album accessories

ADVANTAGE STOCK SHEETS
Advantage stock sheets fit directly in your 2-post or 3-ring National or Specialty album. Available with 1 to 8 pockets.
Sheets are sold in packages of 10.
- Stock sheets match album pages in every respect, including size, border, and color.
- Punched to fit perfectly in binder.
- Ideal for storing minor varieties and collateral material. A great place to keep new issues until the next supplement is available.
- Provides the protection of clear acetate pockets on heavyweight pages.

NATIONAL BORDER

Item			Retail	AA*
AD11	1 Pocket	242mm	$19.99	$17.99
AD12	2 Pockets	119mm	$19.99	$17.99
AD13	3 Pockets	79mm	$19.99	$17.99
AD14	4 Pockets	58mm	$19.99	$17.99
AD15	5 Pockets	45mm	$19.99	$17.99
AD16	6 Pockets	37mm	$19.99	$17.99
AD17	7 Pockets	34mm	$19.99	$17.99
AD18	8 Pockets	31mm	$19.99	$17.99

SPECIALTY BORDER

Item			Retail	AA*
AD21	1 Pocket	242mm	$19.99	$17.99
AD22	2 Pockets	119mm	$19.99	$17.99
AD23	3 Pockets	79mm	$19.99	$17.99
AD24	4 Pockets	58mm	$19.99	$17.99
AD25	5 Pockets	45mm	$19.99	$17.99
AD26	6 Pockets	37mm	$19.99	$17.99
AD27	7 Pockets	34mm	$19.99	$17.99
AD28	8 Pockets	31mm	$19.99	$17.99

BLANK PAGES
Ideal for developing your own album pages to be integrated with your album.

SPECIALTY SERIES PAGES (BORDER A)
(20 per pack)

Item		Retail	AA*
ACC110		$8.99	$6.99
ACC111	Quadrille*	$13.99	$11.99

Graph pattern printed on page.

SPECIALTY/NATIONAL SERIES BINDERS
National series pages are punched for 3-ring and 2-post binders. The 3-ring binder is available in two sizes. The 2-post binder comes in one size. All Scott binders are covered with a tough green leatherette material that is washable and reinforced at stress points for long wear.

3-RING BINDERS & SLIPCASES
With the three ring binder, pages lay flat and the rings make turning the pages easy. The locking mechanism insure that the rings won't pop open even when the binder is full.

Item			Retail	AA*
ACBR01D	Small 3-Ring Binder	Holds up to 100 pages	$41.99	$34.99
ACBR03D	Large 3-Ring Binder	Holds up to 250 pages	$41.99	$34.99
ACSR01	Small 3-Ring Slipcase.		$37.50	$26.99
ACSR03	Large 3-Ring Slipcase.		$37.50	$26.99

LARGE 2-POST BINDER & SLIPCASE
For the traditional Scott collector, we offer the standard hinge post binder. Scott album pages are punched with rectangular holes that fit on rectangular posts. The posts and pages are held by a rod that slides down from the top. With the post binder pages do not lie flat. However, filler strips are available for a minimal cost.

Item			Retail	AA*
ACBS03	Large 2-Post Binder	Holds up to 250 pages	$54.99	$46.99
ACSS03	Large 2-Post Slipcase		$37.50	$26.99

ALBUM PAGE DIVIDERS
Postage, air post, semi-postals; they're all right at your fingertips with Specialty Album Page Dividers. The dividers are a great way to keep your albums organized and save wear and tear on your pages.

Item		Retail	AA*
ACC145	Package of 10	$4.49	$3.49

NATIONAL SERIES PAGES (BORDER B)
(20 per pack)

Item		Retail	AA*
ACC120		$8.99	$6.99
ACC121	Quadrille*	$13.99	$11.99

PAGE PROTECTORS
Protect your stamps and album pages with a clear archival quality plastic sleeve. Sleeves fits over the entire page and protects pages from creases, fingerprints and tears. Scott Page protectors are pvc free and thin enough that they won't make your binder bulge. Page Protectors are available in two sizes. Sold in packages of 25.

2-Post Minuteman/International Pg Protectors

Item	Retail	AA*
ACC165	$13.99	$11.75

National/Specialty Series Pg Protectors*

Item	Retail	AA*
ACC166	$13.99	$11.75

*Punched to fit 2-post and 3-ring binder.

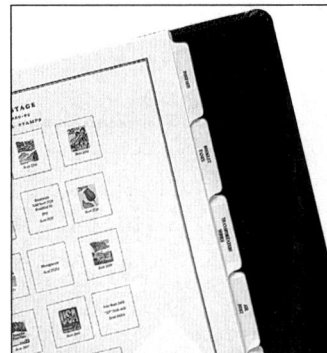

To Order Call 1-800-572-6885
AmosAdvantage.com

1. AA* prices apply to paid subscribers or orders placed online.
2. Prices, terms and product availability subject to change.
3. **Shipping & Handling:**
   United States: 10% of order total. Minimum charge $7.99 Maximum charge $45.00.
   Canada: 20% of order total. Minimum charge $19.99 Maximum charge $200.00.
   Foreign orders are shipped via FedEx Intl. and billed actual freight. Credit cards only.

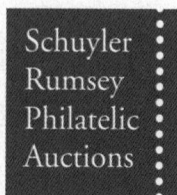

SCOTT

2015
Classic Specialized
Catalogue

TWENTY-FIRST EDITION

STAMPS AND COVERS
OF THE WORLD INCLUDING U.S.
1840–1940
(BRITISH COMMONWEALTH TO 1952)

EDITOR	Charles Snee
MANAGING EDITOR	Donna Houseman
EDITOR EMERITUS	James E. Kloetzel
SENIOR EDITOR /NEW ISSUES & VALUING	Martin J. Frankevicz
SENIOR EDITOR	David Akin
SENIOR VALUING ANALYST	Steven R. Myers
ADMINISTRATIVE ASSISTANT/CATALOGUE LAYOUT	Eric Wiessinger
PRINTING AND IMAGE COORDINATOR	Stacey Mahan
SENIOR GRAPHIC DESIGNER	Cinda McAlexander
ADVERTISING	Angela Nolte
CIRCULATION /PRODUCT PROMOTION MANAGER	Tim Wagner
VICE PRESIDENT	Dean Horowitz
PRESIDENT	Jeff Greisch

SPECIAL EDITORIAL CONSULTANT   **Sergio Sismondo**

Released November 2014

Copyright© 2014 by

Scott Publishing Co.

911 Vandemark Road, Sidney, OH 45365-0828

A division of AMOS MEDIA CO., publishers of *Linn's Stamp News*, *Linn's Stamp News Monthly*, *Coin World* and *Coin World Monthly*.

Table of Contents

See Volumes 1 – 6 of the *Scott Standard Postage Stamp Catalogue*
for stamps issued from 1941 to 2014
(British Commonwealth 1953-2014)

Scott Publishing Mission Statement

The Scott Publishing Team exists to serve the recreational,
educational and commercial hobby needs of stamp collectors and dealers.

We strive to set the industry standard for philatelic information and products by developing and
providing goods that help collectors identify, value, organize and present their collections.

Quality customer service is, and will continue to be, our highest priority.
We aspire toward achieving total customer satisfaction.

Scott Publishing Co.

SCOTT

911 VANDEMARK ROAD, SIDNEY, OHIO 45365   937-498-0802

Fellow Scott Catalogue User:

Hundreds of new listings, thousands of value changes in the 2015 Scott Classic Specialized catalogue.

Welcome to the 2015 edition of the *Scott Classic Specialized Catalogue of Stamps and Covers 1840-1940*, widely regarded as the best single-volume catalogue for the classic-era stamps of the world.

As you scan the pages, you will find thousands of value changes, hundreds of new listings and myriad editorial improvements, including many hundreds of revised and expanded listings. The additions include separate listings for never-hinged stamps, values for on-cover uses, and values for multiples that are popular with collectors, such as pairs, strips of three and four, and blocks of four. Such listings are found only in the Classic Specialized catalogue.

Once again, Scott managing editor Donna Houseman and special editorial consultant Sergio Sismondo worked tirelessly to expand the editorial content and listed values in the Classic Specialized catalogue. Bill Jones, a former Scott associate editor, also provided substantial input by updating thousands of values and making significant editorial enhancements throughout the catalogue. Their collective efforts may be seen on almost every page of this year's edition.

There are a number of editorial additions that bear mentioning. But before doing so, let's go over some of the highlights concerning value changes. The 2015 edition contains slightly more than 15,000 Classic-only value changes — more than double the total recorded last year. Among the value changes made in the six-volume 2015 Scott Standard Postage Stamp Catalogue, 14,800 were carried over into the 2015 Classic, for a grand total of almost 30,000 value changes.

When considering individual countries, the Aegean Islands came in at No. 1, with 2,095 value changes, not including never-hinged and on-cover values. Generally modest increases are seen across all sections. The 1932 St. Anthony of Padua stamps (Scott 12-18) each rise from $30 unused last year to $32.50 in the 2015 catalogue.

A total of 1,665 value changes were made for Italy. Pay particular attention to on-cover values; some of the increases in this category are substantial. Each of the three 1923 Fascist Oath semipostals (Scott B17-B19) is valued at $550 on cover, a $200 jump from the 2014 value of $350.

Speaking of Italy, there also was much activity in Italian Offices Abroad. Here the editors found almost 1,400 value changes. Please note that in some cases unused and never-hinged values were adjusted to reflect accurately market values for stamps in true Very Fine condition, the benchmark grade that Scott values.

Other countries with significant numbers of value changes include: Russia (1,386), Germany (1,367), Eritrea (1,039) and Libya (1,035).

Never-hinged values were added or updated for numerous countries. In Kuwait, the first two definitive sets overprinted "Kuwait" (Scott 1-15, 17-35) are now valued never hinged. Likewise, the first two definitive sets of Oman (1-15, 16-24) also have new never-hinged values.

Numerous never-hinged, on-cover and minor-listing values have been updated for Finland.

In the catalogue introduction, we provide an extensive list of countries with listings for stamps on covers. This year, two countries were added: Dalmatia and, under British Offices Abroad, Eritrea. If you collect covers, it would be well worth your time to read the section titled "Catalogue Values for Stamps on Covers" in the introduction.

British Guiana 1¢ Magenta now valued. Colombia Cubiertas return to the Scott catalogue for the first time since 1941.

For the first time in three decades, the unique British Guiana 1¢ Magenta (Scott 13), often called the world's rarest stamp, is valued in the Scott catalogue. A value of $9.5 million has been assigned to the rare stamp. A footnote explains that the value is based on an auction realization achieved at a sale in New York City in June 2014. The new value also will appear in the British Guiana listings of the 2016 Scott Standard catalogue.

The decision to assign a value was made after some discussion among the Scott editors. Given the attendant media blitz before the sale and the notoriety of the stamp itself, some felt that it would be better to leave a dash in the used column for the iconic stamp. Nonetheless, it was felt that an actual value would be of more use to catalogue users.

For the first time since the 1941 edition of the Scott catalogue, the Colombia Cubiertas are listed and valued once again. The Cubiertas stamps were affixed to the back of letters that contained valuables (typically money) and were insured through the post office.

The origin and date of dispatch were written in the appropriate lines, and a description of the values enclosed and destination were written in the appropriate cartouche below. The denomination indicated the payment of insurance and functioned as a receipt. The recipient often signed the stamp and handed it back to the postman, indicating completed delivery.

A well-kept secret is that the Scott Classic Specialized catalogue includes the most complete listings of treaty port stamps. The 2003 Scott Classic introduced the listings of the China Treaty Port stamps, complete with values. The 2015 catalog lists Hong Kong Treaty Port stamps for the first time.

The postal operations in the treaty ports were operated by the General Post Office in London, England, until 1868, when administration of the program was turned over to Hong Kong. Stamps of Hong Kong were canceled with Hong Kong postmarks or circular datestamps.

For many years, these stamps have been popular with China collectors, but because most catalogs do not list them, they are relatively unknown to most collectors.

In response to an article that appeared in the journal of the Lithuanian Philatelic Society and following Scott's history of listing occupation stamps under the occupied country, the "Ob. Ost" stamps formerly listed as Lithuania 1N1-1N12 have been moved to Russia N1-N12. The author presented convincing evidence that the stamps were used in nine guberniyas of the Russian Empire.

In Belgium, the provisional handstamped "T" stamps have been added to the Postage Due section.

The reorganization of the Ceres issues of Portugal and Portuguese colonies that began in the 2013 Scott Classic catalogue is now complete. The 2015 Classic includes revised listings for Portuguese Congo, Portuguese Guinea, Portuguese India, St. Thomas and Prince Islands, Tete and Timor.

For a summary of these and the many other listing-related changes not specifically mentioned here, you are encouraged to look over the hundreds of number additions, deletions and changes, which may be found on pages 47A-49A in this volume.

Curtain comes down on a successful catalogue season.

Publication of this year's Classic Specialized catalogue officially brings to a close the 2015 season for Scott. Looking back, I would be remiss if I did not acknowledge what a privilege and honor it is to lead the dedicated, motivated members of the Scott editorial staff. They are: managing editor Donna Houseman, senior editors Dave Akin and Martin Frankevicz, and senior valuing analyst Steven Myers. We make it our mission each year to bring you accurate, up-to-date information to help you enjoy the hobby and make informed collecting decisions. Occasionally, though, we do overlook something. If you notice a problem that needs fixing, or if you have suggestions for future editions of the Scott catalogues, please contact me at csnee@amosmedia.com.

Now grab a favorite stamp album, pick up your tongs, settle in with your copy of the Scott Classic catalogue, and bask in the pleasures of the world's greatest hobby. Cheers!

Charles Snee/Catalogue Editor

Acknowledgments

Our appreciation and gratitude go to the following individuals who have assisted us in preparing information included in this year's Scott Catalogues. Some helpers prefer anonymity. These individuals have generously shared their stamp knowledge with others through the medium of the Scott Catalogue.

Those who follow provided information that is in addition to the hundreds of dealer price lists and advertisements and scores of auction catalogues and realizations that were used in producing the catalogue values. It is from those noted here that we have been able to obtain information on items not normally seen in published lists and advertisements. Support from these people goes beyond data leading to catalogue values, for they also are key to editorial changes.

A special acknowledgment to Liane and Sergio Sismondo of The Classic Collector for their extraordinary assistance and knowledge sharing that has aided in the preparation of this year's Standard and Classic Specialized Catalogues.

Roland Austin
Robert Ausubel (Great Britain Collectors Club)
Jack Hagop Barsoumian (International Stamp Co.)
John Birkinbine II
Brian M. Bleckwenn
Roger S. Brody
Keith & Margie Brown
Tina & John Carlson (JET Stamps)
Henry Chlanda
Frank D. Correl
Tony L. Crumbley (Carolina Coin & Stamp, Inc.)
Stephen R. Datz
Tony Davis
Charles Deaton
Ubaldo Del Toro
Bob & Rita Dumaine (Sam Houston Duck Co.)
Sister Theresa Durand
Mark Eastzer (Markest Stamp Co.)
Paul G. Eckman
Dave Elsmore (ozrevenues.com)
George Epstein (Allkor Stamp Co.)
Mehdi Esmaili
George Eveleth (Spink Shreves Galleries)
Henry Fisher
Jeffrey M. Forster
Ernest E. Fricks (France & Colonies Philatelic Society)
Richard Friedberg
Frank Geiger (Worldstamps.com)
Bob Genisol (Sultan Stamp Center)

Stan Goldfarb
Allan Grant (Rushstamps, Ltd.)
Daniel E. Grau
Jan E. Gronwall
Grosvenor Auctions
Chris Harmer (Harmer-Schau Auctions)
Robin Harris
Bruce Hecht (Bruce L. Hecht Co.)
Clifford O. Herrick (Fidelity Trading Co.)
Peter Hoffman
Guanlun Hong (Jade Crown International Stamp Co.)
Armen Hovsepian (Armenstamp)
Philip J. Hughes
John Jamieson (Saskatoon Stamp and Coin)
Peter Jeannopoulos
Stephen Joe (International Stamp Service)
William A. Jones
Andrew Kapochunas
John Kardos
Allan Katz (Ventura Stamp Co.)
Stanford M. Katz
Patricia A. Kaufmann (Confederate Stamp Alliance)
George Krieger
Ingert Kuzych
Frederick P. Lawrence
John R. Lewis (The William Henry Stamp Co.)
Ulf Lindahl
Ignacio Llach (Filatelia Llach S.L.)

George Luzitano
Robert L. Markovits (Quality Investors, Ltd.)
Larry Martin (Crown Colony Stamp Co.)
Marilyn R. Mattke
William K. McDaniel
Gary N. McLean
Mark S. Miller
Allen Mintz
William E. Mooz
Gary Morris (Pacific Midwest Co.)
Bruce M. Moyer (Moyer Stamps & Collectibles)
Richard H. Muller
Scott Murphy (Professional Stamp Experts)
Behruz Nassre
Robert P. Odenweller
Nik & Lisa Oquist
Dr. Everett Parker
Donald J. Peterson (International Philippine Philatelic Society)
Stanley M. Piller (Stanley M. Piller & Associates)
Todor Drumev Popov
Philippe & Guido Poppe (Poppe Stamps, Inc.)
Peter W. W. Powell
Siddique Mahmudur Rahman
Ghassan D. Riachi
Eric Roberts
Robert G. Rufe
Mehrdad Sadri (Persiphila)
Theodosios Sampson PhD
Alex Schauss (Schauss Philatelics)
Jacques C. Schiff, Jr. (Jacques C. Schiff, Jr., Inc.)

Michael Schreiber
Guy Shaw
Jeff Siddiqui
Ray Simrak
Sergio & Liane Sismondo (The Classic Collector)
Jay Smith
Merle Spencer (The Stamp Gallery)
Frank J. Stanley, III
Peter Thy
Scott R. Trepel (Siegel Auction Galleries)
Dan Undersander (United Postal Stationery Society)
Philip T. Wall
Kristian Wang
Daniel C. Warren
Giana Wayman
William R. Weiss, Jr. (Weiss Expertizing)
Don White (Dunedin Stamp Centre)
Kirk Wolford (Kirk's Stamp Company)
Ralph Yorio
Val Zabijaka
Michal Zika
Steven Zirinsky
Alfonso G. Zulueta

Addresses, Telephone Numbers, Web Sites, E-Mail Addresses of General & Specialized Philatelic Societies

Collectors can contact the following groups for information about the philately of the areas within the scope of these societies, or inquire about membership in these groups. Aside from the general societies, we limit this list to groups that specialize in particular fields of philately, particular areas covered by the Scott Standard Postage Stamp Catalogue, and topical groups. Many more specialized philatelic societies exist than those listed below. These addresses were compiled in January 2001, and are, to the best of our knowledge, correct and current. Groups should inform the editors of address changes whenever they occur. The editors also want to hear from other such specialized groups not listed. **Unless otherwise noted all website addresses begin with http://**

American Philatelic Society
100 Match Factory Place
Bellefonte PA 16823-1367
Ph: (814) 933-3803
www.stamps.org
E-mail: apsinfo@stamps.org

American Stamp Dealers Association, Inc.
P.O. Box 692
Leesport PA 19553
Ph: (800) 369-8207
www.americanstampdealer.com
E-mail: asda@americanstampdealer.com

National Stamp Dealers Association
Dick Keiser, President
2916 NW Bucklin Hill Road #136
Silverdale WA 98383-8514
Ph: (800) 875-6633
www.nsdainc.org
E-mail: gail@nsdainc.org

International Society of Worldwide Stamp Collectors
Joanne Berkowitz, MD
P.O. Box 19006
Sacramento CA 95819
www.iswsc.org
E-mail: executivedirector@iswsc.org

Royal Philatelic Society
41 Devonshire Place
London, W1G 6JY
UNITED KINGDOM
www.rpsl.org.uk
E-mail: secretary@rpsl.org.uk

Royal Philatelic Society of Canada
P.O. Box 929, Station Q
Toronto, ON, M4T 2P1
CANADA
Ph: (888) 285-4143
www.rpsc.org
E-mail: info@rpsc.org

Young Stamp Collectors of America
Janet Houser
100 Match Factory Place
Bellefonte PA 16823-1367
Ph: (814) 933-3820
www.stamps.org/ysca/intro.htm
E-mail: ysca@stamps.org

Philatelic Research Resources

(The Scott editors encourage any additional research organizations to submit data for inclusion in this listing category)

American Philatelic Research Library
Tara Murray
100 Match Factory Place
Bellefonte PA 16823
Ph: (814) 933-3803
www.stamplibrary.org
E-mail: aprl@stamps.org

Institute for Analytical Philately, Inc.
P.O. Box 8035
Holland MI 49422-8035
Ph: (616) 399-9299
www.analyticalphilately.org
E-mail: info@analyticalphilately.org

The Western Philatelic Library
P.O. Box 2219
1500 Partridge Ave.
Sunnyvale CA 94087
Ph: (408) 733-0336
www.fwpf.org

Groups focusing on fields or aspects found in worldwide philately (some might cover U.S. area only)

American Air Mail Society
Stephen Reinhard
P.O. Box 110
Mineola NY 11501
www.americanairmailsociety.org
E-mail: sreinhard1@optonline.net

American First Day Cover Society
Douglas Kelsey
P.O. Box 16277
Tucson AZ 85732-6277
Ph: (520) 321-0880
www.afdcs.org
E-mail: afdcs@afdcs.org

American Revenue Association
Eric Jackson
P.O. Box 728
Leesport PA 19533-0728
Ph: (610) 926-6200
www.revenuer.org
E-mail: eric@revenuer.com

American Topical Association
Vera Felts
P.O. Box 8
Carterville IL 62918-0008
Ph: (618) 985-5100
www.americantopicalassn.org
E-mail: americantopical@msn.com

Christmas Seal & Charity Stamp Society
John Denune
234 E. Broadway
Granville OH 43023
Ph: (740) 587-0276
www.seal-society.org
E-mail: jdenune@roadrunner.com

Errors, Freaks and Oddities Collectors Club
Don David Price
5320 Eastchester Drive
Sarasota FL 34134-2711
Ph: (717) 445-9420
www.efocc.org
E-mail: ddprice98@hotmail.com

First Issues Collectors Club
Kurt Streepy, Secretary
3128 E. Mattatha Drive
Bloomington IN 47401
www.firstissues.org
E-mail: secretary@firstissues.org

International Society of Reply Coupon Collectors
Peter Robin
P.O. Box 353
Bala Cynwyd PA 19004
E-mail: peterrobin@verizon.net

The Joint Stamp Issues Society
Richard Zimmermann
124, Avenue Guy de Coubertin
Saint Remy Les Chevreuse, F-78470
FRANCE
www.jointstampissues.net
E-mail: contact@jointstampissues.net

National Duck Stamp Collectors Society
Anthony J. Monico
P.O. Box 43
Harleysville PA 19438-0043
www.ndscs.org
E-mail: ndscs@ndscs.org

No Value Identified Club
Albert Sauvanet
Le Clos Royal B, Boulevard des Pas Enchantes
St. Sebastien-sur Loire, 44230
FRANCE
E-mail: alain.vailly@irin.univ nantes.fr

The Perfins Club
Jerry Hejduk
P.O. Box 490450
Leesburg FL 34749-0450
Ph: (352) 326-2117
E-mail: flprepers@comcast.net

Postage Due Mail Study Group
John Rawlins
13, Longacre
Chelmsford, CM1 3BJ
UNITED KINGDOM
E-mail: john.rawlins2@ukonline.co.uk.

Post Mark Collectors Club
Beverly Proulx
7629 Homestead Drive
Baldwinsville NY 13027
Ph: (315) 638-0532
www.postmarks.org
E-mail: stampdance@yahoo.com

Postal History Society
Joseph F. Frasch, Jr.
P.O. Box 20387
Columbus OH 43220-0387
www.stampclubs.com
E-mail: jfrasch@ix.netcom.com

Precancel Stamp Society
Jerry Hejduk
P.O. Box 490450
Leesburg FL 34749-0450
Ph: (352) 326-2117
www.precancels.com
E-mail: psspromosec@comcast.net

United Postal Stationery Society
Stuart Leven
P.O. Box 24764
San Jose CA 95154-4764
www.upss.org
E-mail: poststat@gmail.com

United States Possessions Philatelic Society
David S. Durbin
3604 Darice Lane
Jefferson City MO 65109
Ph: (573) 230-6921
www.uspps.net
E-mail: patlabb@aol.com

Groups focusing on U.S. area philately as covered in the Standard Catalogue

Canal Zone Study Group
Tom Brougham
737 Neilson St.
Berkeley CA 94707
www.CanalZoneStudyGroup.com
E-mail: czsgsecretary@gmail.com

Carriers and Locals Society
Martin Richardson
P.O. Box 74
Grosse Ile MI 48138
www.pennypost.org
E-mail: martinr362@aol.com

Confederate Stamp Alliance
Patricia A. Kaufman
10194 N. Old State Road
Lincoln DE 19960
Ph: (302) 422-2656
www.csalliance.org
E-mail: trishkauf@comcast.net

Hawaiian Philatelic Society
Kay H. Hoke
P.O. Box 10115
Honolulu HI 96816-0115
Ph: (808) 521-5721

Plate Number Coil Collectors Club
Gene Trinks
16415 W. Desert Wren Court
Surprise AZ 85374
Ph: (623) 322-4619
www.pnc3.org
E-mail: gctrinks@cox.net

Ryukyu Philatelic Specialist Society
Laura Edmonds, Secy.
P.O. Box 240177
Charlotte NC 28224-0177
Ph: (336) 509-3739
www.ryukyustamps.org
E-mail: secretary@ryukyustamps.org

United Nations Philatelists
Blanton Clement, Jr.
P.O. Box 146
Morrisville PA 19067-0146
www.unpi.com
E-mail: bclemjr@yahoo.com

United States Stamp Society
Executive Secretary
P.O. Box 6634
Katy TX 77491-6631
www.usstamps.org
E-mail: webmaster@usstamps.org

U.S. Cancellation Club
Roger Rhoads
6160 Brownstone Court
Mentor OH 44060
bob.trachimowicz.org/uscchome.htm
E-mail: rrrhoads@aol.com

U.S. Philatelic Classics Society
Rob Lund
2913 Fulton St.
Everett WA 98201-3733
www.uspcs.org
E-mail: membershipchairman@uspcs.org

Groups focusing on philately of foreign countries or regions

Aden & Somaliland Study Group
Gary Brown
P.O. Box 106
Briar Hill, Victoria, 3088
AUSTRALIA
E-mail: garyjohn951@optushome.com.au

American Society of Polar Philatelists (Antarctic areas)
Alan Warren
P.O. Box 39
Exton PA 19341-0039
www.polarphilatelists.org

Andorran Philatelic Study Circle
D. Hope
17 Hawthorn Drive
Stalybridge, Cheshire, SK15 1UE
UNITED KINGDOM
apsc.free.fr
E-mail: apsc@free.fr

Australian States Study Circle of The Royal Sydney Philatelic Club
Ben Palmer
GPO 1751
Sydney, N.S.W., 2001
AUSTRALIA

Austria Philatelic Society
Ralph Schneider
P.O. Box 23049
Belleville IL 62223
Ph: (618) 277-6152
www.austriaphilatelicsociety.com
E-mail: rschneiderstamps@att.net

Baltic States Philatelic Society
Anatoly Chlenov
5719 Drysdale Court
San Jose CA 95124
Ph: (650) 863-1552
www.baltic-philately.com
E-mail: achlenov@localstamps.com

American Belgian Philatelic Society
Edward de Bary
11 Wakefield Drive Apt. 2105
Asheville NC 28803

Bechuanalands and Botswana Society
Neville Midwood
69 Porlock Lane
Furzton, Milton Keynes, MK4 1JY
UNITED KINGDOM
www.nevsoft.com
E-mail: bbsoc@nevsoft.com

Bermuda Collectors Society
John Pare
405 Perimeter Road
Mount Horeb WI 53572
www.bermudacollectorssociety.org
E-mail: science29@comcast.net

Brazil Philatelic Association
William V. Kriebel
1923 Manning St.
Philadelphia PA 19103-5728
Ph: (215) 735-3697
www.brazilphilatelic.org
E-mail: info@brazilphilatelic.org

British Caribbean Philatelic Study Group
Bob Stewart
7 West Dune Lane
Long Beach Township NJ 08008
www.bcpsg.org
E-mail: stewartlbi9@comcast.net

The King George VI Collectors Society (British Commonwealth)
Brian Livingstone
21 York Mansions, Prince of Wales Drive
London, SW11 4DL
UNITED KINGDOM
www.kg6.info
E-mail: livingstone484@btinternet.com

British North America Philatelic Society (Canada & Provinces)
David G. Jones
184 Larkin Drive
Nepean, ON, K2J 1H9
CANADA
www.bnaps.org
E-mail: shibumi.management@gmail.com

British West Indies Study Circle
John Seidl
4324 Granby Way
Marietta GA 30062
Ph: (770) 642-6424
www.bwisc.org
E-mail: john.seidl@gmail.com

Burma Philatelic Study Circle
Michael Whittaker
1, Ecton Leys, Hillside
Rugby, Warwickshire, CV22 5SL
UNITED KINGDOM
www.burmastamps.homecall.co.uk
E-mail: manningham8@mypostoffice.co.uk

Cape and Natal Study Circle
Dr. Guy Dillaway
P.O. Box 181
Weston MA 02493
www.nzsc.demon.co.uk

Ceylon Study Circle
R. W. P. Frost
42 Lonsdale Road, Cannington
Bridgewater, Somerset, TA5 2JS
UNITED KINGDOM
www.ceylonsc.org
E-mail: rodney.frost@tiscali.co.uk

Channel Islands Specialists Society
Moira Edwards
86, Hall Lane, Sandon
Chelmsford, Essex, CM2 7RQ
UNITED KINGDOM
www.ciss1950.org.uk
E-mail: membership@ciss1950.org.uk

China Stamp Society
Paul H. Gault
P.O. Box 20711
Columbus OH 43220
www.chinastampsociety.org
E-mail: secretary@chinastampsociety.org

Colombia/Panama Philatelic Study Group (COPAPHIL)
Thomas P. Myers
P.O. Box 522
Gordonsville VA 22942
www.copaphil.org
E-mail: tpmphil@hotmail.com

Association Filatelic de Costa Rica
Giana Wayman
c/o Interlink 102, P.O. Box 52-6770
Miami FL 33152
E-mail: scotland@racsa.co.cr

Society for Costa Rica Collectors
Dr. Hector R. Mena
P.O. Box 14831
Baton Rouge LA 70808
www.socorico.org
E-mail: hrmena@aol.com

International Cuban Philatelic Society
Ernesto Cuesta
P.O. Box 34434
Bethesda MD 20827
www.cubafil.org
E-mail: ecuesta@philat.com

Cuban Philatelic Society of America Æ
P.O. Box 141656
Coral Gables FL 33114-1656
www.cubapsa.com
E-mail: cpsa.usa@gmail.com

Cyprus Study Circle
Colin Dear
10 Marne Close, Wem
Shropshire, SY4 5YE
UNITED KINGDOM
www.cyprusstudycircle.org/index.htm
E-mail: colindear@talktalk.net

Society for Czechoslovak Philately
Tom Cassaboom
P.O. Box 4124
Prescott AZ 86302
www.csphilately.org
E-mail: klfck1@aol.com

Danish West Indies Study Unit of the Scandinavian Collectors Club
Arnold Sorensen
7666 Edgedale Drive
Newburgh IN 47630
Ph: (812) 480-6532
www.scc-online.org
E-mail: valbydwi@hotmail.com

East Africa Study Circle
Michael Vesey-Fitzgerald
Vernalls Orchard, Gosport Lane
Lyndhurst, SO43 7BP
UNITED KINGDOM
www.easc.org.uk
E-mail: secretary@easc.org.uk

Egypt Study Circle
Mike Murphy
109 Chadwick Road
London, SE15 4PY
UNITED KINGDOM
Trent Ruebush: North American Agent
E-mail: truebrush@usaid.gov
egyptstudycircle.org.uk
E-mail: egyptstudycircle@hotmail.com

Estonian Philatelic Society
Juri Kirsimagi
29 Clifford Ave.
Pelham NY 10803
Ph: (914) 738-3713

Ethiopian Philatelic Society
Ulf Lindahl
21 Westview Place
Riverside CT 06878
Ph: (203) 866-3540
home.comcast.net/~fbheiser/ethiopia5.htm
E-mail: ulindahl@optonline.net

Falkland Islands Philatelic Study Group
Carl J. Faulkner
Williams Inn, On-the-Green
Williamstown MA 01267-2620
Ph: (413) 458-9371
www.fipsg.org.uk

Faroe Islands Study Circle
Norman Hudson
40 Queenis Road, Vicaris Cross
Chester, CH3 5HB
UNITED KINGDOM
www.faroeislandssc.org
E-mail: jntropics@hotmail.com

Former French Colonies Specialist Society
COLFRA
BP 628
75367 Paris, Cedex 08
FRANCE
www.colfra.com
E-mail: clubcolfra@aol.com

France & Colonies Philatelic Society
Edward Grabowski
111 Prospect St., 4C
Westfield NJ 07090
www.drunkenboat.net/frandcol/
E-mail: edjjg@alum.mit.edu

Germany Philatelic Society
P.O. Box 6547
Chesterfield MO 63006
www.germanyphilatelicusa.org

Gibraltar Study Circle
David R. Stirrups
10 Crescent Lodge
The Crescent
Middlesbrough, TS5 6SF
UNITED KINGDOM
www.gibraltarstudycircle.wordpress.com
E-mail: stirrups@btinternet.com

Great Britain Collectors Club
Steve McGill
10309 Brookhollow Circle
Highlands Ranch CO 80129
www.gbstamps.com/gbcc
E-mail: steve.mcgill@comcast.net

International Society of Guatemala Collectors
Jaime Marckwordt
449 St. Francis Blvd.
Daly City CA 94015-2136
www.guatemalastamps.com

Haiti Philatelic Society
Ubaldo Del Toro
5709 Marble Archway
Alexandria VA 22315
www.haitiphilately.org
E-mail: u007ubi@aol.com

Hong Kong Stamp Society
Ming W. Tsang
P.O. Box 206
Glenside PA 19038
www.hkss.org
E-mail: hkstamps@yahoo.com

Society for Hungarian Philately
Robert Morgan
2201 Roscomare Road
Los Angeles CA 90077-2222
Ph; (253) 759-4078
www.hungarianphilately.org
E-mail: ruthandlyman@nventure.com

India Study Circle
John Warren
P.O. Box 7326
Washington DC 20044
Ph: (202) 564-6876
www.indiastudycircle.org
E-mail: warren.john@epa.gov

Indian Ocean Study Circle
E. S. Hutton
29 Paternoster Close
Waltham Abby, Essex, EN9 3JU
UNITED KINGDOM
www.indianoceanstudycircle.com
E-mail:
secretary@indianoceanstudycircle.com

Society of Indo-China Philatelists
Ron Bentley
2600 N. 24th St.
Arlington VA 22207
www.sicp-online.org
E-mail: ron.bentley@verizon.net

Iran Philatelic Study Circle
Mehdi Esmaili
P.O. Box 750096
Forest Hills NY 11375
www.iranphilatelic.org
E-mail: m.esmaili@earthlink.net

Eire Philatelic Association (Ireland)
David J. Brennan
P.O. Box 704
Bernardsville NJ 07924
www.eirephilatelicassoc.org
E-mail: brennan704@aol.com

Society of Israel Philatelists
Howard Rotterdam
P.O. Box 507
Northfield OH 44067
www.israelstamps.com
E-mail: israelstamps@gmail.com

Italy and Colonies Study Circle
Richard Harlow
7 Duncombe House, 8 Manor Road
Teddington, TW11 8BE
UNITED KINGDOM
www.icsc.pwp.blueyonder.co.uk
E-mail: harlowr@gmail.com

International Society for Japanese Philately
William Eisenhauer
P.O. Box 230462
Tigard OR 97281
www.isjp.org
E-mail: secretary@isjp.org

Korea Stamp Society
John E. Talmage
P.O. Box 6889
Oak Ridge TN 37831
www.pennfamily.org/KSS-USA
E-mail: jtalmage@usit.net

Latin American Philatelic Society
Jules K. Beck
30½ St. #209
St. Louis Park MN 55426-3551

Liberian Philatelic Society
William Thomas Lockard
P.O. Box 106
Wellston OH 45692
Ph: (740) 384-2020
E-mail: tlockard@zoomnet.net

Liechtenstudy USA (Liechtenstein)
Paul Tremaine
410 SW Ninth St.
Dundee OR 97115
Ph: (503) 538-4500
www.liechtenstudy.org
E-mail: editor@liechtenstudy.org

Lithuania Philatelic Society
John Variakojis
3715 W. 68th St.
Chicago IL 60629
Ph: (773) 585-8649
lithuanianphilately.com/lps
E-mail: variakojis@sbcglobal.net

Luxembourg Collectors Club
Gary B. Little
7319 Beau Road
Sechelt, BC, V0N 3A8
CANADA
lcc.luxcentral.com
E-mail: gary@luxcentral.com

Malaya Study Group
David Tett
P.O. Box 34
Wheathampstead, Herts, AL4 8JY
UNITED KINGDOM
www.m-s-g.org.uk
E-mail: davidtett@aol.com

Malta Study Circle
Alec Webster
50 Worcester Road
Sutton, Surrey, SM2 6QB
UNITED KINGDOM
E-mail: alecwebster50@hotmail.com

Mexico-Elmhurst Philatelic Society International
Thurston Bland
1022 Ramona Ave.
Corona CA 92879-2123
www.mepsi.org

Asociacion Mexicana de Filatelia
AMEXFIL
Jose Maria Rico, 129, Col. Del Valle
Mexico City DF, 03100
MEXICO
www.amexfil.mx
E-mail: alejandro.grossmann@gmail.com

Society for Moroccan and Tunisian Philately
206, bld. Pereire
75017 Paris
FRANCE
members.aol.com/Jhaik5814
E-mail: splm206@aol.com

Nepal & Tibet Philatelic Study Group
Roger D. Skinner
1020 Covington Road
Los Altos CA 94024-5003
Ph: (650) 968-4163
www.fuchs-online.com/ntpsc/
E-mail: colinhepper@hotmail.co.uk

American Society for Netherlands Philately
Hans Kremer
50 Rockport Court
Danville CA 94526
Ph: (925) 820-5841
www.asnp1975.com
E-mail: hkremer@usa.net

New Zealand Society of Great Britain
Keith C. Collins
13 Briton Crescent
Sanderstead, Surrey, CR2 0JN
UNITED KINGDOM
www.cs.stir.ac.uk/~rgc/nzsgb
E-mail: rgc@cs.stir.ac.uk

Nicaragua Study Group
Erick Rodriguez
11817 SW 11th St.
Miami FL 33184-2501
clubs.yahoo.com/clubs/
nicaraguastudygroup
E-mail: nsgsec@yahoo.com

Society of Australasian Specialists/ Oceania
David McNamee
P.O. Box 37
Alamo CA 94507
www.sasoceania.org
E-mail: dmcnamee@aol.com

Orange Free State Study Circle
J. R. Stroud
24 Hooper Close
Burnham-on-sea, Somerset, TA8 1JQ
UNITED KINGDOM
orangefreestatephilately.org.uk
E-mail: richardstroudph@gofast.co.uk

Pacific Islands Study Circle
John Ray
24 Woodvale Ave.
London, SE25 4AE
UNITED KINGDOM
www.pisc.org.uk
E-mail: info@pisc.org.uk

Pakistan Philatelic Study Circle
Jeff Siddiqui
P.O. Box 7002
Lynnwood WA 98046
E-mail: jeffsiddiqui@msn.com

Centro de Filatelistas Independientes de Panama
Vladimir Berrio-Lemm
Apartado 0823-02748
Plaza Concordia Panama
PANAMA
E-mail: panahistoria@gmail.com

Papuan Philatelic Society
Steven Zirinsky
P.O. Box 49, Ansonia Station
New York NY 10023
Ph: (718) 706-0616
www.communigate.co.uk/york/pps
E-mail: szirinsky@cs.com

International Philippine Philatelic Society
Donald J. Peterson
7408 Alaska Ave., NW
Washington DC 20012
Ph: (202) 291-6229
www.theipps.info
E-mail: dpeterson@comcast.net

Pitcairn Islands Study Group
Dr. Everett L. Parker
249 NW Live Oak Place
Lake City FL 32055-8906
Ph: (386) 754-8524
www.pisg.net
E-mail: eparker@hughes.net

Polonus Philatelic Society (Poland)
Robert Ogrodnik
P.O. Box 240428
Ballwin MO 63024-0428
Ph: (314) 821-6130
www.polonus.org
E-mail: rvo1937@gmail.com

International Society for Portuguese Philately
Clyde Homen
1491 Bonnie View Road
Hollister CA 95023-5117
www.portugalstamps.com
E-mail: cjh1491@sbcglobal.net

Rhodesian Study Circle
William R. Wallace
P.O. Box 16381
San Francisco CA 94116
www.rhodesianstudycircle.org.uk
E-mail: bwall8rscr@earthlink.net

Rossica Society of Russian Philately
Alexander Kolchinsky
1506 Country Lake Drive
Champaign IL 6821-6428
www.rossica.org
E-mail: alexander.kolchinsky@rossica.
org

St. Helena, Ascension & Tristan Da Cunha Philatelic Society
Dr. Everett L. Parker
249 NW Live Oak Place
Lake City FL 32055-8906
Ph: (386) 754-8524
www.atlanticislands.org
E-mail: eparker@hughes.net

St. Pierre & Miquelon Philatelic Society
James R. (Jim) Taylor
2335 Paliswood Road SW
Calgary, AB, T2V 3P6
CANADA

Associated Collectors of El Salvador
Joseph D. Hahn
1015 Old Boalsburg Road Apt G-5
State College PA 16801-6149
www.elsalvadorphilately.org
E-mail: jdhahn2@gmail.com

Fellowship of Samoa Specialists
Donald Mee
23 Leo St.
Christchurch, 8051
NEW ZEALAND
www.samoaexpress.org
E-mail: donanm@xtra.co.nz

Sarawak Specialists' Society
Stu Leven
P.O. Box 24764
San Jose CA 95154-4764
Ph: (408) 978-0193
www.britborneostamps.org.uk
E-mail: stulev@ix.netcom.com

Scandinavian Collectors Club
Steve Lund
P.O. Box 16213
St. Paul MN 55116
www.scc-online.org
E-mail: steve88h@aol.com

Slovakia Stamp Society
Jack Benchik
P.O. Box 555
Notre Dame IN 46556

Philatelic Society for Greater Southern Africa
Alan Hanks
34 Seaton Drive
Aurora, ON, L4G 2KI
CANADA
Ph: (905) 727-6993
www.psgsa.thestampweb.com
Email: alan.hanks@sympatico.ca

South Sudan Philatelic Society
William Barclay
134A Spring Hill Road
South Londonerry VT 05155
E-mail: bill.barclay@wfp.org

Spanish Philatelic Society
Robert H. Penn
1108 Walnut Drive
Danielsville PA 18038
Ph: (610) 760-8711
E-mail: roberthpenn@aol.com

Sudan Study Group
David Sher
5 Ellis Park Road
Toronto, ON, M6S 2V2
CANADA
www.sudanstamps.org

American Helvetia Philatelic Society (Switzerland, Liechtenstein)
Richard T. Hall
P.O. Box 15053
Asheville NC 28813-0053
www.swiss-stamps.org
E-mail: secretary2@swiss-stamps.org

Tannu Tuva Collectors Society
Ken R. Simon
P.O. Box 385
Lake Worth FL 33460-0385
Ph: (561) 588-5954
www.tuva.tk
E-mail: yurttuva@yahoo.com

Society for Thai Philately
H. R. Blakeney
P.O. Box 25644
Oklahoma City OK 73125
E-mail: HRBlakeney@aol.com

Transvaal Study Circle
Jeff Woolgar
c/o 9 Meadow Road
Gravesend, DA11 7LR
UNITED KINGDOM
www.transvaal.org.uk

Ottoman and Near East Philatelic Society (Turkey and related areas)
Bob Stuchell
193 Valley Stream Lane
Wayne PA 19087
www.oneps.com
E-mail: rstuchell@msn.com

Ukrainian Philatelic & Numismatic Society
Michael G. Matus
157 Lucinda Lane
Wyomissing PA 19610-1026
Ph: (610) 927 3838
www.upns.org
E-mail: michael.matus@verizon.net

Vatican Philatelic Society
Sal Quinonez
1 Aldersgate, Apt. 1002
Riverhead NY 11901-1830
Ph: (516) 727-6426
www.vaticanphilately.org

British Virgin Islands Philatelic Society
Giorgio Migliavacca
P.O. Box 7007
St. Thomas VI 00801-0007
www.islandsun.com/FEATURES/
bviphil9198.html
E-mail: issun@candwbvi.net

West Africa Study Circle
Martin Bratzel
1233 Virginia Ave.
Windsor, ON, N8S 2Z1
CANADA
www.wasc.org.uk/
E-mail: marty_bratzel@yahoo.com.ca

Western Australia Study Group
Brian Pope
P.O. Box 423
Claremont, Western Australia, 6910
AUSTRALIA
www.wastudygroup.com
E-mail: black5swan@yahoo.com.au

Yugoslavia Study Group of the Croatian Philatelic Society
Michael Lenard
1514 N. Third Ave.
Wausau WI 54401
Ph: (715) 675-2833
E-mail: mjlenard@aol.com

Topical Groups

Americana Unit
Dennis Dengel
17 Peckham Road
Poughkeepsie NY 12603-2018
www.americanaunit.org
E-mail: info@americanaunit.org

Astronomy Study Unit
John W. G. Budd
29203 Coharie Loop
San Antonio FL 33576-4643
Ph: (352) 588-4706
www.astronomystudyunit.com
E-mail: jwgbudd@earthlink.net

Bicycle Stamp Club
Tony Teideman
P.O. Box 90
Baulkham Hills, NSW, 1755
AUSTRALIA
members.tripod.com/~bicyclestamps
E-mail: tonimaur@bigpond.com

Biology Unit
Alan Hanks
34 Seaton Drive
Aurora, ON, L4G 2K1
CANADA
Ph: (905) 727-6993

Bird Stamp Society
Graham Horsman
23A E. Main St.
Blackburn West Lothian
Scotland, EH47 7QR
UNITED KINGDOM
www.bird-stamps.org/bss
E-mail: graham_horsman7@msn.com

Canadiana Study Unit
Robert Haslewood
5140 Cumberland Ave.
Montreal, Quebec, H4V 2N8
CANADA
E-mail: robert.haslewood058@sympatico.ca

Captain Cook Study Unit
Brian P. Sandford
173 Minuteman Drive
Concord MA 01742-1923
www.captaincooksociety.com
E-mail: US@captaincooksociety.com

Casey Jones Railroad Unit
Roy W. Menninger MD
85 SW Pepper Tree Lane
Topeka KS 66611-2072
www.uqp.de/cjr/index.htm
E-mail: roymenn@sbcglobal.net

Cats on Stamps Study Unit
Mary Ann Brown
3006 Wade Road
Durham NC 27705
www.catsonstamps.org
E-mail: mabrown@nc.rr.com

Chemistry & Physics on Stamps Study Unit
Dr. Roland Hirsch
20458 Water Point Lane
Germantown MD 20874
www.cpossu.org
E-mail: rfhirsch@cpossu.org

Chess on Stamps Study Unit
Ray C. Alexis
608 Emery St.
Longmont CO 80501
E-mail: chessstuff911459@aol.com

Christmas Philatelic Club
Jim Balog
P.O. Box 774
Geneva OH 44041
www.web.295.ca/cpc/
E-mail: jpbstamps@windstream.net

Christopher Columbus Philatelic Society
Donald R. Ager
P.O. Box 71
Hillsboro NH 03244-0071
Ph: (603) 464-5379
ccps.maphist.nl/
E-mail: meganddon@tds.net

Collectors of Religion on Stamps
James Bailey
P.O. Box 937
Brownwood TX 76804
www.coros-society.org
E-mail: corosec@directtv.net

Dogs on Stamps Study Unit
Morris Raskin
202A Newport Road
Monroe Township NJ 08831
Ph: (609) 655-7411
www.dossu.org
E-mail: mraskin@cellurian.com

Earth's Physical Features Study Group
Fred Klein
515 Magdalena Ave.
Los Altos CA 94024
epfsu.jeffhayward.com

Ebony Society of Philatelic Events and Reflections, Inc. (African-American topicals)
Manuel Gilyard
800 Riverside Drive, Suite 4H
New York NY 10032-7412
www.esperstamps.org
E-mail: gilyardmani@aol.com

Europa Study Unit
Tonny E. Van Loij
3002 S. Xanthia St.
Denver CO 80231-4237
www.europastudyunit.org/
E-mail: tvanloij@gmail.com

Fine & Performing Arts
Deborah L. Washington
6922 S. Jeffery Blvd., #7 - North
Chicago IL 60649
E-mail: brasslady@comcast.net

Fire Service in Philately
John Zaranek
81 Hillpine Road
Cheektowaga NY 14227-2259
Ph: (716) 668-3352
E-mail: jczaranek@roadrunner.com

Gay & Lesbian History on Stamps Club
Joe Petronie
P.O. Box 190842
Dallas TX 75219-0842
www.glhsc.org
E-mail: glhsc@aol.com

Gems, Minerals & Jewelry Study Unit
George Young
P.O. Box 632
Tewksbury MA 01876-0632
Ph: (978) 851-8283
www.rockhounds.com/rockshop/gmjsuapp.txt
E-mail: george-young@msn.com

Graphics Philately Association
Mark H. Winnegrad
P.O. Box 380
Bronx NY 10462-0380
www.graphics-stamps.com
E-mail: indybruce1@yahoo.com

Journalists, Authors & Poets on Stamps
Ms. Lee Straayer
P.O. Box 6808
Champaign IL 61826
E-mail: lstraayer@dcbnet.com

Lighthouse Stamp Society
Dalene Thomas
8612 W. Warren Lane
Lakewood CO 80227-2352
Ph: (303) 986-6620
www.lighthousestampsociety.org
E-mail: dalene@lighthousestampsociety.org

Lions International Stamp Club
John Bargus
108-2777 Barry Road RR 2
Mill Bay, BC, V0R 2P2
CANADA
Ph: (250) 743-5782

Mahatma Gandhi On Stamps Study Circle
Pramod Shivagunde
Pratik Clinic, Akluj
Solapur, Maharashtra, 413101
INDIA
E-mail: drnanda@bom6.vsnl.net.in

Masonic Study Unit
Stanley R. Longenecker
930 Wood St.
Mount Joy PA 17552-1926
Ph: (717) 669-9094
E-mail: natsco@usa.net

Mathematical Study Unit
Monty J. Strauss
4209 88th St.
Lubbock TX 79423-2041
www.mathstamps.org
E-mail: montystrauss@gmail.com

Medical Subjects Unit
Dr. Frederick C. Skvara
P.O. Box 6228
Bridgewater NJ 08807
E-mail: fcskvara@optonline.net

Military Postal History Society
Ed Dubin
1 S. Wacker Drive, Suite 3500
Chicago IL 60606
www.militaryPHS.org
E-mail: dubine@comcast.net

Mourning Stamps and Covers Club
James Bailey, Jr.
P.O. Box 937
Brownwood TX 76804
E-mail: jfbailey238@directtv.net

Napoleonic Age Philatelists
Ken Berry
7513 Clayton Drive
Oklahoma City OK 73132-5636
Ph: (405) 721-0044
www.nap-stamps.org
E-mail: krb2@earthlink.net

Old World Archeological Study Unit
Caroline Scannell
11 Dawn Drive
Smithtown NY 11787-1761
www.owasu.org
E-mail: editor@owasu.org

Petroleum Philatelic Society International
Dr. Chris Coggins
174 Old Bedford Road
Luton, England, LU2 7HW
UNITED KINGDOM
E-mail: WAMTECH@Luton174.fsnet.co.uk

Philatelic Computing Study Group
Robert de Violini
P.O. Box 5025
Oxnard CA 93031-5025
www.pcsg.org
E-mail: dviolini@adelphia.net

Rotary on Stamps Unit
Gerald L. Fitzsimmons
105 Calla Ricardo
Victoria TX 77904
rotaryonstamps.org
E-mail: glfitz@suddenlink.net

Scouts on Stamps Society International
Lawrence Clay
P.O. Box 6228
Kennewick WA 99336
Ph: (509) 735-3731
www.sossi.org
E-mail: lclay3731@charter.net

Ships on Stamps Unit
Les Smith
302 Conklin Ave.
Penticton, BC, V2A 2T4
CANADA
Ph: (250) 493-7486
www.shipsonstamps.org
E-mail: lessmith440@shaw.ca

Space Unit
Carmine Torrisi
P.O. Box 780241
Maspeth NY 11378
Ph: (917) 620-5687
stargate.1usa.com/stamps/
E-mail: ctorrisi1@nyc.rr.com

Sports Philatelists International
Mark Maestrone
2824 Curie Place
San Diego CA 92122-4110
www.sportstamps.org
Email: president@sportstamps.org

Stamps on Stamps Collectors Club
Alf Jordan
156 W. Elm St.
Yarmouth ME 04096
www.stampsonstamps.org
E-mail: ajordan1@maine.rr.com

Windmill Study Unit
Walter J. Hollien
P.O. Box 346
Long Valley NJ 07853-0346
Ph: (862) 812-0030
E-mail: whollien@earthlink.net

Wine On Stamps Study Unit
Bruce L. Johnson
115 Raintree Drive
Zionsville IN 46077
www.wine-on-stamps.org
E-mail: indybruce@yahoo.com

Women on Stamps Study Unit
Hugh Gottfried
2232 26th St.
Santa Monica CA 90405-1902
E-mail: hgottfried@adelphia.net

Expertizing Services

The following organizations will, for a fee, provide expert opinions about stamps submitted to them. Collectors should contact these organizations to find out about their fees and requirements before submitting philatelic material to them. The listing of these groups here is not intended as an endorsement by Scott Publishing Co.

General Expertizing Services

American Philatelic Expertizing Service (a service of the American Philatelic Society)
100 Match Factory Place
Bellefonte PA 16823-1367
Ph: (814) 237-3803
Fax: (814) 237-6128
www.stamps.org
E-mail: ambristo@stamps.org
Areas of Expertise: Worldwide

B. P. A. Expertising, Ltd.
P.O. Box 1141
Guildford, Surrey, GU5 0WR
UNITED KINGDOM
E-mail: sec@bpaexpertising.org
Areas of Expertise: British Commonwealth, Great Britain, Classics of Europe, South America and the Far East

Philatelic Foundation
70 W. 40th St., 15th Floor
New York NY 10018
Ph: (212) 221-6555
Fax: (212) 221-6208
www.philatelicfoundation.org
E-mail: philatelicfoundation@verizon.net
Areas of Expertise: U.S. & Worldwide

Philatelic Stamp Authentication and Grading, Inc.
P.O. Box 56-2111
Miami FL 33256-2111
Customer Service: (305) 345-9864
www.stampauthentication.com
E-mail: info@stampauthentication.com
Areas of Expertise: U.S., Canal Zone, Hawaii, Philippines, Canada & Provinces

Professional Stamp Experts
P.O. Box 6170
Newport Beach CA 92658
Ph: (877) STAMP-88
Fax: (949) 833-7955
www.collectors.com/pse
E-mail: pseinfo@collectors.com
Areas of Expertise: Stamps and covers of U.S., U.S. Possessions, British Commonwealth

Royal Philatelic Society Expert Committee
41 Devonshire Place
London, W1N 1PE
UNITED KINGDOM
www.rpsl.org.uk/experts.html
E-mail: experts@rpsl.org.uk
Areas of Expertise: Worldwide

Expertizing Services Covering Specific Fields Or Countries

China Stamp Society Expertizing Service
1050 W. Blue Ridge Blvd.
Kansas City MO 64145
Ph: (816) 942-6300
E-mail: hjmesq@aol.com
Areas of Expertise: China

Confederate Stamp Alliance Authentication Service
Gen. Frank Crown, Jr.
P.O. Box 278
Capshaw AL 35742-0396
Ph: (302) 422-2656
Fax: (302) 424-1990
www.csalliance.org
E-mail: csaas@knology.net
Areas of Expertise: Confederate stamps and postal history

Errors, Freaks and Oddities Collectors Club Expertizing Service
138 East Lakemont Drive
Kingsland GA 31548
Ph: (912) 729-1573
Areas of Expertise: U.S. errors, freaks and oddities

Estonian Philatelic Society Expertizing Service
39 Clafford Lane
Melville NY 11747
Ph: (516) 421-2078
E-mail: esto4@aol.com
Areas of Expertise: Estonia

Hawaiian Philatelic Society Expertizing Service
P.O. Box 10115
Honolulu HI 96816-0115
Areas of Expertise: Hawaii

Hong Kong Stamp Society Expertizing Service
P.O. Box 206
Glenside PA 19038
Fax: (215) 576-6850
Areas of Expertise: Hong Kong

International Association of Philatelic Experts United States Associate members:

Paul Buchsbayew
119 W. 57th St.
New York NY 10019
Ph: (212) 977-7734
Fax: (212) 977-8653
Areas of Expertise: Russia, Soviet Union

William T. Crowe
P.O. Box 2090
Danbury CT 06813-2090
E-mail: wtcrowe@aol.com
Areas of Expertise: United States

John Lievsay
(see American Philatelic Expertizing Service and Philatelic Foundation)
Areas of Expertise: France

Robert W. Lyman
P.O. Box 348
Irvington on Hudson NY 10533
Ph and Fax: (914) 591-6937
Areas of Expertise: British North America, New Zealand

Robert Odenweller
P.O. Box 401
Bernardsville NJ 07924-0401
Ph and Fax: (908) 766-5460
Areas of Expertise: New Zealand, Samoa to 1900

Sergio Sismondo
10035 Carousel Center Drive
Syracuse NY 13290-0001
Ph: (315) 422-2331
Fax: (315) 422-2956
Areas of Expertise: British East Africa, Camerouns,.Cape of Good Hope, Canada, British North America

International Society for Japanese Philately Expertizing Committee
132 North Pine Terrace
Staten Island NY 10312-4052
Ph: (718) 227-5229
Areas of Expertise: Japan and related areas, except WWII Japanese Occupation issues

International Society for Portuguese Philately Expertizing Service
P.O. Box 43146
Philadelphia PA 19129-3146
Ph and Fax: (215) 843-2106
E-mail: s.s.washburne@worldnet.att.net
Areas of Expertise: Portugal and Colonies

Mexico-Elmhurst Philatelic Society International Expert Committee
P.O. Box 1133
West Covina CA 91793
Areas of Expertise: Mexico

Ukrainian Philatelic & Numismatic Society Expertizing Service
30552 Dell Lane
Warren MI 48092-1862
Areas of Expertise: Ukraine, Western Ukraine

V. G. Greene Philatelic Research Foundation
P.O. Box 204, Station Q
Toronto, ON, M4T 2M1
CANADA
Ph: (416) 921-2073
Fax: (416) 921-1282
www.greenefoundation.ca
E-mail: vggfoundation@on.aibn.com
Areas of Expertise: British North America

Information on Catalogue Values, Grade and Condition

Catalogue Value

The Scott Catalogue value is a retail value; that is, an amount you could expect to pay for a stamp in the grade of Very Fine with no faults. Any exceptions to the grade valued will be noted in the text. The general introduction on the following pages and the individual section introductions further explain the type of material that is valued. The value listed for any given stamp is a reference that reflects recent actual dealer selling prices for that item.

Dealer retail price lists, public auction results, published prices in advertising and individual solicitation of retail prices from dealers, collectors and specialty organizations have been used in establishing the values found in this catalogue. Scott Publishing Co. values stamps, but Scott is not a company engaged in the business of buying and selling stamps as a dealer.

Use this catalogue as a guide for buying and selling. The actual price you pay for a stamp may be higher or lower than the catalogue value because of many different factors, including the amount of personal service a dealer offers, or increased or decreased interest in the country or topic represented by a stamp or set. An item may occasionally be offered at a lower price as a "loss leader," or as part of a special sale. You also may obtain an item inexpensively at public auction because of little interest at that time or as part of a large lot.

Stamps that are of a lesser grade than Very Fine, or those with condition problems, generally trade at lower prices than those given in this catalogue. Stamps of exceptional quality in both grade and condition often command higher prices than those listed.

Values for pre-1900 unused issues are for stamps with approximately half or more of their original gum. Stamps with most or all of their original gum may be expected to sell for somewhat more, and stamps with less than half of their original gum may be expected to sell for somewhat less than the values listed. On rarer stamps, it may be expected that the original gum will be somewhat more disturbed than it will be on more common issues. Unused stamps issued from 1900 to the present are assumed to have full original gum. From breakpoints in most countries' listings, stamps are valued as never hinged, due to the wide availability of stamps in that condition. These notations are prominently placed in the listings and in the country information preceding the listings. Some countries also feature listings with dual values for hinged and never-hinged stamps.

Values for early and valuable stamps are for examples with certificates of authenticity from acknowledged expert committees, or examples sold with the buyer having the right of certification. This applies to examples with original gum as well as examples without gum. Beware of stamps offered "as is," as the gum on some unused stamps offered with "original gum" may be fraudulent, and stamps offered as unused without gum may in some cases be altered used stamps.

Grade

A stamp's grade and condition are crucial to its value. The accompanying illustrations show examples of Very Fine stamps from different time periods, along with examples of stamps in Fine to Very Fine and Extremely Fine grades as points of reference. When a stamp seller offers a stamp in any grade from fine to superb without further qualifying statements, that stamp should not only have the centering grade as defined, but it also should be free of faults or other condition problems.

FINE-VERY FINE stamps may be somewhat off center on one side, or slightly off center on two sides. Imperforate stamps will have two full margins, and the design will not touch any edge. For perforated stamps, the perfs are well clear of the design, but are still noticeably off center. *However, early issues of a country may be printed in such a way that the design naturally is very close to the edges. In these cases, the perforations may cut into the design very slightly.* Used stamps will not have a cancellation that detracts from the design.

VERY FINE stamps may be slightly off center on one or two sides, but the design will be well clear of the edge. The stamp will present a nice, balanced appearance. Imperforate stamps will have four full margins. *However, early issues of many countries may be printed in such a way that the perforations may touch the design on one or more sides. Where this is the case, a boxed note will be found defining the*

centering and margins of the stamps being valued. Used stamps will have light or otherwise neat cancellations. This is the grade used to establish Scott Catalogue values.

EXTREMELY FINE stamps are close to being perfectly centered. Imperforate stamps will have even margins that are larger than full margins. *Even the earliest perforated issues will have perforations clear of the design on all sides.*

Scott Publishing Co. recognizes that there is no formally enforced grading scheme for postage stamps, and that the final price you pay or obtain for a stamp will be determined by individual agreement at the time of transaction.

Full Margins

The spacing of the designs of classic stamps on their plates differ widely between countries and often between issues of a single country or sometimes even between stamps within a single issue. Because margin size is a significant determinant of grade and value, the *Scott Classic Specialized Catalogue* often includes the dimensions of "full margins" in millimeters in the listings. "Full margin" (a term coined by Edwin Mueller in his catalogue of imperforate European stamps) is defined as half the space between two stamps on the plate. It is the margin that would result from a stamp being cut from its neighbor exactly in the center of the margin space between the stamps. Since the spacing of many early classics is somewhat irregular, the average spacing is used. The horizontal and vertical margins may not be equal on the plate, and in such instances both measurements are given, vertical margins first followed by horizontal margins. In instances where different printings of a single issue were made from plates differing in spacing, the smallest existing spacing is given. Scott has adopted the Mueller convention of giving 1/4mm as the smallest "full margin" measurement even in those cases where there was almost no space between the designs on a plate.

Condition

Grade addresses only centering and (for used stamps) cancellation. *Condition* refers to factors other than grade that affect a stamp's desirability.

Factors that can increase the value of a stamp include exceptionally wide margins, particularly fresh color, the presence of selvage, and plate or die varieties. Unusual cancels on used stamps (particularly those of the 19th century) can greatly enhance their value as well.

Factors other than faults that decrease the value of a stamp include loss of original gum, regumming, a hinge remnant or foreign object adhering to the gum, natural inclusions, straight edges, and markings or notations applied by collectors or dealers.

Faults include missing pieces, tears, pin or other holes, surface scuffs, thin spots, creases, toning, short or pulled perforations, clipped perforations, oxidation or other forms of color changelings, soiling, stains, and such man-made changes as reperforations or the chemical removal or lightening of a cancellation.

Grading Illustrations

On the following seven pages are illustrations of various stamps from countries appearing in *The Classic Specialized Catalogue*. These stamps are arranged by country, and they represent early or important issues that are often found in widely different grades in the marketplace. The editors believe the illustrations will prove useful in showing the margin size and centering that will be seen on the various issues.

Use this Illustrated Grading Chart in conjunction with the Illustrated Gum Chart that follows it to better understand the grade and gum condition of stamps valued in the Scott Catalogues.

In addition to the matters of margin size, centering and original gum, collectors are reminded that the very fine stamps valued in the Scott catalogues also will possess fresh color and intact perforations, and they will be free from defects.

The three grades shown for each stamp are computer manipulated using single digitized master illustrations.

Fine-Very Fine ➡️

SCOTT
CATALOGUES
VALUE
STAMPS IN
THIS GRADE

Very Fine ➡️

Extremely Fine ➡️

Fine-Very Fine ➡️

SCOTT
CATALOGUES
VALUE
STAMPS IN
THIS GRADE

Very Fine ➡️

Extremely Fine ➡️

Fine-Very Fine →

SCOTT
CATALOGUES
VALUE
STAMPS IN
THIS GRADE

Very Fine →

Extremely Fine →

Fine-Very Fine →

SCOTT
CATALOGUES
VALUE
STAMPS IN
THIS GRADE

Very Fine →

Extremely Fine →

Fine-Very Fine →

SCOTT CATALOGUES VALUE STAMPS IN THIS GRADE

Very Fine →

Extremely Fine →

Fine-Very Fine →

SCOTT CATALOGUES VALUE STAMPS IN THIS GRADE

Very Fine →

Extremely Fine →

Fine-Very Fine

SCOTT CATALOGUES VALUE STAMPS IN THIS GRADE

Very Fine

Extremely Fine

Fine-Very Fine

SCOTT CATALOGUES VALUE STAMPS IN THIS GRADE

Very Fine

Extremely Fine

Fine-Very Fine

SCOTT
CATALOGUES
VALUE
STAMPS IN
THIS GRADE

Very Fine

Extremely Fine

Fine-Very Fine

SCOTT
CATALOGUES
VALUE
STAMPS IN
THIS GRADE

Very Fine

Extremely Fine

For purposes of helping to determine the gum condition and value of an unused stamp, Scott Publishing Co. presents the following chart which details different gum conditions and indicates how the conditions correlate with the Scott values for unused stamps. Used together, the Illustrated Grading Chart on the previous pages and this Illustrated Gum Chart should allow catalogue users to better understand the grade and gum condition of stamps valued in the *Scott Classic Specialized Catalogue.*

Gum Categories:	MINT N.H.	ORIGINAL GUM (O.G.)				NO GUM
	Mint Never Hinged *Free from any disturbance*	**Lightly Hinged** *Faint impression of a removed hinge over a small area*	**Hinge Mark or Remnant** *Prominent hinged spot with part or all of the hinge remaining*	**Large part o.g.** *Approximately half or more of the gum intact*	**Small part o.g.** *Approximately less than half of the gum intact*	**No gum** *Only if issued with gum*
Commonly Used Symbol:	★★	★	★	★	★	(★)
Pre-1900 Issues (Pre-1879 for U.S.)	Very fine pre-1900 stamps in these categories trade at a premium over Scott value			Scott Value for "Unused"		Scott "No Gum" listings for selected unused classic stamps
From 1900 to break-points for listings of never-hinged stamps	Scott "Never Hinged" listings for selected unused stamps	Scott Value for "Unused" (Actual value will be affected by the degree of hinging of the full o.g.)				
From breakpoints noted for many countries	Scott Value for "Unused"					

Never Hinged (NH; ★★): A never-hinged stamp will have full original gum that will have no hinge mark or disturbance. The presence of an expertizer's mark does not disqualify a stamp from this designation.

Original Gum (OG; ★): Pre-1900 stamps should have approximately half or more of their original gum. On rarer stamps, it may be expected that the original gum will be somewhat more disturbed than it will be on more common issues. Stamps issued from 1900 to the present should have full original gum. Original gum will show some disturbance caused by a previous hinge(s) which may be present or entirely removed. The actual value of a stamp issued from 1900 to the present will be affected by the degree of hinging of the full original gum.

Disturbed Original Gum: Gum showing noticeable effects of humidity, climate or hinging over more than half of the gum. The significance of gum disturbance in valuing a stamp in any of the Original Gum categories depends on the degree of disturbance, the rarity and normal gum condition of the issue and other variables affecting quality.

Regummed (RG; (★)): A regummed stamp is a stamp without gum that has had some type of gum privately applied at a time after it was issued. This normally is done to deceive collectors and/or dealers into thinking that the stamp has original gum and therefore has a higher value. A regummed stamp is considered the same as a stamp with none of its original gum for purposes of grading.

Catalogue Values for Stamps on Covers

Definition of a Cover

Covers are philatelically defined as folded letters, folded covers or envelopes, with or without postage stamps, that have passed through the mail and bear postal or other markings of philatelic interest. Before the introduction of envelopes about 1840, people folded letters and wrote the address on the outside. Many people covered their letters with an extra sheet of paper on the outside for the address, producing the term "cover." Used stamped envelopes and wrappers and other items of postal stationery also are considered covers. Additionally, a newspaper stamp properly used on a newspaper or newspaper wrapper is considered to be an "on cover" usage, as is a postage stamp used on a post card. Occasionally, the term "newsprint" is used; this refers to either a newspaper or a one-page printed leaflet.

Catalogue Value

The Scott Catalogue value for a stamp on cover, as for a stamp off cover, is a retail value; that is, an amount you could expect to pay for that cover in a grade of Very Fine, as defined below. Folded letters, folded covers, envelopes, stationery entires and newspapers are valued as whole and complete, not as fronts of letter sheets or envelopes or as fragments of newspapers or circulars. Values given are for covers bearing stamps that are "tied on" by the cancellation. A stamp is said to be "tied" to a cover when the cancellation or postmark falls on both the stamp and the cover. Exceptions, such as some of the listings for newspaper stamps used on newspapers, always will be noted. Values for bisected, trisected, etc. stamps on cover are for items on which the cancellation ties the stamp across the cut. Values for U.S. patriotic covers of the Civil War period (bearing pictorial designs of a patriotic nature) are for the most common designs.

It should be noted that conventions observed for calculating the catalogue value of a cover with several different stamps vary somewhat between countries and types of covers. In a general way, however, the most common procedure may be summarized as follows: the stamp which has the highest "value on cover" is counted with its on-cover value, while the other stamps are added on to the total with their normal value as used stamps "off cover."

The value generally is given for the stamps as they are most commonly found on a cover. In some cases a stamp is most commonly found alone, paying a specified rate for the envelope, given its weight, destination and method of intended delivery. For instance, a one-half ounce letter sent internally in England by ordinary first class mail during the 19th century needed one penny of postage. Since such letters were very common, it follows that stamps with denominations of one penny are most often found on envelopes or folded letters paying that one-half ounce internal rate. One penny stamps also are found on letters together with other stamps making up different rates. A pair of one penny stamps may pay for a double weight envelope, four one penny stamps for an envelope addressed to France, six one penny stamps for an envelope addressed to Prussia, Italy or Spain, and so forth. Since letters addressed abroad are less common than letters addressed internally, the value of the one penny stamps given refers to the single usage. That is not true across the board, as there are many stamps issued during the 19th century that are more scarce used singly than in combination with other stamps. In all these other cases, the value given is intended to reflect the least scarce of the combinations.

If the value of a single stamp on a cover is of particular philatelic

---

Countries with listings for stamps on covers in the *Scott Classic Specialized Catalogue of Stamps & Covers*

United States	Chile	Prussia	Liechtenstein	Somali Coast
Confederate States	Cochin-China	Saxony	Luxembourg	South Africa
Guam	Corfu	Schleswig-Holstein	Madagascar (French Offices)	Southern Rhodesia
Hawaii	Cuba	Thurn and Taxis	Madeira	South West Africa
Aden	Cyrenaica	Wurttemberg	Malta	Spain
La Aguera	Dahomey	North German Confederation	Mariana Islands	Straits Settlements
Aitutaki	Dalmatia	Germany	Marienwerder	Swaziland
Alaouites	Danish West Indies	German Offices Abroad	Marshall Islands	Sweden
Albania	Danzig	China	Martinique	Switzerland
Algeria	Diego-Suarez	Morocco	Mauritania	Tahiti
Allenstein	Denmark	Turkish Empire	Mauritius	Tannu Tuva
Spanish Andorra	Ecuador	Grand Comoro	Mayotte	Togo
French Andorra	Epirus	Great Britain	Memel	Transvaal
Anjouan	Eritrea	Great Britain Offices Abroad	Moheli	Tripolitania
Antigua	Ethiopia	Eritrea	Monaco	Tunisia
Argentina	Fiji	Morocco	Morocco	Ubangi-Shari
Buenos Aires	Fiume	Turkish Empire	Netherlands	Upper Senegal & Niger
Cordoba	Finland	Greece	New Brunswick	Upper Silesia
Corrientes	France	Greenland	New Caledonia	Upper Volta (Burkina Faso)
Ascension	French Offices Abroad	Guadeloupe	Newfoundland	Uruguay
Australia	China	Heligoland	New Hebrides, French	Wallis & Futuna Islands
Austria	Crete	Hong Kong	New Zealand	Vatican City
Lombardy-Venetia	Egypt-Alexandria	Iceland	Nicaragua	Venezuela
Austrian	Egypt-Port Said	India	Niger	Zanzibar
Offices in Crete	French Colonies	Indo-China	Northern Rhodesia	
Offices in the Turkish Empire	French Congo	Inini	Norway	
Barbados	French Equatorial Africa	Iran	Nossi Be	
Basutoland	French Guiana	Italian Colonies	Nova Scotia	
Batum	French Guinea	Italian East Africa	Nyasaland Protectorate	
Bechuanaland Protectorate	French India	Italian States	Obock	
Belgian Congo	French Morocco	Modena	Oltre Giuba	
Belgium	French Polynesia	Parma	Paraguay	
Benin	French Sudan	Romagna	Peru	
Bermuda	Gabon	Roman States	Philippines	
Bolivia	German East Africa	Sardinia	Portugal	
Bosnia and Herzegovina	German New Guinea	Tuscany	Prince Edward Island	
Brazil	German South West Africa	Two Sicilies	Puerto Rico	
British Columbia and	German States	Italy	Reunion	
Vancouver Island	Baden	Italian Offices Abroad	Ruanda-Urundi	
British Guiana	Bavaria	China	Russia	
British Honduras	Bergedorf	Africa	Saar	
Bulgaria	Bremen	Crete	Ste.-Marie de Madagascar	
Cameroun	Brunswick	Turkish Empire	St. Pierre & Miquelon	
Canada	Hamburg	Aegean Islands	Samoa	
Cape Juby	Hanover	Ivory Coast	San Marino	
Caroline Islands	Lubeck	Kiauchau	Saudi Arabia	
Castellorizo	Mecklenburg-Schwerin	Labuan	Senegal	
Ceylon	Mecklenburg-Strelitz	Latakia	Senegambia & Niger	
Chad	Oldenburg	Libya	Somalia	

importance, as in the case of the stamps that pay for reduced rates for the delivery of newspapers or other printed matter, then their different value for this usage is indicated in footnotes or as a separate listing. It clearly is impossible to add to a catalogue of worldwide stamps the detailed information regarding the relative scarcity and value of all rates and combinations. We have limited ourselves to some of the more noteworthy and important cases.

In the majority of cases, the value of a cover assumes that the stamps on it have been used in the period contemporaneous with their issuance. Late uses are sometimes considered premium items, but in most cases late and very late usages are of no significance in postal history and detract from the value of the cover.

Condition

When evaluating a cover, care must be given to the factors that determine the overall condition of the item. It is generally more difficult to grade and evaluate a cover than a stamp. The condition of the stamps affixed to the cover must be taken into account — always in relation to the criteria for the particular issue. The Scott Catalogue does specify the grade and condition of the stamps for which a value is given, so it is important to consult this information. In addition, the condition of the cover must be taken into account. Values are for covers that are reasonably well preserved given the period of usage and the country of origin. A tiny nick or tear, or slight reduction from opening, are normal for 19th century covers. Folded letters may be expected to have tears on the reverse from opening, and often they will have file folds. Unless these factors affect the stamps or postal markings, they should not detract from the on-cover values given in the catalogue.

Just as with stamps, various factors can lower the value of a cover. Missing pieces, serious tears, holes, creases, toning, stains and alterations of postal markings are examples of factors that lower the value of a cover. The necessity of considering these factors for the cover, as well as having to consider the condition of the stamps on the cover, helps to explain why it is more difficult to determine the value of a cover than a stamp off cover.

Factors Enhancing the Value of a Cover

A further difficulty in the valuation of covers is the necessity of considering factors other than the stamps used on a cover and the condition of the stamps and the cover. As stated previously, catalogue values listed herein generally reflect the most common uses of stamps on covers that are reasonably well preserved given the period of usage. Consideration of factors that may enhance the value of covers for the most part is beyond the scope of the Scott Catalogue. However, it is critical to understand that there are many such factors. Following is a list of many of the factors that often will increase the value of a cover.

- postal markings indicating origin, transit and arrival;
- postal markings indicating rates paid, which include postage, registration, acknowledgment of receipt, express charges, insurance, postage due, forwarding and many others;
- postal markings indicating carriers such as stagecoaches, trains, ships, aircraft, etc.;
- markings applied by censors, other civilian or military authorities, and others;

- scarce or rare destinations and routings;
- interruptions in the delivery system due to accidents, wars, natural calamities, etc.;
- unusual combinations of stamps;
- printed or hand-drawn pictorial, advertising or patriotic cover designs;
- unusual quality of stamps, postal markings or cover;
- and, outside of postal history, particularly noteworthy addressee, sender or contents.

Catalogue Listing Policy

It is the intent of Scott Publishing Co. to list all postage stamps of the world in the *Scott Standard Postage Stamp Catalogue*. The only strict criteria for listing is that stamps be decreed legal for postage by the issuing country and that the issuing country actually have an operating postal system. Whether the primary intent of issuing a given stamp or set was for sale to postal patrons or to stamp collectors is not part of our listing criteria. Scott's role is to provide basic comprehensive postage stamp information. It is up to each stamp collector to choose which items to include in a collection.

It is Scott's objective to seek reasons why a stamp should be listed, rather than why it should not. Nevertheless, there are certain types of items that will not be listed. These include the following:

1. Unissued items that are not officially distributed or released by the issuing postal authority. If such items are officially issued at a later date by the country, they will be listed. Unissued items consist of those that have been printed and then held from sale for reasons such as change in government, errors found on stamps or something deemed objectionable about a stamp subject or design.

2. Stamps "issued" by non-existent postal entities or fantasy countries, such as Nagaland, Occusi-Ambeno, Staffa, Sedang, Torres Straits and others. Also, stamps "issued" in the name of legitimate stamp-issuing countries that are not authorized by those countries.

3. Semi-official or unofficial items not required for postage. Examples include items issued by private agencies for their own express services. When such items are required for delivery, or are valid as prepayment of postage, they are listed.

4. Local stamps issued for local use only. Postage stamps issued by governments specifically for "domestic" use, such as Haiti Scott 219-228, or the United States non-denominated stamps, are not considered to be locals, since they are valid for postage throughout the country of origin.

5. Items not valid for postal use. For example, a few countries have issued souvenir sheets that are not valid for postage. This area also includes a number of worldwide charity labels (some denominated) that do not pay postage.

6. Intentional varieties, such as imperforate stamps that look like their perforated counterparts and are issued in very small quantities. Also, other egregiously exploitative issues such as stamps sold for far more than face value, stamps purposely issued in artificially small quantities or only against advance orders, stamps awarded only to a selected audience such as a philatelic bureau's standing order customers, or stamps sold only in conjunction with other products. All of these kinds of items are usually controlled issues and/or are intended for speculation. These items normally will be included in a footnote.

7. Items distributed by the issuing government only to a limited group, such as a stamp club, philatelic exhibition or a single stamp dealer or other private company. These items normally will be included in a footnote.

The fact that a stamp has been used successfully as postage, even on international mail, is not in itself sufficient proof that it was legitimately issued. Numerous examples of so-called stamps from non-existent countries are known to have been used to post letters that have successfully passed through the international mail system.

There are certain items that are subject to interpretation. When a stamp falls outside our specifications, it may be listed along with a cautionary footnote.

A number of factors are considered in our approach to analyzing how a stamp is listed. The following list of factors is presented to share with you, the catalogue user, the complexity of the listing process.

Additional printings — "Additional printings" of a previously issued stamp may range from an item that is totally different to cases where it is impossible to differentiate from the original. At least a minor number (a small-letter suffix) is assigned if there is a distinct change in stamp shade, noticeably redrawn design, or a significantly different perforation measurement. A major number (numeral or numeral and capital-letter combination) is assigned if the editors feel the "additional printing" is sufficiently different from the original that it constitutes a different issue.

Commemoratives — Where practical, commemoratives with the same theme are placed in a set. Occasionally, however, stamp sets that were released over a period of years have been separated. Appropriately placed footnotes will guide you to each set's continuation.

Definitive sets — Blocks of numbers generally have been reserved for definitive sets, based on previous experience with any given country. If a few more stamps were issued in a set than originally expected, they often have been inserted into the original set with a capital-letter suffix, such as U.S. Scott 634A. If many more stamps than the originally allotted block were released before the set was completed, two or more blocks of numbers may have been needed to accomodate the entire set or series. Appropriately placed footnotes will guide you to each set's continuation.

Overprints — The color of an overprint is always noted if it is other than black. Where more than one color of ink has been used on overprints of a single set, the color used is noted. Early overprint and surcharge illustrations were altered to prevent their use by forgers.

Understanding the Listings

On the opposite page is an enlarged "typical" listing from this catalogue. Below are detailed explanations of each of the highlighted parts of the listing.

1 Scott number — Scott catalogue numbers are used to identify specific items when buying, selling or trading stamps. Each listed postage stamp from every country has a unique Scott catalogue number. Therefore, Germany Scott 99, for example, can only refer to a single stamp. Although the Scott catalogue usually lists stamps in chronological order by date of issue, there are exceptions. When a country has issued a set of stamps over a period of time, those stamps within the set are kept together without regard to date of issue. This follows the normal collecting approach of keeping stamps in their natural sets.

When a country issues a set of stamps over a period of time, a group of consecutive catalogue numbers is reserved for the stamps in that set, as issued. If that group of numbers proves to be too few, capital-letter suffixes, such as "A" or "B," may be added to existing numbers to create enough catalogue numbers to cover all items in the set. A capital-letter suffix indicates a major Scott catalogue number listing. Scott uses a suffix letter only once. Therefore, a catalogue number listing with a capital-letter suffix will not also be found with the same letter (lower case) used as a minor-letter listing. If there is a Scott 16A in a set, for example, there will not also be a Scott 16a. However, a minor-letter "a" listing may be added to a major number containing an "A" suffix (Scott 16Aa, for example).

Suffix letters are cumulative. A minor "b" variety of Scott 16A would be Scott 16Ab, not Scott 16b.

There are times when a reserved block of Scott catalogue numbers is too large for a set, leaving some numbers unused. Such gaps in the numbering sequence also occur when the catalogue editors move an item's listing elsewhere or have removed it entirely from the catalogue. Scott does not attempt to account for every possible number, but rather attempts to assure that each stamp is assigned its own number.

Scott numbers designating regular postage normally are only numerals. Scott numbers for other types of stamps, such as air post, semi-postal, postal tax, postage due, occupation and others have a prefix consisting of one or more capital letters or a combination of numerals and capital letters.

2 Illustration number — Illustration or design-type numbers are used to identify each catalogue illustration. For most sets, the lowest face-value stamp is shown. It then serves as an example of the basic design approach for other stamps not illustrated. Where more than one stamp use the same illustration number, but have differences in design, the design paragraph or the description line clearly indicates the design on each stamp not illustrated. Where there are both vertical and horizontal designs in a set, a single illustration may be used, with the exceptions noted in the design paragraph or description line.

When an illustration is followed by a lower-case letter in parentheses, such as "A2(b)," the trailing letter indicates which overprint or surcharge illustration applies.

Illustrations normally are 70 percent of the original size of the stamp. Oversized stamps, blocks and souvenir sheets are reduced even more. Overprints and surcharges are shown at 100 percent of their original size if shown alone, but are 70 percent of original size if shown on stamps. In some cases, the illustration will be placed above the set, between listings or omitted completely. Overprint and surcharge illustrations are not placed in this catalogue for purposes of expertizing stamps.

3 Paper color — The color of a stamp's paper is noted in italic type when the paper used is not white.

4 Listing styles — There are two principal types of catalogue listings: major and minor.

Major listings are in a larger type style than minor listings. The catalogue number is a numeral that can be found with or without a capital-letter suffix, and with or without a prefix.

Minor listings are in a smaller type style and have a small-letter suffix or (if the listing immediately follows that of the major number) may show only the letter. These listings identify a variety of the major

item. Examples include perforation, color, watermark or printing method differences, multiples (some souvenir sheets, booklet panes and se-tenant combinations), and singles of multiples.

Examples of major number listings include 16, 28A, B97, C13A, 10N5, and 10N6A. Examples of minor numbers are 16a and C13Ab.

5 Basic information about a stamp or set — Introducing each stamp issue is a small section (usually a line listing) of basic information about a stamp or set. This section normally includes the date of issue, method of printing, perforation, watermark and, sometimes, some additional information of note. *Printing method, perforation and watermark apply to the following sets until a change is noted.* Stamps created by overprinting or surcharging previous issues are assumed to have the same perforation, watermark, printing method and other production characteristics as the original. Dates of issue are as precise as Scott is able to confirm and often reflect the dates on first-day covers, rather than the actual date of release.

6 Denomination — This normally refers to the face value of the stamp; that is, the cost of the unused stamp at the post office at the time of issue. When a denomination is shown in parentheses, it does not appear on the stamp. This includes the non-denominated stamps of the United States, Brazil and Great Britain, for example.

7 Color or other description — This area provides information to solidify identification of a stamp. In many recent cases, a description of the stamp design appears in this space, rather than a listing of colors.

8 Year of issue — In stamp sets that have been released in a period that spans more than a year, the number shown in parentheses is the year that stamp first appeared. Stamps without a date appeared during the first year of the issue. Dates are not always given for minor varieties.

9 Value unused and Value used — The Scott catalogue values are based on stamps that are in a grade of Very Fine unless stated otherwise. Unused values refer to items that have not seen postal, revenue or any other duty for which they were intended. Pre-1900 unused stamps that were issued with gum must have at least most of their original gum. Later issues are assumed to have full original gum. From breakpoints specified in most countries' listings, stamps are valued as never hinged. Stamps issued without gum are noted. Modern issues with PVA or other synthetic adhesives may appear ungummed. Self-adhesive stamps are valued as appearing undisturbed on their original backing paper. For a more detailed explanation of these values, please see the "Catalogue Value," "Condition" and "Understanding Valuing Notations" sections elsewhere in this introduction.

In some cases, where used stamps are more valuable than unused stamps, the value is for an example with a contemporaneous cancel, rather than a modern cancel or a smudge or other unclear marking. For those stamps that were released for postal and fiscal purposes, the used value represents a postally used stamp. Stamps with revenue cancels generally sell for less. Scott values for used self-adhesive stamps are for examples either on piece or off piece.

Stamps separated from a complete se-tenant multiple usually will be worth less than a pro-rated portion of the se-tenant multiple, and stamps lacking the attached labels that are noted in the listings will be worth less than the values shown.

10 Changes in basic set information — Bold type is used to show any changes in the basic data given for a set of stamps. These basic categories include perforation gauge measurements, paper type, printing method and watermark.

11 Total value of a set — The total value of sets of three or more stamps issued after 1900 are shown. The set line also notes the range of Scott numbers and total number of stamps included in the grouping. The actual value of a set consisting predominantly of stamps having the minimum value of twenty cents may be less than the total value shown. Similarly, the actual value or catalogue value of se-tenant pairs or of blocks consisting of stamps having the minimum value of twenty cents may be less than the catalogue values of the component parts.

SCOTT NUMBER ❶

ILLUS. NUMBER ❷

PAPER COLOR ❸

LISTING STYLES ❹ MAJORS / MINORS

BASIC INFORMATION ON STAMP OR SET ❺

DENOMINATION ❻

COLOR OR OTHER DESCRIPTION ❼

YEAR OF ISSUE ❽

CATALOGUE VALUES ❾ UNUSED / USED

CHANGES IN BASIC SET INFORMATION ❿

TOTAL VALUE OF SET ⓫

A6

King George VI
A7

1938-44		Engr.		Perf. 12½	
54	A6	½p	green	.25	2.00
54A	A6	½p	dk brown ('42)	.25	2.25
55	A6	1p	dark brown	2.50	.35
55A	A6	1p	green ('42)	.25	1.75
56	A6	1½p	dark carmine	4.00	6.00
56A	A6	1½p	gray ('42)	.25	5.75
57	A6	2p	gray	5.00	1.25
57A	A6	2p	dark car ('42)	.25	2.00
58	A6	3p	blue	.60	1.00
59	A6	4p	rose lilac	1.60	2.00
60	A6	6p	dark violet	2.00	2.00
61	A6	9p	olive bister	2.00	4.75
62	A6	1sh	orange & blk	2.10	3.25

Typo.
Perf. 14
Chalky Paper

63	A7	2sh	ultra & dl vio, *bl*	7.00	17.50
64	A7	2sh6p	red & blk, *bl*	8.00	19.50
65	A7	5sh	red & grn, *yel*	35.00	30.00
a.		5sh	dk red & dp grn, *yel* ('44)	55.00	140.00
66	A7	10sh	red & grn, *grn*	35.00	70.00

Wmk. 3

67	A7	£1	blk & vio, *red*	30.00	45.00
		Nos. 54-67 (18)		136.05	216.35
		Set, never hinged		220.00	

Special Notices

Classification of stamps

The *Scott Standard Postage Stamp Catalogue* lists stamps by country of issue. The next level of organization is a listing by section on the basis of the function of the stamps. The principal sections cover regular postage, semi-postal, air post, special delivery, registration, postage due and other categories. Except for regular postage, catalogue numbers for all sections include a prefix letter (or number-letter combination) denoting the class to which a given stamp belongs.

The following is a listing of the most commonly used catalogue prefixes.

Prefix	Category
C	Air Post
M	Military
P	Newspaper
N	Occupation - Regular Issues
O	Official
Q	Parcel Post
J	Postage Due
RA	Postal Tax
B	Semi-Postal
E	Special Delivery
MR	War Tax

Other prefixes used by more than one country include the following:

H	Acknowledgment of Receipt
CO	Air Post Official
CQ	Air Post Parcel Post
RAC	Air Post Postal Tax
CF	Air Post Registration
CB	Air Post Semi-Postal
CBO	Air Post Semi-Postal Official
CE	Air Post Special Delivery
EY	Authorized Delivery
S	Franchise
G	Insured Letter
GY	Marine Insurance
I	Late Fee
MC	Military Air Post
MQ	Military Parcel Post
NC	Occupation - Air Post
NL	Occupation - Local Post
NO	Occupation - Official
NJ	Occupation - Postage Due
NRA	Occupation - Postal Tax
NB	Occupation - Semi-Postal
NE	Occupation - Special Delivery
QY	Parcel Post Authorized Delivery
AR	Postal-fiscal
RAJ	Postal Tax Due
RAB	Postal Tax Semi-Postal
F	Registration
EB	Semi-Postal Special Delivery
EO	Special Delivery Official
QE	Special Handling

Number changes

A listing of catalogue number additions, deletions and changes from the previous edition of the catalogue appears in each volume. Only number changes affecting the *Classic Specialized Catalogue* have been included in this volume. See *Classic Catalogue* Number Additions, Deletions & Changes in the table of contents for the location of this list.

Understanding valuing notations

The *minimum catalogue value* of an individual stamp or set is 25 cents. This represents a portion of the costs incurred to a dealer when he prepares an individual stamp for resale. As a point of philatelic-economic fact, the lower the value shown for an item in this catalogue, the greater the percentage of that value is attributed to dealer mark up and profit margin. In many cases, such as the 25-cent minimum value, that price does not cover the labor or other costs involved with stocking it as an individual stamp. The sum of minimum values in a set does not properly represent the value of a complete set primarily composed of a number of minimum-value stamps, nor does the sum represent the actual value of a packet made up of minimum-value stamps. Thus a packet of 1,000 different common stamps — each of which has a catalogue value of 25 cents — normally sells for considerably less than 250 dollars!

The *absence of a retail value* for a stamp does not necessarily suggest that a stamp is scarce or rare. In the U.S. listings, a dash in the value column means that the stamp is known in a stated form or variety, but information is either lacking or insufficient for purposes of establishing a usable catalogue value.

Stamp values in *italics* generally refer to items that are difficult to value accurately. For expensive items, such as those priced at $1,000 or higher, a value in italics indicates that the affected item trades very seldom. For inexpensive items, a value in italics represents a warning. One example is a "blocked" issue where the issuing postal administration may have controlled one stamp in a set in an attempt to make the whole set more valuable. Another example is an item that sold at an extreme multiple of face value in the marketplace at the time of its issue.

One type of warning to collectors that appears in the catalogue is illustrated by a stamp that is valued considerably higher in used condition than it is as unused. In this case, collectors are cautioned to be certain the used version has a genuine and contemporaneous cancellation. The type of cancellation on a stamp can be an important factor in determining its sale price. Catalogue values do not apply to fiscal or telegraph cancels, unless otherwise noted.

Some countries have released back issues of stamps in canceled-to-order form, sometimes covering as much as a 10-year period. The Scott Catalogue values for used stamps reflect canceled-to-order material when such stamps are found to predominate in the marketplace for the issue involved. Notes frequently appear in the stamp listings to specify which items are valued as canceled-to-order, or if there is a premium for postally used examples.

Many countries sell canceled-to-order stamps at a marked reduction of face value. Countries that sell or have sold canceled-to-order stamps at *full* face value include Australia, Netherlands, France and Switzerland. It may be almost impossible to identify such stamps if the gum has been removed, because official government canceling devices are used. Postally used copies of these items on cover, however, are usually worth more than the canceled-to-order stamps with original gum.

Abbreviations

Scott Publishing Co. uses a consistent set of abbreviations throughout this catalogue to conserve space, while still providing necessary information.

COLOR ABBREVIATIONS

amb..... amber	crim..... crimson	ol .... olive
anil...... aniline	cr .... cream	olvn ..... olivine
ap........ apple	dk .... dark	org....... orange
aqua ... aquamarine	dl .... dull	pck ...... peacock
az .... azure	dp .... deep	pnksh .. pinkish
bis .... bister	db .... drab	Prus ..... Prussian
bl .... blue	emer.... emerald	pur....... purple
bld....... blood	gldn .... golden	redsh... reddish
blk .... black	grysh .. grayish	res .... reseda
bril...... brilliant	grn....... green	ros .... rosine
brn....... brown	grnsh... greenish	ryl........ royal
brnsh... brownish	hel ...... heliotrope	sal .... salmon
brnz..... bronze	hn .... henna	saph..... sapphire
brt........ bright	ind....... indigo	scar ..... scarlet
brnt...... burnt	int .... intense	sep ...... sepia
car .... carmine	lav .... lavender	sien ..... sienna
cer .... cerise	lem ...... lemon	sil......... silver
chlky.... chalky	lil .... lilac	sl.......... slate
cham... chamois	lt .... light	stl......... steel
chnt ..... chestnut	mag..... magenta	turq...... turquoise
choc..... chocolate	man..... manila	ultra...... ultramarine
chr .... chrome	mar...... maroon	Ven ..... Venetian
cit........ citron	mv .... mauve	ver .... vermilion
cl......... claret	multi.....multicolored	vio........ violet
cob ...... cobalt	mlky .... milky	yel........ yellow
cop ...... copper	myr ...... myrtle	yelsh.... yellowish

When no color is given for an overprint or surcharge, black is the color used. Abbreviations for colors used for overprints and surcharges include: "(B)" or "(Blk)," black; "(Bl)," blue; "(R)," red; and "(G)," green.

Additional abbreviations in this catalogue are shown below:

Adm. ....Administration
AFL..................American Federation of Labor
Anniv...............Anniversary
APS ....American Philatelic Society
Assoc. ....Association
ASSR...............Autonomous Soviet Socialist Republic
b. ....Born
BEP..................Bureau of Engraving and Printing
Bicent..............Bicentennial
Bklt. ....Booklet
Brit..................British
btwn. ....Between
Bur. ....Bureau
c. or ca.............Circa
Cat. ....Catalogue
Cent. ....Centennial, century, centenary
CIO ....Congress of Industrial Organizations
Conf. ....Conference
Cong. ....Congress
Cpl. ....Corporal
CTO ....Canceled to order
d. ....Died
Dbl. ....Double
EDU.................Earliest documented use
Engr.................Engraved
Exhib...............Exhibition
Expo.................Exposition
Fed. ....Federation
GB ....Great Britain
Gen. ....General
GPO ....General post office
Horiz. ....Horizontal
Imperf. ....Imperforate
Impt.................Imprint

Intl. ....International
Invtd. ....Inverted
L ....Left
Lieut., lt............Lieutenant
Litho. ....Lithographed
LL ....Lower left
LR ....Lower right
mm ....Millimeter
Ms. ....Manuscript
Natl..................National
No....................Number
NY ....New York
NYC..................New York City
Ovpt. ....Overprint
Ovptd. ....Overprinted
P ....Plate number
Perf. ....Perforated, perforation
Phil. ....Philatelic
Photo................Photogravure
PO ....Post office
Pr. ....Pair
P.R. ....Puerto Rico
Prec. ....Precancel, precanceled
Pres. ....President
PTT ....Post, Telephone and Telegraph
Rio...................Rio de Janeiro
Sgt...................Sergeant
Soc. ....Society
Souv. ....Souvenir
SSR ....Soviet Socialist Republic, see ASSR
St.....................Saint, street
Surch. ....Surcharge
Typo. ....Typographed
UL....................Upper left
Unwmkd. ....Unwatermarked
UPU ....Universal Postal Union
UR ....Upper right
US ....United States
USPOD ....United States Post Office Department
USSR ....Union of Soviet Socialist Republics
Vert..................Vertical
VP ....Vice president
Wmk..................Watermark
Wmkd. ....Watermarked
WWI ....World War I
WWII ....World War II

Examination

Scott Publishing Co. will not comment upon the genuineness, grade or condition of stamps, because of the time and responsibility involved. Rather, there are several expertizing groups that undertake this work for both collectors and dealers. Neither will Scott Publishing Co. appraise or identify philatelic material. The company cannot take responsibility for unsolicited stamps or covers sent by individuals.

How to order from your dealer

When ordering stamps from a dealer, it is not necessary to write the full description of a stamp as listed in this catalogue. All you need is the name of the country, the Scott catalogue number and whether the desired item is unused or used. For example, "Japan Scott 422 unused" is sufficient to identify the unused stamp of Japan listed as "422 A206 5y brown."

Basic Stamp Information

A stamp collector's knowledge of the combined elements that make a given stamp issue unique determines his or her ability to identify stamps. These elements include paper, watermark, method of separation, printing, design and gum. On the following pages each of these important areas is briefly described.

Paper

Paper is an organic material composed of a compacted weave of cellulose fibers and generally formed into sheets. Paper used to print stamps may be manufactured in sheets, or it may have been part of a large roll (called a web) before being cut to size. The fibers most often used to create paper on which stamps are printed include bark, wood, straw and certain grasses. In many cases, linen or cotton rags have been added for greater strength and durability. Grinding, bleaching, cooking and rinsing these raw fibers reduces them to a slushy pulp, referred to by paper makers as "stuff." Sizing and, sometimes, coloring matter is added to the pulp to make different types of finished paper.

After the stuff is prepared, it is poured onto sieve-like frames that allow the water to run off, while retaining the matted pulp. As fibers fall onto the screen and are held by gravity, they form a natural weave that will later hold the paper together. If the screen has metal bits that are formed into letters or images attached, it leaves slightly thinned areas on the paper. These are called watermarks.

When the stuff is almost dry, it is passed under pressure through smooth or engraved rollers - dandy rolls - or placed between cloth in a press to be flattened and dried.

Stamp paper falls broadly into two types: wove and laid. The nature of the surface of the frame onto which the pulp is first deposited causes the differences in appearance between the two. If the surface is smooth and even, the paper will be of fairly uniform texture throughout. This is known as *wove paper*. Early papermaking machines poured the pulp onto a continuously circulating web of felt, but modern machines feed the pulp onto a cloth-like screen made of closely interwoven fine wires. This paper, when held to a light, will show little dots or points very close together. The proper name for this is "wire wove," but the type is still considered wove. Any U.S. or British stamp printed after 1880 will serve as an example of wire wove paper.

Closely spaced parallel wires, with cross wires at wider intervals, make up the frames used for what is known as *laid paper*. A greater thickness of the pulp will settle between the wires. The paper, when held to a light, will show alternate light and dark lines. The spacing and the thickness of the lines may vary, but on any one sheet of paper they are all alike. See Russia Scott 31-38 for examples of laid paper.

Batonne, from the French word meaning "a staff," is a term used if the lines in the paper are spaced quite far apart, like the printed ruling on a writing tablet. Batonne paper may be either wove or laid. If laid, fine laid lines can be seen between the batons. The laid lines, which are a form of watermark, may be geometrical figures such as squares, diamonds, rectangles or wavy lines.

Quadrille is the term used when the lines in the paper form little squares. *Oblong quadrille* is the term used when rectangles, rather than squares, are formed. See Mexico-Guadalajara Scott 35-37 for examples of oblong quadrille paper.

Paper also is classified as thick or thin, hard or soft, and by color if dye is added during manufacture. Such colors may include yellowish, greenish, bluish and reddish.

Brief explanations of other types of paper used for printing stamps, as well as examples, follow.

Pelure — Pelure paper is a very thin, hard and often brittle paper that is sometimes bluish or grayish in appearance. See Serbia Scott 169-170.

Native — This is a term applied to handmade papers used to produce some of the early stamps of the Indian states. Stamps printed on native paper may be expected to display various natural inclusions that are normal and do not negatively affect value. Japanese paper, originally made of mulberry fibers and rice flour, is part of this group. See Japan Scott 1-18.

Manila — This type of paper is often used to make stamped envelopes and wrappers. It is a coarse-textured stock, usually smooth on one side and rough on the other. A variety of colors of manila paper exist, but the most common range is yellowish-brown.

Silk — Introduced by the British in 1847 as a safeguard against counterfeiting, silk paper contains bits of colored silk thread scattered throughout. The density of these fibers varies greatly and can include as few as one fiber per stamp or hundreds. U.S. revenue Scott R152 is a good example of an easy-to-identify silk paper stamp.

Silk-thread paper has uninterrupted threads of colored silk arranged so that one or more threads run through the stamp or postal stationery. See Great Britain Scott 5-6 and Switzerland Scott 14-19.

Granite — Filled with minute cloth or colored paper fibers of various colors and lengths, granite paper should not be confused with either type of silk paper. Austria Scott 172-175 and a number of Swiss stamps are examples of granite paper.

Chalky — A chalk-like substance coats the surface of chalky paper to discourage the cleaning and reuse of canceled stamps, as well as to provide a smoother, more acceptable printing surface. Because the designs of stamps printed on chalky paper are imprinted on what is often a water-soluble coating, any attempt to remove a cancellation will destroy the stamp. *Do not soak these stamps in any fluid.* To remove a stamp printed on chalky paper from an envelope, wet the paper from underneath the stamp until the gum dissolves enough to release the stamp from the paper. See St. Kitts-Nevis Scott 89-90 for examples of stamps printed on this type of chalky paper.

India — Another name for this paper, originally introduced from China about 1750, is "China Paper." It is a thin, opaque paper often used for plate and die proofs by many countries.

Double — In philately, the term double paper has two distinct meanings. The first is a two-ply paper, usually a combination of a thick and a thin sheet, joined during manufacture. This type was used experimentally as a means to discourage the reuse of stamps.

The design is printed on the thin paper. Any attempt to remove a cancellation would destroy the design. U.S. Scott 158 and other Banknote-era stamps exist on this form of double paper.

The second type of double paper occurs on a rotary press, when the end of one paper roll, or web, is affixed to the next roll to save time feeding the paper through the press. Stamp designs are printed over the joined paper and, if overlooked by inspectors, may get into post office stocks.

Goldbeater's Skin — This type of paper was used for the 1866 issue of Prussia, and was a tough, translucent paper. The design was printed in reverse on the back of the stamp, and the gum applied over the printing. It is impossible to remove stamps printed on this type of paper from the paper to which they are affixed without destroying the design.

Ribbed — Ribbed paper has an uneven, corrugated surface made by passing the paper through ridged rollers. This type exists on some copies of U.S. Scott 156-165.

Various other substances, or substrates, have been used for stamp manufacture, including wood, aluminum, copper, silver and gold foil, plastic, and silk and cotton fabrics.

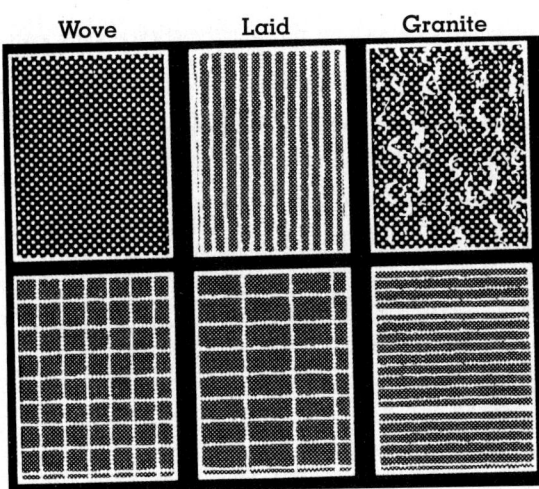

Wove   Laid   Granite

Quadrille   Oblong Quadrille   Laid Battone

Watermarks

Watermarks are an integral part of some papers. They are formed in the process of paper manufacture. Watermarks consist of small designs, formed of wire or cut from metal and soldered to the surface of the mold or, sometimes, on the dandy roll. The designs may be in the form of crowns, stars, anchors, letters or other characters or symbols. These pieces of metal - known in the paper-making industry as "bits" - impress a design into the paper. The design sometimes may be seen by holding the stamp to the light. Some are more easily seen with a watermark detector. This important tool is a small black tray into which a stamp is placed face down and dampened with a fast-evaporating watermark detection fluid that brings up the watermark image in the form of dark lines against a lighter background. These dark lines are the thinner areas of the paper known as the watermark. Some watermarks are extremely difficult to locate, due to either a faint impression, watermark location or the color of the stamp. There also are electric watermark detectors that come with plastic filter disks of various colors. The disks neutralize the color of the stamp, permitting the watermark to be seen more easily.

Multiple watermarks of Crown Agents and Burma

Watermarks of Uruguay, Vatican City and Jamaica

WARNING: Some inks used in the photogravure process dissolve in watermark fluids (Please see the section on Soluble Printing Inks). Also, see "chalky paper."

Watermarks may be found normal, reversed, inverted, reversed and inverted, sideways or diagonal, as seen from the back of the stamp. The relationship of watermark to stamp design depends on the position of the printing plates or how paper is fed through the press. On machine-made paper, watermarks normally are read from right to left. The design is repeated closely throughout the sheet in a "multiple-watermark design." In a "sheet watermark," the design appears only once on the sheet, but extends over many stamps. Individual stamps may carry only a small fraction or none of the watermark.

"Marginal watermarks" occur in the margins of sheets or panes of stamps. They occur on the outside border of paper (ostensibly outside the area where stamps are to be printed). A large row of letters may spell the name of the country or the manufacturer of the paper, or a border of lines may appear. Careless press feeding may cause parts of these letters and/or lines to show on stamps of the outer row of a pane.

Soluble Printing Inks

WARNING: Most stamp colors are permanent; that is, they are not seriously affected by short-term exposure to light or water. Some colors may fade from excessive exposure to light. There are stamps printed with inks that dissolve easily in water or in fluids used to detect watermarks. Use of these inks was intentional to prevent the removal of cancellations. Water affects all aniline inks, those on so-called safety paper and some photogravure printings - all such inks are known as *fugitive colors. Removal from paper of such stamps requires care and alternatives to traditional soaking.*

Separation

"Separation" is the general term used to describe methods used to separate stamps. The three standard forms currently in use are perforating, rouletting and die-cutting. These methods are done during the stamp production process, after printing. Sometimes these methods are done on-press or sometimes as a separate step. The earliest issues, such as the 1840 Penny Black of Great Britain (Scott 1), did not have any means provided for separation. It was expected the stamps would be cut apart with scissors or folded and torn. These are examples of imperforate stamps. Many stamps were first issued in imperforate formats and were later issued with perforations. Therefore, care must be observed in buying single imperforate stamps to be certain they were issued imperforate and are not perforated copies that have been altered by having the perforations trimmed away. Stamps issued imperforate usually are valued as singles. However, imperforate varieties of normally perforated stamps should be collected in pairs or larger pieces as indisputable evidence of their imperforate character.

PERFORATION

The chief style of separation of stamps, and the one that is in almost universal use today, is perforating. By this process, paper between the stamps is cut away in a line of holes, usually round, leaving little bridges of paper between the stamps to hold them together. Some types of perforation, such as hyphen-hole perfs, can be confused with roulettes, but a close visual inspection reveals that paper has been removed. The little perforation bridges, which project from the stamp when it is torn from the pane, are called the teeth of the perforation.

As the size of the perforation is sometimes the only way to differentiate between two otherwise identical stamps, it is necessary to be able to accurately measure and describe them. This is done with a perforation gauge, usually a ruler-like device that has dots or graduated lines to show how many perforations may be counted in the space of two centimeters. Two centimeters is the space universally adopted in which to measure perforations.

Perforation gauge

To measure a stamp, run it along the gauge until the dots on it fit exactly into the perforations of the stamp. If you are using a graduated-line perforation gauge, simply slide the stamp along the surface until the lines on the gauge perfectly project from the center of the bridges or holes. The number to the side of the line of dots or lines that fit the stamp's perforation is the measurement. For example, an "11" means that 11 perforations fit between two centimeters. The description of the stamp therefore is "perf. 11." If the gauge of the perforations on the top and bottom of a stamp differs from that on the sides, the result is what is known as *compound perforations*. In measuring compound perforations, the gauge at top and bottom is always given first, then the sides. Thus, a stamp that measures 11 at top and bottom and 10 1/2 at the sides is "perf. 11 x 10 1/2." See U.S. Scott 632-642 for examples of compound perforations.

Stamps also are known with perforations different on three or all four sides. Descriptions of such items are clockwise, beginning with the top of the stamp.

A perforation with small holes and teeth close together is a "fine perforation." One with large holes and teeth far apart is a "coarse perforation." Holes that are jagged, rather than clean-cut, are "rough perforations." *Blind perforations* are the slight impressions left by the perforating pins if they fail to puncture the paper. Multiples of stamps showing blind perforations may command a slight premium over normally perforated stamps.

The term *syncopated perfs* describes intentional irregularities in the perforations. The earliest form was used by the Netherlands from 1925-33, where holes were omitted to create distinctive patterns. Beginning in 1992, Great Britain has used an oval perforation to help prevent counterfeiting. Several other countries have started using the oval perfs.

perce en arc   perce en lignes

perce en points   oblique roulette

perce en scie   perce serpentin

ROULETTING

In rouletting, the stamp paper is cut partly or wholly through, with no paper removed. In perforating, some paper is removed. Rouletting derives its name from the French roulette, a spur-like wheel. As the wheel is rolled over the paper, each point makes a small cut. The number of cuts made in a two-centimeter space determines the gauge of the roulette, just as the number of perforations in two centimeters determines the gauge of the perforation.

The shape and arrangement of the teeth on the wheels varies. Various roulette types generally carry French names:

Perce en lignes - rouletted in lines. The paper receives short, straight cuts in lines. This is the most common type of rouletting. See Mexico Scott 500.

Perce en points - pin-rouletted. This differs from a small perforation because no paper is removed, although round, equidistant holes are pricked through the paper. See Mexico Scott 242-256.

Perce en arc and perce en scie - pierced in an arc or saw-toothed designs, forming half circles or small triangles. See Hanover (German States) Scott 25-29.

Perce en serpentin - serpentine roulettes. The cuts form a serpentine or wavy line. See Brunswick (German States) Scott 13-18.

Once again, no paper is removed by these processes, leaving the stamps easily separated, but closely attached.

DIE-CUTTING

The third and most recently developed major form of stamp separation is die-cutting. This is a method where a die in the pattern of separation is created that later cuts the stamp paper in a stroke motion. Although some standard stamps bear die-cut perforations, this process is primarily used for modern self-adhesive postage stamps.

Printing Processes

ENGRAVING (Intaglio, Line-engraving, Etching)

Master die - The initial operation in the process of line engraving is making the master die. The die is a small, flat block of softened steel upon which the stamp design is recess engraved in reverse.

Master die

Photographic reduction of the original art is made to the appropriate size. It then serves as a tracing guide for the initial outline of the design. The engraver lightly traces the design on the steel with his graver, then slowly works the design until it is completed. At various points during the engraving process, the engraver hand-inks the die and makes an impression to check his progress. These are known as progressive die proofs. After completion of the engraving, the die is hardened to withstand the stress and pressures of later transfer operations.

Transfer roll

Transfer roll — Next is production of the transfer roll that, as the name implies, is the medium used to transfer the subject from the master die to the printing plate. A blank roll of soft steel, mounted on a mandrel, is placed under the bearers of the transfer press to allow it to roll freely on its axis. The hardened die is placed on the bed of the press and the face of the transfer roll is applied to the die, under pressure. The bed or the roll is then rocked back and forth under increasing pressure, until the soft steel of the roll is forced into every engraved line of the die. The resulting impression on the roll is known as a "relief" or a "relief transfer." The engraved image is now positive in appearance and stands out from the steel. After the required number of reliefs are "rocked in," the soft steel transfer roll is hardened.

Different flaws may occur during the relief process. A defective relief may occur during the rocking in process because of a minute piece of foreign material lodging on the die, or some other cause. Imperfections in the steel of the transfer roll may result in a breaking away of parts of the design. This is known as a relief break, which will show up on finished stamps as small, unprinted areas. If a damaged relief remains in use, it will transfer a repeating defect to the plate. Deliberate alterations of reliefs sometimes occur. "Altered reliefs" designate these changed conditions.

Plate — The final step in pre-printing production is the making of the printing plate. A flat piece of soft steel replaces the die on the bed of the transfer press. One of the reliefs on the transfer roll is positioned over this soft steel. Position, or layout, dots determine the correct position on the plate. The dots have been lightly marked on the plate in advance. After the correct position of the relief is determined, the design is rocked in by following the same method used in making the transfer roll. The difference is that this time the image is being transferred from the transfer roll, rather than to it. Once the design is entered on the plate, it appears in reverse and is recessed. There are as many transfers entered on the plate as there are subjects printed on the sheet of stamps. It is during this process that double and shifted transfers occur, as well as re-entries. These are the result of improperly entered images that have not been properly burnished out prior to rocking in a new image.

Transferring the design to the plate

Following the entering of the required transfers on the plate, the position dots, layout dots and lines, scratches and other markings generally are burnished out. Added at this time by the siderographer are any required *guide lines, plate numbers* or other *marginal markings.* The plate is then hand-inked and a proof impression is taken. This is known as a plate proof. If the impression is approved, the plate is machined for fitting onto the press, is hardened and sent to the plate vault ready for use.

On press, the plate is inked and the surface is automatically wiped clean, leaving ink only in the recessed lines. Paper is then forced under pressure into the engraved recessed lines, thereby receiving the ink. Thus, the ink lines on engraved stamps are slightly raised, and slight depressions (debossing) occur on the back of the stamp. Prior to the advent of modern high-speed presses and more advanced ink formulations, paper had to be dampened before receiving the ink. This sometimes led to uneven shrinkage by the time the stamps were perforated, resulting in improperly perforated stamps, or misperfs. Newer presses use drier paper, thus both *wet* and *dry printings* exist on some stamps.

Rotary Press — Until 1914, only flat plates were used to print engraved stamps. Rotary press printing was introduced in 1914, and slowly spread. Some countries still use flat-plate printing.

After approval of the plate proof, older *rotary press plates* require additional machining. They are curved to fit the press cylinder. "Gripper slots" are cut into the back of each plate to receive the "grippers," which hold the plate securely on the press. The plate is then hardened. Stamps printed from these bent rotary press plates are longer or wider than the same stamps printed from flat-plate presses. The stretching of the plate during the curving process is what causes this distortion.

Re-entry — To execute a re-entry on a flat plate, the transfer roll is re-applied to the plate, often at some time after its first use on the press. Worn-out designs can be resharpened by carefully burnishing out the original image and re-entering it from the transfer roll. If the original impression has not been sufficiently removed and the transfer roll is not precisely in line with the remaining impression, the resulting double transfer will make the re-entry obvious. If the registration is true, a re-entry may be difficult or impossible to distinguish. Sometimes a stamp printed from a successful re-entry is identified by having a much sharper and clearer impression than its neighbors. With the advent of rotary presses, post-press re-entries were not possible. After a plate was curved for the rotary press, it was impossible to make a re-entry. This is because the plate had already been bent once (with the design distorted).

Double Transfer — This is a description of the condition of a transfer on a plate that shows evidence of a duplication of all, or a portion of the design. It usually is the result of the changing of the registration between the transfer roll and the plate during the rocking in of the original entry. Double transfers also occur when only a portion of the design has been rocked in and improper positioning is noted. If the worker elected not to burnish out the partial or completed design, a strong double transfer will occur for part or all of the design.

It sometimes is necessary to remove the original transfer from a plate and repeat the process a second time. If the finished re-worked image shows traces of the original impression, attributable to incomplete burnishing, the result is a partial double transfer.

Re-engraved — Alterations to a stamp design are sometimes necessary after some stamps have been printed. In some cases, either the original die or the actual printing plate may have its "temper" drawn (softened), and the design will be re-cut. The resulting impressions from such a re-engraved die or plate may differ slightly from the original issue, and are known as "re-engraved." If the alteration was made to the master die, all future printings will be consistently different from the original. If alterations were made to the printing plate, each altered stamp on the plate will be slightly different from each other, allowing specialists to reconstruct a complete printing plate.

Dropped Transfers — If an impression from the transfer roll has not been properly placed, a dropped transfer may occur. The final stamp image will appear obviously out of line with its neighbors.

Short Transfer — Sometimes a transfer roll is not rocked its entire length when entering a transfer onto a plate. As a result, the finished transfer on the plate fails to show the complete design, and the finished stamp will have an incomplete design printed. This is known as a "short transfer." U.S. Scott No. 8 is a good example of a short transfer.

TYPOGRAPHY (Letterpress, Surface Printing, Flexography, Dry Offset, High Etch)

Although the word "Typography" is obsolete as a term describing a printing method, it was the accepted term throughout the first century of postage stamps. Therefore, appropriate Scott listings in this catalogue refer to typographed stamps. The current term for this form of printing, however, is "letterpress."

As it relates to the production of postage stamps, letterpress printing is the reverse of engraving. Rather than having recessed areas trap the ink and deposit it on paper, only the raised areas of the design are inked. This is comparable to the type of printing seen by inking and using an ordinary rubber stamp. Letterpress includes all printing where the design is above the surface area, whether it is wood, metal or, in some instances, hardened rubber or polymer plastic.

For most letterpress-printed stamps, the engraved master is made in much the same manner as for engraved stamps. In this instance, however, an additional step is needed. The design is transferred to another surface before being transferred to the transfer roll. In this way, the transfer roll has a recessed stamp design, rather than one done in relief. This makes the printing areas on the final plate raised, or relief areas.

For less-detailed stamps of the 19th century, the area on the die not used as a printing surface was cut away, leaving the surface area raised. The original die was then reproduced by stereotyping or electrotyping. The resulting electrotypes were assembled in the required number and format of the desired sheet of stamps. The plate used in printing the stamps was an electroplate of these assembled electrotypes.

Once the final letterpress plates are created, ink is applied to the raised surface and the pressure of the press transfers the ink impression to the paper. In contrast to engraving, the fine lines of letterpress are impressed on the surface of the stamp, leaving a

debossed surface. When viewed from the back (as on a typewritten page), the corresponding line work on the stamp will be raised slightly (embossed) above the surface.

PHOTOGRAVURE (Gravure, Rotogravure, Heliogravure)

In this process, the basic principles of photography are applied to a chemically sensitized metal plate, rather than photographic paper. The design is transferred photographically to the plate through a halftone, or dot-matrix screen, breaking the reproduction into tiny dots. The plate is treated chemically and the dots form depressions, called cells, of varying depths and diameters, depending on the degrees of shade in the design. Then, like engraving, ink is applied to the plate and the surface is wiped clean. This leaves ink in the tiny cells that is lifted out and deposited on the paper when it is pressed against the plate.

Gravure is most often used for multicolored stamps, generally using the three primary colors (red, yellow and blue) and black. By varying the dot matrix pattern and density of these colors, virtually any color can be reproduced. A typical full-color gravure stamp will be created from four printing cylinders (one for each color). The original multicolored image will have been photographically separated into its component colors.

For examples of the first photogravure stamps printed (1914), see Bavaria Scott 94-114.

LITHOGRAPHY (Offset Lithography, Stone Lithography, Dilitho, Planography, Collotype)

The principle that oil and water do not mix is the basis for lithography. The stamp design is drawn by hand or transferred from engraving to the surface of a lithographic stone or metal plate in a greasy (oily) substance. This oily substance holds the ink, which will later be transferred to the paper. The stone (or plate) is wet with an acid fluid, causing it to repel the printing ink in all areas not covered by the greasy substance.

Transfer paper is used to transfer the design from the original stone or plate. A series of duplicate transfers are grouped and, in turn, transferred to the final printing plate.

Photolithography — The application of photographic processes to lithography. This process allows greater flexibility of design, related to use of halftone screens combined with line work. Unlike photogravure or engraving, this process can allow large, solid areas to be printed.

Offset — A refinement of the lithographic process. A rubber-covered blanket cylinder takes the impression from the inked lithographic plate. From the "blanket" the impression is *offset* or transferred to the paper. Greater flexibility and speed are the principal reasons offset printing has largely displaced lithography. The term "lithography" covers both processes, and results are almost identical.

EMBOSSED (Relief) Printing

Embossing, not considered one of the four main printing types, is a method in which the design first is sunk into the metal of the die. Printing is done against a yielding platen, such as leather or linoleum. The platen is forced into the depression of the die, thus forming the design on the paper in relief. This process is often used for metallic inks.

Embossing may be done without color (see Sardinia Scott 4-6); with color printed around the embossed area (see Great Britain Scott 5 and most U.S. envelopes); and with color in exact registration with the embossed subject.

INK COLORS

Inks or colored papers used in stamp printing often are of mineral origin, although there are numerous examples of organic-based pigments. As a general rule, organic-based pigments are far more subject to varieties and change than those of mineral-based origin.

The appearance of any given color on a stamp may be affected by many aspects, including printing variations, light, color of paper, aging and chemical alterations.

Numerous printing variations may be observed. Heavier pressure or inking will cause a more intense color, while slight interruptions in the ink feed or lighter impressions will cause a lighter appearance. Stamps printed in the same color by water-based and solvent-based inks can differ significantly in appearance. Hand-mixed ink formulas (primarily from the 19th century) produced under different conditions (humidity and temperature) account for notable color variations in early printings of the same stamp (see U.S. Scott 248-250, 279B, for example). Different sources of pigment can also result in significant differences in color.

Light exposure and aging are closely related in the way they affect stamp color. Both eventually break down the ink and fade colors, so that a carefully kept stamp may differ significantly in color from an identical copy that has been exposed to light. If stamps are exposed to light either intentionally or accidentally, their colors can be faded or completely changed in some cases.

Papers of different quality and consistency used for the same stamp printing may affect color appearance. Most pelure papers, for example, show a richer color when compared with wove or laid papers. See Russia Scott 181a, for an example of this effect.

The very nature of the printing processes can cause a variety of differences in shades or hues of the same stamp. Some of these shades are scarcer than others, and are of particular interest to the advanced collector.

Gum

The Illustrated Gum Chart in the first part of this introduction shows and defines various types of gum condition. Because gum condition has an important impact on the value of unused stamps, we recommend studying this chart and the accompanying text carefully.

The gum on the back of a stamp may be shiny, dull, smooth, rough, dark, white, colored or tinted. Most stamp gumming adhesives use gum arabic or dextrine as a base. Certain polymers such as polyvinyl alcohol (PVA) have been used extensively since World War II.

The *Scott Standard Postage Stamp Catalogue* does not list items by types of gum. The *Scott Specialized Catalogue of United States Stamps* does differentiate among some types of gum for certain issues.

Reprints of stamps may have gum differing from the original issues. In addition, some countries have used different gum formulas for different seasons. These adhesives have different properties that may become more apparent over time.

Many stamps have been issued without gum, and the catalogue will note this fact. See, for example, United States Scott 40-47. Sometimes, gum may have been removed to preserve the stamp. Germany Scott B68, for example, has a highly acidic gum that eventually destroys the stamps. This item is valued in the catalogue with gum removed.

Reprints and Reissues

These are impressions of stamps (usually obsolete) made from the original plates or stones. If they are valid for postage and reproduce obsolete issues (such as U.S. Scott 102-111), the stamps are *reissues*. If they are from current issues, they are designated as *second*, *third*, etc., *printing*. If designated for a particular purpose, they are called *special printings*.

When special printings are not valid for postage, but are made from original dies and plates by authorized persons, they are *official reprints*. *Private reprints* are made from the original plates and dies by private hands. An example of a private reprint is that of the 1871-1932 reprints made from the original die of the 1845 New Haven, Conn., postmaster's provisional. *Official reproductions* or imitations

are made from new dies and plates by government authorization. Scott will list those reissues that are valid for postage if they differ significantly from the original printing.

The U.S. government made special printings of its first postage stamps in 1875. Produced were official imitations of the first two stamps (listed as Scott 3-4), reprints of the demonetized pre-1861 issues (Scott 40-47) and reissues of the 1861 stamps, the 1869 stamps and the then-current 1875 denominations. Even though the official imitations and the reprints were not valid for postage, Scott lists all of these U.S. special printings.

Most reprints or reissues differ slightly from the original stamp in some characteristic, such as gum, paper, perforation, color or watermark. Sometimes the details are followed so meticulously that only a student of that specific stamp is able to distinguish the reprint or reissue from the original.

Remainders and Canceled to Order

Some countries sell their stock of old stamps when a new issue replaces them. To avoid postal use, the *remainders* usually are canceled with a punch hole, a heavy line or bar, or a more-or-less regular-looking cancellation. The most famous merchant of remainders was Nicholas F. Seebeck. In the 1880s and 1890s, he arranged printing contracts between the Hamilton Bank Note Co., of which he was a director, and several Central and South American countries. The contracts provided that the plates and all remainders of the yearly issues became the property of Hamilton. Seebeck saw to it that ample stock remained. The "Seebecks," both remainders and reprints, were standard packet fillers for decades.

Some countries also issue stamps *canceled-to-order (CTO)*, either in sheets with original gum or stuck onto pieces of paper or envelopes and canceled. Such CTO items generally are worth less than postally used stamps. In cases where the CTO material is far more prevalent in the marketplace than postally used examples, the catalogue value relates to the CTO examples, with postally used examples noted as premium items. Most CTOs can be detected by the presence of gum. However, as the CTO practice goes back at least to 1885, the gum inevitably has been soaked off some stamps so they could pass as postally used. The normally applied postmarks usually differ slightly from standard postmarks, and specialists are able to tell the difference. When applied individually to envelopes by philatelically minded persons, CTO material is known as *favor canceled* and generally sells at large discounts.

Cinderellas and Facsimiles

Cinderella is a catch-all term used by stamp collectors to describe phantoms, fantasies, bogus items, municipal issues, exhibition seals, local revenues, transportation stamps, labels, poster stamps and many other types of items. Some cinderella collectors include in their collections local postage issues, telegraph stamps, essays and proofs, forgeries and counterfeits.

A *fantasy* is an adhesive created for a nonexistent stamp-issuing authority. Fantasy items range from imaginary countries (Occusi-Ambeno, Kingdom of Sedang, Principality of Trinidad or Torres Straits), to non-existent locals (Winans City Post), or nonexistent transportation lines (McRobish & Co.'s Acapulco-San Francisco Line).

On the other hand, if the entity exists and could have issued stamps (but did not) or was known to have issued other stamps, the items are considered *bogus* stamps. These would include the Mormon postage stamps of Utah, S. Allan Taylor's Guatemala and Paraguay inventions, the propaganda issues for the South Moluccas and the adhesives of the Page & Keyes local post of Boston.

Phantoms is another term for both fantasy and bogus issues.

Facsimiles are copies or imitations made to represent original stamps, but which do not pretend to be originals. A catalogue illustration is such a facsimile. Illustrations from the Moens catalogue of the 19th century were occasionally colored and passed off as stamps. Since the beginning of stamp collecting, facsimiles have been made for collectors as space fillers or for reference. They often carry the word "facsimile," "falsch" (German), "sanko" or "mozo" (Japanese), or "faux" (French) overprinted on the face or stamped on the back. Unfortunately, over the years a number of these items have had fake cancels applied over the facsimile notation and have been passed off as genuine.

Forgeries and Counterfeits

Forgeries and counterfeits have been with philately virtually from the beginning of stamp production. Over time, the terminology for the two has been used interchangeably. Although both forgeries and counterfeits are reproductions of stamps, the purposes behind their creation differ considerably.

Among specialists there is an increasing movement to more specifically define such items. Although there is no universally accepted terminology, we feel the following definitions most closely mirror the items and their purposes as they are currently defined.

Forgeries (also often referred to as *Counterfeits*) are reproductions of genuine stamps that have been created to defraud collectors. Such spurious items first appeared on the market around 1860, and most old-time collections contain one or more. Many are crude and easily spotted, but some can deceive experts.

An important supplier of these early philatelic forgeries was the Hamburg printer Gebruder Spiro. Many others with reputations in this craft included S. Allan Taylor, George Hussey, James Chute, George Forune, Benjamin & Sarpy, Julius Goldner, E. Oneglia and L.H. Mercier. Among the noted 20th-century forgers were Francois Fournier, Jean Sperati and the prolific Raoul DeThuin.

Forgeries may be complete replications, or they may be genuine stamps altered to resemble a scarcer (and more valuable) type. Most forgeries, particularly those of rare stamps, are worth only a small fraction of the value of a genuine example, but a few types, created by some of the most notable forgers, such as Sperati, can be worth as much or more than the genuine. Fraudulently produced copies are known of most classic rarities and many medium-priced stamps.

In addition to rare stamps, large numbers of common 19th- and early 20th-century stamps were forged to supply the early packet trade. Many can still be easily found. Few new philatelic forgeries have appeared in recent decades. Successful imitation of well-engraved work is virtually impossible. It has proven far easier to produce a fake by altering a genuine stamp than to duplicate a stamp completely.

Counterfeit (also often referred to as *Postal Counterfeit* or *Postal Forgery*) is the term generally applied to reproductions of stamps that have been created to defraud the government of revenue. Such items usually are created at the time a stamp is current and, in some cases, are hard to detect. Because most counterfeits are seized when the perpetrator is captured, postal counterfeits, particularly used on cover, are usually worth much more than a genuine example to specialists. The first postal counterfeit was of Spain's 4-cuarto carmine of 1854 (the real one is Scott 25). Apparently, the counterfeiters were not satisfied with their first version, which is now very scarce, and they soon created an engraved counterfeit, which is common. Postal counterfeits quickly followed in Austria, Naples, Sardinia and the Roman States. They have since been created in many other countries as well, including the United States.

An infamous counterfeit to defraud the government is the 1-shilling Great Britain "Stock Exchange" forgery of 1872, used on telegraph forms at the exchange that year. The stamp escaped detection until a stamp dealer noticed it in 1898.

Fakes

Fakes are genuine stamps altered in some way to make them more desirable. One student of this part of stamp collecting has estimated that by the 1950s more than 30,000 varieties of fakes were known.

That number has grown greatly since then. The widespread existence of fakes makes it important for stamp collectors to study their philatelic holdings and use relevant literature. Likewise, collectors should buy from reputable dealers who guarantee their stamps and make full and prompt refunds should a purchased item be declared faked or altered by some mutually agreed-upon authority. Because fakes always have some genuine characteristics, it is not always possible to obtain unanimous agreement among experts regarding specific items. These students may change their opinions as philatelic knowledge increases. More than 80 percent of all fakes on the philatelic market today are regummed, reperforated (or perforated for the first time), or bear forged overprints, surcharges or cancellations.

Stamps can be chemically treated to alter or eliminate colors. For example, a pale rose stamp can be re-colored to resemble a blue shade of high market value. In other cases, treated stamps can be made to resemble missing color varieties. Designs may be changed by painting, or a stroke or a dot added or bleached out to turn an ordinary variety into a seemingly scarcer stamp. Part of a stamp can be bleached and reprinted in a different version, achieving an inverted center or frame. Margins can be added or repairs done so deceptively that the stamps move from the "repaired" into the "fake" category.

Fakers have not left the backs of the stamps untouched either. They may create false watermarks, add fake grills or press out genuine grills. A thin India paper proof may be glued onto a thicker backing to create the appearance an issued stamp, or a proof printed on cardboard may be shaved down and perforated to resemble a stamp. Silk threads are impressed into paper and stamps have been split so that a rare paper variety is added to an otherwise inexpensive stamp. The most common treatment to the back of a stamp, however, is regumming.

Some in the business of faking stamps have openly advertised fool-proof application of "original gum" to stamps that lack it, although most publications now ban such ads from their pages. It is believed that very few early stamps have survived without being hinged. The large number of never-hinged examples of such earlier material offered for sale thus suggests the widespread extent of regumming activity. Regumming also may be used to hide repairs or thin spots. Dipping the stamp into watermark fluid, or examining it under longwave ultraviolet light often will reveal these flaws.

Fakers also tamper with separations. Ingenious ways to add margins are known. Perforated wide-margin stamps may be falsely represented as imperforate when trimmed. Reperforating is commonly done to create scarce coil or perforation varieties, and to eliminate the naturally occurring straight-edge stamps found in sheet margin positions of many earlier issues. Custom has made straight-edged stamps less desirable. Fakers have obliged by perforating straight-edged stamps so that many are now uncommon, if not rare.

Another fertile field for the faker is that of overprints, surcharges and cancellations. The forging of rare surcharges or overprints began in the 1880s or 1890s. These forgeries are sometimes difficult to detect, but experts have identified almost all. Occasionally, overprints or cancellations are removed to create non-overprinted stamps or seemingly unused items. This is most commonly done by removing a manuscript cancel to make a stamp resemble an unused example. "SPECIMEN" overprints may be removed by scraping and repainting to create non-overprinted varieties. Fakers use inexpensive revenues or pen-canceled stamps to generate unused stamps for further faking by adding other markings. The quartz lamp or UV lamp and a high-powered magnifying glass help to easily detect removed cancellations.

The bigger problem, however, is the addition of overprints, surcharges or cancellations - many with such precision that they are very difficult to ascertain. Plating of the stamps or the overprint can be an important method of detection.

Fake postmarks may range from many spurious fancy cancellations to a host of markings applied to transatlantic covers, to adding normally appearing postmarks to definitives of some countries with stamps that are valued far higher used than unused. With the increased popularity of cover collecting, and the widespread interest in postal history, a fertile new field for fakers has come about. Some have tried to create entire covers. Others specialize in adding stamps, tied by fake cancellations, to genuine stampless covers, or replacing less expensive or damaged stamps with more valuable ones. Detailed study of postal rates in effect at the time a cover in question was mailed, including the analysis of each handstamp used during the period, ink analysis and similar techniques, usually will unmask the fraud.

Restoration and Repairs

Scott Publishing Co. bases its catalogue values on stamps that are free of defects and otherwise meet the standards set forth earlier in this introduction. Most stamp collectors desire to have the finest copy of an item possible. Even within given grading categories there are variances. This leads to a controversial practice that is not defined in any universal manner: stamp *restoration*.

There are broad differences of opinion about what is permissible when it comes to restoration. Carefully applying a soft eraser to a stamp or cover to remove light soiling is one form of restoration, as is washing a stamp in mild soap and water to clean it. These are fairly accepted forms of restoration. More severe forms of restoration include pressing out creases or removing stains caused by tape. To what degree each of these is acceptable is dependent upon the individual situation. Further along the spectrum is the freshening of a stamp's color by removing oxide build-up or the effects of wax paper left next to stamps shipped to the tropics.

At some point in this spectrum the concept of *repair* replaces that of restoration. Repairs include filling thin spots, mending tears by reweaving or adding a missing perforation tooth. Regumming stamps may have been acceptable as a restoration or repair technique many decades ago, but today it is considered a form of fakery.

Restored stamps may or may not sell at a discount, and it is possible that the value of individual restored items may be enhanced over that of their pre-restoration state. Specific situations dictate the resultant value of such an item. Repaired stamps sell at substantial discounts from the value of sound stamps.

When the purchaser of an item has any reason to suspect that an item has been repaired, and the detection of such a repair is beyond his own ability, he should seek expert advice. There are services that specialize in giving such advice.

Terminology

Booklets — Many countries have issued stamps in small booklets for the convenience of users. This idea continues to become increasingly popular in many countries. Booklets have been issued in many sizes and forms, often with advertising on the covers, the panes of stamps or on the interleaving.

The panes used in booklets may be printed from special plates or made from regular sheets. All panes from booklets issued by the United States and many from those of other countries contain stamps that are straight edged on the sides, but perforated between. Others are distinguished by orientation of watermark or other identifying features. Any stamp-like unit in the pane, either printed or blank, that is not a postage stamp is considered to be a *label* in the catalogue listings.

Scott lists and values booklet panes only. Complete booklets are listed and valued in only a few cases, such as Grenada Scott 1055 and some forms of British prestige booklets. Individual booklet panes are listed only when they are not fashioned from existing sheet stamps and, therefore, are identifiable from their sheet stamp counterparts.

Panes usually do not have a used value assigned to them because there is little market activity for used booklet panes, even though many exist used and there is some demand for them.

Cancellations — The marks or obliterations put on stamps by postal authorities to show that they have performed service and to prevent their reuse are known as cancellations. If the marking is made with a pen, it is considered a "pen cancel." When the location of the post office appears in the marking, it is a "town cancellation." A "postmark" is technically any postal marking, but in practice the term generally is applied to a town cancellation with a date. When calling attention to a cause or celebration, the marking is known as a "slogan cancellation." Many other types and styles of cancellations exist, such as duplex, numerals, targets, fancy and others. See also "precancels," below.

Coil Stamps — These are stamps that are issued in rolls for use in dispensers, affixing and vending machines. Those coils of the United States, Canada, Sweden and some other countries are perforated horizontally or vertically only, with the outer edges imperforate. Coil stamps of some countries, such as Great Britain and Germany, are perforated on all four sides and may in some cases be distinguished from their sheet stamp counterparts by watermarks, counting numbers on the reverse or other means.

Errors — Stamps that have some major, consistent, unintentional deviation from the normal are considered errors. Errors include, but are not limited to, missing or wrong colors, wrong paper, wrong watermarks, inverted centers or frames on multicolor printing, inverted or missing surcharges or overprints, double impressions, missing perforations and others. Factually wrong or misspelled information, if it appears on all examples of a stamp, are not considered errors in the true sense of the word. They are errors of design. Inconsistent or randomly appearing items, such as misperfs or color shifts, are classified as freaks.

Overprints and Surcharges — Overprinting involves applying wording or design elements over an already existing stamp. Overprints can be used to alter the place of use (such as "Canal Zone" on U.S. stamps), to adapt them for a special purpose ("Porto" on Denmark's 1913-20 regular issues for use as postage due stamps, Scott J1-J7) or to commemorate a special occasion (United States Scott 647-648).

A *surcharge* is a form of overprint that changes or restates the face value of a stamp or piece of postal stationery.

Surcharges and overprints may be handstamped, typeset or, occasionally, lithographed or engraved. A few hand-written overprints and surcharges are known. The world's first surcharge was a handstamped "2" on the United States City Despatch Post stamps of 1846.

Precancels — Stamps that are canceled before they are placed in the mail are known as precancels. Precanceling usually is done to expedite the handling of large mailings and generally allow the affected mail pieces to skip certain phases of mail handling.

In the United States, precancellations generally identified the point of origin; that is, the city and state. This information appeared across the face of the stamp, usually centered between parallel lines. More recently, bureau precancels retained the parallel lines, but the city and state designations were dropped. Recent coils have a service inscription that is present on the original printing plate. These show the mail service paid for by the stamp. Since these stamps are not intended to receive further cancellations when used as intended, they are considered precancels. Such items often do not have parallel lines as part of the precancellation.

In France, the abbreviation *Affranchts* in a semicircle together with the word *Postes* is the general form of precancel in use. Belgian precancellations usually appear in a box in which the name of the city appears. Netherlands precancels have the name of the city enclosed between concentric circles, sometimes called a "lifesaver." Precancellations of other countries usually follow these patterns, but may be any arrangement of bars, boxes and city names.

Precancels are listed in the Scott catalogues only if the precancel changes the denomination (Belgium Scott 477-478); if the precanceled stamp is different from the non-precanceled version (such as untagged U.S. precancels); or if the stamp exists only precanceled (France Scott 1096-1099, U.S. Scott 2265).

Proofs and Essays — Proofs are impressions taken from an approved die, plate or stone in which the design and color are the same as the stamp issued to the public. Trial color proofs are impressions taken from approved dies, plates or stones in colors that vary from the final version. An essay is the impression of a design that differs in some way from the issued stamp. "Progressive die proofs" generally are considered to be essays.

Provisionals — These are stamps that are issued on short notice and intended for temporary use pending the arrival of regular issues. They usually are issued to meet such contingencies as changes in government or currency, shortage of necessary postage values or military occupation.

During the 1840s, postmasters in certain American cities issued stamps that were valid only at specific post offices. In 1861, postmasters of the Confederate States also issued stamps with limited validity. Both of these examples are known as "postmaster's provisionals."

Se-tenant — This term refers to an unsevered pair, strip or block of stamps that differ in design, denomination or overprint.

Unless the se-tenant item has a continuous design (see U.S. Scott 1451a, 1694a) the stamps do not have to be in the same order as shown in the catalogue (see U.S. Scott 2158a).

Specimens — The Universal Postal Union required member nations to send samples of all stamps they released into service to the International Bureau in Switzerland. Member nations of the UPU received these specimens as samples of what stamps were valid for postage. Many are overprinted, handstamped or initial-perforated "Specimen," "Canceled" or "Muestra." Some are marked with bars across the denominations (China-Taiwan), punched holes (Czechoslovakia) or back inscriptions (Mongolia).

Stamps distributed to government officials or for publicity purposes, and stamps submitted by private security printers for official approval, also may receive such defacements.

The previously described defacement markings prevent postal use, and all such items generally are known as "specimens."

Tete Beche — This term describes a pair of stamps in which one is upside down in relation to the other. Some of these are the result of intentional sheet arrangements, such as Morocco Scott B10-B11. Others occurred when one or more electrotypes accidentally were placed upside down on the plate, such as Colombia Scott 57a. Separation of the tete-beche stamps, of course, destroys the tete beche variety.

British Colonial and Crown Agents Watermarks

Watermarks 1 to 4, 314, 373, and 384, common to many British territories, are illustrated here to avoid duplication.

The letters "CC" of Wmk. 1 identify the paper as having been made for the use of the Crown Colonies, while the letters "CA" of the others stand for "Crown Agents." Both Wmks. 1 and 2 were used on stamps printed by De La Rue & Co.

Wmk. 3 was adopted in 1904; Wmk. 4 in 1921; Wmk. 314 in 1957; Wmk. 373 in 1974; and Wmk. 384 in 1985.

In Wmk. 4a, a non-matching crown of the general St. Edwards type (bulging on both sides at top) was substituted for one of the Wmk. 4 crowns which fell off the dandy roll. The non-matching crown occurs in 1950-52 printings in a horizontal row of crowns on certain regular stamps of Johore and Seychelles, and on various postage due stamps of Barbados, Basutoland, British Guiana, Gold Coast, Grenada, Northern Rhodesia, St. Lucia, Swaziland and Trinidad and Tobago. A variation of Wmk. 4a, with the non-matching crown in a horizontal row of crown-CA-crown, occurs on regular stamps of Bahamas, St. Kitts-Nevis and Singapore.

Wmk. 314 was intentionally used sideways, starting in 1966. When a stamp was issued with Wmk. 314 both upright and sideways, the sideways varieties usually are listed also – with minor numbers. In many of the later issues, Wmk. 314 is slightly visible.

Wmk. 373 is usually only faintly visible.

Wmk. 1
Crown and C C

Wmk. 2
Crown and C A

Wmk. 3
Multiple Crown
and C A

Wmk. 4
Multiple Crown
and Script C A

Wmk. 4a

Wmk. 314
St. Edward's Crown
and C A Multiple

Wmk. 373

Wmk. 384

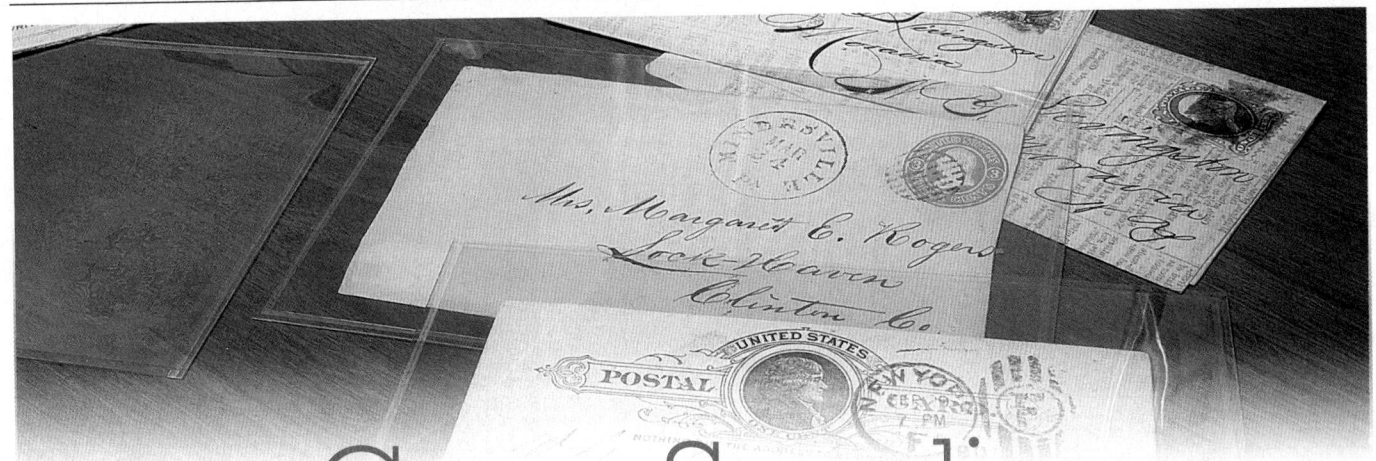

Cover Supplies

COVER SLEEVES

Protect your covers with clear polyethylene sleeves.
Sold in packages of 100.

U.S. POSTAL CARD

3¹¹⁄₁₆"

5¾"

Item	Retail	AA*
CVB05	$2.75	$2.25

U.S. FIRST DAY COVER #6

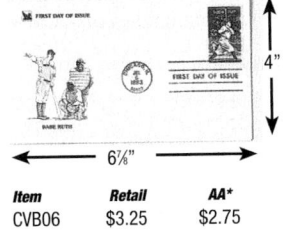

4"

6⅞"

Item	Retail	AA*
CVB06	$3.25	$2.75

CONTINENTAL POSTCARD

4⅜"

6"

Item	Retail	AA*
CVB07	$3.50	$2.99

EUROPEAN FIRST DAY COVER

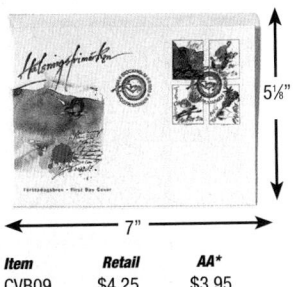

5⅛"

7"

Item	Retail	AA*
CVB09	$4.25	$3.95

#10 BUSINESS ENVELOPE

4¼"

9⅝"

Item	Retail	AA*
CVB10	$5.75	$4.95

COVER BINDERS AND PAGES

Padded, durable, 3-ring binders will hold up to 100 covers. Features the "D" ring mechanism on the right hand side of album so you don't have to worry about creasing or wrinkling covers when opening or closing binder. Cover pages sold separately. Available in black with 1 or 2 pockets. Sold in packages of 10.

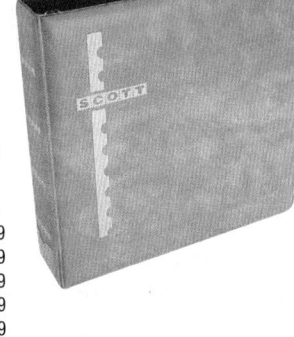

Item		Retail	AA*
CBRD	Burgundy	$11.99	$9.59
CBBL	Blue	$11.99	$9.59
CBCA	Candy Apple	$11.99	$9.59
CBGY	Gray	$11.99	$9.59
CBBK	Black	$11.99	$9.59
SS2PGB	Pgs. 2-Pock.	$5.75	$4.75
SS2PG1B	Pgs. 1-Pock.	$5.75	$4.75

MINT SHEET BINDERS & PAGES

Keep those mint sheets intact in a handsome, 3-ring binder. Just like the cover album, the Mint Sheet album features the "D" ring mechanism on the right hand side of binder so you don't have to worry about damagaing your stamps when turning the pages.

Item			Retail	AA*
MBRD	Red (Burgundy)		$18.99	$15.25
MBBL	Blue		$18.99	$15.25
MBGY	Gray		$18.99	$15.25
MBBK	Black		$18.99	$15.25
SSMP3B	Mint Sheet Pages	(Black 12 per pack)	$9.95	$8.95
SSMP3C	Mint Sheet Pages	(Clear 12 per pack)	$9.95	$8.95

PRINZ CORNER MOUNTS

Clear, self-adhesive corner mounts are ideal for postal cards and covers. Mounts measure ⅞" each side and are made from transparent glass foil. There are 250 mounts in each pack.

Item	Retail	AA*
ACC176	$9.95	**$7.96**

1. AA* prices apply to orders placed online.

2. Prices, terms and product availability subject to change.

3. Shipping & Handling:

United States: 10% of order total. Minimum charge $7.99 Maximum charge $45.00.
Canada: 20% of order total. Minimum charge $19.99 Maximum charge $200.00.
Foreign orders are shipped via FedEx Intl and billed actual freight. Credit cards only.

Call 1-800-572-6885
AmosAdvantage.com

Dies of British Colonial Stamps

DIE A:
1. The lines in the groundwork vary in thickness and are not uniformly straight.
2. The seventh and eighth lines from the top, in the groundwork, converge where they meet the head.
3. There is a small dash in the upper part of the second jewel in the band of the crown.
4. The vertical color line in front of the throat stops at the sixth line of shading on the neck.

DIE B:
1. The lines in the groundwork are all thin and straight.
2. All the lines of the background are parallel.
3. There is no dash in the upper part of the second jewel in the band of the crown.
4. The vertical color line in front of the throat stops at the eighth line of shading on the neck.

DIE I:
1. The base of the crown is well below the level of the inner white line around the vignette.
2. The labels inscribed "POSTAGE" and "REVENUE" are cut square at the top.
3. There is a white "bud" on the outer side of the main stem of the curved ornaments in each lower corner.
4. The second (thick) line below the country name has the ends next to the crown cut diagonally.

DIE Ia.	DIE Ib.
1 as die II.	1 and 3 as die II.
2 and 3 as die I.	2 as die I.

DIE II:
1. The base of the crown is aligned with the underside of the white line around the vignette.
2. The labels curve inward at the top inner corners.
3. The "bud" has been removed from the outer curve of the ornaments in each corner.
4. The second line below the country name has the ends next to the crown cut vertically.

scott**mounts**

Crowned Circle Handstamps and Great Britain Stamps Used Abroad

Crowned Circle Handstamps

Prior to the introduction of postage stamps in a number of British colonies, British postal authorities furnished post offices in these colonies with crowned circle handstamps. Crowned circle handstamps also were issued to a number of British post offices in foreign countries. These handstamps were to be used on mail sent to foreign countries or on mail between two foreign ports. The postage paid by the sender was to be noted in manuscript on the cover.

Crowned circle handstamps from the colonies of British America are listed. Similar handstamps were also furnished to post offices in British possessions outside of British America, such as New Zealand, Lagos and the Ionian Islands; areas where Britain maintained consular offices, such as Cairo, Egypt; and British Postal Agency offices, such as Rio de Janeiro, Brazil and San Juan, Puerto Rico. These items are not listed at this time, but such expansion is planned for future editions.

Some of these handstamps were used for various purposes after the advent of postage stamps. Values are for covers with clearly legible handstamps, produced prior to the advent of the colony's stamps. The color of the handstamp is black unless otherwise noted.

Types of Crowned Circle Handstamps

Type I   Type II   Type III   Type IV   Type V

Type VI   Type VII   Type VIII   Type IX

Great Britain Stamps Used Abroad

In some British colonies, postage stamps of Great Britain were used prior to the introduction of the colony's own postage stamps. Special cancels, most of which show an alphanumeric code, were furnished to the postmasters in these colonies to be used on these Great Britain stamps. Cancels and Great Britain stamps were furnished to colonies outside of the British America area as well as to British consular offices and British Postal Agency offices, but only the obliterators of British colonies in British America are listed at this time.

Cancel numbers assigned and used by post offices in the British American colonies were numbered A01-A15, A18, A27-A37, A39-A49, A51-A62 and A64-A78. A typical example of these cancels is shown below. Similar cancels with different alphanumeric codes, not listed in this catalogue, were assigned to the other colonies, consular offices and Postal Agency offices, as were cancels that are not similar in appearance.

The values quoted are for very fine off cover examples of the Great Britain stamps specified in parentheses in the listing with a legible and clearly identifiable alphanumeric combination. Such examples on cover sell for more.

These listings generally are limited to off cover stamps only. Other stamps that may have been sent to these offices may exist on covers that bear these cancels, but the cancel may not be on the stamp. Such items would need to be collected as complete covers.

Any valid Great Britain stamp brought to these colonies prior to the introduction of the colony's own postage stamps would have received these cancels if properly posted, but in virtually all instances the Great Britain stamps specified in these listings are those that were sent to these colonies by British postal officals during the years noted in the listings.

These canceling devices were returned to Great Britain and put to use there, so some of these cancels may be found on other Great Britain stamps from later periods.

Type A   Type B

For a list of Crowned Circle handstamps and Great Britain stamps used abroad, see end of Index and Identifier.

The British Commonwealth of Nations

Dominions, Colonies, Territories, Offices and Independent Members

Comprising stamps of the British Commonwealth and associated nations.

1. Great Britain

Great Britain: Including England, Scotland, Wales and Northern Ireland.

2. The Dominions, Present and Past

AUSTRALIA

The Commonwealth of Australia was proclaimed on January 1, 1901. It consists of six former colonies as follows:

New South Wales | South Australia | Tasmania
Queensland | Victoria | Western Australia

Territories belonging to, or administered by Australia: Nauru, New Guinea, Papua.

CANADA

The Dominion of Canada was created by the British North America Act in 1867. The following provinces were former sepa- rate colonies and issued postage stamps:

British Columbia and Vancouver Island | Newfoundland
New Brunswick | Nova Scotia
| Prince Edward Island

INDIA

The Republic of India was inaugurated on January 26, 1950. It succeeded the Dominion of India which was proclaimed August 15, 1947, when the former Empire of India was divided into Pakistan and the Union of India. The Republic is composed of about 40 predominantly Hindu states of three classes: governor's provinces, chief commissioner's provinces and princely states. India also has various territories, such as the Andaman and Nicobar Islands.

The old Empire of India was a federation of British India and the native states. The more important princely states were autonomous. Of the more than 700 Indian states, these 43 are familiar names to philatelists because of their postage stamps.

CONVENTION STATES

Chamba | Gwalior | Nabha
Faridkot | Jhind | Patiala

NATIVE FEUDATORY STATES

Alwar | Faridkot (1879-86) | Las Bela
Bamra | Hyderabad | Morvi
Barwani | Idar | Nandgaon
Bhopal | Indore | Nowanuggur
Bhor | Jaipur | Orchha
Bijawar | Jammu | Poonch
Bundi | Jammu and Kashmir | Rajasthan
Bussahir | Jasdan | Rajpeepla
Charkhari | Jhalawar | Sirmoor
Cochin | Jind (1875-76) | Soruth
Dhar | Kashmir | Tonk
Dungarpur | Kishangarh | Travancore
Duttia | Kotah | Wadhwan

NEW ZEALAND

Became a dominion on September 26, 1907. The following islands and territories are, or have been, administered by New Zealand:

Aitutaki | Penrhyn
Cook Islands (Rarotonga) | Samoa (Western Samoa)
Niue

SOUTH AFRICA

Under the terms of the South African Act (1909) the self-governing colonies of Cape of Good Hope, Natal, Orange River Colony and Transvaal united on May 31, 1910, to form the Union of South Africa. It became an independent republic May 3, 1961.

Under the terms of the Treaty of Versailles, South-West Africa, formerly German South-West Africa, was mandated to the Union of South Africa.

3. Colonies, Past and Present; Controlled Territory and Independent Members of the Commonwealth

Aden
Antigua
Ascension
Bahamas
Bahrain
Barbados
Barbuda
Basutoland
Batum
Bechuanaland
Bechuanaland Prot.
Bermuda
British Central
  Africa
British East Africa
British Guiana
British Honduras
British New Guinea
British Solomon
  Islands
British Somaliland
Brunei
Bushire
Cameroons
Cape of Good Hope
Cayman Islands
Ceylon
Crete, British
  Administration
Cyprus
Dominica
East Africa &
  Uganda
  Protectorates
Egypt
Falkland Islands
Fiji
Gambia
German East Africa
Gibraltar
Gilbert & Ellice
  Islands
Gold Coast
Grenada
Griqualand West
Heligoland
Hong Kong
Ionian Islands
Jamaica
Kenya, Uganda &
  Tanzania
Kuwait

Labuan
Lagos
Leeward Islands
Madagascar
Malaya
  Federated Malay
    States
  Johore
  Kedah
  Kelantan
  Negri Sembilan
  Pahang
  Perak
  Selangor
  Sungei Ujong
  Trengganu
Maldive Islands
Malta
Mauritius
Mesopotamia
Montserrat
Natal
Nevis
New Britain
New Hebrides
Niger Coast
  Protectorate
Nigeria
North Borneo
Northern Nigeria
Northern Rhodesia
North West Pacific
  Islands
Nyasaland
  Protectorate
Orange River
  Colony
Palestine
Pitcairn Islands
Rhodesia
St. Christopher
St. Helena
St. Kitts-Nevis-
  Anguilla
St. Lucia
St. Vincent
Samoa
Sarawak
Seychelles
Sierra Leone
Solomon Islands

Somaliland
  Protectorate
Southern Nigeria
Southern Rhodesia
Straits Settlements
Sudan
Swaziland
Tanganyika
Tasmania
Tobago
Togo
Tonga
Transvaal
Trinidad
Trinidad and
  Tobago
Turks and Caicos
Turks Islands
Uganda
Virgin Islands
Zanzibar
Zululand

POST OFFICES IN FOREIGN COUNTRIES

Africa
  East Africa Forces
  Middle East Forces
Bangkok
China
Morocco
Turkish Empire

Colonies, Former Colonies, Offices, Territories Controlled by Parent States

Belgium
Belgian Congo
Ruanda-Urundi

Denmark
Danish West Indies
Faroe Islands
Greenland
Iceland

France

COLONIES PAST AND PRESENT, CONTROLLED TERRITORIES
Alaouites
Alexandretta
Algeria
Alsace & Lorraine
Anjouan
Annam & Tonkin
Benin
Cameroun
Castellorizo
Chad
Cilicia
Cochin China
Dahomey
Diego Suarez
Djibouti (Somali Coast)
French Congo
French Equatorial Africa
French Guiana
French Guinea
French India
French Morocco
French Sudan
Gabon
Grand Comoro
Guadeloupe
Indo-China
Inini
Ivory Coast
Latakia
Lebanon
Madagascar
Martinique
Mauritania
Mayotte
Memel
Middle Congo
Moheli
New Caledonia
New Hebrides
Niger Territory
Nossi-Be
Obock
Oceania (French Polynesia)
Reunion
Rouad, Ile
Ste.-Marie de Madagascar
St. Pierre & Miquelon
Senegal
Senegambia & Niger
Somali Coast
Syria
Tahiti
Togo
Tunisia
Ubangi-Shari

Upper Senegal & Niger
Upper Volta
Wallis & Futuna Islands

POST OFFICES IN FOREIGN COUNTRIES
China
Crete
Egypt
Turkish Empire
Zanzibar

Germany

EARLY STATES
Baden
Bavaria
Bergedorf
Bremen
Brunswick
Hamburg
Hanover
Lubeck
Mecklenburg-Schwerin
Mecklenburg-Strelitz
Oldenburg
Prussia
Saxony
Schleswig-Holstein
Wurttemberg

FORMER COLONIES
Cameroun (Kamerun)
Caroline Islands
German East Africa
German New Guinea
German South-West Africa
Kiauchau
Mariana Islands
Marshall Islands
Samoa
Togo

Italy

EARLY STATES
Modena
Parma
Romagna
Roman States
Sardinia
Tuscany
Two Sicilies
  Naples
  Neapolitan Provinces
  Sicily

FORMER COLONIES, CONTROLLED TERRITORIES, OCCUPATION AREAS
Aegean Islands
  Calimno (Calino)
  Caso
  Cos (Coo)
  Karki (Carchi)
  Leros (Lero)
  Lipso
  Nisiros (Nisiro)
  Patmos (Patmo)
  Piscopi

  Rodi (Rhodes)
  Scarpanto
  Simi
  Stampalia
Castellorizo
Corfu
Cyrenaica
Eritrea
Ethiopia (Abyssinia)
Fiume
Italian East Africa
Libya
Oltre Giuba
Saseno
Somalia (Italian Somaliland)
Tripolitania

POST OFFICES IN FOREIGN COUNTRIES "ESTERO"*
Austria
Bengasi
China
  Peking
  Tientsin
Crete
Tripoli
Turkish Empire
  Constantinople
  Durazzo
  Janina
  Jerusalem
  Salonika
  Scutari
  Smyrna
  Valona
*Stamps overprinted "ESTERO" were used in various parts of the world.

Netherlands
Netherlands Antilles (Curacao)
Netherlands Indies
Netherlands New Guinea
Surinam (Dutch Guiana)

Portugal

COLONIES PAST AND PRESENT, CONTROLLED TERRITORIES
Angola
Angra
Azores
Cape Verde
Funchal
Horta
Inhambane
Kionga
Lourenco Marques
Macao
Madeira
Mozambique
Mozambique Co.
Nyassa
Ponta Delgada
Portuguese Africa
Portuguese Congo
Portuguese Guinea
Portuguese India
Quelimane

St. Thomas & Prince Islands
Tete
Timor
Zambezia

Russia

ALLIED TERRITORIES AND REPUBLICS, OCCUPATION AREAS
Armenia
Aunus (Olonets)
Azerbaijan
Batum
Estonia
Far Eastern Republic
Georgia
Karelia
Latvia
Lithuania
North Ingermanland
Ostland
Russian Turkestan
Siberia
South Russia
Tannu Tuva
Transcaucasian Fed. Republics
Ukraine
Wenden (Livonia)
Western Ukraine

Spain

COLONIES PAST AND PRESENT, CONTROLLED TERRITORIES
Aguera, La
Cape Juby
Cuba
Elobey, Annobon & Corisco
Fernando Po
Mariana Islands
Philippines
Puerto Rico
Rio de Oro
Spanish Guinea
Spanish Morocco
Spanish Sahara

POST OFFICES IN FOREIGN COUNTRIES
Morocco
Tangier
Tetuan

COMMON DESIGN TYPE

PORTUGAL & COLONIES

Pictured in this section are issues where one illustration has been used for a number of countries in the Catalogue. Not included in this section are over-printed stamps or those issues which are illustrated in each country.

Vasco da Gama

Fleet Departing
CD20

Fleet Arriving at Calicut — CD21

Embarking at Rastello
CD22

Muse of History
CD23

San Gabriel, da Gama and Camoens
CD24

Archangel Gabriel, the Patron Saint — CD25

Flagship San Gabriel — CD26

Vasco da Gama — CD27

Fourth centenary of Vasco da Gama's discovery of the route to India.

1898

Azores	93-100
Macao	67-74
Madeira	37-44
Portugal	147-154
Port. Africa	1-8
Port. Congo	75-98
Port. India	189-196
St. Thomas & Prince Islands	170-193
Timor	45-52

Nos. 93-100 (8)	122.00	76.25
Nos. 67-74 (8)	136.00	96.75
Nos. 37-44 (8)	44.55	34.00
Nos. 147-154 (8)	169.30	43.45
Nos. 1-8 (8)	23.95	21.70
Nos. 75-98 (24)	34.45	34.45
Nos. 189-196 (8)	20.25	12.95

Nos. 170-193 (24)	37.85	34.30
Nos. 45-52 (8)	21.50	10.45
Set total (104) Stamps	609.85	364.30

Pombal
POSTAL TAX
POSTAL TAX DUES

Marquis de Pombal — CD28

Planning Reconstruction of Lisbon, 1755 — CD29

Pombal Monument, Lisbon — CD30

Sebastiao Jose de Carvalho e Mello, Marquis de Pombal (1699-1782), statesman, rebuilt Lisbon after earthquake of 1755. Tax was for the erection of Pombal monument. Obligatory on all mail on certain days throughout the year.

Postal Tax Dues are inscribed 'Multa'

1925

Angola	RA1-RA3, RAJ1-RAJ3
Azores	RA9-RA11, RAJ2-RAJ4
Cape Verde	RA1-RA3, RAJ1-RAJ3
Macao	RA1-RA3, RAJ1-RAJ3
Madeira	RA1-RA3, RAJ1-RAJ3
Mozambique	RA1-RA3, RAJ1-RAJ3
Portugal	RA11-RA13, RAJ2-RAJ4
Port. Guinea	RA1-RA3, RAJ1-RAJ3
Port. India	RA1-RA3, RAJ1-RAJ3
St. Thomas & Prince Islands	RA1-RA3, RAJ1-RAJ3
Timor	RA1-RA3, RAJ1-RAJ3

Nos. RA1-RA3,RAJ1-RAJ3 (6)	7.50	6.00
Nos. RA9-RA11 (3)	3.30	3.30
Nos. RA9-RA11,RAJ2-RAJ4 (6)	6.60	9.30
Nos. RA1-RA3,RAJ1-RAJ3 (6)	6.00	5.40
Nos. RA1-RA3,RAJ1-RAJ3 (6)	19.50	4.20
Nos. RA1-RA3,RAJ1-RAJ3 (6)	4.35	12.45
Nos. RA1-RA3,RAJ1-RAJ3 (6)	2.55	2.70
Nos. RA11-RA13,RAJ2-RAJ4 (6)	52.50	38.25
Nos. RA1-RA3,RAJ1-RAJ3 (6)	5.80	5.20
Nos. RA1-RA3,RAJ1-RAJ3 (6)	3.30	2.70
Nos. RA1-RA3,RAJ1-RAJ3 (6)	3.45	3.45
Nos. RA1-RA3,RAJ1-RAJ3 (6)	3.60	3.60
Nos. RA1-RA3,RAJ1-RAJ3 (6)	2.10	3.90
Set total (75) Stamps	120.55	100.45

Vasco da Gama
CD34

Mousinho de Albuquerque
CD35

Dam
CD36

Prince Henry the Navigator
CD37

Affonso de Albquerque
CD38

Plane over Globe
CD39

1938-39

Angola	274-291, C1-C9
Cape Verde	234-251, C1-C9
Macao	289-305, C7-C15
Mozambique	270-287, C1-C9
Port. Guinea	233-250, C1-C9
Port. India	439-453, C1-C8
St. Thomas & Prince Islands	302-319, C1-C18
Timor	223-239, C1-C9

Nos. 274-291,C1-C9 (27)	141.35	22.25
Nos. 234-251,C1-C9 (27)	100.00	31.20
Nos. 256-258A (4)	875.00	297.50
Nos. 270-287 (18)	43.30	6.75
Nos. 270-287,C1-C9 (27)	60.95	11.20
Nos. 233-250,C1-C9 (27)	86.05	30.70
Nos. 439-453,C1-C8 (23)	74.75	25.50
Nos. 302-319,323-340,C1-C18 (54)	319.25	190.35
Nos. 223-239,C1-C9 (26)	149.25	73.15
Set total (233) Stamps	1,850.	688.60

FRENCH COMMUNITY

Colonial Exposition

People of French Empire
CD70

Women's Heads
CD71

France Showing Way to Civilization
CD72

"Colonial Commerce"
CD73

International Colonial Exposition, Paris.

1931

Cameroun	213-216
Chad	60-63
Dahomey	97-100
Fr. Guiana	152-155
Fr. Guinea	116-119
Fr. India	100-103

Fr. Polynesia	76-79
Fr. Sudan	102-105
Gabon	120-123
Guadeloupe	138-141
Indo-China	140-142
Ivory Coast	92-95
Madagascar	169-172
Martinique	129-132
Mauritania	65-68
Middle Congo	61-64
New Caledonia	176-179
Niger	73-76
Reunion	122-125
St. Pierre & Miquelon	132-135
Senegal	138-141
Somali Coast	135-138
Togo	254-257
Ubangi-Shari	82-85
Upper Volta	66-69
Wallis & Futuna Isls.	85-88

Nos. 213-216 (4)	23.00	18.25
Nos. 60-63 (4)	22.00	22.00
Nos. 97-100 (4)	25.00	25.00
Nos. 152-155 (4)	22.00	22.00
Nos. 116-119 (4)	20.00	20.00
Nos. 100-103 (4)	18.00	18.00
Nos. 76-79 (4)	30.00	30.00
Nos. 102-105 (4)	19.00	19.00
Nos. 120-123 (4)	17.50	17.50
Nos. 138-141 (4)	19.00	19.00
Nos. 140-142 (4)	11.50	11.50
Nos. 92-95 (4)	22.50	22.50
Nos. 169-172 (4)	7.90	5.00
Nos. 129-132 (4)	21.00	21.00
Nos. 65-68 (4)	24.50	24.50
Nos. 61-64 (4)	18.50	18.50
Nos. 176-179 (4)	24.00	24.00
Nos. 73-76 (4)	22.50	22.50
Nos. 122-125 (4)	22.00	22.00
Nos. 132-135 (4)	24.00	24.00
Nos. 138-141 (4)	18.00	18.00
Nos. 135-138 (4)	26.00	26.00
Nos. 254-257 (4)	26.00	26.00
Nos. 82-85 (4)	22.00	22.00
Nos. 66-69 (4)	19.00	19.00
Nos. 85-88 (4)	35.00	35.00
Set total (103) Stamps	559.90	552.25

Paris International Exposition
Colonial Arts Exposition

"Colonial Resources"
CD74   CD77

Overseas Commerce
CD75

Exposition Building and Women
CD76

"France and the Empire"
CD78

Cultural Treasures of the Colonies
CD79

Souvenir sheets contain one imperf. stamp.

1937

Cameroun	217-222A
Dahomey	101-107

Fr. Equatorial Africa 27-32, 73
Fr. Guiana 162-168
Fr. Guinea 120-126
Fr. India 104-110
Fr. Polynesia............................117-123
Fr. Sudan.................................106-112
Guadeloupe 148-154
Indo-China..............................193-199
Inini 41
Ivory Coast 152-158
Kwangchowan 132
Madagascar.............................191-197
Martinique...............................179-185
Mauritania...................................69-75
New Caledonia.........................208-214
Niger 72-83
Reunion...................................167-173
St. Pierre & Miquelon..............165-171
Senegal....................................172-178
Somali Coast...........................139-145
Togo 258-264
Wallis & Futuna Isls. 89

Nos. 217-222A (7)	18.95	20.45
Nos. 101-107 (7)	19.95	21.20
Nos. 27-32, 73 (7)	25.60	26.60
Nos. 162-168 (7)	22.50	24.50
Nos. 120-126 (7)	22.55	23.55
Nos. 104-110 (7)	21.15	24.40
Nos. 117-123 (7)	58.50	75.00
Nos. 106-112 (7)	19.95	21.70
Nos. 148-154 (7)	19.55	21.05
Nos. 193-199 (7)	17.70	19.70
No. 41 (1)	19.00	22.50
Nos. 152-158 (7)	19.95	21.20
No. 132 (1)	9.25	11.00
Nos. 191-197 (7)	17.55	18.30
Nos. 179-185 (7)	19.95	21.70
Nos. 180-185 (6)	11.20	11.20
Nos. 69-75 (7)	19.95	21.70
Nos. 208-214 (7)	39.00	50.50
Nos. 73-83 (11)	42.70	44.20
Nos. 167-173 (7)	21.70	23.20
Nos. 165-171 (7)	49.60	64.00
Nos. 172-178 (7)	19.95	21.70
Nos. 139-145 (7)	25.95	27.95
Nos. 258-264 (7)	19.40	20.90
No. 89 (1)	28.50	37.50
Set total (160) Stamps	610.05	695.70

Curie

Pierre and Marie Curie CD80

40th anniversary of the discovery of radium. The surtax was for the benefit of the Intl. Union for the Control of Cancer.

1938

Cameroun.................................... B1
Cuba.......................................B1-B2
Dahomey B2
France.. B76
Fr. Equatorial Africa B1
Fr. Guiana B3
Fr. Guinea B2
Fr. India B6
Fr. Polynesia............................... B5
Fr. Sudan.................................... B1
Guadeloupe B3
Indo-China................................ B14
Ivory Coast B2
Madagascar................................ B2
Martinique.................................. B2
Mauritania.................................. B3
New Caledonia............................ B4
Niger B1
Reunion...................................... B4
St. Pierre & Miquelon................ B3
Senegal....................................... B3
Somali Coast.............................. B2
Togo B1

No. B1 (1)	10.00	10.00
Nos. B1-B2 (2)	8.50	2.40
No. B2 (1)	9.50	9.50
No. B76 (1)	21.00	12.50
No. B1 (1)	24.00	24.00
No. B3 (1)	13.50	13.50
No. B2 (1)	9.00	9.00
No. B6 (1)	10.00	10.00
No. B5 (1)	20.00	20.00
No. B1 (1)	12.50	12.50
No. B3 (1)	11.00	10.50
No. B14 (1)	12.00	12.00
No. B2 (1)	11.00	9.50
No. B2 (1)	11.00	11.00
No. B2 (1)	13.00	13.00
No. B3 (1)	8.75	8.75
No. B4 (1)	16.50	17.50
No. B1 (1)	17.00	17.00
No. B4 (1)	14.00	14.00
No. B3 (1)	21.00	22.50

No. B3 (1)	13.00	13.00
No. B2 (1)	8.75	8.75
No. B1 (1)	20.00	20.00
Set total (24) Stamps	315.00	300.90

Caillie

Rene Calle and Map of Northwestern Africa — CD81

Death centenary of Rene Caillie (1799-1838), French explorer.
All three denominations exist with colony name omitted.

1939

Dahomey 108-110
Fr. Guinea 161-163
Fr. Sudan...................................113-115
Ivory Coast 160-162
Mauritania.................................109-111
Niger 84-86
Senegal......................................188-190
Togo 265-267

Nos. 108-110 (3)	3.90	3.90
Nos. 161-163 (3)	3.20	3.20
Nos. 113-115 (3)	3.15	3.15
Nos. 160-162 (3)	3.20	3.20
Nos. 109-111 (3)	3.90	3.90
Nos. 84-86 (3)	3.20	3.20
Nos. 188-190 (3)	3.20	3.20
Nos. 265-267 (3)	3.15	3.15
Set total (24) Stamps	26.90	26.90

New York World's Fair

Natives and New York Skyline CD82

1939

Cameroun...................................223-224
Dahomey 111-112
Fr. Equatorial Africa 78-79
Fr. Guiana 169-170
Fr. Guinea 164-165
Fr. India 111-112
Fr. Polynesia..............................124-125
Fr. Sudan...................................116-117
Guadeloupe 155-156
Indo-China................................203-204
Inini 42-43
Ivory Coast 163-164
Kwangchowan 121-122
Madagascar...............................209-210
Martinique.................................186-187
Mauritania.................................112-113
New Caledonia..........................215-216
Niger 87-88
Reunion.....................................174-175
St. Pierre & Miquelon..............205-206
Senegal......................................191-192
Somali Coast.............................179-180
Togo 268-269
Wallis & Futuna Isls. 90-91

Nos. 223-224 (2)	2.80	2.40
Nos. 111-112 (2)	2.40	2.40
Nos. 78-79 (2)	3.65	3.65
Nos. 169-170 (2)	2.60	2.60
Nos. 164-165 (2)	2.80	2.80
Nos. 111-112 (2)	3.00	3.00
Nos. 124-125 (2)	4.80	4.80
Nos. 116-117 (2)	2.40	2.40
Nos. 155-156 (2)	2.50	2.50
Nos. 203-204 (2)	2.05	2.05
Nos. 42-43 (2)	7.50	9.00
Nos. 163-164 (2)	3.00	3.00
Nos. 133-134 (2)	2.50	2.50
Nos. 209-210 (2)	3.75	3.75
Nos. 186-187 (2)	2.35	2.35
Nos. 112-113 (2)	1.60	1.60
Nos. 215-216 (2)	3.35	3.35
Nos. 87-88 (2)	2.40	2.40
Nos. 174-175 (2)	2.80	2.80
Nos. 205-206 (2)	4.80	6.00
Nos. 191-192 (2)	2.00	2.00
Nos. 179-180 (2)	2.90	2.90
Nos. 268-269 (2)	2.50	2.50
Nos. 90-91 (2)	6.00	6.00
Set total (48) Stamps	76.45	78.75

French Revolution

Storming of the Bastille — CD83

French Revolution, 150th anniv. The surtax was for the defense of the colonies.

1939

Cameroun.................................B2-B6
Dahomey B3-B7
Fr. Equatorial Africa B4-B8, CB1
Fr. Guiana B4-B8, CB1
Fr. Guinea B3-B7
Fr. India B7-B11
Fr. Polynesia............... B6-B10, CB1
Fr. Sudan.................................B2-B6
Guadeloupe B4-B8
Indo-China............... B15-B19, CB1
Inini B1-B5
Ivory Coast B3-B7
Kwangchowan B1-B5
Madagascar.................. B3-B7, CB1
Martinique...............................B3-B7
Mauritania...............................B4-B8
New Caledonia.............. B5-B9, CB1
Niger B2-B6
Reunion......................... B5-B9, CB1
St. Pierre & Miquelon.............B4-B8
Senegal.......................... B4-B8, CB1
Somali Coast...........................B3-B7
Togo B2-B6
Wallis & Futuna Isls. B1-B5

Nos. B2-B6 (5)	60.00	60.00
Nos. B3-B7 (5)	47.50	47.50
Nos. B4-B8,CB1 (6)	107.50	107.50
Nos. B4-B8,CB1 (6)	79.50	79.50
Nos. B3-B7 (5)	48.75	48.75
Nos. B7-B11 (5)	45.00	45.00
Nos. B6-B10,CB1 (6)	122.50	122.50
Nos. B2-B6 (5)	50.00	50.00
Nos. B4-B8 (5)	50.00	50.00
Nos. B15-B19,CB1 (6)	85.00	85.00
Nos. B1-B5 (5)	80.00	87.50
Nos. B3-B7 (5)	43.75	43.75
Nos. B1-B5 (5)	46.25	46.25
Nos. B3-B7,CB1 (6)	65.50	65.50
Nos. B3-B7 (5)	52.50	52.50
Nos. B4-B8 (5)	47.50	47.50
Nos. B5-B9,CB1 (6)	101.50	101.50
Nos. B2-B6 (5)	60.00	60.00
Nos. B5-B9,CB1 (6)	87.50	87.50
Nos. B4-B8 (5)	67.50	72.50
Nos. B4-B8,CB1 (6)	63.00	63.00
Nos. B3-B7 (5)	52.50	52.50
Nos. B2-B6 (5)	47.50	47.50
Nos. B1-B5 (5)	95.00	95.00
Set total (128) Stamps	1,606.	1,618.

Plane over Coastal Area CD85

All five denominations exist with colony name omitted.

1940

Dahomey C1-C5
Fr. Guinea C1-C5
Fr. Sudan.................................. C1-C5
Ivory Coast C1-C5
Mauritania................................ C1-C5
Niger C1-C5
Senegal.................................. C12-C16

Nos. C1-C5 (5)	4.00	4.00
Nos. C1-C5 (5)	4.90	4.90
Nos. C1-C5 (5)	3.95	3.95
Nos. C1-C5 (5)	4.05	4.05
Nos. C1-C5 (5)	3.90	3.90
Nos. C1-C5 (5)	4.00	4.00
Nos. C12-C16 (5)	4.05	4.05
Set total (40) Stamps	32.85	32.85

BRITISH COMMONWEALTH OF NATIONS

The listings follow established trade practices when these issues are offered as units by dealers. The Peace issue, for example, includes only one stamp from the Indian state of Hyderabad. The U.P.U. issue includes the Egypt set. Pairs are included for those varieties issues with bilingual designs se-tenant.

Silver Jubilee

Windsor Castle and King George V CD301

Reign of King George V, 25th anniv.

1935

Antigua 77-80
Ascension 33-36
Bahamas 92-95
Barbados 186-189
Basutoland......................................11-14
Bechuanaland Protectorate.....117-120
Bermuda 100-103
British Guiana...............................223-226
British Honduras...........................108-111
Cayman Islands.............................81-84
Ceylon 260-263
Cyprus 136-139
Dominica 90-93
Falkland Islands 77-80
Fiji 110-113
Gambia 125-128
Gibraltar 100-103
Gilbert & Ellice Islands................33-36
Gold Coast 108-111
Grenada 124-127
Hong Kong 147-150
Jamaica 109-112
Kenya, Uganda, Tanzania...........42-45
Leeward Islands 96-99
Malta 184-187
Mauritius.......................................204-207
Montserrat 85-88
Newfoundland...............................226-229
Nigeria 34-37
Northern Rhodesia........................18-21
Nyasaland Protectorate...............47-50
St. Helena 111-114
St. Kitts-Nevis...............................72-75
St. Lucia 91-94
St. Vincent 134-137
Seychelles 118-121
Sierra Leone 166-169
Solomon Islands...........................60-63
Somaliland Protectorate.............77-80
Straits Settlements 213-216
Swaziland 20-23
Trinidad & Tobago 43-46
Turks & Caicos Islands 71-74
Virgin Islands.................................69-72

The following have different designs but are included in the omnibus set:

Great Britain.................................226-229
Offices in Morocco (Sp. Curr.)....67-70
Offices in Morocco.......................226-229
Offices in Morocco (Fr. Curr.) 422-425
Offices in Morocco (Tangier)....508-510
Australia..152-154
Canada 211-216
Cook Islands 98-100
India 142-148
Nauru 31-34
New Guinea 46-47
New Zealand 199-201
Niue 67-69
Papua 114-117
Samoa 163-165
South Africa 68-71
Southern Rhodesia.......................33-36
South-West Africa 121-124

Nos. 77-80 (4)	21.50	22.75
Nos. 33-36 (4)	61.00	113.00
Nos. 92-95 (4)	25.00	43.00
Nos. 186-189 (4)	35.75	54.60
Nos. 11-14 (4)	13.35	20.00
Nos. 117-120 (4)	13.75	23.00
Nos. 100-103 (4)	18.00	58.25
Nos. 223-226 (4)	18.35	35.50
Nos. 108-111 (4)	15.25	15.35
Nos. 81-84 (4)	16.95	17.75

Nos. 260-263 (4) 12.60 23.35
Nos. 136-139 (4) 39.75 34.40
Nos. 90-93 (4) 18.85 19.85
Nos. 77-80 (4) 50.00 13.35
Nos. 110-113 (4) 15.25 29.00
Nos. 125-128 (4) 19.60 28.75
Nos. 100-103 (4) 32.90 47.50
Nos. 33-36 (4) 39.50 53.50
Nos. 108-111 (4) 26.75 62.85
Nos. 124-127 (4) 16.60 39.50
Nos. 147-150 (4) 76.50 21.00
Nos. 109-112 (4) 21.80 35.00
Nos. 42-45 (4) 9.00 11.00
Nos. 96-99 (4) 31.00 34.60
Nos. 184-187 (4) 25.00 34.70
Nos. 204-207 (4) 47.60 58.25
Nos. 85-88 (4) 10.25 30.25
Nos. 226-229 (4) 17.00 12.05
Nos. 34-37 (4) 12.55 59.75
Nos. 18-21 (4) 15.75 16.25
Nos. 47-50 (4) 37.25 80.25
Nos. 111-114 (4) 31.15 33.25
Nos. 72-75 (4) 11.55 18.50
Nos. 91-94 (4) 16.00 20.80
Nos. 134-137 (4) 9.45 21.25
Nos. 118-121 (4) 17.50 31.00
Nos. 166-169 (4) 18.50 55.00
Nos. 60-63 (4) 27.50 38.00
Nos. 77-80 (4) 17.75 46.00
Nos. 213-216 (4) 15.00 25.10
Nos. 20-23 (4) 6.05 13.00
Nos. 43-46 (4) 12.30 27.75
Nos. 71-74 (4) 9.25 16.25
Nos. 69-72 (4) 22.20 47.50

Nos. 226-229 (4) 7.25 7.45
Nos. 67-70 (4) 14.35 26.10
Nos. 226-229 (4) 8.20 28.90
Nos. 422-425 (4) 3.90 2.00
Nos. 508-510 (3) 18.80 23.85
Nos. 152-154 (3) 45.75 60.35
Nos. 211-216 (6) 27.85 13.35
Nos. 98-100 (3) 6.75 14.00
Nos. 142-148 (7) 23.25 11.80
Nos. 31-34 (4) 12.60 13.85
Nos. 46-47 (2) 4.10 1.70
Nos. 199-201 (3) 21.75 31.75
Nos. 67-69 (3) 7.80 22.50
Nos. 114-117 (3) 9.20 17.00
Nos. 163-165 (3) 4.40 5.50
Nos. 68-71 (4) 62.50 167.00
Nos. 33-36 (4) 29.00 45.25
Nos. 121-124 (4) 14.50 36.10
Set total (245) Stamps 1,351. 2,070.

Coronation

Queen Elizabeth and King George VI
CD302

1937

Aden 13-15
Antigua 81-83
Ascension 37-39
Bahamas 97-99
Barbados 190-192
Basutoland 15-17
Bechuanaland Protectorate......121-123
Bermuda 115-117
British Guiana..............................227-229
British Honduras........................112-114
Cayman Islands 97-99
Ceylon 275-277
Cyprus 140-142
Dominica 94-96
Falkland Islands 81-83
Fiji 114-116
Gambia 129-131
Gibraltar 104-106
Gilbert & Ellice Islands................37-39
Gold Coast 112-114
Grenada 128-130
Hong Kong 151-153
Jamaica 113-115
Kenya, Uganda, Tanzania 60-62
Leeward Islands 100-102
Malta 188-190
Mauritius 208-210
Montserrat 89-91
Newfoundland 230-232
Nigeria 50-52
Northern Rhodesia.........................22-24
Nyasaland Protectorate.................51-53
St. Helena 115-117
St. Kitts-Nevis.................................76-78
St. Lucia 107-109
St. Vincent 138-140
Seychelles 122-124
Sierra Leone 170-172
Solomon Islands 64-66
Somaliland Protectorate 81-83
Straits Settlements 235-237
Swaziland 24-26
Trinidad & Tobago 47-49

Turks & Caicos Islands 75-77
Virgin Islands..................................73-75

The following have different designs but are included in the omnibus set:

Great Britain 234
Offices in Morocco (Sp. Curr.)...........82
Offices in Morocco (Fr. Curr.)...........439
Offices in Morocco (Tangier)...........514
Canada 237
Cook Islands 109-111
Nauru 35-38
Newfoundland 233-243
New Guinea 48-51
New Zealand 223-225
Niue 70-72
Papua 118-121
South Africa 74-78
Southern Rhodesia 38-41
South-West Africa 125-132

Nos. 13-15 (3) 3.00 6.10
Nos. 81-83 (3) 2.00 4.50
Nos. 37-39 (3) 2.75 2.75
Nos. 97-99 (3) 1.15 3.05
Nos. 190-192 (3) 1.10 1.95
Nos. 15-17 (3) 1.25 3.00
Nos. 121-123 (3) .95 3.35
Nos. 115-117 (3) 1.25 5.00
Nos. 227-229 (3) .80 3.05
Nos. 112-114 (3) 1.20 2.35
Nos. 97-99 (3) 1.10 2.30
Nos. 275-277 (3) 8.25 10.35
Nos. 140-142 (3) 3.75 6.50
Nos. 94-96 (3) .85 2.40
Nos. 81-83 (3) 2.90 2.30
Nos. 114-116 (3) 1.35 5.75
Nos. 129-131 (3) 1.00 4.70
Nos. 104-106 (3) 2.60 6.45
Nos. 37-39 (3) .95 2.00
Nos. 112-114 (3) 3.10 10.00
Nos. 128-130 (3) 1.00 .85
Nos. 151-153 (3) 27.00 12.50
Nos. 113-115 (3) 1.35 1.25
Nos. 60-62 (3) 1.05 1.60
Nos. 100-102 (3) 1.55 3.90
Nos. 188-190 (3) 1.35 1.65
Nos. 208-210 (3) 2.05 3.75
Nos. 89-91 (3) 1.00 3.35
Nos. 230-232 (3) 7.00 2.80
Nos. 50-52 (3) 3.25 8.50
Nos. 22-24 (3) 1.35 2.00
Nos. 51-53 (3) 1.05 1.30
Nos. 115-117 (3) 1.45 2.05
Nos. 76-78 (3) .95 2.05
Nos. 107-109 (3) 1.05 2.05
Nos. 138-140 (3) .80 4.75
Nos. 122-124 (3) 1.20 1.90
Nos. 170-172 (3) 1.95 5.65
Nos. 64-66 (3) .90 2.00
Nos. 81-83 (3) 1.10 3.40
Nos. 235-237 (3) 3.25 1.60
Nos. 24-26 (3) 1.05 1.75
Nos. 47-49 (3) 1.00 1.00
Nos. 75-77 (3) 1.30 1.55
Nos. 73-75 (3) 1.20 5.00

Nos. 264-265 (2) .50 .70
No. 82 (1) .80 .80
No. 439 (1) .35 .25
No. 514 (1) .55 .55
No. 237 (1) .30 .25
Nos. 109-111 (3) .85 .80
Nos. 35-38 (4) 1.15 5.50
Nos. 233-243 (11) 33.20 29.90
Nos. 48-51 (4) 1.40 7.90
Nos. 223-225 (3) 1.40 2.75
Nos. 70-72 (3) .80 2.05
Nos. 118-121 (4) 1.60 5.25
Nos. 74-78 (5) 9.25 11.05
Nos. 38-41 (4) 4.00 16.25
Nos. 125-132 (8) 5.50 8.45
Set total (190) Stamps 169.15 258.50

Peace

King George VI and Parliament Buildings, London
CD303

Return to peace at the close of World War II.

1945-46

Aden 28-29
Antigua 96-97
Ascension 130-131
Bahamas 130-131
Barbados 207-208
Bermuda 131-132
British Guiana..............................242-243
British Honduras........................127-128
Cayman Islands 112-113
Ceylon 293-294
Cyprus 156-157
Dominica 112-113
Falkland Islands 97-98
Falkland Islands Dep.............1L9-1L10

Fiji 137-138
Gambia 144-145
Gibraltar 119-120
Gilbert & Ellice Island 52-53
Gold Coast 128-129
Grenada 143-144
Jamaica 136-137
Kenya, Uganda, Tanzania 90-91
Leeward Islands 116-117
Malta 206-207
Mauritius 223-224
Montserrat 104-105
Nigeria 71-72
Northern Rhodesia.........................46-47
Nyasaland Protectorate.................82-83
Pitcairn Islands 9-10
St. Helena 128-129
St. Kitts-Nevis.................................91-92
St. Lucia 127-128
St. Vincent 152-153
Seychelles 149-150
Sierra Leone 186-187
Solomon Islands 80-81
Somaliland Protectorate...........108-109
Trinidad & Tobago 62-63
Turks & Caicos Islands 90-91
Virgin Islands..................................88-89

The following have different designs but are included in the omnibus set:

Great Britain 264-265
Offices in Morocco (Tangier)....523-524
Aden
 Kathri State of Seiyun.............12-13
 Qu'aiti State of Shihr and
  Mukalla...................................12-13
Australia 200-202
Basutoland 29-31
Bechuanaland Protectorate......137-139
Burma 66-69
Cook Islands 127-130
Hong Kong 174-175
India 195-198
 Hyderabad...51
New Zealand 247-257
Niue 90-93
Pakistan-Bahawalpur.......................O16
Samoa 191-194
South Africa 100-102
Southern Rhodesia 67-70
South-West Africa 153-155
Swaziland 38-40
Zanzibar..222-223

Nos. 28-29 (2) .70 2.30
Nos. 96-97 (2) .50 .80
Nos. 50-51 (2) .90 1.75
Nos. 130-131 (2) .50 1.40
Nos. 131-132 (2) .55 .55
Nos. 242-243 (2) 1.05 1.40
Nos. 127-128 (2) .50 .50
Nos. 112-113 (2) .60 .80
Nos. 293-294 (2) .60 2.10
Nos. 156-157 (2) 1.00 .70
Nos. 112-113 (2) .50 .50
Nos. 97-98 (2) .90 1.35
Nos. 1L9-1L10 (2) 1.40 1.00
Nos. 137-138 (2) .50 1.75
Nos. 144-145 (2) .50 .95
Nos. 119-120 (2) .75 1.00
Nos. 52-53 (2) .50 .50
Nos. 128-129 (2) 1.85 3.75
Nos. 143-144 (2) .50 .95
Nos. 136-137 (2) 7.30 7.50
Nos. 90-91 (2) .65 .65
Nos. 116-117 (2) .50 .50
Nos. 206-207 (2) .65 2.00
Nos. 223-224 (2) .50 1.05
Nos. 104-105 (2) .50 .50
Nos. 71-72 (2) .70 2.25
Nos. 46-47 (2) 1.25 2.00
Nos. 82-83 (2) .50 .50
Nos. 9-10 (2) 1.40 1.40
Nos. 128-129 (2) .65 .70
Nos. 91-92 (2) .50 .50
Nos. 127-128 (2) .50 .60
Nos. 152-153 (2) .50 .50
Nos. 149-150 (2) .55 .50
Nos. 186-187 (2) .50 .50
Nos. 80-81 (2) .50 1.30
Nos. 108-109 (2) .50 .50
Nos. 62-63 (2) .50 .50
Nos. 90-91 (2) .50 .50
Nos. 88-89 (2) .50 .50

Nos. 264-265 (2) .50 .70
Nos. 523-524 (2) 1.50 3.00
Nos. 12-13 (2) .50 .90
Nos. 12-13 (2) .50 1.05
Nos. 200-202 (3) 1.60 3.00
Nos. 29-31 (3) 2.10 2.60
Nos. 137-139 (3) 2.05 4.75
Nos. 66-69 (4) 1.60 1.30
Nos. 127-130 (4) 2.20 2.00
Nos. 174-175 (2) 5.15 3.15
No. 51 (1) .25 .25
Nos. 223-225 (3) 1.40 2.75
Nos. 90-93 (4) 1.70 2.00
No. O16 (1) 5.50 7.00
Nos. 191-194 (4) 2.05 1.00

Nos. 100-102 (3) 1.20 4.00
Nos. 67-70 (4) 1.40 1.75
Nos. 153-155 (3) 2.55 3.50
Nos. 38-40 (3) 2.40 5.50
Nos. 222-223 (2) .65 1.00
Set total (135) Stamps 70.75 100.40

Silver Wedding Issue

King George VI and Queen Elizabeth
CD304　　CD305

1948-49

Aden 30-31
 Kathri State of Seiyun.............14-15
 Qu'aiti State of Shihr and
  Mukalla...................................14-15
Antigua 98-99
Ascension 52-53
Bahamas 148-149
Barbados 210-211
Basutoland 39-40
Bechuanaland Protectorate......147-148
Bermuda 133-134
British Guiana..............................244-245
British Honduras........................129-130
Cayman Islands 116-117
Cyprus 158-159
Dominica 114-115
Falkland Islands 99-100
Falkland Islands Dep..........1L11-1L12
Fiji 139-140
Gambia 146-147
Gibraltar 121-122
Gilbert & Ellice Islands................54-55
Gold Coast 142-143
Grenada 145-146
Hong Kong 178-179
Jamaica 138-139
Kenya, Uganda, Tanzania 92-93
Leeward Islands 118-119
Malaya
 Johore 128-129
 Kedah 55-56
 Kelantan 44-45
 Malacca 1-2
 Negri Sembilan 36-37
 Pahang 44-45
 Penang 1-2
 Perak 99-100
 Perlis 1-2
 Selangor 74-75
 Trengganu 47-48
Malta 223-224
Mauritius 229-230
Montserrat 106-107
Nigeria 73-74
North Borneo 238-239
Northern Rhodesia.........................48-49
Nyasaland Protectorate.................85-86
Pitcairn Islands 11-12
St. Helena 130-131
St. Kitts-Nevis.................................93-94
St. Lucia 129-130
St. Vincent 154-155
Sarawak 174-175
Seychelles 151-152
Sierra Leone 188-189
Singapore 21-22
Solomon Islands 82-83
Somaliland Protectorate...........110-111
Swaziland 48-49
Trinidad & Tobago 64-65
Turks & Caicos Islands 92-93
Virgin Islands..................................90-91
Zanzibar..224-225

The following have different designs but are included in the omnibus set:

Great Britain 267-268
Offices in Morocco (Sp. Curr.) 93-94
Offices in Morocco (Tangier) 525-526
Bahrain 62-63
Kuwait 82-83
Oman 25-26
South Africa 106

South-West Africa 159

Nos. 30-31 (2)	37.90	47.50
Nos. 14-15 (2)	21.50	16.00
Nos. 14-15 (2)	22.00	18.50
Nos. 98-99 (2)	15.00	14.25
Nos. 52-53 (2)	58.15	60.60
Nos. 148-149 (2)	45.25	40.30
Nos. 210-211 (2)	18.35	13.05
Nos. 39-40 (2)	50.30	50.25
Nos. 147-148 (2)	42.85	47.75
Nos. 133-134 (2)	47.75	55.25
Nos. 244-245 (2)	24.25	28.45
Nos. 129-130 (2)	22.75	53.20
Nos. 116-117 (2)	22.75	28.50
Nos. 158-159 (2)	58.50	78.05
Nos. 114-115 (2)	25.25	32.75
Nos. 99-100 (2)	112.10	83.60
Nos. 1L11-1L12 (2)	4.25	6.00
Nos. 139-140 (2)	18.20	10.75
Nos. 146-147 (2)	25.25	26.25
Nos. 121-122 (2)	71.00	90.50
Nos. 54-55 (2)	15.25	24.25
Nos. 142-143 (2)	35.25	37.75
Nos. 145-146 (2)	26.25	26.25
Nos. 178-179 (2)	363.90	136.60
Nos. 138-139 (2)	32.85	75.25
Nos. 92-93 (2)	52.75	72.75
Nos. 118-119 (2)	6.75	6.75
Nos. 128-129 (2)	29.25	53.25
Nos. 55-56 (2)	35.25	50.25
Nos. 44-45 (2)	35.75	62.75
Nos. 1-2 (2)	35.40	49.75
Nos. 36-37 (2)	28.10	38.20
Nos. 44-45 (2)	28.00	38.05
Nos. 1-2 (2)	40.50	37.80
Nos. 99-100 (2)	27.80	37.75
Nos. 1-2 (2)	33.50	58.00
Nos. 74-75 (2)	30.25	25.30
Nos. 47-48 (2)	35.25	62.75
Nos. 223-224 (2)	40.55	45.25
Nos. 229-230 (2)	17.75	45.25
Nos. 106-107 (2)	9.25	18.25
Nos. 73-74 (2)	13.85	20.30
Nos. 238-239 (2)	35.30	45.75
Nos. 48-49 (2)	92.80	80.25
Nos. 85-86 (2)	19.25	32.75
Nos. 11-12 (2)	56.75	53.50
Nos. 130-131 (2)	32.80	42.80
Nos. 93-94 (2)	11.25	7.25
Nos. 129-130 (2)	22.25	45.25
Nos. 154-155 (2)	27.75	30.25
Nos. 174-175 (2)	52.90	55.40
Nos. 151-152 (2)	16.25	45.75
Nos. 188-189 (2)	24.75	26.25
Nos. 21-22 (2)	146.25	55.40
Nos. 82-83 (2)	13.40	13.40
Nos. 110-111 (2)	7.00	8.25
Nos. 48-49 (2)	40.30	47.75
Nos. 64-65 (2)	32.75	38.25
Nos. 92-93 (2)	15.25	20.30
Nos. 90-91 (2)	18.85	21.35
Nos. 224-225 (2)	29.60	38.00
Nos. 235-248 (14)	21.95	8.60
Nos. 93-94 (2)	20.10	25.35
Nos. 525-526 (2)	23.10	29.25
Nos. 62-63 (2)	38.45	72.50
Nos. 82-83 (2)	45.50	45.50
Nos. 25-26 (2)	46.00	47.50
No. 106 (1)	.70	1.25
No. 159 (1)	1.25	.35
Set total (148) Stamps	2,609.	2,762.

U.P.U. Issue

Mercury and Symbols of Communications — CD306

Plane, Ship and Hemispheres — CD307

Mercury Scattering Letters over Globe CD308

U.P.U. Monument, Bern CD309

Universal Postal Union, 75th anniversary.

1949

Aden 32-35
Kathiri State of Seiyun..............16-19
Qu'aiti State of Shihr and
  Mukalla................16-19
Antigua 100-103
Ascension 57-60
Bahamas 150-153
Barbados 212-215
Basutoland...................41-44
Bechuanaland Protectorate....149-152
Bermuda....................138-141
British Guiana.................246-249
British Honduras.............137-140
Brunei...........................79-82
Cayman Islands 118-121
Cyprus 160-163
Dominica......................116-119
Falkland Islands 103-106
Falkland Islands Dep..........1L14-1L17
Fiji 141-144
Gambia 148-151
Gibraltar 123-126
Gilbert & Ellice Islands.............56-59
Gold Coast 144-147
Grenada 147-150
Hong Kong 180-183
Jamaica 142-145
Kenya, Uganda, Tanzania 94-97
Leeward Islands 126-129
Malaya
  Johore......................151-154
  Kedah......................57-60
  Kelantan...................46-49
  Malacca....................18-21
  Negri Sembilan 59-62
  Pahang....................46-49
  Penang....................23-26
  Perak.....................101-104
  Perlis......................3-6
  Selangor...................76-79
  Trengganu 49-52
Malta.......................225-228
Mauritius....................231-234
Montserrat 108-111
New Hebrides, British 62-65
New Hebrides, French 79-82
Nigeria 75-78
North Borneo................240-243
Northern Rhodesia..............50-53
Nyasaland Protectorate...........87-90
Pitcairn Islands................13-16
St. Helena 132-135
St. Kitts-Nevis................95-98
St. Lucia 131-134
St. Vincent 170-173
Sarawak....................176-179
Seychelles 153-156
Sierra Leone 190-193
Singapore 23-26
Solomon Islands 84-87
Somaliland Protectorate 112-115
Southern Rhodesia 71-72
Swaziland....................50-53
Tonga.......................87-90
Trinidad & Tobago 66-69
Turks & Caicos Islands 101-104
Virgin Islands 92-95
Zanzibar....................226-229

The following have different designs but are included in the omnibus set:

Great Britain 276-279
Offices in Morocco (Tangier) 546-549
Australia......................223
Bahrain 68-71
Burma......................116-121
Ceylon.....................304-306
Egypt......................281-283
India.......................223-226
Kuwait......................89-92
Oman......................31-34
Pakistan-Bahawalpur 26-29, O25-O28
South Africa.................109-111
South-West Africa 160-162

Nos. 32-35 (4)	6.60	8.95
Nos. 16-19 (4)	2.40	6.80
Nos. 16-19 (4)	2.55	3.25
Nos. 100-103 (4)	3.95	6.60
Nos. 57-60 (4)	10.90	7.75
Nos. 150-153 (4)	5.60	9.55
Nos. 212-215 (4)	4.40	14.15
Nos. 41-44 (4)	4.75	10.00
Nos. 149-152 (4)	3.35	7.25
Nos. 138-141 (4)	1.70	5.55
Nos. 246-249 (4)	2.65	4.20
Nos. 137-140 (4)	3.35	4.75
Nos. 79-82 (4)	7.75	6.75
Nos. 118-121 (4)	4.00	6.40
Nos. 116-119 (4)	2.30	5.65
Nos. 103-106 (4)	15.65	18.10
Nos. 1L14-1L17 (4)	15.50	14.00
Nos. 141-144 (4)	3.35	14.00
Nos. 148-151 (4)	3.50	7.85
Nos. 123-126 (4)	6.75	9.50
Nos. 56-59 (4)	4.85	8.75
Nos. 144-147 (4)	3.05	6.95
Nos. 147-150 (4)	2.30	3.55
Nos. 180-183 (4)	74.25	23.60
Nos. 142-145 (4)	2.70	6.00
Nos. 94-97 (4)	2.90	3.40
Nos. 126-129 (4)	3.05	3.75
Nos. 151-154 (4)	4.70	8.90
Nos. 57-60 (4)	4.80	10.25
Nos. 46-49 (4)	4.25	11.15
Nos. 18-21 (4)	4.25	17.30
Nos. 59-62 (4)	3.50	10.75
Nos. 46-49 (4)	3.00	7.25
Nos. 23-26 (4)	5.10	11.75
Nos. 101-104 (4)	3.65	10.75
Nos. 3-6 (4)	3.95	14.25
Nos. 76-79 (4)	4.90	12.30
Nos. 49-52 (4)	4.95	9.75
Nos. 225-228 (4)	4.50	5.35
Nos. 231-234 (4)	4.35	6.70
Nos. 108-111 (4)	3.40	3.85
Nos. 62-65 (4)	1.60	4.10
Nos. 79-82 (4)	24.25	24.25
Nos. 75-78 (4)	2.80	9.25
Nos. 240-243 (4)	7.15	6.50
Nos. 50-53 (4)	5.00	6.50
Nos. 87-90 (4)	4.05	4.05
Nos. 13-16 (4)	24.00	18.75
Nos. 132-135 (4)	4.85	7.10
Nos. 95-98 (4)	3.35	4.70
Nos. 131-134 (4)	2.55	3.85
Nos. 170-173 (4)	2.20	5.05
Nos. 176-179 (4)	9.00	11.10
Nos. 153-156 (4)	3.25	4.10
Nos. 190-193 (4)	3.00	5.10
Nos. 23-26 (4)	24.25	14.20
Nos. 84-87 (4)	4.35	4.90
Nos. 112-115 (4)	2.45	7.95
Nos. 71-72 (2)	1.95	2.25
Nos. 50-53 (4)	2.80	4.65
Nos. 87-90 (4)	3.25	5.25
Nos. 66-69 (4)	3.15	3.15
Nos. 101-104 (4)	3.65	4.00
Nos. 92-95 (4)	2.60	4.60
Nos. 226-229 (4)	5.45	13.50
Nos. 276-279 (4)	1.85	2.40
Nos. 546-549 (4)	3.20	10.15
No. 223 (1)	.60	.55
Nos. 68-71 (4)	5.00	16.75
Nos. 116-121 (6)	7.15	5.30
Nos. 304-306 (3)	3.35	4.25
Nos. 281-283 (3)	5.75	2.70
Nos. 223-226 (4)	35.50	10.50
Nos. 89-92 (4)	6.10	10.25
Nos. 31-34 (4)	5.55	15.75
Nos. 26-29, O25-O28 (8)	2.00	42.00
Nos. 109-111 (3)	3.00	3.00
Nos. 160-162 (3)	3.95	6.00
Set total (309) Stamps	500.40	675.80

University Issue

Arms of University College CD310

Alice, Princess of Athlone CD311

1948 opening of University College of the West Indies at Jamaica.

1951

Antigua 104-105
Barbados 228-229
British Guiana.................250-251
British Honduras..............141-142
Dominica......................120-121
Grenada 164-165
Jamaica 146-147
Leeward Islands 130-131
Montserrat 112-113
St. Kitts-Nevis................105-106
St. Lucia 149-150
St. Vincent 174-175

Trinidad & Tobago 70-71
Virgin Islands.............................96-97

Nos. 104-105 (2)	1.35	3.25
Nos. 228-229 (2)	1.85	1.55
Nos. 250-251 (2)	1.10	1.25
Nos. 141-142 (2)	1.40	2.15
Nos. 120-121 (2)	1.40	1.75
Nos. 164-165 (2)	1.20	1.60
Nos. 146-147 (2)	.95	.85
Nos. 130-131 (2)	1.35	2.00
Nos. 112-113 (2)	.85	1.50
Nos. 105-106 (2)	.90	1.50
Nos. 149-150 (2)	1.40	1.50
Nos. 174-175 (2)	1.00	2.15
Nos. 70-71 (2)	.75	.75
Nos. 96-97 (2)	1.50	3.40
Set total (28) Stamps	17.00	25.20

Classic Specialized Additions, Deletions & Number Changes

Number in 2014 Catalogue	Number in 2015 Catalogue
United States	
Postage	
new	374b
Postage Dues	
J78b	J78
J78	J78b
J80b	J80
J80	J80b
J81b	J81
J81	J81b
J82b	J82
J82	J82b
J83b	J83
J83	J83b
J84b	J84
J84	J84b
Revenues – Stock Transfer	
new	RD67a
new	RD68a
new	RD70a
RD71a	RD71b
new	RD71b
new	RD73a
new	RD74a
new	RD75a
new	RD76a
new	RD77a
new	RD78a
new	RD80a
new	RD81a
new	RD82a
new	RD83a
new	RD84a
new	RD85a
Confederate States of America	
new	148XU1
Alaouites	
new	25g
new	27f
new	29f
new	29g
new	C5b
C6b	C6c
new	C6b
new	C7b
new	C8b
new	J9a
Algeria	
new	B26b
Annam & Tonkin	
new	1c
Barbados	
new	132a
new	186a
new	187a
new	188a
new	189a
new	209c
Belgium	
new	J16C-J16D
British East Africa	
new	15d
new	54d
new	55d
58d	deleted
58e	deleted
new	58d
63b (Afr1)	63c
63a (Br1)	63b
new	71c
Canadian Provinces-Newfoundland	
130b	deleted
Canada	
new	23b
Costa Rica	
new	RA1A-RA1E

Number in 2014 Catalogue	Number in 2015 Catalogue
Fiume	
new	148A
new	148B
new	148Bc
French Guiana	
new	97a
French Guinea	
new	63a
new	64a
new	70a
French India	
new	54a
new	55b
French Morocco	
new	120a
new	120b
new	122c
new	123b
French Oceania (French Polynesia)	
new	24a
new	48a
new	54a
new	125Ac
Germany	
new	2b
new	90a
new	337a
new	370b
new	B105a
new	CL5
new	CL6
Greece	
new	N168
Guadeloupe	
new	26f
new	27a
new	27b
new	27c
new	32a
new	33b (2015)
new	47d
new	47e (2015)
new	52a (2015)
new	52b (2015)
new	53a (2015)
new	J4e
Haiti	
new	72c
new	110a
new	111a
new	112a
new	113a
new	114a
new	115a
new	116a
new	117a
new	118a
new	119a
new	119b
new	119c
new	120a
new	120b
new	121a
new	123a
new	124a
Heligoland	
10a	deleted
Hong Kong	
new	29c
new	33a
new	33b
new	48a
new	63a
new	64b
new	64c
new	65a
new	65b
new	66f

Number in 2014 Catalogue	Number in 2015 Catalogue
Treaty Ports	
Amoy	
new	LAM1-LAM108
new	LAM1a
Anping	
new	LAP1-LAP6
Canton	
new	LCA1-LCA99
Chefoo	
new	LCH1-LCH55
new	LCH12a
Foochow	
new	LFO1-LFO90
Hankow	
new	LHA1-LHA91
Kiungchow (Hoihao)	
new	LKC1-LKC85
Ningpo	
new	LNG1-LNG76
new	LNG3a
Shanghai	
new	LSH1-LSH118
Swatow	
new	LSW1-LSW96
new	LSW3a
Tientsin	
new	LTS1-LTS41
Wei Hai Wei (Liu Kung Tau)	
new	LWH1-LWH47
Port Edward	
new	LPE1-LPE35
British Offices in Japan	
Hiogo (Kobe)	
new	LHG1-LHG14
Nagasaki	
new	LNA1-LNA16
Yokohama	
new	LYO1-LYO21
new	LYO3a
new	LYO4a
new	LYO5a
new	LYO6a
new	LYO7a
new	LYO8a
new	LYO9a
new	LYO10a
new	LYO11a
new	LYO12a
new	LYO13a
new	LYO15a
new	LYO20a
new	LYO21a
India	
new	50a
Travancore-Cochin	
new	1m
new	1n
new	2m
new	2n
new	2o
new	3m
new	3n
new	3o
new	3p
new	4m
new	5m
5a	5n
new	5o
new	6m
new	7m
new	7n
new	1g

Number in 2014 Catalogue	Number in 2015 Catalogue
Travancore-Cochin	
new	1h
new	1i
new	2g
new	2h
new	2i
new	2j
new	2k
new	2l
new	3g
new	3h
new	3i
new	3j
new	3k
new	4g
new	4h
new	5g
new	5h
new	6g
new	6h
new	6i
new	7g
new	7h
new	1a
new	1b
new	1c
new	1d
new	1e
new	1f
new	2a
new	2b
new	2c
new	2d
new	2e
new	3a
new	3b
3a	3c
3b	3d
new	3e
new	4a
new	4b
new	4c
new	5a
new	7a
new	1q
new	3q
new	2r
new	4r
new	1s
new	2s
new	3s
new	4s
new	5s
new	6s
new	6t
new	7s
new	7t
new	1u
new	2u
new	3u
new	4u
new	7u
new	9a
new	9b
new	9c
new	13a
new	15b
new	15c
new	15d
new	15e
new	18a
new	18b
new	18c
new	20a
new	20b
new	20c
new	21a
new	21b
new	21c
new	O1j
new	O1k
new	O1l
new	O2j
new	O2k
new	O3j
new	O3k
new	O3l
new	O3m
new	O4j

Columns are headed: **Number in 2014 Catalogue** → **Number in 2015 Catalogue**

Travancore-Cochin

2014	2015
new	O4k
new	O4l
new	O5j
new	O6j
new	O6k
new	O7j
new	O7k
new	O1f
new	O1g
new	O2f
new	O2g
new	O3f
new	O3g
new	O3h
new	O3i
new	O4f
new	O4g
new	O5f
new	O5g
new	O6f
new	O6g
new	O7f
new	O1a
new	O1b
new	O1c
new	O2a
new	O2b
new	O3a
new	O3b
new	O3c
new	O5a
new	O6a
new	O6b
new	O6c
new	O6d
new	O6e
new	O7a
new	O7b
new	O7c
new	O1n
new	O2n
new	O3n
new	O5n
new	O1o
new	O5o
new	O6o
new	O7o
new	O8b
new	O8c
new	O9a
new	O9b
new	O9c
new	O9d
new	O12d
new	O13d
new	O13e
new	O14d
new	O15d
new	O16d
new	O17d
new	O12b
new	O13b
new	O13c
new	O14b
new	O15b
new	O16b
new	O17b
new	O12f
new	O13f
new	O13g
new	O14f
new	O15f
new	O16f
new	O17f
new	O12h
new	O13h
new	O14h
new	O16h
new	O18a
new	O18b
new	O18c
new	O19a
new	O19b
new	O19c
new	O19d
new	O22a
new	O22b
new	O22c
new	O23b
new	O23c
new	O23d
new	O24a

Indo-China

2014	2015
1a	deleted
new	1a
new	1b
new	2d

Iran

2014	2015
new	72c

Italy

2014	2015
new	168a
new	Q16a
new	Q16b

Lebanon

2014	2015
new	72b
new	86b
C6b	C6c
new	C6b

Libya

2014	2015
new	20d-31d

Lithuania

2014	2015
1N1-1N12	Russia N1-N12

Malaya - Johore

2014	2015
6	deleted

Malaya - Kelantan

2014	2015
N16	N16a
N16a	N16

Malaya - Perak

2014	2015
new	11A
17	deleted
new	67b

Malaya - Selangor

2014	2015
4	deleted
5h	deleted

Mozambique Company

2014	2015
new	116a

Natal

2014	2015
new	47a
new	51a
new	72a
77d	77e
new	77d
new	77f

Nevis

2014	2015
new	11a
new	23a
new	31c
new	32b
new	32c

New Britain

2014	2015
new	53
new	53a
new	54
new	54a
new	55
new	55a
new	56
new	56a
new	57
new	58
new	59
new	60
new	61
new	61a
new	62
new	63
new	63a
new	64
new	64a
new	65
new	65a
new	66
new	66a
new	67
new	67a

New Caledonia

2014	2015
new	66b
new	67a
new	68b
new	69a
new	70a
new	71a
new	72a
new	73a
new	74a
new	75b
new	76a
new	77a
new	78b
new	79b
new	80b
new	81c
new	82a
new	83b
new	84b
new	85a
new	86a
new	87a

New Republic

2014	2015
new	4b
new	50Bd

Nicaragua

2014	2015
new	133A
new	133B
new	133C
new	133D
new	133E
new	133F
new	133G
new	C206a
new	2L48a

Niger Coast Protectorate

2014	2015
7d	7e
new	7d
new	7f
new	7g
new	8a
new	8b
new	10a
new	10b
new	20a
new	21a
new	21b
new	25a
new	26a
new	26b
new	29a
new	29b
new	30a
new	31a
new	32a
new	33a
new	34a

North West Pacific Islands

2014	2015
new	3c
new	3d
new	3e
new	11b
deleted	31c
new	34a
new	47a
new	48a

Obock

2014	2015
new	J5a-J11a
new	J15a-J17a
new	J5b
new	J6b
new	J10b
new	J11b
new	J12b
new	J13b

Philippines

2014	2015
new	155a

Portuguese Congo

2014	2015
new	115
new	116

Portuguese Guinea

2014	2015
new	140
new	141
new	142
new	143
new	144
new	145
151	146
new	147
new	148
new	149
159	150
new	151
164	152
166	153
168	154
173	155
140	156
new	157
142	158
new	159
new	160
141	161
143	162
144	163
145	164
146	165
147	166
148	167
149	168
150	169
152	170
153	171
154	172
155	173
156	174
157	175
159	176
160	177
161	178
162	179
163	179A
165	179B
167	179C
169	179D
170	179E
171	179F
172	179G
175	179H
174	179I
176	179J
177	179K
178	179L
179	179M

Portuguese India

2014	2015
new	357
new	358
new	359
new	360
new	361
new	362
new	363
new	364
new	365
new	366
new	367
new	368

Reunion

2014	2015
new	3b
new	5c

Rhodesia (British South Africa)

2014	2015
131	deleted

Ruanda-Urundi

2014	2015
new	J1a
new	J3a

Russia

2014	2015
new	811A
new	812A
new	813A
new	814A
new	815A
new	816A
N1-N8	N13-N20
Lithuania 1N1-1N12	Russia N1-N12
N9-N28	N21-N40
N29-N48	N41-N59

Russia Offices Abroad – Offices in China

2014	2015
new	51a
new	57a

Russia Offices Abroad – Offices in the Turkish Empire

2014	2015
new	113a
new	115a
new	190
new	202a
new	204a

Number in 2014 Catalogue	Number in 2015 Catalogue

Saar

new	1A
new	17f
new	17g
new	17h

St. Vincent

new	33a
new	117e

Samoa

new	23b
new	24c
new	25d
26a	26b
26b	26a
new	29a

San Marino

new	43a
new	46a
79a	79b
new	79a
new	79c
new	82a
new	82b
new	104a
new	105a
new	106a
new	104b
new	105b
new	106b
new	104c
new	106d

Switzerland

new	82c
new	83b
new	84c
new	86b
new	87c
new	88c
new	88d
new	95b

Thrace

new	5c
new	5d
new	6c
new	6d
new	7a
new	7b
new	7c
new	7d
new	8a
new	8b
new	8c
new	16a
new	16b
new	16c
new	16d
new	16e
new	17d
new	17e
new	17f
new	18b
20a	20b
new	20a
new	26A
new	27C
new	31b
new	N8c
new	N9c
new	N9d
new	N9e
new	N10c
new	N10d
new	N10e
new	N23d
new	N24b
new	N24c
new	N24d
new	N25b
new	N24b
new	N24c
new	N24d
new	N25b
new	N36a
new	N44a
new	N47c
new	N56d
new	N73a

Tripolitania

new	2a
new	2b
new	9a
new	13a
new	14a
new	15a
new	16a
new	24a
new	26b
new	EY1a

Turkey

547D	deleted
new	608a
new	605b
new	606b
new	607b
new	607d
new	609b
new	609d
new	610b
new	612b
new	613b
new	614b
new	615b
new	617b
new	605c
new	606c
new	607c
new	609c
new	610c
new	613c
new	615c
new	615d
new	P10c
new	P11b
new	P12b

Uganda

new	2a
new	5a
new	19a
new	38a
new	38b

Vatican City

new	72a

Zanzibar

new	3d
new	6e
new	6f
new	7e
new	7f
new	16d
new	17f
new	17g
new	19a
new	24d
new	26a
new	26b
new	26c
new	27a
new	30a
new	30b
new	30c
new	30d
new	31b
new	31c
new	31d
new	31e
new	31f
new	33a
new	33b
new	34a
new	36a

STOCKBOOKS

Stockbooks are a classic and convenient storage alternative for many collectors. These 9" x 12" Lighthouse stockbooks feature heavyweight archival quality paper with 9 pockets on each page and include double glassine interleaving between the pages for added protection.

Item	Color	Pg Count	Retail	AA*
LS4/8BK	Black	16 pgs	$17.95	**$15.95**
LS4/8BL	Blue	16 pgs	$17.95	**$15.95**
LS4/8GR	Green	16 pgs	$17.95	**$15.95**
LS4/8RD	Red	16 pgs	$17.95	**$15.95**
LS4/16BK	Black	32 pgs	$29.95	**$24.95**
LS4/16BL	Blue	32 pgs	$29.95	**$24.95**
LS4/16GR	Green	32 pgs	$29.95	**$24.95**
LS4/16RD	Red	32 pgs	$29.95	**$24.95**

Item	Color	Pg Count	Retail	AA*
LS4/32BK	Black	64 pgs	$56.95	**$49.95**
LS4/32BL	Blue	64 pgs	$56.95	**$49.95**
LS4/32GR	Green	64 pgs	$56.95	**$49.95**
LS4/32RD	Red	64 pgs	$56.95	**$49.95**

To Order Call:

1-800-572-6885

AmosAdvantage.com

1. *AA prices apply to paid subscribers of Amos Hobby publications, or orders placed online.
2. Prices, terms and product availability subject to change.
3. **Shipping & Handling:**
   United States: 10% of order total.
   Minimum charge $7.99 Maximum charge $45.00
   Canada: 20% of order total.
   Minimum charge $19.99 Maximum charge $200.00

   Foreign orders are shipped via FedEx Intl. and billed actual freight. Credit cards only.

UNITED STATES

yu-ˌnī-təd ˈstāts

GOVT. — Republic
AREA — 3,615,211 sq. mi.
POP. — 226,545,805 (1980)
CAPITAL — Washington, DC

In addition to the 48 States and the District of Columbia, the Republic includes Alaska, Hawaii, Guam, the Commonwealth of Puerto Rico, the Virgin Islands, American Samoa, Wake, Midway, and a number of small islands in the Pacific Ocean, all of which use stamps of the United States.

100 Cents = 1 Dollar

Catalogue values for unused stamps in this country are for Never Hinged items, beginning with Scott 772 in the regular postage section, Scott C19 in the air post section, Scott RW1 in the hunting permit stamps section.

Watermarks

Wmk. 190 — "USPS" in Single-lined Capitals

Wmk. 191 — Double-lined "USPS" in Capitals

Wmk. 190PI — PIPS, used in the Philippines
Wmk. 191PI — PIPS, used in the Philippines
Wmk. 191C — US-C, used for Cuba
Wmk. 191R — USIR

POSTMASTERS' PROVISIONALS

Values for Envelopes are for entires.

Alexandria, Va.

A1

Type I — 40 asterisks in circle.
Type II — 39 asterisks in circle.

1846		Typeset		Imperf.
1X1	A1	5c black, *buff, type I*		325,000.
a.		5c black, *buff,* type II	625,000.	
		On cover (I or II)		500,000.
1X2	A1	5c black, *blue,* type I, on cover		—

All known examples of Nos. 1X1-1X2 are cut to shape.

Annapolis, Md.

ENVELOPE

E1

Printed in upper right corner of envelope

1846			
2XU1	E1	5c carmine red, *white*	600,000.

Handstamped impressions of the circular design with "2" in blue or red exist on envelopes and letter sheets. Values: blue $20,000, red $30,000.
A letter sheet exists with circular design and "5" handstamped in red. Values: blue $10,000, red $12,500.
A similar circular design in blue was used as a postmark.

Baltimore, Md.

Signature of Postmaster — A1

Printed from a plate of 12 (2x6) containing nine 5c stamps (Pos. 1-6, 8, 10, 12) and three 10c (Pos. 7, 9, 11).

1845		Engr.		Imperf.
3X1	A1	5c black		6,000.
		On cover		15,000.
		Vertical pair on cover		150,000.
3X2	A1	10c black, on cover		80,000.
3X3	A1	5c black, *bluish*	65,000.	6,000.
		On cover		13,500.
3X4	A1	10c black, *bluish*		50,000.
		On cover		—

Nos. 3X1-3X4 were printed from a plate of 12 (2x6) containing nine 5c and three 10c.

Off cover values are for stamps canceled by either pen or handstamp. Stamps on covers tied by handstamps command premiums.

ENVELOPES

E1

Three Separate Handstamps

The color given is that of the "PAID 5" and oval. "James M. Buchanan" is handstamped in black, blue or red. The paper is manila, buff, white, salmon or grayish.

1845			Handstamped
Various Papers			
3XU1	E1	5c blue	6,500.
3XU2	E1	5c red	10,000.
3XU3	E1	10c blue	20,000.
3XU4	E1	10c red	20,000.

On the formerly listed "5+5" envelopes, the second "5" in oval is believed not to be part of the basic prepaid marking.

Boscawen, N. H.

A1

1846 (?)		Typeset	Imperf.
4X1	A1	5c dull blue, *yellowish,* on cover	300,000.

Brattleboro, Vt.

Initials of Postmaster (FNP) — A1

Plate of 10 (5x2).

1846		Engr.		Imperf.
Thick Softwove Paper Colored Through				
5X1	A1	5c black, *buff*		9,000.
		On cover		30,000.
		Two singles on cover		—

Lockport, N. Y.

A1

Handstamped, "5" in Black Ms

1846			Imperf.
6X1	A1	5c red, *buff,* on cover	300,000.

Millbury, Mass.

George Washington—A1

Printed from a Woodcut

1846			Imperf.
7X1	A1	5c black, *bluish*	— 50,000.
		On cover	200,000.

New Haven, Conn.

ENVELOPES

E1

1845			Handstamped
Signed in Blue, Black, Magenta or Red			
8XU1	E1	5c red (M)	100,000.
8XU2	E1	5c red, *light bluish* (Bk)	125,000.
8XU3	E1	5c dull blue, *buff* (Bl)	75,000.
8XU4	E1	5c dull blue (Bl)	60,000.

Values of Nos. 8XU1-8XU4 are a guide to value. They are based on auction realizations and retail sales and take condition into consideration. All New Haven envelopes are of equal rarity (each is unique), with the exception of No. 8XU2, of which two exist. An entire of No. 8XU2 is the finest example known, and this is reflected in the value shown. The other envelopes are valued according to condition as much as rarity.

Reprints were made at various times between 1871 and 1932. They differ in shade and paper from the originals.

New York, N. Y.

George Washington — A1

Plate of 40 (5x8). Nos. 9X1d, 9X2, 9X2d and 9X3 unused are valued without gum.

Nos. 9X1-9X3 and varieties unused are valued without gum. Examples with original gum are extremely scarce and will command higher prices.

1845-46		Engr.		Imperf.
Bluish Wove Paper				
9X1	A1	5c black, signed ACM, connected, *1846*	1,500.	500.
		On cover		625.
		On cover to France or England		2,250.
		On cover to other European countries		5,000.
		Pair	5,750.	1,500.
		Pair on cover		2,000.
		Pair on cover to England		4,500.
		Pair on cover to Canada		5,500.
		Vertical pair, 9X1 and 9X1e	85,000.	
		Strip of 3 on cover		9,000.
		Strip of 4 on cover		100,000.
a.		Signed ACM, AC connected	1,750.	575.
		On cover		725.
		On cover to France or England		2,250.
		On cover to other European countries		6,000.
		Pair, Nos. 9X1 and 9X1a, on cover		15,000.
b.		Signed A.C.M.	4,500.	700.
		On cover		850.
		On cover to France or England		2,750.
		On cover to other European countries		6,000.
		Pair		2,400.
		Pair on cover		3,250.
c.		Signed MMJr		10,000.
		On cover		—
		Pair on cover front		26,500.
d.		Signed RHM	13,000.	3,500.
		On cover		5,500.
		On cover from New Hamburgh, N.Y.		12,500.
e.		Without signature	3,750.	950.
		On cover		1,400.
		On cover to France or England		2,500.
		On cover to other European countries		6,000.
		On cover, July 15, 1845		27,500.
		Pair on cover		2,900.

These stamps were usually initialed "ACM" in magenta ink, as a control, before being sold or passed through the mails.

A plate of 9 (3x3) was made from which proofs were printed in black on white and deep blue papers; also in blue, green, brown and red on white bond paper. Stamps from this plate were not issued, and it is possible that it is an essay, as the design differs slightly from the issued stamps from the sheet of 40. No examples from the plate of nine are known used.

1847		Engr.		Imperf.
Blue Wove Paper				
9X2	A1	5c black, signed ACM connected	6,500.	3,500.
		On cover		5,750.
		Pair on cover		—
a.		Signed RHM		—
b.		Signed ACM, AC connected		8,000.
d.		Without signature	11,000.	7,500.

On the listing example of No. 9X2a the "R" is illegible and does not match those of the other "RHM" signatures.
No. 9X2b is unique.

1847		Engr.		Imperf.
Gray Wove Paper				
9X3	A1	5c black, signed ACM connected	5,250.	2,250.
		On cover		5,250.
		On cover to Europe		8,500.
		Pair		7,750.
		Pair on cover		8,750.
a.		Signed RHM		7,000.
b.		Without signature		13,000.

Providence, R.I.

A1 & A2

1846		Engr.		*Imperf.*
10X1	A1	5c gray black	350.	1,900.
	No gum		225.	
	On cover, tied by post-			
	mark			21,500.
	On cover, pen canceled			6,500.
	Two on cover			
10X2	A2	10c gray black	1,150.	16,500.
	No gum		725.	
	On cover, pen canceled			50,000.
a.	Se-tenant with 5c		2,000.	

Plate of 12 (3x4) contains 11-5c and 1-10c.
*Reprints were made in 1898. Each stamp
bears one of the following letters on the back:
B. O. G. E. R. T. D. U. R. B. I. N. Value of 5c,
$65; 10c, $160; sheet, $1,000.
Reprint singles or sheets without back print
sell for more.*

St. Louis, Mo.

A1   A2   A3
Missouri Coat of Arms

Nos. 11X1-11X8 unused are valued without
gum.

**Nos. 11X1-11X8 unused are valued with-
out gum.**

Wove Paper Colored Through

1845-46		Engr.		*Imperf.*
		Greenish Wove Paper		
11X1	A1	5c black,		
		greenish	50,000.	8,000.
	On cover			17,500.
	Two on cover			25,000.
	Strip of 3 plus single on			
	cover			45,000.
11X2	A2	10c black,		
		greenish	50,000.	8,000.
	On cover			14,000.
	Pair on cover			22,500.
	Strip of 3 on cover			40,000.
11X3	A3	20c black,		
		greenish	160,000.	—
	On cover, #11X5, two			
	#11X3			325,000.

Three varieties of 5c, 3 of 10c, 2 of 20c.

1846		**Gray Lilac Paper**		
11X4	A1	5c black, (III),		
		gray lilac	—	55,000.
	On cover			—
11X5	A2	10c black, gray		
		lilac	50,000.	10,000.
	On cover			13,500.
	Strip of 3 on cover			160,000.
11X6	A3	20c black, gray		
		lilac	100,000.	60,000.
	On cover			70,000.
	Pair on cover			145,000.

One variety of 5c, 3 of 10c, 2 of 20c.
No. 11X6 unused is unique. It is in the grade
of fine and valued thus.

1847		**Pelure Paper**		
11X7	A1	5c black, blu-		
		ish	—	11,000.
	On cover			16,000.
	Two on cover			37,500.
11X8	A2	10c black, blu-		
		ish	17,500.	15,000.
	On cover			20,000.
a.	Impression of 5c on			
	back			77,500.

Three varieties of 5c, 3 of 10c.
Values of Nos. 11X7-11X8 reflect the usual
poor condition of these stamps, which were
printed on fragile pelure paper. Attractive
examples with minor defects sell for considerably more.
Used values are for pen-canceled stamps.
No. 11X8a is unique.

Please Note:
Stamps are valued in the grade of
very fine unless otherwise indicated.
Values for early and valuable
stamps are for examples with certificates of authenticity from acknowledged expert committees, or examples sold with the buyer having the
right of certification. This applies to
examples with original gum as well
as examples without gum. Beware of
stamps offered "as is," as the gum
on some unused stamps offered with
"original gum" may be fraudulent,
and stamps offered as unused without gum may in some cases be
altered or faintly canceled used
stamps.

**Manuscript Cancels on Used
Stamps**
Manuscript (pen) cancels reduce the
value of used stamps by about 50%.
See the Scott U.S. Specialized Cata-
logue for individual valuations.

GENERAL ISSUES
**All Issues from 1847 to 1894 are
Unwatermarked.**

Benjamin Franklin — A1

1847, July 1		Engr.		*Imperf.*
		Thin Bluish Wove Paper		
1	A1	5c red brn, blu-		
		ish	6,750.	400.
	No gum		2,400.	
	Pen Cancel			230.
	On cover			475.
a.	5c dark brown		8,750.	900.
	No gum		3,250.	
	On cover			975.
b.	5c orange brown		10,000.	800.
	No gum		3,500.	
	On cover			900.
c.	5c red orange		25,000.	9,500.
	No gum		9,500.	
	On cover			10,500.
d.	5c brown orange		—	1,000.
	No gum		4,500.	
	On cover			1,150.

George
Washington — A2

2	A2	10c black, bluish	35,000.	925.
	No gum		15,000.	
	Pen Cancel			575.
	On cover			1,250.
a.	Diagonal half used as 5c			
	on cover			12,500.
b.	Vertical half used as 5c			
	on cover			30,000.
c.	Horizontal half used as			
	5c on cover			—

A3   A4

REPRODUCTIONS of 1847 ISSUE
**Actually, official imitations made
from new plates of 50 subjects made
by the Bureau of Engraving and
Printing by order of the Post Office
Department. These were not valid for
postal use.**

*5c. On the originals the left side of
the white shirt frill touches the oval on a
level with the top of the "F" of "Five." On
the reproductions it touches the oval
about on a level with the top of the figure "5." On the originals, the bottom of
the right leg of the "N" in "CENTS" is
blunt. On the reproductions, the "N"
comes to a point at the bottom.*

---

*10c. On the reproductions, line of
coat at left points to right tip of "X" and
line of coat at right points to center of
"S" of CENTS. On the originals, line of
coat points to "T" of TEN and between
"T" and "S" of CENTS. The bottom of
the right leg of the "N" of "CENTS"
shows the same difference as on the 5c
originals and reproductions. On the
reproductions, the gap between the bottom legs of the left "X" is noticeably
wider than the gap on the right "X." On
the originals, the gaps are of equal
width. On the reproductions the eyes
have a sleepy look, the line of the
mouth is straighter, and in the curl of
hair near the left cheek is a strong black
dot, while the originals have only a faint
one.*

1875				*Imperf.*
		Bluish paper, without gum		
3	A3	5c red brown	825.	
4	A4	10c black	1,000.	

In Nos. 5-17, the 1¢, 3¢ and 12¢ have
very small margins between the
stamps. The 5¢ and 10¢ have moderate
size margins. The values of these
stamps take the margin size into
consideration.
Values for Nos. 5A, 6b and 19b are
for the less distinct positions. Best
examples sell for more.
Values for No. 16 are for outer line
recut at top. Other recuts sell for more.

Franklin — A5

Type I

Type Ib

ONE CENT.
Type I. Has complete curved lines outside
the labels with "U. S. Postage" and "One
Cent." The scrolls below the lower label are
turned under, forming little balls. The ornaments at top are substantially complete.
Values for type I are for stamps showing the
marked characteristics plainly. Copies of type I
showing the balls indistinctly sell for much
lower prices.

Type Ib. As type I, but balls below bottom
label are not as clear. Plume-like scrolls at
bottom are incomplete.

1851-57				*Imperf.*
5	A5	1c blue, type I		
		(7R1E)	225,000.	70,000.
	On cover			90,000.

Values for No. 5 are for examples with margins touching or cutting slightly into the design.
Value for No. 5 unused is for a stamp with
no gum.

5A	A5	1c blue, type 1b	32,500.	9,000.
	No gum		12,000.	
	On cover			10,500.

A6

Type Ic

Type Ia. Same as type I at bottom, but top
ornaments and outer line at top are partly cut
away.
Type Ic. Same as type Ia, but bottom right
plume and ball ornament incomplete. Bottom
left plume complete or nearly complete.

6	A6	1c blue, type 1a		
		('57)	45,000.	11,000.
	No gum		20,000.	
	On cover			15,000.
	Strip of 3 on cover			75,000.
6b	A6	1c blue, type 1c	7,000.	3,250.
	No gum		3,000.	
	On cover			4,250.

A7

Type II — Same as Type I at top, but the little
balls of the bottom scrolls and the bottoms of
the lower plume ornaments are missing. The
side ornaments are substantially complete.

7	A7	1c blue, type II	1,050.	145.
	No gum		400.	
	On cover			170.

A8

Type IIIa

Type III. The top and bottom curved lines outside the labels are broken in the middle. The side ornaments are substantially complete.

Type IIIa. Similar to type III with the outer line broken at top or bottom but not both.

8	A8	1c blue, type III	25,000.	2,250.
	No gum		7,500.	
	On cover			2,500.

Values for type III are for at least a 2mm break in each outer line. Examples of type III with wider breaks in outer lines command higher prices; those with smaller breaks sell for much less.

8A	A8	1c blue, type IIIa	6,000.	900.
	No gum		2,250.	
	On cover			1,000.

Stamps of type IIIa with bottom line broken command higher prices than those with top line broken. See note after No. 8 on width of break of outer lines.

A9

Type IV. Similar to type II, but with the curved lines outside the labels recut at top or bottom or both.

9	A9	1c blue, type IV ('52)	750.00	95.00
	No gum		275.00	
	On cover			115.00
a.	Printed on both sides, reverse inverted		50,000.	
b.	Diagonal half used as ½c on cover		60,000.	

No. 9a is unique.

The No. 9b cover, a printed-matter circular mailed in 1853, is unique. The circular likely should have been sent at the 1c rate for printed matter in effect at the time. However, both the sending (New Haven, Conn.) and receiving (Hartford, Conn.) post offices treated

---

it as fully prepaid with c postage applied. Value is based on 2013 auction realization.

Washington — A10

All of the 3c stamps of the 1851 and 1857 issues were recut at least to the extent of the outer frame lines, sometimes the inner lines at the sides (type II stamps), and often other lines in triangles, diamond blocks, label blocks and/or top/bottom frame lines.

OUTER FRAME LINE

Type I

THREE CENTS.
Type I — There is an outer frame line on all four sides. The outer frame lines at the sides are always recut, but the inner lines at the sides are not.

10	A10	3c org brown, type I	4,000.	200.00
	No gum		1,500.	
	On cover			280.00

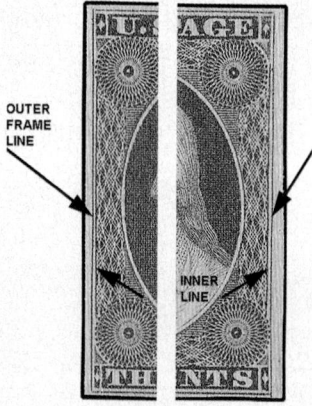

OUTER FRAME LINE

INNER LINE

Type II

Type II — As type I, but with the inner lines at the sides also recut.

10A	A10	3c org brown, type II	3,250.	160.00
	No gum		1,250.	
	On cover			210.00
b.	Printed on both sides		55,000.	

Only one example of No. 10Ab is recorded.

11	A10	3c dull red, type I ('55)	275.00	15.00
	No gum		85.00	
	On cover			17.50
11A	A10	3c dull red, type II ('53-'55)	275.00	15.00
	No gum		85.00	
	On cover			17.50
c.	Vertical half used as 1c on cover			5,000.
d.	Diagonal half used as 1c on cover			5,000.
e.	Double impression			30,000.

Thomas
Jefferson — A11

FIVE CENTS.
Type I — Projections on all four sides.

12	A11	5c red brown, type I ('56)	30,000.	700.
	No gum		11,000.	
	On domestic cover			1,200.

Washington — A12

A13

TEN CENTS
Type I — The "shells" at the lower corners are practically complete. The outer line below the label is very nearly complete. The outer lines are broken above the middle of the top label and the "X" in each upper corner.

13	A12	10c green, type I ('55)	19,000.	925.
	No gum		8,500.	
	On cover			1,050.

Type II — The design is complete at the top. The outer line at the bottom is broken in the middle. The shells are partly cut away, as shown.

14	A13	10c green, type II ('55)	5,000.	160.
	No gum		1,800.	
	On domestic cover			210.

A14

Type III — The outer lines are broken above the top label and the "X" numerals. The outer line at the bottom and the shells are partly cut away, as shown, similar to type II.

15	A14	10c green, type III ('55)	5,000.	160.
	No gum		1,800.	
	On domestic cover			210.

A15

Type IV. The outer lines have been recut at top or bottom or both.

Types I, II, III and IV have complete ornaments at the sides of the stamps and three pearls at each outer edge of the bottom panel.

16	A15	10c green, type IV ('55)	35,000.	1,650.
	No gum		15,000.	
	On domestic cover			1,900.

Washington — A16

17	A16	12c gray black	6,250.	250.
	No gum		2,200.	
	Single, on cover			1,500.
a.	Diagonal half used as 6c on cover			2,500.
b.	Vertical half used as 6c on cover			8,500.
c.	Printed on both sides			40,000.

SAME DESIGNS AS 1851-57 ISSUES

Nos. 18-39 have small or very small margins. The values take into account the margin size.

1857-61   *Perf. 15½*

18	A5	1c blue, type I ('61)	2,100.	550.
	No gum		800.	
	On cover			700.
	Short ornaments at either top or bottom			—
19	A6	1c blue, type Ia	42,500.	9,000.
	No gum		20,000.	
	On cover			9,500.
b.	blue, type Ic		4,250.	2,500.
	No gum		1,750.	
	On cover			3,500.
20	A7	1c blue, type II	900.	275.
	No gum		375.	
	On cover			325.
21	A8	1c blue, type III	17,500.	1,800.
	No gum		7,000.	
	On cover			2,250.
a.	Horiz. pair, imperf between			23,000.

22	A8	1c blue, type IIIa	2,400.	500.
	No gum		850.	
	On cover			550.
b.	Horizontal pair, imperf. between			10,000.

One pair of No. 22b is reported. Beware of numerous pairs that have blind perforations. These are not to be confused with No. 22b.

23	A9	1c blue, type IV	10,000.	900.
	No gum		4,250.	
	On cover			1,100.

Franklin — A20

ONE CENT

Type V — Similar to type III of 1851-57 but with side ornaments partly cut away. About one-half of all positions have side scratches. Wide breaks in top and bottom framelines.

Type Va — Stamps from Plate 5 with almost complete ornaments at right side and no side scratches. Many, but not all, stamps from Plate 5 are Type Va, the remainder being Type V.

24	A20	1c blue, type V	140.00	40.00
	No gum		55.00	
	On cover			47.50
	On cover			150.00
b.	Laid paper			7,500.
25	A10	3c rose, type I	2,750.	125.00
	No gum		950.	
	On cover			140.00
b.	Vert. pair, imperf. horizontally			10,000.
25A	A10	3c rose, type II	8,000.	950.00
	No gum		3,500.	
	On cover			1,000.

CONTINUOUS FRAME LINE — CONTINUOUS FRAME LINE

Washington Type III — A21

THREE CENTS

Type III — There are no outer frame lines at top and bottom. The side frame lines were recut so as to be continuous from the top to the bottom of the plate. Stamps from the top or bottom rows show the ends of the side frame lines and may be mistaken for Type IV.

26	A21	3c dull red, type III	65.00	9.00
	No gum		22.50	
	On cover			10.50
b.	Horiz. pair, imperf. vertically		14,000.	
c.	Vert. pair, imperf. horizontally			16,000.
d.	Horizontal pair, imperf. between			—
e.	Double impression			15,000.
	On cover			—

BROKEN FRAME LINE — BROKEN FRAME LINE

Washington (Type IV) — A21a

Type IV — As type III, but the side frame lines extend only to the top and bottom of the stamp design. All Type IV stamps are from plates 10 and 11 (each of which exists in three states), and these plates produced only Type

IV. The side frame lines were recut individually for each stamp, thus being broken between the stamps vertically.

Beware of type III stamps with frame lines that stop at the top of the design (from top row of plate) or bottom of the design (from bottom row of plate). These are often mistakenly offered as No. 26A.

26A	A21a	3c dull red, type IV	600.00	150.00
	No gum		225.00	
	On cover			190.00
f.	Horiz. strip of 3, imperf. vert., on cover			14,500.

No. 26Af is unique.

27	A11	5c brick red, type I ('58)	80,000.	1,600.
	No gum		20,000.	
	On cover			2,000.
	N.Y. Ocean Mail			+1,000.
28	A11	5c red brown, type I	60,000.	1,100.
	No gum		15,000.	
	On cover			1,300.
b.	Bright red brown		70,000.	2,400.
	No gum		20,000.	
28A	A11	5c Indian red, type I ('58)	175,000.	3,500.
	No gum		40,000.	
	On cover			5,000.

No. 28A unused is valued in the grade of fine. Only four examples are recorded with any amount of gum.

29	A11	5c brown, type I ('59)	5,500.	400.
	No gum		1,750.	
	On cover			525.

Jefferson — A22

FIVE CENTS.

Type II — The projections at top and bottom are partly cut away.

30	A22	5c org brn, type II ('61)	1,250.	1,400.
	No gum		500.	
	On cover			2,400.
30A	A22	5c brown, type II ('60)	2,200.	300.
	No gum		825.	
	On cover			350.
b.	Printed on both sides			45,000.
31	A12	10c green, type I	35,000.	1,200.
	No gum		11,500.	
	On domestic cover			1,400.
32	A13	10c green, type II	6,000.	200.
	No gum		2,150.	
	On domestic cover			250.
33	A14	10c green, type III	6,000.	200.
	No gum		2,150.	
	On domestic cover			250.
34	A15	10c green, type IV	50,000.	2,100.
	No gum		20,000.	
	On domestic cover			2,500.

Example I   Example II

Washington (Two typical examples) — A23

TEN CENTS

Type V — The side ornaments are slightly cut away. Usually only one pearl remains at each end of the lower label, but some copies

show two or three pearls at the right side. At the bottom the outer line is complete and the shells nearly so. The outer lines at top are complete except over the right "X."

35	A23	10c green, type V ('59)	225.00	65.00
	No gum		85.00	
	On domestic cover			77.50

No. 36 outer frame lines recut on plate

TWELVE CENTS. Printed from two plates.
Plate 1 (No. 36) — Outer frame lines are recut on the plate and are complete. Very narrow spacing of stamps on the plate.

36	A16	12c black (Plate 1)	1,900.	350.
	No gum		575.	
	Single on cover			750.
a.	Diagonal half used as 6c on cover			17,500.
c.	Horizontal pair, imperf. between			12,500.

Typical No. 36B, outer frame lines not recut

Plate III (No. 36B) — Weak outer frame lines from the die were not recut and are noticeably uneven or broken, sometimes partly missing. Somewhat wider spacing of stamps on the plate.

36B	A16	12c black, plate III ('59)	700.	275.
	No gum		325.	
	Single on cover			1,200.

Washington   Franklin
A17   A18

37	A17	24c gray lilac ('60)	1,400.	375.
a.	24c gray		1,400.	375.
	No gum		525.	
	On cover to England			1,000.
38	A18	30c orange ('60)	2,150.	425.
	No gum		800.	
	On cover to Germany or France			1,350.

Washington — A19

39	A19	90c blue ('60)	3,000.	11,000.
	No gum		1,100.	
	On cover			225,000.

See Die and Plate proofs in the Scott United States Specialized Catalogue for imperfs. of the 12c, 24c, 30c, 90c.

Genuine cancellations on the 90c are rare. Used examples must be accompanied by certificates of authenticity issued by recognized expertizing committees.

REPRINTS OF 1857-60 ISSUE
White paper, without gum.

1875				**Perf. 12**
40	A5	1c bright blue	575.	
41	A10	3c scarlet	3,000.	
42	A22	5c org brown	1,200.	
43	A12	10c blue green	2,500.	13,000.
44	A16	12c greenish black	2,750.	
45	A17	24c blackish violet	3,000.	10,000.
46	A18	30c yel orange	3,000.	
47	A19	90c deep blue	4,000.	

Nos. 41-46 are valued in the grade of fine.

Nos. 40-47 exist imperforate. Very infrequent sales preclude establishing a value at this time. One set of imperforate pairs is recorded and it sold for $110,000 in a 2009 auction.

Essays-Trial Color Proofs

The paper of former Nos. 55-62 (Nos. 63E11e, 65-E15h, 67-E9e, 69-E6e, 72-E7h, Essay section, Nos. 70eTC, 71bTC, Trial Color Proof section, Scott U.S. Specialized) is thin and semitransparent. That of the postage issues is thicker and more opaque, except Nos. 62B, 70c and 70d.

Franklin — A24

A24

Washington — A25

A25

Jefferson — A26

A26

Washington — A27

A27

A27a

Washington — A28

A28

Washington
A29

Franklin
A30

Washington — A31

A31

1c — There is a dash under the tip of the ornament at right of the numeral in upper left corner.

3c — Ornaments at corners end in a small ball.

5c — There is a leaflet in the foliated ornaments at each corner.

10c (A27a) — A heavy curved line has been cut below the stars and an outer line added to the ornaments above them.

12c — There are corner ornaments consisting of ovals and scrolls.

90c — Parallel lines form an angle above the ribbon with "U. S. Postage"; between these lines there is a row of dashes and a point of color at the apex of the lower line.

1861			Perf. 12	
62B	A27a	10c dark green	8,000.	1,600.
	No gum		3,250.	
	On cover			2,100.
	On patriotic cover			3,000.

1861-62			Perf. 12	
63	A24	1c blue	300.00	50.00
	No gum		100.00	
	On cover (single)			57.50
	On patriotic cover			225.00
a.	1c ultramarine		2,500.	800.00
	No gum		1,000.	
b.	1c dark blue		800.00	800.00
	No gum		300.00	
c.	Laid paper, horiz. or vert.		8,500.	5,000.
d.	Vertical pair, imperf. horiz.			—
e.	Printed on both sides, reverse inverted		—	50,000.
64	A25	3c pink	14,000.	750.00
	No gum		5,000.	
	On cover			900.00
	On patriotic cover			1,500.
a.	3c pigeon blood pink		50,000.	4,750.
	No gum		15,000.	
	On cover			5,500.
	On patriotic cover			7,750.
b.	3c rose pink		600.00	150.00
	No gum		225.00	
	On cover			180.00
	On patriotic cover			250.00
65	A25	3c rose	125.00	3.00
	No gum		40.00	
	On cover			3.50
	On patriotic cover			75.00
b.	Laid paper, horiz. or vert.		—	1,250.
d.	Vertical pair, imperf. horiz.		15,000.	1,500.
e.	Printed on both sides, reverse inverted		40,000.	8,000.
f.	Double impression			15,000.

The 3c lake can be found under No. 66 in the Trial Color Proofs section of the Scott U.S. Specialized Catalogue. The imperf 3c lake under No. 66P in the same section. The imperf 3c rose can be found in the Die and Plate Proofs section of the Specialized.

67	A26	5c buff	27,500.	900.
	No gum		10,500.	
	On cover			1,150.
	On patriotic cover			3,750.
a.	5c brown yellow		30,000.	1,100.
	No gum		11,500.	
b.	5c olive yellow			4,000.

Values of Nos. 67, 67a, 67b reflect the normal small margins.

68	A27	10c green	1,000.	60.00
	No gum		375.	
	On cover			75.00
	On patriotic cover			375.00
	On cover to Canada			100.00
a.	10c dark green		1,400.	85.00
	No gum		525.	
b.	Vertical pair, imperf. horiz.			30,000.
69	A28	12c black	1,800.	100.00
	No gum		725.	
	On domestic cover			140.00
	On patriotic cover			850.00
	On cover to France or Germany with #65			160.00
70	A29	24c red lilac ('62)	3,000.	300.00
	No gum		1,150.	
	On cover			350.00
	On patriotic cover			3,000.
a.	24c brown lilac		3,250.	325.00
	No gum		1,250.	
b.	24c steel blue ('61)		16,500.	850.00
	No gum		6,250.	
c.	24c violet, thin paper		35,000.	1,300.
	No gum		13,500.	2,250.
d.	24c pale gray violet, thin paper		25,000.	3,000.
	No gum		6,000.	

There are numerous shades of the 24c stamp in this and the following issue.

Nos. 70c and 70d are on a thinner, harder and more transparent paper than Nos. 70, 70a, 70b or the latter Nos. 78, 78a, 78b and 78c.

71	A30	30c orange	2,600.	190.
	No gum		1,000.	
	On cover to France or Germany			380.
	On patriotic cover			3,500.
a.	Printed on both sides			

Values for No. 71 are for examples with small margins, especially at sides. Large-margined examples sell for much more.

72	A31	90c blue	3,250.	600.
	No gum		1,300.	
	On cover			25,000.
a.	90c pale blue		3,250.	650.
	No gum		1,300.	
b.	90c dark blue		4,000.	1,000.
	No gum		1,600.	

Please Note:

Stamps are valued in the grade of very fine unless otherwise indicated.

Values for early and valuable stamps are for examples with certificates of authenticity from acknowledged expert committees, or examples sold with the buyer having the right of certification.

This applies to examples with original gum as well as examples without gum.

Beware of stamps offered "as is," as the gum on some unused stamps offered with "original gum" may be fraudulent, and stamps offered as unused without gum may in some cases be altered or faintly canceled used stamps.

DESIGNS AS 1861 ISSUE

Andrew
Jackson
A32

Abraham
Lincoln
A33

1861-66			Perf. 12	
73	A32	2c black ('63)	375.00	65.00
	No gum		140.00	
	On cover			85.00
	On patriotic cover			2,000.
a.	Diagonal half used as 1c as part of 3c rate on cover			1,500.
b.	Diagonal half used alone as 1c on cover			3,000.
c.	Horiz. half used as 1c as part of 3c rate on cover			3,500.
d.	Vert. half used as 1c as part of 3c rate on cover			2,000.
e.	Vert. half used alone as 1c on cover			4,000.
f.	Printed on both sides, reverse not inverted			30,000.
g.	Laid paper		—	12,500.

No. 73f unused is unique. It has perfs cut off on two sides and is valued thus.

The 3c scarlet can be found under No. 74 in the Scott U.S. Specialized Catalogue Trial Color Proofs section.

75	A26	5c red brown ('62)	5,750.	450.
	No gum		2,200.	
	On cover			725.
	On patriotic cover			4,000.

Values for No. 75 reflect the normal small margins.

76	A26	5c brown ('63)	1,400.	120.
	No gum		525.	
	On cover			450.
	On patriotic cover			2,000.
a.	5c black brown		2,250.	400.
	No gum		850.	
b.	Laid paper			—

Values of Nos. 76, 76a reflect the normal small margins.

77	A33	15c black ('66)	4,750.	180.
	No gum		1,750.	
	On cover to France or Germany			200.
78	A29	24c lilac ('62)	2,750.	350.
	No gum		950.	
	On cover, #78, 78a or 78b			400.
a.	24c grayish lilac		2,900.	425.
	No gum		1,000.	
b.	24c gray		2,900.	450.
	No gum		1,000.	
c.	24c blackish violet		100,000.	20,000.
	No gum		30,000.	
	On cover			25,000.

Only three examples are recorded of No. 78c unused with original gum. No. 78c unused with and without gum are valued in the grade of fine-very fine.

d.	Printed on both sides, reverse inverted		22,500.
	On cover		35,000.

SAME DESIGNS AS 1861-66 ISSUES

Grill

Embossed with grills of various sizes. Some authorities believe that more than one size of grill probably existed on one of the grill rolls.

A peculiarity of the United States issues from 1867 to 1870 is the grill or embossing. The object was to break the fiber of the paper so that the ink of the canceling stamp would soak in and make washing for a second using impossible. The exact date at which grilled stamps came into use is unsettled. Luff's "Postage Stamps of the United States" places the date as probably August 8, 1867.

Horizontal measurements are given first.

GRILL WITH POINTS UP

Grills A and C were made by a roller covered with ridges shaped like an inverted V. Pressing the ridges into the stamp paper forced the paper into the pyramidal pits between the ridges, causing irregular breaks in the paper. Grill B was made by a roller with raised bosses.

A. GRILL COVERING THE ENTIRE STAMP

1867			Perf. 12	
79	A25	3c rose	8,500.	1,500.
	No gum		2,750.	
	On cover			2,000.
b.	Printed on both sides			

Nos. 79, 79b, are valued for fine-very fine centering but with minor perforation faults.

An essay which is often mistaken for No. 79 (#79-E15) shows the points of the grill as small squares faintly impressed in the paper, but not cutting through it.

On No. 79 the grill breaks through the paper. Examples free from defects are rare.

80	A26	5c brown		260,000.
a.	5c dark brown			260,000.
81	A30	30c orange		210,000.

Four examples of Nos. 80 and 80a (two of each shade), and eight examples of No. 81 (one in the New York Public Library Miller collection and not available to collectors) are known. All are more or less faulty and/or off center. Values are for off-center examples with small perforation faults.

B. GRILL ABOUT 18x15mm (22x18 POINTS)

82	A25	3c rose	1,000,000.

The four known examples of No. 82 are valued in the grade of fine.

C. GRILL ABOUT 13x16mm (16 TO 17 BY 18 TO 21 POINTS)

The grilled area on each of four C grills in the sheet may total about 18x15mm when a normal C grill adjoins a fainter grill extending to the right or left edge of the stamp.

This is caused by a partial erasure on the grill roller when it was changed to produce C grills instead of the all-over A grill.

The imperf. can be found under No. 74 in the Scott U.S. Specialized Catalogue Die and Plate Proofs section.

83	A25	3c rose	6,000.	1,100.
	No gum		2,150.	
	On cover			1,300.

GRILL WITH POINTS DOWN

The grills were produced by rollers with the surface covered, or partly covered, by pyramidal bosses. On the D, E and F grills the tips of the pyramids are vertical ridges. On the Z grill the ridges are horizontal.

D. GRILL ABOUT 12x14mm (15 BY 17 TO 18 POINTS)

84	A32	2c black	16,000.	4,500.
	No gum		6,500.	
	On cover			5,000.

No. 84 is valued in the grade of fine.

85	A25	3c rose	6,000.	1,050.
	No gum		2,150.	
	On cover			1,200.

Z. GRILL ABOUT 11x14mm (13 TO 14 BY 18 POINTS)

85A	A24	1c blue	3,000,000.

Two examples of No. 85A are known. One is contained in the New York Public Library collection, which is on long-term loan to the Smithsonian National Postal Museum.

85B	A32	2c black	17,500.	1,300.
		No gum	6,750.	
		On cover		1,500.
85C	A25	3c rose	25,000.	3,500.
		No gum	9,000.	
		On cover		4,000.
85D	A27	10c green		650,000.

Six examples of No. 85D are known. One is contained in the New York Public Library collection. Value is for a well-centered example with small faults.

85E	A28	12c intense black	17,500.	2,500.
		No gum	6,500.	
		On cover		3,000.
85F	A33	15c black		2,000,000.

Two examples of No. 85F are documented, one in the grade of very good, the other extremely fine. Value is for the extremely fine example.

E. GRILL ABOUT 11x13mm (14 BY 15 TO 17 POINTS)

86	A24	1c blue	3,250.	475.
		No gum	1,250.	
a.		1c dull blue	3,250.	450.
		No gum	1,250.	
		On cover, #86 or 86a		575.
87	A32	2c black	1,750.	200.
		No gum	675.	
		On cover		300.
a.		Diagonal half used as 1c on cover		2,000.
b.		Vertical half used as 1c on cover		2,000.
88	A25	3c rose	1,000.	27.50
		No gum	375.	
		On cover		32.50
a.		3c lake red	1,250.	50.00
		No gum	475.	
b.		Two diagonal halves from different stamps used as 3c stamp (fraudulent use), one half having grill with points up, on cover		—
89	A27	10c green	5,250.	350.
		No gum	2,100.	
		On cover		450.
90	A28	12c black	4,750.	400.
		No gum	1,900.	
		On cover		550.
91	A33	15c black	12,500.	650.
		No gum	4,500.	
		On cover		750.

F. GRILL ABOUT 9x13mm (11 TO 12 BY 15 TO 17 POINTS)

92	A24	1c blue	3,000.	475.
		No gum	1,000.	
a.		1c pale blue	2,500.	425.
		No gum	750.	
		On cover		525.
93	A32	2c black	450.	60.00
		No gum	170.	
		On cover		75.00
a.		Vertical half used as 1c as part of 3c rate on cover		1,250.
b.		Diagonal half used as 1c as part of 3c rate on cover		1,250.
c.		Horizontal half used alone as 1c on cover		2,500.
d.		Diagonal half used alone as 1c on cover		2,500.
94	A25	3c red	350.	10.00
a.		3c rose	350.	10.00
		No gum	140.	
		On cover, #94 or 94a		11.00
c.		Vertical pair, imperf. horiz.	15,000.	
d.		Printed on both sides	9,000.	

The imperf. 3c can be found in the Scott U.S. Specialized Catalogue Die and Plate Proofs section.

95	A26	5c brown	3,500.	900.
		No gum	1,300.	
		On cover		950.
a.		5c brown	4,750.	2,250.
		No gum	1,800.	

Values of Nos. 95, 95a reflect the normal small margins.

96	A27	10c yel grn	2,750.	250.
		No gum	900.	
		On cover		300.
97	A28	12c black	3,000.	260.
		No gum	1,100.	
		On cover		300.
98	A33	15c black	4,250.	275.
		No gum	1,600.	
		On cover		300.
99	A29	24c gray lilac	8,500.	1,600.
		No gum	3,250.	
		On cover		2,600.
100	A30	30c orange	8,500.	950.
		No gum	3,250.	
		On cover		2,000.

Values for No. 100 are for examples with small margins, especially at sides. Large-margined examples sell for much more.

101	A31	90c blue	14,500.	2,250.
		No gum	5,500.	
		On cover		100,000.

RE-ISSUE OF 1861-66 ISSUES
Without Grill, Hard White Paper
White Crackly Gum

1875   *Perf. 12*

102	A24	1c blue	800.	1,500.
		No gum	350.	
		On cover		—
103	A32	2c black	3,500.	15,000.
		No gum	1,650.	
104	A25	3c brown red	4,000.	17,500.
		No gum	1,850.	
105	A26	5c brown	2,600.	8,000.
		No gum	1,225.	
106	A27	10c green	3,300.	125,000.
		No gum	1,550.	
107	A28	12c black	4,000.	15,000.
		No gum	1,850.	
108	A33	15c black	4,500.	35,000.
		No gum	2,100.	
109	A29	24c deep violet	5,750.	20,000.
		No gum	2,700.	
110	A30	30c brownish org	6,000.	25,000.
		No gum	2,800.	
111	A31	90c blue	6,750.	225,000.
		No gum	3,250.	

These stamps can be distinguished from the 1861-66 issues by the shades and the paper which is hard and very white instead of yellowish. The gum is white and crackly.

Five examples are recorded of No. 111 used, one of which has a non-contemporaneous cancel. Value is for centered and sound example (two are known thus).

Franklin — A34   Post Horse and Rider — A35

G. Grill measuring 9½x9mm (12 by 11 to 11½ points)

1869   **Hard Wove Paper**   *Perf. 12*

112	A34	1c buff	650.	150.
		No gum	225.	
		On cover, single		280.
b.		Without grill	35,000.	
113	A35	2c brown	550.	85.
		No gum	200.	
		On cover, single		140.
b.		Without grill	14,000.	
c.		Half used as 1c on cover, diagonal, vertical or horizontal		6,000.
d.		Printed on both sides		9,000.

Locomotive A36   Washington A37

114	A36	3c ultramarine	250.	17.50
		No gum	80.	
		On cover		25.00
a.		Without grill	13,000.	18,000.
		Without grill, gray paper		3,750.
b.		Vert. one-third used as 1c on cover		—
c.		Vert. two-thirds used as 2c on cover		10,000.
d.		Double impression		15,000.
e.		Printed on both sides, reverse inverted		100,000.

No. 114a used on normal paper and 114a used on gray paper are each unique. No. 114a was lifted from a cover, original gum adhering, examined, and placed back. With 2011 Philatelic Foundation certificate. No. 114a on gray paper is a strip of three on piece, mostly detached from piece, with full gum. It is very good to fine and has 1978 and 2006 Philatelic Foundation certificates.

Nos. 114d and 114e each are unique. No. 114d has a pre-printing paper fold.

115	A37	6c ultramarine	2,750.	225.
		No gum	950.	
b.		Vertical half used as 3c on cover		50,000.

Shield and Eagle — A38   S. S. Adriatic — A39

116	A38	10c yellow	2,000.	130.
		No gum	750.	
		On cover		400.

117	A39	12c green	1,900.	130.
		No gum	700.	
		On cover		450.

Landing of Columbus — A40

Type I. Picture unframed.
No. 118 has horizontal shading lines at the left and right sides of the vignette.

118	A40	15c brn & bl, type I	9,500.	800.
		No gum	3,250.	
		On cover		1,900.
a.		Without grill	13,000.	

A40a

Type II. Picture framed.
No. 119 has diagonal shading lines at the left and right sides of the vignette.

119	A40a	15c brn & bl, type II	3,250.	225.
		No gum	1,150.	
		On cover		850.
b.		Center inverted	1,000,000.	22,500.
		No gum	700,000.	
c.		Center double, one inverted		80,000.

"The Declaration of Independence" A41

120	A41	24c green & vio	8,000.	675.
		No gum	2,800.	
		On domestic cover		12,500.
a.		Without grill	15,000.	
b.		Center inverted	750,000.	37,500.
		On cover		130,000.

Shield, Eagle and Flags — A42   Lincoln — A43

121	A42	30c ultra & carmine	5,250.	450.
		No gum	1,750.	
		On domestic cover		17,500.
a.		Without grill	11,000.	
b.		Flags inverted	800,000.	105,000.
		On cover		300,000.

122	A43	90c carmine & black	12,000.	2,000.
		No gum	4,000.	
		On cover		430,000.
a.		Without grill	24,000.	

Seven examples of No. 121b unused are recorded. Only one has part of its original gum.

Values of varieties of Nos. 112-122 without grill are for examples with original gum. Most examples of Nos. 119b, 120b are faulty. Values are for stamps with fine centering and only minimal faults. No. 120b unused is valued without gum, as all of the three examples available to collectors are without gum.

RE-ISSUE OF 1869 ISSUE
Produced by the National Bank Note Co.
Without grill, hard white paper, with white crackly gum.

The gum is almost always somewhat yellowed with age, and unused stamps with original gum are valued with such gum.

A new plate of 150 subjects was made for the 1c. The plate for the frame of the 15c was made using the same die as that used to make the type I frame for No. 118. For No. 118, the lines on each side of the vignette area were entered onto the plate itself, one position at a time. Upon close examination, each stamp position will be found to exhibit minute differences in these horizontal fringe lines.

1875   *Perf. 12*

123	A34	1c buff	550.	400.
		No gum	230.	
		On cover		3,000.
124	A35	2c brown	650.	800.
		No gum	260.	
		On cover		12,500.
125	A36	3c blue	5,000.	27,500.
		No gum	2,500.	
		On cover		—

Used value for No. 125 is for an attractive fine to very fine example with minimal faults.

126	A37	6c blue	1,650.	*3,250.*
		No gum	725.	
127	A38	10c yellow	1,650.	2,000.
		No gum	725.	
		On cover		22,500.
128	A39	12c green	2,250.	3,250.
		No gum	1,025.	
129	A40	15c brn & bl, Type III	1,350.	1,250.
		No gum	600.	
		On cover		22,500.
a.		Imperf. horizontally, single	14,000.	20,000.
		No gum	5,000.	

Two used examples of No. 129a are recorded. Both have faults and are valued thus.

130	A41	24c grn & violet	2,100.	1,750.
		No gum	900.	
		On cover		27,500.
131	A42	30c ultra & car	2,500.	3,000.
		No gum	1,100.	
132	A43	90c car & blk	3,750.	*6,250.*
		No gum	1,500.	

Soft Porous Paper

1880-82

133	A34	1c buff, issued with gum	325.	*450.*
		No gum	140.	
		On cover		1,900.
a.		1c brown orange, issued without gum ('81 and '82)	250.	*350.*

PRODUCED BY THE NATIONAL BANK NOTE COMPANY

Franklin — A44

A44

A45

Jackson — A45

A45

Washington — A46

A46

Lincoln — A47

A47

Edwin M.
Stanton — A48

A48

Jefferson — A49

A49

Henry Clay — A50

A50

Daniel Webster — A51

A51

Gen. Winfield
Scott
A52

Alexander
Hamilton
A53

Commodore O.H.
Perry — A54

H. GRILL ABOUT 10x12mm
(11 TO 13 BY 14 TO 16 POINTS)

The "H" grills can be separated into early state and late state, based on the shape of the tip of the grill. Early-state grills show a point or very small vertical line at the tip of the pyramid, while late-state grills show the pyramid tips truncated and flat.

Early-state "H" grills tend to be on vertical-mesh wove paper, while later printings and all late-state grills were printed on horizontal-mesh wove paper, resulting in stamp designs being approximately ¼mm shorter than the designs printed on vertical-mesh wove paper. The late-stage "H" grills virtually all seem to have been used only after Jan. 1873.

Poor printing quality often resulted in grills that show only a few grill points or a very few rows of points. This is especially true of the "H" grills. When there are not enough grill points to clearly identify whether the grill is an "H" or an "I," it must be assumed it is the lower-valued "H" grill variety. Authentication is advised for these stamps with high catalogue values.

White Wove Paper, Thin to Medium Thick.

1870-71   *Perf. 12*

134	A44	1c ultra	2,000. 200.00
	No gum		700.
	On cover		240.00
b.	Pair, one without grill		—
135	A45	2c red brown	1,000. 80.00
	No gum		360.
	On cover		105.00
b.	Diagonal half used as 1c on cover		—
c.	Vertical half used as 1c on cover		—
136	A46	3c green	575. 32.50
	No gum		190.
	On cover		37.50
b.	Printed on both sides		—

The imperf. 3c can be found in the Scott U.S. Specialized Catalogue Die and Plate Proofs section.

137	A47	6c carmine	5,000. 500.00
	No gum		1,750.
	On cover		575.00
b.	Pair, one without grill		—
138	A48	7c vermilion ('71)	4,250. 500.
	No gum		1,550.
	On cover		675.
139	A49	10c brown	7,000. 850.
	No gum		2,550.
	On cover		1,050.
b.	Pair, one without grill, one with split grill, on cover		—
140	A50	12c dull vio	27,500. 3,750.
	No gum		13,000.
	On cover		7,000.
141	A51	15c orange	7,500. 1,400.
	No gum		2,500.
	On cover		2,100.
142	A52	24c purple	— 7,000.
143	A53	30c black	20,000. 4,000.
	No gum		7,500.
	On cover		5,000.
144	A54	90c carmine	25,000. 2,500.
	No gum		10,000.

I. GRILL ABOUT 8½x10mm
(10 TO 11 BY 10 TO 13 POINTS)

The "I" grills can be separated into early state and late state, based on the shape of the tip of the grill. Early state grills show small tips of the pyramid, while late state grills show the pyramid tips truncated and flat.

Early state "I" grills tend to be on vertical-mesh wove paper, while later printings and all late-state grills were printed on horizontal-mesh wove paper, resulting in stamp designs being approximately ¼mm shorter than the designs printed on vertical-mesh wove paper. The late-stage "I" grills all seem to have been used only after Jan. 1873.

Values are for stamps with grills that are clearly identifiable. Poor printing quality often resulted in grills that show only a few grill points or a very few rows of points. When there are not enough grill points to clearly

identify whether the grill is an "H" or an "I," it must be assumed it is the lower-valued "H" grill variety. Authentication is advised for these stamps with high catalogue values.

134A	A44	1c ultramarine	2,750. 275.00
	No gum		800.00
135A	A45	2c red brown	2,000. 225.00
	On cover		—
136A	A46	3c green	1,000. 100.00
	On cover		—
a.	Pair, one without grill, on cover		—
137A	A47	6c carmine	7,000. 900.00
138A	A48	7c vermilion ('71)	6,500. 1,400.
	No gum		2,400.
139A	A49	10c brown	15,000. 8,500.
	Pair, on cover		—

The unused No. 139A is unique, and it is valued in the grade of fine.

140A	A50	12c dull violet	30,000.

The unused No. 140A is unique, and it is valued in the grade of fine.

141A	A51	15c orange	17,500. 8,000.
143A	A53	30c black	75,000.

Only one recorded example of No. 143A, which is valued in the grade of fine-very fine.

144A	A54	90c carmine	— 15,000.

The unused No. 144A has a vertically split grill and is unique.

White Wove Paper Without Grill.

1870-71   *Perf. 12*

145	A44	1c ultra	675. 25.00
	No gum		250.
	On cover		27.50
146	A45	2c red brown	325. 20.00
	No gum		115.
	On cover		22.50
a.	Diagonal half used as 1c on cover		700.00
b.	Vertical half used as 1c on cover		800.00
c.	Horiz. half used as 1c on cover		800.00
d.	Double impression		9,000.
147	A46	3c green	225. 2.00
	No gum		80.
	On cover		2.40
a.	Printed on both sides, reverse inverted		17,500.
b.	Double impression		30,000.

Nos. 147a and 147b are valued in the grade of fine.

The imperf. 3c can be found in the Scott U.S. Specialized Catalogue Die and Plate Proofs section.

148	A47	6c carmine	1,000. 25.00
	No gum		320.
	On cover		30.00
a.	Vertical half used as 3c on cover		6,500.
b.	Double impression, on cover		20,000.
c.	Double paper		100.00

No. 148b is unique.

149	A48	7c vermilion ('71)	1,000. 100.00
	No gum		320.
	On cover		160.00
150	A49	10c brown	2,250. 35.00
	No gum		850.
	On cover		50.00
151	A50	12c dull violet	2,750. 220.00
	No gum		1,000.
	On cover		475.00
152	A51	15c brt org	3,500. 220.00
	No gum		1,300.
	On cover		375.00
a.	Double impression		11,000.

No. 152a is unique.

153	A52	24c purple	1,800. 230.00
	No gum		625.
	On cover		1,500.
a.	Double paper		—
154	A53	30c black	7,500. 300.00
	No gum		2,750.
	On cover		900.00
155	A54	90c carmine	5,000. 350.00
	No gum		1,900.
	On cover		—

PRINTED BY THE CONTINENTAL BANK NOTE COMPANY

Designs of the 1870-71 Issue with secret marks on the values from 1c to 15c, as described and illustrated:

The object of secret marks was to provide a simple and positive proof that these stamps were produced by the Continental Bank Note Company and not by their predecessors.

Almost all of the stamps of the Continental Bank Note Co. printing including the Department stamps and some of the Newspaper stamps may be found upon a paper that shows more or less the characteristics of a ribbed paper. The ribbing may be oriented either vertically or horizontally, with horizontal ribbing being far more common than vertical ribbing. Values are for the most common varieties.

Franklin — A44a

1c. In the pearl at the left of the numeral "1" there is a small crescent.

Jackson — A45a

2c. Under the scroll at the left of "U. S." there is a small diagonal line. This mark seldom shows clearly. The stamp, No. 157, can be distinguished by its color.

Washington — A46a

3c. The under part of the upper tail of the left ribbon is heavily shaded.

Lincoln — A47a

6c. The first four vertical lines of the shading in the lower part of the left ribbon have been strengthened.

Stanton — A48a

7c. Two small semi-circles are drawn around the ends of the lines that outline the ball in the lower right hand corner.

Jefferson — A49a

10c. There is a small semi-circle in the scroll at the right end of the upper label.

Clay — A50a

12c. The balls of the figure "2" are crescent shaped.

Webster — A51a

15c. In the lower part of the triangle in the upper left corner two lines have been made heavier forming a "V." This mark can be found on some of the Continental and American (1879) printings, but not all stamps show it.

Secret marks were added to the dies of the 24c, 30c and 90c but new plates were not made from them. The various printings of the 30c and 90c can be distinguished only by the shades and paper.

Experimental J. Grill about 7x9½mm exists on all values except 24c and 90c. Grill was composed of truncated pyramids and was so strongly impressed that some points often broke through the paper.

White Wove Paper, Thin to Thick Without Grill

1873, July (?)   *Perf. 12*

156	A44a	1c ultra	225.	6.00
		No gum	85.	
		On cover		7.50
a.		Double paper	2,000.	500.00
e.		With grill	2,000.	
f.		Imperf., pair	—	1,500.
157	A45a	2c brown	350.	25.00
		No gum	125.	
		On cover		30.00
a.		Double paper	1,500.	200.00
c.		With grill	1,850.	750.00
d.		Double impression		16,500.
e.		Vertical half used as 1c on cover		1,000.

No. 157d is unique.

158	A46a	3c green	110.	1.00
		No gum	30.	
		On cover		1.20
a.		Double paper	600.	100.00
e.		With grill	550.	
h.		Horizontal pair, imperf. vert.		—
i.		Horizontal pair, imperf. between		1,300.
j.		Double impression		7,500.
k.		Printed on both sides		20,000.

Nos. 158j and 158k are valued in the grade of fine.

The imperf 3c, with and without grill, can be found in the Scott U.S. Specialized Catalogue Die and Plate Proofs section.

159	A47a	6c dull pink	400.	20.00
		No gum	130.	
		On cover		30.00
a.		Diagonal half used as 3c on cover		7,250.
b.		With grill	1,800.	
c.		Double paper	—	900.00
160	A48a	7c org ver	1,150.	90.00
		No gum	400.	
		On cover		175.00
a.		With grill	3,500.	
b.		Double paper		—
161	A49a	10c brown	900.	27.50
		No gum	275.	
		On cover		42.50
a.		Double paper		—
c.		With grill	3,750.	
d.		Horizontal pair, imperf. between		25,000.
162	A50a	12c blk vio	2,400.	145.00
		No gum	800.	
		On cover		325.00
a.		With grill	5,500.	
163	A51a	15c yel org	2,250.	160.00
		No gum	750.	
		On cover		350.00
a.		With grill	5,750.	
b.		Double paper		—
164	A52	24c purple		357,500.

The Philatelic Foundation has certified as genuine a 24c on vertically ribbed paper, and that is the unique stamp listed as No. 164. Specialists believe that only Continental used ribbed paper. It is not known for sure whether or not Continental also printed the 24c value on regular paper; if it did, specialists currently are not able to distinguish these from No. 153. The catalogue value represents a 2004 auction sale price realized.

165	A53	30c gray blk	4,000.	140.
		No gum	1,300.	
		On cover		725.
a.		Double paper		—
c.		With grill	22,500.	
166	A54	90c rose car	2,250.	300.00
		No gum	750.	
		On cover		7,500.

Special Printing of the 1873 Issue
Hard, White Wove Paper Without Gum

1875   *Perf. 12*

167	A44a	1c ultramarine	16,000.
168	A45a	2c dark brown	7,250.
169	A46a	3c blue green	25,000.
170	A47a	6c dull rose	21,500.
171	A48a	7c reddish ver	4,750.
172	A49a	10c pale brown	20,000.
173	A50a	12c dark violet	6,750.
174	A51a	15c bright org	18,000.
175	A52	24c dull purple	4,000. 22,500.
176	A53	30c greenish blk	14,500.
177	A54	90c vio carmine	21,500.

Although perforated, these stamps were usually cut apart with scissors. As a result, the perforations are often much mutilated and the design is frequently damaged.

These can be distinguished from the 1873 issue by the shades; also by the paper, which is very white instead of yellowish.

These and the subsequent issues listed under the heading of "Special Printings" are

---

special printings of stamps then in current use which, together with the reprints and re-issues, were made for sale to collectors. They were available for postage except for the Officials, Newspaper and Periodical, and demonetized issues.

Only three examples of No. 175 used have been certified. They all have small faults and are valued thus.

Yellowish Wove Paper

1875   *Perf. 12*

178	A45a	2c vermilion	350.	15.00
		No gum	110.	
		On cover		17.50
a.		Double paper	—	
b.		Half used as 1c on cover		750.00
c.		With grill	900.	2,750.

The imperf 2c can be found in the Scott U.S. Specialized Catalogue Die and Plate Proofs section.

Zachary Taylor — A55

179	A55	5c blue	700.	25.00
		No gum	225.	
		On cover		40.00
a.		Double paper	950.	
c.		With grill	4,500.	

SPECIAL PRINTING OF 1875 ISSUE
Hard, White Wove Paper Without Gum

1875

180	A45a	2c carmine ver	70,000.
181	A55	5c bright blue	450,000.

Unlike Nos. 167-177, Nos. 180-181 were not cut apart with scissors.

IMPORTANT INFORMATION REGARDING VALUES FOR NEVER-HINGED STAMPS

Collectors should be aware that the values given for never-hinged stamps from No. 182 on are for stamps in the grade of very fine, just as the values for all stamps in the catalogue are for very fine stamps unless indicated otherwise. The never-hinged premium as a percentage of value will be larger for stamps in extremely fine or superb grades, and the premium will be smaller for fine-very fine, fine or poor examples. This is particularly true of the issues of the late-19th and early-20th centuries. For example, in the grade of very fine, an unused stamp from this time period may be valued at $100 hinged and $200 never hinged. The never-hinged premium is thus 100%. But in a grade of extremely fine, this same stamp will not only sell for more hinged, but the never-hinged premium will increase, perhaps to 200%-400% or more over the higher extremely fine value. In the grade of superb, a hinged stamp will sell for much more than a very fine stamp, and additionally the never-hinged premium will be much larger, perhaps as large as 500%-1,000%. On the other hand, the same stamp in a grade of fine or fine-very fine not only will sell for less than a very fine stamp in hinged condition, but additionally the never-hinged premium will be smaller than the never-hinged premium on a very fine stamp, perhaps as small as 40%-60%.

Please note that the above statements and percentages are NOT a formula for arriving at the values of stamps in hinged or never-hinged condition in the grades of very good, fine, fine to very fine, extremely fine or superb. The percentages given apply only to the size of the premium for never-hinged condition that might be added to the stamp value for hinged condition. Further, the percentages given are only generalized estimates. Some stamps or grades may have percentages for never-hinged condition that are higher or lower than the ranges given.

VALUES FOR NEVER-HINGED STAMPS PRIOR TO SCOTT 182

This catalogue does not value pre-1879 stamps in never-hinged condition. Premiums for never-hinged condition in the classic era invariably are even larger than those premiums listed for the 1879 and later issues. Generally speaking, the earlier the stamp is listed in the catalogue, the larger will be the never-hinged premium. On some early classics, the premium will be several multiples of the unused, hinged values given in the catalogue.

For values of the most popular U.S. stamps in the grades of very good, fine, fine to very fine, very fine, very fine to extremely fine, extremely fine, extremely fine to superb, and superb, see the *Scott Stamp Values U.S. Specialized by Grade*, updated and issued each year as part of the U.S. specialized catalogue.

PRINTED BY THE AMERICAN BANK NOTE COMPANY
Identification by Paper Type:

Collectors traditionally have identified American Bank Note Co. issues by the soft, porous paper on which they were printed. However, the Continental Bank Note Co. used some intermediate papers as early as 1877 and a soft paper from August 1878 through early 1879, before the consolidation of the companies. When the consolidation occurred in the late afternoon of Feb. 4, 1879, American Bank Note Co. took over the presses, plates, paper, ink, and the employees of Continental. Undoubtedly they also acquired panes of finished stamps and sheets of printed stamps that had not yet been gummed and/or perforated. Since the soft paper that was in use at the time of the consolidation and after is approximately the same texture and thickness as the soft paper that American Bank Note Co. began using regularly in June or July of 1879, all undated soft paper stamps have traditionally been classified as American Bank Note Co. printings.

However, if a stamp bears a dated cancellation or is on a dated cover from Feb. 4, 1879 or earlier, collectors (especially specialist collectors) must consider the stamp to be a Continental Bank Note Co. printing. Undated stamps off cover, and stamps and covers dated Feb. 5 or later, traditionally have been considered to be American Bank Note Co. printings since that company held the contract to print U.S. postage stamps beginning on that date. The most dedicated and serious specialist students sometimes attempt to determine the stamp printer of the issues on soft, porous paper in an absolute manner (by scientifically testing the paper and/or comparing printing records).

SAME AS 1870-75 ISSUES
Soft Porous Paper
Varying from Thin to Thick

1879   *Perf. 12*

182	A44a	1c dark ultra	225.	6.00
		Never hinged	775.	
		No gum	75.	
		On cover		6.50
183	A45a	2c vermilion	100.	5.00
		Never hinged	370.	
		No gum	35.	
		On cover		5.50
a.		Double impression	—	5,500.
b.		Half used as 1c on cover		750.00

No. 183a is valued in the grade of fine.

184	A46a	3c green	90.	1.00
		Never hinged	330.	
		No gum	28.	
		On cover		1.10
b.		Double impression		5,000.

No. 184b is valued in the grade of fine.

The imperf 3c can be found in the Scott U.S. Specialized Catalogue Die and Plate Proofs section.

185	A55	5c blue	450.	17.50
		Never hinged	1,500.	
		No gum	140.	
		On cover		30.00
186	A47a	6c pink	900.	25.00
		Never hinged	3,100.	
		No gum	275.	
		On cover		30.00
187	A49	10c brn, without secret mark	3,250.	42.50
		Never hinged	11,000.	
		No gum	1,100.	
		On cover		60.00
a.		Double paper	8,500.	—
188	A49a	10c brn, with secret mark	1,800.	32.50
		Never hinged	6,500.	
		No gum	625.	
		On cover		47.50
189	A51a	15c red orange	200.	30.00
		Never hinged	675.	
		No gum	80.	
		On cover		87.50
190	A53	30c full black	900.	95.00
		Never hinged	3,000.	
		No gum	325.	
		On cover		450.00
191	A54	90c carmine	2,000.	360.00
		Never hinged	7,000.	
		No gum	650.	
		On cover		5,000.

The Continental Bank Note Co. was consolidated with the American Bank Note Co. on February 4, 1879. The American Bank Note Company used many plates of the Continental Bank Note Company to print the ordinary postage, Departmental and Newspaper stamps. Therefore, stamps bearing the Continental Company's imprint were not always its product.

The A. B. N. Co. also used the 30c and 90c plates of the N. B. N. Co. Some of No. 190 and all of No. 217 were from A. B. N. Co. plate 405.

Early printings of No. 188 were from Continental plates 302 and 303 which contained the normal secret mark of 1873. After those plates were re-entered by the A. B. N. Co. in 1880, pairs or multiple pieces contained combinations of normal, hairline or missing marks. The pairs or other multiples usually found contain at least one hairline mark which tended to disappear as the plate wore.

A. B. N. Co. plates 377 and 378 were made in 1881 from the National transfer roll of 1870. No. 187 from these plates has no secret mark.

The imperf. 90c can be found in the Scott U.S. Specialized Catalogue Die and Plate Proofs section.

Special Printing of the 1879 Issue
Soft Porous Paper
Without Gum

1880 *Perf. 12*

192	A44a	1c dark ultra	65,000.	
193	A45a	2c black brown	20,000.	
194	A46a	3c blue green	115,000.	
195	A47a	6c dull rose	76,000.	
196	A48a	7c scarlet vermilion	8,000.	
197	A49a	10c deep brown	40,000.	
198	A50a	12c blackish purple	11,000.	
199	A51a	15c orange	33,500.	
200	A52	24c dark violet	10,500.	
201	A53	30c greenish black	22,500.	
202	A54	90c dull carmine	33,500.	
203	A45a	2c scarlet vermilion	115,000.	
204	A55	5c deep blue	290,000.	

Nos. 192 and 194 are valued in the grade of fine.

No. 197 was printed from Continental plate 302 (or 303) after plate was re-entered. Therefore, the stamp may show normal, hairline or missing secret mark.

Unlike the 1875 hard-paper Special Printings (Nos. 167-177), the 1880 soft-paper Special Printings were never cut apart with scissors.

James A. Garfield — A56

1882

205	A56	5c yellow brown	240.	12.00
		Never hinged	775.	
		No gum	80.	
		On cover		25.00

Special Printing
1882 *Perf. 12*
Soft porous paper, without gum

205C	A56	5c gray brown	70,000.

DESIGNS OF 1873 RE-ENGRAVED

Franklin — A44b

1c — The vertical lines in the upper part of the stamp have been so deepened that the background often appears to be solid. Lines of shading have been added to the upper arabesques.

1881-82

206	A44b	1c gray blue	70.00	1.00
		Never hinged	225.00	
		No gum	21.00	
		On cover		1.75
a.		Double impression		

No. 206a is a partial double impression, with "ONE 1 CENT," etc. at bottom doubled.
Earliest documented use: Oct. 11, 1881.

Washington — A46b

3c. The shading at the sides of the central oval appears only about one-half the previous width. A short horizontal dash has been cut about 1mm below the "TS" of "CENTS."

207	A46b	3c blue green	70.00	.80
		Never hinged	225.00	
		No gum	20.00	
		On cover		.95
c.		Double impression	5,000.	
		On cover	5,500.	

Lincoln — A47b

6c. On the original stamps four vertical lines can be counted from the edge of the panel to the outside of the stamp. On the re-engraved stamps there are but three lines in the same place.

208	A47b	6c rose	775.	110.00
		Never hinged	2,400.	
		No gum	225.	
		On Cover		140.00
a.		6c deep brown red	550.	175.00
		Never hinged	1,600.	
		No gum	150.	
		On cover		425.00

Jefferson — A49b

10c. On the original stamps there are five vertical lines between the left side of the oval and the edge of the shield. There are only four lines on the re-engraved stamps. In the lower part of the latter, also, the horizontal lines of the background have been strengthened.

209	A49b	10c brown ('82)	160.	6.00
		Never hinged	475.	
		No gum	50.	
		On cover		11.00
b.		10c black brown	3,000.	350.00
		Never hinged	6,000.	
		No gum	950.	
		On cover		550.00
c.		Double impression		

Specimen stamps (usually overprinted "Sample") without overprint exist in a brown shade that differs from No. 209. The unoverprinted brown specimen is cheaper than No. 209. Expertization is recommended.

Washington A57   Jackson A58

Nos. 210-211 were issued to meet the reduced first class rate of 2 cents for each half ounce, and the double rate, which Congress approved Mar. 3, 1883, effective Oct. 1, 1883.

1883, Oct. 1 *Perf. 12*

210	A57	2c red brown	42.50	.75
		Never hinged	130.00	
		No gum	12.50	
		On cover		.85
211	A58	4c blue green	250.	27.50
		Never hinged	900.	
		No gum	80.	
		On cover		55.00

Imperfs can be found in the Scott U.S. Specialized Catalogue Die and Plate Proofs section.

Special Printing
1883-85 Soft porous paper *Perf. 12*

211B	A57	2c pale red brown, with gum ('85)	375.	—
		Never hinged	1,000.	
		No gum	130.	
c.		Horizontal pair, imperf. between	2,000.	
		On cover	3,000.	
211D	A58	4c deep blue grn	60,000.	

No. 211D is without gum.

Franklin — A59

1887 *Perf. 12*

212	A59	1c ultramarine	90.00	2.50
		Never hinged	290.00	
		No gum	30.00	
		On cover		3.25
213	A57	2c green	40.00	.60
		Never hinged	120.00	
		No gum	12.00	
b.		Printed on both sides		.75

Imperf 1c, 2c can be found in the Scott U.S. Specialized Catalogue Die and Plate Proofs section.

214	A46b	3c vermilion	60.00	55.00
		Never hinged	180.00	
		No gum	20.00	
		On cover (single)		95.00
		Nos. 212-214 (3)	190.00	58.10

1888 *Perf. 12*

215	A58	4c carmine	190.	27.50
		Never hinged	550.	
		No gum	55.	
		On cover		50.00
216	A56	5c indigo	225.	17.50
		Never hinged	700.	
		No gum	75.	
		On cover		35.00
217	A53	30c orange brn	250.	100.00
		Never hinged	900.	
		No gum	80.	
		On cover		1,400.
218	A54	90c purple	900.	250.00
		Never hinged	2,750.	
		No gum	275.	
		On cover		10,000.
		Nos. 215-218 (4)	1,565.	395.00

Imperfs can be found in the Scott U.S. Specialized Catalogue Die and Plate Proofs section.

Franklin A60

Washington A61

Jackson A62

Lincoln A63

Grant A64

Garfield A65

William T. Sherman A66

Daniel Webster A67

Henry Clay A68

Jefferson A69

Perry — A70

1890-93 *Perf. 12*

219	A60	1c dull blue	20.	.75
		On cover		.80
219D	A61	2c lake	175.	5.50
		Never hinged	550.	
		On cover		7.50
220	A61	2c carmine	20.00	.70
		Never hinged	60.00	
		On cover		.75
a.		Cap on left "2"	150.00	12.50
		Never hinged	425.00	
c.		Cap on both "2's"	650.00	35.00
		Never hinged	1,800.	
221	A62	3c purple	65.00	9.00
		Never hinged	200.00	
		On cover		17.50
222	A63	4c dark brown	90.00	4.75
		Never hinged	275.00	
		On cover		10.00
223	A64	5c chocolate	70.00	4.75
		Never hinged	220.00	
		On cover		12.50
224	A65	6c brown red	65.00	25.00
		Never hinged	200.00	
		On cover		40.00
225	A66	8c lilac ('93)	50.00	17.00
		On cover		32.50
226	A67	10c green	175.00	5.00
		On cover		10.00
227	A68	15c indigo	225.00	27.50
		Never hinged	675.00	
		On cover		65.00
228	A69	30c black	325.00	35.00
		Never hinged	975.00	
		On cover		600.00
229	A70	90c orange	475.00	150.00
		Never hinged	1,450.	
		On cover		—
		Nos. 219-229 (12)	1,755.	284.95

The No. 220 with "cap on right 2" variety is due to imperfect inking, not a plate defect.

Imperfs. can be found in the *Scott U.S. Specialized Catalogue* Die and Plate Proofs section.

COLUMBIAN EXPOSITION ISSUE

Columbus in Sight of Land — A71

Landing of Columbus A72

Flagship of Columbus A73

Fleet of Columbus A74

Columbus Soliciting Aid from Isabella A75

Columbus Welcomed at Barcelona A76

Columbus
Restored to
Favor — A77

Columbus
Presenting
Natives
A78

Columbus
Announcing
his Discovery
A79

Columbus at
La Rábida
A80

Recall of
Columbus
A81

Isabella
Pledging her
Jewels
A82

Columbus in
Chains
A83

Columbus
Describing
his Third
Voyage
A84

Isabella &
Columbus
A85

Columbus
A86

1893   *Perf. 12*

230	A71	1c deep blue	14.00	.40
		Never hinged	35.00	
		On cover		.90
231	A72	2c brown violet	14.00	.30
		Never hinged	35.00	
		On cover		.35
232	A73	3c green	37.50	17.50
		dull green	37.50	17.50
		dark green	37.50	17.50
		Never hinged	105.00	
		On cover		35.00
233	A74	4c ultra	55.00	9.00
		Never hinged	160.00	
		On cover		24.00
a.		4c blue (error)	17,500.	16,500.
		Never hinged	32,500.	

No. 233a exists in two shades. No. 233a used is valued with small faults, as almost all examples come thus.

234	A75	5c chocolate	55.00	9.50
		Never hinged	160.00	
		On cover		24.00

235	A76	6c purple	55.00	25.00
		Never hinged	160.00	
a.		6c red violet	55.00	25.00
		Never hinged	160.00	
		On cover, #235 or 235a		50.00
236	A77	8c magenta	52.50	12.00
		Never hinged	160.00	
		On cover		24.00
237	A78	10c black brown	100.00	9.00
		Never hinged	285.00	
		On cover		32.50
238	A79	15c dark green	225.00	82.50
		Never hinged	675.00	
		On cover		230.00
239	A80	30c orange brown	240.00	100.00
		Never hinged		400.00
240	A81	50c slate blue	500.00	200.00
		Never hinged	1,450.	
		No gum	225.	
		On cover		625.00
241	A82	$1 salmon	1,100.	600.
		Never hinged	3,750.	
		No gum	500.	
		On cover		1,900.
242	A83	$2 brown red	1,150.	600.
		Never hinged	3,800.	
		No gum	525.	
		On cover		2,000.
243	A84	$3 yellow green	1,500.	825.
		Never hinged	4,750.	
		No gum	750.	
a.		$3 olive green	1,500.	825.
		Never hinged	4,750.	
		No gum	750.	
		On cover, #243 or 243a		2,500.
244	A85	$4 crimson lake	2,000.	1,050.
		Never hinged	7,000.	
		No gum	1,000.	
a.		$4 rose carmine	2,000.	1,050.
		Never hinged	7,000.	
		No gum	1,000.	
		On cover		4,000.
245	A86	$5 black	2,400.	1,200.
		Never hinged	10,000.	
		No gum	1,200.	
		On cover		4,750.

World's Columbia Expo., Chicago, May 1-Oct. 30, 1893.

Nos. 230-245 are known imperf., but were not regularly issued.

See Scott U.S. Specialized Catalogue Die and Plate Proofs section for the 2c.

Never-Hinged Stamps

See note before No. 182 regarding premiums for never-hinged stamps.

Bureau Issues

Starting in 1894, the Bureau of Engraving and Printing at Washington produced most U.S. postage stamps.

Until 1965 Bureau-printed stamps were engraved except Nos. 525-536 which were offset.

The combination of lithography and engraving (see #1253) was first used in 1964, and photogravure (see #1426) in 1971.

Franklin
A87

Washington
A88

Jackson
A89

Lincoln
A90

Grant
A91

Garfield
A92

Sherman
A93

Webster
A94

Clay
A95

Jefferson
A96

Perry
A97

James
Madison
A98

John Marshall — A99

1894   **Unwmk.**   *Perf. 12*

246	A87	1c ultramarine	30.00	7.00
		Never hinged	90.00	
		On cover		22.50
247	A87	1c blue	65.00	4.00
		Never hinged	190.00	
		On cover		18.50

TWO CENTS:

Triangle A
(Type I)

Type I (Triangle A). The horizontal lines of the ground work run across the triangle and are of the same thickness within it as without.

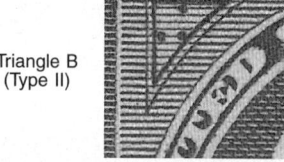

Triangle B
(Type II)

Type II (Triangle B). The horizontal lines cross the triangle but are thinner within it than without. Other minor design differences exist, but the change to Triangle B is a sufficient determinant.

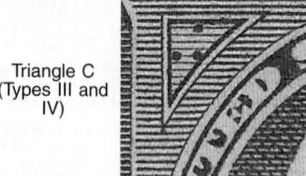

Triangle C
(Types III and IV)

Type III (Triangle C). The horizontal lines do not cross the double lines of the triangle. The lines within the triangle are thin, as in Type II. The rest of the design is the same as Type II, except that most of the designs had the dot in the "S" of "CENTS" removed. Stamps with this dot present are listed; some specialists refer to them as "Type IIIa" varieties.

Type IV

Type IV (Triangle C). See No. 279B and its varieties. Type IV is from a new die with many major and minor design variations including, (1) re-cutting and lengthening of hairline, (2) shaded toga button, (3) strengthening of lines on sleeve, (4) additional dots on ear, (5) "T" of "TWO" straight at right, (6) background lines extend into white oval opposite "U" of "UNITED." Many other differences exist.

248	A88	2c pink, type I	30.00	9.00
		Never hinged	90.00	
		On cover		16.00
249	A88	2c car lake, type I	150.00	7.00
		Never hinged	450.00	
		On cover		12.50
a.		Double impression	5,500.	—
250	A88	2c carmine, type I	30.00	3.00
		Never hinged	90.00	
		On cover		4.00
a.		2c rose, type I	37.50	6.00
		Never hinged	110.00	
		On cover		7.25
b.		2c scarlet, type I	27.50	3.00
		Never hinged	82.50	
		On cover		6.00
d.		Horizontal pair, imperf. between	2,000.	
251	A88	2c carmine, type II	375.00	15.00
		Never hinged	1,100.	
		On cover		22.50
a.		2c scarlet, type II	350.00	14.00
		Never hinged	1,050.	
		On cover		21.00
252	A88	2c carmine, type III	125.00	14.00
		Never hinged	375.00	
		On cover		22.50
a.		2c scarlet, type III	110.00	16.00
		Never hinged	325.00	
		On cover		20.00
b.		Horiz. pair, imperf. vert.	5,000.	
c.		Horiz. pair, imperf. between	5,500.	

Former Nos. 252a, 252b are now Nos. 252b, 252c.

253	A89	3c purple	110.00	13.00
		Never hinged	325.00	
		On cover		27.50
254	A90	4c dark brn	190.00	12.50
		Never hinged	550.00	
		On cover		22.50
255	A91	5c chocolate	110.00	10.00
		Never hinged	325.00	
		On cover		22.50
c.		Vert. pair, imperf. horiz.	4,000.	
256	A92	6c dull brown	160.00	30.00
		Never hinged	475.00	
		On cover		50.00
a.		Vert. pair, imperf. horiz.	3,000.	
		P# block of 6, Impt., T I	30,000.	
257	A93	8c vio brn ('95)	160.00	22.50
		Never hinged	475.00	
		On cover		50.00
258	A94	10c dark green	275.00	22.50
		Never hinged	850.00	
		On cover		37.50
259	A95	15c dark blue	275.00	70.00
		Never hinged	850.00	
		On cover		125.00
260	A96	50c orange	500.	150.
		Never hinged	1,500.	
		On cover		950.

Type I

Type II

ONE DOLLAR

Type I. The circles enclosing "$1" are broken where they meet the curved line below "One Dollar."

Type II. The circles are complete.

261	A97	$1 black, type I	1,000.	375.
	Never hinged		3,150.	
	No gum		325.	
	On cover			2,750.
261A	A97	$1 black, type II	2,100.	825.
	Never hinged		6,500.	
	No gum		675.	
	On cover			4,500.
262	A98	$2 bright blue	2,750.	1,250.
	Never hinged		8,750.	
	No gum		1,100.	
	On cover			5,000.
263	A99	$5 dark green	4,500.	2,750.
	Never hinged		15,000.	
	No gum		2,200.	
	On cover			—

For imperfs. and the 2c pink, vert. pair, imperf. hoirz., see Scott U.S. Specialized Catalogue Die and plate Proofs.

Same as 1894 Issue
Wmk. 191 Horizontally or Vertically
1895   *Perf. 12*

264	A87	1c blue	6.00	.60
	Never hinged		17.50	
	On cover			1.25
265	A88	2c car, type I	27.50	3.50
	Never hinged		82.50	
	On cover			5.50
266	A88	2c car, type II	32.50	5.50
	Never hinged		100.00	
	On cover			8.50
267	A88	2c car, type III	5.50	.50
	Never hinged		16.00	
	On cover			.65
a.	2c pink, type III		20.00	5.00
	Never hinged		60.00	
	On cover			6.00
b.	2c vermilion, type III ('99)		50.00	15.00
c.	2c rose carmine, type III ('99)		—	—

The three left vertical rows from plate 170 are type II, the balance being type III.

268	A89	3c purple	37.50	2.25
	Never hinged		115.00	
	On cover			8.00
269	A90	4c dark brown	42.50	3.50
	Never hinged		125.00	
	On cover			8.00
270	A91	5c chocolate	35.00	3.50
	Never hinged		105.00	
	On cover			8.00
271	A92	6c dull brown	120.00	8.50
	Never hinged		360.00	
	On cover			27.50
a.	Wmkd. USIR		15,000.	8,500.
272	A93	8c violet brown	70.00	2.75
	Never hinged		210.00	
	On cover			14.00
a.	Wmkd. USIR		6,000.	1,000.
273	A94	10c dark green	95.00	2.25
	Never hinged		280.00	
	On cover			15.00
274	A95	15c dark blue	210.00	17.50
	Never hinged		625.00	
	On cover			55.00
275	A96	50c orange	260.	40.00
	Never hinged		775.	
	On cover			400.00
a.	50c red orange		350.	47.50
	Never hinged		1,050.	
	On cover			425.00
276	A97	$1 black, type I	600.	100.
	Never hinged		1,800.	
	No gum		175.	
	On cover			2,250.
276A	A97	$1 black, type II	1,250.	210.
	Never hinged		3,750.	
	No gum		375.	
	On cover			3,750.
277	A98	$2 bright blue	900.	425.
	Never hinged		2,900.	
	No gum		260.	
a.	$2 dark blue		900.	425.
	Never hinged		2,900.	
	No gum		260.	
	On cover			3,500.
278	A99	$5 dark green	2,000.	625.
	Never hinged		6,250.	
	No gum		625.	
	On cover			10,000.

For imperfs. and the 1c horiz. pair, imperf. vert., see Scott U.S. Specialized Catalogue Die and Plate Proofs.
For "I.R." overprints see Nos. R155, R156-R158.
No. 271a unused is valued in the grade of fine.

Wmk. 191 Horizontally or Vertically
1897-1903   *Perf. 12*

279	A87	1c dp grn, horiz. wmk ('98)	9.00	.50
	Never hinged		25.00	
	On cover			.60
a.	Vert. wmk (error)		50.00	7.50
	Never hinged		150.00	
	On cover			22.50
279B	A88	2c red, type IV ('99)	9.00	.40
	Never hinged		25.00	
	On cover			.50
c.	2c rose carmine, type IV ('99)		275.00	200.00
	Never hinged		850.00	
d.	2c orange red, type IV, horiz. wmk. ('00)		11.50	2.00
	Never hinged		32.50	
	On cover			2.50
e.	2c orange red, type IV, vert. wmk.		35.00	10.00

			110.00	
	On cover			20.00
f.	2c carmine, type IV reddish carmine, *Dec. 1898*		10.00	2.00
	Never hinged		27.50	
	On cover			2.25
g.	2c pink, type IV		50.00	5.00
	Never hinged		150.00	
	On cover			5.50
h.	2c vermilion, type IV ('99)		11.00	3.00
	Never hinged		30.00	
	On cover			5.00
i.	2c brown org, type IV ('99)		250.00	50.00
	Never hinged		675.00	
j.	Booklet pane of 6, red, type IV, horiz. wmk. ('00)		500.00	3,000.
	Never hinged		1,000.	
k.	Booklet pane of 6, red, type IV, vertical watermark ('02)		500.00	—
	Never hinged		1,000.	
l.	As No. 279B, all color missing (FO)		500.00	
280	A90	4c rose brn ('98)	25.00	3.25
	Never hinged		75.00	
a.	4c lilac brown		25.00	3.25
	Never hinged		75.00	
b.	4c orange brown		25.00	3.00
	Never hinged		75.00	
	On cover, #280, 280a or 280b			7.50
281	A91	5c dk blue ('98)	32.50	2.25
	Never hinged		100.00	
	On cover			10.00
282	A92	6c lake ('98)	45.00	6.50
	Never hinged		140.00	
	On cover			17.50
a.	6c purple lake		70.00	15.00
	Never hinged		210.00	

Type I. The tips of the foliate ornaments do not impinge on the white curved line below "ten cents."

282C	A94	10c brown, type I ('98)	175.00	6.50
	Never hinged		525.00	
	On cover			18.00

Type II. The tips of the ornaments break the curved line below the "e" of "ten" and the "t" of "cents."

283	A94	10c org brn, type II, horiz. wmk.	150.00	6.00
	Never hinged		450.00	
	On cover			17.50
a.	Vert. wmk. ('00)		225.00	12.50
	Never hinged		700.00	
	On cover			35.00
284	A95	15c olive grn ('98)	150.00	13.00
	Never hinged		475.00	
	On cover			32.50

Nos. 279-284 (8)			*595.50*	*38.40*

For "I.R." overprints, see Nos. R153-R155A.

TRANS-MISSISSIPPI EXPOSITION ISSUE

Marquette on the Mississippi A100

Farming in the West — A101

Indian Hunting Buffalo A102

Frémont on the Rocky Mountains A103

Troops Guarding Wagon Train — A104

Hardships of Emigration A105

Western Mining Prospector A106

Western Cattle in Storm A107

Mississippi River Bridge A108

1898, June 17   **Wmk. 191**   *Perf. 12*

285	A100	1c dk yel grn	25.00	7.00
	Never hinged		67.50	
	On cover			10.00
286	A101	2c copper red	25.00	2.75
	Never hinged		67.50	
	On cover			3.75
287	A102	4c orange	110.00	27.50
	Never hinged		300.00	
	On cover			60.00
288	A103	5c dull blue	100.00	25.00
	Never hinged		275.00	
	On cover			50.00
289	A104	8c violet brown	150.00	50.00
	Never hinged		425.00	
	On cover			120.00
a.	Vert. pair, imperf. horiz.		27,500.	
290	A105	10c gray vio	150.00	35.00
	Never hinged		425.00	
	On cover			90.00
291	A106	50c sage grn	600.00	200.00
	Never hinged		1,800.	
	On cover			1,750.
292	A107	$1 black	1,400.	725.
	Never hinged		3,500.	
	No gum		800.	
	On cover			4,500.
293	A108	$2 org brn	1,900.	1,100.
	Never hinged		6,000.	
	No gum		875.	
	On cover			12,500.

Nos. 285-293 (9)			*4,460.*	*2,172.*

Trans-Mississippi Exposition, Omaha, Neb., June 1 to Nov. 1, 1898.
For "I.R" overprints see #R158A-R158B.

Never-Hinged Stamps
See note before No. 182 regarding premiums for never-hinged stamps.

PAN-AMERICAN EXPOSITION ISSUE

Fast Lake Navigation A109

"Empire State" Express A110

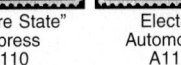

Electric Automobile A111

Bridge at Niagara Falls — A112

Canal Locks at Sault Ste. Marie — A113

Fast Ocean Navigation — A114

1901, May 1   **Wmk. 191**   *Perf. 12*

294	A109	1c grn & blk	16.50	3.00
	Never hinged		42.50	
	On cover			4.50
a.	Center inverted		12,500.	20,000.
	Never hinged		22,500.	
	On cover			—
295	A110	2c car & blk	15.50	1.00
	Never hinged		40.00	
	On cover			1.50
a.	Center inverted		55,000.	60,000.
296	A111	4c dp red brn & blk	70.00	19.00
	Never hinged		170.00	
	On cover			42.50
a.	Center inverted		85,000.	
297	A112	5c ultra & black	75.00	18.00
	Never hinged		180.00	
	On cover			45.00
298	A113	8c brn vio & blk	90.00	55.00
	Never hinged		230.00	
	On cover			110.00
299	A114	10c yel brn & blk	115.00	32.50
	Never hinged		300.00	
	On cover			125.00

Nos. 294-299 (6)			*382.00*	*128.50*
Nos. 294-299, never hinged			*962.50*	

No. 296a was a special printing.
Almost all unused examples of Nos. 295a and 296a have partial or disturbed gum. Values are for examples with full original gum that is slightly disturbed.

Franklin A115

Washington A116

Jackson A117

Grant A118

Lincoln A119

Garfield A120

Martha Washington A121

Webster A122

Benjamin Harrison A123

Clay A124

Jefferson
A125

David G.
Farragut
A126

Madison
A127

Marshall
A128

Many stamps of this issue are known with blurred printing due to having been printed on dry paper.

1902-03   Wmk. 191   Perf. 12

300	A115 1c blue grn ('03)	11.00	.25
	Never hinged	27.50	
	On cover		.30
b.	Booklet pane of 6	600.00	11,500.
	Never hinged	1,150.	
	Wmk. horiz.	2,000.	
301	A116 2c car ('03)	15.00	.50
	Never hinged	37.50	
	On cover		.55
c.	Booklet pane of 6	500.00	6,000.
	Never hinged	950.00	
302	A117 3c brt vio ('03)	50.00	4.00
	Never hinged	130.00	
	On cover		11.00
303	A118 4c brn ('03)	55.00	2.50
	Never hinged	140.00	
	On cover		12.50
304	A119 5c blue ('03)	60.00	2.25
	Never hinged	150.00	
	On cover		6.00
305	A120 6c claret ('03)	60.00	5.75
	Never hinged	150.00	
	On cover		16.00
306	A121 8c vio black	40.00	3.50
	Never hinged	100.00	
	On cover		8.00
307	A122 10c pale red brn ('03)	00.00	3.25
	Never hinged	150.00	
	On cover		9.50
308	A123 13c purple blk	40.00	11.00
	Never hinged	100.00	
	On cover		37.50
309	A124 15c ol grn ('03)	180.00	14.00
	Never hinged	475.00	
	On cover		80.00
310	A125 50c org ('03)	375.	37.50
	deep orange	375.	37.50
	Never hinged	1,150.	
	On cover		700.00
311	A126 $1 black ('03)	600.00	95.00
	Never hinged	1,900.	
	No gum	125.00	
	On cover		1,500.
312	A127 $2 dk bl ('03)	850.00	200.00
	Never hinged	2,650.	
	No gum	190.00	
	On cover		2,500.
313	A128 $5 dk grn ('03)	2,100.	700.00
	Never hinged	6,250.	
	No gum	475.00	
	On cover		5,000.
	Nos. 300-313 (14)	4,496.	1,079.

For listings of designs A127 and A128 with Perf. 10 see Nos. 479 and 480.

1906-08   Imperf.

314	A115 1c blue green	15.00	20.00
	Never hinged	32.50	
314A	A118 4c brn ('08)	100,000.	52,500.
	Never hinged	200,000.	
	On cover		140,000.
315	A119 5c blue ('08)	325.00	1,250.
	Never hinged	600.00	
	On cover, pair		70,000.

No. 314A was issued imperforate but all examples were privately perforated with large oblong perforations at the sides (Schermack type III).

Beware of examples of No. 303 with trimmed perforations and fake private perfs added.

Used examples of Nos. 314 and 315 must have contemporaneous cancels.

COIL STAMPS

Warning! Imperforate stamps are known fraudulently perforated to resemble coil stamps and part-perforate varieties. Fully perforated stamps and booklet stamps also are known with perforations fraudulently trimmed off to resemble coil stamps.

1908   Perf. 12 Horizontally

316	A115 1c blue green	115,000.	
	Pair	240,000.	

317	A119 5c blue	5,750.	—
	Never hinged	12,000.	
	Pair	15,000.	
	Never hinged	45,000.	

Perf. 12 Vertically

318	A115 1c blue green	4,250.	
	Never hinged	9,500.	
	Pair	11,000.	

Coil stamps for use in vending and affixing machines are perforated on two sides only, either horizontally or vertically.

They were first issued in 1908, using perf. 12. This was changed to 8½ in 1910, and to 10 in 1914.

Imperforate sheets of certain denominations were sold to the vending machine companies which applied a variety of private perforations and separations.

Several values of the 1902 and later issues are found on an apparently coarse ribbed paper caused by worn blankets on the printing press and are not true paper varieties.

All examples of Nos. 316-318 must be accompanied by certificates of authenticity issued by recognized expertizing committees.

No. 318 mint never hinged is valued in the grade of fine.

Washington — A129

Type I

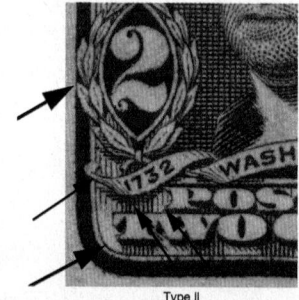
Type II

The two large arrows in the illustrations highlight the two major differences of the type II stamps: closing of the thin left border line next to the laurel leaf, and strengthening of the inner frame line at the lower left corner. The small arrows point out three minor differences that are not always easily discernible: strengthening of shading lines under the ribbon just above the "T" of "TWO," a shorter shading line to the left of the "P" in "POSTAGE," and shortening of a shading line in the left side ribbon.

Type I

1903, Nov. 12   Wmk. 191   Perf. 12

319	A129 2c carmine, type I	6.00	.25
	Never hinged	15.00	
	On cover		.30
a.	2c lake	—	
b.	2c carmine rose	15.00	.40
	Never hinged	45.00	
	On cover		.60
c.	2c scarlet	10.00	.30
	Never hinged	25.00	
	On cover		.40
d.	Vert. pair, imperf. horiz., No. 319	7,500.	
	Never hinged	17,500.	
e.	Vert. pair, imperf. between		
r.	Vert. pair, rouletted between	3,250.	

During the use of No. 319, the postmaster of San Francisco discovered in his stock panes that had the perforations missing between the top two rows of stamps. To facilitate their separation, the imperf rows were rouletted, and the

---

stamps were sold over the counter. These vertical pairs with regular perfs all around and rouletted between are No. 319r. No 319e is from a different source. One example has been authenticated, and collectors are warned that other pairs exist with faint blind perfs or indentations from the perforating machine.

g.	Booklet pane of 6, carmine	125.00	450.00
	Never hinged	240.00	
n.	Booklet pane of 6, carmine rose	275.00	700.00
	Never hinged	500.00	
p.	Booklet pane of 6, scarlet	185.00	625.00
	Never hinged	350.00	

Type II

1908   Wmk. 191   Perf. 12

319F	A129 2c lake	10.00	.30
	Never hinged	25.00	
	On cover		.35
i.	2c carmine	65.00	50.00
	Never hinged	150.00	
	On cover		150.00
j.	2c carmine rose	85.00	1.75
	Never hinged	185.00	
k.	2c scarlet	70.00	2.00
	Never hinged	160.00	
h.	Booklet pane of 6, carmine	900.00	—
	Never hinged	1,500.	
q.	Booklet pane of 6, lake	300.00	800.00
	Never hinged	575.00	

Type I

1906, Oct. 2   Wmk. 191   Imperf.

320	A129 2c carmine	15.00	19.00
	Never hinged	32.50	
	On cover		25.00
b.	2c scarlet	17.50	15.00
	Never hinged	37.50	
	On cover		22.50
c.	2c carmine rose	75.00	42.50
	Never hinged	150.00	

Type II

1908   Wmk. 191   Imperf.

320A	A129 2c lake	45.00	50.00
	Never hinged	100.00	
	On cover		100.00
d.	2c carmine	120.00	2,500.
	Never hinged	175.00	
	On cover		—

No. 320Ad was issued imperforate, but all examples were privately perforated with large oblong perforations at the sides (Schermack type III).

COIL STAMPS

1908   Perf. 12 Horizontally

321	A129 2c car, type I, pair	450,000.	250,000.
	On cover, single		250,000.

Four authenticated unused pairs of No. 321 are known and available to collectors. A fifth, unauthenticated pair is in the New York Public Library Miller collection, which is on long-term loan to the Smithsonian National Postal Museum. The value for an unused pair is for a fine-very fine example. Two fine pairs are recorded and one very fine pair.

There are no authenticated unused single stamps recorded. The used value is for a single on cover, of which two authenticated examples are known, both used from Indianapolis in 1908.

Numerous counterfeits exist.

Perf. 12 Vertically

322	A129 2c carmine, type II	7,000.	—
	Never hinged	15,000.	
	Pair	17,500.	

This Government Coil Stamp should not be confused with those of the International Vending Machine Co., which are perforated 12½.

All examples of Nos. 321-322 must be accompanied by certificates of authenticity issued by recognized expertizing committees.

LOUISIANA PURCHASE EXPOSITION ISSUE

St. Louis, Mo., Apr. 30 - Dec. 1, 1904

Robert R. Livingston
A130

Thomas Jefferson
A131

James Monroe
A132

William McKinley
A133

Map of Louisiana Purchase
A134

1904, Apr. 30   Wmk. 191   Perf. 12

323	A130 1c green	25.00	5.00
	Never hinged	65.00	
	On cover		7.00
324	A131 2c carmine	25.00	2.00
	Never hinged	65.00	
	On cover		3.00
a.	Vertical pair, imperf. horiz.	25,000.	
325	A132 3c violet	70.00	30.00
	Never hinged	185.00	
	On cover		65.00
326	A133 5c dark blue	75.00	25.00
	Never hinged	200.00	
	On cover		50.00
327	A134 10c red brown	130.00	30.00
	Never hinged	310.00	
	On cover		125.00
	Nos. 323-327 (5)	325.00	92.00
	Nos. 323-327, never hinged	845.00	

JAMESTOWN EXPOSITION ISSUE

Hampton Roads, Va., Apr. 26 - Dec. 1, 1907

Captain John Smith — A135

Founding of Jamestown
A136

Pocahontas
A137

1907   Wmk. 191   Perf. 12

328	A135 1c green	22.50	5.00
	Never hinged	60.00	
	On cover		8.00
329	A136 2c carmine	25.00	4.50
	Never hinged	70.00	
	On cover		6.00
a.	2c carmine lake	—	
330	A137 5c blue	115.00	32.50
	Never hinged	285.00	
	On cover		85.00
	Nos. 328-330 (3)	162.50	42.00
	Nos. 328-330, never hinged	405.00	

Franklin
A138

Washington
A139

There are several types of some of the 2c and 3c stamps of this and succeeding issues. These types are described under the dates at which they first appeared.

Illustrations of Types I-VII of the 2c (A140) and Types I-IV of the 3c (A140) are reproduced by permission of H. L. Lindquist.

1908-09   Wmk. 191   Perf. 12

331	A138	1c green	6.75	.40
		Never hinged	17.00	
		On cover		.55
a.		Booklet pane of 6	150.00	700.00
		Never hinged	300.00	

No. 331 exists in horizontal pair, imperforate between, a variety resulting from booklet experiments. Not regularly issued. Value in the grade of fine, $3,750.

No. 331a used is valued with a contemporaneous cancel. A certificate of authenticity is advised.

332	A139	2c carmine	6.25	.35
		Never hinged	15.00	
		On cover		.40
a.		Booklet pane of 6	135.00	500.00
		Never hinged	240.00	
b.		2c lake	4,250.	

No. 332a used is valued with a contemporaneous cancel. A certificate of authenticity is advised.

No. 332b is valued in the grade of fine.

Washington — A140

TYPE I

THREE CENTS.
Type I. The top line of the toga rope is weak and the rope shading lines are thin. The 5th line from the left is missing. The line between the lips is thin. (For descriptions of 3c types II, III and IV, see notes and illustrations preceding Nos. 484, 529-530.)

Used on both flat plate and rotary press printings.

333	A140	3c deep violet, type I	30.00	3.00
		Never hinged	75.00	
		On cover		8.50
334	A140	4c orange brown	37.50	1.50
		Never hinged	92.50	
		On cover		7.00
335	A140	5c blue	50.00	2.50
		Never hinged	120.00	
		On cover		8.50
336	A140	6c red orange	65.00	6.50
		Never hinged	150.00	
		On cover		22.50
337	A140	8c olive green	45.00	3.00
		Never hinged	105.00	
		On cover		18.00
338	A140	10c yellow ('09)	67.50	2.00
		Never hinged	160.00	
		On cover		10.00
339	A140	13c bl green ('09)	37.50	19.00
		Never hinged	90.00	
		On cover		110.00
340	A140	15c pale ultra ('09)	65.00	6.50
		Never hinged	150.00	
		On cover		125.00
341	A140	50c violet ('09)	300.00	22.50
		Never hinged	700.00	
		On cover		5,000.
342	A140	$1 violet brn ('09)	500.00	100.00
		Never hinged	1,150.	
		On cover		6,000.
		Nos. 331-342 (12)	1,210.	167.25

For listings of other perforated sheet stamps of A138, A139 and A140 see:
Nos. 357-366 Bluish paper
Nos. 374-382, 405-407 Single line wmk. Perf. 12
Nos. 423A-423C Single line wmk. Perf 12x10
Nos. 423D-423E Single line wmk. Perf 10x12
Nos. 424-430 Single line wmk. Perf. 10
Nos. 461 Single line wmk. Perf. 11
Nos. 462-469 unwmk. Perf. 10
Nos. 498-507 unwmk. Perf. 11
Nos. 519 Double line wmk. Perf. 11
Nos. 525-530 and 536 Offset printing
Nos. 538-546 Rotary press printing

Imperf

343	A138	1c green	4.00	5.50
		Never hinged	8.50	
		On cover		12.00
344	A139	2c carmine	4.75	3.25
		Never hinged	10.00	
		On cover		8.25
345	A140	3c dp violet, type I	9.00	22.50
		Never hinged	19.00	
		On cover		65.00
346	A140	4c org brn ('09)	13.50	25.00
		Never hinged	29.00	
		On cover		100.00

347	A140	5c blue ('09)	27.50	37.50
		Never hinged	60.00	
		On cover		140.00
		Nos. 343-347 (5)	58.75	93.75
		Nos. 343-347, never hinged	126.50	

For listings of other imperforate stamps of designs A138, A139 and A140 see Nos. 383, 384, 408, 409 and 459 Single line wmk.
Nos. 481-485 unwmk.
Nos. 531-535 Offset printing

COIL STAMPS

1908-10   Perf. 12 Horizontally

348	A138	1c green	35.00	50.00
		Never hinged	75.00	
		On cover		90.00
349	A139	2c carmine ('09)	90.00	100.00
		Never hinged	210.00	
		On cover		175.00
350	A140	4c org brn ('10)	140.00	210.00
		Never hinged	325.00	
		On cover		375.00
351	A140	5c blue ('09)	140.00	300.00
		Never hinged	325.00	
		On cover		625.00
		Nos. 348-351 (4)	405.00	660.00

1909   Perf. 12 Vertically

352	A138	1c green	95.00	190.00
		Never hinged	220.00	
		On cover		350.00
353	A139	2c carmine	90.00	220.00
		Never hinged	200.00	
		On cover		375.00
354	A140	4c org brn	190.00	275.00
		Never hinged	400.00	
		On cover		450.00
355	A140	5c blue	210.00	300.00
		Never hinged	450.00	
		On cover		475.00
356	A140	10c yellow	3,500.	4,500.
		Never hinged	8,500.	
		On cover		10,000.

For listings of other coil stamps of designs A138, A139 and A140, see #385-396, 410-413, 441-458 (single line wmk.), #486-496 (unwatermarked).

Beware of stamps offered as No. 356 which may be examples of No. 338 with perfs. trimmed at top and/or bottom. Beware also of plentiful fakes in the marketplace of Nos. 348-355, made by fraudulently perforating imperforate stamps or by fraudulently trimming perforations off fully perforated stamps. Authentication of all these coils is advised.

BLUISH PAPER

This was made with 35 percent rag stock instead of all wood pulp. The "bluish" color (actually grayish blue) goes through the paper showing clearly on the back as well as on the face.

1909   Perf. 12

357	A138	1c green	85.00	150.00
		Never hinged	180.00	
		On cover		220.00
358	A139	2c carmine	80.00	150.00
		Never hinged	170.00	
		On cover		190.00
359	A140	3c dp violet, type I	1,800.	9,000.
		Never hinged	4,000.	
		On cover		—
360	A140	4c org brn	27,500.	
		Never hinged	80,000.	
		On cover		—
361	A140	5c blue	5,750.	17,500.
		Never hinged	14,500.	
		On cover		27,500.
362	A140	6c red org	1,250.	12,500.
		Never hinged	3,000.	
		On cover		22,500.
363	A140	8c olive green	30,000.	
		Never hinged	85,000.	
		On cover		—
364	A140	10c yellow	1,600.	10,000.
		Never hinged	4,000.	
		On cover		—
365	A140	13c blue green	2,600.	4,000.
		Never hinged	6,000.	
		On cover		—
366	A140	15c pale ultra	1,250.	12,500.
		Never hinged	3,000.	
		On cover		—

Nos. 360 and 363 were not regularly issued. Used examples of Nos. 357-366 must bear contemporaneous cancels, and Nos. 359-366 used must be accompanied by certificates of authenticity issued by recognized expertizing committees.

LINCOLN CENTENARY OF BIRTH ISSUE

Lincoln — A141

1909, Feb. 12   Wmk. 191   Perf. 12

367	A141	2c carmine	5.00	2.00
		Never hinged	10.50	
		On cover		4.00

Imperf

368	A141	2c carmine	14.00	22.50
		Never hinged	25.00	
		On cover		40.00

BLUISH PAPER
Perf. 12

369	A141	2c carmine	150.00	250.00
		Never hinged	320.00	
		On cover		375.00

ALASKA-YUKON-PACIFIC EXPOSITION ISSUE

William H. Seward — A142

1909, June 1   Wmk. 191   Perf. 12

370	A142	2c carmine	7.50	2.25
		Never hinged	16.00	
		On cover		5.00

Imperf

371	A142	2c carmine	16.00	24.00
		Never hinged	32.50	
		On cover		42.50
		On cover, Expo. station machine canc.		450.00

Seattle, Wash., June 1 to Oct. 16.

HUDSON-FULTON CELEBRATION ISSUE

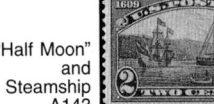

"Half Moon" and Steamship A143

1909, Sept. 25   Wmk. 191   Perf. 12

372	A143	2c carmine	10.00	4.75
		Never hinged	21.00	
		On cover		8.50

Imperf

373	A143	2c carmine	20.00	27.50
		Never hinged	40.00	
		On cover		40.00

Tercentenary of the discovery of the Hudson River and Centenary of Robert Fulton's steamship.

DESIGNS OF 1908-09 ISSUES

1910-11   Wmk. 190   Perf. 12

374	A138	1c green	6.50	.25
		Never hinged	15.00	
		On cover		.30
a.		Booklet pane of 6	225.00	400.00
		Never hinged	375.00	
b.		Double impression		300.00
375	A139	2c carmine	6.50	.25
		Never hinged	15.00	
		On cover		.30
a.		Booklet pane of 6	125.00	300.00
		Never hinged	200.00	
b.		2c lake	800.00	
		Never hinged	1,750.	
c.		As "b," booklet pane of 6	10,000.	
d.		Double impression	750.00	—
		Never hinged	1,500.	
376	A140	3c deep violet, type I ('11)	20.00	2.00
		Never hinged	45.00	
		On cover		8.00
377	A140	4c brown ('11)	30.00	1.00
		Never hinged	70.00	
		On cover		7.50
378	A140	5c blue ('11)	30.00	.75
		Never hinged	70.00	
		On cover		5.25
379	A140	6c red org ('11)	40.00	1.25
		Never hinged	90.00	
		On cover		13.00
380	A140	8c ol grn ('11)	100.00	15.00
		Never hinged	225.00	
		On cover		45.00
381	A140	10c yellow ('11)	95.00	6.00
		Never hinged	220.00	
		On cover		22.50
382	A140	15c pale ultra ('11)	240.00	22.50
		Never hinged	525.00	
		On cover		100.00
		Nos. 374-382 (9)	568.00	49.00

1910, Dec.   Imperf.

383	A138	1c green	2.00	2.25
		Never hinged	4.25	
		On cover		5.50
384	A139	2c carmine	3.25	2.75
		Never hinged	7.00	
		On cover		4.00

COIL STAMPS

1910, Nov. 1   Perf. 12 Horizontally

385	A138	1c green	45.00	45.00
		Never hinged	100.00	
		On cover		90.00
386	A139	2c carmine	130.00	100.00
		Never hinged	280.00	
		On cover		175.00

1910-11   Perf. 12 Vertically

387	A138	1c green	190.00	140.00
		Never hinged	390.00	
		On cover		250.00
388	A139	2c carmine	1,300.	2,250.
		Never hinged	3,100.	
		On cover		3,000.

Stamps offered as No. 388 frequently are privately perforated examples of No. 384, or examples of No. 375 with top and/or bottom perfs trimmed.

389	A140	3c dp violet, type I ('11)	110,000.	10,500.
		Never hinged	240,000.	
		On cover		27,500.

No. 389 is valued in the grade of fine. Stamps offered as No. 389 sometimes are examples of No. 376 with top and/or bottom perfs trimmed.

Beware also of plentiful fakes in the marketplace of Nos. 385-387.

Expertization by competent authorities is recommended.

1910   Perf. 8½ Horizontally

390	A138	1c green	4.50	14.00
		Never hinged	10.00	
		On cover		17.50
391	A139	2c carmine	42.50	50.00
		Never hinged	90.00	
		On cover		70.00

1910-13   Perf. 8½ Vertically

392	A138	1c green	27.50	55.00
		Never hinged	60.00	
		On cover		75.00
393	A139	2c carmine	45.00	45.00
		Never hinged	105.00	
		On cover		80.00
394	A140	3c dp violet, type I ('11)	60.00	67.50
		Never hinged	135.00	
		On cover		125.00
395	A140	4c brown ('12)	60.00	70.00
		Never hinged	135.00	
		On cover		125.00
396	A140	5c blue ('13)	60.00	67.50
		Never hinged	135.00	
		On cover		120.00
		Nos. 392-396 (5)	252.50	305.00

Beware also of plentiful fakes in the marketplace of Nos. 390-393.

PANAMA-PACIFIC EXPOSITION ISSUE
San Francisco, Cal., Feb. 20 - Dec. 4, 1915

Vasco Nunez de Balboa — A144

Pedro Miguel Locks, Panama Canal — A145

Golden Gate — A146

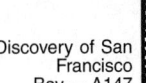

Discovery of San Francisco Bay — A147

1913   Wmk. 190   Perf. 12

397	A144	1c green	16.50	2.00
		Never hinged	40.00	
		On cover		3.50
398	A145	2c carmine	18.00	1.00
		Never hinged	40.00	
		On cover		1.75
a.		2c carmine lake	1,500.	
		Never hinged	2,500.	
b.		2c lake	5,000.	
		Never hinged	8,500.	
399	A146	5c blue	70.00	10.00
		Never hinged	160.00	
		On cover		27.50

400	A147	10c orange yel	120.00	22.50
		Never hinged	270.00	
		On cover		57.50
400A	A147	10c orange	180.00	20.00
		Never hinged	400.00	
		On cover		75.00
		Nos. 397-400A (5)	404.50	55.50
		Nos. 397-400A, never hinged	910.00	

1914-15   **Perf. 10**

401	A144	1c green	25.00	7.00
		Never hinged	60.00	
		On cover		16.00
402	A145	2c car ('15)	70.00	2.75
		Never hinged	170.00	
		On cover		6.50
403	A146	5c blue ('15)	160.00	20.00
		Never hinged	390.00	
		On cover		55.00
404	A147	10c orange ('15)	700.00	75.00
		Never hinged	1,700.	
		On cover		175.00
		Nos. 401-404 (4)	955.00	104.75
		Nos. 401-404, never hinged	2,320.	

1912-14   **Wmk. 190**   **Perf. 12**

405	A140	1c green	6.50	.25
		Never hinged	15.00	
		On cover		.30
a.		Vert. pair, imperf. horiz.	2,000.	
b.		Booklet pane of 6	65.00	75.00
		Never hinged	110.00	
c.		Double impression	6,000.	

TYPE I

TWO CENTS
Type I. There is one shading line in the first curve of the ribbon above the left "2" and one in the second curve of the ribbon above the right "2."
The button of the toga has only a faint outline.
The top line of the toga rope, from the button to the front of the throat, is also very faint.
The shading lines of the face terminate in front of the ear with little or no joining, to form a lock of hair.
Used on both flat plate and rotary press printings.

406	A140	2c car, type I	6.50	.25
		Never hinged	15.00	
		On cover		.30
a.		Booklet pane of 6	65.00	90.00
		Never hinged	110.00	
b.		Double impression	1,250.	
c.		2c lake, type I	2,000.	6,000.
		Never hinged	3,500.	
407	A140	7c black ('14)	70.00	14.00
		Never hinged	160.00	
		On cover		75.00
		Nos. 405-407 (3)	83.00	14.50

1912   **Imperf.**

408	A140	1c green	1.00	1.00
		Never hinged	2.00	
		On cover		1.75
409	A140	2c car, type I	1.20	1.20
		Never hinged	2.40	
		On cover		2.00

COIL STAMPS
1912   **Perf. 8½ Horizontally**

410	A140	1c green	6.00	12.50
		Never hinged	13.00	
		On cover		17.50
411	A140	2c carmine, type I	10.00	15.00
		Never hinged	22.50	
		On cover		20.00

Perf. 8½ Vertically

412	A140	1c green	25.00	25.00
		Never hinged	55.00	
		On cover		35.00
413	A140	2c carmine, type I	50.00	25.00
		Never hinged	110.00	
		On cover		32.50
		Nos. 410-413 (4)	91.00	77.50

Beware also of plentiful fakes in the marketplace of Nos. 410-413.

Franklin — A148

1912-14   **Wmk. 190**   **Perf. 12**

414	A148	8c pale ol grn	42.50	2.00
		Never hinged	100.00	
		On cover		15.00
415	A148	9c sal red ('14)	52.50	14.00
		Never hinged	120.00	
		On cover		50.00
416	A148	10c orange yellow	42.50	.90
		Never hinged	100.00	
		On cover		2.75
a.		10c brown yellow	1,250.	
		Never hinged	2,750.	
417	A148	12c cl brn ('14)	42.50	5.00
		Never hinged	100.00	
		On cover		25.00
418	A148	15c gray	85.00	4.50
		Never hinged	190.00	
		On cover		17.50
419	A148	20c ultra ('14)	190.00	19.00
		Never hinged	400.00	
		On cover		150.00
420	A148	30c org red ('14)	115.00	19.00
		Never hinged	250.00	
		On cover		250.00
421	A148	50c violet ('14)	350.00	30.00
		Never hinged	775.00	
		On cover		2,000.
		Nos. 414-421 (8)	920.00	94.30

No. 421 almost always has an offset of the frame lines on the back under the gum. No. 422 does not have this offset.

VALUES FOR VERY FINE STAMPS
Please note: Stamps are valued in the grade of Very Fine unless otherwise indicated.

1912, Feb. 12   **Wmk. 191**   **Perf. 12**

422	A148	50c violet	225.00	25.00
		Never hinged	500.00	
		On cover		2,000.
423	A148	$1 violet brown	475.00	80.00
		Never hinged	1,000.	
		On cover		7,000.

Perforated sheet stamps of type A148: #431-440 (single line wmk., perf. 10), #460 (double line wmk., perf. 10), #470-478 (unwmkd., perf. 10), #508-518 (unwmkd., perf. 11).

1914 Compound Perforations

As the Bureau of Engraving and Printing made the changeover to perf 10 from perf 12, in the normal course of their stamp production they perforated limited quantities of 1c, 2c and 5c stamps with the old 12-gauge perforations in one direction and the new 10-gauge perforations in the other direction. These were not production errors. These compound-perforation stamps previously were listed as Nos. 424a, 424b, 425c, 425d and 428a.

All examples of Nos. 423A-423E must be accompanied by certificates of authenticity issued by a recognized expertizing committee. Fakes made from perf 12, perf 10 and imperfs exist.

1914   **Wmk. 190**   **Perf. 12x10**

423A	A140	1c green	15,000.	6,000.
		Never hinged		
		On cover, pair		17,500.

Formerly No. 424a. Seventeen unused and 52 used examples are recorded. Value for unused is for a sound stamp with perfs touching or just cutting the design. Value for used is for a sound stamp in the grade of fine-very fine. Of the used examples, 23 are precanceled Quincy IL (very scarce) or Chicago (usually inverted). The unused block of four, used block of four and pair on cover are each unique (top stamp of pair on cover with small piece missing and valued thus). The block of 4 has perfs slightly cutting at top and is valued thus.

423B	A140	2c rose red, type I	175,000.	17,500.
		Never hinged		

Formerly No. 425d. One unused (a plate #7082 single) and 31 used examples are recorded. Value for used is for a sound stamp in the grade of fine-very fine. There are no precancels known on this issue.

423C	A140	5c blue		20,000.

Formerly No. 428a. 25 used examples are recorded. No unused examples are recorded. Three examples are precanceled: Tampa FL (2) and Rahway NJ (1). Value is for a sound stamp in the grade of fine-very fine. The pair is unique (one stamp creased, the other with a small tear).
Earliest documented use: April 14, 1915 (dated cancel on off-cover stamp).

1914   **Wmk. 190**   **Perf. 10x12**

423D	A140	1c green	12,500.	
		On postcard	22,500.	

Formerly No. 424b. 42 used examples are recorded. No unused examples are recorded. 37 examples are precanceled: Dayton OH (34), Buffalo NY (2) and Elkhart IN (1). Value is for a sound stamp in the grade of fine-very fine. The use on postcard is unique.
Earliest documented use: Dec. 19, 1914.

423E	A140	2c rose red, type I	—	

Formerly No. 425c. Only one used example has been certified (by the Philatelic Foundation). It is well centered, has a machine cancel, and has small thinning and a crease.

1913-15   **Wmk. 190**   **Perf. 10**

424	A140	1c green	2.50	.25
		Never hinged	5.25	
		On cover		.25
c.		Vert. pair, imperf. horiz.	3,000.	2,500.
		Never hinged	4,500.	
d.		Booklet pane of 6 ('13)	5.25	7.50
		Never hinged	8.75	
e.		As "d," imperf.	1,600.	
f.		Vert. pair, imperf. between and with straight edge at top	13,000.	

For former Nos. 424a and 424b, see Nos. 423A and 423D.
All known examples of No. 424e are without gum.
The unique example of No. 424f is never hinged, and it is valued thus.

425	A140	2c rose red, type I	2.30	.25
		Never hinged	4.75	
		On cover		.25
e.		Booklet pane of 6, *1913*	17.50	25.00
		Never hinged	25.00	

For former Nos. 425c and 425d, see Nos. 423A and 423D.

426	A140	3c dp vio, type I	14.00	1.50
		Never hinged	32.50	
		On cover		3.50
427	A140	4c brown	32.50	1.00
		Never hinged	75.00	
		On cover		5.25
428	A140	5c blue	32.50	1.00
		Never hinged	75.00	
		On cover		3.00

For former No. 428a, see No. 423C.

429	A140	6c red orange	45.00	2.00
		Never hinged	105.00	
		On cover		9.00
430	A140	7c black	90.00	5.00
		Never hinged	200.00	
		On cover		37.50
431	A148	8c pale olive grn	35.00	3.00
		Never hinged	82.50	
		On cover		8.00
a.		Double impression	—	
432	A148	9c salmon red	45.00	9.00
		Never hinged	105.00	
		On cover		27.50
433	A148	10c org yellow	45.00	1.00
		Never hinged	105.00	
		On cover		7.75
434	A148	11c dk grn ('15)	22.50	8.50
		Never hinged	55.00	
		On cover		25.00
435	A148	12c claret brown	25.00	6.00
		Never hinged	60.00	
		On cover		17.50
		Block of 4	110.00	45.00
a.		12c copper red	30.00	7.00
		Never hinged	72.50	
		On cover		20.00
437	A148	15c gray	125.00	7.25
		Never hinged	280.00	
		On cover		52.50
438	A148	20c ultra	190.00	6.00
		Never hinged	430.00	
		On cover		150.00
439	A148	30c orange red	220.00	20.00
		Never hinged	500.00	
		On cover		250.00
440	A148	50c violet ('15)	450.00	20.00
		Never hinged	1,050.	
		On cover		1,750.
		Nos. 424-440 (16)	1,376.	91.75

COIL STAMPS
1914   **Perf. 10 Horizontally**

441	A140	1c green	1.00	1.50
		Never hinged	2.00	
		On cover		2.75
442	A140	2c carmine, type I	10.00	45.00
		Never hinged	22.50	
		On cover		60.00

1914   **Perf. 10 Vertically**

443	A140	1c green	30.00	45.00
		Never hinged	65.00	
		On cover		60.00
444	A140	2c carmine, type I	45.00	35.00
		Never hinged	110.00	
		On cover		52.50
a.		2c lake	2,000.	
445	A140	3c violet, type I	210.00	250.00
		Never hinged	500.00	
		On cover		500.00
446	A140	4c brown	130.00	150.00
		Never hinged	280.00	
		On cover		200.00
447	A140	5c blue	45.00	115.00
		Never hinged	100.00	
		On cover		125.00
		Nos. 443-447 (5)	460.00	595.00

Beware also of plentiful fakes in the marketplace of Nos. 441-447.

ROTARY PRESS STAMPS

The Rotary Press Stamps are printed from plates that are curved to fit around a cylinder. This curvature produces stamps that are slightly larger, either horizontally or vertically, than those printed from flat plates. Designs of stamps from flat plates measure about 18½-19mm wide by 22mm high.

When the impressions are placed sidewise on the curved plates the designs are 19½-20mm wide; when they are placed vertically the designs are 22½ to 23mm high. A line of color (not a guide line) shows where the curved plates meet or join on the press.

ROTARY PRESS COIL STAMPS
Stamp designs: 18½-19x22½mm
1915-16   **Perf. 10 Horizontally**

448	A140	1c green	7.50	17.50
		Never hinged	16.00	
		On cover		30.00

Type II

TWO CENTS.
Type II. Shading lines in ribbons as on type I.
The toga button, rope and rope shading lines are heavy.
The shading lines of the face at the lock of hair end in a strong vertical curved line.
Used on rotary press printings only.

Type III

Type III. Two lines of shading in the curves of the ribbons.
Other characteristics similar to type II.
Used on rotary press printings only.

Fraudulently altered examples of type III (Nos. 455, 488, 492 and 540) have had one line of shading scraped off to make them resemble type II (Nos. 454, 487, 491 and 539).

449	A140	2c red, type I	2,500.	600.00
		Never hinged	5,500.	
		On cover, type I		1,500.
450	A140	2c carmine, type III ('16)	12.50	22.50
		Never hinged	27.50	
		On cover, type III		45.00

Stamp designs: 19½-20x22mm
1914-16   **Perf. 10 Vertically**

452	A140	1c green	10.00	17.50
		Never hinged	21.00	
		On cover		30.00
453	A140	2c carmine rose, type I	140.00	17.50
		Never hinged	300.00	
		On cover, type I		30.00
454	A140	2c red, type II	70.00	22.50
		Never hinged	160.00	
		On cover, type II		50.00
455	A140	2c carmine, type III	8.00	3.50
		Never hinged	18.00	
		On cover, type III		8.00
456	A140	3c vio, type I ('16)	225.00	170.00
		Never hinged	475.00	
		On cover		250.00
457	A140	4c brown ('16)	25.00	30.00
		Never hinged	55.00	
		On cover		50.00
458	A140	5c blue ('16)	27.50	30.00
		Never hinged	60.00	
		On cover		50.00
		Nos. 452-458 (7)	505.50	291.00

Horizontal Coil

1914, June 30   *Imperf.*
459 A140 2c carmine, type I   175.   *1,300.*
   Never hinged   275.

When the value for a used stamp is higher than the unused value, the stamp must have a contemporaneous cancel. Valuable stamps of this type should be accompanied by certificates of authenticity issued by recognized expertizing committees. The used value for No. 459 is for an example with such a certificate.

Beware of examples of No. 453 with perforations fraudulently trimmed to resemble single examples of No. 459.

FLAT PLATE PRINTINGS

1915, Feb. 8   Wmk. 191   *Perf. 10*
460 A148 $1 violet black   650.   140.
   Never hinged   1,450.
   On cover   12,000.

1915, June 17   Wmk. 190   *Perf. 11*
461 A140 2c pale carmine red, type I   125.   360.
   Never hinged   325.
   On cover   1,200.

Beware of fraudulently perforated examples of No. 409 being offered as No. 461.
See note on used stamps following No. 459.

Unwatermarked

From 1916 onward all postage stamps except Nos. 519 and 832b are on unwatermarked paper.

1916-17   Unwmk.   *Perf. 10*
462 A140 1c green   7.00   .35
   Never hinged   16.00
   On cover   .50
a. Booklet pane of 6   9.50   12.50
   Never hinged   16.00
463 A140 2c carmine, type I   4.50   .40
   Never hinged   10.00
   On cover   .45
a. Booklet pane of 6   110.00   110.00
   Never hinged   180.00
464 A140 3c violet, type I   70.00   19.00
   Never hinged   175.00
   On cover   42.50

Beware of fraudulently perforated examples of No. 483 being offered as No. 464.

465 A140 4c org brn   40.00   2.50
   Never hinged   90.00
   On cover   11.00
466 A140 5c blue   70.00   2.50
   Never hinged   160.00
   On cover   13.00
467 A140 5c car (error in plate of 2c, '17)   450.00   *1,500.*
   Never hinged   850.00
   On cover   5,000.

No. 467 is an error caused by using a 5c transfer roll in re-entering three subjects: 7942 UL 74, 7942 UL 84, 7942 LR 18; the balance of the subjects on the plate being normal 2c entries. No. 467 imperf. is listed as No. 485. The error perf 11 on unwatermarked paper is No. 505.

468 A140 6c red orange   85.00   9.00
   Never hinged   190.00
   On cover   37.50
469 A140 7c black   120.00   15.00
   Never hinged   270.00
   On cover   45.00
470 A148 8c olive green   55.00   8.00
   Never hinged   125.00
   On cover   27.50
471 A148 9c salmon red   55.00   18.50
   Never hinged   125.00
   On cover   42.50
472 A148 10c orange yel   100.00   2.50
   Never hinged   230.00
   On cover   8.50
473 A148 11c dark green   40.00   18.50
   Never hinged   90.00
   On cover   47.50
474 A148 12c claret brn   50.00   7.50
   Never hinged   115.00
   On cover   22.50
475 A148 15c gray   180.00   16.00
   Never hinged   400.00
   On cover   87.50
476 A148 20c lt ultra   225.00   20.00
   Never hinged   525.00
   On cover   725.00
476A A148 30c orange red   2,500.
   Never hinged   4,750.

No. 476A is valued in the grade of fine.

477 A148 50c lt violet ('17)   900.   85.00
   Never hinged   1,450.
   On cover   2,250.
478 A148 $1 violet black   625.00   30.00
   Never hinged   1,450.
   On cover   3,000.
Nos. 462-466,468-476,477-478 (16)   2,626.   254.75

TYPES OF 1903 ISSUE

1917, Mar. 22   Unwmk.   *Perf. 10*
479 A127 $2 dark blue   210.00   40.00
   Never hinged   475.00
   On cover (other than first flight or Zeppelin)   *1,250.*
480 A128 $5 light green   170.00   35.00
   Never hinged   375.00
   On cover   *1,250.*

1916-17   *Imperf.*
481 A140 1c green   .95   .95
   Never hinged   1.90
   On cover   1.50

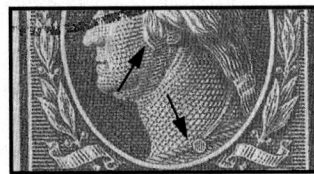

Type Ia

TWO CENTS
Type Ia. The design characteristics are similar to type I except that all of the lines of the design are stronger.
The toga button, toga rope and rope shading lines are heavy.
The latter characteristics are those of type II, which, however, occur only on impressions from rotary plates.
Used only on flat plates 10208 and 10209.

482 A140 2c carmine, type I   1.30   1.30
   Never hinged   2.60
   On cover   2.50
482A A140 2c deep rose, type Ia   —   *65,000.*
   On cover   70,000.

No. 482A was issued imperforate but all examples were privately perforated with large oblong perforations at the sides (Schermack type III).

Type II

THREE CENTS
Type II. The top line of the toga rope is strong and the rope shading lines are heavy and complete.
The line between the lips is heavy.
Used on both flat plate and rotary press printings.

483 A140 3c violet, type I ('17)   10.00   10.00
   Never hinged   22.00
   On cover   25.00
484 A140 3c violet, type II   8.00   8.00
   Never hinged   18.00
   On cover   14.00
485 A140 5c car (error in plate of 2c) ('17)   *8,000.*
   Never hinged   *14,000.*

Although No. 485 is valued as a single stamp, such examples are seldom seen in the marketplace.
No. 485 usually is seen as the center stamp in a block of 9 with 8 No. 482 (value with #485 never hinged, $22,500.) or as two center stamps in a block of 12 (value with both No. 485 never hinged, $42,500).

ROTARY PRESS COIL STAMPS
(See note over No. 448)

1916-18   *Perf. 10 Horizontally*
Stamp designs: 18½-19x22½mm
486 A140 1c green ('18)   .85   .85
   Never hinged   1.75
   On cover   1.15
487 A140 2c carmine, type II   12.50   14.00
   Never hinged   27.50
   On cover   19.00
488 A140 2c carmine, type III   3.00   *5.00*
   Never hinged   6.50
   On cover   7.00
489 A140 3c vio, type I ('17)   4.50   2.25
   Never hinged   10.00
   On cover   3.50
Nos. 486-489 (4)   20.85   22.10

1916-22   *Perf. 10 Vertically*
Stamp designs: 19½-20x22mm
490 A140 1c green   .50   *.60*
   Never hinged   1.05
   On cover   .80

491 A140 2c carmine, type II   2,500.   800.00
   Never hinged   5,250.
   On cover, type II   1,100.
492 A140 2c carmine, type III   9.00   1.00
   Never hinged   19.00
   On cover, type III   1.40
493 A140 3c vio, type I ('17)   14.00   4.50
   Never hinged   30.00
   On cover, type I   8.00
494 A140 3c vio, type II ('18)   10.00   2.50
   Never hinged   21.50
   On cover, type II   4.00
495 A140 4c org brn ('17)   10.00   7.00
   Never hinged   21.50
   On cover   10.00
496 A140 5c blue ('19)   3.25   2.50
   Never hinged   7.00
   On cover   3.00
497 A148 10c org yel ('22)   17.50   17.50
   Never hinged   35.00
   On cover   22.50

Blind Perfs
Listings of imperforate-between varieties are for examples which show no trace of "blind perfs," traces of impressions from the perforating pins which do not cut into the paper.
Some unused stamps have had the gum removed to eliminate the impressions from the perforating pins. These stamps do not qualify as the listed varieties.

FLAT PLATE PRINTINGS
TYPES OF 1913-15 ISSUE

1917-19   Unwmk.   *Perf. 11*
498 A140 1c green   .35   .25
   Never hinged   .75
   On cover   .30
a. Vertical pair, imperf. horiz.   800.00
   Never hinged   1,600.
b. Horizontal pair, imperf. between   650.00
   Never hinged   1,450.
c. Vertical pair, imperf. between   700.00   —
   Never hinged   1,450.
d. Double impression   250.00   3,750.
e. Booklet pane of 6   2.50   2.00
   Never hinged   4.25
f. Booklet pane of 30   1,050.   12,500.
   Never hinged   1,700.
g. Perf. 10 at top or bottom   17,500.   20,000.
   Never hinged   27,500.

No. 498g used is valued in the grade of fine.

499 A140 2c rose, type I   .35   .25
   Never hinged   .75
   On cover, type I   .30
a. Vertical pair, imperf. horiz., type I   1,000.
   Never hinged   2,000.
b. Horiz. pair, imperf. vert., type I   550.00   225.00
   Never hinged   1,100.
c. Vert. pair, imperf. btwn., type I   900.00   300.00
   Never hinged   1,100.
e. Booklet pane of 6, type I   4.00   2.50
   Never hinged   6.75
f. Booklet pane of 30, type I   22,500.   —
   Never hinged   32,500.
g. Double impression, type I   200.00   2,000.
   Never hinged   400.00
h. 2c lake, type I   500.00   800.00
   Never hinged   1,000.
   On cover   —

No. 499b is valued in the grade of fine. No 499c used is valued in the grade of fine.

500 A140 2c deep rose, type Ia   250.00   240.00
   Never hinged   550.00
   On cover, type Ia   650.00

No. 500 exists with imperforate top sheet margin. Examples have been altered by trimming perforations. Some also have faked Schermack perfs.

501 A140 3c lt vio, type I   10.00   .40
   Never hinged   22.50
   On cover, type I   .50
a. Booklet pane of 6, type I   75.00   80.00
   Never hinged   125.00
b. Vert. pair, imper. horiz., type I   2,000.
   Never hinged   3,250.
d. Double impression   3,500.   3,500.
   Never hinged   5,000.

No. 501d is valued in the grade of fine.

502 A140 3c dark violet, type II   13.00   .75
   Never hinged   30.00
   On cover, type II   1.00
b. Bklt. pane of 6, type II   60.00   75.00
   Never hinged   100.00
c. Vert. pair, imperf. horiz., type II   1,400.   750.00
   Never hinged   2,750.
   On cover   1,400.
d. Double impression   800.00   1,000.
   Never hinged   1,000.
e. Perf. 10 at top or bottom   15,000.   30,000.
   Never hinged   21,500.
503 A140 4c brown   9.00   .40
   Never hinged   20.00
   On cover   2.10
b. Double impression   —
504 A140 5c blue   8.00   .35
   Never hinged   18.00
   On cover   .45
a. Horizontal pair, imperf. between   20,000.   —
b. Double impression   1,750.   1,600.

505 A140 5c rose (error in plate of 2c)   300.00   *600.00*
   Never hinged   625.00
   On cover   2,250.
506 A140 6c red orange   12.00   .40
   Never hinged   27.50
   On cover   2.50
a. Perf. 10 at top or bottom   30,000.   8,000.
b. Double impression, never hinged

No. 506a also exists as a transitional stamp gauging partly perf 10 and partly perf 11 at top. Value thus the same as normal 506a.
No. 506b is a partial double impression. Two authenticated examples are documented.

507 A140 7c black   26.00   1.25
   Never hinged   60.00
   On cover   7.75
508 A148 8c olive bister   12.00   .65
   Never hinged   27.50
   On cover   2.75
b. Vertical pair, imperf. between   —
c. Perf. 10 at top or bottom   10,000.
509 A148 9c salmon red   12.00   1.75
   Never hinged   27.50
   On cover   13.00
a. Perf. 10 at top or bottom   7,500.
   Never hinged   37,500.

No. 509a also exists as a transitional stamp gauging partly perf 10 and partly perf 11 at top or bottom. Value thus the same as normal 509a.

510 A148 10c orange yellow   16.00   .25
   Never hinged   36.00
   On cover   2.00
a. 10c brown yellow   1,400.
   Never hinged   3,250.
511 A148 11c lt green   8.00   2.50
   Never hinged   18.00
   On cover   8.50
a. Perf. 10 at top or bottom   4,000.   3,750.
   Never hinged   7,500.

No. 511a also exists as a transitional stamp gauging partly perf 10 and partly perf 11 at top or bottom. Value thus the same as normal 511a.

512 A148 12c claret brown   8.00   .40
   Never hinged   18.00
   On cover   4.00
a. 12c brown carmine   9.00   .50
   Never hinged   20.00
b. Perf. 10 at top or bottom   27,500.   15,000.
   On cover   4.50
513 A148 13c apple grn ('19)   10.00   6.00
   Never hinged   22.00
   On cover   19.00
   Block of 4   42.50   45.00
514 A148 15c gray   35.00   1.50
   Never hinged   80.00
   On cover   25.00
a. Perf. 10 at bottom   10,000.
515 A148 20c lt ultra   42.50   .45
   Never hinged   90.00
   On cover   75.00
b. Vertical pair, imperf. between   2,500.   3,250.
c. Double impression   1,250.
   Never hinged   2,500.
d. Perf. 10 at top or bottom   12,500.

No. 515b is valued in the grade of fine.
Beware of pairs with blind perforations inside the design of the top stamp that are offered as No. 515b.
No. 515c is a partial double impression.

516 A148 30c orange red   30.00   1.50
   Never hinged   70.00
   On cover   150.00
a. Perf. 10 at top or bottom   20,000.   8,500.
   Never hinged   37,500.
b. Double impression   —

No. 516a used is valued in the grade of fine.

517 A148 50c red violet   47.50   .75
   Never hinged   115.00
   On cover   400.00
b. Vertical pair, imperf. between & with natural straight edge at bottom   6,000.
c. Perf. 10 at top or bottom   17,500.

No. 517b is valued in average condition and may be a unique used pair (precancelled). The editors would like to see authenticated evidence of an unused pair.

518 A148 $1 violet brown   37.50   1.50
   Never hinged   95.00
   On cover   550.00
b. $1 deep brown   1,900.   1,250.
   Never hinged
Nos. 498-504,506-518 (20)   587.20   261.30

No. 518b is valued in the grade of fine to very fine.

TYPE OF 1908-09 ISSUE

1917, Oct. 10   Wmk. 191   *Perf. 11*
519 A139 2c carmine   400.00   *1,750.*
   Never hinged   850.00
   On cover   3,500.

Beware of examples of No. 344 fraudulently perforated and offered as No. 519. Obtaining a certificate from a recognized expertizing committee is strongly recommended.
Warning: See note following No. 459 regarding used stamps.

Franklin A140

1918, Aug.   Unwmk.   Perf. 11

523	A149 $2 org red & blk	525.	250.
	Never hinged	1,150.	
	On cover		2,000.
524	A149 $5 dp grn & blk	170.	35.00
	Never hinged	360.	
	On cover		2,500.

See No. 547 for $2 carmine & black.

TYPES OF 1917-19 ISSUE
OFFSET PRINTING

1918-20   Unwmk.   Perf. 11

525	A140 1c gray green	2.50	.90
	Never hinged	6.00	
	On cover		1.75
a.	1c dark green	10.00	1.75
	Never hinged	25.00	
c.	Horizontal pair, imperf.		
	between	500.00	650.00
d.	Double impression	40.00	750.00
	Never hinged	90.00	

No. 525c is valued in the grade of fine and with natural straight edge at right, as all recorded examples come thus. No. 525d used is valued in the grade of very good.

Type IV

TWO CENTS

Type IV — Top line of the toga rope is broken.

The shading lines in the toga button are so arranged that the curving of the first and last form "D (reversed) D."

The line of color in the left "2" is very thin and usually broken.

Used on offset printings only.

Type V

Type V — Top line of the toga is complete.

There are five vertical shading lines in the toga button.

The line of color in the left "2" is very thin and usually broken.

The shading dots on the nose are as shown on the diagram.

Used on offset printings only.

Type Va

Type Va — Characteristics are the same as type V except in the shading dots of the nose. The third row of dots from the bottom has four dots instead of six. The overall height is ⅓mm shorter than the other types.

Used on offset printings only.

Type VI

Type VI — General characteristics the same as type V except that the line of color in the left "2" is very heavy.

Used on offset printings only.

TYPE VII

Type VII — The line of color in the left "2" is invariably continuous, clearly defined and heavier than in type V or Va but not as heavy as type VI.

An additional vertical row of dots has been added to the upper lip.

Numerous additional dots have been added to the hair on top of the head.

Used on offset printings only.

526	A140 2c car, type IV		
	('20)	25.00	4.00
	Never hinged	57.50	
	On cover, type IV		11.00
527	A140 2c car, type V		
	('20)	18.00	1.25
	Never hinged	40.00	
	On cover, Type V		2.75
a.	Double impression	75.00	—
	Never hinged	160.00	
b.	Vert. pair, imperf.		
	horiz.	850.00	
c.	Horiz. pair, imperf.		
	vert.	1,000.	—
528	A140 2c car, type Va		
	('20)	8.00	.40
	Never hinged	20.00	
	On cover, type Va		.75
c.	Double impression	55.00	
	Never hinged	125.00	
g.	Vert. pair, imperf. be-		
	tween	3,500.	
528A	A140 2c car, type VI		
	('20)	47.50	2.00
	Never hinged	115.00	
	On cover, type VI		3.75
d.	Double impression	180.00	900.00
	Never hinged	400.00	
f.	Vert. pair, imperf.		
	horiz.	—	
h.	Vert. pair, imperf. be-		
	tween	5,000.	
528B	A140 2c car, type VII		
	('20)	20.00	.75
	Never hinged	50.00	
	On cover, type VII		1.00
e.	Double impression	77.50	400.00

No. 528Be used is valued in the grade of very good to fine.

TYPE III

THREE CENTS

Type III — The top line of the toga rope is strong but the 5th shading line is missing as in type I.

Center shading line of the toga button consists of two dashes with a central dot.

The "P" and "O" of "POSTAGE" are separated by a line of color.

The frame line at the bottom of the vignette is complete.

Used on offset printings only.

529	A140 3c vio, type III	3.50	.50
	Never hinged	7.75	
	On cover, type III		.60
a.	Double impression	45.00	800.00
	Never hinged	100.00	
b.	Printed on both sides	2,500.	

No. 529a used is valued in the grade of very good.

530	A140 3c pur, type IV	2.00	.30
a.	Double impression	35.00	750.00
	On cover		1,500.
b.	Printed on both sides	600.00	
	Never hinged	1,100.	
c.	Triple impression	1,750.	—
	Nos. 525-530 (8)	126.50	10.10

No. 530a used is valued in the grade of fine.

1918-20   Imperf.

531	A140 1c green ('19)	10.00	12.00
	Never hinged	21.00	
	On cover		17.50
532	A140 2c car rose,		
	type IV		
	('20)	32.50	37.50
	Never hinged	70.00	
	On cover		70.00
533	A140 2c car, type V		
	('20)	85.00	125.00
	Never hinged	175.00	
	On cover		210.00
534	A140 2c car, type		
	Va ('20)	12.00	15.00
	Never hinged	26.00	
	On cover		17.50
534A	A140 2c car, type VI		
	('20)	35.00	37.50
	Never hinged	75.00	
	On cover		45.00
534B	A140 2c car, type		
	VII ('20)	1,850.	1,400.
	Never hinged	3,500.	
	On cover		5,000.
535	A140 3c vio, type IV	8.00	5.00
	Never hinged	18.00	
	On cover		11.00
a.	Double impression	95.00	—
	Never hinged	200.00	
	Nos. 531-534A,535 (6)	182.50	232.00

1919, Aug. 15   Perf. 12½

536	A140 1c gray green	20.00	35.00
	Never hinged	45.00	
	On postcard, single		225.00
	On cover, pair		300.00
a.	Horiz. pair, imperf. vert.	1,200.	

VICTORY ISSUE

"Victory" and Flags of the Allies — A150

FLAT PLATE PRINTING
Unwmk.

1919, Mar. 3   Engr.   Perf. 11

537	A150 3c violet	10.00	3.25
	Never hinged	20.00	
	On cover		11.00
a.	3c deep red violet	1,250.	1,750.
	Never hinged	2,300.	
b.	3c light reddish violet	150.00	50.00
	Never hinged	300.00	
	On cover		250.00
c.	3c red violet	200.00	60.00
	Never hinged	400.00	
	On cover		275.00

Victory of the Allies in World War I.

No. 537a is valued in the grade of fine.

ROTARY PRESS PRINTINGS

1919   Unwmk.   Perf. 11x10

Stamp designs: 19½-20x22-22¼mm

538	A140 1c green	10.00	9.00
	Never hinged	23.00	
	On cover		22.50
a.	Vert. pair, imperf. horiz.	60.00	125.00
	Never hinged	125.00	
539	A140 2c carmine		
	rose, type		
	II	2,700.	17,500.
	Never hinged	4,250.	
	On cover, type II		60,000.
540	A140 2c car rose,		
	type III	12.00	9.50
	Never hinged	27.50	
	On cover, type III		25.00
a.	Vert. pair, imperf horiz.	60.00	140.00
	Never hinged	125.00	
b.	Horiz. pair, imperf. vert.	2,000.	
541	A140 3c vio, type II	40.00	32.50
	Never hinged	100.00	
	On cover		100.00

The part perforate varieties of Nos. 538a and 540a were issued in sheets and may be had in blocks; similar part perforate varieties, Nos. 490 and 492, are from coils and are found only in strips.

See note over No. 448 regarding No. 539.

No. 539 is valued in the grade of fine.

No. 540b is valued in the grade of fine.

1920, May 26   Perf. 10x11

Stamp design: 19x22½-22¾mm

542	A140 1c green	12.50	1.50
	Never hinged	30.00	
	On cover		5.50

1921   Perf. 10

Stamp design: 19x22½mm

543	A140 1c green	.70	.40
	Never hinged	1.75	
	On cover		.45
a.	Horizontal pair, imperf.		
	between	5,000.	

1922   Perf. 11

Stamp design: 19x22½mm

544	A140 1c green	22,500.	3,750.
	Never hinged	35,000.	
	On cover		7,500.

No. 544 is valued in the grade of fine.

1921

Stamp designs: 19½-20x22mm

545	A140 1c green	170.00	200.00
	Never hinged	400.00	
	On cover		1,800.
546	A140 2c carmine		
	rose,		
	type III	105.00	190.00
	Never hinged	230.00	
	On cover		800.00
a.	Perf. 10 on left side	7,500.	17,500.

No. 546a used is valued in the grade of very good. It is unique used.

FLAT PLATE PRINTING

1920, Nov. 1   Perf. 11

547	A149 $2 carmine &		
	black	125.	40.
	Never hinged	270.	
	On cover (commercial)		1,000.
a.	$2 lake & black	200.	40.
	Never hinged	425.	

PILGRIM TERCENTENARY ISSUE

"Mayflower" A151

Landing of the Pilgrims — A152

Signing of the Compact — A153

1920, Dec. 21   Unwmk.   Perf. 11

548	A151	1c green	4.00	2.25
	Never hinged		10.00	
	On cover			3.50
549	A152	2c carmine rose	5.25	1.60
	Never hinged		12.50	
	On cover			2.50
550	A153	5c deep blue	35.00	14.00
	Never hinged		75.00	
	On cover			22.50
	Nos. 548-550 (3)		44.25	17.85
	Nos. 548-550, never hinged		107.50	

Tercentenary of the landing of the Pilgrims at Plymouth, Mass.

Nathan Hale
A154

Franklin
A155

Harding
A156

Washington
A157

Lincoln
A158

Martha
Washington
A159

Theodore
Roosevelt
A160

Garfield
A161

McKinley
A162

Grant
A163

Jefferson
A164

Monroe
A165

Rutherford B.
Hayes
A166

Grover
Cleveland
A167

American
Indian
A168

Statue of
Liberty
A169

Golden
Gate — A170

Niagara
Falls — A171

American
Buffalo
A172

Arlington
Amphitheater
A173

Lincoln
Memorial
A174

US Capitol
A175

Head of Freedom
Statue, Capitol
Dome — A176

FLAT PLATE PRINTINGS

1922-25   Unwmk.   Perf. 11

551	A154	½c olive brown ('25)	.25	.25
	Never hinged		.50	
552	A155	1c dp green ('23)	1.40	.25
	Never hinged		3.00	
a.	Booklet pane of 6		7.50	4.00
	Never hinged		12.50	
553	A156	1½c yel brn ('25)	2.25	.25
	Never hinged		4.60	
554	A157	2c carmine ('23)	1.30	.25
	Never hinged		3.00	
	On cover			.25
a.	Horiz. pair, imperf. vert.		250.00	
b.	Vert. pair, imperf. horiz.		6,000.	
	Never hinged		10,000.	
c.	Booklet pane of 6		7.00	3.00
	Never hinged		12.00	
d.	Perf. 10 at top or bottom		17,500.	10,000.
	On cover			25,000.

No. 554d unused is unique. It is never hinged and has a natural straight edge at left. Value represents the sale price at 2001 auction.

555	A158	3c violet ('23)	14.00	1.20
	Never hinged		30.00	
556	A159	4c yel brn ('23)	17.50	.50
	Never hinged		37.50	
	On cover			9.00
a.	Vert. pair, imperf. horiz.		12,500.	
b.	Perf. 10 at top or bottom		3,500.	22,500.

No. 556a is unique. It resulted from a sheet that was damaged and patched during production.

No. 556b used also exists as a transitional stamp gauging 10 at left top and 11 at right top. Value the same.

557	A160	5c dark blue	17.50	.30
	Never hinged		37.50	
a.	Imperf., pair		2,000.	
	Never hinged		3,750.	
b.	Horiz. pair, imperf. vert.		—	
c.	Perf. 10 at top or bottom		—	9,500.
	On cover			17,500.
558	A161	6c red orange	32.50	1.00
	Never hinged		70.00	
559	A162	7c black ('23)	7.75	.75
	Never hinged		16.50	
560	A163	8c olive grn ('23)	40.00	1.00
	Never hinged		90.00	
561	A164	9c rose ('23)	12.50	1.25
	Never hinged		27.00	
562	A165	10c orange ('23)	15.00	.35
	Never hinged		32.50	
a.	Vert. pair, imperf. horiz.		2,250.	
	Never hinged		3,500.	
b.	Imperf., pair		2,250.	
c.	Perf. 10 at top or bottom		70,000.	15,000.

No. 562a is valued in the grade of fine, with gum and without blue defacing lines. No. 562b is valued without gum and without blue pencil defacing lines. No. 562c is valued in the grade of fine.

563	A166	11c greenish blue	1.40	.60
	Never hinged		3.00	
a.	11c light bluish green		1.40	.60
	Never hinged		3.00	
d.	Imperf., pair		20,000.	

Many other intermediate shades exist for Nos. 563 and 563a, all falling within the blue or green color families.

564	A167	12c brn vio ('23)	5.25	.35
	Never hinged		11.50	
a.	Horiz. pair, imperf. vert.		4,250.	
565	A168	14c blue ('23)	4.75	.90
	Never hinged		10.50	
566	A169	15c gray ('23)	17.50	.30
	Never hinged		37.50	
567	A170	20c car rose ('23)	17.50	.30
	Never hinged		37.50	
a.	Horiz. pair, imperf. vert.		2,750.	
	Never hinged		5,250.	
568	A171	25c yel grn ('23)	15.00	.75
	Never hinged		32.50	
b.	Vert. pair, imperf. horiz.		3,250.	
c.	Perf. 10 at one side		5,000.	11,000.
	Never hinged		7,500.	

No. 568b is valued in the grade of fine. No. 568c used is valued in the grade of fine.

569	A172	30c ol brn ('23)	25.00	.60
	Never hinged		55.00	
570	A173	50c lilac ('23)	35.00	.40
	Never hinged		75.00	
571	A174	$1 vio brn ('23)	37.50	.80
	Never hinged		80.00	
572	A175	$2 dp blue ('23)	65.00	9.00
	Never hinged		140.00	
573	A176	$5 car & bl ('23)	100.00	15.00
	Never hinged		210.00	
a.	$5 car lake & dk bl		190.00	30.00
	Never hinged		350.00	
	Nos. 551-573 (23)		485.85	36.35
	Nos. 551-573, never hinged		1,075.	

For other listings of perforated stamps of designs A154 to A173 see:
Nos. 578 & 579, Perf. 11x10
Nos. 581-591, Perf. 10
Nos. 594-596, Perf. 11
Nos. 632-642, 653, 692-696, Perf. 11x10½
Nos. 697-701, Perf. 10½x11
This series also includes #622-623 (perf. 11), 684-687 & 720-723.

1923-25   Imperf.

Stamp design 19¼x22¼mm

575	A155	1c green	5.00	5.00
	Never hinged		11.00	
576	A156	1½c yel brn ('25)	1.25	1.50
	Never hinged		2.70	

The 1½c A156 Rotary press imperforate is listed as No. 631.

577	A157	2c carmine	1.30	1.25
	Never hinged		2.90	
a.	2c carmine lake		—	—
	Nos. 575-577 (3)		7.55	7.75
	Nos. 575-577, never hinged		16.60	

ROTARY PRESS PRINTINGS
(See note over No. 448)

1923   Perf. 11x10

578	A155	1c green	75.00	160.00
	Never hinged		170.00	
	On cover			700.00
579	A157	2c carmine	70.00	140.00
	Never hinged		160.00	
	On cover			400.00

Nos. 578-579 were made from coil waste of Nos. 597, 599 and measure approximately 19¾x22¼mm.

1923-26   Perf. 10

581	A155	1c green	10.00	.75
	Never hinged		22.50	
582	A156	1½c brown ('25)	6.00	.65
	Never hinged		13.50	
583	A157	2c car ('24)	3.00	.30
	Never hinged		6.50	
	On cover			2.50
a.	Booklet pane of 6		110.00	150.00
	Never hinged		200.00	
584	A158	3c violet ('25)	27.50	3.00
	Never hinged		62.50	
585	A159	4c yel brn ('25)	17.50	.65
	Never hinged		37.50	
	On cover			15.00
586	A160	5c blue ('25)	17.50	.40
	Never hinged		37.50	
a.	Horizontal pair, imperf. vertically		8,000.	

No. 586a is unique, precanceled, with average centering and small faults, and it is valued as such.

587	A161	6c red org ('25)	9.25	.60
	Never hinged		21.00	
588	A162	7c black ('26)	12.50	6.25
	Never hinged		27.50	
589	A163	8c ol grn ('26)	27.50	4.50
	Never hinged		60.00	
590	A164	9c rose ('26)	6.00	2.50
	Never hinged		13.50	
591	A165	10c orange ('25)	45.00	.50
	Never hinged		90.00	
	Nos. 581-591 (11)		181.75	20.10
	Nos. 581-591, never hinged		402.00	

1923   Perf. 11

594	A155	1c green	35,000.	10,500.
	With gum		65,000.	
	On cover			20,000.

The main listing for No. 594 unused is for an example without gum; both unused and used

are valued with perforations just touching frameline on one side.

595	A157	2c carmine	240.00	375.00
	Never hinged		475.00	
	On cover			550.00

Nos. 594-595 were made from coil waste of Nos. 597 and 599, and measure approximately 19¾x22¼mm.

596	A155	1c green		150,000.
	Precanceled			100,000.

No. 596 was made from rotary press sheet waste and measures approximately 19¼x22½mm. A majority of the examples carry the Bureau precancel "Kansas City, Mo." No. 596 is valued in the grade of fine.

COIL STAMPS
ROTARY PRESS

1923-29   Perf. 10 Vertically

Stamp designs approximately 19¾x22¼mm

597	A155	1c green	.30	.25
	Never hinged		.60	
	Three on cover			2.25
598	A156	1½c brown ('25)	.90	.25
	Never hinged		1.80	

Type I

Type II

Type I   Type II

TYPE I. No line outlining forehead. No heavy hair lines at top center of head. Outline of left acanthus scroll generally faint at top and toward base at left side.

TYPE II. Thin line outlining forehead. Three heavy hair lines at top center of head; two being outstanding in the white area. Outline of left acanthus scroll very strong and clearly defined at top (under left edge of lettered panel) and at lower curve (above and to left of numeral oval). This type appears only on Nos. 599A and 634A.

599	A157	2c car, type I	.35	.25
	Never hinged		.70	
	On cover			1.10
b.	2c carmine lake, type I, never hinged		200.00	
	Never hinged		650.00	
599A	A157	2c car, type II ('29)	105.00	17.50
	Never hinged		200.00	
	On cover			32.50
600	A158	3c violet ('24)	6.25	.25
	Never hinged		12.50	
	On cover			6.00
601	A159	4c yel brn	3.75	.35
	Never hinged		7.50	
	On cover			14.00
602	A160	5c dk blue ('24)	1.75	.25
	Never hinged		3.50	
603	A165	10c orange ('24)	3.50	.25
	Never hinged		7.00	

The 6c design A161 coil stamp is listed as No. 723.

1923-25   Perf. 10 Horizontally

Stamp designs: 19¼x22½mm

604	A155	1c green ('24)	.40	.25
	Never hinged		.80	
	Three on cover			6.00
605	A156	1½c yel brn ('25)	.40	.25
	Never hinged		.80	
606	A157	2c carmine	.40	.25
	Never hinged		.80	
	On cover			3.50
a.	2c carmine lake		45.00	
	Never hinged		90.00	
	Nos. 597-599, 600-606 (10)		18.00	2.60
	Nos. 597-599, 600-606, never hinged		36.00	

HARDING MEMORIAL ISSUE

Warren G.
Harding — A177

FLAT PLATE PRINTING
Stamp designs: 19¼x22¼mm

1923   *Perf. 11*
610 A177 2c black   .55 .25
   Never hinged   1.10
   On cover   .30
a. Horiz. pair, imperf. vert.   1,750.
b. Imperf, P#14870 block of 6   25,000.

No. 610a is valued in the grade of fine.
No. 610b comes from left side error panes found in a normal pad of No. 610 stamps before No. 611 was issued. Two left side plate blocks and one top position plate block are recorded. Plate #14870 was not used to print No. 611. Loose stamps separated from the top and left plate blocks are indistinguishable from No. 611.

Imperf
611 A177 2c black   4.75 4.00
   Never hinged   9.50

ROTARY PRESS PRINTING
Stamp designs: 19¼x22½mm
Perf. 10
612 A177 2c black   15.00 1.75
   Never hinged   32.50
   On cover   3.25

Perf. 11
613 A177 2c black   40,000.

Tribute to President Warren G. Harding, who died August 2, 1923.
No. 613 was produced from rotary press sheet waste. It is valued in the grade of fine.

HUGUENOT-WALLOON TERCENTENARY ISSUE
Tercentary of the settling of the Walloons and in honor of the Huguenots.

"New Netherland" A178

Landing at Fort Orange A179

Monument to Jan Ribault at Duvall County, Fla. — A180

FLAT PLATE PRINTINGS
1924, May 1   *Perf. 11*
614 A178 1c dark green   2.40 *3.25*
   Never hinged   4.75
   On cover   4.50
615 A179 2c carmine rose   4.00 2.25
   Never hinged   8.00
   On cover   3.50
616 A180 5c dark blue   16.00 13.00
   Never hinged   32.50
   Nos. 614-616 (3)   22.40 18.50
   Nos. 614-616, never hinged   45.25

LEXINGTON-CONCORD ISSUE
150th anniv. of the Battle of Lexington-Concord.

Washington at Cambridge A181

"Birth of Liberty," by Henry Oandham A182

The Minute Man, by Daniel Chester French A183

1925, Apr. 4   *Perf. 11*
617 A181 1c deep green   2.10 2.50
   Never hinged   4.25
   On cover   3.75
618 A182 2c carmine rose   3.75 4.00
   Never hinged   7.50
   On cover   5.50
619 A183 5c dark blue   15.00 30.00
   Never hinged   30.00
   Nos. 617-619 (3)   20.85 19.50
   Nos. 617-619, never hinged   41.75

150th anniv. of the Battle of Lexington-Concord.

NORSE-AMERICAN ISSUE

Sloop "Restaurationen" A184   Viking Ship A185

1925, May 18   *Perf. 11*
620 A184 2c carmine & black   3.25 3.00
   Never hinged   6.50
   On cover   4.50
621 A185 5c dark blue & black   10.00 10.00
   Never hinged   20.00

100th anniv. of the arrival in NY on Oct. 9, 1825, of the sloop "Restaurationen" with the first group of immigrants from Norway to the U.S.

Benjamin Harrison A186   Woodrow Wilson A187

1925-26   *Perf. 11*
622 A186 13c green ('26)   10.00 .75
   Never hinged   20.00
623 A187 17c black   10.00 .30
   Never hinged   20.00

SESQUICENTENNIAL EXPOSITION ISSUE

Liberty Bell — A188

1926, May 10   *Perf. 11*
627 A188 2c carmine rose   2.25 .50
   Never hinged   4.25
   On cover   1.00

150th anniv. of the Declaration of Independence, Philadelphia, June 1-Dec. 1.

ERICSSON MEMORIAL ISSUE

Statue of John Ericsson — A189

1926, May 29   *Perf. 11*
628 A189 5c gray lilac   5.25 3.25
   Never hinged   9.00

John Ericsson, builder of the "Monitor."

BATTLE OF WHITE PLAINS ISSUE

Alexander Hamilton's Battery — A190

1926, Oct. 18   *Perf. 11*
629 A190 2c carmine rose   1.75 1.70
   Never hinged   3.00
   On cover   2.25

Battle of White Plains, NY, 150th anniv.

INTERNATIONAL PHILATELIC EXHIBITION ISSUE
Souvenir Sheet

A190a

Condition valued:
Centering: Overall centering will average very fine, but individual stamps may be better or worse.
Perforations: No folds along rows of perforations.
Gum: There may be some light gum bends but no gum creases.
Hinging: There may be hinge marks in the selvage and on up to two or three stamps, but no heavy hinging or hinge remnants (except in the ungummed portion of the wide selvage).
Margins: Top panes should have about ½ inch bottom margin and 1 inch top margin. Bottom panes should have about ½ inch top margin and just under ¾ inch bottom margin. Both will have one wide side (usually 1 inch plus) and one narrow (½ inch) side margin. The wide margin corner will have a small diagonal notch on top panes.

1926, Oct. 18   *Perf. 11*
630 A190a 2c carmine rose, pane of 25   350.00 *475.00*
   Never hinged   600.00
   On cover   —

Issued in panes measuring 158-160¼x136-146½mm containing 25 stamps with inscription "International Philatelic Exhibition, Oct. 16th to 23rd, 1926" in top margin.

VALUES FOR VERY FINE STAMPS
Please note: Stamps are valued in the grade of Very Fine unless otherwise indicated.

TYPES OF 1922-26 ROTARY PRESS PRINTINGS
(See note over No. 448.)
1926, Aug. 27   *Imperf.*
631 A156 1½c yellow brown   2.00 1.70
   Never hinged   3.50

1926-34   *Perf. 11x10½*
632 A155 1c green ('27)   .25 .25
   Never hinged   .35
   Three on cover   1.25
a. Booklet pane of 6   5.00 4.00
   Never hinged   8.00
b. Vertical pair, imperf. between   3,000. —
   Never hinged   5,500.
c. Horiz. pair, imperf. between   5,500. —

No. 632b is valued in the grade of fine. No. 632c is valued in the grade of fine and never hinged. It is possibly unique.

633 A156 1½c yel brn ('27)   1.70 .25
   Never hinged   2.60
634 A157 2c car, type I   .25 .25
   Never hinged   .30
   On cover   .25
b. 2c carmine lake   190.00 500.00
   Never hinged   400.00
c. Horiz. pair, imperf. btwn.   6,000.
d. Booklet pane of 6, carmine   1.50 1.50

e. Never hinged   2.50
   As "d," carmine lake   400.00 1,000.
   Never hinged   900.00
f. 2c lake, type I, on cover   —
   Shades of the carmine exist.
No. 634c is valued in the grade of fine.

634A A157 2c car, type II ('28)   325.00 13.50
   Never hinged   650.00
   On cover   21.00
635 A158 3c violet ('27)   .60 .25
   Never hinged   .90
   On cover   2.00
a. 3c bright violet ('34)   .25 .25
   Never hinged   .30
   On cover   .25
636 A159 4c yel brn ('27)   1.90 .25
   Never hinged   3.00
   On cover   8.00
637 A160 5c dk blue ('27)   1.90 .25
   Never hinged   3.00
638 A161 6c red org ('27)   2.00 .25
   Never hinged   3.20
639 A162 7c black ('27)   2.00 .25
   Never hinged   3.20
a. Vertical pair, imperf. between   575.00 250.00
   Never hinged   1,000.
640 A163 8c ol grn ('27)   2.00 .25
   Never hinged   3.20
641 A164 9c rose ('27)   1.90 .25
   Never hinged   3.00
642 A165 10c org ('27)   3.25 .25
   Never hinged   5.50
   Nos. 632-634,635-642 (11)   17.75 2.75
   Nos. 632-634, 635-642 never hinged   28.00

The 1½c, 2c, 4c, 5c, 6c, 8c imperf. (dry print) are printer's waste.
For ½c, 11c-50c see Nos. 653, 692-701.

VERMONT SESQUICENTENNIAL ISSUE
Battle of Bennington, 150th anniv. and State independence.

Green Mountain Boy — A191

FLAT PLATE PRINTING
1927, Aug. 3   *Perf. 11*
643 A191 2c carmine rose   1.20 .80
   Never hinged   2.00
   On cover   1.50

BURGOYNE CAMPAIGN ISSUE
Battles of Bennington, Oriskany, Fort Stanwix and Saratoga.

"The Surrender of General Burgoyne at Saratoga," by John Trumbull A192

1927, Aug. 3   *Perf. 11*
644 A192 2c carmine rose   3.10 2.10
   Never hinged   5.50
   On cover   3.00

VALLEY FORGE ISSUE
150th anniversary of Washington's encampment at Valley Forge, Pa.

Washington at Prayer — A193

1928, May 26   *Perf. 11*
645 A193 2c carmine rose   1.20 .50
   Never hinged   1.90
   On cover   .75
a. 2c lake   —
   Never hinged

BATTLE OF MONMOUTH ISSUE
150th anniv. of the Battle of Monmouth, N.J., and "Molly Pitcher" (Mary Ludwig Hayes), the heroine of the battle.

No. 634 Overprinted

ROTARY PRESS PRINTING
1928, Oct. 20   *Perf. 11x10½*

646	A157	2c carmine	1.00	1.00
		Never hinged	1.60	
		On cover		1.60
a.		"Pitcher" only	675.00	
b.		2c carmine lake		2,500.

No. 646a is valued in the grade of fine. Normally the overprints were placed 18mm apart vertically, but pairs exist with a space of 28mm between the overprints.

HAWAII SESQUICENTENNIAL ISSUE

Sesquicentennial Celebration of the discovery of the Hawaiian Islands.

Nos. 634 and 637 Overprinted

ROTARY PRESS PRINTING
1928, Aug. 13   *Perf. 11x10½*

647	A157	2c carmine	4.00	4.00
		Never hinged	7.25	
		On cover		5.75
648	A160	5c dark blue	11.00	12.50
		Never hinged	21.50	
		On cover		20.00

Nos. 647-648 were sold at post offices in Hawaii and at the Postal Agency in Washington, D.C. They were valid throughout the nation.

Normally the overprints were placed 18mm apart vertically, but pairs exist with a space of 28mm between the overprints.

AERONAUTICS CONFERENCE ISSUE

Intl. Civil Aeronautics Conf., Washington, D.C., Dec. 12 - 14, 1928, and 25th anniv. of the 1st airplane flight by the Wright Brothers, Dec. 17, 1903.

Wright Airplane A194

Globe and Airplane A195

FLAT PLATE PRINTING
1928, Dec. 12   *Perf. 11*

649	A194	2c carmine rose	1.10	.80
		Never hinged	1.75	
		On cover		1.50
650	A195	5c blue	4.50	3.25
		Never hinged	7.25	

GEORGE ROGERS CLARK ISSUE

150th anniv. of the surrender of Fort Sackville, the present site of Vincennes, Ind., to Clark.

Surrender of Fort Sackville A196

1929, Feb. 25   *Perf. 11*

651	A196	2c carmine & black	.75	.50
		Never hinged	1.20	
		On cover		1.00

Type of 1922-26 Issue
ROTARY PRESS PRINTING
1929, May 25   *Perf. 11x10½*

653	A154	½c olive brown	.25	.25
		Never hinged	.35	

Edison's First Lamp A197   Maj. Gen. John Sullivan A198

ELECTRIC LIGHT'S GOLDEN JUBILEE ISSUE

Invention of the 1st incandescent electric lamp by Thomas Alva Edison, Oct. 21, 1879, 50th anniv.

FLAT PLATE PRINTING
1929   *Perf. 11*

654	A197	2c carmine rose	.70	.65
		Never hinged	1.20	
		On cover		1.10
a.		2c lake	—	

ROTARY PRESS PRINTING
Perf. 11x10½

655	A197	2c carmine rose	.65	.25
		Never hinged	1.10	
				.25

ROTARY PRESS COIL STAMP
Perf. 10 Vertically

656	A197	2c carmine rose	11.00	1.75
		Never hinged	21.00	
				2.75

Issued: #654, June 5; #655-656, June 11.

SULLIVAN EXPEDITION ISSUE

150th anniversary of the Sullivan Expedition in New York State during the Revolutionary War.

FLAT PLATE PRINTING
1929, June 17   *Perf. 11*

657	A198	2c carmine rose	.60	.60
		Never hinged	1.00	
		On cover		1.00
a.		2c lake	350.00	250.00
		Never hinged	625.00	
b.		Vert. pair, imperf. btwn.	4,000.	

The unique No. 657b resulted from a paper foldover before perfing, and it has angled errant perfs from another row of horiz. perfs through the left side of the stamps.

Nos. 632-634, 635-642 Overprinted

This special issue was authorized as a measure of preventing losses from post office burglaries. Approximately a year's supply was printed and issued to postmasters. The P.O. Dept. found it desirable to discontinue the State overprinted stamps after the initial supply was used.

ROTARY PRESS PRINTING
1929, May 1   *Perf. 11x10½*

658	A155	1c green	2.50	2.00
		Never hinged	5.00	
a.		Vertical pair, one without ovpt.	300.00	
		Never hinged	500.00	
659	A156	1½c brown	3.25	2.90
		Never hinged	6.50	
a.		Vertical pair, one without ovpt.	475.00	
660	A157	2c carmine	4.00	1.00
		Never hinged	7.50	
661	A158	3c violet	17.50	15.00
		Never hinged	35.00	
a.		Vertical pair, one without ovpt.	600.00	
		Never hinged	800.00	
662	A159	4c yellow brown	17.50	9.00
		Never hinged	35.00	
a.		Vertical pair, one without ovpt.	500.00	
		Never hinged		
663	A160	5c deep blue	12.50	9.75
		Never hinged	25.00	
664	A161	6c red orange	25.00	18.00
		Never hinged	50.00	
665	A162	7c black	25.00	27.50
		Never hinged	50.00	
666	A163	8c olive green	72.50	65.00
		Never hinged	145.00	
667	A164	9c light rose	14.00	11.50
		Never hinged	27.50	

668	A165	10c org yel	22.50	12.50
		Never hinged	45.00	
		Nos. 658-668 (11)	216.25	174.15
		Nos. 658-668, never hinged	431.50	

See notes following No. 679.

Overprinted

1929, May 1

669	A155	1c green	3.25	2.25
		Never hinged	6.50	
b.		No period after "Nebr." (19338, 19339 UR 26, 36)	50.00	
670	A156	1½c brown	3.00	2.50
		Never hinged	6.00	
671	A157	2c carmine	3.00	1.30
		Never hinged	6.00	
672	A158	3c violet	11.00	12.00
		Never hinged	22.00	
a.		Vertical pair, one without ovpt.	500.00	
673	A159	4c yellow brown	17.50	15.00
		Never hinged	35.00	
674	A160	5c deep blue	15.00	15.00
		Never hinged	30.00	
675	A161	6c red orange	35.00	24.00
		Never hinged	70.00	
676	A162	7c black	22.50	18.00
		Never hinged	45.00	
677	A163	8c olive green	30.00	25.00
		Never hinged	60.00	
678	A164	9c light rose	35.00	27.50
		Never hinged	70.00	
a.		Vertical pair, one without ovpt.	750.00	
679	A165	10c org yel	90.00	22.50
		Never hinged	180.00	
		Nos. 669-679 (11)	265.25	165.05
		Nos. 669-679, never hinged	530.50	

Nos. 658-661, 669-673, 677-678 are known with the overprints on vertical pairs spaced 32mm apart instead of the normal 22mm.

Important: Nos. 658-679 with original gum have either one horizontal gum breaker ridge per stamp or portions of two at the extreme top and bottom of the stamps, 21mm apart. Multiple complete gum breaker ridges indicate a fake overprint. Absence of the gum breaker ridge indicates either regumming or regumming and a fake overprint.

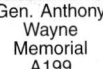

Gen. Anthony Wayne Memorial A199   Lock No. 5, Monongahela River A200

BATTLE OF FALLEN TIMBERS ISSUE

Memorial to Gen. Anthony Wayne and for 135th anniv. of the Battle of Fallen Timbers, Ohio.

FLAT PLATE PRINTING
1929, Sept. 14   *Perf. 11*

680	A199	2c carmine rose	.70	.70
		Never hinged	1.10	
		On cover		1.10

OHIO RIVER CANALIZATION ISSUE

Completion of the Ohio River Canalization Project, between Cairo, Ill. and Pittsburgh, Pa.

1929, Oct. 19   *Perf. 11*

681	A200	2c carmine rose	.60	.60
		Never hinged	.95	
		On cover		1.10
a.		2c lake	425.00	
		Never hinged	650.00	
b.		2c carmine lake, never hinged		

Mass. Bay Colony Seal — A201   Gov. Joseph West and Chief Shadoo, a Kiowa — A202

MASSACHUSETTS BAY COLONY ISSUE

300th anniversary of the founding of the Massachusetts Bay Colony.

1930, Apr. 8   *Perf. 11*

682	A201	2c carmine rose	.70	.50
		Never hinged	1.00	
		On cover		1.00

CAROLINA-CHARLESTON ISSUE

260th anniv. of the founding of the Province of Carolina and the 250th anniv. of the city of Charleston, S.C.

1930, Apr. 10   *Perf. 11*

683	A202	2c carmine rose	1.05	1.05
		On cover	1.65	
				1.40

Warren G. Harding A203   William H. Taft A204

Type of 1922-26 Issue
ROTARY PRESS PRINTING
1930   *Perf. 11x10½*

684	A203	1½c brown	.40	.25
		Never hinged	.55	
685	A204	4c brown	.80	.25
		Never hinged	1.25	
				5.00

ROTARY PRESS COIL STAMPS
Perf. 10 Vertically

686	A203	1½c brown	1.75	.25
		Never hinged	2.60	
687	A204	4c brown	3.00	.45
		Never hinged	4.50	
		On cover		10.00

Statue of Col. George Washington A205   General von Steuben A206

BRADDOCK'S FIELD ISSUE

175th anniversary of the Battle of Braddock's Field, otherwise the Battle of Monongahela.

FLAT PLATE PRINTING
1930, July 9   *Perf. 11*

688	A205	2c carmine rose	.90	.85
		Never hinged	1.40	
		On cover		1.00

VON STEUBEN ISSUE

Baron Friedrich Wilhelm von Steuben (1730-1794), participant in the American Revolution.

FLAT PLATE PRINTING
1930, Sept. 17   *Perf. 11*

689	A206	2c carmine rose	.50	.50
		Never hinged	.75	
		On cover		1.05
a.		Imperf., pair	2,250.	
		Never hinged	3,250.	

General Casimir Pulaski A207   "The Greatest Mother" A208

PULASKI ISSUE

150th anniversary (in 1929) of the death of Gen. Casimir Pulaski, Polish patriot and hero of the American Revolutionary War.

1931, Jan. 16   *Perf. 11*
690 A207 2c carmine rose   .30 .25
   Never hinged   .40
   On cover   .50

TYPE OF 1922-26 ISSUES
ROTARY PRESS PRINTING

1931   *Perf. 11x10½*
692 A166 11c light blue   2.50 .25
   Never hinged   3.75
693 A167 12c brown violet   5.00 .25
   Never hinged   8.00
694 A186 13c yellow green   2.25 .25
   Never hinged   3.50
695 A168 14c dark blue   4.00 .60
   Never hinged   6.25
696 A169 15c gray   7.75 .25
   Never hinged   12.00

         Perf. 10½x11
697 A187 17c black   4.75 .25
   Never hinged   7.25
698 A170 20c carmine rose   7.75 .25
   Never hinged   12.50
699 A171 25c blue green   8.00 .25
   Never hinged   13.00
700 A172 30c brown   13.00 .25
   Never hinged   22.50
701 A173 50c lilac   30.00 .25
   Never hinged   52.50
   Nos. 692-701 (10)   85.00 2.85
   Nos. 692-701, never hinged 141.25

RED CROSS ISSUE

50th anniversary of the founding of the American Red Cross Society.

FLAT PLATE PRINTING

1931, May 21   *Perf. 11*
702 A208 2c black & red   .25 .25
   Never hinged   .35
a.   Red cross missing (FO)   40,000.

One example of No. 702a is documented; believed to be unique. Value reflects most recent sale price at auction in 1994.

YORKTOWN ISSUE

Surrender of Cornwallis at Yorktown, 1781.

Count de Rochambeau, Washington, Count de Grasse — A209

1931, Oct. 19   *Perf. 11*
703 A209 2c carmine rose &
         black   .35 .25
   Never hinged   .50
a.   2c lake & black   4.50 .75
   Never hinged   6.25
b.   2c dark lake & black   400.00
   Never hinged   750.00
c.   Horiz. pair, imperf. vertically   7,000.
   Never hinged   8,500.

No. 703c is valued in the grade of fine.

WASHINGTON BICENTENNIAL ISSUE

200th anniversary of the birth of George Washington. Various Portraits of George Washington.

A210   A211

A212   A213

A214   A215

A216   A217

A218   A219

A220   A221

ROTARY PRESS PRINTINGS

1932, Jan. 1   *Perf. 11x10½*
704 A210 ½c olive brown   .25 .25
   Never hinged   .35
705 A211 1c green   .25 .25
   Never hinged   .35
706 A212 1½c brown   .45 .25
   Never hinged   .60
707 A213 2c carmine rose   .30 .25
   Never hinged   .45
708 A214 3c deep violet   .55 .25
   Never hinged   .80
709 A215 4c light brown   .60 .25
   Never hinged   .85
710 A216 5c blue   1.50 .25
   Never hinged   2.25
711 A217 6c red orange   3.00 .25
   Never hinged   4.50
712 A218 7c black   .60 .25
   Never hinged   .85
713 A219 8c olive bister   2.75 .50
   Never hinged   4.00
714 A220 9c pale red   2.25 .25
   Never hinged   3.25
715 A221 10c orange yellow   10.00 .25
   Never hinged   15.00
   Nos. 704-715 (12)   22.50 3.25
   Nos. 704-715, never hinged 33.25

Skier — A222   Boy and Girl Planting Tree — A223

OLYMPIC WINTER GAMES ISSUE

3rd Olympic Winter Games, held at Lake Placid, N.Y., Feb. 4-13, 1932.

FLAT PLATE PRINTING

1932, Jan. 25   *Perf. 11*
716 A222 2c carmine rose   .40 .25
   Never hinged   .55
a.   2c lake   500.00
   Never hinged   1,000.

ARBOR DAY ISSUE
ROTARY PRESS PRINTING

1932, Apr. 22   *Perf. 11x10½*
717 A223 2c carmine rose   .25 .25
   Never hinged   .35

60th anniv. of the 1st observance of Arbor Day in Nebr., April, 1872.
Birth centenary of Julius Sterling Morton, who conceived the plan and the name "Arbor Day," while a member of the Nebr. State Board of Agriculture.

OLYMPIC GAMES ISSUE

Issued in honor of the 10th Olympic Games, held at Los Angeles, Calif., July 30 to Aug. 14, 1932.

Runner at   Myron's
Starting Mark   Discobolus
A224   A225

ROTARY PRESS PRINTING

1932, June 15   *Perf. 11x10½*
718 A224 3c violet   1.50 .25
   Never hinged   2.00
719 A225 5c blue   2.25 .25
   Never hinged   2.90

Washington — A226

ROTARY PRESS PRINTING

1932, June 16   *Perf. 11x10½*
720 A226 3c deep violet   .25 .25
   Never hinged   .30
b.   Booklet pane of 6   35.00 12.50
   Never hinged   60.00
c.   Vertical pair, imperf. between   700.00 1,350.
   Never hinged   1,400.

ROTARY PRESS COIL STAMPS

1932   *Perf. 10 Vertically*
721 A226 3c deep violet   2.75 .25
   Never hinged   3.50
   Perf. 10 Horizontally
722 A226 3c deep violet   1.50 .35

Issued: #721, 6/24; #722, 10/12.

TYPE OF 1922-26 ISSUES

1932, Aug. 18   *Perf. 10 Vertically*
723 A161 6c deep orange   11.00 .30
   Never hinged   15.00

William Penn   Daniel
A227   Webster
                A228

WILLIAM PENN ISSUE

250th anniv. of the arrival in America of Penn (1644-1718), English Quaker and founder of Pennsylvania.

FLAT PLATE PRINTING

1932, Oct. 24   *Perf. 11*
724 A227 3c violet   .45 .25
   Never hinged   .60
a.   Vert. pair, imperf. horiz.   —

DANIEL WEBSTER ISSUE
FLAT PLATE PRINTING

1932, Oct. 24   *Perf. 11*
725 A228 3c violet   .45 .25
   Never hinged   .60

Daniel Webster (1782-1852), statesman.

Gen. James Edward Oglethorpe — A229

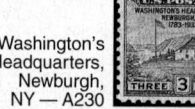

Washington's Headquarters, Newburgh, NY — A230

GEORGIA BICENTENNIAL ISSUE

200th anniv. of the founding of the Colony of Georgia, and honoring Oglethorpe, who landed from England, Feb.

12, 1733, and personally supervised the establishing of the colony.

FLAT PLATE PRINTING

1933, Feb. 12   *Perf. 11*
726 A229 3c violet   .50 .25
   Never hinged   .65

PEACE OF 1783 ISSUE

150th anniv. of the issuance by George Washington of the official order containing the Proclamation of Peace marking officially the ending of hostilities in the War for Independence.

ROTARY PRESS PRINTING

1933, Apr. 19   *Perf. 10½x11*
727 A230 3c violet   .25 .25
   Never hinged   .30

See No. 752.

CENTURY OF PROGRESS ISSUES

"Century of Progress" Intl. Exhibition, Chicago, which opened June 1, 1933, and centenary of the incorporation of Chicago as a city.

Restoration of   Federal Building
Fort Dearborn   at Chicago,
A231   1933
                A232

ROTARY PRESS PRINTING

1933, May 25   *Perf. 10½x11*
728 A231 1c yellow green   .25 .25
   Never hinged   .30
729 A232 3c violet   .25 .25
   Never hinged   .35

AMERICAN PHILATELIC SOCIETY ISSUE
SOUVENIR SHEETS

Restoration of Fort Dearborn — A231a

Federal Building at Chicago, 1933 — A232a

Illustrations reduced.

FLAT PLATE PRINTING

1933, Aug. 25   *Imperf.*
     Without Gum
730 A231a 1c deep yellow
       green, pane of
       25   22.50 25.00
a.   Single stamp   .75 .50
731 A232a 3c deep violet,
       pane of 25   20.00 22.50
a.   Single stamp   .65 .50

Issued in panes measuring 134x120mm.
See Nos. 766-767.

NATIONAL RECOVERY ACT ISSUE

Issued to direct attention to and arouse the support of the nation for the National Recovery Act.

Group of Workers — A233

ROTARY PRESS PRINTING

1933, Aug. 15   *Perf. 10½x11*
732 A233 3c violet   .25   .25
   Never hinged   .30

BYRD ANTARCTIC ISSUE

Issued in connection with the Byrd Antarctic Expedition of 1933 and for use on letters mailed through the Little America Post Office established at the Base Camp of the Expedition in the territory of the South Pole.

World Map on van der Grinten's Projection — A234

FLAT PLATE PRINTING

1933, Oct. 9   *Perf. 11*
733 A234 3c dark blue   .50   .50
   Never hinged   .60

See Nos. 735, 753.

KOSCIUSZKO ISSUE

Kosciuszko (1746-1807), Polish soldier and statesman served in the American Revolution, on the 150th anniv. of the granting to him of American citizenship.

Statue of Gen. Tadeusz Kosciuszko — A235

FLAT PLATE PRINTING

1933, Oct. 13   *Perf. 11*
734 A235 5c blue   .55   .25
   Never hinged   .65
a. Horiz. pair, imperf. vert.   1,750.
   Never hinged   2,750.

NATIONAL STAMP EXHIBITION ISSUE
SOUVENIR SHEET

A235a

Illustration reduced.

1934, Feb. 10   *Imperf.*
Without Gum
735 A235a 3c dark blue, pane
   of 6   11.00   9.00
a. Single stamp   1.75   1.25

Issued in panes measuring 87x93mm.
See No. 768.

MARYLAND TERCENTENARY ISSUE

300th anniversary of the founding of Maryland.

"The Ark" and "The Dove" — A236

FLAT PLATE PRINTING

1934, Mar. 23   *Perf. 11*
736 A236 3c carmine rose   .30   .25
   Never hinged   .40
a. Horizontal pair, imperf between   4,000.
b. 3c lake   —
c. 3c carmine lake, never hinged   —

The unique No. 736a resulted from a paper foldover before perfing, and it has angled errant perfs from another column of vert. perfs through the upper-left corner of the left stamp.

MOTHERS OF AMERICA ISSUE

Issued to commemorate Mother's Day.

Adaptation of Whistler's Portrait of his Mother A237

ROTARY PRESS PRINTING

1934, May 2   *Perf. 11x10½*
737 A237 3c deep violet   .25   .25
   Never hinged   .30

FLAT PLATE PRINTING
Perf. 11
738 A237 3c deep violet   .25   .25
   Never hinged   .30

See No. 754.

WISCONSIN TERCENTENARY ISSUE

Arrival of Jean Nicolet, French explorer, on the shores of Green Bay, 300th anniv. According to historical records, Nicolet was the 1st white man to reach the territory now comprising the State of Wisconsin.

Nicolet's Landing A238

FLAT PLATE PRINTING

1934, July 7   *Perf. 11*
739 A238 3c deep violet   .25   .25
   Never hinged   .40
a. Vert. pair, imperf. horiz.   575.00
   Never hinged   1,050.
b. Horiz. pair, imperf. vert.   1,000.
   Never hinged   1,850.

See No. 755.

NATIONAL PARKS YEAR ISSUE

El Capitan, Yosemite (California) A239

Old Faithful, Yellowstone (Wyoming) A243

Grand Canyon (Arizona) A240

Mt. Rainier and Mirror Lake (Washington) — A241

Mesa Verde (Colorado) A242

Crater Lake (Oregon) A244

Great Head, Acadia Park (Maine) A245

Great White Throne, Zion Park (Utah) A246

Great Smoky Mts. (North Carolina) A248

Mt. Rockwell (Mt. Sinopah) and Two Medicine Lake, Glacier Natl. Park (Montana) A247

FLAT PLATE PRINTING

		Perf. 11
1934 **Unwmk.**		
740 A239 1c green	.30	.25
Never hinged	.40	
a. Vert. pair, imperf. horiz., with gum	1,750.	
Never hinged	3,250.	
741 A240 2c red	.30	.25
Never hinged	.40	
a. Vert. pair, imperf. horiz., with gum	900.00	
Never hinged	1,600.	
b. Horiz. pair, imperf. vert., with gum	1,000.	
Never hinged	1,850.	
742 A241 3c deep violet	.40	.25
Never hinged	.50	
a. Vert. pair, imperf. horiz., with gum	1,000.	
Never hinged	1,850.	
743 A242 4c brown	.50	.40
Never hinged	.70	
a. Vert. pair, imperf. horiz., with gum	2,500.	
Never hinged	6,000.	
744 A243 5c blue	.80	.65
Never hinged	1.10	
a. Horiz. pair, imperf. vert., with gum	1,500.	
Never hinged	4,000.	
745 A244 6c dark blue	1.20	.85
Never hinged	1.65	
746 A245 7c black	.80	.75
Never hinged	1.10	
a. Horiz. pair, imperf. vert., with gum	1,250.	
Never hinged	2,000.	
747 A246 8c sage green	1.75	1.50
Never hinged	2.70	
748 A247 9c red orange	1.60	.65
Never hinged	2.40	
749 A248 10c gray black	3.25	1.25
Never hinged	5.00	
Nos. 740-749 (10)	10.90	6.80

Nos. 740-749, never hinged   15.95
Nos. 740-749, P# blocks of 6   100.00

Beware of fakes of the part-perforate errors of Nos. 740-749, including those with gum (see "without gum" note before No. 752).
See Nos. 750-751, 756-765, 769-770, 797.

AMERICAN PHILATELIC SOCIETY ISSUE
SOUVENIR SHEET

A248a

Illustration reduced.

1934, Aug. 28   *Imperf.*
750 A248a 3c deep violet, pane of 6   25.00   27.50
   Never hinged   37.50
a. Single stamp   3.75   3.25
   Never hinged   4.75

Issued in panes measuring approximately 98x93mm.
See No. 770.

TRANS-MISSISSIPPI PHILATELIC EXPOSITION ISSUE
SOUVENIR SHEET

A248b

Illustration reduced.

1934, Oct. 10   *Imperf.*
751 A248b 1c green, pane of 6   11.00   12.50
   Never hinged   15.00
a. Single stamp   1.75   1.60
   Never hinged   2.40

Issued in panes measuring approximately 92x99mm.
See No. 769.

SPECIAL PRINTING
(Nos. 752-771 inclusive)

"Issued for a limited time in full sheets as printed, and in blocks thereof, to meet the requirements of collectors and others who may be interested." — From Postal Bulletin No. 16614.

Issuance of the following 20 stamps in complete sheets resulted from the protest of collectors and others at the practice of presenting, to certain government officials, complete sheets of unsevered panes, imperforate (except Nos. 752 and 753) and generally ungummed.

Designs of Commemorative Issues
Without Gum

NOTE: In 1940 the P.O. Department offered to and did gum full sheets of Nos. 756-765 and 769-770 sent in by owners. No other Special Printings were accepted for gumming.

TYPE OF PEACE ISSUE
Issued in sheets of 400
ROTARY PRESS PRINTING
Perf. 10½x11

1935, Mar. 15		**Unwmk.**	
752	A230 3c violet	.25	.25

TYPE OF BYRD ISSUE
Issued in sheets of 200
FLAT PLATE PRINTING
Perf. 11

753	A234 3c dark blue	.50	.45

No. 753 is similar to No. 733. Positive identification is by blocks or pairs showing guide line between stamps. These lines between stamps are found only on No. 753.

TYPE OF MOTHERS OF AMERICA ISSUE
Issued in sheets of 200
FLAT PLATE PRINTING
Imperf

754	A237 3c deep violet	.60	.60

TYPE OF WISCONSIN ISSUE
Issued in sheets of 200
FLAT PLATE PRINTING
Imperf

755	A238 3c deep violet	.60	.60

TYPES OF NATIONAL PARKS ISSUE
Issued in sheets of 200
FLAT PLATE PRINTING
Imperf

756	A239	1c green	.25	.25
757	A240	2c red	.25	.25
758	A241	3c deep violet	.50	.45
759	A242	4c brown	1.00	.95
760	A243	5c blue	1.60	1.40
761	A244	6c dark blue	2.40	2.25
762	A245	7c black	1.60	1.40
763	A246	8c sage green	1.90	1.50
764	A247	9c red orange	2.00	1.75
765	A248	10c gray black	4.00	3.50
	Nos. 756-765 (10)		15.50	13.70
	Nos. 756-765, with original gum, never hinged		136.25	
	Nos. 756-765, P# blocks of 6		274.25	

SOUVENIR SHEETS
Note: Single items from these sheets are identical with other varieties, 766 and 730, 766a and 730a, 767 and 731, 767a and 731a, 768 and 735, 768a and 735a, 769a and 756, 770a and 758.

Positive identification is by blocks or pairs showing wide gutters between stamps. These wide gutters occur only on Nos. 766-770 and measure, horizontally, 13mm on Nos. 766-767; 16mm on No. 768, and 23mm on Nos. 769-770.

TYPE OF CENTURY OF PROGRESS ISSUE
Issued in sheets of 9 panes of 25 stamps each
FLAT PLATE PRINTING
Imperf

766	A231a 1c yellow green, pane of 25	25.00	25.00
a.	Single stamp	.70	.50
767	A232a 3c violet, pane of 25	23.50	23.50
a.	Single stamp	.60	.50

NATIONAL EXHIBITION ISSUE
TYPE OF BYRD ISSUE
Issued in sheets of 25 panes of 6 stamps each
FLAT PLATE PRINTING
Imperf

768	A235a 3c dark blue, pane of six	20.00	15.00
a.	Single stamp	2.80	2.40

TYPES OF NATIONAL PARKS ISSUE
Issued in sheets of 20 panes of 6 stamps each
FLAT PLATE PRINTING
Imperf

769	A248b 1c green, pane of six	12.50	11.00
a.	Single stamp	1.85	1.80
770	A248a 3c deep violet, pane of six	30.00	24.00
a.	Single stamp	3.25	3.10

TYPE OF AIR POST SPECIAL DELIVERY
Issued in sheets of 200
FLAT PLATE PRINTING
Imperf

771	APSD1 16c dark blue	2.75	2.60

> **Catalogue values for unused stamps in this section, from this point to the end, are for Never Hinged items.**

VALUES FOR HINGED STAMPS AFTER NO. 771
This catalogue does not value unused stamps after No. 771 in hinged condition. Hinged unused stamps from No. 772 to the present are worth considerably less than the values given for unused stamps, which are for never-hinged examples.

CONNECTICUT TERCENTENARY ISSUE
300th anniv. of the settlement of Connecticut.

Charter Oak A249

ROTARY PRESS PRINTING
Perf. 11x10½

1935, Apr. 26		**Unwmk.**	
772	A249 3c violet	.35	.25

CALIFORNIA PACIFIC EXPOSITION ISSUE
California Pacific Exposition at San Diego.

View of San Diego Exposition A250

Perf. 11x10½

1935, May 29		**Unwmk.**	
773	A250 3c purple	.35	.25

BOULDER DAM ISSUE
Dedication of Boulder Dam.

Boulder Dam — A251

FLAT PLATE PRINTING

1935, Sept. 30	**Unwmk.**	*Perf. 11*	
774	A251 3c purple	.35	.25

MICHIGAN CENTENARY ISSUE
Advance celebration of Michigan Statehood centenary.

Michigan State Seal A252

ROTARY PRESS PRINTING

1935, Nov. 1	**Unwmk.**	*Perf. 11x10½*	
775	A252 3c purple	.35	.25

TEXAS CENTENNIAL ISSUE
Centennial of Texas independence.

Sam Houston, Stephen F. Austin and the Alamo A253

1936, Mar. 2	**Unwmk.**	**Perf. 11x10½**	
776	A253 3c purple	.35	.25

RHODE ISLAND TERCENTENARY ISSUE
300th anniv. of the settlement of Rhode Island.

Statue of Roger Williams — A254

1936, May 4	**Unwmk.**	**Perf. 10½x11**	
777	A254 3c purple	.35	.25

THIRD INTERNATIONAL PHILATELIC EXHIBITION ISSUE
SOUVENIR SHEET

A254a

Illustration reduced.

FLAT PLATE PRINTING

1936, May 9	**Unwmk.**	*Imperf.*	
778	A254a violet, pane of 4	1.75	1.25
b.	3c Type A249	.40	.30
b.	3c Type A250	.40	.30
c.	3c Type A252	.40	.30
d.	3c Type A253	.40	.30

Issued in panes measuring 98x66mm containing four stamps, inscribed in the margins: "Printed by the Treasury Department, Bureau of Engraving and Printing, under authority of James A. Farley, Postmaster General, in compliment to the third International Philatelic Exhibition of 1936. New York, N. Y., May 9-17, 1936. Plate No. 21557 (or 21558)."

ARKANSAS CENTENNIAL ISSUE
100th anniv. of the State of Arkansas.

Arkansas Post, Old and New State Houses A255

ROTARY PRESS PRINTING
Perf. 11x10½

1936, June 15		**Unwmk.**	
782	A255 3c purple	.35	.25

OREGON TERRITORY ISSUE
Opening of the Oregon Territory, 1836, 100th anniv.

Map of Oregon Territory A256

Perf. 11x10½

1936, July 14		**Unwmk.**	
783	A256 3c purple	.35	.25

SUSAN B. ANTHONY ISSUE
Susan Brownell Anthony (1820-1906), woman-suffrage advocate, and 16th anniv. of the ratification of the 19th Amendment which grants American women the right to vote.

Susan B. Anthony — A257

Perf. 11x10½

1936, Aug. 26		**Unwmk.**	
784	A257 3c violet	.25	.25

ARMY ISSUE
Issued in honor of the United States Army.

George Washington, Nathanael Greene and Mount Vernon — A258

Andrew Jackson, Winfield Scott and the Hermitage A259

Generals Sherman, Grant and Sheridan A260

Generals Robert E. Lee, "Stonewall" Jackson and Stratford Hall A261

US Military Academy, West Point A262

1936-37		**Unwmk.**	**Perf. 11x10½**	
785	A258	1c green	.30	.25
786	A259	2c carmine ('37)	.30	.25
787	A260	3c purple ('37)	.40	.25
788	A261	4c gray ('37)	.60	.25
789	A262	5c ultra ('37)	.75	.25
	Nos. 785-789 (5)		2.35	1.25

NAVY ISSUE
Issued in honor of the United States Navy.

John Paul Jones and John Barry A263

Stephen Decatur and Thomas
MacDonough — A264

Admirals
David G.
Farragut
and David
D. Porter
A265

Admirals William T. Sampson, George
Dewey and Winfield S. Schley
A266

Seal of US
Naval
Academy
and Naval
Cadets
A267

1936-37   Unwmk.   Perf. 11x10½
790 A263 1c green   .30   .25
791 A264 2c carmine ('37)   .30   .25
792 A265 3c purple ('37)   .40   .25
793 A266 4c gray ('37)   .60   .25
794 A267 5c ultra ('37)   .75   .25
  Nos. 790-794 (5)   2.35   1.25

ORDINANCE OF 1787 SESQUICENTENNIAL ISSUE

150th anniv. of the adoption of the Ordinance of 1787 and the creation of the Northwest Territory.

Manasseh Cutler, Rufus Putnam and
Map of Northwest Territory
A268

Perf. 11x10½
1937, July 13   Unwmk.
795 A268 3c red violet   .30   .25

VIRGINIA DARE ISSUE

350th anniv. of the birth of Virginia Dare, 1st child born in America of English parents (Aug. 18, 1587), and the settlement at Roanoke Island.

Virginia Dare and
Parents — A269

FLAT PLATE PRINTING

1937, Aug. 18   Unwmk.   Perf. 11
796 A269 5c gray blue   .35   .25

SOCIETY OF PHILATELIC AMERICANS ISSUE
SOUVENIR SHEET

A269a

Illustration reduced.

TYPE OF NATIONAL PARKS ISSUE
1937, Aug. 26   Unwmk.   Imperf.
797 A269a 10c blue green   .60   .40
  Issued in panes measuring 67x78mm.

CONSTITUTION SESQUICENTENNIAL ISSUE

150th anniversary of the signing of the Constitution on September 17, 1787.

Signing of
the
Constitution
A270

Perf. 11x10½
1937, Sept. 17   Unwmk.
798 A270 3c bright red violet   .40   .25

TERRITORIAL ISSUES
Hawaii

Statue of
Kamehameha I,
Honolulu — A271

Alaska

Landscape
with Mt.
McKinley
A272

Puerto Rico

La
Fortaleza,
San Juan
A273

Virgin Islands

Charlotte
Amalie
A274

1937   Unwmk.   Perf. 10½x11
799 A271 3c violet   .35   .25

Perf. 11x10½
800 A272 3c violet   .40   .25
801 A273 3c bright violet   .40   .25
802 A274 3c light violet   .40   .25
  Nos. 799-802 (4)   1.55   1.00

PRESIDENTIAL ISSUE

Benjamin
Franklin
A275

George
Washington
A276

Martha
Washington
A277

John Adams
A278

Thomas
Jefferson
A279

James
Madison
A280

White House
A281

James
Monroe
A282

John Q.
Adams
A283

Andrew
Jackson
A284

Martin Van
Buren
A285

William H.
Harrison
A286

John
Tyler — A287

James K.
Polk — A288

Zachary
Taylor
A289

Millard
Fillmore
A290

Franklin
Pierce
A291

James
Buchanan
A292

Abraham
Lincoln
A293

Andrew
Johnson
A294

Ulysses S.
Grant
A295

Rutherford B.
Hayes
A296

James A.
Garfield
A297

Chester A.
Arthur
A298

Grover
Cleveland
A299

Benjamin
Harrison
A300

William
McKinley
A301

Theodore
Roosevelt
A302

William
Howard Taft
A303

Woodrow
Wilson
A304

Warren G.
Harding
A305

Calvin
Coolidge
A306

1938   Unwmk.
803 A275 ½c deep orange   .25   .25
804 A276 1c green   .25   .25
  b. Booklet pane of 6   2.00   .50
  c. Horiz. pair, imperf between
      (from booklet pane)   —
805 A277 1½c bister brown   .25   .25
  b. Horiz. pair, imperf. be-
      tween   100.00 20.00

No. 805b unused is not precanceled. Precanceled examples are considered used and are valued in the used column. They are valued with gum; pairs without gum are worth less.

806	A278	2c rose carmine	.25	.25
b.		Booklet pane of 6	5.50	1.00
807	A279	3c deep violet	.25	.25
a.		Booklet pane of 6	8.50	2.00
b.		Horiz. pair, imperf. between	2,000.	
c.		Imperf., pair	—	
d.		As "a," imperf between vert.	—	

No. 807c is believed to be unique and has two certificates of authentication. Some specialists question the existence of No. 807c as a genuine error and believe the documented pair to be a counterfeit. The editors would like to examine the pair and would like to see documented evidence of the pair's existence, to include a new certificate of authenticity from a recognized expertizing body.

808	A280	4c red violet	.75	.25
809	A281	4½c dark gray	.40	.25
810	A282	5c bright blue	.35	.25
811	A283	6c red orange	.40	.25
812	A284	7c sepia	.40	.25
813	A285	8c olive green	.40	.25
814	A286	9c rose pink	.45	.25
815	A287	10c brown red	.45	.25
816	A288	11c ultramarine	.75	.25
817	A289	12c bright violet	1.00	.25
818	A290	13c blue green	1.30	.25
819	A291	14c blue	1.00	.25
820	A292	15c blue gray	.90	.25
821	A293	16c black	1.50	.25
822	A294	17c rose red	1.00	.25
823	A295	18c brown carmine	2.25	.25
824	A296	19c bright violet	1.30	.35
825	A297	20c bright blue green	1.20	.25
826	A298	21c dull blue	1.30	.25
827	A299	22c vermilion	1.20	.40
828	A300	24c gray black	3.50	.25
829	A301	25c deep red lilac	1.20	.25
830	A302	30c deep ultramarine	4.00	.25
a.		30c blue	15.00	—
b.		30c deep blue	240.00	—
831	A303	50c light red violet	5.50	.25

FLAT PLATE PRINTING

1938   **Perf. 11**

832	A304	$1 purple & black	7.00	.25
a.		Vert. pair, imperf. horiz.	1,250.	
b.		Watermarked USIR ('51)	200.00	65.00
		Hinged	120.00	
c.		$1 red violet & black ('54)	6.00	.25
d.		As "c," vert. pair, imperf. horiz.	1,000.	
e.		Vert. pair, imperf. btwn.	2,750.	
f.		As "c," vert. pair, imperf. btwn.	8,500.	
g.		As "c," bright magenta & black	75.00	—
h.		As No. 832, red violet & black	—	

No. 832c is dry printed from 400-subject flat plates on thick white paper with smooth, colorless gum.

No. 832g is the far end of the color spectrum for the No. 832c stamp, trending toward a more pinkish shade, but the shade is not pink. No. 832g is known in bright magenta and in deep bright magenta; both shades qualify as No. 832g. No. 832h is the wet-printed first printing, but the shade essentially matches the red violet normally seen on No. 832c.

833	A305	$2 yellow green & black	17.50	3.75
834	A306	$5 carmine & black	85.00	3.00
a.		$5 red brown & black	2,750.	7,000.
		Hinged	1,850.	
	Nos. 803-834 (32)		143.25	14.50
	Nos. 803-834, P# blocks of 4		670.95	

No. 834 can be chemically altered to resemble No. 834a. No. 834a should be purchased only with competent expert certification.

Watermarks

All stamps from No. 835 on are unwatermarked.

CONSTITUTION RATIFICATION ISSUE

150th anniversary of the ratification of the United States Constitution.

Old Court House, Williamsburg, Va. — A307

ROTARY PRESS PRINTING

1938, June 21   **Perf. 11x10½**

835	A307	3c deep violet	.45	.25

SWEDISH-FINNISH TERCENTENARY ISSUE

Tercentenary of the founding of the Swedish and Finnish Settlement at Wilmington, Delaware.

Landing of the Swedes and Finns — A308

FLAT PLATE PRINTING

1938, June 27   **Perf. 11**

836	A308	3c red violet	.35	.25

NORTHWEST TERRITORY SESQUICENTENNIAL

Statue Symbolizing Colonization of the West — A309

ROTARY PRESS PRINTING

1938, July 15   **Perf. 11x10½**

837	A309	3c bright violet	.30	.25

IOWA TERRITORY CENTENNIAL ISSUE

Old Capitol, Iowa City A310

1938, Aug. 24   **Perf. 11x10½**

838	A310	3c violet	.40	.25

ROTARY PRESS COIL STAMPS
Types of 1938

1939, Jan. 20   **Perf. 10 Vertically**

839	A276	1c green	.30	.25
840	A277	1½c bister brown	.30	.25
841	A278	2c rose carmine	.40	.25
842	A279	3c deep violet	.50	.25
843	A280	4c red violet	7.50	.40
844	A281	4½c dark gray	.70	.40
845	A282	5c bright blue	5.00	.35
846	A283	6c red orange	1.10	.25
847	A287	10c brown red	11.00	1.00

1939, Jan. 27   **Perf. 10 Horizontally**

848	A276	1c green	.85	.25
849	A277	1½c bister brown	1.25	.30
850	A278	2c rose carmine	2.50	.40
851	A279	3c deep violet	2.50	.40
	Nos. 839-851 (13)		33.90	4.75
	Nos. 839-851, joint line pairs (13)		139.90	29.65

"Tower of the Sun" A311   Trylon and Perisphere A312

GOLDEN GATE INTL. EXPOSITION, SAN FRANCISCO
ROTARY PRESS PRINTING

1939, Feb. 18   **Perf. 10½x11**

852	A311	3c bright purple	.30	.25

NEW YORK WORLD'S FAIR ISSUE

1939, Apr. 1   **Perf. 10½x11**

853	A312	3c deep purple	.30	.25

WASHINGTON INAUGURATION ISSUE

Sesquicentennial of the inauguration of George Washington as First President.

George Washington Taking Oath of Office — A313

FLAT PLATE PRINTING

1939, Apr. 30   **Perf. 11**

854	A313	3c bright red violet	.60	.25

BASEBALL CENTENNIAL ISSUE

Sand-lot Baseball Game A314

ROTARY PRESS PRINTING

1939, June 12   **Perf. 11x10½**

855	A314	3c violet	1.75	.25

PANAMA CANAL ISSUE

25th anniv. of the opening of the Panama Canal.

Theodore Roosevelt, Gen. George W. Goethals and Gaillard Cut — A315

FLAT PLATE PRINTING

1939, Aug. 15   **Perf. 11**

856	A315	3c deep red violet	.40	.25

PRINTING TERCENTENARY ISSUE

Issued in commemoration of the 300th anniversary of printing in Colonial America. The Stephen Daye press is in the Harvard University Museum.

Stephen Daye Press — A316

ROTARY PRESS PRINTING

1939, Sept. 25   **Perf. 10½x11**

857	A316	3c violet	.25	.25

50th ANNIVERSARY OF STATEHOOD ISSUE

Map of North and South Dakota, Montana and Washington A317

1939, Nov. 2   **Perf. 11x10½**

858	A317	3c rose violet	.35	.25

FAMOUS AMERICANS ISSUES
AMERICAN AUTHORS

Washington Irving — A318   James Fenimore Cooper — A319

Ralph Waldo Emerson A320   Louisa May Alcott A321

Samuel L. Clemens (Mark Twain) — A322

1940   **Perf. 10½x11**

859	A318	1c bright blue green	.25	.25
860	A319	2c rose carmine	.25	.25
861	A320	3c bright red violet	.25	.25
862	A321	5c ultramarine	.35	.25
863	A322	10c dark brown	1.75	1.20
	Nos. 859-863 (5)		2.85	2.20

AMERICAN POETS

Henry W. Longfellow A323   John Greenleaf Whittier A324

James Russell Lowell A325   Walt Whitman A326

James Whitcomb Riley — A327

864	A323	1c bright blue green	.25	.25
865	A324	2c rose carmine	.25	.25
866	A325	3c bright red violet	.25	.25
867	A326	5c ultramarine	.50	.25
868	A327	10c dark brown	1.75	1.25
	Nos. 864-868 (5)		3.00	2.25

AMERICAN EDUCATORS

Horace Mann — A328   Mark Hopkins — A329

Charles W.
Eliot — A330

Frances E.
Willard — A331

Booker T.
Washington — A332

869	A328	1c bright blue green	.25	.25
870	A329	2c rose carmine	.25	.25
871	A330	3c bright red violet	.25	.25
872	A331	5c ultramarine	.50	.25
873	A332	10c dark brown	2.25	1.10
		Nos. 869-873 (5)	3.50	2.10

AMERICAN SCIENTISTS

John James
Audubon
A333

Dr. Crawford W.
Long
A334

Luther
Burbank — A335

Dr. Walter
Reed — A336

Jane
Addams — A337

874	A333	1c bright blue green	.25	.25
875	A334	2c rose carmine	.25	.25
876	A335	3c bright red violet	.25	.25
877	A336	5c ultramarine	.50	.25
878	A337	10c dark brown	1.50	.85
		Nos. 874-878 (5)	2.75	1.85

AMERICAN COMPOSERS

Stephen Collins
Foster — A338

John Philip
Sousa — A339

Victor Herbert
A340

Edward
MacDowell
A341

Ethelbert
Nevin — A342

879	A338	1c bright blue green	.25	.25
880	A339	2c rose carmine	.25	.25
881	A340	3c bright red violet	.25	.25
882	A341	5c ultramarine	.50	.25
883	A342	10c dark brown	3.75	1.35
		Nos. 879-883 (5)	5.00	2.35

AMERICAN ARTISTS

Gilbert Charles
Stuart — A343

James A.
McNeill
Whistler — A344

Augustus Saint-
Gaudens
A345

Daniel Chester
French
A346

Frederic
Remington — A347

884	A343	1c bright blue green	.25	.25
885	A344	2c rose carmine	.25	.25
886	A345	3c bright red violet	.30	.25
887	A346	5c ultramarine	.50	.25
888	A347	10c dark brown	1.75	1.25
		Nos. 884-888 (5)	3.05	2.25

AMERICAN INVENTORS

Eli
Whitney — A348

Samuel F. B.
Morse — A349

Cyrus Hall
McCormick
A350

Elias Howe
A351

Alexander Graham
Bell — A352

889	A348	1c bright blue green	.25	.25
890	A349	2c rose carmine	.30	.25
891	A350	3c bright red violet	.30	.25
892	A351	5c ultramarine	1.10	.30
893	A352	10c dark brown	11.00	2.00
		Nos. 889-893 (5)	12.95	3.05
		Nos. 859-893 (35)	33.10	16.05

PONY EXPRESS, 80th ANNIV. ISSUE

Pony
Express
Rider
A353

1940, Apr. 3   *Perf. 11x10½*
894 A353   3c henna brown   .50   .25

PAN AMERICAN UNION ISSUE

Founding of the Pan American Union,
50th anniv.

The Three Graces
from Botticelli's
"Spring" — A354

1940, Apr. 14   *Perf. 10½x11*
895 A354   3c light violet   .30   .25

IDAHO STATEHOOD, 50th ANNIV.

Idaho
Capitol,
Boise
A355

1940, July 3   *Perf. 11x10½*
896 A355   3c bright violet   .35   .25

WYOMING STATEHOOD, 50th ANNIV.

Wyoming State
Seal — A356

1940, July 10   *Perf. 10½x11*
897 A356   3c brown violet   .35   .25

CORONADO EXPEDITION, 400th ANNIV.

"Coronado
and His
Captains,"
painted by
Gerald
Cassidy
A357

1940, Sept. 7   *Perf. 11x10½*
898 A357   3c violet   .35   .25

NATIONAL DEFENSE ISSUE

Statue of
Liberty — A358

90-millimeter Anti-
aircraft Gun — A359

Torch of
Enlightenment — A360

1940, Oct. 16   *Perf. 11x10½*

899	A358	1c bright blue green	.25	.25
a.		Vertical pair, imperf. between	600.00	—
b.		Horizontal pair, imperf. between	32.50	—
900	A359	2c rose carmine	.25	.25
a.		Horizontal pair, imperf. between	37.50	—
901	A360	3c bright violet	.25	.25
a.		Horizontal pair, imperf. between	22.50	—
		Nos. 899-901 (3)	.75	.75

THIRTEENTH AMENDMENT ISSUE

75th anniv. of the 13th Amendment to
the Constitution abolishing slavery.

"Emancipation,"
Statue of Lincoln and
Slave, by Thomas
Ball — A361

1940, Oct. 20   *Perf. 10½x11*
902 A361   3c deep violet   .50   .25

AIR POST STAMPS

Curtiss Jenny — AP1

FLAT PLATE PRINTINGS
Plates of 100 subjects.

1918   **Unwmk.**   **Engr.**   *Perf. 11*

C1	AP1	6c orange	60.	30.
		Never hinged	120.	
		On cover		50.
C2	AP1	16c green	65.	35.
		Never hinged	130.	
		On cover		55.
C3	AP1	24c car rose & blue	70.	35.
		Never hinged	140.	
		On cover		75.
a.		Center inverted	350,000.	
		Never hinged	700,000.	
		Nos. C1-C3 (3)	195.00	100.00
		Nos. C1-C3, never hinged	390.00	

Wooden
Propeller and
Radiator — AP2

Emblem of Air
Service — AP3

De Havilland
Biplane — AP4

1923   **Unwmk.**   *Perf. 11*

C4	AP2	8c dark green	20.00	15.00
		Never hinged	40.00	
		On cover		22.50
C5	AP3	16c dark blue	65.00	30.00
		Never hinged	130.00	
		On cover		47.50
C6	AP4	24c carmine	70.00	30.00
		Never hinged	140.00	
		On cover		42.50
		Nos. C4-C6 (3)	155.00	75.00
		Nos. C4-C6, never hinged	310.00	

Map of US and Two Mail
Planes — AP5

1926-27   **Unwmk.**   **Perf. 11**
C7   AP5 10c dark blue   2.50   .35
    Never hinged   4.50
C8   AP5 15c olive brown   2.75   2.50
    Never hinged   5.25
C9   AP5 20c yellow green   7.00   2.00
    Never hinged   13.50
    Nos. C7-C9 (3)   12.25   4.85
    Nos. C7-C9, never hinged   23.25

Lindbergh's Airplane "Spirit of St.
Louis" — AP6

1927, June 18   **Unwmk.**   **Perf. 11**
C10   AP6 10c dark blue   7.00   2.50
    Never hinged   13.00
a.   Booklet pane of 3   75.00   65.00
    Never hinged   120.00
b.   Double impression   16,500.

Singles from No. C10a are imperf. at sides
or imperf. at sides and bottom.
Only one example is recorded of No. C10b.

Nos. C1-C10 were available for ordinary postage.

Beacon on
Rocky
Mountains
AP7

1928, July 25   **Unwmk.**   **Perf. 11**
C11   AP7 5c carmine and blue   5.00   .75
    Never hinged   9.50
a.   Vert. pair, imperf. between   7,000.

No. C11a is unique. It is torn and valued
thus.

Winged Globe — AP8

1930, Feb. 10   **Unwmk.**   **Perf. 11**
Stamp design: 46½x19mm
C12   AP8 5c violet   9.50   .50
    Never hinged   18.00
a.   Horiz. pair, imperf. between   4,500.
    See Nos. C16-C17, C19.

GRAF ZEPPELIN ISSUE

Zeppelin over Atlantic Ocean — AP9

Zeppelin between Continents — AP10

Zeppelin Passing Globe — AP11

1930, Apr. 19   **Unwmk.**   **Perf. 11**
C13   AP9   65c green   180.   165.
    Never hinged   275.
    On cover or card   175.
C14   AP10 $1.30 brown   400.   375.
    Never hinged   650.
    On cover   400.
C15   AP11 $2.60 blue   575.   600.
    Never hinged   975.
    On cover   625.
    Nos. C13-C15 (3)   1,155.   1,140.
    Nos. C13-C15, never hinged   1,900.

Issued for use on mail carried on the first
Europe-Pan-America round trip flight of the
Graf Zeppelin in May, 1930. They were withdrawn from sale June 30, 1930.

ROTARY PRESS PRINTING
1931-32   **Unwmk.**   **Perf. 10½x11**
Stamp design: 47½x19mm
C16   AP8 5c violet   5.00   .60
    Never hinged   8.75
C17   AP8 8c olive bister ('32)   2.25   .40
    Never hinged   4.00

CENTURY OF PROGRESS ISSUE

Airship "Graf Zeppelin" — AP12

FLAT PLATE PRINTING
1933, Oct. 2   **Unwmk.**   **Perf. 11**
C18   AP12 50c green   50.00   47.50
    Never hinged   90.00
    On cover   80.00

Issued in connection with the flight of the
airship "Graf Zeppelin" in October, 1933, to
Miami, Akron and Chicago and from the last
city to Europe.

> **Catalogue values for unused stamps in this section, from this point to the end, are for Never Hinged items.**

Type of 1930 Issue
ROTARY PRESS PRINTING
Perf. 10½x11
1934, June 30   **Unwmk.**
C19   AP8 6c dull orange   3.50   .25

TRANSPACIFIC ISSUES

The "China
Clipper"
over the
Pacific
AP13

FLAT PLATE PRINTING
1935, Nov. 22   **Unwmk.**   **Perf. 11**
C20   AP13 25c blue   1.40   1.00

Issued to pay postage on mail transported
by the Transpacific air mail service, inaugurated Nov. 22, 1935.

The "China
Clipper"
over the
Pacific
AP14

FLAT PLATE PRINTING
1937, Feb. 15   **Unwmk.**   **Perf. 11**
C21   AP14 20c green   11.00   1.75
C22   AP14 50c carmine   11.00   5.00

Eagle
Holding
Shield, Olive
Branch and
Arrows
AP15

FLAT PLATE PRINTING
1938, May 14   **Unwmk.**   **Perf. 11**
C23   AP15 6c dark blue &
              carmine   .70   .25
a.   Vert. pair, imperf. horiz.   300.00   —
    On cover   1,750.
b.   Horiz. pair, imperf. vert.   12,500.
c.   6¢ ultra & car   150.00   1,500.
    On cover   1,750.

TRANSATLANTIC ISSUE

Winged Globe — AP16

FLAT PLATE PRINTING
1939, May 16   **Unwmk.**   **Perf. 11**
C24   AP16 30c dull blue   12.00   1.50

AIR POST SPECIAL DELIVERY STAMPS

To provide for the payment of both the
postage and the special delivery fee in
one stamp.

Great Seal
of United
States
APSD1

FLAT PLATE PRINTING
1934, Aug. 30   **Unwmk.**   **Perf. 11**
CE1   APSD1 16c dark blue   .70   .80
    blue   .70   .80
    Never hinged   .90

For imperforate variety see No. 771.

Type of 1934
1936, Feb. 10
CE2   APSD1 16c red & blue   .45   .35
    Never hinged   .60
a.   Horiz. pair, imperf. vert.   4,250.
    Never hinged   5,250.

SPECIAL DELIVERY STAMPS

When affixed to any letter or article of
mailable matter, secured immediate
delivery, between 7 A. M. and midnight,
at any post office.

Messenger Running — SD1

Flat Plate Printing
1885   **Unwmk.**   **Perf. 12**
E1   SD1 10c blue   550.00   80.00
    Never hinged   1,250.
    On cover   225.00

Messenger
Running
SD2

1888, Sept. 6
E2   SD2 10c blue   500.00   45.00
    Never hinged   1,150.
    On cover   135.00

COLUMBIAN EXPOSITION ISSUE

Though not issued expressly for the
Exposition, No. E3 is considered to be
part of that issue.

1893, Jan. 24
E3   SD2 10c orange   300.00   50.00
    Never hinged   675.00
    On cover   200.00

Messenger
Running
SD3

1894, Oct. 10
Line under "TEN CENTS"
E4   SD3 10c blue   900.00   100.00
    Never hinged   2,250.
    On cover   300.00

No. E5a

1895, Aug. 16   **Wmk. 191**
E5   SD3 10c blue   210.00   12.50
    Never hinged   500.00
    On cover   25.00
a.   Dots in curved frame
    above messenger (Pl.
    882)   350.00   45.00
    Never hinged   700.00
b.   Printed on both sides

Messenger
on Bicycle
SD4

1902, Dec. 9
E6   SD4 10c ultramarine   230.00   10.00
    Never hinged   525.00
    On cover   22.50
a.   10c blue   300.00   12.50
    Never hinged   800.00
    On cover   65.00

Helmet of Mercury
and Olive
Branch — SD5

1908, Dec. 12
E7   SD5 10c green   65.00   50.00
    Never hinged   140.00
    On cover   400.00

1911, Jan.   **Wmk. 190**   **Perf. 12**
E8   SD4 10c ultramarine   110.00   10.00
    Never hinged   240.00
    On cover   30.00
b.   10c violet blue   140.00   14.00
    Never hinged   300.00
    On cover   25.00

1914, Sept.   **Perf. 10**
E9   SD4 10c ultramarine   190.00   12.00
    Never hinged   425.00
    On cover   65.00
a.   10c blue   250.00   15.00
    Never hinged   550.00
    On cover   65.00

1916, Oct. 19   **Unwmk.**   **Perf. 10**
E10   SD4 10c pale ultramarine   320.00   50.00
    Never hinged   700.00
    On cover   200.00
a.   10c blue   375.00   50.00
    Never hinged   800.00
    On cover   110.00

1917, May 2   **Perf. 11**
E11   SD4 10c ultramarine   20.00   .75
    Never hinged   45.00
    On cover   4.00
b.   10c gray violet   30.00   3.00
    Never hinged   65.00
    On cover   4.00
c.   10c blue   90.00   5.00
    Never hinged   190.00
    On cover   30.00
d.   Perf. 10 at left   —

Postman and Motorcycle SD6

Post Office Truck SD7

1922, July 12
E12	SD6	10c gray violet	45.00	3.00
		Never hinged	95.00	
		On cover		3.50
a.		10c deep ultramarine	55.00	3.50
		Never hinged	130.00	
		On cover		5.00

FLAT PLATE PRINTING
1925
E13	SD6	15c deep orange	40.00	3.75
		Never hinged	75.00	
		On cover		55.00
E14	SD7	20c black	2.00	1.00
		Never hinged	4.00	
		On cover		25.00
		Nos. E12-E14 (3)	87.00	7.75

Motorcycle Type of 1922
ROTARY PRESS PRINTING
1927-31   Unwmk.   Perf. 11x10½
E15	SD6	10c gray violet	.65	.25
		Never hinged	1.20	
		On cover		.50
a.		10c red lilac	.80	.25
		Never hinged	1.40	
b.		10c gray lilac	.90	.25
		Never hinged	1.55	
c.		Horizontal pair, imperf. between	300.00	
		Never hinged	500.00	
E16	SD6	15c orange ('31)	.60	.25
		Never hinged	.90	
		On cover		1.50

REGISTRATION STAMP

Issued for the prepayment of registry fees; not usable for postage.

Eagle — RS1

ENGRAVED
1911, Dec. 1   Wmk. 190   Perf. 12
F1	RS1	10c ultramarine	80.00	15.00
		Never hinged	175.00	
		On cover		85.00

POSTAGE DUE STAMPS

For affixing, by a postal clerk to any piece of mailable matter, to denote the amount to be collected from the addressee because of insufficient prepayment of postage.

D1

Printed by the American Bank Note Co.
Plates of 200 subjects in two panes of 100 each.

1879   Unwmk.   Engr.   Perf. 12
J1	D1	1c brown	90.00	14.00
		Never hinged	260.00	
J2	D1	2c brown	400.00	25.00
		Never hinged	1,050.	
J3	D1	3c brown	100.00	6.00
		Never hinged	280.00	
J4	D1	5c brown	775.00	70.00
		Never hinged	1,900.	
J5	D1	10c brown	900.00	70.00
		Never hinged	2,500.	
a.		Imperf., pair	2,500.	
J6	D1	30c brown	350.00	65.00
		Never hinged	800.00	
J7	D1	50c brown	600.00	90.00
		Never hinged	1,600.	
		Nos. J1-J7 (7)	3,215.	340.00

SPECIAL PRINTING
1879
J8	D1	1c deep brown	22,500.	
		Never hinged		
J9	D1	2c deep brown	19,000.	
		Never hinged		
J10	D1	3c deep brown	25,000.	
		Never hinged		
J11	D1	5c deep brown	15,000.	
		Never hinged		
J12	D1	10c deep brown	8,500.	
		Never hinged		
J13	D1	30c deep brown	9,750.	
		Never hinged		
J14	D1	50c deep brown	8,750.	
		Never hinged		

1884   Unwmk.   Perf. 12
J15	D1	1c red brown	70.00	7.00
		Never hinged	190.00	
J16	D1	2c red brown	80.00	6.00
		Never hinged	225.00	
J17	D1	3c red brown	1,050.	350.00
		Never hinged	2,500.	
J18	D1	5c red brown	600.00	50.00
		Never hinged	1,450.	
J19	D1	10c red brown	600.00	35.00
		Never hinged	1,450.	
J20	D1	30c red brown	200.00	70.00
		Never hinged	500.00	
J21	D1	50c red brown	1,750.	250.00
		Never hinged	3,750.	
		Nos. J15-J21 (7)	4,350.	768.00

1891   Unwmk.   Perf. 12
J22	D1	1c bright claret	30.00	2.00
		Never hinged	85.00	
J23	D1	2c bright claret	32.50	2.00
		Never hinged	85.00	
J24	D1	3c bright claret	67.50	16.00
		Never hinged	180.00	
J25	D1	5c bright claret	100.00	16.00
		Never hinged	290.00	
J26	D1	10c bright claret	165.00	30.00
		Never hinged	500.00	
J27	D1	30c bright claret	575.00	225.00
		Never hinged	1,700.	
J28	D1	50c bright claret	600.00	225.00
		Never hinged	1,750.	
		Nos. J22-J28 (7)	1,570.	516.00

See Die and Plate Proofs in the Scott U.S. Specialized catalog for imperfs. on stamp paper.

The color on Nos. J29-J44 will run when immersed in water. Extreme caution is advised.

D2

Printed by the Bureau of Engraving and Printing.

1894   Perf. 12
J29	D2	1c vermilion	2,250.	725.
		Never hinged	5,750.	
J30	D2	2c vermilion	775.	350.
		Never hinged	1,900.	

1894-95
J31	D2	1c deep claret	72.50	12.00
		Never hinged	260.00	
b.		Vertical pair, imperf. horiz.	—	
J32	D2	2c deep claret	62.50	10.00
		Never hinged	240.00	
J33	D2	3c deep claret ('95)	200.00	50.00
		Never hinged	575.00	
J34	D2	5c deep claret ('95)	300.00	55.00
		Never hinged	850.00	
J35	D2	10c deep claret	350.00	40.00
		Never hinged	1,000.	
J36	D2	30c deep claret ('95)	550.00	250.00
		Never hinged	1,250.	
a.		30c carmine	675.00	275.00
		Never hinged	1,600.	
b.		30c pale rose	450.00	200.00
		Never hinged	1,100.	
J37	D2	50c deep claret ('95)	1,800.	800.00
		Never hinged	4,250.	
a.		50c pale rose	1,600.	725.00
		Never hinged	3,750.	
		Nos. J31-J37 (7)	3,335.	1,217.

Shades are numerous in the 1894 and later issues.
See Die and Plate Proofs in the Scott U.S. Specialized for 1c imperf. on stamp paper.

1895-97   Wmk. 191   Perf. 12
J38	D2	1c deep claret	13.50	1.00
		Never hinged	40.00	
J39	D2	2c deep claret	13.50	1.00
		Never hinged	40.00	
J40	D2	3c deep claret	100.00	5.00
		Never hinged	225.00	
J41	D2	5c deep claret	110.00	5.00
		Never hinged	280.00	
J42	D2	10c deep claret	110.00	7.50
		Never hinged	280.00	
J43	D2	30c deep claret ('97)	600.00	75.00
		Never hinged	1,500.	
J44	D2	50c deep claret ('96)	375.00	60.00
		Never hinged	925.00	
		Nos. J38-J44 (7)	1,322.	154.50

1910-12   Wmk. 190   Perf. 12
J45	D2	1c deep claret	40.00	5.00
		Never hinged	115.00	
a.		1c rose carmine	35.00	5.00
		Never hinged	105.00	
J46	D2	2c deep claret	40.00	2.00
		Never hinged	115.00	
a.		2c rose carmine	35.00	2.00
		Never hinged	105.00	
J47	D2	3c deep claret	625.00	60.00
		Never hinged	1,600.	
J48	D2	5c deep claret	120.00	12.00
		Never hinged	275.00	
a.		5c rose carmine	120.00	12.00
		Never hinged	275.00	
J49	D2	10c deep claret	125.00	20.00
		Never hinged	280.00	
a.		10c rose carmine	125.00	20.00
		Never hinged	280.00	
J50	D2	50c deep claret ('12)	1,100.	175.00
		Never hinged	2,900.	
a.		50c rose carmine	1,150.	190.00
		Never hinged	2,900.	
		Nos. J45-J50 (6)	2,050.	274.00

1914   Perf. 10
J52	D2	1c carmine lake	80.00	15.00
		Never hinged	220.00	
a.		1c dull rose	85.00	15.00
		Never hinged	230.00	
J53	D2	2c carmine lake	62.50	1.00
		Never hinged	170.00	
a.		2c dull rose	67.50	2.00
		Never hinged	180.00	
b.		2c vermilion	67.50	2.00
		Never hinged	180.00	
J54	D2	3c carmine lake	1,050.	75.00
		Never hinged	3,000.	
a.		3c dull rose	1,000.	75.00
		Never hinged	2,900.	
J55	D2	5c carmine lake	50.00	6.00
		Never hinged	140.00	
a.		5c dull rose	45.00	4.00
		Never hinged	130.00	
J56	D2	10c carmine lake	75.00	4.00
		Never hinged	200.00	
a.		10c dull rose	80.00	5.00
		Never hinged	210.00	
J57	D2	30c carmine lake	225.00	55.00
		Never hinged	525.00	
J58	D2	50c carmine lake	11,500.	1,600.
		Never hinged	21,000.	
		Nos. J52-J58 (7)	13,042.	1,756.

No. J58 unused is valued in the grade of fine to very fine.

1916   Unwmk.   Perf. 10
J59	D2	1c rose	4,000.	750.00
		Never hinged	9,000.	
J60	D2	2c rose	275.00	85.00
		Never hinged	750.00	

1917   Unwmk.   Perf. 11
J61	D2	1c carmine rose	2.75	.25
		Never hinged	9.00	
		Never hinged	15.00	
a.		1c rose red	2.75	.25
		Never hinged	9.00	
b.		1c deep claret	2.75	.25
		Never hinged	9.00	
		Never hinged	42.50	
J62	D2	2c carmine rose	2.75	.25
		Never hinged	9.00	
a.		2c rose red	2.75	.25
		Never hinged	9.00	
b.		2c deep claret	2.75	.25
		Never hinged	9.00	
J63	D2	3c carmine rose	13.50	.80
		Never hinged	35.00	
a.		3c rose red	13.50	.80
		Never hinged	35.00	
b.		3c deep claret	13.50	.80
		Never hinged	35.00	
J64	D2	5c carmine	11.00	.80
		Never hinged	32.50	
a.		5c rose red	11.00	.80
		Never hinged	32.50	
b.		5c deep claret	11.00	.80
		Never hinged	32.50	
J65	D2	10c carmine rose	22.50	1.00
		Never hinged	65.00	
a.		10c rose red	22.50	1.00
		Never hinged	65.00	
b.		10c deep claret	22.50	1.00
		Never hinged	65.00	
J66	D2	30c carmine rose	80.00	2.00
		Never hinged	220.00	
a.		30c deep claret	80.00	2.00
		Never hinged	220.00	
b.		As "a," perf 10 at top, precanceled		21,000.

No. J66b is valued with small faults and fine centering, as the two recorded examples are in this condition and grade. One is precanceled St. Louis, Mo., and the other is precanceled Minneapolis, Minn.

J67	D2	50c carmine rose	140.00	1.00
		Never hinged	325.00	
a.		50c rose red	140.00	1.00
		Never hinged	325.00	
b.		50c deep claret	140.00	1.00
		Never hinged	325.00	
		Nos. J61-J67 (7)	272.50	6.10

1925, Apr. 13
J68	D2	½c dull red	1.00	.25
		Never hinged	1.75	

D3   D4

1930   Unwmk.
J69	D3	½c carmine	4.25	1.90
		Never hinged	9.50	
J70	D3	1c carmine	2.75	.35
		Never hinged	6.25	
J71	D3	2c carmine	3.75	.35
		Never hinged	8.50	
J72	D3	3c carmine	20.00	2.75
		Never hinged	47.50	
J73	D3	5c carmine	18.00	5.00
		Never hinged	42.50	
J74	D3	10c carmine	42.50	2.00
		Never hinged	95.00	
J75	D3	30c carmine	125.00	4.00
		Never hinged	275.00	
J76	D3	50c carmine	175.00	2.00
		Never hinged	375.00	
J77	D4	$1 carmine	32.50	.35
		Never hinged	65.00	
a.		$1 scarlet	27.50	.35
		Never hinged	55.00	
J78	D4	$5 scarlet	37.50	.35
		Never hinged	85.00	
b.		carmine	37.50	.35
		Never hinged	70.00	
		Nos. J69-J78 (10)	461.25	19.05

Type of 1930-31 Issue
Rotary Press Printing
1931   Unwmk.   Perf. 11x10½
J79	D3	½c dull carmine	.90	.25
		Never hinged	1.30	
a.		½c scarlet	.90	.25
		Never hinged	1.30	
J80	D3	1c scarlet	.25	.25
		Never hinged	.30	
b.		dull carmine	.25	.25
		Never hinged	.30	
J81	D3	2c scarlet	.25	.25
		Never hinged	.30	
b.		dull carmine	.25	.25
		Never hinged	.30	
J82	D3	3c scarlet	.30	.25
		Never hinged	.45	
b.		dull carmine	.25	.25
		Never hinged	.40	
J83	D3	5c scarlet	.50	.25
		Never hinged	.75	
b.		dull carmine	.40	.25
		Never hinged	.60	
J84	D3	10c scarlet	1.25	.25
		Never hinged	1.90	
b.		dull carmine	1.10	.25
		Never hinged	1.80	
J85	D3	30c dull carmine	7.50	.25
		Never hinged	11.50	
a.		30c scarlet	7.50	.25
		Never hinged	11.50	
J86	D3	50c dull carmine	9.00	.25
		Never hinged	15.00	
a.		50c scarlet	9.00	.25
		Never hinged	15.00	

UNITED STATES OFFICES IN CHINA

Issued for sale by the postal agency at Shanghai, at their surcharged value in local currency. Valid to the amount of their original values for the prepayment of postage on mail dispatched from the U.S. postal agency at Shanghai to addresses in the U.S.

Nos. 498-499, 502-504, 506-510, 512, 514-518 Surcharged

1919   Unwmk.   Perf. 11
K1	A140	2c on 1c green	25.00	70.00
		Never hinged	70.00	
K2	A140	4c on 2c rose, type I	25.00	70.00
		Never hinged	70.00	
K3	A140	6c on 3c vio, type II	60.00	140.00
		Never hinged	150.00	
K4	A140	8c on 4c brown	60.00	140.00
		Never hinged	150.00	
K5	A140	10c on 5c blue	65.00	140.00
		Never hinged	170.00	
K6	A140	12c on 6c red org	85.00	210.00
		Never hinged	220.00	
K7	A140	14c on 7c black	87.50	210.00
		Never hinged	225.00	
K8	A148	16c on 8c ol bis	70.00	160.00
		Never hinged	180.00	
a.		16c on 8c ol grn	60.00	140.00
		Never hinged	160.00	
K9	A148	18c on 9c sal red	65.00	175.00
		Never hinged	170.00	
K10	A148	20c on 10c org yel	60.00	140.00
		Never hinged	160.00	

K11 A148 24c on 12c brn car — 80.00 / 160.00
Never hinged — 200.00
a. 24c on 12c cl brn — 110.00 / 225.00
Never hinged — 275.00
K12 A148 30c on 15c gray — 87.50 / 230.00
Never hinged — 210.00
K13 A148 40c on 20c deep ultra — 130.00 / 325.00
Never hinged — 300.00
K14 A148 60c on 30c org red — 120.00 / 275.00
Never hinged — 280.00
K15 A148 $1 on 50c lt vio — 575.00 / 1,000.
Never hinged — 1,300.
K16 A148 $2 on $1 vio brn — 450.00 / 750.00
Never hinged — 1,000.
a. Double surcharge — 10,500. / 12,500.
Never hinged — 17,500.
Nos. K1-K16 (16) — 2,045. / 4,195.

Fake surcharges exist, but most are rather crudely made.

Nos. 498 and 528B
Surcharged

1922, July 3
K17 A140 2c on 1c green — 110.00 / 225.00
Never hinged — 250.00
K18 A140 4c on 2c car, type VII — 100.00 / 200.00
Never hinged — 230.00
a. "SHANGHAI" omitted — 7,500.
b. "CHINA" only — 15,000.

OFFICIAL STAMPS

The franking privilege having been abolished, as of July 1, 1873, these stamps were provided for each of the departments of Government for the prepayment of postage on official matter.

Penalty franks were first authorized in 1877, and their expanded use after 1879 reduced the need for official stamps, the use of which was finally abolished on July 5, 1884.

Designs, except Post Office, resemble those illustrated but are not identical. Each bears the name of Department. Portraits are as follows: 1c, Franklin; 2c, Jackson; 3c, Washington; 6c, Lincoln; 7c, Stanton; 10c, Jefferson; 12c, Clay; 15c, Webster; 24c, Scott; 30c, Hamilton; 90c, Perry.

Special printings overprinted "SPECIMEN" follow No. O120.

Printed by the Continental Bank Note Co.
Thin Hard Paper

O1   Franklin—O2

AGRICULTURE

1873   Engr.   Unwmk.   Perf. 12
O1 O1 1c yellow — 280.00 / 200.00
Never hinged — 600.00
No gum — 160.00
On wrapper — 2,500.
O2 O1 2c yellow — 240.00 / 100.00
Never hinged — 500.00
No gum — 100.00
On cover — 4,000.
O3 O1 3c yellow — 220.00 / 17.50
Never hinged — 460.00
No gum — 80.00
On cover — 900.00
O4 O1 6c yellow — 260.00 / 60.00
Never hinged — 550.00
No gum — 95.00
On cover — 7,500.
O5 O1 10c yellow — 525.00 / 200.00
Never hinged — 1,150.
No gum — 220.00
On cover (parcel label) — 6,000.
O6 O1 12c yellow — 450.00 / 260.00
Never hinged — 950.00
No gum — 250.00
On cover — 12,000.

O7 O1 15c yellow — 425.00 / 230.00
Never hinged — 950.00
No gum — 225.00
O8 O1 24c yellow — 425.00 / 250.00
Never hinged — 950.00
No gum — 225.00
On parcel label — —
O9 O1 30c yellow — 550.00 / 280.00
Never hinged — 1,200.
No gum — 275.00
Nos. O1-O9 (9) — 3,375. / 1,597.

EXECUTIVE

1873
O10 O2 1c carmine — 850.00 / 475.00
Never hinged — 2,250.
No gum — 450.00
On cover, single franking — 3,000.
O11 O2 2c carmine — 550.00 / 240.00
Never hinged — 1,250.
No gum — 240.00
On cover, single franking — 3,750.
O12 O2 3c carmine — 700.00 / 210.00
Never hinged — 1,600.
No gum — 270.00
On cover — 1,200.
a. 3c violet rose — 1,000. / 250.00
Never hinged — 2,250.
No gum — 375.00
O13 O2 6c carmine — 900.00 / 550.00
Never hinged — —
No gum — 325.00
On cover — 5,000.
O14 O2 10c carmine — 1,200. / 650.00
Never hinged — —
No gum — 600.00
Nos. O10-O14 (5) — 4,200. / 2,125.

O3   O4

INTERIOR

1873
O15 O3 1c vermilion — 75.00 / 10.00
Never hinged — 170.00
No gum — 30.00
On cover — 160.00
O16 O3 2c vermilion — 70.00 / 12.00
Never hinged — 160.00
No gum — 30.00
On cover — 65.00
O17 O3 3c vermilion — 80.00 / 6.00
Never hinged — 175.00
No gum — 35.00
On cover — 40.00
O18 O3 6c vermilion — 70.00 / 10.00
Never hinged — 160.00
No gum — 27.50
On cover — 95.00
O19 O3 10c vermilion — 70.00 / 20.00
Never hinged — 160.00
No gum — 27.50
On cover — 600.00
O20 O3 12c vermilion — 90.00 / 12.00
Never hinged — 200.00
No gum — 35.00
On cover — 575.00
O21 O3 15c vermilion — 200.00 / 25.00
Never hinged — 450.00
No gum — 80.00
On cover — 650.00
O22 O3 24c vermilion — 180.00 / 20.00
Never hinged — 400.00
No gum — 60.00
On cover — 2,500.
a. Double impression — —
O23 O3 30c vermilion — 290.00 / 20.00
Never hinged — 625.00
No gum — 110.00
O24 O3 90c vermilion — 325.00 / 50.00
Never hinged — 700.00
No gum — 120.00
Nos. O15-O24 (10) — 1,450. / 185.00

JUSTICE

1873
O25 O4 1c purple — 250.00 / 100.00
Never hinged — 550.00
No gum — 100.00
On cover — 1,750.
O26 O4 2c purple — 310.00 / 110.00
Never hinged — 700.00
No gum — 120.00
On cover — 1,500.
O27 O4 3c purple — 320.00 / 35.00
Never hinged — 725.00
No gum — 110.00
On cover — 575.00
O28 O4 6c purple — 310.00 / 45.00
Never hinged — 700.00
No gum — 110.00
On cover — 1,200.
O29 O4 10c purple — 310.00 / 100.00
Never hinged — 700.00
No gum — 120.00
On cover — 3,750.
O30 O4 12c purple — 260.00 / 75.00
Never hinged — 575.00
No gum — 95.00
On cover — 1,750.
O31 O4 15c purple — 475.00 / 200.00
Never hinged — 1,050.
No gum — 210.00
On cover — 1,250.

O32 O4 24c purple — 1,250. / 425.00
Never hinged — —
No gum — 550.00
On cover — 8,000.
O33 O4 30c purple — 1,300. / 350.00
Never hinged — —
No gum — 550.00
O34 O4 90c purple — 1,900. / 900.00
Never hinged — —
No gum — 800.00
On cover with No. O33 — 26,000.
Nos. O25-O34 (10) — 6,685. / 2,340.

O5   O6

NAVY

1873
O35 O5 1c ultramarine — 160.00 / 50.00
Never hinged — 350.00
No gum — 65.00
On cover — 750.00
a. 1c dull blue — 160.00 / 50.00
Never hinged — 350.00
No gum — 65.00
O36 O5 2c ultramarine — 160.00 / 25.00
Never hinged — 350.00
No gum — 65.00
On cover — 500.00
a. 2c dull blue — 160.00 / 25.00
Never hinged — 350.00
No gum — 65.00
O37 O5 3c ultramarine — 170.00 / 15.00
Never hinged — 375.00
No gum — 60.00
On cover — 250.00
a. 3c dull blue — 170.00 / 15.00
Never hinged — 375.00
No gum — 60.00
O38 O5 6c ultramarine — 150.00 / 25.00
Never hinged — 325.00
No gum — 55.00
On cover — 750.00
a. 6c dull blue — 150.00 / 25.00
Never hinged — 325.00
No gum — 55.00
O39 O5 7c ultramarine — 650.00 / 230.00
Never hinged — —
No gum — 250.00
On cover — 3,000.
a. 7c dull blue — 650.00 / 230.00
Never hinged — —
No gum — 250.00
O40 O5 10c ultramarine — 210.00 / 45.00
Never hinged — 475.00
No gum — 75.00
On cover — 6,500.
a. 10c dull blue — 210.00 / 45.00
Never hinged — 475.00
No gum — 75.00
O41 O5 12c ultramarine — 220.00 / 45.00
Never hinged — 500.00
No gum — 80.00
O42 O5 15c ultramarine — 375.00 / 75.00
Never hinged — —
No gum — 135.00
On cover — 21,000.
O43 O5 24c ultramarine — 400.00 / 85.00
Never hinged — —
No gum — 160.00
On cover — 30,000.
a. 24c dull blue — 375.00 / 80.00
Never hinged — —
No gum — 150.00
Violet — +5.00
O44 O5 30c ultramarine — 325.00 / 50.00
Never hinged — —
No gum — 125.00
On cover — 30,000.
O45 O5 90c ultramarine — 1,050. / 375.00
Never hinged — —
No gum — 450.00
a. Double impression — 20,000.
Nos. O35-O45 (11) — 3,870. / 1,020.

POST OFFICE

Stamps of the Post Office Department are often on paper with a gray surface. This is essentially a wiping problem, caused by an over-milled carbon black pigment that released acid and etched the plates. There is no premium for stamps on paper with a gray surface.

1873
O47 O6 1c black — 25.00 / 12.00
Never hinged — 60.00
No gum — 12.00
On cover — 75.00
O48 O6 2c black — 30.00 / 10.00
Never hinged — 75.00
No gum — 13.00
On cover — 175.00
a. Double impression — 700.00 / 400.00
O49 O6 3c black — 10.00 / 2.00
Never hinged — 25.00
No gum — 3.00
On cover — 25.00
Printed on both sides — 7,500.
O50 O6 6c black — 30.00 / 8.00
Never hinged — 75.00
No gum — 12.00
On cover — 85.00
a. Diagonal half used as 3c on cover — 5,000.
b. Double impression — 3,000.

O51 O6 10c black — 140.00 / 55.00
Never hinged — 325.00
No gum — 60.00
On cover — 400.00
O52 O6 12c black — 120.00 / 12.00
Never hinged — 275.00
No gum — 40.00
On cover — 1,000.
O53 O6 15c black — 140.00 / 20.00
Never hinged — 325.00
No gum — 50.00
On cover — 5,000.
O54 O6 24c black — 200.00 / 25.00
Never hinged — 450.00
No gum — 70.00
O55 O6 30c black — 200.00 / 25.00
Never hinged — 450.00
No gum — 70.00
O56 O6 90c black — 220.00 / 25.00
Never hinged — 500.00
No gum — 80.00
Nos. O47-O56 (10) — 1,115. / 194.00

STATE

Franklin — O7   Seward — O8

1873
O57 O7 1c dark green — 260.00 / 75.00
Never hinged — 575.00
No gum — 110.00
O58 O7 2c dark green — 310.00 / 100.00
Never hinged — —
No gum — 120.00
On cover — 1,000.
O59 O7 3c dark green — 220.00 / 25.00
Never hinged — 500.00
No gum — 85.00
On cover — 600.00
O60 O7 6c dark green — 220.00 / 30.00
Never hinged — 600.00
No gum — 85.00
On cover — 800.00
O61 O7 7c dark green — 290.00 / 65.00
Never hinged — 650.00
No gum — 95.00
On cover — 1,000.
O62 O7 10c dark green — 230.00 / 55.00
Never hinged — 525.00
No gum — 100.00
On cover — 2,000.
Block of 4 — 1,150.
O63 O7 12c dark green — 310.00 / 125.00
Never hinged — 700.00
No gum — 140.00
On cover — 1,500.
O64 O7 15c dark green — 320.00 / 90.00
Never hinged — 725.00
No gum — 130.00
On cover — 5,750.
O65 O7 24c dark green — 525.00 / 230.00
Never hinged — —
No gum — 275.00
On cover — 17,500.
O66 O7 30c dark green — 500.00 / 180.00
Never hinged — —
No gum — 240.00
On cover — 12,500.
O67 O7 90c dark green — 1,050. / 325.00
Never hinged — —
No gum — 525.00
O68 O8 $2 green & black — 1,600. / 3,000.
Never hinged — 3,300.
No gum — 800.00
On cover (parcel label) — 175,000.

The No. O68 on parcel label is unique.

O69 O8 $5 green & black — 7,500. / 13,000.
Never hinged — —
No gum — 3,500.
O70 O8 $10 green & black — 4,500. / 7,500.
Never hinged — 10,500.
No gum — 2,500.
O71 O8 $20 green & black — 5,000. / 5,500.
Never hinged — 11,500.
No gum — 2,250.

No. O71 used is valued with a blue or red handstamp favor cancel. Nos. O68-O71 with pen cancels sell for approximately 25-40% of the values shown.

TREASURY

O9

1873

O72	O9 1c brown	120.00	10.00
	Never hinged	250.00	
	No gum	45.00	
	On cover		100.00
O73	O9 2c brown	125.00	8.00
	Never hinged	275.00	
	No gum	45.00	
	On cover		75.00
O74	O9 3c brown	110.00	2.00
	Never hinged	230.00	
	No gum	40.00	
	On cover		100.00
a.	Double impression		5,000.
O75	O9 6c brown	120.00	4.00
	Never hinged	250.00	
	No gum	45.00	
	On cover		75.00
O76	O9 7c brown	250.00	35.00
	Never hinged	550.00	
	No gum	95.00	
	On cover		750.00
O77	O9 10c brown	240.00	12.00
	Never hinged	525.00	
	No gum	90.00	
	On cover		450.00
O78	O9 12c brown	300.00	10.00
	Never hinged	650.00	
	No gum	100.00	
	On cover		600.00
O79	O9 15c brown	300.00	12.00
	Never hinged	650.00	
	No gum	100.00	
	On cover		850.00
O80	O9 24c brown	675.00	100.00
	Never hinged	—	
	No gum	270.00	
O81	O9 30c brown	400.00	12.00
	Never hinged	—	
	No gum	140.00	
	On cover		5,000.
O82	O9 90c brown	400.00	15.00
	Never hinged	—	
	No gum	140.00	

Nos. O72-O82 (11) 3,040. 220.00

WAR

O10

1873

O83	O10 1c rose	240.00	15.00
	Never hinged	525.00	
	No gum	90.00	
	On cover		140.00
O84	O10 2c rose	240.00	15.00
	Never hinged	525.00	
	No gum	90.00	
	On cover		70.00
O85	O10 3c rose	240.00	5.00
	Never hinged	525.00	
	No gum	90.00	
	On cover		40.00
O86	O10 6c rose	625.00	10.00
	Never hinged	1,350.	
	No gum	250.00	
	On cover		60.00
O87	O10 7c rose	160.00	90.00
	Never hinged	360.00	
	No gum	80.00	
	On cover		2,000.
O88	O10 10c rose	140.00	25.00
	Never hinged	300.00	
	No gum	45.00	
	On cover		2,000.
O89	O10 12c rose	275.00	12.00
	Never hinged	600.00	
	No gum	110.00	
	On cover		450.00
O90	O10 15c rose	85.00	15.00
	Never hinged	190.00	
	No gum	30.00	
	On cover		3,250.
O91	O10 24c rose	85.00	12.00
	Never hinged	190.00	
	No gum	30.00	
	On cover		20,000.
O92	O10 30c rose	130.00	12.00
	Never hinged	275.00	
	No gum	45.00	
	On cover		20,000.
O93	O10 90c rose	225.00	60.00
	Never hinged	500.00	
	No gum	80.00	
	On parcel label		3,500.

Nos. O83-O93 (11) 2,445. 271.00

Printed by the American Bank Note Co.

1879   Soft Porous Paper

AGRICULTURE

O94	O1 1c yel, no gum	6,000.	
O95	O1 3c yellow	550.00	150.00
	Never hinged	1,250.	
	No gum	240.00	

INTERIOR

O96	O3 1c vermilion	300.00	275.00
	Never hinged	550.00	
	No gum	160.00	
O97	O3 2c vermilion	10.00	3.00
	Never hinged	17.50	
	No gum	3.00	
	On cover		150.00
O98	O3 3c vermilion	10.00	3.00
	Never hinged	22.50	
	No gum	3.00	
	On cover		30.00

O99	O3 6c vermilion	10.00	12.50
	Never hinged	17.50	
	No gum	3.00	
	On cover		200.00
O100	O3 10c vermilion	110.00	75.00
	Never hinged	250.00	
	No gum	60.00	
	On cover		1,200.
O101	O3 12c vermilion	230.00	115.00
	Never hinged	525.00	
	No gum	130.00	
	On cover		—
O102	O3 15c pale vermilion	400.00	260.00
	Never hinged	900.00	
	No gum	200.00	
	On cover		6,500.
O103	O3 24c pale vermilion	4,500.	—
	Never hinged	10,000.	
	No gum	2,100.	

Nos. O96-O103 (8) 5,570. 743.50

JUSTICE

O106	O4 3c bluish pur	190.00	125.00
	Never hinged	425.00	
	No gum	80.00	
	On cover		1,250.
O107	O4 6c bluish pur	475.00	300.00
	Never hinged	1,050.	
	No gum	210.00	
	On cover		1,000.

No. O107 on cover is unique, but the stamp is damaged. It is valued thus.

POST OFFICE

O108	O6 3c black	30.00	10.00
	Never hinged	70.00	
	No gum	10.00	
	On cover		—

TREASURY

O109	O9 3c brown	80.00	10.00
	Never hinged	175.00	
	No gum	35.00	
	On cover		110.00
O110	O9 6c brown	200.00	50.00
	Never hinged	450.00	
	No gum	65.00	
	On cover		300.00
O111	O9 10c brown	260.00	80.00
	Never hinged	575.00	
	No gum	90.00	
	On cover		750.00
O112	O9 30c brown	2,400.	425.00
	Never hinged	—	
	No gum	875.00	
O113	O9 90c brown	5,500.	750.00
	Never hinged	—	
	No gum	2,000.	

Nos. O109-O113 (5) 8,440. 1,315.

WAR

O114	O10 1c rose red	6.00	4.00
	Never hinged	11.00	
	No gum	2.50	
	On cover		55.00
O115	O10 2c rose red	12.00	4.00
	Never hinged	22.50	
	No gum	4.00	
	On cover		40.00
	Purple		+.50
O116	O10 3c rose red	12.00	2.00
	Never hinged	22.50	
	No gum	4.00	
	On cover		35.00
a.	Imperf., pair	5,000.	
b.	Double impression	7,500.	
O117	O10 6c rose red	11.00	3.00
	Never hinged	20.00	
	No gum	4.00	
	On cover		50.00

Cancellations

O118	O10 10c rose red	65.00	50.00
	Never hinged	120.00	
	No gum	26.00	
	On cover		1,800.
O119	O10 12c rose red	60.00	14.00
	Never hinged	110.00	
	No gum	20.00	
	On cover		—
O120	O10 30c rose red	225.00	100.00
	Never hinged	450.00	
	No gum	90.00	

Nos. O114-O120 (7) 391.00 177.00

SPECIAL PRINTINGS

Special printings of Official stamps were made in 1875 at the time the other Reprints, Re-issues and Special Printings were printed. They are ungummed.

Although perforated, these stamps were sometimes (but not always) cut apart with scissors. As a result the perforations may be mutilated and the design damaged.

All values exist imperforate.

Printed by the Continental Bank Note Co.

Overprinted in Block Letters

SPECIMEN

Type D
AGRICULTURE
Carmine Overprint

1875   *Perf. 12*
Thin, hard white paper

O1S	D 1c yellow	32.50	
a.	"Specimen" error	2,500.	
b.	Horiz. ribbed paper	37.50	
c.	As "b," small dotted "i" in "Specimen"	500.00	
O2S	D 2c yellow	55.00	
a.	"Sepcimen" error	3,000.	
O3S	D 3c yellow	400.00	
a.	"Sepcimen" error	12,500.	
O4S	D 6c yellow	400.00	
a.	"Sepcimen" error	20,000.	
O5S	D 10c yellow	400.00	
a.	"Sepcimen" error	17,500.	
O6S	D 12c yellow	400.00	
a.	"Sepcimen" error	12,500.	
O7S	D 15c yellow	400.00	
a.	"Sepcimen" error	12,500.	
O8S	D 24c yellow	400.00	
a.	"Sepcimen" error	12,500.	
O9S	D 30c yellow	400.00	
a.	"Sepcimen" error	13,500.	

Nos. O1S-O9S (9) 2,887.

EXECUTIVE
Blue Overprint

O10S	D 1c carmine	32.50	
a.	Horiz. ribbed paper	40.00	
b.	As "a," small dotted "i" in "Specimen"	500.00	
O11S	D 2c carmine	55.00	
O12S	D 3c carmine	67.50	
O13S	D 6c carmine	67.50	
O14S	D 10c carmine	67.50	

Nos. O10S-O14S (5) 290.00

INTERIOR
Blue Overprint

O15S	D 1c vermilion	60.00	
O16S	D 2c vermilion	140.00	
a.	"Sepcimen" error	12,500.	
O17S	D 3c vermilion	2,500.	
O18S	D 6c vermilion	2,500.	
O19S	D 10c vermilion	2,500.	
O20S	D 12c vermilion	2,500.	
O21S	D 15c vermilion	2,500.	
O22S	D 24c vermilion	2,500.	
O23S	D 30c vermilion	2,500.	
O24S	D 90c vermilion	2,500.	

Nos. O15S-O24S (10) 20,200.

JUSTICE
Blue Overprint

O25S	D 1c purple	32.50	
a.	"Sepcimen" error	1,900.	
b.	Horiz. ribbed paper	35.00	
c.	As "b," small dotted "i" in "Specimen"	500.00	
O26S	D 2c purple	55.00	
a.	"Sepcimen" error	2,500.	
O27S	D 3c purple	1,250.	
a.	"Sepcimen" error	11,000.	
O28S	D 6c purple	1,250.	
O29S	D 10c purple	1,250.	
O30S	D 12c purple	1,250.	
a.	"Sepcimen" error	17,500.	
O31S	D 15c purple	1,250.	
a.	"Sepcimen" error	17,500.	
O32S	D 24c purple	1,250.	
a.	"Sepcimen" error	20,000.	
O33S	D 30c purple	1,250.	
a.	"Sepcimen" error	15,000.	
O34S	D 90c purple	1,250.	

Nos. O25S-O34S (10) 10,087.

NAVY
Carmine Overprint

O35S	D 1c ultramarine	35.00	
a.	"Sepcimen" error	2,500.	
b.	Double "Specimen" overprint	1,900.	
O36S	D 2c ultramarine	75.00	
a.	"Sepcimen" error	3,250.	
O37S	D 3c ultramarine	1,400.	
O38S	D 6c ultramarine	1,400.	
O39S	D 7c ultramarine	550.00	
a.	"Sepcimen" error	10,000.	
O40S	D 10c ultramarine	1,400.	
a.	"Sepcimen" error	17,500.	
O41S	D 12c ultramarine	1,400.	
a.	"Sepcimen" error	17,500.	
O42S	D 15c ultramarine	1,400.	
a.	"Sepcimen" error	15,000.	
O43S	D 24c ultramarine	1,400.	
a.	"Sepcimen" error	15,000.	
O44S	D 30c ultramarine	1,400.	
a.	"Sepcimen" error	17,500.	
O45S	D 90c ultramarine	1,400.	

Nos. O35S-O45S (11) 11,860.

POST OFFICE
Carmine Overprint

O47S	D 1c black	45.00	
a.	"Sepcimen" error	2,750.	
b.	Inverted overprint	2,750.	
O48S	D 2c black	325.00	
a.	"Sepcimen" error	9,000.	
O49S	D 3c black	1,600.	
a.	"Sepcimen" error	—	
O50S	D 6c black	1,600.	
O51S	D 10c black	1,100.	
a.	"Sepcimen" error	15,000.	
O52S	D 12c black	1,600.	
O53S	D 15c black	1,600.	
a.	"Sepcimen" error	20,000.	
O54S	D 24c black	1,600.	
a.	"Sepcimen" error	20,000.	
O55S	D 30c black	1,600.	
O56S	D 90c black	1,600.	
a.	"Sepcimen" error	20,000.	

Nos. O47S-O56S (10) 12,670.

STATE
Carmine Overprint

O57S	D 1c bluish green	32.50	
a.	"Sepcimen" error	1,900.	
b.	Horiz. ribbed paper	35.00	
c.	As "b," small dotted "i" in "Specimen"	550.00	
d.	Double "Specimen" overprint	3,850.	
O58S	D 2c bluish green	90.00	
a.	"Sepcimen" error	2,500.	
O59S	D 3c bluish green	140.00	
a.	"Sepcimen" error	6,000.	
O60S	D 6c bluish green	350.00	
a.	"Sepcimen" error	11,000.	
O61S	D 7c bluish green	140.00	
a.	"Sepcimen" error	8,250.	
O62S	D 10c bluish green	550.00	
a.	"Sepcimen" error	17,500.	
O63S	D 12c bluish green	550.00	
a.	"Sepcimen" error	17,500.	
O64S	D 15c bluish green	600.00	
O65S	D 24c bluish green	600.00	
a.	"Sepcimen" error	17,500.	
O66S	D 30c bluish green	600.00	
a.	"Sepcimen" error	17,500.	
O67S	D 90c bluish green	600.00	
a.	"Sepcimen" error	15,000.	
O68S	D $2 green & blk	25,000.	
O69S	D $5 green & blk	30,000.	
O70S	D $10 green & blk	60,000.	
O71S	D $20 green & blk	100,000.	

Nos. O57S-O67S (11) 4,252.

TREASURY
Blue Overprint

O72S	D 1c dark brown	80.00	
O73S	D 2c dark brown	450.00	
O74S	D 3c dark brown	1,600.	
O75S	D 6c dark brown	1,600.	
O76S	D 7c dark brown	950.00	
O77S	D 10c dark brown	1,600.	
O78S	D 12c dark brown	1,600.	
O79S	D 15c dark brown	1,600.	
O80S	D 24c dark brown	1,600.	
O81S	D 30c dark brown	1,600.	
O82S	D 90c dark brown	1,650.	

Nos. O72S-O82S (11) 14,330.

WAR
Blue Overprint

O83S	D 1c deep rose	35.00	
a.	"Sepcimen" error	2,750.	
O84S	D 2c deep rose	125.00	
a.	"Sepcimen" error	3,250.	
O85S	D 3c deep rose	1,300.	
a.	"Sepcimen" error	25,000.	
O86S	D 6c deep rose	1,300.	
a.	"Sepcimen" error	27,500.	
O87S	D 7c deep rose	425.00	
a.	"Sepcimen" error	17,500.	
O88S	D 10c deep rose	1,400.	
a.	"Sepcimen" error	30,000.	
O89S	D 12c deep rose	1,400.	
a.	"Sepcimen" error	30,000.	
O90S	D 15c deep rose	1,400.	
a.	"Sepcimen" error	30,000.	
O91S	D 24c deep rose	1,400.	
a.	"Sepcimen" error	30,000.	
O92S	D 30c deep rose	1,400.	
a.	"Sepcimen" error	30,000.	
O93S	D 90c deep rose	1,400.	
a.	"Sepcimen" error	30,000.	

Nos. O83S-O93S (11) 11,585.

Printed by the American Bank Note Co.
SOFT POROUS PAPER
EXECUTIVE

1881   **Blue Overprint**

O10xS	D 1c violet rose	95.00

NAVY
Carmine Overprint

O35xS	D 1c gray blue	100.00
a.	Double overprint	1,200.

STATE

O57xS	D 1c yellow green	180.00

OFFICIAL POSTAL SAVINGS MAIL

These stamps were used to prepay postage on official correspondence of the Postal Savings Division of the POD. Discontinued Sept. 23, 1914.

O11

Printed by the Bureau of Engraving & Printing

1910-11   Engr.   Wmk. 191

O121	O11 2c black	17.50	2.00
	Never hinged	40.00	
	On cover		12.50
O122	O11 50c dark green	160.00	60.00
	Never hinged	375.00	
	On cover		225.00
O123	O11 $1 ultramarine	200.00	15.00
	Never hinged	450.00	

	On cover			110.00
	Wmk. 190			
O124	O11	1c dark violet	10.00	2.00
	Never hinged		22.50	
	On cover			15.00
	Never hinged		350.00	
O125	O11	2c black	55.00	7.00
	Never hinged		106.00	
	On cover			25.00
O126	O11	10c carmine	20.00	2.00
	Never hinged		50.00	
	On cover			20.00
	Nos. O121-O126 (6)		462.50	88.00

NEWSPAPER STAMPS

For the prepayment of postage on bulk shipments of newspapers and periodicals. From 1875 on, the stamps were affixed to pages of receipt books, sometimes canceled and retained by the post office. Discontinued on July 1, 1898.

Virtually all used stamps of Nos. PR1-PR4 are canceled by blue brush strokes. All are rare. Most used stamps of Nos. PR9-PR32, PR57-PR79 and PR81-PR89 are pen canceled (or uncanceled), with some of Nos. PR9-PR32 also known canceled by a thick blue brush stroke.

Handstamp cancellations on any of these issues are rare and sell for much more than catalogue values which are for pen-canceled examples.

Used values for Nos. PR90-PR125 are for stamps with handstamp cancellations.

Washington — N1

Franklin — N2

Lincoln — N3

Values for Nos. PR1-PR8 are for examples with perforations on all four sides. Examples with natural straight edges sell for somewhat less. Some panes were fully perforated, while others have natural straight edges either at top or bottom affecting five stamps in the pane of ten.

Printed by the National Bank Note Co.
Typographed and Embossed
1865   Unwmk.   *Perf. 12*
Thin hard paper, without gum
Size of design: 51x95mm
Colored Border

PR1	N1	5c dark blue	750.00	*2,000.*
a.		5c light blue	1,250.	*4,250.*
PR2	N2	10c blue green	300.00	*2,000.*
a.		10c green	300.00	*2,000.*
b.		Pelure paper	400.00	*2,000.*
PR3	N3	25c orange red	400.00	*2,500.*
a.		25c carmine red	425.00	*2,500.*
b.		Pelure paper	450.00	

Nos. PR1-PR3 used are valued with faults.

White Border
Yellowish paper

PR4	N1	5c light blue	600.00	*5,000.*
a.		5c dark blue	600.00	—
b.		Pelure paper	650.00	—
	Nos. PR1-PR4 (4)		2,050.	

No. PR4 used is valued with faults.

REPRINTS of 1865 ISSUE
Printed by the Continental Bank Note Co. using the original National Bank Note Co. plates
1875   *Perf. 12*
Hard white paper, without gum
5c White Border, 10c and 25c Colored Border

PR5	N1	5c dull blue	225.00
a.		Printed on both sides	*5,750.*
PR6	N2	10c dark bluish green	250.00
a.		Printed on both sides	*4,250.*
PR7	N3	25c dark carmine	300.00
	Nos. PR5-PR7 (3)		775.00

The 5c has white border, 10c and 25c have colored borders.

Many fakes exist of Nos. PR1-PR7, some of high quality. Certification is highly recommended.

The Continental Bank Note Co. made another special printing from new plates, which did not have the colored border. These exist imperforate and perforated, but they were not regularly issued. Value, imperf. set $3,750.

Printed by the American Bank Note Co.
Soft porous paper, without gum
White Border
1881

PR8	N1	5c dark blue	650.00

Statue of Freedom — N4

"Justice" — N5

Ceres — N6

"Victory" — N7

Clio — N8

Minerva — N9

Vesta — N10

"Peace" N11

"Commerce" N12

Hebe — N13

Indian Maiden — N14

Values for used examples of Nos. PR9-PR113 are for fine-very fine examples for denominations to $3, and fine for denominations of $5 or higher. Used examples of some Scott numbers might not exist without faults.

Printed by the Continental Bank Note Co.
Size of design: 24x35mm
1875, Jan. 1   Engr.
Thin hard paper

PR9	N4	2c black	300.00	40.00
	No gum		120.00	
PR10	N4	3c black	300.00	45.00
	No gum		120.00	
PR11	N4	4c black	300.00	40.00
	No gum		120.00	
PR12	N4	6c black	300.00	45.00
	No gum		120.00	

PR13	N4	8c black	350.00	65.00
	No gum		135.00	
PR14	N4	9c black	500.00	125.00
	No gum		185.00	
PR15	N4	10c black	375.00	60.00
	No gum		135.00	
PR16	N5	12c rose	600.00	100.00
	No gum		325.00	
PR17	N5	24c rose	850.00	125.00
	No gum		350.00	
PR18	N5	36c rose	850.00	150.00
	No gum		350.00	
PR19	N5	48c rose	1,250.	400.00
	No gum		450.00	
PR20	N5	60c rose	1,250.	115.00
	No gum		450.00	
PR21	N5	72c rose	1,500.	375.00
	No gum		550.00	
PR22	N5	84c rose	1,850.	375.00
	No gum		650.00	
PR23	N5	96c rose	1,350.	250.00
	No gum		525.00	
PR24	N6	$1.92 dk brn	1,650.	250.00
	No gum		650.00	
PR25	N7	$3 ver	1,800.	450.00
	No gum		700.00	
PR26	N8	$6 ultra	3,600.	550.00
	No gum		1,400.	
PR27	N9	$9 yel org	4,000.	*2,000.*
	No gum		1,400.	
PR28	N10	$12 bl grn	4,500.	*1,100.*
	No gum		1,750.	
PR29	N11	$24 dk gray vio	4,750.	*1,200.*
	No gum		1,850.	
PR30	N12	$36 brn rose	5,000.	*1,400.*
	No gum		2,000.	
PR31	N13	$48 red brn	7,000.	*1,600.*
	No gum		2,600.	
PR32	N14	$60 violet	6,500.	*1,750.*
	No gum		2,400.	

SPECIAL PRINTING of 1875 ISSUE
Printed by the Continental Bank Note Co.
Hard white paper, without gum
1875

PR33	N4	2c gray black	650.00
a.		Horiz. ribbed paper	500.00
PR34	N4	3c gray black	650.00
a.		Horiz. ribbed paper	500.00
PR35	N4	4c gray black	700.00
		Horiz. ribbed paper	1,000.
PR36	N4	6c gray black	900.00
PR37	N4	8c gray black	975.00
PR38	N4	9c gray black	1,050.
PR39	N4	10c gray black	1,400.
PR40	N5	12c pale rose	1,500.
PR41	N5	24c pale rose	2,100.
PR42	N5	36c pale rose	2,800.
PR43	N5	48c pale rose	4,000.
PR44	N5	60c pale rose	4,000.
PR45	N5	72c pale rose	4,500.
PR46	N5	84c pale rose	5,500.
PR47	N5	96c pale rose	8,500.
PR48	N6	$1.92 dk bn	22,500.
PR49	N7	$3 vermilion	45,000.
PR50	N8	$6 ultra	80,000.
PR51	N9	$9 yellow org	250,000.
PR52	N10	$12 blue green	125,000.
PR53	N11	$24 dk gray vio	500,000.
PR54	N12	$36 brn rose	250,000.
PR55	N13	$48 red brown	—
PR56	N14	$60 violet	—

Although four examples of No. PR51 were sold, only one is currently documented.

No. PR54 is valued in the grade of fine.

Although two stamps were sold, only one is currently documented.

All values of this issue, Nos. PR33 to PR56, exist imperforate but were not regularly issued thus. Value, set $60,000.

Printed by the American Bank Note Co.
Soft porous paper
1879   Unwmk.   *Perf. 12*

PR57	N4	2c black	75.00	15.00
	No gum		30.00	
PR58	N4	3c black	85.00	20.00
	No gum		35.00	
PR59	N4	4c black	85.00	20.00
	No gum		35.00	
a.		Double paper	—	
PR60	N4	6c black	125.00	35.00
	No gum		50.00	
PR61	N4	8c black	135.00	35.00
	No gum		55.00	
PR62	N4	10c black	135.00	35.00
	No gum		55.00	
PR63	N5	12c red	500.00	125.00
	No gum		210.00	
PR64	N5	24c red	500.00	125.00
	No gum		210.00	
PR65	N5	36c red	1,000.	325.00
	No gum		475.00	
PR66	N5	48c red	1,000.	300.00
	No gum		450.00	
PR67	N5	60c red	1,000.	275.00
	No gum		450.00	
a.		Imperf., pair	*4,000.*	
PR68	N5	72c red	1,250.	425.00
	No gum		575.00	
PR69	N5	84c red	1,250.	350.00
	No gum		575.00	
PR70	N5	96c red	1,200.	275.00
	No gum		525.00	
PR71	N6	$1.92 pale brn	550.00	175.00
	No gum		225.00	
PR72	N7	$3 red ver	625.00	200.00
	No gum		250.00	

PR73 N8	$6 blue	1,050.	300.00
No gum		400.00	
PR74 N9	$9 orange	800.00	225.00
No gum		325.00	
PR75 N10	$12 yel grn	850.00	250.00
No gum		325.00	
PR76 N11	$24 dk vio	800.00	300.00
No gum		300.00	
PR77 N12	$36 Indian red	850.00	350.00
No gum		350.00	
PR78 N13	$48 yel brn	900.00	450.00
No gum		350.00	
PR79 N14	$60 purple	850.00	400.00
No gum		350.00	
Nos. PR57-PR70 (14)		8,340.	2,360.

See the Scott U.S. Specialized Catalogue Die and Plate Proof section for imperforates.

SPECIAL PRINTING of 1879 ISSUE
Printed by the American Bank Note Co. Without gum

1883

PR80 N4	2c intense black	1,700.	

REGULAR ISSUE
With gum

1885, July 1   Unwmk.   Perf. 12

PR81 N4	1c black	95.00	12.50
No gum		42.50	
PR82 N5	12c carmine	200.00	30.00
No gum		85.00	
PR83 N5	24c carmine	200.00	32.50
No gum		85.00	
PR84 N5	36c carmine	300.00	57.50
No gum		125.00	
PR85 N5	48c carmine	425.00	75.00
No gum		180.00	
PR86 N5	60c carmine	550.00	100.00
No gum		240.00	
PR87 N5	72c carmine	550.00	110.00
No gum		240.00	
PR88 N5	84c carmine	850.00	250.00
No gum		325.00	
PR89 N5	96c carmine	750.00	190.00
No gum		300.00	
Nos. PR81-PR89 (9)		3,920.	857.50

See the Scott U.S. Specialized Catalogue Die and Plate Proof section for imperforates.

Printed by the Bureau of Engraving and Printing

1894

Soft wove paper, with pale, whitish gum

PR90 N4	1c intense black	425.00	5,000.
Never hinged		1,000.	
No gum		175.00	
PR91 N4	2c intense black	500.00	
Never hinged		1,200.	
No gum		210.00	
PR92 N4	4c intense black	550.00	13,500.
Never hinged		1,400.	
No gum		225.00	
PR93 N4	6c intense black	4,500.	
Never hinged		11,500.	
No gum		1,900.	
PR94 N4	10c intense black	1,200.	
No gum		525.00	
PR95 N5	12c pink	2,600.	4,500.
No gum		1,100.	
PR96 N5	24c pink	3,750.	4,750.
No gum		1,850.	
PR97 N5	36c pink	50,000.	
PR98 N5	60c pink	55,000.	16,000.
PR99 N5	96c pink	52,500.	
PR100 N7	$3 scarlet	60,000.	—
PR101 N8	$6 pale blue	60,000.	
No gum		30,000.	

Nos. PR90, PR95-PR98 used are valued with fine centering and small faults.

No. PR97 unused is valued in the grade of very good to fine. No. PR98 unused is valued in the grade of fine. Nos. PR99-PR100 unused are valued in the grade of fine-very fine.

"Statue of Freedom N15"

"Justice" N16

"Victory" — N17

Clio — N18

Vesta — N19

"Peace" — N20

"Commerce" N21

Indian Maiden N22

1895, Feb. 1
Size of designs: 1c-50c, 21x34mm
$2-$100, 24x35mm

PR102 N15	1c black	230.00	125.00
Never hinged		500.00	
No gum		90.00	
PR103 N15	2c black	230.00	125.00
Never hinged		500.00	
No gum		90.00	
PR104 N15	5c black	300.00	300.00
Never hinged		650.00	
No gum		125.00	
PR105 N15	10c black	550.00	400.00
Never hinged		1,150.	
No gum		225.00	
PR106 N16	25c car	750.00	500.00
Never hinged		1,650.	
No gum		300.00	
PR107 N16	50c car	2,750.	800.00
Never hinged		6,250.	
No gum		875.00	
PR108 N17	$2 scarlet	1,500.	1,100.
Never hinged		3,250.	
No gum		575.00	
PR109 N18	$5 ultra	2,100.	1,750.
Never hinged		4,500.	
No gum		800.00	
PR110 N19	$10 green	2,500.	2,000.
Never hinged		5,250.	
No gum		900.00	
PR111 N20	$20 slate	3,250.	2,500.
Never hinged		6,750.	
No gum		1,200.	
PR112 N21	$50 dull rose	2,900.	750.00
Never hinged		6,250.	
No gum		1,100.	
PR113 N22	$100 purple	3,500.	7,000.
Never hinged		7,250.	
No gum		1,400.	
Nos. PR102-PR113 (12)		20,560.	17,350.

1895-97   Wmk. 191

PR114 N15	1c black	8.00	25.00
Never hinged		20.00	
No gum		2.75	
PR115 N15	2c black	8.00	25.00
Never hinged		20.00	
No gum		2.75	
PR116 N15	5c black	13.00	40.00
Never hinged		27.50	
No gum		4.25	
PR117 N15	10c black	13.00	25.00
Never hinged		27.50	
No gum		4.25	
PR118 N16	25c carmine	20.00	65.00
Never hinged		45.00	
No gum		7.00	
PR119 N16	50c carmine	25.00	75.00
Never hinged		55.00	
No gum		8.50	
PR120 N17	$2 scarlet	30.00	110.00
Never hinged		75.00	
No gum		10.00	
PR121 N18	$5 dark bl	40.00	175.00
Never hinged		100.00	
No gum		13.50	
a.	$5 light blue	200.00	500.00
Never hinged		500.00	
No gum		67.50	
PR122 N19	$10 green	42.50	160.00
Never hinged		105.00	
No gum		14.00	
PR123 N20	$20 slate	45.00	180.00
Never hinged		110.00	
No gum		15.00	

PR124 N21	$50 dull rose	75.00	225.00
Never hinged		170.00	
No gum		27.50	
PR125 N22	$100 purple	65.00	240.00
Never hinged		150.00	
No gum		22.50	
Nos. PR114-PR125 (12)		384.50	1,345.
Nos. PR114-PR125, never hinged		905.00	

In 1899 the Government sold 26,989 sets of these stamps, but, as the stock of high values was not sufficient to make up the required number, an additional printing was made of the $5, $10, $20, $50 and $100. These are virtually indistinguishable from earlier printings.

For overprints, see Nos. R159-R160.

PARCEL POST STAMPS

Issued for the prepayment of postage on parcel post packages only.

Post Office Clerk — PP1

City Carrier PP2

Railway Postal Clerk — PP3

Rural Carrier PP4

Mail Train — PP5

Steamship and Mail Tender PP6

Automobile Service PP7

Airplane Carrying Mail — PP8

Manufacturing — PP9

Dairying PP10

Harvesting PP11

Fruit Growing PP12

1913   Wmk. 190   Engr.   Perf. 12

Q1 PP1	1c carmine rose	4.50	1.75
Never hinged		11.00	
On cover, 1913-25			6.00
Q2 PP2	2c carmine rose	5.25	1.40
Never hinged		12.50	
On cover, 1913-25			5.75
a.	2c lake	1,750.	
b.	2c carmine lake	350.00	

No. Q2a is valued in the grade of fine to very fine.

Q3 PP3	3c carmine	9.50	6.50
Never hinged		26.00	
On cover, 1913-25			19.00
Q4 PP4	4c carmine rose	30.00	3.50
Never hinged		85.00	
On cover, 1913-25			65.00
Q5 PP5	5c carmine rose	25.00	2.50
Never hinged		67.50	
On cover, 1913-25			42.50
Q6 PP6	10c carmine rose	42.50	3.50
Never hinged		95.00	
On cover, 1913-25			55.00
Q7 PP7	15c carmine rose	62.50	15.00
Never hinged		175.00	
On cover, 1913-25			400.00
Q8 PP8	20c carmine rose	120.00	30.00
Never hinged		280.00	
On cover, 1913-25			850.00
Q9 PP9	25c carmine rose	57.50	8.50
Never hinged		160.00	
On cover, 1913-25			300.00
Q10 PP10	50c carmine rose	235.00	50.00
Never hinged		600.00	
On cover, 1913-25			—
Q11 PP11	75c carmine rose	85.00	40.00
Never hinged		200.00	
On cover, 1913-25			—
Q12 PP12	$1 carmine rose	280.00	45.00
Never hinged		650.00	
On cover, 1913-25			1,250.
Nos. Q1-Q12 (12)		956.75	207.65
Nos. Q1-Q12, never hinged		2,468.	

PARCEL POST POSTAGE DUE STAMPS

For affixing by a postal clerk to any parcel post package, to denote the amount to be collected from the addressee because of insufficient pre-payment of postage.

PPD1

1913   Wmk. 190   Engr.   Perf. 12

JQ1 PPD1	1c dark green	8.50	4.25
Never hinged		21.00	
On cover, 1913-25			160.00
JQ2 PPD1	2c dark green	65.00	18.00
Never hinged		160.00	
On cover, 1913-25			225.00
JQ3 PPD1	5c dark green	10.00	5.00
Never hinged		25.00	
On cover, 1913-25			200.00
JQ4 PPD1	10c dark green	120.00	45.00
Never hinged		300.00	
On cover, 1913-25			650.00
JQ5 PPD1	25c dark green	75.00	4.75
Never hinged		190.00	
On cover, 1913-25			—
Never hinged		6,500.	
Nos. JQ1-JQ5 (5)		278.50	77.00
Nos. JQ1-JQ5, never hinged		696.00	

SPECIAL HANDLING STAMPS

For use on fourth-class mail to secure the same expeditious handling accorded to first-class mail matter.

PP13

FLAT PLATE PRINTING

1925-28   Engr.   Unwmk.   *Perf. 11*

QE1	PP13	10c yel grn ('28)	2.00	1.00
		Never hinged	4.25	
QE2	PP13	15c yel grn ('28)	2.25	.90
		Never hinged	4.75	
QE3	PP13	20c yel grn ('28)	3.75	1.50
		Never hinged	7.75	
QE4	PP13	25c dp grn ('25)	20.00	3.75
		Never hinged	37.50	
a.		yel grn ('28)	16.50	22.50
		Never hinged	32.50	
		Nos. QE1-QE4 (4)	28.00	7.15
		Nos. QE1-QE4, never hinged	54.25	

CARRIERS' STAMPS

GENERAL ISSUE CARRIER STAMPS

Issued by the U.S. Government to facilitate payment of fees for delivering and collecting letters.

Franklin — OC1

1851   Engr.   Unwmk.   *Imperf.*

LO1	OC1	(1c) dull blue, *rose*	7,000.	8,000.
		On cover from Philadelphia		17,500.
		On cover from New York		30,000.
		On cover from New Orleans with 3c #10 (a 2nd #LO1 removed)		30,000.
LO2	OC2	1c blue (shades)	50.00	80.00
		On cover, used alone		500.00
		On cover, precanceled		600.00
		On cover, pair or 2 singles		1,500.
		On cover with 1c #9		8,500.
		On cover with three 1c #9		4,500.
		On cover with 3c #11		400.
		On cover with 3c #25		
		On cover with 3c #26		600.
		On cover with strip of 3, 3c #26		—
		On cover with 5c #30A and 10c #32		33,000.
		On cover, tied by town handstamp, with 3c #65 (Washington, D.C.)		4,500.
		On 3c envelope #U1, #LO2 pen canceled		—
		On 3c envelope #U2, #LO2 pen canceled		—
		Pair on cover (Cincinnati)		1,250.

1875   *Imperf.*

LO3	OC1	(1c) blue, *rose*	50.

Perf. 12

LO4	OC1	(1c) blue	16,000.

No. LO4 is valued in the grade of average to fine.

Eagle Reprints
Imperf.

LO5	OC2	1c blue	25.

Perf. 12

LO6	OC2	1c blue	175.

Reprints of the Franklin Carrier are printed in dark blue, instead of the dull blue or deep blue of the originals. Two reprintings of 10,000 each were made in 1875 on the same rose paper as the originals. A third reprinting of 5,000 in 1881 is on soft wove paper.

The first two reprintings of 10,000 each of the Eagle carrier are on hard white paper, ungummed and sometimes perforated. A third reprinting of 10,000 stamps in 1881 is on soft wove paper. Originals are on yellowish paper with brown gum.

No. LO6 is valued with the perfs cutting slightly into the design.

CITY CARRIER DEPARTMENT STAMPS

Issued by officials or employees of the U.S. Government for the purpose of securing or indicating payment of carriers' fees.

All are imperforate.
Baltimore, Md.

C1

1850-55   Typo.
Settings of 10 (2x5) varieties

1LB1	C1	1c red, *bluish*	180.	160.
		On cover, tied by handstamp		1,000.
		On cover with 1c #9		
		On cover (tied) with 3c #11		500.
		On cover (tied) with 3c #11A		500.
1LB2	C1	1c blue, *bluish*	200.	150.
		On cover, tied		1,000.
		On cover (tied) with 3c #11		500.
		On cover, uncanceled, with 3c #11A		225.
a.		Bluish laid paper		
1LB3	C1	1c blue	160.	100.
		On cover, tied by handstamp		1,500.
		On cover, tied by ms.		250.
a.		Laid paper	200.	150.
		On cover, tied by handstamp		1,000.
b.		Block of 14 containing three tete-beche gutter pairs (unique)	4,000.	
1LB4	C1	1c green	—	1,000.
		On cover, tied by handstamp		5,000.
		On cover, not tied		1,200.
		On cover with 1c #7, tied by handstamp		2,250.
		On cover, not tied, with 3c #10A		2,000.
		On cover with 3c #11, ms. tied		—
		On 3c envelope #U10		3,500.
1LB5	C1	1c red	2,250.	1,750.
		On cover, tied by handstamp		4,500.
		On cover, not tied		3,000.
		On cover (tied) with 3c #10 or 10A		5,000.

C2

1856   Typo.

1LB6	C2	1c blue (shades)	130.	90.
		On cover		400.
		On cover with 3c #11 or 11A		1,000.
		On cover with 3c #25 (both tied)		1,350.
		On cover with 3c #26		1,250.
		On cover with 3c #26A		
1LB7	C2	1c red (shades)	130.	90.
		On cover		300.
		On cover (tied) with 3c #25		350.
		On cover (tied) with 3c #26		350.

C3

Plate of 10 (2x5); 10 Varieties

The sheet consisted of at least four panes of 10 placed horizontally, the two center panes tete beche. This makes possible five horizontal tete beche gutter pairs.

1857   Typo.

1LB8	C3	1c black (shades)	65.	50.
		On cover, tied by handstamp		125.
		On cover (tied) with 3c #26		225.
		On 3c envelope #U9, tied		225.
		On 3c envelope #U10		225.
		Strip of 3 (not tied), on cover		4,000.
a.		"SENT"	100.	75.
		On cover, tied by handstamp		175.
		On cover (tied) with 3c #26		250.
		On 3c envelope #U9, tied		250.
		On 3c envelope #U10, tied		250.
b.		Short rays	100.	75.
		On cover (tied) with 3c #26		600.
1LB9	C3	1c red	100.	90.
		On cover		175.
		On cover (tied) with 3c #26		300.
		On 3c envelope #U9		325.
		On 3c envelope #U10		325.
a.		"SENT"	140.	110.
		On cover (tied) with 3c #26		500.
b.		Short rays	140.	110.
c.		As "b," double impression		800.

Boston, Mass.

C6

Several Varieties

1849-50   Pelure Paper   Typeset

3LB1	C6	1c blue	375.	180.
		On cover, tied by handstamp		300.
		On cover, uncanceled		150.
		On cover with 5c #1		4,500.
		On cover with two 5c #1		8,750.
		On cover with 3c #10		450.
a.		Wrong ornament at left		400.
		On cover, not tied, with certificate		—

C7

1851   Typeset
Several Varieties
Wove Paper Colored Through

3LB2	C7	1c blue (shades), *slate*	190.	100.
		On cover		220.
		On cover with 5c #1		12,500.
		On cover with 3c #10		500.
		On cover with 3c #11A		325.
		On 3c envelope #U2, #U5 or #U9		350.

Charleston, S. C.
Honour's City Express

C8

1849   Typo.
Wove Paper Colored Through

4LB1	C8	2c blk, *brn rose*	10,000.	
		Cut to shape	4,000.	4,000.
		On cover, not canceled, with certificate		17,000.
		On cover, cut to shape, tied, with 10c #2		40,000.
4LB2	C8	2c blk, *yel*, cut to shape	—	
		On cover, not tied, with certificate		12,500.
		On cover, cut to shape, uncanceled		—
		On cover, rectangular-cut, tied, with 10c #2		—

No. 4LB1 unused is a unique uncanceled stamp on piece. The used cut-to-shape stamp is also unique. In addition two covers exist bearing No. 4LB1.

No. 4LB2 unused (uncanceled) off cover is unique; three known on cover.

See the Scott U.S. Specialized Catalogue.

4LB2A	C8	2c blk, *bl gray*, on cover, cut to shape	—	

No. 4LB2A is unique.

C10

1854   Wove Paper   Typeset

4LB3	C10	2c black	1,500.	
		On cover, tied by pen cancel		3,000.
		On cover with 3c #11 or 11A, tied		4,000.
		On cover with 3c #11 or 11A, not tied		3,250.

C11

Several Varieties

1849-50   Typeset
Wove Paper Colored Through

4LB5	C11	2c black, *bluish*, pelure	750.	500.
		On cover (not tied)		3,500.
		On cover with pair 5c #1b		
		On cover with two 5c #1b		
		On cover (tied) with 3c #11 or 11A		4,500.
a.		"Ceuts"	5,750.	

4LB7	C11	2c black, *yellow*	750.	1,000.
		On cover, tied by handstamp		9,000.
		On cover, not canceled		2,000.
a.		"Ccnts," ms. tied on cover		14,500.

No. 4LB5a is unique. It is without gum and is valued thus. No. 4LB7a also is unique.

C13

C14

C15

Several varieties of each type

1851-58   Typeset
Wove Paper Colored Through

4LB8	C13	2c black, *bluish*	350.	175.
		On cover, tied by handstamp		700.
		On cover, not tied		300.
		On cover with 10c #2		5,500.
		On cover, tied, with 3c #10		1,500.
		On cover, tied, with 3c #11 or 11A		1,500.
		On cover, tied, with 3c #26		1,500.
a.		Period after "PAID"	500.	250.
		On cover		650.
		On cover, ms. tied, with 3c #11 or 11A		750.
b.		"Cens"	700.	900.
		On cover, ms. tied, with 3c #11 or 11A		3,250.
c.		"Conours" and "Bents"		

The No. 4LB8 with No. 2 combination cover is unique. It is a cover front only and is valued thus.

4LB9	C13	2c black, *bluish*, pelure	850.	950.
4LB10	C13	2c black, *pink*, pelure, on cover	—	7,000.
4LB11	C14	(2c) black, *bluish*	—	375.
		On cover, tied by handstamp, with 3c #11 or 11A		12,500.
		On cover, ms. tied, with 3c #11 or 11A		3,000.
		On cover, tied, to foreign destination (Ireland), unique		25,000.
4LB12	C14	(2c) black, *bluish*, pelure		
4LB13	C15	(2c) black, *bluish* ('58)	750.	400.
		On cover with 3c #11A, Aiken, S.C. postmark, tied by handstamp (unique)		6,000.
		On cover with 3c #26, tied by pen cancel		4,500.
		On cover with 3c #26, tied by handstamp cancel		3,750.
a.		Comma after "PAID"	1,100.	
b.		No period after "Post"	1,400.	

Kingman's City Post

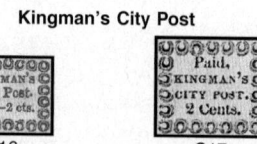

C16   C17

Several varieties of each

1851(?)-58(?)   Typeset
Wove Paper Colored Through

4LB14	C16	2c black, *bluish*	1,400.	900.
		On cover with 3c #11		7,000.
		On cover with 3c #26		6,000.
a.		"Kingman's" erased		5,000.
4LB15	C17	2c black, *bluish*	800.	800.
		On cover		—
a.		"Kingman's" erased, on cover with 3c #11, tied by pen cancel (unique)		4,500.

Martin's City Post

C18

Several varieties

1858   Typeset
Wove Paper Colored Through

4LB16	C18	2c black, *bluish*	8,000.	

Beckman's City Post
Same as C19, but inscribed
"Beckmann's City Post."

1860

4LB17 C19 2c black, on cover — —

No. 4LB17 is unique.

Steinmeyer's City Post

C19   C20

Several varieties of Type C19
Type C20 printed from plate of 10
(2x5) varieties

1859   **Typeset**
Wove Paper Colored Through

4LB18	C19 2c black, *bluish*	21,000.	
	On cover, uncanceled	—	
4LB19	C20 2c black, *bluish*	4,500.	—
4LB20	C20 2c black, *pink*	200.	—
4LB21	C20 2c black, *yellow*	200.	

Cincinnati, Ohio
Williams' City Post

C20a

1854   **Wove Paper**   **Litho.**

9LB1	C20a 2c brown	—	4,000.
	On cover, tied by handstamp		4,500.
	On cover, tied by pen cancel		7,500.
	On cover with 1c #9		

Cleveland, Ohio
Bishop's City Post

C20b   C20c

1854   **Wove Paper**   **Litho.**

10LB1	C20b blue	5,000.	4,000.
	On cover, tied by handstamp		15,000.
	Pair on cover, canceled by pencil, with 3c #11, with certificate		17,000.

Vertically Laid Paper

10LB2	C20c 2c black, *bluish*	4,000.	6,000.
	On cover		
	Pair on cover, canceled by pencil, with 3c #11		14,000.

No. 10LB2 unused is unique. It is cut in at
bottom and without gum, and is valued thus.

Louisville, Ky.
Wharton's U.S.P.O. Despatch

C21

1857   **Lithographed**

5LB1	C21 (2c) bluish green (shades)	125.	

Brown & McGill's U. S. P. O.
Despatch

C22

1858, Nov.-1860   **Lithographed**

5LB2	C22 (2c) blue (shades)	250.	750.
	On cover, not tied, with 3c #26		750.
	On cover with #26, tied by handstamp		6,250.

1858, Feb.-Aug.

5LB3	C22 (2c) black	4,500.	15,000.
	On cover, not tied, with 3c #26		17,500.

The value for No. 5LB3 used refers to the
finer of the two known used (canceled) examples; it is extremely fine and on a piece with a
3c #26.

New York, N. Y.
United States City Despatch Post

C23

Wove Paper Colored Through

1842   **Engr.**

6LB1	C23 3c black, *grayish*	2,000.	
	On cover, tied by handstamp		12,000.
	On cover, not tied		10,000.

Used examples are Carriers' stamps only
when canceled with the regular government
cancellation "U.S." in octagonal frame (see
illustration), "U.S.CITY DESPATCH POST," or
New York circular postmark.

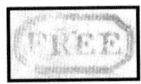

When canceled "FREE" in frame they were
used as local stamps. See No. 40L1 in the
Scott Specialized Catalogue of United States
Stamps.

C24

Wove Paper (unsurfaced) Colored
Through

1842-45

6LB2	C24 3c black, *rosy buff*	5,000.	
6LB3	C24 3c black, *light blue*	1,500.	750.
	On cover, tied by handstamp		2,500.
	On cover, not tied		1,000.
6LB4	C24 3c black, *green*	11,500.	

Some authorities consider No. 6LB2 to be
an essay, and No. 6LB4 a color changeling.
No. 6LB2 unused is valued without gum.

Glazed Paper, Surface Colored

6LB5		C24 3c black, *blue green* (shades)	200.	175.
		On cover, tied by handstamp		600.
		Five on cover		20,000.
a.		Double impression		1,500.
b.		3c black, *blue*	650.	300.
		On cover		750.
c.		As "b," double impression		850.
d.		3c black, *green black, apple green*	1,000.	750.
		On cover		2,000.
e.		As "d," double impression		1,250.
		On cover		—
6LB6		C24 3c black, *pink,* on cover front		14,500.

No. 6LB6 is unique.

No. 6LB5 Surcharged in Red — C25

1846   No. 6LB5 Surcharged in Red

6LB7	C25 2c on 3c black, *bluish grn,* on cover		14,000.

The City Despatch 2c red is listed in the
Scott U.S. Specialized Catalogue as a Local
stamp.

U.S. MAIL

C27

1849   **Typo.**
Wove Paper, Colored Through

6LB9	C27 1c black, *rose*	100.	100.
	On cover, tied by handstamp		350.
	On cover with 5c #1		2,000.

1849-50   **Glazed Surface Paper**

6LB10	C27 1c black, *yellow*	100.	100.
	On cover, tied by handstamp		350.
	On cover with 5c #1		1,500.
6LB11	C27 1c black, *buff*	100.	100.
	On cover		250.
	On cover, not tied, with 5c #1, with certificate		3,000.
a.	Pair, one stamp sideways		2,850.

Philadelphia, Pa.

C28

Several Varieties
Thick Wove Paper Colored Through

1849-50   **Typeset**

7LB1	C28 1c black, *rose* (with "L P")	450.	
	On cover, tied by handstamp		3,000.
	On cover, not canceled		2,000.
	On cover with 5c #1 or 1a		6,000.
7LB2	C28 1c black, *rose* (with "S")	3,000.	
	On cover, not canceled		4,500.
7LB3	C28 1c black, *rose* (with "H")	275.	
	On cover, tied by handstamp		3,750.
	On cover, not canceled		1,000.
	On cover with 5c #1		3,500.
7LB4	C28 1c black, *rose* (with "L S")	400.	500.
	On cover, not canceled		3,000.
7LB5	C28 1c black, *rose* (with "J J")	7,500.	
	On cover with 5c #1, uncanceled		70,000.

The unique used No. 7LB5 is an uncanceled
stamp on a cover front.

C29

Several Varieties

7LB6	C29 1c black, *rose*	300.	250.
	On cover, tied by handstamp		2,500.
	On cover, uncanceled		500.
7LB7	C29 1c black, *blue, glazed*	1,000.	
	On cover, tied by handstamp		6,500.
	On cover, uncanceled		1,250.
	On cover with 5c #1		3,500.
7LB8	C29 1c blk, *ver, glazed*	700.	
	On cover, tied by handstamp		1,500.
	On cover, uncanceled		900.
	On cover with 5c dark brown #1a, uncanceled		12,500.
	On cover with 5c orange brown #1b, uncanceled		21,000.
7LB9	C29 1c blk, *yel, glazed*	2,750.	2,250.
	On cover, not canceled		4,000.
	On cover with 3c #10, un-canceled		2,000.

Cancellations on Nos. 7LB1-7LB9: Normally
these stamps were left uncanceled on the letter, but occasionally were accidentally tied by
the Philadelphia town postmark which was
normally struck in blue ink.
A 1c black on buff (unglazed) of type C29 is
believed to be a color changeling.

C30

Settings of 25 (5x5) varieties (Five
basic types)

1850-52   **Litho.**

7LB11	C30 1c gold, *black, glazed*	175.	110.
	On cover, tied by handstamp		600.
	On cover, uncanceled		325.
	On cover (tied) with 5c #1		3,500.
	On cover (tied) with 3c #10		800.
	On cover (uncanceled) with 3c #10		250.
7LB12	C30 1c blue	400.	275.
	On cover, tied by handstamp		1,250.
	On cover, not tied		400.
	On cover (tied) with 3c #10		1,750.
	On cover (tied) with 3c #11		1,250.
7LB13	C30 1c black	750.	550.
	On cover, tied by handstamp		2,500.
	On cover, uncanceled		1,250.
	On cover (tied) with 3c #10		—
	On cover (not tied) with 3c #11		3,250.

25 varieties of C30.

C31

Handstamped

7LB14	C31 1c blue, *buff*	3,250.	

1855(?)

7LB16	C31 1c black	5,000.	
	On cover with strip of 3, 1c #9		—
	On cover with 3c 1851 stamp removed, tied by handstamp		7,000.

C32

1856(?)   **Handstamped**

7LB18	C32 1c black	1,250.	2,000.
	On cover (cut diamond-shaped) with pair 1c #7 and single 1c #9		—
	On cover with strip of 3, 1c #7		17,000.
	On cover with 3c #11		9,500.
	On 3c envelope #U5		
	On 3c envelope #U10, not canceled		9,000.

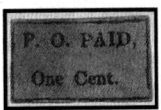

Labels of these designs are believed
by most specialists not to be carrier
stamps. Those seen are uncanceled,
either off cover or affixed to stampless
covers of the early 1850s. Some students believe they should be given carrier status.

St. Louis, Mo.

C36   C37

Illustrations enlarged to show details of the
two types (note upper corners especially).
Sizes of actual designs are 17 1/2x22mm.

1849   **White Wove Paper**   **Litho.**
Two Types

8LB1	C36 2c black	7,000.	3,000.
8LB2	C37 2c black	6,000.	—

Cancellation on Nos. 8LB1-8LB2: Black town.

C38

1857   **Litho.**
8LB3 C38 2c blue   *22,500.*
   On cover, tied by hand-
   stamp   *55,000.*

The used example off cover is unique. Five covers are recorded.
Cancellations on No. 8LB3: Black boxed "1ct," "Paid" in arc, black pen.

STAMPED ENVELOPES AND WRAPPERS

VALUES

Unless otherwise noted, values are for cut squares in a grade of very fine. Very fine cut squares will have the design well centered within moderately large margins. Precanceled cut squares must include the entire precancellation.

Values for unused entires are for those without printed or manuscript address. Values for letter sheets are for folded entires. Unfolded examples sell for more. A "full corner" includes back and side flaps and commands a premium.

Wrappers are listed with envelopes of corresponding designs, and indicated by prefix letter "W" instead of "U."

An ALBINO impression is where two or more envelope blanks are fed into the printing press. The one adjacent to the printing die receives the color and the embossing, while the others are embossed only. Albinos are printing errors and are sometimes worth more than normal, inked impressions. Because of the nature of the printing process, many albinos were produced, and most collectors will not pay much, or any, premium for most of them. Albinos of earlier issues, canceled while current, are scarce.

The papers of these issues vary greatly in texture, and in color from yellowish to bluish white and from amber to dark buff.

"+" Some authorities claim that Nos. U37, U48, U49, U110, U124, U125, U130, U133A, U137A, U137B, U137C, W138, U145, U162, U178A, U185, U220, U285, U286, U298, U299, UO3, UO32, UO38, UO45 and UO45A (each with "+" before number) were not regularly issued and are not known to have been used.

U1

"THREE" in short label with curved ends; 13mm wide at top. Twelve varieties.

Washington — U2

"THREE" in short label with straight ends; 15½mm wide at top. Three varieties.

U3

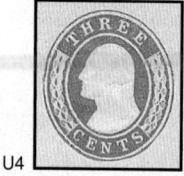

U4

"THREE" in short label with octagonal ends. Two varieties.

"THREE" in wide label with straight ends; 20mm wide at top.

U5

"THREE" in medium wide label with curved ends; 14½mm wide at top. Ten varieties. A sub-variety shows curved lines at either end of label omitted; both T's have longer cross stroke; R is smaller (20 varieties).

U6

Four varieties.

U7

"TEN" in short label; 15½mm wide at top.

U8

"TEN" in wide label; 20mm wide at top.

1853-55
On Diagonally Laid Paper (Early printings of No. U1 on Horizontally Laid Paper)

U1	U1	3c red	350.00	35.00
		Entire	1,600.	45.00
U2	U1	3c red, *buff*	90.00	30.00
		Entire	850.00	40.00
U3	U2	3c red	950.00	50.00
		Entire	3,500.	100.00
U4	U2	3c red, *buff*	425.00	45.00
		Entire	3,250.	95.00
U5	U3	3c red ('54)	5,750.	500.00
		Entire	26,000.	850.00
U6	U3	3c red, *buff* ('54)	4,250.	100.00
		Entire	—	150.00
U7	U4	3c red	5,000.	150.00
		Entire	—	325.00
U8	U4	3c red, *buff*	8,250.	175.00
		Entire	—	325.00
U9	U5	3c red ('54)	40.00	4.00
		Entire	140.00	11.00
U10	U5	3c red, *buff* ('54)	20.00	4.00
		Entire	70.00	6.00
U11	U6	6c red	300.00	90.00
		Entire	375.00	175.00
U12	U6	6c red, *buff*	145.00	90.00
		Entire	350.00	200.00
U13	U6	6c green	260.00	150.00
		Entire	575.00	400.00
U14	U6	6c green, *buff*	200.00	125.00
		Entire	375.00	225.00
U15	U7	10c green ('55)	425.00	100.00
		Entire	700.00	175.00
U16	U7	10c green, *buff* ('55)	175.00	90.00
		Entire	425.00	175.00
a.		10c pale green, *buff*	135.00	70.00
		Entire	375.00	125.00
U17	U8	10c green ('55)	375.00	140.00
		Entire	700.00	225.00
a.		10c pale green	275.00	125.00
		Entire	675.00	200.00

U18	U8	10c green, *buff* ('55)	375.00	100.00
		Entire	625.00	190.00
a.		10c pale green, *buff*	350.00	100.00
		Entire	600.00	190.00

Nos. U9, U10, U11, U12, U13, U14, U17, and U18 have been reprinted on white and buff papers, wove or vertically laid, and are not known entire. The originals are on diagonally laid paper. Value, set of 8 reprints on laid, $225. Reprints on wove sell for more.

The first printings of Nos. U1, U2, U3, U4 and U7 have G.F. Nesbitt crests printed on the envelope flaps. These sell for a premium. Such examples of Nos. U1-U4 with 1853-dated cancels sell for a very large premium.

No. U1 with watermark having a space between lines and on horizontally laid paper sells for a substantial premium.

U9

Period after "POSTAGE." (Eleven varieties.)

Franklin, Period after "POSTAGE." — U10

Bust touches inner frame-line at front and back.

No period after "POSTAGE" — U11

No period after "POSTAGE." (Two varieties.)

Washington — U12

Nine varieties of type U12.

Envelopes are on diagonally laid paper. Wrappers on vert. or horiz. laid paper, or on unwatermarked white paper (Nos. W22, W25).

1860-61

W18B	U9	1c blue ('61)	5,500.	
		Entire		
U19	U9	1c blue, *buff*	35.00	12.50
		Entire	85.00	30.00
W20	U9	1c bl, *buff* ('61)	65.00	50.00
		Entire	120.00	75.00
W21	U9	1c bl, *man* ('61)	55.00	45.00
		Entire	125.00	100.00
U21A	U9	1c bl, *org*		350.00
		Entire	1,800.	
W22	U9	1c bl, *org* ('61)	3,000.	
		Entire		
U23	U10	1c bl, *org*	625.00	350.00
		Entire	850.00	600.00
U24	U11	1c bl, *amb*	350.00	110.00
		Entire	700.00	350.00
W25	U11	1c bl, *man* ('61)	6,750.	1,750.
		Entire	17,500.	5,500.
U26	U12	3c red	27.50	17.50
		Entire	55.00	22.50
U27	U12	3c red, *buff*	22.50	12.50
		Entire	45.00	22.50
U28	U12+U9	3c +1c red & bl	250.00	225.00
		Entire	700.00	400.00
U29	U12+U9	3c +1c red & bl, *buff*	250.00	250.00
		Entire	700.00	450.00
U30	U12	6c red	2,500.	1,500.
		Entire	3,750.	
U31	U12	6c red, *buff*	3,500.	1,450.
		Entire	5,000.	15,000.
U32	U12	10c green	1,250.	450.00
		Entire	10,000.	650.00

U33	U12	10c green, *buff*	1,450.	400.00
		Entire	3,250.	600.00

Nos. U26, U27, U30 to U33 have been reprinted on the same vertically laid paper as the reprints of the 1853-55 issue, and are not known entire. Value, Nos. U26-U27, $75 each; Nos. U30-U33, $75 each.

U13

17 varieties for Nos. U34-U35; 2 varieties for No. U36.

U14

U15

Washington — U16

Envelopes are on diagonally laid paper.

U36 and U45 come on vertically or horizontally laid paper.

1861

U34	U13	3c pink	27.50	5.00
		Entire	60.00	12.50
U35	U13	3c pink, *buff*	32.50	6.00
		Entire	62.50	12.00
U36	U13	3c pink, *blue* (Letter Sheet)	70.00	70.00
		Entire	230.00	*500.00*
+U37	U13	3c pink, *orange*	4,000.	
		Entire	5,500.	
U38	U14	6c pink	100.00	80.00
		Entire	200.00	190.00
U39	U14	6c pink, *buff*	60.00	60.00
		Entire	210.00	160.00
U40	U15	10c yellow green	40.00	30.00
		Entire	77.50	60.00
a.		10c blue green	40.00	30.00
		Entire	77.50	60.00
U41	U15	10c yel grn, *buff*	40.00	30.00
		Entire	77.50	52.50
a.		10c blue green, *buff*	40.00	30.00
		Entire	77.50	52.50
U42	U16	12c red & brn, *buff*	180.00	180.00
		Entire	475.00	650.00
a.		12c lake & brown, *buff*	1,250.	
U43	U16	20c red & bl, *buff*	250.00	225.00
		Entire	450.00	1,250.
U44	U16	24c red & grn, *buff*	210.00	210.00
		Entire	625.00	1,500.
a.		24c lake & green, *salmon*	260.00	225.00
		Entire	750.00	1,750.
U45	U16	40c blk & red, *buff*	300.00	400.00
		Entire	700.00	4,500.

Nos. U38 and U39 have been reprinted on the same papers as the reprints of the 1853-55 issue, and are not known entire. Value, set of 2 reprints, $60.

Jackson — U17

"U.S. POSTAGE" above. Downstroke and tail of "2" unite near the point (seven varieties).

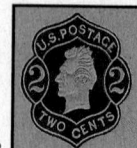

Jackson — U18

"U.S. POSTAGE" above. The downstroke and tail of the "2" touch but do not merge.

Jackson — U19

"U.S. POST" above. Stamp 24-25mm wide (Sixteen varieties).

Jackson — U20

"U.S. POST" above. Stamp 25½-26¼mm wide. (Twenty-five varieties.)
Envelopes are on diagonally laid paper. Wrappers on vertically or horizontally laid paper.

Envelopes are on diagonally laid paper.
Wrappers on vertically or horizontally laid paper.

1863-64

U46	U17 2c black, *buff*		50.00	24.00
	Entire		80.00	37.50
W47	U17 2c black, *dark manila*		90.00	65.00
	Entire		120.00	90.00
+U48	U18 2c black, *buff*		2,250.	
	Entire		4,500.	
+U49	U18 2c black, *orange*		1,900.	
	Entire			
U50	U19 2c black, *buff* ('64)		17.50	11.00
	Entire		40.00	21.00
W51	U19 2c black, *buff* ('64)		450.00	275.00
	Entire		675.00	400.00
U52	U19 2c black, *orange* ('64)		20.00	11.00
	Entire		37.50	18.00
W53	U19 2c black, *dark manila* ('64)		47.50	40.00
	Entire		175.00	140.00
U54	U20 2c black, *buff* ('64)		17.50	9.50
	Entire		37.50	16.00
W55	U20 2c black, *buff* ('64)		95.00	65.00
	Entire		160.00	120.00
U56	U20 2c black, *orange* ('64)		22.50	10.00
	Entire		34.00	16.00
W57	U20 2c black, *light manila* ('64)		22.50	14.00
	Entire		37.50	24.00

Washington — U21

Washington U22

1864-65

U58	U21 3c pink		10.00	1.60
	Entire		20.00	3.25
U59	U21 3c pink, *buff*		10.00	1.25
	Entire		20.00	3.00
U60	U21 3c brown ('65)		65.00	40.00
	Entire		130.00	125.00
U61	U21 3c brown, *buff* ('65)		50.00	30.00
	Entire		115.00	80.00
U62	U21 6c pink		90.00	29.00
	Entire		180.00	85.00
U63	U21 6c pink, *buff*		45.00	27.50
	Entire		100.00	50.00
U64	U21 6c purple ('65)		55.00	26.00
	Entire		100.00	55.00
U65	U21 6c purple, *buff* ('65)		45.00	20.00
	Entire		70.00	55.00
U66	U22 9c lemon, *buff* ('65)		375.00	250.00
	Entire		575.00	1,000.

U67	U22 9c orange, *buff* ('65)		125.00	90.00
	Entire		210.00	300.00
a.	9c orange yellow, *buff*		125.00	90.00
	Entire		210.00	300.00
U68	U22 12c brown, *buff* ('65)		275.00	275.00
	Entire		600.00	1,200.
U69	U22 12c red brown, *buff* ('65)		125.00	55.00
	Entire		180.00	450.00
U70	U22 18c red, *buff* ('65)		80.00	95.00
	Entire		180.00	800.00
U71	U22 24c blue, *buff* ('65)		80.00	95.00
	Entire		225.00	700.00
U72	U22 30c green, *buff* ('65)		100.00	80.00
	Entire		220.00	1,500.
a.	30c yellow green, *buff*		95.00	80.00
	Entire		220.00	1,500.
U73	U22 40c rose, *buff* ('65)		100.00	250.00
	Entire		360.00	2,000.

Printed by George H. Reay, Brooklyn, N. Y.
The engravings in this issue are finely executed.

Franklin — U23

Bust points to the end of the "N" of "ONE."

Jackson — U24

Bust narrow at back. Small, thick figures of value.

Washington — U25

Queue projects below bust.

Lincoln — U26

Neck very long at the back.

Stanton — U27

Bust pointed at the back; figures "7" are normal.

Jefferson — U28

Queue forms straight line with the bust.

Clay — U29

Ear partly concealed by hair, mouth large, chin prominent.

Webster — U30

Has side whiskers.

Scott — U31

Straggling locks of hair at top of head; ornaments around the inner oval end in squares.

Hamilton — U32

Back of bust very narrow, chin almost straight; labels containing figures of value are exactly parallel.

Perry — U33

Front of bust very narrow and pointed; inner lines of shields project very slightly beyond the oval.

1870-71

U74	U23 1c blue		37.50	30.00
	Entire		77.50	45.00
a.	1c ultramarine		65.00	35.00
	Entire		135.00	60.00
U75	U23 1c blue, *amber*		30.00	27.50
	Entire		57.50	40.00
a.	1c ultramarine, *amber*		62.50	30.00
	Entire		95.00	55.00
U76	U23 1c blue, *orange*		17.00	15.00
	Entire		35.00	22.50
W77	U23 1c blue, *manila*		37.50	35.00
	Entire		80.00	70.00
U78	U24 2c brown		35.00	16.00
	Entire		57.50	22.50
U79	U24 2c brown, *amber*		17.50	10.00
	Entire		40.00	17.50
U80	U24 2c brown, *orange*		10.00	6.50
	Entire		17.00	11.00
W81	U24 2c brown, *manila*		25.00	20.00
	Entire		60.00	57.50
U82	U25 3c green		7.00	1.00
	Entire		16.00	4.00
a.	3c brown (error), entire		8,500.	
U83	U25 3c green, *amber*		6.00	2.00
	Entire		17.50	5.00
U84	U25 3c green, *cream*		8.00	4.50
	Entire		16.00	10.00
U85	U26 6c dark red		25.00	16.00
	Entire		57.50	21.00
a.	6c vermilion		25.00	16.00
	Entire		70.00	21.00
U86	U26 6c dark red, *amber*		37.50	20.00
	Entire		75.00	30.00
a.	6c vermilion, *amber*		37.50	30.00
	Entire		75.00	30.00
U87	U26 6c dark red, *cream*		37.50	25.00
	Entire		75.00	30.00
a.	6c vermilion, *cream*		32.50	20.00
	Entire		75.00	30.00

U88	U27 7c vermilion, *amber* ('71)		55.00	175.00
	Entire		80.00	900.00
U89	U28 10c olive black		800.00	900.00
	Entire		1,000.	1,200.
U90	U28 10c olive black, *amber*		800.00	800.00
	Entire		1,100.	1,200.
U91	U28 10c brown		82.50	70.00
	Entire		130.00	125.00
U92	U28 10c brown, *amber*		85.00	52.50
	Entire		120.00	125.00
a.	10c dark brown, *amber*		85.00	125.00
	Entire		120.00	125.00
U93	U29 12c plum		100.00	82.50
	Entire		225.00	450.00
U94	U29 12c plum, *amber*		110.00	100.00
	Entire		225.00	650.00
U95	U29 12c plum, *cream*		225.00	200.00
	Entire		300.00	
U96	U30 15c red orange		75.00	75.00
	Entire		165.00	
a.	15c orange		75.00	
	Entire		200.00	
U97	U30 15c red orange, *amber*		160.00	275.00
	Entire		350.00	
a.	15c orange, *amber*		170.00	
	Entire		350.00	
U98	U30 15c red orange, *cream*		325.00	375.00
	Entire		450.00	
a.	15c orange, *cream*		325.00	
	Entire		450.00	
U99	U31 24c purple		125.00	125.00
	Entire		180.00	
U100	U31 24c purple, *amber*		200.00	300.00
	Entire		375.00	
U101	U31 24c purple, *cream*		260.00	450.00
	Entire		450.00	
U102	U32 30c black		65.00	120.00
	Entire		310.00	750.00
U103	U32 30c black, *amber*		250.00	450.00
	Entire		650.00	
U104	U32 30c black, *cream*		190.00	450.00
	Entire		450.00	
U105	U33 90c carmine		140.00	300.00
	Entire		260.00	
U106	U33 90c carmine, *amber*		350.00	900.00
	Entire		800.00	4,500.
U107	U33 90c carmine, *cream*		175.00	2,250.
	Entire		450.00	5,000.

Printed by Plimpton Manufacturing Co.
The profiles in this issue are inferior to the fine engraving of the Reay issue.

U34

Bust forms an angle at the back near the frame. Lettering poorly executed. Distinct circle in "O" of "Postage."

U35

Lower part of bust points to the end of the "E" in "ONE." Head inclined downward.

U36

Bust narrow at back. Thin numerals. Head of "P" narrow. Bust broad at front, ending in sharp corners.

U37

Bust broad. Figures of value in long ovals.

U38

Similar to U37 but the figure "2" at the left touches the oval.

U39

Similar to U37 but the "O" of "TWO" has the center netted instead of plain and the "G" of "POSTAGE" and the "C" of "CENTS" have diagonal crossline.

U40

Bust broad: numerals in ovals short and thick.

U41

Similar to U40 but the ovals containing the numerals are much heavier. A diagonal line runs from the upper part of the "U" to the white frame-line.

U42

Similar to U40 but the middle stroke of "N" in "CENTS" is as thin as the vertical strokes.

U43

Bottom of bust cut almost semi-circularly.

U44

Thin lettering, long thin figures of value.

U45

Thick lettering, well-formed figures of value, queue does not project below bust.

U46

Top of head egg-shaped; knot of queue well marked and projects triangularly.

Taylor — U47

Die 1   Die 2

Die 1: Figures of value with thick, curved tops.
Die 2: Figures of value with long, thin tops.

U48

Neck short at back.

U49

Figures of value turned up at the ends.

U50

Very large head.

U51

Knot of queue stands out prominently.

U52

Ear prominent, chin receding.

U53

No side whiskers, forelock projects above head.

U54

Hair does not project; ornaments around the inner oval end in points.

U55

Back of bust rather broad, chin slopes considerably; labels containing figures of value are not exactly parallel.

U56

Front of bust sloping; inner lines of shields project considerably into the inner oval.

1874-86

Design U34

U108	1c dark blue	175.00	70.00
	Entire	250.00	110.00
a.	1c light blue	175.00	70.00
	Entire	250.00	125.00
U109	1c dk bl, amb	150.00	75.00
	Entire	200.00	140.00
+U110	1c dk blue, cr	1,100.	
U111	1c dk blue, org	15.00	17.50
	Entire	30.00	25.00
a.	dk blue, org	12.50	12.50
	Entire	30.00	25.00
W112	1c dk blue, man	62.50	40.00
	Entire	105.00	72.50

Design U35

U113	1c light blue	2.25	1.00
	Entire	4.00	2.00
a.	1c dark blue	8.00	7.00
	Entire	29.00	20.00
U114	1c lt blue, amb	3.25	3.25
	Entire	8.25	6.00
a.	dk blue, amb	17.50	10.00
	Entire	30.00	20.00
U115	1c blue, cr	4.75	4.25
	Entire	10.50	6.50
a.	dk blue, cr	17.50	8.50
	Entire	32.50	20.00

U116	1c lt blue, org	.75	.40
	Entire	1.25	1.00
a.	dk blue, org	4.00	2.50
	Entire	16.00	8.00
U117	1c lt bl, bl ('80)	7.50	5.00
	Entire	13.50	9.00
U118	1c lt bl, fawn ('79)	7.50	5.00
	Entire	15.00	10.00
U119	1c lt bl, man ('86)	8.00	3.25
	Entire	17.00	5.00
W120	1c lt bl, man	1.25	1.10
	Entire	2.75	1.75
a.	dk bl, man	8.00	7.00
	Entire	16.00	15.00
U121	1c lt bl, amb man	17.50	10.00
	Entire	29.00	20.00

Design U36

U122	2c brown	140.00	65.00
	Entire	190.00	85.00
U123	2c brown, amb	67.50	40.00
	Entire	125.00	70.00
+U124	2c brn, crm	1,100.	
+U125	2c brn, org	18,000.	
	Entire	35,000.	
W126	2c brn, man	140.00	85.00
	Entire	300.00	160.00
W127	2c ver, man	2,500.	500.00
	Entire	3,250.	5,000.

Design U37

U128	2c brown	60.00	35.00
	Entire	110.00	75.00
U129	2c brn, amb	80.00	45.00
	Entire	125.00	77.50
+U130	2c brn, cr	35,000.	
W131	2c brn, man	17.50	15.00
	Entire	29.00	26.00

Design U38

U132	2c brown	70.00	27.50
	Entire	120.00	80.00
U133	2c brn, amb	325.00	70.00
	Entire	550.00	140.00
+U133A	2c brn, cr	70,000.	

Design U39

U134	2c brown	900.00	160.00
	Entire	1,500.	300.00
U135	2c brn, amb	425.00	150.00
	Entire	650.00	160.00
U136	2c brn, org	50.00	27.50
	Entire	80.00	37.50
W137	2c brn, man	75.00	40.00
	Entire	125.00	55.00
+U137A	2c ver	32,500.	
+U137B	2c ver, amb	30,000.	
	Entire	—	
+U137C	2c ver, org	70,000.	
+W138	2c ver, man	25,000.	

Design U40

U139	2c brn ('75)	57.50	37.50
	Entire	82.50	47.50
U140	2c brn, amb ('75)	85.00	62.50
	Entire	130.00	77.50
+U140A	2c reddish brn, org ('75)	17,500.	
	Entire	32,500.	
W141	2c brn, man ('75)	32.50	25.00
	Entire	45.00	32.50
U142	2c ver ('75)	8.00	5.00
	Entire	16.00	9.00
a.	2c pink	8.00	5.00
	Entire	16.00	9.00
U143	2c ver, amb ('75)	9.00	5.00
	Entire	16.00	9.00
U144	2c ver, cr ('75)	17.50	7.00
	Entire	25.00	12.50
+U145	2c ver, org ('75)	35,000.	
U146	2c ver, bl ('80)	110.00	40.00
	Entire	200.00	140.00
U147	2c ver, fawn ('75)	8.00	5.00
	Entire	16.00	7.00
W148	2c ver, man ('75)	4.00	3.50
	Entire	9.00	6.50

Design U41

U149	2c ver ('78)	45.00	25.00
	Entire	90.00	40.00
a.	2c pink	52.50	27.00
	Entire	90.00	42.50
U150	2c ver, amb ('78)	35.00	15.00
	Entire	60.00	22.50
U151	2c ver, bl ('80)	10.00	8.00
	Entire	20.00	15.00
a.	2c pink, blue	11.00	8.00
	Entire	17.50	12.50
U152	2c ver, fawn ('78)	10.00	4.00
	Entire	17.50	9.00

Design U42

U153	2c ver ('76)	75.00	30.00
	Entire	115.00	40.00
U154	2c ver, amb ('76)	300.00	90.00
	Entire	450.00	175.00
W155	2c ver, man ('76)	20.00	10.00
	Entire	45.00	20.00

Design U43

U156	2c ver ('81)	1,250.	175.00
	Entire	2,000.	500.00
U157	2c ver, amb ('81)	42,500.	27,500.
	Entire	60,000.	

W158 2c ver, *man* ('81) 90.00 55.00 / Entire 200.00 200.00

Design U44
U159 3c green 35.00 10.00 / Entire 60.00 17.50
U160 3c grn, *amb* 35.00 10.00 / Entire 60.00 20.00
U161 3c grn, *cr* 35.00 12.00 / Entire 65.00 30.00
+U162 3c grn, *bl* 75,000.

Design U45
U163 3c green 1.40 .30 / Entire 4.25 2.25
U164 3c grn, *amb* 1.50 .70 / Entire 4.25 2.00
U165 3c grn, *cr* 8.50 6.50 / Entire 19.00 9.00
U166 3c grn, *bl* 7.50 6.00 / Entire 17.00 11.00
U167 3c grn, *fawn* ('75) 4.75 3.50 / Entire 9.25 5.00

Design U46
U168 3c grn ('81) 1,000. 80.00 / Entire 3,500. 275.00
U169 3c grn, *amb* 450.00 140.00 / Entire 700.00 300.00
U170 3c grn, *bl* ('81) 11,500. 2,750. / Entire 20,000. 4,250.
U171 3c grn, *fawn* ('81) 40,000. 2,750. / Entire 10,000.

Design U47
U172 5c bl, die I ('75) 12.50 10.00 / Entire 21.00 16.00
U173 5c bl, die I, *amb* ('75) 12.50 11.00 / Entire 21.00 17.00
U174 5c bl, die I, *cr* ('75) 95.00 45.00 / Entire 175.00 95.00
U175 5c bl, die I, *bl* ('75) 30.00 17.50 / Entire 50.00 27.50
U176 5c bl, die I, *fawn* ('75) 160.00 65.00 / Entire 300.00
U177 5c bl, die 2 ('75) 11.00 9.00 / Entire 18.00 18.00
U178 5c bl, die 2, *amb* ('75) 9.00 8.00 / Entire 20.00 19.00
+U178A 5c bl, die 2, *cr* ('76) 10,000. / Entire 17,500.
U179 5c bl, die 2, *bl* ('75) 25.00 12.50 / Entire 45.00 30.00
U180 5c bl, die 2, *fawn* ('75) 125.00 50.00 / Entire 225.00 140.00

Design U48
U181 6c red 8.00 6.50 / Entire 15.00 12.50
a. 6c vermilion 8.00 6.50 / Entire 15.00 12.50
U182 6c red, amber 12.50 6.50 / Entire 24.00 15.00
a. 6c ver, amb 12.50 6.50 / Entire 24.00 15.00
U183 6c red, cream 50.00 17.50 / Entire 85.00 40.00
a. 6c ver, cr 45.00 15.00 / Entire 82.50 40.00
U184 6c red, *fawn* ('75) 17.50 12.50 / Entire 32.50 29.00

Design U49
+U185 7c vermilion 1,200.
U186 7c ver, *amb* 125.00 75.00 / Entire 225.00

Design U50
U187 10c brown 40.00 20.00 / Entire 65.00
U188 10c brn, *amb* 75.00 35.00 / Entire 150.00

Design U51
U189 10c choc ('75) 6.00 4.00 / Entire 12.00 9.25
a. 10c bister brown 7.00 5.00 / Entire 12.50 10.50
b. 10c yellow ocher 3,000. / Entire 5,250.
U190 10c choc, *amb* ('75) 7.00 6.00 / Entire 13.00 11.50
a. 10c bis brn, amb 7.00 6.00 / Entire 13.00 11.50
b. 10c yel ocher, amb 3,000. / Entire 5,250.
U191 10c brn, *oriental buff* ('86) 12.50 8.75 / Entire 20.00 11.50
U192 10c brn, *bl* ('86) 12.50 8.00 / Entire 20.00 15.00
a. 10c gray blk, bl 12.50 7.50 / Entire 20.00 15.00
b. 10c red brn, bl 12.50 7.50 / Entire 20.00 15.00
U193 10c brn, *man* ('86) 12.50 10.00 / Entire 22.50 16.00
a. 10c red brn, man 12.50 10.00 / Entire 22.50 16.00

U194 10c brn, *amb man* ('86) 17.50 9.00 / Entire 26.00 17.50
a. 10c red brn, amb man 17.50 9.00 / Entire 26.00 17.50

Design U52
U195 12c plum 300.00 100.00 / Entire 625.00
U196 12c plum, *amb* 200.00 160.00 / Entire 350.00
U197 12c plum, *cr* 180.00 130.00 / Entire 850.00

Design U53
U198 15c orange 50.00 35.00 / Entire 100.00 55.00
U199 15c org, *amb* 140.00 130.00 / Entire 300.00
U200 15c org, *cr* 500.00 300.00 / Entire 850.00

Design U54
U201 24c purple 175.00 150.00 / Entire 260.00
a. Printed on both sides, one inverted and overlapping, cut to shape 450.00
U202 24c pur, *amb* 180.00 100.00 / Entire 270.00
U203 24c pur, *cr* 170.00 100.00 / Entire 750.00

Design U55
U204 30c black 60.00 25.00 / Entire 95.00 65.00
U205 30c blk, *amb* 70.00 60.00 / Entire 130.00 250.00
U206 30c blk, *cr* ('75) 325.00 325.00 / Entire 625.00
U207 30c blk, *oriental buff* ('81) 100.00 80.00 / Entire 170.00
U208 30c blk, *blue* ('81) 100.00 80.00 / Entire 180.00
U209 30c blk, *man* ('81) 90.00 70.00 / Entire 200.00
U210 30c blk, *amb man* ('86) 180.00 100.00 / Entire 260.00

Design U56
U211 90c carmine ('75) 95.00 75.00 / Entire 150.00 100.00
U212 90c car, *amb* ('75) 175.00 250.00 / Entire 250.00
U213 90c car, *cr* ('75) 1,100. / Entire 2,100.
U214 90c car, *oriental buff* ('86) 140.00 250.00 / Entire 300.00 300.00
U215 90c car, *bl* ('86) 175.00 250.00 / Entire 275.00 325.00
U216 90c car, *man* ('86) 140.00 225.00 / Entire 250.00 275.00
U217 90c car, *amb man* ('86) 160.00 200.00 / Entire 240.00 300.00

Note: No. U206 has watermark #2; No. U207 watermark #6 or #7. No U213 has watermark #2; No. U214 watermark #7. These envelopes cannot be positively identified except by the watermark.

Single line under "POSTAGE" U57

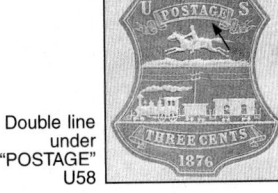
Double line under "POSTAGE" U58

1876
U218 U57 3c red 35.00 25.00 / Entire 67.50 50.00
U219 U57 3c green 35.00 17.50 / Entire 60.00 40.00
+U220 U58 3c red 27,500. / Entire 42,500.
U221 U58 3c green 35.00 25.00 / Entire 80.00 50.00

Cent. of the U.S., and the World's Fair at Philadelphia.
Used examples of Nos. U218-U221 with exposition cancels and/or typed addresses sell for a premium.
See No. U582.

Garfield — U59

1882-86
U222 U59 5c brown 5.00 3.00 / Entire 10.00 7.50
U223 U59 5c brn, *amb* 5.25 3.50 / Entire 11.00 10.00
+U224 U59 5c brn, *oriental buff* ('86) 140.00 / Entire 210.00
+U225 U59 5c brn, *bl* 75.00 / Entire 120.00
U226 U59 5c brn, *fawn* 325.00 / Entire 450.00

Washington — U60

1883, October
U227 U60 2c red 5.50 2.25 / Entire 11.00 4.00
a. 2c brown (error), entire 4,000.
U228 U60 2c red, *amb* 6.50 2.75 / Entire 12.00 6.00
U229 U60 2c red, *blue* 8.00 5.00 / Entire 12.50 8.00
U230 U60 2c red, *fawn* 9.00 5.25 / Entire 14.00 7.00

Wavy lines fine and clear — U61

1883, November
Four Wavy Lines in Oval
U231 U61 2c red 5.00 2.50 / Entire 9.50 4.00
U232 U61 2c red, *amb* 6.00 3.75 / Entire 11.00 5.75
U233 U61 2c red, *blue* 10.00 7.50 / Entire 19.00 10.00
U234 U61 2c red, *fawn* 7.50 4.75 / Entire 11.00 6.00
W235 U61 2c red, *man* 20.00 6.25 / Entire 30.00 12.50

Wavy lines thick and blurred — U62

Retouched die.

1884, June
U236 U62 2c red 15.00 4.00 / Entire 20.00 7.75
U237 U62 2c red, amber 20.00 10.00 / Entire 30.00 11.00
U238 U62 2c red, blue 29.00 12.00 / Entire 40.00 15.00
U239 U62 2c red, fawn 20.00 11.00 / Entire 32.50 12.50

See Nos. U260-W269.

3 ½ links over left "2" — U63

U240 U63 2c red 90.00 45.00 / Entire 150.00 72.50
U241 U63 2c red, *amb* 675.00 300.00 / Entire 2,000. 750.00
U242 U63 2c red, *fawn* 25,000. / Entire 47,500.

2 links below right "2" — U64

U243 U64 2c red 130.00 75.00 / Entire 165.00 100.00
U244 U64 2c red, *amb* 325.00 100.00 / Entire 450.00 125.00
U245 U64 2c red, *blue* 375.00 210.00 / Entire 575.00 225.00
U246 U64 2c red, *fawn* 375.00 200.00 / Entire 625.00 275.00

Round "O" in "TWO." White lines above "WO" of "TWO" joined to form thick white dash. — U65

U247 U65 2c red 2,000. 400.00 / Entire 3,000. 1,100.
U248 U65 2c red, *amb* 3,750. 750.00 / Entire 5,500. 1,650.
U249 U65 2c red, *fawn* 1,100. 500.00 / Entire 1,500. 750.00

See Nos. U270-U276.

Jackson — U66

Die 1   Die 2

Die 1: Numeral at left is 2¾mm wide. Die 2: Numeral at left is 3¼mm wide.

1883-86
U250 U66 4c green, die 1 4.00 3.50 / Entire 6.50 6.00
U251 U66 4c grn, die 1, *amb* 5.00 3.50 / Entire 7.50 5.25
U252 U66 4c grn, die 1, *oriental buff* ('86) 13.00 9.00 / Entire 18.00 12.50
U253 U66 4c green, die 1, *blue* ('86) 13.00 6.50 / Entire 18.00 8.00
U254 U66 4c grn, die 1, *man* ('86) 16.00 7.50 / Entire 21.00 15.00
U255 U66 4c grn, die 1, *amb man* ('86) 22.50 10.00 / Entire 32.50 15.00
U256 U66 4c green, die 2 10.00 5.00 / Entire 17.50 6.75
U257 U66 4c grn, die 2, *amb* 12.50 7.00 / Entire 22.50 10.00
U258 U66 4c grn, die 2, *man* ('86) 12.50 7.50 / Entire 22.50 12.50
U259 U66 4c grn, die 2, *amb man* ('86) 12.50 7.50 / Entire 22.50 12.50

1884, May
U260 U61 2c brown 17.50 5.75 / Entire 20.00 9.00
U261 U61 2c brown, amber 17.50 6.50 / Entire 20.00 7.50
U262 U61 2c brown, blue 20.00 10.00 / Entire 26.00 14.00

U263	U61 2c brown, *fawn*	17.50	9.25
	Entire	20.00	12.50
W264	U61 2c brown, *manila*	18.00	11.50
	Entire	25.00	19.00

1884, June
Retouched Die

U265	U62 2c brown	18.00	6.50
	Entire	25.00	12.00
U266	U62 2c brn, *amb*	60.00	40.00
	Entire	70.00	50.00
U267	U62 2c brown, *blue*	22.50	9.00
	Entire	30.00	15.00
U268	U62 2c brown, *fawn*	17.00	11.00
	Entire	21.00	15.00
W269	U62 2c brn, *man*	27.50	15.00
	Entire	32.50	24.00

2 Links Below Right "2"

U270	U64 2c brown	130.00	50.00
	Entire	160.00	110.00
U271	U64 2c brn, *amb*	425.00	125.00
	Entire	575.00	350.00
U272	U64 2c brown, *fawn*		2,000.
	Entire	8,500.	4,000.

Round "O" in "Two"

U273	U65 2c brown	250.00	100.00
	Entire	375.00	190.00
U274	U65 2c brn, *amb*	250.00	100.00
	Entire	375.00	190.00
U275	U65 2c brown, *blue*		12,500.
	Entire		47,500.
U276	U65 2c brown, *fawn*	800.00	750.00
	Entire	1,250.	1,200.

U67

Extremity of bust below the queue forms a point.

Washington — U68

Extremity of bust is rounded.

Similar to U61
Two wavy lines in oval

1884-86

U277	U67 2c brown	.50	.25
	Entire	1.00	.40
a.	2c brown lake, die 1	22.50	21.00
	Entire	27.50	26.00
U278	U67 2c brn, *amb*	.65	.50
	Entire	1.75	.75
a.	2c brown lake, amber	35.00	35.00
	Entire	42.50	32.50
U279	U67 2c brn, *oriental buff* ('86)	7.00	2.10
	Entire	9.50	3.00
U280	U67 2c brown, *blue*	3.00	2.10
	Entire	4.50	3.50
U281	U67 2c brown, *fawn*	3.75	2.40
	Entire	5.50	4.00
U282	U67 2c brn, *man* ('86)	13.00	4.00
	Entire	17.50	6.50
W283	U67 2c brn, *man*	8.00	5.00
	Entire	11.00	6.50
U284	U67 2c brn, *amb man* ('86)	9.00	5.75
	Entire	15.00	7.00
+U285	U67 2c red	650.00	
	Entire	1,300.	
+U286	U67 2c red, *blue*	275.00	
	Entire	350.00	
W287	U67 2c red, *manila*	150.00	
	Entire	210.00	
U288	U68 2c brown	275.00	50.00
	Entire	700.00	150.00
U289	U68 2c brn, *amb*	20.00	13.00
	Entire	25.00	17.00
U290	U68 2c brown, *blue*	1,000.	325.00
	Entire	1,750.	450.00
U291	U68 2c brown, *fawn*	35.00	25.00
	Entire	45.00	32.50
W292	U68 2c brn, *man*	35.00	19.00
	Entire	45.00	22.50

Grant — US1

1886
Letter Sheet, 160x271mm
Creamy White Paper

U293	US1 2c green, entire	30.00	20.00

See the Scott U.S. Specialized Catalogue for perforation and inscription varieties.

Franklin — U69   Washington U70

Bust points between third and fourth notches of inner oval "G" of "POSTAGE" has no bar.

U71

Bust points between second and third notches of inner oval; "G" of "POSTAGE" has a bar; ear is indicated by one heavy line; one vertical line at corner of mouth.

U72

Frame same as U71; upper part of head more rounded; ear indicated by two curved lines with two locks of hair in front; two vertical lines at corner of mouth.

Jackson — U73

Grant — U74

There is a space between the beard and the collar of the coat. A button is on the collar.

U75

The collar touches the beard and there is no button.

1887-94
Design U69

U294	1c blue	.55	.25
	Entire	1.00	.50
U295	1c dk bl ('94)	7.00	2.50
	Entire	10.00	6.50
U296	1c bl, *amb*	3.25	1.25
	Entire	5.50	3.50
U297	1c dk bl, *amb* ('94)	47.50	22.50
	Entire	60.00	27.50
+U298	1c bl, *oriental buff*	10,000.	
	Entire	16,000.	
+U299	1c bl, *bl*	12,500.	
	Entire	21,000.	
U300	1c bl, *man*	.65	.35
	Entire	1.25	.75
W301	1c bl, *man*	.45	.30
	Entire	1.25	.60
U302	1c dk bl, *man* ('94)	27.50	12.50
	Entire	35.00	20.00
W303	1c DK bl, *man* ('94)	16.00	10.00
	Entire	22.50	15.00

U304	1C bl, *amb man*	12.50	5.00
	Entire	17.50	7.50

Design U70

U305	2c green	15.00	10.00
	Entire	32.50	15.00
U306	2c grn, *amb*	40.00	17.50
	Entire	55.00	22.50
U307	2c grn, *oriental buff*	100.00	40.00
	Entire	130.00	50.00
U308	2c grn, *bl*		3,500.
	Entire		22,000.
U309	2c grn, *man*	12,500.	1,000.
	Entire	25,000.	1,200.
U310	2c grn, *amb man*	27,500.	2,500.
	Entire	—	3,500.

Design U71

U311	2c green	.30	.25
	Entire	.70	.25
a.	2c dark green ('94)	.45	.30
	Entire	1.00	.85
U312	2c grn, *amb*	.40	.25
	Entire	.75	.30
a.	Double impression	—	
b.	2c dk grn ('94)	.55	.35
	Entire	1.00	.85
U313	2c grn, *oriental buff*	.55	.25
	Entire	1.10	.40
a.	2c dk grn, oriental buff ('94)	2.00	1.00
	Entire	4.00	4.00
b.	Double impression	150.00	
U314	2c grn, *bl*	.60	.30
	Entire	1.20	.40
a.	2c dk grn, bl ('94)	.80	.40
	Entire	1.60	1.50
U315	2c grn, *man*	2.00	.50
	Entire	3.00	1.00
a.	2c dk grn, man ('94)	2.75	.75
	Entire	4.00	1.50
W316	2c grn, *man*	3.50	2.50
	Entire	10.00	7.00
U317	2c grn, *amb man*	2.50	1.90
	Entire	5.50	3.00
a.	2c dk grn, amb man ('94)	3.50	3.00
	Entire	7.00	4.00

Design U72

U318	2c green	125.00	12.50
	Entire	190.00	50.00
U319	2c grn, *amb*	175.00	27.50
	Entire	260.00	50.00
U320	2c grn, *oriental buff*	140.00	40.00
	Entire	260.00	70.00
U321	2c grn, *bl*	175.00	70.00
	Entire	280.00	90.00
U322	2c grn, *man*	240.00	70.00
	Entire	300.00	110.00
U323	2c grn, *amb man*	400.00	100.00
	Entire	700.00	175.00

Design U73

U324	4c carmine	3.25	2.00
	Entire	6.00	2.10
a.	4c lake	3.50	2.00
	Entire	7.00	3.75
b.	4c scarlet ('94)	3.50	2.00
	Entire	7.00	3.75
U325	4c car, *amb*	3.50	3.50
	Entire	7.00	4.00
a.	4c lake, amber	3.50	3.50
	Entire	7.25	4.00
b.	4c scarlet, amber ('94)	4.00	3.75
	Entire	8.00	4.25
U326	4c car, *oriental buff*	7.50	3.50
	Entire	15.00	6.25
a.	4c lake, oriental buff	7.50	3.50
	Entire	15.00	6.25
U327	4c car, *bl*	6.00	4.00
	Entire	12.00	7.00
a.	4c lake, blue	6.50	4.00
	Entire	13.00	6.00
U328	4c car, *man*	9.00	7.00
	Entire	13.00	7.50
a.	4c lake, manila	9.00	6.00
	Entire	13.00	7.50
b.	4c pink, manila	15.00	10.00
	Entire	21.00	12.50
U329	4c car, *amb man*	7.00	3.25
	Entire	12.50	5.00
a.	4c lake, amb man	7.00	3.25
	Entire	12.50	5.00
b.	4c pink, amb man	15.00	10.00
	Entire	21.00	12.50

Design U74

U330	5c blue	3.75	4.00
	Entire	7.50	11.00
U331	5c bl, *amb*	5.00	2.50
	Entire	11.00	14.00
a.	Double impression, entire		
U332	5c bl, *oriental buff*	5.50	4.00
	Entire	16.00	18.00
U333	5c blue, *blue*	9.00	6.00
	Entire	18.00	15.00

Design U75

U334	5c blue ('94)	25.00	12.50
	Entire	40.00	22.50
U335	5c bl, *amb* ('94)	12.50	7.50
	Entire	20.00	40.00

Design U55

U336	30c red brn	50.00	45.00
	Entire	65.00	475.00
a.	30c yellow brown	50.00	45.00
	Entire	65.00	475.00
b.	30c chocolate	50.00	45.00
	Entire	65.00	475.00
U337	30c red brn, *amb*	50.00	45.00
	Entire	65.00	475.00
a.	30c yel brn, amb	50.00	45.00
	Entire	65.00	475.00
b.	30c choc, amb	50.00	45.00
	Entire	65.00	475.00

U338	30c red brn, *oriental buff*	50.00	45.00
	Entire	65.00	475.00
a.	30c yel brn, oriental buff	65.00	475.00
U339	30c red brn, *bl*	50.00	45.00
	Entire	95.00	475.00
a.	30c yel brn, bl	50.00	45.00
	Entire	65.00	475.00
U340	30c red brn, *man*	50.00	45.00
	Entire	65.00	475.00
a.	30c brown, manila	50.00	45.00
	Entire	65.00	475.00
U341	30c red brn, *amb man*	50.00	45.00
	Entire	85.00	475.00
a.	30c yel brn, amb man	50.00	45.00
	Entire	85.00	475.00

Design U56

U342	90c purple	67.50	85.00
	Entire	110.00	1,050.
U343	90c pur, *amb*	82.50	85.00
	Entire	130.00	1,050.
U344	90c pur, *oriental buff*	82.50	85.00
	Entire	140.00	1,050.
U345	90c pur, *bl*	82.50	85.00
	Entire	140.00	1,050.
U346	90c pur, *man*	85.00	85.00
	Entire	150.00	1,050.
U347	90c pur, *amb man*	85.00	85.00
	Entire	150.00	1,050.

Columbus and Liberty — U76

1893

U348	U76 1c deep blue	2.25	1.25
	Entire	3.00	2.00
U349	U76 2c violet	1.75	.50
	Entire	3.50	.60
a.	2c dark slate (error)	2,500.	
	Entire	5,000.	
U350	U76 5c chocolate	7.50	7.00
	Entire	12.00	10.00
a.	5c slate brown (error)	850.00	950.00
	Entire	1,200.	1,500.
U351	U76 10c slate brown	30.00	27.50
	Entire	65.00	57.50
	Nos. U348-U351 (4)	41.50	36.25

Franklin U77   Washington U78

Bust points to first notch of inner oval and is only slightly concave below.

U79

Bust points to middle of second notch of inner oval and is quite hollow below. Queue has ribbon around it.

U80

Same as die 2, but hair flowing. No ribbon on queue.

Lincoln — U81

Bust pointed but not draped.

U82

Bust broad and draped.

U83

Head larger, inner oval has no notches.

Grant — U84

Similar to design of 1887-95 but smaller.

1899

U352	U77 1c green	2.00	.25
	Entire	4.75	.50
U353	U77 1c green, *amber*	5.50	1.50
	Entire	9.00	2.75
U354	U77 1c green, *oriental buff*	10.00	2.75
	Entire	17.50	3.75
U355	U77 1c green, *blue*	12.50	7.50
	Entire	20.00	12.50
U356	U77 1c green, *manila*	2.50	.95
	Entire	6.50	2.00
W357	U77 1c green, *manila*	2.75	1.10
	Entire	9.00	4.00
U358	U78 2c carmine	3.00	1.75
	Entire	8.00	3.25
U359	U78 2c car, *amb*	20.00	12.50
	Entire	30.00	21.00
U360	U78 2c carmine, *oriental buff*	20.00	11.00
	Entire	30.00	15.00
U361	U78 2c carmine, *blue*	60.00	35.00
	Entire	80.00	52.50
U362	U79 2c carmine	.35	.25
	Entire	.65	.30
a.	2c dark lake	30.00	30.00
	Entire	37.50	35.00
U363	U79 2c car, *amb*	1.75	.25
	Entire	2.75	.60
U364	U79 2c carmine, *oriental buff*	1.20	.25
	Entire	3.00	.60
U365	U79 2c carmine, *blue*	1.50	.55
	Entire	3.50	2.00
W366	U79 2c car, *man*	9.00	3.25
	Entire	15.00	7.50
U367	U80 2c carmine	6.00	2.75
	Entire	11.00	6.75
U368	U80 2c car, *amb*	10.00	6.50
	Entire	15.00	12.00
U369	U80 2c carmine, *oriental buff*	22.50	12.50
	Entire	30.00	20.00
U370	U80 2c carmine, *blue*	12.50	10.00
	Entire	26.00	15.00
U371	U81 4c brown	15.00	12.50
	Entire	27.50	18.00
U372	U81 4c brown, *amber*	15.00	12.50
	Entire	30.00	24.00
U373	U82 4c brown	7,500.	1,100.
		12,000.	
U374	U83 4c brown	12.50	8.00
	Entire	26.00	12.50
U375	U83 4c brown, *amber*	60.00	25.00
	Entire	80.00	40.00
W376	U83 4c brown, *manila*	20.00	12.50
	Entire	40.00	37.50
U377	U84 5c blue	11.00	9.00
	Entire	16.00	16.00
U378	U84 5c blue, *amber*	12.50	10.00
	Entire	22.50	17.00

Franklin — U85

Washington — U86

"D" of "UNITED" contains vertical line at right that parallels the left vertical line. One short and two long vertical lines at the right of "CENTS."

Grant — U87

Lincoln — U88

1903

U379	U85 1c green	.75	.25
		1.20	.35
U380	U85 1c green, *amber*	12.50	2.00
		20.00	7.00
U381	U85 1c green, *oriental buff*	16.00	2.50
		24.00	3.00
U382	U85 1c green, *blue*	20.00	2.50
		32.50	3.00
U383	U85 1c green, *manila*	4.00	.90
		5.50	1.25
W384	U85 1c green, *manila*	2.50	.40
		4.50	.80
U385	U86 2c carmine	.40	.25
		.85	.35
a.	2c pink	2.00	1.50
		3.00	2.00
b.	2c red	2.00	1.50
		3.00	2.00
U386	U86 2c carmine, *amber*	2.00	.50
	Entire	3.50	.80
a.	2c pink, *amber*	5.50	3.00
	Entire	7.50	4.00
b.	2c red, *amber*	12.50	7.00
	Entire	20.00	10.00
U387	U86 2c carmine, *oriental buff*	2.00	.30
	Entire	3.25	.80
a.	2c pink, *oriental buff*	3.50	2.00
	Entire	5.00	3.00
b.	2c red, *oriental buff*	4.00	2.25
	Entire	5.50	3.25
U388	U86 2c carmine, *blue*	1.75	.50
	Entire	2.75	.60
a.	2c pink, *blue*	20.00	14.00
	Entire	30.00	18.00
b.	2c red, *blue*	20.00	14.00
	Entire	30.00	18.00
W389	U86 2c carmine, *manila*	17.50	9.00
	Entire	25.00	14.00
U390	U87 4c choc	19.00	11.00
	Entire	30.00	14.00
U391	U87 4c choc, *amber*	20.00	11.00
	Entire	32.50	14.00
W392	U87 4c choc, *manila*	22.50	12.50
	Entire	45.00	35.00
U393	U88 5c blue	17.50	11.00
	Entire	30.00	16.00
U394	U88 5c blue, *amber*	17.50	11.00
	Entire	30.00	18.00

U89

Re-cut die — "D" of "UNITED" is well rounded at right. The three lines at the right of "CENTS" and at the left of "TWO" are usually

all short; the lettering is heavier and the ends of the ribbons slightly changed.

1904

Re-cut Die

U395	U89 2c carmine	.75	.25
	Entire	1.75	.45
a.	2c pink	5.50	2.50
U396	U89 2c carmine, *amber*	8.00	1.00
	Entire	12.50	2.00
a.	2c pink, *amber*	9.00	3.00
U397	U89 2c carmine, *oriental buff*	5.50	1.10
	Entire	8.00	1.50
a.	2c pink, *oriental buff*	7.00	2.75
U398	U89 2c carmine, *blue*	4.00	.90
	Entire	5.50	1.40
a.	2c pink, *blue*	5.50	2.50
W399	U89 2c carmine, *manila*	12.50	8.00
	Entire	30.00	24.00
a.	2c pink, *manila*	25.00	17.50
	Entire	70.00	85.00
b.	Double impression, entire	375.00	

Franklin — U90

U90 Die 1

U90 Die 2

U90 Die 3

U90 Die 4

Die 1 — Wide "D" in "UNITED."
Die 2 — Narrow "D" in "UNITED."
Die 3 — Wide "S-S" in "STATES" (1910).
Die 4 — Sharp angle at back of bust, "N" and "E" of "ONE" are parallel (1912).

1907-16 Die 1

U400	U90 1c green	.35	.25
		.60	.30
a.	Die 2	.85	.25
		1.25	.45
b.	Die 3	.85	.35
		1.40	.65
c.	Die 4	.90	.30
		1.40	.45
U401	U90 1c green, *amber*	2.00	.40
		2.75	.60
a.	Die 2	2.50	.70
		3.50	.80
b.	Die 3	3.25	.75
		4.00	.80
c.	Die 4	2.00	.65
		4.00	2.00
U402	U90 1c green, *oriental buff*	9.00	1.00
	Entire	13.00	5.00
a.	Die 2	12.00	1.50
	Entire	18.50	1.75
b.	Die 3	14.00	1.50
	Entire	20.00	2.50
c.	Die 4	9.00	1.50
	Entire	13.00	2.25
U403	U90 1c green, *blue*	9.00	1.50
	Entire	13.00	2.25
a.	Die 2	12.00	3.00
	Entire	16.50	4.00
b.	Die 3	11.50	3.00
	Entire	16.00	7.00
c.	Die 4	8.50	1.25
	Entire	13.50	3.00
U404	U90 1c green, *manila*	3.00	1.90
	Entire	5.50	2.75
a.	Die 2	4.50	3.00
	Entire	7.00	4.50
W405	U90 1c green, *manila*	1.00	.25
		2.25	1.00
a.	Die 2	60.00	25.00
	Entire	90.00	30.00
b.	Die 3	11.00	4.00
	Entire	36.00	25.00
c.	Die 4	85.00	—
	Entire	—	—
d.	Double impression, entire	175.00	

Washington — U91

U91 Die 1 — carmine

U91 Die 2

U91 Die 3

U91 Die 4

U91 Die 5

U91 Die 6

U91 Die 7

U91 Die 8

Die 1 — Oval "O" in "TWO" and "C" in "CENTS." Front of bust broad.
Die 2 — Similar to 1 but hair re-cut in two distinct locks at top of head.
Die 3 — Round "O" in "TWO" and "C" in "CENTS," coarse lettering.
Die 4 — Similar to 3 but lettering fine and clear, hair lines clearly embossed. Inner oval thin and clear.
Die 5 — All "S's" wide (1910).

Die 6 — Similar to 1 but front of bust narrow (1913).

Die 7 — Similar to 6 but upper corner of front of bust cut away (1916).

Die 8 — Similar to 7 but lower stroke of "S" in "CENTS" is a straight line. Hair as in Die 2 (1916).

Die 1

U406	U91 2c brown red	.90	.25
	Entire	2.60	.30
a.	Die 2	40.00	7.00
	Entire	95.00	50.00
b.	Die 3	.80	.25
	Entire	2.50	1.00
U407	U91 2c brown red, *amber*	6.50	2.00
	Entire	9.00	6.00
a.	Die 2	350.00	65.00
	Entire	700.00	200.00
b.	Die 3	4.50	1.25
	Entire	7.00	6.00
U408	U91 2c brown red, *oriental buff*	8.75	1.50
	Entire	12.00	3.75
a.	Die 2	300.00	125.00
	Entire	500.00	300.00
b.	Die 3	7.50	2.50
	Entire	11.00	6.00
U409	U91 2c brn red, *blue*	5.75	2.00
	Entire	8.00	3.75
a.	Die 2	375.00	100.00
	Entire	550.00	500.00
b.	Die 3	5.75	1.75
	Entire	8.00	3.50
W410	U91 2c brn red, *man*	37.50	35.00
	Entire	52.50	45.00
U411	U91 2c carmine	.35	.25
	Entire	1.25	.35
a.	Die 2	.90	.35
	Entire	2.25	1.50
b.	Die 3	.80	.35
	Entire	1.50	.50
c.	Die 4	.65	.25
	Entire	1.25	.35
d.	Die 5	.65	.30
	Entire	1.75	.50
e.	Die 6	.60	.25
	Entire	1.50	.30
f.	Die 7	37.50	25.00
	Entire	52.50	30.00
g.	Die 8	37.50	25.00
	Entire	52.50	30.00
h.	#U411 with added impression of #U400, entire	475.00	
i.	#U411 with added impression of #U416a, entire	475.00	
k.	As No. U411, double impression, entire	175.00	
U412	U91 2c carmine, *amb*	.30	.25
	Entire	1.10	.25
a.	Die 2	2.10	.25
	Entire	5.00	3.00
b.	Die 3	2.25	.45
	Entire	3.00	.75
c.	Die 4	.55	.25
	Entire	1.25	.40
d.	Die 5	.90	.35
	Entire	1.50	.55
e.	Die 6	.70	.35
	Entire	1.10	.30
f.	Die 7	35.00	25.00
	Entire	50.00	32.50
U413	U91 2c car, *oriental buff*	.55	.25
	Entire	.75	.25
a.	Die 2	2.25	.45
	Entire	5.00	3.75
b.	Die 3	9.00	3.00
	Entire	15.00	5.50
c.	Die 4	.55	.25
	Entire	1.25	.40
d.	Die 5	3.50	1.25
	Entire	5.00	3.25
e.	Die 6	.70	.35
	Entire	1.25	.55
f.	Die 7	100.00	45.00
	Entire	135.00	62.50
g.	Die 8	25.00	17.50
	Entire	40.00	22.50
U414	U91 2c carmine, *blue*	.60	.25
	Entire	1.40	.25
a.	Die 2	2.25	.35
	Entire	5.50	5.00
b.	Die 3	2.75	.60
	Entire	4.00	.70
c.	Die 4	.70	.25
	Entire	1.25	.45
d.	Die 5	2.25	.30
	Entire	3.00	.40
e.	Die 6	.65	.30
	Entire	1.10	.40
f.	Die 7	37.50	25.00
	Entire	50.00	35.00
g.	Die 8	37.50	25.00
	Entire	50.00	35.00
W415	U91 2c car, *manila*	5.00	2.00
	Entire	8.00	12.00
a.	Die 2	5.50	1.25
	Entire	8.00	20.00
b.	Die 5	5.50	2.50
	Entire	8.00	18.00
c.	Die 7	120.00	97.50
	Entire	175.00	125.00

U90 4c Die 1   U90 4c Die 2

Die 1 — "F" close to (1mm) left "4."
Die 2 — "F" far from (1¾mm) left "4."

U416	U90 4c black, die 2	7.50	3.00
	Entire	12.00	5.00
a.	Die 1	7.50	3.00
	Entire	12.00	5.00

U417	U90 4c black, *amb*, die 2	7.50	2.50
	Entire	12.00	4.00
a.	Die 1	7.50	2.50
	Entire	12.00	4.00

Die 1 — Tall "F" in "FIVE"

Die 2 — Short "F" in "FIVE"

Die 1 — Tall "F" in "FIVE."
Die 2 — Short "F" in "FIVE."

U418	U91 5c blue, die 2	7.00	2.25
	Entire	13.50	6.50
a.	Die 1	7.00	2.25
	Entire	13.50	6.50
b.	5c blue, *buff*, die 2 (error)	3,500.	
c.	5c blue, *blue*, die 2 (error)	3,250.	
d.	As "c," die 1 (error), entire	6,250.	
U419	U91 5c blue, *amber*, die 2	17.50	12.00
	Entire	25.00	14.00
a.	Die 1	15.00	12.00
	Entire	25.00	14.00

Franklin — U92

Die 1   Die 2

Die 3   Die 4   Die 5

(The 1c and 4c dies are the same except for figures of value.)

Die 1 — UNITED nearer inner circle than outer circle.

Die 2 — Large U; large NT closely spaced.

Die 3 — Knob of hair at back of neck. Large NT widely spaced.

Die 4 — UNITED nearer outer circle than inner circle.

Die 5 — Narrow oval C, (also O and G).

Printed by Middle West Supply Co.
and
International Envelope Corp., Dayton, Ohio.

1915-32   Die 1

U420	U92 1c green ('17)	.25	.25
	Entire	.40	.25
a.	Die 2	100.00	55.00
	Entire, size 8	200.00	70.00
b.	Die 3	.35	.25
	Entire	.50	.25
c.	Die 4	.55	.40
	Entire	.80	.50
d.	Die 5	.45	.35
	Entire	.75	.45
U421	U92 1c grn, *amber* ('17)	.55	.30
	Entire	.80	.45
a.	Die 2	400.00	175.00
	Entire, size 8	675.00	300.00
b.	Die 3	1.40	.65
	Entire	2.00	.95
c.	Die 4	1.90	.85
	Entire	2.50	1.25
d.	Die 5	1.10	.55
	Entire	1.75	.80
U422	U92 1c grn, *oriental buff* ('17)	2.40	.90
	Entire	3.25	1.40
a.	Die 4	5.50	1.25
	Entire	8.00	2.75
U423	U92 1c grn, *bl* ('17)	.50	.35
	Entire	1.00	.50
a.	Die 3	.80	.45
	Entire	1.25	.70
b.	Die 4	1.40	.65
	Entire	2.50	.95
c.	Die 5	.85	.35
	Entire	1.60	.65
U424	U92 1c grn, *manila* (unglazed) ('16)	6.50	4.00
	Entire	8.00	5.00

W425	U92 1c grn, *manila* (unglazed) ('16)	.30	.25
	Entire	1.00	.25
a.	Die 3	175.00	125.00
	Entire	250.00	200.00
U426	U92 1c grn, *brown* (glazed) ('20)	45.00	16.00
	Entire	57.50	27.50
W427	U92 1c grn, *brown* (glazed) ('20)	65.00	35.00
	Entire	80.00	60.00
a.	Printed on unglazed side	400.00	
b.	Unglazed on both sides	750.00	
		150.00	
U428	U92 1c grn, *brown* (unglazed) ('20)	12.50	7.50
	Entire	22.50	24.00
W428A	U92 1c grn, *brn* (unglazed) ('20), entire	3,000.	

Washington — U93

Die 1

Die 2

Die 3

Die 4

Die 5

Die 6

Die 7

Die 8

Die 9

(The 1½c, 2c, 3c, 5c, and 6c dies are the same except for figures of value.)

Die 1 — Letters broad. Numerals vertical. Large head (9¼mm). from tip of nose to back of neck. E closer to inner circle than N of cents.

Die 2 — Similar to 1; but U far from left circle.

Die 3 — Similar to 2; but all inner circles very thin (Rejected die).

Die 4 — Large head as in Die 1. C of CENTS close to circle. Baseline of right numeral "2" slants downward to right. Left numeral "2" is larger.

Die 5 — Small head (8¾mm) from tip of nose to back of neck. T and S of CENTS close at bottom.

Die 6 — Similar to 5; but T and S of CENTS far apart at bottom. Left numeral slopes to right.

Die 7 — Large head. Both numerals slope to right. Clean cut lettering. All letters T have short top strokes.

Die 8 — Similar to 7; but all letters T have long top strokes.

Die 9 — Narrow oval C (also O and G).

1915-32   Die 1

U429	U93 2c carmine	.25	.25
	Entire	.40	.25
a.	Die 2	15.00	7.00
	Entire	25.00	10.00
b.	Die 3	45.00	50.00
	Entire	85.00	200.00
c.	Die 4	27.50	15.00
	Entire	42.50	20.00
d.	Die 5	.55	.35
	Entire	1.00	.45
e.	Die 6	.65	.30
	Entire	1.25	.60
f.	Die 7	.70	.25
	Entire	1.25	.75
g.	Die 8	.50	.25
	Entire	1.00	.50
h.	Die 9	.50	.25
	Entire	1.00	.45
i.	2c green (error), die 1, entire	12,500.	
j.	#U429 with added impression of #U420	600.00	
	Entire	1,000.	
k.	#U429 with added impression of #U416a, entire	3,500.	
l.	#U429 with added impression of #U400, entire	950.00	
m.	#U429, double impression, entire	1,750.	
n.	As "f," double impression, entire	750.00	
o.	As "e," triple impression	—	
p.	As "m," second impression on side flap, entire	250.00	
U430	U93 2c car, *amber* ('16)	.30	.25
	Entire	.50	.25
a.	Die 2	20.00	12.50
	Entire	30.00	15.00
b.	Die 4	50.00	25.00
	Entire	70.00	30.00
c.	Die 5	1.60	.60
	Entire	2.25	.60
d.	Die 6	1.25	.40
	Entire	2.25	.75
e.	Die 7	.75	.35
	Entire	1.75	.95
f.	Die 8	.70	.30
	Entire	1.10	.45
g.	Die 9	.65	.25
	Entire	1.10	.35
h.	As No. U430, with added impression of 4c black (#U416a), entire	650.00	

i. As "g," with added impression of 2c car. die 1 on side flap, entire —

U431	U93 2c car, *oriental buff* ('16)	2.25	.65
	Entire	4.75	1.40
a.	Die 2	180.00	75.00
	Entire	260.00	250.00
b.	Die 4	75.00	60.00
	Entire	100.00	75.00
c.	Die 5	3.50	2.00
	Entire	6.00	2.75
d.	Die 6	3.50	2.00
	Entire	7.00	2.75
e.	Die 7	3.50	2.00
	Entire	6.00	3.25
U432	U93 2c car, *blue* ('16)	.30	.25
	Entire	.60	.25
a.	Die 2	40.00	25.00
	Entire	55.00	35.00
c.	Die 3	160.00	90.00
	Entire	200.00	400.00
d.	Die 4	65.00	50.00
	Entire	95.00	55.00
e.	Die 5	1.10	.30
	Entire	2.00	.75
f.	Die 6	1.10	.40
	Entire	2.00	.60
g.	Die 7	.85	.35
	Entire	1.75	.65
h.	Die 8	.65	.25
	Entire	1.50	.50
i.	Die 9	1.00	.30
	Entire	2.75	.55
j.	2c purple (error), die 9	—	
U432A	U93 2c car, *manila*, die 7, entire	50,000.	
W433	U93 2c car, *manila*, ('16)	.25	.25
	Entire	.50	.30
W434	U93 2c car, *brn* (glazed) ('20)	70.00	45.00
	Entire	95.00	55.00
W435	U93 2c car, *brn* (unglazed) ('20)	90.00	60.00
	Entire	115.00	150.00
U436	U93 3c purple ('32)	.30	.25
	Entire	.55	.25
a.	3c dark violet, die 1 ('17)	.60	.25
	Entire	1.00	.25
b.	3c dark violet, die 5 ('17)	1.75	.75
	Entire	3.25	.90
c.	3c dark violet, die 6 ('17)	2.10	1.40
	Entire	3.25	1.50
d.	3c dark violet, die 7 ('17)	1.50	.95
	Entire	3.00	1.00
e.	3c purple, die 7 ('32)	.70	.30
	Entire	1.75	.75
f.	3c purple, die 9 ('32)	.45	.25
	Entire	.60	.30
g.	3c carmine (error), die 1	35.00	35.00
	Entire	60.00	70.00
h.	3c carmine (error), die 5	30.00	—
	Entire	55.00	
i.	#U436 with added impression of #U420, entire	900.00	
j.	#U436 with added impression of #U429, entire	900.00	950.00
k.	As "f," double impression, preprinted, entire	600.00	
U437	U93 3c purple, *amb* ('32)	.35	.25
	Entire	.60	.35
a.	3c dk vio, die 1 ('17)	5.50	1.25
	Entire	9.00	2.25
b.	3c dk vio, die 5 ('17)	8.50	2.50
	Entire	12.00	3.00
c.	3c dk vio, die 6 ('17)	8.50	2.50
	Entire	12.00	3.00
d.	3c dk vio, die 7 ('17)	8.50	2.25
	Entire	12.00	2.50
e.	3c pur, die 7 ('32)	.75	.25
	Entire	1.25	.50
f.	3c pur, die 9 ('32)	.55	.25
	Entire	1.00	.30
g.	3c carmine (error), die 5	425.00	400.00
	Entire	475.00	750.00
h.	3c black (error), die 1	190.00	—
	Entire	300.00	375.00
U438	U93 3c dk vio, *oriental buff* ('17)	22.50	5.50
	Entire	32.50	21.00
a.	Die 5	22.50	5.50
	Entire	32.50	27.50
b.	Die 6	30.00	8.00
	Entire	45.00	35.00
c.	Die 7	30.00	10.00
	Entire	45.00	45.00
U439	U93 3c purple, *bl* ('32)	.35	.25
	Entire	.75	.25
a.	3c dark violet, die 1 ('17)	7.00	2.00
	Entire	14.00	6.00
b.	3c dark violet, die 5 ('17)	7.50	6.00
	Entire	15.00	7.50
c.	3c dark violet, die 6 ('17)	7.50	6.00

	Entire	15.00	7.50
d.	3c dark violet, die 7 ('17)	10.00	6.00
	Entire	17.50	7.50
e.	3c purple, die 7 ('32)	.75	.25
	Entire	1.50	.50
f.	3c purple, die 9 ('32)	.60	.25
	Entire	1.50	.45
g.	3c carmine (error), die 5	250.00	300.00
	Entire	425.00	725.00
U440	U92 4c black ('18)	1.75	.60
	Entire	3.25	2.00
a.	With added impression of 2c carmine (#U429), die 1, entire	450.00	
U441	U92 4c black, *amb* ('18)	3.00	.85
	Entire	5.00	2.00
a.	4c black, *amb*, with added impression of 2c car (#U429), die 1	175.00	
U442	U92 4c blk, *bl* ('21)	3.25	.85
	Entire	5.75	1.75
U443	U93 5c blue ('18)	3.25	2.75
	Entire	5.75	3.25
U444	U93 5c blue, *amber* ('18)	4.00	1.60
	Entire	6.50	3.50
U445	U93 5c bl, *blue* ('21)	3.75	3.25
	Entire	8.00	4.25

For 1½c and 6c see Nos. U481-W485, U529-U531.

Double or triple surcharge listings of 1920-25 are for examples with surcharge directly or partly upon the stamp.

Surcharged on 1874-1920 Envelopes indicated by Numbers in Parentheses

Type 1

1920-21

Surcharged in Black

U446	U93 2c on 3c dark vio (U436a, die 1)	15.00	10.00
	Entire	24.00	12.50
a.	On No. U436b (die 5)	15.00	10.00
	Entire	24.00	12.50
b.	As "a," double surcharge	140.00	—
	Entire	425.00	

Surcharged

Type 2

Rose Surcharge

U447	U93 2c on 3c dark vio (U436a, die 1)	9.00	7.50
	Entire	16.00	10.00
b.	On No. U436c (die 6)	13.00	8.50
	Entire	27.50	10.00

Black Surcharge

U447A	U92 2c on 1c green (U420, die 1) Entire	3,500.	
U447C	U93 2c on 2c carmine (U429, die 1)	—	
U447D	U93 2c on 2c car, *amb* (U430, die 1)	15,000.	
U448	U93 2c on 3c dark vio (U436a, die 1)	2.75	2.00
	Entire	4.00	2.50
a.	On No. U436b (die 5)	2.75	2.00
	Entire	4.00	2.50
b.	On No. U436c (die 6)	3.50	2.00
	Entire	5.00	2.50
c.	On No. U436d (die 7)	2.75	2.00
	Entire	4.00	2.50

U449	U93 2c on 3c dk vio (U437a, die 1)	7.50	6.00
	Entire	10.00	7.50
a.	On No. U437b (die 5)	13.00	7.50
	Entire	17.50	10.00
b.	On No. U437c (die 6)	9.50	6.00
	Entire	13.50	7.50
c.	On No. U437d (die 7)	8.50	6.50
	Entire	12.00	8.00
U450	U93 2c on 3c dk vio, *oriental buff* (U438, die 1)	17.50	15.00
	Entire	22.50	18.00
a.	On No. U438a (die 5)	17.50	15.00
	Entire	22.50	18.00
b.	On No. U438b (die 6)	17.50	15.00
	Entire	22.50	18.00
c.	On No. U438c (die 7)	130.00	90.00
	Entire	160.00	125.00
U451	U93 2c on 3c dk vio, *blue* (U439a, die 1)	15.00	10.50
	Entire	20.00	11.50
b.	On No. U439b (die 5)	15.00	10.50
	Entire	20.00	11.50
c.	On No. U439c (die 6)	15.00	10.50
	Entire	20.00	11.50
d.	On No. U439d (die 7)	27.50	22.50
	Entire	40.00	27.50

Type 2 exists in three city sub-types.

Surcharged

Type 3

Bars 2mm apart, 25 to 26mm in length

U451A	U90 2c on 1c green (U400, die 1)	25,000.	—
	Entire		
U452	U92 2c on 1c green (U420, die 1)	2,500.	
	Entire	4,000.	
a.	On No. U420b (die 3)	3,000.	
	Entire	4,000.	
b.	As No. U452, double surcharge	3,750.	
	Entire	4,500.	
U453	U91 2c on 2c car (U411b, die 3)	4,500.	
	Entire	7,000.	
a.	On No. U411 (die 1)	4,500.	
	Entire	7,000.	
U453B	U91 2c on 2c car, *bl* (U414e, die 6)	2,000.	750.00
	Entire	3,000.	
U453C	U91 2c on 2c car, *oriental buff* (U413e, die 6)	1,600.	750.00
	Entire	2,000.	
d.	On No. U413 (die 1)	1,600.	
	Entire	2,000.	
U454	U93 2c on 2c car (U429e, die 6)	150.00	
	Entire	225.00	
a.	On No. U429 (die 1)	325.00	
	Entire	375.00	
b.	On No. U429d (die 5)	500.00	
	Entire	650.00	
c.	On No. U429f (die 7)	150.00	
	Entire	200.00	
U455	U93 2c on 2c car, *amb* (U430, die 1)	1,600.	
	Entire	3,500.	
a.	On No. U430d (die 6)	1,750.	
	Entire	3,500.	
b.	On No. U430e (die 7)	1,750.	
	Entire	3,500.	
U456	U93 2c on 2c car, *oriental buff* (U431a, die 2)	250.00	
	Entire	375.00	
a.	On No. U431c (die 5)	250.00	
	Entire	550.00	
b.	On No. U431e (die 7)	800.00	
	Entire	950.00	
c.	As No. U456, double surcharge	700.00	
U457	U93 2c on 2c car, *bl* (U432f, die 6)	375.00	
	Entire	425.00	
a.	On No. U432e (die 5)	325.00	
	Entire	500.00	
b.	On No. U432g (die 7)	800.00	
	Entire	850.00	
U458	U93 2c on 3c dark vio (U436a, die 1)	.50	.35
a.	On No. U436b (die 5)	.75	.40
	Entire	.75	.50
b.	On No. U436c (die 6)	.75	.35
	Entire	.75	.50
c.	On No. U436d (die 7)	.75	.35
	Entire	.75	.45

d.	As #U458, double surcharge	25.00	7.50
	Entire	35.00	10.00
e.	As #U458, triple surcharge	100.00	
	Entire	150.00	
f.	As #U458, dbl. surch., 1 in magenta	100.00	
	Entire	150.00	
g.	As #U458, dbl. surch., types 2 & 3	140.00	
	Entire	190.00	
h.	As "a," double surcharge	27.50	15.00
	Entire	37.50	20.00
i.	As "a," triple surcharge	110.00	
	Entire	160.00	
j.	As "a," double surch., both magenta	110.00	
	Entire	150.00	
k.	As "b," double surcharge	25.00	8.00
	Entire	35.00	11.00
l.	As "c," double surcharge	25.00	8.00
	Entire	35.00	11.00
m.	As "c," triple surcharge	110.00	
	Entire	150.00	
n.	Double impression of indicia, single surcharge, entire	450.00	
U459	U93 2c on 3c dk vio, *amb* (U437c, die 6)	3.00	1.00
	Entire	4.50	1.75
a.	On No. U437a (die 1)	4.00	1.00
	Entire	5.50	1.75
b.	On No. U437b (die 5)	4.00	1.00
	Entire	5.50	1.75
c.	On No. U437d (die 7)	3.00	1.00
	Entire	5.50	1.75
d.	As #U459, double surcharge	35.00	
	Entire	50.00	
e.	As "a," double surcharge	35.00	
	Entire	50.00	
f.	As "b," double surcharge	35.00	
	Entire	50.00	
g.	As "b," double surcharge, types 2 & 3	125.00	
	Entire	175.00	
h.	As "c," double surcharge	35.00	
	Entire	50.00	
U460	U93 2c on 3c dk vio, *oriental buff* (U438a, die 5)	3.50	2.00
	Entire	4.50	2.50
a.	On No. U438 (die 1)	3.50	2.50
	Entire	4.50	2.50
b.	On No. U438b (die 6)	4.00	2.50
	Entire	5.50	2.50
c.	As #U460, double surcharge	20.00	
	Entire	30.00	
d.	As "a," double surcharge	20.00	
	Entire	30.00	
e.	As "b," double surcharge	20.00	
	Entire	30.00	
f.	As "b," triple surcharge	150.00	
	Entire	250.00	
U461	U93 2c on 3c dk vio, *bl* (U439a, die 1)	6.00	1.00
	Entire	8.25	1.50
a.	On No. U439b (die 5)	6.00	1.50
	Entire	8.25	1.50
b.	On No. U439c (die 6)	6.00	2.50
	Entire	8.25	3.50
c.	On No. U439d (die 7)	12.50	7.50
	Entire	17.50	15.00
d.	As #U461, double surcharge	20.00	
	Entire	40.00	30.00
e.	As "a," double surcharge	20.00	
	Entire	40.00	30.00
f.	As "b," double surcharge	20.00	
	Entire	40.00	30.00
g.	As "c," double surcharge	20.00	
	Entire	50.00	40.00
U462	U87 2c on 4c choc (U390)	525.00	260.00
	Entire	825.00	500.00
U463	U87 2c on 4c choc, *amb* (U391)	850.00	350.00
	Entire	1,250.	500.00
U463A	U90 2c on 4c black (U416, die 2)	900.00	400.00
	Entire	1,600.	
U464	U93 2c on 5c blue (U443)	1,000.	—
	Entire	1,750.	

Surcharged

Type 4

Bars 1 mm apart, 21 to 23 mm in length

U465 U92 2c on 1c green (U420, die 1) 1,000.
Entire 1,900.
a. On No. U420b (die 3) 1,400.
Entire 2,750.
U466 U91 2c on 2c car (U411e, die 6), entire 22,500.
U466A U93 2c on 2c carmine (U429, die 1) 800.00
Entire 1,250.
c. On No. U429d (die 5) 900.00
Entire 1,350.
d. On No. U429e (die 6) 900.00
Entire 1,350.
e. On No. U429f (die 7) 900.00
Entire 1,350.
U466B U93 2c on 2c car, amb (U430) 14,000.
Entire 22,500.
U466C U93 2c on 2c car, oriental buff (U431), entire 20,000.
U466D U25 2c on 3c green, die 2 (U82) 7,500.
U467 U45 2c on 3c green, die 2 (U163) 350.00
Entire 525.00
U468 U93 2c on 3c dark vio (U436a, die 1) .70 .45
Entire 1.00 .75
a. On No. U436b (die 5) .70 .50
Entire 1.00 .75
b. On No. U436c (die 6) .70 .50
Entire 1.00 .75
c. On No. U436d (die 7) .70 .50
Entire 1.00 .75
d. As #U468, double surcharge 20.00
Entire 30.00
e. As #U468, triple surcharge 100.00
Entire 150.00
f. As #U468, dbl. surch., types 2 & 4 125.00
Entire 175.00
g. As "a," double surcharge 20.00
Entire 30.00
h. As "b," double surcharge 20.00
Entire 30.00
i. As "c," double surcharge 20.00
Entire 30.00
j. As "c," triple surcharge 100.00
Entire 150.00
k. As "c," inverted surcharge 75.00
Entire 125.00
l. 2c on 3c carmine (error), (U436h) 650.00
Entire 1,500.
m. As #U468, triple surcharge, one inverted, entire 700.00
U469 U93 2c on 3c dk vio, amb (U437a, die 1) 3.75 2.25
Entire 5.00 2.75
a. On No. U437b (die 5) 5.00 2.75
Entire 5.00 2.75
b. On No. U437c (die 6) 5.00 2.75
Entire 5.00 2.75
c. On No. U437d (die 7) 3.75 2.25
Entire 5.00 2.75
d. As #U469, double surcharge 30.00
Entire 40.00
e. As "a," double surcharge 30.00
Entire 40.00
f. As "a," double surcharge, types 2 & 4 100.00
Entire 150.00
g. As "b," double surcharge 30.00
Entire 40.00
h. As "c," double surcharge 30.00
Entire 40.00
U470 U93 2c on 3c dk vio, oriental buff (U438, die 1) 6.00 2.50
Entire 10.00 5.00
a. On No. U438a (die 5) 6.00 2.50
Entire 10.00 6.00
b. On No. U438b (die 6) 6.00 2.50
Entire 10.00 6.00
c. On No. U438c (die 7) 42.50 32.50
Entire 70.00 70.00
d. As #U470, double surcharge 25.00
Entire 35.00
e. As #U470, double surch., types 2 & 4 90.00
Entire 140.00
f. As "a," double surcharge 25.00
Entire 35.00
g. As "b," double surcharge 25.00
Entire 35.00

U471 U93 2c on 3c dk vio, bl (U439a, die 1) 6.75 1.75
Entire 12.50 3.50
a. On No. U439b (die 5) 7.50 1.75
Entire 13.00 6.00
b. On No. U439c (die 6) 7.50 1.75
Entire 13.00 3.50
c. On No. U439d (die 7) 12.00 10.00
Entire 35.00 30.00
d. As #U471, double surcharge 30.00
Entire 40.00
e. As #U471, double surch., types 2 & 4 175.00
Entire 275.00
f. As "a," double surcharge 30.00
Entire 40.00
g. As "b," double surcharge 30.00
Entire 40.00
U471A U83 2c on 4c brown, (U374), entire 625.00
U472 U87 2c on 4c choc (U390) 15.00 12.00
Entire 27.50 16.00
a. Double surcharge 150.00
U473 U87 2c on 4c choc, amb (U391) 17.00 10.00
Entire 27.50 13.50

Surcharged

Double Surcharge, Type 4 and 1c as above

U474 U93 2c on 1c on 3c dark violet (U436a, die 1) 250. 500.
Entire 350.
a. On No. U436b (die 5) 250.
Entire 525.
b. On No. U436d (die 7) 900.
Entire 1,150.
U475 U93 2c on 1c on 3c dk vio, amb (U437a, die 1) 225.
Entire 425.

Surcharged

Type 5

U476 U93 2c on 3c dk vio, amb (U437a, die 1) 225.
Entire 475. 450.
a. On No. U437c (die 6) 800.
Entire 1,100.
b. As #U476, double surcharge —

Surcharged

Type 6

U477 U93 2c on 3c dark vio (U436a, die 1) 130.
Entire 175.
a. On No. U436b (die 5) 250.
Entire 300.
b. On No. U436c (die 6) 250.
Entire 300.
c. On No. U436d (die 7) 250.
Entire 300.
U478 U93 2c on 3c dk vio, amb (U437a, die 1) 290.
Entire 400.

Handstamped Surcharge in Black or Violet — Type 7

U479 U93 2c on 3c dark violet (Bk) (U436a, die 1) 250. —
Entire 550.
a. On No. U436b (die 5) 650.
Entire 1,000.
b. On No. U436d (die 7) 450.
Entire 550.
U480 U93 2c on 3c dark violet (V) (U436d, die 7) 5,000.
Entire 7,000.
a. Double overprint —

Expertization by competent authorities is required for Nos. U476-U480.

1925-34

Type of 1916-32 Issue
Die 1

U481 U93 1½c brown .25 .25
Entire .60 .25
Entire, 1st day cancel 60.00
a. Die 8 .70 .25
Entire 1.00 .50
b. 1½c purple, die 1 (error) ('34) 70.00
Entire 110.00 —
U482 U93 1½c brown, amber .90 .40
Entire 1.50 .60
a. Die 8 1.75 .75
Entire 2.25 .80
U483 U93 1½c brown, bl 1.60 .95
Entire 2.50 1.25
a. Die 8 2.40 1.25
Entire 3.25 1.40
U484 U93 1½c brown, manila 6.50 3.00
Entire 12.00 6.00
W485 U93 1½c brown, manila .85 .25
Entire 2.00 .45
a. With added impression of #W433 120.00 —

Surcharged Type 8

1925

On Envelopes of 1887

U486 U71 1½c on 2c grn (U311) 600.
Entire 1,250.
U487 U71 1½c on 2c green, amb (U312) 1,000.
Entire 1,500.

On Envelopes of 1899

U488 U77 1½c on 1c green (U352) 450.
Entire 850.
U489 U77 1½c on 1c grn, amb (U353) 110. 60.
Entire 200. 90.

On Envelopes of 1907-16

U490 U90 1½c on 1c green (U400, die 1) 6.25 3.50
Entire 10.00 5.50
a. On No. U400a (die 2) 17.00 9.00
Entire 22.50 12.00
b. On No. U400b (die 3) 40.00 17.50
Entire 52.50 22.50
c. On No. U400c (die 4) 9.00 2.50
Entire 13.00 4.00
U491 U90 1½c on 1c grn, amb (U401c, die 4) 8.00 3.00
Entire 12.50 8.50
a. On No. U401 (die 1) 12.50 3.50
Entire 17.50 8.50
b. On No. U401a (die 2) 120.00 70.00
Entire 140.00 140.00
c. On No. U401b (die 3) 60.00 50.00
Entire 100.00 100.00
U492 U90 1½c on 1c grn, oriental buff (U402a, die 2) 500.00 150.00
Entire 800.00 175.00
a. On No. U402c (die 4) 750.00 250.00
Entire 1,500. 300.00
U493 U90 1½c on 1c grn, bl (U403c, die 4) 110.00 65.00
Entire 140.00 70.00
a. On No. U403a (die 2) 110.00 67.50
Entire 140.00 90.00
U494 U90 1½c on 1c grn, man (U404, die 1) 300.00 100.00
Entire 550.00 150.00
a. On No. U404a (die 3) 1,250.

Entire 1,500.

On Envelopes of 1916-20

U495 U92 1½c on 1c green (U420, die 1) .80 .25
Entire 1.10 .45
a. On No. U420a (die 2) 85.00 52.50
Entire 125.00 90.00
b. On No. U420b (die 3) 2.10 .70
Entire 3.00 .85
c. On No. U420c (die 4) 2.10 .85
Entire 3.00 1.15
d. As #U495, double surcharge 10.00 3.00
Entire 15.00 5.00
e. As "b," double surcharge 10.00 3.00
Entire 15.00 5.00
f. As "c," double surcharge 10.00 3.00
Entire 15.00 5.00
U496 U92 1½c on 1c grn, amb (U421, die 1) 18.00 12.50
Entire 27.50 15.00
a. On No. U421b (die 3) 725.00
Entire 1,500.
b. On No. U421c (die 4) 18.00 12.50
Entire 27.50 15.00
U497 U92 1½c on 1c grn, oriental buff (U422, die 1) 3.75 1.90
Entire 7.00 2.25
a. On No. U422b (die 4) 67.50
Entire 100.00
U498 U92 1½c on 1c grn, bl (U423c, die 4) 1.40 .75
Entire 2.25 1.00
a. On No. U423 (die 1) 2.40 1.50
Entire 4.25 2.00
b. On No. U423b (die 3) 1.75 1.50
Entire 3.25 2.00
U499 U92 1½c on 1c grn, man (U424) 12.50 6.00
Entire 17.50 7.00
U500 U92 1½c on 1c grn, brn (unglazed) (U428) 75.00 30.00
Entire 90.00 35.00
U501 U92 1½c on 1c grn, brn (glazed) (U426) 75.00 30.00
Entire 90.00 35.00
U502 U93 1½c on 2c car (U429, die 1) 225.00 —
Entire 450.00
a. On No. U429d (die 5) 275.00
Entire 500.00
b. On No. U429f (die 7) 275.00
Entire 500.00
c. On No. U429e (die 6) 350.00
Entire 500.00
d. On No. U429g (die 8) 475.00
U503 U93 1½c on 2c car, oriental buff (U431c, die 5) 225.00 —
Entire 500.00
a. Double surcharge
b. Double surcharge, one inverted 700.00
U504 U93 1½c on 2c car, bl (U432, die 1) 400.00 —
Entire 500.00
a. On No. U432g (die 7) 400.00
Entire 500.00
b. As "a," double surcharge, entire —
c. On No. U432f (die b), entire 450.00

On Envelopes of 1925

U505 U93 1½c on 1½c brn (U481, die 1) 325.00
Entire 550.00
a. On No. U481a (die 8) 325.00
Entire 500.00
b. As No. U505, double surcharge, entire 2,000.
U506 U93 1½c on 1½c brn, bl (U483a, die 8) 225.00
Entire 550.00
a. On No. U483 (die 1) 325.00

The paper of No. U500 is not glazed and appears to be the same as that used for the wrappers of 1920.

Surcharged Type 9

Black Surcharge

U507 U69 1½c on 1c blue (U294) 2,000.
Entire 2,750.
U507A U69 1½c on 1c blue, amb (U296) —

U507B U69 1½c on 1c
blue,
manila
(U300)   5,000.
Entire   6,000.
U508 U77 1½c on 1c
grn,
amb
(U353)   65.00
Entire   90.00
U508A U85 1½c on 1c grn
(U379)   3,500.
                                    5,750.
U509 U85 1½c on 1c
grn,
amb
(U380)   15.00   10.00
Entire   27.50   *35.00*
a. Double surcharge   75.00
Entire   100.00
U509B U85 1½c on 1c
green,
*oriental
buff*
(U381)   45.00   40.00
Entire   60.00   50.00
U510 U90 1½c on 1c
green
(U400,
die 1)   2.75   1.25
Entire   4.75   1.50
b. On No. U400a (die 2)   9.00   4.00
Entire   13.50   6.00
c. On No. U400b (die 3)   37.50   8.00
Entire   50.00   11.00
d. On No. U400c (die 4)   3.50   1.25
Entire   7.50   2.00
e. As No. U510, double
    surcharge   25.00
Entire   50.00
U511 U90 1½c on 1c
grn,
amb
(U401,
die 1)   210.00 100.00
Entire   325.00 150.00
U512 U90 1½c on 1c
grn,
*oriental
buff*
(U402,
die 1)   8.00   4.00
Entire   15.00   6.50
a. On No. U402c (die 4)   21.00   14.00
Entire   30.00   17.00
U513 U90 1½c on 1c
grn, *bl*
(U403,
die 1)   6.00   4.00
Entire   9.50   4.50
a. On No. U403c (die 4)   6.00   4.00
Entire   9.50   5.00
U514 U90 1½c on 1c
grn,
man
(U404,
die 1)   35.00   9.00
Entire   45.00   22.50
a. On No. U404a (die 3)   77.50   40.00
Entire   100.00 95.00
U515 U92 1½c on 1c
green
(U420,
die 1)   .40   .25
Entire   .75   .30
a. On No. U420a (die 2)   20.00   15.00
Entire   30.00   20.00
b. On No. U420b (die 3)   .40   .25
Entire   .75   .30
c. On No. U420c (die 4)   .40   .25
Entire   .75   .30
d. As #U515, double
    surcharge   10.00
Entire   15.00
e. As #U515, inverted
    surcharge   20.00
Entire   30.00
f. As #U515, triple
    surcharge   20.00
Entire   30.00
g. As #U515, dbl.
    surch., one invtd.,
    entire   —
h. As "b," double
    surcharge   10.00
Entire   15.00
i. As "b," inverted
    surcharge   20.00
Entire   30.00
j. As "b," triple
    surcharge   30.00
Entire   40.00
k. As "c," double
    surcharge   10.00
Entire   15.00
l. As "c," inverted
    surcharge   20.00
Entire   30.00
U516 U92 1½c on 1c
grn,
amb
(U421c,
die 4)   55.00   27.50
Entire   70.00   37.50
a. On No. U421 (die 1)   60.00   32.50
Entire   75.00   42.50
U517 U92 1½c on 1c
grn,
*oriental
buff*
(U422,
die 1)   6.25   1.25
Entire   9.00   1.50
a. On No. U422a (die 4)   7.25   1.50
Entire   10.00   2.00

U518 U92 1½c on 1c
grn, *bl*
(U423b,
die 4)   5.00   1.50
Entire   7.50   5.00
a. On No. U423 (die 1)   8.25   4.50
Entire   27.50   18.00
b. On No. U423a (die 3)   27.50   7.50
Entire   40.00   9.00
c. As "a," double
    surcharge   30.00
Entire   42.50
U519 U92 1½c on 1c
grn,
man
(U424,
die 1)   30.00   12.00
Entire   42.50   15.00
a. Double surcharge   100.00
U520 U93 1½c on 2c
car
(U429,
die 1)   325.00 —
Entire   475.00 —
a. On No. U429d (die 5)   300.00
Entire   450.00
b. On No. U429e (die 6)   300.00
Entire   475.00
c. On No. U429f (die 7)   350.00
Entire   600.00
U520D U93 1½c on 2c
car,
amber
(U430c,
die 5),
entire   —
U520E U92 1½c on 4c
black
(U440,
die 1),
entire   —

Magenta Surcharge

U521 U92 1½c on 1c
grn
(U420b,
die 3)   4.25   3.50
Entire   6.50   5.50
Entire, 1st day can-
cel, Washington,
D.C.   100.00
a. Double surcharge   75.00
Entire   125.00

Sesquicentennial Exposition Issue

150th anniversary of the Declaration
of Independence.

Liberty Bell — U94

Die 1. The center bar of "E" of "postage" is
shorter than top bar.
Die 2. The center bar of "E" of "postage" is
of same length as top bar.

1926, July 27

U522 U94 2c carmine, die 1   1.00   .50
Entire   1.50   .95
a. Die 2   6.50   3.75
Entire   10.00   5.50

Washington Bicentennial Issue

200th anniversary of the birth of
George Washington.

Mount
Vernon — U95

2c Die 1 — "S" of "Postage" normal.
2c Die 2 — "S" of "Postage" raised.

1932

U523 U95 1c olive green   1.00   .80
Entire   1.50   1.75
U524 U95 1½c chocolate   2.00   1.50
Entire   2.75   2.50
U525 U95 2c car, die 1   .40   .25
Entire   .50   .25
a. 2c carmine, die 2   70.00   20.00
Entire   85.00   27.50
b. 2c carmine, *blue*, die 1
    (error) entire   30,000.
U526 U95 3c violet   1.75   .35
Entire   2.25   .40
U527 U95 4c black   17.50   17.50
Entire   22.50   *35.00*
U528 U95 5c dark blue   3.50   3.50
Entire   4.25   *20.00*
Nos. U523-U528 (6)   26.15   23.90

1932, Aug. 18

U529 U93 6c orange, die 7   6.00   4.00
Entire   9.50   7.50

U530 U93 6c orange, *amber,*
die 7   12.00   10.00
Entire   15.00   12.50
U531 U93 6c orange, *blue,* die
7   12.00   10.00
Entire   15.00   12.50

AIR POST STAMPED ENVELOPES AND AIR LETTER SHEETS

UC1

5c — Vertical rudder is not semi-circular but
slopes down to the left. The tail of the plane
projects into the G of POSTAGE.

UC2

Die 2 (5c and 8c): Vertical rudder is semi-
circular. The tail of the plane touches but does
not project into the G of POSTAGE.
Die 2 (6c) — Same as UC2 except three
types of numeral.
2a — The numeral "6" is 6½mm wide.
2b — The numeral "6" is 6mm wide.
2c — The numeral "6" is 5½mm wide.
Die 3 (6c): Vertical rudder leans forward. S
closer to O than to T of POSTAGE. E of
POSTAGE has short center bar. Border types
b and d, also without border.

1929-44

UC1 UC1 5c blue   3.25   2.00
a. Orange and blue bor-
    der, type b   375.00 450.00
UC2 UC2 5c blue, die 2   11.00   5.00
UC3 UC2 6c orange, die
    2a ('34)   1.25   .40
a. With added impression
    of 3c purple
    (#U436a), entire
    without border   4,000.
UC4 UC2 6c orange, die
    2b ('42)   3.00   2.00
UC5 UC2 6c orange, die
    2c ('44)   .70   .30
UC6 UC2 6c orange, die
    3 ('42)   1.00   .35
a. 6c orange, *blue*, die 3
    (error) Entire, without
    border   15,000. 10,000.
UC7 UC2 8c olive green,
    die 2 ('32)   12.50   3.50

OFFICIAL STAMPED ENVELOPES

By the Act of Congress, January 31,
1873, the franking privilege of officials
was abolished as of July 1, 1873 and
the Postmaster General was authorized
to prepare official envelopes. At the
same time official stamps were prepared for all Departments. Department
envelopes became obsolete July 5,
1884. After that, government offices
began to use franked envelopes of
varied design. These indicate no
denomination and lie beyond the scope
of this Catalogue.

Post Office Department

"2" 9mm high — UO1

"3" 9mm high — UO2

"6" 9½mm
high — UO3

1873

UO1 UO1 2c black, *lemon*   25.00   10.00
Entire   40.00   15.00
UO2 UO2 3c black, *lemon*   20.00   6.50
Entire   37.50   11.00
+UO3 UO2 3c black   27,500.
UO4 UO3 6c black, *lemon*   27.50   17.50
Entire   40.00   25.00

The No. UO3 entire is unique. It has a tear
through the stamp that has been profession-
ally repaired. Value based on auction sale in
1999.

"2" 9¼mm
high — UO4

"3" 9¼mm
high — UO5

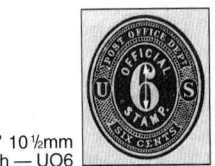

"6" 10½mm
high — UO6

1874-79

UO5 UO4 2c black, *lemon*   11.00   4.25
Entire   20.00   7.00
UO6 UO4 2c black   140.00 37.50
Entire   190.00 57.50
UO7 UO5 3c black, *lemon*   2.75   .85
Entire   4.25   1.50
UO8 UO5 3c black   2,250. 1,200.
Entire   4,250.
UO9 UO5 3c black, *amber*   140.00 40.00
Entire   175.00 60.00
UO10 UO5 3c black, *blue*   37,500.
Entire   42,500.
UO11 UO5 3c blue, *blue*
    ('75)   27,500.
Entire   32,500.
UO12 UO6 6c black, *lemon*   15.00   6.50
Entire   26.00   12.50
UO13 UO6 6c black   2,000. 2,100.
Entire   4,250.

Fakes exist of Nos. UO3, UO8 and UO13.

Postal Service

UO7

1877

UO14 UO7 black   6.00   4.50
Entire   11.00   6.00
UO15 UO7 black, *amber*   200.00 50.00
Entire   650.00 65.00
UO16 UO7 blue, *amber*   200.00 40.00
Entire   650.00 65.00
UO17 UO7 blue, *blue*   8.50   6.75
Entire   13.00   10.50

War Department

Franklin — UO8

Bust points to the end of "N" of "ONE".

Jackson — UO9

Bust narrow at the back.

Washington — UO10

Queue projects below the bust.

Lincoln — UO11

Neck very long at the back.

Jefferson — UO12

Queue forms straight line with bust.

Clay — UO13

Ear partly concealed by hair, mouth large, chin prominent.

Webster — UO14

Has side whiskers.

Scott UO15   Hamilton UO16

Back of bust very narrow; chin almost straight; the labels containing the letters "U S" are exactly parallel.

Printed by George H. Reay.

Reay Issue

1873

No.	Die	Denom	Color	Value 1	Value 2
UO18	UO8	1c	dk red	575.00	300.00
			Entire	1,100.	325.00
WO18A	UO8	1c	dk red, *man, entire*	—	
UO19	UO9	2c	dk red	1,750.	400.00
			Entire	2,500.	
UO20	UO10	3c	dk red	60.00	42.50
			Entire	85.00	70.00
UO21	UO10	3c	dk red, *amb*	32,500.	
			Entire	42,500.	
UO22	UO10	3c	dk red, *cr*	650.00	300.00
			Entire	850.00	350.00

No.	Die	Denom	Color	Value 1	Value 2
UO23	UO11	6c	dk red	300.00	100.00
			Entire	500.00	250.00
UO24	UO11	6c	dk red, *cr*	6,000.	425.00
			Entire	8,500.	3,500.
UO25	UO12	10c	dk red	15,000.	2,250.
			Entire	25,000.	4,000.
UO26	UO13	12c	dk red	175.00	60.00
			Entire	250.00	
UO27	UO14	15c	dk red	150.00	55.00
			Entire	210.00	375.00
UO28	UO15	24c	dk red	160.00	50.00
			Entire	225.00	1,500.
UO29	UO16	30c	dk red	300.00	150.00
			Entire	550.00	725.00
UO30	UO8	1c	ver	200.00	
			Entire	375.00	
WO31	UO8	1c	ver, *man*	20.00	14.00
			Entire	35.00	25.00
+UO32	UO9	2c	ver	375.00	
			Entire	22,500.	
WO33	UO9	2c	ver, *man*	250.00	
			Entire	700.00	
UO34	UO10	3c	ver	90.00	40.00
			Entire	160.00	125.00
UO35	UO10	3c	ver, *amb*	110.00	
			Entire	360.00	
UO36	UO10	3c	ver, *cr*	15.00	12.50
			Entire	37.50	26.00
UO37	UO11	6c	ver	100.00	
			Entire	175.00	
+UO38	UO11	6c	ver, *cr*	500.00	
			Entire	22,500.	
UO39	UO12	10c	ver	350.00	
			Entire	700.00	
UO40	UO13	12c	ver	140.00	
			Entire	200.00	
UO41	UO14	15c	ver	275.00	
			Entire	4,000.	
UO42	UO15	24c	ver	350.00	
			Entire	600.00	
UO43	UO16	30c	ver	325.00	
			Entire	500.00	

UO17

Bottom serif on "S" is thick and short; bust at bottom below hair forms a sharp point.

UO18

Bottom serif on "S" is thick and short; front part of bust is rounded.

UO19

Bottom serif on "S" is short; queue does not project below bust.

UO20

Neck very short at the back.

UO21

Knot of queue stands out prominently.

UO22

Ear prominent, chin receding.

UO23

Has no side whiskers; forelock projects above head.

UO24

Back of bust rather broad; chin slopes considerably; the label containing letters "U S" are not exactly parallel.

Plimpton Issue

1875

No.	Die	Denom	Color	Value 1	Value 2
UO44	UO17	1c	red	175.00	85.00
			Entire	240.00	175.00
+UO45	UO17	1c	red, *amb*	900.00	
+UO45A	UO17	1c	red, *org*	37,500.	
WO46	UO17	1c	red, *man*	4.50	2.75
			Entire	9.50	6.50
UO47	UO18	2c	red	125.00	
			Entire	175.00	
UO48	UO18	2c	red, *amber*	22.50	17.50
			Entire	30.00	37.50
UO49	UO18	2c	red, *orange*	45.00	17.50
			Entire	65.00	30.00
WO50	UO18	2c	red, *manila*	120.00	50.00
			Entire	225.00	
UO51	UO19	3c	red	15.00	10.00
			Entire	22.50	17.50
UO52	UO19	3c	red, *amber*	19.00	10.00
			Entire	27.50	16.00
UO53	UO19	3c	red, *cream*	6.50	3.75
			Entire	10.00	6.50
UO54	UO19	3c	red, *blue*	3.75	2.75
			Entire	6.00	4.50
UO55	UO19	3c	red, *fawn*	6.50	2.75
			Entire	11.50	4.00
UO56	UO20	6c	red	65.00	30.00
			Entire	100.00	
UO57	UO20	6c	red, *amber*	85.00	40.00
			Entire	120.00	
UO58	UO20	6c	red, *cream*	175.00	85.00
			Entire	450.00	
UO59	UO21	10c	red	180.00	80.00
			Entire	225.00	
UO60	UO21	10c	red, *amber*	950.00	
			Entire	1,250.	
UO61	UO22	12c	red	55.00	40.00
			Entire	180.00	250.00
UO62	UO22	12c	red, *amber*	525.00	
			Entire	750.00	
UO63	UO22	12c	red, *cream*	450.00	
			Entire	700.00	
UO64	UO23	15c	red	240.00	140.00
			Entire	300.00	
UO65	UO23	15c	red, *amber*	825.00	
			Entire	1,050.	
UO66	UO23	15c	red, *cream*	525.00	
			Entire	850.00	
UO67	UO24	30c	red	175.00	140.00
			Entire	225.00	
UO68	UO24	30c	red, *amber*	650.00	
			Entire	1,800.	
UO69	UO24	30c	red, *cream*	700.00	
			Entire	1,100.	

POSTAL SAVINGS ENVELOPES

Issued under the Act of Congress, approved June 25, 1910, in lieu of penalty or franked envelopes. Unused remainders, after mid-October 1914, were overprinted with the Penalty Clause. Regular stamped envelopes, redeemed by the Government, were also overprinted for official use.

UO25

1911

No.	Die	Denom	Color	Value 1	Value 2
UO70	UO25	1c	green	85.00	25.00
			Entire	125.00	42.50
UO71	UO25	1c	green, *oriental buff*	225.00	85.00
			Entire	325.00	100.00
UO72	UO25	2c	carmine	13.00	4.00
			Entire	21.00	12.00
a.		2c	carmine, *manila (error)*	1,750.	1,000.
			Entire	2,500.	1,400.

REVENUE STAMPS

Nos. R1-R102 were used to pay taxes on documents and proprietary articles including playing cards. Until Dec. 25, 1862, the law stated that a revenue stamp could be used only for payment of the tax upon the particular instrument or article specified on its face. After that date stamps, except the Proprietary, could be used indiscriminately.

Values quoted are for pen-canceled stamps. Stamps with handstamped cancellations sell at higher prices. Stamps canceled with cuts, punches or holes sell for less. See the Scott U.S. Specialized Catalogue.

General Issue
First Issue

Head of Washington in Oval. Various Frames as Illustrated.

Nos. R1b to R42b, part perforate, occur perforated sometimes at sides only and sometimes at top and bottom only. The higher values, part perforate, are perforated at sides only. Imperforate and part perforate revenues often bring much more in pairs or blocks than as single stamps. Part perforate revenues with an asterisk (*) after the value exist imperforate horizontally or vertically.

The experimental silk paper is a variety of the old paper and has only a very few minute fragments of fiber.

Some of the stamps were in use eight years and were printed several times. Many color variations occurred, particularly when unstable pigments were used and the color was intended to be purple or violet, such as the 4c Proprietary, 30c and $2.50 stamps. Before 1868 dull colors predominate on these and the early red stamps. In later printings of the 4c Proprietary, 30c and $2.50 stamps, red predominates in the mixture, and on the dollar values the red is brighter. The early $1.90 stamp is dull purple, imperf. or perforated. In a later printing, perforated only, the purple is darker.

R1   R2

Old Paper

1862-71	Engr.	*Perf. 12*
R1	R1 1c Express, red	
a.	Imperf.	75.00
b.	Part perf.	55.00*
c.	Perf.	1.50
d.	Silk paper	150.00
e.	As No. R1c, vertical pair, imperf. between	200.00
R2	R1 1c Playing Cards, red	
a.	Imperf.	3,250.
b.	Part perf.	2,000.
c.	Perf.	210.00
R3	R1 1c Proprietary, red	
a.	Imperf.	1,250.
b.	Part perf.	275.00*
c.	Perf.	.50
d.	Silk paper	57.50

R4 R1 1c Telegraph, red
a. Imperf. 800.00
c. Perf. 20.00

R5 R2 2c Bank Check, blue
a. Imperf. 1.50
b. Part perf. 5.50*
c. Perf. .50
e. As No. R5c, Double impression 800.00
f. As No. R5c, pair imperf between 400.00

R6 R2 2c Bank Check, orange
b. Part perf. 60.00*
c. Perf. .45
d. Silk paper 275.00
e. As No. R6c, orange, *green* 700.00
f. As No. R6c, vert. half used as 1c on document —

R7 R2 2c Certificate, blue
a. Imperf. 17.50
c. Perf. 32.50

R8 R2 2c Certificate, orange
c. Perf. 45.00

R9 R2 2c Express, blue
a. Imperf. 15.00
b. Part perf. 35.00*
c. Perf. .40

R10 R2 2c Express, orange
b. Part perf. 800.00
c. Perf. 14.00
d. Silk paper 160.00

R11 R2 2c Playing Cards, blue
a. Imperf. 1,500.
b. Part perf. 325.00
c. Perf. 4.50

R12 R2 2c Playing Cards, org
c. Perf. 55.00

R13 R2 2c Proprietary, blue
a. Imperf. 1,200.
b. Part perf. 350.
c. Perf. .40
d. Silk paper 175.00
e. ultramarine 300.00
f. As No. R13c, horiz. half used as 1c on document —

R14 R2 2c Proprietary, orange
c. Perf. 65.00

R15 R2 2c U.S. Internal Revenue, orange ('64)
a. Imperf —
b. Part perf. —
c. Perf. .35
d. Silk paper .40
e. As No. R15c, orange, *green* 1,500.
f. As No. R15c, half used as 1c on document —

R3

R16 R3 3c Foreign Exchange, green
b. Part perf. 950.00
c. Perf. 5.00
d. Silk paper 175.00

R17 R3 3c Playing Cards, green ('63)
a. Imperf. 40,000.
c. Perf. 175.00

R18 R3 3c Proprietary, green
b. Part perf. 1,250.
c. Perf. 9.00
d. Silk paper 125.00
e. As No. R18c, double impression 1,000.
f. As No. R18c, printed on both sides 3,500.

R19 R3 3c Telegraph, green
a. Imperf. 100.00
b. Part perf. 30.00
c. Perf. 3.00

R20 R3 4c Inland Exchange, brown ('63)
c. Perf. 2.25
d. Silk paper 175.00

R21 R3 4c Playing Cards, slate ('63)
c. Perf. 800.00

R22 R3 4c Proprietary, purple
a. Imperf. —
b. Part perf. 650.00
c. Perf. 8.50
d. Silk paper 250.00

There are shade and color variations of Nos. R21-R22.

R23 R3 5c Agreement, red
c. Perf. .50
d. Silk paper 4.50
e. As No. R23c, diag. half used as 2c on document 2,500.

R24 R3 5c Certificate, red
a. Imperf. 4.00
b. Part perf. 15.00
c. Perf. .50
d. Silk paper 1.10
e. As No. R24c, half used as 2c on document —
f. As No. R24d, impression of No. R3 on back 2,750.

R25 R3 5c Express, red
a. Imperf. 8.00
b. Part perf. 8.00*
c. Perf. .40

R26 R3 5c Foreign Exchange, red
b. Part perf. .50
c. Perf. 500.00
d. Silk paper

R27 R3 5c Inland Exchange, red
a. Imperf. 10.00
b. Part perf. 6.75
c. Perf. .60
d. Silk paper 17.50
e. As No. R27c, double impression —

R28 R3 5c Playing Cards, red ('63)
c. Perf. 40.00
d. Silk paper 750.00
e. Double impression 1,200.

R29 R3 5c Proprietary, red ('64)
c. Perf. 30.00
d. Silk paper 300.00

R30 R3 6c Inland Exchange, orange ('63)
c. Perf. 2.25
d. Silk paper 160.00

R31 R3 6c Proprietary, orange ('71)
c. Perf. 2,000.

Nearly all examples of No. R31 are faulty or repaired and poorly centered. The catalogue value is for a fine centered stamp with minor faults which do not detract from its appearance.

R32 R3 10c Bill of Lading, blue
a. Imperf. 55.00
b. Part perf. 500.00
c. Perf. 1.75
e. As No. R32c, half used as 5c on document 300.00

R33 R3 10c Certificate, blue
a. Imperf. 400.00
b. Part perf. 950.00*
c. Perf. .35
d. Silk paper 6.00
e. As No. R33c, half used as 5c on document 300.00

R34 R3 10c Contract, blue
b. Part perf. 575.00
be. As No. R34b, ultramarine 800.00
c. Perf. .50
ce. As No. R34c, ultramarine 1.00
d. Silk paper 4.25
f. As No. R34c, vertical half used as 5c on document 300.00

R35 R3 10c Foreign Exchange, blue
c. Perf. 14.00
d. Silk paper
e. As No. R35c, ultramarine 20.00

R36 R3 10c Inland Exchange, blue
a. Imperf. 500.00
b. Part perf. 4.50*
c. Perf. .30
d. Silk paper 100.00
e. As No. R36c, half used as 5c on document 300.00

R37 R3 10c Power of Attorney, blue
a. Imperf. 1,100.
b. Part perf. 30.00
c. Perf. 1.00
e. As No. R37c, half used as 5c on document 300.00

R38 R3 10c Proprietary, blue ('64)
c. Perf. 19.00

R39 R3 15c Foreign Exchange, brown ('63)
c. Perf. 17.00
e. Double impression 1,000.

R40 R3 15c Inland Exchange, brown
a. Imperf. 45.00
b. Part perf. 14.00
c. Perf. 2.00
e. As No. R40b, double impression 1,900.
f. As No. R40c, double impression 550.00

R41 R3 20c Foreign Exchange, red
a. Imperf. 95.00
c. Perf. 80.00
d. Silk paper 350.00

R42 R3 20c Inland Exchange, red
a. Imperf. 17.00
b. Part perf. 22.50
c. Perf. .45
d. Silk paper
e. As No. R42c, half used as 5c on document 300.00

R4

R5

R43 R4 25c Bond, red
a. Imperf. 300.00
b. Part perf. 6.75
Pair 60.00
c. Perf. 3.75

R44 R4 25c Certificate, red
a. Imperf. 11.00
b. Part perf. 6.75*
c. Perf. .50
d. Silk paper 2.75
e. As No. R44c, printed on both sides 3,500.
f. As No. R44c, impression of No. R48 on back 6,000.

R45 R4 25c Entry of Goods, red
a. Imperf. 22.50
b. Part perf. 300.00*
c. Perf. 1.50
d. Silk paper 90.00

R46 R4 25c Insurance, red
a. Imperf. 12.50
b. Part perf. 19.00
c. Perf. .30
d. Silk paper 7.00
e. As No. R46c, double impression 500.00

R47 R4 25c Life Insurance, red
a. Imperf. 50.00
b. Part perf. 1,000.
c. Perf. 11.00

R48 R4 25c Power of Attorney, red
a. Imperf. 10.00
b. Part perf. 45.00
c. Perf. 1.00

R49 R4 25c Protest, red
a. Imperf. 35.00
b. Part perf. 1,100.
c. Perf. 10.00

R50 R4 25c Warehouse Receipt, red
a. Imperf. 55.00
b. Part perf. 1,200.
c. Perf. 45.00

R51 R4 30c Foreign Exchange, lilac
a. Imperf. 200.00
b. Part perf. 5,000.
c. Perf. 60.00
d. Silk paper 600.00

R52 R4 30c Inland Exchange, lilac
a. Imperf. 72.50
b. Part perf. 90.00
c. Perf. 8.50
d. Silk paper

There are shade and color variations of Nos. R51-R52.

R53 R4 40c Inland Exchange, brown
a. Imperf. 2,500.
b. Part perf. 9.00
c. Perf. 8.00
d. Silk paper 575.00
f. As No. R53c, double impression —

R54 R5 50c Conveyance, blue
a. Imperf. 20.00
b. Part perf. 3.50
c. Perf. .35
ce. As No. R54c, ultramarine .50
d. Silk paper, blue 3.00
de. As No. R54d, ultramarine

R55 R5 50c Entry of Goods, blue
b. Part perf. 17.50
c. Perf. .60
d. Silk paper 110.00

R56 R5 50c Foreign Exchange, blue
a. Imperf. 75.00
b. Part perf. 125.00
c. Perf. 7.50
e. As No. R56c, double impression 500.00
f. As No. R56c, half used as 25c on document 300.00

R57 R5 50c Lease, blue
a. Imperf. 35.00
b. Part perf. 250.00
c. Perf. 10.00

R58 R5 50c Life Insurance, blue
a. Imperf. 45.00
b. Part perf. 200.00
c. Perf. 1.75
e. As No. R58c, double impression 800.00

R59 R5 50c Mortgage, blue
a. Imperf. 22.50
b. Part perf. 5.00
c. Perf. .70
d. Silk paper —

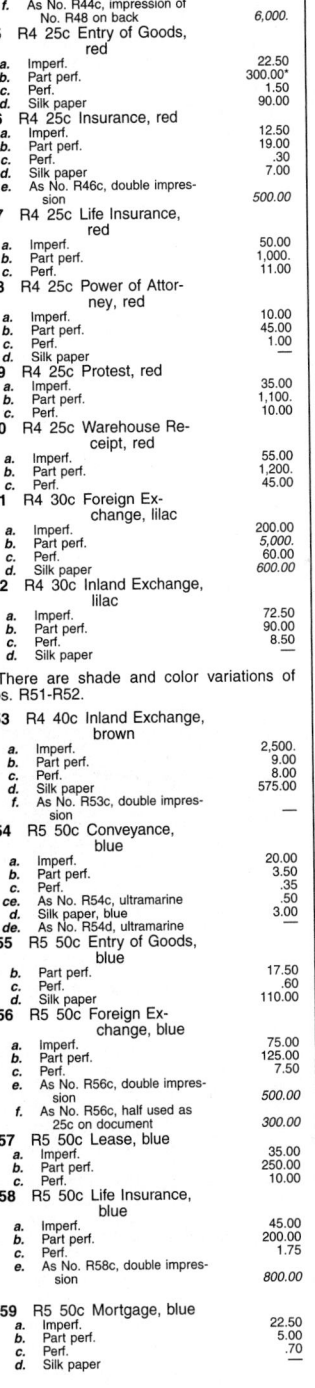

e. As No. R59a, double impression —
f. As No. R59c, double impression —

R60 R5 50c Original Process, blue
a. Imperf. 5.50
b. Part perf. 650.00
c. Perf. 1.00
d. Silk paper 7.50
e. As No. R60c, half used as 25c on document —

R61 R5 50c Passage Ticket, blue
a. Imperf. 140.00
b. Part perf. 500.00
c. Perf. 2.25

R62 R5 50c Probate of Will, blue
a. Imperf. 55.00
b. Part perf. 250.00
c. Perf. 22.50

R63 R5 50c Surety Bond, blue
a. Imperf. 400.00
b. Part perf. 2.75
c. Perf. .30
e. As No. R63c, ultramarine .75

R64 R5 60c Inland Exchange, orange
a. Imperf. 110.00
b. Part perf. 82.50
c. Perf. 9.00
d. Silk paper 85.00

R65 R5 70c Foreign Exchange, green
a. Imperf. 725.00
b. Part perf. 200.00
c. Perf. 14.00
d. Silk paper 110.00

R6

R7

R66 R6 $1 Conveyance, red
a. Imperf. 27.50
b. Part perf. 3,000.
c. Perf. 27.50
d. Silk paper 175.00

R67 R6 $1 Entry of Goods, red
a. Imperf. 50.00
c. Perf. 2.75
d. Silk paper 150.00

R68 R6 $1 Foreign Exchange, red
a. Imperf. 90.00
c. Perf. .75
d. Silk paper 125.00
e. As No. R68d, diagonal half used as 50c on document 300.00

R69 R6 $1 Inland Exchange, red
a. Imperf. 17.00
b. Part perf. 3,000.*
c. Perf. .70
Pair 2.00
d. Silk paper 6.00
e. As No. R69c, horiz. pair, imperf. vert.

No. R69e is an error from a pane of stamps that was intended to be issued fully perforated. It can be differentiated from No. R69b by the color, paper and date of cancel. Expertization is strongly recommended.

R70 R6 $1 Lease, red
a. Imperf. 50.00
c. Perf. 4.50
e. As No. R70c, half used as 50c on document —

R71 R6 $1 Life Insurance, red
a. Imperf. 300.00
c. Perf. 10.00
d. Silk paper 500.00
e. As No. R71c, half used as 50c on document —

R72 R6 $1 Manifest, red
a. Imperf. 47.50
c. Perf. 40.00

R73 R6 $1 Mortgage, red
a. Imperf. 27.50
c. Perf. 300.00

R74 R6 $1 Passage Ticket, red
a. Imperf. 350.00
c. Perf. 350.00

R75 R6 $1 Power of Attorney, red
a. Imperf. 100.00
c. Perf. 2.75
e. As No. R75c, horiz. half used as 50c on document —

R76 R6 $1 Probate of Will, red
a. Imperf. 100.00
Pair 300.00
c. Perf. 55.00

R77 R7 $1.30 Foreign Exchange,
                 orange ('63)
  a. Imperf. 9,000.
  c. Perf. 85.00
R78 R7 $1.50 Inland Ex-
                 change, blue
  a. Imperf. 32.50
  c. Perf 7.00
R79 R7 $1.60 Foreign Ex-
                 change, green
                 ('63)
  a. Imperf. 1,400.
  c. Perf. 180.00
R80 R7 $1.90 Foreign Ex-
                 change, pur-
                 ple ('63)
  a. Imperf. 12,500.
  c. Perf. 200.00
  d. Silk paper 300.00

There are many shade and color variations of No. R80.

R8

R81 R8 $2 Conveyance, red
  a. Imperf. 225.00
  b. Part perf. 2,750.
  c. Perf. 4.00
  d. Silk paper 40.00
  e. As No. R81c, half used as $1 on
                 document 600.00
R82 R8 $2 Mortgage, red
  a. Imperf. 150.00
  c. Perf. 7.00
  d. Silk paper 60.00
  e. As No. R82c, half used as $1 on
                 document —
R83 R8 $2 Probate of Will,
                 red ('63)
  a. Imperf. 7,750.
  c. Perf. 90.00
  e. As No. R83c, horiz. half used as
                 $1 on document 750.00
R84 R8 $2.50 Inland Exchange,
                 purple ('63)
  a. Imperf. 10,000.
  c. Perf. 22.50
  d. Silk paper 30.00
  e. As No. R84c, double impression 1,400.

There are many shade and color variations of Nos. R84c and R84d.

R85 R8 $3 Charter Party,
                 green
  a. Imperf. 200.00
  c. Perf. 11.00
  d. Silk paper 175.00
  e. As No. R85c, printed on both
                 sides 7,000.
  f. As No. R85c, half used as $1.50
                 on document —
  g. As No. R85c, impression of No.
                 RS208 on back 17,000.
R86 R8 $3 Manifest, green
  a. Imperf. 200.00
  c. Perf. 55.00
R87 R8 $3.50 Inland Exchange,
                 blue ('63)
  a. Imperf. 9,000.
  c. Perf. 70.00
  e. As No. R87c, printed on both
                 sides 4,000.

The $3.50 has stars in upper corners.

R9

R10

R88 R9 $5 Charter Party, red
  a. Imperf. 300.00
  c. Perf. 10.00
  d. Silk paper 100.00
R89 R9 $5 Conveyance, red
  a. Imperf. 50.00
  c. Perf. 11.00
  d. Silk paper 140.00
R90 R9 $5 Manifest, red
  a. Imperf. 250.00
  c. Perf. 120.00
R91 R9 $5 Mortgage, red
  a. Imperf. 200.00
  c. Perf. 25.00
R92 R9 $5 Probate of Will, red
  a. Imperf. 800.00
  c. Perf. 27.50
R93 R9 $10 Charter Party,
                 green
  a. Imperf. 900.00
  c. Perf. 37.50
R94 R9 $10 Conveyance, green
  a. Imperf. 175.00
  c. Perf. 77.50
R95 R9 $10 Mortgage, green
  a. Imperf. 900.00
  c. Perf. 40.00
R96 R9 $10 Probate of Will,
                 green
  a. Imperf. 3,500.
  c. Perf. 45.00
R97 R10 $15 Mortgage, blue
  a. Imperf. 3,750.
  c. Perf. 300.00
  e. As No. R97c, ultramarine 325.00
  f. As No. R97c, milky blue 350.00
R98 R10 $20 Conveyance, or-
                 ange
  a. Imperf. 175.00
  c. Perf. 125.00
  d. Silk paper 175.00
R99 R10 $20 Probate of Will, or-
                 ange
  a. Imperf. 3,250.
  c. Perf. 3,000.
R100 R10 $25 Mortgage, red ('63)
  a. Imperf. 2,500.
  c. Perf. 250.00
  d. Silk paper 275.00
  e. As No. R100c, horiz. pair, im-
                 perf. between 2,250.
R101 R10 $50 U.S. Internal Reve-
                 nue, green ('63)
  a. Imperf. 325.00
  c. Perf. 210.00

R11

Illustration R11 reduced.
R102 R11 $200 U.S. Int. Rev.,
                 green & red ('64)
  a. Imperf. 3,000.
  c. Perf. 1,000.

DOCUMENTARY STAMPS
Second Issue

After release of the First Issue revenue stamps, the Bureau of Internal Revenue received many reports of fraudulent cleaning and re-use. The Bureau ordered a Second Issue with new designs and colors, using a patented "chameleon" paper which is usually violet or pinkish, with silk fibers.

While designs are different from those of the first issue, stamp sizes and make up of the plates are the same as for corresponding denominations.

R12

R12a

George Washington
Various Frames and Numeral
Arrangements

1871   *Perf. 12*
R103 R12 1c blue & black 90.00
     Cut cancel 35.00
  a. Inverted center 1,600.
R104 R12 2c blue & black 2.75
     Cut cancel .30
  a. Inverted center 5,000.
R105 R12a 3c blue & black 50.00
     Cut cancel 20.00
R106 R12a 4c blue & black 125.00
     Cut cancel 45.00
  a. Horiz. half used as 2c on
                 document 500.00
  b. Vert. half used as 2c on
                 document 1,000.
R107 R12a 5c blue & black 2.00
     Cut cancel .50
  a. Inverted center 4,000.
R108 R12a 6c blue & black 250.00
     Cut cancel 80.00
R109 R12a 10c blue & black 1.50
     Cut cancel .30
  a. Inverted center 2,000.
  b. Double impression of
                 center —
  c. Half used as 5c on docu-
                 ment 300.00

No. R109a is valued in the grade of fine.

R110 R12a 15c blue & black 85.00
     Cut cancel 30.00
R111 R12a 20c blue & black 8.00
     Cut cancel 3.00
  a. Inverted center 7,000.

No. R111a is valued in the grade of fine and with small faults, as almost all examples have faults.

R13

R13a

R112 R13 25c blue & black 1.50
     Cut cancel .30
  a. Inverted center 12,500.
  b. Sewing machine perf. 150.00
     Cut cancel 80.00
  c. Perf. 8 475.00
R113 R13 30c blue & black 160.00
     Cut cancel 60.00
R114 R13 40c blue & black 130.00
     Cut cancel 40.00
R115 R13a 50c blue & black 1.40
     Cut cancel .35
  a. Sewing machine perf. 450.00
  b. Inverted center 1,250.
     Punch cancel 350.00
R116 R13a 60c blue & black 225.00
     Cut cancel 70.00
R117 R13a 70c blue & black 85.00
     Cut cancel 27.50
  a. Inverted center 4,000.
     Cut cancel 1,250.

R13b

R118 R13b $1 blue & black 10.00
     Cut cancel 2.25
  a. Inverted center 5,000.
     Punch cancel 900.00
R119 R13b $1.30 blue & black 700.00
     Cut cancel 160.00
R120 R13b $1.50 blue & black 22.50
     Cut cancel 9.00
  a. Sewing machine perf. 2,500.

R121 R13b $1.60 blue & black 800.00
     Cut cancel 350.00
R122 R13b $1.90 blue & black 550.00
     Cut cancel 150.00

R13c

R123 R13c $2 blue & black 22.50
     Cut cancel 10.00
R124 R13c $2.50 blue & black 50.00
     Cut cancel 25.00
R125 R13c $3 blue & black 65.00
     Cut cancel 30.00
R126 R13c $3.50 blue & black 500.00
     Cut cancel 130.00

R13d

R127 R13d $5 blue & black 32.50
     Cut cancel 11.00
  a. Inverted center 3,000.
     Punch cancel 1,100.
R128 R13d $10 blue & black 230.00
     Cut cancel 80.00

R13e

R129 R13e $20 blue & black 1,200.
     Cut cancel 350.00
R130 R13e $25 blue & black 1,150.
     Cut cancel 390.00
R131 R13e $50 blue & black 1,500.
     Cut cancel 400.00

R13f

R132 R13f $200 red, blue &
black 9,000.
Cut cancel 3,500.
Printed in sheets of one.

R13g

R133 R13g $500 red orange,
green &
black 17,500.

Printed in sheets of one.
Value for No. R133 is for a very fine appearing example with a light circular cut cancel or with minor flaws.

Inverted Centers: Fraudulently produced inverted centers exist, some excellently made.

Confusion resulting from the fact that all 1c through $50 denominations of the Second Issue were uniform in color, caused the ordering of a new printing with values in distinctive colors.

Plates used were those of the preceding issue.

Third Issue
Various Frames and Numeral Arrangements.
Violet "Chameleon" Paper with Silk Fibers.

1871-72			**Perf. 12**	
R134	R12	1c claret & black ('72)	55.00	
		Cut cancel	25.00	
R135	R12	2c orange & black	.40	
			.25	
a.		2c vermilion & black (error)	800.00	
b.		Inverted center	700.00	—
c.		Imperf., pair	1,500.	
d.		As No. R135, double impression of frame	1,500.	
e.		As No. R135, frame printed on both sides	1,600.	
f.		As No. R135, double impression of center	150.00	
R136	R12a	4c brown & black ('72)	95.00	
		Cut cancel	35.00	
R137	R12a	5c orange & black	.35	
			.25	
a.		Inverted center	4,500.00	

No. R137a is valued in the grade of fine.

R138	R12a	6c orange & black ('72)	110.00	
		Cut cancel	35.00	
R139	R12a	15c brown & black ('72)	22.50	
		Cut cancel	6.75	
a.		Inverted center	16,000.	
		Cut cancel	9,000.	
R140	R13	30c orange & black ('72)	40.00	
		Cut cancel	10.00	
a.		Inverted center	3,500.	
		Cut cancel	1,750.	
R141	R13	40c brown & black ('72)	90.00	
		Cut cancel	25.00	
R142	R13a	60c orange & black ('72)	125.00	
		Cut cancel	45.00	
R143	R13a	70c green & black ('72)	90.00	
		Cut cancel	30.00	
R144	R13b	$1 green & black ('72)	3.00	
		Cut cancel	.80	
a.		Inverted center	15,000.	

No. R144a is valued in the grade of fine.

R145	R13c	$2 vermilion & black ('72)	45.00	
		Cut cancel	18.00	
R146	R13c	$2.50 claret & black ('72)	90.00	
		Cut cancel	27.50	
a.		Inverted center	22,500.	
R147	R13c	$3 green & black ('72)	85.00	
		Cut cancel	27.50	
R148	R13d	$5 vermilion & black ('72)	42.50	
		Cut cancel	15.00	
R149	R13d	$10 green & black ('72)	400.00	
		Cut cancel	85.00	
R150	R13e	$20 orange & black ('72)	800.00	
		Cut cancel	325.00	
a.		$20 vermilion & black (error)	1,200.	

See note on Inverted Centers after No. R133.

1874			**Perf. 12**	
R151	R12	2c orange & black, *green*	.25	
		Cut cancel	.25	
a.		Inverted center	600.00	
		Cut cancel	350.00	

Liberty — R14

1875-78			**Perf. 12**	
R152	R14	2c bl, *blue*	.45	
a.		silk paper	.35	
b.		Wmk. 191R ('78)		
c.		Wmk. 191R, rouletted 6	32.50	
d.		As "a," vert. pair, imperf. horiz.	525.00	
e.		As "b," imperf., pair	350.00	
f.		As "b," vert. pair, imperf. horiz.	350.00	

The watermarked paper came into use in 1878. The rouletted stamps probably were introduced in 1881.

Nos. 279, 267a, 267, 279Bg, 279B, 272-274 Overprinted in Red or Blue

a   b

1898		**Wmk. 191**	**Perf. 12**	

For Nos. R153-R160, values in the first column are for unused examples, values in the second column are for used.

R153	A87 (a)	1c green (R)	5.00	2.75
R154	A87 (b)	1c green (R)	.35	.35
a.		Overprint inverted	35.00	22.50
b.		Overprint on back instead of face, inverted	4,000.	
c.		Pair, one without overprint	10,000.	
R155	A88 (b)	2c pink, III (Bl)	.30	.25
b.		2c carmine, type III (Bl)	.35	.25
c.		As No. R155, overprint inverted	6.50	4.50
d.		Vertical pair, one without overprint	1,750.	
e.		Horiz. pair, one without overprint	—	

f.		As No. R155, overprint on back instead of face, inverted	350.00	
i.		Double ovt., one split	750.00	
R155A	A88 (b)	2c pink, IV (Bl)	.25	.25
g.		2c carmine, type IV (Bl)	.25	.25
h.		As No. R155A, overprint inverted	2.75	2.00

Handstamped Type "b" in Magenta

R156	A93	8c violet brown	5,500.
R157	A94	10c dark green	4,250.
R158	A95	15c dark blue	6,500.

Nos. R156-R158 were emergency provisionals, privately prepared, not officially issued.

Privately Prepared Provisionals

No. 285
Overprinted
in Red

1898		**Wmk. 191**	**Perf. 12**	
R158A	A100	1c dark yellow green	12,500.	12,500.

Same Overprinted "I.R./P.I.D. & Son" in Red

R158B	A100	1c dark yellow green	30,000.	30,000.

No. R158B is valued with small faults as each of the four recorded examples have faults.

Nos. R158A-R158B were overprinted with federal government permission by the Purvis Printing Co. upon order of Capt. L. H. Chapman of the Chapman Steamboat Line. Both the Chapman Line and P. I. Daprix & Son operated freight-carrying steamboats on the Erie Canal. The Chapman Line touched at Syracuse, Utica, Little Falls and Fort Plain; the Daprix boat ran between Utica and Rome. Overprintings of 250 of each stamp were made.

Dr. Kilmer & Co. provisional overprints and St. Louis provisional proprietary stamps are listed under "Private Die Medicine Stamps" in the Scott U.S. Specialized Catalogue.

Newspaper Stamp
No. PR121
Surcharged Vertically
in Red

1898			**Perf. 12**	
R159	N18	$5 dark blue, surcharge reading down	550.00	325.00
R160	N18	$5 dark blue, surcharge reading up	150.00	140.00

Battleship — R15

Inscribed: "Series of 1898" and "Documentary."

There are 2 styles of rouletting for the 1898 proprietary and documentary stamps, an ordinary roulette 5½ and one where small rectangles of the paper are cut out, called hyphen hole perf. 7.

1898		**Wmk. 191R**	**Rouletted 5½**	
R161	R15	½c orange	4.00	17.50
R162	R15	½c dark gray	.30	.25
a.		Vert. pair, imperf. horiz.	100.00	
R163	R15	1c pale blue	.25	.25
a.		Vert. pair, imperf. horiz.	8.00	
b.		Imperf., pair	500.00	
c.		Diagonal half used as ½c, on piece		800.00

R164	R15	2c car rose	.30	.30
a.		Vert. pair, imperf. horiz.	100.00	
b.		Imperf., pair	300.00	
c.		Horiz. pair, imperf. vert.	325.00	
R165	R15	3c dark blue	3.50	.35
R166	R15	4c pale rose	2.50	.35
a.		Vert. pair, imperf. horiz.	175.00	
R167	R15	5c lilac	.65	.35
a.		Pair, imperf. horiz. or vert.	275.00	175.00
b.		Horiz. pair, imperf. btwn.		650.00
R168	R15	10c dark brown	2.00	.25
a.		Vert. pair, imperf. horiz.	40.00	35.00
b.		Horiz. pair, imperf. btwn.		
R169	R15	25c pur brown	5.00	.50
R170	R15	40c blue lilac	125.00	1.50
		Cut cancel		.35
R171	R15	50c slate violet	30.00	.25
a.		Imperf., pair		
b.		Horiz. pair, imperf. btwn.	325.00	375.00
R172	R15	80c bister	110.00	.50
		Cut cancel		.25

No. R167b may not be genuine.

Hyphen Hole Perf. 7

R163p		1c	.30	.25
R164p		2c	.35	.25
R165p		3c	35.00	1.40
R166p		4c	13.00	1.60
R167p		5c	13.00	.35
R168p		10c	7.50	.25
R169p		25c	15.00	.50
R170p		40c	175.00	30.00
		Cut cancel		12.50
R171p		50c	60.00	1.00
b.		Horiz. pair, imperf. btwn.	—	250.00
R172p		80c	210.00	50.00
		Cut cancellation		20.00

Commerce — R16

1898			**Rouletted 5½**	
R173	R16	$1 dark green	25.00	.25
a.		Vert. pair, imperf. horiz.	800.00	
b.		Horiz. pair, imperf. vert.	—	325.00
p.		Hyphen hole perf. 7	37.50	2.00
		Cut cancel		.75
R174	R16	$3 dark brown	45.00	1.25
a.		Horiz. pair, imperf. vert.		500.00
p.		Hyphen hole perf. 7	80.00	3.50
		Cut cancel		.40
R175	R16	$5 orange red	75.00	2.00
		Cut cancel		.30
R176	R16	$10 black	160.00	3.50
		Cut cancel		.65
a.		Horiz. pair, imperf. vert.		
R177	R16	$30 red	500.00	160.00
		Cut cancel		47.50
R178	R16	$50 gray brown	275.00	7.00
		Cut cancel		2.50

See Nos. R182-R183.

John
Marshall — R17

Alexander
Hamilton — R18

James
Madison — R19

1899 — Without Gum — Imperf.

R179	R17	$100 yel brn & blk	300.00	40.00
		Cut cancel		22.50
R180	R18	$500 car lake & blk	?,100.	800.00
		Cut cancel		350.00
R181	R19	$1000 grn & blk	1,500.	400.00
		Cut cancel		160.00

1900 — Hyphen-hole perf. 7
Allegorical Figure of Commerce

R182	R16	$1 carmine	45.00	.55 / .30
R183	R16	$3 lake (fugitive ink)	300.00	60.00
		Cut cancel		10.00

Warning: The ink on No. R183 will run in water.

a

Surcharged type "a"
1900

R184	R16	$1 gray	35.00	.40
		Cut cancel		.30
a.		Horiz. pair, imperf. vert	—	
b.		Surcharge omitted	140.00	
		As "b," cut cancel		82.50
R185	R16	$2 gray	35.00	.40
		Cut cancel		.25
R186	R16	$3 gray	175.00	15.00
		Cut cancel		6.00
R187	R16	$5 gray	85.00	11.00
		Cut cancel		1.60
R188	R16	$10 gray	225.00	25.00
		Cut cancel		4.50
R189	R16	$50 gray	2,000.	575.00
		Cut cancel		140.00

b

Surcharged type "b"

Warning: If Nos. R190-R194 are soaked, the center part of the surcharged numeral may wash off. Before the surcharging, a square of soluble varnish was applied to the middle of some stamps.

1902

R190	R16	$1 green	50.00	3.50
		Cut cancel		.30
a.		Inverted surcharge	190.00	
R191	R16	$2 green	50.00	2.50
		Cut cancel		.45
a.		Surcharged as No. R185	150.00	90.00
b.		Surcharged as No. R185, in violet	2,000.	—
c.		As "a," double surcharge	150.00	
d.		As "a," triple surcharge	850.00	
e.		Pair, Nos. R191c and R191d	1,650.	
R192	R16	$5 green	240.00	42.50
		Cut cancel		5.00
a.		Surcharge omitted	300.00	
b.		Pair, one without surcharge	500.00	
R193	R16	$10 green	525.00	225.00
		Cut cancel		80.00
R194	R16	$50 green	2,750.	1,250.
		Cut cancel		325.00

R20

Inscribed "Series of 1914"
Offset Printing
1914 — Wmk. 190 — Perf. 10

R195	R20	½c rose	14.00	5.00
R196	R20	1c rose	2.75	.30
R197	R20	2c rose	4.00	.30
R198	R20	3c rose	100.00	40.00
R199	R20	4c rose	30.00	2.50
R200	R20	5c rose	10.00	.40
R201	R20	10c rose	8.00	.25
R202	R20	25c rose	50.00	.60
R203	R20	40c rose	32.50	3.00
R204	R20	50c rose	13.00	.35
R205	R20	80c rose	210.00	17.00
		Nos. R195-R205 (11)	474.25	69.70

Wmk. 191R

R206	R20	½c rose	1.60	.50
R207	R20	1c rose	.25	.25
R208	R20	2c rose	.30	.25
R209	R20	3c rose	1.50	.25
R210	R20	4c rose	4.50	.50
R211	R20	5c rose	2.00	.35
R212	R20	10c rose	.80	.25
R213	R20	25c rose	8.00	1.50
R214	R20	40c rose	125.00	15.00
		Cut cancel		.50
R215	R20	50c rose	27.50	.40 / .25
R216	R20	80c rose	200.00	35.00
		Cut cancel		1.25
		Nos. R206-R216 (11)	371.45	54.25

Liberty — R21

Inscribed "Series 1914"
Engr.

R217	R21	$1 green	75.00	.55
		Cut cancel		.25
a.		$1 yellow green	50.00	.25
		Cut cancel		.25
R218	R21	$2 carmine	125.00	1.00
		Cut cancel		.25
R219	R21	$3 purple	150.00	5.00
		Cut cancel		.80
R220	R21	$5 blue	105.00	4.50
		Cut cancel		.65
R221	R21	$10 yellow orange	325.00	7.50
		Cut cancel		1.10
R222	R21	$30 vermilion	775.00	21.00
		Cut cancel		2.25
R223	R21	$50 violet	2,000.	1,200.
		Cut cancel		450.00

See Nos. R240-R245, R257-R259, R276-R281.

Portrait Types of 1899 Inscribed "Series of 1915" (#R224), or "Series of 1914"
1914-15 — Without Gum — Perf. 12

R224	R19	$60 brown (Lincoln)	250.00	150.00
		Cut cancel		70.00
R225	R17	$100 green (Washington)	77.50	45.00
		Cut cancel		16.00
R226	R18	$500 blue (Hamilton)	—	700.00
		Cut cancel		275.00
R227	R19	$1000 orange (Madison)	—	800.00
		Cut cancel		300.00

The stamps of types R17, R18 and R19 in this and subsequent issues were issued in vertical strips of 4 which are imperforate at the top, bottom and right side; therefore, single stamps are always imperforate on one or two sides.

R22

Offset Printing
1917 — Wmk. 191R — Perf. 11

R228	R22	1c carmine rose	.35	.25
R229	R22	2c carmine rose	.25	.25
R230	R22	3c carmine rose	1.75	.40
R231	R22	4c carmine rose	.75	.25
R232	R22	5c carmine rose	.30	.25
R233	R22	8c carmine rose	3.00	.35
R234	R22	10c carmine rose	.40	.25
R235	R22	20c carmine rose	.75	.25
R236	R22	25c carmine rose	1.75	.25
R237	R22	40c carmine rose	2.25	.50
R238	R22	50c carmine rose	2.50	.20
R239	R22	80c carmine rose	9.00	.35
		Nos. R228-R239 (12)	23.05	3.60

Liberty Type of 1914 without "Series 1914"
1917-33 — Engr.

R240	R21	$1 yellow green	10.00	.30
a.		$1 green	7.25	.25
R241	R21	$2 rose	17.50	.25
R242	R21	$3 violet	60.00	1.50
		Cut cancel		.30
R243	R21	$4 yellow brown ('33)	40.00	2.00
		Cut cancel		.30
R244	R21	$5 dark blue	27.50	.35
		Cut cancel		.25
R245	R21	$10 orange	60.00	1.40
		Cut cancel		.30

Portrait Types of 1899 without "Series of" and Date
Portraits: $30, Grant. $60, Lincoln. $100, Washington. $500, Hamilton. $1,000, Madison.

1917 — Without Gum — Perf. 12

R246	R17	$30 dp org, green numerals	55.00	13.00
		Cut cancel		2.25
a.		As "b," imperf. pair	750.00	
b.		Numerals in blue	125.00	3.50
		Cut cancel		1.50
R247	R19	$60 brown	65.00	8.00
		Cut cancel		.85
R248	R17	$100 green	45.00	2.00
		Cut cancel		.50
R249	R18	$500 blue, red numerals	375.00	50.00
		Cut cancel		15.00
a.		Numerals in orange	425.00	65.00
		Cut cancel		.75
R250	R19	$1000 orange	175.00	20.00
		Cut cancel		7.50
a.		Imperf., pair	2,000.	

See note after No. R227.

1928-29 — Offset Printing — Perf. 10

R251	R22	1c carmine rose	2.10	1.60
R252	R22	2c carmine rose	.60	.30
R253	R22	4c carmine rose	7.00	4.00
R254	R22	5c carmine rose	1.75	.55
R255	R22	10c carmine rose	2.75	1.25
R256	R22	20c carmine rose	6.00	4.50

Engr.

R257	R21	$1 green	200.00	45.00
		Cut cancel		5.00
R258	R21	$2 rose	90.00	14.00
R259	R21	$10 orange	325.00	75.00
		Cut cancel		30.00

1929 — Offset Printing — Perf. 11x10

R260	R22	2c carmine rose ('30)	3.00	2.75
R261	R22	5c carmine rose ('30)	2.00	1.90
R262	R22	10c carmine rose	9.25	6.75
R263	R22	20c carmine rose	15.00	8.25

Used values for Nos. R264-R310 are for stamps which are neither cut nor perforated with initials. Examples with cut cancellations or perforated initials are valued in the Scott U. S. Specialized Catalogue.

Types of 1917-33 Overprinted in Black
SERIES 1940

Offset Printing
1940 — Wmk. 191R — Perf. 11

R264	R22	1c rose pink	3.75	2.40
R265	R22	2c rose pink	5.00	2.25
R266	R22	3c rose pink	11.00	5.00
R267	R22	4c rose pink	5.00	.80
R268	R22	5c rose pink	5.00	.25
R269	R22	8c rose pink	22.50	17.00
R270	R22	10c rose pink	2.50	.65
R271	R22	20c rose pink	3.25	.80
R272	R22	25c rose pink	8.00	1.50
R273	R22	40c rose pink	6.75	.90
R274	R22	50c rose pink	11.00	.55
R275	R22	80c rose pink	14.00	1.75

Engr.

R276	R21	$1 green	75.00	1.25
R277	R21	$2 rose	75.00	2.00
R278	R21	$3 violet	100.00	37.50
R279	R21	$4 yellow brown	190.00	35.00
R280	R21	$5 dark blue	85.00	20.00
R281	R21	$10 orange	240.00	50.00

Types of 1917 Handstamped "Series 1940" like R264-R281 in Blue (Nos. R282-R283), Green (Nos. R283-R284, R286) or Violet (No. R285)
1940 — Wmk. 191R — Perf. 12 — Without Gum

R282	R17	$30 vermilion	1,250.	
a.		With black 2-line handstamp in larger type	22,500.	
R283	R19	$60 brown	2,400.	
a.		As #R282a, cut cancel	12,500.	
R284	R17	$100 green	4,250.	
R285	R18	$500 blue	3,000.	
a.		As #R282a	3,250.	4,250.
b.		Blue handstamp; double transfer	—	
R286	R19	$1000 orange	1,250.	
a.		Double overprint, cut cancel	—	

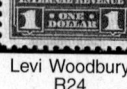

Alexander Hamilton R23	Levi Woodbury R24

Overprinted in Black — SERIES 1940

Various Portraits: 2c, Oliver Wolcott, Jr. 3c, Samuel Dexter. 4c, Albert Gallatin. 5c. G. W. Campbell. 8c, Alexander Dallas. 10c, William H. Crawford. 20c, Richard Rush. 25c, S. D. Ingham. 40c. Louis McLane. 50c, William J. Duane. 80c, Roger B. Taney. $2, Thomas Ewing. $3, Walter Forward. $4, J. C. Spencer. $5, G. M. Bibb. $10, R. J. Walker. $20, William M. Meredith.

1940 — Engr. — Wmk. 191R — Perf. 11

R288	R23	1c carmine	5.75	4.50
a.		Imperf, pair, without gum	250.00	
R289	R23	2c carmine	8.50	4.00
a.		Imperf, pair, without gum	250.00	
R290	R23	3c carmine	30.00	12.00
a.		Imperf, pair, without gum	250.00	
R291	R23	4c carmine	62.50	27.50
a.		Imperf, pair, without gum	250.00	
R292	R23	5c carmine	4.75	.80
a.		Imperf, pair, without gum	250.00	
R293	R23	8c carmine	85.00	60.00
a.		Imperf, pair, without gum	250.00	
R294	R23	10c carmine	4.25	.60
a.		Imperf, pair, without gum	250.00	
R295	R23	20c carmine	5.50	4.25
a.		Imperf, pair, without gum	250.00	
R296	R23	25c carmine	5.00	.75
a.		Imperf, pair, without gum	250.00	
R297	R23	40c carmine	75.00	30.00
a.		Imperf, pair, without gum	250.00	
R298	R23	50c carmine	8.00	.60
a.		Imperf, pair, without gum	250.00	
R299	R23	80c carmine	175.00	100.00
a.		Imperf, pair, without gum	475.00	
R300	R24	$1 carmine	42.50	.60
a.		Imperf, pair, without gum	250.00	
R301	R24	$2 carmine	80.00	.90
a.		Imperf, pair, without gum	1,400.	
R302	R24	$3 carmine	190.00	95.00
a.		Imperf, pair, without gum	700.00	
R303	R24	$4 carmine	125.00	50.00
R304	R24	$5 carmine	70.00	3.00
R305	R24	$10 carmine	125.00	10.00
R305A	R24	$20 carmine	3,000.	1,100.
b.		Imperf, pair, without gum	700.00	

Thomas Corwin — R25

Various Frames and Portraits: $50, James Guthrie. $60, Howell Cobb. $100, P. F. Thomas. $500, J. A. Dix. $1,000, S. P. Chase.

Perf. 12 — Without Gum

R306	R25	$30 carmine	200.00	75.00
R306A	R25	$50 carmine		10,000.
R307	R25	$60 carmine	375.00	80.00
a.		Vert. imperf. btwn.	2,750.	1,450.
R308	R25	$100 carmine	300.00	100.00
R309	R25	$500 carmine		5,500.
R310	R25	$1000 carmine		550.00

The $30 to $1,000 denominations in this and following similar issues, and the $2,500, $5,000 and $10,000 stamps of 1952-58 have straight edges on one or two sides. They were issued without gum through No. R723.

PROPRIETARY STAMPS

Stamps for use on proprietary articles were included in the first general issue of 1862-71. They are Nos. R3, R13-R14, R18, R22, R29, R31, R38.

Washington — RB1

RB1a

Various Frame Designs

1871-74   Engr.   Perf. 12

RB1	RB1	1c grn & blk	
a.		Violet paper ('71)	8.00
b.		Green paper ('74)	14.00
c.		As "a," Imperf.	80.00
d.		As "a." Inverted center	5,250.
RB2	RB1	2c grn & blk	
a.		Violet paper ('71)	8.75
b.		Green paper ('74)	30.00
c.		As "a," Invtd. center	45,000.
d.		As "b," Invtd. center	8,000.
e.		As "b," vert. half used as 1c on document	—

Only two examples recorded of the inverted center on violet paper, No. RB2c. Value is for example with very good to fine centering and very small faults.
RB2d is valued with fine centering and small faults.

RB3	RB1a	3c grn & blk	
a.		Violet paper ('71)	32.50
b.		Green paper ('74)	67.50
c.		As "a," sewing machine perf.	650.00
d.		As "a," inverted center	14,000.

No. RB3d is valued with small faults as 7 of the 8 recorded examples have faults.

RB4	RB1a	4c grn & blk	
a.		Violet paper ('71)	16.00
b.		Green paper ('74)	25.00
c.		As "a." inverted center	15,000.
d.		As "b," vert. half used as 2c on document	—

No. RB4c is valued with small faults as 6 of the 7 recorded examples have faults.

RB5	RB1a	5c grn & blk	
a.		Violet paper ('71)	175.00
b.		Green paper ('74)	250.00
c.		As "a," inverted center	130,000.

No. RB5c is unique. Value represents price realized in 2000 auction sale.

RB6	RB1a	6c grn & blk	
a.		Violet paper ('71)	57.50
b.		Green paper ('74)	140.00
RB7	RB1a	10c grn & blk ('73)	
a.		Violet paper ('71)	300.00
b.		Green paper ('74)	65.00

See note on Inverted Centers after No. R133.

RB1b

RB8	RB1b	50c grn & blk ('73)	
a.		Violet paper ('71)	1,000.
b.		Green paper ('74)	850.00

RB9	RB1b	$1 grn & blk ('73)	
a.		Violet paper ('71)	3,500.
b.		Green paper ('74)	12,500.

RB1c

RB10	RB1c	$5 grn & blk ('73)	
a.		Violet paper ('71)	11,000.
b.		Green paper ('74)	85,000.

No. RB10b is valued with small faults.

Washington — RB2

RB2a

Various Frame Designs
Green Paper

1875-81   Perf.
Unmwkd. (Silk Paper), Wmk. 191R

RB11	RB2	1c green	
a.		Silk paper	2.25
b.		Wmk 191R	.50
c.		Rouletted 6	160.00
d.		As No. RB11b, vert. pair, imperf btwn.	300.00
RB12	RB2	2c brown	
a.		Silk paper	3.25
b.		Wmk 191R	2.00
c.		Rouletted 6	175.00
RB13	RB2a	3c orange	
a.		Silk paper	14.00
b.		Wmk 191R	4.00
c.		Rouletted 6	140.00
d.		As No. RB13c, horiz. pair, imperf. between	—
e.		As No. RB13c, vert. pair, imperf. between	1,900.
RB14	RB2a	4c red brown	
a.		Silk paper	10.00
b.		Wmk 191R	9.00
c.		Rouletted 6	21,000.
RB15	RB2a	4c red	
b.		Wmk 191R	6.00
c.		Rouletted 6	400.00
RB16	RB2a	5c black	
a.		Silk paper	200.00
b.		Wmk 191R	125.00
c.		Rouletted 6	1,850.
RB17	RB2a	6c violet blue	
a.		Silk paper	35.00
b.		Wmk 191R	25.00
c.		Rouletted 6	900.00
RB18	RB2a	6c violet	
b.		Wmk 191R	35.00
c.		Rouletted 6	1,500.
RB19	RB2a	10c blue ('81)	
b.		Wmk 191R	400.00

Many fraudulent roulettes exist.

Battleship — RB3

Inscribed "Series of 1898." and "Proprietary."
See note on rouletting preceding No. R161.

Rouletted 5½

1898	**Wmk. 191R**		**Engr.**	
RB20	RB3	⅛c yellow green	.25	.25
a.		Vert. pair, imperf. horiz.	—	
b.		Vert. pair, imperf. btwn.	800.00	
RB21	RB3	¼c brown	.25	.25
a.		¼c red brown	.25	.25
b.		¼c yellow brown	.25	.25
c.		¼c orange brown	.25	.25
d.		¼c bister	.25	.25
e.		Vert. pair, imperf. horiz.	—	
f.		Printed on both sides	—	
RB22	RB3	⅜c deep orange	.30	.30
a.		Horiz. pair, imperf. vert.	12.50	
b.		Vert. pair, imperf. horiz.	—	
RB23	RB3	⅜c deep ultra	.25	.25
		Double transfer	1.50	
a.		Vert. pair, imperf. horiz.	85.00	
b.		Horiz. pair, imperf. btwn.	350.00	200.00
RB24	RB3	1c dark green	2.25	.50
a.		Vert. pair, imperf. horiz.	325.00	
RB25	RB3	1¼c violet	.35	.25
a.		1¼c brown violet	.25	.25
b.		Vert. pair, imperf. btwn.	—	
RB26	RB3	1⅞c dull blue	15.00	2.00
RB27	RB3	2c violet brown	1.40	.35
a.		Horiz. pair, imperf. vert.	60.00	
RB28	RB3	2½c lake	5.00	.35
a.		Vert. pair, imperf. horiz.	225.00	
RB29	RB3	3¾c olive gray	42.50	15.00
RB30	RB3	4c purple	16.00	1.50
RB31	RB3	5c brown orange	15.00	1.50
a.		Vert. pair, imperf. horiz.	—	400.00
b.		Horiz. pair, imperf. vert.	—	425.00
Nos. RB20-RB31 (12)			*98.55*	*22.50*

Hyphen Hole Perf. 7

RB20p		⅛c	.30	.25
RB21p		¼c	.25	.25
b.		¼c yellow brown	.25	.25
c.		¼c orange brown	.25	.25
d.		¼c bister	.25	.25
RB22p		⅜c	.50	.35
RB23p		⅜c	.30	.25
RB24p		1c	30.00	15.00
RB25p		1¼c	.30	.30
a.		1¼c brown violet	.25	.25
RB26p		1⅞c	35.00	9.00
RB27p		2c	7.25	1.00
RB28p		2½c	6.00	.40
RB29p		3¾c	90.00	27.50
RB30p		4c	62.50	22.50
RB31p		5c	75.00	25.00

See note before No. R161.

RB4

Inscribed "Series of 1914"

Offset Printing

1914	**Wmk. 190**		**Perf. 10**	
RB32	RB4	⅛c black	.25	.35
		Block of 4	1.25	1.60
RB33	RB4	¼c black	4.00	1.50
RB34	RB4	⅜c black	.35	.35
RB35	RB4	⅝c black	7.75	3.00
RB36	RB4	1¼c black	5.00	1.75
RB37	RB4	1½c black	67.50	22.50
RB38	RB4	2½c black	16.00	3.50
RB39	RB4	3⅛c black	200.00	67.50
RB40	RB4	3¾c black	65.00	27.50
RB41	RB4	4c black	90.00	45.00
RB42	RB4	4⅜c black	3,000.	
RB43	RB4	5c black	175.00	110.00
Nos. RB32-RB41,RB43 (11)			*630.85*	*282.95*

Wmk. 191R				
RB44	RB4	⅛c black	.35	.30
RB45	RB4	¼c black	.25	.25
RB46	RB4	⅜c black	.75	.45
RB47	RB4	½c black	4.25	3.75
RB48	RB4	⅝c black	.30	.25
RB49	RB4	1c black	5.50	5.50
RB50	RB4	1¼c black	.65	.40
RB51	RB4	1½c black	4.25	3.00
RB52	RB4	1⅞c black	1.35	.90
RB53	RB4	2c black	7.50	6.00
RB54	RB4	2½c black	2.00	1.40
RB55	RB4	3c black	6.00	4.00
RB56	RB4	3⅛c black	8.00	5.00
RB57	RB4	3¾c black	17.50	11.00
RB58	RB4	4c black	.50	.30
RB59	RB4	4⅜c black	20.00	11.00
RB60	RB4	5c black	4.50	3.75
RB61	RB4	6c black	80.00	52.50
RB62	RB4	8c black	25.00	16.00
RB63	RB4	10c black	18.00	11.00
RB64	RB4	20c black	35.00	24.00
Nos. RB44-RB64 (21)			*241.65*	*160.75*

RB5

1919	**Offset Printing**		**Perf. 11**	
RB65	RB5	1c dark blue	.25	.25
RB66	RB5	2c dark blue	.35	.25
RB67	RB5	3c dark blue	1.50	.75
RB68	RB5	4c dark blue	2.25	.75
RB69	RB5	5c dark blue	3.00	1.25
RB70	RB5	8c dark blue	22.50	16.00
RB71	RB5	10c dark blue	11.00	4.25
RB72	RB5	20c dark blue	17.50	6.00
RB73	RB5	40c dark blue	65.00	20.00
Nos. RB65-RB73 (9)			*123.35*	*49.50*

FUTURE DELIVERY STAMPS

Issued to facilitate the collection of a tax upon each sale, agreement of sale or agreement to sell any products or merchandise at any exchange or board of trade, or other similar place for future delivery.

Documentary Stamps of 1917
Overprinted in Black or Red

Type I

Offset Printing
1918-34   Wmk. 191R   Perf. 11
Overprint Horizontal (Lines 8mm apart)

Left Value — Unused
Right Value — Used

RC1	R22	2c carmine rose	8.75	.25
RC2	R22	3c carmine rose ('34)	47.50	37.50
		Cut cancel		20.00
RC3	R22	4c carmine rose	15.00	.25
		Cut cancel		.25
b.		Double impression of stamp		10.00
RC3A	R22	5c carmine rose ('33)	90.00	7.50
RC4	R22	10c carmine rose	24.00	.25
a.		Double overprint		5.25
b.		"FUTURE" omitted	—	325.00
		"DELIVERY FUTURE"		37.50
RC5	R22	20c carmine rose	35.00	.25
		Cut cancel		.25
a.		Double overprint		21.00
RC6	R22	25c carmine rose	75.00	.60
				.30
RC7	R22	40c carmine rose	85.00	1.25
				.35
RC8	R22	50c carmine rose	22.50	.35
		Cut cancel		.25
a.		"DELIVERY" omitted	—	110.00
RC9	R22	80c carmine rose	175.00	15.00
		Cut cancel		4.00
a.		Double overprint		37.50

Engr.
Overprint Vertical, Reading Up
(Lines 2mm apart)

RC10	R21	$1 green (R)	65.00	.35
		Cut cancel		.25
a.		Overprint reading down		300.00
b.		Black overprint		125.00
		Cut cancel		125.00
RC11	R21	$2 rose	75.00	.45
		Cut cancel		.25
RC12	R21	$3 violet (R)	225.00	3.50
		Cut cancel		.30
a.		Overprint reading down	—	52.50
RC13	R21	$5 dark blue (R)	125.00	.60
		Cut cancel		.25
RC14	R21	$10 orange	150.00	1.35
		Cut cancel		.30
a.		"DELIVERY FUTURE"		110.00
RC15	R21	$20 olive bister	400.00	9.00
		Cut cancel		.80

Overprint Horizontal (Lines 11⅔mm apart)
Perf. 12
Without Gum

RC16	R17	$30 vermilion, green numerals	125.00	5.50
		Cut cancel		1.75
a.		Numerals in blue	110.00	4.75
		Cut cancel		2.00
b.		Imperf., blue numerals		110.00

RC17	R19	$50 olive green (Cleveland)	100.00	3.00
		Cut cancel		.90
a.		$50 olive bister	100.00	2.75
		Cut cancel		2.50
RC18	R19	$60 brown	140.00	9.00
		Cut cancel		1.20
a.		Vert. pair, imperf. horiz.		550.00
RC19	R17	$100 yellow green ('34)	225.00	37.50
				9.00
RC20	R18	$500 blue, red numerals (R)	275.00	25.00
		Cut cancel		9.00
a.		Numerals in orange	—	60.00
		Cut cancel		12.50
RC21	R19	$1000 orange	200.00	7.50
		Cut cancel		2.00
a.		Vert. pair, imperf. horiz.		1,350.

See note after No. R227.

1923-24 Offset Printing Perf. 11
Overprint Horizontal (Lines 2mm apart)

RC22	R22	1c carmine rose	1.25	.25
RC23	R22	80c carmine rose	175.00	3.50
		Cut cancel		.70

Type II

1925-34   Engr.

RC25	R21	$1 green (R)	85.00	2.00
		Cut cancel		.45
RC26	R21	$10 orange (Bk) ('34)	225.00	29.00
		Cut cancel		18.00

Overprint Type I

1928-29 Offset Printing Perf. 10

RC27	R22	1c carmine rose		5,000.
RC28	R22	20c carmine rose		5,000.

Some specialists have questioned the status of No. RC28, believing known examples to be either fraudulently reperforated examples of No. RC5, or examples of No. R256 with fake overprints applied. The editors would like to see authenticated evidence of the existence of No. RC28.

STOCK TRANSFER STAMPS

Issued to facilitate the collection of a tax on all sales or agreements to sell, or memoranda of sales or delivery of, or transfers of legal title to shares or certificates of stock.

Documentary Stamps
Nos. R228 to R259
Overprinted in Black or Red

Offset Printing
1918-22 Wmk. 191R Perf. 11
Overprint Horizontal (Lines 8mm apart)

RD1	R22	1c carmine rose	1.00	.25
a.		Double overprint	—	.25
RD2	R22	2c carmine rose	.25	.25
a.		Double overprint	—	15.00
		Double overprint, cut cancel		7.50
RD3	R22	4c carmine rose	.25	.25
a.		Double overprint	—	4.25
		Double overprint, cut cancel		2.10
b.		"STOCK" omitted		10.50
d.		Ovpt. lines 10mm apart	—	
RD4	R22	5c carmine rose	.30	.25
a.		Ovpt. lines 7mm apart		.25
RD5	R22	10c carmine rose	.30	.25
a.		Double overprint	—	5.25
		Double overprint, cut cancel		2.75
b.		"STOCK" omitted		
RD6	R22	20c carmine rose	.55	.25
a.		Double overprint	—	6.25
b.		"STOCK" double		
RD7	R22	25c carmine rose	2.25	.30
		Cut cancel		.25

RD8	R22	40c carmine rose ('22)	2.25	.25
RD9	R22	50c carmine rose	.80	.25
a.		Double overprint	—	
RD10	R22	80c carmine rose	9.00	.45
		Cut cancel		.25

Engr.
Overprint Vertical, Reading Up (Lines 2mm apart)

RD11	R21	$1 green (R)	190.00	35.00
		Cut cancel		9.50
a.		Overprint reading down	225.00	35.00
		Overprint reading down, cut cancel		10.00
RD12	R21	$1 green (Bk)	3.00	.30
a.		Pair, one without overprint	—	160.00
b.		Overprinted on back instead of face, inverted	—	110.00
c.		Overprint reading down	—	7.50
d.		$1 yellow green	3.00	.25
RD13	R21	$2 rose	3.00	.25
a.		Overprint reading down		11.50
		Overprint reading down, cut cancel		1.50
b.		Vert. pair, imperf. horiz.	500.00	
RD14	R21	$3 violet (R)	27.50	6.00
		Cut cancel		.30
RD15	R21	$4 yellow brown	12.00	.30
		Cut cancel		.25
RD16	R21	$5 dark blue (R)	8.00	.30
a.		Overprint reading down	42.50	1.35
		Overprint reading down, cut cancel		.25
RD17	R21	$10 orange	30.00	.45
		Cut cancel		.25
RD18	R21	$20 olive bister ('21)	130.00	18.00
		Cut cancel		4.50
a.		Overprint reading down	—	

Overprint Horizontal (Lines 11½mm apart)
1918   Without Gum   Perf. 12

RD19	R17	$30 ver, grn numerals	42.50	6.50
		Cut cancel		2.25
a.		Numerals in blue	175.00	75.00
RD20	R19	$50 ol grn, Cleveland	140.00	62.50
		Cut cancel		26.00
RD21	R19	$60 brown	300.00	25.00
		Cut cancel		10.50
RD22	R17	$100 green	45.00	7.50
		Cut cancel		3.00
RD23	R18	$500 blue (R)	425.00	150.00
		Cut cancel		75.00
a.		Numerals in orange		150.00
RD24	R19	$1,000 orange	375.00	95.00
		Cut cancel		32.50

See note after No. R227.

1928 Offset Printing Perf. 10
Overprint Horizontal (Lines 8mm apart)

RD25	R22	2c carmine rose	5.50	.30
RD26	R22	4c carmine rose	5.50	.30
RD27	R22	10c carmine rose	5.50	.30
a.		Inverted overprint		1,400.
b.		Ovpt. lines 9½mm apart		
RD28	R22	20c carmine rose	6.50	.35
RD29	R22	50c carmine rose	10.00	.50

Engr.
Overprint Vertical, Reading Up (Lines 2mm apart)

RD30	R21	$1 green	50.00	.35
		Cut cancel		.25
a.		$1 yellow green	50.00	.50
RD31	R21	$2 carmine rose	45.00	.35
a.		Pair, one without overprint	225.00	190.00
RD32	R21	$10 orange	45.00	.50
		Cut cancel		.25

Overprinted Horiz. in Black

1920   Offset Printing Perf. 11

RD33	R22	2c carmine rose	12.50	1.00
RD34	R22	10c carmine rose	3.00	.35
b.		Inverted overprint	1,500.	1,250.
RD35	R22	20c carmine rose	5.75	.25
a.		Horiz. pair, one without overprint	175.00	
d.		Inverted overprint (perf. initials)	—	
RD36	R22	50c carmine rose	5.00	.30

Engr.

RD37	R21	$1 green	70.00	13.50
		Cut cancel		2.50
RD38	R21	$2 rose	80.00	13.50
		Cut cancel		2.50

Offset Printing
Perf. 10

RD39	R22	2c carmine rose	13.00	1.10
RD40	R22	10c carmine rose	5.25	.55
RD41	R22	20c carmine rose	6.00	.25
		Cut cancel		.25

Used values for Nos. RD42-RD372 are for stamps which are neither cut nor perforated with initials. Stamps with cut cancellations or perforated initials are valued in the Scott U.S. Specialized Catalogue.

Documentary Stamps of 1917-33 Overprinted in Black

Offset Printing
1940   Wmk. 191R   Perf. 11

RD42	R22	1c rose pink	4.50	.65
a.		"Series 1940" inverted	600.00	450.00

No. RD42a always comes with a natural straight edge at left.

RD43	R22	2c rose pink	4.75	.65
RD45	R22	4c rose pink	5.50	.35
RD46	R22	6c rose pink	6.00	.25
RD48	R22	10c rose pink	11.00	.35
RD49	R22	20c rose pink	12.50	.35
RD50	R22	25c rose pink	12.50	1.10
RD51	R22	40c rose pink	9.25	1.00
RD52	R22	50c rose pink	10.50	.35
RD53	R22	80c rose pink	250.00	100.00

Engr.

RD54	R21	$1 green	42.50	.60
RD55	R21	$2 rose	47.50	1.00
RD56	R21	$3 violet	300.00	18.00
RD57	R21	$4 yellow brown	110.00	1.60
RD58	R21	$5 dark blue	85.00	2.00
RD59	R21	$10 orange	250.00	10.00
RD60	R21	$20 olive bister	500.00	150.00

Nos. RD19-RD24 Handstamped in Blue "Series 1940"

1940   Wmk. 191R   Perf. 12
Without Gum

RD61	R17	$30 vermilion	1,250.	1,250.
RD62	R19	$50 olive green	2,250.	2,250.
		Cut cancel		1,000.
a.		Double ovpt., perf. initial		1,000.
RD63	R19	$60 brown	3,000.	3,000.
RD64	R17	$100 green	2,000.	950.
RD65	R18	$500 blue		3,250.
RD66	R19	$1,000 orange		
		Cut cancel		5,000.

Alexander Hamilton ST1

Levi Woodbury ST2

Overprinted in Black   SERIES 1940

Same Portraits as Nos. R288-R310.

1940 Engr. Wmk. 191R Perf. 11

RD67	ST1	1c brt grn	14.00	3.25
a.		Imperf. pair, without gum	250.00	
RD68	ST1	2c brt grn	9.00	1.75
a.		Imperf. pair, without gum	250.00	
RD70	ST1	4c brt grn	16.00	4.50
a.		Imperf. pair, without gum	250.00	
RD71	ST1	5c brt grn	10.00	1.75
a.		Imperf. pair, without gum	250.00	
b.		Without overprint, cut cancel	400.00	
RD73	ST1	10c brt grn	14.00	2.10
a.		Imperf. pair, without gum	250.00	

RD74	ST1	20c brt grn	16.00	2.40
a.		Imperf. pair, without gum	250.00	
RD75	ST1	25c brt grn	55.00	10.50
a.		Imperf. pair, without gum	250.00	
RD76	ST1	40c brt grn	110.00	16.00
a.		Imperf. pair, without gum	250.00	
RD77	ST1	50c brt grn	14.00	2.10
a.		Imperf. pair, without gum	250.00	
RD78	ST1	80c brt grn	160.00	65.00
a.		Imperf. pair, without gum	250.00	
RD79	ST2	$1 brt grn	60.00	4.25
a.		Without overprint, perf. initial	400.00	
RD80	ST2	$2 brt grn	65.00	12.00
a.		Imperf. pair, without gum	250.00	
RD81	ST2	$3 brt grn	90.00	15.00
a.		Imperf. pair, without gum	250.00	
RD82	ST2	$4 brt grn	500.00	275.00
a.		Imperf. pair, without gum	250.00	
RD83	ST2	$5 brt grn	90.00	16.00
a.		Imperf. pair, without gum	250.00	
RD84	ST2	$10 brt grn	225.00	60.00
a.		Imperf. pair, without gum	250.00	
RD85	ST2	$20 brt grn	1,250.	125.00
a.		Imperf. pair, without gum	250.00	

Nos. RD67-RD85 exist imperforate, without overprint. Value, set of pairs, $1,100.

Thomas Corwin — ST3

Overprinted "SERIES 1940"

Various frames and portraits as Nos. R306-R310.

Perf. 12
Without Gum

RD86	ST3	$30 brt grn	1,750.	175.00
RD87	ST3	$50 brt grn	800.00	500.00
RD88	ST3	$60 brt grn	3,000.	1,750.
RD89	ST3	$100 brt grn	600.00	375.00
RD90	ST3	$500 brt grn	—	2,750.
RD91	ST3	$1,000 brt grn	—	3,750.

Nos. RD86-RD91 exist as unfinished imperforates with complete receipt tabs, without overprints or serial numbers. Known in singles, pairs (Nos. RD86-RD88 and Nos. RD90-RD91, value $300 per pair; No. RD89, value $150 per pair), panes of four with plate number, uncut sheets of four panes (with two plate numbers), cross gutter blocks of eight, and blocks of four with vertical gutter between and plate number.

HUNTING PERMIT STAMPS

Catalogue values for all unused stamps in this section are for stamps with never-hinged original gum. Minor natural gum skips and bends are normal on Nos. RW1-RW20. No-gum stamps are without signature or other cancel.

Department of Agriculture
Various Designs Inscribed "U. S. Department of Agriculture"

Mallards Alighting — HP1

Engraved: Flat Plate Printing

1934   Unwmk.   *Perf. 11*
Inscribed "Void after June 30, 1935"
RW1   HP1 $1 blue   700.   150.
     Hinged   350.
     No gum   160.
   a.   Imperf., vertical pair   —
   b.   Vert. pair, imperf. horiz.   —

Used value is for stamp with handstamp or manuscript cancel.

It is almost certain that No. RW1a is No. RW1b with vertical perfs trimmed off. No horizontal pairs of No. RW1a are known. All recorded pairs are vertical, with narrow side margins. Both varieties probably are printer's waste since examples exist with gum on front or without gum.

1935
Inscribed "Void after June 30, 1936"
RW2   HP2 $1 rose lake   700.00   160.00
     deep rose lake
     Hinged   350.
     No gum   180.

1936
Inscribed "Void after June 30, 1937"
RW3   HP3 $1 brown black   325.   90.00
     Hinged   160.
     No gum   90.

1937
Inscribed "Void after June 30, 1938"
RW4   HP4 $1 light green   300.   70.00
     Hinged   140.
     No gum   85.

1938
Inscribed "Void after June 30, 1939"
RW5   HP5 $1 light violet   400.   75.00
     Hinged   190.
     No gum   85.

Department of the Interior
Various Designs Inscribed
"U. S. Department of the Interior"

Green-Winged Teal — HP6

1939
Inscribed "Void after June 30, 1940"
RW6   HP6 $1 chocolate   225.   45.00
     Hinged   100.
     No gum   45.

1940
Inscribed "Void after June 30, 1941"
RW7   HP7 $1 sepia   210.   45.00
     Hinged   105.
     No gum   45.

CONFEDERATE STATES OF AMERICA

3¢ 1861 POSTMASTERS' PROVISIONALS

With the secession of South Carolina from the Union on Dec. 20, 1860, a new era began in U.S. history as well as its postal history. Other Southern states quickly followed South Carolina's lead, which in turn led to the formation of the provisional government of the Confederate States of America on Feb. 4, 1861.

President Jefferson Davis' cabinet was completed Mar. 6, 1861, with the acceptance of the position of Postmaster General by John H. Reagan of Texas. The provisional government had already passed regulations that required payment for postage in cash and that effectively carried over the U.S. 3c rate until the new Confederate Post Office Department took over control of the system.

Soon after entering on his duties, Reagan directed the postmasters in the Confederate States and in the newly seceded states to "continue the performance of their duties as such, and render all accounts and pay all moneys

(sic) to the order of the Government of the U.S. as they have heretofore done, until the Government of the Confederate States shall be prepared to assume control of its postal affairs."

As coinage was becoming scarce, postal patrons began having problems buying individual stamps or paying for letters individually, especially as stamp stocks started to run short in certain areas. Even though the U.S. Post Office Department was technically in control of the postal system and southern postmasters were operating under Federal authority, the U.S.P.O. was hesitant in re-supplying seceded states with additional stamps and stamped envelopes.

The U.S. government had made the issuance of postmasters' provisionals illegal many years before, but the southern postmasters had to do what they felt was necessary to allow patrons to pay for postage and make the system work. Therefore, a few postmasters took it upon themselves to issue provisional stamps in the 3c rate then in effect.

Interestingly, these were stamps and envelopes that the U.S. government did not recognize as legal, but they did do postal duty unchallenged in the Confederate States. Yet the proceeds were to be remitted to the U.S. government in Washington! Six authenticated postmasters' provisionals in the 3c rate have been recorded.

On May 13, 1861, Postmaster General Reagan issued his proclamation "assuming control and direction of postal service within the limits of the Confederate States of America on and after the first day of June," with new postage rates and regulations.

The Federal government suspended operations in the Confederate States (except for western Virginia and the seceding state of Tennessee) by a proclamation issued by Postmaster General Montgomery Blair on May 27, 1861, effective from May 31, 1861, and June 10 for western and middle Tennessee.

As Tennessee did not join the Confederacy until July 2, 1861, the unissued 3c Nashville provisional was produced in a state that was in the process of seceding, while the other provisionals were issued in the Confederacy before the June 1 assumption of control of postal service by the Confederate States of America.

Illustrations are reduced in size.
XU numbers are envelope entires.

HILLSBORO, N.C.

A1

Handstamped Adhesive
1AX1   A1   3c bluish black,
       on cover   —

No. 1AX1 is unique. This is the same handstamp as used for No. 39X1. 3c usage is determined from the May 27, 1861 circular date stamp.

JACKSON, MISS.

E1

Handstamped Envelope
2AXU1   E1   3c black   3,500.
     See Nos. 43XU1-43XU4.

MADISON COURT HOUSE, FLA.

A1   "CNETS"

Typeset Adhesive
3AX1   A1   3c gold   —   20,000.
     On cover   65,000.
   a.   "CNETS"   25,000.

No. 3AX1a is unique.
See No. 137XU1.

NASHVILLE, TENN.

A1

Typeset Adhesive (5 varieties)
4AX1   A1   3c carmine   350.

No. 4AX1 was prepared by Postmaster McNish with the U.S. rate, but the stamp was never issued.
See Nos. 61X2-61XU2.

SELMA, ALA.

E1

Handstamped Envelope
5AXU1   E1   3c black   2,500.
     See Nos. 77XU1-77XU3.

TUSCUMBIA, ALA.

E1

Handstamped Envelope, impression at upper right
6AXU1   E1   3c dull red,
        buff   17,500.

Dangerous forgeries exist of No. 6AXU1.
See Nos. 84XU1-84XU3.

PROVISIONAL ISSUES

These stamps and envelopes were issued by individual postmasters generally between June 1, 1861, when the use of U.S. stamps stopped in the Confederacy, and Oct. 16, 1861, when the 1st Confederate Government stamps were issued.

They were occasionally issued at later periods, especially in Texas, when regular issues of Government stamps were unavailable.

Canceling stamps of the post offices were often used to produce envelopes, some of which were supplied in advance by private citizens.

These envelopes and other stationery therefore may be found in a wide variety of papers, colors, sizes & shapes, including patriotic and semi-official types.

It is often difficult to determine whether the impression made by the canceling stamp indicates provisional usage or merely postage paid at the time the letter was deposited in the post office. Occasionally the same mark was used for both purposes.

The *press-printed* provisional envelopes are in a different category. They were produced in quantity, using envelopes procured in advance by the postmaster, such as those of Charleston, Lynchburg, Memphis, etc.

The press-printed envelopes are listed and valued on all known papers.

The handstamped provisional envelopes are listed and valued according to type and variety of handstamp, but not according to paper. Many exist on such a variety of papers that they defy accurate, complete listing.

The value of a handstamped provisional envelope is determined *primarily* by the clarity of the markings and its overall condition and attractiveness, rather than type of paper.

All handstamped provisional envelopes, when used, should also show the postmark of the town of issue.

Most handstamps are impressed at top right, although they exist from some towns in other positions.

Illustrations in this section are reduced in size.

XU numbers are envelope entires.

ABERDEEN, MISS.

E1

Handstamped Envelopes
1XU1   E1   5c black   7,000.
   a.   10c (ms.) on 5c black   10,000.

No. 1XU1a is unique.

ABINGDON, VA.

E1

Handstamped Envelopes
2XU1   E1   2c black   12,500.
   a.   5c (ms.) on 2c black   15,000.
2XU2   E1   5c black   1,750.
     On patriotic cover   3,000.
2XU3   E1   10c black   2,200.   3,500.

No. 2XU1 is unique. No. 2XU3 unused and used are each unique.

ALBANY, GA.

E1

E2

E3

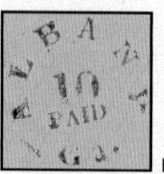

E4

Handstamped Envelopes

3XU1	E1	5c greenish blue		1,000.
	On patriotic cover			
3XU2	E2	10c greenish blue		1,750.
a.	10c on 5c greenish blue			3,500.
3XU5	E3	5c greenish blue		
3XU6	E4	10c greenish blue		3,500.

Only one example each recorded of Nos. 3XU2, 3XU2a and 3XU6. No. 3XU2 is a cover front only and is valued as such. No. 3XU2a is the unique Confederate example of one provisional marking revaluing another.

The existence of No. 3XU5 is in question. The editors would like to see an authenticated example of this marking.

ANDERSON COURT HOUSE, S.C.

E1

E2

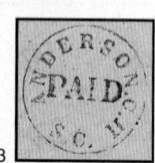

E3

Handstamped Envelopes

4XU1	E1	5c black	1,000.	2,250.
4XU2	E2	10c (ms.) black		2,500.
4XU3	E3	(2c) black, denomi- nation omit- ted (circular rate)		2,250.

ATHENS, GA

A1 — Type I

A1 — Type II

E1

Typographed Adhesives
(from woodcuts of two types)

Pairs, both horizontal and vertical, always show one of each type.

5X1	A1	5c purple		
		(shades)	1,000.	1,750.
	Pair		—	4,500.
	On cover			2,500.
	Pair on cover			7,500.
	Strip of 4 on cover (horiz.)			10,000.
a.	Tete beche pair (vertical)			7,500.
	Tete beche pair on cover			20,000.
5X2	A1	5c red	5,750.	5,500.
	On cover			5,500.
	Pair on cover			17,500.

The colorless ornaments in the four corners of No. 5X2 were recut making them wider than those in No. 5X1.

Dangerous fakes exist of Nos. 5X1 and 5X2. Certificates of authenticity from recognized committees are strongly recommended.

Handstamped Envelopes

5XU1	E1	10c black, on pa- triotic cover	2,500.

The markings on No. 5XU1 are the same as those used on stampless envelopes. On the unique listed example of No. 5XU1, there is a handwritten note on the inside of the flap: 'Andrew had these envelopes stamped & I am obliged to use them or loose the postage.' Two or more similar covers from the same correspondence are known, but without the note under the flap. While these also may be provisional use, it cannot be proven, and these covers are considered handstamp paid covers.

ATLANTA, GA.

E1

E2

E2

Handstamped Envelopes

6XU1	E1	5c red		5,000.
6XU2	E1	5c black	175.	1,000.
	On patriotic cover			3,500.
a.	10c on 5c black			2,500.
	On patriotic cover			
6XU3	E2	PAID, black		1,000.

No. 6UX3 was probably used for drop letters and circulars.

6XU4	E3	2c black		3,000.
6XU5	E3	5c black		1,500.
	On patriotic cover			3,500.
a.	10c on 5c black			2,500.
6XU6	E3	10c black		950.
	On patriotic cover			

Only one example recorded of No. 6XU1.

E3

Handstamped Envelopes

6XU8	E3	5c black	3,500.
6XU9	E3	10c black ("10" up- right)	3,250.

Only one example recorded of No. 6XU8.

AUSTIN, MISS.

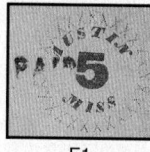

E1

Press-printed Envelope (typeset)

8XU1	E1	5c red, *amber*	75,000.

One example recorded.

AUSTIN, TEX.

E1a

Handstamped Adhesive

9X1	E1a	10c black, *white* or *buff*	—
	On cover, uncanceled		18,000.
	On cover, tied		

Only one example of No. 9X1 tied on cover is recorded.

Handstamped Envelope

9XU1	E1a	10c black	2,500.

AUTAUGAVILLE, ALA.

E1

E2

Handstamped Envelopes

10XU1	E1	5c black	20,000.
10XU2	E2	5c black	20,000.

No. 10XU2 is unique.

BALCONY FALLS, VA.

E1

Handstamped Envelope

122XU1	E1	10c blue	2,000.

The use of No. 122XU1 as a provisional marking is in question. The editors would like to see authenticated evidence of its use as a provisional.

BARNWELL COURT HOUSE, S. C.

E1

Handstamped Envelope

123XU1	E1	5c black	3,000.

These are two separate handstamps. All recorded uses are on addressed covers without postmarks.

BATON ROUGE, LA.

A1

A2

Typeset Adhesives
Ten varieties of each

11X1	A1	2c green	8,250.	5,000.
	On cover			50,000.
a.	"McCcrmick"	40,000.	40,000.
	On cover			55,000.
11X2	A2	5c **green & carmine**	1,500.	1,400.
	On cover			5,000.
a.	"McCcrmick"	10,000.	3,500.
	On cover			15,000.

Only one example each is recorded of No. 11X1a unused, used and on cover.

A3

A4

Ten varieties of each

11X3	A3	5c green & carmine	10,000.	2,750.
	On cover			10,000.
a.	"McCcrmick"			6,000.
11X4	A4	10c blue		50,000.
	On cover			75,000.

No. 11X4 on cover is unique.

BEAUMONT, TEX.

A1

A2

Typeset Adhesives
Several varieties of each

12X1	A1	10c black, *yellow*		12,500.
	On cover			55,000.
12X2	A1	10c black, *pink*		12,500.

No. 12X1 is smaller than No. 12X2.

12X3	A2	10c black, *yellow,*		27,500.
	on cover			90,000.

One example recorded of No. 12X3.

BLUFFTON, S. C.

E1

Handstamped Envelope

124XU1 E1 5c black   *4,250.*

Only one example recorded of No. 124XU1.

BRIDGEVILLE, ALA.

A1

**Handstamped Adhesive in black
within red pen-ruled squares**

13X1 A1 5c black & red,
pair on cover   *20,000.*

CAMDEN, S. C.

E1   E2

Handstamped Envelopes

125XU1 E1 5c black   *2,500.*
125XU2 E2 10c black   *750.*

No. 125XU2 unused was privately carried and is addressed but has no postal markings. No. 125XU2 is indistinguishable from a handstamp paid cover when used.

CANTON, MISS.

E1

"P" in star is initial of Postmaster William Priestly.

Handstamped Envelopes

14XU1 E1 5c black   *4,000.*
  a. 10c (ms.) on 5c black   *5,000.*

CAROLINA CITY, N. C.

E1

Handstamped Envelope

118XU1 E1 5c black   *5,000.*

CARTERSVILLE, GA.

E1

Handstamped Envelope

126XU1 E1 (5c) red   *1,500.*

CHAPEL HILL, N. C.

E1

Handstamped Envelope

15XU1 E1 5c black   *4,000.*

CHARLESTON, S. C.

A1   E1

E2

Lithographed Adhesive

16X1 A1 5c blue   *1,400.   850.*
          On cover   *2,500.*
          Pair, on cover   *5,000.*

Values are for stamps showing parts of the outer frame lines on at least 3 sides. The vast majority of this stamp small faults and are valued thus. Completely sound examples are scarce and sell for more.

**Press-printed Envelopes
(typographed from woodcut)**

16XU1 E1 5c blue   *1,250.   2,750.*
16XU2 E1 5c blue, *amber* *1,250.   2,750.*
16XU3 E1 5c blue, *orange* *1,250.   2,750.*
16XU4 E1 5c blue, *buff* *1,250.   2,750.*
16XU5 E1 5c blue, *blue* *1,250.   2,750.*
16XU6 E2 10c blue, *orange*   *80,000.*

The No. 16XU6 used entire is unique; value based on 1997 auction sale.
Beware of fakes of the E1 design.

Handstamped Cut Square

16XU7 E2 10c black   *3,000.*

There is only one example of No. 16XU7. It is a cutout, not an entire. It may not have been mailed from Charleston, and it may not have paid postage.

CHARLOTTE, N. C.

E1

146XU1 E1 5c blue, "5" in
circle and
straight line
"PAID"   *3,500.*

CHARLOTTESVILLE, VA.

Control

E1

**Handstamped Envelopes,
Manuscript Initials**

127XU1 E1 5c blue   —
127XU2 E1 10c blue   —

The control initials appear at the upper right on the front of the envelope.

CHATTANOOGA, TENN.

E1

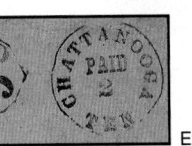

E2

Handstamped Envelopes

17XU2 E1 5c black   *2,500.*
17XU3 E2 5c on 2c black   *5,000.*

No. 17XU3 is unique.

CHRISTIANSBURG, VA.

E1

Handstamped Envelopes
Impressed at top right

99XU1 E1 5c black   *2,250.*
99XU2 E1 5c blue   *2,000.*
99XU4 E1 5c green on U.S.
          envelope No.
          U27   *4,500.*
99XU5 E1 10c blue   *3,500.*

The absence of 5c and 10c handstamped paid markings from this town suggests that Nos. 99XU1-99XU5 were used as both provisional and handstamped paid markings.

COLAPARCHEE, GA.

E1

Control

Handstamped Envelope

119XU1 E1 5c black   *3,500.*

There are only two recorded examples of No. 119XU1, and both are used from Savannah with a general issue stamp.
The control appears on the front of the envelope.

COLUMBIA, S. C.

Oval Control

Circular
Control

E1

E2

E3

E4

E5

E6

E7

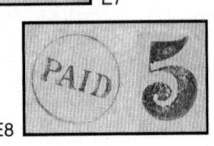

E8

Handstamped Envelopes

18XU1 E1 5c blue   *550.   900.*
  a. 10c on 5c blue   *3,500.*
18XU2 E1 5c black   *600.   1,250.*
18XU4 E2 5c blue, oval
          control on
          front   *7,500.*
  a. Oval control on back   *1,250.*
18XU7 E3 5c blue, oval
          control on
          back   *1,000.*
18XU8 E4 5c blue oval
          control on
          back   *1,000.*
  a. Circular control on
          back   *1,500.*
18XU9 E4 10c blue oval
          control on
          back   *1,250.*
18XU10 E5 10c blue oval
          control on
          back   *1,250.*
18XU11 E6 5c blue oval
          control on
          front   *2,500.*
18XU12 E6 10c blue oval
          control on
          back   *1,250.*
18XU13 E7 5c blue oval
          control on
          back   *1,000.*
  a. Circular control on
          back   *1,500.*
18XU14 E8 5c blue oval
          control on
          back   *1,000.*
  a. No control (unused)   —

COLUMBIA, TENN.

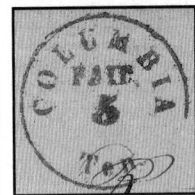

E1

Handstamped Envelope

113XU1 E1 5c red   *6,000.*

One example recorded.

COLUMBUS, GA.

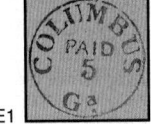

E1

Handstamped Envelopes
19XU1 E1 5c blue   1,200.
19XU2 E1 10c red   3,250.

COURTLAND, ALA.

 E1

Handstamped Envelopes (from woodcut)
103XU1 E1 5c red   37,500.

CUTHBERT, GA

 E1

Handstamped Envelope
95XU1 E1 10c black   750.

The unique example of No. 95XU1 was used by having a C.S.A. 10c #12c placed over it.

DALTON, GA

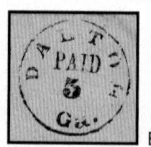 E1

Handstamped Envelopes
20XU1 E1 5c black   750.
  a. Denomination omitted (5c rate)
  b. 10c (ms.) on 5c black   875.
  c. 20c (ms.) on 5c black   1,500.
20XU2 E1 10c black   1,250.

DANVILLE, VA.

 A1

Design measures 60x37mm — E1

 E2   E3

 E4

Typeset Adhesive
Wove Paper
21X1 A1 5c red   6,500.
  On cover   32,500.
  Cut to shape   5,500.
  On cover, cut to shape   27,500.
  Two varieties known.
  Cancellation: blue town.

Laid Paper
21X2 A1 5c red   10,000.

Press-printed Envelopes (typographed)
Two types: "SOUTHERN" in straight or curved line
Impressed (usually) at top left
21XU1 E1 5c black   9,000.
21XU2 E1 5c black, amber   —
21XU3 E1 5c black, dark buff   9,000.

The existence of No. 21XU2 is in question. The editors would like to see authenticated evidence of its existence.
Unissued 10c envelopes (type E1, in red) are known. All recorded examples are envelopes that show evidence of added stamps being torn off.
Dangerous forgeries exist of No. 21XU1.

Handstamped Envelopes
21XU3A E4 5c black (ms "WBP" initials)   1,000.
21XU4 E2 10c black   2,500.
21XU6 E3 10c black   2,750.
21XU7 E4 10c black (ms "WBP" initials)   —

Types E2 and E3 both exist on one cover.

DEMOPOLIS, ALA.

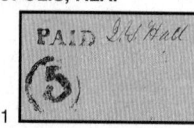 E1

Handstamped Envelopes, Signature in ms.
22XU1 E1 5c black ("Jno. Y. Hall")   3,500.
22XU2 E1 5c black ("J. Y. Hall")   3,500.
22XU3 E1 5c (ms.) black ("J. Y. Hall") 4,000.

EATONTON, GA.

 E1

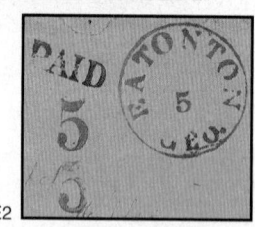 E2

Handstamped Envelopes
23XU1 E1 5c black   3,000.
  a. 10 (ms) on 5c black   —
23XU2 E2 5c + 5c black   5,000.

EMORY, VA.

 A1

Handstamped Adhesives ("PAID" and "5" in circle on selvage of U.S. 1c 1857 issue)
Perf. 15 on three sides
24X1 A1 5c blue, on cover, tied   27,500.
Also known with "5" above "PAID."

 E1

 E2

Handstamped Envelopes
24XU1 E1 5c blue   4,000.
24XU2 E2 10c blue   5,000.
One example each recorded of Nos. 24XU1 and 24XU2.

FINCASTLE, VA.

 E1

Press-printed Envelope (typeset)
Impressed at top right
104XU1 E1 10c black   20,000.
One example recorded of No. 104XU1.

FORSYTH, GA.

 E1   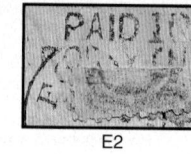 E2

Handstamped Envelope
120XU1 E1 10c black   2,000.
120XU2 E2 10c black   1,250.
Only one example each recorded of Nos. 120XU1 and 120XU2.

FORT VALLEY, GA.

 E1   E2

Handstamped Envelope
148XU1 E1 5c on 3c black   —
Black circle control on front of envelope. Unique.

FRANKLIN, N. C.

 E1   E2

Press-printed Envelope (typeset) (No. 25XU1)
Impressed at top right
25XU1 E1 5c blue, buff   30,000.
25XU2 E2 5c black, large "5" woodcut in 31mm circular town mark   2,500.

The one known No. 25XU1 envelope shows black circular Franklin postmark with manuscript date.

FRAZIERSVILLE, S. C.

 E1

Handstamped Envelope, "5" manuscript
128XU1 E1 5c black   5,000.
Only one example recorded of No. 128XU1.

FREDERICKSBURG, VA.

 A1

Sheets of 20, two panes of 10 varieties each

Typeset Adhesives
Thin bluish paper
26X1 A1 5c blue, bluish   900.   1,250.
  On cover   5,500.
  Pair on cover   12,000.
26X2 A1 10c red (shades), bluish   2,250.

GAINESVILLE, ALA.

 E1   E2

 E3

Handstamped Envelopes
27XU1 E1 5c black   4,500.
27XU2 E2 5c black   5,000.
27XU3 E3 10c ("01") black   7,500.

GALVESTON, TEX.

 E1

Handstamped Envelopes
98XU1 E1 5c black   500. 1,500.
98XU2 E1 10c black   2,000.

 E2

E3

Handstamped Envelopes

98XU3	E2	10c black	550.	2,750.
98XU4	E2	20c black		3,500.
98XU5	E3	5c black		4,500.

GASTON, N. C.

E1

Handstamped Envelope

129XU1	E1	5c black	6,000.

Only one example recorded of No. 129XU1.

GEORGETOWN, S. C.

E1   Control

E2

Handstamped Envelopes

28XU1	E1	5c black	3,500.	
28XU2	E2	5c black, separate "5" and straightline "PAID" handstamps, control on reverse	—	2,000.

GOLIAD, TEX.

A1   A2

Typeset Adhesives

29X1	A1	5c black	15,000.	
29X2	A1	5c black, gray	11,500.	
29X3	A1	5c black, rose	12,000.	
		On cover front	—	47,500.
29X4	A1	10c black	25,000.	
29X5	A1	10c black, rose	12,000.	

Type A1 stamps are signed "Clarke-P.M." vertically in black or red.

29X6	A2	5c black, gray	22,500.	
a.		"GOILAD"	12,000.	
		Pair, left stamp the error		
29X7	A2	10c black, buff	12,000.	
		On cover		40,000.
a.		"GOILAD"	15,000.	
		On cover		30,000.
29X8	A2	5c black, dark blue, on cover		18,000.
29X9	A2	10c black, dark blue		27,500.

GONZALES, TEX.

Colman & Law were booksellers when John B. Law (of the firm) was appointed Postmaster. The firm used a

small lithographed label on drugs and on the front or inside of books they sold.

A1

Lithographed Adhesives on colored glazed paper

30X1	A1	(5c) gold, dark blue, pair on cover, 1861	15,000.	
30X2	A1	(10c) gold, garnet, on cover, 1864	25,000.	
30X3	A1	(10c) gold, black, on cover, 1865	50,000.	

No. 30X1 must bear double-circle town cancel as validating control. The control was applied to the labels in the sheet before their sale as stamps. When used, the stamps bear an additional Gonzales double-circle postmark.

GREENSBORO, ALA.

E1

E2

E3

Handstamped Envelopes

31XU1	E1	5c black	3,000.
31XU2	E1	10c black	2,750.
31XU3	E2	10c black	6,000.
31XU4	E3	10c on 5c black, on cover	3,000.

GREENSBORO, N. C.

E1

Handstamped Envelope

32XU1	E1	10c red	1,250.

GREENVILLE, ALA.

A1   A2

Typeset Adhesives On pinkish surface-colored glazed paper.

33X1	A1	5c blue & red	25,000.	
		On cover		47,500.
33X2	A2	10c red & blue, on cover		47,500.

Two used examples each are known of Nos. 33X1-33X2, and all are on covers. Covers bear a postmark but it was not used to cancel the stamps.

The former No. 33X1a has been identified as a fake.

GREENVILLE, TENN.

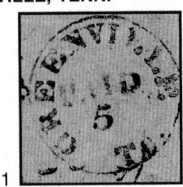

E1

144XU1	E1	5c black	5,000.

Only one example of No. 144XU1 is recorded.

GREENVILLE COURT HOUSE, S. C.

E1

E2

Control A   Control B

Control C

Handstamped Envelopes (Several types)

34XU1	E1	5c black	2,000.	
34XU2	E2	10c black	2,000.	
a.		20c (ms.) on 10c black	3,000.	

Envelopes must bear one of three different postmark controls on the back. When the control postmark is dated, the date must be the same or prior to the date of the postmark on the front of the envelope.

GREENWOOD DEPOT, VA.

A1

"PAID" Handstamped Adhesive ("PAID" with value and signature in ms.) Laid Paper

35X1	A1	10c black, gray blue, on cover	22,500.	
		On cover, tied		

Six examples recorded of No. 35X1, all on covers. One of these is in the British Library collection. Of the remaining five, only one has the stamp tied to the cover.

GRIFFIN, GA.

E1

Handstamped Envelopes

102XU1	E1	5c black	2,250.
102XU2	E1	10c black	5,000.

No. 102XU2 is on a large piece of an envelope with July 25 postmark at left. It is unique.

GROVE HILL, ALA.

A1

Handstamped Adhesive (from woodcut)

36X1	A1	5c black	—
		On cover, tied	75,000.

Two examples are recorded. One is on cover tied by the postmark. The other is canceled by magenta pen on a cover front.

HALLETTSVILLE, TEX.

A1

Handstamped Adhesive Ruled Letter Paper

37X1	A1	10c black, gray blue, on cover	15,000.

One example known.

HAMBURGH, S. C.

E1

Handstamped Envelope

112XU1	E1	5c black	8,000.

HARRISBURGH (Harrisburg), TEX.

E1

E2

Handstamped Envelope

130XU1	E1	5c black	5,500.
130XU2	E2	10c black	—

The unused 5c entire is the only example recorded of No. 130XU1

HELENA, TEX.

A1

Typeset Adhesives
Several varieties
38X1 A1 5c black, *buff* 22,500. 20,000.
38X2 A1 10c black, *gray* 40,000.

On 10c "Helena" is in upper and lower case italics.

Used examples are valued with small faults or repairs, as all recorded have faults.

HILLSBORO, N. C.

A1

Handstamped Adhesive
39X1 A1 5c black, on cover 15,000.

See 3c 1861 Postmaster's Provisional No. 1AX1.

Ms./Handstamped Envelope
39XU1 E1 10c "paid 10" in manuscript with undated blue town cancel as control on face —

HOLLANDALE, TEX.

E1

Handstamped Envelope
132XU1 E1 5c black —

HOUSTON, TEX.

E1

No. 40XU1a

Handstamped Envelopes
40XU1 E1 5c red — 750.
  a. On patriotic cover
       10c (ms.) on 5c red 11,000.
40XU2 E1 10c red — 2,000.
40XU3 E1 10c black 2,250.
40XU4 E1 5c +10c red 2,500.
40XU5 E1 10c +10c red 2,500.

Nos. 40XU2-40XU5 show "TEX" instead of "TXS."

HUNTSVILLE, TEX.

E1

Control

Handstamped Envelope
92XU1 E1 5c black 5,000.

No. 92XU1 exists with "5" outside or within control circle.

INDEPENDENCE, TEX.

A1

A2

Handstamped Adhesives
41X1 A1 10c black, *buff*, on cover, uncanceled, cut to shape 20,000.
41X2 A1 10c black, *dull rose*, on cover —

With small "10" and "Pd" in manuscript
41X3 A2 10c black, *buff*, on cover, uncanceled, cut to shape 32,500.

No. 41X1 is unique.

All known examples of Nos. 41X1-41X3 are uncanceled on covers with black "INDEPENDENCE TEX." (sic) postmark.

The existence of No. 41X2 has been questioned by specialists. The editors would like to see authenticated evidence of the existence of this item.

ISABELLA, GA.

E1

Handstamped Envelope, Manuscript "5"
133XU1 E1 5c black 5,000.

Only one example recorded of No. 133XU1.

IUKA, MISS.

E1

Handstamped Envelope
42XU1 E1 5c black 1,750.

JACKSON, MISS.

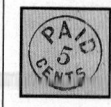
E1

Handstamped Envelopes
Two types of numeral
43XU1 E1 5c black 750.
  a. 10c on 5c black 2,750.
43XU2 E1 10c black 2,000.
  a. 5c on 10c black 3,750.
43XU4 E1 10c on 5c blue 2,750.

The 5c also exists on a lettersheet.

See 3c 1861 Postmaster's Provisional No. 2AXU1.

JACKSONVILLE, ALA.

E1

Handstamped Envelope
110XU1 E1 5c black — 3,000.

JACKSONVILLE, FLA.

E1

Control

Handstamped Envelope
134XU1 E1 5c black —

Undated double circle postmark control on reverse.

JETERSVILLE, VA.

A1

Handstamped Adhesive
("5" with ms. "AHA." initials)
Laid Paper
44X1 A1 5c black, vertical pair on cover, uncanceled 16,000.

JONESBORO, TENN.

E1

Handstamped Envelopes
45XU1 E1 5c black 6,000.
45XU2 E1 5c dark blue 5,000.

KINGSTON, GA.

E1

E2

E3

KINGSTON, GA. (continued)

E4

Typeset Envelopes
(design types E1-E2, E4 are handstamps; typeset design E3 probably impressed by hand but possibly press printed)
46XU1 E1 5c black 3,000.
46XU2 E2 5c black 3,250.
46XU4 E3 5c black 12,500.
46XU5 E4 5c black 2,000.

There is only one recorded example of No. 46XU4.

KNOXVILLE, TENN.

A1

Typographed Adhesives
(stereotype from woodcut)
Grayish Laid Paper
47X1 A1 5c brick red 1,750. 1,400.
       On cover, tied by hand-stamp 8,000.
       Pair on cover 7,500.
47X2 A1 5c carmine 2,750. 2,250.
       On cover, tied by hand-stamp 7,500.
47X3 A1 10c green, on cover 57,750.

The #47X3 cover is unique. Value is based on 1997 auction sale.

E1

E2

Press-printed Envelopes
(typographed)
47XU1 E1 5c blue 2,500.
47XU2 E1 5c blue, *orange* 5,000.
47XU3 E1 10c red (cut to shape) 7,500.
47XU4 E1 10c red, *orange* (cut to shape) 7,500.

Only one example each recorded of Nos. 47XU3 and 47XU4.

Dangerous fakes exist of Nos. 47XU1 and 47XU2.

Handstamped Envelopes
47XU5 E2 5c black 1,500.
  a. 10c on 5c black 3,500.

Type E2 exists with "5" above or below "PAID."

LA GRANGE, TEX.

E1

Handstamped Envelopes
48XU1 E1 5c black — 2,250.
48XU2 E1 10c black 3,250.

LAKE CITY, FLA.

E1

Control

Handstamped Envelope

96XU1 E1 10c black *3,500.*

Envelopes have black circle control mark, or printed name of E. R. Ives, postmaster, on back.

LAURENS COURT HOUSE, S. C.

E1

E2

Control

Handstamped Envelopes

116XU1 E1 5c black *2,250.*
116XU2 E2 5c black *2,250.*

Envelopes have a 25mm undated control mark on reverse. No. 116XU1 is unique.

LENOIR, N. C.

A1

E1

Handstamped Adhesive (from woodcut)

White wove paper with cross-ruled orange lines

49X1 A1 5c blue & orange *7,250.* *6,750.*
    On cover, pen canceled *15,000.*
    On cover, tied by handstamp *22,500.*

Cancellations: blue town, blue "Paid" in circle, black pen.

Handstamped Envelopes

49XU1 A1 5c blue *4,000.*
49XU2 A1 10c (5c+5c) blue *25,000.*
49XU3 E1 5c blue *4,500.*
49XU4 E1 5c black *4,500.*

No. 49XU2 is unique.

LEXINGTON, MISS.

E1

Handstamped Envelopes

50XU1 E1 5c black *5,000.*
50XU2 E1 10c black *6,000.*

Only one example is recorded of No. 50XU2.

LEXINGTON, VA.

E1

Handstamped Envelopes

135XU1 E1 5c blue *500.*
135XU2 E1 10c blue *750.*

Nos. 135XU1-135XU2 by themselves are indistinguishable from stampless covers when used.

LIBERTY, VA. (and Salem, Va.)

  A1

Typeset Adhesive (probably impressed by hand)

Laid Paper

74X1 A1 5c black, on cover, uncanceled *35,000.*
    On cover, uncanceled, with Salem postmark *40,000.*

Two known on covers with Liberty, Va. postmark; one cover known with the nearby Salem, Va. office postmark.

LIMESTONE SPRINGS, S. C.

A1

Handstamped Adhesive

121X1 A1 5c black, *light blue*, on cover *10,000.*
    Two on cover *15,000.*
121X2 A1 5c black, *white*, two on cover *32,500.*

Stamps are cut round or rectangular. Covers are not postmarked. The No. 121X2 cover bears the only two recorded examples of this stamp.

LIVINGSTON, ALA.

  A1

Lithographed Adhesive

51X1 A1 5c blue *15,000.*
    On cover *75,000.*
    Pair on cover *120,000.*

The pair on cover is unique.

LYNCHBURG, VA.

  A1

  E1

Typographed Adhesive
(stereotype from woodcut)

52X1 A1 5c blue (shades) *1,800.* *1,500.*
    On cover *7,000.*
    Pair on cover *20,000.*

Press-printed Envelopes (typographed)
Impressed at top right or left

52XU1 E1 5c black *700.00* *4,000.*
52XU2 E1 5c black, *amber* *4,000.*
52XU3 E1 5c black, *buff* *4,000.*
52XU4 E1 5c black, *brown* *4,000.*
    On patriotic cover —

MACON, GA.

A1

A2

A3

A4

Typeset Adhesives
Several varieties of type A1, 10 of A2, 5 of A3

Wove Paper

53X1 A1 5c black, *light blue green* (shades) *1,250.* *1,000.*
    On cover *6,000.*
    Pair on cover *14,000.*

Warning: Dangerous forgeries exist of the normal variety and the Comma after "OFFICE" variety. Certificates of authenticity from recognized committees are strongly recommended.

53X3 A2 5c black, *yellow* *2,500.* *1,250.*
    On cover *6,500.*
    Pair on cover *11,000.*
    Pair on patriotic cover *25,000.*
53X4 A3 5c black, *yellow* (shades) *3,000.* *1,750.*
    On cover *7,000.*
    Pair on cover *10,000.*
  a. Vertical tête bêche pair —
53X5 A4 2c black, *gray green* —
    On cover *50,000.*

Laid Paper

53X6 A2 5c black, *yellow* *6,000.* *6,000.*
    On cover *8,000.*
53X7 A3 5c black, *yellow* *6,000.*
    On cover *9,000.*
53X8 A1 5c black, *light blue green* *1,750.* *2,250.*
    On cover *4,500.*

No. 53X4a is unique.

E1

Handstamped Envelope

Two types: "PAID" over "5," "5" over "PAID"

53XU1 E1 5c black *250.* *650.*
    On patriotic cover *1,900.*

Values are for "PAID" over "5" variety. "5" over "PAID" is much scarcer.

MADISON, GA.

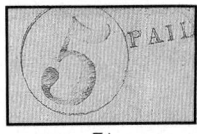

E1

Handstamped Envelope

136XU1 E1 5c red *600.*

No. 136XU1 is indistinguishable from a handstamp paid cover when used.

MADISON COURT HOUSE, FLA.

E1

Typeset Envelope

137XU1 E1 5c black, *yellow* *25,000.*

No. 137XU1 is unique.
See 3c 1861 Postmaster's Provisional No. 3AX1.

MARIETTA, GA.

E1

Control

E2

Handstamped Envelopes

54XU1 E1 5c black *500.*
  a. 10c on 5c black *1,750.*

With Double Circle Control

54XU3 E1 10c black *2,000.*
54XU4 E2 5c black *2,000.*

The existence of No. 54XU3 has been questioned by specialists. The editors would like to see authenticated evidence that verifies this listing.

MARION, VA.

A1

Adhesives with Typeset frame and Handstamped numeral in center

55X1 A1 5c black *7,500.*
    On cover *20,000.*
55X2 A1 10c black *16,500.* *10,000.*
    On cover *35,000.*
55X3 A1 5c black, *bluish,* laid paper —

The 2c, 3c, 15c and 20c are believed to be bogus items printed later using the original typeset frame.

MARS BLUFF, S. C.

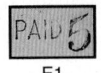

E1

145XU1 E1 5c black

The No. 145XU1 marking is a provisional only when unused, used from another town or used under a general issue.

MEMPHIS, TENN.

A1

56X1a
Partial Print

A2

Typographed Adhesives
(stereotyped from woodcut)

56X1 A1 2c blue

		100.	1,250.
(shades)			
On cover			12,500.
a. Partial print		250.	

On No. 56X1, a "draubing off" (breaking off) of the plate at the right edge caused incomplete printing (approximately 2/3 of the stamp) on stamps in positions 5, 10, 15, 20 and 50.

56X2 A2 5c red (shades) 150. 250.

On cover			2,000.
Pair on cover			4,000.
Strip of 4 on cover			9,000.
On patriotic cover			9,000.
Pair on patriotic cover			15,000.
a. Tête bêche pair			1,500.
Pair on cover			9,500.
b. Pair, one sideways	2,500.		
c. Pelure paper		—	

Press-printed Envelopes
(typographed)

56XU1 A2 5c red		3,000.
(shades)		
56XU2 A2 5c red, amber		3,000.
56XU3 A2 5c red, orange		3,000.
56XU4 A2 5c red, cream	5,750.	

Only one example of No. 56XU4 is recorded. It is on a cover on which a C.S.A. No. 11 is affixed over the provisional to pay the postage.

MICANOPY, FLA.

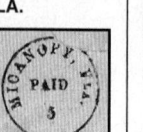

E1

Handstamped Envelope

105XU1 E1 5c black   11,500.

One example recorded.

MILLEDGEVILLE, GA.

E1

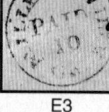

E2   E3

Handstamped Envelopes

Two types of No. 57XU5: Type I, tall, thin "1" and "0" of "10"; Type II, short, fat "1" and "0" of "10."

57XU1 E1 5c black		500.	
a. Wide spacing between "I" and "D" of "PAID"		600.	
b. 10c on 5c black		1,000.	
57XU2 E1 5c blue		800.	
57XU3 E2 10c black	375.	1,200.	
a. Wide spacing between "I" and "D" of "PAID"		1,200.	
57XU5 E3 10c black, type I	125.	800.	
a. Type II		1,500.	

On No. 57XU4, the "PAID/10" virtually always falls outside the Milledgeville control marking (as in illustration E1).

The existence of No. 57XU2 as a provisional has been questioned by specialists. The editors would like to see authenticated evidence of provisional use of this marking.

MILTON, N. C.

E1

Handstamped Envelope, "5" Manuscript

138XU1 E1 5c black   3,000.

MOBILE, ALA.

A1

Lithographed Adhesives

58X1 A1 2c black 2,250. 1,200.

On cover			6,000.
Pair on cover			20,000.
Three singles on one cover			20,000.
Five stamps on one cover			24,000.

58X2 A1 5c blue 350. 450.

On cover			2,000.
Pair on cover			2,750.
Strip of 3 on cover			10,000.
Strip of 4 on cover			25,000.

The existence of a strip of 5 of No. 58X2 has been questioned by specialists. The editors would like to see authenticated evidence of the existence of this strip either on or off cover.

MONTGOMERY, ALA.

E1   E1a

Handstamped Envelopes

59XU1 E1 5c red		1,100.
a. 10c on 5c red		2,750.
59XU2 E1 5c blue	400.	1,000.
59XU3 E1a 10c red		1,000.
59XU4 E1a 10c blue		1,500.
59XU5 E1a 10c black		850.

E2   E3

59XU7 E2 2c red		2,500.
59XU7A E2 2c blue		3,500.
59XU8 E2 5c black		2,250.
59XU9 E3 10c black		3,250.
59XU10 E3 10c red		1,750.

The existence of No. 59XU10 is in question. The editors would like to see an authenticated example of this marking.

MT. LEBANON, LA.

A1

Woodcut Adhesive (mirror image of design)

60X1 A1 5c red brown, on cover   255,000.

One example known. Value represents sale price at 2009 auction.

NASHVILLE, TENN.

A2   E1

Typographed Adhesives
(stereotyped from woodcut)
Gray Blue Ribbed Paper

61X2 A2 5c carmine

		1,000.	650.
(shades)			
On cover			1,000.
Pair on cover			6,000.
a. Vertical tête bêche pair			4,000.
On cover			25,000.

61X3 A2 5c brick red

		1,000.	1,000.
(shades)			
Pair on cover			3,500.
On cover			7,500.

61X4 A2 5c gray (shades) 1,250. 1,500.

On cover			5,750.
Pair on cover			7,500.

61X5 A2 5c violet brown

		1,250.	750.
(shades)			
On cover			4,250.
Pair on cover			6,000.
a. Vertical tete bêche pair	5,000.		7,500.

61X6 A2 10c green

		—	7,500.
On cover			22,500.
On cover with No. 61X2			27,500.

E1

Handstamped Envelopes

61XU1 E1 5c blue		900.
61XU2 E1 10c on 5c blue		2,750.

See 3c Postmaster's Provisional No. 4AX1.

NEW ORLEANS, LA.

A1   A2

Typographed Adhesives
(stereotyped from woodcut)
Plate of 40

62X1 A1 2c blue 225. 550.

On cover			5,000.
Pair on cover			10,000.
Three singles on one cover			20,000.
Three singles + #62X4, on cover			—
Five singles on one cover			12,500.
Strip of 5 on cover			30,000.
a. Printed on both sides, On cover			10,500.

62X2 A1 2c red

		190.	1,000.
(shades)			
On cover			25,000.

62X3 A2 5c brown, white 300. 200.

On cover			450.
Pair on cover			850.
Strip of 5 on cover			5,000.
a. Printed on both sides On cover			7,500.
b. 5c ocher	700.		625.
On cover			2,750.
Pair on cover			3,500.
c. 5c chocolate brown			1,500.

62X4 A2 5c red brn, bluish 325. 200.

On cover			425.
Pair on cover			700.
Block of 4 on cover			5,000.
a. Printed on both sides			3,250.
On cover			9,000.

62X5 A2 5c yel brn, off-white 160. 250.

On cover			850.
Pair on cover			1,200.
Strip of 5 on cover			

62X6 A2 5c red

		—	14,000.
(shades)			

62X7 A2 5c red

			15,000.
(shades), bluish			

E1

Handstamped Envelopes

62XU1 E1 5c black   4,500.

62XU2 E1 10c black   11,500.

"J. L. RIDDELL, P. M." omitted

62XU3 E1 2c black   9,500.

Some authorities question the use of No. 62XU3 as a provisional.

NEW SMYRNA, FLA.

A1

Handstamped Adhesive

On white paper with blue ruled lines

63X1 A1 10c ("O1") on 5c black   50,000.

One example known. It is uncanceled on a postmarked patriotic cover.

NORFOLK, VA.

E1

Manuscript Signature

Handstamped Envelopes
Ms Signature on Back

139XU1 E1 5c blue	—	1,500.
139XU2 E1 10c blue		1,750.

OAKWAY, S. C.

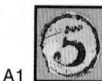

A1

Handstamped Adhesive (from woodcut)

115X1 A1 5c black, on cover   60,000.

Two used examples of No. 115X1 are recorded, both on cover. Value represents 2012 auction realization for the cover on which the stamp is tied by manuscript "Paid."

PENSACOLA, FLA.

E1

Handstamped Envelopes

106XU1 E1 5c black		4,250.
a. 10c (ms.) on 5c black		4,750.

PETERSBURG, VA.

A1

Typeset Adhesive
Ten varieties
Thick white paper

65X1 A1 5c red

		2,250.	750.
(shades)			
On cover			2,500.
Pair on cover			12,500.

PITTSYLVANIA COURT HOUSE, VA.

A1

Typeset Adhesives

66X1	A1	5c dull red, wove paper	7,500.	6,500.
		Octagonally cut		5,000.
		On cover		40,000.
		On cover, octagonally cut		20,000.
66X2	A1	5c dull red, laid paper		5,500.
		On cover		
		Octagonally cut		4,500.
		On cover, octagonally cut		50,000.

PLAINS OF DURA, GA.

E1

Handstamped Envelopes, Ms. Initials

140XU1	E1	5c black	—
140XU2	E1	10c black	5,000.

No. 140XU2 is unique.

PLEASANT SHADE, VA.

A1

Typeset Adhesive
Five varieties

67X1	A1	5c blue	5,000.	20,000.
		On cover		40,000.
		Pair on cover		55,000.

PLUM CREEK, TEX.

E1

Manuscript Adhesive

141X1	E1	10c black, *blue*, on cover	—

The stamps have ruled lines with the value "10" in manuscript. Size and shape vary.

PORT GIBSON, MISS.

E1

Manuscript Signature

Handstamped Envelope, Ms Signature

142XU1	E1	5c black	—

PORT LAVACA, TEX.

A1

Typeset Adhesive

107X1	A1	10c black, on cover	25,000.

One example known. It is uncanceled on a postmarked cover.

RALEIGH, N. C.

E1

Handstamped Envelopes

68XU1	E1	5c red	600.
68XU2	E1	5c blue	3,000.

RHEATOWN, TENN.

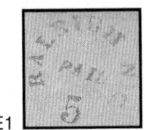

A1

Typeset Adhesive
Three varieties

69X1	A1	5c red	6,000.	6,500.
		On cover, ms. cancel		20,000.
		On cover, tied by handstamp		37,500.
		Pair	15,000.	

RICHMOND, TEX.

E1

Handstamped Envelopes or Letter Sheets

70XU1	E1	5c red		2,500.
a.		10c on 5c red		5,000.
70XU2	E1	10c red		2,000.
a.		15c (ms.) on 10c red		5,000.

RINGGOLD, GA.

E1

Handstamped Envelope

71XU1	E1	5c blue black	9,000.

RUTHERFORDTON, N. C.

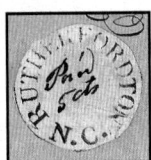

A1

Handstamped Adhesive, Ms. "Paid 5cts"

72X1	A1	5c black, cut round, on cover (uncanceled)	35,000.

No. 72X1 is unique.

SALEM, N. C.

"Paid 5" in Ms. — E1   "Paid 5" Handstamped — E2

Handstamped Envelopes

73XU1	E1	5c black	1,750.
73XU2	E1	10c black	2,250.
73XU3	E2	5c black	2,250.
a.		10c on 5c black	2,800.

Reprints exist on various papers. They either lack the "Paid" and value or have them counterfeited.

SALISBURY, N. C.

E1

Press-printed Envelope (typeset)
Impressed at top left

75XU1	E1	5c black, greenish	15,000.

One example known. Part of the envelope was torn away (now repaired), leaving part of design missing.

SAN ANTONIO, TEX.

E1   E2

Control

Handstamped Envelopes

76XU1	E1	10c black	500.	2,000.
76XU1A	E2	5c black		1,500.
76XU2	E2	10c black		1,500.

Black circle control mark is on front or back.

SAVANNAH, GA.

E1   Control

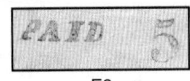

E2

Handstamped Envelopes

101XU1	E1	5c black	400.
a.		10c on 5c black	1,500.
101XU2	E2	5c black	600.
a.		20c on 5c black	2,000.
101XU3	E1	10c black	750.
101XU4	E2	10c black	750.

Envelopes must have octagonal control mark. One example is known of No.101XU2a.

SELMA, ALA.

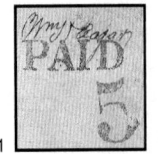

E1

Handstamped Envelopes; Signature in Ms.

77XU1	E1	5c black	1,250.
a.		10c on 5c black	3,000.
77XU2	E1	10c black	2,500.

Signature is that of Postmaster William H. Eagar.

See 3c 1861 Postmaster's Provisional No. 5AX1.

SPARTA, GA.

E1

Handstamped Envelopes

93XU1	E1	5c red	—	2,250.
93XU2	E1	10c red		5,000.

Only one example recorded of No. 93XU2.

SPARTANBURG, S. C.

A1   A2

Handstamped Adhesives
(on ruled or plain wove paper)

78X1	A1	5c black, cut to shape	
		Cut square	27,500.
		On cover, cut to shape	20,000.
		Pair on cover	30,000.
a.		"Paid" instead of denomination, revalued to 5c with "PAID" and "5" in small circle handstamps	
78X2	A2	5c black, *bluish*	4,000.
		On cover	15,000.
78X3	A2	5c black, *brown*	4,000.
		On cover	18,000.

Most examples of Nos. 78X1-78X3 are cut round. Cut square examples in sound condition are worth much more.

E1

Control

Handstamped Envelopes

78XU1	E1	10c black (control on reverse)	5,000.

STATESVILLE, N. C.

E1

Handstamped Envelopes
79XU1 E1 5c black   1,000.
  a.   10c on 5c black   2,500.

Unused examples of No. 79XU1 are reprints.

SUMTER, S. C.

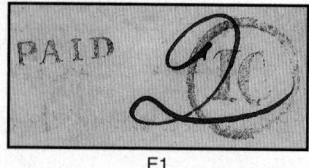

E1

Handstamped Envelopes
80XU1 E1 5c black   500.
  a.   10c on 5c black   900.
80XU2 E1 10c black   600.
  a.   2c (ms.) on 10c black   1,100.

Used examples of Nos. 80XU1-80XU2 are indistinguishable from handstamped "Paid" covers.

TALBOTTON, GA.

E1

Handstamped Envelopes
94XU1 E1 5c black   1,000.
  a.   10c on 5c black   2,000.
94XU2 E1 10c black   1,000.

TALLADEGA, ALA.

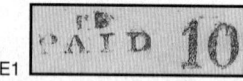

E1

Handstamped Envelopes
143XU1 E1 5c black   1,500.   —
143XU2 E1 10c black   1,500.   —

These same markings were used on hand-stamped "Paid" covers.

TELLICO PLAINS, TENN.

A1

Typeset Adhesives
Settings of two 5c and one 10c
Laid Paper
81X1 A1 5c red   2,500.   —
  On cover   40,000.
81X2 A1 10c red   4,000.

THOMASVILLE, GA.

E1

Control

Handstamped Envelopes
82XU1 E1 5c black   750.
  On patriotic cover   2,750.

On No. 82XU1, the control is on the reverse of the cover. The dated control is known with four different dates, including June 18, June 01 and August 23. The patriotic cover use is unique.

E2

82XU2 E2 5c black   1,000.

TULLAHOMA, TENN.

 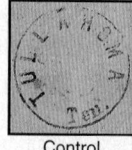

E1   Control

Handstamped Envelope
111XU1 E1 10c black   6,000.

The control appears either on the front or the back of the envelope.

TUSCALOOSA, ALA.

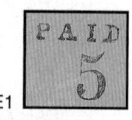

E1

Handstamped Envelopes
83XU1 E1 5c black   250.
83XU2 E1 10c black   250.

Used examples of Nos. 83XU1-83XU2 are indistinguishable from handstamped "Paid" covers.

TUSCUMBIA, ALA.

E1

Handstamped Envelopes
84XU1 E1 5c black   4,000.
84XU2 E1 5c red   5,000.
84XU3 E1 10c black   5,250.

See 3c 1861 Postmaster's Provisional No. 6AXU1.

UNIONTOWN, ALA.

A1

Typeset Adhesives
(settings of 4 (2x2), 4 varieties of each value)
Laid Paper
86X1 A1 2c dark blue,
             gray blue,
             on cover   —
86X2 A1 2c dark blue,
             sheet of 4   40,000.
86X3 A1 5c green, gray
             blue   4,000.   3,250.
  On cover   15,000.
86X4 A1 5c green   4,000.   3,250.
  On cover   15,000.
  Pair on cover   22,500.

86X5 A1 10c red, gray
             blue   —
  On cover   40,000.

Two examples known of No. 86X1, both on cover (drop letters), one uncanceled and one pen canceled.
The only recorded examples of No. 86X2 are in a unique sheet of 4.
The item listed as No. 86X5 used is an uncanceled stamp on a large piece with part of addressee's name in manuscript.

UNIONVILLE, S. C.

A1

Handstamped Adhesive
"PAID" and "5" applied separately
Paper with Blue Ruled Lines
87X1 A1 5c black, grayish   —
  On cover, uncanceled   17,500.
  On cover, tied
  Pair on patriotic cover   32,500.

The pair on patriotic cover is the only pair recorded.

VALDOSTA, GA.

 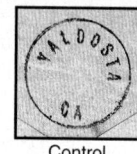

E1   Control

Handstamped Envelopes
100XU1 E1 10c black   9,000.
100XU2 E1 5c +5c black   —

The black circle control must appear on front of the No. 100XU2 envelope and on the back of the No. 100XU1 envelope.
There is one recorded cover each of Nos. 100XU1-100XU2.

VICTORIA, TEX.

A1   A2

Typeset Adhesives
Surface colored paper
88X1 A1 5c red brown,
             green   20,000.
88X2 A1 10c red brown,
             green   22,500.
  On cover   115,000.
88X3 A2 10c red brown,
             green,
             pelure
             paper   32,500. 30,000.

WALTERBOROUGH, S. C.

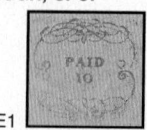

E1

Handstamped Envelopes
108XU1 E1 10c black, buff   —
108XU2 E1 10c carmine   4,250.

The existence of No. 108XU1 is in question. The editors would like to see authenticated evidence of its existence.

WARRENTON, GA.

E1

Handstamped Envelopes
89XU1 E1 5c black   2,100.
  a.   10c (ms.) on 5c black   1,000.

Fakes of the Warrenton provisional marking based on the illustration shown are known on addressed but postally unused covers.

WASHINGTON, GA.

E1

Handstamped Envelope
117XU1 E1 10c black   2,000.

Envelopes must have black circle postmark control on the back. Examples with the undated control on the front are not considered provisional unless a dated postmark is also present.

WEATHERFORD, TEX.

E1

Handstamped Envelopes
(woodcut with "PAID" inserted in type)
109XU1 E1 5c black   2,000.
109XU2 E1 5c +5c black   11,000.

One example is known of No. 109XU2.

WILKESBORO, N. C.

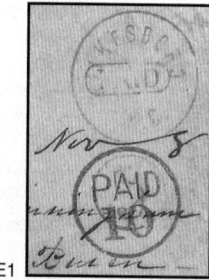

E1

Handstamped Envelope
147XU1 E1 5c black, revalued to
             10c   —

No. 147XU1 is unique.

WINNSBOROUGH, S. C.

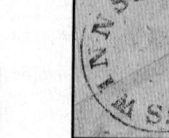

E1   Control

Handstamped Envelopes
97XU1 E1 5c black   2,000.
  On patriotic cover   3,750.
97XU2 E1 10c black   3,500.

Envelopes must have black circle control on front or back.

WYTHEVILLE, VA.

E1   Control

Handstamped Envelope

114XU1 E1 5c black   900.

For later additions, listed out of numerical sequence, see:
- #74X1, Liberty, Va.
- #92XU1, Huntsville, Tex.
- #93XU1, Sparta, Ga.
- #94XU1, Talbotton, Ga.
- #95XU1, Cuthbert, GA
- #96XU1, Lake City, Fla.
- #97XU1, Winnsborough, S.C.
- #98XU1, Galveston, Tex.
- #99XU1, Christiansburg, Va.
- #100XU1, Valdosta, Ga.
- #101XU1, Savannah, Ga.
- #102XU1, Griffin, Ga.
- #103XU1, Courtland, Ala.
- #104XU1, Fincastle, Va.
- #105XU1, Micanopy, Fla.
- #106XU1, Pensacola, Fla.
- #107X1, Port Lavaca, Tex.
- #108XU1, Walterborough, S.C.
- #109XU1, Weatherford, Tex.
- #110XU1, Jacksonville, Ala.
- #111XU1, Tullahoma, Tenn.
- #112XU1, Hamburgh, S.C.
- #113XU1, Columbia, Tenn.
- #114XU1, Wytheville, Va.
- #115X1, Oakway, S.C.
- #116XU1, Laurens Court House, S.C.
- #117XU1, Washington, Ga.
- #118XU1, Carolina City, N.C.
- #119XU1, Colaparchee, Ga.
- #120XU1, Forsyth, Ga.
- #121XU1, Limestone Springs, S.C.
- #122XU1, Balcony Falls, Va.
- #123XU1, Barnwell Court House, S.C.
- #124XU1, Bluffton, S.C.
- #125XU1, Camden, S.C.
- #126XU1, Cartersville, Ga.
- #127XU1, Charlottesville, Va.
- #128XU1, Fraziersville, S.C.
- #129XU1, Gaston, N.C.
- #130XU1, Harrisburg, Tex.
- #132XU1, Hollandale, Tex.
- #133XU1, Isabella, Ga.
- #134XU1, Jacksonville, Fla.
- #135XU1, Lexington, Va.
- #136XU1, Madison, Ga.
- #137XU1, Madison Court House, Fla.
- #138XU1, Milton, N.C.
- #139XU1, Norfolk, Va.
- #140XU1, Plains of Dura, Ga.
- #141X1, Plum Creek, Tex.
- #142XU1, Port Gibson, Miss.
- #143XU1, Talladega, Ala.
- #144XU1, Greenville, Tenn.
- #145XU1, Mars Bluff, S.C.
- #146XU1, Charlotte, N.C.
- #147XU1, Wilkesboro, N.C.
- #148XU1, Fort Valley, Ga.

GENERAL ISSUES

Jefferson Davis — A1

1861   **Unwmk.**   **Litho.**   *Imperf.*

1	A1	5c green (shades)	300.	175.
	No gum		175.	
	On cover			300.
a.	5c light green		275.	175.
	No gum		160.	
b.	5c dark green		375.	250.
	No gum		225.	
c.	5c olive green		400.	250.
	No gum		240.	
	On cover			300.

Thomas Jefferson — A2

1861-62

2	A2 10c blue		275.	180.
	No gum		150.	
	On cover			325.
a.	10c light blue		300.	200.
	No gum		175.	
b.	10c dark blue		700.	300.
	No gum		400.	
c.	10c indigo		5,000.	7,500.
	No gum		2,500.	
d.	Printed on both sides			1,750.
e.	light milky blue		1,250.	325.
	No gum		700.	
	On cover			400.

The earliest printings of No. 2 were made by Hoyer & Ludwig, the later ones by J. T. Paterson & Co.

Stamps of the later printings usually have a small colored dash below the lowest point of the upper left spandrel.

See Nos. 4-5.

Andrew Jackson — A3

1862

3	A3 2c green		950.	750.
	No gum		550.	
	On cover			3,500.
a.	2c bright yellow green		2,000.	
	No gum		1,300.	
	On cover			4,000.
4	A1 5c blue		225.	125.
	No gum		130.	
	On cover			275.
a.	5c dark blue		275.	175.
	No gum		150.	
b.	5c light milky blue		300.	200.
	No gum		170.	
5	A2 10c rose (shades)		2,000.	475.
	No gum		1,150.	
	On cover			800.
a.	10c carmine		3,500.	1,900.
	No gum		2,100.	
	On cover			5,000.
	On patriotic cover			—

Jefferson Davis — A4

Typo.

6	A4 5c light blue		16.	28.
	No gum		7.	
	Pair on cover			100.
7	A4 5c blue (De La Rue thin paper)		20.	22.
	No gum		10.	
	Pair on cover			95.
a.	5c deep blue		25.	30.
	No gum		12.	
b.	Printed on both sides		2,500.	1,400.
	Pair on cover			4,000.

No. 6 has fine, clear impression. No. 7 has coarser impression and the color is duller and often blurred.

Both 2c and 10c stamps, types A4 and A10, were privately printed in various colors.

Andrew Jackson — A5

1863   **Engr.**

8	A5 2c brown red		75.	350.
	No gum		40.	
a.	2c pale red		90.	450.
	No gum		45.	
	Single on cover, #8 or 8a			1,500.

A6

Thick or Thin Paper

9	A6 10c blue		900.	550.
	No gum		575.	
a.	10c milky blue (first printing)		950.	600.
	No gum		575.	

---

b.	10c gray blue		1,000.	650.
	No gum		625.	
	On cover			1,600.

Jefferson Davis — A6a

10	A6a 10c blue (with frame line)		5,000.	1,900.
	No gum		3,500.	
a.	10c milky blue		5,000.	1,900.
	No gum		3,500.	
b.	10c greenish blue		5,500.	1,900.
	No gum		4,000.	
c.	10c dark blue		5,500.	1,900.
	No gum		4,000.	
	On cover			3,000.

Values of Nos. 10, 10a, 10b and 10c are for examples showing parts of lines on at least three sides. Used stamps showing 4 complete lines sell for approximately 3 to 4 times the values given. Unused stamps showing 4 complete lines are exceedingly rare (only two recorded), and the one sound example is valued at $25,000.

A7

There are many slight differences between A7 and A8, the most noticeable being the additional line outside the ornaments at the four corners of A8.

1863-64

11	A7 10c blue		16.	20.
	No gum		7.	
	On cover			125.
a.	10c milky blue		50.	60.
	No gum		27.	
b.	10c dark blue		25.	30.
	No gum		12.	
c.	10c greenish blue		30.	20.
	No gum		17.	
d.	10c green		75.	80.
	No gum		45.	
e.	Officially perforated 12½ (A. & D.)		350.	350.
	On cover			900.

A8

12	A8 10c blue		20.	25.
	No gum		9.	
	On cover			135.
a.	10c milky blue		50.	60.
	No gum		25.	
b.	10c light blue		19.	22.
	No gum		9.	
c.	10c greenish blue		40.	55.
	No gum		20.	
d.	10c dark blue		22.	25.
	No gum		11.	
e.	10c green		125.	140.
	No gum		75.	

f.	Officially perforated 12½ (A. & D.)		375.	375.
	On cover			900.

The paper of Nos. 11 and 12 varies from thin hard to thick soft. The so-called laid paper is probably due to thick streaky gum.

George Washington — A9

1863

13	A9 20c green		45.	400.
	No gum		27.	
	On cover			1,250.
a.	20c yellow green		70.	450.
	No gum		45.	
b.	20c dark green		65.	500.
	No gum		40.	
c.	20c bluish green		100.	—
	No gum		65.	
d.	Diagonal half used as 10c on cover			2,000.
e.	Horizontal half used as 10c on cover			3,500.

John C. Calhoun — A10

1862   **Typo.**

14	A10 1c orange		100.	
	No gum		60.	
a.	1c deep orange		130.	
	No gum		75.	

No. 14 was never put in use.

CANAL ZONE

kə-'nal 'zōn

LOCATION — A strip of land 10 miles wide, extending through the Republic of Panama, between the Atlantic and Pacific Oceans.

GOVT. — From 1904-79 a U.S. Government Reservation; from 1979-99 under joint control of the Republic of Panama and the U.S.

AREA — 552.8 sq. mi.

POP. — 41,800 (est. 1976)

The Canal Zone, site of the Panama Canal, was leased in perpetuity to the U.S. for a cash payment of $10,000,000 and a yearly rental. Treaties between the two countries provided for joint jurisdiction by the U.S. and Panama, 1979-1999, with Panama handling postal service. At the end of 1999, the canal, in its entirety, reverted to Panama.

100 Centavos = 1 Peso
100 Centesimos = 1 Balboa
100 Cents = 1 Dollar

> **Catalogue values for unused stamps in this country are for Never Hinged items, beginning with Scott 118 in the regular postage section and Scott C6 in the air post section.**

Watermarks

Wmk. 190 — "USPS" in Single-lined Capitals

Wmk. 191 — Double-lined "USPS" in Capitals

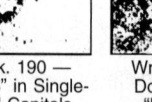

Map of Panama — A1

Violet to Violet-Blue Handstamp on Panama Nos. 72, 72a-72c, 78, 79.

On the 2c "PANAMA" is normally 13mm long. On the 5c and 10c it measures about 15mm.

On the 2c, "PANAMA" reads up on the upper half of the sheet and down on the lower half. On the 5c and 10c, "PANAMA" reads up at left and down at right on each stamp.

On the 2c only, varieties exist with inverted "V" for "A," accent on "A," inverted "N," etc., in "PANAMA."

Unwmk.

1904, June 24   **Engr.**   *Perf. 12*

1	A1	2c rose, both "PAN-AMA" reading up or down	650.	400.
a.		"CANAL ZONE" inverted	1,000.	850.
b.		"CANAL ZONE" double	3,250.	2,000.
c.		"CANAL ZONE" double, both inverted	20,000.	
d.		"PANAMA" reading down and up	750.	650.
e.		As "d," "CANAL ZONE" invtd.	9,000.	9,000.
f.		Vert. pair, "PANAMA" reading up on top 2c, down on other	2,100.	2,100.
g.		As "f," "CANAL ZONE" inverted	20,000.	
2	A1	5c blue	300.	190.
a.		"CANAL ZONE" inverted	775.	600.
b.		"CANAL ZONE" double	2,250.	1,500.
c.		Pair, one without "CANAL ZONE" overprint	5,000.	5,000.
d.		"CANAL ZONE" overprint diagonal, reading down to right	800.	700.
3	A1	10c yellow	400.	230.
a.		"CANAL ZONE" inverted	775.	600.
b.		"CANAL ZONE" double		14,000.

c.	Pair, one without "CANAL ZONE" overprint	6,000.	5,000.
	Nos. 1-3 (3)	1,350.	820.00

Cancellations consist of town and/or bars in magenta or black, or a mixture of both colors. Nos. 1-3 were withdrawn July 17, 1904. Forgeries of the "Canal Zone" overprint and cancellations are numerous.

United States Nos. 300, 319, 304, 306 and 307 Overprinted in Black

1904, July 18   **Wmk. 191**

4	A115	1c blue green	40.00	22.50
5	A129	2c carmine	35.00	25.00
a.		2c scarlet	35.00	30.00
6	A119	5c blue	95.00	65.00
7	A121	8c violet black	150.00	85.00
8	A122	10c pale red brown	140.00	90.00
		Nos. 4-8 (5)	460.00	287.50

Beware of fake overprints.

A2

A3

CANAL ZONE	CANAL ZONE
Regular Type	Antique Type

1904-06   **Unwmk.**

Black Overprint on Stamps of Panama

9	A2	1c green	2.75	2.00
a.		"CANAL" in antique type	100.00	100.00
b.		"ZONE" in antique type	70.00	70.00
c.		Inverted overprint	7,500.	6,000.
d.		Double overprint	2,750.	2,000.
10	A2	2c rose	4.50	2.75
a.		Inverted overprint	225.00	275.00
b.		"L" of "CANAL" sideways	2,500.	2,500.

"PANAMA" (15mm long) reading up at left, down at right

Overprint "CANAL ZONE" in Black, "PANAMA" and Bar in Red

11	A3	2c rose	7.00	5.00
a.		"ZONE" in antique type	200.00	200.00
b.		"PANAMA" overprint inverted, bar at bottom	600.00	675.00
12	A3	5c blue	8.00	3.25
a.		"CANAL" in antique type	75.00	65.00
b.		"ZONE" in antique type	75.00	65.00
c.		"CANAL ZONE" double	800.00	800.00
d.		"PANAMA" double	1,100.	1,000.
e.		"PANAMA" inverted, bar at bottom	1,000.	2,000.
13	A3	10c yellow	18.00	12.00
a.		"CANAL" in antique type	190.00	200.00
b.		"ZONE" in antique type	175.00	160.00
c.		"PANAMA" ovpt. double	650.00	650.00
d.		"PANAMA" overprint in red brown	27.50	25.00
		Nos. 11-13 (3)	33.00	20.25

With Added Surcharge in Red

a

14	A3	8c on 50c bister brn	30.00	27.50
a.		"ZONE" in antique type	1,150.	1,150.
b.		"CANAL ZONE" inverted	450.00	425.00
c.		"PANAMA" overprint in rose brown	37.50	37.50
d.		As "c," "CANAL" in antique type	1,750.	850.00
e.		As "c," "ZONE" in antique type	1,750.	

f.	As "c," "8 cts" double	1,100.	
g.	As "c," "8" omitted	4,500.	
h.	As "c," "cts 8"		

Nos. 11-14 are overprinted or surcharged on Panama Nos. 77, 77e, 78, 78c, 78d, 78f, 78g, 78h, 79 79c, 79e 79g and 81 respectively.

On No. 14 with original gum, the gum is almost always disturbed. Unused stamps are valued thus.

Panama No. 74a, 74b Overprinted "CANAL ZONE" in Regular Type in Black and Surcharged Type "a" in Red Both "PANAMA" (13mm long) Reading Up

15	A3(a)	8c on 50c bister brown	2,000.	4,750.
a.		"PANAMA" reading down and up		6,750.

On No. 15 with original gum, the gum is almost always disturbed. Unused stamps are valued thus.

Map of Panama — A4

Panama Nos. 19 and 21 Surcharged in Black

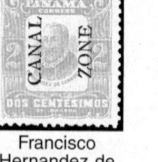

a

b

c

d

e

f

CANAL ZONE 1 ct.

CANAL ZONE 1 ct.

CANAL ZONE 1 ct.

CANAL ZONE 2 cts.

CANAL ZONE 2 cts.

CANAL ZONE 2 cts.

1906

There were three printings of each denomination, differing principally in the relative position of the various parts of the surcharges. Varieties occur with inverted "V" for final "A" in "PANAMA," "CA" spaced, "ZO" spaced,

"2c" spaced, accents in various positions, and with bars shifted so that two bars appear on top or bottom of the stamp (either with or without the corresponding bar on top or bottom) and sometimes with only one bar at top or bottom.

16	A4	1c on 20c violet, type a	1.90	1.60
a.		Type b	1.90	1.60
b.		Type c	2.00	1.50
c.		As No. 16, double surcharge		2,000.
17	A4	2c on 1p lake, type d	2.75	2.75
a.		Type e	2.75	2.75
b.		Type f	20.00	20.00

Panama Nos. 74, 74a and 74b Overprinted "CANAL ZONE" in Regular Type in Black and Surcharged in Red

b

c

1905-06

Both "PANAMA" Reading Up

18	A3(b)	8c on 50c bister brown	50.00	50.00
a.		"ZONE" in antique type	200.00	180.00
b.		"PANAMA" reading down and up	175.00	160.00
19	A3(c)	8c on 50c bister brown	55.00	40.00
a.		"CANAL" in antique type	210.00	180.00
b.		"ZONE" in antique type	210.00	180.00
c.		"8 cts" double	1,100.	1,100.
d.		"PANAMA" reading down and up	110.00	90.00

On Nos. 18-19 with original gum, the gum is usually disturbed. Unused stamps are valued thus.

Panama No. 81 Overprinted "CANAL ZONE" in Regular Type in Black and Surcharged in Red Type "c" plus Period "PANAMA" reading up and down

20	A3(c)	8c on 50c bister brown	35.00	37.50
a.		"CANAL" antique type	200.00	180.00
b.		"ZONE" in antique type	200.00	180.00
c.		"8 cts" omitted	800.00	800.00
d.		"8 cts" double	1,500.	
e.		"cts 8"		

Nos. 14 and 18-20 exist without CANAL ZONE overprint but were not regularly issued and are considered printer's waste. Forgeries of the overprint varieties of Nos. 9-15 and 18-20 are known.

On No. 20 with original gum, the gum is usually disturbed. Unused stamps are valued thus.

Francisco Hernandez de Cordoba — A5

Vasco Nunez de Balboa — A6

Fernández de Córdoba A7

Justo Arosemena A8

Manuel J. Hurtado — A9

Jose de Obaldia — A10

Stamps of Panama Overprinted in Black

1906-07   *Perf. 12*

Overprint Reading Up

21	A5	2c red & black	27.50	27.50
a.		"CANAL" only	4,000.	

Overprint Reading Down

22	A6	1c green & black	2.00	1.00
a.		Horiz. pair, imperf. btwn.	1,100.	1,100.
b.		Vert. pair, imperf. btwn.	2,000.	2,000.
c.		Vert. pair, imperf. horiz.	2,250.	1,750.
d.		Inverted overprint reading up	550.00	550.00
e.		Double overprint	275.00	275.00
f.		Double overprint, one inverted	1,750.	1,600.
g.		Invtd. center, ovpt. reading up	3,750.	4,750.
h.		Horiz. pair, imperf vert.	5,000.	
23	A7	2c red & black	3.00	1.10
a.		Horizontal pair, imperf. between	2,250.	2,000.
b.		Vertical pair, one without overprint	2,500.	2,500.
c.		Double overprint	700.00	700.00
d.		Double overprint, one diagonal	800.00	800.00
e.		Double overprint, one diagonal, in pair with normal	2,500.	
f.		2c carmine red & black	5.00	2.75
g.		As "f," inverted center and overprint reading up	14,000.	
h.		As "d," one "ZONE CANAL"	4,000.	
i.		"CANAL" double	5,000.	
24	A8	5c ultramarine & black	5.75	2.25
c.		Double overprint	500.00	400.00
d.		"CANAL" only	5,500.	
e.		"ZONE CANAL"	5,000.	
25	A9	8c purple & black	20.00	8.00
a.		Horizontal pair, imperf. between and at left margin	1,750.	4,000.
26	A10	10c violet & black	20.00	7.00
a.		Dbl. ovpt., one reading up	5,000.	
b.		Overprint reading up	5,500.	
		Nos. 22-26 (5)	50.75	19.35

Nos. 22-25 occur with "CA" of "CANAL" spaced ½mm further apart on position No. 50 of the setting.

The used pair of No. 25a is unique.

Cordoba A11

Arosemena A12

Hurtado — A13

Jose de Obaldia — A14

1909

Overprint Reading Down

27	A11	2c vermilion & black	12.00	5.00
a.		Horizontal pair, one without overprint	2,600.	
b.		Vert. pair, one without ovpt.	3,500.	
28	A12	5c deep blue & black	40.00	12.50
29	A13	8c violet & black	37.50	14.00
30	A14	10c violet & black	40.00	14.00
a.		Horizontal pair, one with "ZONE" omitted	3,000.	
b.		Vertical pair, one without overprint	4,000.	
		Nos. 27-30 (4)	129.50	45.50

Nos. 27-30 occur with "CA" spaced (position 50).

Do not confuse No. 27 with Nos. 39d or 53a. On No. 30a, the stamp with "ZONE" omitted is also missing most of "CANAL."

For designs A11-A14 with overprints reading up, see Nos. 32-35, 39-41, 47-48, 53-54, 56-57.

Black Overprint Reading Up

Vasco Nunez de Balboa — A15

Type I

Type I Overprint: "C" with serifs both top and bottom. "L," "Z" and "E" with slanting serifs.

Compare Type I overprint with Types II to V illustrated before Nos. 38, 46, 52 and 55.

1909-10

31	A15	1c dark green & black	4.25	1.25
a.		Inverted center and overprint reading down		22,500.
c.		Bklt. pane of 6, handmade, perf. margins	500.00	
32	A11	2c vermilion & black	4.50	1.25
a.		Vert. pair, imperf. horiz.	1,000.	1,000.
c.		Bklt. pane of 6, handmade, perf. margins	800.00	
d.		Double overprint (I)		6,000.
33	A12	5c deep blue & black	17.00	3.50
a.		Double overprint	375.00	375.00
34	A13	8c violet & black	11.00	5.00
a.		Vertical pair, one without overprint	1,750.	
35	A14	10c violet & black	47.50	20.00
		Nos. 31-35 (5)	84.25	31.00

No. 32d is unique and has small faults. See Nos. 38, 46, 52, 55.

A16

A17

Black Surcharge

1911, Jan. 14

36	A16	10c on 13c gray	6.00	2.00
a.		"10 cts" inverted	350.00	300.00
b.		"10 cts" omitted	350.00	

Many used stamps offered as No. 36b are merely No. 36 from which the surcharge has been chemically removed.

1914, Jan. 6

37	A17	10c gray	47.50	11.00

Black Overprint Reading Up

Type II: "C" with serif at top only. "L" and "E" with vertical serifs. "O" tilts to left

1912-16

38	A15	1c green & black	10.00	3.00
a.		Vertical pair, one without overprint	1,750.	1,750.
b.		Booklet pane of 6, imperf. margins	575.00	
c.		Booklet pane of 6, handmade, perf. margins	1,000.	
39	A11	2c vermilion & black	8.00	1.10
a.		Horiz. pair, right stamp without overprint	1,250.	
b.		Horiz. pair, left stamp without overprint	1,750.	
c.		Booklet pane of 6, imperf. margins	550.00	
d.		Overprint reading down	200.00	
e.		As "d," inverted center	650.00	750.00
f.		As "e," booklet pane of 6, handmade, perf. margins	8,000.	
g.		As "c," handmade, perf. margins	900.00	800.00
h.		As No. 39, "CANAL" only		1,100.
40	A12	5c deep blue & black	20.00	2.50
a.		With Cordoba portrait of 2c	12,500.	
41	A14	10c violet & black	60.00	7.50
		Nos. 38-41 (4)	98.00	14.10

Map of Panama Canal A18

Balboa Takes Possession of the Pacific Ocean A19

Gatun Locks — A20

Culebra Cut — A21

1915, Mar. 1

Blue Overprint, Type II

42	A18	1c dark green & black	8.75	6.50
43	A19	2c carmine & black	12.00	4.25
44	A20	5c blue & black	10.00	5.75
45	A21	10c orange & black	19.00	11.00
		Nos. 42-45 (4)	49.75	27.50

Black Overprint Reading Up

Type III Overprint: Similar to Type I but letters appear thinner, particularly the lower bar of "L," "Z" and "E." Impressions are often light, rough and irregular, and not centered.

1915-20

46	A15	1c green & black	175.00	125.00
a.		Overprint reading down	375.00	
b.		Double overprint	225.00	
c.		"ZONE" double	6,500.	
d.		Double overprint, one reads "ZONE CANAL"	2,000.	
47	A11	2c orange vermilion & black	2,750.	60.00
48	A12	5c deep blue & black	450.00	130.00
		Nos. 46-48 (3)	3,375.	315.00

Spacing between words of overprint on Nos. 46-48 is 9¼mm; spacing varieties are not known. This should not be confused with a fairly common 9¼mm spacing of the 2c value of type I, nor with an uncommon 9¼mm spacing variety of the 5c of type I.

S.S. "Panama" in Culebra Cut — A22

S.S. "Panama" in Culebra Cut — A23

S.S. "Cristobal" in Gatun Locks — A24

1917, Jan. 23

Blue Overprint, Type II

49	A22	12c purple & black	17.50	5.25
50	A23	15c bright blue & black	50.00	17.50

51	A24	24c yellow brown & black	35.00	13.00
		Nos. 49-51 (3)	102.50	35.75

Black Overprint Reading Up

Type IV: "C" thick at bottom, "E" with center bar same length as top and bottom bars

1918-20

52	A15	1c green & black	32.50	10.00
a.		Overprint reading down	175.00	—
b.		Booklet pane of 6	600.00	
c.		Booklet pane of 6, left vertical row of 3 without overprint	7,500.	
d.		Booklet pane of 6, right vertical row of 3 with double overprint	7,500.	
e.		Horiz. bkt. pair, left stamp without overprint	3,000.	
f.		Horiz. bkt. pair, right stamp with double overprint	3,000.	
g.		Double overprint, booklet single		3,000.
53	A11	2c vermilion & black	110.00	6.00
a.		Overprint reading down	150.00	150.00
b.		Horiz. pair, right stamp without ovpt. (from misregistered overprints)	2,000.	
c.		Booklet pane of 6	1,050.	
d.		Booklet pane of 6, left vertical row of 3 without overprint	15,000.	
e.		Horiz. bkt. pair, left stamp without overprint	3,000.	
f.		Horiz. sheet pair, one without overprint (from foldover)	1,750.	
54	A12	5c deep blue & black	150.00	32.50
		Nos. 52-54 (3)	292.50	48.50

No. 53e used is unique and is on cover.

Black Overprint Reading Up

Type V: Smaller block type 1¾mm high. "A" with flat top

1920-21

55	A15	1c light green & black	22.50	3.25
a.		Overprint reading down	300.00	225.00
b.		Horiz. pair, right stamp without ovpt.	1,750.	
c.		Horiz. pair, left stamp without ovpt.	1,000.	
d.		"ZONE" only	4,000.	—
e.		Booklet pane of 6	2,250.	
f.		As No. 55, "CANAL" double	2,000.	
56	A11	2c orange vermilion & black	8.50	1.75
a.		Double overprint	600.00	
b.		Double overprint, one reading down	650.00	
c.		Horiz. pair, right stamp without overprint	1,500.	
d.		Horiz. pair, left stamp without overprint	1,000.	
e.		Vertical pair, one without overprint	1,500.	
f.		"ZONE" double	1,000.	
g.		Booklet pane of 6	900.00	
h.		As No. 56, "CANAL" double	800.	
57	A12	5c deep blue & black	300.00	45.00
a.		Horiz. pair, right stamp without overprint	2,250.	
b.		Horiz. pair, left stamp without overprint	2,250.	
		Nos. 55-57 (3)	331.00	50.00

Drydock at Balboa A25

Ship in Pedro Miguel Locks — A26

1920, Sept.

Black Overprint Type V

58	A25	50c orange & black	250.00	160.00
59	A26	1b dark violet & black	175.00	50.00

Jose
Vallarino — A27

The "Land
Gate" — A28

Bolivar's
Tribute — A29

Municipal
Building in 1821
and 1921 — A30

Statue of
Balboa — A31

Tomas
Herrera — A32

Jose de
Fabrega — A33

Type V overprint in black, reading up, on all values except the 5c which is overprinted with larger type in red

1921, Nov. 13

60	A27	1c green	3.75	1.50
a.		"CANAL" double	2,250.	
b.		Booklet pane of 6	900.00	
61	A28	2c carmine	2.75	1.00
a.		Overprint reading down	200.00	225.00
b.		Double overprint	900.00	
c.		Vertical pair, one without overprint	3,500.	
d.		"CANAL" double	1,900.	
f.		Booklet pane of 6	2,000.	
62	A29	5c blue (R)	10.00	3.00
a.		Overprint reading down (R)	60.00	
63	A30	10c violet	18.00	7.50
a.		Overprint, reading down	90.00	
64	A31	15c light blue	47.50	17.50
65	A32	24c black brown	67.50	22.50
66	A33	50c black	145.00	85.00
		Nos. 60-66 (7)	294.50	138.00

Experts question the status of the 5c with a small type V overprint in red or black.

Type III overprint in black, reading up

1924, Jan. 28

67	A27	1c green	500.	200.
a.		"ZONE CANAL" reading down	800.	
b.		"ZONE" only, reading down	1,900.	
c.		Se-tenant pair, #67a and 67b	2,750.	

Coat of Arms — A34

1924, Feb.

68	A34	1c dark green	10.00	4.50
69	A34	2c carmine	2.00	2.75

The 5c to 1b values were prepared but never issued. See listing in the Scott U.S. specialized catalogue.

United States Nos. 551-554, 557, 562, 564-566, 569, 570 and 571 Overprinted in Red (No. 70) or Black (all others)

Type A: Letters "A" with Flat Tops

1924-25   Unwmk.   Perf. 11

70	A154	½c olive brown	.25	.70
		Never hinged	.40	
71	A155	1c deep green	1.40	1.00
		Never hinged	2.50	
a.		Inverted overprint	500.00	500.00
b.		"ZONE" inverted	350.00	325.00
c.		"CANAL" only	1,250.	
d.		"ZONE CANAL"	500.00	
e.		Booklet pane of 6	80.00	
72	A156	1½c yellow brown	2.00	1.70
		Never hinged	3.25	
73	A157	2c carmine	6.75	1.70
		Never hinged	10.50	
a.		Booklet pane of 6	175.00	
74	A160	5c dark blue	16.00	7.00
		Never hinged	25.00	
75	A165	10c orange	40.00	20.00
		Never hinged	65.00	
76	A167	12c brown violet	32.50	30.00
		Never hinged	62.50	
a.		"ZONE" inverted	3,750.	2,250.
77	A168	14c dark blue	27.50	22.50
		Never hinged	45.00	
78	A169	15c gray	45.00	37.50
		Never hinged	70.00	
79	A172	30c olive brown	32.50	20.00
		Never hinged	52.50	
80	A173	50c lilac	75.00	45.00
		Never hinged	150.00	
81	A174	$1 violet brown	225.00	95.00
		Never hinged	400.00	
		Nos. 70-81 (12)	503.90	282.10

Normal spacing between words of the overprint is 9¼mm. Minor spacing variations are known.

All examples of Nos. 71b and 76a have a natural straight edge at right.

Type B: Letters "A" with Sharp Pointed Tops

1925-28

84	A157	2c carmine	27.50	8.00
		Never hinged	45.00	
a.		"CANAL" only	2,250.	
b.		"ZONE CANAL"	475.00	
c.		Horizontal pair, one without overprint	3,500.	
d.		Booklet pane of 6	175.00	
e.		Vertical pair, "a" and "b" se-tenant	3,500.	
85	A158	3c violet	3.75	3.00
		Never hinged	6.00	
a.		"ZONE ZONE"	550.00	550.00
86	A160	5c dark blue	3.50	2.75
		Never hinged	6.00	
a.		"ZONE ZONE" (LR18)	1,000.	
b.		"CANAL" inverted (LR7)	950.00	
c.		Inverted overprint	500.00	
d.		Horizontal pair, one without overprint	3,250.	
e.		Overprinted "ZONE CANAL"	350.00	
f.		"ZONE" only	2,000.	
g.		Vertical pair, one without overprint, other overprint inverted	2,500.	
h.		"CANAL" only	2,250.	
87	A165	10c orange	35.00	12.00
		Never hinged	52.50	
a.		"ZONE ZONE" (LR18)	3,000.	
88	A167	12c brown violet	20.00	12.50
		Never hinged	34.00	
a.		"ZONE ZONE" (LR18)	5,000.	
89	A168	14c dark blue	27.50	15.00
		Never hinged	42.50	
90	A169	15c gray	7.50	4.50
		Never hinged	12.00	
a.		"ZONE ZONE" (LR18)	5,500.	
91	A187	17c black	4.50	2.75
		Never hinged	7.50	
a.		"ZONE" only	1,000.	
b.		"CANAL" only	2,000.	
c.		"ZONE CANAL"	275.00	
92	A170	20c carmine rose	7.25	3.25
		Never hinged	12.00	
a.		"CANAL" inverted (UR48)	6,500.	
b.		"ZONE" inverted (LL76)	4,750.	
c.		"ZONE CANAL" (LL91)	4,750.	
93	A172	30c olive brown	5.75	3.75
		Never hinged	9.00	
94	A173	50c lilac	230.00	165.00
		Never hinged	400.00	
95	A174	$1 violet brown	120.00	55.00
		Never hinged	250.00	
		Nos. 84-95 (12)	492.25	287.50

1926

96	A188	2c carmine rose	4.50	3.75
		Never hinged	6.75	

On this stamp there is a space of 5mm instead of 9mm between the two words of the overprint.

Overprint Type B in Black on U.S. Nos. 583, 584, 591

1926-27   Perf. 10

97	A157	2c carmine	45.00	11.00
		Never hinged	75.00	
a.		Pair, one without overprint	2,750.	
b.		Booklet pane of 6	500.00	
c.		"CANAL" only	2,000.	
d.		"ZONE" only	2,750.	
98	A158	3c violet	7.50	4.25
		Never hinged	11.00	
99	A165	10c orange	18.00	7.50
		Never hinged	27.50	
		Nos. 97-99 (3)	70.50	22.75

No. 97d is valued in the grade of fine. Very fine examples are not known.

Overprint Type B in Black on U.S. Nos. 632, 634 (Type I), 635, 637, 642

1927-31   Perf. 11x10½

100	A155	1c green	1.75	1.40
		Never hinged	2.60	
a.		Vertical pair, one without overprint	3,750.	
101	A157	2c carmine	1.75	1.00
		Never hinged	2.50	
a.		Booklet pane of 6	200.00	
102	A158	3c violet	4.25	2.75
		Never hinged	6.25	
a.		Booklet pane of 6, hand-made, perf. margins	6,500.	
103	A160	5c dark blue	25.00	10.00
		Never hinged	45.00	
104	A165	10c orange	17.50	10.00
		Never hinged	26.00	
		Nos. 100-104 (5)	50.25	25.15

> **Wet and Dry Printings**
> Canal Zone stamps printed by both the "wet" and "dry" process are Nos. 105, 108-109, 111-114, 117, J25, J27.

Maj. Gen.
William
Crawford
Gorgas
A35

Maj. Gen.
George
Washington
Goethals
A36

Gaillard
Cut — A37

Maj. Gen.
Harry Foote
Hodges
A38

Lt. Col. David
DuB. Gaillard
A39

Maj. Gen.
William L.
Sibert — A40

Jackson
Smith — A41

Rear Adm.
Harry H.
Rousseau
A42

Col. Sydney
B. Williamson
A43

J.C.S.
Blackburn — A44

1928-40   Perf. 11

105	A35	1c green	.25	.25
		(22,392,147)		
		Never hinged	.25	
106	A36	2c carmine	.25	.25
		Never hinged	.30	
a.		Booklet pane of 6	15.00	20.00
		Never hinged	22.50	
107	A37	5c blue	1.00	.40
		Never hinged	1.30	
108	A38	10c orange	.25	.25
		Never hinged	.25	
109	A39	12c brown violet	.75	.60
		Never hinged	1.00	
110	A40	14c blue	.85	.85
		Never hinged	1.20	
111	A41	15c gray black	.40	.35
		Never hinged	.55	
112	A42	20c dark brown	.60	.25
		Never hinged	.80	
113	A43	30c black	.80	.70
		Never hinged	1.10	
114	A44	50c rose lilac	1.50	.65
		Never hinged	2.00	
		Nos. 105-114 (10)	6.65	4.55

For surcharges and overprints, see Nos. J21-J24, O1-O8.
Coils are listed as Nos. 160-161.

United States Nos. 720
and 695 Overprinted
type B

1933, Jan. 14   Perf. 11x10½

115	A226	3c deep violet	2.75	.25
		Never hinged	4.00	
b.		"CANAL" only	2,600.	
c.		Booklet pane of 6, hand-made, perf. margins	80.00	
116	A168	14c dark blue	4.50	3.50
		Never hinged	7.00	
a.		"ZONE CANAL"	1,500.	

Gen. George Washington
Goethals — A45

20th anniversary of the opening of the Panama Canal.

1934   Perf. 11

117	A45	3c red violet	.25	.25
		Never hinged	.30	
a.		Booklet pane of 6	12.50	32.50
b.		As "a," handmade, perf. margins	160.00	—

Coil is listed as No. 153.

> **Catalogue values for unused stamps in this section, from this point to the end, are for Never Hinged items.**

United States Nos.
803 and 805
Overprinted in Black

1939, Sept. 1   *Perf. 11x10½*
| 118 | A275 | ½c red orange | .25 | .25 |
| 119 | A277 | 1½c bister brown | .25 | .25 |

Panama Canal Anniversary Issue

Balboa-Before — A46

Balboa-After — A47

Gaillard Cut-Before A48

Gaillard Cut-After A49

Bas Obispo-Before — A50

Bas Obispo-After A51

Gatun Locks-Before — A52

Gatun Locks-After A53

Canal Channel-Before A54

Canal Channel-After — A55

Gamboa-Before A56

Gamboa-After — A57

Pedro Miguel Locks-Before — A58

Pedro Miguel Locks-After A59

Gatun Spillway-Before A60

Gatun Spillway-After — A61

25th anniversary of the opening of the Panama Canal.

1939, Aug. 15
120	A46	1c yellow green	.60	.30
121	A47	2c rose carmine	.70	.35
122	A48	3c purple	.70	.25
123	A49	5c dark blue	2.00	1.25
124	A50	6c red orange	4.50	3.00
125	A51	7c black	4.75	3.00
126	A52	8c green	7.00	3.25
127	A53	10c ultramarine	5.50	5.00
128	A54	11c blue green	11.00	8.00
129	A55	12c brown carmine	11.00	7.50
130	A56	14c dark violet	11.00	7.00
131	A57	15c olive green	12.50	5.75
132	A58	18c rose pink	15.00	8.50
133	A59	20c brown	14.00	7.00
134	A60	25c orange	27.50	17.50
135	A61	50c violet brown	30.00	6.00
		Nos. 120-135 (16)	157.75	83.65

AIR POST STAMPS

Nos. 105-106 Surcharged in Dark Blue

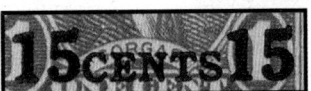

Type I - Flag of "Five" pointing up

Type II - Flag of "5" curved

1929-31   **Engr.**   **Unwmk.**   *Perf. 11*
C1	A35	15c on 1c green, type I	7.50	4.75
C2	A35	15c on 1c yellow green, type II	60.00	47.50
C3	A36	25c on 2c carmine	3.50	2.00
		Nos. C1-C3 (3)	71.00	54.25

Nos. 114 and 106 Surcharged

1929, Dec. 31
C4	A44	10c on 50c lilac	8.00	5.75
C5	A36	20c on 2c carmine	4.50	1.25
a.		Dropped "2" in surcharge	85.00	60.00

> Catalogue values for unused stamps in this section, from this point to the end, are for Never Hinged items.

Gaillard Cut — AP1

1931-49
C6	AP1	4c red violet	.75	.65
C7	AP1	5c yellow green	.60	.30
C8	AP1	6c yellow brown	.75	.35
C9	AP1	10c orange	1.00	.35
C10	AP1	15c blue	1.25	.30
C11	AP1	20c red violet	2.00	.25
C12	AP1	30c rose lake	6.50	1.50
C13	AP1	40c red violet	3.50	1.10
C14	AP1	$1 black	9.00	1.60
		Nos. C6-C14 (9)	25.35	6.40

For overprints, see Nos. CO1-CO14.

Douglas Plane over Sosa Hill — AP2

Planes and Map of Central America AP3

Pan American Clipper and Scene near Fort Amador AP4

Pan American Clipper at Cristobal Harbor AP5

Pan American Clipper over Gaillard Cut — AP6

Pan American Clipper Landing AP7

10th anniversary of Air Mail service and the 25th anniversary of the opening of the Panama Canal.

1939, July 15
C15	AP2	5c greenish black	3.75	2.25
C16	AP3	10c dull violet	3.50	3.00
C17	AP4	15c light brown	5.00	1.00
C18	AP5	25c blue	17.50	8.00
C19	AP6	30c rose carmine	17.50	6.00
C20	AP7	$1 green	45.00	27.50
		Nos. C15-C20 (6)	92.25	47.75

POSTAGE DUE STAMPS

Prior to 1914, many of the postal issues were handstamped "Postage Due" and used as postage due stamps.

Postage Due Stamps of the U.S. Nos. J45a, J46a and J49a Overprinted in Black

1914, Mar.   **Wmk. 190**   *Perf. 12*
J1	D2	1c rose carmine	85.00	15.00
J2	D2	2c rose carmine	250.00	42.50
J3	D2	10c rose carmine	1,000.	40.00
		Nos. J1-J3 (3)	1,335.	97.50

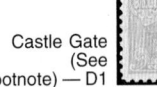

Castle Gate (See footnote) — D1

Statue of Columbus D2   Pedro J. Sosa D3

1915, Mar.   **Unwmk.**
Blue Overprint, Type II, on Postage Due Stamps of Panama
J4	D1	1c olive brown	11.00	5.00
J5	D2	2c olive brown	225.00	17.50
J6	D3	10c olive brown	50.00	10.00
		Nos. J4-J6 (3)	286.00	32.50

Type D1 was intended to show a gate of San Lorenzo Castle, Chagres, and is so labeled. By error the stamp actually shows the main gate of San Geronimo Castle, Portobelo.

Surcharged in Red

1915, Nov.
J7	D1	1c on 1c olive brown	110.00	14.00
J8	D2	2c on 2c olive brown	22.50	7.50
J9	D3	10c on 10c olive brown	22.50	5.00
		Nos. J7-J9 (3)	155.00	26.50

Columbus Statue - D4   Capitol, Panama City — D5

1919, Dec.
Surcharged in Carmine by Panama Canal Press, Mount Hope, C. Z.
"Canal Zone" Type III
J10	D4	2c on 2c olive brown	30.00	11.00
J11	D5	4c on 4c olive brown	35.00	12.50
a.		"ZONE" omitted	9,250.	
b.		"4" omitted	8,500.	

Blue Overprint, Type V, on Postage Due Stamp of Panama

1922

J11C	D1	1c dark olive brown	—	10.00
d.		"CANAL ZONE" reading	£88.00	

Type A
Letters "A" with Flat Tops

1924, July 1			**Perf. 11**	
J12	D2	1c carmine rose	110.00	27.50
J13	D2	2c deep claret	55.00	15.00
J14	D2	10c deep claret	250.00	50.00
		Nos. J12-J14 (3)	415.00	92.50

U.S. Postage Stamps Nos. 552, 554 and 562 Overprinted Type A and additional Overprint in Red or Blue

1925, Feb.

J15	A155	1c deep green (R)	90.00	15.00
J16	A157	2c carmine (Bl)	22.50	7.00
J17	A165	10c orange (R)	55.00	11.00
a.		"POSTAGE DUE" double	800.00	
b.		"E" of "POSTAGE" omitted	750.00	
c.		As "b," "POSTAGE DUE" double	3,250.	
		Nos. J15-J17 (3)	167.50	33.00

Overprinted Type B
Letters "A" with Sharp Pointed Tops
On U.S. Postage Due Stamps Nos. J61, J62, J65, J65a

1925, June 24

J18	D2	1c carmine rose	8.00	2.75
a.		"ZONE ZONE" (LR18)	1,500.	
J19	D2	2c carmine rose	15.00	2.75
a.		"ZONE ZONE" (LR18)	1,500.	
J20	D2	10c carmine rose	50.00	20.00
a.		Vert. pair, one without ovpt.	3,000.	
b.		10c rose red	250.00	150.00
c.		As "b," double overprint	450.00	—
		Nos. J18-J20 (3)	173.00	25.50

Regular Issue of 1928-29 Surcharged

1929-30

J21	A37	1c on 5c blue	3.75	1.75
		Never hinged	7.50	
a.		"POSTAGE DUE" missing	5,500.	
J22	A37	2c on 5c blue	6.50	2.50
		Never hinged	13.00	
J23	A37	5c on 5c blue	6.50	2.75
		Never hinged	13.00	
J24	A37	10c on 5c blue	6.50	2.75
		Never hinged	13.00	
		Nos. J21-J24 (4)	23.25	9.75

On No. J23 the three short horizontal bars in the lower corners of the surcharge are omitted.

Canal Zone Seal — D6

1932-41

J25	D6	1c claret	.25	.25
		Never hinged	.30	
J26	D6	2c claret	.25	.25
		Never hinged	.30	
J27	D6	5c claret	.35	.25
		Never hinged	.50	
J28	D6	10c claret	1.75	1.50
		Never hinged	2.25	
J29	D6	15c claret	1.25	1.00
		Never hinged	1.60	
		Nos. J25-J29 (5)	3.85	3.25

GUAM
'gwäm

LOCATION — One of the Mariana Islands in the Pacific Ocean, about 1450 miles east of the Philippines
GOVT. — United States Possession
AREA — 206 sq. mi.
POP. — 9,000 (est. 1899)
CAPITAL — Agaña

Formerly a Spanish possession, Guam was ceded to the United States in 1898 following the Spanish-American War. Stamps overprinted "Guam" were superseded by the regular postage stamps of the United States in 1901.

100 Cents = 1 Dollar

United States Nos. 279, 279B, 279Bc, 268, 280a, 281, 282, 272, 282C, 283, 284, 275, 275a, 276 and 276A Overprinted

1899		**Wmk. 191**	**Perf. 12**	
		Black Overprint		
1	A87	1c deep green	20.00	25.00
		Never hinged	40.00	
		On cover		200.00

A bogus inverted overprint exists.

2	A88	2c red, type IV	17.50	25.00
		On cover		200.00
		Never hinged	35.00	
a.		rose carmine, type IV	30.00	30.00
		Never hinged	60.00	
		On cover		225.00
3	A89	3c purple	140.00	175.00
		Never hinged	275.00	
		On cover		400.00
4	A90	4c lilac brown	125.00	175.00
		Never hinged	250.00	
		On cover		450.00
5	A91	5c blue	32.50	45.00
		Never hinged	65.00	
		On cover		200.00
6	A92	6c lake	125.00	190.00
		Never hinged	250.00	
		On cover		450.00
7	A93	8c violet brown	125.00	160.00
		Never hinged	250.00	
		On cover		450.00
8	A94	10c brown, type I	45.00	55.00
		Never hinged	90.00	
		On cover		275.00
9	A94	10c brown, type II	2,750.	
		Never hinged	5,500.	—
10	A95	15c olive green	150.00	140.00
		Never hinged	300.00	
		On cover		900.00
11	A96	50c orange	350.00	400.00
		Never hinged	700.00	
		On cover		1,500.
a.		50c red orange	550.00	—
		Never hinged	1,100.	
		Red Overprint		
12	A97	$1 black, type I	350.00	400.00
		Never hinged	700.00	
		On cover		3,500.
13	A97	$1 black, type II	4,250.	
		Never hinged	—	
		Nos. 1-8,10-12 (11)	1,480.	1,790.

Counterfeits of the overprint exist.
No. 13 exists only in the special printing.

SPECIAL DELIVERY STAMP

United States No. E5 Overprinted in Red

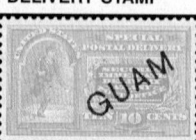

1899		**Wmk. 191**	**Perf. 12**	
E1	SD3	10c blue	150.	200.00
		Never hinged	275.	
		On cover		1,500.
a.		Dots in curved frame above messenger (Plate 882)	200.	
		Never hinged	400.	

Counterfeits of the overprint exist.
The special stamps for Guam were replaced by the regular issues of the United States. Guam Guard Mail stamps of 1930 are listed in the Scott U.S. specialized catalogue.

HAWAII
hə-'wä-yē

LOCATION — Group of 20 islands in the Pacific Ocean, about 2,000 miles southwest of San Francisco.
GOVT. — Former Kingdom and Republic
AREA — 6,435 sq. mi.
POP. — 150,000 (est. 1899)
CAPITAL — Honolulu

Until 1893 an independent kingdom, from 1893 to 1898 a republic, the Hawaiian Islands were annexed to the US in 1898.

100 Cents = 1 Dollar

Values for Nos. 1-4 are for examples with minor damage that has been skillfully repaired.

Values of Hawaii stamps vary considerably according to condition. For Nos. 1-4, values are for examples with minor damage that has been skillfully repaired.

A1

A2

A3

1851-52		**Unwmk.**	**Typeset**	*Imperf.*	
		Pelure Paper			
1	A1	2c blue	660,000.	250,000.	
		On cover		2,250,000.	
2	A1	5c blue	55,000.	35,000.	
		On cover		90,000.	
3	A2	13c blue	37,000.	28,000.	
		On cover		75,000.	
4	A3	13c blue	52,500.	35,000.	
		On cover		80,000.	

Nos. 1-4 are known as the "Missionaries." Two varieties of each. Nos. 1-4, off cover, are almost invariably damaged.
No. 1 unused and on cover are each unique; the on-cover value is based on a 2013 auction sale.

King Kamehameha III

A4

A5

Printed in Sheets of 20 (4x5)

1853				**Engr.**	
		Thick White Wove Paper			
5	A4	5c blue	1,900.	1,900.	
		On cover		5,000.	
		On cover with U.S. #17		12,000.	
a.		Line through "Honolulu" (Pos. 2)	3,000.	3,000.	
6	A5	13c dark red	850.	1,700.	
		On cover		25,000.	
		On cover with #5		12,500.	
		On cover with U.S. #11 (pair)		25,000.	
		On cover with U.S. #17		32,500.	

	On cover with #5 and U.S. #17			32,500.
	On cover with #8 and U.S. #36b			38,500.

See Nos. 8-11.

A6

1857				
7	A6	5c on 13c dark red	7,000.	10,000.
		On cover with pair U.S. #7 and 14		57,500.
		On cover with pair U.S. #11, 14		55,000.
		On cover with U.S. #14		50,000.
		On cover with U.S. #17		45,000.

1857			**Thin White Wove Paper**	
8	A4	5c blue	700.	750.
		On cover with U.S. #11		—
		On cover with U.S. #7, 15		—
		On cover with U.S. #17		10,000.
		On cover with U.S. #26		—
		On cover with U.S. #35		11,000.
		On cover with U.S. #36		10,000.
		On cover with U.S. #69		12,500.
		On cover with U.S. #76		—
a.		Line through "Honolulu" (Pos. 2)	1,350.	1,350.
		On cover with U.S. #17		7,500.
b.		Double impression	3,500.	4,750.

1861			**Thin Bluish Wove Paper**	
9	A4	5c blue	375.	375.
		On cover		5,000.
		On cover with U.S. #36b		3,250.
		On cover with U.S. #65		3,000.
		On cover with U.S. #65, 73		6,500.
		On cover with U.S. #68		4,250.
		On cover with U.S. #76		7,000.
a.		Line through "Honolulu" (Pos. 2)	950.	1,000.

1868

RE-ISSUE
Ordinary White Wove Paper

10	A4	5c blue	27.50	
a.		Line through "Honolulu" (Pos. 2)	75.	
11	A5	13c dull rose	325.	

Remainders of Nos. 10 and 11 were overprinted "SPECIMEN." See Nos. 10S-11Sb in the Scott U.S. Specialized catalogue.

Nos. 10 and 11 were never placed in use but stamps (both with and without overprint) were sold at face value at the Honolulu post office.

REPRINTS (Official Imitations)

Original   Reprint

Original   Reprint

5c — Originals have two small dots near the left side of the square in the upper right corner. These dots are missing in the reprints.
13c — The bottom of the 3 of 13 in the upper left corner is flattened in the originals and rounded in the reprints. The "t" of "Cts" on the left side is as tall as the "C" in the reprints, but shorter in the originals.

Buying, Selling, Expertizations, Hawaii & World Classics
PHOTOGRAPHIC CERTIFICATES OF AUTHENTICITY • Reliable and Fast • Recognized • Competitively Priced
Further information at www.sismondostamps.com Or, contact us for terms and prices

SEND STAMPS OR COVERS WITH CONFIDENCE.. NO INK MARKS, NO RUBBER STAMPS, NO ENCASING

LIANE & SERGIO SISMONDO
10035 Destiny USA Drive • Syracuse, NY 13290-0001
T. 315-422-2331 • F. 315-422-2956
EMAIL: sergio@sismondostamps.com

HELPING COLLECTORS AVOID THE MINEFIELDS

ASDA • PTS • CNEP • CSDA • AFIP

1889
10R A4 5c blue — 65.
  Block of 4 — 280.
11R A5 13c orange red — 300.
  Block of 4 — 1,450.

On August 19, 1892, the remaining supply of reprints was overprinted in black "REPRINT." The reprints (both with and without overprint) were sold at face value. See the Scott U.S. Specialized Catalogue.

Values for the Numeral stamps, Nos. 12-26, are for four-margin examples. Unused values are for stamps without gum.

A7 A8

A9

1859-62 Typeset
12 A7 1c light blue, bluish white — 17,500. 15,000.
  a. "1 Ce" omitted — — 22,500.
  b. "nt" omitted — —

No. 12a is unique.

13 A7 2c light blue, bluish white — 6,250. 5,000.
  On cover — 12,500.
  a. 2c dark blue, grayish white — 6,750. 5,000.
  b. Comma after "Cents" — 6,750.
    On cover — 12,500.
  c. No period after "LETA" — —
14 A7 2c black, greenish blue ('62) — 8,000. 6,000.
  On cover — 10,000.
  a. "2-Cents." — —

1859-63
15 A7 1c black, grayish ('63) — 650. 2,750.
  On cover — 9,000.
  a. Tête bêche pair — —
  b. "NTER" —
  c. Period omitted after "Postage" — 850.
16 A7 2c black, grayish — 1,000. 850.
  On cover — 5,000.
  a. "2" at top of rectangle — 3,750. 3,750.
  b. Printed on both sides — 21,000.
  c. "NTER" — 3,250. 6,500.
  d. 2c black, grayish white — 1,000. 850.
  e. Period omitted after "Cents" — —
  f. Overlapping impressions — —
  g. "TAGE" — —
17 A7 2c dark blue, bluish ('63) — 12,000. 8,750.
  a. "ISL" — —
18 A7 2c black, blue gray ('63) — 3,500. 6,000.
  On cover — 18,000.

1864-65
19 A7 1c black — 550. 10,000.
20 A7 2c black — 775. 1,500.
  On cover — 19,000.
21 A8 5c blue, blue ('65) — 900. 700.
  On cover with U.S. #65 — —
  On cover with U.S. #68 — —
  On cover with U.S. #76 — 8,250.
  a. Tête bêche pair — 10,500.
  b. 5c bluish black, grayish white — 14,000. 3,750.

No. 21b unused is unique. No. 21b used is also unique but defective.

1864
22 A9 5c blue, blue ('65) — 575. 900.
  On cover — 13,000.
  On cover with U.S. #76 — 9,250.
  On cover with U.S. #63 and 76 — —
  a. Tête bêche pair — 20,000.
  b. 5c blue, grayish white — —
  c. Overlapping impressions — —

1864 Laid Paper
23 A7 1c black — 300. 2,500.
  On cover with U.S. #76 — 12,000.
  a. "HA" instead of "HAWAI-IAN" — 3,500.
  b. Tête bêche pair — 6,250.
  c. Tête bêche pair, Nos. 23, 23a — 18,000.
24 A7 2c black — 325. 1,050.
  a. "NTER" — 3,500.
  b. "S" of "POSTAGE" omitted — 1,500.
  c. Tête bêche pair — 7,000.

A10

1865 Wove Paper
25 A10 1c dark blue — 350.
  a. Double impression — —
  b. With inverted impression of No. 21 on face — 18,500.
26 A10 2c dark blue — 350.

Nos. 12 to 26 were typeset and were printed in settings of ten, each stamp differing from the others.

King Kamehameha IV A11

1861-63 Litho.
Horizontally Laid Paper
27 A11 2c pale rose — 350. 350.
  On cover — 1,000.
  a. 2c carmine rose ('63) — 3,000. 2,850.
Vertically Laid Paper
28 A11 2c pale rose — 325. 325.
  On cover — 1,500.
  a. 2c carmine rose ('63) — 350. 400.
    On cover — 2,000.

RE-ISSUE
1869 Engr. Thin Wove Paper
29 A11 2c red — 45.00 —

No. 29 was not issued for postal purposes although canceled examples are known. It was sold only at the Honolulu post office, at first without overprint and later with overprint "CANCELLED." See No. 29S in the Scott U.S. Specialized Catalogue.

See Nos. 50-51 and note following No. 51.

Princess Victoria Kamamalu — A12

King Kamehameha IV — A13

A14

King Kamehameha V — A15

Mataio Kekuanaoa — A16

1864-86 Engr. Perf. 12
Wove Paper
30 A12 1c purple ('86) — 11.00 8.00
  Never hinged — 27.50
  On cover — 150.00
  a. 1c mauve ('71) — 60.00 20.00
    Never hinged — 100.00
  b. 1c violet ('78) — 20.00 10.00
    Never hinged — 50.00
31 A13 2c rose vermilion — 65.00 10.00
  Never hinged — 160.00
  a. 2c vermilion ('86) — 50.00 20.00
    Never hinged — 120.00
  b. Half used as 1c on cover with #32 — 8,500.
    On cover — 500.00
32 A14 5c blue ('66) — 175.00 30.00
  Never hinged — 400.00
  On cover — 250.00
  On cover with any U.S. issues of 1861-67 — 5,000.
  On cover with U.S. #116 — 15,000.
  On cover with U.S. #116 and 69 — 25,000.
33 A15 6c yellow green ('71) — 45.00 10.00
  Never hinged — 110.00
  On cover — 300.00
  a. 6c bluish green ('78) — 35.00 10.00
    Never hinged — 85.00
    On cover — 300.00
    On cover with U.S. #179 — 1,500.
    On cover with U.S. #185 — 1,000.
  b. As "a," horiz. pair, imperf. — 2,250.
34 A16 18c dull rose ('71) — 95.00 37.50
  Never hinged — 225.00
  On cover — 350.00
  Nos. 30-34 (5) — 391.00 95.50
  Set, never hinged — 922.50

No. 32 has traces of rectangular frame lines surrounding the design. Nos. 39 and 52C have no such frame lines.
For overprints see Nos. 53, 58-60, 65, 66C, 71.

King David Kalakaua A17

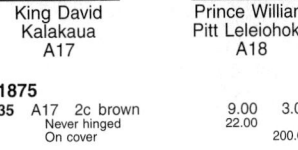
Prince William Pitt Leleiohoku A18

1875
35 A17 2c brown — 9.00 3.00
  Never hinged — 22.00
  On cover — 200.00

36 A18 12c black — 65.00 27.50
  Never hinged — 165.00
  On cover — 400.00

See Nos. 38, 43, 46. For overprints see Nos. 56, 62-63, 66, 69.

Princess Likelike A19

King David Kalakaua A20

Queen Kapiolani — A21

Statue of King Kamehameha I — A22

King William Lunalilo — A23

Queen Emma Kaleleonalani — A24

1882
37 A19 1c blue — 11.00 6.00
  Never hinged — 29.00
  On cover — 60.00
38 A17 2c lilac rose — 125.00 45.00
  Never hinged — 275.00
  On cover — 150.00
39 A14 5c ultramarine — 15.00 3.00
  Never hinged — 37.50
  On cover — 27.50
  a. Vert. pair, imperf. horiz. — 5,000. 6,000.
40 A20 10c black — 47.50 22.50
  Never hinged — 120.00
  On cover — 160.00
41 A21 15c red brown — 65.00 25.00
  Never hinged — 160.00
  On cover — 200.00
  Nos. 37-41 (5) — 263.50 101.50
  Set, never hinged — 621.50

1883-86
42 A19 1c green — 3.00 2.00
  Never hinged — 8.00
  On cover — 25.00
43 A17 2c rose ('86) — 5.00 1.00
  Never hinged — 12.00
  On cover — 25.00
  a. 2c dull red — 62.50 21.00
    Never hinged — 140.00
44 A20 10c red brown ('84) — 37.50 10.00
  Never hinged — 95.00
  On cover — 125.00
45 A20 10c vermilion — 42.50 12.50
  Never hinged — 105.00
  On cover — 125.00
46 A18 12c red lilac — 85.00 35.00
  Never hinged — 225.00
  On cover — 425.00
47 A22 25c dark violet — 150.00 60.00
  Never hinged — 350.00
  On cover — 375.00

48	A23 50c red	190.00	85.00
	Never hinged	425.00	
	On cover		525.00
49	A24 $1 rose red	275.00	250.00
	Never hinged	625.00	
	On cover		8,000.
	Maltese cross cancellation		100.00
	Nos. 48-49 (8)	788.00 466.50	
	Set, never hinged	1,845.	

Other fiscal cancellations exist on No. 49.
Nos. 48-49 are valued used with postal cancels. Canceled-to-order cancels exist and are worth less.

REPRODUCTION and REPRINT
Yellowish Wove Paper

1886-89	**Engr.**	*Imperf.*
50	A11 2c orange vermilion	160.00
	Never hinged	275.00
51	A11 2c carmine ('89)	30.00
	Never hinged	50.00

In 1885, the Postmaster General wished to have on sale complete sets of Hawaii's portrait stamps, but was unable to find either the stone from which Nos. 27 and 28 were printed, or the plate from which No. 29 was printed. He therefore sent an example of No. 29 to the American Bank Note Company, with an order to engrave a new plate like it and print 10,000 stamps therefrom, of which 5000 were overprinted "SPECIMEN" in blue.

The original No. 29 was printed in sheets of fifteen (5x3), but the plate of these "Official Imitations" was made up of fifty stamps (10x5). Later, in 1887, the original die for No. 29 was discovered, and, after retouching, a new plate was made and 37,500 stamps were printed (No. 51). These, like the originals, were printed in sheets of fifteen. They were delivered during 1889 and 1890. In 1892, all remaining unsold in the Post Office were overprinted "Reprint".

No. 29 is red in color, and printed on very thin white wove paper. No. 50 is orange vermilion in color, on medium, white to buff paper. In No. 50 the vertical line on the left side of the portrait touches the horizontal line over the label "Elua Keneta", while in the other two varieties, Nos. 29 and 51, it does not touch the horizontal line by half a millimeter. In No. 51 there are three parallel lines on the left side of the King's nose, while in No. 29 and No. 50 there are no such lines. No. 51 is carmine in color and printed on thick, yellowish to buff, wove paper.

It is claimed that both Nos. 50 and 51 were available for postage, although not made to fill a postal requirement. They exist with favor cancellation. No. 51 also is known postally used. See Nos. 50S-51S in the Scott U.S. specialized catalogue.

Queen
Liliuokalani — A25

1890-91		*Perf. 12*
52	A25 2c dull violet ('91)	15.00	1.50
	Never hinged	25.00	
	On cover		25.00
a.	Vert. pair, imperf. horiz.	3,750.	
52C	A14 5c deep indigo	120.00	150.00
	Never hinged	275.00	
	On cover		500.00

Stamps of 1864-91
Overprinted in Red

Three categories of double overprints:
I. Both overprints heavy.
II. One overprint heavy, one of moderate strength.
III. One overprint heavy, one of light or weak strength.

1893		**Overprinted in Red**
53	A12 1c purple	9.00	13.00
	Never hinged	21.00	
	On cover		35.00
a.	"189" instead of "1893"	600.00	—
b.	No period after "GOVT"	265.00	250.00
f.	Double overprint (III)	600.00	
54	A19 1c blue	9.00	15.00
	Never hinged	21.00	
	On cover		40.00
b.	No period after "GOVT"	140.00	140.00
e.	Double overprint (II)	1,500.	
f.	Double overprint (III)	400.00	
55	A19 1c green	2.00	3.00
	Never hinged	4.50	
	On cover		25.00
d.	Double overprint (I)	650.00	650.00

f.	Double overprint (III)	225.00	250.00
g.	Pair, one without ovpt.	10,000.	
56	A17 2c brown	12.00	20.00
	Never hinged	28.50	
	On cover		60.00
b.	No period after "GOVT"	300.00	
57	A25 2c dull violet	1.50	1.10
	Never hinged		
	On cover		25.00
a.	"18 3" instead of "1893"	850.00	950.00
d.	Double overprint (I)	1,300.	700.00
f.	Double overprint (III)	190.00	190.00
g.	Inverted overprint	4,000.	4,750.
58	A14 5c deep indigo	13.00	25.00
	Never hinged	32.00	
	On cover		100.00
b.	No period after "GOVT"	250.00	250.00
f.	Double overprint (III)	1,250.	675.00
59	A14 5c ultramarine	7.00	3.00
	Never hinged	15.00	
	On cover		40.00
d.	Double overprint (I)	6,500.	
e.	Double overprint (II)	4,000.	4,000.
f.	Double overprint (III)		600.00
g.	Inverted overprint	1,500.	1,500.
60	A15 6c green	17.50	25.00
	Never hinged	40.00	
	On cover		140.00
d.	Double overprint (II)	1,100.	
61	A20 10c black	13.00	20.00
	Never hinged	30.00	
	On cover		125.00
d.	Double overprint (I)	1,000.	750.00
f.	Double overprint (III)	225.00	
61B	A20 10c red brown	17,500.	29,000.
62	A18 12c black	12.00	20.00
	Never hinged	30.00	
	On cover		150.00
d.	Double overprint (I)	2,000.	
e.	Double overprint (II)	1,750.	
63	A18 12c red lilac	165.00	250.00
	Never hinged	400.00	
	On cover		550.00
64	A22 25c dark violet	32.00	40.00
	Never hinged	72.00	
	On cover		225.00
b.	No period after "GOVT"	350.00	350.00
f.	Double overprint (III)	1,100.	
	Nos. 53-61,62-64 (12)	293.00	435.10
	Nos. 53-61, 62-64 never hinged	697.00	

Virtually all known examples of No. 61B are cut in at the top.

Overprinted in Black

65	A13 2c vermilion	80.00	85.00
	Never hinged	200.00	
	On cover		450.00
b.	No period after "GOVT"	275.00	275.00
66	A17 2c rose	1.75	2.25
	Never hinged	3.00	
	On cover		25.00
b.	No period after "GOVT"	65.00	65.00
d.	Double overprint (I)	4,000.	
e.	Double overprint (II)	2,750.	
f.	Double overprint (III)	300.00	
66C	A15 6c green	17,500.	29,000.
	On cover		
67	A20 10c vermilion	20.00	30.00
	Never hinged	50.00	
	On cover		125.00
f.	Double overprint (III)	1,250.	
68	A20 10c red brown	10.00	13.00
	Never hinged	25.00	
	On cover		100.00
f.	Double overprint (III)	4,000.	
69	A18 12c red lilac	325.00	500.00
	Never hinged	575.00	
	On cover		950.00
70	A21 15c red brown	25.00	35.00
	Never hinged	55.00	
	On cover		300.00
e.	Double overprint (II)	2,000.	
71	A16 18c dull rose	35.00	35.00
	Never hinged	75.00	
	On cover		225.00
a.	"18 3" instead of "1893"	525.00	525.00
b.	No period after "GOVT"	325.00	300.00
d.	Double overprint (I)	650.00	
f.	Double overprint (III)	275.00	—
g.	Pair, one without ovpt.	3,500.	
h.	As "b," double overprint (II)	1,750.	
72	A23 50c red	80.00	110.00
	Never hinged	175.00	
	On cover		600.00
b.	No period after "GOVT"	475.00	475.00
	Never hinged	725.00	
f.	Double overprint (III)	1,000.	
73	A24 $1 rose red	150.00	175.00
	Never hinged	325.00	
	On cover		775.00
b.	No period after "GOVT"	475.00	450.00
	Nos. 65-66,67-73 (9)	726.75	985.25
	Nos. 65-66, 67-73 never hinged	1,483.	

Coat of
Arms — A26

View of
Honolulu — A27

Statue of
Kamehameha
I — A28

Stars and
Palms — A29

S. S.
"Arawa" — A30

Pres. Sanford
Ballard
Dole — A31

"CENTS"
Added — A32

1894			
74	A26 1c yellow	2.00	1.50
	Never hinged	5.00	
	On cover		25.00
75	A27 2c brown	2.00	.60
	Never hinged	5.00	
	On cover		25.00
76	A28 5c rose lake	5.00	2.00
	Never hinged	13.00	
	On cover		25.00
77	A29 10c yellow green	8.00	5.00
	Never hinged	22.50	
	On cover		45.00
78	A30 12c blue	17.50	20.00
	Never hinged	42.50	
	On cover		150.00
79	A31 25c deep blue	22.50	16.00
	Never hinged	55.00	
	On cover		100.00
	Nos. 74-79 (6)	57.00	45.10
	Set, never hinged	144.00	

Numerous double transfers exist on Nos. 75 and 81.

1899			
80	A26 1c dark green	2.00	1.50
	Never hinged	5.00	
	On cover		25.00
81	A27 2c rose	1.50	1.00
	Never hinged	4.00	
	On cover		20.00
a.	2c salmon	1.50	1.50
	Never hinged	4.00	
b.	Vert. pair, imperf. horiz.	4,250.	
82	A32 5c blue	8.00	3.50
	Never hinged	20.00	
	On cover		25.00
	Nos. 80-82 (3)	11.50	6.00
	Set, never hinged	29.00	

OFFICIAL STAMPS

Lorrin Andrews
Thurston — O1

1896	**Engr.**	**Unwmk.**	*Perf. 12*
O1	O1 2c green	45.00	20.00
	Never hinged	110.00	
	On cover		400.00
O2	O1 5c black brown	45.00	20.00
	Never hinged	110.00	
	On cover		425.00
O3	O1 6c deep ultramarine	45.00	20.00
	Never hinged	110.00	
	On cover		—
O4	O1 10c bright rose	45.00	20.00
	Never hinged	110.00	
	On cover		475.00
O5	O1 12c orange	55.00	22.50
	Never hinged	135.00	
	On cover		—

O6	O1 25c gray violet	65.00	22.50
	Never hinged	160.00	
	On cover		—
	Nos. O1-O6 (6)	300.00	125.00
	Set, never hinged	735.00	

Used values for Nos. O1-O6 are stamps canceled-to-order "FOREIGN OFFICE/HONOLULU H.I." in double circle without date. Values of postally used stamps: Nos. O1-O2, O4, $40 each; No. O3, $110; No. O5, $140; No. O6, $175.

The stamps of Hawaii were replaced by those of the United States.

ADEN

'ä-d°n

LOCATION — Southern Arabia
GOVT. — British colony and
protectorate
AREA — 112,075 sq. mi.
POP. — 48,338
CAPITAL — Aden

Aden used India stamps before 1937.

12 Pies = 1 Anna
16 Annas = 1 Rupee

> Catalogue values for unused
> stamps in this country are for
> Never Hinged items.

STAMPS OF INDIA USED IN ADEN

Type A

Type B

Stamps of India with Types A or B cancellations associated with circular datestamps of
"ADEN," "ADEN CAMP," "ADEN STEAMER
POINT" OR "ADEN CANTONMENT". Many
other cancellations exist. Values shown are for
the most common cancellation.

1854
A1	½a blue, Die I (#2)	250.00
	Pair (#2)	900.00
	Strip or block of 4 (#2)	5,000.
A4	1a red (#4)	350.00
	1a Pair (#4), #132 cancel	2,000.
A7	2a green (#5)	500.00
	Pair (#5)	2,000.
A11	4a bl & car (#6, 6a)	425.00
	Pair (#6, 6a)	1,500.
	Strip of 3 (#6, 6a)	

Values for #A11 are for stamps and covers
bearing stamps that are cut to shape. Examples with complete margins sell for much
more. Multiples will have a cancellation on
each stamp.

> **Virtually all stamps of British
> India, including officials from 1854
> to 1937, may be found used in
> Aden. The listings below include
> issues from 1855 to 1936. Values
> are for clear strikes of the more
> common postmarks.**

1855-64   Unwmk.
Blue Glazed Paper
A13	4a black (#9)	90.00
A14	8a rose (#10)	90.00

1855-64   Unwmk.   White Paper
A15	½p blue (#11)	15.00
A16	1a brown (#12)	17.50
A17	2a dull rose (#13)	65.00
A18	2a buff (#15)	65.00
a.	2a orange (#15a)	75.00
A19	4a black (#16)	25.00
A20	4a green (#17)	25.00
A21	8a rose (#18)	75.00

1860-64   Unwmk.
A22	8p lilac (#19)	25.00
A23	8p lilac, *bluish* (#19C)	—

1865-67   Wmk. 38
A24	½a blue (#20)	10.00
A25	8p lilac (#21)	35.00
A26	1a brown (#22)	10.00

A27	2a orange (#23)	12.50
a.	2a yellow (#23a)	17.50
A28	4a green (#24)	75.00
A29	8a rose (#25)	

1866-68   Wmk. 38
A30	4a green (#26)	15.00
A31	4a blue green (#26B)	12.00
A32	6a8p slate (#27)	75.00
A33	8a rose ('68)(#28)	25.00

1866   Wmk. 36
A34	6a violet (#29)	—
A35	6a violet (#30)	—

1873-76   Wmk. 38
A36	½a blue (#31)	10.00
A37	9p lilac (#32)	—
A38	6a bister (#33)	12.00
A39	12a red brown (#34)	50.00
A40	1r slate (#35)	75.00

1882-87   Wmk. 39
A41	½a green (#36)	8.00
A42	9p rose (#37)	12.00
A43	1a maroon (#38)	7.00
A44	1a6p bister brown (#39)	12.00
A45	2a ultra (#40)	7.00
A46	3a brown orange (#41)	10.00
A47	4a olive green (#42)	10.00
A48	4a6p green (#43)	20.00
A49	8a red violet (#44)	14.00
A50	12a violet, *red* (#45)	15.00
A51	1r gray (#46)	25.00

1891
A52	2½a on 4a6p green (#47)	12.50

1892
A53	2a6p green (#48)	10.00
A54	1r aniline car & grn (#49)	15.00
A55	1r car rose & green (#49a)	25.00

1895
A56	2r brown & rose (#50)	—
A57	3r green & brown (#51)	—
A58	5r vio & ultra (#52)	—

1898
A59	¼a on ½a green (#53)	10.00

1899-1900
A60	3p car rose (#54)	7.00
A61	3p gray (#55)	10.00
A62	½a light green (#56)	7.00
A63	1a carmine rose (#57)	7.00
A64	2a violet (#58)	8.00
A65	2a6p ultramarine (#59)	10.00

1902-09
A68	3p gray (#60)	7.00
A69	½a green (#61)	8.00
A70	1a carmine rose (#62)	7.00
A71	2a violet (#63)	7.00
A72	2a6p ultramarine (#64)	9.00
A73	3a brown orange (#65)	9.00
A74	4a olive green (#66)	9.00
A75	6a bister (#67)	25.00
A76	8a red violet (#68)	10.00
A77	12a red (#69)	20.00
A78	1r car rose & grn (#70)	15.00
A79	2r brown & rose (#71)	20.00
A80	3r green & brown ('04) (#72)	75.00
A81	5r vio & ultra ('04) (#73)	100.00
A82	10r car rose & grn ('09) (#74)	—
A83	15r ol gray & ultra ('09) (#75)	—
A84	25r ultra & org brn (#76)	—

1905
A85	¼p on ½a green (#77)	8.00

1906
A86	½a green (#78)	7.50
A87	1a carmine rose (#79)	7.50

1911-23
A88	3p gray (#80)	7.50
A89	½a green (#81)	7.50
A90	1a carmine rose (#82)	7.50
A91	1a dk brown (#83)	7.50
A92	2a dull violet (#84)	7.50
A93	2a6p ultramarine (#85)	17.50
A94	3a brown orange (#86)	7.50
A95	3a ultramarine (#87)	7.50
A96	4a olive green (#88)	7.50
A97	6a yel bister (#89)	7.50
A98	6a bister (#90)	7.50
A99	8a red violet (#91)	10.00
A100	12a claret (#92)	12.50
A101	1r grn & red brn (#93)	12.50

A102	2r brn & car rose (#94)	15.00
A103	5r vio & ultra (#95)	25.00
A104	10r car rose & grn (#96)	—
A105	15r ol grn & ultra (#97)	—
A106	25r ultra & brn org (#98)	—

1913-26
A107	2a6p ultramarine (#99)	7.50
A108	2a6p orange ('26) (#100)	17.50

1919
A109	1½a chocolate (#101)	8.00

1921-26
A110	1½a chocolate (#102)	20.00
A111	1½a rose ('26) (#103)	8.00

1921
A112	9p on 1a rose (#104)	7.50

1922
A113	¼p on ½a green (#105)	7.50

1926-36
A114	3p slate (#106)	7.50
A115	½a green (#107)	7.50
A116	1a dark brown (#108)	7.50
A117	1½a car rose ('29) (#109)	7.50
A118	2a dull violet (#110)	7.50
A119	2a vermilion ('34) (#111)	17.50
A120	2a6p violet (#112)	7.50
A121	3a ultramarine (#113)	7.50
A122	3a blue ('30) (#114)	7.50
A123	3a car rose ('32) (#115)	7.50
A124	4a olive green (#116)	7.50
A125	6a bister ('35) (#117)	10.00
A126	8a red violet (#118)	7.50
A127	12a claret (#119)	7.50
A128	1r grn & brn (#120)	7.50
A129	2r brn org & car rose (#121)	9.00
A130	5r dk vio & ultra (#122)	20.00
A131	10r carmine & green (#123)	—
A132	15r ol grn & ultra (#124)	—
A133	25r ultra & brn (#125)	—

1926-32
A134	2a dull violet (#126)	7.50
A135	2a vermilion ('32) (#127)	—
A136	4a olive green (#128)	7.50

1931, Feb. 9
A137	¼a brn & olive grn (#129)	12.50
A138	½a grn & vio (#130)	10.00
A139	1a choc & red vio (#131)	10.00
A140	2a blue green (#132)	30.00
A141	3a car & choc (#133)	40.00
A142	1r deep blue (#134)	75.00

1932
A143	9p dark green (#135)	7.50
A144	1a3p violet (#136)	7.50
A145	3a6p dark green (#137)	7.50

1934
A146	½a green (#138)	7.50
A147	1a dark brown (#139)	7.50

1935
A148	½a lt grn & blk (#142)	10.00
A149	9p dull grn & blk (#143)	10.00
A150	1a brn & blk (#144)	10.00
A151	1½a vio & blk (#145)	10.00
A152	2½a brn org & blk (#146)	10.00
A153	3½a blue & blk (#147)	15.00
A154	8a rose lil & blk (#148)	30.00

A cancellation reading "Support the Jubilee
Fund / Aden" exists and is very scarce. Values
on postcards or covers from $250.

OFFICIAL STAMPS OF INDIA USED IN ADEN

1866   Unwmk.
AO1	½a blue (#O1)	—
AO2	1a brown (#O3)	—
AO3	8a rose (#O4)	—

Wmk. 38
AO4	½a blue (#O5)	55.00
AO5	1a lilac (#O6)	—
AO6	1a brown (#O7)	55.00
AO7	2a yellow (#O8)	—
AO8	4a green (#O9)	—
AO9	4a green (#O10)	—

1866-73   Wmk. 38
AO10	½a blue (#O16)	10.00
AO11	½a blue, re-engraved (#O17)	—
AO12	1a brown (#O18)	10.00
AO13	2a orange (#O19)	17.50
AO14	4a green (#O20)	15.00
AO15	8a rose (#O21)	15.00

1874-82
AO16	½a blue, re-engraved (#O22)	10.00
AO17	1a brown (#O23)	8.00
AO18	2a orange (#O24)	50.00
AO19	4a green (#O25)	22.50
AO20	8a rose (#O26)	25.00

1883-87   Wmk. 39
AO21	½a green (#O27)	10.00
AO22	1a maroon (#O28)	10.00
AO23	2a ultra (#O29)	15.00
AO24	4a ol green (#O30)	10.00
AO25	8a red violet (#O31)	10.00
AO26	1r car rose & green (#O32)	10.00

1899-1900
AO28	3p car rose (#O33)	10.00
AO29	½a light green (#O34)	12.50
AO30	1a car rose (#O35)	10.00
AO31	2a violet (#O36)	12.50

1902-05
AO32	3p gray (#O37)	10.00
AO33	½a green (#O38)	10.00
AO34	1a carmine rose (#O39)	10.00
AO35	2a violet (#O40)	10.00
AO36	4a olive green (#O41)	10.00
AO37	6a bister (#O42)	10.00
AO38	8a red lilac (#O43)	12.50
AO39	1r car rose & grn ('05) (#O44)	15.00

1906-07
AO40	½a green (#O45)	10.00
AO41	1a carmine rose (#O46)	10.00

1909
AO42	2r brn & rose (#O47)	—
AO43	5r vio & ultra (#O48)	—
AO44	10r car rose & grn (#O49)	—
AO44a	10r red & grn (#O49a)	—
AO45	15r ol gray & ultra (#O50)	—
AO46	25r ultra & org brn (#O51)	—

1911-23
AO47	3p gray (#O52)	7.50
AO48	½a green (#O53)	7.50
AO49	1a carmine rose (#O54)	7.50
AO50	1a dk brown (#O55)	7.50
AO51	2a dull violet (#O56)	7.50
AO52	4a olive green (#O57)	7.50
AO53	6a bister (#O58)	10.00
AO54	8a red violet (#O59)	7.50
AO55	1r grn & brn (#O60)	12.50
AO56	2r brn & car rose (#O61)	25.00
AO57	5r vio & ultra (#O62)	—
AO58	10r car rose & grn (#O63)	—
AO59	15r ol grn & ultra (#O64)	—
AO60	25r ultra & brn org (#O65)	—

While only stamps of India were sold
in Aden, stamps from other countries
were canceled there. Aden was a major
transfer point for mail from the Far East,
Indian Ocean and East Africa and it
was not uncommon for ships to arrive
with uncanceled mail aboard. This
included mail not canceled in the country of origin and letters posted at sea
prior to the 1894 use of Paquebot markings. Such mail appropriately received
Aden postmarks as it transited the
country.

STAMPS OF CEYLON USED IN ADEN

Type A cancellation with associated
circular datestamp.

1857-66
A167	6p plum (#2)	—
A168	1p blue (#3)	—
A169	2p deep green (#4)	300.00
a.	2p yellow green (#4a)	375.00
A170	5p org brn (#6)	—
A171	6p bis brn (#28)	—
A172	9p deep brn (#32)	—
A173	10p vermilion (#33)	—
A174	1sh violet (#34)	—
A175	1p blue (#46)	—

A176	6p chocolate brn (#53)	—		
A177	9p brown (#55)	—		

STAMPS OF GREAT BRITAIN USED IN ADEN

Type A cancellation with associated circular datestamp.

1856-62

A190	1p rose red (#20)	—	
A191	4p rose (#26)	—	
A192	6p lilac (#39)	—	
A193	1sh green (#42)	—	

STAMPS OF MAURITIUS USED IN ADEN

Type A cancellation with associated circular datestamp.

1848-63

A200	1p org red (#5b)	900.00	
A201	9p magenta (#11)	—	
A202	2p blue (#14c)	—	
A203	2p blue (#15)	—	
A204	6p blue (#18)	—	
A205	1sh vermilion (#19)	—	
A206	2p blue (#25)	—	
A207	4p rose (#26)	—	

ISSUES UNDER BRITISH ADMINISTRATION

Dhow — A1

Perf. 13x11½

1937, Apr. 1   Engr.   Wmk. 4

1	A1	½a lt green	4.50	2.50
		On cover		17.00
2	A1	9p dark green	4.25	3.50
		On cover		18.50
3	A1	1a black brown	4.25	2.00
		On cover		10.00
4	A1	2a red	4.75	3.00
		On cover		18.50
5	A1	2½a blue	6.75	2.00
		On cover		12.00
6	A1	3a carmine rose	11.00	9.00
		On cover		52.50
7	A1	3½a gray blue	8.50	5.75
		On cover		28.50
8	A1	8a rose lilac	30.00	10.00
		On cover		50.00
9	A1	1r brown	60.00	12.00
		On cover		60.00
10	A1	2r orange yellow	110.00	40.00
		On cover		165.00
11	A1	5r rose violet	240.00	150.00
		On cover		400.00
a.		5r reddish purple, aniline	200.00	200.00
		On cover		400.00
12	A1	10r olive green	625.00	550.00
		On cover		600.00
		Nos. 1-12 (12)	1,109.	789.75
		Set, hinged	800.00	
		Set, perforated "SPECI-MEN"	475.00	

Covers: Values for Nos. 10-12 are for overfranked covers, usually philatelic.

Common Design Types pictured following the introduction.

Coronation Issue
Common Design Type

1937, May 12   Perf. 13½x14

13	CD302	1a black brown	.80	1.25
		On cover		4.00
14	CD302	2½a blue	.95	1.60
		On cover		6.00
15	CD302	3½a gray blue	1.25	3.25
		On cover		12.50
		Nos. 13-15 (3)	3.00	6.10
		Set, hinged	2.00	
		Set, perforated "SPECI-MEN"	120.00	

Values are for covers with correct frankings. Philatelic covers sell for less.

Aidrus Mosque — A2

¾a, 5r, Camel Corpsman. 1a, 2r, Aden Harbor. 1½a, 1r, Adenese dhow. 2½a, 8a, Mukalla. 3a, 14a, 10r, Capture of Aden, 1839.

1939-48   Engr.   Wmk. 4   Perf. 12½

16	A2	½a green (7/42)	1.75	.60
a.		½a yellow green	.55	.65
b.		½a blue green (9/48)	3.50	4.25
17	A2	¾a red brn	3.00	1.40
a.		¾a brn vio	2.25	2.25
18	A2	1a brt lt blue	1.00	.60
a.		1a light blue	1.75	.25
19	A2	1½a red	2.75	.65
20	A2	2a dark brown	1.25	.40
a.		2a sepia	3.75	2.25
21	A2	2½a brt ultra	2.00	.45
22	A2	3a rose car & dk brn	1.90	.30
23	A2	8a orange	2.25	.40
b.		8a red orange	1.00	.45
23A	A2	14a lt bl & brn blk ('45)	4.25	1.25
24	A2	1r bright green	5.25	2.75
a.		1r emerald green	2.75	2.50
25	A2	2r dp mag & bl blk ('44)	11.00	3.00
a.		2r rose vio & indigo	7.00	3.00
26	A2	5r dp ol & lake brn (1/44)	30.00	15.00
a.		5r olive grn & red brn	12.50	8.75
27	A2	10r brt vio & brn	30.00	12.50
a.		10r dark pur & lake brn	45.00	17.50
		Nos. 16-27 (13)	96.15	39.15
		Set, cheapest shades, hinged	70.00	
		Set, perforated "SPECI-MEN"	250.00	

Peace Issue
Common Design Type

1946, Oct. 15   Engr.   Wmk. 4

28	CD303	1½a carmine	.25	1.50
29	CD303	2½a deep blue	.45	.80
a.		Wmk. inverted	950.00	
		Hinged	675.00	
		Set, perforated "SPECIMEN"	90.00	

Return to peace at end of World War II.

Silver Wedding Issue
Common Design Types

1949, Jan. 17   Photo.   Perf. 14x14½

30	CD304	1½a scarlet	.40	2.50

Engraved; Name Typographed   Perf. 11½x11

31	CD305	10r purple	37.50	45.00

25th anniv. of the marriage of King George VI and Queen Elizabeth.

UPU Issue
Common Design Types

Srchd. in Annas and Rupees

Engr.; Name typo. on Nos. 33-34

1949, Oct. 10   Perf. 13½, 11x11½

32	CD306	2½a on 20c dp ultra	.70	1.60
33	CD307	3a on 30c dp car	2.25	1.60
34	CD308	8a on 50c org	1.75	1.75
35	CD309	1r on 1sh blue	1.90	4.00
		Nos. 32-35 (4)	6.60	8.95

75th anniv. of the formation of the UPU.

Nos. 18 and 20-27 Surcharged in Black or Carmine

1951, Oct. 1   Wmk. 4   Perf. 12½

36	A2	5c on 1a #18a	.35	.50
a.		On #18	.50	.50
37	A2	10c on 2a #20a	.35	.55
a.		On #20	.50	.50
b.		On 2a sepia brown	.60	.60
38	A2	15c on 2½a	.45	1.50
a.		Double surcharge	1,600.	
		Hinged	950.00	
39	A2	20c on 3a	.50	.50
a.		On 3a dp sepia & car rose	1.25	1.25
40	A2	30c on 8a #23b (C)	.55	.70
41	A2	50c on 8a #23b	.75	.50
a.		Double surcharge, one albino		
			2,500.	
42	A2	70c on 14a (#23A)	2.50	1.75
a.		On 14a dk sepia & br lt blue	1.25	1.75
43	A2	1sh on 1r #24a	3.00	.40
44	A2	2sh on 2r #25	14.00	3.50
a.		On #25a	7.50	6.50
b.		On #25, albino surcharge	850.00	
		Hinged	850.00	

45	A2	5sh on 5r #26	27.50	14.00
a.		On 5r lake brown & sage green	16.50	12.50
46	A2	10sh on 10r #27	37.50	15.50
		Nos. 36-46 (11)	87.45	39.40

Surcharge on No. 40 includes 2 bars.

Number 38a occured when one sheet was fed through the printing press twice, one time at a slight angle. Values for No. 38a are for examples with the surcharges clearly separated. Some positions have the 2nd overprint almost directly over the 1st, and, while rare, are in less demand and sell for less.

Nos. 37b, 39a, 42a and 45a are surcharged on stamps especially produced for this purpose and were not issued in these shades without surcharge.

KATHIRI

LOCATION — In Eastern Aden Protectorate
GOVT. — Sultanate
CAPITAL — Seiyun

The stamps of the Kathiri State of Seiyun were valid for use throughout Aden. Used stamps generally bear Aden GPO or Aden Camp cancels. Examples with cancels from offices in the Eastern Protectorate command a premium.

Sultan Ja'far bin Mansur al Kathiri — A1   Seiyun — A2

Minaret at Tarim — A3

Designs: 2½a, Mosque at Seiyun. 3a, Palace at Tarim. 8a, Mosque at Seiyun, horiz. 1r, South Gate, Tarim. 2r, Kathiri House. 5r, Mosque at Tarim.

1942   Engr.   Wmk. 4   Perf. 13¾x14

1	A1	½a dark green	.25	1.75
a.		Perf. 14 line	.50	3.00
2	A1	¾a copper brown	.45	4.00
a.		Perf. 14 line	.55	1.00
3	A1	1a deep blue	.80	2.00
a.		Perf. 14 line	.75	1.00

Perf. 13x11½, 11½x13

4	A2	1½a dark car rose	.80	2.50
a.		1½a dp car rose, aniline	1.60	2.00
5	A3	2a sepia brown	.50	2.50
a.		2a sepia	1.25	2.00
6	A3	2½a deep blue	1.50	2.25
7	A2	3a dk car rose & dull brn	2.00	4.00
a.		3a car & sepia brn	2.00	2.50
8	A2	8a orange red	2.50	1.00
9	A3	1r green	6.00	4.50
10	A2	2r rose vio & dk blue	12.00	22.50
a.		2r dp pur & dk bl	10.00	12.50
11	A3	5r gray green & fawn	32.50	30.00
		Nos. 1-11 (11)	59.30	77.00
		Set, perforated "SPECI-MEN"	210.00	

For surcharges see Nos. 20-27.

Nos. 4, 6 Ovptd. in Black or Red

a

Perf. 13x11½, 11½x13

1946, Oct. 15   Wmk. 4

12	A2 (a)	1½a dark car rose	.25	.65
13	A3 (b)	2½a deep blue (R)	.25	.25
a.		Inverted overprint	1,100.	
		Hinged	700.	
b.		Double overprint	1,500.	
		Hinged	1,000.	
		Set, perforated "SPECI-MEN"	90.00	

Victory of the Allied Nations in WWII. All examples of No. 13b have the 2nd overprint almost directly over the 1st.

Silver Wedding Issue
Common Design Types

1949, Jan. 17   Photo.   Perf. 14x14½

14	CD304	1½a scarlet	.50	3.00

Engraved; Name Typo.   Perf. 11½x11

15	CD305	5r green	21.00	13.00

25th anniv. of the marriage of King George VI and Queen Elizabeth.

UPU Issue
Common Design Types

Srchd. in Annas and Rupees

Engr.; Name Typo. on Nos. 17-18

1949, Oct. 10   Perf. 13½, 11x11½

16	CD306	2½a on 20c dp ultra	.25	.80
17	CD307	3a on 30c dp car	1.25	2.00
18	CD308	8a on 50c orange	.40	2.75
19	CD309	1r on 1sh blue	.50	1.25
		Nos. 16-19 (4)	2.40	6.80

75th anniv. of the formation of the UPU.

Nos. 3 and 5-11 Srchd. in Carmine or Black

Perf. 14, 13x11½, 11½x13

1951, Oct. 1   Wmk. 4

20	A1	5c on 1a (C)	.25	1.75
21	A3	10c on 2a #5a	.30	1.25
a.		On #5	.40	1.00
22	A3	15c on 2½a	.30	2.25
23	A2	20c on 3a #7	.25	2.75
a.		On #7a	.50	1.50
24	A2	50c on 8a	.30	1.25
25	A3	1sh on 1r	1.25	3.00
26	A2	2sh on 2r #10	11.00	37.50
a.		On #10a	12.50	45.00
27	A3	5sh on 5r	32.50	50.00
		Nos. 20-27 (8)	46.15	99.75

QUAITI

LOCATION — In Eastern Aden Protectorate
GOVT. — Sultanate
CAPITAL — Mukalla

The stamps of the Quaiti State of Shihr and Mukalla were valid for use throughout Aden. Used stamps generally bear Aden GPO or Aden Camp cancels. Examples with cancels from offices in the Eastern Protectorate command a premium.

Sultan Sir
Saleh bin
Ghalib al
Qu'aiti — A1

Mukalla
Harbor — A2

Buildings at
Shibam — A3

Designs: 2a, Gateway of Shihr. 3a, Outpost of Mukalla. 8a, View of 'Einat. 1r, Governor's Castle, Du'an. 2r, Mosque in Hureidha. 5r, Meshhed.

1942   Engr.   Wmk. 4   Perf. 13¾x14

1	A1	½a blue green	1.50	.50
a.		½a olive green	27.50	37.50
b.		Perf. 14 line	.75	.50
2	A1	¾a copper brown	2.50	.40
a.		Perf. 14 line	1.25	1.00
3	A1	1a deep blue	1.00	1.00
a.		Perf. 14 line	1.25	1.25
b.		1a blue	2.00	2.00

Perf. 13x11½, 11½x13

4	A2	1½a dk car rose	2.00	.50
a.		1½a car rose, aniline	1.50	1.25
5	A2	2a black brown	2.00	2.00
a.		2a yellowish brown	25.00	35.00
b.		2a sepia	2.00	2.00
6	A3	2½a deep blue	.50	.30
7	A2	3a dk car rose & dl brn	1.25	1.00
a.		3a dp car & sepia	2.00	1.50
8	A3	8a orange red	1.25	.40
9	A2	1r green	7.50	4.25
a.		Missing "A" in "CA" of watermark	1,200.	1,100.
10	A3	2r rose vio & dk blue	16.00	12.00
a.		2r dp pur & dp bl	15.00	12.50
11	A3	5r gray green & fawn	32.50	17.00
		Nos. 1-11 (11)	68.00	39.35
		Set, perforated "SPECIMEN"	225.00	

For surcharges see Nos. 20-27.

Nos. 4, 6 Ovptd. in Black or Carmine like Kathiri Nos. 12-13

1946, Oct. 15   Perf. 11½x13, 13x11½

12	A2 (b)	1½a dk car rose	.25	.80
13	A3 (a)	2½a deep blue (C)	.25	.25
		Set, perforated "SPECIMEN"	90.00	

Victory of the Allied Nations in WWII.

Silver Wedding Issue
Common Design Types

1949, Jan. 17   Photo.   Perf. 14x14½

14	CD304	1½a scarlet	1.00	4.50

Engraved; Name Typo.
Perf. 11½x11

15	CD305	5r green	21.00	14.00

25th anniv. of the marriage of King George VI and Queen Elizabeth.

UPU Issue
Common Design Types
Surcharged with New Values in Annas and Rupees

Engr.; Name Typo. on Nos. 17 and 18

1949, Oct. 10   Perf. 13½, 11x11½

16	CD306	2½a on 20c dp ultra	.25	.25
17	CD307	3a on 30c dp car	1.50	1.25
18	CD308	8a on 50c org	.35	1.25
19	CD309	1r on 1sh blue	.45	.50
a.		Surcharge omitted	4,000.	
		Hinged	3,250.	
		Nos. 16-19 (4)	2.55	3.25

Nos. 3, 5-11 &
Types Srchd.
in Carmine or
Black

Perf. 14, 13x11½, 11½x13

1951, Oct. 1   Engr.   Wmk. 4

20	A1	5c on 1a (C)	.25	.25
21	A2	10c on 2a	.25	.25
a.		On #5a (12/18/46)	20.00	30.00
b.		On #5b	.50	.75
22	A3	15c on 2½a	.25	.25
23	A2	20c on 3a #7	.35	.90
a.		20c on 3a #7a	.40	.25
b.		Double surcharge, one albino	375.00	
24	A3	50c on 8a org red	.60	2.50
a.		50c on 8a scarlet	.25	.40
25	A2	1sh on 1r	2.25	.60
26	A3	2sh on 2r	8.50	25.00
27	A3	5sh on 5r	17.50	32.50
		Nos. 20-27 (8)	29.95	62.25

AFGHANISTAN

af-'ga-nə-ˌstan

LOCATION — Central Asia, bounded by Iran, Russian Turkestan, India, Baluchistan and China
GOVT. — Constitutional Monarchy
AREA — 251,773 sq. mi.
POP. — 10,000,000
CAPITAL — Kabul

12 Shahi = 6 Sanar = 3 Abasi =
2 Krans = 1 Rupee Kabuli
60 Paisas = 1 Rupee (1921)
100 Pouls = 1 Rupee Afghani (1927)

CHARACTERS OF VALUE.

From 1871 to 1892 and 1898, the Moslem year date appears on the stamp. Numerals as follows:

Until 1891, cancellation consisted of cutting or tearing a piece from the stamps. Such examples should not be considered as damaged.

Values are for cut square examples of good color. Cut to shape or faded examples sell for much less, particularly Nos. 2-10.

Nos. 2-108 are on laid paper of varying thickness except where wove is noted.

Until 1907, all stamps were issued ungummed.

The tiger's head on types A2 to A11 symbolizes the name of the contemporary amir, Sher (Tiger) Ali.

Kingdom of Kabul

Tiger's Head, Type I — A2

Tiger's Head, Type II — A2a

Both circles dotted. Type I: has well-defined inner and outer circles with evenly spaced dots.
Type II: has no well-defined inner and outer circles, and the dots are randomly spaced.

1871   Unwmk.   Litho.   Imperf.
Dated "1288"

2	A2	1sh black	550.00	25.00
		On cover		800.00
2A	A2a	1sh black	525.00	35.00
3	A2	1sa black	650.00	32.50
		On cover		800.00
3A	A2a	1sa black	210.00	55.00
4	A2	1ab black	250.00	50.00
		On cover		900.00
4A	A2a	1ab black	100.00	32.50
		Nos. 2-4 (3)	1,450.	107.50

Thirty varieties of the shahi, 10 of the sanar and 5 of the abasi.
Similar designs without the tiger's head in the center are revenues.

A3

Outer circle dotted
Dated "1288"

5	A3	1sh black	525.00	35.00
6	A3	1sa black	300.00	50.00
7	A3	1ab black	110.00	32.50
		Nos. 5-7 (3)	935.00	117.50

Five varieties of each.

A4

Toned Wove Paper

1872   Dated "1289"

8	A4	6sh violet	1,350.	800.
		On cover		12,500.
9	A4	1rup violet	1,750.	1,250.

Two varieties of each. Date varies in location. Printed in sheets of 4 (2x2) containing two of each denomination.
Most used examples are smeared with a greasy ink cancel.

A4a

White Laid Paper

1873   Dated "1290"

10	A4a	1sh black	25.00	12.00
		On cover		325.00
a.		Corner ornament missing	550.00	500.00
b.		Corner ornament retouched	75.00	40.00

15 varieties. Nos. 10a, 10b are the sixth stamp on the sheet.

A5

1873

11	A5	1sh black	22.50	11.00
		On cover		300.00
11A	A5	1sh violet	550.00	

Sixty varieties of each.

1874   Dated "1291"

12	A5	1ab black	90.00	55.00
13	A5	½rup black	37.50	20.00
14	A5	1rup black	40.00	24.00
		On cover		200.00
		Nos. 12-14 (3)	167.50	99.00

Five varieties of each.
Nos. 12-14 were printed on the same sheet. Se-tenant varieties exist.

A6   A7

1875   Dated "1292"

15	A6	1sa black	375.00	350.00
		On cover		1,100.
a.		Wide outer circle	1,200.	750.00
16	A6	1ab black	425.00	400.00
17	A6	1sa brown violet	75.00	30.00
a.		Wide outer circle	300.00	185.00
18	A6	1ab brown violet	115.00	67.50

Ten varieties of the sanar, five of the abasi.
Nos. 15-16 and 17-18 were printed in the same sheets. Se-tenant pairs exist.

1876   Dated "1293"

19	A7	1sh black	325.00	175.00
		On cover		2,500.
20	A7	1sa black	375.00	200.00
		On cover		1,000.
21	A7	1ab black	750.00	425.00
22	A7	½rup black	450.00	275.00
23	A7	1rup black	875.00	275.00
24	A7	1sh violet	450.00	275.00
25	A7	1sa violet	425.00	275.00
		On cover		2,000.
26	A7	1ab violet	525.00	275.00
27	A7	½rup violet	225.00	60.00
28	A7	1rup violet	225.00	75.00

12 varieties of the shahi and 3 each of the other values.

A8

1876 Dated "1293"

29	A8	1sh gray		16.00	6.00
		On cover			300.00
30	A8	1sa gray		16.00	8.00
31	A8	1ab gray		42.50	20.00
32	A8	½rup gray		50.00	25.00
33	A8	1rup gray		37.50	17.50
34	A8	1sh olive blk		140.00	80.00
35	A8	1sa olive blk		190.00	100.00
36	A8	1ab olive blk		400.00	250.00
37	A8	½rup olive blk		275.00	275.00
38	A8	1rup olive blk		375.00	400.00
39	A8	1sh green		30.00	8.00
40	A8	1sa green		40.00	24.00
41	A8	1ab green		80.00	60.00
42	A8	½rup green		125.00	80.00
43	A8	1rup green		110.00	125.00
44	A8	1sh ocher		32.50	15.00
45	A8	1sa ocher		40.00	24.00
		On cover			400.00
46	A8	1ab ocher		80.00	50.00
47	A8	½rup ocher		90.00	65.00
48	A8	1rup ocher		140.00	125.00
49	A8	1sh violet		37.50	15.00
50	A8	1sa violet		37.50	15.00
51	A8	1ab violet		50.00	15.00
52	A8	½rup violet		70.00	27.50
53	A8	1rup violet		100.00	40.00

24 varieties of the shahi, 4 of which show denomination written:

12 varieties of the sanar, 6 of the abasi and 3 each of the ½ rupee and rupee.

A9

1877 Dated "1294"

54	A9	1sh gray		10.00	15.00
55	A9	1sa gray		6.00	6.00
56	A9	1ab gray		11.00	9.00
57	A9	½rup gray		14.50	20.00
58	A9	1rup gray		14.50	20.00
59	A9	1sh black		18.00	27.50
60	A9	1sa black		25.00	10.00
61	A9	1ab black		42.50	12.00
62	A9	½rup black		45.00	30.00
63	A9	1rup black		45.00	30.00
64	A9	1sh green		32.50	32.50
		On cover			300.00
a.		Wove paper		35.00	
65	A9	1sa green		12.00	12.00
a.		Wove paper		16.00	15.00
66	A9	1ab green		16.00	16.00
a.		Wove paper		30.00	
67	A9	½rup green		27.50	30.00
a.		Wove paper		32.50	42.50
68	A9	1rup green		27.50	30.00
a.		Wove paper		32.50	42.50
69	A9	1sh ocher		11.00	5.25
70	A9	1sa ocher		8.00	7.25
71	A9	1ab ocher		32.50	24.50
72	A9	½rup ocher		40.00	35.00
73	A9	1rup ocher		45.00	35.00
74	A9	1sh violet		11.00	5.00
75	A9	1sa violet		11.00	5.00
76	A9	1ab violet		19.00	12.00
77	A9	½rup violet		27.50	30.00
78	A9	1rup violet		27.50	30.00

25 varieties of the shahi, 8 of the sanar, 3 of the abasi and 2 each of the ½ rupee and rupee.

Some examples of Nos. 54-78 show a "94" year date. These are valued less.

A10

A11

1878 Dated "1295"

79	A10	1sh gray		5.00	10.00
		On cover			300.00
80	A10	1sa gray		7.00	10.00
81	A10	1ab gray		7.00	10.00
82	A10	½rup gray		12.00	15.00
83	A10	1rup gray		12.00	15.00
84	A10	1sh black		9.50	

85	A10	1sa black		9.50	
86	A10	1ab black		32.50	
87	A10	½rup black		35.00	
88	A10	1rup black		35.00	
89	A10	1sh green		32.50	55.00
90	A10	1sa green		8.00	9.00
91	A10	1ab green		22.11	25.00
92	A10	½rup green		32.50	30.00
93	A10	1rup green		60.00	40.00
		On cover			200.00
94	A10	1sh ocher		24.00	8.00
95	A10	1sa ocher		12.00	15.00
		On cover			50.00
96	A10	1ab ocher		45.00	35.00
97	A10	½rup ocher		65.00	45.00
98	A10	1rup ocher		27.50	30.00
99	A10	1sh violet		8.00	15.00
100	A10	1sa violet		30.00	25.00
101	A10	1ab violet		16.00	15.00
102	A10	½rup violet		55.00	35.00
103	A10	1rup violet		45.00	30.00
104	A11	1sh gray		5.50	5.00
105	A11	1sh black		90.00	50.00
106	A11	1sh ocher		8.00	4.00
107	A11	1sh ocher		8.00	7.25
		On cover			300.00
108	A11	1sh violet		6.50	5.00
		On cover			300.00

40 varieties of the shahi, 30 of the sanar, 6 of the abasi and 2 each of the ½ rupee and 1 rupee.

Some examples of Nos. 79-108 show a "95" year date. These are valued less.

The 1876, 1877 and 1878 issues were printed in separate colors for each main post office on the Peshawar-Kabul-Khulm (Tashkurghan) postal route. Some specialists consider the black printings to be proofs or trial colors.

There are many shades of these colors.

1ab, Type I (26mm) — A12

1ab, Type II (28mm) — A13

A14

A15

Dated "1298", numerals scattered through design
Handstamped, in watercolor
1881-90
Thin White Laid Batonne Paper

109	A12	1ab violet		4.00	2.00
		On cover			100.00
109A	A13	1ab violet		8.00	3.00
		On cover			150.00
110	A12	1ab black brn		5.00	2.00
		On cover			100.00
111	A12	1ab rose		12.00	3.00
		On cover			50.00
b.		Se-tenant with No. 111A		16.00	
111A	A13	1ab rose		6.00	2.00
		On cover			100.00
112	A14	2ab violet		8.00	2.00
		On cover			50.00
113	A14	2ab black brn		10.00	6.00
		On cover			50.00
114	A14	2ab rose		20.00	10.00
		On cover			75.00
115	A15	1rup violet		10.00	2.00
116	A15	1rup black brn		12.00	8.00
117	A15	1rup rose		11.00	6.00

Thin White Wove Batonne Paper

118	A12	1ab violet		12.00	5.00
		On cover			200.00
119	A12	1ab vermilion		30.00	9.00
120	A12	1ab rose		30.00	25.00

121	A14	2ab violet		30.00	25.00
		On cover			600.00
122	A14	2ab vermilion		30.00	16.00
122A	A14	2ab black brn			
		On cover			200.00
123	A15	1rup violet		15.00	8.00
124	A15	1rup		11.00	7.00
125	A15	1rup black brn		19.00	8.00

Thin White Laid Batonne Paper

126	A12	1ab brown org		20.00	8.00
		On cover			300.00
126A	A13	1ab brn org (II)		20.00	8.00
		On cover			50.00
127	A12	1ab carmine lake		20.00	8.00
		On cover			100.00
a.		Laid paper		20.00	8.00
128	A14	2ab brown org		20.00	8.00
129	A14	2ab carmine lake		20.00	8.00
		On cover			70.00
130	A15	1rup brown org		35.00	15.00
131	A15	1rup car lake		35.00	15.00

Yellowish Laid Batonne Paper

132	A12	1ab purple		10.00	10.00
133	A12	1ab red		10.00	5.00

1884 Colored Wove Paper

133A	A13	1ab purple, yel (II)		17.50	17.50
134	A12	1ab purple, grn		20.00	
135	A12	1ab purple, blue		32.50	21.00
136	A12	1ab red, grn		37.50	
137	A12	1ab red, yel		30.00	
139	A12	1ab red, rose		50.00	
140	A14	2ab red, yel		30.00	
142	A14	2ab red, rose		30.00	
143	A15	1rup red, yel		55.00	20.00
145	A15	1rup red, rose		65.00	25.00

Thin Colored Ribbed Paper

146	A14	2ab red, yellow		40.00	
147	A15	1rup red, yellow		80.00	
148	A12	1ab lake, lilac		40.00	
149	A14	2ab lake, lilac		40.00	
150	A15	1rup lake, lilac		40.00	
151	A12	1ab lake, green		40.00	
152	A14	2ab lake, green		40.00	
153	A15	1rup lake, green		40.00	

1886-88 Colored Wove Paper

155	A12	1ab black, magenta		60.00	
156	A12	1ab claret brn, org		50.00	
156A	A12	1ab red, org		40.00	
156B	A14	2ab red, org		40.00	
156C	A15	1rup red, org		40.00	

Laid Batonné Paper

157	A12	1ab black, lavender		40.00	
158	A12	1ab cl brn, grn		40.00	
159	A12	1ab black, pink		60.00	
160	A14	2ab black, pink		100.00	
161	A15	1rup black, pink		70.00	

Laid Paper

162	A12	1ab black, pink		80.00	
163	A14	2ab black, pink		80.00	
164	A15	1rup black, pink		80.00	
165	A12	1ab brown, yel		80.00	
166	A14	2ab brown, yel		80.00	
167	A15	1rup brown, yel		80.00	
168	A12	1ab blue, grn		80.00	
169	A14	2ab blue, grn		80.00	
170	A15	1rup blue, grn		80.00	

1891 Colored Wove Paper

175	A12	1ab green, rose		100.00	
176	A15	1rup pur, grn batonne		100.00	

Nos. 109-176 fall into three categories:

1. Those regularly issued and in normal postal use from 1881 on, handstamped on thin white laid or wove paper in strip sheets containing 12 or more impressions of the same denomination arranged in two irregular rows, with the impressions often touching or overlappng.

2. The 1884 postal issues provisionally printed on smooth or ribbed colored wove paper as needed to supplement low stocks of the normal white paper stamps.

3. The "special" printings made in a range of colors on several types of laid or wove colored papers, most of which were never used for normal printings. These were produced periodically from 1886 to 1891 to meet philatelic demands. Although nominally valid for postage, most of the special printings were exported directly to fill dealers' orders, and few were ever postally used. Many of the sheets contained all three denominations with impressions separated by ruled lines. Sometimes different colors were used, so se-tenant multiples of denomination or color exist. Many combinations of stamp and paper colors exist besides those listed.

Various shades of each color exist.

Type A12 is known dated "1297."

Counterfeits, lithographed or typographed, are plentiful.

Kingdom of Afghanistan

A16

A17

A18

Dated "1309"

1891			Pelure Paper		Litho.
177	A16	1ab slate blue		2.00	2.00
a.		Tete beche pair		19.00	
178	A17	2ab slate blue		12.00	12.00
179	A18	1rup slate blue		27.50	27.50
		Nos. 177-179 (3)		41.50	41.50

Revenue stamps of similar design exist in various colors.

Nos. 177-179 were printed in panes on the same sheet, so se-tenant gutter pairs exist. Examples in black or red are proofs.

A Mosque Gate and Crossed Cannons (National Seal) — A19

Dated "1310" in Upper Right Corner

1892			Flimsy Wove Paper		
180	A19	1ab black, green		3.50	3.00
181	A19	1ab black, orange		4.50	4.50
182	A19	1ab black, yellow		3.50	3.00
183	A19	1ab black, pink		4.00	3.25
184	A19	1ab black, lil rose		4.00	4.00
185	A19	1ab black, blue		6.00	5.50
186	A19	1ab black, salmon		4.50	3.75
187	A19	1ab black, magenta		4.00	4.00
188	A19	1ab black, violet		4.00	4.00
188A	A19	1ab black, scarlet		4.00	3.00

Many shades exist.

A20

A21

Undated

1894			Flimsy Wove Paper		
189	A20	2ab black, green		12.00	8.00
190	A21	1rup black, green		14.50	13.00

24 varieties of the 2 abasi and 12 varieties of the rupee.

Nos. 189-190 and F3 were printed se-tenant in the same sheet. Pairs exist.

A21a

Dated "1316"

1898 **Flimsy Wove Paper**
191 A21a 2ab black, *pink* 3.00
192 A21a 2ab black, *magenta* 3.00
193 A21a 2ab black, *yellow* 1.40
193A A21a 2ab black, *salmon* 3.50
194 A21a 2ab black, *green* 1.75
195 A21a 2ab black, *purple* 2.40
195A A21a 2ab black, *blue* 22.50
Nos. 191-195A (7) 37.55

Nos. 191-195A were not regularly issued. Genuinely used examples are scarce. No. 195A was found in remainder stocks and probably was never released.

A22

A23

A24

1907 **Engr.** **Imperf.**
Medium Wove Paper
196 A22 1ab blue green 50.00 30.00
a. 1ab emerald 75.00 20.00
b. Double impression 550.00
c. Printed on both sides 500.00
197 A22 1ab brt blue 35.00 35.00
198 A23 2ab deep blue 45.00 25.00
a. Double impression 550.00
199 A24 1rup green 100.00 75.00
a. 1rup blue green 100.00 75.00

Zigzag Roulette 10
200 A22 1ab green 2,750. 350.00
a. Double impression 1,500.
b. Printed on both sides 1,750.
c. Double impression and printed on both sides 2,500.
d. 1ab blue green 3,250. 350.00
201 A23 2ab blue 2,750. —

1908 **Serrate Roulette 13**
201A A22 1ab green — —
b. 1ab emerald green, on cover 1,250.
On cover 1,250.
201B A23 2ab blue 3,500.

Nos. 201A and 201Ab are only known used on cover.
No. 201B is known only unused.

Perf. 12 on 2, 3 or 4 Sides
202 A22 1ab green — 65.00
a. 1ab yellow-green — 65.00
203 A23 2ab deep blue 35.00 20.00
a. Horiz. pair, imperf between 450.00
204 A24 1rup blue green 125.00 65.00
a. 1rub turquoise blue 125.00 65.00
b. 1rub dull yellowish green 125.00 65.00
Nos. 202-204 (3) 160.00 150.00

Twelve varieties of the 1 abasi, 6 of the 2 abasi, 4 of the 1 rupee.
Nos. 196-204 were issued in small sheets containing 3 or 4 panes. Gutter pairs, normal and tete beche, exist.
Two plates were used for the 1 abasi: plate I, inner vert. lines extend into lower left panel; plate II, inner vert. lines do not extend into lower left panel.

A25

A26

A27

1909-19 **Typo.** **Perf. 12**
205 A25 1ab ultra 5.00 2.00
a. Imperf., pair 48.00
206 A25 1ab red ('16) 1.60 1.25
a. Imperf. 30.00
207 A25 1ab rose ('18) 1.60 1.00
208 A26 2ab green 2.75 2.25
a. Imperf., pair 48.00
b. Horiz. pair, imperf. btwn.
208C A26 2ab yellow ('16) 3.25 2.75
209 A26 2ab bis ('18-'19) 3.25 3.25
210 A27 1rup lilac brn 7.50 6.50
a. 1rup red brown 7.50 7.50
211 A27 1rup ol bis ('16) 10.00 8.00
Nos. 205-211 (8) 34.95 27.00

A28

1913
212 A28 2pa drab brown 20.00 6.00
a. 2pa red brown 20.00 6.00

No. 212 is inscribed "Tiket waraq dak" (Postal card stamps). It was usable only on postcards and not accepted for postage on letters.
Nos. 196-212 sometimes show letters of a papermaker's watermark, "Howard & Jones, London."

Royal Star — A29

1920, Aug. 24 **Perf. 12**
Size: 39x46mm
214 A29 10pa rose 175.00 100.00
On cover 450.00
215 A29 20pa red brown 275.00 175.00
On cover 700.00
216 A29 30pa green 375.00 250.00
On cover 1,200.
Nos. 214-216 (3) 825.00 525.00

2nd Independence Day. Issued to commemorate the first anniversary of the signing of the armistice that ended the war of independence (Third Afghan War).
Issued in sheets of two.
No. 214 exists in two sizes: 38.5mmx45mm, position 1 in sheet; 38.5mmx46mm, position 2.

1921, Mar. **Size: 22½x28¼mm**
217 A29 10pa rose 2.50 1.25
a. Perf. 11 ('27) 22.50 13.00
218 A29 20pa red brown 4.50 2.50
219 A29 30pa yel green 6.50 3.00
a. Tete beche pair 55.00 32.50
b. 30pa green 6.50 3.50
c. As "b," Tete beche pair 55.00 32.50
Nos. 217-219 (3) 13.50 6.75

3rd Independence Day.
Two types of the 10pa, three of the 20pa.

Hstmpd. in black on Nos. 217-219

1923, Feb. 26
219D A29a 10pa rose — 125.00
219E A29a 20pa red brown — 125.00
219F A29a 30pa yel green 400.00 —

5th Independence Day.
Two types of handstamp exist.
Forgeries exist.
See No. Q13B-Q13E.

These handstamps were used by Afghan post offices on incoming foreign mail from 1921 until Afghanistan joined the Universal Postal Union April 1, 1928. Afghan stamps were applied to foreign mail arriving in the country and were canceled with these postage-due handstamps to indicate that postage was to be collected from the addressee. The handstamps were applied primarily to Nos. 217-219, 227-235, 236, and 237-246. Values are the same as for stamps with postal cancellations. A third type of handstamp exists with no distinctive outer border.

A30

1924, Feb. 26 **Perf. 12**
220 A30 10pa chocolate 45.00 30.00
a. Tete beche pair 150.00 100.00

6th Independence Day.
Printed in sheets of four consisting of two tete beche pairs, and in sheets of two. Two types exist.

Some authorities believe that Nos. Q15-Q16 were issued as regular postage stamps.

Crest of King Amanullah A32

Size: 29x37mm

1925, Feb. 26 **Perf. 12**
222 A32 10pa light brown 75.00 35.00

7th Independence Day.
Printed in sheets of 8 (two panes of 4).

Wove Paper

1926, Feb. 28 **Size: 26x33mm**
224 A32 10pa dark blue 8.00 8.00
a. Imperf., pair 32.50
b. Horiz. pair, imperf. btwn. 75.00
c. Vert. pair, imperf. btwn.
d. Laid paper 40.00 13.00

7th anniv. of Independence. Printed in sheets of 4, and in sheets of 8 (two panes of 4). Tete beche gutter pairs exist.

Tughra and Crest of Amanullah A33

1927, Feb.
225 A33 10pa magenta 14.00 12.00
a. Vertical pair, imperf. between 75.00

Dotted Background
226 A33 10pa magenta 20.00 13.00
a. Horiz. pair, imperf. between 75.00

The surface of No. 226 is covered by a net of fine dots.
8th anniv. of Independence. Printed in sheets of 8 (two panes of 4).
Tete-beche gutter pairs exist. Value, pair $85.

National Seal — A34
A35

A35a

A36

1927, Oct. **Imperf.**
227 A34 15p pink 1.40 1.40
228 A35 30p Prus green 2.75 1.25
229 A36 60p light blue 3.75 3.25
a. Tete beche pair 12.00
Nos. 227-229 (3) 7.90 5.90

1927-30 **Perf. 11, 12**
230 A34 15p pink 1.75 1.40
231 A34 15p ultra ('29) 1.75 1.40
232 A35 30p Prus green 3.25 1.40
233 A35a 30p dp green ('30) 1.75 1.25
234 A36 60p bright blue 3.50 2.00
a. Tete beche pair 17.50 17.50
235 A36 60p black ('29) 4.00 2.25
Nos. 230-235 (6) 16.00 9.70

Nos. 230, 232 and 234 are usually imperforate on one or two sides.
No. 233 has been redrawn. A narrow border of pearls has been added and "30," in European and Arabic numerals, inserted in the upper spandrels.

Tughra and Crest of Amanullah — A37

1928, Feb. 27

236	A37 15p pink	5.00	5.00
a.	Tete beche pair	12.00	10.00
b.	Horiz. pair, imperf. vert.	22.50	19.00
c.	As "a," imperf. vert., block of 4	75.00	

9th anniv. of Independence. This stamp is always imperforate on one or two sides.

A 15p blue of somewhat similar design was prepared for the 10th anniv., but was not issued due to Amanullah's dethronement. Value, $15.

A38

A39

A40

A41

A42

1928-30   *Perf. 11, 12*

237	A38 2p dull blue	7.75	4.50
a.	Vertical pair, imperf. between	20.00	
238	A38 2p lt rose ('30)	.65	.55
239	A39 10p gray green	1.90	.40
a.	Tete beche pair	14.00	6.50
b.	Vert. pair, imperf. between	11.00	11.00
c.	Vertical pair, imperf. between		
240	A39 10p choc ('30)	3.00	1.25
a.	10p brown purple ('29)	8.50	4.00
241	A40 25p car rose	2.25	.40
242	A40 25p Prus green ('29)	4.00	1.25
243	A41 40p ultra	3.00	.75
a.	Tete beche pair	15.00	16.00
244	A41 40p rose ('29)	3.50	1.25
a.	Tete beche pair	14.50	
b.	Vert. pair, imperf. horiz.	11.00	
245	A42 50p red	3.75	1.00
246	A42 50p dk blue ('29)	5.00	1.50
	Nos. 237-246 (10)	34.80	12.85

The sheets of these stamps are often imperforate at the outer margins.
Nos. 237-238 are newspaper stamps.

This handstamp was used for ten months by the Revolutionary Gov't in Kabul as a control mark on outgoing mail. It occasionally fell on the stamps but there is no evidence that it was officially used as an overprint. Unused examples were privately made.

Independence Monument A46

Laid Paper
Without Gum
Wmk. Large Seal in the Sheet
1931, Aug.   Litho.   Perf. 12

262	A46 20p red	2.50	1.25

13th Independence Day.

National Assembly Chamber A47

A48

A50

National Assembly Building A49

National Assembly Chamber A51

National Assembly Building A52

Wove Paper
1932   Unwmk.   Typo.   Perf. 12

263	A47 40p olive	1.15	.40
264	A48 60p violet	1.50	.80
265	A49 80p dark red	2.00	1.25
266	A50 1af black	16.00	7.50
267	A51 2af ultra	7.00	4.00
268	A52 3af gray green	7.50	3.50
	Nos. 263-268 (6)	35.15	17.45

Formation of the Natl. Council. Imperforate or perforated examples on ungummed chalky paper are proofs.
See Nos. 304-305.

Mosque at Balkh — A53

Kabul Fortress A54

Parliament House, Darul Funun — A55

Parliament House, Darul Funun — A56

Arch of Qalai Bist — A57

Memorial Pillar of Knowledge and Ignorance A58

Independence Monument A59

Minaret at Herat — A60

Arch of Paghman A61

Ruins at Balkh — A62

Minarets of Herat — A63

Great Buddha at Bamian — A64

1932   Typo.   Perf. 12

269	A53 10p brown	.80	.25
270	A54 15p dk brown	.60	.30
271	A55 20p red	.95	.25
272	A56 25p dk green	1.35	.25
273	A57 30p red	1.35	.25
274	A58 40p orange	1.75	.50
275	A59 50p blue	2.40	1.40
a.	Tete beche pair	12.00	
276	A60 60p blue	2.25	.90
277	A61 80p violet	4.00	2.00
278	A62 1af dark blue	7.00	.80
279	A63 2af dk red violet	7.75	2.25
280	A64 3af claret	9.50	3.00
	Nos. 269-280 (12)	39.70	12.15

Counterfeits of types A53-A65 exist.
See Nos. 290-295, 298-299, 302-303.

Entwined 2's — A65

Two types:
Type I — Numerals shaded. Size about 21x29mm.
Type II — Numerals unshaded. Size about 21¾x30mm.

1931-38   Perf. 12, 11x12

281	A65 2p red brn (I)	.40	.50
282	A65 2p olive blk (I) ('34)	.30	.80
283	A65 2p grnsh gray (I) ('34)	.40	.75
283A	A65 2p black (II) ('36)	.25	.75
284	A65 2p salmon (II) ('38)	.50	.75
284A	A65 2p rose (I) ('38)	.50	.90
b.	Imperf., pair	10.00	

Imperf

285	A65 2p black (II) ('37)	.75	.75
286	A65 2p salmon (II) ('38)	.75	.75
	Nos. 281-286 (8)	3.85	5.95

The newspaper rate was 2 pouls.

A66

1932, Aug.   Perf. 12

287	A66 1af Independence Monument	5.50	3.25

14th Independence Day.

A67

1929 Liberation Monument, Kabul.

1932, Oct.   Typo.

288	A67 80p red brown	2.00	1.50

Arch of Paghman — A68

1933, Aug.
289 A68 50p light ultra 3.00 1.50
15th Independence Day.
No. 289 exists imperf. Value, $5.

Types of 1932 and

Royal Palace, Kabul A69

Darrah- Shikari Pass, Hindu Kush — A70

1934-38 **Typo.** **Perf. 12**
290 A53 10p deep violet .30 .25
291 A54 15p turq green .50 .25
292 A55 20p magenta .50 .25
293 A56 25p deep rose .60 .25
294 A57 30p orange .65 .30
295 A58 40p blue black .75 .30
296 A69 45p dark blue 2.75 1.50
297 A59 45p red ('38) .50 .25
298 A59 50p orange .80 .25
299 A60 60p purple 1.00 .45
300 A70 75p red 4.00 2.00
301 A70 75p dk blue ('38) 1.00 .65
302 A61 80p brown vio 1.60 .80
303 A62 1af red violet 3.25 1.60
304 A51 2af gray black 5.25 2.40
305 A52 3af ultra 6.00 3.00
  Nos. 290-305 (16) 29.45 14.50

Nos. 290, 292, 300, 304, 305 exist imperf.

Independence Monument — A71

1934, Aug. **Litho.** **Without Gum**
306 A71 50p pale green 3.25 2.75
a. Tete beche pair 11.50 11.50
16th year of Independence. Each sheet of 40 (4x10) included 4 tete beche pairs as lower half of sheet was inverted.

Independence Monument — A74

1935, Aug. 15 **Laid Paper**
309 A74 50p dark blue 3.50 2.40
17th year of Independence.

Fireworks Display A75

Wove Paper
1936, Aug. 15 **Perf. 12**
310 A75 50p red violet 3.25 2.50
18th year of Independence.

Independence Monument and Nadir Shah — A76

1937
311 A76 50p vio & bis brn 2.75 2.10
a. Imperf., pair 9.50 9.50
19th year of Independence.

Mohammed Nadir Shah
A77 A78
1938 **Without Gum** **Perf. 11x12**
315 A77 50p brt blue & sepia 2.75 2.40
a. Imperf. pair 24.00 19.00
20th year of Independence.

1939 **Perf. 11, 12x11**
317 A78 50p deep salmon 2.40 1.50
21st year of Independence.

National Arms A79

Parliament House, Darul Funun — A80

Royal Palace, Kabul A81

Independence Monument — A82

Perf. 12, 12x11, 11
1939, Oct. 1 **Typo.** **Unwmk.**
C1 AP1 5af orange 6.00 4.50
a. Imperf., pair ('47) 29.00 29.00
b. Horiz. pair, imperf. vert. 32.50 32.50

Independence Monument and Nadir Shah — A83

Mohammed Zahir Shah — A84

Mohammed Zahir Shah A85

Perf. 11, 11x12, 12x11, 12
1939-61 **Typo.**
318 A79 2p intense blk .30 .70
318A A79 2p brt pink ('61) .30 .70
  Size: 36.5x24mm
319 A80 10p brt purple .30 .25
  Size: 31.5x21mm
320 A80 15p brt green .35 .25
  Size: 34x22.5mm
321 A80 20p red lilac .50 .25
322 A81 25p rose red .60 .30
322A A81 25p green ('41) .35 .25
323 A81 30p orange .50 .25
a. Vert. pair, imperf between
324 A81 40p dk gray 1.00 .50
325 A82 45p brt carmine 1.00 .40
326 A82 50p dp orange .80 .25
327 A82 60p violet 1.00 .25
328 A83 75p ultra 3.00 .80
328A A83 75p red vio ('41) 2.25 1.60
328C A83 75p brt red ('44) 4.00 3.00
328D A83 75p chnt brn ('49) 4.00 3.00
329 A83 80p chocolate 2.00 1.00
a. 80p dull red violet (error)
330 A84 1af brt red violet 2.25 .80
330A A85 1af brt red vio ('44) 2.25 .90
331 A85 2af copper red 3.00 1.00
a. 2af deep rose red 4.25 1.75
332 A84 3af deep blue 5.00 2.40
  Nos. 318-332 (21) 34.75 18.65

Many shades exist in this issue.
On No. 332 the King faces slightly left.
No. 318A issued with and without gum.
See #795A-795B in *Scott Standard Postage Stamp Catalogue*, Vol. 1. For similar design see #907A in Scott Standard catalogue, Vol. 1.

Mohammed Nadir Shah — A86

1940, Aug. 23 **Perf. 11**
333 A86 50p gray green 2.00 1.50
22nd year of Independence.

AIR POST STAMPS

Plane over Kabul AP1

C2 AP1 10af blue 6.50 4.50
a. 10af lt bl 8.00 6.00
b. Imperf., pair ('47) 29.00
c. Horiz. pair, imperf. vert. 32.50
C3 AP1 20af emerald 12.00 7.50
a. Imperf., pair ('47) 29.00
b. Horiz. pair, imperf. vert. 32.50
c. Vert. pair, imperf. horiz. 35.00
  Nos. C1-C3 (3) 24.50 16.50

These stamps come with clean-cut or rough perforations. Counterfeits exist.

REGISTRATION STAMPS

R1

Dated "1309"
Pelure Paper
1891 **Unwmk.** **Litho.** **Imperf.**
F1 R1 1r slate blue 2.40
a. Tete beche pair 13.50
Genuinely used examples of No. F1 are rare. Counterfeit cancellations exist.

R2

Dated "1311"
1893 **Thin Wove Paper**
F2 R2 1r black, *green* 2.00
Genuinely used examples of No. F2 are rare. Counterfeit cancellations exist.

R3

1894 **Undated**
F3 R3 2ab black, *green* 9.50 11.00
12 varieties. See note below Nos. 189-190.

R4

1898-1900 **Undated**
F4 R4 2ab black, *deep rose* 4.50 4.50
F5 R4 2ab black, *lilac rose* 6.50 5.00
F6 R4 2ab black, *magenta* 8.00 5.00
F7 R4 2ab black, *salmon* 4.50 4.50
F8 R4 2ab black, *orange* 4.50 4.50
F9 R4 2ab black, *yellow* 4.50 3.50
F10 R4 2ab black, *green* 4.50 3.50
  Nos. F4-F10 (7) 37.00 30.50

Many shades of paper.
Nos. F4-F10 come in two sizes, measured between outer frame lines: 52x36mm, 1st printing; 46x33mm, 2nd printing. The outer frame line (not pictured) is 3-6mm from inner frame line.
Used on P.O. receipts.

OFFICIAL STAMPS

(Used only on interior mail.)

Coat of
Arms
O1

1909   Unwmk.   Typo.   Perf. 12
Wove Paper

O1	O1 red	1.25	1.25
a.	Carmine ('19?)	2.50	6.50

Later printings of No. O1 in scarlet, vermilion, claret, etc., on various types of paper, were issued until 1927.

Coat of Arms — O2

1939-68?   Typo.   Perf. 11, 12

O3	O2 15p emerald	1.10	.80
O4	O2 30p ocher ('40)	1.50	1.50
O5	O2 45p dark carmine	1.25	1.25
O6	O2 50p brt car ('68)	.70	.70
a.	50p carmine rose ('55)	1.25	.70
O7	O2 1af brt red violet	2.00	1.75
	Nos. O3-O7 (5)	6.55	6.00

Size of 50p, 24x31mm, others 22½x28mm.

PARCEL POST STAMPS

Coat of
Arms — PP1

PP2

PP3

PP4

1909   Unwmk.   Typo.   Perf. 12

Q1	PP1 3sh bister	1.25	2.25
a.	Imperf., pair		—
Q2	PP2 1kr olive gray	3.50	3.50
a.	Imperf., pair		—
Q3	PP3 1r orange	3.25	3.25
Q4	PP3 1r olive green	24.00	4.50
Q5	PP4 2r red	4.00	4.00
	Nos. Q1-Q5 (5)	36.00	17.50

1916-18

Q6	PP1 3sh green	1.75	3.50
Q7	PP2 1kr pale red	3.00	1.50
a.	1kr rose red ('18)	4.00	4.00
Q8	PP3 1r brown org	3.50	1.75
a.	1r deep brown ('18)	12.00	3.00
Q9	PP4 2r blue	6.25	6.50
	Nos. Q6-Q9 (4)	14.50	13.25

Nos. Q1-Q9 sometimes show letters of the papermaker's watermark "HOWARD & JONES LONDON."
Ungummed stamps are remainders. They sell for one-third the price of mint stamps.

Old Habibia College, Near
Kabul — PP5

1921   Wove Paper

Q10	PP5 10pa chocolate	5.00	5.75
a.	Tete beche pair	22.50	22.50
Q11	PP5 15pa light brn	7.00	7.50
a.	Tete beche pair	27.50	27.50
Q12	PP5 30pa red violet	12.50	7.50
a.	Tete beche pair	40.00	40.00
b.	Laid paper	15.00	15.00
Q13	PP5 1r brt blue	14.00	14.00
a.	Tete beche pair	65.00	65.00
	Nos. Q10-Q13 (4)	38.50	34.75

Stamps of this issue are usually perforated on one or two sides only.
The laid paper of No. Q12b has a papermaker's watermark in the sheet.

Handstamped in black on Nos. Q10-Q13

PP5a

1923, Feb. 26

Q13B	PP5a 10pa chocolate	—	—
Q13C	PP5a 15pa light brn	—	—
Q13D	PP5a 30pa red violet	—	—
Q13E	PP5a 1r brt blue	—	—

5th Independence Day.
Two types of handstamp exist.
Forgeries exist.

PP6

1924-26   Wove Paper

Q15	PP6 5kr ultra ('26)	50.00	50.00
Q16	PP6 5r lilac	20.00	25.00

A 15r rose exists, but is not known to have been placed in use. Value, unused $350.

PP7

PP8

1928-29   Perf. 11, 11xImperf.

Q17	PP7 2r yellow orange	8.00	7.00
Q18	PP7 2r green ('29)	7.50	7.50
Q19	PP8 3r deep green	10.50	10.50
Q20	PP8 3r brown ('29)	9.50	10.50
	Nos. Q17-Q20 (4)	35.50	35.50

POSTAL TAX STAMPS

Aliabad Hospital near Kabul PT1

Pierre and Marie Curie PT2

Perf. 12x11½, 12

1938, Dec. 22   Typo.   Unwmk.

RA1	PT1 10p peacock grn	3.25	5.00
RA2	PT2 15p dull blue	3.25	5.00

Obligatory on all mail Dec. 22-28, 1938. The money was used for the Aliabad Hospital. See note with CD80.

AGÜERA, LA

ä-gwä'rä

LOCATION — An administrative district in southern Rio de Oro on the northwest coast of Africa.
GOVT. — Spanish possession
AREA — Because of indefinite political boundaries, figures for area and population are not available.

100 Centimos = 1 Peseta

Type of 1920 Issue of Rio de Oro Overprinted **LA AGÜERA**

1920, June   Typo.   Unwmk.   *Perf. 13*

1	A8	1c blue green	2.60	2.60
		Never hinged	5.75	
		On cover		65.00
2	A8	2c olive brown	2.60	2.60
		Never hinged	5.75	
		On cover		65.00
3	A8	5c deep green	2.60	2.60
		Never hinged	5.75	
		On cover		65.00
4	A8	10c light red	2.60	2.60
		Never hinged	5.75	
		On cover		65.00
5	A8	15c yellow	2.60	2.60
		Never hinged	5.75	
		On cover		65.00
6	A8	20c lilac	2.60	2.60
		Never hinged	5.75	
		On cover		65.00
7	A8	25c deep blue	2.60	2.60
		Never hinged	5.75	
		On cover		75.00
8	A8	30c dark brown	2.60	2.60
		Never hinged	5.75	
		On cover		75.00
9	A8	40c pink	2.60	2.60
		Never hinged	5.75	
		On cover		75.00
10	A8	50c bright blue	8.50	8.50
		Never hinged	17.50	
		On cover		125.00
11	A8	1p red brown	15.50	15.50
		Never hinged	30.00	
		On cover		250.00
12	A8	4p dark violet	50.00	50.00
		Never hinged	100.00	
		On cover		650.00
13	A8	10p orange	95.00	95.00
		Never hinged	200.00	
		On cover		1,300.
		Nos. 1-13 (13)	192.40	192.40
		Set, never hinged	400.00	

Values for Nos. 1-13 are for stamps with fine centering. Exceptional examples with very fine centering are scarce and command at least 50% premium.
Commercial covers are scarce. Philatelic covers sell for less.

Values for stamps in blocks of 4

1	A8	1c blue green	14.00	15.00
2	A8	2c olive brown	14.00	15.00
3	A8	5c deep green	14.00	15.00
4	A8	10c light red	14.00	15.00
5	A8	15c yellow	14.00	15.00
6	A8	20c lilac	14.00	15.00
7	A8	25c deep blue	14.00	15.00
8	A8	30c dark brown	14.00	15.00
9	A8	40c pink	14.00	15.00
10	A8	50c bright blue	32.50	60.00
11	A8	1p red brown	77.50	82.50
12	A8	4p dark violet	260.00	275.00
13	A8	10p orange	490.00	525.00

Values for Specimen Stamps (numbered A.000.000 on reverse)

1S	A8	1c blue green	8.25
2S	A8	2c olive brown	8.25
3S	A8	5c deep green	8.25
4S	A8	10c light red	8.25
5S	A8	15c yellow	8.25
6S	A8	20c lilac	8.25
7S	A8	25c deep blue	8.25
8S	A8	30c dark brown	8.25
9S	A8	40c pink	8.25
10S	A8	50c bright blue	21.00
11S	A8	1p red brown	21.00
12S	A8	4p dark violet	77.50
13S	A8	10p orange	150.00

King Alfonso XIII — A2

Two Types of 1c:
Type I: Two dots above "U" of "AGUERA," large letters.
Type II: No dots above "U" of "AGUERA," smaller letters.

1922, June

14	A2	1c turquoise bl (I)	1.25	1.10
		Never hinged	2.50	
		On cover		45.00
a.		Type II		95.00
15	A2	2c dark green	1.40	1.10
		Never hinged	2.50	
		On cover		45.00
16	A2	5c blue green	1.40	1.10
		Never hinged	2.50	
		On cover		45.00
17	A2	10c red	1.40	1.10
		Never hinged	2.50	
		On cover		45.00
18	A2	15c red brown	1.40	1.10
		Never hinged	2.50	
		On cover		45.00
19	A2	20c yellow	1.40	1.10
		Never hinged	2.50	
		On cover		45.00
20	A2	25c deep blue	1.40	1.10
		Never hinged	2.50	
		On cover		45.00
21	A2	30c dark brown	1.40	1.10
		Never hinged	2.50	
		On cover		52.50
22	A2	40c rose red	1.60	1.40
		Never hinged	3.50	
		On cover		57.50
23	A2	50c red violet	5.50	4.50
		Never hinged	12.00	
		On cover		77.50
24	A2	1p rose	11.00	9.25
		Never hinged	24.00	
		On cover		140.00
25	A2	4p violet	30.00	24.00
		Never hinged	55.00	
		On cover		350.00
26	A2	10p orange	45.00	37.50
		Never hinged	85.00	
		On cover		575.00
		Nos. 14-26 (13)	104.15	85.45
		Set, never hinged	200.00	

Values for stamps in blocks of 4

14	A2	1c turquoise bl (I)	8.00
15	A2	2c dark green	8.00
16	A2	5c blue green	8.00
17	A2	10c red	8.00
18	A2	15c red brown	8.00
19	A2	20c yellow	8.00
20	A2	25c deep blue	8.00
21	A2	30c dark brown	9.25
22	A2	40c rose red	9.25
23	A2	50c red violet	29.00
24	A2	1p rose	57.50
25	A2	4p violet	165.00
26	A2	10p orange	250.00

Values for Specimen Stamps (numbered A.000.000 on reverse)

14S	A2	1c turquoise bl (I)	6.25
15S	A2	2c dark green	6.25
16S	A2	5c blue green	6.25
17S	A2	10c red	6.25
18S	A2	15c red brown	6.25
19S	A2	20c yellow	6.25
20S	A2	25c deep blue	6.25
21S	A2	30c dark brown	9.25
22S	A2	40c rose red	9.25
23S	A2	50c red violet	12.00
24S	A2	1p rose	12.00
25S	A2	4p violet	37.50
26S	A2	10p orange	62.50

For later issues, see Spanish Sahara.

AITUTAKI

ī̆t-ə-'tăk-ē

LOCATION — One of the larger Cook Islands, in the South Pacific Ocean northeast of New Zealand
GOVT. — A dependency of the British dominion of New Zealand
AREA — 7 sq. mi.
POP. — 1,719

The Cook Islands were attached to New Zealand in 1901. Stamps of Cook Islands were used in 1932-72.

12 Pence = 1 Shilling

Watermark

Wmk. 61- Single-lined NZ and Star Close Together

Stamps of New Zealand Surcharged in Red or Blue

a   b

1903   Engr.   Wmk. 61   *Perf. 14*

1	A18(a)	½p green (R)	5.00	7.25
		On cover		140.00
2	A35(b)	1p rose (Bl)	5.25	6.25
		On cover		140.00

c

d   e

f

Perf. 11

3	A22(c)	2½p blue (R)	17.00	13.00
		On cover		140.00
4	A23(d)	3p yellow brn (Bl)	20.00	16.50
		On cover		160.00
5	A26(e)	6p red (Bl)	32.50	27.50
		On cover		190.00
6	A29(f)	1sh scarlet (Bl)	60.00	95.00
		On cover		375.00
a.		1sh orange red (Bl)	77.50	105.00
		On cover		400.00
b.		1sh orange brown (Bl)	160.00	165.00
		On cover		825.00
c.		As #6, no period after "Tiringi"	675.00	900.00
d.		As #6a, no period after "Tiringi"	850.00	1,000.
e.		As #6b, no period after "Tiringi"	1,300.	1,500.

Values for covers are for commercially used and properly franked items. Philatelic usages also exist and sell for less.

1911, Sept.   Typo.   *Perf. 14x15*

7	A41(a)	½p yellow grn (R)	1.10	6.50

Engr.   *Perf. 14*

9	A22(c)	2½p deep blue (R)	8.75	20.00
a.		No period after "Ava"	175.00	250.00

g   h

1913-16   Typo.

10	A42(b)	1p rose (Bl)	3.25	14.00

Engr.

12	A41(g)	6p car rose (Bl) ('16)	50.00	140.00
13	A41(h)	1sh ver (Bl) ('14)	60.00	160.00

1916-17   *Perf. 14x14½*

17	A45(g)	6p car rose (Bl)	9.00	29.00
a.		Perf 14x13½	13.50	57.50
b.		Vert. pair, #17, 17a	57.50	175.00
18	A45(h)	1sh ver (Bl) ('17)	14.00	100.00
a.		Perf 14x13½	16.00	100.00
b.		Vert. pair, #18, 18a	140.00	450.00
c.		No dot on"i" of "Tai"	250.00	750.00
d.		No dot on second "i" of "Tiringi"	325.00	850.00
e.		No dot on third "i" in "Tir- ingi"	475.00	1,100.
		Nos. 1-18 (13)	285.85	635.00

New Zealand Stamps of 1909-19 Overprinted in Red or Dark Blue

1917-20   Typo.   *Perf. 14x15*

19	A43	½p yellow grn ('20)	1.10	6.50
20	A42	1p car (Bl) ('20)	4.75	32.50
21	A47	1½p gray black	4.25	32.50
22	A47	1½p brown org ('19)	.90	7.75
23	A43	3p choc (Bl) ('19)	3.75	19.00

Engr.   *Perf. 14x14½*

24	A44	2½p dull blue ('18)	1.90	17.50
a.		Perf 14x13½	2.25	20.00
b.		Vert. pair, #24, 24a	40.00	150.00
25	A45	3p vio brn (Bl) ('18)	1.75	29.00
a.		Perf 14x13½	2.00	30.00
b.		Vert. pair, #25, 25a	35.00	175.00
26	A45	6p car rose (Bl)	5.25	22.50
a.		Perf 14x13½	7.25	24.00
b.		Vert. pair, #26, 26a	65.00	225.00
27	A45	1sh vermilion (Bl)	13.00	35.00
a.		Perf 14x13½	16.00	50.00
b.		Vert. pair, #26, 26a	75.00	225.00
		Nos. 19-27 (9)	36.65	202.25

Landing of Capt. Cook A15   Avarua Waterfront A16

Capt. James Cook — A17   Palm — A18

Houses at Arorangi — A19

Avarua Harbor — A20

1920   Engr.   Unwmk.   *Perf. 14*

28	A15	½p green & black	4.00	27.50
29	A16	1p carmine & black	4.00	19.00
		Double derrick flaw	12.50	
30	A17	1½p brown & blk	6.50	13.00
31	A18	3p dp blue & blk	2.75	15.00
32	A19	6p slate & red brn	6.25	15.00
33	A20	1sh claret & blk	10.50	22.50
		Nos. 28-33 (6)	34.00	112.00

Inverted centers, double frames, etc. are from printers waste.

Rarotongan Chief (Te Po) — A21

1924-27   Wmk. 61   *Perf. 14*

34	A15	½p green & blk ('27)	2.25	20.00
35	A16	1p carmine & blk	6.50	8.25
		Double derrick flaw	17.00	
36	A21	2½p blue & blk ('27)	8.25	77.50
		Nos. 34-36 (3)	17.00	105.75

ALAOUITES

'al-au-ˌwītz

LOCATION — A division of Syria, in Western Asia.
GOVT. — Under French Mandate
AREA — 2,500 sq. mi.
POP. — 278,000 (approx. 1930)
CAPITAL — Latakia

This territory became an independent state in 1924, although still administered under the French Mandate. In 1930 it was renamed Latakia and Syrian stamps overprinted "Lattaquie" superseded the stamps of Alaouites. For these and subsequent issues see Latakia and Syria.

100 Centimes = 1 Piaster

Issued under French Mandate
Stamps of France Surcharged

Nos. 1-6, 16-18   Nos. 7-15, 19-21

1925   Unwmk.   Perf. 14x13½

Two types of surcharge , 4p on 85c: type 1, 1¼-1½mm between "4" and "P"; type 2, 2mm between "4" and "P."
Two types of surcharge, 5p, 10p, 25p: type 1, 1-1¾mm between value and "Piastres"; type 2, 3mm between value and "Piastres."

1	A16	10c on 2c vio brn	3.50	3.50
		Never hinged	4.50	
		On cover		32.50
b.		Grayish (GC) paper (#110b)	4.00	4.00
		Never hinged	6.00	
		On cover		35.00
c.		"0" before "P" omitted	40.00	40.00
		Never hinged	70.00	
2	A22	25c on 5c orange	3.50	3.50
		Never hinged	4.50	
		On cover		32.50
3	A20	75c on 15c gray grn	6.50	6.50
		Never hinged	9.00	
		On cover		60.00
b.		Wide spacing between "7" and "5"	25.00	25.00
		Never hinged	40.00	
4	A22	1p on 20c red brn	3.50	3.50
		Never hinged	4.00	
		On cover		32.50
5	A22	1.25p on 25c blue	4.00	4.00
		Never hinged	4.50	
		On cover		32.50
6	A22	1.50p on 30c red	12.50	12.50
		Never hinged	16.00	
		On cover		90.00
7	A22	2p on 35c violet	4.00	4.00
		Never hinged	5.25	
		On cover, single franking		32.50 / 50.00
b.		Arabic surcharge inverted	40.00	40.00
		Never hinged	60.00	
8	A18	2p on 40c red & pale bl	4.75	4.75
		Never hinged	6.00	
		On cover		42.50
		On cover, single franking		65.00
b.		Grayish (GC) paper (#121b)	5.50	5.50
		Never hinged	8.50	
		On cover		32.50
		On cover, single franking		57.50
9	A18	2p on 45c grn & bl	17.00	17.00
		Never hinged	26.00	
		On cover		125.00
		On cover, single franking		250.00
10	A18	3p on 60c vio & ultra	7.50	7.50
		Never hinged	10.00	
		On cover		70.00
		On cover, single franking		95.00
11	A20	3p on 60c lt vio	12.00	12.00
		Never hinged	14.50	
		On cover		95.00
		On cover, single franking		150.00
b.		Double surcharge	155.00	155.00
		Never hinged	235.00	
c.		Small and raised figure "3"	175.00	175.00
		Never hinged	270.00	
12	A20	4p on 85c vermilion, type 1 surcharge	3.50	3.00
		Never hinged	4.50	
		On cover		65.00
		On cover, single franking		70.00
b.		Type 2 surcharge	3.00	3.00
		Never hinged	4.50	
		On cover		35.00
		On cover, single franking		45.00
c.		As "b," inverted surcharge	47.50	47.50
		Never hinged	75.00	

13	A18	5p on 1fr cl & ol grn, type 1 surcharge	7.50	7.50
		Never hinged	10.00	
		On cover		70.00
		On cover, single franking		130.00
b.		Type 2 surcharge	11.00	11.00
		Never hinged		
c.		Type 2, ARABIC value omitted	62.50	62.50
		Never hinged	95.00	
14	A18	10p on 2fr org & pale bl, type 1 surcharge	11.00	11.00
		Never hinged	15.00	
		On cover		85.00
		On cover, single franking		145.00
b.		Surcharge type 2	70.00	70.00
		Never hinged	105.00	
		On cover		100.00
		On cover, single franking		175.00
15	A18	25p on 5fr bl & buff, type 1	14.00	14.00
		Never hinged	19.00	
		On cover		80.00
		On cover, single franking		160.00
b.		Surcharged Type 2	25.00	20.00
		Never hinged	37.50	
		On cover		110.00
		On cover, single franking		225.00
		Nos. 1-15 (15)	115.00	99.75

For overprints, see Nos. C1-C4.

Same Surcharges on Pasteur Stamps of France

16	A23	50c on 10c green	3.00	3.00
		Never hinged	4.50	
		On cover		30.00
17	A23	75c on 15c green	3.75	3.75
		Never hinged	5.50	
		On cover		37.50
18	A23	1.50p on 30c red	3.00	3.00
		Never hinged	4.50	
		On cover		25.00
19	A23	2p on 45c red	3.75	3.75
		Never hinged	5.50	
		On cover		37.50
		On cover, single franking		50.00
b.		Arabic inscription in surcharge inverted	47.50	47.50
		Never hinged	72.50	
20	A23	2.50p on 50c blue	5.25	5.25
		Never hinged	7.00	
		On cover		37.50
		On cover, single franking		62.50
21	A23	4p on 75c blue, type 1	9.00	9.00
		Never hinged	13.00	
		On cover		50.00
		On cover, single franking		80.00
b.		Surcharge type 2	7.00	7.00
		Never hinged	10.50	
		On cover		55.00
		On cover, single franking		100.00
		Nos. 16-21 (6)	27.75	27.75

Inverted Surcharges

1a	A16	10c on 2c vio brn	32.50
		Never hinged	50.00
2a	A22	25c on 5c orange	32.50
		Never hinged	50.00
3a	A20	75c on 15c gray grn	40.00
		Never hinged	60.00
4a	A22	1p on 20c red brn	32.50
		Never hinged	50.00
5a	A22	1.25p on 25c blue	32.50
		Never hinged	50.00
6a	A22	1.50p on 30c red	47.50
		Never hinged	75.00
7a	A22	2p on 35c violet	47.50
		Never hinged	75.00
8a	A18	2p on 40c red & pale bl	47.50
		Never hinged	75.00
9a	A18	2p on 45c grn & bl	47.50
		Never hinged	75.00
10a	A18	3p on 60c vio & ultra	45.00
		Never hinged	75.00
11a	A20	3p on 60c lt vio	47.50
		Never hinged	75.00
12a	A20	4p on 85c vermilion	37.50
		Never hinged	57.50
13a	A18	5p on 1fr cl & ol grn	47.50
		Never hinged	57.50
14a	A18	10p on 2fr org & pale bl	37.50
		Never hinged	75.00
15a	A18	25p on 5fr bl & buff	37.50
		Never hinged	75.00
16a	A23	50c on 10c green	30.00
		Never hinged	45.00
17a	A23	75c on 15c green	37.50
		Never hinged	45.00
18a	A23	1.50p on 30c red	45.00
		Never hinged	77.50
19a	A23	2p on 45c red	35.00
		Never hinged	57.50
20a	A23	2.50p on 50c blue	30.00
		Never hinged	45.00
21a	A23	4p on 75c blue	35.00
		Never hinged	50.00

Stamps of Syria, 1925, Overprinted in Red, Black or Blue

On A3, A5

On A4

1925, Mar. 1   Perf. 12½, 13½

25	A3	10c dk violet (R)	1.50	2.25
		Never hinged	2.25	
		On cover		20.00
a.		Double overprint	42.50	42.50
		Never hinged	65.00	
b.		Inverted overprint	35.00	
		Never hinged	57.50	
c.		Black overprint	37.50	37.50
		Never hinged	57.50	
d.		On Lebanon #50 (error)	125.00	
		Never hinged	150.00	
e.		"ALAOUITES," instead of "ALAOUITES"	30.00	30.00
		Never hinged	45.00	
f.		Surcharge on front and back	45.00	
		Never hinged	90.00	
g.		Pair, one without overprint	175.00	
26	A4	25c olive black (R)	2.25	3.00
		Never hinged	3.00	
		On cover		19.00
a.		Inverted overprint	40.00	
		Never hinged	60.00	
b.		Blue overprint	50.00	50.00
		Never hinged	75.00	
c.		Red overprint	50.00	50.00
		Never hinged	75.00	
d.		"ALAOUITE," instead of "ALAOUITES"	50.00	50.00
		Never hinged	75.00	
e.		Double overprint	50.00	50.00
		Never hinged	75.00	
f.		Pair, one without overprint	275.00	
27	A4	50c yellow green	1.75	1.75
		Never hinged	3.00	
		On cover		15.00
a.		Inverted overprint	40.00	40.00
		Never hinged	60.00	
b.		Blue overprint	50.00	50.00
		Never hinged	75.00	
c.		Red overprint	50.00	50.00
		Never hinged	75.00	
d.		"ALAOUITE," instead of "ALAOUITES"	50.00	50.00
		Never hinged	75.00	
e.		Double overprint	50.00	50.00
		Never hinged	75.00	
f.		Pair, one without overprint	275.00	
28	A4	75c brown orange	2.00	2.25
		Never hinged	3.00	
		On cover		15.00
a.		Inverted overprint	45.00	60.00
		Never hinged	67.50	
b.		Double overprint	47.50	65.00
		Never hinged	72.50	
29	A5	1p magenta	2.75	2.75
		Never hinged	4.25	
		On cover		19.00
a.		Inverted overprint	40.00	47.50
		Never hinged	60.00	
b.		"ALACUITES," instead of "ALAOUITES"	30.00	30.00
		Never hinged	45.00	
c.		"ALAOCITES," instead of "ALAOUITES"	35.00	45.00
		Never hinged	52.50	
d.		"ALAO ITES," instead of "ALAOUITES"	40.00	40.00
		Never hinged	45.00	
e.		"ALAOU ES," instead of "ALAOUITES"	60.00	45.00
		Never hinged	45.00	
f.		Double overprint, one inverted	70.00	
g.		Overprint vertical	120.00	
30	A4	1.25p deep green	3.25	3.50
		Never hinged	4.50	
		On cover		15.00
a.		Red overprint	50.00	50.00
		Never hinged	75.00	
b.		Double overprint		75.00
31	A4	1.50p rose red (Bl)	2.75	3.00
		Never hinged	4.25	
		On cover		15.00
a.		Inverted overprint	45.00	45.00
		Never hinged	67.50	
b.		Black overprint	40.00	40.00
		Never hinged	60.00	
c.		As "b," inverted	80.00	
		Never hinged	120.00	
32	A4	2p dk brown (R)	2.75	3.50
		Never hinged	4.25	
		On cover, single franking		19.00 / 25.00
a.		Blue overprint	65.00	65.00
		Never hinged	100.00	
b.		Inverted overprint	40.00	40.00
		Never hinged	60.00	
33	A4	2.50p pck blue (R)	4.00	4.50
		Never hinged	5.75	
		On cover, single franking		22.50 / 32.50
a.		Black overprint	65.00	65.00
		Never hinged	100.00	
b.		Blue overprint	70.00	70.00
		Never hinged	105.00	
c.		Double overprint		90.00
34	A4	3p orange brown	2.50	2.75
		Never hinged	3.50	
		On cover, single franking		22.50 / 37.50
a.		Inverted overprint	40.00	40.00
		Never hinged	60.00	
b.		Blue overprint	70.00	70.00
		Never hinged	105.00	
c.		Double overprint		90.00
35	A4	5p violet	3.50	4.00
		Never hinged	5.50	
		On cover, single franking		25.00 / 45.00
a.		Red overprint	70.00	70.00
		Never hinged	105.00	
b.		Inverted overprint	42.50	
		Never hinged	65.00	
c.		On Lebanon #60 (error)	175.00	
		Never hinged	200.00	
d.		Surcharge on front and back	40.00	
		Never hinged	60.00	
36	A4	10p violet brown	5.00	6.00
		Never hinged	6.50	
		On cover, single franking		32.50 / 50.00
37	A4	25p ultra (R)	8.00	10.00
		Never hinged	9.00	
		On cover, single franking		37.50 / 95.00
		Nos. 25-37 (13)	42.00	49.25

For overprints see Nos. C5-C19.

Stamps of Syria, 1925, Surcharged in Black or Red

Nos. 38-42

Nos. 43-45

1926

38	A4	3.50p on 75c brn org	2.50	2.75
		Never hinged	3.50	
		On cover		19.00
a.		Surcharged on face and back	22.50	22.50
		Never hinged	35.00	
39	A4	4p on 25c ol blk, type 1 (R)	2.50	2.50
		Never hinged	3.75	
		On cover		19.00
a.		Type 2 surcharge	70.00	70.00
		Never hinged	105.00	
				175.00
b.		As "a," inverted surcharge	105.00	105.00
		Never hinged	160.00	
40	A4	6p on 2.50p pck bl (R)	3.00	3.25
		Never hinged	3.75	
		On cover		25.00
41	A4	12p on 1.25p dp grn	3.25	3.50
		Never hinged	4.00	
		On cover		32.50
a.		Inverted surcharge	35.00	35.00
		Never hinged	55.00	
42	A4	20p on 1.25p dp grn	5.25	5.25
		Never hinged	7.25	
		On cover		62.50
43	A4	4.50p on 75c brn org	5.25	3.25
		Never hinged	7.25	
		On cover		25.00
a.		Inverted surcharge	60.00	60.00
		Never hinged	90.00	
b.		Double surcharge	55.00	55.00
		Never hinged	87.50	
44	A4	7.50p on 2.50p pck bl	4.75	3.25
		Never hinged	6.75	
		On cover		25.00
45	A4	15p on 25p ultra	8.75	5.50
		Never hinged	16.00	
		On cover		45.00
		Nos. 38-45 (8)	35.25	29.25

For overprint see No. C21.

Syria No. 199 Ovptd. in Red like No. 25

1928

46	A3	5c on 10c dk violet	2.00	1.75
		Never hinged	5.00	
		On cover		19.00
a.		Double surcharge	40.00	
		Never hinged	60.00	

Syria Nos. 178 and 174 Surcharged like Nos. 43-45 in Red

47	A4	2p on 1.25p dp green	16.00	8.00
		Never hinged	32.50	
		On cover		62.50
a.		Double surcharge	60.00	
		Never hinged	90.00	
b.		Inverted surcharge	50.00	50.00
		Never hinged	90.00	
48	A4	4p on 25c olive black	11.00	6.50
		Never hinged	27.50	
		On cover		50.00
a.		Double surcharge	50.00	50.00
		Never hinged	75.00	
b.		Inverted surcharge	50.00	50.00
		Never hinged	75.00	

For overprint see No. C20.

49	A4	4p on 25c olive black	82.50	50.00
		Never hinged	150.00	
		On cover		—
a.		Double impression	150.00	
		Never hinged	225.00	
		Nos. 46-49 (4)	111.50	66.25

AIR POST STAMPS

Nos. 8, 10, 13 & 14 with Additional Ovpt. in Black

1925, Jan. 1 Unwmk. Perf. 14x13½

C1	A18	2p on 40c, type 1	30.00	30.00
		Never hinged	47.50	
		On cover		100.00
		On cover, single franking		110.00
a.		Inverted overprint	110.00	110.00
		Never hinged	165.00	
b.		on 40c, type 2	15.00	15.00
		Never hinged	22.50	
		On cover		75.00
		On cover, single franking		95.00
C2	A18	3p on 60c, type 1	20.00	17.50
		Never hinged	30.00	
		On cover		67.50
		On cover, single franking		80.00
a.		Inverted overprint	125.00	125.00
		Never hinged	190.00	
b.		on 60c, type 2	15.00	15.00
		Never hinged	26.00	
		On cover		77.50
		On cover, single franking		90.00
C3	A18	5p on 1fr, type 1	15.00	12.00
		Never hinged	22.50	
		On cover		75.00
		On cover, single franking		110.00
a.		Inverted overprint	37.50	37.50
		Never hinged	57.50	
b.		on 1fr, type 2	12.50	12.50
		Never hinged	26.00	
		On cover		100.00
		On cover, single franking		150.00
C4	A18	10p on 2fr, type 1	19.00	15.00
		Never hinged	30.00	
		On cover		60.00
		On cover, single franking		100.00
a.		Inverted overprint	35.00	35.00
		Never hinged	52.50	
b.		on 1fr, type 2	15.00	15.00
		Never hinged	26.00	
		On cover		115.00
		On cover, single franking		150.00
		Nos. C1-C4 (4)	84.00	74.50

Nos. 32, 34, 35 & 36 With Additional Ovpt. in Green

1925, Mar. 1 Perf. 13½

C5	A4	2p dark brown	6.00	5.00
		Never hinged	12.00	
		On cover		37.50
		On cover, single franking		50.00
a.		Inverted overprint	75.00	75.00
		Never hinged	115.00	
b.		Red overprint	125.00	
		Never hinged	190.00	
C6	A4	3p orange brown	6.00	5.00
		Never hinged	12.00	
		On cover		37.50
		On cover, single franking		55.00
a.		Inverted overprint	75.00	75.00
		Never hinged	110.00	
b.		Red overprint	100.00	
		Never hinged	150.00	
c.		On Lebanon #59 (error)	325.00	
		Never hinged	450.00	
C7	A4	5p violet	6.00	5.00
		Never hinged	12.00	
		On cover		42.50
		On cover, single franking		65.00
a.		Inverted overprint	75.00	75.00
		Never hinged	110.00	
b.		Red overprint	100.00	
		Never hinged	150.00	
C8	A4	10p violet brown	6.00	5.00
		Never hinged	12.00	
		On cover		50.00
		On cover, single franking		95.00
a.		Inverted overprint	75.00	75.00
		Never hinged	110.00	
b.		Red overprint	100.00	
		Never hinged	150.00	
		Nos. C5-C8 (4)	24.00	20.00

Nos. 32, 34, 35 & 36 With Additional Ovpt. in Red

1926, May 1

C9	A4	2p dark brown	6.50	6.50
		Never hinged	14.00	
		On cover		37.50
		On cover, single franking		50.00
a.		Red overprint double	175.00	175.00
		Never hinged	265.00	
b.		Black overprint double	175.00	175.00
		Never hinged	265.00	
c.		Black overprint inverted	70.00	70.00
		Never hinged	105.00	
C10	A4	3p orange brown	6.50	6.50
		Never hinged	14.00	
		On cover		37.50
		On cover, single franking		55.00
a.		Black overprint inverted	70.00	70.00
		Never hinged	105.00	

C11	A4	5p violet	7.50	7.50
		Never hinged	14.00	
		On cover		50.00
		On cover, single franking		75.00
a.		Black overprint inverted	70.00	70.00
		Never hinged	105.00	
C12	A4	10p violet brown	7.50	7.50
		Never hinged	14.00	
		On cover		55.00
		On cover, single franking		100.00
a.		Black overprint inverted	70.00	70.00
		Never hinged	105.00	
		Nos. C9-C12 (4)	28.00	28.00

No. C9 has the original overprint in black. The red plane overprint was also applied to Nos. C5-C8. These are believed to have been essays, and were not regularly issued.

Nos. 27c, 37 and Syria No. 177 With Addtl. Ovpt. of Airplane in Red or Black

1929, June-July

C17	A4	50c yel grn (R)	5.00	5.00
		Never hinged	11.50	
		On cover		17.50
a.		Plane overprint double	250.00	
		Never hinged	375.00	
b.		Plane ovpt. on face and	60.00	
		back Never hinged	95.00	
c.		Pair with plane overprint		
		Tête-bêche	325.00	
		Never hinged	490.00	
d.		Double overprint	225.00	225.00
		Never hinged	340.00	
e.		Overprint inverted	125.00	
		Never hinged	190.00	
f.		Plane only inverted	250.00	
		Never hinged	375.00	
g.		Red surcharge on Lebanon	200.00	
		#52 (error) Never hinged	250.00	
C18	A5	1p magenta (Bk)	9.00	9.00
		Never hinged	15.00	
		On cover		40.00
a.		Red overprint	50.00	
		Never hinged	75.00	
C19	A4	25p ultra (R)	52.50	40.00
		Never hinged	80.00	
		On cover		125.00
a.		Plane overprint inverted	125.00	125.00
		Never hinged	190.00	
b.		Surcharge double	150.00	150.00
		Never hinged	225.00	
		Nos. C17-C19 (3)	66.50	54.00

Nos. 28 and 30 exist with additional overprint of airplane in red. These stamps were never issued. Value, each $100.

Nos. 47 and 45 With Additional Ovpt. of Airplane in Red

1929-30

C20	A4	2p on 1.25p ('30)	7.25	7.25
		Never hinged	12.00	
		On cover		45.00
a.		Surcharge inverted	50.00	50.00
		Never hinged	75.00	
b.		Double surcharge	75.00	75.00
		Never hinged	110.00	
c.		Triple surcharge	175.00	
		Never hinged	265.00	
C21	A4	15p on 25p (Bk + R)	55.00	47.50
		Never hinged	90.00	
		On cover		110.00
a.		Plane overprint inverted	225.00	225.00
		Never hinged	275.00	

POSTAGE DUE STAMPS

Postage Due Stamps of France, 1893-1920, Surcharged Like No. 1 (Nos. J1-J2) or No. 7 (Nos. J3-J5)

1925 Unwmk. Perf. 14x13½

J1	D2	50c on 10c choc	8.50	8.50
		Never hinged	13.00	
		On cover		70.00
J2	D2	1p on 20c ol grn	8.50	8.50
		Never hinged	13.00	
		On cover		70.00
J3	D2	2p on 30c red	8.50	8.50
		Never hinged	13.00	
		On cover		80.00
J4	D2	3p on 50c vio brn	8.50	8.50
		Never hinged	13.00	
		On cover		95.00
J5	D2	5p on 1fr red brn,	8.50	8.50
		straw Never hinged	13.00	
		On cover		95.00
		Nos. J1-J5 (5)	42.50	42.50

Postage Due Stamps of Syria, 1925, Overprinted Like No. 26 (Type D5) or No. 25 (Type D6) in Black, Blue or Red

1925 Perf. 13½

J6	D5	50c brown, *yel*	5.00	5.00
		Never hinged	7.25	
		On cover		32.50
a.		Blue overprint	42.50	
		Never hinged	65.00	
b.		Red overprint	42.50	
		Never hinged	65.00	
c.		Overprint inverted	30.00	30.00
		Never hinged	45.00	
J7	D6	1p vio, *rose* (Bl)	4.50	4.50
		Never hinged	6.50	
		On cover		32.50
a.		Black overprint	150.00	150.00
		Never hinged	200.00	
b.		Double overprint (Bk + Bl)	175.00	175.00
		Never hinged	225.00	
c.		Overprint inverted	40.00	40.00
		Never hinged	60.00	
J8	D5	2p blk, *blue* (R)	6.00	6.00
		Never hinged	8.50	
		On cover		25.00
a.		Blue overprint	45.00	
		Never hinged	55.00	
J9	D5	3p blk, *red org*	8.00	8.00
		Never hinged	11.00	
		On cover		37.50
a.		Overprint inverted	30.00	
		Never hinged	45.00	
J10	D5	5p blk, *bl grn* (R)	10.00	10.00
		Never hinged	14.50	
		On cover		50.00
a.		Overprint inverted	30.00	30.00
		Never hinged	45.00	
b.		Black overprint	45.00	
		Never hinged	70.00	
		Nos. J6-J10 (5)	33.50	33.50

The stamps of Alaouites were superseded in 1930 by those of Latakia.

ALBANIA

al-'bā-nē-ə

LOCATION — Southeastern Europe
GOVT. — Monarchy
AREA — 11,101 sq. mi.
POP. — 1,003,124
CAPITAL — Tirana

After the outbreak of World War I, the country fell into a state of anarchy when the Prince and all members of the International Commission left Albania. Subsequently, General Ferrero, in command of Italian troops, declared Albania an independent country. A constitution was adopted and a republican form of government was instituted, which continued until 1928 when, by constitutional amendment, Albania was declared to be a monarchy. The President of the republic, Ahmed Zogu, became king of the new state. Many unlisted varieties or surcharges and lithographed labels are said to have done postal duty in Albania and Epirus during this unsettled period.

On April 7, 1939, Italy invaded Albania. King Zog fled but did not abdicate. The king of Italy acquired the crown.

40 Paras = 1 Piaster = 1 Grossion
100 Centimes = 1 Franc (1917)
100 Qintar = 1 Franc

AUSTRIAN POST IN ALBANIA

The Austrian Empire maintained post offices in various coastal towns in Albania beginning in 1854, in conjunction with the operations of the Austrian Lloyd shipping line. The nine offices, with opening and closing dates, are listed in the table below. Since Italian was the official operational language, the names are shown in Italian with the modern equivalent in parentheses.

Post Office	Open	Close
Antivari (Bar)	1854	1878
Durazzo (Durres)	1854	1915
Janina (Ioannina)	1857	1914
Prevesa (Preveza)	1854	1914
Santi Quaranta (Sarande)	1870	1915
Sajada (Sayiadha)	1858	1912
San Giovanni Di Medua (Shengjin)	1879	1915
Scutari (Shkoder)	1901	1915
Valona (Vlore)	1854	1915

Values in the first column for Nos. 2A1-2A353 are for stamps without defects tied to piece with legible partial strikes of town cancellations; values in the second column are for stamps without defects tied to cover by complete strikes of town cancellations. Stamps with legible town cancellations off cover sell for 25-50% of the on-piece value.

Issue dates refer to dates of stamps' issue, not necessarily to their usage with specific Albanian postal markings.

ANTIVARI

Stamps of Lombardy-Venetia
Canceled in black with single circle date stamp with post office name, month and date, without year

1863				**Perf. 14**
2A1		2s yellow (#15)	575.00	2,000.
2A2		3s green (#16)	525.00	2,200.
2A3		5s rose (#17)	525.00	2,000.
2A4		10s blue (#18)	500.00	1,750.
2A5		15s yel brn (#19)	575.00	1,850.
1864-65				**Perf. 9½**
2A6		2s yellow (#20)	450.00	1,500.
2A7		3s green (#21)	200.00	850.00
2A8		5s rose (#22)	150.00	700.00
2A9		10s blue (#23)	125.00	500.00
2A10		15s yel brn (#24)	160.00	600.00

Stamps of Austrian Offices in the Turkish Empire
Canceled in black or red brown with single circle date stamp with post office name, month and date, without year

1867-83				**Coarse Print**
2A11		2s yellow (#1)	87.50	650.00
2A12		3s green (#2)	110.00	600.00
2A13		5s red (#3)	75.00	350.00
2A14		10s blue (#4)	70.00	300.00
2A15		15s brown (#5)	75.00	300.00
2A16		25s gray lilac (#6)	100.00	900.00
2A17		50s brown (#7)	110.00	4,000.
				Fine Print
2A18		2s yellow (#7C)	1,200.	—
2A19		3s green (#7D)	85.00	475.00
2A20		5s red (#7E)	82.50	350.00
2A21		10s blue (#7F)	70.00	290.00
2A22		15s org brown (#7I)	175.00	975.00
2A23		25s gray lilac (#7J)	300.00	5,250.

Stamps of Lombardy-Venetia
Canceled in blue with single circle date stamp with post office name, month and date, without year

1863				**Perf. 14**
2A24		2s yellow (#15)	800.00	2,750.
2A25		3s green (#16)	750.00	2,850.
2A26		5s rose (#17)	750.00	1,650.
2A27		10s blue (#18)	700.00	2,400.
2A28		15s yel brn (#19)	800.00	2,500.
1864-65				**Perf. 9½**
2A29		2s yellow (#20)	525.00	1,650.
2A30		3s green (#21)	275.00	1,050.
2A31		5s rose (#22)	150.00	700.00
2A32		10s blue (#23)	190.00	675.00
2A33		15s yel brn (#24)	225.00	800.00

Stamps of Austrian Offices in the Turkish Empire
Canceled in blue with single circle date stamp with post office name, month and date, without year

1867-83				**Coarse Print**
2A34		2s yellow (#1)	125.00	825.00
2A35		3s green (#2)	150.00	750.00
2A36		5s red (#3)	120.00	500.00
2A37		10s blue (#4)	115.00	450.00
2A38		15s brown (#5)	120.00	475.00
2A39		25s gray lilac (#6)	145.00	1,100.
2A40		50s brown (#7)	150.00	4,250.
				Fine Print
2A41		2s yellow (#7C)	1,250.	—
2A42		3s green (#7D)	125.00	625.00
2A43		5s red (#7E)	125.00	525.00
2A44		10s blue (#7F)	115.00	450.00
2A45		15s org brown (#7I)	225.00	1,125.
2A46		25s gray lilac (#7J)	350.00	5,500.

Stamps of Austria
Canceled in blue with single circle date stamp with post office name, month and date, without year

1863-64			
2A47	2kr yellow (#22)	*1,150.*	—
2A48	3kr green (#23)	*1,150.*	—
2A49	5kr red (#24)	*1,150.*	—
2A50	10kr blue (#25)	*1,150.*	—
2A51	15kr yel brown (#26)	*1,150.*	—

DURAZZO
Stamps of Lombardy-Venetia
Canceled in black with single circle date stamp with post office name, month and date, without year

1863			*Perf. 14*
2A52	2s yellow (#15)	350.00	1,250.
2A53	3s green (#16)	300.00	1,350.
2A54	5s rose (#17)	300.00	1,100.
2A55	10s blue (#18)	250.00	850.00
2A56	15s yel brn (#19)	325.00	1,000.
1864-65			*Perf. 9½*
2A57	2s yellow (#20)	425.00	1,275.
2A58	3s green (#21)	160.00	675.00
2A59	5s rose (#22)	110.00	525.00
2A60	10s blue (#23)	85.00	325.00
2A61	15s yel brn (#24)	115.00	450.00

Stamps of Austrian Offices in the Turkish Empire
Canceled in black or red brown with single circle date stamp with post office name, month and date, without year

1867-83			*Coarse Print*
2A62	2s yellow (#1)	87.50	650.00
2A63	3s green (#2)	110.00	600.00
2A64	5s red (#3)	75.00	350.00
2A65	10s blue (#4)	70.00	300.00
2A66	15s brown (#5)	75.00	300.00
2A67	25s gray lilac (#6)	100.00	900.00
2A68	50s brown (#7)	110.00	4,000.
Fine Print			
2A69	2s yellow (#7C)	1,200.	—
2A70	3s green (#7D)	85.00	475.00
2A71	5s red (#7E)	82.50	350.00
2A72	10s blue (#7F)	70.00	290.00
2A73	15s org brown (#7I)	175.00	975.00
2A74	25s gray lilac (#7J)	300.00	5,250.

Stamps of Lombardy-Venetia
Canceled in blue with single circle date stamp with post office name, month and date, without year

1863			*Perf. 14*
2A75	2s yellow (#15)	*1,300.*	*4,500.*
2A76	3s green (#16)	*1,250.*	*4,500.*
2A77	5s rose (#17)	*1,250.*	*4,250.*
2A78	10s blue (#18)	*1,200.*	*4,000.*
2A79	15s yel brn (#19)	*1,300.*	*4,100.*
1864-65			*Perf. 9½*
2A80	2s yellow (#20)	625.00	*1,950.*
2A81	3s green (#21)	375.00	*1,350.*
2A82	5s rose (#22)	325.00	*1,200.*
2A83	10s blue (#23)	300.00	*1,000.*
2A84	15s yel brn (#24)	325.00	*1,100.*

Stamps of Austrian Offices in the Turkish Empire
Canceled in blue with single circle date stamp with post office name, month and date, without year

1867-83			*Coarse Print*
2A85	2s yellow (#1)	125.00	825.00
2A86	3s green (#2)	150.00	750.00
2A87	5s red (#3)	120.00	500.00
2A88	10s blue (#4)	115.00	450.00
2A89	15s brown (#5)	120.00	475.00
2A90	25s gray lilac (#6)	145.00	1,100.
2A91	50s brown (#7)	150.00	4,250.
Fine Print			
2A92	2s yellow (#7C)	1,250.	—
2A93	3s green (#7D)	125.00	625.00
2A94	5s red (#7E)	125.00	525.00
2A95	10s blue (#7F)	115.00	450.00
2A96	15s org brown (#7I)	225.00	1,125.
2A97	25s gray lilac (#7J)	350.00	5,500.

Stamps of Austrian Offices in the Turkish Empire
Canceled in black with "thimble" (diameter 20mm or less) circular date stamp with post office name and date

1867-83			*Coarse Print*
2A99	2s yellow (#1)	200.00	1,000.
2A100	3s green (#2)	215.00	950.00
2A101	5s red (#3)	185.00	700.00
2A102	10s blue (#4)	175.00	650.00
2A103	15s brown (#5)	175.00	650.00
2A104	25s gray lilac (#6)	200.00	1,250.
2A105	50s brown (#7)	215.00	4,400.

Fine Print			
2A106	2s yellow (#7C)	1,300.	
2A107	3s green (#7D)	200.00	825.00
2A108	5s red (#7E)	190.00	700.00
2A109	10s blue (#7F)	175.00	650.00
2A110	15s org brown (#7I)	290.00	1,325.
2A111	25s gray lilac (#7J)	400.00	6,750.

Use of this cancellation is known beginning in 1877.

Stamps of Austrian Offices in the Turkish Empire
Canceled in blue with "thimble" (diameter 20mm or less) circular date stamp with post office name and date

1867-83			*Coarse Print*
2A112	2s yellow (#1)	300.00	1,325.
2A113	3s green (#2)	325.00	1,250.
2A114	5s red (#3)	285.00	1,000.
2A115	10s blue (#4)	275.00	950.00
2A116	15s brown (#5)	280.00	975.00
2A117	25s gray lilac (#6)	300.00	1,575.
2A118	50s brown (#7)	325.00	4,750.
Fine Print			
2A119	2s yellow (#7C)	1,400.	
2A120	3s green (#7D)	300.00	1,125.
2A121	5s red (#7E)	285.00	1,000.
2A122	10s blue (#7F)	275.00	950.00
2A123	15s org brown (#7I)	385.00	1,625.
2A124	25s gray lilac (#7J)	500.00	6,000.

Use of this cancellation is known beginning in 1872.
Austrian Offices in Turkish Empire issues canceled in black with circular Durazzo date stamp with post office name, month, date and year date exist but are very rare.

JANINA
Stamps of Lombardy-Venetia
Canceled in black with single circle date stamp with post office name, month and date, without year

1863			*Perf. 14*
2A126	2s yellow (#15)	240.00	1,000.
2A127	3s green (#16)	200.00	1,200.
2A128	5s rose (#17)	200.00	900.00
2A129	10s blue (#18)	160.00	625.00
2A130	15s yel brn (#19)	225.00	725.00
1864-65			*Perf. 9½*
2A131	2s yellow (#20)	375.00	1,150.
2A132	3s green (#21)	125.00	550.00
2A133	5s rose (#22)	80.00	400.00
2A134	10s blue (#23)	50.00	200.00
2A135	15s yel brn (#24)	85.00	325.00

Stamps of Austrian Offices in the Turkish Empire
Canceled in black or red brown with single circle date stamp with post office name, month and date, without year

1867-83			*Coarse Print*
2A136	2s yellow (#1)	57.50	525.00
2A137	3s green (#2)	75.00	475.00
2A138	5s red (#3)	47.50	215.00
2A139	10s blue (#4)	40.00	165.00
2A140	15s brown (#5)	42.50	175.00
2A141	25s gray lilac (#6)	67.50	775.00
2A142	50s brown (#7)	75.00	4,000.
Fine Print			
2A143	2s yellow (#7C)	1,175.	
2A144	3s green (#7D)	55.00	350.00
2A145	5s red (#7E)	50.00	225.00
2A146	10s blue (#7F)	40.00	165.00
2A147	15s org brown (#7I)	150.00	850.00
2A148	25s gray lilac (#7J)	275.00	5,250.

Stamps of Austria
Canceled in black or red brown with single circle date stamp with post office name, month and date, without year

1867-83			*Coarse Print*
2A149	2kr yellow (#27)	625.00	
2A150	3kr green (#28)	625.00	—
2A151	5kr red (#29)	625.00	—
2A152	10kr blue (#30)	625.00	2,250.
2A153	15kr brown (#31)	625.00	2,250.
2A154	25kr gray lilac (#32)	625.00	—
2A155	50kr brown (#33)	700.00	—
Fine Print			
2A156	2kr yellow (#34)	625.00	—
2A157	3kr green (#35)	625.00	—
2A158	5kr red (#36)	625.00	—
2A159	10kr blue (#37)	625.00	2,250.
2A160	15kr org brown (#38)	625.00	2,250.
2A161	25kr gray (#39)	725.00	
2A162	50kr brown (#40)	750.00	

Stamps of Austrian Offices in the Turkish Empire
Canceled in black with circular date stamp with post office name, month and date, with year date

1867-83			*Coarse Print*
2A163	2s yellow (#1)	57.50	525.00
2A164	3s green (#2)	75.00	475.00
2A165	5s red (#3)	47.50	215.00
2A166	10s blue (#4)	40.00	165.00
2A167	15s brown (#5)	42.50	175.00
2A168	25s gray lilac (#6)	67.50	775.00
2A169	50s brown (#7)	75.00	4,000.
Fine Print			
2A170	2s yellow (#7C)	1,175.	—
2A171	3s green (#7D)	55.00	350.00
2A172	5s red (#7E)	50.00	225.00
2A173	10s blue (#7F)	40.00	165.00
2A174	15s org brown (#7I)	150.00	850.00
2A175	25s gray lilac (#7J)	275.00	5,250.

Use of this cancellation is known beginning in 1880.

PREVESA
Stamps of Lombardy-Venetia
Canceled in black with single circle date stamp with post office name, month and date, without year

1863			*Perf. 14*
2A176	2s yellow (#15)	275.00	1,000.
2A177	3s green (#16)	225.00	1,150.
2A178	5s rose (#17)	225.00	900.00
2A179	10s blue (#18)	200.00	675.00
2A180	15s yel brn (#19)	275.00	800.00
1864-65			*Perf. 9½*
2A181	2s yellow (#20)	375.00	1,150.
2A182	3s green (#21)	125.00	550.00
2A183	5s rose (#22)	80.00	400.00
2A184	10s blue (#23)	50.00	200.00
2A185	15s yel brn (#24)	85.00	325.00

Stamps of Austrian Offices in the Turkish Empire
Canceled in black with single circle date stamp with post office name, month and date, without year

1867-83			*Coarse Print*
2A186	2s yellow (#1)	37.50	450.00
2A187	3s green (#2)	57.50	400.00
2A188	5s red (#3)	27.50	140.00
2A189	10s blue (#4)	20.00	92.50
2A190	15s brown (#5)	24.00	145.00
2A191	25s gray lilac (#6)	50.00	700.00
2A192	50s brown (#7)	57.50	3,850.
Fine Print			
2A193	2s yellow (#7C)	1,150.	—
2A194	3s green (#7D)	35.00	275.00
2A195	5s red (#7E)	32.50	150.00
2A196	10s blue (#7F)	20.00	87.50
2A197	15s org brown (#7I)	135.00	775.00
2A198	25s gray lilac (#7J)	250.00	5,000.

Stamps of Lombardy-Venetia
Canceled in blue with single circle date stamp with post office name, month and date, without year

1863			*Perf. 14*
2A199	2s yellow (#15)	575.00	2,000.
2A200	3s green (#16)	525.00	2,200.
2A201	5s rose (#17)	525.00	2,000.
2A202	10s blue (#18)	500.00	1,750.
2A203	15s yel brn (#19)	575.00	1,850.
1864-65			*Perf. 9½*
2A204	2s yellow (#20)	525.00	1,650.
2A205	3s green (#21)	275.00	1,050.
2A206	5s rose (#22)	220.00	875.00
2A207	10s blue (#23)	190.00	675.00
2A208	15s yel brn (#24)	225.00	800.00

Stamps of Austrian Offices in the Turkish Empire
Canceled in black with circular date stamp with post office name, month and date, with year date

1867-83			*Coarse Print*
2A209	2s yellow (#1)	57.50	525.00
2A210	3s green (#2)	75.00	475.00
2A211	5s red (#3)	47.50	215.00
2A212	10s blue (#4)	40.00	165.00
2A213	15s brown (#5)	42.50	175.00
2A214	25s gray lilac (#6)	67.50	775.00
2A215	50s brown (#7)	75.00	4,000.
Fine Print			
2A216	2s yellow (#7C)	1,175.	
2A217	3s green (#7D)	55.00	340.00
2A218	5s red (#7E)	50.00	225.00
2A219	10s blue (#7F)	40.00	165.00
2A220	15s org brown (#7I)	150.00	850.00
2A221	25s gray lilac (#7J)	275.00	5,250.

Use of this cancellation is known beginning in 1874.

DULCIGNO / S. GIOVANNI DI MEDUA
Stamps of Austrian Offices in the Turkish Empire
Canceled in black with circular date stamp with post office name, month and date, with year date

1867-83			*Coarse Print*
2A222	2s yellow (#1)	650.00	2,500.
2A223	3s green (#2)	675.00	2,450.
2A224	5s red (#3)	640.00	2,200.
2A225	10s blue (#4)	40.00	165.00
2A226	15s brown (#5)	625.00	2,150.
2A227	25s gray lilac (#6)	650.00	2,750.
2A228	50s brown (#7)	675.00	5,750.
Fine Print			
2A229	2s yellow (#7C)	1,750.	
2A230	3s green (#7D)	650.00	2,350.
2A231	5s red (#7E)	640.00	2,200.
2A232	10s blue (#7F)	625.00	2,150.
2A233	15s org brown (#7I)	725.00	2,800.
2A234	25s gray lilac (#7J)	850.00	7,250.

Stamps of Austrian Offices in the Turkish Empire
Canceled in blue with circular date stamp with post office name, month and date, with year date

1867-83			*Coarse Print*
2A235	2s yellow (#1)	1,150.	4,250.
2A236	3s green (#2)	1,150.	4,000.
2A237	5s red (#3)	1,150.	3,900.
2A238	10s blue (#4)	1,150.	3,800.
2A239	15s brown (#5)	1,150.	3,750.
2A240	25s gray lilac (#6)	1,150.	4,375.
2A241	50s brown (#7)	1,200.	7,500.
Fine Print			
2A242	2s yellow (#7C)	2,250.	
2A243	3s green (#7D)	1,100.	4,000.
2A244	5s red (#7E)	1,150.	3,900.
2A245	10s blue (#7F)	1,150.	3,800.
2A246	15s org brown (#7I)	1,250.	4,400.
2A247	25s gray lilac (#7J)	1,350.	8,750.

SAN GIOVANNI DI MEDUA
Stamps of Austrian Offices in the Turkish Empire
Canceled in black with circular date stamp with post office name, month and date, with year date

1867-83			*Coarse Print*
2A248	2s yellow (#1)	440.00	1,825.
2A249	3s green (#2)	450.00	1,750.
2A250	5s red (#3)	425.00	1,500.
2A251	10s blue (#4)	415.00	1,450.
2A252	15s brown (#5)	420.00	1,475.
2A253	25s gray lilac (#6)	450.00	2,100.
2A254	50s brown (#7)	450.00	5,250.
Fine Print			
2A255	2s yellow (#7C)	1,400.	
2A256	3s green (#7D)	300.00	1,625.
2A257	5s red (#7E)	285.00	1,500.
2A258	10s blue (#7F)	275.00	1,450.
2A259	15s org brown (#7I)	385.00	2,150.
2A260	25s gray lilac (#7J)	500.00	6,500.

Use of this cancellation is known beginning in March, 1881.

SANTI QUARANTA
Stamps of Austrian Offices in the Turkish Empire
Canceled in black with circular date stamp with post office name, month and date, with year date

1867-83			*Coarse Print*
2A261	2s yellow (#1)	200.00	1,000.
2A262	3s green (#2)	215.00	950.00
2A263	5s red (#3)	185.00	700.00
2A264	10s blue (#4)	175.00	650.00
2A265	15s brown (#5)	180.00	650.00
2A266	25s gray lilac (#6)	200.00	1,250.
2A267	50s brown (#7)	215.00	
Fine Print			
2A268	2s yellow (#7C)	1,300.	
2A269	3s green (#7D)	200.00	825.00
2A270	5s red (#7E)	190.00	700.00
2A271	10s blue (#7F)	175.00	650.00
2A272	15s org brown (#7I)	290.00	1,325.
2A273	25s gray lilac (#7J)	400.00	5,750.

Use of this cancellation is known beginning in March 28, 1870.

Stamps of Austrian Offices in the Turkish Empire
Canceled in black with 23mm circular date stamp with post office name, month and date, with year date

1867-83			*Coarse Print*
2A274	2s yellow (#1)	300.00	1,325.
2A275	3s green (#2)	325.00	1,250.
2A276	5s red (#3)	285.00	1,000.
2A277	10s blue (#4)	275.00	950.00

2A278	15s brown (#5)	280.00	975.00
2A279	25s gray lilac (#6)	300.00	1,575.
2A280	50s brown (#7)	325.00	—

Fine Print

2A281	2s yellow (#7C)	1,400.	—
2A282	3s green (#7D)	300.00	1,125.
2A283	5s red (#7E)	285.00	1,000.
2A284	10s blue (#7F)	275.00	950.00
2A285	15s org brown (#7I)	385.00	1,625.
2A286	25s gray lilac (#7J)	500.00	6,000.

Use of this cancellation is known beginning in November, 1878.

SCUTARI D'ALBANIA
Stamps of Lombardy-Venetia
Canceled in black with "thimble" (diameter 20mm or less) circular date stamp with post office name and date

1864-65			Perf. 9½
2A287	2s yellow (#20)		
2A288	3s green (#21)		
2A289	5s rose (#22)	3,000.	—
2A290	10s blue (#23)	3,000.	11,500.
2A291	15s yel brn (#24)	3,000.	—

Stamps of Austrian Offices in the Turkish Empire
Canceled in black with "thimble" circular date stamp with post office name and date

1867-83		Coarse Print	
2A292	2s yellow (#1)	1,700.	—
2A293	3s green (#2)	1,750.	—
2A294	5s red (#3)	1,700.	—
2A295	10s blue (#4)	1,700.	6,250.
2A296	15s brown (#5)	1,700.	—
2A297	25s gray lilac (#6)	1,700.	—
2A298	50s brown (#7)	1,750.	—

Fine Print

2A299	2s yellow (#7C)	2,800.	—
2A300	3s green (#7D)	1,700.	—
2A301	5s red (#7E)	1,700.	—
2A302	10s blue (#7F)	1,700.	6,250.
2A303	15s org brown (#7I)	1,800.	—
2A304	25s gray lilac (#7J)	1,950.	—

Also known on Ottoman stamps, and on covers franked with Ottoman stamps.

VALONA
Stamps of Lombardy-Venetia
Canceled in black with single circle date stamp with post office name, month and date, without year

1863			Perf. 14
2A305	2s yellow (#15)	800.00	2,750.
2A306	3s green (#16)	750.00	2,850.
2A307	5s rose (#17)	750.00	1,650.
2A308	10s blue (#18)	700.00	2,400.
2A309	15s yel brn (#19)	800.00	2,500.

1864-65			Perf. 9½
2A310	2s yellow (#20)	625.00	1,950.
2A311	3s green (#21)	375.00	1,350.
2A312	5s rose (#22)	325.00	1,200.
2A313	10s blue (#23)	300.00	1,000.
2A314	15s yel brn (#24)	325.00	1,100.

Stamps of Austrian Offices in the Turkish Empire
Canceled in black or red brown with single circle date stamp with post office name, month and date, without year

1867-83		Coarse Print	
2A315	2s yellow (#1)	87.50	650.00
2A316	3s green (#2)	110.00	600.00
2A317	5s red (#3)	77.50	340.00
2A318	10s blue (#4)	70.00	300.00
2A319	15s brown (#5)	75.00	300.00
2A320	25s gray lilac (#6)	100.00	900.00
2A321	50s brown (#7)	110.00	4,000.

Fine Print

2A322	2s yellow (#7C)	1,200.	—
2A323	3s green (#7D)	85.00	475.00
2A324	5s red (#7E)	82.50	350.00
2A325	10s blue (#7F)	70.00	290.00
2A326	15s org brown (#7I)	180.00	975.00
2A327	25s gray lilac (#7J)	300.00	5,250.

Stamps of Austrian Offices in the Turkish Empire
Canceled in blue with single circle date stamp with post office name, month and date, without year

1867-83		Coarse Print	
2A328	2s yellow (#1)	125.00	825.00
2A329	3s green (#2)	150.00	750.00
2A330	5s red (#3)	120.00	500.00
2A331	10s blue (#4)	115.00	450.00
2A332	15s brown (#5)	120.00	475.00
2A333	25s gray lilac (#6)	145.00	1,100.
2A334	50s brown (#7)	150.00	4,250.

Fine Print

2A335	2s yellow (#7C)	1,250.	—
2A336	3s green (#7D)	125.00	625.00
2A337	5s red (#7E)	125.00	525.00
2A338	10s blue (#7F)	115.00	450.00
2A339	15s org brown (#7I)	225.00	1,125.
2A340	25s gray lilac (#7J)	350.00	5,500.

Stamps of Austrian Offices in the Turkish Empire
Canceled in black with circular date stamp with post office name, month and date, with year date

1867-83		Coarse Print	
2A341	2s yellow (#1)	57.50	525.00
2A342	3s green (#2)	75.00	475.00
2A343	5s red (#3)	47.50	215.00
2A344	10s blue (#4)	40.00	165.00
2A345	15s brown (#5)	42.50	175.00
2A346	25s gray lilac (#6)	67.50	775.00
2A347	50s brown (#7)	75.00	4,000.

Fine Print

2A348	2s yellow (#7C)	1,175.	—
2A349	3s green (#7D)	55.00	340.00
2A350	5s red (#7E)	50.00	225.00
2A351	10s blue (#7F)	40.00	165.00
2A352	15s org brown (#7I)	150.00	850.00
2A353	25s gray lilac (#7J)	275.00	5,250.

GREEK CONSULAR POST IN EPIRUS
The Greek Postal Administration maintained facilities within the consular office at Ioannina, and in the postal agencies at Arta and Preveza.

Post Office	Open	Close
Arta (105)	1852	1881
Ioannina (99)	1852	1881
Preveza (104)	1853	1881

The post office of Arta became a regular Greek post office after annexation of that city on June 24, 1881.

Additional premiums for stamps of Greece with postmarks of the consular office in Epirus. The first column contains values for single stamps or for single stamps on piece; the second, for stamps on cover.

Rhombus of Dots with Numeral

Numeral 99	+25.	+150.
Numeral 104	+650.	+2,000.
Numeral 105	+275.	—

Circular Datestamps

Ioannina	+80.	+375.
Preveza	+800.	—
Arta (105) (until 6/23/81)	+80.	+375.
Arta (105) (after 6/24/81)	+20.	+150.

Greece annexed Arta on June 24, 1881. Greek stamps used from that date on are not "Used in Albania."

Watermarks

Wmk. 125 — Lozenges

Wmk. 220 — Double Headed Eagle

Issues of 1908 Turkey Stamps Handstamped

Perf. 12, 13½ and Compound
1913, June		Unwmk.
1	A19 2½pi violet brown	750.00 650.00

With Additional Overprint in Carmine

| 2 | A19 10pa blue green | 675.00 | 650.00 |

Handstamped on Issue of 1909

4	A21	5pa ocher	450.00	450.00
5	A21	10pa blue green	350.00	225.00
6	A21	20pa car rose	350.00	250.00
7	A21	1pi ultra	325.00	250.00
	On newspaper or wrapper		450.00
8	A21	2pi blue black	500.00	450.00
10	A21	5pi dark violet	1,400.	1,500.
11	A21	1pi dull red	5,000.	4,750.

For surcharge see No. 19.
Additional values of 25pi dark green and 50pi red brown were overprinted and sold only to dealers. Values, 25pi $8,000, 50pi $16,000.

With Additional Overprint in Blue or Carmine

13A	A21	10pa blue green	900.00	850.00
14	A21	20pa car rose		
		(Bl)	800.00	850.00
15	A21	1pi brt blue (C)	1,900.	1,750.

Handstamped on Newspaper Stamp of 1911

| 17 | A21 2pa olive green | 425.00 | 425.00 |

Handstamped on Postage Due Stamp of 1908

| 18 | A19 1pi black, dp | | |
| | rose | 3,000. | 2,500. |

No. 18 was used for regular postage.

No. 6 Surcharged With New Value

| 19 | A21 10pa on 20pa | | |
| | car rose | 1,250. | 1,250. |

The overprint on Nos. 1-19 was handstamped and is found inverted, double, etc.
Nos. 6, 7 and 8 exist with the handstamp in red, blue or violet, but these varieties are not known to have been regularly issued.
A 2pi black was overprinted and sold to dealers. Values, $3,500 unused, $3,250 used.
A 2pa on 5pa newspaper stamp and a 2pi postage due stamp exist with the handstamp, but these are not known to have been regularly issued. Values, $1,800 and $725, respectively.
Covers: Commercial covers of Nos. 1-19 are very scarce.
Excellent counterfeits exist of Nos. 1 to 19.

A1

Handstamped on White Laid Paper Without Eagle and Value Issued Without Gum

1913, July		Imperf.
20	A1 (1pi) black	325.00 525.00
a.	Cut to shape	190.00 275.00
a.	Sewing machine perf.	575.00 725.00

Value Typewritten in Violet Issued Without Gum

1913, Aug.		With Eagle
21	A1 10pa violet	16.00 16.00
a.	Double impression	
22	A1 20pa red & black	22.00 18.00
a.	"2p para"	
23	A1 1gr black	22.00 22.00
24	A1 2gr blue & violet	27.00 21.00

25	A1 5gr violet & blue	32.50	27.00
26	A1 10gr blue	32.50	27.00
	Nos. 21-26 (6)	152.00	131.00

Nos. 21-26 exist with the eagle inverted or omitted and with numerous errors in the figures of value and the spelling of the word "grosh."

A2

Skanderbeg (George Castriota) — A3

Handstamped on White Laid Paper Eagle and Value in Black Issued Without Gum

1913, Nov.			Perf. 11½
27	A2 10pa green	5.50	4.25
b.	Eagle and value in green	2,350.	2,300.
c.	10pa red (error)	32.50	32.50
d.	10pa violet (error)	32.50	32.50
29	A2 20pa red	8.25	6.25
b.	20pa green (error)	42.50	32.50
30	A2 30pa green	8.25	6.25
a.	30pa ultramarine (error)	32.50	32.50
b.	30pa red (error)	32.50	32.50
31	A2 1gr ultramarine	11.00	9.50
a.	1gr green (error)	32.50	32.50
b.	1gr black (error)	32.50	32.50
c.	1gr violet (error)	32.50	32.50
33	A2 2gr black	16.00	10.50
a.	2gr violet (error)	40.00	40.00
b.	2gr blue (error)	40.00	40.00
	Nos. 27-33 (5)	49.00	36.75

The stamps of this issue are known with eagle or value inverted or omitted.
1st anniv. of Albanian independence.
Counterfeits exist.

1913, Dec.		Typo.	Perf. 14
35	A3 2q orange brn & buff	5.50	2.50
36	A3 5q green & blue grn	5.50	2.50
37	A3 10q rose red	5.50	2.50
38	A3 25q dark blue	5.50	2.50
39	A3 50q violet & red	13.00	5.25
40	A3 1fr deep brown	30.00	16.00
	Nos. 35-40 (6)	65.00	31.25

For overprints and surcharges see Nos. 41-52, 105, J1-J9.

Nos. 35-40 Handstamped in Black or Violet

1914, Mar. 7			
41	A3 2q orange brn & buff	75.00	85.00
42	A3 5q grn & bl grn (V)	75.00	85.00
43	A3 10q rose red	75.00	85.00
44	A3 25q dark blue (V)	75.00	85.00
45	A3 50q violet & red	75.00	85.00
46	A3 1fr deep brown	75.00	85.00
	Nos. 41-46 (6)	450.00	510.00

Issued to celebrate the arrival of Prince Wilhelm zu Wied on Mar. 7, 1914.

Nos. 35-40 Surcharged in Black

a

b

1914, Apr. 2			
47	A3 (a) 5pa on 2q	3.25	3.25
48	A3 (a) 10pa on 5q	3.25	3.25
49	A3 (a) 20pa on 10q	5.50	4.25
50	A3 (b) 1gr on 25q	5.50	4.25
51	A3 (b) 2gr on 50q	5.50	5.25
52	A3 (b) 5gr on 1fr	22.00	16.00
	Nos. 47-52 (6)	45.00	36.25

For overprints see Nos. 105, J6-J9.

Inverted Surcharge

47a	A3 (a)	5pa on 2q	24.00	24.00
48a	A3 (a)	10pa on 5q	22.50	22.50
49a	A3 (a)	20pa on 10q	24.00	24.00
50a	A3 (b)	1gr on 25q	24.00	24.00
51a	A3 (b)	2gr on 50q	28.00	28.00
52b	A3 (b)	5gr on 1fr	90.00	90.00
	Nos. 47a-52b (6)		212.50	212.50

Korce (Korytsa) Issues

A4

1914   Handstamped   *Imperf.*

52A	A4	10pa violet & red	200.00	200.00
c.		10pa black & red	325.00	325.00
53	A4	25pa violet & red	200.00	200.00
a.		25pa black & red	425.00	425.00

Nos. 52A-53a were handstamped directly on the cover, so the paper varies. They were also produced in sheets; these are rarely found. Nos. 52A-53a were issued by Albanian military authorities.

Counterfeits exists of Nos. 52A and 53.

A5

1917   Typo. & Litho.   *Perf. 11½*

54	A5	1c dk brown & grn	17.50	12.00
55	A5	2c red & green	17.50	12.00
56	A5	3c gray grn & grn	17.50	12.00
57	A5	5c green & black	16.00	8.00
58	A5	10c rose red & black	16.00	8.00
59	A5	25c blue & black	16.00	8.00
60	A5	50c violet & black	16.00	10.00
61	A5	1fr brown & black	16.00	10.00
	Nos. 54-61 (8)		132.50	80.00

A6

1917-18

62	A6	1c dk brown & grn	2.75	2.40
63	A6	2c red brown & grn	2.75	2.40
a.		"CTM" for "CTS"	72.50	120.00
64	A6	3c black & green	2.75	2.40
a.		"CTM" for "CTS"	80.00	135.00
65	A6	5c green & black	4.00	4.00
66	A6	10c dull red & black	4.00	4.00
67	A6	50c violet & black	7.25	6.50
68	A6	1fr red brn & black	20.00	17.50
	Nos. 62-68 (7)		43.50	39.20

Counterfeits abound of Nos. 54-68, 80-81.

No. 65 Surcharged in Red

1918

80	A6	25c on 5c green & blk	275.00	*325.00*

A7

1918

81	A7	25c blue & black	72.50	95.00

General Issue

A8

A9

Handstamped in Rose or Blue   XV I MCMXIX

1919   *Perf. 12½*

84	A8	(2)q on 2h brown	15.00	15.00
85	A8	5q on 16h green	15.00	15.00
86	A8	10q on 8h rose (Bl)	15.00	15.00
87	A8	25q on 64h blue	15.00	15.00
88	A9	25q on 64h blue	375.00	375.00
89	A8	50q on 32h violet	15.00	15.00
90	A8	1fr on 1.28k org, bl	15.00	15.00
	Nos. 84-90 (7)		465.00	465.00

See Nos. J10-J13. Compare with types A10-A14. For overprints see Nos 91-104.

Handstamped in Rose or Blue

1919, Jan. 16

91	A8	(2)q on 2h brown	16.00	16.00
92	A8	5q on 16h green	12.00	12.00
93	A8	10q on 8h rose (Bl)	12.00	12.00
94	A8	25q on 64h blue	160.00	160.00
95	A9	25q on 64h blue	52.50	60.00
96	A8	50q on 32h violet	16.00	16.00
97	A8	1fr on 1.28k org, bl	16.00	16.00
	Nos. 91-97 (7)		284.50	292.00

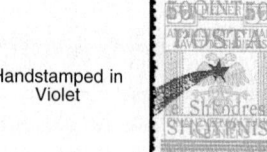

Handstamped in Violet

1919

98	A8	(2)q on 2h brown	20.00	20.00
99	A8	5q on 16h green	20.00	20.00
100	A8	10q on 8h rose	20.00	20.00
101	A8	25q on 64h blue	20.00	20.00
102	A9	25q on 64h blue	160.00	160.00
103	A8	50q on 32h violet	20.00	20.00
104	A8	1fr on 1.28k org, bl	20.00	20.00
	Nos. 98-104 (7)		280.00	280.00

No. 50 Overprinted in Violet

1919   *Perf. 14*

105	A3	1gr on 25q blue	32.50	25.00

A10

A11

1919, June 5   *Perf. 11½, 12½*

106	A10	10q on 2h brown	8.00	6.00
107	A11	15q on 8h rose	8.00	6.00
108	A11	20q on 16h green	8.00	6.00
109	A10	25q on 64h blue	8.00	6.00
110	A11	50q on 32h violet	8.00	6.00
111	A11	1fr on 96h orange	8.00	6.00
112	A10	2fr on 1.60k vio, buff	29.00	24.00
	Nos. 106-112 (7)		77.00	60.00

Nos. 106-108, 110 exist with inverted surcharge.

A12

A13

Surcharged in Black or Violet

1919

113	A12	10q on 8h car	8.00	6.00
114	A12	15q on 8h car (V)	8.00	6.00
115	A13	20q on 16h green	8.00	6.00
116	A13	25q on 32h violet	8.00	6.00
117	A13	50q on 64h blue	22.50	16.00
118	A13	1fr on 96h orange	9.75	8.00
119	A12	2fr on 1.60k vio, buff	16.00	12.00
	Nos. 113-119 (7)		80.25	60.00

A14

Overprinted in Blue or Black Without New Value

1920   *Perf. 12½*

120	A14	1q gray (Bl)	100.00	95.00
121	A14	10q rose (Bk)	14.00	*32.50*
a.		Double overprint	150.00	*150.00*
122	A14	20q brown (Bl)	45.00	47.50
123	A14	25q blue (Bk)	525.00	600.00
124	A14	50q brown vio (Bk)	60.00	*80.00*
	Nos. 120-124 (5)		744.00	855.00

Counterfeit overprints exist of Nos. 120-128.

Surcharged in Black with New Value

125	A14	2q on 10q rose (R)	16.00	*24.00*
126	A14	5q on 10q rose (G)	16.00	*20.00*
127	A14	25q on 10q rose (Bl)	16.00	*24.00*
128	A14	50q on 10q rose (Br)	16.00	*32.50*
	Nos. 125-128 (4)		64.00	100.50

Stamps of type A14 (Portrait of the Prince zu Wied) were not placed in use without overprint or surcharge.

A15

Post Horn Overprinted in Black

1920   *Perf. 14x13*

129	A15	2q orange	12.00	9.75
130	A15	5q deep green	20.00	17.50
131	A15	10q red	35.00	35.00
132	A15	25q light blue	65.00	35.00
133	A15	50q gray green	14.50	12.00
134	A15	1fr claret	14.50	12.00
	Nos. 129-134 (6)		161.00	121.25

Type A15 was never placed in use without post horn or "Besa" overprint.

Stamps of Type A15 (No Post Horn) Overprinted

1921

135	A15	2q orange	8.00	8.00
136	A15	5q deep green	8.00	8.00
137	A15	10q red	16.00	14.00
138	A15	25q light blue	29.00	24.00
139	A15	50q gray green	16.00	14.00
140	A15	1fr claret	16.00	14.00
	Nos. 135-140 (6)		93.00	82.00

For surcharge & overprints see Nos. 154, 156-157.

Stamps of these types, and with "TAKSE" overprint, were unauthorized and never placed in use. They are common.

Gjirokaster A18

Korcha A19

Designs: 5q, Kanina. 10q, Berati. 25q, Bridge at Vezirit. 50q, Rozafat. 2fr, Dursit.

1923   Typo.   *Perf. 12½, 11½*

147	A18	2q orange	1.25	2.10
148	A18	5q yellow green	1.10	1.60
149	A18	10q carmine	1.10	1.60
150	A18	25q dark blue	1.10	1.60
151	A18	50q dark green	1.10	1.60
152	A19	1fr dark violet	1.10	1.60
153	A19	2fr olive green	6.50	8.25
	Nos. 147-153 (7)		13.25	18.35

For overprints & surcharges see Nos. 158-185, B1-B8.

No. 135 Surcharged

1922   *Perf. 14x13*

154	A15	1q on 2q orange	3.25	*8.00*

Stamps of Type A15 (No Post Horn) Overprinted

1922

156	A15	5q deep green	5.00	*8.00*
157	A15	10q red	5.00	*8.00*

Nos. 147-151 Ovptd. in Black and Violet

1924, Jan.   Perf. 12½

158	A18	2q red orange	10.00	20.00
159	A18	5q yellow green	10.00	20.00
160	A18	10q carmine	7.50	14.50
161	A18	10q dark blue	7.50	14.50
162	A18	50q dark green	11.50	20.00
		Nos. 158-162 (5)	46.50	89.00

The words "Mbledhje Kushtetuese" are in taller letters on the 25q than on the other values. Opening of the Constituent Assembly. Counterfeits of Nos. 158 and 161 are plentiful.

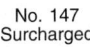

No. 147 Surcharged

1924

163	A18	1q on 2q red orange	3.00	8.00

Nos. 163, 147-152 Overprinted

1924

164	A18	1q on 2q orange	2.75	7.25
165	A18	2q orange	2.75	7.25
166	A18	5q yellow green	2.75	7.25
167	A18	10q carmine	2.75	7.25
168	A18	25q dark blue	2.75	7.25
169	A18	50q dark green	6.25	14.00
170	A19	1fr dark violet	6.25	17.50
		Nos. 164-170 (7)	26.25	67.75

Issued to celebrate the return of the Government to the Capital after a revolution.

Nos. 163, 147-152 Overprinted

1925

171	A18	1q on 2q orange	3.25	8.00
172	A18	2q orange	3.25	8.00
173	A18	5q yellow green	3.25	8.00
174	A18	10q carmine	3.25	8.00
175	A18	25q dark blue	3.25	8.00
176	A18	50q dark green	3.25	12.00
177	A19	1fr dark violet	6.25	16.00
		Nos. 171-177 (7)	25.75	68.00

Proclamation of the Republic, Jan. 21, 1925. The date "1921" instead of "1925" occurs once in each sheet of 50. Counterfeits exist.

Nos. 163, 147-153 Overprinted

1925

178	A18	1q on 2q orange	1.10	1.60
a.		Inverted overprint	12.50	12.50
179	A18	2q orange	1.10	1.60
180	A18	5q yellow green	1.10	1.60
a.		Inverted overprint	12.50	12.50
181	A18	10q carmine	1.10	1.60
182	A18	25q dark blue	1.10	1.60
183	A18	50q dark green	1.10	1.60
184	A19	1fr dark violet	5.00	4.00
185	A19	2fr olive green	7.50	4.00
		Nos. 178-185 (8)	19.10	17.60

Counterfeits exist.

President Ahmed Zogu
A25   A26

1925   Perf. 13½, 13½x13

186	A25	1q orange	.25	.25
187	A25	2q red brown	.25	2.00
188	A25	5q green	.25	.25
189	A25	10q rose red	.25	.25
190	A25	15q gray brown	.75	2.00
191	A25	25q dark blue	.25	.25
192	A25	50q blue green	.85	1.50
193	A26	1fr red & ultra	1.75	2.00
194	A26	2fr green & orange	1.90	2.00
195	A26	3fr brown & violet	4.00	5.00
196	A26	5fr violet & black	4.50	6.75
		Nos. 186-196 (11)	15.00	22.25

No. 193 in ultramarine and brown, and No. 194 in green and brown were not regularly issued. Value, set $15.

For overprints and surcharges see Nos. 197-209, 238-248.

Nos. 186-196 Overprinted in Various Colors

1927

197	A25	1q orange (V)	.60	1.00
198	A25	2q red brn (G)	.25	.30
199	A25	5q green (R)	1.25	.50
200	A25	10q rose red (Bl)	.25	.30
201	A25	15q gray brn (G)	7.00	14.00
202	A25	25q dk blue (R)	.50	.40
203	A25	50q blue grn (Bl)	.50	.40
204	A26	1fr red & ultra (Bk)	1.40	.55
205	A26	2fr green & org (Bk)	1.50	.80
206	A26	3fr brown & vio (Bk)	2.40	1.60
207	A26	5fr violet & blk (Bk)	3.50	2.75
		Nos. 197-207 (11)	19.15	22.60

No. 200 exists perf. 11.
For surcharges see Nos. 208-209, 238-240.

Nos. 200, 202 Surcharged in Black or Red

1928

208	A25	1q on 10q rose red	.50	.55
a.		Inverted surcharge	4.00	4.00
209	A25	5q on 25q dk blue (R)	.50	.55
a.		Inverted surcharge	4.00	4.00

A27   King Zog I — A28

Black Overprint

1928   Perf. 14x13½

210	A27	1q orange brown	5.00	9.50
211	A27	2q slate	5.00	9.50
212	A27	5q blue green	5.00	12.00
213	A27	10q rose red	4.00	12.00
214	A27	15q bister	15.00	47.50
215	A27	25q deep blue	6.00	12.00
216	A27	50q lilac rose	10.00	15.00

Red Overprint
Perf. 13½x14

217	A28	1fr blue & slate	10.00	12.00
		Nos. 210-217 (8)	60.00	129.50

Compare with types A29-A32.

A29   A30

Black or Red Overprint

1928   Perf. 14x13½

218	A29	1q orange brown	12.50	25.00
219	A29	2q slate (R)	12.50	25.00
220	A29	5q blue green	10.00	20.00
221	A29	10q rose red	10.00	16.00
222	A29	15q bister	15.00	27.50
223	A29	25q deep blue (R)	10.00	16.00
224	A29	50q lilac rose	10.00	16.00

Perf. 13½x14

225	A30	1fr blue & slate (R)	12.50	20.00
226	A30	2fr green & slate (R)	12.50	20.00
		Nos. 218-226 (9)	105.00	185.50

Proclamation of Ahmed Zogu as King of Albania.

A31   A32

Black Overprint

1928   Perf. 14x13½

227	A31	1q orange brown	.40	1.25
228	A31	2q slate	.40	1.25
229	A31	5q blue green	2.75	3.50
230	A31	10q rose red	.40	1.25
231	A31	15q bister	15.00	24.00
232	A31	25q deep blue	.40	1.25
233	A31	50q lilac rose	.75	2.00

Perf. 13½x14

234	A32	1fr blue & slate	1.50	2.50
235	A32	2fr green & slate	1.50	4.00
236	A32	3fr dk red & ol bis	7.50	12.00
237	A32	5fr dull vio & gray	7.50	16.00
		Nos. 227-237 (11)	38.10	69.00

The overprint reads "Kingdom of Albania."

Nos. 203, 202, 200 Surcharged in Black

1929   Perf. 13½x13, 11½

238	A25	1q on 50q blue green	.40	.55
239	A25	2q on 25q dark blue	.40	.55
240	A25	15q on 10q rose red	.60	1.00
		Nos. 238-240 (3)	1.40	2.10

Nos. 186-189, 191-194 Overprinted in Black or Red

1929   Perf. 11½, 13½

241	A25	1q orange	7.50	20.00
242	A25	2q red brown	7.50	20.00
243	A25	5q green	7.50	20.00
244	A25	10q rose red	7.50	20.00
245	A25	25q dark blue	7.50	20.00
246	A25	50q blue green (R)	10.00	24.00
247	A26	1fr red & ultra	14.00	35.00
248	A26	2fr green & orange	14.00	35.00
		Nos. 241-248 (8)	75.50	194.00

34th birthday of King Zog. The overprint reads "Long live the King."

Lake Butrinto — A33   King Zog I — A34

Zog Bridge — A35   Ruin at Zog Manor — A36

Perf. 14, 14½

1930, Sept. 1   Photo.   Wmk. 220

250	A33	1q slate	.25	.25
251	A33	2q orange red	.25	.25
252	A34	5q yellow green	.25	.25
253	A33	10q carmine	.25	.25
254	A33	15q dark brown	.25	.25
255	A33	25q dark ultra	.25	.25
256	A33	50q slate green	.70	.55
257	A35	1fr violet	1.10	1.00
258	A35	2fr indigo	1.50	1.10
259	A36	3fr gray green	3.50	2.25
260	A36	5fr orange brown	4.50	3.50
		Nos. 250-260 (11)	12.80	9.90

2nd anniversary of accession of King Zog I.
For overprints see Nos. 261-270, 299-309, J39. For surcharges see Nos. 354-360 in Scott Standard Postage Stamp Catalogue, Vol. 1.

Nos. 250-259 Overprinted in Black

1934, Dec. 24

261	A33	1q slate	8.50	12.00
262	A33	2q orange red	8.50	12.00
263	A34	5q yellow green	8.50	9.50
264	A34	10q carmine	9.25	12.00
265	A33	15q dark brown	9.25	12.00
266	A34	25q dark ultra	9.25	12.00
267	A33	50q slate green	10.00	16.00
268	A35	1fr violet	11.00	20.00
269	A35	2fr indigo	12.00	25.00
270	A36	3fr gray green	15.00	35.00
		Nos. 261-270 (10)	101.25	165.50

Tenth anniversary of the Constitution.

Allegory of Death of Skanderbeg A37   Albanian Eagle in Turkish Shackles A38

5q, 25q, 40q, 2fr, Eagle with wings spread.

1937   Unwmk.   Perf. 14

271	A37	1q brown violet	.25	.25
272	A38	2q brown	.50	.35
273	A38	5q lt green	.50	.50
274	A37	10q olive brown	.50	.80
275	A38	15q rose red	.80	1.00
276	A38	25q blue	1.50	2.00
277	A37	50q deep green	3.75	3.25
278	A37	1fr violet	9.00	6.00
279	A38	2fr orange brown	12.00	9.00
		Nos. 271-279 (9)	28.80	23.15

Souvenir Sheet

280		Sheet of 3	17.50	150.00
a.	A37	20q red violet	3.50	6.25
b.	A38	30q olive brown	3.50	6.25
c.	A38	40q olive brown	3.50	6.25

25th anniv. of independence from Turkey, proclaimed Nov. 26, 1912.

 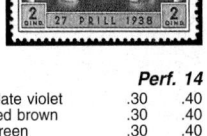

Queen Geraldine and King Zog — A40

1938   Perf. 14

281	A40	1q slate violet	.30	.40
282	A40	2q red brown	.30	.40
283	A40	5q green	.30	.40
284	A40	10q olive brown	1.10	.80
285	A40	15q rose red	1.10	.80
286	A40	25q blue	2.75	2.00

287 A40 50q Prus green 5.75 4.00
288 A40 1fr purple 11.50 8.00
   Nos. 281-288 (8) 23.10 16.80

Souvenir Sheet
289 Sheet of 4 35.00 *175.00*
  a. A40 20q dark red violet 7.75 *9.75*
  b. A40 30q brown olive 7.75 ...

Wedding of King Zog and Countess Geraldine Apponyi, Apr. 27, 1938.
No. 289 contains 2 each of Nos. 289a, 289b.

Queen Geraldine — A42   National Emblems — A43

Designs: 10q, 25q, 30q, 1fr, King Zog.

1938
290 A42 1q dp red violet .25 .55
291 A43 2q red orange .25 .55
292 A42 5q deep green .50 .50
293 A42 10q red brown .50 1.00
294 A42 15q deep rose 1.00 1.25
295 A42 25q deep blue 1.40 1.40
296 A43 50q gray black 8.50 6.00
297 A42 1fr slate green 12.50 9.00
   Nos. 290-297 (8) 24.90 20.25

Souvenir Sheet
298 Sheet of 3 22.50 *100.00*
  b. A43 20q Prussian green 7.00 *12.00*
  c. A42 30q deep violet 7.00 *12.00*

10th anniv. of royal rule. They were on sale for 3 days (Aug. 30-31, Sept. 1) only, during which their use was required on all mail.
No. 298 contains Nos. 294, 298b, 298c.

Issued under Italian Dominion

Nos. 250-260 Overprinted in Black

1939   Wmk. 220   Perf. 14
299 A33 1q slate 1.25 *1.25*
  Never hinged 3.25
300 A33 2q orange red 1.25 *1.25*
  Never hinged 3.25
301 A34 5q yellow green 1.25 *1.25*
  Never hinged 3.25
302 A34 10q carmine 1.25 *1.25*
  Never hinged 3.25
303 A34 15q dark brown 2.00 *3.75*
  Never hinged 4.75
304 A34 25q dark ultra 2.00 *3.75*
  Never hinged 4.75
305 A33 50q slate green 2.50 *5.00*
  Never hinged 6.50
306 A35 1fr violet 2.50 *5.00*
  Never hinged 6.50
307 A35 2fr indigo 3.25 *9.50*
  Never hinged 8.00
308 A36 3fr gray green 7.75 *22.50*
  Never hinged 19.00
309 A36 5fr orange brown 10.00 *25.00*
  Never hinged 24.00
   Nos. 299-309 (11) 35.00 *79.50*
  Set, on overfranked philatelic cover 160.00

Resolution adopted by the Natl. Assembly, Apr. 12, 1939, offering the Albanian Crown to Italy.

A46   A47

Native Costumes — A48

King Victor Emmanuel III
A49   A50

Native Costume — A51

Monastery A52

Designs: 2fr, Bridge at Vezirit. 3fr, Ancient Columns. 5fr, Amphitheater.

1939   Unwmk.   Photo.   Perf. 14
310 A46 1q blue gray 1.25 .50
  Never hinged 3.25
311 A47 2q olive green 1.25 .50
  Never hinged 3.25
312 A48 3q golden brown 1.25 .50
  Never hinged 3.25
313 A49 5q green 1.25 .25
  Never hinged 3.25
314 A50 10q brown 1.25 .25
  Never hinged 3.25
315 A50 15q crimson 1.25 .25
  Never hinged 3.25
316 A50 25q sapphire 2.00 .80
  Never hinged 4.75
317 A50 30q brt violet 2.50 1.40
  Never hinged 6.50
318 A51 50q dull purple 3.25 3.25
  Never hinged 8.00
319 A49 65q red brown 5.00 11.50
  Never hinged 13.00
320 A52 1fr myrtle green 7.50 9.50
  Never hinged 19.00
321 A52 2fr brown lake 11.50 19.00
  Never hinged 29.00
322 A52 3fr brown black 19.00 35.00
  Never hinged 47.50
323 A52 5fr gray violet 25.00 *50.00*
  Never hinged 65.00
   Nos. 310-323 (14) 83.25 132.70
  Set, on overfranked philatelic cover 275.00

For overprints and surcharges see Nos. 331-353 in *Scott Standard Postage Stamp Catalogue*, Vol. 1.

SEMI-POSTAL STAMPS

Nos. 148-151 Surcharged in Red and Black

1924, Nov. 1
B1 A18 5q + 5q yel grn 11.00 *30.00*
B2 A18 10q + 5q carmine 11.00 *30.00*
B3 A18 25q + 5q dark blue 11.00 *30.00*
B4 A18 50q + 5q dark grn 11.00 *30.00*
   Nos. B1-B4 (4) 44.00 *120.00*

Nos. B1 to B4 with Additional Surcharge in Red and Black

1924
B5 A18 5q + 5q + 5q yel grn 11.00 *26.00*
B6 A18 10q + 5q + 5q car 11.00 *26.00*
B7 A18 25q + 5q + 5q dk bl 11.00 *26.00*
B8 A18 50q + 5q + 5q dk grn 11.00 *26.00*
   Nos. B5-B8 (4) 44.00 *104.00*

AIR POST STAMPS

Airplane Crossing Mountains AP1

Wmk. 125
1925, May 30   Typo.   Perf. 14
C1 AP1 5q green 2.25 *3.50*
C2 AP1 10q rose red 2.25 *3.50*
C3 AP1 25q deep blue 2.25 *3.50*
C4 AP1 50q dark green 3.50 *6.00*
C5 AP1 1fr dk vio & blk 6.25 *10.50*
C6 AP1 2fr ol grn & vio 10.50 *17.50*
C7 AP1 3fr brn org & dk grn 10.50 *17.50*
   Nos. C1-C7 (7) 39.50 *62.00*
Nos. C1-C7 exist imperf. Value $3,000.
For overprint see Nos. C8-C28.

Nos. C1-C7 Overprinted

1927, Jan. 18
C8 AP1 5q green 5.25 *10.50*
  a. Dbl. overprint, one invtd. 50.00
C9 AP1 10q rose red 5.25 *10.50*
  a. Dbl. overprint, one invtd. 50.00
C10 AP1 25q deep blue 4.75 *9.50*
  a. Inverted overprint 45.00
C11 AP1 50q dark grn 3.25 *6.50*
  a. Inverted overprint 45.00
C12 AP1 1fr dk vio & blk 3.25 *6.50*
  a. Inverted overprint 45.00
  b. Double overprint 45.00
C13 AP1 2fr ol grn & vio 7.50 *10.50*
C14 AP1 3fr brn org & dk grn 10.50 *15.00*
   Nos. C8-C14 (7) 39.75 *69.00*

Nos. C1-C7 Overprinted

1928, Apr. 21
C15 AP1 5q green 5.25 *10.50*
  a. Inverted overprint 70.00
C16 AP1 10q rose red 5.25 *10.50*
C17 AP1 25q deep blue 5.25 *10.50*
C18 AP1 50q dark green 10.00 *21.00*
C19 AP1 1fr dk vio & blk 55.00 *110.00*
C20 AP1 2fr ol grn & vio 55.00 *110.00*
C21 AP1 3fr brn org & dk grn 55.00 *110.00*
   Nos. C15-C21 (7) 190.75 *382.50*

First flight across the Adriatic, Valona to Brindisi, Apr. 21, 1928.
The variety "SHQYRTARE" occurs once in the sheet for each value. Value 3 times normal.

Nos. C1-C7 Overprinted in Red Brown

1929, Dec. 1
C22 AP1 5q green 6.00 *8.75*
C23 AP1 10q rose red 6.00 *8.75*
C24 AP1 25q deep blue 6.00 *8.75*
C25 AP1 50q dk grn 125.00 *175.00*
C26 AP1 1fr dk vio & blk 225.00 *350.00*
C27 AP1 2fr ol grn 225.00 *350.00*
C28 AP1 3fr brn org & dk grn 225.00 *350.00*
   Nos. C22-C28 (7) 818.00 *1,251.*
Excellent counterfeits exist.

King Zog and Airplane over Tirana AP2

AP3

1930, Oct. 8   Photo.   Unwmk.
C29 AP2 5q yellow green 1.00 *1.75*
C30 AP2 15q rose red 1.00 *1.75*
C31 AP2 20q slate blue 1.00 *1.75*
C32 AP2 50q olive green 2.00 *2.75*
C33 AP3 1fr dark blue 3.00 *5.25*
C34 AP3 2fr olive brown 10.00 *17.50*
C35 AP3 3fr purple 22.50 *17.50*
   Nos. C29-C35 (7) 40.50 *48.25*
For overprints and surcharges see Nos. C36-C45.

Nos. C29-C35 Overprinted

1931, July 6
C36 AP2 5q yellow grn 5.25 *10.50*
  a. Double overprint 140.00
C37 AP2 15q rose red 5.25 *10.50*
C38 AP2 20q slate blue 5.25 *10.50*
C39 AP2 50q olive grn 5.25 *10.50*
C40 AP3 1fr dark blue 30.00 *60.00*
C41 AP3 2fr olive brn 30.00 *60.00*
C42 AP3 3fr purple 30.00 *60.00*
   Nos. C36-C42 (7) 111.00 *222.00*

1st air post flight from Tirana to Rome.
Only a very small part of this issue was sold to the public. Most of the stamps were given to the Aviation Company to help provide funds for conducting the service.

Issued under Italian Dominion

Nos. C29-C30 Overprinted in Black

1939, Apr. 19   Unwmk.   Perf. 14
C43 AP2 5q yel green 2.50 *7.00*
  Never hinged 6.50
C44 AP2 15q rose red 2.50 *7.00*
  Never hinged 6.50

No. C32 With Additional Surcharge

C45 AP2 20q on 50q ol grn 5.00 *11.50*
  Never hinged 13.00
  a. Inverted overprint —
   Nos. C43-C45 (3) 10.00 *25.50*
  Set on flown cover 95.00
See note after No. 309.

King Victor Emmanuel III and Plane over Mountains AP4

1939, Aug. 4   Photo.
C46 AP4 20q brown 32.50 15.00
  Never hinged 80.00
  On commercial cover 40.00

Shepherds AP5

Map of Albania
Showing Air
Routes — AP6

Designs: 20q, Victor Emmanuel III and harbor view. 50q, Woman and river valley. 1fr, Bridge at Vezirit. 2fr, Ruins. 3fr, Women waving to plane.

1940, Mar. 20			Unwmk.	
C47	AP5	5q green	1.25	1.25
		Never hinged	3.25	
C48	AP6	15q rose red	1.25	1.90
		Never hinged	3.25	
C49	AP5	20q deep blue	2.50	3.25
		Never hinged	3.25	
C50	AP6	50q brown	3.25	9.50
		Never hinged	8.00	
C51	AP5	1fr myrtle green	6.50	12.50
		Never hinged	8.00	
C52	AP6	2fr brown black	9.50	19.00
		Never hinged	24.00	
C53	AP6	3fr rose violet	16.00	25.00
		Never hinged	40.00	
		Nos. C47-C53 (7)	40.25	72.40
		Set on overfranked philatelic cover		175.00

SPECIAL DELIVERY STAMPS

Issued under Italian Dominion

King Victor
Emmanuel
III — SD1

1940		Unwmk.	Photo.	Perf. 14	
E1	SD1	25q bright violet		4.50	7.50
		Never hinged		11.00	
E2	SD1	50q red orange		11.50	18.00
		Never hinged		29.00	
		Set on overfranked philatelic cover			55.00

POSTAGE DUE STAMPS

Nos. 35-39
Handstamped in
Various Colors

1914, Feb. 23		Unwmk.	Perf. 14	
J1	A3	2q org brn & buff (Bl)	10.50	4.50
J2	A3	5q green (R)	10.50	4.50
J3	A3	10q rose red (Bl)	15.00	4.50
J4	A3	25q dark blue (R)	17.50	4.50
J5	A3	50q vio & red (Bk)	26.00	14.00
		Nos. J1-J5 (5)	79.50	32.00

The two parts of the overprint are handstamped separately. Stamps exist with one or both handstamps inverted, double, omitted or in wrong color.

Nos. 48-51
Overprinted in Black

1914, Apr. 16				
J6	A3	(a) 10pa on 5q green	5.25	4.50
J7	A3	(a) 20pa on 10q rose red	5.25	4.50
J8	A3	(b) 1gr on 25q blue	5.25	4.50
J9	A3	(b) 2gr on 50q vio & red	5.25	4.50
		Nos. J6-J9 (4)	21.00	18.00

Same Design as
Regular Issue of
1919, Overprinted

1919, Feb. 10			Perf. 11½, 12½	
J10	A8	(4)q on 4h rose	13.00	10.50
J11	A8	(10)q on 10k red, grn	13.00	10.50
J12	A8	20q on 2k org, gray	13.00	10.50
J13	A8	50q on 5k brn, yel	13.00	10.50
		Nos. J10-J13 (4)	52.00	42.00

Fortress at
Scutari — D3

Post Horn Overprinted in Black

1920, Apr. 1			Perf. 14x13	
J14	D3	4q olive green	.75	4.50
J15	D3	10q rose red	1.50	6.50
J16	D3	20q bister brn	1.50	6.50
J17	D3	50q black	4.00	17.50
		Nos. J14-J17 (4)	7.75	35.00

D5

Background of Red Wavy Lines

1922			Perf. 12½, 11½	
J23	D5	4q black, red	1.10	4.50
J24	D5	10q black, red	1.10	4.50
J25	D5	20q black, red	1.10	4.50
J26	D5	50q black, red	1.10	4.50
		Nos. J23-J26 (4)	4.40	18.00

Same Overprinted in
White

1925				
J27	D5	4q black, red	1.90	4.50
J28	D5	10q black, red	1.90	4.50
J29	D5	20q black, red	1.90	4.50
J30	D5	50q black, red	1.90	4.50
		Nos. J27-J30 (4)	7.60	18.00

The 10q with overprint in gold was a trial printing. It was not put in use.

D7

Overprinted "QIND. AR" in Red

1926, Dec. 24			Perf. 13½x13	
J31	D7	10q dark blue	.75	3.50
J32	D7	20q green	.75	3.50
J33	D7	30q red brown	1.50	7.00
J34	D7	50q dark brown	2.75	13.00
		Nos. J31-J34 (4)	5.75	27.00

Coat of Arms — D8

Wmk. Double Headed Eagle (220)

1930, Sept. 1		Photo.	Perf. 14, 14½	
J35	D8	10q dark blue	6.75	21.00
J36	D8	20q rose red	2.75	13.00
J37	D8	30q violet	2.75	13.00
J38	D8	50q dark green	2.75	13.00
		Nos. J35-J38 (4)	15.00	60.00

Nos. J36-J38 exist with overprint "14 Shtator 1943" (see Nos. 332-344 in *Scott Standard Postage Stamp Catalogue*, Vol. 1) which is private and fraudulent on these stamps.

No. 253 Overprinted

1936			Perf. 14	
J39	A34	10q carmine	15.00	45.00
a.		Hyphens on each side of "Takse" ('39)	100.00	200.00

Issued under Italian Dominion

Coat of Arms — D9

1940		Unwmk.	Photo.	Perf. 14	
J40	D9	4q red orange		37.50	75.00
		Never hinged		95.00	
J41	D9	10q bright violet		37.50	75.00
		Never hinged		95.00	
J42	D9	20q brown		37.50	75.00
		Never hinged		95.00	
J43	D9	30q dark blue		37.50	75.00
		Never hinged		95.00	
J44	D9	50q carmine rose		37.50	75.00
		Never hinged		95.00	
		Nos. J40-J44 (5)		187.50	375.00

ALEXANDRETTA

ˌa-lig-ˌzan-ˈdre-tə

LOCATION — A political territory in northern Syria, bordering on Turkey
GOVT. — French mandate
AREA — 10,000 sq. mi. (approx.)
POP. — 220,000 (approx.)

Included in the Syrian territory mandated to France under the Versailles Treaty, the name was changed to Hatay in 1938. The following year France returned the territory to Turkey in exchange for certain concessions. See Hatay.

100 Centimes = 1 Piaster

Stamps of Syria, 1930-36, Overprinted or Surcharged in Black or Red

a

b

c

d

e

1938		Unwmk.	Perf. 12x12½	
1	A6 (a)	10c vio brn	3.50	3.50
2	A6 (a)	20c brn org	3.50	3.00
		Perf. 13½		
3	A9 (b)	50c vio (R)	4.50	3.50
4	A10 (b)	1p bis brn	4.50	3.00
5	A9 (b)	2p yel grn	5.75	3.50
6	A13 (b)	3p yel grn (R)	9.00	7.00
7	A10 (b)	4p yel org	10.00	7.00
8	A16 (b)	6p grnsh blk (R)	12.00	8.00
9	A18 (b)	25p vio brn	25.00	25.00
10	A15 (c)	75c org red	9.00	9.00
11	A10 (d)	2.50p on 4p yel org	7.50	4.00
12	AP2 (e)	12.50p on 15p org red	20.00	15.00
		Nos. 1-12 (12)	114.25	91.50
		Set, never hinged		260.00

Issue dates: Nos. 1-9, Apr. 14, Nos. 10-12, Sept. 2.

Covers: Values for commercial covers begin at about $75.

Nos. 4, 7,
10-12
Ovptd. in
Black

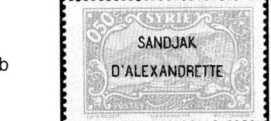

1938, Nov. 10				
13	A15	75c	57.50	57.50
14	A10	1p	35.00	35.00
15	A10	2.50p on 4p	30.00	30.00
16	A10	4p	35.00	35.00
17	AP2	12.50p on 15p	85.00	85.00
		Nos. 13-17 (5)	242.50	242.50
		Set, never hinged		425.00

Death of Kemal Ataturk, pres. of Turkey.

AIR POST STAMPS

Air Post Stamps of Syria, 1937, Overprinted Type "b" in Red or Black

1938, Apr. 14		Unwmk.	Perf. 13	
C1	AP14	½p dark vio (R)	3.25	3.75
C2	AP15	1p black (R)	3.25	3.75
C3	AP14	2p blue grn (R)	4.50	5.50
C4	AP15	3p deep ultra	4.75	6.00
C5	AP14	5p rose lake	9.00	14.00
C6	AP15	10p red brown	9.50	14.00
C7	AP14	15p lake brown	12.50	16.00
C8	AP15	25p dk blue (R)	18.00	22.50
		Nos. C1-C8 (8)	64.75	85.50
		Set, never hinged		200.00

POSTAGE DUE STAMPS

Postage Due Stamps of Syria, 1925-31, Ovptd. Type "b" in Black or Red

1938, Apr. 14		Unwmk.	Perf. 13½	
J1	D5	50c brown, yel	5.50	5.50
J2	D6	1p violet, rose	6.00	6.00
J3	D5	2p blk, blue (R)	7.50	7.50
J4	D5	3p blk, red org	9.00	9.00
J5	D5	5p blk, bl grn (R)	14.50	14.50
J6	D7	8p blk, gray bl (R)	20.00	20.00
		Nos. J1-J6 (6)	62.50	62.50
		Set, never hinged		200.00

On No. J2, the overprint is vertical, reading up, other denominations, horizontal.
Stamps of Alexandretta were discontinued in 1938 and replaced by those of Hatay.

ALGERIA

al-'jir-ē-ə

LOCATION — North Africa

GOVT. — French Colony

AREA — 847,552 sq. mi.

POP. — 7,234,684

CAPITAL — Algiers

100 Centimes = 1 Franc

Catalogue values for unused stamps in this country are for Never Hinged items, beginning with Scott 109 in the regular postage section, and Scott B27 in the semi-postal section.

STAMPS OF FRANCE USED IN ALGERIA

Stamps of France used in Algeria
From 1849 to 1924, stamps of France were used at post offices in Algeria. From 1849 to 1862, stamps were canceled by a lozenge-shaped canceler with small numeral identifiers between 3710 and 4448, each of 83 post offices being identified by its number. From 1862 to 1876, similar cancelers, with larger numerals ranging from 5000 to 5177, were used by 156 post offices. After 1876, each post office used its own circular date stamp.

Grill and Town Cancels

Canceled with grill, on large piece with Algerian town name (first column) or on cover with town name on envelope (second column).

1849   On France No. 6
A6G A1 25c lt blue, *bluish*

Alger	70.00	310.00
Arzew	625.00	3,100.
Bouffarich	625.00	3,100.
Constantine	87.50	400.00
Cherchell	87.50	400.00
Dellys	87.50	400.00
Djidjeli	110.00	460.00
Douera	87.50	400.00
Douera + Coleah	625.00	3,100.
Mostaganem	77.50	350.00
Orleans-ville	240.00	1,200.
Philippeville	77.50	350.00
Tenez	77.50	350.00

The 25c value is the least expensive of the French stamps used in Algeria. Other values of the first issue exist used in Algeria and are worth more than the values shown.

Small Figures in Dotted Lozenge

Single (first column) or on cover (second column).

1849   On France No. 6
A6S A1 25c lt blue, *bluish*

3710 — Alger,	*from*	52.50	150.00
3711 — L'Àrba,	*from*	400.00	3,100.
3712 — Arzew,	*from*	275.00	2,000.
3713 — Aumale,	*from*	130.00	875.00
3714 — Batna,	*from*	110.00	800.00
3715 — Blidah,	*from*	70.00	240.00
3716 — Bone,	*from*	62.50	200.00

3717 — Bouffarich,	*from*	240.00	1,750.
3718 — Bougie,	*from*	110.00	800.00
3719 — Cherchell,	*from*	120.00	825.00
3720 — Coleah,	*from*	300.00	2,400.
3721 — Constantine,			
	from	62.50	200.00
3722 — Dellys,	*from*	220.00	1,550.
3723 — Dely-Ibrahim,			
	from	110.00	3,300.
3724 — Djidjeli,	*from*	225.00	1,625.
3725 — Douera,	*from*	225.00	1,625.
3726 — Mascara,	*from*	100.00	750.00
3727 — Medeah,	*from*	80.00	350.00
3728 — Mers-el-Kebir,			
	from	240.00	1,750.
3729 — Milianah,	*from*	100.00	750.00
3730 — Mostaganem,			
	from	70.00	275.00
3731 — Nemours,	*from*	130.00	875.00
3732 — Oran,	*from*	65.00	225.00
3733 — Orleansville,			
	from	87.50	700.00
3734 — Philippeville,			
	from	75.00	275.00
3735 — Setif,	*from*	87.50	440.00
3736 — Sidi-Bel-Abbes,			
	from	75.00	300.00
3737 — Stora,	*from*	650.00	
3738 — Tenez,	*from*	87.50	440.00
3739 — Tlemcen,	*from*	80.00	350.00

All other values of the set exist used in Algeria. They are worth more than the values shown above, which are for cancellations on the 25c value.

1849   On France No. 15
A15S A3 25c blue, *bluish*
      (I)

3710 — Alger,	*from*	1.75	8.75
3711 — L'Àrba,	*from*	57.50	425.00
3712 — Arzew,	*from*	40.00	265.00
3713 — Aumale,	*from*	20.00	120.00
3714 — Batna,	*from*	17.50	95.00
3715 — Blidah,	*from*	3.50	22.50
3716 — Bone,	*from*	3.50	17.50
3717 — Bouffarik,	*from*	40.00	250.00
3718 — Bougie,	*from*	17.50	100.00
3719 — Cherchell,	*from*	22.50	105.00
3720 — Coleah,	*from*	47.50	310.00
3721 — Constantine,			
	from	13.00	10.00
3722 — Dellys,	*from*	35.00	200.00
3723 — Dely-Ibrahim,			
	from	52.50	440.00
3724 — Djidjeli,	*from*	35.00	225.00
3725 — Douera,	*from*	40.00	225.00
3726 — Mascara,	*from*	12.50	87.50
3727 — Medeah,	*from*	12.50	87.50
3728 — Mers-el-Kebir,			
	from	40.00	275.00
3729 — Milianah,	*from*	13.00	87.50
3730 — Mostaganem,			
	from	4.50	26.00
3731 — Nemours,	*from*	22.50	120.00
3732 — Oran,	*from*	2.25	13.50
3733 — Orleansville,			
	from	13.00	95.00
3734 — Philippeville,			
	from	4.50	20.00
3735 — Setif,	*from*	10.50	65.00
3736 — Sidi-Bel-Abbes,			
	from	4.50	26.50
3737 — Stora,	*from*	165.00	2,500.
3738 — Tenez,	*from*	13.50	175.00
3739 — Tlemcen,	*from*	4.40	35.00
3751 — El Arrouch,	*from*	65.00	650.00
3752 — Biskra,	*from*	40.00	275.00
3753 — Boghar,	*from*	52.50	550.00
3754 — La Calle,	*from*	35.00	325.00
3755 — Gudiel,	*from*	200.00	4,250.
3756 — Guelma,	*from*	13.50	110.00
3757 — Lambese,	*from*	120.00	1,225.
3758 — Milah,	*from*	—	—
3759 — Saida,	*from*	62.50	575.00
3760 — Smendou,	*from*	75.00	625.00
3761 — St. Denis-du-Sig,	*from*	17.50	120.00
3762 — Tebessa,	*from*	52.50	400.00
3763 — Teniet-el-Haad,			
	from	52.50	550.00
3764 — Tiaret,	*from*	50.00	325.00
3774 — El Affroun,	*from*	105.00	3,500.
3774 — Mouzaiaville,			
	from	105.00	650.00
3775 — Ain Benian,	*from*	—	—
3776 — Bou-Medfa,	*from*	77.50	650.00
3777 — Marengo,	*from*	35.00	275.00
3793 — Miserghin,	*from*	62.50	625.00
3795 — Valmy d'Algerie,			
	from	80.00	575.00
3846 — Penthievre,	*from*	105.00	925.00
3912 — La Maison Caree,	*from*	52.50	775.00
4005 — Soukaras,	*from*	52.50	500.00
4007 — Laghouat,	*from*	77.50	575.00
4104 — Jemmapes,	*from*	40.00	325.00
4106 — La Reghaia,			
	from	200.00	2,000.
4116 — Ain-Benida,	*from*	35.00	300.00
4120 — Pont-l'Oued Djer,	*from*	65.00	775.00
4122 — Staoueli,	*from*	77.50	850.00
4187 — Gastonville,			
	from	75.00	700.00
4189 — Lalla Maghrnia,			
	from	75.00	600.00
4190 — Tizi-Ouzou,	*from*	62.50	550.00
4361 — Bou Tkelis,	*from*	77.50	750.00
4362 — Le tlelat,	*from*	100.00	900.00
4363 — Ain-Temouchent			
	from	52.50	475.00
4364 — Relizane	*from*	75.00	625.00
4365 — Assi-Ameur,			
	from	100.00	1,000.
4366 — Aboukir,	*from*	300.00	3,150.
4367 — Ain Tedeles,			
	from	75.00	625.00
4368 — La Stidia,	*from*	225.00	3,000.
4369 — Fondouk,	*from*	95.00	1,000.
4370 — Kouba,	*from*	200.00	2,300.
4371 — Fort Napoleon,			
	from	77.50	700.00
4372 — Dra-el-Mizan,			
	from	115.00	1,150.
4373 — Rouiba,	*from*	190.00	2,500.
4374 — Cheragas,	*from*	190.00	4,250.
4446 — Geryville,	*from*	275.00	3,500.

4447 — Oued-el-Hamman,	*from*	225.00	3,500.
4448 — Sebdou,	*from*		

All other values of the set exist used in Algeria. They are worth more than the values shown above, which are for cancellations on the 25c value.

Large Figures in Dotted Lozenge

Single (first column) or on cover (second column).

1870-76   On France No. 58
A58L A13 25c blue, *bluish*

5000 — Aboukir,	*from*	62.50	625.00
5001 — Ain Beida,	*from*	75.00	650.00
5002 — Ain Beniam,			
	from	—	—
5002 — Saint-Charles,			
	from	77.50	775.00
5003 — Ain Tedeles,			
	from	40.00	350.00
5004 — Ain Temouchena,	*from*	17.50	110.00
5005 — Alger,	*from*	1.75	4.50
5006 — L'Àrba,	*from*	17.50	125.00
5007 — El Arrouch	*from*	22.00	130.00
5008 — Arzew,	*from*	17.50	110.00
5009 — Assi-Ameur,			
	from	75.00	550.00
5010 — Aumale,	*from*	13.00	62.50
5011 — Batna,	*from*	4.50	20.00
5012 — Biskra,	*from*	11.50	52.50
5013 — Blidah,	*from*	2.75	21.50
5014 — Boghar,	*from*	35.00	225.00
5015 — Bone,	*from*	4.50	13.50
5016 — Bou-Tletis,	*from*	52.50	500.00
5017 — Bouffarik,	*from*	11.50	52.50
5018 — Bougie,	*from*	21.00	17.50
5019 — La Calle,	*from*	52.50	175.00
5020 — Cheragas,	*from*	62.50	1,000.
5020 — Palestro,	*from*	62.50	550.00
5021 — Cherchell,	*from*	13.50	75.00
5022 — Coleah,	*from*	22.50	120.00
5023 — Constantine,			
	from	2.75	10.50
5024 — Dellys,	*from*	13.00	80.00
5025 — Dely-Ibrahim,			
	from	35.00	265.00
5026 — Djidjeli,	*from*	16.00	87.50
5027 — Douera,	*from*	22.50	125.00
5028 — Dra-el-Mizan,			
	from	52.50	550.00
5029 — Fondouk,	*from*	40.00	465.00
5030 — Fort Napoleon,			
	from	35.00	310.00
5030 — Fort National,			
	from	35.00	225.00
5031 — Gastonville,			
	from	47.50	475.00
5031 — Robertville,	*from*	47.50	500.00
5032 — Geryville,	*from*	62.50	625.00
5033 — Gudiel,			
	from	—	—
5033 — Guyotville,	*from*	62.50	750.00
5034 — Guelma,	*from*	10.50	35.00
5035 — Jemmapes,	*from*	11.50	65.00
5036 — Kouba,	*from*	35.00	300.00
5037 — Laghouat	*from*	35.00	225.00
5038 — Lalla Maghrnia,			
	from	35.00	275.00
5039 — Lambese,	*from*	35.00	300.00
5040 — La Maison Caree,	*from*	35.00	240.00
5041 — Marengo,	*from*	30.00	200.00
5042 — Mascara,	*from*	4.50	17.50
5043 — Medeah,	*from*	4.50	17.50
5044 — Mers-el-Kebir,			
	from	35.00	225.00
5045 — Milah,	*from*	—	—
5045 — Col des Beni Aicha,	*from*	77.50	775.00
5046 — Milianah,	*from*	5.00	22.50
5047 — Miserghin,	*from*	35.00	300.00
5048 — Mostaganem,			
	from	4.50	17.50
5049 — Mouzaiaville,			
	from	47.50	500.00
5050 — Nemours,	*from*	10.50	55.00
5051 — Oran,	*from*	1.75	6.50
5052 — Orleansville,			
	from	4.50	17.50
5053 — Oued-el-Hammam,	*from*	65.00	625.00
5054 — Penthievre,	*from*	62.50	575.00
5055 — Philippeville,			
	from	1.75	9.00
5056 — Pont de la Oued Djer,	*from*	52.50	625.00
5056 — Bou Medfa,	*from*	52.50	625.00
5057 — La Reghaia	*from*	62.50	625.00
5057 — L'Alma,	*from*	62.50	750.00
5058 — Relizane,	*from*	13.50	75.00
5059 — Rouiba,	*from*	45.00	675.00
5060 — Saida,	*from*	13.50	110.00
5061 — Sebdou,	*from*	62.50	550.00
5062 — Setif,	*from*	4.50	17.50
5063 — Sidi-bel Abbes,			
	from	3.50	13.50
5064 — Smendou,	*from*	52.50	450.00
5065 — Soukaras,	*from*	22.50	120.00
5066 — Staoueli,	*from*	65.00	550.00
5067 — La Stidia,	*from*	65.00	750.00
5068 — Stora,	*from*	275.00	—
5069 — St-Cloud-d'Algerie,	*from*	35.00	400.00
5070 — St. Denis-du-Sig,	*from*	13.50	65.00

5071 — Tebessa,	*from*	35.00	300.00
5072 — Tenez,	*from*	13.50	75.00
5073 — Teniet-el-Haad,			
	from	26.50	175.00
5074 — Le Tlelat,	*from*	40.00	340.00
5075 — Tlemcen,	*from*	4.50	17.50
5076 — Tiaret,	*from*	10.50	62.50
	from	25.00	135.00
5078 — Valmy,	*from*	62.50	500.00
5081 — Beni Mancour,			
	from	75.00	850.00
5093 — Ain el Arba,			
	from	75.00	775.00
5108 — Sidi-Moussa,			
	from	100.00	925.00
5109 — Djelfa,	*from*	17.50	200.00
5110 — Bou Kanifis,			
	from	62.50	550.00
5111 — Collo,	*from*	50.00	400.00
5112 — Duzerville,	*from*	50.00	550.00
5113 — Mondovi,	*from*	70.00	625.00
5114 — Barral,	*from*	80.00	625.00
5115 — Hussein Dey,			
	from	57.50	625.00
5116 — Birtouta,	*from*	57.50	700.00
5117 — Berrouaghia,			
	from	75.00	750.00
5117 — Gue de Constantine,	*from*	75.00	2,100.
5120 — El Kantours,			
	from	65.00	750.00
5122 — Les Trembles,			
	from	65.00	775.00
5123 — Perregaux,	*from*	65.00	700.00
5124 — Bizot,	*from*	45.00	425.00
5125 — Bordj Bou-Arreridj,	*from*	45.00	375.00
5126 — Ouled Mimoun,			
	from	75.00	625.00
5126 — Lamoriciere,			
	from	75.00	925.00
5127 — Gar Rouban,			
	from	75.00	925.00
5128 — Daya,	*from*	57.50	650.00
5130 — Oued-el-Halleg,			
	from	57.50	550.00
5131 — Le Affroun,	*from*	80.00	3,250.
5131 — Bou Saada,			
	from	80.00	750.00
5133 — Kroubs,	*from*	70.00	625.00
5134 — Bouguirat,	*from*	75.00	625.00
5135 — L'Hilil	*from*	57.50	550.00
5136 — Ammi-Moussa,			
	from	75.00	625.00
5137 — Sidi-Ali-ben-Youd,	*from*	75.00	750.00
5138 — Oued-Zenati,			
	from	57.50	700.00
5140 — Affreville,	*from*	62.50	650.00
5141 — Duperre,	*from*	62.50	650.00
5142 — Boghari,	*from*	75.00	700.00
5143 — Akbou,	*from*	95.00	775.00
5144 — Khenchela,	*from*	75.00	750.00
5145 — Zemmorah,	*from*	80.00	775.00
5146 — Bordj Menaiel,			
	from	75.00	700.00
5147 — La Chiffa,	*from*	75.00	775.00
5148 — Rebeval,	*from*	80.00	1,050.
5149 — La Senia,			
	from	—	—
5150 — Oued-Athmenia,			
	from	75.00	775.00
5151 — Birkadem,	*from*	80.00	850.00
5152 — Pontebba,	*from*	80.00	850.00
5157 — Oued-Slyt,	*from*	95.00	1,000.
5158 — Oued-Fodda,			
	from	95.00	1,000.
5159 — Akib-Zamoun,			
	from	175.00	1,350.
5160 — Attatba,	*from*	115.00	1,275.
5161 — Ain-Arnat,	*from*	—	—
5162 — Sidi-Brahim,			
	from	100.00	1,150.
5163 — Oued-Riou,	*from*	105.00	1,750.
5164 — Henneya,	*from*	275.00	3,500.
5165 — Ain Fekarin,			
	from	165.00	2,750.
5166 — Bourkika,	*from*	110.00	1,550.
5167 — Sidi-Ali, *from*			
— Sidi-Ali straight-line cancellation, *from*			3,600.
5168 — Blad-el-Hadjadj,	*from*	130.00	2,000.
5169 — Bordj-Bouira,			
	from	300.00	4,750.
5171 — Beni Saf,	*from*	400.00	5,000.
5172 — Bir Rabalou,			
	from	400.00	5,000.

ISSUES OF FRENCH ALGERIA

Stamps of France Overprinted in Red, Blue or Black

a

b

c

d

1924-26   Unwmk.   Perf. 14x13½

1	A16(a)	1c dk gray (R)	.30 .30
	Never hinged		.50
	On cover		10.00
2	A16(a)	2c violet brn	.35 .30
	Never hinged		.45
	On cover		10.00
3	A16(a)	3c orange	.45 .30
	Never hinged		.60
	On cover		10.00
a.	Grayish paper		.35 .25
	Never hinged		.50
	On cover		10.00
4	A16(a)	4c yel brn (Bl)	.50 .30
	Never hinged		.65
	On cover		8.00
5	A22(a)	5c orange (Bl)	.40 .30
	Never hinged		.55
	On cover		1.75
6	A16(a)	5c green ('25)	.70 .55
	Never hinged		1.00
	On cover		1.75
7	A23(a)	10c green	.65 .40
	Never hinged		1.25
	On cover		2.25
b.	Booklet pane of 10		—
	Complete booklet, 2 #7b		250.00
8	A22(a)	10c green ('25)	.95 .40
	Never hinged		1.40
	On cover		2.25
a.	Pair, one without overprint		1,750.
	Never hinged		2,350.
9	A20(a)	15c slate grn	.50 .30
	Never hinged		.65
	On cover		1.50
10	A23(a)	15c green ('25)	1.10 .40
	Never hinged		1.50
	On cover		2.25
11	A22(a)	15c red brn (Bl) ('26)	.30 .30
	Never hinged		.50
	On cover		1.50
12	A22(a)	20c red brn (Bl)	.50 .30
	Never hinged		.70
	On cover		1.50
a.	Pair, one without overprint		1,750.
	Never hinged		2,500.
13	A22(a)	25c blue (R)	.65 .30
	Never hinged		.90
	On cover		1.50
a.	Booklet pane of 10		—
	Complete booklet, 2 #13a		1,100.
b.	Pair, one without overprint		2,100.
	Never hinged		2,600.
14	A23(a)	30c red (Bl)	2.00 .65
	Never hinged		2.90
	On cover		4.00
15	A22(a)	30c cerise ('25)	1.20 .80
	Never hinged		1.50
a.	"ALGERIE" double		225.00 150.00
	Never hinged		275.00
16	A22(a)	30c lt bl (R) ('25)	.65 .40
	Never hinged		.90
	On cover		6.50
a.	Booklet pane of 10		—
	Complete booklet, 2 #16a		425.00
17	A22(a)	35c violet	.70 .50
	Never hinged		1.00
	On cover		7.00
18	A18(b)	40c red & pale bl	1.00 .40
	Never hinged		1.40
	On cover		3.25
19	A22(a)	40c ol brn (R) ('25)	1.40 .85
	Never hinged		1.90
	On cover		4.00
20	A18(b)	45c grn & bl (R)	.90 .65
	Never hinged		1.25
	On cover		9.00
a.	Double overprint		350.00
	Never hinged		490.00
21	A23(a)	45c red (Bl) ('25)	1.25 .65
	Never hinged		1.75
	On cover		7.00
22	A23(a)	50c blue (R)	1.00 .65
	Never hinged		1.40
	On cover		6.25
23	A20(a)	60c lt violet	1.10 .65
	Never hinged		1.60
	On cover		10.00
a.	Inverted overprint		3,900.
24	A20(a)	65c rose (Bl)	.95 .65
	Never hinged		1.40
	On cover		5.00
25	A23(a)	75c blue (R)	1.25 .75
	Never hinged		1.60
	On cover		10.00
a.	Double overprint		325.00 325.00
	Never hinged		475.00

26	A20(a)	80c ver ('26)	1.90 .90
	Never hinged		2.60
	On cover		20.00
27	A20(a)	85c ver (Bl)	1.60 .90
	Never hinged		2.25
	On cover		9.00
	On cover, single franking		16.00
28	A18(b)	1fr cl & ol grn	1.90 .80
	Never hinged		2.60
	On cover		4.50
	On cover, single franking		10.50
a.	Olive green omitted		325.00 325.00
	Never hinged		475.00
29	A22(a)	1.05fr ver ('26)	1.75 .90
	Never hinged		2.60
	On cover		22.00
	On cover, single franking		75.00
30	A18(c)	2fr org & pale bl	2.25 1.25
	Never hinged		3.50
	On cover		15.00
	On cover, single franking		70.00
31	A18(b)	3fr vio & bl ('26)	4.50 2.00
	Never hinged		6.75
	On cover		40.00
	On cover, single franking		110.00
a.	Blue omitted		350.00
	Never hinged		500.00
32	A18(d)	5fr bl & buff (R)	14.50 9.50
	Never hinged		20.00
	On cover		50.00
	On cover, single franking		185.00
	Nos. 1-32 (32)		49.15 28.30

No. 15 was issued precanceled only. Values for precanceled stamps in first column are for those which have not been through the post and have original gum. Values in second column are for postally used, gumless stamps. For surcharges see Nos. 75, P1.

Street in Kasbah, Algiers A1

Mosque of Sidi Abd-er-Rahman A2

La Pêcherie Mosque — A3

Marabout of Sidi Yacoub A4

1926-39   Typo.   Perf. 14x13½

33	A1	1c olive	.25 .25
	Never hinged		.40
	On cover		6.50
a.	Imperforate		120.00
	Never hinged		160.00
34	A1	2c red brown	.25 .25
	Never hinged		.40
	On cover		6.50
35	A1	3c orange	.25 .25
	Never hinged		.40
	On cover		6.25
36	A1	5c blue green	.25 .25
	Never hinged		.40
	On cover		2.25
37	A1	10c brt violet	.40 .25
	Never hinged		.55
	On cover		2.25
a.	Booklet pane of 10		—
	Complete booklet, 2 #37a		325.00
38	A2	15c orange brn	.40 .25
	Never hinged		.55
	On cover		1.75
a.	Imperforate		120.00
	Never hinged		160.00
b.	Booklet pane of 10		—
	Complete booklet, 2 #38b		275.00
39	A2	20c green	.40 .25
	Never hinged		.55
	On cover		4.50
a.	yel grn, precanceled ('38)		1.40 .75
	Never hinged		1.80
40	A2	20c deep rose	.25 .25
	Never hinged		.40
	On cover		7.00
a.	Imperforate		130.00
	Never hinged		190.00
41	A2	25c blue grn	.40 .25
	Never hinged		.55
	On cover		2.75
42	A2	25c blue ('27)	.65 .40
	Never hinged		.90
	On cover		2.75
a.	Imperforate		130.00
	Never hinged		190.00

43	A2	25c vio bl ('39)	.25 .25
	Never hinged		.40
	On cover		2.75
44	A2	30c blue	.55 .40
	Never hinged		.80
	On cover		10.00
a.	Imperforate		130.00
	Never hinged		190.00
45	A2	30c bl grn ('27)	1.50 .80
	Never hinged		2.00
	On cover		5.25
46	A2	35c dp violet	1.90 1.40
	Never hinged		2.50
	On cover		14.00
47	A2	40c olive green	.55 .30
	Never hinged		.80
	On cover		3.00
a.	Booklet pane of 10		—
	Complete booklet, 2 #47a		250.00
b.	Imperforate		140.00
	Never hinged		200.00
48	A3	45c violet brn	1.00 .40
	Never hinged		1.40
	On cover		3.50
49	A3	50c blue	.55 .40
	Never hinged		.80
	On cover		1.75
a.	Booklet pane of 10		—
	Complete booklet, 2 #49a		325.00
b.	Imperforate		140.00
	Never hinged		190.00
c.	Vert. pair, #49 and 49b		225.00
	Never hinged		320.00
50	A3	50c dk red ('30)	.40 .25
	Never hinged		.55
	On cover		1.75
a.	Booklet pane of 10		—
	Complete booklet, 2 #50a		350.00
b.	Imperforate		140.00
	Never hinged		200.00
51	A3	60c yellow grn	.55 .30
	Never hinged		.80
	On cover		5.00
52	A3	65c blk brn ('27)	3.50 2.50
	Never hinged		4.75
	On cover		10.00
53	A1	65c ultra ('38)	.50 .30
	Never hinged		.65
	On cover		3.00
a.	Booklet pane of 10		—
	Complete booklet, 2 #53a		135.00
54	A3	75c carmine	1.30 .70
	Never hinged		1.75
	On cover		4.00
a.	Imperforate		150.00
	Never hinged		210.00
b.	Vert. pair, #54 and 54a		240.00
	Never hinged		350.00
55	A3	75c blue ('29)	5.25 .75
	Never hinged		7.50
	On cover		2.25
56	A3	80c orange red	1.10 .75
	Never hinged		1.50
	On cover		10.00
57	A3	90c red ('27)	9.50 4.25
	Never hinged		12.50
	On cover		7.50
	On cover, single franking		17.50
a.	Imperforate		130.00
	Never hinged		190.00
58	A4	1fr gray grn & red brn	1.30 .75
	Never hinged		2.00
	On cover		7.00
a.	Imperforate		180.00
	Never hinged		250.00
59	A3	1.05fr lt brown	1.20 .80
	Never hinged		1.60
	On cover		10.00
	On cover, single franking		22.00
60	A3	1.10fr mag ('27)	9.50 3.50
	Never hinged		12.50
	On cover		22.50
	On cover, single franking		87.50
61	A4	1.25fr dk bl & ultra	1.50 1.10
	Never hinged		2.10
	On cover		14.00
	On cover, single franking		24.00
62	A4	1.50fr dk bl & ultra ('27)	6.25 1.00
	Never hinged		8.50
	On cover		10.50
	On cover, single franking		20.00
a.	Imperforate		425.00
	Never hinged		590.00
63	A4	2fr prus bl & blk brn	4.50 1.00
	Never hinged		6.75
	On cover		8.50
	On cover, single franking		11.50
a.	Imperforate		140.00
	Never hinged		195.00
b.	2fr Prus blue & black		7.25 2.60
	Never hinged		10.50
64	A4	3fr violet & org	8.00 2.00
	Never hinged		13.00
	On cover		14.00
	On cover, single franking		25.00
65	A4	5fr red & violet	14.50 5.00
	Never hinged		24.00
	On cover		28.00
	On cover, single franking		50.00
	"ALCERIE," instead of "AL-GERIE"		52.50 40.00
	Never hinged		140.00
66	A4	10fr ol brn & rose ('27)	85.00 45.00
	Never hinged		120.00
	On cover		100.00
	On cover, single franking		160.00
a.	Imperforate		1,000.
	Never hinged		1,500.
b.	10fr sepia brn & dark red		65.00 35.00
	Never hinged		120.00
	On cover		95.00
	On cover, single franking		170.00
67	A4	20fr vio & grn ('27)	8.50 4.00
	Never hinged		11.50
	On cover		17.50
	On cover, single franking		35.00
	Nos. 33-67 (35)		172.15 82.55

A 90c red, design A1, was prepared but not issued. Value, unused $1,000.

Type A4, 50c blue and rose red, inscribed "CENTENAIRE-ALGERIE" is France No. 255.

See design A24 in *Scott Standard Postage Stamp Catalogue*, Vol. 1. For stamps and types surcharged see Nos. 68-74, 131, 136, 187, B1-B13, J27, P2 in this catalogue and Scott Standard catalogue, Vol. 1.

Five Trees Instead of Four (Position 53)

58d	A4	1fr gray grn & red brn	26.50 16.00
	Never hinged		35.00
61d	A4	1.25fr dk blue & ultra	32.50 22.00
	Never hinged		50.00
62d	A4	1.50fr dk blue & ultra ('27)	32.50 16.00
	Never hinged		50.00
63d	A4	2fr prus blue & blk	32.50 24.00
	Never hinged		52.50
64d	A4	3fr violet & orange	45.00 27.50
	Never hinged		65.00
65d	A4	5fr red & violet	130.00 120.00
	Never hinged		200.00
66d	A4	10fr olive brn & rose ('27)	650.00 600.00
	Never hinged		925.00
67d	A4	20fr violet & green ('27)	650.00 600.00
	Never hinged		925.00

Stamps of 1926 Surcharged

1927

68	A2	10c on 35c dp violet	.25 .25
	Never hinged		.40
	On cover		5.50
69	A2	25c on 30c blue	.25 .25
	Never hinged		.40
	On cover		2.40
70	A2	30c on 25c blue grn	.40 .25
	Never hinged		.55
	On cover		4.75
71	A3	65c on 60c yel grn	1.75 1.25
	Never hinged		2.40
	On cover		2.75
72	A3	90c on 80c org red	1.50 1.10
	Never hinged		1.90
	On cover		6.75
73	A3	1.10fr on 1.05fr lt brn	1.00 .50
	Never hinged		1.40
	On cover		20.00
74	A4	1.50fr on 1.25fr dk bl & ultra	3.25 1.50
	Never hinged		4.75
	On cover		9.50
	Nos. 68-74 (7)		8.40 5.10

Bars cancel the old value on Nos. 68, 69, 73, 74.

No. 4 Surcharged

1927

75	A16	5c on 4c yellow brown	.50 .25
	Never hinged		.75
	On cover		7.00
a.	Blue surcharge		1,400. 1,650.
	Never hinged		1,900.

Bay of Algiers A5

1930, May 4   Engr.   Perf. 12½

78	A5	10fr red brown	22.50 22.50
	Never hinged		27.50
	On cover		47.50
a.	Imperf., pair		150.00
b.	Perf 11		22.50 22.50
	Never hinged		31.00
	On cover		52.50

Cent. of Algeria and for Intl. Phil. Exhib. of North Africa, May, 1930.

One example of No. 78 was sold with each 10fr admission.

Travel across the Sahara A6

Arch of Triumph, Lambese A7

Admiralty Building, Algiers A8

Kings' Tombs near Touggourt A9

El-Kebir Mosque, Algiers A10

Oued River at Colomb-Bechar A11

Sidi Bon Medine Cemetery at Tlemcen A13

View of Ghardaia A12

1936-41   Engr.   Perf. 13

79	A6	1c ultra	.25	.25
		Never hinged	.30	
		On cover		5.25
80	A11	2c dk violet	.25	.25
		Never hinged	.30	
		On cover		5.25
81	A7	3c dk blue grn	.25	.25
		Never hinged	.30	
		On cover		5.25
82	A12	5c red violet	.25	.25
		Never hinged	.30	
		On cover		4.00
83	A8	10c emerald	.25	.25
		Never hinged	.30	
		On cover		3.00
84	A9	15c red	.25	.25
		Never hinged	.30	
		On cover		2.75
85	A13	20c dk blue grn	.55	.25
		Never hinged	.70	
		On cover		2.75
86	A10	25c rose vio	1.40	.50
		Never hinged	1.75	
		On cover		1.75
87	A12	30c yellow grn	1.00	.25
		Never hinged	1.20	
		On cover		4.00
88	A9	40c brown vio	.50	.25
		Never hinged	.75	
		On cover		1.75
89	A13	45c deep ultra	2.10	1.40
		Never hinged	2.90	
		On cover		5.00
90	A8	50c red	1.00	.30
		Never hinged	1.25	
		On cover		1.75
91	A6	65c red brn	7.50	4.25
		Never hinged	10.00	
		On cover		10.00
92	A6	65c rose car ('37)	.85	.30
		Never hinged	1.20	
		On cover		1.25
93	A6	70c red brn ('39)	.30	.30
		Never hinged	.40	
		On cover		2.25
94	A11	75c slate bl	.85	.30
		Never hinged	1.20	
		On cover		2.25
95	A7	90c henna brn	2.50	1.40
		Never hinged	3.25	
		On cover		2.75

96	A10	1fr brown	.85	.25
		Never hinged	1.10	
		On cover		2.75
97	A8	1.25fr lt violet	1.45	.90
		Never hinged	2.00	
		On cover		1.75
		On cover, single franking		10.00
98	A8	1.25fr car rose ('39)	.90	.90
		Never hinged	1.10	
		On cover		7.00
		On cover, single franking		12.50
99	A11	1.50fr turq blue	2.60	.75
		Never hinged	3.40	
		On cover		3.25
		On cover, single franking		6.50
99A	A11	1.50fr rose ('40)	1.00	.60
		Never hinged	1.25	
		On cover		6.25
		On cover, single franking		22.50
100	A12	1.75fr henna brn	.55	.25
		Never hinged	.70	
		On cover		3.25
		On cover, single franking		7.50
101	A7	2fr dk brown	.85	.25
		Never hinged	1.10	
		On cover		2.75
		On cover, single franking		6.50
102	A6	2.25fr yellow grn	24.50	15.00
		Never hinged	34.00	
		On cover		32.50
		On cover, single franking		45.00
103	A12	2.50fr dk ultra ('41)	.90	.60
		Never hinged	1.25	
		On cover		6.25
		On cover, single franking		22.50
104	A13	3fr magenta	1.20	.40
		Never hinged	1.50	
		On cover		5.25
		On cover, single franking		13.50
105	A10	3.50fr pck blue	6.50	5.00
		Never hinged	8.50	
		On cover		15.00
		On cover, single franking		27.50
106	A8	5fr slate blue	1.50	.50
		Never hinged	2.25	
		On cover		4.00
		On cover, single franking		11.00
107	A11	10fr henna brn	1.20	.65
		Never hinged	1.50	
		On cover		7.00
		On cover, single franking		16.00
108	A9	20fr turq blue	1.75	1.20
		Never hinged	2.40	
		On cover		9.00
		On cover, single franking		20.00
		Nos. 79-108 (31)	65.70	37.65

See Nos. 124-125, 162 in *Scott Standard Postage Stamp Catalogue*, Vol. 1.

Nos. 82 and 100 with surcharge "E. F. M. 30frs" (Emergency Field Message) were used in 1943 to pay cable tolls for US and Canadian servicemen.

For other surcharges see Nos. 122, B27.

> **Catalogue values for unused stamps in this section, from this point to the end of the section, are for Never Hinged items.**

Algerian Pavilion — A14

1937   Perf. 13

109	A14	40c brt green	1.75	1.10
		On cover		2.00
110	A14	50c rose carmine	1.75	.60
		On cover		1.60
111	A14	1.50fr blue	2.50	1.20
		On cover		2.75
		On cover, single franking		6.50
112	A14	1.75fr brown black	2.50	1.75
		On cover		4.50
		On cover, single franking		4.75
		Nos. 109-112 (4)	8.50	4.65

Paris International Exposition.

Constantine in 1837 — A15

1937

113	A15	65c deep rose	1.10	.85
		On cover		2.00
114	A15	1fr brown	10.00	1.75
		On cover		4.00
		On cover, single franking		7.25
115	A15	1.75fr blue green	1.40	.85
		On cover		3.25
		On cover, single franking		5.50

116	A15	2.15fr red violet	1.75	.85
		On cover		2.75
		On cover, single franking		4.00
		Nos. 113-116 (4)	14.25	4.30

Taking of Constantine by the French, cent.

Ruins of a Roman Villa — A16

1938

117	A16	30c green	1.75	.85
		On cover		4.50
118	A16	65c ultra	.75	.40
		On cover		6.00
119	A16	75c rose violet	1.75	.90
		On cover		12.50
120	A16	3fr carmine rose	5.00	4.00
		On cover		17.50
		On cover, single franking		32.50
121	A16	5fr yellow brown	7.50	6.00
		On cover		21.00
		On cover, single franking		35.00
		Nos. 117-121 (5)	16.75	12.15

Centenary of Philippeville.

No. 90 Surcharged in Black

1938

122	A8	25c on 50c red	.60	.35
		On cover		4.00
a.		Double surcharge	110.00	65.00
b.		Inverted surcharge	75.00	50.00
c.		Pair, one without surcharge	425.00	

Types of 1936 Numerals of Value on Colorless Background

1939

124	A7	90c henna brown	.90	.30
		On cover		1.60
125	A10	2.25fr blue green	1.00	.65
		On cover		5.50
		On cover, single franking		9.50

For surcharge see No. B38 in *Scott Standard Postage Stamp Catalogue*, Vol. 1.

American Export Liner Unloading Cargo A17

1939

126	A17	20c green	2.60	1.25
		On cover		3.25
127	A17	40c red violet	2.75	1.25
		On cover		3.25
128	A17	90c brown black	1.60	.80
		On cover		2.00
129	A17	1.25fr rose	9.00	3.00
		On cover		6.50
		On cover, single franking		11.00
130	A17	2.25fr ultra	2.75	2.10
		On cover		5.50
		On cover, single franking		9.50
		Nos. 126-130 (5)	18.70	8.40

New York World's Fair.

Type of 1926, Surcharged in Black

Two types of surcharge:
I — Bars 6mm
II — Bars 7mm

1939-40   Perf. 14x13½

131	A1	1fr on 90c crimson (I)	.50	.35
		On cover		1.75
a.		Booklet pane of 10		
		Complete booklet, 2 #131a	625.00	
b.		Double surcharge (I)	175.00	
c.		Inverted surcharge (I)	95.00	
d.		Pair, one without surch. (I)	2,000.	
e.		Type II ('40)	7.50	.80

		On cover		3.50
f.		Inverted surcharge (II)	100.00	
g.		Pair, one without surch. (II)	2,000.	

SEMI-POSTAL STAMPS

Regular Issue of 1926 Surcharged in Black or Red

1927   Unwmk.   Perf. 14x13½

B1	A1	5c +5c bl grn	1.25	1.25
		Never hinged	2.10	
		On cover		40.00
B2	A1	10c +10c lilac	1.25	1.25
		Never hinged	2.10	
		On cover		40.00
B3	A2	15c +15c org brn	1.25	1.25
		Never hinged	2.10	
		On cover		35.00
B4	A2	20c +20c car rose	1.25	1.25
		Never hinged	2.10	
		On cover		55.00
B5	A2	25c +25c bl grn	1.25	1.25
		Never hinged	2.10	
		On cover		25.00
B6	A2	30c +30c lt bl	1.25	1.25
		Never hinged	2.10	
		On cover		35.00
B7	A2	35c +35c dp vio	1.25	1.25
		Never hinged	2.10	
		On cover		55.00
B8	A2	40c +40c ol grn	1.25	1.25
		Never hinged	2.10	
		On cover		20.00
B9	A3	50c +50c dp bl (R)	1.30	1.30
		Never hinged	2.10	
		On cover		20.00
a.		Double surcharge	475.00	
		Never hinged	700.00	
B10	A3	80c +80c red org	1.30	1.30
		Never hinged	2.10	
		On cover		55.00
B11	A4	1fr +1fr gray grn & red brn	1.30	1.30
		Never hinged	2.10	
		On cover		35.00
B12	A4	2fr +2fr Prus bl & blk brn	30.00	30.00
		Never hinged	47.50	
		On cover		70.00
B13	A4	5fr +5fr red & vio	40.00	40.00
		Never hinged	57.50	
		On cover		100.00
		Nos. B1-B13 (13)	83.90	83.90

The surtax was for the benefit of wounded soldiers. Government officials speculated in this issue.

Railroad Terminal, Oran SP1

 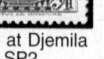

Ruins at Djemila SP2

Mosque of Sidi Abd-er-Rahman SP3

Designs: 10c+10c, Rummel Gorge, Constantine. 15c+15c, Admiralty Buildings, Algiers. 25c+25c, View of Algiers. 30c+30c, Trajan's Arch, Timgad. 40c+40c, Temple of the North, Djemila. 75c+75c Mansourah Minaret, Tlemcen. 1f+1f, View of Ghardaia. 1.50f+1.50f, View of Tolga. 2f+2f, Tuareg warriors. 3f+3f, Kasbah, Algiers.

1930   Engr.   Perf. 12½

B14	SP1	5c +5c orange	8.75	8.75
		Never hinged	12.00	
		On cover		20.00
B15	SP1	10c +10c ol grn	9.50	9.50
		Never hinged	13.50	
		On cover		20.00
B16	SP1	15c +15c dk brn	9.50	9.50
		Never hinged	13.50	
		On cover		20.00
B17	SP1	25c +25c black	9.50	9.50
		Never hinged	13.50	
		On cover		20.00
B18	SP1	30c +30c dk red	9.50	9.50
		Never hinged	13.50	
		On cover		25.00

B19	SP1	40c +40c ap grn	9.50	9.50
		Never hinged	13.50	
		On cover		17.50
B20	SP2	50c +50c ultra	9.50	9.50
		Never hinged	13.50	
		On cover		17.50
B21	SP2	75c +75c red pur	9.50	9.50
		Never hinged	13.50	
		On cover		17.50
B22	SP2	1fr +1fr org red	9.50	9.50
		Never hinged	13.50	
		On cover		20.00
B23	SP2	1.50fr +1.50fr deep ultra	9.50	9.50
		Never hinged	13.50	
		On cover		30.00
B24	SP2	2fr +2fr dk car	9.50	9.50
		Never hinged	13.50	
		On cover		20.00
B25	SP2	3fr +3fr dk grn	9.50	9.50
		Never hinged	13.50	
		On cover		40.00
B26	SP3	5fr +5fr grn & car	22.50	22.50
		Never hinged	30.00	
		On cover		45.00
a.		Center inverted	750.00	
		Never hinged	1,000.	
b.		Center brown	500.00	
		Nos. B14-B26 (13)	135.75	135.75

Centenary of the French occupation of Algeria. The surtax on the stamps was given to the funds for the celebration.

Nos. B14-B26 exist imperf. Value, set in pairs, $800.

> **Catalogue values for unused stamps in this section, from this point to the end of the section, are for Never Hinged items.**

No. 102 Surcharged in Red

1938   **Perf. 13**

B27	A6	65c +35c on 2.25fr yel grn	1.50	1.10
		On cover		40.00
a.		Inverted surcharge	375.00	
b.		Pair, one without surcharge	1,875.	

20th anniversary of Armistice.

No. 79 with surcharge is considered an essay. Value, $300.

René Caillié, Charles Lavigerie and Henri Duveyrier SP14

1939   **Engr.**

B28	SP14	30c +20c dk bl grn	2.40	1.60
		On cover		6.00
B29	SP14	90c +60c car rose	2.40	1.60
		On cover		5.00
B30	SP14	2.25fr +75c ultra	19.00	14.50
		On cover		30.00
		On cover, single franking		75.00
B31	SP14	5fr +5fr brn blk	40.00	30.00
		On cover		50.00
		On cover, single franking		85.00
		Nos. B28-B31 (4)	63.80	47.70

Pioneers of the Sahara.

French and Algerian Soldiers SP15

1940   **Photo.**   **Perf. 12**

B32	SP15	1fr +1fr bl & car	1.60	1.20
		On cover		5.00
a.		Double surcharge	625.00	
B33	SP15	1fr +2fr brn rose & blk	1.60	1.20
		On cover		5.00
B34	SP15	1fr +4fr dp grn & red	2.40	2.00
		On cover		6.00
B35	SP15	1fr +9fr brn & car	3.25	2.00
		On cover		85.00
		Nos. B32-B35 (4)	8.85	6.40

The surtax was used to assist the families of mobilized men.

Nos. B32-B35 exist without surcharge. Value set, $290.

POSTAGE DUE STAMPS

D1

Perf. 14x13½

1926-27   **Typo.**   **Unwmk.**

J1	D1	5c light blue	.40	.30
		Never hinged	.65	
		On cover		4.75
J2	D1	10c dk brn	.40	.30
		Never hinged	.65	
		On cover		4.75
J3	D1	20c olive grn	.85	.30
		Never hinged	1.10	
		On cover		4.75
J4	D1	25c car rose	.95	.70
		Never hinged	1.40	
		On cover		5.50
J5	D1	30c rose red	1.50	.50
		Never hinged	2.25	
		On cover		5.50
J6	D1	45c blue grn	1.90	.90
		Never hinged	3.00	
		On cover		5.50
J7	D1	50c brn vio	.40	.25
		Never hinged	.65	
		On cover		4.50
J8	D1	60c green ('27)	3.50	1.10
		Never hinged	4.50	
		On cover		6.50
J9	D1	1fr red brn, straw	.55	.30
		Never hinged	.75	
		On cover		4.75
J10	D1	2fr lil rose ('27)	.90	.40
		Never hinged	1.20	
		On cover		5.50
J11	D1	3fr deep blue ('27)	.85	.40
		Never hinged	1.10	
		On cover		5.50
		Nos. J1-J11 (11)	12.20	5.45

See Nos. J25-J26, J28-J32 in *Scott Standard Postage Stamp Catalogue*, Vol 1. For surcharges, see Nos. J18-J20.

D2

1926-27

J12	D2	1c olive grn	.40	.30
		Never hinged	.60	
		On cover		4.50
J13	D2	10c violet	1.50	.60
		Never hinged	2.40	
		On cover		5.50
J14	D2	30c bister	1.50	.50
		Never hinged	2.40	
		On cover		5.50
J15	D2	60c dull red	1.00	.50
		Never hinged	1.50	
		On cover		5.50
J16	D2	1fr brt vio ('27)	20.00	4.25
		Never hinged	30.00	
		On cover		13.50
J17	D2	2fr lt bl ('27)	17.50	1.60
		Never hinged	27.00	
		On cover		10.50
		Nos. J12-J17 (6)	41.90	7.75

See note below France No. J51. For surcharges, see Nos. J21-J24.

Stamps of 1926 Surcharged

1927

J18	D1	60c on 20c olive grn	2.25	.80
		Never hinged	3.00	
		On cover		8.00
J19	D1	2fr on 45c blue grn	3.00	1.60
		Never hinged	4.25	
		On cover		9.50
J20	D1	3fr on 25c car rose	1.75	.80
		Never hinged	2.60	
		On cover		8.00
		Nos. J18-J20 (3)	7.00	3.20

Recouvrement Stamps of 1926 Surcharged

1927-32

J21	D2	10c on 30c bis ('32)	5.00	4.00
		Never hinged	7.50	
		On cover		13.50
J22	D2	1fr on 1c olive grn	3.25	1.75
		Never hinged	5.00	
		On cover		9.50
J23	D2	1fr on 60c dl red ('32)	25.00	.95
		Never hinged	37.50	
		On cover		7.25
J24	D2	2fr on 10c violet	16.00	12.00
		Never hinged	26.00	
		On cover		35.00
		Nos. J21-J24 (4)	49.25	18.70

NEWSPAPER STAMPS

Nos. 1 and 33 Surcharged in Red

1924-26   **Unwmk.**   **Perf. 14x13½**

P1	A16	½c on 1c dk gray	.40	.40
		Never hinged	.50	
		On cover		47.50
a.		Triple surcharge	400.00	
		Never hinged	425.00	
P2	A1	½c on 1c olive ('26)	.45	.45
		Never hinged	.60	
		On cover		40.00

ALLENSTEIN

ˈa-lən-ˌshtin

LOCATION — In East Prussia
AREA — 4,457 sq. mi.
POP. — 540,000 (estimated 1920)
CAPITAL — Allenstein

Allenstein, a district of East Prussia, held a plebiscite in 1920 under the Versailles Treaty, voting to join Germany rather than Poland. Later that year, Allenstein became part of the German Republic.

100 Pfennig = 1 Mark

Stamps of Germany, 1906-20, Overprinted

PLÉBISCITE OLSZTYN ALLENSTEIN

Perf. 14, 14½, 14x14½, 14½x14

1920   **Wmk. 125**

1	A16	5pf green	.40	.90
		Never hinged	.85	
		On cover		13.00
		On cover, single franking		150.00
2	A16	10pf carmine	.40	.90
		Never hinged	.85	
		On cover		13.00
		On cover, single franking		22.50
3	A22	15pf dk vio	.40	.90
		Never hinged	.85	
		On cover		13.00
		On cover, single franking		14.00
4	A22	15pf vio brn	5.50	9.50
		Never hinged	12.00	
		On cover		42.50
a.		15pf red brown	65.00	350.00
		Never hinged	150.00	
		On cover		440.00
5	A16	20pf bl vio	.40	1.25
		Never hinged	1.10	
		On cover		13.00
		On cover, single franking		16.00
a.		20pf ultramarine	26.00	105.00
		Never hinged	105.00	
		On cover		450.00
		On cover, single franking		150.00
6	A16	30pf org & blk, buff	.40	1.25
		Never hinged	1.10	
		On cover		13.00
7	A16	40pf lake & blk	.40	.90
		Never hinged	.85	
		On cover		13.00
		On cover, single franking		15.00
8	A16	50pf pur & blk, buff	.40	.90
		Never hinged	.85	
		On cover		13.00
		On cover, single franking		32.50
9	A16	75pf grn & blk	.40	.90
		Never hinged	.85	
		On cover		17.50
		On cover, single franking		85.00
10	A17	1m car rose	1.60	3.75
		Never hinged	3.00	
		On cover		35.00

---

a.		On cover, single franking	—	—
		Double overprint	—	—
11	A17	1.25m green	1.60	3.75
		Never hinged	3.50	
		On cover		40.00
		On cover, single franking		65.00
a.		Double overprint	12.00	35.00
b.		1.25m bluish green	12.00	35.00
		Never hinged	24.00	
		On cover		85.00
		On cover, single franking		210.00
12	A17	1.50m yel brn	.95	3.25
		Never hinged	2.60	
		On cover		42.50
		On cover, single franking		85.00
a.		1.50m red brown	26.00	60.00
		Never hinged	60.00	
		On cover		105.00
		On cover, single franking		160.00
b.		1.50m dark brown	40.00	120.00
		Never hinged	110.00	
		On cover		150.00
		On cover, single franking		225.00
13	A21	2.50m lilac rose (shades)	2.40	10.50
		Never hinged	4.75	
		On cover		35.00
		On cover, single franking		140.00
14	A19	3m blk vio	2.40	3.75
		Never hinged	4.75	
		On cover		52.50
a.		Double overprint	325.00	1,150.
		Never hinged	650.00	
b.		Inverted overprint	—	—
		Nos. 1-14 (14)	17.65	42.40
		Set, never hinged	45.00	

The 5pf brown (Germany No. 118), 10pf orange (No. 119), 20pf green (No. 121), 30pf blue (No. 123) and 40pf (No. 124) exist with this overprint but were not regularly issued. Value, each: $75 hinged, $145 never hinged.

Overprinted

15	A16	5pf green	.40	.90
		Never hinged	.85	
		On cover		13.00
16	A16	10pf carmine	.40	.90
		Never hinged	.85	
		On cover		13.00
		On cover, single franking		15.00
17	A22	15pf dark vio	.40	.90
		Never hinged	.85	
		On cover		13.00
a.		15pf blackish violet	14.00	95.00
		Never hinged	35.00	
		On cover		175.00
18	A22	15pf vio brn	20.00	40.00
		Never hinged	52.50	
		On cover		85.00
a.		15pf red brown	70.00	350.00
		Never hinged	140.00	
19	A16	20pf blue vio	.65	1.50
		Never hinged	1.40	
		On cover		13.00
		On cover, single franking		30.00
a.		20pf ultramarine	100.00	150.00
		Never hinged	260.00	
		On cover		220.00
20	A16	30pf org & blk, buff	.40	.90
		Never hinged	.85	
		On cover		13.00
		On cover, single franking		20.00
21	A16	40pf lake & blk	.40	.90
		Never hinged	.85	
		On cover		13.00
		On cover, single franking		19.00
22	A16	50pf pur & blk, buff	.40	.90
		Never hinged	.85	
		On cover		17.00
		On cover, single franking		32.50
23	A16	75pf grn & blk	.65	1.50
		Never hinged	1.40	
		On cover		17.00
a.		75pf blue green & brownish black	13.00	25.00
		Never hinged	26.00	
		On cover		85.00
24	A17	1m car rose	1.60	3.00
		Never hinged	3.00	
		On cover		35.00
		On cover, single franking		125.00
a.		Inverted overprint	600.00	800.00
		Never hinged	800.00	
25	A17	1.25m green	1.60	3.00
		Never hinged	3.00	
		On cover		35.00
		On cover, single franking		55.00
a.		1.25m bluish green	10.00	17.50
		Never hinged	22.50	
		On cover		65.00
		On cover, single franking		100.00
26	A17	1.50m yel brn	1.25	3.00
		Never hinged	2.25	
		On cover		35.00
		On cover, single franking		75.00
a.		1.50m red brown	13.00	60.00
		Never hinged	30.00	
		On cover		100.00
		On cover, single franking		150.00
b.		1.50m dark brown	15.00	80.00
		Never hinged	35.00	
		On cover		130.00
		On cover, single franking		175.00
27	A21	2.50m lilac rose (shades)	2.75	7.50
		Never hinged	5.25	
		On cover		35.00
		On cover, single franking		125.00
28	A19	3m blk vio	1.75	3.00
		Never hinged	3.00	
		On cover		42.50
		On cover, single franking		160.00

a.	Inverted overprint	400.00	975.00
	Never hinged	725.00	
b.	Double overprint	200.00	600.00
	Never hinged	600.00	
	Nos. 15-28 (14)	32.65	67.90
	Set, never hinged	75.00	

The 40pf carmine rose (Germany No. 124) ̶w̶a̶s̶ ̶w̶i̶t̶h̶ ̶t̶h̶i̶s̶ ̶o̶v̶e̶r̶ ̶o̶v̶e̶r̶p̶r̶i̶n̶t̶,̶ ̶b̶u̶t̶ ̶i̶t̶ ̶i̶s̶ ̶d̶o̶u̶b̶t̶f̶u̶l̶ whether it was regularly issued. Value $105 hinged, $210 never hinged.

ANDORRA, SPANISH ADMINISTRATION

an-'dor-ə

LOCATION — On the southern slope of the Pyrenees Mountains between France and Spain.
GOVT. — Co-principality
AREA — 179 sq. mi.
POP. — 5,231
CAPITAL — Andorre

Andorra is subject to the joint control of France and the Spanish Bishop of Urgel and pays annual tribute to both. The country has no monetary unit of its own, the peseta and franc both being in general use.

100 Centimos = 1 Peseta
100 Centimes = 1 Franc

A majority of the Spanish Andorra stamps issued to about 1950 are poorly centered. The fine examples that are valued will be somewhat off center. Very poorly centered examples (perfs cutting design) sell for less. Well centered very fine stamps are scarce and sell for approximately twice the values shown (Nos. 1-24, E1-E3), or 50% more (Nos. 25-49, E4-E5).

Stamps of Spain, 1922-26, Overprinted in Red or Black

Perf. 13½x12½, 12½x11½, 14

	1928			Unwmk.
1	A49	2c olive green	.55	.55
		Never hinged	2.10	
		On cover		27.50
a.		2c bronze green	2.75	2.75
		Never hinged	8.50	

Control Numbers on Back

2	A49	5c car rose (Bk)	.80	.80
		Never hinged	2.60	
		On cover		27.50
a.		5c rose	5.50	5.25
		Never hinged	17.50	
3	A49	10c green	.80	.80
		Never hinged	3.50	
		On cover		27.50
a.		10c bluish green	22.50	—
		Never hinged	42.50	
4	A49	15c slate blue	3.25	3.25
		Never hinged	7.00	
		On cover		37.50
a.		15c dk slate green	10.00	10.00
		Never hinged	16.50	
5	A49	20c violet	3.25	3.50
		Never hinged	7.00	
		On cover		37.50
a.		20c violet	16.50	
		Never hinged	35.00	
6	A49	25c rose red (Bk)	3.25	3.50
		Never hinged	8.00	
		On cover		37.50
7	A49	30c black brown	18.00	16.50
		Never hinged	45.00	
		On cover		82.50
a.		30c grayish brown	21.00	21.00
		Never hinged	55.00	
b.		As "a," inverted overprint	160.00	160.00
8	A49	40c deep blue	18.00	11.00
		Never hinged	52.50	
		On cover		70.00
a.		40c grayish blue	37.50	32.50
		Never hinged	100.00	
9	A49	50c orange (Bk)	18.00	14.50
		Never hinged	52.50	
		On cover		72.50
a.		50c yellow orange	37.50	32.50
		Never hinged	100.00	
c.		Inverted ovpt., perf 14	160.00	—
10	A49a	1p blue blk	23.00	23.50
		Never hinged	60.00	
		On cover		87.50
11	A49a	4p lake (Bk)	150.00	175.00
		Never hinged	350.00	
		On cover		650.00

12	A49a	10p brown (Bk)	275.00	275.00
		Never hinged	600.00	
		On cover		—
a.		Double overprint	1,000.	
		Never hinged	2,000.	
		Nos. 1-12 (12)	513.90	527.90
		Set, never hinged	1,200.	

Counterfeit overprints exist.

Covers: Values for covers are for commercial items with proper frankings. Overfranked items and other philatelic covers sell for much less.

Values for blocks of 4

1	A49	2c olive green	3.00	3.00
a.		2c bronze green	14.50	15.50
2	A49	5c carmine rose (Bk)	3.50	3.50
a.		5c rose	32.50	32.50
3	A49	10c green	3.50	3.50
a.		10c bluish green	120.00	
4	A49	15c slate blue	16.50	17.50
a.		15c dk slate green	55.00	57.50
5	A49	20c lilac	14.50	19.00
a.		20c violet	87.50	
6	A49	25c rose red (Bk)	16.50	19.00
7	A49	30c brown	110.00	120.00
a.		30c grayish brown	105.00	—
8	A49	40c deep blue	110.00	77.50
a.		40c grayish blue	165.00	165.00
9	A49	50c orange (Bk)	105.00	100.00
a.		50c yellow orange	190.00	190.00
10	A49	1p blue black	275.00	140.00
11	A49	4p lake (Bk)	850.00	1,000.
12	A49	10p brown (Bk)	1,750.	1,900.

Specimen Stamps, Numbered A.000.000 on Reverse

2S	A49	5c rose (Bk)	180.00
		Never hinged	250.00
3S	A49	10c dark green	180.00
		Never hinged	250.00
4S	A49	15c dk slate blue	180.00
		Never hinged	250.00
5S	A49	20c grayish lilac (R)	180.00
		Never hinged	250.00
6S	A49	25c rose red (Bk)	180.00
		Never hinged	250.00
7S	A49	30c brown	240.00
		Never hinged	325.00
8S	A49	40c dark blue	240.00
		Never hinged	325.00
9S	A49	50c orange (Bk)	240.00
		Never hinged	325.00
10S	A49	1p blue black	275.00
		Never hinged	400.00
10aS	A49	1p blue black, perf 14	350.00
11aS	A49	4p lake	350.00
		Never hinged	450.00
12bS	A49	10p brown (Bk)	375.00
		Never hinged	525.00

	1928			Perf. 14
1b	A49	2c olive green	12.50	12.50
		Never hinged	18.00	
		On cover		75.00
		On cover, single franking		250.00
2b	A49	5c rose (Bk)	575.00	700.00
		Never hinged	800.00	
3b	A49	10c green	4.00	4.50
		Never hinged	8.00	
		On cover		65.00
		On cover, single franking		200.00
3c	A49	10c dark green	4.50	4.50
		Never hinged	9.00	
		On cover		75.00
		On cover, single franking		200.00
4b	A49	15c dk slate blue	12.50	12.50
		Never hinged	17.50	
		On cover		75.00
		On cover, single franking		250.00
5b	A49	20c grayish lilac (R)	250.00	300.00
		Never hinged	350.00	
5c	A49	20c lilac (C)	180.00	225.00
		Never hinged	275.00	
6a	A49	25c rose red (Bk)	—	—
b.		As "a," inverted overprint	125.00	65.00
7c	A49	30c brown	27.50	27.50
		Never hinged	40.00	
		On cover		125.00
		On cover, single franking		300.00
8b	A49	40c deep blue	32.50	32.50
		Never hinged	50.00	
		On cover		125.00
		On cover, single franking		300.00
8c	A49	40c dark blue	—	—
9b	A49	50c orange (Bk)	600.00	700.00
c.		As "b," inverted overprint	150.00	80.00
10a	A49	1p blue black	600.00	700.00
		Never hinged	775.00	
11a	A49	4p carmine lake (Bk)	375.00	400.00
		Never hinged	500.00	
11b	A49	4p reddish violet (Bk)	—	—
12b	A49	10p brown (Bk)	450.00	550.00
		Never hinged	650.00	

La Vall — A1

St. Juan de Caselles — A2

St. Julia de Loria — A3

St. Coloma — A4

General Council — A5

1929, Nov. 25	Engr.		Perf. 14
13	A1	2c olive green	1.10	.60
		Never hinged	2.25	

Control Numbers on Back

14	A2	5c carmine lake	3.50	1.25
		Never hinged	8.00	
15	A3	10c yellow green	3.50	4.50
		Never hinged	8.50	
16	A4	15c slate green	3.50	4.50
		Never hinged	9.00	
17	A3	20c violet	3.50	4.50
		Never hinged	8.50	
18	A4	25c carmine rose	7.75	6.25
		Never hinged	16.00	
19	A1	30c olive brown	115.00	175.00
		Never hinged	290.00	
20	A2	40c dark blue	4.50	3.00
		Never hinged	16.00	
21	A3	50c deep orange	5.50	4.50
		Never hinged	15.00	
22	A5	1p slate	12.50	14.50
		Never hinged	40.00	
23	A5	4p deep rose	90.00	110.00
		Never hinged	190.00	
24	A5	10p bister brown	100.00	140.00
		Never hinged	200.00	
		Nos. 13-24 (12)	350.35	468.60
		Set, never hinged	800.00	

Nos. 13-24 exist imperforate. Value, $950.

1931-38				Perf. 11½
13a	A1	2c	6.25	.80
		Never hinged	11.00	

Control Numbers on Back

14a	A2	5c	10.00	2.25
		Never hinged	17.50	
15a	A3	10c	10.00	2.00
		Never hinged	17.50	
16a	A4	15c	30.00	25.00
		Never hinged	41.00	
17a	A3	20c	10.00	6.00
		Never hinged	17.50	
18a	A4	25c	10.00	6.00
		Never hinged	17.50	
19a	A1	30c ('33)	175.00	65.00
		Never hinged	225.00	
20a	A2	40c ('35)	17.00	13.00
		Never hinged	25.00	
22a	A5	1p ('38)	40.00	25.00
		Never hinged	65.00	
		Nos. 13a-22a (9)	308.25	145.05
		Set, never hinged	500.00	

Without Control Numbers

1936-43				Perf. 11½x11
25	A1	2c red brown ('37)	2.00	1.60
		Never hinged	3.75	
26	A2	5c dark brown	2.00	1.60
		Never hinged	3.75	
27	A3	10c blue green	13.00	3.25
		Never hinged	35.00	
a.		10c yellow green	120.00	62.50
		Never hinged	165.00	
28	A4	15c blue green ('37)	7.50	3.50
		Never hinged	14.50	
a.		15c yellow green	8.00	5.75
		Never hinged	8.50	
29	A3	20c violet	7.00	3.50
		Never hinged	10.00	
30	A4	25c deep rose ('37)	3.25	3.25
		Never hinged	4.25	
31	A1	30c carmine	5.50	3.25
		Never hinged	6.25	
31A	A2	40c dark blue	800.00	—
		Never hinged	1,400.	
b.		Perf 14	250.00	
		Never hinged	350.00	
32	A1	45c rose red ('37)	2.00	1.60
		Never hinged	2.90	
33	A3	50c deep orange	10.00	5.75
		Never hinged	14.00	
34	A1	60c deep blue ('37)	7.00	3.50
		Never hinged	10.00	
34A	A5	1p slate	1,000.	
		Never hinged	2,000.	
35	A5	4p deep rose ('43)	40.00	47.50
		Never hinged	70.00	
36	A5	10p bister brn ('43)	52.50	57.50
		Never hinged	65.00	
		Nos. 25-31,32-34,35-36 (12)	151.75	135.80
		Set, never hinged	325.00	

Nos. 26, 28, 32 exist imperforate. Value hinged, $290.

Beware of counterfeits of Nos. 31A and 34A. Purchase of stamps with certificates is strongly advised.

AIR POST STAMPS

A set of 12 stamps, inscribed "CORREU AER / SOBRETAXA" was authorized in 1932 for a proposed private air service between Andorra and Barcelona. These stamps were prepared but not issued. Value, set $40. The stamps were also overprinted "FRANQUICIA DEL CONSELL" for official use. Value, set $140.

SPECIAL DELIVERY STAMPS

Special Delivery Stamp of Spain, 1905 Overprinted

1928	Unwmk.		Perf. 14
Without Control Number on Back			
E1	SD1 20c red	80.00	95.00
	Never hinged	150.00	
	On cover		800.00
With Control Number on Back			
E2	SD1 20c pale red	50.00	50.00
	Never hinged	90.00	
	On cover		120.00

Eagle over Mountain Pass — SD2

1929			Perf. 14
With Control Number on Back			
E3	SD2 20c scarlet	25.00	20.00
	Never hinged	35.00	

Perf 11½ examples are numbered A000.000 and are specimens. Value, $400.

1937			Perf. 11½x11
Without Control Number on Back			
E4	SD2 20c red	7.75	9.50
	Never hinged	8.75	

ANDORRA, FRENCH ADMINISTRATION

Stamps and Types of France, 1900-1929, Overprinted

Perf. 14x13½

1931, June 16   Unwmk.

1	A16	1c gray	1.25	1.25
		Never hinged	1.40	
		On cover		21.00
		On cover, single franking		250.00
a.		Double overprint	2,000.	2,000.
		Never hinged	2,750.	
2	A16	2c red brown	1.60	1.60
		Never hinged	1.75	
		On cover		21.00
		On cover, single franking		160.00
3	A16	3c orange	1.60	1.60
		Never hinged	1.75	
		On cover		21.00
		On cover, single franking		160.00
4	A16	5c green	2.40	2.40
		Never hinged	3.25	
		On cover		21.00
		On cover, single franking		160.00
5	A16	10c lilac	4.00	4.75
		Never hinged	6.00	
		On cover		21.00
		On cover, single franking		160.00
6	A22	15c red brown	5.50	5.50
		Never hinged	9.25	
		On cover		27.50
		On cover, single franking		87.50
7	A22	20c red violet	8.75	9.50
		Never hinged	14.00	
		On cover		37.50
		On cover, single franking		160.00
8	A22	25c yellow brn	9.50	10.00
		Never hinged	17.50	
		On cover		50.00
		On cover, single franking		160.00
9	A22	30c green	9.50	10.00
		Never hinged	16.00	
		On cover		50.00
		On cover, single franking		160.00
10	A22	40c ultra	10.00	12.00
		Never hinged	17.50	
		On cover		42.50
		On cover, single franking		70.00
11	A20	45c lt violet	20.00	21.50
		Never hinged	32.50	
		On cover		55.00
		On cover, single franking		140.00
12	A20	50c vermilion	13.50	15.00
		Never hinged	19.00	
		On cover		55.00
a.		Pair, one without overprint	525.00	
		Never hinged	800.00	
		On cover, single franking		140.00
13	A20	65c gray green	28.00	28.00
		Never hinged	42.50	
		On cover		100.00
		On cover, single franking		250.00
14	A20	75c rose lilac	32.50	28.00
		Never hinged	46.00	
		On cover		100.00
		On cover, single franking		325.00
15	A22	90c red	40.00	45.00
		Never hinged	56.00	
		On cover		125.00
		On cover, single franking		350.00
16	A20	1fr dull blue	40.00	45.00
		Never hinged	62.50	
		On cover		125.00
		On cover, single franking		350.00
17	A22	1.50fr light blue	45.00	47.50
		Never hinged	80.00	
		On cover		140.00
		On cover, single franking		350.00

Overprinted

18	A18	2fr org & pale bl	87.50	95.00
		Never hinged	95.00	
		On cover		140.00
		On cover, single franking		325.00
19	A18	3fr brt vio & rose	110.00	125.00
		Never hinged	160.00	
		On cover		250.00
		On cover, single franking		350.00
20	A18	5fr dk bl & buff	135.00	145.00
		Never hinged	200.00	
		On cover		290.00
		On cover, single franking		500.00
21	A18	10fr grn & red	275.00	350.00
		Never hinged	450.00	
		On cover, single franking		1,250.
22	A18	20fr mag & grn	375.00	575.00
		Never hinged	750.00	
		On cover, single franking		2,150.
		Nos. 1-22 (22)	1,255.	1,578.

See No. P1 for ½c on 1c gray.
Nos. 9, 15 and 17 were not issued in France without overprint.

Chapel of Meritxell
A50

Bridge of St. Anthony
A51

St. Miguel d'Engolasters
A52

Gorge of St. Julia
A53

Old Andorra
A54

1932-43   Engr.   **Perf. 13**

23	A50	1c gray blk	.55	.65
		Never hinged	.70	
		On cover		5.00
		On cover, single franking		35.00
24	A50	2c violet	.90	.90
		Never hinged	.70	
		On cover		5.00
		On cover, single franking		35.00
25	A50	3c brown	.90	.95
		Never hinged	.70	
		On cover		5.00
		On cover, single franking		35.00
26	A50	5c blue green	.90	.95
		Never hinged	1.00	
		On cover		5.00
		On cover, single franking		35.00
27	A51	10c dull lilac	1.40	1.40
		Never hinged	1.50	
		On cover		5.00
		On cover, single franking		35.00
28	A50	15c deep red	2.00	2.00
		Never hinged	3.00	
		On cover		8.50
		On cover, single franking		35.00
29	A51	20c lt rose	13.50	11.00
		Never hinged	21.00	
		On cover		50.00
		On cover, single franking		100.00
30	A52	25c brown	6.50	5.50
		Never hinged	7.75	
		On cover		60.00
		On cover, single franking		175.00
31	A51	25c brn car ('37)	11.00	14.00
		Never hinged	16.00	
		On cover		27.50
		On cover, single franking		55.00
32	A51	30c emerald	4.75	4.75
		Never hinged	5.75	
		On cover		30.00
		On cover, single franking		77.50
33	A51	40c ultra	13.50	11.00
		Never hinged	21.00	
		On cover		35.00
		On cover, single franking		70.00
34	A51	40c brn blk ('39)	1.25	1.25
		Never hinged	1.75	
		On cover		7.00
		On cover, single franking		55.00
35	A51	45c lt red	13.50	11.00
		Never hinged	21.00	
		On cover		55.00
		On cover, single franking		100.00
36	A51	45c bl grn ('39)	6.00	5.25
		Never hinged	9.00	
		On cover		35.00
		On cover, single franking		70.00
37	A52	50c lilac rose	14.50	13.00
		Never hinged	21.00	
		On cover		42.50
		On cover, single franking		85.00
38	A51	50c lt vio ('39)	6.00	5.50
		Never hinged	8.75	
		On cover		35.00
		On cover, single franking		70.00
38A	A51	50c grn ('40)	2.40	2.40
		Never hinged	3.00	
		On cover		37.50
		On cover, single franking		100.00
39	A51	55c lt vio ('38)	24.00	16.00
		Never hinged	37.50	
		On cover		70.00
		On cover, single franking		110.00
40	A51	60c yel brn ('38)	1.60	1.60
		Never hinged	2.25	
		On cover		7.00
		On cover, single franking		70.00

41	A52	65c yel grn	55.00	52.50
		Never hinged	87.50	
		On cover		110.00
		On cover, single franking		160.00
42	A51	65c blue ('38)	18.50	14.50
		Never hinged	25.00	
		On cover		70.00
		On cover, single franking		140.00
43	A51	70c red ('39)	2.40	2.40
		Never hinged	3.50	
		On cover		14.00
		On cover, single franking		70.00
44	A52	75c violet	11.00	8.75
		Never hinged	17.50	
		On cover		42.50
		On cover, single franking		140.00
45	A51	75c ultra ('39)	4.50	4.75
		Never hinged	6.50	
		On cover		35.00
		On cover, single franking		70.00
46	A51	80c green ('38)	27.50	23.00
		Never hinged	45.00	
		On cover		110.00
		On cover, single franking		210.00
46A	A53	80c bl grn ('40)	.40	.40
		Never hinged	.50	
		On cover		27.50
		On cover, single franking		90.00
47	A53	90c deep rose	6.50	6.50
		Never hinged	10.50	
		On cover		52.50
		On cover, single franking		140.00
48	A53	90c dk grn ('39)	3.50	3.50
		Never hinged	5.25	
		On cover		27.50
		On cover, single franking		110.00
49	A53	1fr blue grn	20.00	14.50
		Never hinged	32.50	
		On cover		55.00
		On cover, single franking		90.00
50	A53	1fr scarlet ('38)	32.50	24.00
		Never hinged	47.50	
		On cover		140.00
		On cover, single franking		350.00
51	A53	1fr dp ultra ('39)	.40	.40
		Never hinged	.40	
		On cover		7.00
		On cover, single franking		70.00
51A	A53	1.20fr brt vio ('42)	.40	.40
		Never hinged	.50	
		On cover		5.00
		On cover, single franking		42.50
52	A50	1.25fr rose car ('33)	55.00	45.00
		Never hinged	87.50	
		On cover		55.00
		On cover, single franking		110.00
52A	A50	1.25fr rose ('38)	5.50	4.00
		Never hinged	7.00	
		On cover		27.50
		On cover, single franking		110.00
52B	A53	1.30fr sepia ('40)	.40	.40
		Never hinged	.50	
		On cover		60.00
		On cover, single franking		160.00
53	A54	1.50fr ultra	24.00	19.50
		Never hinged	35.00	
		On cover		60.00
		On cover, single franking		110.00
53A	A53	1.50fr crim ('40)	.40	.40
		Never hinged	.50	
		On cover		55.00
		On cover, single franking		140.00
54	A53	1.75fr violet ('33)	110.00	120.00
		Never hinged	175.00	
		On cover		135.00
		On cover, single franking		165.00
55	A53	1.75fr dk bl ('38)	47.50	40.00
		Never hinged	70.00	
		On cover		150.00
		On cover, single franking		350.00
56	A53	2fr red violet	13.00	11.50
		Never hinged	17.50	
		On cover		27.50
		On cover, single franking		90.00
56A	A50	2fr rose red ('40)	1.60	1.60
		Never hinged	2.40	
		On cover		32.50
		On cover, single franking		70.00
56B	A50	2fr dk bl grn ('42)	.40	.40
		Never hinged	.50	
		On cover		3.50
		On cover, single franking		40.00
57	A50	2.15fr dk vio ('38)	65.00	52.50
		Never hinged	100.00	
		On cover		175.00
		On cover, single franking		375.00
58	A50	2.25fr ultra ('39)	8.75	8.75
		Never hinged	14.00	
		On cover		35.00
		On cover, single franking		110.00
58A	A50	2.40fr red ('42)	.80	.40
		Never hinged	.80	
		On cover		9.00
		On cover, single franking		140.00
59	A50	2.50fr gray blk ('39)	8.00	8.00
		Never hinged	14.00	
		On cover		42.50
		On cover, single franking		115.00
59A	A50	2.50fr dp ultra ('40)	2.75	2.75
		Never hinged	4.00	
		On cover		35.00
		On cover, single franking		70.00
60	A53	3fr orange brn	13.50	10.50
		Never hinged	21.00	
		On cover		32.50
		On cover, single franking		90.00
60A	A50	3fr red brn ('40)	.40	.40
		Never hinged	.50	
		On cover		35.00
		On cover, single franking		70.00
60B	A50	4fr sl bl ('42)	.40	.40
		Never hinged	.50	
		On cover		10.00
		On cover, single franking		70.00
60C	A50	4.50fr dp vio ('42)	2.00	2.00
		Never hinged	2.25	
		On cover		7.75
		On cover, single franking		60.00
61	A54	5fr brown	.90	.80
		Never hinged	1.00	
		On cover		8.50
		On cover, single franking		705.00

62	A54	10fr violet	1.00	.80
		Never hinged	1.25	
		On cover		8.50
		On cover, single franking		70.00
62B	A54	15fr dp ultra ('42)	1.20	1.20
		Never hinged	1.40	
		On cover		12.00
		On cover, single franking		70.00
63	A54	20fr rose lake	1.20	.80
		Never hinged	1.40	
		On cover		8.50
		On cover, single franking		62.50
63A	A51	50fr turq bl ('43)	1.60	1.20
		Never hinged	2.25	
		On cover		13.00
		On cover, single franking		70.00
		Nos. 23-63A (56)	673.05	598.00

A 20c ultra exists but was not issued. Value: unused, $27,500; never hinged $42,500.

No. 37 Surcharged with Bars and New Value in Black

1935, Sept. 18

64	A52	20c on 50c lil rose	18.50	17.00
a.		Double surcharge	6,000.	
		Never hinged	8,750.	

Coat of Arms — A55

1936-42   **Perf. 14x13**

65	A55	1c black ('37)	.25	.25
66	A55	2c blue	.25	.25
67	A55	3c brown	.25	.25
68	A55	5c rose lilac	.25	.25
69	A55	10c ultra ('37)	.25	.25
70	A55	15c red violet	2.75	2.25
71	A55	20c emerald ('37)	.25	.25
72	A55	30c cop red ('38)	.80	.80
72A	A55	30c blk brn ('42)	.40	.40
73	A55	35c Prus grn ('38)	65.00	67.50
74	A55	40c cop red ('42)	.80	.80
75	A55	50c Prus grn ('42)	.80	.80
76	A55	60c turq bl ('42)	.80	.80
77	A55	70c vio ('42)	.80	.80
		Nos. 65-77 (14)	73.65	75.65
		Set, never hinged	135.00	

POSTAGE DUE STAMPS

Postage Due Stamps of France, 1893-1931, Overprinted

On Stamps of 1893-1926

1931-33   Unwmk.   **Perf. 14x13½**

J1	D2	5c blue	2.40	2.40
J2	D2	10c brown	2.40	2.40
J3	D2	30c rose red	1.60	1.60
J4	D2	50c violet brn	2.40	2.40
J5	D2	60c green	34.00	34.00
J6	D2	1fr red brn, *straw*	2.40	2.40
J7	D2	2fr brt violet	16.00	16.00
J8	D2	3fr magenta	3.25	3.25
		Nos. J1-J8 (8)	64.45	64.45

On Stamps of 1927-31

J9	D4	1c olive grn	3.25	3.25
J10	D4	10c rose	5.50	6.50
J11	D4	60c red	27.50	26.50
J12	D4	1fr Prus grn ('32)	110.00	120.00
J13	D4	1.20fr on 2fr bl	80.00	80.00
J14	D4	2fr ol brn ('33)	200.00	225.00
J15	D4	5fr on 1fr vio	120.00	120.00
		Nos. J9-J15 (7)	546.25	581.25

D5   D6

1935-41   Typo.

J16	D5	1c gray green	3.25	3.25
J17	D6	5c light blue ('37)	6.75	6.75
J18	D6	10c brown ('41)	4.00	5.50
J19	D6	2fr violet ('41)	11.00	8.75
J20	D6	5fr red orange ('41)	19.00	11.00
		Nos. J16-J20 (5)	44.00	35.25

NEWSPAPER STAMP

France No. P7
Overprinted

1931   Unwmk.   Perf. 14x13½

P1	A16	½c on 1c gray	1.25	1.25
		On cover	40.00	
		On cover, single franking	60.00	
a.		Double overprint	3,000.	
		Never Hinged	4,000.	

ANGOLA

aŋ-ˈgō-lə

LOCATION — Southwestern Africa between Belgian Congo and South West Africa.
GOVT. — Portuguese colony
AREA — 481,351 sq. mi.
POP. — 3,484,300
CAPITAL — Luanda

1000 Reis = 1 Milreis
100 Centavos = 1 Escudo (1913)
100 Centavos = 1 Angolar (1932)

Watermark

Wmk. 232 — Maltese Cross

Portuguese Crown — A1

1870-77 Typo. Unwmk. Perf. 12½
Thin to Medium Paper

1	A1	5r gray black	3.00	1.75
b.		5r black	2.25	1.40
2	A1	10r yellow	30.00	20.00
a.		10r orange	32.50	16.00
3	A1	20r bister	3.00	2.50
b.		20r pale bister	2.25	2.00
4	A1	25r red	15.00	11.00
a.		25r rose	225.00	175.00
5	A1	40r blue ('77)	150.00	100.00
6	A1	50r green	50.00	15.00
a.		50r page green	50.00	14.00
7a	A1	100r lilac	9.75	4.75
b.		100r pale lilac	11.50	4.75
8a	A1	200r orange ('77)	6.00	4.00
9a	A1	300r choc ('77)	20.00	12.00

Perf. 13½

1a	A1	5r gray black	8.00	4.25
1c	A1	5r black	8.00	4.25
2b	A1	10r yellow	21.00	11.50
2c	A1	10r orange yellow	25.00	20.00
3a	A1	20r bister	450.00	375.00
4b	A1	25r red	21.00	20.00
4c	A1	25r rose	30.00	27.50
5a	A1	40r blue ('77)	225.00	160.00
6b	A1	50r green	1,400.	800.00
7	A1	100r lilac	8.00	5.00
7c	A1	100r lilac	4.75	3.25
8	A1	200r orange ('77)	7.00	3.25
9	A1	300r choc ('77)	8.00	5.00

Perf. 14

4d	A1	25r rose	800.00	460.00

Thick Paper
Perf. 12½

1d	A1	5r black	80.00	67.50
2d	A1	10r orange yellow	110.00	85.00
3c	A1	20r bister	110.00	85.00

4e	A1	25r red	55.00	50.00
6c	A1	50r green	80.00	67.50
7d	A1	100r lilac	110.00	65.00

1881-85   Perf. 12½, 13½

10	A1	10r green ('83)	10.00	4.75
a.		Perf. 12½	37.50	22.50
11	A1	20r carmine rose ('85)	21.00	17.50
12	A1	25r violet ('85)	14.00	5.00
a.		Perf. 13½	12.00	6.75
13	A1	40r buff ('82)	13.00	4.75
a.		Perf. 13½	10.50	4.75
15	A1	50r blue	52.50	14.00
a.		Perf. 13½	77.50	12.00
		Nos. 10-15 (5)	110.50	46.00

Two types of numerals are found on Nos. 2, 11, 13, 15.

The cliche of 40r in plate of 20r error, was discovered before the stamps were issued. All examples were defaced by a blue pencil mark. Values, $2,100 unused; in pair with 20r, $2,400.

In perf. 12½, Nos. 1-4, 4a and 6, as well as 7a, were printed in 1870 on thicker paper and 1875 on normal paper. Stamps of the earlier printing sell for 2 to 5 times more than those of the 1875 printing.

Some reprints of the 1870-85 issues are on a smooth white chalky paper, ungummed and perf. 13½.

Other reprints of these issues are on thin ivory paper with shiny white gum and clear-cut perf. 13½.

Covers: covers bearing Nos. 1-15 are rare; values start at about $1,800.

King Luiz — A2   King Carlos — A3

1886   Embossed   Perf. 12½

16	A2	5r black	15.00	6.25
a.		Perf. 13½	12.50	10.50
17	A2	10r green	15.00	6.25
a.		Perf. 13½	16.00	8.25
b.		10r deep green, perf 12½	7.75	4.25
18	A2	20r rose	22.50	12.50
a.		Perf. 13½	13.00	8.25
b.		20r carmine rose, Perf. 13½	13.00	8.25
c.		As "a," printed on reverse side	55.00	65.00
19	A2	25r red violet	15.00	4.00
a.		Double impression	36.00	42.50
b.		Triple impression	85.00	100.00
20	A2	40r chocolate	21.00	7.50
21	A2	50r blue	26.00	4.00
a.		Double impression	37.50	42.50
22	A2	100r yellow brn	35.00	10.00
23	A2	200r gray violet	50.00	13.00
24	A2	300r orange	50.00	14.00
		Nos. 16-24 (9)	249.50	77.50

For surcharges see Nos. 61-69, 172-174, 208-210.
Reprints of 5r, 20r & 100r have cleancut perf. 13½.

1893-94 Typo. Perf. 11½, 12½, 13½
Chalk-Surfaced Paper
Perf. 12½

25	A3	5r yellow	3.75	1.50
26	A3	10r redsh violet	5.00	3.00
27	A3	15r chocolate	5.25	2.25
30	A3	50r light blue	5.25	2.25
31	A3	75r carmine	17.50	12.00
32	A3	80r lt green	17.50	9.00
33	A3	100r brown, buff	17.50	9.00
34	A3	150r car, rose	27.50	17.50
35	A3	200r dk blue, lt bl	27.50	17.50
36	A3	300r dk blue, sal	30.00	17.50

Perf. 11½

25a	A3	5r yellow	3.00	1.25
27a	A3	15r chocolate	7.00	3.00
28	A3	20r lavender	7.00	3.00
29	A3	25r green	3.25	1.60
30a	A3	50r light blue	3.75	2.00
31a	A3	75r carmine	13.25	9.50
33a	A3	100r brown, buff	55.00	47.50
34a	A3	150r car, rose	16.00	10.00

Perf. 13½

35a	A3	200r dk blue, lt bl	14.00	12.00
36a	A3	300r dk blue, sal	14.00	12.00

Enamel Paper
Perf. 12½

29a	A3	25r green	3.00	1.50
30b	A3	50r light blue	9.00	4.00

Perf. 11½

25b	A3	5r yellow	2.25	1.60
26a	A3	10r redsh violet	2.50	1.80
29b	A3	25r green	3.25	3.00
31b	A3	75r carmine	9.25	7.75

Perf. 13½

25c	A3	5r yellow	1.80	1.50
29c	A3	25r green	7.00	3.75
30c	A3	50r light blue	7.75	6.25
31c	A3	75r carmine	7.75	6.25

For surcharges see Nos. 70-81, 175-179, 213-216, 234.

No. P1 Surcharged in Blue

1894, Aug.

37	N1	25r on 2½r brown	95.00	70.00

King Carlos — A5

1898-1903   Perf. 11½
Name and Value in Black except 500r

38	A5	2½r gray	.65	.50
39	A5	5r orange	.65	.50
40	A5	10r yellow grn	.65	.50
41	A5	15r violet brn	3.00	1.60
42	A5	15r gray green ('03)	1.50	1.40
43	A5	20r gray violet	.60	.50
44	A5	25r sea green	1.60	.65
45	A5	25r car ('03)	.75	.45
46	A5	50r blue	2.75	1.00
47	A5	50r brown ('03)	8.00	3.75
48	A5	65r dull blue ('03)	12.00	5.75
49	A5	75r rose	11.00	6.00
50	A5	75r red violet ('03)	3.00	2.00
51	A5	80r violet	10.00	3.00
52	A5	100r dk blue, blue	2.00	1.25
53	A5	115r org brn, pink ('03)	13.00	7.50
54	A5	130r brn, straw ('03)	12.00	7.50
55	A5	150r brn, straw	11.00	6.00
56	A5	200r red vio, pink	8.00	1.75
57	A5	300r dk blue, rose	9.00	5.50
58	A5	400r dull bl, straw ('03)	9.00	3.50
59	A5	500r blk & red, bl ('01)	12.00	5.00
60	A5	700r vio, yelsh ('01)	35.00	17.50
		Nos. 38-60 (23)	167.15	83.10

For surcharges and overprints see Nos. 83-102, 113-117, 159-171, 181-183, 217-218, 221-225.

Stamps of 1886-94 Surcharged in Black or Red

Two types of surcharge:
I — 3mm between numeral and REIS.
II — 4½mm spacing.

1902   Perf. 12½

61	A2	65r on 40r choc	12.00	7.50
62	A2	65r on 300r org, I	12.00	7.50
a.		Type II	12.00	7.50
63	A2	115r on 10r green	10.00	6.75
a.		Inverted surcharge	90.00	50.00
b.		Perf. 13½	75.00	45.00
64	A2	115r on 200r gray vio	11.00	6.75
65	A2	130r on 50r blue	15.00	5.75
66	A2	130r on 100r brown	10.00	5.75
67	A2	400r on 70r rose	110.00	65.00
a.		Perf. 13½	225.00	125.00
68	A2	400r on 25r violet	27.50	13.00
69	A2	400r on 5r black (R)	22.50	12.00
a.		Double surcharge	75.00	50.00
		Nos. 61-69 (9)	230.00	130.00

For surcharges see Nos. 172-174, 208-210.

Chalk-Surfaced Paper
Perf. 11½

70	A3	65r on 5r yel, I	10.00	8.00
72	A3	65r on 20r lav	12.50	7.50
75a	A3	115r on 100r brn, buff	400.00	225.00
76	A3	115r on 150r car, rose	22.50	15.00
77a	A3	130r on 15r choc, I	11.00	6.00
77b	A3	130r on 15r choc, II	11.00	6.00
78	A3	130r on 75r carmine	12.00	9.00
80a	A3	400r on 50r lt bl, I	40.00	17.50

Perf. 12½

71	A3	65r on 10r red vio, I	9.00	6.75
71a	A3	65r on 10r red vio, II	9.00	6.75
73	A3	65r on 25r green	9.00	6.50
74	A3	115r on 80r lt grn	18.00	10.00
75	A3	115r on 100r brn, buff	17.50	9.00
76b	A3	115r on 150r car, rose	29.00	20.00
77	A3	130r on 15r choc	9.00	9.00
78b	A3	130r on 75r carmine	14.00	10.00
79	A3	130r on 300r dk bl, sal	25.00	20.00
80	A3	400r on 50r lt bl, I	14.00	7.00
81	A3	400r on 200r bl, bl	12.00	11.00

Perf. 13½

75b	A3	115r on 100r brn, buff	80.00	45.00
76a	A3	115r on 150r car, rose	25.00	20.00
79a	A3	130r on 300r dk bl, sal	42.50	20.00
81a	A3	400r on 200r bl, bl	425.00	225.00

Enamel Paper
Perf. 11½

70a	A3	65r on 5r yel, II	10.00	10.00
70b	A3	65r on 5r yel, I	10.00	10.00
71b	A3	65r on 10r red vio, I	14.00	8.00
71c	A3	65r on 10r red vio, II	14.00	8.00
72a	A3	65r on 20r lav	14.00	11.00
78c	A3	130r on 75r carmine	12.00	7.00

Enamel Paper
Perf. 12½

73a	A3	65r on 25r green	12.50	12.50
80b	A3	400r on 50r lt bl, I	10.00	10.00
80c	A3	400r on 50r lt bl, II	10.00	10.00

Perf. 13½

73b	A3	65r on 25r green	15.00	10.00
78a	A3	130r on 75r carmine	70.00	60.00
80d	A3	400r on 50r lt bl, I	400.00	—

Wove Paper
Perf. 11½

82b	N1	400r on 2½r brn, II	3.25	2.75

Perf. 12½

82	N1	400r on 2½r brn, I	2.25	2.00
82a	N1	400r on 2½r brn, II	2.25	2.00

Perf. 13½

82c	N1	400r on 2½r brn, II	6.00	4.00
		Nos. 70-82 (13)	167.75	120.75

For surcharges see Nos. 175-180, 211-216, 234-235.
Reprints of Nos. 65, 67, 68 and 69 have clean-cut perforation 13½.

Stamps of 1898 Overprinted — a

1902   Perf. 11½

83	A5	15r brown	2.75	1.75
84	A5	25r sea green	2.25	1.00
85	A5	50r blue	5.00	2.25
86	A5	75r rose	8.00	6.00
		Nos. 83-86 (4)	18.00	11.00

For surcharge see No. 116.

No. 48 Surcharged in Black

1905

87	A5	50r on 65r dull blue	7.00	3.50

For surcharge see No. 183.

Stamps of 1898-1903 Overprinted in Carmine or Green — b

1911

88	A5	2½r gray	.60	.45
89	A5	5r orange yel	.60	.45
90	A5	10r light green	.60	.45
91	A5	15r gray green	.85	.70
92	A5	20r gray violet	1.00	.75
93	A5	25r car (G)	1.00	.75
94	A5	50r brown	3.75	2.00
95	A5	75r lilac	6.75	3.25
96	A5	100r dk blue, *bl*	6.75	4.00
97	A5	115r org brn, *pink*	4.25	2.25
98	A5	130r brn, *straw*	4.25	2.25
99	A5	200r red lil, *pnksh*	4.75	2.75
100	A5	400r dull bl, *straw*	4.75	2.00
101	A5	500r blk & red, *bl*	4.75	2.25
102	A5	700r violet, *yelsh*	4.75	2.50
		Nos. 88-102 (15)	49.40	26.80

Inverted and double overprints of Nos. 88-102 were made intentionally.
For surcharges see Nos. 217-218, 221-222, 224.

King Manuel II — A6

Overprinted in Carmine or Green

1912   Perf. 11½x12

103	A6	2½r violet	.75	.40
104	A6	5r black	.75	.40
105	A6	10r gray green	.75	.40
106	A6	20r carmine (G)	.75	.40
107	A6	25r violet brown	.75	.40
108	A6	50r dk blue	1.75	1.25
109	A6	75r bister brown	2.00	1.75
110	A6	100r brown, *lt green*	3.50	2.25
111	A6	200r dk green, *salm-on*	3.50	2.25
112	A6	300r black, *azure*	3.50	2.25
		Nos. 103-112 (10)	18.00	11.75

For surcharges see Nos. 219-220, 226-227.

No. 91 Surcharged in Black

1912, June   Perf. 11½

113	A5	2½r on 15r gray green	5.50	3.25
114	A5	5r on 15r gray green	6.00	3.25
115	A5	10r on 15r gray green	4.50	3.25
		Nos. 113-115 (3)	16.00	9.75

Inverted and double surcharges of Nos. 113-115 were made intentionally.

Nos. 86 and 50 Surcharged in Black and Overprinted in Violet — c

1912

116	A5	25r on 75r rose	100.00	55.00
117	A5	25r on 75r red violet	5.75	5.50
a.		"REUPBLICA"	110.00	70.00
b.		"25" omitted	110.00	70.00
c.		"REPUBLICA" omitted	110.00	70.00

Ceres — A7

With Imprint
Chalky Paper
1914   Perf. 15x14
Name and Value in Black

118	A7	¼c olive brown	2.25	.80
		Never hinged	3.50	
119	A7	½c black	2.25	.80
		Never hinged	3.50	
120	A7	1c blue green	2.25	.80
		Never hinged	3.50	
121	A7	1½c lilac brown	4.50	2.75
		Never hinged	7.25	
122	A7	2c carmine	8.00	3.75
		Never hinged	13.00	
123	A7	2½c violet	1.60	.70
		Never hinged	2.50	
124	A7	5c blue	3.50	.80
		Never hinged	5.50	
125	A7	7½c yellow brn	4.50	2.75
		Never hinged	7.25	
126	A7	8c slate	4.50	2.75
		Never hinged	7.25	
127	A7	10c orange brn	4.50	2.75
		Never hinged	7.25	
128	A7	15c brown rose	7.00	3.00
		Never hinged	11.00	
129	A7	20c yel green	3.50	1.75
		Never hinged	5.50	
130	A7	30c brown, *green*	2.75	2.50
		Never hinged	4.50	
131	A7	40c brown, *pink*	2.75	2.50
		Never hinged	4.50	
132	A7	50c orange, *sal*	11.00	7.50
		Never hinged	17.50	
133	A7	1e green, *blue*	8.00	5.00
		Never hinged	13.00	
		Nos. 118-133 (16)	72.85	40.90

1915-22   Ordinary Paper

134	A7	¼c olive brown	.40	.35
		Never hinged	.65	
a.		Thick carton paper	1.25	1.10
		Never hinged	2.00	
135	A7	½c black	.40	.35
		Never hinged	.65	
a.		Thick carton paper	1.25	1.10
		Never hinged	2.00	
136	A7	1c blue green	.40	.35
		Never hinged	.65	
a.		1c dark green	.40	.35
		Never hinged	.65	
137	A7	1c yellow green ('18)	.40	.35
		Never hinged	.65	
138	A7	1½c lilac brown	.40	.35
		Never hinged	.65	
a.		Thick carton paper	1.25	1.10
		Never hinged	2.00	
139	A7	2c carmine	.40	.35
		Never hinged	.65	
140	A7	2½c dark violet	.35	.35
		Never hinged	.55	
a.		2½ pale violet ('18)	.45	.40
		Never hinged	.70	
141	A7	3c orange	37.50	29.00
		Never hinged	60.00	
142	A7	4c dull rose ('21)	.40	.35
		Never hinged	.65	
143	A7	5c blue	1.50	1.25
		Never hinged	2.50	
a.		5c pale blue ('18)	.40	.35
		Never hinged	.65	
144	A7	6c lilac ('21)	.40	.35
		Never hinged	.65	
145	A7	7c ultra ('21)	.40	.35
		Never hinged	.65	
146	A7	7½c yellow brn ('20)	.40	.40
		Never hinged	.65	
147	A7	8c slate	.40	.40
		Never hinged	.65	
148	A7	10c orange brn ('18)	.40	.35
		Never hinged	.65	
149	A7	12c olive brown ('21)	.75	.50
		Never hinged	1.20	
150	A7	15c plum ('20)	.60	.35
		Never hinged	.95	
151	A7	15c brown rose ('21)	.40	.35
		Never hinged	.65	
152	A7	20c yel green ('18)	6.25	5.25
		Never hinged	10.00	
153	A7	30c gray green ('21)	.60	.55
		Never hinged	.95	
154	A7	80c pink ('21)	2.10	1.00
		Never hinged	3.25	
a.		80c bright rose	2.10	1.00
		Never hinged	3.25	
155	A7	2e dark violet ('22)	3.50	3.25
		Never hinged	5.50	
		Nos. 134-155 (22)	58.35	46.15

1921-26   Perf. 12x11½

156	A7	¼c olive brown ('24)	.40	.35
		Never hinged	.65	
157	A7	½c black	.40	.35
		Never hinged	.65	
158	A7	1c blue green ('24)	.40	.35
		Never hinged	.65	
a.		1c dark green	.40	.35
		Never hinged	.65	
b.		1c pale yellow green ('21)	.40	.35
		Never hinged	.65	
158C	A7	1½c lilac brown ('24)	.40	.35
		Never hinged	.65	
158D	A7	2c carmine	.40	.35
		Never hinged	.65	
a.		2c carmine-red	.40	.35
		Never hinged	.65	
158E	A7	2c gray ('25)	.75	.55
		Never hinged	1.20	
158F	A7	2½c lt violet ('24)	.40	.35
		Never hinged	.65	
158G	A7	3c orange	.35	.30
		Never hinged	.55	
158H	A7	4c dull rose	.35	.30
		Never hinged	.55	
a.		4c pink	.35	.30
		Never hinged	.55	
158I	A7	4½c gray	.35	.30
		Never hinged	.55	
158J	A7	5c blue ('24)	.35	.30
		Never hinged	.55	
a.		5c pale blue	.35	.30
		Never hinged	.55	
158K	A7	6c lilac	.35	.30
		Never hinged	.55	
158L	A7	7c ultra	.35	.30
		Never hinged	.55	
158M	A7	7½c yellow brown ('24)	.45	.40
		Never hinged	.70	
158N	A7	8c slate ('24)	.45	.40
		Never hinged	.70	
158O	A7	10c orange brn ('24)	.40	.35
		Never hinged	.65	
158P	A7	12c olive brn	.75	.50
		Never hinged	1.20	
158Q	A7	12c dp green ('25)	.75	.50
		Never hinged	1.20	
158R	A7	15c plum ('24)	1.00	.35
		Never hinged	.95	
158S	A7	20c yel green	2.00	1.60
		Never hinged	3.25	
158T	A7	24c ultra ('25)	1.75	1.40
		Never hinged	2.75	
158U	A7	25c choc ('25)	1.75	1.25
		Never hinged	2.75	
158V	A7	30c gray grn	.70	.55
		Never hinged	1.10	
a.		deep green	.70	.55
		Never hinged	1.10	
158W	A7	40c turq blue	1.40	.75
		Never hinged	2.25	
158X	A7	50c lt violet ('25)	1.40	.70
		Never hinged	2.25	
158Y	A7	60c dk blue ('22)	1.75	.90
		Never hinged	3.00	
158Z	A7	60c dp rose ('26)	90.00	60.00
		Never hinged	145.00	
159A	A7	80c pink ('22)	1.90	1.00
		Never hinged	3.00	
159B	A7	1e rose ('22)	2.00	1.00
		Never hinged	3.25	
		Nos. 156-159B (29)	113.30	76.20

Glazed Paper
1921-25   Perf. 12x11½

159C	A7	1e rose	2.10	1.00
		Never hinged	3.25	
159D	A7	1e deep blue ('25)	3.50	2.00
		Never hinged	5.50	
159E	A7	2e dark violet ('22)	2.75	2.00
		Never hinged	4.50	
159F	A7	5e buff ('25)	16.50	12.50
		Never hinged	27.00	
159G	A7	10e pink ('25)	75.00	27.50
		Never hinged	120.00	
159H	A7	20e pale turq ('25)	150.00	75.00
		Never hinged	250.00	
		Nos. 159C-159H (6)	249.85	120.00

For surcharges see Nos. 228-229, 236-239.

Stamps of 1898-1903 Overprinted type "c" in Red or Green

1914   Perf. 11½, 12

159	A5	10r yel green (R)	6.50	5.25
160	A5	15r gray green (R)	6.00	5.25
161	A5	20r gray violet (G)	2.50	1.75
163	A5	75r red violet (G)	2.00	1.25
164	A5	100r blue, *blue* (R)	4.00	3.50
165	A5	115r org brn, *pink* (R)	125.00	
167	A5	200r red vio, *pnksh* (G)	2.50	1.75
169	A5	400r dl bl, *straw* (R)	47.50	47.50
170	A5	500r blk & red, *bl* (R)	6.00	5.50
171	A5	700r vio, *yelsh* (G)	40.00	25.00

Inverted and double overprints were made intentionally. No. 165 was not regularly issued. Red overprints on the 20r, 75r, 200r were not regularly issued. The 130r was not regularly issued without surcharge (No. 225).

On Nos. 63-65, 74-76, 78-79, 82
Perf. 11½, 12½, 13½

172	A2	115r on 10r (R)	17.00	17.00
a.		Perf. 13½		
173	A2	115r on 200r (R)	24.00	24.00
174	A2	130r on 50r (R)	32.50	32.50
175	A3	115r on 80r (R)	225.00	225.00
176	A3	115r on 100r (R)	250.00	225.00
a.		Perf. 11½	300.00	300.00
b.		Perf. 13½	850.00	850.00
177	A3	115r on 150r (G)	250.00	210.00
a.		Perf. 12½	275.00	225.00
b.		Perf. 13½	825.00	825.00
178	A3	130r on 75r (G)	4.50	4.00
a.		Perf. 12½	9.00	7.50
179	A3	130r on 300r (R)	9.75	9.00
a.		Perf. 13½	17.50	16.00
180	N1	400r on 2½r (R)	1.00	.75
a.		Perf. 11½	4.75	4.00
		Nos. 172-180 (9)	813.75	747.25

Nos. 85-87 Overprinted in Red or Green

On Stamps of 1902
Perf. 11½, 12

181	A5	50r blue (R)	2.50	2.00
182	A5	75r rose (G)	5.75	4.00

On No. 87

183	A5	50r on 65r dull blue (R)	5.50	3.50
		Nos. 181-183 (3)	13.75	9.50

Inverted and double surcharges of Nos. 181-183 were made intentionally.

Common Design Types pictured following the introduction.

Vasco da Gama Issue of Various Portuguese Colonies

Common Design Types CD20-CD27 Srchd.

On Stamps of Macao
1913   Perf. 12½ to 16

184	¼c on ½a blue grn	2.75	2.25
185	½c on 1a red	2.75	2.25
186	1c on 2a red violet	2.75	2.25
187	2½c on 4a yel green	2.25	1.60
188	5c on 8a dk blue	2.25	1.60
189	7½c on 12a vio brn	9.00	5.75
190	10c on 16a bister brn	3.25	2.50
191	15c on 24a bister	4.25	2.50
	Nos. 184-191 (8)	29.25	20.70

On Stamps of Portuguese Africa
Perf. 14 to 15

192	¼c on 2½r blue grn	1.25	.85
193	½c on 5r red	1.25	.85
194	1c on 10r red violet	1.25	.85
195	2½c on 25r yel grn	1.25	.85
196	5c on 50r dk blue	1.25	.85
197	7½c on 75r vio brn	7.50	6.50
198	10c on 100r bister brn	3.00	2.00
199	15c on 150r bister	3.50	2.25
	Nos. 192-199 (8)	20.25	15.00

On Stamps of Timor

200	¼c on ½a blue grn	2.75	2.10
201	½c on 1a red	2.75	2.10
202	1c on 2a red vio	2.75	2.10
203	2½c on 4a yel grn	2.25	1.50
204	5c on 8a dk blue	2.25	1.50
205	7½c on 12a vio brn	9.00	6.00
206	10c on 16a bis brn	3.25	2.40
207	15c on 24a bister	4.25	2.40
	Nos. 200-207 (8)	29.25	20.10
	Nos. 184-207 (24)	78.75	55.80

Provisional Issue of 1902 Overprinted in Carmine

1915   Perf. 11½, 12½, 13½

208	A2	115r on 10r green	2.25	2.25
209	A2	115r on 200r gray vio	2.75	2.25
210	A3	130r on 100r brown	2.25	1.75
211	A3	115r on 80r lt green	2.00	1.75
212	A3	115r on 100r brn, *buff*	2.25	2.00
a.		Perf. 11½	100.00	95.00
b.		Perf. 13½	17.50	15.00
213	A3	115r on 150r car, *rose*	1.75	1.75
a.		Perf. 12½	4.25	3.50
b.		Perf. 13½	3.00	2.25
214	A3	130r on 15r choc	2.00	1.75
a.		Perf. 12½	9.00	8.00
215	A3	130r on 75r carmine	3.50	2.75
a.		Perf. 13½	6.00	4.75
216	A3	130r on 300r dk bl, *sal*	2.25	1.75
a.		Perf. 13½	4.50	2.75
		Nos. 208-216 (9)	21.00	18.00

Stamps of 1911-14 Surcharged in Black

d   e

On Stamps of 1911
1919   Perf. 11½

217	A5 (d)	½c on 75r red lilac	3.25	3.00
218	A5 (d)	2½c on 100r blue, *grysh*	3.50	3.00

On Stamps of 1912
Perf. 11½x12

219	A6 (e)	½c on 75r bis brn	2.00	2.00
220	A6 (e)	2½c on 100r brn, *lt grn*	3.50	3.00

On Stamps of 1914

221	A5 (d)	½c on 75r red lil	2.00	2.00
222	A5 (d)	2½c on 100r bl, grysh	2.75	2.50
		Nos. 217-222 (6)	17.00	15.50

Inverted and double surcharges were made for sale to collectors.

Nos. 163, 98 and Type of 1914 Surcharged with New Values and Bars in Black

1921

223	A5 (c)	00.5c on 75r	350.00	350.00
224	A5 (b)	4c on 130r		
		(#98)	2.75	2.00
225	A5 (c)	4c on 130r brn, *straw*	8.00	7.50
a.		Without surcharge	240.00	

Nos. 109 and 108 Surcharged with New Values and Bars in Black

226	A6	00.5c on 75r	2.00	1.75
227	A6	1c on 50r	2.25	2.00

Nos. 133 and 138 Surcharged with New Values and Bars in Black

228	A7	00.5c on 7½c	2.50	2.25
		Never hinged	4.00	
229	A7	04c on 15c	2.50	2.00
		Never hinged	4.00	
		Nos. 224-229 (6)	20.00	17.50
		Nos. 223-229 (7)	370.00	367.50

The 04c surcharge exists on the 15c brown rose, perf 12x11½, No. 139.
Some authorities question the status of No. 223.

Nos. 81-82
Surcharged

1925   *Perf. 12½*

234	A3	40c on 400r on 200r bl, bl	1.25	1.00
a.		Perf. 13½	6.75	4.50
235	N1	40c on 400r on 2½r brn	.95	.95
a.		Perf. 13½	.95	.95

Nos. 150-151, 154-155
Surcharged

1931   *Perf. 12x 11½*

236	A7	50c on 60c deep rose	3.00	2.00
		Never hinged	4.00	
237	A7	70c on 80c pink	5.00	3.00
		Never hinged	8.00	
238	A7	70c on 1e deep blue	5.00	3.00
		Never hinged	7.25	
239	A7	1.40e on 2e dark violet	4.00	2.00
		Never hinged	5.25	
		Nos. 236-239 (4)	17.00	10.00

Ceres — A14

Perf. 12x11½

1932-46		**Typo.**	**Wmk. 232**	
243	A14	1c bister brn	.30	.25
244	A14	5c dk brown	.35	.30
245	A14	10c dp violet	.35	.30
246	A14	15c black	.35	.30
247	A14	20c gray	.40	.30
248	A14	30c myrtle grn	.40	.30
249	A14	35c yel grn ('46)	9.25	4.25
250	A14	40c dp orange	.45	.25
251	A14	45c lt blue	1.75	1.40
252	A14	50c lt brown	.40	.25
253	A14	60c olive grn	1.00	.30
254	A14	70c orange brn	1.10	.30
255	A14	80c emerald	.75	.25
256	A14	85c rose	5.50	2.25
257	A14	1a claret	1.00	.30
258	A14	1.40a dk blue	11.50	2.25
258A	A14	1.75a dk blue ('46)	20.00	5.25
259	A14	2a dull vio	5.25	.60
260	A14	5a pale yel grn	11.50	2.00

261	A14	10a olive bis	22.50	5.75
262	A14	20a orange	57.50	5.75
		Nos. 243-262 (21)	151.60	32.90
		Set, never hinged	275.00	

For surcharges see Nos. 263-267, 271-273; see 294A-300, J31-J36 in *Scott Standard Postage Stamp Catalogue, Vol. 1.*

Surcharged in Black

5½mm between bars and new value.

1934

263	A14	10c on 45c lt bl	4.00	2.75
264	A14	20c on 85c rose	4.00	2.75
265	A14	30c on 1.40a dk bl	4.00	2.75
266	A14	70c on 2a dl vio	6.00	2.75
267	A14	80c on 5a pale yel grn	9.00	2.75
		Nos. 263-267 (5)	27.00	13.75
		Set, never hinged	45.00	

See Nos. 294A-300 in *Scott Standard Postage Stamp Catalogue, Vol. 1.*

Nos. J26, J30
Surcharged in Black

1935   **Unwmk.**   *Perf. 11½*

268	D2	5c on 6c lt brown	2.50	1.75
269	D2	30c on 50c gray	2.50	1.75
270	D2	40c on 50c gray	2.50	1.75
		Nos. 268-270 (3)	7.50	5.25
		Set, never hinged	14.00	

No. 255 Surcharged in Black

1938   **Wmk. 232**   *Perf. 12x11½*

271	A14	5c on 80c emerald	1.10	.60
272	A14	10c on 80c emerald	1.90	.90
273	A14	15c on 80c emerald	2.50	.90
		Nos. 271-273 (3)	5.50	2.40
		Set, never hinged	10.00	

Vasco da Gama Issue
Common Design Types
Engr.; Name & Value Typo. in Black
Perf. 13½x13

1938, July 26			**Unwmk.**	
274	CD34	1c gray green	.30	.25
275	CD34	5c orange brn	.40	.35
276	CD34	10c dk carmine	.45	.35
277	CD34	15c dk violet brn	.45	.35
278	CD34	20c slate	.45	.35
279	CD35	30c rose violet	.55	.40
280	CD35	35c brt green	1.10	.80
281	CD35	40c brown	.40	.25
282	CD35	50c brt red vio	.55	.25
283	CD36	60c gray black	1.25	.35
284	CD36	70c brown vio	1.25	.35
285	CD36	80c orange	1.25	.35
286	CD36	1a red	1.25	.35
287	CD37	1.75a blue	2.25	1.00
288	CD37	2a brown car	3.50	1.10
289	CD37	5a olive grn	16.00	1.25
290	CD38	10a blue vio	32.50	1.25
291	CD38	20a red brown	45.00	4.00
		Nos. 274-291 (18)	108.90	13.35
		Set, never hinged	190.00	

For surcharges see Nos. 301-304 in *Scott Standard Postage Stamp Catalogue, Vol. 1.*

Marble Column and
Portuguese Arms
with Cross — A20

261	A14	10a olive bis	22.50	5.75

1938, July 29   *Perf. 12½*

292	A20	80c blue green	3.75	2.25
293	A20	1.75a deep blue	22.50	6.25
294	A20	20a dk red brown	65.00	22.50
		Nos. 292-294 (3)	91.25	31.00
		Set, never hinged	175.00	

Visit of the President of Portugal to this colony in 1938.

AIR POST STAMPS

Plane Over Globe
Common Design Type
Perf. 13½x13

1938, July 26		**Engr.**		**Unwmk.**
		Name and Value in Black		
C1	CD39	10c red orange	.55	.45
C2	CD39	20c purple	.55	.40
C3	CD39	50c orange	.55	.45
C4	CD39	1a ultra	.55	.45
C5	CD39	2a lilac brn	1.25	.40
C6	CD39	3a dk green	2.25	.75
C7	CD39	5a red brown	5.75	1.00
C8	CD39	9a rose carmine	8.50	2.00
C9	CD39	10a magenta	12.50	3.00
		Nos. C1-C9 (9)	32.45	8.90

No. C7 exists with overprint "Exposicao Internacional de Nova York, 1939-1940" and Trylon and Perisphere. Value; used & unused $110., never hinged, $175.

POSTAGE DUE STAMPS

D1

1904   **Unwmk.**   **Typo.**   *Perf. 11½x12*

J1	D1	5r yellow grn	.55	.45
J2	D1	10r slate	.55	.45
J3	D1	20r yellow brn	1.00	.70
J4	D1	30r orange	1.00	.70
J5	D1	50r gray brown	1.40	1.00
J6	D1	60r red brown	11.50	7.00
J7	D1	100r lilac	5.00	3.50
J8	D1	130r dull blue	5.00	3.50
J9	D1	200r carmine	14.00	9.00
J10	D1	500r gray violet	12.00	7.75
		Nos. J1-J10 (10)	52.00	34.05

Postage Due Stamps of 1904 Overprinted in Carmine or Green

1911

J11	D1	5r yellow grn	.40	.35
J12	D1	10r slate	.40	.35
J13	D1	20r yellow brn	.40	.35
J14	D1	30r orange	.55	.45
J15	D1	50r gray brown	.55	.45
J16	D1	60r red brown	1.50	1.00
J17	D1	100r lilac	1.50	1.00
J18	D1	130r dull blue	1.75	1.25
J19	D1	200r carmine (G)	2.25	1.25
J20	D1	500r gray violet	2.50	2.25
		Nos. J11-J20 (10)	11.80	8.70

D2

1921   *Perf. 11½*

J21	D2	½c yellow green	.40	.35
J22	D2	1c slate	.40	.35
J23	D2	2c orange brown	.40	.35
J24	D2	3c orange	.40	.35
J25	D2	5c gray brown	.40	.35
J26	D2	6c lt brown	.40	.35
J27	D2	10c red violet	.60	.40
J28	D2	13c dull blue	1.10	.95

J29	D2	20c carmine	1.10	.95
J30	D2	50c gray	1.10	.95
		Nos. J21-J30 (10)	6.30	5.35

For surcharges see Nos. 268-270.

NEWSPAPER STAMP

N1

Perf. 11½, 12½, 13½

1893		**Typo.**	**Unwmk.**	
P1	N1	2½r brown	3.50	1.50

No. P1 was also used for ordinary postage.
For surcharges see Nos. 37, 82, 180, 235.

POSTAL TAX STAMPS

Pombal Issue
Common Design Types

1925, May 8		**Unwmk.**	*Perf. 12½*	
RA1	CD28	15c lilac & black	1.25	1.00
RA2	CD29	15c lilac & black	1.25	1.00
RA3	CD30	15c lilac & black	1.25	1.00
		Nos. RA1-RA3 (3)	3.75	3.00

"Charity"
PT1

Coat of Arms
PT2

1929		**Litho.**	*Perf. 11*	
		Without Gum		
RA4	PT1	50c dark blue	7.25	2.25

1939		**Without Gum**	*Perf. 10½*	
RA5	PT2	50c turq green	3.75	.35
RA6	PT2	1a red	8.50	2.50

A 1.50a, type PT2, was issued for fiscal use. Value, $5.

POSTAL TAX DUE STAMPS

Pombal Issue
Common Design Types

1925, May 8		**Unwmk.**	*Perf. 12½*	
RAJ1	CD28	30c lilac & black	1.25	1.00
RAJ2	CD29	30c lilac & black	1.25	1.00
RAJ3	CD30	30c lilac & black	1.25	1.00
		Nos. RAJ1-RAJ3 (3)	3.75	3.00

See note after Portugal No. RAJ4.

ANGRA

'aŋ-grə

LOCATION — An administrative district of the Azores, consisting of the islands of Terceira, Sao Jorge and Graciosa.
GOVT. — A district of Portugal
AREA — 275 sq. mi.
POP. — 70,000 (approx.)
CAPITAL — Angra do Heroismo

1000 Reis = 1 Milreis

STAMPS OF PORTUGAL USED IN ANGRA

Barred Numeral "48"

1853			**Queen Maria II**
A1	5r org brn (#1)		1,350.
A2	25r blue (#2)		75.00
A3	50r dp yel grn (#3)		1,400.
a.	50r blue grn (#3a)		2,000.
A4	100r lilac (#4)		3,750.

1855		**King Pedro V (Straight Hair)**	
A5	5r red brn (#5)		1,450.
A6	25r blue, type II (#6)		67.50
a.	Type I (#6a)		75.00
A7	50r green (#7)		110.00
A8	100r lilac (#8)		140.00

1856-58		**King Pedro V (Curled Hair)**	
A9	5r red brn (#9)		175.00
A10	25r blue, type II (#10)		120.00
a.	Type I (#10a)		85.00
A11	25r rose, type II (#11; '58)		27.50

1862-64			**King Luiz**
A12	5r brown (#12)		85.00
A13	10r orange (#13)		95.00
A14	25r rose (#14)		20.00
A15	50r yel green (#15)		125.00
A16	100r lilac (#16; '64)		140.00

1866-67			**King Luiz**
	Imperf.		
A17	5r black (#17)		120.00
A18	10r yellow (#18)		200.00
A19	20r bister (#19)		200.00
A20	25r rose (#20)		52.50
A21	50r green (#21)		160.00
A22	80r orange (#22)		160.00
A23	100r dk lilac (#23; '67)		210.00
A24	120r blue (#24)		150.00
	Perf. 12½		
A28	25r rose (#28)		120.00

King Carlos — A1

Enamel surfaced paper

			1892-93 Typo. Unwmk.	**Perf. 12½**	
1	A1	5r yellow		5.00	2.75
		Never hinged		5.75	
2	A1	10r redsh violet		5.00	2.75
		Never hinged		5.75	
3	A1	15r chocolate		7.00	4.00
		Never hinged		6.50	
4	A1	20r lavender		9.0	3.00
		Never hinged		7.50	
5	A1	25r green		5.00	.80
		Never hinged		5.75	
7	A1	50r blue		11.00	4.50
		Never hinged		11.00	
8	A1	75r carmine		12.00	6.00
		Never hinged		14.50	
9	A1	80r yellow green		15.00	11.50
		Never hinged		17.50	
10a	A1	100r brown, *yellow*		175.00	150.00
		Never hinged		210.00	
11	A1	150r car, *rose* ('93)		65.00	45.00
		Never hinged		90.00	
12	A1	200r dk blue, *bl* ('93)		65.00	45.00
		Never hinged		90.00	
13	A1	300r dk blue, *sal* ('93)		65.00	45.00
		Never hinged		90.00	
		Nos. 1-13 (11)		264.00	170.30

Enamel surfaced paper, Perf 13½

1b	A1	5r yellow		4.00	2.75
		Never hinged		3.75	

2a	A1	10r reddish violet		5.75	4.00
		Never hinged		5.00	
3a	A1	15r chocolate		7.00	4.00
		Never hinged		5.00	
4a	A1	20r lavender		9.00	3.25
		Never hinged		14.00	
7a	A1	50r blue		7.00	7.00
		Never hinged		15.00	
10	A1	100r brown, *yellow*		55.00	16.00
		Never hinged		52.50	
11a	A1	150r carmine, *rose*		75.00	60.00
		Never hinged		85.00	
12a	A1	200r dark blue, *blue*		75.00	60.00
		Never hinged ('93)		85.00	
13a	A1	300r dark blue, *salmon*		75.00	60.00
		Never hinged		85.00	

Enamel surfaced paper, perf 11½

1a	A1	5r yellow		14.00	7.00
		Never hinged		17.00	
5b	A1	25r green		6.00	1.25
		Never hinged		7.50	

Chalky surfaced paper with lozenges, Perf 12½

1c	A1	5r yellow		4.25	1.40
		Never hinged		5.25	

Chalky surfaced paper with lozenges, Perf 13½

1d	A1	5r yellow		4.50	1.60
		Never hinged		6.50	
5a	A1	25r green		10.00	6.00
		Never hinged		12.00	
7b	A1	50r blue		—	30.00
		Never hinged		—	

Reprints of 50r, 150r, 200r and 300r, made in 1900, are perf. 11½ and ungummed. Value, each $50. Reprints of all values, made in 1905, have shiny white gum and clean-cut perf. Value, each $22.50.

King Carlos — A2

Name and Value in Black except Nos. 26 and 35

		1897-1905	**Perf. 11½**	
14	A2	2½r gray	.75	.50
		Never hinged	.90	
15	A2	5r orange	.75	.50
		Never hinged	.90	
a.		Diagonal half used as 2½r on newspaper or circular		32.50
16	A2	10r yellow grn	.75	.50
		Never hinged	.90	
17	A2	15r brown	10.00	7.00
		Never hinged	12.00	
18	A2	15r gray grn ('99)	1.00	.70
		Never hinged	1.90	
19	A2	20r gray violet	2.00	1.50
		Never hinged	2.40	
20	A2	25r sea green	3.25	1.40
		Never hinged	4.00	
21	A2	25r car rose ('99)	.75	.70
		Never hinged	1.00	
22	A2	50r dark blue	6.00	2.00
		Never hinged	7.25	
23	A2	50r ultra ('05)	20.00	12.50
		Never hinged	25.00	
24	A2	65r slate bl ('98)	1.40	.70
		Never hinged	1.60	
25	A2	75r rose	4.00	1.90
		Never hinged	4.75	
26	A2	75r gray brn & car, *straw* ('05)	20.00	12.50
		Never hinged	25.00	
27	A2	80r violet	1.60	1.40
		Never hinged	2.00	
28	A2	100r dk blue, *bl*	3.50	2.00
		Never hinged	3.75	
29	A2	115r org brn, *pink* ('98)	4.00	2.25
		Never hinged	3.50	
30	A2	130r gray brn, *straw* ('98)	4.00	2.25
		Never hinged	3.50	
31	A2	150r lt brn, *straw*	3.50	2.00
		Never hinged	3.50	
32	A2	180r sl, *pnksh* ('98)	5.00	3.25
		Never hinged	4.50	
33	A2	200r red vio, *pnksh*	6.00	5.50
		Never hinged	7.25	
34	A2	300r blue, *rose*	12.00	8.00
		Never hinged	14.00	
35	A2	500r blk & red, *bl*	20.00	16.00
		Never hinged	24.00	
a.		Perf. 12½	35.00	20.00
		Never hinged	35.00	
		Nos. 14-35 (22)	130.25	85.05

Yellowish paper

15b	A2	5r orange	.65	.45
		Never hinged	.85	
21b	A2	25r carmine rose		
		('99)	1.00	.50
		Never hinged	1.20	
24b	A2	65r slate blue ('98)	1.10	.55
		Never hinged	1.50	
29a	A2	115r orange, *yellowish*	6.75	3.75
		Never hinged	9.00	

Azores stamps were used in Angra from 1906 to 1931, when they were superseded by those of Portugal.

ANJOUAN

'an-jü-wän

LOCATION — One of the Comoro Islands in the Mozambique Channel between Madagascar and Mozambique.
GOVT. — French Colony.
AREA — 89 sq. mi.
POP. — 20,000 (approx. 1912)
CAPITAL — Mossamondu
See Comoro Islands.

100 Centimes = 1 Franc

PRE-STAMP POSTAL MARKINGS

Three-line handstamp:
Perçu (*Manuscript denomination*)
pour affranchissement
Le Receveur de la Poste

1892, Feb.-Mar.

A1	0f25 on cover		9,500.
A2	0f50 on cover		9,500.

This handstamp was used provisionally, when stocks of French Colonies General Issue stamps had run out, and supplies of the first Anjouan issue had not yet arrived.

Navigation and Commerce — A1

Perf. 14x13½

		1892-1907 Typo.	**Unwmk.**	
		Name of Colony in Blue or Carmine		
1	A1	1c black, *blue*	1.75	1.75
		Never hinged	2.50	
		On cover		250.00
2	A1	2c brown, *buff*	2.75	1.75
		Never hinged	4.25	
		On cover		250.00
3	A1	4c claret, *lav*	5.50	4.00
		Never hinged	7.00	
		On cover		275.00
4	A1	5c green, *grnsh*	9.50	6.25
		Never hinged	16.50	
		On cover		150.00
		On newspaper or wrapper, single franking		550.00
5	A1	10c blk, *lavender*	11.50	6.75
		Never hinged	21.00	
		On cover		150.00
6	A1	10c red ('00)	37.50	30.00
		Never hinged	65.00	
		On cover		300.00
7	A1	15c blue, quadrille paper	17.00	11.50
		Never hinged	27.50	
		On cover		125.00
8	A1	15c gray, *lt gray* ('00)	27.50	22.50
		Never hinged	52.50	
		On cover		250.00
9	A1	20c red, *green*	17.50	11.00
		Never hinged	30.00	
		On cover		225.00
		On cover, single franking		300.00
10	A1	25c black, *rose*	17.50	14.00
		Never hinged	30.00	
		On cover		250.00
		On cover, single franking		375.00
11	A1	25c blue ('00)	30.00	22.50
		Never hinged	56.00	
		On cover		275.00
		On cover, single franking		440.00
12	A1	30c brn, *bister*	35.00	22.50
		Never hinged	60.00	
		On cover		190.00
		On cover, single franking		250.00
13	A1	35c blk, *yel* ('06)	18.00	10.00
		Never hinged	30.00	
		On cover		150.00
		On cover, single franking		250.00
14	A1	40c red, *straw*	37.50	32.50
		Never hinged	75.00	
		On cover		300.00
		On cover, single franking		440.00
15	A1	45c blk, *gray grn* ('07)	140.00	115.00
		Never hinged	280.00	
		On cover		650.00
		On cover		800.00
a.		Perf 11	425.00	
		Never hinged	575.00	
16	A1	50c car, *rose*	42.50	32.50
		Never hinged	82.50	
		On cover		375.00
		On cover, single franking		550.00
17	A1	50c brn, *az* ('00)	32.50	32.50
		Never hinged	62.50	
		On cover		375.00
		On cover, single franking		500.00
18	A1	75c vio, *orange*	37.50	27.50
		Never hinged	77.50	
		On cover		350.00
		On cover, single franking		525.00

19	A1	1fr brnz grn, *straw*	85.00	77.50
		Never hinged	180.00	
		On cover		550.00
		On cover, single franking		700.00
		Nos. 1-19 (19)	606.00	482.00

Perf. 13½x14 stamps are counterfeits.
Covers: Values are for commercial covers used at Anjouan.

Issues of 1892-1907 Surcharged in Black or Carmine

1912

Spacing between figures of surcharge 1.5mm (5c), 2mm (10c)

20	A1	5c on 2c brn, *buff*	1.25	1.25
		Never hinged	1.90	
		On cover		110.00
21	A1	5c on 4c cl, *lav* (C)	1.40	*1.50*
		Never hinged	2.40	
		On cover		105.00
a.		Pair, one without surcharge	*1,000.*	*1,100.*
22	A1	5c on 15c blue (C)	1.40	1.40
		Never hinged	2.25	
		On cover		110.00
a.		Pair, one without surcharge	*1,100.*	*1,000.*
23	A1	5c on 20c red, *green*	1.40	1.40
		Never hinged	2.25	
		On cover		110.00
a.		Pair, one without surcharge	*1,100.*	*1,100.*
24	A1	5c on 25c blk, *rose* (C)	1.50	*1.75*
		Never hinged	2.75	
		On cover		100.00
25	A1	5c on 30c brn, *bis* (C)	2.00	*2.10*
		Never hinged	3.25	
		On cover		110.00
26	A1	10c on 40c red, *straw*	2.00	*2.25*
		Never hinged	3.25	
		On cover		150.00
27	A1	10c on 45c black, *gray green* (C)	2.40	2.40
		Never hinged	3.75	
		On cover		150.00
28	A1	10c on 50c car, *rose*	5.75	*6.50*
		Never hinged	8.00	
		On cover		210.00
29	A1	10c on 75c vio, *org*	4.00	*4.50*
		Never hinged	6.25	
		On cover		190.00
30	A1	10c on 1fr brnz grn, *straw*	5.25	*5.75*
		Never hinged	7.25	
		On cover		210.00
a.		Pair, one without surcharge	*1,250.*	*1,200.*
		Nos. 20-30 (11)	28.35	30.80

Spacing between figures of surcharge 2.25mm (5c), 2.75mm (10c)

20a	A1	5c on 2c brn, *buff*	12.50	12.50
		Never hinged	24.00	
21b	A1	5c on 4c cl, *lav* (C)	12.50	12.50
		Never hinged	24.00	
22b	A1	5c on 15c blue (C)	14.00	14.00
		Never hinged	21.00	
23b	A1	5c on 20c red, *green*	14.00	14.00
		Never hinged	30.00	
24a	A1	5c on 25c blk, *rose* (C)	14.00	14.00
		Never hinged	30.00	
25a	A1	5c on 30c brn, *bis* (C)	14.00	14.00
		Never hinged	30.00	
26a	A1	10c on 40c red, *straw*	45.00	45.00
		Never hinged	97.50	
27a	A1	10c on 45c black, *gray green* (C)	57.50	57.50
		Never hinged	110.00	
28a	A1	10c on 50c car, *rose*	95.00	95.00
		Never hinged	160.00	
29a	A1	10c on 75c vio, *org*	87.50	87.50
		Never hinged	150.00	
30b	A1	10c on 1fr brnz grn, *straw*	95.00	95.00
		Never hinged	160.00	
		Nos. 20a-30b (11)	461.00	461.00

Nos. 20-30 were available for use in Madagascar and the Comoro archipelago.

The stamps of Anjouan were superseded by those of Madagascar, and in 1950 by those of Comoro Islands.

ANNAM & TONKIN

a-'nam and 'tän-'kin

LOCATION — In French Indo-China bordering on the China Sea on the east and Siam on the west.
GOVT. — French Protectorate
AREA — 97,503 sq. mi.
POP. — 14,124,000 (approx. 1890)
CAPITAL — Annam: Hue; Tonkin: Hanoi

For administrative purposes, the Protectorates of Annam, Tonkin, Cambodia, Laos and the Colony of Cochin-China were grouped together and were known as French Indo-China.

100 Centimes = 1 Franc

Catalogue values for unused stamps are for examples without gum as most stamps were issued in that condition.

Stamps of French Colonies, 1881-86 Handstamped Surcharged in Black

Perf. 14x13½

1888, Jan. 21				**Unwmk.**	
1	A9	1c on 2c brn, *buff*		47.50	50.00
		On cover			150.00
a.		Inverted surcharge		200.00	200.00
b.		Sideways surcharge		200.00	210.00
c.		Pair, one surcharge inverted		250.00	
2	A9	1c on 4c claret, *lav*		37.50	35.00
		On cover			125.00
a.		Inverted surcharge		200.00	210.00
b.		Double surcharge		275.00	225.00
c.		Sideways surcharge		200.00	200.00
3	A9	5c on 10c blk, *lav*		47.50	37.50
		On cover			125.00
a.		Inverted surcharge		200.00	200.00
b.		Double surcharge		225.00	225.00

Hyphen between "A" and "T"

7	A9	1c on 2c brn, *buff*		325.00	400.00
		On cover			1,000.
a.		Inverted surcharge		750.00	775.00
b.		Sideways surcharge		750.00	775.00
c.		Pair, Nos. 1, 7		9,000.	
8	A9	1c on 4c claret, *lav*		525.00	625.00
		On cover			1,000.
9	A9	5c on 10c blk, *lav*		220.00	240.00
		On cover			600.00

A 5c on 2c was prepared but not issued. Value $8,500.

In these surcharges there are different types of numerals and letters.

There are numerous other errors in the placing of the surcharges, including double one inverted, double both inverted, double one sideways, and pair one without surcharge. Such varieties command substantial premiums.

These stamps were superseded in 1892 by those of Indo-China.

ANTIGUA

an-'tēg-ˌwˌə

LOCATION — In the West Indies, southeast of Puerto Rico
GOVT. — Presidency of the Leeward Islands Colony
AREA — 171 sq. mi.
POP. — 34,523
CAPITAL — St. John's

Antigua stamps were discontinued in 1890 and resumed in 1903. In the interim, stamps of Leeward Islands were used. Between 1903-1956,

---

stamps of Antigua and Leeward Islands were used concurrently.

12 Pence = 1 Shilling
20 Shillings = 1 Pound

> **Catalogue Values for unused stamps in this country are for Never Hinged items, beginning with Scott 96.**

Watermark

Wmk. 5 — Star

PRE-STAMP POSTAL MARKINGS

Crowned Circle handstamp types I and IV are pictured in the Crowned Circle Handstamps and Great Britain Used Abroad section.

St. John's

1850				
A1	I	"Antigua" crowned circle handstamp in red, on cover		800.

Covers used from 1860-1869 are valued at $650.

English Harbor

1857				
A2	IV	"English Harbor" crowned circle handstamp, on cover		10,000.

STAMPS OF GREAT BRITAIN USED IN ANTIGUA

Numeral cancellation type A is pictured in the Crowned Circle Handstamps and Great Britain Used Abroad section.

1858-60				
		A02 (St. John's)		
A3	A	1p rose red (#20)		775.
A4	A	2p blue (#17)		1,750.
A5	A	2p blue (#29, P8, 9)		1,100.
		Plate 7		1,350.
A6	A	4p rose (#26)		675.
A7	A	6p lilac (#27)		210.
A8	A	1sh green (#28)		3,500.
		A18 (English Harbor)		
A9		2p blue (#29, P7)		11,500.
A10	A	4p rose (#26)		11,500.
A11	A	6p lilac (#27)		2,500.
A12	A	1sh green (#28)		—

Forged cancellations exist.

Values for unused stamps are for examples with original gum as defined in the catalogue introduction. Any exceptions will be noted. Very fine examples of Nos. 1-8, 11, 18-20 will have perforations touching the design on at least one frameline due to the narrow spacing of the stamps on the plates. Stamps with perfs clear of the framelines on all four sides are extremely scarce and will command higher prices.

Queen Victoria
A1   A2

Rough Perf. 14-16

1862		**Engr.**		**Unwmk.**	
1	A1	6p blue green		950.00	600.00
		On cover			5,000.
a.		Perf. 11-13		8,500.	

---

b.		Perf. 11-13x14-16		3,750.	
c.		Perf. 11-13 compound with 14-16		3,750.	

There is a question whether Nos. 1a-1c ever did postal duty.
Values for No. 1 are for stamps with perfs cutting into the design. Values for No. 1b are for examples without gum.

1863-67				**Wmk. 5**	
2	A1	1p dull rose		140.00	60.00
a.		Vert. pair, imperf. btwn.		37,500.	
b.		Imperf., pair			2,750.
c.		1p lilac rose		150.00	82.50
		On cover			650.00
3	A1	1p vermilion ('67)		275.00	32.50
		On cover			450.00
a.		Horiz. pair, imperf. btwn.		37,500.	
4	A1	6p green		775.00	30.00
		On cover			800.00
a.		6p yellow green		4,750.	110.00
		On cover			2,350.
b.		Pair, imperf. btwn.		—	
c.		6p dark green		850.00	30.00
		On cover			900.00

1872		**Wmk. 1**		**Perf. 12½**	
5	A1	1p lake		220.00	22.50
		On cover			800.00
6	A1	1p vermilion		225.00	26.50
		On cover			800.00
7	A1	6p blue green		600.00	12.50
		On cover			800.00

1873-79				**Perf. 14**	
8	A1	1p lake		250.00	12.50
		On cover			625.00
a.		Half used as ½p on cover			9,500.
b.		1p lake rose		250.00	12.50
		On cover			625.00

		Typo.			
9	A2	2½p red brown ('79)		700.00	210.00
		On cover			2,250.
a.		Large "2" with slanting bottom line		12,500.	3,100.
10	A2	4p blue ('79)		290.00	18.00

		Engr.			
11	A1	6p blue green ('76)		400.00	19.00
		On cover			1,000.

No. 9a is the result of damage to the plate.

1882-86		**Typo.**		**Wmk. 2**	
12	A2	½p green		4.00	20.00
		On cover			250.00
13	A2	2½p red brown		225.00	67.50
		On cover			750.00
a.		Large "2" with slanting bottom line		4,000.	1,400.
14	A2	2½p ultra ('86)		8.50	17.00
		On cover			200.00
a.		Large "2" with slanting bottom line		475.00	300.00
15	A2	4p blue		350.00	19.00
		On cover			200.00
16	A2	4p brown org ('86)		2.50	3.75
		On cover			50.00
17	A2	1sh violet ('86)		190.00	175.00
		On cover			2,000.

		Engr.			
18	A1	1p carmine ('84)		2.50	4.50
		On cover			50.00
a.		1p rose		67.50	14.50
		On cover			150.00
19	A1	6p deep green		77.50	150.00
		On cover			1,600.

No. 13a is the result of damage to the plate.
Nos. 18 and 18a were used for a time in St. Christopher and are identified by the "A12" cancellation.

1884				**Perf. 12**	
20	A1	1p rose red		65.00	19.00
		On cover			1,000.

Seal of the Colony — A3   King Edward VII — A4

1903		**Typo. Wmk. 1**		**Perf. 14**	
21	A3	½p blue grn & blk		4.00	7.50
a.		Bluish paper ('09)		100.00	100.00
22	A3	1p car & black		11.00	1.50
a.		Bluish paper ('09)		92.50	92.50
23	A3	2p org brn & vio		8.25	27.50
24	A3	2½p ultra & black		14.00	19.00
25	A3	3p ocher & gray green		12.00	24.00
26	A3	6p black & red vio		35.00	60.00
27	A3	1sh violet & ultra		55.00	65.00

28	A3	2sh pur & gray green		90.00	120.00
29	A3	2sh6p red vio & blk		27.50	65.00
30	A4	5sh pur & gray green		110.00	160.00
		Nos. 21-30 (10)		366.75	549.50
		Set, overprinted "SPECIMEN"		225.00	

The 2½p, 1sh and 5sh exist on both ordinary and chalky paper.

1907				**Chalky Paper**	
21b	A3	½p		4.00	5.00
24a	A3	2½p		32.50	70.00
27a	A3	1sh		60.00	140.00
30a	A4	5sh		150.00	190.00

1908-20				**Wmk. 3**	
31	A3	½p green		4.75	5.25
a.		½p blue green ('17)		5.00	7.50
b.		½p dk grn, thick paper ('20)		3.00	5.00
32	A3	1p carmine		11.00	2.75
a.		1p scarlet ('15)		7.50	3.75
33	A3	2p org brn & dull vio ('12)		5.25	35.00
34	A3	2½p ultra		21.00	19.00
a.		2½p bright blue		25.00	24.00
35	A3	3p ocher & grn ('12)		7.00	21.00
a.		3p orange & dp grn ('18)		8.00	24.00
36	A3	6p blk & red vio ('11)		8.25	47.50
a.		6p grnsh black & magenta ('15)		8.50	50.00
37	A3	1sh vio & ultra		24.00	80.00
a.		1sh dk violet & dk blue ('15)		20.00	75.00
38	A3	2sh vio & green		110.00	130.00
		Nos. 31-38 (8)		191.25	340.50

Nos. 33, 35 to 38 are on chalky paper.
For overprints see Nos. MR1-MR3.

George V — A6

1913					
41	A6	5sh violet & green, chalky paper		95.00	150.00
a.		5sh dull violet & bright green, ordinary paper		85.00	125.00
		Overprinted "SPECIMEN"		90.00	

St. John's Harbor — A7

1921-29				**Wmk. 4**	
42	A7	½p green		3.25	.60
43	A7	1p rose red		4.50	.60
a.		1p bright scarlet ('29)		30.00	4.50
44	A7	1p dp violet ('23)		6.50	1.75
a.		1p mauve ('25)		20.00	8.00
45	A7	1½p orange ('22)		6.00	8.00
46	A7	1½p rose red ('26)		10.00	2.00
47	A7	1½p fawn ('29)		3.25	.75
48	A7	2p gray		4.50	.90
49	A7	2½p ultra		7.50	5.00
a.		2½p bright blue ('22)		7.00	20.00
50	A7	2½p orange ('23)		2.75	20.00

		Chalky Paper			
51	A7	3p violet, *yel* ('25)		11.00	9.50
52	A7	6p vio & red vio		7.00	6.00
53	A7	1sh black, *emer* ('29)		6.50	5.75
54	A7	2sh vio & ultra, *blue* ('27)		12.00	65.00
55	A7	2sh6p blk & red, *blue* ('27)		47.50	35.00
56	A7	3sh grn & vio ('22)		52.50	105.00
57	A7	4sh blk & red ('22)		52.50	77.50
		Nos. 42-57 (16)		237.25	343.35
		Set, overprinted or perforated "SPECIMEN"		450.00	

				Wmk. 3	
		Chalky Paper			
58	A7	3p violet, *yel*		5.00	14.00
59	A7	4p black & red, *yel* ('22)		2.50	6.50
60	A7	1sh black, *emerald*		4.75	10.50
61	A7	2sh vio & ultra, *bl*		14.50	27.50
62	A7	2sh6p blk & red, *bl*		19.00	65.00
63	A7	5sh grn & red, *yel* ('22)		9.25	60.00
64	A7	£1 vio & black, *red* ('22)		275.00	425.00
		Nos. 58-64 (7)		330.00	608.50
		Set, overprinted "SPECIMEN"		200.00	

Old Dockyard, English Harbour — A8

Govt. House, St. John's — A9

Nelson's "Victory," 1805 — A10

Sir Thomas Warner's Ship, 1632 — A11

Perf. 12½

1932, Jan. 27 Engr. Wmk. 4

67	A8	½p green	4.50	8.75
68	A8	1p scarlet	6.00	8.75
69	A8	1½p lt brown	3.75	5.50
70	A9	2p gray	7.50	9.00
71	A9	2½p ultra	7.50	9.75
72	A9	3p orange	7.50	14.00
73	A10	6p violet	16.00	14.00
74	A10	1sh olive green	21.00	32.50
75	A10	2sh6p claret	55.00	77.50
76	A11	5sh red brown & black	110.00	150.00
		Nos. 67-76 (10)	238.75	346.75
		Set, never hinged	600.00	
		Set, perforated "SPECI-MEN"	250.00	

Tercentenary of the colony.
Forged cancellations abound, especially dated "MY 18 1932."

Common Design Types pictured following the introduction.

Silver Jubilee Issue
Common Design Type

1935, May 6 Perf. 13½x14

77	CD301	1p car & blue	2.50	2.75
78	CD301	1½p gray blk & ultra	3.00	1.25
79	CD301	2½p blue & brn	7.00	1.75
80	CD301	1sh brt vio & ind	9.00	17.00
a.		Double frame, one albino	2,000.	
		Nos. 77-80 (4)	21.50	22.75
		Set, never hinged	35.00	
		Set, perforated "SPECI-MEN"	110.00	

Coronation Issue
Common Design Type

1937, May 12 Perf. 11x11½

81	CD302	1p carmine	.50	1.25
82	CD302	1½p brown	.50	1.25
83	CD302	2½p deep ultra	1.00	2.00
		Nos. 81-83 (3)	2.00	4.50

Set, never hinged	3.25
Set, perforated "SPECI-MEN"	100.00

English Harbour — A14

Nelson's Dockyard — A15

Fort James — A16

St. John's Harbor — A17

1938-51 Engr. Perf. 12½

84	A14	½p yel green	.30	1.50
		Never hinged	.45	
a.		½p green ('42)	.30	1.50
		Never hinged	.45	
85	A15	1p scarlet	2.50	2.50
		Never hinged	3.25	
a.		1p red ('42)	2.00	3.25
		Never hinged	4.25	
86	A15	1½p red brown ('43)	2.00	2.25
		Never hinged	3.00	
a.		1½p chocolate brown	4.25	2.00
		Never hinged	6.75	
b.		1½p lake brown ('49)	18.00	15.00
		Never hinged	34.00	
87	A14	2p gray	.70	1.00
		Never hinged	1.10	
a.		2p slate ('51)	4.50	5.75
		Never hinged	9.00	
88	A15	2½p ultra ('43)	.75	.90
		Never hinged	1.10	
a.		2½p deep ultramarine	.60	1.00
		Never hinged	1.10	
89	A16	3p pale orange ('44)	.75	1.10
		Never hinged	1.10	
a.		3p orange	.50	1.00
		Never hinged	1.10	
90	A17	6p purple	2.75	1.40
		Never hinged	3.25	
91	A17	1sh brown & blk	3.75	2.00
		Never hinged	6.00	
a.		1sh red brown & black ('49)	22.50	12.50
		Never hinged	34.00	
b.		As "a," double frame, one albino	4,250.	
		Never hinged	6,000.	
92	A16	2sh6p dp claret ('42)	18.00	18.00
		Never hinged	26.00	
a.		2sh6p brown purple	30.00	17.50
		Never hinged	50.00	
93	A17	5sh grayish olive green ('44)	10.00	10.00
		Never hinged	15.00	
a.		5sh olive green	15.00	12.50
		Never hinged	25.00	
94	A15	10sh red vio ('48)	12.00	35.00
		Never hinged	17.00	
95	A16	£1 Prussian blue ('48)	22.50	55.00
		Never hinged	27.50	
		Nos. 84-95 (12)	76.00	130.65
		Set, never hinged	120.00	
		Set, overprinted "SPECI-MEN"	275.00	

See Nos. 107-113, 115-116, 118-121, 136-142, 144-145 in *Scott Standard Postage Stamp Catalogue*, Vol. 1.
For overprint see Nos. 125-126 in Scott Standard catalogue, Vol. 1.

Catalogue values for unused stamps in this section, from this point to the end of the section, are for Never Hinged items.

Peace Issue
Common Design Type

1946, Nov. 1 Wmk. 4 Perf. 13½x14

96	CD303	1½p brown	.25	.25
97	CD303	3p dp orange	.25	.55
		Set, overprinted "SPECI-MEN"	90.00	

Silver Wedding Issue
Common Design Types

1949, Jan. 3 Photo. Perf. 14x14½

98	CD304	2½p bright ultra	1.00	2.75

Engraved; Name Typographed Perf. 11½x11

99	CD305	5sh dk brown olive	14.00	11.50

UPU Issue
Common Design Types
Perf. 13½, 11x11½

1949, Oct. 10 Wmk. 4
Engr.; Name Typo. on 3p and 6p

100	CD306	2½p deep ultra	.45	.60
101	CD307	3p orange	2.00	2.75
102	CD308	6p purple	.75	2.00
103	CD309	1sh red brown	.75	1.25
		Nos. 100-103 (4)	3.95	6.60

University Issue
Common Design Types
Perf. 14x14½

1951, Feb. 16 Engr. Wmk. 4

104	CD310	3c chocolate & blk	.45	1.50
105	CD311	12c purple & blk	.90	1.75

WAR TAX STAMPS

No. 31 and Type A3 Overprinted in Black or Red

1916-18 Wmk. 3 Perf. 14

MR1	A3	½p green	3.50	3.25
a.		Thick paper	4.00	
MR2	A3	½p green (R) ('17)	1.60	3.25
a.		Thick paper	7.50	
MR3	A3	1½p orange ('18)	1.10	1.60
a.		½p orange & yellow ('19)	1.10	2.00
b.		½p deep orange & yellow ('20)	1.10	2.00
		Nos. MR1-MR3 (3)	6.20	8.10
		Set, overprinted "SPECI-MEN"	110.00	

ARGENTINA

ăr-jən-'tē-nə

LOCATION — In South America
GOVT. — Republic
AREA — 1,084,120 sq. mi.
POP. — 12,760,880
CAPITAL — Buenos Aires

100 Centavos = 1 Peso

Watermarks

Wmk. 84 — Italic RA

Wmk. 85 — Small Sun, 4½mm

Wmk. 86 — Large Sun, 6mm

Wmk. 87 — Honeycomb

Wmk. 88 — Multiple Suns

Wmk. 89 — Large Sun

In this watermark the face of the sun is 7mm in diameter, the rays are heavier than in the large sun watermark of 1896-1911 and the watermarks are placed close together, so that parts of several frequently appear on one stamp. This paper was intended to be used for fiscal stamps and is usually referred to as "fiscal sun paper."

Wmk. 90 — RA in Sun

In 1928 watermark 90 was slightly modified, making the diameter of the Sun 9mm instead

of 10mm. Several types of this watermark exist.

Wmk. 205 — AP in Oval

The letters "AP" are the initials of "AHORRO POSTAL." This paper was formerly used exclusively for Postal Savings stamps.

Wmk. 287 — Double Circle and Letters in Sheet

Wmk. 288 — RA in Sun with Straight Rays

PRE-STAMP POSTAL MARKINGS

Crowned Circle handstamp types I and VII are pictured in the Crowned Circle Handstamps and Great Britain Used Abroad section.

Buenos Aires
Crowned Circle Handstamps Types I or VII

1851, Jan. 5

A1	In red, on cover	900.00
A2	In black, on cover	900.00

Values are for clear cancellations on sound, fault-free stamps, with average to fine centering. In many cases, very fine examples are rare or non-existent.

STAMPS OF GREAT BRITAIN USED IN ARGENTINA
Canceled with barred oval "B32" obliterator

Black B32 Cancel — No. A29   Blue B32 Cancel — No. A29

1860-73

A3	1p rose red (#20)	55.00
A4	1p rose red (#33, see footnote), value from	45.00

#A4 plate numbers P71-74, 76, 78-81, 85, 87, 89-97, 99, 101, 103-104, 107-108, 110, 112-114, 117-121, 123, 125, 127, 129-131, 135-136, 138-140, 142-143, 145, 147, 149-151, 155, 159, 163-164, 166, 169, 172.

A5	2p blue (#29, P8-9) value from	55.00
A6	2p blue, (#30, P12-14) value from	55.00
A7	3p rose (#37)	325.00
A8	3p rose (#44)	125.00
A9	3p rose (#49, P4-10) value from	55.00
A10	4p rose (#26)	125.00
A11	4p vermilion (#34, P3)	120.00
a.	vermilion (#34a, P4)	125.00
A12	4p vermilion, plates 10-12 (#43), value from	60.00
a.	4p dull vermilion, plates 7-9, 13 (#43a), value from	60.00
A13	6p lilac (#27)	120.00
A14	6p lilac (#39, P3)	—
a.	6p lilac (#39b, P4)	—
A15	6p lilac (#45, P5)	95.00
	Plate 6	175.00
A16	6p dull violet (#50, P6)	105.00
A17	6p violet (#51, P8-9)	85.00
A18	6p brown, (#59, P11)	55.00
a.	6p pale buff, #59b, P11)	100.00
A19	9p straw (#40)	350.00
a.	9p bister (#40a)	400.00
A20	9p straw (#46)	575.00
A21	9p bister (#52)	350.00
A22	10p red brown (#53)	400.00
A23	1sh green (#28)	325.00
A24	1sh green (#42)	200.00
A25	1sh green (#48, P4)	190.00
A26	1sh green (#54, P4-6) value from	55.00
	Plate 7	90.00
A27	1sh green (#64, P8)	—
A28	2sh blue (#55)	250.00
A29	5sh rose (#57)	600.00

STAMPS OF ITALIAN OFFICES ABROAD USED IN ARGENTINA

Between 1874 and 1878, the Italian Consulate in Buenos Aires operated postal facilities for handling mail addressed to Italy. Stamps of the Italian Offices Abroad general issue were sold locally for franking this mail. These stamps were canceled on arrival at Genoa with a two-line italic postmark.

2A1	"Da Buenos-Aires coi Postali Italiani" on Italian stamps overprinted "ESTERO," from	300.00
	On cover, with stamps optd. "ESTERO," from	9,000.
2A2	"Da Buenos-Aires coi Postali Italiani" on cover, unpaid and with Italian Postage Due, from	1,500.

Mail could also be consigned to the Consular Agencies without prepayment of postage, in which case it was taxed upon arrival in Italy.

Mail could also be sent through the Consular Agencies to Europe by the English or French Paquet systems. Generally, these countries did not recognize the prepayment of postage by italian stamps, and such letters were assessed postage due charges and penalties upon arrival. Such covers are very rare.

Values for Unused
Unused values for Nos. 5-17 are for examples without gum. Examples with original gum command higher prices. Unused values of Nos. 1-4B and stamps after No. 17 are for examples with original gum as defined in the catalogue introduction.

Argentine Confederation

Symbolical of the Argentine Confederation
    A1   A2

Unwmk.

1858, May 1   Litho.   Imperf.

1	A1	5c red	1.50	40.00
a.		On cover		200.00
		Colon after "5"	1.75	35.00
		On cover		200.00
		On cover		200.00
		Horiz. strip with all 9 types	25.00	
2	A1	10c green	2.50	90.00
		On cover		700.00
a.		With period after "10" (55R1)	20.00	225.00
		On cover		750.00
b.		10c dark green	3.25	75.00
		On cover		600.00
c.		As "a," dark green	30.00	225.00
		On cover		750.00
d.		10c pale green on thick paper	5.00	110.00
		On cover		600.00
e.		Horiz. strip with all 9 types	40.00	
f.		Diagonal half used as 5c on cover		725.00
g.		Horiz. half used as 5c on cover		3,000.
3	A1	15c blue	18.00	250.00
		On cover		3,000.
a.		15c dark blue	200.00	500.00
		On cover		4,500.
b.		Horiz. strip with all 9 types	200.00	
c.		Horiz. third used as 5c on cover		10,000.
d.		Vert. third used as 5c on cover		10,000.
e.		Diagonal third used as 5c on cover		10,000.
f.		Diagonal two-thirds used as 10c on cover		—
g.		As "a," dark blue, horiz. strip with all 9 types	3,000.	—
		Nos. 1-3 (3)	22.00	380.00

There are nine varieties of Nos. 1, 2 and 3. Counterfeits and forged cancellations of Nos. 1-3 are plentiful.

1860, Jan.

4	A2	5c red	3.25	100.00
		On cover		900.00
c.		Strip with all 8 types	30.00	
f.		5c blood red	450.00	
g.		As "f," strip with all 8 types	4,500.	
4A	A2	10c green	7.00	
d.		Strip with all 8 types	70.00	
h.		10c dark green	8.00	
4B	A2	15c blue	30.00	
e.		Strip with all 8 types	300.00	
i.		15c dark blue	35.00	
		Nos. 4-4B (3)	40.25	

Nos. 4A and 4B were never placed in use. Some compositions of Nos. 4-4B contain 8 different types across the sheet. Other settings exist with minor variations. Counterfeits and forged cancellations of Nos. 4-4B are plentiful.

Argentine Republic

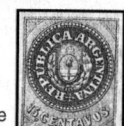

Seal of the Republic — A3

Broad "C" in "CENTAVOS," Accent on "U" of "REPUBLICA"

1862, Jan. 11

5	A3	5c rose	49.00	37.50
		On cover		200.00
a.		5c rose lilac	150.00	35.00
		On cover		200.00
6	A3	10c green	175.00	80.00
		On cover		500.00
b.		Diagonal half used as 5c on cover		7,000.
c.		10c dark green on ribbed paper		400.00
7	A3	15c blue	350.00	225.00
		On cover		3,000.
a.		Without accent on "U"	8,000.	5,000.
b.		Tete beche pair	150,000.	120,000.
i.		15c ultramarine	500.00	350.00
j.		Diagonal third used as 5c on cover		12,000.
k.		15c dark blue	600.00	350.00
				3,500.

Only one used example of No. 7b is known. It has faults. Two unused examples are known. One is sound with original gum, the other is in a block, without gum, and has tiny faults.

Broad "C" in "CENTAVOS," No Accent on "U"

1863

7C	A3	5c rose	20.00	21.00
		On cover		150.00
d.		5c rose lilac	200.00	250.00
		On cover		1,300.
e.		5c carmine rose	175.00	25.00
		On cover		180.00
m.		Worn plate (rose)	500.00	52.50
		On cover		250.00
n.		Worn plate (red)	250.00	60.00
		On cover		200.00
o.		Worn plate (lilac rose)	250.00	250.00
		On cover		1,000.
p.		Accent between "P" and "U"	250.00	90.00
		On cover		500.00
7F	A3	10c yellow green	1,000.	250.00
		On cover		1,500.
g.		10c olive green	1,500.	400.00
		On cover		2,000.

q.	10c green, ribbed paper	1,200.	350.00
	On cover		2,000.
r.	Worn plate (green)	1,200.	375.00
	On cover		2,000.
s.	Worn plate (olive green)	650.00	500.00
	On cover		2,500.

**Narrow "C" in "CENTAVOS." No
Accent on "U"**

1864

7H	A3 5c rose red	225.00	32.50
	On cover		300.00
t.	5c carmine rose	325.00	50.00
	On cover		450.00
u.	5c lilac rose	250.00	35.00
	On cover		250.00
v.	5c brick red	325.00	50.00
	On cover		300.00

The so-called reprints of 10c and 15c are
counterfeits. They have narrow "C" and
straight lines in shield. Nos. 7C and 7H have
been extensively counterfeited.

Rivadavia Issue

Bernardino Rivadavia
A4   A5

Rivadavia — A6

1864-67 Engr. Wmk. 84 *Imperf.*
Clear Impressions

8	A4 5c brown rose	2,500.	250.
	On cover		3,000.
a.	5c orange red ('67)	2,500.	250.
	On cover		2,000.
b.	Partial double impression	—	500.
9	A5 10c green	3,000.	1,750.
	On cover		16,000.
10	A6 15c blue	13,500.	6,500.
	On cover		80,000.

Perf. 11½
Dull to Worn Impressions

11	A4 5c brown rose ('65)	40.00	16.00
	On cover		100.00
11B	A4 5c lake	100.00	22.50
	On cover		150.00
12	A5 10c green	150.00	70.00
	On cover		350.00
a.	Diagonal half used as 5c on cover		2,000.
b.	Vert. half used as 5c on cover		3,000.
c.	Horiz. pair, imperf vert.		5,000.
13	A6 15c blue	450.00	150.00
	On cover		1,500.

1867-72 Unwmk. *Imperf.*

14	A4 5c carmine ('72)	350.	100.
	On cover		600.
15	A4 5c rose	350.	100.
	On cover		600.
15A	A5 10c green	3,000.	3,200.
16	A6 15c blue	3,000.	2,700.
	On cover		

Nos. 15A-16 issued without gum.

1867 Perf. 11½

17	A4 5c carmine	1,000.	200.00
	On cover		1,200.
a.	5c dark carmine rose	1,000.	200.00
	On cover		1,200.
b.	Double impression	—	500.00

Nos. 14, 15 and 17 exist with part of
papermaker's wmk. Unused values, $1,200,
$2,000 and $2,000, respectively.

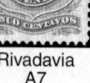

Rivadavia   Manuel
A7   Belgrano
A8

José de San
Martin — A9

Groundwork of Horizontal Lines

1867-68 Perf. 12

18	A7 5c vermilion	225.00	17.50
	On cover		75.00
c.	Double impression		75.00
	On cover		—
18A	A8 10c green	50.00	7.50
	On cover		50.00
b.	Diag. half used as 5c on cover		2,500.
19	A9 15c blue	100.00	22.50
	On cover		250.00

Groundwork of Crossed Lines

20	A7 5c vermilion	15.00	1.25
	On cover		15.00
a.	Double impression		25.00
	On cover		—
21	A9 15c blue	120.00	15.00
	On cover		250.00

See Nos. 27, 33-34, 39 and types A19, A33,
A34, A37. For surcharges and overprints see
Nos. 30-32, 41-42, 47-51, O6-O7, O26.

Gen. Antonio   Mariano
G. Balcarce   Moreno
A10   A11

Carlos Maria   Gervasio
de Alvear   Antonio
A12   Posadas
A13

Cornelio
Saavedra — A14

1873

22	A10 1c purple	6.00	2.25
	On cover		20.00
	On cover, single franking		100.00
a.	1c gray violet	10.00	2.25
	On cover		20.00
	On cover, single franking		100.00
23	A11 4c brown	6.00	.75
	On cover		6.00
a.	4c red brown	15.00	2.00
	On cover		20.00
24	A12 30c orange	140.00	25.00
	On cover		400.00
a.	Vert. pair, imperf horiz.	4,000.	
25	A13 60c black	160.00	5.00
	On cover		1,400.
26	A14 90c blue	60.00	3.00
	On cover		5,000.
	Nos. 22-26 (5)	372.00	36.00

For overprints see Nos. O5, O12-O14, O19-
O21, O25, O29.
Four examples of No. 24a are known. Three
examples of No. 26 are known on cover.

1873 Laid Paper

27	A8 10c green	325.00	32.50
	On cover		250.00

Nos. 18, 18A Surcharged in Black

Nos. 30-31   No. 32

1877, Feb. Wove Paper

30	A7 1c on 5c vermilion	75.00	25.00
	On cover		600.00
a.	Inverted surcharge	1,000.	300.00
31	A7 2c on 5c vermilion	125.00	75.00
	On cover		1,500.
a.	Inverted surcharge		
32	A8 8c on 10c green	160.00	40.00
	On cover		250.00
b.	Inverted surcharge	2,500.	1,000.
	Nos. 30-32 (3)	360.00	140.00

Varieties also exist with double and triple
surcharges, surcharge on reverse, 8c on No.
27, all made clandestinely from the original
cliches of the surcharges.
Forgeries of these surcharges include the
inverted and double varieties.

1876-77 Rouletted

33	A7 5c vermilion	200.00	85.00
	On cover		600.00
34	A7 8c lake ('77)	35.00	.65
	On cover		75.00

Belgrano   Dalmacio
A17   Vélez Sarsfield
A18

San Martín — A19

1878 Rouletted

35	A17 16c green	12.00	1.10
	On cover		22.50
a.	Vert. pair without horiz. roulettes	1,500.	
36	A18 20c blue	20.00	2.25
	On cover		150.00
37	A19 24c blue	30.00	3.50
	On cover		75.00
	Nos. 35-37 (3)	62.00	6.85

See No. 56. For overprints see Nos. O9-
O10, O15-O17, O22, O28.

Vicente   Alvear — A21
Lopez — A20

1877-80 Perf. 12

38	A20 2c yellow green	5.00	.75
	On cover		15.00
39	A7 8c lake ('80)	4.50	.75
	On cover		3.00
a.	8c brown lake	52.50	.75
	On cover		30.00
40	A21 25c lake ('78)	30.00	6.00
	On cover		1,500.
	Nos. 38-40 (3)	39.50	7.50

For overprints see Nos. O4, O11, O18, O24.

No. 18 Surcharged in Black

Large "P"   Small "P"

1882

**Large "P" and Wide "V" in
"PROVISORIO"**

41	A7 ½c on 5c ver	2.75	2.75
	On cover		100.00
a.	Double surcharge	100.00	100.00
	On cover		500.00
b.	Inverted surcharge	50.00	50.00
	On cover		500.00
c.	"PROVISORIO" omitted	110.00	110.00
	On cover		750.00
d.	Fraction omitted	100.00	
e.	"PROVISOBIO"	50.00	50.00
	On cover		500.00

---

f.	Pair, one without surcharge	250.00	

Perforated across Middle of Stamp

42b	A7 ½c on 5c ver	40.00	30.00
	On cover		900.00

**Small "P" and Narrow "V" in
"PROVISORIO"**

41g	A7 ½c on 5c ver	2.75	2.75
	On cover		100.00
41h	Double surcharge	50.00	50.00
	On cover		700.00
41i	Inverted surcharge	75.00	75.00
	On cover		700.00
41j	Fraction omitted	30.00	50.00
	On cover		300.00

Perforated across Middle of Stamp

42	A7 ½c on 5c ver	6.00	6.00
	On cover		400.00
a.	"PROVISORIQ"	50.00	50.00

A23

1882 Typo. Perf. 12½

43	A23 ½c brown	2.25	1.50
	On cover		10.00
a.	Imperf., pair	100.00	80.00
b.	½c chestnut	100.00	50.00
44	A23 1c red	15.00	6.00
	On cover		15.00
45	A23 12c ultra	90.00	14.00
	On cover		50.00

Perf. 14¼

44A	A23 1c red	3.50	1.50
	On cover		5.00
45A	A23 12c ultra	65.00	12.00
	On cover		50.00

Engr.

46	A23 12c grnsh blue	225.00	16.00
	On cover		250.00
	Nos. 43-46 (6)	400.75	51.00

See type A29. For overprints see Nos. O2,
O8, O23, O27.

No. 21 Surcharged in Red

a   b

c

1884 Engr. Perf. 12

47	A9 (a) ½c on 15c blue	3.00	2.00
	On cover		50.00
a.	Groundwork of horiz. lines	150.00	90.00
	On cover		700.00
b.	Inverted surcharge	35.00	25.00
	On cover		300.00
48	A9 (b) 1c on 15c blue	22.50	16.50
	On cover		250.00
a.	Groundwork of horiz. lines	13.00	11.50
	On cover		250.00
b.	Inverted surcharge	100.00	62.50
c.	Double surcharge	50.00	40.00
	On cover		500.00
d.	Triple surcharge	400.00	

Nos. 20-21 Surcharged in Black

49	A7 (a) ½c on 5c ver	5.00	4.50
	On cover		100.00
a.	Inverted surcharge	200.00	150.00
	On cover		1,000.
b.	Date omitted	200.00	—
c.	Pair, one without surcharge	500.00	
d.	Double surcharge	550.00	
50	A9 (a) ½c on 15c blue	15.00	12.00
	On cover		250.00
a.	Groundwork of horiz. lines	50.00	35.00
	On cover		500.00
b.	Inverted surcharge	90.00	70.00
c.	Pair, one without surcharge	400.00	
51	A7 (c) 4c on 5c ver	12.00	9.00
	On cover		100.00
a.	Inverted surcharge	35.00	28.00
	On cover		300.00
b.	Double surcharge	700.00	350.00
	On cover		1,250.
c.	Pair, one without surcharge but with "4" in manuscript	750.00	650.00

A29

1884-85		**Engr.**	**Perf. 12**
52	A29	½c red brown	1.50	.65
		On wrapper or newsprint		15.00
a.		Horiz. pair, imperf vert.		1,200.
53	A29	1c rose red	7.00	.65
		On cover		5.00
a.		Horiz. pair, imperf vert.	300.00	250.00
54	A29	12c deep blue	35.00	1.50
		On cover		10.00
a.		12c grnsh blue ('85)	50.00	1.50
		On cover		10.00
b.		Horiz. pair, imperf vert.	300.00	250.00
		Nos. 52-54 (3)	43.50	2.80

For overprints see Nos. O1, O3, O9.

San Martin Type of 1878

1887			**Engr.**
56	A19	24c blue	20.00	1.40
		On cover		75.00

Justo Jose de
Urquiza — A30

Lopez — A31

Miguel Juarez
Celman — A32

Rivadavia
(Large
head) — A33

Rivadavia (Small
head)
A34

Domingo F.
Sarmiento
A35

Nicolas
Avellaneda — A36

San Martin —
A37

Julio A.
Roca — A37a

Belgrano —
A37b

Manuel
Dorrego — A38

Moreno — A39

Bartolome
Mitre — A40

CINCO CENTAVOS.

A33 — Shows collar on left side only.

A34 — Shows collar on both sides. Lozenges in background larger and clearer than in A33.

1888-90		**Litho.**	**Perf. 11½**
57	A30	½c blue	1.75	.75
		On cover		75.00
b.		Vert. pair, imperf. horiz.	200.00	200.00
c.		Horiz. pair, imperf. vert.	200.00	200.00
58	A31	2c yel grn	20.00	10.00
		On cover		150.00
b.		Vert. pair, imperf. horiz.	130.00	
c.		Horiz. pair, imperf. vert.	250.00	
59	A32	3c blue green	3.50	1.50
		On cover		15.00
b.		Horiz. pair, imperf. vert.	60.00	
c.		Horiz. pair, imperf. btwn.	130.00	
d.		Vert. pair, imperf. btwn.	25.00	25.00
60	A33	5c carmine	18.00	.75
		On cover		30.00
b.		Vert. pair, imperf. horiz.	175.00	
61	A34	5c carmine	26.00	2.25
		On cover		50.00
b.		Horiz. pair, imperf. btwn.	200.00	
		Vert. pair, imperf. horiz.		400.00
62	A35	6c red	50.00	20.00
		On cover		250.00
b.		Vert. pair, imperf. btwn.	150.00	
c.		Perf. 12	100.00	50.00
		On cover		350.00
63	A36	10c brown	26.00	1.50
		On cover		50.00
64	A37	15c orange	27.50	2.25
		On cover		150.00
d.		Vert. pair, imperf. btwn.		600.00
64A	A37a	20c green	25.00	1.50
		On cover		150.00
64B	A37b	25c purple	45.00	4.00
				2,500.
65	A38	30c brown	40.00	4.00
				2,000.
b.		30c reddish chocolate brown	400.00	80.00
		On cover		1,000.
c.		Horiz. pair, imperf. btwn.	700.00	500.00
66	A39	40c slate, perf. 12	150.00	3.00
		On cover		2,500.
a.		Perf. 11½	300.00	4.00
		On cover		2,500.
b.		Horiz. pair, imperf. btwn. (#66)		800.00
67	A40	50c blue	350.00	3.00
		On cover		3,500.
		Nos. 57-67 (13)	782.75	71.50

In this issue there are several varieties of each value, the difference between them being in the relative position of the head to the frame.

Imperf., Pairs

57a	A30	½c	85.00	67.50
58a	A31	2c	100.00	
59a	A32	3c	45.00	27.50
61a	A34	5c		100.00
62a	A35	6c	150.00	150.00
63a	A36	10c	55.00	
64c	A37	15c		200.00
65a	A38	30c	325.00	225.00

Values for Stamps with "MUESTRA" Overprint

59S		3c blue green	30.00
63S		10c brown	30.00
64S		15c orange	30.00
64AS		20c green	30.00
64BS		25c purple	30.00
65S		30c brown	30.00
66S		40c slate	30.00

Urquiza
A41

Velez
Sarsfield
A42

Miguel Juarez
Celman
A43

Rivadavia
(Large head)
A44

Sarmiento
A45

Juan Bautista
Alberdi
A46

1888-89		**Engr.**	**Perf. 11½, 11½x12**
68	A41	½c ultra	.75	.45
		On newspaper, single franking		50.00
a.		Vert. pair, imperf. horiz.	—	
b.		Imperf., pair	30.00	
69	A42	1c brown	1.50	.75
		On cover		3.00
a.		Vert. pair, imperf. horiz.	65.00	
b.		Vert. pair, imperf. btwn.		
c.		Imperf., pair	30.00	
d.		Horiz. pair, imperf. btwn.	100.00	
70	A43	3c blue green	6.00	1.75
		On cover		6.00
71	A44	5c rose	4.50	.75
		On cover		2.50
a.		Imperf., pair	50.00	
72	A45	6c blue black	3.00	.90
		On cover		8.00
b.		Perf. 11½x12	15.00	4.50
		On cover		15.00
73	A46	12c blue	8.75	3.75
		On cover		12.00
a.		Imperf., pair	45.00	
b.		bluish paper	9.50	3.75
		On cover		12.00
c.		Perf. 11½	14.00	3.00
		On cover		15.00
		Nos. 68-73 (6)	24.50	8.35

Nos. 69-70 exist with papermakers' watermarks.
See No. 77, types A50, A61. For surcharges see Nos. 83-84.

Jose Maria
Paz — A48

Santiago
Derqui — A49

Rivadavia
A57

Jose de San
Martin
A58

Rivadavia
(Small head)
A50

Avellaneda
A51

Moreno
A53

Mitre
A54

Posadas — A55

1890		**Engr.**	**Perf. 11½**
75	A48	¼c green	.65	.45
		On wrapper or newspaper, single franking		50.00
76	A49	2c violet	1.50	.75
		On cover		2.00
a.		2c purple	2.00	.75
		On cover		2.00
b.		2c slate	2.00	.75
		On cover		2.50
c.		Horiz. pair, imperf. btwn.	30.00	25.00
d.		Imperf., pair	37.50	
e.		Perf. 11½	9.00	.75
		On cover		3.00
77	A50	5c carmine	3.50	.45
		On cover		2.50
a.		Imperf., pair	70.00	32.50
b.		Perf. 11½x12	10.00	1.25
		On cover		2.50
c.		Vert. pair, imperf. btwn.	75.00	60.00
d.		Horiz. pair, imperf. btwn.	75.00	60.00
78	A51	10c brown	4.50	.75
		On cover		6.00
b.		Imperf., pair	150.00	
c.		Vert. pair, imperf. btwn.	225.00	

80	A53	40c olive green	8.00	1.50
		On cover		450.00
a.		Imperf., pair	55.00	
b.		Horiz. pair, imperf. btwn.		250.00
81	A54	50c orange	9.00	1.50
		On cover		450.00
a.		Imperf., pair	80.00	
b.		Perf. 11½x12	40.00	3.00
		50c lemon yellow	50.00	
82	A55	60c black	20.00	4.50
		Imperf., pair		
a.		Vert. pair, imperf. btwn.	125.00	100.00
c.		60c blue black	25.00	2.50
		Nos. 75-82 (7)	47.15	9.90

Type A50 differs from type A44 in having the head smaller, the letters of "Cinco Centavos" not as tall, and the curved ornaments at sides close to the first and last letters of "Republica Argentina."

Lithographed Surcharge
on No. 73 in Black or
Red

1890			**Perf. 11½x12**
83	A46	¼c on 12c blue	.75	.75
		On wrapper, single franking		15.00
a.		Perf. 11½	50.00	40.00
b.		Double surcharge	75.00	47.50
c.		Inverted surcharge		
84	A46	¼c on 12c blue (R)	.75	.75
		On wrapper, single franking		15.00
a.		Double surcharge	55.00	50.00
b.		Perf. 11½	8.00	3.00
		On wrapper, single franking		45.00

Surcharge is different on Nos. 83 and 84.
Nos. 83-84 exist as pairs, one without surcharge. These were privately produced.

Rivadavia
A57

Jose de San
Martin
A58

Gregorio
Araoz de
Lamadrid
A59

Admiral
Guillermo
Brown
A60

1891		**Engr.**	**Perf. 11½**
85	A57	8c carmine rose	1.50	.65
		On cover		2.00
a.		Imperf., pair	130.00	
86	A58	1p deep blue	50.00	12.00
		On cover		
87	A59	5p ultra	325.00	45.00
		On cover		
88	A60	20p green	500.00	100.00
		Nos. 85-88 (4)	876.50	157.65

Nos. 86-88 with violet oval or black boxed cancellations were used on parcels. Stamps so used are worth about 25% less than the values shown.

A 10p brown and a 50p red were prepared but not issued. Values: 10p $2,250 for fine, 50p $1,000 with rough or somewhat damaged perfs.

Velez Sarsfield
A61

"Santa Maria,"
"Nina" and "Pinta"
A62

1890 — Perf. 11½

89 A61 1c brown — 1.25 / .65
  On cover — 2.50
  b. Horiz. pair, imperf. btwn. — 550.00

Type A61 is a re-engraving of A42. The figure "1" in each upper corner has a short horizontal serif instead of a long one pointing ... In type A61 the first and last letters of "Correos y Telegrafos" are closer to the curved ornaments below than in type A42. Background is of horizontal lines (cross-hatching on No. 69).

1892, Oct. 12 — Wmk. 85 — Perf. 11½

90 A62 2c light blue — 8.50 / 3.00
  On cover — 30.00
  a. Double impression — 225.00
91 A62 5c dark blue — 9.50 / 4.00
  On cover, #90, 91 — 50.00

Discovery of America, 400th anniv. Counterfeits of Nos. 90-91 are litho.

Rivadavia A63 — Belgrano A64

San Martin — A65

1892-95 — Wmk. 85 — Perf. 11½

92 A63 ½c dull blue — 1.00 / .35
  Never hinged — 1.50
  On wrapper — 10.00
  a. ½c bright ultra — 80.00 / 40.00
    Never hinged — 120.00
    On wrapper — 100.00
93 A63 1c brown — .65 / .50
  Never hinged — .95
  On cover — 1.00
94 A63 2c green — 1.00 / .35
  Never hinged — 1.50
  On cover — 1.00
95 A63 3c orange ('95) — 1.75 / .35
  Never hinged — 2.50
  On cover — 1.50
96 A63 5c carmine — 1.75 / .35
  Never hinged — 2.50
  On cover — 1.00
  b. 5c green (error) — 700.00 / 700.00
    On cover — 3,500.
98 A64 10c carmine rose — 13.50 / .60
  Never hinged — 20.00
  On cover — 1.50
99 A64 12c deep blue ('93) — 10.00 / .60
  Never hinged — 15.00
  On cover — 1.50
100 A64 16c gray — 16.50 / .65
  Never hinged — 25.00
  On cover — 2.00
101 A64 24c gray brown — 16.50 / .65
  Never hinged — 25.00
  On cover — 3.00
102 A64 50c blue green — 27.50 / .75
  Never hinged — 42.50
  On cover — 10.00
103 A65 1p lake ('93) — 12.00 / 1.00
  Never hinged — 18.00
  On cover — 100.00
  a. 1p red brown — 20.00 / 5.00
    Never hinged — 30.00
    On cover — 175.00
104 A65 2p dark green — 27.50 / 3.50
  Never hinged — 42.50
  On cover — 150.00
105 A65 5p dark blue — 37.50 / 3.50
  Never hinged — 55.00
  On cover — 250.00
Nos. 92-105 (13) — 167.15 / 13.15

Perf. 12

92E A63 ½c dull blue — 6.00 / 1.00
  Never hinged — 9.00
  On wrapper — 10.00
93E A63 1c brown — 10.00 / 2.00
  Never hinged — 15.00
  On cover — 1.00
94E A63 2c green — 10.00 / 3.00
  Never hinged — 15.00
  On cover — 1.00
95E A63 3c orange ('95) — 30.00 / 5.00
  Never hinged — 45.00
  On cover — 1.50
96E A63 5c carmine — 35.00 / 1.00
  Never hinged — 52.50
  On cover — 1.00
98E A64 10c carmine rose — 21.00 / 3.50
  Never hinged — 32.50
  On cover — 1.50
99E A64 12c deep blue ('93) — 40.00 / 4.00
  Never hinged — 60.00
  On cover — 1.50
100E A64 16c gray — 40.00 / 4.00
  Never hinged — 60.00
  On cover — 2.00
101E A64 24c gray brown — 30.00 / 17.00
  Never hinged — 45.00
  On cover — 50.00
102E A64 50c blue green — 30.00 / 6.00
  Never hinged — 45.00
  On cover — 50.00
104E A65 2p dark green — 125.00 / 40.00
  Never hinged — 190.00
  On cover — 150.00
Nos. 92E-104E (11) — 377.00 / 86.50

Perf. 11½x12

92F A63 ½c dull blue — 18.00 / 10.00
  Never hinged — 27.50
  On wrapper — 10.00
93F A63 1c brown — 15.00 / 8.00
  Never hinged — 22.50
  On cover — 1.00
94F A63 2c green — 40.00 / 15.00
  Never hinged — 60.00
  On cover — 1.00
95F A63 3c orange ('95) — 55.00 / 22.50
  Never hinged — 82.50
  On cover — 1.50
96F A63 5c carmine — 20.00 / 4.00
  Never hinged — 30.00
  On cover — 1.00
98F A64 10c carmine rose — 30.00 / 7.50
  Never hinged — 45.00
  On cover — 1.50
99F A64 12c deep blue ('93) — 60.00 / 27.50
  Never hinged — 90.00
  On cover — 1.50
100F A64 16c gray — 60.00 / 27.50
  Never hinged — 90.00
  On cover — 2.00
102F A64 50c blue green — 60.00 / 10.00
  Never hinged — 90.00
  On cover — 50.00
103F A64 1p red brown — 60.00 / 10.00
  Never hinged — 90.00
  On cover — 50.00
104F A65 2p dark green — 175.00 / 75.00
  Never hinged — 260.00
  On cover — 150.00
Nos. 92F-104F (11) — 593.00 / 217.00

Part-perforate varieties of Nos. 92-99 include vert. and/or horiz. pairs, imperf. between. Valued from $45.

The high values of this and succeeding issues are frequently punched with the word "INUTILIZADO," parts of the letters showing on each stamp. These punched stamps sell for only a small fraction of the catalogue values.

Examples of No. 95 in yellow shades are changelings.

Reprints of No. 96b have white gum. The original stamp has yellowish gum. Value $125.

Imperf., Pairs

92b A63 ½c — 60.00
  Never hinged — 90.00
93a A63 1c — 60.00
  Never hinged — 90.00
94a A63 2c — 30.00
  Never hinged — 45.00
96a A63 5c — 30.00
  Never hinged — 45.00
98a A64 10c — 60.00
  Never hinged — 90.00
99a A64 12c — 60.00
  Never hinged — 90.00
100a A64 16c — 60.00
  Never hinged — 90.00
101a A64 24c — 60.00
  Never hinged — 90.00
102a A64 50c — 60.00
  Never hinged — 90.00
103b A65 1p — 60.00
  Never hinged — 90.00
105a A65 5p — 150.00
  Never hinged — 225.00

Nos. 102a, 103b and 105a exist only without gum; the other imperfs are found with or without gum, and values are the same for either condition.

Vertical Pairs, Imperf. Between

92c A63 ½c — 125.00
  Never hinged — 190.00
93b A63 1c — 100.00
  Never hinged — 150.00
94b A63 2c — 50.00
  Never hinged — 75.00
95a A63 3c — 250.00
  Never hinged — 375.00
96c A63 5c — 45.00 / —
  Never hinged — 67.50
98b A64 10c — 100.00
  Never hinged — 150.00
99b A64 12c — 100.00
  Never hinged — 150.00

Horizontal Pairs, Imperf. Between

93c A63 1c — 110.00
  Never hinged — 170.00
94c A63 2c — 55.00
  Never hinged — 82.50
96d A63 5c — 55.00 / 45.00
  Never hinged — 82.50
98c A64 10c — 110.00
  Never hinged — 170.00

1896-97 — Wmk. 86 — Perf. 11½

106 A63 ½c slate — .65 / .30
  Never hinged — .95
  On wrapper — 10.00
  a. ½c gray blue — .65 / .30
    Never hinged — .95
    On wrapper — 10.00
  b. ½c indigo — .65 / .30
    Never hinged — .95
    On cover — 10.00
107 A63 1c brown — .65 / .30
  Never hinged — .95
  On cover — 1.00
108 A63 2c yellow green — .65 / .30
  Never hinged — .95
  On cover — 1.00
109 A63 3c orange — .65 / .30
  Never hinged — .95
  On cover — 1.50
110 A63 5c carmine — .65 / .30
  Never hinged — .95
  On cover — 1.00
111 A64 10c carmine rose — 10.00 / .30
  Never hinged — 15.00
  On cover — 1.50
  a. Imperf., pair — 100.00
112 A64 12c deep blue — 5.00 / .30
  Never hinged — 7.50
  On cover — 1.50
  a. Imperf., pair — —
113 A64 16c gray — 13.50 / .90
  Never hinged — 20.00
  On cover — 5.00
114 A64 24c gray brown — 13.50 / 1.25
  Never hinged — 20.00
  On cover — 6.00
  a. Imperf., pair — 100.00 / —
115 A64 30c orange ('97) — 13.50 / .70
  Never hinged — 20.00
  On cover — 5.00
116 A64 50c blue green — 13.50 / .70
  Never hinged — 20.00
  On cover — 10.00
117 A64 80c dull violet — 20.00 / .90
  Never hinged — 30.00
  On cover — 20.00
118 A65 1p lake — 30.00 / 1.60
  Never hinged — 45.00
  On cover — 40.00
119 A65 1p20c black ('97) — 13.50 / 3.50
  Never hinged — 20.00
  On cover — 125.00
120 A65 2p dark green — 20.00 / 10.00
  Never hinged — 30.00
  On cover — 150.00
121 A65 5p dark blue — 135.00 / 13.50
  Never hinged — 200.00
  On cover — 250.00
Nos. 106-121 (16) — 290.75 / 35.15

Perf. 12

106E A63 ½c slate — 2.00 / 1.00
  Never hinged — 3.00
  On wrapper — 10.00
  a. ½c gray blue — 10.00 / 4.00
    Never hinged — 15.00
    On wrapper — 10.00
  b. ½c indigo — 10.00 / 4.00
    Never hinged — 15.00
    On wrapper — 10.00
107E A63 1c brown — 1.75 / 1.00
  Never hinged — 2.50
  On cover — 1.00
108E A63 2c yellow green — 2.50 / 1.00
  Never hinged — 3.75
  On cover — 1.00
109E A63 3c orange — 45.00 / 2.00
  Never hinged — 67.50
  On cover — 1.50
110E A63 5c carmine — 3.50 / 1.00
  Never hinged — 5.25
  On cover — 1.00
111E A64 10c carmine rose — 15.00 / 1.00
  Never hinged — 22.50
  On cover — 1.50
112E A64 12c deep blue — 11.00 / 2.00
  Never hinged — 16.50
  On cover — 1.50
113E A64 16c gray — 35.00 / 5.50
  Never hinged — 52.50
  On cover — 6.00
114E A64 24c gray brown — 52.50 / 11.00
  Never hinged — 77.50
  On cover — 5.00
115E A64 30c orange ('97) — 52.50 / 2.50
  Never hinged — 77.50
  On cover — 5.00
116E A64 50c blue green — 65.00 / .80
  Never hinged — 97.50
  On cover — 10.00
117E A64 80c dull violet — 65.00 / 22.50
  Never hinged — 97.50
  On cover — 20.00
118E A65 1p lake — 65.00 / 3.50
  Never hinged — 97.50
  On cover — 40.00
119E A65 1p20c black ('97) — 65.00 / 22.50
  Never hinged — 97.50
  On cover — 125.00
121E A65 5p dark blue — 800.00 / 20.00
  Never hinged — 1,200.
  On cover — 250.00
Nos. 106E-121E (15) — 1,280. / 97.30

Perf. 11½x12

106F A63 ½c slate — 20.00 / 11.00
  Never hinged — 30.00
  On wrapper — 10.00
107F A63 1c brown — 30.00 / 25.00
  Never hinged — 45.00
  On cover — 1.00
108F A63 2c yellow green — 20.00 / 11.00
  Never hinged — 30.00
  On cover — 1.00
109F A63 3c orange — 13.00 / 8.00
  Never hinged — 19.50
  On cover — 1.50
110F A63 5c carmine — 26.00 / 4.50
  Never hinged — 40.00
  On cover — 1.50
111F A64 10c carmine rose — 45.00 / 18.00
  Never hinged — 67.50
  On cover — 1.50
112F A64 12c deep blue — 47.50 / 15.00
  Never hinged — 72.50
  On cover — 1.50
113F A64 16c gray — 60.00 / 20.00
  Never hinged — 90.00
  On cover — 5.00
115F A64 30c orange ('97) — — / 75.00
  Never hinged —
  On cover — 0.00
116F A64 50c blue green — — / 75.00
  Never hinged —
  On cover — 10.00
117F A64 80c dull violet — — / 75.00
  Never hinged —
  On cover — 20.00
119F A65 1p20c black ('97) — 100.00 / 60.00
  Never hinged — 150.00
  On cover — 125.00
Nos. 106F-119F (12) — 361.50 / 397.50

Vertical Pairs, Imperf. Between

106c A63 ½c — 200.00
  Never hinged — 300.00
107a A63 1c — 125.00
  Never hinged — 190.00
108a A63 2c — 125.00
  Never hinged — 190.00
109a A63 3c — 200.00
  Never hinged — 300.00
110b A63 5c — 125.00 / 125.00
  Never hinged — 190.00
112b A64 12c — 125.00 / 100.00
  Never hinged — 190.00

Horizontal Pairs, Imperf. Between

107b A63 1c — 125.00
  Never hinged — 190.00
108b A63 2c — 125.00
  Never hinged — 190.00
110c A63 5c — 125.00 / 80.00
  Never hinged — 190.00
111a A64 10c — 125.00
  Never hinged — 190.00
112c A64 12c — 125.00
  Never hinged — 190.00

Allegory, Liberty Seated
A66 — A67

1899-1903 — Perf. 11½

122 A66 ½c yellow brown — .40 / .30
  Never hinged — .60
  On cover, single franking — 20.00
123 A66 1c green — .60 / .30
  Never hinged — .90
  On cover — 1.00
124 A66 2c slate — .60 / .30
  Never hinged — .90
  On cover — 1.00
125 A66 3c orange ('01) — .80 / .50
  Never hinged — 1.20
  On cover — 1.50
126 A66 4c yellow ('03) — 1.40 / .60
  Never hinged — 2.10
  On cover — 2.00
127 A66 5c carmine rose — .60 / .30
  Never hinged — .90
  On cover — 1.00
128 A66 6c black ('03) — .90 / .60
  Never hinged — 1.35
  On cover — 2.00
129 A66 10c dark green — 1.40 / .40
  Never hinged — 2.10
  On cover — 1.50
130 A66 12c dull blue — .95 / .60
  Never hinged — 1.40
  On cover — 2.00
131 A66 12c olive grn ('01) — .95 / .60
  Never hinged — 1.40
  On cover — 2.00
132 A66 15c sea green ('01) — 2.50 / .60
  Never hinged — 3.75
  On cover — 2.50
132B A66 15c dull blue ('01) — 2.50 / .60
  Never hinged — 3.75
  On cover — 2.50
133 A66 16c orange — 8.00 / 8.00
  Never hinged — 12.00
  On cover — 25.00
134 A66 20c claret — 1.90 / .30
  Never hinged — 2.75
  On cover — 1.00
135 A66 24c violet — 4.00 / 1.00
  Never hinged — 6.00
  On cover — 5.00
136 A66 30c rose — 7.25 / .60
  Never hinged — 11.00
  On cover — 5.00
137 A66 30c vermilion ('01) — 4.00 / .50
  Never hinged — 6.00
  On cover — 5.00
  a. 30c scarlet — 47.50 / 3.00
    Never hinged — 72.50
    On cover — 12.50
138 A66 50c brt blue — 4.50 / .50
  Never hinged — 6.75
  On cover — 10.00

139 A67 1p bl & blk 15.00 1.25
 Never hinged 22.50
 On cover 225.00
 a. Center inverted 2,000. 1,000.
 b. Perf. 12 500.00 160.00
140 A67 5p orange & blk 57.50 11.00
 Never hinged 22.50
 Punch cancellation 3.00
 a. Center inverted 2,750. 2,500.
141 A67 10p green & blk 70.00 18.00
 Punch cancellation 3.00
 a. Center inverted 5,000.
 Punch cancellation 675.00
142 A67 20p red & black 200.00 35.00
 Never hinged 300.00
 Punch cancellation 3.00
 a. Center invtd. (punch cancel) 4,000.
 Nos. 122-142 (22) 385.75 81.85

Nos. 139-142 used are valued with violet oval or black boxed parcel cancels. Examples with letter cancels are worth ⅓rd more.
Part-perforate varieties of Nos. 122-129, 132, 138 include vert. and/or horiz. pairs, imperf. between. Valued from $3.

Perf. 12

122E A66 ½c yellow brown 1.50 1.20
 Never hinged 2.25
 On cover, single franking 20.00
123E A66 1c green 2.00 .60
 Never hinged 3.00
 On cover 1.00
124E A66 2c slate 1.50 .60
 Never hinged 2.25
 On cover 1.00
125E A66 3c orange ('01) 3.50 1.75
 Never hinged 5.25
 On cover 1.50
126E A66 4c yellow ('03) 10.00 3.50
 Never hinged 15.00
 On cover 2.00
127E A66 5c carmine rose 5.25 .60
 Never hinged 7.75
 On cover 1.00
128E A66 6c black ('03) 8.50 2.00
 Never hinged 13.00
 On cover 2.00
129E A66 10c dark green 8.50 1.75
 Never hinged 13.00
 On cover 1.50
130E A66 12c dull blue 8.50 2.00
 Never hinged 13.00
 On cover 2.00
131E A66 12c olive grn ('01) 8.50 2.00
 Never hinged 13.00
 On cover 2.00
132E A66 15c sea green ('01) 17.00 1.75
 Never hinged 26.00
 On cover 2.50
133E A66 16c orange 10.00 9.50
 Never hinged 15.00
 On cover 25.00
134E A66 20c claret 12.00 9.50
 Never hinged 18.00
 On cover 1.00
135E A66 24c violet 11.00 8.50
 Never hinged 16.50
 On cover 5.00
136E A66 30c rose 28.00 3.50
 Never hinged 42.50
 On cover 5.00
137E A66 30c vermilion ('01) 60.00 4.00
 Never hinged 90.00
 On cover 5.00
 a. 30c scarlet 47.50 3.00
 Never hinged 72.50
 On cover 12.50
138E A66 50c brt blue 27.50 3.50
 Never hinged 42.50
 On cover 10.00
139E A67 1p bl & blk 500.00 160.00
 Never hinged 750.00
 On cover 225.00
 Nos. 122E-139E (18) 723.25 216.25

Perf. 11½x12

122F A66 ½c yellow brown 25.00 15.00
 Never hinged 37.50
 On cover, single franking 20.00
123F A66 1c green 25.00 15.00
 Never hinged 37.50
 On cover 1.00
124F A66 2c slate 12.00 3.00
 Never hinged 18.00
 On cover 1.00
125F A66 3c orange ('01) 47.50 18.00
 Never hinged 72.50
 On cover 1.50
127F A66 5c carmine rose 12.00 6.00
 Never hinged 18.00
 On cover 1.00
128F A66 6c black ('03) 32.50 20.00
 Never hinged 13.00
 On cover 2.00
129F A66 10c dark green 30.00 6.50
 Never hinged 45.00
 On cover 1.50
130F A66 12c dull blue 50.00 15.00
 Never hinged 75.00
 On cover 2.00
131F A66 12c olive grn ('01) 50.00 10.00
 Never hinged 75.00
 On cover 2.00
132F A66 15c sea green ('01) 50.00 8.00
 Never hinged 75.00
 On cover 2.50
134F A66 20c claret 60.00 12.00
 Never hinged 90.00
 On cover 1.00

135F A66 24c violet 50.00 10.00
 Never hinged 75.00
 On cover 5.00
136F A66 30c rose 120.00 20.00
 Never hinged 175.00
 On cover 5.00
137F A66 30c vermilion ('01) 140.00 25.00
 Never hinged 210.00
138F A66 50c brt blue 120.00 20.00
 Never hinged 175.00
 On cover 10.00
 Nos. 122F-138F (15) 824.00 203.50

Imperf., Pairs

122a A66 ½c 35.00
 Never hinged 52.50
123a A66 1c 50.00
 Never hinged 75.00
124a A66 2c 17.50
 Never hinged 26.00
125a A66 3c 325.00
 Never hinged 490.00
127a A66 5c 17.50
 Never hinged 26.00
128a A66 6c 60.00
 Never hinged 90.00
129a A66 10c 50.00
 Never hinged 75.00
132a A66 15c 50.00
 Never hinged 75.00

Vertical Pairs, Imperf. Between

122b A66 ½c 10.00 9.50
 Never hinged 15.00
123b A66 1c 10.00 9.50
 Never hinged 15.00
124b A66 2c 5.00 4.50
 Never hinged 7.50
125b A66 3c 325.00 200.00
 Never hinged 490.00
126a A66 4c 400.00 275.00
 Never hinged 600.00
127b A66 5c 4.50 2.50
 Never hinged 6.75
128b A66 6c 13.50 10.00
 Never hinged 20.00
129b A66 10c 85.00
 Never hinged 130.00
132c A66 15c 15.00 10.00
 Never hinged 22.50

Horizontal Pairs, Imperf. Between

122c A66 ½c 30.00 19.00
 Never hinged 45.00
123c A66 1c 47.50 27.50
 Never hinged 72.50
124c A66 2c 10.00 5.00
 Never hinged 15.00
125c A66 3c 325.00 200.00
 Never hinged 490.00
126b A66 4c 400.00
 Never hinged 600.00
127c A66 5c 10.00 5.00
 Never hinged 15.00
128c A66 6c 17.00 10.00
 Never hinged 26.00
129c A66 10c 17.00 10.00
 Never hinged 26.00
132d A66 15c 40.00 23.00
 Never hinged 60.00
138a A66 50c 165.00
 Never hinged 250.00

River Port of Rosario
A68

1902, Oct. 26   Perf. 11½, 11½x12

143 A68 5c deep blue 4.75 2.00
 Never hinged 7.00
 On cover 20.00
 a. Imperf., pair 95.00
 Never hinged 140.00
 b. Vert. pair, imperf. btwn. 60.00
 Never hinged 90.00
 c. Horiz. pair, imperf. btwn. 90.00
 Never hinged 135.00

Completion of port facilities at Rosario.

San Martin
A69   A70

1908-09   Typo.   Perf. 13½x12½

144 A69 ½c violet .50 .30
 Never hinged .75
145 A69 1c brnsh buff .50 .30
 Never hinged .75
146 A69 2c chocolate .60 .30
 Never hinged .75
147 A69 3c green .65 .40
 Never hinged .95
148 A69 4c redsh violet 1.25 .40
 Never hinged 1.90
149 A69 5c carmine .60 .30
 Never hinged .90
150 A69 6c olive bister .75 .40
 Never hinged 1.10
151 A69 10c gray green 1.75 .30
 Never hinged 2.50
152 A69 12c yellow buff 1.00 .60
 Never hinged 1.50

153 A69 12c dk blue ('09) 1.75 .30
 Never hinged 2.50
155 A69 20c ultra 1.25 .30
 Never hinged 1.90
156 A69 24c red brown 3.50 .60
 Never hinged 5.25
157 A69 30c dull rose 6.00 .60
 Never hinged 9.00
158 A69 50c black 6.00 .50
 Never hinged 9.00
159 A70 1p sl bl & pink 18.00 2.50
 Never hinged 27.50
 Nos. 144-159 (15) 44.10 8.10

The 1c blue was not issued. Value $500.
Wmk. 86 appears on ½, 1, 6, 20, 24 and 50c. Other values have similar wmk. with wavy rays.
Stamps lacking wmk. are from outer rows printed on sheet margin.

Perf. 13½

146A A69 2c chocolate 1.20 .25
 Never hinged 1.75
147A A69 3c green 2.00 1.00
 Never hinged 3.00
148A A69 4c redsh violet 1.30 .50
 Never hinged 2.00
149A A69 5c carmine 1.00 .30
 Never hinged 1.50
 c. rose carmine 1.00 .30
 Never hinged 1.50
151A A69 10c gray green 6.25 2.25
 Never hinged 9.50
152A A69 12c yellow buff 1.20 .70
 Never hinged 1.75
153A A69 12c dk blue ('09) 4.25 1.00
 Never hinged 6.50
154A A69 15c apple green .60 .50
 Never hinged .90
156A A69 24c red brown 4.75 1.30
 Never hinged 7.00
157A A69 30c dull rose 9.50 1.30
 Never hinged 14.00
159A A70 1p sl bl & pink 20.00 3.00
 Never hinged 30.00
 b. 1p rose & indigo 300.00 100.00
 Never hinged 450.00

Pyramid of May — A71

Nicolas Rodriguez Pena and Hipolito Vieytes — A72

Meeting at Pena's Home — A73

Designs: 3c, Miguel de Azcuenaga (1754-1833) and Father Manuel M. Alberti (1763-1811). 4c, Viceroy's house and Fort Buenos Aires. 5c, Cornelio Saavedra (1759-1829). 10c, Antonio Luis Beruti (1772-1842) and French distributing badges. 12c, Congress building. 20c, Juan Jose Castelli (1764-1812) and Domingo Matheu (1765-1831). 24c, First council. 30c, Manuel Belgrano (1770-1820) and Juan Larrea (1782-1847). 50c, First meeting of republican government, May 25, 1810. 1p, Mariano Moreno (1778-1811) and Juan Jose Paso (1758-1833). 5p, Oath of the Junta. 10p, Centenary Monument. 20p, Jose Francisco de San Martin (1778-1850).

Inscribed "1810 1910"
Various Frames

1910, May 1   Engr.   Perf. 11½

160 A71 ½c bl & gray bl .30 .25
161 A72 1c blue grn & blk .30 .30
 b. Horiz. pair, imperf. btwn. 65.00
162 A73 2c olive & gray .25 .30
163 A72 3c green .70 .40
164 A73 4c dk blue & grn .70 .40
165 A71 5c carmine .40 .25
166 A73 10c yel brn & blk 1.10 .50
167 A73 12c brt blue 1.10 .50
168 A72 20c gray brn & blk 3.25 .60
169 A73 24c org brn & bl 1.75 1.25
170 A72 30c lilac & blk 1.75 1.00
171 A71 50c carmine & blk 4.50 1.25
172 A72 1p brt blue 9.50 3.25
173 A73 5p orange & vio 72.50 35.00
 Punch cancel 5.00

174 A71 10p orange & blk 90.00 62.50
 Punch cancel 10.00
175 A71 20p dp blue & ind 150.00 100.00
 Punch cancel 15.00
 Nos. 160-175 (16) 338.10 207.75
Centenary of the republic.

Center Inverted

160a A71 ½c 1,000.
161a A72 1c 1,000.
162a A73 2c 800.00
164a A73 4c 650.00
167a A73 12c 1,000.
171a A71 50c 1,000.
173a A73 5p 750.00

Domingo F. Sarmiento A87

Agriculture A88

1911, May 15   Typo.   Perf. 13½

176 A87 5c gray brn & blk .80 .40
Domingo Faustino Sarmiento (1811-88), pres. of Argentina, 1868-74.

Size: 19x25mm
Wmk. 86, without Face

1911   Engr.   Perf. 12

177 A88 5c vermilion .40 .25
178 A88 5c deep blue 5.00 .50

Size: 18x23mm
Wmk. 86, with Face

1911   Typo.   Perf. 13½x12½

179 A88 ½c violet .50 .30
180 A88 1c brown ocher .30 .30
181 A88 2c chocolate .30 .25
 a. Perf. 13½ 15.00 4.00
 b. Imperf., pair 40.00
182 A88 3c green .50 .50
183 A88 4c brown violet .50 .30
184 A88 10c gray green .50 .30
185 A88 20c ultra 4.00 .95
186 A88 24c red brown 6.00 3.75
187 A88 30c claret 3.00 .50
188 A88 50c black 6.00 .80
 Nos. 179-188 (10) 21.60 7.95

The 5c dull red is a proof. In this issue Wmk. 86 comes: straight rays (4c, 20c, 24c) and wavy rays (2c). All other values exist with both forms.

Wmk. 87 (Horiz. or Vert.)

1912-14   Perf. 13½x12½

189 A88 ½c violet .30 .30
190 A88 1c ocher .30 .30
191 A88 2c chocolate .50 .30
192 A88 3c green .50 .50
193 A88 4c brown violet .50 .30
194 A88 5c red .40 .30
195 A88 10c deep green 1.75 .30
196 A88 12c deep blue .60 .30
197 A88 20c ultra 3.00 .50
198 A88 24c red brown 6.00 2.00
199 A88 30c claret 5.00 7.00
200 A88 50c black 9.00 .90
 Nos. 189-200 (12) 27.85 13.30

See Nos. 208-212. For overprints see Nos. OD1-OD8, OD47-OD54, OD102-OD108, OD146-OD152, OD183-OD190, OD235-OD241, OD281-OD284, OD318-OD323.

Perf. 13½

189a A88 ½c 1.00 .30
190a A88 1c 1.00 .30
191a A88 2c 1.00 .30
192a A88 3c 150.00 30.00
193a A88 4c 2.50 1.25
194a A88 5c .90 .90
196a A88 12c 3.50 1.50
197a A88 20c 9.00 .90
 Nos. 189a-197a (8) 168.90 34.85

A89

1912-13   Perf. 13½

201 A89 1p dull bl & rose 10.00 1.10
 Punch cancel .30
202 A89 5p slate & ol grn 19.00 7.00
 Punch cancel 1.00

203	A89	10p violet & blue	75.00	17.50
		Punch cancel		1.40
204	A89	20p blue & claret	210.00	80.00
		Punch cancel		2.00
		Nos. 201-204 (4)	314.00	105.60

1915   Unwmk.   Perf. 13½x12½

208	A88	1c ocher	.50	.30
209	A88	2c chocolate	.90	.30
212	A88	5c red	.50	.30
		Nos. 208-212 (3)	1.90	.90

Only these denominations were printed on paper without watermark.

Other stamps of the series are known unwatermarked but they are from the outer rows of sheets the other parts of which are watermarked.

Francisco Narciso de Laprida A90

Declaration of Independence A91

A92   A92a

Jose de San Martin

Perf. 13½, 13½x12½

1916, July 9   Litho.   Wmk. 87

215	A90	½c violet	.60	.30
216	A90	1c buff	.50	.30

Perf. 13½x12½

217	A90	2c chocolate	.60	.30
218	A90	3c green	.60	.60
219	A90	4c red violet	.60	.60

Perf. 13½

220	A91	5c red	.50	.30
a.		Imperf., pair	40.00	
221	A91	10c gray green	1.50	.30
222	A92	12c blue	.90	.35
223	A92	20c ultra	.70	.70
224	A92	24c red brown	2.75	1.40
225	A92	30c claret	2.75	1.60
226	A92	50c gray black	6.75	1.60
227	A92a	1p slate bl & red	10.00	10.00
		Punch cancel		.50
a.		Imperf., pair	325.00	
228	A92a	5p black & gray grn	100.00	80.00
		Punch cancel		15.00
229	A92a	10p violet & blue	150.00	135.00
		Punch cancel		9.00
230	A92a	20p dull blue & cl	150.00	100.00
		Punch cancel		7.00
a.		Imperf., pair	650.00	
		Nos. 215-230 (16)	428.75	333.35

Cent. of Argentina's declaration of independence of Spain, July 9, 1816.

The watermark is either vert. or horiz. on Nos. 215-220, 222; only vert. on No. 221, and only horiz. on Nos. 223-230.

For overprints see Nos. OD9, OD55-OD56, OD109, OD153, OD191-OD192, OD285, OD324.

A93   A94

A94a

1917   Perf. 13½

231	A93	½c violet	.30	.30
		Never hinged	.45	
a.		Imperf. pair	70.00	
		Never hinged	105.00	

232	A93	1c buff	.30	.30
		Never hinged	.45	
a.		Imperf., pair	70.00	
		Never hinged	105.00	
233	A93	2c brown	.30	.30
		Never hinged	.45	
a.		Imperf., pair	70.00	
		Never hinged	105.00	
234	A93	3c lt green	.70	.30
		Never hinged	1.05	
a.		imperf., pair	70.00	
		Never hinged	105.00	
235	A93	4c red violet	.70	.30
		Never hinged	1.05	
a.		Imperf., pair	70.00	
		Never hinged	105.00	
236	A93	5c red	.30	.30
		Never hinged	.45	
a.		Imperf., pair	15.00	
		Never hinged	22.50	
237	A93	10c gray green	.30	.30
		Never hinged	.45	
a.		Imperf., pair	70.00	
		Never hinged	105.00	
		Nos. 231-237 (7)	2.90	2.10

Perf. 13½x12½

231B	A93	½c violet	.30	.30
		Never hinged	.45	
232B	A93	1c buff	.40	.40
		Never hinged	.60	
233B	A93	2c brown	.40	.40
		Never hinged	.60	
234B	A93	3c lt green	.70	.30
		Never hinged	1.05	
235B	A93	4c red violet	.70	.30
		Never hinged	1.05	
236B	A93	5c red	.30	.30
		Never hinged	.45	
237B	A93	10c gray green	.30	.30
		Never hinged	.45	
		Nos. 231B-237B (7)	3.10	2.30

Perf. 13½

238	A94	12c blue	1.00	.25
		Never hinged	1.50	
239	A94	20c ultra	2.50	.30
		Never hinged	3.75	
240	A94	24c red brown	6.00	3.00
		Never hinged	9.00	
241	A94	30c claret	6.00	1.50
		Never hinged	9.00	
242	A94	50c gray black	6.00	.60
		Never hinged	9.00	
243	A94a	1p slate bl & red	6.00	.60
		Never hinged	9.00	
244	A94a	5p black & gray grn	19.00	3.00
		Never hinged	29.00	
		Punch cancel		1.50
245	A94a	10p violet & blue	47.50	12.00
		Never hinged	72.50	
		Punch cancel		1.50
246	A94a	20p dull blue & cl	90.00	50.00
		Never hinged	135.00	
		Punch cancel		1.00
a.		Center inverted	1,500.	1,500.
		Nos. 231-246 (16)	186.90	73.35

The watermark is either vert. or horiz. on Nos. 231-236, 238 and 231B-236B, 238B; only vert. on No. 237 and 237B, and only horiz. on Nos. 239-246.

All known examples of No. 246a are off-center to the right.

Juan Gregorio Pujol — A95

1918, June 15   Litho.   Perf. 13½

247	A95	5c bister & gray	.60	.30

Cent. of the birth of Juan G. Pujol (1817-61), lawyer and legislator.

1918-19   Unwmk.   Perf. 13½

248	A93	½c violet	.30	.25
249	A93	1c buff	.30	.25
		Never hinged	.45	
a.		Imperf., pair	14.00	
		Never hinged	21.00	
250	A93	2c brown	.30	.25
		Never hinged	.45	
251	A93	3c lt green	.50	.25
		Never hinged	.75	
252	A93	4c red violet	.50	.25
		Never hinged	.75	
253	A93	5c red	.30	.25
		Never hinged	.75	
254	A93	10c gray green	.80	.25
		Never hinged	1.20	
255	A94	12c blue	1.25	.25
		Never hinged	1.90	
256	A94	20c ultra	1.40	.25
		Never hinged	2.10	
257	A94	24c red brown	2.40	.25
		Never hinged	3.50	
258	A94	30c claret	3.00	.30
		Never hinged	4.50	
259	A94	50c gray black	6.00	.50
		Never hinged	9.00	
		Nos. 248-259 (12)	17.05	3.30

Perf. 13½x12½

248B	A93	½c violet	.30	.25
		Never hinged	.45	
249B	A93	1c buff	.30	.25
		Never hinged	.45	
250B	A93	2c brown	.30	.25
		Never hinged	.45	
251B	A93	3c lt green	.50	.25
		Never hinged	.75	
252B	A93	4c red violet	.50	.25
		Never hinged	.75	
253B	A93	5c red	.30	.25
		Never hinged	.75	
254B	A93	10c gray green	1.10	.25
		Never hinged	1.60	
		Nos. 248B-254B (7)	3.30	1.75

The stamps of this issue sometimes show letters of papermakers' watermarks.

There were two printings, in 1918 and 1923, using different ink and paper.

1920   Wmk. 88

264	A93	½c violet	.50	.25
		Never hinged	.75	
265	A93	1c buff	.50	.25
		Never hinged	.75	
266	A93	2c brown	.50	.25
		Never hinged	.75	
267	A93	3c green	1.50	1.00
		Never hinged	2.25	
268	A93	4c red violet	2.00	1.50
		Never hinged	3.00	
269	A93	5c red	.50	.25
		Never hinged	.75	
270	A93	10c gray green	4.50	.25
		Never hinged	6.75	

Perf. 13½

264A	A93	½c violet	.80	.30
		Never hinged	1.20	
265A	A93	1c buff	.80	.30
		Never hinged	1.20	
266A	A93	2c brown	1.00	.30
		Never hinged	1.50	
267A	A93	3c green	2.00	1.00
		Never hinged	3.00	
269A	A93	5c red	4.00	.30
		Never hinged	6.00	
270A	A93	10c gray green	55.00	15.00
		Never hinged	82.50	
271	A94	12c blue	3.00	.30
		Never hinged	4.50	
272	A94	20c ultra	4.25	.40
		Never hinged	6.50	
274	A94	30c claret	15.00	3.00
		Never hinged	22.50	
275	A94	50c gray black	10.00	3.00
		Never hinged	15.00	
		Nos. 264-275 (17)	105.85	27.65

See Nos. 292-300, 304-307A, 310-314, 318, 322.

For overprints see Nos. OD10-OD20, OD57-OD71, OD74, OD110-OD121, OD154-OD159, OD161-OD162, OD193-OD207, OD209-OD211, OD242-OD252, OD254-OD255, OD286-OD290, OD325-OD328, OD330.

Belgrano's Mausoleum A96

Creation of Argentine Flag A97

Gen. Manuel Belgrano — A98

1920, June 18

280	A96	2c red	1.00	.30
a.		Perf. 13½x12½	2.00	.50
281	A97	5c rose & blue	1.00	.30
282	A98	12c green & blue	2.00	1.00
		Nos. 280-282 (3)	4.00	1.60

Belgrano (1770-1820), Argentine general, patriot and diplomat.

Gen. Justo Jose de Urquiza — A99

Bartolome Mitre — A100

1920, Nov. 11

283	A99	5c gray blue	.60	.30

Gen. Justo Jose de Urquiza (1801-70), pres. of Argentina, 1854-60. See No. 303.

1921, June 26   Unwmk.

284	A100	2c violet brown	.50	.30
285	A100	5c light blue	.50	.30

Bartolome Mitre (1821-1906), pres. of Argentina, 1862-65.

Allegory, Pan-America — A101

1921, Aug. 25   Perf. 13½

286	A101	3c violet	.55	.30
287	A101	5c blue	2.00	.30
288	A101	10c vio brown	2.50	.50
289	A101	12c rose	3.00	1.00
		Nos. 286-289 (4)	8.05	2.10

Inscribed "Buenos Aires-Agosto de 1921" A102

Inscribed "Republica Argentina" A103

1921, Oct.   Perf. 13½x12½

290	A102	5c rose	.60	.30
		Never hinged	.90	
291	A103	5c rose	2.50	.30
		Never hinged	3.75	

Perf. 13½

290A	A102	5c rose	6.00	.50
		Never hinged	9.00	
291A	A103	5c rose	2.50	.30
		Never hinged	3.75	

1st Pan-American Postal Cong., Buenos Aires, Aug., 1921.

See Nos. 308-309, 319. For overprints see Nos. OD72, OD160, OD208, OD253, OD329.

1920   Wmk. 89   Perf. 13½x12½

292	A93	½c violet	1.60	.80
		Never hinged	2.50	
293	A93	1c buff	4.50	1.50
		Never hinged	6.75	
294	A93	2c brown	3.50	.50
		Never hinged	5.25	
297	A93	5c red	4.50	.35
		Never hinged	6.75	
298	A93	10c gray green	4.50	.35
		Never hinged	6.75	
		Nos. 292-298,300 (6)	30.60	4.50

Perf. 13½

294A	A93	2c brown	7.00	1.50
		Never hinged	11.00	
297A	A93	5c red	52.50	9.00
		Never hinged	75.00	
298A	A93	10c gray green	40.00	2.00
		Never hinged	60.00	
299	A94	12c blue	*3,000.*	200.00
		Never hinged	4,500.	
300	A94	20c ultra	12.00	1.00
		Never hinged	18.00	

1920

303	A99	5c gray blue	450.00	300.00
		Never hinged	675.00	

1922-23   Wmk. 90   Perf. 13½

304	A93	½c violet	.60	.25
		Never hinged	675.00	
305	A93	1c buff	1.00	.30
		Never hinged	1.50	

306	A93	2c brown	1.00	.30
		Never hinged	1.50	
307	A93	3c green	.60	.40
		Never hinged	.90	
307A	A93	4c red violet	1.50	1.00
		Never hinged	2.25	
308	A102	5c rose	10.00	3.00
		Never hinged	15.00	
309	A103	5c red	5.00	.80
		Never hinged	7.50	
310	A93	10c gray green	9.00	1.00
		Never hinged	13.50	
311	A94	12c blue	1.00	
		Never hinged	1.50	
312	A94	20c ultra	2.00	.50
		Never hinged	3.00	
313	A94	24c red brown	20.00	10.00
		Never hinged	30.00	
314	A94	30c claret	10.00	1.00
		Never hinged	15.00	

Perf. 13½x12½

304B	A93	½c violet	.50	.30
		Never hinged	.75	
305B	A93	1c buff	.50	.30
		Never hinged	.75	
306B	A93	2c brown	.50	.30
		Never hinged	.75	
307B	A93	3c green	1.00	.80
		Never hinged	1.50	
307C	A93	4c red violet	22.50	10.00
		Never hinged	35.00	
308B	A102	5c rose	3.00	.60
		Never hinged	4.50	
309B	A103	5c red	.50	.25
		Never hinged	.75	
310B	A93	10c gray green	2.25	.25
		Never hinged	3.50	
		Nos. 304-310B (20)	92.45	31.75

Paper with Gray Overprint RA in Sun

1922-23   Unwmk.   *Perf. 13½*

318	A93	2c brown	3.00	1.00
		Never hinged	4.50	
319	A103	5c red	10.00	1.00
		Never hinged	15.00	
322	A94	20c ultra	30.00	1.50
		Never hinged	45.00	
		Nos. 318-322 (3)	43.00	3.50

Perf. 13½x12½

318A	A93	2c brown	3.00	1.00
		Never hinged	4.50	
319A	A103	5c red	3.00	.30
		Never hinged	4.50	

San Martín
A104   A105

With Period after Value

Perf. 13½x12½

1923, May   Litho.   Wmk. 90

323	A104	½c red violet	.50	.30
		Never hinged	.75	
324	A104	1c buff	.50	.30
		Never hinged	.75	
325	A104	2c dark brown	.50	.30
		Never hinged	.75	
326	A104	3c lt green	.50	.40
		Never hinged	.75	
327	A104	4c red brown	.50	.40
		Never hinged	.75	
328	A104	5c red	.50	.30
		Never hinged	.75	
329	A104	10c dull green	3.50	.30
		Never hinged	5.25	
330	A104	12c deep blue	.50	.30
		Never hinged	.75	
331	A104	20c ultra	1.50	.30
		Never hinged	2.25	
332	A104	24c lt brown	3.50	3.00
		Never hinged	5.25	
333	A104	30c claret	15.00	.50
		Never hinged	22.50	
334	A104	50c black	7.50	.50
		Never hinged	11.00	

Perf. 13½

323A	A104	½c red violet	.50	.30
		Never hinged	.75	
324A	A104	1c buff	.50	.30
		Never hinged	.75	
325A	A104	2c dark brown	.50	.30
		Never hinged	.75	
326A	A104	3c lt green	.50	.40
		Never hinged	.75	
327A	A104	4c red brown	.50	.40
		Never hinged	.75	
328A	A104	5c red	.50	.30
		Never hinged	.75	
329A	A104	10c dull green	3.50	.30
		Never hinged	5.25	
330A	A104	12c deep blue	.50	.30
		Never hinged	.75	
331A	A104	20c ultra	1.50	.30
		Never hinged	2.25	
332A	A104	24c lt brown	3.50	3.00
		Never hinged	5.25	

333A	A104	30c claret	15.00	.50
		Never hinged	22.50	
334A	A104	50c black	7.50	.50
		Never hinged	11.00	

Without Period after Value
Wmk. 87
Perf. 13½

335	A105	1p blue & red	10.00	.50
		Never hinged	15.00	
336	A105	5p gray lilac & grn	30.00	6.00
		Never hinged	45.00	
		Punch cancel		1.00
337	A105	10p claret & blue	90.00	15.00
		Never hinged	135.00	
		Punch cancel		2.00
338	A105	20p sl & brn lake	120.00	45.00
		Never hinged	175.00	
		Punch cancel		1.25
a.		Center inverted		
		Nos. 323-338 (28)	319.00	80.30

Nos. 335-338 and 353-356 canceled with round or oval killers in purple (revenue cancellations) sell for one-fifth to one-half as much as postally used copies.
For overprints see Nos. 399-404.

Design of 1923
Without Period after Value
Perf. 13½x12½

1923-24   Litho.   Wmk. 90

340	A104	½c red violet	.50	.30
		Never hinged	.75	
341	A104	1c buff	.50	.30
		Never hinged	.75	
342	A104	2c dk brown	.50	.30
		Never hinged	.75	
343	A104	3c green	.60	.30
		Never hinged	.90	
a.		Imperf., pair	8.00	
			12.00	
344	A104	4c red brown	.60	.30
		Never hinged	.90	
345	A104	5c red	.50	.30
		Never hinged	.75	
346	A104	10c dull green	.50	.30
		Never hinged	.75	
347	A104	12c deep blue	.60	.30
		Never hinged	.90	
348	A104	20c ultra	.90	.30
		Never hinged	1.35	
349	A104	24c lt brown	2.50	1.25
		Never hinged	3.75	
350	A104	25c purple	1.25	.30
		Never hinged	1.90	
351	A104	30c claret	2.50	.30
		Never hinged	3.75	
352	A104	50c black	6.00	.30
		Never hinged	9.00	

Perf. 13½

340B	A104	½c red violet	125.00	40.00
		Never hinged	190.00	
345B	A104	5c red	55.00	22.50
		Never hinged	82.50	
346B	A104	10c dull green	55.00	22.50
		Never hinged	82.50	
349B	A104	24c lt brown	92.50	30.00
		Never hinged	135.00	
353	A105	1p blue & red	6.00	.30
		Never hinged	9.00	
354	A105	5p dk vio & grn	30.00	1.50
		Never hinged	45.00	
		Punch cancel		1.00
355	A105	10p claret & blue	75.00	6.00
		Never hinged	110.00	
		Punch cancel		2.00
356	A105	20p slate & lake	105.00	15.00
		Never hinged	160.00	
		Punch cancel		1.25
		Nos. 340-356 (21)	560.95	142.65

1931-33   Typo.

343b	A104	3c	3.00	.50
345a	A104	5c	4.50	.50
346a	A104	10c	7.50	.50
347a	A104	12c	15.00	3.00
348a	A104	20c	50.00	2.50
350a	A104	25c	40.00	1.75
351a	A104	30c	21.00	1.25
		Nos. 343b-351a (7)	141.00	10.00

The typographed stamps were issued only in coils and have a rough impression with heavy shading about the eyes and nose. Nos. 343 and 346 are known without watermark.
Nos. 343-345, 347-349, 351a may be found in pairs, one with period.
See note after No. 338. See Nos. 362-368.
For overprints see Nos. OD21-OD33, OD75-OD87, OD122-OD133, OD163-OD175, OD212-OD226, OD256-OD268, OD291-OD304, OD331-OD345.

Rivadavia — A106

1926, Feb. 8   *Perf. 13½*

357	A106	5c rose	.60	.30

Presidency of Bernardino Rivadavia, cent.

Rivadavia
A108

San Martin
A109

General Post Office,
1926 — A110

General Post Office,
1826 — A111

1926, July 1   *Perf. 13½x12½*

358	A108	3c gray green	.40	.30
359	A109	5c red	.40	.30

Perf. 13½

360	A110	12c deep blue	1.25	.40
361	A111	25c chocolate	1.60	.25
a.		"1326" for "1826"	15.00	5.00
		Nos. 358-361 (4)	3.65	1.25

Centenary of the Post Office.
For overprints see Nos. OD34, OD88, OD134, OD227-OD228, OD269, OD305, OD346.

Type of 1923-31 Issue
Without Period after Value

1927   Wmk. 205   *Perf. 13½x12½*

362	A104	½c red violet	.50	.50
a.		Pelure paper	2.50	2.50
363	A104	1c buff	.50	.50
364	A104	2c dark brown	.50	.30
a.		Pelure paper	.70	.70
365	A104	5c red	.50	.30
a.		Period after value	9.00	6.00
b.		Pelure paper	.70	.70
366	A104	10c dull green	5.00	3.00
367	A104	20c ultra	47.50	4.75

Perf. 13½

368	A105	1p blue & red	36.00	6.00
		Nos. 362-368 (7)	90.50	15.35

Arms of Argentina and Brazil
A112

Wmk. RA in Sun (90)

1928, Aug. 27   *Perf. 12½x13*

369	A112	5c rose red	1.50	.40
370	A112	12c deep blue	2.50	.70

Cent. of peace between the Empire of Brazil and the United Provinces of the Rio de la Plata.

Allegory, Discovery of the New World — A113

"Spain" and "Argentina" — A114

"America" Offering Laurels to Columbus
A115

1929, Oct. 12   Litho.   *Perf. 13½*

371	A113	2c lilac brown	2.00	.40
372	A114	5c light red	2.00	.40
373	A115	12c dull blue	6.00	1.00
		Nos. 371-373 (3)	10.00	1.80

Discovery of America by Columbus, 437th anniv.

Spirit of Victory Attending Insurgents — A116

March of the Victorious Insurgents
A117

Perf. 13½x12½ (A116), 12½x13 (A117)

1930

374	A116	½c violet gray	1.00	.50
375	A116	1c myrtle green	1.00	.50
376	A117	2c dull violet	1.00	.50
377	A116	3c green	.50	.50
378	A116	4c violet	.80	.70
379	A116	5c rose red	.70	.30
380	A116	10c gray black	1.00	.70
381	A117	12c dull blue	1.50	.70
382	A117	20c ocher	1.50	.80
383	A117	24c red brown	5.00	2.00
384	A117	25c green	6.00	2.00
385	A117	30c deep violet	8.00	3.00
386	A117	50c black	10.00	4.00
387	A117	1p sl bl & red	24.00	8.00
388	A117	2p black & org	30.00	12.00
389	A117	5p dull grn & blk	92.50	35.00
390	A117	10p dp red brn & dull blue	120.00	40.00
391	A117	20p yel grn & dl bl	210.00	90.00
392	A117	50p dk grn & vio	750.00	650.00
		Nos. 374-390 (17)	304.50	111.20

Revolution of 1930.
Nos. 387-392 with oval (parcel post) cancellation sell for less.
For overprint see No. 405.

1931   *Perf. 12½x12½*

393	A117	½c red violet	.50	.50
394	A117	1c gray black	1.50	1.00
395	A117	3c green	1.50	.70
396	A117	4c red brown	.80	.50
397	A117	5c red	.70	.50
a.		Plane omitted, top left corner	3.00	1.50
398	A117	10c dull green	1.50	.70
		Nos. 393-398 (6)	6.50	3.90

Revolution of 1930.

Stamps of 1924-25 Overprinted in Red or Green

1931, Sept. 6   *Perf. 13½, 13½x12½*

399	A104	3c green	.40	.40
400	A104	5c dull green	.60	.60
401	A104	30c claret (G)	4.50	2.50
402	A104	50c black	4.50	3.00

Overprinted in Blue

403	A105	1p blue & red	5.50	3.00
404	A105	5p dk violet & grn	60.00	20.00

No. 388 Overprinted in Blue

Perf. 12½x13

405	A117	2p black & orange	10.00	7.50
		Nos. 399-405 (7)	85.50	37.00

1st anniv. of the Revolution of 1930.
See Nos. C30-C34.

Compressor — A118

Perf. 13½x12½

1932, Aug. 29   **Litho.**
406 A118   3c green   1.00   .50
407 A118 10c scarlet   2.00   .40
408 A118 12c gray blue   7.00 1.10
     Nos. 406-408 (3)   10.00 2.00
6th Intl. Refrigeration Congress.

Port of La
Plata
A119

Pres. Julio A.
Roca — A120

Municipal
Palace
A121

Cathedral of
La
Plata — A122

Dardo Rocha
A123

Perf. 13½x13, 13x13½ (10c)
1933, Jan.
409 A119   3c green & dk brn   .40   .30
410 A120 10c orange & dk vio .60   .30
411 A121 15c dk bl & dp bl   2.50 1.50
412 A122 20c violet & yel brn 1.75   .90
413 A123 30c dk grn & vio brn 13.00 6.00
     Nos. 409-413 (5)   18.25 9.00
50th anniv. of the founding of the city of La
Plata, Nov. 19th, 1882.

Christ of the
Andes — A124

Buenos Aires
Cathedral
A125

1934, Oct. 1   Perf. 13x13½, 13½x13
414 A124 10c rose & brown 1.00   .30
415 A125 15c dark blue   3.00   .60

32nd Intl. Eucharistic Cong., Oct. 10-14.

"Liberty" with   Symbolical of
Arms of Brazil   "Peace" and
and Argentina   "Friendship"
A126   A127

1935, May 15   Perf. 13x13½
416 A126 10c red   1.00   .30
417 A127 15c blue   2.00   .60
Visit of Pres. Getulio Vargas of Brazil.

Belgrano   Sarmiento
A128   A129

Urquiza — A130   Louis
                       Braille — A131

San   Brown — A133
Martin — A132

Moreno   Alberdi
A134   A135

Nicolas   Rivadavia
Avellaneda   A137
A136

Mitre   Bull (Cattle
A138   Breeding)
                       A139

Perf. 13, 13½x13, 13x13½
1935-51   Litho.   Wmk. 90
418 A128 ½c red violet   .30   .25
419 A129   1c buff   .30   .25
   a.   Typo.   .80   .25

Martin Güemes   Agriculture
A140   A141

Merino
Sheep (Wool)
A142

Sugar Cane
A143

Oil Well
(Petroleum) — A144

Map of South America
A145   A146

Fruit — A147

Iguacu Falls   Grapes
(Scenic   (Vineyards)
Wonders)   A149
A148

Cotton — A150

Two types of A140:
Type I — Inscribed Juan Martin Guemes.
Type II — Inscribed Martin Güemes.

420 A130   2c dark brown   .50   .25
421 A131 2½c black ('39)   .30   .25
422 A132   3c green   .50   .25
423 A132   3c lt gray ('39)   .50   .25
424 A132   3c lt gray ('46)   .50   .25
425 A133   4c sage green
              ('39)   .40   .25
427 A134   5c yel brn, typo. .25   .25
   a. Tete beche pair, typo.   20.00 10.00
   b. Booklet pane of 8, typo.
   c. Booklet pane of 4, typo.
   d. Litho.   5.00   .50
428 A135   6c olive green   .40   .25
429 A136   8c orange ('39)   .40   .25
430 A137 10c car, perf.
              13½ (typo.)   .25   .25
   a. Perf. 13½x13   2.00   .25
431 A137 10c brown ('42)   .25   .25
432 A138 12c brown   1.00   .25
433 A138 12c red ('39)   .25   .25
434 A139 15c slate bl ('36) 1.50   .25
435 A139 15c pale ultra
              ('39)   1.00   .25
436 A140 15c lt gray bl (II)
              ('42)   45.00 2.00
437 A140 20c lt ultra (I)   1.00   .25
438 A140 20c lt ultra (II)
              ('36)   1.00   .25
439 A140 20c bl gray (II)
              ('39)   .35   .25
439A A139 20c dk bl & pale
             bl, ('42)
             22x33mm   1.00   .25
   a. Typo.   .25   .25
440 A139 20c blue ('51)   .25   .25
441 A141 25c car & pink
              ('36)   .50   .25
442 A142 30c org brn & yel
             brown ('36)   .80   .25
443 A143 40c dk vio ('36)   .70   .25
444 A144 50c red & org
              ('36)   .70   .25
445 A145   1p brn blk & lt bl
              ('36)   25.00 1.00
446 A146   1p brn blk & lt bl
              ('37)   15.00   .30
   a. Chalky paper   100.00 2.00
447 A147   2p brn lake & dk
             ultra ('36)   1.00   .25
448 A148   5p ind & ol grn
              ('36)   3.00   .25
449 A149 10p brn lake &
             blk ('36)   15.00 1.00
450 A150 20p bl grn & brn
              ('36)   25.00 3.00
     Nos. 418-450 (34)   144.40 14.55

See Nos. 485-500, 523-540, 659, 668 in
Scott Standard Postage Stamp Catalogue,
Vol. 1. For overprints see Nos. O37-O41, O43-
O51, O53-O56, O58-O78, O108, O112,
OD35-OD46, OD89-OD101, OD135-OD145,
OD176-OD182C, OD229-OD234F, OD270-
OD280, OD306-OD317, OD347-OD357 in this
catalogue or Scott Standard catalogue, Vol. 1.
   No. 439A exists with attached label showing
medallion. Value $42.50 unused, $22.50 used.

Souvenir Sheet

A151

Without Period after Value

1935, Oct. 17   Litho.   Imperf.
452 A151   Sheet of 4   75.00 35.00
   a.   10c dull green   16.50 7.50

Phil. Exhib. at Buenos Aires, Oct. 17-24,
1935. The stamps were on sale during the 8
days of the exhibition only. Sheets measure
83x101mm.

Plaque — A152

1936, Dec. 1   *Perf. 13x13½*
453   A152   10c rose   .80   .40
Inter-American Conference for Peace.

Domingo Faustino
Sarmiento — A153

1938, Sept. 5
454   A153   3c sage green   .50   .50
455   A153   5c red   .50   .50
456   A153   15c deep blue   1.00   .50
457   A153   50c orange   4.00   1.00
          Nos. 454-457 (4)   6.00   2.50
50th anniv. of the death of Domingo Faustino Sarmiento, pres., educator and author.

"Presidente
Sarmiento" — A154

1939, Mar. 16
458   A154   5c greenish blue   .50   .30
Final voyage of the training ship "Presidente
Sarmiento."

Allegory of the   Coat of
UPU — A155   Arms — A157

Post Office,
Buenos
Aires — A156

Iguacu
Falls — A158

Bonete Hill,
Nahuel
Huapi
Park — A159

Allegory of   Argentina, Land
Modern   of Promise
Communications   A161
A160

Lake Frias,
Nahuel
Huapi
Park — A162

Perf. 13x13½, 13½x13
1939, Apr. 1   **Photo.**
459   A155   5c rose carmine   .70   .25
460   A156   15c grnsh black   .70   .40
461   A157   20c brt blue   .70   .25
462   A158   25c dp blue grn   1.10   .40
463   A159   50c brown   1.60   .90
464   A160   1p brown violet   4.25   2.40
465   A161   2p magenta   18.50 15.00
466   A162   5p purple   42.50 30.00
          Nos. 459-466 (8)   70.05 49.60
Universal Postal Union, 11th Congress.

Souvenir Sheets

A163

A164

1939, May 12   Wmk. 90   Imperf.
467   A163   Sheet of 4   6.50   5.00
  a.   5c rose carmine (A155)   1.40   1.00
  b.   20c bright blue (A157)   1.40   1.00
  c.   25c deep blue green (A158) 1.40   1.00
  d.   50c brown (A159)   1.40   1.00
468   A164   Sheet of 4   6.50   5.00

Issued in four forms:
  a.   Unsevered horizontal pair of
       sheets, type A163 at left,
       A164 at right   27.50 16.00
  b.   Unsevered vertical pair of
       sheets, type A163 at top,
       A164 at bottom   27.50 16.00
  c.   Unsevered block of 4 sheets,
       type A163 at left, A164 at
       right   55.00 55.00
  d.   Unsevered block of 4 sheets,
       type A163 at top, A164 at
       bottom   55.00 55.00
11th Cong. of the UPU and the Argentina
Intl. Phil. Exposition (C.Y.T.R.A.).
No. 468 contains Nos. 467a-467d.

Family and
New House
A165

Perf. 13½x13
1939, Oct. 2   Litho.   Wmk. 90
469   A165   5c bluish green   .50   .25
1st Pan-American Housing Congress.

Bird Carrying   Head of Liberty
Record   and Arms of
A166   Argentina
                        A167

Record and
Winged
Letter
A168

Perf. 13x13½, 13½x13 (#472)
1939, Dec. 11
470   A166   1.18p indigo   14.00 10.00
471   A167   1.32p bright blue   14.00 10.00
472   A168   1.50p dark brown   52.50 35.00
          Nos. 470-472 (3)   80.50 55.00
These stamps were issued for the recording
and mailing of flexible phonograph records.

Map of the
Americas — A169

1940, Apr. 14   Perf. 13x13½
473   A169   15c ultramarine   .50   .25
50th anniv. of the Pan American Union.

Souvenir Sheet

Reproductions of Early Argentine
Stamps — A170

Wmk. RA in Sun (90)
1940, May 25   Litho.   Imperf.
474   A170   Sheet of 5   11.00   8.00
  a.   5c dark blue (Corrientes A2) 1.75   1.50
  b.   5c red (Argentina A1)   1.75   1.50
  c.   5c dark blue (Cordoba #1)   1.75   1.50
  d.   5c red (Argentina A3)   1.75   1.50
  e.   10c dark blue (Buenos Aires
       A1)   1.75   1.50
100th anniv. of the first postage stamp.

AIR POST STAMPS

Airplane Circles   Eagle — AP2
the
Globe — AP1

Wings Cross
the
Sea — AP3

Condor on
Mountain
Crag — AP4

Perforations of Nos. C1-C37 vary from
clean-cut to rough and uneven, with many
skipped perfs.

Perf. 13x13½, 13½x13
1928, Mar. 1   Litho.   Wmk. 90
C1   AP1   5c lt red   1.50   .60
C2   AP1   10c Prus blue   2.50   1.10
C3   AP2   15c lt brown   2.50   1.00
C4   AP1   18c lilac gray   4.00   3.00
  a.   18c brown lilac   375.00
  b.   Double impression
C5   AP2   20c ultra   3.00   1.00
C6   AP2   24c deep blue   5.00   3.00
C7   AP3   25c brt violet   5.00   1.60
C8   AP3   30c rose red   6.00   1.25
C9   AP4   35c rose   5.00   1.10
C10   AP1   36c bister brn   3.00   1.60
C11   AP4   50c gray black   5.00   .75
C12   AP2   54c chocolate   5.00   2.25
C13   AP2   72c yellow grn   6.00   2.25
  a.   Double impression   350.00
C14   AP3   90c dk brown   11.00   2.00
C15   AP3   1p slate bl & red   13.00   .90
C16   AP3   1.08p rose & dk bl   18.00   5.00
C17   AP4   1.26p dull vio & grn 25.00 10.00
C18   AP4   1.80p blue & lil rose 25.00 10.00
C19   AP4   3.60p gray & blue   50.00 22.00
          Nos. C1-C19 (19)   195.50 70.40
The watermark on No. C4a is larger than on
the other stamps of this set, measuring 10mm
across Sun.

Zeppelin First Flight

Air Post Stamps of
1928 Overprinted in
Blue

1930, May
C20   AP2   20c ultra   10.00   5.00
C21   AP4   50c gray black   20.00 10.00
  a.   Inverted overprint   475.00
C22   AP3   1p slate bl &
             red   25.00 12.50
  a.   Inverted overprint   650.00
C23   AP4   1.80p blue & lil
             rose   70.00 30.00
C24   AP4   3.60p gray & blue   200.00 90.00
          Nos. C20-C24 (5)   325.00 147.50

Overprinted in Green
C25   AP2   20c ultra   13.00   8.00
C26   AP4   50c gray black   15.00 10.00
C27   AP3   90c dark brown   13.00   8.00
C28   AP3   1p slate bl &
             red   25.00 15.00
C29   AP4   1.80p blue & lil
             rose   700.00 500.00
  a.   Thick paper   850.00
          Nos. C25-C29 (5)   766.00 541.00

Air Post Stamps of 1928 Overprinted in Red or Blue

On AP1-AP2

On AP3-AP4

1931

C30	AP1	18c lilac gray	2.00	1.50
C31	AP2	72c yellow green	14.00	10.50
C32	AP3	90c dark brown	14.00	10.50
C33	AP4	1.80p bl & lil rose (Bl)	30.00	22.50
C34	AP4	3.60p gray & blue	57.50	40.00
		Nos. C30-C34 (5)	117.50	85.00

1st anniv. of the Revolution of 1930.

Zeppelin Issue

Nos. C1, C4, C4a, C14 Overprinted in Blue or Red

On AP1

On AP3

1932, Aug. 4

C35	AP1	5c lt red (Bl)	3.00	2.00
C36	AP1	18c lilac gray (R)	12.50	9.00
a.		18c brown lilac (R)	100.00	60.00
C37	AP3	90c dark brown (R)	32.50	26.00
		Nos. C35-C37 (3)	48.00	37.00

Plane and Letter — AP5

Mercury — AP6   Plane in Flight — AP7

Perf. 13½x13, 13x13½

			Wmk. 90	
1940, Oct. 23		Photo.		
C38	AP5	30c deep orange	5.00	.25
C39	AP6	50c dark brown	7.50	.25
C40	AP5	1p carmine	1.75	.25
C41	AP7	1.25p deep green	.50	.25
C42	AP5	2.50p bright blue	1.25	.25
		Nos. C38-C42 (5)	16.00	1.25

OFFICIAL STAMPS

Regular Issues
Overprinted in Black — a

1884-87		**Unwmk.**	**Perf. 12, 14**	
O1	A29	½c brown	40.00	25.00
O2	A23	1c red	12.00	8.00
b.		Perf. 12	100.00	80.00
O3	A29	1c red	1.00	.50
		On cover		
b.		Double overprint	100.00	100.00
O4	A20	2c green	1.00	.50
		On cover		
b.		Double overprint	120.00	120.00
O5	A11	4c brown	1.00	.50
		On cover		
O6	A7	8c lake	1.00	1.00
		On cover		
O7	A8	10c green	100.00	50.00
O8	A23	12c ultra (#45)	1.50	1.00
a.		Perf. 14	1,000.	250.00
O9	A29	12c grnsh blue	1.50	1.00
		On cover		
O10	A19	24c blue	2.00	1.50
		On cover		
O11	A21	25c lake	30.00	25.00
O12	A12	30c orange	80.00	70.00
O13	A13	60c black	50.00	40.00
O14	A14	90c black	30.00	25.00
b.		Double overprint	120.00	120.00
		Nos. O1-O14 (14)	351.00	249.00

Inverted Overprint

O1a	A29	½c	30.00	20.00
O2a	A23	1c Perf. 14	100.00	80.00
c.		Perf. 12	75.00	—
O3a	A29	1c	2.50	1.25
O4a	A20	2c	120.00	120.00
O5a	A11	4c	60.00	50.00
O6a	A7	8c (Inverted overprint on reverse)	500.00	—
O8b	A23	12c Perf. 12	—	—
O9a	A29	12c	300.00	250.00
O10a	A19	24c	6.00	5.00
O13a	A13	60c	150.00	120.00
O14a	A14	90c	120.00	120.00

1884			**Rouletted**	
O15	A17	16c green	3.00	2.00
a.		Double overprint	25.00	
b.		Inverted overprint	300.00	
O16	A18	20c blue	15.00	12.00
a.		Inverted overprint	120.00	80.00
O17	A19	24c blue	2.00	1.50
a.		Inverted overprint	6.00	5.00
b.		Double ovpt., one inverted	250.00	
		Nos. O15-O17 (3)	20.00	15.50

Overprinted Diagonally in Red

1885			**Perf. 12**	
O18	A20	2c green	3.00	2.00
a.		Inverted overprint	100.00	100.00
O19	A11	4c brown	3.00	2.00
a.		Inverted overprint	100.00	
b.		Double overprint	100.00	100.00
O20	A13	60c black	50.00	40.00
O21	A14	90c blue	450.00	275.00

1885			**Rouletted**	
O22	A19	24c blue	27.50	20.00

On all of these stamps, the overprint is found reading both upwards and downwards. Counterfeits exist of No. O21 overprint and others.

Regular Issues Handstamped Horizontally in Black — b

1884			**Perf. 12, 14**	
O23	A23	1c red	100.00	50.00
a.		Perf. 12	400.00	300.00
O24	A20	2c green, diagonal overprint	60.00	40.00
a.		Horizontal overprint	450.00	300.00
O25	A11	4c brown	25.00	20.00
O26	A7	8c lake	25.00	10.00
O27	A23	12c ultra	50.00	

Overprinted Diagonally

O28	A19	24c bl, rouletted	50.00	35.00
O29	A13	60c black	30.00	15.00

Counterfeit overprints exist.

Liberty Head — O1

Perf. 11½, 12 and Compound

1901, Dec. 1			**Engr.**	
O31	O1	1c gray	.40	.25
b.		On cover		20.00
		Vert. pair, imperf. horiz.	50.00	
c.		Horiz. pair, imperf. vert.	50.00	
O32	O1	2c orange brown	.40	.25
		On cover		25.00
O33	O1	5c red	.45	.25
		On cover		25.00
b.		Vert. pair, imperf. horiz.	50.00	
O34	O1	10c dark green	.90	.25
		On cover		35.00
O35	O1	30c dark blue	5.00	1.60
		On cover		50.00
O36	O1	50c orange	3.00	1.40
		On cover		75.00
		Nos. O31-O36 (6)	10.15	4.00

Imperf, Pairs

O31a	O1	1c	80.00	
O32a	O1	2c	80.00	
O33a	O1	5c	100.00	
O34a	O1	10c	80.00	
O35a	O1	30c	100.00	
O36a	O1	50c	150.00	

Regular Stamps of 1935-51 Overprinted in Black — c

SERVICIO OFICIAL

Perf. 13x13½, 13½x13, 13

1938-54		**Wmk. RA in Sun (90)**		
O37	A129	1c buff ('40)	.40	.25
O38	A130	2c dk brn ('40)	.40	.25
O39	A132	3c grn ('39)	1.00	.25
O40	A132	3c lt gray ('39)	.40	.25
O41	A134	5c yel brn	.40	.25
O42	A195	5c car ('53)	.40	.25
O43	A137	10c carmine	.55	.25
O44	A137	10c brn ('39)	.45	.25
O45	A140	15c lt gray bl, type II ('47)	.40	.25
O46	A139	15c slate blue	.75	.25
O47	A139	15c pale ultra ('39)	.45	.25
O48	A139	20c blue ('53)	1.10	.40
O49	A141	25c carmine	.40	.25
a.		Overprint 11mm	.55	.25
O49B	A143	40c dk violet	1.50	.35
O50	A144	50c red & org	.40	.25
a.		Overprint 11mm	.40	.25
O51	A146	1p brn blk & lt bl ('40)	.45	.25
a.		Overprint 11mm	.45	.40
O52	A224	1p choc & lt bl ('51)	1.50	.25
a.		Overprint 11mm	.40	.25
O53	A147	2p brn lake & dk ultra (ovpt. 11mm) ('54)	1.50	.25
		Nos. O37-O53 (18)	12.45	4.75

OFFICIAL DEPARTMENT STAMPS

Regular Issues of 1911-38 Overprinted in Black
Ministry of Agriculture

No. OD1

1913		**Type I**	**Perf. 13½x12½**	
OD1	A88	2c chocolate (#181)	.50	.25
OD2	A88	1c ocher (#190)	.50	.25
OD3	A88	2c chocolate (#191)	1.00	.50
OD4	A88	5c red (#194)	1.00	.50
a.		Perf. 13½ (#194a)	3.00	1.00
OD5	A88	12c deep blue (#196)	1.00	.50
a.		Perf. 13½ (#196a)	3.00	.50
		Nos. OD2-OD5 (4)	3.50	1.75

1915				
OD6	A88	1c ocher (#208)	1.50	.50
OD7	A88	2c chocolate (#209)	1.00	.50
OD8	A88	5c red (#212)	1.00	.50
		Nos. OD6-OD8 (3)	3.50	1.50

No. OD9

1916			**Perf. 13½**	
OD9	A91	5c red (#220)	.50	.25

No. OD11   No. OD15

1918				
OD10	A94	12c blue (#238)	1.50	.50
OD11	A93	1c buff (#249)	.50	.25
OD12	A93	2c brown (#250)	.50	.25
OD13	A93	5c red (#253)	.50	.25
OD14	A94	12c blue (#255)	.50	.25
OD15	A94	20c ultra (#256)	.50	.25
		Nos. OD10-OD15 (6)	4.00	1.75

1920			**Perf. 13½, 13½x12½**	
OD16	A93	1c buff (13½x12½) (#265)	1.00	.50
OD17	A93	2c brown (#266A)	4.00	1.00
OD18	A93	5c red (#269A)	.70	.30
a.		Perf. 13½x12½ (#269)	.70	.30
		Nos. OD16-OD18 (3)	5.70	1.80

1922			**Perf. 13½**	
OD19	A94	12c blue (#311)	2.00	.75
OD20	A94	20c ultra (#312)	75.00	

No. OD23

1923			**Perf. 13½x12½**	
OD21	A104	1c buff (#324)	1.00	.50
a.		Perf. 13½ (#324A)	5.00	2.00
OD22	A104	2c dark brown (#325)	.50	.25
OD23	A104	5c red (#328)	1.00	.50
a.		Perf. 13½ (#328A)	.50	.25
OD24	A104	12c deep blue (#330)	.80	.25
OD25	A104	20c ultra (#331)	.80	.25
a.		Perf. 13½ (#331A)	6.00	2.00
		Nos. OD21-OD25 (5)	3.60	1.50

1924				
OD26	A104	1c buff (#341)	.50	.25
a.		Inverted ovpt.	20.00	15.00
OD27	A104	2c dk brown (#342)	.50	.25
a.		Pair, one with period	16.00	16.00
OD29	A104	5c red (#345)	.50	.25
a.		Pair, one with period	20.00	20.00
OD30	A104	10c dull green (#346)	.50	.25
OD31	A104	12c deep blue (#347)	.50	.25
OD32	A104	20c deep blue (#348)	.50	.25
a.		Inverted ovpt.	80.00	60.00
		Nos. OD26-OD32 (6)	3.00	1.50

No. OD34

1926				
OD34	A110	12c deep blue (#360)	.50	.25

No. OD28B

Type II
1931-36   *Perf. 13x13½, 13½x13*
OD27B	A104	2c dark brown (#342)	5.00	2.00
OD28B	A104	3c green (#343)	.50	.25
OD29B	A104	5c red (#345)	.50	.25
OD30B	A104	10c dull green (#346)	.50	.25
c.		Typo (coil) (#346a)	.50	.25
OD32B	A104	20c ultra (#348)	1.00	.50
c.		Typo (coil) (#348a)	.50	.25
OD33B	A104	30c claret (#351)	.50	.25
c.		Typo (coil) (#351a)	.50	.25

No. OD36

1936-38   **Litho.**
OD35	A129	1c buff (#419)	.50	.25
OD36	A130	2c dark brown (#420)	.50	.25
OD37	A132	3c green (#422)	.50	.25
OD38	A134	5c yel brn (#427)	.50	.25
OD40	A139	15c lt gray bl (#436)	2.50	.30
OD41	A140	20c lt ultra (#437)	3.00	.30
OD42	A140	20c lt ultra (#438)	.80	.25
OD43	A141	25c car & pink (#441), perf. 13x13½	.50	.25
OD44	A142	30c org brn & yel brown (#442)	.50	.25
OD45	A145	1p brn blk & Lt bl (#445)	3.50	1.50
OD46	A146	1p brn blk & lt bl (#446)	.60	.30
		Nos. OD35-OD46 (11)	13.40	4.15

Typo.   *Perf. 13½*
OD38A	A134	5c yel brn (#427)	.50	.25
OD39A	A137	10c carmine (#430)	.50	.25
b.		Perf. 13½x13 (#430a)	1.00	.50

Ministry of War

No. OD47

1913   **Type I**   *Perf. 13½x12½*
OD47	A88	2c chocolate (#181)	.80	.30
OD48	A88	1c ocher (#190)	.30	.25
OD49	A88	2c chocolate (#191)	4.00	.50
a.		Perf. 13½ (#191a)	15.00	5.00
OD50	A88	5c red (#194)	1.00	.50
a.		Inverted ovpt.	50.00	—
OD51	A88	12c deep blue (#196)	.50	.25
a.		Perf. 13½ (#196a)	5.00	1.00
		Nos. OD48-OD51 (4)	5.80	1.50

1915
OD52	A88	1c ocher (#208)	30.00	6.00
OD53	A88	2c chocolate (#209)	4.00	.80
OD54	A88	5c red (#212)	4.00	.80
		Nos. OD52-OD54 (3)	38.00	7.60

1916   *Perf. 13½*
OD55	A91	5c red (#220)	3.00	.50
OD56	A92	12c blue (#222)	3.00	.50

1918
OD57	A93	1c buff (#232)	1.00	.50
a.		Perf. 13½x12½ (#232B)	8.00	1.00
OD58	A93	2c brown (#233)	5.00	.80
a.		Perf. 13½x12½ (#233B)	1.50	.50
OD59	A93	5c red (#236B) (Perf. 13½x12½)	1.50	.50
OD60	A94	12c blue (#238)	2.00	.80
		Nos. OD57-OD60 (4)	9.50	2.60

1918
OD61	A93	1c buff (#249)	1.50	.50
a.		Perf. 13½x12½ (#249B)	6.00	5.00

OD62	A93	2c brown (#250)	.50	.25
a.		Perf. 13½x12½ (#250B)	1.00	1.00
OD63	A93	5c red (#253)	1.00	.50
a.		Perf. 13½x12½ (#253B)	.50	.25
OD64	A94	12c blue (#255)	1.50	.50
OD65	A94	20c ultra (#256)	4.00	.60
		Nos. OD61-OD65 (5)	8.50	2.35

1920
OD66	A93	2c brown (#266A)	2.50	.50
a.		Perf. 13½x12½ (#266)	.50	.25
OD67	A93	5c red (#269A)	1.50	.50
a.		Perf. 13½x12½ (#269)	1.00	.25
OD68	A94	12c blue (#271)	1.00	.50
		Nos. OD66-OD68 (3)	5.00	1.50

1921
OD69	A94	12c blue (#299)	5.00	1.00

No. OD72

1922
OD70	A93	1c buff (#305)	3.00	.30
OD71	A93	2c brown (13½x12½) (#306B)	5.00	1.00
OD72	A103	5c red (#309)	2.00	.50
OD73	A94	20c ultra (#312)	1.00	.50
		Nos. OD70-OD73 (4)	11.00	2.30

Perf. 13½x12½
OD74	A93	2c brown (#318A)	5.00	1.00

1923   *Perf. 13½x12½*
OD75	A104	1c buff (#324)	1.00	.50
a.		Inverted ovpt.	20.00	18.00
b.		Perf. 13½ (#324A)	5.00	1.50
OD76	A104	2c dark brown (#325)	.50	.25
a.		Perf. 13½ (#325A)	2.00	.50
OD77	A104	5c red (#328)	.50	.25
a.		Inverted ovpt.	20.00	18.00
b.		Perf. 13½ (#328A)	1.50	.50
OD78	A104	12c deep blue (#330)	1.00	.50
OD79	A104	20c ultra (#331)	2.00	.50
a.		Perf. 13½ (#331A)	3.00	.25
b.		As "a.," inverted ovpt.	20.00	18.00
		Nos. OD75-OD79 (5)	5.00	2.00

1924
OD80	A104	1c buff (#341)	5.00	1.00
OD81	A104	2c dark brown (#342)	.50	.25
a.		Pair, one with period	15.00	—
OD82	A104	3c green (#343)	.80	.25
OD83	A104	5c red (#345)	.50	.25
a.		Pair, one with period	15.00	—
OD84	A104	10c dull green (#346)	2.00	.25
OD85	A104	20c ultra (#348)	.50	.25
a.		Pair, one with period	15.00	—
OD86	A104	30c claret (#351)	5.00	.50
OD87	A105	1p blue & red (#353)	5.00	.30
		Nos. OD80-OD87 (8)	19.30	3.05

No. OD88

1926
OD88	A109	5c red (#359)	1.50	.25

No. OD82B

Type II
1931-36   *Perf. 13½x12½, 13*
OD82B	A104	3c green (#343)	1.50	.50
OD83B	A104	5c red (#345)	.60	.25
c.		Inverted overprint	—	60.00
OD84B	A104	10c dull green (#346)	.50	.25
c.		Typo (coil) (#346a)	1.50	.50
OD85B	A104	20c ultra (#348)	1.00	.30
c.		Typo (coil) (#348a)	5.00	.50
OD86B	A104	30c claret (#351)	.80	.25
c.		Typo (coil) (#351a)	2.00	.50

OD87B	A105	1p blue & red (#353) (Perf. 13)	5.00	.30
		Nos. OD82B-OD87B (6)	9.40	1.85

No. OD90

1936-38   **Litho.**
OD89	A129	1c buff (#419)	.50	.25
OD90	A130	2c dark brown (#420)	.50	.25
OD91	A132	3c green (#422)	.50	.25
OD92	A134	5c yel brn (#427)	.50	.25
OD93	A137	10c carmine (#430)	.50	.25
OD94	A139	15c slate bl (#434)	.80	.25
OD95	A140	20c lt ultra (#437)	7.00	.50
OD96	A140	20c lt ultra (#438)	.50	.25
OD97	A141	25c car & pink (#441)	.50	.25
OD98	A142	30c org brn & yel brown (#442)	.50	.25
OD99	A144	50c red & org (#444)	.70	.25
OD100	A145	1p brn blk & lt bl (#445)	2.00	.60
OD101	A146	1p brn blk & lt bl (#446)	1.00	.50
		Nos. OD89-OD101 (13)	15.50	4.10

Typo.   *Perf. 13½*
OD92B	A134	5c yel brn (#427)	.50	.25
c.		Inverted ovpt.	20.00	15.00
OD93B	A137	10c car (#430)	.50	.25
c.		Inverted ovpt.	50.00	35.00
d.		Perf. 13½x13 (#430a)	1.00	.50

Ministry of Finance

No. OD102

1913   **Type I**   *Perf. 13½x12½*
OD102	A88	2c chocolate (#181)	.50	.25
OD103	A88	1c ocher (#190)	.50	.25
OD104	A88	2c chocolate (#191)	.50	.25
OD105	A88	5c red (#194)	.50	.25
OD106	A88	12c deep blue (#196)	.50	.25
a.		Perf. 13½ (#196a)	90.00	35.00
		Nos. OD103-OD106 (4)	2.00	1.00

1915
OD107	A88	2c chocolate (#209)	.50	.25
OD108	A88	5c red (#212)	.50	.25

1916   *Perf. 13½*
OD109	A91	5c red (#220)	.70	.30

1917
OD110	A93	2c brown (#233)	.50	.25
OD111	A93	5c red (#236)	4.00	.50
OD112	A94	12c blue (#238)	.50	.25
		Nos. OD110-OD112 (3)	5.00	1.00

1918
OD113	A93	2c brown (#250)		100.00
OD114	A93	5c red (#253)	.50	.25
a.		Perf. 13½x12½ (#253B)	.70	.25
OD115	A94	12c blue (#255)	.70	.25
OD116	A94	20c ultra (#256)	1.00	.50
		Nos. OD113-OD116 (4)	2.20	101.00

1920
OD117	A93	1c buff (#265)	3.00	1.00
OD118	A93	2c brown (#266)	4.50	1.50
OD119	A93	5c #269	6.00	1.50
a.		Perf. 13½ (#269A)	1.50	.30
OD120	A94	12c blue (perf. 13½) (#271)	1.50	.30
		Nos. OD117-OD120 (4)	15.00	4.30

1922
OD121	A94	20c ultra (#312)	40.00	7.00

1923   *Perf. 13½x12½, 13½*
OD122	A104	1c buff (#324)	20.00	10.00
a.		Perf. 13½ (#324A)	2.00	1.00

OD123	A104	2c dark brown (#325)	.50	.25
a.		Perf. 13½ (#325A)	10.00	1.00
OD124	A104	5c red (#328)	.50	—
a.		Inverted ovpt.	—	35.00
b.		Perf. 13½ (#328A)	1.00	.50
OD125	A104	12c deep blue (#330)	.70	.25
a.		Perf. 13½ (#330A)	3.00	.30
OD126	A104	20c ultra (#331)	.50	.25
a.		Perf. 13½ (#331A)	2.50	.30
		Nos. OD122-OD126 (5)	22.20	11.00

1924   *Perf. 13½x12½*
OD127	A104	2c dark brown (#342)	250.00	250.00
OD128	A104	5c red (#345)	1.00	.25
OD130	A104	12c deep blue (#347)	40.00	17.50
OD131	A104	20c ultra (#348)	.50	.25
		Nos. OD127-OD131 (4)	291.50	268.00

1926
OD134	A110	12c deep blue (#360)	30.00	12.50

No. OD129B   No. OD133B

1931-36   **Type II**
OD127B	A104	3c green (#343)	25.00	10.00
OD129B	A104	10c dull green (#346)	.50	.25
c.		Typo (coil) (#346a)	.60	.25
OD131B	A104	20c ultra (#348)	.50	.25
c.		Typo (coil) (#348a)	.50	.25
OD132B	A104	30c claret (#351)	.50	.25
c.		Typo (coil) (#351a)	1.50	.25

Perf. 13
OD133B	A105	1p blue & red (#353)	1.00	.50
		Nos. OD127B-OD133B (5)	28.00	11.50

No. OD135

1936-38   **Litho.**   *Perf. 13½x13*
OD135	A129	1c buff (#419)	.50	.25
OD136	A130	2c dark brown (#420)	.50	.25
OD137	A132	3c green (#422)	.50	.25
OD138	A134	5c yel brn (Perf. 13½) (#427d)	.50	.25
OD139	A137	10c carmine (#430)	.50	.30
OD140	A139	15c slate blue (#434) ('36)	2.00	.80
a.		Inverted ovpt.	—	80.00
OD141	A140	20c lt ultra (#437)	2.50	.25
OD142	A140	20c lt ultra (#438)	.50	.25
OD143	A142	30c org brn & yel brown (#442)	.50	.25
OD144	A145	1p brn blk & lt bl (#445)	5.00	1.50
OD145	A146	1p brn blk & lt bl (#446)	.60	.30
		Nos. OD135-OD145 (11)	13.60	4.65

Typo.   *Perf. 13½*
OD138A	A134	5c yel brn (#427)	.50	.25
b.		Inverted ovpt.	50.00	50.00
OD139A	A137	10c car (#430)	.50	.25
b.		Perf. 13½x13 (#430a)	18.00	1.50

Ministry of the Interior

No. OD147

1913 — Type I — Perf. 13½x12½

OD146	A88	2c chocolate (#181)	.90	.30
OD147	A88	1c ocher (#190)	.50	.25
OD148	A88	2c chocolate (#191)	2.50	.50
OD149	A88	5c red (#194)	1.00	.40
OD150	A88	12c deep blue (#196)	1.20	.50
a.		Perf. 13½ (#196a)	6.00	1.50
		Nos. OD146-OD150 (5)	6.10	1.95

1915

OD151	A88	2c chocolate (#209)	2.00	.60
OD152	A88	5c red (#212)	2.00	.60

1916 — Perf. 13½

OD153	A91	5c red (#220)	2.00	.80

1918

OD154	A93	5c red (#236B)	5.00	.50
OD155	A93	2c brown (#250)	.50	.25
OD156	A93	5c red (#253)	.70	.30
a.		Perf. 13½x12½ (#253B)	.50	.25
		Nos. OD154-OD156 (3)	6.20	1.05

1920

OD157	A93	1c buff (13½x12½) (#265)	10.00	3.00
OD158	A93	5c red (#269)	5.00	1.00

1922

OD160	A103	5c red (#309)	6.00	2.00
OD161	A94	12c blue (#311)	2.00	.50
OD162	A94	20c ultra (#312)	2.00	.50
		Nos. OD160-OD162 (3)	10.00	3.00

1923 — Perf. 13½x12½

OD163	A104	1c buff (#324)	1.50	.50
a.		Perf. 13½ (#324A)	1.00	.50
OD164	A104	2c dark brown (#325)	.50	.25
a.		Perf. 13½ (#325A)	50.00	30.00
OD165	A104	5c red (#328)	.60	.25
a.		Perf. 13½ (#328A)	4.00	.50
OD166	A104	12c deep blue (#330)	6.00	.80
a.		Perf. 13½ (#330A)	45.00	20.00
OD167	A104	20c ultra (#331)	9.00	1.00
a.		Perf. 13½ (#331A)	7.00	1.00
		Nos. OD163-OD167 (5)	17.60	2.80

1924

OD168	A104	1c buff (#341)	.50	.25
OD169	A104	2c dk brown (#342)	.50	.25
a.		Pair, one with period	15.00	—
OD170	A104	3c green (#343)	3.00	.60
OD171	A104	5c red (#345)	.50	.25
OD173	A104	12c deep blue (#347)	1.00	.25
OD174	A104	20c ultra (#348)	10.00	8.00
		Nos. OD168-OD174 (6)	15.50	9.60

No. OD172B

Type II

1931-36 — Perf. 13½x12½

OD170B	A104	3c green (#343)	.70	.25
OD171B	A104	5c red (#345)	.70	.25
OD172B	A104	10c dull green (#346)	.50	.25
c.		Typo (coil) (#346b)	.50	.25
OD174B	A104	20c ultra (#348)	.50	.25
c.		Typo (coil) (#348a)	1.00	.50
OD175B	A104	30c claret (#351)	3.00	.50
c.		Typo (coil) (#351a)	6.00	2.00
		Nos. OD170B-OD175B (5)	5.40	1.50

No. OD182A

1936-38 — Litho. — Perf. 13½x13

OD176	A129	1c buff (#419)	.50	.25
OD177	A130	2c dark brown (#420)	.50	.25
OD178	A132	3c green (#422)	.50	.25
OD178A	A134	5c yel brn (#427d)	.50	.25
OD180	A139	15c slate bl (#434) ('36)	.70	.30

OD181	A140	20c lt ultra (#437)	3.00	.50
OD182	A140	20c lt ultra (#438)	.50	.25
OD182A	A142	30c org brn & yel brown (#442)	.50	.25
OD182B	A145	1p brn blk & lt blue (#445)	5.00	2.00
OD182C	A146	1p brn blk & lt bl (#446) ('37)	.60	.30
		Nos. OD176-OD182C (10)	12.30	4.60

Typo. — Perf. 13½

OD178D	A134	5c yel brn (#427)	.60	.25
e.		Inverted ovpt.		75.00
OD179D	A137	10c car (#430)	.80	.30
e.		Perf. 13½x13 (#430a)	.50	.25

Ministry of Justice and Instruction

M. J. I.
No. OD184

1913 — Type I — Perf. 13½x12½

OD183	A88	2c chocolate (#181)	3.00	.50
OD184	A88	1c ocher (#190)	4.00	.50
OD185	A88	2c chocolate (#191)	2.50	.50
a.		Perf. 13½ (#191a)	30.00	10.00
OD186	A88	5c red (#194)	1.00	.50
OD187	A88	12c deep blue (#196)	1.50	.50
		Nos. OD184-OD187 (4)	9.00	2.00

1915

OD188	A88	1c ocher (#208)	1.00	.50
OD189	A88	2c chocolate (#209)	1.00	.50
OD190	A88	5c red (#212)	2.00	.80
		Nos. OD188-OD190 (3)	4.00	1.80

1916 — Perf. 13½

OD191	A91	5c red (#220)	1.00	.50
OD192	A92	12c blue (#222)	2.00	.80

1918

OD193	A93	1c buff (#232)	1.00	.50
a.		Perf. 13½x12½ (#232B)	1.00	.50
OD194	A93	2c brown (#233)	4.00	.50
a.		Perf. 13½x12½ (#233B)	2.00	.50
OD195	A93	5c red (#236)	9.00	1.00
a.		Perf. 13½x12½ (#236B)	1.00	.50
OD196	A94	12c blue (#238)	45.00	10.00
		Nos. OD193-OD196 (4)	59.00	12.00

OD197	A93	1c buff (#249)	.60	.30
a.		Perf. 13½x12½ (#249B)	20.00	7.00
OD198	A93	2c brown (#250)	.30	.25
a.		Perf. 13½x12½ (#250B)	.50	.25
OD199	A93	5c red (#253)	.50	.25
a.		Perf. 13½x12½ (#253B)	.60	.30
OD200	A94	12c blue (#255)	.50	.25
OD201	A94	20c ultra (#256)	.70	.30
		Nos. OD197-OD201 (5)	2.60	1.35

1920 — Perf. 13½x12½

OD202	A93	1c buff (#265)	.50	.25
OD203	A93	2c brown (#266)	.50	.25
OD204	A93	5c red (#269)	.50	.25
a.		Perf. 13½ (#269A)	8.00	2.50
OD205	A94	12c blue (Perf. 13½) (#271)	1.00	.50
		Nos. OD202-OD205 (4)	2.70	1.25

1922 — Perf. 13½

OD206	A93	1c buff (#305)	3.00	1.00
a.		Perf. 13½x12½ (#305B)	.70	.25
OD207	A93	2c brown, perf. 13½x12½ (#306B)	4.00	1.00
a.		Perf. 13½x12½ (#309B)	.50	.25
OD208	A103	5c red (#309)	.70	.25
OD209	A94	12c blue (#311)	20.00	4.00
OD210	A94	20c ultra (#312)	4.00	.60
		Nos. OD206-OD210 (5)	31.70	6.85

1922 — Perf. 13½x12½

OD211	A93	2c brown (#318A)	3.50	.70

1923

OD212	A104	1c buff (#324)	.60	.25
a.		(#324A)	1.20	.50
OD213	A104	2c dark brown (#325)	.50	.25
a.		Perf. 13½ (#325A)	1.00	.50
b.		As "a," inverted ovpt.	25.00	20.00
OD214	A104	5c red (#328)	.50	.25
a.		Perf. 13½ (#328A)	.50	.25
OD215	A104	12c deep blue (#330)	.50	.25
OD216	A104	20c ultra (#331)	.50	.25
a.		Perf. 13½ (#331A)	1.20	.30
		Nos. OD212-OD216 (5)	2.60	1.25

1924

OD218	A104	1c buff (#341)	.50	.25
OD219	A104	2c dark brown (#342)	.50	.25
a.		Pair, one with period	15.00	—
OD220	A104	3c green (#343)	.60	.25
OD221	A104	5c red (#345)	.50	.25
a.		Pair, one with period	15.00	—
OD222	A104	10c dull green (#346)	1.00	.50
OD223	A104	12c deep blue (#347)	.50	.25
OD224	A104	20c ultra (#348)	.50	.25
		Nos. OD218-OD224 (7)	4.10	2.00

1926

OD227	A109	5c red (#359)	.50	.25
a.		Inverted ovpt.	35.00	30.00
OD228	A110	12c deep blue (#360)	.50	.25

M.J.I.
No. OD217B

Type II

1931-36 — Perf. 13½x12½, 13

OD217B	A104	½c red violet (#340)	5.00	2.00
OD218B	A104	1c buff (#341)	.50	.25
OD220B	A104	3c green (#343)	.50	.25
c.		Typo (coil) (#343b)	.50	.25
OD221B	A104	5c red (#345)	.50	.25
OD222B	A104	10c dull green (#346)	.50	.25
c.		Typo (coil) (#346a)	.50	.25
OD223B	A104	12c deep blue (#347)	1.20	.30
OD224B	A104	20c ultra (#348)	.50	.25
c.		Typo (coil) (#348a)	.50	.25
OD225B	A104	30c claret (#351)	.50	.25
c.		Typo (coil) (#351a)	1.30	.50
OD226B	A105	1p blue & red (Perf. 13½) (#353)	1.00	.50
		Nos. OD217B-OD226B (9)	10.20	4.30

M. J. I.
No. OD229

1936-38 — Perf. 13½x13

OD229	A129	1c buff (#419)	.50	.25
OD230	A130	2c dark brown (#420)	.50	.25
OD231	A132	3c green (#422)	.50	.25
OD232	A134	5c yel brn (#427d)	.50	.25
OD234	A139	15c slate bl (#434)	1.00	.25
OD234A	A140	20c lt ultra (#437)	.50	.25
OD234B	A140	20c lt ultra (#438)	.60	.25
OD234C	A141	25c car & pink (#441)	.50	.25
OD234D	A142	30c org brn & yel brown (#442)	.50	.25
OD234E	A145	1p brn blk &lt bl (#445)	2.00	.60
OD234F	A146	1p brn blk & lt bl (#446)	3.00	.30
		Nos. OD229-OD234F (11)	10.10	3.15

Typo. — Perf. 13½

OD232A	A134	5c yel brn (#427)	.50	.25
OD233	A137	10c car (#430)	.50	.25
a.		Perf. 13½x13 (#430a)	.50	.25

Ministry of Marine

M. M.
No. OD236

1913 — Type I — Perf. 13½x12½

OD235	A88	2c chocolate (#181)	.60	.25
a.		Perf. 13½ (#181a)	150.00	75.00

OD236	A88	1c ocher (#190)	.50	.25
OD237	A88	2c chocolate (#191)	8.00	.50
OD238	A88	5c red (#194)	.50	.25
a.		Perf. 13½ (#194a)	40.00	8.00
OD239	A88	12c deep blue (#196)	.60	.30
		Nos. OD236-OD239 (4)	9.60	1.30

1915

OD240	A88	2c chocolate (#209)	3.00	.50
OD241	A88	5c red (#212)	2.00	.50

1918

OD242	A93	1c buff (#232)	.70	.30
OD243	A93	2c brown (#233)	.70	.25
OD244	A93	5c red (#236)	.70	.25
a.		Perf. 13½ (#236B)	1.00	.50
		Nos. OD242-OD244 (3)	2.10	.80

1920 — Perf. 13½

OD245	A93	1c buff (#249)	.50	.25
OD246	A93	2c brown (#250)	.70	.25
a.		Perf. 13½x12½ (#250)	1.00	.50
OD247	A93	5c red (#253)	3.50	.25
a.		Perf. 13½x12½ (#253B)	.50	.25
OD248	A94	12c blue (#255)	2.50	.30
OD249	A94	20c ultra (#256)	8.00	1.50
		Nos. OD245-OD249 (5)	15.20	2.55

1920

OD250	A93	1c buff Perf. 13½x12½ (#265A)	.50	.25
OD251	A93	2c brown (#266A)	.70	.30
a.		Perf. 13½ (#266)	.80	.30
OD252	A93	5c red (#269A)	.80	.25
		Nos. OD250-OD252 (3)	2.00	.80

1922

OD253	A103	5c red (#309)	3.00	.50
a.		Perf. 13½x12½ (#309B)	1.50	.30
OD254	A94	12c blue (#311)	30.00	10.00
OD255	A94	20c ultra (#312)	45.00	8.00
		Nos. OD253-OD255 (3)	78.00	18.50

1923 — Perf. 13½x12½

OD256	A104	1c buff (#324)	.50	.25
a.		Perf. 13½ (#324A)	87.50	50.00
OD257	A104	2c dark brown (#325)	1.00	.50
a.		Inverted overprint	—	75.00
b.		Perf. 13½ (#325A)	1.00	.50
OD258	A104	5c red (#328)	2.50	.25
a.		Inverted overprint	—	75.00
b.		Perf. 13½ (#328A)	15.00	.50
c.		As "b," inverted overprint	—	75.00
OD259	A104	12c deep blue (#330)	1.20	.40
a.		Perf. 13½ (#330A)	10.00	1.50
OD260	A104	20c ultra (#331)	2.00	.40
a.		Perf. 13½ (#331A)	3.50	1.00
		Nos. OD256-OD260 (5)	7.20	1.80

1924

OD261	A104	1c buff (#341)	3.00	1.00
OD262	A104	2c dk brown (#342)	.50	.25
a.		Pair, one with period	15.00	—
OD264	A104	5c red (#345)	.50	.25
a.		Pair, one with period		40.00
OD266	A104	20c ultra (#348)	3.50	.25
		Nos. OD261-OD266 (4)	7.50	1.75

1926

OD269	A109	5c red (#359)	.50	.25

M. M.
No. OD264B

Type II

1931-36 — Perf. 13½x12½, 13

OD263B	A104	3c green (#343)	1.50	.40
OD264B	A104	5c red (#345)	1.50	.25
OD265B	A104	10c dull green (#346)	2.00	.50
c.		Typo (coil) (#346a)	.60	.25
OD266B	A104	20c ultra (#348)	7.00	1.00
c.		Typo (coil) (#348a)	5.00	.25
OD267B	A104	30c claret (#351)	3.00	.50
OD268B	A105	1p blue & red (Perf. 13½) (#353)	40.00	20.00

No. OD270

1936-38　　　　　　　　***Perf. 13½x13***
OD270　A129　1c buff (#419)　　　.50　.25
OD271　A130　2c dark brown
　　　　　　　　(#420)　　　　　.50　.25
OD272　A132　3c green (#422)　　.50　.25
OD273　A134　5c yel brn
　　　　　　　　(#427d)　　　　　.50　.25
OD275　A139　15c slate bl (#434)
　　　　　　　　('36)　　　　　　1.00　.30
OD276　A140　20c lt ultra (#437)　1.20　.30
OD277　A140　20c lt ultra (#438)　1.00　.30
OD278　A142　30c org brn & yel
　　　　　　　　brn (#442)
　　　　　　　　('36)　　　　　　.60　.25
OD279　A145　1p brn blk & lt bl
　　　　　　　　(#445) ('36)　　8.00　2.00
OD280　A146　1p brn blk & lt bl
　　　　　　　　(#446) ('37)　　2.00　.50
　　Nos. OD270-OD280 (10)　　15.80　4.65

Typo.　　　　　　　***Perf. 13½***
OD273A A134　5c yel brn
　　　　　　　　(#427)　　　　　.50　.25
　　b.　Inverted overprint　　25.00　25.00
OD274A A137　10c car (#430)　　2.00　.25
　　b.　Perf. 13½x13 (#430a)　.60　.25

Ministry of Public Works

No. OD281

1913　　**Type I**　　***Perf. 13½x12½***
OD281　A88　2c chocolate
　　　　　　　(#181)　　　　　1.00　.25
　　a.　Perf. 13½ (#181a)　　4.00　1.00
OD282　A88　1c ocher (#190)　1.00　.25
OD283　A88　5c red (#194)　　.80　.25
OD284　A88　12c deep blue
　　　　　　　(#196)　　　　　5.00　1.00
　　a.　Perf. 13½ (#196a)　　15.00　6.00
　　Nos. OD282-OD284 (3)　6.80　1.50

1916　　　　　　　***Perf. 13½***
OD285　A91　5c red (#220)　　35.00　10.00

1918　　　　　***Perf. 13½x12½***
OD286　A93　2c brown (#233)　30.00　20.00
OD287　A93　5c red (#236)　　18.00　9.00

1920　　　　　　***Perf. 13½***
OD288　A93　2c brown (#266)　35.00　8.00
OD289　A93　5c red (#269)　　5.00　1.00
OD290　A94　12c blue (#271)　50.00　20.00
　　Nos. OD288-OD290 (3)　90.00　29.00

1923　　　　　***Perf. 13½x12½***
OD291　A104　1c buff (#324)　　.60　.25
　　a.　Perf. 13½ (#324A)　　40.00　15.00
OD292　A104　2c dark brown
　　　　　　　(#325)　　　　　.50　.25
　　a.　Perf. 13½ (#325A)　　.80　.25
OD293　A104　5c red (#328)　　.60　.30
　　a.　Perf. 13½ (#328A)　　.80　.25
OD294　A104　12c deep blue
　　　　　　　(#330)　　　　　.80　.30
　　a.　Perf. 13½ (#330A)　　2.00　.50
OD295　A104　20c ultra #331　　2.00　.50
　　a.　Perf. 13½ (#331A)　　2.50　.50
　　Nos. OD291-OD295 (5)　4.50　1.60

1924
OD296　A104　1c buff (#341)　　.50　.25
OD297　A104　2c dk brown
　　　　　　　(#342)　　　　　.50　.25
　　a.　Pair, one with period　15.00　—
OD299　A104　5c red (#345)　　.50　.25
OD301　A104　12c deep blue
　　　　　　　(#347)　　　　　30.00　8.00
OD302　A104　20c ultra (#348)　.50　.25
　　Nos. OD296-OD302 (5)　32.00　9.00

1926
OD305　A109　5c red (#359)　　.60　.25

No. OD299B

Type II
1931-36　　　***Perf. 13½x12½, 13***
OD298B A104　3c green
　　　　　　　(#343)　　　　　.50　.25
　　c.　Typo (coil) (#343b)　25.00　5.00
OD299B A109　5c red (#345)　.60　.25
OD300B A104　10c dull green
　　　　　　　(#346)　　　　　.60　.25
　　a.　Typo (coil) (#346a)　2.00　.25
OD301B A104　20c ultra typo
　　　　　　　(coil)
　　　　　　　(#348b)　　　　50.00　10.00
OD303B A104　30c claret
　　　　　　　(#351)　　　　　1.00　.25
OD304B A105　1p blue & red
　　　　　　　(13½)
　　　　　　　(#353)　　　　　70.00　20.00
　　Nos. OD298B-OD304B (6)　122.70　31.00

No. OD307

1936-38　　　　　　***Perf. 13½x13***
OD306　A129　1c buff (#419)　　.50　.25
OD307　A130　2c dark brown
　　　　　　　(#420)　　　　　.50　.25
OD308　A132　3c green (#422)　.50　.25
OD309　A134　5c yel brn
　　　　　　　(#427d)　　　　　.50　.25
OD311　A139　15c slate bl (#434)　1.50　.25
OD312　A140　20c lt ultra (#437)　2.00　.30
OD313　A140　20c lt ultra (#438)　.50　.25
OD314　A142　30c org brn & yel
　　　　　　　brown (#442)
　　　　　　　('36)　　　　　　.60　.25
OD315　A144　50c red & org
　　　　　　　(#444) ('36)　　.60　.30
OD316　A145　1p brn blk & lt bl
　　　　　　　(#445) ('36)　　4.00　1.00
OD317　A146　1p brn blk & lt bl
　　　　　　　(#446) ('37)　　1.20　.40
　　Nos. OD306-OD317 (11)　12.40　3.75

Typo.　　　　　　***Perf. 13½***
OD309A A134　5c yel brn
　　　　　　　(#427)　　　　　.60　.25
　　b.　Inverted overprint　　—　75.00
OD310　A137　10c car (#430)　1.00　.30
　　a.　Perf. 13½x13 (#430a)　1.00　.30

Ministry of Foreign Affairs and Religion

No. OD318

1913　　**Type I**　　***Perf. 13½x12½***
OD318　A88　2c chocolate
　　　　　　　(#181)　　　　　45.00　9.00
OD319　A88　1c ocher (#190)　.50　.25
OD320　A88　2c chocolate
　　　　　　　(#191)　　　　　.50　.25
OD321　A88　5c red (#194)　　1.20　.30
OD322　A88　12c deep blue
　　　　　　　(#196)　　　　　.60　.25
　　a.　Perf. 13½ (#196a)　　50.00　20.00
　　Nos. OD319-OD322 (4)　2.80　1.05

1915
OD323　A88　5c red (#212)　　1.00　.50

1916　　　　　　***Perf. 13½***
OD324　A91　5c red (#220)　　1.20　.50

1918
OD325　A94　20c ultra (#256)　5.00　2.00

1922
OD326　A93　1c buff, perf.
　　　　　　　13½x12½ (#265)　1.00　.40
OD327　A93　5c red (#269)　　.50　.30

1922-23　　　　　***Perf. 13½x12½***
OD328　A93　2c brown
　　　　　　　(#306)　　　　40.00　15.00
OD329　A103　5c red
　　　　　　　(#309B)　　　100.00
　　　　　　Perf. 13½
OD330　A93　12c blue
　　　　　　　(#311)　　　　100.00
OD330A A94　20c ultra
　　　　　　　(#312)　　　　100.00

1923　　　　　　***Perf. 13½x12½***
OD331　A104　1c buff (#324)　.60　.25
　　a.　Perf. 13½ (#324A)　　25.00　10.00
OD332　A104　2c dark brown
　　　　　　　(#325)　　　　　.50　.25
　　a.　Perf. 13½ (#325A)　　5.00　2.00
OD333　A104　5c red (#328)　.50　.25
　　a.　Perf. 13½ (#328A)　　2.00　.30
OD334　A104　12c deep blue
　　　　　　　(#330)　　　　　.50　.25
　　a.　Perf. 13½ (#330A)　　1.50　.50
OD335　A104　20c ultra (#331)　.50　.25
　　Nos. OD331-OD335 (5)　2.60　1.30

No. OD344

1924
OD337　A104　1c buff (#341)　　.60　.25
OD338　A104　2c dark brown
　　　　　　　(#342)　　　　　.50　.25
　　a.　Pair, one with period　15.00　—
OD339　A104　3c green (#343)　.50　.25
OD340　A104　5c red (#345)　　.50　.25
　　a.　Pair, one with period　15.00　—
OD341　A104　10c dull green
　　　　　　　(#346)　　　　　4.00　.50
OD342　A104　12c deep blue
　　　　　　　(#347)　　　　　.60　.30
OD343　A104　20c ultra (#348)　.60　.30
OD344　A104　30c claret (#351)　.70　.30
　　Nos. OD337-OD344 (8)　8.00　2.40

1926
OD346　A110　12c deep blue
　　　　　　　(#360)　　　　　.50　.25

Type II
1931-36　　　***Perf. 13½x12½, 13½***
OD336B A104　½c red violet
　　　　　　　(#340)　　　　2.50　1.00
OD341B A104　10c dull green
　　　　　　　(#346)　　　　　.60　.30
OD343B A104　20c ultra (typo,
　　　　　　　coil) (#348a)　　.60　.30
OD344B A104　30c claret (typo,
　　　　　　　coil) (#351a)　　.60　.30
OD345B A105　1p blue & red,
　　　　　　　perf. 13½
　　　　　　　(#353)　　　　　.60　.30
　　Nos. OD336B-OD345B (5)　4.90　2.20

No. OD347

1935-37　　**Typo.**　　***Perf. 13x13½***
OD347　A129　1c buff (#419)　.50　.25
OD348　A130　2c dark brown
　　　　　　　(#420)　　　　　.50　.25
OD349　A132　3c green (#422)　.50　.25
OD350　A134　5c yel brn
　　　　　　　#427d　　　　　.50　.25
OD352　A139　15c slate bl
　　　　　　　(#434)　　　　　.70　.30
OD353　A140　20c lt ultra
　　　　　　　(#437)　　　　1.00　.50
OD354　A140　20c lt ultra #438　.50　.25
OD355　A142　30c org brown &
　　　　　　　yel brown
　　　　　　　(#442)　　　　　.50　.25
OD356　A145　1p brn blk & lt
　　　　　　　bl (#445)　　　6.00　2.50
OD357　A146　1p brn blk & lt
　　　　　　　bl (#446)　　　.70　.50
　　Nos. OD347-OD357 (10)　11.40　5.30

Typo.　　　　　　***Perf. 13½***
OD350B A134　5c yel brn (#427)　.60　.25
OD351B A137　10c car (#430)　.50　.25
　　c.　Perf. 13½x13 (#430a)　2.00　.25

BUENOS AIRES

The central point of the Argentine struggle for independence. At intervals Buenos Aires maintained an independent government but after 1862 became a province of the Argentine Republic.

8 Reales = 1 Peso

Values of Buenos Aires Nos. 1-8 vary according to condition. Quotations are for fine examples. Very fine to superb specimens sell at much higher prices, and inferior or poor stamps sell at reduced values, depending on the condition of the individual specimen.

Nos. 1-8 are normally found without gum, and the values below are for such items. Examples with original gum sell for higher prices.

Steamship — A1

1858　**Unwmk.**　**Typo.**　***Imperf.***
1　A1　1 (in) pesos lt
　　　　brn　　　　　500.00　300.
　　a.　Double impression　　　1,800.
　　　　　　　　　　　　　　　　700.
2　A1　2 (dos) pesos
　　　　blue　　　　300.00　150.
　　　　　　　　　　　　　　　　1,000.
　　a.　2p indigo　　450.00　220.
　　　　On cover　　　　　　　1,500.
　　b.　Diag. half used as 1p
　　　　on cover　　　　　　　7,500.
3　A1　3 (tres) pe-
　　　　sos grn　　1,500.　950.
　　　　On cover　　　　　　　6,500.
　　a.　3p dark green　2,000.　1,500.
　　　　On cover　　　　　　　8,000.
　　b.　3p emerald green　2,000.　1,500.
　　　　On cover　　　　　　　—
4　A1　4 (cuatro) pe-
　　　　sos ver　　5,000.　4,500.
　　　　On cover　　　　　　　20,000.
　　a.　Half used as 2p on
　　　　cover　　　　　　　　25,000.
　　b.　4p chestnut brown (er-
　　　　ror)　　　30,000.　40,000.
5　A1　5 (cinco) pe-
　　　　sos org　　5,000.　3,000.
　　　　On cover　　　　　　　29,000.
　　a.　5p ocher　5,000.　3,000.
　　　　On cover　　　　　　　29,000.
　　b.　5p olive yellow　5,000.　3,000.
　　　　On cover　　　　　　　29,000.

Issued: Nos. 2-5, Apr. 29; No. 1, Oct. 26.

1858, Oct. 26
6　A1　4 (cuatro) reales
　　　　brown　　350.00　300.
　　　　On cover　　　　　　　1,500.
　　a.　4r gray brown　400.00　300.
　　　　On cover　　　　　　　1,500.
　　b.　4r chestnut　350.00　300.
　　　　On cover　　　　　　　1,500.

1859, Jan. 1
7　A1　1 (in) pesos
　　　　blue　　　　200.　100.
　　　　On cover　　　　　　　1,500.
　　a.　1p indigo　　300.　150.
　　　　On cover　　　　　　　2,000.
　　b.　Impression on re-
　　　　verse of stamp in
　　　　blue　　　28,500.
　　c.　Double impression　2,800.　700.
　　d.　Vert. tête-bêche pair　　675,000.
　　e.　Horiz. tête-bêche
　　　　pair　　　　　　　　　—
　　f.　Half used as 4r on
　　　　cover　　　　　　　　7,500.

A canceled vertical tête-bêche pair, No. 7d, sold at a New York City auction in 2008 for $661,250.

8　A1　1 (to) pesos
　　　　blue　　　　600.　325.
　　　　On cover　　　　　　　2,500.
　　a.　1 (to) deep blue　650.　300.
　　　　On cover　　　　　　　2,750.
　　b.　Partial double im-
　　　　pression　　800.　500.
　　　　On cover　　　　　　　2,750.

No. 7e is valued with faults.
Nos. 1, 2, 3 and 7 have been reprinted on very thick, hand-made paper. The same four stamps and No. 8 have been reprinted on thin, hard, white wove paper.
Counterfeits of Nos. 1-8 are plentiful.

Liberty Head — A2

1859, Sept. 3

9	A2	4r green, *bluish*	400.00	275.00
		On cover, pair		1,000.
		On cover, single franking		2,000.
a.		4r green, blurred impression	200.00	100.00
		On cover		2,000.
b.		4r olive green, blurred impression	400.00	250.00
		On cover		3,000.
10	A2	1p blue, fine impression	40.00	30.00
		On cover		200.00
a.		1p milky blue, blurred impression	250.00	125.00
		On cover		750.00
b.		1p indigo	250.00	125.00
		On cover		750.00
c.		1p greenish blue, blurred impression	250.00	125.00
		On cover		750.00
d.		Double impression	600.00	400.00
		On cover		—
e.		Partial double impression	325.00	175.00
		On cover		—
11	A2	2p vermilion, fine impression	500.00	300.00
		On cover		2,000.
a.		2p red, blurred impression	375.00	125.00
		On cover		1,200.
b.		Vert. half used as 1p on cover		4,000.

Both fine and blurred impressions of these stamps may be found. They have generally been called Paris and Local prints, respectively, but the opinion now obtains that the differences are due to the impression and that they do not represent separate issues. Values are for fine impressions. Rough or blurred impressions sell for less.

Many shades exist of Nos. 1-11.

1862, Oct. 4

12	A2	1p rose	350.00	150.00
		On cover		1,500.
a.		1p carmine	425.00	200.00
		On cover		2,000.
b.		1p rose, blurred impression	100.00	40.00
		On cover		500.00
c.		As "a," blurred impression	200.00	80.00
		On cover		1,000.
13	A2	2p blue	350.00	90.00
		On cover		900.00
a.		2p blue, blurred impression	220.00	50.00
		On cover		700.00
b.		2p indigo, blurred impression	—	500.00

All three values have been reprinted in black, brownish black, blue and red brown on thin hard white paper. The 4r has also been reprinted in green on bluish paper.
Values are for fine impressions. Rough or blurred impressions sell for less.
No. 13 exists with papermaker's wmk.

CORDOBA

A province in the central part of the Argentine Republic.
100 Centavos = 1 Peso

Arms of Cordoba — A1

Unwmk.
1858, Oct. 28　　Litho.　　*Imperf.*
Laid Paper

1	A1	5c blue	150.	
		On cover, pen canceled		1,250.
2	A1	10c black	3,000.	

Cordoba stamps were printed on laid paper, but stamps from edges of the sheets sometimes do not show any laid lines and appear to be on wove paper. Counterfeits are plentiful.

CORRIENTES

The northeast province of the Argentine Republic.

---

1 Real M(oneda) C(orriente) =
12 ½ Centavos M.C. = 50 Centavos
100 Centavos Fuertes = 1 Peso
Fuerte

Nos. 1-2 were issued without gum. Nos. 3-8 were issued both with and without gum (values the same).

Ceres
A1　　　　　A2

Unwmk.
1856, Aug. 21　Typo.　*Imperf.*

1	A1	1r black, *blue*	100.00	40.00
		On cover		450.00

No. 1 used is valued with pen cancellation.

Pen Stroke Through "Un Real"

1860, Feb. 8

2	A1	(3c) black, *blue*	600.00	120.00
		On cover		1,250.

No. 2 used is valued with pen cancellation.

1860-80

3	A2	(3c) black, *blue*	9.50	30.00
		On cover		150.00
4	A2	(2c) blk, *yel grn* ('64)	50.00	100.00
		On cover		250.00
a.		(2c) black, *blue green*	92.50	150.00
		On cover		750.00
5	A2	(2c) blk, *yel* ('67)	7.50	19.00
		On cover		100.00
6	A2	(3c) blk, *dk bl* ('71)	3.00	19.00
		On cover		100.00
7	A2	(3c) blk, *rose red* ('76)	150.00	70.00
		On cover		275.00
a.		(3c) black, *lil rose* ('75)	200.00	100.00
		On cover		400.00
8	A2	(3c) blk, *dk rose* ('79)	8.00	35.00
		On cover		200.00
a.		(3c) black, *red vio* ('77)	75.00	50.00
		On cover		200.00
		Nos. 3-8 (6)	228.00	273.00

Pen canceled examples of Nos. 3-8 that do not indicate the town of origin sell for much less.
Printed from settings of 8 varieties, 3 or 4 impressions constituting a sheet. Some impressions were printed inverted and tete beche pairs may be cut from adjacent impressions.
From Jan. 1 to Feb. 24, 1864, No. 4 was used as a 5 centavos stamp but examples so used can only be distinguished when they bear dated cancellations.
The reprints show numerous spots and small defects which are not found on the originals. They are printed on gray blue, dull blue, gray green, dull orange and light magenta papers.

ARMENIA

är-'mē-nē-ə

LOCATION — South of Russia bounded by Georgia, Azerbaijan, Iran and Turkey
GOVT. — Republic
AREA — 11,306 sq. mi.
POP. — 1,109,200
CAPITAL — Yerevan

With Azerbaijan and Georgia, Armenia made up the Transcaucasian Federation of Soviet Republics.
Stamps of Armenia were replaced in 1923 by those of Transcaucasian Federated Republics.

100 Kopecks = 1 Ruble

Counterfeits abound of all overprinted and surcharged stamps.

Watermark

Diamonds — Wmk. 171

Perforations

Perforations are the same as the basic Russian stamps.

National Republic
Russian Stamps of 1902-19
Handstamped

At least thirteen types exist of both framed and unframed overprints ("a" and "c"). The device is the Armenian "H," initial of Hayasdan (Armenia). Inverted and double overprints are found.

Surcharged

Type I — Without periods (two types).
Type II — Periods after 1st "K" and "60."

Black Surcharge

				Perf. 14x14½	
1919		Unwmk.			
1	A14	60k on 1k orange (II)		2.75	2.75
a.		Imperf. (I)		5.00	5.00
b.		Imperf. (II)		1.25	1.25

Violet Surcharge

2	A14	60k on 1k orange (II)		1.00	1.00

Handstamped in Violet
a

				Perf.	
6	A15	4k carmine		3.50	3.50
7	A14	5k claret, imperf.		9.00	9.00
a.		Perf.		8.00	6.00
9	A14	10k on 7k lt blue		6.00	6.00
10	A11	15k red brn & bl		3.50	3.50
11	A8	20k blue & car		2.50	2.50
13	A11	35k red brn & grn		4.75	4.75
14	A8	50k violet & green		4.25	4.25
15	A14	60k on 1k orange (II)		3.50	3.50
a.		Imperf. (I)		6.00	6.00
b.		Imperf. (II)		10.00	10.00
18	A13	5r dk bl, grn & pale bl		18.00	18.00
a.		Imperf.		9.00	9.00
19	A12	7r dk green & pink		35.00	15.00
20	A13	10r scar, yel & gray		40.00	15.00

Handstamped in Black

31	A14	2k green, imperf.		3.00	3.00
a.		Perf.		6.00	6.00
32	A14	3k red, imperf.		3.00	3.00
a.		Perf.		10.00	10.00

33	A15	4k carmine		5.00	5.00
a.		Imperf.		10.00	10.00
34	A14	5k claret		1.25	1.25
a.		Imperf.		10.00	10.00
36	A15	10k dark blue		2.50	2.50
37	A14	10k on 7k lt blue		2.00	5.00
38	A11	15k red brn & bl		1.00	5.00
a.		Imperf.		15.00	15.00
39	A8	20k blue & car		2.00	5.00
40	A11	25k green & gray vio		2.00	5.00
41	A11	35k red brn & grn		2.00	4.00
42	A8	50k violet & green		3.00	5.00
43	A14	60k on 1k orange (II)		5.00	5.00
43A	A11	70k brown & org		3.00	3.00
b.		Imperf.		2.00	4.00
44	A9	1r pale brn, dk brn & org		3.00	5.00
a.		Imperf.		8.00	8.00
45	A12	3½r mar & lt grn, imperf.		3.00	6.00
a.		Perf.		6.00	6.00
46	A13	5r dk bl, grn & pale bl		6.00	6.00
a.		Imperf.		10.00	10.00
47	A12	7r dk green & pink		7.25	7.25
48	A13	10r scar, yel & gray		35.00	50.00

Handstamped in Violet
c

				Unwmk.	Perf.
				Wove Paper	
62	A14	2k green, imperf.		12.00	12.00
a.		Perf.		18.00	18.00
63	A14	3k red, imperf.		2.50	2.50
a.		Perf.		15.00	15.00
64	A15	4k carmine		10.00	10.00
65	A14	5k claret		3.50	3.50
a.				3.50	3.50
67	A15	10k dark blue		5.00	10.00
68	A14	10k on 7k lt bl		3.50	3.50
69	A11	15k red brn & bl		3.00	3.00
70	A8	20k blue & car		3.00	5.00
71	A11	25k grn & gray vio		7.50	15.00
72	A11	35k red brn & grn		15.00	14.00
73	A8	50k violet & grn		5.00	10.00
74	A14	60k on 1k org (II)		6.00	8.00
a.		Imperf. (II)		6.00	8.00
b.		Imperf. (II)		6.00	8.00
75	A9	1r pale brn, dk brn & org		12.50	12.50
a.		Imperf.		10.00	10.00
76	A12	3½r mar & lt grn, imperf.		5.00	5.00
a.		Perf.		6.00	6.00
77	A13	5r dk bl, grn & pale bl, imperf.		12.50	12.50
a.		Perf.		8.00	8.00
78	A12	7r dk green & pink		20.00	20.00
79	A13	10r scar, yel & gray		20.00	20.00

Imperf

85	A11	70k brown & org		6.00	6.00

Handstamped in Black
Perf.

90	A14	1k orange		8.00	8.00
a.		Imperf.		10.00	10.00
91	A14	2k green, imperf.		1.25	1.25
a.		Perf.		8.00	8.00
92	A14	3k red, imperf.		5.00	10.00
a.		Perf.		2.00	2.00
93	A15	4k carmine		3.00	3.00
94	A14	5k claret		1.25	1.25
a.				3.50	5.00
95	A14	7k light blue		10.00	15.00
96	A15	10k dark blue		10.00	15.00
97	A14	10k on 7k lt bl		1.00	2.00
98	A11	15k red brn & bl		2.00	4.00
99	A8	20k blue & car		1.75	3.00
100	A11	25k grn & gray vio		2.00	5.00
101	A11	35k red brn & grn		2.00	4.00
102	A8	50k violet & grn		2.00	5.00
102A	A14	60k on 1k org, imperf. (I)		5.00	5.00
b.		Imperf. (II)		5.00	5.00
c.		Perf. (II)		5.00	5.00
103	A9	1r pale brn, dk brn & org		2.00	5.00
a.		Imperf.		2.00	5.00
104	A12	3½r maroon & lt grn		4.75	8.00
a.		Imperf.		15.00	15.00
105	A13	5r dk bl, grn & pale bl		15.00	15.00
a.		Imperf.		6.00	6.00
106	A12	7r dk green & pink		5.00	10.00
107	A13	10r scar, yel & gray		20.00	45.00

Imperf

113	A11	70k brown & org		2.50	4.00

Handstamped in Violet or Black

f

g

Violet Surcharge, Type f

1920				Perf.	
120	A14	3r on 3k red, imperf.		10.00	15.00
a.		Perf.		10.00	15.00
121	A14	5r on 3k red		10.00	10.00
122	A15	5r on 4k car		10.00	12.00
123	A14	5r on 5k claret, imperf.		5.00	12.00
a.		Perf.		12.00	20.00
124	A15	5r on 10k dk blue		20.00	30.00
125	A14	5r on 10k on 7k lt bl		20.00	30.00
126	A8	5r on 20k bl & car		10.00	15.00

Imperf

127	A14	5r on 2k green		12.00	12.00
128	A11	5r on 35k red brn & grn		12.00	12.00

Black Surcharge, Type f or Type g (#130)
Perf.

130	A14	1r on 1k orange		10.00	12.00
a.		Imperf.		15.00	15.00
131	A14	3r on 3k red		10.00	10.00
a.		Imperf.		5.00	5.00
132	A15	3r on 4k carmine		25.00	25.00
133	A14	5r on 2k grn, imperf.		2.50	2.50
a.		Perf.		5.00	5.00
134	A14	5r on 3k red		10.00	10.00
a.		Imperf.		5.00	5.00
135	A15	5r on 4k carmine		4.00	4.00
a.		Imperf.		10.00	10.00
136	A14	5r on 5k claret		4.00	4.00
a.		Imperf.		2.00	2.00
137	A14	5r on 7k lt blue		3.00	3.00
138	A15	5r on 10k dk blue		2.00	2.00
139	A14	5r on 10k on 7k lt bl		2.00	2.00
140	A11	5r on 14k bl & rose		2.50	2.50
141	A11	5r on 15k red brn & blue		1.00	1.00
a.		Imperf.		2.50	2.50
142	A8	5r on 20k bl & car		1.00	5.00
a.		Imperf.		30.00	30.00
143	A11	5r on 20k on 14k bl & rose		75.00	100.00
144	A11	5r on 25k grn & gray vio		10.00	15.00

Black Surcharge, Type g or Type f (#148A, 151)

145	A14	10r on 1k org, imperf.		1.10	1.10
a.		Perf.		125.00	125.00
146	A14	10r on 3k red		175.00	175.00
147	A14	10r on 5k claret		18.00	18.00
a.		Imperf.		15.00	
148	A8	10r on 20k bl & car		15.00	15.00
148A	A11	10r on 25k grn & gray vio		10.00	10.00
149	A11	10r on 25k grn & gray vio		5.00	6.00
a.		Imperf.		10.00	20.00
150	A11	10r on 35k red brn & grn		2.00	2.00
151	A8	10r on 50k brn vio & grn		50.00	50.00
152	A8	10r on 50k brn vio & grn		3.00	4.00
152A	A11	10r on 70k brn & org, imperf.		5.00	5.00
b.		Perf.		240.00	240.00
152C	A8	25r on 20k bl & car		4.75	4.75
153	A11	25r on 25k grn & gray vio		5.00	5.00
154	A11	25r on 35k red brn & grn		20.00	20.00
a.		Imperf.		4.00	4.00
155	A8	25r on 50k vio & grn		5.00	5.00
a.		Imperf.		6.00	6.00
156	A11	25r on 70k brn & org		8.00	8.00
a.		Imperf.		5.00	5.00
157	A9	50r on 1r pale brn, dk brn & org, imperf.		2.00	2.00
a.		Perf.		10.00	15.00
158	A13	50r on 5r dk bl, grn & lt bl		25.00	25.00
a.		Imperf.		45.00	45.00
159	A12	100r on 3½r mar & lt grn		10.00	15.00
a.		Imperf.		10.00	10.00
160	A13	100r on 5r dk bl, grn & pale bl		12.00	12.00
a.		Imperf.		25.00	25.00
161	A12	100r on 7r dk grn & pink		12.00	15.00
a.		Imperf.		42.00	42.00
162	A13	100r on 10r scar, yel & gray		15.00	20.00

Wmk. Wavy Lines (168)
Perf. 11½
Vertically Laid Paper

163	A12	100r on 3½r blk & gray		120.00	120.00
164	A12	100r on 7r blk & yel		120.00	120.00

1920		Unwmk.		Imperf.	
		Wove Paper			
166	A14	(g) 1r on 60k on 1k org (I)		12.00	14.50
168	A14	(f) 5r on 1k orange		12.00	12.00
173	A11	(f) 5r on 35k red brn & org		12.00	12.00
177	A11	(g) 50r on 70k brn & org		6.00	10.00
179	A12	(g) 50r on 3½r mar & lt grn		20.00	20.00
181	A9	(g) 100r on 1r pale brn, dk brn & org		20.00	20.00

Romanov Issues Surcharged Type g or Type f (#185-187, 190) on Stamps of 1913

1920				Perf. 13½	
184	A16	1r on 1k brn org		175.00	175.00
185	A18	3r on 3k rose red		24.00	24.00
186	A19	5r on 4k dull red		12.00	12.00
187	A22	5r on 14k blue grn		50.00	50.00
187A	A19	10r on 4k dull red		40.00	
187B	A26	10r on 35k gray vio & dk grn			
187C	A19	25r on 4k dull red		20.00	20.00
188	A26	25r on 35k gray vio & dk grn		3.25	3.25
189	A28	25r on 70k yel grn & brn		3.25	3.25
190	A31	50r on 3r dk vio		2.50	2.50
190A	A16	100r on 1k brn org		125.00	125.00
190B	A17	100r on 2k green		125.00	125.00
191	A30	100r on 2r brown		12.50	12.50
192	A31	100r on 3r dk vio		12.50	12.50

On Stamps of 1915, Type g
Thin Cardboard
Inscriptions on Back
Perf. 12

193	A21	100r on 10k blue		20.00	
194	A23	100r on 15k brn		20.00	
195	A24	100r on 20k ol grn		18.00	

On Stamps of 1916, Type f
Perf. 13½

196	A20	5r on 10k on 7k brown		8.00	8.00
197	A22	5r on 20k on 14k bl grn		15.00	25.00

Srch. Type f or Type g (#204-205A, 207-207C, 210-211) over Type c
Type c in Violet
Perf.

200	A15	5r on 4k car		6.00	8.00
201	A15	5r on 10k dk bl		25.00	25.00
202	A11	5r on 15k red brn & bl		5.00	5.00
203	A8	5r on 20k blue & car		10.00	10.00
204	A11	10r on 25k grn & gray vio		12.00	12.00
205	A11	10r on 35k red brn & grn		3.50	3.50
205A	A8	10r on 50k brn vio & grn		12.00	12.00
206	A8	25r on 50k brn vio & grn		150.00	150.00
207	A9	50r on 1r pale brn, dk brn & org, imperf.		30.00	30.00
a.		Perf.		30.00	30.00
207B	A12	100r on 3½r mar & lt grn		50.00	50.00
207C	A12	100r on 7r dk grn & pink		60.00	60.00

Imperf

208	A14	5r on 2k green		30.00	30.00
209	A14	5r on 5k claret		30.00	30.00
210	A11	25r on 70k brn & org		40.00	50.00
211	A13	100r on 5r dk bl, grn & pale bl		100.00	110.00

Surcharged Type g or Type f (212-213, 215, 219-219A, 221-222) over Type c
Type c in Black
Perf.

212	A14	5r on 7k lt bl		150.00	150.00
213	A14	5r on 10k on 7k lt bl		6.00	6.00
214	A11	5r on 15k red brn & bl		5.00	7.00
215	A8	5r on 20k blue & car		3.50	3.50

116

ARMENIA

215A	A11	10r on 5r on 25k grn & gray vio	50.00	50.00
216	A11	10r on 35k red brn & grn	50.00	60.00
217	A8	10r on 50k brn vio & grn	12.00	15.00
217A	A9	50r on 1r pale brn, dk brn & org	35.00	50.00
b.		Imperf.	40.00	50.00
217C	A12	100r on 3½r mar & lt grn	30.00	30.00
218	A13	100r on 5r dk bl, grn & pale bl	35.00	40.00
a.		Imperf.	45.00	55.00
219	A12	100r on 7r dk grn & pink	35.00	50.00
219A	A13	100r on 10r scar, yel & gray	45.00	55.00

Imperf

220	A14	1r on 60k on 1k org (I)	35.00	35.00
221	A14	5r on 2k green	6.00	6.00
222	A14	5r on 5k claret	10.00	12.00
223	A11	10r on 70k brn & org	30.00	40.00
224	A11	25r on 70k brn & org	25.00	30.00

Surcharged Type g or Type f (#233) over Type a
Type a in Violet
Imperf

231	A9	50r on 1r pale brn, dk brn & org	170.00	170.00
232	A13	100r on 5r dk bl, grn & pale bl	100.00	110.00

Type a in Black
Perf.

233	A8	5r on 20k blue & car	6.00	6.00
233A	A11	10r on 25k grn & gray vio	20.00	20.00
234	A11	10r on 35k red brn & grn	175.00	175.00
235	A12	100r on 3½r mar & lt grn	10.00	10.00
a.		Imperf.	10.00	10.00

Imperf

237	A14	5r on 2k green	150.00	150.00
237A	A11	10r on 70k brn & org		

Surcharged Type a and New Value
Type a in Violet
Perf.

238	A11	10r on 15k red brn & blue	30.00	30.00

Type a in Black

239	A8	5r on 20k blue & car	4.00	5.00
239A	A8	10r on 20k blue & car	20.00	20.00
239B	A8	10r on 50k brn red & grn	30.00	40.00

Imperf

240	A12	100r on 3½r mar & lt grn	50.00	60.00

Surcharged Type c and New Value
Type c in Black
1920
Perf.

241	A15	5r on 4k red	6.00	8.00
242	A11	5r on 15k red brn & bl	4.00	6.00
243	A8	10r on 20k blue & car	20.00	20.00
243A	A11	10r on 25k grn & gray vio	12.00	15.00
244	A11	10r on 35k red brn & grn	45.00	50.00
a.		With additional surch. "5r"	—	—
245	A12	100r on 3½r mar & lt grn	10.00	15.00

Imperf

247	A14	3r on 3k red	10.00	15.00
248	A14	5r on 2k green	3.00	7.00
249	A9	50r on 1r pale brn, dk brn & org	20.00	20.00

Type c in Violet

249A	A14	5r on 2k green	8.00	12.00

Russia AR1-AR3 Surcharged

A1   A2   A3

Perf. 14½x15
Wmk. 171

250	A1	60k on 1k red & buff	60.00	60.00
251	A2	1r on 1k red & buff	60.00	60.00
252	A3	5r on 5k green & buff	60.00	60.00
253	A3	5r on 10k brn & buff	60.00	60.00

Russian Semi-Postal Stamps of 1914-18 Surcharged with Armenian Monogram and New Values like Regular Issues
On Stamps of 1914
Unwmk.   *Perf.*

255	SP5	25r on 1k red brn & dk grn, *straw*	72.50	72.50
256	SP5	25r on 3k mar & gray grn, *pink*	72.50	72.50
257	SP5	50r on 7 dk brn & dk grn, *buff*	90.00	90.00
258	SP5	100r on 1k red brn & dk grn, *straw*	90.00	90.00
259	SP5	100r on 3k mar & gray grn, *pink*	90.00	90.00
260	SP5	100r on 7k dk brn & dk grn, *buff*	90.00	90.00

On Stamps of 1915-19

261	SP5	25r on 1k org brn & gray	100.00	100.00
262	SP5	25r on 3k car & gray	90.00	90.00
263	SP5	50r on 10k dk bl & brn	50.00	50.00
264	SP5	100r on 1k org brn & gray	90.00	90.00
265	SP5	100r on 10k dk bl & brn	90.00	90.00

These surcharged semi-postal stamps were used for ordinary postage.

A set of 10 stamps in the above designs was prepared in 1920, but not issued for postal use, though some were used fiscally. Value of set, $10. Exist imperf with "SPECIMEN" overprint. Value of set, $40. Reprints exist.

Soviet Socialist Republic

Hammer and Sickle — A7

Mythological Monster — A8

Symbols of Soviet Republics on Designs from old Armenian Manuscripts A9

Ruined City of Ani — A10

Mythological Monster — A11

Armenian Soldier — A12

Mythological Monster A13

Soviet Symbols, Armenian Designs — A14

Mt. Alagöz and Plain of Shirak A15

Fisherman on River Aras — A16

Post Office in Erevan and Mt. Ararat A17

Ruin in City of Ani — A18

Street in Erevan — A19

Lake Sevan and Sevan Monastery — A20

Mythological Subject from old Armenian Monument — A21

Mt. Ararat — A22

1921   Unwmk.   Perf. 11½, Imperf.

278	A7	1r gray green	.50	
279	A8	2r slate gray	.50	
280	A9	3r carmine	.50	
281	A10	5r dark brown	.50	
282	A11	25r gray	.50	.50
283	A12	50r red	.30	
284	A13	100r orange	.30	
285	A14	250r dark blue	.30	
286	A15	500r brown vio	.30	
287	A16	1000r sea green	.40	
288	A17	2000r bister	1.75	
289	A18	5000r dark brown	1.00	
290	A19	10,000r dull red	1.00	
291	A20	15,000r slate blue	1.25	
292	A21	20,000r lake	1.50	
293	A22	25,000r gray blue	2.00	
294	A22	25,000r brown olive	8.00	
		Nos. 278-294 (17)	20.60	

Except the 25r, Nos. 278-294 were not regularly issued and used. Counterfeits exist. For surcharges see Nos. 347-390.

Russian Stamps of 1909-17 Surcharged

Wove Paper
Lozenges of Varnish on Face
1921, Aug.   *Perf. 13½*

295	A9	5000r on 1r	25.00
296	A12	5000r on 3½r	25.00
297	A13	5000r on 5r	25.00
298	A12	5000r on 7r	25.00
299	A13	5000r on 10r	25.00
		Nos. 295-299 (5)	125.00

Nos. 295-299 were not officially issued. Counterfeits abound.

A23

Mt. Ararat & Soviet Star — A24

Soviet
Symbols — A25

Crane — A26

Peasant — A27

Harpy — A28

Peasant
Sowing — A29

Soviet
Symbols — A30

Forging — A31

Plowing
A32

1922   **Perf. 11½**
300	A23	50r green & red	.85
301	A24	300r slate bl & buff	1.00
302	A25	400r blue & pink	1.00
303	A26	500r vio & pale lil	1.00
304	A27	1000r dull bl & pale bl	1.00
305	A28	2000r black & gray	1.25

306	A29	3000r black & grn		1.25
307	A30	4000r black & lt brn		1.25
308	A31	5000r blk & dull red		1.25
309	A32	10,000r black & pale rose		1.25
a.		Tête-bêche pair		42.50
		Nos. 300-309 (10)		11.10

Nos. 300-309 were not issued without surcharge.

Stamps of types A23 to A32, printed in other colors than Nos. 300 to 309, are essays.

Nos. 300-309 with
Hstmpd. Srch. in
Rose, Violet or
Black

1922
310		10,000 on 50r (R)	90.00	90.00
311		10,000 on 50r (V)	60.00	60.00
312		10,000 on 50r	30.00	30.00
313		15,000 on 300r (R)	120.00	120.00
314		15,000 on 300r (V)	90.00	90.00
315		15,000 on 300r	30.00	30.00
316		25,000 on 400r (V)	60.00	60.00
317		25,000 on 400r	30.00	30.00
318		30,000 on 500r (R)	120.00	120.00
319		30,000 on 500r (V)	60.00	60.00
320		30,000 on 500r	30.00	30.00
321		50,000 on 1000r (R)	120.00	120.00
322		50,000 on 1000r (V)	60.00	60.00
323		50,000 on 1000r	25.00	25.00
324		75,000 on 3000r	30.00	30.00
325		100,000 on 2000r (R)	120.00	275.00
326		100,000 on 2000r (V)	60.00	60.00
327		100,000 on 2000r	25.00	25.00
328		200,000 on 4000r (V)	12.00	12.00
329		200,000 on 4000r	12.00	12.00
330		300,000 on 5000r (V)	60.00	60.00
331		300,000 on 5000r	25.00	25.00
332		500,000 on 10,000r (V)	60.00	60.00
333		500,000 on 10,000r	12.00	12.00
		Nos. 310-333 (24)	*1,341.*	*1,496.*

Forgeries exist.

Goose — A33

Armenian Woman
at Well — A35

Armenian
Village
Scene
A34

Mt. Ararat
A36

Mt.
Ararat
A37

New Values in Gold Kopecks, Handstamped Surcharge in Black

1922   *Imperf.*
334	A33	1(k) on 250r rose	18.00	18.00
335	A33	1(k) on 250r gray	24.00	24.00
336	A34	2(k) on 500r rose	10.00	10.00
337	A34	3(k) on 500r gray	10.00	10.00
338	A35	4(k) on 1000r rose	10.00	10.00
339	A35	4(k) on 1000r gray	18.00	18.00
340	A36	5(k) on 2000r gray	10.00	10.00
341	A36	10(k) on 2000r rose	10.00	10.00
342	A37	15(k) on 5000r rose	62.50	62.50
343	A37	20(k) on 5000r gray	10.00	10.00
		Nos. 334-343 (10)	*182.50*	*182.50*

Nos. 334-343 were issued for postal tax purposes.

Nos. 334-343 exist without surcharge but are not known to have been issued in that condition. Counterfeits exist of both sets.

Regular Issue of 1921 Handstamped with New Values in Black or Red Short, Thick Numerals

1922   *Imperf.*
347	A8	2(k) on 2r (R)	60.00	60.00
350	A11	4(k) on 25r (R)	100.00	100.00
353	A13	10(k) on 100r (R)	24.00	24.00
354	A14	15(k) on 250r	3.50	3.50
355	A15	20(k) on 500r	18.00	18.00
a.		With "k" written in red	12.00	12.00
357	A22	50(k) on 25,000r bl (R)	300.00	300.00
358	A22	50(k) on 25,000r brn ol (R)	150.00	150.00
359	A22	50(k) on 25,000r brn ol		
		Nos. 347-358 (7)	655.50	655.50

Perf. 11½
360	A7	1(k) on 1r, imperf.	75.00	75.00
a.		Perf.	50.00	50.00
361	A7	1(k) on 1r (R)	45.00	45.00
a.		Imperf.	50.00	70.00
362	A8	2(k) on 2r, imperf.	47.50	47.50
a.		Perf.	50.00	50.00
363	A15	2(k) on 500r	100.00	125.00
a.		Imperf.	100.00	100.00
364	A15	2(k) on 500r (R)	150.00	150.00
365	A11	4(k) on 25r, imperf.	30.00	30.00
a.		Perf.	50.00	50.00
366	A12	5(k) on 50r, imperf.	24.00	36.00
a.		Perf.	100.00	100.00
367	A13	10(k) on 100r	24.00	24.00
a.		Imperf.	50.00	50.00
368	A21	35(k) on 20,000r, imperf.	90.00	100.00
a.		With "k" written in violet	90.00	90.00
b.		Perf.	90.00	90.00
c.		As "a," perf.	90.00	90.00
d.		With "kop" written in violet, imperf.	90.00	90.00
		Nos. 360-368 (9)	585.50	632.50

Manuscript Surcharge in Red
Perf. 11½
371	A14	1k on 250r dk bl	50.00	50.00

Handstamped in Black or Red Tall, Thin Numerals

No. 381

Imperf
377	A11	4(k) on 25r (R)	5.00	5.00
379	A13	10(k) on 100r	90.00	100.00
380	A15	20(k) on 500r	7.25	7.25
381	A22	50k on 25,000r bl	20.00	90.00
a.		Surcharged "50" only	60.00	60.00
382	A22	50k on 25,000r bl (R)	14.50	14.50
382A	A22	50k on 25,000r brn ol	29.00	29.00
		Nos. 377-382A (6)	*165.75*	*245.75*

On Nos. 381, 382 and 382A the letter "k" forms part of the surcharge.

Perf. 11½
383	A7	1(k) on 1r (R)	40.00	40.00
a.		Imperf.	100.00	
384	A14	1(k) on 250r	60.00	60.00
385	A15	2(k) on 500r	10.00	10.00
a.		Imperf.	24.00	24.00
386	A15	2(k) on 500r (R)	24.00	24.00
387	A9	3(k) on 3r	35.00	35.00
a.		Imperf.	40.00	40.00
388	A21	3(k) on 20,000r, imperf.	12.00	12.00
a.		Perf.	60.00	60.00
389	A11	4(k) on 25r	30.00	30.00
a.		Imperf.	120.00	120.00

390	A12	5(k) on 50r, imperf.	12.00	12.00
a.		Perf.	18.00	75.00
		Nos. 383-390 (8)	223.00	223.00

ASCENSION

ə-'sen͡t͜-shən

LOCATION — An island in the South Atlantic Ocean, 900 miles from Liberia
GOVT. — A part of the British Crown Colony of St. Helena
AREA — 34 sq. mi.
POP. — 188 (1931 census)

In 1922 Ascension was placed under the administration of the Colonial Office and annexed to the British Crown Colony of St. Helena. The only post office is at Georgetown.

12 Pence = 1 Shilling
20 Shillings = 1 Pound

STAMPS OF GREAT BRITAIN USED IN ASCENSION

Stamps of Great Britain with clearly legible circular or oval datestamps of Ascension.

1855-86
A1	1p red brown (#16), from		7,000.
A2	6p lilac, (#27)		—
A3	1p rose red (#33), from		2,750.
A4	6p lilac (#45, P5), from		7,000.
A5	1sh green (#48)		—
A6	1sh green (#54, P7)		—
A7	6p gray (#62, P15, 16), from		5,500.
A8	1p lilac (#89), from		80.00
A9	6p on 6p violet (#95)		—

Values for Nos. A1-A7 are for complete covers with the Great Britain stamps canceled on arrival in England with an Ascension postmark struck elsewhere on the cover.

No. A3 exists with plate numbers 71, 74, 76, 78, 83, 85, 96, 100, 102-104, 122, 134, 154, 155, 157, 160, 168, 178. Value is for the most common plate numbers.

1887-92 — Victoria Jubilee
A10	½p ver (#111)		105.00
A11	1½p vio & grn (#112)		650.00
A12	2p grn & car rose (#113)		275.00
A13	2½p vio, blue (#114)		125.00
A14	3p vio, yel (#115)		525.00
A15	4p brn & grn (#116)		400.00
A16	4½p car rose & grn (#117)		950.00
A17	5p lil & bl (#118)		400.00
A18	6p vio, rose (#119)		325.00
A19	9p bl & lil (#120)		850.00
A20	10p car rose & lil (#121)		1,000.
A21	1sh green (#122)		900.00

1900
A22	½p blue grn (#125)		125.00
A23	1sh car rose & green (#126)		950.00

1902-11 — King Edward VII
A24	½p gray grn (#127)		85.00
A25	1p carmine (#128)		30.00
	On cover		200.00
A26	1½p vio & grn (#129)		300.00
A27	2p grn & car (#130)		180.00
A28	2½p ultra (#131)		190.00
A29	3p vio, yel (#132)		300.00
A30	4p brn & grn (#133)		850.00
A31	4p orange (#144)		325.00
A32	5p lil & ultra (#134)		325.00
A33	6p dull vio (#135)		300.00
A34	7p gray (#145)		450.00
A35	9p ultra & vio (#136)		500.00
A36	10p car rose & vio (#137)		650.00
A37	1sh car rose & green (#138)		170.00
A38	2sh 6p dull vio (#139)		1,275.
A39	5sh car rose (#140)		1,750.
A40	10sh ultra (#141)		3,250.
A41	£1 green (#142)		8,000.

Only one example is known of No. A41.

1911-12 — King George V
A42	½p green (#151)		195.00
A43	½p yel grn (#153)		85.00
A44	1p scarlet (#154)		90.00

1912
A45	½p green (#157)		90.00
A46	1p scarlet (#158)		85.00

1912-22
A47	½p green (#159)		70.00
A48	1p scarlet (#160)		35.00
	On cover		225.00
A49	1½p red brn (#161)		95.00
A50	2p org, die 1 (#162)		80.00
a.	Die II (#162a)		800.00
A51	2½p ultra (#163)		105.00
A52	3p bluish vio (#164)		150.00
A53	4p slate grn (#165)		190.00
A54	5p yel brn (#166)		240.00
A55	6p rose lil (#167)		160.00
A56	7p olive grn (#168)		650.00
A57	8p black, yel (#169)		700.00
A58	9p blk brn (#170)		600.00
A59	9p olive grn (#183)		1,400.
A60	10p lt blue (#171)		650.00
A61	1sh bister (#172)		190.00
A62	2sh 6p gray brn (#179)		1,700.
A63	5sh car rose (#180)		3,000.

Catalogue values for unused stamps in this country are for Never Hinged items, beginning with Scott 50.

Stamps and Types of St. Helena, 1912-22 Overprinted in Black or Red

1922 — Wmk. 4 — Perf. 14
1	A9	½p green & blk		6.50	26.00
		On cover			110.00
2	A10	1p green		6.50	25.00
		On cover			110.00
3	A10	1½p rose red		21.00	60.00
		On cover			325.00
4	A9	2p gray & blk		21.00	16.00
		On cover			110.00
5	A9	3p ultra		16.00	26.00
		On cover			110.00
6	A10	8p dl vio & blk		34.00	62.50
					190.00
7	A10	2sh ultra & blk, blue		120.00	150.00
		On cover			225.00
8	A10	3sh vio & blk		175.00	200.00
		On cover			265.00

Wmk. 3
9	A9	1sh blk, gray grn (R)		35.00	60.00
		On cover			275.00
		Nos. 1-9 (9)		435.00	625.50
		Set, never hinged		675.00	
		Set, overprinted "SPECIMEN"		800.00	

Covers: Values for Nos. 7-8 on covers are for overfranked covers, usually philatelic.

All values are known with forged cancellations, many of them dated "MY 24 23."

Nos. 1, 4, 6 and 8 are from special printings, made expressly to be overprinted, and do not exist without overprint.

Seal of Colony — A3

1924-33 — Typo. — Wmk. 4 — Perf. 14
Chalky Paper
10	A3	½p black & gray		6.00	19.00
11	A3	1p green & blk		7.00	12.50
a.		1p br bl grn & gray blk ('33)		135.00	625.00
12	A3	1½p rose red		10.00	42.50
13	A3	2p bluish gray & gray		21.00	12.00
14	A3	3p ultra		10.00	19.00
15	A3	4p blk & gray, yel		60.00	100.00
16	A3	5p ol & blk ('27)		19.00	29.00
17	A3	6p rose lil & gray		62.50	125.00
18	A3	8p violet & gray		19.00	52.50
19	A3	1sh brown & gray		25.00	62.50
20	A3	2sh ultra & gray, blue		75.00	110.00
21	A3	3sh blk & gray, blue		100.00	110.00
		Nos. 10-21 (12)		414.50	694.00
		Set, never hinged		675.00	
		Set, overprinted "SPECIMEN"		850.00	

View of Georgetown — A4

Map of Ascension — A5

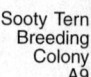

Sooty Tern Breeding Colony A9

Designs: 1½p, Pier at Georgetown. 3p, Long Beach. 5p, Three Sisters. 5sh, Green Mountain.

1934, July 2 — Engr.
23	A4	½p violet & blk		1.10	1.00
24	A5	1p lt grn & blk		2.25	1.60
25	A4	1½p red & black		2.25	2.75
26	A5	2p org & black		2.25	3.00
27	A4	3p ultra & blk		2.25	1.90
28	A4	5p blue & black		2.75	4.00
29	A5	8p dk brn & blk		5.25	6.00
30	A9	1sh carmine & blk		22.50	11.00
31	A5	2sh6p violet & blk		57.50	47.50
32	A4	5sh brown & blk		62.50	70.00
		Nos. 23-32 (10)		160.60	148.75
		Set, never hinged		240.00	
		Set, perforated "SPECIMEN"		425.00	

Common Design Types pictured following the introduction.

Silver Jubilee Issue — Common Design Type
1935, May 6 — Perf. 11x12
33	CD301	1½p car & dk blue		3.50	10.50
34	CD301	2p blk & ultra		11.00	30.00
35	CD301	5p ind & grn		22.50	32.50
36	CD301	1sh brn vio & indigo		24.00	40.00
		Nos. 33-36 (4)		61.00	113.00
		Set, never hinged		100.00	
		Set, perforated "SPECIMEN"		375.00	

25th anniv. of the reign of King George V.

Coronation Issue — Common Design Type
1937, May 19 — Perf. 13½x14
37	CD302	1p deep green		.75	1.50
38	CD302	2p deep orange		1.00	.65
39	CD302	3p bright ultra		1.00	.60
		Nos. 37-39 (3)		2.75	2.75
		Set, never hinged		3.50	
		Set, perforated "SPECIMEN"		400.00	

Georgetown — A11

Designs: No. 41, 41A, 2p, 4p, Green Mountain. No. 41D, 6p, 10sh, Three Sisters. 1½p, 2sh6p, Pier at Georgetown. 3p, 5sh, Long Beach.

Perf. 13, 13½ (#41, 44, 45), 14 (#43C)
1938-53 — Center in Black
40	A11	½p violet ('44)		.70	3.25
		Never hinged		1.40	
a.		Perf. 13½		3.00	3.25
		Never hinged		6.00	
41	A11	1p green		25.00	13.00
		Never hinged		52.50	
41A	A11	1p org yel, ('42)		.25	.60
		Never hinged		.50	
b.		Perf. 14 ('49)		.40	16.00
		Never hinged		.70	

---

c.		Perf. 13½		7.00	9.00
		Never hinged		14.00	
41D	A11	1p green ('49)		.35	1.50
		Never hinged		.60	
42	A11	1½p red, ('44)		.45	.80
		Never hinged		.95	
a.		Perf. 14 ('49)		1.30	12.50
		Never hinged		2.50	
b.		Perf. 13½		2.50	1.40
		Never hinged		4.75	
42C	A11	1½p lilac rose ('53)		.30	6.50
		Never hinged		.55	
d.		Perf. 14 ('49)		.75	1.00
		Never hinged		1.50	
e.		1½p carmine, perf 14		6.00	6.50
		Never hinged		12.00	
43	A11	2p orange ('44)		.40	.40
		Never hinged		.85	
a.		Perf. 14 ('49)		1.50	45.00
		Never hinged		2.75	
b.		Perf. 13½		3.50	1.00
		Never hinged		7.00	
43C	A11	2p red ('49)		.65	2.00
		Never hinged		1.25	
44	A11	3p ultra		55.00	29.00
		Never hinged		125.00	
44A	A11	3p black, ('44)		.35	.80
		Never hinged		.85	
c.		Perf. 13½ ('40)		10.00	3.50
		Never hinged		20.00	
44B	A11	4p ultra, ('44)		2.50	3.00
		Never hinged		5.00	
d.		Perf. 13½		9.00	3.25
		Never hinged		17.50	
45	A11	6p gray blue		5.50	2.50
		Never hinged		10.00	
a.		Perf. 13 ('44)		6.00	7.00
		Never hinged		12.00	
46	A11	1sh dk brn ('44)		3.25	2.00
		Never hinged		5.50	
a.		Perf. 13½		11.00	2.25
		Never hinged		22.00	
47	A11	2sh6p car ('44)		19.00	35.00
		Never hinged		37.50	
a.		Perf. 13½		29.00	10.50
		Never hinged		50.00	
b.		Frame printed doubly, one albino		3,750.	
		Never hinged		5,250.	
48	A11	5sh yel brn ('44)		25.00	40.00
		Never hinged		50.00	
a.		Perf. 13½		60.00	9.50
		Never hinged		100.00	
49	A11	10sh red vio ('44)		30.00	60.00
		Never hinged		45.00	
		Never hinged		72.50	47.50
		Never hinged		115.00	
b.		10sh brt aniline red pur, perf 13		60.00	47.50
		Never hinged		110.00	
		Nos. 40-49 (16)		168.70	200.35
		Set, never hinged		350.00	

Catalogue values for unused stamps in this section, from this point to the end of the section, are for Never Hinged items.

Peace Issue — Common Design Type
Perf. 13½x14
1946, Oct. 21 — Engr. — Wmk. 4
50	CD303	2p deep orange		.45	1.10
51	CD303	4p deep blue		.45	.65
		Set, perforated "SPECIMEN"		400.00	

Silver Wedding Issue — Common Design Types
1948, Oct. 20 — Photo. — Perf. 14x14½
52	CD304	3p black		.65	.60

Engraved; Name Typographed
Perf. 11½x11
53	CD305	10sh red violet		57.50	60.00

The stamps formerly listed as Nos. 54-56 have been merged into the rest of the George VI definitive series as Nos. 41//43C.

UPU Issue — Common Design Types
Engr.; Name Typo. on Nos. 58, 59
1949, Oct. 10 — Perf. 13½, 11x11½
57	CD306	3p rose carmine		1.40	1.75
58	CD307	4p indigo		4.75	1.25
59	CD308	6p olive		1.75	2.75
60	CD309	1sh slate		3.00	2.00
		Nos. 57-60 (4)		10.90	7.75

AUSTRALIAN STATES

NEW SOUTH WALES

'nü sauth 'wā͟ə͟lz

LOCATION — Southeast coast of Australia in the South Pacific Ocean
GOVT. — British Crown Colony
AREA — 309,432 sq. mi.
POP. — 1,500,000 (estimated, 1900)
CAPITAL — Sydney

In 1901 New South Wales united with five other British colonies to form the Commonwealth of Australia. Stamps of Australia are now used.

12 Pence = 1 Shilling
20 Shillings = 1 Pound

Watermarks

Wmk. 12 — Crown and Single-lined A

Wmk. 13 — Large Crown and Double-lined A

Wmk. 49 — Double-lined Numerals Corresponding with the Value

Wmk. 50 — Single-lined Numeral

Wmk. 51 — Single-lined Numeral

Wmk. 52 — Single-lined Numeral

Wmk. 53 — 5/-

Wmk. 54 — Small Crown and NSW

Wmk. 55 — Large Crown and NSW

Wmk. 56 — NSW

Wmk. 57 — 5/- NSW in Diamond

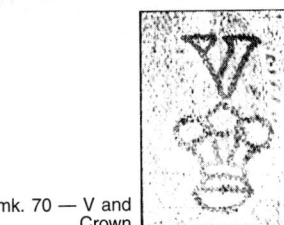

Wmk. 58 — 20/- NSW in Circle

Wmk. 70 — V and Crown

Wmk. 199 — Crown and A in Circle

Values for unused stamps are for examples with original gum as defined in the catalogue introduction except for Nos. 1-20 which are rarely found with gum and are valued without gum. Very fine examples of Nos. 35-100, F3-F5, J1-J10 and O1-O40 will have perforations touching the framelines or design on one or more sides due to the narrow spacing of the stamps on the plates and imperfect perforation methods. Stamps with perfs clear of the design on all four sides are scarce and will command higher prices.

Seal of the Colony
A1   A2

A1 has no clouds. A2 has clouds added to the design, except in pos. 15.

Unwmk.

1850, Jan. 1   Engr.   *Imperf.*

Yellowish Wove Paper

1	A1	1p red	9,500.	725.00
a.		1p brownish red	10,000.	725.00
c.		1p carmine	10,000.	725.00
d.		1p crimson lake	10,000.	725.00

Bluish Wove Paper

1b.	A1	1p red	9,500.	725.00
1e.	A1	1p lake	10,000.	725.00

Re-engraved, with Clouds

1850, Aug.   Yellowish Wove Paper

2	A2	1p red carmine	7,000.	600.00
f.		Hill unshaded (Pos. 2/3)	10,500.	925.00
g.		No clouds (Pos. 3/5)	10,500.	925.00
h.		No trees (Pos. 2/2)	10,500.	925.00
2i	A2	1p vermilion	7,000.	750.00

Bluish Wove Paper

2c	A2	1p carmine red	5,000.	750.00
j.		Hill unshaded	10,000.	650.00
k.		No clouds	10,000.	650.00
l.		No trees	10,000.	650.00
2m	A2	1p brownish lake	5,500.	800.00
2n	A2	1p crimson lake	6,000.	800.00
2o	A2	1p gooseberry red	10,000.	800.00

Laid Paper

2b	A2	1p carmine red, *yellowish*	10,000.	800.00
p.		Hill unshaded	—	1,100.
q.		No clouds	—	1,100.
r.		No trees	—	1,100.
2e	A2	1p carmine red, *bluish*		
2s	A2	1p vermilion, *bluish*	10,500.	600.00

Printed in panes of 25 (5x5). Twenty-five varieties.

Stamps from early impressions of the plate sell at considerably higher prices.

No. 1 was reproduced by the collotype process in a souvenir sheet distributed at the London International Stamp Exhibition 1950. The paper is white.

Plate I — A3   Plate II — A4

Plate I: Vertically lined background.
Plate I re-touched: Lines above and below "POSTAGE" and "TWO PENCE" deepened. Outlines of circular band around picture also deepened.

Plate II (First re-engraving of Plate I): Horizontally lined background; the bale on the left side is dated and there is a dot in the star in each corner.
Plate II retouched: Dots and dashes added in lower spandrels.

Plate I

1850, Jan. 1   Early Impressions

3a	A3	2p gray blue, *yelsh wove*	12,500.	550.00
b.		Double line on bale (Pos. 2/7)		1,000.
3c	A3	2p deep blue, *yelsh wove*	11,000.	550.00

Intermediate Impressions

3d	A3	2p gray blue, *yelsh wove*	8,000.	450.00
3e	A3	2p deep blue, *yelsh wove*	9,000.	500.00

Late (worn plate) Impressions

3	A3	2p blue, *yelsh wove*	4,500.	300.00
3f	A3	2p deep blue, *yelsh wove*	6,000.	225.00

Printed in panes of 24 (12x2). Twenty-four varieties.

Plate I, Retouched

4	A3	2p blue, *yelsh wove*	6,500.	400.00
4a	A3	2p gray blue, *yelsh wove*	6,000.	500.00

Twelve varieties.

Plate II

1850, Apr.   Early Impressions

5h	A3	2p gray blue, *yelsh wove*	8,500.	375.00
j.		"CREVIT" omitted (Pos. 2/1)	—	1,000.
k.		Pick & shovel omitted (Pos. 1/10)	—	600.00
l.		No whip (Pos. 1/4, 1/8, 2/8)	—	500.00
5m	A3	2p bright blue, *bluish wove*	8,500.	375.00
5n	A3	2p indigo blue, *yelsh wove*	8,500.	375.00
5o	A3	2p lilac blue, *yelsh wove*		2,000.

Late (worn plate) Impressions

5	A4	2p blue, *yelsh wove*	4,500.	165.00
5a	A4	2p blue, *bluish wove*	4,250.	165.00
5b	A4	2p blue, *grayish wove*	4,250.	165.00
5p	A4	2p prussian blue, *bluish wove*	4,750.	225.00
c.		"CREVIT" omitted	—	575.00
d.		Pick and shovel omitted	—	450.00
e.		No whip	6,500.	325.00

Plate II, Retouched

5F	A4	2p blue, *bluish wove*	6,000.	300.00
g.		No whip		475.00
i.		"CREVIT" omitted		1,500.
5q	A4	2p prussian blue, *bluish wove*	6,750.	350.00

Eleven varieties.

Plate III   Plate IV
A5   A6

Plate III (Second re-engraving of Plate I): The bale is not dated and, with the exception of Nos. 7, 10 and 12, it is single-lined. There are no dots in the stars.
Plate IV (Third re-engraving of Plate I): The bale is double-lined and there is a circle in the center of each star.

1850-51   **Wove Paper**
6   A5   2p bl, *grayish wove*   6,000.   300.00
  a. Fan with 6 segments — 650.00
  b. Double-lined bale — 500.00
  c. No whip — 475.00
6d   A5   2p ultramarine   6,250.   300.00
7   A6   2p blue, *bluish wove* ('51)   5,500.   250.00
7b   A6   2p blue, *grayish wove*   5,750.   275.00
  c. Fan with 6 segments (Pos. 2/8) — 425.00
  d. No clouds (Pos. 2/10) — 425.00
  e. Hill not shaded (Pos. 1/12) — 450.00
  f. No waves (Pos. 1/9, 2/5) — 300.00
7g   A6   2p 2p ultramarine   6,000.   300.00
7h   A6   2p 2p prussian blue   5,000.   250.00

Laid Paper
7a   A6   2p ultramarine   7,000.   275.00
7i   A6   2p prussian blue   7,750.   375.00
  j. Fan with 6 segments (Pos. 2/8) — 350.00
  k. No clouds (Pos. 2/10) — 350.00
  l. Hill not shaded (Pos. 1/12) — 350.00
  m. No waves (Pos. 1/9, 2/5) — 300.00
  n. "PENOE" (Pos. 1/10, 2/12) — 375.00

Twenty-four varieties.

Plate V — A7

Plate V (Fourth re-engraving of Plate I): There is a pearl in the fan-shaped ornament below the central design.

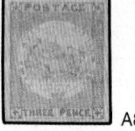

A8

1850-51   **Wove Paper**
8   A7   2p blue, *grayish wove* ('51)   5,500.   300.00
  b. Fan with 6 segments (Pos. 2/8) — 500.00
  c. Pick and shovel omitted (Pos. 2/5) — 525.00
8d   A7   2p ultramarine   5,500.   300.00

Laid Paper
8a   A7   2p ultramarine   8,500.   425.00
  e. Fan with 6 segments (Pos. 2/8) — 600.00
  f. Pick and shovel omitted (Pos. 2/5) — 575.00

Yellowish Wove Paper
9a   A8   3p green   7,000.   3575.00
9h   A8   3p emerald green   8,500.   350.00
  e. No whip (Pos. 4/3, 4/4) — 600.00
  f. "SIGIIIUM" for "SIGILLUM" (Pos. 5/3) — 650.00
9g   A8   3p myrtle green   20,000.   1,500.

Bluish Wove Paper
9   A8   3p yellow green   6,250.   325.00
9d   A8   3p emerald green   7,500.   350.00
  i. No whip (Pos. 4/3, 4/4) — 500.00
  j. "SIGIIIUM" for "SIGILLUM" (Pos. 5/3) — 650.00

Laid Paper
9b   A8   3p green, *yellowish laid*   12,000.   925.00
  k. No whip (Pos. 4/3, 4/4) — 1,100.
  l. "SIGIIIIUM" for "SIGILLUM" (Pos. 5/3) — 1,200.
9c   A8   3p green, *bluish laid*   12,000.   925.00
9m   A8   3p bright green, *yellowish laid*   12,000.

Twenty-four varieties of No. 8, twenty-five of No. 9.

Queen Victoria
A9   A10

TWO PENCE
Plate I — Background of wavy lines.
Plate II — Stars in corners.
Plate III (Plate I re-engraved) — Background of crossed lines.

SIX PENCE
Plate I — Background of fine lines.
Plate II (Plate I re-engraved) — Background of coarse lines.

1851   **Yellowish Wove Paper**
10   A9   1p carmine   4,000.   400.00
  b. No leaves to right of "SOUTH"   5,500.   1,000.
  c. Two leaves to right of "SOUTH"   5,500.   1,100.
  d. "WALE"   5,500.   1,100.
11   A9   2p ultra, Plate I   1,600.   125.00

1852   **Bluish Laid Paper**
12   A9   1p orange brown   6,000.   600.00
  a. 1p claret   6,000.   1,100.
  b. As "a," no leaves to right of "SOUTH"   1,250.
  c. As "a," two leaves to right of "SOUTH"   1,300.
  d. As "a," "WALE"   1,300.

1852-55   **Bluish or Grayish Wove Paper**
13   A9   1p red   1,750.   200.00
  a. 1p carmine   1,900.   200.00
  b. 1p scarlet   1,900.   250.00
  c. 1p brick red   1,750.   200.00
  d. As "c," no leaves to right of "SOUTH"   4,000.   400.00
  e. As "c," two leaves to right of "SOUTH"   475.00
  f. As "c," "WALE"   550.00
14   A9   2p blue, Plate I   1,150.   45.00
  a. 2p ultramarine   1,350.   45.00
  b. 2p slate   1,750.   45.00
  c. 2p chalky blue   1,150.   45.00
  d. 2p prussian blue   1,000.   45.00
15   A10   2p blue, Plate II ('53)   2,000.   125.00
  a. "WAEES"   3,000.   550.00
  b. 2p deep ultramarine   2,150.   160.00
  c. 2p prussian blue   2,150.   135.00
  d. As "c," "WAEES" — 550.00
16   A9   2p blue, Plate III ('55)   925.00   90.00
  a. "WALES" partly covered with wavy lines — 325.00
  b. 2p blue, *white paper* ('55)   900.00   95.00
  c. As "b," "WALES" partly covered with wavy lines — 300.00
17   A9   3p green   2,600.   210.00
  a. 3p emerald   3,750.   300.00
  b. As "a," "WACES" — 900.00
  c. 3p deep green   3,250.   300.00
  d. 3p yellow green   3,000.   275.00
  e. As "d," "WACES" — 625.00
  f. 3p blue green, *thick paper* — 325.00
  g. As "f," "WACES"   3,000.   900.00
18   A9   6p brown, Plate I   3,200.   450.00
  a. "WALLS"   4,500.   1,500.
  b. 6p black brown   4,500.   1,250.
  c. 6p yellow brown   3,750.   350.00
  d. 6p chocolate brown   3,500.   350.00
  e. 6p yellow brown, *white paper* — 1,350.
  f. As "e," "WALLS" — 2,400.
19   A9   6p brown, Plate II   3,600.   425.00
  a. 6p bister brown   3,500.   425.00
20   A9   8p yellow ('53)   10,000.   1,100.
  a. 8p orange   9,500.   1,100.
  b. No leaves to right of "SOUTH" — 2,250.
  c. No bow at back of head — 2,250.
  d. No lines in spandrel — 1,350.

The plates of the 1, 2, 3 and 8p each contained 50 varieties and those of the 6p 25 varieties.

The 2p, plate II, 6p, plate II, and 8p have been reprinted on grayish blue wove paper. The reprints of the 2p have the spandrels and background much worn. Most of the reprints of the 6p have no floreate ornaments to the right and left of "South." On all the values the wreath has been retouched.

Type of 1851 and

A11   A12

A13   A14

1854-55   **Wmk. 49**   **Imperf.**
23   A9   1p orange   450.00   57.50
  a. No leaves to right of "SOUTH"   975.00   225.00
  b. Two leaves to right of "SOUTH"   1,125.   240.00
  c. "WALE"   1,150.   240.00
  d. 1d orange vermilion   450.00   57.50
24   A9   2p blue   400.00   27.50
  a. 2p ultramarine   400.00   27.50
  b. 2p Prussian blue   400.00   27.50
25   A9   3p green   525.00   57.50
  a. "WACES"   1,400.   225.00
  b. Watermarked "2"   6,000.   2,250.

Value for No. 25b is for copy with the design cut into.

26   A11   5p green   1,600.   800.00
27   A12   6p sage green   1,600.   125.00
28   A12   6p brown   900.00   42.50
  a. Watermarked "8"   4,600.   175.00
29   A12   6p gray   1,250.   125.00
  a. 6p greenish gray   1,250.   125.00
  b. 6p bluish gray   1,100.   225.00

  c. 6p deep slate   1,400.   125.00
  d. As "c," wmk sideways   1,200.
  e. 6p fawn   1,150.   190.00
  f. As "e," watermarked "8"   4,500.   175.00
  g. As "f," wmk sideways   600.00
30   A13   8p orange ('55)   15,500.   1,900.
  a. 8p yellow   16,750.   1,600.
31   A14   1sh pale red brown   2,250.   140.00
  a. 1sh red   2,200.   110.00
  b. 1sh rose vermilion   2,200.   110.00
  c. As "b," watermarked "8"   6,500.   250.00

See Nos. 38-42, 56, 58, 65, 67.
Nos. 38-42 exist with wide margins. Stamps with perforations trimmed are often offered as Nos. 26, 30, and 30a.

A15

1856   **Imperf.**
32   A15   1p red   400.00   57.50
  a. 1p orange red   400.00   57.50
  b. As "a," printed on both sides   4,200.   2,500.
  c. Watermarked "2"   8,000.
  d. 1p carmine vermilion   400.00   57.50
33   A15   2p blue   325.00   27.50
  a. Watermarked "1"   8,750.
  b. Watermarked "5"   1,000.   110.00
  c. Watermarked "8"   8,250.
  d. 2p dp turquoise blue   275.00   25.00
  e. 2p ultramarine   325.00   27.50
  f. 2p pale blue   325.00   27.50
34   A15   3p green   1,350.   125.00
  a. 3p yellow green   1,350.   125.00
  b. Watermarked "2"   5,000.
  c. 3p bluish green ('56)   1,350.   125.00
  Nos. 32-34 (3)   2,075.   210.00

The two known examples of No. 33c are in museums. Both are used.

The 1p has been reprinted in orange on paper watermarked Small Crown and NSW, and the 2p in deep blue on paper watermarked single lined "2." These reprints are usually overprinted "SPECIMEN."
See Nos. 34C-37, 54, 63, 90.

1859   **Litho.**
34C   A15   2p light blue — 1,250.
  On cover   4,500.

1860-63   **Engr.**   **Wmk. 49**   **Perf. 13**
35   A15   1p red   175.00   20.00
  a. 1p orange   225.00   42.50
  b. Perf. 12x13   2,100.
  c. Perf. 12   325.00   42.50
36   A15   2p blue, perf. 12   325.00   29.00
  a. Watermarked "1"   4,500.
  c. Perf. 12x13   3,400.   250.00
37   A15   3p blue green   100.00   29.00
  a. 3p yellow green   140.00   25.00
  b. 3p deep green   140.00   24.00
  c. Watermarked "6"   225.00   32.50
  d. Perf. 12   1,300.   92.50
38   A11   5p dark green   110.00   29.00
  a. 5p yellow green   200.00   87.50
  b. Perf. 12   400.00   175.00
39   A12   6p brown, perf. 12   750.00   97.50
  a. 6p gray, perf. 12   750.00   110.00
40   A12   6p violet   325.00   14.00
  a. 6p aniline lilac   1,600.   170.00
  b. Watermarked "5"   850.00   65.00
  c. Watermarked "12"   850.00   32.50
  e. Perf. 12   775.00   32.50
  f. As "b," wmk sideways   800.00
41   A13   8p yellow   450.00   92.50
  a. 8p orange   500.00   92.50
  b. As "a," perf. 12   6,000.   1,450.
  c. 8p red orange   500.00   92.50
  d. As "c," perf 12   6,000.   1,450.
42   A14   1sh rose   325.00   20.00
  a. 1sh carmine   275.00   22.50
  b. As "a," perf. 12   1,350.   100.00
  c. 1sh crimson lake   250.00   22.50
  d. 1sh brownish red, perf 12   1,300.   100.00
  Nos. 35-42 (8)   2,560.   331.00

1864   **Wmk. 50**   **Perf. 13**
43   A15   1p red   100.00   40.00

A16

1861-80   **Wmk. 53**   **Perf. 13**
44   A16   5sh dull violet   350.00   77.50
  a. 5sh purple   450.00   105.00
  b. 5sh dull violet, perf. 12   2,100.   400.00
  c. 5sh purple, perf. 12 — 110.00
  d. 5sh purple, perf. 10   325.00   110.00
  e. 5sh purple, perf. 12x10   475.00   110.00
  f. 5sh royal purple, perf 13 ('72)   575.00   97.50
  g. 5sh deep rose lilac, perf 13 ('75)   225.00   57.50
  h. 5sh rose lilac, perf 10 ('83)   260.00   75.00

  i. 5sh purple, perf 10x12 ('85) — 260.00
  j. 5sh reddish purple, perf 10 ('86)   260.00   75.00
  k. 5sh rose lilac, perf 11 ('88) — 225.00

See No. 101. For overprint see No. O11.
Reprints are perf. 10 and overprinted "REPRINT" in black.

A17   A18

1862-65   **Typo.**   **Unwmk.**   **Perf. 13**
45   A17   1p red ('65)   200.00   60.00
  a. Perf. 14   200.00   90.00
  b. 1p brick red ('65)   115.00   62.50
46   A18   2p blue   160.00   29.00
  a. Perf. 14   175.00   105.00

1863-64   **Wmk. 50**   **Perf. 13**
47   A17   1p red   57.50   20.00
  a. Watermarked "2"   225.00   35.00
  b. 1p dark red brown   260.00   35.00
  c. 1p brick red   57.50   6.25
  d. 1p brick red, shiny surfaced paper ('65)   425.00
  e. Horiz. pair, imperf between   1,500.
48   A18   2p blue   35.00   6.00
  a. Watermarked "1"   375.00   13.00
  b. 2p cobalt blue   35.00   6.00
  c. 2p Prussian blue   57.50   8.50

1862   **Wmk. 49**   **Perf. 13**
49   A18   2p blue   140.00   20.00
  a. Watermarked "5"   200.00   25.00
  b. Perf. 12x13   975.00   500.00
  c. Perf. 12   400.00   85.00

See Nos. 52-53, 61-62, 70-71.

A19   A20

1867, Sept.   **Wmk. 51, 52**   **Perf. 13**
50   A19   4p red brown   105.00   10.50
  a. Imperf.
  b. 4p pale red brown   105.00   10.50
51   A20   10p lilac   32.50   10.50
  Ovptd. "SPECIMEN"   45.00
  b. Horiz. pair, imperf between   2,500.

See Nos. 55, 64, 91, 97, 117, 129.

A21   A22

A23

Typo.; Engr. (3p, 5p, 8p)
1871-84   **Wmk. 54**   **Perf. 13**
52   A17   1p red   22.50   2.50
  a. Perf. 10   375.00   57.50
  b. Perf. 13x10   35.00   1.90
  c. Horiz. pair, imperf between   2,250.
53   A18   2p blue   30.00   2.25
  a. Imperf.
  b. Horiz. pair, imperf vert.   2,500.
  c. Perf. 10   525.00   42.50
  d. Perf. 13x10   30.00   1.75
  e. Perf. 12x13
  f. Perf. 11x12   450.00   72.50
54   A15   3p green ('74)   60.00   9.50
  a. Perf. 10   250.00   140.00
  b. Perf. 12 — 400.00
  c. Perf. 10x12   250.00   57.50
  d. Perf. 11x12   200.00   45.00
  e. Perf. 10   175.00   17.50
  f. Perf. 13x10   200.00   25.00
55   A19   4p red brown ('77)   125.00   20.00
  a. Perf. 10   275.00   105.00
  b. Perf. 13x10   175.00   12.00
56   A11   5p dk grn, perf. 10 ('84)   35.00   29.00
  a. Horiz. pair, imperf between   2,250.
  b. Perf. 12   375.00   200.00
  c. Perf. 10x12   250.00   92.50
  d. Perf. 10x13

57 A21 6p lilac ('72) — 105.00 — 3.50
- a. Imperf. — —
- b. Perf. 13x10 — 125.00 — 3.50
- c. Perf. 10 — 325.00 — 21.00

58 A13 8p yellow ('77) — 250.00 — 35.00
- a. Imperf. — —
- b. Perf. 10 — 625.00 — 50.00
- c. Perf. 13x10 — 400.00 — 47.50

59 A22 9p on 10p red brown, perf. 12 (Bk) — 32.50 — 13.00
- a. Double surcharge, blk & bl — 325.00
- b. Perf. 12x10 — 525.00 — 400.00
- c. Perf. 10 — 25.00 — 11.00
- d. Perf. 12x11 — 35.00 — 12.00
- e. Perf. 11x12 — 65.00 — 15.00
- f. Perf. 11 — 72.50 — 15.00
- g. Perf. 10x11 — 105.00 — 25.00

60 A23 1sh black ('76) — 80.00 — 3.75
- a. Perf. 13x10 — 425.00 — 14.00
- c. Perf. 10 — 450.00 — 14.00
- d. Perf. 11 — —
- e. Vert. pair, imperf between — 2,250.
- f. Pair, imperf — 2,000.
- Nos. 52-60 (9) — 740.00 — 118.50

The surcharge on No. 59 measures 15mm.
See Nos. 66, 68. For overprints see Nos. O1-O10.

Typo.; Engr. (3p, 5p, 8p)
1882-91   Wmk. 55   *Perf. 11x12*

61 A17 1p red — 13.00 — 1.10
- a. Perf. 10 — 19.00 — 1.25
- b. Perf. 10x13 — 240.00 — 14.00
- c. Perf. 10x12 — 525.00 — 140.00
- d. Perf. 12x11 — 250.00
- e. Perf. 10x11 — 1,100. — 225.00
- f. Perf. 11 — 350.00
- g. Perf. 13 — 1,100. — 475.00
- h. Perf. 13x10 — 87.50 — 3.50
- i. Perf. 12x10 — 525.00 — 135.00
- j. Perf. 11x10 — 1,100. — 225.00
- k. Horiz. pair, imperf between — 2,100.

62 A18 2p blue — 24.00 — 1.10
- a. Perf. 10 — 45.00 — 1.25
- b. Perf. 13x10 — 140.00 — 6.25
- c. Perf. 13 — 1,100. — 250.00
- d. Perf. 12x10 — 750.00 — 140.00
- e. Perf. 11 — 250.00
- f. Perf. 12x11 — 950.00 — 250.00
- g. Perf. 11x10 — 1,100. — 325.00
- h. Perf. 12 — 525.00

63 A15 3p green — 18.00 — 7.00
- a. Imperf., pair — 700.00
- b. Vert. pair, imperf. btwn. — —
- c. Horiz. pair, imperf. vert. — 700.00
- d. Double impression — —
- e. Perf. 10 — 21.00 — 5.00
- f. Perf. 11 — 21.00 — 5.00
- g. Perf. 12 — 24.00 — 5.25
- h. Perf. 12x11 — 22.50 — 5.00
- i. Perf. 10x12 — 97.50 — 9.25
- m. Perf. 10x11 — 50.00 — 6.50
- n. Perf. 12x10 — 97.50 — 9.25
- o. Wmk sideways — 20.00 — 6.00

64 A19 4p red brown — 95.00 — 5.75
- a. Perf. 10 — 105.00 — 8.00
- b. Perf. 10x12 — 425.00 — 125.00
- c. Perf. 12 — 700.00 — 400.00

65 A11 5p dk blue green — 21.00 — 3.50
- a. Imperf., pair — 625.00
- b. Perf. 11 — 22.50 — 3.50
- c. Perf. 10 — 32.50 — 3.50
- d. Perf. 12 — 42.50 — 4.25
- e. Perf. 10x12 — 57.50
- f. 5p green, perf. 12x11 — 15.00 — 2.50
- g. 5p green, perf. 11x10 — 105.00 — 13.25
- h. 5p green, perf. 12x10 — 240.00 — 140.00
- i. 5p green, perf. 10x11 — 120.00 — 10.50
- j. 5p green, perf. 11 — 16.00 — 2.50
- k. Wmk sideways — 25.00 — 8.00

66 A21 6p lilac, perf. 10 — 105.00 — 5.25
- a. Horiz. pair, imperf. between — 2,000.
- b. Perf. 10x12 — 105.00 — 5.75
- c. Perf. 11x12 — 200.00 — 25.00
- d. Perf. 12 — 200.00 — 20.00
- e. Perf. 11x10 — 140.00 — 6.25
- f. Perf. 11 — 200.00 — 18.00
- g. Perf. 10x13 — 700.00

67 A13 8p yellow, perf. 10 — 200.00 — 32.50
- a. Perf. 11 — 200.00 — 42.50
- b. Perf. 12 — 350.00 — 57.50
- c. Perf. 10x12 — 250.00 — 100.00

68 A23 1sh black — 175.00 — 18.00
- a. Perf. 10x13 — —
- b. Perf. 10 — 175.00 — 14.00
- c. Perf. 11 — 450.00 — 29.00
- d. Perf. 10x12 — 525.00
- Nos. 61-68 (8) — 651.00 — 74.20

Nos. 63 and 65 exist with two types of watermark 55 — spacings of 1mm or 2mm between crown and NSW.
See Nos. 92-94, O12-O19.
The 1, 2, 4, 6, 8p and 1sh have been reprinted on paper watermarked Large Crown and NSW. The 1, 2, 4p and 1sh are perforated 11x12, the 6p is perforated 10 and the 8p 11. All are overprinted "REPRINT," the 1sh in red and the others in black.

Perf. 11x12
1886-87   Typo.   Wmk. 56
Bluish Revenue Stamp Paper

70 A17 1p scarlet — 13.00 — 6.00
- a. Perf. 10 — 35.00 — 13.00

71 A18 2p dark blue — 32.50 — 6.00
- a. Perf. 10 — 105.00 — 15.00

For overprint, see No. O20.

A24

Perf. 12 (#73-75), 12x10 (#72, 75A) and Compound
1885-86   **"POSTAGE" in Black**

72 A24 5sh green & vio — 850.00 — 125.00
- a. Perf. 10 — —
- b. Perf. 13 — —

73 A24 10sh rose & vio — 1,750. — 275.00
- a. Perf. 13 — —

74 A24 £1 rose & vio — 9,000.
- a. Perf. 13 — 5,250.

"POSTAGE" in Blue
Bluish Paper

75 A24 10sh rose & vio — 325.00 — 80.00
- b. Perf. 10 — 1,350. — 300.00
- c. Perf. 12x11 — —

White Paper

75A A24 £1 rose & vio — 6,750. — 4,250.

For overprints, see Nos. O21-O23.
The 5sh with black overprint and the £1 with blue overprint have been reprinted on paper watermarked NSW. They are perforated 12x10 and are overprinted "REPRINT" in black.

"POSTAGE" in Blue
1894   White Paper

76 A24 10sh rose & violet, perf 12 — 450.00 — 105.00
- a. Double overprint — —
- b. 10sh mauve & claret, perf 10 — 850.00 — 275.00
- c. 10sh mauve & violet, perf 11 — 750.00 — 190.00
- d. 10sh mauve & violet, perf 12x11 — 425.00 — 125.00

See No. 108B.

View of Sydney A25

Emu A26

Captain Cook — A27

Victoria and Coat of Arms — A28

Lyrebird A29

Kangaroo A30

1888-89   Wmk. 55   *Perf. 11x12*

77 A25 1p violet — 10.00 — 1.40
- a. Perf. 12 — 14.00 — 1.10
- b. Perf. 12x11½ — 42.50 — 2.40

78 A26 2p blue — 16.00 — 1.40
- a. Imperf., pair — 400.00
- b. Perf. 12 — 25.00 — .95
- c. Perf. 12x11½ — 29.00 — .95

79 A27 4p brown — 25.00 — 8.75
- a. Perf. 12x11½ — 87.50 — 20.00
- b. Perf. 12 — 72.50 — 10.00
- c. Perf. 11 — 700.00 — 200.00
- d. Imperf. — —

80 A28 6p carmine rose — 57.50 — 8.75
- a. Perf. 12 — 47.50 — 15.00
- b. Perf. 12x11½ — 57.50 — 8.75

81 A29 8p red violet — 42.50 — 9.50
- a. Perf. 12 — 42.50 — 9.50
- b. Perf. 12x11½ — 75.00 — 20.00

82 A30 1sh maroon ('89) — 57.50 — 8.75
- a. Imperf., pair — 1,000.
- b. Perf. 12x11½ — 57.50 — 4.25
- c. Perf. 12 — 72.50 — 4.25
- d. 1sh violet brown, perf 11x12 — 40.00 — 9.25
- e. 1sh violet brown, perf 12x11½ — 75.00 — 11.50
- f. 1sh violet brown, perf 12 — 75.00 — 11.50
- Nos. 77-82 (6) — 208.50 — 38.55
- Set, ovptd. "SPECIMEN" — 290.00

First British settlement in Australia, cent.
For overprints see Nos. O24-O29.

1888   Wmk. 56   *Perf. 11x12*
83 A25 1p violet — 35.00 — 4.00
84 A26 2p blue — 115.00 — 6.00
See Nos. 104B-106C, 113-115, 118, 125-127, 130.

Map of Australia — A31

Governors Capt. Arthur Phillip (above) and Lord Carrington — A32

1888-89   Wmk. 53   *Perf. 10*
85 A31 5sh violet ('89) — 475.00 — 105.00
- a. 5sh deep purple — 450.00 — 105.00

86 A32 20sh ultra — 600.00 — 225.00
See Nos. 88, 120. For overprints see Nos. O30-O31.

1890   Wmk. 57   *Perf. 10*
87 A31 5sh violet — 400.00 — 77.50
- a. Perf. 11 — 450.00 — 100.00
- b. Perf. 10x11 — 550.00 — 77.50
- c. Perf. 12 — 700.00 — 115.00
- d. 5sh mauve, perf 10 — 425.00 — 77.50
- e. 5sh mauve, perf 11 — 425.00 — 92.50
- f. Horiz. pair, imperf btwn. — —

Perf. 11x12, 12x11 Wmk. 58
88 A32 20sh ultra — 225.00 — 90.00
- a. Perf. 11 — 275.00 — 90.00
- b. Perf. 12 — 700.00 — 275.00
- c. 20sh cobalt blue, perf 10 — 525.00 — 275.00
- d. As "c," perf 11 — 350.00 — 90.00
- Nos. 87-88, ovptd. "SPECIMEN" — 260.00

For overprints see Nos. O32-O33.

"Australia" — A33

1890, Dec. 22   Wmk. 55   *Perf. 11x12*
89 A33 2½p ultra — 14.00 — 5.75
- a. Perf. 12 — 29.00 — 5.75
- b. Perf. 12x11½ — 87.50
- Overprinted "SPECIMEN" — 27.50

For overprint see No. O35.

Type of 1856
1891   Engr.   Wmk. 52   *Perf. 10*
90 A15 3p green — 15.00 — 100.00
- a. Double impression — —
- b. 3p light green — 22.50 — 125.00

Type of 1867
1893   Typo.   *Perf. 11*
91 A20 10p lilac — 35.00 — 11.50
- a. Perf. 10 — 42.50 — 14.00
- b. Perf. 11x10 or 10x11 — 47.50 — 18.00
- c. Perf. 12x11 — 250.00 — 35.00

Types of 1862-84 Surcharged in Black

a   b

1891, Jan. 5   Wmk. 55   *Perf. 11x12*
92 A17(a) ½p on 1p gray — 21.00 — 14.00
- a. Imperf. — —
- b. Surcharge omitted — —
- c. Double surcharge — 550.00

93 A21(b) 7½p on 6p brown — 21.00 — 14.00
- a. Perf. 10 — 21.00 — 14.00
- b. Perf. 11 — 20.00 — 11.50
- c. Perf. 12 — 24.00 — 14.00
- d. Perf. 10x12 — 24.00 — 14.00

Perf. 12x11½
94 A23(b) 12½p on 1sh red — 14.00 — 12.00
- a. Perf. 11x12 — 22.50 — 22.50
- b. Perf. 10 — 29.00 — 25.00
- c. Perf. 11 — 30.00 — 25.00
- d. Perf. 12 — 30.00 — 25.00
- Nos. 92-94 (3) — 56.00 — 40.00
- Nos. 92-94 overprinted "SPECIMEN" — 80.00

For overprints see Nos. O34, O36-O37.

Victoria — A37

1892-97   *Perf. 11x12*
95 A37 ½p slate ('97) — 5.75 — .85
- a. Perf. 12x11½ — 5.75 — .85
- b. Perf. 12 — 5.50 — .85
- c. As #95, horiz. pair, imperf between — 1,350.
- d. ½p gray, pearl — 80.00 — 7.25
- e. As "d," perf. 10x12 — 140.00 — 18.00
- f. As "d," perf. 11 — 160.00 — 14.00
- g. As "d," perf. 11x12 — 2.25 — .50
- As "g," overprinted "SPECIMEN" — 22.50

See Nos. 102, 109, 121. For overprint see No. O38.

Types of 1867-71
1897   *Perf. 11x12*
96 A22 9p on 10p red brn (Bk) — 20.00 — 17.50
- a. 9p on 10p org brn (Bk) — 20.00 — 17.50
- b. Surcharge omitted — —
- c. Double surcharge — 375.00 — 375.00
- d. Perf. 11 — 25.00 — 24.00
- e. Perf. 12 — 25.00 — 22.50

97 A20 10p violet — 25.00 — 16.00
- a. Perf. 12x11½ — 25.00 — 16.00
- b. Perf. 11 — 47.50 — 22.50
- c. Perf. 12 — 35.00 — 17.50
- Nos. 96-97, overprinted "SPECIMEN" — 75.00

The surcharge on No. 96 measures 13½mm.
For overprints see Nos. O39-O40.

Seal A38   Victoria A39

A40

ONE PENNY:
Die I — The first pearl in the crown at the left is merged into the arch, the shading under the fleur-de-lis is indistinct, and the "s" of "WALES" is open.
Die II — The first pearl is circular, the vertical shading under the fleur-de-lis is clear, and the "s" of "WALES" not so open.

2½ PENCE:
Die I — There are 12 radiating lines in the star on the Queen's breast.
Die II — There are 16 radiating lines in the star. The eye is nearly full of color.

1897   *Perf. 12*
98 A38 1p rose red, II — 4.75 — .50
- a. Imperf., pair — 5.75 — .50
- b. Imperf. horiz., pair — 700.00
- c. Die I, perf. 12x11½ — —
- d. Die I, perf. 12 — 11.50 — 1.75
- e. Die I, perf. 12x11½ — 4.75 — .50
- f. Die II, perf. 12x11½ — 4.75 — .50
- g. Die II, perf. 11x12 — 4.75 — .50

99 A39 2p deep blue — 13.50 — .65
- a. Perf. 11x12 — 9.00 — .65
- b. Perf. 12x11½ — 7.75 — .65

100 A40 2½p dp purple, II — 20.00 — 4.25
- a. Die I, perf. 12x11 — 22.50 — 4.25
- b. Die I, perf. 11 — 25.00 — 7.75
- c. Die I, perf. 11½x12 — 25.00 — 4.25
- d. Die II, perf. 11x12 — 21.00 — 4.25
- e. Die II, perf. 11½x12 — 25.00 — 4.25
- Nos. 98-100 (3) — 38.25 — 5.40
- Nos. 98-100 overprinted "SPECIMEN" — 70.00

Sixtieth year of Queen Victoria's reign.
See Nos. 103-104, 110-112, 122-124.

Type of 1861
1897   Engr.   Wmk. 53   Perf. 11

101 A16	5sh red violet	105.00	29.00
a.	Horiz. pair, imperf. btwn.	11,000.	
b.	Perf. 11x12 or 12x11	130.00	42.50
c.	Perf. 12	140.00	52.50

Perf. 12x11½, 11½x12
1899, Oct.   Typo.   Wmk. 55

HALF PENNY:
Die I — Narrow "H" in "HALF."

102 A37	½p blue green, I	3.50	.95
a.	Imperf., pair	190.00	325.00
103 A39	2p ultra	5.75	.95
a.	Imperf., pair	325.00	
104 A40	2½p dk blue, II	8.00	3.25
a.	Imperf., pair	325.00	
104B A27	4p org brown	22.50	13.50
c.	4p red brown	24.00	12.00
d.	As "c," imperf. pair	750.00	
105 A28	6p emerald	135.00	52.50
a.	Imperf., pair	600.00	
106 A28	6p orange	29.00	6.75
a.	Imperf., pair	475.00	
b.	6p yellow	26.00	10.75
106C A29	8p magenta	42.50	8.00
	Nos. 102-106C (7)	246.25	85.90

Lyrebird A41   "Australia" A42

1903   Perf. 12x11½

107 A41	2sh6p blue green	87.50	42.50
	Overprinted "SPECIMEN"	85.00	

See Nos. 119, 131.

1903   Wmk. 70   Perf. 12½

108 A42	9p org brn & ultra	29.00	7.25
	Overprinted "SPECIMEN"	52.50	
a.	Perf. 11	5,250.	1,850.

See No. 128.

Type of 1885-86
1904   Wmk. 56   Perf. 12x11
"POSTAGE" in Blue

108B A24	10sh brt rose & vio	325.00	125.00
c.	Perf. 11	525.00	200.00
d.	Perf. 14	400.00	135.00
e.	10sh aniline crimson & violet, perf 12	650.00	200.00
f.	As "e," perf 12x11	475.00	130.00
g.	10sh claret & violet, chalky paper, perf 12x11	475.00	175.00

The watermark (NSW) of No. 108B is 20x7mm, with rounded angles in "N" and "W." On No. 75, the watermark is 21x7mm, with sharp angles in the "N" and "W."

HALF PENNY:
Die II — Wide "H" in "HALF."

Perf. 11, 11x12½, 12x11½ and Compound
1905-06   Wmk. 12

109 A37	½p blue grn, II	6.00	1.10
a.	½p blue green, I	6.25	1.10
b.	Booklet pane of 12	—	
110 A38	1p car rose, II	4.75	.50
a.	Booklet pane of 6	—	
b.	Booklet pane of 12	—	
111 A39	2p deep ultra	4.75	.50
112 A40	2½p dk blue, II	9.00	5.25
113 A27	4p org brown	21.00	8.75
a.	4p red brown	27.50	7.00
114 A28	6p orange	29.00	6.00
a.	6p yellow	35.00	6.00
b.	Perf. 11	525.00	
115 A29	8p magenta	52.50	11.00
117 A20	10p violet	32.50	10.00
118 A30	1sh vio brown	57.50	5.75
119 A41	2sh6p blue green	77.50	40.00

Wmk. 199
Perf. 12x11 or 11x12

120 A32	20sh ultra	225.00	87.50
a.	Perf 12	300.00	97.50
b.	Perf 11	225.00	80.50
	Nos. 109-115,117-120 (11)	519.50	176.35

1906-07   Wmk. 13

121 A37	½p green, I	8.75	3.25
122 A38	1p rose, II	17.00	2.25
123 A39	2p ultra	17.00	2.25
124 A40	2½p blue, II	110.00	200.00
125 A27	4p org brown	29.00	25.00
126 A28	6p orange	67.50	37.50
127 A29	8p red violet	42.50	37.50

128 A42	9p org brn & ultra, perf. 12x12½ ('06)	22.50	4.50
a.	Perf. 11	175.00	140.00
b.	9p org brn & ultra, perf. 12x12½	27.50	4.00
129 A20	10p violet	62.50	87.50
130 A30	1sh vio brown	92.50	18.00
a.	Perf. 11		
131 A41	2sh6p blue green	125.00	105.00
	Nos. 121-131 (11)	594.25	522.75

Portions of some of the sheets on which the above are printed show the watermark "COMMONWEALTH OF AUSTRALIA." Stamps may also be found from portions of the sheet without watermark.

SEMI-POSTAL STAMPS

SP1

Allegory of Charity SP2

1897, June   Wmk. 55   Perf. 11

B1 SP1	1p (1sh) grn & brn	72.50	72.50
B2 SP2	2½p (2sh6p) rose, bl & gold	350.00	350.00
	Nos. B1-B2 overprinted "SPECIMEN"	275.00	

Diamond Jubilee of Queen Victoria. The difference between the postal and face values of these stamps was donated to a fund for a home for consumptives.

REGISTRATION STAMPS

Queen Victoria — R1

Unwmk.
1856, Jan. 1   Engr.   Imperf.

F1 R1	(6p) orange & blue	1,400.	250.00
F2 R1	(6p) red & blue	1,400.	210.00
a.	Frame printed on back	7,000.	4,000.

1860   Perf. 12, 13

F3 R1	(6p) orange & blue	900.00	190.00
F4 R1	(6p) red & blue	625.00	90.00

Nos. F1 to F4 exist also on paper with papermaker's watermark in sheet.

1863   Wmk. 49

F5 R1	(6p) red & blue	250.00	47.50
a.	(6p) red & Prussian blue	275.00	40.00
b.	(6p) red & indigo	400.00	55.00
c.	Double impression of frame	—	800.00

Fifty varieties.
Nos. F1-F2 were reprinted on thin white wove unwatermarked paper and on thick yellowish wove unwatermarked paper; the former are usually overprinted "SPECIMEN."
No. F4 was reprinted on thin white wove unwatermarked paper; perf. 10 and overprinted "REPRINT" in black.

POSTAGE DUE STAMPS

D1

Perf. 10, 11, 11½, 12 and Compound
1891-92   Typo.   Wmk. 55

J1 D1	½p green, perf 10	10.00	10.00
a.	Chalky paper		
J2 D1	1p green	21.00	3.75
a.	Perf 12	45.00	9.00
b.	Chalky paper	19.00	6.25
J3 D1	2p green	29.00	5.75
a.	Perf 12x10	47.50	7.00
b.	Chalky paper	22.50	9.25
J4 D1	3p green	47.50	21.00
a.	Chalky paper	55.00	37.50
J5 D1	4p green	42.50	11.50
a.	Chalky paper	45.00	20.00
J6 D1	6p green, perf 10	27.50	17.50
J7 D1	8p green, perf 10	160.00	42.50
J8 D1	5sh green, perf 10	325.00	105.00
a.	Perf 11	575.00	175.00
b.	Perf 11x12	—	300.00

Perf. 12x10

J9 D1	10sh green	600.00	300.00
a.	Perf. 10	600.00	140.00
J10 D1	20sh green	700.00	300.00
a.	Perf. 10	1,000.	225.00
b.	Perf. 12	1,050.	
	Nos. J1-J10 (10)	1,962.	817.00

Used values for Nos. J8-J10 are for c-t-o stamps.

OFFICIAL STAMPS

Regular Issues Overprinted in Black or Red

Perf. 10, 11, 12, 13 and Compound
1879-80   Wmk. 54

O1 A17	1p red	30.00	5.75
a.	Perf. 10	350.00	65.00
b.	Perf. 10x13	72.50	9.50
O2 A18	2p blue	47.50	5.25
a.	Perf. 11x12	525.00	
b.	Perf. 10	525.00	77.50
O3 A15	3p green (R)	1,200.	700.00
O4 A15	3p green	350.00	60.00
a.	Watermarked "6"	—	925.00
b.	Double overprint		
c.	3p yel grn, perf 10	350.00	60.00
d.	3p yel grn, perf 12	425.00	175.00
O5 A19	4p red brown	400.00	21.00
a.	Perf. 10x13	450.00	190.00
O6 A11	5p dark green	42.50	27.50
O7 A21	6p lilac	600.00	20.00
a.	Perf. 10	800.00	75.00
b.	Perf. 13x10	450.00	90.00
O8 A13	8p yellow (R)	1,500.	400.00
O9 A13	8p yellow	—	52.50
a.	Perf. 10	625.00	175.00
O10 A23	1sh black (R)	600.00	17.50
a.	Perf. 10	—	35.00
b.	Perf. 10x13	—	77.50
c.	Perf. 13x10	—	29.00

1880   Wmk. 53

O11 A16	5sh lilac, perf. 11	475.00	175.00
a.	Double overprint	4,500.	2,400.
b.	Perf. 10	1,150.	375.00
c.	Perf. 12x10	1,000.	250.00
d.	Perf. 13	1,350.	225.00
e.	Perf. 10x12		

Two No. O14 overprint types: Type I, "O" and "S" 7mm apart. Type II, "O" and "S" 5.5mm apart.

1881   Wmk. 55

O12 A17	1p red	35.00	6.00
a.	Perf. 10x13	—	200.00
O13 A18	2p blue	21.00	2.40
a.	Perf. 10	400.00	200.00
O14 A15	3p green (I)	17.50	8.50
a.	Double overprint (I)	—	1,200.
b.	Perf. 12	325.00	200.00
c.	Perf. 11		
d.	Type II ovpt	25.00	15.00
e.	As "b," type II ovpt	350.00	250.00
f.	Wmk sideways	25.00	8.00
O15 A19	4p red brown	35.00	7.50
a.	Perf. 10x12	350.00	200.00
b.	Perf. 12	350.00	350.00

O16 A11	5p dark green	32.50	35.00
a.	Perf. 12	250.00	
b.	Perf. 12x10	—	—
c.	Perf. 12x11 ('85)	65.00	16.00
O17 A21	6p lilac	50.00	11.50
a.	Perf. 12	—	105.00
b.	Perf. 11x12	—	—
c.	Perf. 12x11 ('85)	100.00	27.50
O18 A13	8p yellow	57.50	25.00
a.	Double overprint	—	—
b.	Perf. 12	350.00	525.00
c.	Perf. 11 ('85)	52.50	32.50
d.	Perf. 10x12 or 12x10 ('85)	52.50	25.00
e.	Triple overprint		
O19 A23	1sh black (R)	72.50	21.00
a.	Double overprint	—	525.00
b.	Perf. 10x13	—	140.00
c.	Perf. 11x12, comb.	—	21.00
	Nos. O12-O19 (8)	321.00	116.90

Beware of other red overprints on watermark 55 stamps.

1881   Wmk. 56

O20 A17	1p red	105.00	17.50

1887-90

O21 A24	10sh on #75	—	3,200.
O22 A24	£1 on #75A	19,500.	9,250.

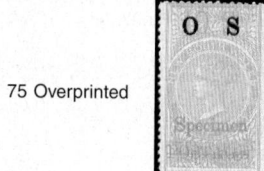

No. 75 Overprinted

1889

O23 A24	10sh rose & vio	4,500.	1,500.
	Overprinted "SPECIMEN"	125.00	
a.	Perf. 10	7,000.	2,750.

Overprinted

1888-89   Wmk. 55

O24 A25	1p violet	6.25	2.00
a.	Overprinted "O" only		
O25 A26	2p blue	9.50	1.40
O26 A27	4p red brown	25.00	9.50
O27 A28	6p carmine	18.00	12.00
O28 A29	8p red lilac	47.50	32.50
a.	Perf 12	60.00	40.00
O29 A30	1sh vio brown	45.00	9.50
a.	Double overprint		
b.	1sh purple brown, perf 12	45.00	9.50
c.	1sh maroon, perf 11x12 ('90)	45.00	9.50
d.	1sh maroon, perf 12	45.00	9.50
	Nos. O24-O29 (6)	151.25	66.90

Wmk. 53

O30 A31	5sh violet (R)	1,500.	650.00
O31 A32	20sh ultra	3,750.	1,100.

1890   Wmk. 57

O32 A31	5sh violet	425.00	175.00
a.	5sh, dull lilac, perf. 12	1,200.	325.00
b.	5sh lilac, perf 10	425.00	160.00

Wmk. 58

O33 A32	20sh ultra	4,000.	3,500.
	O32b, O33 ovptd. "SPECIMEN"	325.00	

Centenary of the founding of the Colony (Nos. O24-O33).

1891   Wmk. 55

O34 A17(a)	½p on 1p gray & black	125.00	125.00
a.	Double overprint		
O35 A33	2½p ultra	24.00	14.00
O36 A21(b)	7½p on 6p brn & black	72.50	85.00
O37 A23(b)	12½p on 1sh red & black	125.00	140.00

1892

O38 A37	½p gray, perf 11x12	12.50	24.00
a.	Perf 10	16.00	27.50
b.	Perf 12	15.00	20.00
c.	Perf 12x11½	27.50	22.50
	Overprinted "SPECIMEN"	45.00	

1894   **Wmk. 54**

O39	A22	9p on 10p red brn	800.00 675.00
		Overprinted "SPECI-MEN"	85.00

Wmk. 52

O40	A20	10p lilac, perf. 13	325.00 *175.00*
a.		Perf. 11x10 or 10x11	475.00 *450.00*
b.		Perf 10	400.00
c.		Double overprint, one albino	
		Overprinted "SPECI-MEN"	75.00

The official stamps became obsolete on Dec. 31, 1894. In Aug., 1895, sets of 32 varieties of "O.S." stamps, together with some envelopes and postal cards, were placed on sale at the Sydney post office at £2 per set.

These sets contained most of the varieties listed above and a few which are not known in the original issues. An obliteration consisting of the letters G.P.O. or N.S.W. in three concentric ovals was lightly applied to the center of each block of four stamps.

It is understood that the earlier stamps and many of the overprints were reprinted to make up these sets.

QUEENSLAND

ˈkwēnzˌland

LOCATION — Northeastern part of Australia
GOVT. — British Crown Colony
AREA — 670,500 sq. mi.
POP. — 498,129 (1901)
CAPITAL — Brisbane

Originally a part of New South Wales, Queensland was constituted a separate colony in 1859. It was one of the six British Colonies that united in 1901 to form the Commonwealth of Australia.

12 Pence = 1 Shilling
20 Shillings = 1 Pound

MORETON BAY

Until 1860, Queensland, then known as Moreton Bay, utilized the postal service of New South Wales, and stamps of New South Wales were used until November 1, 1860. The New South Wales post offices in Queensland, with their opening dates and assigned canceler numbers, were:

Post Office	Opened
Brisbane	1834 (#95)
Burnett's Inn (became Goodes Inn)	1850 (#108)
Callandoon	1850 (#74)
Condamine	1856 (#151)
Dalby	1854 (#133)
Drayton	1846 (#85)
Gayndah	1850 (#86)
Gladstone	1854 (#131)
Goodes Inn	1858 (#108)
Ipswich	1846 (#87)
Maryborough	1849 (#96)
Rockhampton	1858 (#201)
Surat	1852 (#110)
Taroom	1856 (#152)
Toowoomba	1858 (#214)
Warwick	1848 (#81)

Values for unused stamps are for examples with original gum as defined in the catalogue introduction. Very fine examples of Nos. 4-73, 84-125, 128-140, and F1-F3b will have perforations touching the design on at least one or more sides due to the narrow spacing of the stamps on the plates. Stamps with perfs clear of the design on all four sides are scarce and will command higher prices.

Watermarks

Wmk. 5 — Small Star

Wmk. 6 — Large Star

Wmk. 12 — Crown and Single-lined A

Wmk. 13 — Crown and Double-lined A

Wmk. 65 — "Queensland Postage Stamps" in Sheet in Script Capitals

Wmk. 66

Wmks. 66 & 67 — "Queensland" in Large Single-lined Roman Capitals in the Sheet and Short-pointed Star to Each Stamp (Stars Vary Slightly in Size and Shape)

Wmk. 68 — Crown and Q

Wmk. 69 — Large Crown and Q

There are two varieties of the watermark 68, differing slightly in the position and shape of the crown and the tongue of the "Q."

Wmk. 70 — V and Crown

Queen Victoria — A1

Wmk. 6

		1860, Nov. 1 Engr.	Imperf.
1	A1	1p deep rose	4,500. 1,050.
2	A1	2p deep blue	12,000. 2,250.
3	A1	6p deep green	8,500. 1,050.

Clean-Cut Perf. 14 to 16

4	A1	1p deep rose	2,750. 375.
5	A1	2p deep blue	1,050. 140.
a.		Horiz. pair, imperf between	— 4,250.
6	A1	6p deep green	1,050. 110.

Clean-Cut Perf. 14 to 16

		1860-61	Wmk. 5
6A	A1	2p blue	925.00 135.00
b.		Horiz. pair, imperf. vert	— 4,000.
6D	A1	3p brown ('61)	550.00 110.00
6E	A1	6p deep green	1,000. 95.00
6F	A1	1sh gray violet	1,050. 120.00

Regular Perf. 14

6H	A1	1p rose	225.00 62.50
6I	A1	2p deep blue	625.00 105.00

Rough Perf. 14 to 16

7	A1	1p deep rose	115.00 57.50
8	A1	2p blue	185.00 52.50
a.		Horiz. pair, imperf between	5,250. —
9	A1	3p brown ('61)	105.00 60.00
a.		Horiz. pair, imperf. vert.	5,250. —
10	A1	6p deep green	275.00 52.50
a.		6p yellow green	400.00 42.50
11	A1	1sh dull violet	800.00 140.00

Thick Yellowish Paper

Square Perf. 12½ to 13

		1862-67	Unwmk.
12	A1	1p Indian red	575.00 115.00
13	A1	1p orange ('63)	140.00 22.50
a.		Perf. 13, round holes ('67)	160.00 42.50
b.		Horiz. pair, imperf. between	— 2,000.
c.		Imperf., pair	— 2,000.
14	A1	2p deep blue	100.00 15.00
a.		2p pale blue	200.00 60.00
b.		Perf. 13, round holes ('67)	100.00 27.50
c.		Imperf., pair	— 2,000.
e.		Horiz. pair, imperf. between	— 2,400.
f.		Vert. pair, imperf. between	4,500. —
15	A1	3p brown ('63)	105.00 62.50
a.		Imperf.	—
b.		Perf. 13, round holes ('67)	130.00 60.00
16	A1	6p yellow grn ('63)	195.00 32.50
a.		6p green	240.00 100.00
b.		Perf. 13, round holes ('67)	200.00 32.50
c.		Imperf., pair	— 2,400.
d.		Horiz. pair, imperf. between	— 2,400.
e.		6p apple green ('63)	225.00 37.50
17	A1	1sh gray ('63)	500.00 47.50
b.		Imperf. horizontally	—
c.		Horiz. pair, imperf. between	— 3,500.
d.		Perf. 13, round holes ('67)	500.00 47.50
e.		Vert. pair, imperf between	—

White Wove Paper

		1865 Wmk. 5	Rough Perf. 13
18	A1	1p orange	120.00 40.00
a.		Horiz. pair, imperf. between	1,600.
19	A1	2p light blue	130.00 30.00
a.		Vert. pair, imperf. between	2,750.
b.		Half used as 1p on cover	4,500.
20	A1	6p yellow green	180.00 45.00
		Nos. 18-20 (3)	430.00 115.00

		1865	Perf. 12½x13
18B	A1	1p orange vermilion	140.00 75.00
19C	A1	2p blue	175.00 75.00

Perf. 13, Round Holes

		1866	Wmk. 65
21	A1	1p orange vermilion	250.00 52.50
22	A1	2p blue	100.00 32.50
b.		Diagonal half used as 1p on cover	—

		1865	Perf. 12½x13
21A	A1	1p orange vermilion	250.00 75.00
22C	A1	2p blue	250.00 75.00

		1866 Unwmk. Litho.	Perf. 13
23	A1	4p lilac	240.00 42.50
a.		4p slate	325.00 42.50
		Handstamped "SPECI-MEN"	65.00

24	A1	5sh pink	975.00 250.00
a.		5sh bright rose	400.00 92.50
		Handstamped "SPECI-MEN"	67.50
b.		Vert. pair, imperf between	— 3,500.

Wmk. 66, 67

		1868-74 Engr.	Perf. 13
25	A1	1p orange ('71)	87.50 9.25
26	A1	2p blue	72.50 6.00
a.		2p pale blue	75.00 6.50
b.		2p bright blue	82.50 4.75
c.		2p greenish blue	175.00 4.25
d.		2p dark blue	75.00 4.25
27	A1	3p grnsh brn ('71)	175.00 12.50
a.		3p brown	115.00 11.50
b.		3p olive brown	180.00 11.50
28	A1	6p yel green ('71)	250.00 14.00
a.		6p deep green	325.00 35.00
b.		6p green	240.00 18.00
30	A1	1sh grnsh gray ('72)	750.00 175.00
31	A1	1sh violet ('74)	400.00 37.50
a.		1sh brownish gray	750.00 175.00

Perf. 12

32	A1	1p orange	600.00 47.50
33	A1	2p blue	140.00 75.00
34	A1	3p brown	875.00 325.00
a.		3p greenish gray	— 325.00
35	A1	6p deep green	1,600. 52.50
36	A1	1sh violet	900.00 87.50

Perf. 13x12

36A	A1	1p orange	250.00
37	A1	2p blue	*1,600.* 50.00
37A	A1	3p brown	*1,250.*

The reprints are perforated 13 and the colors differ slightly from those of the originals.

		1868-75 Wmk. 68	Perf. 13
38	A1	1p orange	115.00 8.75
a.		Imperf pair	575.00
39	A1	1p rose ('74)	105.00 17.00
a.		1p deep rose red	175.00 16.00
40	A1	2p blue	62.50 4.00
a.		Vert. pair, imperf between	—
b.		Imperf., pair	725.00
c.		2p pale blue ('74)	92.50 8.50
41	A1	3p brown ('75)	140.00 21.00
42	A1	6p yel green ('69)	185.00 14.00
a.		6p apple green	240.00 17.50
b.		6p deep green	225.00 17.50
c.		As "a," imperf pair	725.00
43	A1	1sh violet ('75)	375.00 87.50
		Nos. 38-43 (6)	*982.50* 152.25

		1876-78	Perf. 12
44	A1	1p orange	72.50 9.50
a.		Imperf.	775.00
b.		1p pale org vermilion	85.00 9.75
c.		Vert. pair, imperf. between	—
45	A1	1p rose	90.00 20.00
a.		1p salmon	115.00 20.00
46	A1	2p blue	70.00 2.40
a.		2p pale blue	160.00 29.00
b.		2p deep blue	70.00 3.50
47	A1	3p brown	125.00 17.50
48	A1	6p yellow green	250.00 9.50
a.		6p apple green	300.00 15.50
b.		6p deep green	250.00 16.00
c.		6p green	290.00 9.25
49	A1	1sh violet	75.00 17.50
m.		Vert. pair, imperf between	—
n.		1sh purple	240.00 9.75
		Nos. 44-49 (6)	682.50 76.40

Nos. 44, 49 exist in vertical pairs, imperf. between.

Perf. 13x12

49B	A1	1p orange	300.00
49C	A1	2p blue	*1,500.* 325.00
49D	A1	4p yellow	575.00
49E	A1	6p deep green	575.00

Perf. 12½x13

49G	A1	1p orange vermilion	700.00
49H	A1	2p deep blue	700.00

The reprints are perforated 12 and are in paler colors than the originals.

		1879 Unwmk.	Perf. 12
50	A1	6p pale emerald	450.00 40.00
a.		Horiz. pair, imperf. vert.	2,250.

A2

		1875-81 Litho. Wmk. 68	Perf. 13
50B	A1	4p yellow ('75)	1,250. 100.00
a.		Handstamped "SPECI-MEN"	100.00

Perf. 12

51	A1	4p buff ('76)	1,000. 30.00
a.		4p yellow	1,000. 32.00

52	A1	2sh pale blue ('81)	180.00	57.50
		Fiscal cancellation		5.75
a.		2sh deep blue	200.00	57.50
b.		Imperf.		
c.		2sh blue	190.00	57.50
53	A2	2sh6p lt red ('81)	325.00	175.00
		Fiscal cancellation		5.75
a.		2sh6p bright scarlet	325.00	150.00
54	A1	5sh orange brn ('81)	425.00	200.00
		Fiscal cancellation		7.00
a.		5sh fawn	425.00	200.00
55	A1	10sh brown ('81)	875.00	400.00
		Fiscal cancellation		7.00
a.		Imperf., pair	1,750.	
b.		10sh bister brown	750.00	350.00
56	A1	20sh rose ('81)	2,900.00	675.00
		Fiscal cancellation		9.25
		Nos. 50B-56 (7)	6,955.	1,637.

Nos. 53-56, 62-64, 74-83 with pen (revenue) cancellations removed are often offered as unused.

A3

1879-81   Typo.   Wmk. 68   Perf. 12

57	A3	1p rose red	62.50	14.00
a.		1p red orange	87.50	21.00
b.		1p brown orange	115.00	29.00
c.		"QUEENSLAND"	1,375.	—
d.		Imperf.		—
e.		Vert. pair, imperf. horiz.		1,100.
58	A3	2p gray blue	115.00	7.25
a.		2p deep ultra	120.00	7.25
b.		Imperf.		—
c.		"PENGE"	800.00	125.00
d.		"TW" joined	87.50	7.25
e.		Vert. pair, imperf. horiz.		1,750.
59	A3	4p orange yellow	350.00	42.50
a.		Imperf.		—
60	A3	6p yellow green	125.00	12.50
a.		Imperf.		—
61	A3	1sh pale violet ('81)	140.00	15.00
a.		1sh deep violet	125.00	14.00
		Nos. 57-61 (5)	792.50	91.25

The stamps of type A3 were electrotyped from plates made up of groups of four types, differing in minor details. Two dies were used for the 1p and 2p, giving eight varieties for each of those values.
Nos. 59-60 exist imperf. vertically.
For surcharge see No. 65.

Moiré on Back

1878-79   Unwmk.

62	A3	1p brown org ('79)	725.00	100.00
a.		"QOEENSLAND"	2,000.	
63	A3	2p deep ultra ('79)	650.00	57.50
a.		"PENGE"	4,750.	900.00
64	A1	1sh red violet	250.00	115.00
		Nos. 62-64 (3)	1,625.	272.50

No. 57b Surcharged
Vertically in Black

1880   Wmk. 68

65	A3	½p on 1p brn org	600.00	1,850.
a.		"QUEENSLAND"	2,000.	1,100.

On No. 65, the surcharge reads from bottom to top. Stamps with surcharges reading downward are fakes.

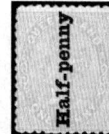

A4

1882-83   Typo.   Perf. 12

66	A4	1p pale red	8.50	1.10
a.		1p rose	9.00	1.10
b.		Imperf. pair		—
c.		1p deep vermilion	8.50	1.15
67	A4	2p gray blue	12.00	1.10
a.		2p deep ultra	13.00	1.10
b.		Horiz. pair, imperf between		—
68	A4	4p yellow ('83)	35.00	4.75
a.		"PENGE"	325.00	70.00
b.		Imperf., single		—
69	A4	6p yellow green	26.50	3.25
70	A4	1sh violet ('83)	35.00	7.25
a.		1sh lilac	17.50	4.50
b.		1sh deep purple	35.00	7.25
c.		1sh pale mauve	20.00	4.00
		Nos. 66-70 (5)	117.00	17.45

There are eight minor varieties of the 1p, twelve of the 2p and four each of the other values. On the 1p there is a period after

"PENNY." On all values the lines of shading on the neck extend from side to side.
Compare design A4 with A6, A10, A11, A15, A16.

1883   Perf. 9½x12

71	A4	1p rose	250.00	77.50
72	A4	2p gray blue	850.00	92.50
73	A4	1sh pale violet	425.00	95.00
		Nos. 71-73 (3)	1,525.	265.00

Beware of faked perfs.
See Nos. 94, 95, 100.

A5

Wmk. 68 Twice Sideways
1882-85   Engr.   Perf. 12
Thin Paper

74	A5	2sh ultra	225.00	60.00
75	A5	2sh6p vermilion	160.00	32.50
76	A5	5sh car rose ('85)	125.00	35.00
77	A5	10sh brown	425.00	110.00
78	A5	£1 dk grn ('83)	650.00	250.00
		Nos. 74-78 (5)	1,585.	487.50

The 2sh, 5sh and £1 exist imperf.
There are two varieties of the watermark on Nos. 74-78, as in the 1879-81 issue.
Stamps with revenue cancels sell for $3.25-6.50.

1886   Wmk. 69   Perf. 12
Thick Paper

79	A5	2sh ultra	250.00	52.50
80	A5	2sh6p vermilion	87.50	35.00
81	A5	5sh car rose	80.00	62.50
82	A5	10sh dark brown	185.00	70.00
83	A5	£1 dark green	425.00	125.00
		Nos. 79-83 (5)	1,027.	345.00

High value stamps with cancellations removed are offered as unused.
Stamps with revenue cancels sell for $3.25-6.50.
See Nos. 126-127, 141-144.

A6

Redrawn
1887-89   Typo.   Wmk. 68   Perf. 12

84	A6	1p orange	9.50	1.40
85	A6	2p gray blue	14.00	1.40
a.		2p deep ultra	18.00	1.75
b.		Half used as 1c on cover		—
86	A6	2sh red brown ('89)	130.00	72.50
		Perf. 9½x12		
88	A6	2p deep ultra	775.00	125.00
		Nos. 84-88 (4)	928.50	200.30

The 1p has no period after the value.
In the redrawn stamps the shading lines on the neck are not completed at the left, leaving an irregular white line along that side.
Variety "LA" joined exists on Nos. 84-86, 88, 90, 91, 93, 97, 98, 102.
On No. 88 beware of faked perfs.

A7   A8

1890-92   Perf. 12½, 13

89	A7	½p green	9.50	3.25
a.		½p green	9.75	3.25
b.		½p deep blue green	8.50	3.25
90	A6	1p orange red	6.25	1.00
a.		Imperf., pair	275.00	275.00
b.		Double impression		650.00
91	A6	2p gray blue	11.50	.70
a.		2p pale blue	11.50	.70
92	A8	2½p rose carmine	24.00	7.25
93	A6	3p brown ('92)	17.50	5.75
94	A4	4p orange	27.50	4.75
a.		"PENGE" for "PENCE"	125.00	42.50
b.		4p orange yellow	37.50	4.75
c.		As "b," "PENGE" for "PENCE"	160.00	42.50
d.		4p yellow	42.50	4.75
e.		As "d," "PENGE" for "PENCE"	180.00	52.50
95	A6	6p green	21.00	3.25
96	A6	2sh red brown	105.00	57.50
a.		2sh pale brown	115.00	62.50
		Nos. 89-96 (8)	222.25	83.45

The ½p and 3p exist imperf.

1895   Wmk. 69   Perf. 12½, 13
Thick Paper

98	A6	1p orange	8.75	.95
a.		1p reddish vermilion	11.50	1.15
99	A6	2p gray blue	4.50	.50
		Perf. 12		
100	A4	1sh pale violet	25.00	11.50
		Nos. 98-100 (3)	38.25	12.95

A9   A10

Moiré on Back
1895   Unwmk.   Perf. 12½, 13

101	A9	½p green	8.75	4.50
a.		Without moire	80.00	
b.		½p deep green	8.50	4.50
102	A6	1p orange	4.75	1.10
a.		"PE" missing	350.00	350.00
b.		1p reddish vermilion	4.75	1.10
		Wmk. 68		
103	A9	½p green	4.50	2.00
a.		½p deep green	4.50	2.00
b.		Printed on both sides	200.00	
c.		Double impression		—
104	A10	1p orange	4.75	.70
a.		1p pale red	6.25	.70
105	A10	2p gray blue	14.00	1.40
		Wmk. 69		
		Thick Paper		
106	A9	½p green, perf 12½	6.00	3.75
a.		Perf 13	6.00	3.25
b.		Perf 12	27.50	
c.		1p deep green, perf 12	32.50	

1895-96   Unwmk.   Thin Paper
Crown and Q Faintly Impressed

107	A9	½p green	4.50	4.50
108	A10	1p orange	6.00	3.75
108A	A6	2p gray blue	22.50	250.00

A11   A12

A13

1895-96   Wmk. 68

109	A11	1p red	11.50	1.05
110	A12	2½p blue green	27.50	9.25
a.		2½p carmine	27.50	9.25
111	A13	5p violet brown	35.00	9.25
111A	A11	6p yellow green	22,500.	

Only a few used examples of No. 111A are known, and readable cancels are from 1902. It is suggested that this otherwise unissued design was accidentally included in the plate of No. 120.

A14   A15

A16   A17

A18   A19

TWO PENCE:
Type I — Point of bust does not touch frame.
Type II — First redrawing. The top of the crown, the chignon and the point of the bust touch the frame. The forehead is completely shaded.
Type III — Second redrawing. The top of crown does not touch the frame, though the chignon and the point of the bust do. The forehead and the bridge of the nose are not shaded.

1897-1900   Perf. 12½, 13

112	A14	½p deep green	10.00	10.00
a.		Perf. 12		225.00
113	A15	1p red	4.75	.60
a.		Perf. 12	15.00	5.75
114	A16	2p gray blue (I)	6.25	.60
a.		Perf. 12	1,000.	7.00
115	A17	2½p rose	47.50	37.50
116	A17	2½p violet, *blue*	18.00	4.50
117	A15	3p brown	21.00	4.50
118	A15	4p bright yellow	21.00	4.50
119	A18	5p violet brown	17.50	4.50
120	A15	6p yellow green	17.50	4.50
121	A19	1sh lilac	26.00	4.75
a.		1sh light violet	32.50	7.25
122	A19	2sh turq blue	65.00	45.00
		Nos. 112-122 (11)	254.50	120.95

See Nos. 130-140.

1898   Serrated Roulette 13

123	A15	1p scarlet	12.00	7.75
a.		Serrated and perf. 13	16.00	11.50
b.		Serrated in black	24.00	17.50
c.		Serrated without color and in black	24.00	35.00
d.		Same as "b," and perf. 13	125.00	175.00
e.		Same as "c," and perf. 13	125.00	175.00

Victoria — A20

1899   Typo.   Perf. 12, 12½, 13

124	A20	½p blue green	5.25	4.00
a.		½p green, perf 12	175.00	87.50
b.		½p pale green	5.25	4.00

Unwatermarked stamps are proofs.

"Australia" — A21

NINE PENCE:
Type I — "QUEENSLAND" 18x1½mm.
Type II — "QUEENSLAND" 17½x1¼mm.

1903   Wmk. 70   Perf. 12½

125	A21	9p org brn & ultra, II	35.00	7.75
a.		Type I	35.00	7.75

See No. 128.

Type of 1882
1903-06   Wmk. 68   Perf. 12, 12½-13
Typographed, Perf. 12½-13 Irreg. ('03)

125B	A5	5sh rose	200.00	92.50
125C	A5	£1 dark green	2,250.	750.00

Lithographed, Perf. 12 ('05-'06)

126	A5	5sh rose	120.00	92.50
127	A5	£1 dark green	550.00	140.00
c.		Perf. 12½-13 Irreg.	1,250.	210.00

1907   Typo.   Wmk. 13   Perf. 12½

128	A21	9p yel brn & ultra,	25.00	6.50
a.		Type I	77.50	7.75
b.		Perf. 11, type II	5,500.	750.00

1907   Wmk. 68   Perf. 12½, 13

129	A16	2p ultra, type II	17.50	7.25
129A	A18	5p dark brown	16.00	6.50
b.		5p olive brown	12.50	4.75

Queensland (continued)

1907-09   **Wmk. 12**

130	A20	½p deep green	3.50	5.75
131	A15	1p red	5.75	.85
a.		Imperf., pair	475.00	
132	A16	2p ultra, II	14.00	2.40
133	A16	2p ultra, III	7.25	.75
134	A15	3p pale brown	24.00	4.50
135	A15	4p bright yellow	21.00	5.75
136	A15	4p gray black ('09)	32.50	9.00
137	A18	5p brown	20.00	11.50
a.		5p olive brown	25.00	12.50
138	A15	6p yellow green	21.00	7.75
139	A19	1sh violet	22.50	6.00
140	A19	2sh turquoise bl	55.00	37.50

Wmk. 12 Sideways
Litho.

141	A5	2sh6p deep orange	77.50	60.00
a.		2sh6p dull orange ('10)	125.00	115.00
b.		2sh6p reddish orange ('12)	325.00	375.00
142	A5	5sh rose	120.00	82.50
a.		5sh deep rose ('10)	140.00	115.00
b.		5sh carmine red ('12)	350.00	425.00
143	A5	10sh dark brown	225.00	120.00
a.		10sh sepia ('12)	725.00	575.00
144	A5	£1 blue green	400.00	140.00
a.		£1 dp blue green ('10)	600.00	400.00
b.		£1 yellow green ('12)	2,200.	1,350.
		Nos. 130-144 (15)	1,049.	494.25

POSTAL FISCAL STAMPS

Authorized for postal use from Jan. 1, 1880. Authorization withdrawn July 1, 1892.

Used values are for examples with postal cancellations used from Jan. 1, 1880 through June 30, 1892.

Beware of stamps with a pen cancellation removed and a fake postmark added.

Queen Victoria
PF1   PF2

1866-74   **Engr.**   **Unwmk.**   **Perf. 13**

AR1	PF1	1p blue	105.00	47.50
AR2	PF1	6p violet	250.00	175.00
AR3	PF1	1sh green	240.00	140.00
AR4	PF1	2sh brown	260.00	140.00
AR5	PF1	2sh 6p red	475.00	275.00
AR6	PF1	5sh yellow	925.00	375.00
AR7	PF1	6sh yellow	1,250.	
AR8	PF1	10sh yellow green	925.00	325.00
AR9	PF1	20sh rose	1,250.	500.00

Wmk. 68

AR10	PF1	1p blue	52.50	47.50
AR11	PF1	6p violet	115.00	115.00
AR12	PF1	6p blue	425.00	325.00
AR13	PF1	1sh green	125.00	92.50
AR14	PF1	2sh brown	200.00	110.00
AR15	PF1	5sh yellow	650.00	225.00
AR16	PF1	10sh yellow green	925.00	325.00
AR17	PF1	20sh rose	1,250.	500.00

1872-73   **Wmk. 69**   **Perf. 13**

AR18	PF2	1p lilac	35.00	29.00
AR19	PF2	6p brown	175.00	87.50
AR20	PF2	1sh green	200.00	105.00
AR21	PF2	2sh blue	325.00	140.00
AR22	PF2	2sh 6p vermilion	400.00	200.00
AR23	PF2	5sh orange brown	275.00	120.00
AR24	PF2	10sh brown	600.00	225.00
AR25	PF2	20sh rose	1,100.	325.00

Perf. 12

AR26	PF2	1p lilac	35.00	29.00
AR27	PF2	6p brown	175.00	87.50
AR28	PF2	2sh blue	325.00	140.00
AR29	PF2	2sh 6p vermilion	200.00	100.00
AR30	PF2	5sh orange brown	275.00	125.00
AR31	PF2	10sh brown	600.00	225.00
AR32	PF2	20sh rose	1,100.	325.00

Unwmk.
Perf. 13

AR33	PF2	1p lilac	40.00	20.00
AR34	PF2	6p lilac	200.00	100.00
AR35	PF2	6p brown	175.00	77.50
AR36	PF2	1sh green	115.00	47.50
AR37	PF2	2sh blue	140.00	115.00
AR38	PF2	2sh 6p vermilion	250.00	125.00
AR39	PF2	5sh orange brown	400.00	140.00
AR40	PF2	10sh brown	650.00	225.00
AR41	PF2	20sh rose	1,100.	325.00

Perf. 12

AR42	PF2	1p lilac	40.00	20.00
AR43	PF2	6p lilac	200.00	100.00
AR44	PF2	6p brown	175.00	77.50
AR45	PF2	1sh green	115.00	47.50
AR46	PF2	2sh blue	140.00	115.00
AR47	PF2	2sh 6p vermilion	250.00	125.00
AR48	PF2	5sh orange brown	400.00	140.00
AR49	PF2	10sh brown	650.00	225.00
AR50	PF2	20sh rose	1,100.	325.00

Queen Victoria — PF3

1878-79   **Engr.**   **Unwmk.**   **Perf. 12**

AR51	PF3	1p violet	275.00	140.00

Wmk. 68

AR52	PF3	1p violet	175.00	105.00

SEMI-POSTAL STAMPS

Queen Victoria, Colors and Bearers — SP1

SP2

Perf. 12, 12½
1900, June 19   **Wmk. 68**

B1	SP1	1p red lilac	225.00	200.00
		On cover		575.00
B2	SP2	2p deep violet	600.00	525.00
		On cover		700.00
		Nos. B1-B2 on one cover		1,000.

These stamps were sold at 1sh and 2sh respectively. The difference was applied to a patriotic fund in connection with the Boer War.

REGISTRATION STAMPS

R1

Clean-Cut Perf. 14 to 16
1861   **Wmk. 5**   **Engr.**

F1	R1	(6p) olive yellow	675.00	125.00
a.		Horiz. pair, imperf. vert.	8,000.	

Rough Perf. 14 to 16

F2	R1	(6p) dull yellow	110.00	72.50

1864   **Perf. 12½ to 13**

F3	R1	(6p) golden yellow	125.00	50.00
a.		Imperf.		
b.		Double impression	2,750.	2,750.

The reprints are watermarked with a small truncated star and perforated 12.

SOUTH AUSTRALIA

'sauth o-'strāl-yə

LOCATION — Central part of southern Australia
GOVT. — British Colony
AREA — 380,070 sq. mi.
POP. — 358,346 (1901)
CAPITAL — Adelaide

South Australia was one of the six British colonies that united in 1901 to form the Commonwealth of Australia.

12 Pence = 1 Shilling
20 Shillings = 1 Pound

Values for unused stamps are for examples with original gum as defined in the catalogue introduction.

Very fine examples of Nos. 10-60 and O1-O60 will have perforations slightly cutting into the framelines or design on one or more sides due to the narrow spacing of the stamps on the plates.

Stamps with perfs clear on all sides are scarce to rare and will command higher to substantially higher prices.

Watermarks

Wmk. 6 — Star with Long Narrow Points   Wmk. 7 — Star with Short Broad Points

Wmk. 70 — Crown and V   Wmk. 72 — Crown and SA

Wmk. 73 — Crown and SA, Letters Close

Wmk. 74 — Crown and Single-lined A

Queen Victoria — A1

1855-56   **Engr.**   **Wmk. 6**   *Imperf.*
London Print

1	A1	1p dark green	7,500.	525.
2	A1	2p dull carmine	750.	100.
3	A1	6p deep blue	2,800.	200.
4	A1	1sh violet ('56)	15,000.	

No. 4 was never put in use. Nos. 1 and 3 without watermark are proofs.

Six examples each of Nos. 1-4 were hand-stamped "CANCELLED" in oval in 1855-56 by the printers, Perkins Bacon, for presentation to members of Sir Rowland Hill's family. Values, from $12,500.

1856-59   **Local Print**

5	A1	1p deep yel grn ('58)	10,000.	675.00
a.		1p yellow green ('58)	8,500.	800.00
6	A1	2p blood red	2,250.	90.00
a.		Printed on both sides		1,100.
b.		2p orange red ('56)	2,250.	97.50
7	A1	2p pale red ('57)	800.	55.00
a.		Printed on both sides		900.00
8	A1	6p slate blue ('57)	3,750.	210.00
9	A1	1sh orange ('57)	7,500.	500.00
a.		Printed on both sides	—	625.00
b.		1sh red orange		

1858-59   *Rouletted*

10	A1	1p yellow grn ('59)	1,150.	110.00
a.		Horiz. pair, imperf. between	—	—
b.		1p pale yellow green ('59)	1,150.	115.00
11	A1	2p pale red ('59)	180.00	37.50
a.		Printed on both sides		1,150.
12	A1	6p slate blue	650.00	70.00
13	A1	1sh orange ('59)	1,500.	55.00
c.		Printed on both sides		1,600.

See Nos. 14-16, 19-20, 25-26, 28-29, 32, 35-36, 41-43, 47, 51-52, 69-70, 73, 113, 118. For overprints see Nos. O1-O2, O5, O7, O9, O11-O13, O17, O20, O27, O30, O32, O39-O40, O42, O52, O76, O85.

A2   A3

Surcharge on #22-24, 34, 49-50

1860-69   *Rouletted*

14	A1	1p dull blue green	100.00	57.50
a.		1p deep green	525.00	92.50
b.		1p bright green	110.00	47.50
15	A1	1p sage green	130.00	57.50
a.		1p deep yellow green ('69)	200.00	
b.		1p pale sage green ('65)	100.00	
16	A1	2p vermilion ('62)	120.00	7.25
a.		Horiz. pair, imperf. btwn.	3,100.	650.00
b.		Rouletted and perf. all around	2,100.	550.00
c.		2p pale red	120.00	5.75
d.		As "c," printed on both sides	—	750.00
e.		2p bright vermilion ('64)	200.00	5.25
18	A2	4p dull violet ('67)	130.00	40.00
19	A1	6p grnsh bl ('63)	140.00	7.25
20	A1	6p dull blue ('62)	200.00	11.50
a.		6p sky blue	200.00	11.50
b.		6p Prussian blue	1,100.	9,000.
c.		Horiz. pair, imperf btwn.		2,000.
d.		6p ultramarine	140.00	7.25
e.		Horiz. pair, imperf. btwn. (#20f)	—	1,600.
f.		6p indigo blue		100.00
g.		Rouletted and perf. all around (#20f)		575.00
h.		6p violet blue	260.00	10.00
i.		6p violet ultramarine ('68)	240.00	9.25
21	A3	9p gray lilac ('69)	100.00	16.00
a.		Double impression	—	
b.		Horiz. pair, imperf between		2,500.
c.		Rouletted and perf. all around	2,150.	250.00
22	A3	10p on 9p red org (Bl) ('66)	350.00	62.50
23	A3	10p on 9p yel (Bl) ('67)	625.00	47.50

No.	Design	Description	Unused	Used
24	A3	10p on 9p yel (Blk) ('69)	2,800.	72.50
a.		Inverted surcharge		5,000.
c.		Printed on both sides		1,250.
d.		Rouletted x perf. 10		
24E	A1	1sh yellow ('61)	900.00	52.50
f.		Vert. pair, imperf. btwn.		2,700.
25	A1	1sh lake brn ('65)	200.00	21.50
a.		Horiz. pair, imperf. btwn.	—	1,300.
26	A1	1sh brown ('63)	275.00	35.00
a.		1sh chestnut ('64)	290.00	16.00
b.		1sh gray brown ('63)	425.00	62.50
27	A2	2sh carmine ('67)	350.00	52.50
a.		Vert. pair, imperf. btwn.		1,600.

There are six varieties of the surcharge "TEN PENCE" in this and subsequent issues. Nos. 16b, 20g, 21c, 28a, 32c, 33a are rouletted remainders that were later perforated.

See Nos. 31, 33, 46, 48, 53, 63, 68, 72, 74, 112, 113B, 119-120. For surcharges & overprints see Nos. 34, 44-45, 49-50, 59, 67, 71, O4, O6, O8, O10, O16-O19, O18, O21, O26, O28-O29, O31, O33, O36-O38, O41, O41B, O43, O53. Compare with design A6a.

1867-72 Perf. 11½ to 12½xRoulette

No.	Design	Description	Unused	Used
28	A1	1p blue green	475.00	77.50
a.		Rouletted and perf. all around		975.00
29	A1	1p grayish green ('70)	345.00	45.00
a.		1p bright green ('68)	345.00	45.00
b.		1p pale bright green ('67)	300.00	32.50
31	A2	4p dull violet ('68)	2,250.	185.00
a.		4p purple ('69)		185.00
32	A1	6p Prus blue	750.00	35.00
a.		6p sky blue	900.00	35.00
b.		Printed on both sides		
c.		Rouletted and perf. all around		475.00
d.		6p indigo blue ('69)	1,000.	47.50
e.		As "d," rouletted and perf. all around	—	600.00
33	A3	9p gray lilac ('72)	—	525.00
34	A3	10p on 9p yel (Bl) ('68)	975.00	62.50
a.		Printed on both sides		1,100.
35	A1	1sh chestnut ('68)	475.00	32.50
36	A1	1sh lake brown ('69)	475.00	35.00
a.		Rouletted and perf. all around	—	

Nos. 44-45 Surcharged

3-PENCE

1867-74 Perf. 11½-12½

No.	Design	Description	Unused	Used
41	A1	1p yellow green	130.00	40.00
42	A1	1p blue green	140.00	40.00
a.		Printed on both sides		
b.		Horiz. pair, imperf between		2,400.
c.		1p pale bright green ('68)	290.00	47.50
d.		1p gray green ('68)	290.00	80.00
43	A1	2p vermilion		1,250.
44	A2	3p on 4p sky blue (Blk) ('70)	550.00	22.50
a.		3p on 4p ultra, black surcharge	140.00	16.00
b.		Surcharge omitted	30,000.	15,000.
c.		Double surcharge		4,500.
d.		Surcharged on both sides		3,500.
e.		Rouletted	—	1,200.
f.		3p on 4p Prussian blue ('71)		1,100.
46	A2	4p dull violet	115.00	14.00
a.		4p dull purple ('68)	120.00	24.00
47	A1	6p Prussian blue	200.00	10.00
a.		6p sky blue	450.00	15.00
b.		Imperf. vert., pair	—	
c.		Horiz. pair, imperf x perf 11½		1,500.
d.		6p indigo ('69)	230.00	27.50
48	A3	9p red lilac ('72)	100.00	14.00
a.		9p violet	200.00	14.00
b.		9p red violet	200.00	11.50
c.		Printed on both sides		925.00
49	A3	10p on 9p yel (Bl) ('68)	1,600.	50.00
50	A3	10p on 9p yel (Blk) ('69)	350.00	55.00
51	A1	1sh deep brown	185.00	21.00
52	A1	1sh red brown	155.00	21.00
a.		1sh chestnut	225.00	29.00
b.		1sh lake brown ('68)	290.00	17.00
53	A2	2sh carmine	125.00	18.00
a.		Printed on both sides		700.00
b.		Horiz. pair, imperf. vert.	—	
c.		2sh pale rose pink ('69)	1,850.	210.00
d.		2sh deep rose pink ('69)	—	170.00
e.		2sh carmine red ('69)	160.00	27.50

Perf. 10

No.	Design	Description	Unused	Used
42e	A1	1p bright green ('71)	240.00	26.00
42f	A1	1p pale br green ('70)	240.00	26.00
42g	A1	1p gray green ('70)	240.00	26.00
44g	A2	3p on 4p pale ultra (Blk) ('71)	525.00	32.50
44h	A2	3p on 4p ultra (Blk) ('71)	230.00	35.00
44i	A2	3p on 4p Pruss bl (Blk) ('71)		1,100.
45	A2	3p on 4p sl bl (Red) ('70)	1,050.	160.00
46b	A2	4p dull violet ('70)	200.00	17.00
46c	A2	4p dull pur ('71)	160.00	17.00
47e	A1	6p br blue ('70)	290.00	24.00
47f	A1	6p indigo ('71)	400.00	22.50
52c	A1	1sh chestnut ('71)	260.00	40.00

Perf. 10x11½-12½, 11½-12½x10, or Compound

No.	Design	Description	Unused	Used
42h	A1	1p pale br grn	290.00	22.50
i		Printed on both sides		
42j	A1	1p deep green	145.00	15.00
42k	A1	1p gray green	260.00	24.00
44j	A2	3p on 4p ultra (Blk)	400.00	80.00
46d	A2	4p dull lilac	—	30.00
46e	A2	4p slate lilac	170.00	22.50
47g	A1	6p Prussian blue	240.00	12.50
47h	A1	6p br Pruss blue	260.00	16.00
50a	A3	10p on 9p yel (Blk)	460.00	72.50
52d	A1	1sh chestnut	375.00	80.00
53f	A2	2sh carmine	240.00	57.50
53g	A2	2sh rose pink	—	275.00

See Nos. 67, O14, O28, O36.

A6   A6a

1868 Typo. Wmk. 72 Rouletted

No.	Design	Description	Unused	Used
54	A6a	2p orange red	125.00	4.00
a.		Imperf.		
b.		Printed on both sides		725.00
c.		Horiz. pair, imperf. btwn.		1,100.
d.		2p deep brick red	145.00	7.75

1869 Perf. 11½ to 12½xRoulette

| 55 | A6a | 2p orange red | 250.00 | |

1870 Perf. 10xRoulette

| 56 | A6a | 2p orange red | 700.00 | 47.50 |

Perf. 10, 11½, 12½ and Compound
1868-75

No.	Design	Description	Unused	Used
57	A6	1p bl grn ('75)	82.50	10.00
58	A6a	2p orange red	22.50	1.90
a.		Printed on both sides		575.00
b.		Horiz. pair, imperf. vert.		

Engr.

| 59 | A3 | 10p on 9p yel (Bl) | | 1,550. |

1869 Typo. Wmk. 6 Rouletted

60	A6a	2p orange red	140.00	32.50
a.		Imperf.		
b.		Printed on both sides		

Perf. 11½ to 12½xRoulette

| 61 | A6a | 2p orange red | 2,500. | 125.00 |

Perf. 11½ to 12½

| 61B | A6a | 2p orange red | — | 1,350. |

See Nos. 62, 64-66, 97-98, 105-116, 115-116, 133-134, 145-146. For surcharges & overprints see Nos. 75, O3, O22-O25, O34-O35, O44-O47, O49, O55-O56, O62-O63, O68-O69, O74, O78-O79.

1871 Wmk. 70 Perf. 10

| 62 | A6a | 2p orange red | 140.00 | 40.00 |

Engr.

| 63 | A2 | 4p dull violet | 3,750. | 325.00 |
| a. | | Printed on both sides | | 4,500. |

Examples of the 4p from edge of sheet sometimes lack watermark.

Perf. 10, 11½, 12½ and Compound
1876-80 Typo. Wmk. 73

No.	Design	Description	Unused	Used
64	A6	1p green	27.50	.95
65	A6a	2p orange	29.00	.70
66	A6a	2p blood red ('80)	325.00	7.75
		Nos. 64-66 (3)	381.50	9.40

See Nos. 97-98, 105-106, 115-116, 133-134, 145-146.

8 PENCE — No. 71   HALF-PENNY — No. 75

1876-84 Engr. Wmk. 7

No.	Design	Description	Unused	Used
67	A2	3p on 4p ultra (Blk)	140.00	35.00
a.		3p on 4p deep blue	140.00	22.50
b.		Double surcharge		1,850.
68	A2	4p reddish violet	110.00	10.00
a.		4p dull violet	110.00	12.00
b.		4p slate violet ('79)	185.00	27.50
69	A1	6p deep ultra	130.00	7.00
a.		Horiz. pair, imperf. between	—	
b.		Imperf.	—	
c.		6p bright blue, perf 10	200.00	24.00
d.		6p Prussian blue, perf 10	170.00	24.00
70	A1	6p pale ultra ('84)	95.00	3.75
71	A3	8p on 9p bister brn	160.00	12.00
a.		8p on 9p yellow brown	140.00	12.00
b.		8p on 9p gray brown ('80)	130.00	12.00
d.		Double surcharge		1,950.
e.		Vert. pair, imperf between	1,850.	
72	A3	9p rose lilac	20.00	5.75
a.		Printed on both sides		700.00
73	A1	1sh red brown	72.50	4.50
a.		1sh brown	92.50	6.00
b.		1sh chocolate	40.00	4.75
c.		As "b," horiz. pair, imperf. btwn.	400.00	
d.		1sh sepia	40.00	4.75
e.		As "d," vert. pair, imperf. btwn.	400.00	
f.		1sh reddish lake brown, perf 10	490.00	
74	A2	2sh carmine	70.00	9.25
a.		Horiz. pair, imperf. vert.		2,000.
b.		Imperf., pair		

For overprint see No. O41.

1882 Wmk. 73 Perf. 10
Black Surcharge

| 75 | A6 | ½p on 1p green | 22.50 | 15.00 |

A9   A10

A11   A12

Perf. 10, 11½, 12½ and Compound
1883-93 Typo.

No.	Design	Description	Unused	Used
76	A9	½p chocolate brown	11.50	2.50
a.		½p red brown ('89)	7.50	2.25
b.		½p bister brown	6.25	2.25
78	A10	3p deep green ('93)	17.00	4.75
a.		3p olive green ('90)	24.00	4.75
b.		3p sage green ('86)	24.00	3.25
79	A11	4p violet ('90)	37.50	4.50
a.		4p aniline violet ('93)	45.00	4.00
80	A12	6p pale blue ('87)	37.50	3.50
a.		6p blue ('87)	32.50	1.40
		Nos. 76-80 (4)	103.50	15.25

See Nos. 96, 100-101, 104, 108-109, 111. For surcharges & overprints see Nos. 94-95, 99, O48, O50-O51, O54, O57-O61, O64, O66-O67, O71, O73, O75, O81-O82.

A13

1886-96 Perf. 11½ to 12½

No.	Design	Description	Unused	Used
81	A13	2sh6p violet	67.50	12.50
a.		2sh6p bright aniline violet	70.00	11.00
82	A13	5sh rose	85.00	22.50
83	A13	10sh green	210.00	60.00
84	A13	15sh buff	675.00	225.00
85	A13	£1 blue	475.00	160.00
86	A13	£2 red brown	2,500.	475.00
87	A13	50sh rose red	3,250.	550.00
88	A13	£3 olive green	3,500.	550.00
89	A13	£4 lemon	5,750.	1,000.
90	A13	£5 gray	6,000.	
90A	A13	£5 brown ('96)	4,300.	1,000.
91	A13	£10 bronze	5,000.	1,000.
92	A13	£15 silver	19,000.	1,850.
93	A13	£20 lilac	22,000.	2,000.

Perf. 10

81b	A13	2sh6p violet	87.50	13.00
82a	A13	5sh rose	110.00	22.50
83a	A13	10sh green	240.00	67.50
84a	A13	15sh buff	600.00	350.00
85a	A13	£1 blue	525.00	175.00
86a	A13	£2 red brown	2,750.	525.00
87a	A13	50sh rose red	3,750.	675.00
88a	A13	£3 olive green	4,000.	625.00
89a	A13	£4 lemon	7,500.	
90b	A13	£5 gray	6,000.	
91a	A13	£10 bronze	6,000.	1,250.
92a	A13	£15 silver	21,000.	
93a	A13	£20 lilac	24,500.	

For overprints see Nos. O83-O84.

2½d. #94, 99   5D. #95

Perf. 10, 11½x12½ and Compound
1891 Brown Surcharge

No.	Design	Description	Unused	Used
94	A11	2½p on 4p green	14.00	4.00
a.		"½" nearer the "2"	47.50	35.00
b.		Pair, imperf. between		2,150.
c.		Fraction bar omitted	175.00	130.00

Carmine Surcharge

| 95 | A12 | 5p on 6p red brn | 24.00 | 9.25 |
| a. | | No period after "D" | 300.00 | |

See No. 99. For overprints see Nos. O48, O57, O59.

Many stamps of the issues of 1855-91 have been reprinted; they are all on paper watermarked Crown and SA, letters wide apart, and are overprinted "REPRINT."

1893 Typo. Perf. 15

No.	Design	Description	Unused	Used
96	A9	½p brown	9.50	2.00
a.		Horiz. pair, imperf. btwn	290.00	
b.		Pair, perf. 12 btwn; perf. 15 around	350.00	87.50
97	A6	1p green	24.00	2.00
98	A6a	2p orange	22.50	1.40
a.		Vert. pair, imperf. between	700.00	
99	A11	2½p on 4p green	42.50	5.25
a.		"½" nearer the "2"	110.00	42.50
b.		Fraction bar omitted		
100	A11	4p gray violet	35.00	4.75
101	A12	6p blue	72.50	6.25
		Nos. 96-101 (6)	206.00	21.65

Kangaroo, Palm — A16   Coat of Arms — A17

1894, Mar. 1

| 102 | A16 | 2½p blue violet | 42.50 | 4.75 |
| 103 | A17 | 5p dull violet | 37.50 | 4.75 |

See Nos. 107, 110, 117, 135-136, 147, 151. For overprints see Nos. O65, O70, O72, O80.

1895-97 Perf. 13

No.	Design	Description	Unused	Used
104	A9	½p pale brown	5.25	.60
105	A6	1p green	14.00	.70
a.		Vert. pair, imperf. between		
106	A6a	2p orange	11.50	.35
107	A16	2½p blue violet	35.00	1.60
108	A10	3p olive green ('97)	12.00	3.50
109	A11	4p bright violet	11.50	1.00
110	A17	5p dull violet	13.00	2.00

111	A12	6p blue		14.00	2.75
a.		6p pale blue ('96)		12.00	2.50
		Nos. 104-111 (8)		116.25	12.50

Some authorities regard the so-called redrawn 1p stamps with thicker lettering (said to have been issued in 1897) as impressions from a new or cleaned plate.

Perf. 11½, 12½, Clean-Cut, Compound

1896 **Engr.** **Wmk. 7**

112	A3	9p lilac rose		18.00	8.75
113	A1	1sh dark brown		45.00	7.50
a.		Horiz. pair, imperf. vert.		350.00	
c.		Vert. pair, imperf. btwn.		475.00	
113B	A2	2sh carmine		57.50	12.00
		Nos. 112-113B (3)		120.50	28.25

Adelaide Post
Office — A18

1899 **Typo.** **Wmk. 73** **Perf. 13**

114	A18	½p yellow green		5.25	1.25
115	A6	1p carmine		9.00	.70
a.		1p scarlet		7.75	.85
116	A6a	2p purple		7.55	.40
117	A16	2½p dark blue		11.50	3.50
		Nos. 114-117 (4)		33.30	5.85

See Nos. 132, 144. For overprint see No. O77.

Perf. 11½, 12½

1901 **Engr.** **Wmk. 72**

118	A1	1sh dark brown		40.00	18.00
a.		1sh red brown		45.00	25.00
b.		Horiz. pair, imperf. vert.			
119	A2	2sh carmine		45.00	17.50

1902

120	A3	9p magenta		25.00	25.00

A19   A20

The measurements given in parentheses are the length of the value inscription in the bottom panel.

Perf. 11½, 12½ and Compound

1902-03 **Typo.** **Wmk. 73**

121	A19	3p olive grn (18.5mm)	12.00	2.75
a.		3p olive grn (20mm), perf 12	24.00	3.50
b.		Wmk sideways		1,900.
122	A19	4p red org (17mm)	20.00	3.50
a.		4p red org (17.5-18mm), perf 12	20.00	2.90
123	A19	6p blue grn (16-16.5mm)	14.00	2.60
a.		6p blue grn (15mm), perf 12	42.50	10.00
124	A19	8p ultra (value 19mm long)	15.00	13.00
124A	A19	8p ultra (value 16½mm long) ('03)	18.00	15.00
b.		"EIGNT"	2,000.	3,000.
125	A19	9p claret	15.00	8.75
a.		Vert. pair, imperf. between	1,750.	
b.		Horiz. pair, imperf. between		
c.		9p claret, perf 12	115.00	20.00
126	A19	10p org buff	22.50	14.00
127	A19	1sh brn ('03)	30.00	8.75
a.		Horiz. pair, imperf. btwn.		
b.		Vert. pair, imperf. btwn.	1,850.	
c.		"Postage" and denomination in red brown	1,100.	1,000.
128	A19	2sh6p purple	37.50	24.00
a.		2sh6p blue violet	72.50	45.00
129	A19	5sh rose	130.00	82.50
130	A19	10sh grn ('03)	180.00	130.00
131	A19	£1 blue	525.00	290.00
		Nos. 121-131 (12)	1,019.	594.85

1904 **Perf. 12x11½**

132	A18	½p yellow green		7.50	2.40
133	A6	1p rose		11.50	.85
134	A6a	2p purple		12.00	1.40
135	A16	2½p dark blue		15.00	4.50
136	A17	5p dull violet		25.00	3.75
		Nos. 132-136 (5)		71.00	12.90

1904-08 **Perf. 12 and 12x11½**

137	A20	6p blue green	27.50	5.75
a.		Vert. pair, imperf. between	4,250.	
138	A20	8p ultra ('06)	17.50	15.00
139	A20	9p claret	25.00	9.00
139A	A20	10p org buff ('07)	30.00	24.00
b.		Vert. pair, imperf. between	3,750.	
c.		Horiz. pair, imperf. between	2,000.	1,850.
140	A20	1sh brown	35.00	5.75
a.		Vert. pair, imperf. between	1,750.	
b.		Horiz. pair, imperf. between	2,000.	
141	A20	2sh6p purple ('05)	110.00	32.50
142	A20	5sh scarlet	100.00	60.00
a.		5sh pale rose, Perf 12½, small holes ('10)	125.00	70.00
142B	A20	10sh green ('08)	225.00	260.00
143	A20	£1 deep blue	350.00	200.00
a.		Perf 12½, small holes ('10)	260.00	200.00
		Nos. 137-143 (9)	920.00	612.00

See Nos. 148-150, 152-157.

1906-12 **Wmk. 74**

144	A18	½p green	10.50	1.60
145	A6	1p carmine	9.25	.60
146	A6a	2p purple	8.75	.60
a.		Horiz. pair, imperf. between	2,500.	
147	A16	2½p dk blue ('11)	17.50	11.50
148	A20	3p ol grn (value 19mm long)	22.50	6.25
a.		Horiz. pair, imperf. between		5,500.
149	A20	3p ol grn (value 17mm long) ('09)	13.00	6.25
150	A20	4p red orange	18.00	4.75
151	A17	5p dull vio ('08)	30.00	7.25
152	A20	6p blue grn ('07)	14.00	4.75
a.		Vert. pair, imperf. between	1,850.	1,750.
153	A20	8p ultra ('09)	20.00	22.50
154	A20	9p claret	20.00	8.75
a.		Vert. pair, imperf. between	1,600.	
b.		Horiz. pair, imperf. btwn.	4,250.	
155	A20	1sh brown	21.00	9.00
a.		Horiz. pair, imperf. between	3,100.	
b.		Vert. pair, imperf. between	2,500.	
156	A20	2sh6p purple ('09)	105.00	25.00
a.		2sh6p pale violet, perf 12 ('10)	145.00	22.50
b.		2sh6p pale violet, perf 12½ ('12)	85.00	55.00
157	A20	5sh lt red ('12)	140.00	105.00
		Nos. 144-157 (14)	449.50	213.80

OFFICIAL STAMPS

For Departments
Regular Issues Overprinted in Red, Black or Blue:

A. (Architect), A. G. (Attorney General), A. O. (Audit Office), B. D. (Barracks Department), B. G. (Botanical Gardens), B. M. (Bench of Magistrates), C. (Customs), C. D. (Convict Department), C. L. (Crown Lands), C. O. (Commissariat Officer), C. S. (Chief Secretary), C. Sgn. (Colonial Surgeon), C. P. (Commissioner of Police), C. T. (Commissioner of Titles), D. B. (Destitute Board), D. R. (Deed Registry), E. (Engineer), E. B. (Education Board), G. P. (Government Printer), G. S. (Government Storekeeper), G. T. (Goolwa Tramway), G. F. (Gold Fields), H. (Hospital), H. A. (House of Assembly), I. A. (Immigration Agent), I. E. (Intestate Estates), I. S. (Inspector of Sheep), L. A. (Lunatic Asylum), L. C. (Legislative Council), L. L. (Legislative Library), L. T. (Land Titles), M. (Military), M. B. (Marine Board), M. R. (Manager of Railways), M. R. G. (Main Roads Gambierton), N. T. (Northern Territory), O. A. (Official Assignee), P. (Police), P. A. (Protector of Aborigines), P. O. (Post Office),

P. S. (Private Secretary), P. W. (Public Works), R. B. (Road Board), R. G. (Registrar General of Births, &c.), S. (Sheriff), S. C. (Supreme Court), S.G. (Surveyor General), S. M. (Stipendiary Magistrate), S. T. (Superintendent of Telegraph), T. (Treasurer), T. R. (Titles Registry), V. (Volunteers), V. A. (Valuator), V. N. (Vaccination), W. (Waterworks).

1868-74 **Wmk. 6** **Rouletted**

O1	A1	1p green	350.00
O2	A1	2p pale red	275.00
O3	A6a	2p vermilion	120.00
O4	A2	4p dull violet	275.00
O5	A1	6p slate blue	275.00
O6	A3	9p gray lilac	500.00
O7	A1	1sh brown	275.00
O8	A2	2sh carmine	275.00

Perf. 11½ to 12½ x Roulette

O9	A1	1p green	275.00
O10	A2	4p dull violet	850.00
O11	A1	6p blue	210.00
O12	A1	1sh brown	200.00

Perf. 10, 11½, 12½ and Compound

O13	A1	1p green	160.00
O14	A2	3p on 4p slate blue (Red)	750.00
O15	A2	3p on 4p slate blue (Blk)	275.00
O16	A2	4p dull violet	200.00
O17	A1	6p deep blue	275.00
O18	A3	9p violet	500.00
O19	A3	10p on 9p yellow (Blk)	500.00
O20	A1	1sh brown	140.00	160.00
O21	A2	2sh carmine	100.00

Rouletted
Wmk. 72

O22	A6a	2p orange	120.00

Perf. 11 ½ x Roulette

O23	A6a	2p orange	160.00
a.		Perf 10 x Roulette	275.00

Perf. 10, 11½, 12½ and Compound

O24	A6a	2p orange	22.50

Wmk. 70
Perf. 10

O25	A6a	2p orange	110.00
O26	A2	4p dull violet	275.00

For General Use

Overprinted in Black

Perf. 10, 11½, 12½ and Compound

1874 **Wmk. 6**

O27	A1	1p green	—	400.00
a.		1p dp yel green, perf 11½-12½x10	2,500.	400.00
b.		As "a," printed on both sides		1,100.
O28	A2	3p on 4p ultra	6,750.	2,150.
a.		No period after "S"		3,000.
O29	A2	4p dull violet	92.50	17.50
a.		Inverted overprint		62.50
b.		No period after "S"		400.00
c.		Perf. 11½-12½x10	2,000.	
O30	A1	6p deep blue	175.00	24.00
a.		No period after "S"		95.00
b.		6p Prussian blue, perf 11½-12½x10	130.00	15.00
O31	A3	9p violet	3,000.	1,200.
a.		No period after "S"	4,000.	1,750.
O32	A1	1sh red brown	130.00	16.00
a.		Double overprint		225.00
b.		No period after "S"	350.00	95.00
O33	A2	2sh carmine	275.00	30.00
a.		Double overprint		
b.		No period after "S"		125.00
c.		2sh carmine, perf 11½-12½x10		175.00

1874-75 **Wmk. 72**

O34	A6	1p blue green	175.00	42.50
a.		Inverted overprint		
O35	A6a	2p orange	40.00	6.00

1876-86 **Wmk. 7**

O37	A2	4p dull violet	130.00	12.00
O38	A2	4p reddish vio	57.50	5.25
a.		Double overprint		225.00
b.		Inverted overprint		
c.		Dbl. ovpt., one inverted		
O39	A1	6p dark blue	1,350.	10.00
a.		Double overprint		140.00
b.		Inverted overprint		
O40	A1	6p ultramarine	130.00	8.75
a.		Double overprint		
b.		Inverted overprint		
O41B	A1	6p violet	7,500.	
O42	A1	1sh red brown	70.00	14.00
a.		Inverted overprint	625.00	180.00
O43	A2	2sh carmine	225.00	15.00
a.		Double overprint		225.00
b.		Inverted overprint		250.00
c.		No period after "S"		175.00

1880-91 **Wmk. 73**

O44	A6	1p blue green	27.50	2.00
a.		Inverted overprint		95.00
b.		Double overprint	130.00	85.00
c.		Dbl. ovpt., one inverted		750.00
O45	A6	1p yellow green	35.00	2.00
O46	A6a	2p orange	17.00	2.00
a.		Inverted overprint		42.50
b.		Double overprint	130.00	62.50
c.		Overprinted sideways		
d.		Dbl. ovpt., one inverted		
e.		Dbl. ovpt., both inverted		240.00
O47	A6a	2p blood red	110.00	22.50
O48	A11	2½p on 4p green	130.00	14.00
a.		"½" nearer the "2"		100.00
b.		Double overprint		
c.		Pair, one without ovpt.		
		Nos. O44-O48 (5)	319.50	42.50

1882-90 **Perf. 10**

O49	A6	½p on 1p green	130.00	30.00
a.		Inverted overprint		
O50	A11	4p violet	135.00	9.25
O51	A12	6p blue	37.50	2.40
a.		Double overprint		
b.		No period after "S"		
		Nos. O49-O51 (3)	302.50	41.65

Overprinted in Black

Perf. 10, 11½, 12½ and Compound

1891 **Wmk. 7**

O52	A1	1sh red brown	70.00	10.50
a.		No period after "S"		115.00
b.		1sh lake brown, perf 11½-12½	105.00	27.50
O53	A2	2sh carmine	140.00	20.00
a.		Double overprint		
b.		No period after "S"		

1891-95 **Wmk. 73**

O54	A9	½p brown	40.00	10.50
a.		No period after "S"	87.50	52.50
O55	A6	1p blue green	45.00	3.75
a.		Double overprint	140.00	77.50
b.		No period after "S"	75.00	17.50
O56	A6a	2p orange	42.50	3.25
a.		No period after "S"		45.00
O57	A11	2½p on 4p green	77.50	25.00
a.		"½" nearer the "2"	175.00	57.50
b.		Inverted overprint	400.00	
O58	A11	4p violet	92.50	6.50
a.		Double overprint		
O59	A12	5p on 6p red brn	80.00	35.00
O60	A12	6p blue	40.00	4.50
a.		Double overprint		
b.		No period after "S"		
		Nos. O54-O60 (7)	417.50	88.50

1893 **Perf. 15**

O61	A9	½p brown	77.50	18.00
O62	A6	1p green	24.00	2.40
O63	A6a	2p orange	27.50	.85
a.		Inverted overprint		40.00
b.		Double overprint		57.50
O64	A11	4p gray violet	115.00	8.75
a.		Double overprint	375.00	77.50
O65	A17	5p dull violet	125.00	22.50
O66	A12	6p blue	52.50	5.75
		Nos. O61-O66 (6)	421.50	58.25

1896 **Perf. 13**

O67	A9	½p brown	40.00	11.50
a.		Triple overprint	375.00	
O68	A6	1p green	42.50	1.10
a.		Inverted overprint	125.00	18.00
O69	A6a	2p orange	42.50	1.10
a.		No period after "S"	115.00	18.00
O70	A16	2½p blue violet	75.00	9.50
a.		No period after "S"		70.00
O71	A11	4p brt violet	100.00	5.75
a.		Double overprint	300.00	57.50
b.		No period after "S"	300.00	42.50
O72	A17	5p dull violet	130.00	27.50
O73	A12	6p blue	62.50	3.75
a.		No period after "S"	180.00	105.00
		Nos. O67-O73 (7)	492.50	60.20

On No. O67a, one overprint is upright, two sideways.

Same Overprint in Dark Blue

1891-95 **Perf. 10**

O74	A6	1p green	375.00	1,100.
O75	A12	6p blue		

Black Overprint
Perf. 11½, 12½, Clean-Cut

1897 **Wmk. 7**

O76	A1	1sh brown	62.50	11.00
a.		Double overprint		
b.		No period after "S"		375.00

Overprinted in Black

O. S.

1900   Wmk. 73   Perf. 13

O77	A18	½p yellow green	22.50	11.50
a.		Inverted overprint	110.00	
b.		No period after "S"	62.50	
c.		As "b," inverted overprint		
O78	A6	1p carmine rose	27.50	2.25
a.		Inverted overprint	115.00	72.50
b.		Double overprint	475.00	
c.		No period after "S"	82.50	22.50
O79	A6a	2p purple	35.00	1.40
a.		Inverted ovpt.	95.00	72.50
b.		No period after "S"	77.50	21.00
O80	A16	2½p dark blue	105.00	35.00
a.		Inverted overprint		140.00
b.		No period after "S"	225.00	
O81	A11	4p violet	92.50	10.50
a.		Inverted overprint	325.00	
b.		No period after "S"	200.00	
O82	A12	6p blue	42.50	10.50
a.		No period after "S"	110.00	
		Nos. O77-O82 (6)	325.00	71.15

1901   Perf. 10

O83	A13	2sh6p violet	6,000.	5,000.
O84	A13	5sh rose	6,000.	5,000.

On Nos. O77-O82 the letters "O.S." are 11½mm apart; on Nos. O83-O84, 14½mm apart.

Overprinted in Black

1903   Wmk. 72   Perf. 11½, 12½

O85	A1	1sh red brown	105.00	27.50

TASMANIA

taz-'mā-nē-ə

LOCATION — An island off the south-eastern coast of Australia
GOVT. — British Colony
AREA — 26,215 sq. mi.
POP. — 172,475 (1901)
CAPITAL — Hobart

Tasmania was one of the six British colonies that united in 1901 to form the Commonwealth of Australia. The island was originally named Van Diemen's Land by its discoverer, Abel Tasman, the present name having been adopted in 1853. Stamps of Australia are now used.

12 Pence = 1 Shilling
20 Shillings = 1 Pound

Watermarks

Wmk. 6 — Large Star

Wmk. 49 Double-lined Numeral

Wmk. 75 Double-lined Numeral

Wmk. 50 Single-lined "2"

Wmk. 51 Single-lined "4"

Wmk. 52 — Single-lined "10"

Wmk. 70 — V and Crown

Wmk. 13 — Crown & Double-lined A

Wmk. 76 — TAS

Wmk. 77 — TAS

Wmk. 78 — Multiple TAS

Values for unused stamps are for examples with original gum as defined in the catalogue introduction except for Nos. 1-2b and 10 which are valued without gum as few examples exist with any remaining original gum. Very fine examples of Nos. 17-75a will have perforations touching the design on one or more sides due to the narrow spacing of the stamps on the plates. Stamps with perfs clear of the design on all four sides are scarce and command higher prices.

Queen Victoria
A1   A2

Unwmk.

1853, Nov. 1   Engr.   Imperf.

1		A1 1p blue, fine impression, soft paper	7,500.	1,350.
a.		1p blue, blurred impression, hard paper	7,500.	1,200.
2		A2 4p red orange	3,750.	550.00
a.		4p yellow orange	3,500.	450.00
		Cut to shape		25.00
b.		4p orange, blurred impression ('55)	3,500.	450.00
		Cut to shape		25.00

Twenty-four varieties of each.

No. 1 is the first printing, which was printed on a soft yellowish paper. Background lines are clear and distinct. The second printing, No. 1a, was done on hard white paper and demonstrates a wearing of the plate, with blurred background lines.

Two plates were made for No. 2. Plate I (Nos. 2, 2a) is finely engraved, with all lines clear and sharp. Plate II (No. 2b) is more coarsely done, with blurred impressions and thicker background lines.

The 4p on vertically laid paper is believed to be a proof. Value, unused, $7,500.

The reprints are made from defaced plates and show marks across the face of each stamp. They are on thin and thick, unwatermarked paper and thin cardboard; only the first are perforated. Nearly all the reprints of Tasmania may be found with and without the overprint "REPRINT."

Nos. 1-47A with pen or revenue cancellations sell for a small fraction of the price of postally used examples. Stamps are found with pen cancellation removed.

Queen Victoria — A3

1855   Wmk. 6   Wove Paper

4	A3	1p dark carmine	9,000.	1,000.
5	A3	2p green	4,000.	550.00
a.		2p deep green	4,000.	625.00
6	A3	4p deep blue	3,250.	125.00
a.		4p blue	3,250.	125.00

1856-57   Unwmk.

7	A3	1p pale red	10,500.	750.00
8	A3	2p emerald ('57)	13,000.	1,100.
9	A3	4p blue ('57)	1,700.	135.00
a.		4p deep blue ('57)	1,700.	135.00
b.		4p pale blue ('57)		175.00

1856   Pelure Paper

10	A3	1p brown red	7,250.	925.00

1857-69   Wmk. 49, 75

11	A3	1p carmine ('67)	180.00	72.50
a.		1p orange red ('65)	325.00	57.50
b.		1p brown red	650.00	52.50
c.		Double impression	860.00	300.00
d.		1p brick red ('63)	325.00	60.00
e.		Wmk. 50 (error) ('69)		—
12	A3	2p sage green ('60)	275.00	115.00
a.		2p yellow green	750.00	160.00
b.		2p green		95.00
c.		2p dull emerald green		185.00
d.		As "b," double impression		325.00
13	A3	4p pale blue	275.00	42.50
a.		4p blue	290.00	45.00
b.		Printed on both sides		—
c.		4p deep blue		170.00
d.		As "a," double impression		275.00
e.		As "c," double impression		315.00
g.		4p cobalt blue		145.00
		Nos. 11-13 (3)	730.00	230.00

See Nos. 17-19, 23-25, 29-31, 35-37, 39-41, 45-47A.

 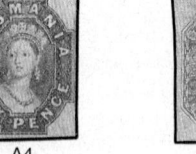

A4   A4a

1858-67

14	A4	6p gray lilac ('63)	375.00	85.00
a.		6p red violet ('67)	875.00	180.00
b.		Double impression ('63)		450.00
c.		6p dull lilac	875.00	105.00
15	A4	6p blue gray ('65)	700.00	135.00
16	A4a	1sh vermilion	675.00	90.00
		Nos. 14-16 (3)	1,750.	310.00

No. 15 watermarked large star was not regularly issued.

Issued: No. 14c, 16, 1/58; No. 14, 4/63; No. 15, 2/65; No. 14a, 4/67.

1864   Rouletted

17	A3	1p carmine	750.00	275.00
a.		1p brick red		425.00
18	A3	2p yellow grn	—	1,250.
19	A3	4p blue	—	400.00
21	A4	6p gray lilac	—	475.00
22	A4a	1sh vermilion	—	1,300.

Values for Nos. 17-22 are for stamps showing rouletting on two or three sides. Examples with full roulettes on all four sides are rare.

1864-69   Perf. 10

23	A3	1p brick red	140.00	62.50
a.		1p carmine	125.00	55.00
b.		1p orange red	140.00	45.00
c.		As "b," double impression		—
24	A3	2p yellow green	800.00	225.00
		2p sage green	625.00	225.00
25	A3	4p blue	275.00	27.50
a.		Double impression		240.00
26	A4	6p lilac	425.00	40.00
		6p red lilac	600.00	140.00
27	A4	6p slate blue	650.00	125.00
28	A4a	1sh vermilion	325.00	40.00
a.		Horiz. pair, imperf. vert.		
		Nos. 23-28 (6)	2,615.	520.00

1864-91   Perf. 12

29	A3	1p carmine	130.00	27.50
a.		1p orange red	115.00	40.00
b.		1p brick red	140.00	62.50
c.		Double impression		—
d.		Wmkd. "2"		2,750.
		As "d," pen cancel		275.00
30	A3	2p yellow green	400.00	115.00
31	A3	4p pale blue	225.00	40.00
a.		4p deep blue	225.00	35.00
b.		4p cobalt blue	—	92.50
32	A4	6p red lilac	130.00	57.50
a.		Horiz. pair, imperf between		—
b.		Vert. pair, imperf between		—
c.		6p violet	260.00	40.00
d.		As "c," Vert. pair, imperf between		—
e.		6p purple ('84)	175.00	57.50
f.		Horiz. pair, imperf between	1,650.	
g.		6p dull claret ('91)	45.00	20.00
34	A4a	1sh vermilion	325.00	175.00
a.		Double impression	—	325.00
b.		Horiz. pair, imperf. vert.		

Perf. 10x12

29e	A3	1p carmine		2,750.
31c	A3	4p blue		2,250.

Perf. 12½

29f	A3	1p carmine	85.00	22.50
29g	A3	1p orange red	145.00	52.50
29h	A3	1p brick red	160.00	65.00
30a	A3	2p yellow green	725.00	240.00
30b	A3	2p sage green	600.00	275.00
31d	A3	4p blue	345.00	92.50
31e	A3	4p bright blue	345.00	92.50
32h	A4	6p purple	750.00	225.00
32i	A4	6p slate violet	460.00	100.00
33	A4	6p slate blue	625.00	175.00
34c	A4a	1sh vermilion	600.00	185.00

Perf. 11½

32j	A4	6p dull lilac	200.00	37.50
32k	A4	6p lilac	185.00	37.50
l.		Pair, imperf between		1,350.
32m	A4	6p deep slate lilac ('75)	185.00	37.50
n.		Imperf, pair		1,200.
32o	A4	6p bright violet ('78)	185.00	55.00
p.		Double impression		230.00
q.		Horiz. pair, imperf between	2,200.	
32r	A4	6p dull reddish lilac ('79)	170.00	70.00
34d	A4a	1sh dull vermilion ('73)	240.00	85.00
e.		Horiz. pair, imperf between		
34f	A4a	1sh brownish vermilion ('73)	230.00	85.00

The reprints are on unwatermarked paper, perforated 11½, and on thin cardboard, imperforate and perforated.

1867   Pin-perf. 5½ to 9½

35	A3	1p carmine	1,000.	250.00
36	A3	2p yellow green		975.00
37	A3	4p blue		475.00
38	A4	6p gray		450.00
38A	A4	6p red lilac		1,250.
38B	A4a	1sh vermilion		

Pin-perf. 13½ to 14½

35a	A3	1p brick red		575.00
35b	A3	1p dull vermilion		575.00
35c	A3	1p carmine		
36a	A3	2p yellow green		975.00
37a	A3	4p pale blue		490.00
38Ac	A4	6p gray violet		1,300.
38Bd	A4a	1sh vermilion		

Oblique Roulette 14-15

39	A3	1p carmine		850.00
a.		1p brick red		850.00
b.		1p dull vermilion		850.00
40	A3	2p yellow green		1,150.
41	A4	4p blue		850.00
42	A4	6p gray		1,450.
43	A4	6p red lilac		—
44	A4a	1sh vermilion		1,800.

Oblique Roulette 10-10½

39c	A3	1p carmine	2,000.	625.00
39d	A3	1p brick red		725.00
40a	A3	2p yellow green		1,050.
41a	A4	4p blue		850.00
43a	A4	6p gray lilac		1,450.

Oblique Roulette Imperf 10-10½

41b	A3	4p blue		850.00

1868　　　　　　*Serrate Perf. 19*
45	A3	1p carmine	575.00	200.00
46	A3	2p yellow green		800.00
47	A3	4p blue	1,350.	200.00
47A	A3	6p purple	—	1,150.
47B	A3	1sh vermilion	—	—

Queen Victoria — A5

1870-71　Typo.　Wmk. 50　Perf. 11½
48	A5	2p blue green	130.00	8.75
a.		Double impression	4,500.	1,750.
b.		Perf. 12	155.00	13.00
c.		2p green	250.00	13.00
d.		As "c," perf. 12	140.00	13.00
e.		As "d," imperf. pair	—	

See Nos. 49-75, 98, 108-109.

Wmk. 51
49	A5	1p rose ('71)	110.00	27.50
a.		Imperf., pair	1,300.	1,300.
50	A5	4p blue	1,100.	525.00

Wmk. 52
51	A5	1p rose	75.00	17.50
a.		Imperf. pair	1,300.	1,300.
c.		Perf. 11½	1,400.	
52	A5	10p black	42.50	42.50
a.		Imperf. pair	625.00	
b.		Perf. 11½	47.50	47.50

The reprints are on unwatermarked paper. The 4p has also been reprinted on thin cardboard, imperf and perf.

1871-76　Wmk. 76　Perf. 11½
53	A5	1p rose	14.00	1.90
a.		Imperf.		
c.		Perf. 12	185.00	22.50
d.		1p carmine	15.00	1.60
e.		1p pink	18.00	3.50
f.		As "d," perf. 12	185.00	16.00
g.		As "e," perf. 12	170.00	14.00
53B	A5	1p vermilion ('73)	375.00	130.00
54	A5	2p deep green ('72)	62.50	2.40
a.		2p yellow green	300.00	5.75
b.		2p blue green	57.50	2.25
c.		Imperf. pair		1,700.
d.		2p green, perf. 12	1,050.	260.00
e.		Double impression		
55	A5	3p brown	90.00	6.00
a.		3p purple brown	90.00	7.25
b.		As "a," imperf. pair		1,150.
c.		3p brownish purple	90.00	7.75
56	A5	3p red brown ('71)	90.00	7.50
a.		3p indian red	90.00	7.75
b.		Imperf. pair	140.00	
c.		Vert. pair, imperf. horiz.		
d.		Perf. 12	175.00	30.00
e.		3p deep red brown, perf. 12	170.00	30.00
f.		As "e," imperf. between		
57	A5	4p dull yellow ('76)	120.00	32.50
a.		Perf. 12	450.00	32.50
b.		4p ocher	145.00	20.00
c.		4p buff	115.00	22.50
58	A5	9p blue	32.50	14.00
a.		Imperf. pair	450.00	
b.		Perf. 12	52.50	52.50
c.		Double impression		
59	A5	5sh bright violet	450.00	240.00
a.		Imperf.		
b.		Horiz. pair, imperf. vert.		
c.		Perf. 12	650.00	475.00
d.		5sh purple	490.00	260.00
e.		5sh purple, perf. 12	775.00	
		Pen cancel		11.00
		Nos. 53-59 (8)	1,234.	434.30

The reprints are on unwatermarked paper, the 5sh has also been reprinted on thin cardboard; all are perforated.

1878　Wmk. 77　Perf. 14
60	A5	1p rose	7.50	3.00
61	A5	2p deep green	9.00	3.00
62	A5	8p violet brown	30.00	14.00
		Nos. 60-62 (3)	46.50	20.00

The 8p has been reprinted on thin unwatermarked paper, perforated 11½.

1880-83　　　　Perf. 12, 11½
63	A5	3p indian red, perf. 12	20.00	6.50
a.		Imperf. pair	400.00	
b.		Horiz. pair, imperf. between	1,750.	
c.		Perf. 11½	25.00	7.75
64	A5	4p lem, perf. 11½ ('83)	87.50	42.50
a.		4p olive yellow, perf. 11½	175.00	35.00
b.		Printed on both sides	1,100.	
c.		Imperf.		
d.		4p deep yellow, perf. 12	105.00	20.00

Type of 1871
Surcharged in Black

1889　　　　　　　Perf. 14
65	A5	½p on 1p carmine	27.50	27.50
a.		"al" sideways in surcharge	1,450.	1,200.

No. 65 has been reprinted on thin cardboard, perforated 12, with the surcharge "Halfpenny" 19mm long.

1889-96　　　　　Perf. 11½
66	A5	½p red orange	5.75	5.25
a.		½p yellow orange	5.75	5.25
b.		Perf. 12	5.25	7.25
67	A5	1p dull red	11.50	4.50
a.		1p vermilion	10.50	4.50
68	A5	1p car, perf. 12	25.00	6.00
a.		1p pink, perf. 12	29.00	9.00
b.		1p salmon rose, perf. 12	32.50	7.75
c.		Imperf. pair	350.00	375.00

Perf. 12
69	A5	4p bister ('96)	29.00	20.00
70	A5	9p chalky bl ('96)	15.00	5.75
		Nos. 66-70 (5)	86.25	41.50

1891　　Wmk. 76　　Perf. 11½
71	A5	½p orange	57.50	35.00
a.		½p brown orange	45.00	22.50
b.		Imperf. pair	240.00	
c.		Perf. 12	47.50	35.00
72	A5	1p salmon rose	32.50	15.00
a.		1p carmine, perf. 12	40.00	29.00
73	A5	4p ol bis, perf. 12	32.50	21.00
		Nos. 71-73 (3)	122.50	71.00

See Nos. 98, 108-109.

Surcharged in Black

1891　　Wmk. 77　　Perf. 11½
Surcharge 14mm High
74	A5	2½p on 9p lt blue	17.50	9.25
a.		Dbl. surcharge, one invtd.	850.00	950.00
b.		Imperf. pair	—	

Perf. 12
Surcharge 15mm High
75	A5	2½p on 9p lt blue	8.50	7.75
a.		Surcharged in blue	10.00	6.50

No. 74 has been reprinted on thin unwatermarked paper, imperforate. There is also a reprint on thin cardboard, in deep ultramarine, with surcharge 16½mm high, and perforated 12.

A8　　　　　　A9

1892-99　　Typo.　　Perf. 14
76	A8	½p orange & vio	4.25	4.25
77	A9	2½p magenta	7.25	7.25
78	A8	5p pale bl & brn	11.50	7.25
79	A8	6p blue vio & blk	15.00	7.25
80	A8	10p red brn & grn ('99)	29.00	21.00
81	A8	1sh rose & green	15.00	7.25
82	A8	2sh6p brown & blue	47.50	35.00
83	A8	5sh brn vio & red	92.50	42.50
84	A8	10sh brt vio & brn	160.00	115.00
85	A8	£1 green & yel	700.00	450.00
		Nos. 76-85 (10)	1,082.	696.75

No. 80 shows the numeral on white tablet.
See Nos. 99, 110-111.

Lake
Marion — A10

Mt.
Wellington — A11

View of
Hobart — A12

Tasman's
Arch — A13

Spring River,
Port
Davey — A14

Russell
Falls — A15

Mt. Gould and
Lake St.
Clair — A16

Dilston
Falls — A17

1899-1900　Engr.　Wmk. 78　Perf. 14
86	A10	½p dark green	16.00	12.00
87	A11	1p carmine	10.50	3.00
88	A12	2p violet	25.00	3.50
89	A13	2½p dark blue	35.00	17.50
90	A14	3p dark brown	18.00	9.00
91	A15	4p ocher	42.50	12.00
92	A16	5p ultramarine	47.50	29.00
93	A17	6p lake	45.00	37.50
		Nos. 86-93 (8)	239.50	123.50

See Nos. 94-97, 102-107, 114-117.

Perf. 11, 12½, 11x12½
1902-03　　Litho., Typo.　　Wmk. 70
94	A10	½p green	8.00	2.75
95	A11	1p carmine	15.00	2.40
96	A11	1p dull red	22.50	3.00
97	A12	2p violet	14.00	1.40
98	A5	9p blue	15.00	7.25
a.		9p ultramarine	750.00	
b.		9p indigo	240.00	
c.		Perf. 11	15.00	15.00
d.		Perf 12½, wmkd. sideways	40.00	17.00
99	A8	1sh rose & green	32.50	10.50
a.		Perf. 11	75.00	75.00
		Nos. 94-99 (6)	107.00	27.30

Nos. 94, 97 are litho., Nos. 96, 98-99 typo.
No. 95 was printed both ways.

No. 78 Surcharged in
Black

1904　　Wmk. 77　　Perf. 14
100	A8	1½p on 5p blue & brn	2.75	2.75

Perf. 11, 12, 12½ and Compound
1905-08　　Typo.　　Wmk. 13
102	A10	½p dull green	4.25	.95
a.		Booklet pane of 12		
103	A11	1p carmine	3.50	.60
a.		Booklet pane of 18		
104	A12	2p violet	18.00	.80
105	A14	3p dark brown	15.00	9.00
106	A15	4p ocher	25.00	7.25
107	A17	6p lake	70.00	12.50
108	A5	8p violet brown	35.00	16.00
109	A5	9p blue	130.00	8.00
110	A8	1sh rose & green	24.00	9.25
111	A8	10sh brt vio & brn	325.00	350.00
a.		Perf. 11	475.00	475.00
		Nos. 102-111 (10)	649.75	414.35

Nos. 104-107 also printed litho.

1911　　　　　　　Redrawn
114	A12	2p bright violet	10.00	7.50
a.		Perf. 11	17.00	8.50
b.		Compound perf. 11, 12½	85.00	27.50
c.		Compound perf. 12, 12½	575.00	
115	A15	4p dull yellow	72.50	72.50
a.		Perf. 11	82.50	
116	A17	6p lake	35.00	55.00
a.		Perf. 11	52.50	
b.		Compound perf. 11, 12½	525.00	
		Nos. 114-116 (3)	122.50	135.00

The redrawn 2p measures 33½x25mm instead of 32½x24½mm. There are many slight changes in the clouds and other parts of the design.

The 4p is much lighter, especially the waterfall and trees above it. This appears to be a new or cleaned plate rather than a redrawn one.

In the redrawn 6p there are more colored lines in the waterfall and the river and more white dots in the trees.

No. 114
Surcharged in
Red

1912
117	A12	1p on 2p bright violet	2.75	2.75
a.		Perf. 11	3.50	3.50
b.		Compound perf. 12½ 11	240.00	260.00

POSTAL FISCAL STAMPS

Authorized for postal use by Act of November 1, 1882. Authorization withdrawn Nov. 30, 1900.

Used values are for examples with postal cancellations used from Nov. 1, 1882 through Nov. 30, 1900.

Beware of stamps with a pen cancellation removed, often regummed or with a fake postmark added.

PF1　　　　　　PF2

St. George and the Dragon
PF3　　　　PF4

1863-80   Engr.   Wmk. 139   *Imperf.*

AR1	PF1	3p green	450.00	200.00
AR2	PF2	2sh 6p car	450.00	180.00
AR3	PF3	5sh green	525.00	250.00
AR4	PF3	5sh brown	900.00	550.00
AR5	PF4	10sh salmon ('80)	900.00	575.00
a.		10sh orange	1,200.	550.00

For overprint see No. AR32.

Perf. 10
AR6	PF1	3p green	475.00	300.00
AR7	PF2	2sh 6p car	450.00	
AR8	PF3	5sh brown	650.00	475.00
AR9	PF4	10sh orange	525.00	

Perf. 12
AR10	PF1	3p green	500.00	375.00
AR11	PF2	2sh 6p car	500.00	425.00
AR12	PF3	5sh brown	500.00	350.00
AR13	PF3	5sh brown	950.00	
AR14	PF4	10sh orange	600.00	375.00

Perf. 12½
AR15	PF1	3p green	800.00	
AR16	PF2	2sh 6p car	375.00	
AR17	PF3	5sh brown	650.00	
AR18	PF4	10sh orange	575.00	

Perf. 11½
AR19	PF1	3p green		
AR20	PF2	2sh 6p car	750.00	425.00
AR21	PF3	5sh brown	300.00	200.00
AR22	PF4	10sh salmon	350.00	300.00
a.		10sh orange	300.00	140.00

Wmk. 77
Perf. 12
AR23	PF2	2sh 6p car	72.50	52.50

For overprint see No. AR33.

Duck-billed Platypus — PF5

1880   Engr.   Wmk. 77   *Perf. 14*
AR24	PF5	1p slate	42.50	12.00
AR25	PF5	3p brown	29.00	7.75
AR26	PF5	6p lilac	140.00	21.00
AR27	PF5	1sh rose	200.00	35.00

For overprints see Nos. AR28-AR31.

Nos. AR24-AR27, AR2, AR23, 85
Overprinted "REVENUE"
1900, Nov. 15
AR28	PF5	1p slate	42.50	42.50
AR29	PF5	3p brown	42.50	45.00
AR30	PF5	6p lilac	300.00	140.00
AR31	PF5	1sh rose	500.00	240.00
AR32	PF2	2sh 6p car (#AR2)	675.00	525.00
AR33	PF2	2sh 6p car (#AR23)	450.00	
AR34	PF4	10sh orange	950.00	950.00
AR35	A8	£1 grn & yel (#85)	375.00	350.00

Nos. AR28-AR35 were not supposed to be postally used. Because of imprecise terminology, postal use was tolerated until all postal use of revenues ceased on Nov. 30, 1900.

Other denominations and watermarks were overprinted after postal use was no longer allowed.

VICTORIA

vik-'tōr-ē-ə

LOCATION — In the extreme southeastern part of Australia
GOVT. — British Colony
AREA — 87,884 sq. mi.
POP. — 1,201,341 (1901)
CAPITAL — Melbourne

Victoria was one of the six former British colonies which united on Jan. 1, 1901, to form the Commonwealth of Australia.

12 Pence = 1 Shilling
20 Shillings = 1 Pound

Unused values for Nos. 1-16 are for stamps without gum as these stamps are seldom found with original gum. Otherwise, unused values are for stamps with original gum as defined in the catalogue introduction.

Very fine examples of all rouletted, perforated and serrate perforated stamps from Nos. 9-109 and F2 will have roulettes, perforations or serrate perforations touching the design. Examples clear on four sides range from scarce to rare and will command higher prices.

Watermarks

Wmk. 6 — Large Star   Wmk. 80

Wmk. 50   Wmk. 80a

Wmk. 81   Wmk. 139

Wmk. 49   Wmk. 75

Wmk. 70 — V and Crown   Wmk. 13 — Crown & Double-lined A

Queen Victoria — A1

A1 TYPES

1p:
Type I — "VICTORIA" very close to top of design, with very thin line of color between "VICTORIA" and frameline.
Type II — Thicker line of color between "VICTORIA" and frameline at top.

2p:
Type I — Border, two sets of nine wavy lines crisscrossing. Background, 22 groups of wavy triple lines below "VICTORIA."
Type II — Border, same. Background, 15 groups of wavy triple lines below "VICTORIA."
Type III — Border, two sets of five wavy lines crisscrossing. Background, same as type II.

3p:
Type I — Orb poorly defined, with white area at right and thicker at left. Central band of orb does not protrude at left.
Type II — Orb clearly defined, with white outlines at left and right. Central band of orb protrudes at left.

1850   Litho.   Unwmk.   *Imperf.*
1	A1	1p dull red, II	3,750.	225.00
a.		1p dull org ver, II	5,000.	750.00
b.		1p brownish red, II ('51)	1,500.	210.00
c.		1p dull brown, I	19,000.	2,500.
d.		1p orange vermilion, I	30,000.	5,500.
e.		1p orange brown, I		2,100.
2	A1	1p rose, II	3,000.	200.00
a.		1p pink, II	1,750.	190.00
b.		1p reddish brown, II ('51)	5,000.	190.00
3	A1	3p blue, I	6,000.	450.00
a.		3p light blue, II ('52)	2,100.	110.00
b.		3p bright blue, II	7,250.	625.00
4	A1	3p indigo, II	3,000.	100.00
a.		3p pale grnsh blue, II ('52)	3,500.	210.00
		Nos. 1-4 (4)	15,750.	975.00

Nos. 1-4 exist with and without frame line.

5	A1	2p lilac, I	7,500.	550.00
a.		2p brn lilac, I	7,000.	550.00
b.		2p orange brown, I		2,500.
6	A1	2p brn lilac, II	2,500.	250.00
a.		2p gray lilac, II	6,000.	200.00
7	A1	2p brn lilac, III	7,250.	200.00
a.		2p gray lilac, III	11,000.	500.00
b.		Value omitted, III		17,500.
8	A1	2p yel brn, III	3,000.	200.00

A used pair of No. 5b, the 2 pence, type I, orange brown shade, issued in January 1850, realized the equivalent of U.S. $10,400 at an Australian auction in 2004.
A used example of No. 7b, with "butterfly" cancellation, realized the equivalent of U.S. $12,910 at an Australian auction in 2004.

Rouletted 7
9	A1	1p vermilion		3,350.
10	A1	3p blue	2,500.	250.00
a.		3p deep blue	2,500.	300.00

Perf. 12
12	A1	3p blue	2,000.	175.00
a.		3p deep blue	2,000.	175.00

Victoria on Throne — A2

1852   Engr.   *Imperf.*
14	A2	2p reddish brn	400.00	45.00
a.		2p chestnut		175.00
b.		2p purple brown	575.00	30.00

No. 14 was reprinted on paper with watermark 70, imperf. & perf. 12½, overprinted "REPRINT."

1854   Litho.
15	A2	2p gray brown	450.00	45.00
a.		2p purple black		37.50
16	A2	2p brown lilac	300.00	40.00
a.		2p purple black		37.50
b.		As "a," "TVO" for "TWO"	10,000.	1,500.

Fifty varieties.

A3   A4

1854-58   Typo.
17	A3	6p yellow orange	375.00	32.50
a.		6p dull orange	375.00	32.50
b.		6p reddish brown	725.00	72.50

See Nos. 19-20, 22-24A, 26-28

Lithographed
18	A4	1sh blue	1,100.	35.00
a.		1sh greenish blue	1,250.	35.00
b.		1sh indigo blue	—	180.00

See Nos. 21, 25.

Typographed
19	A3	2sh green	3,000.	250.00

1857-58   *Rouletted 7, 9½*
20	A3	6p orange	—	87.50
a.		6p yellow orange	—	100.00
b.		6p reddish brown	—	115.00

Lithographed
21	A4	1sh blue	—	160.00
a.		1sh greenish blue	—	160.00

Typographed
22	A3	2sh green ('58)	7,000.	675.00

Small Serrate Perf. 19
23	A3	6p orange	—	125.00

Large Serpentine Perf. 10½
24	A3	6p orange	—	125.00

Serrate x Serpentine Perf.
24A	A3	6p orange	—	200.00

1859   Litho.   *Perf. 12*
25	A4	1sh blue	250.00	25.00
a.		1sh greenish blue	275.00	27.50
b.		1sh indigo blue	—	52.50

Typographed
26	A3	2sh green	525.00	70.00

1861   Wmk. "SIX PENCE" (80)
27	A3	6p black	300.00	80.00

Wmk. Single-lined "2" (50)
1864   *Perf. 12, 13*
28	A3	2sh blue, *green*	350.00	13.00

A5

Wmk. Large Star (6)
1856, Oct.   Engr.   *Imperf.*
29	A5	1p green	250.00	42.50

1858   *Rouletted 5½-6½*
30	A5	6p blue	350.00	28.00
a.		6p light blue	450.00	45.00

Nos. 29 and 30 have been reprinted on paper watermarked V and Crown. They are imperforate and overprinted "REPRINT."

A6

1857-61   Typo.   *Imperf.*
Wove Paper
31	A6	1p yellow green	175.00	25.00
a.		Printed on both sides		2,750.
b.		1p deep green	230.00	47.50
32	A6	4p vermilion	450.00	15.00
a.		Printed on both sides		2,750.
b.		4p brownish vermilion	425.00	15.00
33	A6	4p rose	375.00	15.00
a.		4p dull red	260.00	12.00

Rouletted 7 to 9½
34	A6	1p yellow green	625.00	140.00
35	A6	4p rose		57.50
a.		4p vermilion		160.00
b.		4p dull red		60.00
35A	A6	4p vermilion		575.00

Perf. 12
36	A6	1p yellow green	—	500.00

Unwmk.   *Imperf.*
37	A6	1p blue green	425.00	22.50
a.		1p emerald green		22.50
38	A6	2p lilac	400.00	21.00
a.		2p gray lilac	400.00	20.00
39	A6	4p rose	575.00	47.50
a.		4p rose pink	575.00	42.50
b.		4p reddish pink		47.50

Examples of No. 39 printed in dull carmine on thin paper are regarded as printer's waste and of little value. They are also found printed on both sides.

Rouletted 7 to 9½

40	A6	1p emerald green	575.00	37.50
a.		1p pale emerald	525.00	35.00
41	A6	2p lilac	1,150.	725.00
42	A6	4p rose pink	400.00	11.50
a.		Vert. pair, imperf. btwn.		750.00
b.		4p reddish pink		20.00
c.		4p bright rose	400.00	11.50

Perf. 12

43	A6	1p blue green	225.00	20.00
a.		1p yellow green	325.00	24.00
b.		Horiz. pair, imperf. btwn.		
c.		As "a," on thin, glazed "Bordeaux" paper		240.00
44	A6	2p lilac		450.00
a.		2p gray lilac		400.00
45	A6	4p rose	300.00	8.00
b.		Vert. pair, imperf. btwn.		—

Rouletted 5½-6½

45C	A6	4p dull rose		1,250.

Serrate Rouletted 19

45A	A6	2p lilac	1,100.	600.00

Laid Paper
Imperf

46	A6	4p rose	825.00	35.00

Rouletted 5 to 7

47	A6	2p violet	275.00	10.50
a.		2p brown lilac	225.00	15.00
b.		2p dark lilac	300.00	25.00
48	A6	4p rose	250.00	7.25
a.		4p pale dull red, vertically laid paper	260.00	7.25
b.		4p pale dull red, horizontally laid paper		1,250.
c.		4p dull rose red	225.00	6.25

Serrate Rouletted 19

48D	A6	4p rose red		825.00

Perf. 12

49	A6	1p green	300.00	25.00
a.		Laid lines close together		35.00
50	A6	1p rose	200.00	15.00
a.		Laid lines close together		13.00

Wove Paper
1860   Wmk. Value in Words (80)

51	A6	1p pale yellowish green	130.00	10.50
a.		Wmk. "FOUR PENCE" (error)		9,750.
b.		1p yellow green	125.00	7.25
52	A6	2p gray lilac	200.00	10.00
a.		2p brown lilac ('61)		52.50
b.		2p bluish slate ('61)	200.00	9.50
c.		2p slate gray ('62)		9.50
d.		2p bluish gray ('63)	230.00	35.00

Wmk. "THREE PENCE" (80)

53	A6	2p bluish gray ('63)	225.00	25.00
a.		2p gray lilac ('62)	325.00	22.50

Single-lined "2" (50)

54	A6	2p lilac	300.00	18.00
a.		2p gray lilac	275.00	22.50
b.		2p brown lilac	225.00	21.00
c.		As "a," wmkd. single-lined "6"		7,750.
d.		6p pale violet ('63)	220.00	20.00
e.		2p slate ('63)	290.00	35.00

A7

1860   Unwmk.   Laid Paper

56	A7	3p deep blue	625.00	77.50

Wmk. Value in Words (80)
Perf. 11½ to 12

1860-64   Wove Paper

57	A7	3p blue ('63)	240.00	12.50
a.		"TRREE" instead of "THREE" in watermark		800.00
b.		3p pale blue ('61)	240.00	45.00
c.		3p bright blue ('61)	225.00	12.50
d.		3p deep blue ('64)	230.00	10.00
58	A7	3p claret	180.00	37.50
a.		Perf. 13	240.00	47.50
59	A7	4p rose	200.00	7.75
a.		4p rose pink		12.50
b.		4p rose red	170.00	7.00
c.		4p rose carmine		12.50
60	A7	6p orange	5,750.	350.00
61	A7	6p black	250.00	10.50
a.		6p gray black	275.00	9.25

Wmk. "FIVE SHILLINGS" (80)

62	A7	4p rose	3,000.	30.00

Wmk. Single-lined "4" (80a)
1863   Imperf.

63	A7	4p rose	—	175.00

Rouletted

64	A7	4p rose	3,250.	350.00

Perf. 11½ to 12

65	A7	4p rose	180.00	10.50

1863   Unwmk.   Perf. 12

66	A7	4p rose	625.00	10.50
a.		4p rose pink, thin glazed "Bordeaux" paper		22.50
b.		4p rose, thick coarse paper	600.00	22.50

A8   A9

1861-63   Wmk. 80   Perf. 11½ to 12

67	A8	1p green	140.00	17.00
a.		1p olive green		16.00
68	A9	6p black	140.00	15.00
a.		6p gray black	145.00	17.00
b.		6p jet black	160.00	18.00

Wmk. Double-lined "1" (139)

69	A8	1p green	250.00	18.00
a.		1p dull green	—	15.00
b.		Horiz. pair, imperf between		

Wmk. Single-lined Figures (50)

70	A8	1p green	115.00	11.50
a.		1p apple green	115.00	11.50
b.		1p olive green	100.00	17.00
71	A9	6p gray black	140.00	10.00
a.		6p jet black	—	11.50
b.		6p jet black, perf 13	170.00	11.50
c.		6p gray black, perf 13	170.00	11.50

The 1p and 6p of 1861-63 are known on paper without watermark but were probably impressions on the margins of watermarked sheets.

A10   A11

A12   A13

Wmk. Single-lined Figures (50, 80a, 81)

1863-67   Perf. 11½ to 13

74	A10	1p green	120.00	8.50
a.		Double impression		1,500.
75	A10	2p gray lilac	120.00	15.00
a.		2p violet	115.00	11.50
76	A10	4p rose	140.00	14.00
a.		Double impression		1,500.
77	A11	6p blue	115.00	4.25
78	A11	8p orange	700.00	115.00
79	A12	10p brn, rose	200.00	10.50
80	A13	1sh blue, blue	200.00	6.50
		Nos. 74-80 (7)	1,595.	164.75

See Nos. 81-82, 84-96, 99-101, 108-112, 115-119, 124-126, 144, 188. Compare type A11 with type A54.

A14

Wmk. Double-lined "1" (139)

81	A10	1p green	125.00	7.00
82	A10	2p gray lilac	325.00	10.50
83	A14	3p lilac	325.00	100.00
84	A11	6p blue	115.00	9.50
		Nos. 81-84 (4)	890.00	127.00

See Nos. 97, 113, 114, 155, 186. Compare type A14 with type A51.

Wmk. Double-lined "2" (49)

85	A11	6p blue		4,250.

Wmk. Single-lined "4" (80a)

86	A10	1p green	200.00	30.00
87	A10	2p gray lilac	250.00	10.50
88	A11	6p blue		2,750.

Wmk. Double-lined "4" (75)

89	A10	1p green	2,500.	160.00
90	A10	2p gray lilac	250.00	8.00
91	A10	4p rose	300.00	9.50
92	A11	6p blue	325.00	35.00

Wmk. Single-lined "6" (50)

93	A10	1p green	325.00	42.50
94	A10	2p gray lilac	350.00	11.50

Wmk. Single-lined "8" (50)

95	A10	1p green	300.00	27.50
96	A10	2p gray lilac	325.00	10.50
97	A14	3p lilac	250.00	57.50
99	A12	10p slate	1,000.	200.00

Wmk. "SIX PENCE" (80)

100	A10	1p green	1,150.	57.50
100A	A10	2p slate gray	16,000.	
101	A11	6p blue	800.00	42.50
a.		6p indigo blue		42.50

All values of the 1864-67 series except the 3p and 8p are known on unwatermarked paper. They are probably varieties from watermarked sheets which have been so placed on the printing press that some of the stamps escaped the watermark.

One example of the 2p gray lilac, type A10, is reported to exist with only "PENCE" of watermark 80 showing. Some believe this is part of the "SIX PENCE" watermark.

1870   Wmk. "THREE PENCE" (80)

108	A11	6p blue	475.00	17.50

Wmk. "FOUR PENCE" (80)

109	A11	6p blue	800.00	52.50

A15

1867-78   Wmk. (70)   Perf. 11½ to 13

110	A10	1p green	115.00	5.75
a.		1p bright olive green	125.00	5.75
111	A10	2p gray lilac	110.00	5.25
a.		2p gray lilac	125.00	9.50
112	A10	2p lilac, lilac	130.00	14.00
113	A14	3p red lilac	400.00	65.00
a.		3p lilac	475.00	72.50
114	A14	3p orange	47.50	6.50
a.		3p yellow	77.50	7.75
b.		3p org brn, glazed paper ('78)	52.50	17.00
115	A10	4p rose	130.00	11.50
a.		4p dl rose, glazed paper ('79)	125.00	6.00
b.		Wmk sideways		200.00
116	A11	6p blue	60.00	4.75
117	A11	6p ultra	72.50	5.00
a.		6p lilac blue	130.00	17.50
b.		6p light Prussian blue ('75)	145.00	4.75
118	A10	8p brn, rose	140.00	10.50
a.		8p choc, pink ('78)	160.00	11.50
b.		Perf. 13x12		460.00
119	A13	1sh bl, blue	325.00	17.50
120	A15	5sh bl, yel	3,250.	500.00
121	A15	5sh bl & rose	400.00	32.50
a.		Without blue line under crown	375.00	30.00
b.		5sh ind bl & car	425.00	42.50
122	A15	5sh ultra & rose	325.00	42.50

See Nos. 126, 144, 188. For surcharge see No. 124.

For additional stamps of type A15, see No. 191. Compare type A15 with type A58.

A16

1870   Perf. 13

123	A16	2p lilac	115.00	2.60
a.		Perf. 12	125.00	3.50

No. 110 Surcharged in Red

1873, July 19   Perf. 13, 12

124	A10	½p on 1p green	100.00	24.00
a.		Perf. 12	125.00	24.00

No. 79 Surcharged in Blue

1871   Wmk. Single-lined "10" (81)

125	A12	9p on 10p brn, rose	650.00	25.00
a.		Double surcharge		2,500.

A19

1873-78   Typo.

126	A10	8p brown, rose ('78)	175.00	10.50
127	A19	9p brown, rose	175.00	27.50

For additional stamps of type A19, see Nos. 128-129, 174-175. Compare type A19 with type A55.

1875   Wmk. V and Crown (70)

128	A19	9p brown, rose	200.00	27.50

No. 128 Surcharged in Blue

1876

129	A19	8p on 9p brn, rose	350.00	32.50

A21   A22

A23   A24

A25

1873-81   Perf. 13, 12

130	A21	½p rose ('74)	24.00	2.00
a.		½p pink, glazed paper ('80)	24.00	2.00
b.		½p lil rose ('74)	27.50	2.90
131	A21	½p rose, rose ('78)	70.00	42.50
132	A22	1p grn ('75)	52.50	3.25
a.		1p yel grn, glazed paper ('78)	52.50	3.50
133	A22	1p grn, gray ('78)	240.00	110.00
134	A22	1p grn, yel ('78)	160.00	30.00
135	A23	2p violet	77.50	1.30
a.		2p pale mv ('80)	77.50	1.25
b.		2p pale mv, glazed paper ('79)	77.50	1.60
136	A23	2p vio, grnsh ('78)	325.00	40.00
137	A23	2p vio, buff ('78)	300.00	40.00
137A	A23	2p vio, lil ('78)	—	1,200.
138	A24	1sh bl, bl ('76)	130.00	6.75
a.		1sh brt bl, bl, glazed paper ('83)	145.00	12.00
139	A25	2sh bl, grn ('81)	240.00	35.00
a.		2sh ultra, grnsh, glazed paper ('84)		45.00
b.		Wmk sideways		50.00

See Nos. 140, 156A-158, 184, 189-190. Compare design A21 with design A46, A24 with A56, A25 with A57.

1878 — Double-lined Outer Oval
140 A23 2p violet — 77.50 — 3.75
b. Vert. pair, lower stamp imperf horiz. — 3,000.

 A26
 A27

 A28

1880-84 — Perf. 12½
141 A26 1p green ('84) — 140.00 — 22.50
142 A27 2p brown — 50.00 — 1.40
143 A27 2p lilac — 37.50 — 2.25
144 A10 4p car rose — 260.00 — 15.00
   4p lilac rose — 125.00 — 11.50
145 A28 4p car rose ('81) — 115.00 — 10.00
a. 4p pink ('82) — 115.00 — 9.50
Nos. 141-145 (5) — 602.50 — 51.15

See Nos. 156, 185, 187. Compare design A26 with design A47, A27 with A49, A28 with A52.

 A29
 A30

A31
A32

A33
A34

1884-86
146 A29 ½p rose — 22.50 — 2.25
a. ½p salmon ('85) — 26.00 — 2.40
147 A30 1p green — 29.00 — 2.40
a. 1p pea green — 35.00 — 3.25
148 A31 2p violet — 32.50 — 1.25
a. 2p lilac rose — 32.50 — 1.25
149 A30 3p bister — 20.00 — 2.40
a. 3p ocher — 20.00 — 2.40
150 A32 4p magenta — 110.00 — 6.25
a. 4p violet (error) — 6,000. — 1,250.
151 A30 6p bright blue ('85) — 125.00 — 5.00
a. 6p ultramarine ('85) — 85.00 — 4.75
b. 6p gray blue ('85) — 82.50 — 4.75
152 A33 8p rose, rose — 52.50 — 14.00
153 A34 1sh blue, yel — 175.00 — 24.00
154 A33 2sh olive, grn — 115.00 — 6.25
Nos. 146-154 (9) — 681.50 — 63.80

See Nos. 177-178, 192A. Compare designs A31-A32 with designs A37-A38.

Nos. 114, 145, 138-139 Ovptd. Vertically in Blue or Black

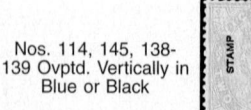 (STAMP DUTY)

1885
155 A14 3p orange (Bl) — 115.00 — 47.50
156 A28 4p car rose (Bl) — 105.00 — 72.50
156A A24 1sh bl, bl (Bl) — 3,500.
   Revenue cancel — 1,250.

157 A24 1sh bl, bl (Bk) — 175.00 — 37.50
158 A25 2sh bl, grn (Bk) — 175.00 — 35.00
a. Wmk sideways — 100.00 — 25.00
Nos. 155-156,157-158 (4) — 570.00 — 192.50

Reprints of 4p and 1sh have brighter colors than originals. They lack the overprint "REPRINT."

 A35
 A36

 A37
A38

 A39
A40

1886-87 — Perf. 12½
159 A35 ½p lilac — 37.50 — 9.50
160 A35 ½p rose — 17.50 — 1.40
160A A35 ½p scarlet — 7.75 — 1.40
161 A36 1p green — 16.00 — 2.25
162 A37 2p violet — 20.00 — .55
a. 2p red lilac — 11.50 — .70
b. Imperf. — 1,100.
163 A38 4p red — 22.50 — 2.40
164 A39 6p blue — 37.50 — 3.25
165 A39 6p ultra — 32.50 — 1.10
166 A40 1sh lilac brown — 37.50 — 3.75
Nos. 159-166 (9) — 228.75 — 25.60

See No. 180.

 A41

1889
167 A41 1sh6p blue — 260.00 — 140.00
168 A41 1sh6p orange — 35.00 — 15.00

 A42

 Southern Cross — A43

 Queen Victoria — A44

1890-95 — Perf. 12½
169 A42 1p org brn — 10.00 — .75
a. 1p chocolate brown — 12.50 — 1.10
170 A42 1p yel brn — 12.50 — .55
171 A42 1p brn org, pink ('91) — 10.50 — 4.50
172 A43 2½p brn red, yel — 19.00 — 1.75
173 A44 5p choc ('91) — 15.00 — 3.75
174 A19 9p green ('92) — 45.00 — 16.00
175 A19 9p rose red — 32.50 — 6.00
a. 9p rose ('95) — 37.50 — 11.50
176 A40 1sh deep claret — 37.50 — 2.40
a. 1sh red brown — 32.50 — 1.40
b. 1sh maroon — 87.50 — 5.25
177 A33 2sh yel grn — 37.50 — 17.50
178 A33 2sh emerald — 35.00 — 19.00
Nos. 169-178 (10) — 254.50 — 72.20

In 1891 many stamps of the early issues were reprinted. They are on paper watermarked V and Crown, perforated 12, 12½, and overprinted "REPRINT."

 A45

See Nos. 181, 183, 192. Compare type A43 with type A50, A44 with A53.

1897
179 A45 1½p yellow green — 6.00 — 6.50

See No. 182. Compare type A45 with type A48.

1899
180 A35 ½p emerald — 25.00 — 5.75
181 A42 1p brt rose — 11.50 — .55
182 A45 1½p red, yel — 5.75 — 3.50
183 A43 2½p dark blue — 15.00 — 15.00
Nos. 180-183 (4) — 57.25 — 24.80

1901
184 A21 ½p blue green — 3.75 — 3.25
a. "VICTORIA" — 110.00 — 62.50
185 A27 2p violet — 14.00 — 3.00
186 A14 3p brown org — 22.50 — 50.00
187 A28 4p bister — 42.50 — 25.00
188 A11 6p emerald — 17.50 — 13.00
189 A24 1sh orange yel — 87.50 — 65.00
190 A25 2sh blue, rose — 72.50 — 55.00
191 A15 5sh rose red & bl — 90.00 — 72.50
Nos. 184-191 (8) — 350.25 — 286.75

1901
192 A42 1p olive green — 11.50 — 7.50
192A A30 3p sage green — 40.00 — 19.00

Nos. 192-192A were available for postal use until June 30, 1901, and thereafter restricted to revenue use.

 A46
 A47

 A48
A49

 A50
A51

 A52
A53

 A54
A55

 A56
A57

 A58

1901 — Perf. 11, 12½ and Compound
193 A46 ½p blue green — 5.75 — 1.40
194 A47 1p rose red — 4.50 — .65
a. 1p rose — 14.00 — 1.00
b. Wmk sideways — 10.00 — 5.00
195 A48 1½p red, yellow — 3.75 — 1.25
a. Perf. 11 — 110.00 — 110.00
196 A49 2p violet — 21.00 — 1.10
197 A50 2½p blue — 15.00 — 1.10
198 A51 3p brown org — 15.00 — 2.50
a. Wmk sideways — 20.00 — 8.00
199 A52 4p bister — 10.50 — 1.25
200 A53 5p chocolate — 17.50 — 1.10
201 A54 6p emerald — 21.00 — 2.40
202 A55 9p rose — 26.00 — 4.00
a. Wmk sideways — 30.00 — 10.00
203 A56 1sh org yel — 29.00 — 5.00
204 A57 2sh blue, rose — 40.00 — 5.00
205 A58 5sh rose red & bl — 110.00 — 35.00
a. 5sh carmine & blue — 110.00 — 26.00
Nos. 193-205 (13) — 319.00 — 61.75

See Nos. 209-229, 232.

King Edward VII
A59   A60

1901-05
206 A59 £1 deep rose — 350.00 — 150.00
a. Perf. 11 ('05) — 475.00 — 225.00
208 A60 £2 dk blue ('02) — 700.00 — 450.00
a. Perf. 11 ('05) — 2,250. — 1,400.

See Nos. 230-231.

1903 — Redrawn
209 A56 1sh yellow — 35.00 — 5.75
a. 1sh orange — 32.50 — 4.75

No. 209 has the network lighter than No. 203. In the latter the "P" and "E" of "POSTAGE" are in a position more nearly horizontal than on No. 209.

Perf. 11, 12x12½, 12½, 12½x11
1905-10 — Wmk. 13
218 A46 ½p blue green — 4.75 — .75
219 A47 1p rose red — 2.40 — .35
a. 1p carmine rose — 15.00 — 3.00
b. Wmk sideways — 10.00 — 5.00
220 A49 2p violet — 9.25 — .75
a. 2p purple — 10.00 — .90
221 A50 2½p blue — 5.75 — 1.00
222 A51 3p brown org — 15.00 — 3.00
a. 3p dull yellow — 17.50 — 3.00
223 A52 4p bister — 12.50 — 1.75
224 A53 5p chocolate — 12.50 — 4.75
225 A54 6p emerald — 24.00 — 5.00
226 A55 9p orange brown — 24.00 — 5.00
a. 9p brown rose — 26.00 — 5.25
227 A55 9p car rose — 17.50 — 3.00
228 A56 1sh yellow ('08) — 24.00 — 4.50
229 A58 5sh orange red & ultra — 130.00 — 26.00
a. 5sh rose red & ultra — 140.00 — 32.50
230 A59 £1 pale red ('07) — 450.00 — 240.00
a. £1 rose ('10) — 350.00 — 240.00
231 A60 £2 dull blue — 1,150. — 725.00
Nos. 218-229 (12) — 281.65 — 52.85

 (ONE PENNY surcharge)

No. 220 Surcharged in Red

1912, July 1
232 A49 1p on 2p violet — 1.75 — 1.25

POSTAL-FISCAL STAMPS

On Jan. 1, 1884, all postage and fiscal stamps were made available for either purpose. Fiscal stamps became invalid after June 30, 1901.

Used values are for examples with postal cancellations used from Jan. 1, 1884 through June 30, 1901.

Beware of stamps with a pen cancellation removed, often regummed or with a fake postmark added.

Stamps inscribed "Stamp Duty" that were issued primarily in postal rates in the normal postage stamp size are listed in the postage section (Nos. 146-178, 180-183, 192-192A). The stamps meeting primarily fiscal rates and in the larger fiscal stamp size, are listed here in the Postal-Fiscal section.

Stamps Inscribed "Stamp Statute"

Victoria — PF1

PF1a (AR3)

PF1b (AR5)   PF1c (AR6)

Coat of Arms — PF2

PF3

Wmk. V and Crown (70)

1870-83		**Typo.**		**Perf. 13**
AR1	PF1a	1p green	90.00	75.00
		Revenue cancel		7.25
a.		Perf. 12½	140.00	120.00
AR2	PF1	3p lilac	1,150.	600.00
		Revenue cancel		140.00
AR3	PF1a	4p red	1,000.	500.00
		Revenue cancel		125.00

AR4	PF1a	6p blue	125.00	45.00
		Revenue cancel		14.00
a.		Perf. 12	140.00	35.00
		Revenue cancel		10.50
AR5	PF1b	1sh blue, blue	140.00	45.00
		Revenue cancel		14.00
a.		Perf. 12	140.00	50.00
		Revenue cancel		17.50
b.		Perf. 12½	140.00	45.00
		Revenue cancel		14.00
c.		Wmk. 50, perf. 13	140.00	32.50
		Revenue cancel		11.50
d.		Wmk. 50, perf. 12	160.00	37.50
		Revenue cancel		13.00
AR6	PF1c	2sh blue, grn	225.00	130.00
		Revenue cancel		30.00
a.		Perf. 12	225.00	—
		Revenue cancel		35.00
b.		Wmk. 50, perf. 13	300.00	125.00
		Revenue cancel		17.50
c.		Wmk. 50, perf. 12	325.00	125.00
		Revenue cancel		21.00
AR7	PF2	2sh 6p orange, yel	650.00	260.00
		Revenue cancel		72.50
a.		Perf. 12	650.00	260.00
		Revenue cancel		72.50
b.		Perf. 12½	—	300.00
		Revenue cancel		87.50
AR8	PF1a	5sh blue, yel	600.00	140.00
		Revenue cancel		72.50
a.		Perf. 12	650.00	—
b.		Perf. 12½	650.00	140.00
		Revenue cancel		72.50
AR9	PF1a	10sh brn, rose	1,600.	375.00
		Revenue cancel		90.00
a.		Perf. 12	—	—
		Revenue cancel		90.00
b.		Wmk. 50, perf. 13	1,600.	350.00
		Revenue cancel		75.00
c.		Wmk. 50, perf. 12		
AR10	PF1a	£1 lilac, yel	1,250.	350.00
		Revenue cancel		90.00
a.		Perf. 12	1,150.	325.00
		Revenue cancel		90.00
b.		Perf. 12½	1,150.	325.00
		Revenue cancel		90.00
AR11	PF3	£5 black, grn	10,000.	1,900.
		Revenue cancel		135.00
a.		Perf. 12	—	—
b.		Perf. 12½	10,000.	1,900.
		Revenue cancel		150.00

Nos. AR1-AR12 distributed for postal use from Jan. 1, 1884 through Apr. 23, 1884.

No. AR1 Surcharged "½d/HALF"

1879-96				
AR12	PF1	½p on 1p grn	120.00	105.00
		Revenue cancel		42.50

Stamps Inscribed "Stamp Duty"

PF4   PF5

PF6   PF7

PF8   PF9

PF10   PF11

PF12   PF13

PF14   PF15

PF16   PF17

PF18   PF19

PF20   PF21

PF22

PF23

PF24

PF25

PF26

PF27

PF28

Wmk. V and Crown (70)

1879-96		**Litho.**		**Perf. 13**
AR13	PF4	1p green	140.00	45.00
		Revenue cancel		14.00
a.		Perf. 12	140.00	45.00
		Revenue cancel		14.00
b.		Perf. 12½	—	—
AR14	PF8	1sh 6p pink	375.00	50.00
		Revenue cancel		21.00
a.		Perf. 12	—	65.00
		Revenue cancel		26.00
b.		Perf. 12½	—	—
AR15	PF11	3sh violet, blue	875.00	85.00
		Revenue cancel		21.00
a.		Perf. 12	1,000.	100.00
		Revenue cancel		21.00
b.		Perf. 12½		
AR16	PF12	4sh orange	175.00	35.00
		Revenue cancel		11.00
a.		Perf. 12	175.00	35.00
		Revenue cancel		11.00
b.		Perf. 12½		
AR17	PF14	6sh green	575.00	70.00
		Revenue cancel		12.50
a.		Perf. 12½	—	—
AR18	PF15	10sh brown, pink	925.00	175.00
		Revenue cancel		62.50
a.		Perf. 12	—	—
b.		Perf. 12½	—	—
AR19	PF16	15sh lilac	1,750.	325.00
		Revenue cancel		125.00
AR20	PF17	£1 orange	800.00	110.00
		Revenue cancel		25.00
a.		Perf. 12½	800.00	110.00
AR21	PF18	£1 5sh pink	2,400.	450.00
		Revenue cancel		125.00
AR22	PF19	£1 10sh olive	2,750.	275.00
		Revenue cancel		75.00
AR23	PF20	35sh lilac	10,000.	
		Revenue cancel		350.00
AR24	PF21	£2 blue	—	240.00
		Revenue cancel		37.50
AR25	PF22	45sh violet	5,000.	425.00
		Revenue cancel		92.50
AR26	PF23	£5 rose	9,000.	1,000.
		Revenue cancel		125.00

AR27	PF24	£6 blue,		
		pink	—	1,500.
		Revenue cancel		175.00
AR28	PF25	£7 violet,		
		blue	—	1,500.
		Revenue cancel		175.00
AR29	PF26	£8 scarlet,		
		yel	—	1,700.
		Revenue cancel		200.00
AR30	PF27	£9 green,		
		grn	—	1,700.
		Revenue cancel		200.00

Typo.

AR31	PF4	1p green	105.00	45.00
		Revenue cancel		8.75
a.		Perf. 12	105.00	45.00
		Revenue cancel		8.75
b.		Perf. 12½	—	
AR32	PF5	1p brown	40.00	7.75
		Revenue cancel		1.40
a.		Perf. 12	40.00	9.25
		Revenue cancel		1.40
b.		Perf. 12½	—	
AR33	PF6	6p blue	140.00	22.50
		Revenue cancel		5.75
a.		Perf. 12	140.00	37.50
		Revenue cancel		5.75
b.		Perf. 12½	—	
AR34	PF7	1sh blue,		
		blue	140.00	11.50
		Revenue cancel		5.75
a.		Perf. 12	140.00	14.00
		Revenue cancel		5.75
b.		Perf. 12½	140.00	13.00
		Revenue cancel		5.75
AR35	PF7	1sh blue,		
		yel,		
		perf		
		12½	200.00	45.00
		Revenue cancel		17.50
AR36	PF8	1sh 6p pink	260.00	50.00
		Revenue cancel		17.50
AR37	PF9	2sh blue,		
		grn	325.00	45.00
		Revenue cancel		13.00
a.		Perf. 12	—	50.00
		Revenue cancel		13.00
b.		Perf. 12½	350.00	52.50
		Revenue cancel		13.00
AR38	PF10	2sh 6p org,		
		perf		
		12½	175.00	37.50
a.		2sh6p yellow ('85)	115.00	17.50
b.		2sh6p lemon yellow		
		('92)	115.00	18.00
		Revenue cancel		5.75
AR39	PF11	3sh violet,		
		bl,		
		perf		
		12½	700.00	65.00
		Revenue cancel		14.00
AR40	PF11	3sh bister	125.00	29.00
		Revenue cancel		21.00
AR41	PF12	4sh org,		
		perf		
		12½	140.00	26.00
		Revenue cancel		7.25
AR42	PF13	5sh claret,		
		yel	110.00	11.50
		Revenue cancel		5.75
a.		Perf. 12	125.00	22.50
		Revenue cancel		5.75
b.		Perf. 12½	100.00	22.50
		Revenue cancel		5.75
AR43	PF13	5sh car		
		rose	140.00	35.00
		Revenue cancel		7.25
AR44	PF14	6sh green	200.00	85.00
		Revenue cancel		16.00
AR45	PF15	10sh brn,		
		pink	—	175.00
		Revenue cancel		57.50
a.		Perf. 12	—	
b.		Perf. 12½	—	
AR46	PF15	10sh green	325.00	65.00
		Revenue cancel		20.00
AR47	PF16	15sh brown	1,200.	145.00
		Revenue cancel		42.50
AR48	PF17	£1 org,		
		yel,		
		perf		
		12½	875.00	80.00
		Revenue cancel		25.00
a.		Perf. 12	1,100.	95.00
		Revenue cancel		30.00
AR49	PF18	£1 5sh		
		pink	2,250.	160.00
		Revenue cancel		75.00
AR50	PF19	£1 10sh		
		olive	1,750.	135.00
		Revenue cancel		50.00
AR51	PF21	£2 blue	1,350.	125.00
		Revenue cancel		27.50
a.		Perf. 12	—	200.00
		Revenue cancel		27.50
AR52	PF22	45sh gray li-		
		lac	5,000.	180.00
		Revenue cancel		62.50
AR53	PF23	£5 rose,		
		perf.		
		12	—	900.00
		Revenue cancel		105.00
a.		perf. 12½	—	1,100.
		Revenue cancel		150.00
AR54	PF28	£10 lilac	5,500.	210.00
		Revenue cancel		62.50
a.		Perf. 12	5,500.	325.00
		Revenue cancel		62.50

Nos. AR49-AR52, AR54, used, are valued cto.

PF29

PF30

PF31

Wmk. V and Crown (70)

1879-1900		Engr.		Perf. 12½
AR55	PF29	£25 green	—	900.00
		Revenue cancel		110.00
a.		Perf. 13		—
b.		Perf. 12		—
AR56	PF30	£50 violet	—	975.00
		Revenue cancel		125.00
a.		Perf. 13		—
AR57	PF31	£100 red	—	1,000.
		Revenue cancel		225.00
a.		Perf. 13		—
b.		Perf. 12		225.00

Typo.

AR58	PF29	£25 green	—	325.00
a.		Lithographed		100.00
		Revenue cancel		100.00
AR59	PF30	£50 violet	—	500.00
a.		Lithographed		140.00
		Revenue cancel		140.00
AR60	PF31	£100 red	—	650.00
a.		Lithographed		225.00
		Revenue cancel		225.00

Nos. AR55-AR60, used, are valued cto.

PF32

1887-90				Typo.
AR61	PF32	£5 cl & ultra	4,000.	175.00
		Revenue cancel		82.50
AR62	PF32	£6 blue & yel	5,000.	200.00
		Revenue cancel		90.00
AR63	PF32	£7 blk & red	5,500.	225.00
		Revenue cancel		110.00
AR64	PF32	£8 org & lil	6,000.	250.00
		Revenue cancel		110.00
AR65	PF32	£9 red & green	6,500.	275.00
		Revenue cancel		135.00

Nos. AR61-AR65, used, are valued cto.

SEMI-POSTAL STAMPS

SP1

Queen Victoria and Figure of Charity SP2

Wmk. V and Crown (70)

1897, Oct.		Typo.		Perf. 12½
B1	SP1	1p deep blue	27.50	27.50
B2	SP2	2½p red brown	140.00	110.00

These stamps were sold at 1sh and 2sh6p respectively. The premium was given to a charitable institution.

Victoria Cross — SP3

Scout Reporting SP4

1900				
B3	SP3	1p brown olive	125.00	75.00
B4	SP4	2p emerald	225.00	225.00

These stamps were sold at 1sh and 2sh respectively. The premium was given to a patriotic fund in connection with the South African War.

REGISTRATION STAMPS

R1

Unwmk.

1854, Dec. 1		Typo.		Imperf.
F1	R1	1sh rose & blue	2,500.	225.00

1857				Rouletted 7
F2	R1	1sh rose & blue	8,750.	425.00

LATE FEE STAMP

LF1

Unwmk.

1855, Jan. 1		Typo.		Imperf.
I1	LF1	6p lilac & green	1,900.	275.00

POSTAGE DUE STAMPS

D1

Wmk. V and Crown (70)

1890		Typo.	Perf. 12½	
J1	D1	½p claret & blue	8.00	7.00
J2	D1	1p claret & blue	11.50	2.60
J3	D1	2p claret & blue	18.00	3.25
J4	D1	4p claret & blue	27.50	4.75
J5	D1	5p claret & blue	26.00	3.50
J6	D1	6p claret & blue	27.50	6.50
J7	D1	10p claret & blue	140.00	90.00
J8	D1	1sh claret & blue	90.00	14.00
J9	D1	2sh claret & blue	200.00	92.50
J10	D1	5sh claret & blue	300.00	140.00
		Nos. J1-J10 (10)	848.50	364.10

1891-94				
J11	D1	½p lake & blue	5.50	7.75
J12	D1	1p brown red & blue		
		('93)	15.00	2.75
J13	D1	2p brown red & blue		
		('93)	26.00	2.00
J14	D1	4p lake & blue ('94)	22.50	11.50
		Nos. J11-J14 (4)	69.00	24.00

1894-96				
J15	D1	½p bl grn & rose	9.50	3.00
J16	D1	1p bl grn & rose	9.00	3.00
J17	D1	2p bl grn & rose	18.00	3.50
J18	D1	4p bl grn & rose	18.00	3.00
J19	D1	5p bl grn & rose	22.50	22.50
J20	D1	6p bl grn & rose	20.00	14.00
J21	D1	10p bl grn & rose	45.00	20.00
J22	D1	1sh bl grn & rose	32.50	6.00
J23	D1	2sh yel green &		
		rose	115.00	37.50
J24	D1	5sh yel green &		
		rose	200.00	75.00
		Nos. J15-J24 (10)	489.50	187.50

1897-99				
J15a	D1	½p yel grn & pale		
		scar	9.00	1.75
J16a	D1	1p yel grn & pale		
		scar	10.00	1.25
J17a	D1	2p yel grn & pale		
		scar	13.50	1.25
J18a	D1	4p yel grn & pale		
		scar	27.50	2.25
J19a	D1	5p yel grn & pale		
		scar	27.50	7.00
J20a	D1	6p yel grn & pale		
		scar	12.00	4.50
		Nos. J15a-J20a (6)	99.50	18.00

1905-09				Wmk. 13
J25	D1	½p yel grn & rose	10.00	*13.00*
a.		½p pale green & pink	24.00	22.50
J26	D1	1p yel grn & rose	12.00	4.50
a.		1p pale green & pink	92.50	11.50
J27	D1	2p yel grn & rose	29.00	5.25
J28	D1	4p yel grn & rose	35.00	21.00
		Nos. J25-J28 (4)	86.00	43.75

A 5p with wmk. 13 exists but was not issued.

WESTERN AUSTRALIA

ˈwes-tərn o-ˈstrāl-yə

LOCATION — Western part of Australia, occupying about a third of that continent
GOVT. — British Colony
AREA — 975,920 sq. mi.
POP. — 184,124 (1901)
CAPITAL — Perth

Western Australia was one of the six British colonies that united on January

1, 1901, to form the Commonwealth of Australia.

12 Pence = 1 Shilling
20 Shillings = 1 Pound

Unused values for Nos. 1-10 are for stamps without gum as these stamps are seldom found with original gum. Otherwise, unused values are for stamps with original gum as defined in the catalogue introduction.

Very fine examples of all rouletted and perforated stamps from Nos. 6-34 have roulettes or perforations touching the design. Examples clear on all four sides range from scarce to rare and will command higher prices.

Watermarks

Wmk. 82 — Swan

Wmk. 83 — Crown and W A

Wmk. 70 — V and Crown

Wmk. 13 — Crown & Double-lined A

Wmk. 74 — Crown and Single-lined A

Swan

A1   A2

1854-57   Engr.   Wmk. 82   Imperf.

1	A1	1p black	1,350.	275.

Litho.

2	A2	2p brown, *red* ('57)	4,000.	800.
a.		2p brown, *deep red* ('57)	4,250.	1,100.
b.		Printed on both sides	4,250.	950.

See Nos. 4, 6-7, 9, 14-39, 44-52, 54, 59-61. For surcharges see Nos. 41, 55-56.

A3   A4

3	A3	4p blue	450.	275.
a.		Frame inverted		95,000.
		As "a," cut to shape		27,500.
b.		4p slate blue	3,750.	1,350.
4	A2	6p bronze ('57)	6,000.	900.
5	A4	1sh pale brown	550.	400.
a.		1sh dark brown	700.	450.
b.		1sh dark red brown	2,250.	1,000.
c.		1sh pale red brown	26,500.	4,000.

Engraved
Rouletted

6	A1	1p black	3,200.	750.

Lithographed

7	A2	2p brown, *red* ('57)	9,500.	1,900.
a.		Printed on both sides		2,300.
8	A3	4p blue	—	675.
9	A2	6p bronze ('57)	12,500.	2,000.
10	A4	1sh brown	4,750.	1,000.

The 1p, 2p, 4p and 6p are known with pin-perforation but this is believed to be unofficial. No. 7a is only recorded used and with pin perforations.

1860   Engr.   Imperf.

14	A1	2p vermilion	140.00	130.00
a.		2p pale orange	140.00	130.00
15	A1	4p blue	325.	2,000.
16	A1	6p dull green	2,100.	875.00

Rouletted

17	A1	2p vermilion	800.00	250.00
a.		2p pale orange	650.00	250.00
18	A1	4p deep blue	5,000.	—
19	A1	6p dull green	4,500.	750.00

1861   Clean-Cut Perf. 14 to 16

20	A1	1p rose	700.00	200.00
a.		Imperf.		
21	A1	2p blue	140.00	45.00
a.		Imperf., pair		
b.		Horiz. pair, imperf. vert.		
22	A1	4p vermilion	1,550.	2,400.
a.		Imperf.		
23	A1	6p purple brn	525.00	92.50
a.		Imperf.		
24	A1	1sh green	875.00	140.00
a.		Imperf.		

Rough Perf. 14 to 16

24B	A1	1p rose	300.00	65.00
24C	A1	6p pur brn, *blu-ish*	3,500.	525.00
24D	A1	1sh deep green	2,500.	425.00

Perf. 14

25	A1	1p rose	400.00	110.00
25A	A1	2p blue	180.00	72.50
25B	A1	4p vermilion	450.00	300.00

Unwmk.   Perf. 13

26	A1	1p lake	115.00	7.75
28	A1	6p violet	240.00	77.50

1865-79   Wmk. 1   Perf. 12½

29	A1	1p bister	110.00	10.00
30	A1	1p yel ocher	130.00	15.00
31	A1	2p yellow	125.00	4.75
a.		2p lilac (error) ('79)	20,000.	17,500.
b.		2p chrome yellow	160.00	11.00
32	A1	4p carmine	120.00	8.75
a.		Double impression	42,500.	
33	A1	6p violet	160.00	11.50
a.		6p lilac	300.00	11.50
b.		6p red lilac	300.00	11.50
c.		Double impression		27,500.
34	A1	1sh bright green	200.00	21.00
		Handstamped "SPECIMEN"	175.00	
a.		1sh sage green	525.00	45.00
		Nos. 29-34 (6)	845.00	71.00

An unused example of No. 31a realized the equivalent of U.S. $12,330 at an Australian auction in 2005.

A used example of No. 31a realized the equivalent of U.S. $16,180 at an Australian auction in 2005.

An unused example of No. 32a, with short perforations, realized the equivalent of U.S. $38,530 at an Australian auction in 2005.

A used example of No. 33c realized the equivalent of U.S. $27,740 at an Australian auction in 2005.

1872-78   Perf. 14

35	A1	1p bister	180.00	7.25
36	A1	1p yellow ocher	115.00	5.00
37	A1	2p yellow	115.00	2.40

38	A1	4p carmine	750.00	140.00
39	A1	6p lilac	200.00	6.50
		Nos. 35-39 (5)	1,360.	161.15

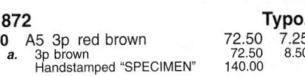

A5

1872   Typo.

40	A5	3p red brown	72.50	7.25
a.		3p brown	72.50	8.50
		Handstamped "SPECIMEN"	140.00	

See Nos. 53, 92. For surcharges see Nos. 57, 69-72A.

No. 31 Surcharged in Green

1875   Engr.   Perf. 12½

41	A1	1p on 2p yellow	625.00	80.00
a.		Pair, one without surcharge		
b.		"O" of "ONE" omitted		
c.		Triple surcharge		5,500.

Forged surcharges exist.

1882   Wmk. 2   Perf. 12

44	A1	1p ocher yellow	125.00	8.00
46	A1	2p yellow	160.00	7.75
47	A1	4p carmine	300.00	60.00
48	A1	6p pale violet	575.00	60.00
		Nos. 44-48 (4)	1,160.	135.75

1882   Perf. 14

49	A1	1p ocher yellow	45.00	3.00
50	A1	2p yellow	50.00	3.00
51	A1	4p carmine	180.00	17.50
52	A1	6p pale violet	140.00	5.25
a.		6p violet	140.00	6.50
		Handstamped "SPECIMEN"	160.00	

Typographed

53	A5	3p red brown	14.00	4.50
a.		3p brown	29.00	4.50
		Nos. 49-53 (5)	429.00	33.25

1883   Engr.   Perf. 12x14

54	A1	1p ocher yellow	4,000.	300.00

Nos. 44 and 49 Surcharged in Red

1884   Perf. 12

55	A1	½p on 1p ocher yel	18.00	32.50

Perf. 14

56	A1	½p on 1p ocher yel	30.00	40.00
a.		Thin fraction bar	97.50	115.00

No. 40 Surcharged in Green

1885   Typo.   Wmk. 1

57	A5	1p on 3p red brown	87.50	26.00
a.		1p on 3p brown	115.00	27.50
b.		"1" with straight top	240.00	75.00
c.		As "a," "1" with straight top	275.00	75.00

A8

Wmk. Crown and C A (2)

1885   Typo.   Perf. 14

58	A8	½p green	7.25	1.25

See No. 89.

1888   Engr.

59	A1	1p rose	35.00	5.75
60	A1	2p slate	90.00	2.75
61	A1	4p red brown	130.00	37.50
		Nos. 59-61 (3)	255.00	46.00

A9   A10

A11   A12

1890-93   Typo.

62	A9	1p carmine rose	35.00	2.00
63	A10	2p slate	37.50	3.00
64	A11	2½p blue	20.00	3.25
65	A12	4p orange brown	14.00	2.75
66	A12	5p bister	15.00	5.00
67	A12	6p violet	21.00	6.50
68	A12	1sh olive green	26.00	7.50
		Nos. 62-68 (7)	168.50	30.00

See Nos. 73-74, 76, 80, 90, 94.

Nos. 40 and 53a Surcharged in Green

1893   Wmk. Crown and C C (1)

69	A5	1p on 3p red brown	16.00	7.75
a.		1p on 3p brown	16.00	7.50
b.		Double surcharge	1,600.	

Wmkd. Crown and C A (2)

70	A5	1p on 3p brown	77.50	10.50

Nos. 40a and 53a Surcharged in Green

1895   Wmk. Crown and C C (1)

71	A5	½p on 3p brown	13.00	35.00
a.		Double surcharge	1,250.	

No. 72 Surcharged in Green and Red

72   A5   ½p on 3p brown   140.00   350.00

Wmk. Crown and C A (2)

72A	A5	½p on 3p brown	100.00	225.00

After the supply of paper watermarked Crown and C C was exhausted, No. 72A was printed. Ostensibly this was to provide samples for Postal Union distribution, but a supply for philatelic demands was also made.

Types of 1890-93 and

A15

1899-1901   Typo.   Wmk. 83

73	A9	1p carmine rose	7.75	1.75
74	A10	2p yellow	29.00	3.50
75	A15	2½p blue ('01)	14.00	4.75
		Nos. 73-75 (3)	50.75	10.00

A16   A17

A18   A19

A20

A21

A22

Southern
Cross — A23

Queen Victoria
A24   A25

Perf. 12½, 12x12½

1902-05				**Wmk. 70**
76	A9	1p car rose	22.00	1.00
a.		1p salmon		
b.		Perf. 11	400.00	35.00
c.		Perf. 12½x11	1,200.	675.00
77	A16	2p yellow	22.50	4.75
a.		Perf. 11	400.00	57.50
b.		Perf. 12½x11	1,750.	1,100.
79	A17	4p orange brn	29.00	4.00
a.		Perf. 11	1,400.	450.00
80	A12	5p ol bis, perf 12½ ('05)	175.00	115.00
a.		Perf. 11	90.00	100.00
81	A18	8p pale yel grn	30.00	4.75
82	A19	9p orange	50.00	17.50
b.		Perf. 11	175.00	185.00
83	A20	10p red	57.50	13.00
84	A21	2sh orange red, *yel* ('06)	115.00	32.50
a.		Perf. 11	500.00	225.00
b.		2sh orange brown, *yel* ('11)	77.50	19.00
c.		2sh bright red	130.00	19.00
d.		As "c", perf. 11	350.00	200.00
85	A22	2sh6p dk bl, *rose*	77.50	14.00
86	A23	5sh blue green	125.00	45.00
87	A24	10sh violet	300.00	130.00
a.		10sh bright purple	725.00	400.00
88	A25	£1 brown org	450.00	225.00
a.		£1 orange	750.00	425.00
		Nos. 76-88 (12)	1,453.	606.50

Perf. 12½, 12x12½

1905-12				**Wmk. 13**
89	A8	½p dp green ('10)	8.00	9.25
a.		Perf 11	2,750.	
90	A9	1p rose	18.00	1.75
e.		Perf. 11	55.00	21.00
f.		Perf. 12½x11	1,100.	475.00
91	A16	2p yellow	11.50	3.25
a.		Perf. 11	65.00	32.50
b.		Perf. 12½x11	925.00	525.00
92	A5	3p brown	37.50	4.75
a.		Perf. 11	29.00	9.50
b.		Perf. 12½x11	—	1,200.
93	A17	4p orange brn	35.00	12.00
a.		4p bister brown	37.50	13.00
b.		Perf. 11	1,100.	290.00
94	A12	5p olive bis	29.00	15.00
a.		Perf. 11, pale olive bister	52.50	18.00
b.		Perf. 11, olive green	32.50	24.00
95	A18	8p pale yel grn ('12)	32.50	82.50
96	A19	9p orange	45.00	8.75
b.		Perf. 11	200.00	240.00
97	A20	10p red orange	37.50	35.00
98	A23	5s blue green	240.00	180.00
		Nos. 89-98 (10)	494.00	352.25

For surcharge see No. 103.

A26   A27

1906-07		**Wmk. 83**		**Perf. 14**
99	A26	6p bright violet	40.00	3.25
100	A27	1sh olive green	50.00	6.50

1912		**Wmk. 74**		**Perf. 11½x12**
101	A26	6p bright violet	21.00	19.00
102	A27	1sh gray green	45.00	29.00
a.		Perf. 12½		2,750.

No. 91 Surcharged

ONE PENNY

1912		**Wmk. 13**		**Perf. 12½**
103	A16	1p on 2p yellow	2.00	2.50
a.		Perf compound 12½x11	750.00	500.00

Stamps of Western Australia were replaced by those of Australia.

POSTAL-FISCAL STAMPS

Postal use of the 1p telegraph stamp was authorized beginning Oct. 25, 1886.

Used values are for examples with postal cancellations.

Beware of stamps with a pen cancellation removed and a fake postmark added.

PF1

1886		**Wmk. 1**		**Perf. 14**
AR1	PF1	1p bister	65.00	9.25
			Perf. 12½	
AR2	PF1	1p bister	65.00	7.75

Authorized for postal use by the Post and Telegraph Act of Sept. 5, 1893 were the current revenue stamps through the 1sh value.

Beware of stamps with a pen cancellation removed and a fake postmark added.

Because the Act specified current stamps, postally used examples from the provisional issue of of 1881 are not included here.

PF2

1882		**Wmk. 2**		**Perf. 14**
AR3	PF2	1p purple	26.00	4.00
AR4	PF2	2p purple	260.00	100.00
AR5	PF2	3p purple	90.00	5.75
AR6	PF2	6p purple	105.00	7.75
AR7	PF2	1sh purple	180.00	15.00

The 6p is known postally used but was not authorized.

Wmk. 83

AR8	PF2	1p purple	22.50	4.50
AR9	PF2	3p purple	85.00	5.75
AR10	PF2	6p purple	85.00	6.00
AR11	PF2	1sh purple	180.00	22.50

Nos. AR7, AR11 have a rectangular outer frame and a circular frame around the swan.

Higher values are known with postal cancels, some postally used, but these were not authorized.

AUSTRALIA

o-'strāl-yə

LOCATION — Oceania, south of Indonesia, bounded on the west by the Indian Ocean
GOVT. — Self-governing dominion of the British Commonwealth
AREA — 2,967,909 sq. mi.
POP. — 6,866,590
CAPITAL — Canberra

Australia includes the former British colonies of New South Wales, Victoria, Queensland, South Australia, Western Australia and Tasmania.

12 Pence = 1 Shilling
20 Shillings = 1 Pound

> **Catalogue values for unused stamps in this country are for Never Hinged items, beginning with Scott 197 in the regular postage section, Scott C6 in the air post section, and Scott J71 in the postage due section.**

Watermarks

Wmk. 8 — Wide Crown and Wide A

Wmk. 9 — Wide Crown and Narrow A

Wmk. 10 — Narrow Crown and Narrow A

Wmk. 11 — Multiple Crown and A

Wmk. 12 — Crown and Single-lined A

Wmk. 13 — Large Crown and Double-lined A

Wmk. 55 — Large Crown and NSW

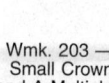

Wmk. 203 — Small Crown and A Multiple

Wmk. 228 — Small Crown and C of A Multiple

Kangaroo and Map — A1

Die I — The inside frameline has a break at left, even with the top of the letters of the denomination.
Die II — The frameline does not show a break (repaired die).
Die III — The left inside frameline shows a break opposite the face of the kangaroo.
Die IV — As Die III, with a break in the top outside frameline above the "ST" of "AUSTRALIA." The upper right inside frameline has an incomplete corner.

Dies are only indicated when there are more than one for any denomination.

1913	**Typo.**	**Wmk. 8**	**Perf. 11½, 12**	
1	A1	½p green	11.50	7.50
		Never hinged	17.00	
		On cover		30.00
a.		½p yellow green	10.00	6.50
b.		½p deep green	10.00	6.50
c.		Wmk. sideways, crown pointing to left		18,000.
d.		Wmk. sideways, crown pointing to right		30,000.
e.		Wmk. inverted	52.50	17.50
f.		Printed on gummed side	2,250.	
2	A1	1p car (I)	15.00	1.75
		Never hinged	24.00	
		On cover		7.00
a.		1p red (I)	12.50	1.75
b.		1p pale red (I)	12.50	1.75
		Never hinged	22.50	
c.		1p rose red (I)	12.50	1.75
d.		1p carmine (II)	12.50	1.75
		Never hinged	22.50	
		On cover		8.00
e.		1p red (II)	14.00	1.75
f.		1p pale red (II)	14.00	1.75
g.		1p rose red (II)	14.00	1.75
h.		1p carmine (III)	24.00	2.25
		Never hinged	40.00	
		On cover		9.75
i.		1p red (III)	22.50	1.75
j.		1p pale red (III)	22.50	1.75
k.		1p rose red (III)	22.50	1.75
l.		As #2, wmk. sideways	1,200.	300.00
m.		As "d", wmk. sideways	1,300.	325.00
n.		As #2, wmk. inverted	47.50	16.00
o.		As "d", wmk. inverted	47.50	16.00
p.		As "h", wmk. inverted	70.00	12.00
3	A1	2p gray	70.00	10.00
		Never hinged	175.00	
		On cover		37.50
a.		2p deep gray	62.50	10.00
b.		2p slate	62.50	10.00
c.		As #3, wmk. inverted	110.00	29.00
4	A1	2½p dark blue	70.00	22.50
		Never hinged	190.00	
		On cover		62.50
a.		2½p indigo	62.50	22.50
5	A1	3p ol bis, die I	140.00	17.50
		Never hinged	310.00	
		On cover		90.00
a.		Die II	450.00	225.00
		Never hinged	850.00	
		On cover		170.00
b.		Pair, #5-5a	725.00	325.00
c.		3p pale olive green (I)	125.00	17.50
		Never hinged	300.00	
d.		As "c", (II)	275.00	90.00
		Never hinged	625.00	
e.		Pair, #5c-5d	725.00	350.00
f.		3p green (I)	115.00	13.50
		Never hinged	290.00	
g.		As "f", (II)	275.00	85.00
		Never hinged	625.00	
h.		As #3, wmk. inverted	180.00	55.00
i.		As "a", wmk. inverted	630.00	220.00
j.		Pair, #5f-5g	800.00	400.00
6	A1	4p orange	150.00	40.00
		Never hinged	700.00	
		On cover		115.00
a.		4p deep orange	130.00	40.00
		Never hinged	630.00	
b.		4p yellow orange	460.00	97.50
		Never hinged	1,035.	
		On cover		275.00

Many examples offered as No. 6b are either Nos. 6 or 6a with faded color.

7	A1	5p orange brown	150.00 50.00
		Never hinged	375.00
		On cover	160.00
8	A1	6p ultra (II)	140.00 30.00
		Never hinged	450.00
		On cover	160.00
a.		6p blue (II)	125.00 32.50
		Never hinged	430.00
		On cover	195.00
b.		As #8, (III)	4,000. 1,300.
c.		As #8, wmk. inverted	150.00 65.00
d.		As "a", wmk. inverted	150.00 65.00
e.		As "b", wmk. inverted	2,250. 750.00
9	A1	9p purple	160.00 37.50
		Never hinged	575.00
		On cover	170.00
a.		9p violet	140.00 37.50
b.		9p deep violet	140.00 37.50
10	A1	1sh blue green	130.00 29.00
		Never hinged	700.00
		On cover	220.00
a.		1sh emerald	115.00 22.50
b.		As "a," aniline ink	140.00 29.00
c.		As "a," wmk. inverted	1,150. 97.50
11	A1	2sh brown	300.00 140.00
		Never hinged	1,250.
		On telegram form or parcel	300.00
a.		2sh dark brown	315.00 145.00
12	A1	5sh yellow & gray	550.00 260.00
		Never hinged	2,000.
		On cover	—
a.		5sh chrome yel & gray	550.00 260.00
13	A1	10sh pink & gray	1,600. 800.00
		Never hinged	4,250.
		On cover	—
a.		10sh pink & slate	1,150. 800.00
14	A1	£1 ultra & brown	4,000. 2,400.
		Never hinged	9,250.
		On cover	—
a.		£1 ultra & red brn	3,300. 2,100.
15	A1	£2 dp rose & blk	8,500. 3,750.
		Never hinged	16,000.
		On cover	—
a.		£2 rose & gray	5,750. 3,250.
		Never hinged	12,500.
b.		£2 rose & jet black	5,750. 3,250.
		Never hinged	12,500.
		Nos. 1-12 (12)	1,886. 645.75

On No. 4, "2½d" is colorless in solid blue background.

See Nos. 38-59, 96-102, 121-129, 206.

King George V
A2

Kookaburra
(Kingfisher)
A3

1913-14   Unwmk.   Engr.   Perf. 11

17	A2	1p carmine	5.25 7.00
		Never hinged	8.00
a.		Vert. pair, imperf. between	3,250.
18	A3	6p lake brown ('14)	115.00 70.00
		Never hinged	260.00

See No. 95.

A4

ONE PENNY
Die I — Normal die, having outside the oval band with "AUSTRALIA" a white line and a heavy colored line.
Die Ia — As die I with a small white spur below the right serif at foot of the "1" in left tablet.
Die II — A heavy colored line between two white lines back of the emu's neck. A white scratch crossing the vertical shading lines at the lowest point of the bust.
TWO PENCE
Die I — The numeral "2" is thin. The upper curve is 1mm. across and a very thin line connects it with the foot of the figure.
Die II — The "2" is thicker than in die I. The top curve is 1½mm across and a strong white line connects it with the foot of the figure. There are thin vertical lines across the ends of the groups of short horizontal lines at each side of "TWO PENCE."
THREE PENCE
Die I — The ends of the thin horizontal lines in the background run into the solid color of the various parts of the design. The numerals are thin and the letters of "THREE PENCE" are thin and irregular.

horizontal background lines. The numerals are thick and the letters of "THREE PENCE" are heavy and regular.
FIVE PENCE
Die I — The top of the flag of the "5" is slightly curved.
Die II — The top of the flag of the "5" is flat. There are thin white vertical lines across the ends of the short horizontal lines at each side of "FIVE PENCE."

1914-24   Typo.   Wmk. 9   Perf. 14

19	A4	½p emerald ('15)	3.75 1.75
		Never hinged	8.50
a.		Thin "½" at right	20,000. 5,750.
20	A4	½p orange ('23)	4.00 4.00
		Never hinged	7.00
21	A4	1p red (I)	9.00 1.75
		Never hinged	15.00
a.		1p carmine rose (I)	22.50 4.00
		Never hinged	40.00
b.		1p red (Ia)	550.00 9.75
		Never hinged	1,150.
c.		1p carmine (II) ('18)	85.00 35.00
		Never hinged	175.00
d.		1p scar (I), rough paper	22.50 9.75
e.		1p rose red (Ia), rough paper	800.00 29.00
f.		1p brt rose (Ia), rough paper	750.00 115.00
22	A4	1p vio (I) ('22)	7.00 1.75
		Never hinged	11.50
a.		1p red violet	10.50 5.25
		Never hinged	14.00
23	A4	1p green (I) ('24)	5.75 2.50
		Never hinged	10.50
24	A4	1½p choc ('18)	7.50 2.25
		Never hinged	12.50
a.		1½p red brown	8.00 2.50
		Never hinged	18.00
b.		1½p black brown	7.00 2.50
		Never hinged	11.50
25	A4	1½p emerald ('23)	7.50 2.75
		Never hinged	12.50
a.		Rough paper	260.00 160.00
26	A4	1½p scarlet ('24)	4.25 1.10
		Never hinged	7.00
27	A4	2p brn org (I) ('20)	17.50 3.25
		Never hinged	32.50
a.		2p orange (I) ('20)	17.50 2.50
		Never hinged	32.50
b.		Booklet pane of 6	
28	A4	2p red (I) ('22)	17.50 3.25
		Never hinged	30.00
29	A4	2p red brn (I) ('24)	22.50 12.50
		Never hinged	37.50
30	A4	3p ultra (I) ('24)	32.50 7.75
		Never hinged	70.00
31	A4	4p orange ('15)	45.00 4.00
		Never hinged	92.50
a.		4p yellow	140.00 32.50
		Never hinged	600.00
32	A4	4p violet ('21)	22.50 21.00
		Never hinged	37.50
33	A4	4p lt ultra ('22)	67.50 13.00
		Never hinged	140.00
34	A4	4p ol bis ('24)	35.00 13.00
		Never hinged	70.00
35	A4	4½p violet ('24)	27.50 6.75
		Never hinged	60.00
36	A4	5p org brn (I) ('15)	37.50 6.75
		Never hinged	110.00
37	A4	1sh4p lt blue ('20)	140.00 35.00
		Never hinged	475.00
		Nos. 19-37 (19)	513.75 144.10

See Nos. 60-76, 113-120, 124.

1915   Perf. 11½, 12

38	A1	2p gray	160.00 17.00
		Never hinged	325.00
a.		Wmk. inverted	1,250.
39	A1	2½p dark blue	140.00 37.50
		Never hinged	300.00
40	A1	6p ultra (II)	325.00 29.00
		Never hinged	875.00
a.		Die III	4,250. 1,450.
b.		6p bright blue (II)	350.00 85.00
c.		As "b," Die III	4,000. 1,500.
d.		As #40, wmk. inverted	2,500.
41	A1	9p violet	325.00 60.00
		Never hinged	1,400.
a.		Wmk. inverted	3,500. 2,000.
42	A1	1sh blue green	275.00 35.00
		Never hinged	1,250.
43	A1	2sh brown	1,050. 125.00
		Never hinged	4,750.
44	A1	5sh yellow & gray	1,500. 475.00
		Never hinged	3,250.
a.		Wmk. inverted	1,250. 425.00
b.		Yellow double	15,000. 4,000.
		Nos. 38-44 (7)	3,775. 778.50

1915-24   Wmk. 10

45	A1	2p gray (I)	37.50 10.50
		Never hinged	62.50
a.		Die II, shiny paper	45.00 17.50
		Never hinged	62.50
46	A1	2½p dark blue	30.00 17.50
		Never hinged	47.50
a.		"1" of fraction omitted	45,000. 50,000.

47	A1	3p olive bister (I)	37.50 9.50
		Never hinged	72.50
a.		Die II	175.00 57.50
		Never hinged	325.00
b.		3p lt olive (IV)	52.50 14.00
		Never hinged	92.50
48	A1	6p ultra (II)	120.00 17.50
		Never hinged	275.00
a.		6p chalky blue (III)	125.00 22.50
		Never hinged	250.00
b.		6p ultra (III)	1,600. 500.00
c.		6p ultra (IV)	120.00 20.00
		Never hinged	250.00
49	A1	6p yel brn (IV, '23)	32.50 7.25
		Never hinged	62.50
50	A1	9p violet (IV)	80.00 22.50
		Never hinged	190.00
a.		9p lilac (II)	82.50 22.50
		Never hinged	200.00
51	A1	1sh blue grn (II, '16)	72.50 14.00
		Never hinged	190.00
b.		Die IV	75.00 14.00
52	A1	2sh brown ('16)	325.00 27.50
		Never hinged	975.00
53	A1	2sh vio brn (II, '24)	140.00 37.50
		Never hinged	325.00
54	A1	5sh yel & gray ('18)	325.00 125.00
		Never hinged	850.00
55	A1	10sh brt pink & gray ('17)	1,050. 400.00
		Never hinged	1,750.
56	A1	£1 ultra & brn org ('16)	3,450. 2,100.
		Never hinged	9,250.
a.		£1 ultra & brn ('16)	3,250. 2,100.
		Never hinged	10,500.
57	A1	£1 gray (IV, '24)	900.00 425.00
		Never hinged	2,250.
58	A1	£2 dp rose & blk ('19)	7,000. 3,250.
		Never hinged	14,000.
59	A1	£2 rose & vio brn ('24)	5,250. 3,250.
		Never hinged	12,500.
		Nos. 45-54 (10)	1,200. 288.75

Perf. 14, 14½, 14½x14

1918-23   Wmk. 11

60	A4	½p emerald	3.50 3.25
		Never hinged	8.00
a.		Thin "½" at right	140.00 160.00
61	A4	1p rose (I)	27.50 19.00
		Never hinged	45.00
62	A4	1p dl grn (I) ('24)	9.25 9.25
		Never hinged	17.50
63	A4	1½p choc ('19)	8.00 4.25
		Never hinged	17.50
a.		1½p red brown ('19)	12.50 4.50
		Never hinged	26.00
		Nos. 60-63 (4)	48.25 35.75

1924   Unwmk.   Perf. 14

64	A4	1p green (I)	5.75 6.25
		Never hinged	12.50
65	A4	1½p carmine	9.25 7.50
		Never hinged	17.50

Perf. 14, 13½x12½

1926-30   Wmk. 203

66	A4	½p orange	3.75 2.25
		Never hinged	7.00
a.		Perf. 14 ('27)	7.50 8.25
		Never hinged	11.50
67	A4	1p green (I)	3.75 1.10
		Never hinged	8.00
a.		1p green (Ia)	55.00 70.00
		Never hinged	75.00
b.		Perf. 14	4.50 1.75
		Never hinged	9.25

68	A4	1½p rose red ('27)	4.50 2.00
		Never hinged	9.25
c.		Perf. 14 ('26)	11.50 2.00
		Never hinged	22.50
69	A4	1½p red brn ('30)	6.25 4.50
		Never hinged	9.75
70	A4	2p red brn (II, '28)	9.25 5.75
		Never hinged	22.50
a.		Perf. 14 (I, '27)	45.00 29.00
		Never hinged	85.00
71	A4	2p red (II) ('30)	11.50 3.25
		Never hinged	22.50
a.		Tête bêche pair	175,000.
b.		2p red (I) ('30)	7.00 3.50
		Never hinged	12.00
c.		Unwmkd. (II) ('31)	2,000. 2,500.
72	A4	3p ultra (II) ('29)	35.00 5.50
		Never hinged	57.50
a.		3p ultra (I)	70.00 22.50
		Never hinged	150.00
b.		Perf. 14	45.00 11.50
		Never hinged	80.00
73	A4	4p ol bis ('29)	29.00 6.75
		Never hinged	52.50
a.		Perf. 14 ('28)	125.00 50.00
		Never hinged	300.00
74	A4	4½p dk vio ('27)	26.00 10.50
		Never hinged	45.00
a.		Perf. 13½x12½ ('28)	85.00 32.50
		Never hinged	150.00
75	A4	5p brn buff (II) ('30)	45.00 14.00
		Never hinged	85.00
76	A4	1sh4p pale turq bl ('28)	200.00 37.50
		Never hinged	500.00
a.		Perf. 14 ('27)	260.00 140.00
		Never hinged	775.00
		Nos. 66-76 (11)	374.00 93.10

For surcharges & overprints see Nos. 106-107, O3-O4.

Parliament House, Canberra
A5

Unwmk.

1927, May 9   Engr.   Perf. 11

94	A5	1½p brown red	1.10 1.10
		Never hinged	2.00
a.		Vert. pair, imperf. btwn.	4,500. 4,250.
b.		Horiz. pair, imperf. btwn.	7,500. 7,500.

Opening of Parliament House at Canberra.

Melbourne Exhibition Issue
Kookaburra Type of 1914

1928, Oct. 29

95	A3	3p deep blue	5.50 8.00
		Never hinged	8.25
a.		Pane of 4	200.00 260.00
		Never hinged	300.00

No. 95a was issued at the Melbourne Intl. Phil. Exhib. No marginal inscription. Printed in sheets of 60 stamps (15 panes). No. 95a exists imperf. Value, $300,000.
No. 95 was printed in sheets of 120 and issued Nov. 2 throughout Australia.

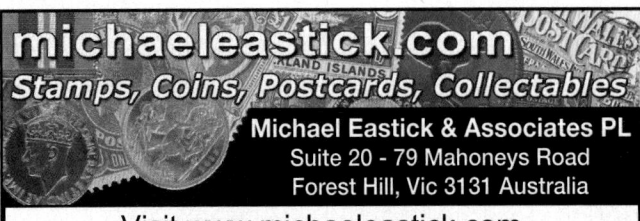

Kangaroo-Map Type of 1913
Perf. 11½, 12

1929-30	Wmk. 203		Typo.	
96	A1	6p brown	35.00	22.50
	Never hinged		57.50	
97	A1	9p violet	75.00	26.00
	Never hinged		160.00	
98	A1	1sh blue green	70.00	14.50
	Never hinged		165.00	
99	A1	2sh red brown	150.00	29.00
	Never hinged		425.00	
100	A1	5sh yel & gray	475.00	150.00
	Never hinged		1,000.	
101	A1	10sh pink & gray	1,000.	725.00
	Never hinged		2,000.	
102	A1	£2 dl red & blk		
		('30)	5,250.	925.00
	Never hinged		11,500.	
	Nos. 96-102 (7)		7,055.	1,892.

For overprint see No. O5.

Black Swan — A6

Unwmk.
1929, Sept. 28	Engr.		Perf. 11	
103	A6	1½p dull red	1.60	2.00
	Never hinged		2.75	

Centenary of Western Australia.

Capt. Charles Sturt — A7

1930, June 2
104	A7	1½p dark red	1.25	1.25
	Never hinged		2.50	
105	A7	3p dark blue	7.50	10.00
	Never hinged		11.00	

Capt. Charles Sturt's exploration of the Murray River, cent.

Nos. 68 and 74a surcharged

FIVE PENCE

1930   Wmk. 203   Perf. 13½x12½
106	A4	2p on 1½p rose red	1.90	1.25
	Never hinged		3.50	
107	A4	5p on 4½p dark violet	11.00	14.00
	Never hinged		18.00	

"Southern Cross" over Hemispheres A8

Perf. 11, 11½
1931, Mar. 19			Unwmk.	
111	A8	2p dull red	1.25	1.25
	Never hinged		2.50	
112	A8	3p blue	6.25	6.25
	Never hinged		10.00	
	Nos. 111-112,C2 (3)		15.50	15.50

Trans-oceanic flights (1928-1930) of Sir Charles Edward Kingsford-Smith (1897-1935). See No. C3 for similar design. For overprints see Nos. CO1, O1-O2.

Types of 1913-23 Issues
Perf. 13½x12½
1931-36	Typo.		Wmk. 228	
113	A4	½p orange		
		('32)	7.50	7.50
	Never hinged		11.50	
114	A4	1p green (I)	2.50	.40
	Never hinged		4.50	
115	A4	1½p red brn		
		('36)	8.00	15.00
	Never hinged		12.50	
116	A4	2p red (II)	2.50	.30
	Never hinged		4.50	

117	A4	3p ultra (II)		
		('32)	32.50	2.25
	Never hinged		75.00	
118	A4	4p ol bis ('33)	29.00	2.25
	Never hinged		55.00	
120	A4	5p brn buff (II)		
		('32)	22.50	2.25
	Never hinged		35.00	

Perf. 11½, 12; 13½x12½ (1sh4p)
121	A1	6p yel brn		
		('36)	30.00	37.50
	Never hinged		52.50	
122	A1	9p violet ('32)	42.50	9.00
	Never hinged		115.00	
124	A4	1sh4p lt blue ('32)	115.00	11.00
	Never hinged		160.00	
125	A1	2sh red brn		
		('35)	7.50	5.25
	Never hinged		12.50	
126	A1	5sh yel & gray		
		('32)	350.00	27.50
	Never hinged		925.00	
127	A1	10sh pink & gray		
		('32)	600.00	225.00
	Never hinged		2,000.	
128	A1	£1 gray ('35)	1,400.	375.00
	Never hinged		2,000.	
129	A1	£2 dl rose &		
		blk ('34)	4,500.	800.00
	Never hinged		9,250.	
	Nos. 113-129 (15)		7,149.	1,520.

For redrawn 2sh see No. 206. For overprints see Nos. O6-O11.

Sydney Harbor Bridge — A9

Unwmk.
1932, Mar. 14	Engr.		Perf. 11	
130	A9	2p red	4.50	5.25
	Never hinged		7.00	
131	A9	3p blue	7.50	9.50
	Never hinged		11.50	
132	A9	5sh gray green	575.00	350.00
	Never hinged		1,600.	

Wmk. 228
Perf. 10½
Typo.
133	A9	2p red	4.00	2.25
	Never hinged		5.75	

Opening of the Sydney Harbor Bridge on Mar. 19, 1932.
Value for 5sh, used, is for CTO examples.
For overprints see Nos. O12-O13.

Kookaburra — A14

1932, June 1   Perf. 13½x12½
139	A14	6p light brown	17.00	1.10
	Never hinged		27.50	

Male Lyrebird — A16

1932, Feb. 15   Unwmk.   Perf. 11
Size: 21½x25mm
141	A16	1sh green	42.50	4.50
	Never hinged		65.00	

See No. 175. See No. 300 in Scott Standard Postage Stamp Catalogue, Vol. 1. For overprint see No. O14.

Yarra Yarra Tribesman, Yarra River and View of Melbourne A17

Wmk. 228
1934, July 2	Engr.		Perf. 10½	
142	A17	2p vermilion	3.00	1.75
	Never hinged		4.50	
a.	Perf. 11½		10.50	4.50
	Never hinged		20.00	
143	A17	3p blue	4.00	6.50
	Never hinged		10.00	
a.	Perf. 11½		5.00	9.00
	Never hinged		9.00	
144	A17	1sh black	55.00	27.50
	Never hinged		110.00	
a.	Perf. 11½		65.00	32.50
	Never hinged		120.00	
	Nos. 142-144 (3)		62.00	35.75

Centenary of Victoria.

Merino Sheep — A18

1934, Nov. 1   Perf. 11½
147	A18	2p copper red	8.00	2.00
	Never hinged		11.50	
a.	Die II		15.00	5.75
	Never hinged		29.00	
148	A18	3p dark blue	15.00	19.00
	Never hinged		20.00	
149	A18	9p dark violet	35.00	50.00
	Never hinged		75.00	
	Nos. 147-149 (3)		58.00	71.00

Capt. John Macarthur (1767-1834), "father of the New South Wales woolen industry."
Two dies of 2p: I, shading on hill in background uneven from light to dark. II, shading is uniformly dark.

Cenotaph in Whitehall, London — A19

George V on His Charger "Anzac" — A20

1935, Mar. 18   Perf. 13½x12½
150	A19	2p red	2.50	.50
	Never hinged		5.25	

Perf. 11
151	A19	1sh black	50.00	45.00
	Never hinged		100.00	

Anzacs' landing at Gallipoli, 20th anniv.
The 1sh perf 13½x12½ is a plate proof. Value, unused $2,250, mint never hinged $3,500.

1935, May 2   Perf. 11½
152	A20	2p red	2.75	.35
	Never hinged		5.00	
153	A20	3p blue	8.00	12.50
	Never hinged		17.50	
154	A20	2sh violet	35.00	47.50
	Never hinged		85.00	
	Nos. 152-154 (3)		45.75	60.35

25th anniv. of the reign of King George V.

Amphitrite Joining Cables between Australia and Tasmania A21

1936, Apr. 1
157	A21	2p red	1.25	.60
	Never hinged		2.75	
158	A21	3p dark blue	3.75	3.50
	Never hinged		5.50	

Australia/Tasmania telephone link.

Proclamation Tree and View of Adelaide, 1936 — A22

1936, Aug. 3
159	A22	2p red	1.00	.60
	Never hinged		2.25	
160	A22	3p dark blue	3.75	3.75
	Never hinged		5.75	
161	A22	1sh green	14.00	10.00
	Never hinged		27.50	
	Nos. 159-161 (3)		18.75	14.35

Centenary of South Australia.

Gov. Arthur Phillip at Sydney Cove — A23

1937, Oct. 1   Perf. 13x13½
163	A23	2p red	1.00	.45
	Never hinged		3.25	
164	A23	3p ultra	3.75	3.25
	Never hinged		6.50	
165	A23	9p violet	15.00	13.00
	Never hinged		25.00	
	Nos. 163-165 (3)		19.75	16.70

150th anniversary of New South Wales.

Kangaroo A24

Queen Elizabeth A25

King George VI A26

A27

Koala — A28

Merino Sheep — A29

Kookaburra (Kingfisher) A30

Platypus A31

Queen Elizabeth and King George VI in Coronation Robes A32   A33

King George VI and Queen Elizabeth A34

Type I   **Type II**

Two Types of A25 and A26:

Type I — Highlighted background. Lines around letters of Australia Postage and numerals of value.

Type II — Background of heavy diagonal lines without the highlighted effect. No lines around letters and numerals.

Perf. 13½x14, 14x13½

1937-46   Engr.   Wmk. 228

166	A24	½p org, perf.		
		15x14 ('42)	.85	.70
		Never hinged	2.25	
a.		Perf. 13½x14 ('38)	1.40	.60
		Never hinged	3.50	
167	A25	1p emerald (I)	1.10	1.00
		Never hinged	2.25	
168	A26	1½p dull red brn		
		(II)	6.25	5.75
		Never hinged	11.50	
a.		Perf. 15x14 ('41)	4.75	14.00
		Never hinged	8.00	
169	A26	2p scarlet (I)	1.10	.60
		Never hinged	2.25	
170	A27	3p ultramarine	40.00	24.00
		Never hinged	75.00	
a.		3p dp ultra, thin paper ('38)	40.00	4.50
		Never hinged	75.00	
171	A28	4p grn, perf.		
		15x14 ('42)	1.10	.30
		Never hinged	2.25	
a.		Perf. 13½x14 ('38)	3.25	3.00
		Never hinged	9.00	
172	A29	5p pale rose		
		vio, perf.		
		14x15 ('46)	1.40	1.10
		Never hinged	2.25	
a.		Perf. 14x13½ ('38)	3.00	.90
		Never hinged	4.50	
173	A30	6p vio brn, perf.		
		15x14 ('42)	1.25	.30
		Never hinged	3.00	
a.		Perf. 13½x14	12.50	2.25
		Never hinged	26.00	
b.		6p chocolate, perf. 15x14	1.40	.55
		Never hinged	2.25	
174	A31	9p sep, perf.		
		14x15 ('43)	2.00	.45
		Never hinged	3.00	
a.		Perf. 14x13½ ('38)	4.50	2.25
		Never hinged	9.75	
175	A16	1sh gray grn,		
		perf. 15x14		
		('41)	1.40	.40
		Never hinged	2.00	
a.		Perf. 13½x14	27.50	3.50
		Never hinged	72.50	
176	A27	1sh4p magenta		
		('38)	1.60	3.25
		Never hinged	3.50	

Perf. 13½

177	A32	5sh dl red brn		
		('38)	9.75	4.50
		Never hinged	26.00	
a.		Thin paper ('48)	4.00	3.50
		Never hinged	5.25	
178	A33	10sh dl gray vio		
		('38)	35.00	20.00
		Never hinged	57.50	
a.		Thin paper ('48)	35.00	29.00
		Never hinged	45.00	
179	A34	£1 bl gray ('38)	70.00	42.50
		Never hinged	115.00	
a.		Thin paper ('48)	70.00	62.50
		Never hinged	100.00	
		Nos. 166-179 (14)	172.80	104.85

No. 175 measures 17½x21½mm.

Nos. 177-179 were issued on chalk-surfaced paper. Nos. 177a-179a were printed on a thin, rough ordinary paper. The watermark is more distinct on Nos. 177a-179a, while impressions are not as sharp as on Nos. 177-179.

See Nos. 223A, 293, 295, 298, 300 in this catalogue or *Scott Standard Postage Stamp Catalogue*, Vol. 1. For surch. & overprints see Nos. 190, M1, M4-M5, M7.

1938-42   Perf. 15x14

180	A25	1p emerald (II)	1.00	.70
181	A25	1p dl red brn (II)		
		('41)	.70	.60
181B	A26	1½p bl grn (II) ('41)	.70	2.25
182	A26	2p scarlet (II)	1.00	.30
182B	A26	2p red vio (II) ('41)	.40	.30
183	A27	3p dk ultra ('40)	29.00	4.50
		Never hinged	57.50	
183A	A27	3p dk vio brn ('42)	.40	.30
		Nos. 180-183A (7)	33.20	8.95
		Set, never hinged		

No. 183 differs from Nos. 170-170a in the shading lines on the king's left eyebrow which go downward, left to right, instead of the reverse. Also, more of the left epaulette shows.

For surcharges & ovpt. see Nos. 188-189, M3.

Coil Perforation

A special perforation was applied to stamps intended for use in coils to make separation easier. It consists of small and large holes (2 small, 10 large, 2 small) on the stamps' narrow side. Some of the stamps so perforated were sold in sheets.

This coil perforation may be found on Nos. 166, 181, 182, 182B, 193, 215, 223A, 231. See *Scott Standard Postage Stamp Catalogue Vol. 1* for Nos. 257, 315-316, 319, 319a and others.

Nurse, Sailor, Soldier and Aviator — A35

Perf. 13½x13

1940, July 15   Engr.   Wmk. 228

184	A35	1p green	1.10	3.25
		Never hinged	2.50	
185	A35	2p red	1.10	1.90
		Never hinged	2.50	
186	A35	3p ultra	8.00	12.50
		Never hinged	16.00	
187	A35	6p chocolate	17.00	27.50
		Never hinged	32.50	
		Nos. 184-187 (4)	27.20	45.15

Australia's participation in WWII.

No. 182 Surcharged in Blue

1941, Dec. 10   Perf. 15x14

188	A26	2½p on 2p red	.75	1.00
		Never hinged	1.50	

No. 183 Surcharged in Black and Yellow

189	A27	3½p on 3p dk ultra	.90	2.25
		Never hinged	1.75	

No. 172a Surcharged in Purple

Perf. 14x13½

190	A29	5½p on 5p pale rose		
		vio	3.25	6.50
		Never hinged	5.00	
		Nos. 188-190 (3)	4.90	9.75

Queen Elizabeth
A36   A37

King George VI
A38   A39

George VI and Blue Wrens
A40

Emu
A41

1942-44   Engr.   Perf. 15x14

191	A36	1p brown vio ('43)	.45	.25
192	A37	1½p green	.70	.25
193	A38	2p lt rose vio ('44)	.70	.25
194	A39	2½p red	.70	.30
195	A40	3½p ultramarine	.95	.70
196	A41	5½p indigo	1.75	.35
		Nos. 191-196 (6)	5.25	2.10
		Set, never hinged	9.00	

See Nos. 224-225. For overprint see No. M2.

> **Catalogue values for unused stamps in this section, from this point to the end of the section, are for Never Hinged items.**

Duke and Duchess of Gloucester
A42

1945, Feb. 19   Engr.   Perf. 14½

197	A42	2½p brown red	.30	.25
198	A42	3½p bright ultra	.45	1.25
199	A42	5½p indigo	.55	1.25
		Nos. 197-199 (3)	1.30	2.75

Inauguration of the Duke of Gloucester as Governor General.

Official Crest and Inscriptions
A43

Dove and Australian Flag
A44

Angel of Peace; "Motherhood" and "Industry"
A45

1946, Feb. 18   Wmk. 228   Perf. 14½

200	A43	2½p carmine	.25	.25
201	A44	3½p deep ultra	.65	1.75
202	A45	5½p deep yellow green	.70	1.00
		Nos. 200-202 (3)	1.60	3.00

End of WWII. See Nos. 1456-1458 in *Scott Standard Postage Stamp Catalogue*, Vol. 1.

Sir Thomas Mitchell and Map of Queensland
A46

1946, Oct. 14

203	A46	2½p dark carmine	.25	.25
204	A46	3½p deep ultra	.75	1.60
205	A46	1sh olive green	.75	.60
		Nos. 203-205 (3)	1.75	2.45

Sir Thomas Mitchell's exploration of central Queensland, cent.

Kangaroo-Map Type of 1913 Redrawn

1945, Dec.   Typo.   Perf. 11½

206	A1	2sh dk red brown	5.50	5.50

The R and A of AUSTRALIA are separated at the base and there is a single line between the value tablet and "Two Shillings." On No.

---

125 the tail of the R touches the A, while two lines appear between value tablet and "Two Shillings." There are many other minor differences in the design.

For overprint see No. M6.

John Shortland
A47

Pouring Steel
A48

Loading Coal — A49

1947, Sept.   Engr.   Perf. 14½x14

207	A47	2½p brown red	.35	.25

Perf. 14½

208	A48	3½p deep blue	.65	1.50
209	A49	5½p deep green	.65	.75
		Nos. 207-209 (3)	1.65	2.50

150th anniv. of the discovery of the Hunter River estuary, site of Newcastle by Lieut. John Shortland. By error the 2½p shows his father, Capt. John Shortland.

Princess Elizabeth — A50

Perf. 14x14½

1947, Nov. 20   Wmk. 228

210	A50	1p brown violet	.40	.45

See No. 215.

Hereford Bull
A51

Crocodile
A52

1948, Feb. 16   Perf. 14½

211	A51	1sh3p violet brown	2.25	1.40
212	A52	2sh chocolate	2.25	.35

See No. 302 in *Scott Standard Postage Stamp Catalogue*, Vol. 1.

William J. Farrer — A53

Design: No. 214, Ferdinand von Mueller.

1948   Perf. 14½x14

213	A53	2½p red	.50	.25
214	A53	2½p dark red	.45	.25

William J. Farrer (1845-1906), wheat researcher, and Ferdinand von Mueller (1825-1896), German-born botanist.

Issue dates: No. 213, July 12. No. 214, Sept. 13.

Elizabeth Type of 1947

1948, Aug.   Unwmk.   Perf. 14x14½

215	A50	1p brown violet	.40	.25

Scout in
Uniform — A55

Arms of
Australia — A56

1948, Nov. 15   Engr.   Wmk. 228
216 A55 2½p brown red   .45   .25

Pan-Pacific Scout Jamboree, Victoria, Dec. 29, 1948 to Jan. 9, 1949. See No. 249.

1949-50   Wmk. 228   Perf. 14x13½
218 A56   5sh dark red   4.50   .85
219 A56   10sh red violet   29.00   2.00
220 A56   £1 deep blue   45.00   8.50
221 A56   £2 green ('50)   200.00 26.00
  Nos. 218-221 (4)   278.50 37.35

Henry Hertzberg
Lawson (1867-1922),
Author and Poet — A57

Perf. 14½x14
1949, June 17   Unwmk.
222 A57 2½p rose brown   .50   .25

Outback Mail
Carrier and
Plane — A58

1949, Oct. 10
223 A58 3½p violet blue   .60   .55

UPU, 75th anniv.

Types of 1938, 1942-44 and

Aborigine — A59

1948-50   Unwmk.   Perf. 14½x14
223A A24 ½p orange ('49)   .45   .25
224 A37 1½p green ('49)   .35   .45
225 A38 2p lt rose violet   1.00 .55

Wmk. 228
226 A59 8½p dark brown ('50)   .55   .45
  Nos. 223A-226 (4)   2.35 1.70

Issued: 2p, Dec.; ½p, Sept.; 1½p, 8/29; 8½p, 8/14.
See No. 248; No. 303 in *Scott Standard Postage Stamp Catalogue*, Vol. 1.

John Forrest — A60

1949, Nov. 28   Wmk. 228
227 A60 2½p brown red   .50   .25

Forrest (1847-1918), explorer & statesman.

New South
Wales
A61

Victoria
A62

First stamp designs.

Perf. 14½x14
1950, Sept. 27   Unwmk.
228 A61 2½p rose brown   .45   .25
229 A62 2½p rose brown   .45   .25
  a. Pair, #228-229   1.40 1.10

Cent. of Australian adhesive postage stamps. Issued in sheets of 160 stamps containing alternate copies of Nos. 228 and 229.

Elizabeth
A63

George VI
A64

1950-51   Engr.   Unwmk.
230 A63 1½p deep green   .85   .75
231 A63 2p yellow grn ('51)   .30   .30
232 A64 2½p violet brn ('51)   .30   .45
233 A64 3p dull green ('51)   .35   .25
  Nos. 230-233 (4)   1.80 1.70

Issued: 1½p, 6/19; 2p, 3/28; 2½p, 5/23; 3p, 11/14.

A65

A66

1950-52   Wmk. 228
234 A64 2½p red   .25   .25
235 A64 3p red ('51)   .35   .45
236 A65 3½p red brown ('51)   .35   .25
237 A65 4½p scarlet ('52)   .45   .90
238 A65 6½p choc ('52)   .35   .55
238A A65 6½p blue green ('52) .45   .25
239 A66 7½p deep blue ('51)   .50   .55
  Nos. 234-239 (7)   2.70 3.20

Issued: 2½p, 4/12; 3p, 2/28; 7½p, 10/31; 3½p, 11/28; 4½p, No. 238, 2/20; No. 238A, 4/9.

A67

Founding of the Commonwealth of
Australia, 50th Anniv. — A68

Designs: No. 240, Sir Edmund Barton. No. 241, Sir Henry Parkes. 5½p, Duke of York opening first Federal Parliament. 1sh6p, Parliament House, Canberra.

Perf. 14½x14
1951, May 1   Engr.   Unwmk.
240   3p carmine   1.60 .25
241   3p carmine   1.60 .25
  a. A67 Pair, #240, 241   3.50 3.50
242 A68 5½p deep blue   .90   3.00
243 A68 1sh6p red brown   1.40 1.40
  Nos. 240-243 (4)   5.50 4.90

Edward Hammond
Hargraves — A69

Design: No. 245, Charles Joseph Latrobe (1801-1875), first governor of Victoria.

1951, July 2
244 A69 3p rose brown   1.00 .25
245 A69 3p rose brown   1.00 .25
  a. Pair, #244, 245   2.50 2.50

Discovery of gold in Australia, cent. (No. 244); Establishment of representative government in Victoria, cent. (No. 245). Sheets contain alternate rows of Nos. 244 and 245.

King George
VI — A70

1952, Mar. 19   Wmk. 228   Perf. 14½
247 A70 1sh½p slate blue   2.50 .85

Aborigine Type of 1950 Redrawn
Size: 20½x25mm
248 A59 2sh6p dark brown   5.75 1.10

Portrait as on A59; lettering altered and value repeated at lower left. See No. 303 in *Scott Standard Postage Stamp Catalogue*, Vol. 1.

Scout Type of 1948
Dated "1952-53"
Perf. 14x14½
1952, Nov. 19   Wmk. 228
249 A55 3½p red brown   .45   .25

Pan-Pacific Scout Jamboree, Greystanes, Dec. 30, 1952, to Jan. 9, 1953.

AIR POST STAMPS

Airplane over
Bush
Lands — AP1

Unwmk.
1929, May 20   Engr.   Perf. 11
C1 AP1 3p deep green   9.25 8.50
      Never hinged   14.50
  a. Booklet pane of 4 ('30)   450.00

Kingsford-Smith Type of 1931
1931, Mar. 19
C2 A8 6p gray violet   8.00 8.00
      Never hinged   11.50

AP3

1931, Nov. 4
C3 AP3 6p olive brown   17.00 14.00
      Never hinged   35.00

For overprint see No. CO1.

Mercury and
Hemispheres
AP4

1934, Dec. 1   Perf. 11
C4 AP4 1sh6p violet brown   40.00 8.00
      Never hinged   97.50

Perf. 13½x14
1937, Oct. 22   Wmk. 228
C5 AP4 1sh6p violet brown   8.50 1.40
      Never hinged   14.50

Catalogue values for unused stamps in this section, from this point to the end of the section, are for Never Hinged items.

Mercury and
Globe — AP5

1949, Sept. 1   Perf. 14½
C6 AP5 1sh6p sepia   2.25 .60

AIR POST OFFICIAL STAMP

No. C3
Overprinted

Perf. 11, 11½
1931, Nov. 17   Unwmk.
CO1 AP3 6p olive brown   35.00 35.00
      Never hinged   57.50

Issued primarily for official use, but to prevent speculation, a quantity was issued for public distribution.

POSTAGE DUE STAMPS

Very fine examples of Nos. J1-J38 will have perforations touching the design on one or more sides due to the narrow spacing of the stamps on the plates. Stamps with perfs clear of the design on all four sides are scarce and will command higher prices.

D1   D2

1902 Typo. Wmk. 55 Perf. 11½, 12
J1 D1 ½p emerald   11.50   11.50
J2 D1 1p emerald   17.50   11.50
  a. Perf. 11   2,800. 1,400.
  b. Perf. 11x11½   450.00 250.00
J3 D1 2p emerald   32.00   11.50
  a. Perf. 11x11½   600.00 200.00
J4 D1 3p emerald   32.00   21.00
J5 D1 4p emerald   45.00   25.00
J6 D1 6p emerald   70.00   17.00
J7 D1 8p emerald   180.00 140.00
J8 D1 5sh emerald   400.00 125.00
  Nos. J1-J8 (8)   788.00 362.50

Perf. 11½, 12, Compound with 11
1902-04
J9   D2 ½p emerald   17.50   11.50
  a. Perf. 11   775.00 400.00
J10 D2 1p emerald, Perf
              12x11   17.00   5.75
  a. Perf. 11   200.00 42.50
  b. Perf. 11x11½   400.00 20.00
  c. Perf 11x11½   37.50   11.50
J11 D2 2p emerald   23.00   5.75
  a. Perf. 11   260.00 57.50
  b. Perf. 12   —   225.00
  c. Perf 11x11½   120.00 37.50
  d. Perf 11x12   140.00 45.00
J12 D2 3p emerald   160.00 26.00
  a. Perf. 11   225.00 63.00
  b. Perf. 12   450.00 170.00
J13 D2 4p emerald   140.00 32.00
  a. Perf. 11   400.00 115.00
J14 D2 5p emerald   140.00 35.00
  a. Perf. 11   500.00 86.00
  b. Perf. 12   100.00 23.00
J15 D2 6p emerald   160.00 29.00
  a. Perf. 11   260.00 32.00
J16 D2 8p emerald   325.00 120.00
J17 D2 10p emerald   175.00 29.00
  a. Perf 12x11½   150.00 29.00
J18 D2 1sh emerald   160.00 29.00
  a. Perf. 11   500.00 90.00
  b. Perf 12x11½   125.00 32.00
J19 D2 2sh emerald   200.00 32.00
  a. Perf 11½, 12   200.00 40.00
J20 D2 5sh emerald   500.00 57.50
  a. Perf. 11   1,700. 600.00
  Nos. J9-J20 (12)   2,017. 412.50

Perf. 11
J21 D2 10sh emerald   4,000. 3,200.
J22 D2 20sh emerald   8,500. 5,500.
  Nos. J9-J20 (12)   2,017. 412.50

Perf. 11½, 12 Compound with 11

1906			Wmk. 12	
J23	D2	½p emerald	16.00	16.00
J24	D2	1p emerald	35.00	5.75
a.		Perf. 11	3,500.	1,450.
J25	D2	2p emerald	62.50	11.50
J26	D2	3p emerald	1,150.	450.00
J27	D2	4p emerald	140.00	27.50
a.		Perf. 11	4,600.	2,900.
J28	D2	6p emerald	490.00	35.00
		Nos. J23-J28 (6)	1,893.	545.75

1907		Wmk. 13	Perf. 11½x11	
J29	D2	½p emerald	42.50	85.00
J30	D2	1p emerald	260.00	140.00
J31	D2	2p emerald	375.00	290.00
J32	D2	4p emerald	500.00	290.00
J33	D2	6p emerald	550.00	400.00
		Nos. J29-J33 (5)	1,727.	1,205.

D3   D4

Perf. 11 (2sh, 10sh, 20sh), 11½x11 (1sh, 5sh)

1908-09			Wmk. 12	
J34	D3	1sh emer ('09)	225.00	29.00
J35	D3	2sh emerald	1,800.	—
J36	D3	5sh emerald	775.00	75.00
J37	D3	10sh emerald	5,200.	—
J38	D3	20sh emerald	13,000.	—

1909-23		Wmk. 13	Perf. 12x12½	
J39	D3	½p green & car	32.00	45.00
a.		Perf 11, green & rose ('14)	20.00	17.00
b.		Perf 12½, green & scarlet ('13)	37.50	29.00
c.		Perf 14 ('19)	20.00	17.00
J40	D4	1p green & car	23.00	9.75
a.		Perf 11, yel grn & rose, thicker paper, thick yellowish gum	4,600.	1,725.
b.		Perf 11, bright apple green & rose, thin paper, thin white gum ('14)	20.00	8.50
c.		Perf 14 ('14)	70.00	17.00
J41	D4	2p green & car	32.00	5.75
a.		Perf 11	—	—
b.		Perf 14 ('18)	29.00	7.50
J42	D4	3p green & car	35.00	14.50
a.		Perf 14, green & rose ('16)	150.00	52.00
J43	D4	4p green & car	24.00	11.50
a.		Perf 14 ('21)	200.00	70.00
J44	D4	6p green & car	35.00	14.00
a.		Perf 11	—	—
J45	D4	1sh green & car	33.00	9.25
a.		Perf 14, yel grn & scarlet ('23)	45.00	23.00
J46	D4	2sh green & car	115.00	16.00
J47	D4	5sh green & car	175.00	17.00
J48	D4	10sh green & car	450.00	325.00
a.		Perf 14, yel grn & scarlet ('21)	2,600.	
J49	D4	£1 green & car	1,100.	575.00
a.		Perf 14, yel grn & scarlet ('21)	1,600.	
		Nos. J39-J49 (11)	2,054.	1,042.

Nos. J39-J48 and J40a, J41a, J44a are from the 1909 printings and have thicker paper and thick yellowish gum. The other listings are from the 1912-23 printings on thinner paper with thin white gum.

1922-30		Wmk. 10	Perf. 14, 11 (4p)	
J50	D4	½p grn & car ('23)	9.25	7.50
J51	D4	1p green & car	7.50	2.25
J52	D4	1½p green & rose ('25)	4.25	7.50
J53	D4	2p green & car	9.25	4.25
J54	D4	3p green & car	17.00	3.25
J55	D4	4p green & car ('30)	17.00	8.00
a.		Perf 14	52.00	23.00
J56	D4	6p green & car	37.50	18.50
		Nos. J50-J56 (7)	101.75	51.25
		Set, never hinged	200.00	

1931-36		Wmk. 228	Perf. 11	
J57	D4	½p yel green & rose ('34)	23.00	23.00
J58	D4	1p yel grn & rose ('32)	9.00	2.25
a.		Perf 14	14.00	11.50
J59	D4	2p yel grn & rose ('33)	10.50	2.25
a.		Perf 14	11.50	11.50
J60	D4	3p yel green & rose ('36)	140.00	115.00
J61	D4	4p yel green & rose ('34)	29.00	4.50
J62	D4	6p yel green & rose ('36)	550.00	500.00
J63	D4	1sh yel green & rose ('34)	70.00	30.00
		Nos. J57-J63 (7)	831.50	677.00
		Set, never hinged	1,400.	

D5

Engraved; Value Typo.

1938			Perf. 14½x14	
J64	D5	½p green & car	3.50	3.50
J65	D5	1p green & car	12.50	1.10
J66	D5	2p green & car	12.50	2.25
J67	D5	3p green & car	55.00	23.00
J68	D5	4p green & car	16.00	1.10
J69	D5	6p green & car	100.00	45.00
J70	D5	1sh green & car	57.50	20.00
		Nos. J64-J70 (7)	257.00	95.95
		Set, never hinged	400.00	

> Catalogue values for unused stamps in this section, from this point to the end of the section, are for Never Hinged items.

Type of 1938 Value Tablet Redrawn

Original

Redrawn

Pence denominations: "D" has melon-shaped center in redrawn tablet. The redrawn 3p differs slightly, having semi-melon-shaped "D" center, with vertical white stroke half filling it.

1sh. 1938: Numeral "1" narrow, with six background lines above.

1sh. 1947: Numeral broader, showing more white space around dotted central ornament. Three lines above.

1946-57			Wmk. 228	
J71	D5	½p grn & car ('56)	7.00	5.75
J72	D5	1p grn & car ('47)	4.50	1.10
J73	D5	2p green & car	8.00	1.10
J74	D5	3p green & car	10.00	1.10
J75	D5	4p grn & car ('52)	14.00	1.40
J76	D5	5p grn & car ('48)	18.50	2.25
J77	D5	6p grn & car ('47)	18.50	2.90
J78	D5	7p grn & car ('53)	8.00	7.00
J79	D5	8p grn & car ('57)	26.00	23.00
J80	D5	1sh grn & car ('47)	29.00	4.50
		Nos. J71-J80 (10)	143.50	50.10

MILITARY STAMPS

Nos. 166, 191, 183A, 173, 175, 206 and 177 Overprinted in Black

a   b

B.C.O.F.
JAPAN
1946

c

1946 (Wrong font "6")

AN AN

Normal & Narrow "N"

1946-47			Wmk. 228	
M1	A24(a)	½p orange	3.50	3.50
		Never hinged	5.75	
a.		Wrong font "6" in ovpt.	90.00	170.00
b.		Narrow "N"	97.50	185.00
M2	A36(b)	1p brown vio	3.50	3.50
		Never hinged	5.75	
a.		Blue overprint	115.00	77.50
		Never hinged	140.00	
M3	A27(b)	3p dk vio brn	3.50	3.50
		Never hinged	5.75	
a.		Double overprint	850.00	
M4	A30(a)	6p brn violet	12.00	11.50
		Never hinged	18.00	
a.		Wrong font "6" in ovpt.	160.00	240.00
b.		Narrow "N"	160.00	240.00
M5	A16(a)	1sh gray green	12.00	11.50
		Never hinged	18.00	
a.		Wrong font "6" in ovpt.	200.00	290.00
b.		Narrow "N"	200.00	290.00
M6	A1(c)	2sh dk red brn	35.00	45.00
		Never hinged	50.00	
M7	A32(c)	5sh dl red brn	140.00	200.00
		Never hinged	250.00	
a.		Thin paper (#177a) ('48)	115.00	200.00
		Never hinged	185.00	
		Nos. M1-M7 (7)	209.50	278.50

"B.C.O.F." stands for "British Commonwealth Occupation Force."

Issue dates: Nos. M1-M3, Oct. 11, 1946, Nos. M4-M7, May 8, 1947.

OFFICIAL STAMPS

OVERPRINTED AND PERFORATED OFFICIAL STAMPS

Overprinted and perforated Official stamps are comparatively more difficult to find well centered than the basic issues on which they are printed. This is because poorly centered sheets that had been discarded were purposely chosen to be overprinted to save money.

Perforated Initials

In 1913-31, postage stamps were perforated "OS" for official Australian Federal and State government use. The first of such issues were punched with large initials 14mm high and containing 18 and 17 holes in the O and S, respectively. When stamps with this size initial fell apart, a smaller size was used. This was 8.5mm high and had 12 or 11 holes in the O and S. A third size OS, 9mm high was also used for a short time. Stamps exist with double or triple perforatioins. The system of perforated initials was replaced in 1931 by printed initials.

PERFORATED LARGE OS

OA Plus Scott Number

1913			Wmk. 8	
OA1	A1	½p green	20.00	11.00
		Never hinged	35.00	
		On newspaper, postal card		75.00
e.		Wmk. inverted		92.50
OA2	A1	1p car (I)	18.00	4.00
		Never hinged	37.50	
		On circular, cover		35.00
d.		Die II	24.00	6.50
		Never hinged	40.00	
		On circular, cover		37.50
n.		As #OA2, wmk. inverted	92.50	9.00
o.		As "d," wmk. inverted	92.50	9.00
OA3	A1	2p gray	35.00	14.50
		Never hinged	55.00	
		On cover		97.50
OA4	A1	2½p dark blue	335.00	145.00
		Never hinged	600.00	
		On cover		400.00
OA5	A1	3p ol bis (I)	185.00	82.50
		Never hinged	315.00	
		On cover		200.00
a.		Die II	345.00	92.50
		Never hinged	690.00	
		On cover		290.00
b.		Pair, #OA5-OA5a	850.00	
h.		As #OA5, wmk. inverted	125.00	57.50
i.		As "a," wmk. inverted	460.00	110.00
OA6	A1	4p orange	185.00	25.00
		Never hinged	345.00	
		On cover		97.50
b.		4p yellow orange	260.00	110.00
OA7	A1	5p org brn	160.00	37.50
		Never hinged	315.00	
		On cover		185.00
OA8	A1	6p ultra (I)	160.00	30.00
		Never hinged	375.00	
		On cover		185.00
c.		Wmk. inverted	260.00	92.50
OA9	A1	9p purple	145.00	55.00
		Never hinged	345.00	
		On cover		230.00
c.		Wmk. inverted		3,100.

All examples of the 9p purple with inverted watermark were released as #OA9c, of which 6 used specimens are known.

OA10	A1	1sh blue green	185.00	33.00
		Never hinged	350.00	
		On cover		290.00
c.		Wmk. inverted	690.00	220.00
OA11	A1	2sh brown	400.00	185.00
		Never hinged	1,380.	
OA12	A1	5sh yel & gray	1,000.	575.00
		Never hinged	1,750.	
OA13	A1	10sh pink & gray	2,300.	1,450.
		Never hinged	3,800.	
OA14	A1	£1 ultra & brn	3,600.	2,650.
		Never hinged	5,500.	
OA15	A1	£2 dp rose & blk	6,600.	3,500.
		Never hinged	9,700.	

PERFORATED SMALL OS

OB Plus Scott Number

1914			Wmk. 8	
OB1	A1	½p green	16.00	11.00
		Never hinged	35.00	
		On newspaper, postcard		115.00
e.		Wmk. inverted		55.00
OB2	A1	1p car (I)	18.50	7.25
		Never hinged	35.00	
		On circular, cover		52.50
d.		Die II	25.00	4.00
		Never hinged	45.00	
		On circular, cover		29.00
h.		Die III	20.00	2.75
		Never hinged	40.00	
		On circular, cover		29.00
OB3	A1	2p gray	65.00	6.00
		Never hinged	105.00	
		On cover		75.00
c.		Wmk. inverted	105.00	16.00
OB4	A1	2½p dark blue	335.00	125.00
		Never hinged	690.00	
		On cover		350.00
OB5	A1	3p ol bis (I)	90.00	8.00
		Never hinged	185.00	
		On cover		115.00
a.		Die II	240.00	57.50
		Never hinged	460.00	
		On cover		170.00
b.		Pair, #OB5-OB5a	—	
h.		As # OB5, wmk. inverted		
i.		As "a," wmk. inverted	360.00	92.50
OB6	A1	4p orange	200.00	92.50
		Never hinged	400.00	
		On cover		275.00
b.		4p yellow orange	260.00	115.00
OB7	A1	5p org brn	160.00	55.00
		Never hinged	315.00	
		On cover		230.00
OB8	A1	6p ultra (II)	97.50	16.00
		Never hinged	230.00	
		On cover		145.00
c.		Wmk. inverted	240.00	87.50
OB9	A1	9p purple	97.50	30.00
		Never hinged	230.00	
		On cover		170.00
OB10	A1	1sh blue green	115.00	30.00
		Never hinged	290.00	
		On cover		315.00
OB11	A1	2sh brown	260.00	125.00
		Never hinged	860.00	
		On cover		—
OB12	A1	5sh yel & gray	1,250.	660.00
		Never hinged	2,200.	
OB13	A1	10sh pink & gray	2,600.	1,600.
		Never hinged	4,900.	
OB14	A1	£1 ultra & brn	4,300.	2,650.
		Never hinged	6,000.	
		On cover		—
OB15	A1	£2 dp rose & black	7,200.	4,300.
		Never hinged	12,000.	
		On cover		—

1914-24			Wmk. 9	
OB19	A4	½p emerald	13.00	3.50
OB20	A4	1p orange	21.00	13.00
OB21	A4	1p red (I)	14.50	1.00
c.		1p carmine (II)	400.00	18.00
d.		1p scarlet (I), rough paper	27.50	8.00
e.		1p rose red (Ia), rough paper	290.00	18.00
f.		1p brt rose (Ia), rough paper	550.00	52.50
OB22	A4	1p violet (I)	30.00	17.50
OB23	A4	1p green (I)	10.00	2.75
OB24	A4	2p choc	35.00	3.50
a.		1½p red brown	27.50	2.50
OB25	A4	1½p emerald	18.00	1.60
OB26	A4	1½p scarlet	8.00	.80
OB27	A4	2p brn org (I)	17.50	1.60
OB28	A4	2p scarlet	22.50	5.25
OB29	A4	2p red brn (I)	25.00	5.00
OB30	A4	3p ultra (I)	40.00	8.00
OB31	A4	4p orange	52.50	4.50
a.		4p yellow	290.00	65.00
OB32	A4	4p violet	55.00	17.50
OB33	A4	4p ultra	80.00	14.50
OB34	A4	4p ol bis	52.50	8.00
OB35	A4	4½p violet	140.00	16.00
OB36	A4	5p org brn (I)	65.00	11.50
a.		5p chestnut (I), rough paper	1,700.	160.00

All examples of the 5p chestnut on rough paper were released as #OB36a.

| OB37 | A4 | 1sh4p light blue | 70.00 | 22.50 |

1915			Wmk. 9	
OB38	A1	2p gray	105.00	14.50
OB40	A1	6p ultra (II)	170.00	20.00
a.		Die III	1,800.	500.00
OB41	A1	9p violet	240.00	87.50
OB42	A1	1sh blue green	240.00	52.50
OB43	A1	2sh brown	720.00	125.00
OB44	A1	5sh yellow & gray	920.00	170.00

1915-24   **Wmk. 10**

OB45	A1	2p gray (I)	25.00	6.50
a.	Die II		40.00	20.00
OB46	A1	2½p dark blue	62.50	16.00
OB47	A1	3p ol bis (I)	32.50	5.75
a.	Die II		115.00	55.00
b.	Die IV		32.50	18.50
OB48	A1	6p ultra (II)	45.00	8.00
b.	Die III		1,450.	450.00
c.	Die IV		62.50	18.50
OB49	A1	6p yel brn (IV)	29.00	3.50
OB50	A1	9p violet (II)	35.00	16.00
a.	9p lilac (III)		35.00	16.00
OB51	A1	1sh blue grn (I)	30.00	3.50
a.	Die IV		30.00	4.50
OB52	A1	2sh brown	145.00	20.00
OB53	A1	2sh vio brn (II)	72.50	16.00
OB54	A1	5sh yel & gray	230.00	60.00
OB55	A1	10sh brt pink & gray	525.00	80.00
OB56	A1	£1 ultra & brn	2,650.	1,600.
OB57	A1	£1 gray (IV)	920.00	460.00
OB58	A1	£2 rose & blk	2,650.	1,150.

1918-20   **Wmk. 11**

OB60	A4	½p emerald	20.00	8.00
OB61	A4	1p rose (I)	140.00	52.50
OB62	A4	1p green (I)	20.00	20.00
OB63	A4	1½p chocolate	24.00	3.50
a.	1½p red brown		29.00	3.00

1924   **Unwmk.**

OB64	A4	1p green	92.50	87.50
OB65	A4	1½p carmine	97.50	87.50

Perf. 14, 13½x12½

1926-30   **Wmk. 203**

OB66	A4	½p orange	5.25	1.60
a.	Perf. 14		230.00	97.50
OB67	A4	1p green (I)	5.25	1.60
a.	Die Ia		125.00	160.00
b.	Perf. 14		13.00	1.60
OB68	A4	1½p rose red	9.75	2.50
c.	Perf. 14		27.50	2.50
OB69	A4	1½p red brn	21.00	5.00
OB70	A4	2p red brn (II)	35.00	18.00
a.	Die I, perf. 14		160.00	52.50
OB71	A4	2p red (II)	21.00	5.00
OB72	A4	3p ultra (I)	37.50	6.50
a.	Die II		29.00	5.00
b.	Perf. 14		80.00	17.00
OB73	A4	4p ol bis	29.00	5.00
a.	Perf. 14		170.00	52.50
OB74	A4	4½p violet	170.00	45.00
a.	Perf. 13½x12½		125.00	125.00
OB75	A4	5p brown buff (II)	65.00	9.25
OB76	A4	1sh4p pale turq bl	300.00	32.50
a.	Perf. 14		400.00	100.00

1928

OB95	A3	3p deep blue	17.50	11.50

1928-30   **Wmk. 203**

OB96	A1	6p brown	30.00	5.25
OB97	A1	9p violet	57.50	7.25
OB98	A1	1sh blue green	30.00	5.25
OB99	A1	2sh red brown	87.50	11.50
OB100	A1	5sh yel & gray	260.00	97.50
OB101	A1	10sh pink & gray	2,300.	
OB102	A1	£2 dl red & blk	4,300.	

1930

OB104	A7	1½p dark red	13.00	9.25
OB105	A7	3p dark blue	18.00	11.00

PERFORATED MEDIUM OS

OC Plus Scott Number

1927

OC94	A5	1½p brown red	20.00	10.00

1929

OC103	A6	1½p dull red	20.00	13.00

1929

OCC1	AP1	3p deep green	30.00	16.00

OVERPRINTED OFFICIAL STAMPS

See note at beginning of section.

Overprinted

On Regular Issue of 1931

1931, May 4   **Unwmk.**   *Perf. 11, 11½*

O1	A8	2p dull red	160.00	45.00
O2	A8	3p blue	450.00	80.00

These stamps were issued primarily for official use but to prevent speculation a quantity was issued for public distribution.
Used values are for CTO examples.
Counterfeit overprints exist.

On Regular Issues of 1928-32

1932   **Wmk. 203**   *Perf. 13½x12½*

O3	A4	2p red (II)	25.00	13.00
O4	A4	4p olive bister	40.00	26.00

Perf. 11½, 12

O5	A1	6p brown	97.50	90.00

1932-33   **Wmk. 228**   *Perf. 13½x12½*

O6	A4	½p orange	9.25	6.00
a.	Inverted overprint		—	—
O7	A4	1p green (I)	6.00	2.00
O8	A4	2p red (II)	13.00	6.50
a.	Inverted overprint		—	—
O9	A4	3p ultra (II) ('33)	18.00	9.25
O10	A4	5p brown buff	57.50	52.50

Perf. 11½, 12

O11	A1	6p yellow brown	45.00	35.00
a.	Inverted overprint		—	—
	Nos. O6-O11 (6)		148.75	111.25
	Set, never hinged		275.00	

1932   **Unwmk.**   *Perf. 11, 11½*

O12	A9	2p red	7.25	6.00
O13	A9	3p blue	24.00	24.00
O14	A16	1sh gray green	72.50	52.50
	Nos. O12-O14 (3)		103.75	82.50
	Set, never hinged		160.00	

AUSTRIA

ˈȯs-trē-ə

LOCATION — Central Europe
AREA — 32,378 sq. mi.
POP. — 6,760,233
CAPITAL — Vienna

Before 1867 Austria was an absolute monarchy, which included Hungary and Lombardy-Venetia. In 1867 the Austro-Hungarian Monarchy was established, with Austria and Hungary as equal partners. After World War I, in 1918, the different nationalities established their own states and only the German-speaking parts remained, forming a republic under the name "Deutschoster-reich" (German Austria), which name was shortly again changed to "Austria." In 1938 German forces occupied Austria, which became part of the German Reich.

60 Kreuzer = 1 Gulden
100 Neu-Kreuzer = 1 Gulden (1858)
100 Heller = 1 Krone (1899)
100 Groschen = 1 Schilling (1925)

Unused stamps without gum sell for about one-third or less of the values quoted.

Watermarks

Wmk. 91 — "BRIEF-MARKEN" In Double-lined Capitals Across the Middle of the Sheet

Wmk. 109 — Webbing   Wmk. 125 — Lozenges

Wmk. 140 — Crown

Wmk. 237 — Swastikas

Issues of the Austrian Monarchy (including Hungary)

Coat of Arms — A1

NINE KREUZER
Type I. One heavy line around coat of arms center. On the 9kr the top of "9" is about on a level with "Kreuzer" and not near the top of the label. Each cliche has the "9" in a different position.
Type IA. As type I, but with 1 ¼mm between "9" and "K."
Type II. One heavy line around coat of arms center. On the 9kr the top of "9" is much higher than the top of the word "Kreuzer" and nearly touches the top of the label.
Type III. As type II, but with two, thinner, lines around the center.

Wmk. K.K.H.M. in Sheet or Unwmk.
1850   Typo.   Imperf.

The stamps of this issue were at first printed on a rough hand-made paper, varying in thickness and having a watermark in script letters K.K.H.M., the initials of Kaiserlich Königliches Handels-Ministerium (Imperial and Royal Ministry of Commerce), vertically in the gutter between the panes. Parts of these letters show on margin stamps in the sheet. From 1854 a thick, smooth machine-made paper without watermark was used.

Thin to Thick Paper

1	A1	1kr yellow	1,650.	115.00
		No gum	425.00	
		On cover		425.00
a.		Printed on both sides	2,000.	150.00
b.		1kr orange	2,350.	150.00
		No gum	590.00	
		On cover		475.00
c.		1kr brown orange	3,475.	625.00
		No gum	875.00	
		On cover		2,300.
e.		1kr cadmium yellow	2,250.	130.00
		No gum	650.00	
		On cover		500.00
2	A1	2kr black	1,375.	82.50
		No gum	350.00	
		On cover		290.00
a.		Ribbed paper	—	4,550.
		On cover		13,500.
b.		2kr gray black	2,350.	120.00
		No gum	600.00	
		On cover		375.00
d.		Half used as 1kr on cover		52,500.
		Half used as 1kr on cover, single franking		—

A cover bearing one example of the 2 kreuzer and a diagonally bisected example of the same stamp realized the equivalent of U.S. $50,950 at a Zurich auction in 2003.

A faulty cover bearing one example of the 2 kreuzer diagonally bisected, paying a 1 kreuzer rate, realized the equivalent of U.S. $41,520 at a Zurich auction in 2004.

e.		2kr silver gray ('50, 1st printing)	3,600.	650.00

		No gum	900.00	
		On cover		1,550.
3	A1	3kr red	825.00	4.00
		No gum	210.00	
		On cover		25.00
a.		Ribbed paper	4,000.	160.00
		No gum	1,000.	
		On cover		500.00
b.		Laid paper	—	19,000.
		On cover		23,500.
c.		Printed on both sides		10,000.
d.		3kr dark carmine	1,750.	25.00
		No gum	450.00	
		On cover		100.00
4	A1	6kr brown	1,000.	6.00
		No gum	250.00	
		On cover		30.00
a.		Ribbed paper		2,450.
		On cover		6,750.
c.		Diagonal half used as 3kr on cover		20,000.
d.		6kr black brown	—	210.00
		On cover		400.00
e.		6kr pale reddish brown	1,500.	11.00
		No gum	375.00	
		On cover		42.50
5	A1	9kr blue, type II	2,350.	9.00
		No gum	590.00	
		On cover		50.00
a.		9kr blue, type I	2,250.	19.00
		No gum	550.00	
		On cover		100.00
b.		9kr blue, type IA	15,000.	1,250.
				2,500.
c.		Laid paper, type III		15,000.
d.		Printed on both sides, type II		9,250.
f.		9kr pale blue, type I	2,000.	13.00
		No gum	500.00	
		On cover		90.00
g.		9kr very dark blue, type III	2,700.	57.50
		No gum	675.00	
		On cover		160.00

1854
Machine-made Paper, Type III

1d	A1	1kr yellow	1,450.	100.00
		No gum	360.00	
		On cover		300.00
1f	A1	1kr cadmium yellow	2,000.	140.00
		No gum	525.00	
		On cover		375.00
1g	A1	1kr yellow ocher	2,300.	140.00
		No gum	590.00	
		On cover		425.00
1h	A1	1kr golden yellow	3,850.	250.00
		No gum	1,000.	
		On cover		575.00
1i	A1	1kr mustard yellow		475.00
1j	A1	1kr lemon yellow	1,500.	110.00
		No gum	375.00	
		On cover		325.00
2c	A1	2kr black	1,750.	80.00
		No gum	450.00	
		On cover		275.00
3e	A1	3kr red	475.00	4.25
		No gum	115.00	
		On cover		16.50
f.		3kr red, type I	4,650.	52.50
		No gum	1,150.	
		On cover		200.00
4b	A1	6kr brown	975.00	8.25
		No gum	240.00	
		On cover		32.50
4f	A1	6kr reddish brown	1,050.	7.75
		No gum	260.00	
		On cover		40.00
5e	A1	9kr blue	1,025.	4.25
		No gum	260.00	
		On cover		21.00
5h	A1	9kr dark slate blue	1,450.	13.50
		No gum	360.00	
		On cover		82.50

Full margins = 1 ½mm.

In 1852-54, Nos. 1-5, rouletted 14, were used in Tokay and Homonna. A 12kr blue exists, but was not issued. Value, $100,000.
The reprints are type III in brighter colors, some on paper watermarked "Briefmarken" in the sheet.
For similar design see Lombardy-Venetia A1.

Values for used pairs
Hand-made Paper

1	A1	1kr yellow	375.00
		On cover	1,000.
1b	A1	1kr orange	390.00
		On cover	1,100.
1c	A1	1kr brown orange	1,300.
		On cover	2,900.
1e	A1	1kr cadmium yellow	425.00
		On cover	1,100.
2	A1	2kr black	310.00
		On cover	3,200.
2b	A1	2kr gray black	315.00
		On cover	2,900.
2e	A1	2kr silver gray	1,800.
		On cover	
3	A1	3kr red	21.00
		On cover	82.50

3d	A1	3kr dark carmine	57.50
		On cover	190.00
4	A1	6kr brown	90.00
		On cover	310.00
5	A1	9kr blue, type II	32.50
		On cover	525.00
5a	A1	9kr blue, type I	140.00
		On cover	400.00
5f	A1	9kr pale blue, type I	140.00
		On cover	400.00

Machine-made Paper, Type III

1d	A1	1kr yellow	300.00
		On cover	875.00
1f	A1	1kr cadmium yellow	540.00
		On cover	1,500.
1g	A1	1kr yellow ocher	435.00
		On cover	1,250.
1h	A1	1kr golden yellow	540.00
		On cover	1,500.
1j	A1	1kr lemon yellow	325.00
		On cover	875.00
2c	A1	2kr black	275.00
		On cover	2,700.
3e	A1	3kr red	16.50
		On cover	110.00
3f	A1	3kr red, type I	130.00
		On cover	300.00
4b	A1	6kr brown	75.00
		On cover	200.00
5e	A1	9kr blue	32.50
		On cover	105.00

Values for used strips of 3
Hand-made Paper

1	A1	1kr yellow	900.00
		On cover	1,900.
1b	A1	1kr orange	1,000.
		On cover	2,100.
1c	A1	1kr brown orange	2,300.
		On cover	4,800.
1e	A1	1kr cadmium yellow	1,050.
		On cover	2,100.
2	A1	2kr black	950.00
		On cover	2,150.
2b	A1	2kr gray black	1,000.
		On cover	1,900.
2e	A1	2kr silver gray	3,500.
3	A1	3kr red	70.00
		On cover	275.00
3d	A1	3kr dark carmine	200.00
		On cover	540.00
4	A1	6kr brown	440.00
		On cover	900.00
5	A1	9kr blue, type II	175.00
		On cover	825.00
5a	A1	9kr blue, type I	400.00
		On cover	950.00
5f	A1	9kr pale blue, type I	375.00

Machine-made Paper, Type III

1d	A1	1kr yellow	800.00
		On cover	1,750.
1f	A1	1kr cadmium yellow	1,300.
		On cover	2,750.
1g	A1	1kr yellow ocher	1,050.
		On cover	2,750.
1h	A1	1kr golden yellow	1,300.
		On cover	2,650.
1j	A1	1kr lemon yellow	800.00
		On cover	1,700.
2c	A1	2kr black	875.00
		On cover	1,850.
3e	A1	3kr red	45.00
		On cover	400.00
3f	A1	3kr red, type I	350.00
		On cover	750.00
4b	A1	6kr brown	325.00
		On cover	800.00
5e	A1	9kr blue	140.00
		On cover	400.00

Values for used blocks of 4
Hand-made Paper

1	A1	1kr yellow		8,000.
1b	A1	1kr orange		8,750.
1c	A1	1kr brown orange		
1e	A1	1kr cadmium yellow		8,750.
2	A1	2kr black		13,750.
2b	A1	2kr gray black		15,000.
2e	A1	2kr silver gray		
3	A1	3kr red	14,500.	3,500.
3d	A1	3kr dark carmine	16,500.	5,750.
4	A1	6kr brown	16,500.	7,000.
4d	A1	6kr black brown		
5	A1	9kr blue, type II	45,000.	6,750.
5a	A1	9kr blue, type I	55,000.	7,000.
5f	A1	9kr pale blue, type I		7,000.

Machine-made Paper, Type III

1d	A1	1kr yellow		7,500.
1f	A1	1kr cadmium yellow		
1g	A1	1kr yellow ocher		9,000.
1h	A1	1kr golden yellow		6,500.
1j	A1	1kr lemon yellow		6,500.
2c	A1	2kr black	50,000.	13,750.
3e	A1	3kr red	10,000.	1,650.
3f	A1	3kr red, type I		5,750.
4b	A1	6kr brown	10,000.	5,750.
5e	A1	9kr blue	13,000.	2,750.

Values for stamps used in Lombardy-Venetia

Hand-made Paper

1	A1	1kr yellow, *from*	365.00
		On cover, *from*	5,800.
1b	A1	1kr orange, *from*	425.00
		On cover, *from*	7,000.
2	A1	2kr black, *from*	625.00
		On cover, *from*	4,000.
3	A1	3kr red, *from*	57.50
		On cover, *from*	375.00
3a	A1	3kr red (ribbed paper), *from*	250.00
		On cover, *from*	1,600.
4	A1	6kr brown, *from*	62.50
		On cover, *from*	475.00
5	A1	9kr blue (II)(from)	250.00
		On cover, *from*	2,100.
5a	A1	9kr blue (I)(from)	100.00
		On cover, *from*	1,100.

Machine-made Paper, Type III

1d	A1	1kr yellow, *from*	650.00
		On cover, *from*	16,500.
2c	A1	2kr black, *from*	575.00
		On cover, *from*	11,250.
3e	A1	3kr red, *from*	325.00
		On cover, *from*	2,100.
4b	A1	6kr brown, *from*	375.00
		On cover, *from*	3,750.
5e	A1	9kr blue, *from*	500.00
		On cover, *from*	4,100.

Values for Stamps Cancelled First Day of Issue (June 1, 1850)

1	A1	1kr yellow	—
		On cover	—
2	A1	2kr black	—
		On cover	67,500.
3	A1	3kr red	1,300.
		On cover	25,000.
4	A1	6kr brown	1,450.
		On cover	30,000.
5a	A1	9kr blue, type I	1,450.
		On cover	25,000.

Values for Stamps with Red Cancellations

Hand-Made Paper

1	A1	1kr yellow	3,500.
2	A1	2kr black	1,300.
3	A1	3kr red	675.00
4	A1	6kr brown	625.00
5	A1	9kr blue, type II	875.00

Machine-Made Paper

1a	A1	1kr yellow	1,250.
2c	A1	2kr black	475.00
3e	A1	3kr red	240.00
4b	A1	6kr brown	90.00
5e	A1	9kr blue	60.00

Values for Stamps with Blue Cancellations

Hand-Made Paper

1	A1	1kr yellow	1,075.
2	A1	2kr black	1,000.
3	A1	3kr red	250.00
4	A1	6kr brown	275.00
5	A1	9kr blue, type II	300.00

Machine-Made Paper

1a	A1	1kr yellow	800.00
2c	A1	2kr black	825.00
3e	A1	3kr red	120.00
4b	A1	6kr brown	120.00
5e	A1	9kr blue	160.00

Rouletted 14

1	A1	1kr yellow	—
		On cover, Tokay cancellation	—
2	A1	2kr black	—
		On cover, Tokay cancellation	—
3	A1	3kr red	1,575.
		On cover, Tokay cancellation	11,500.
4	A1	6kr brown	2,150.
		On cover, Tokay cancellation	30,000.
5a	A1	9kr blue, type I	1,850.
		On cover, Tokay cancellation	21,000.

This roulette was applied to stamps by the postmasters of the Tokay and Hommona post offices (now in Hungary) post offices during 1852-54.

A2

A3

Emperor Franz Josef — A4

A5

A6

Two Types of Each Value.

Type I. Loops of the bow at the back of the head broken, except the 2kr. In the 2kr, the "2" has a flat foot, thinning to the right. The frame line in the UR corner is thicker than the line below. In the 5kr the top frame line is unbroken.

Type II. Loops complete. Wreath projects further at top of head. In the 2kr, the "2" has a more curved foot of uniform thickness, with a shading line in the upper and lower curves. The frame line UR is thicker than the line below. In the 5kr the top frame line is broken.

1858-59　　Embossed　　*Perf. 14½*

6	A2	2kr yellow, type II	1,225.	55.00
		No gum	200.00	
		On cover		125.00
a.		2kr yellow, type I	3,000.	400.00
		No gum	400.00	
		On cover		725.00
b.		2kr orange, type II	3,750.	450.00
		No gum	600.00	
		On cover		900.00
c.		Half used as 1kr on cover		41,500.
d.		2kr dark orange, type II	7,250.	725.00
		No gum	1,450.	
		On cover		1,350.
7	A3	3kr black, type II	2,500.	175.00
		No gum	400.00	
		On cover		400.00
a.		3kr black, type I	2,000.	240.00
		No gum	275.00	
		On cover		475.00
b.		3kr gray black, type I		600.00
		On cover		1,350.
8	A3	3kr green, type II ('59)	1,350.	140.00
		No gum	240.00	
		On cover		325.00
a.		3k bluish green, type II ('59)	2,000.	175.00
		No gum	275.00	
		On cover		350.00
9	A4	5kr red, type II	475.00	2.40
		No gum	80.00	
		On cover		6.50
a.		5kr red, type I	2,000.	20.00
		No gum	360.00	
		On cover		55.00
b.		5kr red, type II with type I frame	950.00	32.50
		No gum	175.00	
		On cover		72.50
10	A5	10kr brown, type II	875.00	4.75
		No gum	140.00	
		On cover		12.00
a.		10kr brown, type I	2,400.	24.00
		No gum	400.00	
		On cover		95.00
b.		Half used as 5kr on cover, single franking		16,000.
c.		Half used as 5kr on 15kr rate cover		20,000.
11	A6	15kr blue, type II	800.00	2.00
		No gum	140.00	
		On cover		14.50
a.		Type I	2,400.	24.00
		No gum	400.00	
		On cover		47.50
b.		Half used as 7kr on cover		—
c.		15k deep blue, Type I	2,750.	65.00
		No gum	475.00	
		On cover		65.00

The reprints are of type II and are perforated 10½, 11, 12, 12½ and 13. There are also imperforate reprints of Nos. 6 to 8.

For similar designs see Lombardy-Venetia A2-A6.

Values for used pairs

6	A2	2kr yellow, type II	125.00
		On cover	1,300.
6a	A2	2kr yellow, type I	875.00
		On cover	3,250.
6b	A2	2kr orange, type II	675.00
7	A3	3kr black, type II	525.00
		On cover	2,350.
7a	A3	3kr black, type I	600.00
		On cover	2,500.
7b	A3	3kr gray black, type I	1,325.
8	A3	3kr green, type II ('59)	400.00
		On cover	2,200.
9	A4	5kr red, type II	5.50
		On cover	20.00
9a	A4	5kr red, type I	47.50
		On cover	95.00
9b	A4	5kr red, type II with type I frame	75.00
10	A5	10kr brown, type II	16.00
		On cover	40.000
10a	A5	10kr brown, type I	95.00
		On cover	160.00
11	A6	15kr blue, type II	14.00
		On cover	30.00

11a	A6	15kr blue, type I		50.00
		On cover		145.00

Values for used strips of 3

6	A2	2kr yellow, type II		200.00
		On cover		2,500.
6a	A2	2kr yellow, type I		1,450.
		On cover		4,750.
7	A3	3kr black, type II		800.00
		On cover		—
7a	A3	3kr black, type I		950.00
		On cover		—
7b	A3	3kr gray black, type I		3,000.
		On cover		—
8	A3	3kr green, type II ('59)		650.00
		On cover		—
9	A4	5kr red, type II		20.00
		On cover		125.00
9a	A4	5kr red, type I		80.00
		On cover		240.00
9b	A4	5kr red, type II with type 1 frame		125.00
		On cover		—
10	A5	10kr brown, type II		45.00
		On cover		275.00
10a	A5	10kr brown, type I		160.00
		On cover		375.00
11	A6	15kr blue, type II		32.50
		On cover		140.00
11a	A6	15kr blue, type I		110.00
		On cover		250.00

Values for used strips of 4

6	A2	2kr yellow, type II		535.00
6a	A2	2kr yellow, type I		2,350.
7	A3	3kr black, type II		1,325.
7a	A3	3kr black, type I		1,650.
7b	A3	3kr gray black, type II		3,250.
8	A3	3kr green, type II ('59)		1,250.
9	A4	5kr red, type II		65.00
9a	A4	5kr red, type I		215.00
9b	A4	5kr red, type II with type I frame		—
10	A5	10kr brown, type II		175.00
10a	A5	10kr brown, type I		375.00
11	A6	15kr blue, type II		110.00
11a	A6	15kr blue, type I		325.00

Values for blocks of 4

6	A2	2kr yellow, type II		2,750.
6a	A2	2kr yellow, type I		7,250.
7	A3	3kr black, type II		4,000.
7a	A3	3kr black, type I	15,000.	4,750.
7b	A3	3kr gray black, type I		—
8	A3	3kr green, type II ('59)		4,000.
9	A4	5kr red, type II	3,900.	400.00
		On cover		950.00
9a	A4	5kr red, type I		725.00
		On cover		1,800.
9b	A4	5kr red, type II with type 1 frame		—
10	A5	10kr brown, type II		825.00
		On cover		1,850.
10a	A5	10kr brown, type I		1,500.
		On cover		3,300.
11	A6	15kr blue, type II		575.00
		On cover		1,500.
11a	A6	15kr blue, type I		1,200.
		On cover		2,700.

Values for stamps, covers used in Lombardy-Venetia

6	A2	2kr yellow, type II, *from*	900.00	
		On cover, *from*	14,500.	
6a	A2	2kr yellow, type I, *from*	1,750.	
		On cover, *from*	—	
6b	A2	2kr orange, type II, *from*	2,750.	
		On cover, *from*	—	
7	A3	3kr black, type II, *from*	350.00	
		On cover, *from*	3,750.	
7a	A3	3kr black, type I, *from*	450.00	
		On cover, *from*	5,000.	
7b	A3	3kr gray black, type I, *from*	—	
		On cover, *from*	—	
8	A3	3kr green, type II ('59)(from)	450.00	
		On cover, *from*	6,250.	
9	A4	5kr red, type II, *from*	200.00	
		On cover, *from*	1,550.	
9a	A4	5kr red, type I, *from*	200.00	
		On cover, *from*	1,800.	
9b	A4	5kr red, type II with type I frame, *from*	—	
10	A5	10kr brown, type II, *from*	200.00	
		On cover, *from*	2,500.	
10a	A5	10kr brown, type I, *from*	250.00	
		On cover, *from*	3,500.	
11	A6	15kr blue, type II, *from*	275.00	
		On cover, *from*	5,000.	
11a	A6	15kr blue, type I, *from*	400.00	
		On cover, *from*	5,500.	

Values for Stamps with Red Cancellations

6	A2	2kr yellow, type II	160.00
6a	A2	2kr yellow, type I	750.00
6b	A2	2kr orange, type II	4,750.
7	A3	3kr black, type II	240.00
7a	A3	3kr black, type I	290.00
8	A3	3kr green, type II ('59)	250.00
9	A4	5kr red, type II	30.00
9a	A4	5kr red, type I	200.00
10	A5	10kr brown, type II	25.00
10a	A5	10kr brown, type I	115.00
11	A6	15kr blue, type II	12.50
11a	A6	15kr blue, type I	110.00

Values for Stamps with Blue Cancellations

6	A2	2kr yellow, type II	1,250.
6a	A2	2kr yellow, type I	1,950.
6b	A2	2kr orange, type II	2,300.
7	A3	3kr black, type II	1,150.
7a	A3	3kr black, type I	1,325.
8	A3	3kr green, type II ('59)	675.00
9	A4	5kr red, type II	100.00
9a	A4	5kr red, type I	115.00
10	A5	10kr brown, type II	110.00
10a	A5	10kr brown, type I	210.00
11	A6	15kr blue, type II	115.00
11a	A6	15kr blue, type I	200.00

Values for Stamps on Cover Cancelled First Day of Issue (Nov. 1, 1858)

6a	A2	2kr yellow, type I		25,000.
7a	A3	3kr black, type I		11,000.
9a	A4	5kr red, type I		10,000.
10a	A5	10kr brown, type I		11,000.
11a	A6	15kr blue, type I		12,500.

Franz Josef — A7

Coat of Arms — A8

1860-61　　Embossed　　*Perf. 14*

12	A7	2kr yellow	450.00	35.00
		No gum	90.00	
		On cover		65.00
a.		Half used as 1kr on cover		25,000.
13	A7	3kr green	375.00	30.00
		No gum	90.00	
		On cover		75.00
a.		3kr yellow green	500.00	35.00
		No gum	125.00	
		On cover		72.50
14	A7	5kr red	290.00	1.00
		No gum	72.50	
		On cover		4.00
a.		5kr deep red	375.00	3.00
		No gum	90.00	
		On cover		11.00
15	A7	10kr brown	325.00	3.00
		No gum	80.00	
		On cover		7.25
a.		Half used as 5kr on cover		9,000.
b.		10kr deep brown	500.00	8.50
		No gum	125.00	
		On cover		20.00
16	A7	15kr blue	475.00	3.00
		No gum	115.00	
		On cover		5.50
a.		15k deep blue	650.00	4.75
		No gum	160.00	
		On cover		11.00

Values for Pairs

12	A7	2kr yellow	1,300.	70.00
		On cover		700.00
13	A7	3kr green	1,250.	72.50
		On cover		975.00
14	A7	5kr red	800.00	4.00
		On cover		18.00
15	A7	10kr brown	900.00	7.50
		On cover		32.50
16	A7	15kr blue	1,050.	5.00
		On cover		25.00

Values for Strips of 3

12	A7	2kr yellow		140.00
		On cover		2,400.
13	A7	3kr green		130.00
		On cover		2,250.
14	A7	5kr red		18.00
		On cover		70.00
15	A7	10kr brown		35.00
		On cover		190.00
16	A7	15kr blue		30.00
		On cover		130.00

Values for Strips of 4

12	A7	2kr yellow	250.00
13	A7	3kr green	240.00
14	A7	5kr red	42.50
15	A7	10kr brown	105.00
16	A7	15kr blue	75.00

Values for Blocks of 4

12	A7	2kr yellow	4,800.	1,750.
13	A7	3kr green	4,700.	1,750.
		On cover		4,700.
14	A7	5kr red	2,650.	250.00
		On cover		775.00
15	A7	10kr brown	3,500.	500.00
		On cover		1,400.
16	A7	15kr blue	4,400.	375.00
		On cover		1,100.

Values for stamps, covers used in Lombardy-Venetia

12	A7	2kr yellow, *from*	550.00
		On cover, *from*	13,750.
13	A7	3kr green, *from*	460.00
		On cover, *from*	12,500.
14	A7	5kr red, *from*	165.00
		On cover, *from*	1,850.
15	A7	10kr brown, *from*	220.00
		On cover, *from*	2,100.
16	A7	15kr blue, *from*	375.00
		On cover, *from*	5,750.

The reprints are perforated 9, 9½, 10, 10½, 11, 11½, 12, 12½, 13 and 13½.
There are also imperforate reprints of the 2 and 3kr.
For similar design see Lombardy-Venetia A7.

1863

17	A8	2kr yellow	675.00	110.00
		No gum	140.00	
		On cover		225.00
a.		Half used as 1kr on cover		—
18	A8	3kr green	525.00	100.00
		No gum	125.00	
		On cover		225.00
a.		3kr yellow green	800.00	120.00
		No gum	200.00	
		On cover		300.00
19	A8	5kr rose	625.00	15.00
		No gum	115.00	
		On cover		40.00
a.		5kr carmine rose	650.00	22.00

		No gum	160.00	
		On cover		60.00
20	A8	10kr blue	1,650.	18.50
		No gum	350.00	
		On cover		47.50
a.		10kr deep blue	1,600.	22.00
		No gum	400.00	
		On cover		60.00
21	A8	15kr yellow brown	1,650.	18.00
		No gum	300.00	
		On cover		54.00
a.		15kr deep brown	1,700.	24.00
		No gum	425.00	
		On cover		72.50

Values for used pairs

17	A8	2kr yellow	290.00
18	A8	3kr green	250.00
19	A8	5kr rose	30.00
20	A8	10kr blue	40.00
21	A8	15kr yellow brown	47.50

Values for Stamps with Red Cancellations

17	A8	2kr yellow	2,000.
18	A8	3kr green	200.00
19	A8	5kr rose	54.00
20	A8	10kr blue	47.50
21	A8	15kr yellow brown	47.50

Values for Stamps with Blue Cancellations

17	A8	2kr yellow	550.00
18	A8	3kr green	325.00
19	A8	5kr rose	57.50
20	A8	10kr blue	115.00
21	A8	15kr yellow brown	105.00

For similar design see Lombardy-Venetia A1.

Wmk. 91, or, before July 1864, Unwmkd.

1863-64 — Perf. 9½

22	A8	2kr yellow ('64)	190.00	15.00
		No gum	35.00	
		On cover		45.00
a.		Ribbed paper	550.00	
		On cover		1,500.
b.		Half used as 1kr on cover		27,500.
c.		2kr deep yellow	235.00	22.00
		No gum	57.50	
		On cover		60.00
23	A8	3kr green ('64)	190.00	15.00
		No gum	45.00	
		On cover		54.00
a.		3kr deep green ('64)	275.00	22.00
		No gum	55.00	
		On cover		72.50
24	A8	5kr rose	55.00	.75
		No gum	12.50	
		On cover		5.40
a.		Ribbed paper	775.00	
		On cover		2,100.
b.		5kr carmine rose	175.00	3.75
		No gum	45.00	
		On cover		8.00
25	A8	10kr blue	250.00	3.50
		No gum	55.00	
		On cover		12.00
a.		Half used as 5kr on cover		22,500.
b.		10kr greenish blue	290.00	8.50
		No gum	72.50	
		On cover		14.00
26	A8	15kr yellow brown	225.00	2.25
		No gum	50.00	
		On cover		8.75
a.		15kr deep brown	275.00	3.50
		No gum	65.00	
		On cover		12.00
		Nos. 22-26 (5)	910.00	36.50

Values for Pairs

22	A8	2kr yellow ('64)	40.00
23	A8	3kr green ('64)	40.00
24	A8	5kr rose	1.75
25	A8	10kr blue	9.50
26	A8	15kr yellow brown	9.00

Values for Stamps with Red Cancellations

22	A8	2kr yellow ('64)	525.00
23	A8	3kr green ('64)	42.50
24	A8	5kr rose	22.00
25	A8	10kr blue	14.00
26	A8	15kr yellow brown	9.00

Values for Stamps with Blue Cancellations

22	A8	2kr yellow ('64)	130.00
23	A8	3kr green ('64)	35.00
24	A8	5kr rose	7.25
25	A8	10kr blue	19.00
26	A8	15kr yellow brown	11.00

Values for Stamps with Green Cancellations

22	A8	2kr yellow ('64)	1,100.
23	A8	3kr green ('64)	1,100.
24	A8	5kr rose	375.00

The reprints are perforated 10½, 11½, 13 and 13½. There are also imperforate reprints of the 2 and 3kr.

Issues of Austro-Hungarian Monarchy

From 1867 to 1871 the independent postal administrations of Austria and Hungary used the same stamps.

A9   A10

5 kr:

Type I. In arabesques in lower left corner, the small ornament at left of the curve nearest the figure "5" is short and has three points at bottom.

Type II. The ornament is prolonged within the curve and has two points at bottom. The corresponding ornament at top of the lower left corner does not touch the curve (1872).

Type III. Similar to type II but the top ornament is joined to the curve (1881). Two different printing methods were used for the 1867-74 issues. The first produced stamps on which the hair and whiskers were coarse and thick, from the second they were fine and clear.

1867-72   Wmk. 91   Typo.   Perf. 9½

Coarse Print

27	A9	2kr yellow	120.00	3.00
		Never hinged	240.00	
		On cover		13.00
a.		Half used as 1kr on cover		—
b.		2kr lemon yellow	190.00	6.00
		Never hinged	350.00	
		On cover		21.00
c.		2kr ochre yellow	190.00	8.75
		Never hinged	350.00	
		On cover		45.00
d.		2kr yellowish orange	120.00	2.75
		Never hinged	225.00	
		On cover		15.00
e.		2kr deep orange	190.00	6.00
		Never hinged	390.00	
		On cover		30.00
f.		2kr brown orange	290.00	17.50
		Never hinged	575.00	
		On cover		77.50
28	A9	3kr green	140.00	2.90
		Never hinged	240.00	
		On cover		16.50
a.		3kr pale yellow green	140.00	3.00
		Never hinged	275.00	
		On cover		18.00
b.		3kr blue green	190.00	4.00
		Never hinged	350.00	
		On cover		30.00
c.		3kr deep green	250.00	6.00
		Never hinged	475.00	
		On cover		42.50
d.		3kr emerald green	300.00	15.00
		Never hinged	600.00	
		On cover		90.00
29	A9	5kr rose, type II	87.50	.25
		Never hinged	165.00	
		On cover		3.00
a.		5kr rose, type I	95.00	.25
		Never hinged	175.00	
		On cover		3.00
b.		Perf. 10½, type II	190.00	6.00
		Never hinged	300.00	
c.		Cliché of 3kr in plate of 5kr		37,500.
d.		5kr lilac rose, type I	95.00	1.20
		Never hinged	175.00	
		No gum	20.00	
		On cover		4.25
e.		5kr brick red, type II	150.00	1.75
		Never hinged	275.00	
		No gum	22.00	
		On cover		8.00
f.		5kr violet red, type I	260.00	2.75
		Never hinged	450.00	
		On cover		14.50
30	A9	10kr blue	290.00	2.40
		Never hinged	500.00	
		On cover		42.50
		On cover, single franking		54.00
a.		Half used as 5kr on cover		—
b.		10kr pale milky blue	325.00	6.00
		Never hinged	600.00	
		On cover		42.50
c.		10kr deep blue	325.00	3.00
		Never hinged	540.00	
		On cover		45.00
31	A9	15kr brown	290.00	6.50
		Never hinged	550.00	
		On cover		20.00
a.		15kr deep brown	440.00	29.00
		Never hinged	800.00	
		On cover		60.00
b.		15kr yellowish brown	325.00	7.75
		Never hinged	600.00	
		On cover		29.00
c.		15kr gray brown	300.00	8.75
		Never hinged	600.00	
		On cover		40.00
d.		15kr reddish brown	350.00	13.00
		Never hinged	650.00	
		On cover		54.00
32	A9	25kr lilac	87.50	21.00
		Never hinged	165.00	
		On cover		165.00
a.		25kr gray lilac	47.50	17.50
		Never hinged	95.00	
		On cover		165.00
b.		25kr brown violet	325.00	65.00
		Never hinged	650.00	
		On cover		350.00
c.		25kr violet	52.50	19.00
		Never hinged	105.00	
		On cover		160.00
d.		25kr brownish lilac	87.50	40.00
		Never hinged	165.00	
		On cover		240.00
e.		25kr dull gray	900.00	350.00

		Never hinged	1,500.	
		On cover		1,200.

Perf. 12

33	A10	50kr light brown	40.00	130.00
		Never hinged	70.00	
		On cover		3,000.
a.		50kr pale red brown	500.00	210.00
		Never hinged	850.00	
		On cover		3,400.

A cover bearing a 50 kreuzer red brown, with 2 kreuzer yellow, 10 kreuzer blue and 15 kreuzer dark brown, addressed to Aden, realized the equivalent of U.S. $18,300 at a German auction in 2003.

b.		50kr brownish rose	500.00	325.00
		Never hinged	850.00	
		On cover		3,750.
c.		Pair, imperf. btwn., vert. or horizontal	725.00	1,700.

There are 3 known examples of No. 29c. Each has small defects. The value for No. 29c is for a defective example. An undamaged example believed to be unique was sold at a German auction in 2013 for the equivalent of US $275,000.00.

Issues for Austria only

1874-80   Perf. 9½

Fine Print

34	A9	2kr yellow ('76)	14.50	.90
		Never hinged	30.00	
		On cover		13.00
f.		2kr lemon yellow	19.00	12.00
		Never hinged	45.00	
		On cover		21.00
35	A9	3kr green ('76)	65.00	.90
		Never hinged	130.00	
		On cover		17.50
f.		3kr yellow green	95.00	.90
		Never hinged	165.00	
		On cover		18.50
36	A9	5kr rose, type III	4.50	.25
		Never hinged	9.50	
		On cover		3.50
f.		5kr carmine rose	4.75	.25
		Never hinged	16.50	
		On cover		4.75
37	A9	10kr blue ('75)	160.00	.60
		Never hinged	350.00	
		On cover		29.00
f.		10kr pale blue	210.00	.90

		Never hinged	450.00	
		On cover		24.00
38	A9	15kr brown ('77)	8.75	7.75
		Never hinged	21.00	
		On cover		60.00
f.		15kr deep chestnut brown	20.00	13.00
		Never hinged	42.50	
		On cover		47.50
39	A9	25kr gray lil ('78)	1.10	190.00
		Never hinged	3.00	
		On cover		10,000.
f.		25kr gray violet	22.50	225.00
		Never hinged	47.50	
		On cover		10,000.
40	A10	50kr red brown	14.50	190.00
		Never hinged	40.00	
		On cover		12,500.

Perf. 9

34a	A9	2kr	250.00	65.00
		On cover		600.00
35a	A9	3kr	225.00	30.00
		On cover		600.00
36a	A9	5kr	87.50	3.50
		On cover		150.00
37a	A9	10kr	440.00	35.00
		On cover		775.00
38a	A9	15kr	625.00	130.00
		On cover		1,100.

Perf. 10½

34b	A9	2kr	60.00	4.50
		On cover		57.50
35b	A9	3kr	100.00	2.75
		On cover		57.50
36b	A9	5kr	14.50	.90
		On cover		30.00
37b	A9	10kr	225.00	2.75
		On cover		65.00
38b	A9	15kr	250.00	27.50
		On cover		210.00

Perf. 12

34c	A9	2kr	275.00	160.00
		On cover		525.00
35c	A9	3kr	250.00	27.50
		On cover		425.00
36c	A9	5kr	60.00	5.00
		On cover		130.00
37c	A9	10kr	525.00	130.00
		On cover		725.00
38c	A9	15kr	825.00	190.00
		On cover		1,150.
40b	A10	50kr brown ('80)	19.00	190.00
		On cover		13,750.
c.		Perf. 10½x12	325.00	

Perf. 13

34d	A9	2kr	325.00	360.00
		On cover		950.00
35d	A9	3kr	225.00	36.00
		On cover		425.00
36d	A9	5kr	130.00	21.00
		On cover		115.00
37d	A9	10kr	275.00	100.00
		On cover		600.00
38d	A9	15kr	625.00	475.00
		On cover		—
40a	A10	50kr	30.00	250.00

Perf. 9x10½

34e	A9	2kr	440.00	87.50
		On cover		
35e	A9	3kr	360.00	77.50
		On cover		
36e	A9	5kr	140.00	18.00
		On cover		
37e	A9	10kr	410.00	105.00
		On cover		

Various compound perforations exist.
Values are for stamps that do not show the watermark. Stamps showing the watermark often sell for more.
For similar designs see Offices in the Turkish Empire A1-A2.

A11

Perf. 9, 9½, 10, 10½, 11½, 12, 12½
1883　　Inscriptions in Black

41	A11	2kr brown	6.00	.45
		Never hinged	16.00	
		On cover		12.00
42	A11	3kr green	6.00	.35
		Never hinged	24.00	
		On cover		12.00
43	A11	5kr rose	75.00	.30
		Never hinged	190.00	
		On cover		3.00
a.		Vert. pair, imperf. btwn.	190.00	425.00
		Never hinged	325.00	
44	A11	10kr blue	4.50	.35
		Never hinged	16.00	
		On cover		15.00
45	A11	20kr gray	55.00	4.25
		Never hinged	165.00	
		On cover		240.00
c.		Perf 9		1,650.
46	A11	50kr red lilac, perf 9½	375.00	80.00
		Never hinged	1,200.	
		On cover		3,400.
		On parcel post receipt card		390.00
a.		50kr brown lilac & black, perf 10	350.00	120.00
		On cover		4,000.
		On parcel post receipt card		425.00

The last printings of Nos. 41-46 are watermarked "ZEITUNGS-MARKEN" instead of "BRIEF-MARKEN." Values are for stamps that do not show watermark.
The 5kr has been reprinted in a dull red rose, perforated 10½.
For similar design see Offices in the Turkish Empire A3.
For surcharges see Offices in the Turkish Empire Nos. 15-19.

Values for stamps with "BRIEF-MARKEN" watermark

41a	A11	2kr brown	8.75	.70
42a	A11	3kr green	8.75	.70
43b	A11	5kr rose	110.00	.55
44a	A11	10kr blue	6.50	.60
45a	A11	20kr gray	82.50	6.50
46b	A11	50kr red lilac	465.00	120.00

Values for stamps with "ZEITUNGS-MARKEN" watermark

41b	A11	2kr brown	30.00	13.00
42b	A11	3kr green	30.00	13.00
43c	A11	5kr rose	120.00	10.50
44b	A11	10kr blue	30.00	10.50
45b	A11	20kr gray	92.50	40.00
46c	A11	50kr red lilac	500.00	190.00

A12　　　　　　A13

Perf. 9 to 13½, also Compound
1890-96　Unwmk.　Granite Paper
Numerals in black, Nos. 51-61

51	A12	1kr dark gray	1.50	.30
		Never hinged	4.25	
		On cover		6.50
a.		Pair, imperf. between	225.00	540.00
		Never hinged	400.00	
b.		Half used as ½kr on cover		150.00
		As "b," on postcard		120.00
52	A12	2kr light brown	.35	.30
		Never hinged	2.90	
		On cover		2.40
53	A12	3kr gray green	.45	.30
		Never hinged	3.25	
		On cover		3.00
a.		Pair, imperf. between	325.00	650.00
		Never hinged	475.00	
54	A12	5kr rose	.45	.30
		Never hinged	3.25	
		On cover		1.50
a.		Pair, imperf. between	260.00	450.00
		Never hinged	390.00	
55	A12	10kr ultramarine	1.10	.30
		Never hinged	6.00	
		On cover		6.50
a.		Pair, imperf. between	360.00	650.00
		Never hinged	575.00	
56	A12	12kr claret	2.60	.40
		Never hinged	12.00	
		On cover		47.50
		On parcel post receipt card		11.00
a.		Pair, imperf. between	—	800.00
57	A12	15kr lilac	2.60	.40
		Never hinged	12.00	
		On cover		15.00
		On parcel post receipt card		13.00
a.		Pair, imperf. between	475.00	900.00
		Never hinged	700.00	
58	A12	20kr olive green	37.50	2.40
		Never hinged	115.00	
		On cover		350.00
		On parcel post receipt card		16.00
59	A12	24kr gray blue	2.25	1.50
		Never hinged	11.50	
		On cover		600.00
		On parcel post receipt card		16.00
a.		Pair, imperf. between	475.00	700.00
		Never hinged	900.00	
60	A12	30kr dark brown	2.75	.80
		Never hinged	11.50	
		On cover		210.00
		On parcel post receipt card		16.00
61	A12	50kr violet, perf 10	6.00	11.00
		Never hinged	15.00	
		On cover		3,750.
		On parcel post receipt card		36.00
a.		Perf 9½	26.00	15.00
		Never hinged	65.00	
		On cover		4,700.
		On parcel post receipt card		36.00

Engr.

62	A13	1gld dark blue	3.00	3.00
		Never hinged	9.50	
		On cover		1,400.
		On parcel post receipt card		37.50
63	A13	1gld pale lilac ('96)	45.00	4.50
		Never hinged	120.00	
		On cover		1,250.
		On parcel post receipt card		80.00
64	A13	2gld carmine	3.25	24.00
		Never hinged	12.00	
		On cover		2,500.
		On parcel post receipt card		130.00
65	A13	2gld gray green ('96)	15.00	47.50
		Never hinged	47.50	
		On cover		2,600.
		On parcel post receipt card		200.00
		Nos. 51-65 (15)	123.80	97.00

Nearly all values of the 1890-1907 issues are found with numerals missing in one or more corners, some with numerals printed on the back.
For surcharges see Offices in the Turkish Empire Nos. 20-25, 28-31.

A14

Perf. 9 to 13½, also Compound
1891　Typo.　Numerals in black

66	A14	20kr olive green	1.90	.30
		Never hinged	11.00	
		On cover		18.00
		On parcel post receipt card		9.50
67	A14	24kr gray blue	3.25	.95
		Never hinged	12.00	
		On cover		240.00
		On parcel post receipt card		9.50
68	A14	30kr brown	1.90	.30
		Never hinged	12.00	
		On cover		37.50
		On parcel post receipt card		9.50
a.		Pair, imperf. between	275.00	700.00
		Never hinged	600.00	
b.		Perf. 9	110.00	55.00
		On cover		—
69	A14	50kr violet	1.90	.40
		Never hinged	15.00	
		On cover		475.00
		On parcel post receipt card		12.00
		Nos. 66-69 (4)	8.95	1.95

For surcharges see Offices in the Turkish Empire Nos. 26-27.

A15　　　　　　A16

A17　　　　　　A18

Perf. 10½ to 13½ and Compound
1899　Without Varnish Bars
Numerals in black, Nos. 70-82

70	A15	1h lilac	.75	.25
		Never hinged	2.40	
		On cover		4.75
		On parcel post receipt card		9.50
b.		Imperf.	60.00	150.00
		Never hinged	130.00	
		Imperf, pair	150.00	325.00
		Never hinged	290.00	
c.		Perf. 10½	32.50	8.00
		On cover		150.00
d.		Numerals inverted	2,250.	3,400.
71	A15	2h dark gray	2.75	.65
		Never hinged	19.00	
		On cover		6.00
		On parcel post receipt card		9.50
72	A15	3h bister brown	6.50	.25
		Never hinged	21.00	
		On cover		1.75
		On parcel post receipt card		9.50
b.		"3" in lower right corner sideways		3,000.
73	A15	5h blue green	7.25	.25
		Never hinged	21.00	
		On cover		1.20
		On parcel post receipt card		9.50
c.		Perf. 10½	22.50	4.75
		Never hinged	42.50	
		On cover		47.50
74	A15	6h orange	.75	.25
		Never hinged	2.40	
		On cover		3.25
		On parcel post receipt card		9.50
75	A16	10h rose	16.00	.25
		Never hinged	57.50	
		On cover		1.20
		On parcel post receipt card		9.50
b.		Perf. 10½	875.00	210.00
		Never hinged	1,450.	
		On cover		—
76	A16	20h brown	5.25	.25
		Never hinged	20.00	
		On cover		4.50
		On parcel post receipt card		9.50
77	A16	25h ultramarine	60.00	.35
		Never hinged	190.00	
		On cover		5.40
		On parcel post receipt card		9.50
78	A16	30h red violet	19.00	2.75
		Never hinged	72.50	
		On cover		22.50
		On parcel post receipt card		15.00
b.		Horiz. pair, imperf. btwn.	600.00	—
		Never hinged	925.00	
80	A17	40h green	32.50	3.50
		Never hinged	100.00	
		On cover		30.00
		On parcel post receipt card		15.00
81	A17	50h gray blue	17.50	4.25
		Never hinged	60.00	
		On cover		45.00
		On parcel post receipt card		15.00
b.		All four "50's" parallel		3,100.

82	A17	60h brown	50.00	1.25
		Never hinged	150.00	
		On cover		35.00
		On parcel post receipt card		15.00
b.		Horiz. pair, imperf. btwn.	550.00	1,050.
		Never hinged		
c.		Perf. 10½	105.00	5.40
		Never hinged	175.00	
		On cover		32.50

Engr.

83	A18	1k carmine rose	6.00	.45
		Never hinged	21.00	
		On cover		175.00
		On parcel post receipt card		15.00
a.		1k carmine	6.00	.25
		Never hinged	21.00	
		On cover		240.00
		On parcel post receipt card		18.00
b.		Vert. pair, imperf. btwn.	250.00	350.00
		Never hinged	425.00	
84	A18	2k gray lilac	52.50	.45
		Never hinged	165.00	
		On cover		1,350.
		On parcel post receipt card		24.00
a.		Vert. pair, imperf. btwn.	440.00	725.00
		Never hinged	800.00	
85	A18	4k gray green	10.50	18.00
		Never hinged	40.00	
		On cover		1,100.
		On parcel post receipt card		90.00
		Nos. 70-85 (15)	287.25	33.15

For surcharges see Offices in Crete Nos. 1-7, Offices in the Turkish Empire Nos. 32-45.

1901　　With Varnish Bars

70a	A15	1h lilac	1.60	.45
		Never hinged	7.50	
		On cover		4.75
71a	A15	2h dark gray	6.50	.40
		Never hinged	37.50	
		On cover		5.75
72a	A15	3h bister brown	.80	.25
		Never hinged	2.60	
		On cover		2.40
73a	A15	5h blue green	.80	.25
		Never hinged	2.60	
		On cover		1.20
74a	A15	6h orange	.80	.25
		Never hinged	2.60	
		On cover		3.25
75a	A16	10h rose	.80	.25
		Never hinged	3.50	
		On cover		1.20
76a	A16	20h brown	.80	.25
		Never hinged	5.00	
		On cover		4.75
77a	A16	25h ultra	.80	.25
		Never hinged	5.00	
		On cover		4.75
78a	A16	30h red violet	3.25	.80
		Never hinged	11.00	
		On cover		13.00
79	A17	35h green	.80	.25
		Never hinged	2.50	
		On cover		11.00
80a	A17	40h green	3.25	4.75
		Never hinged	12.00	
		On cover		22.50
81a	A17	50h gray blue	4.75	11.00
		Never hinged	12.50	
		On cover		45.00
82a	A17	60h brown	3.25	1.60
		Never hinged	12.00	
		On cover		27.00
		Nos. 70a-78a,79,80a-82a (13)	28.20	20.75

The diagonal yellow bars of varnish were printed across the face to prevent cleaning.

A19　　　　　　A20

A21

Perf. 12½ to 13½ and Compound
1905-07　　　　Typo.
Without Varnish Bars
Colored Numerals

86	A19	1h lilac	.25	.35
		Never hinged	.40	
		On cover		4.00
87	A19	2h dark gray	.25	.25
		Never hinged	.40	
		On cover		4.75
88	A19	3h bister brown	.25	.25
		Never hinged	1.60	
		On cover		2.00
89	A19	5h dk blue green	12.00	.25
		Never hinged	26.00	
		On cover		1.20
90	A19	5h yellow grn ('06)	.25	.25
		Never hinged	.80	
		On cover		.70

91 A19 6h deep orange .25 .25
  Never hinged 2.40
  On cover 2.40
92 A20 10h carmine ('06) .50 .25
  Never hinged 1.60
  On cover .70
93 A20 12h violet ('07) 1.20 .80
  Never hinged 4.25
  On cover 130.00
  On parcel post receipt card 9.50
94 A20 20h brown ('06) 4.00 .25
  Never hinged 11.50
  On cover 7.50
95 A20 25h ultra ('06) 4.00 .40
  Never hinged 10.50
  On cover 9.25
96 A20 30h red violet ('06) 8.00 .40
  Never hinged 22.00
  On cover 22.50

Black Numerals
97 A20 10h carmine 16.00 .25
  Never hinged 80.00
  On cover .90
98 A20 20h brown 40.00 1.60
  Never hinged 130.00
  On cover 9.00
99 A20 25h ultra 40.00 2.40
  Never hinged 120.00
  On cover 16.50
100 A20 30h red violet 55.00 4.75
  Never hinged 175.00
  On cover 30.00

White Numerals
101 A21 35h green 2.00 .25
  Never hinged 12.00
  On cover 9.50
102 A21 40h deep violet 2.00 .80
  Never hinged 12.00
  On cover 18.00
103 A21 50h dull blue 2.00 3.50
  Never hinged 12.00
  On cover 25.00
104 A21 60h yellow brown 2.00 .80
  Never hinged 12.00
  On cover 18.00
105 A21 72h rose 2.00 1.75
  Never hinged 16.00
  On cover 350.00
Nos. 86-105 (20) 191.95 19.80
Set, never hinged 650.00

For surcharges see Offices in Crete Nos. 8-14.

1904   *Perf. 13x13½*
With Varnish Bars
86a A19 1h lilac .35 .95
  Never hinged 1.60
  On cover 4.75
87a A19 2h dark gray 1.40 .95
  Never hinged 6.50
  On cover 13.00
88a A19 3h bister brown 2.00 .25
  Never hinged 6.50
  On cover 1.75
89a A19 5h dk blue green 3.25 .25
  Never hinged 9.50
  On cover 1.20
91a A19 6h deep orange 8.00 .30
  Never hinged 30.00
  On cover 2.75
97a A20 10h carmine 1.75 .25
  Never hinged 14.50
  On cover 1.20
98a A20 20h brown 29.00 1.20
  Never hinged 100.00
  On cover 8.00
99a A20 25h ultra 29.00 .80
  Never hinged 92.50
  On cover 8.00
100a A20 30h red violet 45.00 1.60
  Never hinged 145.00
  On cover 16.00
101a A21 35h green 29.00 .55
  Never hinged 97.50
  On cover 80.00
102a A21 40h deep violet 27.50 4.00
  Never hinged 97.50
  On cover 80.00
103a A21 50h dull blue 29.00 9.50
  Never hinged 97.50
  On cover 80.00
104a A21 60h yellow brown 40.00 1.60
  Never hinged 160.00
  On cover 30.00
105a A21 72h rose 2.00 2.25
  Never hinged 16.00
  On cover 325.00
Nos. 86a-105a (14) 247.25 24.45
Set, never hinged 875.00

Stamps of the 1901, 1904 and 1905 issues perf. 9 or 10½, also compound with 12½, were not sold at any post office, but were supplied only to some high-ranking officials. This applies also to the contemporaneous issues of Austrian Offices Abroad.

1904   *Perf. 13x12½*
With Varnish Bars
86b A19 1h lilac .80 .95
  Never hinged 3.00
  On cover 4.75
87b A19 2h dark gray 2.00 .55
  Never hinged 7.00
  On cover 13.00
88b A19 3h bister brown 2.00 .25
  Never hinged 8.00
  On cover 1.75
89b A19 5h dk blue green 4.50 .25
  Never hinged 12.00
  On cover 1.20
91b A19 6h deep orange 9.50 .30
  Never hinged 35.00
  On cover 3.00
97b A20 10h carmine 2.40 .25
  Never hinged 20.00
  On cover 1.20

98b A20 20h brown 29.00 .80
  Never hinged 110.00
  On cover 8.00
99b A20 25h ultra 29.00 .80
  Never hinged 95.00
  On cover 8.00
100b A20 30h red violet 45.00 1.60
  Never hinged 145.00
  On cover 16.00
101b A21 35h green 29.00 2.00
  Never hinged 100.00
  On cover 80.00
102b A21 40h deep violet 28.00 9.50
  Never hinged 100.00
  On cover 80.00
103b A21 50h dull blue 30.00 10.00
  Never hinged 100.00
  On cover 105.00
104b A21 60h yellow brown 40.00 1.20
  Never hinged 165.00
  On cover 30.00
Nos. 86b-104b (13) 251.20 28.45
Set, never hinged 900.00

Stamps of the 1901, 1904 and 1905 issues perf. 9 or 10½, also compound with 12½, were not sold at any post office, but were supplied only to some high-ranking officials. This applies also to the contemporaneous issues of Austrian Offices Abroad.

Karl VI — A22   Franz Josef — A23

Schönbrunn Palace — A24

Franz Josef — A25

Designs: 2h, Maria Theresa. 3h, Joseph II. 5h, 10h, 25h, Franz Josef. 6h, Leopold II. 12h, Franz I. 20h, Ferdinand I. 30h, Franz Josef as youth. 35h, Franz Josef in middle age. 60h, Franz Josef on horseback. 1k, Franz Josef in royal robes. 5k, Hofburg, Vienna.

1908-16   *Typo.*   *Perf. 12½*
Ordinary paper ('08-'13)
110 A22 1h gray black .35 .95
  Never hinged .75
  On cover 4.75
111 A22 2h blue violet .25 .70
  Never hinged .75
  On cover 4.75
112 A22 3h magenta .25 .25
  Never hinged .75
  On cover 4.50
113 A22 5h yellow green .25 .25
  Never hinged .50
  On cover .90
  a. Booklet pane of 6 27.50
114 A22 6h orange brown 1.50 2.10
  Never hinged 7.00
  On cover 16.00
115 A22 10h rose .25 .25
  Never hinged .50
  On cover .90
  a. Booklet pane of 6 82.50
116 A22 12h scarlet 1.50 2.10
  Never hinged 8.00
  On cover 20.00
117 A22 20h choc. 1.90 .25
  Never hinged 10.00
  On cover 11.50
118 A22 25h ultramarine 2.75 .45
  Never hinged 12.00
  On cover 3.25
119 A22 30h olive green 11.00 .65
  Never hinged 24.00
  On cover 12.00
120 A22 35h slate 2.40 .25
  Never hinged 26.00
  On cover 9.50

Engr.
121 A23 50h dark green .55 .25
  Never hinged 11.00
  On cover 32.50
  a. Vert. pair, imperf. btwn. 200.00 400.00
    Never hinged 475.00
  b. Horiz. pair, imperf. btwn. 200.00 400.00
    Never hinged 475.00

122 A23 60h deep carmine .25 .25
  Never hinged 1.75
  On cover 20.50
  a. Vert. pair, imperf. btwn. 160.00 400.00
    Never hinged 475.00
  b. Horiz. pair, imperf. btwn. 160.00 400.00
    Never hinged 475.00
123 A23 72h dk brown 1.60 .40
  Never hinged 14.50
  On cover 100.00
124 A23 1k purple 12.00 .25
  Never hinged 37.50
  On cover 54.00
  On cover, value declared 240.00
  a. Vert. pair, imperf. btwn. 200.00 350.00
    Never hinged 470.00
  b. Horiz. pair, imperf. btwn. 200.00 350.00
    Never hinged 410.00
125 A24 2k lake & olive grn 20.00 .40
  Never hinged 80.00
  On cover 95.00
  On cover, value declared 475.00
126 A24 5k bister & dk vio 40.00 6.00
  Never hinged 140.00
  On cover (value declared) 925.00
127 A25 10k blue, bis & dp brn 190.00 65.00
  Never hinged 500.00
  On cover (value declared) 1,550.
Nos. 110-127 (18) 286.80 80.75
Set, never hinged 875.00

Chalky Paper ('08-'13)
110a A22 1h gray black .25 .25
  Never hinged 4.00
  On cover 4.25
111a A22 2h violet .25 .25
  Never hinged 6.50
  On cover 4.50
112a A22 3h magenta .50 .25
  Never hinged 4.00
  On cover 3.50
113b A22 5h yellow green .25 .25
  Never hinged 2.00
  On cover .90
  c. Booklet pane of 6 25.00
114a A22 6h buff ('13) .55 .80
  Never hinged 8.00
  On cover 16.00
115b A22 10h rose .25 .25
  Never hinged 4.00
  On cover .90
  c. Booklet pane of 6 75.00
116a A22 12h scarlet .80 1.20
  Never hinged 12.00
  On cover 18.50
117a A22 20h chocolate 4.75 .45
  Never hinged 35.00
  On cover 10.50
118a A22 25h deep blue 2.00 .45
  Never hinged 24.00
  On cover 3.00
119a A22 30h olive green 9.50 .65
  Never hinged 47.50
  On cover 32.50
120a A22 35h slate 2.40 .25
  Never hinged 24.00
  On cover 12.00

Wartime Printings on Grayish Paper ('16)
122c A23 60h deep carmine 1.40 1.90
  Never hinged 6.50
  On cover 80.00
123a A23 72h dk brown 3.50 2.75
  Never hinged 24.00
124c A23 1k purple 20.00 1.75
  Never hinged 72.50
125a A24 2k lake & olive grn 28.00 4.50
  Never hinged 100.00
  On cover (value declared) —
126a A24 5k bister & dk vio 55.00 11.00
  Never hinged 320.00
  On cover (value declared) —

Definitive set issued for the 60th year of the reign of Emperor Franz Josef.
Nos. 110a-120a, 121, and 123-127 were issued in 1908. Nos. 110-20 and 122 were issued in 1913.
All values exist imperforate. They were not sold at any post office, but presented to a number of high government officials. This applies also to all imperforate stamps of later issues, including semi-postals, etc., and those of the Austrian Offices Abroad.
Litho. forgeries of No. 127 exist.
For overprint and surcharge see #J47-J48.
For similar designs see Offices in Crete A5-A6, Offices in the Turkish Empire A16-A17.

Birthday Jubilee Issue

No. 144

Similar to 1908 Issue, but designs enlarged by labels at top and bottom bearing dates "1830" and "1910"
1910   *Typo.*
128 A22 1h gray black 4.00 *8.00*
  Never hinged 12.50
  On cover 40.00
129 A22 2h violet 4.75 *16.00*
  Never hinged 20.00
  On cover 65.00
130 A22 3h magenta 4.00 *12.00*
  Never hinged 15.00
  On cover 40.00
131 A22 5h yellow green .25 .35
  Never hinged 2.25
  On cover 9.00
132 A22 6h buff 3.25 *12.00*
  Never hinged 12.50
  On cover 60.00
133 A22 10h rose .25 .35
  Never hinged 2.25
  On cover 9.00
134 A22 12h scarlet 3.25 *12.00*
  Never hinged 15.00
  On cover 65.00
135 A22 20h chocolate 3.25 *12.00*
  Never hinged 30.00
  On cover 92.50
136 A22 25h deep blue 1.60 *2.40*
  Never hinged 10.00
  On cover 16.00
137 A22 30h olive green 3.25 *12.00*
  Never hinged 18.00
  On cover 92.50
138 A22 35h slate 3.25 *12.00*
  Never hinged 18.00
  On cover 120.00

Engr.
139 A23 50h dark green 5.50 *12.00*
  Never hinged 18.00
  On cover 180.00
140 A23 60h deep carmine 5.50 *12.00*
  Never hinged 18.00
  On cover 165.00
141 A23 1k purple 5.50 *16.00*
  Never hinged 18.00
  On cover 375.00
142 A24 2k lake & ol grn 140.00 *225.00*
  Never hinged 280.00
  On cover (value declared) *1,250.*
143 A24 5k bister & dk vio 110.00 *225.00*
  Never hinged 200.00
  On cover (value declared) *2,000.*
144 A25 10k blue, bis & dp brn 175.00 *325.00*
  Never hinged 360.00
  On cover (value declared) *2,750.*
Nos. 128-144 (17) 472.60 *914.10*
Set, never hinged 1,050.

80th birthday of Emperor Franz Josef. All values exist imperforate. Litho. forgeries of Nos. 142-144 exist.

Austrian Crown — A37   Franz Josef — A38

Coat of Arms
A39   A40

Two sizes of Type A40:
Type I: 25x30mm
Type II: 26x29mm

1916-18   *Typo.*
145 A37 3h brt violet .25 .25
  Never hinged .25
  On cover 4.25
146 A37 5h lt green .25 .25
  Never hinged .30
  On cover 1.20
  a. Booklet pane of 6 15.50
  b. Booklet pane of 4 + 2 labels 30.00
147 A37 6h deep orange .25 .25
  Never hinged .85
  On cover 24.00
148 A37 10h magenta .25 .25
  Never hinged .30
  On cover 1.20
  a. Booklet pane of 6 30.00
149 A37 12h light blue .25 *.90*
  Never hinged 1.30
  On cover 40.00

150	A38	15h rose red	.40	.25
		Never hinged	2.25	
		On cover		2.10
a.		Booklet pane of 6	16.50	
151	A38	20h chocolate	4.00	.25
		Never hinged	14.00	
		On cover		12.00
152	A38	25h blue	4.00	.80
		Never hinged	21.00	
		On cover		13.00
153	A38	30h slate	6.50	.65
		Never hinged	21.00	
		On cover		16.00
154	A39	40h olive green	.25	.25
		Never hinged	1.60	
		On cover		6.00
155	A39	50h blue green	.25	.25
		Never hinged	1.60	
		On cover		18.00
156	A39	60h deep blue	.25	.25
		Never hinged	1.60	
		On cover		25.00
157	A39	80h orange brown	.25	.25
		Never hinged	1.60	
		On cover		32.50
158	A39	90h red violet	.25	.25
		Never hinged	1.60	
		On cover		80.00
159	A39	1k car, yel ('18)	.25	.25
		Never hinged	1.60	
		On cover		100.00

Engr.

160	A40	2k dark blue (I)	4.00	.40
		Never hinged	6.50	
		On cover		130.00
a.		Type II	11.00	1.20
		Never hinged	32.50	
161	A40	3k claret (I)	24.00	1.20
		Never hinged	57.50	
		On cover		200.00
a.		Type II	92.50	18.00
		Never hinged	290.00	
162	A40	4k deep green (I)	8.00	2.40
		Never hinged	13.50	
a.		Type II	4.40	3.50
		Never hinged	24.00	
163	A40	10k deep violet (I)	27.50	52.50
		Never hinged	92.50	
a.		Type II	120.00	240.00
		Never hinged	290.00	
		On cover		400.00
		Nos. 145-163 (19)	81.15	62.40
		Set, never hinged	240.00	

Stamps of type A38 have two varieties of the frame. Stamps of type A40 have various decorations about the shield.

Nos. 145-163 exist imperf. Value set, $475 hinged, $875 never hinged.

1917   **Ordinary Paper**

164	A40	2k light blue (I)	2.00	.80
		Never hinged	5.50	
		On cover		140.00
a.		Type II	2.60	.55
		Never hinged	5.75	
165	A40	3k carmine rose (I)	47.50	.80
		Never hinged	125.00	
		On cover		210.00
a.		Type II	250.00	165.00
		Never hinged	2,000.	
166	A40	4k yellow green (I)	3.25	1.25
		Never hinged	9.00	
a.		Type II	22.50	22.50
		Never hinged	80.00	
167	A40	10k violet (I)	140.00	110.00
		Never hinged	335.00	
a.		Type II	5,500.	—
		Never hinged	8,100.	
		Nos. 164-167 (4)	192.75	112.85
		Set, never hinged	475.00	

Nos. 164-167 exist imperf. Value set, $325 unused, $650 never hinged.

See Nos. 172-175 (granite paper). For overprints and surcharges see Nos. 181-199, C1-C3, J60-J63, N1-N5, N10-N19, N33-N37, N42-N51. Western Ukraine 2-7, 11-15, 19-28, 57-58, 85-89, 94-103, N3-N14, NJ13.

Emperor Karl I — A42

1917-18   **Typo.**

168	A42	15h dull red	.40	.40
		Never hinged	2.00	
		On cover		3.25
a.		Booklet pane of 6	16.50	
169	A42	20h dk green ('18)	.40	.40
		Never hinged	2.00	
		On cover		5.40
a.		20h green ('17)	.80	.65
		Never hinged	7.50	
		On cover		16.50
170	A42	25h blue	.40	.40
		Never hinged	5.50	
		On cover		14.00
171	A42	30h dull violet	2.00	.40
		Never hinged	4.00	
		On cover		18.00
		Nos. 168-171 (4)	3.20	1.60
		Set, never hinged	13.50	

Nos. 168-171 exist imperf. Value set, $160 unused, $400 never hinged.

For overprints and surcharges see Nos. N6-N9, N20, N38-N41, N52, N64. Western Ukraine 1, 8, 16-18, 90-93, N15-N18.

1918-19   **Engr.**   **Granite Paper**

172	A40	2k light blue (II)	1.20	.45
		Never hinged	2.00	
		On cover		150.00
a.		Perf. 11½	725.00	1,200.
		Never hinged	1,600.	
b.		Type I	1.75	2.90
		Never hinged	3.50	
		On cover		180.00
173	A40	3k carmine rose (II)	.40	.80
		Never hinged	.75	
		On cover		300.00
a.		Type I	1.90	2.90
		Never hinged	3.50	
		On cover		425.00
174	A40	4k yellow green (II) ('19)	4.00	20.00
		Never hinged	11.00	
		On cover		350.00
a.		Type I	14.00	29.00
		Never hinged	47.50	
		On cover		475.00
175	A40	10k lt violet (II) ('19)	8.00	32.50
		Never hinged	26.00	
		On cover		690.00
a.		Type I ('19)	44.00	140.00
		Never hinged	140.00	
		Nos. 172-175 (4)	13.60	53.75
		Set, never hinged	40.00	

Issues of the Republic

Austrian Stamps of 1916-18 Overprinted

1918-19   **Unwmk.**   **Perf. 12½**

181	A37	3h bright violet	.25	.25
		Never hinged	.70	
		On cover		4.25
182	A37	5h light green	.25	.25
		Never hinged	.70	
		On cover		1.20
183	A37	6h deep orange	.80	3.25
		Never hinged	3.75	
		On cover		24.00
184	A37	10h magenta	.25	.25
		Never hinged	.70	
		On cover		.90
185	A37	12h light blue	.40	2.40
		Never hinged	3.75	
		On cover		40.00
a.		12h deep greenish blue	30.00	
		Never hinged	105.00	
186	A42	15h dull red	.80	2.00
		Never hinged	3.00	
		On cover		3.50
187	A42	20h deep green	.40	.25
		Never hinged	1.40	
		On cover		1.20
188	A42	25h blue	.80	.25
		Never hinged	3.00	
		On cover		5.40
189	A42	30h dull violet	.80	.25
		Never hinged	3.00	
		On cover		2.40
190	A39	40h olive green	.80	.25
		Never hinged	3.00	
		On cover		8.00
191	A39	50h deep green	.80	2.00
		Never hinged	3.00	
		On cover		12.00
192	A39	60h deep blue	1.20	2.00
		Never hinged	3.75	
		On cover		16.00
193	A39	80h orange brown	.40	.80
		Never hinged	1.40	
		On cover		16.00
a.		Inverted overprint	275.00	325.00
		Never hinged	650.00	
194	A39	90h red violet	1.20	.80
		Never hinged	3.75	
		On cover		24.00
195	A39	1k carmine, yel	1.40	.80
		Never hinged	4.50	
		On cover		24.00

Granite Paper

196	A40	2k light blue (II)	.25	.25
		Never hinged	.35	
		On cover		40.00
a.		Horiz. pair, imperf. between	240.00	
		Never hinged	400.00	
b.		Vert. pair, imperf. between	400.00	
		Never hinged	1,200.	
c.		Perf. 11½	95.00	110.00
		Never hinged	175.00	
		On cover		350.00
197	A40	3k carmine rose (II)	.35	.80
		Never hinged	.75	
		On cover		165.00
198	A40	4k yellow green (II)	1.60	3.25
		Never hinged	3.00	
		On cover		290.00
a.		Perf. 11½	16.00	35.00
		Never hinged	32.50	
199	A40	10k deep violet (II)	9.50	20.00
		Never hinged	19.00	
		On cover		575.00

a.		Type I	100.00	190.00
		Never hinged	225.00	
		Nos. 181-199 (19)	22.25	40.10
		Set, never hinged	62.50	

Nos. 181, 182, 184, 187-191, 194, 197 and 199 exist imperforate. Value: 181//194, each $18; 197, $150; 199, $225.

Post Horn — A43   Coat of Arms — A44

Allegory of New Republic — A45

1919-20   **Typo.**   **Perf. 12½**

Ordinary Paper

200	A43	3h gray	.25	.25
		Never hinged	.30	
		On cover		4.25
a.		3h deep gray	2.25	4.75
		Never hinged	4.75	
b.		3h gray black	150.00	225.00
		Never hinged	325.00	
		On cover		400.00
201	A44	5h yellow green	.25	.25
		Never hinged	.30	
		On cover		4.25
202	A44	5h gray ('20)	.25	.25
		Never hinged	.30	
		On cover		4.25
a.		5h deep gray	9.00	18.50
		Never hinged	18.50	
b.		5h gray black	290.00	400.00
		Never hinged	475.00	
		On cover		—
203	A43	6h orange	.25	.50
		Never hinged	.45	
		On cover		24.00
204	A44	10h deep rose	.25	.25
		Never hinged	.30	
		On cover		1.20
205	A44	10h red ('20)	.25	.25
		Never hinged	.30	
		On cover		1.20
a.		Thick grayish paper ('20)	.25	.40
		Never hinged	.30	
206	A43	12h grnsh blue	.25	4.00
		Never hinged	.40	
		On cover		40.00
a.		12h deep greenish blue	52.50	210.00
		Never hinged	210.00	
		On cover		—
207	A43	15h bister ('20)	.35	.80
		Never hinged	.65	
		On cover		4.25
a.		Thick grayish paper ('20)	.25	.40
		Never hinged	.30	
		On cover		1.60
208	A45	20h dark green	.25	.25
		Never hinged	.30	
		On cover		1.00
a.		20h yellow green	.25	.25
		Never hinged	.30	
		On cover		1.50
b.		As "a," thick grysh paper ('20)	1.60	4.00
		Never hinged	2.10	
		On cover		9.00
209	A44	25h blue	.25	.25
		Never hinged	.30	
		On cover		4.75
a.		25h pale blue	16.50	27.50
		Never hinged	40.00	
		On cover		45.00
b.		25h deep blue	210.00	290.00
		Never hinged	390.00	
		On cover		—
210	A43	25h violet ('20)	.25	.25
		Never hinged	.30	
		On cover		2.40
211	A45	30h dark brown	.25	.25
		Never hinged	.30	
		On cover		3.00
212	A45	40h violet	.25	.25
		Never hinged	.30	
		On cover		4.50
213	A45	40h lake ('20)	.25	.25
		Never hinged	.35	
		On cover		3.25
214	A44	45h olive green	.30	.80
		Never hinged	.40	
		On cover		24.00
215	A45	50h dark blue	.25	.25
		Never hinged	.30	
		On cover		2.40
a.		Thick grayish paper ('20)	.40	.95
		Never hinged	.85	
216	A43	60h olive green ('20)	.25	.25
		Never hinged	.30	
		On cover		5.75
217	A44	1k carmine, yel	.25	.25
		Never hinged	.30	
		On cover		16.00

218	A44	1k light blue ('20)	.25	.25
		Never hinged	.35	
		On cover		10.50
a.		1k deep blue	155.00	290.00
		Never hinged	350.00	
		Nos. 200-218 (19)	4.90	9.85

All values exist imperf. (For regularly issued imperfs, see Nos. 227-235.)

For overprints and surcharge see Nos. B11-B19, B30-B38, J102, N21, N27, N53, N58, N65, N71.

Parliament Building A46

1919-20   **Engr.**   **Perf. 12½, 11½**

Granite Paper

219	A46	2k ver & blk	.25	.80
		Never hinged	1.25	
		On cover		80.00
a.		Center inverted	2,750.	
		Never hinged	6,500.	
b.		Perf. 11½	1.60	3.25
		Never hinged	1.80	
		On cover		47.50
220	A46	2½k olive bis ('20)	.30	.25
		Never hinged	.60	
		On cover		8.00
221	A46	3k blue & blk brn	.25	.25
		Never hinged	.60	
		On cover		12.00
a.		Perf. 11½	5.75	20.00
		Never hinged	10.50	
		On cover		29.00
222	A46	4k carmine & blk	.25	.25
		Never hinged	.60	
		On cover		16.00
a.		Center inverted	950.00	3,250.
		Never hinged	2,400.	
b.		Perf. 11½	2.00	6.50
		Never hinged	4.50	
		On cover		20.00
223	A46	5k black ('20)	.25	.25
		Never hinged	.60	
		On cover		8.00
a.		Perf. 11½x12½	55.00	87.50
		Never hinged	160.00	
b.		Perf. 11½	2.75	7.25
		Never hinged	6.00	
		On cover		21.00
224	A46	7½k plum	.30	.40
		Never hinged	1.25	
		On cover		8.00
a.		Perf. 11½	120.00	240.00
		Never hinged	290.00	
b.		Perf. 11½x12½	80.00	240.00
		Never hinged	240.00	
225	A46	10k olive grn & blk brn	.30	.40
		Never hinged	1.25	
		On cover		16.00
a.		Perf. 11½x12½	160.00	300.00
		Never hinged	475.00	
b.		Perf. 11½	13.50	30.00
		Never hinged	32.50	
		On cover		72.50
226	A46	20k lilac & red ('20)	.25	.40
		Never hinged	.60	
		On cover		24.00
a.		Center inverted	60,000.	40,000.
b.		Perf. 11½	72.50	175.00
		Never hinged	175.00	
		On cover		325.00
		Nos. 219-226 (8)	2.15	3.00
		Set, never hinged	6.75	

Nos. 220-222, 225-226 exist imperforate between. Values, per pair: unused $200-$350; never hinged $400-$725.

See No. 248. For overprints and surcharge see Nos. B23-B29, B43-B49.

1920   **Typo.**   **Imperf.**

Ordinary Paper

227	A44	5h yellow green	.35	.95
		Never hinged	.65	
		On cover		12.00
228	A44	5h gray	.25	.25
		Never hinged	.30	
		On cover		4.25
229	A44	10h deep rose	.25	.25
		Never hinged	.30	
		On cover		1.80
230	A44	10h red	.25	.25
		Never hinged	.30	
		On cover		1.80
231	A43	15h bister	.25	.25
		Never hinged	.30	
		On cover		4.75
232	A43	25h violet	.25	.25
		Never hinged	.30	
		On cover		3.50
233	A45	30h dark brown	.25	.25
		Never hinged	.30	
		On cover		4.25
234	A45	40h violet	.25	.25
		Never hinged	.35	
		On cover		3.50
235	A43	60h olive green	.25	.25
		Never hinged	.35	
		On cover		4.75
		Nos. 227-235 (9)	2.35	2.95

Arms
A47   A48

1920-21   Typo.   Perf. 12½
White Paper

238	A47	80h rose	.25	.25
		Never hinged	.35	
		On cover		.90
a.		Thick grayish paper	.25	.25
		Never hinged	.35	
		On cover		.90
239	A47	1k black brown	.25	.25
		Never hinged	.35	
		On cover		.90
a.		Thick grayish paper	.25	.25
		Never hinged	.35	
		On cover		.90
241	A47	1½k green ('21)	.30	.25
		Never hinged	1.15	
		On cover		2.10
a.		Thick grayish paper	.45	.25
		Never hinged	.90	
		On cover		1.50
242	A47	2k blue	.25	.30
		Never hinged	.35	
		On cover		1.20
a.		Thick grayish paper	.25	.25
		Never hinged	.35	
		On cover		1.50
243	A48	3k yel grn & dk grn ('21)	.25	.30
		Never hinged	.50	
		On cover		1.20
a.		Thick grayish paper	.25	.35
		Never hinged	.35	
		On cover		1.20
b.		3k pale green & blue green, white paper	8.75	35.00
		Never hinged	21.00	
		On cover		70.00
c.		3k pale green & blue green, thick grayish paper	12.00	32.50
		Never hinged	34.00	
		On cover		70.00
d.		3k dark green & blackish green, thick grayish paper	325.00	575.00
		Never hinged	650.00	
		On cover		—
244	A48	4k red & claret ('21)	.25	.25
		Never hinged	.50	
		On cover		2.40
a.		Thick grayish paper	.45	.35
		Never hinged	.65	
		On cover		2.40
245	A48	5k vio & claret ('21)	.25	.25
		Never hinged	.50	
		On cover		2.10
a.		Thick grayish paper	.45	.35
		Never hinged	.85	
		On cover		2.10
246	A48	7½k yellow & brown ('21)	.25	.30
		Never hinged	.50	
		On cover		2.75
247	A48	10k ultra & blue ('21)	.25	.25
		Never hinged	.50	
		On cover		2.75
a.		Thick grayish paper	.45	.40
		Never hinged	.85	
		On cover		3.00
		Nos. 238-247 (9)	2.30	2.40
		Set, never hinged	4.75	

For overprints and surcharges see Nos. B20-B22, B39-B42.

1921   Engr.

248	A46	50k dk violet, *yel*	.95	*1.60*
		Never hinged	1.60	
		On cover		80.00
a.		Perf. 11½	14.50	77.50
		Never hinged	23.00	
		On cover		240.00

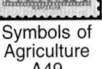

Symbols of   Symbols of
Agriculture   Labor and
A49   Industry
                    A50

1922-24   Typo.   Perf. 12½

250	A49	½k olive bister	.25	*.65*
		Never hinged	.30	
		On cover		24.00
251	A50	1k brown	.25	.25
		Never hinged	.30	
		On cover		8.00
252	A50	2k cobalt blue	.25	.25
		Never hinged	.30	
		On cover		7.25
253	A49	2½k orange brown	.25	.25
		Never hinged	.30	
		On cover		8.00

254	A50	4k dull violet	.25	*1.00*
		Never hinged	.25	
		On cover		40.00
255	A50	5k gray green	.25	.25
		Never hinged	.30	
		On cover		1.20
256	A49	7½k gray violet	.25	.25
		Never hinged	.30	
		On cover		1.40
257	A50	10k claret	.25	.25
		Never hinged	.30	
		On cover		1.20
258	A49	12½k gray green	.25	.25
		Never hinged	.30	
		On cover		1.20
259	A49	15k bluish green	.25	.25
		Never hinged	.30	
		On cover		9.50
260	A49	20k dark blue	.25	.25
		Never hinged	.30	
		On cover		1.20
261	A49	25k claret	.25	.25
		Never hinged	.30	
		On cover		1.20
262	A50	30k pale gray	.25	.25
		Never hinged	.30	
		On cover		8.00
263	A50	45k pale red	.25	.25
		Never hinged	.30	
		On cover		7.25
264	A50	50k orange brown	.25	.25
		Never hinged	.30	
		On cover		1.80
265	A50	60k yellow green	.25	.25
		Never hinged	.30	
		On cover		8.00
266	A50	75k ultramarine	.25	.25
		Never hinged	.30	
		On cover		6.00
267	A50	80k yellow	.25	.25
		Never hinged	.30	
		On cover		1.40
268	A49	100k gray	.25	.25
		Never hinged	.30	
		On cover		1.20
269	A49	120k brown	.25	.25
		Never hinged	.30	
		On cover		9.00
270	A49	150k orange	.25	.25
		Never hinged	.30	
		On cover		4.25
271	A49	160k light green	.25	.25
		Never hinged	.30	
		On cover		3.50
272	A49	180k red	.25	.25
		Never hinged	.30	
		On cover		10.50
273	A49	200k pink	.25	.25
		Never hinged	.30	
		On cover		1.20
274	A49	240k dark violet	.25	.25
		Never hinged	.35	
		On cover		4.25
275	A49	300k light blue	.25	.25
		Never hinged	.30	
		On cover		1.20
276	A49	400k deep green	1.20	.80
		Never hinged	4.00	
		On cover		1.20
a.		400k gray green	.90	.40
		Never hinged	2.40	
		On cover		1.20
277	A49	500k yellow	.25	.25
		Never hinged	.35	
		On cover		1.20
278	A49	600k slate	.25	.25
		Never hinged	.40	
		On cover		2.40
279	A49	700k brown ('24)	2.40	.25
		Never hinged	12.00	
		On cover		2.40
280	A49	800k violet ('24)	1.60	*2.10*
		Never hinged	8.00	
		On cover		29.00
281	A50	1000k violet ('23)	2.40	.25
		Never hinged	10.00	
		On cover		1.20
282	A50	1200k car rose ('23)	.80	.50
		Never hinged	11.00	
		On cover		9.50
283	A50	1500k orange ('24)	2.00	.25
		Never hinged	7.25	
		On cover		1.80
284	A50	1600k slate ('23)	3.25	*3.25*
		Never hinged	18.00	
		On cover		16.00
285	A50	2000k dp bl ('23)	4.75	2.75
		Never hinged	21.00	
		On cover		4.25
286	A50	3000k lt blue ('23)	12.00	2.40
		Never hinged	42.50	
		On cover		8.00
287	A50	4000k dk bl, *bl* ('24)	6.00	2.75
		Never hinged	35.00	
		On cover		16.00
		Nos. 250-287 (38)	43.40	23.45
		Set, never hinged	175.00	

Nos. 250-287 exist imperf. Value set, $600 unused, $1,200 never hinged.

Symbols of Art
and
Science — A51

1922-24   Engr.   Perf. 12½

288	A51	20k dark brn	.25	.25
		Never hinged	.30	
		On cover		8.00
a.		Perf. 11½	1.60	*1.60*
		Never hinged	5.50	
		On cover		24.00

289	A51	25k blue	.25	.25
		Never hinged	.30	
		On cover		3.50
a.		Perf 11½	1.25	*1.25*
		Never hinged	4.00	
		On cover		30.00
b.		25k deep blue	.45	.25
		Never hinged	.95	
		On cover		4.75
c.		As "b," perf 11½	.75	*1.40*
		Never hinged	3.25	
		On cover		32.50
290	A51	50k brown red	.25	.25
		Never hinged	.30	
		On cover		4.25
a.		Perf. 11½	1.60	*1.60*
		Never hinged	6.25	
		On cover		42.50
b.		Vert. pair, imperf. btwn.	250.00	350.00
		Never hinged	475.00	
c.		Perf 12½x11½	—	*1,400.*
d.		50k deep brownish red	4.50	4.50
		Never hinged	9.50	
		On cover		32.50
291	A51	100k deep grn	.25	.25
		Never hinged	.30	
		On cover		8.00
a.		Perf. 11½	4.75	*4.75*
		Never hinged	16.00	
		On cover		54.00
b.		Vert. pair, imperf. btwn.	—	*475.00*
		Never hinged	—	
c.		100k pale olive green	1.20	*2.40*
		Never hinged	2.75	
		On cover		12.00
292	A51	200k dark violet	.25	.25
		Never hinged	.30	
		On cover		12.00
a.		Perf. 11½	5.50	*5.50*
		Never hinged	20.00	
		On cover		80.00
b.		Vert. pair, imperf. btwn.	250.00	
		Never hinged	475.00	
293	A51	500k dp orange	.25	*.25*
		Never hinged	1.20	
		On cover		35.00
294	A51	1000k blk vio, *yel*	.25	.25
		Never hinged	.30	
		On cover		8.00
a.		Perf. 11½	240.00	*240.00*
		Never hinged	475.00	
		On cover		*1,200.*
b.		Vert. pair, imperf. btwn.	360.00	
		Never hinged	500.00	
c.		Horiz. pair, imperf. btwn.	360.00	
		Never hinged	500.00	
295	A51	2000k olive grn, *yel*	.25	.25
		Never hinged	.35	
		On cover		12.00
a.		Vert. pair, imperf. btwn.	360.00	
		Never hinged	475.00	
b.		2000k yellow green, *yel*	8.00	
		Never hinged	16.00	
296	A51	3000k claret brn ('23)	10.00	.40
		Never hinged	40.00	
		On cover		20.00
297	A51	5000k gray black ('23)	1.60	.80
		Never hinged	12.00	
		On cover		65.00

Granite Paper

298	A51	10,000k red brown ('24)	4.50	*4.50*
		Never hinged	14.00	
		On cover		575.00
		Nos. 288-298 (11)	18.10	7.70
		Set, never hinged	72.50	

On Nos. 281-287, 291-298 "kronen" is abbreviated to "k" and transposed with the numerals.

Nos. 288-298 exist imperf. Value set, $410 hinged, $750 never hinged.

Numeral   Fields
A52   Crossed by
                 Telegraph
                 Wires
                 A53

White-Shouldered
Eagle — A54

Church of Minorite
Friars — A55

1925-32   Typo.   Perf. 12

303	A52	1g dark gray	.40	.25
		Never hinged	1.05	
		On cover		2.10

304	A52	2g claret	.40	.25
		Never hinged	1.45	
		On cover		1.80
a.		2g red lilac ('32)	.55	.25
		Never hinged	3.25	
		On cover		1.80
305	A52	3g scarlet	.40	.25
		Never hinged	1.45	
		On cover		1.50
306	A52	4g grnsh blue ('27)	1.20	.25
		Never hinged	4.25	
		On cover		2.40
307	A52	5g brown orange	1.60	.25
		Never hinged	5.00	
		On cover		2.10
308	A52	6g ultramarine	1.60	.25
		Never hinged	5.75	
		On cover		3.25
a.		6g violet blue	1.90	.25
		Never hinged	8.00	
		On cover		4.25
309	A52	7g chocolate	1.60	.25
		Never hinged	6.50	
		On cover		2.10
310	A52	8g yellow green	4.00	.25
		Never hinged	17.00	
		On cover		1.80
311	A53	10g orange	.80	.25
		Never hinged	1.05	
		On cover		1.80
313	A53	15g red lilac	.80	.25
		Never hinged	1.05	
		On cover		1.50
314	A53	16g dark blue	.80	.25
		Never hinged	1.05	
		On cover		1.80
315	A53	18g olive green	1.20	*.80*
		Never hinged	3.75	
		On cover		2.40
316	A54	20g dark violet	1.20	.25
		Never hinged	5.75	
		On cover		1.20
317	A54	24g carmine	1.20	.40
		Never hinged	5.75	
		On cover		2.10
318	A54	30g dark brown	1.20	.25
		Never hinged	5.75	
		On cover		3.00
319	A54	40g ultramarine	1.20	.25
		Never hinged	5.75	
		On cover		3.00
320	A54	45g yellow brown	1.60	.25
		Never hinged	6.50	
		On cover		5.00
321	A54	50g gray	1.60	.30
		Never hinged	6.50	
		On cover		5.40
322	A54	80g turquoise blue	3.50	*4.50*
		Never hinged	27.50	
		On cover		36.00

Perf. 12½
Engr.

323	A55	1s deep green	20.00	1.60
		Never hinged	80.00	
		On cover		15.00
a.		1s light green	375.00	24.00
		Never hinged	1,750.	
		On cover		100.00
b.		As "a," pair, imperf between	925.00	
		Never hinged	675.00	
324	A55	2s brown rose	8.00	*10.50*
		Never hinged	27.00	
		On cover		47.50
		Nos. 303-324 (21)	54.30	*21.85*
		Set, never hinged	225.00	

Nos. 303-324 exist imperf. Value, set unused $475; never hinged $2,000.

For type A52 surcharged see No. B118.

Güssing — A56   National Library,
                       Vienna — A57

15g, Hochosterwitz. 16g, 20g, Durnstein. 18g, Traunsee. 24g, Salzburg. 30g, Seewiesen. 40g, Innsbruck. 50g, Worthersee. 60g, Hohenems. 2s, St. Stephen's Cathedral, Vienna.

1929-30   Typo.   Perf. 12½
Size: 25½x21½mm

326	A56	10g brown orange	.65	.25
		Never hinged	6.50	
		On cover		1.80
327	A56	10g bister ('30)	.65	.25
		Never hinged	9.00	
		On cover		1.80
328	A56	15g violet brown	.65	*1.40*
		Never hinged	4.00	
		On cover		11.00
329	A56	16g dark gray	.25	.25
		Never hinged	1.00	
		On cover		5.00
330	A56	18g blue green	.40	.50
		Never hinged	9.00	
		On cover		11.00
331	A56	20g dark gray ('30)	.80	.25
		Never hinged	22.50	
		On cover		7.25
332	A56	24g maroon	6.50	*8.00*
		Never hinged	35.00	
		On cover		11.50
333	A56	24g lake ('30)	6.50	.50
		Never hinged	45.00	
		On cover		3.00

334 A56 30g dark violet	6.50	.25	
Never hinged	47.50		
On cover			3.25
335 A56 40g dark blue	8.00	.25	
Never hinged	80.00		
On cover			3.00
336 A56 50g gray violet ('30)	27.50	.25	
Never hinged	160.00		
On cover			5.75
337 A56 60g olive green	17.50	.25	
Never hinged	145.00		
On cover			4.75

Engr.
Size: 21x26mm

338 A57 1s black brown	8.00	.25	
Never hinged	45.00		
On cover			15.00
a. Horiz. pair, imperf. btwn.	260.00		
Never hinged	450.00		
b. Vert. pair, imperf. btwn.	260.00		
Never hinged	450.00		
339 A57 2s dark green	16.00	12.00	
Never hinged	65.00		
a. Horiz. pair, imperf. btwn.	325.00		
Never hinged	575.00		
Nos. 326-339 (14)	99.90	24.65	
Set, never hinged	675.00		

Nos. 326, 328-330 and 332-339 exist imperf. Values, set of 12 unused hinged $1,450, never hinged $2,000.

Type of 1929-30 Issue

Designs: 12g, Traunsee. 64g, Hohenems.

1932 **Perf. 12**
Size: 21x16½mm

340 A56 10g olive brown	.80	.25	
Never hinged	3.00		
On cover			2.40
341 A56 12g blue green	1.60	.25	
Never hinged	5.50		
On cover			2.50
342 A56 18g blue green	1.60	3.25	
Never hinged	4.50		
On cover			6.00
343 A56 20g dark gray	.80	.25	
Never hinged	6.50		
On cover			2.40
344 A56 24g carmine rose	8.00	.25	
Never hinged	24.00		
On cover			2.10
345 A56 24g dull violet	4.75	.25	
Never hinged	16.00		
On cover			2.10
346 A56 30g dark violet	20.00	.25	
Never hinged	60.00		
On cover			3.00
347 A56 30g carmine rose	8.00	.25	
Never hinged	24.00		
On cover			3.00
a. Vert. pair, imperf. btwn.	45.00		
Never hinged, #347a	60.00		
348 A56 40g dark blue	24.00	1.60	
Never hinged	95.00		
On cover			4.25
349 A56 40g dark violet	8.00	.40	
Never hinged	35.00		
On cover			4.25
350 A56 50g gray violet	24.00	.40	
Never hinged	95.00		
On cover			15.00
351 A56 50g dull blue	8.00	.40	
Never hinged	32.50		
On cover			4.75
352 A56 60g gray green	65.00	4.00	
Never hinged	250.00		
On cover			8.00
353 A56 64g gray green	24.00	.40	
Never hinged	100.00		
On cover			12.00
Nos. 340-353 (14)	198.55	12.20	
Set, never hinged	750.00		

For overprints and surcharges see Nos. B87-B92, B119-B121.
Nos. 340-353 exist imperf. Values, set unused hinged, $575, never hinged $1,200.

> Used values for Nos. 354-389 are for stamps with philatelic favor cancels. Values for postally used examples are 50%-100% more.

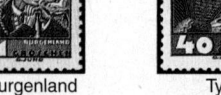

Burgenland A67

Tyrol A68

Costumes of various districts: 3g, Burgenland. 4g, 5g, Carinthia. 6g, 8g, Lower Austria. 12g, 20g, Upper Austria. 24g, 25g, Salzburg. 30g, 35g, Styria. 45g, Tyrol. 60g, Vorarlberg bridal couple. 64g, Vorarlberg. 1s, Viennese family. 2s, Military.

1934-35 **Typo.** **Perf. 12**

354 A67 1g dark violet	.25	.25	
Never hinged	.30		
On cover			—

355 A67 3g scarlet	.25	.25	
Never hinged	.30		
On cover			1.50
356 A67 4g olive green	.25	.25	
Never hinged	.30		
On cover			4.25
357 A67 5g red violet	.25	.25	
Never hinged	.30		
On cover			2.40
358 A67 6g ultramarine	.25	.25	
Never hinged	.75		
On cover			3.00
359 A67 8g green	.25	.25	
Never hinged	.35		
On cover			2.40
360 A67 12g dark brown	.25	.25	
Never hinged	.35		
On cover			1.50
361 A67 20g yellow brown	.25	.25	
Never hinged	.35		
On cover			4.25
362 A67 24g grnsh blue	.25	.25	
Never hinged	.35		
On cover			1.50
363 A67 25g violet	.25	.25	
Never hinged	.80		
On cover			3.25
364 A67 30g maroon	.25	.25	
Never hinged	.75		
On cover			1.80
365 A67 35g rose carmine	.35	.35	
Never hinged	1.75		
On cover			4.25

Perf. 12½

366 A68 40g slate gray	.30	.25	
Never hinged	2.50		
On cover			1.80
367 A68 45g brown red	.30	.25	
Never hinged	2.50		
On cover			4.25
368 A68 60g ultramarine	.55	.40	
Never hinged	4.00		
On cover			3.25
369 A68 64g brown	.80	.25	
Never hinged	4.75		
On cover			6.50
370 A68 1s deep violet	1.20	.65	
Never hinged	10.50		
On cover			9.25
371 A68 2s dull green	45.00	45.00	
Never hinged	160.00		
On cover			150.00

Designs Redrawn
Perf. 12 (6g), 12½ (2s)

372 A67 6g ultra ('35)	.25	.25	
Never hinged	.50		
On cover			2.40
373 A68 2s emerald ('35)	3.50	3.50	
Never hinged	8.50		
On cover			30.00
Nos. 354-373 (20)	55.00	53.65	
Set, never hinged	200.00		

The design of No. 358 looks as though the man's ears were on backwards, while No. 372 appears correctly.
On No. 373 there are seven feathers on each side of the eagle instead of five.
Nos. 354-373 exist imperf. Values, set unused hinged $410, never hinged $700.
For surcharges see Nos. B128-B131.

Dollfuss Mourning Issue

Engelbert Dollfuss — A85

1934-35 **Engr.** **Perf. 12½**

374 A85 24g greenish black	.35	.35	
Never hinged	1.60		
On overfranked cover			4.25
375 A85 24g indigo ('35)	.80	.80	
Never hinged	3.25		
On cover			6.00

Nos. 374-375 exist imperf. Value, each unused hinged $200, never hinged $400.

"Mother and Child," by Joseph Danhauser A86

1935, May 1

376 A86 24g dark blue	.80	.35	
Never hinged	2.00		
On cover			3.25
a. Vert. pair, imperf. btwn.	300.00		
Never hinged	425.00		
b. Horiz. pair, imperf. btwn.	275.00		
Never hinged	400.00		

Mother's Day. No. 376 exists imperf. Value, unused hinged $200, never hinged $475.

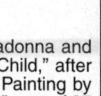

"Madonna and Child," after Painting by Dürer — A87

1936, May 5 **Photo.**

377 A87 24g violet blue	.65	.55	
Never hinged	1.75		
On cover			5.00

Mother's Day. No. 377 exists imperf. Value, unused hinged $250, never hinged $400.

Farm Workers — A88

Design: 5s, Construction workers.

1936, June **Engr.** **Perf. 12½**

378 A88 3s red orange	13.50	13.50	
Never hinged	32.50		
On cover			47.50
379 A88 5s brown black	32.50	32.50	
Never hinged	52.50		
On cover			120.00

Nos. 378-379 exist imperf. Values, set unused hinged $350, never hinged $800.

Engelbert Dollfuss — A90

1936, July 25

380 A90 10s dark blue	725.00	725.00	
Never hinged	1,100.		
On cover			1,750.

Second anniv. of death of Engelbert Dollfuss, chancellor.
Value, used, is for CTO examples.
Exists imperf. Value, $1,900, never hinged $3,250.

Mother and Child — A91

1937, May 5 **Photo.** **Perf. 12**

381 A91 24g henna brown	.65	.80	
Never hinged	1.60		
On cover			5.40

Mother's Day. Exists imperf. Values, unused hinged $200, never hinged $325.

S.S. Maria Anna A92

Steamships: 24g, Uranus, 64g, Oesterreich.

1937, June 9

382 A92 12g red brown	1.10	.55	
Never hinged	5.50		
On cover			5.40
383 A92 24g deep blue	1.10	.55	
Never hinged	5.50		
On cover			4.25

384 A92 64g dark green	1.10	.55	
Never hinged	3.50		
On cover			13.00
Nos. 382-384 (3)	3.30	1.65	
Set, never hinged	14.50		

Centenary of steamship service on Danube River. Exist imperf. Value, set never hinged $3,500.

First Locomotive, "Austria" A95

Designs: 25g, Modern steam locomotive. 35g, Modern electric train.

1937, Nov. 22

385 A95 12g black brown	.25	.25	
Never hinged	3.00		
On cover			3.00
386 A95 25g dark violet	.65	.65	
Never hinged	4.00		
On cover			7.00
387 A95 35g brown red	2.00	2.00	
Never hinged	8.00		
On cover			11.00
Nos. 385-387 (3)	2.90	2.90	
Set, never hinged	15.00		

Centenary of Austrian railways. Exist imperf. Value, set never hinged $325.

Rose and Zodiac Signs — A98

1937 **Engr.** **Perf. 13x12½**

388 A98 12g dark green	.25	.25	
Un cover	.80		
On cover			2.10
389 A98 24g dark carmine	.25	.25	
Never hinged	.80		
On cover			2.10
Set, never hinged	1.60		

Nos. 388-389 exist imperf. Value, set never hinged $275.

> Austria was incorporated into Germany on March 13, 1938, and German stamps were introduced on April 4. Austrian stamps remained valid for use until Sept. 30, 1938, at the rate of 1 mark = 1.50 schilling.
> The listings below are for German stamps used in Austria after annexation, bearing clear Austrian cancellations. The catalogue numbers assigned are those of the basic German stamp, preceded by the letter "A." The numbers of one German set, listed under Danzig, are prefixed "AD."

German and Austrian Carrying Nazi Flag — A95

Wmk. Swastikas (237)
1938, Apr. 8 **Photo.** **Perf. 14x13½**
Size: 23x28mm

A484 A95 6pf dark green	1.20	
On cover		2.50

Unwmk. **Perf. 12½**
Size: 21½x26mm

A485 A95 6pf deep green	.85	
On cover		2.25
On propaganda cover		2.50

Union of Austria and Germany.

Cathedral Island — A96

Hermann Goering Stadium — A97

Town Hall, Breslau — A98

Centennial Hall, Breslau — A99

1938, June 21   Engr.   Perf. 14
A486 A96 3pf dark brown   1.00
  On cover   4.25
A487 A97 6pf deep green   .85
  On cover   2.50
A488 A98 12pf copper red   .85
  On cover   2.50
A489 A99 15pf violet brown   1.40
  On cover   8.25
  Set, on philatelic cover   10.00

16th German Gymnastic and Sports Festival held at Breslau, July 23-31, 1938.

Nazi Emblem — A100

1939, Apr. 4   Photo.   Wmk. 237
A490 A100 6pf dark green   5.00
  On cover   16.50
A491 A100 12pf deep carmine   5.00
  On cover   16.50
  Set, on philatelic cover   16.50

Young Workers' Professional Competitions.

St. Mary's Church — A101

The Krantor, Danzig — A102

1939, Sept. 18
A492 A101 6pf dark green   1.00
  On cover   3.25
A493 A102 12pf orange red   1.00
  On cover   3.25
  Set on philatelic cover   3.25

Unification of Danzig with the Reich.

Stamps of Danzig, 1925-39, Surcharged in Black

a   b

c

1939   Wmk. 109   Perf. 14
AD241 A19(b) 4rpf on 35pf ultra   9.00
  On cover   35.00
AD242 A19(b) 12rpf on 7pf yel
       grn   5.75
  On cover   16.50

AD243 A19(a) 20rpf gray   —
  On cover   —
Wmk. 237
AD244 A19(a) 3rpf brown   8.25
  On cover   50.00
AD245 A19(a) 5rpf orange   9.00
  On cover   22.50
AD246 A19(a) 8pf yellow grn   10.00
  On cover   25.00
AD247 A19(a) 10rpf blue grn   11.00
  On cover   27.50
AD248 A19(a) 15rpf scarlet   —
AD249 A19(a) 25rpf carmine   —
AD250 A19(a) 30rpf dk violet   —
AD251 A19(a) 40rpf dk blue   —
AD252 A19(a) 50rpf brt bl & red   —
  On cover   —
Thick Paper
AD253 A20(c) 1rm on 1g red
       org & blk   —
  On cover   —
Wmk. 125
Thin White Paper
AD254 A20(c) 2rm on 2g rose &
       blk   —
  On cover   —

Johannes Gutenberg and Library at Leipzig — A103

6pf, "High House," Leipzig. 12pf, Old Town Hall, Leipzig. 25pf, View of Leipzig Fair.

Inscribed "Leipziger Messe"
Perf. 10½
1940, Mar. 3   Photo.   Unwmk.
A494 A103 3pf dark brown   .85
  On cover   3.75
A495 A103 6pf dk gray green   .85
  On cover   2.50
A496 A103 12pf henna brown   .85
  On cover   2.50
A497 A103 25pf ultra   2.50
  On cover   8.25
  Set, on philatelic cover   8.25

Leipzig Fair.

SEMI-POSTAL STAMPS

Adolf Hitler — SP101

1938, Apr. 13   Engr.   Unwmk.
AB118 SP101 12 + 38pf copper
       red   3.25
  On cover   8.25
  On commemorative cover,
    from   12.50

Hitler's 49th birthday.

Horsewoman — SP102

1938, July 20
AB119 SP102 42 + 108pf dp
       brn   67.50
  On cover   120.00

5th "Brown Ribbon" at Munich.

Adolf Hitler — SP103

Theater at Saarbrücken — SP104

1938, Sept. 1
AB120 SP103 6 + 19pf deep grn   5.00
  On cover   12.50

1938 Nazi Congress at Nuremberg. The surtax was for Hitler's National Culture Fund.

1938, Oct. 9   Photo.   Wmk. 237
AB121 SP104 6 + 4pf blue grn   3.00
  On cover   10.00
AB122 SP104 12 + 8pf dk car   4.25
  On cover   14.00

Inauguration of the theater of the District of Saarpfalz at Saarbrücken. The surtax was for Hitler's National Culture Fund.

Castle of Forchtenstein — SP105

Designs (scenes in Austria and various flowers): 4pf+3pf, Flexenstrasse in Vorarlberg. 5pf+3pf, Zell am See, Salzburg. 6pf+4pf, Grossglockner. 8pf+4pf, Ruins of Aggstein. 12pf+6pf, Prince Eugene Monument, Vienna. 15pf+10pf, Erzberg. 25pf+15pf, Hall, Tyrol. 40pf+35pf, Braunau.

Unwmk.
1938, Nov. 18   Engr.   Perf. 14
AB123 SP105 3 + 2pf olive brn   .50
  On cover   2.50
AB124 SP105 4 + 3pf indigo   2.50
  On cover   5.75
AB125 SP105 5 + 3pf emerald   .85
  On cover   3.25
AB126 SP105 6 + 4pf dk grn   .40
  On cover   2.10
AB127 SP105 8 + 4pf red org   2.50
  On cover   7.50
AB128 SP105 12 + 6pf dk car   .65
  On cover   2.50
AB129 SP105 15 + 10pf dp cl   7.50
  On cover   21.00
AB130 SP105 25 + 15pf dk blue   7.50
  On cover   16.50
AB131 SP105 40 + 35pf plum   12.50
  On cover   42.50
  Set, on philatelic cover   50.00

The surtax was for "Winter Help."

Sudeten Couple — SP114

1938, Dec. 2   Photo.   Wmk. 237
AB132 SP114 6 + 4pf blue grn   5.00
  On cover   15.00
AB133 SP114 12 + 8pf dk car   4.50
  On cover   16.50
  Set, on philatelic cover   18.50

Annexation of the Sudeten Territory. The surtax was for Hitler's National Culture Fund.

Early Types of Automobiles — SP115

Designs: 12pf+8pf, Racing cars. 25pf+10pf, Modern automobile.

1939
AB134 SP115 6 + 4pf dk grn   12.50
  On cover   25.00
AB135 SP115 12 + 8pf brt car   12.50
  On cover   25.00

AB136 SP115 25 + 10pf dp blue   21.00
  On cover   37.50
  Set, on philatelic cover   57.50

Berlin Automobile and Motorcycle Exhibition. The surtax was for Hitler's National Culture Fund. For overprints see Nos. B141-B143.

Adolf Hitler — SP118

Exhibition Building — SP119

Unwmk.
1939, Apr. 13   Engr.   Perf. 14
AB137 SP118 12 + 38pf carmine   6.75
  On cover   16.50
  On philatelic cover   14.00

Hitler's 50th birthday. The surtax was for Hitler's National Culture Fund.

1939, Apr. 22   Photo.   Perf. 12½
AB138 SP119 6 + 4pf dk green   4.25
  On cover   14.00
AB139 SP119 15 + 5pf dp plum   4.25
  On cover
  Set, on philatelic cover   16.50

Horticultural Exhib. held at Stuttgart. Surtax for Hitler's National Culture Fund.

Adolf Hitler — SP120

Perf. 14x13½
1939, Apr. 28   Wmk. 237
AB140 SP120 6 + 19pf black
       brn   6.75
  On cover   16.50

Day of National Labor. The surtax was for Hitler's National Culture Fund. See No. AB147.

Nos. B134-B136 Overprinted in Black

1939, May 18   Perf. 14
AB141 SP115 6 + 4pf dk green   57.50
  On cover   150.00
AB142 SP115 12 + 8pf brt car   57.50
  On cover   150.00
AB143 SP115 25 + 10pf dp blue   57.50
  On cover   150.00
  Set, on philatelic cover   225.00

Nurburgring Auto Races, 5/21, 7/23/39.

Racehorse "Investment" and Jockey — SP121

1939, June 18   Engr.   Unwmk.
AB144 SP121 25 + 50pf ultra   30.00
  On cover   82.50

70th anniv. of the German Derby. The surtax was divided between Hitler's National Culture Fund and the race promoters.

Man Holding
Rearing Horse
— SP122

"Venetian Woman"
by Albrecht Dürer
— SP123

1939, July 12
AB145 SP122 42 + 108pf dp
brown 35.00
On cover 90.00

6th "Brown Ribbon" at Munich.

1939, July 12   Photo.   Wmk. 237
AB146 SP123 6 + 19pf dk
green 15.00
On cover 35.00

Day of German Art. The surtax was used for
Hitler's National Culture Fund.

Hitler Type of 1939
Inscribed "Reichsparteitag 1939"

1939, Aug. 25   Perf. 14x13½
AB147 SP120 6 + 19pf black brn 13.00
On cover 30.00

1939 Nazi Congress at Nuremberg.

Meeting in
German
Hall, Berlin
— SP124

Designs: 4pf+3pf, Meeting of postal and telegraph employees. 5pf+3pf, Professional competitions. 6pf+4pf, 6pf+9pf, Professional camp.
8pf+4pf, 8pf+12pf, Gold flag competitions.
10pf+5pf, Awarding prizes. 12&f+6pf,
12pf+18pf, Automobile race. 15pf+10pf,
Sports. 16pf+10pf, 16pf+24pf, Postal police.
20pf+10pf, 20pf+30pf, Glider workshops.
24pf+10pf, 24pf+36pf, Mail coach. 25pf+15pf,
Convalescent home, Konigstein.

Perf. 13½x14
1939-41   Unwmk.   Photo.
AB148 SP124 3 + 2pf bister
brn 7.50
On cover 25.00
AB149 SP124 4 + 3pf slate
blue 7.50
On cover 25.00
AB150 SP124 5 + 3pf brt bl
grn 3.00
On cover 9.00
AB151 SP124 6 + 4pf myrtle
grn 1.75
On cover 6.75
AB151A SP124 6 + 9pf dk grn
('41) 2.10
On cover 5.75
AB152 SP124 8 + 4pf dp or-
ange 2.10
On cover 8.25
AB152A SP124 8 + 12pf hn brn
('41) 2.10
On cover 8.25
AB153 SP124 10 + 5pf dk
brown 2.50
On cover 8.25
AB154 SP124 12 + 6pf rose
brown 1.60
On cover 6.75
AB154A SP124 12 + 18pf dk car
rose ('41) 1.60
On cover 5.75
AB155 SP124 15 + 10pf dp red
lilac 4.25
On cover 16.50
AB156 SP124 16 + 10pf slate
grn 5.75
On cover 18.50
AB156A SP124 16 + 24pf black
('41) 5.75
On cover 16.50
AB157 SP124 20 + 10pf ultra 5.75
On cover 19.00
AB157A SP124 20 + 30pf ultra
('41) 5.75
On cover 22.50
AB158 SP124 24 + 10pf ol grn 8.25
On cover 23.00

AB158A SP124 24 + 36pf pur
('41) 13.50
On cover 35.00
AB159 SP124 25 + 15pf dk
blue 8.25
On cover 25.00
Set, '39 issues (12) on phil-
atelic cover(s) 95.00
Set, '41 issues (6) on phila-
telic cover 50.00

The surtax was used for Hitler's National
Culture Fund and the Postal Employees' Fund.

Elbogen Castle
— SP136

Buildings: 4pf+3pf, Drachenfels on the
Rhine. 5pf+3pf, Kaiserpfalz at Goslar. 6pf+4pf,
Clocktower at Graz. 8pf+4pf, Town Hall, Frankfurt. 12pf+6pf, Guild House, Klagenfurt.
15pf+10pf, Ruins of Schreckenstein Castle.
25pf+15pf, Fortress of Salzburg. 40pf+35pf,
Castle of Hohentwiel.

1939   Unwmk.   Engr.   Perf. 14
AB160 SP136 3 + 2pf dk brn .40
On cover 3.00
AB161 SP136 4 + 3pf gray blk 3.25
On cover 8.25
AB162 SP136 5 + 3pf emerald .85
On cover 3.00
AB163 SP136 6 + 4pf slate grn .60
On cover 1.75
AB164 SP136 8 + 4pf red org 2.10
On cover 4.50
AB165 SP136 12 + 6pf dk car .65
On cover 1.75
AB166 SP136 15 + 10pf brn vio 7.50
On cover 16.50
AB167 SP136 25 + 15pf ultra 7.50
On cover 16.50
AB168 SP136 40 + 35pf rose vio 9.00
On cover 25.00
Set, on philatelic cover 42.50

Hall of Honor at
Chancellery,
Berlin — SP145

1940, Mar. 28
AB169 SP145 24 + 76pf dk grn 25.00
On cover 37.50

2nd National Stamp Exposition, Berlin.

Child Greeting
Hitler — SP146

Perf. 14x13½
1940, Apr. 10   Photo.   Wmk. 237
AB170 SP146 12 + 38pf cop red 7.50
On cover 18.50

51st birthday of Adolf Hitler.

Armed Warrior
— SP147   Horseman — SP148

1940, Apr. 30   Unwmk.   Perf. 14
AB171 SP147 6 + 4pf sl grn & lt
grn 1.75
On cover 5.50

Issued to commemorate May Day.

Perf. 14x13½
1940, June 22   Wmk. 237
AB172 SP148 25 + 100pf dp ultra 15.00
On cover 30.00

Blue Ribbon race, Hamburg, June 30, 1940.
Surtax for Hitler's National Culture Fund.

Chariot —
SP149

Unwmk.
1940, July 20   Engr.   Perf. 14
AB173 SP149 42 + 108pf brown 45.00
On cover 82.50

7th "Brown Ribbon" at Munich.
The surtax was for Hitler's National Culture
Fund and the promoters of the race.

View of
Malmedy —
SP150

Design: 12pf+8pf, View of Eupen.

Perf. 14x13½
1940, July 25   Photo.   Wmk. 237
AB174 SP150 6 + 4pf dk green 4.25
On cover 8.25
AB175 SP150 12 + 8pf org red 4.25
On cover 8.25
Set, on philatelic cover 8.50

Issued on the occasion of the reunion of
Eupen-Malmedy with the Reich.

Rocky Cliffs of
Heligoland —
SP152

1940, Aug. 9   Unwmk.
AB176 SP152 6 + 94pf brt bl grn
& red org 15.00
On cover 24.00

Heligoland's 50th year as part of Germany.

Artushof in Danzig
— SP153

Buildings: 4pf+3pf, Town Hall, Thorn.
5pf+3pf, Castle at Kaub. 6pf+4pf, City Theater, Poznan. 8pf+4pf, Castle at Heidelberg.
12pf+6pf, Porta Nigra Trier. 15pf+10pf, New
German Theater, Prague. 25pf+15pf, Town
Hall, Bremen. 40pf+35pf, Town Hall, Munster.

1940, Nov. 5   Engr.   Perf. 14
AB177 SP153 3 + 2pf dk brn .85
On cover 4.25
AB178 SP153 4 + 3pf bluish blk 1.25
On cover 6.75
AB179 SP153 5 + 3pf yel grn .85
On cover 2.50
AB180 SP153 6 + 4pf dk grn .85
On cover 1.75
AB181 SP153 8 + 4pf dp org 2.50
On cover 6.75
AB182 SP153 12 + 6pf carmine .85
On cover 1.75
AB183 SP153 15 + 10pf dk vio
brn 5.00
On cover 11.00
AB184 SP153 25 + 15pf dp ultra 5.00
On cover 11.50
AB185 SP153 40 + 35pf red lil 8.25
On cover 18.50
Set, on philatelic cover 30.00

von Behring — SP162

1940, Nov. 26   Photo.
AB186 SP162 6 + 4pf dp
green 3.00
On cover 7.50
AB187 SP162 25 + 10pf brt ul-
tra 3.75
On cover 10.00
Set, on philatelic cover 10.00

Dr. Emil von Behring (1854-1917),
bacteriologist.

AIR POST STAMPS

Count Zeppelin

Airship Gondola

1938, July 5   Unwmk.   Perf. 13½
AC59 AP11 25pf dull blue 3.00
On cover 10.00
AC60 AP12 50pf green 3.00
On cover 10.00
Set, on philatelic cover 13.50

Count Ferdinand von Zeppelin (1838-1917),
airship inventor and builder.

SEMI-POSTAL STAMPS

Issues of the Monarchy

Emperor Franz
Josef — SP1

Perf. 12½
1914, Oct. 4   Typo.   Unwmk.
B1 SP1 5h green .40 .80
Never hinged 1.00
B2 SP1 10h rose .80 1.60
Never hinged 1.75
Set, never hinged 2.75

Nos. B1-B2 were sold at an advance of 2h
each over face value. Exist imperf.; value, set
$120.

The Firing
Step — SP2

Designs: 5h+2h, Cavalry. 10h+2h, Siege
gun. 20h+3h, Battleship. 35h+3h, Airplane.

1915, May 1
B3 SP2 3h + 1h violet brn 1.20 .40
Never hinged 1.50
B4 SP2 5h + 2h green .25 .25
Never hinged .50
B5 SP2 10h + 2h deep rose .25 .25
Never hinged .50
B6 SP2 20h + 3h Prus blue 4.00 2.40
Never hinged 10.00

B7	SP2 35h + 3h ultra	6.50	5.50	
	Never hinged	22.50		
	Nos. B3-B7 (5)	12.20	8.80	
	Set, never hinged	35.00		

Exist imperf. Value, set $325 hinged and $525 never hinged.

Issues of the Republic

Types of Austria, 1919-20, Overprinted in Black

1920, Sept. 16 Perf. 12½

B11	A44 5h gray, *yellow*	.55	1.60	
	Never hinged	1.20		
B12	A44 10h red, *pink*	.55	1.25	
	Never hinged	1.20		
B13	A43 15h bister, *yel*	.25	.80	
	Never hinged	.95		
B14	A45 20h dark grn, *bl*	.25	.65	
	Never hinged	.80		
B15	A43 25h violet, *pink*	.25	.75	
	Never hinged	.80		
B16	A45 30h brown, *buff*	1.40	2.90	
	Never hinged	3.50		
B17	A45 40h carmine, *yel*	.25	.80	
	Never hinged	.95		
B18	A45 50h dark bl, *blue*	.25	.65	
	Never hinged	.80		
B19	A43 60h ol grn, *azure*	1.40	2.75	
	Never hinged	3.25		
B20	A47 80h red	.35	.75	
	Never hinged	.80		
B21	A47 1k orange brown	.35	.80	
	Never hinged	.80		
B22	A47 2k pale blue	.35	.80	
	Never hinged	.80		

Granite Paper
Imperf

B23	A46 2½k brown red	.40	1.00	
	Never hinged	1.20		
B24	A46 3k dk blue & green	.50	1.25	
	Never hinged	1.20		
B25	A46 4k carmine & violet	.65	1.50	
	Never hinged	1.60		
B26	A46 5k blue	.55	1.25	
	Never hinged	1.20		
B27	A46 7½k yellow green	.55	1.25	
	Never hinged	1.20		
B28	A46 10k gray grn & red	.55	1.40	
	Never hinged	1.60		
B29	A46 20k lilac & orange	.75	1.75	
	Never hinged	1.20		
	Nos. B11-B29 (19)	10.15	23.90	
	Set, never hinged	26.00		

Carinthia Plebiscite. Sold at three times face value for the benefit of the Plebiscite Propaganda Fund.
Nos. B11-B19 exist imperf. Values, set unused hinged $290, never hinged $400.

Types of Regular Issues of 1919-21 Overprinted

1921, Mar. 1 Perf. 12½

B30	A44 5h gray, *yellow*	.25	.80	
	Never hinged	.55		
B31	A44 10h orange brown	.25	.80	
	Never hinged	.55		
B32	A43 15h gray	.25	.80	
	Never hinged	.55		
B33	A45 20h green, *yellow*	.25	.80	
	Never hinged	.55		
B34	A43 25h blue, *yellow*	.25	.80	
	Never hinged	.55		
B35	A45 30h violet, *bl*	.50	1.60	
	Never hinged	1.10		
B36	A45 40h org brn, *pink*	.55	2.00	
	Never hinged	1.40		
B37	A45 50h green, *blue*	1.25	3.25	
	Never hinged	2.25		
B38	A43 60h lilac, *yellow*	.50	1.60	
	Never hinged	1.05		
B39	A47 80h pale blue	.50	1.60	
	Never hinged	1.20		
B40	A47 1k red org, *blue*	.40	1.60	
	Never hinged	.80		
B41	A47 1½k green, *yellow*	.25	.80	
	Never hinged	.50		
B42	A47 2k lilac brown	.25	.80	
	Never hinged	.50		

Overprinted

B43	A46 2½k light blue	.25	.80	
	Never hinged	.55		
B44	A46 3k ol grn & brn red	.25	.80	
	Never hinged	.55		
B45	A46 4k lilac & orange	.80	2.75	
	Never hinged	1.65		
B46	A46 5k olive green	.25	1.60	
	Never hinged	.55		
B47	A46 7½k brown red	.30	1.60	
	Never hinged	.70		
B48	A46 10k blue & olive grn	.30	1.60	
	Never hinged	.65		
B49	A46 20k car rose & vio	.50	2.40	
	Never hinged	1.20		
	Nos. B30-B49 (20)	8.10	28.80	
	Set, never hinged	18.00		

Nos. B30-B49 were sold at three times face value, the excess going to help flood victims. Exists imperf. Values, set unused hinged $300, never hinged $525.

Nos. B50-B76, B93-B98, B112-B117, B122-B127, B132-B137 and B146-B164 exist imperf. on handmade paper, printed in black or in colors other than those of the issued stamps. These are proofs.

Franz Joseph Haydn — SP9

Musicians: 5k, Mozart. 7½k, Beethoven. 10k, Schubert. 25k, Anton Bruckner. 50k, Johann Strauss (son). 100k, Hugo Wolf.

1922, Apr. 24 Engr. Perf. 12½

B50	SP9 2½k brown, perf. 11½	7.25	7.25	
	Never hinged	22.50		
a.	Perf. 12½	11.00	12.00	
	Never hinged	30.00		
B51	SP9 5k dark blue	1.25	1.25	
	Never hinged	2.40		
B52	SP9 7½k black	2.00	2.00	
	Never hinged	4.00		
a.	Perf. 11½	110.00	110.00	
	Never hinged	240.00		
B53	SP9 10k dark violet	2.75	2.40	
	Never hinged	9.50		
a.	Perf. 11½	3.25	3.25	
	Never hinged	18.00		
B54	SP9 25k dark green	4.75	4.75	
	Never hinged	12.50		
a.	Perf. 11½	4.75	4.75	
	Never hinged	16.00		
B55	SP9 50k claret	2.40	2.40	
	Never hinged	5.50		
B56	SP9 100k brown olive	8.00	8.00	
	Never hinged	16.00		
a.	Perf. 11½	10.50	10.50	
	Never hinged	47.50		
	Nos. B50-B56 (7)	28.40	28.05	
	Set, never hinged	72.50		

These stamps were sold at 10 times face value, the excess being given to needy musicians.
Used values are for examples with philatelic favor cancels. Postally used stamps are worth 50%-100% more.
All values exist imperf. Values, set unused hinged $900, never hinged $1,750.
A 1969 souvenir sheet without postal validity contains reprints of the 5k in black, 7½k in claret and 50k in dark blue, each overprinted "NEUDRUCK" in black at top. It was issued for the Vienna State Opera Centenary Exhibition.

View of Bregenz — SP16

Designs: 120k, Mirabelle Gardens, Salzburg. 160k, Church at Eisenstadt. 180k, Assembly House, Klagenfurt. 200k, "Golden Roof," Innsbruck. 240k, Main Square, Linz. 400k, Castle Hill, Graz. 600k, Abbey at Melk. 1000k, Upper Belvedere, Vienna.

Various Frames

1923, May 22 Perf. 12½

B57	SP16 100k dk green	4.00	4.00	
	Never hinged	9.00		
B58	SP16 120k deep blue	4.00	4.00	
	Never hinged	9.00		
B59	SP16 160k dk violet	4.00	4.00	
	Never hinged	9.00		
B60	SP16 180k red violet	4.00	4.00	
	Never hinged	9.00		
B61	SP16 200k lake	4.00	4.00	
	Never hinged	9.00		
B62	SP16 240k red brown	4.00	4.00	
	Never hinged	9.00		
B63	SP16 400k dark brown	4.00	4.00	
	Never hinged	9.00		
B64	SP16 600k olive brn	4.00	4.00	
	Never hinged	14.00		
B65	SP16 1000k black	4.00	4.00	
	Never hinged	24.00		
	Nos. B57-B65 (9)	36.00	36.00	
	Set, never hinged	100.00		

Nos. B57-B65 were sold at five times face value, the excess going to needy artists.
Used values are for examples with philatelic favor cancels. Values for postally used: Nos. B57-B64, each $8; No. B65 $14.
All values exist imperf. on both regular and handmade papers. Values, set hinged $700, never hinged $1,000.

Feebleness — SP25

Designs: 300k+900k, Aid to industry. 500k+1500k, Orphans and widow. 600k+1800k, Indigent old man. 1000k+3000k, Alleviation of hunger.

1924, Sept. 6 Photo.

B66	SP25 100k + 300k yel grn	4.00	4.00	
	Never hinged	9.00		
B67	SP25 300k + 900k red brn	4.00	4.00	
	Never hinged	9.00		
B68	SP25 500k + 1500k brn vio	4.00	4.00	
	Never hinged	9.00		
B69	SP25 600k + 1800k pck bl	8.00	6.50	
	Never hinged	17.50		
B70	SP25 1000k + 3000k brn org	9.50	8.00	
	Never hinged	23.00		
	Nos. B66-B70 (5)	29.50	26.50	
	Set, never hinged	67.50		

The surtax was for child welfare and anti-tuberculosis work.
Used values are for examples with philatelic favor cancels. Values for postally used are 2-2.5 times values shown.
Set exists imperf. Values, set unused hinged $350, never hinged $525.

Siegfried Slays the Dragon — SP30

Designs: 8g+2g, Gunther's voyage to Iceland. 15g+5g, Brunhild accusing Kriemhild. 20g+5g, Nymphs telling Hagen the future. 24g+6g, Rudiger von Bechelaren welcomes the Nibelungen. 40g+10g, Dietrich von Bern vanquishes Hagen.

1926, Mar. 8 Engr.
Design size 27½x28½mm

B71	SP30 3g + 2g olive blk	.95	.80	
	Never hinged	1.75		
	On cover			8.00
B72	SP30 8g + 2g indigo	.40	.40	
	Never hinged	.45		
	On cover			8.00
B73	SP30 15g + 5g dk claret	.35	.35	
	Never hinged	.45		
	On cover			8.00
B74	SP30 20g + 5g olive grn	.50	.50	
	Never hinged	.70		
	On cover			12.00
B75	SP30 24g + 6g dk violet	.50	.50	
	Never hinged	.75		
	On cover			12.00
B76	SP30 40g + 10g red brn	2.40	2.40	
	Never hinged	11.00		
	On cover			16.00
	Nos. B71-B76 (6)	5.10	4.95	

	Set, never hinged	15.00		

Design size 28½x27½mm

B72a	SP30 8g + 2g indigo	2.25	2.00	
	Never hinged	7.00		
	On cover			8.00
B73a	SP30 15g + 5g dk claret	2.00	4.00	
	Never hinged	4.75		
	On cover			12.00
B74a	SP30 20g + 5g olive grn	40.00	40.00	
	Never hinged	95.00		
	On cover			200.00
B75a	SP30 24g + 6g dk violet	2.75	7.25	
	Never hinged	6.50		
	On cover			18.00
B76a	SP30 40g + 10g red brn	7.25	12.00	
	Never hinged			
	On cover			24.00
	Nos. B72a-B76a (5)	54.25	65.25	
	Set, never hinged	130.00		

Nibelungen issue. The surtax was for child welfare.
Used values are for examples with philatelic favor cancels. Values for postally used are 1.5 times values shown.
Nos. B71-B76 exist imperf. Values, set unused hinged $350, never hinged $500.

Pres. Michael Hainisch — SP36

1928, Nov. 5

B77	SP36 10g dark brown	5.50	4.75	
	Never hinged	9.50		
B78	SP36 15g red brown	5.50	4.75	
	Never hinged	9.50		
B79	SP36 30g black	5.50	4.75	
	Never hinged	9.50		
B80	SP36 40g indigo	5.50	4.75	
	Never hinged	9.50		
	Nos. B77-B80 (4)	22.00	19.00	
	Set, never hinged	37.50		

Tenth anniversary of Austrian Republic. Sold at double face value, the premium aiding war orphans and children of war invalids.
Used values are for examples with philatelic favor cancels. Values for postally used are 2.5 times values shown.
Set exists imperf, without gum. Value, set $625.

Pres. Wilhelm Miklas — SP37

1930, Oct. 4

B81	SP37 10g light brown	7.25	7.25	
	Never hinged	21.00		
B82	SP37 20g red	7.25	7.25	
	Never hinged	21.00		
B83	SP37 30g brown violet	7.25	7.25	
	Never hinged	21.00		
B84	SP37 40g indigo	7.25	7.25	
	Never hinged	21.00		
B85	SP37 50g dark green	7.25	7.25	
	Never hinged	21.00		
B86	SP37 1s black brown	7.25	7.25	
	Never hinged	21.00		
	Nos. B81-B86 (6)	43.50	43.50	
	Set, never hinged	125.00		

Nos. B81-B86 were sold at double face value. The excess aided the anti-tuberculosis campaign and the building of sanatoria in Carinthia.
Used values are for examples with philatelic favor cancels. Values for postally used are 3 times values shown.
Set exists imperf, without gum. Value, set $950.

Regular Issue of 1929-30 Overprinted in Various Colors

1931, June 20

B87	A56 10g bister (Bl)	27.50	27.50	
	Never hinged	95.00		
B88	A56 20g dk gray (R)	27.50	27.50	
	Never hinged	95.00		
B89	A56 30g dk violet (Gl)	27.50	27.50	
	Never hinged	95.00		
B90	A56 40g dk blue (Gl)	27.50	27.50	
	Never hinged	95.00		
B91	A56 50g gray vio (O)	27.50	27.50	
	Never hinged	95.00		

B92 A57   1s black brn (Bk)   27.50   27.50
   Never hinged   95.00
   Nos. B87-B92 (6)   165.00   165.00
   Set, never hinged   550.00

Rotary convention, Vienna.
Nos. B87 to B92 were sold at double their
face values. The excess was added to the
beneficent funds of Rotary International.
Used values are for examples with philatelic
favor cancels. Values for postally used are 2
times values shown.
Exists imperf.

Ferdinand
Raimund — SP38

Poets: 20g, Franz Grillparzer. 30g, Johann
Nestroy. 40g, Adalbert Stifter. 50g, Ludwig
Anzengruber. 1s, Peter Rosegger.

1931, Sept. 12
B93 SP38 10g dark violet   13.50   11.00
   Never hinged   27.50
B94 SP38 20g gray black   13.50   11.00
   Never hinged   27.50
B95 SP38 30g orange red   13.50   11.00
   Never hinged   27.50
B96 SP38 40g dull blue   13.50   11.00
   Never hinged   27.50
B97 SP38 50g gray green   13.50   11.00
   Never hinged   27.50
B98 SP38 1s yellow brown   13.50   11.00
   Never hinged   27.50
   Nos. B93-B98 (6)   81.00   66.00
   Set, never hinged   160.00

Nos. B93-B98 were sold at double face
value. The surtax aided unemployed young
people.
Used values are for examples with philatelic
favor cancels. Values for postally used are 3
times values shown.
Set exists imperf, without gum. Value, set
$950.

Chancellor Ignaz
Seipel — SP44

1932, Oct. 12   **Perf. 13**
B99 SP44 50g ultra   12.00   9.50
   Never hinged   27.50

Msgr. Ignaz Seipel, Chancellor of Austria,
1922-29. Sold at double face value, the excess
aiding wounded veterans of World War I.
Used value is for a cancelled-to-order example. Value for postally used $27.50.
Exists imperf, without gum. Value $800.

Ferdinand Georg
Waldmüller
SP45

Artists: 24g, Moritz von Schwind. 30g,
Rudolf von Alt. 40g, Hans Makart. 64g, Gustav
Klimt. 1s, Albin Egger-Lienz.

1932, Nov. 21
B100 SP45 12g slate green   20.00   16.00
   Never hinged   45.00
B101 SP45 24g dp violet   20.00   16.00
   Never hinged   45.00
B102 SP45 30g dark red   20.00   16.00
   Never hinged   45.00
B103 SP45 40g dark gray   20.00   16.00
   Never hinged   45.00
B104 SP45 64g dark brown   20.00   16.00
   Never hinged   45.00
B105 SP45 1s claret   20.00   16.00
   Never hinged   45.00
   Nos. B100-B105 (6)   120.00   96.00
   Set, never hinged   260.00

Nos. B100 to B105 were sold at double their
face values. The surtax was for the assistance
of charitable institutions.

Used values are for examples with philatelic
favor cancels. Values for postally used, each
$60.
Set exists imperf, without gum. Value, set
$1,200.

Mountain
Climbing
SP51

Designs: 24g, Ski gliding. 30g, Walking on
skis. 50g, Ski jumping.

1933, Jan. 9   Photo.   Perf. 12½
B106 SP51 12g dark green   6.50   6.50
   Never hinged   20.00
B107 SP51 24g dark violet   95.00 75.00
   Never hinged   245.00
B108 SP51 30g brown red   12.00 12.00
   Never hinged   32.50
B109 SP51 50g dark blue   95.00 75.00
   Never hinged   230.00
   Nos. B106-B109 (4)   208.50 168.50
   Set, never hinged   525.00

Meeting of the Intl. Ski Federation, Innsbruck, Feb. 8-13.
These stamps were sold at double their face
value. The surtax was for the benefit of "Youth
in Distress."
Used values are for examples with philatelic
favor cancels. Values for postally used, 25%-
80% higher.
Set exists imperf, without gum. Value, set
$4,000.

Stagecoach, after Painting by Moritz
von Schwind — SP55

1933, June 23   Engr.   Perf. 12½
Ordinary Paper
B110 SP55 50g deep ul-
       tra   150.00 150.00
   Never hinged   260.00
   On cover   260.00
a. Granite paper   325.00 325.00
   Never hinged   600.00
   On cover   725.00

Sheets of 25.
Used values are for examples with philatelic
favor cancels. Values for postally used, 50%
higher.
Nos. B110 and B110a exist imperf. Value,
No. B110 unused hinged, $2,400.

Souvenir Sheet
Perf. 12
Granite Paper
B111 Sheet of 4   2,500.   2,400.
   Never hinged   3,050.
a. SP55 50g deep ultra   475.00 475.00
   Never hinged   650.00
   On cover   950.00

Intl. Phil. Exhib., Vienna, 1933. In addition to
the postal value of 50g the stamp was sold at
a premium of 50g for charity and of 1.60s for
the admission fee to the exhibition.
Size of No. B111: 126x103mm.
Used values are for examples with philatelic
favor cancels. Values for postally used, 35%
higher.
A 50g dark red in souvenir sheet, with dark
blue overprint ("NEUDRUCK WIPA 1965"),
had no postal validity.
Even though the margins No. B111 have no
gum, the sheet sells for a premium when defi-
nitely never hinged.
No. B111 exists imperf.

St. Stephen's   Marco d'Aviano,
Cathedral in   Papal
1683 — SP56   Legate — SP57

Designs: 30g, Count Ernst Rudiger von
Starhemberg. 40g, John III Sobieski, King of
Poland. 50g, Karl V, Duke of Lorraine. 64g,
Burgomaster Johann Andreas von
Liebenberg.

1933, Sept. 6   Photo.   Perf. 12½
B112 SP56 12g dark green   24.00 20.00
   Never hinged   55.00
B113 SP57 24g dark violet   20.00 16.00
   Never hinged   52.50
B114 SP57 30g brown red   20.00 16.00
   Never hinged   52.50
B115 SP57 40g blue black   32.50 20.00
   Never hinged   75.00
B116 SP57 50g dark blue   20.00 16.00
   Never hinged   52.50
B117 SP57 64g olive brown   27.50 16.00
   Never hinged   67.50
   Nos. B112-B117 (6)   144.00 104.00
   Set, never hinged   350.00

Deliverance of Vienna from the Turks, 250th
anniv., and Pan-German Catholic Congress,
Sept. 6, 1933.
The stamps were sold at double their face
value, the excess being for the aid of Catholic
works of charity.
Used values are for examples with philatelic
favor cancels. Values for postally used, 2-3
times values shown.

**Types of Regular Issue of 1925-30
Surcharged**

a   b

c

1933, Dec. 15
B118 A52(a) 5g + 2g ol grn   .25   .25
   Never hinged   .80
B119 A56(b) 12g + 3g lt blue .25   .25
   Never hinged   .95
B120 A56(b) 24g + 6g brn org .25   .25
   Never hinged   .80
B121 A57(c) 1s + 50g org
       red   35.00 32.50
   Never hinged   77.50
   Nos. B118-B121 (4)   35.75 33.25
   Set, never hinged   75.00

Winterhelp.
Used values are for examples with philatelic
favor cancels. Values for postally used, 2-3
times values shown.

Anton
Pilgram — SP62

Architects: 24g, J. B. Fischer von Erlach.
30g, Jakob Prandtauer. 40g, A. von Siccard-
sburg & E. van der Null. 60g, Heinrich von
Ferstel. 64g, Otto Wagner.

1934, Dec. 2   Engr.   Perf. 12½
Thick Yellowish Paper
B122 SP62 12g black   9.50   8.00
   Never hinged   20.00
B123 SP62 24g dull violet   9.50   8.00
   Never hinged   20.00
B124 SP62 30g carmine   9.50   8.00
   Never hinged   20.00
B125 SP62 40g brown   9.50   8.00
   Never hinged   20.00
B126 SP62 60g blue   9.50   8.00
   Never hinged   20.00
B127 SP62 64g dull green   9.50   8.00
   Never hinged   20.00
   Nos. B122-B127 (6)   57.00 48.00
   Set, never hinged   120.00

Used values are for examples with philatelic
favor cancels. Values for postally used, each
$20.
Exist imperf. Values, set unused hinged
$650, never hinged $850.
Nos. B124-B127 exist in horiz. pairs imperf.
between. Value, each $250-$325.

These stamps were sold at double their face
value. The surtax on this and the following
issues was devoted to general charity.

**Types of Regular Issue of 1934
Surcharged in Black**

c   d

1935, Nov. 11   Perf. 12, 12½
B128 A67(d) 5g + 2g emerald   .50   .80
   Never hinged   1.60
B129 A67(d) 12g + 3g blue   .95   .95
   Never hinged   2.40
B130 A67(d) 24g + 6g lt brown .50   .80
   Never hinged   1.60
B131 A68(c) 1s + 50g ver   32.50 32.50
   Never hinged   80.00
   Nos. B128-B131 (4)   34.45 35.05
   Set, never hinged   80.00

Winterhelp. Set exists imperf. Values, set
unused hinged $175, never hinged $260.
Set without surcharge unused hinged $250,
never hinged $325.

Prince Eugene of
Savoy — SP68

Military Leaders: 24g, Field Marshal
Laudon. 30g, Archduke Karl. 40g, Field Mar-
shal Josef Radetzky. 60g, Admiral Wilhelm
Tegetthoff. 64g, Field Marshal Franz Conrad
Hotzendorff.

1935, Dec. 1   Perf. 12½
B132 SP68 12g brown   10.50   9.50
   Never hinged   21.00
B133 SP68 24g dark green   10.50   9.50
   Never hinged   21.00
B134 SP68 30g claret   10.50   9.50
   Never hinged   21.00
B135 SP68 40g slate   10.50   9.50
   Never hinged   21.00
B136 SP68 60g deep ultra   10.50   9.50
   Never hinged   21.00
B137 SP68 64g dark violet   10.50   9.50
   Never hinged   21.00
   Nos. B132-B137 (6)   63.00 57.00
   Set, never hinged   125.00

These stamps were sold at double their face
value.
Used values are for examples with philatelic
favor cancels. Values for postally used, each
$20.
Set exists imperf. Values, set unused hinged
$650, never hinged $850.

Slalom
Turn — SP74

Designs: 24g, Jumper taking off. 35g, Slalom turn. 60g, Innsbruck view.

1936, Feb. 20   Photo.
B138 SP74 12g Prus green   1.60   1.60
   Never hinged   4.75
B139 SP74 24g dp violet   2.40   2.40
   Never hinged   6.50
B140 SP74 35g rose car   24.00 24.00
   Never hinged   60.00
B141 SP74 60g sapphire   24.00 24.00
   Never hinged   60.00
   Nos. B138-B141 (4)   52.00 52.00
   Set, never hinged   130.00

Ski concourse issue. These stamps were
sold at twice face value.
Used values are for examples with philatelic
favor cancels. Value for postally used set,
$110.
Set exists imperf. Values, set unused hinged
$600, never hinged $750.

St. Martin of Tours — SP78

Designs: 12g+3g, Medical clinic. 24g+6g, St. Elizabeth of Hungary. 1s+1s, "Flame of Charity."

1936, Nov. 2   **Unwmk.**

B142 SP78 5g + 2g dp green	.25	.25	
Never hinged	.40		
B143 SP78 12g + 3g dp violet	.25	.25	
Never hinged	.40		
B144 SP78 24g + 6g dp blue	.35	.35	
Never hinged	.40		
B145 SP78 1s + 1s dk car	7.50	7.50	
Never hinged	13.00		
Nos. B142-B145 (4)	8.35	8.35	
Set, never hinged	14.00		

Winterhelp.
Used values are for examples with philatelic favor cancels. Values for postally used: Nos. B142-B144, each 80¢; No. B145, $19.
Set exists imperf. Values, set unused hinged $400, never hinged $500.

Josef Ressel — SP82

Inventors: 24g, Karl von Ghega. 30g, Josef Werndl. 40g, Carl Auer von Welsbach. 60g, Robert von Lieben. 64g, Viktor Kaplan.

1936, Dec. 6   **Engr.**

B146 SP82 12g dk brown	2.75	2.75	
Never hinged	8.00		
B147 SP82 24g dk violet	2.75	2.75	
Never hinged	8.00		
B148 SP82 30g dp claret	2.75	2.75	
Never hinged	8.00		
B149 SP82 40g gray violet	2.75	2.75	
Never hinged	8.00		
B150 SP82 60g vio blue	2.75	2.75	
Never hinged	8.00		
B151 SP82 64g dk slate green	2.75	2.75	
Never hinged	8.00		
Nos. B146-B151 (6)	16.50	16.50	
Set, never hinged	47.50		

These stamps were sold at double their face value.
Used values are for examples with philatelic favor cancels. Values for postally used: each $6.75.
Exists imperf, without gum. Value, set unused hinged $800, never hinged $1,000.

Nurse and Infant — SP88

12g+3g, Mother and child. 24g+6g, Nursing the aged. 1s+1s, Sister of Mercy with patient.

1937, Oct. 18   **Photo.**

B152 SP88 5g + 2g dk green	.30	.25	
Never hinged	.80		
B153 SP88 12g + 3g dk brown	.30	.25	
Never hinged	.80		
B154 SP88 24g + 6g dk blue	.30	.25	
Never hinged	.80		
B155 SP88 1s + 1s dk car-			
mine	4.00	3.50	
Never hinged	8.75		
Nos. B152-B155 (4)	4.90	4.25	
Set, never hinged	11.00		

Winterhelp.
Used values are for examples with philatelic favor cancels. Values for postally used: Nos. B152-B154, each 40¢; No. B155, $13.50.
Set exists imperf. Values, set unused hinged $125, never hinged $160.

Gerhard van Swieten — SP92

Physicians: 8g, Leopold Auenbrugger von Auenbrugg. 12g, Karl von Rokitansky. 20g, Joseph Skoda. 24g, Ferdinand von Hebra. 30g, Ferdinand von Arlt. 40g, Joseph Hyrtl. 60g, Theodor Billroth. 64g, Theodor Meynert.

1937, Dec. 5   **Engr.**   **Perf. 12½**

B156 SP92 5g choc	2.40	2.00	
Never hinged	5.50		
B157 SP92 8g dk red	2.40	2.00	
Never hinged	5.50		
B158 SP92 12g brown blk	2.40	2.00	
Never hinged	5.50		
B159 SP92 20g dk green	2.40	2.00	
Never hinged	5.50		
B160 SP92 24g dk violet	2.40	2.00	
Never hinged	5.50		
B161 SP92 30g brown car	2.40	2.00	
Never hinged	5.50		
B162 SP92 40g dp olive grn	2.40	2.00	
Never hinged	5.50		
B163 SP92 60g indigo	2.40	2.00	
Never hinged	5.50		
B164 SP92 64g brown vio	2.40	2.00	
Never hinged	5.50		
Nos. B156-B164 (9)	21.60	18.00	
Set, never hinged	52.50		

These stamps were sold at double their face value.
Used values are for examples with philatelic favor cancels. Values for postally used: each $5.25.
Set exists imperf, without gum. Value, set $2,250.

AIR POST STAMPS

Issues of the Monarchy

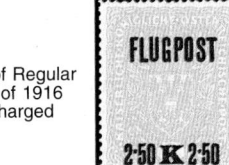

Types of Regular Issue of 1916 Surcharged

1918, Mar. 30   **Unwmk.**   **Perf. 12½**
Grayish paper

C1 A40 1.50k on 2k lilac	1.60	7.50	
Never hinged	4.00		
On cover		95.00	
C2 A40 2.50k on 3k ocher	10.50	32.50	
Never hinged	25.00		
On cover		110.00	
a. Inverted surcharge	1,200.		
Never hinged	2,400.		
b. Perf. 11½	725.00	1,100.	
Never hinged	1,600.		
On cover		1,350.	
c. Perf. 12½x11½	65.00	140.00	
Never hinged	160.00		
On cover		160.00	

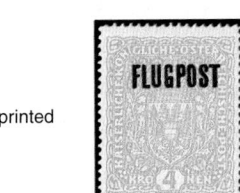

Overprinted

C3 A40 4k gray	4.75	20.00	
Never hinged	8.00		
On cover		—	
Nos. C1-C3 (3)	16.85	60.00	
Set, never hinged	40.00		

Exist imperf, without gum. Value, set $450.

White paper

C1a A40 1.50k on 2k lilac	2.40	8.50	
Never hinged	5.75		
On cover		160.00	
C2d A40 2.50k on 3k ocher	8.00	24.00	
Never hinged	16.00		
On cover		175.00	
C3a A40 4k gray	18.40	24.00	
Never hinged	16.00		
On cover		120.00	
On cover, overfranked		120.00	
Nos. C1a-C3a (3)	18.40	56.50	
Set, never hinged	37.75		

Set exists imperf. Values, set unused hinged $325, never hinged $525.

Nos. C1-C3 also exist without surcharge or overprint. Values, set perf unused hinged $475, never hinged $1,050. Values, set imperf, unused hinged $425, never hinged $850.
A 7k on 10k red brown was prepared but not regularly issued. Values: perf, $550 unused hinged, $1,600 never hinged; imperf, without gum, $1,050.

Issues of the Republic

Hawk — AP1

Wilhelm Kress — AP2

1922-24   **Typo.**   **Perf. 12½**

C4 AP1 300k claret	.35	.35	
Never hinged	.70		
On cover		77.50	
C5 AP1 400k green ('24)	5.00	4.75	
Never hinged	12.00		
On cover		160.00	
C6 AP1 600k bister	.25	.25	
Never hinged	.40		
On cover		77.50	
C7 AP1 900k brn orange	.25	.25	
Never hinged	.40		
On cover		77.50	

Engr.

C8 AP2 1200k brn violet	.25	.25	
Never hinged	.40		
On cover		77.50	
C9 AP2 2400k slate	.25	.25	
Never hinged	.40		
On cover		77.50	
C10 AP2 3000k dp brn ('23)	3.25	2.75	
Never hinged	8.00		
On cover		120.00	
C11 AP2 4800k dark bl ('23)	2.75	2.75	
Never hinged	6.50		
On cover		120.00	
Nos. C4-C11 (8)	12.35	11.60	
Set, never hinged	29.00		

Values for used are for stamps with philatelic favor cancels. Postally used value, set $45.
Set exists imperf. Values, set unused hinged $350, never hinged $500.

Plane and Pilot's Head — AP3

Airplane Passing Crane — AP4

1925-30   **Typo.**   **Perf. 12½**

C12 AP3 2g gray brown	.40	.40	
Never hinged	.80		
On cover		12.00	
C13 AP3 5g red	.40	.40	
Never hinged	.80		
On cover		8.00	
a. Horiz. pair, imperf. btwn.	800.00		
Never hinged	1,250.		
C14 AP3 6g dark blue	.80	.80	
Never hinged	2.75		
On cover		12.00	
C15 AP3 8g yel green	.80	.80	
Never hinged	2.75		
On cover		12.00	
C16 AP3 10g dp org ('26)	.80	.80	
Never hinged	4.00		
On cover		16.00	
a. Horiz. pair, imperf. btwn.	800.00		
Never hinged	1,250.		
C17 AP3 15g red vio ('26)	.40	.40	
Never hinged	.80		
On cover		12.00	
a. Horiz. pair, imperf. btwn.	800.00		
Never hinged	1,250.		
C18 AP3 20g org brn ('30)	11.00	11.00	
Never hinged	32.50		
On cover		16.00	
C19 AP3 25g blk vio ('30)	4.75	4.75	
Never hinged	9.50		
On cover		55.00	
C20 AP3 30g bister ('26)	8.00	8.00	
Never hinged	27.50		
On cover		47.50	
C21 AP3 50g bl gray ('26)	13.50	13.50	
Never hinged	40.00		
On cover		47.50	
C22 AP3 80g dk grn ('30)	2.40	2.40	
Never hinged	8.00		
On cover		32.50	

Photo.

C23 AP4 10g orange red	.80	.80	
Never hinged	2.00		
On cover		12.00	
a. Horiz. pair, imperf. btwn.	800.00		
Never hinged	1,250.		
C24 AP4 15g claret	.80	.80	
Never hinged	1.60		
On cover		9.50	
C25 AP4 30g brn violet	.80	.80	
Never hinged	1.60		
On cover		12.00	
C26 AP4 50g gray black	.80	.80	
Never hinged	1.60		
On cover		12.00	
C27 AP4 1s deep blue	8.00	8.00	
Never hinged	40.00		
On cover		16.00	
C28 AP4 2s dark green	1.60	1.60	
Never hinged	6.50		
On cover		20.00	
a. Vertical pair, imperf.			
btwn.	800.00		
C29 AP4 3s red brn ('26)	52.50	52.50	
Never hinged	105.00		
On cover		90.00	
C30 AP4 5s indigo ('26)	13.50	13.50	
Never hinged	27.50		
On cover		60.00	

Size: 25½x32mm

C31 AP4 10s blk brown,			
gray ('26)	8.00	8.00	
Never hinged	16.00		
On cover		400.00	
Nos. C12-C31 (20)	130.05	130.05	
Set, never hinged	325.00		

Values for used are for stamps with philatelic favor cancels. Postally used value, set $200.
Exists imperf. Values, set unused hinged $850, never hinged $1,100.

Airplane over Güssing Castle — AP5

Airplane over the Danube — AP6

Designs (each includes plane): 10g, Maria-Worth. 15g, Durnstein. 20g, Hallstatt. 25g, Salzburg. 30g, Upper Dachstein and Schladminger Glacier. 40g, Lake Wetter. 50g, Arlberg. 60g, St. Stephen's Cathedral. 80g, Church of the Minorites. 2s, Railroad viaduct, Carinthia. 3s, Gross Glockner mountain. 5s, Aerial railway. 10s, Seaplane and yachts.

1935, Aug. 16   **Engr.**   **Perf. 12½**

C32 AP5 5g rose violet	.25	.25	
Never hinged	.80		
On cover		4.00	
C33 AP5 10g red orange	.25	.25	
Never hinged	.80		
On cover		4.00	
C34 AP5 15g yel green	.80	.80	
Never hinged	1.60		
On cover		8.00	
C35 AP5 20g gray blue	.25	.25	
Never hinged	.80		
On cover		6.50	
C36 AP5 25g violet brn	.25	.25	
Never hinged	.80		
On cover		6.50	
C37 AP5 30g brn orange	.25	.25	
Never hinged	.80		
On cover		6.50	
C38 AP5 40g gray green	.25	.25	
Never hinged	.80		
On cover		8.00	
C39 AP5 50g light sl bl	.25	.25	
Never hinged	.80		
On cover		12.00	
C40 AP5 60g black brn	.35	.35	
Never hinged	.80		
On cover		12.00	
C41 AP5 80g light brown	.40	.40	
Never hinged	.80		
On cover		12.00	
C42 AP6 1s rose red	.35	.35	
Never hinged	.80		
On cover		12.00	
C43 AP6 2s olive green	2.40	2.00	
Never hinged	6.50		
On cover		40.00	
C44 AP6 3s yellow brn	12.00	8.00	
Never hinged	27.50		
On cover		55.00	
C45 AP6 5s dark green	4.00	2.75	
Never hinged	16.00		
On cover		160.00	

C46 AP6 10s slate blue   52.50   52.50
Never hinged   95.00
On cover   325.00
Nos. C32-C46 (15)   74.55   68.90
Set, never hinged   150.00

Values for used are for stamps with philatelic favor cancels. Postally used value, set $175.

Set exists imperf. Values, set unused hinged $375, never hinged $475.

POSTAGE DUE STAMPS

Issues of the Monarchy

D1   D2

Perf. 10 to 13½

1894-95	Typo.	Wmk. 91	
J1 D1 1kr brown		2.00	1.25
Never hinged		8.75	
On cover		20.00	
Single franking on postcard		90.00	
Single franking on printed matter		95.00	
a. Perf. 13½		45.00	62.50
Never hinged		95.00	
On cover		75.00	
b. Half used as ½kr on cover		80.00	
J2 D1 2kr brown ('95)		2.75	2.40
Never hinged		10.50	
On cover		24.00	
a. Pair, imperf. btwn.		200.00	300.00
Never hinged		350.00	
b. Half used as 1kr on cover		200.00	
J3 D1 3kr brown		3.25	1.25
Never hinged		11.00	
On cover		11.00	
On cover, single franking		13.00	
a. Half used as 1½kr on cover		160.00	
J4 D1 5kr brown		3.25	.80
Never hinged		12.00	
On cover		8.00	
On cover, single franking		9.50	
a. Perf. 13½		25.00	25.00
Never hinged		60.00	
On cover		65.00	
b. Pair, imperf. btwn.		160.00	250.00
Never hinged		275.00	
J5 D1 6kr brown ('95)		2.75	6.50
Never hinged		8.75	
On cover		72.50	
a. Half used as 3kr on cover		200.00	
J6 D1 7kr brown ('95)		.80	6.00
Never hinged		4.75	
On cover		110.00	
a. Vert. pair, imperf. btwn.		275.00	550.00
Never hinged		475.00	
b. Horiz. pair, imperf. btwn.		275.00	550.00
Never hinged		475.00	
J7 D1 10kr brown		4.75	.95
Never hinged		20.00	
On cover		16.00	
a. Half used as 5kr on cover		140.00	
J8 D1 20kr brown		.80	6.00
Never hinged		4.75	
On cover		240.00	
J9 D1 50kr brown		35.00	72.50
Never hinged		80.00	
On cover			2,400.
Nos. J1-J9 (9)		55.35	97.65

Values for Nos. J1-J9 are for stamps that do not show the watermark. Stamps showing the watermark often sell for more.
See Nos. J204-J231 in *Scott Standard Postage Stamp Catalogue,* Vol. 1.

1899-1900			*Imperf.*
J10 D2 1h brown		.25	*.40*
Never hinged		2.40	
On cover		11.00	
J11 D2 2h brown		.25	*.55*
Never hinged		2.40	
On cover		12.00	
J12 D2 3h brown ('00)		.25	*.40*
Never hinged		2.40	
On cover		11.00	
J13 D2 4h brown		2.00	2.00
Never hinged		9.00	
On cover		14.50	
J14 D2 5h brown ('00)		1.60	*1.25*
Never hinged		12.00	
On cover		9.50	
J15 D2 6h brown		.25	*.50*
Never hinged		3.25	
On cover		35.00	
J16 D2 10h brown		.25	*.50*
Never hinged		3.25	
On cover		6.50	
J17 D2 12h brown		.35	*2.40*
Never hinged		4.00	
On cover		65.00	
J18 D2 15h brown		.35	*1.60*
Never hinged		3.25	
On cover		40.00	
J19 D2 20h brown		24.00	4.75
Never hinged		77.50	
On cover		16.00	
J20 D2 40h brown		2.40	*2.60*
Never hinged		16.00	
On cover			275.00
J21 D2 100h brown		4.75	3.25
Never hinged		24.00	
On cover			1,300.
Nos. J10-J21 (12)		36.70	20.20

Perf. 10½, 12½, 13½ and Compound			
J22 D2 1h brown		.55	.25
Never hinged		2.40	
On cover		5.50	
J23 D2 2h brown		.40	.25
Never hinged		2.40	
On cover		4.75	
J24 D2 3h brown ('00)		.40	.25
Never hinged		2.40	
On cover		12.00	
J25 D2 4h brown		.65	.25
Never hinged		2.40	
On cover		13.00	
J26 D2 5h brown ('00)		.55	.25
Never hinged		3.25	
On cover		4.75	
J27 D2 6h brown		.40	.25
Never hinged		3.25	
On cover		6.50	
J28 D2 10h brown		.55	.25
Never hinged		4.00	
On cover		4.00	
J29 D2 12h brown		.55	.75
Never hinged		5.50	
On cover		47.50	
J30 D2 15h brown		.80	.80
Never hinged		5.50	
On cover		24.00	
J31 D2 20h brown		.95	.25
Never hinged		8.00	
On cover		12.00	
J32 D2 40h brown		1.25	.75
Never hinged		12.00	
On cover		240.00	
J33 D2 100h brown		24.00	2.00
Never hinged		87.50	
On cover			1,050.
Nos. J22-J33 (12)		31.05	6.30

Nos. J10-J33 exist on unwmkd. paper.
For surcharges see Offices in the Turkish Empire Nos. J1-J5.

D3

Ordinary Thin Paper

1910-13	Unwmk.		*Perf. 12½*
J34b D3 1h carmine		3.25	2.00
Never hinged		12.00	
On cover		55.00	
J35 D3 2h carmine		.50	.35
Never hinged		1.60	
On cover		8.00	
d. Half used as 1h on cover		95.00	
J36 D3 4h carmine		.50	.25
Never hinged		1.60	
On cover		8.00	
c. Half used as 2h on cover		95.00	
d. Used as 5h with manuscript "5" on cover		175.00	
J37 D3 6h carmine		.50	.25
Never hinged		1.60	
On cover		8.00	
c. Used as 5h with manuscript "5" on cover		175.00	
J38 D3 10h carmine		.50	.25
Never hinged		1.60	
On cover		1.60	
c. Half used as 5h on cover		47.50	
J39 D3 14h carmine ('13)		4.00	2.75
Never hinged		16.00	
On cover		325.00	
J40b D3 20h carmine		5.50	2.00
Never hinged		32.50	
On cover		8.00	
c. Half used as 10h on cover		95.00	
J41 D3 25h carmine ('10)		8.00	6.50
Never hinged		40.00	
On cover			1,100.
J42 D3 30h carmine		8.00	.35
Never hinged		24.00	
On cover		55.00	
J43 D3 50h carmine		12.00	.40
Never hinged		87.50	
On cover		80.00	
J44 D3 100h carmine		16.00	.80
Never hinged		65.00	
On cover			1,100.
Nos. J34-J44 (9)		53.25	11.55
Nos. J34b-J44 (11)		58.75	14.15

All values exist on ordinary paper, Nos. J34-J38, J40, J42-J44 on chalky paper and Nos. J34-J38, J40, J44 on thin ordinary paper. In most cases, values are for the least expensive stamp of the types. Some of the expensive types sell for considerably more.
All values exist imperf.
See Offices in the Turkish Empire type D3.

1908-13			**Chalky Paper**
J34a D3 1h carmine		1.60	*4.75*
Never hinged		4.00	
On cover		24.00	
J35a D3 2h carmine		4.00	*9.50*
Never hinged		12.00	
On cover		35.00	
J36a D3 4h carmine		2.40	*2.40*
Never hinged		8.00	
On cover		8.00	
J37a D3 6h carmine		1.20	*2.75*
Never hinged		8.00	
On cover		12.00	
J38a D3 10h carmine		8.00	.55
Never hinged		24.00	
On cover		4.00	
J40 D3 20h carmine		8.00	.25
Never hinged		35.00	
On cover		35.00	

J42a D3 30h carmine		8.00	3.25
Never hinged		40.00	
On cover		72.50	
J43a D3 50h carmine		12.00	9.50
Never hinged		52.50	
On cover		120.00	
J44a D3 100h carmine		16.00	16.00
Never hinged		65.00	
On cover			1,100.

1909		**Thin Translucent Paper**	
J34 D3 1h carmine		.80	*1.60*
Never hinged		2.40	
On cover		24.00	
J35b D3 2h carmine		2.00	1.20
Never hinged		8.00	
On cover		9.50	
J36b D3 4h carmine		9.50	1.20
Never hinged		20.00	
On cover		12.00	
J37b D3 6h carmine		.50	*.80*
Never hinged		1.60	
On cover		12.00	
J38b D3 10h carmine		.50	.55
Never hinged		3.25	
On cover		4.00	
J40a D3 20h carmine		42.50	7.50
Never hinged		1.20	
On cover		95.00	
J44b D3 100h carmine		85.00	50.00
Never hinged		220.00	
On cover			—

See Offices in the Turkish Empire type D3.

1911, July 16			
J45 D3 5k violet		80.00	12.50
Never hinged		250.00	
On cover			—
J46 D3 10k violet		240.00	4.00
Never hinged		750.00	
On cover			—

Nos. J45-J46 exist imperf. Value set: unused hinged $900; never hinged $1,200.

Regular Issue of 1908 Overprinted or Surcharged in Carmine or Black

a   b

1916, Oct. 21			
J47 A22 1h gray (C)		.25	.25
Never hinged		.40	
On cover		14.50	
a. Pair, one without overprint		210.00	
Never hinged		300.00	
J48 A22 15h on 2h vio (Bk)		.25	*.55*
Never hinged		1.20	
On cover		25.00	
a. Inverted surcharge		400.00	
Never hinged		750.00	
Set, never hinged		1.60	

D4   D5

Perf. 12½, 12½x13 (#J57-J59)			
1916, Oct. 1			
J49 D4 5h rose red		.25	.25
Never hinged		.40	
On cover		8.00	
J50 D4 10h rose red		.25	.25
Never hinged		.40	
On cover		5.50	
a. Half used as 5h on cover		65.00	
J51 D4 15h rose red		.25	.25
Never hinged		.40	
On cover		16.00	
J52 D4 20h rose red		.25	.25
Never hinged		.40	
On cover		6.50	
J53 D4 25h rose red		.25	*.95*
Never hinged		.80	
On cover		325.00	
J54 D4 30h rose red		.25	*.40*
Never hinged		.40	
On cover		22.50	
a. Half used as 15h on cover		160.00	
J55 D4 40h rose red		.25	*.40*
Never hinged		.40	
On cover		16.00	
a. Half used as 20h on cover		140.00	
J56 D4 50h rose red		.95	*3.25*
Never hinged		2.40	
On cover		160.00	
J57 D5 1k ultramarine		.25	*.40*
Never hinged		4.00	
On cover			550.00
a. Horiz. pair, imperf. btwn.		250.00	550.00
Never hinged		550.00	
b. Perf 12½		30.00	7.50
Never hinged		80.00	
On cover			850.00

J58 D5 5k ultramarine		2.75	*3.25*
Never hinged		8.00	
a. Perf 12½		75.00	57.50
Never hinged		200.00	
J59 D5 10k ultramarine		3.50	1.60
Never hinged		14.50	
a. Perf 12½		150.00	80.00
Never hinged		375.00	
Nos. J49-J59 (11)		9.20	11.25
Set, never hinged		32.50	

Exists imperf. Value set: unused hinged $150, never hinged $400.
For overprints see J64-J74, Western Ukraine Nos. 54-55, NJ1-NJ6, Poland Nos. J1-J10.

Type of Regular Issue of 1916 Surcharged

1917			
J60 A38 10h on 24h blue		1.60	.55
Never hinged		8.00	
J61 A38 15h on 36h violet		.50	.25
Never hinged		2.00	
J62 A38 20h on 54h orange		.25	*.40*
Never hinged		2.00	
J63 A38 50h on 42h chocolate		.35	.35
Never hinged		2.00	
Nos. J60-J63 (4)		2.70	1.55
Set, never hinged		14.00	

All values of this issue are known imperforate, also without surcharge, perforated and imperforate. Values, set imperf unused hinged $160, never hinged $250. Value of set without surcharge imperf unused hinged $200, never hinged $350. Same values for set without surcharge, perf 12½.
For surcharges see Poland Nos. J11-J12

Issues of the Republic

Postage Due Stamps of 1916 Overprinted

1919			
J64 D4 5h rose red		.25	.25
Never hinged		.40	
a. Inverted overprint		250.00	325.00
Never hinged		325.00	
J65 D4 10h rose red		.25	.25
Never hinged		.40	
J66 D4 15h rose red		.25	*.40*
Never hinged		.80	
J67 D4 20h rose red		.25	*.40*
Never hinged		8.00	
J68 D4 25h rose red		8.00	*27.50*
Never hinged		21.00	
J69 D4 30h rose red		.25	*.40*
Never hinged		.40	
J70 D4 40h rose red		.25	*.80*
Never hinged		.80	
J71 D4 50h rose red		.30	*1.25*
Never hinged		1.20	
J72 D5 1k ultramarine		4.50	*16.00*
Never hinged		14.50	
J73 D5 5k ultramarine		8.75	*16.00*
Never hinged		24.00	
J74 D5 10k ultramarine		10.50	4.00
Never hinged		32.50	
Nos. J64-J74 (11)		33.55	67.25
Set, never hinged		100.00	

Nos. J64, J65, J67, J70 exist imperf. Value, 4 values hinged $325.

D6   D7

1920-21			*Perf. 12½*
J75 D6 5h bright red		.25	*.35*
J76 D6 10h bright red		.25	.25
J77 D6 15h bright red		.25	*1.60*
J78 D6 20h bright red		.25	.25
J79 D6 25h bright red		.25	*1.60*
J80 D6 30h bright red		.25	*.35*
J81 D6 40h bright red		.25	*.35*
J82 D6 50h bright red		.25	*.35*
J83 D6 1k bright red		.25	*.45*
J84 D7 1k ultramarine		.25	*.35*
a. Thick grayish paper		.25	*.40*

J85	D7	1½k ultra ('21)	.25	.35
a.		Thick grayish paper	.25	.40
J86	D7	2k ultra ('21)	.25	.35
a.		Thick grayish paper	.25	.40
J87	D7	3k ultra ('21)	.25	.95
a.		Thick grayish paper	.25	.40
J88	D7	4k ultra ('21)	.25	.95
a.		Thick grayish paper	.25	.65
J89	D7	5k ultramarine	.25	.35
			.80	4.00
J90	D7	8k ultra ('21)	.25	.95
			.25	1.20
J91	D7	10k ultramarine	.25	.45
			.30	2.00
J92	D7	20k ultra ('21)	.30	2.00
a.		Thick grayish paper	.40	2.40
		Nos. J75-J92 (18)		12.25
		Set, never hinged	4.75	

Nos. J84 to J92 exist imperf. Values, set unused hinged $150, never hinged $250.

Imperf

J93	D6	5h bright red	.25	.65
J94	D6	10h bright red	.25	.40
J95	D6	15h bright red	.25	1.60
J96	D6	20h bright red	.25	.40
J97	D6	25h bright red	.25	1.60
J98	D6	30h bright red	.25	1.25
J99	D6	40h bright red	.25	.65
J100	D6	50h bright red	.25	1.10
J101	D6	80h bright red	.25	.85
		Nos. J93-J101 (9)		8.50
		Set, never hinged	3.25	

No. 207a Surcharged in Dark Blue

1921, Dec. — Perf. 12½

J102	A43	7½k on 15h bister	.25	.25
		Never hinged	.25	
		On cover		8.00
a.		Inverted surcharge	450.00	500.00
		Never hinged	575.00	

D8

1922

J103	D8	1k reddish buff	.25	.35
J104	D8	2k reddish buff	.25	.40
J105	D8	4k reddish buff	.25	.65
J106	D8	5k reddish buff	.25	.35
J107	D8	7½k reddish buff	.25	1.20
J108	D8	10k blue green	.25	.50
J109	D8	15k blue green	.25	.75
J110	D8	20k blue green	.25	.55
J111	D8	25k blue green	.25	1.25
J112	D8	40k blue green	.25	.40
J113	D8	50k blue green	.25	1.25
		Nos. J103-J113 (11)		7.65
		Set, never hinged	5.25	

Issue date: Nos. J108-J113, June 2.

D9

D10

1922-24

J114	D9	10k cobalt blue	.25	.40
		Never hinged	.25	
J115	D9	15k cobalt blue	.25	.55
		Never hinged	.25	
J116	D9	20k cobalt blue	.25	.55
		Never hinged	.25	
J117	D9	50k cobalt blue	.25	.55
		Never hinged	.25	
J118	D10	100k plum	.25	.25
		Never hinged	.50	
J119	D10	150k plum	.25	.25
		Never hinged	.50	
J120	D10	200k plum	.25	.25
		Never hinged	.50	

J121	D10	400k plum	.25	.25
		Never hinged	.50	
J122	D10	600k plum ('23)	.25	.40
		Never hinged	1.60	
J123	D10	800k plum	.25	.25
		Never hinged	.50	
J124	D10	1,000k plum ('23)	.25	.25
		Never hinged	1.60	
J125	D10	1,200k plum ('23)	1.00	4.75
		Never hinged	3.25	
J126	D10	1,500k plum ('24)	.25	.80
		Never hinged	1.60	
J127	D10	1,800k plum ('24)	3.25	12.00
		Never hinged	9.50	
J128	D10	2,000k plum ('23)	.40	1.60
		Never hinged	3.25	
J129	D10	3,000k plum ('24)	5.50	24.00
		Never hinged	16.00	
J130	D10	4,000k plum ('24)	3.25	20.00
		Never hinged	9.50	
J131	D10	6,000k plum ('24)	3.25	27.50
		Never hinged	22.50	
		Nos. J114-J131 (18)	19.65	94.60
		Set, never hinged	70.00	

J103-J131 sets exist imperf. Values, both sets unused hinged $450, never hinged $650.

D11 D12

1925-34 — Perf. 12½

J132	D11	1g red	.25	.25
		Never hinged	.25	
J133	D11	2g red	.25	.25
		Never hinged	.25	
J134	D11	3g red	.25	.25
		Never hinged	.30	
J135	D11	4g red	.25	.25
		Never hinged	.30	
J136	D11	5g red ('27)	.25	.25
		Never hinged	.30	
J137	D11	6g red	.25	.25
		Never hinged	.55	
J138	D11	8g red	.25	.25
		Never hinged	.55	
J139	D11	10g dark blue	.25	.25
		Never hinged	3.25	
J140	D11	12g dark blue	.25	.25
		Never hinged	.40	
J141	D11	14g dark blue ('27)	.25	.25
		Never hinged	.55	
J142	D11	15g dark blue	.25	.25
		Never hinged	.40	
J143	D11	16g dark blue ('29)	.25	.25
		Never hinged	1.20	
J144	D11	18g dark blue ('34)	1.25	2.75
		Never hinged	2.00	
J145	D11	20g dark blue	.25	.25
		Never hinged	1.20	
J146	D11	23g dark blue	.40	.25
		Never hinged	2.00	
J147	D11	24g dark blue ('32)	1.60	.25
		Never hinged	9.50	
J148	D11	28g dark blue ('27)	1.60	.25
		Never hinged	9.50	
J149	D11	30g dark blue	.25	.25
		Never hinged	3.25	
J150	D11	31g dark blue ('29)	1.25	.25
		Never hinged	9.50	
J151	D11	35g dark blue ('30)	1.25	.25
		Never hinged	9.50	
J152	D11	39g dark blue ('32)	1.60	.25
		Never hinged	12.00	
J153	D11	40g dark blue	2.00	2.50
		Never hinged	5.50	
J154	D11	60g dark blue	2.00	2.00
		Never hinged	5.50	
J155	D12	1s dark green	2.75	1.25
		Never hinged	24.00	
J156	D12	2s dark green	25.00	4.00
		Never hinged	105.00	
J157	D12	5s dark green	87.50	45.00
		Never hinged	240.00	
J158	D12	10s dark green	35.00	8.00
		Never hinged	120.00	
		Nos. J132-J158 (27)	166.70	70.50
		Set, never hinged	575.00	

Issues of 1925-27 exist imperf. Values, set of 18 unused hinged $600, never hinged $800.

Issued: 3g, 2s-10s, Dec; 5g, 28g, 1/1; 14g, June; 31g, 2/1; 35g, Jan; 24g, 39g, Sept; 16g, May; 18g, 6/25; others, 6/1.

Coat of Arms

D13 D14

1935, June 1

J159	D13	1g red	.25	.25
		Never hinged	.30	
J160	D13	2g red	.25	.25
		Never hinged	.30	
J161	D13	3g red	.25	.25
		Never hinged	.30	
J162	D13	5g red	.25	.25
		Never hinged	.30	
J163	D13	10g blue	.25	.25
		Never hinged	.30	

J164	D13	12g blue	.25	.25
		Never hinged	.30	
J165	D13	15g blue	.25	.50
		Never hinged	.55	
J166	D13	20g blue	.25	.25
		Never hinged	.55	
J167	D13	24g blue	.25	.25
		Never hinged	1.20	
J168	D13	30g blue	.25	.25
		Never hinged	1.20	
J169	D13	39g blue	.35	.25
		Never hinged	1.60	
J170	D13	60g blue	.50	1.25
		Never hinged	1.60	
J171	D14	1s green	.80	.35
		Never hinged	3.50	
J172	D14	2s green	1.50	1.00
		Never hinged	8.00	
J173	D14	5s green	3.00	4.00
		Never hinged	16.00	
J174	D14	10s green	4.75	.65
		Never hinged	20.00	
		Nos. J159-J174 (16)	13.40	10.25
		Set, never hinged	55.00	

On Nos. J163-J170, background lines are horiz.

Nos. J159-J174 exist imperf. Values, set unused hinged $160, never hinged $350.

MILITARY STAMPS

Issues of the Austro-Hungarian Military Authorities for the Occupied Territories in World War I

See Bosnia and Herzegovina for similar designs inscribed "MILITARPOST" instead of "FELDPOST."

Stamps of Bosnia of 1912-14 Overprinted

1915 — Unwmk. — Perf. 12½

M1	A23	1h olive green	.25	.40
		Never hinged	.40	
		On cover		35.00
M2	A23	2h bright blue	.25	.40
		Never hinged	.40	
		On cover		32.50
M3	A23	3h claret	.25	.40
		Never hinged	.40	
		On cover		35.00
M4	A23	5h green	.25	.25
		Never hinged	.25	
		On cover		20.00
M5	A23	6h dark gray	.25	.40
		Never hinged	.45	
		On cover		47.50
M6	A23	10h rose carmine	.25	.25
		Never hinged	.25	
		On cover		20.00
M7	A23	12h deep ol grn	.25	.80
		Never hinged	.80	
		On cover		35.00
M8	A23	20h orange brn	.35	.80
		Never hinged	.80	
		On cover		55.00
M9	A23	25h ultramarine	.35	.80
		Never hinged	.80	
		On cover		55.00
M10	A23	30h orange red	3.25	6.50
		Never hinged	6.50	
		On cover		65.00
M11	A24	35h myrtle grn	2.50	4.75
		Never hinged	5.00	
		On cover		150.00
M12	A24	40h dark violet	2.50	4.75
		Never hinged	5.00	
		On cover		175.00
M13	A24	45h olive brown	2.50	4.75
		Never hinged	5.00	
		On cover		200.00
M14	A24	50h slate blue	2.50	4.75
		Never hinged	5.00	
		On cover		225.00
M15	A24	60h brn violet	.40	.80
		Never hinged	.80	
		On cover		160.00
M16	A24	72h dark blue	2.50	4.75
		Never hinged	5.00	
		On cover		—
M17	A25	1k brn vio, *straw*	2.50	4.75
		Never hinged	5.00	
		On cover		—
M18	A25	2k dk gray, *blue*	2.50	4.75
		Never hinged	5.00	
		On postal money order or receipt		100.00
M19	A26	3k car, *green*	20.00	47.50
		Never hinged	50.00	
		On cover		—
		On postal money order or receipt		—
M20	A26	5k dk vio, *gray*	20.00	40.00
		Never hinged	40.00	
		On cover		—
		On postal money order or receipt		—
		On overfranked philatelic cover		—

M21	A25	10k dk ultra, *gray*	150.00	300.00
		Never hinged	310.00	
		On cover		—
		On postal money order or receipt		—
		On overfranked philatelic cover		—
		Nos. M1-M21 (21)	213.50	432.55
		Set, never hinged	420.00	

Exists imperf. Values, set unused hinged $450, never hinged $875.

Nos. M1-M21 also exist with overprint double, inverted and in red. These varieties were made by order of an official but were not regularly issued. Values, each set: unused $325; never hinged $650.

Covers: On cover values are for stamps on postal money order receipts.

M1 M2

Emperor Franz Josef

Perf. 11½, 12½ and Compound

1915-17 — Engr.

M22	M1	1h olive green	.25	.25
		Never hinged	.30	
		On cover		9.50
M23	M1	2h dull blue	.25	.35
		Never hinged	.40	
		On cover		9.50
		Single franking on printed matter		25.00
M24	M1	3h claret	.25	.25
		Never hinged	.25	
		On cover		9.50
M25	M1	5h green	.25	.25
		Never hinged	.25	
		On cover		4.00
a.		Perf. 11½	100.00	150.00
		Never hinged	200.00	
b.		Perf. 11½x12½	150.00	240.00
		Never hinged	325.00	
c.		Perf. 12½x11½	200.00	325.00
		Never hinged	400.00	
M26	M1	6h dark gray	.25	.35
		Never hinged	.25	
		On cover		14.50
M27	M1	10h rose carmine	.25	.25
		Never hinged	.80	
		On cover		4.00
M28	M1	10h gray bl ('17)	.25	.35
		Never hinged	1.20	
		On cover		12.00
M29	M1	12h deep olive grn	.25	.40
		Never hinged	.65	
		On cover		20.00
M30	M1	15h car rose ('17)	.25	.40
		Never hinged	.25	
		On cover		8.00
a.		Perf. 11½	8.00	27.50
		Never hinged	27.50	
M31	M1	20h orange brn	.35	.40
		Never hinged	3.00	
		On cover		10.00
M32	M1	20h ol green ('17)	.25	.50
		Never hinged	2.00	
		On cover		15.00
M33	M1	25h ultramarine	.25	.35
		Never hinged	1.60	
		On cover		12.50
M34	M1	30h vermilion	.35	.50
		Never hinged	1.60	
		On cover		21.00
M35	M1	35h dark green	.35	.65
		Never hinged	3.00	
		On cover		35.00
M36	M1	40h dark violet	.35	.65
		Never hinged	3.00	
		On cover		35.00
M37	M1	45h olive brown	.35	.65
		Never hinged	3.00	
		On cover		50.00
M38	M1	50h myrtle green	.35	.65
		Never hinged	3.00	
		On cover		32.50
M39	M1	60h brown violet	.35	.65
		Never hinged	3.00	
		On cover		85.00
M40	M1	72h dark blue	.35	.65
		Never hinged	3.00	
		On cover		100.00
M41	M1	80h org brn ('17)	.35	.35
		Never hinged	3.00	
		On cover		67.50
M42	M1	90h magenta ('17)	.80	1.25
		Never hinged	5.00	
		On cover		125.00
M43	M2	1k brn vio, *straw*	1.60	2.50
		Never hinged	10.00	
		On cover		85.00
M44	M2	2k dk gray, *blue*	.80	1.60
		Never hinged	8.50	
		On cover		85.00
M45	M2	3k car, *green*	.80	6.50
		Never hinged	6.75	
		On cover		250.00
M46	M2	4k dark violet, *gray* ('17)	.80	8.00
		Never hinged	5.00	
		On cover		500.00
M47	M2	5k dk vio, *gray*	20.00	37.50
		Never hinged	50.00	
		On cover		675.00

M48 M2 10k dk ultra, *gray*   4.00   16.00
  Never hinged   10.00
  On cover   1,000.
  Nos. M22-M48 (27)   34.70   82.20
  Set, never hinged   125.00

Nos. M22-M48 exist imperf. Values, set unused hinged $250, never hinged $475.

Emperor Karl I
   M3   M4

1917-18   *Perf. 12½*
M49 M3 1h grnsh blue
   ('18)   .25   .25
  Never hinged   .40
  On cover   6.50
  a. Perf. 11½   5.50   16.00
  Never hinged   16.00
M50 M3 2h red org ('18)   .25   .25
  Never hinged   .40
  On cover   6.50
M51 M3 3h olive gray   .25   .25
  Never hinged   .40
  On cover   6.50
  a. Perf. 11½   20.00   47.50
  Never hinged   47.50
  b. Perf. 11½x12½   32.50   80.00
  Never hinged   80.00
M52 M3 5h olive green   .25   .25
  Never hinged   .75
  On cover   4.25
M53 M3 6h violet   .25   .25
  Never hinged   .40
  On cover   12.50
M54 M3 10h orange brn   .25   .25
  Never hinged   .65
  On cover   4.25
M55 M3 12h blue   .25   .25
  Never hinged   .40
  On cover   17.00
  a. Perf. 11½   4.00   12.00
  Never hinged   12.00
M56 M3 15h bright rose   .25   .25
  Never hinged   .40
  On cover   5.00
M57 M3 20h red brown   .25   .25
  Never hinged   .40
  On cover   6.75
M58 M3 25h ultramarine   .25   .55
  Never hinged   1.75
  On cover   8.50
M59 M3 30h slate   .25   .25
  Never hinged   .85
  On cover   12.50
M60 M3 40h olive bister   .25   .25
  Never hinged   .40
  On cover   10.00
  a. Perf. 11½   2.50   6.50
  Never hinged   6.50
M61 M3 50h deep green   .25   .25
  Never hinged   .85
  On cover   21.00
  a. Perf. 11½   8.00   32.50
  Never hinged   32.50
M62 M3 60h car rose   .25   .40
  Never hinged   .85
  On cover   17.00
M63 M3 80h dull blue   .25   .25
  Never hinged   .40
  On cover   25.00
M64 M3 90h dk violet   .35   .80
  Never hinged   2.50
  On cover   85.00
M65 M4 2k rose, *straw*   .25   .25
  Never hinged   .85
  On cover   42.50
  a. Perf. 11½   4.00   12.00
  Never hinged   12.00
M66 M4 3k green, *blue*   1.25   2.75
  Never hinged   5.00
  On cover   210.00
M67 M4 4k rose, *green*   16.00   24.00
  Never hinged   85.00
  On cover   —
  a. Perf. 11½   40.00   80.00
  Never hinged   80.00
M68 M4 10k dl vio, *gray* 1.25   8.00
  Never hinged   8.50
  On cover   850.00
  a. Perf. 11½   16.00   47.50
  Never hinged   47.50
  Nos. M49-M68 (20)   22.85   40.00
  Set, never hinged   87.50

Nos. M49-M68 exist imperf. Values, set unused hinged $160, never hinged $325. Also exist in pairs, imperf between. Values, each: unused $60, never hinged $120.

See No. M82. For surcharges and overprints see Italy Nos. N1-N19, Western Ukraine Nos. 44-63, 75, 95-101, Poland Nos. 30-40, Romania Nos. 1N1-1N17.

Emperor Karl I — M5

1918   **Typo.**   *Perf. 12½*
M69 M5 1h grnsh blue   24.00
  Never hinged   60.00
M70 M5 2h orange   9.50
  Never hinged   25.00
M71 M5 3h olive gray   9.50
  Never hinged   25.00
M72 M5 5h yellow green   .40
  Never hinged   .85
M73 M5 10h dark brown   .40
  Never hinged   .85
M74 M5 20h red   .80
  Never hinged   2.50
M75 M5 25h blue   .80
  Never hinged   2.50
M76 M5 30h bister   95.00
  Never hinged   210.00
M77 M5 45h dark slate   95.00
  Never hinged   210.00
M78 M5 50h deep green   47.50
  Never hinged   125.00
M79 M5 60h violet   95.00
  Never hinged   250.00
M80 M5 80h rose   65.00
  Never hinged   170.00
M81 M5 90h brown violet   1.60
  Never hinged   4.25

      Engr.
M82 M4 1k ol bister, *blue* .40
  Never hinged   .85
  Nos. M69-M82 (14)   444.90
  Set, never hinged   1,050.

Nos. M69-M82 were on sale at the Vienna post office for a few days before the Armistice signing. They were never issued at the Army Post Offices. They exist imperf. Values, set unused hinged $800, never hinged $1,600.

For surcharges see Italy Nos. N20-N33, Romania 1N35-1N47.

MILITARY SEMI-POSTAL STAMPS

Emperor Karl   Empress
I — MSP7   Zita — MSP8

     Perf. 12½x13
1918, July 20 **Unwmk.** **Typo.**
MB1 MSP7 10h gray green   .40   .80
  Never hinged   1.00
MB2 MSP8 20h magenta   .40   .80
  Never hinged   1.00
MB3 MSP7 45h blue   .40   .80
  Never hinged   1.00
  Nos. MB1-MB3 (3)   1.20   2.40
  Set, never hinged   3.00

These stamps were sold at a premium of 10h each over face value. The surtax was for "Karl's Fund."

For overprints see Western Ukraine Nos. 31-33.

Exist imperf. Values, set hinged unused $95, never hinged $240.

MILITARY NEWSPAPER STAMPS

Mercury — MN1

1916 **Unwmk.**   **Typo.**   *Perf. 12½*
MP1 MN1 2h blue   .25   .35
  Never hinged   .40
  On newspaper   30.00
  a. Perf. 11½   1.25   2.00
  Never hinged   3.25
  On newspaper   —
  b. Perf. 12½x11½   240.00 240.00
  Never hinged   450.00
  On newspaper   —
MP2 MN1 6h orange   .50   1.50
  Never hinged   2.00
  On newspaper   250.00
MP3 MN1 10h carmine   .55   1.50
  Never hinged   2.50
  On newspaper   250.00
MP4 MN1 20h brown   1.25   1.50
  Never hinged   3.00
  On newspaper   425.00
  a. Perf. 11½   4.00   8.00

  Never hinged   8.00
  On newspaper   —
  Nos. MP1-MP4 (4)   2.55   4.85
  Set, never hinged   8.00

Exist imperf. Values, Nos. MP2-MP3, unused hinged each $1.60, never hinged $6.50; Nos. MP1, MP4, unused hinged each $40, never hinged $120.

For surcharges see Italy Nos. NP1-NP4.

NEWSPAPER STAMPS

From 1851 to 1866, the Austrian Newspaper Stamps were also used in Lombardy-Venetia.

> Values for unused stamps 1851-67 are for fine examples with original gum. Examples without gum sell for about a third or less of the figures quoted.

Issues of the Monarchy

Mercury — N1

Three Types
Type I — The "G" has no crossbar.
Type II — The "G" has a crossbar.
Type IIa — as type II but the rosette is deformed. Two spots of color in the "G."

1851-56 **Unwmk.** **Typo.** *Imperf.*
    Machine-made Paper
P1 N1 (0.6kr) bl, type IIa 175.00 110.00
  No gum   30.00
  On newspaper   340.00
  On wrapper   250.00
  a. Blue, type I   250.00 130.00
  No gum   50.00
  On newspaper   425.00
  On wrapper   325.00
  b. Ribbed paper   625.00 240.00
  No gum   110.00
  On newspaper   500.00
  On wrapper   375.00
  c. Blue, type II   600.00 250.00
  No gum   125.00
  On newspaper   750.00
  On wrapper   750.00
P2 N1 (6kr) yel, type I 31,000. 10,000.
  No gum   22,500.
  On newspaper   19,500.
  On wrapper   18,500.
  a. (6kr) brown orange, type I — 12,000.
P3 N1 (30kr) rose, type I   —   13,000.
  No gum   34,000.
  On newspaper   24,500.
  On wrapper   23,500.
P4 N1 (6kr) scar, type II
    ('56)   85,000. 13,500.
  No gum   32,500.

Full margins = 1½mm at top and bottom, ½mm at sides.

Values for pairs
P1   N1 (0.6kr) blue, type IIa   375.00   500.00
  On newspaper   600.00
P1a N1 (0.6kr) blue, type I   525.00   400.00
  On newspaper   650.00
P1b N1 (0.6kr) blue, type I,
   ribbed paper   1,300.   475.00
  On newspaper   800.00
P1c N1 (0.6kr) blue, type II   1,250.   750.00
  On newspaper   —

Values for strips of 3
P1   N1 (0.6kr) blue, type IIa   600.00   725.00
  On newspaper   900.00
P1a N1 (0.6kr) blue, type I   825.00   750.00
  On newspaper   1,350.
P1b N1 (0.6kr) blue, type I,
   ribbed paper   2,100.   900.00
  On newspaper   1,350.
P1c N1 (0.6kr) blue, type II   —   1,450.
  On newspaper   —

Values for blocks of 4
P1   N1 (0.6kr) blue, type IIa   2,000.   1,700.
P1a N1 (0.6kr) blue, type I   2,250.   3,000.
P1b N1 (0.6kr) blue, type I,
   ribbed paper   4,500.   3,250.
P1c N1 (0.6kr) blue, type II

From 1852 No. P3 and from 1856 No. P2 were used as 0.6 kreuzer values.

Values for Nos. P2-P3 unused are for stamps without gum. Pale shades sell at considerably lower values.

Originals of Nos. P2 and P3 are usually in pale colors and poorly printed. Values are for stamps clearly printed and in bright colors. Numerous reprints of Nos. P1 to P4 were made between 1866 and 1904. Those of Nos. P2 and P3 are always well printed and in much deeper colors. All reprints are in type I, but occasionally show faint traces of a crossbar on "G" of "ZEITUNGS."

   N2   N3

Two Types of the 1858-59 Issue
Type I — Loops of the bow at the back of the head broken.
Type II — Loops complete. Wreath projects further at top of head.

1858-59   **Embossed**
P5 N2 (1kr) blue, type I   650.00 625.00
  No gum   75.00
  On newspaper   1,100.
  On wrapper   1,100.
  a. (1kr) deep blue, type I 800.00 700.00
  No gum   150.00
  On newspaper   1,100.
  On wrapper   875.00
P6 N2 (1kr) lilac, type II
    ('59)   875.00 300.00
  No gum   100.00
  On newspaper   600.00
  On wrapper   575.00
  a. (1kr) dark lilac, type II 1,650. 450.00
  No gum   250.00
  On newspaper   575.00
  On wrapper   550.00
  b. (1kr) dark slate lilac, type
    II   —   650.00
  On wrapper   1,300.
  c. (1kr) gray, type II 2,400. 725.00
  No gum   375.00
  On newspaper   1,000.
  On wrapper   950.00

Values for pairs
P5   N2 (1kr) blue, type I   1,400.   1,750.
P6   N2 (1kr) lilac, type II   1,900.   1,200.
P6a N2 (1kr) dark lilac, type II   —   900.00

Values for strips of 3
P5   N2 (1kr) blue, type I   2,100.   2,250.
P6   N2 (1kr) lilac, type II   3,000.   1,400.
P6a N2 (1kr) dark lilac, type II

Values for blocks of 4
P5   N2 (1kr) blue, type I   3,250.   4,750.
P6   N2 (1kr) lilac, type II   5,500.   3,500.
P6a N2 (1kr) dark lilac, type II   —   5,500.

1861
P7 N3 (1kr) gray   175.00 175.00
  No gum   25.00
  On newspaper   375.00
  On wrapper   350.00
  a. (1kr) gray lilac   625.00 240.00
  No gum   120.00
  On newspaper   525.00
  On wrapper   475.00
  b. (1kr) deep lilac   2,500. 800.00
  No gum   475.00
  On newspaper   1,500.
  On wrapper   1,450.
  c. (1kr) brownish lilac 550.00 275.00
  No gum   140.00
  On newspaper   600.00
  On wrapper   575.00

Values for pairs
P7   N3 (1kr) gray   350.00   425.00
  On newspaper   800.00
  On wrapper   750.00
P7a N3 (1kr) gray lilac   —   525.00
P7b N3 (1kr) deep lilac

The embossing on the reprints of the 1858-59 and 1861 issues is not as sharp as on the originals.

   N4

Wmk. 91, or, before July 1864, Unwmkd.
1863
P8 N4 (1.05kr) gray   45.00   16.50
  No gum   8.00
  On newspaper   125.00
  On wrapper   110.00
  a. Tete beche pair   125,000.
  b. (1.05kr) gray lilac 100.00   20.00
  No gum   25.00
  On newspaper   100.00
  On wrapper   90.00
  c. (1.05kr) brownish lilac 57.50 21.00
  On newspaper   100.00
  On wrapper   85.00

Values for pairs
P8   N4 (1.05kr) gray   125.00   42.50
P8b N4 (1.05kr) gray lilac   150.00   75.00

Values are for stamps that do not show the watermark. Stamps showing the watermark often sell for more.

The embossing of the reprints is not as sharp as on the originals.

Mercury

N5   N6

Three Types.
Type I — Helmet not defined at back, more or less blurred. Two thick short lines in front of wing of helmet. Shadow on front of face not separated from hair.
Type II — Helmet distinctly defined. Four thin short lines in front of wing. Shadow on front of face clearly defined from hair.
Type III — Outer white circle around head is open at top (closed on types I and II). Greek border at top and bottom is wider than on types I and II.

Coarse Print

1867-73		**Typo.**		**Wmk. 91**
P9	N5 (1kr) vio, type I	75.00	8.50	
	On newspaper		50.00	
	On wrapper		25.00	
a.	(1kr) violet, type II ('73)	225.00	25.00	
	On newspaper		190.00	
	On wrapper		95.00	

1874-76				**Fine Print**
P9B	N5 (1kr) violet, type III ('76)	.55	.40	
	On newspaper		7.00	
	On wrapper		4.50	
c.	(1kr) gray lilac, type I ('76)	225.00	32.50	
	On newspaper		145.00	
	On wrapper		90.00	
d.	(1kr) violet, type II	65.00	8.50	
	On newspaper		80.00	
	On wrapper		50.00	
e.	Double impression, type III		175.00	

Stamps of this issue, except No. P9Bc, exist in many shades, from gray to lilac brown and deep violet. Stamps in type III exist also privately perforated or rouletted.

1880			
P10	N6 ½kr blue green	8.50	1.25
	On newspaper		30.00
	On wrapper		16.00
a.	½kr yellow green	5.00	.95
	On newspaper		32.50
	On wrapper		17.50

Nos. P9B and P10 also exist on thicker paper without sheet watermark and No. P10 exists with unofficial perforation.

N7

Without Varnish Bars

1899		**Unwmk.**		**Imperf.**
P11	N7 2h dark blue	.25	.25	
	Never hinged	.85		
	On newspaper		4.25	
	On wrapper		4.50	
P12	N7 6h orange	1.60	2.00	
	Never hinged	5.00		
	On newspaper		85.00	
	On wrapper		80.00	
P13	N7 10h brown	1.60	.95	
	Never hinged	8.00		
	On newspaper		42.50	
	On wrapper		40.00	
P14	N7 20h rose	1.60	2.00	
	Never hinged	8.00		
	On newspaper		175.00	
	On wrapper		165.00	
	Nos. P11-P14 (4)	5.05	5.20	

1901		**With Varnish Bars**		
P11a	N7 2h dark blue	2.40	.25	
	Never hinged	12.00		
	On newspaper		8.50	
	On wrapper		8.50	
P12a	N7 6h orange	16.00	24.00	
	Never hinged	50.00		
	On newspaper		250.00	
	On wrapper		250.00	
P13a	N7 10h brown	16.00	8.00	
	Never hinged	50.00		
	On newspaper		210.00	
	On wrapper		200.00	
P14a	N7 20h rose	20.00	65.00	
	Never hinged	60.00		
	On newspaper		425.00	
	On wrapper		400.00	
	Nos. P11a-P14a (4)	54.40	97.25	

Nos. P11-P14 were re-issued in 1905. They exist privately perforated.

Mercury

N8   N9

1908			**Imperf.**
P15	N8 2h dark blue	.80	.25
	Never hinged	4.00	
	On newspaper		8.50
	On wrapper		8.00
a.	Tete beche pair	200.00	325.00
	Never hinged	425.00	
P16	N8 6h orange	3.25	.50
	Never hinged	11.00	
	On newspaper		65.00
	On wrapper		60.00
P17	N8 10h carmine	3.25	.40
	Never hinged	14.00	
	On newspaper		65.00
	On wrapper		60.00
P18	N8 20h brown	3.25	.40
	Never hinged	14.00	
	On newspaper		100.00
	On wrapper		90.00
	Nos. P15-P18 (4)	10.55	1.55

All values are found on chalky, regular and thin ordinary paper. They exist privately perforated.

1916			**Imperf.**
P19	N9 2h brown	.25	.40
	Never hinged	1.00	
	On newspaper		9.00
	On wrapper		8.50
P20	N9 4h green	.35	1.25
	Never hinged	2.00	
	On newspaper		130.00
	On wrapper		125.00
P21	N9 6h dark blue	.55	1.25
	Never hinged	2.00	
	On newspaper		130.00
	On wrapper		125.00
P22	N9 10h orange	.60	1.25
	Never hinged	2.50	
	On newspaper		130.00
	On wrapper		125.00
P23	N9 30h claret	.55	1.60
	Never hinged	2.00	
	On newspaper		210.00
	On wrapper		200.00
	Nos. P19-P23 (5)	2.30	5.75
	Set, never hinged	9.50	

Nos. P19-P23 exist privately perforated.

Issues of the Republic

Newspaper Stamps
of 1916 Overprinted

1919			
P24	N9 2h brown	.25	.80
	Never hinged	.35	
	On newspaper		5.00
	On wrapper		4.25
P25	N9 4h green	.40	6.50
	Never hinged	.95	
	On newspaper		32.50
	On wrapper		30.00
P26	N9 6h dark blue	.25	8.00
	Never hinged	.50	
	On newspaper		45.00
	On wrapper		42.50
P27	N9 10h orange	.40	9.50
	Never hinged	.95	
	On newspaper		62.50
	On wrapper		60.00
P28	N9 30h claret	.25	16.00
	Never hinged	.50	
	On newspaper		77.50
	On wrapper		75.00
	Nos. P24-P28 (5)	1.55	40.80
	Set, never hinged	3.25	

Nos. P24-P28 exist privately perforated.

Mercury

N10   N11

1920-21			**Imperf.**
P29	N10 2h violet	.25	.25
	Never hinged		
P30	N10 4h brown	.25	.25
	Never hinged		
P31	N10 5h slate	.25	.25
	Never hinged		
P32	N10 6h turq blue	.25	.25
	Never hinged		
P33	N10 8h green	.25	.40
	Never hinged		

P34	N10 9h yellow ('21)	.25	.25
	Never hinged		.25
P35	N10 10h red	.25	.25
	Never hinged		.25
P36	N10 12h blue	.25	.40
	Never hinged		.25
P37	N10 15h lilac ('21)	.25	.25
	Never hinged		.25
a.	Thick grayish paper	.35	2.50
	Never hinged	3.25	
P38	N10 18h blue grn ('21)	.25	.25
	Never hinged		.25
a.	Thick grayish paper	.25	.40
	Never hinged		.25
P39	N10 20h orange	.25	.25
	Never hinged		.25
a.	Thick grayish paper	.25	.45
	Never hinged		.25
P40	N10 30h yellow brn ('21)	.25	.25
	Never hinged		.25
a.	Thick grayish paper	.25	.45
	Never hinged		.35
P41	N10 45h green ('21)	.25	.40
	Never hinged		.35
P42	N10 60h claret	.25	.25
	Never hinged		.35
a.	Thick grayish paper	.25	1.30
	Never hinged		.35
P43	N10 72h chocolate ('21)	.25	.40
	Never hinged		.35
P44	N10 90h violet ('21)	.25	.80
	Never hinged		.35
a.	Thick grayish paper	.25	1.25
	Never hinged		.40
P45	N10 1.20k red ('21)	.25	.80
	Never hinged		.40
P46	N10 2.40k yellow grn ('21)	.25	.80
	Never hinged		.40
P47	N10 3k gray ('21)	.25	.80
	Never hinged		.35
a.	Thick grayish paper	.25	.80
	Never hinged		.25
	Nos. P29-P47 (19)		7.55
	Set, never hinged	4.00	

Nos. P29-P47 exist privately perforated.

1921-22			
P48	N11 45h gray	.25	.25
P49	N11 75h brown org ('22)	.25	.25
P50	N11 1.50k ol bister ('22)	.25	.25
P51	N11 1.80k gray blue ('22)	.25	.25
P52	N11 2.25k light brown	.25	.25
P53	N11 3k dull green ('22)	.25	.25
P54	N11 6k claret ('22)	.25	.25
P55	N11 7.50k bister	.25	.40
	Nos. P48-P55 (8)		2.15
	Set, never hinged	4.75	

Used values are for cancelled-to-order stamps. Postally used examples are worth much more.
Nos. P48-P55 exist privately perforated.

NEWSPAPER TAX STAMPS

Values for unused stamps 1853-59 are for examples in fine condition with gum. Examples without gum sell for about one-third or less of the figures quoted.

Issues of the Monarchy

NT1

		Unwmk.	
1853, Mar. 1		**Typo.**	**Imperf.**
PR1	NT1 2kr green	1,800.	57.50
	No gum	350.00	
	On newspaper		300.00
a.	2kr deep green	2,000.	72.50
	No gum	400.00	
	On newspaper		325.00
b.	2kr yellow green	2,150.	100.00
	No gum	450.00	
	On newspaper		350.00
c.	2kr blue green	2,100.	65.00
	No gum	450.00	
	On newspaper		325.00

Full margins = 1 ¼mm at top and bottom, ¾mm at sides.

The reprints are in finer print than the more coarsely printed originals, and on a smooth toned paper.

Values for Nos. PR2-PR9 are for stamps that do not show the watermark. Stamps showing the watermark often sell for more.

NT2

Two Types.
Type I — The banderol on the Crown of the left eagle touches the beak of the eagle.
Type II — The banderol does not touch the beak.

Wmk. 91, or, before July 1864, Unwmkd.

1858-59			
PR2	NT2 1kr blue, type II ('59)	50.00	5.50
	No gum	10.00	
	On newspaper		17.50
a.	1kr blue, type I	1,225.	190.00
	No gum	250.00	
	On newspaper		425.00
b.	Printed on both sides, type II		—
PR3	NT2 2kr brown, type II ('59)	47.50	6.75
	No gum	10.00	
	On newspaper		16.00
a.	2kr red brown, type II	600.00	240.00
	No gum	125.00	
	On newspaper		475.00
PR4	NT2 4kr brn, type I	425.00	1,100.
	No gum	115.00	
	On newspaper		3,000.
a.	4kr deep brown, type I	650.00	3,250.
	No gum	145.00	
	On newspaper		3,250.

Nos. PR2a, PR3a, and PR4 were printed only on unwatermarked paper. Nos. PR2 and PR3 exist on unwatermarked and watermarked paper.
Nos. PR2 and PR3 exist in coarse and (after 1874) in fine print, like the contemporary postage stamps.
The reprints of the 4kr brown are of type II and on a smooth toned paper.
Issue date: 4kr, Nov. 1.
See Lombardy-Venetia for the 1kr in black and the 2kr, 4fk in red.

NT3

1877			**Redrawn**
PR5	NT3 1kr blue	12.50	1.40
	No gum	1.50	
	On newspaper		5.50
a.	1kr pale ultramarine		2,900.
	On newspaper		11,500.
PR6	NT3 2kr brown	14.00	6.75
	No gum	1.75	
	On newspaper		10.00

In the redrawn stamps the shield is larger and the vertical bar has eight lines above the white square and nine below, instead of five.
Nos. PR5 and PR6 exist also watermarked "WECHSEL" instead of "ZEITUNGS-MARKEN."

NT4

1890, June 1			
PR7	NT4 1kr brown	9.00	1.00
	No gum	1.35	
	On newspaper		6.00
PR8	NT4 2kr green	10.00	1.50
	No gum	1.75	
	On newspaper		8.00

#PR5-PR8 exist with private perforation.

NT5

1890, June 1	**Wmk. 91**		**Perf. 12½**
PR9	NT5 25kr carmine	95.00	200.00
	Never hinged	160.00	
	No gum	22.50	
	On newspaper		47.50

	Fiscal cancellation		425.00
a.	Perf 13	125.00	240.00
	Never hinged	220.00	

Nos. PR1-PR9 did not pay postage, but were a fiscal tax, collected by the postal authorities on newspapers.

Values for stamps in pairs

PR1	NT1	2kr green	5,000.	—
PR2	NT2	1kr blue, type II	125.00	35.00
PR2a	NT2	1kr blue, type I	3,000.	700.00
PR2b	NT2	1kr blue, printed on both sides		—
PR3	NT2	2kr brown, type II	125.00	
PR3a	NT2	2kr red brown, type II	1,500.	—
PR4	NT2	4kr brown, type I	1,000.	—
PR5	NT3	1kr blue	60.00	5.00
PR6	NT3	2kr brown	50.00	50.00
PR7	NT4	1kr brown	40.00	5.00
PR8	NT4	2kr green	40.00	6.00
PR9	NT5	25kr carmine	225.00	500.00

SPECIAL HANDLING STAMPS

(For Printed Matter Only)
Issues of the Monarchy

Mercury
SH1

1916		**Unwmk.**	**Perf. 12½**	
QE1	SH1	2h claret, *yellow*	1.20	4.00
		Never hinged	3.25	
		On cover		50.00
QE2	SH1	5h dp green, *yellow*	1.20	4.00
		Never hinged	3.25	
		On cover		50.00
		Set, never hinged	6.50	

SH2

1917		SH2 2h claret, *yellow*	**Perf. 12½**	
QE3	SH2	2h claret, *yellow*	.25	.40
		Never hinged	.80	
		On cover		35.00
a.		Pair, imperf. between	325.00	650.00
		Never hinged	650.00	
b.		Perf. 11½x12½	150.00	260.00
		Never hinged	800.00	
		On cover		250.00
c.		Perf. 12½x11½	225.00	325.00
		Never hinged	950.00	
		On cover		340.00
d.		Perf. 11½	1.60	4.00
		Never hinged	4.00	
		On cover		42.50
QE4	SH2	5h dp green, *yellow*	.25	.40
		Never hinged	.80	
		On cover		42.50
a.		Pair, imperf. between	325.00	650.00
		Never hinged	650.00	
b.		Perf. 11½x12½	120.00	150.00
		Never hinged	800.00	
		On cover		250.00
c.		Perf. 12½x11½	190.00	260.00
		Never hinged	950.00	
		On cover		340.00
d.		Perf. 11½	1.60	4.00
		Never hinged	4.00	
		On cover		42.50
		Set, never hinged	1.60	

Nos. QE1-QE4 exist imperforate.

Issues of the Republic

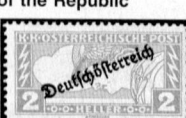

Nos. QE3
and QE4
Overprinted

1919				
QE5	SH2	2h claret, *yellow*	.35	.25
		Never hinged	.80	
		On cover		17.00
a.		Inverted overprint	325.00	
		Never hinged	650.00	
b.		Perf. 11½x12½	6.00	12.00
		Never hinged	10.50	
		On cover		125.00
c.		Perf. 12½x11½	110.00	290.00
		Never hinged	325.00	
		On cover		375.00
d.		Perf. 11½	.40	1.25
		Never hinged	1.25	
		On cover		30.00
QE6	SH2	5h deep green, *yellow*	.35	.25
		Never hinged	.80	
		On cover		21.00
a.		Perf. 11½x12½	1.60	4.50
		Never hinged	4.00	
		On cover		125.00
b.		Perf. 12½x11½	40.00	95.00

	Never hinged	87.50	
	On cover		375.00
c.	Perf. 11½	.35	.80
	Never hinged	.80	
	On cover		35.00
	Set, never hinged	1.60	

Nos. QE5 and QE6 exist imperforate. Value, set unused hinged $175; never hinged $360.

Dark Blue
Surcharge —
SH3

1921				
QE7	SH3	50h on 2h claret, *yel*	.25	.80
		Never hinged	.80	
		On cover		75.00

SH4

1922			**Perf. 12½**	
QE8	SH4	50h lilac, *yellow*	.25	.25
		Never hinged	.40	
		On cover		210.00

Nos. QE5-QE8 exist in vertical pairs, imperf between. No. QE8 exists imperf. Value: unused hinged $125; never hinged $250.

OCCUPATION STAMPS

Issued under Italian Occupation

Issued in Trieste

Austrian Stamps of
1916-18 Overprinted

Regno d'Italia
Venezia Giulia
3. XI. 18.

1918		**Unwmk.**	**Perf. 12½**	
N1	A37	3h bright vio	1.60	1.60
		Never hinged	3.25	
a.		Double overprint	57.50	57.50
b.		Inverted overprint	57.50	57.50
N2	A37	5h light grn	1.60	1.60
		Never hinged	3.25	
a.		Inverted overprint	57.50	57.50
c.		Double overprint	—	57.50
N3	A37	6h dp orange	2.50	2.50
		Never hinged	5.00	
N4	A37	10h magenta	25.00	4.00
		Never hinged	50.00	
a.		Inverted overprint	57.50	57.50
N5	A37	12h light bl	3.25	3.25
		Never hinged	6.50	
a.		Double overprint	57.50	57.50
N6	A42	15h dull red	1.60	1.60
		Never hinged	3.25	
a.		Inverted overprint	57.50	57.50
b.		Double overprint	57.50	57.50
N7	A42	20h dark green	1.60	1.60
		Never hinged	3.25	
a.		Inverted overprint	57.50	57.50
c.		Double overprint	140.00	
N8	A42	25h deep blue	12.50	12.50
		Never hinged	25.00	
a.		Inverted overprint	225.00	225.00
N9	A42	30h dl violet	3.25	3.25
		Never hinged	6.50	
N10	A39	40h olive grn	275.00	290.00
		Never hinged	550.00	
N11	A39	50h dark green	12.50	12.50
		Never hinged	25.00	
N12	A39	60h deep blue	29.00	29.00
		Never hinged	57.50	
N13	A39	80h orange brn	20.00	20.00
		Never hinged	40.00	
a.		Inverted overprint	—	
N14	A39	1k car, *yel*	20.00	20.00
		Never hinged	40.00	
a.		Inverted overprint	130.00	
N15	A40	2k light bl	450.00	500.00
		Never hinged	900.00	
N16	A40	4k yellow grn	1,050.	1,250.
		Never hinged	2,600.	

Handstamped

N17	A40	10k dp violet	30,000.	52,000.
		Never hinged	45,000.	

Granite Paper

N18	A40	2k light blue	675.00	
		Never hinged	1,350.	
N19	A40	3k car rose	650.00	700.00
		Never hinged	1,300.	
		Nos. N1-N14 (14)	409.40	403.40
		Set, never hinged	975.00	

Some authorities question the authenticity of No. N18.
Counterfeits of Nos. N10, N15-N19 are plentiful.

A variety of N19 exists on ordinary paper. Only 50 examples are known. Values, $8,250 unused, $12,250 never hinged.

A 90h stamp was printed but not issued because the Austrian stamps were replaced by Italian stamps. Only 50 90h were printed. Values, $4,100 unused, $8,000 never hinged.

Italian Stamps of 1901-
18 Overprinted

Venezia
Giulia

			Wmk. 140	**Perf. 14**	
N20	A42	1c brown	3.25	8.25
		Never hinged	8.00	
a.		Inverted overprint	32.50	32.50
N21	A43	2c orange brn	3.25	8.25
		Never hinged	8.00	
a.		Inverted overprint	29.00	29.00
N22	A48	5c green	2.50	2.50
		Never hinged	6.25	
a.		Inverted overprint	57.50	57.50
b.		Double overprint	140.00	
N23	A48	10c claret	2.50	2.50
		Never hinged	6.25	
a.		Inverted overprint	85.00	85.00
b.		Double overprint	140.00	
N24	A50	20c brn orange	2.50	3.25
		Never hinged	6.25	
a.		Inverted overprint	110.00	110.00
b.		Double overprint	130.00	130.00
N25	A49	25c blue	2.50	4.00
		Never hinged	6.25	
b.		Double overprint	130.00	130.00
N26	A49	40c brown	16.00	29.00
		Never hinged	40.00	
a.		Inverted overprint		
N27	A45	45c olive grn	6.50	10.00
		Never hinged	16.00	
a.		Inverted overprint	160.00	160.00
N28	A49	50c violet	12.50	12.50
		Never hinged	30.00	
N29	A49	60c brown car	85.00	160.00
		Never hinged	210.00	
b.		Double overprint	375.00	
N30	A46	1 l brn & green	40.00	57.50
		Never hinged	100.00	
a.		Inverted overprint		
		Nos. N20-N30 (11)	176.50	297.75
		Set, never hinged	525.00	

Italian Stamps of 1901-
18 Surcharged

Venezia
Giulia
5 Heller

N31	A48	5h on 5c green	1.60	3.25
		Never hinged	4.00	
a.		"5" omitted	125.00	125.00
b.		Inverted surcharge	125.00	125.00
N32	A50	20h on 20c brn org	1.60	3.25
		Never hinged	4.00	
a.		Double surcharge	125.00	125.00

Issued in the Trentino

Austrian Stamps of
1916-18 Overprinted

Regno d'Italia
Trentino
3 nov. 1918

1918		**Unwmk.**	**Perf. 12½**	
N33	A37	3h bright vio	12.50	12.50
		Never hinged	19.00	
a.		Double overprint	130.00	130.00
b.		Inverted overprint	125.00	125.00
N34	A37	5h light grn	10.00	5.00
		Never hinged	15.00	
a.		"8 nov. 1918"	3,400.	
b.		Inverted overprint	125.00	125.00
N35	A37	6h dp orange	125.00	110.00
		Never hinged	190.00	
N36	A37	10h magenta	10.00	8.25
		Never hinged	15.00	
a.		"8 nov. 1918"	250.00	250.00
N37	A37	12h light blue	325.00	290.00
		Never hinged	490.00	
N38	A42	15h dull red	12.50	10.00
		Never hinged	19.00	
N39	A42	20h dark green	8.25	8.25
		Never hinged	12.50	
a.		"8 nov. 1918"	325.00	325.00
b.		Double overprint	130.00	130.00
c.		Inverted overprint	57.50	57.50
d.		20h pale green	1,250.	3,000.
		Never hinged	1,900.	
N40	A42	25h deep blue	75.00	65.00
		Never hinged	110.00	
N41	A42	30h dl violet	29.00	25.00
		Never hinged	42.50	
N42	A39	40h olive grn	100.00	90.00
		Never hinged	150.00	

N43	A39	50h dark green	65.00	50.00
		Never hinged	97.50	
a.		Inverted overprint	325.00	325.00
N44	A39	60h deep blue	110.00	90.00
		Never hinged	165.00	
a.		Double overprint	325.00	325.00
N45	A39	80h orange brn	160.00	130.00
		Never hinged	240.00	
N46	A39	90h red violet	2,250.	3,100.
		Never hinged	4,500.	
N47	A39	1k car, *yel*	150.00	125.00
		Never hinged	225.00	
N48	A40	2k light blue	750.00	900.00
		Never hinged	1,500.	
N49	A40	4k yel green	3,400.	4,100.
		Never hinged	6,750.	
N50	A40	10k dp violet, black ovpt.	235,000.	
a.		dp violet, gray ovpt.	25,000.	25,000.
		Never hinged	37,500.	
		On cover		42,500.
b.		10k pale violet, gray ovpt.	27,500.	25,000.
		Never hinged	37,500.	
		On cover		42,500.

Granite Paper

N51	A40	2k light blue	1,650.	2,250.
		Never hinged	3,300.	

Counterfeits of Nos. N33-N51 are plentiful.

Italian Stamps of 1901-
18 Overprinted

Venezia
Tridentina

			Wmk. 140	**Perf. 14**	
N52	A42	1c brown	4.00	11.50
		Never hinged	10.00	
a.		Inverted overprint	110.00	110.00
b.		Double overprint	125.00	
N53	A43	2c orange brn	4.00	11.50
		Never hinged	10.00	
a.		Inverted overprint	110.00	110.00
N54	A48	5c green	4.00	11.50
		Never hinged	10.00	
a.		Inverted overprint	110.00	110.00
b.		Double overprint	125.00	125.00
N55	A48	10c claret	4.00	11.50
		Never hinged	10.00	
a.		Inverted overprint	160.00	160.00
b.		Double overprint	125.00	125.00
N56	A50	20c brn orange	4.00	11.50
		Never hinged	10.00	
a.		Inverted overprint	160.00	160.00
N57	A49	40c brown	130.00	85.00
		Never hinged	325.00	
N58	A45	45c olive grn	65.00	85.00
		Never hinged	160.00	
a.		Double overprint	375.00	375.00
N59	A49	50c violet	65.00	85.00
		Never hinged	160.00	
N60	A46	1 l brn & green	65.00	85.00
		Never hinged	160.00	
a.		Double overprint	375.00	375.00
		Nos. N52-N60 (9)	345.00	397.50

Italian Stamps of 1906-
18 Surcharged

Venezia
Tridentina
5 Heller

N61	A48	5h on 5c green	2.50	4.00
		Never hinged	6.25	
N62	A48	10h on 10c claret	2.50	4.00
		Never hinged	6.25	
a.		Inverted overprint	110.00	110.00
N63	A50	20h on 20c brn org	2.50	4.00
		Never hinged	6.25	
a.		Double surcharge	110.00	110.00
		Nos. N61-N63 (3)	7.50	12.00

General Issue

Italian Stamps of 1901-
18 Surcharged

5
centesimi
di corona

1919				
N64	A42	1c on 1c brown	1.60	4.00
		Never hinged	4.00	
a.		Inverted surcharge	25.00	25.00
N65	A43	2c on 2c org brn	1.60	4.00
		Never hinged	4.00	
a.		Double surcharge	375.00	
b.		Inverted surcharge	20.00	20.00
c.		Ovptd. "cerona"	67.50	67.50
N66	A48	5c on 5c green	1.60	1.60
		Never hinged	4.00	
a.		Inverted surcharge	65.00	65.00
b.		Double surcharge	125.00	
N67	A48	10c on 10c claret	1.60	1.60
		Never hinged	4.00	
a.		Inverted surcharge	65.00	65.00
b.		Double surcharge	125.00	125.00
c.		Ovptd. "oorona"	120.00	

	Never hinged	300.00		
d.	Ovptd. "corena"	120.00	120.00	
N68	A50 20c on 20c brn org	1.60	1.60	
	Never hinged	4.00		
a.	Double surcharge	160.00	160.00	
b.	Half used as 10c on cover		400.00	
N69	A49 25c on 25c blue	1.60	2.50	
	Never hinged	4.00		
a.	Double surcharge	160.00		
N70	A49 40c on 40c brown	1.60	4.00	
	Never hinged	4.00		
a.	"ccrona"	150.00	150.00	
N71	A45 45c on 45c ol grn	1.60	4.00	
	Never hinged	4.00		
a.	Inverted surcharge	180.00	180.00	
N72	A49 50c on 50c violet	1.60	4.00	
	Never hinged	4.00		
N73	A49 60c on 60c brn car	1.60	4.00	
	Never hinged	4.00		
a.	"00" for "60"	180.00	180.00	

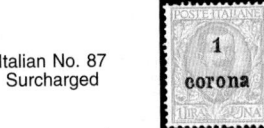

Italian No. 87
Surcharged

N74	A46 1cor on 1 l brn & green	5.00	10.00	
	Never hinged	12.50		
	Nos. N64-N74 (11)	21.00	41.30	

Surcharges similar to these but differing in style or arrangement of type were used in Dalmatia.

OCCUPATION SPECIAL DELIVERY STAMPS

Issued in Trieste

Special Delivery Stamp of Italy of 1903 Overprinted

1918	Wmk. 140		Perf. 14
NE1	SD1 25c rose red	75.00	130.00
	Never hinged	190.00	
a.	Inverted overprint	400.00	400.00

General Issue

Special Delivery Stamps of Italy of 1903-09 Surcharged

1919			
NE2	SD1 25c on 25c rose	2.50	3.25
	Never hinged	6.25	
a.	Double surcharge	130.00	130.00
NE3	SD2 30c on 30c bl & rose	4.00	6.50
	Never hinged	10.00	
a.	Pair, on stamp without surcharge		1,500.

OCCUPATION POSTAGE DUE STAMPS

Issued in Trieste

Postage Due Stamps of Italy, 1870-94, Overprinted

1918	Wmk. 140		Perf. 14
NJ1	D3 5c buff & mag	1.60	1.60
	Never hinged	4.00	
a.	Inverted overprint	29.00	29.00
b.	Double overprint	260.00	
NJ2	D3 10c buff & mag	1.60	1.60
	Never hinged	4.00	
a.	Inverted overprint	110.00	110.00
NJ3	D3 20c buff & mag	3.25	3.25
	Never hinged	8.00	
a.	Double overprint	260.00	
b.	Inverted overprint	110.00	110.00
NJ4	D3 30c buff & mag	6.50	6.50
	Never hinged	16.00	
NJ5	D3 40c buff & mag	50.00	60.00
	Never hinged	125.00	
a.	Inverted overprint	375.00	375.00

NJ6	D3 50c buff & mag	110.00	160.00	
	Never hinged	275.00		
a.	Inverted overprint	450.00	450.00	
NJ7	D3 1 l bl & mag	250.00	500.00	
	Never hinged	625.00		
	Nos. NJ1-NJ7 (7)	422.95	732.95	

General Issue

Postage Due Stamps of Italy, 1870-1903 Surcharged

1919			
Buff & Magenta			
NJ8	D3 5c on 5c	2.50	2.50
	Never hinged	6.25	
a.	Inverted overprint	37.50	37.50
NJ9	D3 10c on 10c	2.50	2.50
	Never hinged	6.25	
a.	Center and surcharge invtd.	260.00	260.00
NJ10	D3 20c on 20c	4.00	2.50
	Never hinged	10.00	
a.	Double overprint	260.00	260.00
NJ11	D3 30c on 30c	4.00	5.00
	Never hinged	10.00	
NJ12	D3 40c on 40c	4.00	5.00
	Never hinged	10.00	
NJ13	D3 50c on 50c	6.50	8.25
	Never hinged	16.00	

Surcharged			una corona	

NJ14	D3 1cor on 1 l bl & mag	6.50	12.50	
	Never hinged	16.00		
NJ15	D3 2cor on 2 l bl & mag	75.00	160.00	
	Never hinged	190.00		
NJ16	D3 5cor on 5 l bl & mag	75.00	160.00	
	Never hinged	190.00		
	Nos. NJ8-NJ16 (9)	180.00	358.25	

AUSTRIAN OFFICES ABROAD

These stamps were on sale and usable at all Austrian post-offices in Crete and in the Turkish Empire.

100 Centimes = 1 Franc

OFFICES IN CRETE

Used values are italicized for stamps often found with false cancellations.

Stamps of Austria of 1899-1901 Issue, Surcharged in Black

a   b

c   d

On Nos. 73a, 75a, 77a, 81a
Granite Paper
With Varnish Bars

1903-04	Unwmk.	Perf. 12½, 13½	
1	A15(a) 5c on 5h blue green	1.20	4.75
	Never hinged	4.25	
	On cover		37.50
a.	Perf 13x12½	45.00	125.00
	Never hinged	160.00	
	On cover		160.00

2	A16(b) 10c on 10h rose	.80	4.75	
	Never hinged	2.50		
	On cover		50.00	
3	A16(b) 25c on 25h ultra	40.00	32.50	
	Never hinged	110.00		
	On cover		425.00	
a.	Perf 13x12½	95.00	120.00	
	Never hinged	250.00		
	On cover		—	
4	A17(c) 50c on 50h gray blue	10.50	160.00	
	Never hinged	35.00		
	On cover		1,250.	
a.	Perf 13x12½	24.00		
	Never hinged	62.50		
	On cover		—	

On Nos. 83, 83a, 84, 85
Without Varnish Bars

5	A18(d) 1fr on 1k car rose	1.20	140.00	
	Never hinged	1.75		
	On cover		1,800.	
a.	1fr on 1k carmine	9.50		
	Never hinged	35.00		
b.	Horiz. or vert. pair, imperf. between	225.00		
	Never hinged	425.00		
6	A18(d) 2fr on 2k ('04)	8.00	400.00	
	Never hinged	26.00		
7	A18(d) 4fr on 4k ('04)	12.00	650.00	
	Never hinged	42.50		
	Nos. 1-7 (7)	73.70	1,392.	

Surcharged on Austrian Stamps of 1904-05
On Nos. 89, 97

1905	Without Varnish Bars		
8a	A19(a) 5c on 5h blue green	55.00	55.00
	Never hinged	110.00	
	On cover		190.00
9	A20(b) 10c on 10h car	.55	16.00
	Never hinged	1.10	
	On cover		6.00

On Nos. 89a, 97a, 99a, 103a
With Varnish Bars

8	A19(a) 5c on 5h bl grn	2.40	5.50	
	Never hinged	5.75		
	On cover		42.50	
b.	Perf 13x12½	17.00	85.00	
	Never hinged	75.00		
	On cover		170.00	
9a	A20(b) 10c on 10h carmine	32.50	65.00	
	Never hinged	115.00		
	On cover		170.00	
10	A20(b) 25c on 25h ultra	.55	140.00	
	Never hinged	3.00		
	On cover		850.00	
b.	Perf 13x12½	.60	1.50	
	Never hinged	1.50		
	On cover		850.00	
11	A21(b) 50c on 50h dl bl	.80	650.00	
	Never hinged	1.60		
	On cover		—	
b.	Perf 13x12½	8.50	12.50	
	Never hinged	17.00		
	On cover		—	

Surcharged on Austrian Stamps and Type of 1906-07
Without Varnish Bars

1907		Perf. 12½, 13½	
12	A19(a) 5c on 5h yel green (#90)	.80	4.00
	Never hinged	2.50	
	On cover		32.50
13	A20(b) 10c on 10h car (#92)	1.00	40.00
	Never hinged	3.25	
	On cover		150.00
14	A20(b) 15c on 15h vio	.80	40.00
	Never hinged	2.50	
	On cover		240.00
	Nos. 12-14 (3)	2.60	84.00

A5   A6

1908	Typo.	Perf. 12½	
15	A5 5c green, yellow	.25	1.00
	Never hinged	.65	
	On cover		12.50
16	A5 10c scarlet, rose	.35	1.20
	Never hinged	.75	
	On cover		13.50
17	A5 15c brown, buff	.45	8.00
	Never hinged	1.50	
	On cover		210.00
18	A5 25c dp blue, blue	16.00	6.50
	Never hinged	47.50	
	On cover		110.00
a.	25c deep blue, greenish blue paper	25.00	42.50
	Never hinged	62.50	
	On cover		100.00

Engr.

19	A6 50c lake, yellow	4.00	32.50	
	Never hinged	10.00		
	On cover		425.00	

20	A6 1fr brown, gray	8.00	60.00	
	Never hinged	17.00		
	On cover		1,350.	
a.	Vert pair, imperf. btwn.	200.00		
	Never hinged	325.00		
	Nos. 15-20 (6)	29.05	109.20	

Nos. 15-18 are on paper colored on the surface only. All values exist imperforate.

60th year of the reign of Emperor Franz Josef, for permanent use.

Paper Colored Through

1914		Typo.	
21	A5 10c rose, rose	1.25	2,300.
	Never hinged	2.75	
	On cover		4,250.
22	A5 25c ultra, blue	.80	190.00
	Never hinged	1.60	
	On cover		1,250.
	On parcel post receipt card		650.00

Nos. 21 and 22 exist imperforate.

STAMPS OF LOMBARDY-VENETIA USED IN AUSTRIAN OFFICES IN THE TURKISH EMPIRE

From 1863 to 1867 the stamps of Lombardy-Venetia (Nos. 15 to 24) were used at the Austrian Offices in the Turkish Empire. Values for stamps are for examples with neat and legible town cancellations of the most common types from the larger post offices. Values for scarcer cancellation types and for cancellations from smaller post offices are much higher. Values for covers are also for the most common frankings. Covers bearing unusual frankings and unusual combinations of stamps are also worth much more.

Aegean Islands: Leros
Meteline
Rhodes
Scio
Scio-Cesme
Albania: Dulcigno San
Giovanni di Me-
dusa
Durazzo
Santi Quaranta
San Giovanni
Scutari
Valona
Bulgaria: Burgas
Kustendje
Philippoli
Rustschuk
Sofia
Varna
Widdin
Crete: Candia
La Canea
Rettimo
Cyprus: Larnaca
Egypt: Alexandria
Port Said
Greece: Cavalla
Corfu
Janina
Lagos
Prevesa
Salonica
Sayada
Serres
Volo
Moldavia- Bakau
Walachia: Berlad
Bottuschan
Bukarest
Czernawoda
Fokschan
Galatz
giurgevo
Ibralia
Jassy
Piatra
Ploeschti
Roman
Sulina
Tekutsch
Tultscha
Montenegro: Antivari
Serbia: Belgrade
Turkey (Otto- Adrianopoli
man Empire): Alexandrette
Beyrut
Haifa (Caifa)
Cesme
Constantinople
Dardanelles
Gallipoli
Ineboli
Jaffa
Jerusalem
Kerassunda
Latakia
Mersina
Rodosto
Samsun
Sinope
Smyrna
Tenedos
Trebizonde
Tripoli in Syria

				Perf. 14
1863				
A15	A8	2s yellow, *value from*	220.00	
		On cover, *value from*	875.00	
		Single franking, on cover, *value from*		5,200.
A16	A8	3s green, *value from*	130.00	
		On cover, *value from*	1,000.	
		Single franking, on cover, *value from*		4,500.
A17	A8	5s rose, *value from*	130.00	
		On cover, *value from*	675.00	
		Single franking, on cover, *value from*		2,800.
A18	A8	10s blue, *value from*	82.50	
		On cover, *value from*	330.00	
A19	A8	15s yellow brown, *value from*	175.00	
		On cover, *value from*	550.00	

Values for Pairs, with legible cancellations

A15	A8	2s yellow, *value from*	450.00
		On cover, *value from*	1,575.
A16	A8	3s green, *value from*	675.00
		On cover, *value from*	2,850.
A17	A8	5s rose, *value from*	300.00
		On cover, *value from*	1,250.
A18	A8	10s blue, *value from*	165.00
		On cover, *value from*	675.00
A19	A8	15s yellow brown, *value from*	350.00
		On cover, *value from*	1,175.

1864-65		**Wmk. 91**		**Perf. 9½**
A20	A8	2s yellow ('65), *value from*	400.00	
		On cover, *value from*	1,475.	
		Single franking, on cover	—	
A21	A8	3s green, *value from*	100.00	
		On cover, *value from*	600.00	
		Single franking, on cover, *value from*		2,750.
A22	A8	5s rose, *value from*	47.50	
		On cover, *value from*	375.00	
		Single franking, on cover, *value from*		1,850.
A23	A8	10s blue, *value from*	16.00	
		On cover, *value from*	67.50	
A24	A8	15s yellow brown, *value from*	55.00	
		On cover, *value from*	240.00	

Only one example is known of No. A20 on single franking cover.

Values for Pairs, with legible cancellations

A20	A8	2s yellow ('65), *value from*		800.00
		On cover, *value from*		2,750.
A21	A8	3s green, *value from*		340.00
		On cover, *value from*		2,750.
A22	A8	5s rose, *value from*		165.00
		On cover, *value from*		825.00
A23	A8	10s blue, *value from*		50.00
		On cover, *value from*		235.00
A24	A8	15s yellow brown, *value from*		110.00
		On cover, *value from*		475.00

OFFICES IN THE TURKISH EMPIRE

100 Soldi = 1 Florin
40 Paras = 1 Piaster

> **Values for unused stamps are for examples with gum. Examples without gum sell for about one-third or less of the figures quoted. Used values are italicized for stamps often found with false cancellations.**

For similar designs in Kreuzers, see early Austria.

A1   A2

Two different printing methods were used, as in the 1867-74 issues of Austria. They may be distinguished by the coarse or fine lines of the hair and whiskers and by the paper, which is more transparent on the later issue.

1867		**Typo. Wmk. 91**		**Perf. 9½**
		Coarse Print		
1	A1	2sld orange	2.40	27.50
		Never hinged	4.00	
		On cover		3,000.
a.		2sld yellow	65.00	80.00
		Never hinged	115.00	
		On cover		1,000.
2	A1	3sld green	150.00	67.50
		Never hinged	275.00	
		On cover		775.00
a.		3sld dark green	325.00	200.00
		Never hinged	550.00	
		On cover		425.00
3	A1	5sld red	240.00	14.00
		Never hinged	575.00	
		On cover		1,000.
a.		5sld carmine	325.00	40.00
		Never hinged	975.00	
		On cover		900.00
b.		5sld red lilac	275.00	24.00
		Never hinged	675.00	
		On cover		—
4	A1	10sld blue	200.00	2.40
		Never hinged	300.00	
		On cover		27.50
a.		10sld light blue	275.00	3.25
		Never hinged	400.00	
		On cover		35.00
b.		10sld dark blue	240.00	3.25
		Never hinged	375.00	
		On cover		37.50
5	A1	15sld brown	24.00	8.00
		Never hinged	37.50	
		On cover		50.00
a.		15sld dark brown	95.00	65.00
		Never hinged	250.00	
		On cover		125.00
b.		15sld reddish brown	40.00	16.00
		Never hinged	60.00	
		On cover		60.00
c.		15sld gray brown	80.00	16.00
		Never hinged	150.00	
		On cover		55.00

6	A1	25sld violet	24.00	40.00
		Never hinged	40.00	
		On cover		1,500.
a.		25sld brown violet	40.00	60.00
		Never hinged	72.50	
		On cover		1,500.
b.		25sld gray lilac	120.00	47.50
		Never hinged	250.00	
		On cover		1,650.
7	A2	50sld brn, perf. 10½	1.25	65.00
		Never hinged	1.75	
		On cover		8,750.
a.		Perf. 12	100.00	110.00
		Never hinged	160.00	
b.		Perf. 13	325.00	—
		Never hinged	650.00	
k.		Perf. 9	27.50	140.00
		Never hinged	65.00	
l.		50sld pale red brn, perf. 12	160.00	160.00
		Never hinged	275.00	
		On cover		8,500.
m.		Vert. pair, imperf. btwn.	300.00	550.00
		Never hinged	425.00	
n.		Horiz. pair, imperf. btwn.	300.00	550.00
		Never hinged	425.00	
o.		Perf. 10½x9	85.00	160.00
		Never hinged	120.00	

		Perf. 9, 9½, 10½ and Compound		
1876-83				**Fine Print**
7C	A1	2sld yellow ('83)	.40	3,000.
		Never hinged	.75	
7D	A1	3sld green ('78)	1.20	27.50
		Never hinged	2.75	
		On cover, single franking		275.00
p.		Perf. 10½x9	—	450.00
		Never hinged		
7E	A1	5sld red ('78)	.40	24.00
		Never hinged	1.35	
		On cover		—
q.		Perf. 9		350.00
		On cover		
7F	A1	10sld blue	100.00	1.25
		Never hinged	210.00	
		On cover, single franking		21.00
r.		Perf. 10½	190.00	15.50
		Never hinged	350.00	
		On cover, single franking		77.50
s.		Perf. 9	150.00	250.00
		Never hinged	280.00	
		On cover, single franking		750.00
t.		Perf. 10½x9	—	165.00
		On cover, single franking		575.00
7I	A1	15sld org brn ('81)	12.00	160.00
		Never hinged	27.50	
		On cover, single franking		1,900.
u.		Perf. 10½		425.00
		On cover		
7J	A1	25sld gray lilac ('83)	.80	360.00
		Never hinged	1.60	
		On cover, single franking		15,000.
		Nos. 7C-7J (6)	114.80	3,572.

The 10 soldi was reprinted in deep dull blue, perforated 10½. Value, $6.50.

A3

1883				**Perf. 9½**
8	A3	2sld brown	.25	190.00
		Never hinged	.45	
		On cover		—
9	A3	3sld green	1.20	35.00
		Never hinged	6.00	
		On cover, single franking		300.00
10	A3	5sld rose	.25	20.00
		Never hinged	.45	
		On cover, single franking		225.00
a.		Perf. 10	5.50	135.00
		Never hinged	17.00	
11	A3	10sld blue	.80	.80
		Never hinged	2.40	
		On cover, single franking		22.50
a.		Perf. 10½	1.60	200.00
		On cover		—
12	A3	20sld gray, perf. 10	6.50	600.00
		Never hinged	18.00	
a.		Perf. 9½	1.60	9.50
		Never hinged	3.75	
		On cover, single franking		750.00
13	A3	50sld red lilac	1.25	20.00
		Never hinged	3.75	
		On cover, single franking		2,250.
		Nos. 8-13 (6)	10.25	865.80

No. 9 Surcharged

10 PARAS ON 3 SOLDI:
Type I — Surcharge 16½mm across. "PARA" about ½mm above bottom of "10." 2mm space between "10" and "P;" 1½mm between "A" and "10." Perf. 9½ only.
Type II — Surcharge 15¼ to 16mm across. "PARA" on same line with figures or slightly higher or lower. 1½mm space between "10" and "P;" 1mm between "A" and "10." Perf. 9½ and 10.

1886				**Perf. 9½, 10**
14	A4	10pa on 3sld green, type II, perf. 10	.35	8.00
		Never hinged	.60	
		On cover		150.00
a.		10pa on 3sld green, type I	200.00	500.00
		Never hinged	350.00	
b.		Inverted surcharge, type I		2,000.
c.		As #14, perf. 9½	.95	20.00
		Never hinged	2.50	
		On cover		150.00

Nos. 14 and 14c were overprinted in Vienna. Nos. 14a and 14b were overprinted in Constantinople.

Same surcharge on Austria Nos. 42-46

1888				
15	A11	10pa on 3kr grn	4.00	12.00
		Never hinged	12.00	
		On cover		77.50
a.		"01 PARA 10"		1,200.
16	A11	20pa on 5kr rose	.40	12.00
		Never hinged	1.75	
		On cover		90.00
a.		Double surcharge	400.00	
		Never hinged	1,200.	
17	A11	1pi on 10kr blue	65.00	1.60
		Never hinged	135.00	
		On cover		17.00
a.		Perf. 13½		800.00
b.		Double surcharge		
18	A11	2pi on 20kr gray	1.60	6.50
		Never hinged	4.75	
		On cover		340.00
19	A11	5pi on 50kr vio	2.00	20.00
		Never hinged	4.00	
		On cover		1,350.
		Nos. 15-19 (5)	73.00	52.10

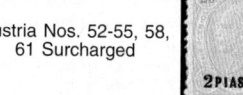

Austria Nos. 52-55, 58, 61 Surcharged

1890-92		**Unwmk. Perf. 9 to 13½**		
		Granite Paper		
20	A12	8pa on 2kr brn ('92)	.25	.65
		Never hinged	.50	
		On cover		17.50
a.		Perf. 9½	12.00	16.00
		Never hinged	32.50	
		On cover		95.00
21	A12	10pa on 3kr green	.55	.65
		Never hinged	1.25	
		On cover		13.00
a.		Pair, imperf. between		550.00
22	A12	20pa on 5kr rose	.35	.65
		Never hinged	.65	
		On cover		6.00
a.		Perf 13½x11½	110.00	110.00
		Never hinged	225.00	
23	A12	1pi on 10kr ultra	.40	.25
		Never hinged	.95	
		On cover		8.50
a.		Pair, imperf. between		550.00
24	A12	2pi on 20kr ol grn	8.00	32.50
		Never hinged	16.00	
		On cover		700.00
a.		Perf. 9½	185.00	
		Never hinged	300.00	
25	A12	5pi on 50kr violet	12.00	72.50
		Never hinged	24.00	
		On cover		1,850.
a.		Perf. 9½	185.00	
		Never hinged	300.00	
		Nos. 20-25 (6)	21.55	107.20

Values on cover for Nos. 20-25 are for covers paying the correct rate. Overfranked covers are usually philatelic and are valued at 25 percent more than the combined values of the used stamps attached.

See note after Austria No. 65 on missing numerals, etc.

Austria Nos. 66, 69 Surcharged

1891				**Perf. 10 to 13½**
26	A14	2pi on 20kr green	6.50	1.60
		Never hinged	16.00	
		On cover		42.50
a.		Perf. 9¼	200.00	160.00
		Never hinged	400.00	
		On cover		2,250.
27	A14	5pi on 50kr violet	3.25	3.25
		Never hinged	8.00	
		On cover		450.00

Two types of the surcharge on No. 26 exist.

Austria Nos. 62-65
Surcharged

1892   **Perf. 10½, 11½**
28   A13 10pi on 1gld blue   12.00   32.50
   Never hinged   37.50
   On cover   125.00
29   A13 20pi on 2gld car   16.00   60.00
   Never hinged   50.00
   On cover   125.00
   a.   Double surcharge

Values on cover for Nos. 28-29 are for over-franked complete covers, usually philatelic.

1896   **Perf. 10½, 11½, 12½**
30   A13 10pi on 1gld pale li-
     lac   18.50   22.50
   Never hinged   52.50
   On cover   1,700.
   On overfranked cover   95.00
   a.   Perf. 12½   45.00 375.00
   Never hinged   120.00
31   A13 20pi on 2gld gray
     grn   37.50   75.00
   Never hinged   110.00
   On overfranked cover   130.00
   a.   Perf. 12½   45.00 375.00
   Never hinged   120.00

Austria Nos. 73, 75, 77, 81, 83-85
Surcharged

#32-35   #36-38

Perf. 12½, 13½ and Compound
1900   **Without Varnish Bars**
32   A15 10pa on 5h bl grn   4.75   .80
   Never hinged   21.00
   On cover   15.00
33   A16 20pa on 10h rose   5.50   .80
   Never hinged   28.00
   On cover   15.00
   b.   Perf. 12½x10½   400.00 350.00
   Never hinged   1,200.
34   A16 1pi on 25h ultra   3.25   .40
   Never hinged   16.00
   On cover   8.00
   b.   Perf. 10½   24.00   16.00
   Never hinged   80.00
   On cover   100.00
35   A17 2pi on 50h gray
     bl   8.00   4.00
   Never hinged   40.00
   On cover   37.50
   a.   Perf. 10½   50.00   42.50
   Never hinged   160.00
   On cover   200.00
36   A18 5pi on 1k car
     rose   .55   .40
   Never hinged   4.50
   On cover   425.00
   a.   5pi on 1k carmine   .80   1.20
   Never hinged   8.00
   On cover   500.00
   b.   Horiz. or vert. pair, imperf.
     btwn.   160.00
   Never hinged   300.00
37   A18 10pi on 2k gray lil   2.00   3.50
   Never hinged   13.00
   On cover   1,000.
   On parcel post receipt card   200.00
   a.   Horiz. pair, imperf. btwn.
38   A18 20pi on 4k gray
     grn   1.60   8.00
   Never hinged   12.00
   On cover   2,100.
   On parcel post receipt card   500.00
   Nos. 32-38 (7)   25.65   17.90

In the surcharge on Nos. 37 and 38 "piaster" is printed "PIAST."

1901   **With Varnish Bars**
32a A15 10pa on 5h blue
     green   1.60   2.75
   Never hinged   12.50
   On cover   16.50
33a A16 20pa on 10h rose   2.40 400.00
   Never hinged   12.00
   On cover   600.00
34a A16 1pi on 25h ultra   1.20   .80
   Never hinged   8.00
   On cover   21.00
35b A17 2pi on 50h gray blue   2.75   8.00
   Never hinged   17.50
   On cover   42.50
   Nos. 32a-35b (4)   7.95 411.55

A4   A5

A6

1906   **Perf. 12½ to 13½**
Without Varnish Bars
39   A4   10pa dark green   12.00   4.00
   Never hinged   32.50
   On cover   17.00
40   A5   20pa rose   .80   1.20
   Never hinged   4.75
   On cover   15.00
41   A5   1pi ultra   .80   .40
   Never hinged   4.00
   On cover   15.00
42   A6   2pi gray blue   .80   1.20
   Never hinged   4.00
   On cover   32.50
   Nos. 39-42 (4)   14.40   6.80

1903   **With Varnish Bars**
39a A4   10pa dark green   4.75   2.00
   Never hinged   12.00
   On cover   15.00
40a A5   20pa rose   3.25   .80
   Never hinged   10.50
   On cover   15.00
41a A5   1pi ultra   2.40   .40
   Never hinged   8.00
   On cover   15.00
42a A6   2pi gray blue   160.00   3.25
   Never hinged   325.00
   On cover   37.50
   Nos. 39a-42a (4)   170.40   6.45

1907   **Without Varnish Bars**
43   A4   10pa yellow green   .55   2.00
   Never hinged   1.60
   On cover   32.50
45   A5   30pa violet   .55   4.00
   Never hinged   1.60
   On cover   97.50

A7   A8

1908   **Typo.**   **Perf. 12½**
46   A7   10pa green, yellow   .25   .40
   Never hinged   .75
   On cover   15.00
47   A7   20pa scarlet, rose   .25   .40
   Never hinged   .75
   On cover   15.00
48   A7   30pa brown, buff   .40   2.00
   Never hinged   1.25
   On cover   65.00
49   A7   1pi deep bl, blue   14.50   .25
   Never hinged   65.00
   On cover   12.50
   a.   1pi greenish blue, blue 15.00   1.50
   Never hinged   67.50
   On cover   13.50
50   A7   60pa vio, bluish   .65   5.50
   Never hinged   1.60
   On cover   250.00

Engr.
51   A8   2pi lake, yellow   .65   .25
   Never hinged   3.25
   On cover   110.00
52   A8   5pi brown, gray   .65   .95
   Never hinged   4.00
   On cover   625.00
53   A8   10pi green, yellow   .95   2.40
   Never hinged   5.00
   On cover   1,250.
54   A8   20pi blue, gray   2.40   4.75
   Never hinged   9.50
   On cover   1,750.
   Nos. 46-54 (9)   20.70   16.90

Nos. 46-50 are on paper colored on the surface only. 60th year of the reign of Emperor Franz Josef I, for permanent use.

Nos. 46-50 exist imperforate. Values, set: unused $275, never hinged $650.

Paper Colored Through

1913-14   **Typo.**
57   A7   20pa rose, rose ('14)   .55 650.00
   Never hinged   2.00
   On cover   2,750.

58   A7   1pi ultra, blue   .35   .55
   Never hinged   .90
   On cover   12.50
   Nos. 57 and 58 exist imperforate.

POSTAGE DUE STAMPS

Type of Austria D2
Surcharged in Black

1902   **Unwmk.**   **Perf. 12½, 13½**
J1   D2   10pa on 5h gray
     green   1.60   8.00
   Never hinged   8.00
   On cover   575.00
   a.   10pa on 5h yellow green 6.50
   Never hinged   16.00
J2   D2   20pa on 10h gray
     green   1.60   12.00
   Never hinged   11.00
   On cover   425.00
   a.   20pa on 10h yellow green 4.00
   Never hinged   10.00
J3   D2   1pi on 20h gray
     green   1.60   12.00
   Never hinged   10.00
   On cover   425.00
   a.   1pi on 20h yellow green   4.00
   Never hinged   10.00
J4   D2   2pi on 40h gray
     green   1.60   12.00
   Never hinged   13.00
   On cover   700.00
   a.   2pi on 40h yellow green 16.00
   Never hinged   42.50
J5   D2   5pi on 100h gray
     green   1.60   8.00
   Never hinged   8.00
   On cover   1,000.
   a.   5pi on 100h yellow green 8.00
   Never hinged   35.00
   Nos. J1-J5 (5)   8.00   52.00

Shades of Nos. J1-J5 exist, varying from yellowish to dark green.

D3

1908   **Typo.**   **Perf. 12½**
Chalky Paper
J6   D3   ¼pi pale green   3.25   13.50
   Never hinged   12.00
   On cover   750.00
J7   D3   ½pi pale green   2.00   11.00
   Never hinged   8.00
   On cover   325.00
J8   D3   1pi pale green   2.40   8.00
   Never hinged   8.00
   On cover   325.00
J9   D3   1½pi pale green   1.20   24.00
   Never hinged   8.00
   On cover   425.00
J10 D3   2pi pale green   1.60   20.00
   Never hinged   12.00
   On cover   675.00
J11 D3   5pi pale green   2.40   14.50
   Never hinged   9.50
   On cover   1,250.
J12 D3   10pi pale green   16.00 150.00
   Never hinged   65.00
J13 D3   20pi pale green   11.00 160.00
   Never hinged   35.00
J14 D3   30pi pale green   16.00   14.50
   Never hinged   72.50
   Nos. J6-J14 (9)   55.85 415.50

Chalky paper
J6a D3   ¼pi dark green   2.50   21.00
   Never hinged   7.25
   On cover   825.00
J7a D3   ½pi dark green   1.75   21.00
   Never hinged   7.25
   On cover   825.00
J8a D3   1pi dark green   1.75   21.00
   Never hinged   7.25
   On cover   825.00
J9a D3   1½pi dark green   1.75   21.00
   Never hinged   6.50
   On cover   825.00
J10a D3   2pi dark green   6.00   30.00
   Never hinged   13.00
J12a D3   10pi dark green   60.00 625.00
   Never hinged   160.00
J13a D3   20pi dark green   55.00 650.00
   Never hinged   135.00
   On cover

J14a D3   30pi dark green   100.00   40.00
   Never hinged   275.00
   On cover   —
   Nos. J6a-J14a (8)   228.75 1,429.

Thin ordinary paper
J6b D3   ¼pi dark green   4.00   37.50
   Never hinged   12.00
   On cover   1,000.
J7b D3   ½pi dark green   1.60   37.50
   Never hinged   8.00
   On cover   1,000.
J8b D3   1pi dark green   1.60   32.50
   Never hinged   8.00
   On cover   1,000.
J9b D3   1½pi dark green   2.50   85.00
   Never hinged   8.00
   On cover   —
J10b D3   2pi dark green   3.25   90.00
   Never hinged   12.00
   On cover   —
J11b D3   5pi dark green   6.50   50.00
   Never hinged   16.00
   On cover   —
J12b D3   10pi dark green   60.00 625.00
   Never hinged   145.00
   On cover   —
J13b D3   20pi dark green   47.50 625.00
   Never hinged   120.00
   On cover   —
J14b D3   30pi dark green   32.50 170.00
   Never hinged   87.50
   Nos. J6b-J14b (9)   159.45 1,752.

Thick ordinary paper
J6c D3   ¼pi dark green   4.00   37.50
   Never hinged   16.00
   On cover   750.00
J7c D3   ½pi dark green   1.60   19.00
   Never hinged   8.00
   On cover   750.00
J8c D3   1pi dark green   1.60   19.00
   Never hinged   8.00
   On cover   750.00
J9c D3   1½pi dark green   1.60   75.00
   Never hinged   8.00
   On cover   950.00
J10c D3   2pi dark green   2.50 100.00
   Never hinged   12.00
   On cover   —
J11b D3   5pi dark green   4.00   27.50
   Never hinged   16.00
   On cover   —
J12c D3   10pi dark green   47.50 625.00
   Never hinged   145.00
   On cover   —
J13c D3   20pi dark green   47.50 625.00
   Never hinged   180.00
   On cover   —
J14c D3   30pi dark green   8.00   27.50
   Never hinged   27.50
   On cover   —
   Nos. J6c-J14c (9)   118.30 1,555.

No. J6-J14 exist imperforate.
Forgeries exist.

LOMBARDY-VENETIA

Formerly a kingdom in the north of Italy forming part of the Austrian Empire. Milan and Venice were the two principal cities. Lombardy was annexed to Sardinia in 1859, and Venetia to the kingdom of Italy in 1866.

100 Centesimi = 1 Lira
100 Soldi = 1 Florin (1858)

Unused examples without gum of Nos. 1-24 are worth approximately 20% of the values given, which are for stamps with original gum as defined in the catalogue introduction.

For similar designs in Kreuzers, see early Austria.

Coat of Arms — A1

15 CENTESIMI:
Type I — "5" is on a level with the "1." One heavy line around coat of arms center.
Type II — As type I, but "5" is a trifle sideways and is higher than the "1."
Type III — As type II, but two, thinner, lines around center.
45 CENTESIMI:
Type I — Lower part of "45" is lower than "Centes." One heavy line around coat of arms center. "45" varies in height and distance from "Centes."
Type II — One heavy line around coat of arms center. Lower part of "45" is on a level with lower part of "Centes."
Type III — As type II, but two, thinner, lines around center.

Wmk. K.K.H.M. in Sheet or Unwmkd.

1850   Typo.   *Imperf.*

Thick to Thin Paper

1	A1	5c buff	6,000.	200.00
		No gum	1,500.	
		On cover		575.00
		On cover, single franking		625.00
		On cover, single franking, printed matter		1,900.
a.		Printed on both sides	21,500.	675.00
		No gum	5,350.	
		On cover		1,700.
b.		5c yellow	11,250.	650.00
		No gum	3,000.	
		On cover		3,350.
		On cover, single franking		3,400.
c.		5c orange	6,500.	225.00
		No gum	1,775.	
		On cover		675.00
		On cover, single franking		700.00
d.		5c lemon yellow	—	2,500.
		On cover		10,000.
		On cover, single franking		10,000.
e.		5c greenish lemon yellow	—	7,500.
		On cover, single franking		22,500.
3	A1	10c black	6,000.	200.00
		No gum	1,500.	
		On cover		575.00
		On cover, single franking		625.00
a.		10c gray black	6,000.	175.00
		No gum	1,500.	
		On cover		575.00
		On cover, single franking		625.00
b.		10c silver gray	16,500.	1,800.
		No gum	4,100.	
		On cover		5,250.
		On cover, single franking		5,250.
e.		10c charcoal black	7,500.	350.00
		No gum	1,900.	
		On cover		1,000.
		On cover, single franking		1,000.
4	A1	15c red, type III	1,900.	7.50
		No gum	650.00	
		On cover		30.00
a.		15c carmine, type III	3,000.	11.50
		No gum	750.00	
		On cover		45.00
b.		15c red, type I	4,500.	29.00
		No gum	1,125.	
		On cover		125.00
c.		Ribbed paper, type II	—	900.00
		No gum	—	
		On cover		2,250.
d.		Ribbed paper, type I	27,500.	275.00
		No gum	7,000.	
		On cover		675.00
f.		15c red, type II	2,400.	30.00
		No gum	600.00	
		On cover		120.00
h.		Laid paper, type III	19,000.	75,000.
		On cover		75,000.
i.		15c carmine, type I	4,500.	57.50
		No gum	1,125.	
		On cover		225.00
5	A1	30c brown	6,750.	26.50
		No gum	1,600.	
		On cover		110.00
a.		Ribbed paper	13,500.	175.00
		No gum	3,400.	
		On cover		425.00
c.		30c pale brown	7,500.	57.50
		No gum	1,900.	
		On cover		225.00
d.		30c reddish brown	8,250.	30.00
		No gum	2,100.	
		On cover		125.00
6	A1	45c blue, type III	20,000.	60.00
		No gum	5,000.	
		On cover		250.00
a.		45c blue, type I	21,250.	60.00
		No gum	5,500.	
		On cover		250.00
b.		Ribbed paper, type I	—	750.00
		No gum	—	
		On cover		1,900.
c.		45c blue, type II	190,000.	75.00
		No gum	50,000.	
		On cover		300.00
e.		45c ultramarine, type III	20,000.	650.00
		No gum	5,250.	
		On cover		2,650.
f.		45c pale grayish blue, type III	34,000.	375.00
		No gum	9,000.	
		On cover		1,500.
g.		45c pale grayish ultramarine, type III	—	1,050.
		On cover		4,250.
h.		45c sky blue, type I	24,500.	100.00
		No gum	6,500.	
		On cover		425.00

A cover bearing one example of the 15 centesimi, Type III, on laid paper (Scott 4h), sold for the equivalent of U.S. $40,500 at a Torino auction in 2003.

A mint example of the 45 centesimi blue, Type I, on hand-made paper (Scott No. 6a), was sold at a German auction for the equivalent of U.S. 16,755 in January, 2003.

1854

Machine-made Paper, Type III

3c	A1	10c black	12,250.	500.00
		No gum	3,100.	
		On cover		1,500.
3d	A1	10c gray black	15,000.	1,400.
		No gum	3,750.	
		On cover		4,250.
4g	A1	15c pale red	2,100.	6.00
		No gum	525.00	
		On cover		25.00
4j	A1	15c salmon	2,100.	6.00
		No gum	525.00	
		On cover		25.00
5b	A1	30c brown ('55)	7,500.	26.50
		No gum	1,900.	
		On cover		110.00
5e	A1	30c grayish brown, rough impression	15,000.	75.00
		No gum	3,750.	
		On cover		300.00
6d	A1	45c blue	18,000.	75.00
		No gum	4,500.	
		On cover		300.00
6i	A1	45c cobalt	18,000.	75.00
		No gum	4,500.	
		On cover		300.00

Full margins = 1½mm.

See note about the paper of the 1850 issue of Austria. *The reprints are type III, in brighter colors.*

Values for pairs
Thick to Thin Hand-made Paper

1	A1	5c buff	13,500.	400.00
		On cover		1,200.
1a	A1	5c buff, printed on both sides		1,500.
		On cover		3,750.
3	A1	10c black	13,500.	400.00
		On cover		1,200.
4	A1	15c red, type III	4,200.	27.50
		On cover		100.00
4b	A1	15c red, type I	10,000.	90.00
		On cover		325.00
4c	A1	15c Ribbed paper, type II		6,000.
4d	A1	15c Ribbed paper, type I		600.00
		On cover		1,700.
4f	A1	15c red, type II	5,250.	90.00
		On cover		275.00
4h	A1	15c red, type III, laid paper		—
5	A1	30c brown	14,750.	125.00
		On cover		350.00
5a	A1	30c Ribbed paper		550.00
		On cover		1,500.
6	A1	45c blue, type III		200.00
		On cover		725.00
6a	A1	45c blue, type I		200.00
		On cover		725.00
6h	A1	45c Ribbed paper, type I		1,650.
		On cover		4,500.
6c	A1	45c blue, type II		250.00
		On cover		1,000.

Machine-made Paper

3c	A1	10c black		1,050.
		On cover		3,250.
4g	A1	15c pale red	4,500.	15.00
		On cover		67.50
5b	A1	30c brown	16,500.	75.00
		On cover		300.00
6d	A1	45c blue	39,500.	250.00
		On cover		1,000.

Values for strips of 3
Thick to Thin Hand-made Paper

1	A1	5c buff	20,000.	675.00
		On cover		2,250.
1a	A1	5c buff, printed on both sides		1,500.
		On cover		7,250.
3	A1	10c black	20,000.	675.00
		On cover		2,250.
4	A1	15c red, type III	6,250.	210.00
		On cover		650.00
4b	A1	15c red, type I	15,000.	425.00
		On cover		1,500.
4d	A1	15c Ribbed paper, type I		2,650.
		On cover		7,500.
4f	A1	15c red, type II	8,000.	425.00
		On cover		1,500.
5	A1	30c brown		575.00
		On cover		2,000.
5a	A1	30c Ribbed paper		3,000.
		On cover		9,000.
6	A1	45c blue, type III		1,000.
		On cover		3,250.
6a	A1	45c blue, type I		1,000.
		On cover		3,250.
6b	A1	45c Ribbed paper, type I		3,750.
		On cover		12,000.
6c	A1	45c blue, type II		1,200.
		On cover		4,400.

Machine-made Paper

3c	A1	10c black		2,000.
		On cover		6,000.
4g	A1	15c pale red	6,900.	140.00
		On cover		425.00
5b	A1	30c brown		625.00
		On cover		2,100.
6d	A1	45c blue		1,150.
		On cover		3,600.

Values for strips of 4

1	A1	5c buff	26,500.	3,400.
				11,500.
3	A1	10c black	20,000.	4,250.
				13,500.
4	A1	15c red, type III		
4b	A1	15c red, type I	20,000.	1,000.
				2,850.
4f	A1	15c red, type II	10,500.	1,000.
		On cover		2,850.
5	A1	30c brown		1,150.
		On cover		3,250.

5a	A1	30c ribbed paper		5,000.
				14,000.
6	A1	45c blue, type III		1,800.
		On cover		5,500.
6a	A1	45c blue, type I		1,800.
		On cover		5,500.
6b	A1	45c blue, type I, ribbed paper		5,750.
		On cover		17,000.
6c	A1	45c blue, type II		2,250.
		On cover		6,750.

Machine-made Paper

3c	A1	10c black		10,500.
4g	A1	15c pale red		575.00
		On cover		1,750.
5b	A1	30c grown		1,250.
6d	A1	45c blue		3,750.
				2,200.
				6,500.

Values for blocks of 4
Thick to Thin Hand-made Paper

1	A1	5c buff	100,000.	32,500.
		On cover		112,500.
1a	A1	5c 5c buff, printed on both sides, on cover		82,500.
3	A1	10c black	50,000.	95,000.
4	A1	15c red, type III	16,500.	8,000.
				29,000.
4b	A1	15c red, type I		25,000.
				82,500.
4f	A1	15c red, type II	22,500.	21,000.
				52,500.
5	A1	30c brown	90,000.	30,000.
				82,500.
6	A1	45c blue, type III		26,500.
				82,500.
6a	A1	45c blue, type I		52,500.
				180,000.
6c	A1	45c blue, type II		100,000.

Machine-made Paper

3c	A1	10c black		—
4g	A1	15c pale red	10,000.	4,750.
				11,500.
5b	A1	30c brown	37,500.	14,000.
				42,500.
6d	A1	45c blue	82,500.	22,500.
				67,500.

Values for stamps used in Austria
Thick to Thin Hand-made Paper

1	A1	5c buff (from)		575.
		On cover (from)		13,250.
3	A1	10c black (from)		275.
		On cover (from)		2,100.
4	A1	15c red, type III (from)		225.
		On cover (from)		2,250.
4b	A1	15c red, type I (from)		155.
		On cover (from)		1,250.
4c	A1	15c Ribbed paper, type II (from)		1,450.
		On cover (from)		7,000.
4d	A1	15c Ribbed paper, type I (from)		450.
		On cover (from)		2,650.
4f	A1	15c red, type II (from)		200.
		On cover (from)		210.
5	A1	30c brown (from)		155.
		On cover (from)		1,250.
5a	A1	30c Ribbed paper (from)		310.
		On cover (from)		2,300.
6	A1	45c blue, type III (from)		425.
		On cover (from)		3,750.
6a	A1	45c blue, type I (from)		275.
		On cover (from)		2,350.
6b	A1	45c Ribbed paper, type I (from)		1,250.
6c	A1	45c blue, type II (from)		375.
		On cover (from)		2,900.

Machine-made Paper

3c	A1	10c black (from)		675.
		On cover (from)		6,500.
4g	A1	15c pale red (from)		210.
		On cover (from)		2,000.
5b	A1	30c brown (from)		300.
		On cover (from)		2,500.
6d	A1	45c blue (from)		500.
		On cover (from)		4,750.

A2

A3

A4

A5

A6

Two Types of Each Value.
Type I — Loops of the bow at the back of the head broken.

Type II — Loops complete. Wreath projects further at top of head.

1858-62   Embossed   *Perf. 14½*

7	A2	2s yel, type II	2,400.	150.00
		No gum	600.00	
		On cover, single franking		375.00
				425.00
a.		2s yellow, type I	12,000.	900.00
		No gum	3,000.	
		On cover, single franking		2,250.
				2,500.
b.		2s bright yellow, type I	13,000.	1,000.
		No gum	3,500.	
				2,600.
8	A3	3s black, type II	18,000.	190.00
		No gum	4,500.	
		On cover, single franking		475.00
				525.00
a.		3s black, type I	6,750.	375.00
		No gum	1,700.	
		On cover, single franking		950.00
				1,050.
b.		Perf. 16, type I	—	2,250.
		On cover		5,750.
c.		Perf. 15x16 or 16x15, type I	12,500.	750.00
		No gum	3,100.	
				1,900.
d.		3s gray black, type II	13,000.	1,000.
		No gum	3,500.	
		On cover		2,500.
9	A3	3s grn, type II ('62)	1,325.	140.00
		No gum	350.00	
		On cover, single franking		285.00
				650.00
a.		3s bluish green	1,800.	190.00
		No gum	450.00	
		On cover		375.00
10	A4	5s red, type II	750.00	12.00
		No gum	190.00	
		On cover		32.50
a.		5s red, type I	2,400.	45.00
		No gum	600.00	
		On cover		120.00
b.		Printed on both sides, type II		6,750.
c.		5s bright red, type I	2,400.	45.00
		No gum	600.00	
		On cover		115.00
11	A5	10s brown, type II	5,250.	24.00
		No gum	1,350.	
		On cover		60.00
a.		10s brown, type I	1,500.	140.00
		No gum	375.00	
		On cover		350.00
b.		10s dark brown, type I	2,250.	210.00
		No gum	575.00	
		On cover		525.00
12	A6	15s blue, type II	6,000.	125.00
		No gum	1,500.	
		On cover		300.00
a.		15s blue, type I	12,000.	225.00
		No gum	4,000.	
		On cover		575.00
b.		Printed on both sides, type II		18,750.
c.		15s bright blue, type I	13,250.	275.00
		No gum	3,400.	
		On cover		650.00
d.		15s bright blue, type II	6,750.	150.00
		No gum	1,700.	
		On cover		375.00

The reprints are of type II and are perforated 10½, 11, 11½, 12, 12½ and 13. There are also imperforate reprints of Nos. 7-9.

Values for pairs

7	A2	2s yellow, type II	5,250.	325.00
		On cover		950.00
		On cover, pair only (4 soldi rate)		—
7a	A2	2s yellow, type I	26,000.	1,900.
		On cover, pair only (4 soldi rate)		4,750.
8	A3	3s black, type II	40,000.	400.00
		On cover		1,000.
		On cover, pair only (6 soldi rate)		—
8a	A3	3s black, type I	15,000.	800.00
		On cover		1,900.
8b	A3	3s Perf. 16, type I		3,100.
9	A3	3s green, type II	2,900.	300.00
		On cover		600.00
10	A4	5s red, type II	1,650.	27.50
		On cover		82.50
10a	A4	5s red, type I	5,250.	95.00
		On cover		275.00
11	A5	10s brown, type II	11,500.	52.50
		On cover		175.00
11a	A5	10s brown, type I	3,250.	290.00
		On cover		750.00
12	A6	15s blue, type II	13,000.	275.00
		On cover		750.00
12a	A6	15s blue, type I	26,500.	500.00
		On cover		1,500.

Values for used strips of 3

7	A2	2s yellow, type II		575.
				2,100.
7a	A2	2s yellow, type I		2,800.
		On cover		8,250.
8	A3	3s black, type II		750.
				2,800.
8a	A3	3s black, type I		1,500.
				4,500.
9	A3	3s green, type II		750.
				3,750.
10	A4	5s red, type II		82.50
				375.
10a	A4	5s red, type I		375.
				1,400.
11	A5	10s brown, type II		250.
				1,000.
11a	A5	10s brown, type I		950.
				3,000.
12	A6	15s blue, type II		600.
		On cover		2,750.

12a	A6	15s blue, type I		1,300.
		On cover		5,250.

A strip of three of the 3 soldi green (Scott No. 9), with another single example, and a 3 soldi black stamp (Scott No. 8) on a cover sent from Peschiera to Vienna sold for the equivalent of US $20,380 at a Zurich auction in 2004.

Values for strips of 4

7	A2	2s yellow, type II		1,500.
		On cover		5,100.
7a	A2	2s yellow, type I		4,500.
		On cover		12,000.
8	A3	3s black, type II		1,750.
		On cover		5,750.
8a	A3	3s black, type I		3,000.
		On cover		9,500.
9	A3	3s green, type II		2,750.
		On cover		6,750.
10	A4	5s red, type II		375.
		On cover		1,500.
10a	A4	5s red, type I		1,250.
		On cover		3,600.
11	A5	10s brown, type II		675.
		On cover		2,100.
11a	A5	10s brown, type I		1,750.
		On cover		5,100.
12	A6	15s blue, type II		1,300.
		On cover		5,250.
12a	A6	15s blue, type I		2,650.
		On cover		12,000.

Values for blocks of 4

7	A2	2s yellow, type II	11,000.	13,250.
		On cover		—
7a	A2	2s yellow, type I		—
8a	A3	3s black, type I		—
9	A3	3s green, type II	4,500.	26,000.
10	A4	5s red, type II	4,000.	2,500.
		On cover		12,500.
10a	A4	5s red, type I	11,500.	9,500.
		On cover		26,500.
11	A5	10s brown, type II	30,000.	10,000.
		On cover		—
11a	A5	10s brown, type I	6,750.	19,500.
12	A6	15s blue, type II	33,750.	9,500.
		On cover		45,000.
12a	A6	15s blue, type I		25,000.

Values for stamps used in Austria

7	A2	2s yellow, type II (from)		1,000.
		On cover (from)		16,500.
7a	A2	2s yellow, type I (from)		2,100.
8	A3	3s black, type II (from)		250.
		On cover (from)		1,450.
8a	A3	3s black, type I (from)		525.
		On cover (from)		2,250.
9	A3	3s green, type II (from)		500.
		On cover (from)		2,900.
10	A4	5s red, type II (from)		200.
		On cover (from)		2,100.
10a	A4	5s red, type I (from)		225.
		On cover (from)		2,700.
11	A5	10s brown, type II (from)		225.
		On cover (from)		2,700.
11a	A5	10s brown, type I (from)		325.
		On cover (from)		3,700.
12	A6	15s blue, type II (from)		350.
		On cover (from)		5,600.
12a	A6	15s blue, type I (from)		575.
		On cover (from)		8,250.

A7

1861-62   *Perf. 14*

13	A7	5s red	7,125.	7.00
		No gum	1,800.	
		On cover		26.00
14	A7	10s brown ('62)	13,000.	75.00
		No gum	3,250.	
		On cover		190.00

The reprints are perforated 9, 9 ½, 10½, 11, 12, 12½ and 13. There are also imperforate reprints of the 2 and 3s.

The 2, 3 and 15s of this type exist only as reprints.

Values for pairs

13	A7	5s red	15,000.	22.50
		On cover		72.50
14	A7	10s brown	28,500.	265.00
		On cover		1,300.

Values for strips of 3

13	A7	5s red		75.00
		On cover		325.00
14	A7	10s brown		1,050.
		On cover		3,400.

Values for strips of 4

13	A7	5s red		265.00
		On cover		1,200.
14	A7	10s brown		2,650.
		On cover		8,250.

Values for blocks of 4

13	A7	5s red	30,000.	2,250.
		On cover		8,250.
14	A7	10s brown		26,500.
		On cover		90,000.

Values for stamps used in Austria

13	A7	5s red		250.00
		On cover		2,500.
14	A7	10s brown		1,125.
		On cover		—

A8

1863

15	A8	2s yellow	425.00	225.00
		No gum	165.00	
		On cover		675.00
		On cover, single franking		750.00
16	A8	3s green	5,250.	125.00
		No gum	1,325.	
		On cover		375.00
		On cover, single franking		1,500.
17	A8	5s rose	6,750.	37.50
		No gum	1,700.	
		On cover		95.00
18	A8	10s blue	14,000.	90.00
		No gum	3,500.	
		On cover		225.00
		On cover, single franking		250.00
19	A8	15s yellow brown	12,000.	340.00
		No gum	3,000.	
		On cover		1,000.

Values for pairs

15	A8	2s yellow	925.00	475.00
		On cover		1,500.
16	A8	3s green	11,500.	265.00
		On cover		850.00
		On cover, alone (6 soldi rate)		
17	A8	5s rose	15,000.	82.50
		On cover		225.00
18	A8	10s blue	31,000.	215.00
		On cover		700.00
19	A8	15s yellow brown	26,500.	725.00
		On cover		2,250.

Values for strips of 3

15	A8	2s yellow		825.
		On cover		3,000.
16	A8	3s green		1,300.
		On cover		4,750.
17	A8	5s rose		300.00
		On cover		1,250.
18	A8	10s blue		650.00
		On cover		2,500.
19	A8	15s yellow brown		1,600.
		On cover		6,000.

Values for strips of 4

15	A8	2s yellow		1,900.
		On cover		6,750.
16	A8	3s green		2,750.
		On cover		10,000.
17	A8	5s rose		675.00
		On cover		1,800.
18	A8	10s blue		2,500.
		On cover		6,500.
19	A8	15s yellow brown		3,750.
		On cover		10,500.

Values for blocks of 4

15	A8	2s yellow	1,950.	18,000.
		On cover		40,000.
16	A8	3s green	26,500.	
		On cover		
17	A8	5s rose		4,100.
		On cover		12,000.
18	A8	10s blue		
19	A8	15s yellow brown	60,000.	22,500.
		On cover		64,000.

Values for stamps used in Austria

15	A8	2s yellow		750.00
		On cover		19,000.
16	A8	3s green		200.00
		On cover		2,400.
17	A8	5s rose		250.00
		On cover		2,700.
18	A8	10s blue		500.00
		On cover		6,500.
19	A8	15s yellow brown		650.00
		On cover		10,000.

1864-65   **Wmk. 91**   *Perf. 9½*

20	A8	2s yellow ('65)	640.00	900.00
		No gum	160.00	
		On cover		2,650.
		On cover, single franking		2,900.
21	A8	3s green	55.00	52.50
		No gum	14.00	
		On cover		105.00
		On cover, single franking		375.00
22	A8	5s rose	9.00	11.50
		No gum	2.25	
		On cover		27.50
23	A8	10s blue	110.00	22.50
		No gum	27.50	
		On cover		45.00
		On cover, single franking		60.00
24	A8	15s yellow brown	1,250.	210.00
		No gum	310.00	
		On cover		625.00

Nos. 15-24 reprints are perforated 10½ and 13. There are also imperforate reprints of the 2s and 3s.

Values for pairs

20	A8	2s yellow	1,400.	1,900.
		On cover		8,250.
21	A8	3s green	120.00	115.00
		On cover		260.00
		On cover alone (6 soldi rate)		
22	A8	5s rose	20.00	24.50
		On cover		67.50
23	A8	10s blue	240.00	47.50
		On cover		125.00

24	A8	15s yellow brown	2,750.	450.00
		On cover		1,400.

Values for strips of 3

20	A8	2s yellow		5,300.
		On cover		10,250.
21	A8	3s green		300.00
		On cover		2,300.
22	A8	5s rose		60.00
		On cover		240.00
23	A8	10s blue		160.00
		On cover		800.00
24	A8	15s yellow brown		725.00
		On cover		2,300.

Values for strips of 4

20	A8	2s yellow		12,500.
21	A8	3s green		1,300.
		On cover		6,000.
22	A8	5s rose		325.00
		On cover		1,100.
23	A8	10s blue		1,200.
		On cover		4,000.
24	A8	15s yellow brown		2,500.
		On cover		7,500.

Values for blocks of 4

20	A8	2s yellow	2,850.	17,000.
21	A8	3s green	250.00	
22	A8	5s rose	40.00	1,500.
		On cover		4,850.
23	A8	10s blue	500.00	11,250.
		On cover		36,000.
24	A8	15s yellow brown	5,500.	9,500.
		On cover		32,500.

Value for No. 20 in used block of four is for an example with faults.

Values for stamps used in Austria

20	A8	2s yellow		1,500.
21	A8	3s green		145.00
				1,650.
22	A8	5s rose		160.00
				2,500.
23	A8	10s blue		330.00
				4,500.
24	A8	15s yellow brown		500.00
				6,750.

NEWSPAPER TAX STAMPS

From 1853 to 1858 the Austrian Newspaper Tax Stamp 2kr green (No. PR1) was also used in Lombardy-Venetia, at the value of 10 centesimi.

NT1

Type I — The banderol of the left eagle touches the beak of the eagle.
Type II — The banderol does not touch the beak.

1858-59   **Unwmk.**   **Typo.**   *Imperf.*

PR1	NT1	1kr black, type I ('59)	3,750.	4,750.
		No gum	1,400.	
		On newspaper		17,500.
PR2	NT1	2kr red, type II ('59)	500.00	75.00
		No gum	200.00	
		On newspaper		425.00
a.		Watermark 91	1,650.	115.00
		On newspaper		—
PR3	NT1	4kr red, type I	150,000.	5,500.
		No gum	23,000.	
		On newspaper		26,000.

The reprints are on a smooth toned paper and are all of type II.

Values for blocks of 4

PR1	NT1	1kr black, type I		50,000.
PR2	NT1	2kr red, type II		3,750.

Values for stamps used in Austria

PR1	NT1	1kr black, type I		5,500.
PR2	NT1	2kr red, type II		1,250.

AZERBAIJAN

ˌa-zər-ˌbī-ˈjän

(Azerbaidjan)

LOCATION — Southernmost part of Russia in Eastern Europe, bounded by Georgia, Dagestan, Caspian Sea, Persia and Armenia
GOVT. — A Soviet Socialist Republic
AREA — 32,686 sq. mi.
POP. — 2,096,973 (1923)
CAPITAL — Baku

100 Kopecks = 1 Ruble

National Republic

Standard Bearer — A1

Farmer at Sunset — A2

Baku — A3

Temple of Eternal Fires — A4

1919   **Unwmk.**   **Litho.**   *Imperf.*

1	A1	10k multicolored	.25	.30
2	A1	20k multicolored	.25	.30
3	A2	40k green, yellow & blk	.25	.30
4	A2	60k red, yellow & blk	.25	.35
5	A2	1r blue, yellow & blk	.45	.50
6	A3	2r red, bister & blk	.45	.50
7	A3	5r blue, bister & blk	1.90	1.75
8	A3	10r olive grn, bis & blk	1.90	1.75
9	A4	25r blue, red & black	3.25	40.00
10	A4	50r ol grn, red & black	4.50	4.75
		Nos. 1-10 (10)	13.45	50.50

The two printings of Nos. 1-10 are distinguished by the grayish or thin white paper. Both have yellowish gum. White paper examples are worth five times the above values.
For surcharges see Nos. 57-64, 75-80.

Soviet Socialist Republic

Symbols of Labor — A5

Oil Well — A6

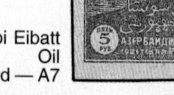

Bibi Eibatt Oil Field — A7

Khan's Palace, Baku — A8

Globe and Workers — A9

Maiden's Tower,
Baku — A10

Goukasoff
House
A11

Blacksmiths — A12

Hall of
Judgment,
Baku — A13

1922

15	A5	1r gray green	.25	.35
16	A6	2r olive black	.60	.60
17	A7	5r gray brown	.25	.35
18	A8	10r gray	.60	.70
19	A9	25r orange brown	.25	.40
20	A10	50r violet	.25	.40
21	A11	100r dull red	.35	.50
22	A12	150r blue	.35	.50
23	A9	250r violet & buff	.35	.50
24	A13	400r dark blue	.40	.50
25	A12	500r gray vio & blk	.40	.50
26	A13	1000r dk blue & rose	.40	.60
27	A8	2000r blue & black	.40	.50
28	A7	3000r brown & blue	.45	.50
a.		Tete beche pair	18.00	18.00
29	A11	5000r black, ol grn	.75	.90
		Nos. 15-29 (15)	6.05	7.80

Counterfeits exist of Nos. 1-29. They generally sell for more than genuine examples.
For overprints and surcharges see Nos. 32-41, 43, 45-55, 65-72, 300-304, 307-333.

Nos. 15, 17, 23, 28, 27 Handstamped from Metal Dies in a Numbering Machine

1922

32	A5	10,000r on 1r	19.50	17.50
33	A7	15,000r on 5r	19.50	27.50
34	A9	33,000r on 250r	6.25	6.25
35	A7	50,000r on 3000r	32.50	10.00
36	A8	66,000r on 2000r	19.50	12.00
		Nos. 32-36 (5)	97.25	73.25

Same Surcharges on Regular Issue and Semi-Postal Stamps of 1922

1922-23

36A	A7	500r on 5r	180.00	190.00
37	A6	1000r on 2r	30.00	36.00
38	A8	2000r on 10r	18.00	9.00
39	A7	5000r on 2000r	9.00	3.75
40	A11	15,000r on 5000r	15.00	12.00
41	A5	20,000r on 1r	24.00	14.50
42	SP1	25,000r on 500r	60.00	—

43	A7	50,000r on 5r	60.00	60.00
44	SP2	50,000r on 1000r	60.00	—
45	A11	50,000r on 5000r	18.00	18.00
45A	A8	60,000r on 2000r	120.00	225.00
46	A11	70,000r on 5000r	150.00	47.50
47	A6	100,000r on 2r	18.00	18.00
48	A8	200,000r on 10r	12.00	12.00
49	A9	200,000r on 25r	18.00	19.00
50	A7	300,000r on 3000r	50.00	50.00
51	A8	500,000r on 2000r	30.00	30.00

Regular Issue Stamps of 1922-23 Surcharged

52	A7	500r on #33	650.00	700.00
53	A11	15,000r on #46	650.00	700.00
54	A7	300,000r on #35	750.00	800.00
55	A8	500,000r on #36	650.00	700.00

The surcharged semi-postal stamps were used for regular postage.

Same Surcharges on Stamps of 1919

57	A1	25,000r on 10k	.85	1.50
58	A1	50,000r on 20k	.85	1.50
59	A2	75,000r on 40k	2.00	4.00
60	A2	100,000r on 60k	.85	1.50
61	A2	200,000r on 1r	.85	1.50
62	A3	300,000r on 2r	1.10	1.50
63	A3	500,000r on 5r	1.10	1.50
64	A2	750,000r on 40k	4.25	5.50
		Nos. 57-64 (8)	11.85	18.50

Handstamped from Settings of Rubber Type in Black or Violet

 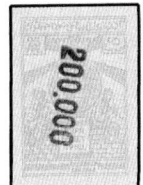

Nos. 65-66, 72-80	Nos. 67-70

On Stamps of 1922

65	A6	100,000r on 2r	27.50	27.50
66	A8	200,000r on 10r	80.00	80.00
67	A8	200,000r on 10r (V)	80.00	80.00
68	A9	200,000r on 25r (V)	80.00	80.00
a.		Black surcharge	80.00	80.00
69	A7	300,000r on 3000r (V)	40.00	40.00
70	A8	500,000r on 2000r (V)	72.50	72.50
a.		Black surcharge	90.00	90.00
72	A11	1,500,000r on 5000r (V)	140.00	140.00
a.		Black surcharge	120.00	120.00

On Stamps of 1919

75	A1	50,000r on 20k	4.00
76	A2	75,000r on 40k	4.00
77	A2	100,000r on 60k	4.00
78	A2	200,000r on 1r	4.00
79	A3	300,000r on 2r	4.00
80	A3	500,000r on 5r	4.00

Inverted and double surcharges of Nos. 32-80 sell for twice the normal price.
Counterfeits exist of Nos. 32-80.

Baku Province

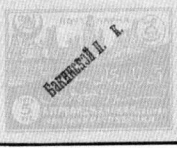

Regular and Semi-Postal Stamps of 1922 Handstamped in Violet or Black

The overprint reads "Bakinskoi P(ochtovoy) K(ontory)," meaning Baku Post Office.

1922		Unwmk.	Imperf.	
300	A5	1r gray green	100.00	
301	A7	5r gray brown	100.00	200.00
302	A12	150r blue	100.00	100.00
303	A9	250r violet & buff	100.00	200.00
304	A13	400r dark blue	75.00	75.00
305	SP1	500r bl & pale bl	100.00	150.00

306	SP2	1000r brown & bis	100.00	
307	A8	2000r blue & black	120.00	150.00
308	A7	3000r brown & blue	100.00	
309	A11	5000r black, ol grn	120.00	
		Nos. 300-309 (10)	1,015.	

Stamps of 1922 Handstamped in Violet

Бакинскаго Г.·П.·Т.О.№1

Ovpt. reads: Baku Post, Telegraph Office No. 1.

1924 Overprint 24x2mm

312	A12	150r blue	65.00
313	A9	250r violet & buff	65.00
314	A13	400r dark blue	65.00
317	A8	2000r blue & black	65.00
318	A7	3000r brn & blue	65.00
319	A11	5000r black, ol grn	200.00

Overprint 30x3½mm

323	A12	150r blue	100.00	125.00
324	A9	250r violet & buff	100.00	
325	A13	400r dark blue	100.00	100.00
328	A8	2000r blue & black	100.00	100.00
329	A7	3000r brn & blue	100.00	150.00
330	A11	5000r black, ol grn	100.00	

Overprinted on Nos. 32-33, 35

331	A5	10,000r on 1r	500.00
332	A7	15,000r on 5r	500.00
333	A7	50,000r on 3000r	500.00
		Nos. 312-333 (15)	2,625.

The overprinted semipostal stamps were used for regular postage.
A 24x2mm handstamp on #17, B1-B2, and 30x3½mm on Nos. 15, 17, B1-B2, was of private origin.

SEMI-POSTAL STAMPS

Carrying
Food to
Sufferers
SP1

1922		Unwmk.	Imperf.	
B1	SP1	500r blue & pale blue	.40	.75

For overprint and surcharge see Nos. 42, 305.

Widow and
Orphans — SP2

1922				
B2	SP2	1000r brown & bister	.75	1.25

Counterfeits exist.
For overprint and surcharge see Nos. 44, 306.

Russian stamps of 1909-18 were privately overprinted as above in red, blue or black by a group of Entente officers working with Russian soldiers returning from Persia. Azerbaijan was not occupied by the Allies. There is evidence that existing covers (some seemingly postmarked at Baku, dated Oct. 19, 1917, and at Tabriz, Russian Consulate, Apr. 25, 1917) are fakes.

AZORES

'ä-‚zōrz

LOCATION — Group of islands in the North Atlantic Ocean, due west of Portugal

GOVT. — Integral part of Portugal, former colony

AREA — 922 sq. mi.

POP. — 253,935 (1930)

CAPITAL — Ponta Delgada

Azores stamps were supplanted by those of Portugal in 1931.

1000 Reis = 1 Milreis
100 Centavos = 1 Escudo (1912)

Stamps of Portugal Overprinted in Black or Carmine

A

B

C

There are three types of surcharge. Type A: "C" and "O" rounded; "C" and "O" thinner; "C" and "O" raised. Type B: "C" and "O" rounded; "C" and "O" close together. Type C: "C" and "O" almost rectangular.

Type A

				1868		Unwmk.	Imperf.
1	A14	5r	black			3,500.	2,400.
2	A14	10r	yellow			13,750.	10,000.
3	A14	20r	bister			200.00	140.00
4	A14	50r	green			200.00	140.00
5	A14	80r	orange			200.00	150.00
6	A14	100r	lilac			200.00	150.00

The reprints are on thick chalky white wove paper, ungummed, and on thin ivory paper with shiny white gum. Value $35-42.50 each.

1868-70   **Perf. 12½**

5 REIS:
Type I — The "5" at the right is 1mm from end of label.
Type II — The "5" is 1½mm from end of label.

7	A14	5r	black, type I (C)		60.00	30.00
a.			Type II		70.00	70.00
b.			As "a," double impression of stamp		125.00	110.00
8	A14	10r	yellow		100.00	40.00
a.			Inverted overprint		250.00	150.00
b.			10r orange yellow		92.50	70.00
9	A14	20r	bister		50.00	65.00
10	A14	25r	rose		50.00	11.00
a.			Inverted overprint		—	—
b.			25r deep rose		70.00	11.00
11	A14	50r	green		160.00	150.00
a.			50r pale green		200.00	190.00
12	A14	80r	orange		160.00	150.00
13	A14	100r	lilac ('69)		160.00	150.00
a.			100r pale mauve		200.00	200.00
14	A14	120r	blue		150.00	130.00
a.			120r deep blue		175.00	150.00
15	A14	240r	violet		700.00	400.00

The reprints are on thick chalky white paper ungummed, perf 13½, and on thin ivory paper with shiny white gum, perf 13½. Value $30 each.

Overprint Type B

1871-75   **Perf. 12½**

21	A15	5r	black (C)		13.50	8.75
a.			Inverted overprint		47.50	42.50
23	A15	10r	yellow		30.00	25.00
a.			Inverted overprint		—	—
b.			Double overprint		60.00	47.50
24	A15	20r	bister		30.00	26.00
a.			Ribbed paper		52.50	35.00

25	A15	25r	rose		17.00	4.25
a.			Inverted overprint		—	—
b.			Double overprint		40.00	
c.			Perf. 14		190.00	85.00
d.			Dbl. impression of stamp		—	—
26	A15	50r	green		85.00	42.50
e.			Ribbed paper		85.00	42.50
27	A15	80r	orange		90.00	50.00
28	A15	100r	lilac		90.00	60.00
a.			Perf. 14		195.00	150.00
29	A15	120r	blue		175.00	125.00
a.			Inverted overprint		—	—
b.			Ribbed paper		325.00	260.00

Nos. 21-29 exist with overprint "b."

Perf. 13½

21b	A15	5r	black (C)		12.50	6.50
23c	A15	10r	yellow		40.00	25.00
24b	A15	20r	bister		60.00	30.00
25e	A15	25r	rose		25.00	3.75
26a	A15	50r	green		100.00	57.50
27a	A15	80r	orange		125.00	62.50

Perf. 14

| 25c | A15 | 25r | rose | | 165.00 | 57.50 |

Overprint Type A

Perf. 12½

21c	A15	5r	black (C)		20.00	9.50
23d	A15	10r	yellow		27.50	20.00
24c	A15	20r	yellow		55.00	30.00
24d	A15	20r	olive bister		32.50	21.00
24e	A15	20r	yellow bister		32.50	21.00
24f	A15	20r	bister, ribbed paper		37.50	24.00
25f	A15	25r	rose		18.00	4.50
b.			Double overprint		37.50	27.50
25g	A15	25r	rose, ribbed paper		30.00	7.75
26b	A15	50r	green		100.00	27.50
27b	A15	80r	orange		110.00	60.00
28b	A15	100r	lilac		110.00	70.00
29c	A15	120r	blue		150.00	95.00
30	A15	240r	violet		850.00	675.00
30a	A15	240r	violet, ribbed paper		1,000.	725.00

Overprint Type C

Perf. 12½

21d	A15	5r	black (C)		13.00	6.75
23e	A15	10r	yellow		27.50	12.50
24g	A15	20r	bister		27.50	12.50
25h	A15	25r	rose		16.00	3.25
26c	A15	50r	green		80.00	25.00
27c	A15	80r	orange		100.00	50.00
28c	A15	100r	lilac		80.00	37.50
29d	A15	120r	blue		160.00	80.00

Perf. 13½

21e	A15	5r	black (C)		13.00	6.75
21f	A15	5r	double impression of stamp		125.00	80.00
23f	A15	10r	yellow		50.00	25.00
24h	A15	20r	bister		50.00	25.00
25i	A15	25r	rose		17.00	3.25
26d	A15	50r	green		92.50	52.50
27d	A15	80r	orange		140.00	62.50
28d	A15	100r	lilac		110.00	45.00
29e	A15	120r	blue		160.00	80.00

Perf. 14

| 28e | A15 | 100r | lilac | | 175.00 | 100.00 |

The reprints are of type "b." All values exist are on thick chalky white paper ungummed, perf 13½ (value, each $29) and also on thin white paper with shiny white gum and perforated 13½ (value, each $30). The 5r, 10r, 15r, 50r and 120r also exist on thick chalky white paper ungummed, perf 12½. Value, each $80.

Overprint Type C in Black

15 REIS:
Type I — The figures of value, 1 and 5, at the right in upper label are close together.
Type II — The figures of value at the right in upper label are spaced.

1875-80   **Perf. 13½**

32	A15	10r	yellow green		150.00	125.00
33c	A15	15r	lilac brown		70.00	47.50
a.			Inverted overprint		150.00	
34	A15	50r	blue		140.00	60.00
a.			50r pale blue		175.00	95.00
35	A15	150r	blue		200.00	175.00
36	A15	150r	yellow		300.00	175.00
37	A15	300r	violet		95.00	65.00

Perf. 12½

31	A15	10r	blue green		150.00	125.00
32a	A15	10r	yellow green		130.00	95.00
33b	A15	15r	lilac brown		20.00	18.00
34b	A15	50r	pale blue		175.00	95.00
35a	A15	150r	blue		200.00	150.00

Overprint Type B

Perf. 13½

37a	A15	300r	violet		100.00	67.50

Perf. 12½

33	A15	15r	lilac brown		30.00	21.00
35b	A15	150r	blue		210.00	150.00

The reprints have the same papers, gum and perforations as those of the preceding issue.

Overprint Type C in Black

1880   **Perf. 12½**

38	A17	25r	gray		150.00	95.00
a.			Perf. 13½		150.00	42.50
39	A18	25r	red lilac		60.00	9.50
a.			Perf. 13½		60.00	9.50
b.			25r gray		—	—
c.			As "b," perf 13½		50.00	9.50
d.			As "c," double overprint		—	—

Overprint Type C in Carmine or Black
Ordinary Paper

1881-82

40	A16	5r	black (C)		29.00	12.00
a.			perf 13½		29.00	12.00
41	A23	25r	brown ('82)		55.00	8.00
a.			Double overprint		—	—
b.			perf 13½		55.00	8.00
42	A19	50r	blue		190.00	47.50
a.			perf 13½		190.00	47.50
			Nos. 40-42 (3)		274.00	67.50

Enamel Surfaced Paper

40b	A16	5r	black (C)		160.00	95.00
41c	A16	25r	brown ('82)		55.00	8.00
d.			perf 13½		55.00	8.00

Reprints of Nos. 38, 39, 39a, 40 and 42 have the same papers, gum and perforations as those of preceding issues.

Overprinted in Red or Black — d

15, 20 REIS

Type I — The figures of value are some distance apart and close to the end of the label.
Type II — The figures are closer together and farther from the end of the label. On the 15 reis this is particularly apparent in the upper right figures.

1882-85   **Ordinary Paper**   **Perf. 12½**

43	A16	5r	black (R)		20.00	10.00
45	A15	10r	green		90.00	50.00
a.			Inverted overprint		—	—
47	A15	15r	lilac brn		35.00	20.00
b.			Inverted overprint		—	—
48	A15	20r	bister		70.00	40.00
a.			Inverted overprint		—	—
50	A23	25r	brown		30.00	4.50
51	A15	50r	blue		2,000.	1,250.
52	A24	50r	blue		24.00	3.50
a.			Double overprint		—	—
53a	A15	80r	orange		125.00	110.00
b.			Double overprint		—	—
54	A15	100r	lilac		125.00	95.00
55	A15	150r	blue		1,800.	900.00
56	A15	150r	yellow		125.00	110.00
57	A15	300r	violet		125.00	110.00
58	A21	5r	slate (R)		25.00	6.00
60	A15	1000r	black		150.00	125.00

Perf. 13½

43a	A16	5r	black (R)		29.00	14.00
45b	A15	10r	green		97.50	62.50
47c	A15	15r	lilac brown		75.00	65.00
48b	A15	20r	bister		150.00	85.00
50a	A23	25r	brown		26.00	4.50
51a	A15	50r	blue		1,100.	925.00
52b	A24	50r	blue		42.50	4.50
53c	A15	80r	orange		175.00	110.00
54a	A15	100r	lilac		150.00	110.00
55a	A15	150r	blue		900.00	800.00
56a	A15	150r	yellow		110.00	85.00
57a	A15	300r	violet		110.00	85.00
60a	A15	1000r	black ('85) (R)		140.00	125.00

Perf. 11½

50b	A23	25r	brown		26.00	4.50

Enamel Surfaced Paper
Perf. 12½

43b	A16	5r	black (R)		70.00	47.50
44	A21	5r	slate		19.00	4.50
a.			Double overprint		—	—
c.			Inverted overprint		—	—
45d	A15	10r	green		125.00	110.00
46	A22	10r	green ('84)		32.50	14.00
a.			Double overprint		—	—
47d	A15	15r	lilac brown		87.50	75.00
48c	A15	20r	bister		87.50	75.00
49	A15	20r	carmine ('85)		150.00	125.00
a.			Double overprint		190.00	
50c	A23	25r	brown		27.50	4.50
52c	A24	50r	blue		27.50	4.50
53	A15	80r	yellow		80.00	62.50
53b	A15	80r	orange		80.00	62.50
54b	A15	100r	lilac		62.50	55.00
56b	A15	150r	yellow		65.00	57.50
57b	A15	300r	violet		87.50	77.50
59	A24a	500r	black (R)		195.00	175.00

Perf. 13½

44b	A21	5r	slate		32.50	11.00
45e	A15	10r	green		125.00	100.00
46b	A22	10r	green ('84)		32.50	14.00
47e	A15	15r	lilac brown		95.00	75.00
48e	A15	20r	bister		900.00	55.00
49b	A15	20r	carmine ('85)		150.00	125.00
50d	A23	25r	brown		30.00	4.50
52d	A24	50r	blue		37.50	14.00
53d	A15	80r	orange		95.00	75.00
56c	A15	150r	yellow		110.00	92.50
57c	A15	300r	violet		110.00	92.50

Perf. 11½

44d	A21	5r	slate		37.50	22.50
46c	A22	10r	green ('84)		32.50	14.00
50e	A23	25r	brown		27.50	4.50
52e	A24	50r	blue		27.50	4.50
58a	A21	5r	slate (R)		15.00	3.00

Reprints of the 1882-85 issues have the same papers, gum and perforations as those of preceding issues.

1887   **Black Overprint**

61	A25	20r	pink		50.00	19.00
a.			Inverted overprint		—	—
b.			Double overprint		—	—
62	A26	25r	lilac rose		60.00	3.00
a.			Inverted overprint		—	—
b.			Double ovpt., one invtd.		—	—
63	A26	25r	red violet		60.00	3.00
a.			Double overprint		—	—
64	A24a	500r	red violet		200.00	110.00
a.			Perf. 13½		400.00	240.00
			Nos. 61-64 (4)		370.00	135.00

Nos. 58-64 inclusive have been reprinted on thin white paper with shiny white gum and perforated 13½. Value: Nos. 58, 61-64, each $22.50; No. 59, $85; No. 60, $50.

Prince Henry the Navigator Issue

Portugal Nos. 97-109 Overprinted

1894, Mar. 4   **Perf. 14**

65	A46	5r	orange yel		3.50	3.00
			Never hinged		7.00	
a.			Inverted overprint		60.00	60.00
66	A46	10r	violet rose		3.50	3.00
			Never hinged		7.00	
a.			Double overprint		—	—
b.			Inverted overprint		—	—
67	A46	15r	brown		4.25	4.00
			Never hinged		8.25	
68	A46	20r	violet		4.50	4.25
			Never hinged		8.50	
a.			Double overprint		—	—
69	A47	25r	green		5.00	4.50
			Never hinged		9.50	
a.			Double overprint		75.00	75.00
b.			Inverted overprint		75.00	75.00
70	A47	50r	blue		12.50	6.75
			Never hinged		24.00	
71	A47	75r	dp carmine		22.50	9.50
			Never hinged		47.50	
72	A47	80r	yellow grn		27.50	10.00
			Never hinged		52.50	
73	A47	100r	lt brn, pale buff		27.50	8.00
			Never hinged		52.50	
a.			Double overprint		—	—
74	A48	150r	lt car, pale rose		40.00	19.00
			Never hinged		77.50	
75	A48	300r	dk bl, sal buff		60.00	30.00
			Never hinged		82.50	
76	A48	500r	brn vio, pale lil		90.00	45.00
			Never hinged		150.00	
77	A48	1000r	gray blk, yelsh		200.00	70.00
			Never hinged		300.00	
a.			Double overprint		700.00	500.00
			Nos. 65-77 (13)		500.75	217.00

St. Anthony of Padua Issue

Portugal Nos. 132-146 Overprinted in Red or Black

1895, June 13   **Perf. 12**

78	A50	2½r	black (R)		3.00	1.25
79	A51	5r	brown yel		9.50	3.00
80	A51	10r	red lilac		9.50	4.50
81	A51	15r	red brown		14.50	7.00
82	A51	20r	gray lilac		16.00	9.50
83	A51	25r	green & vio		10.00	3.00
84	A52	50r	blue & brn		32.50	15.00
85	A52	75r	rose & brn		47.50	40.00
86	A52	80r	lt green & brn		55.00	47.50
87	A52	100r	choc & blk		55.00	42.50
88	A53	150r	vio rose & bis		125.00	100.00
89	A53	200r	blue & bis		100.00	100.00
90	A53	300r	slate & bis		200.00	110.00
91	A53	500r	vio brn & grn		350.00	150.00
92	A53	1000r	violet & grn		600.00	225.00
			Nos. 78-92 (15)		1,677.	858.25

7th cent. of the birth of Saint Anthony of Padua.

Common Design Types
pictured following the introduction.

Vasco da Gama Issue
Common Design Types

1898, Apr. 1   *Perf. 14, 15*

93	CD20	2½r blue green	3.50	1.25
		Never hinged	5.00	
94	CD21	5r red	3.50	1.50
		Never hinged	5.00	
95	CD22	10r gray lilac	7.00	3.00
		Never hinged	10.00	
96	CD23	25r yellow green	7.00	3.00
		Never hinged	10.00	
97	CD24	50r dark blue	10.00	9.50
		Never hinged	15.00	
98	CD25	75r violet brown	21.00	14.00
		Never hinged	32.50	
99	CD26	100r bister brown	27.50	14.00
		Never hinged	40.00	
100	CD27	150r bister	42.50	30.00
		Never hinged	62.50	
		Nos. 93-100 (8)	122.00	76.25

For overprints and surcharges see Nos. 141-148.

King Carlos — A28

1906   **Typo.**   *Perf. 11½x12*

101	A28	2½r gray	.45	.40
		Never hinged	.50	
a.		Inverted overprint	35.00	35.00
102	A28	5r orange yel	.45	.40
		Never hinged	.50	
a.		Inverted overprint	35.00	35.00
103	A28	10r yellow grn	.45	.40
		Never hinged	.50	
104	A28	20r gray vio	.70	.50
		Never hinged	.80	
105	A28	25r carmine	.70	.40
		Never hinged	.80	
106	A28	50r ultra	6.00	4.75
		Never hinged	6.75	
107	A28	75r brown, *straw*	2.10	*1.25*
		Never hinged	2.40	
108	A28	100r dk blue, *bl*	2.10	*1.40*
		Never hinged	2.40	
109	A28	200r red lilac, *pnksh*	2.25	*1.40*
		Never hinged	2.60	
110	A28	300r dk blue, *rose*	6.75	*5.75*
		Never hinged	8.00	
111	A28	500r black, *blue*	16.00	14.00
		Never hinged	18.00	
		Nos. 101-111 (11)	37.95	30.65

"Acores" and letters and figures in the corners are in red on the 2½, 10, 20, 75 and 500r and in black on the other values.

King Manuel II — A29

1910, Apr. 1   *Perf. 14x15*

112	A29	2½r violet	.50	.40
113	A29	5r black	.50	.40
114	A29	10r dk green	.50	.40
115	A29	15r lilac brn	.90	.65
116	A29	20r carmine	1.25	1.00
117	A29	25r violet brn	.50	.50
a.		Perf. 11½	3.00	1.60
118	A29	50r blue	3.00	1.60
119	A29	75r bister brn	3.00	1.60
120	A29	80r slate	3.00	1.60
121	A29	100r brown, *lt grn*	5.00	3.75
122	A29	200r green, *sal*	5.00	3.75
123	A29	300r black, *blue*	3.00	2.75
124	A29	500r olive & brown	9.50	10.00
125	A29	1000r blue & black	21.00	19.00
		Nos. 112-125 (14)	56.65	47.40

The errors of color 10r black, 15r dark green, 25r black and 50r carmine are considered to be proofs.

Stamps of 1910 Overprinted in Carmine or Green

1910

126	A29	2½r violet	.40	.35
a.		Inverted overprint	12.50	12.50
127	A29	5r black	.40	.35
a.		Inverted overprint	12.50	12.50
128	A29	10r dk green	.40	.35
a.		Inverted overprint	12.50	12.50
129	A29	15r lilac brn	1.90	1.40
a.		Inverted overprint	12.50	12.50
130	A29	20r carmine (G)	1.90	1.40
a.		Inverted overprint	22.50	22.50
b.		Double overprint	22.50	22.50
131	A29	25r violet brn	.40	.30
a.		Perf. 11½	65.00	57.50
132	A29	50r blue	1.40	1.25
133	A29	75r bister brn	1.40	.95
a.		Double overprint	12.50	12.50
134	A29	80r slate	1.40	.95
135	A29	100r brown, *grn*	1.10	.90
136	A29	200r green, *sal*	1.10	*.95*
137	A29	300r black, *blue*	3.50	2.25
138	A29	500r olive & brn	4.50	*3.25*
139	A29	1000r blue & blk	11.00	*7.00*
		Nos. 126-139 (14)	30.80	21.65

Vasco da Gama Issue Overprinted or Surcharged in Black

e	
f	
g	

1911   *Perf. 14, 15*

141	CD20(e)	2½r blue green	.65	.50
142	CD21(f)	15r on 5r red	.65	.50
143	CD23(e)	25r yellow grn	.65	.50
144	CD24(e)	50r dk blue	2.25	1.40
145	CD25(e)	75r violet brn	1.90	1.75
146	CD27(f)	80r on 150r bister	2.00	1.90
147	CD26(e)	100r yellow brn	2.10	1.90
a.		Double surcharge	40.00	40.00
148	CD22(g)	1000r on 10r lilac	20.00	15.00
		Nos. 141-148 (8)	30.20	23.45

Postage Due Stamps of Portugal Overprinted or Surcharged in Black

1911   *Perf. 12*

149	D1	5r black	1.25	1.10
150	D1	10r magenta	2.75	1.10
a.		"Acores" double	20.00	15.00
151	D1	20r orange	5.25	3.75
152	D1	200r brn, *buff*	30.00	20.00
a.		"Acores" inverted	75.00	
153	D1	300r on 50r slate	30.00	19.00
154	D1	500r on 100r car, *pink*	30.00	18.00
		Nos. 149-154 (6)	99.25	62.95

Ceres Issue of Portugal Overprinted in Black or Carmine

With Imprint
Chalky Paper

1912-21   *Perf. 15x14*

155	A64	¼c olive brown	3.00	1.25
		Never hinged	4.50	
156	A64	½c black (C)	3.00	1.25
		Never hinged	4.50	
157	A64	1c deep green ('13)	3.00	1.25
		Never hinged	4.50	
158	A64	1½c choc ('13)	4.00	3.00
		Never hinged	6.00	
159	A64	2c carmine ('13)	6.00	3.00
		Never hinged	9.00	
160	A64	2½c violet	5.00	1.10
		Never hinged	7.00	
161	A64	5c dp blue ('13)	5.00	1.10
		Never hinged	7.00	
162	A64	7½c yel brn ('13)	12.00	7.00
		Never hinged	18.00	
163	A64	8c slate ('13)	12.00	7.00
		Never hinged	18.00	
164	A64	10c org brn ('13)	13.00	7.50
		Never hinged	20.00	
165	A64	15c plum ('13)	17.00	7.50
		Never hinged	26.00	
166	A64	20c vio brn, *grn* ('13)	15.00	7.00
		Never hinged	22.50	
a.		20c pale brown, *green*	15.00	7.00
		Never hinged	22.50	
167	A64	30c brn, *pink* ('13)	80.00	60.00
		Never hinged	120.00	
168	A64	30c brn, *yel* ('19)	2.25	1.90
		Never hinged	3.50	
169	A64	50c org, *sal* ('13)	6.50	2.75
		Never hinged	10.00	
170	A64	50c org, *yellow* ('13)	6.50	2.75
		Never hinged	10.00	
171	A64	1e dp grn, *bl* ('13)	7.00	6.00
		Never hinged	11.00	

Nos. 155 and 160 also exist on glazed non-chalky paper.

Perf. 12x11½

172	A64	14c dk bl, *yel* ('21)	3.00	*1.90*
		Never hinged	4.50	
		Nos. 155-172 (18)	203.25	123.25

Nos. 155 and 160 exist on glazed paper.

Ordinary Paper

1917-21   *Perf. 15x14*

173	A64	¼c olive brown	.55	.40
		Never hinged	.85	
a.		Inverted overprint	12.50	9.50
		Never hinged	19.00	
b.		Thick carton paper	3.50	3.25
		Never hinged	5.25	
174	A64	½c black (C)	.55	.40
		Never hinged	.85	
a.		Thick carton paper	2.25	1.75
		Never hinged	3.50	
175	A64	1c deep green	1.10	.80
		Never hinged	1.60	
a.		Inverted overprint	12.50	
		Never hinged	19.00	
176	A64	1c deep brown ('18)	.55	.40
		Never hinged	.85	
a.		Inverted overprint	17.50	
		Never hinged	27.00	
177	A64	1½c choc	1.10	.80
		Never hinged	1.50	
a.		Inverted overprint	13.00	
		Never hinged	19.00	
178	A64	1½c deep green ('18)	.55	.50
		Never hinged	.85	
a.		Inverted overprint	17.50	
		Never hinged	26.00	
179	A64	2c carmine	.80	.65
		Never hinged	1.20	
a.		Inverted overprint	20.00	
		Never hinged	30.00	
180	A64	2c orange ('19)	.55	.50
		Never hinged	.85	
a.		Inverted overprint	25.00	
		Never hinged	37.50	
181	A64	2½c violet	.80	.65
		Never hinged	1.20	
182	A64	3c rose ('18)	.80	.65
		Never hinged	1.20	
183	A64	3½c lt grn ('18)	.55	.50
		Never hinged	.85	
184	A64	4c lt grn ('19)	.55	.50
		Never hinged	.85	
185	A64	5c deep blue	.80	.65
		Never hinged	1.20	
186	A64	5c yellow brown ('21)	.75	.65
		Never hinged	1.15	
187	A64	6c dull rose ('20)	.55	.50
		Never hinged	.85	
188	A64	7½c yellow brown	6.75	3.75
		Never hinged	10.00	
189	A64	7½c dp bl ('19)	1.90	1.75
		Never hinged	2.75	
190	A64	8c slate	.80	.70
		Never hinged	1.20	
191	A64	10c orange brown	8.00	4.00
		Never hinged	12.00	
192	A64	15c plum	.85	.65
		Never hinged	1.25	
193	A64	30c gray brn ('21)	1.90	1.60
		Never hinged	2.75	
194	A64	60c blue ('21)	1.90	1.50
		Never hinged	2.75	
		Nos. 173-194 (22)	32.65	22.50

1918-26   *Perf. 12x11½*

195	A64	¼c olive brown	.55	.55
		Never hinged	.75	
a.		Thick carton paper	2.25	1.75
		Never hinged	3.25	
196	A64	½c black (R)	.55	.40
		Never hinged	.75	
197	A64	1c deep brown	.55	.40
		Never hinged	.75	
198	A64	1½c deep green	.90	.70
		Never hinged	1.25	
199	A64	2c orange ('19)	.55	.50
		Never hinged	.75	
a.		Inverted overprint	24.00	
		Never hinged	35.00	
b.		Thick carton paper	13.00	12.00
		Never hinged	18.00	
200	A64	3c rose	.90	.65
		Never hinged	1.25	
201	A64	3c dull ultra ('25)	.40	.30
		Never hinged	.55	
202	A64	4c lt grn ('19)	.55	.50
		Never hinged	.55	
a.		Inverted overprint	21.00	
		Never hinged	30.00	
203	A64	5c olive brown ('21)	.55	.50
		Never hinged	.75	
204A	A64	6c dull rose ('20)	.55	.50
		Never hinged	.75	
b.		Thick carton paper	1.25	1.00
		Never hinged	1.90	
204	A64	6c choc ('25)	.55	.50
		Never hinged	.75	
205	A64	7½c dp bl ('19)	75.00	50.00
		Never hinged	105.00	
206	A64	8c bl grn ('24)	.80	.55
		Never hinged	1.10	
207	A64	8c orange ('25)	1.00	.95
		Never hinged	1.40	
208	A64	10c orange brown	.55	.50
		Never hinged	.75	
209	A64	12c bl gray ('20)	2.75	1.75
		Never hinged	3.75	
210	A64	12c dp grn ('22)	.90	.75
		Never hinged	1.25	
a.		Inverted overprint	20.00	
		Never hinged	28.00	
211	A64	13½c chlky bl ('20)	2.75	1.90
		Never hinged	3.75	
212	A64	15c blk (R) ('24)	.55	.50
		Never hinged	.75	
213	A64	16c brt ultra ('26)	.95	.90
		Never hinged	1.35	
214	A64	20c choc ('21)	.90	.75
		Never hinged	1.25	
a.		Thick carton paper	7.00	6.00
		Never hinged	10.00	
215	A64	20c deep green ('24)	1.25	.95
		Never hinged	1.75	
a.		Double overprint	22.50	22.50
		Never hinged	30.00	
216	A64	20c gray ('24)	.80	.60
		Never hinged	1.10	
217	A64	24c grnsh bl ('21)	.90	.55
		Never hinged	1.25	
218	A64	25c salmon ('23)	.70	.50
		Never hinged	1.00	
219	A64	30c gray brn ('21)	1.90	1.60
		Never hinged	2.75	
220	A64	32c dp grn ('26)	2.75	2.40
		Never hinged	3.75	
221	A64	36c red ('21)	.85	.65
		Never hinged	1.20	
222	A64	40c dp blue ('23)	1.00	.70
		Never hinged	1.40	
a.		"CORREIC" for "CORREIO"	67.50	67.50
		Never hinged	95.00	
223	A64	40c blk brn ('24)	1.90	1.00
		Never hinged	2.75	
a.		"CORREIC" for "CORREIO"	67.50	67.50
		Never hinged	95.00	
224	A64	48c brt rose ('26)	5.00	3.00
		Never hinged	7.00	
225	A64	50c yellow ('23)	1.90	1.50
		Never hinged	2.75	
226	A64	60c blue ('21)	1.90	1.50
		Never hinged	2.75	
227	A64	64c pale ultra ('26)	5.00	2.25
		Never hinged	7.00	
228	A64	75c dull rose ('24)	5.00	4.00
		Never hinged	7.00	
229	A64	80c dull rose ('21)	2.50	2.10
		Never hinged	3.50	
230	A64	80c violet ('24)	2.50	1.90
		Never hinged	3.50	
231	A64	90c chlky bl ('21)	2.50	2.10
		Never hinged	3.50	
232	A64	96c dp rose ('26)	7.50	3.50
		Never hinged	11.00	
233	A64	1e violet ('21)	2.50	2.10
		Never hinged	3.50	
234	A64	1.10e yel brn ('21)	2.75	2.10
		Never hinged	3.75	
235	A64	1.20e yel grn ('22)	3.25	2.10
		Never hinged	4.50	

236	A64	2e slate grn ('22)	10.00	6.50
		Never hinged	14.00	
		Nos. 195-236 (42)	156.55	107.15

1924-30 *Perf. 12x11½*

Glazed Paper

237	A64	1e gray vio	3.75	3.25
		Never hinged	5.75	
237A	A64	1.20e buff	8.25	6.00
		Never hinged	12.50	
237B	A64	1.50e blk vio	9.75	6.75
		Never hinged	14.50	
237C	A64	1.50e lilac ('25)	8.50	6.75
		Never hinged	13.00	
237D	A64	1.60e dp bl ('25)	8.50	7.00
		Never hinged	13.00	
237E	A64	2.40e apple grn ('30)	100.00	60.00
		Never hinged	150.00	
237F	A64	3e lil pink ('28)	120.00	60.00
		Never hinged	180.00	
237G	A64	3.20e gray grn ('26)	9.75	9.50
		Never hinged	14.50	
237H	A64	5e emer ('25)	19.00	10.00
		Never hinged	29.00	
237I	A64	10e pink ('25)	90.00	27.50
		Never hinged	135.00	
237J	A64	20e pale turq ('25)	175.00	82.50
		Never hinged	260.00	
		Nos. 237-237J (11)	552.50	279.25

For same overprint on surcharged stamps, see Nos. 300-306. For same design without imprint see Nos. 307-313.

Castello-Branco Issue

Stamps of Portugal, 1925, Overprinted in Black or Red

1925, Mar. 29 *Perf. 12½*

238	A73	2c orange	.25	.25
239	A73	3c green	.25	.25
240	A73	4c ultra (R)	.25	.25
241	A73	5c scarlet	.25	.25
242	A74	10c pale blue	.25	.25
243	A74	16c red orange	.40	.30
244	A75	25c car rose	.40	.30
245	A75	32c green	.50	.50
246	A75	40c grn & blk (R)	.50	.50
247	A74	48c red brn	1.10	1.10
248	A76	50c blue green	1.10	1.00
249	A76	64c orange brn	1.10	1.00
250	A76	75c gray blk (R)	1.10	1.00
251	A75	80c brown	1.10	1.00
252	A76	96c car rose	1.40	1.10
253	A77	1.50e dk bl, *bl* (R)	1.40	1.10
254	A75	1.60e indigo (R)	1.50	1.40
255	A77	2e dk grn, *grn* (R)	2.50	2.10
256	A77	2.40e red, *org*	3.25	2.40
257	A77	3.20e blk, *grn* (R)	6.00	5.25
		Nos. 238-257 (20)	24.60	21.30

First Independence Issue

Stamps of Portugal, 1926, Overprinted in Red

1926, Aug. 13 *Perf. 14, 14½*

Center in Black

258	A79	2c orange	.35	.35
259	A80	3c ultra	.35	.35
260	A79	4c yellow grn	.35	.35
261	A80	5c black brn	.35	.35
262	A79	6c ocher	.35	.35
263	A80	15c dk green	.75	.70
264	A81	20c dull violet	.75	.70
265	A82	25c scarlet	.75	.70
266	A81	32c deep green	.75	.70
267	A82	40c yellow brn	.75	.70
268	A82	50c olive bis	2.00	2.00
269	A82	75c red brown	2.10	2.10
270	A83	1e black violet	3.00	3.00
271	A84	4.50e olive green	10.00	10.00
		Nos. 258-271 (14)	22.60	22.35

The use of these stamps instead of those of the regular issue was obligatory on Aug. 13th and 14th, Nov. 30th and Dec. 1st, 1926.

Second Independence Issue

Same Overprint on Stamps of Portugal, 1927, in Red

1927, Nov. 29 **Center in Black**

272	A86	2c lt brown	.30	.30
273	A87	3c ultra	.30	.30
274	A86	4c orange	.30	.30
275	A88	5c dk brown	.30	.30
276	A89	6c orange brn	.30	.30
277	A87	15c black brn	.30	.30
278	A86	25c gray	1.25	1.25
279	A89	32c blue grn	1.25	1.25
280	A90	40c yellow grn	1.00	.90
281	A90	96c red	4.00	3.25
282	A88	1.60e myrtle grn	4.00	3.25
283	A91	4.50e bister	10.00	8.75
		Nos. 272-283 (12)	23.30	20.30

Third Independence Issue

Same Overprint on Stamps of Portugal, 1928, in Red

1928, Nov. 27 **Center in Black**

284	A93	2c lt blue	.30	.30
285	A94	3c lt green	.30	.30
286	A95	4c lake	.30	.30
287	A96	5c olive grn	.30	.30
288	A97	6c orange brn	.30	.30
289	A94	15c slate	.65	.60
290	A95	16c dk violet	.75	.75
291	A93	25c ultra	.75	.75
292	A97	32c dk green	.80	.80
293	A96	40c olive brn	.80	.80
294	A95	50c red orange	1.75	1.75
295	A97	80c lt gray	1.75	1.75
296	A97	96c carmine	3.00	3.00
297	A96	1e claret	3.00	3.00
298	A93	1.60e dk blue	3.00	3.00
299	A98	4.50e yellow	8.75	8.50
		Nos. 284-299 (16)	26.50	26.20

A31

A32

Black Overprint

1929-30 *Perf. 12x11½, 15x14*

300	A31	4c on 25c pink ('30)	.75	.75
		Never hinged	1.15	
301	A31	4c on 60c dp blue	1.40	1.40
		Never hinged	2.10	
a.		Perf. 15x14	4.75	4.75
		Never hinged	7.25	
302	A31	10c on 25c pink	1.50	1.50
		Never hinged	2.25	
303	A31	12c on 25c pink	1.40	1.40
		Never hinged	2.10	
304	A31	15c on 25c pink	1.40	1.40
		Never hinged	2.10	
305	A31	20c on 25c pink	2.50	2.40
		Never hinged	3.75	
306	A31	40c on 1.10e yel brn	5.00	4.75
		Never hinged	7.50	
		Nos. 300-306 (7)	13.95	13.60

Black or Red Overprint

1930 *Perf. 14*

Without Imprint at Foot

307	A32	4c orange	.90	.70
		Never hinged	1.35	
308	A32	5c dp brown	3.00	2.75
		Never hinged	4.50	
309	A32	10c vermilion	1.50	1.10
		Never hinged	2.25	
310	A32	15c black (R)	1.50	1.10
		Never hinged	2.25	
311	A32	40c brt green	1.40	.90
		Never hinged	2.10	
312	A32	80c violet	15.00	12.00
		Never hinged	22.50	
313	A32	1.60e dk blue	4.00	1.75
		Never hinged	6.00	
		Nos. 307-313 (7)	27.30	20.30

Black or Red Overprint

1930-31 *Perf. 12x11½*

With Imprint at Foot

313A	A64	4c orange	.55	.50
		Never hinged	.85	
313B	A64	5c black brown ('31)	4.00	3.25
		Never hinged	6.00	
313C	A64	6c red brown ('31)	.40	.30
		Never hinged	.60	
313D	A64	15c black (R)	.95	.70
		Never hinged	1.45	
313E	A64	16c deep blue ('31)	2.75	1.90
		Never hinged	4.25	
313F	A64	32c deep green	3.25	2.25
		Never hinged	5.00	
313G	A64	40c bright green ('31)	1.50	.75
		Never hinged		
313H	A64	48c dull pink ('31)	3.50	3.00
		Never hinged	5.25	
313I	A64	50c bister ('31)	4.75	3.50
		Never hinged	7.25	

313J	A64	50c red brown ('31)	4.75	3.50
		Never hinged	7.25	
313K	A64	64c brown rose ('31)	9.00	5.00
		Never hinged	16.00	
313L	A64	75c carmine rose ('31)	4.75	3.50
		Never hinged	7.25	
313M	A64	80c dk grn ('31)	4.75	3.00
		Never hinged	7.25	
313N	A64	1e brn lake	40.00	27.50
		Never hinged	60.00	
313O	A64	1.25e dk blue	2.75	2.25
		Never hinged	4.25	
		Nos. 313A-313O (15)	87.65	60.90

The original stamps (Portugal Nos. 496A-496R) were printed at the Lisbon Mint from new plates produced from the original dies. The paper is whiter than the paper used for earlier Ceres stamps. The gum is white.

POSTAGE DUE STAMPS

Portugal Nos. J7-J13 Overprinted in Black — D2

1904 **Unwmk.** *Perf. 12*

J1	D2	5r brown	1.25	1.10
J2	D2	10r orange	1.40	1.10
J3	D2	20r lilac	2.25	1.10
J4	D2	30r gray green	2.25	1.75
a.		Double overprint		
J5	D2	40r gray violet	4.00	2.40
J6	D2	50r carmine	6.75	4.50
J7	D2	100r dull blue	8.50	8.25
		Nos. J1-J7 (7)	26.40	20.20

Same Overprinted in Carmine or Green (Portugal Nos. J14-J20)

1911

J8	D2	5r brown	.75	.65
J9	D2	10r orange	.75	.65
J10	D2	20r lilac	.95	.85
J11	D2	30r gray green	.95	.85
J12	D2	40r gray violet	1.50	1.10
J13	D2	50r carmine (G)	7.75	7.50
J14	D2	100r dull blue	2.75	2.75
		Nos. J8-J14 (7)	15.40	14.35

Portugal Nos. J21-J27 Overprinted in Black — D3

1918

J15	D3	½c brown	.75	.75
a.		Inverted overprint	6.00	
b.		Double overprint	6.00	
J16	D3	1c orange	.75	.75
a.		Inverted overprint	6.00	
b.		Double overprint	6.00	
J17	D3	2c red lilac	.95	.85
a.		Inverted overprint	4.00	
b.		Double overprint	6.00	
J18	D3	3c green	.75	.75
a.		Inverted overprint	6.00	
b.		Double overprint	6.00	
J19	D3	4c gray	.75	.75
a.		Inverted overprint	6.00	
b.		Double overprint	6.00	
J20	D3	5c rose	.75	.75
a.		Inverted overprint	6.00	
J21	D3	10c dark blue	.75	.75
		Nos. J15-J21 (7)	5.45	5.35

Stamps and Type of Portugal Postage Dues, 1921-27, Overprinted in Black

1922-24 *Perf. 11½x12*

J30	D3	½c gray green ('23)	.35	.35
J31	D3	1c gray green ('23)	.55	.45
J32	D3	2c gray green ('23)	.55	.45
J33	D3	3c gray green ('24)	.90	.45
J34	D3	8c gray green ('24)	.90	.45
J35	D3	10c gray green ('24)	.90	.45
J36	D3	12c gray green ('24)	.90	.45
J37	D3	16c gray green ('24)	.95	.45
J38	D3	20c gray green ('24)	.95	.45
J39	D3	24c gray green ('24)	.95	.45
J40	D3	32c gray green ('24)	.95	.45

J41	D3	36c gray green	.95	.60
J42	D3	40c gray green ('24)	.95	.60
J43	D3	48c gray green ('24)	.95	.60
J44	D3	50c gray green	.95	.60
J45	D3	60c gray green	1.30	.70
J46	D3	72c gray green	1.50	.70
J47	D3	80c gray green ('24)	5.00	4.25
J48	D3	1.20e gray green	5.75	4.75
		Nos. J30-J48 (19)	26.40	17.65

NEWSPAPER STAMPS

Newspaper Stamps of Portugal, Nos. P1, P1a, Overprinted Types c & d in Black or Red and

N3

Perf. 12½, 13½ (#P4)

1876-88 **Unwmk.**

P1	N1	2½r (c) olive	13.00	5.50
a.		Inverted overprint		
b.		Perf 13½	8.00	3.50
P2	N1	2½r (d) olive ('82)	5.75	1.90
a.		Inverted overprint	—	
b.		Double overprint	—	
c.		Perf 13½	3.00	1.00
d.		2½r emerald green	3.00	1.00
e.		As "d," perf 13½	3.00	1.00
f.		As "d," perf 11½	20.00	3.00
g.		As "d," ribbed paper	3.00	1.00
P3	N3	2r black ('85)	6.00	3.00
a.		Inverted overprint		
b.		Double overprint, one inverted		
c.		Perf 13½	3.00	1.50
P4	N1	2½r (d) bister ('82)	5.75	1.90
a.		Double overprint	9.00	
b.		Perf 11½	20.00	3.00
c.		Perf 13½, ribbed paper	3.00	1.00
d.		Perf 11½, enamel paper	3.00	1.00
P5	N3	2r black (R) ('88)	19.00	16.00
a.		Perf 13½	10.00	6.00
		Nos. P1-P5 (5)	49.50	28.30

Reprints of the newspaper stamps have the same papers, gum and perforations as reprints of the regular issues. Value $2 each.

PARCEL POST STAMPS

Portugal Nos. Q1-Q17 Ovptd. in Black or Red

1921-22 **Unwmk.** *Perf. 12*

Q1	PP1	1c lilac brown	.50	.45
a.		Inverted overprint	6.00	
Q2	PP1	2c orange	.50	.45
a.		Inverted overprint	6.00	
Q3	PP1	5c light brown	.50	.45
a.		Inverted overprint	6.00	
b.		Double overprint	6.00	
Q4	PP1	10c red brown	.75	.45
a.		Inverted overprint	6.00	
b.		Double overprint	6.00	
Q5	PP1	20c gray blue	.75	.45
a.		Inverted overprint	6.00	
b.		Double overprint	6.00	
Q6	PP1	40c carmine	.75	.45
a.		Double overprint	8.00	
Q7	PP1	50c black (R)	1.00	*1.90*
Q8	PP1	60c black (R)	1.00	*1.90*
Q9	PP1	70c gray brown	2.50	1.25
a.		Double overprint	6.00	
Q10	PP1	80c ultra	2.50	1.25
Q11	PP1	90c light violet	2.50	1.25
Q12	PP1	1e light green	2.50	1.25
Q13	PP1	2e pale lilac	5.00	3.50
Q14	PP1	3e olive	10.00	3.75
Q15	PP1	4e ultra	12.00	3.75
Q16	PP1	5e gray	12.00	7.25
Q17	PP1	10e chocolate	50.00	25.00
		Nos. Q1-Q17 (17)	104.75	54.75

POSTAL TAX STAMPS

These stamps represent a special fee for the delivery of postal matter on certain days in the year. The money derived from their sale is applied to works of public charity.

Nos. 128 and 157
Overprinted in
Carmine

1911-13   Unwmk.   Perf. 14x15
RA1   A29 10r dark green   1.50   1.10

The 20r of this type was for use on telegrams. Value $2.25 unused, $1.90 used.

Perf. 15x14
RA2   A64 1c deep green   5.00   3.75

The 2c of this type was for use on telegrams. Value $7.00 unused, $5.00 used.

Portugal No. RA4
Overprinted in
Black

1915   Perf. 12
RA3   PT2 1c carmine   .65   .35

The 2c of this type was for use on telegrams. Value $1.10 unused, 85c used.

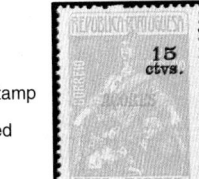

Postal Tax Stamp
of 1915
Surcharged

1924
RA4   PT2 15c on 1c rose   1.10   .90

The 30c on 2c of this type was for use on telegrams. Value $3.00 unused, $1.90 used.

Comrades of the Great War Issue

Postal Tax
Stamps of
Portugal,
1925,
Overprinted

1925, Apr. 8   Perf. 11
RA5   PT3 10c brown   1.10   1.10
RA6   PT3 10c green   1.10   1.10
RA7   PT3 10c rose   1.10   1.10
RA8   PT3 10c ultra   1.10   1.10
      Nos. RA5-RA8 (4)   4.40   4.40

The use of Nos. RA5-RA11 in addition to the regular postage was compulsory on certain days. If the tax represented by these stamps was not prepaid, it was collected by means of Postal Tax Due Stamps.

Pombal Issue
Common Design Types

1925   Perf. 12½
RA9   CD28 20c dp grn & blk   1.10   1.10
RA10 CD29 20c dp grn & blk   1.10   1.10
RA11 CD30 20c dp grn & blk   1.10   1.10
      Nos. RA9-RA11 (3)   3.30   3.30

POSTAL TAX DUE STAMPS

Portugal No. RAJ1
Ovptd. in Black

1925, Apr. 8   Unwmk.   Perf. 11x11½
RAJ1   PTD1 20c brown orange   1.10   .95
      See note after No. RA8.

Pombal Issue
Common Design Types

1925, May 8   Perf. 12½
RAJ2   CD28 40c dp grn & blk   1.10   2.00
RAJ3   CD29 40c dp grn & blk   1.10   2.00
RAJ4   CD30 40c dp grn & blk   1.10   2.00
      Nos. RAJ2-RAJ4 (3)   3.30   6.00
      See note after No. RA8.

BAHAMAS

bə-'hä-mə

LOCATION — A group of about 700 islands and 2,000 rocks in the West Indies, off the coast of Florida. Only 30 islands are inhabited.
GOVT. — British Colony
AREA — 5,353 sq. mi.
POP. — 209,505 (1980)
CAPITAL — Nassau

The principal island, on which the capital is located, is New Providence.

12 Pence = 1 Shilling
20 Shillings = 1 Pound

> **Catalogue values for unused stamps in this country are for Never Hinged items, beginning with Scott 130.**

PRE-STAMP POSTAL MARKINGS

Crowned Circle handstamp type III is pictured in the Crowned Circle Handstamps and Great Britain Used Abroad section.

Nassau

1846-58
A1   III "Bahamas" crowned circle handstamp in red,
      on cover   2,850.

This handstamp, in black, was used from 1899-1935 denoting payment of postage for official mail.

STAMPS OF GREAT BRITAIN USED IN BAHAMAS

Numeral cancellation type A is pictured in the Crowned Circle Handstamps and Great Britain Used Abroad section.

1858-60

A05 (Nassau)
A2   A 1p rose red (#20)   2,850.
A3   A 2p blue (#29, P8)   1,650.
  a.   Plate 7   1,650.
A4   A 4p rose (#26)   575.
A5   A 6p lilac (#27)   450.
A6   A 1sh green (#28)   2,850.

Values for unused stamps are for examples with original gum as defined in the catalogue introduction. Very fine examples of Nos. 2-26 will have perforations touching the design or frameline on at least one side due to the narrow spacing of the stamps on the plates. Stamps with perfs clear of the design or framelines on all four sides are extremely scarce and will command higher prices.

Pen cancellations usually indicate revenue use. Such stamps sell for much less than postally canceled examples. Beware of stamps with revenue or pen cancellations removed and forged postal cancellations added.

Queen Victoria
A1   A2

1859-60   Unwmk.   Engr.   Imperf.
1   A1 1p dull lake, thin
             paper ('60)   75.00   1,900.
  a. 1p reddish lake, thick
         paper   6,000.   2,850.
  b. 1p brownish lake, thick
         paper   6,000.   2,850.
      On cover   17,500.
  c. As "b," thin paper   325.

Most unused examples of No. 1 are remainders, and false cancellations are plentiful.
Stamps with pen cancellations may be postally used on inter-island mail. Certificates of authenticity are recommended.

1861   Rough Perf. 14 to 16
2   A1 1p lake   925.00   425.00
  a. Clean-cut perf. ('60) 7,250.   950.
3   A2 4p dull rose   1,800.   500.
  a. Imperf. between, pair 37,500.
4   A2 6p gray lilac   5,500.   750.
  a. Pale lilac   4,250.   650.

No. 2 exists perf 11 to 12½. This is a trial perforation by Perkins, Bacon and was not sent to the colony. Value, $2,850.

1862   Perf. 11½, 12
5   A1 1p lake   1,250.   225.
  a. Pair, imperf. between 6,250.
  b. 1p carmine lake   1,900.   325.
  c. Perf. 11½x11 or 12x11 2,850.   1,200.
  d. As "b," perf. 11½x11 or
         12x11   2,600.   1,100.
6   A2 4p dull rose   4,500.   500.
  a. Perf. 11½x11 or 12x11 24,500. 1,400.
7   A2 6p gray violet   13,500. 625.
  a. Perf. 11½x11 or 12x11 24,500. 2,500.

No. 5a was not issued in the Bahamas. It is unique and faulty.

Perf. 13
8   A1 1p brown lake   950.   160.
  a. 1p carmine lake   1,150.   200.
9   A2 4p rose   3,500.   475.
10   A2 6p gray violet   4,250.   600.
  a. 6p dull violet   3,500.   575.

Queen Victoria — A3

Engr., Typo. (A3)
1863-65   Wmk. 1   Perf. 12½
11   A1 1p lake   140.00 90.00
  a. 1p brown lake   120.00 85.00
  b. 1p rose lake   160.00 95.00
  c. 1p rose red   70.00 55.00
  d. 1p red   75.00 55.00
12   A1 1p vermilion   90.00 57.50
13   A2 4p rose   375.00 75.00
  a. 4p rose lake   575.00 100.00
  b. 4p bright rose   375.00 75.00
14   A2 6p dk violet   200.00 85.00
  a. 6p violet   325.00 115.00
  b. 6p rose lilac   8,500. 3,500.
  c. 6p lilac   475.00 90.00
15   A3 1sh green ('65)   3,250. 375.00

For surcharge see No. 26.

1863-81   Engr., Typo. (A3)   Perf. 14
16   A1 1p vermilion   70.00 20.00
17   A1 1p car lake (anil.) 1,500.
18   A2 4p rose   475.00 50.00
  a. 4p deep rose ('76)   550.00 50.00
  b. 4p dull rose   1,900. 50.00
19   A3 1sh green ('80)   10.00 10.00
  a. 1sh dark green   350.00 50.00

Some examples of No. 16 show a light aniline appearance and care should be taken not to confuse these with No. 17. All known used examples of No. 17 bear fiscal cancels.

Engr., Typo. (A3)
1882-98   Wmk. 2
20   A1 1p vermilion   575.00 75.00
21   A2 4p rose   1,500. 75.00
22   A3 1sh rose   50.00 18.00
23   A3 1sh blue grn ('98)   45.00 37.50

Perf. 12
24   A1 1p vermilion   60.00 22.50
25   A2 4p rose   700.00 60.00

No. 14a Surcharged in
Black

1883   Engr.   Wmk. 1   Perf. 12½
26   A2 4p on 6p violet   725.   500.
  a. Inverted surcharge   25,000. 12,000.

The surcharge, being handstamped, is found in various positions. Counterfeit overprints exist.

Queen   Queen's
Victoria — A5   Staircase — A6

1884-90   Typo.   Wmk. 2   Perf. 14
27   A5 1p carmine rose   9.00   3.25
  a. 1p pale rose   95.00   16.00
  b. 1p car (aniline)   4.00   8.50
28   A5 2½p ultra   12.50   3.00
  a. 2½p dull blue   95.00   22.50
  b. 2½p bright blue   55.00   9.50
29   A5 4p yellow   12.50   5.00
30   A5 6p violet   7.50   37.50
31   A5 5sh olive green   85.00   95.00
32   A5 £1 brown   350.00 275.00
      Revenue cancellation   55.00
      Nos. 27-32 (6)   476.50 418.75

Cleaned fiscally used examples of No. 32 are often found with forged postmarks of small post offices added, especially dated "AU 29 94."

1901-03   Engr.   Wmk. 1
33   A6 1p carmine & blk   15.00   4.00
34   A6 5p org & blk ('03) 11.00   66.00
35   A6 2sh ultra & blk ('03) 35.00 65.00
36   A6 3sh green & blk ('03) 50.00 75.00
      Nos. 33-36 (4)   111.00 210.00
      Set, overprinted "SPECI-
      MEN"   165.00

See Nos. 48, 58-62, 71, 78, 81-82.

Edward VII   George V
A7   A8

1902   Wmk. 2   Typo.
37   A7 1p carmine rose   2.00   3.25
38   A7 2½p ultra   8.50   1.75
39   A7 4p orange   20.00   77.50
  a. 4p yellow ('10)   30.00   90.00
40   A7 6p bister brn   5.00   30.00
41   A7 1sh gray blk & car 26.00   65.00
  a. 1sh brownish gray & car-
        mine ('07)   28.00   65.00

42 A7 5sh violet & ultra 85.00 110.00
43 A7 £1 green & blk 325.00 425.00
Nos. 37-43 (7) 471.50 712.50
Set, overprinted "SPECI-MEN" 350.00

Beware of forged postmarks, especially dated "2 MAR 10."

1906-11 **Wmk. 3**
44 A7 ½p green 6.25 4.00
Overprinted "SPECIMEN" 70.00
45 A7 1p car rose 32.50 1.75
46 A7 2½p ultra ('07) 32.50 32.50
47 A7 6p bister brn ('11) 30.00 60.00
Nos. 44-47 (4) 101.25 98.25

1911-19 **Engr.**
48 A6 1p red & gray blk ('16) 6.00 3.25
a. 1p carmine & black ('11) 23.00 3.50
b. 1p carmine & gray black ('19) 10.00 7.50

For overprints see Nos. B1-B2.

1912-19 **Typo.**
49 A8 ½p green 1.00 12.50
a. ½p yellow green 3.25 19.00
50 A8 1p car rose (aniline) 4.50 .45
b. 1p deep rose 10.00 3.00
c. 1p rose 14.00 3.75
d. Inverted watermark 250.00 115.00
50A A8 1p gray ('19) 3.00 3.75
51 A8 2½p ultra 6.00 35.00
a. 2½p deep blue 20.00 50.00
52 A8 4p orange 3.25 20.00
a. 4p orange yellow 7.00 25.00
53 A8 6p bister brown 2.25 7.00

Chalky Paper
54 A8 1sh black & car 2.25 11.50
a. 1sh jet black & carmine 17.50 27.50
55 A8 5sh violet & ultra 50.00 90.00
a. 5sh pale violet & deep blue 65.00 95.00
56 A8 £1 dull grn & blk 250.00 425.00
a. £1 bright green & black 225.00 375.00
Nos. 49-56 (9) 322.25 605.20
Set, overprinted "SPECI-MEN" 375.00

1917-19 **Engr.**
58 A6 3p reddish pur, *buff* 7.00 6.25
a. 3p purple, *yellow* 6.00 37.50
59 A6 3p brown & blk ('19) 2.75 5.00
60 A6 5p violet & blk 3.50 9.00
61 A6 2sh ultra & black 37.50 70.00
62 A6 3sh green & black 82.50 70.00
Nos. 58-62 (5) 133.25 160.25

Peace Commemorative Issue

King George V and Seal of Bahamas — A9

1920, Mar. 1 **Engr.** **Perf. 14**
65 A9 ½p gray green 1.25 7.00
66 A9 1p deep red 3.50 1.25
67 A9 2p gray 3.50 9.50
68 A9 3p brown 3.50 11.50
69 A9 1sh dark green 22.50 45.00
Nos. 65-69 (5) 34.25 74.25
Set, overprinted "SPECI-MEN" 225.00

Types of 1901-12
Typo., Engr. (A6)
1921-34 **Wmk. 4**
70 A8 ½p green ('24) .65 .50
71 A6 1p car & black 3.50 2.75
72 A8 1p car rose 1.25 .25
73 A8 1½p fawn ('34) 13.00 1.25
74 A8 2p gray ('27) 1.90 3.00
75 A8 2½p ultra ('22) 1.25 3.00
76 A8 3p violet, *yel* ('13) 8.25 20.00
77 A8 4p yellow ('24) 1.90 5.25
78 A6 5p red vio & gray blk ('29) 5.50 57.50
79 A8 6p bister brn ('22) 1.25 3.00
80 A8 1sh blk & red ('26) 6.00 7.25
81 A6 2sh ultra & blk ('22) 30.00 27.50
82 A8 3sh grn & blk ('24) 60.00 82.50
83 A8 5sh vio & ultra ('24) 45.00 85.00
84 A8 £1 grn & blk ('26) 215.00 425.00
Nos. 70-84 (15) 394.45 723.75
Set, ovptd/perf "SPECI-MEN" 500.00

The 3p, 1sh, 5sh and £1 are on chalky paper.

Seal of Bahamas — A10

1930, Jan. 2 **Engr.** **Perf. 12**
85 A10 1p red & black 3.50 3.50
86 A10 3p dp brown & blk 5.50 19.00
87 A10 5p dk vio & blk 5.50 19.00
88 A10 2sh ultra & black 22.50 62.50
89 A10 3sh dp green & blk 52.50 110.00
Nos. 85-89 (5) 89.50 214.00
Set, perforated "SPECI-MEN" 190.00

The dates on the stamps commemorate important events in the history of the colony. The 1st British occupation was in 1629. The Bahamas were ceded to Great Britain in 1729 and a treaty of peace was signed by that country, France and Spain.

Type of 1930 Issue
Without Dates at Top
1931-46
90 A10 2sh ultra & black 15.00 9.00
a. 2sh ultra & slate purple 30.00 37.50
b. 2sh ind bl & slate purple 115.00 50.00
c. 2sh steel bl & slate pur 18.00 3.25
91 A10 3sh dp green & blk 10.00 7.00
a. 3sh deep grn & slate purple 37.50 35.00
b. 3sh deep grn & brownish blk 10.00 6.25
Nos. 90a, 91a perf "SPECI-MEN" 92.50

Nos. 90a-91a are on thicker paper with yellowish gum, Later printings are on thinner white paper with colorless gum.
Issued: No. 90a, 91a, 7/14/31; No. 90b, 9/42; nos. 90, 91b, 4/13/43; No. 90c 6/44; No. 91, 1946.
For overprints see Nos. 126-127.

Common Design Types pictured following the introduction.

Silver Jubilee Issue
Common Design Type
1935, May 6 **Perf. 13½x14**
92 CD301 1½p car & blue 1.25 4.00
93 CD301 2½p blue & brn 6.25 10.00
94 CD301 6p ol grn & lt bl 8.75 15.00
95 CD301 1sh brt vio & ind 8.75 14.00
Nos. 92-95 (4) 25.00 43.00
Set, never hinged 35.00
Set, perforated "SPECI-MEN" 150.00

Flamingos in Flight A11

1935, May 22 **Perf. 12½**
96 A11 8p car & ultra 7.25 4.25
Never hinged 10.00
Perforated "SPECIMEN" 62.50

Coronation Issue
Common Design Type
1937, May 12 **Perf. 13½x14**
97 CD302 ½p dp green .25 .25
98 CD302 1½p brown .35 1.40
99 CD302 2½p brt ultra .55 1.40
Nos. 97-99 (3) 1.15 3.05
Set, never hinged 1.75
Set, perforated "SPECI-MEN" 110.00

George VI — A12

Sea Gardens, Nassau A13

Fort Charlotte A14

Flamingos in Flight A15

1938-46 **Typo.** **Wmk. 4** **Perf. 14**
100 A12 ½p green 1.00 1.60
Never hinged 1.60
a. ½p bluish grn 1.50 2.75
Never hinged 2.25
b. ½p myrtle grn 5.50 8.75
Never hinged 8.75
101 A12 1p carmine 7.00 4.50
Never hinged 10.00
Complete booklet, 12 #101 in blocks of 6 and 8 #102 in folded block —
101A A12 1p pale gray ('41) .50 .90
Never hinged .75
b. 1p olive gray 2.75 4.00
Never hinged 4.00
102 A12 1½p pred brown 1.25 1.60
Never hinged 1.90
a. 1½p pale red brn 5.75 3.25
Never hinged 8.00
103 A12 2p gray 14.00 5.75
Never hinged 21.00
103B A12 2p carmine ('41) .85 .85
Never hinged 1.25
c. "TWO PENCE" double 15,000.
d. 2p pale rose red 2.75 4.00
Never hinged 4.00
104 A12 2½p ultra 2.75 1.90
Never hinged 4.00
104A A12 2½p plt violet ('43) 1.10 1.60
Never hinged 1.60
b. "2½ PENNY" double 3,250. —
Never hinged 4,750.
105 A12 3p lt violet 13.00 5.00
Never hinged 19.00
105A A12 3p ultra ('43) .50 1.60
Never hinged .75
b. 3p bright ultra 3.75 6.00
Never hinged 5.50

Engr.
Perf. 12½
106 A13 4p red org & blue .80 1.25
Never hinged 1.25
107 A14 6p blue & ol grn .65 1.25
Never hinged 1.00
108 A15 8p car & ultra 7.25 3.25
Never hinged 10.50

Typo.
Perf. 14
109 A12 10p yel org ('46) 2.25 .55
Never hinged 3.25

Ordinary Paper
110 A12 1sh black & bright red 11.50 1.00
Never hinged 16.00
a. 1sh gray blk & car, thick chalky paper 18.00 7.50
Never hinged 30.00
c. 1sh black & car 16.00 8.75
Never hinged 27.50
d. 1sh brownish gray & scar, thin chalky paper 375.00 100.00
Never hinged 575.00
e. 1sh pale brownish gray & crim 12.50 1.90
Never hinged 17.50
112 A12 5sh pur & ultra 17.50 17.50
Never hinged 26.00
a. 5sh lilac & blue 22.00 27.50
Never hinged 35.00
b. 5sh lilac & blue, thick chalky paper 150.00 125.00
Never hinged 215.00
c. 5sh reddish lil & bl, thin chalky paper 1,750. 750.00
Never hinged 2,850.
d. 5sh dull mauve & dp bl 80.00 75.00
Never hinged 125.00
e. 5sh brn pur & dp brt bl 30.00 15.00
Never hinged 65.00
113 A12 £1 bl grn & blk 45.00 60.00
Never hinged 67.50
a. £1 dp gray grn & blk, thick chalky paper 225.00 175.00
Never hinged 325.00
b. £1 gray grn & blk 135.00 120.00
Never hinged 200.00
Nos. 100-113 (17) 126.90 110.10
Set, never hinged 190.00

See Nos. 154-156. For overprints see Nos. 116-125, 128-129.

No. 104 Surcharged in Black

1940, Nov. 28 **Perf. 14**
115 A12 3p on 2½p ultra 1.25 2.75
Never hinged 1.90

Stamps of 1931-42 Overprinted in Black

1942, Oct. 12 **Perf. 14, 12½, 12**
116 A12 ½p green .25 .75
Never hinged .40
a. Double overprint 1,400.
Never hinged 2,000.
117 A12 1p gray .25 .75
Never hinged .40
118 A12 1½p red brn .35 .75
Never hinged .50
119 A12 2p carmine .40 .80
Never hinged .65
120 A12 2½p ultra .40 .80
Never hinged .65
121 A12 3p ultra .25 .80
Never hinged .35
122 A13 4p red org & blue .35 1.10
Never hinged .50
123 A14 6p blue & ol grn .35 2.10
Never hinged .70
124 A15 8p car & ultra 1.10 .85
Never hinged 1.90
125 A12 1sh blk & car (#110c) 6.50 11.00
Never hinged 9.50
a. On No. 110d 6.50 5.00
Never hinged 9.50
b. On No. 110 12.00 11.00
Never hinged 19.00
126 A10 2sh dk ultra & blk 6.75 11.50
Never hinged 10.00
a. On No. 90b 13.50 27.50
Never hinged 20.00
b. On No. 90c 25.00 32.50
Never hinged 37.50
127 A10 3sh dp grn & sl pur(#91a) 6.50 8.00
Never hinged 10.00
a. On No. 91b 35.00 45.00
Never hinged 52.50
128 A12 5sh lilac & ultra (#112a) 17.50 16.00
Never hinged 30.00
a. On No. 112c 40.00 21.00
Never hinged 60.00
129 A12 £1 green & black 22.50 27.50
Never hinged 37.50
a. On No. 113a 67.50 110.00
Never hinged 100.00
Nos. 116-129 (14) 63.45 82.70
Set, never hinged 95.00
Set, perforated "SPECI-MEN" 600.00

450th anniv. of the discovery of America by Columbus.
Nos. 125, 128-129 printed on chalky and ordinary paper.
Two printings of the basic stamps were overprinted, the first with dark gum, the second with white gum.

> **Catalogue values for unused stamps in this section, from this point to the end of the section, are for Never Hinged items.**

Peace Issue
Common Design Type
Perf. 13½x14
1946, Nov. 11 **Engr.** **Wmk. 4**
130 CD303 1½p brown .25 .70
131 CD303 3p deep blue .25 .70
Set, perforated "SPECI-MEN" 95.00

Infant Welfare Clinic A16

Designs: 1p, Modern agriculture. 1½p, Sisal. 2p, Native straw work. 2½p, Modern dairying. 3p, Fishing fleet. 4p, Out island settlement. 6p, Tuna fishing. 8p, Paradise Beach. 10p, Modern hotel. 1sh, Yacht racing. 2sh, Water skiing. 3sh, Shipbuilding. 5sh, Modern transportation. 10sh, Modern salt production. £1, Parliament Building.

1948, Oct. 11		Unwmk.		Perf. 12
132	A16	½p orange	.40	1.60
133	A16	1p olive green	.40	.45
134	A16	1½p olive bister	.40	1.00
135	A16	2p vermilion	.40	.50
136	A16	2½p red brown	.85	1.00
137	A16	3p brt ultra	3.25	1.10
138	A16	4p gray black	.75	.90
139	A16	6p emerald	2.75	1.00
140	A16	8p violet	1.25	.90
141	A16	10p rose car	1.25	.75
142	A16	1sh olive brn	3.00	1.25
143	A16	2sh claret	6.25	11.00
144	A16	3sh brt blue	12.50	11.00
145	A16	5sh purple	20.00	6.50
146	A16	10sh dk gray	15.00	13.00
147	A16	£1 red orange	16.50	18.00
		Nos. 132-147 (16)	84.95	69.95

300th anniv., in 1947, of the settlement of the colony.

Silver Wedding Issue
Common Design Type
Perf. 14x14½

1948, Dec. 1		Wmk. 4		Photo.
148	CD304	1½p red brown	.25	.30

Engr.; Name Typo.
Perf. 11½x11

| 149 | CD305 | £1 gray green | 45.00 | 40.00 |

UPU Issue
Common Design Types
Engr.; Name Typo. on #151 & 152

1949, Oct. 10			Perf. 13½, 11x11½
150	CD306	2½p rose car	.45	.80
151	CD307	3p indigo	2.75	3.75
152	CD308	6p blue gray	.90	3.50
153	CD309	1sh rose car	1.50	1.50
		Nos. 150-153 (4)	5.60	9.55

George VI Type of 1938
Perf. 13½x14

1951-52		Wmk. 4		Typo.
154	A12	½p claret ('52)	1.25	3.25
a.		Wmk. 4a (error)	4,750.	
		Lightly hinged	3,250.	
b.		Crown missing in wmk.	11,500.	
		Lightly hinged	8,250.	
155	A12	2p green	1.60	1.00
156	A12	3p rose red ('52)	.75	4.00
		Nos. 154-156 (3)	3.60	8.25

SEMI-POSTAL STAMPS

No. 48 Overprinted in Red

1917, May 18		Wmk. 3		Perf. 14
B1	A6	1p car & black	.50	2.50
		Overprinted "SPECIMEN"	85.00	

Type of 1911 Overprinted in Red

1919, Jan. 1				
B2	A6	1p red & black	.40	3.25
a.		Double overprint	2,750.	
		Overprinted "SPECIMEN"	70.00	

This stamp was originally scheduled for release in 1918.

SPECIAL DELIVERY STAMPS

No. 34 Overprinted

1916		Wmk. 1		Perf. 14
E1	A6	5p orange & black	7.50	47.50
a.		Double overprint	1,000.	1,500.
b.		Inverted overprint	1,750.	1,800.
c.		Double ovpt., one invtd.	1,550.	1,750.
d.		Pair, one without overprint	35,000.	50,000.

The No. E1 overprint exists in two types. Type I (illustrated) is much scarcer. Type II shows "SPECIAL" farther right, so that the letter "I" is slightly right of the vertical line of the "E" below it.

The first printing of 600 of no. E1 was sold in Canada from May 1, 1916, and under an agreement with the Canadian Post Office were used in combination with Canadian stamps and postmarked in Canada. Values for covers showing such use (canceled before December 13, 1916): from Toronto, $750; from Montreal, $800; from Ottawa, $1,200; from Winnipeg, $2,000.

Type of Regular Issue of 1903 Overprinted

1917, July 2				Wmk. 3
E2	A6	5p orange & black	.80	11.00
		Overprinted "SPECIMEN"	82.50	

No. 60 Overprinted in Red

1918				
E3	A6	5p violet & black	.60	4.00
		Overprinted "SPECIMEN"	82.50	

WAR TAX STAMPS

Stamps of 1912-18 Overprinted

1918, Feb. 21		Wmk. 3		Perf. 14
MR1	A8	½p green	11.50	55.00
a.		Double overprint	—	—
b.		Inverted overprint	—	—
MR2	A8	1p car rose	1.25	1.00
a.		Double overprint	—	—
b.		Inverted overprint	—	—
MR3	A6	3p brown, yel	3.75	3.50
a.		Double overprint	1,400.	1,500.
b.		Inverted overprint	2,000.	2,150.
MR4	A8	1sh black & red	125.00	175.00
a.		Double overprint	—	—
		Nos. MR1-MR4 (4)	141.50	234.50

Same Overprint on No. 48a

1918, July 10				
MR5	A6	1p car & black	4.50	6.50
a.		Double overprint	2,150.	2,400.
b.		Double ovpt., one invtd.	1,100.	—
c.		Inverted overprint	1,900.	2,000.

Nos. 49-50, 54 Overprinted in Black or Red

MR6	A8	½p green	2.25	2.25
MR7	A8	1p car rose	2.25	.45
a.		Watermarked sideways	600.00	
MR8	A8	1sh black & red (R)	11.50	3.50
		Nos. MR6-MR8 (3)	16.00	6.20
		Set, overprinted "SPECIMEN"	175.00	

Nos. 58-59 Overprinted

1918-19				
MR9	A6	3p brown, yel	.90	3.25
MR10	A6	3p brown & blk ('19)	.90	3.75
		Set, overprinted "SPECIMEN"	95.00	

Nos. 49-50, 54 Overprinted in Red or Black

1919, July 14				
MR11	A8	½p green (R)	.40	1.60
MR12	A8	1p car rose	1.90	1.90
MR13	A8	1sh black & red (R)	27.50	55.00
		Nos. MR11-MR13 (3)	29.80	58.50

No. 59 Overprinted

MR14	A6	3p brown & black	1.00	10.00
		Nos. MR11-MR14, overprinted "SPECIMEN"	175.00	

BAHRAIN
bä-'rän

LOCATION — An archipelago in the Persian Gulf, including the islands of Bahrain, Muharraq, Sitra, Nebi Saleh, Kasasifeh and Arad.
GOVT. — British-protected territory
AREA — 255 sq. mi.
POP. — 350,798 (1981)
CAPITAL — Manama

12 Pies = 1 Anna
16 Annas = 1 Rupee

> Catalogue values for unused stamps in this country are for Never Hinged items, beginning with Scott 62 in the regular postage section.

Indian Postal Administration

Stamps of India, 1926-32, Overprinted in Black — a

Wmk. Multiple Stars (196)				
1933, Aug. 10				Perf. 14
1	A46	3p gray	7.50	.75
		Never hinged	13.00	
2	A47	½a green	12.00	4.00
		Never hinged	21.00	
3	A68	9p dark green	8.00	3.50
		Never hinged	14.00	
4	A48	1a dark brown	11.00	3.00
		Never hinged	19.00	
5	A69	1a3p violet	12.00	2.75
		Never hinged	21.00	
6	A60	2a vermilion	15.00	20.00
		Never hinged	26.00	
7	A51	3a blue	29.00	67.50
		Never hinged	50.00	
8	A70	3a6p deep blue	7.00	.50
		Never hinged	12.00	
9	A61	4a olive green	27.50	65.00
		Never hinged	47.50	
10	A54	8a red violet	10.00	.50
		Never hinged	18.00	
11	A55	12a claret	12.50	1.75
		Never hinged	22.00	

Overprinted in Black — b

12	A56	1r green & brown	25.00	11.00
		Never hinged	45.00	
13	A56	2r brn org & car rose	40.00	42.50
		Never hinged	70.00	
14	A56	5r dk violet & ultra	190.00	165.00
		Never hinged	325.00	
		Nos. 1-14 (14)	406.50	387.75

Stamps of India, 1926-32, Overprinted Type "a" in Black

1934				
15	A72	1a dark brown	15.00	.60
		Never hinged	26.00	
a.		Complete booklet, containing 16 #15, wmk inverted, in four blocks of 4	1,500.	
16	A51	3a carmine rose	8.50	.75
		Never hinged	15.00	
17	A52	4a olive green	9.75	.70
		Never hinged	18.00	
		Nos. 15-17 (3)	33.25	2.05

The cover of No. 15a is red and black on tan, with Mysore Sandal Soup advertisement on front.

India Nos. 138, 111, 111a Overprinted Type "a" in Black

1935-37			Perf. 13½x14, 14
18	A71	½a green	8.50	2.25
19	A49	2a vermilion	65.00	10.00
a.		Small die ('37)	100.00	.30

India Stamps of 1937 Overprinted Type "a" in Black

1938-41		Wmk. 196		Perf. 13½x14
20	A80	3p slate	12.00	8.00
		Never hinged	19.00	
21	A80	½a brown	7.00	.30
		Never hinged	9.25	
22	A80	9p green	9.00	14.00
		Never hinged	11.50	
23	A80	1a carmine	8.00	.30
		Never hinged	11.00	
24	A81	2a scarlet	4.00	6.00
		Never hinged	5.00	
26	A81	3a yel grn ('41)	8.00	12.00
		Never hinged	10.00	
27	A81	3a6p ultra	4.00	10.00
		Never hinged	6.00	
28	A81	4a dk brn ('41)	125.00	90.00
		Never hinged	190.00	
30	A81	8a bl vio ('40)	180.00	42.50
		Never hinged	200.00	
31	A81	12a car lake ('40)	105.00	55.00
		Never hinged	140.00	

Overprinted Type "b" in Black

32	A82	1r brn & slate	4.75	2.50
		Never hinged	5.75	
33	A82	2r dk brn & dk vio	12.00	11.00
		Never hinged	16.50	
34	A82	5r dp ultra & dk grn	10.00	16.00
		Never hinged	19.00	
35	A82	10r rose car & dk vio ('41)	60.00	60.00
		Never hinged	80.00	
36	A82	15r dk grn & dk brn ('41)	60.00	90.00
		Never hinged	175.00	
37	A82	25r dk vio & bl vio ('41)	95.00	110.00
		Never hinged	125.00	
		Nos. 20-37 (16)	703.75	527.60
		Set, never hinged	1,000.	

India Stamps of 1941-43 Overprinted Type "a" in Black

			1942-44	Wmk. 196	Perf. 13½x14
38	A83	3p slate		2.00	2.50
		Never hinged		3.50	
39	A83	½a rose vio ('44)		3.00	4.50
		Never hinged		0.00	
40	A83	9p lt green ('43)		11.00	24.00
		Never hinged		17.50	
41	A83	1a car rose ('44)		5.00	1.00
		Never hinged		8.50	
42	A84	1a3p bister ('43)		6.50	22.50
		Never hinged		11.00	
43	A84	1½a dk pur ('43)		4.25	8.50
		Never hinged		8.50	
45	A84	2a scarlet ('43)		4.25	2.00
		Never hinged		8.25	
46	A84	3a violet ('43)		14.00	8.00
		Never hinged		24.00	
47	A84	3½a ultra		4.50	27.50
		Never hinged		6.75	
48	A85	4a chocolate		2.00	2.50
		Never hinged		5.00	
49	A85	6a peacock blue		14.00	13.00
		Never hinged		21.00	
50	A85	8a blue vio ('43)		7.00	4.50
		Never hinged		7.50	
51	A85	12a car lake		10.00	6.50
		Never hinged		12.00	
		Nos. 38-51 (13)		88.50	127.00
		Set, never hinged		135.00	

British Postal Administration

See Oman (Muscat) for similar stamps with surcharge of new value only.

Great Britain Nos. 258 to 263, 243 and 248 Surcharged in Black — c

			1948-49	Wmk. 251	Perf. 14½x14
52	A101	½a on ½p green		.50	1.75
		Never hinged		.75	
53	A101	1a on 1p vermilion		.50	3.50
		Never hinged		.75	
54	A101	1½a on 1½p lt red brn		.50	4.75
		Never hinged		.75	
55	A101	2a on 2p lt orange		.50	.30
		Never hinged		.75	
56	A101	2½a on 2½p ultra		.75	7.00
		Never hinged		1.10	
57	A101	3a on 3p violet		.50	.30
		Never hinged		.75	
58	A102	6a on 6p rose lilac		.50	.30
		Never hinged		.75	
59	A103	1r on 1sh brown		1.25	.35
		Never hinged		1.75	

Great Britain Nos. 249A, 250 and 251A Surcharged in Black

				Wmk. 259	Perf. 14
60	A104	2r on 2sh6p yel grn		4.50	8.00
		Never hinged		7.50	
61	A104	5r on 5sh dull red		4.75	8.50
		Never hinged		7.50	
61A	A105	10r on 10sh ultra		65.00	70.00
		Never hinged		95.00	
		Nos. 52-61A (11)		79.25	104.75
		Set, never hinged		115.00	

Surcharge bars at bottom on No. 61A.
Issued: 10r, 7/4/49; others, 4/1/48.

Catalogue values for unused stamps in this section, from this point to the end of the section, are for Never Hinged items.

Silver Wedding Issue
Great Britain Nos. 267 and 268 Surcharged in Black

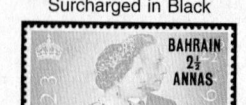

			Perf. 14½x14, 14x14½
1948, Apr. 26			**Wmk. 251**
62	A109	2½a on 2½p	.95	2.50
		Never hinged	1.45	
63	A110	15r on £1	37.50	70.00
		Never hinged	60.00	

Three bars obliterate the original denomination on No. 63.

Olympic Issue
Great Britain Nos. 271 to 274 Surcharged "BAHRAIN" and New Value in Black

1948, July 29			**Perf. 14½x14**
64	A113	2½a on 2½p brt ultra	1.40	4.75
		Never hinged	2.25	
a.		Double surcharge	3,250.	4,000.
65	A114	3a on 3p dp vio	1.10	4.25
		Never hinged	1.75	
66	A115	6a on 6p red vio	1.75	4.25
		Never hinged	2.75	
67	A116	1r on 1sh dk brn	2.75	4.25
		Never hinged	4.25	
		Nos. 64-67 (4)	7.00	17.50

A square of dots obliterates the original denomination on No. 67.

UPU Issue
Great Britain Nos. 276 to 279 Surcharged "BAHRAIN," New Value and Square of Dots in Black

1949, Oct. 10	Photo.		**Perf. 14½x14**
68	A117	2½a on 2½p brt ultra	.90	3.50
		Never hinged	1.35	
69	A118	3a on 3p brt vio	1.10	5.25
		Never hinged	1.60	
70	A119	6a on 6p red vio	1.00	4.25
		Never hinged	1.50	
71	A120	1r on 1sh brown	2.00	3.75
		Never hinged	3.00	
		Nos. 68-71 (4)	5.00	16.75

Great Britain Nos. 280-285 Surcharged Type "c" in Black

1950-51			**Wmk. 251**
72	A101	½a on ½p lt org	3.00	3.00
		Never hinged	4.50	
73	A101	1a on 1p ultra	3.50	.35
		Never hinged	5.25	
74	A101	1½a on 1½p green	3.50	17.50
		Never hinged	5.25	
75	A101	2a on 2p lt red brn	2.00	.35
		Never hinged	3.00	
76	A101	2½a on 2½p ver	3.75	16.00
		Never hinged	5.75	
77	A102	4a on 4p ultra	3.75	1.90
		Never hinged	5.75	

Great Britain Nos. 286-288 Surcharged in Black

Three types of surcharge on No. 78: Type I, "2" level with "RUPEES;" Type II, "2" raised higher than "RUPEES," 15mm between "BAHRAIN" and "2 RUPEES;" Type III, as type II, but 16mm between "BAHRAIN" and "2 RUPEES."

Perf. 11x12			**Wmk. 259**
78	A121	2r on 2sh6p green, type I ('51)	40.00	15.00
		Never hinged	52.50	
a.		2r on 2sh6p, type II ('53)	140.00	55.00
b.		2r on 2sh6p, type III ('55)	1,350.	140.00
79	A121	5r on 5sh dl red	17.50	6.50
		Never hinged	27.00	
80	A122	10r on 10sh ultra	40.00	10.50
		Never hinged	60.00	
		Nos. 72-80 (9)	117.00	71.10

Longer bars, at lower right, on No. 80.
Issued: 4a, Nov. 2, 1950; others, May 3, 1951.

Stamps of Great Britain, 1952-54, Surcharged "BAHRAIN" and New Value in Black or Dark Blue

1952-54	Wmk. 298		**Perf. 14½x14**
81	A126	½a on ½p red org ('53)	.45	.25
a.		"½" omitted	400.00	375.00
82	A126	1a on 1p ultra	.45	.25
83	A126	1½a on 1½p grn	.45	.25
84	A126	2a on 2p red brn	.45	.25

85	A127	2½a on 2½p scar	.90	1.75
86	A127	3a on 3p dk pur (Dk Bl)	1.60	.25
87	A128	4a on 4p ultra	8.25	.50
88	A129	6a on 6p lil rose	6.00	.45
89	A132	12a on 1sh3p grn	6.00	.75
90	A131	1r on 1sh6p dk bl	6.00	1.00
		Nos. 81-90 (10)	30.55	5.70

Issued: Nos. 83, 85, 12/5; Nos. 81-82, 84, 8/31/53; Nos. 87, 89-90, 11/2/53; Nos. 86, 88, 1/18/54.

BANGKOK

ˈbaŋˌkäk

LOCATION — Capital of Siam (Thailand).

Stamps were issued by Great Britain under rights obtained in the treaty of 1855. These were in use until July 1, 1885, when the stamps of Siam were designated as the only official postage stamps to be used in the kingdom.

100 Cents = 1 Dollar

STAMPS OF STRAITS SETTLEMENTS USED IN BANGKOK

Oval postmark: "BRITISH CONSULATE BANGKOK" with Royal Arms in center

1877-82			
A1	2c bister brown (#10)	475.00	
A2	4c rose (#11)	475.00	
A3	6c violet (#12)	525.00	
A4	8c orange yellow (#13)	475.00	
A5	10c on 30c claret (#22)	1,200.	
A6	10c on 30c claret (#23)	1,200.	
A8	12c blue (#14)	725.00	

Excellent counterfeits of Nos. 1-22 are plentiful.

Stamps of Straits Settlements Overprinted in Black

1882			**Wmk. 1**	**Perf. 14**
1	A2	2c brown	4,500.	1,950.
2	A2	4c rose	4,250.	1,650.
b.		Double overprint		9,750.
3	A6	5c brown violet	475.	500.
4	A2	6c violet	325.	150.
5	A3	8c yel orange	3,250.	290.
6	A7	10c slate	575.	190.
7	A3	12c blue	1,200.	600.
8	A3	24c green	900.	190.
9	A4	30c claret	57,500.	39,000.
10	A5	96c olive gray	9,750.	4,000.

See note after No. 20.

1882-83			**Wmk. 2**	
11	A2	2c brown	600.00	450.00
12	A2	2c rose ('83)	75.00	57.50
a.		Inverted overprint	19,000.	14,000.
b.		Double overprint	3,500.	3,500.
c.		Triple overprint	13,000.	
13	A2	4c rose	800.00	400.00
14	A2	4c brown ('83)	100.00	90.00
a.		Double overprint	4,500.	
15	A6	5c ultra ('83)	325.00	210.00
16	A2	6c violet ('83)	250.00	140.00
a.		Double overprint	9,000.	
17	A3	8c yel orange	200.00	82.50
a.		Inverted overprint	27,000.	15,000.
18	A7	10c slate	225.00	110.00
19	A3	12c violet brn ('83)	375.00	190.00
20	A3	24c green	7,500.	3,750.

Double overprints must have two clear impressions. Partial double overprints exist on a number of these issues. They sell for a modest premium over catalogue value depending on how much of the impression is present.

1883			**Wmk. 1**	
21	A5	2c on 32c pale red	3,500.	3,500.

On Straits Settlements No. 9

1885			**Wmk. 38**
22	A7	32c on 2a yel (B+B)	45,000.	—

BARBADOS

bär-'bā-ₔdōs

LOCATION — A West Indies island east of the Windwards
GOVT. — British Colony
AREA — 166 sq. mi.
POP. — 270,500 (1981)
CAPITAL — Bridgetown

4 Farthings = 1 Penny
12 Pence = 1 Shilling
20 Shillings = 1 Pound
100 Cents = 1 Dollar (1950)

Catalogue values for unused stamps in this country are for Never Hinged items, beginning with Scott 207 in the regular postage section, and Scott J1 in the postage due section.

Watermarks

Wmk. 5 — Small Star   Wmk. 6 — Large Star

PRE-STAMP POSTAL MARKINGS

Crowned Circle handstamp type I is pictured in the Crowned Circle Handstamps and Great Britain Used Abroad section.

1849

A1	I	"Barbados" crowned circle handstamp in red, on cover		525.00
a.		Used with 1p stamp paying local postage, #A1 the overseas postage		4,000.

This handstamp was used 2/17/93 to 3/15/93 as a ½p stamp, 1/23/96 to 5/4/96 as a ¼p stamp. Value $105.

Values for unused stamps are for examples with original gum as defined in the catalogue introduction. Very fine examples of Nos. 10-42a, 44-59a will have perforations touching the design on at least one side due to the narrow spacing of the stamps on the plates and imperfect perforation methods. Stamps with perfs clear of the design on all four sides are extremely scarce and will command higher prices.

Britannia
A1   A2

1852-55   Unwmk.   Engr.   Imperf.
Blued Paper

1	A1	(½p) deep green	150.00	375.00
a.		(½p) yellow green	9,000.	800.00
2	A1	(1p) dark blue	40.00	80.00
		On cover		300.00
		Pair, on cover		500.00
a.		(1p) blue	65.00	225.00
		On cover		400.00
3	A1	(2p) slate blue	30.00	
a.		(2p) grayish slate	315.00	1,375.
b.		As "a," vert. half used as 1p on cover		9,000.
c.		(2p) deep slate	275.00	
4	A1	(4p) brown red ('55)	125.00	325.00
		Nos. 1-4 (4)	345.00	

No. 3, 3c were not placed in use. No. 3c differs from No. 3a in the thickness and color of the gum which is yellowish and blotchy, as well as in shade. Beware of color changelings of Nos. 2-3 that may resemble No. 3a. Certificates of authenticity are required for Nos. 3a and 3b.
Use of No. 3b was authorized from 8/4-9/21/1854.

1855-58   White Paper

5	A1	(½p) deep green ('58)	190.00	230.00
a.		(½p) yellow green ('57)	600.00	125.00
6	A1	(1p) blue	90.00	70.00
a.		(1p) pale blue	170.00	80.00

It is believed that the (4p) brownish red on white paper exists only as No. 17b.

1859

8	A2	6p rose red	850.00	140.00
a.		6p deep rose red	850.00	210.00
9	A2	1sh black	260.00	85.00
a.		1sh brownish black	290.00	125.00

Pin-perf. 14

10	A1	(½p) pale yel grn	2,900.	500.00
11	A1	(1p) blue	2,400.	175.00
a.		1p deep blue	2,650.	195.00

Pin-perf. 12½

12	A1	(½p) pale yel grn	9,500.	800.00
12A	A1	(1p) blue	—	1,725.

Pin-perf. 14x12½

12B	A1	(½p) pale yel grn		8,500.

1861   Clean-Cut Perf. 14 to 16

13	A1	(½p) dark blue grn	190.00	21.00
14	A1	(1p) pale blue	800.00	85.00
a.		(1p) blue	925.00	90.00
b.		Half used as ½p on cover		—

Rough Perf. 14 to 16

15	A1	(½p) green	30.00	47.50
a.		(½p) blue green	62.50	85.00
b.		Imperf., pair	800.00	
c.		(½p) deep green	37.50	47.50
16	A1	(1p) blue	75.00	4.25
a.		Diagonal half used as ½p on cover		—
b.		Imperf., pair	850.00	650.00
c.		(1p) deep blue	75.00	4.25
17	A1	(4p) rose red	160.00	75.00
a.		(4p) brown red	190.00	80.00
b.		As "a," imperf., pair	1,700.	
c.		(4p) rose red, imperf., pair	1,150.	
d.		(4p) lake rose	190.00	100.00
e.		As "d," imperf pair	1,800.	
18	A1	(4p) vermilion	350.00	105.00
a.		Imperf., pair	1,575.	
19	A2	6p rose red	400.00	24.00
a.		6p orange red ('64)	180.00	32.50
20	A2	6p orange ver	160.00	34.00
a.		6p vermilion	180.00	30.00
b.		Imperf., pair	800.00	1,100.
c.		6p orange ('70)	200.00	52.50

21	A2	1sh brownish black	77.50	10.50
a.		1sh black	75.00	10.50
b.		Horiz. pair, imperf. btwn.	9,500.	
c.		1sh blue (error)	20,000.	

No. 21c was never placed in use. All examples are pen-marked (some have been removed) and have clipped perfs on one or more sides.
Use of No. 14b, 16a was authorized from 4/63-11/66. Only two full covers are known with bisected 1p stamps. The bisected stamps (Nos. 14b, 16a, 33a, 51b) are typically found on fragments or partial covers.

Perf. 11 to 13

22	A1	(½p) deep green	16,000.	
23	A1	(1p) blue	2,500.	

Nos. 22 and 23 were never placed in use.

1870   Wmk. 6   Rough Perf. 14 to 16

24	A1	(½p) deep green	180.00	10.00
a.		Imperf., pair (#24)	1,200.	
b.		(½p) yellow green	240.00	52.50
25	A1	(1p) blue	2,600.	67.50
a.		Imperf., pair	3,000.	
b.		1p blue, blue	4,250.	135.00
26	A1	(4p) dull red	1,675.	125.00
27	A2	6p vermilion	1,050.	90.00
28	A2	1sh black	475.00	21.00

1871   Wmk. 5

29	A1	(1p) blue	190.00	4.25
30	A1	(4p) rose red	1,375.	67.50
31	A2	6p vermilion	750.00	26.00
32	A2	1sh black	275.00	16.75

1872   Clean-Cut Perf. 14½ to 16

33	A1	(1p) blue	350.00	3.25
a.		Diagonal half used as ½p on cover		—
34	A2	6p vermilion	1,000.	90.00
35	A2	1sh black	200.00	17.00

Perf. 11 to 13x14½ to 16

36	A1	(½p) blue green	400.00	67.50
37	A1	(4p) vermilion	850.00	125.00

1873   Perf. 14

38	A2	3p claret	375.00	140.00

Wmk. 6
Clean-Cut Perf. 14½ to 16

39	A1	(½p) blue green	475.00	27.50
40	A1	(4p) rose red	1,475.	265.00
41	A2	6p vermilion	950.00	95.00
a.		Imperf., pair	105.00	1,750.
42	A2	1sh black	170.00	22.50
a.		Horiz. pair, imperf. btwn.	9,500.	

No. 41 perf 11 to 12 was prepared, but not issued. Value, $10,000.

Britannia — A3

1873   Wmk. 5   Perf. 15½x15

43	A3	5sh dull rose	1,200.	375.00
		Handstamped "SPECIMEN"	375.00	

For surcharged bisects see Nos. 57-59.

1874   Wmk. 6   Perf. 14

44	A2	½p blue green	57.50	16.00
45	A2	1p blue	137.50	5.00

Clean-Cut Perf. 14½ to 16

45A	A2	1p blue		20,000.

1875   Wmk. 1   Perf. 12½

46	A2	½p yellow green	90.00	8.50
47	A2	4p scarlet	350.00	27.50
48	A2	6p orange	750.00	80.00
a.		6p bright yellow	1,150.	105.00
49	A2	1sh purple	575.00	5.00
		Nos. 46-49 (4)	1,765.	121.00

1875-78   Perf. 14

50	A2	½p yel green ('76)	24.00	1.00
51	A2	1p ultramarine	135.00	2.25
a.		Half used as ½p on cover		1,350.
b.		1p gray blue	135.00	1.60
c.		Watermarked sideways		1,000.
52	A2	3p violet ('78)	170.00	15.00
53	A2	4p rose red	160.00	15.00
a.		4p scarlet	240.00	4.50
b.		As "a," perf. 14x12½	9,000.	
54	A2	4p lake	575.00	4.50
55	A2	6p chrome yel	160.00	2.40
a.		6p yellow, wmkd. sideways	400.00	11.00
56	A2	1sh purple ('76)	170.00	8.50
a.		1sh violet	7,750.	45.00
b.		1sh dull mauve	575.00	5.75
c.		Half used as ½p on cover		—

Nos. 48, 49, 55, 56 have the watermark sideways.
No. 53b was never placed in use.

A mint example of the one shilling aniline violet (Scott No. 56a) sold for the equivalent of U.S. $15,340 in a Singapore auction in 2003.

A4   A5

Large Surcharge, ("1" 7mm High, "D" 2¾mm High)

1878   Wmk. 5   Perf. 15½x15
Slanting Serif

57	A4	1p on half of 5sh	6,250.	850.00
a.		Unsevered pair	27,500.	2,750.
b.		Unsevered horiz. pair, #57 + 58		5,500.
d.		Unsevered horiz. pair, #57 + 58, imperf. between		42,500.
e.		Unsevered horiz. pair, #57 + 59	42,500.	9,000.
f.		No period after "D"	18,750.	2,250.

Straight Serif

58	A4	1p on half of 5sh	7,500.	1,050.
a.		Unsevered pair		4,750.

Small Surcharge, ("1" 6mm, "D" 2½mm High)

59	A5	1p on half of 5sh	9,500.	1,175.
a.		Unsevered pair	37,500.	5,250.

On Nos. 57, 58 and 59 the surcharge is found reading upwards or downwards.
The perforation, which divides the stamp into halves, measures 11½ to 13.
The old denomination has been cut off the bottom of the stamps.

Queen Victoria — A6

1882-85   Typo.   Wmk. 2   Perf. 14

60	A6	½p green	31.50	2.25
a.		½p dull green	30.00	2.25
61	A6	1p carmine rose	52.50	1.35
a.		1p rose	90.00	2.75
b.		Half used as ½p on cover		1,800.
62	A6	2½p dull blue	145.00	1.70
a.		2½p ultramarine	125.00	1.70
63	A6	3p magenta	8.50	30.00
a.		3p lilac	125.00	50.00
64	A6	4p slate	375.00	4.75
65	A6	4p brown ('85)	16.00	2.25
a.		4p pale brown ('85)	31.50	5.25
66	A6	6p olive gray	85.00	52.50
67	A6	1sh orange brown	32.50	24.00
68	A6	5sh bister	180.00	215.00
		Nos. 60-68 (9)	926.00	333.80

No. 65 Surcharged in
Black

1892

69	A6	½p on 4p brown	2.75	6.50
a.		Without hyphen	21.00	40.00
b.		Double surcharge, one albino	—	
c.		Double surch., red & black	950.00	1,275.
d.		As "c," without hyphen	3,750.	4,250.
e.		Surcharged "PENNY HALF"	400.00	240.00

A8   Badge of Colony — A9

1892-1903   Wmk. 2

70	A8	1f sl & car ('96)	2.75	.25
71	A8	½p green	2.75	.25
72	A8	1p carmine rose	5.50	.25
73	A8	2p sl & org ('99)	10.50	1.25
74	A8	2½p ultramarine	20.00	.25
75	A8	5p olive brn	8.00	5.25
76	A8	6p vio & car	18.50	3.00
77	A8	8p org & ultra	4.50	32.50
78	A8	10p bl grn & car	9.50	10.00
79	A8	2sh6p slate & org	55.00	70.00
80	A8	2sh6p pur & grn ('03)	160.00	325.00
		Nos. 70-80 (11)	297.00	448.00
		Set, ovptd. "SPECIMEN"	300.00	

See Nos. 90-101. For surcharge see No B1.

Victoria Jubilee Issue

1897   Wmk. 1

81	A9	1f gray & car	9.50	.75
82	A9	½p gray green	9.50	.75
83	A9	1p carmine rose	10.50	.75
84	A9	2½p ultra	15.00	1.00
85	A9	5p dk olive brn	34.00	21.50
86	A9	6p vio & car	45.00	27.50
87	A9	8p org & ultra	24.00	28.50
88	A9	10p bl grn & car	70.00	62.50
89	A9	2sh6p slate & org	100.00	65.00
		Nos. 81-89 (9)	317.50	208.25
		Set, ovptd. "SPECIMEN"	240.00	

Bluish Paper

81a	A9	1f gray & car	32.50	35.00
82a	A9	½p gray green	32.50	35.00
83a	A9	1p carmine rose	44.00	47.50
84a	A9	2½p ultra	45.00	52.50
85a	A9	5p dk olive brn	260.00	300.00
86a	A9	6p vio & car	150.00	165.00
87a	A9	8p org & ultra	160.00	175.00
88a	A9	10p bl grn & car	215.00	275.00
89a	A9	2sh6p slate & org	150.00	150.00
		Nos. 81a-89a (9)	1,089.	1,235.

Badge Type of 1892-1903

1904-10   Wmk. 3

90	A8	1f gray & car	13.75	3.25
91	A8	1f brown ('09)	10.75	.35
92	A8	½p green	27.50	.25
a.		½p blue green ('09)	27.50	1.75
93	A8	1p carmine rose	27.50	.25
94	A8	1p carmine ('09)	27.50	.25
95	A8	2p gray ('09)	10.00	21.00
96	A8	2½p ultramarine	28.50	.35
a.		2½p bright blue ('10)	60.00	11.00
97	A8	6p vio & car	32.50	32.50
98	A8	6p dl vio & vio ('10)	22.50	35.00
99	A8	8p org & ultra	70.00	135.00
100	A8	1sh blk, grn ('09)	17.00	18.00
101	A8	2sh6p pur & green	70.00	160.00
		Nos. 90-101 (12)	357.50	406.20

Nelson Centenary Issue

Lord Nelson
Monument — A10

1906   Engr.   Wmk. 1

102	A10	1f gray & black	17.00	2.50
103	A10	½p green & black	12.00	.40
104	A10	1p car & black	15.00	.25
105	A10	2p org & black	2.75	5.50
106	A10	2½p ultra & black	4.50	1.50
107	A10	6p lilac & black	22.50	30.00
108	A10	1sh rose & black	26.00	62.50
		Nos. 102-108 (7)	99.75	102.65

See Nos. 110-112.

The "Olive
Blossom"
A11

1906, Aug. 15   Wmk. 3

109	A11	1p blk, green & blue	18.00	.30

Tercentenary of the 1st British landing.

Nelson Type of 1906

1907, July 6   Wmk. 3

110	A10	1f gray & black	6.25	10.00
111	A10	2p org & black	32.50	47.50
112	A10	2½p ultra & black	10.00	50.00
a.		2½p indigo & black	825.00	1,000.
		Nos. 110-112 (3)	48.75	107.50

A12   A13

1912   Typo.

116	A12	¼p brown	1.90	1.90
117	A12	½p green	4.75	.25
a.		Booklet pane of 6		
118	A12	1p carmine	12.00	.25
a.		1p scarlet	45.00	4.25
b.		Booklet pane of 6		
119	A12	2p gray	7.00	21.00
120	A12	2½p ultramarine	1.90	.75
121	A13	3p violet, yel	2.25	17.50
122	A13	4p blk & scar, yel	4.50	25.00
123	A13	6p vio & red vio	15.00	15.00
124	A14	1sh black, green	14.00	25.00
125	A14	2sh vio & ultra, bl	65.00	70.00
126	A14	3sh grn & violet	115.00	130.00
		Nos. 116-126 (11)	243.30	306.65

King
George V — A14

Seal of the
Colony — A15

1916-18   Engr.

127	A15	¼p brown	.90	.50
128	A15	½p green	3.00	.25
129	A15	1p red	3.00	.25
130	A15	2p gray	12.75	37.50
131	A15	2½p ultramarine	6.50	3.75
132	A15	3p violet, yel	9.50	14.75
a.		3p deep purple, yel, thick paper	45.00	65.00
133	A15	4p red, yel	1.35	17.50
134	A15	4p red & black ('18)	1.00	4.50

135	A15	6p claret	10.50	8.00
136	A15	1sh black, green	12.75	13.50
137	A15	2sh violet, blue	20.00	9.25
138	A15	3sh dark violet	75.00	180.00
139	A15	3sh dk vio & grn ('18)	30.00	115.00
a.		3sh bright violet & green ('18)	300.00	450.00
		Nos. 127-139 (13)	186.25	404.75

Nos. 134 and 139 are from a re-engraved die. The central medallion is not surrounded by a line and there are various other small alterations.

Victory Issue

Victory

A16   A17

1920, Sept. 9   Wmk. 3

140	A16	¼p bister & black	.35	.85
141	A16	½p yel green & blk	1.05	.25
a.		Booklet pane of 2		
142	A16	1p org red & blk	5.00	.25
a.		Booklet pane of 2		
143	A16	2p gray & black	3.25	17.00
144	A16	2½p ultra & dk bl	3.50	28.50
145	A16	3p red lilac & blk	3.75	8.00
146	A16	4p grn grn & blk	4.00	8.75
147	A16	6p orange & blk	5.00	24.00
148	A17	1sh yel green & blk	20.00	52.50
149	A17	2sh brown & blk	52.50	80.00
150	A17	3sh green & blk	57.50	100.00
		Set, ovptd. "SPECIMEN"	300.00	

1921, Aug. 22   Wmk. 4

151	A16	1p orange red & blk	21.00	.35
		Nos. 140-151 (12)	177.70	320.45

A18   A19

1921-24   Wmk. 4

152	A18	¼p brown	.30	.25
		Never hinged	.50	
153	A18	½p green	1.90	1.00
		Never hinged	3.00	
154	A18	1p carmine	1.00	.25
		Never hinged	1.75	
155	A18	2p gray	2.00	.25
		Never hinged	3.50	
156	A18	2½p ultramarine	1.90	10.00
		Never hinged	3.00	
158	A18	6p claret	4.35	7.50
		Never hinged	7.00	
159	A18	1sh blk, emer ('24)	60.00	160.00
		Never hinged	100.00	
160	A18	2sh dk vio, blue	12.50	24.00
		Never hinged	20.00	
161	A18	3sh dark violet	25.00	90.00
		Never hinged	37.50	

Wmk. 3

162	A18	3p violet, yel	2.50	10.00
		Never hinged	4.00	
163	A18	4p red, yel	2.25	25.00
		Never hinged	3.50	
164	A18	1sh black, green	7.00	24.00
		Never hinged	11.00	
		Nos. 152-164 (12)	120.70	352.25
		Set, ovptd. "SPECIMEN"	215.00	

1925-35   Wmk. 4   Perf. 14

165	A19	¼p brown	.30	.25
		Never hinged	.50	
166	A19	½p green	.65	.25
		Never hinged	1.00	
a.		Perf. 13½x12½ ('32)	9.50	.25
		Never hinged	18.00	
b.		Booklet pane of 10		
167	A19	1p carmine	.65	.25
		Never hinged	1.00	
a.		Perf. 13½x12½ ('32)	10.50	.60
		Never hinged	19.00	
b.		Booklet pane of 10		
168	A19	1p org, perf. 13½x12½ ('32)	6.50	1.25
		Never hinged	10.00	
a.		Booklet pane of 6		
b.		Perf. 14	17.50	4.00
		Never hinged	27.50	
169	A19	2p gray	.80	4.00
		Never hinged	1.20	

170	A19	2½p ultramarine	.60	1.00
		Never hinged	1.00	
a.		Perf. 13½x12½ ('32)	19.00	8.50
		Never hinged	30.00	
171	A19	3p vio brn, yel	1.25	.55
		Never hinged	2.00	
172	A19	3p red brn, yel ('35)	7.50	7.50
		Never hinged	12.00	
173	A19	4p red, yel	.95	1.25
		Never hinged	1.50	
174	A19	6p claret	1.25	1.10
		Never hinged	2.00	
175	A19	1sh blk, emerald	2.50	8.50
		Never hinged	4.00	
a.		Perf. 13½x12½ ('32)	75.00	50.00
		Never hinged	130.00	
176	A19	1sh brn blk, yel grn ('32)	6.00	12.50
		Never hinged	9.00	
177	A19	2sh violet, bl	8.75	9.00
		Never hinged	14.00	
178	A19	2sh6p car, blue ('32)	25.00	45.00
		Never hinged	52.50	
179	A19	3sh dark violet	14.00	21.00
		Never hinged	22.50	
		Nos. 165-179 (15)	84.20	113.40

Charles I
and
George
V — A20

1927, Feb. 17   Perf. 12½

180	A20	1p carmine lake	1.25	.90
		Never hinged	2.25	
		Overprinted "SPECIMEN"	5.00	

Tercentenary of the settlement of Barbados.

Common Design Types
pictured following the introduction.

Silver Jubilee Issue
Common Design Type

1935, May 6   Perf. 11x12

186	CD301	1p car & dk bl	2.25	.35
a.		Damaged turret	600.00	350.00
187	CD301	1½p blk & ultra	5.50	9.75
a.		Damaged turret	700.00	
188	CD301	2½p ultra & brn	3.00	7.00
a.		Bird by turret	325.00	400.00
189	CD301	1sh brn vio & ind	25.00	37.50
a.		Kite and horizontal log	750.00	800.00
		Nos. 186-189 (4)	35.75	54.60
		Set, never hinged	45.00	

Coronation Issue
Common Design Type

1937, May 14   Perf. 13½x14

190	CD302	1p carmine	.25	.25
191	CD302	1½p brown	.40	.80
192	CD302	2½p bright ultra	.45	.90
		Nos. 190-192 (3)	1.10	1.95
		Set, never hinged	2.50	
		Set, perf "SPECIMEN"	95.00	

A21

1938-47   Perf. 13-14 & Compound

193	A21	½p green	5.00	.25
		Never hinged	7.00	
b.		Perf. 14	55.00	1.50
		Never hinged	75.00	
c.		Booklet pane of 10		
193A	A21	½p bister ('42)	.25	.45
		Never hinged	.25	
194	A21	1p carmine	14.00	.25
		Never hinged	20.00	
b.		Perf. 13½x13	195.00	5.00
		Never hinged	300.00	
c.		Booklet pane of 10		
194A	A21	1p green ('42)	.25	.25
		Never hinged	.25	
d.		Perf. 13½x13	3.50	1.00
		Never hinged	5.25	
195	A21	1½p red orange	.25	.65
		Never hinged	.25	
c.		Perf. 14	4.75	.80
		Never hinged	7.00	
d.		Booklet pane of 6		
195A	A21	2p rose lake ('41)	.90	3.75
		Never hinged	1.35	
195B	A21	2p bright rose red ('43)	.50	1.00
		Never hinged	.85	
e.		Perf. 14	.50	2.10
		Never hinged	.85	
196	A21	2½p ultramarine	.65	.95
		Never hinged	1.05	

197	A21	3p brown	.65	*3.50*
		Never hinged	1.10	
b.		Perf. 14	.25	.75
		Never hinged	.35	
197A	A21	3p deep bl ('47)	.65	*2.50*
		Never hinged	1.05	
198	A21	4p black	.25	.25
		Never hinged	.35	
a.		Perf. 14	.65	*6.50*
		Never hinged	1.05	
199	A21	6p violet	.65	.65
		Never hinged	1.00	
199A	A21	8p red vio ('46)	.45	*3.25*
		Never hinged	.60	
200	A21	1sh brn olive	1.40	.25
		Never hinged	2.25	
a.		1sh olive green	12.50	*3.00*
		Never hinged	17.00	
201	A21	2sh6p brown vio	7.00	*2.25*
		Never hinged	9.50	
201A	A21	5sh indigo ('41)	6.50	*11.00*
		Never hinged	9.50	
		Nos. 193-201A (16)	39.35	31.20
		Set, never hinged	57.50	
		Set, perf "SPECIMEN"	450.00	

For surcharge see No. 209.

Kings Charles I, George VI Assembly Chamber and Mace
A22

Perf. 13½x14

			Wmk. 4	
1939, June 27		Engr.		
202	A22	½p deep green	2.15	2.00
		Never hinged	3.25	
203	A22	1p scarlet	2.15	1.35
		Never hinged	3.25	
204	A22	1½p deep orange	2.25	.65
		Never hinged	3.50	
205	A22	2½p ultramarine	3.25	9.00
		Never hinged	5.25	
206	A22	3p yellow brown	3.25	6.00
		Never hinged	5.25	
		Nos. 202-206 (5)	13.05	*19.00*
		Set, never hinged	21.00	
		Set, perf "SPECIMEN"	190.00	

Tercentenary of the General Assembly.

Catalogue values for unused stamps in this section, from this point to the end of the section, are for Never Hinged items.

Peace Issue
Common Design Type

1946, Sept. 18				
207	CD303	1½p deep orange	.25	.55
208	CD303	3p brown	.25	.55

Nos. 195e, 195B, Surcharged in Black

1947, Apr. 21			**Perf. 14**	
209	A21	1p on 2p brt rose red	2.40	5.25
b.		Perf. 13½x13	3.25	*6.50*
c.		As "b.," double surcharge	*3,250.*	

Silver Wedding Issue
Common Design Types
Perf. 14x14½

			Wmk. 4	
1948, Nov. 24		Photo.		
210	CD304	1½p orange	.35	.55

Engraved; Name Typographed
Perf. 11½x11

211	CD305	5sh dark blue	18.00	12.50

UPU Issue
Common Design Types

1949, Oct. 10			**Perf. 13½, 11x11½**	
212	CD306	1½p red orange	.55	2.15
213	CD307	3p indigo	2.75	7.50
214	CD308	4p gray	.55	3.50
215	CD309	1sh olive	.55	1.00
		Nos. 212-215 (4)	4.40	14.15

Dover
Fort — A23

Admiral Nelson Statue — A24

Designs: 2c, Sugar cane breeding. 3c, Public buildings. 6c, Casting net. 8c, Intercolonial schooner. 12c, Flying Fish. 24c, Old Main Guard Garrison. 48c, Cathedral. 60c, Careenage. $1.20, Map. $2.40, Great Seal, 1660.

Perf. 11x11½ (A23), 13x13½ (A24)

			Wmk. 4	
1950, May 1		Engr.		
216	A23	1c slate	.35	4.75
217	A23	2c emerald	.25	3.25
218	A23	3c slate & brown	1.25	4.25
219	A24	4c carmine	.30	.40
220	A23	6c blue	.35	2.50
221	A23	8c choc & blue	1.60	4.00
222	A23	12c olive & aqua	1.25	1.85
223	A23	24c gray & red	1.25	.55
224	A24	48c violet	11.00	9.00
225	A23	60c brn car & bl grn	14.00	13.75
226	A24	$1.20 olive & car	14.00	5.50
227	A23	$2.40 gray	27.50	45.00
		Nos. 216-227 (12)	73.10	94.80

University Issue
Common Design Types

1951, Feb. 16			**Perf. 14x14½**	
228	CD310	3c turq bl & choc	.60	.30
229	CD311	12c ol brn & turq bl	1.25	1.25

Stamp of 1852
A25

Perf. 13½

			Wmk. 4	Engr.
1952, Apr. 15				
230	A25	3c slate bl & dp grn	.40	.30
231	A25	4c rose pink & bl	.50	1.00
232	A25	12c emer & slate bl	.50	1.00
233	A25	24c gray blk & red brn	1.00	.80
		Nos. 230-233 (4)	2.40	3.10

Centenary of Barbados postage stamps.

SEMI-POSTAL STAMP

No. 73 Surcharged in Red

Perf. 14

			Typo.	Wmk. 2
1907, Jan. 25				
B1	A8	1p on 2p sl & org	3.75	10.00
a.		No period after 1d	55.00	*92.50*
b.		Inverted surcharge	2.00	*7.50*
c.		Inverted surcharge, no period after 1d	47.50	*105.00*
d.		Double surcharge	925.00	*1,000.*
e.		Dbl. surch., both invtd.	925.00	
f.		Dbl. surch., one invtd.	*1,200.*	
g.		Vert. pair, one normal, one surcharge double		*1,200.*
h.		Pair with surcharges tête-bêche	1,500.	

POSTAGE DUE STAMPS

Catalogue values for unused stamps in this section are for Never Hinged items.

D1

1934-47	**Typo.**	**Wmk. 4**	**Perf. 14**	
J1	D1	½p green ('35)	1.60	8.50
		On cover		75.00
J2	D1	1p black	1.60	1.75
		On cover		75.00
a.		Half used as ½p on cover		2,500.
J3	D1	3p dk car rose ('47)	26.00	23.00
		On cover		200.00
		Nos. J1-J3 (3)	29.20	33.25
		Set, perf. "SPECIMEN"	100.00	

A 2nd die of the 1p was introduced in 1947.

Use of #J2a was authorized from Mar. 1934 through Feb. 1935. Some examples have "½d" written on the bisect in black or red ink.

On cover values are for properly franked commercial covers. Philatelic usages also exist and sell for less.

1950				
J4	D1	1c green	3.75	*32.50*
		On cover		75.00
J5	D1	2c black	7.00	*17.00*
		On cover		75.00
J6	D1	6c carmine rose	16.00	*17.50*
		On cover		150.00
		Nos. J4-J6 (3)	26.75	*67.00*

Values are for 1953 chalky paper printing. Values on ordinary paper, unused $30, used $65.

Wmk. 4a (error)

J4a	D1	1c green		425.00
J5a	D1	2c black		800.00
J6a	D1	6c carmine rose		175.00
		Nos. J4a-J6a (3)		1,400.

WAR TAX STAMP

No. 118 Overprinted

1917		**Wmk. 3**	**Perf. 14**	
MR1	A12	1p carmine	.55	.25
a.		Imperf., pair	2,500.	

BARBUDA

bär-'büd-ə

LOCATION — Northernmost of the Leeward Islands, West Indies
GOVT. — Dependency of Antigua
AREA — 63 sq. mi.
POP. — 1,000 (estimated)
See Antigua.

12 Pence = 1 Shilling

Leeward Islands
Stamps of 1912-22
Ovptd. in Black or Red

BARBUDA

Die II

For description of dies I and II, see Dies of British Colonial Stamps in the catalogue introduction.

1922, July 13   Wmk. 4   Perf. 14

1	A5	½p green	1.75	13.00
2	A5	1p rose red	1.75	13.00
3	A5	2p gray	1.75	10.50
4	A5	2½p ultramarine	1.75	11.00
5	A5	6p vio & red vio	2.40	23.00
6	A5	2sh vio & ultra, *bl*	16.00	62.50
7	A5	3sh green & violet	35.00	100.00
8	A5	4sh blk & scar (R)	42.50	100.00

Wmk. 3

9	A5	3p violet, *yel*	2.10	17.00
10	A5	1sh blk, *emer* (R)	1.90	12.00
11	A5	5sh grn & red, *yel*	87.50	200.00
		Nos. 1-11 (11)	194.40	562.00
		Set, never hinged	400.00	
		Set, overprinted "SPECI- MEN"	260.00	

Beware of forgeries, especially used examples dated June 1, 1923.
Covers: Values for commercial covers with the 1p, 2p or 3p stamps begin at about $50. Other stamps are very scarce to rare on cover.

BASUTOLAND

bə-'sü-tə-ˌland

LOCATION — An enclave in the state of South Africa
GOVT. — British Crown Colony
AREA — 11,716 sq. mi.
POP. — 733,000 (est. 1964)
CAPITAL — Maseru

The Colony, a former independent native state, was annexed to the Cape Colony in 1871. In 1883 control was transferred directly to the British Crown. Stamps of the Cape of Good Hope were used from 1871 to 1910 and those of the Union of South Africa from 1910 to 1933.

12 Pence = 1 Shilling

Catalogue values for unused stamps in this country are for Never Hinged items, beginning with Scott 29 in the regular postage section and Scott J1 in the postage due section.

George V — A1

Crocodile and River Scene

Perf. 12½

1933, Dec. 1   Engr.   Wmk. 4

1	A1	½p emerald	1.50	2.40
		On cover		8.00
2	A1	1p carmine	1.25	1.75
		On cover		6.00

3	A1	2p red violet	1.50	1.10
		On cover		6.00
4	A1	3p ultra	1.25	1.40
		On cover		8.00
5	A1	4p slate	2.75	9.50
		On cover		30.00
6	A1	6p yellow	3.00	2.40
		On cover		9.00
7	A1	1sh red orange	3.50	5.00
		On cover		24.00
8	A1	2sh6p dk brown	35.00	57.50
		On cover		200.00
9	A1	5sh violet	67.50	87.50
		On cover		275.00
10	A1	10sh olive green	200.00	200.00
		On cover		500.00
		Nos. 1-10 (10)	317.25	368.55
		Set, never hinged	700.00	

Common Design Types pictured following the introduction.

Silver Jubilee Issue
Common Design Type

1935, May 4   Perf. 13½x14

11	CD301	1p car & blue	.85	3.00
12	CD301	2p gray blk & ultra	1.25	3.00
13	CD301	3p blue & brown	5.50	7.00
14	CD301	6p brt vio & indigo	5.75	7.00
		Nos. 11-14 (4)	13.35	20.00
		Set, never hinged	20.00	

Coronation Issue
Common Design Type

1937, May 12   Perf. 13½x14

15	CD302	1p carmine	.25	1.00
16	CD302	2p rose violet	.45	1.00
17	CD302	3p bright ultra	.55	1.00
		Nos. 15-17 (3)	1.25	3.00
		Set, never hinged	1.75	

George VI — A2

1938, Apr. 1   Perf. 12½

18	A2	½p emerald	.25	1.25
19	A2	1p rose car	.75	.85
20	A2	1½p light blue	.40	.65
21	A2	2p rose lilac	.30	.80
22	A2	3p ultra	.30	1.50
23	A2	4p gray	1.50	4.25
24	A2	6p yel ocher	2.00	1.75
25	A2	1sh red orange	2.00	1.40
26	A2	2sh6p black brown	11.50	9.00
27	A2	5sh violet	25.00	10.00
28	A2	10sh olive green	25.00	22.50
		Nos. 18-28 (11)	69.00	53.95
		Set, never hinged	110.00	

Catalogue values for unused stamps in this section, from this point to the end of the section, are for Never Hinged items.

Peace Issue

South Africa Nos. 100-102 Overprinted

Basic stamps inscribed alternately in English and Afrikaans.

1945, Dec. 3   Wmk. 201   Perf. 14

29	A42	1p rose pink & choc, pair	.70	.90
a.		Single, English	.25	.25
b.		Single, Afrikaans	.25	.25
30	A43	2p vio & slate blue, pair	.70	.75
a.		Single, English	.25	.25
b.		Single, Afrikaans	.25	.25
31	A43	3p ultra & dp ultra, pair	.70	.95
a.		Single, English	.25	.25
b.		Single, Afrikaans	.25	.25
		Nos. 29-31 (3)	2.10	2.60

King George VI — A3

King George VI and Queen Elizabeth A4

Princess Margaret Rose and Princess Elizabeth A5

Royal British Family A6

Perf. 12½

1947, Feb. 17   Wmk. 4   Engr.

35	A3	1p red	.25	.25
36	A4	2p green	.25	.25
37	A5	3p ultra	.25	.25
38	A6	1sh dark violet	.25	.25
		Nos. 35-38 (4)	1.00	1.00

Visit of the British Royal Family, Mar. 11-12, 1947.

Silver Wedding Issue
Common Design Types

1948, Dec. 1   Photo.   Perf. 14x14½

39	CD304	1½p brt ultra	.30	.25

Engr.; Name Typo.
Perf. 11½

40	CD305	10sh dk brown olive	50.00	50.00

UPU Issue
Common Design Types

Engr.; Name Typo. on 3p, 6p
Perf. 13½, 11x11½

1949, Oct. 10   Wmk. 4

41	CD306	1½p blue	.50	1.50
42	CD307	3p indigo	2.25	2.00
43	CD308	6p orange yel	1.25	5.00
44	CD309	1sh red brown	.75	1.50
		Nos. 41-44 (4)	4.75	10.00

POSTAGE DUE STAMPS

Catalogue values for all unused stamps in this section are for Never Hinged items.

D1

1933-52   Wmk. 4   Typo.   Perf. 14
Chalky Paper

J1	D1	1p dark red ('51)	2.00	8.00
		On cover		80.00
a.		1p carmine, ordinary paper	3.00	13.00
		On cover		80.00
b.		1p dk car, ordinary paper ('38)	50.00	60.00
		On cover		150.00
c.		Wmk. 4a (error)	140.00	
d.		Wmk. 4, crown missing (error)	350.00	
J2	D1	2p lt violet ('52)	.40	25.00
		On cover		80.00
a.		2p lt violet, ordinary paper	9.50	24.00
		On cover		80.00

---

b.	Wmk. 4a (error)		150.00
c.	Wmk. 4, crown missing (error)		375.00

For surcharge see No. J7 in *Scott Standard Postage Stamp Catalogue*, Vol. 1.
On cover values are for properly franked commercial covers. Philatelic usages also exist and sell for less.

OFFICIAL STAMPS

Nos. 1-3 and 6 Overprinted "OFFICIAL"

1934   Wmk. 4   Engr.   Perf. 12½

O1	A1	½p emerald	14,000.	7,500.
O2	A1	1p carmine	5,000.	3,750.
O3	A1	2p red violet	5,500.	1,250.
O4	A1	6p yellow	14,000.	5,000.

Counterfeits exist.

BATUM

bä-'tūm

LOCATION — A seaport on the Black Sea.

Batum is the capital of Adzhar, a territory which, in 1921, became an autonomous republic of the Georgian Soviet Socialist Republic.

Stamps of Batum were issued under the administration of British forces which occupied Batum and environs between December, 1918, and July, 1920, following the Treaty of Versailles.

100 Kopecks = 1 Ruble

Counterfeits of Nos. 1-65 abound.

A1

1919		Unwmk. Litho.	Imperf.	
1	A1	5k green	8.00	24.00
		On cover		500.00
2	A1	10k ultramarine	8.00	24.00
		On cover		500.00
3	A1	50k yellow	4.75	9.00
		On cover		350.00
4	A1	1r red brown	6.50	8.50
		On cover		375.00
a.		Printed on both sides		50.00
5	A1	3r violet	11.50	20.00
		On cover		625.00
6	A1	5r brown	12.00	35.00
		On cover		675.00
		Nos. 1-6 (6)	50.75	120.50

For overprints and surcharges see Nos. 13-20, 51-65.

Nos. 7-12, 21-50: numbers in parentheses are those of the basic Russian stamps.

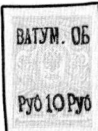

Russian Stamps of 1909-17 Surcharged

1919		On Stamps of 1917		
7		10r on 1k orange (#119)	75.00	75.00
		On cover		750.00
8		10r on 3k red (#121)	26.50	32.50
		On cover		700.00

On Stamp of 1909-12
Perf. 14x14½

| 9 | | 10r on 5k claret (#77) | 950.00 | 950.00 |
| | | On cover | | |

On Stamp of 1917

10		10r on 10k on 7k light blue (#117)	975.00	725.00
		On cover		
		Nos. 7-10 (4)	2,026.	1,782.

Russian Stamps of 1909-13 Surcharged

1919				
11		35k on 4k carmine (#76)	1,950.	6,000.
		Unused on complete postcard	5,000.	
		On complete postcard		—
12		35k on 4k dull red (#91)	6,500.	13,000.
		Unused on complete postcard	11,500.	
		On complete postcard		—

This surcharge was intended for postal cards. A few cards which bore adhesive stamps were also surcharged.

Values are for stamps off card and without gum.

Type of 1919 Issue Overprinted

1919		Unwmk.	Imperf.	
13	A1	5k green	22.50	15.00
		On cover		400.00
14	A1	10k dark blue	15.00	17.50
		On cover		400.00
15	A1	25k orange	22.50	17.50
		On cover		350.00
16	A1	1r pale blue	5.50	17.50
		On cover		325.00
17	A1	2r salmon pink	1.25	7.00
		On cover		325.00
18	A1	3r violet	1.25	7.00
		On cover		325.00
19	A1	5r brown	1.50	7.00
		On cover		325.00
20	A1	7r dull red	5.00	9.50
		On cover		350.00
a.		"CCUPATION"	475.00	475.00
		Nos. 13-20 (8)	74.50	98.00

Russian Stamps of 1909-17 Surcharged in Various Colors

10r & 50r   15r

On Stamps of 1917

1919-20		Imperf.	
21	10r on 3k red (#121)	25.00	27.50
a.	Inverted overprint	500.00	
22	15r on 1k org (R) (#119)	60.00	100.00
23	15r on 1k org (Bk) (#119)	100.00	150.00
a.	Inverted overprint	750.00	750.00
24	15r on 1k org (V) (#119)	75.00	95.00
25	50r on 1k org (#119)	975.00	675.00
26	50r on 2k green (#120)	975.00	1,100.

On Stamps of 1909-17
Perf. 14x14½

27	50r on 2k green (#74)	975.00	850.00
28	50r on 3k red (#75)	1,700.	2,500.
29	50r on 4k car (#76)	1,500.	1,500.
30	50r on 5k claret (#77)	975.00	975.00
31	50r on 10k dk blue (R) (#79)	2,250.	3,500.
32	50r on 15k red brn & blue (#81)	700.00	850.00

Surcharged

On Stamps of 1909-17

33	25r on 5k cl (Bk) (#77)	100.00	150.00
34	25r on 5k cl (Bl) (#77)	100.00	150.00
a.	Inverted overprint	250.00	
35	25r on 10k on 7k lt blue (Bk) (#117)	150.00	175.00
36	25r on 10k on 7k lt blue (Bl) (#117)	100.00	87.50
37	25r on 20k on 14k bl & rose (Bk) (#118)	95.00	150.00
38	25r on 20k on 14k bl & rose (Bl) (#118)	200.00	110.00
39	25r on 25k grn & gray vio (Bk) (#83)	160.00	175.00
a.	Inverted overprint	250.00	
40	25r on 25k grn & gray vio (Bl) (#83)	100.00	135.00
41	25r on 50k vio & green (Bk) (#85a)	100.00	110.00
a.	Inverted overprint		250.00

42	25r on 50k vio & green (Bl) (#85a)	100.00	105.00
43	50r on 2k green (#74)	200.00	145.00
44	50r on 3k red (#75)	200.00	145.00
45	50r on 4k car (#76)	200.00	250.00
46	50r on 5k claret (#77)	200.00	100.00

On Stamps of 1917
Imperf

47	50r on 2k green (#120)	975.00	650.00
48	50r on 3k red (#121)	975.00	675.00
49	50r on 5k claret (#123)	1,500.	1,650.

On Stamp of 1913
Perf. 13½

| 50 | 50r on 4k dull red (Bl) (#91) | 100.00 | 95.00 |

Nos. 3, 13 and 15 Surcharged in Black or Blue

1920		Imperf.	
51	A1 25r on 5k green	75.00	100.00
52	A1 25r on 5k grn (Bl)	250.00	70.00
53	A1 25r on 25k orange	35.00	45.00
54	A1 25r on 25k org (Bl)	125.00	140.00
55	A1 50r on 50k yellow	30.00	30.00
a.	"50" cut in pieces	18.00	19.00
56	A1 50r on 50k yel (Bl)	100.00	125.00
a.	"50" cut in pieces	200.00	200.00
	Nos. 51-56 (6)	615.00	510.00

The figures of value in the surcharge on Nos. 55a and 56a were file-cut as a counterforgery measure. Typically, the "5" is cut at bottom and on the right side of the loop. The zero is shorn at top and bottom, leaving the side bars intact. Nos. 55 and 56 are from early printings, before the handstamps were cut.

The surcharges on Nos. 21-56 inclusive are handstamped and are known double, inverted, etc.

Tree Type of 1919 Overprinted Like Nos. 13-20

1920				
57	A1	1r orange brown	2.25	12.00
58	A1	2r gray blue	2.25	12.00
59	A1	3r rose	2.25	12.00
60	A1	5r black brown	2.25	12.00
61	A1	7r yellow	2.25	12.00
62	A1	10r dark green	2.25	12.00
63	A1	15r violet	2.75	17.50
64	A1	25r vermilion	2.50	16.00
65	A1	50r dark blue	2.75	20.00
		Nos. 57-65 (9)	21.50	125.50

The variety "BPITISH" occurs on Nos. 57-65. The "P" is actually a broken "R" and appears in Row 1, Pos. 19, in each sheet. Value, about $150 each.

Nos. 57-65 exist without overprint.

BECHUANALAND

ˌbech-'wä-nə-ˌland

(British Bechuanaland)

LOCATION — Southern Africa
GOVT. — A British Crown Colony, which included the area of the former Stellaland, annexed in 1895 to the Cape of Good Hope Colony.
AREA — 51,424 sq. mi.
POP. — 72,700 (1891)
CAPITAL — Vryburg

British Bechuanaland stamps were also used in Bechuanaland Protectorate until 1897.

12 Pence = 1 Shilling
20 Shillings = 1 Pound

Except for the first issue of British Bechuanaland, which was canceled in manuscript, many of the pen cancellations are fiscal cancellations.

Watermarks

Wmk. 29 — Orb   Wmk. 14 — VR in Italics

Stellaland was annexed by Great Britain in 1885 and became part of British Bechuanaland. Stamps issued by the short-lived republic from 1884-1885 are listed in Volume 6 under Stellaland.

Cape of Good Hope Stamps of 1871-85 Overprinted

British Bechuanaland

1885-87		Wmk. 1	Perf. 14	
		Black Overprint		
1	A6	4p blue ('86)	85.00	85.00
		Wmk. 2		
		Black Overprint		
3	A6	3p claret	50.00	60.00
		Red Overprint		
4	A6	½p black	30.00	35.00
a.		Overprint in lake	5,500.	10,000.
b.		Double overprint in lake & blk	900.00	1,100.
		Wmk. Anchor (16)		
		Black Overprint		
5	A6	½p black ('87)	12.00	25.00
a.		"ritish"	2,500.	2,600.
b.		Double overprint	4,250.	
6	A6	1p rose	25.00	11.00
a.		"ritish"	7,500.	4,250.
b.		Double overprint		2,200.
c.		Missing dot in first "i" of "British"	175.00	175.00
7	A6	2p bister	45.00	11.00
a.		"ritish"	9,000.	5,500.
b.		Double overprint		2,500.
c.		Missing dot in first "i" of "British"	425.00	175.00
8	A3	6p violet	175.00	47.50
a.		Missing dot in first "i" of "British"	1,250.	575.00
9	A3	1sh green ('86)	325.00	190.00
a.		"ritish"	22,500.	18,000.

There is no period after Bechuanaland on the genuine stamps.
Covers: Values for commercial covers begin at $400.

Black Ovpt. on Great Britain #111

1887		Wmk. 30		
10	A54	½p vermilion	1.50	1.50
		Handstamped "SPECIMEN"	100.00	
a.		Double overprint	2,700.	

For overprints see Bechuanaland Protectorate Nos. 51-53.

A1   A2

A3

1887   **Typo.**   **Wmk. 29**
Country Name in Black

11	A1	1p lilac	22.50	3.50
12	A1	2p lilac	100.00	2.75
a.		2p pale dull lilac	50.00	27.50
13	A1	3p lilac	8.00	7.00
a.		3p pale reddish lilac	72.50	22.50
14	A1	4p lilac	60.00	2.75
15	A1	6p lilac	72.50	3.00

Wmk. 14

16	A2	1sh green	37.50	8.50
17	A2	2sh green	60.00	47.50
18	A2	2sh6p green	72.50	72.50
19	A2	5sh green	110.00	180.00
		Pen cancellation		4.50
20	A2	10sh green	225.00	400.00
		Pen cancellation		30.00

Wmk. 29

21	A3	£1 lilac	1,100.	900.00
		Pen cancellation		47.50
22	A3	£5 lilac	4,000.	1,900.
		Pen cancellation		200.00

Nos. 11-22 handstamped "SPECIMEN"   1,050.

The corner designs and central oval differs on No. 22.
For overprints see Bechuanaland Protectorate Nos. 54-58, 60-66. For surcharges see Nos. 23-28, 30, AR2, Cape of Good Hope No. 171.
Beware of cleaned pen (fiscal) cancellations and forged postmarks on Nos. 21-22.

Nos. 11-12, 14-16 Surcharged

1888
Country Name in Black
Black Surcharge

23	A1	1p on 1p lilac	9.25	8.00
a.		Double surcharge		
24	A1	6p on 6p lilac	145.00	20.00

Red Surcharge

25	A1	2p on 2p lilac	55.00	3.75
a.		"2" with curved tail	325.00	180.00
b.		On 2p pale dull lilac (#12a)	100.00	60.00
26	A1	4p on 4p lilac	425.00	550.00

Green Surcharge

27	A1	2p on 2p lilac	4,000.	
a.		"2" with curved tail		—

Blue Surcharge

27A	A1	6p on 6p lilac	25,000.	

Wmk. 14
Black Surcharge

28	A2	1sh on 1sh green	220.00	100.00

Cape of Good Hope No.41 Overprinted in Green

1889   **Wmk. 16**

29	A4	½p black	4.75	35.00
a.		Double ovpt., one inverted	3,500.	
b.		Double ovpt., one vertical	1,200.	
c.		Pair, one stamp without ovpt.	10,000.	

Exists with "British" missing from shifted overprint.

No. 13 Surcharged in Black

1888   **Wmk. 29**

30	A1	½p on 3p lilac & blk	250.00	300.00

Stamps with errors of spelling in the surcharge are fakes.

Cape of Good Hope Nos. 43-44 Overprinted in Black, Reading Up

1891   **Wmk. 16**

31	A4	1p rose	12.00	15.00
a.		Horiz. pair, one without overprint	25,000.	
b.		"British" omitted	3,000.	—
c.		"Bechuanaland" omitted		—
32	A4	2p bister	5.50	2.75
a.		Without period	325.00	390.00

Nos. 31-32 handstamped "SPECIMEN"   150.00

See Nos. 38-39.

Stamps of Great Britain Overprinted in Black

1891-94   **Wmk. 30**

33	A40	1p lilac	7.25	1.90
34	A56	2p green & car	21.00	5.00
35	A59	4p brown & green	3.75	.80
a.		Half used as 2p on cover		3,000.
36	A62	6p violet, *rose*	7.50	2.50
37	A65	1sh green ('94)	16.00	19.50
a.		Half used as 6p on cover		—

Nos. 33-37 (5)   55.50   29.70
Nos. 33-36 handstamped "SPECIMEN"   200.00

No. 35a was used at the Palapye Post Office in Nov. 1899. No. 37a was used at the Kanye Post Office in Dec. 1904.
For surcharges see Cape of Good Hope Nos. 172, 176-177.

Cape of Good Hope Nos. 43-44 Overprinted, Reading Down

1893-95   **Wmk. 16**

38	A6	1p rose	3.50	3.00
a.		No dots over the "i"s of "British"	150.00	155.00
c.		As "a," reading up	4,000.	
d.		Pair, one without overprint		
39	A6	2p bister ('95)	10.00	3.00
a.		Double overprint	1,700.	850.00
b.		No dots over the "i"s of "British"	275.00	160.00
d.		As "b," reading up	4,500.	

The missing dot-over-i variety exists only on this issue. Nos. 38c and 39d resulted from the sheets being fed into the press upside down. Nos. 38-39 exist with "British" missing (from shifted overprint).

Cape of Good Hope No. 42 Overprinted

"BECHUANALAND" 16mm Long Overprint Lines 13mm Apart

1897

40	A6	½p light green	3.25	17.00

"BECHUANALAND" 15mm Long Overprint Lines 10½mm Apart

41	A6	½p light green	17.00	65.00

"BECHUANALAND" 15mm Long Overprint Lines 13½mm Apart

42	A6	½p light green	35.00	95.00

Nos. 40-42 (3)   55.25   177.00

Nos. 40-42 actually are issues of Bechuanaland Protectorate.

BECHUANALAND PROTECTORATE

ˌbech-ˈwä-nə-ˌland prə-ˈtek-t̬ə-ˌrət

LOCATION — In central South Africa, north of the Republic of South Africa, east of South West Africa and bounded on the north by the Caprivi Strip of South West Africa and on the east by Southern Rhodesia
GOVT. — British Protectorate
AREA — 222,000 sq. mi.
POP. — 540,400 (1964)
CAPITAL — Vryburg (to 1895), Mafeking

12 Pence = 1 Shilling
20 Shillings = 1 Pound

Catalogue values for unused stamps in this country are for Never Hinged items, beginning with Scott 137 in the regular postage section.

Additional Overprint in Black on Bechuanaland No. 10

a

b

c

1888-90   **Wmk. 30**   *Perf. 14*

51	A54(a)	½p vermilion ('90)	225.00	425.00
a.		Double overprint	1,800.	2,200.
b.		"Protectorre"		
c.		As "b," double overprint	20,000.	
52	A54(b)	½p vermilion ('88)	12.00	50.00
		Handstamped "SPECIMEN"	100.00	
a.		Double overprint	375.00	
53	A54(c)	½p vermilion ('90)	200.00	225.00
a.		Inverted overprint	87.50	110.00
b.		Double overprint	125.00	190.00
c.		As "a," double	700.00	850.00
d.		"Portectorate"		—
e.		As "a," "Portectorate"	20,000.	—

For surcharge see No. 68.

Bechuanaland Nos. 16-20 Overprinted Type "b" in Black

Wmk. 14
Country Name in Black

54	A2	1sh green	120.00	60.00
		Handstamped "SPECIMEN"	125.00	
a.		First "o" omitted	6,750.	3,750.
55	A2	2sh green	700.00	1,200.
a.		First "o" omitted	20,000.	
56	A2	2sh6p green	650.00	1,100.
a.		First "o" omitted	18,000.	
57	A2	5sh green	1,400.	2,750.
a.		First "o" omitted	25,000.	
58	A2	10sh green	5,250.	6,500.
a.		First "o" omitted	25,000.	

Bechuanaland Nos. 11-15 Ovptd. Type "b" and Srchd. in Black

1888   **Wmk. 29**
Country Name in Black

60	A1	1p on 1p lilac	17.50	16.00
a.		Short "1"	475.00	550.00
61	A1	2p on 2p lilac	37.50	20.00
a.		"2" with curved tail	900.00	550.00
63	A1	3p on 3p reddish lilac	180.00	225.00
64	A1	4p on 4p lilac	450.00	475.00
a.		Small "4"	5,500.	5,500.
65	A1	6p on 6p lilac	100.00	50.00

In #60 the "1" is 2½mm high; in #60a, 2mm.

Value Surcharged in Red

66	A1	4p on 4p lilac	120.00	50.00

Cape of Good Hope Type of 1886 Overprinted in Green

1889   **Wmk. 16**

67	A6	½p black	6.00	55.00
a.		Double overprint	600.00	800.00

No. 67 exists with "Bechuanaland" missing and with ovpt. words reversed (from shifted overprint).

Bechuanaland Protectorate No. 52 Surcharged in Black

Wmk. 30

68	A54	4p on ½p ver	40.00	6.00
		Handstamped "SPECIMEN"	150.00	
a.		Inverted surcharge		4,500.
b.		"rpence" omitted		7,000.
c.		"ourpence" omitted	12,500.	
d.		As "c," inverted surcharge		17,500.

Stamps of Great Britain 1881-87, Overprinted in Black

1897, Oct.

69	A54	½p vermilion	1.75	2.50
70	A40	1p lilac	4.50	.85
71	A56	2p green & car	9.50	4.00
72	A58	3p violet, *yel*	6.25	10.00
73	A59	4p brown & green	24.00	22.50
74	A62	6p violet, *rose*	25.00	12.50

Nos. 69-74 (6)   71.00   52.35
Set, handstamped "SPECIMEN"   250.00

For surcharges see Cape of Good Hope Nos. 167-170, 173-175.

Same on Great Britain No. 125

1902, Feb. 25

75	A54	½p blue green	1.75	4.00
		Handstamped "SPECIMEN"	37.50	

Stamps of Great Britain, 1902, Overprinted in Black

1904-12

76	A66	½p gray green ('06)	2.75	3.25
77	A66	1p car ('05)	10.00	.65
78	A66	2½p ultra	12.00	7.50
a.		Period after "P" of "Protectorate"	1,100.	1,400.
79	A74	1sh scar & grn ('12)	55.00	170.00
a.		1sh carmine & green	50.00	125.00

Nos. 76-79 (4)   79.75   181.40

Same on Great Britain No. 143
1908
80 A66 ½p pale yel green 4.25 4.00

Transvaal No. 274 overprinted "Bech-uanaland Protectorate," formerly listed as No. 81, now appears as No. AR1 in the Postal-Fiscal Stamps section.

Great Britain No. 154 Overprinted Like Nos. 76-79
1912, Sept. Wmk. 30 Perf. 15x14
82 A81 1p scarlet 3.50 .90
a. No cross on crown 175.00 87.50
b. 1p aniline scarlet ('14) 190.00 92.50

Great Britain Stamps of 1912-13 Overprinted Like Nos. 76-79
Wmk. Crown and GvR (33)
1913-24
83 A82 ½p green 1.40 2.00
84 A83 1p scarlet ('15) 3.25 .85
a. 1p carmine ('22) 30.00 3.00
85 A84 1½p red brn ('20) 7.00 3.50
86 A85 2p reddish orange (I) 13.00 4.25
a. 2p orange (I) ('21) 22.50 4.50
b. 2p orange (II) ('24) 47.50 4.00
87 A86 2½p ultra 4.00 27.50
a. 2½p blue ('15) 16.00 27.50
88 A87 3p bluish violet 6.75 13.50
89 A88 4p slate green 7.25 32.50
90 A89 6p dull violet 9.00 24.00
a. Double overprint, one albino 30.00
91 A90 1sh bister 20.00 37.50
a. 1sh bister brown ('23) 30.00 35.00
Overprinted "SPECIMEN" 85.00
Nos. 83-91 (9) 71.65 145.60

The dies of No. 86 are the same as in Great Britain 1912-13 issue.

Wmk. 34 Perf. 11x12
92 A91 2sh6p dark brown ('15) 150.00 300.00
a. 2sh6p light brown ('16) 125.00 300.00
b. 2sh6p sepia brown ('17) 150.00 260.00
c. Double overprint, one albino, on #92 350.00
d. Triple overprint, one albino, on #92b —
93 A91 5sh rose carmine ('14) 180.00 450.00
a. 5sh carmine ('19) 350.00 500.00
b. Double overprint, one albino, on #93 450.00
c. Double overprint, one albino, on #93a 525.00

Nos. 92, 93 were printed by Waterlow Bros. & Layton; Nos. 92a, 93a were printed by Thomas De La Rue & Co.

Same Overprint On Retouched Seahorses Stamps of 1919 (Great Britain Nos. 179, 180)
1920-23
94 A91 2sh6p gray brown 100.00 200.00
95 A91 5sh car rose 140.00 325.00

Nos. 94-95 measure 22.5-23mm vertically. Most examples have a small dot of color at top center, outside of frameline. Perforation holes are larger and usually are evenly spaced.

Great Britain Stamps of 1924 Overprinted like Nos. 76-79
Wmk. Crown and Block GvR Multiple (35)
1925-27 Perf. 15x14
96 A82 ½p green ('27) 1.65 2.00
97 A83 1p scarlet 2.25 1.00
99 A85 2p deep org (II) 2.50 1.25
101 A87 3p violet ('26) 5.50 25.00
102 A88 4p slate green ('26) 8.00 55.00
103 A89 6p dull violet, chalky paper 70.00 100.00
a. 6p purple, ordinary paper 55.00 57.50
104 A90 1sh bister ('26) 11.00 30.00
Nos. 96-104 (7) 100.90 214.25

George V — A11

Perf. 12½
1932, Dec. 12 Engr. Wmk. 4
105 A11 ½p green 2.75 .35
a. Horiz. pair, imperf between 27,000.
106 A11 1p carmine 1.75 .40
107 A11 2p red brown 1.75 .45
108 A11 3p ultra 4.00 4.00
109 A11 4p orange 4.00 9.00
110 A11 6p red violet 5.50 7.00
111 A11 1sh blk & ol grn 4.00 8.00
112 A11 2sh black & org 27.50 70.00
113 A11 2sh6p black & car 26.00 50.00
114 A11 3sh black & red vio 47.50 60.00
115 A11 5sh black & ultra 100.00 125.00
116 A11 10sh blk & red brown 250.00 275.00
Nos. 105-116 (12) 474.75 609.20

Common Design Types pictured following the introduction.

Silver Jubilee Issue
Common Design Type
1935, May 4 Perf. 11x12
117 CD301 1p car & blue 1.25 5.50
118 CD301 2p black & ultra 1.50 5.50
119 CD301 3p ultra & brown 3.25 6.00
120 CD301 6p brown vio & ind 7.75 6.00
Nos. 117-120 (4) 13.75 23.00
Set, never hinged 21.00

Coronation Issue
Common Design Type
1937, May 12 Perf. 13½x14
121 CD302 1p carmine .25 .50
122 CD302 2p brown .30 1.25
123 CD302 3p bright ultra .40 1.60
Nos. 121-123 (3) .95 3.35
Set, never hinged 1.75

George VI, Cattle and Baobab Tree — A12

1938, Apr. 1 Perf. 12½
124 A12 ½p green 2.00 3.50
125 A12 1p rose car .70 .65
126 A12 1½p light blue 1.25 1.25
127 A12 2p brown .60 .75
128 A12 3p ultra .75 3.00
129 A12 4p orange 1.75 4.50
130 A12 6p rose violet 3.00 3.50
131 A12 1sh blk & ol grn 3.25 8.50
133 A12 2sh6p black & car 9.00 18.00
135 A12 5sh black & ultra 22.50 27.50
136 A12 10sh black & brn 17.50 32.50
Nos. 124-136 (11) 62.30 103.65
Set, never hinged 95.00

> Catalogue values for unused stamps in this section, from this point to the end of the section, are for Never Hinged items.

Peace Issue

South Africa Nos. 100-102 Overprinted

Basic stamps inscribed alternately in English and Afrikaans.

1945, Dec. 3 Wmk. 201 Perf. 14
137 A42 1p rose pink & choc, pair .75 1.50
a. Single, English .25 .25
b. Single, Afrikaans .25 .25
138 A43 2p vio & slate blue, pair .55 1.50
a. Single, English .25 .25
b. Single, Afrikaans .25 .25
139 A43 3p ultra & dp ultra, pair .75 1.75
a. Single, English .25 .25
b. Single, Afrikaans .25 .25
Nos. 137-139 (3) 2.05 4.75

World War II victory of the Allies.

Royal Visit Issue
Types of Basutoland, 1947
Perf. 12½
1947, Feb. 17 Wmk. 4 Engr.
143 A3 1p red .25 .25
144 A4 2p green .25 .25
145 A5 3p ultra .25 .25
146 A6 1sh dark violet .25 .25
Nos. 143-146 (4) 1.00 1.00

Visit of the British Royal Family, 4/17/47.

Silver Wedding Issue
Common Design Types
1948, Dec. 1 Photo. Perf. 14x14½
147 CD304 1½p brt ultra .35 .25
Engr.; Name Typo.
Perf. 11½x11
148 CD305 10sh gray black 42.50 47.50

UPU Issue
Common Design Types
Engr.; Name Typo. on 3p and 6p
1949, Oct. 10 Perf. 13½, 11x11½
149 CD306 1½p blue .30 1.00
150 CD307 3p indigo 1.50 1.50
151 CD308 6p red lilac .80 2.75
152 CD309 1sh olive .75 2.00
Nos. 149-152 (4) 3.35 7.25

POSTAL-FISCAL STAMPS

Transvaal No. 274 Overprinted

1910, July Wmk. 3
AR1 A27 12sh6p brn org & blk 190.00 375.00

This stamp was issued for fiscal use in January 1907, but the "POSTAGE" inscription was not obliterated, and examples were accepted for postal use during 1910-11.

Bechuanaland No. 16 surcharged "£5"

1918 Wmk. 29
AR2 A1 £5 on 1sh green 18,000.

The known used examples of AR2 are all fiscally used.

South Africa No. 3 Overprinted in two lines

1922 Wmk. 177
AR3 A2 1p rose red 50.00 155.00
a. Double ovpt, one albino 160.00

POSTAGE DUE STAMPS

Postage Due Stamps of Great Britain Overprinted

On Stamp of 1914-22
1926 Wmk. 33 Perf. 14x14½
J1 D1 1p carmine 11.00 125.00
On Stamps of 1924-30
Wmk. 35
J2 D1 ½p emerald 11.00 75.00

Overprinted

J3 D1 2p black brown 11.00 100.00
Nos. J1-J3 (3) 33.00 300.00
Set, never hinged 52.50

D2

1932 Wmk. 4 Typo. Perf. 14½
J4 D2 ½p olive green 6.75 60.00
On cover 300.00
J5 D2 1p carmine rose 8.00 10.00
On cover 275.00
J6 D2 2p dull violet 10.00 55.00
On cover 300.00
b. Thick "d" 120.00
Nos. J4-J6 (3) 24.75 125.00
Set, never hinged 40.00
Set, perforated "SPECIMEN" 80.00

Chalky Paper
1958, Nov. 27
J5a D2 1p carmine 1.50 27.50
On cover 275.00
J6a D2 2p violet 1.75 22.00
On cover 300.00
c. Thick "d" 42.50

On cover values are for properly franked commercial covers. Philatelic usages also exist and sell for less.

BELGIAN CONGO

ˈbel-jən ˈkäŋ‿gō

LOCATION — Central Africa
GOVT. — Belgian colony
AREA — 902,082 sq. mi. (estimated)
POP. — 12,660,000 (1956)
CAPITAL — Léopoldville

Congo was an independent state, founded by Leopold II of Belgium, until 1908 when it was annexed to Belgium as a colony.

100 Centimes = 1 Franc

Independent State

A1   A2

King Leopold II — A3

1886   Unwmk.   Typo.   Perf. 15

1	A1	5c green	14.00	25.00
		Never hinged	30.00	
		On cover		
2	A1	10c rose	5.50	6.00
		Never hinged	9.25	
		On cover		550.00
3	A2	25c blue	55.00	45.00
		Never hinged	130.00	
		On cover		450.00
a.		25c greenish blue	55.00	45.00
		Never hinged	130.00	
		On cover		450.00
b.		25c ultramarine	80.00	—
		Never hinged	150.00	
4	A3	50c olive green	9.00	9.00
		Never hinged	13.50	
		On cover		750.00
a.		50c dark olive	27.50	25.00
		Never hinged	55.00	
5	A1	5fr lilac	400.00	325.00
		Never hinged	925.00	
		On cover		—
a.		Perf. 14	1,100.	650.00
		Never hinged		
b.		5fr deep lilac	850.00	525.00
		Never hinged	—	
c.		Imperforate	875.00	

Counterfeits exist.
Postal stationery with stamps added sell for considerably less.
For surcharge see No. Q1.

King Leopold II — A4

1887-94

6	A4	5c grn ('89)	1.00	1.25
		Never hinged	1.50	
		On cover		125.00
7	A4	10c rose ('89)	1.75	1.75
		Never hinged	2.50	
		On cover		125.00
8	A4	25c blue ('89)	1.75	1.75
		Never hinged	2.25	
		On cover		300.00
9	A4	50c reddish brown	65.00	30.00
		Never hinged	120.00	
		On cover		500.00
a.		50c deep brown	105.00	47.50
		Never hinged	190.00	
		On cover		500.00
10	A4	50c gray ('94)	4.00	22.50
		Never hinged	5.00	
		On cover		2,000.
11	A4	5fr violet	1,300.	550.00
		Never hinged	—	
		On cover		6,750.
12	A4	5fr gray ('92)	165.00	140.00
		Never hinged	250.00	
		On cover, overfranked		1,000.
		On portion of parcel wrapper		1,250.
13	A4	10fr buff ('91)	625.00	425.00
		Never hinged	950.00	
		On cover, overfranked		2,000.

The 25fr and 50fr in gray were not issued. Values, each $30., never hinged $40.
Counterfeits exist of Nos. 10-13, 25fr and 50fr, unused, used, genuine stamps with faked

---

cancels and counterfeit stamps with genuine cancels.
Covers: Postal stationery with stamps added sell for considerably less. Values for Nos. 12-13 are for overfranked covers, usually philatelic.
For surcharges see Nos. Q3-Q6.

Port Matadi — A5

River Scene on the Congo, Stanley Falls — A6

Inkissi Falls — A7

Railroad Bridge on M'pozo River — A8

Hunting Elephants A9

Bangala Chief and Wife — A10

1894-1901   Engr.   Perf. 12½ to 15

14	A5	5c pale bl & blk	19.00	19.00
		Never hinged	37.50	
		On cover		50.00
15	A5	5c red brn & blk ('95)	4.25	1.75
		Never hinged	7.50	
		On cover		25.00
16	A5	5c grn & blk ('00)	2.25	.60
		Never hinged	5.00	
		On cover		27.50
a.		Retouched	4.50	1.50
		Never hinged	13.50	
		On cover		50.00
17	A6	10c red brn & blk	19.00	19.00
		Never hinged	42.50	
		On cover		50.00
18	A6	10c grnsh bl & blk ('95)	3.50	1.90
		Never hinged	7.50	
		On cover		25.00
a.		Center inverted	3,000.	2,750.
		On cover		10,000.
19	A6	10c car & blk ('00)	4.50	1.10
		Never hinged	7.00	
		On cover		60.00
20	A7	25c yel org & blk	5.00	3.50
		Never hinged	8.75	
		On cover		25.00
21	A7	25c lt bl & blk ('00)	5.25	2.50
		Never hinged	8.75	
		On cover		12.50
a.		Redrawn frame	1,350.	775.00
22	A8	50c grn & blk	2.00	2.00
		Never hinged	3.50	
		On cover		80.00
23	A8	50c ol & blk ('00)	5.00	1.25
		Never hinged	8.75	
		On cover		60.00
24	A9	1fr lilac & blk	32.50	19.00
		Never hinged	55.00	
		On cover		375.00
a.		1fr rose lilac & black	475.00	37.50
		Never hinged	850.00	
		On cover		375.00
25	A9	1fr car & blk ('01)	400.00	9.50
		Never hinged	750.00	
		On cover		300.00
26	A10	5fr lake & blk	55.00	40.00
		Never hinged	160.00	
		On cover		200.00
a.		5fr carmine rose & black	125.00	62.50

	Never hinged	225.00	
	On cover		300.00
	Nos. 14-26 (13)	557.25	121.10

No. 16a has a small circle touching the the frameline, about 2mm from the lower right corner
The frameline has been strenghtened at the top and bottom of No. 21a. It is thicker and more regular than on No. 21.
Covers: Postal stationery with stamps added sell for considerably less. Values for Nos. 26, 26a are for overfranked covers, usually philatelic.
For overprints see Nos. 31-32, 34, 36-37, 39.

Climbing Oil Palms — A11

Congo Canoe A12

1896

27	A11	15c ocher & blk	5.00	1.25
		Never hinged	8.75	
		On cover		25.00
28	A12	40c bluish grn & blk	5.00	4.00
		Never hinged	8.75	
		On cover		30.00

For overprints see Nos. 33, 35.

Congo Village A13

River Steamer on the Congo A14

1898

29	A13	3.50fr red & blk	200.00	140.00
		Never hinged	325.00	
		On cover		—
a.		Perf. 14x12	550.00	350.00
		Never hinged	850.00	
30	A14	10fr yel grn & blk	190.00	50.00
		Never hinged	225.00	
a.		Center inverted	25,000.	
b.		Perf. 12	725.00	52.50
		Never hinged		
c.		Perf. 12x14	475.00	—
		Never hinged		
		As "c," pen canceled		21.00

Nos. 29-30 exist imperf. Value, set $850.
For overprints see Nos. 38, 40.

Belgian Congo

Overprinted

1908

31	A5	5c green & blk	8.75	8.75
		Never hinged	30.00	
		On cover		45.00
a.		Handstamped	5.50	3.25
		Never hinged	10.00	
		On cover		45.00
32	A6	10c car & blk	16.00	16.00
		Never hinged	47.50	
		On cover		45.00
a.		Handstamped	5.50	3.25
		Never hinged	10.00	
		As "a," on cover		30.00
33	A11	15c ocher & blk	8.75	8.75
		Never hinged	30.00	
		On cover		35.00
a.		Handstamped	5.50	5.50
		Never hinged	20.00	
		As "a," on cover		35.00

34	A7	25c lt blue & blk	5.75	3.25
		Never hinged	13.50	
		On cover		35.00
a.		Handstamped	12.50	5.00
		Never hinged	32.50	
b.		As "a," redrawn frame (#21a)		37.50
		Never hinged	30.00	17.50
			62.50	
c.		Double overprint (#34)	300.00	
35	A12	40c bluish grn & blk	3.25	3.25
		Never hinged	10.50	
		On cover		45.00
a.		Handstamped	16.00	9.25
		Never hinged	32.50	
		As "a," on cover		50.00
36	A8	50c olive & blk	6.25	3.25
		Never hinged	13.50	
		On cover		25.00
a.		Handstamped	8.00	5.50
		Never hinged	20.00	
		As "a," on cover		25.00
b.		As #36, inverted overprint	775.00	
37	A9	1fr car & blk	27.50	8.75
		Never hinged	75.00	
		On cover		100.00
a.		Handstamped	75.00	17.50
		Never hinged	120.00	
		As "a," on cover		85.00
38	A13	3.50fr red & blk	40.00	32.50
		Never hinged	105.00	
		On cover		125.00
a.		Handstamped	450.00	200.00
		Never hinged	825.00	
		As "a," on cover		250.00
b.		As #38, inverted overprint	750.00	
39	A10	5fr car & blk	72.50	37.50
		Never hinged	160.00	
		On cover		125.00
a.		Handstamped	150.00	80.00
		Never hinged	325.00	
		As "a," on cover		150.00
40	A14	10fr yel grn & blk	140.00	35.00
		Never hinged	310.00	
		On cover		150.00
a.		Perf. 14 ½	375.00	
		Never hinged	750.00	
b.		Handstamped	275.00	92.50
		Never hinged	550.00	
		As "a," on cover		150.00
c.		Handstamped, perf. 14 ½	575.00	325.00
		Never hinged	1,050.	
d.		As #40a, double overprint	600.00	
		Nos. 31-40 (10)	328.75	157.00

Most of the above handstamps are also found inverted and double.
There are two types of handstamped overprints, those applied in Brussels and those applied locally. There are eight types of each overprint. Values listed are the lowest for each stamp.
Covers: Values for Nos. 39, 39a, 40, 40b are for overfranked covers, usually philatelic. Counterfeits of the handstamped overprints exist.

Port Matadi A15

River Scene on the Congo, Stanley Falls — A16

Climbing Oil Palms — A17

Railroad Bridge on M'pozo River — A18

1909   Perf. 14

41	A15	5c green & blk	1.00	1.00
		Never hinged	3.75	
		On cover		22.50
42	A16	10c carmine & blk	1.00	.65
		Never hinged	3.75	
		On cover		35.00
43	A17	15c ocher & blk	37.50	20.00
		Never hinged	175.00	
		On cover		37.50
44	A18	50c olive & blk	4.25	2.75
		Never hinged	17.50	
		On cover		92.50
		Nos. 41-44 (4)	43.75	24.40

Port Matadi
A19

River Scene
on the Congo,
Stanley
Falls — A20

Climbing Oil
Palms — A21

Inkissi
Falls — A22

Congo
Canoe
A23

Railroad
Bridge on
M'pozo
River — A24

Hunting
Elephants
A25

Congo
Village
A26

Bangala Chief and
Wife — A27

River
Steamer on
the Congo
A28

1910-15	**Engr.**		**Perf. 14, 15**	
45	A19	5c green & blk	.75	.30
	Never hinged		1.75	
	On cover			10.00
46	A20	10c carmine & blk	.75	.30
	Never hinged		1.75	
	On cover			10.00
a.	10c lake & black		62.50	62.50
	Never hinged		125.00	—
47	A21	15c ocher & blk	.70	.30
	Never hinged		1.50	
	On cover			20.00

48	A21	15c grn & blk ('15)	.60	.25
	Never hinged		.95	
	On cover			10.00
a.	Booklet pane of 10		25.00	
49	A22	25c blue & blk	2.25	.60
	Never hinged		5.00	
	On cover			11.00
50	A23	40c bluish grn & blk	3.25	3.00
	Never hinged		5.00	
	On cover			20.00
51	A23	40c brn red & blk ('15)	5.50	3.25
	Never hinged		17.50	
	On cover			110.00
52	A24	50c olive & blk	5.00	2.75
	Never hinged		11.00	
	On cover			35.00
53	A24	50c brn lake & blk ('15)	9.50	3.00
	Never hinged		26.00	
	On cover			25.00
54	A25	1fr carmine & blk	4.50	4.00
	Never hinged		9.75	
	On cover			105.00
55	A25	1fr ol bis & blk ('15)	3.50	1.25
	Never hinged		11.00	
	On cover			80.00
56	A26	3fr red & blk	22.50	14.50
	Never hinged		50.00	
	On cover			100.00
57	A27	5fr carmine & blk	32.50	32.50
	Never hinged		130.00	
	On cover			100.00
58	A27	5fr ocher & blk ('15)	2.50	1.25
	Never hinged		6.25	
	On cover			75.00
59	A28	10fr green & blk	27.50	27.50
	Never hinged		90.00	
	On cover			100.00
	Nos. 45-59 (15)		121.30	94.75

Nos. 48, 51, 53, 55 and 58 exist imperforate.
Value, set $150.
Covers: Value for No. 59 is for overfranked
cover, usually philatelic.
For overprints and surcharges see Nos. 64-
76, 81-86, B5-B9.

Port Matadi
A29

Stanley Falls,
Congo
River — A30

Inkissi
Falls — A31

TEN CENTIMES.
Type I — Large white space at top of picture
and two small white spots at lower edge.
Vignette does not fill frame.
Type II — Vignette completely fills frame.

1915				
60	A29	5c green & blk	.30	.25
	Never hinged		1.00	
	On cover			6.25
a.	Booklet pane of 10		19.00	
61	A30	10c car & blk (II)	.30	.30
	Never hinged		2.00	
	On cover			6.25
a.	10c carmine & black (I)		.30	.25
	Never hinged		.95	
	On cover			6.25
d.	Booklet pane of 10 (II)		25.00	
62	A31	25c blue & blk	1.50	.50
	Never hinged		5.00	
	On cover			12.50
a.	Booklet pane of 10		125.00	
	Nos. 60-62 (3)		2.10	1.00
	Set, never hinged		8.00	

Nos. 60-62 exist imperforate. Value, set $15.
For surcharges see Nos. 77-80, 87, B1-B4.

Stamps of
1910 Issue
Surcharged
in Red or
Black

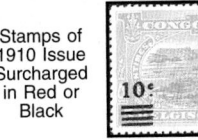

1921				
64	A23	5c on 40c bluish grn & blk (R)	.40	.40
	Never hinged		.70	
	On cover			7.50

65	A19	10c on 5c grn & blk (R)	.40	.40
	Never hinged		.70	
	On cover			6.25
66	A24	15c on 50c ol & blk (R)	.40	.40
	Never hinged		.70	
	On cover			7.50
a.	Inverted surcharge			275.00
67	A21	25c on 15c ocher & blk (R)	2.75	1.60
	Never hinged		4.25	
	On cover			25.00
68	A20	30c on 10c car & blk	.75	.75
	Never hinged		1.40	
	On cover			9.50
69	A22	50c on 25c bl & blk (R)	2.75	1.60
	Never hinged		5.25	
	On cover			15.00
	Nos. 64-69 (6)		7.45	5.15
	Set, never hinged		13.00	

The position of the new value and the bars
varies on Nos. 64 to 69.

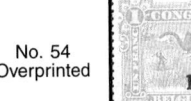

No. 54
Overprinted

1921				
70	A25	1fr carmine & blk	1.60	1.60
	Never hinged		4.00	
	On cover			110.00
a.	Double overprint		125.00	
71	A26	3fr red & blk	4.00	4.00
	Never hinged		10.00	
	On cover			100.00
72	A27	5fr carmine & blk	11.00	11.00
	Never hinged		27.50	
73	A28	10fr green & blk (R)	8.75	6.25
	Never hinged		26.00	
	Nos. 70-73 (4)		25.35	22.85
	Set, never hinged		67.50	

Belgian Surcharges

Nos. 51, 53,
60-62
Surcharged
in Black or
Red

1922				
74	A24	5c on 50c	.65	.65
	Never hinged		1.25	
	On cover			11.00
75	A29	10c on 5c (R)	.65	.50
	Never hinged		1.25	
	On cover			11.00
76	A23	25c on 40c (R)	3.75	.60
	Never hinged		9.50	
	On cover			30.00
77	A30	30c on 10c (II)	.40	.40
	Never hinged		.75	
	On cover			7.50
a.	30c on 10c (I)		.65	.35
	Never hinged		1.25	
b.	Double surcharge		6.00	6.00
78	A31	50c on 25c (R)	1.25	.45
	Never hinged		3.25	
	On cover			25.00
	Nos. 74-78 (5)		6.70	2.60
	Set, never hinged		16.00	

No. 74 has the surcharge at each side.

Congo Surcharges
Nos. 60, 51 Surcharged in Red or
Black

a

b

1922				
80	A29	10c on 5c (R)	.70	.70
	Never hinged		2.25	
	On cover			15.00
a.	Inverted surcharge		25.00	25.00
b.	Double surcharge		6.00	
c.	Double surch., one invtd.		50.00	
d.	Pair, one without surcharge		52.50	
e.	On No. 45		325.00	325.00

81	A23	25c on 40c	1.25	.65
	Never hinged		4.00	
	On cover			45.00
a.	Inverted surcharge		25.00	25.00
b.	Double surcharge		6.75	
c.	"25c" double			
d.	25c on 5c, No. 60		225.00	225.00

Nos. 55, 58
Surcharged
in Red

1922				
84	A25	10c on 1fr (R)	.75	.75
	Never hinged		2.25	
	On cover			45.00
a.	Double surcharge		17.50	
b.	Inverted surcharge		25.00	25.00
85	A27	25c on 5fr	2.50	2.50
	Never hinged		7.00	
	On cover			100.00

Nos. 68, 77
Handstamped

86	A20	25c on 30c on 10c	30.00	20.00
	Never hinged		42.50	
	On cover			90.00
87	A30	25c on 30c on 10c (II)	20.00	20.00
	Never hinged		42.50	
	On cover			90.00

Nos. 86-87 exist with handstamp surcharge
inverted.
Counterfeit handstamped surcharges exist.

Ubangi
Woman — A32

Watusi
Cattle — A44

Designs: 10c, Baluba woman. 15c,
Babuende woman. No. 91, 40c, 1.25fr, 1.50fr,
1.75fr, Ubangi man. 25c, Basketmaking. 30c,
35c, No. 101, Weaving. No. 102, Carving
wood. 50c, Archer. Nos. 92, 100, Weaving. 1fr,
Making pottery. 3fr, Working rubber. 5fr, Making palm oil. 10fr, African elephant.

1923-27	**Engr.**		**Perf. 12**	
88	A32	5c yellow	.35	.25
	Never hinged		.60	
89	A32	10c green	.25	.25
	Never hinged		.60	
	On cover			15.00
90	A32	15c olive brown	.25	.25
	Never hinged		.60	
	On cover			6.25
91	A32	20c olive grn ('24)	.25	.25
	Never hinged		.60	
	On cover			15.00
92	A44	20c green ('26)	.50	.25
	Never hinged		.60	
	On cover			7.50
93	A44	25c red brown	.30	.25
	Never hinged		.60	
	On cover			6.25
94	A44	30c rose red ('24)	.65	.65
	Never hinged		1.90	
	On cover			21.00
95	A44	30c olive grn ('25)	.30	.25
	Never hinged		.60	
	On cover			3.00
96	A44	35c green ('27)	.75	.45
	Never hinged		1.10	
	On cover			12.50
97	A32	40c violet ('25)	.30	.25
	Never hinged		1.10	
	On cover			12.50
98	A44	50c gray blue	.30	.25
	Never hinged		.60	
	On cover			6.25
99	A44	50c buff ('25)	.65	.25
	Never hinged		.95	
	On cover			4.00
100	A44	75c red orange	.30	.25
	Never hinged		1.90	
	On cover			21.00
101	A44	75c gray bl ('25)	.65	.35
	Never hinged		1.10	
	On cover			7.50

102	A44	75c salmon red ('26)	.30	.25

102 A44 75c salmon red ('26) .30 .25
　Never hinged .60
　On cover 6.25
103 A44 1fr bister brown 1.00 .40
　Never hinged 1.90
　On cover 27.50
104 A44 1fr dl blue ('25) .65 .25
　Never hinged 1.10
　On cover 6.25
105 A44 1fr rose red ('27) 1.25 .25
　Never hinged 4.25
106 A32 1.25fr dl blue ('26) .95 .40
　Never hinged 1.90
　On cover 12.50
107 A32 1.50fr dl blue ('26) .95 .30
　Never hinged 1.90
　On cover 19.00
108 A32 1.75fr dl blue ('27) 8.00 6.25
　Never hinged 20.00
　On cover 25.00
109 A44 3fr gray brn ('24) 8.00 4.00
　Never hinged 22.00
　On cover 105.00
110 A44 5fr gray ('24) 15.00 8.00
　Never hinged 60.00
111 A44 10fr gray blk ('24) 30.00 15.00
　Never hinged 125.00

1925-26

112 A44 45c dk vio ('26) .70 .40
　Never hinged 1.10
　On cover 9.25
113 A44 60c carmine rose .70 .30
　Never hinged 1.10
　On cover 3.00
　　Nos. 88-113 (26) 73.30 40.00
　Set, never hinged 250.00

For surcharges see Nos. 114, 136-138, 157.

No. 107
Surcharged

1927, June 14
114 A32 1.75fr on 1.50fr dl bl 1.00 1.00
　Never hinged 2.00
　On cover 19.00

Sir Henry Morton
Stanley — A45

1928, June 30   **Perf. 14**
115 A45 5c gray blk .25 .25
　Never hinged .35
116 A45 10c dp violet .25 .25
　Never hinged .35
　On cover 25.00
117 A45 20c orange red .50 .30
　Never hinged .75
　On cover 25.00
118 A45 35c green 1.25 .75
　Never hinged 2.50
　On cover 15.00
119 A45 40c red brown .60 .25
　Never hinged 1.10
　On cover 15.00
120 A45 60c black brn 1.00 .50
　Never hinged 1.50
　On cover 11.00
121 A45 1fr carmine .40 .25
　Never hinged 1.50
　On cover 6.25
122 A45 1.60fr dk gray 10.50 8.75
　Never hinged 35.00
　On cover 50.00
123 A45 1.75fr dp blue 2.25 1.00
　Never hinged 5.00
　On cover 9.25
124 A45 2fr dk brown 1.60 .95
　Never hinged 5.00
　On cover 11.00
125 A45 2.75fr red violet 10.50 .45
　Never hinged 35.00
　On cover 37.50
126 A45 3.50fr rose lake 1.75 1.25
　Never hinged 4.25
　On cover 40.00
127 A45 5fr slate grn 1.50 1.25
　Never hinged 4.25
　On cover 30.00
128 A45 10fr violet blue 2.25 1.25
　Never hinged 5.00
129 A45 20fr claret 10.50 7.50
　Never hinged 35.00
　　Nos. 115-129 (15) 45.10 24.95
　Set, never hinged 140.00

Sir Henry M. Stanley (1841-1904), explorer.

Nos. 118, 121-123,
125-126 Surcharged in
Red, Blue or Black

1931, Jan. 15
130 A45 40c on 35c 1.60 .75
　Never hinged 4.25
　On cover 19.00
131 A45 1.25fr on 1fr (Bl) 1.00 .25
　Never hinged 2.50
　On cover 9.25
132 A45 2fr on 1.60fr 1.60 .50
　Never hinged 4.25
　On cover 30.00
133 A45 2fr on 1.75fr 1.60 .45
　Never hinged 4.25
　On cover 35.00
134 A45 3.25fr on 2.75fr (Bk) 4.50 3.25
　Never hinged 15.00
　On cover 27.50
135 A45 3.25fr on 3.50fr (Bk) 8.75 7.50
　Never hinged 25.00
　On cover 37.50

Nos. 96, 108,
112 Surcharged
in Red

Perf. 12½, 12
136 A44 40c on 35c grn 6.50 5.75
　Never hinged 15.00
　On cover 42.50
137 A44 50c on 45c dk vio 3.75 2.50
　Never hinged 12.50
　On cover 37.50

No. 108
Surcharged

138 A32 2(fr) on 1.75fr dl bl 17.50 15.00
　Never hinged 62.50
　On cover 62.50
　　Nos. 130-138 (9) 46.80 35.95
　Set, never hinged 160.00

View of
Sankuru
River — A46

Flute
Players — A50

Designs: 15c, Kivu Kraal. 20c, Sankuru
River rapids. 25c, Uele hut. 50c, Musicians of
Lake Leopold II. 60c, Batetelas drummers.
75c, Mangbetu woman. 1fr, Domesticated elephant of Api. 1.25fr, Mangbetu chief. 1.50fr,
2fr, Village of Mondimbi. 2.50fr, 3.25fr, Okapi.
4fr, Canoes at Stanleyville. 5fr, Woman preparing cassava. 10fr, Baluba chief. 20fr, Young
woman of Irumu.

1931-37   Engr.   Perf. 11½
139 A46 10c gray brn ('32) .25 .25
　Never hinged .70
　On cover 19.00
140 A46 15c gray ('32) .25 .25
　Never hinged .70
　On cover 19.00
141 A46 20c brn lil ('32) .25 .25
　Never hinged .70
　On cover 19.00
142 A46 25c dp blue ('32) .25 .25
　Never hinged .75
　On cover 11.00

---

143 A50 40c dp grn ('32) .30 .30
　Never hinged .75
　On cover 11.00
144 A46 50c violet ('32) .25 .25
　Never hinged .70
　On cover 11.00
b. 　Booklet pane of 8 6.25
　　Never hinged 15.00
145 A50 60c vio brn ('32) .30 .30
　Never hinged .70
　On cover 5.00
146 A50 75c rose ('32) .30 .30
　Never hinged .70
　On cover 3.00
b. 　Booklet pane of 8 5.50
　　Never hinged 9.25
147 A50 1fr rose red ('32) .30 .30
　Never hinged .70
　On cover 3.00
148 A50 1.25fr red brown .30 .30
　Never hinged .70
b. 　Booklet pane of 8 5.50
　　Never hinged 9.25
149 A46 1.50fr dk ol gray ('37) .30 .30
　Never hinged .80
　On cover 3.75
b. 　Booklet pane of 8 11.00
　　Never hinged 11.00
150 A46 2fr ultra ('32) .35 .30
　Never hinged .80
　On cover 7.50
151 A46 2.50fr dp blue ('37) .50 .30
　Never hinged 1.40
　On cover 7.50
b. 　Booklet pane of 8 15.00
　　Never hinged 15.00
152 A46 3.25fr gray blk ('32) .80 .50
　Never hinged 2.00
　On cover 12.50
153 A46 4fr dl vio ('32) .50 .30
　Never hinged .95
　On cover 12.50
154 A50 5fr dp vio ('32) 1.00 .40
　Never hinged 2.75
　On cover 15.00
155 A50 10fr red ('32) 1.25 1.00
　Never hinged 4.00
156 A50 20fr blk brn ('32) 2.50 1.50
　Never hinged 7.50
　　Nos. 139-156 (18) 9.95 7.35
　Set, never hinged 27.50

No. 109
Surcharged in
Red

1932, Mar. 15   Perf. 12
157 A44 3.25fr on 3fr gray brn 8.75 5.75
　Never hinged 25.00
　On cover 75.00

King Albert Memorial Issue

King Albert — A62

1934, May 7   Photo.   Perf. 11½
158 A62 1.50fr black 1.25 .90
　Never hinged 3.25
　On cover 7.50

No. 158 exists imperf. Value, $67.50.

Leopold I,
Leopold II,
Albert I,
Leopold III
A63

1935, Aug. 15   Engr.   Perf. 12½x12
159 A63 50c green 2.00 1.25
　Never hinged 5.00
　On cover 19.00
160 A63 1.25fr dk carmine 2.00 .40
　Never hinged 6.25
　On cover 9.25
161 A63 1.50fr brown vio 2.00 .40
　Never hinged 6.25
　On cover 9.25
162 A63 2.40fr brown org 6.25 6.25
　Never hinged 17.50
163 A63 2.50fr lt blue 6.25 2.25
　Never hinged 17.50
　On cover 9.25
164 A63 4fr brt violet 6.25 3.25
　Never hinged 17.50
　On cover 15.00

---

165 A63 5fr black brn 6.25 3.25
　Never hinged 17.50
　On cover 20.00
　　Nos. 159-165 (7) 31.00 17.05
　Set, never hinged 87.50

Founding of Congo Free State, 50th anniv.
Nos. 159-165 exist imperf. Value set,
$3,500.
For surcharges see Nos. B21-B22.

Molindi
River — A64

Bamboos — A65

Suza River — A66

Rutshuru
River — A67

Karisimbi
A68

Mitumba
Forest
A69

1937-38   Photo.   Perf. 11½
166 A64 5c purple & blk .30 .25
　Never hinged .50
　On cover 15.00
167 A65 90c car & brn .70 .35
　Never hinged 1.10
168 A66 1.50fr dp red brn & blk .50 .40
　Never hinged 1.10
　On cover 7.50
169 A67 2.40fr ol blk & brn .40 .30
　Never hinged 1.10
170 A68 2.50fr dp ultra & blk .65 .40
　Never hinged 1.10
　On cover 11.00
171 A69 4.50fr dk grn & brn .85 .70
　Never hinged 1.25
　On cover 11.00
172 A69 4.50fr car & sep .40 .30
　Never hinged .95
　On cover 15.00
　　Nos. 166-172 (7) 3.80 2.60
　Set, never hinged 7.50

National Parks.
Nos. 166-171 were issued Mar. 1, 1938.
Exist imperf. Value, set $100.
No. 172 was issued in sheets of four measuring 140x111mm. It was sold by subscription, the subscription closing Dec. 31, 1938.
Value: unused $3.75; never hinged $8. Exists
imperf. Value, $1,250.
See No. B26. For surcharges see Nos. 184,
186 in *Scott Standard Postage Stamp Catalogue*, Vol. 1.

SEMI-POSTAL STAMPS

Types of
1910-15
Issues
Surcharged
in Red

1918, May 15   Unwmk.   Perf. 14, 15
B1 A29 5c + 10c grn & bl .50 .50
　Never hinged 1.25

B2	A30 10c + 15c car & bl (l)	.50	.50
	Never hinged	1.25	
B3	A21 15c + 20c bl grn & bl	.50	.50
	Never hinged	1.25	
B4	A31 25c + 25c dp bl & pale bl	.50	.50
	Never hinged	1.25	
B5	A23 40c + 40c brn red & bl	.75	.75
	Never hinged	1.90	
B6	A24 50c + 50c brn lake & bl	.75	.75
	Never hinged	1.90	
B7	A25 1fr + 1fr ol bis & bl	3.00	3.00
	Never hinged	6.25	
B8	A27 5fr + 5fr ocher & bl	15.00	15.00
	Never hinged	35.00	
B9	A28 10fr + 10fr grn & bl	160.00	160.00
	Never hinged	450.00	
	Nos. B1-B9 (9)	181.50	181.50
	Set, never hinged	500.00	

The position of the cross and the added value varies on the different stamps.
Nos. B1-B9 exist imperforate without gum. Value, set $525.
Perf 15 examples of Nos. B1-B6 are worth approximately twice the values shown.

SP1

Design: No. B11, Inscribed "Belgisch Congo."

1925, July 8   *Perf. 12½*

B10	SP1 25c + 25c carmine & blk	.40	.40
	Never hinged	.60	
B11	SP1 25c + 25c carmine & blk	.40	.40
a.	Pair, Nos. B10-B11	1.00	1.00
	Never hinged	1.60	

Colonial campaigns in 1914-1918.
The surtax helped erect at Kinshasa a monument to those who died in World War I.

Nurse Weighing Child — SP3

First Aid Station SP5

Designs: 20c+10c, Missionary & Child. 60c+30c, Congo hospital. 1fr+50c, Dispensary service. 1.75fr+75c, Convalescent area. 3.50fr+1.50fr, Instruction on bathing infant. 5fr+2.50fr, Operating room. 10fr+5fr, Students.

1930, Jan. 16   **Engr.**   *Perf. 11½*

B12	SP3 10c + 5c ver	1.00	1.00
	Never hinged	1.25	
B13	SP3 20c + 10c dp brn	1.25	1.25
	Never hinged	1.60	
B14	SP5 35c + 15c dp grn	1.90	1.90
	Never hinged	4.00	
B15	SP5 60c + 30c dl vio	2.25	2.25
	Never hinged	4.50	
B16	SP3 1fr + 50c dk car	3.75	3.75
	Never hinged	7.50	
B17	SP5 1.75fr + 75c dp bl	8.75	8.75
	Never hinged	22.50	
B18	SP5 3.50fr + 1.50fr rose lake	11.00	11.00
	Never hinged	22.50	
B19	SP5 5fr + 2.50fr red brn	15.00	15.00
	Never hinged	40.00	
B20	SP5 10fr + 5fr gray blk	17.50	17.50
	Never hinged	52.50	
	Nos. B12-B20 (9)	62.40	62.40
	Set, never hinged	160.00	

The surtax was intended to aid welfare work among the natives, especially the children.

Nos. 161, 163 Surcharged "+50c" in Blue or Red

1936, May 15   *Perf. 12½x12*

B21	A63 1.50fr + 50c (Bl)	8.75	6.25
	Never hinged	18.00	
	On cover		37.50
B22	A63 2.50fr + 50c (R)	4.50	3.00
	Never hinged	7.00	
	On cover		37.50
	Set, never hinged	25.00	

Surtax was for the King Albert Memorial Fund.

Queen Astrid with Congolese Children — SP12

1936, Aug. 29   **Photo.**   *Perf. 12½*

B23	SP12 1.25fr + 5c dark brown	.65	.65
	Never hinged	1.60	
	On cover		19.00
B24	SP12 1.50fr + 10c dull rose	.65	.65
	Never hinged	1.60	
	On cover		19.00
B25	SP12 2.50fr + 25c dark blue	1.25	1.25
	Never hinged	3.75	
	On cover		20.00
	Nos. B23-B25 (3)	2.55	2.55
	Set, never hinged	7.00	

Issued in memory of Queen Astrid. The surtax was for the aid of the National League for Protection of Native Children.

National Park Type of 1937-38
Souvenir Sheet

1938, Oct. 3   *Perf. 11½*
Star in Yellow

B26	Sheet of 6	67.50	67.50
	Never hinged	125.00	
	On first day cover		75.00
a.	A64 5c ultra & light brown	6.50	6.50
b.	A65 90c ultra & light brown	6.50	6.50
c.	A66 1.50fr ultra & light brown	6.50	6.50
d.	A67 2.40fr ultra & light brown	6.50	6.50
e.	A68 2.50fr ultra & light brown	6.50	6.50
f.	A69 4.50fr ultra & light brown	6.50	6.50

Intl. Tourist Cong. A surtax of 3.15fr was for the benefit of the Congo Tourist Service. Exists imperf. Value $1,350.

Marabou Storks and Vultures — SP14

Buffon's Kob — SP15

Designs: 1.50fr+1.50fr, Pygmy chimpanzees. 4.50fr+4.50fr, Dwarf crocodiles. 5fr+5fr, Lioness.

1939, June 6   **Photo.**   *Perf. 14*

B27	SP14 1fr + 1fr dp claret	8.75	8.75
	Never hinged	19.00	
B28	SP15 1.25fr + 1.25fr car	8.75	8.75
	Never hinged	19.00	
B29	SP15 1.50fr + 1.50fr brt pur	8.75	8.75
	Never hinged	19.00	
B30	SP14 4.50fr + 4.50fr sl grn	8.75	8.75
	Never hinged	19.00	
B31	SP15 5fr + 5fr brown	8.75	8.75
	Never hinged	19.00	
	Nos. B27-B31 (5)	43.75	43.75
	Set, never hinged	95.00	

Surtax for the Leopoldville Zoological Gardens. Exists imperf. Value $225.
Sold in full sets by subscription.

AIR POST STAMPS

Wharf on Congo River AP1

Congo "Country Store" AP2

View of Congo River AP3

Stronghold in the Interior — AP4

Unwmk.

1920, July 1   **Engr.**   *Perf. 12*

C1	AP1 50c orange & blk	.75	.25
	Never hinged	1.90	
C2	AP2 1fr dull vio & blk	.80	.25
	Never hinged	2.25	
C3	AP3 2fr blue & blk	1.25	.60
	Never hinged	3.50	
C4	AP4 5fr green & blk	2.25	1.00
	Never hinged	6.25	
	On cover		22.50
	Nos. C1-C4 (4)	5.05	2.10
	Set, never hinged	14.00	

Kraal AP5

Porters on Safari AP6

1930, Apr. 2

C5	AP5 15fr dk brn & blk	3.50	1.25
	Never hinged	11.00	
C6	AP6 30fr brn vio & blk	4.00	2.00
	Never hinged	14.00	
	Set, never hinged	25.00	

Fokker F VII over Congo AP7

1934, Jan. 22   *Perf. 13½x14*

C7	AP7 50c gray black	.35	.25
	Never hinged	.60	
C8	AP7 1fr dk carmine	.60	.25
	Never hinged	.95	
a.	Booklet pane of 8	8.00	
	Never hinged	12.50	
C9	AP7 1.50fr green	.60	.25
	Never hinged	1.60	
C10	AP7 3fr brown	.35	.25
	Never hinged	.95	
	On cover		19.00
C11	AP7 4.50fr brt ultra	.60	.25
	Never hinged	1.60	
	On cover		4.75
a.	Booklet pane of 8	14.00	
	Never hinged	25.00	

C12	AP7 5fr red brown	1.00	.35
	Never hinged	1.25	
	On cover		9.25
C13	AP7 15fr brown vio	1.25	.60
	Never hinged	2.50	
C14	AP7 30fr red orange	2.25	1.90
	Never hinged	6.25	
C15	AP7 50fr violet	6.50	3.50
	Never hinged	15.00	
	Nos. C7-C15 (9)	13.50	7.60
	Set, never hinged	32.50	

The 1fr, 3fr, 4.50fr, 5fr, 15fr exist imperf. Values: 3fr, $37.50; 5fr, $60; 15fr, $32.50.

No. C10 Surcharged in Blue with New Value and Bars

1936, Mar. 25

C16	AP7 3.50fr on 3fr brown	.60	.25
	Never hinged	1.25	
	On cover		9.25

POSTAGE DUE STAMPS

In 1908-23 regular postage stamps handstamped "TAXES" or "TAXE," usually boxed, were used in lieu of postage due stamps.

D1

1923   **Typo.**   **Unwmk.**   *Perf. 14*

J1	D1 5c black brown	.25	.25
	Never hinged	.35	
J2	D1 10c rose red	.25	.25
	Never hinged	.35	
J3	D1 15c violet	.25	.25
	Never hinged	.60	
J4	D1 30c green	.30	.25
	Never hinged	.75	
J5	D1 50c ultramarine	.40	.35
	Never hinged	1.00	
J6	D1 50c blue ('29)	.45	.35
	Never hinged	1.00	
J7	D1 1fr gray	.55	.40
	Never hinged	1.40	
	Nos. J1-J7 (7)	2.45	2.10
	Set, never hinged	6.00	

Nos. J1-J7 exist imperf. Value, set $37.50.

PARCEL POST STAMPS

Handstamped Surcharges in Black or Blue on Nos. 5, 11-12

PP1

PP2

PP3

1887-93   **Unwmk.**   *Perf. 15*

Q1	PP1 3.50fr on 5fr li-lac	1,400.	1,000.
Q3	PP2 3.50fr on 5fr vio	1,200.	675.00
Q4	PP3 3.50fr on 5fr vio ('88)	950.00	550.00
Q6	PP3 3.50fr on 5fr gray ('93)	190.00	190.00
	Never hinged	250.00	

Nos. Q1, Q3-Q4, and Q6 are known with inverted surcharge and double surcharge, and No. Q6 in pair with unsurcharged stamp. These varieties sell for somewhat more than the normal surcharges.
Genuine stamps with counterfeit surcharges, counterfeit stamps with counterfeit surcharges, and both with counterfeit cancels exist.

BELGIUM

'bel-jəm

LOCATION — Western Europe, bordering the North Sea
GOVT. — Constitutional Monarchy
AREA — 11,778 sq. mi.
POP. — 9,853,000 (est. 1983)
CAPITAL — Brussels

100 Centimes = 1 Franc

Watermarks

Wmk. 96
(With Frame)

Wmk. 96a
(No Frame)

King Leopold I
A1   A2

Wmk. Two "L's" Framed (96)

		Engr.		*Imperf.*
1	A1 10c brown		*2,600.*	100.00
	No gum		1,700.	
	On cover			175.00
a.	10c red brown		*4,300.*	425.00
	No gum		2,500.	
	On cover			750.00
b.	10c bister brown		*2,900.*	140.00
	No gum		1,800.	
	On cover			260.00
c.	10c dark brown		*2,650.*	85.00
	No gum		1,800.	
	On cover			210.00
2	A1 20c blue		*2,650.*	57.50
	No gum		1,900.	
	On cover			145.00
a.	20c milky blue		*3,700.*	160.00
	No gum		2,300.	
	On cover			400.00
b.	20c greenish blue		*3,900.*	290.00
	No gum		2,500.	
	On cover			500.00
c.	20c dark blue		*3,100.*	62.50
	No gum		2,000.	
	On cover			150.00

Full margins = ½mm.

The reprints are on thick and thin wove and thick laid paper unwatermarked.

A souvenir sheet containing reproductions of the 10c, 20c and 40c of 1849-51 with black burelage on back was issued Oct. 17, 1949, for the cent. of the 1st Belgian stamps. It was sold at BEPITEC 1949, an intl. stamp exhib. at Brussels, and was not valid. Value, $15.

Values for pairs

1	A1 10c brown		200.
	On cover		450.
2	A1 20c blue		175.
	On cover		425.

Values for strips of 3

1	A1 10c brown		900.
	On cover		2,250.
2	A1 20c blue		675.
	On cover		2,250.

Values for strips of 4

1	A1 10c brown		1,900.
	On cover		10,000.
2	A1 20c blue		1,600.
	On cover		10,000.

A cover sent from Herinnes to Charleroi bearing a strip of four of the 20 centimes blue (Scott No. 2) was sold for the equivalent of U.S. $10,000 in a Brussels auction in 2003.

Values for blocks of 4

1	A1 10c brown		3,500.
	On cover		10,000.
2	A1 20c blue		3,750.
	On cover		10,000.

1849-50   Thin Paper

3	A2 10c brown ('50)		*2,500.*	100.00
	No gum		2,000.	
	On cover			175.00
4	A2 20c blue ('50)		*2,200.*	62.50
	No gum		1,550.	
	On cover			145.00

5	A2 40c carmine rose		*2,000.*	525.00
	No gum		1,500.	
	On cover			1,000.

Full margins = ½mm.

Thick Paper

3a	A2 10c brown ('50)		*2,500.*	100.00
	No gum		2,100.	
	On cover			175.00
4a	A2 20c blue ('50)		*2,200.*	62.50
	No gum		1,550.	
	On cover			145.00
5a	A2 40c carmine rose		*2,000.*	525.00
	No gum		1,550.	
	On cover			1,000.

Values for pairs

3	A2 10c brown ('50)		250.
	On cover		400.
4	A2 20c blue ('50)		175.
	On cover		290.
5	A2 40c carmine rose		1,150.
	On cover		1,425.

Values for strips of 3

3	A2 10c brown ('50)		675.
	On cover		1,000.
4	A2 20c blue ('50)		425.
	On cover		675.
5	A2 40c carmine rose		1,775.
	On cover		2,250.

Values for strips of 4

3	A2 10c brown ('50)		1,400.
	On cover		2,250.
4	A2 20c blue ('50)		900.
	On cover		1,350.
5	A2 40c carmine rose		2,250.
	On cover		2,900.

Values for blocks of 4

3	A2 10c brown ('50)		2,500.
	On cover		3,500.
4	A2 20c blue ('50)		1,600.
	On cover		2,250.
5	A2 40c carmine rose		4,750.
	On cover		5,500.

Wmk. Two "L's" Without Frame (96a)

1851-54   Thick Wove Paper

6	A2 10c brown		625.00	8.50
	No gum		375.00	
	On cover			17.50
a.	Ribbed paper ('54)		1,000.	62.50
7	A2 20c blue		800.00	8.00
	No gum		475.00	
	On cover			17.50
a.	Ribbed paper ('54)		1,000.	62.50
8	A2 40c car rose		*4,250.*	110.00
	No gum		2,300.	
	On cover			160.00
a.	Ribbed paper ('54)		*5,000.*	260.00

Full margins = ½mm.

Nos. 6a, 7a, 8a must have regular and parallel ribs covering the whole stamp.

Thin to Medium Wove Paper

6b	A2 10c brown		675.00	9.00
	No gum		400.00	
	On cover			17.50
7b	A2 20c blue		875.00	8.50
	No gum		500.00	
	On cover			17.50
8b	A2 40c car rose		*4,200.*	110.00
	No gum		2,400.	
	On cover			170.00

Values for used pairs

6	A2 10c brown		22.50
	On cover		65.00
7	A2 20c blue		22.50
	On cover		67.50
8	A2 40c car rose		265.00
	On cover		475.00

Values for strips of 3

6	A2 10c brown		80.00
	On cover		140.00
7	A2 20c blue		85.00
	On cover		145.00
8	A2 40c car rose		575.00
	On cover		900.00

Values for strips of 4

6	A2 10c brown		140.00
	On cover		275.00
7	A2 20c blue		140.00
	On cover		275.00
8	A2 40c car rose		1,350.
	On cover		2,000.

Values for blocks of 4

6	A2 10c brown		300.00
	On cover		800.00
7	A2 20c blue		300.00
	On cover		800.00
8	A2 40c car rose		2,750.
	On cover		3,750.

Stamps 22mm high; Oval 17¼high

1861   Unwmk.

9	A2 1c green ('61)		225.00	125.00
	No gum		140.00	
	On wrapper			900.00
a.	1c pale green		225.00	140.00
	No gum		150.00	
	On wrapper			925.00
b.	1c dark green		225.00	150.00
	No gum		175.00	
	On wrapper			975.00
c.	1c deep bottle green		575.00	375.00
	No gum		425.00	
	On wrapper			1,100.
10	A2 10c brown		475.00	9.00
	No gum		325.00	
	On cover			15.00
a.	10c dark brown		500.00	11.00
	No gum		325.00	
	On cover			15.00

11	A2 20c blue		500.00	9.00
	No gum		325.00	
	On cover			15.00
a.	20c dark blue		525.00	10.50
	No gum		340.00	
	On cover			15.00
12	A2 40c vermilion		*3,750.*	150.00
	No gum		2,100.	
	On cover			160.00
a.	40c carmine rose		*4,000.*	150.00
	No gum		2,250.	
	On cover			160.00

Full margins = ½mm.

Nos. 9 and 13 were valid for postage on newspapers and printed matter only.

Reprints of Nos. 9-12 are on thin wove paper. The colors are brighter than those of the originals. They were made from the dies and show lines outside the stamps.

Values for pairs

9	A2 1c green		290.00
	On cover		975.00
10	A2 10c brown		22.50
	On cover		40.00
11	A2 20c blue		22.50
	On cover		35.00
12	A2 40c vermilion		175.00
	On cover		310.00

Values for strips of 3

9	A2 1c green		450.00
	On cover		1,100.
10	A2 10c brown		57.50
	On cover		90.00
11	A2 20c blue		57.50
	On cover		90.00
12	A2 40c vermilion		575.00
	On cover		1,000.

Values for strips of 4

9	A2 1c green		775.00
	On cover		1,400.
10	A2 10c brown		110.00
	On cover		180.00
11	A2 20c blue		125.00
	On cover		190.00
12	A2 40c vermilion		1,500.
	On cover		1,800.

Values for blocks of 4

9	A2 1c green		1,000.
	On cover		2,250.
10	A2 10c brown		350.00
	On cover		675.00
11	A2 20c blue		350.00
	On cover		725.00
12	A2 40c vermilion		3,600.
	On cover		3,600.

Stamps 21mm high; Oval 16½ high

1858   Unwmk.

10b	A2 10c brown		675.00	10.75
	No gum		375.00	
	On cover			18.00
11b	A2 20c blue		675.00	10.75
	No gum		375.00	
	On cover			18.00
12b	A2 40c vermilion		*4,600.*	110.00
	No gum		3,000.	
	On cover			200.00

Values for pairs

10b	A2 10c brown		35.00
	On cover		150.00
11b	A2 20c blue		35.00
	On cover		150.00
12b	A2 40c vermilion		260.00
	On cover		775.00

Values for strips of 3

10	A2 10c brown		90.00
	On cover		225.00
11	A2 20c blue		90.00
	On cover		225.00
12	A2 40c vermilion		725.00
	On cover		1,350.

Values for strips of 4

10	A2 10c brown		175.00
	On cover		360.00
11	A2 20c blue		175.00
	On cover		375.00
12	A2 40c vermilion		1,750.
	On cover		2,500.

Values for blocks of 4

10	A2 10c brown		350.00
	On cover		725.00
11	A2 20c blue		350.00
	On cover		725.00
12	A2 40c vermilion		5,000.
	On cover		6,750.

Values for Nos. 13-16 are for stamps with perfs cutting into the design. Values for perforated stamps from Nos. 17 through 107 are for examples with perforations touching the design on one or two sides. Stamps with all perforations clear are exceptional and command substantial premiums.

1865, Sept.   Perf. 14½

13	A2 1c green		62.50	26.00
	Never hinged		140.00	
	No gum		30.00	
	On wrapper			450.00
14	A2 10c brown		80.00	3.75
	Never hinged		180.00	
	No gum		35.00	
	On cover			9.00
a.	10c reddish brown		100.00	4.50
	Never hinged		250.00	
	No gum		52.50	
	On cover			9.50
15	A2 20c blue		80.00	3.50
	Never hinged		180.00	
	No gum		40.00	

	On cover			9.00
a.	20c turquoise blue		—	50.00
	On cover			75.00
16	A2 40c carmine rose		450.00	25.00
	Never hinged		975.00	
	No gum		210.00	
	On cover			60.00
a.	40c bright vermilion		525.00	67.50
	Never hinged		1,200.	
	No gum		310.00	
	On cover			90.00
b.	40c pomegranate red		1,100.	110.00
	Never hinged		2,400.	
	No gum		625.00	
	On cover			210.00
	Nos. 13-16 (4)		672.50	58.25

1863   Perf. 12½

13a	A2 1c green		200.00	80.00
	Never hinged		475.00	
	No gum		92.50	
	On wrapper			600.00
14b	A2 10c brown		225.00	5.00
	Never hinged		500.00	
	No gum		92.50	
	On cover			11.00
15b	A2 20c blue		225.00	5.00
	Never hinged		500.00	
	No gum		92.50	
	On cover			12.00
16c	A2 40c carmine rose		1,200.	35.00
	Never hinged		2,800.	
	No gum		600.00	
	On cover			75.00
16d	A2 40c vermilion		1,300.	45.00
	Never hinged		3,000.	
	No gum		600.00	
	On cover			90.00

1863, August   Perf. 12½x13½

13b	A2 1c green		80.00	45.00
	Never hinged		180.00	
	On wrapper		37.50	475.00
13c	A2 1c emerald green		85.00	42.50
	Never hinged		200.00	
	No gum		40.00	
	On wrapper			525.00
14c	A2 10c brown		115.00	4.00
	Never hinged		260.00	
	No gum		47.50	
	On cover			10.00
15c	A2 20c blue		120.00	4.00
	Never hinged		275.00	
	No gum		47.50	
	On cover			10.00
16e	A2 40c carmine rose		650.00	35.00
	Never hinged		1,400.	
	No gum		315.00	
	On cover			67.50
16f	A2 40c bright vermilion		700.00	45.00
	Never hinged		1,600.	
	No gum		375.00	
	On cover			90.00

Values for Nos. 13-16f are for stamps with perfs cutting into design.

King Leopold I — A3a
A3

A4   A4a

A5

London Print

1865   Typo.   Perf. 14

17	A5 1fr pale violet		1,750.	110.00
	Never hinged		3,600.	
	No gum		1,000.	
	On cover			900.00

Brussels Print
Thick (Perf 15) or Thin (Perf 14½x14) Paper

1867   Perf. 15

18	A3 10c slate		185.00	2.25
	Never hinged		400.00	
	No gum		80.00	
	On cover			5.00
19	A3a 20c blue		290.00	2.00
	Never hinged		650.00	
	No gum		125.00	
	On cover			5.00
a.	20c lilac blue		460.00	2.75
	Never hinged		1,100.	
	No gum		140.00	
	On cover			6.50
20	A4 30c brown		625.00	11.00
	Never hinged		1,400.	
	No gum		300.00	
	On cover			24.00

21	A4a 40c rose	775.00	20.00
	Never hinged	1,700.	
	No gum	350.00	
	On cover		110.00
22	A5 1fr violet	2,000.	97.50
	Never hinged	4,500.	
	No gum	850.00	
	On cover		750.00
a.	1fr lilac	2,100.	110.00
	Never hinged	4,750.	
	No gum	850.00	
	On cover		850.00

1865-66 — Perf. 14½x14
18a	A3 10c slate	230.00	2.75
	Never hinged	500.00	
	No gum	100.00	
	On cover		5.50
b.	Pair, imperf. between		—
19b	A3a 20c blue	375.00	4.00
	Never hinged	850.00	
	No gum	170.00	
	On cover		5.50
19c	A3a 20c prussian blue	475.00	7.00
	Never hinged	1,100.	
	No gum	200.00	
	On cover		18.00
20a	A4 30c brown	700.00	11.50
	Never hinged	1,650.	
	No gum	350.00	
	On cover		24.00
b.	Pair, imperf. between	2,000.	
21a	A4a 40c rose	1,050.	20.00
	Never hinged	2,350.	
	No gum	425.00	
	On cover		90.00
22b	A5 1f violet	1,900.	125.00
	Never hinged	4,300.	
	No gum	925.00	
	On cover		700.00
22c	A5 1f dark violet	2,450.	475.00
	Never hinged	5,600.	
	No gum	1,300.	
	On cover		1,250.

The reprints are on thin paper, imperforate and ungummed.

Coat of Arms — A6

1866-67 — Imperf.
23	A6 1c gray	250.00	150.00
	Never hinged	600.00	
	No gum	170.00	
	On wrapper		750.00

Perf. 14½x14
24	A6 1c gray	57.50	16.00
	Never hinged	140.00	
	No gum	40.00	
	On wrapper		67.50
25	A6 2c blue ('67)	190.00	90.00
	Never hinged	475.00	
	No gum	125.00	
	On wrapper		775.00
a.	2c dark blue	200.00	100.00
	Never hinged	500.00	
	No gum	200.00	
	On wrapper		850.00
26	A6 5c brown	240.00	90.00
	Never hinged	550.00	
	No gum	160.00	
	On wrapper		450.00
a.	5c yellowish brown	250.00	92.50
	Never hinged	600.00	
	No gum	170.00	
	On wrapper		525.00

1867 — Perf. 15
24a	A6 1c gray	45.00	16.00
	Never hinged	100.00	
	No gum	30.00	
	On wrapper		55.00
b.	1c bluish gray	300.00	100.00
	Never hinged	650.00	
	No gum	200.00	
	On wrapper		140.00
25b	A6 2c blue	140.00	90.00
	Never hinged	375.00	
	No gum	190.00	
	On wrapper		700.00
c.	2c ultramarine	150.00	110.00
	Never hinged	400.00	
	No gum	100.00	
	On wrapper		825.00
26b	A6 5c brown	175.00	90.00
	Never hinged	440.00	
	No gum	115.00	
	On wrapper		525.00
c.	5c yellowish brown	200.00	92.50
	Never hinged	500.00	
	No gum	130.00	
	On wrapper		625.00
d.	5c bister brown	190.00	95.00
	Never hinged	475.00	
	No gum	125.00	
	On wrapper		625.00
	Nos. 23-26b (2)	390.00	240.00

Nos. 23-26d were valid for postage on newspapers and printed matter only.
Counterfeits exist.
Reprints of Nos. 24-26 are on thin paper, imperforate and without gum.

Imperf. varieties of 1869-1912 (between Nos. 28-105) are without gum.

A7

A8

A9

A10

A11

A12

A13

A14

King Leopold II — A15

1869-70 — Perf. 15
28	A7 1c green	8.25	.40
	Never hinged	37.50	
	On cover, single franking		29.00
29	A7 2c ultra ('70)	25.00	1.65
	Never hinged	70.00	
	On cover, single franking		100.00
30	A7 5c buff ('70)	62.50	.75
	Never hinged	210.00	
	On cover, single franking		20.00
31	A7 8c lilac ('70)	67.50	50.00
	Never hinged	170.00	
	On cover, single franking		725.00
32	A8 10c green	27.50	.40
	Never hinged	75.00	
	On cover		3.75
33	A9 20c lt ultra ('70)	125.00	.90
	Never hinged	325.00	
	On cover		15.00
34	A10 30c buff ('70)	80.00	4.00
	Never hinged	160.00	
	On cover		10.00
a.	30c reddish ocher ('73)	82.50	4.00
	Never hinged	160.00	
	On cover		10.00
35	A11 40c brt rose ('70)	135.00	6.50
	Never hinged	400.00	
	On cover		120.00
a.	40c rose lilac	230.00	10.00
	Never hinged	500.00	
	On cover		120.00
36	A12 1fr dull lilac ('70)	400.00	17.00
	Never hinged	825.00	
	No gum	250.00	
	On cover		700.00
a.	1fr rose lilac	500.00	20.00
	Never hinged	850.00	
	No gum	300.00	
	On cover		775.00
	Nos. 28-36 (9)	930.75	81.60

The frames and inscriptions of Nos. 30, 31 and 42 differ slightly from the illustration.
Minor "broken letter" varieties exist on several values.
Nos. 28-30, 32-33, 35-38 also were printed in aniline colors. These are not valued separately.
Nos. 28-36 exist imperforate, without gum. The 1c and 2c are valued from $55 to $85. The 40c and 1fr stamps are scarcer, valued from $500 to $675. Some denominations exist with gum. Pairs command premiums. Large multiples are scarce.
See Nos. 40-43, 49-51, 55.

1875-78
37	A13 25c olive bister	165.00	1.45
	Never hinged	400.00	
	On cover		8.00
a.	25c ocher	185.00	1.55
	Never hinged	425.00	
	On cover		8.00
38	A14 50c gray	275.00	11.00
	Never hinged	675.00	
	On cover		150.00
	Roller cancel		12.50
a.	50c gray black	325.00	50.00
	Never hinged	700.00	
	On cover		200.00
b.	50c deep black	1,750.	250.00
	Never hinged		

	No gum	1,000.	
	On cover		800.00
39	A15 5fr dp red brown	1,700.	1,450.
	Never hinged	3,100.	
	No gum	1,000.	
	On cover		11,000.
	Roller cancel		700.00
a.	5fr pale brown ('78)	3,750.	1,450.
	Never hinged		
	No gum	2,250.	
	On cover		11,000.
	Roller cancel		700.00

No. 37 exists imperforate, without gum. Value, $250.
Dangerous counterfeits of No. 39 exist.

Printed in Aniline Colors
1881 — Perf. 14
40	A7 1c gray green	18.00	.85
	Never hinged	35.00	
	On cover		32.50
41	A7 2c lt ultra	19.00	3.00
	Never hinged	57.50	
	On cover, single franking		100.00
42	A7 5c orange buff	55.00	1.25
	Never hinged	165.00	
	On cover		30.00
a.	5c red orange	55.00	1.25
	Never hinged	165.00	
	On cover		30.00
43	A8 10c gray green	27.50	1.10
	Never hinged	70.00	
	On cover		5.00
44	A13 25c olive bister	95.00	3.00
	Never hinged	160.00	
	On cover		11.00
	Nos. 40-44 (5)	214.50	9.20

See note following No. 36.

A16

A17

A18

A19

1883
45	A16 10c carmine	27.50	2.50
	Never hinged	62.50	
	On cover		22.00
a.	10c carmine rose	30.00	2.90
	Never hinged	67.50	
	On cover		25.00
46	A17 20c gray	175.00	10.00
	Never hinged	575.00	
	On cover		125.00
a.	20c slate gray	200.00	11.00
	Never hinged	575.00	
	On cover		135.00
47	A18 25c blue	360.00	35.00
	Never hinged	1,200.	
	On cover		190.00
	Roller cancel		15.00
a.	25c dark blue	380.00	35.00
	Never hinged	1,200.	
	On cover		290.00
48	A19 50c violet	325.00	35.00
	Never hinged	800.00	
	On cover		300.00
	Roller cancel		15.00
a.	50c deep violet	350.00	45.00
	Never hinged	1,000.	
	On cover		310.00
	Nos. 45-48 (4)	887.50	82.50

A20

A21

A22

1884-85 — Perf. 14
49	A7 1c olive green	16.00	.75
	Never hinged	47.50	
	On cover, single franking		60.00
50	A7 1c gray	4.25	.40
	Never hinged	11.00	
	On cover, single franking		15.00
51	A7 5c green	37.50	.40
	Never hinged	110.00	
	On cover, single franking		8.00
52	A20 10c rose, bluish	12.50	.40
	Never hinged	37.50	
	On cover		3.50

a.	Grayish paper	13.50	.50
	Never hinged	40.00	
	On cover		5.00
c.	Yellowish paper	225.00	22.50
	Never hinged	500.00	
	On cover		100.00
53	A21 25c blue, pink ('85)	15.00	.75
	Never hinged	37.50	
	On cover		7.25
a.	25c blue, dark rose	16.50	1.00
	Never hinged	37.50	
	On cover		7.00
54	A22 1fr brown, grnsh	750.00	17.50
	Never hinged	2,150.	
	No gum	450.00	
	On cover		550.00
a.	1fr deep brown, dk grn	900.00	20.00
	Never hinged	2,400.	
	No gum	550.00	
	On cover		575.00

The frame and inscription of No. 51 differ slightly from the illustration.
See note after No. 36.
Nos. 50-54 exist imperforate, without gum. The 1c and 10c stamps are valued from $32.50 to $55. The 5c, 25c and 1fr stamps are valued from $160 to $375.

A23

A24

A25

A26

1886-91
55	A7 2c purple brn ('88)	13.50	1.65
	Never hinged	45.00	
	On cover, single franking		70.00
56	A23 20c olive, grnsh	200.00	1.65
	Never hinged	575.00	
	On cover		21.00
b.	20c deep olive, grnsh	210.00	1.90
	Never hinged	590.00	
	On cover		22.50
57	A24 35c vio brn, brnsh ('91)	18.00	3.00
	Never hinged	45.00	
	On cover		20.00
58	A25 50c bister, yelsh	12.50	2.25
	Never hinged	30.00	
	On cover		50.00
59	A26 2fr violet, pale lil	72.50	35.00
	Never hinged	125.00	
	On cover		625.00
	Roller cancel		7.50
a.	2fr vio, brt lilac	67.50	40.00
	Never hinged	140.00	
	On cover		675.00
	Nos. 55-59 (5)	316.50	43.55

Nos. 56 and 57 exist imperforate, without gum. No. 56 is valued at $275. No. 57 is valued at $55.

Values quoted for Nos. 60-107 are for unused and used stamps with label attached. Stamps without label sell for much less.

Coat of Arms
A27

King Leopold
A28

Type A27 has two 1mm high ornamental bands across the top and bottom of the label. These bands do not appear on Type A32.

1893-1900
60	A27 1c gray	1.00	.25
	Never hinged	1.65	
	On cover, single franking, without label		2.75
61	A27 2c yellow	1.00	1.10
	Never hinged	1.65	
	On cover, single franking, without label		160.00
a.	Wmkd. coat of arms in sheet ('95)	—	
62	A27 2c violet brn ('94)	1.65	.40
	Never hinged	7.50	
	On cover, single franking, without label		23.00

```
63  A27  2c red brown ('98)      3.00    .90
      Never hinged               9.00
      On cover, single franking,
        without label                   30.00
64  A27  5c yellow grn           9.00    .30
      Never hinged              29.00
      On cover, without label            2.00
65  A28  10c orange brn          4.00    .30
      Never hinged              20.00
      On cover, without label            4.00
66  A28  10c brt rose ('00)      3.25    .40
      Never hinged              11.50
      On cover, without label            5.50
67  A28  20c olive green        15.00    .60
      Never hinged              37.50
      On cover, without label           18.00
68  A28  25c ultra              10.00    .50
      Never hinged              27.50
      On cover, without label            4.00
  a.  No ball to "5" in upper left
        corner                 32.50   12.50
      Never hinged              92.50
69  A28  35c violet brn         22.50   1.50
      Never hinged              65.00
      On cover, without label           15.00
  a.  35c red brown             35.00   2.40
      Never hinged              80.00
      On cover, without label           17.50
70  A28  50c bister             57.50  20.00
      Never hinged             160.00
      On cover, without label           85.00
71  A28  50c gray ('97)         62.50   2.50
      Never hinged             175.00
      On cover, without label           72.50
72  A28  1fr car, lt grn        80.00  20.00
      Never hinged             225.00
      On cover, without label          175.00
73  A28  1fr orange ('00)      100.00   5.00
      Never hinged             260.00
      On cover, without label          185.00
  a.  1fr yellow orange        105.00   6.00
      Never hinged             275.00
      On cover, without label          200.00
74  A28  2fr lilac, rose        80.00  70.00
      Never hinged             160.00
      On cover, without label          450.00
75  A28  2fr lilac ('00)       160.00  13.50
      Never hinged             350.00
      On cover, without label          425.00
      Nos. 60-75 (16)         610.40 137.25
```

Covers: Values for covers are for commercial items with proper frankings and stamps without labels. Stamps on postcards and printed envelopes sell for less than the values quoted.

Values for stamps with labels attached and perforations clear of the design, and for covers bearing these stamps.

```
60  A27  1c gray                 2.00    .35
      Never hinged               3.25
      On cover                           7.00
61  A27  2c yellow               2.25   2.00
      Never hinged               3.25
      On cover                         400.00
62  A27  2c violet brn           3.25    .75
      Never hinged              15.00
      On cover                          55.00
63  A27  2c red brown            6.00   1.75
      Never hinged              17.50
      On cover                          70.00
64  A27  5c yellow grn          18.00    .55
      Never hinged              57.50
      On cover                           5.00
65  A28  10c orange brn          8.00    .55
      Never hinged              40.00
      On cover                          10.00
66  A28  10c brt rose            6.25    .75
      Never hinged              22.00
      On cover                          15.00
67  A28  20c olive green        30.00   1.10
      Never hinged              75.00
      On cover                          40.00
68  A28  25c ultra              20.00    .90
      Never hinged              55.00
      On cover                          10.00
  a.  No ball to "5" in upper left
        corner                 65.00   24.00
      Never hinged             190.00
69  A28  35c violet brn         45.00   4.00
      Never hinged             130.00
      On cover                          37.50
  a.  35c red brown             70.00   4.50
      Never hinged             160.00
      On cover                          47.50
70  A28  50c bister            115.00  37.50
      Never hinged             310.00
      On cover                         190.00
71  A28  50c gray              125.00   4.50
      Never hinged             350.00
      On cover                         150.00
72  A28  1fr car, lt grn       160.00  37.50
      Never hinged             450.00
      On cover                         425.00
73  A28  1fr orange            200.00   9.00
      Never hinged             520.00
      On cover                         450.00
  a.  1fr yellow orange        210.00  11.50
      Never hinged             550.00
      On cover                         450.00
74  A28  2fr lilac, rose       160.00 135.00
      Never hinged             310.00
      On cover                         950.00
75  A28  2fr lilac             320.00  25.00
      Never hinged             700.00
      On cover                        1,000.
```

Very thin transparent paper (1904-05)

```
60a  A27  1c gray                3.75   2.50
       Never hinged              6.00
62a  A27  2c violet brown        6.00   4.25
       Never hinged             12.00
64a  A27  5c yellow green       11.50  10.00
       Never hinged             35.00
66a  A28  10c bright rose       26.00  18.00
       Never hinged             52.50
68b  A28  25c ultramarine       45.00  30.00
       Never hinged             80.00
69b  A28  35c violet brown      50.00  32.50
       Never hinged             92.50
71a  A28  50c gray             100.00  55.00
       Never hinged            200.00
73b  A28  1fr orange           240.00 145.00
       Never hinged            450.00
```

Antwerp Exhibition Issue

Arms of Antwerp — A29

1894
```
76  A29  5c green, rose          4.75   3.25
      Never hinged              12.50
      On cover, with label              36.00
77  A29  10c carmine, bluish     3.75   2.50
      Never hinged               7.50
      On cover, with label              32.50
78  A29  25c blue, rose          1.00   1.00
      Never hinged               1.00
      On cover, with label              55.00
      Nos. 76-78 (3)             9.50   6.75
```

Brussels Exhibition Issue

St. Michael and Satan
A30   A31

1896-97   **Perf. 14x14**
```
79  A30  5c dp violet            1.00    .60
      Never hinged               1.40
      On cover, with label              27.50
      Sheet of 25               25.00  17.50
        Never hinged            40.00
80  A31  10c orange brown        8.50   3.50
      Never hinged              20.00
      On cover, with label              32.50
      Sheet of 25              425.00 300.00
        Never hinged           550.00
81  A31  10c lilac brown          .50    .35
      Never hinged                .65
      On cover, with label              22.50
      Sheet of 25               12.50  12.50
        Never hinged            16.00
      Nos. 79-81 (3)            10.00   4.45
```

A32   A33

A34   A35

A36   A37

A38   A39

Two types of 1c:
I — Periods after "Dimanche" and "Zondag" in label.

II — No period after "Dimanche." Period often missing after "Zondag."

1905-11   **Perf. 14**
```
82  A32  1c gray (I) ('07)       1.50    .25
      Never hinged               3.60
      On cover, single franking,
        without label                    3.00
  a.  Type II ('08)              2.00    .60
      Never hinged               4.50
      On cover, single franking,
        without label                    5.00
83  A32  2c red brown ('07)     14.50   5.75
      Never hinged              45.00
      On cover, single franking,
        without label                   20.00
84  A32  5c green ('07)         11.50    .60
      Never hinged              32.50
      On cover, without label            3.00
85  A33  10c dull rose           1.75    .60
      Never hinged               4.00
      On cover, without label            5.00
86  A34  20c olive grn          26.00   1.00
      Never hinged              70.00
      On cover, without label            7.25
87  A35  25c ultra              12.00    .85
      Never hinged              32.50
      On cover, without label            5.00
  a.  25c deep blue ('11)       13.50   2.00
      Never hinged              40.00
88  A36  35c red brn            27.50   2.40
      Never hinged              75.00
      On cover, without label           30.00
  a.  35c purple brown ('05)    27.50   2.40
      Never hinged              72.50
      On cover, without label           30.00
89  A37  50c bluish gray        95.00   4.00
      Never hinged             235.00
      On cover, without label           85.00
90  A38  1fr yellow orange     110.00   8.00
      Never hinged             340.00
      On cover, without label          175.00
  a.  1fr orange ('09)         130.00   9.00
      Never hinged             360.00
      On cover, without label          190.00
91  A39  2fr violet             75.00  22.50
      Never hinged             240.00                —
      Bar cancellation                   5.00
      Nos. 82-91 (10)          374.75  45.95
```

Values for covers bearing stamps with labels attached, and perforations clear of the design

```
82  A32  1c gray (I)                    7.00
  a.  Type II                         12.00
83  A32  2c red brown                  45.00
84  A32  5c green                       7.00
85  A33  10c dull rose                 12.00
86  A34  20c olive grn                 40.00
87  A35  25c ultra                     10.00
  a.  25c deep blue                    16.50
88  A36  35c red brn                   65.00
  a.  35c purple brown                 70.00
89  A37  50c bluish gray              185.00
90  A38  1fr yellow orange            425.00
  a.  1fr orange                      450.00
91  A39  2fr violet                       —
```

A40   A41

Lion of Belgium — A42

A43

King Albert I — A44

1912
```
92  A40  1c orange                .25    .25
      Never hinged                .30
      On cover, single franking          2.00
93  A41  2c orange brn            .25    .45
      Never hinged                .40
      On cover, single franking         20.00
94  A42  5c green                 .25    .25
      Never hinged                .30
      On cover                           1.00
95  A43  10c red                  .75    .40
      Never hinged               2.40
      On cover                           4.00
```

```
96  A43  20c olive grn          16.00   4.00
      Never hinged              35.00
      On cover                          22.50
  a.  20c bronze green          90.00  27.50
      Never hinged             200.00
      On cover                         125.00
97  A43  35c bister brn          1.00    .70
      Never hinged               2.00
      On cover                          17.50
98  A43  40c green              16.00  14.50
      Never hinged              40.00
      On cover                          65.00
99  A43  50c gray                1.00    .80
      Never hinged               2.10
      On cover                          30.00
100  A43  1fr orange             4.00   3.00
      Never hinged               8.75
      On cover                         110.00
101  A43  2fr violet            17.50  17.50
      Never hinged              29.00
      On cover                         135.00
102  A44  5fr plum              80.00  25.00
      Never hinged             175.00
      On cover                         150.00
      Nos. 92-102 (11)        137.00  66.85
```

Counterfeits exist of Nos. 97-102. Those of No. 102 are common.

Covers: Values for stamps on cover are for stamps with labels attached. Covers bearing stamps without labels are worth about half of the values given.

For overprints see Nos. Q49-Q50, Q52, Q55-Q55A, Q57-Q60.

A45

With Engraver's Name

1912-13   **Larger Head**
```
103  A45  10c red                .40    .25
       Never hinged             1.25
       On cover                          3.00
  a.  Without engraver's name    .25    .25
       Never hinged              .30
       On cover                          3.00
104  A45  20c olive green ('13)  .40    .40
       Never hinged              .50
       On cover                         13.50
  a.  Without engraver's name   2.00   2.00
       Never hinged             2.40
       On cover                         32.50
105  A45  25c ultramarine       4.25    .30
       Never hinged             7.00
       On cover                          7.00
  a.  Without engraver's name    .25    .40
       Never hinged              .30
       On cover                          6.00
107  A45  40c green ('13)        .50    .60
       Never hinged              .70
       On cover                         42.50
       Nos. 103-107 (4)         5.55   1.55
```

For overprints see Nos. Q51, Q53-Q54, Q56.

Albert I
A46

Cloth Hall of Ypres
A47

Bridge of Dinant — A48

Library of Louvain — A49

Scheldt River at Antwerp
A50

Anti-slavery Campaign in the Congo A51

King Albert I at Furnes A52

Kings of Belgium Leopold I, Albert I, Leopold II A53

1915-20   Typo.   Perf. 14

108	A46	1c orange	.25	.25
		Never hinged	.30	
		On cover, single franking		4.00
109	A46	2c chocolate	.25	.25
		Never hinged	.30	
		On cover, single franking		6.00
110	A46	3c gray blk ('20)	.30	.25
		Never hinged	.80	
		On cover		2.00
111	A46	5c green	1.00	.25
		Never hinged	3.25	
		On cover		1.00
112	A46	10c carmine	.90	.25
		Never hinged	3.00	
		On cover		1.00
a.		10c bright carmine	3.00	.30
		Never hinged	6.75	
		On cover		2.00
113	A46	15c purple	1.50	.25
		Never hinged	4.25	
		On cover		2.00
114	A46	20c red violet	3.00	.25
		Never hinged	10.00	
		On cover		4.00
115	A46	25c blue	.50	.40
		Never hinged	1.10	
		On cover		6.75
a.		25c bright blue	1.10	.50
		Never hinged	3.00	
		On cover		7.75

Engr.

116	A47	35c brown org & blk	.50	.30
		Never hinged	2.40	
		On cover		8.00
117	A48	40c green & black	1.00	.30
		Never hinged	1.40	
		On cover		11.50
a.		Vert. pair, imperf. btwn.		
118	A49	50c car rose & blk	4.50	.30
		Never hinged	12.50	
		On cover		11.00
119	A50	1fr violet	32.50	1.00
		Never hinged	90.00	
		On cover		32.50
120	A51	2fr slate	21.00	2.00
		Never hinged	57.50	
		On cover		55.00
a.		2fr gray black	25.00	2.40
		Never hinged	67.50	
		On cover		57.50
b.		2fr pale gray	42.50	7.75
		Never hinged	97.50	
		On cover		115.00
121	A52	5fr dp blue	275.00	125.00
		Never hinged	775.00	
		On cover		325.00
		Telegraph or railroad cancel		55.00
122	A53	10fr brown	20.00	20.00
		Never hinged	35.00	
		On cover		175.00
		Nos. 108-122 (15)	362.20	151.05

Perf 15

116a	A47	35c brown orange & black	1.60	.80
		Never hinged	5.00	
		On cover		8.00
117b	A48	40c green & black	1.60	.80
		Never hinged	5.00	
		On cover		11.50
118a	A49	50c carmine rose & black	6.00	1.00
		Never hinged	17.50	
		On cover		11.50
119a	A50	1f violet	37.50	4.00
		Never hinged	110.00	
		On cover		35.00
120c	A51	2f slate	27.50	5.75
		Never hinged	77.50	
		On cover		57.50
121a	A52	5f deep blue	350.00	145.00
		Never hinged	1,050.	
		On cover		500.00
122a	A53	10f brown	25.00	25.00
		Never hinged	50.00	
		On cover		175.00

Two types each of the 1c, 10c and 20c; three of the 2c and 15c; four of the 5c, differing in the top left corner.

See No. 138. For surcharges see Nos. B34-B47.

Nos. 111-119 were handstamped "T" for local provisional use. See Nos. J16C-J16K.

Perron of Liege (Fountain) — A54

Size: 18¼x28½mm

1919, July 25   Perf. 11½

123	A54	25c blue	2.40	.35
		Never hinged	8.50	
		On cover		9.00
a.		25c deep blue	3.00	.45

Size: 18½x28mm

1919, July 19

123B	A54	25c blue	400.00	400.00
c.		Sheet of 10	6,000.	6,000.
		Never hinged	7,000.	

No. 123B is the first printing, which was issued in sheets of 10. Nos. 123 and 123a were later printings, issued in sheets of 100.

King Albert in Trench Helmet — A55

Perf. 11, 11½, 11½x11, 11x11½

1919   Size: 18½x22mm

124	A55	1c lilac brn	.25	.25
		Never hinged	.30	
125	A55	2c olive	.25	.25
		Never hinged	.30	
		On cover, single franking		11.00

Size: 22x26

126	A55	5c green	.25	.25
		Never hinged	.45	
		On cover		2.50
127	A55	10c carmine, 22x26¾mm	.25	.25
		Never hinged	.50	
		On cover		2.00
a.		Size: 22½x26mm	1.00	.60
		Never hinged	2.00	
		On cover		6.00
128	A55	15c gray vio, 22x26¾mm	.30	.30
		Never hinged	.60	
		On cover		3.50
a.		Size: 22½x26mm	2.40	.60
		Never hinged	5.50	
		On cover		6.75
129	A55	20c olive blk	1.10	1.10
		Never hinged	2.00	
		On cover		23.50
130	A55	25c deep blue	1.60	1.60
		Never hinged	2.75	
		On cover		14.00
131	A55	35c bister brn	3.00	3.00
		Never hinged	3.50	
132	A55	40c red	5.00	5.00
		Never hinged	11.50	
133	A55	50c red brn	9.50	10.00
		Never hinged	19.00	
		On cover		135.00
134	A55	1fr lt orange	40.00	40.00
		Never hinged	77.50	
135	A55	2fr violet	375.00	375.00
		Never hinged	575.00	

Size: 28x33½mm

136	A55	5fr car lake	100.00	100.00
		Never hinged	175.00	
137	A55	10fr claret	110.00	110.00
		Never hinged	275.00	
		Nos. 124-137 (14)	646.50	647.00
		Set, never hinged	1,150.	

Type of 1915 Inscribed: "FRANK" instead of "FRANKEN"

1919, Dec.   Perf. 14, 15

138	A52	5fr deep blue	1.75	1.25
		Never hinged	3.00	
		On cover		40.00

Town Hall at Termonde — A56

1920   Perf. 11½

139	A56	65c claret & black, 27x22mm	.75	.25
		Never hinged	1.50	
		On cover		12.00
b.		Center inverted	67,500.	
c.		Size: 26¼x22½mm	5.75	2.40
		Never hinged	13.50	
		On cover		16.50

For surcharge see No. 143.

Nos. B48-B50 Surcharged in Red or Black

1921   Perf. 12

140	SP6	20c on 5c + 5c (R)	.60	.25
		Never hinged	1.90	
		On cover		10.00
a.		Inverted surcharge	625.00	625.00
		Never hinged	1,100.	
		On cover		2,200.
141	SP7	20c on 10c + 5c	.40	.25
		Never hinged	1.10	
		On cover		7.75
142	SP8	20c on 15c + 15c (R)	.60	.25
		Never hinged	1.90	
		On cover		10.00
a.		Inverted surcharge	625.00	625.00
		Never hinged	1,100.	
		On cover		2,200.

No. 139 Surcharged in Red

143	A56	55c on 65c claret & blk	1.50	.35
		Never hinged	3.50	
a.		Pair, one without surcharge	2.25	.85
		Never hinged	5.00	
		Nos. 140-143 (4)	3.10	1.10
		Set, never hinged	8.50	

A58

1922-27   Typo.   Perf. 14

144	A58	1c orange	.25	.25
		Never hinged	.30	
		On cover, single franking		10.00
145	A58	2c olive ('26)	.25	.25
		Never hinged	.30	
		On cover, single franking		13.50
146	A58	3c fawn	.25	.25
		Never hinged	.30	
		On cover		2.50
147	A58	5c gray	.25	.25
		Never hinged	.30	
		On cover		1.00
148	A58	10c blue grn	.25	.25
		Never hinged	.30	
		On cover		1.00
149	A58	15c plum ('23)	.25	.25
		Never hinged	.30	
		On cover		1.25
150	A58	20c black brn	.25	.25
		Never hinged	.40	
		On cover		2.00
151	A58	25c magenta	.25	.25
		Never hinged	.40	
a.		25c dull violet ('23)	.50	.25
		Never hinged	1.10	
		On cover		1.25
152	A58	30c vermilion	.50	.25
		Never hinged	.70	
		On cover		4.00
153	A58	30c rose ('25)	.35	.25
		Never hinged	.70	
		On cover		5.00
154	A58	35c red brown	.35	.30
		Never hinged	.50	
		On cover		11.50
155	A58	35c blue grn ('27)	.80	.35
		Never hinged	1.75	
		On cover		6.75
156	A58	40c rose	.50	.25
		Never hinged	.70	
		On cover		6.75
157	A58	50c bister ('25)	.50	.25
		Never hinged	.80	
		On cover		3.00
158	A58	60c olive brn ('27)	3.00	.25
		Never hinged	9.50	
		On cover		1.00
159	A58	1.25fr dp blue ('26)	1.10	1.10
		Never hinged	1.25	
		On cover		50.00
160	A58	1.50fr brt blue ('26)	1.60	.45
		Never hinged	4.00	
		On cover		9.00
a.		1.50fr bright sky blue ('27)	7.75	2.00
		Never hinged	19.50	
		On cover		10.00
b.		1.50fr intense bright blue ('30)	11.50	.40
		Never hinged	48.00	
		On cover		40.00
161	A58	1.75fr ultra ('27)	1.40	.25
		Never hinged	4.00	
		On cover		1.25
a.		Tete beche pair	5.00	5.00

	Never hinged	10.00	
c.	Bklt. pane of 4 + 2 labels	40.00	
	Nos. 144-161 (18)	12.10	5.70
	Set, never hinged	27.50	

See Nos. 185-190. For overprints and surcharges see Nos. 191-195, 197, B56, O1-O6.

A59

1921-25   Engr.

Perf. 11, 11x11½, 11½, 11½x11, 11½x12, 11½x12½, 12½

162	A59	50c dull blue	.30	.25
		Never hinged	1.60	
		On cover		3.00
163	A59	75c scarlet ('22)	.25	.25
		Never hinged	.30	
		On cover		10.00
164	A59	75c ultra ('24)	.45	.25
		Never hinged	.60	
		On cover		5.00
165	A59	1fr black brn ('22)	.80	.25
		Never hinged	2.00	
		On cover		6.50
166	A59	1fr dk blue ('25)	.60	.25
		Never hinged	.80	
		On cover		7.00
167	A59	2fr dk green ('22)	.90	.25
		Never hinged	2.00	
		On cover		15.00
168	A59	5fr brown vio ('23)	13.50	15.00
		Never hinged	18.00	
		On cover		40.00
169	A59	10fr magenta ('22)	9.00	6.50
		Never hinged	25.00	
		On cover		165.00
		Nos. 162-169 (8)	25.80	23.00
		Set, never hinged	52.50	

No. 162 measures 18x20¾mm and was printed in sheets of 100.

Philatelic Exhibition Issues

1921, May 26   Perf. 11½

170	A59	50c dark blue	3.50	3.50
		Never hinged	4.75	
a.		Sheet of 25	200.00	175.00
		Never hinged	225.00	

No. 170 measures 17½x21¼mm, was printed in sheets of 25 and sold at the Philatelic Exhibition at Brussels.

The sheet normally has pin holes and a cancellation-like marking in the margin. These are considered unused and the condition valued here.

Souvenir Sheet

1924, May 24   Perf. 11½

171		Sheet of 4	140.00	140.00
		Never hinged	260.00	
a.		A59 5fr red brown	10.00	10.00
		Never hinged	12.00	
		On cover		35.00

Sold only at the Intl. Phil. Exhib., Brussels. Sheet size: 130x145mm.

The sheet normally has pin holes and a cancellation-like marking in the margin. These are considered unused and the condition valued here.

Kings Leopold I and Albert I — A60

1925   Perf. 14

172	A60	10c dp green	7.25	7.25
		Never hinged	17.50	
173	A60	15c dull vio	3.75	4.50
		Never hinged	7.75	
		On cover		20.00
174	A60	20c red brown	3.75	4.50
		Never hinged	7.75	
175	A60	25c grnsh black	3.75	4.50
		Never hinged	7.75	
		On cover		40.00
176	A60	30c vermilion	3.75	4.50
		Never hinged	7.75	
		On cover		17.50
177	A60	35c lt blue	3.75	4.50
		Never hinged	7.75	
178	A60	40c brnsh blk	3.75	4.50
		Never hinged	7.75	
		On cover		40.00
179	A60	50c yellow brn	3.75	4.50
		Never hinged	7.75	
		On cover		30.00
180	A60	75c dk blue	3.75	4.50
		Never hinged	7.75	
181	A60	1fr dk violet	6.50	6.50
		Never hinged	13.50	

182	A60 2fr ultra	4.00	4.00
	Never hinged	7.75	
183	A60 5fr blue blk	3.75	4.50
	Never hinged	7.75	
184	A60 10fr dp rose	6.50	8.00
	Never hinged	17.50	
	Nos. 172-184 (13)	58.00	66.25
	Set, never hinged	126.00	

75th anniv. of Belgian postage stamps.
Nos. 172-184 were sold only in sets and only by The Administration of Posts, not at post offices.

A61

1926-27   Typo.

185	A61 75c dk violet	.75	.70
	Never hinged	1.60	
	On cover		20.00
186	A61 1fr pale yellow	.60	.35
	Never hinged	.75	
	On cover		15.00
187	A61 1fr rose red ('27)	1.00	.25
	Never hinged	2.40	
	On cover		5.00
a.	Tete beche pair	7.50	4.50
c.	Bklt. pane 4 + 2 labels	25.00	
188	A61 2fr Prus blue	2.50	.45
	Never hinged	5.75	
	On cover		17.50
189	A61 5fr emerald ('27)	27.50	1.60
	Never hinged	77.50	
	On cover		67.50
190	A61 10fr dk brown ('27)	60.00	7.75
	Never hinged	160.00	
	On cover		175.00
	Nos. 185-190 (6)	92.35	11.10
	Set, never hinged	249.00	

For overprints and surcharge see Nos. 196, Q174-Q175.

Stamps of 1921-27
Surcharged in Carmine,
Red or Blue

1927

191	A58 3c on 2c olive (C)	.25	.25
	Never hinged	.30	
	On cover, single franking		18.50
192	A58 10c on 15c plum (R)	.25	.25
	Never hinged	.30	
	On cover		3.00
193	A58 35c on 40c rose (Bl)	.45	.25
	Never hinged	.60	
	On cover		2.50
194	A58 1.75fr on 1.50fr brt bl (C)	2.25	.80
	Never hinged	3.00	
	Nos. 191-194 (4)	3.20	1.55
	Set, never hinged	3.75	

Nos. 153, 185 and 159
Surcharged in Black

1929, Jan. 1

195	A58 5c on 30c rose	.25	.25
	Never hinged	.30	
	On cover		4.50
196	A61 5c on 75c dk violet	.25	.25
	Never hinged	.30	
	On cover		4.50
197	A58 5c on 1.25fr dp blue	.25	.25
	Never hinged	.30	
	On cover		4.50
	Nos. 195-197 (3)	.75	.75
	Set, never hinged	.65	

The surcharge on Nos. 195-197 is a pre-cancelation which alters the value of the stamp to which it is applied.

Values for precanceled stamps in unused column are for those which have not been through the post and have original gum. Values in second column are for postally used, gumless stamps.

1929-32   Typo.   Perf. 14

198	A63 1c orange	.25	.25
	Never hinged	.30	
199	A63 2c emerald ('31)	.45	.45
	Never hinged	.50	
200	A63 3c red brown	.25	.25
	Never hinged	.30	
201	A63 5c slate	.25	.25
	Never hinged	.30	
c.	Bklt. pane of 4 + 2 labels	8.25	
202	A63 10c olive grn	.25	.25
	Never hinged	.30	
	On cover		1.00
c.	Bklt. pane of 4 + 2 labels	4.50	
203	A63 20c brt violet	1.00	.25
	Never hinged	4.00	
	On cover		15.00
204	A63 25c rose red	.45	.25
	Never hinged	1.00	
	On cover		1.00
c.	Bklt. pane of 4 + 2 labels	8.25	
205	A63 35c green	.60	.25
	Never hinged	1.10	
	On cover		2.00
c.	Bklt. pane of 4 + 2 labels	9.75	
206	A63 40c red vio ('30)	.30	.25
	Never hinged	1.25	
	On cover		1.00
c.	Bklt. pane of 4 + 2 labels	9.75	
207	A63 50c dp blue	.45	.25
	Never hinged	.80	
	On cover		1.00
c.	Bklt. pane of 4 + 2 labels	8.25	
208	A63 60c rose ('30)	2.00	.25
	Never hinged	6.75	
	On cover		6.75
c.	Bklt. pane of 4 + 2 labels	30.00	
209	A63 70c org brn ('30)	1.10	.25
	Never hinged	4.25	
	On cover		4.00
c.	Bklt. pane of 4 + 2 labels	22.50	
210	A63 75c dk blue ('30)	2.00	.25
	Never hinged	7.75	
	On cover		2.40
b.	75c blue violet	2.40	.25
	Never hinged	8.75	
	On cover		2.40
211	A63 75c dp brown ('32)	6.00	.25
	Never hinged	26.00	
	On cover		2.00
b.	Bklt. pane of 4 + 2 labels	100.00	
	Nos. 198-211 (14)	15.35	3.70
	Set, never hinged	55.00	

For overprints and surcharges see Nos. 225-226, 240-241, 254-256, 309, O7-O15.

Tete Beche Pairs

201a	A63 5c	.60	.60
	Never hinged	1.10	
202a	A63 10c	.30	.30
	Never hinged	.60	
204a	A63 25c	1.75	1.75
	Never hinged	2.75	
205a	A63 35c	2.75	2.75
	Never hinged	3.75	
206a	A63 40c	2.75	2.75
	Never hinged	3.75	
207a	A63 50c	2.25	2.25
	Never hinged	3.50	
208a	A63 60c	8.00	7.50
	Never hinged	15.00	
209a	A63 70c	6.00	5.00
	Never hinged	8.75	
210a	A63 75c	9.00	8.50
	Never hinged	15.00	
211a	A63 75c	27.50	25.00
	Never hinged	62.50	
	Nos. 201a-211a (10)	60.90	56.40
	Set, never hinged	110.00	

Tete-beche gutter pairs also exist.

A64

1929, Jan. 25   Engr.   Perf. 14½, 14

212	A64 10fr dk brown	15.00	4.00
	Never hinged	37.50	
	On cover		75.00
213	A64 20fr dk green	85.00	20.00
	Never hinged	190.00	
	On cover		175.00
214	A64 50fr red violet	13.50	13.50
	Never hinged	24.00	
a.	Perf. 14½	37.50	40.00
	Never hinged	87.50	
215	A64 100fr brownish lake	13.50	13.50
	Never hinged	25.00	
a.	Perf. 14½	37.50	40.00
	Never hinged	87.50	
	Nos. 212-215 (4)	127.00	51.00
	Set, never hinged	276.50	

Peter Paul
Rubens — A65

Zenobe
Gramme — A66

1930, Apr. 26   Photo.   Perf. 12½x12

216	A65 35c blue green	.40	.25
	Never hinged	1.00	
	On cover		1.00
217	A66 35c blue green	.40	.25
	Never hinged	1.10	
	On cover		1.00
	Set, never hinged	2.10	

No. 216 issued for the Antwerp Exhibition, No. 217 the Liege Exhibition.

Leopold I, by
Lievin de
Winne — A67

Leopold II, by
Joseph
Leempoels — A68

Design: 1.75fr, Albert I.

1930, July 1   Engr.   Perf. 11½

218	A67 60c brown violet	.25	.25
	Never hinged	.35	
	On cover		1.25
219	A68 1fr carmine	1.10	1.10
	Never hinged	2.50	
	On cover		3.50
220	A68 1.75fr dk blue	2.75	1.25
	Never hinged	6.75	
	On cover		4.50
	Nos. 218-220 (3)	4.10	2.60
	Set, never hinged	9.60	

Centenary of Belgian independence.
For overprints see Nos. 222-224.

Antwerp Exhibition Issue
Souvenir Sheet

Arms of
Antwerp
A70

1930, Aug. 9   Perf. 11½

221	A70 4fr Sheet of 1	275.00	240.00
	Never hinged	600.00	
	On cover		140.00
a.	Single stamp	100.00	80.00
			140.00

Size: 142x141mm. Inscription in lower margin "ATELIER DU TIMBRE-1930-ZEGELFABRIEK." Each purchaser of a ticket to the Antwerp Phil. Exhib., Aug. 9-15, was allowed to purchase one stamp. The ticket cost 6 francs.

The sheet normally has pin holes and a cancellation-like marking in the margin. These are considered unused and the condition valued here.

Nos. 218-220
Overprinted in Blue
or Red

B.I.T.
OCT. 1930

1930, Oct.

222	A67 60c brown vio (Bl)	2.00	2.00
	Never hinged	4.00	
	On cover		6.75
223	A68 1fr carmine (Bl)	8.25	7.75
	Never hinged	15.00	
	On cover		24.00
224	A68 1.75fr dk blue (R)	14.50	14.50
	Never hinged	35.00	
	On cover		42.50
	Nos. 222-224 (3)	24.75	24.25
	Set, never hinged	55.00	

50th meeting of the administrative council of the Intl. Labor Bureau at Brussels.

The names of the painters and the initials of the engraver have been added at the foot of these stamps.

Stamps of 1929-30 Surcharged in Blue or Black

1931, Feb. 20   Perf. 14

225	A63 2c on 3c red brown (Bl)	.25	.25
	Never hinged	2.00	
226	A63 10c on 60c rose (Bk)	.50	.25
	Never hinged	1.75	
	On cover		8.50
	Set, never hinged	3.75	

The surcharge on No. 226 is a precancelation which alters the denomination. See note after No. 197.

King Albert — A71a
A71

1931, June 15   Photo.

227	A71 1fr brown carmine	.50	.25
	Never hinged	1.00	
	On cover		3.00

1932, June 1

228	A71a 75c bister brown	1.25	.25
	Never hinged	5.00	
	On cover		1.00
a.	Tete beche pair	6.75	6.75
	Never hinged	17.50	
c.	Bklt. pane 4 + 2 labels	18.00	

See No. 257. For overprint see No. O18.

A72

1931-32   Engr.

229	A72 1.25fr gray black	.75	.50
	Never hinged	2.25	
	On cover		6.75
230	A72 1.50fr brown vio	1.25	.50
	Never hinged	4.75	
	On cover		5.50
231	A72 1.75fr dp blue	.80	.25
	Never hinged	1.60	
	On cover		1.00
232	A72 2fr red brown	1.10	.25
	Never hinged	2.40	
	On cover		5.50
233	A72 2.45fr dp violet	1.90	.40
	Never hinged	8.00	
	On cover		11.50
234	A72 2.50fr black brn ('32)	10.00	.50
	Never hinged	22.50	
	On cover		23.50
235	A72 5fr dp green	18.00	1.10
	Never hinged	67.50	
	On cover		30.00
236	A72 10fr claret	45.00	12.50
	Never hinged	140.00	
	On cover		77.50
	Nos. 229-236 (8)	78.80	16.00
	Set, never hinged	249.00	

Nos. 206 and 209 Surcharged as No. 226, but dated "1932"

1932, Jan. 1

240	A63 10c on 40c red vio	2.50	.30
	Never hinged	7.25	
	On cover		5.00
241	A63 10c on 70c org brn	2.00	.25
	Never hinged	6.25	
	On cover		5.00
	Set, never hinged	22.50	

See note after No. 197.

Gleaner
A73

Mercury
A74

1932, June 1   Typo.   Perf. 13½x14

245	A73 2c pale green	.35	.35
	Never hinged	.50	
246	A74 5c dp orange	.25	.25
	Never hinged	.40	
	On cover, single franking		5.00
247	A73 10c olive grn	.25	.25
	Never hinged	.40	
	On cover		1.00
a.	Tete beche pair	4.00	4.00
	Never hinged	5.75	
c.	Bklt. pane 4 + 2 labels	15.00	
248	A74 20c brt violet	1.00	.25
	Never hinged	3.25	
	On cover		37.50
249	A73 25c deep red	.60	.25
	Never hinged	2.00	
	On cover		1.60
a.	Tete beche pair	3.50	3.50
	Never hinged	5.00	
c.	Bklt. pane 4 + 2 labels	15.00	
250	A74 35c dp green	2.40	.25
	Never hinged	7.75	
	On cover		1.00
	Nos. 245-250 (6)	4.85	1.60
	Set, never hinged	14.50	

For overprints see Nos. O16-O17.

Auguste Piccard's
Balloon — A75

1932, Nov. 26   Engr.   Perf. 11½

251	A75 75c red brown	3.50	.30
	Never hinged	9.50	
	On cover		3.00
252	A75 1.75fr dk blue	13.50	2.10
	Never hinged	37.50	
	On cover		7.25
253	A75 2.50fr dk violet	17.00	11.50
	Never hinged	47.50	
	On cover		27.50
	Nos. 251-253 (3)	34.00	13.90
	Set, never hinged	110.00	

Issued in commemoration of Prof. Auguste Piccard's two ascents to the stratosphere.

Nos. 206 and 209 Surcharged as No. 226, but dated "1933"

1933, Nov.   Perf. 14

254	A63 10c on 40c red vio	14.00	4.00
	Never hinged	32.50	
	On cover		55.00
255	A63 10c on 70c org brn	12.50	1.50
	Never hinged	32.50	
	On cover		7.00
	Set, never hinged	80.00	

No. 206 Surcharged as No. 226, but dated "1934"

1934, Feb.

256	A63 10c on 40c red vio	12.50	1.50
	Never hinged	50.00	
	On cover		8.00

For Nos. 254 to 256 see note after No. 197. Regummed examples of Nos. 254-256 are plentiful.

King Albert Memorial Issue
Type of 1932 with Black Margins

1934, Mar. 10   Photo.

257	A71a 75c black	.30	.25
	Never hinged	.60	
	On cover		3.50

Congo
Pavilion — A76

Designs: 1fr, Brussels pavilion. 1.50fr, "Old Brussels." 1.75fr, Belgian pavilion.

1934, July 1   Perf. 14x13½

258	A76 35c green	.75	.30
	Never hinged	2.50	
	On cover		3.00
259	A76 1fr dk carmine	1.25	.40
	Never hinged	4.25	
	On cover		2.00
260	A76 1.50fr brown	5.00	.80
	Never hinged	18.00	
	On cover		10.00

261	A76 1.75fr blue	5.00	.30
	Never hinged	19.00	
	On cover		5.00
	Nos. 258-261 (4)	12.00	1.80
	Set, never hinged	45.00	

Brussels Intl. Exhib. of 1935.

King Leopold III
A80   A81

1934-35   Perf. 13½x14

262	A80 70c olive blk ('35)	.35	.25
	Never hinged	1.00	
	On cover		1.00
a.	Tete beche pair	1.50	1.00
	Never hinged	2.25	
c.	Bklt. pane 4 + 2 labels	6.25	
263	A80 75c brown	.65	.25
	Never hinged	1.50	
	On cover		3.00

Perf. 14x13½

264	A81 1fr rose car ('35)	3.25	.35
	On cover	7.75	
			6.00
	Nos. 262-264 (3)	4.25	.85
	Set, never hinged	10.00	

For overprint see No. O19.

Coat of Arms — A82

1935-48   Typo.   Perf. 14

265	A82 2c green ('37)	.25	.25
	Never hinged	.30	
a.	2c yellow green ('44)	.25	.25
	Never hinged	.30	
266	A82 5c orange	.25	.25
	Never hinged	.30	
	On cover		.75
267	A82 10c olive bister	.25	.25
	Never hinged	.30	
	On cover		.60
a.	Tete beche pair	.30	.25
	Never hinged	.50	
b.	Bklt. pane 4 + 2 labels	4.50	
268	A82 15c dk violet	.25	.25
	Never hinged	.30	
	On cover		4.00
269	A82 20c lilac	.25	.25
	Never hinged	.30	
	On cover		4.00
270	A82 25c carmine rose	.25	.25
	Never hinged	.30	
	On cover		1.25
a.	Tete beche pair	.30	.40
	Never hinged	.55	
c.	Bklt. pane 4 + 2 labels	4.50	
271	A82 25c yel org ('46)	.25	.25
	Never hinged	.30	
272	A82 30c brown	.25	.25
	Never hinged	.30	
	On cover		4.50
273	A82 35c green	.25	.25
	Never hinged	.30	
	On cover		1.00
a.	Tete beche pair	.30	.30
	Never hinged	.50	
c.	Bklt. pane 4 + 2 labels	3.00	
274	A82 40c red vio ('38)	.25	.25
	Never hinged	.90	
	On cover		1.25
275	A82 50c blue	.40	.25
	Never hinged	.80	
	On cover		1.00
276	A82 60c slate ('41)	.25	.25
	Never hinged	.30	
	On cover		1.00
277	A82 65c red lilac ('46)	.25	.25
	Never hinged	.75	
278	A82 70c lt blue grn ('45)	.25	.25
	Never hinged	.30	
	On cover		7.75
279	A82 75c lilac rose ('45)	.25	.25
	Never hinged	.70	
	On cover		3.00
280	A82 80c green ('48)	3.50	.40
	Never hinged	8.75	
	On cover		8.75
281	A82 90c dull vio ('46)	.25	.25
	Never hinged	.50	
	On cover		2.00
282	A82 1fr red brown ('45)	.25	.25
	Never hinged	.50	
	On cover		2.00
	Nos. 265-282 (18)	7.90	4.65
	Set, never hinged	17.00	

Several stamps of type A82 exist in various shades.
Nos. 265, 361 were privately overprinted and surcharged "+10FR." by the Association Belgo-Americaine for the dedication of the Bastogne Memorial, July 16, 1950. The overprint is in six types. Value $1.50 per set.
See design O1. For overprints and surcharges see Nos. 312-313, 361-364, 390-394, O20-O22, O24, O26-O28, O33 in this

catalogue or *Scott Standard Postage Stamp Catalogue*, Vol. 1.

A83   A83a

Perf. 14, 14x13½, 11½

1936-56   Photo.

Size: 17½x21¾mm

283	A83 70c brown	.30	.25
	Never hinged	.50	
	On cover		.75
a.	Tete beche pair	.80	.80
	Never hinged	1.40	
c.	Bklt. pane 4 + 2 labels	7.50	

Size: 20¾x24mm

284	A83a 1fr rose car	.30	.25
	Never hinged	1.00	
	On cover		1.50
285	A83a 1.20fr dk brown ('51)	.80	.25
	Never hinged	1.50	
	On cover		1.00
a.	Perf. 11½ ('56)	1.20	.25
	Never hinged	2.75	
	On cover		1.00
286	A83a 1.50fr brt red vio ('43)	.40	.30
	Never hinged	1.00	
	On cover		6.75
287	A83a 1.75fr dp ultra ('43)	.25	.25
	Never hinged	.40	
	On cover		16.00
288	A83a 1.75fr dk car ('50)	.25	.25
	Never hinged	.30	
	On cover		.75
289	A83a 2fr dk pur ('43)	1.00	1.00
	Never hinged	1.60	
	On cover		29.00
290	A83a 2.25fr grnsh blk ('43)	.25	.25
	Never hinged	.40	
	On cover		16.00
291	A83a 2.50fr org red ('51)	1.75	.30
	Never hinged	6.50	
	On cover		2.00
a.	Perf. 11½ ('56)	20.00	.25
	Never hinged	60.00	
	On cover		6.00
292	A83a 3.25fr chestnut ('43)	.25	.25
	Never hinged	.30	
	On cover		7.25
293	A83a 5fr dp green ('43)	1.00	.40
	Never hinged	3.25	
	On cover		24.00
	Nos. 283-293 (11)	6.55	3.75
	Set, never hinged	17.00	

Nos. 287-288, 290-291, 293 inscribed "Belgie-Belgique."
See designs A85, A91. For overprints and surcharges see Nos. 314, O23, O25; Nos. O29, O31, O34 in *Scott Standard Postage Stamp Catalogue*, Vol. 1.

A84

1936-51   Engr.   Perf. 14x13½

294	A84 1.50fr rose lilac ('41)	.60	.35
	Never hinged	2.00	
	On cover		8.75
a.	1.50fr magenta ('36)	4.00	2.00
	Never hinged	9.75	
	On cover		14.00
b.	1.50fr rose ('39)	1.00	.40
	Never hinged	3.00	
	On cover		10.00
295	A84 1.75fr dull blue	.25	.25
	Never hinged	.70	
	On cover		5.00
a.	1.75fr ultramarine ('36)	2.00	.40
	Never hinged	4.75	
	On cover		5.00
b.	1.75fr blue black ('37)	2.75	.40
	Never hinged	6.75	
	On cover		5.75
296	A84 2fr dull vio	.40	.30
	Never hinged	1.50	
	On cover		6.75
a.	2fr lilac ('36)	1.50	.60
	Never hinged	4.75	
	On cover		9.00
b.	2fr red violet ('38)	1.00	.35
	Never hinged	6.75	
	On cover		7.75
297	A84 2.25fr gray vio ('41)	.25	.25
	Never hinged	.70	
	On cover		17.50
298	A84 2.45fr black	32.50	.70
	Never hinged	100.00	
	On cover		3.25
299	A84 2.50fr ol blk ('40)	2.00	.25
	Never hinged	8.75	
	On cover		13.50
300	A84 3.25fr org brn ('41)	.30	.25
	Never hinged	.50	
	On cover		5.75

301	A84 5fr dull green	2.40	.50
	Never hinged	7.00	
	On cover		16.50
a.	5fr yellow green ('37)	57.50	11.50
	Never hinged	165.00	
	On cover		16.50
b.	5fr olive green ('38)	2.40	.50
	Never hinged	7.25	
	On cover		1.75
302	A84 10fr vio brn	.60	.25
	Never hinged	.90	
	On cover		10.00
a.	10fr light brown	10.00	.25
	Never hinged	30.00	
	On cover		11.50
303	A84 20fr vermilion	1.00	.30
	Never hinged	2.40	
	On cover		30.00
a.	20fr rose orange ('36)	1.15	.40
	Never hinged	4.00	
	On cover		35.00

Perf. 11½

304	A84 3fr yel brn ('51)	.55	.25
	Never hinged	1.50	
	On cover		4.75
305	A84 4fr bl, bluish ('50)	4.75	.25
	Never hinged	5.00	
	On cover		2.00
a.	White paper	9.00	.25
	Never hinged	14.50	
306	A84 6fr brt rose car ('51)	2.75	.25
	Never hinged	10.00	
	On cover		9.00
307	A84 10fr brn vio ('51)	.55	.25
	Never hinged	1.25	
	On cover		3.00
308	A84 20fr red ('51)	1.10	.25
	Never hinged	2.50	
	On cover		6.75
	Nos. 294-308 (15)	50.00	4.65
	Set, never hinged	150.00	

See No. 1159 in *Scott Standard Postage Stamp Catalogue*, Vol. 1. For overprint and surcharges see Nos. 316-317; No. O32 in Scott Standard catalogue, Vol. 1.

No. 206 Surcharged as No. 226, but dated "1937"

1937   Unwmk.   Perf. 14

309	A63 10c on 40c red vio	.25	.25
	On cover	.30	
			5.75

See note after No. 197.

A85

1938-41   Photo.   Perf. 13½x14

310	A85 75c olive gray	.25	.25
	Never hinged	.60	
	On cover		1.00
a.	Tete beche pair	.75	.80
	Never hinged	1.50	
c.	Bklt. pane 4 + 2 labels	6.75	
311	A85 1fr rose pink ('41)	.25	.25
	Never hinged	.30	
	On cover		1.00
a.	Tete beche pair	.25	.25
	Never hinged	.40	
b.	Booklet pane of 6	2.25	
c.	Bklt. pane 4 + 2 labels	2.25	
	Set, never hinged	.80	

For overprints and surcharges see Nos. 315, O25; Nos. O30, O35 in *Scott Standard Postage Stamp Catalogue*, Vol. 1.

Nos. 272, 274, 283, 310, 299, 298 Srchd. in Blue, Black, Carmine or Red

a   b

c

1938-42

312	A82 (a) 10c on 30c (Bl)	.25	.25
	Never hinged	.30	
			3.50
313	A82 (a) 10c on 40c (Bl)	.25	.25
	Never hinged	.30	
	On cover		4.00

314 A83 (b) 10c on 70c (Bk) .25 .25
　Never hinged .30
　On cover 3.50
315 A85 (b) 50c on 75c (C) .25 .25
　Never hinged .40
　On cover 4.00
316 A84 (c) 2.25fr on 2.50fr .45 .45
　　　　(C)
　Never hinged .70
　On cover 57.50
317 A84 (c) 2.50fr on 2.45fr 11.00 .25
　　　　(R)
　Never hinged 25.00
　On cover 15.00
　Nos. 312-317 (6) 12.45 1.70
　Set, never hinged 26.00

Issue date: No. 317, Oct. 31, 1938.

Basilica and Bell Tower — A86　　Water Exhibition Buildings — A87

Designs: 1.50fr, Albert Canal and Park. 1.75fr, Eygenbilsen Cut in Albert Canal.

1938, Oct. 31　Perf. 14x13½, 13½x14
318 A86 35c dk blue grn .25 .25
　Never hinged .30
　On cover 3.00
319 A87 1fr rose red .45 .30
　Never hinged 1.50
　On cover 2.00
320 A87 1.50fr vio brn 1.10 .60
　Never hinged 4.75
　On cover 5.50
321 A87 1.75fr ultra 1.25 .25
　Never hinged 4.25
　On cover 4.00
　Nos. 318-321 (4) 3.05 1.40
　Set, never hinged 11.00

Intl. Water Exhibition, Liège, 1939.

SEMI-POSTAL STAMPS

Values quoted for Nos. B1-B24 are for stamps with label attached. Stamps without label sell for one-tenth or less.

St. Martin of Tours Dividing His Cloak with a Beggar
SP1　　　　SP2

Unwmk.
1910, June 1　Typo.　Perf. 14
B1 SP1 1c gray .75 .75
B2 SP1 2c purple brn 8.00 8.00
B3 SP1 5c peacock blue 1.90 1.90
B4 SP1 10c brown red 1.90 1.90
B5 SP2 1c gray green 1.90 1.90
B6 SP2 2c violet brn 5.00 5.00
B7 SP2 5c peacock blue 2.25 2.25
B8 SP2 10c carmine 2.25 2.25
　Nos. B1-B8 (8) 23.95 23.95
　Set, never hinged 65.00

Overprinted "1911" in Black
1911, Apr. 1
B9 SP1 1c gray 27.50 16.00
　a.　Inverted overprint
B10 SP1 2c purple brn 125.00 72.50
B11 SP1 5c peacock blue 8.00 5.25
B12 SP1 10c brown red 8.00 5.25
B13 SP2 1c gray green 42.50 27.50
B14 SP2 2c violet brn 60.00 32.50
B15 SP2 5c peacock blue 8.00 5.25
B16 SP2 10c carmine 8.00 5.25
　Nos. B9-B16 (8) 287.00 169.50
　Set, never hinged 600.00

Overprinted "CHARLEROI-1911"
1911, June
B17 SP1 1c gray 4.00 2.50
B18 SP1 2c purple brn 16.00 10.00
B19 SP1 5c peacock blue 9.00 6.50

B20 SP1 10c brown red 9.00 6.50
B21 SP2 1c gray green 4.00 2.50
B22 SP2 2c violet brn 11.00 9.00
B23 SP2 5c peacock blue 9.00 6.50
B24 SP2 10c carmine 9.00 6.50
　Nos. B17-B24 (8) 71.00 50.00
　Set, never hinged 90.00

Nos. B1-B24 were sold at double face value, except the 10c denominations which were sold for 15c. The surtax benefited the national anti-tuberculosis organization.

King Albert I — SP3

1914, Oct. 3　Litho.
B25 SP3 5c green & red 5.00 5.00
B26 SP3 10c red 1.00 1.00
B27 SP3 20c violet & red 15.00 15.00
　Nos. B25-B27 (3) 21.00 21.00
　Set, never hinged 90.00

Counterfeits of Nos. B25-B27 abound. Probably as many as 90% of the stamps on the market are counterfeits. Values are for genuine examples.

Merode Monument — SP4

1914, Oct. 3
B28 SP4 5c green & red *4.50 3.00*
B29 SP4 10c red *7.50 7.50*
B30 SP4 20c violet & red *75.00 75.00*
　Nos. B28-B30 (3) *87.00 85.50*
　Set, never hinged *175.00*

Counterfeits of Nos. B28-B30 abound. Probably as many as 90% of the stamps on the market are counterfeits. Genuine stamps have a tail on the "Q" of "BELGIQUE" at the top of the stamp, counterfeits don't have a tail. Values are for genuine examples.

King Albert I — SP5

1915, Jan. 1　Perf. 12, 14
B31 SP5 5c green & red 5.00 3.00
　a.　Perf. 12x14 16.00 12.00
B32 SP5 10c rose & red 20.00 6.00
B33 SP5 20c violet & red 25.00 14.00
　a.　Perf. 14x12 500.00 250.00
　b.　Perf. 12 50.00 32.50
　Nos. B31-B33 (3) 50.00 23.00
　Set, never hinged 150.00

Nos. B25-B33 were sold at double face value. The surtax benefited the Red Cross.

Types of Regular Issue of 1915 Surcharged in Red

Nos. B34-B40　　Nos. B41-B43

Nos. B44-B47

1918, Jan. 15　Typo.　Perf. 14
B34 A46 1c + 1c dp orange .50 .50
B35 A46 2c + 2c brown .60 .60
B36 A46 5c + 5c blue grn 1.40 1.40
B37 A46 10c + 10c red 2.25 2.25
B38 A46 15c + 15c brt violet 3.25 3.25
B39 A46 20c + 20c plum 7.50 7.50
B40 A46 25c + 25c ultra 7.50 7.50
Engr.
B41 A47 35c + 35c lt vio & blk 10.00 10.00
B42 A48 40c + 40c dull red & blk 10.00 10.00
B43 A49 50c + 50c turq blue & blk 12.00 12.00
B44 A50 1fr + 1fr bluish slate 35.00 35.00
B45 A51 2fr + 2fr dp gray grn 100.00 100.00
B46 A52 5fr + 5fr brown 250.00 250.00
B47 A53 10fr + 10fr dp blue 550.00 500.00
　Nos. B34-B47 (14) 990.00 940.00
　Set, never hinged 2,000.

Discus Thrower — SP6　　Racing Chariot — SP7

Runner — SP8

1920, May 20　Engr.　Perf. 12
B48 SP6 5c + 5c dp green 1.40 1.40
B49 SP7 10c + 5c carmine 1.40 1.40
B50 SP8 15c + 15c dk brown 3.00 3.00
　Nos. B48-B50 (3) 5.80 5.80
　Set, never hinged 17.00

7th Olympic Games, 1920. Surtax benefited wounded soldiers. Exists imperf.
For surcharges see Nos. 140-142.

Allegory: Asking Alms from the Crown SP9　　Wounded Veteran SP10

1922, May 20
B51 SP9 20c + 20c brown 1.40 1.40
　Never hinged 2.75

1923, July 5
B52 SP10 20c + 20c slate gray 2.50 2.50
　Never hinged 7.50

Surtax on Nos. B51-B52 was to aid wounded veterans.

SP11

1925, Dec. 15　Typo.　Perf. 14
B53 SP11 15c + 5c dull vio & red .50 .25
B54 SP11 30c + 5c gray & red .25 .25
B55 SP11 1fr + 10c chalky blue & red 1.25 1.40
　Nos. B53-B55 (3) 2.00 1.90
　Set, never hinged 3.00

Surtax for the Natl. Anti-Tuberculosis League.

SP12

St. Martin, by Van Dyck
SP13　　　　SP14

1926, Feb. 10
B56 SP12 30c + 30c bluish grn (red surch.) .50 .50
B57 SP13 1fr + 1fr lt blue 7.25 7.25
B58 SP14 1fr + 1fr lt blue 1.10 1.25
　Nos. B56-B58 (3) 8.85 9.00
　Set, never hinged 20.00

The surtax aided victims of the Meuse flood.

Lion and Cross of Lorraine — SP15

Queen Elisabeth and King Albert SP16

1926, Dec. 6　Typo.　Perf. 14
B59 SP15 5c + 5c dk brown .25 .25
B60 SP15 20c + 5c red brown .45 .40
B61 SP15 50c + 5c dull violet .30 .25
Engr.　Perf. 11½
B62 SP16 1.50fr + 25c dk blue .75 .70
B63 SP16 5fr + 1fr rose red 6.50 6.00
　Nos. B59-B63 (5) 8.25 7.60
　Set, never hinged 16.00

Surtax was used to benefit tubercular war veterans.

Boat Adrift SP17

1927, Dec. 15　Engr.　Perf. 11½, 14
B64 SP17 25c + 10c dk brn .70 .70
B65 SP17 35c + 10c yel grn .70 .70
B66 SP17 60c + 10c dp violet .60 .40
B67 SP17 1.75fr + 25c dk blue 1.50 *2.00*
B68 SP17 5fr + 1fr plum 4.50 *4.75*
　Nos. B64-B68 (5) 8.00 *8.55*
　Set, never hinged 16.00

The surtax on these stamps was divided among several charitable associations.

Ogives of Orval Abbey — SP18

Monk Carving Capital of Column — SP19

Ruins of Orval Abbey SP20

Design: 60c+15c, 1.75fr+25c, 3fr+1fr, Countess Matilda recovering her ring.

1928, Sept. 15   Photo.   Perf. 11½

B69	SP18	5c + 5c red & gold	.25	.25
B70	SP18	25c + 5c dk vio & gold	.45	.45

Engr.

B71	SP19	35c + 10c dp grn	1.25	1.25
B72	SP19	60c + 15c red brn	.75	.25
B73	SP19	1.75fr + 25c dk blue	3.25	2.10
B74	SP19	2fr + 40c dp vio	25.00	21.00
B75	SP19	3fr + 1fr red	22.50	20.00

Perf. 14

B76	SP20	5fr + 5fr rose lake	15.50	15.50
B77	SP20	10fr + 10fr ol green	15.50	15.50
		Nos. B69-B77 (9)	84.45	76.30
		Set, never hinged	150.00	

Surtax for the restoration of the ruined Orval Abbey.

St. Waudru, Mons — SP22

St. Rombaut, Malines — SP23

Designs: 25c + 15c, Cathedral of Tournal. 60c + 15c, St. Bavon, Ghent. 1.75fr + 25c, St. Gudule, Brussels. 5fr + 5fr, Louvain Library.

1928, Dec. 1   Photo.   Perf. 14, 11½

B78	SP22	5c + 5c carmine	.25	.25
B79	SP22	25c + 15c ol brn	.25	.25

Engr.

B80	SP23	35c + 10c dp grn	1.50	1.50
B81	SP23	60c + 15c red brn	.45	.45
B82	SP23	1.75fr + 25c vio bl	10.50	10.50
B83	SP23	5fr + 5fr red vio	21.00	21.00
		Nos. B78-B83 (6)	33.95	33.95
		Set, never hinged	65.00	

The surtax was for anti-tuberculosis work.

Nos. B69-B77 with this overprint in blue or red were privately produced. They were for the laying of the 1st stone toward the restoration of the ruined Abbey of Orval. Value, set, $650.
Forgeries of the overprint exist.

Waterfall at Coo — SP28

Bayard Rock, Dinant — SP29

Designs: 35c+10c, Menin Gate, Ypres. 60c+15c, Promenade d'Orleans, Spa. 1.75fr+25c, Antwerp Harbor. 5fr+5fr, Quai Vert, Bruges.

1929, Dec. 2   Engr.   Perf. 11½

B93	SP28	5c + 5c red brn	.25	.25
B94	SP29	25c + 15c gray blk	.95	.90
B95	SP28	35c + 10c green	1.25	1.40
B96	SP28	60c + 15c rose lake	.85	.75
B97	SP28	1.75fr + 25c dp blue	6.75	6.75

Perf. 14

B98	SP29	5fr + 5fr dl vio	40.00	40.00
		Nos. B93-B98 (6)	50.05	50.05
		Set, never hinged	70.00	

Bornhem — SP34

Beloeil — SP35

Gaesbeek SP36

25c + 15c, Wynendaele. 70c + 15c, Oydonck. 1fr + 25c, Ghent. 1.75fr + 25c, Bouillon.

1930, Dec. 1   Photo.   Perf. 14

B99	SP34	10c + 5c violet	.25	.30
B100	SP34	25c + 15c olive brn	.60	.60

Engr.

B101	SP35	40c + 10c brn vio	.80	1.00
B102	SP35	70c + 15c gray blk	.55	.55
B103	SP35	1fr + 25c rose lake	5.50	5.50
B104	SP35	1.75fr + 25c dp bl	7.25	4.50
B105	SP36	5fr + 5fr gray grn	45.00	52.50
		Nos. B99-B105 (7)	59.95	64.95
		Set, never hinged	80.00	

Philatelic Exhibition Issue
Souvenir Sheet

Prince Leopold — SP41

1931, July 18   Photo.   Perf. 14

B106	SP41	2.45fr + 55c car brn	225.00	225.00
		Never hinged	650.00	
a.		Single stamp	100.00	

Sold exclusively at the Brussels Phil. Exhib., July 18-21, 1931. Size: 122x159mm. Surtax for the Veterans' Relief Fund.
The sheet normally has pin holes and a cancellation-like marking in the margin. These are considered unused and the condition valued here.

Queen Elisabeth — SP42

1931, Dec. 1   Engr.

B107	SP42	10c + 5c red brn	.30	.50
B108	SP42	25c + 15c dk vio	1.40	1.50
B109	SP42	50c + 10c dk grn	1.10	1.25
B110	SP42	75c + 15c blk brn	.95	.85
B111	SP42	1fr + 25c rose lake	8.00	7.25
B112	SP42	1.75fr + 25c ultra	5.75	4.75
B113	SP42	5fr + 5fr brn vio	65.00	65.00
		Nos. B107-B113 (7)	82.50	81.10
		Set, never hinged	150.00	

The surtax was for the National Anti-Tuberculosis League.

Désiré Cardinal Mercier — SP43

Mercier Protecting Children and Aged at Malines — SP44

Mercier as Professor at Louvain University — SP45

Mercier in Full Canonicals, Giving His Blessing SP46

1932, June 10   Photo.   Perf. 14½x14

B114	SP43	10c + 10c dk violet	1.10	.70
B115	SP43	50c + 30c brt violet	2.75	3.00
B116	SP43	75c + 25c olive brn	2.75	2.75
B117	SP43	1fr + 2fr brown red	7.25	7.25

Engr.   Perf. 11½

B118	SP44	1.75fr + 75c dp blue	85.00	100.00
B119	SP45	2.50fr + 2.50fr dk brn	85.00	85.00
B120	SP44	3fr + 4.50fr dull grn	85.00	85.00
B121	SP45	5fr + 20fr vio brn	95.00	100.00
B122	SP46	10fr + 40fr brn lake	210.00	250.00
		Nos. B114-B122 (9)	573.85	633.70
		Set, never hinged	950.00	

Honoring Cardinal Mercier and to obtain funds to erect a monument to his memory.

Belgian Infantryman SP47

Sanatorium at Waterloo SP48

1932, Aug. 4   Perf. 14½x14

B123	SP47	75c + 3.25fr red brn	80.00	80.00
		Never hinged	125.00	

B124	SP47	1.75fr + 4.25fr dk blue	80.00	80.00
		Never hinged	125.00	

Honoring Belgian soldiers who fought in WWI and to obtain funds to erect a natl. monument to their glory.

1932, Dec. 1   Photo.   Perf. 13½x14

B125	SP48	10c + 5c dk vio	.30	.90
B126	SP48	25c + 15c red vio	1.00	1.25
B127	SP48	50c + 10c red brn	1.00	1.25
B128	SP48	75c + 15c ol	1.00	.80
B129	SP48	1fr + 25c dp red	15.00	12.50
B130	SP48	1.75fr + 25c dp blue	12.00	11.00
B131	SP48	5fr + 5fr gray grn	100.00	110.00
		Nos. B125-B131 (7)	130.30	137.70
		Set, never hinged	250.00	

Surtax for the assistance of the Natl. Anti-Tuberculosis Society at Waterloo.

View of Old Abbey SP49

Ruins of Old Abbey — SP50

Count de Chiny Presenting First Abbey to Countess Matilda SP56

Restoration of Abbey in XVI and XVII Centuries SP57

Abbey in XVIII Century, Maria Theresa and Charles V — SP58

Madonna and Arms of Seven Abbeys SP60

Designs: 25c+15c, Guests, courtyard, 50c+25c, Transept. 75c+50c, Bell Tower. 1fr+1.25fr, Fountain. 1.25fr+1.75fr, Cloisters. 5fr+20fr, Duke of Brabant placing 1st stone of new abbey.

1933, Oct. 15 — *Perf. 14*

B132	SP49	5c + 5c dull grn	57.50	*65.00*
B133	SP50	10c + 15c ol grn	52.50	*57.50*
B134	SP49	25c + 15c dk brn	52.50	*57.50*
B135	SP50	50c + 25c red brn	52.50	*57.50*
B136	SP50	75c + 30c dp grn	52.50	*57.50*
B137	SP50	1fr + 1.25fr cop red	52.50	*57.50*
B138	SP49	1.25fr + 1.75fr gray blk	52.50	*57.50*
B139	SP56	1.75fr + 2.75fr blue	60.00	*65.00*
B140	SP57	2fr + 3fr mag	60.00	*65.00*
B141	SP58	2.50fr + 5fr dull brn	60.00	*65.00*
B142	SP56	5fr + 20fr vio	65.00	*65.00*

Perf. 11½

B143	SP60	10fr + 40fr bl	375.00	*375.00*
	Nos. B132-B143 (12)		992.50	*1,045.*
	Set, never hinged		1,500.	

The surtax was for a fund to aid in the restoration of Orval Abbey. Counterfeits exist.

"Tuberculosis Society" SP61 · Peter Benoit SP62

1933, Dec. 1 — Engr. — *Perf. 14x13½*

B144	SP61	10c + 5c blk	1.50	1.50
B145	SP61	25c + 15c vio	5.00	5.00
B146	SP61	50c + 10c red brn	3.75	3.75
B147	SP61	75c + 15c blk brn	16.00	15.00
B148	SP61	1fr + 25c cl	18.00	18.00
B149	SP61	1.75fr + 25c vio bl	21.00	21.00
B150	SP61	5fr + 5fr lilac	175.00	140.00
	Nos. B144-B150 (7)		240.25	204.25
	Set, never hinged		350.00	

The surtax was for anti-tuberculosis work.

1934, June 1 — Photo.

B151	SP62	75c + 25c olive brn	6.00	6.00
	Never hinged		12.50	

The surtax was to raise funds for the Peter Benoit Memorial.

SP63 · King Leopold III — SP64

1934, Sept. 15

B152	SP63	75c + 25c ol blk	18.00	17.00
	Never hinged		37.50	
a.	Sheet of 20		925.00	925.00
	Never hinged		1,100.	
B153	SP64	1fr + 25c red vio	17.00	16.00
	Never hinged		37.50	
a.	Sheet of 20		925.00	925.00
	Never hinged		1,100.	

The surtax aided the National War Veterans' Fund. Sold for 4.50fra set at the Exhibition of War Postmarks 1914-18, held at Brussels by the Royal Philatelic Club of Veterans. The price included an exhibition ticket. Sold at Brussels post office Sept. 18-22. No. B152 printed in sheets of 20 (4x5) and 100 (10x10). No. B153 printed in sheets of 20 (4x5) and 150 (10x15).

1934, Sept. 24

B154	SP63	75c + 25c violet	1.50	1.50
	Never hinged		2.50	
B155	SP64	1fr + 25c red brn	10.50	10.50
	Never hinged		20.00	

The surtax aided the National War Veterans' Fund. No. B154 printed in sheets of 100 (10x10); No. B155 in sheets of 150 (10x15). These stamps remained in use one year.

Crusader SP65

1934, Nov. 17 — Engr. — *Perf. 13½x14*
Cross in Red

B156	SP65	10c + 5c blk	1.50	1.50
B157	SP65	25c + 15c brn	2.10	2.00
B158	SP65	50c + 10c dull grn	2.10	2.10
B159	SP65	75c + 15c vio brn	1.00	1.00
B160	SP65	1fr + 25c rose	10.50	10.50
B161	SP65	1.75fr + 25c ultra	9.00	9.00
B162	SP65	5fr + 5fr brn vio	125.00	125.00
	Nos. B156-B162 (7)		151.20	151.10
	Set, never hinged		550.00	

The surtax was for anti-tuberculosis work.

Prince Baudouin, Princess Josephine and Prince Albert SP66

1935, Apr. 10 — Photo.

B163	SP66	35c + 15c dk grn	1.25	1.10
B164	SP66	70c + 30c red brn	1.25	.90
B165	SP66	1.75fr + 50c dk blue	4.50	5.25
	Nos. B163-B165 (3)		7.00	7.25
	Set, never hinged		20.00	

Surtax was for Child Welfare Society.

Stagecoach — SP67

1935, Apr. 27

B166	SP67	10c + 10c ol blk	.75	.80
B167	SP67	25c + 25c bis brn	2.25	2.10
B168	SP67	35c + 25c dk green	3.00	2.75
	Nos. B166-B168 (3)		6.00	5.65
	Set, never hinged		15.00	

Printed in sheets of 10. Value, set of 3, $175.

Souvenir Sheet

Franz von Taxis — SP68

1935, May 25 — Engr. — *Perf. 14*

B169	SP68	5fr + 5fr grnsh blk	150.00	150.00
	Never hinged		450.00	
a.	Single stamp		115.00	
	Never hinged		140.00	

Sheets measure 91½x117mm.
Nos. B166-B169 were issued for the Brussels Philatelic Exhibition (SITEB). The sheet normally has pin holes and a cancellation-like marking in the margin. These are considered unused and the condition valued here.

Queen Astrid — SP69

1935 — Photo. — *Perf. 11½*
Borders in Black

B170	SP69	10c + 5c ol blk	.25	.25
B171	SP69	25c + 15c brown	.25	.30
B172	SP69	35c + 5c dk green	.25	.25
B173	SP69	50c + 10c rose lil	.80	.65
B174	SP69	70c + 5c gray blk	.25	.25
B175	SP69	1fr + 25c red	1.00	.85
B176	SP69	1.75fr + 25c blue	2.40	1.75
B177	SP69	2.45fr + 55c dk vio	3.00	*3.25*
	Nos. B170-B177 (8)		8.20	7.55
	Set, never hinged		25.00	

Queen Astrid Memorial issue. The surtax was divided among several charitable organizations.
Issued: No. B174, 10/31; others, 12/1.

Borgerhout Philatelic Exhibition Issue
Souvenir Sheet

Town Hall, Borgerhout SP70

1936, Oct. 3

B178	SP70	70c + 30c pur brn	90.00	62.50
	Never hinged		275.00	
a.	Single stamp		45.00	
	Never hinged		60.00	

Sheet measures 115x126mm.
The sheet normally has pin holes and a cancellation-like marking in the margin. These are considered unused and the condition valued here.

Town Hall and Belfry of Charleroi SP71 · Prince Baudouin SP72

Charleroi Youth Exhibition
Souvenir Sheet

1936, Oct. 18 — Engr.

B179	SP71	2.45fr + 55c gray blue	65.00	60.00
	Never hinged		150.00	
a.	Single stamp		45.00	
	Never hinged		60.00	

Sheet measures 95x120mm.
The sheet normally has pin holes and a cancellation-like marking in the margin. These are considered unused and the condition valued here.

1936, Dec. 1 — Photo. — *Perf. 14x13½*

B180	SP72	10c + 5c dk brown	.25	.25
B181	SP72	25c + 5c violet	.25	*.25*
B182	SP72	35c + 5c dk green	.25	.25
B183	SP72	50c + 5c vio brn	.50	*.60*
B184	SP72	70c + 5c ol grn	.25	.25
B185	SP72	1fr + 25c cerise	1.10	.45
B186	SP72	1.75fr + 25c ultra	1.90	1.10
B187	SP72	2.45fr + 2.55fr vio rose	5.25	*6.75*
	Nos. B180-B187 (8)		9.75	*9.90*
	Set, never hinged		30.00	

The surtax was for the assistance of the National Anti-Tuberculosis Society.

1937, Jan. 10

B188	SP72	2.45fr + 2.55fr slate	2.50	2.50
	Never hinged		6.50	

Intl. Stamp Day. Surtax for the benefit of the Brussels Postal Museum, the Royal Belgian Phil. Fed. and the Anti-Tuberculosis Soc.

Queen Astrid and Prince Baudouin SP73 · Queen Mother Elisabeth SP74

1937, Apr. 15 — *Perf. 11½*

B189	SP73	10c + 5c magenta	.25	.25
B190	SP73	25c + 5c ol blk	.25	*.25*
B191	SP73	35c + 5c dk grn	.25	*.25*
B192	SP73	50c + 5c violet	1.25	*1.25*
B193	SP73	70c + 5c slate	.25	*.30*
B194	SP73	1fr + 25c dk car	1.60	1.40
B195	SP73	1.75fr + 25c dp ultra	2.75	2.75
B196	SP73	2.45fr + 1.55fr dk brn	6.75	6.50
	Nos. B189-B196 (8)		13.35	12.95
	Set, never hinged		45.00	

The surtax was to raise funds for Public Utility Works.

1937, Sept. 15 — *Perf. 14x13½*

B197	SP74	70c + 5c int black	.30	.30
B198	SP74	1.75fr + 25c brt ultra	.70	.70
	Set, never hinged		2.00	

Souvenir Sheet
Perf. 11½

B199		Sheet of 4	45.00	25.00
	Never hinged		125.00	
a.	SP74 1.50fr+2.50fr red brn		4.25	3.75
b.	SP74 2.45fr+3.55fr red vio		3.75	2.25

Issued for the benefit of the Queen Elisabeth Music Foundation in connection with the Eugene Ysaye intl. competition.
No. B199 contains two se-tenant pairs of Nos. B199a and B199b. Size: 111x145mm. On sale one day, Sept. 15, at Brussels.
The sheet normally has pin holes and a cancellation-like marking in the margin. These are considered unused and the condition valued here.

Princess Josephine-Charlotte SP75

1937, Dec. 1 — *Perf. 14x13½*

B200	SP75	10c + 5c sl grn	.25	.25
B201	SP75	25c + 5c lt brn	.25	.25
B202	SP75	35c + 5c yel grn	.25	.25
B203	SP75	50c + 5c ol gray	.70	.60
B204	SP75	70c + 5c brn red	.25	.25
B205	SP75	1fr + 25c red	1.25	.90
B206	SP75	1.75fr + 25c vio bl	1.50	1.25
B207	SP75	2.45fr + 2.55fr mag	5.75	*6.00*
	Nos. B200-B207 (8)		10.20	*9.75*
	Set, never hinged		30.00	

King Albert Memorial Issue
Souvenir Sheet

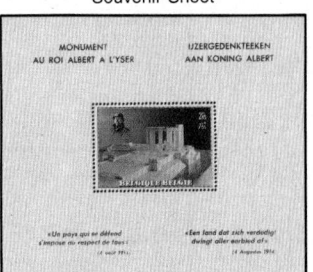

King Albert Memorial — SP76

1938, Feb. 17   *Perf. 11½*
B208 SP76 2.45fr + 7.55fr brn
    vio   20.00   16.50
    Never hinged   62.50

Dedication of the monument to King Albert. The sheet normally has pin holes and a cancellation-like marking in the margin. These are considered unused and the condition valued here. Sheets without the "cancellation" are extremely scarce. Values: unused, $525; never hinged, $1,000.

King Leopold III in Military Plane SP77

1938, Mar. 15
B209 SP77   10c + 5c car brn   .25   .30
B210 SP77   35c + 5c dp grn   .35   .90
B211 SP77   70c + 5c gray blk   .95   .75
B212 SP77   1.75fr + 25c ultra   2.25   2.10
B213 SP77   2.45fr + 2.55fr pur   5.25   4.50
    Nos. B209-B213 (5)   9.05   8.55
    Set, never hinged   22.50

The surtax was for the benefit of the National Fund for Aeronautical Propaganda.

Basilica of Koekelberg SP78

Interior View of the Basilica of Koekelberg SP79

1938, June 1   **Photo.**
B214 SP78   10c + 5c lt brn   .25   .25
B215 SP78   35c + 5c grn   .25   .25
B216 SP78   70c + 5c gray grn   .25   .25
B217 SP78   1fr + 25c car   .70   .60
B218 SP78   1.75fr + 25c ultra   .70   .70
B219 SP78   2.45fr + 2.55fr brn
    vio   3.25   3.75

Engr.
B220 SP79   5fr + 5fr dl grn   12.25   11.50
    Nos. B214-B220 (7)   17.65   17.30
    Set, never hinged   35.00

Souvenir Sheet

1938, July 21   **Engr.**   *Perf. 14*
B221 SP79   5fr + 5fr lt vio   16.00   16.00
    Never hinged   25.00

The surtax was for a fund to aid in completing the National Basilica of the Sacred Heart at Koekelberg.

Nos. B214, B216 and B218 are different views of the exterior of the Basilica.

The sheet normally has pin holes and a cancellation-like marking in the margin. These are considered unused and the condition valued here.

Stamps of 1938 Surcharged in Black

Nos. B222-B223

No. B224

1938, Nov. 10   *Perf. 11½*
B222 SP78   40c on 35c+5c grn   .50   .60
B223 SP78   75c on 70c+5c gray
    grn   .75   .90
B224 SP78   2.50 +2.50fr on
    2.45+2.55fr   6.75   7.50
    Nos. B222-B224 (3)   8.00   9.00
    Set, never hinged   19.00

Prince Albert of Liege — SP81

1938, Dec. 10   **Photo.**   *Perf. 14x13½*
B225 SP81   10c + 5c brown   .25   .25
B226 SP81   30c + 5c mag   .25   .30
B227 SP81   40c + 5c olive
    gray   .25   .30
B228 SP81   75c + 5c slate
    grn   .25   .25
B229 SP81   1fr + 25c dk car   .75   1.10
B230 SP81   1.75fr + 25c ultra   .75   1.10
B231 SP81   2.50fr + 2.50fr dp
    grn   5.25   8.25
B232 SP81   5fr + 5fr brn
    lake   16.00   12.50
    Nos. B225-B232 (8)   23.75   24.05
    Set, never hinged   70.00

Henri Dunant SP82

Florence Nightingale SP83

Queen Mother Elisabeth and Royal Children — SP84

Queen Astrid — SP86

King Leopold and Royal Children SP85

Queen Mother Elisabeth and Wounded Soldier — SP87

1939, Apr. 1   **Photo.**   *Perf. 11½*
    Cross in Carmine
B233 SP82   10c + 5c brn   .25   .25
B234 SP83   30c + 5c brn car   .45   .45
B235 SP84   40c + 5c ol gray   .25   .30
B236 SP85   75c + 5c slate
    blk   .60   .25
B237 SP84   1fr + 25c brt
    rose   3.00   1.60
B238 SP85   1.75fr + 25c brt ul-
    tra   .90   1.25
B239 SP86   2.50fr + 2.50fr dl
    vio   1.90   2.40

B240 SP87   5fr + 5fr gray
    grn   6.50   8.25
    Nos. B233-B240 (8)   13.85   14.75
    Set, never hinged   42.50

75th anniversary of the founding of the International Red Cross Society.

Rubens' House, Antwerp SP88

"Albert and Nicolas Rubens" — SP89

Arcade, Rubens' House SP90

"Helena Fourment and Her Children" — SP91

Rubens and Isabelle Brandt — SP92

Peter Paul Rubens — SP93

"The Velvet Hat" — SP94

"Descent from the Cross" SP95

1939, July 1
B241 SP88   10c + 5c brn   .25   .25
B242 SP89   40c + 5c brn
    car   .25   .25
B243 SP90   75c + 5c ol blk   .65   .65
B244 SP91   1fr + 25c rose   2.50   2.50
B245 SP92   1.50fr + 25c sep   2.75   2.75
B246 SP93   1.75fr + 25c dp
    ultra   4.50   4.50
B247 SP94   2.50fr + 2.50fr brt
    red vio   15.00   15.00
B248 SP95   5fr + 5fr slate
    gray   19.00   19.00
    Nos. B241-B248 (8)   44.90   44.90
    Set, never hinged   140.00

Issued to honor Peter Paul Rubens. The surtax was used to restore Rubens' home in Antwerp.

"Martin van Nieuwenhove" by Hans Memling (1430?-1495), Flemish Painter — SP96

1939, July 1
B249 SP96   75c + 75c olive blk   2.75   2.75
    Never hinged   4.50

Twelfth Century Monks at Work — SP97

Reconstructed Tower Seen through Cloister — SP98

Monks Laboring in the Fields SP99

Orval Abbey, Aerial View SP100

Bishop Heylen of Namur, Madonna and Abbot General Smets of the Trappists — SP101

King Albert I and King Leopold III and Shrine — SP102

1939, July 20
B250 SP97   75c + 75c ol
    blk   3.50   3.75
B251 SP98   1fr + 1fr rose
    red   2.25   2.25
B252 SP99   1.50fr + 1.50fr dl
    brn   2.25   2.25
B253 SP100   1.75fr + 1.75fr
    saph   2.25   2.25
B254 SP101   2.50fr + 2.50fr brt
    red vio   10.00   9.00
B255 SP102   5fr + 5fr brn
    car   10.00   10.00
    Nos. B250-B255 (6)   30.25   29.50
    Set, never hinged   82.50

The surtax was used for the restoration of the Abbey of Orval.

Bruges
SP103

Furnes
SP104

Belfries: 30c+5c, Thuin. 40c+5c, Lierre. 75c+5c, Mons. 1.75fr+25c, Namur. 2.50fr+2.50fr, Alost. 5fr+5fr, Tournai.

1939, Dec. 1   Photo.   Perf. 14x13½
B256	SP103	10c + 5c ol gray	.25 .25
B257	SP103	30c + 5c brn org	.30 .40
B258	SP103	40c + 5c brt red vio	.50 .50
B259	SP103	75c + 5c olive blk	.25 .25

Engr.
B260	SP104	1fr + 25c rose car	1.25 1.50
B261	SP104	1.75fr + 25c dk blue	1.25 1.50
B262	SP104	2.50fr + 2.50fr dp red brn	8.75 9.50
B263	SP104	5fr + 5fr pur	12.00 13.25
		Nos. B256-B263 (8)	24.55 27.15
		Set, never hinged	65.00

Mons
SP111

Ghent
SP112

Coats of Arms: 40c+10c, Arel. 50c+10c, Bruges. 75c+15c, Namur. 1fr+25c, Hasselt. 1.75fr+50c, Brussels. 2.50fr+2.50fr, Antwerp. 5fr+5fr, Liege.

1940-41   Typo.   Perf. 14x13½
B264	SP111	10c + 5c multi	.25 .25
B265	SP112	30c + 5c multi	.25 .25
B266	SP111	40c + 10c multi	.25 .25
B267	SP112	50c + 10c multi	.25 .25
B268	SP112	75c + 15c multi	.25 .25
B269	SP112	1fr + 25c multi	.30 .30
B270	SP111	1.75fr + 50c multi	.45 .40
B271	SP112	2.50fr + 2.50fr multi	1.25 1.25
B272	SP111	5fr + 5fr multi	1.50 1.50
		Nos. B264-B272 (9)	4.75 4.70
		Set, never hinged	8.50

Nos. B264, B269-B272 issued in 1941. Surtax for winter relief. See No. B279 in *Scott Standard Postage Stamp Catalogue*, Vol. 1.

Queen Elisabeth Music Chapel SP120

Bust of Prince Albert of Liege — SP121

1940, Nov.   Photo.   Perf. 11½
B273	SP120	75c + 75c slate	3.50 3.50
B274	SP120	1fr + 1fr rose red	1.25 1.25
B275	SP121	1.50fr + 1.50fr Prus grn	1.25 1.25
B276	SP121	1.75fr + 1.75fr ultra	1.25 1.25
B277	SP120	2.50fr + 2.50fr brn org	3.50 3.50

B278	SP121	5fr + 5fr red vio	3.50 3.50
		Nos. B273-B278 (6)	14.25 14.25
		Set, never hinged	55.00

The surtax was for the Queen Elisabeth Music Foundation. Nos. B273-B278 were not authorized for postal use, but were sold to advance subscribers either mint or canceled to order. See Nos. B317-B318 in *Scott Standard Postage Stamp Catalogue*, Vol. 1.

AIR POST STAMPS

Fokker FVII/3m over Ostend AP1

Designs: 1.50fr, Plane over St. Hubert. 2fr, over Namur. 5fr, over Brussels.

Perf. 11½
1930, Apr. 30   Unwmk.   Photo.
C1	AP1	50c blue	.45 .45
C2	AP1	1.50fr black brn	2.50 2.50
C3	AP1	2fr deep green	2.00 .90
C4	AP1	5fr brown lake	2.00 1.10
		Nos. C1-C4 (4)	6.95 4.95
		Set, never hinged	22.50

Nos. C1-C4 exist imperf.

1930, Dec. 5
C5	AP1	5fr dark violet	30.00 30.00
		Never hinged	65.00

Issued for use on a mail carrying flight from Brussels to Leopoldville, Belgian Congo, starting Dec. 7.
Exists imperf.

Nos. C2 and C4 Surcharged in Carmine or Blue

1935, May 23
C6	AP1	1fr on 1.50fr (C)	.55 .40
C7	AP1	4fr on 5fr (Bl)	8.75 8.00
		Set, never hinged	42.50

SPECIAL DELIVERY STAMPS

From 1874 to 1903 certain hexagonal telegraph stamps were used as special delivery stamps.

Town Hall, Brussels — SD1

2.35fr, Street in Ghent. 3.50fr, Bishop's Palace, Liege. 5.25fr, Notre Dame Cathedral, Antwerp.

1929   Unwmk.   Photo.   Perf. 11½
E1	SD1	1.75fr dark blue	.80 .30
E2	SD1	2.35fr carmine	1.75 .45
E3	SD1	3.50fr dark violet	11.00 10.00
E4	SD1	5.25fr olive green	10.50 10.00

Eupen — SD2

1931
E5	SD2	2.45fr dark green	17.00 2.50
		Nos. E1-E5 (5)	41.05 23.25
		Set, never hinged	110.00

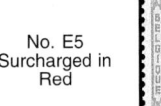

No. E5 Surcharged in Red

1932
E6	SD2	2.50fr on 2.45fr dk grn	18.00 2.00
		Never hinged	60.00

POSTAGE DUE STAMPS

D1

1870   Unwmk.   Typo.   Perf. 15
J1	D1	10c green	3.75 2.00
		Never hinged	10.00
		On cover	110.00
a.		10c deep green	4.50 3.00
		Never hinged	12.50
		On cover	120.00
J2	D1	20c ultra, thin paper	30.00 3.75
		Never hinged	140.00
		On cover	225.00

In 1909 many bisects of Nos. J1-J2 were created. The 10c bisect used as 5c on piece sells for $3.50.

No. J2 was also printed in aniline ink on thin paper. Value about the same.

D2

1895-09   Perf. 14
J3	D2	5c yellow grn	.25 .25
		Never hinged	.40
		On cover	3.50
a.		5c green	.85 .25
		Never hinged	3.00
		On cover	3.50
J4	D2	10c orange brn	17.50 1.75
		Never hinged	57.50
		On cover	15.00
e.		15c black, *deep blue*	75.00 65.00
J5	D2	10c carmine ('00)	.25 .25
		Never hinged	.40
		On cover	2.00
a.		10c rose	1.50 .40
		Never hinged	3.00
		On cover	2.00
J6	D2	20c olive green	.25 .25
		Never hinged	.40
		On cover	3.50
J7	D2	30c pale blue ('09)	.30 .25
		Never hinged	.80
		On cover	17.50
J8	D2	50c yellow brn	17.50 5.00
		Never hinged	57.50
		On cover	85.00
J9	D2	50c gray ('00)	.75 .45
		Never hinged	1.60
		On cover	30.00
a.		50c blackish gray	3.75 1.25
		Never hinged	10.00
		On cover	37.50
J10	D2	1fr carmine	20.00 11.50
		Never hinged	50.00
		On cover	850.00
J11	D2	1fr ocher ('00)	6.50 5.00
		Never hinged	10.00
		On cover	1,000.
		Nos. J3-J11 (9)	63.30 24.70

1916   Redrawn
J12	D2	5c blue grn	25.00 7.00
		Never hinged	72.50
		On cover	22.50
J13	D2	10c carmine	42.50 11.00
		Never hinged	140.00
		On cover	15.00
J14	D2	20c dp gray grn	42.50 15.00
		Never hinged	140.00
		On cover	40.00
J15	D2	30c brt blue	6.00 5.00
		Never hinged	14.00
		On cover	50.00
J16	D2	50c gray	125.00 60.00
		Never hinged	425.00
		On cover	150.00
		Nos. J12-J16 (5)	241.00 98.00

In the redrawn stamps the lions have a heavy, colored outline. There is a thick vertical line at the outer edge of the design on each side.

Stamps handstamped "T" on Nos. 111-119

1919, Oct.-Nov.
J16C	A46	5c green (#111)	1.20 .25
		Never hinged	4.25
		On cover	17.50
J16D	A46	10c carmine (#112)	1.20 .25
		Never hinged	4.25
		On cover	9.00
J16E	A46	15c purple (#113)	2.10 .25
		Never hinged	7.50
		On cover	17.50
J16F	A46	20c red violet (#114)	3.00 .25
		Never hinged	11.00
		On cover	40.00
J16G	A46	25c blue (#115)	1.00 .50
		Never hinged	3.75
		On cover	60.00
J16H	A47	35c brown org & blk (#116)	1.00 .50
		Never hinged	3.00
		On cover	37.50
J16I	A48	40c green & blk (#117)	1.00 .50
		Never hinged	3.00
		On cover	75.00
J16J	A49	50c carmine rose & blk (#118)	5.75 .50
		Never hinged	22.50
		On cover	90.00
J16K	A50	1fr violet (#119)	40.00 3.00
		Never hinged	130.00
		On cover	225.00
		Nos. J16C-J16K (9)	56.25 6.00
		Set, never hinged	190.00

Nos. J16C-J16K were handstamped locally for use as provisionals during a shortage of postage due stamps.

D3

1919   Perf. 14
J17	D3	5c green	.40 .50
J18	D3	10c carmine	.95 .35
J19	D3	20c gray green	7.25 1.25
J20	D3	30c bright blue	1.40 .40
J21	D3	50c gray	2.75 .50
		Nos. J17-J21 (5)	12.75 3.00
		Set, never hinged	40.00

The 5c, 10c, 20c and 50c values also exist perf 14x15.

D4

1922-32
J22	D4	5c dk gray	.25 .25
J23	D4	10c green	.25 .25
J24	D4	20c deep brown	.25 .25
J25	D4	30c ver ('24)	.65 .25
a.		30c rose red	1.00 .45
J26	D4	40c red brn ('25)	.25 .25
J27	D4	50c ultra	1.90 .25
J28	D4	70c red brn ('29)	.30 .25
J29	D4	1fr violet ('25)	.45 .25
J30	D4	1fr rose lilac ('32)	.55 .25
J31	D4	1.20fr ol grn ('29)	.65 .45
J32	D4	1.50fr ol grn ('32)	.65 .45
J33	D4	2fr violet ('29)	.75 .25
J34	D4	3.50fr dp blue ('29)	1.00 .25
		Nos. J22-J34 (13)	7.90 3.65
		Set, never hinged	15.00

1934-46				*Perf. 14x13½*
J35	D4	35c green ('35)	.40	.45
J36	D4	50c slate	.25	.25
J37	D4	60c carmine ('38)	.40	.30
J38	D4	80c slate ('38)	.30	.25
J39	D4	1.40fr gray ('35)	.65	.45
J39A	D4	9fr org brn ('46)	1.30	.60
J39B	D4	7fr brt red vio ('46)	2.25	3.25
		Nos. J35-J39B (7)	5.75	5.55
		Set, never hinged	12.00	

See Nos. J54-J61 in *Scott Standard Postage Stamp Catalogue*, Vol. 1.

MILITARY PARCEL POST STAMP

Type of Parcel Post Stamp of 1938 Srchd. in Blue

1939		Unwmk.	*Perf. 13½*	
MQ1	PP19	3fr on 5.50fr copper red	.30	.25
		Never hinged	.60	

OFFICIAL STAMPS

For franking the official correspondence of the Administration of the Belgian National Railways.

Most examples of Nos. O1-O25 in the marketplace are counterfeits. Values are for genuine examples.

Regular Issue of 1921-27 Overprinted in Black

1929-30		Unwmk.	*Perf. 14*	
O1	A58	5c gray	.25	.25
O2	A58	10c blue green	.30	.40
O3	A58	35c blue green	.40	.30
O4	A58	60c olive green	.45	.30
O5	A58	1.50fr brt blue	8.00	6.25
O6	A58	1.75fr ultra ('30)	1.75	2.00
		Nos. O1-O6 (6)	11.15	9.50

Same Overprint, in Red or Black, on Regular Issues of 1929-30

1929-31				
O7	A63	5c slate (R)	.25	.35
O8	A63	10c olive grn (R)	.50	.40
O9	A63	25c rose red (Bk)	1.50	.85
O10	A63	35c dp green (R)	1.75	.50
O11	A63	40c red vio (Bk)	1.25	.45
O12	A63	50c dp blue (R) ('31)	.80	.35
O13	A63	60c rose (Bk)	10.00	6.00
O14	A63	70c orange brn (Bk)	4.25	1.25
O15	A63	75c black vio (R) ('31)	4.00	.85
		Nos. O7-O15 (9)	24.30	11.00

Overprinted on Regular Issue of 1932

1932				
O16	A73	10c olive grn (R)	.50	.60
O17	A74	35c dp green	9.00	.75
O18	A71a	75c bister brn (R)	1.50	.30
		Nos. O16-O18 (3)	11.00	1.65

Overprinted on No. 262 in Red

1935			*Perf. 13½x14*	
O19	A80	70c olive black	2.75	.25

Regular Stamps of 1935-36 Overprinted in Red

1936-38		*Perf. 13½, 13½x14, 14*		
O20	A82	10c olive bister	.25	.35
O21	A82	35c green	.25	.40
O22	A82	50c dark blue	.45	.35
O23	A82	70c brown	1.50	.65

Overprinted in Black or Red on Regular Issue of 1938

		Perf. 13½x14		
O24	A82	40c red violet (Bk)	.30	.35
O25	A85	75c olive gray (R)	.65	.30
		Nos. O20-O25 (6)	3.40	2.40

NEWSPAPER STAMPS

Most examples of Nos. P1-P40 in the marketplace are counterfeits. Values are for genuine examples.

Parcel Post Stamps of 1923-27 Overprinted

Perf. 14½x14, 14x14½

1928			**Unwmk.**	
P1	PP12	10c vermilion	.25	.40
P2	PP12	20c turq blue	.25	.40
P3	PP12	40c olive grn	.25	.40
P4	PP12	60c orange	.70	.90
P5	PP12	70c dk brown	.45	.40
P6	PP12	80c violet	.60	.70
P7	PP12	90c slate	2.25	2.00
P8	PP13	1fr brt blue	.90	.60
a.		1fr ultramarine	12.00	5.00
P10	PP13	2fr olive grn	1.50	.60
P11	PP13	3fr orange red	1.60	.90
P12	PP13	4fr rose	2.25	1.10
P13	PP13	5fr violet	2.25	1.00
P14	PP13	6fr bister brn	4.50	1.75
P15	PP13	7fr orange	5.00	2.25
P16	PP13	8fr dk brown	6.00	2.75
P17	PP13	9fr red violet	10.00	3.00
P18	PP13	10fr blue green	9.00	2.75
P19	PP13	20fr magenta	15.00	7.00
		Nos. P1-P8,P10-P19 (18)	62.75	28.90

Parcel Post Stamps of 1923-28 Overprinted

1929-31				
P20	PP12	10c vermilion	.25	.25
P21	PP12	20c turq blue	.25	.25
P22	PP12	40c olive green	.30	.25
a.		Inverted overprint		
P23	PP12	60c orange	.55	.35
P24	PP12	70c dk brown	.55	.25
P25	PP12	80c violet	.60	.25
P26	PP12	90c gray	2.00	1.00
P27	PP13	1fr ultra	.60	.25
a.		1fr bright blue	4.00	2.50
P28	PP13	1.10fr org brn ('31)	6.25	1.40
P29	PP13	1.50fr gray vio ('31)	6.25	1.90
P30	PP13	2fr olive green	2.00	.25
P31	PP13	2.10fr sl gray ('31)	17.00	12.00
P32	PP13	3fr orange red	2.25	.45
P33	PP13	4fr rose	2.25	.70
P34	PP13	5fr violet	3.00	.55
P35	PP13	6fr bister brn	3.75	1.00
P36	PP13	7fr orange	3.75	1.00
P37	PP13	8fr dk brown	3.75	1.00
P38	PP13	9fr red violet	5.25	1.50
P39	PP13	10fr blue green	3.75	1.10
P40	PP13	20fr magenta	13.00	4.50
		Nos. P20-P40 (21)	77.35	30.20

PARCEL POST AND RAILWAY STAMPS

Values for used Railway Stamps (Chemins de Fer) stamps are for copies with railway cancellations. Railway Stamps with postal cancellations sell for twice as much.

Coat of Arms — PP1

1879-82		Unwmk. Typo. *Perf. 14*		
Q1	PP1	10c violet brown	110.00	5.75
		No gum	50.00	
Q2	PP1	20c blue	275.00	17.50
		No gum	140.00	
Q3	PP1	25c green ('81)	375.00	10.00
		No gum	175.00	
Q4	PP1	50c carmine	1,750.	10.00
		No gum	1,100.	
Q5	PP1	80c yellow	2,000.	57.50
		No gum	1,150.	
Q6	PP1	1fr gray ('82)	275.00	16.00
		No gum	140.00	

Used examples of Nos. Q1-Q6 with pinholes, a normal state, sell for approximately 40-60 percent of the values given.

Most of the stamps of 1882-1902 (Nos. Q7 to Q28) are without watermark. Twice in each sheet of 100 stamps they have one of three watermarks: (1) A winged wheel and "Chemins de Fer de l'Etat Belge," (2) Coat of Arms of Belgium and "Royaume de Belgique," (3) Larger Coat of Arms, without inscription.

PP2

1882-94			*Perf. 15½x14¼*	
Q7	PP2	10c brown ('86)	20.00	1.50
a.		10c rose brown	21.50	1.60
b.		10c chestnut brown	23.50	3.00
Q8	PP2	15c gray ('94)	8.75	7.25
Q9	PP2	20c blue ('86)	65.00	7.00
a.		20c ultramarine ('90)	75.00	4.00
b.		20c greenish blue ('90)	72.50	3.75
Q10	PP2	25c yel grn ('91)	72.50	4.25
a.		25c blue green ('87)	67.50	4.00
Q11	PP2	50c carmine	72.50	2.50
a.		50c rose ('82)	67.50	.75
b.		50c pomegranate	75.00	5.00
Q12	PP2	80c brnsh buff	72.50	.90
a.		80c bister ('83)	67.50	.80
Q13	PP2	80c lemon	75.00	1.60
Q14	PP2	1fr lavender	350.00	3.00
a.		1fr gray	385.00	3.50
b.		1fr bronze	425.00	4.50
Q15	PP2	2fr yel buff ('94)	210.00	67.50

Counterfeits exist.

PP3

Name of engraver below frame

1895-97		**Numerals in Black, except 1fr, 2fr**		
Q16	PP3	10c red brown ('96)	11.00	.60
		Never hinged	20.00	
Q17	PP3	15c gray	11.00	7.00
		Never hinged	18.00	
Q18	PP3	20c blue	17.50	1.00
		Never hinged	32.50	
Q19	PP3	25c green	17.50	1.25
		Never hinged	32.50	
Q20	PP3	50c carmine	25.00	.80
		Never hinged	50.00	
Q21	PP3	60c violet ('96)	50.00	1.00
		Never hinged	100.00	
Q22	PP3	80c ol yel ('96)	50.00	1.40
		Never hinged	100.00	
Q23	PP3	1fr lilac brown	175.00	3.00
		Never hinged	350.00	
Q24	PP3	2fr yel buff ('97)	200.00	15.00
		Never hinged	400.00	

Counterfeits exist.

1901-02		**Numerals in Black**		
Q25	PP3	30c orange	21.00	2.00
		Never hinged	37.50	
Q26	PP3	40c green	26.00	1.75
		Never hinged	50.00	
Q27	PP3	70c blue	50.00	1.40
		Never hinged	100.00	
a.		Numerals omitted	750.00	
b.		Numerals printed on reverse	750.00	
Q28	PP3	90c red	65.00	2.00
		Never hinged	140.00	
		Nos. Q25-Q28 (4)	162.00	7.15

Winged Wheel PP4

Without engraver's name

1902-14			*Perf. 15*	
Q29	PP3	10c yel brn & slate	.25	.25
Q30	PP3	15c slate & vio	.25	.25
Q31	PP3	20c ultra & yel brn	.25	.25
Q32	PP3	25c yel grn & red	.25	.25
Q33	PP3	30c orange & bl grn	.25	.25
Q34	PP3	35c bister & bl grn ('12)	.35	.25
Q35	PP3	40c blue grn & vio	.25	.25
Q36	PP3	50c pale rose & vio	.25	.25
Q37	PP3	55c lilac brn & ultra ('14)	.35	.25
Q38	PP3	60c violet & red	.25	.25
Q39	PP3	70c blue & red	.25	.25
Q40	PP3	80c lemon & vio brn	.25	.25
Q41	PP3	90c red & yel grn	.25	.25
Q42	PP4	1fr vio brn & org	.25	.25
Q43	PP4	1.10fr rose & blk ('06)	.25	.25
Q44	PP4	2fr ocher & bl grn	.25	.25
Q45	PP4	3fr black & ultra	.35	.25
Q46	PP4	4fr yel grn & red ('13)	1.25	.70
Q47	PP4	5fr org & bl grn ('13)	.55	.55
Q48	PP4	10fr ol yel & brn vio ('13)	.90	.55
		Nos. Q29-Q48 (20)	7.25	6.05

Regular Issues of 1912-13 Handstamped in Violet

1915			*Perf. 14*	
Q49	A42	5c green	190.00	160.00
		Never hinged	230.00	
Q50	A43	10c red	1,400.	1,400.
		Never hinged	1,850	
Q51	A45	10c red	230.00	200.00
		Never hinged	300.00	
a.		With engraver's name	775.00	775.00
		Never hinged	925.00	
Q52	A43	20c olive grn	1,600.	1,600.
		Never hinged	2,100	
Q53	A45	20c olive grn	260.00	225.00
		Never hinged	350.00	
a.		With engraver's name	775.00	775.00
		Never hinged	925.00	
Q54	A45	25c ultra	260.00	225.00
		Never hinged	350.00	
a.		With engraver's name	775.00	775.00
		Never hinged	925.00	
Q55	A43	35c bister brn	350.00	300.00
		Never hinged	425.00	
Q55A	A43	40c green	2,500.	2,500.
		Never hinged	3,750	
Q56	A45	40c green	325.00	275.00
		Never hinged	425.00	
Q57	A43	50c gray	325.00	275.00
		Never hinged	400.00	
Q58	A43	1fr orange	325.00	275.00
		Never hinged	375.00	
Q59	A43	2fr violet	1,900.	1,650.
		Never hinged	2,200	
Q60	A44	5fr plum	4,000.	3,500.
		Never hinged	4,500.	

Excellent forgeries of this overprint exist.

PP5

PP6

1916			**Litho.**	*Perf. 13½*	
Q61	PP5	10c pale blue	1.10	.25
Q62	PP5	15c olive grn	1.40	.50
Q63	PP5	20c red	2.25	.50
Q64	PP5	25c lt brown	2.25	.50
Q65	PP5	30c lilac	1.40	.50
Q66	PP5	35c gray	1.40	.45
Q67	PP5	40c orange yel	3.00	1.50
Q68	PP5	50c bister	2.25	.45
Q69	PP5	55c brown	3.00	2.25
Q70	PP5	60c gray vio	2.25	.45

Q71	PP5	70c green	2.25	.45
Q72	PP5	80c red brown	2.25	.45
Q73	PP5	90c blue	2.25	.45
Q74	PP6	1fr gray	2.25	.45
Q75	PP6	1.10fr ultra (Franken)	27.50	21.00
Q76	PP6	2fr red	25.00	.45
Q77	PP6	3fr violet	25.00	.45
Q78	PP6	4fr emerald	45.00	1.50
Q79	PP6	5fr brown	45.00	3.00
Q80	PP6	10fr orange	45.00	1.50
		Nos. Q61-Q80 (20)	241.80	37.05

Type of 1916 Inscribed "FRANK" instead of "FRANKEN"

1920

Q81	PP6	1.10fr ultra	2.00	.45

PP7

PP8

1920   *Perf. 14*

Q82	PP7	10c blue grn	1.75	.75
Q83	PP7	15c olive grn	1.75	1.10
Q84	PP7	20c red	1.75	.75
Q85	PP7	25c gray brn	2.50	.75
Q86	PP7	30c red vio	27.00	22.50
Q87	PP7	40c pale org	11.00	.75
Q88	PP7	50c bister	9.00	.75
Q89	PP7	55c pale brown	5.50	4.50
Q90	PP7	60c dk violet	10.00	.75
Q91	PP7	70c green	18.00	1.10
Q92	PP7	80c red brown	40.00	1.50
Q93	PP7	90c dull blue	10.00	.75
Q94	PP8	1fr gray	85.00	1.50
Q95	PP8	1.10fr ultra	26.00	2.00
Q96	PP8	1.20fr dk green	11.00	.75
Q97	PP8	1.40fr black brn	11.00	.75
Q98	PP8	2fr vermilion	110.00	1.25
Q99	PP8	3fr red vio	125.00	.85
Q100	PP8	4fr yel org	125.00	.75
Q101	PP8	5fr bister brn	125.00	.75
Q102	PP8	10fr brown org	125.00	.75
		Nos. Q82-Q102 (21)	881.25	45.30

PP9

PP10

Types PP7 and PP9 differ in the position of the wheel and the tablet above it.

Types PP8 and PP10 differ in the bars below "FR".

There are many other variations in the designs.

1920-21   *Typo.*

Q103	PP9	10c carmine	.30	.25
Q104	PP9	15c yel grn	.30	.25
Q105	PP9	20c blue grn	.70	.25
Q106	PP9	25c ultra	.65	.25
Q107	PP9	30c chocolate	.85	.25
Q108	PP9	35c orange brn	.90	.30
Q109	PP9	40c orange	1.10	.25
Q110	PP9	50c rose	1.10	.25
Q111	PP9	55c yel ('21)	4.50	3.25
Q112	PP9	60c dull rose	1.00	.25
Q113	PP9	70c emerald	3.00	.40
Q114	PP9	80c violet	2.25	.25
Q115	PP9	90c lemon	37.50	21.00
Q116	PP9	90c claret	4.50	.40
Q117	PP10	1fr buff	4.50	.35
Q118	PP10	1fr red brown	4.00	.45
Q119	PP10	1.10fr ultra	1.60	.45
Q120	PP10	1.20fr orange	6.25	.30
Q121	PP10	1.40fr yellow	10.00	1.75
Q122	PP10	1.60fr turq blue	18.00	.70
Q123	PP10	1.60fr emerald	40.00	.70
Q124	PP10	2fr pale rose	26.00	.30
Q125	PP10	3fr dp rose	24.00	.30
Q126	PP10	4fr emerald	24.00	.30
Q127	PP10	5fr lt violet	17.50	.30
Q128	PP10	10fr lemon	110.00	9.00
Q129	PP10	10fr dk brown	22.50	.30
Q130	PP10	15fr dp rose	22.50	.30
Q131	PP10	20fr dk blue	325.00	3.00
		Nos. Q103-Q131 (29)	714.60	45.95

PP11

1922   *Engr.*   *Perf. 11½*

Q132	PP11	2fr black	4.00	.25
Q133	PP11	3fr brown	37.50	.25
Q134	PP11	4fr green	9.00	.25
Q135	PP11	5r claret	9.00	.25
Q136	PP11	10fr yel brown	10.00	.25
Q137	PP11	15fr rose red	10.00	.25
Q138	PP11	20fr blue	67.50	.25
		Nos. Q132-Q138 (7)	147.00	1.75

PP12

PP13

Perf. 14x13½, 13½x14

1923-40   *Typo.*

Q139	PP12	5c red brn	.25	.25
Q140	PP12	10c vermilion	.25	.25
Q141	PP12	15c ultra	.25	.30
Q142	PP12	20c turq blue	.25	.25
Q143	PP12	30c brn vio ('27)	.25	.25
Q144	PP12	40c olive grn	.25	.25
Q145	PP12	50c mag ('27)	.25	.25
Q146	PP12	60c orange	.25	.25
Q147	PP12	70c dk brn ('24)	.25	.25
Q148	PP12	80c violet	.25	.25
Q149	PP12	90c sl ('27)	1.25	.25
Q150	PP13	1fr ultra	.35	.25
Q151	PP13	1fr brt blue ('28)	.55	.25
Q152	PP13	1.10fr orange	3.00	.30
Q153	PP13	1.50fr turq blue	3.25	.30
Q154	PP13	1.70fr dp brown ('31)	.75	.60
Q155	PP13	1.80fr claret	4.25	.60
Q156	PP13	2fr olive grn ('24)	.35	.25
Q157	PP13	2.10fr gray grn	7.50	.85
Q158	PP13	2.40fr dp violet	4.00	.85
Q159	PP13	2.70fr gray ('24)	35.00	1.40
Q160	PP13	3fr org red	.45	.25
Q161	PP13	3.30fr brn ('24)	55.00	1.40
Q162	PP13	4fr rose ('24)	.55	.25
Q163	PP13	5fr vio ('24)	.90	.25
Q163A	PP13	5fr brn vio ('40)	.45	.30
Q164	PP13	6fr bis brn ('27)	.50	.25
Q165	PP13	7fr org ('27)	.90	.25
Q166	PP13	8fr dp brown ('27)	.75	.25
Q167	PP13	9fr red vio ('27)	2.50	.25
Q168	PP13	10fr blue grn ('27)	1.10	.25
Q168A	PP13	10fr blk ('40)	5.75	5.00
Q169	PP13	20fr mag ('27)	1.90	.25
Q170	PP13	30fr turq grn ('31)	6.00	.40
Q171	PP13	40fr gray ('31)	55.00	.75
Q172	PP13	50fr bis ('27)	9.00	.30
		Nos. Q139-Q172 (36)	203.50	18.85

See Nos. Q239-Q262 in *Scott Standard Postage Stamp Catalogue*, Vol. 1. For overprints see Nos. Q216-Q238. Stamps overprinted "Bagages Reisgoed" are revenues.

No. Q158 Srchd.

1924   **Green Surcharge**

Q173	PP13	2.30fr on 2.40fr violet	5.00	.85
		Never hinged	30.00	
a.		Inverted surcharge	57.50	

Type of Regular Issue of 1926-27 Overprinted

1928   *Perf. 14*

Q174	A61	4fr buff	7.50	1.10
Q175	A61	5fr bister	7.50	1.25
		Set, never hinged	55.00	

Central P.O., Brussels PP15

1929-30   *Engr.*   *Perf. 11½*

Q176	PP15	3fr black brn	2.00	.25
Q177	PP15	4fr gray	2.00	.25
Q178	PP15	5fr carmine	2.00	.25
Q179	PP15	6fr vio brn ('30)	29.00	32.50
		Nos. Q176-Q179 (4)	35.00	33.25
		Set, never hinged	115.00	

No. Q179 Surcharged in Blue

1933

Q180	PP15	4(fr) on 6fr vio brn	25.00	.25
		Never hinged	105.00	

Modern Locomotive PP16

1934   *Photo.*   *Perf. 13½x14*

Q181	PP16	3fr dk green	40.00	9.00
Q182	PP16	4fr red violet	9.50	.25
Q183	PP16	5fr dp rose	37.50	.25
		Nos. Q181-Q183 (3)	87.00	9.50
		Set, never hinged	275.00	

Modern Railroad Train — PP17

Old Railroad Train — PP18

1935   *Engr.*   *Perf. 14x13½, 13½x14*

Q184	PP17	10c rose car	.45	.25
Q185	PP17	20c violet	.50	.25
Q186	PP17	30c black brn	.65	.45
Q187	PP17	40c dk blue	.80	.25
Q188	PP17	50c orange red	.80	.25
Q189	PP17	60c green	.90	.25
Q190	PP17	70c ultra	1.00	.25
Q191	PP17	80c olive blk	.90	.25
Q192	PP17	90c rose lake	1.25	.65
Q193	PP18	1fr brown vio	1.25	.25
Q194	PP18	2fr gray blk	2.75	.25
Q195	PP18	3fr red org	3.50	.25
Q196	PP18	4fr violet brn	4.25	.25
Q197	PP18	5fr plum	4.50	.25
Q198	PP18	6fr dp green	5.00	.25
Q199	PP18	7fr dp violet	24.00	.25
Q200	PP18	8fr olive blk	24.00	.25
Q201	PP18	9fr dk blue	24.00	.25
Q202	PP18	10fr car lake	24.00	.25
Q203	PP18	20fr green	125.00	.25
Q204	PP18	30fr violet	125.00	2.75
Q205	PP18	40fr black brn	125.00	3.50
Q206	PP18	50fr rose car	140.00	2.75
Q207	PP18	100fr dull grn	350.00	62.50
		Nos. Q184-Q207 (24)	989.50	77.10
		Set, never hinged	3,375.	

Centenary of Belgian State Railway.

Winged Wheel PP19

Surcharged in Red or Blue

1938   *Photo.*   *Perf. 13½*

Q208	PP19	5fr on 3.50fr dk grn	22.50	1.50
Q209	PP19	5fr on 4.50fr rose vio (Bl)	.25	.25
Q210	PP19	6fr on 5.50fr cop red (Bl)	.50	.25
a.		Half used as 3fr on piece	8.00	
		Nos. Q208-Q210 (3)	23.25	2.00
		Set, never hinged	75.00	

Nos. Q208-Q210 exist without surcharge. Value, set, $750.

See No. MQ1; Nos. Q297-Q299 in *Scott Standard Postage Stamp Catalogue*, Vol. 1.

Symbolizing Unity Achieved Through Railroads PP20

1939   *Engr.*   *Perf. 13½x14*

Q211	PP20	20c redsh brn	5.00	5.25
Q212	PP20	50c vio bl	5.00	5.25
Q213	PP20	2fr rose red	5.00	5.25
Q214	PP20	9fr slate grn	5.00	5.25
Q215	PP20	10fr dk vio	5.00	5.25
		Nos. Q211-Q215 (5)	25.00	26.25
		Set, never hinged	30.00	

Railroad Exposition and Cong. held at Brussels.

Parcel Post Stamps of 1925-27 Overprinted in Blue or Carmine

Perf. 14½x14, 14x14½

1940   *Unwmk.*

Q216	PP12	10c vermilion	.25	.25
Q217	PP12	20c turq bl (C)	.25	.25
Q218	PP12	30c brn vio	.25	.25
Q219	PP12	40c ol grn (C)	.25	.25
Q220	PP12	50c magenta	.25	.25
Q221	PP12	60c orange	.60	.55
Q222	PP12	70c dk brn	.25	.25
Q223	PP12	80c vio (C)	.25	.25
Q224	PP12	90c slate (C)	.25	.25
Q225	PP13	1fr ultra (C)	.25	.25
Q226	PP13	2fr ol grn (C)	.25	.25
a.		Ovpt. inverted	140.00	75.00
Q227	PP13	3fr org red	.25	.25
Q228	PP13	4fr rose	.25	.25
Q229	PP13	5fr vio (C)	.25	.25
Q230	PP13	6fr bis brn	.35	.25
Q231	PP13	7fr orange	.35	.25
Q232	PP13	8fr dp brown	.35	.25
Q233	PP13	9fr red vio	.35	.25
Q234	PP13	10fr bl grn (C)	.35	.25
Q235	PP13	20fr magenta	.60	.25
Q236	PP13	30fr turq grn (C)	1.10	.75
Q237	PP13	40fr gray (C)	2.25	2.10
Q238	PP13	50fr bister	1.60	1.10
		Nos. Q216-Q238 (23)	11.15	9.25
		Set, never hinged	18.00	

ISSUED UNDER GERMAN OCCUPATION

German Stamps of 1906-11 Surcharged

Nos. N1-N6

Nos. N7-N9

Wmk. Lozenges (125)

			1914-15	Perf. 14, 14½
N1	A16	3c on 3pf brown	.45	.25
		On cover		5.50
N2	A16	5c on 5pf green	.40	.25
		On cover		2.75
N3	A16	10c on 10pf car	.50	.25
		On cover		2.75
N4	A16	25c on 20pf ultra	.50	.25
		On cover		2.75
		On cover, single franking		4.50
N5	A16	50c on 40pf lake & blk	2.50	1.25
		On cover		4.50
		On cover, single franking		8.50
N6	A16	75c on 60pf mag	.90	*1.25*
		On cover		8.50
		On cover, single franking		22.50
N7	A16	1fr on 80pf lake & blk, *rose*	2.50	1.75
		On cover		12.00
		On cover, single franking		27.50
N8	A17	1fr25c on 1m car	20.00	12.50
		On cover		42.50
		On cover, single franking		85.00
N9	A21	2fr50c on 2m gray bl	18.00	15.00
		On cover		125.00
		Nos. N1-N9 (9)	45.75	32.75
		Set, never hinged	160.00	

German Stamps of 1906-18 Surcharged

Nos. N10-N21   No. N22

Nos. N23-N25

1916-18

N10	A22	2c on 2pf drab	.25	.25
		On cover		8.50
N11	A16	3c on 3pf brn	.35	.25
		On cover		3.00
N12	A16	5c on 5pf grn	.35	.25
		On cover		2.00
		On cover, single franking		3.00
N13	A22	8c on 7½pf org	.65	.35
		On cover		4.50
N14	A16	10c on 10pf car	.25	.25
		On cover		2.50
N15	A22	15c on 15pf yel brn	.65	.25
		On cover		3.00
N16	A22	15c on 15pf dk vio	.65	.45
		On cover		3.00
N17	A16	20c on 25pf org & blk, *yel*	.35	.35
		On cover		8.50
		On cover, single franking		27.50
N18	A16	25c on 20pf ultra	.35	.25
		On cover		5.50
		On cover, single franking		5.00
a.		25c on 20pf blue	.40	.25
		On cover		8.50
		On cover, single franking		17.50
N19	A16	40c on 30pf org & blk, *buff*	.40	.30
		On cover		5.50
		On cover, single franking		7.00
N20	A16	50c on 40pf lake & blk	.35	.30
		On cover		6.00
		On cover, single franking		9.00

N21	A16	75c on 60pf mag	1.00	*12.50*
		On cover		175.00
N22	A16	1fr on 80pf lake & blk, *rose*	2.00	*2.50*
		On cover		70.00
		On cover, single franking		115.00
N23	A17	1fr25c on 1m car	2.00	2.00
		On cover		85.00
		On cover, single franking		150.00
N24	A21	2fr50c on 2m gray bl	27.50	25.00
a.		2fr50c on 1m car (error)		*3,500.*
N25	A20	6fr25c on 5m sl & car	40.00	37.50
		On overfranked cover		450.00
		Nos. N10-N25 (16)	77.10	82.75
		Set, never hinged	145.00	

A similar series of stamps without "Belgien" was used in parts of Belgium and France while occupied by German forces. See France Nos. N15-N26.

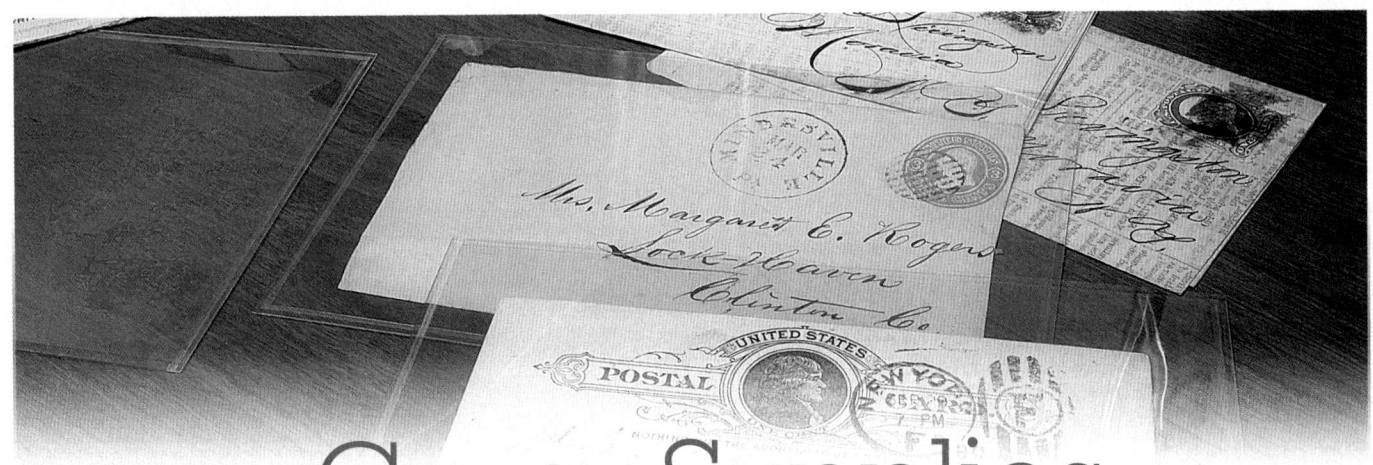

Cover Supplies

COVER SLEEVES

Protect your covers with clear polyethylene sleeves.
Sold in packages of 100.

U.S. POSTAL CARD

3¹¹⁄₁₆"

5¾"

Item	Retail	AA*
CVB05	$2.75	$2.25

U.S. FIRST DAY COVER #6

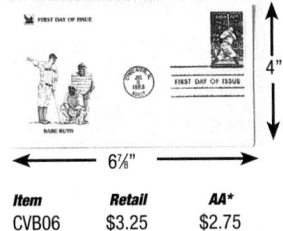

4"

6⅞"

Item	Retail	AA*
CVB06	$3.25	$2.75

CONTINENTAL POSTCARD

4⅜"

6"

Item	Retail	AA*
CVB07	$3.50	$2.99

EUROPEAN FIRST DAY COVER

5⅛"

7"

Item	Retail	AA*
CVB09	$4.25	$3.95

#10 BUSINESS ENVELOPE

4¼"

9⅝"

Item	Retail	AA*
CVB10	$5.75	$4.95

COVER BINDERS AND PAGES

Padded, durable, 3-ring binders will hold up to 100 covers. Features the "D" ring mechanism on the right hand side of album so you don't have to worry about creasing or wrinkling covers when opening or closing binder. Cover pages sold separately. Available in black with 1 or 2 pockets. Sold in packages of 10.

Item		Retail	AA*
CBRD	Burgundy	$11.99	$9.59
CBBL	Blue	$11.99	$9.59
CBCA	Candy Apple	$11.99	$9.59
CBGY	Gray	$11.99	$9.59
CBBK	Black	$11.99	$9.59
SS2PGB	Pgs. 2-Pock.	$5.75	$4.75
SS2PG1B	Pgs. 1-Pock.	$5.75	$4.75

MINT SHEET BINDERS & PAGES

Keep those mint sheets intact in a handsome, 3-ring binder. Just like the cover album, the Mint Sheet album features the "D" ring mechanism on the right hand side of binder so you don't have to worry about damaging your stamps when turning the pages.

Item			Retail	AA*
MBRD	Red (Burgundy)		$18.99	$15.25
MBBL	Blue		$18.99	$15.25
MBGY	Gray		$18.99	$15.25
MBBK	Black		$18.99	$15.25
SSMP3B	Mint Sheet Pages	(Black 12 per pack)	$9.95	$8.95
SSMP3C	Mint Sheet Pages	(Clear 12 per pack)	$9.95	$8.95

PRINZ CORNER MOUNTS

Clear, self-adhesive corner mounts are ideal for postal cards and covers. Mounts measure ⅞" each side and are made from transparent glass foil. There are 250 mounts in each pack.

Item	Retail	AA*
ACC176	$9.95	**$7.96**

1. AA* prices apply to orders placed online.

2. Prices, terms and product availability subject to change.

3. **Shipping & Handling:**
   United States: 10% of order total. Minimum charge $7.99 Maximum charge $45.00.
   Canada: 20% of order total. Minimum charge $19.99 Maximum charge $200.00.
   Foreign orders are shipped via FedEx Intl and billed actual freight. Credit cards only.

Call 1-800-572-6885
AmosAdvantage.com

BENIN

bə-'nin

LOCATION — West Coast of Africa
GOVT. — French Possession
AREA — 8,627 sq. mi.
POP. — 493,000 (approx.)
CAPITAL — Benin

In 1895 the French possessions known as Benin were incorporated into the colony of Dahomey.

100 Centimes = 1 Franc

Handstamped on Stamps of French Colonies

1892   Unwmk.   Perf. 14x13½
Black Overprint

1	A9	1c blk, *bluish*	200.00	170.00
		On cover		625.00
2	A9	2c brn, *buff*	180.00	150.00
		On cover		600.00
3	A9	4c claret, *lav*	80.00	72.50
		Never hinged	160.00	
		On cover		300.00
4	A9	5c grn, *grnsh*	36.00	28.00
		Never hinged	67.50	
		On cover		140.00
		On cover, single franking		500.00
a.		Pair, one without over-		
		print	600.00	640.00
5	A9	10c blk, *lavender*	100.00	72.50
		On cover		250.00
		On cover, single franking		500.00
6	A9	15c blue	40.00	28.00
		Never hinged	67.50	
		On cover		140.00
		On cover, single franking		500.00
a.		Pair, one without over-		
		print	1,000.	
7	A9	20c red, *grn*	250.00	220.00
		On cover		925.00
8	A9	25c blk, *rose*	125.00	72.50
		On cover		400.00
		On cover, single franking		600.00
9	A9	30c brn, *yelsh*	210.00	190.00
		On cover		840.00
10	A9	35c blk, *orange*	210.00	190.00
		On cover		1,000.
11	A9	40c red, *straw*	180.00	170.00
		On cover		750.00
12	A9	75c car, *rose*	500.00	350.00
		On cover		1,250.
13	A9	1fr brnz grn,		
		straw	450.00	375.00
		On cover		1,300.

Red Overprint

14	A9	15c blue	120.00	100.00
		On cover		275.00

Blue Overprint

15	A9	5c grn, *grnsh*	2,600.	1,200.
		On cover		2,900.
15A	A9	15c blue	2,600.	1,200.
		On cover		2,900.

The overprints of Nos. 1-15A are of four types, three without accent mark on "E." They exist diagonal.
Counterfeits exist of Nos. 1-19.

Inverted Overprint

2a	A9	2c brn, *buff*	225.00	225.00
4b	A9	5c grn, *grnsh*	190.00	160.00
5b	A9	10c blk, *lavender*	190.00	160.00
8b	A9	25c blk, *rose*	250.00	225.00
9b	A9	30c brn, *yelsh*	400.00	375.00
10b	A9	35c blk, *orange*	390.00	290.00
11b	A9	40c red, *straw*	375.00	290.00
12b	A9	75c car, *rose*	800.00	675.00
13b	A9	1fr brnz grn, *straw*	800.00	675.00
15b	A9	5c grn, *grnsh*	2,600.	1,250.
15Ac	A9	15c grn, *grnsh*	2,600.	1,250.

Red Overprint

14b	A9	15c blue	110.00	95.00

Double Overprint

4c	A9	5c grn, *grnsh*	160.00	120.00
5c	A9	10c blk, *lavender*	200.00	175.00
8c	A9	25c blk, *rose*	250.00	225.00
10c	A9	35c blk, *orange*	500.00	425.00
11c	A9	40c red, *straw*	425.00	400.00

Red Overprint

14c	A9	15c blue	120.00	110.00

Additional Surcharge in Red or Black

1892

16	A9	01c on 5c grn,	360.00	250.00
		grnsh		
		On cover		950.00
a.		Double surcharge	1,000.	1,000.
17	A9	40c on 15c blue	225.00	120.00
		On cover		500.00
a.		Double surcharge		3,800.
18	A9	75c on 15c blue	1,000.	600.00
		On cover		2,000.
19	A9	75c on 15c bl (Bk)	3,500.	2,800.
		On cover		9,750.

Counterfeits exist.

Navigation and Commerce
A3   A4

1893   Typo.   Perf. 14x13½
Name of Colony in Blue or Carmine

20	A3	1c blk, *bluish*	5.25	3.25
		Never hinged	6.75	
		On cover		200.00
21	A3	2c brn, *buff*	6.75	4.75
		Never hinged	9.00	
		On cover		200.00
22	A3	4c claret, *lav*	6.25	4.75
		Never hinged	8.25	
		On cover		200.00
23	A3	5c grn, *grnsh*	9.00	6.50
		Never hinged	12.00	
		On cover		87.50
24	A3	10c blk, *lavender*	9.75	6.50
		Never hinged	12.50	
		On cover		92.50
a.		Name of country omitted		6,500.
25	A3	15c blue, quadrille		
		paper	45.00	30.00
		Never hinged	67.50	
		On cover		140.00
26	A3	20c red, *grn*	25.00	21.00
		Never hinged	37.50	
		On cover		190.00
		On cover, single franking		300.00
27	A3	25c blk, *rose*	60.00	37.50
		Never hinged	90.00	
		On cover		125.00
		On cover, single franking		200.00
28	A3	30c brn, *bis*	27.50	21.00
		Never hinged	45.00	
		On cover		275.00
		On cover, single franking		375.00
29	A3	40c red, *straw*	6.25	6.25
		Never hinged	8.25	
		On cover		190.00
		On cover, single franking		275.00
30	A3	50c car, *rose*	6.75	7.25
		Never hinged	9.75	
		On cover		190.00
		On cover, single franking		250.00
31	A3	75c vio, *org*	14.00	12.50
		Never hinged	20.00	
		On cover		350.00
		On cover, single franking		500.00
32	A3	1fr brnz grn, *straw*	77.50	77.50
		Never hinged	125.00	
		On cover		500.00
		On cover, single franking		750.00
		Nos. 20-32 (13)	299.00	238.75

Perf. 13½x14 stamps are counterfeits.

1894   Perf. 14x13½

33	A4	1c blk, *bluish*	3.00	3.25
		Never hinged	3.50	
		On cover		140.00
34	A4	2c brn, *buff*	4.00	3.25
		Never hinged	5.25	
		On cover		140.00
35	A4	4c claret, *lav*	4.50	3.75
		Never hinged	6.50	
		On cover		140.00
36	A4	5c grn, *grnsh*	6.50	4.00
		Never hinged	8.25	
		On cover		55.00
37	A4	10c blk, *lavender*	6.75	6.00
		Never hinged	9.00	
		On cover		50.00
38	A4	15c bl, quadrille pa-		
		per	13.50	6.00
		Never hinged	20.00	
		On cover		50.00
39	A4	20c red, *grn*	13.00	9.50
		Never hinged	19.00	
		On cover		100.00
		On cover, single franking		225.00
40	A4	25c blk, *rose*	15.00	7.50
		Never hinged	22.50	
		On cover		60.00
		On cover, single franking		100.00
41	A4	30c brn, *bis*	10.50	10.50
		Never hinged	16.00	
		On cover		92.50
		On cover, single franking		125.00
42	A4	40c red, *straw*	26.00	17.00
		Never hinged	40.00	
		On cover		100.00
		On cover, single franking		140.00
43	A4	50c car, *rose*	32.50	16.00
		Never hinged	47.50	
		On cover		225.00
		On cover, single franking		300.00
44	A4	75c vio, *org*	26.00	15.00
		Never hinged	40.00	
		On cover		350.00
		On cover, single franking		500.00

45	A4	1fr brnz grn, *straw*	7.50	6.50
		Never hinged	10.50	
		On cover		375.00
		On cover, single franking		625.00
		Nos. 33-45 (13)	168.75	108.25

Perf. 13½x14 stamps are counterfeits.

POSTAGE DUE STAMPS

French Colony

Handstamped in Black on Postage Due Stamps of French Colonies

1894   Unwmk.   *Imperf.*

J1	D1	5c black	175.00	70.00
		On cover		550.00
J2	D1	10c black	175.00	70.00
		On cover		550.00
J3	D1	20c black	175.00	70.00
		On cover		550.00
J4	D1	30c black	175.00	70.00
		On cover		550.00
		Nos. J1-J4 (4)	700.00	280.00

Nos. J1-J4 exist with overprint in various positions.

BERMUDA

bər-'myü-də

LOCATION — A group of about 150 small islands of which only 20 are inhabited, lying in the Atlantic Ocean about 580 miles southeast of Cape Hatteras.
GOVT. — British Crown Colony
AREA — 20.5 sq. mi.
POP. — 54,893 (1980)
CAPITAL — Hamilton

4 Farthings = 1 Penny
12 Pence = 1 Shilling
20 Shillings = 1 Pound

> **Catalogue values for unused stamps in this country are for Never Hinged items, beginning with Scott 131.**

PRE-STAMP POSTAL MARKINGS

Crowned Circle handstamp type I is pictured in the Crowned Circle Handstamps and Great Britain Used Abroad section.

1845

A1	I	"Hamilton" crowned circle handstamp in red, on cover	4,250.
A2	I	"St. Georges" crowned circle handstamp in red, on cover	8,000.
A3	I	"Ireland Isle" crowned circle handstamp in red, on cover	8,000.

Earliest known uses: #A1, 11/13/46. #A2, 8/1/45. #A3, 8/1/45.
See Nos. X4-X5 for use as adhesives.

POSTMASTER STAMPS

PM1

1848-56   Unwmk.   *Imperf.*

X1	PM1	1p blk, *bluish*		
		(1848)		170,000.
		On cover		160,000.
a.		Dated 1849		200,000.

X2	PM1	1p red, *bluish*		
		(1856)		225,000.
a.		Dated 1854		375,000.
X3	PM1	1p red (1853)		175,000.

PM2

Same inscribed "ST GEORGES"

1860

X4	PM2	(1p) red, *yellowish*		100,000.

Same inscribed "HAMILTON"

1861

X5	PM2	(1p) red, *bluish*		130,000.
X6	PM2	(1p) red		38,500.

Nos. X1-X3 were produced and used by Postmaster William B. Perot of Hamilton. No. X4 is attributed to Postmaster James H. Thies of St. George's.
Only a few of each stamp exist. Values reflect actual sales figures for stamps in the condition in which they are found.

Values for unused stamps are for examples with original gum as defined in the catalogue introduction. Very fine examples of Nos. 1-1a, 2-15b will have perforations touching the design (or framelines where applicable) on at least one side due to the narrow spacing of the stamps on the plates. Stamps with perfs clear of the design on all four sides are scarce and will command higher prices.

Queen Victoria
A1   A2

A3   A4

A5

1865-74   Typo.   Wmk. 1   Perf. 14

1	A1	1p rose red	110.00	1.75
a.		1p dull rose	140.00	8.00
b.		Imperf.	85,000.00	27,000.
2	A2	2p blue ('66)	450.00	32.00
a.		2p bright blue	475.00	21.00
3	A3	3p buff ('73)	600.00	80.00
		On cover		400.00
a.		3p orange		2,050.
		On cover		550.00
4	A4	6p brown lilac	2,300.	90.00
5	A4	6p lilac ('74)	30.00	17.00
		On cover		600.00
6	A5	1sh green	450.00	70.00
		On cover		600.00
		Nos. 1-6 (6)	3,940.	290.75

See Nos. 7-9, 19-21, 23, 25. For surcharges see Nos. 10-15.
No. 1b is a proof.

1882-1903   Perf. 14x12½

7	A3	3p buff	210.00	75.00
8	A4	6p violet ('03)	17.00	27.50
9	A5	1sh green ('94)	20.00	150.00
		On cover		325.00
a.		Vert. strip of 3, perf. all around & imperf. btwn.	13,750.	
		Nos. 7-9 (3)	247.00	252.50

Handstamped
Diagonally

1874 **Perf. 14**
10 A5 3p on 1sh green   1,700.   950.

Handstamped
Diagonally

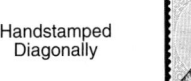

11 A1 3p on 1p rose   19,000. 20,000.
12 A5 3p on 1sh green   2,850.   975.
  a. "P" with top like "R"   2,300. 1,100.
    On cover   5,500.

No. 11 is stated to be an essay, but a few examples are known used. Nos. 10-12 are found with double or partly double surcharges.

Surcharged in Black

1875
13 A2 1p on 2p blue   875.00   475.00
    On cover   3,250.
  a. Without period   27,500. 13,250.
  b. Round "O" in "One"   1,650.   600.
14 A3 1p on 3p buff   550.00   425.00
  a. Round "O" in "One"   800.00 500.00
15 A5 1p on 1sh
     green   675.00   310.00
    On cover   1,750.
  a. Inverted surcharge   — 50,000.
  b. Without period   40,000. 20,000.
  c. Round "O" in "One"   — 450.00

A6   A7

1880 **Wmk. 1**
16 A6 ½p brown   7.50   5.25
17 A7 4p orange   21.00   2.50
    On cover   225.00

See Nos. 18, 24.

A8   A9

1883-1904 **Wmk. 2**
18 A6 ½p deep gray grn
     ('93)   4.50   1.00
  a. ½p green ('92)   7.50   4.50
19 A1 1p aniline car ('89)   17.00   .30
  a. 1p dull rose   200.00   5.25
  b. 1p rose red   100.00   4.00
  c. 1p carmine rose ('86)   75.00   1.00
20 A2 2p blue ('86)   70.00   7.00
21 A2 2p brn pur ('98)   4.75   2.00
  a. 2p aniline pur ('93)   17.50   5.00
22 A8 2½p ultra ('84)   16.00   .50
  a. 2½p deep ultra   24.00   3.75
23 A3 3p gray ('86)   27.50   9.50
24 A7 4p brown org ('04)   37.50 62.50
25 A5 1sh ol bis ('93)   19.00 21.00
  a. 1sh yellow brown   22.00 21.00
    Nos. 18-25 (8)   196.25 103.80

Black Surcharge

1901
26 A9 1f on 1sh gray   5.00   1.25
    Overprinted "SPECIMEN"   92.50
  a. 1f on 1sh bluish gray   4.00   1.10
  b. As "a," "F" in "FARTHING"
     doubled   7,500. 8,500.

The second "F" is inserted by hand.

Dry Dock — A10

1902-03
28 A10 ½p gray grn & blk
     ('03)   15.00   3.75
29 A10 1p car rose &
     brown   10.00   .35
30 A10 3p ol grn & violet   5.00   3.50
    Nos. 28-30 (3)   30.00   7.60
    Set, overprinted "SPECI-
MEN"   160.00

1906-10 **Wmk. 3**
31 A10 ¼p pur & brn ('08)   2.10   1.90
32 A10 ½p gray grn & blk   24.00   1.25
33 A10 ½p green ('09)   17.50   4.25
34 A10 1p car rose & brn   37.50   .25
35 A10 1p carmine ('08)   22.00   .50
36 A10 2p orange & gray   9.25 13.50
37 A10 2½p blue & brown   28.00   9.50
38 A10 2½p ultra ('10)   24.00   9.50
39 A10 4p vio brn & blue
     ('09)   3.75 20.00
    Nos. 31-39 (9)   168.10 60.65

Caravel   King George V
A11   A12

1910-24 **Engr.** **Perf. 14**
40 A11 ¼p brown ('12)   2.10   3.00
  a. ¼p pale brown   2.00   1.75
41 A11 ½p yel green   3.25   .30
  a. ½p dark green ('18)   15.00   1.50
42 A11 1p red (I)   20.00   .35
  a. 1p carmine (I) ('19)   67.50 10.00
  b. 1p rose red (I) ('16)   26.00   .35
43 A11 2p gray ('13)   5.00 19.00
44 A11 2½p ultra (I) ('12)   4.25   .75
45 A11 3p violet, yel
     ('13)   3.00   7.50
46 A11 4p red, yellow
     ('19)   14.00 15.00
47 A11 6p claret ('24)   12.50   9.00
  a. 6p purple ('12)   18.00 23.00
48 A11 1sh blk, green
     ('12)   6.00   5.00
  a. 1sh black, olive ('25)   6.00 21.00
    Nos. 40-48, optd "SPECI-
MEN"   450.00

Typographed
Chalky Paper
49 A12 2sh ultra & dl
     vio, bl ('20)   22.50 62.50
50 A12 2sh6p red & blk, bl   35.00 100.00
51 A12 4sh car & black
     ('20)   75.00 200.00
52 A12 5sh red & grn,
     yellow   75.00 150.00
  a. 5sh dp green & dp red, yellow   75.00 150.00
53 A12 10sh red & grn,
     green   225.00 425.00
  a. 10sh red & green, pale bluish green ('22)   310.00 490.00
54 A12 £1 black & vio,
     red   400.00 700.00
    Nos. 40-54 (15)   902.60 1,697.
    Nos. 49-54, optd "SPECI-
MEN"   900.00

Types I of 1p and 2½p are illustrated above Nos. 81-97.
The 1p was printed from two plates, the 2nd of which, No. 42a, exists only in carmine on opaque paper with a bluish tinge. Compare No. MR1 (as No. 42) and MR2 (as No. 42a). Revenue cancellations are found on Nos. 52-54.
See Nos. 81-97.

Seal of the
Colony and
King George V
A13

1920-21 Wmk. 3 **Ordinary Paper**
55 A13 ¼p brown   4.00 27.00
56 A13 ½p green   9.50 18.00
57 A13 2p gray   17.00 55.00

Chalky Paper
58 A13 3p vio & dl vio,
     yel   15.00 55.00
59 A13 4p red & blk, yel-
low   15.00 42.50
60 A13 1sh blk, gray grn   20.00 60.00

Ordinary Paper
Wmk. 4
67 A13 1p rose red   4.50   .35
68 A13 2½p ultra   19.00 20.00

Chalky Paper
69 A13 6p red vio & dl
     vio   32.50 95.00
    Nos. 55-60,67-69 (9)   136.50 372.85
Issued: 6p, 1/19/21; others, 11/11/20.

King George V
A14

1921, May 12 **Engr.**
71 A14 ¼p brown   4.25   4.50
72 A14 ½p green   3.50   8.50
73 A14 1p carmine   9.00   .45

Wmk. 3
74 A14 2p gray   11.50 50.00
75 A14 2½p ultra   14.00   6.00
76 A14 3p vio, orange   6.90 20.00
77 A14 4p scarlet, org   20.00 32.00
78 A14 6p claret   19.00 65.00
79 A14 1sh blk, green   29.00 65.00
    Nos. 71-79 (9)   117.15 251.45
Tercentenary of "Local Representative Institutions" (Nos. 55-79).

Types of 1910-20 Issue

Type I

Types of 1p

Type II

Type III

Type I, figure "1" has pointed serifs, scroll at top left very weak.
Type II, thick "1" with square serifs, scroll weak.
Type III, thinner "1" with long square serifs, scroll complete with strong line.

Types of 2½p

Type I   Type II

Type I, small "d," short, thick figures of value.
Type II, larger "d," taller, thinner figures of value.

1922-34   Wmk. 4

81	A11	¼p brown ('28)	1.90	*3.75*
82	A11	½p green	1.90	.25
83	A11	1p car, III ('28)	15.00	.35
a.		1p carmine, II ('26)	55.00	7.50
b.		1p carmine, I	21.00	.75
84	A11	1½p red brown ('34)	11.00	.45
85	A11	2p gray ('23)	1.90	1.90
86	A11	2½p ap grn ('23)	3.25	1.90
87	A11	2½p ultra, II ('32)	2.10	.90
a.		2½p ultra, I ('26)	5.00	.60
88	A11	3p ultra ('24)	20.00	*32.50*
89	A11	3p vio, *yellow* ('26)	5.00	1.25
90	A11	4p red, *yellow* ('24)	2.50	1.25
91	A11	6p claret ('24)	1.25	1.00
92	A11	1sh blk, *emer* ('27)	8.00	*11.00*
93	A11	1sh brn blk, *yel grn* ('34)	42.50	*62.50*

Chalky Paper

94	A12	2sh ultra & vio, *bl* ('27)	55.00	*87.50*
a.		2sh bl & dp vio, *dp bl* ('31)	67.50	100.00
95	A12	2sh 6p red & blk, *bl* ('27)	75.00	125.00
a.		2sh6p pale org ver & blk; *gray bl* ('30)	3,500.	3,250.
b.		2sh6p dp ver & blk, *deep blue* ('31)	100.00	*150.00*
96	A12	10sh red & grn, *emer* ('24)	160.00	*300.00*
a.		10sh dp red & pale grn, *dp emer* ('31)	175.00	*350.00*
97	A12	12sh 6p ocher & gray blk ('32)	300.00	*425.00*
		On cover		3,000.
		Nos. 81-97 (17)	706.30	*1,056.*

Revenue cancellations are found on Nos. 94-97.
For the 12sh6p with "Revenue" on both sides, see No. AR1.

Common Design Types pictured following the introduction.

Silver Jubilee Issue
Common Design Type

1935, May 6   *Perf. 11x12*

100	CD301	1p car & dk bl	.60	*2.25*
101	CD301	1½p blk & ultra	.90	*3.50*
102	CD301	2½p ultra & brn	1.50	2.50
103	CD301	1sh brn vio & ind	15.00	*50.00*
		Nos. 100-103 (4)	18.00	*58.25*
		Set, never hinged	35.00	

Hamilton Harbor — A15

South Shore — A16   Yacht "Lucie" — A17

Grape Bay — A18

Typical Cottage — A19

Scene at Par-la-Ville — A20

1936-40   *Perf. 12*

105	A15	½p blue green	.25	.25
106	A16	1p car & black	.55	.35
107	A16	1½p choc & black	1.25	.60
108	A17	2p lt bl & blk	6.00	2.00
109	A17	2p brn blk & turq bl ('38)	55.00	16.00
109A	A17	2p red & ultra ('40)	1.25	1.25
110	A18	2½p dk bl & lt bl	1.25	.30
111	A19	3p car & black	3.25	2.75
112	A20	6p vio & rose lake	1.00	.25
113	A18	1sh deep green	4.00	*19.00*
114	A15	1sh6p brown	.60	.25
		Nos. 105-114 (11)	74.40	43.00
		Set, never hinged	100.00	

No. 108, blue border and black center.
No. 109, black border, blue center.

Coronation Issue
Common Design Type

1937, May 14   *Perf. 13½x14*

115	CD302	1p carmine	.25	*1.50*
116	CD302	1½p brown	.35	*1.75*
117	CD302	2½p bright ultra	.65	*1.75*
		Nos. 115-117 (3)	1.25	*5.00*
		Set, never hinged	1.75	

Hamilton Harbor — A21   Grape Bay — A22

St. David's Lighthouse A23   King George VI A25

Bermudian Water Scene and Yellow-billed Tropic Bird — A24

1938-51   Wmk. 4   *Perf. 12*

118	A21	1p red & blk	.60	.25
a.		1p rose red & black	16.00	1.40
119	A21	1½p vio brn & blue	4.75	1.40
a.		1½p dl vio brn & bl ('43)	4.00	1.40
120	A22	2½p blue & lt bl	8.50	1.00
120A	A22	2½p ol brn & lt bl ('41)	2.50	1.25
b.		2½p dk ol blk & pale blue ('43)	2.50	1.40
121	A23	3p car & blk	16.00	2.25
121A	A23	3p dp ultra & blk ('42)	1.40	.25
c.		3p brt ultra & blk ('41)	1.40	.25
		Complete booklet, 6 each #118, 119, 109A, 120Ab, 121Ac	160.00	
		Complete booklet, 6 #121Ac and 18 #112, in blocks of 6, and 12 air mail labels	180.00	
121D	A24	7½p yel grn, bl & blk ('41)	5.00	2.00

122	A22	1sh green	1.60	.55

Typo.
Perf. 13

123	A25	2sh ultra & red vio, *bl*	13.50	12.00
a.		2sh ultra & vio, *bl*, perf. 14	9.25	3.50
b.		2sh ultra & dl vio, *bl* (mottled paper), perf. 14 ('42)	9.25	3.50
124	A25	2sh 6p red & blk, *bl*	14.50	8.75
a.		Perf. 14	26.00	8.75
125	A25	5sh red & grn, *yel*	17.00	15.00
a.		Perf. 14	60.00	20.00
126	A25	10sh red & grn, *grn* ('51)	40.00	*32.50*
a.		10sh brn lake & grn, *grn*, perf. 14	140.00	100.00
b.		10sh red & grn, *grn*, perf. 14 ('39)	225.00	200.00
127	A25	12sh 6p org & gray blk	87.50	72.50
a.		12sh 6p org & gray, perf. 14	110.00	60.00
b.		12sh 6p yel & gray, perf. 14 ('47)	725.00	600.00
c.		12sh 6p brn org & gray, perf. 14	275.00	100.00

Wmk. 3

128	A25	£1 blk & vio, *red* ('51)	52.50	*62.50*
a.		£1 blk & pur, *red*, perf. 14	300.00	140.00
b.		£1 blk & dk vio, *salmon*, perf. 14 ('42)	87.50	67.50
		Nos. 118-128 (14)	265.35	212.20
		Set, never hinged	450.00	

No. 127b is the so-called "lemon yellow" shade.
Revenue cancellations are found on Nos. 123-128. Stamps with removed revenue cancellations and forged postmarks are abundant.

No. 118a Surcharged in Black

1940, Dec. 20   Wmk. 4   *Perf. 12*

129	A21	½p on 1p rose red & blk	.30	2.40
		Never hinged	1.00	

Catalogue values for unused stamps in this section, from this point to the end of the section, are for Never Hinged items.

Peace Issue
Common Design Type
Perf. 13½x14

1946, Nov. 6		Engr.	Wmk. 4	
131	CD303	1½p brown	.25	.25
132	CD303	3p deep blue	.30	.30

Silver Wedding Issue
Common Design Types
1948, Dec. 1   Photo.   *Perf. 14x14½*

133	CD304	1½p red brown	.25	.25

Engr.; Name Typo.
Perf. 11½x11

134	CD305	£1 rose carmine	47.50	*55.00*

Postmaster Stamp of 1848 — A26

1949, Apr. 11   Engr.   *Perf. 13x13½*

135	A26	2½p dk brown & dp bl	.25	.25
136	A26	3p dp blue & black	.25	.25
137	A26	6p green & rose vio	.45	.45
		Nos. 135-137 (3)	.95	.95

No. 137 shows a different floral arrangement.
Bermuda's first postage stamp, cent.

UPU Issue
Common Design Types
Engr.; Name Typo.
1949, Oct. 10   *Perf. 13½, 11x11½*

138	CD306	2½p slate	.88	*1.10*
139	CD307	3p indigo	1.25	1.00
140	CD308	6p rose violet	1.00	.80
141	CD309	1sh blue green	2.00	2.00
		Nos. 138-141 (4)	4.75	5.55

POSTAL-FISCAL STAMP

"Revenue Revenue" PF1

1936   Typo.   Wmk. 4   *Perf. 14*
Chalky Paper

AR1	PF1	12sh6p org & grayish blk	1,250.	*1,750.*
		Revenue cancel		75.00
		On cover		3,250.

No. AR1 was authorized for postal use from Feb. 1 through May, 1937 and during Nov. and Dec. 1937. Used values are for examples with dated postal cancels indicating usage during the authorized periods. Beware of bogus and improperly dated favor cancels.
Six covers are known properly used during those time periods.

WAR TAX STAMPS

No. 42 Overprinted

1918   Wmk. 3   *Perf. 14*

MR1	A11	1p rose red	1.25	*2.00*

No. 42a Overprinted

1920

MR2	A11	1p carmine	2.40	*3.00*

BOLIVIA

bə-'li-vē-ə

LOCATION — Central South America, separated from the Pacific Ocean by Chile and Peru.
GOVT. — Republic
AREA — 424,165 sq. mi.
POP. — 6,252,250 (est. 1984)
CAPITAL — Sucre (La Paz is the actual seat of government).

100 Centavos = 1 Boliviano

PRE-STAMP POSTAL MARKINGS

BRITISH CONSULAR OFFICES IN BOLIVIA
Crowned Circle handstamp type V is pictured in the Crowned Circle Handstamps and Great Britain Used Abroad section.

Cobija

1862, Mar. 29
A1 V   Crowned circle hand-
         stamp, in red, on cover

STAMPS OF GREAT BRITAIN USED IN BOLIVIA
Numeral cancellation type A is pictured in the Crowned Circle Hanstamps and Great Britain Used Abroad section.

1865-78

C39 (Cobija)

A2	A	1p rose red (#33, P93, 95)	—
A3	A	2p blue (#30, P14)	—
A4	A	3p rose (#49, P6)	—
A5	A	3p rose (#61, P16, 19)	—
A6	A	4p pale ol grn (#70, P15)	650.00
A7	A	6p red violet (#51, P9)	650.00
A8	A	6p pale buff (#59b, P11)	—
A9	A	6p gray (#62, P13-16) (from)	550.00
A10	A	1sh green (#54, P4-5)	550.00
A11	A	1sh pale green (#64, P10-13)	550.00
A12	A	2sh blue (#55)	750.00
A13	A	5sh rose (#57, P2)	1,500.

On Feb. 21, 1863, the Bolivian Government decreed contracts for carrying the mails should be let to the highest bidder, the service to commence on the day the bid was accepted, and stamps used for the payment of postage. The winner of the contract would be responsible for expenses and would keep the profits. On Mar. 18, the contract was awarded to Sr. Justiniano Garcia and was in effect until Apr. 29, 1863, when it was rescinded. Stamps in the form illustrated above were prepared in denominations of ½, 1, 2 and 4 reales. All values exist in black and in blue. The blue are twice as scarce as the black. Value, black, $75 each.

It is said that used examples exist on covers, but the authenticity of these covers remains to be established.

Condor — A1

A2

A3

72 varieties of each of the 5c, 78 varieties of the 10c, 30 varieties of each of the 50c and 100c.

The plate of the 5c stamps was entirely reengraved 4 times and retouched at least 6 times. Various states of the plate have distinguishing characteristics, each of which is typical of most, though not all the stamps in a sheet. These characteristics (usually termed types) are found in the shading lines at the right side of the globe. a, vertical and diagonal lines. b, diagonal lines only. c, diagonal and horizontal with traces of vertical lines. d, diagonal and horizontal lines. e, horizontal lines only. f, no lines except the curved ones forming the outlines of the globe.

1867-68   Unwmk.   Engr.   Imperf.

1	A1	5c yel grn, thin paper (a, b)	11.00	25.00
		Pair, on cover		3,250.
a.		5c blue green (a)	11.00	30.00
b.		5c deep green (a)	11.00	30.00
c.		5c ol grn, thick paper (a)	450.00	450.00
d.		5c yel grn, thick paper (a)	300.00	300.00
e.		5c yel grn, thick paper (b)	300.00	300.00
f.		5c blue green (b)	11.00	30.00
2	A1	5c green (d)	10.00	25.00
a.		5c green (c)	15.00	30.00
b.		5c green (e)	15.00	30.00
c.		5c green (f)	15.00	30.00
3	A1	5c vio ('68)	375.00	375.00
a.		5c rose lilac ('68)	375.00	375.00
		Revenue cancel		150.00
4	A3	10c brown	400.00	350.00
		On cover		10,000.
		Revenue cancel		175.00
5	A2	50c orange	35.00	
		Revenue cancel		15.00
6	A2	50c blue ('68)	500.00	
a.		50c dark blue ('68)	500.00	
		Revenue cancel		250.00
7	A3	100c blue	80.00	
		Revenue cancel		45.00
8	A3	100c green ('68)	250.00	
a.		100c pale blue grn ('68)	250.00	
		Revenue cancel		175.00

Used values are for postally canceled stamps. Pen cancellations usually indicate that the stamps have been used fiscally.

The 500c is an essay.

Reprints of Nos. 3,4, 6 and 8 are common. Value, $10 each. Reprints of Nos. 2 and 5 are scarcer. Value, $25 each.

Coat of Arms
A4   A5

1868-69   Perf. 12

Nine Stars

10	A4	5c green	27.50	18.00
11	A4	10c vermilion	45.00	25.00
12	A4	50c blue	70.00	45.00
13	A4	100c orange	80.00	55.00
14	A4	500c black	1,000.	1,000.

Eleven Stars

15	A5	5c green	18.00	12.00
16	A5	10c vermilion	25.00	20.00
a.		Half used as 5c on cover		600.00
17	A5	50c blue	50.00	40.00
18	A5	100c dp orange	60.00	50.00
19	A5	500c black	3,500.	3,500.

See Nos. 26-27, 31-34.

Arms and "The Law" — A6

1878   Various Frames   Perf. 12

20	A6	5c ultra	15.00	7.00
21	A6	10c orange	12.00	6.00
a.		Half used as 5c on cover		250.00
22	A6	20c green	45.00	10.00
a.		Half used as 10c on cover		200.00
23	A6	50c dull carmine	120.00	30.00
		Nos. 20-23 (4)	192.00	53.00

A7   A8
(11 Stars)   (9 Stars)
Numerals Upright

1887   Rouletted

24	A7	1c rose	4.00	3.00
25	A7	2c violet	4.00	3.00
26	A5	5c blue	14.50	8.00
27	A5	10c blue	14.50	8.00
		Nos. 24-27 (4)	37.00	22.00

See No. 37.

1890   Perf. 12

28	A8	1c rose	3.00	2.00
29	A8	2c violet	8.00	4.00
30	A4	5c blue	6.00	2.00
31	A4	10c orange	12.00	3.00
32	A4	20c dk green	25.00	6.00
33	A4	50c red	12.00	8.00
34	A4	100c yellow	25.00	30.00
		Nos. 28-34 (7)	91.00	55.00

See Nos. 35-36, 38-39.

1893   Litho.   Perf. 11

35	A8	1c rose	6.00	5.00
a.		Imperf. pair	100.00	
b.		Horiz. pair, imperf. vert.	100.00	
c.		Horiz. pair, imperf. btwn.	100.00	
36	A8	2c violet	6.00	5.00
a.		Block of 4 imperf. vert. and horiz. through center	200.00	
b.		Horiz. pair, imperf. btwn.	100.00	
c.		Vert. pair, imperf betwn.	100.00	
37	A5	5c blue	8.00	4.00
a.		Vert. pair, imperf. horiz.	100.00	
b.		Horiz. pair, imperf. vert.	100.00	
38	A8	10c orange	25.00	8.00
a.		Horiz. pair, imperf. btwn.	100.00	
39	A8	20c dark green	100.00	45.00
a.		Imperf. pair, vert. or horiz.	200.00	
b.		Pair, imperf. btwn., vert. or horiz.	175.00	
		Nos. 35-39 (5)	145.00	67.00

Coat of Arms — A9

1894   Unwmk.   Engr.   Perf. 14, 14½
Thin Paper

40	A9	1c bister	1.50	1.25
41	A9	2c red orange	3.00	2.25
42	A9	5c green	1.50	1.25
43	A9	10c yellow brn	1.50	1.25
44	A9	20c dark blue	8.00	8.00
45	A9	50c claret	20.00	20.00
46	A9	100c brown rose	40.00	40.00
		Nos. 40-46 (7)	75.50	74.00

Stamps of type A9 on thick paper were surreptitiously printed in Paris on the order of an official and without government authorization. Some of these stamps were substituted for part of a shipment of stamps on thin paper, which had been printed in London on government order.

When the thick paper stamps reached Bolivia they were at first repudiated but afterwards were allowed to do postal duty. A large quantity of the thick paper stamps were fraudulently canceled in Paris with a cancellation of heavy bars forming an oval. Value of unused set: $5.

To be legitimate, stamps of the thick paper stamps must have genuine cancellations of Bolivia. Value, on cover, each $150.

The 10c blue on thick paper is not known to have been issued.

Some examples of Nos. 40-46 show part of a papermakers' watermark "1011."

For overprints see Nos. 55-59.

President Tomas   President Jose M.
Frias — A10   Linares — A11

Pedro Domingo   Bernardo
Murillo   Monteagudo
A12   A13

Gen. Jose   Gen. Antonio
Ballivian — A14   Jose de
                   Sucre — A15

Simon   Coat of
Bolivar — A16   Arms — A17

1897   Litho.   Perf. 12

47	A10	1c pale yellow grn	2.00	2.00
a.		Vert. pair, imperf. horiz.	100.00	
b.		Vert. pair, imperf. btwn.	100.00	
48	A11	2c red	3.00	2.00
49	A12	5c dk green	2.00	2.00
a.		Horiz. pair, imperf. btwn.	100.00	
50	A13	10c brown vio	2.00	2.00
a.		Vert. pair, imperf. btwn.	100.00	
51	A14	20c lake & blk	10.00	5.00
a.		Imperf., pair	100.00	
52	A15	50c orange	10.00	10.00
53	A16	1b Prus blue	20.00	20.00
54	A17	2b red, yel, grn & blk	60.00	90.00
		Nos. 47-54 (8)	109.00	133.00

Excellent forgeries of No. 54, perf and imperf, exist, some postally used.

Reprint of No. 53 has dot in numeral. Same value.

Nos. 40-44
Handstamped in Violet or Blue

E. F.
1899

1899   Perf. 14½

55	A9	1c yellow bis	30.00	30.00
56	A9	2c red orange	40.00	50.00
57	A9	5c green	17.00	17.00
58	A9	10c yellow brn	30.00	30.00
59	A9	20c dark blue	50.00	75.00
		Nos. 55-59 (5)	167.00	202.00

The handstamp is found inverted, double, etc. Values twice the listed amounts. Forgeries of this handstamp are plentiful. "E.F." stands for Estado Federal.

The 50c and 100c (Nos. 45-46) were overprinted at a later date in Brazil. Value, $500.

Antonio José de Sucre — A18

**   Perf. 11½, 12**
1899   Engr.   Thin Paper

62	A18	1c gray blue	5.00	2.00
63	A18	2c brnsh red	5.00	2.00
64	A18	5c dk green	5.00	2.00
65	A18	10c yellow org	4.00	2.00
66	A18	20c rose pink	5.00	2.00

67	A18	50c bister brn	10.00 5.00
68	A18	1b gray violet	8.00 4.00
		Nos. 62-68 (7)	42.00 19.00

1901

69	A18	5c dark red	3.00 2.00

Col. Adolfo Ballivian
A19

Eliodoro Camacho
A20

President Narciso Campero
A21

Jose Ballivian
A22

Gen. Andres Santa Cruz — A23

Coat of Arms — A24

1901-02 **Engr.**

70	A19	1c claret	.85 .30
71	A20	2c green	1.00 .50
73	A21	5c scarlet	1.00 .30
74	A22	10c blue	3.00 .50
75	A23	20c violet & blk	2.00 1.00
76	A24	2b brown	7.00 5.00
		Nos. 70-71,73-76 (6)	14.85 7.60

Nos. 73-74 exist imperf. Value, pairs, each $50.

For surcharges see Nos. 95-96, 193.

1904 **Litho.**

77	A19	1c claret	3.00 1.00

In No. 70 the panel above "CENTAVO" is shaded with continuous lines. In No. 77 the shading is of dots.

See Nos. 103-105, 107, 110.

Coat of Arms of Dept. of La Paz — A25

Murillo — A26

Jose Miguel Lanza — A27

Ismael Montes — A28

1909 **Litho.** **Perf. 11**

78	A25	5c blue & blk	15.00 11.00
79	A26	10c green & blk	15.00 11.00
80	A27	20c orange & blk	15.00 11.00
81	A28	2b red & black	15.00 11.00
		Nos. 78-81 (4)	60.00 44.00

Centenary of Revolution of July, 1809.

Nos. 78-81 exist imperf. and tête bêche. Values: imperf. pairs, each $80; tête bêche pairs,

---

each $95. Nos. 79-81 exist with center inverted. Value, each $95.

Miguel Betanzos
A29

Col. Ignacio Warnes
A30

Murillo
A31

Monteagudo
A32

Esteban Arce — A33

Antonio Jose de Sucre — A34

Simon Bolivar — A35

Manuel Belgrano — A36

1909 **Dated 1809-1825** **Perf. 11½**

82	A29	1c lt brown & blk	1.00 .40
83	A30	2c green & blk	1.50 .60
84	A31	5c red & blk	1.50 .50
85	A32	10c dull bl & blk	2.00 .50
86	A33	20c violet & blk	1.75 .70
87	A34	50c olive bister & blk	2.00 .80
88	A35	1b gray brn & blk	2.50 1.50
89	A36	2b chocolate & blk	2.50 2.00
		Nos. 82-89 (8)	14.75 7.00

War of Independence, 1809-1825.

Nos. 82-89 exist imperf. Value, set of pairs $400.

For surcharge see No. 97.

Warnes
A37

Betanzos
A38

Arce — A39

Dated 1910-1825

1910 **Perf. 13x13½**

92	A37	5c green & black	.50 .30
a.		Imperf., pair	15.00
93	A38	10c claret & indigo	.60 .50
a.		Imperf., pair	50.00
94	A39	20c dull blue & indigo	1.00 .80
a.		Imperf., pair	20.00
		Nos. 92-94 (3)	2.10 1.60

War of Independence.

Nos. 92-94 may be found with parts of a papermaker's watermark: "A I & Co/EXTRA STRONG/9303."

Both perf and imperf exist with inverted centers.

Nos. 71 and 75 Surcharged in Black

1911 **Perf. 11½, 12**

95	A20	5c on 2c green	.75 .30
a.		Inverted surcharge	10.00 10.00
b.		Double surcharge	12.00 10.00
c.		Period after "1911"	4.50 1.50
d.		Blue surcharge	100.00 80.00
e.		Double dsurch., one invtd.	20.00 20.00
96	A23	5c on 20c vio & blk	30.00 30.00
a.		Inverted surcharge	60.00 60.00
b.		Double surch., one invtd.	80.00
c.		Period after "1911"	40.00 40.00

No. 83 Handstamp Surcharged in Green

97	A30	20c on 2c grn & blk	2,500.

This provisional was issued by local authorities at Villa Bella, a town on the Brazilian border. The 20c surcharge was applied after the stamp had been affixed to the cover. Excellent forgeries of No. 96-97 exist.

"Justice"
A40 A41

1912

Black or Dark Blue Overprint On Revenue Stamps

98	A40	2c green (Bk)	.75 .30
a.		Inverted overprint	15.00
99	A41	10c ver (Bl)	6.00 1.00
a.		Inverted overprint	20.00

A42

A43

Red or Black Overprint

Engr.

100	A42	5c orange (R)	.75 .65
a.		Inverted overprint	20.00
b.		Pair, one without overprint	50.00
c.		Black overprint	35.00

Red or Black Surcharge

101	A43	10c on 1c bl (R)	1.00 .60
a.		Inverted surcharge	25.00
b.		Double surcharge	25.00
c.		Dbl. surcharge, one invtd.	40.00
d.		Black surcharge	200.00 150.00
e.		As "d," inverted	250.00
f.		As "d," double surcharge	225.00
g.		Pair, one without black surch.	800.00

Fakes of No. 101d are plentiful.

Revenue Stamp Surcharged

Type 1 —Serifed "1"s in date

Type 2 — Sans-serif "1"s in date

1917 **Litho.**

102	10c on 1c blue, Type 1	5,000. 1,750.
a.	10c on 1c, Type 2	— 2,000.

Design similar to type A43.

1,000 examples of Nos. 102 and 102a were reportedly produced, with 90 percent of the issue being type 1 and the balance type 2. No. 102a also exists with overprint in black. Value, used, $2,500.

Excellent forgeries exist.

Types of 1901 and

Frias — A45

Sucre — A46

Bolivar — A47

1913 **Engr.** **Perf. 12**

103	A19	1c car rose	.75 .30
104	A20	2c vermilion	.75 .30
105	A21	5c green	1.00 .25
106	A45	8c yellow	1.50 1.00
107	A22	10c gray	1.50 .25
108	A46	50c dull violet	3.00 1.50
109	A47	1b slate blue	6.00 2.00
110	A24	2b black	10.00 5.00
		Nos. 103-110 (8)	24.50 10.60

No. 107, litho., was not regularly issued.

Nine values commemorating the Guaqui-La Paz railroad were printed in 1915 but never issued. Value, set $25.

The original set is engraved. Crude, typographed forgeries exist.

Monolith of Tiahuanacu
A48

Mt. Potosí
A49

Lake Titicaca — A50

Mt. Illimani — A51

Legislature Building — A53

FIVE CENTAVOS.

Type I — Numerals have background of vertical lines. Clouds formed of dots.
Type II — Numerals on white background. Clouds near the mountain formed of wavy lines.

1916-17 **Litho.** *Perf. 11½*
111	A48	½c brown	.40	.30
a.		Horiz. pair, imperf. vert.	50.00	40.00
112	A49	1c gray green	.50	.30
a.		Imperf., pair	40.00	30.00
113	A50	2c car & blk	.50	.30
a.		Imperf., pair	40.00	30.00
b.		Vert. pair, imperf. horiz.	40.00	30.00
c.		Center inverted	150.00	100.00
d.		Imperf., center inverted	250.00	150.00
114	A51	5c dk blue (I)	1.25	.30
a.		Imperf., pair	40.00	30.00
b.		Vert. pair, imperf. horiz.	40.00	30.00
c.		Horiz. pair, imperf. vert.	40.00	30.00
115	A51	5c dk blue (II)	1.00	.50
a.		Imperf., pair	40.00	30.00
116	A53	10c org & bl	1.00	.30
a.		Imperf., pair	60.00	40.00
b.		No period after "Legislativo"	1.00	.30
c.		Center inverted	200.00	125.00
d.		Vertical pair, imperf. between	60.00	50.00
		Nos. 111-116 (6)	4.65	2.00

For surcharges see Nos. 194-196.

Coat of Arms
A54   A55

Printed by the American Bank Note Co.

1919-20 **Engr.** *Perf. 12*
118	A54	1c carmine	.40	.30
119	A54	2c dk violet	8.00	4.00
120	A54	5c dk green	.75	.30
121	A54	10c vermilion	.75	.30
122	A54	20c dk blue	2.25	.40
123	A54	22c lt blue	1.40	.90
124	A54	24c purple	.90	.60
125	A54	50c orange	7.00	.70
126	A55	1b red brown	9.00	2.50
127	A55	2b black brn	13.50	6.75
		Nos. 118-127 (10)	43.95	16.75

Printed by Perkins, Bacon & Co., Ltd.

1923-27 **Re-engraved** *Perf. 13½*
128	A54	1c carmine ('27)	.40	.30
129	A54	2c dk violet	.40	.30
130	A54	5c dp green	1.00	.30
131	A54	10c vermilion	25.00	18.00
132	A54	20c slate blue	2.50	.90
135	A54	50c orange	5.50	1.50
136	A55	1b red brown	1.50	1.00
137	A55	2b black brown	2.00	.60
		Nos. 128-137 (8)	38.30	22.50

There are many differences in the designs of the two issues but they are too minute to be illustrated or described.
Nos. 128-137 exist imperf. Value, $50 each pair.
See Nos. 144-146, 173-177. For surcharges see Nos. 138-143, 160, 162, 181-186, 236-237.

Stamps of 1919-20 Surcharged in Blue, Black or Red

Habilitada
5 cts.

1924 *Perf. 12*
138	A54	5c on 1c car (Bl)	.40	.30
a.		Inverted surcharge	10.00	6.00
b.		Double surcharge	10.00	6.00
139	A54	15c on 10c ver (Bk)	1.00	.70
a.		Inverted surcharge	12.00	6.00
140	A54	15c on 22c lt bl (Bk)	1.00	.75
a.		Inverted surcharge	12.00	6.00
b.		Double surcharge, one inverted	16.00	6.00

No. 140 surcharged in red or blue probably are trial impressions. They appear jointly, and with black in blocks.

Same Surcharge on No. 131
Perf. 13½
142	A54	15c on 10c ver (Bk)	1.00	.30
a.		Inverted surcharge	12.00	6.00

No. 121 Surcharged

Habilitada
15 cts.

Perf. 12
143	A54	15c on 10c ver (Bk)	1.00	.50
a.		Inverted surcharge	12.00	6.00
b.		Double surcharge	12.00	6.00
		Nos. 138-143 (5)	4.40	2.55

Type of 1919-20 Issue
Printed by Waterlow & Sons
Second Re-engraving

1925 **Unwmk.** *Perf. 12½*
144	A54	5c deep green	1.00	.50
145	A54	15c ultra	1.00	.50
146	A54	20c dark blue	1.00	.50
		Nos. 144-146 (3)	3.00	1.50

These stamps may be identified by the perforation.

Miner — A56

Condor Looking Toward the Sea — A57

Designs: 2c, Sower. 5c, Torch of Eternal Freedom. 10c, National flower (kantuta). 15c, Pres. Bautista Saavedra. 50c, Liberty head. 1b, Archer on horse. 2b, Mercury. 5b, Gen. A. J. de Sucre.

1925 **Engr.** *Perf. 14*
150	A56	1c dark green	1.50	
151	A56	2c rose	1.50	
152	A56	5c red, *grn*	1.50	.50
153	A56	10c car, *yel*	2.50	1.00
154	A56	15c red brown	.80	.50
155	A57	25c ultra	2.50	1.00
156	A56	50c dp violet	3.00	1.00
157	A56	1b red	5.00	2.50
158	A57	2b orange	6.00	3.00
159	A56	5b black brn	6.00	3.00
		Nos. 150-159 (10)	30.30	

Cent. of the Republic. The 1c and 2c were not released for general use.
Nos. 150-159 exist imperf. Value, $60 each pair.
For surcharges see Nos. C59-C62.

Stamps of 1919-27 Surcharged in Blue, Black or Red

1927
5
CENTAVOS

1927
160	A54	5c on 1c car (Bl)	4.50	3.25
a.		Inverted surcharge	15.00	15.00
b.		Black surcharge	40.00	40.00

Perf. 12
162	A54	10c on 24c pur (Bk)	4.50	3.25
a.		Inverted surcharge	50.00	50.00
b.		Red surcharge	70.00	70.00

Coat of Arms — A66

Printed by Waterlow & Sons

1927 **Litho.** *Perf. 13½*
165	A66	2c yellow	.50	.35
166	A66	3c pink	.90	.90
167	A66	4c red brown	.75	.75
168	A66	20c lt ol grn	1.00	.35
169	A66	25c deep blue	1.00	.50
170	A66	30c violet	1.50	1.50
171	A66	40c orange	2.00	2.00
172	A66	50c dp brown	2.00	1.00
173	A55	1b red	2.50	2.00
174	A55	2b plum	4.00	3.50
175	A55	3b olive grn	4.50	4.50
176	A55	4b claret	7.50	6.00
177	A55	5b bister brn	8.00	6.50
		Nos. 165-177 (13)	36.15	29.85

For overprints and surcharges see Nos. 178-180, 208, 211-212.

Type of 1927 Issue Overprinted

1927
178	A66	5c dark green	.50	.30
179	A66	10c slate	.75	.30
180	A66	15c carmine	.75	.35
		Nos. 178-180 (3)	2.00	.95

Exist with inverted overprint. Value $30 each.

Stamps of 1919-27 Surcharged

15 cts.
1928

1928 *Perf. 12, 12½, 13½*
Red Surcharge
181	A54	15c on 20c #122	15.00	15.00
a.		Inverted surcharge	22.50	22.50
182	A54	15c on 20c #132	15.00	15.00
a.		Inverted surcharge	25.00	25.00
b.		Black surcharge	45.00	
183	A54	15c on 20c #146	250.00	160.00

Black Surcharge
184	A54	15c on 24c #124	2.25	1.25
a.		Inverted surcharge	8.00	8.00
b.		Blue surcharge	75.00	
185	A54	15c on 50c #125	90.00	*400.00*
a.		Inverted surcharge	120.00	
186	A54	15c on 50c #135	1.75	1.25
a.		Inverted surcharge	10.00	10.00
		Nos. 181-186 (6)	374.00	592.50

Condor — A67   Hernando Siles — A68

Map of Bolivia — A69

Printed by Perkins, Bacon & Co., Ltd.

1928 **Engr.** *Perf. 13½*
189	A67	5c green	1.50	.25
190	A68	10c slate	.50	.25
191	A69	15c carmine lake	3.00	.25
		Nos. 189-191 (3)	5.00	.75

Nos. 104, 111, 113, Surcharged in Various Colors

O.03
Centavos
R. S. 21-4
1930

1930 *Perf. 12, 11½*
193	A20	1c on 2c (Bl)	2.00	2.00
a.		"0.10" for "0.01"	35.00	35.00

194	A50	3c on 2c (Br)	2.00	2.00
195	A48	25c on ½c (Bk)	2.00	2.00
196	A50	25c on 2c (V)	2.00	2.00
		Nos. 193-196 (4)	8.00	8.00

The lines of the surcharges were spaced to fit the various shapes of the stamps. The surcharges exist inverted, double, etc.
Trial printings were made of the surcharges on Nos. 193 and 194 in black and on No. 196 in brown.

Mt. Potosi — A70   Mt. Illimani — A71

Eduardo Abaroa — A72   Map of Bolivia — A73

Sucre — A74   Bolivar — A75

1931 **Engr.** *Perf. 14*
197	A70	2c green	2.00	1.00
198	A71	5c light blue	2.00	.30
199	A72	10c red orange	2.00	.30
200	A73	15c violet	4.50	.40
201	A73	35c carmine	3.00	1.25
202	A73	45c orange	3.00	1.25
203	A74	50c gray	1.50	1.00
204	A75	1b brown	2.50	1.40
		Nos. 197-204 (8)	20.50	6.90

No. 198 exists imperf.
See Nos. 207, 241. For surcharges see Nos. 209-210.

Symbols of 1930 Revolution — A76

1931 **Litho.** *Perf. 11*
205	A76	15c scarlet	6.00	1.00
a.		Pair, imperf. between	25.00	
206	A76	50c brt violet	1.50	1.25
a.		Pair, imperf. between	30.00	

Revolution of June 25, 1930.
For surcharges see Nos. 239-240.

Map Type of 1931 Without Imprint

1932 **Litho.**
207	A73	15c violet	4.00	.35

Habilitada
A 15 Cts.
D. S. 13-7-1933

Stamps of 1927-31 Surcharged

1933 *Perf. 13½, 14*
208	A66	5c on 1b red	1.00	.50
a.		Without period after "Cts"	3.00	3.00
209	A73	15c on 35c car	.50	.50
a.		Inverted surcharge	30.00	20.00
210	A73	15c on 45c orange	.60	.60
a.		Inverted surcharge	30.00	20.00

211 A66 15c on 50c dp brn   2.00   .50
212 A66 25c on 40c orange   1.00   .50
     Nos. 208-212 (5)   5.10   2.60

The hyphens in "13-7-33" occur in three positions: type 1, both hyphens in middle (shown); type 2, both hyphens on base line of numbers; type 3, left hyphen in middle, right hyphen on base line. Values are the same for all types.

Coat of Arms — A77

1933   **Engr.**   **Perf. 12**
213 A77 2c blue green   .50   .30
214 A77 5c blue   .50   .30
215 A77 10c red   1.00   .75
216 A77 15c deep violet   .50   .30
217 A77 25c dark blue   1.50   .75
     Nos. 213-217 (5)   4.00   2.40

For surcharges see Nos. 233-235, 238.

Mariano Baptista — A78   Map of Bolivia — A79

1935
218 A78 15c dull violet   .75   .50

1935
219 A79 2c dark blue   .50   .30
220 A79 3c yellow   .50   .30
221 A79 5c vermilion   .50   .30
222 A79 5c blue grn   .50   .30
223 A79 10c black brn   .50   .30
224 A79 15c deep rose   .50   .30
225 A79 15c ultra   .50   .30
226 A79 20c yellow grn   1.00   .60
227 A79 25c lt blue   1.50   .30
228 A79 30c deep rose   1.00   .60
229 A79 40c orange   2.25   1.00
230 A79 50c gray violet 2.25   1.00
231 A79 1b yellow   1.25   .60
232 A79 2b olive brown   3.00   1.50
     Nos. 219-232 (14)   15.75   7.70

Regular Stamps of 1925-33 Surcharged in Black

1937   **Perf. 11, 12, 13½**
233 A77 5c on 2c bl grn   .30   .30
234 A77 15c on 25c dk bl   .50   .50
235 A77 30c on 25c dk bl   .80   .80
236 A55 45c on 1b red brn 1.00   1.00
237 A55 1b on 2b plum   1.00   1.00
   a. "1" missing   15.00 15.00
238 A77 2b on 25c dk bl   1.00   1.00

"Comunicaciones" on one line
239 A76 3b on 50c brt vio 2.00   2.00
   a. "3" of value missing 20.00 20.00
240 A76 5b on 50c brt vio 3.00   3.00
     Nos. 233-240 (8)   9.60   9.60

Exist inverted, double, etc.

President Siles — A80

1937   **Unwmk.**   **Perf. 14**
241 A80 1c yellow brown   .50   .50

Native School — A81   Oil Wells — A82

Modern Factories A83   Torch of Knowledge A84

Map of the Sucre-Camiri R. R. — A85

Allegory of Free Education — A86   Allegorical Figure of Learning — A87

Symbols of Industry — A88

Modern Agriculture — A89

1938   **Litho.**   **Perf. 10½, 11**
242 A81 2c dull red   .80   .60
243 A82 10c pink   .90   .50
244 A83 15c yellow grn   1.40   .40
245 A84 30c yellow   1.75   .60
246 A85 45c rose red   3.00   1.25
247 A86 60c dk violet   2.50   1.25
248 A87 75c dull blue   2.00   1.75
249 A88 1b lt brown   4.50   1.00
250 A89 2b bister   4.00   1.50
     Nos. 242-250 (9)   20.85   8.85

For surcharge see No. 314 in *Scott Standard Postage Stamp Catalogue*, Vol. 1.

Llamas — A90   Vicuna — A91

Coat of Arms — A92   Cocoi Herons — A93

Chinchilla — A94

Toco Toucan — A95

Condor — A96

Jaguar — A97

1939, Jan. 21   **Perf. 10½, 11½x10½**
251 A90 2c green   1.50   .75
252 A90 4c fawn   1.50   .75
253 A90 5c red violet   1.50   .75
254 A91 10c black   1.50   .75
255 A91 15c emerald   3.00   1.25
256 A91 20c dk slate grn 3.00   1.25
257 A92 25c lemon   1.50   .75
258 A92 30c dark blue   1.50   .75
259 A93 40c vermilion   2.50   1.00
260 A93 45c gray   2.50   1.00
261 A94 60c rose red   2.50   1.00
262 A94 75c slate blue   2.50   1.00
263 A95 90c orange   5.00   1.25
264 A95 1b blue   5.00   1.25
265 A96 2b rose lake   7.00   1.25
266 A96 3b dark violet   10.00   1.75
267 A97 4b brown org   10.00   1.75
268 A97 5b gray brown   11.50   2.00
     Nos. 251-268 (18) 73.50 20.25

All but 20c exist imperf. Value, each pair $40.

Imperf. counterfeits with altered designs exist of some values.

For surcharges see Nos. 315-317 in *Scott Standard Postage Stamp Catalogue*, Vol. 1.

Flags of 21 American Republics — A98

1940, Apr.   **Litho.**   **Perf. 10½**
269 A98 9b multicolored   4.50   2.25

Pan American Union, 50th anniversary.

AIR POST STAMPS

Aviation School
AP1   AP2

1924, Dec. Unwmk. Engr. Perf. 14
C1 AP1 10c ver & blk   1.00   .50
   a. Inverted center   2,500.
C2 AP1 15c carmine & blk   2.00   2.00
C3 AP1 25c dk blue & blk   1.50   1.00
C4 AP1 50c orange & blk   10.00   5.00
C5 AP2 1b red brn & blk   3.00   3.00
C6 AP2 2b blk brn & blk   20.00 10.00
C7 AP2 5b dk vio & blk   25.00 20.00
     Nos. C1-C7 (7)   62.50 41.50

Natl. Aviation School establishment.

These stamps were available for ordinary postage. Nos. C1, C3, C5 and C6 exist imperforate. Value, $400. each pair.

Proofs of the 2b with inverted center exist imperforate and privately perforated. Value, [illegible]

For overprints and surcharges see Nos. C11-C23, C56-C58.

Emblem of Lloyd Aéreo Boliviano AP3

1928   **Litho.**   **Perf. 11**
C8 AP3 15c green   2.50   1.50
   a. Imperf., pair   70.00 60.00
C9 AP3 20c dark blue   4.00   3.25
C10 AP3 35c red brown   3.25   2.50
     Nos. C8-C10 (3)   9.75   7.25

No. C8 exists imperf. between. Value, $60 pair.

For surcharges see Nos. C24-C26, C53-C55.

Graf Zeppelin Issues
Nos. C1-C5 Surcharged or Overprinted in Various Colors

Nos. C11, C19   Nos. C12-C18, C20-C23

1930, May 6   **Perf. 14**
C11 AP1 5c on 10c ver &
            blk (G)   20.00 20.00
C12 AP1 10c ver & blk (Bl) 20.00 20.00
C13 AP1 10c ver & blk (Br) 2,500. 2,500.
C14 AP1 15c car & blk (V) 20.00 20.00
C15 AP1 25c dk bl & blk (R) 20.00 20.00
C16 AP1 50c org & blk (Br) 20.00 20.00
C17 AP1 50c org & blk (R) 1,000. 1,000.
C18 AP2 1b red brn & blk
            (gold)   350.00 350.00

Experts consider the 50c with gold or silver overprint and 5c with black to be trial color proofs.

See notes following No. C23.

Inverted Overprint
C11a AP1 5c on 10c ver & blk
            (G)   50.00 50.00
C12a AP1 10c ver & black (Bl) 150.00 150.00
C14a AP1 15c car & blk (V) 100.00 100.00
C15a AP1 25c dk blue & blk (R) 150.00 150.00
C16a AP1 50c org & blk (Br) 225.00 225.00
C18a AP1 1b red brn & blk(G) 1,750.

Double Overprint
C11b AP1 5c on 10c ver & blk
            (G)   175.00 175.00
C12b AP1 10c ver & black (Bl) 175.00 175.00
C14b AP1 15c car & blk (V) 75.00 75.00
C15b AP1 25c dk blue & blk (R) 550.00
C16b AP1 50c org & blk (Br) 225.00 225.00

Double Overprint, One Inverted
C11c AP1 5c on 10c ver & blk
            (G)   200.00 200.00
C11d AP1 5c Double
            surcharge, one
            sideways   300.00
C12c AP1 10c ver & black (Bl) 200.00 200.00
C14c AP1 15c car & blk (V) 450.00
C15c AP1 25c dk blue & blk (R) 150.00 150.00
C16c AP1 50c org & blk (Br) 250.00 250.00
C16d AP1 50c Double overprint,
            both inverted 450.00

Surcharged or Overprinted in Bronze Inks of Various Colors
C19 AP1 5c on 10c ver &
            blk (G)   120.00 150.00
   a. Inverted surcharge 200.00
C20 AP1 10c ver & blk (Bl) 100.00 150.00
   a. Inverted surcharge 150.00   —
C21 AP1 15c car & blk (V) 100.00 150.00
   a. Inverted surcharge 150.00   —
C22 AP1 25c dk bl & blk
            (cop)   100.00 150.00
   a. Inverted surcharge 150.00   —
C23 AP2 1b red brn & blk
            (gold)   700.00 900.00
   a. Inverted surcharge
     Nos. C19-C23 (5) 1,120. 1,500.

Flight of the airship Graf Zeppelin from Europe to Brazil and return via Lakehurst, NJ. Nos. C19 to C23 were intended for use on postal matter forwarded by the Graf Zeppelin. No. C18 was overprinted with light gold or gilt bronze ink. No. C23 was overprinted with deep gold bronze ink. Nos. C13 and C17 were overprinted with trial colors but were sold with the regular printings. The 5c on 10c is known surcharged in black and in blue.

No. C8-C10
Surcharged

1930, May 6   *Perf. 11*
C24	AP3	1.50b on 15c	80.00	80.00
a.		Inverted surcharge	300.00	300.00
b.		Comma instead of period after "1"	100.00	100.00
C25	AP3	3b on 20c	80.00	80.00
a.		Inverted surcharge	350.00	350.00
b.		Comma instead of period after "3"	125.00	125.00
C26	AP3	6b on 35c	80.00	80.00
a.		Inverted surcharge	375.00	375.00
b.		Comma instead of period after "6"	125.00	125.00
		Nos. C24-C26 (3)	240.00	240.00

Airplane and
Bullock
Cart — AP6

Airplane and
River
Boat — AP7

1930, July 24   **Litho.**   *Perf. 14*
C27	AP6	5c dp violet	1.50	1.10
C28	AP7	15c red	1.50	1.10
C29	AP7	20c yellow	1.10	.90
C30	AP6	35c yellow grn	1.00	.75
C31	AP7	50c deep blue	2.50	1.50
C32	AP6	1b lt brown	3.50	1.75
C33	AP7	2b deep rose	4.50	2.50
C34	AP6	3b slate	8.00	6.00
		Nos. C27-C34 (8)	23.60	15.60

Nos. C27 to C34 exist imperforate. Value,
$60 each pair.
For surcharge see No. C52.

Air
Service
Emblem
AP8

1932, Sept. 16   *Perf. 11*
C35	AP8	5c ultra	3.25	2.40
C36	AP8	10c gray	2.00	1.50
C37	AP8	15c dark rose	2.00	1.50
C38	AP8	25c orange	2.00	1.50
C39	AP8	30c green	1.25	.80
C40	AP8	50c violet	3.25	2.50
C41	AP8	1b dk brown	3.25	2.50
		Nos. C35-C41 (7)	17.00	12.70

Map of
Bolivia — AP9

1935, Feb. 1   **Engr.**   *Perf. 12*
C42	AP9	5c brown red	.30	.30
C43	AP9	10c dk green	.30	.30
C44	AP9	20c dk violet	.30	.30
C45	AP9	30c ultra	.30	.30
C46	AP9	50c orange	.50	.50
C47	AP9	1b bister brn	.50	.50
C48	AP9	1½b yellow	1.25	.75
C49	AP9	2b carmine	1.25	1.00
C50	AP9	5b green	1.50	1.25
C51	AP9	10b dk brown	5.00	1.75
		Nos. C42-C51 (10)	11.20	6.95

Nos. C1, C4,
C10, C30
Srchd. in Red
(#C52-C56) or
Green (#C57-
C58) — c

Correo Aéreo
D. S. 25-2-37
0.05

1937, Oct. 6   *Perf. 11, 14*
C52	AP6	5c on 35c yel grn	.50	.40
a.		"Carreo"	30.00	30.00
b.		Inverted surcharge	20.00	
C53	AP3	20c on 35c red brn	.75	.60
a.		Inverted surcharge	20.00	20.00
C54	AP3	50c on 35c red brn	1.50	1.00
a.		Inverted surcharge	50.00	50.00
C55	AP3	1b on 35c red brn	2.00	1.50
a.		Inverted surcharge	25.00	20.00
C56	AP1	2b on 50c org & blk	2.50	2.00
a.		Inverted surcharge	20.00	15.00
C57	AP1	12b on 10c ver & blk	15.00	10.00
a.		Inverted surcharge	75.00	50.00
C58	AP1	15b on 10c ver & blk	15.00	10.00
a.		Inverted surcharge	75.00	30.00

Regular Postage
Stamps of 1925
Surcharged in
Green or Red — d

Perf. 14
C59	A56 (d)	3b on 50c dp vio (G)	5.00	5.00
C60	A56 (d)	4b on 1b red (G)	5.00	5.00
C61	A57 (c)	5b on 2b org (G)	6.00	6.00
a.		Double surcharge	175.00	
C62	A56 (d)	10b on 5b blk brn	8.50	7.00
a.		Double surcharge	50.00	
		Nos. C52-C62 (11)	61.75	48.50

No. C59-C62 exist with inverted surcharge,
No. C62a with black and black and red
surcharges.

Courtyard of
Potosi
Mint — AP10

Miner — AP11

Emancipated
Woman
AP12

Pincers, Torch
and Good Will
Principles
AP15

Airplane
over Field
AP13

Airplanes
and Liberty
Monument
AP14

Airplane
over River
AP16

Emblem of New
Government
AP17

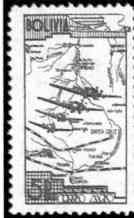

Transport Planes
over Map of
Bolivia
AP18

1938, May   **Litho.**   *Perf. 10½*
C63	AP10	20c deep rose	.60	.30
C64	AP11	30c gray	.60	.30
C65	AP12	40c yellow	.70	.40
C66	AP13	50c yellow grn	.60	.30
C67	AP14	60c dull blue	.75	.40
C68	AP15	1b dull red	.75	.40
C69	AP16	2b bister	1.50	.50
C70	AP17	3b lt brown	2.25	1.00
C71	AP18	5b dk violet	3.00	1.00
		Nos. C63-C71 (9)	10.75	4.60

40c, 1b, 2b exist imperf.

Chalice — AP19

Virgin of
Copacabana
AP20

Jesus
Christ — AP21

Church of
San
Francisco,
La Paz
AP22

St. Anthony of
Padua — AP23

1939, July 19 Litho.   *Perf. 13½, 10½*
C72	AP19	5c dull violet	.75	.50
a.		Pair, imperf. between	80.00	
C73	AP20	30c lt bl grn	1.00	.50
C74	AP21	45c violet bl	1.00	.50
a.		Vertical pair, imperf. between	90.00	
C75	AP22	60c carmine	1.50	.75
C76	AP23	75c vermilion	1.50	1.25
C77	AP23	90c deep blue	1.50	.60
C78	AP22	2b dull brown	2.50	.50
C79	AP21	4b deep plum	3.00	1.00
C80	AP20	5b lt blue	7.00	.80
C81	AP19	10b yellow	12.00	1.25
		Nos. C72-C81 (10)	31.75	7.65

2nd National Eucharistic Congress.

For surcharge see No. C112 in *Scott Standard Postage Stamp Catalogue*, Vol. 1.

POSTAGE DUE STAMPS

D1

1931 Unwmk. Engr.   *Perf. 14, 14½*
J1	D1	5c ultra	1.75	3.50
J2	D1	10c red	2.50	3.50
J3	D1	15c yellow	2.50	5.00
J4	D1	30c deep green	2.50	6.00
J5	D1	40c deep violet	6.00	8.00
J6	D1	50c black brown	12.00	15.00
		Nos. J1-J6 (6)	27.25	41.00

Symbol of Youth
D2

Torch of
Knowledge
D3

Symbol of the
Revolution of May
17, 1936 — D4

1938   **Litho.**   *Perf. 11*
J7	D2	5c deep rose	1.75	1.50
a.		Pair, imperf. between	10.00	
J8	D3	10c green	2.00	1.50
J9	D4	30c gray blue	2.00	1.60
		Nos. J7-J9 (3)	5.75	4.60

POSTAL TAX STAMPS

Worker — PT1

Imprint: "LITO. UNIDAS LA PAZ."
Perf. 13½x10½, 10½, 13½
1939		**Litho.**	**Unwmk.**	
RA1	PT1	5c dull violet	1.00	.50
a.		Double impression	15.00	15.00

Redrawn
Imprint: "TALL. OFFSET LA PAZ."
1940			*Perf. 12x11, 11*	
RA2	PT1	5c violet	.75	.30
a.		Horizontal pair, imperf. between	3.00	2.00
b.		Imperf. horiz., pair	10.00	
c.		Double impression	15.00	10.00

Tax of Nos. RA1-RA2 was for the Workers'
Home Building Fund.

BOSNIA & HERZEGOVINA

'bäz-nē-ə and ˌhert-sə-gō-'vē-nə

LOCATION — Dalmatia and Serbia
GOVT. — Provinces of Turkey under Austro-Hungarian occupation, 1879-1908; provinces of Austria-Hungary 1908-1918
AREA — 19,768 sq. mi.
POP. — 2,000,000 (approx. 1918)
CAPITAL — Sarajevo

Following World War I Bosnia and Herzegovina united with the kingdoms of Montenegro and Serbia, and Croatia, Dalmatia and Slovenia, to form the Kingdom of Yugoslavia (See Yugoslavia.)

100 Novcica (Neukreuzer) = 1 Florin (Gulden)

100 Heller = 1 Krone (1900)

Watermark

Wmk. 91 — BRIEF-MARKEN or (from 1890) ZEITUNGS-MARKEN in Double-lined Capitals, Across the Sheet

Coat of Arms — A1

Type I — The heraldic eaglets on the right side of the escutcheon are entirely blank. The eye of the lion is indicated by a very small dot, which sometimes fails to print.
Type II — There is a colored line across the lowest eaglet. A similar line sometimes appears on the middle eaglet. The eye of the lion is formed by a large dot which touches the outline of the head above it.
Type III — The eaglets and eye of the lion are similar to type I. Each tail feather of the large eagle has two lines of shading and the lowest feather does not touch the curved line below it. In types I and II there are several shading lines in these feathers, and the lowest feather touches the curved line.

Varieties of the Numerals

2 NOVCICA:
A — The "2" has curved tail. All are type I.
B — The "2" has straight tail. All are type II.

15 NOVCICA:
C — The serif of the "1" is short and forms a wide angle with the vertical stroke.
D — The serif of the "1" forms an acute angle with the vertical stroke.
The numerals of the 5n were retouched several times and show minor differences, especially in the flag.

Other Varieties

½ NOVCICA:
There is a black dot between the curved ends of the ornaments near the lower spandrels.
G — This dot touches the curve at its right. Stamps of this (1st) printing are litho.
H — This dot stands clear of the curved lines. Stamps of this (2nd) printing are typo.

10 NOVCICA:
Ten stamps in each sheet of type II show a small cross in the upper section of the right side of the escutcheon.

Perf. 9 to 13½ and Compound
1879-94   Litho.   Wmk. 91
Type I

1	A1	½n blk (type II) ('94)	26.00	50.00
		Never hinged	45.00	
		On wrapper or address label from printed matter		600.00

2	A1	1n gray	16.00	2.50
		Never hinged	27.50	
		On wrapper or address label from printed matter		275.00
c.		1n gray lilac		3.00
4	A1	2n yellow	24.00	1.60
		Never hinged	40.00	
		On postcard		30.00
		On printed matter		210.00
5	A1	3n green	27.50	3.25
		Never hinged	45.00	
		Single franking on local cover		400.00
6	A1	5n rose red	47.50	.55
		Never hinged	70.00	
		On cover		25.00
7	A1	10n blue	160.00	1.60
		Never hinged	345.00	
		On cover		190.00
8	A1	15n brown (D)	160.00	10.25
		Never hinged	270.00	
		On cover		600.00
a.		15n brown (C)	360.00	50.00
		Never hinged	535.00	
		On cover		1,200.
9	A1	20n gray green ('93)	625.00	14.00
		Never hinged	950.00	
		On cover		2,100.
10	A1	25n violet	140.00	12.00
		Never hinged	225.00	
		On cover		5,100.
		On other postal document		850.00
		Nos. 1-10 (9)	1,226.	95.75

No. 2c was never issued. It is usually canceled by blue pencil marks and "mint" examples generally have been cleaned.

> A fine cover sent from Sarajevo to Belgrade bearing a pair of 25n (Scott No. 10) sold for the equivalent of $10,425 at a Geneva auction in 2004.

Perf. 10½ to 13 and Compound
1894-98   Typo.
Type II

1a	A1	½n black	17.50	25.00
		Never hinged	32.50	
		On wrapper or address label from printed matter		625.00
2a	A1	1n gray	5.75	1.60
		Never hinged	9.75	
		On wrapper or address label from printed matter		300.00
4a	A1	2n yellow	3.25	.80
		Never hinged	6.25	
		On postcard		12.50
5a	A1	3n green	5.75	1.75
		Never hinged	11.00	
		Single franking on local cover		300.00
6a	A1	5n rose red	140.00	.90
		Never hinged	27.00	
		On cover		7.25
7a	A1	10n blue	8.00	1.25
		Never hinged	17.50	
		On cover		120.00
b.		Pair, imperf btw, perf 10½ all around		12,500.
8b	A1	15n brown	7.25	4.75
		Never hinged	15.00	
		On cover		225.00
9a	A1	20n gray green	8.00	6.00
		Never hinged	15.00	
		On cover		1,850.
10a	A1	25n violet	9.50	15.00
		Never hinged	20.00	
		On cover		—
		On other postal document		500.00
		Nos. 1a-10a (9)	205.00	57.05

Type III

6b	A1	5n rose red ('98)	8.00	.85
		Never hinged	25.00	
c.		Perf 10½	14.50	1.70
		Never hinged	22.50	
d.		Perf 11½	85.00	3.25
		Never hinged	125.00	

All the preceding stamps exist in various shades.
Nos. 1a to 10a were reprinted in 1911 in lighter colors, on very white paper and perf. 12½. Value, set $32.50.

> A very fine used pair imperforate between of the 10n blue (Scott No. 7b) sold for the equivalent of U.S. $10,425 at a Geneva auction in 2004.

A2

A3

Perf. 10½, 12½ and Compound
1900   Typo.

11	A2	1h gray black	.25	.25
		Never hinged	.60	
		On cover, postcard, newsprint or wrapper		50.00
12	A2	2h gray	.25	.25
		Never hinged	.60	
		On cover, postcard, newsprint or wrapper		30.00
13	A2	3h yellow	.25	.25
		Never hinged	.60	
		On cover		30.00
14	A2	5h green	.25	.25
		Never hinged	.60	
		On cover		3.25
15	A2	6h brown	.40	.25
		Never hinged	.85	
		On cover		45.00
16	A2	10h red	.25	.25
		Never hinged	.60	
		On cover		6.00
17	A2	20h rose	150.00	12.50
		Never hinged	325.00	
		On cover		375.00
18	A2	25h blue	1.20	1.20
		Never hinged	2.50	
		On cover		60.00
19	A2	30h bister brown	150.00	14.50
		Never hinged	325.00	
		On cover		425.00
20	A2	40h orange	200.00	17.00
		Never hinged	425.00	
		On cover		625.00
21	A2	50h red lilac	.80	.80
		Never hinged	2.10	
		On cover		1,250.
22	A3	1k dark rose	1.10	.65
		Never hinged	2.50	
		On cover		—
23	A3	2k ultra	1.60	2.00
		Never hinged	3.75	
		On cover		—
24	A3	5k dull blue grn	3.75	6.75
		Never hinged	8.50	
		On cover		—
		Nos. 11-24 (14)	510.10	56.90

All values of this issue except the 3h exist on ribbed paper.
Nos. 17, 19 and 20 were reprinted in 1911. The reprints are in lighter colors and on whiter paper than the originals. Reprints of Nos. 17 and 19 are perf. 10½ and those of No. 20 are perf. 12½. Value each $5. Reprints also exist imperf.

Numerals in Black
1901-04   Perf. 12½

25	A2	20h pink ('02)	1.00	.60
		Never hinged	2.50	
		On cover		85.00
26	A2	30h bister brn ('03)	1.00	.60
		Never hinged	2.50	
		On cover		85.00
27	A2	35h blue	1.50	.95
		Never hinged	3.25	
		On cover		85.00
a.		35h ultramarine	175.00	9.50
		Never hinged	425.00	
		On cover		175.00
28	A2	40h orange ('03)	1.25	1.00
		Never hinged	3.00	
		On cover		425.00
29	A2	45h grnsh blue ('04)	1.25	1.00
		Never hinged	3.00	
		On cover		625.00
		Nos. 25-29 (5)	6.00	4.15

Nos. 11-16, 18, 21-29 exist imperf. Most of Nos. 11-29 exist perf. 6½; compound with 12½; part perf.; in pairs imperf. between. These were supplied only to some high-ranking officials and never sold at any P.O.

View of Deboj — A4

The Carsija at Sarajevo — A5

Designs: 2h, View of Mostar. 3h, Pliva Gate, Jajce. 5h, Narenta Pass and Prenj River. 6h, Rama Valley. 10h, Vrbas Valley. 20h, Old Bridge, Mostar. 25h, Bey's Mosque, Sarajevo. 30h, Donkey post. 35h, Jezero and tourists' pavilion. 40h, Mail wagon. 45h, Bazaar at Sarajevo. 50h, Postal car. 2k, St. Luke's Campanile, Jajce. 5k, Emperor Franz Josef.

Perf. Perf 12½
1906   Engr.   Unwmk.

30	A4	1h black	.25	.25
		Never hinged	.40	
		On cover		8.50

31	A4	2h violet	.25	.25
		Never hinged	.40	
		On cover		4.25
32	A4	3h olive	.25	.25
		Never hinged	.40	
		On cover		—
33	A4	5h dark green	.35	.25
		Never hinged	1.75	
		On cover		2.50
34	A4	6h brown	.25	.30
		Never hinged	1.25	
		On cover		11.00
35	A4	10h carmine	.45	.25
		Never hinged	2.00	
		On cover		2.50
36	A4	20h dark brown	.90	.45
		Never hinged	3.75	
		On cover		17.50
37	A4	25h deep blue	1.75	1.60
		Never hinged	6.50	
		On cover		35.00
38	A4	30h green	1.75	.80
		Never hinged	6.50	
		On cover		42.50
39	A4	35h myrtle green	1.75	.80
		Never hinged	6.50	
		On cover		37.50
40	A4	40h orange red	1.75	.80
		Never hinged	6.50	
		On cover		47.50
41	A4	45h brown red	1.75	2.00
		Never hinged	6.50	
		On cover		85.00
42	A4	50h dull violet	2.50	2.00
		Never hinged	8.50	
		On cover		175.00
43	A5	1k maroon	6.50	3.50
		Never hinged	17.50	
		On cover		350.00
44	A5	2k gray green	8.00	12.00
		Never hinged	35.00	
		On cover		—
45	A5	5k dull blue	5.00	8.00
		Never hinged	12.50	
		On cover		—
		Nos. 30-45 (16)	33.45	33.50

Perf. 9¼

30a	A4	1h black	.85	.95
		Never hinged	1.75	
31a	A4	2h violet	.85	.95
		Never hinged	1.75	
32a	A4	3h olive	.85	.95
		Never hinged	1.75	
33a	A4	5h dark green	.95	.95
		Never hinged	1.90	
34a	A4	6h brown	.85	1.25
		Never hinged	1.75	
35a	A4	10h carmine	.95	.95
		Never hinged	2.00	
36a	A4	20h dark brown	2.50	3.50
		Never hinged	5.00	
37a	A4	25h deep blue	7.00	10.00
		Never hinged	14.00	
38a	A4	30h green	7.00	7.25
		Never hinged	14.00	
39a	A4	35h myrtle green	7.00	7.25
		Never hinged	14.00	
40a	A4	40h orange red	7.00	7.25
		Never hinged	14.00	
41a	A4	45h brown red	7.00	7.25
		Never hinged	14.00	
42a	A4	50h dull violet	7.00	10.00
		Never hinged	14.00	
43a	A5	1k maroon	14.50	35.00
		Never hinged	29.00	
44a	A5	2k gray green	22.50	52.50
		Never hinged	45.00	
45a	A5	5k dull blue	21.00	50.00
		Never hinged	42.50	
		Nos. 30a-45a (14)	104.45	191.25

Imperf

30b	A4	1h black	.45	.45
		Never hinged	1.00	
31b	A4	2h violet	.50	.45
		Never hinged	1.10	
32b	A4	3h olive	.50	.45
		Never hinged	1.10	
33b	A4	5h dark green	.60	.45
		Never hinged	1.25	
34b	A4	6h brown	.95	.75
		Never hinged	2.10	
35b	A4	10h carmine	.60	.45
		Never hinged	1.25	
36b	A4	20h dark brown	2.50	1.25
		Never hinged	5.50	
37b	A4	25h deep blue	5.50	5.25
		Never hinged	12.00	
38b	A4	30h green	6.25	6.00
		Never hinged	14.00	
39b	A4	35h myrtle green	6.25	6.00
		Never hinged	14.00	
40b	A4	40h orange red	6.25	6.00
		Never hinged	14.00	
41b	A4	45h brown red	7.00	6.75
		Never hinged	15.00	
42b	A4	50h dull violet	7.00	6.75
		Never hinged	15.00	
43b	A5	1k maroon	12.50	14.50
		Never hinged	27.50	
44b	A5	2k gray green	19.00	24.00
		Never hinged	41.00	
45b	A5	5k dull blue	15.50	27.50
		Never hinged	34.00	
		Nos. 30b-45b (16)	91.35	107.00

Perf. 12½ and 9¼ Compound

30c	A4	1h black	4.50	5.50
		Never hinged	8.50	
31c	A4	2h violet	4.50	5.50
		Never hinged	8.50	
32c	A4	3h olive	4.50	5.50
		Never hinged	8.50	
33c	A4	5h dark green	4.50	5.50
		Never hinged	8.50	
34c	A4	6h brown	4.00	6.00
		Never hinged	7.50	
35c	A4	10h carmine	12.00	10.00
		Never hinged	22.50	
36c	A4	20h dark brown	40.00	12.00
		Never hinged	75.00	
37c	A4	25h deep blue	17.50	32.50
		Never hinged	32.50	
38c	A4	30h green	40.00	32.50
		Never hinged	75.00	
39c	A4	35h myrtle green	40.00	32.50
		Never hinged	75.00	

Perf. 12½, 9¼ and 6½ Compound (continued)

40c	A4	40h orange red	42.50	42.50
		Never hinged	80.00	
41c	A4	45h brown red	42.50	42.50
		Never hinged	80.00	
42c	A4	50h dull violet	42.50	42.50
		Never hinged	80.00	
43c	A5	1k maroon	87.50	65.00
		Never hinged	160.00	
44c	A5	2k gray green	140.00	140.00
		Never hinged	275.00	
45c	A5	5k dull blue	140.00	140.00
		Never hinged	275.00	
		Nos. 30c-45c (16)	666.50	620.00

Perf. 12½, 9¼ and 6½ Compound

30d	A4	1h black	2.25	2.25
		Never hinged	5.00	
31d	A4	2h violet	3.25	3.25
		Never hinged	7.00	
32d	A4	3h olive	3.25	3.25
		Never hinged	7.00	
33d	A4	5h dark green	4.50	2.25
		Never hinged	10.00	
34d	A4	6h brown	3.25	3.25
		Never hinged	7.00	
35d	A4	10h carmine	4.50	4.50
		Never hinged	9.50	
36d	A4	20h dark brown	13.00	13.00
		Never hinged	27.50	
37d	A4	25h deep blue	50.00	50.00
		Never hinged	110.00	
38d	A4	30h green	45.00	45.00
		Never hinged	92.50	
39d	A4	35h myrtle green	47.50	47.50
		Never hinged	100.00	
40d	A4	40h orange red	47.50	47.50
		Never hinged	100.00	
41d	A4	45h brown red	47.50	47.50
		Never hinged	100.00	
42d	A4	50h dull violet	50.00	50.00
		Never hinged	110.00	
43d	A5	1k maroon	87.50	87.50
		Never hinged	175.00	
44d	A5	2k gray green	225.00	225.00
		Never hinged	475.00	
45d	A5	5k dull blue	140.00	140.00
		Never hinged	290.00	
		Nos. 30d-45d (16)	774.00	769.75

Perf. 12½ and 6½ Compound

30e	A4	1h black	3.50	3.50
		Never hinged	7.50	
31e	A4	2h violet	3.50	3.50
		Never hinged	7.50	
32e	A4	3h olive	3.50	3.50
		Never hinged	7.50	
33e	A4	5h dark green	3.50	3.50
		Never hinged	7.50	
34e	A4	6h brown	5.50	5.50
		Never hinged	12.00	
35e	A4	10h carmine	6.00	6.00
		Never hinged	13.00	
36e	A4	20h dark brown	14.50	14.50
		Never hinged	30.00	
37e	A4	25h deep blue	20.00	20.00
		Never hinged	45.00	
38e	A4	30h green	21.00	21.00
		Never hinged	45.00	
39e	A4	35h myrtle green	25.00	25.00
		Never hinged	55.00	
40e	A4	40h orange red	19.00	19.00
		Never hinged	40.00	
41e	A4	45h brown red	27.50	27.50
		Never hinged	60.00	
42e	A4	50h dull violet	27.50	27.50
		Never hinged	60.00	
43e	A5	1k maroon	55.00	55.00
		Never hinged	120.00	
44e	A5	2k gray green	95.00	95.00
		Never hinged	200.00	
45e	A5	5k dull blue	87.50	87.50
		Never hinged	190.00	
		Nos. 30e-45e (16)	417.50	417.50

Perf. 9¼ and 6½ Compound

30f	A4	1h black	3.50	3.50
		Never hinged	7.50	
31f	A4	2h violet	3.50	3.50
		Never hinged	7.50	
32f	A4	3h olive	3.50	3.50
		Never hinged	7.50	
33f	A4	5h dark green	3.50	3.50
		Never hinged	7.50	
34f	A4	6h brown	5.50	5.50
		Never hinged	12.00	
35f	A4	10h carmine	6.00	6.00
		Never hinged	13.00	
36f	A4	20h dark brown	14.50	14.50
		Never hinged	30.00	
37f	A4	25h deep blue	20.00	20.00
		Never hinged	45.00	
38f	A4	30h green	21.00	21.00
		Never hinged	45.00	
39f	A4	35h myrtle green	25.00	25.00
		Never hinged	55.00	
40f	A4	40h orange red	19.00	19.00
		Never hinged	40.00	
41f	A4	45h brown red	27.50	27.50
		Never hinged	60.00	
42f	A4	50h dull violet	27.50	27.50
		Never hinged	60.00	
43f	A5	1k maroon	55.00	55.00
		Never hinged	120.00	
44f	A5	2k gray green	95.00	95.00
		Never hinged	200.00	
45f	A5	5k dull blue	87.50	87.50
		Never hinged	190.00	
		Nos. 30f-45f (16)	417.50	417.50

Perf. 13½

34g	A4	6h brown	21.00	35.00
		Never hinged	45.00	
36g	A4	20h dark brown	82.50	150.00
		Never hinged	180.00	

Perf. 6½

30h	A4	1h black	1.75	5.50
		Never hinged	4.00	
31h	A4	2h violet	1.75	5.50
		Never hinged	4.00	
32h	A4	3h olive	1.75	5.50
		Never hinged	4.00	
33h	A4	5h dark green	1.75	5.50
		Never hinged	4.00	
34h	A4	6h brown	10.50	7.00
		Never hinged	22.50	
35h	A4	10h carmine	14.00	5.50
		Never hinged	30.00	
36h	A4	20h dark brown	16.50	10.50
		Never hinged	35.00	
37h	A4	25h deep blue	32.50	32.50
		Never hinged	70.00	
38h	A4	30h green	37.50	16.50
		Never hinged	80.00	
39h	A4	35h myrtle green	40.00	16.50
		Never hinged	85.00	
40h	A4	40h orange red	47.50	16.50
		Never hinged	100.00	
41h	A4	45h brown red	47.50	32.50
		Never hinged	100.00	
42h	A4	50h dull violet	47.50	25.00
		Never hinged	100.00	
43h	A5	1k maroon	87.50	250.00
		Never hinged	180.00	
44h	A5	2k gray green	140.00	375.00
		Never hinged	300.00	
45h	A5	5k dull blue	130.00	440.00
		Never hinged	275.00	
		Nos. 30h-45h (16)	658.00	1,249.

Perf. 10½

30i	A4	1h black	4.50	6.00
		Never hinged	9.00	
31i	A4	2h violet	4.50	7.50
		Never hinged	9.00	
32i	A4	3h olive	4.50	10.00
		Never hinged	9.00	
33i	A4	5h dark green	4.50	10.00
		Never hinged	9.00	
34i	A4	6h brown	10.50	11.00
		Never hinged	21.00	
35i	A4	10h carmine	5.50	7.50
		Never hinged	11.00	
36i	A4	20h dark brown	21.00	32.50
		Never hinged	42.50	
37i	A4	25h deep blue	55.00	87.50
		Never hinged	110.00	
38i	A4	30h green	55.00	120.00
		Never hinged	110.00	
39i	A4	35h myrtle green	55.00	120.00
		Never hinged	110.00	
40i	A4	40h orange red	77.50	130.00
		Never hinged	160.00	
41i	A4	45h brown red	77.50	130.00
		Never hinged	160.00	
42i	A4	50h dull violet	77.50	130.00
		Never hinged	160.00	
43i	A5	1k maroon	160.00	375.00
		Never hinged	325.00	
44i	A5	2k gray green	250.00	450.00
		Never hinged	500.00	
45i	A5	5k dull blue	225.00	440.00
		Never hinged	450.00	
		Nos. 30i-45i (16)	1,087.	2,067.

Perf. 10½ and 9¼ Compound

30j	A4	1h black	6.00	6.00
		Never hinged	12.00	
31j	A4	2h violet	10.50	10.50
		Never hinged	21.00	
32j	A4	3h olive	9.50	9.50
		Never hinged	19.00	
33j	A4	5h dark green	9.50	9.50
		Never hinged	19.00	
34j	A4	6h brown	10.50	10.50
		Never hinged	21.00	
35j	A4	10h carmine	12.00	12.00
		Never hinged	24.00	
36j	A4	20h dark brown	16.50	16.50
		Never hinged	35.00	
37j	A4	25h deep blue	24.00	24.00
		Never hinged	47.50	
38j	A4	30h green	32.50	32.50
		Never hinged	65.00	
39j	A4	35h myrtle green	32.50	32.50
		Never hinged	65.00	
40j	A4	40h orange red	22.50	22.50
		Never hinged	45.00	
41j	A4	45h brown red	35.00	35.00
		Never hinged	70.00	
42j	A4	50h dull violet	50.00	50.00
		Never hinged	100.00	
43j	A5	1k maroon	55.00	55.00
		Never hinged	110.00	
44j	A5	2k gray green	275.00	275.00
		Never hinged	550.00	
45j	A5	5k dull blue	120.00	120.00
		Never hinged	240.00	
		Nos. 30j-45j (16)	721.00	721.00

Perf. 10½ and 12½ Compound

30k	A4	1h black	6.50	6.50
		Never hinged	13.00	
31k	A4	2h violet	9.00	9.00
		Never hinged	18.00	
32k	A4	3h olive	6.50	6.50
		Never hinged	13.00	
33k	A4	5h dark green	6.50	6.50
		Never hinged	13.00	
34k	A4	6h brown	10.50	10.50
		Never hinged	21.00	
35k	A4	10h carmine	12.00	12.00
		Never hinged	24.00	
36k	A4	20h dark brown	14.50	14.50
		Never hinged	29.00	
37k	A4	25h deep blue	29.00	29.00
		Never hinged	57.50	
38k	A4	30h green	32.50	32.50
		Never hinged	65.00	
39k	A4	35h myrtle green	23.00	.2300
		Never hinged	45.00	
40k	A4	40h orange red	22.50	22.50
		Never hinged	45.00	
41k	A4	45h brown red	30.00	30.00
		Never hinged	60.00	
42k	A4	50h dull violet	24.00	24.00
		Never hinged	47.50	
43k	A5	1k maroon	55.00	55.00
		Never hinged	110.00	
44k	A5	2k gray green	140.00	140.00
		Never hinged	275.00	
45k	A5	5k dull blue	140.00	140.00
		Never hinged	275.00	
		Nos. 30k-45k (16)	561.50	538.73

Perf. 10½, 12½ and 9¼ Compound

30l	A4	1h black	4.50	4.50
		Never hinged	9.00	
31l	A4	2h violet	6.50	6.50
		Never hinged	13.00	
32l	A4	3h olive	5.25	5.25
		Never hinged	10.50	
33l	A4	5h dark green	6.50	6.50
		Never hinged	13.00	
34l	A4	6h brown	10.50	10.50
		Never hinged	21.00	
35l	A4	10h carmine	12.00	12.00
		Never hinged	24.00	
36l	A4	20h dark brown	14.50	14.50
		Never hinged	29.00	
37l	A4	25h deep blue	27.50	27.50
		Never hinged	55.00	
38l	A4	30h green	32.50	32.50
		Never hinged	65.00	
39l	A4	35h myrtle green	32.50	32.50
		Never hinged	65.00	
40l	A4	40h orange red	32.50	32.50
		Never hinged	65.00	
41l	A4	45h brown red	35.00	35.00
		Never hinged	70.00	
42l	A4	50h dull violet	35.00	35.00
		Never hinged	70.00	
43l	A5	1k maroon	52.50	52.50
		Never hinged	105.00	
44l	A5	2k gray green	130.00	130.00
		Never hinged	140.00	
45l	A5	5k dull blue	625.00	625.00
		Never hinged	1,250.	
		Nos. 30l-45l (16)	1,062.	1,062.

For overprint and surcharges see Nos. 126, B1-B4, Yugoslavia 1L38, 1LB5-1LB7.

Birthday Jubilee Issue

Designs of 1906 Issue, with "1830-1910" in Label at Bottom

1910 — Perf. 12½

46	A4	1h black	.40	.40
		Never hinged	1.75	
		On cover	65.00	
47	A4	2h violet	.40	.40
		Never hinged	1.75	
		On cover	42.50	
48	A4	3h olive	.40	.40
		Never hinged	1.75	
		On cover	42.50	
49	A4	5h dark green	.40	.40
		Never hinged	1.75	
		On cover	12.50	
50	A4	6h orange brn	.40	.40
		Never hinged	2.50	
		On cover	75.00	
51	A4	10h carmine	.85	.25
		Never hinged	2.50	
		On cover	12.50	
52	A4	20h dark brown	1.60	*2.50*
		Never hinged	5.00	
		On cover	125.00	
53	A4	25h deep blue	2.50	*4.25*
		Never hinged	8.50	
		On cover	150.00	
54	A4	30h green	2.50	*4.25*
		Never hinged	8.50	
		On cover	210.00	
55	A4	35h myrtle grn	2.50	*4.25*
		Never hinged	8.50	
		On cover	210.00	
56	A4	40h orange red	2.50	*5.00*
		Never hinged	8.50	
		On cover	240.00	
57	A4	45h brown red	3.50	*8.50*
		Never hinged	12.50	
		On cover	300.00	
58	A4	50h dull violet	4.25	*8.50*
		Never hinged	17.50	
		On cover	425.00	
59	A5	1k maroon	5.00	*8.50*
		Never hinged	17.50	
		On cover	850.00	
60	A5	2k gray green	16.00	*34.00*
		Never hinged	60.00	
		On cover	—	
61	A5	5k dull blue	1.60	*10.00*
		Never hinged	5.00	
		On cover	—	
		Nos. 46-61 (16)	44.80	92.00

80th birthday of Emperor Franz Josef.

Scenic Type of 1906

Views: 12h, Jaice. 60h, Konjica. 72h, Vishegrad.

1912

62	A4	12h ultra	6.00	*7.25*
		Never hinged	15.00	
		On cover	110.00	
63	A4	60h dull blue	3.50	*5.00*
		Never hinged	8.50	
		On cover	175.00	
64	A4	72h carmine	12.00	*24.00*
		Never hinged	35.00	
		On cover	425.00	
		Nos. 62-64 (3)	21.50	*36.25*

Value, imperf set: hinged $120; never hinged $240.

See Austria for similar designs inscribed "FELDPOST" instead of "MILITARPOST."

Emperor Franz Josef
A23   A24

A25

A26

1912-14 — Various Frames

65	A23	1h olive green	.40	.25
		Never hinged	1.75	
		On cover	6.00	
66	A23	2h brt blue	.40	.25
		Never hinged	1.75	
		On cover	6.00	
67	A23	3h claret	.40	.25
		Never hinged	1.75	
		On cover	6.00	
68	A23	5h green	.40	.25
		Never hinged	1.75	
		On cover	2.10	
69	A23	6h dark gray	.40	.25
		Never hinged	1.75	
		On cover	12.50	
70	A23	10h rose car	.40	.25
		Never hinged	1.75	
		On cover	2.10	
71	A23	12h dp olive grn	.55	.40
		Never hinged	2.50	
		On cover	21.00	
72	A23	20h orange brn	3.00	.25
		Never hinged	12.00	
		On cover	13.00	
73	A23	25h ultra	1.60	.25
		Never hinged	6.75	
		On cover	13.00	
74	A23	30h orange red	1.60	.25
		Never hinged	6.75	
		On cover	30.00	
75	A24	35h myrtle grn	1.90	.25
		Never hinged	8.50	
		On cover	25.00	
76	A24	40h dk violet	5.25	.25
		Never hinged	25.00	
		On cover	21.00	
77	A24	45h olive brn	2.40	.40
		Never hinged	14.50	
		On cover	42.50	
78	A24	50h slate blue	2.75	.25
		Never hinged	17.50	
		On cover	35.00	
79	A24	60h brown vio	1.60	.25
		Never hinged	17.50	
		On cover	35.00	
80	A24	72h dark blue	4.00	*6.00*
		Never hinged	10.00	
		On cover	210.00	
81	A25	1k brn vio, *straw*	9.75	.85
		Never hinged	37.50	
		On cover	250.00	
82	A25	2k dk gray, *bl*	8.50	.85
		Never hinged	25.00	
		On cover	—	
83	A26	3k carmine, *grn*	10.00	*12.00*
		Never hinged	37.50	
		On cover	—	
84	A26	5k dk vio, *gray*	20.00	*32.50*
		Never hinged	55.00	
		On cover	—	
85	A25	10k dk ultra, *gray* ('14)	100.00	*140.00*
		Never hinged	240.00	
		On cover	—	
		Nos. 65-85 (21)	175.30	196.25

Value, imperf set: hinged $375; never hinged $750.

For overprints and surcharges see Nos. 127, B5-B8, Austria M1-M21.

A27

A28

1916-17 — Perf. 12½

86	A27	3h dark gray	.25	.40
		Never hinged	.85	
		On cover	21.00	
87	A27	5h olive green	.25	.60
		Never hinged	1.00	
		On cover	8.50	

88	A27	6h violet	.25	.75
		Never hinged	1.00	
		On cover		25.00
89	A27	10h olive brown	1.60	3.25
		Never hinged	6.00	
		On cover		6.00
a.		10h bister	2.40	3.75
		Never hinged	0.30	
		On cover		20.00
90	A27	12h blue gray	.30	.95
		Never hinged	1.25	
		On cover		25.00
91	A27	15h car rose	.25	.25
		Never hinged	.45	
		On cover		6.00
92	A27	20h brown	.40	.95
		Never hinged	1.50	
		On cover		35.00
93	A27	25h blue	.25	.95
		Never hinged	1.40	
		On cover		35.00
94	A27	30h dark green	.25	.95
		Never hinged	1.40	
		On cover		42.50
95	A27	40h vermilion	.25	.95
		Never hinged	1.40	
		On cover		50.00
96	A27	50h green	.25	.95
		Never hinged	1.40	
		On cover		50.00
97	A27	60h lake	.25	.95
		Never hinged	1.40	
		On cover		85.00
98	A27	80h orange brn	1.50	.80
		Never hinged	6.50	
		On cover		175.00
a.		Perf. 11½	3.50	8.00
		Never hinged	9.00	
		On cover		350.00
99	A27	90h dark violet	1.10	1.60
		Never hinged	6.00	
		On cover		350.00
a.		Perf. 11½	1,050.	—
		Never hinged	1,850.	
101	A28	2k claret, straw	.75	3.25
		Never hinged	2.10	
		On cover		—
102	A28	3k green, bl	1.50	4.00
		Never hinged	4.25	
		On cover		—
103	A28	4k carmine, grn	6.50	13.50
		Never hinged	19.00	
		On cover		—
104	A28	10k dp vio, gray	21.00	40.00
		Never hinged	42.50	
		On cover		—
		Nos. 86-104 (18)	36.90	75.05

Value, imperf set: hinged $275; never hinged $500.
For overprints see Nos. B11-B12.

Emperor Karl I

	A29	A30
1917		**Perf. 12½**

105	A29	3h olive gray	.25	.30
		Never hinged	.65	
		On cover		14.00
a.		Perf. 11½	125.00	250.00
		Never hinged	210.00	
		On cover		—
b.		Perf. 12½x11½	24.00	55.00
		Never hinged	50.00	
		On cover		—
106	A29	5h olive green	.25	.30
		Never hinged	.35	
		On cover		5.00
107	A29	6h violet	.40	.95
		Never hinged	1.90	
		On cover		32.50
108	A29	10h orange brn	.25	.25
		Never hinged	.35	
		On cover		3.50
a.		Perf. 11½x12½	160.00	350.00
		Never hinged	240.00	
		On cover		—
b.		Perf. 11½	160.00	425.00
		Never hinged	240.00	
109	A29	12h blue	.35	.95
		Never hinged	1.90	
		On cover		32.50
110	A29	15h brt rose	.25	.25
		Never hinged	.50	
		On cover		5.00
111	A29	20h red brown	.25	.25
		Never hinged	.75	
		On cover		12.50
112	A29	25h ultra	.65	.80
		Never hinged	2.75	
		On cover		25.00
113	A29	30h gray green	.25	.40
		Never hinged	1.90	
		On cover		55.00
114	A29	40h olive bis	.25	.40
		Never hinged	1.90	
		On cover		17.50
115	A29	50h dp green	.65	.80
		Never hinged	2.75	
		On cover		47.50
116	A29	60h car rose	.55	.80
		Never hinged	2.75	
		On cover		50.00
a.		Perf. 11½	30.00	67.50
		Never hinged	47.50	
		On cover		—
117	A29	80h steel blue	.30	.75
		Never hinged	1.50	
		On cover		150.00

118	A29	90h dull violet	1.25	2.10
		Never hinged	4.25	
		On cover		210.00
119	A30	2k carmine, straw	1.00	.85
		Never hinged	2.00	
		On cover		350.00
120	A30	3k green, bl	91.00	27.00
		Never hinged	67.50	
		On cover		—
121	A30	4k carmine, grn	7.50	16.00
		Never hinged	23.00	
		On cover		—
122	A30	10k dp violet, gray	4.00	14.50
		Never hinged	12.00	
		On cover		12.50
		Nos. 105-122 (18)	39.40	68.15

Value, imperf set: hinged $150; never hinged $325.

Nos. 47 and 66 Overprinted in Red

1918

126	A4	2h violet	.60	1.75
		Never hinged	1.25	
		On cover		50.00
b.		Inverted overprint	60.00	
		Never hinged	95.00	
d.		Double overprint	35.00	
		Never hinged	50.00	
f.		Double overprint, one inverted	30.00	
		Never hinged	60.00	
127	A23	2h bright blue	.60	1.75
		Never hinged	1.25	
		On cover		50.00
a.		Pair, one without overprint		—
b.		Inverted overprint	60.00	
		Never hinged	50.00	
c.		Double overprint	35.00	
		Never hinged	70.00	
d.		Double overprint, one inverted	30.00	
		Never hinged	50.00	

Emperor Karl I — A31

1918	**Typo.**	**Perf. 12½, Imperf.**	
128	A31	2h orange	12.00
		Never hinged	30.00
129	A31	3h dark green	12.00
		Never hinged	30.00
130	A31	5h lt green	12.00
		Never hinged	30.00
131	A31	6h blue green	12.00
		Never hinged	30.00
132	A31	10h brown	12.00
		Never hinged	30.00
133	A31	20h brick red	12.00
		Never hinged	30.00
134	A31	25h ultra	12.00
		Never hinged	30.00
135	A31	45h dk slate	12.00
		Never hinged	30.00
136	A31	50h lt bluish grn	12.00
		Never hinged	30.00
137	A31	60h blue violet	12.00
		Never hinged	30.00
138	A31	70h ocher	12.00
		Never hinged	30.00
139	A31	80h rose	12.00
		Never hinged	30.00
140	A31	90h violet brn	12.00
		Never hinged	30.00

		Engr.	
141	A30	1k ol grn, grnsh	2,100.
		Never hinged	3,250.
		Nos. 128-140 (13)	156.00

Nos. 128-141 were prepared for use in Bosnia and Herzegovina, but were not issued there. They were sold after the Armistice at the Vienna post office for a few days.

Nos. 128-141 exist imperf. Values: Nos. 128-140, hinged $210, never hinged $375; No. 141, hinged $1,950, never hinged $3,000.

SEMI-POSTAL STAMPS

Nos. 33 and 35 Surcharged in Red

T1	T2	T3

1914, Nov. 1	**Unwmk.**	**Perf. 12½**	
B1	A4	7h on 5h dk grn (1)	.45	.85
		Never hinged	.85	
		On cover		25.00
a.		Type 2	3.00	4.25
		Never hinged	5.00	
		On cover		75.00
b.		Type 3	15.00	35.00
		Never hinged	37.50	
		On cover		150.00
B2	A4	12h on 10h car (1)	.45	.85
		Never hinged	.85	
		On cover		25.00
a.		Type 2	3.00	4.25
		Never hinged	5.00	
		On cover		75.00
b.		Type 3	15.00	35.00
		Never hinged	37.50	
		On cover		150.00

Nos. B1-B2 exist with double and inverted surcharges. Values, double surcharge, each: unused $25, never hinged $40. Values, inverted surcharge, each: unused $30, never hinged $50.

Nos. 33, 35 Surcharged in Red or Blue

1915, July 10			**Perf. 12½**	
B3	A4	7h on 5h (R)	12.00	17.00
		Never hinged	25.00	
		On cover		105.00
a.		Perf. 9¼	200.00	250.00
		Never hinged	350.00	
B4	A4	12h on 10h (Bl)	.40	.60
		Never hinged	2.50	
		On cover		50.00

Nos. B3-B4 exist with double and inverted surcharges. Value about $30 each.

Nos. 68, 70 Surcharged in Red or Blue

The overprint on Nos. B5-B6 is found in four types, differing in length of surcharge lines:
I — date 18mm, denomination 14mm.
II — date 16mm, denomination 14mm.
III — date 18mm, denomination 16mm.
IV — date 16mm, denomination 16mm.

1915, Dec. 1				
B5	A23	7h on 5h (R) (I)	.85	2.40
		Never hinged	2.50	
		On cover		50.00
a.		"1915" at top and bottom	42.50	77.50
		Never hinged	75.00	
b.		Type II	.85	2.25
		Never hinged	2.50	
		On cover		50.00
B6	A23	12h on 10h (Bl) (II)	1.75	4.75
		Never hinged	5.00	
		On cover		50.00
a.		Surcharged "7 Heller."	47.50	100.00
		Never hinged	75.00	
b.		Type I	17.50	35.00
		Never hinged	35.00	
		On cover		110.00
c.		Type III	1.40	4.25
		Never hinged	4.50	
		On cover		60.00
d.		Type IV	25.00	45.00
		Never hinged	60.00	
		On cover		150.00

Nos. B5-B6 exist with double and inverted surcharges. Values, each: unused $25, never hinged $42.50.

Nos. B5a and B6a exist double and inverted.

Nos. 68, 70 Surcharged in Red or Blue

The overprint on Nos. B7-B8 is found in two types, differing in length of surcharge lines:
I — date 18mm, denomination 14mm.
II — date 16mm, denomination 14mm.

1916. Feb. 1				
B7	A23	7h on 5h (R) (I)	.85	.85
		Never hinged	1.75	
		On cover		50.00
a.		Type II	.50	.70
		Never hinged	1.75	
		On cover		50.00
B8	A23	12h on 10h (Bl) (I)	.85	.90
		Never hinged	1.75	
a.		Type II	.50	.90
		Never hinged	1.75	
		On cover		50.00

Nos. B7-B8 exist with double and inverted surcharges. Value $20 each.

Wounded Soldier — SP1	Blind Soldier — SP2

1916, July 10			**Engr.**	
B9	SP1	5h (+ 2h) green	1.10	2.10
		Never hinged	2.50	
		On cover		75.00
B10	SP2	10h (+ 2h) magenta	1.75	3.00
		Never hinged	4.25	
		On cover		75.00

Nos. B9-B10 exist imperf. Value, set: hinged $200, never hinged $210.

Nos. 89, 89a, 91 Overprinted

1917, May 9				
B11	A27	10h bister (#89a)	.30	.30
		Never hinged	.90	
		On cover		75.00
a.		On 10h olive brown (#89)	4.00	8.50
		Never hinged	8.50	
		On cover		100.00
B12	A27	15h carmine rose	.30	.60
		Never hinged	.90	
		On cover		8.50

Nos. B11-B12 exist imperf. Value, set: hinged $190, never hinged $250.
Nos. B11-B12 exist with double and inverted overprint. Value $15-20 each.

Design for Memorial Church at Sarajevo SP3

Archduke Francis Ferdinand — SP4

Duchess Sophia and Archduke Francis Ferdinand SP5

1917, June 20 Typo. Perf. 12½

```
B13 SP3 10h violet black          .40    .40
      Never hinged          1.75
      On cover                     92.50
  a.   Perf 11½              3.50   6.50
        Never hinged         8.50
        On cover                   125.00
B14 SP4 15h claret                .40    .40
      Never hinged          1.75
      On cover                     72.50
  a.   Perf 11½              3.50   6.50
        Never hinged         8.50
        On cover                   100.00
B15 SP5 40h deep blue             .40    .40
      Never hinged          1.75
      On cover                     72.50
  a.   Perf 11½              3.50   6.50
        Never hinged         8.50
        On cover                   100.00
      Nos. B13-B15 (3)       1.20   1.20
```

Assassination of Archduke Ferdinand and Archduchess Sophia. Sold at a premium of 2h each, which helped build a memorial church at Sarajevo.

Exist imperf. Value, set: hinged $37.50; never hinged $100.

Blind Soldier — SP6   Emperor Karl I — SP8

Design: 15h, Wounded soldier.

1918, Mar. 1 Engr. Perf. 12½

```
B16 SP6 10h (+ 10h) grnsh bl      .60   1.60
      Never hinged          2.10
      On cover                     72.50
B17 SP6 15h (+ 10h) red brn       .60   1.60
      Never hinged          2.10
      On cover                     72.50
```

#B16-B17 exist imperf. Value, set: hinged $80; never hinged $150.

1918, July 20 Typo. Perf. 12½x13

Design: 15h, Empress Zita.

```
B18 SP8 10h gray green            .50   1.25
      Never hinged          1.25
      On cover                     110.00
B19 SP8 15h brown red             .50   1.25
      Never hinged          1.25
      On cover                     110.00
B20 SP8 40h violet                .50   1.25
      Never hinged          1.25
      On cover                     110.00
      Nos. B18-B20 (3)       1.50   3.75
```

Sold at a premium of 10h each which went to the "Karl's Fund."

Nos. B18-B20 exist imperf. Value, set: hinged $140; never hinged $135.

POSTAGE DUE STAMPS

D1   D2

1904 Unwmk. Perf. 12½

```
J1 D1  1h black, red & yel        .85    .35
      Never hinged          1.40
      On cover                     140.00
J2 D1  2h black, red & yel        .85    .35
      Never hinged          1.40
      On cover                     140.00
J3 D1  3h black, red & yel        .85    .35
      Never hinged          1.40
      On cover                     140.00
J4 D1  4h black, red & yel        .85    .35
      Never hinged          1.40
      On cover                     240.00
J5 D1  5h black, red & yel       4.25    .35
      Never hinged          8.00
      On cover                     100.00
J6 D1  6h black, red & yel        .85    .35
      Never hinged          1.40
      On cover                     160.00
J7 D1  7h black, red & yel       6.00   4.25
      Never hinged         12.00
      On cover                     240.00
J8 D1  8h black, red & yel       6.00   2.60
      Never hinged         12.00
      On cover                     200.00
J9 D1  10h black, red & yel       .85    .35
      Never hinged          2.40
      On cover                     80.00
J10 D1 15h black, red & yel       .85    .35
      Never hinged          2.40
      On cover                     140.00
J11 D1 20h black, red & yel      6.75    .35
      Never hinged         12.00
      On cover                     100.00
J12 D1 50h black, red & yel      3.50    .45
      Never hinged          6.50
      On cover                     600.00
J13 D1 200h black, red &
        grn                     30.00   3.50
      Never hinged         55.00
      On cover
      Nos. J1-J13 (13)       62.45  13.95
      Set, never hinged     140.00
```

For overprints and surcharges see Western Ukraine Nos. 61-72, Yugoslavia Nos. 1LJ23-1LJ26.

Perf. 12½x13

```
J1a D1  1h black, red & yel      1.20    .80
      Never hinged          2.40
J2a D1  2h black, red & yel       .80    .80
      Never hinged          1.60
J3a D1  3h black, red & yel       .80    .80
      Never hinged          1.60
J4a D1  4h black, red & yel       .80    .80
      Never hinged          1.60
J5a D1  5h black, red & yel      3.50    .55
      Never hinged          7.25
J6a D1  6h black, red & yel       .80    .40
      Never hinged          1.60
J7a D1  7h black, red & yel      4.75   4.75
      Never hinged          9.50
J8a D1  8h black, red & yel      4.75   2.00
      Never hinged          9.50
J9a D1  10h black, red & yel     1.20    .40
      Never hinged          2.40
J10a D1 15h black, red & yel     1.20    .40
      Never hinged          2.40
J11a D1 20h black, red & yel     7.25    .80
      Never hinged         14.50
J12a D1 50h black, red & yel     3.25    .80
      Never hinged          6.50
J13a D1 200h black, red & grn   27.50   3.25
      Never hinged         55.00
      Nos. J1a-J13a (13)    57.80  16.55
      Set, never hinged     115.00
```

Perf. 13¼x13

```
J1b D1  1h black, red & yel      2.40   2.75
      Never hinged          5.00
J2b D1  2h black, red & yel       .80    .55
      Never hinged          1.60
J3b D1  3h black, red & yel       .80    .80
      Never hinged          1.60
J4b D1  4h black, red & yel       .80    .55
      Never hinged          1.60
J6b D1  6h black, red & yel       .80    .55
      Never hinged          1.60
J7b D1  7h black, red & yel      4.75   4.75
      Never hinged         10.00
J8b D1  8h black, red & yel      4.75   2.00
      Never hinged         10.00
J10b D1 15h black, red & yel     1.20    .80
      Never hinged          2.50
J11b D1 20h black, red & yel     6.50   1.60
      Never hinged         13.50
J12b D1 50h black, red & yel     4.00   1.20
      Never hinged          8.50
      Nos. J1b-J12b (10)    26.80  15.55
      Set, never hinged      55.00
```

Perf. 10½

```
J1c D1  1h black, red & yel     11.00  11.00
      Never hinged         20.00
J2c D1  2h black, red & yel     11.00  11.00
      Never hinged         20.00
J4c D1  4h black, red & yel     11.00  11.00
      Never hinged         20.00
J5c D1  5h black, red & yel     16.00  16.00
      Never hinged         30.00
J6c D1  6h black, red & yel     20.00  20.00
      Never hinged         37.50
J7c D1  7h black, red & yel     15.00  15.00
      Never hinged         27.50
J8c D1  8h black, red & yel     45.00  45.00
      Never hinged         85.00
J9c D1  10h black, red & yel    17.50  17.50
      Never hinged         32.50
J10c D1 15h black, red & yel    47.50  47.50
      Never hinged         90.00
J11c D1 20h black, red & yel    47.50  47.50
      Never hinged         90.00
J12c D1 50h black, red & yel    47.50  47.50
      Never hinged         90.00
      Nos. J1c-J12c (11)   289.00 289.00
      Set, never hinged    540.00
```

Perf. 9¼

```
J1d D1  1h black, red & yel      4.75
      Never hinged          9.00
J2d D1  2h black, red & yel      4.75
      Never hinged          9.00
J3d D1  3h black, red & yel     22.50
      Never hinged         40.00
J4d D1  4h black, red & yel     22.50
      Never hinged         40.00
J5d D1  5h black, red & yel     22.50
      Never hinged         40.00
J6d D1  6h black, red & yel     20.00
      Never hinged         35.00
J7d D1  7h black, red & yel     16.00
      Never hinged         30.00
J8d D1  8h black, red & yel      6.00
      Never hinged         10.00
J9d D1  10h black, red & yel    13.50
      Never hinged         25.00
J10d D1 15h black, red & yel     6.00
      Never hinged         11.00
J11d D1 20h black, red & yel    24.00
      Never hinged         42.50
J12d D1 50h black, red & yel    21.00
      Never hinged         40.00
J13d D1 200h black, red & grn   25.00
      Never hinged         45.00
      Nos. J1d-J13d (13)   208.50
      Set, never hinged    335.00
```

Perf. 12½, 13 and 10½ Compound

```
J1e D1  1h black, red & yel     12.00
      Never hinged         22.50
J2e D1  2h black, red & yel     12.00
      Never hinged         22.50
J4e D1  4h black, red & yel     21.00
      Never hinged         37.50
J5e D1  5h black, red & yel     21.00
      Never hinged         37.50
J6e D1  6h black, red & yel     21.00
      Never hinged         37.50
J7e D1  7h black, red & yel     21.00
      Never hinged         37.50
J9e D1  10h black, red & yel    27.50
      Never hinged         50.00
J10e D1 15h black, red & yel     7.50
      Never hinged         13.50
J11e D1 20h black, red & yel    65.00
      Never hinged        120.00
J12e D1 50h black, red & yel    25.00
      Never hinged         45.00
      Nos. J1e-J12e (10)   233.00
      Set, never hinged    420.00
```

Perf. 12½, 13 and 9¼ Compound

```
J1f D1  1h black, red & yel     22.50
      Never hinged         40.00
J2f D1  2h black, red & yel     42.50
      Never hinged         75.00
J3f D1  3h black, red & yel      6.00
      Never hinged         11.00
J4f D1  4h black, red & yel     14.50
      Never hinged         25.00
J6f D1  6h black, red & yel     11.00
      Never hinged         20.00
J8f D1  8h black, red & yel     13.00
      Never hinged         22.50
J9f D1  10h black, red & yel    24.00
      Never hinged         45.00
J10f D1 15h black, red & yel    17.50
      Never hinged         32.50
J11f D1 20h black, red & yel    21.00
      Never hinged         37.50
J12f D1 50h black, red & yel    27.50
      Never hinged         50.00
J13f D1 200h black, red & grn   55.00
      Never hinged        100.00
      Nos. J1f-J13f (11)   254.50
      Set, never hinged    455.00
```

Imperf

```
J1g D1  1h black, red & yel      4.50
      Never hinged          8.00
J2g D1  2h black, red & yel      4.50
      Never hinged          8.00
J3g D1  3h black, red & yel      4.50
      Never hinged          8.00
J4g D1  4h black, red & yel      4.50
      Never hinged          8.00
J5g D1  5h black, red & yel      4.50
      Never hinged          8.00
J6g D1  6h black, red & yel      4.50
      Never hinged          8.00
J7g D1  7h black, red & yel     14.50
      Never hinged         25.00
J8g D1  8h black, red & yel     16.00
      Never hinged         27.50
J9g D1  10h black, red & yel     4.50
      Never hinged          8.00
J10g D1 15h black, red & yel     4.50
      Never hinged          8.00
J11g D1 20h black, red & yel    35.00
      Never hinged         62.50
J12g D1 50h black, red & yel    15.00
      Never hinged         27.50
J13g D1 200h black, red & grn   90.00
      Never hinged         90.00
      Nos. J1g-J13g (13)   166.50
      Set, never hinged    295.00
```

1916-18 Perf. 12½

```
J14 D2  2h red ('18)              .40   1.60
      Never hinged           .65
J15 D2  4h red ('18)              .25   1.60
      Never hinged           .65
J16 D2  5h red                    .40   1.60
      Never hinged           .90
J17 D2  6h red ('18)              .25   1.60
      Never hinged           .65
J18 D2  10h red                   .40   1.60
      Never hinged           .65
      On cover                    300.00
J19 D2  15h red                  3.50  10.00
      Never hinged          6.50
J20 D2  20h red                   .45   1.60
      Never hinged           .65
      On cover                    340.00
J21 D2  25h red                  1.25   4.25
      Never hinged          2.75
J22 D2  30h red                  1.00   4.25
      Never hinged          2.50
      On cover                    425.00
J23 D2  40h red                  9.50  24.00
      Never hinged         25.00
J24 D2  50h red                 30.00  72.50
      Never hinged         67.50
J25 D2  1k dark blue             6.25  13.00
      Never hinged         14.50
J26 D2  3k dark blue            22.50  45.00
      Never hinged         60.00
      Nos. J14-J26 (13)     76.15 182.60
      Set, never hinged    200.00
```

Nos. J25-J26 have colored numerals on a white tablet.

Value, imperf. set, $240.

For surcharges see Italy Nos. NJ1-NJ7, Yugoslavia 1LJ1-1LJ13.

NEWSPAPER STAMPS

Bosnian Girl — N1

1913 Unwmk. Imperf.

```
P1 N1  2h ultra                   .85   1.25
      Never hinged          2.00
P2 N1  6h violet                 2.50   3.75
      Never hinged          5.50
P3 N1  10h rose                  3.00   3.75
      Never hinged          6.50
P4 N1  20h green                 3.50   4.25
      Never hinged          8.00
      Nos. P1-P4 (4)         9.85  13.00
```

After Bosnia and Herzegovina became part of Yugoslavia, stamps of type N1 perf., and imperf. copies surcharged with new values, were used as regular postage stamps. See Yugoslavia Nos. 1L21-1L22, 1L43-1L45.

SPECIAL HANDLING STAMPS

"Lightning" — SH1

1916 Unwmk. Engr. Perf. 12½

```
QE1 SH1 2h vermilion              .30    .85
      Never hinged           .55
  a.   Perf. 11½x12½       425.00 250.00
        Never hinged       650.00
QE2 SH1 5h deep green             .45   1.25
      Never hinged          1.25
  a.   Perf. 11½            17.50  42.50
        Never hinged        42.50
```

For surcharges see Italy Nos. NE1-NE2.

BRAZIL

brə-'zil

Brasil (after 1918)

LOCATION — On the north and east coasts of South America, bordering on the Atlantic Ocean.
GOVT. — Republic
AREA — 3,286,000 sq. mi.
POP. — 132,580,000 (est. 1984)
CAPITAL — Brasilia

Brazil was an independent empire from 1822 to 1889, when a constitution was adopted and the country became officially known as The United States of Brazil.

1000 Reis = 1 Milreis

Values for unused stamps are for examples with original gum as defined in the catalogue introduction except for Nos. 1-38 and 42-52 which are valued without gum.

Watermarks

Wmk. 97
"CORREIO
FEDERAL
REPUBLICA
DOS ESTADOS
UNIDOS DO
BRAZIL" in Sheet

Wmk. 98
"IMPOSTO DE
CONSUMO
REPUBLICA DOS
ESTADOS
UNIDOS DO
BRAZIL" in Sheet

Wmk. 99 — "CORREIO"

Wmk. 100 — "CASA DA MOEDA" in Sheet

Because of the spacing of this watermark, a few stamps in each sheet may show no watermark.

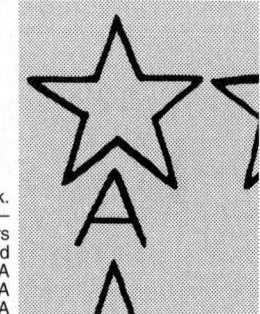

Wmk. 101 — Stars and CASA DA MOEDA

Wmk. 116 — Crosses and Circles

Wmk. 127 — Quatrefoils

Wmk. 193 — ESTADOS UNIDOS DO BRASIL

Wmk. 206 — Star-framed CM, Multiple

Wmk. 218 — E U BRASIL Multiple, Letters 8mm High

Wmk. 221 ESTADOS UNIDOS DO BRASIL, Multiple, Letters 6mm High

Wmk. 222 — CORREIO BRASIL and 5 Stars in Squared Circle

Wmk. 236 — Coat of Arms in Sheet

Watermark (reduced illustration) covers 22 stamps in sheet.

Wmk. 245 — Multiple "CASA DA MOEDA DO BRASIL" and Small Formee Cross

Wmk. 249 — "CORREIO BRASIL" multiple

Wmk. 256 — "CASA+DA+MOEDA+DO+BRAZIL" in 8mm Letters

Wmk. 264 — "*CORREIO*BRASIL*" Multiple, Letters 7mm High

GREAT BRITAIN POST OFFICES IN BRAZIL

PRE-STAMP POSTAL MARKINGS

Crowned Circle handstamp type IX is pictured in the Crowned Circle Handstamps and Great Britain Used Abroad section.

Bahia

1851, Jan. 6

A1	IX	Crowned circle handstamp, on cover	3,000.
A2	IX	Crowned circle handstamp, in red, on cover	5,500.
A3	IX	Crowned circle handstamp, in green, on cover	—

Pernambuco

A4	IX	Crowned circle handstamp, on cover	6,250.
A5	IX	Crowned circle handstamp, in red, on cover	3,000.

Rio de Janeiro

A6	IX	Crowned circle handstamp, on cover	2,900.
A7	IX	Crowned circle handstamp, in red, on cover	800.
A8	IX	Crowned circle handstamp, in green, on cover	—

STAMPS OF GREAT BRITAIN USED IN BRAZIL

Values are for clear cancellations on sound, fault-free stamps, with average to fine centering. In many cases, very fine examples are rare or non-existent.

1860-73
Numeral Cancellation Type B, C81 (Bahia)

A9	A	1p rose red (#33, P90, 93, 96, 108, 113, 117, 135, 140, 147, 155) (from)	50.00
A10	A	1½p lake red (#32, P3)	125.00
A11	A	2p blue (#29, P9, 12)	85.00
A12	A	2p bl (#30, P13-14) (from)	75.00
A13	A	3p rose (#44)	—
A14	A	3p rose (#49, P4, 6, 8-10) (from)	60.00
A15	A	3p rose (#61, P11)	—
A16	A	4p ver (#43, P8-13) (from)	55.00
A17	A	6p lilac (#45, P5)	—
A18	A	6p dull violet (#50, P6)	160.00
A19	A	6p red vio (#51, P8-9) (from)	80.00
A20	A	6p pale buff (#59b, P11-12) (from)	110.00
a.		6p brown (#59, P11)	110.00
A21	A	6p gray (#60, P12)	—
A22	A	6p gray (#62, P13)	—
A23	A	9p straw (#46)	475.00
A24	A	9p bister (#52)	275.00
A25	A	1sh green (#48)	190.00
A26	A	1sh green (#54, P4-6) (from)	55.00
		Plate 7	55.00
A27	A	1sh deep green (#64a, P8-9)	95.00
A28	A	2sh blue (#55)	300.00
A29	A	5sh rose (#57, P1)	550.00

Numeral Cancellation Type B, C82 (Pernambuco)

No. A48

A30	A	1p rose red (#33, P85, 108, 111, 130-132, 149, 157, 159, 160, 187(from)	50.00
A31	A	2p blue (#29, P9, 12)	60.00
A32	A	2p blue (#30, P13-14) (from)	60.00
A33	A	3p rose (#44)	125.00
A34	A	3p rose (#49, P4-7, 10) (from)	60.00
A35	A	3p rose (#61, P11)	—
A36	A	4p vermilion (#43, P9-14) (from)	55.00
A37	A	6p lilac (#45, P5-6)	—
A38	A	6p dull violet (#50, P6)	90.00
A39	A	6p red violet (#51, P8-9) (from)	80.00
A40	A	6p brown (#59, P11)	90.00
a.		6p pale buff (#59b, P11-12)	60.00
A41	A	6p gray (#60, P12)	—
A42	A	9p straw (#46)	475.00
A43	A	9p bister (#52)	250.00
A44	A	10p red brown (#53)	325.00
A45	A	1sh green (#48)	190.00
A46	A	1sh green (#54, P4-6) (from)	55.00
		Plate 7	55.00
A47	A	2sh blue (#55)	275.00
A48	A	5sh rose (#57, P1)	550.00

Numeral Cancellation Type B, C83 (Rio de Janeiro)

A49	A	1p rose red (#20)	50.00
A50	A	1p rose red (#33, P71, 76, 80, 82, 86, 94, 103, 113, 117, 119, 123, 130, 132, 134-135, 146, 148, 159, 161, 166, 185, 200, 204 (from)	42.50
A51	A	2p blue (#29, P9, 12)	42.50
A52	A	2p blue (#30, P13-14) (from)	42.50
A53	A	3p rose (#49, P4-8) (from)	50.00
A54	A	3p rose (#61, P11)	—
A55	A	4p vermilion (#43, P8-13) (from)	55.00
A56	A	6p lilac (#45, P5)	110.00
A57	A	6p dull violet (#50, P6)	82.50
A58	A	6p red violet (#51, P8-9)	77.50
A59	A	6p brown (#59, P11)	82.50
a.		6p pale buff (#59b, P11)	50.00
A60	A	6p gray (#60, P12)	—
A61	A	9p straw (#46)	450.00
A62	A	9p bister (#52)	225.00
A63	A	10p red brown (#53)	300.00
A64	A	1sh green (#48)	150.00
A65	A	1sh green (#54, P4-6) (from)	50.00
		Plate 7	90.00

A66 A 1sh green (#64, P8-9)
    (from) 80.00
A67 A 2sh blue (#55) 150.00
A68 A 5sh rose (#57, P1) 550.00
    Plate 2 700.00

ISSUES OF THE EMPIRE

A1

Fine Impressions
Grayish or Yellowish Paper
Unwmk.

1843, Aug. 1	Engr.	Imperf.
1 A1 30r black	4,500.	550.
On cover		11,000.
On cover, single franking		16,500.
c. Pair, #1-2		950,000.
d. Strip of 3, 2 #1, 1 #2		850,000.
2 A1 60r black	600.	300.
On cover		9,000.
3 A1 90r black	4,000.	1,400.
On cover		14,000.
On cover, single franking		30,000.

Nos. 1-3b were issued with gum, but very few unused examples retain even a trace of their original gum. Stamps with original gum command substantial premiums.

Fine impressions are true black and have background lathework complete.

Most examples of Nos. 1-3b are printed on yellowish or grayish paper. They also exist on white paper, usually thin and somewhat translucent. Such examples are scarce and command premiums.

Nos. 1c and 1d are each unique.

Intermediate Impressions

1a A1 30r	4,250.	525.
On cover		10,500.
On cover, single franking		16,500.
2a A1 60r	1,100.	275.
On cover		8,500.
3a A1 90r	3,750.	1,300.
On cover		13,000.
On cover, single franking		30,000.

Intermediate impressions are grayish black and have weaker lathework in the background.

Worn Impressions

1b A1 30r	4,000.	500.
On cover, pair		10,000.
On cover, single franking		16,500.
2b A1 60r	1,000.	250.
On cover		8,000.
3b A1 90r	3,500.	1,250.
On cover		12,000.
On cover, single franking		30,000.

Worn impressions have white areas in the background surrounding the numerals due to plate wear affecting especially the lathework.

A2   A3

Grayish or Yellowish Paper
1844-46

7 A2 10r black	125.00	25.00
On cover		275.00
On cover, single franking		
8 A2 30r black	160.00	35.00
On cover		300.00
9 A2 60r black	125.00	25.00
On cover		250.00
10 A2 90r black	1,000.	120.00
On cover		750.00
11 A2 180r black	4,500.	1,800.
On cover		11,000.
12 A2 300r black	6,500.	2,000.
On cover		16,000.
13 A2 600r black	6,000.	2,200.
On cover		

Nos. 8, 9 and 10 exist on thick paper and are considerably scarcer.

Grayish or Yellowish Paper
1850, Jan. 1

21 A3 10r black	30.00	42.50
On cover		300.00
On cover, single franking		
22 A3 20r black	92.50	120.00
On cover		575.00
23 A3 30r black	12.00	3.50
On cover		60.00
24 A3 60r black	12.00	3.00
On cover		30.00
25 A3 90r black	100.00	14.50
On cover		120.00
26 A3 180r black	100.00	65.00
On cover		650.00

27 A3 300r black	400.00	72.50
On cover		550.00
28 A3 600r black	500.00	110.00
On cover		1,500.

No. 22 used is generally found precanceled with a single horizontal line in pen or blue crayon or with two diagonal pen lines. Value precanceled without gum, $75.

All values except the 90r were reprinted in 1910 on very thick paper.

1854

37 A3 10r blue	14.50	14.50
On cover		400.00
On cover, single franking		450.00
a. 10r pale blue	17.50	17.50
On cover		450.00
b. 10r steel blue	85.00	50.00
On cover		750.00
38 A3 30r blue	40.00	60.00
On cover		500.00
a. 30r dark blue	70.00	50.00
On cover		500.00
b. 30r steel blue	400.00	100.00
On cover		750.00

A4

1861

39 A4 280r red	175.00	120.00
No gum	100.00	
On cover		750.00
40 A4 430r yellow	250.00	175.00
No gum	160.00	
On cover		1,500.

Nos. 39-40 have been reprinted on thick white paper with white gum. They are printed in aniline inks and the colors are brighter than those of the originals.

1866		Perf. 13½
42 A3 10r blue	125.00	150.00
On cover		—
43 A3 20r black	1,100.	500.00
On cover		—
44 A3 30r black	350.00	190.00
On cover		600.00
45 A3 30r blue	800.00	925.00
On cover		—
46 A3 60r black	140.00	30.00
On cover		600.00
47 A3 90r black	725.00	350.00
On cover		675.00
48 A3 180r black	925.00	350.00
On cover		—
49 A4 280r red	800.00	800.00
On cover		2,500.
50 A3 300r black	750.00	400.00
On cover		—
51 A4 430r yellow	725.00	425.00
On cover		4,000.
52 A3 600r black	725.00	300.00
On cover		3,250.

Fraudulent perforations abound. Purchases should be accompanied by certificates of authenticity.

A 10r black is questioned.

A5   A6

A7   A8

A8a   A9

A10

Emperor Dom Pedro —
A9a

100 reis

Type I — Left frameline weak and incomplete and composed of a single line which never touches the upper ornaments.

Type II — Left frameline incomplete and composed of a double outer line which does not touch the upper ornaments.

Type III — Left frameline complete and composed of two continuous outer lines which meet the upper ornaments.

Thick or Thin White Wove Paper

1866, July 1		Perf. 12
53 A5 10r vermilion	14.50	6.00
On cover		375.00
On cover, single franking		500.00
b. 10r carmine vermilion	35.00	15.00
On cover		375.00
On cover, single franking		500.00
54 A6 20r red lilac	25.00	3.50
On cover		325.00
On cover, single franking		375.00
a. 20r dull violet	80.00	30.00
On cover		400.00
On cover, single franking		500.00
56 A7 50r blue	35.00	3.00
On cover		60.00
On cover, single franking		275.00
57 A8 80r slate violet	92.50	6.00
On cover		160.00
On cover, single franking		550.00
b. 80r rose lilac	100.00	10.00
On cover		175.00
On cover, single franking		600.00
58 A8a 100r blue green, type III	35.00	1.90
On cover		25.00
a. 100r green (shades), type I	35.00	1.90
On cover		35.00
c. 100r green (shades), type II	75.00	5.00
On cover		67.50
59 A9 200r black	120.00	10.00
On cover		80.00
60 A9a 500r orange	250.00	42.50
On cover		425.00
Nos. 53-60 (7)	572.00	72.90

The 10r and 20r exist imperf. on both white and bluish paper. Some authorities consider them proofs.

Nos. 58 and 65 are found in three types.

Bluish Paper

53a A5 10r	600.00	500.00
On cover		—
54b A6 20r	190.00	30.00
On cover		—
56a A7 50r	250.00	30.00
On cover		350.00
57a A8 80r	300.00	35.00
On cover		—
58b A8a 100r Type II	1,000.	140.00
On cover		275.00
d. A8a 100r Type I	9,000.	—

1876-77		Rouletted
61 A5 10r vermilion ('77)	72.50	42.50
On cover		275.00
On cover, single franking		—
62 A6 20r red lilac ('77)	85.00	35.00
On cover		250.00
On cover, single franking		425.00
63 A7 50r blue ('77)	85.00	12.00
On cover		275.00
On cover, single franking		—
64 A8 80r violet ('77)	210.00	25.00
On cover		375.00
65 A8a 100r green	50.00	1.50
On cover		50.00
66 A9 200r black ('77)	100.00	9.25
On cover		140.00
a. Half used as 100r on cover		1,000.
67 A9a 500r orange	225.00	50.00
On cover		700.00
Nos. 61-67 (7)	827.50	175.25

A10   A11

A12   A13

A14   A15

A16   A17

A18   A19

A20

1878-79		Rouletted
68 A10 10r vermilion	14.50	3.50
On cover		275.00
On cover, single franking		500.00
69 A11 20r violet	19.00	3.00
On cover		100.00
On cover, single franking		500.00
a. 20r dark violet	24.00	6.00
On cover		125.00
On cover, single franking		600.00
b. 20r rose lilac	17.50	5.25
On cover		125.00
On cover, single franking		600.00
70 A12 50r blue	30.00	2.50
On cover		100.00
On cover, single franking		175.00
71 A13 80r lake	35.00	12.00
On cover		375.00
On cover, single franking		1,375.
72 A14 100r green	35.00	1.50
On cover		35.00
73 A15 200r black	175.00	21.00
On cover		200.00
a. Half used as 100r on cover		1,000.
74 A16 260r dk brown	100.00	27.50
On cover		550.00
75 A18 300r bister	100.00	7.25
On cover		550.00
a. One-third used as 100r on cover		10,000.
76 A19 700r red brown	190.00	100.00
On cover		3,500.
77 A20 1000r gray lilac	225.00	47.50
On cover		600.00
On cover, single franking		2,500.
Nos. 68-77 (10)	923.50	225.75

1878, Aug. 21		Perf. 12
78 A17 300r orange & grn	100.00	25.00
On cover		600.00

Nos. 68-78 exist imperforate.

A21   A22

A23

Small Heads
Laid Paper
Perf. 13, 13½ and Compound
1881, July 15

79 A21 50r blue	140.00	21.00
On cover		165.00
On cover, single franking		375.00
80 A22 100r olive green	600.00	35.00
On cover		165.00

81	A23	200r pale red brn	600.00	140.00
		On cover		250.00
a.		Half used as 100r on cover		2,100.

On Nos. 79 and 80 the hair above the ear curves forward. On Nos. 83 and 88 it is drawn backward. On the stamps of the 1881 issue the board in smaller than in the 1882 80 issues and fills less of the space between the neck and the frame at the left.
See No. 88.

A24   A25

A26   A27

Two types each of the 100 and 200 reis.

100 REIS:
Type I — Groundwork formed of diagonal crossed lines and horizontal lines.
Type II — Groundwork formed of diagonal crossed lines and vertical lines.

200 REIS:
Type I — Groundwork formed of diagonal and horizontal lines.
Type II — Groundwork formed of diagonal crossed lines.

Larger Heads
Laid Paper
Perf. 12½ to 14 and Compound
1882-84

82	A24	10r black	12.00	25.00
		On cover		275.00
83	A25	100r ol grn, type I	42.50	3.50
		On cover		45.00
b.		100r dark green, type II	250.00	14.50
		On cover		125.00
84	A26	200r pale red brn, type I	100.00	27.50
		On cover		100.00
a.		Half used as 100r on cover		1,300.
85	A27	200r pale rose, type II	55.00	5.50
		On cover		55.00
a.		Diag. half used as 100r on cover		950.00
		Nos. 82-85 (4)	209.50	61.50

See No. 86.

A28   A29

A30

Three types of A29

Type I — Groundwork of horizontal lines.
Type II — Groundwork of diagonal crossed lines.
Type III — Groundwork solid.

Perf. 13, 13½, 14 and Compound
1884-85

86	A24	10r orange	3.00	2.50
		On cover		225.00
		On cover, single franking		250.00
87	A28	20r slate green	35.00	3.50
		On cover		275.00
a.		20r olive green	35.00	3.50
		On cover		275.00
b.		Half used as 10r on newspaper		3,500.
88	A21	50r bl, head larger	35.00	3.50
		On cover		60.00
		On cover, single franking		115.00
90	A29	100r lilac, type I	150.00	3.00
		On cover		65.00
a.		100r lilac, type II	450.00	75.00
		On cover		275.00
b.		100r lilac, type III	325.00	55.00
		On cover		250.00

91	A30	100r lilac	200.00	5.00
		On cover		85.00
		Nos. 86-91 (5)	423.00	17.50

A31   A32

Southern Cross   Crown
A33   A34

Perf. 13, 13½, 14 and Compound
1885

92	A31	100r lilac	125.00	3.00
		On cover		22.50

Compare design A31 with A35.

1887

93	A32	50r chalky blue	35.00	5.00
		On cover		30.00
		On cover, single franking		125.00
94	A33	300r gray blue	250.00	30.00
		On cover		400.00
		On cover, single franking		600.00
95	A34	500r olive	140.00	14.00
		On cover		275.00
		On cover, single franking		450.00
		Nos. 93-95 (3)	425.00	49.00

A35   A36

Entrance to Bay of Rio de Janeiro — A37

1888

96	A35	100r lilac	72.50	1.90
		On cover		16.75
a.		Imperf., pair	150.00	175.00
97	A36	700r violet	80.00	110.00
		On cover		750.00
98	A37	1000r dull blue	300.00	110.00
		On cover		1,500.
		Nos. 96-98 (3)	452.50	221.90

Issues of the Republic

Southern Cross — A38

Wove Paper, Thin to Thick
Perf. 12½ to 14, 11 to 11½, and 12½ to 14x11 to 11½, Rough or Clean-Cut
Engraved; Typographed (#102)
1890-91

99	A38	20r gray green	2.50	1.90
		On postcard		35.00
		On cover, single franking		175.00
a.		20r blue green	2.50	1.90
		On postcard		35.00
		On cover, single franking		175.00
b.		20r emerald	19.00	7.00
		On postcard		40.00
		On cover, single franking		190.00
100	A38	50r gray green	6.25	1.90
		On postcard		35.00
		On cover, single franking		150.00
a.		50r olive green	14.00	7.00
		On postcard		40.00
		On cover, single franking		165.00
b.		50r yellow green	14.00	7.00
		On postcard		40.00
		On cover, single franking		165.00
c.		50r dark slate green	8.25	4.00
		On postcard		40.00
		On cover, single franking		165.00
d.		Horiz. pair, imperf. btwn.		—
101	A38	100r lilac rose	450.00	6.00
		On cover		100.00

102	A38	100r red lil, redrawn	30.00	1.90
		On cover		20.00
a.		Tete beche pair	25,000.	19,000.
		On cover		35,000.
103	A38	200r purple	10.00	1.90
		On cover		30.00
a.		200r violet	12.00	2.50
		On cover		32.50
b.		200r violet blue	27.50	3.50
		On cover		35.00
c.		Half used as 100r on cover		875.00
104	A38	300r dark violet	90.00	6.00
		On cover		175.00
a.		300r gray	90.00	10.00
		On cover		150.00
b.		300r gray blue	100.00	10.00
		On cover		150.00
c.		300r slate violet	175.00	30.00
		On cover		175.00
105	A38	500r olive bister	21.00	9.50
		On cover		150.00
a.		500r olive gray	21.00	11.50
		On cover		165.00
106	A38	500r slate	21.00	13.50
		On cover		175.00
107	A38	700r fawn	19.00	19.00
		On cover		180.00
a.		700r chocolate	24.00	26.00
		On cover		180.00
108	A38	1000r bister	17.50	3.50
		On cover		225.00
a.		1000r yellow buff	35.00	8.50
		On cover		240.00
		Nos. 99-108 (10)	667.25	65.10

The redrawn 100r may be distinguished by the absence of the curved lines of shading in the left side of the central oval. The pearls in the oval are not well aligned and there is less shading at right and left of "CORREIO" and "100 REIS."

A 100 reis stamp of type A38 but inscribed "BRAZIL" instead of "E. U. DO BRAZIL" was not placed in issue but postmarked copies are known. A reprint on thick paper was made in 1910.

No. 101 exists imperf., not regularly issued.
For surcharges see Nos. 151-158.

Liberty Head
A39   A40

Perf. 12½ to 14, 11 to 11½ and 12½ to 14x11 to 11½

1891, May 1				**Typo.**
109	A39	100r blue & red	42.50	1.90
		On cover		15.00
a.		Frame inverted	125.00	100.00
		On cover		500.00
b.		Tete beche pair	850.00	925.00
		On cover		2,500.
c.		100r ultra & red	42.50	1.90
		On cover		15.00

Perf. 11, 11½, 13, 13½, 14 and Compound

1893, Jan. 18				**Litho.**
111	A40	100r rose	75.00	1.75
		On cover, single franking		37.50
a.		100r rose, perf 13	150.00	3.50
		On cover, single franking		40.00

A41   A41a

Sugarloaf Mountain

A42   A42a

Liberty Head

Hermes — A43

Perf. 11 to 11½, 12½ to 14 and 12½ to 14x11 to 11½

1894-97				**Unwmk.**
112	A41	10r rose & blue	2.50	.90
		On postcard, with other stamps		15.00
		On cover, with other stamps		10.00
		Single franking, on newspaper		150.00
113	A41a	10r rose & blue	2.50	.90
		On postcard, with other stamps		15.00
		On cover, with other stamps		10.00
		Single franking, on newspaper		150.00
114	A41a	20r orange & bl ('97)	1.40	.40
		On postcard with other stamps		15.00
		On cover, with other stamps		10.00
		Single franking, on newspaper		50.00
a.		20r reddish orange & blue ('94)	1.75	.75
115	A41a	50r dk blue & blue	13.00	1.60
		On postcard		3.00
		Pair, on cover		10.00
a.		20r blue ('97)	6.00	4.00
116	A42	100r carmine & blk	5.00	.50
		On cover		10.00
a.		Vert. pair, imperf. btwn.	100.00	
b.		100r rose & black ('96)	9.00	.70
118	A42a	200r orange & blk	1.25	.50
a.		Imperf. horiz., pair	80.00	
b.		Vert. pair, imperf. btwn.	80.00	
c.		200r reddish orange & black ('97)	6.00	.60
d.		Half used as 100r on cover		850.00
119	A42a	300r green & blk	19.00	.70
		On cover, single franking		25.00
a.		300r pale green & black ('94)	18.00	1.25
		On cover, single franking		30.00
120	A42a	500r blue & blk	30.00	2.00
		On cover		60.00
a.		500r indigo & black ('94)	190.00	6.00
121	A42a	700r light lilac & blk	20.00	2.00
		On cover		80.00
a.		700r lilac & black ('97)	18.00	1.75
		On cover		80.00
122	A43	1000r green & vio	72.50	2.00
		On cover		100.00
a.		1000r pale green & mauve ('94)	75.00	4.00
		On cover		110.00
124	A43	2000r blk & gray lil	85.00	20.00
		On cover		375.00
a.		2000r black & gray lilac, chalky paper ('94)	60.00	15.00
		On cover		350.00
		Nos. 112-124 (11)	252.15	31.50

Values for Nos. 112-124 are for the most common perforation variety of each stamp. Some perforations and combinations command premiums.

Values for this set are for stamps cut into the design on one or two sides due to the narrow spacing of the stamps in the setting of the plates and imperfect perforation methods. Between 1902 and 1905 these stamps were reissued with wider spacing between subjects and perforated 11½. These are listed as Nos. 113a-122b below.

The head of No. 116 exists in five types. See Nos. 140-150A, 159-161, 166-171d.

Wider Spacing Between Stamps

1902-05				**Perf. 11½**
113a	A41a	10r rose & bl	8.50	12.00
114b	A41a	20r orange & bl	8.00	.50
119b	A42a	300r green & blk	35.00	1.20
120b	A42a	500r blue & blk	35.00	1.20
122b	A43	1000r green & vio	275.00	10.00

1889 Issue of Newspaper Stamps
Surcharged (Type N1)

a

b

c

1898 Green Surcharge *Rouletted*

125	(b)	700r on 500r yel	8.50	12.00
126	(c)	1000r on 700r yel	42.50	35.00
a.		Surcharged "700r"	850.00	1,000.
127	(c)	2000r on 1000r yel	35.00	18.00
128	(c)	2000r on 1000r brn	25.00	7.25

Violet Surcharge

129	(a)	100r on 50r brn yel	2.50	55.00
130	(c)	100r on 50r brn yel	77.50	57.50
131	(c)	300r on 200r blk	4.00	1.40
a.		Double surcharge	190.00	325.00

The surcharge on No. 130 is handstamped. The impression is blurred and lighter in color than on No. 129. The two surcharges differ most in the shapes and serifs of the figures "1."

Counterfeits exist of No. 126a.

Black Surcharge

132	(b)	200r on 100r violet	4.00	1.40
a.		Double surcharge	95.00	200.00
b.		Inverted surcharge	95.00	200.00
132C	(b)	500r on 300r car	6.50	3.50
133	(b)	700r on 500r green	9.50	2.40

Blue Surcharge

134	(b)	500r on 300r car	7.50	6.25

Red Surcharge

135	(c)	1000r on 700r ultra	27.50	17.00
a.		Inverted surcharge	240.00	—

Surcharged on 1890-94 Issues

d e

Perf. 11 to 14 and Compound
Black Surcharge

136	N3(e)	20r on 10r blue	3.75	7.00
137	N2(d)	200r on 100r red lilac	25.00	17.00
a.		Double surcharge	275.00	300.00
b.		200r on 100r pink	175.00	120.00

Surcharge on No. 137 comes blue to deep black.

Blue Surcharge

138	N3(e)	50r on 20r green	9.50	11.50

Red Surcharge

139	N3(e)	100r on 50r green	21.00	24.00
a.		Blue surcharge	15.00	

The surcharge on 139a exists inverted, and in pair, one without surcharge.

Types of 1894-97

1899   Perf. 5½-7 and 11-11½x5½-7

140	A41a	10r rose & bl	6.00	14.00
141	A41a	20r orange & bl	9.25	9.25
142	A41a	50r dk bl & lt bl	12.00	37.50
143	A42	100r carmine & blk	20.00	5.50
144	A42a	200r orange & blk	12.00	3.50
145	A42a	300r green & blk	75.00	8.75
		Nos. 140-145 (6)	134.25	78.50

Perf. 8½-9½, 8½-9½x11-11½

146	A41a	10r rose & bl	6.00	3.50
147	A41a	20r orange & bl	19.00	3.50
147A	A41a	50r dk bl & bl	160.00	35.00
148	A42	100r carmine & blk	37.50	1.75
149	A42a	200r orange & blk	19.00	1.25
150	A42a	300r green & blk	75.00	6.00
150A	A43	1000r green & vio	160.00	15.00
		Nos. 146-150A (7)	476.50	66.00

Nos. 140-150A are valued with perfs just cut into the design on one or two sides. Expect some irregularity of the perforations.

Issue of 1890-93
Surcharged in Violet
or Magenta

Perf. 11 to 11½, 12½ to 14 and Compound

1899, June 25

151	A38	50r on 20r gray grn	2.50	3.50
a.		Double surcharge	150.00	150.00
152	A38	100r on 50r gray grn	2.50	3.50
b.		Double surcharge	125.00	125.00
153	A38	300r on 200r pur	9.25	14.50
a.		Double surcharge	300.00	
b.		Pair, one without surcharge	500.00	—
154	A38	500r on 300r ultra, perf. 13	22.50	8.75
a.		500r on 300r gray lilac	35.00	10.00
b.		Pair, one without surcharge	500.00	575.00
c.		500r on 300r slate violet	45.00	17.00
155	A38	700r on 500r ol bis	30.00	7.00
a.		Pair, one without surcharge	500.00	
156	A38	1000r on 700r choc	22.50	7.00
157	A38	1000r on 700r fawn	22.50	7.00
a.		Pair, one without surcharge	500.00	575.00
158	A38	2000r on 1000r bister (perf 11-11½)	37.50	5.25
a.		2000r on 1000r yel buff (perf 13)	60.00	5.25
b.		Pair, one without surcharge	500.00	575.00
		Nos. 151-158 (8)	149.25	56.50

Types of 1894-97
Perf. 11, 11½, 13 and Compound

1900

159	A41a	50r green	13.00	.70
160	A42	100r rose	25.00	.35
a.		Frame around inner oval	125.00	4.75
161	A42a	200r blue	14.50	.40
		Nos. 159-161 (3)	52.50	1.45

Three types exist of No. 161, all of which have the frame around inner oval.

Cabral Arrives at Brazil — A44

Independence Proclaimed — A45

"Emancipation of Slaves" — A46

Allegory, Republic of Brazil — A47

1900, Jan. 1   Litho.   Perf. 12½

162	A44	100r red	7.25	5.75
a.		Imperf., pair	400.00	500.00
163	A45	200r green & yel	7.25	5.75
164	A46	500r blue	7.25	5.75
165	A47	700r emerald	7.25	5.75
		Nos. 162-165 (4)	29.00	23.00

Discovery of Brazil, 400th anniversary.

Types of 1894-97
Wmk. (97? or 98?)

1905   Perf. 11, 11½

166	A41a	10r rose & bl	7.00	4.75
167	A41a	20r orange & bl	12.50	2.40
168	A41a	50r green	25.00	3.50
169	A42	100r rose	32.50	1.25
170	A42a	200r dark blue	19.00	1.25

171	A42a	300r green & blk	65.00	2.40
		Nos. 166-171 (6)	161.00	15.55

Positive identification of Wmk. 97 or 98 places stamp in specific watermark groups below.

Wmk. 97

166b	A41a	10r rose & blue	37.50	19.00
167b	A41a	20r orange & blue	37.50	9.50
168b	A41a	50r green	72.50	9.50
169b	A42	100r rose	250.00	35.00
170b	A42a	200r dark blue	150.00	4.75
171b	A42a	300r green & blk	450.00	35.00
171A	A43	1000r green & vio	350.00	35.00
		Nos. 166b-171A (7)	1,347.	147.75

Wmk. 98

166c	A41a	10r rose & blue	50.00	50.00
167c	A41a	20r orange & blue	100.00	24.00
168c	A41a	50r green	200.00	35.00
169c	A42	100r rose	100.00	4.75
170c	A42a	200r dark blue	150.00	4.75
171d	A42a	300r green & blk	350.00	35.00
		Nos. 166c-171d (6)	950.00	153.50

Allegory, Pan-American Congress
A48

1906, July 23   Litho.   Unwmk.

172	A48	100r carmine rose	30.00	30.00
173	A48	200r blue	75.00	10.00

Third Pan-American Congress.

Aristides Lobo
A48a

Benjamin Constant
A49

Pedro Alvares Cabral
A50

Eduardo Wandenkolk
A51

Manuel Deodoro da Fonseca
A52

Floriano Peixoto
A53

Prudente de Moraes
A54

Manuel Ferraz de Campos Salles
A55

Francisco de Paula Rodrigues Alves — A56

Liberty Head — A57

A58   A59

1906-16   Engr.   Perf. 12

174	A48a	10r bluish slate	1.10	.25
175	A49	20r aniline vio	1.10	.25
176	A50	50r green	1.10	.25
a.		Booklet pane of 6 ('08)	47.50	150.00
177	A51	100r anil rose	2.50	.25
a.		Imperf. vert., coil ('16)	2.50	.40
b.		Booklet pane of 6 ('08)	95.00	150.00
178	A52	200r blue	2.50	.25
a.		Booklet pane of 6 ('08)	72.50	150.00
179	A52	200r ultra ('15)	2.50	.40
a.		Imperf. vert., coil ('16)	2.50	.40
180	A53	300r gray blk	3.75	.80
181	A54	400r olive grn	37.50	2.40
182	A55	500r dk violet	7.50	.80
183	A54	600r olive grn ('10)	4.25	1.60
184	A56	700r red brown	7.50	3.50
185	A57	1000r vermilion	42.50	1.25
186	A58	2000r yellow grn	25.00	.80
187	A58	2000r Prus blue ('15)	13.00	1.25
188	A59	5000r carmine rose	10.00	2.40
		Nos. 174-188 (15)	161.80	16.45

Allegorical Emblems: Liberty, Peace, Industry, etc. — A60

1908, July 14

189	A60	100r carmine	24.00	1.75

National Exhibition, Rio de Janeiro.

Emblems of Peace Between Brazil and Portugal
A61

1908, July 14

190	A61	100r red	11.00	1.25

Opening of Brazilian ports to foreign commerce, cent. Medallions picture King Carlos I of Portugal and Pres. Affonso Penna of Brazil.

Bonifacio, Bolivar, Hidalgo, O'Higgins, San Martin, Washington — A62

1909

191	A62	200r deep blue	13.50	1.50

For surcharge see No. E1.

Nilo Peçanha
A63

Baron of Rio Branco
A64

1910, Nov. 15

192	A63	10,000r brown	11.00	3.00

1913-16

193	A64	1000r deep green	5.00	.50
194	A64	1000r slate ('16)	29.00	.80

Cabo Frio — A65

Perf. 11½

1915, Nov. 13   Litho.   Wmk. 99
195 A65 100r dk grn, yelsh   5.00 4.00
Founding of the town of Cabo Frio, 300th anniversary.

Bay of Guajara A66

1916, Jan. 5
196 A66 100r carmine   11.00 6.00
City of Belem, 300th anniversary.

Revolutionary Flag — A67

1917, Mar. 6
197 A67 100r deep blue   18.00 8.50
Revolution of Pernambuco, Mar. 6, 1817.

Rodrigues Alves — A68

Unwmk.
1917, Aug. 31   Engr.   Perf. 12
198 A68 5000r red brown   80.00 12.50

Liberty Head A69   A70

Perf. 12½, 13, 13x13½.

			Unwmk.	
1918-20		**Typo.**		
200	A69	10r orange brn	.70	.30
201	A69	20r slate	.70	.30
202	A69	25r ol gray ('20)	.70	.30
203	A69	50r green	40.00	4.00
204	A70	100r rose	2.25	.30
a.		Imperf., pair	—	
205	A70	300r red orange	25.00	4.00
206	A70	500r dull violet	25.00	4.00
		Nos. 200-206 (7)	94.35	13.20

			Wmk. 100	
1918-20				
207	A69	10r red brown	8.00	2.00
a.		Imperf., pair	—	
207B	A69	20r slate	1.90	1.90
c.		Imperf., pair	—	
208	A69	25r ol gray ('20)	1.00	.65
209	A69	50r green	1.90	.65
210	A70	100r rose	62.50	.65
a.		Imperf., pair	—	
211	A70	200r dull blue	8.00	.65
212	A70	300r orange	62.50	5.00
213	A70	500r dull violet	62.50	9.50
214	A70	600r orange	3.50	9.50
		Nos. 207-214 (9)	211.80	30.50

Because of the spacing of this watermark, a few stamps in each sheet may show no watermark.

"Education" — A72

1918   Engr.   Perf. 11½
215 A72 1000r blue   8.00 .30
216 A72 2000r red brown   35.00 10.00
217 A72 5000r dark violet   10.00 10.00
    Nos. 215-217 (3)   53.00 20.30
Watermark note below No. 257 also applies to Nos. 215-217.
    See Nos. 233-234, 283-285, 404, 406, 458, 460. For surcharge see No. C30.

Railroad A73   "Industry" A74

"Aviation" A75   Mercury A76

"Navigation" — A77

Perf. 13½x13, 13x13½

			Unwmk.	
1920-22		**Typo.**		
218	A73	10r red violet	1.00	.50
219	A73	20r olive green	1.00	.50
220	A74	25r brown violet	.90	.50
221	A74	50r blue green	1.10	.50
222	A74	50r orange brn ('22)	1.90	.50
223	A75	100r rose red	3.75	.50
224	A75	100r orange ('22)	10.00	.50
225	A75	150r violet ('21)	1.90	.50
226	A75	200r blue	6.00	.50
227	A75	200r rose red ('22)	10.50	.50
228	A76	300r olive gray	17.00	.65
229	A76	400r dull blue ('22)	30.00	4.25
230	A76	500r red brown	24.00	.65
		Nos. 218-230 (13)	109.05	10.55

See Nos. 236-257, 265-266, 268-271, 273-274, 276-281, 302-311, 316-322, 326-340, 357-358, 431-434, 436-441, 461-463B, 467-470, 472-474, 488-490, 492-494. For surcharges see Nos. 356-358, 376-377.

Perf. 11, 11½

			Wmk. 100	
		Engr.		
231	A77	600r red orange	2.75	.50
232	A77	1000r claret	7.00	.30
a.		Perf. 8½	50.00	9.50
233	A72	2000r dull violet	27.50	.95
234	A72	5000r brown	21.00	11.00
		Nos. 231-234 (4)	58.25	12.75

Nos. 233 and 234 are inscribed "BRASIL CORREIO." Watermark note below No. 257 also applies to Nos. 231-234.
See No. 282.

King Albert of Belgium and President Epitacio Pessoa A78

1920, Sept. 19   Engr.   Perf. 11½x11
235 A78 100r dull red   1.00 1.00
Visit of the King and Queen of Belgium.

Types of 1920-22 Issue
Perf. 13x13½, 13x12½

			Typo.	Wmk. 100	
1922-29					
236	A73	10r red violet		.30	.25
237	A73	20r olive green		.30	.25
238	A75	20r gray violet ('29)		.30	.25
239	A74	25r brown violet		.35	.25
240	A74	50r blue grn		4.25	45.00
241	A74	50r org brn ('23)		.50	.40
242	A75	100r rose red		30.00	.50
243	A75	100r orange ('26)		.65	.25
244	A75	100r turq grn ('28)		.65	.25
245	A75	150r violet		2.50	.50
246	A75	200r blue		400.00	15.00
247	A75	200r rose red		.50	.25
248	A75	200r ol grn ('28)		3.50	3.75
249	A76	300r olive gray		2.50	.30
250	A76	300r rose red ('29)		.40	.30
251	A76	400r blue		2.50	.25
252	A76	400r orange ('29)		1.00	3.25
253	A76	500r red brown		10.00	.65
254	A76	500r ultra ('29)		14.50	.25
255	A76	600r brn org ('29)		12.00	4.50
256	A76	700r dull vio ('29)		12.00	2.50
257	A76	1000r turq bl ('29)		14.50	1.00
		Nos. 236-257 (22)		513.20	79.90

Because of the spacing of the watermark, a few stamps in each sheet show no watermark.
    A booklet exists with panes of 6 (2x3), created from the left margin blocks of sheet stamps of Nos. 241, 243, 247, 249 and 253. Once removed from the booklet, they cannot be separately identified.

"Agriculture" — A79

		Unwmk.	**Perf. 13½x13**	
1922				
258	A79	40r orange brown	.70	.50
259	A79	80r grnsh blue	.50	3.25
		See Nos. 263, 267, 275.		

Declaration of Ypiranga — A80

Dom Pedro I and Jose Bonifacio — A81

National Exposition and President Pessoa — A82

Unwmk.
1922, Sept. 7   Engr.   Perf. 14
260 A80 100r ultra   5.00 .75
261 A81 200r red   7.00 .50
262 A82 300r green   7.00 .50
    Nos. 260-262 (3)   19.00 1.75
Cent. of independence and Natl. Exposition of 1922.

Agriculture Type of 1922
Perf. 13½x12
1923   Wmk. 100   Typo.
263 A79 40r orange brown   .75 7.50

Brazilian Army Entering Bahia — A83

Unwmk.
1923, July 12   Litho.   Perf. 13
264 A83 200r rose   11.00 6.50
Centenary of the taking of Bahia from the Portuguese.

Types of 1920-22 Issue
Perf. 13x13½

			Typo.	Wmk. 193	
1924					
265	A73	10r red violet		8.88	1.00
266	A73	20r olive green		10.50	7.50
267	A79	40r orange brown		7.50	2.75
268	A74	50r orange brown		10.00	30.00
269	A75	100r orange		7.50	.75
270	A75	200r rose		10.50	.75
271	A76	400r blue		8.00	4.75
		Nos. 265-271 (7)		63.00	54.00

Arms of Equatorial Confederation, 1824 — A84

Unwmk.
1924, July 2   Litho.   Perf. 11
272 A84 200r bl, blk, yel, & red   4.00 2.75
a.   Red omitted   350.00 350.00
Centenary of the Equatorial Confederation. Chemically bleached fakes of No. 272a are more common than the genuine error. Expertization is advised.

Types of 1920-22 Issue
Perf. 9½ to 13½ and Compound

			Typo.	Wmk. 101	
1924-28					
273	A73	10r red violet		.75	.35
274	A73	20r olive gray		.75	.35
275	A79	40r orange brn		.75	.35
276	A74	50r orange brn		.75	.35
277	A75	100r red orange		2.25	.35
278	A75	200r rose		1.00	.35
279	A76	300r ol gray ('25)		10.00	1.25
280	A76	400r blue		6.00	.50
281	A76	500r red brown		15.00	.50
		Engr.			
282	A77	600r red orange ('26)		2.50	.35
283	A72	2000r dull vio ('26)		7.50	.75
284	A72	5000r brown ('26)		22.50	.85
285	A72	10,000r rose ('28)		30.00	2.00
		Nos. 273-285 (13)		99.75	8.30

Nos. 283-285 are inscribed "BRASIL CORREIO."

Ruy Barbosa — A85

1925   Wmk. 100   Perf. 11½
286 A85 1000r claret   6.25 1.75

1926   Wmk. 101
287 A85 1000r claret   2.10 .40

"Justice" — A86

Scales of Justice and Map of Brazil — A87

Perf. 13½x13

			Typo.	Wmk. 206	
1927, Aug. 11					
288	A86	100r deep blue		1.10	.65
289	A87	200r rose		.95	.40

Founding of the law courses, cent.

Liberty Holding Coffee Leaves — A88

1928, Feb. 5
290	A88	100r blue green	1.75	.80
291	A88	200r carmine	1.10	.50
292	A88	300r olive black	9.00	.40
		Nos. 290-292 (3)	11.85	1.70

Introduction of the coffee tree in Brazil, bicent.

Official Stamps of 1919 Surcharged in Red or Black

Perf. 11, 11½
			Engr.	
1928		Wmk. 100		
293	O3	700r on 500r org	8.00	8.00
a.		Inverted surcharge	210.00	210.00
294	O3	1000r on 100r rose red (Bk)	4.75	.60
295	O3	2000r on 200r dull bl	6.50	1.00
296	O3	5000r on 50r grn	6.50	1.60
297	O3	10,000r on 10r ol grn	30.00	2.50
		Nos. 293-297 (5)	55.75	13.70

Nos. 293-297 were used for ordinary postage.

Stamps in the outer rows of the sheets are often without watermark.

Ruy Barbosa — A89

Perf. 9, 9½x11, 11, and Compound
			Wmk. 101	
1929				
300	A89	5000r blue violet	20.00	.95

See Nos. 405, 459. For surcharge see No. C29.

Types of 1920-22 Issue
Perf. 13½x12½
			Wmk. 218	
1929		Typo.		
302	A75	20r gray violet	.40	.25
303	A75	50r red brown	.40	.25
304	A75	100r turq green	.55	.25
305	A76	200r olive green	22.50	5.00
306	A76	300r rose red	1.10	.25
307	A76	400r orange	1.25	2.00
308	A76	500r ultra	14.00	.65
309	A76	600r brown org	16.00	1.25
310	A76	700r dp violet	4.25	.25
311	A76	1000r turq blue	7.50	.25
		Nos. 302-311 (10)	67.95	10.40

Wmk. 218 exists both in vertical alignment and in echelon.

Wmk. in echelon
302a	A75	20r	.50	.40
303a	A75	50r	140.00	75.00
306a	A76	300r	1.25	1.25
308a	A76	500r	200.00	47.50
311a	A76	1000r	10.00	11.00

Architectural Fantasies
A90   A91

Architectural Fantasy — A92

Perf. 13x13½
			Wmk. 206	
1930, June 20				
312	A90	100r turq blue	2.00	1.25
313	A91	200r olive gray	3.25	.80
314	A92	300r rose red	5.50	1.25
		Nos. 312-314 (3)	10.75	3.30

Fourth Pan-American Congress of Architects and Exposition of Architecture.

Types of 1920-22 Issue
			Perf. 13x12½	
1930		Wmk. 221		
316	A75	20r gray violet	.40	.35
317	A75	50r red brown	.40	.35
318	A75	100r turq blue	.80	.35
319	A75	200r olive green	4.75	1.25
320	A76	300r rose red	.95	.35
321	A76	500r ultra	2.40	.35
322	A76	700r turq blue	40.00	1.50
		Nos. 316-322 (7)	49.70	4.50

Imperforates
From 1930 to 1947, imperforate or partly perforated sheets of nearly all commemorative and some definitive issues were obtainable.

Types of 1920-22 Issue
Perf. 11, 13½x13, 13x12½
			Wmk. 222	
1931-34		Typo.		
326	A75	10r deep brown	.25	.25
327	A75	20r gray violet	.25	.25
328	A74	25r brn vio ('34)	.25	1.25
330	A75	50r blue green	.25	.25
331	A75	50r red brown	.25	.25
332	A75	100r orange	.50	.25
334	A75	200r dp carmine	1.00	.40
335	A76	300r olive green	1.40	.25
336	A76	400r ultra	3.00	.25
337	A76	500r red brown	6.00	.25
338	A76	600r brown org	6.50	.25
339	A76	700r deep violet	6.50	.25
340	A76	1000r turq blue	21.00	.25
		Nos. 326-340 (13)	47.15	4.40

Getulio Vargas and Joao Pessoa A93

Vargas and Pessoa A94

Oswaldo Aranha
A95   A96

Antonio Carlos A97   Pessoa A98

Vargas — A99

Unwmk.
			Litho.	Perf. 14
1931, Apr. 29				
342	A93	10r + 10r lt bl	.25	13.00
343	A93	20r + 20r yel brn	.25	9.50
344	A95	50r + 50r bl grn, red & yel	.25	.40
a.		Red missing at left	.90	1.60
345	A93	100r + 50r orange	.55	.45
346	A93	200r + 100r green	.55	.45
347	A94	300r + 150r multi	.55	.45
348	A93	400r + 200r dp rose	1.90	1.00
349	A93	500r + 250r dk bl	1.40	1.10
350	A93	600r + 300r brn vio	.95	13.00
351	A94	700r + 350r multi	1.75	.90
352	A96	1000r + 500r brt grn, red & yel	3.75	.55
353	A97	2000r + 1000r gray blk & red	15.00	.80
354	A98	5000r + 2500r blk & red	32.50	13.50
355	A99	10000r + 5000r brt grn & yel	80.00	24.00
		Nos. 342-355 (14)	139.65	79.10

Revolution of Oct. 3, 1930. Prepared as semi-postal stamps, Nos. 342-355 were sold as ordinary postage stamps with stated surtax ignored.

Nos. 306, 320 and 250 Surcharged

Perf. 13½x12½
			Wmk. 218	
1931, July 20				
356	A76	200r on 300r rose red	1.75	1.25
a.		Wmk. in echelon	30.00	30.00
b.		Inverted surcharge	47.50	

Perf. 13x12½
Wmk. 221
357	A76	200r on 300r rose red	.50	.25
a.		Inverted surcharge	55.00	55.00

Perf. 13½x12½
Wmk. 100
358	A76	200r on 300r rose red	92.50	92.50

Map of South America Showing Meridian of Tordesillas — A100

Joao Ramalho and Tibiriça A101

Martim Affonso de Souza A102

King John III of Portugal A103

Disembarkation of M. A. de Souza at Sao Vicente — A104

Wmk. 222
			Typo.	Perf. 13
1932, June 3				
359	A100	20r dk violet	.40	.50
360	A101	100r black	.60	.50
361	A102	200r purple	1.25	.40
362	A103	600r red brown	2.10	2.25

Engr.
Wmk. 101
Perf. 9½, 11, 9½x11
363	A104	700r ultra	3.50	2.75
		Nos. 359-363 (5)	7.85	6.40

1st colonization of Brazil at Sao Vicente, in 1532, under the hereditary captainy of Martim Affonso de Souza.

Revolutionary Issue

Map of Brazil — A105   Soldier and Flag — A106

Allegory: Freedom, Justice, Equality A107   Soldier's Head A108

"LEX" and Sword A109

Symbolical of Law and Order — A110

Symbolical of Justice — A111

Perf. 11½
			Litho.	Unwmk.
1932, Sept.				
364	A105	100r brown org	.55	2.40
365	A106	200r dk car	.45	.85
366	A107	300r gray green	2.40	4.25
367	A108	400r dark blue	8.75	8.75
368	A105	500r blk brn	8.75	8.75
369	A107	600r red	8.75	8.75
370	A106	700r violet	4.25	8.75
371	A108	1000r orange	2.10	8.75
372	A109	2000r dark brn	17.00	24.00
373	A110	5000r yellow grn	21.00	40.00
374	A111	10000r plum	24.00	45.00
		Nos. 364-374 (11)	98.00	160.25

Issued by the revolutionary forces in the state of Sao Paulo during the revolt of September, 1932. Subsequently the stamps were recognized by the Federal Government and placed in general use.

Excellent counterfeits of Nos. 373 and 374 exist. Favor cancels, applied at a later date, abound.

City of Vassouras and Illuminated Memorial — A112

Wmk. 222
1933, Jan. 15 Typo. Perf. 12
375 A112 200r rose red 1.40 1.10
City of Vassouras founding, cent.

Nos. 306, 320
Surcharged

Perf. 13½x12½
1933, July 28 Wmk. 218
376 A76 200r on 300r rose red 1.00 1.00
a. Wmk. 218 in echelon (No. 306a) 19.00 19.00
b. Wmk. 100 (No. 250) 140.00 140.00

Perf. 13x12½
Wmk. 221
377 A76 200r on 300r rose red .65 .65
a. Inverted surcharge 42.50
b. Double surcharge 42.50

Religious Symbols and Inscriptions — A113

Wmk. 222
1933, Sept. 3 Typo. Perf. 13
378 A113 200r dark red 1.00 .85
1st Natl. Eucharistic Congress in Brazil.

"Flag of the Race" A114

1933, Aug. 18
379 A114 200r deep red 2.00 .85
The raising of the "Flag of the Race" and the 441st anniv. of the sailing of Columbus from Palos, Spain, Aug. 3, 1492.

Republic Figure, Flags of Brazil and Argentina — A115

Wmk. 101
1933, Oct. 7 Engr. Perf. 11½
380 A115 200r blue .45 .35

Thick Laid Paper
1933, Dec. Wmk. 236 Perf. 11, 11½
381 A115 400r green 1.50 1.00
382 A115 600r brt rose 5.00 6.75
383 A115 1000r lt violet 7.25 4.75
Nos. 380-383 (4) 14.20 13.10
Visit of President Justo of the Argentina to Brazil, Oct. 2-7, 1933.

Allegory: "Faith and Energy" — A116

Allegory of Flight — A117

1933 Typo. Wmk. 222
384 A116 200r dark red .30 .25
385 A116 200r dark violet .85 .25
See Nos. 435, 471, 491.

Wmk. 236
1934, Apr. 15 Engr. Perf. 12
386 A117 200r blue .80 .65
1st Natl. Aviation Congress at Sao Paulo.

A118

Wmk. 222
1934, May 12 Typo. Perf. 11
387 A118 200r dark olive .40 .40
388 A118 400r carmine 2.25 2.25
389 A118 700r ultra 2.40 2.25
390 A118 1000r orange 6.00 1.00
Nos. 387-390 (4) 11.05 5.90
7th Intl. Fair at Rio de Janeiro.

Christ of Corcovado A119

1934, Oct. 20
392 A119 300r dark red 4.25 4.25
a. Tete beche pair 17.00 17.00
393 A119 700r ultra 17.00 17.00
a. Tete beche pair 72.50 72.50
Visit of Eugenio Cardinal Pacelli, later Pope Pius XII, to Brazil.
The three printings of Nos. 392-393, distinguishable by shades, sell for different prices.

José de Anchieta A120

Thick Laid Paper
1934, Nov. 8 Wmk. 236 Perf. 11, 12
394 A120 200r yellow brown .90 .60
395 A120 300r violet .75 .40
396 A120 700r blue 3.00 3.00
397 A120 1000r lt green 6.00 1.75
Nos. 394-397 (4) 10.65 5.75
Jose de Anchieta, S.J. (1534-1597), Portuguese missionary and "father of Brazilian literature."

A121

"Brazil" and "Uruguay" — A122

Wmk. 222
1935, Jan. 8 Typo. Perf. 11
398 A121 200r orange 1.10 .55
399 A122 300r yellow 1.40 1.25
400 A122 700r ultra 8.00 8.00
401 A121 1000r dk violet 13.00 8.00
Nos. 398-401 (4) 20.50 14.80
Visit of President Terra of Uruguay.

View of Town of Igarassu A123

1935, July 1
402 A123 200r maroon & brn 1.60 .55
403 A123 300r vio & olive brn 1.60 .45
Captaincy of Pernambuco founding, 400th anniv.

Types of 1918-29
Thick Laid Paper
Perf. 9½, 11, 12, 12x11
1934-36 Engr. Wmk. 236
404 A72 2000r violet 12.50 .60
405 A89 5000r blue vio ('36) 17.00 1.25
406 A72 10000r claret ('36) 15.00 1.75
Nos. 404-406 (3) 44.50 3.60
No. 404 is inscribed "BRASIL CORREIO."

Revolutionist A124

Bento Gonçalves da Silva — A125

Duke of Caxias A126

Perf. 11, 12
1935, Sept. 20-1936, Jan.
407 A124 200r black 1.40 1.40
408 A124 300r rose lake 1.40 .80
409 A125 700r dull blue 4.50 6.50
410 A126 1000r light violet 5.00 4.00
Nos. 407-410 (4) 12.30 12.70
Centenary of the "Ragged" Revolution.

Federal District Coat of Arms A127

Wmk. 222
1935, Oct. 19 Typo. Perf. 11
411 A127 200r blue 4.00 4.00
8th Intl. Sample Fair held at Rio de Janeiro.

Coutinho's Ship — A128

Arms of Fernandes Coutinho — A129

1935, Oct. 25
412 A128 300r maroon 3.00 1.25
413 A129 700r turq blue 5.50 3.75
400th anniversary of the establishment of the first Portuguese colony at Espirito Santo by Vasco Fernandes Coutinho.

Gavea, Rock near Rio de Janeiro A130

1935, Oct. 12 Wmk. 245 Perf. 11
414 A130 300r brown & vio 2.75 2.00
415 A130 300r blk & turq bl 2.75 2.00
416 A130 300r Prus bl & ultra 2.75 2.00
417 A130 300r crimson & blk 2.75 2.00
Nos. 414-417 (4) 11.00 8.00
"Child's Day," Oct. 12.

Viscount of Cairu — A131

Perf. 11, 12x11
1936, Jan. 20 Engr. Wmk. 236
418 A131 1200r violet 10.00 6.00
Jose da Silva Lisboa, Viscount of Cairu (1756-1835).

View of Cametá A132

1936, Feb. 26 Perf. 11, 12
419 A132 200r brown orange 1.75 1.40
420 A132 300r green 1.75 1.00
300th anniversary of the founding of the city of Cameta, Dec. 24, 1635.

Coining Press A133

Thick Laid Paper
1936, Mar. 24 Perf. 11
421 A133 300r pur brn, cr 1.25 1.25
1st Numismatic Cong. at Sao Paulo, Mar., 1936.

Carlos Gomes — A134

"Il Guarany" — A135

Thick Laid Paper
1936, July 11   **Perf. 11, 11x12**
422 A134 300r dull rose   1.00 .70
423 A134 300r black brown   1.00 .70
424 A135 700r ocher   3.25 2.00
425 A135 700r blue   3.75 2.75
  Nos. 422-425 (4)   9.00 6.15

Birth cent. of Antonio Carlos Gomes, who composed the opera "Il Guarany."

Scales of Justice — A136

Wmk. 222
1936, July 4   **Typo.**   **Perf. 11**
426 A136 300r rose   2.00 .65

First National Judicial Congress.

Federal District Coat of Arms A137

1936, Nov. 13 **Typo.** **Wmk. 249**
427 A137 200r rose red   1.25 .65

Ninth International Sample Fair held at Rio de Janeiro.

Eucharistic Congress Seal — A138

1936, Dec. 17 **Wmk. 245** **Perf. 11½**
428 A138 300r grn, yel, bl & blk 1.25 .60

2nd Natl. Eucharistic Congress in Brazil.

Botafogo Bay A139

Thick Laid Paper
Wmk. 236
1937, Jan. 2   **Engr.**   **Perf. 11**
429 A139 700r blue   1.60 .80
430 A139 700r black   1.60 .80

Birth cent. of Francisco Pereira Passos, engineer who planned the modern city of Rio de Janeiro.

Types of 1920-22, 1933
Perf. 11, 11½ and Compound
1936-37   **Typo.**   **Wmk. 249**
431 A75 10r deep brown   .25 .25
432 A75 20r dull violet   .25 .25
433 A75 50r blue green   .25 .25
434 A75 100r orange   .50 .25
435 A116 200r dk violet   1.50 .25
436 A76 300r olive green   .50 .25
437 A76 400r ultra   1.25 .25
438 A76 500r lt brown   1.75 .25
439 A76 600r brn org ('37) 9.00 .25
440 A76 700r deep violet   7.00 .25
441 A76 1000r turq blue   7.75 .25
  Nos. 431-441 (11)   30.00 2.75

Massed Flags and Star of Esperanto A140

1937, Jan. 19
442 A140 300r green   1.75 .90

Ninth Brazilian Esperanto Congress.

Bay of Rio de Janeiro A141

1937, June 9 **Unwmk.** **Perf. 12½**
443 A141 300r orange red & blk 1.00 .75
444 A141 700r blue & dk brn   2.50 .75

2nd South American Radio Communication Conf. held in Rio, June 7-19.

Globe — A142

Perf. 11, 12
1937, Sept. 4   **Wmk. 249**
445 A142 300r green   1.50 .65

50th anniversary of Esperanto.

Monroe Palace, Rio de Janeiro A143

Botanical Garden, Rio de Janeiro — A144

1937, Sept. 30 **Unwmk.** **Perf. 12½**
446 A143 200r lt brn & bl   1.00 .50
447 A143 300r org & ol grn   1.00 .50
448 A143 2000r grn & cerise   13.00 13.00
449 A144 10000r lake & indigo 70.00 60.00
  Nos. 446-449 (4)   85.00 74.00

Brig. Gen. Jose da Silva Paes — A145

1937, Oct. 11 **Wmk. 249** **Perf. 11½**
450 A145 300r blue   1.00 .50

Bicentenary of Rio Grande do Sul.

Eagle and Shield — A146

1937, Dec. 2 **Typo.** **Perf. 11**
451 A146 400r dark blue   2.75 .60

150th anniversary of the US Constitution.

Bags of Brazilian Coffee A147

Frame Engraved, Center Typographed
1938, Jan. 17 **Unwmk.** **Perf. 12½**
452 A147 1200r multicolored   6.25 .50

Arms of Olinda A148

Perf. 11, 11x11½
1938, Jan. 24 **Engr.** **Wmk. 249**
453 A148 400r violet   .80 .35

4th cent. of the founding of the city of Olinda.

Independence Memorial, Ypiranga A149

1938, Jan. 24 **Typo.** **Perf. 11**
454 A149 400r brown olive   1.00 .50

Proclamation of Brazil's independence by Dom Pedro, Sept. 7, 1822.

Iguaçu Falls — A150

Perf. 12½
1938, Jan. 10 **Unwmk.** **Engr.**
455 A150 1000r sepia & yel brn   3.00 1.75
456 A150 5000r ol blk & grn   27.50 22.50

Couto de Magalhaes A151

Perf. 11, 11x11½
1938, Mar. 17   **Wmk. 249**
457 A151 400r dull green   .80 .40

General Couto de Magalhaes (1837-1898), statesman, soldier, explorer, writer, developer.

Types of 1918-38
Perf. 11, 12x11, 12x11½, 12
1938   **Engr.**   **Wmk. 249**
458 A72 2000r blue violet   12.00 .30
459 A89 5000r violet blue   45.00 .50
  a. 5000r deep blue   37.50 .50
460 A72 10000r rose lake   55.00 1.50
  Nos. 458-460 (3)   112.00 2.30

No. 458 is inscribed "BRASIL CORREIO."

Types of 1920-22
1938 **Wmk. 245** **Typo.** **Perf. 11**
461 A75 50r blue green   1.40 1.10
462 A75 100r orange   3.25 1.10
463 A76 300r olive green   1.40 3.00
463A A76 400r ultra   225.00 150.00
463B A76 500r red brown   1.40 60.00
  Nos. 461-463B (5)   232.45 215.20

National Archives Building A152

1938, May 20   **Wmk. 249**
464 A152 400r brown   .75 .40

Centenary of National Archives.

Souvenir Sheets

Sir Rowland Hill — A153

1938, Oct. 22   **Imperf.**
465 A153   Sheet of 10   20.00 20.00
  a. 400r dull green, single stamp 1.25 1.25

Brazilian Intl. Philatelic Exposition (Brapex). Issued in sheets measuring 106x118mm. A few perforated sheets exist.

President Vargas — A154

1938, Nov. 10   **Perf. 11**
Without Gum
466 A154   Sheet of 10   27.50 27.50
  a. 400r slate blue, single stamp 1.75 1.75

Constitution of Brazil, set up by President Vargas, Nov. 10, 1937. Size: 113x135½mm.

Types of 1920-33

			Perf. 11	
1939	Typo.	Wmk. 256		
467	A75	10r red brown	1.00	1.00
468	A75	20r dull violet	2.00	.30
469	A75	50r blue green	1.50	.30
470	A75	100r yellow org	1.50	.30
471	A116	200r dk violet	3.00	.30
472	A76	400r ultra	3.00	.30
473	A76	600r dull orange	4.50	.30
474	A76	1000r turq blue	20.00	.30
		Nos. 467-474 (8)	36.50	3.10

View of Rio de Janeiro — A155

1939, June 14   Engr.   Wmk. 249
475 A155 1200r dull violet   2.25   .25

View of Santos — A156

1939, Aug. 23
476 A156 400r dull blue   .50   .40
Centenary of founding of Santos.

Chalice Vine and Blossoms — A157

1939, Aug. 23
477 A157 400r green   1.60   .35
1st South American Botanical Congress held in January, 1938.

Eucharistic Congress Seal — A158

1939, Sept. 3
478 A158 400r rose red   .60   .45
Third National Eucharistic Congress.

Duke of Caxias, Army Patron — A159

1939, Sept. 12   Photo.   Rouletted
479 A159 400r deep ultra   .60   .45
Issued for Soldiers' Day.

A159a

A159b

A159c

A159d

Designs: 400r, George Washington. 800r, Emperor Pedro II. 1200r, Grover Cleveland. 1600r, Statue of Friendship, given by US.

Unwmk.
1939, Oct. 7   Engr.   Perf. 12

480	A159a	400r yellow orange	.70	.30
481	A159b	800r dark green	.35	.25
482	A159c	1200r rose car	.70	.25
483	A159d	1600r dark blue	.70	.30
		Nos. 480-483 (4)	2.45	1.10

New York World's Fair.

Benjamin Constant A160

Fonseca on Horseback A162

Manuel Deodoro da Fonseca and President Vargas A161

Wmk. 249
1939, Nov. 15   Photo.   Rouletted
484 A160 400r deep green   .85   .50
485 A161 1200r chocolate   1.10   .50

Engr.   Perf. 11
486 A162 800r gray black   .65   .50
Nos. 484-486 (3)   2.60   1.50
Proclamation of the Republic, 50th anniv.

President Roosevelt, President Vargas and Map of the Americas A163

1940, Apr. 14
487 A163 400r slate blue   1.00   .55
Pan American Union, 50th anniversary.

Types of 1920-33

1940-41	Typo.	Wmk. 264	Perf. 11	
488	A75	10r red brown	.80	.80
489	A75	20r dull violet	.80	.80
489A	A75	80r blue grn ('41)	1.50	1.75
490	A75	100r yellow org	2.50	.50
491	A116	200r violet	7.50	.50
492	A76	400r ultra	7.50	.50
493	A76	600r dull orange	10.00	.50
494	A76	1000r turq blue	22.50	.50
		Nos. 488-494 (8)	53.10	5.60

Map of Brazil — A164

1940, Sept. 7   Engr.
495 A164 400r carmine   .50   .50
   a.   Unwmkd.   50.00   30.00
9th Brazilian Congress of Geography held at Florianopolis.

Victoria Regia Water Lily — A165

President Vargas — A166

Relief Map of Brazil — A167

1940, Oct. 30   Wmk. 249   Perf. 11
Without Gum

496	A165	1000r dull violet	1.40	1.75
a.		Sheet of 10	14.50	35.00
497	A166	5000r red	10.00	10.00
a.		Sheet of 10	125.00	175.00
498	A167	10,000r slate blue	15.00	7.50
a.		Sheet of 10	160.00	175.00
		Nos. 496-498 (3)	26.40	19.25

New York World's Fair.
All three sheets exist unwatermarked and also with papermaker's watermark of large globe and "AMERICA BANK" in sheet. A few imperforate sheets also exist.

Joaquim Machado de Assis — A168

Pioneers and Buildings of Porto Alegre — A169

1940, Nov. 1
499 A168 400r black   .65   .25
Birth centenary of Joaquim Maria Machado de Assis, poet and novelist.

1940, Nov. 2   Wmk. 264
500 A169 400r green   .60   .30
Colonization of Porto Alegre, bicent.

Proclamation of King John IV of Portugal — A173

1940, Dec. 1   Wmk. 249
501 A173 1200r blue black   2.50   .50
800th anniv. of Portuguese independence and 300th anniv. of the restoration of the monarchy.
No. 501 was also printed on paper with papermaker's watermark of large globe and "AMERICA BANK." Unwatermarked copies are from these sheets. Value of unwatermarked stamps, $150.

Brazilian Flags and Head of Liberty — A175

Wmk. 256
1940, Dec. 18   Engr.   Perf. 11
502 A175 400r dull violet   .70   .25
  b.   Unwmkd.   22.50   22.50

Wmk. 245
502A A175 400r dull violet   75.00   50.00
10th anniv. of the inauguration of President Vargas.

SEMI-POSTAL STAMPS

National Philatelic Exhibition Issue

SP1

Thick Paper
Wmk. Coat of Arms in Sheet (236)
1934, Sept. 16   Engr.   Imperf.

B1	SP1	200r + 100r dp claret	1.25	3.00
B2	SP1	300r + 100r ver	1.25	3.00
B3	SP1	700r + 100r brt bl	8.00	27.50
B4	SP1	1000r + 100r blk	8.00	27.50
		Nos. B1-B4 (4)	18.50	61.00

The surtax was to help defray the expenses of the exhibition. Issued in sheets of 60, inscribed "EXPOSICAO FILATELICA NACIONAL."

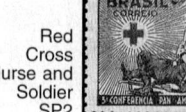

Red Cross Nurse and Soldier SP2

Wmk. 222
1935, Sept. 19   Typo.   Perf. 11

B5	SP2	200r + 100r pur & red	1.75	1.25
B6	SP2	300r + 100r ol brn & red	2.00	.90
B7	SP2	700r + 100r turq bl & red	12.50	7.00
		Nos. B5-B7 (3)	16.25	9.15

3rd Pan-American Red Cross Conf. Exist imperf.

Three Wise Men
and Star of
Bethlehem — SP3

Angel and
Child — SP4

Southern Cross
and
Child — SP5

Mother and
Child — SP6

Wmk. 249

1939-40   Litho.   Perf. 10½

B8	SP3	100r + 100r chlky bl & bl blk	1.60	1.60
a.		Horiz. or vert. pair, imperf. between	40.00	
B9	SP4	200r + 100r brt grnsh bl	2.25	2.10
a.		Horizontal pair, imperf. between	40.00	
B10	SP5	400r + 200r ol grn & ol	1.75	1.10
B11	SP6	1200r + 400r crim & brn red	7.00	3.25
a.		Vertical pair, imperf. between	40.00	
		Nos. B8-B11 (4)	12.60	8.05

Dates of issue: No. B8, 12/20/39; Nos. B9-B11, 2/26/40.

Surtax for charitable institutions.

For surcharges see Nos. C55-C59 in *Scott Standard Postage Stamp Catalogue*, Vol. 1.

AIR POST STAMPS

Nos. O14-O29
Surcharged

1927, Dec. 28   Unwmk.   Perf. 12

C1	O2	50r on 10r	.45	.35
a.		Inverted surcharge	325.00	
b.		Top ornaments missing	75.00	
C2	O2	200r on 1000r	2.25	4.50
a.		Double surcharge	325.00	
C3	O2	200r on 2000r	1.40	10.00
a.		Double surcharge	750.00	
b.		Double surcharge, one inverted	750.00	
C4	O2	200r on 5000r	1.75	1.40
a.		Double surcharge	325.00	
b.		Double surcharge, one inverted	350.00	
c.		Triple surcharge	450.00	
C5	O2	300r on 500r	1.75	2.25
C6	O2	300r on 600r	.85	.90
b.		Pair, one without surch.		
C6A	O2	500r on 10r	400.00	425.00
C7	O2	500r on 50r	1.75	.70
a.		Double surcharge	300.00	
C8	O2	1000r on 20r	1.40	.45
a.		Double surcharge	300.00	
C9	O2	2000r on 100r	3.00	1.75
a.		Pair, one without surcharge		
b.		Double surcharge	300.00	
C10	O2	2000r on 200r	4.00	1.75
C11	O2	2000r on 10,000r	3.50	.70
C12	O2	5000r on 20,000r	10.00	4.00
C13	O2	5000r on 50,000r	10.00	4.00
C14	O2	5000r on 100,000r	32.50	30.00
C15	O2	10,000r on 500,000r	35.00	20.00

C16	O2	10,000r on 1,000,000r	45.00	37.50
		Nos. C1-C6,C7-C16 (16)	154.60	120.25

Nos. C1, C1b, C7, C8 and C9 have small diamonds printed over the numerals in the upper corners.

Monument to de
Gusmao — AP1

Santos-Dumont's
Airship — AP2

Augusto Severo's
Airship "Pax" — AP3

Santos-Dumont's
Biplane "14 Bis" — AP4

Ribeiro de Barros's
Seaplane
"Jahu" — AP5

Perf. 11, 12½x13, 13x13½

1929   Typo.   Wmk. 206

C17	AP1	50r blue grn	.35	.25
C18	AP2	200r red	1.40	.25
C19	AP3	300r brt blue	2.25	.25
C20	AP4	500r red violet	2.50	.25
C21	AP5	1000r orange brn	9.00	.40
		Nos. C17-C21 (5)	15.50	1.40

See Nos. C32-C36. For surcharges see Nos. C26-C27.

Bartholomeu de
Gusmao — AP6

Augusto
Severo — AP7

Alberto Santos-
Dumont
AP8

Perf. 9, 11 and Compound

1929-30   Engr.   Wmk. 101

C22	AP6	2000r lt green ('30)	14.00	.50
C23	AP7	5000r carmine	16.00	1.25
C24	AP8	10,000r olive grn	16.00	1.75
		Nos. C22-C24 (3)	46.00	3.50

Nos. C23-C24 exist imperf.
See Nos. C37, C40.

Allegory: Airmail
Service between
Brazil and the
US — AP9

1929   Typo.   Wmk. 206

C25	AP9	3000r violet	14.00	1.75

Exists imperf. See Nos. C38, C41. For surcharge see No. C28.

Nos. C18-C19
Surcharged in Blue or
Red

1931, Aug. 16   Perf. 12½x13½

C26	AP2	2500r on 200r (Bl)	30.00	25.00
C27	AP3	5000r on 300r (R)	35.00	30.00

No. C25
Surcharged

1931, Sept. 2   Perf. 11

C28	AP9	2500r on 3000r vio	27.50	27.50
a.		Inverted surcharge	160.00	
b.		Surch. on front and back	160.00	

Regular Issues of
1928-29 Surcharged

1932, May Wmk. 101 Perf. 11, 11½

C29	A89	3500r on 5000r gray lil	27.50	27.50
C30	A72	7000r on 10,000r rose	27.50	27.50
b.		Horiz. pair, imperf. between	750.00	

Imperforates

Since 1933, imperforate or partly perforated sheets of nearly all of the airmail issues have become available.

Flag and
Airplane
AP10

Wmk. 222

1933, June 7   Typo.   Perf. 11

C31	AP10	3500r grn, yel & dk bl	6.50	2.00

See Nos. C39, C42.

1934   Wmk. 222

C32	AP1	50r blue grn	2.75	2.75
C33	AP2	200r red	3.25	.85
C34	AP3	300r brt blue	8.00	2.40
C35	AP4	500r red violet	3.25	.85
C36	AP5	1000r orange brn	11.00	.85
		Nos. C32-C36 (5)	28.25	7.70

1934 Wmk. 236 Engr. Perf. 12x11
Thick Laid Paper

C37	AP6	2000r lt green	6.75	1.75

Types of 1929, 1933
Perf. 11, 11½, 12

1937-40   Typo.   Wmk. 249

C38	AP9	3000r violet	25.00	2.25
C39	AP10	3500r grn, yel & dk bl	4.50	2.00

Engr.

C40	AP7	5000r ver ('40)	9.00	2.00
		Nos. C38-C40 (3)	38.50	6.25

Watermark note after No. 501 also applies to No. C40.

Types of 1929-33
Perf. 11, 11½x12

1939-40   Typo.   Wmk. 256

C41	AP9	3000r violet	2.40	.90
C42	AP10	3500r bl, dl grn & yel ('40)	2.40	.80

AIR POST SEMI-OFFICIAL STAMPS

Beginning in 1927, the Brazil government contracted with private companies to establish airmail service within Brazil, and from Brazil to cities in Europe and the United States. From 1927 to 1931, four major commercial airlines, Condor, Varig, Empresa de Transportes Aereos Ltda. (better known as E.T.A.) and Luftschiffbau Zeppelin G.m.b.H., carried mail under contract with the Brazil Post Office. Each company issued semi-official airmail stamps to be used on mail carried on these flights. These stamps paid the airmail fee, but postal regulations required that Brazil stamps also be affixed to the envelopes to pay regular Brazilian postage.

CONDOR SYNDICATE
(Syndicato Condor)

Condor and Southern
Cross — APL1

Wmk. 116

1927, Nov. 8   Litho.   Perf. 14

1CL1	APL1	500r olive	5.50	4.00
		Never hinged	8.25	
1CL2	APL1	700r orange	5.50	2.00
		Never hinged	8.25	
1CL3	APL1	1000r red	5.50	2.00
		Never hinged	8.25	
1CL4	APL1	1300r green	5.50	2.00
		Never hinged	8.25	
1CL5	APL1	2000r dp Prus bl	11.00	2.00
		Never hinged	16.50	
1CL6	APL1	3000r violet	11.00	2.00
		Never hinged	16.50	
1CL7	APL1	10000r org ver	27.50	45.00
		Never hinged	42.50	
		Nos. 1CL1-1CL7 (7)	71.50	59.00

Nos. 1CL1-1CL7 were printed by the Government Printing Office in Berlin. A second printing was never issued to the public. The stamps from the second printing have paler colors than the stamps from the original printing. Values of second-printing set, unused, $32.50; never hinged, $65.00.

Without "Syndicato Condor"

APL1a

1927

1CL8	APL1a	1300r green	135.00	—
		Never hinged	210.00	
a.		1300r pale green ('37)	72.50	—
		Never hinged	110.00	

No. 1CL8 is known with overprints: See Nos. 1CL13, 3CL1-3CL12, 3CLE1-3CLE2, 3CLF1-3CLF2, 4CL6-4CL7.

APL2

1930, Jan. 9   Unwmk.   *Perf. 13*
1CL9 APL2 2000r black   180.00   27.50
   Never hinged   275.00
   On cover   70.00

No. 1CL9 was issued in commemoration of the Rio de Janeiro-Santos-San Francisco-Florianapolis-Itajai flight made January 4, 1927, which included in its list of passengers Dr. Victor Konder, Brazil's minister of transportation and public works. The stamp was printed by Casa da Moneda, Rio de Janeiro.

Nos. 1CL2, 1CL6, 1CL7,1CL8 Surcharged

No. 1CL10   No. 1CL11

No. 1CL12   No. 1CL13

1930, Sept. 10   *Perf. 13*
1CL10 APL1   50r on 700r   9.00   45.00
   Never hinged   14.00
   a. Inverted surcharge *(150)*   275.00   *450.00*
     Never hinged   425.00
   b. Double surcharge *(50)*   550.00   *700.00*
     Never hinged   825.00
   c. Triple surcharge *(50)*   550.00
     Never hinged   825.00
1CL11 APL1   200r on 3000r   9.00   37.50
   Never hinged   14.00
1CL12 APL1   350r on 10000r   9.00   37.50
   Never hinged   14.00
1CL13 APL1   750r on 1300r   19.00   35.00
   Never hinged   27.50
   a. Inverted surcharge *(100)*   375.00   *550.00*
     Never hinged   575.00
     Never hinged   700.00
  Nos. 1CL10-1CL13 (4)   46.00   155.00

Nos. CL10-CL13 were issued to pay the rate for letters weighing 5 grams or less.

REGISTRATION STAMPS

No. 1CLF1 —   No. 1CLF2 —
Block letter   Italic letter

No. 1CLF3 — Italic letter

1930, Sept. 10   *Perf. 13*
1CLF1 APL1 400r on 10000r,
   (15,050)   37.50   55.00
   Never hinged   55.00
1CLF2 APL1 400r on 10000r,
   (10,100)   55.00   72.50
   Never hinged   82.50
1CLF3 APL1 400r on 1300r,
   (5,000)   110.00   600.00
   Never hinged   175.00
   a. Inverted surcharge *(100)*   475.00
     Never hinged   700.00
  Nos. 1CLF1-1CLF3 (3)   202.50   727.50

E.T.A.
Empresa de Transportes Aereos Ltda.

Plane — APL3

Perf. 11½
1929, June 17   Litho.   Unwmk.
2CL1 APL3 200r brown & carmine
   (2,600)   275.00   300.00
2CL2 APL3 300r violet & red, perf 10¾
   (2,000)   135.00   190.00
   a. Plane inverted   2,250.
   b. Block of 4   140.00
2CL3 APL3 1000r blue & red
   (2,600)   135.00   225.00
2CL4 APL3 2000r green & red
   (2,600)   135.00   225.00
2CL5 APL3 5,000r yellow & red
   (2,600)   135.00   225.00
   a. Sheet of 16 stamps   3,250.
  Nos. 2CL1-2CL5 (5)   815.00   1,165.

The first E.T.A. printing was in sheets of 16 stamps (Nos. 2CL1, 2CL3-2CL5) in four horizontal rows of four stamps each. The stamps were printed on thick paper with thick, streaky yellowish to brownish gum. No. 2CL2 was printed in blocks of four. All 300r stamps have two straight edges.

Plane — APL4

1929
2CL6 APL4 200r brown & carmine   90.00
2CL7 APL4 300r violet & red, perf 11¼   90.00
   a. Sheet of 16 stamps   1,650.
   b. Block of 4   375.00
2CL8 APL4 1000r blue & red   90.00
2CL9 APL4 2000r green & red   90.00
2CL10 APL4 5,000r yellow & red   90.00
  Nos. 2CL6-2CL10 (5)   450.00

The second E.T.A. printing was in sheets of 16 stamps (Nos. 2CL6, 2CL8-2CL10) in four horizontal rows of four stamps each. The stamps are printed on thinner paper with whitish gum.

No. 2CL7 was printed in blocks of four. All 300r stamps have two straight edges.

A printing also exists in which the five stamps were in one setting of 20 subjects. Sheets thus printed were separated. Examples of the 300r stamp that can be attributed to this printing are rare. A few vertical strips with all five stamps have survived. Value single stamp, $1,600.

VARIG (Viacao Aerea Riograndense) Overprint in Red on No. 1CL8

No. 3CL1   Large "VARIG"

Small "VARIG"

Wmk. 116
1927, Nov. 9   Litho.   *Perf. 14*
3CL1 APL1a 700r on 1300r green
   (3,050)   70.00   55.00
3CL2 APL1a 1300r green, "VARIG" 12.5mm
   (15,000)   14.00   5.00
3CL3 APL1a 1300r green, "VARIG" 9.5mm
   (3,950)   275.00   45.00
  Nos. 3CL1-3CL3 (3)   359.00   105.00

Surcharge in Black on No. 1CL8

No. 3CL4   No. 3CL5

No. 3CL6   No. 3CL7

No. 3CL8

1928, Nov. 5
3CL4 APL1a   50r on 1300r green
   (4,950)   14.00   55.00
3CL5 APL1a 350r on 1300r green
   (15,000)   10.00   5.00
   a. Inverted overprint   2,250.   550.00
3CL6 APL1a 700r on 1300r green
   (10,000)   14.00   9.00
   a. Inverted overprint   525.00   900.00
3CL7 APL1a 1050r on 1300r green
   (3,000)   110.00   110.00
3CL8 APL1a 1400r on 1300r green
   (7,000)   27.50   14.00

Surcharge in Red on No. 1CL8

No. 3CL9   No. 3CL10

No. 3CL11   No. 3CL12

3CL9 APL1a 500r on 1300r green
   (2,500)   27.50   110.00
3CL10 APL1a 1000r on 1300r green
   (2,500)   65.00   165.00
3CL11 APL1a 1500r on 1300r green
   (2,500)   27.50   110.00
   a. Se-tenant pair (#3CL10 with #3CL11) *(50)*   *3,750.*   *3,750.*
3CL12 APL1a 2000r on 1300r green
   (2,500)   27.50   110.00
  Nos. 3CL4-3CL12 (9)   323.00   688.00

Varig Logo (Icarus) — APL5

Perf. 13½
1931, Apr. 22   Typo.   Unwmk.
3CL13 APL5   50r brn, *buff*
   (30,000)   2.75   7.25
3CL14 APL5 350r red
   (60,000)   5.50   1.00
3CL15 APL5 500r vio, *bluish*
   (20,000)   4.50   4.50
3CL16 APL5 700r red, *yel*
   (40,000)   14.00   2.00
3CL17 APL5 1000r claret, *rose*
   (16,000)   9.00   5.00
3CL18 APL5 1050r grn, *buff*
   (15,000)   9.00   5.50
3CL19 APL5 1400r red brn, *yel*
   (15,000)   25.00   5.50
3CL20 APL5 1500r dk grn, *lt grn*
   (16,000)   5.50   7.50
3CL21 APL5 2000r vio, *rose*
   (10,000)   40.00   11.00
3CL22 APL5 10000r black
   (8,000)   22.50   70.00
  Nos. 3CL13-3CL22 (10)   137.75   119.25

Nos. 3CL13-3CL22 are occasionally found with part of a sheet watermark.

APL6

1932
3CL23 APL6   50r olive grn, *rose*
   (40,000)   7.50   27.50
3CL24 APL6 500r stl blue, *straw*
   (30,000)   9.00   9.00

APL7

1933, June 27
3CL25 APL7   50r dp grn, *pale grn*
   2.00   4.50
3CL26 APL7 350r chestnut   14.00   2.00
3CL27 APL7 500r blue, *grn*   7.50   6.00
3CL28 APL7 1000r chnt, *rose*   35.00   22.50
3CL29 APL7 2000r dk blue, *rose*   27.50   22.50
  Nos. 3CL25-3CL29 (5)   86.00   57.50

APL8

1934, Jan. 18
3CL30 APL8   50r red, *rose*   4.50   1.50
3CL31 APL8 350r yelsh grn   4.50   1.00
3CL32 APL8 500r lilac, *rose*   4.50   2.75
3CL33 APL8 700r grn, *pale grn*   4.50   1.50
3CL34 APL8 1050r org, *pale rose*   2.00   6.00
3CL35 APL8 1400r grnsh blue, *blue*
   (30,000)   2.00   6.00
3CL36 APL8 1500r brn car, *blue*
   (25,000)   4.00   15.00
  Nos. 3CL30-3CL36 (7)   26.00   33.75

APL9

1934, June

3CL37	APL9	50r blue		
		(15,000)	2.75	35.00
3CL38	APL9	1000r olive brown		
		(10,000)	3.75	45.00
3CL39	APL9	1000r bluish grn		
		(15,000)	2.75	82.50
3CL40	APL9	1050r pale chnt		
		(10,000)	3.75	115.00
3CL41	APL9	1400r pale lil rose		
		(10,000)	2.75	70.00
3CL42	APL9	1500r org ver		
		(15,000)	2.75	70.00
3CL43	APL9	2000r red brown		
		(5,880)	37.50	150.00
		Nos. 3CL37-3CL43 (7)	56.00	567.50

SPECIAL DELIVERY
"E" and New Value in Black or Red

No. 3CLE1   No. 3CLE2

1928, Mar. 8

3CLE1	APL1a	700r on 1300r (#3CL1) (R)		
		(9,600)	70.00	70.00

1931, Nov. 23

3CLE2	APL1a	700r on 1300r (#3CL2) (B)		
		(2,000)	135.00	450.00

1933, Aug. 1

3CLE3	APL5	1000r on 1400r (#3CL19) (R)		
		(10,000)	14.00	18.00

1934, Jan. 31

3CLE4	APL5	1000r on 1050r (#3CL34) (R)		
		(17,860)	4.50	15.00

1934, June 16

3CLE5	APL5	1000r on 350r (#3CL31) (R)		
		(9,988)	4.50	60.00
		Nos. 3CLE1-3CLE5 (5)	228.00	613.00

REGISTRATION STAMPS
"R" and New Value in Black or Red

No. 3CLF1   No. 3CLF2

1928, Mar. 8

3CLF1	APL1a	400r on 1300r (#3CL2) (R)		
		(10,800)	70.00	70.00

1931, Nov. 23

3CLF2	APL1a	400r on 1300r (#3CL2) (B)		
		(1,920)	135.00	450.00

1933, Aug. 1

3CLF3	APL5	400r on 1050r (#3CL18) (B)		
		(10,000)	14.00	18.00

1934, Jan. 18

3CLF4	APL5	400r on 700r (#3CL33) (B)		
		(18,354)	5.00	15.00

1934, June 16

3CLF5	APL5	400r on 350r (#3CL31) (R)		
		(9,860)	5.00	60.00
		Nos. 3CLF1-3CLF5 (5)	229.00	613.00

LUFTSCHIFFBAU ZEPPELIN G.M.B.H.
Stamps for Graf Zeppelin Flights

Semi-official airmail stamps of Luftschiffbau Zeppelin G.m.b.H. paid the airmail fee for mail carried on Graf Zeppelin flights from Brazil to North America and Europe. The basic stamps were printed by the Government Printing Office, Berlin.

Graf Zeppelin
APL10

Wmk. 127

1930, May 17   Typo.   Perf. 14

4CL1	APL10	5000r green		
		(11,950)	40.00	45.00
		Never hinged	375.00	
		On cover		100.00
4CL2	APL10	10000r red		
		(11,880)	27.50	45.00
		Never hinged	45.00	
		On cover		100.00
4CL3	APL10	20000r blue		
		(5,865)	90.00	175.00
		Never hinged	175.00	
		On cover		275.00
		Nos. 4CL1-4CL3 (3)	257.50	265.00

No. 4CL3 exists with a surcharge "5" known as the Paraiba (or Parahyba) Provisional. The surcharged stamp was used in Paraiba, Brazil. Experiencing a shortage of 5,000r stamps, the local post office was authorized to surcharge a few of the 20,000r stamps it had on hand. The provisional also was used in Recife, Brazil. Expertization of this stamp is essential.

No. 4CL4   **Rs.5$000**

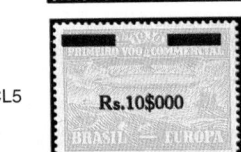

No. 4CL5   **Rs.10$000**

1930, May 17

4CL4	APL6	5000r on 20000r blue		
		(4,013)	225.00	300.00
		Never hinged	450.00	
		On cover		400.00
4CL5	APL6	10000r on 20000r blue		
		(4,975)	175.00	300.00
		Never hinged	375.00	
		On cover		400.00

No. 1CL8 Surcharged in Black

Graf Zeppelin Rs.5$000   **Graf Zeppelin Rs.10$000**

No. 4CL6   No. 4CL7

1930, May 25

4CL6	APL1a	5000r on 1300r green		
		(4,985)	45.00	90.00
		Never hinged	90.00	
		On cover		1,000.

4CL7	APL1a	10000r on 1300r green		
			55.00	
		Never hinged	110.00	

No. 4CL8

1930, May 25

4CL8	APL6	5000r green		
		(7,950)	135.00	100.00
		Never hinged	275.00	
		On cover		150.00
4CL9	APL6	10000r red		
		(8,100)	90.00	100.00
		Never hinged	175.00	
		On cover		150.00
4CL10	APL6	20000r blue		
		(3,390)	140.00	400.00
		Never hinged	275.00	
		On cover		450.00
		Nos. 4CL8-4CL10 (3)	365.00	600.00

The Brazil Post Office issued stamps for use on mail carried on Zeppelin flights. See Nos. C26-C30.

SPECIAL DELIVERY STAMPS

No. 191 Surcharged

1930   Unwmk.   Perf. 12

E1	A62	1000r on 200r dp blue	6.50	2.00
a.		Inverted surcharge	500.00	

POSTAGE DUE STAMPS

D1   D2

1889   Unwmk.   Typo.   Rouletted

J1	D1	10r carmine	2.10	1.40
J2	D1	20r carmine	3.25	2.00
J3	D1	50r carmine	5.50	4.00
J4	D1	100r carmine	2.10	1.40
J5	D1	200r carmine	65.00	15.00
J6	D1	300r carmine	6.75	8.00
J7	D1	500r carmine	6.75	8.00
J8	D1	700r carmine	11.00	14.00
J9	D1	1000r carmine	11.00	10.00
		Nos. J1-J9 (9)	113.45	63.80

Counterfeits are common.

1890

J10	D1	10r orange	.65	.30
J11	D1	20r ultra	.65	.30
J12	D1	50r olive	1.40	.30
J13	D1	200r magenta	6.75	.40
J14	D1	300r blue green	3.25	1.50
J15	D1	500r slate	4.50	3.00
J16	D1	700r purple	5.25	7.75
J17	D1	1000r dk violet	6.50	5.00
		Nos. J10-J17 (8)	28.95	18.75

Counterfeits are common.

Perf. 11 to 11½, 12½ to 14 and Compound

1895-1901

J18	D2	10r dk blue ('01)	2.10	1.25
J19	D2	20r yellow grn	8.75	3.00
J20	D2	50r yellow grn ('01)	11.00	5.50
J21	D2	100r brick red	7.25	1.25
J22	D2	200r violet	6.75	.60
a.		200r gray lilac ('98)	13.00	2.00
J23	D2	300r dull blue	4.00	2.25
J24	D2	2000r brown	13.00	13.00
		Nos. J18-J24 (7)	52.85	26.85

1906   Wmk. 97

J25	D2	100r brick red	8.75	3.00

Wmk. (97? or 98?)

J26	D2	200r violet	8.75	1.25
a.		Wmk. 97	350.00	85.00
b.		Wmk. 98	14.50	50.00

D3   D4

1906-10   Unwmk.   Engr.   Perf. 12

J28	D3	10r slate	.25	.25
J29	D3	20r brt violet	.25	.25
J30	D3	50r dk green	.30	.25
J31	D3	100r carmine	2.00	.60
J32	D3	200r dp blue	1.10	.30
J33	D3	300r gray blk	.40	.60
J34	D3	400r olive grn	1.40	.90
J35	D3	500r dk violet	40.00	40.00
J36	D3	600r violet ('10)	1.40	3.00
J37	D3	700r red brown	35.00	30.00
J38	D3	1000r red	1.60	3.25
J39	D3	2000r green	5.25	5.50
J40	D3	5000r choc ('10)	1.60	24.00
		Nos. J28-J40 (13)	90.55	108.90

Perf. 12½, 11, 11x10½

1919-23   Typo.

J41	D4	5r red brown	.30	.25
J42	D4	10r violet	.60	.25
J43	D4	20r olive gray	.30	.25
J44	D4	50r green ('23)	.30	.25
J45	D4	100r red	1.75	1.10
J46	D4	200r blue	8.75	2.10
J47	D4	400r brown ('23)	1.75	1.60
		Nos. J41-J47 (7)	13.75	5.80

Perf. 12½, 12½x13½

1924-35   Wmk. 100

J48	D4	5r red brown	.25	.25
J49	D4	100r red	.85	.70
J50	D4	200r slate bl ('29)	1.25	.50
J51	D4	400r dp brn ('29)	1.50	1.00
J52	D4	600r dk vio ('29)	1.75	1.10
J53	D4	600r orange ('35)	.75	.50
		Nos. J48-J53 (6)	6.35	4.05

1924   Wmk. 193   Perf. 11x10½

J54	D4	100r red	55.00	55.00
J55	D4	200r slate blue	6.00	6.00

Perf. 11x10½, 13x13½

1925-27   Wmk. 101

J56	D4	20r olive gray	.25	.25
J57	D4	100r red	1.25	.35
J58	D4	200r slate blue	4.50	.50
J59	D4	400r brown	3.25	2.00
J60	D4	600r dk violet	5.50	3.25
		Nos. J56-J60 (5)	14.75	6.35

Wmk. E U BRASIL Multiple (218)

1929-30   Perf. 12½x13½

J61	D4	100r light red	.50	.25
J62	D4	200r blue black	1.75	.50
J63	D4	400r brown	1.75	.50
J64	D4	1000r myrtle grn	1.75	.75
		Nos. J61-J64 (4)	5.75	2.00

Perf. 11, 12½x13, 13

1931-36   Wmk. 222

J65	D4	10r lt violet ('35)	.25	.25
J66	D4	20r black ('33)	.25	.25
J67	D4	50r blue grn ('35)	.50	.25
J68	D4	100r rose red ('35)	.50	.25
J69	D4	200r sl blue ('35)	2.00	.50
J70	D4	400r blk brn ('35)	3.25	2.00
J71	D4	600r dk violet	.50	.25
J72	D4	1000r myrtle grn	.65	.50
J73	D4	2000r brown ('36)	1.10	1.10
J74	D4	5000r indigo ('36)	1.25	1.00
		Nos. J65-J74 (10)	10.25	6.35

1938   Wmk. 249   Perf. 11

J75	D4	200r slate blue	2.75	1.00

1940   Typo.   Wmk. 256

J76	D4	10r light violet	1.10	1.10
J77	D4	20r black	1.10	1.10
J79	D4	100r rose red	1.10	1.10
J80	D4	200r myrtle green	2.40	1.10
		Nos. J76-J80 (4)	5.70	4.40

OFFICIAL STAMPS

Pres. Affonso Penna O1

Pres. Hermes da Fonseca O2

Unwmk.
1906, Nov. 15   Engr.   Perf. 12

O1	O1	10r org & grn	1.00	.30
O2	O1	20r org & grn	1.25	.30
O3	O1	50r org & grn	1.90	.30
O4	O1	100r org & grn	1.00	.30
O5	O1	200r org & grn	1.25	.30
O6	O1	300r org & grn	4.00	.60
O7	O1	400r org & grn	8.25	2.75
O8	O1	500r org & grn	4.00	1.60
O9	O1	700r org & grn	5.25	3.75
O10	O1	1000r org & grn	5.25	1.25
O11	O1	2000r org & grn	7.50	2.25
O12	O1	5000r org & grn	13.50	1.60
O13	O1	10,000r org & grn	13.50	1.40
		Nos. O1-O13 (13)	67.65	16.70

The portrait is the same but the frame differs for each denomination of this issue.

1913, Nov. 15   Center in Black

O14	O2	10r gray	.40	.55
O15	O2	20r ol grn	.40	.55
O16	O2	50r gray	.40	.55
O17	O2	100r ver	1.10	.40
O18	O2	200r blue	2.00	.40
O19	O2	500r orange	3.50	.65
O20	O2	600r violet	4.00	2.50
O21	O2	1000r blk brn	5.00	1.75
O22	O2	2000r red brn	7.50	1.75
O23	O2	5000r brown	8.75	3.50
O24	O2	10,000r black	16.00	7.75
O25	O2	20,000r blue	30.00	30.00
O26	O2	50,000r green	55.00	55.00
O27	O2	100,000r org red	200.00	200.00
O28	O2	500,000r brown	325.00	325.00
O29	O2	1,000,000r dk brn	350.00	350.00
		Nos. O14-O29 (16)	1,009.	980.35

The portrait is the same on all denominations of this series but there are eight types of the frame.

Pres. Wenceslau Braz — O3

Perf. 11, 11½
1919, Apr. 11   Wmk. 100

O30	O3	10r olive green	.50	9.00
O31	O3	50r green	1.25	1.25
O32	O3	100r rose red	2.00	.85
O33	O3	200r dull blue	3.50	.85
O34	O3	500r orange	9.25	40.00
		Nos. O30-O34 (5)	16.50	51.95

The official decree called for eleven stamps in this series but only five were issued.
For surcharges see Nos. 293-297.

NEWSPAPER STAMPS

N1

Rouletted
1889, Feb. 1   Unwmk.   Litho.

P1	N1	10r yellow	3.25	7.25
a.		Pair, imperf. between	125.00	140.00
P2	N1	20r yellow	9.00	9.00
P3	N1	50r yellow	15.00	12.50
P4	N1	100r yellow	7.50	3.00
P5	N1	200r yellow	3.00	2.50
P6	N1	300r yellow	3.00	2.50
P7	N1	500r yellow	30.00	15.00
P8	N1	700r yellow	3.00	20.00
P9	N1	1000r yellow	3.00	20.00
		Nos. P1-P9 (9)	76.75	91.75

For surcharges see Nos. 125-127.

1889, May 1

P10	N1	10r olive	3.00	1.25
P11	N1	20r green	3.00	1.25
P12	N1	50r brn yel	3.00	1.25
P13	N1	100r violet	4.50	3.00
a.		100r deep olive	7.50	20.00
b.		100r lilac	14.00	3.00
P14	N1	200r black	4.50	3.00
P15	N1	300r carmine	17.50	17.50
P16	N1	500r green	75.00	90.00
P17	N1	700r pale blue	50.00	55.00
a.		700r ultramarine	90.00	100.00
b.		700r cobalt	425.00	450.00
P18	N1	1000r brown	17.50	75.00
		Nos. P10-P18 (9)	178.00	247.25

For surcharges see Nos. 128-135.

N2

N3

White Wove Paper Thin to Thick
Perf. 11 to 11½, 12½ to 14 and 12½ to 14x11 to 11½
1890   Typo.

P19	N2	10r blue	22.50	10.00
a.		10r ultramarine	22.50	10.00
P20	N2	20r emerald	70.00	20.00
P21	N2	100r violet	22.50	14.00
		Nos. P19-P21 (3)	115.00	44.00

For surcharge see No. 137.

1890-93

P22	N3	10r ultramarine	5.00	3.00
a.		10r blue	9.00	4.00
P23	N3	10r ultra, *buff*	3.00	3.00
P24	N3	20r green	10.00	3.00
a.		20r emerald	10.00	3.00
P25	N3	50r yel grn ('93)	25.00	15.00
		Nos. P22-P25 (4)	43.00	24.00

For surcharges see Nos. 136, 138-139.

POSTAL TAX STAMPS

Icarus from the Santos-Dumont Monument at St. Cloud, France — PT1

Perf. 13½x12½, 11
1933, Oct. 1   Typo.   Wmk. 222

RA1	PT1	100r deep brown	.75	.25

Honoring the Brazilian aviator, Santos-Dumont. Its use was obligatory as a tax on all correspondence sent to countries in South America, the US and Spain. Its use on correspondence to other countries was optional. The funds obtained were used for the construction of airports throughout Brazil.

BRITISH CENTRAL AFRICA
'bri-tish 'sen-trəl 'a-fri-kə

LOCATION — Central Africa, on the west shore of Lake Nyassa
GOVT. — British territory, under charter to the British South Africa Company
AREA — 37,800 sq. mi.
POP. — 1,639,329
CAPITAL — Zomba

In 1907 the name was changed to Nyasaland Protectorate, and stamps so inscribed replaced those of British Central Africa.

12 Pence = 1 Shilling
20 Shillings = 1 Pound

Rhodesia Nos. 2, 4-19 Overprinted in Black

1891-95   Unwmk.   Perf. 14

1	A1	1p black	12.00	9.00
2	A2	2p gray green & ver	13.00	5.00
a.		Half used as 1p on cover ('95)		7,000.
3	A2	4p red brn & blk	13.00	6.25
4	A1	6p ultramarine	60.00	24.00
5	A1	6p dark blue	16.00	10.00
6	A2	8p rose & blue	20.00	35.00
a.		8p red & ultra	32.50	
7	A1	1sh bis brown	27.50	18.00
8	A1	2sh vermilion	42.50	60.00
9	A1	2sh6p gray lilac	80.00	105.00
a.		2sh6p gray purple	80.00	105.00
10	A1	3sh brn & grn ('95)	85.00	85.00
11	A2	4sh gray & ver ('93)	85.00	105.00
12	A1	5sh yellow	100.00	100.00
13	A1	10sh green	190.00	230.00
14	A3	£1 blue	1,000.	800.00
15	A3	£2 rose red	1,200.	1,500.
16	A3	£5 yel green	2,250.	—
17	A3	£10 red brown	4,500.	5,500.
		Nos. 1-13 (13)	744.00	792.25

High values with fiscal cancellation are fairly common and can be purchased at a small fraction of the above values. This applies to subsequent issues also. The most common fiscal marking consists of an undated double-circle cancel with the words "BRITISH CENTRAL AFRICA" between the circles, and a town name in the center. This cancel exists in various sizes and is usually applied in black.
For surcharge see No. 20.

Rhodesia Nos. 13-14 Surcharged in Black

1892-93

18	A2	3sh on 4sh gray & ver ('93)	400.00	400.00
19	A1	4sh on 5sh yellow	100.00	110.00

No. 2 Surcharged in Black, with Bar

1895

20	A2	1p on 2p	27.50	55.00
a.		Double surcharge	9,500.	7,000.

A double surcharge, without period after "Penny," and measuring 16mm instead of 18mm, is from a trial printing made at Blantyre. Value, $650.

A4

Coat of Arms of the Protectorate — A5

1895   Unwmk.   Typo.   Perf. 14

21	A4	1p black	19.00	16.00
22	A4	2p green & black	45.00	14.50
23	A4	4p org & black	80.00	52.50
24	A4	6p ultra & black	85.00	10.00
25	A4	1sh rose & black	100.00	42.50
26	A5	2sh6p vio & black	325.00	375.00
27	A5	3sh yel & black	190.00	60.00
28	A5	5sh olive & blk	250.00	250.00
29	A5	£1 org & black	1,150.	800.00
30	A5	£10 ver & black	6,750.	4,800.
31	A5	£25 bl grn & blk	14,500.	
		Nos. 21-28 (8)	1,094.	820.50
		Nos. 21-29, overprinted "SPECIMEN"	450.00	

1896   Wmk. 2

32	A4	1p black	4.25	8.00
33	A4	2p green & black	18.00	6.00
34	A4	4p org brown & blk	30.00	21.00
35	A4	6p ultra & black	45.00	16.00
36	A4	1sh rose & black	45.00	22.00

Wmk. 1 Sideways

37	A5	2sh6p vio rose & blk	180.00	160.00
38	A5	3sh yel & black	160.00	67.50
39	A5	5sh olive & blk	225.00	240.00
40	A5	£1 blue & blk	1,100.	600.00
41	A5	£25 bl grn & blk	10,000.	4,800.
		Overprinted "SPECIMEN"	210.00	
42	A5	£25 bl grn & blk	19,000.	—
		Overprinted "SPECIMEN"	390.00	
		Nos. 32-39 (8)	707.25	540.50
		Nos. 32-40, overprinted "SPECIMEN"	450.00	

A6

A7

1897-1901   Wmk. 2

43	A6	1p ultra & black	4.00	1.50
44	A6	1p rose & violet ('01)	3.50	.80
45	A6	2p yel & black	2.50	2.50
46	A6	4p car rose & blk	8.00	2.25
47	A6	4p ol green & violet ('01)	11.00	13.50
48	A6	6p green & black	60.00	5.25
49	A6	6p red brown & violet ('01)	7.00	3.75
50	A6	1sh gray lilac & black	13.50	8.50

Wmk. 1

51	A7	2sh6p ultra & blk	85.00	50.00
52	A7	3sh gray grn & blk	300.00	325.00
53	A7	4sh car rose & blk	100.00	100.00
54	A7	10sh ol & black	250.00	275.00
55	A7	£1 dp vio & blk	425.00	200.00
56	A7	£10 org & black	7,000.	2,500.
		Overprinted "SPECIMEN"	240.00	
		Nos. 43-54 (12)	844.50	788.05
		Nos. 43-55, overprinted "SPECIMEN"	350.00	

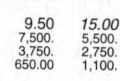
No. 52 Surcharged in Red

1897

57	A7	1p on 3sh	9.50	15.00
a.		"PNNEY"	7,500.	5,500.
b.		"PENN"	3,750.	2,750.
c.		Double surcharge	650.00	1,100.

A8

Type I — The vertical framelines are not continuous between stamps.
Type II — The vertical framelines are continuous between stamps.

1898, Mar. 11   Unwmk.   Imperf.
Type I
Control on Reverse

58	A8	1p ver & ultra	—	145.00
a.		1p ver & deep ultra	5,500.	150.00
b.		No control on reverse	4,750.	220.00
c.		Control double		525.00
d.		Control on front		3,900.
e.		Pair, one without oval	30,000.	

Type II
Control on Reverse

f.		1p ver & ultra	—	800.00

No Control on Reverse

g.		1p grayish blue & ver., initials on back	12,000.	1,100.
h.		No initials	6,000.	
i.		Oval inverted	30,000.	
j.		Oval double	—	
k.		Pair, with 3 ovals	—	

Perf. 12
Type I
Control on Reverse

59	A8	1p ver & ultra	5,000.	30.00
a.		1p ver & deep ultra		47.50
b.		Two diff. controls on reverse	—	800.00

No Control on Reverse

d.		1p ver & ultra	4,750.	115.00

There are 30 types of each setting of Nos. 58-59.
No. 58 issued without gum.
Control consists of figures or letters.
Initials are of Postmaster General (J.G. or J.T.G.).

A9

King Edward VII — A10

1903-04   Wmk. 2

60	A9	1p car & black	9.50	2.25
61	A9	2p vio & dull vio	4.50	2.25
62	A9	4p blk & gray green	3.25	11.00
63	A9	6p org brn & blk	4.00	4.00
64	A9	1sh pale blue & blk ('04)	5.00	15.00

Wmk. 1

65	A10	2sh6p gray green	65.00	100.00
66	A10	4sh vio & dl vio	90.00	105.00
67	A10	10sh blk & gray green	190.00	300.00
68	A10	£1 scar & blk	360.00	260.00
69	A10	£10 ultra & blk	7,750.	4,500.
		Overprinted "SPECIMEN"	475.00	
		Nos. 60-68 (9)	731.25	789.50
		Nos. 60-68, overprinted "SPECIMEN"	390.00	

1907   Wmk. 3

70	A9	1p car & black	8.50	3.50
71	A9	2p vio & dull vio	16,000.	
72	A9	4p blk & gray grn	16,000.	
73	A9	6p org brn & blk	40.00	60.00

Nos. 71-72 were not issued.
British Central Africa stamps were replaced by those of Nyasaland Protectorate in 1908.

A mint example with sheet border at right of the 2 pence violet (Scott No. 71) sold for U.S. $19,250 at a New York City auction in 2003.
A mint example with sheet border at right of the 4 pence gray & green (Scott No. 72) sold for U.S. $19,250 at a New York City auction in 2003.

BRITISH EAST AFRICA

ˈbri-tish ˈēst ˈa-fri-kə

LOCATION — East coast of Africa; modern Kenya. Included all of the territory in East Africa under British control.

Postage stamps were issued by the Imperial British East Africa Company

(IBEAC) in May 1900. Transferred to the Crown as a Protectorate July 1, 1895. Postal administration amalgamated with Uganda in 1901 with new stamps issued in July 1903 inscribed 'East Africa and Uganda Protectorates.'

16 Annas = 1 Rupee

STAMPS OF INDIA USED IN BRITISH EAST AFRICA

1890, July-Oct.

A1	½a green (#36)		600.
A2	1a maroon (#38)		540.
A3	1a6p bister brown (#39)		900.
A4	2a ultramarine (#40)		1,000.
A5	3a brown orange (#41)		1,000.
A6	4a6p green (#43)		325.
A7	8a red violet (#44)		540.
A8	1r gray (#46)		1,000.

As Nos. 1-3 ran out, the Mombasa Post Office utilized unoverprinted Indian stamps for mail. Stamps so used were cancelled with the 21mm Mombasa circular datestamp with indicia C. Indian stamps were also used at Lamu during this period, and stamps with Lamu cancellations are worth much more than the values above.

Stamps of India with British East Africa cancellations at later dates originate on ship mail.

A1

A2

A6

Queen Victoria — A3

1890   Wmk. 30   Perf. 14

1	A1	½a on 1p lilac	350.00	240.00
2	A2	1a on 2p grn & car rose	575.00	350.00
3	A3	4a on 5p lilac & bl	600.00	375.00

Covers: Commercial covers of this issue are rare. Values start at about $2,000.
Fournier and other forgeries exist.

Sun and Crown Symbolical of "Light and Liberty"
A4   A5

1890-94   Unwmk.   Litho.   Perf. 14

14	A4	½a bister brown	1.25	15.00
b.		½a deep brown	1.00	8.50
c.		As "b," horiz. pair, imperf. btwn.	1,925.	775.00
d.		As "b," vert. pair, imperf. btwn.	1,200.	600.00
f.		½a dull brown	6.50	9.00
15	A4	1a blue green	8.00	12.00
b.		1a deep blue green ('95)	1.00	
c.		"ANL" (broken "D" in "AND")	850.00	850.00
d.		As "c," imperf. pair	18,000.	
16	A4	2a vermilion	4.50	5.25
17	A4	2½a black, yel ('91)	5.50	6.00
a.		Horiz. pair, imperf. btwn.	6,000.	
b.		2½a black, pale buff ('92)	110.00	10.50
c.		2½a black, bright yellow ('93)	110.00	30.00
e.		As "c," horiz. pair, imperf. btwn.	1,700.	550.00
f.		As "c," vert. pair, imperf. btwn.	1,700.	725.00
18	A4	3a black, red ('91)	5.50	12.00
b.		Horiz. pair, imperf. btwn.	1,100	525.00
c.		Vert. pair, imperf. btwn.	850.00	450.00
d.		3a black, dull red ('91)	16.50	17.50
19	A4	4a yellow brown	3.00	11.00
20	A4	4½a brown vio ('91)	3.00	21.00
b.		4½a gray violet ('91)	42.50	18.00
c.		Horiz. pair, imperf. btwn.	2,100.	1,200.
d.		Vert. pair, imperf. btwn.	1,200.	600.00
21	A4	5a black, blue ('94)	1.50	13.00
		Handstamped "SPECIMEN"	52.50	

22	A4	7½a black ('94)	1.50	19.00
		Handstamped "SPECIMEN"	52.50	
23	A4	8a blue	6.75	11.50
24	A4	8a gray	350.00	350.00
25	A4	1r rose	7.50	11.00
26	A4	1r gray	275.00	275.00
27	A5	2r brick red	17.00	42.50
28	A5	3r gray violet	12.00	60.00
29	A5	4r ultra	15.00	60.00
30	A5	5r gray green	37.50	85.00
		Nos. 14-30 (17)	754.50	1,009.

Some of the paper used for this issue had a papermaker's watermark and parts of it often can be seen on the stamps.

Values for Nos. 14c, 14d, 17b, 17c, 18b, 18c, 20c, 20d, unused, are for examples with little or no original gum. Stamps with natural straight edges are almost as common as fully perforated stamps from the early printings of Nos. 14-30, and for all printings of the rupee values. Values about the same.

For surcharges and overprints see Nos. 31-53.

1890-93   Imperf.

Values for Pairs except No. 19b.

14a	A4	½a bister brown	1,200.	450.
14e	A4	½a deep brown	1,700.	725.
15a	A4	1a blue green	3,300.	850.
d.		"ANL" (broken "D")	18,000.	
16a	A4	2a vermilion	2,750.	975.
17d	A4	2½a black, bright yellow	1,200.	550.
18a	A4	3a black, red	1,150.	500.
19a	A4	4a yel brown	3,000.	1,350.
19b	A4	4a gray	1,500.	1,700.
20a	A4	4½a dull violet	1,950.	550.
23a	A4	8a blue	5,700.	1,150.
25a	A4	1r rose	14,500.	1,300.

A6

Handstamped Surcharges

1891   Perf. 14

31	A6	½a on 2a ver ("A.D.")	14,000.	1,000.
a.		Double surcharge		10,000.
b.		Original denomination not obliterated		3,000.
32	A6	1a on 4a yel brn ("A.B.")	21,000.	2,300.

Validation initials are shown in parentheses. See note below No. 35.

Manuscript Surcharges

1891-95

33	A6	½a on 2a ver ("A.B.")	17,000.	1,050.
a.		"½ Annas" ("A.B.")		1,200.
b.		Initialed "A.D."		6,500.
34	A6	½a on 3a blk, red ("T.E.C.R.")	700.	60.
b.		Initialed "A.B."	14,000.	2,750.
34A	A6	1a on 3a blk, red ("V.H.M.")	13,000.	2,250.
c.		Initialed "T.E.C.R."	23,000.	3,250.
35	A6	1a on 4a yel brn ("A.B.")	12,000.	2,200.

The manuscript initials on Nos. 31-35, given in parentheses, stand for Andrew Dick, Archibald Brown, Victor H. Mackenzie (1891) and T.E.C. Remington (1895).
Three persons applied the surcharge to No. 33, and two persons applied the surcharge to No. 35, resulting in different types.

A7

1894   Printed Surcharges

36	A7	5a on 8a blue	85.00	110.00
37	A7	7½a on 1r rose	85.00	110.00
		Set, handstamped "SPECIMEN"	100.00	

Stamps of 1890-94 Handstamped in Black

1895

38	A4	½a deep brown	90.00	30.00
b.		Inverted overprint		6,000.
c.		½a bister brown		2,700.
d.		½a pale brown	120.00	50.00
39	A4	1a blue green	200.00	135.00
a.		1a deep blue-green	—	3,250.
b.		"ANL" (broken "D")	3,000.	
40	A4	2a vermilion	220.00	115.00
41	A4	2½a black, yel	220.00	67.50
a.		2½a black, pale buff	—	2,250.
42	A4	3a black, dull red	105.00	60.00
43	A4	4a yel brown	62.50	42.50
44	A4	4½a gray violet	250.00	120.00
a.		4½a brown violet	1,450.	1,150.
45	A4	5a black, blue	300.00	170.00
b.		Inverted overprint		4,500.
46	A4	7½a black	150.00	100.00
47	A4	8a blue	115.00	90.00
b.		Inverted overprint		7,200.
48	A4	1r rose	67.50	60.00
49	A5	2r brick red	550.00	300.00
50	A5	3r gray violet	275.00	160.00
b.		Inverted overprint		85.00
51	A5	4r ultra	250.00	200.00
52	A5	5r gray green	525.00	325.00
		Nos. 38-52 (15)	3,380.	1,975.

Forgeries exist.

Double Overprints

38a	A4	½a	550.	525.
39a	A4	1a	600.	550.
40a	A4	2a	800.	575.
41a	A4	2½a	800.	525.
43a	A4	4a	575.	550.
44b	A4	4½a gray violet	850.	675.
44c	A4	4½a brown violet	3,300.	2,400.
45a	A4	5a	1,100.	1,000.
46a	A4	7½a	800.	675.
47a	A4	8a	725.	725.
48a	A4	1r	675.	675.
50a	A5	3r	1,100.	1,100.
51a	A5	4r	1,000.	1,000.
52a	A5	5r	1,600.	1,600.

Surcharged in Red

1895

53	A4	2½a on 4½a gray vio	225.00	90.00
a.		Double overprint (#44b)	1,200.	1,050.

Stamps of India 1874-95 Overprinted or Surcharged

British East Africa

a

b

c

1895   Wmk. Star (39)

54	A17	½a green	8.50	6.75
55	A19	1a maroon	8.00	7.25
56	A20	1a6p bister brn	5.25	5.00
57	A21	2a ultra	8.50	3.75
58	A28	2a6p green	12.00	3.25
59	A20(a)	2½a on 1a6p bis brn	115.00	57.50
a.		"½" without fraction line	135.00	
d.		As "a," "1" of "½" invtd.	1,100.	725.00
62	A22	3a orange	20.00	13.50
63	A23	4a olive green	50.00	37.50
a.		4a slate green	32.00	26.00
64	A25	8a red violet	35.00	60.00
		8a red lilac	110.00	85.00
65	A26	12a vio, red	27.50	40.00
66	A27	1r gray	115.00	80.00
67	A29	4a car & grn	55.00	160.00
a.		Dbl. ovpt., one sideways	525.00	1,100.
68	A30	2r bis & rose	110.00	180.00
69	A30	3r grn & brn	135.00	200.00

70	A30	5r vio & ul-		
		tra	160.00	200.00
a.		Double overprint	2,750.	

Wmk. Elephant's Head (38)

| 71 | A14 | 6a bister | 50.00 | 60.00 |
| | | Nos. 54-59,62-71 (16) | 914.75 | 1,114. |

"Brit1sh" for "British"

54a	A17	½a	7,250.	6,600.
55a	A19	1a	8,750.	4,750.
57a	A21	2a	7,750.	7,750.
58a	A28	2a6p		5,000.

"Br1tish" for "British"

54b	A17	½a	450.00	
55b	A19	1a	525.00	
56a	A19	1a6p	550.00	
57b	A21	2a	475.00	300.00
58b	A28	2a6p	600.00	325.00
59b	A20(a)	2½a on 1a6p	1,600.	
62a	A22	3a	600.00	600.00
63b	A23	4a	800.00	600.00
64b	A25	8a red vio	900.00	775.00
64c	A25	8a red lilac	1,600.	
65a	A26	12a	825.00	825.00
66a	A27	1r gray	1,900.	
67b	A29	1r carmine		
		& grn	1,600.	
71a	A14	6a	1,450.	

"Afr1ca" for "Africa"

54c	A17	½a	525.00	
55c	A19	1a	600.00	
56b	A19	1a6p	650.00	
57c	A21	2a	550.00	400.00
58c	A28	2a6p	725.00	425.00
59c	A20(a)	2½a on 1a6p	1,600.	
62b	A22	3a	800.00	
63c	A23	4a	900.00	725.00
64d	A25	8a red vio	925.00	800.00
64e	A25	8a red lilac	1,600.	
65b	A26	12a	950.00	
66b	A27	1r gray	1,900.	
67c	A29	1r carmine		
		& grn	1,600.	
71b	A14	6a	1,600.	

Inverted "a" for "t"

64f	A25	8a red lilac		17,000.
67d	A29	1r carmine		
		& grn	11,000.	

"Briti" for "British"

54d	A17	½a	2,000.	
55d	A19	1a	2,000.	
58d	A28	2a6p	2,000.	

"Eas" for "East"

| 58f | A28 | 2a6p | 1,200. | 1,600. |

"E st" for "East"

| 71c | A14 | 6a | | — |

Letter "B" handstamped

68a	A30	2r	7,250.	7,250.
69a	A30	3r	7,250.	7,250.
70b	A30	5r	6,500.	6,000.

No. 59 is surcharged in bright red; surcharges in brown red were prepared for the UPU, but not regularly issued as stamps. See note following No. 93.

Queen Victoria and
British Lions — A8

1896-1903   Engr.   Wmk. 2   Perf. 14

72	A8	½a yel green	5.00	1.00
73	A8	1a carmine	13.00	.50
a.		1a red	11.00	.50
74	A8	1a dp rose ('03)	27.50	5.00
75	A8	2a chocolate	10.00	7.00
76	A8	2½a dark blue	16.00	2.25
a.		Inverted "S" in "ANNAS"	190.00	75.00
b.		2½a violet blue	20.00	2.50
77	A8	3a gray	8.50	12.00
78	A8	4a deep green	8.00	4.25
79	A8	4½a orange	15.00	20.00
80	A8	5a dk ocher	9.25	7.00
81	A8	7½a lilac	9.00	27.00
82	A8	8a olive gray	9.50	7.00
83	A8	1r ultra	130.00	80.00
a.		1r pale blue	75.00	30.00
84	A8	2r red orange	80.00	35.00
85	A8	3r deep violet	80.00	40.00
86	A8	4r lake	72.50	85.00
87	A8	5r dark brown	70.00	50.00
a.		Thin "U" in "RUPEES"	1,650.	1,350.
		Nos. 72-87 (16)	563.25	383.00
		Set, ovptd. "SPECIMEN"	325.00	

Zanzibar Nos. 38-40,
44-46 Overprinted in
Black

1897   Wmk. Rosette (71)

88	A2	½a yel grn & red	67.50	55.00
89	A2	1a indigo & red	115.00	110.00
90	A2	2a red brn & red	47.50	26.00
91	A2	4½a org & red	60.00	37.50
a.		Right serif of left-hand "4" omitted	950.00	
b.		Fraction bar at right omitted	950.00	600.00

92	A2	5a bister & red	67.50	42.50
a.		"tish" omitted	1,900.	1,900.
93	A2	7½a lilac & red	60.00	42.50
a.		Ovptd. on front and back	2,000.	
b.		"tish" omitted	2,000.	
		Nos. 88-93 (6)	417.50	313.50

Nos. 92a and 93b were apparently caused by the presence of foreign matter on the plate during overprinting.

The 1a with red overprint, which includes a period after "Africa", was sent to the UPU, but never placed in use. No. 88, 90-93 and 95-100 also exist with period (in black) in sets sent to the UPU. Some experts consider these essays.

**Black Ovpt. on Zanzibar #39, 42
New Value Surcharged in Red**

1897

95	A2(a)	2½a on 1a	135.00	80.00
a.		Black overprint double	7,800.	
96	A2(b)	2½a on 1a	300.00	130.00
97	A2(c)	2½a on 1a	160.00	90.00
a.		Black overprint double	7,800.	
98	A2(a)	2½a on 3a	135.00	67.50
99	A2(b)	2½a on 3a	300.00	120.00
100	A2(c)	2½a on 3a	160.00	75.00
		Nos. 95-100 (6)	1,190.	562.50

A special printing of the 2½a surcharge on the 1a and 3a stamps was made for submission to the U.P.U. Stamps have a period after "Africa" in the overprint, and the surcharges included a "2" over "1" error in the fraction of the surcharge. These stamps were never placed in use. The fraction error appears on both the 1a and 3a stamps. Value, each, $1,500.

A10

1898   Wmk. 1   Engr.

102	A10	1r gray blue	95.00	42.50
a.		1r dull blue ('01)	95.00	47.50
b.		1r ultramarine ('03)	425.00	300.00
103	A10	2r orange	130.00	130.00
104	A10	3r dk violet	170.00	180.00
105	A10	4r carmine	475.00	550.00
106	A10	5r black brown	425.00	500.00
107	A10	10r bister	425.00	550.00
		Overprinted "SPECI-MEN"	75.00	
108	A10	20r yel green	1,000.	2,000.
		Overprinted "SPECI-MEN"	150.00	
109	A10	50r lilac	2,000.	7,500.
		Overprinted "SPECI-MEN"	300.00	
		Nos. 102a-107 (6)	1,720.	1,952.
		Nos. 102-107 (6)	1,645.	1,877.
		Nos. 102-106 ovptd. "SPECIMEN"	210.00	

Nos. 102-109 are often found with fiscal or Court Fee cancels. Stamps with these cancels can be purchased at a fraction of these values.

The stamps of this country were superseded by the stamps of East Africa and Uganda Protectorate.

BRITISH GUIANA

ˈbri-tish gē-ˈa-nə, -ˈä-nə

LOCATION — On the northeast coast of South America
GOVT. — British Crown Colony
AREA — 83,000 sq. mi.
POP. — 628,000 (estimated 1964)
CAPITAL — Georgetown

100 Cents = 1 Dollar

Catalogue values for unused stamps in this country are for **Never Hinged** items, beginning with Scott 242 in the regular postage section and Scott J1 in the postage due section.

**STAMPS OF GREAT BRITAIN USED
IN BRITISH GUIANA**

Numeral cancellation type A is pictured in the Crowned Circle Handstamps and Great Britain Used Abroad section.

1858-60

A03 (Georgetown/Demerara)

A1	A	1p rose red (#20)	400.	
A2	A	4p rose (#26)	210.	
A3	A	6p lilac (#27)	140.	
a.		6p lilac, blued paper (#27c)	—	
A4	A	1sh green (#28)	2,000.	

A04 (New Amsterdam/Berbice)

A5	A	1p rose red (#20)	1,000.	
A6	A	2p blue (#29, P8)	1,200.	
		Plate 7	1,200.	
A7	A	4p rose (#26)	450.	
A8	A	6p lilac (#27)	300.	
A9	A	1sh green (#28)	2,250.	

Values for unused stamps are for examples with original gum except for Nos. 6-12 and 35-53, which are valued without gum. Very fine examples of all stamps from No. 6 on will have four clear margins. Inferior examples sell at much reduced prices, depending on the condition of the individual stamp.

A1

1850-51   Typeset   Unwmk.   Imperf.

1	A1	2c blk, pale rose, cut to shape ('51)	275,000.	
2	A1	4c black, orange	75,000.	
a.		4c black, yellow	100,000.	
		Cut to shape	12,000.	
		Cut to shape	17,500.	
3	A1	4c blk, yellow (pelure)	110,000.	
		Cut to shape	18,500.	
4	A1	8c black, green	50,000.	
		Cut to shape	12,000.	
5	A1	12c black, blue	21,500.	
		Cut to shape	8,000.	
a.		12c black, pale blue	27,500.	
		Cut to shape	9,750.	
b.		12c black, indigo	27,500.	
		Cut to shape	9,250.	
c.		"1" of "12" omitted, cut to shape	200,000.	
		On cover	950,000.	
d.		"2" of "12" with straight bottom	22,500.	

These stamps were initialed before use by the Deputy Postmaster General or by one of the clerks of the Colonial Postoffice at Georgetown. The following initials are found: — E. T. E. D(alton); E. D. W(ight); G. B. S(mith); H. A. K(illikelley); W. H. L(ortimer). As these stamps are type-set there are several types of each value.

Ship and Motto of
Colony — A2

1852   Litho.

6	A2	1c black, magenta	10,000.	6,750.
		On cover		15,000.
7	A2	4c black, blue	18,500.	10,500.
		On cover		16,000.

Both 1c and 4c are found in two types. Examples with paper cracked or rubbed sell for much less.

Some examples are initialed E. D. W(ight). The reprints are on thicker paper and the colors are brighter. They are perforated 12½ and imperforate. Value $20 each.

Seal of the
Colony — A3

Without Line above Value

1853-59   Imperf.

| 8 | A3 | 1c vermilion | 6,000. | 1,750. |

A proof of No. 8 exists in reddish brown, value about $850.

**Full or Partial White Line Above
Value**

Types of One Cent:
I: Larger "O" in "ONE," 1mm from end of value tablet.
II: Smaller "O" in "ONE," ¾mm from end of tablet.
III: "O" like Type II, "N" and "T" of "CENTS" widely spaced.
IV: Smaller "O" in "ONE," 1¼mm from end of tablet, letters in "ONE" are closely spaced.

9	A3	1c red (I)	4,800.	1,750.
a.		Type II	5,500.	1,850.
b.		Type III	7,500.	2,150.
c.		Type IV	37,500.	15,000.
d.		1c brownish red (I)	10,000.	2,150.
e.		1c brownish red (II)	11,000.	2,500.
f.		1c brownish red (III)	—	3,250.
g.		1c brownish red (IV)	—	
10	A3	4c blue	2,400.	750.00
a.		4c dark blue	4,250.	975.00
b.		4c pale blue	1,750.	650.00

On No. 9, "ONE CENT" varies from 11 to 13mm in width.

**No. 10 Retouched; White Line
above Value Removed**

11	A3	4c blue	3,250.	925.00
a.		4c dark blue	6,000.	1,400.
b.		4c pale blue	2,150.	850.00

Reprints of Nos. 8 and 10 are on thin paper, perf. 12½ or imperf. The 1c is orange red, the 4c sky blue.

1860

Numerals in Corners Framed

| 12 | A3 | 4c blue | 5,500. | 750.00 |

A4

1856   Typeset   Imperf.

13	A4	1c black, magenta		9,500,000.
14	A4	4c black, magenta		15,000.
		With initials "C.A.W." (C.E. Watson)		16,000.
a.		4c black, rose carmine	45,000.	18,500.
15	A4	4c black, blue		100,000.
16	A4	4c black, blue, paper colored through		140,000.

These stamps were initialed before being issued and the following initials are found: — E. T. E. D.; E. D. W.; W. H. L.; C. A. W. No. 13 is unique.

Scott 13 sold for the equivalent of U.S. $9,500,000 in a New York City auction in 2014.

A5

**Wide space between value and
"Cents"**

**1860-61   Litho.   Perf. 12
Thick Paper**

17	A5	1c brown red ('61)	500.00	115.00
18	A5	1c pink	3,500.	300.00
19	A5	2c orange	350.00	65.00
a.		2c deep orange	325.00	60.00
20	A5	8c rose	825.00	130.00
a.		8c brownish rose	1,000.	160.00
21	A5	12c gray	750.00	55.00
a.		12c lilac	850.00	55.00
22	A5	24c green	1,600.	85.00
a.		24c deep green	2,500.	150.00

All denominations of type A5 above four cents are expressed in Roman numerals.
Bisects and trisects are found on covers. These were not officially authorized.
Nos. 21 and 21a are often found with a large red "5d" overprint of the same size as the stamp. This was an accounting marking to indicate postage payable by the Colonial Post Office to Great Britain for the overseas portion of postage collected.

The reprints of the 1c pink are perforated 12½; the other values have not been reprinted.

1862-65 — Thin Paper

23	A5	1c brown	925.00	275.00
24	A5	1c black ('63)	160.00	65.00
25	A5	2c orange	150.00	65.00
26	A5	8c rose ('63)	300.00	85.00
27	A5	12c lilac	400.00	55.00
a.		12c purple	400.00	42.50
b.		12c grayish purple ('63)	375.00	37.50
28	A5	24c green	1,600.	110.00

Perf. 12½ and 13

29	A5	1c black	80.00	25.00
30	A5	2c orange	95.00	27.50
31	A5	8c rose	350.00	97.50
32	A5	12c lilac	1,075.	140.00
33	A5	24c green	875.00	80.00

Medium Paper

33A	A5	1c black ('64)	70.00	55.00
33B	A5	2c deep orange ('64)	90.00	32.50
a.		2c orange ('62)	92.50	30.00
33C	A5	8c pink ('64)	300.00	80.00
33D	A5	12c lilac ('65)	1,250.	130.00
33E	A5	24c green ('64)	375.00	65.00
f.		24c deep green	450.00	90.00

Perf. 10

34	A5	12c gray lilac	800.00	97.50

Imperfs. are proofs. See Nos. 44-62.

A6

A7

A8

A9

A10

A11

1862 — Typeset — Rouletted

35	A6	1c black, *rose*	5,400.	850.
		Unsigned		650.
36	A7	1c black, *rose*	7,000.	1,400.
		Unsigned		750.
37	A8	1c black, *rose*	9,750.	1,400.
		Unsigned		1,200.
38	A6	2c black, *yellow*	5,500.	450.
		Unsigned		2,400.
39	A7	2c black, *yellow*	7,000.	550.
		Unsigned		2,750.
40	A8	2c black, *yellow*	9,750.	925.
		Unsigned		3,500.
41	A9	4c black, *blue*	8,000.	1,400.
		Unsigned		1,400.
42	A10	4c black, *blue*	10,750.	2,000.
a.		Unsigned Without inner lines	8,000.	1,400.
		As "a," unsigned	1,300.	
43	A11	4c black, *blue*	6,000.	1,100.
		Unsigned		1,175.

Nos. 35-43 were typeset, in sheets of 24 each. They were initialed before use "R. M. Ac. R. G.," being the initials of Robert Mather, Acting Receiver General.

The initials are in black on the 1c and in red on the 2c stamps. An alkali was used on the 4c stamps, which, destroying the color of the paper, caused the initials to appear to be written in white.

Uninitialed stamps are remainders, few sheets having been found.

Stamps with roulette on all sides are valued higher.

Narrow space between value and "Cents"

1860 — Thick Paper — Litho. — Perf. 12

44	A5	4c blue	450.00	80.00
c.		4c deep blue	800.00	120.00

Thin Paper

44A	A5	4c pale blue	150.00	42.50
d.		4c blue	170.00	55.00

Perf. 12½ and 13

44B	A5	4c blue	115.00	32.50

Medium Paper

1863-68 — Perf. 12½ and 13

45	A5	1c black ('66)	80.00	40.00
46	A5	2c orange	85.00	10.00
a.		2c orange red ('65)	85.00	10.00
47	A5	4c gray blue ('64)	100.00	25.00
a.		4c blue	130.00	32.50
48	A5	8c rose ('68)	400.00	27.50
a.		8c carmine	500.00	30.00
49	A5	12c lilac ('67)	650.00	50.00
a.		12c brownish lilac	750.00	55.00
		Nos. 45-49 (5)	1,315.	152.50

1866-71 — Perf. 10

50	A5	1c black	24.00	8.50
a.		1c gray black	26.00	17.25
51	A5	2c orange	60.00	5.00
a.		2c red orange	75.00	7.25
52	A5	4c blue	130.00	11.00
a.		Half used as 2c on cover		7,500.
b.		4c slate blue	150.00	15.00
c.		4c pale blue	120.00	11.00
53	A5	8c rose	300.00	37.50
a.		Diagonal half used as 4c on cover		
b.		8c brownish pink	350.00	42.50
c.		8c carmine	425.00	60.00
54	A5	12c lilac	300.00	27.50
a.		Third used as 4c on cover		
b.		12c pale lilac ('67)	325.00	27.50
c.		12c gray lilac	300.00	26.00
d.		12c brownish gray	300.00	27.50
		Nos. 50-54 (5)	814.00	89.50

1875-76 — Perf. 15

58	A5	1c black	65.00	9.00
59	A5	2c orange	185.00	17.00
a.		2c red orange	185.00	17.00
60	A5	4c blue	300.00	120.00
61	A5	8c rose	325.00	110.00
62	A5	12c lilac	925.00	100.00
		Nos. 58-62 (5)	1,800.	356.00

Seal of Colony
A12   A13

1863 — Perf. 12

63	A12	24c yellow green	275.00	15.50
a.		24c green	350.00	25.00

Perf. 12½ to 13

64	A12	6c blue	200.00	72.50
a.		6c milky blue	200.00	72.50
b.		6c greenish blue	200.00	77.50
c.		6c deep blue	300.00	100.00
65	A12	24c green	275.00	16.00
a.		24c yellow green	240.00	16.00
b.		24c blue green	375.00	25.00
66	A12	48c deep red	425.00	80.00
a.		48c rose	450.00	80.00
b.		48c pale red	400.00	80.00
		Nos. 63-66 (4)	1,175.	184.00

1866 — Perf. 10

67	A12	6c blue	200.00	40.00
a.		6c ultramarine	215.00	67.50
b.		6c milky blue ('67)	200.00	37.50
68	A12	24c yellow green	275.00	9.00
a.		24c green	375.00	11.00
b.		24c blue green	350.00	9.50
69	A12	48c rose red	400.00	37.50
a.		48c crimson	425.00	45.00
		Perforated "SPECIMEN"	240.00	
		Handstamped "SPECIMEN"	300.00	
		Nos. 67-69 (3)	875.00	86.50

For surcharges see Nos. 83-92.

1875 — Perf. 15

70	A12	6c ultra	1,075.	150.00
71	A12	24c yellow green	800.00	42.50
a.		24c deep green	1,600.	120.00

1876 — Typo. — Wmk. 1 — Perf. 14

72	A13	1c slate	3.25	1.75
a.		Perf. 14x12½		225.00
73	A13	2c orange	92.50	4.00
74	A13	4c ultra	150.00	15.00
a.		Perf. 12½	1,450.	250.00
75	A13	6c chocolate	100.00	12.75
76	A13	8c rose	160.00	1.00
77	A13	12c lilac	75.00	2.50
78	A13	24c green	80.00	4.00
79	A13	48c red brown	160.00	50.00
80	A13	96c bister	575.00	325.00
		Nos. 72-80 (9)	1,395.	184.00

See Nos. 107-111. For surcharges see Nos. 93-95, 98-101.

Stamps Surcharged by Brush-like Pen Lines

Type a

Type b

Type c

Type d

Surcharge Types:
Type a — Two horiz. lines.
Type b — Two lines, one horiz., one vert.
Type c — Three lines, two horiz., one vert.
Type d — One horiz. line.

On Nos. 75 and 67 — Perf. 10, 14

1878				
82	A13(a)	(1c) on 6c choc	52.50	140.00
83	A12(b)	(1c) on 6c blue	250.00	90.00
84	A13(b)	(1c) on 6c choc	425.00	135.00

On Nos. O3, O8-O10

85	A13(c)	(1c) on 4c ultra	425.00	120.00
a.		Type b	50,000.	6,000.
86	A13(b)	(1c) on 6c choc	650.00	135.00
87	A5(c)	(2c) on 8c rose	4,800.	400.00
88A	A13(b)	(2c) on 8c rose	600.00	240.00

On Nos. O1, O3, O6-O7

89	A5(d)	(1c) on 1c blk	300.00	90.00
89A	A5(d)	(2c) on 8c rose		
90	A13(d)	(1c) on 1c sl	220.00	80.00
91	A13(d)	(2c) on 2c org	450.00	80.00

The provisional values of Nos. 82 to 91 were established by various official decrees. The horizontal lines crossed out the old value, "OFFICIAL," or both.

The existence of No. 89A has been questioned by specialists. The editors would like to see authenticated evidence of its existence.

Nos. 69 and 80 Surcharged with New Values in Black

No. 92

No. 93

No. 94

No. 95

1881				
92	A12	1c on 48c red	55.00	6.00
a.		Without bar	—	725.00
93	A13	1c on 96c bister	6.00	10.00
a.		Without bar	—	
		Bar in red	—	
94	A13	2c on 96c bister	18.50	22.00
a.		Without bar	—	
		Bar in red	—	
95	A13	2c on 96c bister	80.00	150.00
a.		Bar in red	—	
		Nos. 92-95 (4)	159.50	188.00

Nos. O4, O5 and Unissued Official Stamps Surcharged with New Values

No. 96

No. 97

Nos. 98, 100   Nos. 99, 101

No. 102

1881				
96	A5	1c on 12c lilac (#O4)	155.00	85.00
97	A13	1c on 48c red brn	215.00	140.00
98	A13	2c on 12c lilac	700.00	500.00
99	A13	2c on 12c lilac	100.00	55.00
a.		"2" inverted		
b.		"2" double	950.00	550.00
c.		Pair, #98-99	1,600.	1,850.
d.		As "c," "2" doubled	6,000.	
e.		"OFFICIAL" obliterated by bar		—
100	A13	2c on 24c green	925.00	925.00
101	A13	2c on 24c green	110.00	65.00
a.		"2" inverted		
d.		Double surcharge	1,325.	
102	A12	on 24c green (#O5)	375.00	185.00

A27

Typeset

ONE AND TWO CENTS.
Type I — Ship with three masts.
Type II — Brig with two masts.

"SPECIMEN"

Perforated Diagonally across Stamp

1882 — Unwmk. — Perf. 12				
103	A27	1c black, *lil rose*, I	75.00	35.00
a.		Horiz. pair, imperf between		10,000.
b.		Without "Specimen"	1,200.	500.00
104	A27	1c black, *lil rose*, II	75.00	35.00
a.		Without "Specimen"	1,200.	525.00
105	A27	2c black, *yel*, I	95.00	60.00
a.		Without "Specimen"	975.00	650.00
b.		Diagonal half used as 1c on cover		—
106	A27	2c black, *yel*, II	110.00	65.00
a.		Without "Specimen"	975.00	650.00
		Nos. 103-106 (4)	355.00	195.00

Nos. 103-106 were typeset, 12 to a sheet, and, to prevent fraud on the government, the word "Specimen" was perforated across them before they were issued. There were 2 settings of the 1c and 3 settings of the 2c, thus there are 24 types of the former and 36 of the latter.

Type of 1876

1882 — Typo. — Wmk. 2 — Perf. 14				
107	A13	1c slate	16.00	.40
108	A13	2c orange	52.50	.35
a.		"2 CENTS" double		11,500.
109	A13	4c ultra	110.00	6.50
110	A13	6c brown	6.00	8.00
111	A13	8c rose	130.00	1.00
		Nos. 107-111 (5)	314.50	16.25

"INLAND REVENUE" Overprint and Surcharged in Black

A28   A29

4 CENTS and $4
Type I — Figure "4" is 3mm high.
Type II — Figure "4" is 3½mm high.

Type I	Type II

6 CENTS
Type I — Top of "6" is flat.
Type II — Top of "6" turns downward.

1889

112	A28	1c lilac	3.00	.55
113	A28	2c lilac	2.75	2.75
114	A28	3c lilac	1.60	.40
115	A28	4c lilac, I	13.00	.45
116	A28	4c lilac, II	24.00	7.50
117	A28	6c lilac, I	23.00	8.50
118	A28	6c lilac, II	15.00	6.50
119	A28	8c lilac	1.90	.65
120	A28	10c lilac	7.25	3.25
121	A28	20c lilac	26.00	22.50
122	A28	40c lilac	42.50	32.50
123	A28	72c lilac	80.00	72.50
124	A28	$1 green	575.00	650.00
125	A28	$2 green	275.00	300.00
126	A28	$3 green	275.00	300.00
127	A28	$4 green, I	650.00	775.00
127A	A28	$4 green, II	2,200.	2,750.
128	A28	$5 green	400.00	425.00
		Nos. 112-128 (18)	4,615.	5,358.

For surcharges see Nos.129, 148-151B.

No. 113 Surcharged "2" in Red

1889

129	A29	2c on 2c lilac	5.50	.55

Inverted and double surcharges of "2" were privately made.

A30	A31

1889-1903   **Typo.**

130	A30	1c lilac & gray	8.00	3.50
131	A30	1c green ('90)	1.10	.25
131A	A30	1c gray grn ('00)	2.10	6.00
132	A30	2c lilac & org	5.50	.25
133	A30	2c lil & rose ('00)	4.00	.40
134	A30	2c vio & blk, red ('01)	2.00	.25
135	A30	4c lilac & ultra	5.50	4.00
a.		4c lilac & blue	25.00	4.00
136	A30	5c ultra ('91)	3.75	.25
137	A30	6c lilac & mar	8.50	25.00
a.		6c lilac & brown	42.50	27.50
138	A30	6c gray blk & ul-tra ('02)	8.00	13.50
139	A30	8c lilac & rose	18.50	4.00
140	A30	8c lil & blk ('90)	7.50	2.25
141	A30	12c lilac & vio	10.00	4.00
142	A30	24c lilac & grn	7.50	4.00
143	A30	48c lilac & ver	30.00	13.00
144	A30	48c dk gray & lil brn ('01)	35.00	35.00
a.		48c gray & purple brown	60.00	50.00
145	A30	60c gray grn & car ('03)	75.00	250.00
146	A30	72c lil & org brn	34.00	55.00
a.		72c lilac & yellow brown	77.50	90.00
147	A30	96c lilac & car-mine	80.00	85.00
a.		96c lilac & rose	90.00	100.00
		Nos. 130-147 (19)	345.95	505.65

Stamps of the 1889-1903 issue with pen or revenue cancellation sell for a small fraction of the above quotations.
See Nos. 160-177.

1890   **Red Surcharge**

148	A31	1c on $1 grn & blk	3.00	.50
a.		Double surcharge	300.00	170.00
149	A31	1c on $2 grn & blk	2.50	1.10
a.		Double surcharge	120.00	—
150	A31	1c on $3 grn & blk	3.25	1.50
a.		Double surcharge	160.00	—
151	A31	1c on $4 grn & blk, type I	5.50	12.00
a.		Double surcharge	150.00	—
151B	A31	1c on $4 grn & blk, type II	15.00	40.00
c.		Double surcharge		
		Nos. 148-151B (5)	29.25	55.10

Mt. Roraima A32

Kaieteur (Old Man's) Falls — A33

1898   **Wmk. 1**   **Engr.**

152	A32	1c car & gray blk	9.25	2.50
153	A33	2c indigo & brn	35.00	4.50
a.		Horiz. pair, imperf. between	16,500.	
b.		2c blue & brown	40.00	4.50
154	A32	5c brown & grn	57.50	6.50
155	A33	10c red & blue blk	30.00	32.50
156	A32	15c blue & red brn	37.50	26.00
		Nos. 152-156 (5)	169.25	72.00

60th anniv. of Queen Victoria's accession to the throne.

Nos. 154-156 Surcharged in Black

1899

157	A32	2c on 5c brn & grn	4.00	3.25
a.		Without period	185.00	140.00
158	A33	2c on 10c red & bl black	4.00	2.75
a.		"GENTS"	70.00	92.50
b.		Inverted surcharge	750.00	875.00
c.		Without period	25.00	65.00
d.		Inverted surcharge	1,000.	1,000.
159	A32	2c on 15c bl & red brown	4.00	1.50
a.		Without period	80.00	80.00
b.		Double surcharge	1,100.	1,500.
c.		Inverted surcharge	875.00	1,100.
d.		As "a," inverted surcharge		
e.		As "b," one without period	10,000.	
		Nos. 157-159 (3)	12.00	7.50

There are many slight errors in the setting of this surcharge, such as: small "E" in "CENTS"; no period and narrow "C"; comma between "T" and "S"; dash between "TWO" and "CENTS"; comma between "N" and "T."

Ship Type of 1889-1903

1905-10   **Wmk. 3**
Chalky Paper

160	A30	1c gray green	12.00	1.35
a.		Booklet pane of 6		
161	A30	2c vio & blk, red	5.50	.25
162	A30	4c lilac & ultra	8.50	15.00
163	A30	5c lil & blue, bl	4.25	8.00
164	A30	6c gray black & ultra	18.00	50.00
165	A30	12c lilac & vio	27.50	55.00
166	A30	24c lil & grn ('06)	4.50	5.50
167	A30	48c gray & vio brn	17.00	27.50
168	A30	60c gray grn & car rose	17.00	110.00
169	A30	72c lil & org brn ('07)	40.00	85.00
170	A30	96c blk & red, yel('06)	42.50	55.00
		Overprinted "SPECIMEN"	42.50	
		Nos. 160-170 (11)	196.75	412.60

Ordinary Paper

160b	A30	1c gray green	7.50	.35
161a	A30	2c vio & blk, red	17.50	.25
162a	A39	4c lilac & ultra	16.00	22.50
163a	A30	5c lil & blue, bl	20.00	22.50
164a	A30	6c gray black & ultra	21.50	50.00
165a	A30	12c lilac & vio	29.00	50.00
166a	A30	24c lil & grn ('06)	14.00	20.00
167a	A30	48c gray & vio brn	32.50	52.50
168a	A30	60c gray grn & car rose	27.50	110.00

A34

Black Overprint

171	A34	$2.40 grn & vio	210.00	500.00
		Overprinted "SPECIMEN"	95.00	

Ship Type of 1889-1903
Ordinary Paper

Type I	Type II

TWO CENTS
Type I — Only the upper right corner of the flag touches the mast.
Type II — The entire right side of the flag touches the mast.

1907-10

171A	A30	1c blue green ('10)	16.00	3.00
172	A30	2c red, type I	21.00	1.10
b.		2c red, type II	10.50	.25
174	A30	4c brown & vio	3.50	1.35
175	A30	5c blue	18.50	6.00
176	A30	6c gray & black	16.00	8.50
177	A30	12c orange & vio	5.00	6.50
		Nos. 171A177 (6)	80.00	26.45

George V — A35

1913-17   **Perf. 14**

178	A35	1c green	4.50	.90
a.		bl grn ('17)	1.90	.30
179	A35	2c scarlet	3.75	.25
a.		2c carmine	1.60	.25
180	A35	4c brn & red vio	7.50	.40
181	A35	5c ultra	2.25	1.25
182	A35	6c gray & black	3.75	2.75
183	A35	12c org & vio	1.75	1.25

Chalky Paper

184	A35	24c dl vio & grn	4.25	5.00
185	A35	48c blk & vio brn	30.00	21.00
186	A35	60c grn & car	20.00	60.00
187	A35	72c dl vio & org brn	60.00	100.00

Surface Colored Paper

188	A35	96c blk & red, yel	32.50	65.00

Paper Colored Through

189	A35	96c blk & red, yel ('16)	22.50	65.00
		Nos. 178-189 (12)	192.75	322.80

The 72c and late printings of the 2c and 5c are from redrawn dies. The ruled lines behind the value are thin and faint, making the tablet appear lighter than before. The shading lines in other parts of the stamps are also lighter. Several paper shades of No. 189 exist.

1921-27   **Wmk. 4**

191	A35	1c green	5.75	.40
192	A35	2c rose red	6.50	.30
193	A35	2c dp vio ('23)	3.00	.25
194	A35	4c brn & vio	5.75	.25
195	A35	6c ultra	3.75	.40
196	A35	12c org & vio	3.50	2.00

Chalky Paper

197	A35	24c dl vio & grn	2.75	5.50
198	A35	48c blk & vio brn ('26)	12.00	4.50
199	A35	60c grn & car ('26)	12.50	57.50
200	A35	72c dl vio & brn org	37.50	80.00
201	A35	96c blk & red, yel ('27)	27.50	55.00
		Nos. 191-201 (11)	120.50	206.10

Plowing a Rice Field — A36

Indian Shooting Fish — A37	Kaieteur Falls — A38

Georgetown, Public Buildings A39

1931, July 21   **Engr.**   **Perf. 12½**

205	A36	1c blue green	3.00	1.75
206	A37	2c dk brown	2.75	.25
207	A38	4c car rose	2.50	.60
208	A39	6c ultra	3.00	3.50
209	A38	$1 violet	55.00	65.00
		Nos. 205-209 (5)	66.25	71.10
		Set, never hinged	100.00	
		Set, Perf "SPECIMEN"	130.00	

Cent. of the union of Berbice, Demerara and Essequibo to form the Colony of British Guiana.

A40

A41	Gold Mining — A42

Kaieteur Falls — A43

Shooting Logs over Falls — A44

Stabroek Market — A45

Sugar Cane in Punts — A46

Forest Road — A47

Victoria Regia Lilies — A48

Mt.
Roraima — A49

Sir Walter Raleigh
and Son — A50

Botanical
Gardens
A51

1934, Oct. 1   *Perf. 12½*

210	A40	1c green	.75	2.25
211	A41	2c brown	1.75	1.90
212	A42	3c carmine	.50	.25
b.		Perf. 12½x13½ ('43)	1.10	1.10
c.		Perf. 13x13½ ('49)	.75	.25
213	A43	4c vio black	2.50	3.75
a.		Vert. pair, imperf. horiz.	20,000.	20,000.
214	A44	6c dp ultra	5.50	7.50
215	A45	12c orange	.25	.25
a.		Perf. 13½x13 ('51)	.70	1.25
216	A46	24c rose violet	4.50	12.00
217	A47	48c black	10.00	10.00
218	A43	50c green	15.00	22.50
219	A48	60c brown	32.50	32.00
220	A49	72c rose violet	1.60	2.75
221	A50	96c black	37.50	37.50
222	A51	$1 violet	52.50	50.00
	Nos. 210-222 (13)		164.85	182.65
	Set, never hinged		290.00	
	Set, Perf "SPECIMEN"		250.00	

See Nos. 236, 238, 240.

Common Design Types
pictured following the introduction.

Silver Jubilee Issue
Common Design Type

1935, May 6   *Perf. 13½x14*

223	CD301	2c gray blk & ultra	.35	.25
224	CD301	6c blue & brown	1.50	5.50
225	CD301	12c indigo & grn	6.50	9.75
226	CD301	24c brt vio & ind	10.00	20.00
	Nos. 223-226 (4)		18.35	35.50
	Set, never hinged		27.50	
	Set, Perf "SPECIMEN"		140.00	

Coronation Issue
Common Design Type

1937, May 12   *Perf. 13½x14*

227	CD302	2c brown	.25	.25
228	CD302	4c gray black		.65
229	CD302	6c bright ultra	.55	2.15
	Nos. 227-229 (3)		.80	3.05
	Set, never hinged		1.60	
	Set, Perf "SPECIMEN"		130.00	

A52

A53

A54

A55

A56

A57

A58

Victoria Regia
Lilies and
Jacanas — A59

1938-52   **Engr.**   **Wmk. 4**   *Perf. 12½*

230	A52	1c green	.25	.25
		Never hinged	.35	
b.		Perf. 14x13 ('49)	.65	1.00
		Never hinged	1.10	
231	A53	2c violet blk, perf. 13x14 ('49)	.40	.25
		Never hinged	.60	
b.		Perf. 12½	.50	.25
		Never hinged	.65	
232	A54	4c black & rose, perf. 13x14 ('52)	.65	.25
		Never hinged	1.10	
a.		Perf. 12½	.90	.40
		Never hinged	1.50	
c.		Vert. pair, imperf. between	30,000.	30,000.
		Never hinged	37,500.	
233	A55	6c deep ultra, perf. 13x14 ('49)	1.50	.40
		Never hinged	2.15	
a.		Perf. 12½	1.00	.25
		Never hinged	1.35	
234	A56	24c deep green	2.75	.25
		Never hinged	3.75	
a.		Wmk. upright	20.00	12.50
		Never hinged	27.50	
235	A53	36c purple	3.50	.25
		Never hinged	5.00	
a.		Perf. 13x14 ('51)	3.00	.40
		Never hinged	4.50	
236	A47	48c orange yel	.90	.60
		Never hinged	1.35	
a.		Perf. 14x13 ('51)	1.25	2.25
		Never hinged	1.75	
237	A57	60c brown	13.50	10.00
		Never hinged	20.00	
238	A50	96c brown vio	8.00	3.25
		Never hinged	12.00	
a.		Perf. 12½x13½ ('44)	8.75	13.00
		Never hinged	13.00	
239	A58	$1 deep violet	17.50	.55
		Never hinged	27.50	
a.		Perf. 14x13 ('51)	300.00	700.00
		Never hinged	550.00	
240	A49	$2 rose vio ('45)	12.50	27.50
		Never hinged	18.50	
a.		Perf. 14x13 ('50)	16.00	37.50
		Never hinged	24.00	

241	A59	$3 orange brn ('45)	27.50	40.00
		Never hinged	40.00	
a.		Perf. 14x13 ('52)	29.50	55.00
		Never hinged	42.50	
	Nos. 230-241 (12)		88.95	83.55
	Set, never hinged		90.00	
	Set, Perf "SPECIMEN"		300.00	

The watermark on No. 234 is sideways.

> Catalogue values for unused stamps in this section, from this point to the end of the section, are for Never Hinged items.

Peace Issue
Common Design Type

1946, Oct. 21   *Perf. 13½x14*

242	CD303	3c carmine	.25	.45
243	CD303	6c deep blue	.80	.95
	Set, Perf "SPECIMEN"		110.00	

Silver Wedding Issue
Common Design Types

1948, Dec. 20   **Photo.**   *Perf. 14x14½*

244	CD304	3c scarlet	.25	.45

Engr.
Perf. 11½x11

245	CD305	$3 orange brown	24.00	28.00

UPU Issue
Common Design Types

Engr.; Name Typo. on 6c and 12c
Perf. 13½, 11x11½

1949, Oct. 10   **Wmk. 4**

246	CD306	4c rose carmine	.25	.55
247	CD307	6c indigo	1.90	2.00
248	CD308	12c orange	.25	.75
249	CD309	24c blue green	.25	.90
	Nos. 246-249 (4)		2.65	4.20

University Issue
Common Design Types

1951, Feb. 16   **Engr.**   *Perf. 14x14½*

250	CD310	3c carmine & black	.55	.55
251	CD311	6c dp ultra & black	.55	.70

POSTAGE DUE STAMPS

> Catalogue values for unused stamps in this section are for Never Hinged items.

D1

Perf. 13½x14

1940-55   **Typo.**   **Wmk. 4**

J1	D1	1c green, *chalky paper* ('52)	1.50	22.50
		Never hinged	2.25	
		On cover		100.00
a.		Wmk. 4a (error)	140.00	
		Never hinged	175.00	
b.		1c green, *ordinary paper* ('40)	5.00	12.00
		Never hinged	7.00	
J2	D1	2c black, *chalky paper* ('52)	4.00	10.00
		Never hinged	5.00	
		On cover		100.00
a.		Wmk. 4a (error)	145.00	
		Never hinged	175.00	
b.		2c black, *ordinary paper* ('40)	20.00	2.25
		Never hinged	27.50	
J3	D1	4c ultra ('52)	.35	14.00
		Never hinged	.45	
		On cover		200.00
a.		Wmk. 4a (error)	140.00	
		Never hinged	175.00	
J4	D1	12c carmine, *chalky paper* ('55)	17.50	45.00
		Never hinged	22.50	
a.		12c scarlet, *ordinary paper* ('40)	25.00	7.00
		Never hinged	40.00	
		On cover		175.00
	Nos. J1-J4 (4)		23.35	91.50

Cover values are for properly franked commercial items. Philatelic usages exist and sell for less.

WAR TAX STAMP

Regular Issue No. 179
Overprinted

1918, Jan. 4   **Wmk. 3**   *Perf. 14*

MR1	A35	2c scarlet	1.90	.25

The relative positions of "War" and "Tax" vary throughout the sheet.

OFFICIAL STAMPS

> Counterfeit overprints exist.

No. 50 Overprinted in
Red

1875   **Unwmk.**   *Perf. 10*

O1	A5	1c black	75.00	26.00
a.		Horiz. pair, imperf btwn.		22,500.

Nos. 51, 53-54, 68
Overprinted in Black

O2	A5	2c orange	300.00	17.50
O3	A5	8c rose	375.00	150.00
O4	A5	12c lilac	3,500.	600.00
O5	A12	24c green	2,750.	325.00

For surcharges see Nos. 87, 89, 89A, 96, 102.

**Nos. 72-76 Overprinted "OFFICIAL"
Similar to #O2-O5**

1877   **Wmk. 1**   *Perf. 14*

O6	A13	1c slate	350.00	70.00
a.		Vert. pair, imperf btwn.		27,500.
O7	A13	2c orange	160.00	18.00
O8	A13	4c ultramarine	140.00	35.00
O9	A13	6c chocolate	6,600.	725.00
O10	A13	8c rose	2,400.	550.00

The type A13 12c lilac, 24c green and 48c red brown overprinted "OFFICIAL" were never placed in use. A few examples of the 12c and 24c have been seen but the 48c is only known surcharged with new value for provisional use in 1881. See Nos. 97-101.

For surcharges see #85-86, 88A, 90-91.

BRITISH HONDURAS

'bri-tish hän-'dur-əs

LOCATION — Central America bordering on Caribbean on east, Mexico on north and Guatemala on west.
GOVT. — British Crown Colony
AREA — 8,867 sq. mi.
POP. — 130,000 (est. 1972)
CAPITAL — Belmopan

Before British Honduras became a colony (subordinate to Jamaica) in 1862, it was a settlement under British influence. In 1884 it became an independent colony.

12 Pence = 1 Shilling
100 Cents = 1 Dollar (1888)

Catalogue values for unused stamps in this country are for Never Hinged items, beginning with Scott 127 in the regular postage section, Scott J1 in the postage due section.

PRESTAMP POSTAL MARKINGS

Crowned Circle handstamp type II is pictured in the Crowned Circle Handstamps and Great Britain Used Abroad section.

1841
A1 II "Belize" crowned circle handstamp in red, on cover　　　　　4,750.

STAMPS OF GREAT BRITAIN USED IN BRITISH HONDURAS

Numeral cancellation type A is pictured in the Crowned Circle Handstamps and Great Britain Used Abroad section.

1858-60

A06 (Belize)
A2	A	1p rose red (#20)	1,100.
A3	A	4p rose (#26)	475.
A4	A	6p lilac (#27)	450.
A5	A	1sh green (#28)	2,000.

Values for unused stamps are for examples with original gum as defined in the catalogue introduction. Very fine examples of Nos. 1-37 will have perforations touching the design on at least one side due to the narrow spacing of the stamps on the plates. Stamps with perfs clear of the design on all four sides are extremely scarce and will command higher prices.

Queen Victoria — A1

1866　　Unwmk.　Typo.　Perf. 14
1	A1	1p pale blue	72.50	72.50
a.	Horiz. pair, imperf. btwn.			
b.	1p blue		100.00	82.50
2	A1	6p rose	425.00	195.00
3	A1	1sh green	400.00	145.00
a.	Vert. pair, Nos. 1, 3 with gutter btwn.		55,000.	
b.	Horiz. pair, Nos. 2, 3 with gutter btwn.		45,000.	

The 6p and 1sh were printed only in a sheet with the 1p. The 1p was later printed in sheets without the 6p and 1sh.

1872　　Wmk. 1　Perf. 12½
4	A1	1p pale blue	100.00	24.00
a.	1p deep blue ('74)		110.00	24.00
5	A1	3p reddish brn	180.00	90.00
a.	3p chocolate brn ('74)		200.00	110.00
6	A1	6p rose	400.00	55.00
a.	6p carmine rose ('74)		600.00	72.50
7	A1	1sh green	500.00	32.50
a.	Horiz. pair, imperf. btwn.		27,500.	
b.	1sh deep green ('74)		500.00	27.50

For surcharges see Nos. 18-19.
No. 7a is unique and has faults.

1877-79　　　　　Perf. 14
8	A1	1p blue	87.50	22.50
a.	Horiz. strip of 3, imperf. btwn.		27,500.	
b.	1p pale blue ('78)		95.00	21.00
9	A1	3p brown	170.00	24.00
10	A1	4p violet ('79)	300.00	10.00
11	A1	6p rose ('78)	500.00	225.00
12	A1	1sh green	325.00	13.50

For surcharges see Nos. 20-21, 29.

1882-87　　　　　Wmk. 2
13	A1	1p blue ('84)	67.50	18.00
14	A1	1p rose ('84)	27.50	16.00
a.	Overprinted "SPECIMEN"		200.00	
b.	Diagonal half used as ½p on cover			—
c.	1p carmine		60.00	22.50
15	A1	4p violet	100.00	5.75
16	A1	6p yellow ('85)	325.00	240.00
17	A1	1sh gray ('87)	300.00	200.00
a.	Overprinted "SPECIMEN"		75.00	

For surcharges see Nos. 22-26, 28-35.

Stamps of 1872-87 Surcharged in Black

1888　　Wmk. 1　Perf. 12½
18	A1	2c on 6p rose	350.00	275.00
19	A1	3c on 3p brown	20,000.	6,500.

Perf. 14
20	A1	2c on 6p rose	190.00	180.00
a.	Diagonal half used as 1c on cover			300.00
b.	Double surcharge		2,700.	—
c.	"2" with curved tail		3,500.	—
21	A1	3c on 3p brown	110.00	120.00

Wmk. 2
22	A1	2c on 1p rose	11.00	35.00
a.	Diagonal half used as 1c on cover			220.00
b.	Double surcharge		1,100.	1,100.
c.	Inverted surcharge		4,500.	4,000.
23	A1	10c on 4p violet	70.00	20.00
a.	Inverted surcharge			
24	A1	20c on 6p yellow	35.00	42.50
25	A1	50c on 1sh gray	475.00	725.00
a.	"5" for "50"		16,500.	

No. 25 with Additional Surcharge in Red or Black

26	A1	2c (R) on 50c on 1sh gray	60.00	115.00
a.	"TWO" in black		18,750.	15,000.
b.	"TWO" double (Blk + R)		18,750.	16,000.
c.	Diagonal half used as 1c on cover			350.00

A mint example of No. 26a with part of original gum realized the equivalent of U.S. $18,630 at a London auction in 2005.

A mint example of No. 26b with part of original gum realized the equivalent of U.S. $18,630 at a London auction in 2005.

Stamps of 1872-87 Srchd. in Black — c

1888-89
28	A1	2c on 1p rose	.80	2.75
a.	Diagonal half used as 1c on cover			110.00
29	A1	3c on 3p brown	4.00	1.75
30	A1	10c on 4p violet	22.50	1.00
a.	Double surcharge		3,500.	
31	A1	20c on 6p yel ('89)	18.00	50.00
32	A1	50c on 1sh gray	35.00	105.00
		Nos. 28-32 (5)	80.30	125.50

For other examples of this surcharge see Nos. 36, 47. For overprint see No. 51.

No. 30 with Additional Surcharge in Black or Red

1891
33	A1	6c (Blk) on 10c on 4p	1.75	2.25
a.	"6" and bar inverted		4,500.	1,200.
b.	"6" only inverted			6,500.
34	A1	6c (R) on 10c on 4p	1.90	2.50
a.	"6" and bar inverted		725.00	725.00
b.	"6" only inverted			6,500.

Stamps similar to No. 33 but with "SIX" instead of "6," both with and without bar, were prepared but not regularly issued. See No. 37.

No. 29 with Additional Surcharge in Black

35	A1	5c on 3c on 3p brown	1.60	2.00
a.	Double surcharge of "Five" and bar		450.00	850.00
b.	Wide space between "I" and "V" of "FIVE"		72.50	90.00

Black Surcharge, Type "c"
36	A1	6c on 3p blue	4.25	22.00

No. 36 with Additional Surcharge like Nos. 33-34 in Red

1891
37	A1	15c (R) on 6c on 3p blue	16.00	35.00
a.	Double surcharge			—

A8

1891-98　　Wmk. 2　　Perf. 14
38	A8	1c green	3.00	1.50
39	A8	2c carmine rose	4.00	.30
40	A8	3c brown	9.50	5.00
41	A8	5c ultra ('95)	14.50	.90
42	A8	6c ultramarine	13.00	2.50
43	A8	10c vio & grn ('95)	14.00	15.00
a.	10c dull purple & green ('01)		13.00	9.00
44	A8	12c vio & green	3.25	3.00
a.	12c pale mauve & green		24.50	7.50
45	A8	24c yellow & blue	6.75	21.00
a.	24c orange & blue		35.00	65.00
46	A8	25c red brn & grn ('98)	95.00	160.00
		Nos. 38-46 (9)	163.00	209.20

Numeral tablet on Nos. 43-46 has lined background with colorless value and "c."
For overprints see Nos. 48-50.

Type of 1866 Surcharged Type "c"
1892
47	A1	1c on 1p green	1.00	1.90

Regular Issue Overprinted in Black

1899　　　　Overprint 12mm Long
48	A8	5c ultramarine	25.00	3.00
a.	"BEVENUE"		150.00	175.00
49	A8	10c lilac & green	15.00	20.00
a.	"BEVENUE"		300.00	425.00
c.	"REVENU"		725.00	
50	A8	25c red brn & grn	3.75	42.50
a.	"BEVENUE"		175.00	425.00
c.	"REVE UE"		2,700.	
51	A1	50c on 1sh gray (No. 32)	235.00	450.00
a.	"BEVENUE"		5,500.	6,500.
		Nos. 48-51 (4)	278.75	515.50

Two lengths of the overprint are found on the same pane: 12mm (43 to the pane) and 11mm (17 to the pane). The "U" is found in both a tall, narrow type and the more common small type.

A9

Overprint 11mm Long
48b	A8	5c	27.50	10.00
49b	A8	10c	22.50	52.50
49d	A8	10c "REVENU"	850.00	950.00
50b	A8	25c	5.00	85.00
51b	A1	50c		640.00

1899-1901
52	A9	5c gray blk & ultra, bl ('00)	19.50	3.00
53	A9	10c vio & grn ('01)	13.50	9.00
54	A9	50c grn & car rose	30.00	72.50
55	A9	$1 grn & car rose	100.00	155.00
56	A9	$2 green & ultra	150.00	200.00
57	A9	$5 green & black	400.00	500.00
		Nos. 52-57 (6)	713.00	939.50

Numeral tablet on Nos. 53-54 has lined background with colorless value and "c."

King Edward VII — A10

1902-04　　Typo.　Wmk. 2
58	A10	1c gray grn & grn ('04)	2.25	27.50
59	A10	2c vio & blk, red	1.25	.40
60	A10	5c gray blk & ultra, blue	14.00	.70
61	A10	20c dl vio & vio ('04)	12.00	20.00
		Nos. 58-61 (4)	29.50	48.60
	Set, overprinted "SPECIMEN"		65.00	

1904-06　　Chalky Paper　Wmk. 3
62	A10	1c green	2.25	2.75
a.	1c green, ordinary paper		12.00	16.00
63	A10	2c vio & blk, red	1.75	.40
a.	2c vio & blk, red, ordinary paper		3.00	.35
64	A10	5c blk & ultra, bl ('05)	2.10	.25
65	A10	10c vio & grn ('06)	5.25	16.00
67	A10	25c vio & org ('06)	9.50	55.00
68	A10	50c grn & car rose ('06)	24.00	90.00
69	A10	$1 grn & car rose ('06)	70.00	100.00
70	A10	$2 grn & ultra ('06)	150.00	200.00
71	A10	$5 grn & blk ('06)	375.00	425.00
		Nos. 62-71 (9)	639.85	889.40

1909　　　　　Ordinary Paper
72	A10	2c carmine	14.00	.25
73	A10	5c ultramarine	2.50	.25

1911
74	A10	25c black, green	6.50	55.00

Numeral tablet on Nos. 61, 65-68, 74 has lined background with colorless value and "c."

King George V
A11　　　　　A12

1913-17　　Wmk. 3　Perf. 14
75	A11	1c green	4.50	1.75
a.	1c yellow green		9.00	3.00
76	A11	2c scarlet	5.00	1.75
	Complete booklet of 100 #76, in blocks of 10 (5x2)		4,500.	
a.	2c carmine		5.00	1.25
b.	2c bright scarlet ('15)		7.25	1.20
c.	2c red, bluish		15.00	9.50
77	A11	3c orange ('17)	1.25	.25
	Complete booklet of 100 #77, in blocks of 10 (5x2)		—	
78	A11	5c violet	2.50	1.10

Chalky Paper
79	A12	10c dl vio & ol grn	4.50	8.00
a.	10c purple & br green ('17)		20.00	30.00
80	A12	25c blk, gray grn	1.50	14.50
a.	25c black, emerald		2.10	34.00
b.	25c blk, bl grn, olive back		6.00	13.50
81	A12	50c vio & ultra, bl	26.00	17.50
82	A11	$1 black & scar	27.50	65.00
83	A11	$2 grn & dull vio	85.00	100.00
84	A11	$5 vio & blk, red	290.00	325.00
		Nos. 75-84 (10)	447.75	534.85

See No. 91. For overprints see Nos. MR2-MR5.

With Moire Overprint in Violet

1915
85	A11	1c green	4.50	22.00
a.		1c yellow green	.65	19.00
86	A11	2c carmine	4.25	.60
87	A11	5c ultramarine	.40	7.25
	Nos. 85-87 (3)		9.15	29.85

For 'War' overprint see No. MR1.

Peace Commemorative Issue

Seal of Colony and George V A13

1921, Apr. 28   Engr.
89	A13	2c carmine	5.50	1.00
	Never hinged		10.00	

Similar to A13 but without "Peace Peace"

1922   Wmk. 4
90	A13	4c dark gray	11.00	1.25
	Never hinged		18.50	

Type of 1913-17

1921   Typo.   Wmk. 4
91	A11	1c green	7.00	14.00

A14

1922-33   Typo.   Wmk. 4
92	A14	1c green ('29)	14.00	6.50
93	A14	2c dark brown	2.00	2.00
	Complete booklet of 100 #93, in blocks of 10 (5x2)		—	
94	A14	2c rose red ('27)	7.50	2.00
	Complete booklet of 100 #94, in blocks of 10 (5x2)		—	
95	A14	3c orange ('33)	32.50	5.00
96	A14	4c gray ('29)	19.00	1.00
97	A14	5c ultramarine	2.00	.70

Chalky Paper
98	A14	10c olive grn & lil	3.50	.40
99	A14	25c black, emerald	2.00	9.00
100	A14	50c ultra & vio, bl	5.75	16.00
101	A14	$1 scarlet & blk	15.00	27.50
102	A14	$2 red vio & grn	45.00	120.00

Wmk. 3
103	A14	25c black, emerald	8.00	55.00
104	A14	$5 blk & vio, red	275.00	300.00
	Nos. 92-104 (13)		431.25	545.10

For surcharges see Nos. B1-B5.

Common Design Types pictured following the introduction.

Silver Jubilee Issue
Common Design Type
Perf. 11x12

1935, May 6   Engr.   Wmk. 4
108	CD301	3c black & ultra	2.00	.60
109	CD301	4c indigo & grn	4.50	4.25
110	CD301	5c ultra & brn	2.25	2.50
111	CD301	25c brn vio & ind	6.50	8.00
	Nos. 108-111 (4)		15.25	15.35
	Set, never hinged		24.00	

Coronation Issue
Common Design Type
1937, May 12   Perf. 13½x14
112	CD302	3c deep orange	.25	.25
113	CD302	4c gray black	.35	.35
114	CD302	5c bright ultra	.60	1.75
	Nos. 112-114 (3)		1.20	2.35
	Set, never hinged		2.00	

Mayan Figures A15

Chicle Tapping — A16   Cohune Palm — A17

Local Products A18

Grapefruit Industry A19

Mahogany Logs in River — A20

Sergeant's Cay — A21

Dory — A22

Chicle Industry A23

Court House, Belize — A24   Mahogany Cutting — A25

Seal of Colony — A26

1938   Perf. 11x11½, 11½x11
115	A15	1c green & violet	.25	1.75
116	A16	2c car & black	.25	1.25
a.		Perf. 12 ('47)	2.75	1.25

117	A17	3c brown & dk vio	.50	1.00
118	A18	4c green & black	.50	.90
119	A19	5c slate bl & red vio	1.10	1.00
120	A20	10c brown & yel grn	1.25	.80
121	A21	15c blue & brown	2.25	.90
122	A22	25c green & ultra	1.75	1.50
123	A23	50c dk vio & blk	9.00	4.25
124	A24	$1 ol green & car	17.50	10.00
125	A25	$2 rose lake & ind	21.00	25.00
126	A26	$5 brn & carmine	22.50	37.50
	Nos. 115-126 (12)		77.85	85.85
	Set, never hinged		175.00	

Issued: 3c-5c, 1/10; 1c, 2c, 10c-50c, 2/14; $1-$5, 2/28.

Catalogue values for unused stamps in this section, from this point to the end of the section, are for Never Hinged items.

Peace Issue
Common Design Type
Perf. 13½x14

1946, Sept. 9   Engr.   Wmk. 4
127	CD303	3c brown	.25	.25
128	CD303	5c deep blue	.25	.25

Silver Wedding Issue
Common Design Types
1948, Oct. 1   Photo.   Perf. 14x14½
129	CD304	4c dark green	.25	.70

Engraved; Name Typographed
Perf. 11½x11
130	CD305	$5 light brown	22.50	52.50

St. George's Cay — A27

H.M.S. Merlin — A28

1949, Jan. 10   Engr.   Perf. 12½
131	A27	1c green & ultra	.25	1.25
132	A27	3c yel brn & dp blue	.25	1.50
133	A27	4c purple & brn ol	.25	1.75
134	A28	5c dk blue & brown	1.75	.75
135	A28	10c vio brn & blue grn	1.75	.45
136	A28	15c ultra & emerald	1.75	.45
	Nos. 131-136 (6)		6.00	6.15

Battle of St. George's Cay, 150th anniv.

UPU Issue
Common Design Types
Perf. 13½, 11x11½

1949, Oct. 10   Engr.   Wmk. 4
137	CD306	4c blue green	.40	.40
138	CD307	5c indigo	1.50	.60
139	CD308	10c chocolate	.55	3.00
140	CD309	25c blue	.90	.75
	Nos. 137-140 (4)		3.35	4.75

University Issue
Common Design Types
1951, Feb. 16   Engr.   Perf. 14x14½
141	CD310	3c choc & purple	.55	1.50
142	CD311	10c choc & green	.85	.65

SEMI-POSTAL STAMPS

Regular Issue of 1921-29 Surcharged in Black or Red

1932   Wmk. 4   Perf. 14
B1	A14	1c + 1c green	2.00	12.00
B2	A14	2c + 2c rose red	2.00	12.00
B3	A14	3c + 3c orange	2.50	25.00

B4	A14	4c + 4c gray (R)	13.00	27.50
B5	A14	5c + 5c ultra	7.50	15.00
	Nos. B1-B5 (5)		27.00	91.50

The surtax was for a fund to aid sufferers from the destruction of the city of Belize by a hurricane in Sept. 1931.

POSTAGE DUE STAMPS

Catalogue values for unused stamps in this section are for Never Hinged items.

D1

1923-64   Typo.   Wmk. 4   Perf. 14
J1	D1	1c black, chalky paper ('56)	1.25	26.00
	On cover			165.00
a.		1c black, white ordinary paper ('64)	37.50	45.00
b.		1c black, yellowish thin paper ('23)	2.75	21.00
J2	D1	2c black, chalky paper ('56)	1.25	22.50
	On cover			165.00
a.		2c black, yellowish thin paper ('23)	2.75	12.00
J3	D1	4c black, chalky paper ('56)	2.50	19.00
	On cover			275.00
a.		4c black, yellowish thin paper ('23)	1.75	9.50
	Nos. J1-J3 (3)		5.00	67.50

Nos. J1b, J2a, J3a, overprinted "SPECIMEN"   70.00

On cover values are for properly franked commercial covers. Philatelic usages also exist and sell for less.

WAR TAX STAMPS

Nos. 85, 75 and 77 Overprinted

1916-17   Wmk. 3   Perf. 14
With Moire Overprint
MR1	A11	1c green	.80	2.50
a.		"WAR" inverted	300.00	350.00

Without Moire Overprint
MR2	A11	1c green ('17)	1.75	5.50
MR3	A11	3c orange ('17)	5.50	5.50
a.		Double overprint	425.00	425.00
	Nos. MR1-MR3 (3)		8.05	17.50

Nos. 75 and 77 Overprinted

1918
MR4	A11	1c green	.25	.40
MR5	A11	3c orange	1.00	3.00

BRUNEI

'brü-ˌnī

LOCATION — On the northwest coast of Borneo
GOVT. — British Protectorate
AREA — 2,226 sq. mi.
POP. — 191,770 (1981)
CAPITAL — Bandar Seri Begawan

Although Brunei became a British protectorate in 1888, postage stamps were not issued until 1906, when the administration was transferred from the Sultan to the British Resident.

100 Cents (Sen) = 1 Dollar

> **Catalogue values for unused stamps in this country are for Never Hinged items, beginning with Scott 62.**

Star and Local Scene — A1a

Perf. 13 to 13½

			1895, July 22 Litho.	Unwmk.
A1	A1a	½c brown (shades)	4.75	24.00
		Never hinged	7.50	
A2	A1a	1c brown lake (shades)	3.75	17.50
		Never hinged	5.25	
A3	A1a	2c black	4.75	19.00
		Never hinged	7.00	
A4	A1a	3c deep blue	4.50	16.50
		Never hinged	6.50	
A5	A1a	5c deep blue green	7.50	20.00
		Never hinged	10.50	
A6	A1a	8c plum	7.50	37.50
		Never hinged	10.50	
A7	A1a	10c orange red	9.50	35.00
		Never hinged	13.50	
a.		Imperf pair	2,100.	
A8	A1a	25c turquoise	90.00	105.00
		Never hinged	125.00	
A9	A1a	50c yellow green	24.00	130.00
		Never hinged	35.00	
A10	A1a	$1 yellow olive	26.00	130.00
		Never hinged	37.50	
		Nos. A1-A10 (10)	182.25	524.50

These stamps were valid within Brunei and to Labuan. Prior to Brunei's admission to the UPU in 1906, all overseas mail was sent through Labuan, where Labuan stamps were required for despatch abroad.

Covers bearing examples of Nos. A1-A10, mostly in combination with stamps of Labuan, are usually philatelic. Values start at about $425. Commercial uses of these stamps exist.

Labuan Stamps of 1902-03
Overprinted or Surcharged in Red

			1906	Unwmk.	Perf. 12 to 16
1	A38	1c violet & blk		47.50	65.00
a.		Black overprint		2,500.	3,000.
2	A38	2c on 3c brn & blk		6.50	19.00
a.		"BRUNEI." double		4,500.	3,000.
b.		"TWO CENTS." double		6,500.	
3	A38	2c on 8c org & blk		32.50	80.00
a.		"TWO CENTS." double		13,000.	
b.		"TWO CENTS." omitted, in pair with normal		14,500.	
4	A38	3c brown & blk		38.50	100.00
5	A38	4c on 12c yel & black		7.00	6.00
6	A38	5c on 16c org brn & green		55.00	90.00
7	A38	8c orange & blk		14.00	37.50
8	A38	10c on 16c org brn & green		7.75	26.00

9	A38	25c on 16c org brn & green		125.00	150.00
10	A38	30c on 16c org brn & green		125.00	150.00
11	A38	50c on 16c org brn & green		125.00	150.00
12	A38	$1 on 8c org & blk		125.00	150.00
		Nos. 1-12 (12)		708.75	1,023.

The 25c surcharge reads: "25 CENTS."
Covers: Covers bearing this issue are rare.

Scene on Brunei River — A1

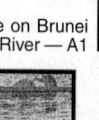

Type I	Type II

Two Types of 1908 1c, 3c:
Type I — Dots form bottom line of water shading. (Double plate.)
Type II — Dots removed. (Single plate.)

			1907-21	Engr.	Wmk. 3	Perf. 14
13	A1	1c yel green & blk			2.75	13.00
14	A1	1c green (II) ('08)			.70	2.50
a.		Type I ('19)			1.00	2.75
c.		Type II, "A" missing from wmk.			260.00	
d.		Type II, "C" missing from wmk.			260.00	
15	A1	2c red & black			3.75	5.25
16	A1	2c brn & blk ('11)			4.75	1.50
17	A1	3c red brn & blk			12.50	26.00
18	A1	3c car (I) ('08)			7.25	1.75
a.		Type II ('17)			120.00	45.00
19	A1	4c lilac & blk			9.00	12.00
a.		4c reddish purple & gray black ('10)			80.00	70.00
20	A1	4c claret ('12)			5.75	.90
21	A1	5c ultra & blk			60.00	110.00
22	A1	5c org & blk ('08)			8.50	8.50
23	A1	5c orange ('16)			19.00	25.00
24	A1	8c orange & blk			9.00	27.50
25	A1	8c blue ('08)			8.50	13.00
26	A1	8c lilac ('16)			7.25	32.50
27	A1	10c dk green & blk			5.25	9.00
28	A1	10c violet, yel ('12)			4.50	2.10
b.		10c violet, pale yellow ('22)			2.00	4.50
29	A1	25c yel brn & blue			37.50	57.50
30	A1	25c violet ('12)			6.75	22.50
b.		25c deep dull purple ('20)			14.00	20.00
31	A1	30c black & pur			30.00	26.00
32	A1	30c org & red vio ('12)			11.00	14.50
33	A1	50c brown & grn			18.00	27.50
34	A1	50c blk, grn ('12)			32.50	77.50
35	A1	50c blk, grnsh bl ('21)			10.00	42.50
36	A1	$1 slate & red			72.50	110.00
37	A1	$1 red & blk, bl ('12)			25.00	57.50
38	A1	$5 lake, grn ('08)			200.00	300.00
39	A1	$25 blk, red ('08)			650.00	1,200.
		Nos. 13-38 (26)			611.70	1,026.

Used value for No. 39 is for a canceled-to-order example dated before December 1941. CTOs dated later are worth about half the value given.

Stamps of 1908-21
Overprinted in Four
Lines in Black

			1922		
14b	A1	1c green		7.75	42.50
16a	A1	2c brown & black		7.75	50.00
18b	A1	3c carmine		8.75	55.00
20a	A1	4c claret		15.50	60.00
23a	A1	5c orange		21.00	65.00
28a	A1	10c violet, yellow		8.00	65.00
30a	A1	25c violet		17.00	100.00
35a	A1	50c greenish blue		60.00	175.00
37a	A1	$1 red & black, blue		90.00	225.00
		Nos. 14b-37a (9)		235.75	837.50

Industrial fair, Singapore, Mar. 31-Apr. 15

Type of 1907 Issue

			1924-37		Wmk. 4
43	A1	1c black ('26)		1.25	.90
44	A1	2c deep brown		1.25	9.00
45	A1	2c green ('33)		2.40	1.25

46	A1	3c green		1.25	7.75
47	A1	4c claret brown		1.75	1.50
48	A1	4c orange ('29)		2.40	1.25
49	A1	5c orange		8.25	2.00
50	A1	5c lt gray ('31)		21.00	14.00
51	A1	5c brown ('33)		21.00	1.20
52	A1	6c ultra ('27)		7.25	6.00
53	A1	8c gray ('33)		19.00	.90
54	A1	10c violet, yel ('37)		21.00	32.50
55	A1	25c dk violet ('31)		14.00	15.00
56	A1	30c org & red vio ('31)		25.00	19.00
57	A1	50c black, grn ('31)		13.00	17.50
58	A1	$1 red & blk, bl ('31)		29.00	90.00
		Nos. 43-58 (16)		188.80	219.75

For overprints see Nos. N1-N20.

Dwellings in Town of Brunei A2

			1924-31		
59	A2	6c black		17.00	12.00
60	A2	6c red ('31)		8.00	13.00
61	A2	12c blue		5.50	11.00
		Nos. 59-61 (3)		30.50	36.00

See note after Nos. N1-N19.

> **Catalogue values for unused stamps in this section, from this point to the end of the section, are for Never Hinged items.**

Types of 1907-24

			1947-51	Engr.	Perf. 14
62	A1	1c brown		.65	2.50
63	A1	2c gray		.75	6.00
a.		Perf. 14½x13½ ('50)		2.40	5.25
64	A2	3c dark green		1.20	6.50
65	A1	5c deep orange		1.00	1.75
a.		Perf. 14½x13½ ('50)		4.75	17.00
66	A2	6c gray black		1.25	6.00
67	A1	8c scarlet		.60	1.50
a.		Perf. 13 ('51)		.65	10.00
68	A1	10c violet		2.25	.40
a.		Perf. 14½x13½ ('50)		2.40	6.50
69	A1	15c brt ultra		2.10	.90
70	A1	25c red violet		3.25	1.25
a.		Perf. 14½x13½ ('51)		3.50	11.00
71	A1	30c dp org & gray blk		3.00	1.25
a.		Perf. 14½x13½ ('51)		2.40	16.00
72	A1	50c black		4.75	1.00
a.		Perf. 13		2.10	19.00
73	A1	$1 scar & gray blk		12.00	.90
74	A1	$5 red org & grn ('48)		20.00	22.50
75	A1	$10 dp claret & gray blk ('48)		85.00	35.00
		Nos. 62-75 (14)		137.80	87.45
		Set, perforated "SPECIMEN"		275.00	

Sultan Ahmed and Pile Dwellings A3

			1949, Sept. 22	Wmk. 4	Perf. 13
76	A3	8c car & black		1.50	1.50
77	A3	25c red orange & pur		1.50	1.90
78	A3	50c blue & black		1.50	1.90
		Nos. 76-78 (3)		4.50	5.30

25th anniv. of the reign of Sultan Ahmed Tajudin Akhazul Khair Wad-din.

Common Design Types pictured following the introduction.

UPU Issue
Common Design Types
Engr.; Name Typo. on 15c and 25c

			1949, Oct. 10	Perf. 13½, 11x11½
79	CD306	8c rose car		1.25	1.75
80	CD307	15c indigo		4.00	2.00
81	CD308	25c red lilac		1.25	1.50
82	CD309	50c slate		1.25	1.50
		Nos. 79-82 (4)		7.75	6.75

Sultan Omar Ali Saifuddin — A4

River Kampong A5

Perf. 13½x13

			1952, Mar. 1	Engr.	Wmk. 4
			Center in Black		
83	A4	1c black		.25	.60
84	A4	2c red orange		.25	.60
85	A4	3c red brown		.25	.35
86	A4	4c green		.25	.25
87	A4	6c gray		.60	.25
88	A4	8c carmine		.60	.60
a.		8c carmine lake & black ('56)		10.00	.25
89	A4	10c olive brown		.25	.25
90	A4	12c violet		6.00	.25
91	A4	15c blue		4.00	.25
92	A4	25c purple		3.00	.25
a.		25c reddish purple & black ('53)		5.50	1.10
93	A4	50c ultramarine		3.00	.35
a.		50c blue & black		7.75	.25
			Perf. 13		
94	A5	$1 dull green		1.75	1.75
a.		$1 bronze green & black ('58)		6.00	3.50
95	A5	$2 red		5.50	3.00
96	A5	$5 dp deep plum		22.50	8.50
a.		$5 brnish purple & black ('56)		26.00	8.50
		Nos. 83-96 (14)		48.20	17.25

See Nos. 101-114 in *Scott Standard Postage Stamp Catalogue*, Vol. 1.

OCCUPATION STAMPS

Issued under Japanese Occupation

Stamps and Types of 1908-37 Hstmpd. in Violet, Red Violet, Blue or Red

No. N1 Surcharged in Red

Perf. 14, 14x11½ (#N7)

			1942-44		Wmk. 4
N1	A1	1c black		11.00	28.00
N2	A1	2c green		75.00	140.00
N3	A1	2c dull orange		7.50	11.00
N4	A1	3c green		45.00	92.50
N5	A1	4c orange		6.00	16.00
N6	A1	5c brown		7.00	16.00
N7	A2	6c slate gray		85.00	275.00
N8	A2	6c red		900.00	775.00
N9	A1	8c gray (RV)		1,200.	1,050.
N10	A2	8c carmine		11.00	15.00
N11	A1	10c violet, yel		14.00	32.50
N12	A2	12c blue		42.50	32.50
N13	A2	15c ultra		32.50	32.50
N14	A1	25c dk violet		40.00	70.00
N15	A1	30c org & red vio		150.00	290.00
N16	A1	50c blk, green		60.00	85.00
N17	A1	$1 red & blk, bl		85.00	110.00
					Wmk. 3
N18	A1	$5 lake, green		1,400.	2,750.
N19	A1	$25 black, red		1,500.	2,750.

Overprints vary in shade. Nos. N3, N7, N10 and N13 without overprint are not believed to have been regularly issued.

			1944	Wmk. 4	Perf. 14
N20	A1	$3 on 1c black		15,000.	7,500.
a.		On No. 43		10,000.	—

BULGARIA

ˌbəl-ˈgar-ē-ə

LOCATION — Southeastern Europe bordering on the Black Sea on the east and the Danube River on the north
GOVT. — Monarchy
AREA — 42,823 sq. mi.
POP. — 8,929,332 (1983)
CAPITAL — Sofia

In 1885 Bulgaria, then a principality under the suzerainty of the Sultan of Turkey, was joined by Eastern Rumelia. Independence from Turkey was obtained in 1908.

100 Centimes = 1 Franc
100 Stotinki = 1 Lev (1881)

Catalogue values for unused stamps in this country are for Never Hinged items, beginning with Scott 293 in the regular postage section, Scott B1 in the semipostal section, Scott C15 in the airpost section, Scott E1 in the special delivery section.

Watermarks

Wmk. 145 — Wavy Lines

Wmk. 168 — Wavy Lines and EZGV in Cyrillic

Wmk. 275 — Entwined Curved Lines

AUSTRIAN POST IN BULGARIA

The Austrian Empire maintained post offices in various cities in Bulgaria. The six offices established are listed below. The Austrian Lloyd Agency operated its own office. Filipopoli was open during two periods, the first while under Austrian occupation during the military campaign of 1854-57.

Burgas (Eastern Rumelia)
Filipopoli
Rustschuck
Sofia
Varna
Varna Lloyd Agency
Widdin

Values for Nos. 2A1-2A23 are for stamps without defects tied to cover by complete strikes of town cancellations. Stamps tied to piece with legible full strikes of town cancellations sell for 5-30% of the on-cover value. Stamps with partial strikes of town cancellations sell for 25-50% of the on-piece value.

Stamps of Lombardy-Venetia canceled with Austrian-Levant postmark of Rustschuck in black

2A1	2s	yellow (#15)	1,250.
2A2	3s	green (#16)	1,400.
2A3	5s	rose (#17)	1,100.
2A4	10s	blue (#18)	825.
2A5	15s	yel brn (#19)	925.

Other Town Cancellations

Burgas (blk)	+2,100.
Burgas (bl)	+2,100.
Filipopoli	+625.
Rustschuck (bl)	+225.
Sofia	+1,250.

2A6	2s	yellow (#20)	1,600.
2A7	3s	green (#21)	825.
2A8	5s	rose (#22)	650.
2A9	10s	blue (#23)	400.
2A10	15s	yel brn (#24)	525.

Other Town Cancellations

Burgas (blk)	+800.
Burgas (bl)	+825.
Filipopoli	+10.
Rustschuck (bl)	+800.
Sofia	+825.
Widdin (blk)	+1,450.
Widdin (bl)	+4,250.

Stamps of Austrian Levant canceled with Austrian-Levant blue circular date stamp of Varna
Course Print

2A11	2s	yellow (#1a)	500.
2A12	3s	green (#2)	425.
2A13	5s	rose (#3)	100.
2A14	10s	blue (#4)	45.
2A15	15s	yel brn (#5)	55.
2A16	25s	gray lilac (#6b)	800.
2A17	50s	brown (#7)	4,750.

Fine Print

2A18	2s	yellow (#7C)	
2A19	3s	green (#7D)	250.
2A20	5s	rose (#7E)	110.
2A21	10s	blue (#7F)	40.
2A22	15s	yel brn (#7I)	875.
2A23	25s	gray lilac (#7J)	6,250.

Other Town Cancellations

Burgas	+525.
Filipopoli	+165.
Rustschuck	+70.
Sofia (blk)	+525.
Sofia (bl)	+2,500.
Varna, straight-line (blk)	+750.
Varna, straight-line (bl)	+1,150.
Varna, thimble (blk)	+325.
Varna, thimble (bl)	+525.
Varna, Bulgaria cancel	+750.
Varna Lloyd Agency	+525.
Widdin, thimble (blk)	+750.
Widdin, thimble (bl)	+1,150.

FRENCH IMPERIAL POST IN BULGARIA

Values for Nos. 3A1-3A8 are for stamps without defects tied to cover by complete strikes of the indicated cancels assigned to the French Post Office in Varna. Stamps off cover sell for 10-20% of the on-cover value.

Stamps of France canceled with small numerals "4018"

3A1	1c	ol grn, pale bl (#12)	—
3A2	5c	grn, grnsh (#13)	—
3A3	10c	bister, yelsh (#14)	475.00
3A4	20c	bl, bluish (#15)	500.00
3A5	40c	org, yelsh (#18)	475.00
3A6	80c	lake, yelsh (#19)	800.00
3A7	80c	rose, pnksh (#20)	750.00

Stamp canceled with large numerals "5103"

3A8	40c	pale org, yelsh (#35)	375.00

Lion of Bulgaria

A1   A2   A3

Perf. 14½x15

1879, May 1			**Wmk. 168**		**Typo.**
Laid Paper					
1	A1	5c black & orange		160.00	57.50
		On cover			2,500.
a.		5c black & yellow		90.00	20.00
		On cover			2,500.
2	A1	10c black & green		900.00	200.00
		On cover			800.00
b.		Vertical half used as 5c on cover			3,750.
3	A1	25c black & violet		440.00	40.00
		On cover			300.00
		On cover, single franking			600.00
a.		Imperf.			
b.		25c black & purple		225.00	17.00
		On cover			300.00
4	A1	50c black & blue		800.00	160.00
		On cover			1,250.
5	A2	1fr black & red		95.00	40.00
		On cover			1,500.

1881, Apr. 10					
6	A3	3s red & silver		32.50	6.50
		On cover			200.00
a.		3s deep carmine & gray		15.00	3.25
		On cover			200.00
7	A3	5s black & orange		32.50	6.50
		On cover			200.00
a.		Background inverted			2,400.
b.		5s black & yellow		15.00	2.50
		On cover			200.00
8	A3	10s black & green		175.00	20.00
		On cover			500.00
a.		10s black & deep green		85.00	10.00
		On cover			500.00
9	A3	15s dp car red & green		175.00	20.00
		On cover			250.00
a.		15s car & pale green		85.00	10.00
		On cover			250.00
10	A3	25s black & violet		900.00	100.00
		On cover			250.00
a.		25s black & purple		350.00	35.00
		On cover			250.00
11	A3	30s blue & fawn		32.50	16.00
		On cover			300.00
a.		30s deep blue & brown		17.50	10.00
		On cover			300.00

1882, Dec. 4					
12	A3	3s orange & yel		1.60	.80
		On cover			20.00
a.		Background inverted		4,000.	4,000.
13	A3	5s green & pale green		12.50	1.20
		On cover			20.00
a.		5s rose & pale rose (error)		3,000.	3,000.
		On cover			4,000.
14	A3	10s rose & pale rose		16.00	1.20
		On cover			20.00
15	A3	15s red vio & pale lil		16.00	1.20
		On cover			25.00
16	A3	25s blue & pale blue		14.50	1.60
		On cover			20.00
17	A3	30s violet & grn		14.50	1.20
		On cover			30.00
18	A3	50s blue & pink		14.50	1.20
		On cover			30.00
		Nos. 12-18 (7)		89.60	8.40

See Nos. 207-210, 286.

Surcharged in Black, Carmine or Vermilion

A4   A5

1884, May 1			**Typo. Surcharge**	
19	A4	3s on 10s rose (Bk)	240.00	80.00
20	A4	5s on 30s blue & fawn (C)	160.00	100.00
20A	A4	5s on 30s bl & fawn (V)	2,800.	2,250.
21	A5	15s on 25s blue (C)	175.00	100.00

On some values the surcharge may be found inverted or double.

1885, Apr. 5			**Litho. Surcharge**	
21B	A4	3s on 10s rose (Bk)	80.00	80.00
21C	A4	5s on 30s bl & fawn (V)	80.00	80.00
21D	A5	15s on 25s blue (V)	145.00	100.00
22	A5	50s on 1fr blk & red (Bk)	550.00	360.00
		On cover		800.00

Forgeries of Nos. 19-22 are plentiful.

Word below left star in oval has 5 letters
A6

Third letter below left star is "A"
A7

1885, May 25				
23	A6	1s gray vio & pale gray	28.00	9.50
		On wrapper or newsprint		110.00
24	A7	2s sl grn & pale gray	28.00	6.75
		On cover		75.00

Word below left star has 4 letters
A8

Third letter below left star is "b" with cross-bar in upper half
A9

A10

1886-87				
25	A8	1s gray vio & pale gray	2.00	.40
26	A9	2s sl grn & pale gray	2.00	.40
27	A10	1 l black & red ('87)	57.50	7.25
		Nos. 25-27 (3)	61.50	8.05

For surcharge see No. 40.

A11

Perf. 10½, 11, 11½, 13, 13½					
1889		**Wove Paper**	**Unwmk.**		
28	A11	1s lilac		1.60	.40
		On wrapper or newspaper			75.00
29	A11	2s gray		2.40	1.20
30	A11	3s bister brown		1.60	.40
31	A11	5s yellow green		12.00	.90
a.		Vert. pair, imperf. btwn.			
32	A11	10s rose		12.00	.80
33	A11	15s orange		80.00	.80
34	A11	25s blue		12.00	.80
35	A11	30s dk brown		13.50	.80
36	A11	50s green		.80	.40
37	A11	1 l orange red		.80	.80
		Nos. 28-37 (10)		136.70	6.70

The 10s orange is a proof.
Nos. 28-34 exist imperforate. Value, set $225.
See Nos. 39, 41-42. For overprints and surcharges see Nos. 38, 55-56, 77-81, 113.

No. 35 Surcharged in Black

1892, Jan. 26				
38	A11	15s on 30s brn	40.00	1.60
a.		Inverted surcharge	70.00	52.50

1894			**Perf. 10½, 11, 11½**	
Pelure Paper				
39	A11	10s red	7.00	2.00
a.		Imperf.	57.50	

No. 26 Surcharged in
Red

Wmk. Wavy Lines (168)
1895, Oct. 25   **Perf. 14½x15**
Laid Paper

40	A9	1s on 2s	1.20	.40
a.		Inverted surcharge	8.00	6.50
b.		Double surcharge	62.50	62.50
c.		Pair, one without surcharge	125.00	125.00

This surcharge on No. 24 is a proof.

Wmk. Coat of Arms in the Sheet
1896, Apr. 30   **Perf. 11½, 13**
Wove Paper

41	A11	2 l rose & pale rose	3.25	2.40
42	A11	3 l black & buff	4.75	5.50

Coat of Arms A14   Cherry Wood Cannon A15

1896, Feb. 2   **Perf. 13**

43	A14	1s blue green	.35	.25
		On wrapper or newspaper		75.00
44	A14	5s dark blue	.35	.25
45	A14	15s purple	.60	.30
46	A14	25s red	5.75	1.00
		Nos. 43-46 (4)	7.05	1.80

Baptism of Prince Boris.
Examples of Nos. 41-46 from sheet edges show no watermark.
Nos. 43, 45-46 were also printed on rough unwatermarked paper.

1901, Apr. 20   **Litho.**   **Unwmk.**

53	A15	5s carmine	1.50	1.10
54	A15	15s yellow green	1.50	1.10

Insurrection of Independence in April, 1876, 25th anniversary.
Exist imperf. Forgeries exist.

Nos. 30 and 36 Surcharged in Black

1901, Mar. 24   **Typo.**

55	A11	5s on 3s bister brn	2.50	1.60
a.		Inverted surcharge	45.00	45.00
b.		Pair, one without surcharge	70.00	70.00
56	A11	10s on 50s green	2.50	1.60
a.		Inverted surcharge	50.00	50.00
b.		Pair, one without surcharge	72.50	72.50

Tsar Ferdinand — A17

Type I   Type II

ONE LEV:
Type I — The numerals in the upper corners have, at the top, a sloping serif on the left side and a short straight serif on the right.
Type II — The numerals in the upper corners are of ordinary shape without the serif at the right.

1901, Oct. 1-1905   **Typo.**   **Perf. 12½**

57	A17	1s vio & gray blk	.25	.25
58	A17	2s brnz grn & ind	.25	.25
a.		Imperf.		
59	A17	3s orange & ind	.25	.25
60	A17	5s emerald & brn	2.25	.25

61	A17	10s rose & blk	1.50	.25
62	A17	15s claret & gray blk	.80	.25
63	A17	25s blue & blk	.80	.25
64	A17	30s bis & gray blk	18.00	.30
65	A17	50s dk blue & brn	1.00	.25
66	A17	1 l red org & brnz grn, type I	0.80	1.20
67	A17	1 l brn red & brnz grn, II ('05)	55.00	4.00
68	A17	2 l carmine & blk	5.00	.85
69	A17	3 l slate & red brn	6.00	2.25
		Nos. 57-69 (13)	93.60	10.65

For surcharges see Nos. 73, 83-85, 87-88.

Fighting at Shipka Pass — A18

1902, Aug. 29   **Litho.**   **Perf. 11½**

70	A18	5s lake	3.00	1.00
71	A18	10s blue green	3.00	1.00
72	A18	15s blue	12.00	5.00
		Nos. 70-72 (3)	18.00	7.00

Battle of Shipka Pass, 1877.
Imperf. copies are proofs.
Excellent forgeries of Nos. 70 to 72 exist.

No. 62 Surcharged in Black

1903, Oct. 1   **Perf. 12½**

73	A17	10s on 15s	6.00	.40
a.		Inverted surcharge	57.50	50.00
b.		Double surcharge	57.50	50.00
c.		Pair, one without surcharge	100.00	100.00
d.		10s on 10s rose & black	325.00	325.00

Ferdinand in 1887 and 1907 — A19

1907, Aug. 12   **Litho.**   **Perf. 11½**

74	A19	5s deep green	17.50	1.75
75	A19	10s red brown	25.00	1.75
76	A19	25s deep blue	60.00	3.50
		Nos. 74-76 (3)	102.50	7.00

Accession to the throne of Ferdinand I, 20th anniversary.
Nos. 74-76 imperf. are proofs. Nos. 74-76 exist in pairs imperforate between.

Stamps of 1889 Overprinted

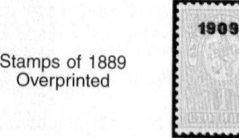

1909

77	A11	1s lilac	1.60	.70
a.		Inverted overprint	21.00	17.50
b.		Double overprint, one inverted	24.00	24.00
78	A11	5s yellow green	1.60	.70
a.		Inverted overprint	25.00	25.00
b.		Double overprint	25.00	25.00

With Additional Surcharge

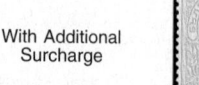

79	A11	5s on 30s brown (Bk)	2.75	.70
a.		"5" double	700.00	550.00
b.		"1990" for "1909"		
80	A11	10s on 15s org (Bk)	2.75	.95
a.		Inverted surcharge	17.50	17.50
b.		"1909" omitted	27.50	27.50

81	A11	10s on 50s dk grn (R)	2.75	.95
a.		"1990" for "1909"	100.00	100.00
b.		Black surcharge	52.50	52.50

Nos. 62 & 64 Surcharged with Value Only

83	A17	5s on 15s (Bl)	2.40	.80
a.		Inverted surcharge	21.00	21.00
84	A17	10s on 15s (Bl)	6.25	.55
a.		Inverted surcharge	21.00	21.00
85	A17	25s on 30s (R)	8.00	1.25
a.		Double surcharge	75.00	75.00
b.		"2" of "25" omitted	87.50	87.50
c.		Blue surcharge	300.00	175.00

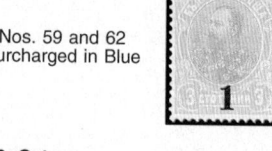

Nos. 59 and 62 Surcharged in Blue

1910, Oct.

87	A17	1s on 3s	4.25	1.60
a.		"1910" omitted	21.00	
88	A17	5s on 15s	4.25	1.60

Tsar Assen's Tower (Crown over lion) A20   Tsar Ferdinand A21

City of Trnovo A22   Tsar Ferdinand A23

Ferdinand A24   Isker River A25

Ferdinand A26   Rila Monastery (Crown at UR) A27

Tsar and Princes — A28   Ferdinand in Robes of Ancient Tsars — A29

Monastery of Holy Trinity — A30

View of Varna — A31

1911, Feb. 14   **Engr.**   **Perf. 12**

89	A20	1s myrtle green	.25	.25
90	A21	2s car & blk	.25	.25
91	A22	3s lake & blk	.45	.25
92	A23	5s green & blk	1.60	.25
93	A24	10s dp red & blk	2.50	.25
94	A25	15s brown bister	5.75	.25
95	A26	25s ultra & blk	.55	.25
96	A27	30s blue & blk	5.75	.25
97	A28	50s ocher & blk	30.00	.25
a.		Center inverted		2,700.
98	A29	1 l chocolate	13.50	.25
99	A30	2 l dull pur & blk	3.25	.50
100	A31	3 l blue vio & blk	15.00	3.75
		Nos. 89-100 (12)	78.85	6.75

See Nos. 114-120, 161-162. For overprints and surcharges see Nos. 104-112, 188, B8, Greece N167-N178, N182-N187, Thrace 16-21, Romania 2N1-2N4.

Tsar Ferdinand — A32

1912, Aug. 2   **Typo.**   **Perf. 12½**

101	A32	5s olive green	15.00	2.00
a.		5s pale green	325.00	150.00
102	A32	10s claret	7.00	3.50
103	A32	25s slate	10.00	5.50
		Nos. 101-103 (3)	32.00	11.00

25th year of reign of Tsar Ferdinand.

Nos. 89-95 Overprinted in Various Colors

1913, Aug. 6   **Engr.**

104	A20	1s myrtle grn (C)	.50	.25
105	A21	2s car & blk (Bl)	2.00	.25
107	A22	3s lake & blk (Bl Bk)	2.00	.25
108	A23	5s grn & blk (R)	.50	.25
109	A24	10s dp red & blk (Bk)	.50	.25
110	A25	15s brown bis (G)	2.50	1.50
111	A26	25s ultra & blk (R)	8.00	2.00
		Nos. 104-111 (7)	16.00	5.25

Victory over the Turks in Balkan War of 1912-1913.

No. 95 Surcharged in Red

1915, July 6

112	A26	10s on 25s	.95	.25

No. 28 Surcharged in Green

113	A11	3s on 1s lilac	9.50	4.50

Types of 1911 Re-engraved
1915, Nov. 7   **Perf. 11½, 14**

114	A20	1s dk bl grn	.25	.25
115	A23	5s grn & brn vio	3.25	.25
116	A24	10s red brn & brnsh blk	.25	.25
117	A25	15s olive green	.25	.25
118	A26	25s indigo & blk	.25	.25
119	A27	30s ol grn & red brn	.25	.25
120	A29	1 l dark brown	.40	.30
		Nos. 114-120 (7)	4.90	1.80

Widths: No. 114 is 19½mm; No. 89, 18½mm. No. 118 is 19¼mm; No. 95, 18¼mm. No. 120 is 20mm; No. 98, 19mm. The re-engraved stamps also differ from the 1911 issue in many details of design. Nos. 114-120 exist imperforate.

The 5s exists in two types: I, 20x29.3mm, green and brown violet; II, 19.5x29mm, dark green and brown. There are a number of minor design differences between the two types. The editors would welcome any information that Bulgarian specialists can provide on this and similar varieties on stamps of this period.

The 5s and 10s exist perf. 14x11½.

For Nos. 114-116 and 118 overprinted with Cyrillic characters and "1916-1917," see Romania Nos. 2N1-2N4.

Coat of Arms — A33

Peasant and Bullock — A34

Soldier and Mt. Sonichka — A35

View of Nish — A36

Town and Lake Okhrida — A37

Demir-Kapiya (Iron Gate) — A37a

View of Gevgeli — A38

Perf. 11½, 12½x13, 13x12½

1917-19   **Typo.**
122	A33	5s green	.30	.25
123	A34	15s slate	.25	.25
124	A35	25s blue	.25	.25
125	A36	30s orange	.25	.25
126	A37	50s violet	.50	.30
126A	A37a	2 l brn org ('19)	.50	.35
127	A38	3 l claret	1.75	1.75
		Nos. 122-127 (7)	3.80	3.40

Liberation of Macedonia. A 1 l dark green was prepared but not issued. Value $1.65.
For surcharges see Nos. B9-B10, B12.

View of Veles — A39

Monastery of St. Clement at Okhrida — A40

1918   **Perf. 13x14**
| 128 | A39 | 1s gray | .25 | .25 |
| 129 | A40 | 5s green | .25 | .25 |

Tsar Ferdinand A41

Plowing with Oxen A42

1918, July 1   **Perf. 12½x13**
130	A41	1s dark green	.80	.25
131	A41	2s dark brown	.80	.25
132	A41	3s indigo	1.60	.25
133	A41	10s brown red	1.60	.25
		Nos. 130-133 (4)	4.80	1.00

Ferdinand's accession to the throne, 30th anniv.

1919   **Perf. 13½x13**
| 134 | A42 | 1s gray | .25 | .25 |

Sobranye Palace — A43   Tsar Boris III — A44

1919   **Perf. 11½x12, 12x11½**
| 135 | A43 | 1s black | .25 | .25 |
| 137 | A43 | 2s olive green | .25 | .25 |

For surcharges see Nos. 186, B1.

1919, Oct. 3
138	A44	3s orange brn	.25	.25
139	A44	5s green	.25	.25
140	A44	10s rose red	.25	.25
141	A44	15s violet	.25	.25
142	A44	25s deep blue	.25	.25
143	A44	30s chocolate	.25	.25
144	A44	50s yellow brn	.25	.25
		Nos. 138-144 (7)	1.75	1.75

1st anniv. of enthronement of Tsar Boris III.
Nos. 135-144 exist imperforate.
For surcharges see Nos. 187, B2-B7.

Birthplace of Vazov at Sopot and Cherrywood Cannon — A47

Ivan Vazov in 1870 and 1920 A49

"The Bear Fighter"-a Character from "Under the Yoke" — A48

Vazov — A50

Homes of Vazov at Plovdiv and Sofia A51

The Monk Paisii — A52

1920, Oct. 20   Photo.   Perf. 11½
147	A47	30s brown red	.25	.25
148	A48	50s dark green	.25	.25
149	A49	1 l drab	.25	.30
150	A50	2 l light brown	1.20	.65
151	A51	3 l black violet	1.90	.75
152	A52	5 l deep blue	2.40	1.50
		Nos. 147-152 (6)	6.25	3.70

70th birthday of Ivan Vazov (1850-1921), Bulgarian poet and novelist.
Several values of this series exist imperforate and in pairs imperforate between.

Tsar Ferdinand A53

A54

Mt. Shar — A55

Bridge over Vardar River — A56

View of Ohrid — A57

Perf. 13x14, 14x13
1921, June 11   **Typo.**
153	A53	10s claret	.25	.25
154	A54	10s claret	.25	.25
155	A55	10s claret	.25	.25
156	A56	10s rose lilac	.25	.25
157	A57	20s blue	.70	.25
		Nos. 153-157 (5)	1.70	1.25

Nos. 153-157 were intended to be issued in 1915 to commemorate the liberation of Macedonia. They were not put in use until 1921. A 50s violet was prepared but never placed in use. Value $1.75.

View of Sofia — A58

"The Liberator," Monument to Alexander II A59

Monastery at Shipka Pass — A62

Tsar Boris III — A63

Harvesting Grain — A64

Tsar Assen's Tower (No crown over lion) — A65

Rila Monastery (Rosette at upper right) — A66

1921-23   Engr.   Perf. 12
158	A58	10s blue gray	.25	.25
159	A59	20s deep green	.25	.25
160	A63	25s blue grn ('22)	.25	.25
161	A22	50s orange	.25	.25
162	A22	50s dk blue ('23)	4.00	2.50
163	A62	75s dull vio	.30	.25
164	A62	75s dp blue ('23)	.30	.25
165	A63	1 l carmine	.30	.25
166	A63	1 l dp blue ('22)	.30	.25
167	A64	2 l brown	.30	1.00
168	A65	3 l brown vio	1.40	1.10
169	A66	5 l lt blue	3.75	1.25
170	A63	10 l violet brn	9.50	2.10
		Nos. 158-170 (13)	21.10	9.95

For surcharge see No. 189.

Bourchier in Bulgarian Costume A67

James David Bourchier A68

View of Rila Monastery A69

1921, Dec. 31
171	A67	10s red orange	.25	.25
172	A67	20s orange	.25	.25
173	A68	30s dp gray	.25	.25
174	A68	50s bluish gray	.25	.25
175	A68	1 l dull vio	.25	.25
176	A69	1½ l olive grn	.25	.25
177	A69	2 l deep green	.25	.25
178	A69	3 l Prus blue	.60	.25
179	A69	5 l red brown	1.00	.50
		Nos. 171-179 (9)	3.35	2.50

Death of James D. Bourchier, Balkan correspondent of the London Times.
For surcharges see Nos. B13-B16.

Postage Due Stamps of 1919-22 Surcharged — a

1924
182	D6	10s on 20s yellow	.25	.25
183	D6	20s on 5s gray grn	.25	.25
a.		20s on 5s emerald	30.00	30.00

238 BULGARIA

|---|---|---|---|---|---|
184	D6	20s on 10s violet		.25	.25
185	D6	20s on 30s orange		.25	.25
		Nos. 182-185 (4)		1.00	1.00

Nos. 182 to 185 were used for ordinary postage.

Regular Issues of 1919-23
Surcharged in Blue or Red

b   c

186	A43 (a)	10s on 1s black (R)	.25	.25
187	A44 (b)	1 l on 5s emer (Bl)	.25	.25
188	A22 (c)	3 l on 50s dk bl (R)	.25	.25
189	A63 (b)	6 l on 1 l car (Bl)	.60	.25
		Nos. 186-189 (4)	1.35	1.00

The surcharge of No. 188 comes in three types: normal, thick and thin.

Nos. 182, 184-189 exist with inverted surcharge.

Lion of Bulgaria
A70   A71

Tsar Boris III — A72   New Sofia Cathedral — A73

Harvesting A74

1925		Typo.	Perf. 13, 11½	
191	A70	10s red & bl, *pink*	.40	.25
192	A70	15s car & org, *blue*	.40	.25
193	A70	30s blk & buff	.40	.25
a.		Cliche of 15s in plate of 30s		
194	A71	50s choc, *green*	.40	.25
195	A72	1 l dull green	.95	.25
196	A73	2 l dk grn & buff	1.90	.25
197	A74	4 l lake & yellow	1.90	.25
		Nos. 191-197 (7)	6.35	1.75

Several values of this series exist imperforate and in pairs imperforate between.
See Nos. 199, 201. For overprint see No. C2.

Cathedral of Sveta Nedelya, Sofia, Ruined by Bomb — A75

1926			Perf. 11½	
198	A75	50s gray black	.25	.25

A76   A77

Type A72 Re-engraved. (Shoulder at left does not touch frame)

1926				
199	A76	1 l gray		.45	.25
a.		1 l green		.45	.25
201	A76	2 l olive brown		.70	.25

Center Embossed

202	A77	6 l dp bl & pale lemon	1.90	.25
203	A77	10 l brn blk & brn org	4.75	1.75
		Nos. 199-203 (4)	7.80	2.50

For overprints see Nos. C1, C3-C4.

Christo Botev — A78

1926, June 2				
204	A78	1 l olive green	.55	.25
205	A78	2 l slate violet	1.20	.25
206	A78	4 l red brown	1.20	.35
		Nos. 204-206 (3)	2.95	.85

Botev (1847-76), Bulgarian revolutionary, poet.

Lion Type of 1881 Redrawn
1927-29			Perf. 13	
207	A3	10s dk red & drab	.25	.25
208	A3	15s blk & org ('29)	.25	.25
209	A3	30s dk bl & bis brn ('28)	.25	.25
a.		30s indigo & buff	.25	
210	A3	50s blk & rose red ('28)	.25	.25
		Nos. 207-210 (4)	1.00	1.00

Scott 207-210 have less detailed scrollwork surrounding the central lion, which is also less detailed than Scott 1-18.

Tsar Boris III — A79

1928, Oct. 3			Perf. 11½	
211	A79	1 l olive green	.90	.25
212	A79	2 l deep brown	1.00	.25

St. Clement A80   Konstantin Miladinov A81

George S. Rakovski A82   Drenovo Monastery A83

Paisii — A84   Tsar Simeon — A85

Lyuben Karavelov A86   Vassil Levski A87

Georgi Benkovski A88   Tsar Alexander II A89

1929, May 12				
213	A80	10s dk violet	.25	.25
214	A81	15s violet brn	.40	.40
215	A82	30s red	.25	.25
216	A83	50s olive grn	.25	.25
217	A84	1 l orange brn	1.00	.25
218	A85	2 l dk blue	1.15	.25
219	A86	3 l dull green	2.50	.45
220	A87	4 l olive brown	4.00	.25
221	A88	5 l brown	2.50	.35
222	A89	6 l Prus green	3.75	.90
		Nos. 213-222 (10)	16.05	3.60

Millenary of Tsar Simeon and 50th anniv. of the liberation of Bulgaria from the Turks.

Royal Wedding Issue

Tsar Boris and Fiancee, Princess Giovanna A90

Queen Ioanna and Tsar Boris — A91

1930, Nov. 12			Perf. 11½	
223	A90	1 l green	.35	.25
224	A91	2 l dull violet	.35	.30
225	A90	4 l rose red	.35	.30
226	A91	6 l dark blue	.35	.40
		Nos. 223-226 (4)	1.40	1.25

Fifty-five copies of a miniature sheet incorporating one each of Nos. 223-226 were printed and given to royal, governmental and diplomatic personages.

Tsar Boris III
A92   A93

Perf. 11½, 12x11½, 13

1931-37			Unwmk.	
227	A92	1 l blue green	.25	.25
228	A92	2 l carmine	.40	.25
229	A92	4 l red org ('34)	.75	.25
230	A92	4 l yel org ('37)	.25	.25
231	A92	6 l deep blue	.70	.25
232	A92	7 l dp bl ('37)	.25	.25
233	A92	10 l slate blk	8.75	.70
234	A92	12 l lt brown	.40	.25
235	A92	14 l lt brn ('37)	.30	.25
236	A93	20 l claret & org brn	1.00	.45
		Nos. 227-236 (10)	13.05	3.15

Nos. 230-233 and 235 have outer bars at top and bottom as shown on cut A92; Nos. 227-229 and 234 are without outer bars.

See Nos. 251, 279-280, 287. For surcharge see No. 252.

Balkan Games Issues

Gymnast A95

Soccer — A96   Riding — A97

Swimmer A100   "Victory" A101

Designs: 6 l, Fencing. 10 l, Bicycle race.

1931, Sept. 18			Perf. 11½	
237	A95	1 l lt green	1.25	.50
238	A96	2 l garnet	1.75	.50
239	A97	4 l carmine	3.25	.75
240	A95	6 l Prus blue	7.50	1.25
241	A95	10 l red org	20.00	3.75
242	A100	12 l dk blue	70.00	16.00
243	A101	50 l olive brn	65.00	36.00
		Nos. 237-243 (7)	168.75	58.75

1933, Jan. 5				
244	A95	1 l blue grn	2.50	.95
245	A96	2 l blue	4.00	1.10
246	A97	4 l brn vio	6.00	1.10
247	A95	6 l brt rose	12.50	1.50
248	A95	10 l olive brn	90.00	20.00
249	A100	12 l orange	150.00	37.50
250	A101	50 l red brown	400.00	160.00
		Nos. 244-250 (7)	665.00	222.15

Nos. 244-250 were sold only at the philatelic agency.

Boris Type of 1931
Outer Bars at Top and Bottom Removed

1933			Perf. 13	
251	A92	6 l deep blue	.80	.25

Type of 1931 Surcharged in Blue

1934				
252	A92	2 (l) on 3 l ol brn	7.25	.25

Soldier Defending Shipka Pass A102   Shipka Battle Memorial A103

Color-Bearer
A104

Veteran of the
War of
Liberation,
1878 — A105

Widow and
Orphans — A106

Perf. 10½, 11½

1934, Aug. 26   Wmk. 145
253	A102	1 l green	.70	.40
254	A103	2 l pale red	.70	.25
255	A104	3 l bister brn	2.40	1.25
256	A105	4 l dk carmine	2.00	.60
257	A104	7 l dk blue	2.75	2.25
258	A106	14 l plum	17.00	8.00
		Nos. 253-258 (6)	25.55	12.75

Shipka Pass Battle memorial unveiling.
An unwatermarked miniature sheet incorporating one each of Nos. 253-258 was put on sale in 1938 in five cities at a price of 8,000 leva. Printing: 100 sheets. Value: $1,500.

1934, Sept. 21
259	A102	1 l bright green	.70	.40
260	A103	2 l dull orange	.70	.25
261	A104	3 l yellow	2.40	1.25
262	A105	4 l rose	2.00	.60
263	A104	7 l blue	2.75	2.25
264	A106	14 l olive bister	17.00	8.00
		Nos. 259-264 (6)	25.55	12.75

An unwatermarked miniature sheet incorporating one each of Nos. 259-263 was issued. Value: $1,500.

Velcho A.   Capt. G. S.
Djamjiyata   Mamarchev
A108   A109

1935, May 5   Perf. 11½
265	A108	1 l deep blue	2.00	.40
266	A109	2 l maroon	2.00	.60

Bulgarian uprising against the Turks, cent.

Soccer   Cathedral of
Game — A110   Alexander
          Nevski — A111

Soccer
Team —
A112

Symbolical of   Player and
Victory — A113   Trophy — A114

The Trophy — A115

1935, June 14
267	A110	1 l green	12.00	.90
268	A111	2 l blue gray	12.00	1.40
269	A112	4 l crimson	12.00	2.25
270	A113	7 l brt blue	20.00	7.00
271	A114	14 l orange	20.00	9.00
272	A115	50 l lilac brn	300.00	125.00
		Nos. 267-272 (6)	376.00	145.55

5th Balkan Soccer Tournament.

Gymnast on   Youth in "Yunak"
Parallel Bars   Costume
A116   A117

Girl in "Yunak"   Pole Vaulting
Costume   A119
A118

Stadium,
Sofia — A120

Yunak
Emblem — A121

1935, July 10
273	A116	1 l green	6.00	1.10
274	A117	2 l lt blue	6.00	1.10
275	A118	4 l carmine	8.00	2.25
276	A119	7 l dk blue	8.00	3.50
277	A120	14 l dk brown	10.00	4.00
278	A121	50 l red	170.00	80.00
		Nos. 273-278 (6)	208.00	91.95

8th tournament of the Yunak Gymnastic Organization at Sofia, July 12-14.

Boris Type of 1931
1935   Wmk. 145   Perf. 12½, 13
279	A92	1 l green	.55	.25
280	A92	2 l carmine	35.00	.25

Janos Hunyadi   King Ladislas
A122   Varnenchik
          A123

Varna
Memorial
A124

King Ladislas
III — A125

Battle of
Varna,
1444 — A126

1935, Aug. 4   Perf. 10½, 11½
281	A122	1 l brown org	3.75	1.50
282	A123	2 l maroon	3.75	1.75
283	A124	4 l vermilion	22.50	6.75
284	A125	7 l dull blue	3.75	2.25
285	A126	14 l green	4.00	2.00
		Nos. 281-285 (5)	37.75	14.25

Battle of Varna, and the death of the Polish King, Ladislas Varnenchik (1424-44). Nos. 281-285 exist imperf. Value, set $50.

Lion Type of 1881
1935   Wmk. 145   Perf. 13
286	A3	10s dk red & drab	.70	.25

Boris Type of 1933
Outer Bars at Top and Bottom Removed
1935
287	A92	6 l gray blue	1.25	.25

Dimitr Monument
A127

Haji
Dimitr — A128

Haji Dimitr
and Stefan
Karaja
A129

Taking the
Oath — A130

Birthplace of
Dimitr
A131

1935, Oct. 1   Unwmk.   Perf. 11½
288	A127	1 l green	2.50	.45
289	A128	2 l brown	3.50	.90
290	A129	4 l car rose	10.00	2.75
291	A130	7 l blue	12.00	6.00
292	A131	14 l orange	15.00	4.50
		Nos. 288-292 (5)	43.00	14.60

67th anniv. of the death of the Bulgarian patriots, Haji Dimitr and Stefan Karaja. Nos. 288-292 exist imperf.

Catalogue values for unused stamps in this section, from this point to the end of the section, are for Never Hinged items.

A132   A133

1936-39   Perf. 13x12½, 13
293	A132	10s red org ('37)	.30	.25
294	A132	15s emerald	.30	.25
295	A133	30s maroon	.30	.25
296	A133	30s yel brn ('37)	.30	.25
297	A133	30s Prus bl ('37)	.30	.25
298	A133	50s ultra	.30	.25
299	A133	50s dk car ('37)	.30	.25
300	A133	50s slate grn ('39)	.30	.25
		Nos. 293-300 (8)	2.40	2.00

Meteorological   Peasant Girl
Station, Mt.   A135
Moussalla
A134

Town of
Nessebr
A136

1936, Aug. 16   Photo.   Perf. 11½
301	A134	1 l purple	4.00	1.90
302	A135	2 l ultra	4.00	2.25
303	A136	7 l dark blue	8.00	3.75
		Nos. 301-303 (3)	16.00	7.90

4th Geographical & Ethnographical Cong., Sofia, Aug. 1936.

Sts. Cyril and
Methodius
A137

Displaying the
Bible to the
People
A138

1937, June 2
304	A137	1 l	dk green	.60	.30
305	A137	2 l	dk plum	.65	.30
306	A138	4 l	vermilion	.80	.30
307	A137	7 l	dk blue	4.25	1.60
308	A138	14 l	rose red	4.75	1.90
	Nos. 304-308 (5)			11.05	4.40

Millennium of Cyrillic alphabet.

Princess
Marie Louise
A139

Tsar Boris III
A140

1937, Oct. 3
310	A139	1 l	yellow green	.70	.25
311	A139	2 l	brown red	.70	.25
312	A139	4 l	scarlet	.70	.40
	Nos. 310-312 (3)			2.10	.90

Issued in honor of Princess Marie Louise.

1937, Oct. 3
313	A140	2 l	brown red	1.00	.45

19th anniv. of the accession of Tsar Boris III
to the throne. See No. B11.

National Products Issue

Peasants
Bundling Wheat
A141

Sunflower
A142

Wheat — A143

Chickens and
Eggs — A144

Cluster of
Grapes — A145

Rose and
Perfume
Flask — A146

Strawberries
A147

Girl Carrying
Grape Clusters
A148

Rose — A149

Tobacco
Leaves — A150

1938   Perf. 13
316	A141	10s	orange	.25	.25
317	A141	10s	red org	.25	.25
318	A142	15s	brt rose	.50	.25
319	A142	15s	deep plum	.50	.25
320	A143	30s	golden brn	.40	.25
321	A143	30s	copper brn	.40	.25
322	A144	50s	black	1.00	.25
323	A144	50s	indigo	1.00	.25
324	A145	1 l	yel grn	1.00	.25
325	A145	1 l	green	1.00	.25
326	A146	2 l	rose pink	1.00	.25
327	A146	2 l	rose brn	1.00	.25
328	A147	3 l	dp red lil	2.00	.25
329	A147	3 l	brn lake	2.00	.25
330	A148	4 l	plum	1.50	.25
331	A148	4 l	golden brn	1.50	.25
332	A149	7 l	vio blue	3.00	1.50
333	A149	7 l	dp blue	3.00	1.50
334	A150	14 l	dk brown	5.00	1.90
335	A150	14 l	red brn	5.00	1.90
	Nos. 316-335 (20)			31.30	10.80

Several values of this series exist
imperforate.

Crown Prince Simeon
A151   A153

Designs: 2 l, Same portrait as 1 l, value at
lower left. 14 l, similar to 4 l, but no wreath.

1938, June 16
336	A151	1 l	brt green	.30	.25
337	A151	2 l	rose pink	.30	.25
338	A153	4 l	dp orange	.40	.25
339	A151	7 l	ultra	1.25	.40
340	A153	14 l	dp brown	1.50	.50
	Nos. 336-340 (5)			3.75	1.65

First birthday of Prince Simeon.
Nos. 336-340 exist imperf. Value, set $15.

Tsar Boris III
A155   A156

Various Portraits of Tsar.

1938, Oct. 3
341	A155	1 l	lt green	.25	.25
342	A156	2 l	rose brown	.95	.25
343	A156	4 l	golden brn	.30	.25
344	A156	7 l	brt ultra	.50	.50
345	A156	14 l	deep red lilac	.55	.50
	Nos. 341-345 (5)			2.55	1.75

Reign of Tsar Boris III, 20th anniv.
Nos. 341-345 exist imperf. Value, set $40.

Early
Locomotive
A160

Designs: 2 l, Modern locomotive. 4 l, Train
crossing bridge. 7 l, Tsar Boris in cab.

1939, Apr. 26
346	A160	1 l	yel green	.50	.30
347	A160	2 l	copper brn	.50	.30
348	A160	4 l	red orange	3.00	1.50
349	A160	7 l	dark blue	9.00	4.00
	Nos. 346-349 (4)			13.00	6.10

50th anniv. of Bulgarian State Railways.

Post Horns and
Arrows — A164

Central Post
Office,
Sofia — A165

1939, May 14   Typo.
350	A164	1 l	yellow grn	.30	.25
351	A165	2 l	brt carmine	.40	.25

Establishment of the postal system, 60th
anniv.

Gymnast on
Bar — A166

Yunak
Emblem — A167

Discus
Thrower — A168

Athletic
Dancer — A169

Weight
Lifter — A170

1939, July 7   Photo.
352	A166	1 l	yel grn & pale grn	.45	.35
353	A167	2 l	brt rose	.50	.35
354	A168	4 l	brn & gldn brn	.90	.45
355	A169	7 l	dk bl & bl	3.00	1.50
356	A170	14 l	plum & rose vio	14.00	10.00
	Nos. 352-356 (5)			18.85	12.65

9th tournament of the Yunak Gymnastic
Organization at Sofia, July 4-8.

Tsar Boris
III — A171

Bulgaria's First
Stamp — A172

1940-41   Typo.
356A	A171	1 l	dl grn ('41)	.80	.25
357	A171	2 l	brt crimson	.80	.25

1940, May 19   Photo.   Perf. 13

20 l, Similar design, scroll dated "1840-
1940."
358	A172	10 l	olive black	2.50	2.00
359	A172	20 l	indigo	2.50	2.00

Cent. of 1st postage stamp.
Nos. 358-359 exist imperf. Value, set $100.

Peasant Couple
and Tsar
Boris — A174

Flags over
Wheat Field and
Tsar
Boris — A175

Tsar Boris
and Map of
Dobrudja
A176

1940, Sept. 20
360	A174	1 l	slate green	.25	.25
361	A175	2 l	rose red	.25	.25
362	A176	4 l	dark brown	.40	.25
363	A176	7 l	dark blue	1.00	.65
	Nos. 360-363 (4)			1.90	1.40

Return of Dobrudja from Romania.

Fruit
A177

Bees and
Flowers
A178

Plowing
A179

Shepherd and
Sheep
A180

Tsar Boris III — A181

Perf. 10, 10½x11½, 11½, 13
1940-44   Typo.   Unwmk.
364	A177	10s	red orange	.25	.25
365	A178	15s	blue	.25	.25
366	A179	30s	olive brn ('41)	.25	.25
367	A180	50s	violet	.25	.25
368	A181	1 l	brt green	.25	.25
369	A181	2 l	rose car	.25	.25
370	A181	4 l	red orange	.25	.25
371	A181	6 l	red vio ('44)	.30	.25

| 372 | A181 | 7 l blue | .30 | .25 |
| 373 | A181 | 10 l blue grn ('41) | .30 | .25 |

Nos. 364-373 (10)   2.65 2.50

See Nos. 373A-377; No. 440 in *Scott Standard Postage Stamp Catalogue*, Vol. 1. For overprints see Nos. 455-463, C31-C32 in Scott Standard catalogue, Vol. 1.

1940-41		**Wmk. 145**	***Perf. 13***	
373A	A180	50s violet ('41)	.25	.25
374	A181	1 l green	.25	.25
375	A181	2 l rose car	.25	.25
376	A181	7 l dull blue	.45	.25
377	A181	10 l blue green	.65	.25

Nos. 373A-377 (5)   1.85 1.25

Watermarked vertically or horizontally.

P. R. Slaveikov
A182

Sofronii, Bishop of Vratza
A183

Saint Ivan Rilski — A184

Martin S. Drinov — A185

Monk Khrabr — A186

Kolio Ficheto — A187

1940, Sept. 23		**Photo.**	**Unwmk.**	
378	A182	1 l brt bl grn	.25	.25
379	A183	2 l brt carmine	.25	.25
380	A184	3 l dp red brn	.25	.25
381	A185	4 l red orange	.25	.25
382	A186	7 l deep blue	1.60	.60
383	A187	10 l dp red brn	2.40	.85

Nos. 378-383 (6)   5.00 2.45

Liberation of Bulgaria from the Turks in 1878.

Johannes Gutenberg
A188

N. Karastoyanov, 1st Bulgarian Printer
A189

1940, Dec. 16				
384	A188	1 l slate green	.35	.35
385	A189	2 l orange brown	.35	.35

500th anniv. of the invention of the printing press and 100th anniv. of the 1st Bulgarian printing press.

SEMI-POSTAL STAMPS

Catalogue values for unused stamps in this section are for Never Hinged items.

Regular Issues of 1911-20 Surcharged

a

b

c

Perf. 11½x12, 12x11½

1920, June 20			**Unwmk.**	
B1	A43 (a)	2s + 1s ol grn	.25	.25
B2	A44 (b)	5s + 2½s grn	.25	.25
B3	A44 (b)	10s + 5s rose	.25	.25
B4	A44 (b)	15s + 7½s vio	.25	.25
B5	A44 (b)	25s + 12½s dp bl	.25	.25
B6	A44 (b)	30s + 15s choc	.25	.25
B7	A44 (b)	50s + 25s yel brn	.25	.25
B8	A29 (c)	1 l + 50s dk brn	.45	.25
B9	A37a (a)	2 l + 1 l brn org	.45	.40
B10	A38 (a)	3 l + 1½ l claret	1.20	.80

Nos. B1-B10 (10)   3.85 3.20

Surtax aided ex-prisoners of war. Value, Nos. B1-B7 imperf., $7.75.

Tsar Boris Type of 1937
Souvenir Sheet

| **1937, Nov. 22** | | **Photo.** | ***Imperf.*** | |
| B11 | A140 | 2 l + 18 l ultra | 10.00 | 20.00 |

19th anniv. of the accession of Tsar Boris III to the throne.

Stamps of 1917-21 Surcharged in Black

1939, Oct. 22			***Perf. 12½, 12***	
B12	A34	1 l + 1 l on 15s slate	.25	.25
B13	A69	2 l + 1 l on 1½ l ol grn	.35	.35
B14	A69	4 l + 2 l on 2 l dp grn	.40	.40
B15	A69	7 l + 4 l on 3 l Prus bl	1.25	1.50
B16	A69	14 l + 7 l on 5 l red brn	1.75	2.00

Nos. B12-B16 (5)   4.00 4.50

Surtax aided victims of the Sevlievo flood. The surcharge on #B13-B16 omits "leva."

AIR POST STAMPS

Regular Issues of 1925-26 Overprinted in Various Colors

1927-28		**Unwmk.**	***Perf. 11½***	
C1	A76	2 l ol (R) ('28)	1.60	1.60
C2	A74	4 l lake & yel (Bl)	3.00	1.60
C3	A77	10 l brn blk & brn org (G) ('28)	47.50	10.00

Overprinted Vertically and Surcharged with New Value

C4	A77	1 l on 6 l dp bl & pale lem (C)	1.60	1.60
a.		Inverted surcharge	340.00	275.00
b.		Pair, one without surcharge	440.00	

Nos. C1-C4 (4)   53.70 14.80

Nos. C2-C4 overprinted in changed colors were not issued, value set $14.

Dove Delivering Message
AP1

Junkers Plane, Rila Monastery
AP2

1931, Oct. 28			**Typo.**	
C5	AP1	1 l dk green	.45	.25
C6	AP1	2 l maroon	.45	.25
C7	AP1	6 l dp blue	.60	.40
C8	AP1	12 l carmine	1.25	.40
C9	AP1	20 l dk violet	1.25	.80
C10	AP1	30 l dp orange	2.40	1.60
C11	AP1	50 l orange brn	3.50	2.75

Nos. C5-C11 (7)   9.90 6.45

Counterfeits exist. See Nos. C15-C18.

1932, May 9				
C12	AP2	18 l blue grn	72.50	40.00
C13	AP2	24 l dp red	50.00	30.00
C14	AP2	28 l ultra	30.00	25.00

Nos. C12-C14 (3)   152.50 95.00

Catalogue values for unused stamps in this section, from this point to the end of the section, are for Never Hinged items.

1938, Dec. 27				
C15	AP1	1 l violet brown	.35	.25
C16	AP1	2 l green	.40	.25
C17	AP1	6 l deep rose	1.25	.50
C18	AP1	12 l peacock blue	1.40	.55

Nos. C15-C18 (4)   3.40 1.55

Counterfeits exist.

Mail Plane — AP3

Plane over Tsar Assen's Tower — AP4

Designs: 4 l, Plane over Bachkovski Monastery. 6 l, Bojurishte Airport, Sofia. 10 l, Plane, train and motorcycle. 12 l, Planes over Sofia Palace. 16 l, Plane over Pirin Valley. 19 l, Plane over Rila Monastery. 30 l, Plane and Swallow. 45 l, Plane over Sofia Cathedral. 70 l, Plane over Shipka Monument. 100 l, Plane and Royal Cipher.

1940, Jan. 15		**Photo.**	***Perf. 13***	
C19	AP3	1 l dk green	.25	.25
C20	AP4	2 l crimson	2.25	.25
C21	AP4	4 l red orange	.25	.25
C22	AP3	6 l dp blue	.50	.25
C23	AP4	10 l dk brown	.50	.25
C24	AP3	12 l dull brown	1.00	.25
C25	AP3	16 l brt bl vio	1.10	.50
C26	AP3	19 l sapphire	1.50	.75
C27	AP4	30 l rose lake	2.25	1.00
C28	AP4	45 l gray violet	5.50	1.25
C29	AP4	70 l rose pink	5.50	1.75
C30	AP4	100 l dp slate bl	18.50	5.00

Nos. C19-C30 (12)   39.10 11.75

SPECIAL DELIVERY STAMPS

Catalogue values for unused stamps in this section are for Never Hinged items.

Postman on Bicycle
SD1

Postman on Motorcycle
SD3

Mail Car — SD2

1939		**Unwmk.**	**Photo.**	***Perf. 13***
E1	SD1	5 l deep blue	1.20	.25
E2	SD2	6 l copper brn	.25	.25
E3	SD3	7 l golden brn	.35	.25
E4	SD2	8 l red orange	1.20	.25
E5	SD1	20 l bright rose	2.50	.40

Nos. E1-E5 (5)   5.50 1.40

POSTAGE DUE STAMPS

D1

Large Lozenge Perf. 5½ to 6½

1884		**Typo.**	**Unwmk.**	
J1	D1	5s orange	875.00	110.00
J2	D1	25s lake	340.00	52.50
J3	D1	50s blue	47.50	32.50

Nos. J1-J3 (3)   1,262. 195.00

1886			***Imperf.***	
J4	D1	5s orange	440.00	20.00
J5	D1	25s lake	640.00	20.00
J6	D1	50s blue	20.00	17.50

Nos. J4-J6 (3)   1,100. 57.50

1887			***Perf. 11½***	
J7	D1	5s orange	60.00	9.50
J8	D1	25s lake	20.00	6.00
J9	D1	50s blue	24.00	16.00

Nos. J7-J9 (3)   104.00 31.50

Same, Redrawn
24 horizontal lines of shading in upper part instead of 30 lines

1892			***Perf. 10½, 11½***	
J10	D1	5s orange	40.00	6.00
J11	D1	25s lake	20.00	6.00

D2

| **1893** | | | **Pelure Paper** | |
| J12 | D2 | 5s orange | 47.50 | 20.00 |

D3

D4

| **1895** | | | ***Imperf.*** | |
| J13 | D3 | 30s on 50s blue | 35.00 | 9.50 |

Perf. 10½, 11½

| J14 | D3 | 30s on 50s blue | 40.00 | 9.50 |

Wmk. Coat of Arms in the Sheet

1896		**Perf. 13**	
J15	D4	5s orange	20.00	3.25
J16	D4	10s purple	12.00	2.75
J17	D4	30s green	9.50	2.40
	Nos. J15-J17 (3)		41.50	8.40

Nos. J15-J17 are also known on unwatermarked paper from the edges of sheets.

In 1901 a cancellation, "T" in circle, was applied to Nos. 60-65 and used provisionally as postage dues.

D5   D6

1901-04		**Unwmk.**	**Perf. 11½**	
J19	D5	5s dl rose	.80	.50
J20	D5	10s yel grn	1.60	.50
J21	D5	20s dl bl ('04)	12.00	.50
J22	D5	30s vio brn	4.00	.50
J23	D5	50s org ('02)	9.50	9.50
	Nos. J19-J23 (5)		27.90	11.50

Nos. J19-J23 exist imperf. and in pairs imperf. between. Value, imperf., $250.

1915		**Unwmk.**	**Perf. 11½**	
Thin Semi-Transparent Paper				
J24	D6	5s green	.50	.25
J25	D6	10s purple	.50	.25
J26	D6	20s dl rose	.50	.25
J27	D6	30s dp org	2.75	.25
J28	D6	50s dp bl	.95	.25
	Nos. J24-J28 (5)		5.20	1.25

1919-21		**Perf. 11½, 12x11½**	
J29	D6	5s emerald	.25	.25
a.	5s gray green ('21)		.30	.25
J30	D6	10s violet	.25	.25
a.	10s light violet ('21)		.25	.25
J31	D6	20s salmon	.25	.25
a.	20s yellow		.25	.25
J32	D6	30s orange	.25	.25
a.	30s red orange ('21)		.65	.65
J33	D6	50s blue	.25	.25
J34	D6	1 l emerald ('21)	.25	.25
J35	D6	2 l rose ('21)	.25	.25
J36	D6	3 l brown org ('21)	.35	.25
	Nos. J29-J36 (8)		2.10	2.00

Stotinki values of the above series surcharged 10s or 20s were used as ordinary postage stamps. See Nos. 182-185.

The 1919 printings are on thicker white paper with clean-cut perforations, the 1921 printings on thicker grayish paper with rough perforations.

Most of this series exist imperforate and in pairs imperforate between.

Heraldic Lion — D7

1932, Aug. 15		**Thin Paper**	
J37	D7	1 l olive bister	1.60	1.00
J38	D7	2 l rose brown	1.60	1.00
J39	D7	6 l brown violet	3.50	1.20
	Nos. J37-J39 (3)		6.70	3.20

Lion of   National
Trnovo — D8   Arms — D9

1933, Apr. 10			
J40	D8	20s dk brn	.25	.25
J41	D8	40s dp bl	.25	.25
J42	D8	80s car rose	.25	.25
J43	D9	1 l org brn	1.60	.50
J44	D9	2 l olive	1.60	.75
J45	D9	6 l dl vio	.80	.30
J46	D9	14 l ultra	1.20	.50
	Nos. J40-J46 (7)		5.95	2.80

POSTAL TAX STAMPS

The use of stamps Nos. RA1 to RA18 was compulsory on letters, etc., to be delivered on Sundays and holidays. The money received from their sale was used toward maintaining a sanatorium for employees of the post, telegraph and telephone services.

View of Sanatorium PT1

Sanatorium, Peshtera PT2

1925-29		**Unwmk. Typo.**	**Perf. 11½**	
RA1	PT1	1 l blk, grnsh bl	2.75	.25
RA2	PT1	1 l chocolate ('26)	2.75	.25
RA3	PT1	1 l orange ('27)	3.00	.30
RA4	PT1	1 l pink ('28)	4.50	.30
RA5	PT1	1 l vio, pnksh ('29)	4.75	.30
RA6	PT2	2 l blue green	.35	.25
RA7	PT2	2 l violet ('27)	.35	.25
RA8	PT2	5 l deep blue	3.00	.80
RA9	PT2	5 l rose ('27)	3.75	.40
	Nos. RA1-RA9 (9)		25.20	3.10

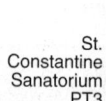

St. Constantine Sanatorium PT3

1930-33			
RA10	PT3	1 l red brn & ol grn	4.00	.25
RA11	PT3	1 l ol grn & yel ('31)	.50	.25
RA12	PT3	1 l red vio & ol brn ('33)	.50	.25
	Nos. RA10-RA12 (3)		5.00	.75

Trojan Rest Home PT4

Sanatorium PT5

1935		**Wmk. 145**	**Perf. 11, 11½**	
RA13	PT4	1 l choc & red org	.30	.25
RA14	PT4	1 l emer & indigo	.30	.25
RA15	PT5	5 l red brn & indigo	1.40	.35
	Nos. RA13-RA15 (3)		2.00	.85

BURMA

ˈbər-mə

LOCATION — Bounded on the north by China; east by China, Laos and Thailand; south and west by the Bay of Bengal, and India.

GOVT. — Self-governing unit of the British Commonwealth

AREA — 261,789 sq. mi.

POP. — 35,313,905 (1983)

CAPITAL — Rangoon

Burma was part of India from 1826 until April 1, 1937, when it became a

self-governing unit of the British Commonwealth and received a constitution.

> 12 Pies = 1 Anna
> 16 Annas = 1 Rupee

> **Catalogue values for unused stamps in this country are for Never Hinged items, beginning with Scott 35 in the regular postage section and Scott O28 in the official section.**

Watermarks

Wmk. 254 —   Wmk. 257 —
Elephant Heads   Curved Wavy Lines

Stamps of India 1926-36 Overprinted

1937, Apr. 1		**Wmk. 196**	**Perf. 14**	
1	A46	3p slate	1.25	.25
	Never hinged		2.25	
2	A71	½a green	.65	.25
	Never hinged		1.15	
3	A68	9p dark green	.65	.25
	Never hinged		1.15	
4	A72	1a dark brown	2.75	.25
	Never hinged		5.25	
5	A49	2a ver (small die)	.65	.25
	Never hinged		1.15	
6	A57	2a6p buff	.55	.25
	Never hinged		1.10	
7	A51	3a carmine rose	2.75	.50
	Never hinged		5.25	
8	A70	3a6p deep blue	4.25	.25
	Never hinged		7.50	
a.	3a6p dull blue		14.50	9.00
	Never hinged		20.00	
9	A52	4a olive green	.75	.25
	Never hinged		1.30	
10	A53	6a bister	.75	.60
	Never hinged		1.30	
11	A54	8a red violet	2.25	.25
	Never hinged		4.00	
12	A55	12a claret	8.50	3.25
	Never hinged		15.00	

Overprinted

13	A56	1r green & brown	35.00	5.00
	Never hinged		57.50	
14	A56	2r brn org & car rose	29.00	40.00
	Never hinged		45.00	
15	A56	5r dk violet & ultra	32.50	45.00
	Never hinged		55.00	
16	A56	10r car & green	135.00	125.00
	Never hinged		230.00	
17	A56	15r ol green & ultra	450.00	225.00
	Never hinged		700.00	
18	A56	25r blue & ocher	750.00	500.00
	Never hinged		1,350.	
	Nos. 1-18 (18)		1,457.	946.60
	Set, never hinged		2,475.	

For overprints see Nos. 1N1-1N3, 1N25-1N26, 1N47.

King George VI
A1   A2

Royal Barge — A3

Elephant Moving Teak Log — A4

Farmer Plowing Rice Field — A5

Sailboat on Irrawaddy River — A6

Peacock — A7

George VI — A8

1938-40		**Litho.**	**Perf. 13½x14** **Wmk. 254**	
18A	A1	1p red org ('40)	2.25	1.10
	Never hinged		3.25	
19	A1	3p violet	.25	2.60
	Never hinged		.35	
20	A1	6p ultramarine	.25	.25
	Never hinged		.30	
21	A1	9p yel green	.90	1.60
	Never hinged		1.25	
22	A2	1a brown violet	.25	.25
	Never hinged		.30	
23	A2	1½a turquoise green	.25	3.25
	Never hinged		.35	
24	A2	2a carmine	1.60	.55
	Never hinged		2.40	
			Perf. 13	
25	A3	2a6p rose lake	10.00	3.25
	Never hinged		15.00	
26	A4	3a dk violet	10.00	3.25
	Never hinged		15.00	
27	A5	3a6p dp bl & brt bl	2.50	7.75
	Never hinged		3.50	
28	A2	4a slate blue, perf. 13½x14	2.00	.25
	Never hinged		2.90	
29	A6	8a slate green	2.75	.60
	Never hinged		4.25	
			Perf. 13½	
30	A7	1r brt ultra & dk violet	3.00	1.00
	Never hinged		4.25	
31	A7	2r dk vio & red brown	16.00	4.75
	Never hinged		22.50	
32	A8	5r car & dull vio	45.00	47.50
	Never hinged		67.50	
33	A8	10r gray grn & brn	50.00	80.00
	Never hinged		75.00	
	Nos. 18A-33 (16)		147.00	157.95
	Set, never hinged		220.00	

See Nos. 51-65. For overprints and surcharges see Nos. 34-50, O15-O27, 1N4-1N11, 1N28-1N30, 1N37-1N46, 1N48-1N49.

No. 25
Surcharged
in Black

1940, May 6   *Perf. 13*
34   A3   1a on 2a6p rose lake   3.00   2.75
      Never hinged   4.50

Centenary of first postage stamp.

> **Catalogue values for unused stamps in this section, from this point to the end of the section, are for Never Hinged items.**

Nos. 18A to 33 Overprinted in Black

a

b

1945
35	A1(a)	1p red orange	.25	.25
a.		Pair, one without overprint	1,850.	
		Hinged	1,275.	
36	A1(a)	3p violet	.25	1.60
37	A1(a)	6p ultramarine	.25	.35
38	A1(a)	9p yel green	.35	1.40
39	A2(a)	1a brown violet	.25	.25
40	A2(a)	1½a turq green	.25	.25
41	A2(a)	2a carmine	.25	.25
42	A3(b)	2a6p rose lake	2.25	2.50
43	A4(b)	3a dk violet	1.75	.25
44	A5(b)	3a6p dp bl & brt bl	.25	.85
45	A2(a)	4a slate blue	.25	.85
46	A6(b)	8a slate green	.25	1.60
47	A7(b)	1r brt ultra & dk vio	.50	.60
48	A7(b)	2r dk vio & red brown	.50	1.50
49	A8(b)	5r car & dull vio	.60	1.50
50	A8(b)	10r gray grn & brn	.60	1.50
		Nos. 35-50 (16)	8.80	15.50

Types of 1938
Perf. 13½x14

1946, Jan. 1   **Litho.**   **Wmk. 254**
51	A1	3p brown	.25	3.75
52	A1	6p violet	.25	.40
53	A1	9p dull green	.25	5.75
54	A2	1a deep blue	.25	.25
55	A2	1½a salmon	.25	.25
56	A2	2a rose lake	.25	.60

Perf. 13
57	A3	2a6p greenish blue	3.25	6.75
58	A4	3a blue violet	7.00	9.50
59	A5	3a6p ultra & gray blk	2.25	4.50
60	A2	4a rose lil, perf. 13½x14	.60	1.00
61	A6	8a deep magenta	2.00	6.25

Perf. 13½
62	A7	1r dp mag & dk vio	2.10	3.25
63	A7	2r salmon & red brn	7.50	6.25
64	A8	5r red brn & dk grn	8.50	25.00
65	A8	10r dk vio & car	21.00	37.50
		Nos. 51-65 (15)	55.70	111.00

For overprints see Nos. 70-84, O28-O42.

Burmese
Man — A9

Burmese
Woman — A10

Mythological
Chinze — A11

Elephant Hauling
Teak — A12

1946, May 2   *Perf. 13*
66	A9	9p peacock green	.30	.25
67	A10	1½a brt violet	.30	.25
68	A11	2a dark green	.30	.25
69	A12	3a6p ultramarine	.70	.55
		Nos. 66-69 (4)	1.60	1.30

Victory of the Allied Nations in WWII.

Nos. 51-65 Overprinted in Black

1947, Oct. 1   *Perf. 13½x14, 13, 13½*
70	A1	3p brown	1.50	.85
71	A1	6p violet	.25	.40
72	A1	9p dull green	.25	.40
a.		Inverted overprint	26.00	32.50
73	A2	1a deep blue	.25	.40
74	A2	1½a salmon	2.10	.25
75	A2	2a rose lake	.40	.30
76	A3	2a6p greenish bl	2.25	1.75
77	A4	3a blue violet	4.00	2.00
78	A5	3a6p ultra & gray blk	1.60	2.75
79	A2	4a rose lilac	2.25	.50
80	A6	8a dp magenta	2.25	3.00
81	A7	1r dp mag & dk vio	7.50	3.00
82	A7	2r sal & red brn	7.50	7.75
83	A8	5r red brn & dk grn	7.50	6.00
84	A8	10r dk vio & car	5.00	6.00
		Nos. 70-84 (15)	44.60	35.35

The overprint is slightly larger on Nos. 76 to 78 and 80 to 84. The Burmese characters read "Interim Government."

Other denominations are known with the overprint inverted or double.

OFFICIAL STAMPS

Stamps of India, 1926-34, Overprinted in Black

1937   **Wmk. 196**   *Perf. 14*
O1	A46	3p gray	4.25	.25
O2	A71	½a green	15.00	.25
O3	A68	9p dark green	5.25	1.60
O4	A72	1a dark brown	8.50	.30
O5	A49	2a vermilion	18.00	.75
O6	A57	2a6p buff	8.50	3.25
O7	A52	4a olive grn	8.50	.30
O8	A53	6a bister	8.50	15.00
O9	A54	8a red violet	8.50	3.25
O10	A55	12a claret	8.50	12.00

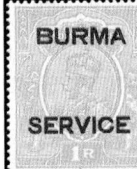
Overprinted

1937   (continued)
O11	A56	1r green & brown	24.00	9.50
O12	A56	2r buff & car rose	47.50	67.50
O13	A56	5r dk vio & ultra	160.00	70.00
O14	A56	10r car & green	450.00	250.00
		Nos. O1-O14 (14)	775.00	433.95
		Set, never hinged	825.00	

For overprint see No. 1N27.

Regular Issue of 1938
Overprinted in Black

Perf. 13½x14, 13, 13½
1939   **Wmk. 254**
O15	A1	3p violet	.35	.45
O16	A1	6p ultramarine	.35	.45
O17	A1	9p yel green	5.00	6.25
O18	A2	1a brown violet	.40	.50
O19	A2	1½a turquoise green	4.50	2.75
O20	A2	2a carmine	1.50	.50
O21	A2	4a slate blue	5.50	4.75

Overprinted

O22	A3	2a6p rose lake	24.00	20.00
O23	A6	8a deep magenta	19.00	5.00
O24	A7	1r brt ultra & dk vio	20.00	7.00
O25	A7	2r dk vio & red brn	37.50	18.00
O26	A8	5r car & dull vio	31.00	40.00
O27	A8	10r gray grn & brn	160.00	50.00
		Nos. O15-O27 (13)	309.10	155.65
		Set, never hinged	420.00	

For overprints see Nos. 1N12-1N16, 1N31-1N36, 1NO1.

> **Catalogue values for unused stamps in this section, from this point to the end of the section, are for Never Hinged items.**

Nos. 51-56, 60 Overprinted Like Nos. O15-O21

1946   *Perf. 13½x14*
O28	A1	3p brown	3.75	5.50
O29	A1	6p violet	2.75	2.75
O30	A1	9p dull green	.70	5.75
O31	A2	1a deep blue	.30	2.50
O32	A2	1½a salmon	.30	.40
O33	A2	2a rose lake	.35	2.25
O34	A2	4a rose lilac	.35	.90

Nos. 57, 61-65 Ovptd. Like Nos. O22-O27
Perf. 13, 13½
O35	A3	2a6p greenish blue	2.50	10.50
O38	A6	8a deep magenta	4.50	6.25
O39	A7	1r dp mag & dk vio	1.90	9.50
O40	A7	2r salmon & red brn	10.00	55.00
O41	A8	5r red brn & dk grn	19.00	67.50
O42	A8	10r dk violet & car	20.00	75.00
		Nos. O28-O42 (13)	66.40	243.80

Nos. O28 to O42 Overprinted in Black

1947
O43	A1	3p brown	2.40	.50
O44	A1	6p violet	4.75	.25
O45	A1	9p dull green	6.25	1.25

O46	A2	1a deep blue	6.25	1.10
O47	A2	1½a salmon	10.50	.60
O48	A2	2a rose lake	6.25	.30
O49	A3	2a6p greenish bl	35.00	18.00
O50	A2	4a rose lilac	24.00	.80
O51	A6	8a dp magenta	24.00	5.00
O52	A7	1r dp mag & dk vio	17.50	3.00
O53	A7	2r sal & red brn	17.50	25.00
O54	A8	5r red brn & dk grn	18.00	25.00
O55	A8	10r dk vio & car	18.00	37.50
		Nos. O43-O55 (13)	190.40	118.30

The overprint is slightly larger on Nos. O49 and O51 to O55. The Burmese characters read "Interim Government."

OCCUPATION STAMPS

Issued by Burma Independence Army (in conjunction with Japanese occupation officials)

Henzada Issue
Stamps of Burma, 1937-40, Overprinted in Black Blue, or Red; Nos. 1, 3, 5 Overprinted in Blue or Black

Henzada Type I

1942, May   **Wmk. 196**   *Perf. 14*
1N1	A46	3p slate	5.00	25.00
1N2	A68	9p dark green	30.00	80.00
1N3	A49	2a vermilion	130.00	220.00

On 1938-40 George VI Issue
Perf. 13½x14
Wmk. 254
1N4	A1	1p red orange	275.00	400.00
1N5	A1	3p violet	45.00	95.00
1N6	A1	6p ultra	30.00	65.00
1N7	A1	9p yel green	1,100.	
1N8	A2	1a brown violet	11.00	50.00
1N9	A2	1½a turq green	25.00	85.00
1N10	A2	2a carmine	25.00	85.00
1N11	A2	4a slate blue	30.00	120.00

On Official Stamps of 1939
1N12	A1	3p violet	150.00	300.00
1N13	A1	6p ultra	175.00	300.00
1N14	A2	1½a turq green	200.00	350.00
1N15	A2	2a carmine	425.00	550.00
1N16	A2	4a slate blue	1,350.	

Authorities believe this overprint was officially applied only to postal stationery and that the adhesive stamps existing with it were not regularly issued. It has been called "Henzada Type II."

Myaungmya Issue
1937 George V Issue Overprinted in Black

Myaungmya Type I

1942, May   **Wmk. 196**   *Perf. 14*
1N25	A68	9p dk green	130.00	
1N26	A70	3a6p deep blue	85.00	

On Official Stamp of 1937, No. O8
1N27	A53	6a bister	95.00	

On 1938-40 George VI Issue
Perf. 13½x14
Wmk. 254
1N28	A1	9p yel green	175.00	
1N29	A2	1a brown vio	650.00	

1N30	A2	4a sl blue (blk ovpt. over red)		190.00	

On Official Stamps of 1939

1N31	A1	3p violet		35.00	110.00
1N32	A1	6p ultra		25.00	80.00
1N33	A1	1a brown vio		25.00	85.00
1N34	A2	1½a turq green		850.00	1,350.
1N35	A2	2a carmine		32.50	120.00
1N36	A2	4a slate blue		32.50	95.00

1938-40 George VI Issue Overprinted

Myaungmya Type II

1942, May

1N37	A1	3p violet		21.00	90.00
1N38	A1	6p ultra		60.00	130.00
1N39	A1	9p yel green		25.00	85.00
1N40	A2	1a brown vio		17.50	80.00
1N41	A2	2a carmine		32.50	100.00
1N42	A2	4a slate blue		57.50	130.00

Nos. 30-31 Overprinted

Myaungmya Type III

1N43	A7	1r brt ultra & dk vio		400.00	650.00
1N44	A7	2r dk vio & red brn		210.00	475.00

Pyapon Issue

No. 5 and 1938-40 George VI Issue Overprinted

1942, May

1N45	A1	6p ultra	100.00	
1N46	A2	1a brown vio	120.00	300.00
1N47	A49	2a vermilion	100.00	
1N48	A2	2a carmine	160.00	350.00
1N49	A2	4a slate blue	850.00	850.00
		Nos. 1N45-1N49 (5)	1,330.	

Nos. 1N47-1N49 are valued in faulty condition.
Counterfeits of the peacock overprints exist.

OCCUPATION OFFICIAL STAMP

Myaungmya Issue
Burma No. O23 Overprinted in Black

1942, May   Wmk. 254   Perf. 13

1NO1	A6	8a slate green	110.00	

Overprint characters translate: "Office use."
Two types of overprint differ mainly in base of peacock which is either 5mm or 8mm.

ISSUED UNDER JAPANESE OCCUPATION

Yano Seal — OS1

Wmk. ABSORBO DUPLICATOR and Outline of Elephant in Center of Sheet Handstamped
1942, June 1   Perf. 12x11
Without Gum

2N1	OS1	1(a) vermilion	50.00	85.00

This stamp is the handstamped impression of the personal chop or seal of Shizuo Yano, chairman of the committee appointed to re-establish the Burmese postal system. It was prepared in Rangoon on paper captured from the Burma Government Offices. Not every stamp shows a portion of the watermark.

Farmer Plowing — OS2

Vertically Laid Paper Without Gum
Wmk. ELEPHANT BRAND and Outline of Trumpeting Elephant Covering Several Stamps
1942, June 15   Litho.   Perf. 11x12

2N2	OS2	1a scarlet	22.50	25.00

See illustration OS4.

Same, Surcharged with New Value
1942, Oct. 15

2N3	OS2	5c on 1a scarlet	22.50	27.50

Stamps of Japan, 1937-42, as shown, Handstamp Surcharged with New Value in Black

Rice Harvest A83

General Nogi A84

Power Plant A85

Admiral Togo A86

Diamond Mountains, Korea — A89

Yomei Gate, Nikko — A91

Mount Fuji and Cherry Blossoms A94

Torii of Miyajima Shrine — A96

1942, Sept.   Wmk. 257   Perf. 13

2N4	A83	¼a on 1s fawn	45.00	52.50
2N5	A84	½a on 2s crim	52.50	55.00
2N6	A85	¾a on 3s green	85.00	90.00
2N7	A86	1a on 5s brn lake	82.50	72.50
2N8	A89	3a on 7s dp green	130.00	150.00
2N9	A86	4a on 4s dk green	65.00	72.50
a.		4a on 4s + 2s dk green (#B5)	190.00	200.00
2N10	A90	8a on 8s dk pur & pale vio	180.00	180.00
a.		Red surcharge	300.00	325.00
2N11	A91	1r on 10s lake	26.00	30.00
2N12	A94	2r on 20s ultra	60.00	60.00
a.		Red surcharge	60.00	60.00
2N13	A96	3r on 30s pck bl	17.50	32.50
a.		Red surcharge	30.00	37.50
		Nos. 2N4-2N13 (10)	743.50	795.00

Numerous double, inverted, etc., surcharges exist.

Re-surcharged in Black
1942, Oct. 15

2N14	A83	1c on ¼a on 1s	65.00	65.00
2N15	A84	2c on ½a on 2s	65.00	65.00
2N16	A85	3c on ¾a on 3s	65.00	65.00
a.		"3C." in blue	225.00	
2N17	A86	5c on 1a on 5s	90.00	77.50
2N18	A89	10c on 3a on 7s	160.00	150.00
2N19	A86	15c on 4a on 4s	55.00	60.00
2N20	A90	20c on 8a on 8s (#2N10)	825.00	750.00
a.		On #2N10a	400.00	300.00
		Nos. 2N14-2N20 (7)	1,325.	1,232.

No. 2N16a was issued in the Shan States. Done locally, numerous different hand-stamps of each denomination can exist.

Stamps of Japan, 1937-42, Handstamp Surcharged with New Value in Black
1942, Oct. 15

2N21	A83	1c on 1s fawn	32.50	24.00
2N22	A84	2c on 2s crim	65.00	42.50
2N23	A85	3c on 3s green	92.50	65.00
a.		"3C." in blue	110.00	120.00
2N24	A86	5c on 5s brn lake	100.00	60.00
a.		"5C." in violet	180.00	60.00
2N25	A89	10c on 7s dp grn	120.00	82.50
2N26	A86	15c on 4s dk grn	30.00	30.00
2N27	A90	20c on 8s dk pur & pale vio	210.00	110.00
		Nos. 2N21-2N27 (7)	650.00	414.00

Nos. 2N23a and 2N24a were issued in the Shan States.

Burma State Government Crest — OS3

Unwmk.
1943, Feb. 15   Litho.   Perf. 12
Without Gum

2N29	OS3	5c carmine	27.50	32.50
a.		Imperf.	27.50	32.50

This stamp was intended to be used to cover the embossed George VI envelope stamp and generally was sold affixed to such envelopes. It is also known used on private envelopes.

Farmer Plowing — OS4

1943, Mar.   Typo.   Without Gum

2N30	OS4	1c deep orange	5.00	10.00
2N31	OS4	2c yel green	1.00	1.20
2N32	OS4	3c blue	4.00	1.20
a.		Laid paper	24.00	35.00
2N33	OS4	5c carmine	4.00	7.50
a.		Small "5c"	27.50	20.00
b.		Imperf.	130.00	

2N34	OS4	10c violet brown	7.75	8.00
2N35	OS4	15c red violet	1.00	4.00
a.		Laid paper	7.25	25.00
2N36	OS4	20c dull purple	1.00	1.20
2N37	OS4	30c blue green	1.00	2.50
		Nos. 2N30-2N37 (8)	24.75	35.60

Small "c" in Nos. 2N34 to 2N37.

Burmese Soldier Carving "Independence" OS5

Farmer Rejoicing OS6

Boy with Burmese Flag — OS7

Hyphen-hole Perf., Pin-Perf. x Hyphen-hole Perf.
1943, Aug. 1   Typo.

2N38	OS5	1c orange	1.50	2.10
a.		Perf. 11	11.50	19.50
2N39	OS6	3c blue	3.00	3.25
a.		Perf. 11	12.00	20.00
2N40	OS7	5c rose	3.00	3.50
a.		Perf. 11	22.50	10.00
		Nos. 2N38-2N40 (3)	7.50	8.85

Declaration of the independence of Burma by the Ba Maw government, Aug. 1, 1943.

Burmese Girl Carrying Water Jar — OS8

Elephant Carrying Teak Log — OS9

Watch Tower of Mandalay Palace — OS10

1943, Oct. 1   Litho.   Perf. 12½

2N41	OS8	1c dp salmon	24.00	18.00
2N42	OS8	2c yel green	1.00	2.40
2N43	OS8	3c violet	1.00	2.75
2N44	OS9	5c rose	1.00	1.00
2N45	OS9	10c blue	2.00	1.25
2N46	OS9	15c vermilion	1.20	3.50
2N47	OS9	20c yel green	1.20	2.10
2N48	OS9	30c brown	1.20	2.40
2N49	OS10	1r vermilion	1.00	2.40
2N50	OS10	2r violet	1.00	2.75
		Nos. 2N41-2N50 (10)	34.60	38.55

No. 2N49 exists imperforate. Canceled to order examples of Nos. 2N42-2N50 same values as unused.

Bullock Cart OS11

Shan Woman OS12

1943, Oct. 1   Perf. 12½

2N51	OS11	1c brown	40.00	47.50
2N52	OS11	2c yel green	45.00	47.50
2N53	OS11	3c violet	7.00	14.00
2N54	OS11	5c ultra	2.75	8.50
2N55	OS12	10c blue	18.00	22.50

2N56	OS12 20c rose	42.50	22.50
2N57	OS12 30c brown	27.50	75.00
	Nos. 2N51-2N57 (7)	182.75	237.50

For use only in the Shan States. Perak No. N34 also used in Shan States. Canceled-to-order stamps are valued at ½ used value.

Surcharged in Black

1944, Nov. 1

2N58	OS11 1c brown	4.25	8.00
2N59	OS11 2c yel green	1.00	5.00
a.	Inverted surcharge	500.00	850.00
2N60	OS11 3c violet	2.75	8.50
2N61	OS11 5c ultra	2.50	3.00
2N62	OS12 10c blue	4.00	3.00
2N63	OS12 20c rose	1.00	2.00
2N64	OS12 30c brown	1.00	2.25
	Nos. 2N58-2N64 (7)	16.50	31.75

Top line of surcharge reads: "Bama naing ngan daw" (Burma State). Bottom line repeats denomination in Burmese. Surcharge applied when the Shan States came under Burmese government administration, Dec. 24, 1943. Canceled-to-order stamps same value as unused.

BUSHIRE

bü-'shir

LOCATION — On Persian Gulf

Bushire is an Iranian port that British troops occupied Aug. 8, 1915.

20 Chahis (or Shahis) = 1 Kran
10 Krans = 1 Toman

Watermark

Wmk. 161 — Lion

ISSUED UNDER BRITISH OCCUPATION

Basic Iranian Designs

Ahmad
Shah — A32

Imperial
Crown — A33

King Darius,
Farvahar overhead
Overhead — A34

Ruins of
Persepolis — A35

Iranian Stamps of 1911-13 Overprinted in Black

BUSHIRE
Under British
Occupation.

Perf. 11½, 11½x11
Typo. & Engr.

1915, Aug. 15   **Unwmk.**

N1	A32 1c green & org	120.00	80.00
N2	A32 2c red & sepia	120.00	80.00
N3	A32 3c gray brn & grn	150.00	100.00
N4	A32 5c brown & car	950.00	800.00
N5	A32 6c green & red brn	120.00	60.00
N6	A32 9c yel brn & vio	130.00	100.00
a.	Double overprint		
N7	A32 10c red & org brn	150.00	120.00
N8	A32 12c grn & ultra	150.00	120.00
N9	A32 1k ultra & car	200.00	150.00
a.	Double overprint	7,500.	
N10	A32 24c vio & grn	180.00	140.00
N11	A32 2k grn & red vio	475.00	350.00
N12	A32 3k vio & blk	500.00	400.00
N13	A32 5k red & ultra	400.00	325.00
N14	A32 10k ol bis & cl	400.00	350.00
	Nos. N1-N14 (14)	4,045.	3,175.

Forged overprints exist of Nos. N1-N29. The Bushire overprint exists on Iran No. 537 but is considered a forgery.

Covers: Covers of this issue are scarce. Values start at $450.

No Period after "OCCUPATION"

N1b	A32 1c green & org	210.00	225.00
N2b	A32 2c red & sepia	210.00	210.00
N3b	A32 3c gray brn & grn	275.00	300.00
N5b	A32 6c green & red brn	210.00	190.00
N6b	A32 9c yel brn & vio	225.00	275.00
N7b	A32 10c red & org brn	225.00	250.00
N8b	A32 12c grn & ultra	275.00	275.00
N9b	A32 1k ultra & car	440.00	185.00
N10b	A32 24c vio & grn	490.00	300.00
N11b	A32 2k grn & red vio	1,200.	750.00
N12b	A32 3k vio & blk	1,050.	1,000.
N13b	A32 5k red & ultra	800.00	650.00
N14b	A32 10k ol bis & cl	750.00	600.00

On Iranian Stamps of 1915
Perf. 11, 11½

1915, Sept.   **Wmk. 161**

N15	A33 1c car & indigo	800.00	700.
N16	A33 2c blue & car	12,000.	12,000.
N17	A33 3c dk grn	950.	950.
N18	A33 5c red	11,000.	11,000.
N19	A33 6c ol grn & car	10,000.	10,000.
N20	A33 9c yel brn & vio	1,500.	1,400.
N21	A33 10c bl grn & yel brn	2,300.	2,300.
N22	A33 12c ultra	2,500.	2,500.
N23	A34 1k sil, yel brn & gray	1,600.	1,300.
N24	A33 24c yel brn & dk brn	1,300.	1,100.
N25	A34 2k sil, bl & rose	1,350.	1,200.
N26	A34 3k sil, vio & brn	1,350.	1,200.
N27	A34 5k sil, brn & grn	1,950.	1,400.
a.	Inverted overprint	—	25,000.
N28	A35 1t gold, pur & blk	2,300.	1,700.
N29	A35 3t gold, cl & red brn	6,500.	6,500.

Persia resumed administration of Bushire post office Oct. 16, 1915.

Covers: Commercial covers of this issue are scarce. Values start at about $1,750.

CAMEROUN

ˌka-mə-'rün

(Kamerun)

LOCATION — On the west coast of Africa, north of the equator
AREA — 456,054 sq. mi.
POP. — 9,060,000 (est. 1983)

CAPITAL — Yaounde

Before World War I, Cameroun (Kamerun) was a German Protectorate. It was occupied during the war by Great Britain and France and in 1922 was mandated to these countries by the League of Nations.

100 Pfennig = 1 Mark
12 Pence = 1 Shilling
100 Centimes = 1 Franc

Watermark

Wmk. 125 — Lozenges

STAMPS OF GERMANY USED IN CAMEROUN

Type A

KAMERUN
Post Office opened 2/1/1887, was redesignated Duala 6/1/1901, and closed 9/27/1914.

1A1	A 3pf green (#37)	1,750.
	On cover	2,500.
1A2	A 5pf violet (#38)	225.00
	On cover	550.00
1A3	A 10pf red (#39)	140.00
	On cover	260.00
a.	10pf rose (#39b)	1,100.
	On cover	4,500.
1A4	A 20pf ultra (#40)	60.00
	On cover	150.00
a.	20pf blue (#40b)	60.00
	On cover	150.00
1A5	A 25pf red brn (#41a)	1,900.
	On cover	3,000.
1A6	A 50pf deep grayish ol grn (#42)	140.00
	On cover	375.00
a.	50pf gray (#42a)	165.00
	On cover	450.00
b.	50pf brt olive (#42b)	1,100.
	On cover	2,250.
c.	50pf dk ol grn (#42c)	225.00
	On cover	600.00
1A7	A 2m dull vio pur (#36b)	750.00
	On cover	3,750.
a.	2m e lilac (#36d)	1,100.
	On cover	4,500.
1A8	A 3pf gray brn (#46)	47.50
	On cover	90.00
a.	3pf brown (#46)	90.00
	On cover	110.00
b.	3pf yel brn (#46a)	50.00
	On cover	80.00
c.	3pf red brn (#46c)	65.00
	On cover	120.00
d.	3pf brown ocher (#46f)	60.00
	On cover	110.00
e.	3pf ol brn (#46e)	60.00
	On cover	110.00
1A9	A 5pf blue green (#47)	25.00
	On cover	45.00
a.	5pf yellow green (#47a)	47.50
	On cover	87.50
b.	5pf deep green (#47b)	62.50
	On cover	110.00
c.	5pf gray green (#47b)	62.50
	On cover	110.00
1A10	A 10pf red (#48)	22.50
	On cover	45.00
a.	10pf dark carmine (#48c)	300.00
	On cover	600.00
b.	10pf brownish red (#48d)	1,050.
	On cover	2,600.
c.	10pf rose carmine (#48e)	37.50
	On cover	67.50
1A11	A 20pf pale ultra (#49)	18.00
	On cover	37.50
a.	20pf Prussian blue (#49a)	360.00
	On cover	875.00
b.	20pf grayish ultra (#49b)	55.00
	On cover	150.00
c.	20pf blue (#49c)	37.50
	On cover	75.00
1A12	A 25pf red orange (#50)	150.00
	On cover	375.00
a.	25pf org yel (#50b)	175.00
	On cover	300.00

1A13	A 50pf lilac brn (#51)	50.00
	On cover	125.00
a.	50pf brown red (#51c)	3,250.
b.	50pf red brown (#51d)	675.00
	On cover	675.00
c.	50pf red lilac brn (#51d)	275.00
d.	50pf dull rose brn (#51e)	72.50
	On cover	190.00
1A14	A 2m brown purple (#36)	72.50
	On cover	1,500.
a.	2m carmine lilac (#36e)	525.00

BIBUNDI
Post Office in operation 7/5/1891-1/8/1897, 5/22/1906-10/8/1914.
Type A Cancel with 2 Stars Below Year Date

2A1	A 3pf gray brn (#46)	240.00
a.	3pf brown (#46)	275.00
2A2	A 5pf blue grn (#47)	125.00
a.	5pf yel grn (#47a)	190.00
2A3	A 10pf red (#48)	110.00
a.	10pf brownish rose (#48e)	140.00
2A4	A 20pf blue (#49c)	140.00
2A5	A 25pf reddish org (#50)	575.00
a.	25pf org yel (#50b)	—
2A6	A 50pf lilac brn (#51)	250.00

Type B

BUEA
Post Office in operation 2/15/00-11/15/14.

3A1	B 3pf yel brn (#46a)	140.00
a.	3pf reddish brn (#46c)	140.00
b.	3pf brown ocher (#46f)	140.00
3A2	B 5pf blue green (#47)	165.00
3A3	B 10pf red (#48)	110.00
3A4	B 20pf pale ultra (#49)	—
3A5	B 50pf lilac brn (#51)	—
3A6	B 2m car lilac (#36e)	1,725.

DUALA/KAMERUN
Post Office in operation 6/1/01-9/27/14.

4A1	B 3pf yel brn (#46a)	50.00
a.	3pf red brn (#46c)	50.00
b.	3pf brn ocher (#46f)	55.00
4A2	B 5pf blue grn (#47)	25.00

GROS-BRATANGA
Post Office in operation 3/1/1893-12/31/1893.

5A1	A 3pf gray brn (#46)	240.00
5A2	A 5pf blue grn (#47)	190.00
a.	5pf yel grn (#47a)	240.00
5A3	A 10pf brownish rose (#48e)	210.00
a.	10pf car rose (#48d)	—
5A4	A 20pf blue (#49c)	175.00
a.	20pf Prussian blue (#49e)	1,725.
5A5	A 25pf reddish org (#50)	575.00
a.	25pf org yel (#50b)	900.00
5A6	A 50pf lilac brn (#51)	—

KRIBI
Post Office in operation 8/10/1894-10/13/1914.
Type A Cancel with 2 Stars Below Date

6A1	A 3pf yel brn (#46a)	70.00
a.	3pf red brn (#46c)	70.00
b.	3pf brn ocher (#46f)	70.00
c.	3pf gray brn (#46)	240.00
6A2	A 5pf blue grn (#47)	47.50
6A3	A 10pf red (#48)	85.00
a.	10pf brn rose (#48e)	110.00
b.	10pf red brn (#48f)	1,000.
6A4	A 20pf pale ultra (#49)	35.00
c.	20pf blue (#49c)	150.00
6A5	A 25pf red org (#50)	290.00
6A6	A 50pf lilac brn (#51)	87.50
a.	50pf dull rose brn (#51e)	210.00
6A7	A 2m brn purple (#36)	190.00
a.	2m car lilac (#36e)	450.00

RIO DEL REY
Post Office in operation 1/9/1897-8/1914.
Type A Cancel with 3 Stars Centered Below Date

7A1	A 3pf gray brown (#46)	240.00
a.	3pf yel brown (#46a)	190.00
b.	3pf red brown (#46c)	190.00
c.	3pf brown ocher (#46f)	190.00
7A2	A 5pf blue green (#47)	140.00
7A3	A 10pf red (#48)	85.00
7A4	A 20pf pale ultra (#49)	72.50
7A5	A 25pf red orange (#50)	575.00
7A6	A 50pf lilac brown (#51)	400.00

Several cancellation types exist. Values are for most common variety.

Type C

VIKTORIA

Post Office in operation 12/12/1888-
9/1914, spelling changed to Victoria
12/1900.

8A1	C	3pf green (#37)	—
8A2	C	5pf violet	1,250.
8A3	C	10pf red (#48)	375.00
8A4	C	20pf ultra (#40)	225.00
8A5	C	20pf blue (#49c)	225.00
8A6	C	50pf deep grayish ol grn (#42)	500.00
a.		50pf dk ol grn (#42c)	650.00
8A7	C	2m rose lilac (#36d)	2,750.
8A8	C	3pf yel brn (#46a)	50.00
a.		3pf red brn (#46c)	50.00
b.		3pf brn ocher (#46f)	55.00
c.		3pf ol brn (#46e)	55.00
d.		3pf brown (#46)	140.00
e.		3pf gray brn (#46)	140.00
8A9	C	5pf bl grn (#47)	42.50
a.		5pf yel grn (#47a)	70.00
b.		5pf deep grn (#47b)	250.00
c.		5pf gray grn (#47b)	250.00
8A10	C	10pf red (#48)	32.50
a.		10pf brnish red (#48c)	1,000.
b.		10pf car rose (#48d)	3,000.
c.		10pf brnish rose (#48e)	110.00
8A11	C	20pf pale ultra (#49)	27.50
a.		20pf grayish ultra (#49b)	425.00
b.		20pf blue (#49c)	110.00
8A12	C	25pf red org (#50)	290.00
a.		25pf org yel (#50b)	550.00
8A13	C	50pf lilac brn (#51)	50.00
a.		50pf dull rose brn (#51e)	210.00
8A14	C	2m brn pur (#36)	250.00

VICTORIA/KAMERUN

8A15	B	3pf yel brn (#46a)	140.00
a.		3pf red brn (#46c)	140.00
b.		3pf brn ocher (#46f)	140.00
8A16	B	2m brn pur (#36)	1,200.

Issued under German Dominion

Stamps of Germany
Overprinted in Black

1897		Unwmk.		Perf. 13½x14½
1	A9	3pf yel brn	11.00	17.00
	Never hinged		25.00	
	On cover			110.00
	On cover, single franking			240.00
a.	3pf red brown		62.50	240.00
	Never hinged		225.00	
	On cover			425.00
	On cover, single franking			500.00
b.	3pf dark brown		18.00	42.50
	Never hinged		60.00	
	On cover			150.00
	On cover, single franking			300.00
c.	3pf olive brown		10.00	42.50
	Never hinged		30.00	
	On cover			85.00
	On cover, single franking			175.00
2	A9	5pf green	6.00	8.50
	Never hinged		14.00	
	On cover			25.00
	On cover, single franking			40.00
3	A10	10pf carmine	4.25	5.00
	Never hinged		12.50	
	On cover			21.00
	On cover, single franking			45.00
4	A10	20pf ultra	4.00	8.00
	Never hinged		13.00	
	On cover			25.00
	On cover, single franking			57.50
a.	Diagonal half used as 10pf on cover			18,750.
5	A10	25pf orange	20.00	42.50
	Never hinged		60.00	
	On cover			120.00
	On cover, single franking			500.00
6	A10	50pf red brn	16.00	29.00
	Never hinged		50.00	
	On cover			67.50
	Nos. 1-6 (6)		61.25	110.00

Covers: Values for Nos. 1-5 are for covers
paying the correct rates. No. 6 is for overfranked complete cover, usually philatelic.

A3

Kaiser's Yacht "Hohenzollern" — A4

1900		Unwmk.	Typo.	Perf. 14
7	A3	3pf brown	1.40	1.75
	Never hinged		3.50	
	On cover			60.00
	On cover, single franking			40.00
8	A3	5pf green	13.50	1.40
	Never hinged		35.00	
	On cover			21.00
	On cover, single franking			18.00
9	A3	10pf carmine	40.00	1.50
	Never hinged		85.00	
	On cover			21.00
10	A3	20pf ultra	25.00	2.40
	Never hinged		60.00	
	On cover			25.00
a.	Vertical half used as 10pf on cover (Longji, '11)			7,500.
11	A3	25pf org & blk, yel	1.50	5.50
	Never hinged		4.25	
	On cover			50.00
12	A3	30pf org & blk, sal	2.00	4.75
	Never hinged		4.25	
	On cover			50.00
13	A3	40pf lake & blk	2.00	4.25
	Never hinged		4.25	
	On cover			50.00
14	A3	50pf pur & blk, sal	2.00	6.25
	Never hinged		4.25	
	On cover			42.50
15	A3	80pf lake & blk, rose	2.75	11.00
	Never hinged		6.25	
	On cover			42.50
		Engr.		Perf. 14½x14
16	A4	1m carmine	67.50	77.50
	Never hinged		170.00	
	On cover			110.00
17	A4	2m blue	5.50	77.50
	Never hinged		17.00	
	On cover			110.00
18	A4	3m blk vio	5.50	125.00
	Never hinged		21.00	
	On cover			175.00
19	A4	5m slate & car	160.00	575.00
	Never hinged		390.00	
	On cover			875.00
	Nos. 7-19 (13)		328.65	893.80

Covers: Values for Nos. 14-19 are for overfranked complete covers, usually philatelic.

1905-18		Wmk. 125		Typo.
20	A3	3pf brown ('18)	.85	
	Never hinged		2.25	
21	A3	5pf green	.85	1.75
	Never hinged		2.25	
	On cover			37.50
a.	Bklt. pane of 6		15.00	
b.	Bklt. pane of 6, 2 #21 + 4 #22		62.50	
c.	Booklet pane of 5 + label		375.00	
22	A3	10pf carmine ('06)	2.40	1.75
	Never hinged		15.50	
	On cover			37.50
a.	Bklt. pane of 6		17.50	
b.	Booklet pane of 5 + label		500.00	
23	A3	20pf ultra ('14)	3.25	125.00
	Never hinged		9.25	
	On cover			425.00
	On cover, single franking			850.00
a.	20pf dull blue ('17)		15.00	
	Never hinged		32.50	
24	A4	1m carmine (26x17 perf holes) ('15)	11.00	
	Never hinged		25.00	
a.	25x17 perf holes ('19)		12.00	
	Never hinged		42.50	
25	A4	5m slate & carmine (26x17 perf holes) ('13)	50.00	4,250.
	Never hinged		130.00	
	On cover			8,500.
a.	5m slate & rose red (26x17 perf holes) ('13)		30.00	
	Never hinged		85.00	
b.	5m slate & rose red (25x17 perf holes) ('19)		30.00	
	Never hinged		85.00	
	Nos. 20-25 (6)		68.35	

The 3pf and 1m were not placed in use.
Nos. 21a, 22a were made from sheet
stamps.

Covers: Value for No. 25 is for overfranked
complete cover, usually philatelic.

Issued under British Occupation
Stamps of German Cameroun
Surcharged

No. 53

No. 62

Wmk. Lozenges (125) (#54-56, 65);
Unwmk. (Other Values)

1915				Perf. 14, 14½
		Blue Surcharge		
53	A3	½p on 3pf brn	15.00	50.00
54	A3	½p on 5pf grn	5.00	16.50
a.	Double surcharge			1,000.
b.	Black surcharge			
55	A3	1p on 10pf car	2.50	12.00
a.	"1" with thin serifs		15.00	75.00
b.	Double surcharge		400.00	
c.	Black surcharge		20.00	82.50
d.	As "c," "1" with thin serifs		275.00	
e.	"C.E.F." omitted		3,200.	
f.	"1d" double		2,100.	
		Black Surcharge		
56	A3	2p on 20pf ultra	5.00	26.00
57	A3	2½p on 25pf org & blk, yel	18.00	65.00
a.	Double surcharge		12,000.	
58	A3	3p on 30pf org & blk, sal	18.00	65.00
a.	Large "3" in "3d"		900.00	
b.	Triple surcharge, two albino		290.00	
59	A3	4p on 40pf lake & blk	18.00	67.50
a.	Short "4" in "4d"		740.00	1,050.
60	A3	6p on 50pf pur & blk, sal	18.00	67.50
61	A3	8p on 80pf lake & blk, rose	18.00	67.50
62	A4	1sh on 1m car	200.00	900.00
a.	"S" inverted		1,000.	3,500.
63	A4	2sh on 2m bl	200.00	900.00
a.	"S" inverted		1,000.	3,500.
64	A4	3sh on 3m blk vio	200.00	900.00
a.	"S" inverted		1,000.	3,500.
b.	Double surcharge		12,000.	
65	A4	5sh on 5m sl & car	275.00	925.00
a.	"S" inverted		1,200.	3,750.
	Nos. 53-65 (13)		992.50	4,062.

The letters "C. E. F." are the initials of "Cameroons Expeditionary Force."
Numerous overprint varieties exist for Nos.
53-65.
Counterfeits exist of Nos. 54a, 54b.

Values for stamp with albino impressions of the surcharge

54c	½p on 5pf, double surcharge, one albino	240.
55g	1p on 10pf, double surcharge, one albino	100.
55h	1p on 10pf, triple surcharge, two albino	260.
56a	2p on 20pf, double surcharge, one albino	225.
57b	2½p on 25pf, double surcharge, one albino	—
58b	3p on 30pf, triple surcharge, two albino	290.
59b	4p on 40pf, triple surcharge, two albino	260.
59c	4p on 40pf, quadruple surcharge, three albino	1,900.
60a	6p on 50pf, double surcharge, one albino	210.
61a	4p on 40pf, double surcharge, two albino	1,250.
63b	8p on 80pf, double surcharge, one albino	1,700.
64c	3s on 3m, double surcharge, one albino	1,700.

See Cameroons for Nos. 66-77.

Issued under French Occupation

Gabon Nos. 37, 49-
52, 54, 57-58, 60,
62-64, 66, 69-70
Overprinted

1915		Unwmk.		Perf. 13½x14
		Inscribed "Congo Français"		
101	A10	10c red & car	32.50	24.00
	Never hinged		65.00	
	On cover			275.00
		Inscribed "Afrique Equatoriale"		
102	A10	1c choc & org	110.00	47.50
	Never hinged		260.00	
	On cover			875.00
103	A10	2c blk & choc	200.00	150.00
	On cover			1,100.
104	A10	4c vio & dp bl	200.00	150.00
	On cover			1,100.

105	A10	5c ol gray & grn	40.00	24.00
	Never hinged		85.00	
	On cover			525.00
105A	A10	10c red & car	22,500.	25,000
106	A10	20c ol brn & blk vio	210.00	210.00
	On cover			1,000.
107	A11	25c dp bl & choc	60.00	47.50
	Never hinged		140.00	
	On cover			675.00
108	A11	30c gray blk & red	200.00	200.00
	On cover			1,100.
109	A11	35c dk vio & grn	67.50	45.00
	Never hinged		150.00	
	On cover			550.00
a.	Double overprint		1,900.	
110	A11	40c choc & ultra	200.00	200.00
	On cover			1,000.
111	A11	45c car & vio	225.00	225.00
	On cover			1,100.
112	A11	50c bl grn & gray	225.00	225.00
	On cover			1,350.
113	A11	75c org & choc	275.00	225.00
	On cover			1,350.
114	A12	1fr dk brn & bis	260.00	225.00
	On cover			1,500.
115	A12	2fr car & brn	300.00	260.00
	On cover			1,700.
	Nos. 101-105,106-115 (15)		2,605.	2,258.

The overprint is vertical, reading up, on Nos.
101-106, 114-115, and horizontal on Nos.
107-113.

Stamps of
Middle
Congo,
Issue of
1907,
Overprinted

1916				Unwmk.
116	A1	1c ol gray & brn	110.00	110.00
	Never hinged		260.00	
	On cover			675.00
117	A1	2c violet & brn	110.00	110.00
	Never hinged		260.00	
	On cover			675.00
118	A1	4c blue & brown	120.00	120.00
	Never hinged		275.00	
	On cover			750.00
119	A1	5c dk green & blue	32.50	32.50
	Never hinged		65.00	
	On cover			325.00
120	A2	35c violet brn & bl	110.00	75.00
	Never hinged		240.00	
	On cover			450.00
121	A2	45c violet & red	87.50	75.00
	Never hinged		200.00	
	On cover			600.00

The overprint is vert., reading down, on Nos.
120-121.

Same Overprint On Stamps of French Congo, 1900

Wmk. Branch of Thistle (122)

Overprint Horizontal

122	A4	15c dull vio & ol grn	120.00	120.00
	On cover			525.00
a.	Inverted overprint		200.00	180.00

Wmk. Branch of Rose Tree (123)

Overprint Reading Up

123	A5	20c yellow grn & org	140.00	92.50
	On cover			600.00
124	A5	30c car rose & org	110.00	87.50
	On cover			750.00
125	A5	40c org brn & brt grn	105.00	80.00
	On cover			550.00
126	A5	50c gray vio & lil	110.00	87.50
	On cover			675.00
127	A5	75c red vio & org	110.00	85.00
	On cover			675.00

Wmk. Branch of Olive (124)

128	A6	1fr gray lilac & ol	125.00	120.00
	On cover			800.00
129	A6	2fr carmine & brn	160.00	120.00
	On cover			875.00
	Nos. 116-129 (14)		1,550.	1,315.

Values are for stamps centered in the grade
of fine.
Counterfeits exist of Nos. 101-129.

Overprint Reading Down

123a	A5	20c yellow grn & org	130.00	82.50
124a	A5	30c car rose & org	105.00	80.00
125a	A5	40c org brn & brt grn	100.00	80.00
126a	A5	50c gray vio & lil	100.00	80.00
127a	A5	75c red vio & org	110.00	85.00
128a	A6	1fr gray lilac & ol	110.00	110.00
129a	A6	2fr carmine & brn	140.00	110.00

Pairs, One Up, One Down

123b	A5	20c yellow grn & org	2,100.	2,100.
124b	A5	30c car rose & org	1,700.	1,700.
125b	A5	40c org brn & brt grn	1,750.	1,750.
126b	A5	50c gray vio & lil	1,700.	1,700.
127b	A5	75c red vio & org	1,700.	1,700.
128b	A6	1fr gray lilac & ol	1,900.	1,900.
129b	A6	2fr carmine & brn	1,900.	1,900.

Stamps of Middle Congo, Issue of 1907 Overprinted

1916-17   Unwmk.
130 A1 1c ol gray & brn   .40   .40
  Never hinged   .65
  On cover   67.50
 a.   Chalky paper   .40   .40
  Never hinged   .65
  On cover   67.50
131 A1 2c violet & brn   .50   .50
  Never hinged   .80
  On cover   67.50
 a.   Chalky paper   .45   .45
  Never hinged   .80
  On cover   67.50
132 A1 4c blue & brn   .85   .55
  Never hinged   1.20
  On cover   67.50
 a.   Chalky paper   .75   .55
  Never hinged   1.20
  On cover   67.50
133 A1 5c dk green & bl   .50   .40
  Never hinged   .80
  On cover   27.50
 a.   Chalky paper   .40   .40
  Never hinged   .80
  On cover   27.50
134 A1 10c carmine & bl   1.25   .80
  Never hinged   1.75
  On cover   16.00
 a.   Chalky paper   1.25   .75
  Never hinged   1.75
  On cover   16.00
135 A1 15c brn vio & rose ('17)   2.25   .80
  Never hinged   3.00
  On cover   19.00
 a.   Chalky paper   2.25   .75
  Never hinged   3.00
  On cover   19.00
136 A1 20c brown & bl   .90   .80
  Never hinged   1.50
  On cover   22.00
 a.   Chalky paper   .80   .70
  Never hinged   1.40
  On cover   22.00
137 A2 25c blue & grn   .90   .80
  Never hinged   1.50
  On cover   32.50
  On cover, single franking   87.50
 a.   Triple overprint   550.00   700.00
 d.   Chalky paper   .80   .60
  Never hinged   1.40
  On cover   32.50
138 A2 30c scarlet & grn   1.25   .80
  Never hinged   1.75
  On cover   40.00
  On cover, single franking   75.00
 a.   Double overprint   400.00   575.00
 b.   Chalky paper   1.25   .80
  Never hinged   1.75
  On cover   40.00
139 A2 35c vio brn & bl   .90   .80
  Never hinged   1.60
  On cover   40.00
  On cover, single franking   75.00
 a.   Chalky paper   .90   .80
  Never hinged   1.60
  On cover   75.00
140 A2 40c dull grn & brn   2.75   1.60
  Never hinged   4.25
  On cover   45.00
  On cover, single franking   87.50
 a.   Chalky paper   2.75   1.25
  Never hinged   4.25
  On cover   45.00
141 A2 45c violet & red   2.75   1.60
  Never hinged   4.25
  On cover   55.00
  On cover, single franking   87.50
 a.   Chalky paper   2.75   1.25
  Never hinged   4.25
  On cover   55.00
142 A2 50c blue grn & red   2.75   1.60
  Never hinged   4.25
  On cover   62.50
  On cover, single franking   125.00
 a.   Chalky paper   2.75   1.40
  Never hinged   4.25
  On cover   62.50
143 A2 75c brown & blue   2.75   1.60
  Never hinged   4.25
  On cover   55.00
  On cover, single franking   125.00
 a.   Chalky paper   2.75   1.50
  Never hinged   4.25
  On cover   55.00
144 A3 1fr dp grn & vio   2.00   1.60
  Never hinged   6.50
  On cover   67.50
  On cover, single franking   150.00
 a.   Chalky paper   2.00   1.60
  Never hinged   6.50
  On cover   67.50
145 A3 2fr vio & gray grn   8.25   6.75
  Never hinged   14.00
  On cover   80.00
  On cover, single franking   160.00
 a.   Chalky paper   8.25   6.00
  Never hinged   14.00
  On cover   80.00
146 A3 5fr blue & rose   13.50   11.00
  Never hinged   19.00
  On cover   100.00
  On cover, single franking   200.00
 a.   Chalky paper   13.50   11.00
  Never hinged   21.00
  On cover   100.00
  Nos. 130-146 (17)   44.45   32.40

No period after "Francaise"
130b A1 1c ol gray & brn   4.00   4.00
  Never hinged   5.25
131b A1 2c violet & brn   4.00   4.00
  Never hinged   5.25
137b A2 25c blue & grn   6.25   6.25
  Never hinged   11.00

138b A2 30c scarlet & grn   6.25   6.25
  Never hinged   11.00
139b A2 35c vio brn & bl   6.25   6.25
  Never hinged   11.00
140b A2 40c dull grn & brn   7.50   7.50
  Never hinged   13.50
141b A2 45c violet & red   7.50   7.50
  Never hinged   13.50
142b A2 50c blue grn & red   7.50   7.50
  Never hinged   13.50
144b A3 1fr dp grn & vio   14.50   14.50
  Never hinged   25.00
  Nos. 130b-144b (9)   63.75   63.75

Letter "s" of "Francaise" inverted
137c A2 25c blue & grn   6.25   6.25
  Never hinged   11.00
138d A2 30c scarlet & grn   6.25   6.25
  Never hinged   11.00
139c A2 35c vio brn & bl   6.25   6.25
  Never hinged   11.00
140c A2 40c dull grn & brn   6.25   6.25
  Never hinged   12.00
141c A2 45c violet & red   8.00   8.00
  Never hinged   13.50
142c A2 50c blue grn & red   8.00   8.00
  Never hinged   13.50
143c A2 75c brown & blue   8.00   8.00
  Never hinged   13.50
144c A3 1fr dp grn & vio   8.00   8.00
  Never hinged   13.50
145c A3 2fr vio & gray grn   32.50   32.50
  Never hinged   55.00
146c A3 5fr blue & rose   32.50   32.50
  Never hinged   55.00
  Nos. 137c-146c (10)   122.00   122.00

On Nos. 137-146 there is 7mm between "Cameroun" and "Occupation."

Provisional French Mandate

Types of Middle Congo, 1907, Overprinted

1921
147 A1 1c ol grn & org   .35   .30
  Never hinged   .50
  On cover   55.00
148 A1 2c brown & rose   .35   .30
  Never hinged   .50
  On cover   55.00
149 A1 4c gray & lt grn   .55   .55
  Never hinged   .80
  On cover   55.00
150 A1 5c dl red & org   .55   .55
  Never hinged   .80
  On cover   21.00
 a.   Double overprint   1,200.
151 A1 10c bl grn & lt grn   1.25   .90
  Never hinged   2.00
  On cover   42.50
152 A1 15c blue & org   .55   .55
  Never hinged   .80
  On cover   25.00
153 A1 20c red brn & ol   .85   .80
  Never hinged   1.25
  On cover   16.00
154 A2 25c slate & org   1.20   .80
  Never hinged   1.75
  On cover   13.50
155 A2 30c rose & ver   1.25   .80
  Never hinged   2.00
  On cover   22.50
  On cover, single franking   50.00
156 A2 35c gray & ultra   .85   .80
  Never hinged   1.25
  On cover   20.00
  On cover, single franking   32.50
157 A2 40c ol grn & org   1.25   .80
  Never hinged   2.00
  On cover   16.00
  On cover, single franking   22.50
158 A2 45c brown & rose   .85   .80
  Never hinged   1.25
  On cover   32.50
  On cover, single franking   75.00
159 A2 50c blue & ultra   1.25   .80
  Never hinged   2.00
  On cover   32.50
  On cover, single franking   67.50
160 A2 75c red brn & lt grn   1.25   .80
  Never hinged   2.00
  On cover   40.00
  On cover, single franking   62.50
161 A3 1fr slate & org   2.40   2.40
  Never hinged   3.50
  On cover   55.00
  On cover, single franking   65.00
162 A3 2fr ol grn & rose   6.50   5.50
  Never hinged   10.50
  On cover   62.50
  On cover, single franking   120.00
163 A3 5fr dull red & gray   9.50   8.00
  Never hinged   15.00
  On cover   67.50
  On cover, single franking   120.00
  Nos. 147-163 (17)   30.75   25.45

The 1c, 2c, 4c, 15c, 20c, 25c and 50c exist with overprint omitted. For listings, see the *Scott Specialized Catalogue of Stamps & Covers.*

Without Overprint
148b A1 2c brown & rose   225.00
  Never hinged   350.00
149b A1 4c gray & lt grn   260.00
  Never hinged   425.00

152b A1 15c blue & org   1,200.
154b A2 25c slate & org   1,200.
159b A2 50c blue & ultra   260.00
  Never hinged   425.00

Nos. 152, 162, 163, 158, 160 Surcharged with New Value and Bars

1924-25
164 A1 25c on 15c bl & org ('25)   1.25   1.25
  Never hinged   2.00
  On cover   16.00
165 A3 25c on 2fr ol grn & rose   1.75   1.75
  Never hinged   2.50
  On cover   16.00
166 A3 25c on 5fr red & gray   1.75   1.75
  Never hinged   2.50
  On cover   16.00
 a.   Pair, one without new value and bars
167 A2 65c on 45c brn & rose ('25)   2.00   2.00
  Never hinged   3.00
  On cover   75.00
  On cover, single franking   160.00
168 A2 85c on 75c red brn & lt grn ('25)   3.00   3.00
  Never hinged   4.50
  On cover   62.50
  On cover, single franking   110.00
  Nos. 164-168 (5)   9.75   9.75

French Mandate

Herder and Cattle Crossing Sanaga River — A5

Tapping Rubber Tree — A6

Rope Suspension Bridge A7

1925-38   Typo.   Perf. 14x13½
170 A5 1c ol grn & brn vio, *lav*   .25   .25
  Never hinged   .40
  On cover   42.50
171 A5 2c rose & grn, *grnsh*   .25   .25
  Never hinged   .40
  On cover   42.50
172 A5 4c blue & blk   .25   .25
  Never hinged   .40
  On cover   42.50
173 A5 5c org & red vio, *lav*   .25   .25
  Never hinged   .40
  On cover   35.00
174 A5 10c red brn & org, *yel*   .45   .40
  Never hinged   .65
  On cover   25.00
175 A5 15c sl grn & grn   .45   .40
  Never hinged   .65
  On cover   19.00
176 A5 15c lilac & red ('27)   1.00   .80
  Never hinged   1.40
  On cover   22.50

Perf. 13½x14
177 A6 20c ol brn & red brn   .70   .40
  Never hinged   1.00
  On cover   15.00
178 A6 20c green ('26)   .65   .50
  Never hinged   .85
  On cover   19.00
179 A6 20c brn red & ol brn ('27)   .65   .65
  Never hinged   .85
  On cover   32.50
180 A6 25c lt green & blk   .95   .50
  Never hinged   1.20
  On cover   15.00
181 A6 30c bluish grn & ver   .50   .30
  Never hinged   .70
  On cover   12.50
182 A6 30c dk grn & grn ('27)   .90   .70
  Never hinged   1.30
  On cover   32.50
183 A6 35c brown & black   1.10   .50
  Never hinged   1.35
  On cover   32.50
  On cover, single franking   50.00
184 A6 35c dl grn & grn ('38)   1.90   1.20
  Never hinged   2.40
  On cover   40.00
185 A6 40c orange & vio   2.00   1.20
  Never hinged   2.75
  On cover   40.00
  On cover, single franking   47.50

---

186 A6 45c dp rose & cer   .80   .50
  Never hinged   1.25
  On cover   22.50
  On cover, single franking   32.50
187 A6 45c vio & org brn ('27)   2.25   1.60
  Never hinged   3.00
  On cover   40.00
  On cover, single franking   62.50
188 A6 50c lt green & cer   .80   .30
  Never hinged   1.25
  On cover   12.50
189 A6 55c ultra & car ('38)   1.60   1.60
  Never hinged   2.10
  On cover   12.50
190 A6 60c red vio & blk   .80   .55
  Never hinged   1.25
  On cover   40.00
  On cover, single franking   67.50
191 A6 60c brown red ('26)   .95   .55
  Never hinged   1.50
  On cover   37.50
  On cover, single franking   75.00
192 A6 65c indigo & brn   1.20   1.20
  Never hinged   1.90
  On cover   67.50
  On cover, single franking   125.00
193 A6 75c indigo & dp bl   .80   .80
  Never hinged   1.25
  On cover   27.50
  On cover, single franking   37.50
194 A6 75c org brn & red vio ('27)   1.40   1.10
  Never hinged   1.90
  On cover   30.00
  On cover, single franking   110.00
195 A6 80c carmine & brn ('38)   1.40   1.20
  Never hinged   1.90
  On cover   62.50
  On cover, single franking   110.00
196 A6 85c dp rose & bl   1.60   1.20
  Never hinged   2.40
  On cover   55.00
  On cover, single franking   120.00
197 A6 90c brn red & cer ('27)   2.75   1.20
  Never hinged   3.75
  On cover   32.50
  On cover, single franking   87.50

Perf. 14x13½
198 A7 1fr indigo & brn   1.20   1.20
  Never hinged   1.60
  On cover   32.50
  On cover, single franking   67.50
199 A7 1fr dull bl ('26)   .80   .55
  Never hinged   1.20
  On cover   42.50
  On cover, single franking   80.00
200 A7 1fr ol brn & red vio ('27)   1.10   .80
  Never hinged   1.50
  On cover   27.50
  On cover, single franking   37.50
201 A7 1fr grn & dk brn ('29)   2.50   1.20
  Never hinged   3.25
  On cover   27.50
  On cover, single franking   40.00
202 A7 1.10fr rose red & dk brn ('28)   4.75   6.50
  Never hinged   7.25
  On cover   190.00
  On cover, single franking   350.00
203 A7 1.25fr gray & dp bl ('33)   5.50   3.50
  Never hinged   7.25
  On cover   32.50
  On cover, single franking   87.50
204 A7 1.50fr dull bl ('27)   1.20   .80
  Never hinged   1.90
  On cover   32.50
  On cover, single franking   75.00
205 A7 1.75fr brn & org ('33)   1.60   1.20
  Never hinged   2.40
  On cover   20.00
  On cover, single franking   27.50
206 A7 1.75fr dk bl & lt bl ('38)   2.50   1.60
  Never hinged   3.25
  On cover   37.50
  On cover, single franking   67.50
207 A7 2fr dl grn & brn org   2.00   1.20
  Never hinged   2.75
  On cover   40.00
  On cover, single franking   75.00
208 A7 3fr ol brn & red vio ('27)   7.25   2.75
  Never hinged   10.00
  On cover   40.00
  On cover, single franking   92.50
209 A7 5fr brn & blk, *bluish*   3.50   2.00
  Never hinged   5.25
  On cover   50.00
  On cover, single franking   87.50
 a.   Cliché of 2fr in plate of 5fr   1,450.
  Never hinged   1,750.
 b.   As "a," in pair with #209   1,700.
  Never hinged   2,250.
210 A7 10fr org & vio ('27)   14.50   7.25
  Never hinged   20.00
  On cover   55.00
  On cover, single franking   100.00
211 A7 20fr rose & ol grn ('27)   21.00   15.00
  Never hinged   32.50
  On cover   67.50
  On cover, single franking   125.00
  Nos. 170-211 (42)   98.00   65.90

Shades exist for several values.

For overprints and surcharge see Nos. 212, 264, 276, 278, 279, B7-B9; No. B21 in *Scott Standard Postage Stamp Catalogue,* Vol. 2.

No. 199 Surcharged with New Value and Bars in Red

1926
212 A7 1.25fr on 1fr dull blue   1.20   .80
  Never hinged   1.90
  On cover   62.50

On cover, single franking   110.00

Common Design Types
pictured following the introduction.

Colonial Exposition Issue
Common Design Types
Name of Country in Black

1931		**Engr.**	**Perf. 12½**	
213	CD70	40c deep green	5.50	4.00
		Never hinged	8.75	
		On cover		105.00
214	CD71	50c violet	5.50	4.75
		Never hinged	8.75	
		On cover		87.50
215	CD72	90c red orange	5.50	4.75
		Never hinged	8.75	
		On cover		150.00
		On cover, single franking		200.00
216	CD73	1.50fr dull blue	6.50	4.75
		Never hinged	9.25	
		On cover		140.00
		On cover, single franking		200.00
		Nos. 213-216 (4)	23.00	18.25

Paris International Exposition Issue
Common Design Types

1937			**Perf. 13**	
217	CD74	20c deep violet	1.75	1.75
		Never hinged	2.75	
		On cover		105.00
218	CD75	30c dark green	1.75	1.75
		Never hinged	2.75	
		On cover		87.50
219	CD76	40c carmine rose	1.75	1.75
		Never hinged	2.75	
		On cover		80.00
220	CD77	50c dark brown	1.90	1.90
		Never hinged	2.75	
		On cover		75.00
221	CD78	90c red	1.90	1.90
		Never hinged	2.75	
		On cover		105.00
		On cover, single franking		190.00
222	CD79	1.50fr ultramarine	1.90	1.90
		Never hinged	2.75	
		On cover		90.00
		On cover, single franking		150.00
		Nos. 217-222 (6)	10.95	10.95

French Colonial Art Exhibition
Common Design Type
Souvenir Sheet

1937			**Imperf.**	
222A	CD77	3fr org red & blk	8.00	9.50
		Never hinged	12.00	
		On cover		110.00
		On cover, single franking		175.00

New York World's Fair Issue
Common Design Type

1939			**Perf. 12½x12**	
223	CD82	1.25fr carmine lake	1.40	1.20
		Never hinged	2.00	
		On cover		80.00
		On cover, single franking		150.00
224	CD82	2.25fr ultra	1.40	1.20
		Never hinged	2.00	
		On cover		80.00
		On cover, single franking		140.00

For overprints and surcharges see Nos. 280-281, B14-B17; Nos. B23, B25 in *Scott Standard Postage Stamp Catalogue, Vol. 2.*

Mandara Woman — A19

Falls on M'bam River near Banyo — A20

Elephants A21

Man in Yaré — A22

1939-40		**Engr.**	**Perf. 13**	
225	A19	2c black brn	.25	.25
		Never hinged	.40	
226	A19	3c magenta ('40)	.25	.25
		Never hinged	.40	
		On cover		37.50
227	A19	4c deep ultra	.25	.25
		Never hinged	.40	
228	A19	5c red brown	.25	.25
		Never hinged	.40	
229	A19	10c dp bl grn	.25	.25
		Never hinged	.40	
230	A19	15c rose red	.30	.30
		Never hinged	.50	
231	A19	20c plum	.30	.30
		Never hinged	.50	
232	A20	25c black brn	.65	.65
		Never hinged	.90	
233	A20	30c dk red	.80	.70
		Never hinged	1.00	
234	A20	40c ultra ('40)	.80	.80
		Never hinged	1.00	
		On cover		17.50
235	A20	45c slate green ('40)	2.60	2.25
		Never hinged	3.50	
		On cover		30.00
236	A20	50c brown car	.90	.70
		Never hinged	1.10	
237	A20	60c pck blue ('40)	.75	.65
		Never hinged	.95	
		On cover		22.50
238	A20	70c plum ('40)	3.25	2.90
		Never hinged	4.50	
		On cover		30.00
239	A21	80c Prus blue	2.60	2.10
		Never hinged	3.25	
240	A21	90c Prus blue	.95	.75
		Never hinged	1.40	
		On cover, single franking	42.50	92.50
241	A21	1fr car rose	1.90	.95
		Never hinged	2.25	
242	A21	1fr choc ('40)	1.40	.80
		Never hinged	1.70	
		On cover		6.75
243	A21	1.25fr car rose	4.00	3.25
		Never hinged	5.50	
		On cover		62.50
		On cover, single franking		110.00
244	A21	1.40fr org red ('40)	1.25	.95
		Never hinged	1.75	
		On cover		40.00
		On cover, single franking		87.50
245	A21	1.50fr chocolate	1.20	.95
		Never hinged	1.35	
246	A21	1.60fr black brn ('40)	2.50	2.25
		Never hinged	3.25	
		On cover		42.50
		On cover, single franking		100.00
247	A21	1.75fr dk blue	1.40	.95
		Never hinged	2.10	
248	A21	2fr dk green	.90	.90
		Never hinged	1.20	
249	A21	2.25fr dk blue	1.40	.90
		Never hinged	2.25	
		On cover		55.00
		On cover, single franking		100.00
250	A21	2.50fr brt red vio ('40)	1.20	1.00
		Never hinged	1.60	
		On cover		32.50
		On cover, single franking		55.00
251	A21	3fr dk violet	1.40	.80
		Never hinged	1.70	
252	A22	5fr black brn	1.40	.95
		Never hinged	1.70	
253	A22	10fr brt red vio	2.00	1.60
		Never hinged	2.60	
254	A22	20fr dk green	4.00	3.25
		Never hinged	5.50	
		Nos. 225-254 (30)	41.10	32.85

For overprints and surcharges see Nos. 255-263, 265-275, 277, 278A, 279A, B10-B13; Nos. B22, B24 in *Scott Standard Postage Stamp Catalogue, Vol. 2.*

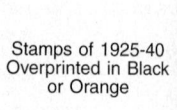

Stamps of 1925-40 Overprinted in Black or Orange

1940		**Perf. 14x13½, 13½x14, 13**		
255	A19	2c blk brn (O)	1.60	1.60
		Never hinged	2.10	
		On cover		67.50
256	A19	3c magenta	2.40	2.40
		Never hinged	3.75	
		On cover		120.00

257	A19	4c dp ultra (O)	1.60	1.60
		Never hinged	2.10	
		On cover		67.50
258	A19	5c red brn	5.50	5.50
		Never hinged	10.50	
		On cover		100.00
259	A19	10c dp bl grn (O)	1.60	1.60
		Never hinged	2.10	
		On cover		67.50
260	A19	15c rose red	2.40	2.40
		Never hinged	3.75	
		On cover		120.00
260A	A19	20c plum (O)	13.50	13.50
		Never hinged	30.00	
		On cover		230.00
261	A20	25c blk brn	1.60	1.60
		Never hinged	2.10	
		On cover		67.50
b.		Inverted overprint	260.00	260.00
		Never hinged	375.00	
261A	A20	30c dk red	14.50	14.50
		Never hinged	28.00	
		On cover		230.00
262	A20	40c ultra	5.50	5.50
		Never hinged	9.25	
		On cover		140.00
263	A20	45c slate green	4.00	4.00
		Never hinged	6.50	
		On cover		125.00
264	A6	50c lt grn & cer	2.40	1.60
		Never hinged	2.75	
		On cover		8.75
a.		Inverted overprint	225.00	
		Never hinged	350.00	
265	A20	60c pck bl	6.50	6.50
		Never hinged	11.00	
		On cover		165.00
266	A20	70c plum	3.25	3.25
		Never hinged	5.50	
		On cover		125.00
267	A21	80c Prus bl (O)	5.50	5.50
		Never hinged	10.50	
		On cover		165.00
268	A21	90c Prus bl (O)	1.60	1.60
		Never hinged	1.70	
		On cover		50.00
269	A21	1.25fr car rose	1.60	1.60
		Never hinged	2.40	
		On cover		105.00
270	A21	1.40fr org red	4.75	4.75
		Never hinged	8.50	
		On cover		140.00
271	A21	1.50fr chocolate	1.60	1.60
		Never hinged	2.40	
		On cover		100.00
272	A21	1.60fr blk brn (O)	3.25	3.25
		Never hinged	5.50	
		On cover		110.00
273	A21	1.75fr dk bl (O)	2.40	2.40
		Never hinged	4.00	
		On cover		100.00
274	A21	2.25fr dk bl (O)	1.60	1.60
		Never hinged	2.40	
		On cover		100.00
275	A21	2.50fr brt red vio	1.60	1.60
		Never hinged	2.40	
		On cover		100.00
276	A7	5fr brn & blk, *bluish*	16.00	14.00
		Never hinged	32.50	
		On cover		200.00
277	A22	5fr black brn	24.00	16.00
		Never hinged	45.00	
		On cover		230.00
278	A7	10fr org & vio	27.50	26.00
		Never hinged	60.00	
		On cover		230.00
278A	A22	10fr brt red vio	65.00	45.00
		Never hinged	140.00	
		On cover		375.00
279	A7	20fr rose & ol grn	52.50	47.50
		Never hinged	120.00	
		On cover		260.00
279A	A22	20fr dk green	190.00	190.00
		Never hinged	300.00	
		On cover		600.00

Same Overprint on Stamps of 1939
Perf. 12½x12

280	CD82	1.25fr car lake	8.75	8.75
		Never hinged	17.00	
		On cover		160.00
281	CD82	2.25fr ultra	8.75	8.75
		Never hinged	17.00	
		On cover		160.00
		Nos. 255-281 (31)	482.75	445.45

Issued to note Cameroun's affiliation with General de Gaulle's "Free France" movement. Numerous overprint varieties exist.

SEMI-POSTAL STAMPS

Curie Issue
Common Design Type

1938		**Unwmk.**	**Perf. 13**	
B1	CD80	1.75fr + 50c brt ultra	10.00	10.00
		Never hinged	15.00	
		On cover		105.00
		On cover, single franking		165.00

French Revolution Issue
Common Design Type
Photogravure; Name and Value Typographed in Black

1939				
B2	CD83	45c + 25c green	11.50	11.50
		Never hinged	17.50	
		On cover		150.00
B3	CD83	70c + 30c brown	11.50	11.50
		Never hinged	17.50	
		On cover		110.00

B4	CD83	90c + 35c red org	11.50	11.50
		Never hinged	17.50	
		On cover		100.00
B5	CD83	1.25fr + 1fr rose pink	11.50	11.50
		Never hinged	17.50	
		On cover		160.00
		On cover, single franking		250.00
B6	CD83	2.25fr + 2fr blue	14.00	14.00
		Never hinged	22.50	
		On cover		150.00
		On cover, single franking		220.00
		Nos. B2-B6 (5)	60.00	60.00

Stamps of 1925-33 Srchd. in Black

1940			**Perf. 14x13½**	
B7	A7	1.25fr + 2fr gray & dp bl	27.50	24.00
		Never hinged	55.00	
		On cover		300.00
B8	A7	1.75fr + 3fr brn & org	27.50	24.00
		Never hinged	55.00	
		On cover		300.00
B9	A7	2fr + 5fr dl grn & brn org	27.50	24.00
		Never hinged	55.00	
		On cover		300.00
		Nos. B7-B9 (3)	82.50	72.00

The surtax was used for war relief work.

Regular Stamps of 1939 Surcharged in Black

1940			**Perf. 13**	
B10	A20	25c + 5fr blk brn	130.00	110.00
		Never hinged	225.00	
		On cover		450.00
B11	A20	45c + 5fr slate grn	130.00	110.00
		Never hinged	225.00	
		On cover		450.00
B12	A20	60c + 5fr peacock bl	130.00	120.00
		Never hinged	225.00	
		On cover		450.00
B13	A20	70c + 5fr plum	130.00	120.00
		Never hinged	225.00	
		On cover		450.00
		Nos. B10-B13 (4)	520.00	460.00

The surtax was used to purchase Spitfire planes for the Free French army.

POSTAGE DUE STAMPS

Man Felling Tree — D1

1925-27		**Unwmk.**		**Typo.**
J1	D1	2c lt bl & blk	.30	.50
		Never hinged	.50	
		On cover		67.50
J2	D1	4c ol bis & red vio	.30	.50
		Never hinged	.50	
		On cover		67.50
J3	D1	5c vio & blk	.65	.80
		Never hinged	.80	
		On cover		67.50
J4	D1	10c red & blk	.65	.80
		Never hinged	.80	
		On cover		75.00
J5	D1	15c gray & blk	.75	.95
		Never hinged	.95	
		On cover		75.00
J6	D1	20c olive grn & blk	.75	.95
		Never hinged	.95	
		On cover		80.00
J7	D1	25c yel & blk	1.40	1.60
		Never hinged	2.10	
		On cover		87.50
J8	D1	30c blue & org	1.60	1.90
		Never hinged	2.25	
		On cover		87.50
J9	D1	50c brn & blk	2.00	2.40
		Never hinged	3.50	
		On cover		92.50
J10	D1	60c bl grn & rose red	2.00	2.40
		Never hinged	3.50	
		On cover		92.50

J11	D1	1fr dl red & grn, *grnsh*	2.40	3.25
		Never hinged	4.00	
		On cover		92.50
J12	D1	2fr red & vio ('27)	4.75	5.50
		Never hinged	7.25	
		On cover		105.00
J13	D1	3fr org brn & ultra		
		('27)	7.25	8.00
		Never hinged	12.00	
		On cover		120.00
		Nos. J1-J13 (13)	24.80	29.55

Shades occur for several values.

Carved Figures — D2

1939		**Engr.**	**Perf. 14x13**	
J14	D2	5c brt red vio	.25	.80
		Never hinged	.40	
		On cover		27.50
J15	D2	10c Prus blue	.75	.90
		Never hinged	.90	
		On cover		27.50
J16	D2	15c car rose	.25	.40
		Never hinged	.40	
		On cover		27.50
J17	D2	20c blk brn	.25	.40
		Never hinged	.40	
		On cover		27.50
J18	D2	30c ultra	.50	.65
		Never hinged	.65	
		On cover		27.50
J19	D2	50c dk grn	.50	.65
		Never hinged	.70	
		On cover		32.50
J20	D2	60c brn vio	.85	1.00
		Never hinged	1.00	
		On cover		32.50
J21	D2	1fr dk vio	1.10	1.20
		Never hinged	1.25	
		On cover		40.00
J22	D2	2fr org red	1.60	1.60
		Never hinged	1.90	
		On cover		40.00
J23	D2	3fr dark blue	2.25	2.40
		Never hinged	2.40	
		On cover		55.00
		Nos. J14-J23 (10)	8.30	10.00

CANADIAN PROVINCES

BRITISH COLUMBIA & VAN-COUVER ISLAND

'bri-tish kə-'ləm-bē-ə

and van-'kü-vər 'i-lənd

LOCATION — On the northwest coast of North America
GOVT. — British Colony
AREA — 355,900 sq. mi.
POP. — 694,300

In 1871 the colony became a part of the Canadian Confederation and the postage stamps of Canada have since been used.

12 Pence = 1 Shilling
20 Shillings = 1 Pound
100 Cents = 1 Dollar (1865)

Values for unused stamps are for examples with original gum as defined in the catalogue introduction. Very fine examples of Nos. 2 and 5-18 will have perforations touching the design on at least one side due to the narrow spacing of the stamps on the plates. Stamps with perfs clear of the design on all four sides are extremely scarce and will command much higher prices.

Queen Victoria — A1

1860		**Unwmk.** **Typo.**	**Imperf.**	
1	A1	2½p dull rose	*30,000.*	

No. 1 was not placed in use and may be a proof or reprint. Most examples are without gum. Value without gum, $20,000.

		Perf. 14		
2	A1	2½p dull rose	*1,000.*	250.
		Never hinged	*1,150.*	
		On cover		1,250.
a.		2½p pale dull rose	450.	250.
		Never hinged	675.	
		On cover		1,250.

Two singles of the 2½ pence (Scott No. 2) on a very fine cover sent to Canada via San Francisco was sold for $10,000 at an American auction in 2003.
Two singles of the 2½ pence (Scott No. 2) on a very fine cover sent to Bergamo, Italy, via San Francisco was sold for $17,250 at an American auction in 2004.

VANCOUVER ISLAND

A2   A3

1865		**Wmk. 1**	**Imperf.**	
3	A2	5c rose	75,000.	12,000.
		Never hinged	90,000.	
		No gum	42,500.	
		On cover		37,500.
4	A3	10c blue	4,500.	1,250.
		Never hinged	7,000.	
		On cover		—
		Perf. 14		
5	A2	5c rose	400.	275.
		Never hinged	600.	
		On cover, *from*		800.
6	A3	10c blue	350.	250.
		Never hinged	625.	
		On cover		—

BRITISH COLUMBIA

Seal of British Columbia — A4

1865, Nov. 1				
7	A4	3p blue	120.00	110.00
		Never hinged	180.00	
		On cover, *from*		325.00
a.		3p pale blue	130.00	110.00
		Never hinged	190.00	
		On cover, *from*		325.00

Type A4 of 1865 Surcharged in Various Colors

1867-69			**Perf. 14**	
8		2c on 3p brown (Bk)	175.00	160.00
		Never hinged	260.00	
		On cover, *from*		1,150.
9		5c on 3p brt red (Bk) ('69)	275.00	250.00
		Never hinged	475.00	
		On cover, *from*		575.00

10		10c on 3p lilac rose (Bl)	1,750.	
		Never hinged	3,750.	
11		25c on 3p orange (V) ('69)	400.00	350.00
		Never hinged	600.00	
		On cover, *from*		850.00
12		50c on 3p violet (R)	875.00	*1,150.*
		Never hinged	1,600.	
13		$1 on 3p green (G)	2,000.	
		Never hinged	3,250.	

Nos. 10 and 13 were not placed in use.

1869			**Perf. 12½**	
14		5c on 3p brt red (Bk)	2,250.	1,400.
		Never hinged	4,250.	
		On cover		—
15		10c on 3p lilac rose (Bl)	1,300.	1,100.
		Never hinged	2,400.	
		On cover		—
16		25c on 3p orange (V)	1,100.	900.00
		Never hinged	2,150.	
		On cover, *from*		1,500.
17		50c on 3p violet (R)	1,600.	1,100.
		Never hinged	3,100.	
		On cover, *from*		2,400.
18		$1 on 3p green (G)	2,500.	2,000.
		Never hinged	4,400.	
		On cover, *from*		—

NEW BRUNSWICK

'nü 'brənz-ₒwik

LOCATION — Eastern Canada, bordering on the Bay of Fundy and the Gulf of St. Lawrence.
GOVT. — British Province
AREA — 27,985 sq. mi.
POP. — 285,594 (1871)
CAPITAL — Fredericton

At one time a part of Nova Scotia, New Brunswick became a separate province in 1784. Upon joining the Canadian Confederation in 1867 its postage stamps were superseded by those of Canada.

12 Pence = 1 Shilling
100 Cents = 1 Dollar (1860)

Crown of Great Britain and Heraldic Flowers of the United Kingdom A1

1851		**Unwmk.** **Engr.**	**Imperf.**	
		Blue Paper		
1	A1	3p red	5,500.	575.
		On cover		950.
a.		3p dark red	5,750.	625.
		On cover		1,100.
b.		Half used as 1½p on cover		4,750.
2	A1	6p olive yellow	7,000.	1,250.
		On cover		1,750.
a.		6p orange yellow	7,000.	1,300.
		On cover		1,750.
b.		Half used as 3p on cover		3,500.
c.		Quarter used as 1½p on cover		30,000.
d.		6p mustard yellow	10,500.	1,500.
3	A1	1sh brt red violet	32,500.	7,000.
		On cover		11,500.
a.		Half used as 6p on cover		24,000.
b.		Quarter used as 3p on cover		24,000.
4	A1	1sh dull violet	40,000.	8,000.
		On cover		18,000.
a.		Half used as 6p on cover		24,000.
b.		Quarter used as 3p on cover		24,000.

The reprints are on stout white paper. The 3p is printed in orange and the 6p and 1sh in violet black. Value about $275 per set of 3.

Charles Connell — A2

1860			**Perf. 12**	
5	A2	5c brown	*15,000.*	
		Pair, no gum	*32,500.*	

No. 5 was prepared for use but not issued. The listed pair is the unique multiple of this issue.
Most examples of No. 5 have creases or other faults. Value of an average example is about half that shown here.

Locomotive   Victoria
A3   A4

A5   A6

Steam and Sailing Ship — A7   Edward VII as Prince of Wales — A8

1860-63		**White Paper**	**Perf. 12**	
6	A3	1c red lilac	37.50	37.50
		Never hinged	80.00	
		On cover		250.00
		On circular, single franking		350.00
a.		1c brown violet	75.00	65.00
		Never hinged	150.00	
		On cover		300.00
		On circular, single franking		425.00
b.		Horiz. pair, imperf. vert.	700.00	
		Never hinged	850.00	
7	A4	2c orange ('63)	15.00	14.00
		Never hinged	42.50	
		On cover		725.00
a.		Vertical pair, imperf. horiz.	750.00	
		Never hinged		
b.		2c deep orange	19.00	19.00
		Never hinged	55.00	
c.		2c yellow orange	19.00	19.00
		Never hinged	55.00	
8	A5	5c yellow green	22.50	22.50
		Never hinged	50.00	
		On cover		47.50
a.		5c blue green	22.50	22.50
		Never hinged	50.00	
		On cover		47.50
		As "a," "elongated earring" plate flaw (Pos. 60)	125.00	125.00
		Never hinged		
		On cover		250.00
b.		5c olive green	150.00	37.50
		Never hinged	340.00	
		On cover		47.50
9	A6	10c vermilion	47.50	47.50
		Never hinged	90.00	
		On cover		100.00
a.		Half used as 5c on cover		800.00
b.		Double impression	*350.00*	*175.00*
10	A7	12½c blue	80.00	80.00
		Never hinged	135.00	
		On cover		250.00
11	A8	17c black	47.50	*65.00*
		Never hinged	90.00	
		On cover		*5,500.*
		Nos. 6-11 (6)	250.00	266.50
		Set, never hinged	487.50	

NEWFOUNDLAND

ˈnü-fən͜d͜-lənd

LOCATION — Island in the Atlantic
Ocean off the coast of Canada, and
Labrador, a part of the mainland
GOVT. — British Dominion
AREA — 42,734 sq. mi.
POP. — 321,177 (1945)
CAPITAL — St. John's

Newfoundland was a self-governing
Dominion of the British Empire from
1855 to 1933, when it became a Crown
Colony. In 1949 it united with Canada.

12 Pence = 1 Shilling
100 Cents = 1 Dollar (1866)

PRE-STAMP POSTAL MARKINGS

Crowned Circle handstamp type VIII is
pictured in the Crowned Circle
Handstamps and Great Britain Used
Abroad section.

St. John's

1846-57
A1 VIII "St. John's" crowned
circle handstamp in
red, on cover .... 1,050.

Issued under British Administration

Values for unused stamps are for
examples with original gum as defined
in the catalogue introduction. However,
very fine examples of Nos. 2-7, 9, 11,
12, 13 and 15 without gum are often
traded at values very close to those for
examples with original gum.

Watermark

Wmk. 224
Coat of
Arms

As the watermark 224 does not show on
every stamp in the sheet, pairs are found one
with and one without watermark. This applies
to all stamps with watermark 224.

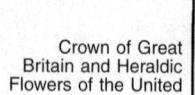

Crown of Great
Britain and Heraldic
Flowers of the United
Kingdom — A1

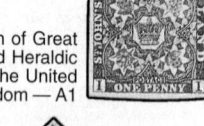

Rose, Thistle and Shamrock — A3

A2   A4

A5   A6

A7   A8

1857 Unwmk. Engr. *Imperf.*
Thick Porous Wove Paper with Mesh

1	A1	1p brown vio	125.00	*200.00*
		Never hinged	210.00	
		On cover		*6,000.*
a.		Half used as ½p on cover		*15,000.*
2	A2	2p scarlet ver	*17,500.*	6,000.
		On cover		*14,000.*
a.		Vert. half used as 1p		*19,000.*
3	A3	3p green	475.00	475.00
		On cover		*4,000.*
4	A4	4p scarlet ver	*12,000.*	3,750.
		On cover		*8,000.*
a.		Half used as 2p on cover		*20,000.*
5	A1	5p brown vio	300.00	400.00
		Never hinged	500.00	
		On cover		*8,000.*
6	A5	6p scarlet ver	*27,500.*	4,750.
		On cover		*24,000.*
7	A6	6½p scarlet ver	*5,000.*	3,750.
		On cover		*10,000.*
8	A7	8p scarlet ver	450.00	475.00
		Never hinged	525.00	
		On cover		*17,500.*
a.		Half used as 4p on cover		*6,000.*
9	A8	1sh scarlet ver	*45,000.*	10,000.
		On cover		*30,000.*
a.		Half used as 6p on cover		*20,000.*

1860
Thin to Thick Wove Paper, No Mesh

11	A2	2p orange	475.00	475.00
		On cover		*2,000.*
11A	A3	3p green	77.50	105.00
		Never hinged	130.00	
		On cover		*2,000.*
12	A4	4p orange	4,250.	1,150.
		On cover		*7,000.*
b.		Half used as 2p on cover		*15,000.*
12A	A1	5p vio brown	77.50	135.00
		Never hinged	130.00	
		On cover		*7,500.*
13	A5	6p orange	5,500.	1,000.
		On cover		*24,000.*
15	A8	1sh orange	35,000.	12,000.
		On cover		—
b.		Half used as 6p on cover		*17,500.*

A 6½p orange exists as a souvenir item.
A 1sh exists in orange on horizontally or
vertically laid paper. Most authorities consider
these to be proofs. Value, $10,500.

1861-62

15A	A1	1p vio brown	175.00	250.00
		Never hinged	425.00	
c.		1p chocolate brown	220.00	325.00
		Never hinged	450.00	
		On cover		—
16	A1	1p reddish brown	*14,000.*	
17	A2	2p rose	175.00	175.00
		Never hinged	425.00	
		On cover		—
18	A4	4p rose	37.50	70.00
		Never hinged	47.50	
		On cover		*5,000.*
a.		Half used as 2p on cover		—
19	A1	5p reddish brown	75.00	77.50
		Never hinged	115.00	
		On cover		*6,500.*
a.		5p orange brown	85.00	100.00
		Never hinged	130.00	
		On cover		*6,500.*
b.		5p chocolate brown	110.00	125.00
		Never hinged	175.00	
		On cover		*7,000.*
20	A5	6p rose	22.50	62.50
		Never hinged	30.00	
		On cover		*9,250.*
a.		Half used as 3p on cover		*10,000.*

21	A6	6½p rose	85.00	*275.00*
		Never hinged	145.00	
		On cover		*7,500.*
22	A7	8p rose	85.00	*300.00*
		Never hinged	145.00	
		On cover		—
23	A8	1sh rose	42.50	*275.00*
		Never hinged	52.50	
		On cover		—
a.		Half used as 6p on cover		*20,000.*

Some sheets of Nos. 11-23 are known with
the papermaker's watermark "STACEY WISE
1858" in large capitals. Values unused and
used about 25% more than values shown,
except about 50% more for unused Nos. 12
and 13, and 75% more for unused No. 16.
No. 16 was prepared but not issued.
False cancellations are found on Nos. 1, 3,
5, 8, 11, 11A, 12A and 17-23.
Forgeries exist of most or all of Nos. 1-23.

Codfish — A9

Harp Seal — A10   Prince
Albert — A11

Victoria — A12   Fishing
Ship — A13

Victoria — A14

1865-94   *Perf. 12*
White Paper(#24, 27, 28)
Thin Yellowish Paper (#25-26, 29-31)

24	A9	2c green	110.00	30.00
		Never hinged	250.00	
		On cover		*400.00*
a.		Thin yellowish paper	140.00	45.00
		Never hinged	325.00	
		On cover		*525.00*
b.		Half used as 1c on cover		*4,000.*
25	A10	5c brown	550.00	375.00
		Never hinged		*750.00*
		On cover		*5,250.*
a.		Half used as 2c on cover		
26	A10	5c black ('68)	400.00	150.00
		Never hinged	900.00	
		On cover		*425.00*
27	A11	10c black	325.00	60.00
		Never hinged	775.00	
		On cover		*325.00*
a.		Thin yellowish paper	375.00	115.00
		Never hinged	875.00	
		On cover		*350.00*
b.		Half used as 5c on cover		*4,250.*
28	A12	12c pale red brn	65.00	47.50
		Never hinged	115.00	
		On cover		*130.00*
a.		Thin yellowish paper	550.00	190.00
		Never hinged		*225.00*
b.		Half used as 6c on cover		*3,250.*
29	A12	12c brn, *white* ('94)	70.00	45.00
		Never hinged	120.00	
		On cover		*120.00*
30	A13	13c orange	250.00	115.00
		Never hinged	550.00	
		On cover		*450.00*
31	A14	24c blue, thin transluscent paper	55.00	30.00
		Never hinged	115.00	
		On cover		*450.00*
a.		Thicker white paper ('70)	375.00	300.00

See Nos. 38, 40.

Edward VII as   Queen
Prince of   Victoria — A16
Wales — A15

1868-94

32	A15	1c violet	75.00	60.00
		Never hinged	160.00	
		On cover		*425.00*
32A	A15	1c brown lilac (re-engr. '71)	115.00	75.00
		Never hinged	350.00	
		On cover		*400.00*
33	A16	3c ver ('70)	400.00	190.00
		Never hinged		*425.00*
34	A16	3c blue ('73)	375.00	75.00
		Never hinged	875.00	
		On cover		*200.00*
35	A16	6c dull rose ('70)	22.50	15.00
		Never hinged	37.50	
		On cover		*55.00*
a.		6c bright rose	37.50	22.50
		Never hinged	75.00	
		On cover		*70.00*
36	A16	6c car lake ('94)	37.50	22.50
		Never hinged	72.50	
		On cover		*50.00*
		Nos. 32-36 (6)	1,000.	437.50

In the re-engraved 1c the top of the letters
"N" and "F" are about ½mm from the ribbon
with "ONE CENT." In No. 32 they are fully
1mm away. There are many small differences
in the engraving.

1876-79   *Rouletted*

37	A15	1c brn lilac ('77)	160.00	52.50
		Never hinged	375.00	
		On cover		*375.00*
38	A9	2c green ('79)	200.00	52.50
		Never hinged	425.00	
		On cover		*375.00*
39	A16	3c blue ('77)	425.00	14.00
		Never hinged	900.00	
		On cover		*87.50*
40	A10	5c blue	275.00	14.00
		Never hinged	575.00	
		On cover		*62.50*
		Nos. 37-40 (4)	1,060.	133.00

A17   A19

A18   A20

1880-96   *Perf. 12*

41	A17	1c violet brown	52.50	11.50
		Never hinged	120.00	
		On cover		*50.00*
42	A17	1c gray brown	52.50	11.50
		Never hinged	120.00	
		On cover		*50.00*
43	A17	1c brown ('96)	125.00	57.50
		Never hinged	225.00	
		On cover		*175.00*
44	A17	1c deep green ('87)	20.00	3.75
		Never hinged	30.00	
		On cover		*19.00*
a.		1c gray green	26.00	5.00
		Never hinged	40.00	
		On cover		*19.00*
45	A17	1c green ('97)	20.00	4.00
		Never hinged	30.00	
		On cover		*25.00*
a.		1c yellow green	25.00	6.00
		Never hinged	35.00	
		On cover		*25.00*
46	A19	2c yellow green	55.00	14.00
		Never hinged	135.00	
		On cover		*45.00*
47	A19	2c green ('96)	100.00	27.50
		Never hinged	225.00	
		On cover		*50.00*
48	A19	2c red org ('87)	32.50	9.50
		Never hinged	52.50	
		On cover		*50.00*
a.		Imperf., pair	325.00	
		Never hinged	510.00	
b.		2c orange	32.50	9.50
		Never hinged	52.50	
		On cover		*50.00*
49	A18	3c blue	55.00	6.75
		Never hinged	110.00	
		On cover		*16.00*
a.		3c pale blue	70.00	6.50
		Never hinged	150.00	
		On cover		*16.00*

b.	3c deep blue	50.00	6.50
	Never hinged	130.00	
	On cover		16.00
51	A18 3c umber brn ('87)	55.00	4.75
	Never hinged	150.00	
	On cover		16.00
a.	3c brown	70.00	4.75
	Never hinged	150.00	
	On cover		24.00
52	A18 3c vio brown ('96)	120.00	90.00
	Never hinged	220.00	
	On cover		100.00
53	A20 5c pale blue	375.00	10.00
	Never hinged	900.00	
	On cover		40.00
54	A20 5c dark blue ('87)	175.00	8.50
	Never hinged	380.00	
	On cover		32.50
55	A20 5c bright bl ('94)	60.00	6.50
	Never hinged	120.00	
	On cover		20.00
	Nos. 41-55 (14)	1,297.	265.75

Newfoundland Dog — A21   Schooner — A22

1887-96

56	A21 ½c rose red	10.00	7.25
	Never hinged	16.00	
	On cover		55.00
a.	½c deep rose red	12.00	9.00
	Never hinged	18.00	
	On cover		60.00
57	A21 ½c orange red ('96)	75.00	45.00
	Never hinged	125.00	
	On cover		110.00
58	A21 ½c black ('94)	15.00	7.25
	Never hinged	27.50	
	On cover		55.00
59	A22 10c black	130.00	67.50
	Never hinged	210.00	
	On cover		175.00
	Nos. 56-59 (4)	230.00	127.00

Queen Victoria — A23

1890

60	A23 3c slate	30.00	1.60
	Never hinged	77.50	
	On cover		8.00
a.	3c gray lilac	30.00	1.60
	Never hinged	75.00	
	On cover		8.00
b.	3c brown lilac	55.00	1.60
	Never hinged	135.00	
	On cover		8.00
c.	3c lilac	30.00	1.60
	Never hinged	75.00	
	On cover		8.00
d.	3c slate violet	75.00	3.00
	Never hinged	175.00	
	On cover		12.00
e.	Vert. pair, imperf. horiz.	700.00	
	Never hinged	1,550.	

Examples of No. 60 on red tinted paper are from a recovered consignment that fell into the sea. Value, used $4.
For surcharges see Nos. 75-77.

Victoria — A24   Cabot (John?) — A25

Cape Bonavista A26   Caribou Hunting A27

Mining — A28   Logging — A29

Fishing — A30

Cabot's Ship "Matthew" A31   Willow Ptarmigan A32

Seals — A33   Salmon Fishing — A34

Colony Seal — A35   Iceberg off St. John's — A36

Henry VII — A37

1897, June 24

61	A24 1c deep green	1.75	1.75
	Never hinged	2.75	
	On cover		8.00
62	A25 2c carmine lake	2.20	1.35
	Never hinged	3.50	
	On cover		8.00
63	A26 3c ultramarine	4.25	1.40
	Never hinged	7.50	
	On cover		12.50
64	A27 4c olive green	5.75	2.75
	Never hinged	11.50	
	On cover		24.00
65	A28 5c violet	12.00	2.75
	Never hinged	21.50	
	On cover		24.00

66	A29 6c red brown	5.75	3.25
	Never hinged	10.50	
	On cover		24.00
67	A30 8c red orange	17.50	14.00
	Never hinged	30.00	
	On cover		80.00
68	A31 10c black brown	17.50	7.50
	Never hinged	30.00	
	On cover		50.00
69	A32 12c dark blue	30.00	14.00
	Never hinged	50.00	
	On cover		80.00
70	A33 15c scarlet	22.50	13.00
	Never hinged	37.50	
	On cover		80.00
71	A34 24c gray violet	30.00	12.00
	Never hinged	47.50	
	On cover		60.00
72	A35 30c slate	55.00	55.00
	Never hinged	82.50	
	On cover		100.00
73	A36 35c red	120.00	60.00
	Never hinged	240.00	
	On cover		225.00
74	A37 60c black	19.00	11.50
	Never hinged	26.00	
	On cover		60.00
	Nos. 61-74 (14)	343.20	200.25
	Set, never hinged	580.75	

400th anniv. of John Cabot's discovery of Newfoundland; 60th year of Victoria's reign. The ship on the 10c was previously used by the American Bank Note Co. as the "Flagship of Columbus" on US No. 232. The portrait on the 2c, intended to be of John Cabot, is said to be a Holbein painting of his son, Sebastian.

Bisects are known of the 2c, 3c and 6c values but were not authorized. Values, on cover, 2c (1c) $300, 3c (1 ½c) $300, 6c (3c) $400.

For surcharges and overprints see Nos. 127-130, C2-C4.

No. 60a Surcharged with Bars and

No. 75   No. 76

No. 77

1897, Oct.

75	A23 1c on 3c gray lilac	65.00	30.00
	Never hinged	120.00	
	On cover		75.00
a.	Dbl. surch., one diagonal	2,250.	
b.	Vert. pair, "ONE CENT" and lower bar omitted on bottom stamp	4,250.	
76	A23 1c on 3c gray lilac	225.00	190.00
	Never hinged	540.00	
	On cover		250.00
77	A23 1c on 3c gray lilac	750.00	700.00
	Never hinged	1,600.	
	On cover		1,600.
a.	Block of 4, #76-77, 2 #75	1,500.	
	Never hinged	3,750.	
	Nos. 75-77 (3)	1,040.	920.00
	Set, never hinged	2,260.	

Most examples of Nos. 75-77 are poorly centered. Fine examples sell for about 60% of the values given. No. 75b is valued in the grade of fine.

Trial surcharges of Nos. 75-77 exist with red surcharge and with double surcharge, one in red and one in black, but these were not issued.

Edward VIII as a Child — A38   Victoria — A39

Edward VII as Prince of Wales — A40   Queen Alexandra as Princess of Wales — A41

Queen Mary as Duchess of York — A42   George V as Duke of York — A43

1897-1901   Engr.

78	A38 ½c olive green	3.75	2.25
	Never hinged	4.75	
	On cover		14.00
79	A39 1c carmine rose	4.75	4.75
	Never hinged	6.75	
	On cover		32.50
80	A39 1c yel grn ('98)	4.50	.25
	Never hinged	7.75	
	On cover		8.00
a.	1c deep green	6.00	.25
	Never hinged	9.50	
	On cover		6.00
b.	Vert. pair, imperf. horiz.	500.00	
	Never hinged	900.00	
81	A40 2c orange	6.25	4.25
	Never hinged	8.50	
	On cover		20.00
82	A40 2c ver ('98)	11.50	.60
	Never hinged	15.00	
	On cover		12.00
b.	Pair, imperf. between	575.00	
	Never hinged	1,025.	
83	A41 3c orange ('98)	27.50	.75
	Never hinged	45.00	
	On cover		12.00
a.	Vert. pair, imperf. horiz.	500.00	
	Never hinged	900.00	
c.	3c red orange, *thin bluish* ('98)	40.00	2.25
	Never hinged	80.00	
84	A42 4c violet ('01)	37.50	4.50
	Never hinged	55.00	
	On cover		5.00
85	A43 5c blue ('99)	47.50	3.00
	Never hinged	77.50	
	On cover		40.00
	Nos. 78-85 (8)	143.25	20.35
	Set, never hinged	222.50	

No. 80b is valued in the grade of fine.

Imperf., Pairs

78a	A38	½c	600.00	800.00
		Never hinged	900.00	
81a	A40	2c		400.00
		On cover		625.00
82a	A40	2c	350.00	
		Never hinged	505.00	
		On cover		950.00
83b	A41	3c	425.00	
		Never hinged	650.00	
84a	A42	4c	700.00	
		Never hinged	1,050.	

No. 82a used is known only on cover. Three such covers are recorded.

Imperf., Pairs

Newfoundland imperforates virtually always are proofs on stamp paper or "postmaster's perquisites." Most part-perforate varieties also are "postmaster's perquisites." These items were not regularly issued, but rather were sold or given to favored persons.

Map of Newfoundland — A44

1908, Sept.

86	A44	2c rose carmine	47.50	1.90
		Never hinged	85.00	
		On cover		60.00
		On postcard		20.00

Guy Issue

James I — A45   Arms of the London and Bristol Co. — A46

John Guy A47   Guy's Ship, the "Endeavour" A48

View of Cupids — A49   Lord Bacon — A50

View of Mosquito — A51

Logging Camp — A52

Paper Mills — A53   Edward VII — A54

George V — A55

Type I	Type II

SIX CENT TYPES
I — "Z" of "COLONIZATION" reversed.
II — "Z" of normal.

1910, Aug. 15   Litho.   Perf. 12

87	A45	1c deep green, perf. 12x11	2.30	1.10
		Never hinged	4.75	
		On cover		4.75
		"NFW" for "NEW"	70.00	60.00
		Never hinged	130.00	
a.		Perf. 12	4.75	1.90
		Never hinged	9.25	
		On cover		7.00
		"NFW" for "NEW"	70.00	60.00
		Never hinged	130.00	
b.		Perf. 12x14	7.50	2.25
		Never hinged	15.00	
		On cover		7.00
		"NFW" for "NEW"	70.00	60.00
c.		Horiz. pair, imperf. btwn., perf 12x11	400.00	—
		Never hinged	525.00	
		"NFW" for "NEW"	600.00	
		Never hinged	1,000.	
d.		Vert. pair, imperf. btwn., perf 12x11	475.00	
		Never hinged	800.00	
e.		Horiz. pair, imperf. btwn., perf 12	475.00	
		Never hinged	800.00	
		"NFW" for "NEW"	750.00	
		Never hinged	1,250.	
f.		Vert. pair, imperf. btwn., perf 12	500.00	
		Never hinged	875.00	
g.		Horiz. pair, imperf. btwn., perf 12x14	800.00	—
		Never hinged	1,300.	
		"NFW" for "NEW"	500.00	
		Never hinged	875.00	
h.		Perf. 12x12x12x11		—
88	A46	2c carmine	8.50	1.15
		Never hinged	15.00	
		On cover		8.00
a.		Perf. 12x14	7.00	.85
		Never hinged	12.50	
		On cover		8.00
b.		As "a," horiz. pair, imperf. between	900.00	
		Never hinged	1,500.	
c.		Perf. 12x11½	800.00	400.00
		Never hinged	1,250.	
89	A47	3c brown olive	20.00	14.00
		Never hinged	37.50	
		On cover		60.00
90	A48	4c dull violet	20.00	11.50
		Never hinged	37.50	
		On cover		40.00
91	A49	5c ultramarine, perf. 14x12	17.50	4.50
		Never hinged	30.00	
		On cover		24.00
a.		Perf. 12	27.50	7.50
		Never hinged	47.50	
		On cover		24.00
92	A50	6c claret, type I	85.00	65.00
		Never hinged	160.00	
		On cover		240.00
92A	A50	6c claret, type II	40.00	37.50
		Never hinged	75.00	
		On cover		80.00
b.		Imperf., pair	450.00	
		Never hinged	800.00	
93	A51	8c pale brown	70.00	55.00
		Never hinged	145.00	
		On cover		200.00
94	A52	9c olive green	70.00	55.00
		Never hinged	145.00	
		On cover		200.00
95	A53	10c vio black	70.00	55.00
		Never hinged	145.00	
		On cover		200.00
96	A54	12c lilac brown	70.00	55.00
		Never hinged	145.00	
		On cover		240.00
a.		Imperf., pair	375.00	
		Never hinged	650.00	
97	A55	15c gray black	77.50	65.00
		Never hinged	160.00	
		On cover		400.00
		Nos. 87-97 (12)	550.80	419.75
		Set, never hinged	1,100.	

Tercentenary of the Colonization of Newfoundland.
On No. 87 printing flaws such as "NFW" and "JANES" exist.

1911   Engr.   Perf. 14

98	A50	6c brown vio	32.50	22.50
		Never hinged	60.00	
		On cover		80.00
b.		Horiz. pair, imperf. btwn.	—	
99	A51	8c blue grn	75.00	57.50
		Never hinged	120.00	
		On cover		200.00
b.		Horiz. pair, imperf. btwn.	1,400.	
100	A52	9c olive grn	75.00	57.50
		Never hinged	125.00	
		On cover		200.00
b.		Horiz. pair, imperf. btwn.	1,400.	
101	A53	10c violet blk	95.00	95.00
		Never hinged	175.00	
		On cover		250.00
b.		Horiz. pair, imperf. btwn.	1,400.	
102	A54	12c red brown	75.00	75.00
		Never hinged	150.00	
		On cover		240.00
b.		Horiz. pair, imperf. btwn.	—	
103	A55	15c slate grn	75.00	75.00
		Never hinged	150.00	
		On cover		575.00
b.		Horiz. pair, imperf. btwn.	1,400.	
		Nos. 98-103 (6)	427.50	392.50
		Set, never hinged	755.00	

Nos. 100 and 103 are known with papermaker's watermark "E. TOWGOOD FINE."

Imperf., Pairs

98a	A50	6c	325.00
		Never hinged	390.00
99a	A51	8c	325.00
		Never hinged	390.00
100a	A52	9c	325.00
		Never hinged	390.00
101a	A53	10c	325.00
		Never hinged	390.00
102a	A54	12c	325.00
		Never hinged	390.00
103a	A55	15c	325.00
		Never hinged	390.00

Nos. 98a-103a were made with and without gum. Values the same.

Royal Family Issue

Queen Mary — A56   George V — A57

Prince of Wales (Edward VIII) — A58   Prince Albert (George VI) — A59

Princess Mary — A60   Prince Henry — A61

Prince George A62   Prince John A63

Queen Alexandra A64   Duke of Connaught A65

Seal of Colony — A66

1911, June 19   Perf. 13½x14, 14

104	A56	1c yellow grn	3.00	.25
		Never hinged	4.50	
		On cover		1.60
b.		1c blue green	4.00	.95
		Never hinged	7.50	
		On cover		1.60
105	A57	2c carmine	2.75	.80
		Never hinged	4.50	
		On cover		1.25
b.		2c rose red (blurred impression)	8.00	.80
		Never hinged	17.50	
		On cover		1.60
106	A58	3c red brown	25.00	19.00
		Never hinged	45.00	
		On cover		24.00
107	A59	4c violet	25.00	13.50
		Never hinged	40.00	
		On cover		20.00
108	A60	5c ultra	15.00	1.90
		Never hinged	24.00	
		On cover		25.00
109	A61	6c black	22.50	22.50
		Never hinged	40.00	
		On cover		25.00
110	A62	8c blue (paper colored through)	75.00	65.00
		Never hinged	125.00	
		On cover		175.00
a.		8c peacock blue	80.00	70.00
		Never hinged	140.00	
		On cover		175.00
111	A63	9c bl violet	25.00	20.00
		Never hinged	45.00	
		On cover		60.00
112	A64	10c dark green	40.00	37.50
		Never hinged	70.00	
		On cover		40.00
113	A65	12c plum	37.50	37.50
		Never hinged	65.00	
		On cover		40.00
114	A66	15c magenta	30.00	37.50
		Never hinged	45.00	
		On cover		80.00
		Nos. 104-114 (11)	300.75	255.45
		Set, never hinged	508.00	

Coronation of King George V.

Imperf., Pairs Without Gum

104a	A56	1c	325.00
105a	A57	2c	325.00
108a	A60	5c	325.00
113a	A65	12c	325.00
114a	A66	15c	125.00

Trail of the Caribou Issue

Caribou

A67   A68

1919, Jan. 2   Perf. 14

115	A67	1c green	2.25	.35
		Never hinged	4.00	
		On cover		.75
116	A68	2c scarlet	2.75	.50
		Never hinged	4.25	
		On cover		.75
b.		2c carmine red	5.00	.75
		Never hinged	8.50	
		On cover		1.20
117	A67	3c red brown	3.00	.30
		Never hinged	4.75	
		On cover		.75
b.		3c brown	3.00	.30
		Never hinged	4.75	
		On cover		.75
118	A67	4c violet	4.50	1.40
		Never hinged	7.50	
		On cover		3.25
b.		4c mauve	6.00	1.40
		Never hinged	10.50	
		On cover		3.25
119	A68	5c ultramarine	7.50	1.40
		Never hinged	11.00	
		On cover		2.40
120	A67	6c gray	22.50	22.50
		Never hinged	35.00	
		On cover		24.00
121	A68	8c magenta	22.50	19.00
		Never hinged	35.00	
		On cover		21.00
122	A67	10c dark green	17.50	5.50
		Never hinged	28.00	
		On cover		6.50
123	A68	12c orange	65.00	45.00
		Never hinged	110.00	
		On cover		50.00
124	A67	15c dark blue	42.50	42.50
		Never hinged	65.00	
		On cover		47.50
b.		15c Prussian blue	225.00	150.00
		Never hinged	400.00	
		On cover		200.00
125	A67	24c bister	45.00	42.50
		Never hinged	80.00	
		On cover		42.50
126	A67	36c olive green	37.50	35.00
		Never hinged	57.50	
		On cover		42.50
		Nos. 115-126 (12)	272.50	215.95
		Set, never hinged	425.00	

Services of the Newfoundland contingent in WWI.

Each denomination of type A67 is inscribed with the name of a different action in which Newfoundland troops took part.

For overprint and surcharge see Nos. C1, C5.

Imperf., Pairs
Without Gum

115a	A67	1c	280.00
116a	A68	2c	280.00
117a	A67	3c red brown	280.00
c.		3c brown	225.00
118a	A67	4c	280.00
119a	A68	5c	280.00
120a	A68	6c	280.00
121a	A68	8c	280.00
122a	A67	10c	280.00
123a	A68	12c	280.00
124a	A67	15c	280.00
125a	A67	24c	280.00
126a	A67	36c	280.00

No. 72 Surcharged in Black

1920 **Perf. 12**

127	A35	2c on 30c slate	5.75	5.50
		Never hinged	8.75	
		On cover		9.00
a.		Inverted surcharge	1,100.	
		Never hinged	1,400.	

No. 127 with red surcharge is an unissued color trial. 25 examples are known. Value, $1,000.

Also known reading "TWO / 2 / CENTS," with surcharge in red. 50 stamps were so surcharged, including examples with double surcharge. Value, $1,000.

Nos. 70 and 73 Surcharged in Black

THREE CENTS
Type I — Bars 10½mm apart.
Type II — Bars 13½mm apart.

128	A33	3c on 15c scar (I)	230.00	225.00
		Never hinged	350.00	
		On cover		300.00
a.		Inverted surcharge	3,000.	
		Never hinged	5,000.	
129	A33	3c on 15c scar (II)	19.00	11.00
		Never hinged	27.50	
		On cover		17.50
130	A36	3c on 35c red	11.50	9.50
		Never hinged	17.50	
		On cover		17.50
a.		Lower bar omitted	135.00	135.00
		Never hinged	175.00	

All examples of the former No. 130c ("THREE" omitted) examined show part of the tops or bottoms of the letters. It is probable that no examples with "THREE" completely omitted exist.

Twin Hills, Tor's Cove — A70

South West Arm, Trinity — A71

War Memorial, St. John's A72

Coast of Trinity — A74

Quidi Vidi, near St. John's — A76

Humber River Canyon A78

Humber River A73

Upper Steadies, Humber River — A75

Caribou Crossing Lake — A77

Shell Bird Island A79

Mt. Moriah, Bay of Islands A80

Placentia, from Mt. Pleasant A82

Humber River near Little Rapids A81

Topsail Falls near St. John's A83

1923-24 **Engr.** **Perf. 14, 13½x14**

131	A70	1c gray green	1.90	.30
		Never hinged	2.90	
		On cover		10.00
a.		Booklet pane of 8	500.00	
		Never hinged	700.00	
132	A71	2c carmine	1.90	.25
		Never hinged	2.90	
		On cover		1.00
a.		Booklet pane of 8	300.00	
		Never hinged	425.00	
133	A72	3c brown	2.50	.25
		Never hinged	2.90	
		On cover		1.00
134	A73	4c brn violet	2.75	1.80
		Never hinged	4.00	
		On cover		3.25
135	A74	5c ultramarine	4.50	2.25
		Never hinged	5.50	
		On cover		3.50

136	A75	6c gray black	5.25 5.25
		Never hinged	7.00
		On cover	12.00
137	A76	8c dull violet	4.50 4.25
		Never hinged	5.50
		On cover	12.00
138	A77	9c slate green	37.50 27.50
		Never hinged	50.00
		On cover	55.00
139	A78	10c dark violet	4.25 2.50
		Never hinged	7.00
		On cover	8.00
b.		10c purple	5.50 2.50
		Never hinged	8.50
		On cover	8.00
140	A79	11c olive green	7.00 7.00
		Never hinged	9.25
		On cover	20.00
141	A80	12c lake	7.50 7.50
		Never hinged	12.00
		On cover	16.00
142	A81	15c deep blue	9.50 8.00
		Never hinged	15.00
		On cover	20.00
143	A82	20c red brn ('24)	13.00 7.50
		Never hinged	24.00
		On cover	18.00
144	A83	24c blk brn ('24)	60.00 45.00
		Never hinged	97.50

Nos. 131-144 (14) 162.05 119.35
Set, never hinged 250.00

For surcharge see No. 160.

Imperf., Pairs

131b	A70	1c	200.00
		Never hinged	250.00
132b	A71	2c	200.00
		Never hinged	250.00
133a	A72	3c	300.00
134a	A73	4c	250.00
135a	A74	5c	250.00
136a	A75	6c	250.00
137a	A76	8c	250.00
138a	A77	9c	250.00
139a	A78	10c	250.00
140a	A79	11c	250.00
141a	A80	12c	250.00
142a	A81	15c	160.00

Nos. 133a-139a, 141a-142a are without gum. Others are either with or without gum; values about the same.

Map of New-
foundland
A84

Steamship
"Caribou"
A85

Queen Mary,
George V — A86

Prince of
Wales — A87

Express
Train — A88

Newfoundland
Hotel, St.
John's — A89

Heart's
Content — A90

Cabot Tower,
St.
John's — A91

War Memorial, St.
John's — A92

GPO, St.
John's — A93

First Nonstop
Transatlantic
Flight,
1919 — A94

Colonial Building,
St. John's — A95

Grand Falls,
Labrador — A96

Perf. 14, 13½x13, 13x13½
1928, Jan. 3

145	A84	1c deep green	1.40 .75
		Never hinged	2.40
		On cover	.80
146	A85	2c deep carmine	2.50 .70
		Never hinged	3.50
		On cover	.80
a.		Imperf., pair	300.00
		Never hinged	450.00
147	A86	3c brown	2.75 .50
		Never hinged	3.50
		On cover	.80
148	A87	4c lilac rose	3.50 1.80
		Never hinged	4.50
		On cover	8.00
a.		4c rose purple ('29)	5.25 2.50
		Never hinged	7.00
		On cover	8.00
149	A88	5c slate green	10.00 4.25
		Never hinged	20.00
		On cover	8.00
150	A89	6c ultramarine	5.75 3.50
		Never hinged	8.25
		On cover	8.00
151	A90	8c lt red brown	7.25 4.50
		Never hinged	10.50
		On cover	12.00
152	A91	9c myrtle green	7.00 6.75
		Never hinged	10.00
		On cover	12.00
153	A92	10c dark violet	9.00 4.25
		Never hinged	14.00
		On cover	12.00
154	A93	12c brn carmine	5.50 4.00
		Never hinged	11.00
		On cover	16.00
155	A91	14c red brown	10.50 6.75
		Never hinged	14.50
		On cover	20.00
156	A94	15c dark blue	9.25 7.00
		Never hinged	16.00
		On cover	16.00
157	A95	20c gray black	11.50 6.00
		Never hinged	22.50
		On cover	16.00
158	A93	28c gray green	27.50 22.50
		Never hinged	50.00
		On cover	55.00
159	A96	30c olive brown	14.00 7.50
		Never hinged	20.00
		On cover	16.00

Nos. 145-159 (15) 127.40 80.75
Set, never hinged 210.65

See Nos. 163-182.

THREE
CENTS

No. 136 Surcharged
in Red or Black

Type I — 5mm between "CENTS" and bar.
Type II — 3mm between "CENTS" and bar.

1929　　　　　　Perf. 14x13½

160	A75	3c on 6c gray black (II) (R)	4.25 4.25
		Never hinged	6.75
		On cover	35.00
a.		Inverted surcharge (II)	1,000.
		Never hinged	1,300.

The stamps with black surcharge, type I and II, were 1st or trial printings, and were not issued. There were 50 examples of each. Value, each $1,750.

Types of 1928 Issue Re-engraved

1c — On No. 145 the lines of the engraving are thinner and the impression is clearer than on No. 163. On the former "C. BAULD" is above "C. NORMAN." On the latter these words are transposed.

2c — On the 1928 stamp the "D" of "NEW-FOUNDLAND" is 1mm from the scroll at the right; the flag at the stern is lower than the top of the boat davit. On the 1929 stamp the "D" is ½mm from the scroll and the flag rises above the davits.

3c — On the 1928 stamp the pearls at the top of the crown, the jewels of the tiara and the pillars flanking the portraits are all unshaded. On the reengraved stamp there are small curved lines inside the pearls, the jewels of the

---

tiara are in solid color, and the pillars have vertical shading lines. On the 1928 stamps the tablets with "THREE" and "CENTS" have a background of crossed lines (vertical and horizontal). On the 1929 stamp the background is of horizontal lines only.

4c — On the 1928 stamp the figures "4" have shading of horizontal and diagonal crossed lines. There are six circles at each side of the portrait.

On the 1929 stamp the "4s" have shading of horizontal lines only. There are five roses at each side of the portrait.

5c — The crossbars of the telegraph pole touch the frame at the left on the 1929 stamp but just clear it on the 1928 stamp. In the 1928 issue the foliate ornaments beside and below the figures "5" end in small scrolls and a small spur. These spurs are omitted on the 1929 stamp.

6c — On the re-engraved stamp the columns at right and left of the picture have heavy wavy outlines on the inner sides. There is no period after "JOHNS." The numerals in the lower corners are 1½mm wide instead of 1¼mm.

8c — The impression of the 1928 stamp is clear, that of 1931 is slightly blurred. The 1928 stamp has three horizontal lines above "EIGHT CENTS" and four berries on the laurel branch at the right side. On the 1931 stamp there are two horizontal lines and three berries.

10c — On the re-engraved stamp there is no period after "ST. JOHN'S." The letters of "TEN CENTS" are slightly larger and the numerals "10" slightly smaller than in 1928. Inside the "0" of "10" at the right there are two vertical lines instead of three. The clouds are fainter in 1929 and the cross upheld by the figure on the monument is more distinct. On the 1928 stamp the torch at the left side terminates in a single tongue of flame. On the 1929-30 stamp it terminates in two tongues.

15c — On the 1928 stamp the "N" of "NEW-FOUNDLAND" is 1½mm from the left frame, the "L" of "LEAVING" is under the first "A" of "AIRPLANE" and the apostrophe in "JOHN'S" breaks the first line above it.

On the 1929 stamp the "N" of "NEW-FOUNDLAND" is 1mm from the left frame, the "L" of "LEAVING" is below the "T" of "FIRST" and the apostrophe in "JOHN'S" does not touch the line above it.

20c — On the 1928 stamp the points of the "W" of "NEWFOUNDLAND" are truncated. The "O" is wide and nearly round. The columns that form the sides of the frame have a shading of evenly spaced horizontal lines at their inner sides.

On the 1929-31 stamp the points of the "W" form sharp angles. The "O" is narrow and has a small opening. Many lines have been added to the shading on the inner sides of the columns, making it almost solid.

30c — 1928 stamp. Size: 19¼x24½mm. At the outer side of the right column there are three strong and two faint vertical lines. Faint period after "FALLS."

1931 stamp. Size: 19x25mm. At the outer side of the right column there are two strong vertical lines and a fragment of the lower end of a faint one. Clear period after "FALLS." A great many of the small lines of the design have been deepened making the whole stamp appear darker.

1929-31　Unwmk.　Perf. 13½ to 14

163	A84	1c green	2.25 .65
		Never hinged	3.25
		On cover	1.20
a.		Double impression	325.00
		Never hinged	475.00
b.		Vert. pair, imperf. btwn.	210.00
		Never hinged	300.00
164	A85	2c deep carmine	2.25 .35
		Never hinged	3.50
		On cover	1.20
165	A86	3c dp red brown	2.50 .35
		Never hinged	4.00
		On cover	1.20
166	A87	4c magenta	3.75 1.25
		Never hinged	6.75
		On cover	4.00
167	A88	5c slate green	7.25 1.60
		Never hinged	12.00
		On cover	8.00
168	A89	6c ultramarine	9.75 9.00
		Never hinged	16.50
		On cover	12.00
169	A92	10c dark violet	8.75 2.25
		Never hinged	15.00
		On cover	8.00
170	A94	15c deep blue ('30)	45.00 37.50
		Never hinged	75.00
		On cover	40.00
171	A95	20c gray blk ('31)	75.00 27.50
		Never hinged	110.00
		On cover	32.50

Nos. 163-171 (9) 156.50 80.45
Set, never hinged 246.00

Imperf., Pairs

163c	A84	1c	120.00
		Never hinged	160.00
164a	A85	2c pale carmine, cream	145.00
		Never hinged	180.00
b.		2c dark carmine	145.00

165a	A86	3c	145.00
		Never hinged	180.00
166a	A87	4c	145.00
		Never hinged	180.00

No. 164b is without gum, others with gum.

Types of 1928 Issue Re-engraved
1931　Wmk. 224　Perf. 13½x14

172	A84	1c green, perf. 13½	2.25 1.25
		Never hinged	3.00
		On cover	2.00
a.		Horiz. pair, imperf. btwn.	425.00
		Never hinged	510.00
173	A85	2c red	6.00 1.30
		Never hinged	9.00
		On cover	1.60
174	A86	3c red brown	3.50 1.25
		Never hinged	5.50
		On cover	2.40
175	A87	4c rose	4.25 2.00
		Never hinged	6.00
		On cover	8.00
176	A88	5c grnsh gray	12.50 7.00
		Never hinged	18.50
		On cover	12.00
177	A89	6c ultramarine	22.50 16.00
		Never hinged	32.50
		On cover	24.00
178	A90	8c lt red brn	22.50 16.00
		Never hinged	32.50
		On cover	20.00
179	A92	10c dk violet	15.00 9.00
		Never hinged	23.00
		On cover	12.00
180	A94	15c deep blue	45.00 27.50
		Never hinged	72.50
		On cover	30.00
181	A95	20c gray black	57.50 17.50
		Never hinged	90.00
		On cover	20.00
182	A96	30c olive brown	45.00 25.00
		Never hinged	70.00
		On cover	25.00

Nos. 172-182 (11) 236.00 123.80
Set, never hinged 361.75

Codfish — A97

George
V — A98

Queen
Mary — A99

Prince of
Wales — A100

Caribou
A101

Princess
Elizabeth
A102

Salmon Leaping
Falls — A103

Newfoundland
Dog — A104

Harp Seal
Pup — A105

Cape
Race — A106

Sealing
Fleet — A107

Fishing Fleet
Leaving for "The
Banks" — A108

| Type I | Type II |

FIVE CENT
Die I — Antlers even, or equal in height.
Die II — Antler under "T" higher.

1932-37   Engr.   Perf. 13½, 14

183	A97	1c green	2.25	.50
		Never hinged	3.25	
		On cover		1.20
a.		Booklet pane of 4, perf. 13	75.00	
		Never hinged	110.00	
c.		Vert. pair, imperf. btwn.	200.00	
		Never hinged	250.00	
184	A97	1c gray black	.35	.25
		Never hinged	.55	
		On cover		.60
a.		Bklt. pane of 4, perf. 13½	57.50	
		Never hinged	80.00	
b.		Booklet pane of 4, perf. 14	72.50	
		Never hinged	90.00	
185	A98	2c rose	2.25	.35
		Never hinged	3.25	
		On cover		1.20
a.		Booklet pane of 4, perf. 13½	35.00	
		Never hinged	50.00	
b.		Booklet pane of 4, perf. 13	47.50	
		Never hinged	60.00	
186	A98	2c green	1.10	.25
		Never hinged	1.75	
		On cover		.60
a.		Bklt. pane of 4, perf. 13½	25.00	
		Never hinged	32.50	
b.		Booklet pane of 4, perf. 14	35.00	
		Never hinged	50.00	
d.		Horiz. pair, imperf. btwn.	160.00	
		Never hinged	225.00	
187	A99	3c orange brn	1.10	.35
		Never hinged	1.75	
		On cover		.60
a.		Bklt. pane of 4, perf. 13½	55.00	
		Never hinged	75.00	
b.		Booklet pane of 4, perf. 14	67.50	
		Never hinged	92.50	
c.		Booklet pane of 4, perf. 13	75.00	
		Never hinged	100.00	
e.		Vert. pair, imperf. btwn.	300.00	
		Never hinged	450.00	
188	A100	4c deep violet	5.50	1.60
		Never hinged	8.25	
		On cover		1.60
189	A100	4c rose lake	.75	.35
		Never hinged	1.10	
		On cover		1.60
b.		Vert. pair, imperf. btwn.	120.00	
		Never hinged	165.00	
c.		Horiz. pair, imperf. btwn.	120.00	
		Never hinged	165.00	
d.		Perf. 14	5.75	4.50
		Never hinged	8.50	
				6.50
190	A101	5c vio brn, perf. 13½ (Die I)	9.50	1.25
		Never hinged	13.00	
				3.25
191	A101	5c dp vio, perf. 13½ (Die II)	1.10	.25
		Never hinged	1.75	
				.40
a.		5c dp vio, perf. 13½ (Die I)	11.00	1.00
		Never hinged	15.00	
		On cover		2.00
c.		Horiz. pair, imperf. btwn. (I)	240.00	
		Never hinged	325.00	
e.		Perf. 14 (Die I)	42.50	20.00
		Never hinged	65.00	
				65.00
f.		Perf. 14 (Die II)	40.00	16.00
		Never hinged	57.50	
				65.00
g.		Horiz. pair, imperf. btwn. (II)	240.00	
		Never hinged	325.00	
192	A102	6c dull blue	11.00	11.00
		Never hinged	17.00	
				24.00
193	A103	10c olive black	1.40	.85
		Never hinged	2.25	
				1.60
194	A104	14c int black	3.25	2.75
		Never hinged	4.50	
		On cover		8.00

195	A105	15c magenta	2.50	2.25
		Never hinged	3.50	
		On cover		8.00
b.		Perf. 14	14.00	7.00
		Never hinged	18.00	
		On cover		12.50
196	A106	20c gray green	2.50	1.00
		Never hinged	3.50	
		On cover		8.00
b.		Perf. 14	55.00	37.50
		Never hinged	77.50	
197	A107	25c gray	2.75	2.00
		Never hinged	4.25	
		On cover		8.00
b.		Horiz. pair, imperf. btwn.	450.00	
		Never hinged	650.00	
c.		Vert. pair, imperf. btwn.	450.00	
		Never hinged	650.00	
d.		Perf. 14	62.50	45.00
		Never hinged	85.00	
198	A108	30c ultra	32.50	24.00
		Never hinged	45.00	
		On cover		55.00
b.		Vert. pair, imperf. btwn.	1,000.	
		Never hinged	1,400.	
c.		Perf. 14	400.00	—
		Never hinged	625.00	
199	A108	48c red brn ('37)	11.00	5.25
		Never hinged	16.50	
		On cover		20.00
		Nos. 183-199 (17)	90.80	54.25
		Set, never hinged	132.75	

Two dies were used for 2c green, one for 2c rose.
See Nos. 253-266.

Imperf., Pairs

183b	A97	1c	240.00
		Never hinged	350.00
184c	A97	1c	47.50
		Never hinged	60.00
185c	A98	2c	250.00
		Never hinged	325.00
186c	A98	2c	47.50
		Never hinged	60.00
187d	A99	3c	95.00
		Never hinged	120.00
189a	A100	4c	60.00
		Never hinged	75.00
190a	A101	5c	160.00
		Never hinged	200.00
191b	A101	5c (II)	60.00
		Never hinged	77.50
191d	A101	5c (I)	95.00
192a	A102	6c	145.00
		Never hinged	180.00
193a	A103	10c	110.00
		Never hinged	140.00
194a	A103	14c	120.00
		Never hinged	150.00
195a	A103	15c	120.00
		Never hinged	150.00
196a	A106	20c	225.00
		Never hinged	280.00
197a	A107	25c	225.00
		Never hinged	280.00
198a	A108	30c	700.00
		Never hinged	900.00
199a	A108	48c	120.00
		Never hinged	160.00

All with gum. Nos. 186c, 187d, 192a, 193a and 196a also made without gum; values about 10% less.

Queen
Elizabeth when
Duchess of
York — A109

Corner Brook
Paper Mills — A110

Loading Iron Ore
at Bell
Island — A111

1932

208	A109	7c red brown	1.40	1.25
		Never hinged	1.75	
		On cover		8.00
a.		Imperf., pair	160.00	
		Never hinged	200.00	
b.		Horiz. pair, imperf. between	600.00	
		Never hinged	775.00	
209	A110	8c orange red	1.40	1.10
		Never hinged	2.00	
		On cover		8.00
a.		Imperf., pair	120.00	
		Never hinged	150.00	
210	A111	24c light blue	2.75	2.75
		Never hinged	4.00	
		On cover		12.00
a.		Imperf., pair	200.00	
		Never hinged	260.00	
b.		Double impression	1,250.	
		Never hinged	1,600.	
		Nos. 208-210 (3)	5.55	5.10
		Set, never hinged	7.75	

No. 208a was made both with and without gum. Values about the same.

See Nos. 259, 264.

No. C9
Overprinted Bars
and

1933, Feb. 9   Wmk. 224   Perf. 14

211	AP6	15c brown	11.00	9.50
		Never hinged	17.00	
		On cover		20.00
a.		Vert. pair, one without overprint	7,000.	
		Never hinged	11,000.	
b.		Overprint reading up	4,750.	
		Never hinged	7,500.	

"L. & S." stands for "Land and Sea."

Sir Humphrey Gilbert Issue

Sir Humphrey
Gilbert — A112

Compton Castle,
Home of the
Gilbert
Family — A113

Gilbert Coat of
Arms — A114

Eton
College — A115

Token from Queen
Elizabeth I — A116

Sir Humphrey
Receiving Royal
Patents for
Colonization
A117

 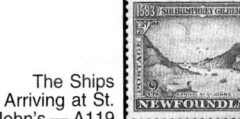

Sir Humphrey's
Ships Leaving
Plymouth,
1583 — A118

The Ships
Arriving at St.
John's — A119

Annexation of
Newfoundland,
Aug. 5,
1583 — A120

Coat of Arms
of England
A121

Sir Humphrey
on the Deck of
the "Squirrel"
A122

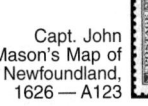

Capt. John
Mason's Map of
Newfoundland,
1626 — A123

Queen
Elizabeth I
A124

Gilbert Statue
at Truro
A125

Wmk. 224

1933, Aug. 3   Engr.   Perf. 13½

212	A112	1c gray black	1.10	.75
		Never hinged	1.50	
		On cover		1.00
213	A113	2c green	1.10	.75
		Never hinged	1.60	
		On cover		1.00
b.		Double impression	600.00	
		Never hinged	900.00	
214	A114	3c yellow brn	1.90	.75
		Never hinged	2.50	
		On cover		3.25
215	A115	4c carmine	1.90	.75
		Never hinged	2.50	
		On cover		3.25
216	A116	5c dull violet	2.75	1.10
		Never hinged	3.00	
		On cover		2.40
217	A117	7c blue	19.00	12.50
		Never hinged	35.00	
		On cover		24.00
b.		Perf. 14	16.00	16.00
		Never hinged	30.00	
		On cover		24.00
218	A118	8c orange red	7.50	7.00
		Never hinged	10.00	
		On cover		24.00
a.		8c brownish red (error), never hinged	525.00	
219	A119	9c ultramarine	8.00	7.50
		Never hinged	11.00	
		On cover		24.00
b.		Perf. 14	75.00	75.00
		Never hinged	110.00	
		On cover		120.00
220	A120	10c red brown	8.00	6.25
		Never hinged	11.00	
		On cover		16.00
b.		Perf. 14	100.00	100.00
		Never hinged	140.00	
		On cover		120.00
221	A121	14c black	16.00	14.00
		Never hinged	20.00	
		On cover		26.00
b.		Perf. 14	20.00	18.00
		Never hinged	30.00	
		On cover		30.00
222	A122	15c claret	14.00	14.00
		Never hinged	19.00	
		On cover		27.50
223	A123	20c deep green	13.00	10.00
		Never hinged	19.00	
		On cover		20.00
b.		Perf. 14	16.50	12.50
		Never hinged	25.00	
		On cover		24.00
224	A124	24c vio brown	22.50	22.50
		Never hinged	32.50	
		On cover		40.00
b.		Perf. 14	24.00	24.00
		Never hinged	35.00	
		On cover		40.00
225	A125	32c gray	22.50	22.50
		Never hinged	35.00	
		On cover		40.00
a.		Perf. 14	24.00	24.00
		Never hinged	35.00	
		On cover		40.00
		Nos. 212-225 (14)	139.25	120.35
		Set, never hinged	203.60	

350th anniv. of annexation of Newfoundland to England, Aug. 5, 1583, by authority of Letters Patent issued by Queen Elizabeth I to Sir Humphrey Gilbert.

Imperf., Pairs

212a	A112	1c	47.50
213a	A113	2c	47.50
214a	A114	3c	300.00
215a	A115	4c	50.00
216a	A116	5c	325.00
219a	A119	9c	425.00
220a	A120	10c	425.00
221a	A120	14c	400.00
222a	A120	15c	200.00
224a	A124	24c	225.00

Common Design Types
pictured following the introduction.

Silver Jubilee Issue
Common Design Type

1935, May 6 Wmk. 4 Perf. 11x12			
226	CD301 4c bright rose	2.00	.70
	Never hinged	2.50	
	On cover		1.60
227	CD301 5c violet	2.00	.85
	Never hinged	2.50	
	On cover		1.60
228	CD301 7c dark blue	4.00	3.50
	Never hinged	5.75	
	On cover		8.00
229	CD301 24c olive green	9.00	7.00
	Never hinged	14.00	
	On cover		10.00
a.	24c dark olive	16.00	12.00
	Never hinged	22.50	
	On cover		14.00
	Nos. 226-229 (4)	17.00	12.05
	Set, never hinged	24.75	

Coronation Issue
Common Design Type

1937, May 12		**Perf. 11x11½**	
230	CD302 2c deep green	1.75	.70
	Never hinged	2.40	
	On cover		1.60
231	CD302 4c carmine rose	1.75	.70
	Never hinged	2.40	
	On cover		1.60
232	CD302 5c dark violet	3.50	1.40
	Never hinged	5.00	
	On cover		3.25
	Nos. 230-232 (3)	7.00	2.80
	Set, never hinged	9.80	

Codfish
A126

Map of Newfoundland — A127

Caribou
A128

Corner
Brook
Paper Mills
A129

Salmon
A130

Newfoundland Dog — A131

Harp Seal
Pup
A132

Cape Race
A133

Loading
Iron Ore at
Bell Island
A134

Sealing
Fleet
A135

Fishing
Fleet
Leaving for
"The
Banks"
A136

Type I   Type II

Two types of the 3c
Type I — Fine impression; no lines on bridge of nose.
Type II — Coarse impression; lines on bridge of nose.

Perf. 13½, 14 (#234-235)

1937, May 12		**Wmk. 224**	
233	A126 1c gray black	.45	.30
	Never hinged	.70	
	On cover		1.00
	"Fish hook" plate flaw (pos. 23)	15.00	12.00
	Never hinged	27.00	
	On cover		16.00
234	A127 3c org brn, die I	2.50	1.10
	Never hinged	3.50	
	On cover		1.60
a.	Die II	1.75	1.10
	Never hinged	2.25	
	On cover		1.60
b.	Vert. pair, imperf. btwn. (I)	750.00	
	Never hinged	1,100.	
c.	Vert. pair, imperf. btwn. (II)	750.00	
	Never hinged	1,100.	
d.	Horiz. pair, imperf. btwn. (I)	575.00	
	Never hinged	850.00	
e.	Horiz. pair, imperf. btwn. (II)	575.00	
	Never hinged	850.00	
f.	Imperf., pair	240.00	
	Never hinged	360.00	
i.	Horiz. pair, imperf. vert., never hinged	1,800.	
235	A128 7c blue	2.50	2.50
	Never hinged	4.00	
	On cover		8.00
236	A129 8c orange red	2.50	2.50
	Never hinged	4.00	
	On cover		8.00
a.	Imperf., pair	275.00	
	Never hinged	400.00	
b.	Vert. pair, imperf. between	1,250.	
	Never hinged	1,850.	
c.	Horiz. pair, imperf. vert.	2,000.	
	Never hinged	3,000.	
237	A130 10c olive gray	4.25	4.25
	Never hinged	5.00	
	On cover		8.00
a.	Double impression	280.00	
	Never hinged	560.00	
238	A131 14c black	3.50	3.50
	Never hinged	3.75	
	On cover		8.00
a.	Imperf., pair	400.00	
	Never hinged	600.00	
239	A132 15c rose lake	3.50	3.50
	Never hinged	4.75	
	On cover		8.00
a.	Vert. pair, imperf. between	1,000.	
	Never hinged	1,500.	
240	A133 20c green	2.75	2.25
	Never hinged	3.75	
	On cover		8.00
a.	Vert. pair, imperf. between	1,500.	
	Never hinged	2,250.	
241	A134 24c turq blue	3.50	3.25
	Never hinged	4.50	
	On cover		8.00
a.	Vert. pair, imperf. between	2,000.	
	Never hinged	3,000.	
242	A135 25c gray	3.50	3.25
	Never hinged	4.50	
	On cover		8.00
a.	Imperf., pair	200.00	
	Never hinged	300.00	
243	A136 48c dark violet	4.25	3.50
	Never hinged	6.50	
	On cover		12.00
a.	Vert. pair, imperf. between	2,000.	
	Never hinged	3,000.	
b.	Imperf., pair	240.00	
	Never hinged	360.00	
	Nos. 233-243 (11)	33.20	29.90
	Set, never hinged	45.10	

Imperfs are with gum. No. 243b also made without gum; value the same.

Two line-perforating machines were used to produce this set, with exact measurements of 13.7 and 14.1 respectively.

Perf. 13½

233a	A126 1c gray black	16.00	22.00
	Never hinged	24.00	
	On cover		40.00
	"Fish hook" plate flaw (pos. 23)	175.00	—
	Never hinged	225.00	—
234g	A127 3c org brn, die I	1.60	1.00
	Never hinged	2.40	
	On cover		1.50
h.	Die II	2.00	1.25
	Never hinged	3.00	
	On cover		1.60
235a	A128 7c blue	400.00	275.00
	Never hinged	550.00	
236d	A129 8c orange red	3.25	3.25
	Never hinged	4.75	
	On cover		10.00
237b	A130 10c olive gray	5.00	6.00
	Never hinged	7.50	
	On cover		10.00
238b	A131 14c black	20,000.	—
	On cover		20.00
239b	A132 15c rose lake	11.00	11.00
	Never hinged	16.00	
	On cover		20.00
240b	A133 20c green	3.25	3.25
	Never hinged	5.00	
	On cover		8.00
241b	A134 24c turq blue	11.00	11.00
	Never hinged	16.50	
	On cover		16.00
242b	A135 25c gray	11.00	11.00
	Never hinged	16.50	
	On cover		16.00
243c	A136 48c dark violet	18.00	18.00
	Never hinged	25.00	
	On cover		24.00

This set was produced with a comb perforator with an exact perforation of 13.3x13.2.

Princess
Elizabeth — A139

Designs: 2c, King George VI. 3c, Queen Elizabeth. 7c, Queen Mother Mary.

1938, May 12		**Perf. 13½**	
245	A139 2c green	1.75	.25
	Never hinged	2.10	
	On cover		1.60
246	A139 3c dark carmine	1.75	.25
	Never hinged	2.10	
	On cover		1.60
b.	Perf. 14	750.00	500.00
	Never hinged	1,100.	
			750.00
247	A139 4c light blue	2.40	.25
	Never hinged	2.90	
	On cover		1.60
248	A139 7c dark ultra	1.60	1.10
	Never hinged	2.40	
	On cover		4.00
	Nos. 245-248 (4)	7.50	1.85
	Set, never hinged	9.50	

See Nos. 254-256, 258, 269.

Imperf., Pairs

245a	A139 2c	120.00	
	Never hinged	175.00	
246a	A139 3c	120.00	
	Never hinged	175.00	
247a	A139 4c	120.00	
	Never hinged	175.00	
248a	A139 7c	120.00	
	Never hinged	175.00	
	Set, never hinged	700.00	

George VI
and Queen
Elizabeth
A141

1939, June 17		**Unwmk.**	
249	A141 5c violet blue	1.25	1.10
	Never hinged	1.60	
	On cover		1.60

Visit of King George and Queen Elizabeth.

No. 249
Surcharged
in Brown or
Red

1939, Nov. 20			
250	A141 2c on 5c vio blue (Br)	1.25	1.00
	Never hinged	1.60	
	On cover		2.40
251	A141 4c on 5c vio blue (R)	1.10	1.00
	Never hinged	1.50	
	On cover		2.40
	Set, never hinged	3.10	

There are many varieties of broken letters and figures in the settings of the surcharges.

Sir Wilfred Grenfell and
"Strathcona II" — A142

1941, Dec. 1		**Perf. 12**	
252	A142 5c dull blue	.40	.30
	Never hinged	.50	
	On cover		1.20

Grenfell Mission, 50th anniv.

Types of 1931-38

1941-44	**Wmk. 224**	**Perf. 12½**	
253	A97 1c dark gray	.35	.25
	Never hinged	.45	
	On cover		.25
a.	Imperf., pair	150.00	
	Never hinged	275.00	
254	A139 2c deep green	.35	.25
	Never hinged	.45	
	On cover		.25
255	A139 3c rose carmine	.45	.25
	Never hinged	.60	
	On cover		.25
256	A139 4c blue	.70	.30
	Never hinged	.80	
	On cover		.40
257	A101 5c violet (Die I)	1.10	.25
	Never hinged	1.40	
	On cover		.25
a.	Imperf., pair	175.00	
	Never hinged	225.00	
b.	Horiz. pair, imperf. vert.	475.00	
	Never hinged	575.00	
c.	Double impression	400.00	
	Never hinged	550.00	
258	A139 7c vio blue ('42)	1.20	1.00
	Never hinged	1.40	
	On cover		1.80
259	A110 8c red	1.30	.65
	Never hinged	1.60	
	On cover		1.20
260	A103 10c brownish blk	1.30	.60
	Never hinged	1.60	
	On cover		1.25
261	A104 14c black	2.10	1.75
	Never hinged	3.00	
	On cover		2.40
a.	Imperf., pair	240.00	
	Never hinged	325.00	
c.	Vert. pair, imperf. horiz.	350.00	
	Never hinged	500.00	
262	A105 15c pale rose vio	2.00	1.40
	Never hinged	2.50	
	On cover		2.25
263	A106 20c green	2.00	1.10
	Never hinged	2.50	
	On cover		1.90
264	A111 24c deep blue	2.25	2.00
	Never hinged	2.75	
	On cover		3.00
265	A107 25c slate	2.25	2.00
	Never hinged	2.75	
	On cover		3.00
266	A108 48c red brown ('44)	3.00	1.75
	Never hinged	3.75	
	On cover		3.00
	Nos. 253-266 (14)	20.35	13.55
	Set, never hinged	25.55	

Nos. 254 and 255 are re-engraved.

Memorial
University
College
A143

1943, Jan. 2	**Unwmk.**	**Perf. 12**	
267	A143 30c carmine	1.40	1.00
	Never hinged	1.85	
	On cover		8.00

No. 267
Surcharged
in Black

1946, Mar. 23			
268	A143 2c on 30c carmine	.30	.30
	Never hinged	.40	
	On cover		2.00

Princess
Elizabeth — A144

Wmk. 224

1947, Apr. 21	**Engr.**		**Perf. 12½**
269	A144 4c light blue	.30	.25
	Never hinged	.40	
	On cover		.80
a.	Imperf., pair	240.00	
	Never hinged	300.00	
b.	Horiz. pair, imperf. vert.	325.00	
	Never hinged	450.00	

Princess Elizabeth's 21st birthday.

Deck of the
Matthew
A145

1947, June 24			
270	A145 5c rose violet	.30	.25
	Never hinged	.40	
	On cover		1.20
a.	Horiz. pair, imperf. between	1,200.	
	Never hinged	1,650.	
b.	Imperf., pair	240.00	
	Never hinged	325.00	

Cabot's arrival off Cape Bonavista, 450th anniv.

AIR POST STAMPS

No. 117 Overprinted
in Black

1919, Apr. 12	**Unwmk.**	**Perf. 14**	
C1	A67 3c red brown	27,500.	16,000.
	Never hinged	37,500.	
	On cover		25,000.

No. C1 was issued for the first attempt to cross the Atlantic by air, by Lt. H. G. Hawker (pilot) and Lt. Cdr. K. M. Grieve (navigator). This flight was ended by a controlled crash landing in the ocean after about 13 hours of flying, the crew being rescued. The plane and mail bag were salvaged about five weeks later by an east-bound ship and the envelopes were delivered to England by sea.

Also in April 1919, W. C. Campbell, the Secretary of the Postal Department, prepared stamps for use on the Raynham-Morgan transatlantic flight attempt that took off shortly after the Hawker flight. Campbell is believed to have applied "Aerial Atlantic Mail" to No. 117 in manuscript and J. A. Robinson, the Postmaster, applied his initials "J.A.R.," also in manuscript. This flight lasted only a few hundred yards, as did a second attempt in July. Mail from these attempts was then taken by sea to London and delivered in January 1920. Value, on cover, $27,500.

No. 70 Surcharged
in Black

1919, June 9		**Perf. 12**	
C2	A33 $1 on 15c scarlet	225.00	225.00
	Never hinged	375.00	
	On cover		1,200.
a.	Without comma after "Post"	240.00	275.00
	Never hinged	360.00	
	On cover		1,200.
b.	As "a," without period after "1919"	450.00	450.00
	Never hinged	675.00	
	On cover		1,400.
c.	As "a," "A" of "AIR" under "a" of "Trans"	450.00	450.00
	Never hinged	675.00	
	On cover		1,400.

No. C2 was issued for the June 14, 1919, flight of Capt. J. Alcock and Lt. A. W. Brown. This became the first successful non-stop

transatlantic flight. No. C2 also was used on mail of other flights.

No. 73
Overprinted in
Black

1921, Nov. 7			
C3	A36 35c red, 2½mm between "AIR" and "MAIL"	145.00	180.00
	Never hinged	250.00	
	On cover		200.00
a.	Inverted overprint	6,000.	
	Never hinged	9,000.	
b.	With period after "1921"	160.00	200.00
	Never hinged	240.00	
	On cover		225.00
c.	As "b," inverted overprint	6,500.	
	Never hinged	9,500.	
d.	"1" of "1921" below "f" of "Halifax"	500.00	500.00
	Never hinged	750.00	
	On cover		550.00
e.	As "d," inverted overprint	25,000.	
	Never hinged	—	
f.	35c red, 1½mm between "AIR" and "MAIL"	350.00	350.00
	Never hinged	500.00	
	On cover		400.00
g.	As "f," inverted overprint	12,500.	
	Never hinged	17,500.	
h.	As "f," with period after "1921"	300.00	300.00
	Never hinged	400.00	
	On cover		260.00
i.	As "h," inverted overprint	10,000.	
	Never hinged	15,000.	
j.	As "f," "1" of "1921" below "f" of "Halifax"	500.00	500.00
	Never hinged	700.00	
	On cover		550.00
k.	As "j," inverted overprint	22,500.	
	Never hinged	—	

No. 74 Overprinted in
Red

1927, May 21			
C4	A37 60c black	45,000.	20,000.
	Never hinged	60,000.	
	On cover		20,000.
a.	Short "7" in "1927"	47,500.	20,000.
	Never hinged	67,500.	
	On cover		24,000.

No. 126 Surcharged
in Black

1930, Sept. 25		**Perf. 14**	
C5	A67 50c on 36c ol grn	9,500.	9,500.
	Never hinged	13,750.	
	On cover		14,000.

Dog Sled and
Airplane — AP6

First Transatlantic Mail Airplane and
Packet Ship — AP7

Routes of Historic Transatlantic
Flights — AP8

1931, Jan. 2	**Engr.**	**Unwmk.**	
C6	AP6 15c brown	11.00	7.50
	Never hinged	16.50	
	On cover		16.00
a.	Horiz. pair, imperf. between	950.00	
	Never hinged	1,400.	
b.	Vert. pair, imperf. between	950.00	
	Never hinged	1,400.	
c.	Imperf., pair	625.00	
	Never hinged	1,500.	
C7	AP7 50c green	35.00	25.00
	Never hinged	60.00	
	On cover		40.00
a.	Horiz. pair, imperf. between	1,350.	825.00
	Never hinged	2,000.	
b.	Vert. pair, imperf. between	1,350.	
	Never hinged	2,000.	
c.	Imperf., pair	725.00	
	Never hinged	1,100.	
C8	AP8 $1 blue	70.00	55.00
	Never hinged	120.00	
	On cover		100.00
a.	Horiz. pair, imperf. between	1,000.	
	Never hinged	1,500.	
b.	Vert. pair, imperf. between	1,000.	
	Never hinged	1,500.	
c.	Imperf., pair	725.00	
	Never hinged	1,100.	
	Nos. C6-C8 (3)	116.00	87.50
	Set, never hinged	195.00	

1931		**Wmk. 224**	
C9	AP6 15c brown	11.00	7.50
	Never hinged	16.00	
	On cover		16.00
a.	Horiz. pair, imperf. between	950.00	
	Never hinged	1,400.	
b.	Vert. pair, imperf. between	1,100.	
	Never hinged	1,650.	
c.	Imperf., pair	600.00	
	Never hinged	900.00	
C10	AP7 50c green	40.00	35.00
	Never hinged	77.50	
	On cover		47.50
a.	Horiz. pair, imperf. between	950.00	
	Never hinged	1,400.	
b.	Vert. pair, imperf. between	950.00	
	Never hinged	1,400.	
c.	Horiz. pair, imperf. vert.	950.00	
C11	AP8 $1 blue	100.00	90.00
	Never hinged	170.00	
	On cover		120.00
a.	Vert. pair, imperf. between	1,000.	
	Never hinged	1,500.	
b.	Horiz. pair, imperf. between	1,000.	
	Never hinged	1,500.	
c.	Imperf., pair	600.00	
	Never hinged	900.00	
d.	Vert. pair, imperf. horiz.	1,000.	
e.	Imperf., pair	600.00	
	Never hinged	900.00	
	Nos. C9-C11 (3)	151.00	132.50
	Set, never hinged	263.50	

As the watermark 224 does not show on every stamp in the sheet, pairs are found one with and one without watermark.

For overprint and surcharge see Nos. 211, C12.

No. C11 Surcharged in Red

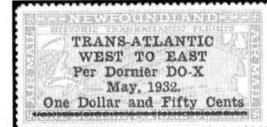

1932, May 19			
C12	AP8 $1.50 on $1 blue	275.00	275.00
	Never hinged	425.00	
	On cover		400.00
a.	Inverted surcharge	20,000.	
	Never hinged	32,500.	

A stamp of this design was produced in the US in 1932 by a private company

under contract with Newfoundland authorities. The government canceled the contract and the stamp was not valid for prepayment of postage. Value, $35.

"Put to
Flight" — AP9

"Land of
Heart's
Delight"
AP10

"Spotting the
Herd"
AP11

"News from
Home"
AP12

"Labrador,
The Land of
Gold"
AP13

Perf. 11½ (10, 60c), 14 (5, 30, 75c)

1933, June 9		**Engr.**	
C13	AP9 5c lt brown	11.00	11.00
	Never hinged	14.00	
	On cover		27.50
b.	Horiz. pair, imperf. between	1,250.	
	Never hinged	1,800.	
c.	Vert. pair, imperf. between	1,250.	
	Never hinged	1,800.	
C14	AP10 10c yellow	19.00	17.50
	Never hinged	26.00	
	On cover		40.00
C15	AP11 30c blue	30.00	30.00
	Never hinged	37.50	
	On cover		47.50
C16	AP12 60c green	65.00	57.50
	Never hinged	100.00	
	On cover		80.00
C17	AP13 75c bister	60.00	57.50
	Never hinged	92.50	
	On cover		80.00
b.	Horiz. pair, imperf. between	2,500.	
	Never hinged	3,500.	
c.	Vert. pair, imperf. between	2,500.	
	Never hinged	3,500.	
	Nos. C13-C17 (5)	185.00	173.50
	Set, never hinged	262.50	

Beware of clever forgeries of Nos. C13b, C13c, C17b and C17c. Certificates of authenticity are highly recommended.

Imperf., Pairs

C13a	AP9 5c	275.00	
	Never hinged	375.00	
C14a	AP10 10c	200.00	
	Never hinged	300.00	
C15a	AP11 30c	600.00	
	Never hinged	825.00	
C16a	AP12 60c	675.00	
	Never hinged	850.00	
C17a	AP13 75c	650.00	
	Never hinged	800.00	
	Set, never hinged	3,150.	

No. C17
Surcharged
in Black

1933, July 24   *Perf. 14*

C18	AP13	$4.50 on 75c bister	325.00	350.00
		Never hinged	500.00	
		On cover		875.00
a.		Inverted surcharge	100,000.	
		Never hinged	130,000.	

Return flight from Chicago to Rome of the squadron of Italian seaplanes under the command of Gen. Italo Balbo.

No. C18a was not regularly issued.

The $4.50 on No. C14, 10c yellow, is a proof. Value, $62,500.

View of St. John's
AP14

1943, June 1   Unwmk.   *Perf. 12*

C19	AP14	7c bright ultra	.35	.30
		Never hinged	.45	
		First day cover		2.75

POSTAGE DUE STAMPS

D1

Perf. 10-10½, Compound

1939-49   Litho.   Unwmk.

J1	D1	1c yellow green, perf. 11 ('49)	4.25	5.50
		Never hinged	8.25	
		On cover		400.00
a.		Perf. 10-10½	7.25	5.50
		Never hinged	9.00	
		On cover		350.00
J2	D1	2c vermilion	7.00	5.50
		Never hinged	10.50	
		On cover		350.00
a.		Perf. 11x9 ('46)	7.00	5.50
		Never hinged	10.50	
		On cover		550.00
J3	D1	3c ultramarine	7.00	5.50
		Never hinged	10.50	
		On cover		450.00
a.		Perf. 11x9 ('49)	7.50	7.50
		Never hinged	10.00	
		On cover		750.00
b.		Perf. 9	2,750.	
		Never hinged	4,000.	
J4	D1	4c yel org, perf. 11x9 ('49)	9.50	9.50
		Never hinged	16.00	
		On cover		750.00
a.		Perf 10-10½	15.00	15.00
		Never hinged	22.50	
		On cover		450.00
J5	D1	5c pale brown	15.00	4.25
		Never hinged	22.50	
		On cover		600.00
J6	D1	10c dark violet	6.00	5.00
		Never hinged	11.00	
		On cover		550.00
		Nos. J1-J6 (6)	48.75	35.25
		Set, never hinged	78.75	

1949   Wmk. 224   *Perf. 11*

J7	D1	10c dark violet	11.00	14.00
		Never hinged	19.00	
		On cover		750.00
		"LUE" instead of "DUE" plate flaw	50.00	50.00
		Never hinged	75.00	
a.		Vert. pair, imperf. between	850.00	
		Never hinged	1,275.	

For used examples of Nos. J1-J7 with dated cancels from 1939-49, triple the values shown.

Covers: Cover values are for proper postage due usages on commercial covers prior to April 1, 1949. Note that multiples and combinations are not additive; therefore, for example, a pair of No. J2 on cover is valued at approximately $355 (cover value plus single used value). Values for philatelic covers range from approximately $55 to $100.

POST OFFICE SEAL

King Edward VII — POS1

1905   Unwmk.   *Perf. 12*

OX1	POS1	black, *blue*	750.	500.
		Never hinged	1,500.	
		On cover		2,750.

No. OX1 used or on cover is valued creased but not torn. Cover value is for presentable cover, with damage to the cover consistent with the application of the seal.

Some examples of No. OX1 show a portion of the papermaker's watermark. Values, unused $1,000, mint never hinged $2,000, used $600.

NOVA SCOTIA

ˌnō-və-ˈskō-shə

LOCATION — Eastern coast of Canada between the Gulf of St. Lawrence and the Atlantic Ocean
GOVT. — British Crown Colony
AREA — 21,428 sq. mi.
POP. — 386,500 (1871)
CAPITAL — Halifax

Nova Scotia joined the Canadian Confederation in 1867 and is now a province of the Dominion. Postage stamps of Canada are used.

12 Pence = 1 Shilling
100 Cents = 1 Dollar (1860)

PRE-STAMP POSTAL MARKINGS

Crowned Circle handstamp type I is pictured in the Crowned Circle Handstamps and Great Britain Used Abroad section.

1845-51

A1	I	"Amherst" crowned circle handstamp in red, on cover		1,150.
A2	I	"St. Margarets Bay" crowned circle handstamp in red, on cover		11,000.

Values for unused stamps are for examples with original gum as defined in the catalogue introduction except for Nos. 4-7, which are rarely found with any remaining original gum.

Queen Victoria — A1

Crown of Great Britain and Heraldic Flowers of the Empire — A2

Blue Paper

1851-57   Unwmk.   Engr.   *Imperf.*

1	A1	1p red brown ('53)	3,500.	650.
		On cover		2,100.
a.		Half used as ½p on cover		—

2	A2	3p bright blue	1,750.	240.
		On cover		325.
a.		Half used as 1½p on cover		3,750.
b.		3p pale blue ('57)	1,750.	275.
		On cover		325.
c.		As "b," half used as 1½p on cover		3,750.
3	A2	3p dark blue	2,000.	300.
		On cover		400.
a.		Half used as 1½p on cover		4,500.
4	A2	6p yellow green	5,000.	675.
		On cover		1,600.
a.		Half used as 3p on cover		4,500.
5	A2	6p dark green ('57)	10,000.	1,750.
		On cover		2,400.
a.		Half used as 3p on cover		5,000.
b.		Quarter used as 1½p on cover		47,500.
6	A2	1sh reddish pur ('57)	25,000.	5,250.
		On cover		16,000.
a.		Half used as 6p on cover		32,500.
b.		1sh deep purple	25,000.	5,750.
		On cover		16,000.
7	A2	1sh dull violet	25,000.	6,500.
		On cover		16,000.
a.		Half used as 6p on cover		47,500.
b.		Quarter used as 3p on cover		60,000.

The 1sh is known with a papermaker's watermark, "T. H. Saunders." Value, $22,500 unused, $7,500 used.

Nos. 2a, 2c, 3a are normally found with a 6p stamp to make up the 7½p rate for a half ounce letter to the United Kingdom.

Reprints are on thin hard white paper. 1p in brown, 3p in blue, 6p dark green, 1sh violet black. Value about $300 per set.

No. 6 was reproduced by the collotype process in a souvenir sheet distributed at the London International Stamp Exhibition 1950.

Queen Victoria — A3   A5

A6

White or Yellowish Paper

1860-63   *Perf. 12*

8	A3	1c black	12.00	7.50
		Never hinged	18.00	
		On cover		200.00
a.		White paper	12.00	7.50
		Never hinged	18.00	
		On cover		200.00
b.		Half used as ½c on cover		5,750.
c.		Horiz. pair, imperf. vert.	325.00	
9	A3	2c lilac	12.00	12.50
		Never hinged	18.00	
		On cover		40.00
a.		Yellowish paper	12.00	12.50
		Never hinged	18.00	
		On cover		40.00
b.		Half used as 1c on cover		3,250.
c.		2c grayish purple	12.50	15.00
		Never hinged	19.00	
10	A3	5c blue	400.00	12.00
		Never hinged	1,300.	
		On cover		37.50
a.		Yellowish paper	400.00	12.00
		Never hinged	1,300.	
		On cover		37.50
b.		Half used as 2½c on cover		5,000.
c.		5c dark blue	400.00	12.00
		Never hinged	1,300.	
11	A5	8½c green	12.00	22.00
		Never hinged	18.00	
		On cover		900.00
a.		White paper	12.00	20.00
		Never hinged	18.00	
		On cover		900.00
12	A5	10c vermilion	12.00	12.00
		Never hinged	18.00	
		On cover		80.00
a.		Yellowish paper	12.00	12.00
		Never hinged	18.00	
		On cover		80.00
b.		Half used as 5c on cover		1,200.
13	A6	12½c black	37.50	37.50
		Never hinged	55.00	
		On cover		325.00
a.		White paper	37.50	37.50
		Never hinged	55.00	
		On cover		325.00
		Nos. 8-13 (6)	485.50	103.50
		Set, never hinged	1,075.	

The stamps of Nova Scotia were replaced by those of Canada.

PRINCE EDWARD ISLAND

ˈprin̪t̪s ˈed-wərd ˈī-lənd

LOCATION — In the Gulf of St. Lawrence, opposite the provinces of New Brunswick and Nova Scotia
GOVT. — British Crown Colony
AREA — 2,184 sq. mi.
POP. — 92,000 (estimated)
CAPITAL — Charlottetown

Originally annexed to Nova Scotia, Prince Edward Island was a separate colony from 1769 to 1873, when it became a part of the Canadian Confederation. Postage stamps of Canada are now used.

12 Pence = 1 Shilling
100 Cents = 1 Dollar (1872)

Values for covers are for examples in fine condition. Very fine covers are extremely scarce and command substantial premiums.

A1   A2

Queen Victoria — A3

1861, Jan. 1   Unwmk.   Typo.   *Perf. 9*

1	A1	2p dull rose	700.	300.
		Never hinged	1,700.	
		On cover		375.
a.		2p deep rose	825.	350.
		Never hinged	2,200.	
		On cover		400.
b.		Rouletted		22,500.
c.		Horiz. pair, imperf. between	6,500.	
d.		Diagonal half used as 1p on cover		1,900.
2	A2	3p blue	2,250.	750.
		Never hinged	5,250.	
		On cover		1,100.
a.		Diagonal half used as 1½p on cover		2,250.
b.		Double impression	4,750.	

No. 2b is valued with very small faults.

3	A3	6p yellow green	2,750.	1,200.
		Never hinged	6,000.	
		On cover		2,800.

A4   A5

White or Yellowish Paper

1862-65   *Perf. 11½-12*

4	A4	1p yellow orange	37.50	35.00
		Never hinged	60.00	
		On cover		350.00
a.		1p brown orange, perf. 11	45.00	35.00
		Never hinged	72.50	
		On cover		375.00
b.		Imperf., pair	200.00	
		Never hinged	300.00	
c.		Half used as ½p on cover		1,500.
d.		Perf. 11x11½-12	75.00	35.00
		Never hinged	150.00	
		On cover		
5	A1	2p rose	8.50	7.50
		Never hinged	12.50	
		On cover		100.00
a.		Yellowish paper	14.00	7.50
		Never hinged	20.00	
		On cover		100.00
b.		Imperf., pair	100.00	
		Never hinged	150.00	
c.		Horiz. pair, imperf. vert.	275.00	
		Never hinged	410.00	
d.		Vert. pair, imperf. horiz.	375.00	
		Never hinged	560.00	
e.		Diagonal half used as 1p on cover		1,900.
f.		"TWC" for "TWO"	60.00	30.00
		Never hinged	90.00	

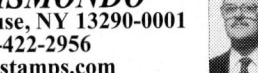

	On cover		175.00
g.	Perf. 11x11½-12	8.00	8.00
	Never hinged	12.50	
	On cover		225.00
6	A2 3p blue	16.00	*15.00*
	Never hinged	25.00	
	On cover		45.00
a.	Yellowish paper	32.50	15.00
	Never hinged	50.00	
	On cover		45.00
b.	Imperf., pair	150.00	
	Never hinged	225.00	
c.	Vert. pair, imperf. horiz.	400.00	
	Never hinged	650.00	
d.	Horiz. pair, imperf. vert.	400.00	
	Never hinged	650.00	
e.	Diagonal half used as 1½p on cover		250.00
f.	Perf. 11x11½-12	45.00	45.00
	Never hinged	67.50	
	On cover		120.00
7	A3 6p yellow green	115.00	95.00
	Never hinged	200.00	
	On cover		475.00
a.	6p blue green	115.00	95.00
	Never hinged	200.00	
	On cover		475.00
b.	Imperf.	—	
c.	Diagonal half used as 3p		*3,000.*
d.	Perf. 11x11½-12	115.00	100.00
	Never hinged	225.00	
	On cover		—
8	A5 9p violet	95.00	80.00
	Never hinged	140.00	
	On cover		600.00
a.	Imperf., pair	300.00	
	Never hinged	475.00	
b.	Horiz. pair, imperf. vert.	325.00	
	Never hinged	510.00	
c.	Diagonal half used as 4½p on cover		*2,250.*
d.	Perf. 11	95.00	80.00
	Never hinged	200.00	
	On cover		*1,200.*
	Nos. 4-8 (5)	272.00	232.50

Some specialists question the existence of No. 7b. The editors would like to see authenticated evidence of the existence of this item.

Queen Victoria
A6   A7

1868

9	A6 4p black	9.50	19.00
	Never hinged	11.50	
	On cover		200.00
a.	Yellowish paper	15.00	22.50
	Never hinged	21.00	
	On cover		200.00
b.	Horiz. pair, imperf. vert.	190.00	
	Never hinged	290.00	
c.	Diagonal half used as 2p on cover		*2,250.*
d.	Imperf., pair	140.00	
	Never hinged	210.00	
e.	Horiz. pair, imperf. between	160.00	
	Never hinged	240.00	
f.	Perf. 11x11½-12	45.00	45.00
	Never hinged	75.00	
	On cover		325.00

1870, June 1   Engr.   Perf. 12

10	A7 4½p brown	125.00	90.00
	Never hinged	250.00	
	On cover		*2,400.*
	Without gum	55.00	
	Block of 4 with horiz. gutter btwn.	550.00	
	Never hinged		*1,100.*
	Without gum	360.00	

A8   A9

A10

A11

A12   A13

1872, Jan. 1   Typo.   Perf. 12, 12½

11	A8 1c brown orange	7.00	*7.50*
	Never hinged	10.50	
	On cover		160.00
a.	Imperf., pair	240.00	
	Never hinged	450.00	
b.	Perf. 12½	9.00	*9.00*
	Never hinged	16.00	
	On cover		160.00
c.	1c orange, perf. 12x12½	16.00	*15.00*
	Never hinged	24.00	
	On cover		160.00
12	A9 2c ultra	24.00	*30.00*
	Never hinged	36.00	
	On cover		800.00
a.	Imperf., pair	350.00	
	Never hinged	800.00	
b.	Diagonal half used as 1c		—
13	A10 3c rose	25.00	22.50
	Never hinged	42.50	
	On cover		60.00
a.	Imperf., pair	325.00	
	Never hinged	600.00	
b.	Diagonal half used as 1½c on cover		—
c.	Horiz. or vert. pair, imperf. between	240.00	
	Never hinged	425.00	
d.	Perf. 12½	22.50	22.50
	Never hinged	35.00	
	On cover		120.00
e.	Perf. 12x12½	24.00	24.00
	Never hinged	40.00	
	On cover		50.00
14	A11 4c green	11.50	*16.00*
	Never hinged	16.50	
	On cover		225.00
a.	Imperf., pair	325.00	
	Never hinged	600.00	
b.	Diagonal half used as 2c		*2,000.*
15	A12 6c black	8.00	*13.00*
	Never hinged	12.00	
	On cover		200.00
a.	Horiz. pair, imperf. btwn.	250.00	
	Never hinged	475.00	
b.	Half used as 3c on cover		*900.00*
c.	Perf. 12½	80.00	*175.00*
	Never hinged	160.00	
	On cover		*375.00*
16	A13 12c violet	7.75	*30.00*
	Never hinged	11.50	
	On cover		*2,000.*
a.	Imperf., pair	325.00	
	Never hinged	600.00	
b.	Half used as 6c on cover		—
	Nos. 11-16 (6)	83.25	*119.00*

CANADA

ˈka-nə-də

LOCATION — Northern part of North American continent, except for Alaska

GOVT. — Self-governing dominion in the British Commonwealth of Nations

AREA — 3,851,809 sq. mi.

POP. — 24,907,100 (est. 1983)

CAPITAL — Ottawa

Included in the dominion are British Columbia, Vancouver Island, Prince Edward Island, Nova Scotia, New

Brunswick and Newfoundland, all of which formerly issued stamps.

12 Pence = 1 Shilling
100 Cents = 1 Dollar (1859)

Catalogue values for unused stamps in this country are for Never Hinged items, beginning with Scott 268 in the regular postage section, Scott C9 in the air post section, Scott CE3 in the air post special delivery section, Scott CO1 in the air post official section, Scott E11 in the special delivery section, Scott EO1 in the special delivery official section, Scott J15 in the postage due section, and Scott O1 in the official section.

Values for unused stamps of Nos. 1-33 are for examples with partial original gum. Stamps without gum often trade at prices very close to those of stamps with partial gum. Examples with full original gum and lightly hinged are extremely scarce and generally sell for substantially more than the values listed.

Very fine examples of the perforated issues between Nos. 11-20 will have perforations touching the design or frameline on at least one side due to the narrow spacing of the stamps on the plates. Stamps with perfs clear of the designs on all four sides are extremely scarce and will command much higher prices.

PRE-STAMP POSTAL MARKINGS

Crown Circle Handstamp

Crowned Circle handstamp type II is pictured in the Crowned Circle Handstamps and Great Britain Used Abroad section.

1842-51

A1 II "Quebec" crowned circle handstamp in red, on cover   200.

Crown Circle handstamps exist also from Amherst, Nova Scotia, and St. Margaret's Bay, Nova Scotia, and St. John's, Newfoundland. These are listed under Nova Scotia and Newfoundland respectively.

POSTMASTER PROVISIONAL
New Carlisle, Gaspé

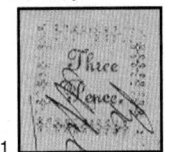

E1

ENVELOPE

1851, Apr.   Typeset

1X1	E1 3p black, entire	

Only one example of No. 1X1 is recorded, an entire postmarked April 7, 1851, to Toronto.

Province of Canada

Beaver — A1   Prince Albert — A2

Queen Victoria — A3

1851   Unwmk.   Engr.   *Imperf.*
Laid Paper

1	A1 3p red	35,000.	1,000.
	No gum	24,000.	
	On cover		*1,900.*
	Double transfer (pos. 47, pane A)		2,700.
	On cover		*3,250.*
a.	3p orange vermilion	30,000.	1,000.
	No gum	24,000.	
	On cover		*1,900.*
2	A2 6p slate violet	40,000.	1,750.
	No gum	27,500.	
	On cover		*3,100.*
a.	Diagonal half used as 3p on cover		*32,500.*
b.	6p grayish purple	40,000.	1,750.
	No gum	27,500.	
	On cover		*3,100.*
3	A3 12p black	175,000.	140,000.
	No gum	87,500.	
	On cover		*300,000.*

On some stamps the laid lines of Nos. 1-3 are practically invisible.

No. 1 double transfer position 47 shows extensive doubling of "EE PEN," above and below "POS," in and below "ANADA THR" and in all four numerals. Pane A is the upper pane.

1852-57   Wove Paper

4	A1 3p red	1,500.	225.
	No gum	1,250.	
	On cover		*460.*
	Double transfer (pos. 47, pane A)	4,250.	750.
	No gum	2,750.	
	On cover		*1,500.*
a.	3p brown red ('53)	1,700.	250.
	No gum	1,550.	
	On cover		*500.*
b.	Diagonal half used as 1½p on cover		*32,500.*
c.	Ribbed paper	4,000.	550.
	No gum	3,500.	
	On cover		*700.00*
d.	Thin paper	1,600.	225.
	No gum	1,450.	
	On cover		*460.*
5	A2 6p slate gray ('55)	30,000.	1,500.
	No gum	23,000.	
	On cover		*1,900.*
a.	6p brownish gray	40,000.	2,000.
	No gum	30,000.	
	On cover		*2,500.*
b.	6p greenish gray	30,000.	1,500.
	No gum	23,000.	
	On cover		*1,900.*
c.	Diagonal half used as 3p on cover		*17,500.*
d.	Thick hard paper (gray vio) ('57)	30,000.	3,000.
	No gum	23,000.	
	On cover		*3,500.*

See note after No. 3 for characteristics of double transfer pos. 47 on No. 4. Pos. 47 is considered the most prominent double transfer, but many others exist. The double transfers exist on all shades and papers; values are for the most common shade and paper.

Most authorities believe the 12p black does not exist on wove paper.

Jacques Cartier — A4

1855

7	A4	10p blue	11,000.	1,750.
	No gum		8,000.	
	On cover			3,250.
a.	Thick paper		12,000.	2,250.
	No gum		9,500.	
	On cover			3,500.

Queen Victoria
A5   A6

1857

8	A5	½p rose	1,100.	700.
	No gum		875.	
	On cover			950.00
	On cover, single franking			1,250.
	On newspaper or circular			1,000.
a.	Horizontally ribbed paper		10,000.	2,500.
	No gum		8,500.	
	On cover			2,750.
b.	Vertically ribbed paper		10,000.	3,750.
	No gum		8,600.	
	On cover			4,000.
9	A6	7½p green	10,000.	3,500.
	No gum		7,000.	
	On cover			6,000.
a.	7½p deep green		20,000.	6,000.
	No gum		8,750.	
	On cover			6,250.

Very Thick Soft Wove Paper

10	A2	6p reddish pur	32,500.	7,500.
	No gum		16,000.	
	On cover			9,000.
a.	Half used as 3p on cover			30,000.

1858-59   Wove Paper   Perf. 12

11	A5	½p rose	3,500.	1,900.
	No gum		3,000.	
	On cover			2,300.
	On cover, single franking			2,500.
	On circular, single franking			2,100.
	On newspaper, single franking			2,500.
12	A1	3p red	17,500.	1,300.
	No gum		12,500.	
	On cover			1,500.
	Double transfer (pos. 47, pane A)			1,500.
	On cover			2,250.
13	A2	6p brown vio ('59)	22,500.	7,500.
	No gum		19,000.	
	On cover			8,750.
a.	6p gray violet		22,500.	7,500.
	No gum		19,000.	
	On cover			8,750.
b.	Diagonal half used as 3p on cover			17,500.

Nos. 11-13 values are for examples with perfs touching the design.

A7   A8

A9   A10

A11   A12

1859

14	A7	1c rose	425.00	90.00
	No gum		325.00	
	On cover			180.00
	On cover, single franking			180.00
	On circular			140.00
	On newspaper			240.00
a.	Imperf., pair		5,000.	
b.	1c deep rose		575.00	140.00
	No gum		350.00	
	On cover			350.00
	On cover, single franking			390.00
	On circular			225.00
	On newspaper			475.00
15	A8	5c ver	525.00	37.50
	No gum		425.00	
	On cover			47.50
	Major re-entry (pos. 28)		2,100.	800.00
	On cover		1,750.	1,200.
a.	Imperf., pair		14,000.	
b.	Diagonal half used as 2½c on cover			6,000.
c.	5c brick red		625.00	42.50
	No gum		410.00	
	On cover			60.00
16	A9	10c black brn, perf. 11¾	22,500.	6,500.
	No gum		17,500.	
	On cover			7,000.
a.	Half used as 5c on cover			8,500.
17	A9	10c red lilac	2,000.	150.00
	No gum		1,600.	
	On cover			240.00
a.	10c violet		2,500.	160.00
	No gum		2,000.	
	On cover			225.00
b.	10c brown		2,000.	140.00
	No gum		1,600.	
	On cover			225.00
c.	Imperf., pair		11,000.	
d.	Diagonal half used as 5c on cover			5,000.
e.	10c deep red purple		3,250.	1,500.
	No gum		2,100.	
	On cover			1,250.
18	A10	12½c yel green	875.00	120.00
	No gum		725.00	
	On cover			300.00
a.	12½c blue green		1,050.	125.00
	No gum		875.00	
	On cover			375.00
b.	Imperf., pair		5,000.	
19	A11	17c blue	1,250.	190.00
	No gum		950.00	
	On cover			475.00
a.	17c slate blue		1,250.	210.00
	No gum		950.00	
	On cover			475.00
b.	Imperf., pair		4,750.	

Values for Nos. 14-19 are for examples with perfs touching the design. Imperfs. are without gum.

Re-entries of the 5c are numerous. Many of them are slight and have only small premium value. The major re-entry has many lines of the design double, especially the outlines of the ovals and frame at left.

Nos. 14b, 15c, 16, 17b, 18a and 19 represent the 1st printings of the stamps. No. 17e is from a 2nd printing. All of these gauge closer to perf. 11¾, and this will aid in their proper identification.

No. 15b was used with a 10c for a 12½c rate.

No. 16 should be accompanied by a certificate of authenticity issued by a recognized expertizing authority. Less expensive dark brown shades of the 10c often are offered as the rare black brown.

1864

20	A12	2c rose	800.00	300.00
	No gum		475.00	
	On cover, single franking			1,600.
	On circular, single franking			1,450.
	On wrapper, single franking			2,700.
a.	2c deep claret rose		850.00	350.00
	No gum		575.00	
	On cover, single franking			1,750.
	On circular, single franking			1,600.
	On wrapper, single franking			2,750.
b.	Imperf., pair		3,500.	

Imperfs. are without gum.
Values are for examples with perfs touching the design.
On cover value is for a single franking on cover, circular or newspaper.

Dominion of Canada

Queen Victoria
A13   A14

A15   A16

A17   A18

A19   A20

1868-76   Perf. 12, 11½x12 (5c)

21	A13	½c black	110.00	80.00
	No gum		80.00	
	On cover			1,100.
	On cover, single franking			2,250.
a.	Perf. 11½x12 ('73)		150.00	90.00
	No gum		92.50	
	On cover			1,250.
	On cover, single franking			2,500.
b.	Watermarked		18,500.	11,000.
	No gum		16,750.	
c.	Thin paper		150.00	80.00
	No gum		100.00	
	On cover			1,250.
	On cover, single franking			2,500.
22	A14	1c brown red	900.00	160.00
	No gum		600.00	
	On cover			200.00
a.	Watermarked		3,250.	500.00
	No gum		2,150.	
	On cover			—
b.	Thin paper		950.00	140.00
	No gum		625.00	
	On cover			210.00
23	A14	1c yellow org	1,750.	225.00
	No gum		1,400.	
	On cover			240.00
a.	1c deep orange		2,500.	260.00
	No gum		1,900.	
	On cover			275.00
b.	1c yellow		2,000.	260.00
	No gum		1,500.	
	On cover			325.00
24	A15	2c green	900.00	100.00
	No gum		725.00	
	On cover			275.00
a.	Watermarked		3,250.	425.00
	No gum		2,500.	
	On cover			—
b.	Thin paper		950.00	110.00
	No gum		800.00	
	On cover			320.00
c.	Diagonal half used as 1c on cover			4,000.
25	A16	3c red	2,250.	40.00
	No gum		1,900.	
	On cover			50.00
a.	Watermarked		5,250.	475.00
	No gum		4,250.	
	On cover			—
b.	Thin paper		2,500.	47.50
	No gum		2,100.	
	On cover			50.00
26	A17	5c ol grn ('75)	2,000.	225.00
	No gum		1,600.	
	On cover			400.00
a.	Perf. 12		8,000.	1,000.
	No gum		7,250.	
	On cover			1,300.
b.	Imperf., pair		32,500.	
27	A18	6c dark brown	2,250.	140.00
	No gum		1,800.	
	On cover			190.00
a.	6c yellow brown		2,000.	140.00
	No gum		1,550.	
	On cover			190.00
b.	Watermarked		24,000.	2,500.
	No gum		7,500.	
	On cover			—
c.	Thin paper		2,100.	175.00
	No gum		1,650.	
	On cover			225.00
d.	Diagonal half used as 3c on cover			3,000.
e.	Vert. half used as 3c on cover			
f.	6c black brown, thin paper (Mar. '68, 1st printing)		3,250.	260.00
	No gum		2,600.	
	On cover			425.00
28	A19	12½c blue	1,250.	125.00
	No gum		950.00	
	On cover			225.00
a.	Watermarked		7,500.	425.00
	No gum		3,750.	
	On cover			2,000.
b.	Thin paper		1,200.	150.00
	No gum		950.00	
	On cover			225.00

c.	Horiz. pair, imperf. vert.		—
d.	Vert. pair, imperf. horiz.		16,000.
29	**A20 15c gray violet**	**110.00**	**65.00**
	No gum	85.00	
	On cover		550.00
a.	Perf. 11½x12 ('74)	1,750.	425.00
	No gum	1,500.	
	On cover		850.00
b.	15c red lilac	1,050.	130.00
	No gum	800.00	
	On cover		850.00
c.	Watermarked	12,500.	1,250.
	No gum	7,000.	
	On cover		—
d.	Imperf., pair		1,500.
	Never hinged		3,000.
	No gum		875.00
e.	Thin paper	800.00	150.00
	No gum	600.00	
	On cover		1,750.
30	**A20 15c gray**	**110.00**	**65.00**
	No gum	85.00	
	On cover		750.00
a.	Perf. 11½x12 ('73)	1,350.	425.00
	No gum	1,050.	
	On cover		1,500.
b.	15c blue gray ('75)	130.00	75.00
	No gum	95.00	
	On cover		675.00
c.	Very thick paper (dp vio)	5,250.	1,600.
	No gum	4,000.	
	On cover		1,900.
d.	Script wmk., Perf. 11½x12, ('76)	25,000.	9,000.
	No gum	18,500.	
	On cover		—
e.	15c deep blue	1,750.	425.00
	No gum	1,400.	
	On cover		800.00

The watermark on Nos. 21b, 22a, 24a, 25a, 27b, 28a and 29c consists of double-lined letters reading: "E. & G. BOTHWELL CLUTHA MILLS." The script watermark on No. 30d reads in full: "Alexr. Pirie & Sons." Values for all these watermarked stamps are for fine examples. Very fine examples are rare, seldom traded, and generally command premiums of about 100% over the values listed.

No. 26a unused is valued in the grade of fine. No. 26b is a unique pair.

The existence of No. 28c has been questioned.

Nos. 21-21c on cover values are for single frankings on cover or circular.

1868			**Laid Paper**
31	**A14 1c brown red**	**40,000.**	**10,000.**
	No gum	17,500.	
	On cover		11,000.
32	**A15 2c green**		**200,000.**
33	**A16 3c bright red**	**25,000.**	**2,250.**
	No gum	17,500.	
	On cover		3,000.

Only three examples of No. 32 are recorded, none being very fine.

Montreal and Ottawa Printings

A21

A22

A23

A24

A25

A26

A27

1870-89		**Wove Paper**	**Perf. 12**
34	**A21 ½c black ('82)**	**17.50**	**10.00**
	Never hinged	32.50	
	On cover		250.00
	On newspaper		275.00
	On unaddressed circular		325.00
	Pair with vertical gutter between	300.00	—
	Never hinged	550.00	
	On cover		1,500.
a.	Imperf., pair	750.00	
	Never hinged	1,100.	
b.	Horiz. pair, imperf. between	850.00	
	Never hinged	1,275.	
35	**A22 1c yellow**	**55.00**	**1.25**
	Never hinged	110.00	
	On cover		8.00
a.	1c orange ('70)	225.00	11.00
	Never hinged	450.00	
	On cover		12.00
b.	Imperf., pair	550.00	
	Never hinged	725.00	
c.	Diagonal half used as ½c on circular		4,500.
36	**A23 2c green ('72)**	**85.00**	**2.50**
	Never hinged	170.00	
	On cover		12.00
a.	Imperf., pair	800.00	
	Never hinged	1,300.	
b.	Diagonal half used as 1c on cover		2,000.
c.	Vertical half used as 1c on cover		2,000.
d.	2c blue green ('89)	110.00	5.00
	Never hinged	200.00	
	On cover		12.00
f.	Double impression	—	
37	**A24 3c orange red ('73)**	**140.00**	**2.00**
	Never hinged	280.00	
	On cover		8.00
a.	3c rose ('71)	675.00	17.50
	Never hinged	1,400.	
	On cover		19.00
b.	3c copper red ('70)	1,750.	65.00
	Never hinged	3,750.	
	On cover		70.00
c.	3c dull red ('72)	140.00	3.25
	Never hinged	280.00	
	On cover		10.00
38	**A25 5c sl green ('76)**	**1,000.**	**27.50**
	Never hinged	2,000.	
	On cover		62.50
39	**A26 6c yel brn ('72)**	**800.00**	**27.50**
	Never hinged	1,600.	
	On cover		40.00
a.	Diagonal half used as 3c on cover		4,500.
c.	Imperf., pair	4,500.	
d.	6c brown ('75)	725.00	22.50
	Never hinged	1,450.	
	On cover		40.00
40	**A27 10c dull rose lilac ('77)**	**1,750.**	**100.00**
	Never hinged	3,000.	
	On cover		450.00
a.	10c magenta ('80)	2,000.	100.00
	Never hinged	3,000.	
	On cover		450.00
b.	10c deep lilac rose	1,750.	100.00
	Never hinged	3,000.	
	On cover		450.00

No. 34 on cover value is for single franking paying the circular rate.

No. 34a was made with and without gum; values the same.

Examples of Nos. 36b and 36c postmarked "Halifax" are a private speculation.

No. 39c is unique and in the form of a strip of three.

1870			**Perf. 12½**
37d	A24 3c copper red (Ottawa)	11,000.	1,500.
	Never hinged	22,500.	
	On cover		1,700.

1873-79			**Perf. 11½x12**
35d	A22 1c orange	500.00	20.00
	Never hinged	1,000.	
	On cover		60.00
36e	A23 2c green	750.00	25.00
	Never hinged	1,500.	
	On cover		27.50
37e	A24 3c red	325.00	12.50
	Never hinged	650.00	
	On cover		13.00
38a	A25 5c slate green	1,250.	52.50
	Never hinged	2,500.	
	On cover		60.00
39b	A26 6c yellow brown	1,100.	65.00
	Never hinged	2,200.	
	On cover		60.00
40c	A27 10c dull rose lilac	2,000.	260.00
	Never hinged	3,500.	
	On cover		500.00
40d	A27 10c magenta	2,000.	240.00
	Never hinged	1,500.	
	On cover		500.00

40e	A27	10c pale milky rose lilac ('74)	3,000.	700.00
		Never hinged	5,500.	
		On cover		850.00

The gum on Nos. 35d-40c is always dull and usually blotchy or streaky. It is distinct from the earlier clean, smooth gum and from the bright shiny gums of the later periods.

Nos. 38 and 40 were printed at Montreal. Printings of Nos. 34 to 37, and 39 were made at Ottawa or Montreal and can be separated only by differences in paper and gum.

Ottawa Printing

A28   A29

1888-97   Perf. 12

41	A24	3c brt vermilion	70.00	.85
		Never hinged	145.00	
		On cover		8.00
a.		3c rose carmine	525.00	12.50
		Never hinged	1,150.	
		On cover		12.50
42	A25	5c gray	230.00	5.25
		Never hinged	500.00	
		On cover		35.00
43	A26	6c red brown	240.00	12.50
		Never hinged	525.00	
		On cover		40.00
a.		6c chocolate ('90)	300.00	32.50
		Never hinged	625.00	
		On cover		65.00
c.		5c on 6c re-entry	4,000.	3,250.
44	A28	8c violet black ('93)	260.00	6.50
		Never hinged	550.00	
		On cover		25.00
a.		8c blue gray	425.00	8.50
		Never hinged	900.00	
		On cover		27.50
b.		8c slate	300.00	6.50
		Never hinged	650.00	
		On cover		25.00
c.		8c gray	300.00	6.50
		Never hinged	650.00	
		On cover		25.00
45	A27	10c brown red ('97)	725.00	65.00
		Never hinged	1,400.	
		On cover		225.00
a.		10c dull rose	675.00	60.00
		Never hinged	1,300.	
		On cover		225.00
b.		10c pink	750.00	65.00
		Never hinged	1,450.	
		On cover		240.00
46	A29	20c ver ('93)	475.00	125.00
		Never hinged	1,100.	
		On cover		1,000.
47	A29	50c dp blue ('93)	475.00	85.00
		Never hinged	1,100.	
		On cover		1,000.

Stamps of the 1870-93 issues are found on paper varying from very thin to thick, also occasionally on paper showing a distinctly ribbed surface.

The gum on Nos. 41-47 appears bright and shiny, often with a yellowish tint.

Values for Nos. 46-47 on cover are for single frankings paying the correct rate.

Imperf., Pairs

41b	A24	3c	600.
		Never hinged	925.
42a	A25	5c	900.
		Never hinged	1,425.
43b	A26	6c	750.
		Never hinged	1,050.
44d	A28	8c	1,000.
		Never hinged	1,400.
45c	A27	10c	750.
		Never hinged	1,050.
46a	A29	20c	1,600.
		Never hinged	2,600.
47a	A29	50c	1,600.
		Never hinged	2,600.

Nos. 41b-45c made with and without gum. Without gum sell for the same as the unused hinged price.

The value for No. 44d is for the pair in the blue gray shade. The imperf. pair also is known in the violet black shade without gum. Value thus, $1,250.

Imperforates and Part-Perforates

From 1859 through 1943 (Nos. 14a/262a), imperforate stamps were printed. The earliest imperforates through perhaps 1917 most likely were from imprimatur sheets (i.e. the first sheets from the approved plates, normally kept in government files) or proof sheets on stamp paper that once were in the post office archives. The imperforates from approximately 1927 to 1943 (often made both with and without gum) were specially created and traded for classic stamps needed for the post office museum, given as gifts to governmental or other dignitaries, or sold or given to favored persons.

The only imperforates from this entire period that were issued to the public were Nos. 90a and 136-138.

Similarly, almost all stamps that are known part-perforate (i.e., horizontal pairs imperforate vertically and vertical pairs imperforate horizontally) were specially made for trading purposes or as presentation items to be given to favored persons. Part-perforate error stamps that are believed to have been actually issued to the public are listed in this catalogue.

See the similar imperforates in the air post, Nos. CE1a and CE2a, special delivery, No. F2c (but not No. F1c which was an issued error), postage dues, and Nos. MR4b and MR4c.

Jubilee Issue

Queen Victoria, "1837" and "1897" — A30

1897, June 19   Unwmk.   Perf. 12

50	A30	½c black	120.00	120.00
		Never hinged	300.00	
		On cover		500.00
51	A30	1c orange	22.50	8.00
		Never hinged	57.50	
		On cover		18.00
52	A30	2c green	35.00	15.00
		Never hinged	87.50	
		On cover		25.00
53	A30	3c bright rose	22.50	2.50
		Never hinged	57.50	
		On cover		7.50
54	A30	5c deep blue	70.00	45.00
		Never hinged	180.00	
		On cover		100.00
55	A30	6c yellow brown	230.00	175.00
		Never hinged	575.00	
		On cover		325.00
56	A30	8c dark violet	120.00	65.00
		Never hinged	300.00	
		On cover		200.00
57	A30	10c brown violet	120.00	120.00
		Never hinged	300.00	
		On cover		300.00
58	A30	15c steel blue	275.00	190.00
		Never hinged	675.00	
		On cover		350.00
59	A30	20c vermilion	275.00	190.00
		Never hinged	650.00	
		On cover		450.00
60	A30	50c ultra	375.00	190.00
		Never hinged	775.00	
		On cover		450.00
61	A30	$1 lake	1,000.	700.00
		Never hinged	2,900.	
		On cover		1,750.
62	A30	$2 dk purple	1,400.	600.00
		Never hinged	4,000.	
		On cover		1,200.
63	A30	$3 yel bister	1,400.	1,100.
		Never hinged	4,000.	
		On cover		2,200.
64	A30	$4 purple	1,400.	1,100.
		Never hinged	4,000.	
		On cover		2,200.
65	A30	$5 olive green	1,500.	1,100.
		Never hinged	4,250.	
		On cover		2,000.
		Nos. 50-60 (11)	1,665.	1,120.
		Nos. 50-60, never hinged	3,850.	

60th year of Queen Victoria's reign.

Roller and smudged cancels on Nos. 61-65 sell for less.

Covers: Value for No. 50 is for a single franking paying the correct rate. In combination with other postage it is worth much less. Values for Nos. 61-65 are for overfranked items, usually philatelic.

A31

1897-98

66	A31	½c black	13.00	7.50
		Never hinged	32.50	
		On cover		240.00
67	A31	1c blue green	40.00	2.00
		Never hinged	100.00	
		On cover		3.50
68	A31	2c purple	40.00	2.25
		Never hinged	100.00	
		On cover		6.50
69	A31	3c carmine ('98)	65.00	2.00
		Never hinged	165.00	
		On cover		4.00
70	A31	5c dk bl, bluish	150.00	9.00
		Never hinged	375.00	
		On cover		47.50
71	A31	6c brown	130.00	40.00
		Never hinged	325.00	
		On cover		550.00
72	A31	8c orange	300.00	20.00
		Never hinged	750.00	
		On cover		55.00
73	A31	10c brown vio ('98)	600.00	80.00
		Never hinged	1,500.	
		On cover		800.00
		Nos. 66-73 (8)	1,338.	162.75
		Nos. 66-73, never hinged	3,248.	

Values for Nos. 66, 71 and 73 on cover are for single frankings paying correct rates.

For surcharge see No. 87.

Imperf., Pairs

66a	A31	½c	500.
		Never hinged	950.
67a	A31	1c	400.
		Never hinged	750.
68a	A31	2c	500.
		Never hinged	950.
69a	A31	3c	800.
		Never hinged	1,450.
70a	A31	5c	500.
		Never hinged	750.
71a	A31	6c	800.
		Never hinged	1,450.
72a	A31	8c	600.
		Never hinged	1,100.
73a	A31	10c	600.
		Never hinged	1,100.

Nos. 66a, 67a, 68a and 70a made with and without gum. Specialists can distinguish printings made with and without gum by shade and paper quality. Without gum sell for about 95% of the unused hinged price.

A32

Type I   Type II

TWO CENTS:
Type I — Frame of four very thin lines.
Type II — Frame of a thick line between two thin ones.

1898-1902

74	A32	½c black	10.00	2.25
		Never hinged	20.00	
		On cover		250.00
75	A32	1c gray green	40.00	.75
		Never hinged	80.00	
		On cover		2.00
76	A32	2c purple (I)	37.50	.75
		Never hinged	75.00	
		On cover		2.00
a.		Thick paper ('99)	175.00	12.00
		Never hinged	350.00	
		On cover		24.00
77	A32	2c car (I) ('99)	40.00	.75
		Never hinged	80.00	
		On cover		2.00
a.		2c carmine (II) ('99)	50.00	.60
		Never hinged	100.00	
		On cover		2.50
b.		Booklet pane of 6 (II) ('00)	1,600.	—
		Never hinged	3,000.	
78	A32	3c carmine	90.00	1.10
		Never hinged	180.00	
		On cover		1.75

79	A32	5c blue, bluish ('99)	220.00	3.00
		Never hinged	440.00	
		On cover		47.50
b.		Whiter paper ('99)	260.00	3.25
		Never hinged	525.00	
		On cover		47.50
80	A32	6c brown	200.00	55.00
		Never hinged	400.00	
		On cover		550.00
81	A32	7c ol yel ('02)	150.00	22.50
		Never hinged	300.00	
		On cover		67.50
82	A32	8c orange	350.00	25.00
		Never hinged	700.00	
		On cover		80.00
83	A32	10c brown vio	425.00	25.00
		Never hinged	850.00	
		On cover		550.00
84	A32	20c ol grn ('00)	600.00	110.00
		Never hinged	1,200.	
		On cover		1,100.
		Nos. 74-84 (11)	2,162.	246.10
		Nos. 74-84, never hinged	4,245.	

Values for Nos. 74, 80, 83-84 on cover are for single frankings paying correct rates. For surcharges see Nos. 88-88C.

Imperf., Pairs

74a	A32	½c	475.	
		Never hinged	775.	
75a	A32	1c	1,400.	
		Never hinged	2,500.	
77c	A32	2c (I)	475.	
		Never hinged	775.	
77d	A32	2c (I)	1,800.	
e.		As No. 77b, imperf., 2 panes tete beche ('00)	15,000.	
79a	A32	5c	1,200.	
		Never hinged	1,900.	
80a	A32	6c	1,200.	
		Never hinged	1,900.	
81a	A32	7c	600.	
		Never hinged	1,200.	
82a	A32	8c	1,200.	
		Never hinged	1,900.	
83a	A32	10c	1,200.	
		Never hinged	1,900.	
84a	A32	20c	4,500.	

Nos. 77d, 77e, 81a and 84a were made only without gum. No. 80a was made only with gum. Others either with or without gum and of these those without gum sell for about ⅔ of the values shown for unused hinged. Specialists can distinguish printings made with and without gum by shade and paper quality.

Imperial Penny Postage Issue

Map of British Empire on Mercator Projection A33

No. 86

1898, Dec. 7   Engr. & Typo.

85	A33	2c black, lav & car	45.00	9.00
		Never hinged	90.00	
		On cover		25.00
a.		Imperf., pair	550.00	
86	A33	2c black, bl & car	40.00	9.00
		Never hinged	80.00	
		On cover		25.00
a.		Imperf., pair	550.00	
b.		2c black, deep bl & car	50.00	11.50
		Never hinged	100.00	
		On cover		27.50

Imperfs. are without gum, and known in both the blue and deep blue shades of No. 86 and 86b; values the same.

Nos. 69 and 78 Surcharged in

1899, July

87	A31	2c on 3c carmine	17.50	7.50
		Never hinged	45.00	
		On cover		11.00
88	A32	2c on 3c carmine	32.50	6.00
		Never hinged	82.50	
		On cover		10.50

No. 78 Surcharged in Blue or Violet

A32a   A32b

1899, Jan. 5

88B	A32a	1(c)	on ⅓ of 3c, on cover (Bl)	
88C	A32b	2(c)	on ⅔ of 3c, on cover (V)	7,750.
				7,750.

Nos. 88B-88C were prepared and used at Port Hood, Nova Scotia, without official authorization.

Nos. 88B-88C must be accompanied by certificates from recognized expertizing organizations.

King Edward VII — A34

1903-08   **Engr.**

89	A34	1c green	35.00	.40
		Never hinged	87.50	
		On cover		1.75
90	A34	2c carmine	37.50	.40
		Never hinged	95.00	
		On cover		1.75
		"Hairlines" plate cracks	70.00	7.50
		Never hinged	140.00	
				10.00
b.		Booklet pane of 6	1,600.	1,250.
		Never hinged	2,750.	
91	A34	5c blue, *blue*	220.00	5.50
		Never hinged	550.00	
		On cover		30.00
b.		Whiter paper	220.00	7.00
		Never hinged	440.00	
		On cover		42.50
92	A34	7c olive bister	225.00	5.50
		Never hinged	550.00	
		On cover		20.00
93	A34	10c brown lilac	400.00	15.00
		Never hinged	1,000.	
		On cover		350.00
94	A34	20c olive green ('04)	700.00	50.00
		Never hinged	1,750.	
		On cover		450.00
95	A34	50c purple ('08)	900.00	175.00
		Never hinged	2,250.	
		On cover		1,500.
		Nos. 89-95 (7)	2,517.	251.80
		Nos. 89-95, never hinged	6,282.50	

Values for Nos. 94 and 95 used are for examples with contemporary circular datestamps. Stamps with heavy cancellations or parcel cancellations sell for much less.

Hairlines: a pattern of fine lines across the face of the stamp caused by plate cracks. The values are for stamps with prominent and extensive lines. Values will be less for stamps with less prominent and less extensive cracks. See similar listings for Nos. 104, 104a, 106a, 106c.

Covers: values for Nos. 93-95 are for single frankings paying the correct rate.
Issued: 1c-10c, 7/1/03; 20c, 9/27/04; 50c, 11/19/08.

Imperf., Pairs

89a	A34	1c	725.00	
90a	A34	2c	45.00	45.00
		Never hinged	95.00	
		On cover		50.00
c.		As No. 90b, imperf, 2 panes tete beche	14,500.	
91a	A34	5c	1,200.	
92a	A34	7c	800.	
93a	A34	10c	1,200.	

All imperfs except No. 90a were made without gum.

No. 90a issued to the public with gum from plates 13 and 14. Also made without gum from plates 1 and 2, which are distinguishable by experts. Value, pair, plates 1 and 2 with certificate of authenticity, $850. Imperfs with black or red defacing lines are from experimental printings and are considered to be proofs.

Quebec Tercentenary Issue

Prince and Princess of Wales, 1908 — A35

Jacques Cartier and Samuel de Champlain A36

Queen Alexandra and King Edward A37

Champlain's Home in Quebec A38

Generals Montcalm and Wolfe — A39

View of Quebec in 1700 — A40

Champlain's Departure for the West — A41

Arrival of Cartier at Quebec A42

1908, July 16

96	A35	½c black brown	7.50	5.00
		Never hinged	18.50	
		On cover		275.00
		Re-entry (line through "CANADA" - pos. 44)	55.00	55.00
		Never hinged	130.00	
		On cover		350.00
97	A36	1c blue green	25.00	6.00
		Never hinged	62.50	
		On cover		8.00
98	A37	2c carmine	32.50	3.00
		Never hinged	82.50	
		On cover		8.00
99	A38	5c dark blue	75.00	70.00
		Never hinged	190.00	
		On cover		190.00
100	A39	7c olive green	150.00	100.00
		Never hinged	375.00	
		On cover		120.00
101	A40	10c dark violet	200.00	125.00
		Never hinged	500.00	
		On cover		325.00
102	A41	15c red orange	225.00	160.00
		Never hinged	550.00	
		On cover		400.00
103	A42	20c yellow brown	250.00	225.00
		Never hinged	625.00	
		On cover		500.00
		Nos. 96-103 (8)	965.00	694.00
		Nos. 96-103, never hinged	2,404.	

Covers: values for Nos. 96-103 are for properly franked items in the correct period of use.

Imperf., Pairs

96a	A35	½c	650.
		Never hinged	1,150.
97a	A36	1c	650.
		Never hinged	1,150.
98a	A37	2c	650.
		Never hinged	1,150.
99a	A38	5c	650.
		Never hinged	1,150.
100a	A39	7c	650.
		Never hinged	1,150.
101a	A40	10c	650.
		Never hinged	1,150.
102a	A41	15c	650.
		Never hinged	1,150.
103a	A42	20c	650.
		Never hinged	1,150.

100 pairs of imperfs made, 50 with gum and 50 without. Due to demand, pairs without gum generally sell for 90-95% of the unused hinged price.

WET and DRY PRINTINGS

Before 1922, stamps were printed using dampened paper (wet printing). As the paper dried, it shrank slightly across the grain. In 1922, a new process was introduced that used much drier paper (dry printing) with little or no shrinkage. Additionally, on wet printings the gum does not extend to the edges of the pane and the design is more flat from the gummed side; on dry printings the gum extends to the edges of the pane and the designs shows some embossing effect when viewed from the gummed side.

The King George V Admiral issue, design A43, was printed from 1911 to 1925, and the earlier wet printings generally show a narrower design due to paper shrinkage

King George V — A43

Type I

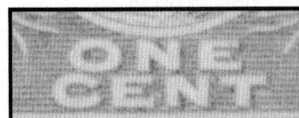

Type II

Two types of 1c.
Type I — The "N" of "ONE" is separated from the oval above it.
Type II — The "N" of "ONE" almost touches the oval above it.

Type I   Type II

Two types of 3c carmine.
Type I — The "R" of "THREE" is separated from the oval above it. The bottom line of the vignette does not touch the heavy diagonal stroke at right.
Type II — The "R" of "THREE" almost touches the oval above it. The bottom horizontal line of the vignette touches the heavy diagonal stroke at right.

1911-25

		Un	Used
104	A43 1c green	22.50	.25
	Never hinged	55.00	
	On cover		1.60
	"Hairlines" plate cracks (horiz.)	37.50	25.00
	Never hinged	82.50	
a.	Booklet pane of 6	35.00	35.00
	Never hinged	70.00	
b.	1c blue green	30.00	.25
	Never hinged	72.50	
	On cover		1.60
	Major double transfer at lower right (35 LR 12)	2,500.	1,250.
	On cover		2,500.
c.	1c deep blue green	40.00	.25
	Never hinged	95.00	
	On cover		1.60
	As "c," "hairlines" plate cracks	60.00	7.50
	Never hinged	120.00	
	On cover		8.00
105	A43 1c yellow, wet printing (I) ('22)	25.00	.25
	Never hinged	60.00	
	On cover		1.75
a.	Booklet pane of 4 + 2 labels	55.00	55.00
	Never hinged	110.00	
b.	Booklet pane of 6	62.50	62.50
	Never hinged	125.00	
d.	1c orange yellow, dry printing (II)	20.00	.25
	Never hinged	50.00	
	On cover		1.75
e.	1c lemon yellow, wet printing (I)	37.50	6.50
	Never hinged	105.00	
	On cover		13.00
f.	1c yellow, dry printing (I)	30.00	.50
	Never hinged	82.50	
	On cover		—
106	A43 2c carmine	20.00	.25
	Never hinged	50.00	
	On cover		1.75
a.	Booklet pane of 6	40.00	40.00
	Never hinged	80.00	
	As "a," "hairlines" plate cracks	52.50	52.50
	Never hinged	90.00	
b.	2c pink	150.00	18.00
	Never hinged	350.00	
	On cover		25.00
c.	2c rose carmine	20.00	.25
	Never hinged	50.00	
	On cover		1.75
	As "c," "hairlines" plate cracks	45.00	4.50
	Never hinged	75.00	
	On cover		8.00
d.	As "c," booklet pane of 6	160.00	160.00
	Never hinged	320.00	
107	A43 2c yel green, wet printing ('22)	25.00	.25
	Never hinged	60.00	
	On cover		2.50

		Un	Used
a.	Thin paper, wet printing ('24)	20.00	2.50
	Never hinged	50.00	
	On cover		5.00
b.	Booklet pane of 4 + 2 labels ('22)	70.00	80.00
	Never hinged	119.99	
c.	Booklet pane of 6, wet printing ('22)	350.00	325.00
	Never hinged	625.00	
e.	2c green, dry printing ('23)	25.00	.25
	Never hinged	60.00	
	On cover		2.50
f.	As "c," dry printing	300.00	300.00
	Never hinged	550.00	
108	A43 3c brown, wet printing ('18)	20.00	.25
	Never hinged	50.00	
	On cover		2.50
a.	Booklet pane of 4 + 2 labels	90.00	95.00
	Never hinged	180.00	
b.	3c yellow brown, wet printing	27.50	.25
	Never hinged	65.00	
	On cover		2.50
c.	3c brown, dry printing ('23)	16.00	.25
	Never hinged	40.00	
	On cover		2.50
109	A43 3c car (I) ('23)	15.00	.25
	Never hinged	37.50	
	On cover		2.50
a.	Booklet pane of 4 + 2 labels	70.00	75.00
	Never hinged	140.00	
c.	Die II ('24)	32.50	.25
	Never hinged	82.50	
	On cover		4.00
d.	3c rose carmine (I) ('23)	35.00	3.50
	Never hinged	90.00	
	On cover		12.00
110	A43 4c ol bis, wet printing ('22)	47.50	4.50
	Never hinged	120.00	
	On cover, single franking		27.50
b.	4c olive yellow, wet printing	50.00	4.50
	Never hinged	125.00	
	On cover, single franking		20.00
c.	4c golden yellow, wet printing	140.00	10.00
	Never hinged	350.00	
	On cover, single franking		27.50
d.	4c yellow ocher, dry printing ('25)	55.00	4.75
	Never hinged	140.00	
	On cover, single franking		20.00
111	A43 5c dark blue ('12)	160.00	1.40
	Never hinged	400.00	
	On cover		40.00
a.	5c indigo	375.00	2.10
	Never hinged	825.00	
	On cover		40.00
b.	5c gray blue	180.00	1.40
	Never hinged	425.00	
	On cover		40.00
112	A43 5c violet, wet printing ('22)	40.00	1.00
	Never hinged	100.00	
	On cover		32.50
a.	Thin paper ('24)	35.00	7.50
	Never hinged	87.50	
	On cover		40.00
c.	Dry printing ('25)	52.50	1.60
	Never hinged	115.00	
	On cover		40.00
113	A43 7c yel ocher ('12)	45.00	3.00
	Never hinged	110.00	
	On cover		16.00
a.	7c olive bister ('15)	75.00	3.25
	Never hinged	190.00	
	On cover		16.00
b.	7c straw	175.00	14.00
	Never hinged	410.00	
	On cover		47.50
c.	7c sage green ('14)	600.00	27.50
	Never hinged	1,500.	
	On cover		60.00
114	A43 7c red brown, dry printing ('24)	20.00	10.00
	Never hinged	50.00	
	On cover		20.00
	On cover, single franking		40.00
b.	7c red brown, wet printing	30.00	14.50
	Never hinged	80.00	
	On cover		20.00
	On cover, single franking		40.00
115	A43 8c blue ('25)	32.50	10.00
	Never hinged	80.00	
	On cover		22.50
	On cover, single franking		52.50
116	A43 10c plum ('12)	275.00	4.00
	Never hinged	675.00	
	On cover		27.50
	On cover, single franking		55.00
a.	10c reddish purple	310.00	4.00
	Never hinged	850.00	
	On cover		27.50
	On cover, single franking		55.00
117	A43 10c blue, wet printing ('22)	45.00	2.00
	Never hinged	110.00	
	On cover, single franking		32.50
a.	Dry printing	42.50	2.25
	Never hinged	110.00	
	On cover, single franking		32.50
118	A43 10c bis brn ('25)	40.00	2.00
	Never hinged	95.00	
	On cover, single franking		32.50
b.	10c yellow brown	60.00	2.25
	Never hinged	150.00	
	On cover, single franking		32.50
119	A43 20c ol grn, dry printing ('25)	100.00	1.75
	Never hinged	250.00	
	On cover, single franking		200.00
b.	20c sage green, wet printing	225.00	6.00
	Never hinged	550.00	
	On cover, single franking		200.00
c.	20c dk olive green, wet printing ('12)	140.00	2.50

		Un	Used
	Never hinged	300.00	
	On cover, single franking		200.00
d.	20c gray green, wet printing	150.00	5.50
	Never hinged	375.00	
	On cover, single franking		200.00
120	A43 50c blk brn, dry printing ('25)	80.00	3.75
	Never hinged	200.00	
	On cover, single franking		325.00
a.	50c black, wet printing ('12)	225.00	12.00
	Never hinged	550.00	
	On cover, single franking		325.00
122	A43 $1 orange, dry printing ('23)	95.00	10.00
	Never hinged	240.00	
	On cover, single franking		450.00
b.	$1 deep orange, wet printing	200.00	14.00
	Never hinged	450.00	
	On cover, single franking		450.00
	Nos. 104-122 (18)	1,107.	54.90
	Nos. 104-122, never hinged	2,683.	

For type A43 perforated 12x8 see No. 184.
For surcharges see Nos. 139-140.
Issued: Nos. 104, 106, 12/22/11; No. 105, 6/7/22; No. 108, 8/6/18; No. 109, 12/18/23; 4c, 7/7/22; No. 111, 1/17/12; No. 112, 2/2/22; Nos. 113, 116, 1/12/12; No. 114, 12/12/24; 8c, 9/1/25; No. 117, 2/20/22; No. 118, 8/1/25; 20c, 1/23/12; 50c, 1/26/12; $1, 7/22/23.

Imperf., Panes

105c	As No. 105b, imperf, 2 panes tete beche	12,500.	
107d	As No. 107c, imperf, 2 panes tete beche	12,500.	
109b	As No. 109a, imperf, 2 panes tete beche	12,500.	

Imperf., Pairs

110a	A43 4c	2,000.	
	Never hinged	3,600.	
112b	A43 5c	2,000.	
	Never hinged	3,600.	
114a	A43 7c	2,000.	
	Never hinged	3,600.	
115a	A43 8c	2,000.	
	Never hinged	3,600.	
118a	A43 10c	2,000.	
	Never hinged	3,600.	
119a	A43 20c	2,000.	
	Never hinged	3,600.	
120b	A43 50c	3,000.	
	Never hinged	5,250.	
122a	A43 $1	2,000.	
	Never hinged	3,600.	

Nos. 105c and 109b made without gum, others with gum. About half of the No. 120b pairs have creases; value thus $500.
Two pairs of tete beche singles are known from No. 107d; value, unused, $1,750.

Coil Stamps

1913   Perf. 8 Horizontally

		Un	Used
123	A43 1c dark green	100.00	60.00
	Never hinged	250.00	
	On cover		65.00
	Pair	210.00	125.00
	Never hinged	425.00	
	On cover		140.00
	Paste-up pair	275.00	140.00
	Never hinged	550.00	
	On cover		160.00
124	A43 2c carmine	120.00	60.00
	Never hinged	300.00	
	On cover		75.00
	Pair	250.00	210.00
	Never hinged	500.00	
	On cover		225.00
	Paste-up pair	325.00	210.00
	Never hinged	650.00	
	On cover		225.00

1912-24   Perf. 8 Vertically

		Un	Used
125	A43 1c green	25.00	2.00
	Never hinged	50.00	
	On cover		4.00
	Pair	50.00	4.50
	Never hinged	100.00	
	On cover		11.00
	Paste-up pair	60.00	30.00
	Never hinged	120.00	
	On cover		40.00
	Major double transfer at lower right (35 LR 12)		—
126	A43 1c orange yellow, dry printing (II) ('23)	12.00	7.50
	Never hinged	24.00	
	On cover		8.50
	Pair	24.00	19.00
	Never hinged	48.00	
	On cover		22.50
	Paste-up pair	37.50	31.00
	Never hinged	62.50	
	On cover		32.50
a.	As #126, block of 4 (II)	65.00	50.00
	Never hinged	100.00	
	On cover, block of 4		62.50
	On cover, vert. pair, commercial		27.50
	On cover, vert. pair, 1st flight		16.00
b.	1c orange yellow, wet printing (I)	25.00	11.00
	Never hinged	50.00	
	On cover		16.00
	Pair	55.00	27.50
	Never hinged	100.00	
	On cover		27.50
	Paste-up pair	62.50	30.00
	Never hinged	115.00	
	On cover		40.00
c.	As "b," block of 4 (I)	450.00	
	Never hinged	750.00	
d.	1c yellow, dry printing (I)	100.00	10.00
	Never hinged	50.00	
	On cover		15.00
	Pair	62.50	22.50

		Un	Used
	Never hinged	105.00	
	On cover		25.00
	Paste-up pair	125.00	50.00
	Never hinged	200.00	
	On cover		40.00
127	A43 2c carmine	10.00	2.00
	Never hinged	80.00	
	On cover		4.00
	Pair	80.00	7.00
	Never hinged	160.00	
	On cover		24.00
	Paste-up pair	100.00	40.00
	Never hinged	185.00	
	On cover		42.50
128	A43 2c green ('22)	25.00	1.10
	Never hinged	50.00	
	On cover		3.75
	Pair	50.00	3.25
	Never hinged	95.00	
	On cover		24.00
	Paste-up pair	65.00	16.00
	Never hinged	110.00	
	On cover		27.50
a.	Block of 4	65.00	60.00
	Never hinged	100.00	
	On cover, block of 4		65.00
	On cover, vert. pair, commercial		22.50
	On cover, vert. pair, 1st flight		15.00
129	A43 3c brown ('18)	27.50	1.30
	Never hinged	55.00	
	On cover		4.00
	Pair	55.00	4.50
	Never hinged	110.00	
	On cover		32.50
	Paste-up pair	67.50	22.50
	Never hinged	140.00	
	On cover		25.00
130	A43 3c carmine, wet printing (I) ('24)	75.00	9.00
	Never hinged	150.00	
	On cover		16.00
	Pair	150.00	40.00
	Never hinged	260.00	
	On cover, pair alone		65.00
	Paste-up pair	190.00	80.00
	Never hinged	300.00	
	On cover		95.00
a.	Block of 4 (I)	950.00	750.00
	Never hinged	1,500.	
	On cover, block of 4		—
	On cover, vert. pair, commercial		325.00
	On cover, vert. pair, 1st flight		250.00
b.	Dry printing, die II	100.00	10.00
	Never hinged	200.00	
	On cover		16.00
	Pair	160.00	50.00
	Never hinged	325.00	
	On cover, pair alone		60.00
	Paste-up pair	190.00	90.00
	Never hinged	375.00	
	On cover		110.00
	Nos. 125-130 (6)	204.50	22.90
	Nos. 125-130, never hinged	381.50	

Nos. 126a and 128a were issued to the public. Nos. 126c and 130a were issued "by favor" as were the various other imperf and part-perfs of this era.
The used example of No. 125 with major double transfer is unique; it is defective.
Beware of fakes of No. 130a made from No. 138.

1915-24   Perf. 12 Horizontally

		Un	Used
131	A43 1c dark green	7.50	6.50
	Never hinged	15.00	
	On cover		9.00
	Pair	15.00	15.00
	Never hinged	30.00	
	On cover, pair alone		24.00
	Paste-up pair	19.00	19.00
	Never hinged	37.50	
	On cover		27.50
132	A43 2c carmine	40.00	10.00
	Never hinged	80.00	
	On cover		15.00
	Pair	80.00	27.50
	Never hinged	160.00	
	On cover, pair alone		50.00
	Paste-up pair	100.00	40.00
	Never hinged	200.00	
	On cover		55.00
133	A43 2c yellow grn ('24)	75.00	75.00
	Never hinged	150.00	
	On cover		80.00
	Pair	150.00	125.00
	Never hinged	300.00	
	On cover, pair alone		160.00
	Paste-up pair	190.00	175.00
	Never hinged	375.00	
	On cover		210.00
134	A43 3c brown ('21)	11.00	6.50
	Never hinged	22.00	
	On cover		12.00
	Pair	22.00	15.00
	Never hinged	45.00	
	On cover, pair alone		27.50
	Paste-up pair	29.00	19.00
	Never hinged	57.50	
	On cover		35.00
	Nos. 131-134 (4)	133.50	98.00
	Nos. 131-134, never hinged	242.00	

"The Fathers of Confederation" — A44

1917, Sept. 15 — Perf. 12

135	A44	3c brown	47.50	2.25
		Never hinged	120.00	
		On commercial cover		8.00
		1st day cover		325.00
a.		Imperf., pair	600.00	

50th anniv. of the Canadian Confederation.
Imperfs. are without gum.
Value for No. 135 on commercial cover is for an example with stamp in grade of very fine.
Value for grades below very fine are much less than the value shown.

1924 — Imperf.

136	A43	1c orange yellow (I)	35.00	35.00
		Never hinged	65.00	
		On cover, single franking		40.00
		Pair	87.50	87.50
		Never hinged	160.00	
		On cover		80.00
137	A43	2c green	35.00	35.00
		Never hinged	65.00	
		On cover, single franking		40.00
		Pair	87.50	87.50
		Never hinged	160.00	
		On cover		80.00
138	A43	3c carmine (I)	17.50	17.50
		Never hinged	32.50	
		On cover, single franking		20.00
		Pair	42.50	42.50
		Never hinged	77.50	
		On cover		45.00
		Nos. 136-138 (3)	87.50	87.50
		Nos. 136-138, never hinged	162.50	

Plate Number Blocks

Before 1958, plate blocks consist of the printer's name and a plate number. As with single stamps, all plate blocks are valued in the grade of very fine, with listings for both hinged and never hinged through Nos. 262, C8, CE2, E10, and J14, and never hinged only from Nos. 268, B1, C9, CE3, C01, E11, EO1, J15, and O1. Some plate numbers and/or positions are worth more than others; only the most common are valued here.

No. 109 Surcharged

a   b

1926 — Perf. 12

139	A43(a)	2c on 3c carmine (I)	55.00	55.00
		Never hinged	90.00	
		On commercial cover		90.00
		On 1st flight cover		62.50
		Plate block of 8	600.00	
		Never hinged	950.00	
a.		Pair, one without surcharge	375.00	
		Never hinged	600.00	
b.		Double surcharge	225.00	
		Never hinged	350.00	
c.		Die II	800.00	
		Never hinged	1,400.	
140	A43(b)	2c on 3c carmine	25.00	30.00
		Never hinged	42.50	
		On commercial cover		55.00
		On 1st flight cover		37.50
		Plate block of 8	350.00	
		Never hinged	550.00	
a.		Double surcharge	250.00	250.00
		Never hinged	400.00	
b.		Triple surcharge	275.00	250.00
		Never hinged	450.00	
c.		Double surch., one invtd.	375.00	
		Never hinged	550.00	

First Day Covers

Values for first day covers are for addressed non-cacheted covers through No. 190, addressed cacheted covers from No. 191 to No. 277, and unaddressed covers with the most common cachets from No. 282 and later.

Sir John A. Macdonald A45   Sir Wilfrid Laurier A48

"The Fathers of Confederation" — A46

Parliament Building at Ottawa A47

Map of Canada A49

1927, June 29

141	A45	1c orange	3.50	1.30
		Never hinged	6.50	
		1st day cover		120.00
		Plate block of 8	42.50	
		Never hinged	65.00	
142	A46	2c green	1.90	.25
		Never hinged	3.50	
		1st day cover		120.00
		Plate block of 4	45.00	
		Never hinged	67.50	
		Plate block of 6	25.00	
		Never hinged	35.00	
143	A47	3c brown carmine	10.00	6.50
		Never hinged	18.00	
		1st day cover		120.00
		Plate block of 4	70.00	
		Never hinged	105.00	
		Plate block of 6	90.00	
		Never hinged	135.00	
144	A48	5c violet	4.50	3.50
		Never hinged	8.25	
		1st day cover		120.00
		Plate block of 8	60.00	
		Never hinged	95.00	
145	A49	12c dark blue	25.00	6.50
		Never hinged	45.00	
		1st day cover		160.00
		Plate block of 6	200.00	
		Never hinged	300.00	
		Nos. 141-145 (5)	44.90	18.05
		#141-145, never hinged	81.25	
		Set of 5 stamps on one 1st day cover		375.00

60th year of the Canadian Confederation.

Imperf., Pairs

141a	A45	1c	125.00
	Never hinged		180.00
142a	A46	2c	125.00
	Never hinged		180.00
143a	A47	3c	125.00
	Never hinged		180.00
144a	A48	5c	125.00
	Never hinged		180.00
145a	A49	12c	125.00
	Never hinged		180.00

Horizontal Pairs, Imperf. Vertically

141b	A45	1c	125.00
	Never hinged		180.00
142b	A46	2c	125.00
	Never hinged		180.00
143b	A47	3c	125.00
	Never hinged		180.00
144b	A48	5c	125.00
	Never hinged		180.00
145b	A49	12c	125.00
	Never hinged		180.00

Vertical Pair, Imperf. Horizontally

141c	A45	1c	125.00
	Never hinged		180.00
142c	A46	2c	125.00
	Never hinged		180.00
143c	A47	3c	125.00
	Never hinged		180.00
144c	A48	5c	125.00
	Never hinged		180.00
145c	A49	12c	125.00
	Never hinged		180.00

Thomas d'Arcy
McGee — A50

Laurier and
Macdonald
A51

Robert
Baldwin and
Sir Louis
Hypolyte
Lafontaine
A52

1927, June 29

146	A50	5c violet	4.00	3.00
	Never hinged		7.25	
	1st day cover			120.00
	Plate block of 8 (UR)		60.00	
	Never hinged		90.00	
	Plate block of 10 (UL)		72.50	
	Never hinged		110.00	
147	A51	12c green	10.00	5.50
	Never hinged		18.00	
	1st day cover			140.00
	Plate block of 6		100.00	
	Never hinged		150.00	
148	A52	20c brown carmine	27.50	6.50
	Never hinged		50.00	
	1st day cover			140.00
	Plate block of 4		135.00	
	Never hinged		225.00	
	Plate block of 6		200.00	
	Never hinged		325.00	
	Nos. 146-148 (3)		41.50	15.00
	#146-148, never hinged		75.25	

Nos. 146-148 were to have been issued in July, 1926, as a commemorative series, but were withheld and issued June 29, 1927.

Imperf., Pairs

146a	A50	5c	125.00
	Never hinged		180.00
147a	A51	12c	125.00
	Never hinged		180.00
148a	A52	20c	125.00
	Never hinged		180.00

Horizontal Pairs, Imperf. Vertically

146b	A50	5c	125.00
	Never hinged		180.00
147b	A51	12c	125.00
	Never hinged		180.00
148b	A52	20c	125.00
	Never hinged		180.00

Vertical Pairs, Imperf. Horizontally

146c	A50	5c	125.00
	Never hinged		180.00
147c	A51	12c	125.00
	Never hinged		180.00
148c	A52	20c	125.00
	Never hinged		180.00

King George V — A53

Mt. Hurd from Bell-Smith's Painting
"The Ice-crowned Monarch of the
Rockies"
A54

Quebec
Bridge
A55

Harvesting
Wheat
A56

Schooner
"Bluenose"
A57

Parliament
Building
A58

1928-29

149	A53	1c orange	3.50	.35
	Never hinged		6.50	
	1st day cover (10/29/28)			275.00
	Plate block of 8		32.50	
	Never hinged		55.00	
a.	Booklet pane of 6		27.50	25.00
	Never hinged		40.00	
150	A53	2c green	1.90	.25
	Never hinged		3.50	
	1st day cover (10/17/28)			275.00
	Plate block of 8		20.00	
	Never hinged		37.50	
a.	Booklet pane of 6		27.50	25.00
	Never hinged		40.00	
151	A53	3c dk carmine	30.00	12.50
	Never hinged		55.00	
	1st day cover (12/12/28)			350.00
	Plate block of 8		225.00	
	Never hinged		425.00	
152	A53	4c bister ('29)	27.50	6.00
	Never hinged		50.00	
	1st day cover (8/16/29)			425.00
	Plate block of 8		175.00	
	Never hinged		310.00	
153	A53	5c dp violet	16.00	3.00
	Never hinged		30.00	
	1st day cover (12/12/28)			350.00
	Plate block of 8		90.00	
	Never hinged		175.00	
a.	Booklet pane of 6		200.00	140.00
	Never hinged		280.00	
154	A53	8c blue	19.00	7.50
	Never hinged		35.00	
	1st day cover (12/21/28)			425.00
	Plate block of 8		180.00	
	Never hinged		300.00	
155	A54	10c green	22.50	2.50
	Never hinged		42.50	
	1st day cover (12/5/28)			500.00
	Plate block of 6		150.00	
	Never hinged		300.00	
156	A55	12c gray ('29)	45.00	7.50
	Never hinged		85.00	
	1st day cover (1/8/29)			500.00
	Plate block of 6		225.00	
	Never hinged		450.00	
157	A56	20c dk car ('29)	60.00	12.00
	Never hinged		110.00	
	1st day cover (1/8/29)			550.00
	Plate block of 6		300.00	
	Never hinged		575.00	
158	A57	50c dk blue ('29)	225.00	65.00
	Never hinged		450.00	
	1st day cover (1/8/29)			5,000.
	Plate block of 4		1,800.	
	Never hinged		2,700.	
	Plate block of 6		2,250.	
	Never hinged		3,750.	
	"Man on the Mast" plate flaw		1,500.	1,750.
159	A58	$1 olive grn ('29)	300.00	80.00
	Never hinged		600.00	
	1st day cover (1/8/29)			3,500.

	Plate block of 6	2,800.	
	Never hinged	4,500.	
	Nos. 149-159 (11)	750.40	196.60
	Nos. 149-159, never hinged	1,467.	

Imperf., Panes

149c	As No. 149a, imperf, 2 panes tete beche	1,050.	
	Never hinged	1,550.	
150c	As No. 150a, imperf, 2 panes tete beche	1,050.	
	Never hinged	1,550.	
153c	As No. 153a, imperf, 2 panes tete beche	1,050.	
	Never hinged	1,550.	

Imperf., Pairs

149b	A53	1c	100.00
	Never hinged		140.00
150b	A53	2c	100.00
	Never hinged		140.00
151a	A53	3c	120.00
	Never hinged		170.00
152a	A53	4c	120.00
	Never hinged		170.00
153b	A53	5c	100.00
	Never hinged		140.00
154a	A53	8c	120.00
	Never hinged		170.00
155a	A54	10c	200.00
	Never hinged		280.00
156a	A55	12c	200.00
	Never hinged		280.00
157a	A56	20c	200.00
	Never hinged		280.00
158a	A57	50c	800.00
	Never hinged		1,150.
159a	A58	$1	725.00
	Never hinged		1,050.

Horizontal Pairs, Imperf. Vertically

149d	A53	1c	100.00
	Never hinged		140.00
150d	A53	2c	100.00
	Never hinged		140.00
151b	A53	3c	120.00
	Never hinged		170.00
152b	A53	4c	120.00
	Never hinged		170.00
153d	A53	5c	120.00
	Never hinged		170.00
154b	A53	8c	120.00
	Never hinged		170.00
155b	A54	10c	200.00
	Never hinged		280.00
156b	A55	12c	200.00
	Never hinged		280.00
157b	A56	20c	200.00
	Never hinged		280.00
158b	A57	50c	800.00
	Never hinged		1,150.
159b	A58	$1	725.00
	Never hinged		1,050.

Vertical Pairs, Imperf. Horizontally

149e	A53	1c	100.00
	Never hinged		140.00
150e	A53	2c	100.00
	Never hinged		140.00
151c	A53	3c	120.00
	Never hinged		170.00
152c	A53	4c	120.00
	Never hinged		170.00
153e	A53	5c	120.00
	Never hinged		170.00
154c	A53	8c	100.00
	Never hinged		140.00
155c	A54	10c	200.00
	Never hinged		280.00
156c	A55	12c	200.00
	Never hinged		280.00
157c	A56	20c	200.00
	Never hinged		280.00
158c	A57	50c	800.00
	Never hinged		1,150.
159c	A58	$1	725.00
	Never hinged		1,050.

Coil Stamps

1929   Perf. 8 Vertically

160	A53	1c orange	40.00	22.50
	Never hinged		75.00	
	On commercial cover			22.50
	Pair		80.00	22.50
	Never hinged		160.00	
	On commercial cover			55.00
	Paste-up pair		100.00	67.50
	Never hinged		200.00	
	On commercial cover			67.50
	Precanceled			22.50
161	A53	2c green	40.00	3.50
	Never hinged		75.00	
	On commercial cover			8.00
	Pair		80.00	10.00
	Never hinged		160.00	
	On commercial cover			22.50
	Paste-up pair		100.00	35.00
	Never hinged		200.00	
	On commercial cover			37.50

King George
V
A59

Library of
Parliament
A60

The Citadel
at Quebec
A61

Harvesting
Wheat
A62

Museum at
Grand Pré
and
Monument to
Evangeline
A63

Mt. Edith
Cavell
A64

Type I   Type II

Two types of 1c.
Type I — Three thick and one thin colored lines between "P" at right and ornament above it.
Type II — Four thick colored lines. Curved line in ball of ornament at right is longer than in die I.

Type I   Type II

Two types of 2c.
Type I — The top of the letter "P" encloses a tiny dot of color.
Type II — The top of the "P" encloses a larger spot of color than in die I. The "P" appears almost like a "D."

1930-31   Perf. 11

162	A59	1c orange	1.25	.60
	Never hinged		2.50	
	1st day cover (7/17/30)			150.00
	Plate block of 4		9.00	
	Never hinged		18.00	
163	A59	1c deep green (II)	2.00	.25
	Never hinged		4.00	
	On commercial cover			1.75
	Plate block of 4		9.00	
	Never hinged		18.00	
a.	Booklet pane of 4 + 2 labels (II)		120.00	110.00
	Never hinged		180.00	
b.	Die I (12/6/30)		2.00	.25
	Never hinged		4.00	
	1st day cover (12/6/30)			140.00
c.	Booklet pane of 6 (I)		22.50	20.00
	Never hinged		35.00	
164	A59	2c dull green (I)	1.50	.25
	Never hinged		3.00	
	1st day cover (6/6/30)			140.00
	Plate block of 4		10.00	
	Never hinged		20.00	
a.	Booklet pane of 6		32.50	32.50
	Never hinged		47.50	
165	A59	2c deep red (I)	1.75	.25
	Never hinged		3.50	
	On commercial cover			2.50

	Plate block of 4	10.00	
	Never hinged	20.00	
a.	Die II	2.10	.25
	Never hinged	4.20	
	1st day cover (11/17/30)	12.00	—
	Plate block of 4	12.00	
	Never hinged	24.00	
	"Extended mustache" variety (65LR8)	75.00	55.00
	Never hinged	150.00	
	On commercial cover		90.00
b.	Booklet pane of 6 (I)	25.00	25.00
	Never hinged	37.50	
166	A59 2c dk brn (II) ('31)	2.00	.25
	Never hinged	4.00	
	On commercial cover		1.60
	Plate block of 4	9.50	
	Never hinged	19.00	
	"Extended mustache" variety (65LR8)	75.00	55.00
	Never hinged	150.00	
	On commercial cover		90.00
a.	Booklet pane of 4 + 2 labels (II)	130.00	130.00
	Never hinged	200.00	
b.	Die I	5.00	4.25
	Never hinged	10.00	
	1st day cover (7/4/31)	30.00	—
	Plate block of 4	30.00	
	Never hinged	60.00	
c.	Booklet pane of 6 (I)	57.50	57.50
	Never hinged	87.50	
167	A59 3c deep red ('31)	3.25	.25
	Never hinged	6.50	
	1st day cover (7/13/31)		210.00
	Plate block of 4	17.50	
	Never hinged	35.00	
a.	Booklet pane of 4 + 2 labels	40.00	40.00
	Never hinged	60.00	
168	A59 4c yel bister	14.00	7.50
	Never hinged	28.00	
	1st day cover (11/5/30)		210.00
	Plate block of 4	75.00	
	Never hinged	150.00	
169	A59 5c dl vio, rotary press	7.50	5.00
	Never hinged	15.00	
	On commercial cover		16.00
	Plate block of 4	45.00	
	Never hinged	90.00	
a.	Flat plate printing	11.00	
	Never hinged	22.00	
	1st day cover (6/18/30)		210.00
170	A59 5c dull blue	6.00	1.25
	Never hinged	12.00	
	1st day cover (11/13/30)		150.00
	On commercial cover		12.00
	Plate block of 4	35.00	
	Never hinged	70.00	
171	A59 8c dark blue	27.50	13.50
	Never hinged	55.00	
	1st day cover (8/13/30)		250.00
	Plate block of 4	135.00	
	Never hinged	275.00	
172	A59 8c red orange	6.50	5.50
	Never hinged	13.00	
	1st day cover (11/5/30)		110.00
	Plate block of 4	52.50	
	Never hinged	105.00	
173	A60 10c olive green	12.50	1.30
	Never hinged	25.00	
	1st day cover (9/15/30)		250.00
	Plate block of 4	75.00	
	Never hinged	150.00	
174	A61 12c gray black	27.50	6.50
	Never hinged	55.00	
	1st day cover (12/4/30)		400.00
	On commercial cover		12.50
	1st flight cover		7.50
	Plate block of 4	135.00	
	Never hinged	275.00	
175	A62 20c brown red	42.50	1.40
	Never hinged	85.00	
	1st day cover (12/4/30)		400.00
	Plate block of 4	250.00	
	Never hinged	500.00	
176	A63 50c dull blue	175.00	14.00
	Never hinged	350.00	
	1st day cover (12/4/30)		1,000.
	Plate block of 4	1,500.	
	Never hinged	3,000.	
177	A64 $1 dk ol green	175.00	27.50
	Never hinged	350.00	
	1st day cover (12/4/30)		1,000.
	Plate block of 4	1,500.	
	Never hinged	3,000.	
	Nos. 162-177 (16)	*505.75*	*85.30*
	Nos. 162-177, never hinged	1,012.	

No. 169 rotary printing is distinguished unused from No. 169a flat plate printing by the former having gum ridges about 5mm apart.

See No. 201. For surcharge see No. 191. For overprint see No. 203.

Imperf., Pairs

163d	A59 1c (II)	1,600.	
	Never hinged	2,400.	
173a	A60 10c	1,600.	
	Never hinged	2,400.	
174a	A61 12c	725.	
	Never hinged	1,050.	
175a	A62 20c	725.	
	Never hinged	1,050.	
176a	A63 50c	1,000.	
	Never hinged	1,500.	
177a	A64 $1	1,000.	
	Never hinged	1,500.	

Coil Stamps

1930-31   *Perf. 8½ Vertically*

178	A59 1c orange	15.00	9.00
	Never hinged	30.00	
	On commercial cover		11.00
	Pair	30.00	21.00
	Never hinged	60.00	
	On cover		24.00
	Joint line pair	45.00	26.00
	Never hinged	90.00	
	On cover		32.50

179	A59 1c deep green	9.00	5.75
	Never hinged	18.00	
	On commercial cover		7.00
	Pair	18.00	16.00
	Never hinged	36.00	
	On cover		17.00
	Joint line pair	27.50	22.50
	Never hinged	55.00	
	On cover		25.00
180	A59 2c dull green	6.00	3.00
	Never hinged	12.00	
	On commercial cover		3.75
	"Cockeyed King" variety	52.50	
	Never hinged	105.00	
	On cover		50.00
	Pair	12.00	7.50
	Never hinged	24.00	
	On cover		8.00
	Joint line pair	20.00	14.00
	Never hinged	40.00	
	On cover		17.50
	"Cockeyed King" variety, left stamp in line pair	75.00	67.50
	Never hinged	150.00	
	On cover		80.00
181	A59 2c deep red	25.00	2.50
	Never hinged	50.00	
	On commercial cover		4.00
	"Cockeyed King" variety	60.00	52.50
	Never hinged	120.00	
	On cover		55.00
	Pair	50.00	6.00
	Never hinged		12.50
	On cover		15.00
	Joint line pair	67.50	15.00
	Never hinged	135.00	
	On cover		17.50
	"Cockeyed King" variety, left stamp in line pair	90.00	75.00
	Never hinged	180.00	
	On cover		85.00
182	A59 2c dark brown ('31)	12.00	.70
	Never hinged	24.00	
	On commercial cover		5.50
	"Cockeyed King" variety	55.00	45.00
	Never hinged	110.00	
	On cover		47.50
	Pair	24.00	2.10
	Never hinged	47.50	
	On cover		12.50
	Joint line pair	34.00	6.00
	Never hinged	67.50	
	On cover		14.00
	"Cockeyed King" variety, left stamp in line pair	82.50	67.50
	Never hinged	165.00	
	On cover		75.00
183	A59 3c deep red ('31)	18.00	.70
	Never hinged	36.00	
	On commercial cover		2.00
	Pair	36.00	1.75
	Never hinged	72.50	
	On cover		20.00
	Joint line pair	55.00	7.50
	Never hinged	110.00	
	On cover		25.00
	Nos. 178-183 (6)	*85.00*	*21.65*
	Nos. 178-183, never hinged	170.00	

A vertical "jump" in spacing invariably occurs at the line in line pairs of Nos. 178-183. Therefore, a very fine line pair will not contain perfectly centered stamps, but it should show attractive balanced centering, This also applies to the "cockeyed king" variety in a line pair, as this variety occurs on the stamp to the left of the joint line.

George V Type of 1912-25

1931, June 24   *Perf. 12x8*

184	A43 3c carmine	8.00	4.50
	Never hinged	20.00	
	1st day cover		650.00
	Plate block of 8	90.00	
	Never hinged	180.00	

Sir Georges Etienne Cartier — A65

1931, Sept. 30   *Perf. 11*

190	A65 10c dark green	14.00	.25
	Never hinged	30.00	
	1st day cover		650.00
	Plate block of 4	75.00	
	Never hinged	150.00	
a.	Imperf., pair	500.00	
	Never hinged	750.00	

First Day Covers

Values for first day covers are for addressed non-cacheted covers through No. 190, addressed cacheted covers from No. 191 to No. 277, and unaddressed covers with the most common cachets from No. 282 and later.

Nos. 165, 165a
Surcharged

1932, June 21

191	A59 3c on 2c dp red (II)	1.40	.25
	Never hinged	2.25	
	1st day cover		17.50
	Plate block of 4	7.50	
	Never hinged	15.00	
	"Extended mustache" variety (65LR8)	75.00	60.00
	Never hinged	150.00	
	On commercial cover		90.00
a.	Die I	2.75	1.90
	Never hinged	4.50	
	1st day cover		190.00
	Plate block of 4	11.00	
	Never hinged	22.00	

King George V — A66

Edward, Prince of Wales — A67

Allegory of British Empire A68

1932, July 12

192	A66 3c deep red	1.25	.25
	Never hinged	2.50	
	1st day cover		9.00
	Plate block of 4	6.50	
	Never hinged	13.00	
193	A67 5c dull blue	7.00	3.00
	Never hinged	14.00	
	1st day cover		12.00
	Plate block of 4	52.50	
	Never hinged	105.00	
194	A68 13c deep green	10.00	7.00
	Never hinged	20.00	
	1st day cover		24.00
	Plate block of 4	90.00	
	Never hinged	180.00	
	Nos. 192-194 (3)	*18.25*	*10.25*
	Nos. 192-194, never hinged	36.50	

Imperial Economic Conference, Ottawa.

Type of 1930 and

King George V — A69

Type I   Type II

Two types of 3c.
Type I — Upper left tip of "3" level with horizontal line to its left.
Type II — Raised "3"; upper left tip of "3" is above horizontal line.

1932, Dec. 1

195	A69 1c dk grn, rotary press	1.25	.25
	Never hinged	2.50	
	1st day cover		16.00
	Plate block of 4	6.75	
	Never hinged	13.50	
a.	Booklet pane of 4 + 2 labels ('33)	80.00	80.00
	Never hinged	120.00	
b.	Booklet pane of 6 ('33)	47.50	47.50
	Never hinged	72.50	
d.	Flat plate printing	4.25	
	Never hinged	6.00	
	Plate block of 4	19.00	
	Never hinged	37.50	
196	A69 2c black brown	1.40	.25
	Never hinged	2.80	
	1st day cover		16.00
	Plate block of 4	7.50	
	Never hinged	15.00	
a.	Booklet pane of 4 + 2 labels ('33)	110.00	110.00
	Never hinged	165.00	
b.	Booklet pane of 6 ('33)	70.00	70.00
	Never hinged	105.00	
197	A69 3c deep red (I)	1.40	.25
	Never hinged	2.80	
	1st day cover		15.00
	Plate block of 4	16.00	
	Never hinged	32.50	
c.	Die II	1.40	.25
	Never hinged	2.80	
	On commercial cover		2.40
	Plate block of 4	10.50	
	Never hinged	21.00	
d.	Booklet pane of 4 + 2 labels, die II ('33)	37.50	37.50
	Never hinged	75.00	
198	A69 4c ocher	50.00	7.00
	Never hinged	100.00	
	1st day cover		24.00
	Plate block of 4	260.00	
	Never hinged	525.00	
199	A69 5c dark blue	14.00	.50
	Never hinged	28.00	
	1st day cover		24.00
	Plate block of 4	75.00	
	Never hinged	150.00	
a.	Horiz. pair, imperf. vert.	1,600.	
	Never hinged	2,250.	
200	A69 8c red orange	45.00	3.50
	Never hinged	90.00	
	1st day cover		27.50
	On commercial cover, single franking		55.00
	Plate block of 4	210.00	
	Never hinged	420.00	
201	A61 13c dull violet	42.50	3.50
	Never hinged	85.00	
	1st day cover		35.00
	Plate block of 4	225.00	
	Never hinged	450.00	
	Nos. 195-201 (7)	*155.55*	*15.25*
	Nos. 195-201, never hinged	311.10	
	Set of 7, #195-201 on one 1st day cover		35.00

Type A66 has at the foot of the stamp "OTTAWA-CONFERENCE 1932". This inscription does not appear on the stamps of type A69.

No. 195 was printed from both flat and rotary press plates. Unused examples of No. 195 will show gum ridges about 5mm apart. The gum on No. 195d is flat.

Imperf., Pairs

195c	A69	1c	240.00	
		Never hinged	360.00	
196c	A69	2c	240.00	
		Never hinged	360.00	
197b	A69	3c (I)	240.00	
		Never hinged		
197e	A69	3c (II)	*2,000.*	
198a	A69	4c	240.00	
		Never hinged	360.00	
199b	A69	5c	240.00	
		Never hinged	360.00	
200a	A69	8c	240.00	
		Never hinged	360.00	
201a	A69	13c	800.00	
		Never hinged	1,200.	

No. 197e exists as one unused block of 4.

Government Buildings, Ottawa — A70

1933, May 18 *Perf. 11*

202	A70	5c dark blue	10.00	3.75
		Never hinged	18.50	
		1st day cover		27.50
		Plate block of 4	65.00	
		Never hinged	125.00	
a.		Imperf., pair	625.00	
		Never hinged	950.00	

Meeting of the Executive Committee of the UPU at Ottawa, May and June, 1933.

No. 175 Overprinted in Blue

1933, July 24

203	A62	20c brown red	45.00	14.00
		Never hinged	80.00	
		1st day cover		55.00
		Plate block of 4	225.00	
		Never hinged	450.00	
		Broken "X" in "Exhibition" variety (pos. 19)	110.00	60.00
		Never hinged	225.00	
		1st day cover		80.00
a.		Imperf., pair	650.00	
		Never hinged	1,000.	
		Imperf., pair with one broken "X"	4,500.	
		Never hinged	6,750.	

World's Grain Exhibition and Conference at Regina.
Three examples are known of No. 203a with one stamp having the broken "X" variety. Two of these pairs are never hinged.

Steamship Royal William — A71

1933, Aug. 17

204	A71	5c dark blue	10.00	3.75
		Never hinged	18.50	
		1st day cover		26.00
		Plate block of 4	55.00	
		Never hinged	110.00	
a.		Imperf., pair	625.00	
		Never hinged	950.00	

Centenary of the linking by steam of the Dominion, then a colony, with Great Britain, the mother country. The Royal William's 1833 voyage was the first Trans-Atlantic passage under steam all the way.

George V Type of 1932
Coil Stamps

1933 *Perf. 8½ Vertically*

205	A69	1c dark green	15.00	3.00
		Never hinged	26.00	
		On commercial cover		7.25
		Pair	28.00	6.00
		Never hinged	56.00	
		On cover		8.00
		Joint line pair	37.50	7.50
		Never hinged	75.00	
		On cover		19.00
206	A69	2c black brown	20.00	1.10
		Never hinged	35.00	
		On commercial cover		6.50
		Pair	40.00	2.25
		Never hinged	70.00	
		On cover		10.00
		Joint line pair	47.50	7.00
		Never hinged	80.00	
		On cover		24.00
207	A69	3c deep red	17.50	.40
		Never hinged	30.00	
		On commercial cover		6.50
		Pair	35.00	1.20
		Never hinged	60.00	
		On cover		10.00
		Joint line pair	40.00	3.00
		Never hinged	60.00	
		On cover		24.00
		Nos. 205-207 (3)	52.50	4.50
		Nos. 205-207, never hinged	91.00	

Cartier's Arrival at Quebec — A72

1934, July 1 *Perf. 11*

208	A72	3c blue	4.50	1.40
		Never hinged	9.00	
		1st day cover		20.00
		Plate block of 4	30.00	
		Never hinged	60.00	
		Horiz. strip of 4 with wide vert. gutter btwn. center stamps	300.00	
		Never hinged	600.00	
a.		Imperf., pair	625.00	
		Never hinged	950.00	

Landing of Jacques Cartier, 400th anniv.

Group from Loyalists Monument, Hamilton, Ontario A73

1934, July 1

209	A73	10c olive green	28.00	7.50
		Never hinged	52.50	
		1st day cover		20.00
		Plate block of 4	175.00	
		Never hinged	350.00	
a.		Imperf., pair	1,400.	
		Never hinged	2,100.	

Emigration of the United Empire Loyalists from the US to Canada, 150th anniv.

Seal of New Brunswick — A74

1934, Aug. 16

210	A74	2c red brown	3.25	2.25
		Never hinged	6.00	
		1st day cover		12.00
		Plate block of 4	17.50	
		Never hinged	35.00	
a.		Imperf., pair	700.00	
		Never hinged	1,100.	

150th anniv. of the founding of the Province of New Brunswick.

Princess Elizabeth A75　　Duke of York A76

King George V and Queen Mary — A77

Prince of Wales — A78

Windsor Castle A79

Royal Yacht Britannia A80

1935, May 4 *Perf. 12*

211	A75	1c green	.75	.35
		Never hinged	1.10	
		1st day cover		6.50
		Plate block of 6	10.00	
		Never hinged	20.00	
		"Weeping Princess" plate flaw (21UR1)	125.00	85.00
		Never hinged	190.00	
				225.00
212	A76	2c brown	1.10	.25
		Never hinged	1.60	
		1st day cover		6.50
		Plate block of 6	10.00	
		Never hinged	15.00	
213	A77	3c carmine	2.00	.25
		Never hinged	3.25	
		1ct day cover		6.50
		Plate block of 6	20.00	
		Never hinged	30.00	
214	A78	5c blue	5.50	3.00
		Never hinged	9.00	
		1st day cover		16.00
		Plate block of 6	65.00	
		Never hinged	95.00	
215	A79	10c green	8.50	3.00
		Never hinged	13.50	
		1st day cover		20.00
		Plate block of 6	72.50	
		Never hinged	105.00	
216	A80	13c dark blue	10.00	6.50
		Never hinged	16.00	
		1st day cover		27.50
		Plate block of 6	95.00	
		Never hinged	140.00	
		Plate block of 10 (LL position)	150.00	
		Never hinged	225.00	
		"Shilling mark" plate flaw between "1" and "3" of left "13" (78UR1)	450.00	375.00
		Never hinged	600.00	
		On cover		350.00
		Nos. 211-216 (6)	27.85	13.35
		Nos. 211-216, never hinged	44.45	
		Set of 6, Nos. 211-216 on one 1st day cover		47.50

25th anniv. of the accession to the throne of George V.

Imperf., Pairs

211a	A75	1c	275.00	
		Never hinged	425.00	
212a	A76	2c	275.00	
		Never hinged	425.00	
213a	A77	3c	275.00	
		Never hinged	425.00	
214a	A78	5c	275.00	
		Never hinged	425.00	
215a	A79	10c	275.00	
		Never hinged	425.00	
216b	A80	13c	275.00	
		Never hinged	425.00	

King George V — A81

Royal Canadian Mounted Police — A82

Confederation Conference at Charlottetown, 1864 — A83

Niagara Falls — A84

Parliament Buildings, Victoria, B.C. — A85

Champlain Monument, Quebec A86

1935, June 1 *Perf. 12*

217	A81	1c green	.30	.25
		Never hinged	.40	
		1st day cover		5.50
		Plate block of 6	6.00	
		Never hinged	9.00	
		Plate block of 8 (pl. 3)	7.50	
		Never hinged	11.00	
a.		Bklt. pane of 4 + 2 labels	70.00	70.00
		Never hinged	105.00	
b.		Booklet pane of 6	55.00	55.00
		Never hinged	82.50	
218	A81	2c brown	.45	.25
		Never hinged	.65	
		1st day cover		5.50
		Plate block of 6	6.00	
		Never hinged	9.00	
		Plate block of 8	7.50	
		Never hinged	11.00	
a.		Bklt. pane of 4 + 2 labels	70.00	70.00
		Never hinged	105.00	
b.		Booklet pane of 6	55.00	55.00
		Never hinged	82.50	
219	A81	3c dk carmine	.70	.25
		Never hinged	1.05	
		1st day cover		5.50
		Plate block of 6	11.00	
		Never hinged	16.50	
		Plate block of 8	15.00	
		Never hinged	22.50	
a.		Bklt. pane of 4 + 2 labels	40.00	40.00
		Never hinged	60.00	
c.		Printed on gummed side	600.00	
220	A81	4c yellowish orange	2.50	.55
		Never hinged	3.75	
		1st day cover		8.00
		Plate block of 6	52.50	
		Never hinged	80.00	
221	A81	5c blue	3.25	.35
		Never hinged	5.00	
		1st day cover		8.00
		Plate block of 6	52.50	
		Never hinged	80.00	
a.		Horiz. pair, imperf. vert.	225.00	
		Never hinged	340.00	
222	A81	8c dp orange	3.00	2.25
		Never hinged	4.50	
		1st day cover		12.00
		On commercial cover		27.50
		On commercial cover, single franking		65.00
		Plate block of 6	52.50	
		Never hinged	80.00	
223	A82	10c car rose	7.00	.25
		Never hinged	10.50	
		1st day cover		12.00
		Plate block of 6	75.00	
		Never hinged	110.00	
		"Broken leg" on mountie variety	1,650.	1,350.
		Never hinged	2,500.	
224	A83	13c violet	7.50	.75
		Never hinged	11.00	
		1st day cover		24.00
		Plate block of 6	67.50	
		Never hinged	100.00	
225	A84	20c olive green	17.50	.75
		Never hinged	25.00	
		1st day cover		27.50
		On commercial cover		16.00
		Plate block of 6	190.00	
		Never hinged	275.00	
226	A85	50c dull violet	27.50	6.00
		Never hinged	40.00	
		1st day cover		60.00
		Plate block of 6	225.00	
		Never hinged	340.00	
227	A86	$1 deep blue	62.50	11.00
		Never hinged	95.00	
		1st day cover		160.00
		Plate block of 6	600.00	
		Never hinged	900.00	
		Nos. 217-227 (11)	132.20	22.65

Nos. 217-227, never
hinged   196.85
Set of 11, Nos. 217-227 on one 1st
day cover   160.00

No. 219c is valued in the grade of fine. Very
fine examples are rare and sell for much more.

Imperf., Pairs

217c	A81	1c	150.00	
		Never hinged	220.00	
218c	A81	2c	150.00	
		Never hinged	220.00	
219b	A81	3c	150.00	
		Never hinged	220.00	
220a	A81	4c	150.00	
		Never hinged	220.00	
221b	A81	5c	150.00	
		Never hinged	220.00	
222a	A81	8c	150.00	
		Never hinged	220.00	
223a	A82	10c	225.00	
		Never hinged	340.00	
224a	A83	13c	225.00	
		Never hinged	340.00	
225a	A84	20c	225.00	
		Never hinged	340.00	
226a	A85	50c	225.00	
		Never hinged	340.00	
227a	A86	$1	300.00	
		Never hinged	450.00	

Coil Stamps

1935   **Perf. 8 Vertically**

228	A81	1c green	15.00	3.25
		Never hinged	22.50	
		On commercial cover		6.50
		Pair	30.00	6.50
		Never hinged	45.00	
		On cover		9.50
229	A81	2c brown	19.00	1.00
		Never hinged	28.50	
		On commercial cover		6.50
		Pair	38.00	2.25
		Never hinged	57.50	
		On cover		16.00
230	A81	3c dark carmine	16.00	.60
		Never hinged	24.00	
		On commercial cover		6.50
		Pair	30.00	2.50
		Never hinged	45.00	
		On cover		16.00
		Nos. 228-230 (3)	50.00	4.85
		Nos. 228-230, never hinged	75.00	

George VI — A87

George VI
and Queen
Elizabeth
A88

1937   **Perf. 12**

231	A87	1c green	.25	.25
		Never hinged	.40	
		1st day cover (4/1/37)		4.75
		Plate block of 4	2.75	
		Never hinged	4.10	
a.		Booklet pane of 4 + 2 labels	20.00	25.00
		Never hinged	30.00	
b.		Booklet pane of 6	7.50	20.00
		Never hinged	11.50	
232	A87	2c brown	.60	.25
		Never hinged	.90	
		1st day cover (4/1/37)		4.75
		Plate block of 4	3.50	
		Never hinged	5.25	
a.		Booklet pane of 4 + 2 labels	20.00	22.50
		Never hinged	30.00	
b.		Booklet pane of 6	12.00	15.00
		Never hinged	18.00	
233	A87	3c carmine	.65	.25
		Never hinged	1.00	
		1st day cover (4/1/37)		4.75
		Plate block of 4	4.25	
		Never hinged	6.50	
a.		Booklet pane of 4 + 2 labels	7.00	14.00
		Never hinged	10.50	
234	A87	4c yellow	2.75	.25
		Never hinged	4.00	
		1st day cover (5/10/37)		7.25
		Plate block of 4	22.50	
		Never hinged	34.00	
235	A87	5c blue	3.50	.25
		Never hinged	5.00	
		1st day cover (5/10/37)		7.25
		Plate block of 4	22.50	
		Never hinged	34.00	
236	A87	8c orange	2.75	.45
		Never hinged	4.00	
		1st day cover (5/10/37)		7.25
		On commercial cover		8.50
		On commercial cover, single franking		60.00
		Plate block of 4	22.50	
		Never hinged	32.50	
		Nos. 231-236 (6)	10.50	1.70
		Nos. 231-236, never hinged	15.30	

Imperf., Pairs

231c	A87	1c	300.00	
		Never hinged	450.00	
232c	A87	2c	300.00	
		Never hinged	450.00	
233b	A87	3c	300.00	
		Never hinged	450.00	
234a	A87	4c	300.00	
		Never hinged	450.00	

235a	A87	5c	300.00	
		Never hinged	450.00	
236a	A87	8c	300.00	
		Never hinged	450.00	

1937, May 10

237	A88	3c carmine	.30	.25
		Never hinged	.35	
		1st day cover		3.25
		Plate block of 4	3.00	
		Never hinged	4.50	
a.		Imperf., pair	625.00	
		Never hinged	950.00	

Coronation of King George VI and Queen
Elizabeth.

George VI Types of 1937
Coil Stamps

1937   **Perf. 8 Vertically**

238	A87	1c green	3.00	1.10
		Never hinged	4.50	
		On commercial cover		6.50
		Pair	6.00	2.25
		Never hinged	9.00	
		On cover		8.00
239	A87	2c brown	5.50	.40
		Never hinged	8.25	
		On commercial cover		7.25
		Pair	11.00	1.60
		Never hinged	16.50	
		On cover		12.50
240	A87	3c carmine	9.00	.25
		Never hinged	13.50	
		On commercial cover		4.50
		Pair	13.00	.80
		Never hinged	27.50	
		On cover		13.50
		Nos. 238-240 (3)	17.50	1.75
		Nos. 238-240, never hinged	26.25	

Memorial Chamber,
Parliament Building,
Ottawa — A89

Entrance to
Halifax
Harbor
A90

Fort Garry
Gate,
Winnipeg
A91

Vancouver
Harbor
A92

Chateau de
Ramezay,
Montreal
A93

1938   **Perf. 12**

241	A89	10c dk carmine	9.00	.25
		Never hinged	13.50	
		1st day cover (7/28/38)		80.00
		Plate block of 4	55.00	
		Never hinged	82.50	
a.		10c carmine rose	9.00	.25
		Never hinged	13.50	
		1st day cover (6/15/38)		24.00
		Plate block of 4	40.00	
		Never hinged	60.00	
242	A90	13c deep blue	12.00	.60
		Never hinged	18.00	
		1st day cover (11/15/38)		24.00
		Plate block of 4	75.00	
		Never hinged	110.00	
243	A91	20c red brown	16.00	.45
		Never hinged	24.00	
		1st day cover (6/15/38)		27.50
		Plate block of 4	110.00	
		Never hinged	165.00	
244	A92	50c green	37.50	6.00
		Never hinged	55.00	
		1st day cover (6/15/38)		55.00
		Plate block of 4	195.00	
		Never hinged	290.00	
245	A93	$1 dull violet	80.00	7.75
		Never hinged	120.00	
		1st day cover (6/15/38)		100.00

		Plate block of 4	450.00	
		Never hinged	675.00	
a.		Vert. pair, imperf., horiz.	4,500.	
		Never hinged	6,250.	
		Nos. 241-245 (5)	154.50	15.05
		Nos. 241-245, never hinged	230.50	

Imperf., Pairs

241b	A89	10c dark carmine	450.00	
		Never hinged	675.00	
241c	A89	10c carmine rose	450.00	
		Never hinged	675.00	
242a	A90	13c	450.00	
		Never hinged	675.00	
243a	A91	20c	450.00	
		Never hinged	675.00	
244a	A92	50c	450.00	
		Never hinged	675.00	
245b	A93	$1	600.00	
		Never hinged	900.00	

Princess
Elizabeth
and Princess
Margaret
Rose — A94

War Memorial,
Ottawa — A95

King George
VI and
Queen
Elizabeth
A96

Unwmk.

1939, May 15   Engr.   **Perf. 12**

246	A94	1c green & black	.30	.25
		Never hinged	.35	
		1st day cover		2.40
		Plate block of 4	2.25	
		Never hinged	3.25	
247	A95	2c brown & black	.30	.25
		Never hinged	.35	
		1st day cover		2.40
		Plate block of 4	2.25	
		Never hinged	3.25	
248	A96	3c dk car & black	.30	.25
		Never hinged	.35	
		1st day cover		2.40
		Plate block of 4	2.25	
		Never hinged	3.25	
		Nos. 246-248 (3)	.90	.75
		Nos. 246-248, never hinged	1.05	
		Set of 3, #246-248 on 1 1st day cover		3.75

Visit of George VI and Queen Elizabeth to
Canada and the US.

This is the first issue of Canada that
required the use of two separate plates, and
each plate block shows two plate numbers
(one for the frame and one for the vignette).
165 different plate number combinations are
known, with a few being extremely scarce to
rare. The scarcer plate combinations are
worth large premiums.

Imperf., Pairs

246a	A94	1c	550.00	
		Never hinged	800.00	
247a	A95	2c	550.00	
		Never hinged	800.00	
248a	A96	3c	550.00	
		Never hinged	800.00	

A97

A98

1949, June 21   Unwmk.
283 A118 4c purple   .30   .25
    1st day cover   2.40
    Plate block of 4   1.25

200th anniv. of the founding of Halifax, Nova Scotia.

A119

A120

A121

A122

A123

1949, Nov. 15
284 A119 1c green   .25   .25
    1st day cover   6.50
    Plate block of 4   1.10
a.   Booklet pane of 3 ('50)   .80   1.25
285 A120 2c sepia   .30   .25
    1st day cover   6.50
    Plate block of 4   1.40
286 A121 3c rose violet   .35   .25
    1st day cover   6.50
    Plate block of 4   1.40
a.   Booklet pane of 3 ('50)   2.50   6.50
b.   Booklet pane of 4 + 2 labels ('50)   3.25   3.75
287 A122 4c dk carmine   .60   .25
    1st day cover   6.50
    Plate block of 4   2.50
a.   Booklet pane of 3 ('50)   12.50   12.50
b.   Booklet pane of 6 ('50)   18.00   18.00
288 A123 5c deep blue   1.25   .30
    1st day cover   6.50
    Plate block of 4   6.25
    Nos. 284-288 (5)   2.75   1.30
Set of 5, #284-288 on one 1st day cover   12.00

Stamps from booklet panes of 3 are imperf. on 2 or 3 sides.

"POSTES POSTAGE" Omitted
1950, Jan. 19
289 A119 1c green   .25   .25
    1st day cover   27.50
    Plate block of 4   1.10
290 A120 2c sepia   .30   .25
    1st day cover   27.50
    Plate block of 4   2.75
291 A121 3c rose violet   .30   .25
    1st day cover   27.50
    Plate block of 4   1.90
292 A122 4c dark carmine   .30   .25
    1st day cover   27.50
    Plate block of 4   1.90
293 A123 5c deep blue   1.40   1.00
    1st day cover   27.50
    Plate block of 4   7.00
    Nos. 289-293 (5)   2.55   2.00
Set of 5, #289-293 on one 1st day cover   45.00

See Nos. 295-300, 305-306, 309-310. For overprints see Nos. O12-O20.

Oil Wells, Alberta
A124

1950, Mar. 1   Engr.   **Perf. 12**
294 A124 50c dull green   9.00   1.40
    1st day cover   32.50
    Plate block of 4   50.00

Development of oil wells in Canada. For overprints see Nos. O11, O24.

Types of 1949
"POSTES POSTAGE" Omitted
Coil Stamps
1950   **Perf. 9½ Vertically**
295 A119 1c green   .75   .30
    On commercial cover   4.50
    Pair   1.50   .60
     On cover   7.50

296 A121 3c rose violet   1.25   .60
    On commercial cover   5.25
    Pair   2.50   1.20
     On cover   8.50

With "POSTES POSTAGE"
Perf. 9½ Vertically
297 A119 1c green   .45   .25
    On commercial cover   4.50
    Pair   .80   .50
     On cover   8.00
298 A120 2c sepia   3.75   1.30
    On commercial cover   6.00
    Pair   7.50   2.75
     On cover   12.50
299 A121 3c rose violet   2.50   .25
    On commercial cover   4.50
    Pair   5.00   .50
     On cover   11.00
300 A122 4c dark carmine   20.00   .70
    On commercial cover   12.50
    Pair   40.00   2.25
     On cover   32.50
    Nos. 297-300 (4)   26.70   2.50

See note after No. 288.

Indians Drying Skins on Stretchers
A125

1950, Oct. 2   **Perf. 12**
301 A125 10c black brown   .90   .25
    1st day cover   5.50
    Plate block of 4   5.50

Canada's fur resources. For overprint see No. O26.

Fishing
A126

1951, Feb. 1   Unwmk.
302 A126 $1 bright ultra   45.00   10.00
    1st day cover   72.50
    Plate block of 4   225.00

Canada's fish resources. For overprint see No. O27.

Sir Robert Laird Borden
A127

William L. Mackenzie King
A128

1951, June 25   **Perf. 12**
303 A127 3c turquoise green   .30   .25
    1st day cover   2.40
    Plate block of 4   1.60
304 A128 4c rose pink   .35   .25
    1st day cover   2.40
    Plate block of 4   1.65

George VI Types of 1949
1951   **Perf. 12**
305 A120 2c olive green   .25   .25
    On commercial cover   .75
    Plate block of 4   1.10
306 A122 4c orange vermilion   .30   .25
    On commercial cover   .75
    Plate block of 4   1.10
a.   Booklet pane of 3   5.25   2.75
b.   Booklet pane of 6   5.00   5.00

For overprints see Nos. O28-O29.

Coil Stamps
Perf. 9½ Vertically
309 A120 2c olive green   1.50   .60
    On commercial cover   5.50
    Pair   2.80   1.50
     On cover   9.50
310 A122 4c orange vermilion   3.00   .70
    On commercial cover   6.50
    Pair   5.50   1.60
     On cover   20.00

Trains of 1851 and 1951 — A129

"Threepenny Beaver" of 1851 — A130

Designs: 5c, Steamships City of Toronto and Prince George. 7c, Stagecoach and Plane.

1951, Sept. 24   Unwmk.   **Perf. 12**
311 A129 4c dark gray   .60   .25
    1st day cover   2.75
    Plate block of 4   4.00
312 A129 5c purple   1.80   1.25
    1st day cover   4.00
    Plate block of 4   9.50
313 A129 7c deep blue   1.10   .30
    1st day cover   4.00
    Plate block of 4   5.50
314 A130 15c bright red   1.20   .30
    1st day cover   4.00
    Plate block of 4   6.50
    Nos. 311-314 (4)   4.70   2.10
Set of 4, #311-314 on one 1st day cover   8.00

Centenary of British North American postal administration.

Princess Elizabeth and Duke of Edinburgh
A131

1951, Oct. 26   Engr.
315 A131 4c violet   .25   .25
    1st day cover   2.40
    Plate block of 4   1.10

Visit of Princess Elizabeth, Duchess of Edinburgh and the Duke of Edinburgh to Canada and the US.

Symbols of Newsprint Paper Production
A132

1952, Apr. 1   Unwmk.   **Perf. 12**
316 A132 20c gray   1.70   .25
    1st day cover   6.75
    Plate block of 4   9.50

Canada's paper production. For overprint see No. O30.

Red Cross on Sun — A133

1952, July 26   Engr. and Litho.
317 A133 4c blue & red   .25   .25
    1st day cover   2.40
    Plate block of 4   1.30

18th Intl. Red Cross Conf., Toronto, July 1952.

Sir John J. C. Abbott
A134

Alexander Mackenzie
A135

1952, Nov. 3   Engr.
318 A134 3c rose lilac   .25   .25
    1st day cover   2.40
    Plate block of 4   1.10
319 A135 4c orange vermilion   .30   .25
    1st day cover   2.40
    Plate block of 4   1.25

Canada Goose
A136

1952, Nov. 3
320 A136 7c blue   .40   .25
    1st day cover   6.75
    Plate block of 4   2.10

For overprint see No. O31.

AIR POST STAMPS

Allegory of Flight — AP1

Unwmk.
1928, Sept. 21   Engr.   **Perf. 12**
C1 AP1 5c brown olive   15.00   5.00
    Never hinged   27.50
    1st day cover   100.00
    Plate block of 6   125.00
     Never hinged   250.00
    "Swollen breast" variety (4UR2)   75.00   60.00
     Never hinged   150.00
     On commercial cover   80.00
    Plate block of 6 (UR2)   190.00
     Never hinged   375.00
a.   Imperf., pair   275.00
     Never hinged   375.00
b.   Horiz. pair, imperf. vert.   225.00
     Never hinged   340.00
c.   Vert. pair, imperf. horiz.   225.00
     Never hinged   340.00

For surcharge see No. C3.

For information on imperforate and part-perforate varieties, see note following No. 47a.

Allegory-Air Mail Circles Globe
AP2

1930, Dec. 4   **Perf. 11**
C2 AP2 5c olive brown   85.00   27.50
    Never hinged   140.00
    1st day cover   160.00
    Plate block of 6   600.00
     Never hinged   1,200.

For surcharge see No. C4.

No. C1 Surcharged

1932, Feb. 22   **Perf. 12**
C3 AP1 6c on 5c brown olive   12.50   4.00
    Never hinged   22.00
    1st day cover   14.50
    Plate block of 6   110.00
     Never hinged   165.00
    "Swollen breast" variety (4UR2)   75.00   60.00
     Never hinged   150.00
     On commercial cover   80.00
    Plate block of 6 (UR2)   190.00
     Never hinged   375.00
a.   Inverted surcharge   200.00
     Never hinged   280.00
b.   Double surcharge   675.00
     Never hinged   950.00
c.   Triple surcharge   400.00
     Never hinged   550.00
d.   Pair, one without surcharge   950.00
     Never hinged   1,350.

Counterfeit surcharges exist.
No. C3b is valued in the grade of fine.

No. C2 Surcharged in Dark Blue

1932, July 12   *Perf. 11*

C4	AP2 6c on 5c olive brown	40.00	12.50
	Never hinged	70.00	
	1st day cover		17.50
	Plate block of 4	225.00	
	Never hinged	450.00	

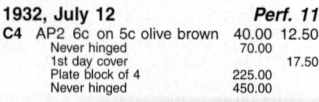

Daedalus
AP3

1935, June 1   *Perf. 12*

C5	AP3 6c red brown	4.25	1.25
	Never hinged	6.00	
	1st day cover		17.50
	Plate block of 6	32.50	
	Never hinged	50.00	
a.	Horiz. pair, imperf. vert.	6,000.	
b.	Imperf., pair	650.00	
	Never hinged	1,000.	

No. C5a is believed to be unique and is the result of a pre-perforating paper foldover. It is valued in the grade of fine.

Mackenzie River Steamer and Seaplane AP4

1938, June 15

C6	AP4 6c blue	3.75	.40
	Never hinged	5.25	
	1st day cover		16.00
	Plate block of 4	22.50	
	Never hinged	32.50	
a.	Imperf., pair	650.00	
	Never hinged	950.00	

Planes and Student Flyers AP5

1942-43

C7	AP5 6c deep blue	5.25	1.20
	Never hinged	7.50	
	1st day cover (7/1/42)		12.00
	Plate block of 4	26.00	
	Never hinged	40.00	
a.	Imperf., pair	650.00	
	Never hinged	950.00	
C8	AP5 7c deep blue ('43)	1.00	.25
	Never hinged	1.40	
	1st day cover (4/16/43)		8.00
	Plate block of 4	6.50	
	Never hinged	9.75	
a.	Imperf., pair	650.00	
	Never hinged	950.00	

Canada's contribution to the war effort of the Allied Nations.

Catalogue values for unused stamps in this section, from this point to the end of the section, are for Never Hinged items.

Canada Geese in Flight — AP6

1946, Sept. 16

C9	AP6 7c deep blue	1.25	.25
	1st day cover		6.00
	Plate block of 4	6.00	
a.	Booklet pane of 4	5.00	5.00
	1st day cover		45.00

For overprints see Nos. CO1, CO2.

AIR POST SPECIAL DELIVERY STAMPS

Trans-Canada Airplane and Aerial View of a City — APSD1

1942-43   Unwmk.   Engr.   *Perf. 12*

CE1	APSD1 16c bright ultra	2.50	2.00
	Never hinged	3.50	
	1st day cover (7/1/42)		14.50
	Plate block of 4	13.50	
	Never hinged	20.00	
a.	Imperf., pair	750.00	
	Never hinged	1,100.	
CE2	APSD1 17c brt ultra ('43)	3.25	3.00
	Never hinged	4.75	
	1st day cover (4/17/43)		35.00
	Plate block of 4	18.00	
	Never hinged	27.50	
a.	Imperf., pair	650.00	
	Never hinged	950.00	

Canada's contribution to the war effort of the Allied Nations.

Catalogue values for unused stamps in this section, from this point to the end of the section, are for Never Hinged items.

DC-4 Transatlantic Mail Plane Over Quebec — APSD2

1946, Sept. 16

CE3	APSD2 17c bright ultra	6.00	4.25
	1st day cover		14.50
	Plate block of 4	30.00	

Circumflex accent on second "E" of "EXPRES."

1946, Dec. 3   Corrected Die

CE4	APSD2 17c bright ultra	6.00	4.25
	1st day cover		140.00
	Plate block of 4	30.00	

Grave accent on the 2nd "E" of "EXPRES."

AIR POST OFFICIAL STAMPS

Catalogue values for unused stamps in this section are for Never Hinged items.

All cover values in this section are for uses on commercial covers.

No. C9 Overprinted in Black

1949   Unwmk.   *Perf. 12*

CO1	AP6 7c deep blue	12.00	4.75
	On cover		24.00
	Plate block of 4	50.00	
a.	No period after "S"	110.00	60.00
	On cover		90.00
	Plate block of 4 (LL1, LL2)	150.00	

Same Overprinted

1950

CO2	AP6 7c deep blue	17.50	15.00
	On cover		32.50
	Plate block of 4	100.00	

AIR POST SEMI-OFFICIAL STAMPS

Mail was first carried by airplane in Canada in 1912, and air clubs and air transport companies pioneered the delivery of mail by air to remote areas of the country, the latter operating under contract with the Canadian Post Office. During 1918-33, labels were issued by both Aero clubs and private companies to frank mail carried on these private flights. Postal regulations required that such labels be affixed to the back of envelopes, and that regular Canadian postage be paid. Generally, hand-stamped cachets bearing the dates or points of the flight were applied to covers flown.

Approximate quantities printed, where known, are noted in parentheses.

AIR CLUBS & SPECIAL FLIGHTS

AERO CLUB OF CANADA
Toronto-Ottawa

Zeppelin on Fire — APL1

1918, Aug. 24   Litho.   *Perf. 12*

CLP1	APL1 (25c) black & red (194)	1,600.	500.00
	Never hinged	2,000.	
	Cover, Aug. 26, Toronto to Ottawa, green route cancel (100)		3,000.
	Registered cover, Aug. 26, Toronto to Ottawa, green route cancel (26)		4,000.
	Cover, Aug. 27, Ottawa to Toronto, green route cancel (approx. 35)		3,800.
	Cover, Aug. 27, Ottawa to Toronto, black route cancel (2)		4,000.
	Cover, Sept. 4, Toronto to Ottawa, green route cancel		3,400.
	Cover, Sept. 4, Ottawa to Toronto, green route cancel		3,400.
a.	Tête-bêche pair	3,200.	
b.	Red flame omitted (6)	3,600.	

Nos. CLP1 and CLP2 were issued in panes of 2, with the stamps printed tête-bêche. No. CLP1 and a portion of the print run of No. CLP2 were printed on a rough off-white paper. The majority of No. CLP2 was printed on smooth white paper.

A black essay of CLP1 exists on perforated pelure paper, with no gum as issued and no red flame. One recorded. Value, $6,500.

As No. CLP1, Numerals of Value Added — APL2

1918, Aug. 28

CLP2	APL2 25c black & red (2,800)	500.00	
	Never hinged	750.00	
	Cover, Sept. 4, Toronto to Ottawa, green route cancel		4,000.
	Cover, Sept. 4, Ottawa to Toronto, green route cancel		4,000.
a.	Tête-bêche pair	1,200.	
	Never hinged	1,600.	
b.	Red flame omitted	1,800.	
c.	Red flame double (on one stamp in tête-bêche pair)	1,800.	
d.	On rough off-white paper	750.00	
	Never hinged	1,000.	
e.	As "d," tête-bêche	1,000.	1,600.

Sept. 4 flight covers in both directions bore either CLP1 or CLP2, but no record was kept of which variety was affixed. Total covers flown: Toronto to Ottawa, 44; Ottawa to Toronto, 136.

AERO CLUB OF CANADA
Toronto-New York

APL3

1918, Aug. 25

CLP3	APL3 ($1) red & blue (3,000)	350.00	125.00
	Never hinged	550.00	
	No gum	125.00	
	Cover, Aug. 25, Toronto to New York (approx. 300)		850.00
	Return flight, New York to Toronto, without #CLP3		250.00
	Commercial cover		1,000.
a.	On thin paper, design showing through	350.00	

First international air mail service, from the Leaside Aerodrome, Toronto, to Roosevelt Field, Mineola, Long Island, New York. Printed in panes of 10 (5x2). Color shift varieties exist.

GRAND ARMY OF CANADA
Toronto-Hamilton and Return

Denomination blocked out — APL4

1920, May 28
CLP4 APL4 ($1) black 13,000. —
  Never hinged
  Flown cover, *May
    28*, Toronto to
    Hamilton 14,000.
  Flown cover, *May
    28*, Hamilton to
    Toronto 14,000.

Issued in panes of 5, with five stamps in a horizontal strip, surrounded by blank marginal selvage.
Forgeries exist.

ESTEVAN - WINNIPEG PROMOTIONAL ISSUE

APL5

Two types: I, normal spacing between "e" and "w" in "Saskatchewan"; II, wide spacing between "e" and "w" in "Saskatchewan."

1924, Oct. 1   *Imperf.*
CLP5 APL5 ($1) black
  red, type I *(514)* 350.00 150.00
  Never hinged 650.00
  On cover, *Oct. 1,*
    Estevan to Winni-
    peg *(200-250)* 300.00
a. Inscription inverted
    (12) 850.00 1,750.
b. Type II 350.00 150.00
  Never hinged 550.00
  On cover, *Oct. 1,*
    Estevan to Winni-
    peg *(200-250)* 250.00
c. As "b," inscription
    inverted *(12)* 850.00 1,750.
d. Inscription omitted
    (4) 850.00 1,750.
e. As #CLP5d, pane of
    2 2,250.
f. Pane of 2, #CLP5 +
    CLP5b 1,500.
  Never hinged 2,250.
g. Pane of 2, #CLP5a
    + CLP5c 2,500.
h. "Aerial" misspelled
    "Airial" *(2)* 6,500.
  First flight cover
    without #CLP5
    (approx. 1,400) 75.00

Issued for first Saskatchewan flight and to publicize the coal-rich area of Estevan.
Issued in vertical panes of 2.

LONDON (Ontario) to LONDON (UK) FLIGHT

Capt. Terrence B. Tully & Lt. James Medcalf — APL6

1927, Aug.   *Perf. 12*
CLP6 APL6 25c green &
  yellow *(100)* 50,000.
  On cover *(1)* 100,000.

Issued for the attempted first transatlantic flight, aborted on Aug. 29, 1927. A second attempt ended in the crash at sea and death of the pilots on Sept. 6.
Issued in panes of 4. Of the 100 stamps printed, 13 unused single stamps and one example on cover are known.

MOOSE JAW FLYING CLUB
Moose Jaw - Winnipeg

APL7

1927, Aug. 17   *Perf. 11*
CLP7 APL7 ($1) red
  (approx. 200) 2,750.
  Never hinged 3,000.
  Flight cover, *Aug. 17
    (161)* 3,250.
  Pane of 5 12,000.

Issued in vertical panes of 5 stamps (1x5).

PRIVATE COMMERCIAL AIRLINES
LAURENTIDE AIR SERVICE LTD.
Haileybury, Ont. - Rouyn/Angliers, Que.

APL8

1924, Aug. 30   *Rouletted at Left*
CL1 APL8 (25c) green
  (200) 2,000. 1,500.
  Never hinged 3,000.
  First flight cover, *Sept.
    21*, Haileybury to
    Rouyn or return,
    each 3,000.
  Commercial cover 3,500.
a. Booklet pane of 2, with
    tab at left 4,000.
  Never hinged 6,000.
  Complete Booklet, 4
    #CL1a, stapled at left
    (2 known) 20,000.

The cover of the No. CL1 booklet is plain, with no printing on front or back.

1924, Sept. 5   *Rouletted at Top*
CL2 APL8 (25c) green
  (1,220) 150.00 100.00
  Never hinged 250.00
  Sheet of 25 3,750.
  First flight cover, *Sept.
    21*, Haileybury to
    Rouyn or return,
    each 2,500.
  Flight cover, *Oct. 1,*
    Angliers to Rouyn 500.00
  Flight cover, *Oct. 17,*
    Haileybury to Rouyn 450.00
  Cover, *Jan. 22, 1925,*
    Three Rivers to
    Rouyn 250.00
  Commercial cover 600.00
a. Booklet pane of 2, tab
    at top 400.00
  Never hinged 650.00
  Complete Booklet, 4
    #CL2a, stapled at
    top, printing on front
    cover 1,800.
  Complete Booklet, 4
    #CL2a, stapled at
    top, printing on front
    and back covers 1,800.
b. (25c) dk blue green
    (2,400) 200.00
  Never hinged 400.00
  Flight cover, *Jan. 22,
    1925,* Larder Lake to
    Rouyn 375.00
  Commercial cover 600.00
c. As "b," booklet pane of
    2, tab at top 425.00
  Never hinged 600.00
  Complete Booklet, 4
    #CL2b, stapled at
    top, printing on front
    and back covers 3,000.

"Canada 1924" Added — APL9

1924, Oct. 1   *Perf. 11½*
CL3 APL9 (25c) red
  (3,000) 140.00
  Never hinged 210.00
  Pane of 20 2,800.
  Flight cover, *Oct. 3,*
    Haileybury to Rouyn
    or return, *each* 275.00
  Flight cover, *Oct. 24,*
    Haileybury to Rouyn
    or return, *each* 375.00
  Cover, *Jan. 22, 1925,*
    Three Rivers to
    Rouyn Lake 275.00
  Commercial cover 500.00

No. CL3 was issued in panes of 20 (4x5).

1924, Oct. 2   *Rouletted at Top*
CL4 APL9 (25c) red
  (2,160) 175.00
  Never hinged 260.00
  Flight cover, *Oct. 3,*
    Haileybury to Rouyn
    or return, *each* 275.00
  Flight cover, *Oct. 24,*
    Haileybury to Rouyn
    or return, *each* 375.00
  Flight cover, *Jan. 22,
    1925,* Three Rivers
    to Rouyn Lake 275.00
  Commercial cover 525.00
a. Booklet pane of 2, tab
    at top 350.00
  Never hinged 525.00
  Complete booklet, 4
    #CL4a 3,000.
b. As "a," top stamp dark
    red, bottom stamp
    light red 500.00
  Complete booklet, 4
    #CL4b 3,000.

Nos. CL4a and CL4b are stapled at top, with printing on both front and back covers.

NORTHERN AIR SERVICE
Haileybury, Ont. - Rouyn, Que.

APL10

1925, June 27   *Perf. 12*
CL5 APL10 (25c) blue
  (4,000) 175.00
  Never hinged 260.00
  Flight cover, *June 27,*
    Haileybury to Rouyn
    or return, *each* 175.00
  Commercial cover 500.00
a. Tête-bêche pair 700.00
b. Blue dot left of mono-
    gram 200.00

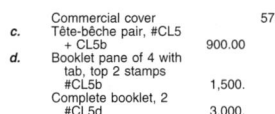

c. Commercial cover 575.00
  Tête-bêche pair, #CL5
    + CL5b 900.00
d. Booklet pane of 4 with
    tab, top 2 stamps
    #CL5b 1,500.
  Complete booklet, 2
    #CL5d 3,000.

No. CL5 was issued both in panes of 25 and in booklet panes of 4.
An experimental flight without No. CL5, but with a special cachet, was made on May 18, 1925, from Haileybury to Rouyn and return. 8 pieces were carried each way. Value, $2,500.

JACK V. ELLIOT AIR SERVICE
Red Lake-Rolling Portage (Hudson) - Sioux Lookout, Ont.

APL11

Yellow background of zig-zag lines

1926, Mar. 6   *Perf. 11½*
CL6 APL11 (25c) red &
  yellow *(2,500)* 55.00
  Never hinged 82.50
  Flight cover, *Mar. 26,*
    Rolling Portage to
    Red Lake or return,
    each 85.00
  Commercial cover 225.00
  Pane of 8 550.00
a. Imperf, pair 400.00
b. Tête-bêche gutter pair
    from sheet of 16 350.00
c. As "b," imperf 700.00
d. Double impression,
    imperf pair *(2
    known)* 1,750.
e. White spot (position 8,
    LR) 150.00
  On cover 175.00
f. As "e," in pane of 8 650.00

Yellow background of swastikas

1926, Mar. 25

CL7	APL11	(25c) red & yellow *(2,000)*	90.00	
		Never hinged	135.00	
		Pane of 8	800.00	
		Sheet of 16	2,250.	
		Flight cover, Mar. 25, Rolling Portage to Red Lake or return, *each*		85.00
		Commercial cover		225.00
a.		Imperf, pair	400.00	
b.		As "a," one stamp with "AIR SERVICE" inverted	550.00	
c.		Tête-bêche gutter pair from sheet of 16	450.00	
d.		As "c," imperf	600.00	

Nos. CL6 and CL7 were printed in sheets of 16, most of which were cut into two panes of 8, each containing two horizontal rows of 4.

One proof of CL6 exists in black. Value, $50,000.

ELLIOT-FAIRCHILD AIR SERVICE
Service to Red Lake and Rouyn Goldfields

APL12

Yellow background of swastikas

1926, Mar. 21

CL8	APL12	(25c) red & yellow *(2,504)*	40.00	
		Never hinged	60.00	
		Pane of 8	350.00	
		Sheet of 16	2,000.	
		Flight cover, Mar. 30, Rolling Portage to Red Lake or return, *each*		275.00
		Flight cover, April 15, Rolling Portage to Red Lake or return, *each*		500.00
		Flight cover, May 27, Rouyn to Haileybury or return, *each*		600.00
		Commercial cover		400.00
a.		Imperf, pair	225.00	
b.		Tête-bêche gutter pair from sheet of 16	300.00	
c.		Tall "r" variety, Pos. 2 and 4	95.00	

No. CL8 was printed in sheets of 16 (4x4), with gutter between rows 2 and 3, and cut into panes of 8 (4x2).

ELLIOT-FAIRCHILD AIR SERVICE

APL13

Yellow background of swastikas

1926, Apr. 7

CL9	APL13	(25c) blue & yellow *(5,600)*	30.00	
		Never hinged	45.00	
		Pane of 8	275.00	
		Flight cover, April 15, Rolling Portage to Red Lake or return, *each*		250.00
		Flight cover, May 27, Rouyn to Haileybury or return, *each*		350.00
		Commercial cover		500.00
a.		Imperf, pair	1,600.	
b.		Horiz. tête-bêche pair	150.00	
c.		Vert. tête-bêche pair	150.00	
d.		Filled-in wing on Pos. 8	100.00	
		On cover		300.00

No. CL9 was printed in sheets of 16 (4x4) and cut into panes of 8 (4x2).

ELLIOT-FAIRCHILD AIR TRANSPORT LTD.
Rouyn - Haileybury

APL14

1926, Aug. 12

CL10	APL14	(25c) dark red large perfs *(3,000)*	80.00	
		Never hinged	120.00	
		Flight cover, Aug. 12, Haileybury to Rouyn or return, *each*		225.00
		Commercial cover		450.00
		White dot over "o" of "Elliot," 4th stamp in vert. strip of 5	95.00	
		First Flight Cover		275.00
		Commercial cover		475.00
b.		(25c) light red with fine perfs *(2,000)*	80.00	
c.		As "b," white dot over "o" of "Elliot," 4th stamp in vert. strip of 5	95.00	
		First Flight Cover		275.00
		Commercial cover		475.00

No. CL10 was printed in sheets of 10 (2x5) and cut into panes of 5 (1x5).

FAIRCHILD AIR TRANSPORT LTD.
Northern Ontario to Rouyn Goldfields

APL15

1926, Oct. 19   *Perf. 12*

CL11	APL15	(25c) deep blue *(5,000)*	40.00	
		Never hinged	60.00	
		Pane of 10	450.00	
		Flight cover, Oct. 20, Haileybury to Rouyn or return, *each*		90.00
		Commercial cover		250.00
a.		Vertical tête-bêche pair	85.00	

No. CL11 was printed in sheets of 10 (2x5). The pairs of stamps in rows 1, 3 and 5 were normally printed upright, while those in rows 2 and 4 were printed inverted.

CL12	APL15	(25c) ultra *(5,000)*	45.00	
		Never hinged	67.50	
		Pane of 10	500.00	
a.		Horiz. tête-bêche pair, inverted on right	95.00	
b.		Horiz. tête-bêche pair, one stamp darker shade	150.00	
		Pane of 10, one column darker shade	1,250.	
c.		Pane with all stamps tete-beche	2,250.	
d.		Horiz. tête-bêche pair, inverted on left (from #C12c)	500.00	
e.		Vert. tête-bêche pair (from #C12c)	350.00	

No. CL12 was normally printed in sheets of 10 (2x5), with one column of 5 inverted (No. CL12a). It was also issued with one column in a darker shade (No. CL12b). Within No. CL12c, stamps in positions 1, 4, 5, 8 and 9 are inverted, so that all stamps form tête-bêche pairs with the stamps with which they are contiguous. No. CL12 was prepared but not issued.

PATRICIA AIRWAYS AND EXPLORATION CO., LTD.
Operated between Sioux Lookout and the Northern Ontario Goldfields, Woman Lake, Pine Ridge, Red Lake, Birch Lake, Ont., and Rouyn, Que.

APL16

Inscribed "Sioux Lookout to Pine Ridge and Red Lake"

1926, July 1

CL13	APL16	(25c) green & red, *yellow (12,800)*	65.00	
		Never hinged	100.00	
		Sheet of 8	700.00	
		First flight cover, July 7, Sioux Lookout to Red Lake		125.00
		Commercial cover		250.00
a.		Imperf, pair	375.00	
b.		Horiz. pair, imperf between, on cover (4 known)		500.00
c.		Small "t" in "TO" (pos. 8)	325.00	
		On cover		575.00
d.		No. CL13c in sheet of 8 with 7 #CL13	1,000.	
e.		Route inscription in black *(488)*	400.00	
		On cover		500.00
f.		As "e," small "t" in "TO"	500.00	
		On cover		650.00
g.		No. CL13f in sheet of 8 with 7 #CL13e	1,200.	
h.		Handstamped "FED" in red (only known on cover)		1,500.
i.		(25c) green & red, *pale yellow*	100.00	
		Sheet of 8	800.00	
		On cover		150.00
j.		As "i," small "t" in "TO"	750.00	
		On cover		750.00
k.		Route inscription inverted	4,000.	
		On cover		2,500.

Printed in sheets of 8 (2x4). Proofs exist in various formats and papers.

No. CL13 Surcharged in Red

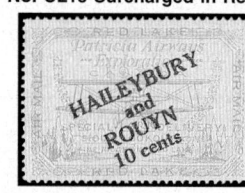

1927, Apr. 1

CL14	APL16	10c on (25c) green & red, *yellow, (1,800)*	135.00	
		Never hinged	200.00	
		Sheet of 8	1,200.	
		Cover, April 9, Rouyn to Haileybury		350.00
a.		On #CL13e	600.00	
		On flown cover		800.00
b.		On #CL13c	1,500.	
		On flown cover		1,500.
c.		Surcharge inverted	550.00	
d.		Double surcharge, one inverted	850.00	
e.		10c on (25c), *buff*	175.00	
		Sheet of 8	1,500.	
		On flown cover		350.00
f.		Broken "N" in "ROUYN"	175.00	
		Sheet of 8	1,500.	
		On flown cover		350.00
g.		Surcharge in light red	135.00	
		Sheet of 8	1,200.	
		On flown cover		350.00

No. CL13 Surcharged in Black

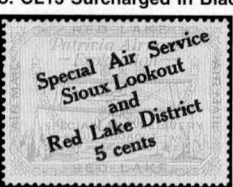

1927, Sept. (?)

CL15	APL16	5c on (25c) green & red, *yellow,* overprint ascending *(200)*	275.00	
		Never hinged	400.00	
		Sheet of 8	3,250.	
		On flown cover		375.00
a.		Overprint descending *(8)*	1,200.	
		On flown cover		1,400.
b.		Overprint in red, descending *(200)*	650.00	
		Sheet of 8	5,200.	
c.		As "b," malformed "O" in "LOOKOUT" (Plate 1, Pos. 7)	800.00	
		Sheet of 8, with 7 #CL15	2,800.	

No. CL13 Surcharged in Black

1927, Sept. (?)

CL16	APL16	10c on (25c) green & red, *yellow,* overprint ascending	800.00	
		Never hinged	1,200.	
		Sheet of 8	5,400.	
		On flown cover		1,600.
a.		Overprint descending	900.00	
		Never hinged	1,250.	
		On flown cover		1,600.
b.		Double overprint, descending	1,100.	
		Never hinged	1,400.	
c.		Inverted overprint	900.00	

200 stamps were overprinted, which included varieties.

No. CL14 Surcharged in Black

(No. CL17a)

1927, Aug.

CL17	APL16	10c on (25c) green & red, *yellow,* black overprint ascending *(200)*	750.00	
		Never hinged	1,050.	
		Sheet of 8	5,500.	
		On flown cover		850.00
a.		Black overprint descending	800.00	
		Never hinged	1,100.	
		On flown cover		1,600.
b.		As "a," inverted overprint	1,250.	
c.		Inverted red overprint, descending	800.00	
		Never hinged	1,600.	

APL17

Inscribed "Woman L Birch L via Sioux Lookout"

1926, July 7

CL18	APL17	(50c) black & red, *blue (1,800)*	200.00	
		Never hinged	300.	
		Sheet of 8	1,600.	
		Flight cover, Aug. 2, Sioux Lookout to Woman Lake or return, *each*		250.
a.		Imperf, pair	325.	
b.		Variety "OTT" in "LOOKOUT"	350.	
		On flown cover		450.
c.		Horiz. pair, imperf between	325.	
d.		As "c," "OTT" variety	450.	
e.		Additional "FED" in green ink	2,000.	
		On flown cover		1,400.
f.		As "e," "OTT" variety	2,500.	
		On flown cover		1,750.
g.		Missing route inscription	1,250.	
		Sheet of 8	10,000.	

No. CL18 on deep blue paper is a trial color proof. Value $500.

No. CL18 Surcharged in Red

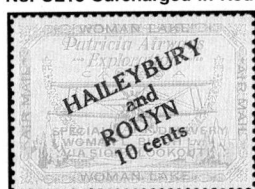

1926, July 7
CL19 APL17   10c on (50c)
       black & red, *blue*
       (770)   325.00
       Never hinged   500.00
       Sheet of 8   2,600.
       On flown cover   450.00
a.   Black overprint   1,200.
b.   Dark red overprint   325.00
       Sheet of 8   2,600.
       On flown cover   450.00
c.   Missing red overprint   5,500.

No. CL18 Surcharged in Black

1926, July 7
CL20 APL17   5c on (50c)   900.00
       black & red, *blue*,
       ovpt. ascending
       (200)   900.00
       Never hinged   1,350.
       Sheet of 8   7,250.
       On flown cover   1,000.
a.   Overprint descending
       (24)   900.00
       Sheet of 8   7,250.
       On flown cover   1,100.
b.   Ovpt. in red, ascending
       (200)   750.00
       Sheet of 8   6,000.
       On flown cover   1,000.
c.   Ovpt. in red, descend-
       ing *(24)*   900.00
       Sheet of 8   7,250.
       On flown cover   1,100.
d.   As "c," malformed "O"
       in "LOOKOUT" (Plate
       1, Position 7)   1,100.
       On flown cover   1,200.
       Sheet of 8, 1 #CL20d
       with 7 #CL20c   *7,500.*

No. CL18 Overprinted in Black

1926, July 7
CL21 APL17   (50c) black
       & red, *blue*, ovpt.
       descending *(24)*   1,300.
       Never hinged   2,000.
       On flown cover   1,350.
a.   Overprint in violet, as-
       cending *(16)*   1,500.
       Never hinged   2,250.
       On flown cover   1,800.
b.   Overprint in violet, de-
       scending *(16)*   1,500.
       Never hinged   2,250.
       Sheet of 8   17,500.
       On flown cover   1,500.
c.   Double overprint in vio-
       let (ascending)   1,800.
       Never hinged   2,750.
d.   Overprinted in violet,
       horizontal   1,600.
       Never hinged   2,400.
       On flown cover   1,800.

No. CL18 Surcharged in Red and Overprinted in Black

1926, July 7
CL22 APL17   10c on (50c)
       black & red, *blue*,
       ovpt. ascending
       (24)   1,000.
       Never hinged   1,500.
       Sheet of 8   8,400.
       On flown cover   1,150.
a.   Overprint descending
       (24)   1,050.
       Sheet of 8   8,500.
       On flown cover   1,050.
b.   Overprint inverted, as-
       cending *(16)*   1,200.
       Sheet of 8   9,600.
       On flown cover   1,300.
c.   Overprint inverted, de-
       scending *(16)*   1,100.
       Sheet of 8   8,800.
       On flown cover   1,300.
d.   As "a," broken "N" in
       "ROUYN"   1,100.
       On flown cover   1,250.
e.   As "a," surcharge in
       light red   1,100.
       On flown cover   1,250.
f.   As "b," broken "N" in
       "ROUYN"   1,400.
       On flown cover   1,500.

Nos. CL18-CL22 on commercially flown covers are very elusive and command premium prices.

APL18

CL23 APL18   (50c) green
       & red, *yellow*   700.00
       Never hinged   1,000.
       Sheet of 8   5,600.
a.   Imperf, pair   750.00
       Never hinged   1,100.

CL23 exists with rouletting doubled.

No. CL23 Surcharged in Red

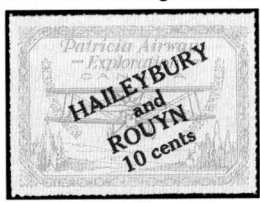

CL24 APL18   10c on (50c)
       green & red, *yel-
       low* *(800)*   135.00
       Never hinged   200.00
       Sheet of 8   1,100.
       On flown cover   250.00

No. CL23 Surcharged in Black

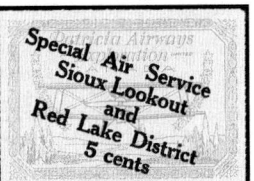

CL25 APL18   5c on
       (50c) green & red,
       yellow, descend-
       ing *(800)*   65.00
       Never hinged   95.00
       Sheet of 8   575.00
       On flown cover   185.00
a.   Overprint in red, de-
       scending *(1368)*   45.00
       Never hinged   65.00
       Sheet of 8   475.00

b.   On flown cover   185.00
       Overprint in green, de-
       scending   45.00
       Never hinged   65.00
       Sheet of 8   475.00
c.   On flown cover   185.00
       Overprint in green, as-
       cending *(4448)*   45.00
       Never hinged   65.00
       Sheet of 8   475.00
d.   On flown cover   185.00
       As "a," *pale yellow*   175.00
e.   As "c," *pale yellow*   175.00

The overprint on Nos. CL25a-CL25c exists with the third "O" in "LOOKOUT" malformed (plate 1, position 7). Values, each: unused $450; on flown cover $500.

No. CL23 Surcharged in Black

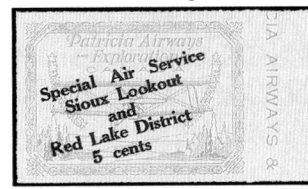

CL26 APL18   5c on
       (50c) green & red,
       yellow, ascending
       (800)   125.00
       Never hinged   175.00
       Sheet of 8   1,100.
       On flown cover   215.00
a.   Inverted overprint   500.00
b.   Horiz. pair, left stamp
       overprinted "RED
       LAKE" in red, de-
       scending   800.00
c.   Overprint in red, as-
       cending *(800)*   125.00
       Sheet of 8   1,150.
       On flown cover   300.00
d.   As "c," overprint invert-
       ed   400.00
e.   Overprint in green
       (800)   135.00
       Sheet of 8   1,200.
       On flown cover   250.00
f.   As "e," overprint in-
       verted   450.00

No. CL24 Surcharged in Black

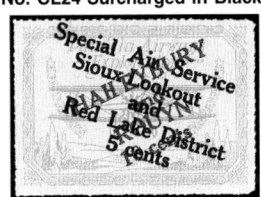

CL27 APL18   5c on 10c
       on (50c) green &
       red, *yellow (400)*   400.00
       Never hinged   600.00
       Sheet of 8   2,800.
       On flown cover   550.00
a.   Pair, one stamp miss-
       ing 5c overprint   850.00

No. CL24 Surcharged in Black

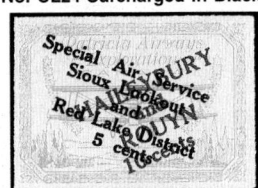

CL28 APL18   5c on 10c
       on (50c) green &
       red, *yellow (400-
       600)*   175.00
       Never hinged   250.00
       Sheet of 8   1,400.
       On flown cover   350.00
a.   Black overprint invert-
       ed   450.00
b.   On *pale yellow*   175.00
       Never hinged   250.00

No. CL24 Ovptd. in Black, Purple or Green

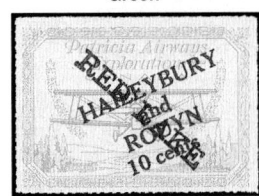

CL29 APL18   10c on (50c)
       green & red, *yel-
       low*, Black ovpt.,
       descending   200.00
       Never hinged   300.00
       Sheet of 8   1,600.
       On flown cover   350.00
a.   Overprint ascending   200.00
       Never hinged   300.00
       Sheet of 8   1,600.
       On flown cover   350.00
b.   As #CL29, overprint
       inverted   250.00
       Never hinged   375.00
       Sheet of 8   2,000.
       On flown cover   375.00
c.   As #CL29a, overprint
       inverted   250.00
       Never hinged   375.00
       Sheet of 8   2,000.
       On flown cover   375.00
d.   Overprint in purple,
       descending   200.00
       Never hinged   300.00
       Sheet of 8   1,600.
       On flown cover   350.00
e.   Overprint in purple,
       ascending   200.00
       Never hinged   300.00
       Sheet of 8   1,600.
       On flown cover   350.00
f.   As #CL29d, overprint
       inverted   250.00
       Never hinged   375.00
       Sheet of 8   2,000.
       On flown cover   375.00
g.   As #CL29e, overprint
       inverted   250.00
       Never hinged   375.00
       Sheet of 8   2,000.
       On flown cover   375.00
h.   Overprint in green, de-
       scending   200.00
       Never hinged   300.00
       Sheet of 8   1,600.
       On flown cover   350.00
i.   Overprint in green, as-
       cending   200.00
       Never hinged   300.00
       Sheet of 8   1,600.
       On flown cover   350.00
j.   As #CL29h, overprint
       inverted   250.00
       Never hinged   375.00
       Sheet of 8   2,000.
       On flown cover   375.00
k.   As #CL29i, overprint
       inverted   250.00
       Never hinged   375.00
       Sheet of 8   2,000.
       On flown cover   375.00

No. CL23 Overprinted in Black

CL30 APL18   50c green &
       red, *yellow*, Black
       ovpt., descending   95.00
       Never hinged   150.00
       Sheet of 8   800.00
       On flown cover   135.00
a.   Overprint ascending   95.00
       Never hinged   150.00
       Sheet of 8   800.00
       On flown cover   135.00
b.   As #CL30, overprint
       inverted   175.00
       Never hinged   225.00
c.   As #CL30a, overprint
       inverted   175.00
       Never hinged   225.00
d.   Imperf, pair   400.00
e.   Overprint in red, de-
       scending   95.00
       Sheet of 8   800.00
       On flown cover   135.00
f.   Overprint in red, as-
       cending   95.00
       Sheet of 8   800.00
       On flown cover   135.00
g.   As #CL30e, overprint
       inverted   175.00
       Never hinged   225.00
h.   As #CL30f, overprint
       inverted   175.00
       Never hinged   225.00
i.   Imperf, pair   400.00
j.   Overprint in green, de-
       scending   95.00
       Never hinged   150.00
       Sheet of 8   800.00
       On flown cover   135.00
k.   As "j," imperf pair   550.00
l.   Overprint in green, as-
       cending   95.00

Never hinged	150.00	
Sheet of 8	800.00	
On flown cover		135.00
m. As #CL30j, overprint inverted	175.00	
Never hinged	225.00	
n. As #CL30k, overprint inverted	550.00	
Never hinged	675.00	
o. Double overprint, one red, one green	450.00	
p. Plane inverted, ovpt. in red, descending	2,250.	
q. Plane inverted, ovpt. in red, ascending	2,250.	
r. As "q," overprint inverted	2,250.	
s. As "q," ovpt. in black	3,000.	
t. As "q," ovpt. in green	2,250.	

Nos. CL23-CL30 on commercially flown covers are very elusive and command premium prices.

WESTERN CANADA AIRWAYS SERVICE

APL19

1927, May 1 — Perf. 12

CL40 APL19 (10c) black & pink (36,600)	7.00	
Never hinged	10.00	
Pane of 50	400.00	
First flight cover, *June 1, 1927, Lac du Bonnet to Long Lake*		250.00
Flight cover, later flight		50.00
Commercial cover		150.00
a. (10c) black & pale rose (10,000)	8.50	
Never hinged	12.50	
Pane of 50	450.00	
b. As "a," black double	300.00	
c. (10c) black & dark red (10,000)	9.00	
d. Vertical pair, imperf between	500.00	
e. Horizontal pair, imperf between	500.00	

Issued in sheets of 200, cut into panes of 50.
The Western Canada Airways Service had bases in northern Ontario, Manitoba, Saskatchewan, Alberta and Northwest Territories. No. CL40 was sold at the Winnipeg post offices and at other Canadian offices, as well as being available from the air service itself.

Jubilee Issue

APL20

1927, July 1 — Thick Paper

CL41 APL20 (10c) black & orange (10,000)	15.00
Never hinged	22.50
Pane of 50	750.00
Jubilee flight cover, *July 1, Rolling Portage to Red Lake*	425.00
Same, printed map on reverse of cover	750.00
Other flight covers, *July 1*	425.00
Commercial cover	600.00
d. Vertical pair, imperf between	550.00

Issued to commemorate the 60th anniversary of Canadian Confederation.
Issued in sheets of 200, cut into panes of 50.
Valid for one day only. Many cachets exist.

YUKON AIRWAYS & EXPLORATION CO., LTD.

APL21

1927, Nov. 11 — Perf. 12

CL42 APL21 25c dark blue (10,000)	45.00	
Never hinged	65.00	
Flight cover, *April 2, 1928, Mayo Landing to White Horse*		175.00
Flight cover, *April 13, 1928*		50.00
Commercial cover		450.00
a. Booklet pane of 10, with tab	500.00	
Complete booklet of 10 #CL42a (2 known)	5,000.	
b. Imperf, pair	5,000.	
c. "ArRWAYS" variety	275.00	
On cover		500.00
d. 25c light blue (1,200)	150.00	
Never hinged	225.00	
On cover		50.00
e. Double print	350.00	
f. As "e," "ArRWAYS" variety	550.00	
g. As "e," strip of 10 with "ArRWAYS" variety, never hinged	4,500.	
h. Horiz. pair, imperf vertically	2,000.	
Never hinged	2,500.	
Horiz. strip of 16 (8x2) with selvage on both sides	19,000.	

No. CL42 was printed in sheets of 80 and cut into vertical strips of 10 for sale in booklets containing 10 strips with a plain brown cover. The No. CL42h strip of 16 proves the sheet size was 80 stamps (8x10) before cutting into panes for booklet sales.
No. CL42g is unique.

PATRICIA AIRWAYS LTD.

APL22

1928, Mar. 5 — Rouletted

CL43 APL22 (10c) green & red, *yellow* (3,200)	50.00
Never hinged	75.00
Sheet of 8	400.00
Flight cover, *Mar. 9, 1928, Sioux Lookout to Gold Pines*	225.00
Flight cover, other flights	225.00
Commercial cover	350.00
a. Plane inverted	1,250.
Never hinged	1,850.
b. Imperf, pair	700.00

Printed in sheets of 8 (2x4)

BRITISH COLUMBIA AIRWAYS LTD.
Operated between Vancouver and Victoria, B.C.

APL23

1928, Aug. 3

CL44 APL23 5c ultra (110,000)	15.00
Never hinged	17.50
First flight cover, *Aug. 3, 1928,, Victoria to Vancouver*	150.00
Covers flown Aug. 4-25	275.00

Issued in sheets of 220, cut into panes of 55.

KLONDIKE AIRWAYS LTD.
Operated between bases in the Yukon

APL24

1928, Oct. 4

CL45 APL24 25c blue (110,000)	65.00	
Never hinged	95.00	
Pane of 4 with tab	300.00	
On cover		400.00

Issued in panes of four (1x4), rouletted between the stamps.

CHERRY RED AIRLINE LTD.
Northern Saskatchewan

APL25

1929, July 3 — Perf. 12

CL46 APL25 10c black & red (24,000)	12.00
Never hinged	15.00
First flight cover, *Dec. 25, 1929, Prince Albert to Ile a la Crosse*	45.00
Other flight covers	40.00

COMMERCIAL AIRWAYS LTD.
Northern Alberta and Northwest Territories

APL26

1929, May 18

CL47 APL26 10c black (3,000)	125.00
Never hinged	175.00
Pane of 10	1,200.
First flight cover, *May 21, 1929, Edmonton to Grande Prairie*	100.00

APL27

1930, June 2

CL48 APL27 10c black (2,000)	15.00	
Never hinged	18.50	
Pane of 10	150.00	
First flight cover, *Dec. 12, 1930, Edmonton to Peace River or return*		50.00
a. 10c deep black on thin paper	15.00	
Pane of 10	150.00	
b. Imperf, pair	300.00	

1930, July 21

CL49 APL27 10c purple (2,000)	200.00	
Never hinged	300.00	
Pane of 10	1,800.	
Flight cover, *July 23, 1930, Edmonton to Ft. McMurray or return*		250.00
a. Imperf, pair	500.00	
Imperf single on cover		450.00
b. Vertical pair, imperf between	1,400.	

Of the 2,000 stamps printed, approximately 700 were destroyed.

1930, Dec. 6

CL50 APL27 10c orange thick paper (5,000)	17.50	
Never hinged	21.00	
Pane of 10	175.00	
Flight cover, *Feb. 24, 1931, Ft. McMurray to Athabaska or return*		70.00
a. On thin paper	17.50	
Pane of 10	175.00	
b. Imperf, pair	300.00	

Nos. CL47-CL50 were printed in panes of 10 (2x5).

CANADIAN AIRWAYS LTD.
Northern Alberta and Northwest Territories, Manitoba Mining Areas

APL28

1932

CL51 APL28 (10c) blue & orange (2,000)	30.00
Never hinged	45.00
Flight cover, *Dec. 30, 1932, Edmonton to Ft. McMurray or return*	70.00
a. Horizontal pair, imperf between (20 pairs)	700.00
b. Vertical pair, imperf between (10 pairs)	700.00

Printed in sheets of 200, cut into panes of 50.

No. CL51 Surcharged in Black

1934

CL52 APL28 10c on (10c) blue & orange	25.00
Never hinged	32.50
Flight cover, *July 19, 1934, Edmonton to Ft. McMurray or return*	75.00
a. Inverted surcharge (50)	1,000.
Never hinged	1,250.
b. Double surcharge (10)	1,000.
c. Pair, one with inverted surcharge	2,000.

SPECIAL DELIVERY STAMPS

All cover values in this section are for uses on commercial covers.

SD1

Unwmk.

1898, June 28 — Engr. — Perf. 12

E1 SD1 10c blue green	110.00	11.00
Never hinged	300.00	
On cover		140.00
Plate block of 4 (pl. 2)	550.00	
Never hinged	950.00	
Plate block of 6 (pl. 1)	750.00	
Never hinged	1,250.	
a. 10c green	110.00	11.00
Never hinged	300.00	
On cover		200.00
Plate block of 4 (pl. 2)	560.00	
Never hinged	950.00	
Plate block of 6 (pl. 1)	750.00	
Never hinged	1,250.	
b. 10c yellow green	150.00	18.50
Never hinged	450.00	
On cover		240.00
Plate block of 4 (pl. 2)	750.00	
Never hinged	1,250.	
Plate block of 6 (pl. 1)	1,100.	
Never hinged	1,900.	

Due to plate wear, the last examples of No. E1 printed show no shading in the value tablet areas. Such examples sell for only slightly more than normal stamps, either unused, used or on cover.

SD2

1922, Aug. 21
E2 SD2 20c carmine, dry printing (42½ wide) 100.00 9.00
Never hinged 220.00
On cover 32.50
Plate block of 4 1,100.
Never hinged 1,900.
a. 20c scarlet, wet printing (41mm wide) 150.00 18.00
Never hinged 250.00
On cover 35.00
Plate block of 4 1,150.
Never hinged 1,800.

Five Stages of Mail Transportation SD3

1927, June 29
E3 SD3 20c orange 35.00 17.50
Never hinged 70.00
On cover 55.00
Plate block of 6 210.00
Never hinged 360.00
a. Imperf., pair 200.00
Never hinged 275.00
b. Horiz. pair, imperf. vert. 190.00
Never hinged 275.00
c. Vert. pair, imperf. horiz. 190.00
Never hinged 275.00

No. E3 forms part of the Confederation Commemorative issue.

SD4

1930, Sept. 2   Perf. 11
E4 SD4 20c henna brown 65.00 15.00
Never hinged 125.00
On cover 67.50
Plate block of 4 300.00
Never hinged 550.00

SD5

1932, Dec. 24
E5 SD5 20c henna brown 60.00 16.00
Never hinged 115.00
On cover 60.00
Plate block of 4 300.00
Never hinged 550.00
a. Imperf., pair 650.00
Never hinged 950.00

Allegory of Progress — SD6

1935, June 1   Perf. 12
E6 SD6 20c dark carmine 14.00 7.50
Never hinged 22.50
On cover 32.50
Plate block of 4 (LL 1) 92.50
Never hinged 140.00
Plate block of 6 120.00
Never hinged 180.00
a. Imperf., pair 650.00
Never hinged 950.00

Arms of Canada — SD7

1938-39
E7 SD7 10c dk green (4/1/39) 7.00 3.25
Never hinged 11.00
On cover 24.00
Plate block of 4 52.50
Never hinged 75.00
a. Imperf., pair 725.00
Never hinged 1,250.
E8 SD7 20c dark carmine (6/15/38) 30.00 25.00
Never hinged 50.00
On cover 50.00
Plate block of 4 (LL 1) 210.00
Never hinged 275.00
Plate block of 6 250.00
Never hinged 325.00
a. Imperf., pair 650.00
Never hinged 950.00

No. E8 Surcharged in Black

1939, Mar. 1
E9 SD7 10c on 20c dk car 8.00 6.50
Never hinged 12.00
On cover 27.50
Plate block of 4 (LL 1) 37.50
Never hinged 50.00
Plate block of 6 52.50
Never hinged 75.00

Coat of Arms and Flags SD8

1942, July 1
E10 SD8 10c green 3.25 2.00
Never hinged 4.50
On cover 9.50
Plate block of 4 22.50
Never hinged 30.00
a. Imperf., pair 650.00
Never hinged 950.00

Canada's contribution to the war effort of the Allied Nations.

> **Catalogue values for unused stamps in this section, from this point to the end of the section, are for Never Hinged items.**

Arms of Canada — SD9

1946, Sept. 16
E11 SD9 10c green 4.25 1.10
On cover 8.00
Plate block of 4 20.00

The laurel and olive branches symbolize Victory and Peace.
For overprints see Nos. EO1, EO2.

SPECIAL DELIVERY OFFICIAL STAMPS

> **Catalogue values for unused stamps in this section are for Never Hinged items.**

> **All cover values in this section are for uses on commercial covers.**

No. E11 Overprinted in Black

1950   Unwmk.   Perf. 12
EO1 SD9 10c green 17.50 15.00
On cover 67.50
Plate block of 4 70.00

Same Overprinted

EO2 SD9 10c green 25.00 20.00
On cover 80.00
Plate block of 4 120.00

REGISTRATION STAMPS

> **All cover values in this section are for uses on commercial covers.**

R1

1875-88   Unwmk.   Engr.   Perf. 12
F1 R1 2c orange 115.00 5.75
Never hinged 250.00
On cover 40.00
a. 2c vermilion 170.00 15.00
Never hinged 375.00
On cover 40.00
b. 2c rose carmine 340.00 110.00
Never hinged 725.00
On cover 85.00
c. As "a," imperf., pair —
d. Perf. 12x11½ 525.00 100.00
Never hinged 1,100.
On cover 160.00
F2 R1 5c dark green 150.00 6.00
Never hinged 300.00
On cover 40.00
a. 5c blue green ('88) 160.00 6.00
Never hinged 325.00
On cover 40.00
b. 5c yellow green 240.00 7.50
Never hinged 475.00
On cover 40.00
c. Imperf., pair 1,200.
Never hinged 1,700.
d. Perf. 12x11½ 1,300. 240.00
Never hinged 2,500.
On cover 325.00
F3 R1 8c dull blue ('76) 600.00 350.00
Never hinged 1,500.
On cover 12,000.
a. 8c bright blue 450.00 350.00
Never hinged 1,050.
On cover 12,000.
Nos. F1-F3 (3) 865.00 361.75

Value for No. F3 on cover is for a correct usage in 1876-1877.
The used No. F1c is unique (fine centering).

POSTAGE DUE STAMPS

> **All cover values in this section are for uses on commercial covers.**
> On cover values are for stamps tied by postal cancellations such as datestamps or rollers. Covers with stamps uncanceled or tied by crayon marks sell for much less.

D1   D2

1906-28   Unwmk.   Engr.   Perf. 12
J1 D1 1c violet 25.00 4.75
Never hinged 40.00
On cover 20.00
a. Thin paper ('24) 45.00 7.50
Never hinged 80.00
b. Imperf., pair 400.00
c. 1c reddish violet ('28) 25.00 4.75
Never hinged 40.00
J2 D1 2c violet 25.00 1.00
Never hinged 40.00
On cover 12.00
a. Thin paper ('24) 45.00 11.00
Never hinged 80.00
b. Imperf., pair 400.00
c. 2c reddish violet ('28) 25.00 1.00
Never hinged 40.00
J3 D1 4c violet ('28) 65.00 22.50
Never hinged 110.00
On cover 40.00
J4 D1 5c violet 25.00 2.00
Never hinged 40.00
On cover 40.00
a. As "c," thin paper 20.00 7.50
Never hinged 35.00
b. Imperf., pair 400.00
c. 5c reddish violet ('28) 25.00 2.00
Never hinged 40.00
J5 D1 10c violet ('28) 85.00 14.00
Never hinged 160.00
On cover 80.00
Nos. J1-J5 (5) 225.00 44.25
#J1-J5, never hinged 390.00

In 1924 there was a printing of Nos. J1, J2 and J4 on thin semi-transparent paper. Imperf pairs are without gum.

1930-32   Perf. 11
J6 D2 1c dark violet 12.50 4.25
Never hinged 22.50
On cover, single franking 20.00
Plate block of 4 225.00
Never hinged 350.00
J7 D2 2c dark violet 7.00 1.10
Never hinged 12.50
On cover, single franking 16.00
Plate block of 4 175.00
Never hinged 260.00
J8 D2 4c dark violet 20.00 5.50
Never hinged 35.00
On cover, single franking 20.00
Plate block of 4 275.00
Never hinged 375.00
J9 D2 5c dark violet 25.00 6.50
Never hinged 42.50
On cover 40.00
Plate block of 4 275.00
Never hinged 375.00
J10 D2 10c dark violet ('32) 110.00 10.00
Never hinged 200.00
On cover 50.00
Plate block of 4 650.00
Never hinged 950.00
a. Vert. pair, imperf. horiz. 1,750. —
Never hinged 2,750.
Nos. J6-J10 (5) 174.50 27.35
#J6-J10, never hinged 312.50

No. J10a is valued in the grade of fine.

D3

1933-34
J11 D3 1c dark violet ('34) 15.00 6.50
Never hinged 27.50
On cover, single franking 20.00
Plate block of 4 80.00
Never hinged 125.00
a. Imperf., pair 400.00
Never hinged 575.00
J12 D3 2c dark violet 7.50 1.25
Never hinged 13.00
On cover, single franking 16.00
Plate block of 4 60.00
Never hinged 90.00
J13 D3 4c dark violet 15.00 8.00
Never hinged 27.50
On cover, single franking 20.00
Plate block of 4 75.00
Never hinged 110.00
J14 D3 10c dark violet 35.00 6.50
Never hinged 57.50
On cover 47.50

Plate block of 4	175.00	
Never hinged	250.00	
Nos. J11-J14 (4)	72.50	22.25
Nos. J11-J14, never hinged	115.50	

Catalogue values for unused stamps in this section, from this point to the end of the section, are for Never Hinged items.

D4

1935-65   *Perf. 12*

J15	D4	1c dark violet	.30	.25
	On cover, single franking			12.00
	Plate block of 4 (LL 1)		1.90	
	Plate block of 6		3.00	
	Plate block of 10		3.75	
a.	Imperf., pair		200.00	
b.	1c red violet ('40)		2.25	.55
	Plate block of 4 (LL 1)		9.00	
	Plate block of 6		15.00	
	Plate block of 10		20.00	
J16	D4	2c dark violet	.30	.25
	On cover, single franking			8.00
	Plate block of 4 (LL 1)		1.90	
	Plate block of 6		3.00	
	Plate block of 10		3.75	
a.	Imperf., pair		200.00	
c.	2c red violet		1.90	.55
	Plate block of 4 (LL 1, LL 2)		9.00	
	Plate block of 6		15.00	
	Plate block of 10		20.00	
J16B	D4	3c dark vio ('65)	2.00	1.50
	On cover, single franking			40.00
	Plate block of 4 (LL 1)		15.00	
	Plate block of 6		22.50	
	Plate block of 10		30.00	
J17	D4	4c dark violet	.35	.25
	On cover, single franking			12.00
	Plate block of 4		2.25	
	Plate block of 6		3.75	
	Plate block of 10		4.50	
a.	Imperf., pair		200.00	
b.	4c red violet		1.50	.55
	Plate block of 4 (LL 1)		9.00	
	Plate block of 6		15.00	
	Plate block of 10		21.00	
J18	D4	5c dark vio ('48)	.40	.35
	On cover, single franking			20.00
	Plate block of 4 (LL 1)		3.00	
	Plate block of 6		4.90	
	Plate block of 10		6.00	
a.	5c red violet		3.00	1.10
	Plate block of 4 (LL 1)		15.00	
	Plate block of 6		22.50	
	Plate block of 10		30.00	
J19	D4	6c dark vio ('57)	2.25	1.75
	On cover, single franking			16.00
	Plate block of 4 (LL 1)		12.00	
	Plate block of 6		19.00	
	Plate block of 10		22.50	
J20	D4	10c dark violet	.40	.25
	On cover, single franking			12.00
	Plate block of 4 (LL 1)		2.60	
	Plate block of 6		4.00	
	Plate block of 10		5.25	
a.	Imperf., pair		200.00	
b.	10c red violet		1.50	.55
	Plate block of 4 (LL 1)		13.00	
	Plate block of 6		19.00	
	Plate block of 10		26.00	
	Nos. J15-J20 (7)		6.00	4.60

WAR TAX STAMPS

All cover values in this section are for uses on commercial covers.

WT1

Unwmk.
1915, Mar. 25   Engr.   *Perf. 12*

MR1	WT1	1c green	25.00	.40
	Never hinged		60.00	
	On cover			1.60
MR2	WT1	2c carmine	25.00	.40
	Never hinged		60.00	
	On cover			4.00
a.	2c rose carmine		30.00	.60
	Never hinged		70.00	
	On cover			4.00

In 1915 postage stamps of 5, 20 and 50 cents were overprinted "WAR TAX" in two lines. These stamps were intended for fiscal use, the war tax on postal matter being 1 cent. A few of these stamps were used to pay postage.

WT2

Type I   Type II

TWO TYPES:

Type I — There is a colored line between two white lines below the large letter "T."

Type II — The right half of the colored line is replaced by two short diagonal lines and five small dots.

1916

MR3	WT2	2c + 1c car		
		(I)	40.00	.25
	Never hinged		100.00	
	On cover			1.60
a.	2c + 1c carmine (II)		275.00	4.50
	Never hinged		625.00	
	On cover			8.00
b.	2c + 1c rose red (I)		45.00	.40
	Never hinged		110.00	
	On cover			1.60
MR4	WT2	2c + 1c brn		
		(II)	25.00	.25
	Never hinged		62.50	
	On cover			1.20
a.	2c + 1c brown (I)		700.00	10.00
	Never hinged		1,300.	
	On cover			16.00
b.	Imperf., pair (I)		200.00	
c.	Imperf., pair (II)		2,250.	

Nos. MR4b and MR4c were made without gum.

Perf. 12x8

MR5	WT2	2c + 1c car		
		(I)	65.00	30.00
	Never hinged		140.00	
	On cover			32.50

Coil Stamps
Perf. 8 Vertically

MR6	WT2	2c + 1c car		
		(I)	150.00	9.00
	Never hinged		350.00	
	On cover			10.00
	Pair		280.00	110.00
	Never hinged		475.00	
	On cover			*150.00*
	Paste-up pair		340.00	—
	Never hinged		550.00	
MR7	WT2	2c + 1c brn		
		(II)	45.00	2.50
	Never hinged		100.00	
	On cover			8.00
	Pair		65.00	15.00
	Never hinged		120.00	
	On cover			15.00
	Paste-up pair		110.00	—
	Never hinged		190.00	
a.	2c + 1c brown (I)		200.00	7.50
	Never hinged		500.00	
	On cover			10.00
	Pair		375.00	75.00
	Never hinged		850.00	
	Paste-up pair		410.00	—
	Never hinged		750.00	

OFFICIAL STAMPS

PERFORATED OFFICIAL STAMPS
Stamps perforated "O.H.M.S." (On His Majesty's Service) were introduced in May 1923 for use in the Receiver General's office of the Finance Department and by the Assistant Receiver Generals' offices in provincial cities. In 1935, the Post Office Department became responsible for perforating these stamps, and on March 28, 1939, the Treasury Board ruled that on and after June 30, 1939, all postage stamps used by government offices had to be perforated "O.H.M.S." These stamps continued to be produced until they were replaced by the overprinted "O.H.M.S." stamps in 1949.

The perforated initials can appear either upright, inverted, or sideways reading up or down on any given stamp, and further can be right-reading either from the front of the stamp or from the reverse. Thus, eight varieties are possible for each stamp, though not all

stamps are known with all possible varieties. This catalogue values only the most common orientation.

The perfins come in two styles, as shown below. Stamps perforated with five holes in the vertical bars of the "H" are valued only used, because unused examples are rarely seen.

Values are for very fine examples with the stamp itself well centered and the perforations undamaged by encroaching perfin holes. Stamps in a grade below very fine and/or with damaged perforations will sell for less.

Beware of forgeries. On used stamps, be aware that ink from cancellations will tend to "bleed" into the perfin holes of genuine examples, whereas it will not on most forgeries, which almost always were made using already canceled stamps. As with all scarce issues that may be forged, dealing with reputable and knowledgable sources and using recognized expertizing authorities is recommended.

Stamps overprinted "O.H.M.S." or "G" follow No. OE11.

5-HOLE PERFINS

Large "O.H.M.S" 5 Holes in Vertical Bars of "H"

(OA plus Scott No.)

For die types of the 1c and 3c see postage.

1912-25   *Perf. 12*

OA104	A43	1c green	50.00
OA105	A43	1c yellow (I)	
		('22)	45.00
d.	1c yellow (II)		45.00
OA106	A43	2c carmine	45.00
OA107	A43	2c yel green	
		('22)	34.00
a.	Thin paper ('24)		45.00
OA108	A43	3c brown ('18)	40.00
OA109	A43	3c car (I) ('23)	34.00
c.	Die II ('24)		40.00
OA110	A43	4c olive bister	
		('22)	45.00
OA111	A43	5c dark blue	50.00
OA112	A43	5c violet ('22)	45.00
a.	Thin paper ('24)		50.00
OA113	A43	7c yellow ocher	72.50
OA114	A43	7c red brn ('24)	62.50
OA115	A43	8c blue ('25)	72.50
OA116	A43	10c plum	72.50
OA117	A43	10c blue ('22)	50.00
OA118	A43	10c bis brn ('25)	34.00
OA119	A43	20c olive grn	
		('25)	50.00
OA120	A43	50c blk brn, dry printing	
		('25)	85.00
a.	50c black, wet printing		120.00
OA122	A43	$1 orange ('23)	125.00

Coil Stamp
1918   *Perf. 8 Vertically*

OA129	A43	3c brown	400.00

50th Anniv. of the Canadian Confederation
1917   *Perf. 12*

OA135	A44	3c brown	400.00

60th Year of the Canadian Confederation
1927

OA141	A45	1c orange	45.00
OA142	A46	2c green	62.50
OA143	A47	3c brown car	72.50
OA144	A48	5c violet	50.00
OA145	A49	12c dark blue	340.00

1927, June 29

OA146	A50	5c violet	45.00
OA147	A51	12c green	250.00
OA148	A52	20c brown car	170.00

Definitives
1928-29

OA149	A53	1c orange	55.00
OA150	A53	2c green	40.00
OA151	A53	3c dk car	85.00
OA152	A53	4c bister ('29)	110.00
OA153	A53	5c dp violet	40.00
OA154	A53	8c blue	110.00
OA155	A54	10c green	35.00

OA156	A55	12c gray ('29)	340.00
OA157	A56	20c dk car ('29)	100.00
OA158	A57	50c dk blue ('29)	525.00
OA159	A58	$1 olive grn ('29)	125.00

1930-31   *Perf. 11*
For die types of the 1c and 2c see postage.

OA162	A59	1c orange	55.00
OA163	A59	1c deep green (II)	28.00
b.	Die I (12/6/30)		34.00
OA164	A59	2c dull green (I)	140.00
OA165	A59	2c deep red (I)	45.00
a.	Die II		40.00
OA166	A59	2c dk brn (II) ('31)	45.00
b.	Die I		50.00
OA167	A59	3c deep red ('31)	35.00
OA168	A59	4c yel bister	95.00
OA169	A59	5c dull violet	67.50
OA170	A59	5c dull blue	55.00
OA171	A59	8c dark blue	95.00
OA172	A59	8c red orange	85.00
OA173	A60	10c olive green	45.00
OA174	A61	12c gray black	225.00
OA175	A62	20c brown red	100.00
OA176	A63	50c dull blue	150.00
OA177	A64	$1 dk ol green	350.00

George V Type of 1912-25
1931   *Perf. 12x8*

OA184	A43	3c carmine	110.00

Sir Georges Etienne Cartier
1931   *Perf. 11*

OA190	A65	10c dark green	57.50

Nos. 165, 165a Surcharged
1932

OA191	A59	3c on 2c dp red (II)	55.00
a.	Die I		62.50

Imperial Economic Conference, Ottawa
1932

OA192	A66	3c deep red	40.00
OA193	A67	5c dull blue	75.00
OA194	A68	13c deep green	375.00

Type of 1930 and King George V
For die types of the 3c see postage.
1932

OA195	A69	1c dark green	35.00
OA196	A69	2c black brown	35.00
OA197	A69	3c deep red (I)	35.00
OA198	A69	4c ocher	110.00
OA199	A69	5c dark blue	55.00
OA200	A69	8c red orange	110.00
OA201	A61	13c dull violet	110.00

UPU Executive Meeting, Ottawa
1933

OA202	A70	5c dark blue	110.00

World's Grain Exhibition and Conference at Regina
1933

OA203	A62	20c brown red	160.00

Steamship Royal William
1933

OA204	A71	5c dark blue	110.00

Landing of Jacques Cartier, 400th Anniv.
1934

OA208	A72	3c blue	140.00

Emigration of the United Empire Loyalists from the US to Canada, 150th anniv.
1934

OA209	A73	10c olive green	160.00

150th anniv. of the Founding of the Province of New Brunswick
1934

OA210	A74	2c red brown	160.00

25th anniv. of the accession to the throne of George V
1935   *Perf. 12*

OA211	A75	1c green	67.50
OA212	A76	2c brown	77.50
OA213	A77	3c carmine	100.00
OA214	A78	5c blue	100.00
OA215	A79	10c green	260.00
OA216	A80	13c dark blue	260.00

Definitives
1935

OA217	A81	1c green	40.00	
OA218	A81	2c brown	67.50	
OA219	A81	3c dk carmine	62.50	
OA220	A81	4c yellow	105.00	
OA221	A81	5c blue	62.50	
OA222	A81	8c dp orange	105.00	
OA223	A82	10c car rose	85.00	
OA224	A83	13c violet	105.00	
OA225	A84	20c olive green	110.00	
OA226	A85	50c dull violet	77.50	
OA227	A86	$1 deep blue	210.00	

King George VI
1937

OA231	A87	1c green	5.00	
OA232	A87	2c brown	6.25	
OA233	A87	3c carmine	5.00	
OA234	A87	4c yellow	16.00	
OA235	A87	5c blue	12.50	
OA236	A87	8c orange	35.00	

Coronation of King George VI and Queen Elizabeth
1937

OA237	A88	3c carmine	95.00	

George VI Types of 1937
Coil Stamp
1937 — Perf. 8 Vertically

OA240	A87	3c carmine	150.00	

Pictorials
1938 — Perf. 12

OA241	A89	10c dk carmine	55.00	
a.		10c carmine rose	45.00	
OA242	A90	13c deep blue	55.00	
OA243	A91	20c red brown	67.50	
OA244	A92	50c green	140.00	
OA245	A93	$1 dull violet	225.00	

Visit of George VI and Queen Elizabeth to Canada and the U.S.
1939

OA246	A94	1c green & black	110.00	
OA247	A95	2c brown & black	110.00	
OA248	A96	3c dk car & black	110.00	

Air Post Issues
1928

OAC1	AP1	5c brown olive	225.00	

1930 — Perf. 11

OAC2	AP2	5c olive brown	340.00	

No. C1 Surcharged
1932 — Perf. 12

OAC3	AP1	6c on 5c brn olive	225.00	

No. C2 Surcharged in Dark Blue
1932 — Perf. 11

OAC4	AP2	6c on 5c olive brn	280.00	

Daedalus
1935 — Perf. 12

OAC5	AP3	6c red brown	195.00	

Mackenzie River Steamer and Seaplane
1938

OAC6	AP4	6c blue	55.00	

Special Delivery Stamps

OAE1	SD1	10c blue green	340.00	

1922

OAE2	SD2	20c carmine	280.00	

1927

OAE3	SD3	20c orange	310.00	

1930 — Perf. 11

OAE4	SD4	20c henna brown	280.00	

1933

OAE5	SD5	20c henna brown	225.00	

1935 — Perf. 12

OAE6	SD6	20c dark carmine	225.00	

Arms of Canada
1938-39

OAE7	SD7	10c dk green ('39)	85.00	
OAE8	SD7	20c dark carmine	140.00	

No. E8 Surcharged in Black
1939

OAE9	SD7	10c on 20c dk car	125.00	

4-HOLE PERFINS

Small "O.H.M.S" 4 Holes in Vertical Bars of "H"

(O plus Scott No.)
Definitives
1935 — Perf. 12

O223	A82	10c car rose	170.00	100.00
		Never hinged	250.00	
O224	A83	13c violet	170.00	85.00
		Never hinged	250.00	
O225	A84	20c olive green	170.00	100.00
		Never hinged	250.00	
O226	A85	50c dull violet	170.00	100.00
		Never hinged	250.00	
		Nos. O223-O226 (4)	680.00	385.00

George VI and Queen Elizabeth
1937

O231	A87	1c green	2.25	.25
		Never hinged	3.40	
O232	A87	2c brown	2.80	.25
		Never hinged	4.25	
O233	A87	3c carmine	2.80	.25
		Never hinged	4.25	
O234	A87	4c yellow	6.75	4.00
		Never hinged	10.00	
O235	A87	5c blue	4.50	.25
		Never hinged	6.75	
O236	A87	8c orange	22.50	9.00
		Never hinged	34.00	
		Nos. O231-O236 (6)	41.60	14.00

Coronation of King George VI and Queen Elizabeth
1937

O237	A88	3c carmine	110.00	95.00
		Never hinged	165.00	

George VI Types of 1937
Coil Stamps
1937 — Perf. 8 Vertically

O239	A87	2c brown	110.00	85.00
		Never hinged	165.00	
O240	A87	3c carmine	110.00	85.00
		Never hinged	165.00	

Pictorials
1938 — Perf. 12

O241	A89	10c dk carmine	11.00	.55
		Never hinged	16.50	
a.		10c carmine rose	80.00	6.75
		Never hinged	120.00	
O242	A90	13c deep blue	17.00	2.75
		Never hinged	26.00	
O243	A91	20c red brown	50.00	3.40
		Never hinged	75.00	
O244	A92	50c green	85.00	17.00
		Never hinged	125.00	
O245	A93	$1 dull violet	180.00	67.50
		Never hinged	275.00	
		Nos. O241-O245 (5)	343.00	91.20

Visit of George VI and Queen Elizabeth to Canada and the US.
1939

O246	A94	1c grn & blk	140.00	90.00
		Never hinged	210.00	
O247	A95	2c brn & blk	140.00	90.00
		Never hinged	210.00	
O248	A96	3c dk car & blk	140.00	90.00
		Never hinged	210.00	
		Nos. O246-O248 (3)	420.00	270.00

Canada's Contribution to the War Effort of the Allied Nations
1942-43

O249	A97	1c green	.55	.25
		Never hinged	.80	
O250	A98	2c brown	.80	.25
		Never hinged	1.20	
O251	A99	3c dk carmine	2.00	.65
		Never hinged	3.00	
O252	A99	3c rose violet ('43)	1.10	.25
		Never hinged	1.60	
O253	A100	4c greenish black	4.00	1.40
		Never hinged	6.00	
O254	A98	4c dk car ('43)	.90	.25
		Never hinged	1.40	
O255	A97	5c deep blue	1.75	.25
		Never hinged	2.60	
O256	A101	8c red brown	11.00	4.00
		Never hinged	16.50	
O257	A102	10c brown	6.75	.35
		Never hinged	10.00	
O258	A103	13c dull green	8.00	6.75
		Never hinged	12.00	
O259	A103	14c dull grn ('43)	10.00	1.75
		Never hinged	15.00	
O260	A104	20c chocolate	14.00	1.40
		Never hinged	21.00	

O261	A105	50c violet	55.00	9.00
		Never hinged	82.50	
O262	A106	$1 deep blue	170.00	55.00
		Never hinged	250.00	
		Nos. O249-O262 (14)	285.85	81.55

Peace Issue
1946

O268	A107	8c red brown	17.00	5.50
		Never hinged	25.00	
O269	A108	10c olive	4.50	.30
		Never hinged	6.75	
O270	A109	14c blk brn	5.50	1.10
		Never hinged	8.25	
O271	A110	20c slate black	6.75	1.10
		Never hinged	10.00	
O272	A111	50c dk bl grn	40.00	9.50
		Never hinged	60.00	
O273	A112	$1 red violet	100.00	35.00
		Never hinged	150.00	
		Nos. O268-O273 (6)	173.75	52.50

"POSTES POSTAGE"
1949

O285	A120	2c sepia	1.10	1.10
		Never hinged	1.60	
O286	A121	3c rose violet	1.10	1.10
		Never hinged	1.60	

Air Post Issues
1928

OC1	AP1	5c brown olive	28.00	25.00
		Never hinged	42.50	

Daedalus
1935

OC5	AP3	6c red brown	100.00	90.00
		Never hinged	150.00	

Mackenzie River Steamer and Seaplane
1938

OC6	AP4	6c blue	4.50	1.70
		Never hinged	6.75	

Canada's Contribution to the War Effort of the Allied Nations
1942-43

OC7	AP5	6c deep blue	4.50	2.25
		Never hinged	6.75	
OC8	AP5	7c dp bl ('43)	4.50	.55
		Never hinged	6.75	

Canada Geese in Flight
1946

OC9	AP6	7c deep blue	3.50	.85
		Never hinged	5.25	

Air Post Special Delivery
Canada's Contribution to the War Effort of the Allied Nations
1942-43

OCE1	APSD1	16c brt ultra	35.00	28.00
		Never hinged	50.00	
OCE2	APSD1	17c brt ultra ('43)	22.50	22.50
		Never hinged	34.00	

DC-4 Transatlantic Mail Plane
1946-47

OCE3	APSD2	17c bright ultra	55.00	50.00
		Never hinged	82.50	

Circumflex accent on second "E" of "EXPRES."

OCE4	APSD2	17c bright ultra ('47)	110.00	110.00
		Never hinged	165.00	

Corrected Die

Grave accent on the 2nd "E" of "EXPRES."

Special Delivery Stamps
1933 — Perf. 11

OE5	SD5	20c henna brown	280.00	170.00
		Never hinged	425.00	

1935 — Perf. 12

OE6	SD6	20c dark carmine	140.00	85.00
		Never hinged	210.00	

Arms of Canada
1939

OE7	SD7	10c dk green ('39)	22.50	10.00
		Never hinged	34.00	

No. E8 Surcharged in Black
1939

OE9	SD7	10c on 20c dk car	170.00	100.00
		Never hinged	250.00	

Canada's Contribution to the War Effort of the Allied Nations
1942

OE10	SD8	10c green	22.50	13.50
		Never hinged	34.00	

Arms of Canada
1946

OE11	SD9	10c green	11.00	10.00
		Never hinged	16.50	

OVERPRINTED OFFICIAL STAMPS

Catalogue values for unused stamps in this section are for Never Hinged items.

All cover values in this section are for uses on commercial covers.

Nos. 249, 250, 252 and 254 Overprinted in Black

1949-50 — Unwmk. — Perf. 12

O1	A97	1c green	2.00	1.75
		On cover		8.00
		Plate block of 4	13.00	
a.		No period after "S"	150.00	65.00
		On cover		120.00
O2	A98	2c brown	10.00	7.50
		On cover		24.00
		Plate block of 4	160.00	
a.		No period after "S"	150.00	65.00
		On cover		120.00
O3	A99	3c rose violet	2.25	1.25
		On cover		8.00
		Plate block of 4	13.00	
O4	A98	4c dark carmine	2.75	.75
		On cover		8.00
		Plate block of 4	20.00	

Nos. 269 to 273 Overprinted in Black

O6	A108	10c olive	3.50	.60
		On cover		15.00
		Plate block of 4	27.50	
a.		No period after "S"	85.00	60.00
		Plate block of 4 (LL 1, LL 2)	200.00	
O7	A109	14c black brown	4.00	2.25
		On cover		15.00
		Plate block of 4	42.50	
a.		No period after "S"	125.00	75.00
		Plate block of 4 (LL 1)	170.00	
O8	A110	20c slate black	16.00	3.25
		On cover		15.00
		Plate block of 4	100.00	
a.		No period after "S"	150.00	75.00
		Plate block of 4 (LL 1, LL 2)	180.00	
O9	A111	50c dk blue grn	200.00	110.00
		On cover		200.00
		Plate block of 4	1,400.	
a.		No period after "S"	1,000.	600.00
		Plate block of 4 (LL 1)	1,800.	
O10	A112	$1 red violet	70.00	35.00
		On cover		120.00
		Plate block of 4	550.00	
a.		No period after "S"	2,500.	1,750.
		Plate block of 4 (LL 1)	3,250.	
		Nos. O1-O4,O6-O10 (9)	310.50	162.35

The "no period" varieties occur at 47LL1 & 47LL2 on some panes of #O6, O7, O8, on all panes of #O9, and on just a few panes of #O10.

Same Overprint on No. 294
1950

O11	A124	50c dull green	40.00	25.00
		On cover		95.00
		Plate block of 4	225.00	

Nos. 284 to 288 Overprinted in Black

1950

O12	A119	1c green	.40	.30
		On cover		6.50
		Plate block of 4	4.50	
O13	A120	2c sepia	1.10	.75
		On cover		6.50
		Plate block of 4	5.50	
O14	A121	3c rose violet	1.10	.50
		On cover		6.50
		Plate block of 4	7.25	

O15	A122 4c dark carmine	1.10	.25
			6.50
	Plate block of 4	7.25	
b.	No period after "S"	85.00	55.00
	On cover		55.00
O15A	A123 5c deep blue	2.25	1.50
	On cover		6.50
	Plate block of 4	10.50	
c.	No period after "S"	85.00	55.00
	On cover		95.00
	Nos. O12-O15A (5)	5.95	3.30

The "no period" varieties occur at 52LL1 on #O15 and at 52LL1, 78UL1 & 78UL2 on #O15A.

Stamps of 1946-50 Overprinted in Black

a

b

1950

O16	A119(a) 1c grn (#284)	.50	.25
	On cover		5.50
	Plate block of 4	4.50	
O17	A120(a) 2c sep (#285)	1.30	.90
	On cover		5.50
	Plate block of 4	9.00	
O18	A121(a) 3c rose vio (#286)	1.30	.25
	On cover		5.50
	Plate block of 4	9.00	
O19	A122(a) 4c dk car (#287)	1.30	.25
	On cover		5.50
	Plate block of 4	9.00	
O20	A123(a) 5c dp bl (#288)	1.60	.90
	On cover		5.50
	Plate block of 4	17.00	
O21	A108(b) 10c olive	2.50	.50
	On cover		11.00
	Plate block of 4	18.00	
O22	A109(b) 14c black brn	6.50	2.00
	On cover		12.00
	Plate block of 4	42.50	
O23	A110(b) 20c slate blk	14.00	1.00
	On cover		12.00
	Plate block of 4	110.00	
O24	A124(b) 50c dull green	10.00	5.50
	On cover		100.00
	Plate block of 4	72.50	
O25	A112(b) $1 red violet	105.00	80.00
	On cover		120.00
	Plate block of 4	560.00	
	Nos. O16-O25 (10)	144.00	91.55

Nos. 301-302 Overprinted Type "b"
1950-51

O26	A125 10c black brown	1.30	.25
	On cover		9.00
	Plate block of 4	10.00	
a.	Pair, one without "G"	775.00	650.00
O27	A126 $1 brt ultra ('51)	100.00	90.00
	On cover		140.00
	Plate block of 4	560.00	

It is recommended that a certificate of authenticity be acquired for No. O26a.

Nos. 305-306 Overprinted Type "a"

1951-52		Unwmk.	Perf. 12
O28	A120 2c olive green	.60	.25
	On cover		4.75
	Plate block of 4	3.25	
O29	A122 4c orange ver ('52)	.95	.25
	On cover		4.75
	Plate block of 4	5.50	

No. 316 Overprinted Type "b"
1952

O30	A132 20c gray	2.25	.25
	On cover		9.00
	Plate block of 4	18.00	

Nos. 320-321 Overprinted Type "b"
1952-53

O31	A136 7c blue	4.00	1.25
	On cover		16.00
	Plate block of 4	20.00	
O32	A137 $1 gray ('53)	14.00	8.00
	On cover		45.00
	Plate block of 4	85.00	

POST OFFICE SEALS

Values for Nos. OX1-OX4 used are for examples that are creased but not torn. Covers: All cover values in this section are for presentable covers with damage to the covers consistent with the application of the seal, which will be creasd but not torn.

POS1

1879	Unwmk.	Engr.	Perf. 12
OX1	POS1 brown	350.00	150.00
	Never hinged	950.00	
	On cover		2,000.

No. OX1 unused is very scarce with very fine centering, and rare very fine and never hinged; in fine condition values are 25-30% of those given for very fine.

POS2

1902-07			
OX2	POS2 black, bluish	675.00	275.00
	Never hinged	1,750.	
	On cover		2,400.
a.	Imperf., pair	4,000.	
OX3	POS2 black ('07)	125.00	55.00
	Never hinged	280.00	
	On cover		2,400.

No. OX2a is without gum.

POS3

1913			
OX4	POS3 dark brown	100.00	37.50
	Never hinged	225.00	
	On cover		2,400.

CAPE JUBY

'kāp 'jü-bē

LOCATION — Northwest coast of Africa in Spanish Sahara
GOVT. — Spanish administration
AREA — 12,700 sq. mi.
POP. — 9,836
CAPITAL — Villa Bens (Cape Juby)

By agreement with France, Spain's Sahara possessions were extended to include Cape Juby and in 1916 Spanish troops occupied the territory. It is attached for administrative purposes to Spanish Sahara.

100 Centimos = 1 Peseta

STAMPS OF SPANISH MOROCCO USED IN CAPE JUBY

1015

Cancellations from "CABO JUBI" or "VILLA BENS"

A1	¼c blue green (#39)		55.00
	On cover		160.00
A2	2c dark brown (#40)		55.00
	On cover		160.00
A3	5c green (#41)		55.00
	On cover		160.00
A4	10c carmine (#42)		55.00
	On cover		160.00
A5	15c violet (#43)		55.00
	On cover		160.00
A6	20c olive green (#44)		55.00
	On cover		160.00
A7	25c deep blue (#45)		55.00
	On cover		160.00
A8	30c blue green (#46)		55.00
	On cover		160.00
A9	40c rose (#47)		55.00
	On cover		160.00
A10	50c slate blue (#48)		55.00
	On cover		160.00
A11	1p lake (#49)		160.00
	On cover		525.00
A12	4p deep violet (#50)		440.00
	On cover		1,350.
A13	10p orange (#51)		440.00
	On cover		1,350.
A14	20c red (#E2)		110.00
	On cover		275.00

Values for stamps on cover are for philatelic covers, usually overfranked.

1917-19

A15	¼c blue green (#52)		55.00
	On cover		160.00
A16	2c dark brown (#53)		55.00
	On cover		160.00
A17	5c green (#54)		55.00
	On cover		160.00
A18	10c carmine (#55)		65.00
	On cover		190.00
A19	25c deep blue (#58)		65.00
	On cover		190.00
A20	30c blue green (#59)		65.00
	On cover		225.00

Values for stamps on covers are for philatelic covers, usually overfranked.

Stamps of Rio de Oro, 1914 Surcharged in Violet, Red, Green or Blue

Two Types of Surcharge:
I: "CABO JUBI" in letters without serifs.
II: "CABO JUBI" in thin letters with serifs.

1916		Unwmk.	Perf. 13
Type I			
1	A6 5c on 4p rose (V)	240.00	19.00
	Never hinged	315.00	
	On cover		85.00
	On registered cover		125.00
a.	Inverted surcharge	250.00	30.00
d.	Double surcharge	325.00	50.00
e.	As "d," inverted	350.00	
2	A6 10c on 10p dl vio (R)	50.00	19.00
	Never hinged	62.50	
	On cover		85.00
	On registered cover		125.00
a.	Inverted surcharge	55.00	30.00
d.	Double surcharge	75.00	50.00
2E	A6 10c on 10p dl vio (V)	125.00	72.50
	Never hinged	200.00	
f.	Double surcharge (R, V)	150.00	90.00
2G	A6 10c on 10p dl vio (B)	125.00	72.50
	Never hinged	200.00	
3	A6 15c on 50c dk brn (G)	52.50	30.00
	Never hinged	95.00	
a.	Inverted surcharge	57.50	30.00
4	A6 15c on 50c dk brn (R)	50.00	19.00
	Never hinged	62.50	
	On cover		85.00
	On registered cover		140.00
a.	Inverted surcharge	55.00	30.00
5	A6 40c on 1p red vio (G)	87.50	35.00
	Never hinged	145.00	
a.	Inverted surcharge	75.00	37.50
6	A6 40c on 1p red vio (R)	85.00	26.00
	Never hinged	115.00	
	On cover		110.00
	On registered cover		190.00
a.	Inverted surcharge	75.00	42.50
	Nos. 1-6 (8)	815.00	293.00
	Set, never hinged	1,300.	
Type II			
1b	A6 5c on 4p rose (V)	190.00	100.00
c.	Inverted surcharge	425.00	200.00
2b	A6 10c on 10p dl vio (R)	190.00	100.00
c.	Inverted surcharge	425.00	200.00
3b	A6 15c on 50c dk brn (G)	325.00	200.00
c.	Inverted surcharge	425.00	200.00
4b	A6 15c on 50c dk brn (R)	190.00	100.00
c.	Inverted surcharge	425.00	200.00
5b	A6 40c on 1p red vio (G)	425.00	—
c.	Inverted surcharge	425.00	200.00
6b	A6 40c on 1p red vio (R)	190.00	100.00
c.	Inverted surcharge	425.00	200.00

Values for stamps in blocks of 4
Type I

1	A6	5c on 4p rose (V)	1,150.	140.00
2	A6	10c on 10p dl vio (R)	260.00	140.00
4	A6	15c on 50c dk brn (R)	200.00	100.00
6	A6	40c on 1p red viol (R)	425.00	200.00

Very fine examples of Nos. 1-6 will be somewhat off center. Well centered examples are uncommon and will sell for more.
Fakes of Nos. 1-6 are plentiful.

Stamps of Spain, 1876-1917, Overprinted in Red or Black

1919			Imperf.
7	A21 ¼c bl grn (R)	.30	.30
	Never hinged	.45	
	On cover		10.00

	Perf. 13x12½, 14		
8	A46 2c dk brn (Bk)	.30	.30
	Never hinged	.45	
	On cover		10.00
a.	Double overprint	40.00	50.00
b.	Double overprint (Bk + R)	100.00	52.50
c.	Imperf	30.00	22.50
9	A46 5c grn (R)	.75	.65
	Never hinged	1.05	
	On cover		12.50
a.	Double overprint	40.00	50.00
b.	Inverted overprint	30.00	47.50
c.	Imperf (R)	30.00	22.50
d.	Imperf (Bk)	60.00	60.00
10	A46 10c car (Bk)	1.00	.70
	Never hinged	1.30	
	On cover		15.00
a.	Double overprint (Bk + R)	100.00	52.50
b.	Double overprint (Bk)	40.00	50.00
c.	Imperf	30.00	22.50
11	A46 15c ocher (Bk)	3.50	3.00
	Never hinged	5.00	
	On cover		25.00
b.	Double overprint	40.00	50.00
c.	Red control #	6.50	3.75
	As "c," never hinged	9.50	
d.	As "c," inverted overprint	13.00	
e.	Imperf (Bk)	30.00	22.50
f.	Imperf (R)	30.00	22.50
12	A46 20c ol grn (R)	22.00	16.00
	Never hinged	27.50	
	On cover		130.00
a.	Imperf	92.50	92.50
b.	Imperf, control number omitted	190.00	190.00
13	A46 25c dp bl (R)	3.25	3.00
	On cover	5.25	
			40.00
a.	Double overprint	40.00	50.00
b.	Imperf	30.00	22.50
14	A46 30c bl grn (R)	3.25	3.00
	Never hinged	5.25	
			40.00
a.	Imperf	30.00	22.50
15	A46 40c rose (Bk)	3.50	3.25
	Never hinged	5.25	
			40.00
a.	Imperf	30.00	22.50
16	A46 50c sl bl (R)	4.00	3.50
	On cover	6.25	
			55.00
17	A46 1p lake (Bk)	11.00	8.75
	Never hinged	18.00	
			125.00
a.	Imperf	35.00	35.00
18	A46 4p dp vio (R)	45.00	34.00
	Never hinged	72.50	
			350.00
a.	Imperf	40.00	40.00
19	A46 10p org (Bk)	60.00	45.00
	Never hinged	100.00	
			725.00
a.	Imperf	87.50	87.50
	Nos. 7-19 (13)	157.85	121.40
	Set, never hinged	300.00	

Nos. 8-19 have blue control number on back.

Values for stamps in blocks of 4

7	A21	¼c bl grn(R)	1.25	1.50
8	A46	2c dk brn (Bk)	1.25	1.50
9	A46	5c grn (R)	3.25	4.00
10	A46	10c car (Bk)	3.75	4.50
11	A46	15c ocher (Bk)	17.50	24.50
12	A46	20c ol grn (R)	95.00	130.00
13	A46	25c dp bl (R)	16.00	19.00
14	A46	30c bl grn (R)	16.00	19.00
15	A46	40c rose (Bk)	16.00	19.50
16	A46	50c sl bl (R)	20.00	26.00
17	A46	1p lake (Bk)	55.00	67.50
18	A46	4p dp vio (R)	200.00	290.00
19	A46	10p org (Bk)	290.00	360.00

Same on Stamps of Spain, 1920-21

1922			Imperf.
20	A47 1c blue green	25.00	14.00
	Never hinged	45.00	

	Engr.	Perf. 13x12½	
Blue Control Number on Back			
23	A46 20c violet	145.00	42.50
	Never hinged	215.00	
	On cover		230.00

A 2c and a 15c exist, values $400 and $10, respectively, for unused, hinged examples, $600 and $15 for never hinged. Overprint on 2c privately applied.

Same on Stamps of Spain, 1922-23

1925   *Perf. 13½x13*

25	A49	5c red vio	5.25	3.50
	Never hinged		7.00	
	On cover			30.00
26	A49	10c bl grn	13.00	3.50
	Never hinged		22.50	
	On cover			50.00
28	A49	20c violet	27.50	10.00
	Never hinged		42.50	
	On cover			110.00
	Nos. 25-28 (3)		45.75	17.00
	Set, never hinged		72.50	

Exists on Spain No. 331, 2c olive green. Value $350 unused hinged and $600 never hinged. Overprint was privately applied.

Seville-Barcelona Exposition Issue

Stamps of Spain, 1929, Overprinted in Red or Blue

1929   *Perf. 11*

29	A52	5c rose lake (Bl)	.45	.45
	Never hinged		.90	
	On cover			22.50
30	A53	10c green (R)	.45	.45
	Never hinged		.90	
	On cover			22.50
31	A50	15c Prus bl (R)	.45	.45
	Never hinged		.90	
	On cover			22.50
32	A51	20c pur (R)	.45	.45
	Never hinged		.90	
	On cover			22.50
33	A50	25c brt rose (Bl)	.45	.45
	Never hinged		.90	
	On cover			22.50
34	A52	30c blk brn (Bl)	.45	.45
	Never hinged		.90	
	On cover			22.50
35	A53	40c dk bl (R)	.45	.45
	Never hinged		.90	
	On cover			22.50
36	A51	50c dp org (Bl)	.60	.60
	Never hinged		2.25	
	On cover			32.50
37	A52	1p bl blk (R)	21.00	21.00
	Never hinged		40.00	
	On cover			—
38	A53	4p dp rose (Bl)	27.50	27.50
	Never hinged		52.50	
	On cover			—
39	A53	10p brn (Bl)	27.50	27.50
	Never hinged		52.50	
	On cover			—
	Nos. 29-39 (11)		79.75	79.75
	Set, never hinged		150.00	

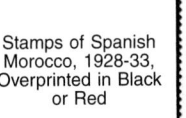

Stamps of Spanish Morocco, 1928-33, Overprinted in Black or Red

1934   *Perf. 14*

40	A7	1c brt rose (Bk)	.55	.55
	Never hinged		.75	
	On cover			18.00
41	A2	2c dk vio (R)	5.00	5.00
	Never hinged		9.00	
	On cover			27.50
42	A2	5c dp bl (R)	5.75	5.75
	Never hinged		9.00	
	On cover			27.50
43	A2	10c dk grn (Bk)	14.00	11.50
	Never hinged		22.50	
	On cover			57.50
43A	A10	10c dk grn (R)	3.50	3.50
	Never hinged		5.50	
	On cover			27.50
44	A2	15c org brn (Bk)	32.50	29.00
	Never hinged		57.50	
	On cover			150.00
45	A7	20c sl grn (R)	13.00	10.00
	Never hinged		17.00	
	On cover			55.00
46	A3	25c cop red (R)	6.00	5.50
	Never hinged		8.50	
	On cover			27.50
47	A10	30c red brn (Bk)	11.00	10.00
	Never hinged		18.00	
	On cover			62.50
48	A13	40c dp bl (R)	40.00	37.50
	Never hinged		65.00	
	On cover			175.00
49	A13	50c red org (Bk)	80.00	70.00
	Never hinged		120.00	
	On cover			375.00
50	A4	1p yel grn (Bk)	57.50	57.50
	Never hinged		97.50	
	On cover			250.00
51	A5	2.50p red vio (Bk)	120.00	115.00
	Never hinged		180.00	
	On cover			600.00

52	A6	4p ultra (R)	160.00	145.00
	Never hinged		290.00	
	On cover			725.00

No. 43A and 1c, 20c, 30c, 40c, 50c, with control numbers.

Same Overprint in Black on Stamp of Spanish Morocco, 1932

53	A2	1c car rose ("Ct")	2.40	2.40
	Never hinged		4.00	
	On cover			27.50
	Nos. 40-53 (15)		551.20	508.20
	Set, never hinged		900.00	

Stamps of Spanish Morocco, 1933-35, Overprinted in Black, Blue or Red

1935-36

54	A8	2c grn (R)	1.25	1.00
55	A9	5c mag (Bk)	3.75	3.50
55A	A10	10c dk grn (R)		
		('36)	22.50	21.00
56	A11	15c yel (Bl)	8.75	8.25
57	A12	25c crim (Bk)	110.00	100.00
58	A8	1p sl blk (R)	14.50	13.50
59	A9	2.50p brn (Bl)	55.00	52.50
60	A11	4p yel grn (R)	95.00	90.00
61	A12	5p blk (R)	75.00	70.00
	Nos. 54-61 (9)		385.75	359.75
	Set, never hinged		750.00	

Same Overprint in Black or Red on Stamps of Spanish Morocco, 1935

1935   *Perf. 13½*

62	A14	25c vio (R)	4.00	4.00
63	A15	30c crim (Bk)	4.00	4.00
64	A14	40c org (Bk)	5.75	5.25
65	A15	50c brt bl (R)	15.00	11.00
66	A14	60c dk bl grn (R)	17.50	14.00
67	A15	2p brn lake (Bk)	95.00	75.00

Same Overprint on Stamps of Spanish Morocco, 1933

Perf. 13½, 14

68	A7	1c brt rose (Bk)	.30	.30

Perf. 14

69	A7	20c slate grn (R)	6.75	6.75
	Nos. 62-69 (8)		148.30	120.30
	Set, never hinged		200.00	

Same Overprint on Stamps of Spanish Morocco, 1937

1937   *Perf. 13½*

70	A21	1c dk bl (Bk)	.50	.50
71	A21	2c org brn (Bk)	.50	.50
72	A21	5c cer (Bk)	.50	.50
73	A21	10c emer (Bk)	.50	.50
74	A21	15c brt bl (Bk)	.50	.50
75	A21	20c red brn (Bk)	.50	.50
76	A21	25c mag (Bk)	.50	.50
77	A21	30c red org (Bk)	.50	.50
78	A21	40c org (Bk)	1.60	1.60
79	A21	50c ultra (R)	1.60	1.60
80	A21	60c yel grn (Bk)	1.60	1.60
81	A21	1p bl vio (Bk)	1.60	1.60
82	A21	2p Prus bl (Bk)	87.50	87.50
83	A21	2.50p gray blk (R)	87.50	87.50
84	A21	4p dk brn (Bk)	87.50	87.50
85	A22	10p vio blk (R)	87.50	87.50
	Nos. 70-85 (16)		360.40	360.40
	Set, never hinged		550.00	

1st Year of the Revolution.

Same Overprint in Black on Types of Spanish Morocco, 1939

Designs: 5c, Spanish quarter. 10c, Moroccan quarter. 15c, Street scene, Larache. 20c, Tetuan.

1939   **Photo.**   *Perf. 13½*

86	A25	5c vermilion	.50	.50
87	A25	10c deep green	.50	.50
88	A25	15c brown lake	.50	.50
89	A25	20c bright blue	.50	.50
	Nos. 86-89 (4)		2.00	2.00
	Set, never hinged		4.00	

Same Overprint in Black or Red on Stamps of Spanish Morocco, 1940

1940   *Perf. 11½x11*

90	A26	1c dk brn (Bk)	.25	.25
91	A27	2c ol grn (R)	.25	.25
92	A28	5c dk bl (R)	.25	.25
93	A29	10c dk red lil (Bk)	.25	.25
94	A30	15c dk grn (Bk)	.25	.25
95	A31	20c pur (R)	.30	.30
96	A32	25c blk brn (R)	.30	.30
97	A33	30c brt grn (Bk)	.35	.35
98	A34	40c slate grn (R)	.85	.75
99	A35	45c org ver (Bk)	.85	.75
100	A36	50c brn org (R)	.90	.90
101	A37	70c saph (R)	2.40	2.25
102	A38	1p ind & brn (Bk)	5.00	5.00

103	A39	2.50p choc & dk grn (Bk)	14.00	12.50
104	A40	5p dk cer & sep (Bk)	14.00	13.00
105	A41	10p dk ol grn & brn org (Bk)	40.00	35.00
	Nos. 90-105 (16)		80.20	72.35
	Set, never hinged		150.00	

Imperfs exist. Value, set $300.

SEMI-POSTAL STAMPS

Types of Semi-Postal Stamps of Spain, 1926, Overprinted

1926   **Unwmk.**   *Perf. 12½, 13*

B1	SP1	1c orange	11.50	11.50
	Never hinged		19.00	
B2	SP2	2c rose	11.50	11.50
	Never hinged		19.00	
B3	SP3	5c blk brn	3.00	3.00
	Never hinged		4.50	
B4	SP4	10c dk grn	1.60	1.60
	Never hinged		2.25	
B5	SP1	15c dk vio	1.10	1.10
	Never hinged		1.40	
B6	SP4	20c vio brn	1.10	1.10
	Never hinged		1.40	
B7	SP5	25c dp car	1.10	1.10
	Never hinged		1.40	
B8	SP1	30c ol grn	1.10	1.10
	Never hinged		1.40	
B9	SP3	40c ultra	.45	.45
	Never hinged		1.40	
B10	SP2	50c red brn	.45	.45
	Never hinged		1.40	
B11	SP4	1p vermilion	.45	.45
	Never hinged		1.40	
B12	SP3	4p bister	2.00	2.00
	Never hinged		3.75	
B13	SP5	10p lt vio	3.00	3.00
	Never hinged		7.25	
	Nos. B1-B13 (13)		38.35	38.35
	Set, never hinged		65.00	

Nos. B12-B13 surcharged "Alfonso XIII" and new value are listed as Spain Nos. B68-B69. See Spain No. B6a.

AIR POST STAMPS

Spanish Morocco, Nos. C1 to C10 Overprinted "CABO JUBY" as on #54-61

1938, June 1   **Unwmk.**   *Perf. 13½*

C1	AP1	5c brown	.25	.25
C2	AP1	10c brt grn	.25	.25
C3	AP1	25c crimson	.25	.25
C4	AP1	40c light blue	2.10	2.10
C5	AP2	50c brt mag	.25	.25
C6	AP2	75c dk bl	.25	.25
C7	AP1	1p sepia	.25	.25
C8	AP1	1.50p dp vio	1.90	1.90
C9	AP1	2p dp red brn	2.75	2.75
C10	AP1	3p brn blk	7.25	7.25
	Nos. C1-C10 (10)		15.50	15.50
	Set, never hinged		45.00	

SPECIAL DELIVERY STAMPS

Special Delivery Stamp of Spain Ovptd. "CABO JUBY" as on #7-28

1919   **Unwmk.**   *Perf. 14*

E1	SD1	20c red (Bk)	3.25	3.25
b.	Double overprint		27.50	13.00

Spanish Morocco #E4 Overprinted "CABO JUBY" as on #40-52 in Red

1934

E2	SD2	20c black	10.00	10.00

Spanish Morocco No. E5 Overprinted "CABO JUBY" as on Nos. 54-61

1935

E3	SD3	20c vermilion	3.50	3.50

Same Ovpt. on Spanish Morocco #E6

1937   *Perf. 13½*

E4	SD4	20c bright carmine	1.10	1.10

1st Year of the Revolution.

Same Ovpt. on Spanish Morocco #E8

1940   *Perf. 11½x11*

E5	SD5	25c scarlet	.65	.65

SEMI-POSTAL SPECIAL DELIVERY STAMP

Type of Semi-Postal Special Delivery Stamp of Spain, 1926, Overprinted "CABO-JUBY" as on Nos. B1-B13

1926   **Unwmk.**   *Perf. 12½, 13*

EB1	SPSD1	20c ultra & black	3.50	3.50

CAPE OF GOOD HOPE

ˈkāp əv ˈgud ˈhōp

LOCATION — In the extreme southern part of South Africa
GOVT. — British Colony
AREA — 276,995 sq mi. (1911)
POP. — 2,564,965 (1911)
CAPITAL — Cape Town

Cape of Good Hope joined with Natal, the Transvaal and the Orange River Colony in 1910, forming the Union of South Africa.

12 Pence = 1 Shilling

Watermarks

Wmk. 15 —   Wmk. 16 —
Anchor   Anchor

"Hope"
Seated
A1

Printed by Perkins, Bacon & Co.
Wmk. 15

			1853, Sept. 1 Engr.	*Imperf.*
1	A1	1p brick red, bluish paper	3,500.	400.00
a.		1p pale brick red, deeply blued paper	4,500.	400.00
b.		1p deep brick red, deeply blued paper	10,500.	425.00
f.		1p deep brick red, bluish paper	3,750.	300.00
2	A1	4p deep blue, lightly blued paper	1,750.	170.00
a.		4p deep blue, deeply blued paper	3,500.	300.00
b.		4p blue, bluish paper	3,250.	200.00

Watermark Sideways

1c	A1	1p As #1	—	385.00
1d	A1	1p As #1a	—	475.00
1e	A1	1p As #1b	—	475.00
1g	A1	1p As #1f	—	385.00
2c	A1	4p As #2	—	325.00
2d	A1	4p As #2a	4,500.	300.00
2e	A1	4p As #2b	—	325.00

Values for pairs

1	A1	1p	—	650.00
1a	A1	1p	—	975.00
1b	A1	1p	—	1,050.
1f	A1	1p	—	740.00
2	A1	4p	4,750.	360.00
2a	A1	4p	9,550.	825.00
2b	A1	4p	8,750.	490.00

Values for Blocks of 4

1	A1	1p	—	1,400.
1a	A1	1p	—	2,200.
1b	A1	1p	—	2,300.
1f	A1	1p	—	1,600.
2	A1	4p	10,500.	800.00
2a	A1	4p	21,000.	1,100.
2b	A1	4p	19,000.	1,150.

Counterfeits exist.

			1855-58	**White Paper**
3	A1	1p rose ('57)	600.00	325.00
a.		1p dull red	850.00	425.00
b.		1p brick red	6,000.	1,050.
		As "b," Rouletted, unofficial		3,600.
4	A1	4p blue	700.00	70.00
		Rouletted, unofficial		2,750.
a.		Half used as 2p on cover		42,000.
b.		4p deep blue	900.00	75.00
c.		4p bright blue	900.00	75.00
5	A1	6p pale lilac ('58)	950.00	240.00
a.		6p rose lilac	2,500.	350.00
		As "a," Rouletted, unofficial		1,750.
b.		6p grayish lilac on bluish paper	5,000.	540.00
c.		6p slate purple on bluish paper	4,150.	1,200.
		Half used as 3p on cover		—
6	A1	1sh yellow grn ('58)	3,250.	250.00
		Rouletted, unofficial		3,850.
a.		1sh dark green	375.00	600.00

		As "a," Rouletted, unofficial		4,150.
b.		Half used as 6p on cover		—

Unofficially rouletted copies of 3b, 4, 5a, 6 and 6a require certificates of authenticity.

Watermark Sideways

3c	A1	1p As #3	—	500.00
3d	A1	1p As #3a	—	500.00
4c	A1	4p As#4	—	225.00
4d	A1	4p As #4b	—	225.00
5e	A1	6p As #5	—	1,100.
6c	A1	1sh As #6	—	1,600.

Values for Pairs

3	A1	1p		1,650.	650.00
3a	A1	1p		2,250.	825.00
3b	A1	1p		16,250.	2,900.
4	A1	4p		1,500.	160.00
4b	A1	4p		2,100.	175.00
4e	A1	4p		2,100.	175.00
5	A1	6p		2,500.	950.00
5a	A1	6p		6,900.	1,400.
5b	A1	6p		14,000.	2,150.
5c	A1	6p		11,500.	4,750.
6	A1	1sh		8,750.	900.00
6a	A1	1sh		825.	2,400.

Values for Blocks of 4

3	A1	1p		3,500.	1,900.
3a	A1	1p		4,750.	2,400.
3b	A1	1p		—	
4	A1	4p		3,300.	450.00
4b	A1	4p		4,700.	475.00
4e	A1	4p		4,500.	475.00
5	A1	6p		5,350.	1,900.
5a	A1	6p		15,000.	2,850.
5b	A1	6p		—	4,250.
5c	A1	6p		—	9,500.
6	A1	1sh		18,000.	1,800.
6a	A1	1sh		1,800.	4,750.

Nos. 3-6 are known rouletted unofficially. Counterfeits exist.

No. 4 was reproduced by the collotype process in an unwatermarked souvenir sheet distributed at the London Intl. Stamp Exhib. 1950.

Printed by Saul Solomon & Co.

			1861 Laid Paper	Unwmk.	Typo.
7	A2	1p vermilion	16,500.	2,650.
a.		1p carmine	42,500.	4,000.
b.		1p red	45,000.	5,000.
c.		1p milky blue (error)	180,000.	32,500.
d.		1p pale blue (error)		36,000.
9	A2	4p milky blue	40,000.	3,000.
a.		4p pale blue	42,000.	3,250.
b.		4p blue	45,000.	3,500.
c.		4p dark blue	112,500.	5,750.
d.		As #9, right corner retouched		7,750.
e.		As #9a, right corner retouched		7,750.
f.		4p vermilion (error)	180,000.	65,000.
g.		4p carmine (error)		112,500.
h.		Tête bêche pair, cliche error		145,000.

Values for Pairs

7	A2	1p	46,000.	8,000.
7a	A2	1p	115,000.	12,000.
7b	A2	1p	120,000.	15,000.
9	A2	4p	110,000.	15,000.
9a	A2	4p	118,000.	15,000.
9b	A2	4p	140,000.	17,500.
9c	A2	4p	575,000.	30,000.

Value for Used Blocks of 4

7	A2	1p	26,000.
7a	A2	1p	40,000.
7b	A2	1p	50,000.
9	A2	4p	29,000.
9a	A2	4p	30,000.
9b	A2	4p	36,000.
9c	A2	4p	59,000.

Nos. 7 and 9 are usually called Wood Blocks. The plates were made locally and composed of clichés mounted on wood. The errors were caused by a cliché of each value being mounted in the plate of the other value.

No. 9h is the unique pair with the two stamps positioned so that the inscription "POSTAGE" on one stamp is aligned next to the inscription "FOUR PENCE" on the adjoining stamp.

In 1883 plate proofs of both values on white paper, usually called "reprints," were made. The 1p is in dull orange red; the 4p in dark blue. These are known canceled, as a few were misused as stamps. The proofs do not include the errors.

Counterfeits exist.

Printed by De La Rue & Co.

			1863-64 Wmk. 15	Engr.
12	A1	1p dark carmine	225.00	270.00
a.		1p reddish brown	500.00	300.00
b.		1p brownish red	500.00	275.00
13	A1	4p dark blue	200.00	90.00
a.		4p slate blue	2,500.	600.00
b.		4p steel blue	2,400.	325.00
c.		4p pale grayish blue	215.00	75.00

14	A1	6p purple	325.00	450.00
15	A1	1sh emerald	475.00	550.00
a.		1sh pale emerald		1,200.

Watermark Sideways

12c	A1	1p As #12	425.00	350.00
12d	A1	1p As #12a	600.00	350.00
12e	A1	1p As #12b	600.00	325.00
13d	A1	4p As #13	750.00	225.00
14a	A1	6p As #14		1,400.

Values for Pairs

12	A1	1p	540.00	875.00
12a	A1	1p	1,200.	975.00
12b	A1	1p	1,200.	875.00
13	A1	4p	475.00	210.00
13a	A1	4p	6,000.	1,900.
13b	A1	4p	6,000.	975.00
13c	A1	4p	500.00	250.00
14	A1	6p	700.00	1,750.
15	A1	1sh	1,200.	2,100.
15a	A1	1sh	3,000.	

Values for Blocks of 4

12	A1	1p	1,200.	2,700.
12a	A1	1p	3,000.	2,950.
12b	A1	1p	2,750.	2,700.
13	A1	4p	1,150.	650.00
13a	A1	4p	—	6,000.
13b	A1	4p	—	3,000.
13c	A1	4p	1,200.	775.00
14	A1	6p	1,450.	5,400.
15	A1	1sh	3,000.	5,400.
15a	A1	1sh	7,250.	

Nos. 12-15 can be distinguished from Nos. 3-6 not only by colors but because Nos. 12-15 often appear in a granular ink or with the background lightly printed in whole or part.

No. 12a, Wmk. 1, is believed to be a proof. Value, $29,000.

Counterfeits exist.

"Hope" and Symbols of
Colony — A3

Frame Line Around Stamp

			1864-65 Typo. Wmk. 1 *Perf.* 14	
16	A3	1p rose ('65)	100.00	30.00
a.		1p car red	100.00	31.00
17	A3	4p blue ('65)	150.00	4.25
a.		4p pale blue	150.00	4.25
b.		4p dull ultramarine	325.00	65.00
c.		4p deep blue ('72)	200.00	4.50
18	A3	6p bright violet	180.00	1.75
a.		6p dull violet	300.00	8.25
b.		6p pale lilac ('84)	160.00	26.00
19	A3	1sh yellow green	170.00	4.50
a.		1sh blue green	180.00	6.00
b.		1sh deep green	650.00	21.50
		Nos. 16-19 (4)	600.00	40.50

Watermark Inverted

16b	A3	1p rose	375.00	150.00
17d	A3	4p blue	500.00	175.00
18c	A3	6p bright violet	—	325.00
19d	A3	1sh blue green	800.00	175.00

Watermark Reversed

19e	A3	1sh yellow green	—	

Imperf. stamps are believed to be proofs.

For surcharges see Nos. 20-21, N3.

For types A3 and A6 with manuscript surcharge of 1d or overprints "G. W." or "G," see Griqualand West listings.

Stamps of 1864 Surcharged in Red or Black

a   b

			1868-74	**Red Surcharge**
20	A3(a)	4p on 6p	450.00	19.00
a.		"Peuce" for "Pence"	2,250.	900.00
b.		"Fonr" for "Four"		850.00
c.		Wmk. inverted		400.00
21	A3(b)	1p on 6p ('74)	650.00	130.00
a.		"E" of "PENNY" omitted		1,600.

Space between words and bars varies from 12½-16mm on No. 20, and 16½-18mm on No. 21.

			1876	**Black Surcharge**
22	A3 (b)	1p on 1sh green	120.00	65.00

"Hope" and Symbols of
Colony — A6

Without Frame Line Around Stamp

			1871-81	*Perf.* 14
23	A6	½p gray black ('75)	27.50	11.00
24	A6	1p rose ('72)	45.00	1.00
25	A6	3p lilac rose ('80)	250.00	31.00
26	A6	3p claret ('81)	150.00	3.50
a.		3p pale claret	175.00	3.25
27	A6	4p blue ('76)	140.00	.90
a.		4p ultramarine	275.00	60.00
28	A6	5sh orange	425.00	20.00
		Nos. 23-28 (6)	1,037.	67.40

Watermark Inverted

23a	A6	½p gray black	—	150.00
24a	A6	1p rose	375.00	160.00
25a	A6	3p lilac rose	—	400.00
26b	A6	3p claret	—	
27b	A6	4p blue	425.00	110.00

For surcharges see Nos. 29-32, 39, 55.

No. 27 Surcharged in
Red

			1879	
29	A6	3p on 4p blue	140.00	3.00
a.		"THE.EE"	3,000.	350.00
b.		"PENCB"	2,500.	275.00
c.		Double surcharge	11,000.	3,900.
d.		As "a," double surcharge	—	—

Type of 1871
Surcharged in Black

			1880	
30	A6	3p on 4p lilac rose	90.00	2.75
a.		Wmk. inverted		300.00

No. 25 Surcharged in Black

e   f

31	A6(e)	3p on 3p lilac rose	300.00	9.50
a.		Inverted surcharge	11,000.	1,200.
b.		Wmk inverted		550.00
32	A6(f)	3p on 3p lilac rose	110.00	2.10
a.		Inverted surcharge	1,300.	47.50
b.		Vert. pair, #31-32	1,200.	475.00
c.		Wmk inverted	—	200.00

			1882-83	**Wmk. 2**
33	A6	½p gray black	32.50	3.25
a.		½p black	32.50	3.25
b.		Wmk. inverted	—	175.00
34	A6	1p rose	75.00	2.50
a.		1p pure red	75.00	2.50
b.		Wmk inverted	—	225.00
35	A6	2p bister	120.00	1.50
a.		2p dp bister	130.00	1.50
b.		Wmk inverted	—	225.00
36	A6	3p claret	9.50	1.50
a.		3p dp claret	16.50	1.50
b.		Wmk. inverted	—	140.00
37	A3	6p bright violet	120.00	1.00
38	A6	5sh orange ('83)	950.00	275.00

For overprint see Rhodesia No. 49.

Nos. 26 and 36
Surcharged in Black

			1882	**Wmk. 1**
39	A6	½p on 3p claret	7,000.	160.00
a.		Hyphen omitted		3,750.

				Wmk. 2
40	A6	½p on 3p claret	45.00	5.00
a.		"ENNY"	2,500.	825.00
b.		"PENN"	1,500.	725.00
c.		Hyphen omitted	825.00	425.00
d.		Wmk. inverted		425.00

			1884-98	**Wmk. 16**
41	A6	½p gray black ('86)	8.00	.25
a.		Wmk. inverted	—	475.00
42	A6	½p yel green ('96)	1.80	.60
a.		½p green	3.25	.60
43	A6	1p rose ('85)	10.00	.25
a.		Wmk inverted	—	225.00

44	A6	2p bister	11.00	.25
a.		2p pale bister ('84)	36.00	1.50
b.		As "a," wmk inverted	—	350.00
45	A6	2p choc brown ('97)	2.50	2.25
46	A6	3p red violet ('98)	15.00	1.20
47	A6	4p blue ('90)	19.00	.60
48	A6	4p pale ol grn ('97)	8.00	3.25
49	A3	6p violet	14.00	.25
a.		6p reddish purple	72.50	2.00
b.		6p bright mauve	13.00	.60
c.		As "a," wmk inverted	—	375.00
50	A3	1sh dull bluish grn ('89)	140.00	.60
a.		1sh green ('85)	165.00	6.00
b.		Wmk. inverted	—	475.00
51	A6	1sh blue grn ('94)	85.00	6.50
52	A6	1sh yel buff ('96)	15.00	2.75
53	A6	5sh orange ('87)	130.00	8.00
54	A6	5sh brown org ('96)	100.00	5.00
		Nos. 41-54 (14)	559.30	31.75

For surcharges see Nos. 58, 162, 165-166.
For overprints see Rhodesia Nos. 43, 45-48.

Type of 1871 Surcharged in Black

1891, Mar.

55	A6	2½p on 3p deep magenta	6.00	.25
a.		"1" of "½" has straight serif	75.00	37.50
b.		2½p on 3p vio rose	13.00	2.00
c.		As "a," vio rose	90.00	60.00

Hope Seated — A13

1892-96

56	A13	2½p sage green	18.00	.25
a.		2½p olive green	18.00	.65
57	A13	2½p ultra ('96)	9.00	.25

For surcharge see No. N4. For overprint see Orange River Colony No. 55.

No. 44 Surcharged in Black

1893, Mar.

58	A6	1p on 2p bister	4.75	.60
a.		Double surcharge		500.00
b.		No period after "PENNY"	85.00	20.00
c.		1p on 2p pale bister (#44a)	10.00	2.50

Hope Standing A15 — Table Mountain and Bay; Coat of Arms A16

1893-1902

59	A15	½p green ('98)	6.50	.25
60	A15	1p rose	2.50	.25
a.		1p carmine	6.00	2.00
b.		Wmk. inverted	—	160.00
61	A15	3p red violet ('02)	5.50	2.50
		Nos. 59-61 (3)	14.50	3.00

For surcharges see Nos. 163-164, N2. For overprints see Orange River Colony Nos. 54, 56, Rhodesia No. 44, Transvaal Nos. 236-236A.

1900, Jan.

62	A16	1p carmine rose	6.00	.25
a.		Wmk. inverted	—	160.00

King Edward VII — A17

Various frames.

1902-04   **Wmk. 16**

63	A17	½p emerald	2.75	.25
64	A17	1p car rose	2.50	.25
a.		Wmk. inverted	—	—
b.		Wmk. inverted and reversed	—	—
65	A17	2p brown ('04)	17.50	.95
a.		Wmk. inverted	—	—
66	A17	2½p ultra ('04)	4.00	9.00
67	A17	3p red violet ('03)	13.00	1.40
68	A17	4p ol green ('03)	16.00	.80
69	A17	6p violet ('03)	24.00	.60
70	A17	1sh bister	17.50	1.25
71	A17	5sh brown org ('03)	130.00	25.00
		Nos. 63-71 (9)	227.25	39.50

Imperf. stamps are proofs.

Cape of Good Hope stamps were replaced by those of Union of South Africa.

OFFICIAL STAMPS

PERFORATED OFFICIAL STAMPS

Stamps of Cape of Good Hope punched with an 11-hole double triangle device were used by the Stationery and Printed Forms Branch of the Cape of Good Hope Colonial Secretary's Department between 1904 and 1906. They are only known used.

1904-06
On Seated Hope Stamps of 1884/1897

OA1	A6	2p pale bister (#44a)	27.50
OA2	A6	2p choc brown (#45)	27.50
OA3	A6	3p red violet (#46)	35.00
OA4	A6	4p pale bister (#48)	35.00
OA5	A3	6p violet (#49)	32.50

On Standing Hope Stamps of 1898/1902

OA6	A15	½p green (#59)	35.00
OA7	A15	3p red violet (#61)	27.50

On Table Mountain Stamp of 1900

OA8	A16	1p carmine rose (#62)	25.00

On King Edward VII issue of 1902-04

OA9	A17	½p emerald (#63)	35.00
OA10	A17	1p car rose (#64)	20.00
OA11	A17	2p brown (#65)	32.50
OA12	A17	3p red violet (#67)	27.50
OA13	A17	4p ol green (#68)	28.00
OA14	A17	6p violet (#69)	30.00
OA15	A17	1sh bister (#70)	37.50
OA16	A17	5sh brown org (#71)	85.00

ISSUED IN MAFEKING

Excellent forgeries of Nos. 162-179 are known.

Stamps of Cape of Good Hope Surcharged

1900, Mar. 24

162	A6	1p on ½p grn	275.00	80.00
163	A15	1p on ½p grn	325.00	100.00
164	A15	3p on 1p rose	275.00	65.00
165	A6	6p on 3p red vio	42,500.	300.00
166	A6	1sh on 4p pale ol green	8,000.	425.00

Stamps of Bechuanaland Protectorate Surcharged

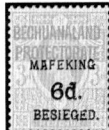

1900   **Wmk. 30**

167	A54	1p on ½p ver	275.00	77.50
a.		Inverted surcharge	—	7,000.
b.		Vert. pair, surcharge tête bêche		36,000.
168	A40	3p on 1p lilac	1,000.	120.00
a.		Double surcharge		30,000.
169	A56	6p on 2p grn & car	2,500.	100.00
170	A58	6p on 3p vio, yel	6,500.	375.00
a.		Inverted surcharge		38,000.
b.		Double surcharge	—	—

The lettering of "Mafeking Besieged" shows varying breaks in various letters, and may have either a period or no punctuation after "Mafeking."

On Stamps of Bechuanaland Wmk. 29

171	A1	6p on 3p violet & black	475.00	85.00

Wmk. 30

172	A59	1sh on 4p brn & grn	1,650.	95.00
a.		Double surch., one inverted	—	27,500.
b.		Triple surcharge	—	27,500.
c.		Inverted surcharge	—	27,500.
d.		Double surcharge	—	27,500.

Stamps of Bechuanaland Protectorate Surcharged

173	A40	3p on 1p lilac	1,050.	95.00
a.		Double surcharge	—	10,750.
174	A56	6p on 2p grn & car	1,300.	95.00
175	A62	1sh on 6p vio, rose	7,250.	120.00

On Stamps of Bechuanaland

176	A62	1sh on 6p vio, rose	45,000.	900.00
177	A65	2sh on 1sh green	14,500.	550.00

A fine mint example of the 1 shilling on 6 pence (Scott No. 176) sold for the equivalent of U.S. $13,077 at a London auction in 2003.

Sgt. Major Goodyear M1 — Gen. Robert S. S. Baden-Powell M2

Wmk. OCEANA FINE
Photographic Print
1900, Apr.   **Perf. 12**
Laid Paper

178	M1	1p blue, *blue*	1,100.	425.00
a.		On cover		10,000.
		Imperf. pair	25,000.	
179	M2	3p blue, *blue*, 18½mm wide	1,400.	400.00
		On cover		7,500.
a.		Horiz. pair, imperf. between	—	85,000.
b.		Double impression	—	26,000.
c.		Reversed design	80,000.	50,000.
180	M2	3p blue, *blue*, 21mm wide	12,000.	1,500.
		On cover		14,000.
a.		3p deep blue	12,000.	1,450.
		On cover		15,000.

The color of the paper varies from pale to deep blue.

OCEANA FINE is a sheet watermark and does not appear on every stamp.

Imperfs of No. 178 are proofs.

There is one used pair of No. 179a privately owned. A single used, partially imperf. example of No. 179 exists. Value, *$37,000.* There are four used examples of No. 179b reported. There are 2 unused and 6 used examples of No. 179c privately owned.

Issued: No. 179, Apr. 6; Nos. 178 and 180, Apr. 10.

ISSUED IN VRYBURG

Under Boer Occupation

Cape of Good Hope Stamps of 1884-96 Surcharged

Two Types of Surcharge:
Type I — Surcharge 10mm high. Space between lines 5½mm.
Type II — Surcharge 12mm high. Space between lines 7½mm.

1899, Nov.   **Wmk. 16**   *Perf. 14*

N1	A6	½p on ½p emer (I)	240.	95.00
	a.	Type II	2,000.	825.
N2	A15	1p on 1p rose (I)	275.	120.
	a.	Double surcharge		
	b.	Type II	2,250.	950.
N3	A3	2p on 6p vio (II)	2,500.	600.
N4	A13	2½p on 2½p ultra (I)	2,000.	500.
	a.	Type II	12,000.	5,000.

Italic Z in "Z.A.R."

N1b	A6	½p on ½p	2,000.	825.00
N2c	A15	1p on 1p	2,250.	950.00
N3a	A3	2p on 6p	13,000.	5,000.
N4b	A13	2½p on 2½p	13,000.	5,000.

"Z.A.R." stands for Zuid Afrikaansche Republiek (South African Republic).

Under British Occupation

Transvaal Stamps of 1895-96 Handstamped

1900   **Unwmk.**   *Perf. 12½*

N5	A13	½p green	—	3,250.
N6	A13	1p rose & grn	10,750.	5,000.
N7	A13	2p brown & grn	—	37,500.
N8	A13	2½p ultra & grn	—	37,500.

CAPE VERDE

'kāp 'vərd

LOCATION — A group of 10 islands and five islets in the Atlantic Ocean, about 500 miles due west of Senegal.
GOVT. — Portuguese Territory
AREA — 1,557 sq. mi.
POP. — 296,093 (1980)
CAPITAL — Praia

1000 Reis = 1 Milreis
100 Centavos = 1 Escudo (1913)

BR. POSTAL AGENCY IN CAPE VERDE

FORERUNNERS — British Postal Agency
Crowned Circle handstamp type VII is pictured in the Crowned Circle Handstamps and Great Britain Used Abroad section.

St. Vincent (San Vicente)
1851
A1 VII Crowned circle handstamp on cover, Type VII, inscribed "PAID AT ST. VICENT C. DE V."   6,000.

Crown of Portugal — A1

1877   **Unwmk.**   **Typo.**   *Perf. 12½*

1	A1	5r black	5.00	2.00
2	A1	10r yellow	50.00	11.00
	b.	10r orange bister	50.00	11.00
3	A1	20r bister	3.00	1.40
	b.	20r pale bister	2.40	1.25
4	A1	25r rose	2.50	1.40
5	A1	40r blue	82.50	50.00
	b.	Cliche of Mozambique in Cape Verde plate, in pair with #5	2,000.	1,400.
	d.	40r pale blue	90.00	50.00
6	A1	50r green	150.00	72.50
	b.	50r yellow green	90.00	50.00
7	A1	100r lilac	8.25	3.50
	b.	100r pale lilac	9.00	2.25

8	A1	200r orange	5.00	3.75
9	A1	300r brown	6.00	5.25
		Nos. 1-9 (9)	312.25	150.80

Perf. 13½

1a	A1	5r black	3.50	1.25
2a	A1	10r yellow	55.00	13.00
3a	A1	20r bister	2.40	1.25
4a	A1	25r rose	9.00	4.75
5a	A1	40r blue	75.00	40.00
	c.	Cliche of Mozambique in Cape Verde plate, in pair with #5a	1,500.	1,500.
6a	A1	50r green	90.00	50.00
7a	A1	100r lilac	7.25	3.75
8a	A1	200r orange	9.00	5.75
		Nos. 1a-8a (8)	251.15	117.75

1881-85   *Perf. 12½*

10	A1	10r green	2.75	2.10
11	A1	20r carmine ('85)	5.50	3.75
12	A1	25r violet ('85)	4.00	3.00
13	A1	40r yellow buff	2.40	1.75
	a.	Imperf.	40.00	
	b.	Cliche of Mozambique in Cape Verde plate, in pair with #13	110.00	110.00
	c.	As "b," imperf.	—	
14	A1	50r blue	6.75	4.25
		Nos. 10-14 (5)	21.40	14.85

Reprints of the 1877-85 issues are on smooth white chalky paper, ungummed, and on thin white paper with shiny white gum. They are perf 13½.

Perf. 13½

10a	A1	10r green	2.40	1.10
11a	A1	20r carmine ('85)	45.00	30.00
13d	A1	40r yellow buff	4.25	3.00
	e.	Cliche of Mozambique in Cape Verde plate, in pair with #13d	100.00	75.00
14a	A1	50r blue	6.50	3.50

King Luiz — A2

1886   **Embossed**   *Perf. 13½*
Chalk-Surfaced Paper

15	A2	5r black	4.50	3.00
	a.	Perf 12½	4.25	3.00
16	A2	10r green	6.75	3.00
	a.	Perf 12½	4.75	2.10

Perf. 12½

17	A2	20r carmine	9.00	5.25
	a.	Perf. 13½	6.50	4.00
18	A2	25r violet	9.00	5.50
19	A2	40r chocolate	9.00	3.50
	a.	Perf. 13½	8.75	4.50
20	A2	50r blue	9.00	3.50
21	A2	100r yel brown	9.00	4.50
22	A2	200r gray lilac	18.00	10.50
23	A2	300r orange	24.00	4.25
		Nos. 15-23 (9)	98.25	43.00

The 25r, 50r and 100r have been reprinted in aniline colors with clean-cut Perf. 13½.
For surcharges see Nos. 59-67, 184-187.

King Carlos — A3

1894-95   **Typo.**   *Perf. 11½*

24	A3	5r orange	1.60	1.25
25	A3	10r redsh violet	1.60	1.25
26	A3	15r chocolate	4.00	2.60
27	A3	20r lavender	4.00	2.60
28	A3	25r dp green	3.50	2.25
29	A3	50r lt blue	3.50	2.25
31	A3	80r yel grn ('95)	12.00	6.50
32	A3	100r brn, buff ('95)	9.00	5.25
33b	A3	150r car, rose	70.00	45.00
35	A3	300r dk blue, sal ('95)	45.00	17.00

Perf. 12½

26a	A3	15r	150.00	120.00
28a	A3	25r	4.00	3.25
30	A3	75r carmine ('95)	11.50	5.75
32a	A3	100r	100.00	55.00
33a	A3	150r	400.00	300.00
34a	A3	200r	150.00	120.00

Perf. 13½

29a	A3	15r	14.00	4.50
30a	A3	75r	55.00	42.00
31a	A3	80r	45.00	35.00
33	A3	150r car, rose ('95)	40.00	27.00
34	A3	200r dk blue, lt blue ('95)	40.00	27.00

For surcharges see Nos. 68-78, 137, 189-193, 201-205.

King Carlos — A4

1898-1903   *Perf. 11½*
Name and Value in Black except 500r

36	A4	2½r gray	.40	.30
37	A4	5r orange	.50	.30
38	A4	10r lt green	.55	.30
39	A4	15r brown	5.50	2.00
40	A4	15r gray green ('03)	1.90	1.25
41	A4	20r gray violet	1.60	1.00
42	A4	25r sea green	3.50	1.25
	a.	Perf 12½	300.00	180.00
43	A4	25r carmine ('03)	1.00	.40
44	A4	50r dark blue	3.50	1.50
45	A4	50r brown ('03)	3.75	2.40
46	A4	65r slate blue ('03)	40.00	30.00
47	A4	75r rose	10.00	3.50
48	A4	75r lilac ('03)	3.50	2.25
49	A4	80r violet	8.50	3.50
50	A4	100r dk blue, blue	3.50	2.00
51	A4	115r org brn, pink ('03)	15.00	13.50
52	A4	130r brown, straw ('03)	15.00	13.50
53	A4	150r brown, straw ('03)	8.50	6.75
54	A4	200r red vio, pnksh	4.00	3.00
55	A4	300r dk blue, rose	10.00	5.00
56	A4	400r dull blue, straw ('03)	16.00	10.50
57	A4	500r blk & red, blue ('01)	10.00	5.00
58	A4	700r violet, yelsh ('01)	28.00	17.50
		Nos. 36-58 (23)	194.20	126.70

For overprints and suecharges see Nos. 80-99, 139, 200.

Regular Issues Surcharged in Red or Black

Two spacing types of surcharge. See note above Angola No. 61.

On Issue of 1886
1902, Dec. 1   *Perf. 12½, 13½*

59	A2	65r on 5r black (R)	7.00	3.75
60	A2	65r on 200r gray lilac	7.00	3.75
61	A2	65r on 300r orange	7.00	3.75
62	A2	115r on 10r green	7.00	3.75
63	A2	115r on 20r rose	7.00	3.75
	a.	Perf 13½	60.00	35.00
64	A2	130r on 50r blue	7.00	3.75
65	A2	130r on 100r brown	7.00	3.75
66	A2	400r on 25r violet	5.00	2.60
67	A2	400r on 40r choc	9.00	3.75
	a.	Perf 13½	50.00	35.00

On Issue of 1894
Perf. 11½, 12½, 13½

68	A3	65r on 10r red violet	7.00	3.75
69	A3	65r on 20r lavender	7.00	3.75
70	A3	65r on 100r brown, buff	8.50	5.25
	a.	Perf 12½	26.00	24.00
71	A3	115r on 5r orange	5.00	3.00
	a.	Inverted surcharge	60.00	60.00
72	A3	115r on 25r blue grn	4.00	2.10
	a.	Perf 11½	55.00	55.00
73	A3	115r on 150r car, rose	9.00	6.50
	a.	Perf 13½	55.00	25.00
74	A3	130r on 75r car	5.00	3.00
	a.	Perf 13½	250.00	200.00
75	A3	130r on 80r yel grn	4.00	2.00
	a.	Perf 11½	2.25	1.90
76	A3	130r on 200r dk blue, blue	4.00	2.60
77	A3	400r on 50r lt blue	9.00	3.00
	a.	Inverted surcharge	65.00	55.00
	b.	Perf 13½	300.00	300.00
78	A3	400r on 300r dk blue, sal	4.00	1.75

On Newspaper Stamp of 1893

79	N1	400r on 2½r brown	1.60	1.50
	a.	Inverted surcharge		27.50
	b.	Perf 12½	225.00	200.00
	c.	Perf 11½	1.25	1.00
		Nos. 59-79 (21)	131.10	70.80

Reprints of Nos. 59, 66, 67, and 77 have shiny white gum and clean-cut perforation 13½.
For overprint and surcharge see Nos. 137, 205-206.

Overprinted in Black
On Nos. 39, 42, 44, 47

1902-03   *Perf. 11½*

80	A4	15r brown	2.00	1.25
81	A4	25r sea green	2.00	1.25
82	A4	50r blue ('03)	2.00	1.25
83	A4	75r rose ('03)	3.75	2.75
	a.	Inverted overprint	42.50	42.50
		Nos. 80-83 (4)	9.75	6.50

For overprint see No. 139.

No. 46 Surcharged in Black

1905, July 1

84	A4	50r on 65r slate blue	4.00	3.00

Stamps of 1898-1903 Overprinted in Carmine or Green

1911, Aug. 20

85	A4	2½r gray	.25	.25
86	A4	5r orange	.25	.25
87	A4	10r lt green	1.00	.80
88	A4	15r gray green	.90	.45
89	A4	20r gray violet	1.50	.80
90	A4	25r carmine (G)	.90	.45
91	A4	50r brown	8.50	6.00
92	A4	75r red lilac	1.40	.80
93	A4	100r dk blue, blue	1.40	.80
94	A4	115r org brn, pink	1.40	.80
95	A4	130r brown, straw	1.40	.80
96	A4	200r red vio, pnksh	6.50	4.00
97	A4	400r dull bl, straw	3.50	1.25
98	A4	500r blk & red, bl	3.50	1.25
99	A4	700r violet, straw	3.50	1.40
		Nos. 85-99 (15)	35.90	20.10

King Manuel II — A5

Overprinted in Carmine or Green

1912   *Perf. 11½x12*

100	A5	2½r violet	.25	.25
101	A5	5r black	.25	.25
102	A5	10r gray grn	.45	.40
103	A5	20r carmine (G)	2.40	1.40
104	A5	25r vio brown	.45	.25
105	A5	50r dk blue	5.00	3.50
106	A5	75r bister brn	1.10	1.00
107	A5	100r brown, lt grn	1.10	1.00
108	A5	200r dk green, sal	1.75	1.10
109	A5	300r black, azure	1.75	1.10

Perf. 14½x15

110	A5	400r black & blue	3.75	3.00
111	A5	500r ol grn & vio brn	3.75	3.00
		Nos. 100-111 (12)	22.00	16.25

Common Design Types pictured following the introduction.

Vasco da Gama Issue of Various Portuguese Colonies

Common Design Types CD20-CD27 Surcharged

On Stamps of Macao
1913, Feb. 13   *Perf. 12½ to 16*

112		¼c on ½a blue grn	2.00	.85
113		½c on 1a red	2.00	.85
114		1c on 2a red violet	2.00	.85

115	2½c on 4a yel grn	2.00	.85
116	5c on 8a dk blue	7.00	6.00
117	7½c on 12a vio brn	5.75	2.40
118	10c on 16a bister brn	2.25	1.60
119	15c on 24a bister	5.75	3.50
	Nos. 112-119 (8)	28.75	16.90

On Stamps of Portuguese Africa
Perf. 14 to 15

120	¼c on 2½r bl grn	1.40	.60
121	½c on 5r red	1.40	.60
122	1c on 10r red vio	1.40	.60
123	2½c on 25r yel grn	1.40	.60
124	5c on 50r dk blue	2.00	1.50
125	7½c on 75r vio brn	3.75	3.00
126	10c on 100r bis brn	2.00	1.90
127	15c on 150r bister	2.50	2.50
	Nos. 120-127 (8)	15.85	11.30

On Stamps of Timor

128	¼c on ½a bl grn	1.40	.85
129	½c on 1a red	1.40	.85
130	1c on 2a red vio	1.40	.85
131	2½c on 4a yel grn	1.40	.85
132	5c on 8a dk blue	7.00	5.50
133	7½c On 12a vio brn	5.50	3.00
134	10c on 16a bis brn	2.25	1.90
135	15c on 24a bister	4.50	2.40
	Nos. 128-135 (8)	24.85	16.20
	Nos. 112-135 (24)	66.90	44.40

For surcharges see Nos. 197-198.

No. 75 Overprinted in
Red

1913   **Perf. 11½, 12½, 13½**
137 A3 130r on 80r yel grn   5.00 3.75

Nos. 73 and 76 overprinted but not issued.
Values, $15, $20.

Same Overprint on No. 83 in Green
1914   **Perf. 12**
139 A4 75r rose   5.50 3.75
   a. "PROVISORIO" double (G and   70.00 57.50
     R)

Ceres — A6

1914   **Typo.**   **Perf. 15x14**
Name and Value in Black
Chalky Paper

144	A6 ¼c olive brn	.75	.55
	Never hinged	1.20	
145	A6 ½c black	.45	.30
	Never hinged	.70	
146	A6 1c blue grn	5.25	4.75
	Never hinged	8.50	
147	A6 1½c lilac brown	.75	.55
	Never hinged	1.20	
148	A6 2c carmine	1.25	.70
	Never hinged	2.00	
149	A6 2½c lt violet	.60	.50
	Never hinged	.95	
150	A6 5c deep blue	1.00	.80
	Never hinged	1.60	
151	A6 7½c yel brn	1.25	.70
	Never hinged	2.00	
152	A6 8c slate	1.25	.75
	Never hinged	2.00	
153	A6 10c orange brn	2.00	.90
	Never hinged	3.25	
154	A6 15c brn rose ('22)	8.50	5.00
	Never hinged	13.50	
155	A6 20c yel grn	2.00	2.00
	Never hinged	3.25	
156	A6 30c brown, *grn*	4.00	3.00
	Never hinged	4.75	
157	A6 40c brown, *pink*	4.00	3.00
	Never hinged	4.75	
158	A6 50c orange, *sal*	4.00	3.00
	Never hinged	4.75	
159	A6 1e green, *blue*	3.00	3.00
	Never hinged	4.75	
	Nos. 144-159 (16)	32.55	24.20

1916

Enamel-Surfaced Paper

160	A6 ¼c olive brn	.45	.30
	Never hinged	.70	
161	A6 5c deep blue	.75	.45
	Never hinged	1.20	

Ordinary Paper

162	A6 ¼c olive brn	.25	.25
	Never hinged	.40	
163	A6 ½c black	.25	.25
	Never hinged	.40	

164	A6 1c blue grn	.85	.75
	Never hinged	1.35	
165	A6 1c yel grn ('22)	.25	.25
	Never hinged	.40	
166	A6 1½c lilac brown	.25	.25
	Never hinged	.40	
167	A6 2c carmine	.25	.25
	Never hinged	.40	
168	A6 2½c lt violet	.25	.25
	Never hinged	.40	
169	A6 3c org ('22)	.30	.25
	Never hinged	.50	
170	A6 4c rose ('22)	.25	*.25*
	Never hinged	.40	
171	A6 12c blue grn ('22)	.35	.25
	Never hinged	.55	
172	A6 15c plum	.90	.75
	Never hinged	1.45	
	Nos. 162-172 (11)	4.15	3.75

1920-26   **Perf. 12x11½**

173	A6 ¼c olive brn	.25	.25
	Never hinged	.40	
174	A6 ½c black	.25	.25
	Never hinged	.40	
175	A6 1c yel grn ('22)	.25	.25
	Never hinged	.40	
176	A6 1½c lilac brown	.25	.25
	Never hinged	.40	
177	A6 2c carmine	.25	.25
	Never hinged	.40	
178	A6 2c gray ('26)	.25	.25
	Never hinged	.40	
179	A6 2½c lt violet	.25	.25
	Never hinged	.40	
180	A6 3c org ('22)	2.40	2.25
	Never hinged	3.75	
181	A6 4c rose ('22)	.35	*.50*
	Never hinged	.55	
182	A6 4½c gray ('22)	.25	*.50*
	Never hinged	.40	
183	A6 5c brt blue ('22)	.25	.25
	Never hinged	.40	
183A	A6 6c lilac ('22)	.25	*.50*
	Never hinged	.40	
183B	A6 7c ultra ('22)	.25	*.50*
	Never hinged	.40	
183C	A6 7½c yel brn	.25	*.50*
	Never hinged	.40	
183D	A6 8c slate	.40	.30
	Never hinged	.65	
183E	A6 10c orange brn	.25	.25
	Never hinged	.40	
183F	A6 12c blue grn ('22)	.35	.25
	Never hinged	.55	
183G	A6 15c plum	.30	.30
	Never hinged	.50	
183H	A6 20c yel grn	.25	.25
	Never hinged	.40	
183I	A6 24c ultra ('26)	1.50	1.40
	Never hinged	2.40	
183J	A6 25c choc ('26)	1.50	1.40
	Never hinged	2.40	
183K	A6 30c gray grn ('22)	.75	.25
	Never hinged	1.20	
183L	A6 40c turq blue ('22)	1.75	.25
	Never hinged	2.75	
183M	A6 50c violet ('26)	1.75	.30
	Never hinged	2.75	
183N	A6 60c dk blue ('22)	1.75	.45
	Never hinged	2.75	
183O	A6 60c rose ('26)	1.75	.45
	Never hinged	2.75	
183P	A6 80c brt rose ('22)	2.00	1.10
	Never hinged	3.25	
	Nos. 173-183P (27)	20.05	13.70

For surcharge see No. 214.

Glazed Paper

183Q	A6 1e rose ('22)	7.00	2.25
	Never hinged	11.00	
183R	A6 1e dp blue ('26)	9.00	1.50
	Never hinged	14.50	
183S	A6 2e dk violet ('22)	10.00	4.00
	Never hinged	16.00	
183T	A6 5e buff ('26)	25.00	12.00
	Never hinged	40.00	
183U	A6 10e pink ('26)	100.00	60.00
	Never hinged	160.00	
183V	A6 20e pale turq ('26)	150.00	80.00
	Never hinged	240.00	
	Nos. 183Q-183V (6)	301.00	144.75

Provisional Issue of
1902 Overprinted in
Carmine

1915   **Perf. 11½, 12½, 13½**
184 A2 115r on 10r green
     (11½)   2.50 2.00
  a. Perf. 13½   100.00 100.00
185 A2 115r on 20r rose
     (12½)   2.75 1.75
  a. Perf. 13½   30.00 30.00
186 A2 130r on 50r blue
     (12½)   2.50 1.25
187 A2 130r on 100r brown
     (12½)   1.60 1.00
188 A3 115r on 5r orange
     (11½)   1.40 .75
  a. Inverted overprint   45.00
189 A3 115r on 25r blue grn
     (12½)   2.50 1.75
  a. Perf. 11½   70.00 70.00
190 A3 115r on 150r car,
     rose (11½)   1.00 .75

191 A3 130r on 75r carmine
     (12½)   2.50 1.00
192 A3 130r on 80r yel grn
     (11½)   2.50 1.00
  a. Inverted overprint   50.00
193 A3 130r on 200r bl, *bl*
     (13½)   2.00 1.00
  a. Perf. 12½   90.00 80.00
   Nos. 184-193 (10)   21.25 12.25

War Tax
Stamps of
Portuguese
Africa
Srchd.

1921, Feb. 3   **Perf. 15x14**
194 WT1 ¼c on 1c green   .60 .40
195 WT1 ½c on 1c green   .70 .50
  a. "1/2" instead of "½" as
     shown   15.00 15.00
196 WT1 1c green   .65 .50

Perf. 12x11½
194B WT1 ¼c on 1c green   1.20 1.00
195B WT1 ½c on 1c green   1.20 1.00
  a. "1/2" instead of "½" as
     shown   19.00 19.00
196B WT1 1c green   1.10 .95

Nos. 194B-196B also exist on enameled
paper. The values are the same.

Nos. 127 and
126
Surcharged

Perf. 14 to 15
197 CD27 2c on 15c on
     150r   2.25 1.50
198 CD26 4c on 10c on
     100r   2.75 2.60
  a. On No. 118 (error)   175.00 175.00
The 4c surcharge also exists on No. 134.
Value, $500.

No. 50 Surcharged

Perf. 12
200 A4 6c on 100r dk bl, *bl*   2.75 2.10
  a. No accent on "U" of surcharge   17.50 15.00
   Nos. 194-200 (6)   9.70 7.60

No. 200 has an accent on the "U" of the
surcharge.

Stamps of 1913-15
Surcharged

1922, Apr.   **Perf. 11½, 12½, 13½**
On No. 137
201 A3 4c on 130r on 80r   1.25 1.25
On Nos. 191-193
202 A3 4c on 130r on 75r   1.60 1.60
203 A3 4c on 130r on 80r   1.25 1.25
204 A3 4c on 130r on 200r   1.00 .80
  a. Perf. 12½   15.00 15.00
   Nos. 201-204 (4)   5.10 4.90

Surcharge of Nos. 201-204 with smaller $
occurs once in sheet of 28. Value eight times
normal.

Nos. 78-79
Surcharged

1925   **Perf. 13½, 11½**
205 A3 40c on 400r on 300r   1.00 .80
206 N1 40c on 400r on 2½r   1.00 .75

No. 176 Surcharged

1931, Nov.   **Perf. 12x11½**
214 A6 70c on 80c brt rose   3.75 2.50

Ceres — A7

1934, May 1   **Wmk. 232**

215	A7 1c bister	.25	*.25*
	Never hinged	.40	
216	A7 5c olive brown	.25	.25
	Never hinged	.40	
217	A7 10c violet	.25	.25
	Never hinged	.40	
218	A7 15c black	.25	.25
	Never hinged	.40	
219	A7 20c gray	.25	.25
	Never hinged	.40	
220	A7 30c dk green	.25	.25
	Never hinged	.40	
221	A7 40c red org	.25	.25
	Never hinged	.40	
222	A7 45c brt blue	2.00	.85
	Never hinged	3.25	
223	A7 50c brown	.90	.55
	Never hinged	1.45	
224	A7 60c olive grn	.90	.55
	Never hinged	1.45	
225	A7 70c brown org	.90	.55
	Never hinged	1.45	
226	A7 80c emerald	.90	.55
	Never hinged	1.45	
227	A7 85c deep rose	4.00	2.60
	Never hinged	6.50	
228	A7 1e maroon	2.75	.50
	Never hinged	4.50	
229	A7 1.40e dk blue	3.75	3.00
	Never hinged	6.00	
230	A7 2e dk violet	4.50	2.60
	Never hinged	7.25	
231	A7 5e apple green	21.00	5.00
	Never hinged	32.50	
232	A7 10e olive bister	32.50	18.00
	Never hinged	52.50	
233	A7 20e orange	60.00	24.00
	Never hinged	95.00	
	Nos. 215-233 (19)	135.85	60.50

For surcharge see No. 256 in *Scott Standard Postage Stamp Catalogue*, Vol. 2.

Vasco da Gama Issue
Common Design Types
1938   **Unwmk.**   **Perf. 13½x13**
Name and Value in Black

234	CD34 1c gray green	.25	.25
235	CD34 5c orange brn	.25	.25
236	CD34 10c dk carmine	.25	.25
237	CD34 15c dk vio brn	1.00	.85
238	CD34 20c slate	.50	.25
239	CD35 30c rose vio	.50	.25
240	CD35 35c brt green	.50	.25
241	CD35 40c brown	.50	.25
242	CD35 50c brt red vio	.50	.25
243	CD36 60c gray blk	.50	.25
244	CD36 70c brown vio	.50	.25
245	CD36 80c orange	.45	.25
246	CD36 1e red	.60	.25
247	CD37 1.75e blue	1.90	.70
248	CD37 2e dk blue grn	3.50	2.00
249	CD37 5e ol grn	8.00	2.00
250	CD38 10e blue vio	13.00	2.60
251	CD38 20e red brown	37.50	5.00
	Nos. 234-251 (18)	70.20	16.15

For surcharges see Nos. 255, 271-276, 288-
292 in *Scott Standard Postage Stamp Catalogue*, Vol. 2.

Outline Map of
Africa — A8

1939, June 23 Litho.   Perf. 11½x12

252	A8	80c vio, *pale rose*	5.00	3.50
253	A8	1.75e blue, *pale bl*	40.00	30.00
254	A8	20e brown, *buff*	85.00	26.00
		Nos. 252-254 (3)	130.00	59.50

Visit of the President of Portugal in 1939.

AIR POST STAMPS

Common Design Type
Name and Value in Black
Perf. 13½x13

1938, July 26   Unwmk.

C1	CD39	10c red orange	.60	.50
C2	CD39	20c purple	.60	.50
C3	CD39	50c orange	.60	.50
C4	CD39	1e ultra	.60	.50
C5	CD39	2e lilac brown	1.40	.80
C6	CD39	3e dk green	1.75	1.40
C7	CD39	5e red brown	5.50	2.10
C8	CD39	9e rose carmine	9.00	3.75
C9	CD39	10e magenta	9.75	5.00
		Nos. C1-C9 (9)	29.80	15.05
		Set, never hinged	50.00	

No. C7 exists with overprint "Exposicao Internacional de Nova York, 1939-1940" and Trylon and Perisphere.

POSTAGE DUE STAMPS

D1

1904   Unwmk.   Typo.   Perf. 12

J1	D1	5r yellow grn	.40	.25
J2	D1	10r slate	.40	.25
J3	D1	20r yellow brn	.50	.40
J4	D1	30r red orange	1.25	.40
J5	D1	50r gray brown	.50	.35
J6	D1	60r red brown	9.25	4.25
J7	D1	100r lilac	1.75	1.25
J8	D1	130r dull blue	1.90	1.25
J9	D1	200r carmine	1.60	1.60
J10	D1	500r dull violet	5.00	3.00
		Nos. J1-J10 (10)	22.55	13.00

Overprinted in Carmine or Green

1911

J11	D1	5r yellow grn	.30	.25
J12	D1	10r slate	.30	.25
J13	D1	20r yellow brn	.35	.25
J14	D1	30r orange	.35	.25
J15	D1	50r gray brown	.65	.40
J16	D1	60r red brown	.65	.40
J17	D1	100r lilac	.65	.40
J18	D1	130r dull blue	.75	.65
J19	D1	200r carmine (G)	2.00	1.50
J20	D1	500r dull violet	2.50	1.75
		Nos. J11-J20 (10)	8.50	6.10

D2

1921   Perf. 11½

J21	D2	½c yellow grn	.30	.25
J22	D2	1c slate	.30	.25
J23	D2	2c red brown	.30	.25
J24	D2	3c orange	.30	.25
J25	D2	5c gray brown	.30	.25
J26	D2	6c lt brown	.30	.25
J27	D2	10c red violet	.30	.25
J28	D2	13c dull blue	.55	.40
J29	D2	20c carmine	.60	.50
J30	D2	50c gray	1.75	1.10
		Nos. J21-J30 (10)	5.00	3.75

NEWSPAPER STAMP

N1

1893   Typo.   Unwmk.   Perf. 11½

P1	N1	2½r brown	1.50	.60
a.		Perf. 12½	3.00	1.50
b.		Perf. 13½	6.50	3.00

For surcharges see Nos. 79, 206.

POSTAL TAX STAMPS

Pombal Issue
Common Design Types

1925   Unwmk.   Engr.   Perf. 12½

RA1	CD28	15c dull vio & blk	1.25	1.10
RA2	CD29	15c dull vio & blk	1.25	1.10
RA3	CD30	15c dull vio & blk	1.25	1.10
		Nos. RA1-RA3 (3)	3.75	3.30

POSTAL TAX DUE STAMPS

Pombal Issue
Common Design Types

1925   Unwmk.   Perf. 12½

RAJ1	CD28	30c dull vio & blk	.75	.70
RAJ2	CD29	30c dull vio & blk	.75	.70
RAJ3	CD30	30c dull vio & blk	.75	.70
		Nos. RAJ1-RAJ3 (3)	2.25	2.10

CAROLINE ISLANDS

'kar-ə-ˌlīn 'ī-ləndz

LOCATION — A group of about 549 small islands in the West Pacific Ocean, north of the Equator.
GOVT. — German colony
AREA — 550 sq. mi.
POP. — 40,000 (approx. 1915)

100 Pfennig = 1 Mark

Watermark

Wmk. 125 — Lozenges

Stamps of Germany 1889-90 Overprinted in Black

#1-6

#1a-6a

Overprinted at 56 degree Angle

1900   Unwmk.   Perf. 13½x14½

1	A9	3pf dk brown	13.00	14.00
		Never hinged	30.00	
		On cover		110.00
		On cover, single franking		125.00
2	A9	5pf green	18.00	18.00
		Never hinged	37.50	
		On cover		70.00
		On cover, single franking		85.00
3	A10	10pf carmine	19.00	19.00
		Never hinged	50.00	
		On cover		70.00
		On cover, single franking		85.00
4	A10	20pf ultra	24.00	30.00
		Never hinged	55.00	
		On cover		150.00
		On cover, single franking		175.00
5	A10	25pf orange	55.00	65.00
		Never hinged	145.00	
		On cover		160.00
		On cover, single franking		375.00
6	A10	50pf red brown	55.00	65.00
		Never hinged	135.00	
		On cover		125.00
		On cover, single franking		160.00
		Nos. 1-6 (6)	184.00	211.00

1899
Overprinted at 48 degree Angle

1a	A9	3pf light brown	625.00	750.00
		Never hinged	1,600.	
		On cover		1,750.
		On cover, single franking		2,100.
2a	A9	5pf green	650.00	650.00
		Never hinged	1,700.	
		On cover		1,400.
		On cover, single franking		1,750.
3a	A10	10pf carmine	65.00	150.00
		Never hinged	175.00	
		On cover		300.00
		On cover, single franking		325.00
4a	A10	20pf ultra	65.00	150.00
		Never hinged	175.00	
		On cover		300.00
		On cover, single franking		375.00
5a	A10	25pf orange	1,650.	3,100.
		Never hinged	3,400.	
		On cover		4,750.
		On cover, single franking		6,750.
6a	A10	50pf red brown	900.00	1,600.
		Never hinged	1,500.	
		On cover		2,750.
		On cover, single franking		3,500.

Covers: Values for Nos. 1-5, 1a-5a are for covers paying the correct rates. Nos. 6, 6a are for overfranked complete covers, usually philatelic.

A3

Kaiser's Yacht "Hohenzollern" — A4

1901, Jan.   Typo.   Perf. 14

7	A3	3pf brown	1.10	1.75
		Never hinged	2.10	
		On cover		13.00
		On cover, single franking		50.00
8	A3	5pf green	1.10	2.10
		Never hinged	2.10	
		On cover		17.00
		On cover, single franking		21.00
9	A3	10pf carmine	1.10	5.00
		Never hinged	2.50	
		On cover		17.50
		On cover, single franking		25.00
a.		Half used as 5pf on cover, back-stamped in Jaluit ('05)		120.00
10	A3	20pf ultra	1.25	9.00
		Never hinged	3.75	
		On cover		40.00
		On cover, single franking		50.00
a.		Half used as 10pf on cover ('10)		8,500.
11	A3	25pf org & blk, *yel*	1.60	14.50
		Never hinged	4.25	
		On cover		75.00
		On cover, single franking		100.00
12	A3	30pf org & blk, *sal*	1.60	14.50
		Never hinged	4.25	
		On cover		75.00
		On cover, single franking		100.00
13	A3	40pf lake & blk	1.60	16.50
		Never hinged	4.25	
		On cover		75.00
		On cover, single franking		100.00
14	A3	50pf pur & blk, *sal*	2.00	22.50
		Never hinged	5.00	
		On cover		52.50
		On cover, single franking		60.00
15	A3	80pf lake & blk, *rose*	3.00	25.00
		Never hinged	6.25	
		On cover		55.00
		On cover, single franking		65.00

Engr.   Perf. 14½x14

16	A4	1m carmine	4.50	62.50
		Never hinged	11.00	
		On cover		110.00
		On cover, single franking		120.00
17	A4	2m blue	7.25	87.50
		Never hinged	18.50	
		On cover		120.00
		On cover, single franking		140.00
18	A4	3m black violet	10.00	150.00
		Never hinged	30.00	
		On cover		275.00
		On cover, single franking		300.00
19	A4	5m slate & carmine	160.00	550.00
		Never hinged	500.00	
		On cover		875.00
		On cover, single franking		1,100.
		Nos. 7-19 (13)	196.10	960.85

No. 9a is known as the "typhoon provisional" the stock of 5pf stamps having been destroyed

during a typhoon. Covers (cards) without backstamp, value about $72.50.
Forged cancellations are found on #7-19.
Covers: Values for Nos. 14-19 are for overfranked complete envelopes, usually philatelic.

No. 7 Handstamp Surcharged

1910, July 12

20	A3	5pf on 3pf brown		5,500.
a.		Inverted surcharge		7,750.
b.		Double surcharge		11,000.

Values are for stamps tied to cover. Stamps on piece sell for about 40% less.

1915-19   Wmk. 125   Typo.

21	A3	3pf brown ('19)	.90
		Never hinged	2.10
22	A3	5pf green	12.50
		Never hinged	32.50

Engr.

23	A4	5m slate & carmine (25x17 holes)	35.00
		Never hinged	120.00
a.		26x17 holes	42.50
		Never hinged	190.00
		Nos. 21-23 (3)	48.40

Nos. 21-23 were not placed in use.

CASTELLORIZO

ˌkäs-tə-ˈlor-ə-ˌzō

(Castelrosso)

LOCATION — A Mediterranean island in the Dodecanese group lying close to the coast of Asia Minor and about 60 miles east of Rhodes.
GOVT. — Italian Colony
AREA — 4 sq. mi.
POP. — 2,238 (1936)

Formerly a Turkish possession, Castellorizo was occupied by the French in 1915 & ceded to Italy after World War I.

25 Centimes = 1 Piaster
100 Centimes = 1 Franc

Issued under French Occupation

Stamps of French Offices in Turkey Overprinted

			1920	Unwmk.	Perf. 14x13½
1	A2	1c gray		55.00	62.50
		Never hinged		100.00	
		On cover			1,000.
a.		Inverted overprint		240.00	240.00
b.		Double overprint		400.00	440.00
2	A2	2c vio brn		60.00	67.50
		Never hinged		105.00	
		On cover			1,000.
a.		Double overprint		350.00	450.00
3	A2	3c red org		55.00	62.50
		Never hinged		100.00	
		On cover			1,000.
a.		Inverted overprint		225.00	225.00
4	A2	5c green		85.00	85.00
		Never hinged		160.00	
		On cover			1,100.
a.		Inverted overprint		275.00	275.00
5	A3	10c rose		97.50	97.50
		Never hinged		190.00	
		On cover			1,350.
6	A3	15c pale red		135.00	135.00
		On cover			2,000.
a.		Inverted overprint		450.00	450.00
7	A3	20c brn vio		135.00	135.00
		On cover			2,000.
8	A5	1pi on 25c blue		125.00	125.00
		On cover			2,000.
a.		Pair, one without overprint		800.00	800.00
9	A3	30c lilac		150.00	150.00
		On cover			2,500.

Overprint Reading Down

10	A4	40c red & pale bl (down)		225.00	225.00
		On cover			3,400.
a.		Inverted ovpt (reading up)		925.00	925.00
11	A6	2pi on 50c bis brn & lav (down)		250.00	275.00
		On cover			3,400.
a.		Inverted ovpt (reading up)		975.00	975.00
b.		Double overprint		1,350.	1,350.
12	A6	4pi on 1fr cl & ol grn (down)		300.00	350.00
		On cover			1,350. / 1,350.
a.		Double overprint		1,350.	1,350.
b.		Inverted ovpt (reading up)		1,050.	1,050.
13	A6	20pi on 5fr dk bl & buff		675.00	750.00
		On cover			—
a.		Double overprint		1,900.	1,900.
		Nos. 1-13 (13)		2,347.	2,520.

"S" instead of "Z" in "CASTELLORIZO"

1c	A2	1c gray		140.00	140.00
2c	A2	2c vio brn		160.00	160.00
3c	A2	3c red org		140.00	140.00
4c	A2	5c green		225.00	225.00
5c	A3	10c rose		240.00	240.00
6c	A3	15c pale red		800.00	800.00
7c	A3	20c brn vio		800.00	800.00
8c	A5	1pi on 25c blue		750.00	750.00
9c	A3	30c lilac		800.00	800.00
10c	A4	40c red & pale bl (down)		725.00	725.00
11c	A6	2pi on 50c bis brn & lav (down)		800.00	800.00
12c	A6	4pi on 1fr cl & ol grn (down)		800.00	800.00
13c	A6	20pi on 5fr dk bl & buff		1,800.	2,000.

"CASTELLORIZO" Inverted

1d	A2	1c gray		200.00	200.00
2d	A2	2c vio brn		225.00	225.00
3d	A2	3c red org		200.00	200.00
4d	A2	5c green		275.00	275.00
5d	A3	10c rose		300.00	300.00
6d	A3	15c pale red		1,000.	1,000.
7d	A3	20c brn vio		1,000.	1,000.
8d	A5	1pi on 25c blue		925.00	925.00
9d	A3	30c lilac		1,000.	1,000.

No Dot after "N"

10e	A4	40c red & pale bl (down)		640.00	640.00
11e	A6	2pi on 50c bis brn & lav (down)		675.00	675.00

12e	A6	4pi on 1fr cl & ol grn (down)		675.00	675.00
13e	A6	20pi on 5fr dk bl & buff		1,600.	1,800.

No. 1-9 were overprinted in blocks of 25. Position 4 had "CASTELLORIZO" inverted and Positions 8 and 18 had "CASTELLORISO." The later variety also occurred in the setting of the form for Nos. 10-13.

"B. N. F." are the initials of "Base Navale Francaise".

Covers: Values for covers are for commercial items. Philatelic covers sell for less.

Overprinted in Black or Red

1920
On Stamps of French Offices in Turkey

14	A2	1c gray		37.50	42.50
		Never hinged		67.50	
		On cover			750.00
15	A2	2c vio brn		42.50	50.00
		Never hinged		75.00	
		On cover			875.00
16	A2	3c red org		72.50	77.50
		Never hinged		120.00	
		On cover			1,100.
17	A2	5c green (R)		37.50	37.50
		Never hinged		67.50	
		On cover			750.00
19	A3	10c rose		47.50	47.50
		Never hinged		82.50	
		On cover			925.00
20	A3	15c pale red		77.50	77.50
		Never hinged		135.00	
		On cover			1,100.
21	A3	20c brn vio		120.00	120.00
		Never hinged			
		On cover			1,750.
22	A5	1pi on 25c bl (R)		72.50	72.50
		Never hinged		120.00	
		On cover			925.00
23	A3	30c lilac (R)		85.00	92.50
		Never hinged		150.00	
		On cover			1,250.
24	A4	40c red & pale bl		77.50	77.50
		Never hinged		135.00	
		On cover			1,100.
25	A6	2pi on 50c bis brn & lav		72.50	72.50
		Never hinged		130.00	
		On cover			1,050.
26	A6	4pi on 1fr claret & ol grn		125.00	140.00
		Never hinged			—
		On cover			2,000.
28	A6	20pi on 5fr dk bl & buff		400.00	450.00
		Never hinged			—
		On cover			2,500.
		Nos. 14-28 (13)		1,267.	1,357.

On Nos. 25, 26 and 28 the two lines of the overprint are set wider apart than on the lower values.

"O.N.F." are the initials of "Occupation Navale Francaise."

Overprint on 5c in black and on 8pi on 2fr (#37) were prepared but not issued. Values: 5c, $1,100; 8pi on 2fr, $1,200.

Covers: Values for covers are for commercial items. Philatelic covers sell for less.

On Stamps of France

30	A22	10c red		50.00	50.00
		Never hinged		95.00	
		On cover			1,000.
a.		Inverted overprint		240.00	240.00
31	A22	25c blue (R)		50.00	50.00
		Never hinged		90.00	
		On cover			1,000.
a.		Inverted overprint		240.00	240.00

"Casetllorizo" instead of "Castellorizo"

14b	A2	1c gray		175.00	175.00
15b	A2	2c vio brn		195.00	195.00
16b	A2	3c red org		240.00	240.00
17b	A2	5c green (R)		190.00	190.00
19b	A3	10c rose		210.00	210.00
20b	A3	15c pale red		300.00	300.00
21b	A3	20c brn vio		325.00	325.00
22b	A5	1pi on 25c bl (R)		195.00	195.00
23b	A3	30c lilac (R)		280.00	280.00

"asetllorizo" instead of "Castellorizo"

14c	A2	1c gray		160.00	160.00
15c	A2	2c vio brn			195.00
16c	A2	3c red org			240.00
17c	A2	5c green (R)		175.00	175.00
19c	A3	10c rose			200.00
20c	A3	15c pale red			260.00
21c	A3	20c brn vio			300.00
22c	A5	1pi on 25c bl (R)		200.00	200.00
23c	A3	30c lilac (R)		260.00	260.00

No dot over "i" of "Castellorizo"

14d	A2	1c gray		175.00	175.00
15d	A2	2c vio brn		195.00	195.00
16d	A2	3c red org		240.00	240.00
17d	A2	5c green (R)		175.00	175.00
19d	A3	10c rose		200.00	200.00
20d	A3	15c pale red		260.00	260.00

Map of Castellorizo; Flag of Italy — A1

1923

60	A1	5c gray green		7.25	40.00
		Never hinged		16.00	
		On cover			450.00

21d	A3	20c brn vio		300.00	300.00
22d	A5	1pi on 25c bl (R)		225.00	225.00
23d	A3	30c lilac (R)		275.00	275.00

This overprint exists on 8 other 1900-1907 denominations of France (5c, 15c, 20c, 30c, 40c, 50c, 1fr, 5fr). These are believed not to have been issued or postally used. Values: 5c, $775; 15c, $775; 20c, $825; 30c, $1,250; 40c, $1,250; 50c, $2,350; 1fr, $1,350; 5fr, $12,500. Varieties exist: 5c, "Casetllorizo" for "Castellorizo," $1,000; 5c, "astellorizo" for "Castellorizo," $1,000; 20c, No dot over "i" of "Castellorizo," $1,200.

Stamps of France, 1900-1907, Handstamped in Black or Violet

1920

33	A22	5c green		190.00	190.00
		On cover			1,400.
34	A22	10c red		190.00	190.00
		On cover			1,400.
35	A22	20c vio brn		190.00	190.00
		On cover			1,000.
a.		Overprint inverted (reading up)		1,500.	
b.		Double overprint			725.00
36	A22	25c blue		190.00	190.00
		On cover			1,400.
37	A18	50c bis brn & lav		1,000.	1,150.
		On cover			2,600.
a.		Double overprint		1,700.	
38	A18	1fr cl & ol grn (V)		1,000.	1,150.
		On cover			2,600.
		Nos. 33-38 (6)		2,760.	3,060.

Forgeries of overprints on Nos. 1-38 exist. They abound for Nos. 33-38.

French Offices in Turkey Nos. 25//38 were hand-stamped "Occupation Francaise Castellorizo" locally by the officers in charge of the French Navy postal facilities but were not issued. Values: 5c, 10c, 15c, 20c, 1pi on 25c, each $1,050; 40c, 2pi on 50c, each $2,000; 4pi on 1fr, $2,350; 20pi on 5fr, $9,250.

Covers: Values for covers are for commercial items. Philatelic covers sell for less.

Issued under Italian Dominion
100 Centesimi = 1 Lira

Italian Stamps of 1906-20 Overprinted

1922			Wmk. 140		Perf. 14
51	A48	5c green		6.50	27.50
		Never hinged		11.00	
		On cover			175.00
52	A48	10c claret		4.00	27.50
		Never hinged		6.50	
		On cover			160.00
53	A48	15c slate		4.75	27.50
		Never hinged		12.00	
		On cover			225.00
54	A50	20c brn org		4.00	27.50
		Never hinged		9.50	
		On cover			160.00
a.		Double overprint		475.00	
b.		Vertical pair, one without overprint		2,100.	
		Never hinged		2,600.	
55	A49	25c blue		4.00	27.50
		Never hinged		9.50	
		On cover			175.00
56	A49	40c brown		55.00	37.50
		Never hinged		130.00	
		On cover			240.00
57	A49	50c violet		55.00	37.50
		Never hinged		130.00	
		On cover			325.00
58	A49	60c carmine		55.00	55.00
		Never hinged		130.00	
		On cover			600.00
a.		Diagonal overprint			725.00
59	A49	85c chocolate		8.00	65.00
		Never hinged		13.00	
		On cover			750.00
		Nos. 51-59 (9)		196.25	332.50
		Set, never hinged		450.00	
		Complete set, on over-franked cover			525.00

Italian Stamps of 1901-20 Overprinted

1924

65	A48	5c green		2.75	32.50
		Never hinged		6.50	
		On cover			275.00
66	A48	10c claret		2.75	32.50
		Never hinged		6.50	
		On cover			150.00
a.		Vertical pair, one stamp with albino overprint		1,250.	
		Never hinged		1,800.	
67	A48	15c slate		2.75	42.50
		Never hinged		6.50	
		On cover			225.00
68	A50	20c brn orange		2.75	42.50
		Never hinged		6.50	
		On cover			225.00
a.		Double overprint		150.00	
69	A49	25c blue		2.75	32.50
		Never hinged		6.50	
		On cover			210.00
70	A49	40c brown		2.75	32.50
		Never hinged		6.50	
		On cover			225.00
71	A49	50c violet		2.75	42.50
		Never hinged		6.50	
		On cover			210.00
72	A49	60c carmine		2.75	52.50
		Never hinged		6.50	
		On cover			320.00
a.		Double overprint		475.00	
73	A49	85c red brown		2.75	60.00
		Never hinged		6.50	
		On cover			550.00
74	A46	1 l brn & green		2.75	60.00
		Never hinged		6.50	
		On cover			675.00
		Nos. 65-74 (10)		27.50	430.00
		Set, never hinged		65.00	
		Complete set, on over-franked cover			750.00

Ferrucci Issue

Italian Stamps of 1930, Ovptd. in Red or Blue

1930

				Wmk. Crowns (140)	
75	A102	20c violet		12.00	12.00
		Never hinged		26.00	
		On cover			180.00
76	A103	25c dark green		12.00	28.00
		Never hinged		26.00	
		On cover			225.00
77	A103	50c black		12.00	12.00
		Never hinged		26.00	
		On cover			165.00
78	A103	1.25 l deep blue		12.00	28.00
		Never hinged		26.00	
		On cover			340.00
79	A104	5 l + 2 l dp car (Bl)		35.00	92.50
		Never hinged		85.00	
		Nos. 75-79 (5)		83.00	172.50
		Set, never hinged		190.00	
		Complete set, on over-franked cover			260.00

Garibaldi Issue
Types of Italian Stamps of 1932, Overprinted like Nos. 75-79 in Red or Blue

1932

80	A138	10c brown		25.00	50.00
		Never hinged		62.50	
		On cover			240.00
81	A138	20c red brn (Bl)		25.00	50.00
		Never hinged		62.50	
		On cover			180.00
82	A138	25c dp grn		25.00	50.00
		Never hinged		62.50	
		On cover			225.00
83	A138	30c bluish slate		25.00	50.00
		Never hinged		62.50	
		On cover			240.00
84	A138	50c red vio (Bl)		25.00	50.00
		Never hinged		62.50	
		On cover			180.00
85	A141	75c cop red (Bl)		25.00	50.00
		Never hinged		62.50	
		On cover			340.00

86	A141	1.25 l dull blue	25.00	50.00
		Never hinged	62.50	
		On cover		490.00
87	A141	1.75 l + 25c brn	25.00	50.00
		Never hinged	62.50	
		On cover		—
88	A144	2.55 l	50o org	25.00	50.00
		(Bl)		
		Never hinged	62.50	
89	A145	5 l + 1 l dl vio	25.00	50.00
		Never hinged	62.50	
		On cover		—
		Nos. 80-89 (10)	250.00	500.00
		Set, never hinged	625.00	
		Complete set, on over-franked cover		675.00

CAYMAN ISLANDS

ˌkā-'man 'ī-lənds

LOCATION — Three islands in the Caribbean Sea, about 200 miles northwest of Jamaica
GOVT. — Dependency of Jamaica
AREA — 100 sq. mi.
POP. — 18,285 (1982)
CAPITAL — George Town, located on Grand Cayman

12 Pence = 1 Shilling
20 Shilling = 1 Pound

STAMPS OF JAMAICA USED IN CAYMAN ISLANDS

Georgetown, Grand Cayman
Stamps of Jamaica canceled in purple with large double oval "GRAND CAYMAN * POST OFFICE" with date in center.

1889-94

A1	½p gray green (#16a)		625.
A2	1p lilac & red vio (#24)		625.
A3	2p slate (#20)		6,600.
A4	2p green (#25)		1,100.
A5	2½p lilac & ultra (#26)		1,350.
A6	4p orange brown (#22a)		3,750.

Official Stamps

A7	½p green, type II, OFFICIAL 17 to 17½mm (#O1)		1,500.
a.	1/2p green, type I, OFFICIAL 16mm (#O1a)		3,750.
A8	1p carmine rose (#O3)		1,500.
A9	2p slate (#O4)		4,600.

Stamps of Jamaica Canceled in purple or black with Single Circle Datestamp "GRAND CAYMAN/P.O." with date in center on two lines

1895-98

A10	½p gray green (#16a)		750.
A11	1p lilac & red vio (#24)		575.
A12	2½p lilac & ultra (#26)		950.
A13	3p olive green (#21)		5,000.

Official Stamps

A14	½p green, type I (#O1a)		3,250.
A15	1p carmine rose (#O3)		4,900.
A16	2p slate (#O4)		5,500.

Stamps of Jamaica Canceled with Double Circle Datestamp "GRAND CAYMAN * CAYMAN ISLANDS" with date in center on two lines

1898-1901

A17	½p blue green (#16)		575.
a.	1/2p gray green (#16a)		575.
A18	1p lilac & red violet (#24)		575.
A19	1p red (#31)		625.
A20	2½p lilac & ultra (#26)		850.

Stake Bay, Cayman Brac
Stamps of Jamaica Canceled with Rectangular Postmark: "CAYMAN BRAC/CAYMAN ISLANDS"

1898-1900

A21	½p gray green (#16a)		4,000.
A22	1p lilac & red vio (#24)		4,300.
A23	2p green (#25)		5,500.
A24	2½p lilac & ultra (#26)		4,300.

Stamps of Jamaica Canceled with Double Circle Datestamp "CAYMAN BRAC * CAYMAN ISLANDS" with date in center in two lines

1000 01

A25	½p gray green (#16a)		4,500.
A26	1p lilac & red violet (#24)		4,750.
A27	1p red (#31)		4,750.
A28	2½p lilac & ultra (#26)		4,250.

> **Catalogue values for unused stamps in this country are for Never Hinged items, beginning with Scott 112.**

Victoria
A1

Edward VII
A2

1900   Typo.   Wmk. 2   Perf. 14

1	A1	½p pale green	13.00	22.50
a.		½p green to deep green	21.00	30.00
2	A1	1p carmine rose	14.00	3.75
a.		6p deep carmine	20.00	17.50
		Set, Ovptd. "SPECIMEN"	160.00	

1901-03

3	A2	½p green ('02)	5.50	30.00
a.		Dented frame under "A" of "CAYMAN" (R1/P6) ('02)	250.00	350.00
4	A2	1p car rose ('03)	12.00	10.00
a.		Dented frame under "A" of "CAYMAN" (R1/P6) ('03)	350.00	350.00
5	A2	2½p ultramarine	12.00	14.50
a.		Dented frame under "A" of "CAYMAN" (R1/P6)	375.00	350.00
6	A2	6p chocolate	35.00	70.00
a.		Dented frame under "A" of "CAYMAN" (R1/P6)	700.00	1,000.
7	A2	1sh brown orange	72.50	125.00
a.		Dented frame under "A" of "CAYMAN" (R1/P6)	850.00	1,350.
		Nos. 3-7 (5)	137.00	249.50
		Set, Ovptd. "SPECIMEN"	230.00	

1905   Wmk. 3

8	A2	½p green	10.00	14.00
a.		Dented frame under "A" of "CAYMAN" (R1/P6)	325.00	350.00
9	A2	1p carmine rose	19.00	20.00
a.		Dented frame under "A" of "CAYMAN" (R1/P6)	475.00	500.00
10	A2	2½p ultramarine	10.00	4.75
a.		Dented frame under "A" of "CAYMAN" (R1/P6)	350.00	350.00
11	A2	6p chocolate	18.00	45.00
a.		Dented frame under "A" of "CAYMAN" (R1/P6)	400.00	600.00
12	A2	1sh brown orange	37.50	55.00
a.		Dented frame under "A" of "CAYMAN" (R1/P6)	600.00	—
		Nos. 8-12 (5)	94.50	138.75

For surcharge see No. 17.

1907, Mar. 13

13	A2	4p brown & blue	37.50	67.50
a.		Dented frame under "A" of "CAYMAN" (R1/P6)	800.00	1,000.
14	A2	6p ol green & rose	40.00	80.00
a.		Dented frame under "A" of "CAYMAN" (R1/P6)	800.00	1,000.
15	A2	1sh violet & green	65.00	95.00
a.		Dented frame under "A" of "CAYMAN" (R1/P6)	950.00	1,250.
16	A2	5sh ver & green	225.00	350.00
a.		Dented frame under "A" of "CAYMAN" (R1/P6)	5,000.	5,500.
		Nos. 13-16 (4)	367.50	592.50
		Set, Ovptd. "SPECIMEN"	240.00	

Numerals of 4p, 1sh and 5sh of type A2 are in color on colorless tablet.
For surcharges see Nos. 18-20.

Nos. 9, 16, 13 Handstamped

One Halfpenny.

No. 17

No. 18

1D

No. 19

2½D

No. 20

1907-08

17	A2	½p on 1p	60.00	92.50
a.		Dented frame under "A" of "CAYMAN" (R1/P6)	950.00	1,450.
18	A2	½p on 5sh	325.00	525.00
a.		Inverted surcharge	85,000.	
b.		Double surcharge	12,750.	12,750.
c.		Double surcharge, one inverted		
d.		Pair, one without surcharge	95,000.	
e.		Dented frame under "A" of "CAYMAN" (R1/P6)	5,000.	
19	A2	1p on 5sh	350.00	525.00
a.		Double surcharge	22,500.	20,000.
b.		Inverted surcharge	150,000.	
c.		Dented frame under "A" of "CAYMAN" (R1/P6)	4,500.	5,000.
20	A2	2½p on 4p ('08)	2,000.	3,750.
a.		Double surcharge	60,000.	30,000.
b.		Dented frame under "A" of "CAYMAN" (R1/P6)	22,500.	5,000.

No. 19b is unique. It exists on the upper left stamp in an upper left corner margin plate no. 1 block of four that is lightly hinged in the top margin only.

The 1p on 4p is a revenue stamp not authorized for postal use, although postally used examples exist. Value for unused is about $300. Varieties exist: surcharge inverted $1,750.; surcharge double $2,750; surcharge double, both inverted $2,750.

A3

A4

1907-09   Perf. 14

21	A3	½p green	4.25	5 50
22	A3	1p carmine rose	2.10	1.10
23	A3	2½p ultramarine	5.50	5.25

Chalky Paper

24	A3	3p violet, yellow	4.50	9.75
25	A3	4p blk & red, yel	67.50	100.00
26	A3	6p purple & br pur	22.50	52.50
a.		6p purple & violet purple	37.50	65.00
27	A3	1sh black, grn	11.00	32.50
28	A3	5sh grn & red, yel	60.00	90.00
		Nos. 21-28 (8)	177.35	296.60

Issued: ½p, 1p, 12/27/07; 2½p, 3p, 4p, 5sh, 3/30/08; 6d, 10/2/08; 1sh, 4/5/09.
Forged cancellations are found on No. 28.

1908, Mar. 30   Wmk. 2

29	A3	1sh black, green	85.00	125.00
30	A3	10sh grn & red, grn	225.00	400.00
		Set of 9, #21-26, 28-30, Ovptd. "SPECIMEN"	375.00	

Numerals of 3p, 4p, 1sh and 5sh of type A3 are in color on plain tablet.
Forged cancellations are found on No. 30.

1908   Wmk. 3   Ordinary Paper

31	A4	¼p brown	6.00	1.00
a.		¼p gray brown ('09)	4.75	1.10
		Ovpted "SPECIMEN"	100.00	

King George V
A5   A6

1912-20

32	A5	¼p brown ('13)	1.25	.50
33	A5	½p green	3.25	6.00
34	A5	1p carmine ('13)	4.00	3.00
35	A5	2p gray	1.25	12.50
36	A5	2½p ultra ('14)	8.50	13.50
a.		2½p deep bright blue ('17)	21.00	29.00

Chalky Paper

37	A5	3p vio, yel ('13)	3.00	22.50
		Ovpted "SPECIMEN"	75.00	
a.		3p purple, yellow ('14)	17.50	45.00
b.		3p purple, pale yellow ('20)	4.00	35.00
c.		3p purple, orange buff ('20)	11.50	35.00
d.		3p purple, buff ('14)		
38	A5	4p blk & red, yel ('13)	1.25	12.50
39	A5	6p vio & red vio ('13)	4.50	9.00
40	A5	1sh blk, grn ('13)	4.25	32.50
		Ovpted "SPECIMEN"	75.00	
41	A5	2sh vio & ultra, bl	14.50	57.50
42	A5	3sh green & vio	22.50	77.50
43	A5	5sh grn & red, yel ('14)	90.00	190.00

44	A5	10sh grn & red, bl grn, olive back ('18)	125.00	225.00
a.		10sh green & red, grn ('13)	130.00	225.00
		Ovptd "SPECIMEN"	110.00	
		Nos. 32-44 (13)	283.25	662.00

The first printings of the 3p, 1sh and 10sh have a white back.
For surcharges, see Nos. MR1-MR7.

1913, Nov. 19
Surface-colored Paper

45	A5	3p violet, yel	4.25	9.50
46	A5	1sh black, grn	4.25	4.25
47	A5	10sh grn & red, grn	100.00	175.00
		Nos. 45-47 (3)	108.50	188.75
		Set, ovptd. "SPECIMEN"	100.00	

Numeral of ¼p, 2p, 3p, 4p, 1sh, 2sh, 3sh and 5sh of type A5 are in color on plain tablet.

1921-26   Wmk. 4   Perf. 14

50	A6	¼p yel brown ('22)	.60	1.75
51	A6	½p gray green ('22)	.60	.35
52	A6	1p rose red ('22)	1.75	1.00
53	A6	1½p orange brn ('22)	2.10	.35
54	A6	2p gray ('22)	2.10	4.75
55	A6	2½p ultramarine ('22)	.60	.60
56	A6	3p violet, yel ('23)	1.75	4.75
57	A6	4½p olive grn ('23)	3.50	3.75
58	A6	6p claret ('22)	6.50	37.50
a.		6p deep claret	21.00	45.00
59	A6	1sh black, grn ('25)	11.50	37.50
60	A6	2sh violet, blue ('22)	17.00	29.00
61	A6	3sh violet ('22)	27.50	19.00
62	A6	5sh green, yel ('25)	29.00	55.00
63	A6	10sh car, green ('26)	72.50	100.00
		Nos. 50-63 (14)	177.00	295.30
		Set, ovptd. "SPECIMEN"	400.00	

Issued: 1½p, 4/4/21; ½p, 1p, 2p, 2½p, 6p, 2sh, 3sh, 4/1/22; 3p, 4½p, 6/29/23; 5sh, 2/15/25; 1sh, 5/15/25; 10sh, 9/5/26.

1921-22   Wmk. 3

64	A6	3p violet, org	1.75	9.50
65	A6	4p red, grn	1.25	4.75
66	A6	1sh black, green	2.25	11.50
67	A6	5sh green, yel	19.00	85.00
68	A6	10sh car, green	75.00	125.00
		Nos. 64-68 (5)	99.25	235.75
		Set, ovptd. "SPECIMEN"	225.00	

Issued: 4p, 4/1/22; others, 4/4/21.

King William IV, King George V
A7

Perf. 12½
1932, Dec. 5   Wmk. 4   Engr.

69	A7	¼p brown	1.90	1.40
70	A7	½p green	3.25	10.50
71	A7	1p carmine	3.25	13.00
72	A7	1½p orange	3.25	3.75
73	A7	2p gray	3.25	4.75
74	A7	2½p ultramarine	3.25	2.00
75	A7	3p olive green	6.00	6.75
76	A7	6p red violet	11.50	30.00
77	A7	1sh brn & black	20.00	42.50
78	A7	2sh ultra & blk	55.00	100.00
79	A7	5sh green & blk	100.00	160.00
80	A7	10sh car & black	350.00	475.00
		Nos. 69-80 (12)	560.65	849.65
		Set, never hinged	1,250.	
		Set, Perf "SPECIMEN"	575.00	

Centenary of the formation of the Cayman Islands Assembly.

Common Design Types pictured following the introduction.

Silver Jubilee Issue
Common Design Type

1935, May 6   Perf. 13½x14

81	CD301	½p green & black	.35	1.50
82	CD301	2½p blue & brown	4.00	1.50
83	CD301	6p ol grn & lt bl	1.60	4.75
84	CD301	1sh brt vio & ind	11.00	10.00
		Nos. 81-84 (4)	16.95	17.75
		Set, never hinged	24.00	
		Set, Perf "SPECIMEN"	160.00	

King George V
A8

Catboat
A9

Red-footed Boobies
A10

Conches and Coconut Palms — A11

Hawksbill Turtles
A12

1935-36   **Perf. 12½**

85	A8	¼p brown & blk	.60	1.25
86	A9	½p yel grn & ultra	1.25	1.25
87	A10	1p car & ultra	5.00	3.00
88	A11	1½p org & black	1.75	2.40
89	A9	2p brown vio & ultra	4.50	1.50
90	A12	2½p dp blue & blk	4.00	1.60
91	A8	3p ol grn & blk	3.00	3.75
92	A12	6p red vio & blk	10.50	6.00
93	A9	1sh org & ultra	7.25	9.25
94	A10	2sh black & ultra	55.00	50.00
95	A12	5sh green & blk	60.00	70.00
96	A11	10sh car & black	125.00	140.00
		Nos. 85-96 (12)	277.85	290.00
		Set, never hinged	525.00	
		Set, perf "SPECIMEN"	300.00	

Issued: No. 86, 2½p, 6p, 1sh, 1/1/36; others, 5/1/35.

Coronation Issue
Common Design Type

1937, May 13   **Perf. 11x11½**

97	CD302	½p deep green	.25	1.50
98	CD302	1p dark carmine	.30	.25
99	CD302	2½p deep ultra	.55	.55
		Nos. 97-99 (3)	1.10	2.30
		Set, never hinged	2.25	
		Set, Perf "SPECIMEN"	110.00	
		Set, Perf "SPECIMEN," never hinged	150.00	

Beach View, Grand Cayman
A13

Dolphin — A14

Map of the Islands
A15

Hawksbill Turtles — A16

Cayman Schooner
A17

Perf. 12½; 11½x13 or 13x11½ (A14, #111); 14 (#104, 107)

1938-43   **Engr.**

100	A13	¼p red orange	.55	.75
a.		Perf. 13½x12½ ('43)	.25	.85
101	A14	½p yel green	.85	.75
a.		Perf. 14 ('43)	1.50	1.75
102	A15	1p carmine	.25	1.00
103	A13	1½p black	.25	.25
104	A16	2p dp violet ('43)	.50	.35
a.		Perf. 11½x13	3.00	.40
105	A17	2½p ultra	.40	.25
106	A15	3p orange	.40	.25
107	A16	6p dk ol grn ('43)	2.50	2.50
a.		Perf. 11½x13	7.25	5.25
108	A14	1sh reddish brown	5.00	2.00
a.		Perf. 14 ('43)	4.00	2.50
109	A13	2sh green	25.00	18.00
110	A17	5sh deep rose	27.50	19.00
111	A16	10sh dark brown	19.00	12.00
a.		Perf. 14 ('43)	19.00	12.00
		Nos. 100-111 (12)	82.20	57.10
		Set, never hinged	325.00	
		Set of 14, #100-111, 114-115, Perf "SPECIMEN"	325.00	
		Set, Perf "SPECIMEN," never hinged	425.00	

See Nos. 114-115.

> **Catalogue values for unused stamps in this section, from this point to the end of the section, are for Never Hinged items.**

Peace Issue
Common Design Type

1946, Aug. 26   **Wmk. 4**   **Perf. 13½**

112	CD303	1½p black	.30	.40
113	CD303	3p orange	.30	.40
		Set, ovptd. "SPECIMEN"	125.00	

Types of 1938

1947, Aug. 25   **Perf. 12½**

114	A17	2½p orange	3.50	.65
115	A15	3p ultramarine	3.50	.45

Silver Wedding Issue
Common Design Types

1948, Nov. 29   **Photo.**   **Perf. 14x14½**

116	CD304	½p dark green	.25	1.00

Perf. 11½x11

Engr.; Name Typo.

117	CD305	10sh blue violet	22.50	27.50

UPU Issue
Common Design Types

Engr.; Name Typo. on #119, 120

1949, Oct. 10   **Perf. 13½, 11x11½**

118	CD306	2½p orange	.40	1.00
119	CD307	3p indigo	1.90	2.50
120	CD308	6p olive	.85	2.50
121	CD309	1sh red brown	.85	.40
		Nos. 118-121 (4)	4.00	6.40

Catboat
A18

Designs: ½p, Coconut grove. 1p, Green turtle. 1½p, Thatch rope industry. 2p, Caymanian

seamen. 2½p, Map. 3p, Parrot fish. 6p, Bluff, Cayman Brac. 9p, George Town harbor. 1sh, Turtle "crawl". 2sh, Cayman schooner. 5sh, Boat-building. 10sh, Government offices.

Perf. 11½x11

1950, Oct. 2   **Wmk. 4**   **Engr.**

122	A18	¼p rose red & blue	.25	.80
123	A18	½p bl grn & red violet	.25	1.75
124	A18	1p dp blue & olive	.75	1.00
125	A18	1½p choc & bl grn	.45	1.00
126	A18	2p rose car & vio	1.75	2.00
127	A18	2½p sepia & aqua	1.75	.85
128	A18	3p bl & blue grn	2.10	2.00
129	A18	6p dp bl & org brn	2.50	1.75
130	A18	9p dk grn & rose red	12.00	2.50
131	A18	1sh red org & brn	4.50	3.75
132	A18	2sh red vio & vio	13.00	14.50
133	A18	5sh vio & olive	22.50	9.50
134	A18	10sh rose red & blk	27.50	20.00
		Nos. 122-134 (13)	89.30	61.40

WAR TAX STAMPS

No. 36 Surcharged

a   b

1917, Feb. 26   **Wmk. 3**   **Perf. 14**

MR1	A5(a)	1½p on 2½p	16.00	17.00
a.		Fraction bar omitted	225.00	250.00
MR2	A5(b)	1½p on 2½p	2.10	7.25
a.		Fraction bar omitted	85.00	150.00

No. 1 exists with missing period. On No. 1 the distance between "WAR STAMP" and "1½" varies.

Surcharged

1917, Sept. 4

MR3	A5	1½p on 2½p ultra	850.00	2,500.

Surcharged

1917, Sept. 4

MR4	A5	1½p on 2½p ultra	.30	.65
a.		Ovpted "SPECIMEN"	125.00	

No. 33 Overprinted

1919, Feb. 4

MR5	A5	½p green	.70	3.00

The "brownish paper" variety comes from the interleaving used for shipment from England.

Type of 1912-16
Surcharged

1919, Feb. 4

MR6	A5	1½p on 2½p orange	1.25	2.50
a.		Ovpted "SPECIMEN"	125.00	

No. 35 Surcharged

1920, Mar. 10

MR7	A5	1½p on 2p gray	4.00	8.50

The "rose-tinted paper" variety comes from the interleaving used for shipment from England.

A surcharge in red was not issued.

CENTRAL LITHUANIA

'sen-trəl ˌli-thə-'wā-nē-ə

LOCATION — North of Poland and east of Lithuania
CAPITAL — Vilnius

At one time Central Lithuania was a grand duchy of Lithuania but at the end of the 18th Century it fell under Russian rule. After World War I, Lithuania regained her sovereignty but certain areas were occupied by Poland. During the Russo-Polish war this territory was seized by Lithuania whose claim was promptly recognized by the Soviet Government. Under the leadership of the Polish General Zeligowski the territory was recaptured and it was during this occupation the stamps of Central Lithuania came into being. Subsequently the territory became a part of Poland.

100 Fennigi = 1 Markka

Coat of Arms — A1

Perf. 11½, Imperf.

		1920-21	Typo.	Unwmk.	
1	A1	25f red		.40	.55
2	A1	25f dark grn ('21)		.40	.55
3	A1	1m blue		.40	.55
a.		Tête-bêche pair		4.75	4.75
4	A1	1m dark brn ('21)		.40	.55
a.		Tête-bêche pair		4.75	4.75
5	A1	2m violet		.40	.55
a.		Tête-bêche pair		4.75	4.75
6	A1	2m orange ('21)		.40	.55
		Nos. 1-6 (6)		2.40	3.30

For surcharges see Nos. B1-B5.

Lithuanian Stamps of 1919 Surcharged in Blue or Black

Perf. 11½x12, 12½x11½, 14

		1920, Nov. 23		Wmk. 145	
13	A5	2m on 15sk lil		47.50	55.00
a.		Inverted surcharge		200.00	900.00
14	A5	4m on 10sk red		47.50	52.50
a.		Inverted surcharge		150.00	
15	A5	4m on 20sk dl bl (Bk)		47.50	52.50
a.		Inverted surcharge		150.00	
16	A5	4m on 30sk buff		47.50	52.50
a.		Inverted surcharge		150.00	
17	A6	6m on 50sk lt grn		47.50	52.50
a.		4m on 50sk (error)		200.00	200.00
b.		10m on 50sk (error)		200.00	
c.		Surcharge inverted			—
18	A6	6m on 60sk vio & red		47.50	52.50
a.		4m on 60sk (error)		200.00	
b.		10m on 60sk (error)		200.00	
19	A6	6m on 75sk bis & red		47.50	52.50
a.		4m on 75sk (error)		200.00	
b.		10m on 75sk (error)		200.00	
20	A8	10m on 1auk gray & red		95.00	110.00
a.		Inverted surcharge		210.00	
21	A8	10m on 3auk lt brn & red		1,400.	1,800.
22	A8	10m on 5auk bl grn & red		1,400.	1,800.
		Nos. 13-20 (8)		427.50	480.00
		Nos. 13-22 (10)		3,227.	4,080.

The overprint on Nos. 17-19 is down-reading, i.e., the top of the overprint is at the right of the original design, the bottom at the left. The inverted overprint on No. 17c is up-reading.

Reprints of Nos. 17a, 17b, 18a, 18b, 19a, 19b. Value, each $45.

Counterfeits of Nos. 21-22 exist.

Lithuanian Girl — A2

Warrior — A3

Holy Gate of Vilnius — A4

Tower and Cathedral, Vilnius — A5

Rector's Insignia — A6

Gen. Lucien Zeligowski — A7

Perf. 11½, Imperf.

		1920	Litho.	Unwmk.	
23	A2	25f gray		.25	.75
24	A3	1m orange		.25	.75
25	A4	2m claret		.50	1.00
26	A5	4m gray grn & buff		.75	1.50
a.		Tête-bêche pair		24.00	32.50
27	A6	6m rose & gray		2.50	3.25
28	A7	10m brown & yellow		3.50	4.75
		Nos. 23-28 (6)		7.75	12.00

For surcharges see Nos. B13-B14, B17-B19.

St. Anne's Church, Vilnius — A8

St. Stanislas Cathedral, Vilnius — A9

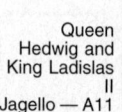

White Eagle, White Knight Vytis — A10

Queen Hedwig and King Ladislas II Jagello — A11

Coat of Arms of Vilnius — A12

Poczobut Astronomical Observatory A13

Union of Lithuania and Poland — A14

Tadeusz Kosciuszko and Adam Mickiewicz A15

1921　　　　Perf. 14, Imperf.

35	A8	1m dk gray & yel		.75	1.25
36	A9	2m rose & green		.75	1.25
37	A10	3m dark green		.75	1.25
38	A11	4m brown & buff		.75	1.25
39	A12	5m red brown		.75	1.25
40	A13	6m slate & buff		.75	1.50
41	A14	10m red vio & buff		1.00	2.50
42	A15	20m blk brn & buff		1.00	2.50
		Nos. 35-42 (8)		6.50	12.75

Set, perf. 13½, $150.

Peasant Girl Sowing — A16

White Eagle and Vytis — A17

Great Theater at Vilnius — A18

Allegory: Peace and Industry — A19

Gen. Zeligowski Entering Vilnius — A20

Gen. Zeligowski — A21

1921-22　　　　Perf. 11½, Imperf.

53	A16	10m brown ('22)		3.25	6.25
54	A17	25m red & yel ('22)		3.50	8.00
55	A18	50m dk blue ('22)		5.00	12.00
56	A19	75m violet ('22)		6.00	22.50
57	A20	100m bl & bister		2.50	5.25
58	A21	150m ol grn & brn		3.50	6.75
		Nos. 53-58 (6)		23.75	60.75

Opening of the Natl. Parliament, Nos. 53-56; anniv. of the entry of General Zeligowski into Vilnius, Nos. 57-58.

SEMI-POSTAL STAMPS

Nos. 1-6 Surcharged in Black or Red

1921　　Unwmk.　　Perf. 11½, Imperf.

B1	A1	25f + 2m red (Bk)		1.25	2.25
B2	A1	25f + 2m dk green		1.25	2.25
B3	A1	1m + 2m blue		1.50	2.25
B4	A1	1m + 2m dk brown		1.50	2.25
B5	A1	2m + 2m violet		1.50	2.25
B6	A1	2m + 2m orange		1.50	2.25
		Nos. B1-B6 (6)		8.50	13.50

The surcharge means "For Silesia 2 marks." The stamps were intended to provide a fund to assist the plebiscite in Upper Silesia.

Nos. 25, 26 Surcharged

a

b

Perf. 11½, Imperf.

B13	A4	(a) 2m + 1(m) claret		1.00	2.00
B14	A5	(b) 4m + 1m gray green & buff		1.00	2.00

Nos. 25-26, 28 with inset

Perf. 11½, Imperf.

B17	A4	2m + 1m claret		.65	1.25
B18	A5	4m + 1m gray green & buff		.65	1.25
B19	A7	10m + 2m brn & yel		.90	1.25
		Nos. B13-B19 (5)		4.20	7.75

POSTAGE DUE STAMPS

University, Vilnius D1

Castle Hill, Vilnius D2

Castle Ruins, Troki — D3

Holy Gate, Vilnius — D4

St. Stanislas Cathedral D5

St. Anne's Church, Vilnius D6

1920-21　Unwmk.　Perf. 11½, Imperf.

J1	D1	50f red violet		.40	1.25
J2	D2	1m green		.40	1.25
J3	D3	2m red violet		.50	1.25
J4	D4	3m red violet		.85	1.60
J5	D5	5m red violet		1.00	2.50
J6	D6	20m scarlet		2.00	3.25
		Nos. J1-J6 (6)		5.15	11.10

CEYLON

si-'län

LOCATION — An island in the Indian Ocean separated from India by the Gulf of Manaar
GOVT. — British Colony
AREA — 25,332 sq. mi.
POP. — 12,670,000 (est. 1971)
CAPITAL — Colombo

12 Pence = 1 Shilling
100 Cents = 1 Rupee (1872)

Values for unused stamps are for examples with original gum as defined in the catalogue introduction except for Nos. 2, 5, 8-9 which seldom have any remaining trace of their original gum. Many unused stamps of Ceylon, especially between Nos. 59 and 274, have toned gum or tropical stains. Values quoted are for stamps with fresh gum. Toned stamps have lower values, and common stamps with toned gum are worth very little.

Very fine examples of Nos. 1-15 will be cut square, will have small margins, but will show an intact design. Inferior examples with the design partly cut away will sell for much less, and examples with large margins will command higher prices. Very fine examples of Nos. 17-58b will have perforations just cutting into the design on one or more sides due to the narrow spacing of the stamps on the plates and to imperfect perforating methods. Stamps with perfs clear on all four sides are extremely scarce and will command substantially higher prices.

> **Catalogue values for unused stamps in this country are for Never Hinged items, beginning with Scott 290 in the regular postage section.**

Watermarks

Wmk. 1a — 22½mm high, Oval Letters   Wmk. 1b — 21mm high, Round Letters

Wmk. 6 — Large Star

Queen Victoria
A1   A2

1857   Engr.   Wmk. 6   Imperf.
Blued Paper

No.	Type	Description	Unused	Used
1	A1	1p blue	—	240.
		On cover		1,750.
		On cover, single franking		2,100.
2	A1	6p plum	12,500.	525.
		On cover		4,700.
		On cover, single franking		5,800.

1857-59   White Paper

No.	Type	Description	Unused	Used
3	A1	1p dp turq	1,150.	45.00
a.		1p blue	1,250.	72.50
		On cover		325.00
		On cover, single franking		575.00
		Rouletted, unofficial	9,000.	
4	A1	2p deep grn	210.00	75.00
		On cover		525.00
		On cover, single franking		4,750.
		Rouletted, unofficial	4,000.	1,750.
a.		2p yellow green	575.00	105.00
		On cover		850.00
		On cover, single franking		—
5	A2	4p dl rose ('59)	70,000.	4,500.
		On cover		26,500.
		On cover, single franking		—
6	A1	5p org brown	1,750.	175.00
		On cover with other values		1,150.
		On cover, single franking		850.00
6A	A1	6p plum	2,850.	170.00
		On cover with other values		725.00
		On cover, single franking		575.00
7	A1	6p brown	9,000.	575.00
		On cover		3,750.
		On cover, single franking		—
a.		6p deep brown	12,500.	1,150.
		On cover		7,250.
		On cover, single franking		—
b.		6p pale brown	—	2,400.
		On cover		—
8	A2	8p brown ('59)	25,000.	1,750.
		On cover		10,500.
		On cover, single franking		—
9	A2	9p lil brn ('59)	62,500.	1,050.
		On cover		8,750.
		On cover, single franking		11,500.
10	A1	10p vermilion	950.00	350.00
		On cover with other values		7,500.
		On cover, single franking		3,750.
11	A1	1sh violet	5,750.	225.00
		On cover with other values		1,425.
		On cover, single franking		1,150.
12	A2	1sh9p green ('59)	950.00	925.00
		On cover, single franking		21,500.
		Rouletted, unofficial	10,000.	
a.		1sh9p yellow green	5,250.	3,500.
13	A2	2sh blue ('59)	6,750.	1,400.
		On cover		

Stamps of type A2 frequently have repaired corners.
Beware of Nos. 17-57 trimmed to resemble Nos. 3-13. Values are for stamps with clear margins on all sides.
No. 5 was reproduced by the collotype process in a souvenir sheet distributed at the London International Stamp Exhibition 1950. The paper is unwatermarked.

A3

1857-58   Typo.   Unwmk.

No.	Type	Description	Unused	Used
14	A3	½p lilac ('58)	200.	240.
		On cover		2,550.
		Rouletted, unofficial	9,000.	
15	A3	½p lilac, bluish	4,250.	625.
		On cover		7,500.
		On cover, single franking		11,500.

No. 14 exists unofficially rouletted.
Nos. 14-15, 38 are printed on surface-glazed paper. Values are for stamps without cracking of the surface, and examples showing cracking should be discounted.

Clean-Cut Perf. 14 to 15½
1861   Wmk. 6   Engr.

No.	Type	Description	Unused	Used
17	A1	1p blue	210.00	18.00
		On cover		425.00
		On cover, single franking		
a.		1p pale blue	2,350.	290.00
		On cover		425.00
18	A1	2p yel grn	260.00	27.50
		On cover		
a.		2p green	260.00	32.50
		On cover with other stamps		750.00
b.		As "b," vert. pair, imperf between		—
19	A2	4p dull rose	2,300.	350.00
		On cover with other stamps		8,000.
20	A1	5p org brown	115.00	10.00
		On cover		215.00
		On cover, single franking		215.00
20A	A1	6p brown	3,200.	160.00
		On cover, single franking		1,275.
b.		6p bister brown	2,250.	240.00
		On cover, single franking		2,750.
21	A2	8p brown	2,350.	575.00
		On cover		—
22	A2	9p lilac brown	16,000.	275.00
		On cover with other stamps		6,500.
23	A1	1sh violet	135.00	17.50
		On cover		650.00
		On cover, single franking		1,000.
24	A2	2sh blue	3,500.	850.00
		On cover with other stamps		25,000.

Rough Perf. 14 to 15½

No.	Type	Description	Unused	Used
25	A1	1p blue	170.00	12.50
		On cover		215.00
		On cover, single franking		215.00
b.		Blued paper	850.00	26.00
26	A1	2p yel green	475.00	92.50
		On cover		900.00
		On cover, single franking		
27	A2	4p rose red	575.00	115.00
		On cover with other stamps		6,600.
a.		4p dp rose red	675.00	145.00
28	A1	6p olive brown	1,150.	105.00
		On cover, single franking		875.00
		On cover with other stamps		—
a.		6p deep brown	1,250.	115.00
		On cover, single franking		1,100.
		On cover with other stamps		1,550.
b.		6p bister brown	2,100.	175.00
		On cover, single franking		1,400.
		On cover with other stamps		1,800.
29	A2	8p brown	1,775.	650.00
		On cover		—
30	A2	8p yel brown	1,800.	425.00
		On cover		—
31	A2	9p olive brown	850.00	85.00
		On cover		1,100.
		On cover, single franking		1,550.
32	A2	9p deep brown	125.00	100.00
		On cover, single franking		1,450.
a.		9p light brown	1,250.	115.00
		On cover		
33	A1	10p vermilion	325.00	28.00
		On cover, single franking		1,000.
		On cover with other stamps		—
a.		Imperf. vert., pair		—
34	A1	1sh violet	300.00	17.50
		On cover		425.00
35	A2	1sh9p green	825.00	
36	A2	2sh blue	800.00	160.00
		On cover		—
a.		2sh deep blue	1,100.	200.00
		On cover		

The 1sh9p green was never placed in use.

1863   Perf. 12½

No.	Type	Description	Unused	Used
37	A1	10p vermilion	325.00	22.00
		On cover		425.00
		On cover, single franking		650.00

1864   Typo.   Unwmk.

No.	Type	Description	Unused	Used
38	A3	½p lilac	260.00	210.00
		On cover, single franking		4,250.

See note following No. 15.

1863   Engr.   Perf. 13

No.	Type	Description	Unused	Used
39	A1	1p blue	170.00	7.00
		On cover		225.00
		On cover, single franking		350.00
40	A1	5p car brown	1,850.	175.00
41	A1	6p deep brown	210.00	30.00
		On cover with other stamps		725.00
		On cover, single franking		650.00
a.		6p brown	190.00	30.00
		On cover with other stamps		725.00
		On cover, single franking		675.00
42	A2	9p brown	1,400.	115.00
		On cover, single franking		5,000.
43	A1	1sh grayish violet	2,100.	92.50

Parts of the papermaker's sheet watermark, "T. H. SAUNDERS 1862," may be found on some stamps of Nos. 39-43.

Perf. 12

No.	Type	Description	Unused	Used
44	A1	1p blue	1,900.	150.00
		On cover with other stamps		1,450.
a.		Horiz. pair, imperf. btwn.		18,000.

Two Types of Watermark Crown and CC (1)

1863-67   Typo.   Wmk. 1a   Perf. 12½

No.	Type	Description	Unused	Used
45	A3	½p lilac	72.50	50.00
		On cover with other stamps		1,200.
		On cover, single franking		—
a.		½p reddish lilac	82.50	62.50
		On cover with other stamps		1,750.
		On cover, single franking		3,600.
b.		½p mauve	50.00	50.00
		On cover		

Engr.

No.	Type	Description	Unused	Used
46	A1	1p blue	170.00	8.50
		On cover		110.00
		On cover, single franking		120.00
		1p dark blue	170.00	8.50
		On cover		110.00
		On cover, single franking		125.00
c.		Perf. 11½	3,650.	350.00
		On cover		1,500.
		On cover, single franking		1,800.
47	A1	2p gray green	100.00	14.50
		On cover		200.00
		On cover, single franking		—
48	A1	2p emerald	190.00	115.00
		On cover		
48A	A1	2p yel green	10,000.	475.00
48B	A1	2p bottle green		4,250.
49	A1	2p olive	325.00	260.00
		On cover		
50	A2	4p rose	525.00	115.00
a.		4p carmine rose	900.00	240.00
		On cover with other stamps		6,750.
51	A1	5p car brown	325.00	95.00
		On cover		1,200.
		On cover, single franking		1,800.
52	A1	5p olive green	1,700.	350.00
		On cover		5,000.
e.		5p deep sage green	2,100.	400.00
		On cover		7,500.
53	A1	6p choc brown	210.00	7.50
		On cover		200.00
		On cover, single franking		275.00
a.		Perf. 13	2,850.	260.00
		On cover, single franking		—
b.		6p black brown	260.00	11.50
		On cover		240.00
		On cover, single franking		360.00
c.		As "b," double impression		4,500.
d.		6p reddish brown	325.00	14.00
		On cover		
54	A2	8p red brown	135.00	62.50
		On cover		3,900.
		On cover, single franking		8,000.
55	A2	9p brown	360.00	52.50
		On cover		3,750.
		On cover, single franking		
c.		Perf. 13	5,250.	900.00
56	A1	10p vermilion	4,200.	70.00
		On cover with other stamps		900.00
		On cover, single franking		700.00
a.		10p orange	6,250.	500.00
		On cover		
58	A2	2sh blue	350.00	42.50
		On cover with other stamps		14,000.

The ½p, 1p blue, 2p olive, 4p and 5p green exist imperf.

Wmk. 1b

No.	Type	Description	Unused	Used
46d	A1	1p blue	275.00	16.00
		On cover		160.00
		On cover, single franking		175.00
e.		1p dark blue	240.00	14.00
		On cover		160.00
		On cover, single franking		175.00
49d	A1	2p orange yellow	135.00	7.50
		On cover		725.00
		On cover, single franking		
e.		2p olive yellow	175.00	14.00
		On cover		850.00
		On cover, single franking		
f.		2p olive green	175.00	30.00
		On cover		2,150.
		On cover, single franking		
50b	A2	4p rose	325.00	65.00
		On cover		1,750.
		On cover, single franking		8,500.
c.		4p carmine rose	125.00	40.00
		On cover		1,750.
		On cover, single franking		

52b	A1	5p myrtle green	150.00	22.50
		On cover		1,100.
c.		5p olive green	150.00	22.50
		On cover		2,300.
		On cover, single frank-ing		2,300.
d.		5p bronze green	55.00	55.00
		On cover		2,150.
		On cover, single frank-ing		2,150.
53e	A1	6p chocolate brown	125.00	11.00
		On cover		575.00
		On cover, single frank-ing		575.00
f.		6p brown	150.00	9.00
		On cover		250.00
		On cover, single frank-ing		900.00
54a	A2	8p red brown	135.00	80.00
		On cover		4,600.
b.		8p chocolate	115.00	72.50
55a	A2	9p dark brown	67.50	7.00
		On cover		350.00
		On cover, single frank-ing		600.00
b.		9p bister brown	950.00	40.00
		On cover		725.00
		On cover, single frank-ing		1,000.
56b	A1	10p orange	135.00	16.00
		On cover		675.00
c.		10p orange red	85.00	18.00
		On cover		650.00
		On cover, single frank-ing		625.00
d.		10p vermilion	5,250.	170.00
		On cover		340.00
		On cover, single frank-ing		2,000.
57	A1	1sh purple	135.00	10.50
		On cover		440.00
		On cover, single frank-ing		450.00
a.		1sh reddish lilac	325.00	32.50
		On cover		1,900.
		On cover, single frank-ing		1,900.
58a	A2	2sh deep blue	160.00	15.00
		On cover		13,500.
		On cover, single frank-ing		17,250.
b.		2sh indigo	300.00	22.50
		On cover		

The 1p blue and 6p brown exist imperf.
For overprints see Nos. O2, O4-O7.

A4

A5

1866 **Typo.** **Wmk. 1** **Perf. 12½**

59	A5	3p rose	300.00	105.00
a.		Imperf., pair	1,000.	

For overprint see No. O3.

1868 **Perf. 14**

61	A4	1p blue	30.00	11.50
62	A5	3p rose	95.00	52.50
a.		3p bright rose	100.00	57.50

No. 61 exists imperf.
For overprint see No. O1.

A6

A7

A8

A10   A11

A12   A13

A14   A15

A16

1872-80 **Perf. 14**

63	A6	2c brown	28.50	4.50
64	A7	4c gray	45.00	1.60
65	A7	4c lil rose ('80)	72.50	1.60
66	A8	8c orange	50.00	7.25
a.		8c orange yellow	42.50	8.00
67	A9	16c violet	125.00	3.00
68	A10	24c green	72.50	2.25
69	A11	32c slate bl ('77)	175.00	16.00
70	A12	36c blue	160.00	28.00
71	A13	48c rose	95.00	9.50
72	A14	64c red brn ('77)	325.00	77.50
73	A15	96c olive gray	300.00	30.00
		Nos. 63-73 (11)	1,448.	181.20

For surcharges see Nos. 83-84, 94A-110, 112-114. For types surcharged see Nos. 124-129.

1872 **Perf. 12½**

74	A6	2c brown	4,000.	260.00
75	A7	4c gray	2,750.	325.00

1879 **Perf. 14x12½**

77	A6	2c brown	425.00	75.00
78	A7	4c gray	2,350.	40.00
79	A8	8c orange	475.00	57.50

Perf. 12½x14

82	A16	2r50c claret	800.00	425.00

The 32c and 64c are known perf. 14x12½, but were not regularly issued.
No. 82, perf. 12½, was not regularly issued.
See Nos. 142, 158. For surcharges see Nos. 111, 115, 130. For types surcharged see Nos. 160-161.

Nos. 68, 72 Surcharged

SIXTEEN
16
CENTS

1882 **Perf. 14**

83	A10	16c on 24c green	37.50	9.00
a.		Inverted surcharge	—	
84	A14	20c on 64c red brn	12.50	9.00
a.		Double surcharge		1,750.

1883-99 **Wmk. 2**

85	A6	2c pale brown	67.50	3.50
86	A6	2c green ('84)	3.00	.25
		Ovptd. "SPECIMEN"	475.00	
a.		Perf. 12	6,750.	
87	A6	2c org brn ('99)	4.75	.40
88	A7	4c lilac rose	5.25	.35
89	A7	4c rose ('84)	6.25	13.50
		Overprinted "SPECIMEN"	450.00	
a.		Perf. 12	6,750.	
90	A7	4c brt rose ('98)	11.50	11.50
91	A7	4c yellow ('99)	3.75	3.75
92	A8	8c orange	6.75	12.50
a.		8c yellow	4.75	11.00
93	A9	16c violet	2,100.	175.00
94	A10	24c purple brown	1,675.	
		Overprinted "SPECIMEN"	725.00	
b.		Perf. 12	7,250.	

Nos. 86a, 89a, 94 and 94b were never placed in use. A 48c brown, perf. 12, was prepared but not issued.
For surcharges and overprints see Nos. 116-123, 143-151D, 155-156. O8-O9.

Issues of 1872-82 Surcharged

a   b

c   d

1885 **Wmk. 1** **Perf. 14**

94A	A9 (a)	5c on 16c		3,250.
95	A10 (a)	5c on 24c	5,250.	115.00
96	A11 (a)	5c on 32c	67.50	20.00
a.		Inverted surcharge		2,200.
97	A12 (a)	5c on 36c	325.00	13.50
a.		Inverted surcharge		2,750.
98	A13 (a)	5c on 48c	2,100.	65.00
99	A14 (a)	5c on 64c	135.00	11.50
a.		Double surcharge		2,900.
100	A15 (a)	5c on 96c	575.00	75.00
101	A9 (b)	10c on 16c	10,500.	3,200.
102	A10 (b)	10c on 24c	525.00	130.00
103	A12 (b)	10c on 36c	450.00	240.00
104	A14 (b)	10c on 64c	475.00	240.00
105	A10 (b)	20c on 24c	80.00	25.00
106	A11 (c)	20c on 32c	85.00	65.00
a.		20c on 32c dark gray	95.00	52.50
107	A11 (c)	25c on 32c	24.00	6.75
108	A13 (c)	25c on 48c	45.00	10.00
a.		Double surcharge		2,350.
109	A12 (b)	30c on 36c	16.00	11.00
a.		Inverted surcharge	325.00	135.00
110	A15 (b)	56c on 96c	32.50	27.50

Perf. 12½

111	A16 (d)	1r12c on 2r50c	750.00	115.00

Perf. 14x12½

112	A11 (a)	5c on 32c	900.00	57.50
113	A14 (a)	5c on 64c	950.00	52.50
114	A14 (b)	10c on 64c	90.00	160.00
a.		Vert. pair, imperf. btwn.	5,000.	

Perf. 12½x14

115	A16 (d)	1r12c on 2r50c	115.00	50.00

Perf. 14
Wmk. 2

117	A7 (a)	5c on 4c rose	26.00	5.00
a.		Inverted surcharge		350.00
118	A8 (a)	5c on 8c org	90.00	12.00
a.		Inverted surcharge		3,750.
b.		Double surcharge		3,250.
119	A9 (a)	5c on 16c vio	160.00	17.00
a.		Inverted surcharge		260.00
120	A10 (a)	5c on 24c pur brn	—	600.00
121	A9 (b)	10c on 16c vio	11,500.	1,800.
122	A10 (b)	10c on 24c pur brn	17.50	9.50
123	A9 (b)	15c on 16c vio	14.50	11.50

A 5c on 4c lilac rose and a 5c on 24c green are known to exist and are considered to be a forgeries.

Types of 1872-80 Surcharged

e   f

g

1885-87

124	A8 (e)	5c on 8c lilac	26.00	1.60
125	A10 (f)	10c on 24c pur brn	12.50	9.00
126	A9 (f)	15c on 16c org	62.50	15.50
127	A11 (f)	28c on 32c sl bl	28.00	2.75
128	A12 (f)	30c on 36c ol grn	30.00	15.50
129	A15 (f)	56c on 96c ol gray	52.50	18.00

Wmk. 1 Sideways

130	A16 (g)	1r12c on 2r50c cl	62.50	135.00
		Nos. 124-130 (7)	274.00	197.35

A23

Type I   Type II

FIVE CENTS
Type I — Thin lines in background. Hair and curl clear.
Type II — Thicker lines in background. Heavier shading under chin.

1886 **Wmk. 2**

131	A23	5c lilac, type I	3.75	.25
a.		Type II	3.75	.25

For overprint see No. O12.

A24

1886-1900

132	A24	3c org brn & green ('93)	5.75	.50
133	A24	3c green ('00)	4.75	.60
134	A24	6c rose & blk ('99)	2.75	.50
135	A24	12c ol grn & car ('00)	5.00	9.00
136	A24	15c olive green	9.00	2.40
137	A24	15c ultra ('00)	8.00	1.50
138	A24	25c brown	5.75	2.00
a.		25c brown, value in ol yel	155.00	90.00
139	A24	28c slate	25.00	1.50
140	A24	30c vio & org brown ('93)	4.75	3.50
141	A24	75c blk & org brown ('00)	9.50	9.50
		Nos. 132-141 (10)	80.25	31.00

Numeral tablet of 3c, 12c and 75c has lined background with colorless value and "c."
For surcharges & overprints see Nos. 152-154, 157, 159, O10-O11, O13-O17.

1887 **Wmk. 1**

142	A16	1r12c claret	30.00	30.00
		Overprinted "SPECIMEN"	160.00	

For overprint see No. O18.

Issue of 1883-84 Surcharged

1888-90 **Wmk. 2**

143	A7	2c on 4c lilac rose	1.60	.95
a.		Inverted surcharge	25.00	24.00
b.		Double surcharge, one invtd.		375.00
144	A7	2c on 4c rose	2.50	.35
a.		Inverted surcharge	20.00	21.00
b.		Double surcharge		400.00

Surcharged

145 A7 2c on 4c lilac rose — 1.10 / .35
- a. Inverted surcharge — 42.50 / 42.50
- b. Double surcharge — 100.00 / 110.00
- c. Double surcharge, one invtd. — 85.00 / 85.00

146 A7 2c on 4c rose — 8.00 / .25
- a. Double surcharge, one invtd. — 105.00 / 125.00
- b. Double surcharge — 110.00 / 125.00
- c. Inverted surcharge — 425.00

Surcharged

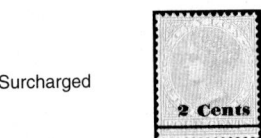

147 A7 2c on 4c lilac rose — 82.50 / 35.00
- a. Inverted surcharge — 175.00 / 47.50
- b. Double surcharge, one inverted — 210.00

148 A7 2c on 4c rose — 4.00 / .90
- a. Inverted surcharge — 17.50 / 10.00
- b. Double surcharge, one inverted — 9.50 / 15.00
- c. Double surcharge — 210.00 / 175.00

Surcharged

149 A7 2c on 4c lilac rose — 65.00 / 27.50
- a. Inverted surcharge — 200.00 / 35.00

150 A7 2c on 4c rose — 3.00 / 1.25
- a. Inverted surcharge — 17.50 / 8.50
- b. Double surcharge — 160.00 / 150.00
- c. Double surcharge, one inverted — 17.50 / 11.00

Surcharged

151 A7 2c on 4c rose — 13.00 / 1.20
- a. Inverted surcharge — 24.00 / 7.50
- b. Double surcharge — 135.00 / 135.00
- c. Double surch., one invtd. — 26.00 / 12.00
- i. "S" of "Cents" inverted — 475.00 / 350.00

151D A7 2c on 4c lilac rose — 65.00 / 35.00
- e. Inverted surcharge — 67.50 / 95.00
- f. Double surcharge — 425.00
- g. Double surch., one invtd. — 135.00 / 135.00
- h. "S" of "Cents" inverted — 675.00
- i. "POSTAGE" spaced between "T" and "A" — 85.00 / 90.00
- j. As "i," inverted surcharge — 1,500.

Counterfeit errors of surcharges of Nos. 143 to 151D are prevalent.

No. 136 Surcharged

POSTAGE / Five Cents / REVENUE

1890
152 A24 5c on 15c ol green — 3.75 / 2.50
- a. "FIve" instead of "Five" — 140.00 / 100.00
- b. "REVENUE" omitted — 200.00 / 190.00
- c. Inverted surcharge — 60.00 / 75.00
- d. Double surcharge — 125.00 / 145.00
- e. As "a," inverted surcharge — — / 1,800.
- f. Inverted "s" in "Cents" — 115.00 / 100.00
- g. As "f," inverted surcharge — 2,200.
- h. As "b," invtd. "s" in "Cents" — 1,700.

Nos. 138-139 Surcharged

FIFTEEN CENTS

1891
153 A24 15c on 25c brown — 19.00 / 18.00
154 A24 15c on 28c slate — 19.00 / 10.00

Nos. 88, 89 and 139 Surcharged

1892
155 A7 3c on 4c lilac rose — 1.20 / 3.75
156 A7 3c on 4c rose — 7.25 / 11.00
157 A24 3c on 28c slate — 6.25 / 5.75
- a. Double surcharge, one invtd. — 180.00

Nos. 155-157 (3) — 14.70 / 20.50

Type of 1879

1898
158 A16 2r50c violet, red — 37.50 / 62.50

No. 136 Surcharged in Black

1899
159 A24 6c on 15c olive green — 1.25 / .85

Surcharged Type "g" in Black

1899 Wmk. 1
160 A16 1r50c on 2r50c gray — 24.00 / 52.50
161 A16 2r25c on 2r50c yel — 47.50 / 95.00

A35

1900 Wmk. 1
162 A35 1r50c car rose — 35.00 / 52.50
163 A35 2r25c dull blue — 37.50 / 52.50

Nos. 166-292 exist in many different shades, representing different printings for each stamp.

King Edward VII
A36 A37

A38 A39

A40

1903-05 Wmk. 2
166 A36 2c org brown — 2.40 / .25
167 A37 3c green — 2.40 / 1.20
168 A37 4c yel & blue — 2.40 / 6.00
169 A38 5c dull lilac — 1.75 / .70
170 A39 6c car rose — 11.00 / 1.75
171 A37 12c ol grn & car — 5.50 / 11.50
172 A40 15c ultra — 6.75 / 3.50
173 A40 25c bister — 4.75 / 12.00
174 A40 30c vio & green — 3.50 / 4.25
175 A40 75c bl & org ('05) — 13.50 / 24.00
176 A40 1r50c gray ('04) — 67.50 / 60.00
177 A40 2r25c brn & grn ('04) — 95.00 / 60.00
Nos. 166-177 (12) — 206.45 / 185.15
Set, never hinged — 400.00

For overprints see Nos. O19-O24.

1904-10 Wmk. 3
178 A36 2c orange brown — 2.00 / .25
- a. 2c orange — 1.60 / .60

179 A37 3c green — 1.60 / .25
180 A37 4c yel & blue — 2.75 / 1.75
181 A38 5c dull lilac — 3.00 / 1.50
- a. Booklet pane of 12 — 6.75 / .75
- b. 5c dull lilac, "chalky paper" — .75

182 A39 6c car rose — 4.00 / .25
183 A40 10c ol grn & vio ('10) — 2.50 / 3.50
184 A37 12c ol grn & car — 1.75 / 2.00
185 A40 15c ultra — 3.25 / .70
186 A40 25c bister ('05) — 6.25 / 4.00
187 A40 25c slate ('10) — 2.75 / 3.00
188 A40 30c vio & grn ('05) — 2.75 / 3.25
189 A40 50c brown ('10) — 4.25 / 7.75
190 A37 75c bl & org ('05) — 5.50 / 8.25
191 A40 1r vio, yel ('10) — 8.50 / 11.50
192 A40 1r50c gray ('05) — 32.50 / 11.50
193 A40 2r scar, yel ('10) — 16.00 / 30.00
194 A40 2r25c brn & grn — 26.00 / 32.50
195 A40 5r blk, grn ('10) — 45.00 / 85.00
196 A40 10r blk, red ('10) — 130.00 / 240.00
Nos. 178-196 (19) — 300.35 / 446.95
Set, never hinged — 600.00

A41 A42

1908
197 A41 5c deep red violet — 5.25 / .25
- a. Booklet pane of 12

198 A42 6c carmine rose — 1.90 / .25

1911, July 5
199 A40 3c green — 1.10 / .85

A44 King George V — A45

Type I Type II

3 AND 6 CENTS
Type I — Small "c" after value, 2 1/4mm wide and 2mm high.
Type II — Large "c" after value, 2 1/2mm wide and 2 1/4mm high.
1, 5 AND 9 CENTS are Type II, other denominations Type I.

For description of dies I and II see "Dies of British Colonial Stamps" in the Table of Contents.

1912-25 Die I Wmk. 3
200 A44 1c dp brn (Die Ib) ('20) — 1.20 / .25
201 A44 2c brown org — .45 / .25
202 A44 3c dp grn (Die Ia, type II) — 5.25 / .50
- a. 3c deep green, die I, type I — 6.75 / 2.40

203 A44 5c red violet — 1.20 / .70
204 A44 6c car (Die Ib, type II) — 1.50 / 1.60
- a. 6c carmine, die I, type I — 20.00 / 1.25
- b. As "a," bklt. pane of 6

205 A44 10c olive green — 3.50 / 2.00
206 A44 15c ultra — 3.00 / 1.50

Chalky Paper
207 A44 25c yel & ultra — 2.10 / 2.10
208 A44 30c green & vio — 4.75 / 3.75
209 A44 50c black & scar — 1.75 / 2.10
210 A44 1r violet, yel — 5.25 / 4.25
211 A44 2r blk & red, yel — 3.75 / 15.00
212 A44 5r blk, green — 20.00 / 40.00
- a. 5r black, bl grn, olive back — 25.00 / 45.00
- b. 5r blk, emer (Die II) ('20) — 52.50 / 120.00

213 A44 10r vio & blk, red — 85.00 / 105.00
- a. Die II ('20) — 95.00 / 165.00

214 A44 20r blk & red, bl — 165.00 / 175.00
215 A45 50r dull violet — 550.00
216 A45 100r gray black — 2,200.

---

217 A45 500r gray green — 7,250.
218 A45 1000r vio, red ('25) — 29,500.
Nos. 200-214 (15) — 303.70 / 354.00
Set, never hinged — 600.00

Although Nos. 217 and 218 were theoretically available for postage it is not probable that they were ever used for other than fiscal purposes.
The 1r through 100r with revenue cancellations sell for minimal prices.
For surcharge & overprints see Nos. 223, MR1-MR3.

Die I
1913-14 Surface-colored Paper
220 A44 1r violet, yellow — 5.00 / 5.75
221 A44 2r black & red, yel — 3.25 / 15.00
222 A44 5r black, green — 26.00 / 37.50
Nos. 220-222 (3) — 34.25 / 58.25

No. 203 Surcharged

1918
223 A44 1c on 5c red violet — .25 / .30

For overprint see No. MR4.

Die I
1921-33 Wmk. 4 Ordinary Paper
225 A44 1c dp brn (Die Ib) ('27) — 1.20 / .40
226 A44 2c brn org (Die II) — .85 / .30
227 A44 3c green (Die Ia, type II) — 4.75 / .90
228 A44 3c slate (Die Ia, type II) ('22) — .90 / .25
229 A44 5c red vio (Die I) — .70 / .25
230 A44 6c carmine (Die Ib, type II) — 2.60 / .90
231 A44 6c vio (Die Ib, type II) ('22) — 2.00 / .25
232 A44 9c red, yel (Die II) ('26) — 2.40 / .35
233 A44 10c olive green — 1.60 / .45
- a. Die II — 2.10 / .70

234 A44 12c scarlet, Die II — 1.20 / 6.00
- a. Die I ('25) — 8.50 / 12.50

235 A44 15c ultramarine — 3.75 / 16.50
236 A44 15c green, yel, Die II — 4.25 / 1.20
- a. Die I ('22) — 4.75 / 6.00

237 A44 20c ultra, Die II ('24) — 4.25 / .50
- a. — 5.25 / 7.25

238 A44 25c yel & blue — 2.40 / 2.25
- a. Die II — 4.50 / 1.50

For surcharges see Nos. 248-249.

Chalky Paper
239 A44 30c green & violet — 1.90 / 4.75
- a. Die I — 5.75 / 1.50

240 A44 50c blk & scar (Die II) — 1.90 / .95
- a. Die I — 65.00 / 100.00

241 A44 1r vio, yel, Die II — 24.00 / 32.50
- a. Die I — 15.00 / 40.00

242 A44 2r blk & red, yel (Die II) — 8.50 / 12.00
243 A44 5r blk, emer, (Die II) — 50.00 / 85.00
244 A44 20r blk & red, bl (Die II) — 260.00 / 350.00
245 A45 50r dull vio — 625.00 / 1,050.
246 A45 100r gray black — 2,750.
247 A45 100r ultra & dl vio ('27) — 2,500.
Nos. 225-244 (20) — 379.15 / 515.70
Set, never hinged — 625.00

Nos. 228, 231 Surcharged

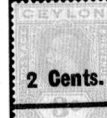

1926
248 A44 2c on 3c slate — 2.40 / 1.20
- a. Double surcharge — 85.00
- b. Bar omitted — 90.00 / 100.00

249 A44 5c on 6c violet — .65 / .45
- a. Double surcharge

A46

1927-29   Chalky Paper   Wmk. 4

254	A46	1r red vio & dl vio ('28)	3.00	1.50
255	A46	2r car & green ('29)	4.50	3.25
256	A46	5r brn vio & grn ('28)	16.00	24.00
257	A46	10r org & green	52.50	115.00
258	A46	20r ultra & dl vio	190.00	340.00
		Nos. 254-258 (5)	266.00	483.75
		Set, never hinged	450.00	

Common Design Types
pictured following the introduction.

Silver Jubilee Issue
Common Design Type

1935, May 6   Engr.   Perf. 13½x14

260	CD301	6c gray blk & ultra	.80	.35
261	CD301	9c indigo & green	.80	3.25
262	CD301	20c blue & green	5.00	3.25
263	CD301	50c brt vio & ind	6.00	16.50
		Nos. 260-263 (4)	12.60	23.35
		Set, never hinged	22.50	

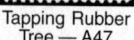

Tapping Rubber Tree — A47

Colombo Harbor — A49

Adam's Peak — A48

Picking Tea — A50

Coconut Palms — A53

Rice Terraces A51

River Scene A52

Temple of the Tooth, Kandy A54

Ancient Reservoir A55

Wild Elephants A56

View of Trincomalee A57

Perf. 11x11½, 11½x11; 11½x13, 13x11½ (A47, A48, A53); 14 (A56)

1935-36   Wmk. 4

264	A47	2c car rose & blk	.45	.55
a.		Perf. 14	12.00	.55
265	A48	3c olive & black	.50	.55
a.		Perf. 14	35.00	.40
266	A49	6c blue & black	.45	.40
267	A50	9c org red & ol grn	1.50	.90
268	A51	10c dk vio & blk	1.75	3.25
269	A52	15c grn & org brn	1.50	.70
270	A53	20c ultra & black	2.50	3.50
271	A54	25c choc & dk ultra	2.00	1.75
272	A55	30c green & lake	3.00	3.75
273	A56	50c dk vio & blk	15.00	2.50
274	A57	1r brown & vio	35.00	24.00
		Nos. 264-274 (11)	63.65	41.85
		Set, never hinged	200.00	

Issued: 2c, 15c, 25c, 5/1/35; 10c, 6/1/35; 1r, 7/1/35; 30c, 8/1/35; 3c, 10/1/35; 6c, 9c, 20c, 50c, 1/1/36.

Coronation Issue
Common Design Type

1937, May 12   Perf. 11x11½

275	CD302	6c dark carmine	.75	1.10
a.		Booklet pane of 10	20.00	
276	CD302	9c deep green	3.00	4.75
a.		Booklet pane of 10	300.00	
277	CD302	20c deep ultra	4.50	4.50
		Nos. 275-277 (3)	8.25	10.35
		Set, never hinged	16.00	

Types of 1935 with "Postage & Revenue Removed" and Picturing George VI and

Sigiriya (Lion Rock) — A61

Ancient Guard Stone — A68

George VI — A69

Perf. 11x11½, 11½x11; 12 (#286)

1938-52   Engr.   Wmk. 4

278	A47	2c car rose & blk ('44)	.45	1.25
a.		Perf. 13½x13 ('38)	100.00	2.00
b.		Perf. 13½ ('38)	2.00	2.00
c.		Perf. 12 ('49)	1.25	4.50
d.		Perf. 11½x13 ('38)	10.00	2.75
279	A48	3c dk grn & blk ('42)	.50	.25
a.		Perf. 13x13½ ('38)	225.00	12.50
b.		Perf. 14 ('41)	100.00	1.10
c.		Perf. 13½ ('38)	3.50	.25
d.		Perf. 12 ('49)	.70	.95
e.		Perf. 13x11½	8.00	2.50
280	A49	6c blue & black	.25	.25
281	A61	10c blue & black	1.75	.25
282	A52	15c red brn & grn	1.25	.25
283	A50	20c dull bl & blk	2.25	.25
284	A54	25c choc & dk ultra	3.25	.30
285	A55	30c dk grn & rose car	8.00	3.75
286	A56	50c dk vio & blk ('46)	2.75	.25
a.		Perf. 14 ('42)	90.00	29.00
b.		Perf. 13x11½ ('38)	140.00	52.50
c.		Perf. 13x13½ ('38)	300.00	3.00
d.		Perf. 13½ ('38)	15.00	.55
e.		Perf. 11½x11 ('42)	4.00	4.25
287	A57	1r dk brn & bl vio	10.50	1.60
288	A68	2r dark car & blk	9.25	4.00

Perf. 14
Typo.

289	A69	5r brn vio & grn	27.50	13.50
289A	A69	10r yel org & dl grn ('52)	50.00	50.00
		Nos. 278-289A (13)	117.70	75.90
		Set, never hinged	360.00	

No. 289A differs from type A69 in having "REVENUE" inscribed vertically at either side of the frame. This revenue 10r was valid for postage Dec. 1, 1952-Mar. 14, 1954.
See Nos. 292, 295. For surcharges see Nos. 290-291.

> Catalogue values for unused stamps in this section, from this point to the end of the section, are for Never Hinged items.

No. 283 Surcharged in Black

3 CENTS

1940, Nov. 5   Perf. 11x11½

290	A50	3c on 20c dull bl & blk	5.00	6.00

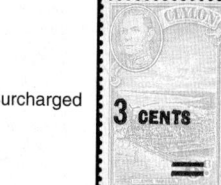

No. 280 Surcharged

3 CENTS

1941, May 10

291	A49	3c on 6c blue & black	.65	1.00

Coconut Palms — A70

1943-47   Wmk. 4   Engr.   Perf. 12

292	A70	5c red org & ol grn ('47)	1.75	.35
a.		Perf. 13½ ('43)	.35	.25

Peace Issue
Common Design Type

1946, Dec. 10   Perf. 13½x14

293	CD303	6c deep blue	.30	.35
294	CD303	15c brown	.30	1.75

Guard Stone Type of 1938

1947, Mar. 15   Perf. 11x11½

295	A68	2r violet & black	2.40	2.75

Parliament Building, Colombo — A71

Adam's Peak A72

Dagoba at Anuradhapura A74

Temple of the Tooth, Kandy A73

1947, Nov. 25   Perf. 11x12, 12x11

296	A71	6c deep ultra & black	.25	.25
297	A72	10c car, orange & black	.25	.40
298	A73	15c red vio & grnsh blk	.25	.80
299	A74	25c brt green & bister	.25	1.75
		Nos. 296-299 (4)	1.00	3.20

New constitution of 1947.

National Flag A75

D. S. Senanayake A76

Engr., Flag Typo. (A75); Engr. (A76)
Perf. 12½x12, 12x12½, 13x12½

1949   Wmk. 4

300	A75	4c org brn, car & yel	.25	.25
301	A76	5c dark green & brn	.25	.25

Wmk. 290

302	A75	15c red org, car & yel	1.00	.40
303	A76	25c dp blue & brown	.25	1.00
		Nos. 300-303 (4)	1.75	1.90

Size of No. 302: 28x22¼mm.
1st anniv. of Ceylon's independence.
Issued: Nos. 300-301, Feb. 4; Nos. 302-303, Apr. 5.

A77

A78

Design: 15c, Lion Rock and UPU symbols.

Wmk. 290

1949, Oct. 10   Engr.   Perf. 12

304	A77	5c dk green & brown	.85	.25
305	A77	15c dark car & black	1.25	2.75
306	A78	25c ultra & black	1.25	1.25
		Nos. 304-306 (3)	3.35	4.25

75th anniv. of the UPU.

Kandyan Dancer A79

Kiri Vehera, Polonnaruwa A80

Vesak Orchid — A81

Sigiriya — A82

Ratmalana, Plane — A83

1950, Feb. 4   *Perf. 12x12½*
307	A79	4c bright red & choc	.25 .25
308	A80	5c green	.25 .25
309	A81	15c pur & blue green	2.75 .50
310	A82	30c carmine & yel	.40 .70

Perf. 11x11½, 11½x11
311	A83	75c red org & blue	8.50 .25
312	A84	1r red brn & dp blue	2.50 .45
		Nos. 307-312 (6)	14.65 2.40

Vatadage Ruins at Madirigiriya A84

See Nos. 340-345 in *Scott Standard Postage Stamp Catalogue*, Vol. 2.

Coconut Palms — A85

Star Orchid — A86

1951-52 Unwmk. Photo.   *Perf. 11½*
313	A85	10c gray & dark green	1.25 .75
314	A86	35c dk grn & rose brn ('52)	1.50 1.50
a.		Corrected inscription ('54)	6.00 .70

On No. 314a a dot has been added above the third character in the second line of the Tamil inscription.

Issue dates: 10c, Aug. 1; 35c, Feb. 1.
See No. 351 in *Scott Standard Postage Stamp Catalogue*, Vol. 2.

Mace and Symbols of Industry A87

1952, Feb. 23   *Perf. 12½x14*   **Wmk. 290**
315	A87	5c green	.25 .30
316	A87	15c brt ultramarine	.40 .60

Colombo Plan Exhibition, February 1952.

WAR TAX STAMPS

Nos. 201, 202, 202a and 203 Overprinted

Die I

1918   **Wmk. 3**   *Perf. 14*
MR1	A44	2c brown orange	.25 .45
a.		Double overprint	35.00 47.50
b.		Inverted overprint	65.00 75.00
MR2	A44	3c dp grn (Die Ia, type II)	3.00 .45
a.		3c dp green (Die I, type I)	.25 .60
b.		Double overprint (Die I)	95.00 110.00
MR3	A44	5c red violet	.60 .35
a.		Double overprint	60.00 70.00
b.		Inverted overprint	120.00

No. 223 Overprinted in Black

MR4	A44	1c on 5c red violet	.25 .30
a.		Double overprint	210.00
		Nos. MR1-MR4 (4)	4.10 1.55

OFFICIAL STAMPS

Regular Issues Overprinted

Black Overprint

1869   **Wmk. 1**   *Perf. 12½, 14*
O1	A4	1p blue	77.50
O2	A1	2p yellow	77.50
O3	A5	3p rose	155.00
O4	A2	8p red brown	77.50
O5	A1	1sh gray lilac	175.00

Red Overprint
O6	A1	6p brown	77.50
O7	A2	2sh blue	125.00
a.		Imperf.	1,150.
		Nos. O1-O7 (7)	765.00

Nos. O1-O7 were never placed in use. The overprint measures 15mm on Nos. O1, O3.

Regular Issues Overprinted in Black or Red

1895-1900   **Wmk. 2**   *Perf. 14*
O8	A6	2c green	16.50 .75
O9	A6	2c org brn ('00)	10.50 .65
O10	A24	3c org brn & grn	11.00 2.50
O11	A24	3c green ('00)	12.50 4.50
O12	A23	5c lilac	5.25 .30
O13	A24	15c olive green	20.00 .55
O14	A24	15c ultra ('00)	25.00 .65
O15	A24	25c brown	13.50 3.00
O16	A24	30c vio & org brn	13.50 .65
O17	A24	75c blk & org brn (R) ('99)	8.50 8.50

Wmk. 1
O18	A16	1r12c claret	100.00 62.50
a.		Double ovpt., one albino	325.00
		Nos. O8-O18 (11)	236.25 84.55

1903-04   **Wmk. 2**
O19	A36	2c orange brown	20.00 1.75
O20	A37	3c green	13.50 2.40
O21	A38	5c dull lilac	28.00 1.60
O22	A40	15c ultramarine	40.00 3.25
O23	A40	25c bister	35.00 22.50
O24	A40	30c violet & green	20.00 2.25
		Nos. O19-O24 (6)	156.50 33.75

CHAD

'chad

(Tchad)

LOCATION — Central Africa, south of Libya
GOVT. — French Colony
AREA — 495,572 sq. mi.
POP. — 5,122,000 (est. 1984)
CAPITAL — N'djamena

A former dependency of Ubangi-Shari, Chad became a separate French colony in 1920. In 1934, the colonies of Chad, Gabon, Middle Congo and Ubangi-Shari were grouped in a single administrative unit known as French Equatorial Africa, with the capital at Brazzaville.

100 Centimes = 1 Franc

Types of Middle Congo, 1907-17, Overprinted

Perf. 14x13½, 13½x14

1922   **Unwmk.**
1	A1	1c red & violet	.40	.55
		Never hinged	.55	
		On cover		75.00
a.		Overprint omitted	225.00	
		Never hinged	340.00	
2	A1	2c ol brn & salmon	.50	.70
		Never hinged	.75	
		On cover		75.00
a.		Overprint omitted	260.00	
		Never hinged	375.00	
3	A1	4c ind & vio	1.10	1.50
		Never hinged	1.75	
		On cover		75.00
4	A1	5c choc & grn	1.25	1.60
		Never hinged	1.75	
		On cover		20.00
5	A1	10c dp grn & gray grn	2.40	2.75
		Never hinged	3.25	
		On cover		50.00
6	A1	15c vio & red	2.50	2.75
		Never hinged	3.50	
		On cover		27.50
7	A1	20c grn & vio	4.00	4.75
		Never hinged	6.00	
		On cover		27.50
8	A2	25c ol brn & brn	9.50	11.00
		Never hinged	14.00	
		On cover		30.00
9	A2	30c rose & pale rose	1.60	2.00
		Never hinged	2.40	
		On cover		40.00
		On cover, single franking		75.00
10	A2	35c dl bl & dl rose	2.75	3.25
		Never hinged	4.50	
		On cover		32.50
		On cover, single franking		50.00
11	A2	40c choc & grn	3.25	4.00
		Never hinged	5.00	
		On cover		32.50
		On cover, single franking		50.00
12	A2	45c vio & grn	2.40	2.75
		Never hinged	3.50	
		On cover		62.50
		On cover, single franking		110.00
13	A2	50c dk bl & pale bl	2.75	3.00
		Never hinged	4.00	
		On cover		32.50
		On cover, single franking		75.00
14	A2	60c on 75c vio, pnksh	4.00	4.75
		Never hinged	6.50	
		On cover		40.00
		On cover, single franking		62.50
a.		"TCHAD" omitted	300.00	
		Never hinged	450.00	
b.		"60" omitted	300.00	
		Never hinged	410.00	
15	A1	75c red & violet	3.25	4.00
		Never hinged	5.00	
		On cover		67.50
		On cover, single franking		105.00
16	A3	1fr indigo & salmon	13.00	13.00
		Never hinged	22.50	
		On cover		87.50
		On cover, single franking		125.00
17	A3	2fr indigo & violet	21.00	24.00
		Never hinged	35.00	
		On cover		105.00
		On cover, single franking		190.00
18	A3	5fr ind & olive brn	21.00	24.00
		Never hinged	35.00	
		On cover		140.00
		On cover, single franking		225.00
		Nos. 1-18 (18)	96.65	110.85

See Nos. 26a, 32a, 38a, 55a.

Stamps of 1922 Overprinted in Various Colors

Nos. 19-28

Nos. 29-50

1924-33
19	A1	1c red & vio	.30	.50
		Never hinged	.50	
		On cover		55.00
a.		"TCHAD" omitted	225.00	250.00
		Never hinged	425.00	
b.		Double overprint	300.00	
		Never hinged	450.00	
c.		Violet omitted	300.00	
		Never hinged	425.00	
20	A1	2c ol brn & sal	.30	.50
		Never hinged	.50	
		On cover		55.00
a.		"TCHAD" omitted	225.00	
		Never hinged	340.00	
b.		Double overprint	240.00	
		Never hinged	350.00	
21	A1	4c ind & vio	.30	.50
		Never hinged	.50	
		On cover		55.00
a.		"TCHAD" omitted	950.00	
22	A1	5c choc & grn (Bl)	1.60	2.00
		Never hinged	2.50	
		On cover		27.50
a.		"TCHAD" omitted	200.00	
		Never hinged	310.00	
23	A1	5c choc & grn	.50	.70
		Never hinged	.75	
		On cover		27.50
a.		"TCHAD" omitted	225.00	
		Never hinged	340.00	
24	A1	10c dp grn & gray grn (Bl)	1.20	1.40
		Never hinged	1.90	
		On cover		21.00
25	A1	10c dp grn & gray grn	1.20	1.40
		Never hinged	1.90	
		On cover		21.00
26	A1	10c red org & blk ('25)	.55	.80
		Never hinged	.80	
		On cover		27.50
a.		"Afrique Equatoriale Fran- caise" omitted	225.00	250.00
		Never hinged	340.00	
b.		"TCHAD" omitted	240.00	260.00
		Never hinged	350.00	
27	A1	15c vio & red	.65	.85
		Never hinged	1.05	
		On cover		17.50
28	A1	20c grn & vio	.80	.80
		Never hinged	1.10	
		On cover		27.50
a.		"TCHAD" omitted	225.00	
		Never hinged	340.00	
b.		"Afrique Equatoriale Fran- caise" doubled	340.00	
		Never hinged	450.00	
29	A2	25c ol brn & brn	.65	.85
		Never hinged	1.05	
		On cover		13.50
a.		"Afrique Equatoriale Fran- caise" doubled	160.00	
		Never hinged	240.00	
30	A2	30c rose & pale rose	.80	1.10
		Never hinged	1.20	
		On cover		32.50
		On cover, single franking		75.00
31	A2	30c gray & bl (R) ('25)	.55	.80
		Never hinged	.80	
		On cover		13.50
32	A2	30c dk grn & grn ('27)	1.20	1.60
		Never hinged	1.90	
		On cover		40.00
a.		"Afrique Equatoriale Fran- caise" omitted	340.00	
		Never hinged	450.00	
33	A2	35c indigo & dl rose	.65	.85
		Never hinged	1.05	
		On cover		40.00
		On cover, single franking		67.50
34	A2	40c choc & grn	1.25	1.60
		On cover		45.00
		On cover, single franking		75.00
a.		Double overprint (R + Bk)	275.00	
		Never hinged	425.00	
35	A2	45c vio & grn	.95	1.40
		Never hinged	1.50	
		On cover		16.00
		On cover, single franking		27.50
a.		Double overprint (R + Bk)	275.00	
		Never hinged	425.00	
36	A2	50c dk bl & pale bl	1.60	1.90
		Never hinged	2.40	
		On cover		16.00
		On cover, single franking		22.50

a.	Inverted overprint		160.00	
	Never hinged		240.00	
37	A2	50c grn & vio ('25)	2.00	2.00
	Never hinged		3.50	
	On cover			13.50
38	A2	65c org brn & bl	2.00	2.40
	('28)			
	Never hinged		3.25	
	On cover			32.50
	On cover, single franking			67.50
a.	"Afrique Equatoriale Fran-caise" omitted		260.00	
	Never hinged		375.00	
39	A2	75c red & vio	1.60	1.90
	Never hinged		2.40	
	On cover			32.50
	On cover, single franking			75.00
40	A2	75c dp bl & lt bl (R) ('25)	.90	1.20
	Never hinged		1.30	
	On cover			21.00
	On cover, single franking			32.50
a.	"TCHAD" omitted		260.00	
	Never hinged		375.00	
41	A2	75c rose & dk brn ('28)	2.75	3.25
	Never hinged		4.25	
	On cover			20.00
	On cover, single franking			32.50
42	A2	90c brn red & pink ('30)	7.25	8.75
	Never hinged		11.50	
	On cover			67.50
	On cover, single franking			160.00
43	A3	1fr ind & salmon	2.00	2.50
	Never hinged		4.50	
	On cover			32.50
	On cover, single franking			75.00
44	A3	1.10fr dl grn & bl ('28)	3.25	4.00
	Never hinged		5.25	
	On cover			160.00
	On cover, single franking			375.00
45	A3	1.25fr org brn & lt bl ('33)	8.00	9.50
	Never hinged		12.00	
	On cover			50.00
	On cover, single franking			125.00
46	A3	1.50fr ultra & bl ('30)	7.25	8.75
	Never hinged		11.00	
	On cover			62.50
	On cover, single franking			150.00
47	A3	1.75fr ol brn & vio ('33)	40.00	45.00
	Never hinged		65.00	
	On cover			190.00
	On cover, single franking			250.00
48	A3	2fr ind & vio	2.75	3.50
	Never hinged		4.75	
	On cover			62.50
	On cover, single franking			110.00
a.	Double impression of frame		550.00	
	Never hinged		875.00	
49	A3	3fr red vio ('30)	10.50	12.00
	Never hinged		16.005	
	On cover			100.00
	On cover, single franking			190.00
50	A3	5fr ind & ol brn	3.50	4.75
	Never hinged		6.00	
	On cover			67.50
	On cover, single franking			125.00
	Nos. 19-50 (32)		108.80	129.05

See No. 58a.

Types of 1922 Overprinted like Nos. 29-50 and Surcharged with New Values

1924-27

51	A2	60c on 75c dk vio, *pnksh*	.95	1.20
	Never hinged		1.40	
	On cover			20.00
	On cover, single franking			32.50
a.	"60" omitted		200.00	
	Never hinged		290.00	
52	A3	65c on 1fr brn & ol grn ('25)	1.60	2.00
	Never hinged		2.40	
	On cover			80.00
	On cover, single franking			175.00
53	A3	85c on 1fr brn & ol grn ('25)	1.60	2.00
	Never hinged		2.40	
	On cover			67.50
	On cover, single franking			140.00
54	A2	90c on 75c brn red & rose red ('27)	1.60	2.00
	Never hinged		2.25	
	On cover			67.50
	On cover, single franking			125.00
55	A3	1.25fr on 1fr dk bl & ultra (R) ('26)	.70	.80
	Never hinged		1.00	
	On cover			75.00
	On cover, single franking			150.00
a.	"Afrique Equatoriale Francaise" omitted		175.00	
			260.00	
56	A3	1.50fr on 1fr ultra & bl ('27)	1.60	2.00
	Never hinged		2.10	
	On cover			62.50
	On cover, single franking			105.00
57	A3	3fr on 5fr org brn & dl red ('27)	5.00	6.00
	Never hinged		7.25	
	On cover			110.00
	On cover, single franking			225.00
58	A3	10fr on 5fr ol grn & cer ('27)	13.00	14.50
	Never hinged		18.50	
	On cover			150.00
	On cover, single franking			310.00
a.	"10fr" omitted	400.00	400.00	
	Never hinged		575.00	

59	A3	20fr on 5fr vio & ver ('27)	18.00	21.00
	Never hinged		27.50	
	On cover			190.00
	On cover, single franking			340.00
	Nos. 51-59 (9)		44.05	51.50

Common Design Types
pictured following the introduction.

Colonial Exposition Issue
Common Design Types

1931		**Engr.**	**Perf. 12½**	
		Name of Country in Black		
60	CD70	40c deep green	5.50	5.50
	Never hinged		8.75	
	On cover			110.00
61	CD71	50c violet	5.50	5.50
	Never hinged		8.75	
	On cover			92.50
62	CD72	90c red orange	5.50	5.50
	Never hinged		8.75	
	On cover			160.00
	On cover, single franking			225.00
63	CD73	1.50fr dull blue	5.50	5.50
	Never hinged		8.75	
	On cover			150.00
	On cover, single franking			200.00
	Nos. 60-63 (4)		22.00	22.00

POSTAGE DUE STAMPS

Postage Due Stamps of France Overprinted

1928		**Unwmk.**	**Perf. 14x13½**	
J1	D2	5c light blue	.40	.50
	Never hinged		.75	
	On cover			100.00
J2	D2	10c gray brown	.40	.50
	Never hinged		.75	
	On cover			100.00
J3	D2	20c olive green	.55	.75
	Never hinged		.95	
	On cover			100.00
J4	D2	25c bright rose	.85	1.10
	Never hinged		1.40	
	On cover			110.00
J5	D2	30c light red	.85	1.10
	Never hinged		1.25	
	On cover			110.00
J6	D2	45c blue green	1.50	1.90
	Never hinged		2.10	
	On cover			120.00
J7	D2	50c brown violet	2.00	2.50
	Never hinged		2.90	
	On cover			125.00
J8	D2	60c yellow brown	2.00	2.50
	Never hinged		2.90	
	On cover			140.00
J9	D2	1fr red brown	2.10	2.75
	Never hinged		3.00	
	On cover			150.00
J10	D2	2fr orange red	4.75	6.50
	Never hinged		7.50	
	On cover			160.00
J11	D2	3fr bright violet	4.00	5.50
	Never hinged		6.50	
	On cover			180.00
	Nos. J1-J11 (11)		19.40	25.60

Huts — D3

Canoe — D4

1930		**Typo.**	**Perf. 14x13½, 13½x14**	
J12	D3	5c dp bl & olive	.50	.40
	Never hinged		.65	
	On cover			50.00
J13	D3	10c dk red & brn	.50	.40
	Never hinged		.65	
	On cover			50.00
J14	D3	20c grn & brn	.80	.65
	Never hinged		1.20	
	On cover			50.00
J15	D3	25c lt bl & brn	1.10	.90
	Never hinged		1.60	
	On cover			55.00

J16	D3	30c bis brn & Prus bl	1.10	.90
			1.60	
	On cover			62.50
J17	D3	45c Prus bl & olive	1.50	1.50
			2.10	
	On cover			62.50
J18	D3	50c red vio & brn	2.25	3.25
			2.60	
	On cover			67.50
J19	D3	60c gray lil & bl blk	3.00	4.25
			4.50	
	On cover			75.00
J20	D4	1fr bis brn & bl blk	3.00	4.25
			4.50	
	On cover			87.50
J21	D4	2fr vio & brn	6.25	8.50
			8.75	
	On cover			100.00
J22	D4	3fr dp red & brn	35.00	50.00
			52.50	
	On cover			250.00
	Nos. J12-J22 (11)		55.00	75.00

In 1934 stamps of Chad were superseded by those of French Equatorial Africa.

CHILE

'chi-lē

LOCATION — Southwest corner of South America
GOVT. — Republic
AREA — 292,135 sq. mi.
POP. — 11,682,260 (est. 1982)
CAPITAL — Santiago

100 Centavos = 1 Peso

STAMPS OF GREAT BRITAIN USED IN CHILE

Values are for clear cancellations on sound, fault-free stamps, with average to fine centering. In many cases, very fine copies are rare or non-existent.

Type A

Numeral Cancellation Type A, C37 (Caldera)

1865-81

A1	1p rose red, plates 71, 72, 88, 90, 95, 195 (#33), *value from*	62.50
A2	1½p lake red, plate 3 (#32a)	
A3	2p blue, plate 9 (#29)	67.50
A4	3p rose (#44)	100.00
A5	3p rose, plates 5, 7 (#49), *value from*	75.00
A6	3p rose, plates 11, 12, 16-19 (#61), *value from*	62.50
A7	4p vermilion (#34a)	—
A8	4p vermilion, plates 8, 11-14 (#43), *value from*	62.50
A9	4p pale olive green, plate 16 (#70)	—
A10	6p lilac, plate 4 (#39b)	110.00
A11	6p lilac, plate 5 (#45)	150.00
	Plate 6	150.00
A12	6p dull lilac, plate 6 (#50)	100.00
A13	6p violet, plates 8, 9 (#51), *value from*	100.00
A14	6p brown, plate 11 (#59)	—
a.	6p pale buff, plate 11 (#59b)	—
A15	6p gray, plate 12 (#60)	—
A16	6p gray, plates 13-17 (#62), *value from*	62.50
A17	8p orange (#73)	400.00
A18	9p bister (#52)	275.00
A19	10p red brown (#53)	300.00
A20	1sh green, plate 4 (#48)	—
A21	1sh green, plates 4-6 (#54), *value from*	62.50
A22	1sh green, plates 8, 10, 11 (#64), *value from*	95.00
	Plates 12, 13, *value from, value from*	95.00
A23	2sh blue (#55)	250.00
a.	2sh cobalt blue (#55c)	
A24	2sh brown (#56)	2,250.
A25	5sh rose, plate 2 (#57)	550.00

Numeral Cancellation Type A, C40 (Coquimbo)

No. A53

1865-81

A26	½p rose red, plate 14 (#58)	—
A27	1p rose red (#20)	—
A28	1p rose red, plates 85, 204 (#33)	—
A29	2p blue, plate 9 (#29)	—
A30	2p blue, plate 14 (#30)	—
A31	3p rose (#44)	—
A32	3p rose, plate 8 (#49)	—
A33	3p rose, plate 9 (#61), *value from*	62.50
A34	4p vermilion, plate 4 (#34a)	—
A35	4p vermilion, plates 12, 14, *value from* (#43)	70.00
A36	4p pale olive green, plates 15, 16 (#70), *value from*	225.00
A37	6p lilac, plate 3 (#39)	95.00
a.	Hair lines, plate 4 (#39b)	—
A38	6p lilac, plate 5 (#45)	—
A39	6p dull lilac, plate 6 (#50)	85.00
A40	6p violet, plates 6, 8, 9 (#51), *value from*	80.00
A41	6p brown, plate 11 (#59)	—
a.	6p pale buff, plate 11 (#59b)	85.00
	Plate 12	240.00
A42	6p gray, plate 12 (#60)	240.00
A43	6p gray, plates 13-16 (#62), *value from*	62.50
A44	8p orange (#73)	—
A45	9p straw (#40)	350.00
A46	9p bister (#52)	250.00
A47	10p red brown (#53)	375.00
A48	1sh green, plate 4 (#48)	190.00
A49	1sh green, plates 4-6 (#54), *value from*	62.50
A50	1sh green, plates 8-13 (#64), *value from*	90.00
A51	2sh blue (#55)	210.00
a.	2sh cobalt blue (#55c)	
A52	2sh brown (#56)	2,250.
A53	5sh rose, plate 1 (#57)	550.00
	Plate 2	700.00

VALPARAISO
Crowned Circle Handstamps

Crowned Circle handstamp types I and III are pictured in the Crowned Circle Handstamps and Great Britain Used Abroad section.

1846

A54	Crowned circle handstamp on cover, Type III, inscribed "PAID AT VALPARAISO"	450.00
A55	Crowned circle handstamp on cover, Type I, inscribed "PAID AT VALPARAISO"	525.00

Earliest known uses: A54, Oct. 31, 1846; A55, July 16, 1846.

Type B

Numeral Cancellation Type B, C30 (Type A)

No. A93

1865-81

A56	½p rose red, plates 6, 11-14 (#58), *value from*		75.00
A57	1p rose red, plates 80, 84, 85, 89, 91, 101, 106, 113, 122, 123, 138, 140, 141, 148, 149, 152, 157, 158, 162, 167, 175, 178, 181, 185-187, 189, 190, 195, 197-201, 207, 209-215, 217 (#33), *value from*		35.00
A58	1p red brown (#79)		
A59	1½p lake red, plate 1 (#32)		90.00
	Plate 3		60.00
A60	1½p red brown (#80)		—
A61	2p blue, plate 9 (#29)		50.00
A62	2p blue, plates 13-15 (#30), *value from*		50.00
A63	2½p claret, plate 2 (#66)		225.00
A64	2½p claret, plates 4, 8 (#67), *value from*		190.00
A65	3p rose (#37)		
A66	3p rose (#44)		
A67	3p rose, plates 5-10 (#49), *value from*		57.50
A68	3p rose, plates 11, 12, 14, 16-19 (#61), *value from*		42.50
A69	4p vermilion, plate 4 (#34a)		—
a.	Hair lines (#34c)		
A70	4p vermilion, plates 9-14 (#43), *value from*		57.50
A71	4p vermilion, plate 15 (#69)		350.00
A72	4p pale olive green, plate 15 (#70), *value from*		225.00
	Plate 16		225.00
A73	4p gray brown, plate 17 (#71)		125.00
A74	6p lilac, plate 3 (#39)		125.00
a.	Hair lines, Plate 4 (#39b)		
A75	6p lilac, plate 5 (#45)		—
	Plate 6		—
A76	6p dull violet, plate 6 (#50)		—
A77	6p violet, plates 6, 8, 9 (#51), *value from*		80.00
A78	6p brown, plates 11, 12 (#59), *value from*		50.00
a.	6p pale buff, plate 11 (#59b)		85.00
	Plate 12		240.00
A79	6p gray, plate 12 (#60)		240.00
A80	6p gray, plates 13-17 (#62), *value from*		50.00
A81	6p gray, plate 17 (#86)		—
A82	8p orange (#73)		350.00
A83	9p straw (#40)		—
a.	9p bister (#40a)		—
A84	9p straw (#46)		225.00
A85	9p bister (#52)		300.00
A86	10p red brown (#53)		—
A87	1sh green, plate 4 (#48)		
A88	1sh green, plates 4-6 (#54), *value from*		42.50
	Plate 7		60.00
A89	1sh green, plates 8-11 (#64), *value from*		75.00
	Plates 12, 13, *value from*		75.00
A90	1sh salmon, plate 13 (#87)		425.00
A91	2sh blue (#55)		150.00
a.	2sh cobalt blue (#55c)		1,700.
A92	2sh brown (#56)		2,250.
A93	5sh rose, plate 1 (#57)		550.00
	Plate 2		700.00
A94	10sh gray green (#74)		3,100.
A95	£1 brown lilac (#75)		4,250.

Issues of the Republic

Values for Nos. 1-14 are for examples with four margins clear of the design. Because these stamps are printed closely together, large margins are not possible, without including portions of adjacent stamps or sheet margin. Values for stamps described as having three margins are for examples with margin touching the design on one side or one corner. Stamps with margins cutting into the design sell for much less than the values shown.

Unused values for Nos. 1-14 are for stamps without gum. Examples with original gum are very scarce and are worth considerably more.

Pen cancellations are common on the 1862-67 issues. Such stamps sell for much less than the quoted values which are for those with handstamped postal cancellations.

Watermarks

Wmk. 215 — Small Star in Shield, Multiple

Christopher Columbus — A1

London Prints
1853   Wmk. b   Engr.   Imperf.
Blued Paper

1	A1	5c brown red		650.00	150.00
		On cover, stamp with three margins			275.00
a.		White paper			250.00

Wmk. e
White Paper

2	A1	10c dp brt bl		1,000.	175.00
		On cover, stamp with three margins			475.00
a.		Blued paper			225.00
b.		Diag. half used as 5c on cover			550.00
c.		Horiz. half used as 5c on cover			550.00
d.		Vert. half used as 5c on cover			550.00

Used examples of Nos. 1-2 with three margins sell for 10-20 percent of the values shown.

Santiago Prints
Impressions Fine and Clear
1854   Wmk. b and e
White Paper

3	A1	5c pale red brn		600.00	67.50
		On cover, stamp with three margins			200.00
a.		5c deep red brown	650.00		67.50
b.		5c chestnut	1,000.		200.00
c.		5c chocolate			275.00
d.		Ribbed paper			110.00
e.		Double impression			275.00
4	A1	5c burnt sienna		1,800.	300.00
		On cover, stamp with three margins			475.00
a.		5c dull chocolate	3,500.		2,000.

5	A1	10c deep blue		1,200.	275.00
		On cover, stamp with three margins			325.00
a.		10c slate blue			275.00
b.		10c greenish blue			475.00
c.		10c sky blue			190.00
d.		Diag. half used as 5c on cover			450.00
e.		Horiz. half used as 5c on cover			450.00
f.		Vert. half used as 5c on cover			450.00
6	A1	10c lt dl bl		800.00	150.00
		On cover, stamp with three margins			325.00
a.		10c pale blue			190.00
b.		Diag. half used as 5c on cover			425.00
c.		Horiz. half used as 5c on cover			425.00
d.		Vert. half used as 5c on cover			425.00

Litho.

7	A1	5c pale brown		1,000.	300.00
		On cover, stamp with three margins			750.00
		5c red brown		1,500.	300.00
		On cover, stamp with three margins			750.00
b.		5c deep brown		1,000.	325.00
		On cover, stamp with three margins			750.00
c.		5c orange brown		1,450.	325.00
		On cover, stamp with three margins			750.00
d.		5c chocolate brown		1,000.	325.00
		On cover, stamp with three margins			750.00
e.		5c deep chocolate brown		1,000.	325.00
		On cover, stamp with three margins			750.00
f.		5c deep red		1,400.	325.00
		On cover, stamp with three margins			750.00

No. 5b is normally found on ribbed paper.
Used examples of Nos. 3, 5-7 with three margins sell for 15 percent of the values shown. Three-margin examples of No. 4 sell for about 20 percent.

London Print
1855   Blued Paper   Wmk. c   Engr.

8	A1	5c brown red		220.00	16.00
		Fiscal cancellation			2.75
		On cover, stamp with three margins			67.50
a.		Thin paper			27.50
b.		Ivory head			40.00
c.		Cream paper without bluing			67.50

Santiago Prints
Impressions Worn and Blurred
1856-62   Wmk. b and e
White Paper

9	A1	5c rose red ('58)		60.00	8.00
		Fiscal cancellation			1.40
		On cover, stamp with three margins			27.50
		On cover, stamp with four margins			55.00
a.		5c carmine red ('62)		90.00	20.00
b.		5c orange red ('61)		225.00	100.00
c.		5c dull redsh brn ('57)		250.00	27.50
d.		5c vermilion		125.00	67.50
e.		5c salmon		125.00	67.50
f.		Printed on both sides		450.00	250.00
g.		Double impression		450.00	140.00
h.		Very worn plate			20.00
i.		Ribbed paper			60.00
10	A1	10c sky blue ('57)		160.00	40.00
		Fiscal cancellation			1.40
		On cover, stamp with three margins			55.00
		On cover, stamp with four margins			110.00
a.		10c deep blue		160.00	40.00
		On cover, stamp with three margins			85.00
		On cover, stamp with four margins			150.00
b.		10c light blue ('59)		160.00	40.00
c.		10c indigo blue ('60)		175.00	50.00
d.		10c deep slate blue ('57)			27.50
e.		10c greenish blue ('58)			27.50
f.		10c deep gray blue ('58)			27.50
g.		10c slate blue ('59)			27.50
h.		10c blue, *bluish* ('59)			40.00
i.		10c dark blue ('60)			40.00
j.		Printed on both sides			350.00
k.		Very worn plate			55.00
l.		10c greenish blue, poor impression			40.00
m.		As "j," half used as 5c on cover			165.00
n.		Any shade, horiz. half used as 5c on cover			200.00
o.		Any shade, vert. half used as 5c on cover			200.00

London Prints
1862   Wmk. a, f and g

11	A1	1c lemon yellow		67.50	40.00
		Fiscal cancellation			1.50
		On cover, stamp with three margins			550.00
		On cover, stamp with four margins			750.00
a.		Double impression, one inverted			200.00
b.		1c greenish yellow			27.50
		Fiscally used			5.00
12	A1	10c bright blue		40.00	15.00
		Fiscally used			1.50
		On cover, stamp with three margins			55.00
		On cover, stamp with four margins			90.00
a.		10c deep blue	32.50		21.00
b.		Blued paper			17.50
c.		Wmkd. "20" (error)	5,000.		5,200.

d.		Diag. half used as 5c on cover			110.00
e.		Horiz. half used as 5c on cover			125.00
f.		Vert. half used as 5c on cover			125.00
13	A1	20c green		160.00	67.50
		Fiscally used			6.75
		On cover, stamp with three margins			400.00
		On cover, stamp with four margins			—
a.		20c yellow green		165.00	67.50
		On cover, stamp with four margins			400.00
b.		20c intense green		—	—
		Nos. 11-13 (3)		267.50	122.50

No. 11a is only known fiscally used.

Santiago Print
1865   Wmk. d

14	A1	5c rose red		80.00	20.00
		Fiscally used			1.50
		On cover, stamp with three margins			35.00
		On cover, stamp with four margins			67.50
a.		5c carmine red		80.00	20.00
		On cover, stamp with four margins			67.50
b.		Printed on both sides		375.00	200.00
c.		Laid paper			90.00
d.		Double impression, entire stamp		825.00	160.00
e.		5c pale red		55.00	13.50
		On cover, stamp with four margins			35.00
f.		5c vermilion		37.50	9.25
		On cover, stamp with four margins			35.00
g.		Vertically laid paper			100.00
h.		Very thin, silky paper			32.50
i.		Thick paper (cardboard)			67.50
j.		Partial double impression			140.00
k.		Very worn plate			21.50

The 5c rose red (shades) on unwatermaked paper, either wove or ribbed, and on paper watermarked Chilean arms in the sheet are reprints made about 1870.
No. 13 has been reprinted in the color of issue and in fancy colors, both from the original engraved plate and from lithographic transfers. The reprints are on paper without watermark or with watermark CHILE and Star.

A2   A3

1867   Unwmk.   Perf. 12

15	A2	1c orange		70.00	15.00
		Never hinged	72.50		
		On cover, with other stamps			32.50
		Pen cancellation			1.25
16	A2	2c black		80.00	30.00
		Never hinged	95.00		
		On cover, with other stamps			50.00
		Pen cancellation			2.00
17	A2	5c red		60.00	2.00
		Never hinged	70.00		
		On cover			16.00
		Pen cancellation			.40
18	A2	10c blue		80.00	6.00
		Never hinged	95.00		
		On cover			20.00
		Pen cancellation			1.25
19	A2	20c green		80.00	8.00
		Never hinged	95.00		
		On cover			60.00
		Pen cancellation			1.00
		Nos. 15-19 (5)		370.00	61.00

Unused values for Nos. 15-19 are for stamps with original gum.
Nos. 15-17 were used during stamp shortages between July 3 and August 28, 1881. So used, they are scarce.

1877   Rouletted

20	A3	1c gray		9.00	3.00
		Never hinged	9.25		
		On cover			18.50
		Pen cancellation			.60
21	A3	2c orange		30.00	4.00
		Never hinged	27.50		
		On cover			15.00
		Pen cancellation			.60
22	A3	5c dull lake		24.00	2.00
		Never hinged	22.50		
		On cover			4.50
		Pen cancellation			.40
23	A3	10c blue		18.00	2.75
		Never hinged	27.50		
		On cover			14.00
a.		Diagonal half used as 5c on cover			—
24	A3	20c green		20.00	4.50
		Never hinged	65.00		
		On cover			37.50
		Nos. 20-24 (5)		101.00	16.25

The panel inscribed "CENTAVO" is straight on No. 22.

A4   A5

Columbus — A6

1878-99   Rouletted

25	A4	1c green ('81)	1.00	.25
		Never hinged	2.50	
		On cover		3.75
26	A4	2c rose ('81)	1.00	.25
		Never hinged	2.50	
		On cover		3.75
27	A5	5c dull lake ('78)	7.25	.90
		Never hinged	18.00	
		On cover		9.00
28	A5	5c ultra ('83)	1.90	.50
		Never hinged	5.50	
		On cover		3.75
29	A5	10c orange ('85)	2.75	.35
		Never hinged	9.25	
		On cover		12.75
a.		10c yellow	9.00	1.90
		Never hinged	27.50	
		On cover		18.50
30	A5	15c dk grn ('92)	3.00	.55
		Never hinged	10.00	
		On cover		9.00
31	A5	20c gray ('86)	3.00	.55
		Never hinged	10.00	
		On cover		14.00
32	A5	25c org brn ('92)	3.00	.55
		Never hinged	10.00	
		On cover		9.00
33	A5	30c rose car ('99)	7.25	3.75
		Never hinged	22.50	
		On cover		27.50
34	A5	50c lilac ('78)	45.00	27.50
		Never hinged	100.00	
		On cover		135.00
35	A5	50c violet ('85)	3.00	2.00
		Never hinged	10.00	
		On cover		14.50
36	A6	1p dk brn & blk ('92)	19.00	2.75
		Never hinged	55.00	
		On cover		225.00
a.		Imperf. horiz. or vert., pair	75.00	
		Never hinged	150.00	
		Nos. 25-36 (12)	97.15	39.90

For surcharge and overprint see Nos. 50, O16.

Columbus — A7

1894   Re-engraved

37	A7	1c blue green	.90	.25
		Never hinged	2.25	
		On cover		3.75
38	A7	2c carmine lake	.90	.25
		Never hinged	2.25	
		On cover		3.75

In type A4 there is a small colorless ornament at each side of the base of the numeral, above the "E" and "V" of "CENTAVO." In type A7 these ornaments are missing, the figure "1" is broader than in type A4 and the head of the figure "2" is formed by a curved line instead of a ball.

Columbus — A8

Type I   Type II

Type I — There is a heavy shading of short horizontal lines below "Chile" and the adjacent ornaments.

Type II — There is practically no shading below "Chile" and the ornaments.

Type I

1900-01

39	A8	1c yel grn	.80	.25
		Never hinged	2.10	
		On cover		4.50
40	A8	2c brn rose	1.25	.25
		Never hinged	2.50	
		On cover		4.50
41	A8	5c dp bl	6.50	.35
		Never hinged	27.50	
		On cover		7.50
42	A8	10c violet	6.50	.70
		Never hinged	18.50	
		On cover		9.25
43	A8	20c gray	6.50	2.50
		Never hinged	16.50	
		On cover		12.75
44	A8	30c dp org ('01)	6.50	2.50
		Never hinged	20.00	
		On cover		18.50
45	A8	50c red brn	7.50	2.50
		Never hinged	24.00	
		On cover		27.50
		Nos. 39-45 (7)	35.55	9.05

Type II

46	A8	1c yel grn ('01)	.85	.25
		Never hinged	2.25	
		On cover		4.50
47	A8	2c rose ('01)	.85	.30
		Never hinged	2.25	
		On cover		4.50
48	A8	5c dull blue ('01)	5.00	.25
		Never hinged	19.00	
		On cover		6.50
a.		Printed on both sides		—
49	A8	10c vio ('01)	6.00	.85
		Never hinged	20.00	
		On cover		13.00
		Nos. 46-49 (4)	12.70	1.65

Nos. 40, 45 and 47 exist in vertical pairs, imperf horizontally, and horizontal pairs, imperf vertically. Nos. 42 and 48 exist in horizontal pairs, imperf between. No.43 exist in vertical pairs, imperf between. Value: unused $22.50, never hinged $45.

For surcharge see No. 57.

No. 33 Surcharged in Black

1900   Black Surcharge

50	A5	5c on 30c rose car	1.25	.35
		Never hinged	2.50	
		On cover		6.50
a.		Inverted surcharge	32.50	24.00
		Never hinged	95.00	
b.		Double surcharge	90.00	60.00
		Never hinged	95.00	
c.		Double surcharge, both invtd.	90.00	60.00
		Never hinged	95.00	
d.		Double surcharge, one invtd.	90.00	60.00
		Never hinged	95.00	

Columbus — A10

1901-02   Perf. 12

51	A10	1c green	.50	.30
52	A10	2c carmine	.65	.25
53	A10	5c ultra	1.50	.25
54	A10	10c red & blk	2.25	.35
55	A10	30c vio & blk	6.75	.85
56	A10	50c red org & blk	7.25	2.25
		Nos. 51-56 (6)	18.90	4.25

No. 44 Surcharged in Dark Blue

1903   Rouletted

57	A8	10c on 30c orange	1.90	.75
a.		Inverted surcharge	18.00	12.00
b.		Double surcharge	25.00	15.00
c.		Double surch., one inverted	25.00	15.00
d.		Double surch., both invtd.	25.00	15.00
e.		Stamp design printed on both sides		

Telegraph Stamps Surcharged or Overprinted in Black

Pedro de Valdivia — A11   Coat of Arms — A12

A13

Type I   Type II

Type I — Animal at left has neither mane nor tail.
Type II — Animal at left has mane and tail.

1904   Perf. 12

58	A11	1c on 20c ultra	.40	.30
a.		Imperf. horiz., pair	40.00	40.00
		Inverted surcharge	50.00	50.00
59	A13	2c yel brn, I	.35	.25
a.		Inverted overprint	20.00	20.00
b.		Pair, one without overprint	50.00	50.00
60	A13	5c red, I	.55	.25
a.		Inverted overprint	20.00	20.00
c.		Pair, one without overprint	50.00	50.00
61	A13	10c ol grn, I	1.50	.50
a.		Inverted overprint	50.00	50.00
		Nos. 58-61 (4)	2.80	1.30

Perf. 12½ to 16

62	A13	2c yel, brn, II	5.25	4.50
63	A11	3c on 5c brn red	37.50	32.50
a.		Inverted surcharge		
64	A12	3c on 1p brn, II	.45	.30
a.		Double surcharge	50.00	50.00
65	A13	5c red, II	6.25	5.50
a.		Inverted overprint		
66	A13	10c ol grn, II	14.50	10.00
67	A11	12c on 5c brn red	1.00	.45
a.		No star at left of "Centavos"	3.00	2.50
b.		Inverted surcharge	40.00	40.00
c.		Double surcharge	50.00	50.00
		Nos. 62-67 (6)	64.95	53.25

Counterfeits exist of the overprint and surcharge varieties of Nos. 57-67.
For overprint see No. O12.

A14   A15

Columbus — A16

1905-09   Perf. 12

68	A14	1c green	.25	.25
69	A14	2c carmine	.30	.25
70	A14	3c yel brn	.65	.30
71	A14	5c ultra	.70	.25
72	A15	10c gray & blk	1.10	.25
73	A15	12c lake & blk	5.50	2.25
74	A15	15c vio & blk	1.25	.25
75	A15	20c org brn & blk	2.25	.25
76	A15	30c bl grn & blk	3.50	.35
77	A15	50c ultra & blk	3.50	.40

78	A16	1p gold, grn & gray	16.00	11.00
		Nos. 68-78 (11)	35.00	15.80

A 20c dull red and black, type A15, was prepared but not issued. Value $125. "Specimen" examples of Nos. 74, 76-78 exist, punched to prevent postal use.
For surcharges and overprints see Nos. 79-82, O9, O11-O15.

Nos. 73, 78 Surcharged in Blue or Red

a   b

1910

79	A15 (a)	5c on 12c (Bl)	.50	.25
80	A16 (b)	10c on 1p (R)	1.10	.30
81	A16 (b)	20c on 1p (R)	1.60	.60
82	A16 (b)	1p (R)	3.00	1.10
		Nos. 79-82 (4)	6.20	2.25

The 1p is overprinted "ISLAS DE JUAN FERNANDEZ" only. The use of these stamps throughout Chile was authorized.

Independence Centenary Issue

Oath of Independence — A17

Monument to O'Higgins — A26   Adm. Lord Thomas Cochrane — A29

Designs: 2c, Battle of Chacabuco. 3c, Battle of Roble. 5c, Battle of Maipu. 10c, Naval Engagement of "Lautaro" and "Esmeralda." 12c, Capturing the "Maria Isabel." 15c, First Sortie of Liberating Forces. 20c, Abdication of O'Higgins. 25c, Chile's First Congress. 50c, Monument to José M. Carrera. 1p, Monument to San Martin. 2p, Gen. Manuel Blanco Encalada. 5p, Gen. José Ignacio Zenteno.

1910   Center in Black

83	A17	1c dk green	.25	.25
a.		Center inverted	7,000.	
84	A17	2c lake	1.10	.75
85	A17	3c red brown	.80	.45
86	A17	5c dp blue	.45	.25
87	A17	10c gray brn	1.20	.30
88	A17	12c vermilion	2.50	1.00
89	A17	15c slate	1.90	.55
90	A17	20c red orange	2.50	.85
91	A17	25c ultra	3.25	2.00
92	A26	30c violet	3.25	1.40
93	A26	50c olive grn	6.75	2.25
94	A26	1p yel org	14.00	5.25
95	A29	2p red	14.00	5.25
96	A29	5p yel grn	37.50	17.50
97	A29	10p dk violet	35.00	16.00
		Nos. 83-97 (15)	124.45	54.05

Columbus A32   De Valdivia A33

Mateo de Toro
Zambrano
A34

Ramón
Freire — A36

Joaquín
Prieto — A38

Manuel
Montt — A40

Federico
Errázuriz
Zanartu — A42

Bernardo
O'Higgins
A35

F. A.
Pinto — A37

Manuel
Bulnes — A39

José Joaquín
Pérez — A41

José de
Balmaceda — A43

Designs: 1p, Anibal Pinto, 2p, Domingo
Santa María. 10p, Federico Errázuriz
Echaurren.

**Outer backgrounds consist of
horizontal and diagonal lines**

1911		Engr.	Perf. 12	
98	A32	1c dp green	.25	.25
99	A33	2c scarlet	.25	.25
100	A34	3c sepia	.75	.25
101	A35	5c dk blue	.25	.25
102	A36	10c gray & blk	.75	.25
a.		Center inverted	800.00	600.00
103	A37	12c carmine & blk	1.00	.25
104	A38	15c violet & blk	.90	.25
a.		Center inverted	1,000.	
105	A39	20c org red & blk	1.75	.25
a.		Center inverted	50.00	50.00
106	A40	25c lt blue & blk	2.75	.60
107	A41	30c bis brn & blk	4.00	.30
108	A42	50c myr grn & blk	5.00	.30
109	A43	1p green & blk	9.00	.40
110	A43	2p ver & blk	17.50	1.75
111	A43	5p ol grn & blk	50.00	9.50
112	A43	10p org yel & blk	45.00	8.50
		Nos. 98-112 (15)	139.15	23.35

See Nos. 117, 121, 123, 127-128, 133-141,
143, 155A, 157-161, 165-169,171-172 and
designs A47-A55, A57. For overprints see
Nos. C6, C6B-C6D, C7-C8, C10-C11, C13-
C21, O19-O22, O24-O27, O30-O34, O40.

Columbus
A47

Toro Zambrano
A48

Freire
A49

O'Higgins
A50

1912-13		Engr.	Perf. 12	
113	A47	2c scarlet	.25	.25
114	A48	4c black brn	.30	.25
115	A49	8c gray	1.00	.25
116	A50	10c blue & blk	1.00	.25
a.		Center inverted	500.00	400.00
b.		Imperf. horiz. or vert., pair	50.00	
117	A37	14c car & blk	1.50	.25
121	A38	40c violet & blk	5.75	.60
123	A40	60c lt blue & blk	14.00	1.75
		Nos. 113-123 (7)	23.80	3.60

See Nos. 125-126, 131, 164, 170, 173. For
overprints see Nos. C6E, O18, O23, O28,
O29.

Cochrane — A52

1915		Engr.	Perf. 13½x14	
124	A52	5c slate blue	.60	.35
a.		Imperf., pair	11.50	

See Nos. 155, 162-163. For overprints see
Nos. O17, O37.

1918
125 A49 8c slate 17.50 .80

No. 125 is from a plate made in Chile to
resemble No. 115. The top of the head is further from the oval, the spots of color enclosed
in the figures "8" are oval instead of round, and
there are many small differences in the design.

1921
126 A49 8c gray **Worn Plate** 20.00 5.00

No. 126 differs from No. 125 in not having
diagonal lines in the frame and only a few
diagonal lines above the shoulders (due to
wear), while No. 125 has diagonal lines in the
oval up to the level of the forehead.

Columbus — A53

1915-25		Typo.	Perf. 13½ to 14½	
127	A32	1c gray green	.25	.25
128	A33	2c red	.25	.25
129	A53	4c brown ('18)	.25	.25

Frame Litho.; Head Engr.

131	A50	10c bl & blk	1.25	.25
a.		10c dark blue & black	1.25	.25
b.		Imperf., pair	110.00	
c.		Center inverted	325.00	
133	A38	15c vio & blk	.90	.25
134	A39	20c org red & blk	1.40	.25
a.		20c brown orange & blk	1.75	.25
135	A40	25c dl bl & blk	.55	.25
136	A41	30c bis brn & blk	1.75	.25
137	A42	50c dp grn & blk	1.75	.25

Perf. 14

138	A43	1p grn & blk	8.00	.25
139	A43	2p red & blk	9.75	.25
a.		2p vermilion & black	32.50	.60
140	A43	5p ol grn & blk ('20)	24.00	.60
141	A43	10p org & blk ('25)	25.00	1.75
		Nos. 127-141 (13)	75.10	5.10

The frames have crosshatching on the 15c,
20c, 30c, 2p, 5p and 10p. They have no cross-
hatching on the 10c, 25c, 50c and 1p.

Nos. 131a and 134a are printed from new
head plates which give blacker and heavier
impressions. No. 131a exists with; (a) frame
litho., head engr.; (b) frame typo., head engr.;
(c) frame typo., head litho. No. 134a is with
frame typo., head engr.

A 4c stamp with portrait of Balmaceda and a
14c with portrait of Manuel de Salas were prepared but not placed in use. Both stamps were
sent to the paper mill at Puente Alto for
destruction. They were not all destroyed as
some were privately preserved and sold.

Columbus
A54

Manuel Rengifo
A55

Types of 1915-20 Redrawn

1918-20			Perf. 13½x14½	
143	A32	1c gray grn ('20)	.30	.25
144	A54	4c brown	.50	.25

No. 143 has all the lines much finer and
clearer than No. 127. The white shirt front is
also much less shaded.

1921
145 A55 40c dk vio & blk 2.00 .40

For overprints see Nos. C6A, C9.

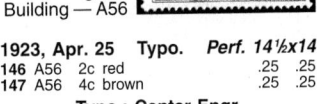

Pan-American
Congress
Building — A56

1923, Apr. 25		Typo.	Perf. 14½x14	
146	A56	2c red	.25	.25
147	A56	4c brown	.25	.25

Typo.; Center Engr.

148	A56	10c blue & blk	.25	.25
149	A56	20c orange & blk	.75	.25
150	A56	40c dl vio & blk	1.00	.25
151	A56	1p green & blk	1.25	.50
152	A56	2p red & blk	5.00	.60
153	A56	5p dk grn & blk	17.00	4.50
		Nos. 146-153 (8)	25.75	6.90

Fifth Pan-American Congress.

Adm. Juan José
Latorre — A57

Typographed; Head Engraved

1927			Perf. 13½x14½	
154	A57	80c dk brn & blk	2.00	.60

**Types of 1915-25 Issues
Inscribed: "Chile Correos"**
Perf. 13½x14½

1928-31		Engr.	Wmk. 215	
155	A52	5c slate blue	1.40	.25

Frame Typo.; Center Engr.

155A	A38	15c violet & blk		2,200.
156	A55	40c dk vio & blk	.60	.25
157	A42	50c dp grn & blk	2.50	.25

Perf. 14

158	A43	1p green & blk	1.00	.25
159	A43	2p red & blk	5.00	.25
160	A43	5p ol grn & blk	9.75	.45
161	A43	10p orange & blk	9.75	1.90
		Nos. 155,156-161 (7)	30.00	3.60

Paper of Nos. 155-161 varies from thin to
thick.

**Types of 1915-25 Issues
Inscribed: "Correos de Chile"**

1928		Engr.	Perf. 13½x14½	
162	A52	5c deep blue	.35	.25

1929			Litho.	
163	A52	5c light green	.50	.25

Frame Litho.; Center Engr.

164	A50	10c blue & blk	2.00	.25
165	A38	15c violet & blk	2.40	.25
166	A39	20c org red & blk	5.75	.25
167	A40	25c blue & blk	.95	.25
168	A41	30c brown & blk	.75	.25
169	A42	50c dp grn & blk	.65	.25
		Nos. 163-169 (7)	13.00	1.75

Redrawn

1929		Frame Typo.; Center Litho.		
170	A50	10c blue & blk	3.00	.25
171	A38	15c violet & blk	2.75	.25
172	A39	20c org red & blk	4.25	.25
		Nos. 170-172 (3)	10.00	.75

1931			Unwmk.	
173	A50	10c blue & blk	.70	.25

In the redrawn stamps the lines behind the
portraits are heavier and completely fill the
ovals. There are strong diagonal lines above
the shoulders. On No. 170 the head is larger
than on Nos. 164, 173.

A58

Prosperity of Saltpeter Trade
A59   A60

Perf. 13½x14

1930, July 21		Litho.	Wmk. 215	
		Size: 20x25mm		
175	A58	5c yellow grn	.60	.40
176	A58	10c red brown	.60	.30
177	A58	15c violet	.60	.30
178	A59	25c deep gray	1.90	.60
179	A60	70c dark blue	4.50	1.50

Perf. 14
Size: 24½x30mm

180	A60	1p dk gray grn	3.75	.75
		Nos. 175-180 (6)	11.95	3.85

Cent. of the 1st shipment of saltpeter from
Chile, July 21, 1830.

Manuel Bulnes
A61

Bernardo
O'Higgins
A62

1931			Perf. 13½, 14	
181	A61	20c dark brown	1.00	.30

For overprints see Nos. O35, O39.

1932				
182	A62	10c deep blue	1.50	.45

For overprints see Nos. O36, O38.

Mariano
Egana — A63

Joaquin
Tocornal — A64

1934			Perf. 13½x14	
183	A63	30c magenta	.60	.25
		Perf. 14		
184	A64	1.20p bright blue	1.00	.25

Centenary of the constitution.

José Joaquín
Pérez — A65

1934   *Perf. 13½x14*
185 A65 30c bright pink   1.60 .35

Atacama
Desert — A66

Designs: 10c, Fishing boats. 20c, Coquito palms. 25c, Sheep. 30c, Mining. 40c, Lonquimay forest. 50c, Colliery at Port Lota. 1p, Shipping at Valparaiso. 1.20p, Puntiagudo volcano. 2p, Diego de Almagro. 5p, Cattle. 10p, Mining saltpeter.

Wmk. 215
1936, Mar. 1   **Litho.**   *Perf. 14*
186 A66   5c vermilion   .60 .30
187 A66   10c violet   .30 .25
188 A66   20c magenta   .40 .25
189 A66   25c grnsh blue   3.00 .80
190 A66   30c lt green   .30 .25
191 A66   40c blk, *cream*   3.00 .85
192 A66   50c bl, *bluish*   1.50 .30

Engr.
193 A66   1p dk green   1.60 .50
194 A66   1.20p dp blue   1.75 .70
195 A66   2p dk brown   2.00 .80
196 A66   5p copper red   5.00 2.25
197 A66   10p dk violet   12.00 8.00
   Nos. 186-197 (12)   31.45 15.25

400th anniv. of the discovery of Chile by Diego de Almagro.

Laja
Waterfall — A78   Fishing in
Chiloé — A84

Designs: 10c, Agriculture. 15c, Boldo tree. 20c, Nitrate Industry. 30c, Mineral spas. 40c, Copper mine. 50c, Mining. 1.80p, Osorno Volcano. 2p, Mercantile marine. 5p, Lake Villarrica. 10p, State railways.

Perf. 13½x14
1938-40   **Litho.**   **Wmk. 215**
198 A78   5c brn car ('39)   .25 .25
199 A78   10c sal pink ('39)   .25 .25
200 A78   15c brn org ('40)   .25 .25
201 A78   20c light blue   .25 .25
202 A78   30c brt pink   .25 .25
203 A78   40c lt grn ('39)   .25 .25
204 A78   50c violet   .25 .25

Engr.   *Perf. 14*
205 A84   1p orange brn   .25 .25
206 A84   1.80p deep blue   .45 .40
207 A84   2p car lake   .25 .25
208 A84   5p dk slate grn   .35 .25
209 A84   10p rose vio ('40)   .90 .25
   Nos. 198-209 (12)   3.95 3.15

See Nos. 217-227 in *Scott Standard Postage Stamp Catalogue*, Vol. 2. For surcharge and overprints see Nos. 253, O41-O66, O70-O71 in this catalogue or Scott Standard catalogue, Vol. 2.

Map of the
Americas — A89

Unwmk.
1940, Sept. 11   **Litho.**   *Perf. 14*
210 A89 40c dl grn & yel grn   .35 .25

Pan American Union, 50th anniversary.

SEMI-POSTAL STAMPS

S. S.
Abtao
and
Captain
Policarpo
Toro
SP1

S. S.
Abtao
and
Brother
Eugenio
Eyraud
SP2

Perf. 14½x15
1940, Mar. 1   **Engr.**   **Unwmk.**
B1 SP1 80c + 2.20p dk grn
    & lake   2.50 2.00
B2 SP2 3.60p + 6.40p lake &
    dk grn   2.50 2.00
  a.   Pair, #B1-B2   10.00 8.00
   Set, never hinged   8.00

50th anniv. of Chilean ownership of Easter Is. Surtax used for charitable institutions.
Sheets containing 15 of each value, with 9 se-tenant pairs.

AIR POST STAMPS

Surcharged in
Black

2 pesos

Lithographed; Center Engraved
1927   **Unwmk.**   *Perf. 13½x14*
Black Brown & Blue
C1 40c on 10c   400.00 50.00
C2 80c on 10c   400.00 65.00
C3 1.20p on 10c   400.00 75.00
C4 1.60p on 10c   400.00 75.00
C5 2p on 10c   400.00 75.00
   Nos. C1-C5 (5)   2,000. 340.00

Issued for air post service between Santiago and Valparaiso. The stamps picture Bernardo O'Higgins and are not known without surcharge.

Regular Issues of
1915-28 Overprinted
or Surcharged in
Black, Red or Blue

Inscribed: "Chile Correos"
1928-29   *Perf. 13½x14, 14*
C6 A39 20c brn org & blk
    (Bk)   .50 .30
C6A A55 40c dk vio & blk
    (R)   .50 .30
C6B A43 1p grn & blk (Bl)   1.60 .70
C6C A43 2p red & blk (Bl)   2.60 .40
  f.   2p ver & blk (Bl)   120.00 30.00
C6D A43 5p ol grn & blk
    (Bl)   4.00 1.10
C6E A50 6p on 10c dp bl
    & blk (R)   65.00 22.50

C7 A43 10p org & blk (Bk)
    ('29)   16.00 4.50
C8 A43 10p org & blk (Bl)   60.00 35.00
   Nos. C6-C8 (8)   150.20 64.80

On Nos. C6B to C6D, C7 and C8 the overprint is larger than on the other stamps of the issue.

Same Overprint or Surcharge on Nos. 155, 156, 158-161
Inscribed: "Chile Correos"
1928-32   **Wmk. 215**
C9 A55 40c vio & blk (R)   .70 .40
C10 A43 1p grn & blk (Bl)   1.90 .60
C11 A43 2p red & blk (Bl)   11.00 2.25
C12 A52 3p on 5c sl bl (R)   65.00 40.00
C13 A43 5p ol grn & blk (Bl)   8.50 2.25
C14 A43 10p org & blk (Bk)   45.00 11.00
   Nos. C9-C14 (6)   132.10 56.50

Same Overprint on Nos. 166-169, 172 and 158 in Black or Red
Inscribed: "Correos de Chile"
1928-30
C15 A39 20c (#166) ('29)   1.20 .70
C16 A39 20c (#172) ('30)   .50 .25
C17 A40 25c bl & blk (R)   .60 .25
C18 A41 30c brn & blk   .40 .25
  a.   Double ovpt., one inverted   250.00 250.00
C19 A42 50c dp grn & blk
    (R)   .50 .25
   Nos. C15-C19 (5)   3.20 1.70

Inscribed: "Chile Correos"
1932   *Perf. 13½x14, 14*
C21 A43 1p yel grn & blk (Bk)   2.75 1.50

Condor on
Andes — AP1a   Airplane
Crossing
Andes — AP3

Los Cerrillos
Airport — AP2

1931   **Litho.**   *Perf. 13½x14, 14½x14*
C22 AP1a 5c yellow grn   .25 .25
C23 AP1a 10c yellow brn   .25 .25
C24 AP1a 20c rose   .25 .25
C25 AP2 50c dark blue   1.50 .50
C26 AP3 50c black brn   .75 .25
C27 AP3 1p purple   .60 .25
C28 AP3 2p blue blk   .90 .30
  a.   2p bluish slate   1.00 .45
C29 AP2 5p lt red   3.00 .30
   Nos. C22-C29 (8)   7.50 2.35

For surcharges see Nos. C51-C53.

Airplane over
City — AP4   Two Airplanes
over Globe — AP9

Designs: 30c, 40c, 50c, Wings over Chile. 60c, Condor. 70c, Airplane and Star of Chile. 80c, Condor and Statue of Canpolican. 3p, 4p, 5p, Seaplane. 6p, 8p, 10p, Airplane. 20p, 30p, Airplane and Southern Cross. 40p, 50p, Airplane and symbols of space.

Perf. 13½x14
1934-39   **Engr.**   **Wmk. 215**
C30 AP4 10c yel grn ('35)   .30 .25
C31 AP4 15c dk grn ('35)   .45 .25
C32 AP4 20c dp bl ('36)   .25 .25
C33 AP4 30c blk brn ('35)   .25 .25
C34 AP4 40c indigo ('38)   .25 .25
C35 AP4 50c dk brn ('36)   .25 .25
C36 AP4 60c vio blk ('35)   .25 .25
C37 AP4 70c blue ('35)   .45 .25
C38 AP4 80c ol blk ('35)   .25 .25

Perf. 14
C39 AP9 1p slate blk   .25 .25
C40 AP9 2p grnsh bl   .25 .25
C41 AP9 3p org brn ('35)   .30 .25
C42 AP9 4p dull ('35)   .30 .25
C43 AP9 5p org red   .30 .25
C44 AP9 6p yel brn ('35)   .45 .25
  a.   6p brown ('39)   2.75 1.90
C45 AP9 8p grn ('35)   .40 .25
C46 AP9 10p brn lake   .45 .25
C47 AP9 20p olive   .45 .25
C48 AP9 30p gray blk   .50 .25
C49 AP9 40p gray vio   1.40 .25
C50 AP9 50p brn vio   1.60 .70
   Nos. C30-C50 (21)   9.35 6.15

Nos. C30-C50 have been re-issued in slightly different colors, with white gum. The first printings are considerably scarcer.
See Nos. C90-C107B, C148-C154 in *Scott Standard Postage Stamp Catalogue*, Vol. 2.

Types of 1931
Surcharged in Black
or Red

Cts.80

Perf. 13½x14, 14½x14
1940   **Wmk. 215**
C51 AP1a 80c on 20c lt rose   .70 .25
C52 AP2 1.60p on 5p lt red   4.25 1.50
C53 AP3 5.10p on 2p sl bl (R)   3.50 1.75
   Nos. C51-C53 (3)   8.45 3.50

The surcharge on No. C52 measures 21½mm.

ACKNOWLEDGMENT OF RECEIPT STAMPS

AR1

1894   **Unwmk.**   *Perf. 11½*
H1 AR1 5c brown   .75 .50
  a.   Imperf., pair   3.00

The black stamp of design similar to AR1 inscribed "Avis de Paiement" was prepared for use on notices of payment of funds but was not regularly issued.

POSTAGE DUE STAMPS

D1   D2

Handstamped
1894   **Unwmk.**   *Perf. 13*
J1 D1 2c black, *straw*   15.00 8.00
J2 D1 4c black, *straw*   15.00 8.00
J3 D1 6c black, *straw*   15.00 8.00
J4 D1 8c black, *straw*   14.00 8.00
J5 D2 10c black, *straw*   15.00 8.00
J6 D1 16c black, *straw*   15.00 8.00
J7 D1 20c black, *straw*   15.00 8.00
J8 D1 30c black, *straw*   15.00 8.00
J9 D1 40c black, *straw*   15.00 8.00
   Nos. J1-J9 (9)   134.00 72.00

J1a D1 2c black, *yellow*   85.00 85.00
J2a D1 4c black, *yellow*   55.00 40.00
J3a D1 6c black, *yellow*   80.00 35.00
J4a D1 8c black, *yellow*   16.00 16.00
J5a D2 10c black, *yellow*   16.00 16.00
J6a D1 16c black, *yellow*   16.00 16.00
J7a D1 20c black, *yellow*   16.00 16.00
J8a D1 30c black, *yellow*   16.00 16.00
J9a D1 40c black, *yellow*   16.00 16.00
   Nos. J1a-J9a (9)   316.00 251.00

Counterfeits exist.

D3

1895 Litho. Perf. 11

J19	D3	1c red, *yellow*		7.50	3.00
J20	D3	2c red, *yellow*		7.50	3.00
J21	D3	4c red, *yellow*		6.00	3.00
J22	D3	6c red, *yellow*		7.50	3.00
J23	D3	8c red, *yellow*		4.50	3.00
J24	D3	10c red, *yellow*		4.50	4.50
J25	D3	20c red, *yellow*		4.50	2.25
J26	D3	40c red, *yellow*		4.50	3.00
J27	D3	50c red, *yellow*		4.50	4.50
J28	D3	60c red, *yellow*		9.00	4.50
J29	D3	80c red, *yellow*		9.00	6.00
J30	D3	1p red, *yellow*		9.50	6.50
		Nos. J19-J30 (12)		78.50	44.75

Nos. J19-J30 were printed in sheets of 100 (10x10) containing all 12 denominations. Counterfeits of Nos. J19-J42 exist.

1896 Perf. 13½

J31	D3	1c red, *straw*		.90	.50
J32	D3	2c red, *straw*		.90	.50
J33	D3	4c red, *straw*		1.10	.50
J34	D3	6c red, *straw*		2.50	1.00
J35	D3	8c red, *straw*		1.10	.60
J36	D3	10c red, *straw*		.90	.60
J37	D3	20c red, *straw*		.90	.60
J38	D3	40c red, *straw*		18.00	15.00
J39	D3	50c red, *straw*		18.00	15.00
J40	D3	60c red, *straw*		18.00	15.00
J41	D3	80c red, *straw*		25.00	17.50
J42	D3	100c red, *straw*		36.00	30.00
		Nos. J31-J42 (12)		123.30	96.80

D4   D5

1898 Perf. 13

J43	D4	1c scarlet	.50	.30
J44	D4	2c scarlet	1.25	.60
J45	D4	4c scarlet	.50	.30
J46	D4	10c scarlet	.50	.30
J47	D4	20c scarlet	.50	.30
		Nos. J43-J47 (5)	3.25	1.80

1924 Perf. 11½, 12½

J48	D5	2c blue & red	1.10	.90
J49	D5	4c blue & red	1.10	.90
J50	D5	8c blue & red	1.10	.90
J51	D5	10c blue & red	1.10	.90
J52	D5	20c blue & red	1.10	.60
J53	D5	40c blue & red	1.10	.90
J54	D5	60c blue & red	1.10	.90
J55	D5	80c blue & red	1.10	.90
J56	D5	1p blue & red	1.50	1.10
J57	D5	2p blue & red	2.60	1.90
J58	D5	5p blue & red	2.60	1.90
		Nos. J48-J58 (11)	15.50	11.80

Nos. J48-J58 were printed in sheets of 150 containing all 11 denominations, and a second printing was printed in sheets of 50 containing the five lower denominations, providing various se-tenants. Stamps from the second printing are of a slightly different shade of red.

All values of this issue exist imperforate, also with center inverted, but are not believed to have been regularly issued. Those with inverted centers sell for about 10 times normal stamps.

OFFICIAL STAMPS

For Domestic Postage

O1

Single-lined frame
Control number in violet

1907 Unwmk. Imperf.

O1	O1	dl bl, "CARTA" org	22.50	17.50
O2	O1	red, "OFICIO" bl	22.50	17.50
O3	O1	vio, "PAQUETE" red	22.50	17.50
O4	O1	org, bl, "EP" vio	22.50	17.50
		Nos. O1-O4 (4)	90.00	70.00

The diagonal inscription in differing color indicates type of usage: CARTA for letters of ordinary weight; OFICIO, heavy letters to 100 grams; PAQUETE, parcels to 100 grams; E P (Encomienda Postal), heavier parcels; C (Certificado), as on No. O8, registration including postage.

Varieties include CARTA, PAQUETE and E P inverted, OFICIO omitted, etc.

Double-lined frame
Large control number in black
Perf. 11

O5	O1	bl, "CARTA" yel	8.00	7.00
O6	O1	red, "OFICIO" bl	8.00	5.25
O7	O1	brn, "PAQUETE" grn	8.00	5.25
O8	O1	grn, "C" red	110.00	82.50
		Nos. O5-O8 (4)	134.00	100.00

Nos. O5-O8 exist in tête bêche pairs; with CARTA, OFICIO or PAQUETE double or inverted, and other varieties.
Counterfeits of Nos. O1-O8 exist.

For Foreign Postage

Regular Issues of 1892-1909 Overprinted in Red — a

On Stamps of 1904-09

1907 Perf. 12

O9	A14	1c green	7.50	7.50
a.		Inverted overprint	17.50	
O10	A12	3c on lp brn	14.00	13.00
a.		Inverted overprint	52.50	
O11	A14	5c ultra	10.00	9.50
a.		Inverted overprint	35.00	
O12	A15	10c gray & blk	10.50	10.50
O13	A15	15c vio & blk	14.00	13.00
O14	A15	20c org brn & blk	14.00	14.00
O15	A15	50c ultra & blk	45.00	45.00

On Stamp of 1892
Rouletted

O16	A6	1p dk brn & blk	110.00	87.50
		Nos. O9-O16 (8)	225.00	200.00

Counterfeits of Nos. O9-O16 exist.

Regular Issues of 1915-25 Overprinted in Red or Blue — b

1926 Perf. 13½x14, 14

O17	A52	5c slate bl (R)	2.50	.50
O18	A50	10c bl & blk (R)	4.00	.75
O19	A39	20c org red & blk (Bl)	2.00	.40
O20	A42	50c dp grn & blk (Bl)	2.00	.40
O21	A43	1p grn & blk (R)	2.75	.70
O22	A43	2p ver & blk (Bl)	4.00	1.00
		Nos. O17-O22 (6)	17.25	3.75

Nos. O21 and O22 are overprinted vertically at each side.
Nos. O17 to O22 were for the use of the Biblioteca Nacional.

Regular Issue of 1915-25 Overprinted in Red — c

1928 Perf. 13½x14, 14

O23	A50	10c bl & blk	6.50	2.00
O24	A39	20c brn org & blk	3.00	1.00
O25	A40	25c dl bl & blk	7.50	1.00
O26	A42	50c dp grn & blk	4.00	1.00
O27	A43	1p grn & blk	5.00	1.50
		Nos. O23-O27 (5)	26.00	6.50

The overprint on Nos. O23 to O26 is 16½mm high; on No. O27 it is 20mm.

Regular Issues of 1928-30 Overprinted in Red — d

On Stamp Inscribed: "Correos de Chile"

1930-31

O28	A50	10c bl & blk	3.00	1.50

Wmk. 215

On Stamps Inscribed: "Correos de Chile"

O29	A50	10c bl & blk	6.00	3.00
O30	A39	20c org red & blk	.75	.50
O31	A40	25c bl & blk	.75	.50
O32	A42	50c dp grn & blk	1.50	.75

On Stamps Inscribed: "Chile Correos"

O33	A42	50c dp grn & blk	1.50	.75
O34	A43	1p grn & blk	1.50	.75
		Nos. O28-O34 (7)	15.00	7.75

Same Overprint on No. 181

1933 Perf. 13½x14

O35	A61	20c dk brn	.75	.25

Same Overprint in Red on No. 182

1935 Wmk. 215

O36	A62	10c deep blue	.75	.50

No. 163 Ovptd. Type "b" in Red
Inscribed: "Correos de Chile"

1934

O37	A52	5c lt grn	.60	.50

Overprint "b" on No. 182

1935

O38	A62	10c dp bl	.50	.50

Same Overprint in Black on No. 181

1936 Wmk. 215 Perf. 13½x14

O39	A61	20c dk brn	10.00	.50

Overprint "b" in Red on No. 158

1938 Perf. 14

O40	A43	1p grn & blk	2.50	1.00

Nos. 204 and 205 Overprinted Type "d" in Black

1939 Perf. 13½x14, 14

O41	A78	50c violet	4.00	2.50
O42	A84	1p org brn	5.00	4.00

Stamps of 1938-40 Overprinted Type "b" in Black, Red or Blue

1940-46 Perf. 13½x14, 14

O43	A78	10c sal pink ('45)	2.00	1.75
O44	A78	15c brn org	1.00	.40
O45	A78	20c lt bl (R) ('42)	1.50	.60
O46	A78	30c brn pink (Bl)	.75	.40
O47	A78	40c lt grn	.75	.40
O48	A78	50c vio ('45)	4.00	.75
O49	A84	1p org brn ('42)	2.00	.75
O50	A84	1.80p dp bl (R) ('45)	10.00	6.00
O51	A84	2p car lake ('42)	2.00	1.25
		Nos. O43-O51 (9)	24.50	12.30

Overprint "b" in Black on Nos. 223, 225

Unwmk.

O58	A84	1p brn org	2.50	1.50
O59	A84	2p car lake ('46)	5.00	2.00

CHINA

ˈchī-nə

LOCATION — Eastern Asia
GOVT. — Republic
AREA — 2,903,475 sq. mi.
POP. — 462,798,093 (1948)

10 Candareen = 1 Mace
10 Mace = 1 Tael
100 Cents = 1 Dollar (Yuan) (1897)

Watermarks

Wmk. 103 —
Yin-Yang Symbol

Wmk. 261 —
Character Yu
(Post) Multiple

Issues of the Imperial Maritime Customs Post

Imperial
Dragon — A1

1878 Unwmk. Typo. Perf. 12½
Thin Paper
Stamps printed 2½-3¼mm apart

1	A1	1c green	700.00	550.00
a.		1c dark green	800.00	575.00
2	A1	3c brown red	825.00	475.00
a.		3c vermilion	900.00	500.00
3	A1	5c orange	900.00	450.00
a.		5c bister orange	1,250.	600.00

Imperforate essays of Nos. 1-3 have an extra circle near the dragon's lower left foot. Examples with the circle completely or mostly removed are proofs or unfinished stamps.

1882
Thin or Pelure Paper
Stamps printed 4½mm apart

4	A1	1c green	775.00	425.00
a.		1c dark green	850.00	475.00
5	A1	3c brown red	1,350.	400.00
6	A1	5c orange yellow	16,000.	1,750.

1883 Rough to smooth Perf. 12½
Medium to Thick Opaque Paper
Stamps printed 2½ to 3¼mm apart

7	A1	1c green	775.00	525.00
a.		1c dark green	900.00	600.00
b.		1c light green	950.00	625.00
c.		Vert. pair, imperf. between	160,000.	
8	A1	3c brown red	1,350.	450.00
a.		3c vermilion	1,650.	450.00
b.		Vert. pair, imperf. between		60,000.
9	A1	5c yellow	2,200.	725.00
a.		5c chrome yellow	2,500.	950.00
b.		Horiz. pair, imperf. btwn.		60,000.

Nos. 1-9 were printed from plates of 25, 20 or 15 individual copper dies, but only No. 5 exists in the 15-die setting. Many different printings and plate settings exist. All values occur in a wide variety of shades and papers. The effect of climate on certain papers has produced the varieties on so-called toned papers in Nos. 1-15.
Value for No. 8b is for a damaged example.
Counterfeits, frequently with forged cancellations, occur in all early Chinese issues.

Imperial Dragon — A2

1885 Wmk. 103 Perf. 12½

10	A2	1c green	225.00	100.00
a.		Vert. pair, imperf. btwn.	20,000.	17,500.
b.		Horiz. pair, imperf. btwn.	24,000.	
11	A2	3c lilac	500.00	140.00
a.		Horiz. pair, imperf. btwn.	22,000.	17,500.
b.		Vert. pair, imperf. btwn.		24,000.
12	A2	5c grnsh yellow	450.00	140.00
a.		5c bister brown	725.00	170.00
b.		Vert. pair, imperf. btwn.	24,000.	24,000.
c.		Horiz. pair, imperf. btwn.		52,500.
		Nos. 10-12 (3)	1,175.	380.00

1888 *Perf. 11½-12*

13	A2	1c green	100.00	55.00
14	A2	3c lilac	250.00	90.00
b.		Double impression		1,100.
15	A2	5c grnsh yellow	450.00	140.00
b.		Double impression		
c.		Horiz. pair, imperf. vert.	1,100.	1,100.
		Nos. 13-15 (3)	800.00	285.00

Nos. 10-15 were printed from plates made of 40 individual copper dies, arranged in two panes of 20 each. Several different settings exist of all values.

Imperforates of Nos. 13-15 are considered proofs by most authorities.

Stamps overprinted "Formosa" in English or Chinese are proofs.

For surcharges see Nos. 25-27, 75-77.

"Shou" and "Wu Fu" — A3

Dragon and Hydrangea Leaves — A4

"Pa Kua" Signs in Corners — A5

Dragon and Peony — A6

Carp, the Messenger Fish — A7

Dragon, "Pa Kua" and Immortelle A8

Dragons and "Shou" A9

Dragons and Giant Peony — A10

Junk on the Yangtse A11

1894　Lithographed in Shanghai

16	A3	1c orange red	65.00	47.50
a.		Vert. pair, imperf. btwn.	2,250.	2,100.
b.		Horiz. pair, imperf. btwn.	17,500.	12,000.
c.		Vert. pair, imperf. horiz.	3,250.	3,250.
17	A4	2c green	70.00	45.00
a.		Horiz. pair, imperf. btwn.	3,750.	3,500.
18	A5	3c orange	60.00	37.50
a.		Vert. pair, imperf. btwn.	3,350.	3,500.
b.		Horiz. pair, imperf. btwn.	5,000.	3,800.
19	A6	4c rose pink	240.00	250.00
a.		Vert. pair, imperf. btwn.	14,000.	
20	A7	5c dull orange	450.00	500.00
a.		Vert. pair, imperf. btwn.	18,000.	18,000.
21	A8	6c dark brown	190.00	60.00
a.		Vert. pair, imperf. btwn.	24,000.	
b.		Horiz. pair, imperf. btwn.	12,500.	
22	A9	9c dark green	325.00	120.00
a.		Imperf., pair	2,250.	
b.		Horiz. pair, imperf. horiz.	4,250.	3,750.
c.		Vert. pair, imperf. horiz.	4,250.	
d.		Vert. pair, imperf. btwn.	4,750.	4,250.
e.		Tete beche pair, vert.	1,650.	1,400.
f.		Tete beche pair, imperf. horiz.	5,500.	
g.		Tete beche pair, imperf. vert.	5,500.	4,750.

h.		Vert. strip of 3, imperf. btwn.	5,500.	
i.		Tete beche pair, imperf. btwn.	1,500.	1,300.
23	A10	12c orange	675.00	350.00
24	A11	24c carmine	900.00	250.00
a.		Vert. pair, imperf. btwn.	30,000.	
		Nos. 16-24 (9)	2,975.	1,660.

60th birthday of Tsz'e Hsi, the Empress Dowager. All values exist in several distinct shades.

On Mar. 20, 1896, the Customs Post was changed, by Imperial Edict, effective Jan. 1, 1897, to a National Post and the dollar was adopted as the unit of currency.

Time was required to work out details of the Imperial Post and design new stamps. As a provisional measure, stocks of Nos. 16-24 were ordered surcharged with new values in dollars and cents. It is believed that only the Shanghai office stock of Nos. 16-24 (plus any reserve stock at the printers) was surcharged with small figures of value. Other post offices throughout China were instructed to return all unoverprinted stocks on receipt of the new surcharges.

Early in the year it was apparent that all stamps would be exhausted before the new issues were ready (Nos. 86-97), and since the stones from which Nos. 16-24 had been printed no longer existed, new stones were made from the original transfers. A printing from the new stones was made early in 1897 and surcharged with large figures of value spaced 2½mm below the Chinese characters. During the surcharging, sheets from the 1894 (original) printing were received from outlying post offices and surcharged as they arrived. A small quantity of the 1897 printing reached the public without surcharge (Nos. 16n-24n).

Additional stamps were still required and another printing was made from the new stones and surcharged with large figures, but in a new setting with 1½mm between the Chinese characters and the value. Additional sheets of the 1894 printing were received from the most distant post offices and were also surcharged with the 1½mm setting. Thus there are four different sets of the large-figure surcharges. All these stamps were regularly issued but no attempt was made by the post office to separate printings. Some values are difficult to distinguish as to printing, particularly in used condition.

See No. 73. For surcharges see Nos. 28-72, 74.

1897　Lithographed in Shanghai

16n	A3	1c pink	725.00	
17n	A4	2c olive green	1,200.	
18n	A5	3c chrome yellow	725.00	
p.		3c yellow buff	1,000.	
19n	A6	4c pale rose	875.00	
20n	A7	5c yellow	875.00	
21n	A8	6c red brown	1,000.	
22n	A9	9c yellowish green	3,750.	
p.		9c emerald green	—	
23n	A10	12c yellowish orange	3,750.	
24n	A11	24c purplish red	2,200.	

The colors of the 1897 printings are pale or dull; the gum is thin and white. The 1894 printing has a thicker, yellowish gum.

The set of 9 values on thick unwatermarked paper is a special printing of 5,000 sets ordered by P. G. von Mollendorf, a Customs official, for presentation purposes. Value, set $2,400.

For surcharges see Nos. 47-55, 65-72.

Issues of the Chinese Government Post

Preceding Issues Surcharged in Black

Small Numerals 2½mm Below Chinese Characters
Surcharged on Nos. 13-15

1897, Jan. 2 *Perf. 11½-12*

25	A2	1c on 1c	72.50	85.00
26	A2	2c on 3c	325.00	120.00
a.		Double surcharge		
27	A2	5c on 5c	110.00	57.50
		Nos. 25-27 (3)	507.50	262.50

Surcharged on Nos. 16-24

28	A5	½c on 3c	45.00	32.50
a.		"1" instead of "½"	350.00	350.00
b.		Horiz. pair, imperf. btwn.	5,000.	
c.		Vert. pair, imperf. horiz.	5,000.	3,000.
d.		Double surcharge	12,000.	11,000.
e.		Vert. pair, imperf. btwn.	5,000.	
29	A3	1c on 1c	27.50	25.00
a.		Inverted surcharge	25,000.	25,000.
30	A4	2c on 2c	32.50	22.50
a.		Horiz. pair, imperf. btwn.	4,000.	
b.		Vert. pair, imperf. btwn.	4,000.	
c.		Double surcharge	14,000.	
d.		Inverted surcharge	—	15,000.
e.		Horiz. pair, imperf. btwn.	2,000.	

31	A6	4c on 4c	35.00	27.50
a.		Double surcharge	30,000.	20,000.
b.		Vert. pair, imperf. btwn.	5,000.	5,000.
c.		Horiz. pair, imperf. btwn.	5,000.	5,000.
32	A7	5c on 5c	42.50	19.00
a.		Vert. pair, imperf. btwn.	15,000.	15,000.
33	A8	6c on 6c	55.00	35.00
a.		Vert. pair, imperf. btwn.	2,750.	2,250.
b.		Vert. strip of 3, imperf.		
c.		Horiz. pair, imperf. btwn.	4,200.	2,100.
34	A8	10c on 6c	90.00	70.00
a.		Vert. pair, imperf. btwn.	7,500.	2,500.
b.		Horiz. pair, imperf. vert.	2,400.	2,400.
35	A9	10c on 9c	500.00	190.00
a.		Double surcharge	40,000.	40,000.
b.		Inverted surcharge	450,000.	—
36	A10	10c on 12c	475.00	190.00
a.		Vert. pair, imperf. horiz.	2,000.	
b.		Horiz. pair, imperf. btwn.	2,200.	2,200.
37	A11	30c on 24c	625.00	250.00
a.		*Nos. 28-37 (10)*	1,927.	861.50

Small Numerals 4mm Below Chinese Characters

25a	A2	1c on 1c green	75.00	85.00
28f	A4	½c on 3c orange	60.00	60.00
29b	A3	1c on 1c vermilion	75.00	75.00
30f	A4	2c on 2c dark green	55.00	55.00
31d	A6	4c on 4c dark pink	55.00	55.00
32b	A7	5c on 5c dull orange	55.00	55.00
33d	A8	8c on 6c brown	55.00	37.50
35c	A9	10c on 9c dark green	425.00	350.00
37b	A11	30c on 24c dark red	500.00	500.00

Preceding Issues Surcharged in Black

Large Numerals
Numerals 2½mm below Chinese characters
Surcharged on Nos. 16-24

1897, Mar.

38	A5	½c on 3c	2,500.	850.00
b.		Inverted surcharge		10,000.
39	A3	1c on 1c	700.00	200.00
40	A4	2c on 2c	375.00	350.00
41	A6	4c on 4c vermilion	475.00	375.00
b.		Horiz. pair, imperf. btwn.		11,000.
42	A7	5c on 5c	225.00	200.00
43	A8	8c on 6c	2,250.	1,750.
44	A9	10c on 9c	800.00	375.00
45	A10	10c on 12c	35,000.	2,750.
46	A11	30c on 24c	1,200.	1,300.
b.		2mm spacing between "30" and "cents."		15,000.

Same Surcharge on Nos. 16n-24n

47	A5	½c on 3c	32.50	40.00
a.		"cen" for "cent"	850.00	850.00
b.		Vert. pair, imperf. btwn.	2,100.	2,100.
c.		Vert. pair, imperf. horiz.	1,750.	1,250.
d.		As "a" and "c"	9,500.	9,500.
e.		As "a" and "b"	7,500.	7,500.
f.		Horiz. pair, imperf. btwn.	1,900.	1,900.
48	A3	1c on 1c	27.50	22.50
a.		Horiz. pair, imperf. btwn.		
b.				2,500.
49	A4	2c on 2c	25.00	17.50
50	A6	4c on 4c	35.00	25.00
a.		Horiz. pair, imperf. btwn.	3,250.	3,250.
b.		Vert. pair, imperf. btwn.		4,000.
51	A7	5c on 5c	47.50	27.50
52	A8	8c on 6c	525.00	300.00
53	A9	10c on 9c	200.00	85.00
a.		10c on 9c emerald	210.00	87.50
b.		Pair, one without surcharge	1,100.	
54	A10	10c on 12c	375.00	90.00
55	A11	30c on 24c	750.00	325.00
a.		2mm spacing btwn "30" and "cents"	1,250.	750.00
b.		Horiz. pair, imperf. btwn.	6,250.	

All recorded unused examples of No. 45 are flawed.

Numerals 1½mm below Chinese characters

1897, May
Surcharged on Nos. 16-24

56	A5	½c on 3c org yel	500.00	425.00
57	A3	1c on 1c	350.00	275.00
58	A4	2c on 2c	—	3,500.
59	A6	4c on 4c	300.00	225.00
60	A7	5c on 5c	175.00	160.00
61	A8	8c on 6c	1,600.	1,350.
62	A9	10c on 9c	350.00	250.00
63	A10	10c on 12c	1,500.	1,100.
64	A11	30c on 24c	60,000.	

Same Surcharge on Nos. 16n-24n

65	A5	½c on 3c	25.00	27.50
a.		Inverted surcharge	3,000.	3,000.
b.		½mm spacing	1,500.	1,200.

66	A3	1c on 1c	27.50	22.50
67	A4	2c on 2c	30.00	25.00
a.		Inverted surcharge	25,500.	8,750.
b.		Vert. pair, imperf. btwn.		8,500.
68	A6	4c on 4c	200.00	100.00
a.		Inverted surcharge	2,500.	1,500.
69	A7	5c on 5c	300.00	140.00
70	A9	10c on 9c	210.00	95.00
a.		Inverted surcharge	1,350.	1,100.
71	A10	10c on 12c	375.00	110.00
72	A11	30c on 24c	13,000.	2,600.

Same Surcharge (1½mm Spacing) on Type A12, and

A12

A12a

Redrawn Designs
Printed from New Stones

1897

73	A12	½c on 3c yel	250.00	200.00
a.		½mm spacing	7,000.	5,000.
74	A12a	2c on 2c yel grn	60.00	45.00
a.		Horiz. pair, imperf. btwn.	6,000.	

Nos. 73 and 74 were surcharged on stamps printed from new stones, which differ slightly from the originals. On No. 73 the numeral "3" and symbols in the four corner panels have been enlarged and strengthened. On No. 74, the numeral "2" has a thick, flat base.

Surcharged on Nos. 13-15

75	A2	1c on 1c green	500.00	625.00
76	A2	2c on 3c lilac	1,000.	1,000.
77	A2	5c on 5c grnsh yel	350.00	500.00

Revenue Stamps Surcharged in Black

A13

a

b

c

d

f

e

g

1897　Unwmk. *Perf. 12 to 15*

78	A13 (a)	1c on 3c red	500.00	300.000
a.		No period after "cent"	525.00	350.00
b.		Central character with large "box"	550.00	525.00
79	A13 (b)	2c on 3c red	825.00	450.00
a.		Inverted surcharge	25,000.	12,000.
b.		Inverted "S" in "CENTS"	900.00	575.00
c.		No period after "CENTS"	900.00	575.00
d.		Comma after "CENTS"	850.00	500.00
e.		Double surcharge	25,000.	25,000.
f.		Dbl. surch., both inverted	50,000.	
g.		Double surch. (blk & grn)	220,000.	
80	A13 (c)	2c on 3c red	550.00	375.00

81	A13 (d)	4c on 3c red	100,000.	75,000.
a.		Double surcharge (blk & vio)	250,000.	250,000.
82	A13 (e)	4c on 3c red	1,650.	600.00
83	A13 (f)	$1 on 3c red	900,000.	—
a.		No period after "r"		
84	A13 (g)	$1 on 3c red	9,000.	3,500.
85	A13 (g)	$5 on 3c red	75,000.	40,000.
a.		Inverted surcharge	110,000.	45,000.

A few examples of the 3c red exist without surcharge; one canceled. Value, unused $60,000. No. 79 with green surcharge is a trial printing. Value for faulty upper left corner block, $190,000.

No. 79g is unique. The only canceled example of No. 83 is in a museum.

Dragon — A14   Carp — A15

Wild Goose — A16

"Imperial Chinese Post"
Lithographed in Japan
Perf. 11, 11½, 12

1897, Aug. 16 — **Wmk. 103**

86	A14	½c purple brn	5.50	4.50
a.		Horiz. pair, imperf. btwn.	650.00	
87	A14	1c yellow	6.50	4.00
88	A14	2c orange	5.75	3.75
a.		Vert. pair, imperf. horiz.	900.00	
89	A14	4c brown	10.50	3.75
a.		Horiz. pair, imperf. btwn.	1,000.	
90	A14	5c rose red	12.00	3.75
91	A14	10c dk green	40.00	3.75
92	A15	20c maroon	85.00	17.50
93	A15	30c red	140.00	32.50
94	A15	50c yellow grn	100.00	45.00
a.		50c black green	1,150.	
b.		50c blue green	1,300.	
95	A16	$1 car & rose	300.00	200.00
a.		Horiz. pair, imperf. vert.	—	
96	A16	$2 orange & yel	2,100.	1,200.
a.		Horiz. pair, imperf. vert.		
97	A16	$5 yel grn & pink	1,600.	1,000.

The inner circular frames and outer frames of Nos. 86-91 differ for each denomination.

No. 97 imperforate was not regularly issued. **Examples have been privately perforated and offered as No. 97.** Shades occur in most values of this issue.

A17   A18

A19

"Chinese Imperial Post"
Engraved in London

1898 — Wmk. 103 — Perf. 12 to 16

98	A17	½c chocolate	6.00	2.75
a.		Vert. pair, imperf. btwn.	850.00	475.00
b.		Vert. pair, imperf. horiz.	850.00	475.00
99	A17	1c ocher	6.50	2.75
a.		Vert. pair, imperf. btwn.	300.00	250.00
b.		Horiz. pair, imperf. btwn.	400.00	350.00
100	A17	2c scarlet	7.25	2.75
a.		Vert. pair, imperf. btwn.	400.00	200.00
b.		Horiz. pair, imperf. vert.	400.00	200.00
101	A17	4c orange brn	7.50	2.75
a.		Vert. pair, imperf. btwn.	575.00	
b.		Horiz. pair, imperf. btwn.	400.00	300.00
c.		Horiz. pair, imperf. btwn.	700.00	600.00
d.		Horiz. strip of 3, imperf. btwn.	2,250.	1,500.
102	A17	5c salmon	11.00	4.75
a.		Vert. pair, imperf. btwn.	400.00	300.00
b.		Horiz. pair, imperf. btwn.	775.00	500.00

c.		Vert. pair, imperf. horiz.	600.00	500.00
d.		5c pale reddish orange	16.00	5.50
e.		As "d," vert pair, imperf.	600.00	500.00
103	A17	10c dk blue grn	17.50	3.00
a.		Vert. or horiz. pair, imperf. btwn		
104	A18	20c claret	70.00	9.00
a.		Horiz. pair, imperf. btwn.	850.00	750.00
b.		Vert. pair, imperf. btwn.	850.00	750.00
c.		Vert. pair, imperf. btwn.	900.00	800.00
105	A18	30c dull rose	60.00	14.00
a.		Horiz. pair, imperf. btwn.	2,000.	
b.		Vert. pair, imperf. btwn.	1,750.	
c.		Vert. pair, imperf. btwn.	1,750.	
106	A18	50c lt green	85.00	19.00
a.		Vert. pair, imperf. btwn.	2,250.	
107	A19	$1 red & pale rose	375.00	45.00
108	A19	$2 brn, red & yel	600.00	85.00
109	A19	$5 dp grn & sal	975.00	300.00
a.		Horiz. pair, imperf. btwn.	8,000.	
b.		Vert. pair, imperf. btwn.	8,500.	
		Nos. 98-109 (12)	2,220.	490.75

No. 98 surcharged "B. R. A.-Five Cents" in three lines in black or green, was surcharged by British military authorities shortly after the Boxer riots for use from military posts in an occupied area along the Peking-Mukden railway. Usually canceled in violet.

See note following No. 122.

1900(?)-06 — Unwmk. — Perf. 12 to 16

110	A17	½c brown	4.00	2.75
a.		Horiz. pair, imperf. btwn.	400.00	400.00
b.		Vert. pair, imperf. btwn.	400.00	400.00
111	A17	1c ocher	4.00	2.75
a.		Horiz. pair, imperf. btwn.	350.00	350.00
b.		Vert. pair, imperf. btwn.	350.00	350.00
c.		Vert. pair, imperf. horiz.	350.00	350.00
112	A17	2c scarlet	5.25	2.75
a.		Horiz. pair, imperf. btwn.	300.00	325.00
b.		Vert. pair, imperf. btwn.	300.00	300.00
c.		Horiz. pair, imperf. horiz.	300.00	300.00
d.		Horiz. pair, imperf. vert.	300.00	300.00
e.		Vert. strip of 3, imperf. btwn.	1,250.	750.00
113	A17	4c orange brn	5.75	2.75
a.		Horiz. pair, imperf. btwn.	300.00	300.00
b.		Vert. pair, imperf. btwn.	300.00	300.00
114	A17	5c rose red	30.00	4.25
a.		Horiz. pair, imperf. btwn.	300.00	300.00
b.		Vert. pair, imperf. horiz.	275.00	275.00
115	A17	5c orange	27.50	4.75
a.		5c yellow	200.00	27.50
b.		Vert. pair, imperf. btwn.	475.00	475.00
c.		Vert. pair, imperf. horiz.	475.00	475.00
116	A17	10c green	20.00	2.75
a.		Horiz. pair, imperf. btwn.	425.00	
b.		Vert. pair, imperf. btwn.	725.00	
c.		Vert. pair, imperf. horiz.	425.00	
d.		Vert. strip of 3, imperf. btwn.	700.00	
117	A18	20c red brown	30.00	2.75
a.		Horiz. pair, imperf. btwn.	600.00	
b.		Vert. pair, imperf. btwn.	500.00	
c.		Vert. pair, imperf. horiz.	500.00	
118	A18	30c dull red	30.00	2.75
a.		Horiz. pair, imperf. btwn.	850.00	
119	A18	50c yellow grn	55.00	2.75
a.		Vert. pair, imperf. btwn.	1,000.	
120	A19	$1 red & pale rose ('06)	175.00	27.50
121	A19	$2 brn red & yel ('06)	400.00	60.00
122	A19	$5 dp grn & sal	650.00	250.00
		Nos. 110-122 (13)	1,436.	368.50

See No. 124-130. For surcharges and overprints see Nos. 123, 134-177, J1-J6, Offices in Tibet 1-11.

Diagonal Half of No. 112 Surcharged on Stamp and Envelope

1903

123	A17	1c on half of 2c scarlet, on cover		1,600.

Used Oct. 22 to Oct. 24. Value is for cover mailed to post office other than sending office (Foochow) and bearing backstamp showing arrival date. Locally addressed or unaddressed covers without backstamps properly used are worth approximately $1,000. Others are worth less.

Forgeries are plentiful, particularly on pieces of cover. Certificates of authenticity are mandatory.

1905-10

124	A17	2c green ('08)	3.00	2.50
a.		Horiz. pair, imperf. btwn.	325.00	325.00
b.		Vert. pair, imperf. btwn.	325.00	325.00
c.		Horiz. pair, imperf. vert.	325.00	325.00
d.		Horiz. strip of 4, imperf. btwn.	725.00	725.00
125	A17	3c slate grn ('10)	5.00	2.50
a.		Horiz. pair, imperf. btwn.	250.00	
b.		Vert. pair, imperf. btwn.	250.00	
126	A17	4c vermilion ('09)	6.00	2.25
127	A17	5c violet	7.50	2.50
a.		5c lilac	8.50	2.50
b.		Horiz. pair, imperf. btwn.	450.00	

c.		Vert. pair, imperf. btwn.	1,000.	
d.		Vert. pair, imperf. horiz.	500.00	
128	A17	7c maroon ('10)	16.00	8.75
129	A17	10c ultra ('08)	21.00	2.75
a.		Horiz. pair, imperf. btwn.	400.00	
b.		Vert. pair, imperf. btwn.	400.00	
c.		Vert. pair, imperf. horiz.	400.00	400.00
130	A18	16c olive grn ('07)	60.00	17.50
		Nos. 124-130 (7)	118.50	38.75

Temple of Heaven, Peking — A20

1909 — Perf. 14

131	A20	2c orange & green	9.00	8.00
132	A20	3c orange & blue	12.00	21.00
133	A20	7c orange & brn vio	17.50	12.00
		Nos. 131-133 (3)	38.50	41.00

1st year of the reign of Hsuan T'ung, who later became Henry Pu-yi and then Emperor Kang Teh of Manchukuo.

Stamps of 1902-10 Overprinted with Chinese Characters
Foochow Issue

Overprinted in Red or Black

1912 — Perf. 12 to 16

134	A17	3c slate grn (R)	300.	160.
135	A19	$1 red & pale rose	2,900.	2,500.
136	A19	$2 brn red & yel	4,400.	3,500.
137	A19	$5 dp grn & sal	5,750.	4,000.

The overprint "Ling Shih Chung Li" or "Provisional Neutrality," signified that the P.O. was conducted neutrally by agreement between the Manchu and opposing forces.

Nanking Issue

Overprinted in Red or Black

138	A17	1c ocher (R)	275.	175.
139	A17	3c slate grn (R)	275.	175.
140	A17	7c maroon	525.	375.
141	A18	16c olive grn (R)	2,750.	2,500.
142	A18	50c yellow grn (R)	3,500.	2,250.
143	A19	$1 red & pale rose	3,750.	1,800.
144	A19	$2 brn red & yel	5,500.	4,400.
145	A19	$5 dp green & sal	12,750.	10,000.

Vertical overprint reads: "Chung Hwa Min Kuo" (Republic of China).

Stamps of this issue were also used in Shanghai and Hankow.

Additional values were overprinted but not issued. Excellent forgeries of the overprints of Nos. 134-145 exist.

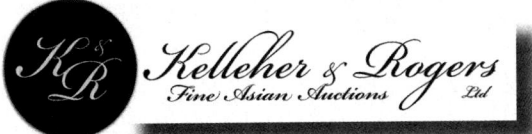

Issues of the Republic

Overprinted in Black ~~or Red~~

Overprinted by the Maritime Customs Statistical Department, Shanghai

146	A17	½c brown	1.50	1.25
a.		Inverted overprint	50.00	50.00
b.		Double overprint	100.00	
147	A17	1c ocher (R)	2.25	1.25
a.		Vert. pair, imperf. horiz.	200.00	200.00
b.		Inverted overprint	175.00	125.00
c.		Double overprint	200.00	175.00
d.		Horiz. pair, imperf. btwn.	300.00	250.00
e.		Horiz. pair, imperf. vert.	175.00	
f.		Pair, one without overprint	175.00	
148	A17	2c green (R)	2.50	1.75
a.		Vert. pair, imperf. btwn.	350.00	300.00
149	A17	3c slate grn (R)	3.00	1.50
a.		Inverted overprint	125.00	75.00
b.		Horiz. pair, imperf. btwn.	300.00	300.00
c.		Vert. pair, imperf btwn.	300.00	300.00
d.		Horiz. pair, imperf. vert.	125.00	
e.		Horiz. strip of 3, imperf btwn.	450.00	
f.		Horiz. strip of 5, imperf btwn.	975.00	
150	A17	4c vermilion	4.75	1.75
a.		Vert. pair, imperf. btwn.	800.00	
151	A17	5c violet (R)	6.25	1.75
a.		Horiz. pair, imperf. btwn.		
152	A17	7c maroon	8.25	3.50
153	A17	10c ultra (R)	8.50	1.75
a.		Double overprint	250.00	
b.		Pair, one without overprint	900.00	
c.		Brownish red overprint	22.50	9.00
d.		Inverted overprint	275.00	275.00
154	A18	16c olive grn (R)	22.50	8.50
155	A18	20c rod brown	19.00	5.00
156	A18	30c rose red	24.00	6.00
157	A18	50c yel grn (R)	40.00	6.00
158	A19	$1 red & pale rose	400.00	35.00
a.		Inverted overprint		27,500.

GRADING MATTERS

PRC # 2131
PSE Grade 100
Catalog Value $2.00
Sold for $75.00

Enough Said!

Professional Stamp Experts
P.O. Box 6170
Newport Beach, CA 92658
(714) 957-1139
www.gradingmatters.com

159	A19	$2 brn red & yel	275.00	70.00
a.		Inverted overprint	600.00	600.00
160	A19	$5 dp grn & sal	650.00	500.00
		Nos. 146-160 (15)	1,467.	645.00

Stamps with blue overprint similar to the preceding were not an official issue but were privately made by a printer in Tientsin.

Overprinted in Red

Overprinted by the Commercial Press, Shanghai

This type differs in that the top character is shifted slightly to right and the bottom character is larger and has small "legs".

161	A17	1c ocher	6.00	1.25
a.		Inverted overprint	375.00	375.00
b.		Vert. pair, imperf. btwn.	450.00	
c.		Double overprint	450.00	
162	A17	2c green	34.00	2.25
a.		Inverted overprint	1,100.	900.00
b.		Vert. pair, imperf. btwn.	260.00	
c.		Horiz. pair, imperf. btwn.	300.00	
d.		Horiz. strip of 3, imperf. btwn.	475.00	

Overprinted in Blue, Carmine or Black

Overprinted by Waterlow & Sons, London

163	A17	½c brown (Bl)	1.75	1.25
a.		Vert. pair, imperf. btwn.	1,400.	1,275.
164	A17	1c ocher (C)	1.75	1.25
a.		Horiz. pair, imperf. btwn.	825.00	
165	A17	2c green (C)	3.25	1.40
166	A17	3c slate grn (C)	3.75	1.50
a.		Inverted overprint		1,750.
167	A17	4c vermilion (Bk)	5.00	1.75
168	A17	5c violet (C)	11.00	1.60
169	A17	7c maroon (Bk)	35.00	37.50
170	A17	10c ultra (C)	17.50	2.75
a.		Vert. pair, imperf. btwn.	1,500.	2,600.
171	A18	16c olive grn (R)	50.00	19.00
172	A18	20c red brn (Bk)	32.50	3.50
173	A18	30c dull red (Bk)	100.00	6.75
174	A18	50c yellow grn (R)	150.00	17.50
175	A19	$1 red & pale rose (Bk)	225.00	20.00
176	A19	$2 brn red & yel (Bk)	475.00	225.00
177	A19	$5 dp grn & sal (C)	750.00	525.00
		Nos. 163-177 (15)	1,861.	865.75

Due to instructions issued to postmasters throughout China at the time of the Revolution, a number of them prepared unauthorized overprints using the same characters as the overprints prepared by the government. While many were made in good faith, some, like the blue overprints from Tientsin, were bogus, and the status of certain others is extremely dubious.

Dr. Sun Yat-sen — A21

1912, Dec. 14   Perf. 14½

178	A21	1c orange	4.75	3.25
179	A21	2c yellow grn	4.75	3.25
180	A21	3c slate grn	4.75	3.25
181	A21	5c rose lilac	9.50	3.25
182	A21	8c dp brown	9.50	5.00
183	A21	10c dull blue	9.50	5.00
184	A21	16c olive grn	27.50	17.50
185	A21	20c maroon	37.50	10.00
186	A21	50c dk green	100.00	40.00
187	A21	$1 brown red	260.00	60.00
188	A21	$2 yellow brn	750.00	300.00
189	A21	$5 gray	275.00	225.00
		Nos. 178-189 (12)	1,492.	675.50

Honoring the leader of the Revolution.

President Yuan Shih-kai — A22

1912, Dec. 14

190	A22	1c orange	2.75	1.75
191	A22	2c yellow green	2.75	1.75
192	A22	3c slate green	2.75	1.75
193	A22	5c rose lilac	3.75	2.00
194	A22	8c deep brown	11.50	4.00
195	A22	10c dull blue	9.50	2.50
196	A22	16c olive green	10.00	12.00
197	A22	20c maroon	9.00	10.00
198	A22	50c dark green	55.00	35.00
199	A22	$1 brown red	160.00	55.00
200	A22	$2 yellow brown	200.00	65.00
201	A22	$5 gray	600.00	290.00
		Nos. 190-201 (12)	1,067.	480.75

Honoring the 1st pres. of the Republic.

Junk — A24

Reaping Rice — A25

Gateway, Hall of Classics, Peking — A26

DESIGN A24

London Printing: Vertical shading lines under top panel fine, junk with clear diagonal shading lines on sails, right pennant of junk usually long, lines in water weak except directly under junk.

Peking Printing: Vertical shading lines under top panel and inner vertical frame line much heavier, water and sails of junk more evenly and strongly colored, white wave over "H" of "CHINA" pointed upward, touching the junk.

DESIGN A25

London: Front hat brim thick and nearly straight, left foot touches shadow.

Peking: Front hat brim thin and strongly upturned, left foot and sickle clearly outlined in white, shadow of middle tree lighter than those of the right and left trees.

DESIGN A26

London: Light colored walk clearly defined almost to the doorway, figure in right doorway "T" shaped with strong horizontal cross-bar, white panel in base of central tower rectangular, vertical stroke in top left character uniformly thick at its base, tree to right of doorway ends in minute dots.

Peking: Walk more heavily shaded near doorway, especially at right; figure in right doorway more like a "Y", white panel at base of central tower is a long oval, right vertical stroke in top left character incurved near its base, tree at right has five prominent dots at top.

London Printing: By Waterlow & Sons, London, perf. 14 to 15.

Peking Printing: By the Chinese Bureau of Engraving and Printing, Peking, perf. 14.

London Printing

1913, May 5   Perf. 14-15

202	A24	½c black brn	.75	.40
a.		Horiz. or vert. pair, imperf. btwn.	200.00	
203	A24	1c orange	.75	.40
a.		Horiz. pair, imperf. btwn.	250.00	
b.		Vert. pair, imperf. btwn.	175.00	
c.		Horiz. strip of 5, imperf. btwn	650.00	
204	A24	2c yellow grn	2.75	.40
a.		Horiz. pair, imperf. btwn.	400.00	
205	A24	3c blue grn	6.75	.45
a.		Horiz. pair, imperf. btwn.	200.00	
b.		Vert. pair, imperf. btwn.		400.00
206	A24	4c scarlet	9.50	.70
207	A24	5c rose lilac	30.00	.60
208	A24	6c gray	5.00	.90
209	A24	7c violet	22.50	8.75
210	A24	8c brown org	42.50	2.50
211	A24	10c dk blue	37.50	1.10
a.		Horiz. pair, imperf. btwn.	375.00	375.00
b.		Vert. pair, imperf. btwn.	400.00	300.00
212	A25	15c brown	32.50	5.75
213	A25	16c olive grn	17.50	2.25
214	A25	20c brown red	30.00	2.75
215	A25	30c brown vio	32.50	2.00
216	A25	50c green	60.00	3.50
217	A26	$1 ocher & blk	150.00	5.00

218	A26	$2 blue & blk	275.00	17.50
219	A26	$5 scarlet & blk	425.00	125.00
220	A26	$10 yel grn & blk	1,375.	925.00
		Nos. 202-220 (19)	2,555.	1,104.

First Peking Printing

1915   Perf. 14

221	A24	½c black brn	.80	.35
222	A24	1c orange	.80	.35
223	A24	2c yellow grn	1.60	.35
224	A24	3c blue grn	1.75	.35
225	A24	4c scarlet	20.00	.35
226	A24	5c rose lilac	8.50	.35
a.		Booklet pane of 4	140.00	
227	A24	6c gray	16.00	.35
228	A24	7c violet	25.00	4.50
229	A24	8c brown org	14.00	.40
230	A24	10c dk blue	15.00	.70
a.		Booklet pane of 4	140.00	
231	A25	15c brown	42.50	4.50
232	A25	16c olive grn	17.50	.70
233	A25	20c brown red	18.50	.70
234	A25	30c brown vio	17.50	.70
235	A25	50c green	42.50	.80
236	A26	$1 ocher & blk	140.00	.85
237	A26	$2 blue & blk	350.00	5.00
a.		Center inverted	185,000.	
238	A26	$5 scarlet & blk	800.00	30.00
239	A26	$10 yel grn & blk	1,300.	250.00
		Nos. 221-239 (19)	2,831.	301.30

1919

240	A24	1½c violet	3.75	.60
241	A25	13c brown	9.50	.70
242	A26	$20 yellow & blk	4,900.	3,250.

Nos. 226 and 230 overprinted in red with five characters in vertical column were for postal savings use.

The higher values of the 1913-19 issues are often overprinted with Chinese characters, which are the names of various postal districts. Stamps were frequently stolen while in transit to post offices. The overprints served to protect them, since the stamps could only be used in the districts for which they were overprinted.

Compare designs A24-A26 with designs A29-A31. For surcharges and overprints see Nos. 247, 288, B1-B3, Sinkiang 1-38.

Yeh Kung-cho, Hsu Shi-chang and Chin Yun-peng A27

1921, Oct. 10

243	A27	1c orange	6.00	1.75
244	A27	3c blue green	6.50	1.50
245	A27	6c gray	7.50	5.00
246	A27	10c blue	8.50	4.00
		Nos. 243-246 (4)	28.50	12.25

National Post Office, 25th anniversary. For overprints see Sinkiang Nos. 39-42.

No. 224 Surcharged in Red

1922

247	A24	2c on 3c blue green	3.50	.70
a.		Inverted surcharge	200,000.	—

Second Peking Printing

A29

A30

A31

Types of 1913-19 Issues Re-engraved

Type A29: Most of the whitecaps in front of the junk have been removed and the water made darker. The shading lines have been removed from the arabesques and pearls above the top inscription. The inner shadings at the top and sides of the picture have been cut away.

Type A30: The heads of rice in the side panels have a background of crossed lines instead of horizontal lines. The Temple of Heaven is strongly shaded and has a door. There are rows of pearls below the Chinese characters in the upper corners. The arabesques above the top inscription have been altered and are without shading lines.

Type A31: The curved line under the inscription at top is single instead of double. There are four vertical lines, instead of eight, at each side of the picture. The trees at the sides of the temple had foliage in the 1913-19 issues, but now the branches are bare. There are numerous other alterations in the design.

1923   **Perf. 14**

248	A29	½c black brown	1.75	.30
a.		Horiz. pair, imperf. btwn.	175.00	175.00
b.		Horiz. pair, imperf. vert.	150.00	150.00
249	A29	1c orange	1.00	.30
a.		Imperf., pair	125.00	
b.		Horiz. pair, imperf. vert.	125.00	
c.		Booklet pane of 6	90.00	
d.		Booklet pane of 4	45.00	
250	A29	1½c violet	3.50	.90
251	A29	2c yellow grn	2.00	.30
252	A29	3c blue green	6.00	.30
a.		Booklet pane of 6	80.00	
253	A29	4c gray	27.50	.80
254	A29	5c claret	4.00	.50
a.		Booklet pane of 4	100.00	
255	A29	6c scarlet	8.50	.50
256	A29	7c violet	8.50	.50
257	A29	8c orange	17.50	.50
258	A29	10c blue	14.50	.30
a.		Booklet pane of 6	120.00	
b.		Booklet pane of 2	150.00	
259	A30	13c brown	32.50	.60
260	A30	15c dp blue	10.00	.60
261	A30	16c olive grn	11.00	.60
262	A30	20c brown red	8.50	.40
263	A30	30c purple	32.50	.40
264	A30	50c dp green	60.00	.55
265	A31	$1 org brn & sep	65.00	.65
266	A31	$2 blue & red brn	85.00	1.00
267	A31	$5 red & slate	140.00	4.25
268	A31	$10 green & claret	675.00	50.00
269	A31	$20 plum & blue	1,300.	175.00
		Nos. 248-269 (22)	2,514.	254.25

Nos. 249 and 275 exist with webbing watermark from experimental printing.

To prevent speculation and theft, the dollar denominations were overprinted with single characters in red for use in Kwangsi ($1-$20) and Kweichow ($1-$5).

See Nos. 275, 324. For surcharges and overprints see Nos. 274, 289, 311, 325, 330, 339-340, Szechwan 1-3, Yunnan 1-20, Manchuria 1-20, Sinkiang 47-69, 114, C1-C4.

Temple of Heaven, Peking — A32

1923, Oct. 17   **Perf. 14**

270	A32	1c orange	5.00	1.00
271	A32	3c blue green	5.50	2.25
272	A32	4c red	10.50	2.50
273	A32	10c blue	16.50	3.50
		Nos. 270-273 (4)	37.50	9.25

Adoption of Constitution, October, 1923.
For overprints see Sinkiang Nos. 43-46.

No. 253 Surcharged in Red

1925

274	A29	3c on 4c gray	3.50	.35
a.		Inverted surcharge	300,000.	275,000.
b.		Vert. pair, imperf. btwn.		

Junk Type of 1923

1926

275	A29	4c olive green	1.60	.25
a.		Horiz. pair, imperf. vert.	200.00	
b.		Horiz. pair, imperf. btwn.	200.00	
c.		Horiz. strip of 3, imperf. btwn.	250.00	

Marshal Chang Tso-lin — A34

1928, Mar. 1   **Perf. 14**

276	A34	1c brown orange	1.50	1.50
277	A34	4c olive green	3.00	3.00
278	A34	10c dull blue	7.50	5.50
279	A34	$1 red	60.00	65.00
		Nos. 276-279 (4)	72.00	75.00

Assumption of office by Marshal Chang Tso-lin. The stamps of this issue were only available for postage in the Provinces of Chihli and Shantung and at the Offices in Manchuria and Sinkiang.

For overprints see Manchuria Nos. 21-24, Sinkiang 70-73.

President Chiang Kai-shek — A35

1929, May

280	A35	1c brown orange	1.00	.40
281	A35	4c olive green	1.50	.75
282	A35	10c dark blue	12.50	1.50
283	A35	$1 dark red	75.00	55.00
		Nos. 280-283 (4)	90.00	57.65

Unification of China.
For overprints see Yunnan Nos. 21-24, Manchuria 25-28, Sinkiang 74-77.

Sun Yat-sen Mausoleum, Nanking — A36

1929, May 30   **Perf. 14**

284	A36	1c brown orange	1.25	.75
285	A36	4c olive green	1.00	1.25
286	A36	10c dark blue	7.00	2.50
287	A36	$1 dark red	70.00	35.00
		Nos. 284-287 (4)	79.25	39.50

The transfer of Dr. Sun Yat-sen's remains from Peiping to the mausoleum at Nanking.
For overprints see Yunnan Nos. 25-28, Manchuria 29-32, Sinkiang 78-81.

Nos. 224 and 252 Surcharged in Red

1930

288	A24	1c on 3c blue green	1.25	2.25
289	A29	1c on 3c blue green	1.00	.40
a.		No period after "Ct"	18.00	18.00

See Nos. 311, 325, 330.

Dr. Sun Yat-sen — A37

Type I   Type II

Type I — Double-lined circle in the sun.
Type II — Heavy, single-lined circle in the sun.

Printed by De la Rue & Co., Ltd., London

Perf. 11½x12½, 12½x13, 12½, 13½

1931, Nov. 12   **Type I**   **Engr.**

290	A37	1c orange	.55	.30
291	A37	2c olive green	.65	.40
292	A37	4c green	1.10	.30
293	A37	20c ultra	1.40	.30
294	A37	$1 org brn & dk brn	12.00	.50
295	A37	$2 blue & org brn	35.00	3.00
296	A37	$5 dull red & blk	50.00	5.00
		Nos. 290-296 (7)	100.70	9.80

Stamps issued prior to 1933 were printed by a wet-paper process, and owing to shrinkage such stamps are 1-1½mm narrower than the later dry-printed stamps.

Early printings are perf. 12½x13. Nos. 304, 305 and 306 were later perf. 11½x12½.

1931-37   **Type II**

297	A37	2c olive grn	.45	.25
298	A37	4c green	.65	.25
299	A37	5c green ('33)	.40	.25
300	A37	15c dk green	4.25	1.25
301	A37	15c scarlet ('34)	.45	.25
302	A37	20c ultra ('37)	.85	.25
303	A37	25c ultra	.45	.65
304	A37	$1 org brn & dk brn	14.00	.50
305	A37	$2 blue & org brn	25.00	1.25
306	A37	$5 dull red & blk	47.50	5.00
		Nos. 297-306 (10)	94.00	9.90

See Nos. 631-635 in *Scott Standard Postage Stamp Catalogue*, Vol. 2. For surcharges and overprints see Nos. 341, 343, 678, 682, 684-685, 689-691, 768, 843, 1N1, 2N1-2N5, 2N57-2N59, 2N83-2N84, 2N101-2N106, 2N116, 2N124-2N126, 3N1-3N5, 4N1-4N5, 5N1-5N4, 6N1-6N5, 7N1-7N4, 7N54, 8N2-8N3, 8N43-8N44, 8N54, 8N57, 8N69-8N71, 8N85, 9N1-9N5, Taiwan 19, 21-22, Northeastern Provinces 44, Szechwan 4-11, Yunnan 29-44, Sinkiang 82-97 in this catalogue or Scott Standard catalogue, Vol. 2.

"Nomads in the Desert" — A38

1932   **Unwmk.**   **Perf. 14**

307	A38	1c deep orange	29.00	29.00
308	A38	4c olive green	29.00	29.00
309	A38	5c claret	29.00	29.00
310	A38	10c deep blue	29.00	29.00
		Nos. 307-310 (4)	116.00	116.00

Northwest Scientific Expedition of Sven Hedin. A small quantity of this issue was sold at face at Peking and several other cities. The bulk of the issue was furnished to Hedin and sold at $5 (Chinese) a set for funds to finance the expedition.

#252 Surcharged in Black Like #288
1932

311	A29	1c on 3c blue green	2.50	1.10

Martyrs Issue

Teng Keng A39   Ch'en Ying-shih A40

Chu Chih-hsin A45   Sung Chiao-jen A46

Huang Hsing A47   Liao Chung-kai A48

1932-34   **Perf. 14**

312	A39	½c black brown	.25	.25
313	A40	1c orange ('34)	.25	.25
314	A39	2½c rose lilac ('33)	.25	.25
315	A48	3c dp brown ('33)	.25	.25
316	A45	8c brown orange	.50	.30
317	A46	10c dull violet	.60	.30
318	A45	13c blue green	.65	.30
319	A46	17c brown olive	.55	.30
320	A47	20c brown red	1.10	.30
321	A48	30c brown violet	1.50	.30
322	A47	40c orange	1.40	.35
323	A40	50c green ('34)	5.00	.50
		Nos. 312-323 (12)	12.30	3.65

Perfs. 12 to 13 and compound and with secret marks are listed as Nos. 402-439. No. 316 re-drawn is No. 485.

For overprints and surcharge see Nos. 342, 472, 474, 478-479, 486-487, 490, 531-536, 539-541, 544-549, 616, 619, 622-624, 647-659, 662-663, 665, 669, 672, 698, 704, 711, 713-715, 720-721, 831, 846-847, 867, 870, 872, 881-882, J120-J121, 1N14-1N15, 1N59, 2N6-2N9, 2N32-2N56, 2N60, 2N76-2N82, 2N85, 2N87-2N90, 2N107-2N115, 2N118, 2N121-2N123, 3N6-3N10, 3N34-3N55, 3N59, 4N6-4N9, 4N39-4N64, 4N69, 5N5-5N8, 5N34-5N60, 5N65, 6N6-6N8, 6N35-6N61, 6N66, 7N5-7N7, 7N30-7N53, 7N55, 7N59, 8N1, 8N4, 8N28-8N42, 8N45, 8N47-8N50, 8N60-8N61, 8N68, 8N73, 8N76-8N79, 8N89, 8N97, 8N99-8N100, 8N103-8N104, 9N72-9N77, Taiwan 14-17, 20, 28A, 74, Northeastern Provinces 6-8, 11, Szechwan 12-23, Yunnan 49-60, Sinkiang 102-113, 140-161, 197 in this catalogue or *Scott Standard Postage Stamp Catalogue*, Vol. 2.

Junk Type of 1923
1933   *Perf. 14*
324 A29 6c brown   20.00 1.25

#275 Surcharged in Red Like #288
1933
325 A29 1c on 4c olive green   1.75 .35
  a. No period after "Ct"   21.00 21.00

Tan Yuan-chang — A49

1933, Jan. 9
326 A49 2c olive green   2.50 1.25
327 A49 5c green   4.00 .40
328 A49 25c ultra   10.00 1.75
329 A49 $1 red   72.50 35.00
  Nos. 326-329 (4)   89.00 38.40

Tan Yuan-chang, more commonly known as Tan Yen-kai, a prominent statesman in China since the revolution of 1912 and Pres. of the Executive Dept. of the Natl. Government. Placed on sale Jan. 9, 1933, the date of the ceremony in celebration of the completion of the Tan Yuan-chang Memorial Hall and Tomb at Mukden.

For overprints see Yunnan Nos. 45-48, Sinkiang 98-101.

#251 Surcharged in Red Like #288
1935   *Perf. 14*
330 A29 1c on 2c yellow grn   2.50 .25

Emblem of New Life Movement A50

Four Virtues of New Life A51

Lighthouse — A52

1936, Jan. 1
331 A50 2c olive green   1.75 .75
332 A50 5c green   2.00 .25
333 A51 20c dark blue   6.00 .70
334 A52 $1 rose red   40.00 11.00
  Nos. 331-334 (4)   49.75 12.70
"New Life" movement.

Methods of Mail Transportation A53

Maritime Scene — A54

Shanghai General Post Office — A55

Ministry of Communications, Nanking — A56

1936, Oct. 10
335 A53 2c orange   3.00 .70
336 A54 5c green   1.50 .25
337 A55 25c blue   4.75 .45
338 A56 $1 dk carmine   27.50 8.50
  Nos. 335-338 (4)   36.75 9.90
Founding of the Chinese PO, 40th anniv.

Nos. 260 and 261 Surcharged in Red

1936, Oct. 11
339 A30 5c on 15c dp blue   1.75 .50
340 A30 5c on 16c olive grn   3.00 1.00

No. 298 Surcharged in Red

1937
341 A37 1c on 4c green, type II   1.25 .50
  a. Upper left character missing

Nos. 322 and 303 Surcharged in Black or Red

1938   *Perf. 12½, 14*
342 A47 8c on 40c orange (Bk)   2.00 .75
343 A37 10c on 25c ultra (R)   1.75 .30

Dr. Sun Yat-sen — A57

Type I   Type II   Type III

Type I — Coat button half circle. Six lines of shading above head. Top frame partially shaded with vertical lines.
Type II — Coat button complete circle. Nine lines of shading above head. Top frame partially shaded with vertical lines.
Type III — Coat button complete circle. Nine lines of shading above head. Top frame line fully shaded with vertical lines.

Printed by the Chung Hwa Book Co.
Type I
1938 Unwmk.   Engr.   *Perf. 12½*
344 A57 $1 henna & dk brn   85.00 12.00
345 A57 $2 dp blue & org brn   17.50 4.25
346 A57 $5 red & grnsh blk   150.00 19.00
  Nos. 344-346 (3)   252.50 35.25

1939   **Type II**
347 A57 $1 henna & dk brn   16.00 1.00
348 A57 $2 dp blue & org brn   18.00 4.00

1939-43   **Type III**
349 A57 2c olive green   .25 .25
350 A57 3c dull claret   .25 .25
351 A57 5c green   .25 .25
352 A57 5c olive green   .25 .25
353 A57 8c olive green   .25 .25
354 A57 10c green   .25 .25
355 A57 15c scarlet   1.25 2.25
356 A57 15c dk vio brn ('43)   17.50 32.50
357 A57 16c olive gray   1.75 .45
358 A57 25c dk blue   .35 .35
359 A57 $1 henna & dk brn   2.00 .75
360 A57 $2 dp blue & org brn   4.50 .55
  a. Imperf., pair   275.00
361 A57 $5 red & grnsh blk   2.75 .50
362 A57 $10 dk green & dull pur   17.50 2.25
363 A57 $20 rose lake & dk blue   60.00 50.00
  Nos. 349-363 (15)   109.10 91.50

Several values exist imperforate, but these were not regularly issued. No. 361 imperforate is printer's waste.

See Nos. 368-401, 506-524; for surcharges and overprints see Nos. 440-448, 473, 475-477, 480-481, 482-484, 489, 537-538, 615, 618, 620, 660-661, 664, 666-668, 673-676, 680-681, 686, 688, 699-703, 707-709, 717, 719, 830, J67-J68, M2, M11-M12, 1N2-1N13, 1N23-1N42, 1N57-1N58, 2N10-2N31, 2N61-2N75, 2N86, 2N91-2N93, 2N117, 2N119-2N120, 3N11-3N33, 3N56-3N58, 3N60-3N61, 4N10-4N38, 4N65-4N68, 4N70-4N71, 5N9-5N33, 5N61-5N64, 5N66-5N68, 6N9-6N34, 6N62-6N65, 6N67-6N69, 7N8-7N29, 7N56-7N58, 7N60-7N61, 8N5-8N27, 8N46, 8N51-8N53, 8N55-8N56, 8N58-8N59, 8N62-8N67, 8N72, 8N74-8N75, 8N80-8N84, 8N86-8N88, 8N90, 8N95-8N96, 8N98, 8N101-8N102, 8N105-8N106, 9N6-9N71, 9N97, 9N99, Taiwan 78, 84, Northeastern Provinces 9-10, Sinkiang 115-139, 174-188, 196, 198 in this catalogue or *Scott Standard Postage Stamp Catalogue*, Vol. 2.

Chinese and American Flags and Map of China — A58
Printed by American Bank Note Co.

Frame Engr., Center Litho.
1939, July 4   Unwmk.   *Perf. 12*
Flag in Deep Rose and Ultramarine
364 A58 5c dark green   1.75 .50
365 A58 25c deep blue   1.75 .90
366 A58 50c brown   4.00 1.10
367 A58 $1 rose carmine   6.50 2.25
  Nos. 364-367 (4)   14.00 4.75
150th anniv. of the US Constitution.

Type of 1939-41 Re-engraved

2c, 1939-41   Re-engraved

8c, 1939-41   Re-engraved

1940   *Perf. 12½*
368 A57 2c olive green   .25 .25
369 A57 8c olive green   .25 .25

Type of 1938-41
Type III
1940   Unwmk.   *Perf. 14*
370 A57 2c olive green   2.50 1.00
371 A57 5c green   5.00 2.10
372 A57 $1 henna & dk brn   110.00 19.00
373 A57 $2 dp blue & org brn   21.00 5.00
374 A57 $5 red & grnsh blk   26.00 16.50
375 A57 $10 dk grn & dull pur   72.50 12.50
  Nos. 370-375 (6)   237.00 56.10
See surcharge note following No. 363.

Type of 1939-41
1940   Wmk. 261   *Perf. 12½*
Type III
376 A57 $1 henna & dk brn   7.00 9.00
377 A57 $2 dp blue & org brn   9.00 9.00
378 A57 $5 red & grnsh blk   10.00 18.00
379 A57 $10 dk green & dull pur   15.00 30.00
380 A57 $20 rose lake & dp blue   19.00 30.00
  Nos. 376-380 (5)   60.00 96.00
See surcharge note following No. 363.

Printed by the Dah Tung Book Co.
Type III with Secret Marks
Five Cent

Type III — Characters joined

Secret Mark — Characters not joined

Eight Cent

Type III — Characters not joined

Secret Mark — Characters joined

Ten Cent

Type III — Characters sharp and well shaped

Secret Mark — Characters coarse and varying in thickness

Dollar Values

Type III   Secret Mark

1940 — Unwmk. — Perf. 14

381	A57	5c green	.25	.25
382	A57	5c olive green	.25	.25
383	A57	8c olive green	.40	.25
a.		Without "star" in uniform button.	1.50	2.50
384	A57	10c green	.25	.25
385	A57	30c scarlet	.35	.25
386	A57	50c dk blue	.45	.25
387	A57	$1 org brn & sepia	2.50	.25
388	A57	$2 dp blue & yel brn	1.00	.35
389	A57	$5 red & slate grn	1.00	.45
390	A57	$10 dk grn & dull pur	4.00	2.25
391	A57	$20 rose lake & dk blue	12.00	3.50
		Nos. 381-391 (11)	22.45	8.30

Type III with Secret Marks

1940 — Wmk. 261 — Perf. 14

392	A57	5c green	.25	.25
393	A57	5c olive green	.25	.25
394	A57	10c green	.35	.25
395	A57	30c scarlet	.25	.25
396	A57	50c dk blue	.55	.25
397	A57	$1 org brn & sepia	4.50	2.75
398	A57	$2 dp blue & yel brn	12.50	13.00
399	A57	$5 red & slate grn	11.50	12.00
400	A57	$10 dk grn & dull pur	16.00	17.00
401	A57	$20 rose lake & dk blue	25.00	20.00
		Nos. 392-401 (10)	71.15	66.00

Nos. 383, 384, 385, 397, 400 and 401 exist perf. 12½, but were not issued with this perforation.

See surcharge note following No. 363.

Types of 1932-34 Martyrs Issue with Secret Mark

1932-34 Issue. In the left Chinese character in bottom row, the two parts are not joined.

Secret Mark, 1940-41 Issue. The two parts are joined.

Perf. 12½, 13 and Compound

1940-41 — Wmk. 261

402	A39	½c olive blk	.25	.25
403	A40	1c orange	.25	.25
404	A46	2c dp blue ('41)	.25	.25
405	A39	2½c rose lilac	.25	.25
406	A48	3c dp yellow brn	.30	.25
407	A39	4c pale vio ('41)	.30	.25
408	A48	5c dull red org ('41)	.30	.25
409	A45	8c dp orange	.25	.25
410	A46	10c dull violet	.25	.25
411	A45	13c dp yellow grn	.35	.25
412	A48	15c brown car	.25	.25
413	A46	17c brown olive	.25	.25
414	A47	20c lt blue	.25	.25
415	A45	21c olive brn ('41)	1.10	1.25
416	A40	25c red vio ('41)	.25	.25
417	A48	28c olive ('41)	.30	.25
418	A40	30c brown car	.25	.25
a.		Vert. pair, imperf. btwn.	125.00	
419	A47	40c orange		.25
420	A40	50c green	.30	.25

Unwmk.

421	A39	½c olive black	.25	.25
422	A40	1c orange	.25	.25
a.		Without secret mark	2.75	2.75
b.		Horiz. pair, imperf. vert.	110.00	
423	A46	2c dp blue	.25	.25
a.		Vert. pair, imperf. horiz.	100.00	
b.		Horiz. pair, imperf. between	160.00	
424	A39	2½c rose lilac	.25	.25
425	A48	3c dp yellow brn	.25	.25
426	A39	4c pale violet	.25	.25
427	A48	5c dull red org	.25	.25
428	A45	8c dp orange	.25	.25
429	A46	10c dull violet	3.25	.40
430	A45	13c dp yel grn	.25	.65
431	A48	15c brown car	.35	.60
432	A46	17c brn olive	.40	.25
433	A47	20c lt blue	.30	.25
a.		Vert. pair, imperf. horiz.	125.00	
b.		Horiz. pair, imperf. vert.	125.00	
434	A45	21c olive brn	.50	.35
435	A40	25c red vio	.35	.50
436	A46	28c olive	.70	.50
437	A48	30c brown car	2.50	2.50

438	A47	40c orange	.35	.35
439	A40	50c green	3.50	.40
		Nos. 402-439 (38)	20.65	14.50

Several values exist imperforate, but they were not regularly issued.

Used values are for favor cancels. Postally used examples sell for more.

See surcharge note following No. 323.

Regional Surcharges.

The regional surcharges, Nos. 440-448, 482-484, 486-491, 525-549, have been listed according to the basic stamps, with black or red surcharges. The surcharges of the individual provinces, plus Hong Kong and Shanghai, are noted in small type. The numeral following each letter is the surcharge denomination. These surcharges are identified by the following letters:

a — Hong Kong	i — Kwangsi
b — Shanghai	j — Kwangtung
bx — Anhwei	k — Western Szechwan
c — Hunan	l — Yunnan
d — Kansu	m — Honan
e — Kiangsi	n — Shensi
f — Eastern Szechwan	o — Kweichow
g — Chekiang	p — Hupeh
h — Fukien	

Regional Surcharges on Stamps of 1939-40

Hong Kong — a4

Shanghai — b3

Hunan — c3

Kansu — d3

Kiangsi — e3

Eastern Szechwan — f3

Chekiang — g3

1940-41 — Unwmk. — Perf. 12½, 14

Carmine Surcharge

440	A57	4c on 5c ol grn (#382)	.60	.60
r.		Lower right character duplicated at left	30.00	32.50

Black Surcharge

441	A57	3c on 5c grn (#351) (b3)	1.25	1.40
442	A57	3c on 5c ol grn (#352) (c3, d3)	.65	2.00
443	A57	3c on 5c grn (#381) (b3)	.60	1.25
444	A57	3c on 5c grn (#382) (e3)	.70	1.00
r.		Lower left character duplicated at right (Kiangsi)	42.50	42.50
		(b3) Shanghai	.65	1.40
		(f3) Eastern Szechwan	.65	1.60

The Kansu surcharges of No. 442 are of 6 types. Differences include formation of top part of fen character (at left of "3"), fen with low right hook, height of "3" (5-4mm), space between upper and lower characters (6-9mm), etc.

1940-41 — Wmk. 261 — Perf. 14

445	A57	3c on 5c grn (#392) (e3)	.60	1.40
r.		Lower left character duplicated at right (Kiangsi)	35.00	35.00
		(b3, c3) Shanghai, Hunan	.60	1.60
446	A57	3c on 5c ol grn (#393) (f3)	.70	1.75
		(b3) Shanghai	.95	1.75
r.		Lower left character duplicated at right (f3)	60.00	65.00

Red Surcharge

447	A57	3c on 5c grn (#392) (g3)	1.25	3.25
448	A57	3c on 5c ol grn (#393) (g3)	6.00	6.00

SEMI-POSTAL STAMPS

SP1

Red or Blue Surcharge

1920, Dec. 1 — Unwmk. — Perf. 14, 15

B1	SP1	1c on 2c green	5.00	2.00
B2	SP1	3c on 4c scar (B)	8.00	3.00
B3	SP1	5c on 6c gray	12.00	5.00
		Nos. B1-B3 (3)	25.00	10.00

The surcharge represents the actual franking value. The extra cent helped victims of the 1919 Yellow River flood.

AIR POST STAMPS

Curtiss "Jenny" over Great Wall (Bars of Republic flag on tail) — AP1

1921, July 1 — Unwmk. — Engr. — Perf. 14

C1	AP1	15c bl grn & blk	52.50	52.50
C2	AP1	30c scar & blk	52.50	52.50
C3	AP1	45c dull vio & blk	52.50	52.50
C4	AP1	60c dk blue & blk	67.50	67.50
C5	AP1	90c ol grn & blk	75.00	75.00
		Nos. C1-C5 (5)	300.00	300.00

(Nationalist sun emblem on tail) — AP2

1929, July 5

C6	AP2	15c blue grn & blk	10.00	3.00
C7	AP2	30c dk red & blk	15.00	5.00
C8	AP2	45c dk vio & blk	25.00	10.00
C9	AP2	60c dk blue & blk	30.00	12.00
C10	AP2	90c ol grn & blk	30.00	18.00
		Nos. C6-C10 (5)	110.00	48.00

Junkers F-13 over Great Wall AP3

1932-37

C11	AP3	15c gray grn	.70	.45
C12	AP3	25c orange ('33)	5.00	3.00
C13	AP3	30c red	10.00	2.50
C14	AP3	45c brown vio	1.00	.45
C15	AP3	50c dk brown ('33)	1.00	.45
C16	AP3	60c dk blue	1.00	.45
C17	AP3	90c olive grn	1.00	.60
C18	AP3	$1 yellow grn ('33)	1.50	.45
C19	AP3	$2 brown ('37)	1.50	.80
C20	AP3	$5 brown car ('37)	4.00	3.00
		Nos. C11-C20 (10)	26.70	12.15

See #C21-C40. For surcharges and overprints see #C41-C52, C54-C60, 9N111-

9N114, 9NC1-9NC7, Szechwan C1, C3-C6, Sinkiang C5-C19.

Type of 1932-37, with secret mark

1932-37 Issue. Lower part of left character joined

Secret Mark, 1940-41 Issue. Separated.

Perf. 12, 12½, 12½x13, 13

1940-41 — Wmk. 261

C21	AP3	15c gray green	1.00	.60
C22	AP3	25c yellow org	1.25	.80
C23	AP3	30c red	1.00	.60
a.		Vert. pair, imperf. between	500.00	
C24	AP3	45c dull rose vio ('41)	1.00	.60
C25	AP3	50c brown	1.00	.60
C26	AP3	60c dp blue ('41)	1.00	.60
C27	AP3	90c olive ('41)	1.00	.70
C28	AP3	$1 apple grn ('41)	1.00	.70
C29	AP3	$2 lt brown ('41)	1.00	.70
C30	AP3	$5 lake	2.50	1.20
		Nos. C21-C30 (10)	11.75	7.10

Perf. 12½, 13, 13½

Unwmk.

C31	AP3	15c gray green ('41)	.70	.30
C32	AP3	25c lt orange ('41)	.70	.30
C33	AP3	30c lt red ('41)	.70	.30
C34	AP3	45c dl rose vio ('41)	.70	.45
C35	AP3	50c brown	.70	.60
C36	AP3	60c blue ('41)	.70	.60
C37	AP3	90c olive ('41)	.70	.60
C38	AP3	$1 apple grn ('41)	.70	.70
C39	AP3	$2 lt brown ('41)	3.00	1.50
C40	AP3	$5 lake ('41)	2.00	1.25
		Nos. C31-C40 (10)	10.60	6.60

For surcharges see note following No. C20.

SPECIAL DELIVERY STAMPS

Used values of Nos. E1-E8 are for mailer's receipts. Complete unused strips of four are exceptionally scarce because the first section (#1) was to remain in the P.O. booklet.

The mailer received the righthand section (#4), usually canceled, as a receipt. The middle two sections were canceled and attached to the letter. Upon arrival at the destination P.O. they were canceled again, usually on the back, with the righthand copy (#3) retained by that P.O. The lefthand copy (#2) was signed by the recipient and returned to the original P.O. as evidence of delivery. Sections 2 and 3 usually are thin or badly damaged.

Unused strips of three (#2-4) can be found of Nos. E3-E8.

Design: Dragon in irregular oval. Stamp 8x2½ inches, divided into four parts by perforation or serrate rouletting.

"Chinese Imperial Post Office" in lines, repeated to form the background which is usually lighter in color than the rest of the design. Dragon's head facing downward Background with period after "POSTOFFICE."

No Date

1905		Unwmk.		Perf. 11
E1		10c grass green	12,000.	500.00

Serrate Roulette in Black

E2		10c deep green	15,000.	500.00

Type, E3-E8

Dragon's head facing forward
Background with no period after
"POSTOFFICE"
No Date

1907-10
E3   10c light bluish green   2,000. 250.00

Background with date at bottom

1909-11
E4   10c green (Feby
     1909)   1,500. 200.00
E5   10c bl grn (Jan.
     1911)   1,600. 150.00

"IMPERIAL POST OFFICE" in
serifed letters repeated to form the
background.
No Date, No Border
Background of 30 or 28 lines

1912
E6   10c green (30 lines)   1,400. 120.00
  a.   28 lines   1,600. 800.00

Background of 35 lines of sans-serif
letters
Colored Border

E8   10c green   1,600. 175.00

On No. E8 the medallion in the third section has Chinese characters in the background instead of the usual English inscriptions. E6 and E8 occur with many types of four-character overprints reading "Republic of China," applied locally but unofficially at various post offices.

Type, E9, E10

Design: Wild Goose. Stamp 7½x2¾
inches, divided into five parts.
"CHINESE POST OFFICE" in sans-
serif letters, repeated to form the
background of 28 lines. With
border.

Serrate Roulette in Black

1913
E9   10c green   900.00 100.00

Unused values for Nos. E9-E10 are for complete strips of five parts. Used values are for single parts.

"CHINESE POST OFFICE" in
antique letters, forming a
background of 29 or 30 lines. No
border.

1914   Serrate Roulette in Green
E10   10c green   300.00 50.00

On No. E9 the background is in sans-serif capitals, the Chinese and English inscriptions are on white tablets and the serial numbers are in black.
On No. E10 the background is in antique capitals and extends under the inscriptions. The serial numbers are in green.

NOTE:

In February, 1916, the Special Delivery Stamps were demonetized and became merely receipts without franking value. To mark this, four of the five sections of the stamp had the letters A, B, C, D either handstamped or printed on them.

POSTAGE DUE STAMPS

Regular Issue of 1902-
03 Overprinted in
Black

D1

1904		**Unwmk.**	*Perf. 14 to 15*	
J1	A17	½c chocolate	14.00	6.00
J2	A17	1c ocher	14.00	5.00
J3	A17	2c scarlet	17.00	6.00
J4	A17	4c red brn	18.00	7.00
J5	A17	5c salmon	20.00	12.00
J6	A17	10c dk blue grn	33.00	20.00
a.		Vert. pair, imperf. btwn.	*2,000.*	*2,000.*
		Nos. J1-J6 (6)	116.00	56.00

1904			**Engr.**	
J7	D1	½c blue	7.00	4.00
a.		Horiz. pair, imperf. btwn.	*3,000.*	*2,000.*
J8	D1	1c blue	12.00	4.00
J9	D1	2c blue	12.00	4.00
a.		Horiz. pair, imperf. btwn.	*2,000.*	*1,800.*
J10	D1	4c blue	15.00	4.00
J11	D1	5c blue	18.00	7.00
J12	D1	10c blue	20.00	9.00
J13	D1	20c blue	50.00	12.00
J14	D1	30c blue	70.00	40.00
		Nos. J7-J14 (8)	204.00	86.00

Arabic numeral of value at left on Nos. J12-J14.

1911				
J15	D1	1c brown	25.00	18.00
J16	D1	2c brown	40.00	32.50

The ½c, 4c, 5c and 20c in brown exist but were not issued as they arrived in China after the downfall of the Ching dynasty.

Issue of 1904 Overprinted
in Red

1912				
J19	D1	½c blue	700.	*1,000.*
J20	D1	4c blue	900.	*1,100.*
J21	D1	5c blue	1,000.	*1,100.*
J22	D1	10c blue	1,500.	*1,500.*
J23	D1	20c blue	3,000.	*3,200.*
J24	D1	30c blue	3,000.	*3,200.*

Nos. J15-J16 exist with this overprint, but were not regularly issued.

Nos. J25-J33

1912			**Overprinted in Red**	
J25	D1	½c blue	5.00	3.00
J26	D1	1c brown	6.00	3.00
a.		Horiz. pair, imperf. btwn.	*3,000.*	*3,000.*
b.		Inverted overprint	550.00	550.00
J27	D1	2c brown	8.00	4.00
J28	D1	4c blue	15.00	6.00
J29	D1	5c blue	275.00	*300.00*
J30	D1	5c brown	20.00	10.00
a.		Inverted overprint	320.00	*340.00*
J31	D1	10c blue	25.00	13.00
J32	D1	20c blue	27.00	17.00
J33	D1	30c blue	35.00	30.00
		Nos. J25-J33 (9)	416.00	386.00

Nos. J34-J42

1912			**Overprinted in Black**	
J34	D1	½c blue	15.00	10.00
J35	D1	½c brown	8.00	3.00
J36	D1	1c brown	8.00	3.00
a.		Inverted overprint	300.00	300.00
J37	D1	2c brown	10.00	5.00
J38	D1	4c brown	20.00	9.50
J39	D1	5c brown	27.50	14.00
a.		Horiz. pair, imperf. btwn.	*3,800.*	*3,800.*
J40	D1	10c blue	45.00	27.50
J41	D1	20c brown	65.00	100.00
J42	D1	30c blue	75.00	65.00
		Nos. J34-J42 (9)	273.50	237.00

D4

Printed by Waterlow & Sons

1913, May			*Perf. 14, 15*	
J43	D4	½c blue	3.00	1.50
a.		Horiz. pair, imperf. btwn.	*4,000.*	*3,000.*
J44	D4	1c blue	3.50	1.50
J45	D4	2c blue	5.00	3.00
J46	D4	4c blue	8.00	3.00
J47	D4	5c blue	12.00	6.00
J48	D4	10c blue	17.50	8.00
J49	D4	20c blue	27.50	13.00
J50	D4	30c blue	35.00	15.00
		Nos. J43-J50 (8)	111.50	51.00

Printed by the Chinese Bureau of
Engraving & Printing

1915		**Re-engraved**	*Perf. 14*	
J51	D4	½c blue	3.00	1.00
J52	D4	1c blue	3.75	65
J53	D4	2c blue	4.00	.65
J54	D4	4c blue	5.00	.75
J55	D4	5c blue	7.00	1.50
J56	D4	10c blue	11.00	2.50
J57	D4	20c blue	17.50	8.00
J58	D4	30c blue	50.00	20.00
		Nos. J51-J58 (8)	101.25	35.05

In the upper part of the stamps of type D4 there is an ornament of five marks like the letter "V". Below this is a curved label with an inscription in Chinese characters. On the 1913 stamps there are two complete background lines between the ornament and the label. The 1915 stamps show only one unbroken line at this place. There are other minute differences in the engraving of the stamps of the two issues.

D5

1932			*Perf. 14*	
J59	D5	½c orange	.60	.30
J60	D5	1c orange	.60	.30
J61	D5	2c orange	.60	.30
J62	D5	4c orange	.60	.30
J63	D5	5c orange	1.50	1.50
J64	D5	10c orange	2.00	2.00
J65	D5	20c orange	2.75	3.00
J66	D5	30c orange	4.00	4.00
		Nos. J59-J66 (8)	12.65	11.70

See Nos. J69-J79. For surcharges see Nos. 1NJ1, 9NJ1-9NJ4.

Regular Stamps of
1939 Overprinted in
Black or Red

1940				
J67	A57	$1 henna & dk brn		
		(Bk)	8.00	25.00
J68	A57	$2 dl bl & org brn (R)	12.00	25.00

Type of 1932
Printed by The Commercial Press,
Ltd.

Perf. 12½, 12½x13, 13

1940-41			**Engr.**	
J69	D5	½c yellow orange	.80	1.00
J70	D5	1c yellow orange	.80	1.00
J71	D5	2c yellow orange		
		('41)	.80	1.00
J72	D5	4c yellow orange	.80	1.00
J73	D5	5c yellow orange		
		('41)	1.20	1.00

J74 D5 10c yellow orange
   ('41)   .80   *1.00*
J75 D5 20c yellow orange
   ('41)   .80   *1.00*
J76 D5 30c yellow orange   .80   *1.00*
J77 D5 50c yellow orange   1.00   *1.00*
J78 D5 $1 yellow orange   1.20   *1.00*
J79 D5 $2 yellow orange   1.50   *2.00*
   Nos. J69-J79 (11)   10.50   *12.00*

For surcharge see No. 1NJ1.

SZECHWAN PROVINCE

Re-engraved Issue of
China, 1923,
Overprinted

1933   **Unwmk.**   **Perf. 14**
1 A29 1c orange   11.00   *1.00*
2 A29 5c claret   11.00   *1.40*
3 A30 50c deep green   32.50   *6.75*
   Nos. 1-3 (3)   54.50   *9.15*

The overprint reads "For use in Szechwan Province exclusively."

Same on Sun Yat-sen Issue of 1931-37
Type II

1933-34   **Perf. 12½**
4 A37 2c olive grn   2.00   *1.00*
5 A37 5c green   22.50   *2.40*
6 A37 15c dk green   7.75   *3.50*
7 A37 15c scar ('34)   9.00   *12.00*
8 A37 25c ultra   7.50   *1.75*
9 A37 $1 org brn & dk brn   22.50   *4.00*
10 A37 $2 bl & org brn   55.00   *6.75*
11 A37 $5 dl red & blk   125.00   *37.50*
   Nos. 4-11 (8)   251.25   *68.90*

Same on Martyrs Issue of 1932-34

1933   **Perf. 14**
12 A39 ½c black brn   .80   *.80*
13 A40 1c orange   1.25   *.55*
14 A39 2½c rose lilac   3.50   *3.75*
15 A48 3c deep brown   3.00   *3.00*
16 A45 8c brown org   1.75   *1.50*
17 A46 10c dull violet   4.50   *.55*
18 A45 13c blue green   5.00   *1.00*
19 A44 17c brown olive   5.50   *1.40*
20 A47 20c brown red   8.50   *1.00*
21 A48 30c brown violet   6.75   *1.00*
22 A47 40c orange   18.00   *1.40*
23 A40 50c green   37.50   *2.10*
   Nos. 12-23 (12)   96.05   *18.05*

YUNNAN PROVINCE

Stamps of China,
1923-26, Overprinted

The overprint reads "For exclusive use in the Province of Yunnan." It was applied to prevent stamps being purchased in the depreciated currency of Yunnan and used elsewhere.

1926   **Unwmk.**   **Perf. 14**
1 A29 ½c blk brn   1.10   *.35*
2 A29 1c orange   1.75   *.35*
3 A29 1½c violet   3.75   *4.25*
4 A29 2c yellow grn   2.75   *.50*
5 A29 3c blue green   2.75   *.50*
6 A29 4c olive grn   3.50   *.50*
7 A29 5c claret   3.50   *.50*
8 A29 6c red   5.25   *1.25*
9 A29 7c violet   5.50   *1.90*
10 A29 8c brown org   4.75   *1.40*
11 A29 10c dark blue   3.00   *.30*
12 A30 13c brown   1.75   *1.90*
13 A30 15c dark blue   1.75   *1.90*
14 A30 16c olive grn   3.50   *1.90*
15 A30 20c brown red   8.50   *3.25*
16 A30 30c brown vio   5.75   *5.75*
17 A30 50c deep green   5.50   *5.75*
18 A31 $1 org brn & sep   20.50   *14.00*
19 A31 $2 blue & red brn   35.00   *14.00*
20 A31 $5 red & slate   240.00   *260.00*
   Nos. 1-20 (20)   359.35   *320.10*

Unification Issue of
China, 1929,
Overprinted in Red

1929   **Perf. 14**
21 A35 1c brown org   2.25   *2.25*
22 A35 4c olive grn   3.75   *5.75*
23 A35 10c dark blue   12.00   *9.00*
24 A35 $1 dark red   120.00   *90.00*
   Nos. 21-24 (4)   138.00   *107.00*

Similar Overprint in Black on Sun Yat-sen Mausoleum Issue
Characters 15½-16mm apart
25 A36 1c brown orange   2.25   *2.00*
26 A36 4c olive green   2.25   *3.75*
27 A36 10c dark blue   9.00   *8.50*
28 A36 $1 dark red   77.50   *67.50*
   Nos. 25-28 (4)   91.00   *81.75*

London Print Issue of
China, 1931-37,
Overprinted

1932-34   **Unwmk.**   **Perf. 12½**
Type I (double circle)
29 A37 1c orange   4.00   *2.75*
30 A37 2c olive grn   5.00   *5.50*
31 A37 4c green   3.25   *5.50*
32 A37 20c ultra   3.25   *3.00*
33 A37 $1 org brn & dk brn   50.00   *55.00*
34 A37 $2 bl & org brn   82.50   *85.00*
35 A37 $5 dl red & blk   250.00   *295.00*
   Nos. 29-35 (7)   398.00   *451.75*

Type II (single circle)
36 A37 2c olive grn   26.00   *26.00*
37 A37 4c green   17.00   *10.75*
38 A37 5c green   15.00   *10.00*
39 A37 15c dk green   8.00   *8.75*
40 A37 15c scar ('34)   8.00   *10.00*
41 A37 25c ultra   11.00   *11.50*
42 A37 $1 org brn & dk brn   67.50   *67.50*
43 A37 $2 bl & org brn   125.00   *125.00*
44 A37 $5 dl red & blk   260.00   *260.00*
   Nos. 36-44 (9)   537.50   *529.50*

Nos. 36-39, 41-44 were overprinted in London as well as in Peking. The London overprints are 11mm in length; the Peking overprints are 12mm in length. There are other minor differences. Value of London overprints is significantly more than the Peking overprints, which are valued above.

Tan Yuan-chang
Issue of China,
1933, Overprinted

1933   **Perf. 14**
45 A49 2c olive green   1.75   *1.75*
46 A49 5c green   3.00   *2.40*
47 A49 25c ultra   5.25   *5.50*
48 A49 $1 red   80.00   *65.00*
   Nos. 45-48 (4)   90.00   *74.65*

Martyrs Issue of
China, 1932-34,
Overprinted

1933
49 A39 ½c blk brown   1.75   *1.60*
50 A40 1c orange   3.50   *2.75*
51 A39 2½c rose lilac   4.00   *4.50*
52 A48 3c deep brown   6.25   *2.25*
53 A45 8c brown org   2.75   *2.25*
54 A46 10c dull vio   4.00   *4.50*
55 A45 13c blue green   2.50   *1.10*
56 A44 17c brn olive   12.50   *12.50*
57 A47 20c brown red   3.25   *3.25*
58 A48 30c brown vio   10.00   *10.00*

59 A47 40c orange   47.50   *47.50*
60 A40 50c green   47.50   *47.50*
   Nos. 49-60 (12)   145.50   *140.20*

China No. 324 was overprinted with characters arranged vertically, like Sinkiang No. 114, but was not issued.

MANCHURIA

Kirin and Heilungkiang Issue

Stamps of China,
1923-26, Overprinted

The overprint reads: "For use in Ki-Hei District" the two names being abbreviated.
  The intention of the overprint was to prevent the purchase of stamps in Manchuria, where the currency was depreciated, and their resale elsewhere.

1927   **Unwmk.**   **Perf. 14**
1 A29 ½c black brn   1.90   *.35*
2 A29 1c orange   1.90   *.35*
3 A29 1½c violet   2.50   *1.90*
4 A29 2c yellow grn   2.50   *1.90*
5 A29 3c blue grn   1.75   *.75*
6 A29 4c olive grn   .85   *.35*
7 A29 5c claret   1.75   *.35*
8 A29 6c red   2.50   *1.90*
9 A29 7c violet   5.25   *1.90*
10 A29 8c brown org   3.50   *1.90*
11 A29 10c dk blue   1.90   *.50*
12 A30 13c brown   4.00   *3.00*
13 A30 15c dk blue   4.00   *3.00*
14 A30 16c olive grn   4.00   *2.75*
15 A30 20c brown red   6.00   *3.50*
16 A30 30c brown vio   8.75   *3.50*
17 A30 50c dp green   12.00   *4.25*
18 A31 $1 org brn & sep   26.00   *8.75*
19 A31 $2 bl & red brn   70.00   *19.00*
20 A31 $5 red & slate   325.00   *325.00*
   Nos. 1-20 (20)   486.05   *384.90*

Several values of this issue exist with inverted overprint, double overprint and in pairs with one overprint omitted. These "errors" were not regularly issued. Forgeries also exist.

Chang Tso-lin
Stamps of 1928
Overprinted in Red
or Blue

1928   **Perf. 14**
21 A34 1c brown org (R)   2.75   *1.75*
22 A34 4c olive grn (R)   1.75   *1.75*
23 A34 10c dull blue (R)   5.00   *3.75*
24 A34 $1 red (Bl)   50.00   *45.00*
   Nos. 21-24 (4)   59.50   *52.25*

Unification Issue of China, 1929,
Overprinted in Red as in 1928
1929
25 A35 1c brown orange   2.00   *2.00*
26 A35 4c olive green   3.75   *3.25*
27 A35 10c dark blue   13.00   *12.50*
28 A35 $1 dark red   110.00   *100.00*
   Nos. 25-28 (4)   128.75   *117.75*

Similar Overprint in Black on Sun Yat-sen Mausoleum Issue of China
Characters 15-16mm apart
1929   **Perf. 14**
29 A36 1c brown orange   2.25   *2.50*
30 A36 4c olive green   2.75   *3.00*
31 A36 10c dark blue   8.50   *5.25*
32 A36 $1 dark red   85.00   *65.00*
   Nos. 29-32 (4)   98.50   *75.75*

SINKIANG

Stamps of China,
1913-19, Overprinted
in Black or Red

The first character of overprint is ½mm out of alignment, to the left, and the overprint measures 16mm.

1915   **Unwmk.**   **Perf. 14**
1 A24 ½c black brn   1.75   *.95*
2 A24 1c orange   1.75   *.70*
3 A24 2c yellow grn   2.40   *1.25*
4 A24 3c slate grn   2.40   *.65*
5 A24 4c scarlet   4.75   *1.10*
6 A24 5c rose lilac   3.50   *.95*
7 A24 6c gray   6.50   *2.75*
8 A24 7c violet   6.50   *8.50*
9 A24 8c brown orange   5.50   *5.50*
10 A24 10c dark blue   5.50   *2.75*
11 A25 15c brown   6.50   *3.50*
12 A25 16c olive grn   13.00   *9.25*
13 A25 20c brown red   13.00   *7.25*
14 A25 30c brown violet   14.50   *11.00*
15 A25 50c deep green   40.00   *18.50*
16 A26 $1 ocher & blk
   (R)   145.00   *62.50*
  a. Second & third characters of overprint transposed   *70,000.*
   Nos. 1-16 (16)   272.55   *137.10*

Stamps of China,
1913-19, Overprinted
in Black or Red

The five characters of overprint are correctly aligned and measure 15½mm.

1916-19
17 A24 ½c black brn   2.00   *2.40*
18 A24 1c orange   3.25   *1.75*
19 A24 1½c violet   4.50   *4.00*
20 A24 2c yellow grn   3.25   *1.75*
21 A24 3c slate grn   5.50   *.70*
22 A24 4c scarlet   5.50   *1.25*
23 A24 5c rose lilac   5.50   *.90*
24 A24 6c gray   8.00   *1.25*
25 A24 7c violet   8.00   *11.00*
26 A24 8c brown org   8.75   *8.50*
27 A24 10c dark blue   8.75   *1.25*
28 A25 13c brown   4.75   *8.00*
29 A25 15c brown   6.00   *8.50*
30 A25 16c olive grn   5.50   *4.00*
31 A25 20c brown red   4.50   *3.00*
32 A25 30c brown vio   6.75   *6.00*
33 A25 50c deep green   9.25   *5.50*
34 A26 $1 ocher & blk
   (R)   29.00   *11.00*
35 A26 $2 dk bl & blk (R)   27.50   *12.00*
36 A26 $5 scar & blk (R)   110.00   *37.50*
37 A26 $10 yel grn & blk
   (R)   275.00   *175.00*
38 A26 $20 yel & blk (R)   1,435.00   *875.00*
   Nos. 17-38 (22)   1,976.   *1,180.*

For overprint see No. C4.

China Nos.
243-246
Overprinted

1921   **Perf. 14**
39 A27 1c orange   1.75   *1.75*
40 A27 3c blue green   3.50   *3.50*
41 A27 6c gray   13.50   *13.50*
42 A27 10c blue   80.00   *80.00*
   Nos. 39-42 (4)   98.75   *98.75*

Constitution Issue
of China, 1923,
Overprinted

1923

43	A32	1c orange	1.55	1.55
44	A32	3c blue green	6.50	6.50
45	A32	4c red	9.75	9.75
46	A32	10c blue	27.50	27.50
		Nos. 43-46 (4)	45.30	45.30

Stamps of China, 1909-23, Overprinted as in 1916-19, in Black or Red

1924
Re-engraved

47	A29	½c black brn	1.50	3.00
48	A29	1c orange	1.50	1.25
49	A29	1½c violet	2.75	5.00
50	A29	2c yellow grn	4.25	1.40
51	A29	3c blue grn	4.25	1.25
52	A29	4c gray	4.25	6.75
53	A29	5c claret	1.40	1.00
54	A29	6c red	7.50	2.75
55	A29	7c violet	8.50	7.50
56	A29	8c org brn	17.00	15.00
57	A29	10c dark blue	6.75	1.90
58	A30	13c red brown	6.00	8.50
59	A30	15c deep blue	8.75	6.75
60	A30	16c olive grn	10.00	9.75
61	A30	20c brown red	8.50	6.25
62	A30	30c brown vio	9.75	6.75
63	A30	50c deep green	10.00	6.75
64	A31	$1 org brn & sep (R)	18.00	8.50
65	A31	$2 bl & red brn (R)	40.00	12.00
66	A31	$5 red & slate (R)	95.00	19.00
67	A31	$10 grn & claret (R)	300.00	170.00
68	A31	$20 plum & bl (R)	425.00	325.00
		Nos. 47-68 (22)	990.65	626.05

See #69, 114. For overprints see #C1-C3.

Same Overprint on China No. 275
1926

69	A29	4c olive green	5.50	5.50

Chang Tso-lin Stamps of China, 1928, Overprinted in Red or Blue

1928
Perf. 14

70	A34	1c brn org (R)	1.75	1.75
71	A34	4c ol grn (R)	2.75	2.75
72	A34	10c dull bl (R)	6.50	6.50
73	A34	$1 red (Bl)	55.00	55.00
		Nos. 70-73 (4)	66.00	66.00

Unification Issue of China, 1929, Overprinted in Red as in 1928
1929

74	A35	1c brown org	2.75	2.75
75	A35	4c olive grn	4.75	4.75
76	A35	10c dk blue	11.50	11.50
77	A35	$1 dk red	90.00	90.00
		Nos. 74-77 (4)	109.00	109.00

Similar Overprint in Black on Sun Yat-sen Mausoleum Issue of China Characters 15mm apart
1929
Perf. 14

78	A36	1c brown org	2.25	2.25
79	A36	4c olive grn	3.50	3.50
80	A36	10c dark blue	8.00	8.00
81	A36	$1 dark red	95.00	95.00
		Nos. 78-81 (4)	108.75	108.75

Stamps of Sun Yat-sen Issue of 1931-37 Overprinted

1932
Type I   Perf. 12½

82	A37	1c orange	1.75	4.00
83	A37	2c olive grn	4.25	5.75
84	A37	4c green	2.50	6.50
85	A37	20c ultra	4.00	8.25
86	A37	$1 org brn & dk brn	12.00	20.00
87	A37	$2 bl & org brn	35.00	42.50
88	A37	$5 dl red & blk	40.00	60.00
		Nos. 82-88 (7)	99.50	147.00

No. 83 was overprinted in Shanghai in 1938. The overprint differs in minor detail.

1932-38
Type II

89	A37	2c olive grn	.45	2.00
90	A37	4c green	1.25	4.00
91	A37	5c green	.80	4.00
92	A37	15c dk green	1.10	4.00
93	A37	15c scar ('34)	1.10	4.00
93A	A37	20c ultra ('00)	.80	2.75
94	A37	25c ultra	1.25	4.00
95	A37	$1 org brn & dk brn	9.50	11.00
96	A37	$2 bl & org brn	20.00	32.50
97	A37	$5 dl red & blk	40.00	65.00
		Nos. 89-97 (10)	76.25	133.25

Nos. 89, 90 and 94 were overprinted in London, Peking and Shanghai. Nos. 92, 95-97 exist with London and Peking overprints. Nos. 91 and 93 exist with Peking and Shanghai overprints. No. 93A is a Shanghai overprint. The overprints differ in minor details.

Tan Yuan-chang Issue of China, 1933, Overprinted as in 1928
1933
Perf. 14

98	A49	2c olive grn	3.75	3.75
99	A49	5c green	4.75	4.75
100	A49	25c ultra	15.00	15.00
101	A49	$1 red	75.00	65.00
		Nos. 98-101 (4)	98.50	88.50

Stamps of China Martyrs Issue of 1932-34 Overprinted

1933-34

102	A39	½c black brown	.25	3.50
103	A40	1c orange	1.10	4.25
104	A39	2½c rose lilac	.25	3.25
105	A48	3c deep brown	.25	3.25
106	A45	8c brown orange	.75	3.50
107	A46	10c dull violet	.25	3.25
108	A45	13c blue green	.25	4.50
109	A46	17c brown olive	.25	2.50
110	A47	20c brown red	1.10	0.50
111	A40	30c brown violet	.40	4.50
112	A47	40c orange	.60	3.25
113	A40	50c green	.70	2.50
		Nos. 102-113 (12)	6.15	44.75

Nos. 102-113 were originally overprinted in Peking. In 1938, Nos. 103-105, 108-112 were overprinted in Shanghai. The two overprints differ in minor details. No. 105, Shanghai overprint, is scarce. Value $35.

China No. 324 Overprinted as in 1916-19
1936
Perf. 14

114	A29	6c brown	20.00	20.00

Stamps of China, 1939-40 Overprinted in Black
Type III
1940-45
Unwmk.   Perf. 12½

115	A57	2c olive green	.85	1.00
116	A57	3c dull claret ('41)	.25	1.50
117	A57	5c green	.25	1.50
118	A57	5c olive green	.25	1.50
119	A57	8c olive green ('41)	.25	.75
120	A57	10c green ('41)	.25	1.10
121	A57	15c scarlet	.55	2.50
122	A57	16c olive gray ('41)	.40	1.00
123	A57	25c dark blue	.55	2.75
124	A57	$1 hn & dk brn (type II)	6.25	11.00
125	A57	$2 dp bl & org brn (type I)	4.50	11.00
126	A57	$5 red & grnsh blk	26.00	32.50
		Nos. 115-126 (12)	40.35	68.10

Perf. 14
With Secret Marks

127	A57	8c ol grn (#383a)	1.10	1.65
a.		On #383	19.00	22.50
128	A57	10c green ('41)	10.00	13.00
129	A57	30c scarlet ('45)	.30	1.10
130	A57	50c dk blue ('45)	.55	1.75
131	A57	$1 org brn & sep	.55	2.25
132	A57	$2 dp bl & org brn	.55	2.25
133	A57	$5 red & sl grn	.65	3.75
134	A57	$10 dk grn & dl pur	1.90	2.75
135	A57	$20 rose lake & dk bl	3.50	5.50
		Nos. 127-135 (9)	19.10	34.00

Wmk. Character Yu (Post) (261)
Perf. 14

136	A57	5c olive green	.30	2.50
137	A57	10c green	.35	3.75
138	A57	30c scarlet	.35	5.00
139	A57	50c dark blue	.45	2.50
		Nos. 136-139 (4)	1.45	13.75

AIR POST STAMPS

Sinkiang Nos. 53, 57, 59, 32 Overprinted in Red

1932-33
Unwmk.   Perf. 14

C1	A29	5c claret ('33)	400.00	290.00
C2	A29	10c dark blue ('33)	400.00	225.00
C3	A30	15c deep blue	2,700.	775.00
C4	A25	30c brown violet	1,170.	990.00

Counterfeits exist of Nos. C1-C4.

OFFICES IN TIBET

12 Pies = 1 Anna
16 Annas = 1 Rupee

Stamps of China, Issues of 1902-10, Surcharged

1911
Unwmk.   Perf. 12 to 16

1	A17	3p on 1c ocher	27.50	45.00
a.		Inverted surcharge	3,500.	
2	A17	½a on 2c grn	27.50	45.00
3	A17	1a on 4c ver	27.50	45.00
4	A17	2a on 7c mar	27.50	45.00
5	A17	2½a on 10c ultra	35.00	55.00
6	A17	3a on 16c ol grn	70.00	80.00
a.		Large "S" in "Annas"	1,250.	
7	A18	4a on 20c red brn	70.00	80.00
8	A18	6a on 30c rose red	125.00	140.00
9	A18	12a on 50c yel grn	325.00	400.00
10	A19	1r on $1 red & pale rose	900.00	900.00
11	A19	2r on $2 red & yel	1,620.	1,800.
		Nos. 1-11 (11)	3,255.	3,635.

Beware of fake overprints.

SHANGHAI
shaṇ-'hī

LOCATION — A city on the Whangpoo River, Kiangsu Province, China
POP. — 3,489,998

During 1842-1860, the Chinese government opened a number of ports for foreign trade, and European mercantile colonies were quickly established in these cities. The most active settlement was at Shanghai, where a British settlement was established in 1843, with French and American settlements soon following. The Shanghai Municipal Council was formed in 1854 to administer the foreign settlement. Virtually independent of Chinese control, the Council performed most government functions in Shanghai. Similar autonomous Western commercial settlements were later established in most of the treaty ports. Lack of confidence in existing Chinese postal services and dissatisfaction with the limited service provided by the British Hong Kong Postal Agency prompted the Shanghai Municipal Council to form the Shanghai Local Post in 1863. The first distinctive stamps for this service appeared in 1865, and Shanghai issues continued until 1897. Many of the other Chinese Treaty Ports joined the Shanghai Postal System, and the System handled more mail during its existence than the Imperial Customs Post, the Hong Kong Agencies, and all of the other foreign post offices. Ten of the ports within the system issued stamps during 1893-1897. On Nov. 1, 1897, the Shanghai

Local Post was absorbed into the Imperial Chinese Post Office.

Cash Coin System
800-1600 Cash = 1 Tael
Dollar System
10 Cash = 1 Cent
10 Cents = 1 Chiao (Hao)
100 Cents = 1 Dollar (Yuan)
1 Dollar = .72 Tael
Tael System
10 Li = 1 Fen (Candereen)
10 Fen (Candereen) = 1 Ch'ien (Mace)
10 Ch'ien (Mace) = 1 Liang (Tael)

Covers: Although authentic used examples exist of many of Nos. 1-41a, covers are not known.
Margins: While unused stamps normally have wide margins and are valued in that condition, almost all known used examples have very narrow margins or are cut into the design, and are valued in that condition.

Watermark

Wmk. 175 — Kung Pu (Municipal Council)

Dragon — A1

Antique Numerals
Roman "I" in "I6"
"Candareens" Plural
1865-66
Unwmk.   Typo.   Imperf.
Wove Paper

1	A1	2ca black	775.00	6,750.
a.		Pelure paper	825.00	
2	A1	4ca yellow	1,000.	5,250.
a.		Pelure paper	1,000.	
b.		Double impression		
3	A1	8ca green	650.00	6,000.
a.		8ca yellow green	775.00	
4	A1	16ca scarlet	2,250.	6,000.
a.		16ca vermilion	2,250.	
b.		Pelure paper	2,250.	
		Nos. 1-4 (4)	4,675.	24,000.

No. 1: top character of three in left panel as illustrated. No. 5: top character is two horiz. lines.
Nos. 2, 3: center character of three in left panel as illustrated. Nos. 6, 7: center character much more complex.

Antique Numerals
"Candareens" Plural
Pelure Paper

5	A1	2ca black	650.00	
a.		Wove paper	650.00	6,250.
6	A1	4ca yellow	825.00	3,750.
7	A1	8ca deep green	875.00	—
		Nos. 5-7 (3)	2,350.	

Antique Numerals
"Candareen" Singular
Laid Paper

8	A1	1ca blue	700.00	5,500.
a.		1ca deep blue	375.00	
9	A1	2ca black	10,000.	
10	A1	4ca yellow	2,750.	
		Nos. 8-10 (3)	13,450.	

Wove Paper

11	A1	1ca blue	500.00	7,750.
12	A1	2ca black	650.00	7,750.
13	A1	4ca yellow	775.00	8,000.
14	A1	8ca olive green	650.00	
15	A1	16ca vermilion	700.00	
a.		"1" of "16" omitted	26,000.	
		Nos. 11-15 (5)	3,275.	

SHANGHAI

311

Roman "I," Antique "2"
"Candareens" Plural Except on 1ca
Wove Paper

16	A1	1ca blue	950.00	3,800.
17	A1	12ca fawn	375.00	
18	A1	12ca choco-late	550.00	
		Nos. 16-18 (3)	1,875.	

Antique Numerals
"Candareens" Plural Except on 1ca
Wove Paper

19	A1	1ca indigo, pelure paper	450.00	5,500.
a.		1ca blue, wove paper	425.00	5,750.
b.		1ca indigo, wove paper	175.00	
20	A1	3ca orange brown	500.00	4,250.
a.		Pelure paper	525.00	3,750.
21	A1	6ca red brown	350.00	
22	A1	6ca fawn	875.00	—
23	A1	6ca vermilion	500.00	
24	A1	12ca orange brown	325.00	
25	A1	16ca vermilion	325.00	1,500.
a.		"1" of "16" omitted	500.00	
		Nos. 19-25 (7)	3,325.	

Examples of No. 22 usually have the straight lines cutting through the paper.

Antique Numerals
Roman "I"
"Candareens" Plural Except on 1ca
Laid Paper

26	A1	1ca blue	32,000.	
27	A1	2ca black	7,000.	
28	A1	3ca red brown	28,000.	—

Examples of No. 28 usually have the straight lines cutting through the paper.

Modern Numerals
"Candareen" Singular

29	A1	1ca slate blue	250.00	4,500.
a.		1ca dark blue	250.00	4,250.
30	A1	3ca red brown	250.00	5,000.

"Candareens" Plural Except the 1c

31	A1	2ca gray	225.00	
a.		2ca black	125.00	
32	A1	3ca red brown	225.00	3,400.

Coarse Porous Wove Paper

33a	A1	1ca blue	160.00	
34a	A1	2ca black	210.00	
b.		Grayish paper	275.00	
35a	A1	3ca red brown	150.00	
36a	A1	4ca yellow	350.00	
b.		4ca orange yellow	80.00	
37a	A1	6ca olive green	190.00	
b.		6ca bronze green	95.00	
38a	A1	8ca emerald	225.00	
b.		8ca green	95.00	
39a	A1	12ca orange vermilion	160.00	
b.		12ca reddish orange	80.00	
40a	A1	16ca brown	250.00	875.00
41a	A1	16ca red brown	225.00	875.00
		Nos. 33a-41a (9)	1,920.	

Chinese characters change on same denomination stamps.

Nos. 1, 2, 11 and 32 exist on thicker paper, usually toned. Most authorities consider these four stamps and Nos. 33a-41a to be official reprints made to present sample sets to other post offices. The tone in this paper is an acquired characteristic, due to various causes. Many shades and minor varieties exist of Nos. 1-41a.

 A2
 A3
 A4
 A5

1866   Litho.   Perf. 12

42	A2	2c rose	27.50	35.00
43	A3	4c lilac	47.50	60.00
44	A4	8c gray blue	52.50	55.00
45	A5	16c green	82.50	110.00
		Nos. 42-45 (4)	210.00	260.00

Nos. 42-45 imperf. are proofs. See No. 50. For surcharges see Nos. 51-61, 67.

 A6
 A7
 A8
 A9

1866   Perf. 15

46	A6	1ca brown	11.00	15.50
a.		"CANDS"	200.00	200.00
47	A7	3ca orange	45.00	60.00
48	A8	6ca slate	47.50	55.00
49	A9	12ca olive gray	72.50	110.00
		Nos. 46-49 (4)	176.00	240.50

See Nos. 69-77. For surcharges see Nos. 62-66, 68, 78-83.

1872

50	A2	2c rose	170.00	200.00

Handstamp Surcharged in Blue, Red or Black — a

1873   Perf. 12

51	A2	1ca on 2c rose	60.00	65.00
52	A3	1ca on 4c lilac	25.00	37.50
a.		Inverted surcharge	625.00	
b.		Double surcharge	725.00	
53	A3	1ca on 4c lilac (R)	9,000.	3,750.
a.		Double surch., 1 blue	15,000.	
54	A3	1ca on 4c lilac (Bk)	25.00	37.50
a.		Inverted surcharge	300.00	
55	A4	1ca on 8c gray bl	52.50	55.00
a.		Double surcharge	625.00	
56	A4	1ca on 8c gray bl (R)	22,000.	16,000.
57	A5	1ca on 16c green	4,250.	3,250.
a.		Double surcharge	10,000.	
58	A5	1ca on 16c green (R)	32,000.	13,500.

Perf. 15

59	A2	1ca on 2c rose	72.50	75.00

1875   Perf. 12

60	A2	3ca on 2c rose	300.00	250.00
61	A5	3ca on 16c green	4,250.	3,250.

Perf. 15

62	A7	1ca on 3ca orange	38,000.	18,000.
63	A8	1ca on 6ca slate	875.00	650.00
64	A8	1ca on 6ca slate (R)	12,000.	4,500.
65	A9	1ca on 12ca ol gray	1,100.	900.00
66	A9	1ca on 12ca ol gray (R)	8,000.	4,000.
67	A2	3ca on 2c rose	875.00	750.00
68	A9	3ca on 12ca olive gray	6,000.	6,000.

Counterfeits exist of Nos. 51-68.

Types of 1866

1875   Perf. 15

69	A6	1ca yel, yel	42.50	37.50
70	A7	3ca rose, rose	42.50	37.50

Perf. 11½

71	A6	1ca yel, yel	900.00	650.00

1876   Perf. 15

72	A6	1ca yellow	25.00	30.00
73	A7	3ca rose	95.00	95.00
74	A8	6ca green	140.00	160.00

75	A9	9ca blue	250.00	300.00
76	A9	12ca light brown	275.00	325.00
		Nos. 72-76 (5)	785.00	910.00

1877   Engr.   Perf. 12½

77	A6	1ca rose	2,250.	3,000.

Stamps of 1875-76 Surcharged type "a" in Blue or Red

1877   Litho.   Perf. 15

78	A7	1ca on 3ca rose, rose	550.00	475.00
79	A7	1ca on 3ca rose	170.00	150.00
a.		Double surcharge	2,250.	
80	A8	1ca on 6ca green	300.00	250.00
81	A9	1ca on 9ca blue	550.00	550.00
82	A9	1ca on 12ca lt brn	3,250.	2,000.
83	A9	1ca on 12ca lt brn (R)	8,500.	5,500.

Counterfeits exist of Nos. 78-83.

 A11
 A12
 A13
 A14

1877   Perf. 15

84	A11	20 cash blue violet	16.50	15.00
a.		20 cash violet	13.00	10.00
85	A12	40 cash rose	22.50	20.00
86	A13	60 cash green	25.00	23.00
87	A14	80 cash blue	32.50	35.00
88	A14	100 cash brown	30.00	32.50
		Nos. 84-88 (5)	126.50	125.50

Handstamp Surcharged in Blue — b

1879   Perf. 15

89	A12	20 cash on 40c rose	45.00	37.50
a.		Inverted surcharge	550.00	
90	A14	60 cash on 80c blue	55.00	70.00
91	A14	60 cash on 100c brn	65.00	65.00
		Nos. 89-91 (3)	165.00	172.50

Types of 1877

1880   Perf. 11½

92	A11	20 cash violet	11.00	11.00
a.		Horiz. pair, imperf. btwn.	800.00	
b.		Vert. pair, imperf. horiz.	850.00	
93	A12	40 cash rose	17.50	15.00
a.		Horiz. pair, imperf. btwn.	900.00	
94	A13	60 cash green	20.00	20.00
95	A14	80 cash blue	21.00	20.00
96	A14	100 cash brown	24.00	22.50

Perf. 15x11½

97	A11	20 cash lilac	170.00	150.00
		Nos. 92-97 (6)	263.50	238.50

Surcharged type "b" in Blue

1884   Perf. 11½

98	A12	20 cash on 40c rose	24.00	22.00
a.		Double surcharge	700.00	
99	A14	60 cash on 80c blue	35.00	36.00
100	A14	60 cash on 100c brn	42.50	42.50
		Nos. 98-100 (3)	101.50	100.50

Types of 1877

1884

101	A11	20 cash green	10.50	10.00

1885   Perf. 15

102	A11	20 cash green	8.25	5.00
103	A12	40 cash brown	10.00	9.00
104	A13	60 cash red violet	17.50	17.00
a.		60 cash red violet	22.50	25.00
b.		Vert. pair, imperf. btwn.	1,000.	
105	A14	80 cash buff	16.50	15.00
a.		Horiz. pair, imperf. btwn.	800.00	

106	A14	100 cash yellow	20.00	20.00

Perf. 11½x15

107	A11	20 cash green	16.50	15.00
108	A13	60 cash red vio	17.50	15.00
		Nos. 102-108 (7)	106.25	96.00

Surcharged type "b" in Blue or Red

1886   Perf. 15

109	A14	40 cash on 80c buff	13.50	12.00
a.		Inverted surcharge	20.00	18.00
b.		Red surcharge	550.00	
110	A14	60 cash on 100c yellow	20.00	18.00
a.		Inverted surcharge	100.00	100.00
b.		Double surcharge	225.00	
c.		Red surcharge	600.00	

Types of 1877

1888   Perf. 15

111	A11	20 cash gray	9.50	5.50
112	A12	40 cash black	9.50	9.50
113	A13	60 cash rose	13.00	12.00
a.		Third character at left lacks dot at top	27.50	20.00
114	A14	80 cash green	14.00	
115	A14	100 cash lt blue	17.50	17.50
		Nos. 111-115 (5)	63.50	54.50

Nos. 106, 103, 105 Handstamp Surcharged in Blue or Red Type "b" or

 c
  d

1888   Perf. 15

116	A14(b)	40 cash on 100c yel	16.50	16.00
a.		Inverted surcharge	125.00	
b.		Double surcharge	140.00	
c.		Red surcharge	32.50	30.00
118	A12(c)	20 cash on 40c brn	27.50	25.00
a.		Inverted surcharge	200.00	175.00
b.		Double surcharge	350.00	
c.		Red surcharge	400.00	
119	A14(c)	20 cash on 80c buff	14.50	12.00
a.		Inverted surcharge	250.00	140.00
b.		Double surcharge	650.00	550.00
c.		Red surcharge	425.00	
120	A12(d)	20 cash on 40c brn	27.50	26.00
a.		Inverted surcharge	300.00	275.00
		Nos. 116-120 (4)	86.00	79.00

Omitted surcharges paired with normal stamp exist on Nos. 116, 119.

Handstamp Surcharged in Black and Red (100 cash) or Red (20 cash) — e

1889   Unwmk.

121	A14(e)	100 cash on 20c on 100c yel	200.00	225.00
a.		Without the surcharge "100 cash"	500.00	
b.		Blue & red surcharge	1,800.	—
122	A14(c)	20 cash on 80c grn	16.50	15.00
a.		Inverted surcharge	140.00	
123	A14(c)	20 cash on 100c bl	16.50	15.00
a.		Double surcharge	350.00	
		Nos. 121-123 (3)	233.00	255.00

Counterfeits exist of Nos. 116-123.

1889   Wmk. 175   Perf. 15

124	A11	20 cash gray	5.75	4.25
125	A12	40 cash black	8.50	7.00
126	A13	60 cash rose	27.50	27.50
a.		Third character at left lacks dot at top	30.00	30.00

Perf. 12

127	A14	80 cash green	11.00	22.00
a.		Horiz. pair, imperf. btwn.	2,000.	
128	A14	100 cash dk bl	17.50	22.00
		Nos. 124-128 (5)	70.25	82.75

Nos. 124-126 are sometimes found without watermark. This is caused by the sheet being misplaced in the printing press, so that the stamps are printed on the unwatermarked margin of the sheet.

Shield with Dragon
Supporters — A20

1890		Unwmk.	Litho.	Perf. 15	
129	A20	2c brown		4.25	4.75
130	A20	5c rose		12.00	8.00
131	A20	15c blue		27.50	15.00

Nos. 129-131 imperforate are proofs.

Wmk. 175

132	A20	10c black		17.50	12.00
a.		Perf. 12		1,000.	550.00
133	A20	15c blue		25.00	18.00
134	A20	20c violet		17.50	14.00
		Nos. 129-134 (6)		103.75	71.75

See Nos. 135-141. For surcharges and overprints see Nos. 142-152, J1-J13.

1891				Perf. 12	
135	A20	2c brown		3.00	2.00
136	A20	5c rose		13.00	7.00

1892					
137	A20	2c green		3.50	2.50
a.		Bisect used as 1c on cover		—	
138	A20	5c red		8.25	7.25
139	A20	10c orange		22.00	22.00
140	A20	15c violet		13.50	10.00
141	A20	20c brown		14.50	13.00
		Nos. 137-141 (5)		61.75	54.75

No. 130 Handstamp
Surcharged in Blue — f

1892		Unwmk.		Perf. 15	
142	A20	2c on 5c rose		130.00	80.00
a.		Inverted surcharge		850.00	750.00

Counterfeits exist of Nos. 142-152.

Stamps of 1892 Handstamp Surcharged in Blue

g   h

1893		Wmk. 175		Perf. 12	
143	A20	½c on 15c violet		20.00	13.00
a.		Double surcharge		375.00	
b.		Vert. pair, imperf. btwn.		350.00	325.00
144	A20	1c on 20c brown		20.00	13.00
a.		½c on 20c brown (error)		26,000.	

Nos. 144 and 144a exist in se-tenant pairs. Example pairs with black surcharge come from a trial printing.

Surcharged in Blue or Red (#152) on Halves of #136 (#145-147), #138 (#148-150), #135 (#151), #137 (#152)

i   j   k   m

145	A20(i)	½c on half of 5c	13.50	10.00
146	A20(j)	½c on half of 5c	13.50	10.00
147	A20(k)	½c on half of 5c	275.00	200.00
148	A20(i)	½c on half of 5c	13.50	10.00
149	A20(j)	½c on half of 5c	13.50	10.00
150	A20(k)	½c on half of 5c	225.00	160.00
151	A20(m)	1c on half of 2c	3.50	3.00
c.		Dbl. surch., one in green	1,600.	350.00
d.		Dbl. surch., one in black	1,700.	350.00
152	A20(m)	1c on half of 2c	16.50	12.00
		Nos. 145-152 (8)	574.00	415.00

The ½c surcharge setting of 20 (2x10) covers a vertical strip of 10 unsevered stamps, with horizontal gutter midway. This setting has 11 of type "i," 8 of type "j" and 1 of type "k." Nos. 145-152 are perforated vertically down the middle.

Inverted surcharges exist on Nos. 145-151. Double surcharges, one inverted, are also found in this issue.

Handstamped provisionals somewhat similar to Nos. 145-152 were issued in Foochow by the Shanghai Agency.

Coat of Arms — A24

Typo. (Dot)

Litho. (No Dot)

Frame Inscriptions in Black

1893		Litho.	Perf. 13½x14	
153	A24	½c orange	7.25	3.00
b.		Horiz. pair, imperf vert.	225.00	
154	A24	1c brown	7.25	1.75
155	A24	2c vermilion	8.00	2.50
a.		Imperf, pair	225.00	
156	A24	5c blue	1.10	.65
a.		Black inscriptions inverted	1,800.	
b.		Black inscriptions double	900.00	
157	A24	10c green	10.00	11.00
158	A24	15c yellow	1.10	.90
159	A24	20c lilac	11.00	9.00
		Nos. 153-159 (7)	45.70	28.80

Typographed

153a	A24	½c orange	.55	.50
154a	A24	1c brown	.55	.50

Typo & Litho

157a	A24	10c green	2.75	3.00
159a	A24	20c lilac	3.00	5.00

On Nos. 157 and 159, frame inscriptions are lithographed, rest of design typographed.

See Nos. 170-172. For overprints and surcharges see Nos. 160-166, 168-169.

Stamps of 1893
Overprinted in Black

1893, Dec. 14				
160	A24	½c (On #153a)	.50	.50
a.		Inverted overprint	165.00	150.00
161	A24	1c (On #154a)	.65	.65
a.		Double overprint	67.50	50.00
162	A24	2c (On #155)	.90	.90
a.		Inverted overprint	165.00	120.00
163	A24	5c (On #156)	3.50	5.00
a.		Inverted overprint	325.00	
164	A24	10c (On #157a)	11.00	12.00
165	A24	15c (On #158)	7.25	6.50
166	A24	20c (On #159)	9.50	10.00
		Nos. 160-166 (7)	33.30	35.55

50th anniv. of the first foreign settlement in Shanghai.

Mercury — A26

1893, Nov. 11		Litho.	Perf. 13½	
167	A26	2c vermilion & black	1.10	1.00

Nos. 158 and 159
Handstamp
Surcharged in Black

1896			Perf. 13½x14	
168	A24	4c on 15c yellow & blk	11.00	8.00
169	A24	6c on 20c lilac & blk (#159)	11.00	8.00
a.		On #159a	55.00	25.00

Surcharge occurs inverted or double on Nos. 168-169.

Arms Type of 1893

1896				
170	A24	2c scarlet & blk	.30	1.60
a.		Black inscriptions inverted	2,000.	1,800.
b.		Black inscriptions double	1,400.	1,200.
171	A24	4c orange & blk, yel	7.25	5.50
172	A24	6c car & blk, rose	8.25	8.50
		Nos. 170-172 (3)	15.80	15.60

POSTAGE DUE STAMPS

Postage Stamps of 1890-92 Handstamped in Black, Red or Blue

1892		Unwmk.	Perf. 15	
J1	A20	2c brown (Bk)	900.00	900.00
a.		Inverted overprint	2,500.	
J2	A20	5c rose (Bk)	25.00	14.00
a.		Inverted overprint	425.00	
J3	A20	15c blue (Bk)	52.50	47.50
a.		Inverted overprint	400.00	
b.		Blue overprint	425.00	

		Wmk. 175		
J4	A20	10c black (R)	35.00	32.50
J5	A20	15c blue (R)	30.00	27.50
a.		Inverted overprint	600.00	
b.		Double overprint	300.00	
c.		Pair, one without ovpt.	1,300.	
J6	A20	20c violet (Bk)	22.50	20.00
		Nos. J1-J6 (6)	1,065.	1,041.

1892-93			Perf. 12	
J7	A20	2c brown (Bk)	3.75	3.75
a.		Inverted overprint	175.00	160.00
b.		Double overprint	400.00	
c.		Pair, one without ovpt.	1,000.	
J8	A20	2c brown (Bl)	3.50	3.00
J9	A20	5c rose (Bl)	15.50	9.00
a.		Inverted overprint	225.00	
J10	A20	10c orange (Bk)	250.00	225.00
J11	A20	10c orange (Bl)	20.00	15.00
a.		Inverted overprint	325.00	
J12	A20	15c violet (R)	32.50	30.00
J13	A20	20c brown (R)	32.50	30.00
		Nos. J7-J13 (7)	357.75	315.75

D2

1893		Litho.	Perf. 13½	
J14	D2	½c orange & blk	.55	.55

			Perf. 14x13½	
J15	D2	1c brown & black	.65	.55
a.		Horiz. pair, imperf. vert.	350.00	
J16	D2	2c vermilion & black	.65	.55
a.		Horiz. pair, imperf. vert.	350.00	
J17	D2	5c blue & black	1.00	.90
J18	D2	10c green & black	6.00	2.00
J19	D2	15c yellow & black	4.75	4.00
J20	D2	20c violet & black	1.75	1.50
		Nos. J14-J20 (7)	15.35	10.05

Stamps of Shanghai were discontinued in 1898.

CHINA TREATY PORTS

Wmk. 402 — Chinese Characters

AMOY

A seaport on an island located off the coast of Fukien Province, in south China. The Shanghai Local Post was handling mail from Amoy as early as 1863, but a formal branch office was not established until 1890. Shanghai stamps were used from 1890 until Mar. 31, 1895, when the post office was taken over by the Amoy Local Council. Amoy stamps were used from June 8, 1895, until Feb. 2, 1897, when mail services came under control of the Imperial Chinese Post Office.

All Amoy issues were printed by Schleicher and Schull, Duren, Germany.

Geese — A1   Type 1

Type 2

		Perf. 11½		
1895, June 8-1896		Unwmk.	Litho.	
1	A1	½c green	5.00	7.00
2	A1	1c rose red	5.00	55.00
a.		1c aniline rose red	6.00	6.00
3	A1	2c blue, Type 1	80.00	85.00
4	A1	2c blue, Type 2	14.00	22.50
5	A1	4c brown	14.00	22.00
6	A1	5c orange	15.00	20.00

Two lithographic stones were made for the ½ cent value, with the first used for the June 8, 1895, printing and the second used for a second printing on May 11, 1896, when Nos. 11-13 were printed. Plating details are needed to differentiate the two printings.

No. 1 also exists with papermaker's watermark "C S & S" in script letters.

Nos. 5 and 6 surcharged in two lines, wide "f"

1896, May 8				
7	A1	Half Cent on 4c brown	60.00	72.50
8	A1	Half Cent on 5c orange	60.00	72.50

Nos. 5 and 6 surcharged "1/2"c, "2" with curved foot

1896, May 9				
9	A1	½c on 4c brown	50.00	52.50
a.		"2" with straight foot	115.00	95.00
10	A1	½c on 5c orange	37.50	52.50
a.		"2" with straight foot	110.00	85.00
b.		Double surcharge	1,600.	
c.		Double surcharge, one red	1,450.	
d.		As "a." double surcharge	1,600.	

1896, May 11		Wmk. 402		
11	A1	15c gray black	22.50	23.00
12	A1	20c violet	27.50	23.00
13	A1	25c lilac rose	32.50	23.00

Nos. 5 and 6 surcharged in two lines, narrow "f"

1896, May 20
Unwmk.

Surcharged in Blue

14	A1	½c on 4c brown	62.50	100.00
a.	"G" instead of "C" in cent		950.00	850.00
15	A1	½c on 5c orange	62.50	100.00
a.	"G" instead of "C" in cent		950.00	850.00

Surcharged in Black

16	A1	½c on 4c brown	17.50	23.00
17	A1	½c on 5c orange	17.50	23.00

Nos. 11-13 surcharged, dropped "C"

1896, Oct. 1
Wmk. 402

18	A1	3c on 15c gray black	20.00	35.00
19	A1	6c on 20c violet	20.00	35.00
20	A1	10c on 25c lilac rose	20.00	35.00
a.	Blue surcharge with bar in black		600.00	
b.	Blue surcharge			
c.	Double surcharge, one blue, one black		—	

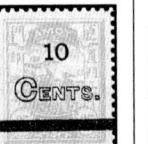

Nos. 11-13 surcharged in red (R) or black, "C" in line with other letters

1896, Oct. 9

21	A1	3c on 15c gray black (R)	20.00	32.00
a.	Brownish red surcharge		35.00	27.50
22	A1	6c on 20c violet (R)	20.00	30.00
23	A1	10c on 25c lilac rose	30.00	30.00
a.	Double surcharge		300.00	

POSTAGE DUE STAMPS
Nos. 1, 3-6 overprinted in red

Normal — "D" under "S"   Variety — "DUE" shifted to right

Perf. 11½
1895, Oct. 14   Unwmk.   Litho.

J1	A1	½c green	30.00	32.50
a.	Vertical pair, one without ovpt.		575.00	
b.	Vertical pair, one with red ovpt., one with black			
c.	"DUE" shifted to right		—	—
J2	A1	2c blue, type 1	525.00	525.00
a.	"DUE" shifted to right		725.00	
J3	A1	2c blue, type 2	30.00	30.00
a.	"DUE" shifted to right		550.00	550.00
J4	A1	4c brown	30.00	30.00
a.	"DUE" shifted to right		550.00	550.00
J5	A1	5c orange	30.00	30.00
a.	"DUE" shifted to right		550.00	550.00

Overprinted in Black

J6	A1	½c green	13.00	12.00
a.	Double overprint		575.00	325.00
b.	Inverted overprint		—	
c.	"DUE" shifted to right		550.00	550.00
J7	A1	1c rose red	9.00	10.00
a.	Double overprint		900.00	
b.	Inverted overprint		550.00	550.00
c.	"DUE" shifted to right		550.00	550.00
J8	A1	2c blue, type 1	525.00	
J9	A1	2c blue, type 2	95.00	75.00
a.	"DUE" shifted to right		550.00	
J10	A1	4c brown	52.50	42.50
a.	"DUE" shifted to right		550.00	550.00
J11	A1	5c orange	52.50	42.50
a.	"DUE" shifted to right		550.00	550.00

No. 2 overprinted in Roman (serifed) Type

1896, June 1

J12	A1	1c rose red	450.00 500.00

CHEFOO

A seaport in Shantung Province, on the Straits of Pechile. It was opened to foreign trade by the Treaty of Peking in 1860 and by the 1890's had become a bustling city. Because of its pleasant climate, Chefoo became a favorite summer vacation area for foreigners in China. The Chefoo Local Post Committee was formed in mid-1893, and the first stamps for Chefoo were issued on Oct. 6, 1893. The Chefoo Local Post's operations were taken over by the Imperial Chinese Post Office on Feb. 2, 1897.

All Chefoo issues were printed by Schleicher and Schull, Duren, Germany. All were impressed with a faux watermark, the Chinese character for Yan, the first half of the Chinese name for Chefoo, Yan-Tai. Nos. 14-16 are impressed with two characters, for the full city name.

Smoke Tower and Semaphore — A1

Type 1: the right bottom of the "H" and the left bottom of the "E" of "CHEFOO" are clearly separated from each other; the ball of the semaphore is clear. Type 2: the "H" and the "E" of "CHEFOO" are nearly touching; the ball of the semaphore is not clear, and the rim is irregular; there is a hairline in the lower right of the outer frame.

Type 1

1893, Oct. 6   Litho.   *Perf. 11½*

1	A1	½c green	30.00	22.50
2	A1	1c red	9.00	7.00
3	A1	2c ultramarine	30.00	23.00
a.	Vertical pair, imperf between		850.00	
b.	2c pale blue		30.00	23.00
4	A1	5c orange	30.00	30.00
a.	Imperforate		325.00	
5	A1	10c brown	30.00	23.00
a.	10c reddish brown		32.50	25.00

Type 2

1894, Jan.

6	A1	½c dark gray green	4.00	3.00
7	A1	5c red orange	9.00	8.00

Type 2; "Yan" Character Impressed on Front of Stamp

1894, March

8	A1	½c green	4.00	3.00
a.	"Yan" impression on back of stamp		11.00	11.00
9	A1	1c scarlet	2.00	2.00
a.	"Yan" impressed on back of stamp		11.00	11.00
10	A1	1c rose red	4.00	7.00
11	A1	2c blue	6.00	6.00
a.	Pair, imperf between		—	
12	A1	5c brown orange	9.00	8.00
a.	"Yan" impression inverted		22.00	
b.	"Yan" impression on back of stamp		11.00	11.00
13	A1	10c brown	9.00	9.00
a.	10c reddish brown		11.00	11.00

Harbor Scene — A2

"Yan Tai" Characters Impressed on Front of Stamp

1896, Jan.

14	A2	15c red brown & green	17.00	22.00
15	A2	20c red brown & violet	27.50	23.00
16	A2	25c violet & red	17.00	22.00

In Jan. 1896 a postal clerk overprinted 56 sets of Nos. 1-5 with a hand-stamped two-line "POSTAGE DUE" overprint, applied either horizontally or diagonally. These were sold from the post office but were never authorized and were later condemned by the Chefoo postmaster.

CHINKIANG

An ancient strategic city on the Yangtze River, 112 miles inland from Shanghai. Chinkiang became a Treaty Port in 1860, and in 1864 a British trading settlement was established in the city. By 1866, Chinkiang was a part of the Shanghai Postal System. On Aug. 6, 1894, postal operations were taken over by the Chinkiang Local Post Office. On Feb. 2, 1897, the Chinkiang mail service was absorbed into the Imperial Chinese Post.

All Chinkiang Local Post stamps were printed by Tokyo Tsukiji Foundry Co., Japan.

Golden Mountain — A1

Perf. 11½
1894, Aug. 6   Unwmk.   Litho.

1	A1	½c rose	4.00	5.00
a.	Horiz. pair, imperf between		150.00	
b.	Horiz. pair, imperf between		130.00	
c.	½c aniline rose		7.00	7.00
2	A1	1c blue	2.00	2.00
a.	Horiz. strip of 3, imperf vert.		275.00	275.00
b.	Perf 11½x11		10.00	10.00
3	A1	2c brown	7.00	8.00
a.	Perf 11½x11		10.00	10.00
4	A1	4c yellow	10.00	10.00
a.	Perf 11		11.00	11.00
5	A1	5c green	10.00	11.00
a.	Perf 11½x11		10.00	10.00
b.	Horiz. pair, imperf between		250.00	
c.	Vert. pair, imperf between		275.00	
6	A1	6c mauve	15.00	13.00
a.	Perf 11		13.00	13.50
b.	Perf 11½x11		10.00	11.00
c.	Perf 11x11½		12.00	12.00
d.	Horiz. pair, imperf between		200.00	
7	A1	10c orange	20.00	15.00
a.	Perf 11½x11		22.00	22.00
b.	Perf 11		14.00	14.00
c.	Perf 11x11½		14.00	14.00

Golden Mountain — A2

Type A2 is similar to A1, but clouds have been added to the sky, and shading added to the river.

1895, Apr. 9

8	A2	½c rose red	8.00	8.00
9	A2	1c blue	10.00	10.00
10	A2	2c brown	35.00	32.50
11	A2	4c yellow	24.00	24.00
12	A2	5c emerald green	24.00	24.00
13	A2	6c mauve	24.00	26.00
a.	Horiz. pair, imperf. vert.		275.00	175.00
b.	Horiz. pair, imperf between		295.00	240.00
c.	Imperf, pair		—	
14	A2	10c orange	20.00	20.00
15	A2	15c carmine red	26.00	27.50

POSTAGE DUE STAMPS

Nos. 1-7 overprinted, narrow (1.5mm) spacing between "DUE" and Chinese characters

Perf. 11½
1894, Dec. 21   Unwmk.   Litho.

J1	A1	½c rose	13.00	12.00
a.	Inverted overprint		82.50	72.50
b.	Double overprint		140.00	85.00
J2	A1	1c blue	13.00	9.00
a.	Inverted overprint		82.50	77.50
b.	Double overprint, one inverted		—	
J3	A1	2c brown	13.00	11.00
a.	Inverted overprint		82.50	77.50
b.	Double overprint		200.00	200.00
J4	A1	4c yellow	13.00	15.00
a.	Inverted overprint		115.00	90.00
b.	Vert. pair, imperf between		115.00	
c.	Perf 11		14.00	14.00
J5	A1	5c green	13.00	13.00
a.	Inverted overprint		100.00	90.00
J6	A1	6c mauve	16.00	15.00
a.	Inverted overprint		115.00	100.00
b.	Perf 11		14.00	14.00
c.	As "b," inverted overprint		115.00	100.00
d.	Perf 11x11½		20.00	20.00
J7	A1	10c orange	11.00	11.00
a.	Inverted overprint		115.00	100.00
b.	Perf 11½x11		13.00	13.00
c.	Perf 11½x11		13.00	13.00
d.	Vert. pair, imperf between		120.00	

Nos. 1-7, 15 overprinted, wide (2.5mm) spacing between "DUE" and Chinese characters

Split "P" Variety

1895, Apr. 9

Overprinted in Red

J8	A1	½c rose	190.00	160.00
a.	Inverted overprint		250.00	250.00
b.	Pair, one with inverted overprint		450.00	450.00
c.	Split "P"		250.00	250.00
d.	Inverted overprint, Split "P"		325.00	325.00

Overprinted in Black over Red

J9	A1	½c rose	275.00	310.00
a.	Both overprints inverted		350.00	350.00
b.	Pair, one with inverted overprint		550.00	550.00
J10	A1	1c blue	275.00	310.00
a.	Both overprints inverted		550.00	550.00
b.	Pair, one with inverted overprint		500.00	500.00
J11	A1	2c brown	275.00	310.00
a.	Both overprints inverted		350.00	350.00
J12	A1	4c yellow	275.00	310.00
a.	"DUE" omitted in red ovpt.		350.00	
b.	Both overprints inverted		550.00	550.00
J13	A1	5c green	275.00	310.00
a.	Both overprints inverted		350.00	350.00
J14	A1	6c mauve	275.00	310.00
a.	Both overprints inverted		550.00	550.00
J15	A1	10c orange	275.00	310.00
a.	Both overprints inverted		650.00	650.00
b.	Perf 11½x11		325.00	325.00
c.	Perf 11x11½		375.00	375.00
J16	A1	15c carmine	275.00	310.00
a.	Both overprints inverted		350.00	350.00
b.	Red overprint double			

Overprinted in Black over Red, Split "P" Variety

J9c	A1	½c rose	350.00	350.00
d.	Both overprints inverted		650.00	650.00
J10c	A1	1c blue	350.00	350.00
d.	Both overprints inverted		650.00	650.00
J11b	A1	2c brown	350.00	350.00
c.	Both overprints inverted		650.00	650.00
J12c	A1	4c yellow	350.00	350.00
d.	Both overprints inverted		650.00	650.00
J13b	A1	5c green	350.00	350.00
c.	Both overprints inverted		650.00	650.00
J14b	A1	6c mauve	350.00	350.00
c.	Both overprints inverted		650.00	650.00
J15d	A1	10c orange	350.00	350.00
f.	Perf 11x11½		350.00	350.00
J16c	A1	15c carmine	350.00	350.00
d.	Both overprints inverted		650.00	650.00

Overprinted in Black

J17	A1	½c rose	9.00	7.00
a.	Inverted overprint		275.00	77.50
b.	Pair, one with inverted overprint		325.00	
c.	"U" of "DUE" omitted		250.00	250.00
d.	"U" of "DUE" handstamped		250.00	
e.	"DU" of "DUE" omitted		325.00	
f.	"DU" handstamped		325.00	
J18	A1	1c blue	9.00	8.00
a.	Inverted overprint		275.00	
b.	Double overprint, one inverted		—	
c.	Pair, one with inverted overprint		300.00	

J19	A1 2c brown	20.00	20.00
a.	Inverted overprint	275.00	
b.	Double overprint	—	
c.	Horiz. pair, imperf between	200.00	200.00
d.	Perf 11½x11	22.50	25.00
J20	A1 4c yellow	15.00	16.00
a.	Inverted overprint	275.00	—
J21	A1 5c green	77.50	82.50
a.	Inverted overprint	—	
J22	A1 6c mauve	19.00	16.50
a.	Inverted overprint	425.00	
b.	Double overprint, one inverted	—	
J23	A1 10c orange	15.00	42.50
a.	Inverted overprint	—	
b.	Perf 11½x11	40.00	40.00
c.	As "b," inverted overprint	275.00	
d.	Perf 11x11½	32.50	32.50
J24	A1 15c carmine	20.00	22.50
a.	Inverted overprint	275.00	
b.	Double overprint, one inverted	350.00	

Overprinted in Black, Split "P" Variety

J17g	A1 ½c rose	65.00	
h.	Inverted overprint	350.00	—
J18d	A1 1c blue	65.00	
e.	Inverted overprint	350.00	—
J19e	A1 2c brown	65.00	—
J20b	A1 4c yellow	77.50	
J21b	A1 5c green	65.00	—
a.	Inverted overprint	190.00	—
J22c	A1 6c mauve	65.00	
	Inverted overprint	500.00	
J23e	A1 10c orange	65.00	—
f.	Inverted overprint	500.00	500.00
g.	Perf 11½x11	65.00	
h.	Perf 11x11½	65.00	
i.	As "h," inverted overprint	350.00	—
J24c	A1 15c carmine	65.00	
d.	Inverted overprint	350.00	

Nos. 8-15 overprinted

POSTAGE DUE

1895

J25	A2 ½c rose	9.00	9.00
a.	Inverted overprint	50.00	50.00
b.	Double overprint	—	
J26	A2 1c blue	9.00	10.00
a.	Inverted overprint	50.00	50.00
b.	Double overprint	—	
J27	A2 2c brown	22.50	24.00
a.	Inverted overprint	75.00	75.00
b.	Double overprint	—	
J28	A2 4c yellow	25.00	27.50
a.	Inverted overprint	75.00	75.00
J29	A2 5c green	27.50	30.00
a.	Inverted overprint	75.00	75.00
J30	A2 6c mauve	27.50	32.50
a.	Inverted overprint	75.00	75.00
J31	A2 10c orange	25.00	27.50
a.	Inverted overprint	75.00	75.00
J32	A2 15c carmine	25.00	27.50
a.	Inverted overprint	75.00	75.00

Split "P" Variety

J25c	A2 ½c rose	50.00	50.00
J26b	A2 1c blue	50.00	50.00
J27c	A2 2c brown	50.00	50.00
J28b	A2 4c yellow	50.00	50.00
J29b	A2 5c green	50.00	50.00
J30b	A2 6c mauve	50.00	50.00
J31b	A2 10c orange	50.00	50.00
J32b	A2 15c carmine	50.00	50.00

D1

Perf. 11, 11½ (#J33, J36, J39)
1895, Apr. 9

J33	D1 ½c rose	9.00	9.00
a.	Imperf	90.00	
J34	D1 1c blue	9.00	9.00
a.	Imperf	100.00	
b.	Vert. pair, imperf between	190.00	190.00
c.	Perf 11½x11	8.00	8.00
J35	D1 2c brown	20.00	20.00
J36	D1 4c yellow	15.00	15.00
J37	D1 5c green	20.00	20.00
a.	Perf 11½	24.00	24.00
J38	D1 6c mauve	20.00	18.00
a.	Imperf	24.00	
b.	Vert. pair, imperf between	65.00	75.00
J39	D1 10c orange	15.00	16.00
J40	D1 15c carmine	20.00	22.50
a.	Perf 11½	21.00	24.00

Nos. J37, J37a surcharged in red

1895, Sept. 11

J41	D1 FIVE CENTS on 5c green (#J37a)	32.50	40.00
a.	Inverted surcharge	200.00	150.00
b.	On #J37	40.00	40.00
c.	Inverted surcharge	250.00	250.00

OFFICIAL STAMPS

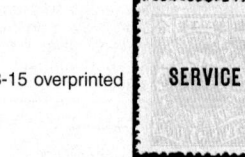

Nos. 8-15 overprinted

1896

O1	A2 ½c rose	10.00	16.00
a.	Inverted overprint	60.00	
O2	A2 1c blue	16.00	20.00
a.	Inverted overprint	60.00	
O3	A2 2c brown	26.00	16.50
a.	Inverted overprint	60.00	
O4	A2 4c yellow	35.00	26.00
a.	Inverted overprint	100.00	
O5	A2 5c green	35.00	32.50
a.	Inverted overprint	100.00	
O6	A2 6c mauve	27.50	26.00
a.	Inverted overprint	100.00	
O7	A2 10c orange	35.00	32.50
a.	Inverted overprint	100.00	
O8	A2 15c carmine	200.00	190.00
a.	Inverted overprint	200.00	

Inverted overprint with period is probably from a trial printing.

CHUNGKING

An ancient port city on the Yangtze River, some 1,500 miles above Shanghai, which served as a main hub for trade between the interior provinces and the coast. Chungking was opened to foreign trade in 1890. Mail service to the outside world was slow and expensive, and on Nov. 1, 1893, the Chunking Local Post was established to provide improved services at lower rates. It opened offices in Ichang and Shanghai and issued its first stamps in Dec. 1893. It was replaced by the Imperial Chinese Post Office on Feb. 2, 1897, but, because of the lack of government service, the local post continued operations for a few months.

Nos. 1 and 2 were lithographed by Kelly and Walsh, Shanghai. Nos. 3-7 were lithographed by Tokyo Tsukiji Type Foundry Co., Tokyo, Japan, in sheets of 50 (10x5).

Forgeries exist of the rarer Chungking stamps and covers. These should be purchased with certificates of authenticity from knowledgeable authorities.

Pagoda and Junk — A1

Perf. 12½
1893, Dec.   Unwmk.   Litho.

1	A1 2c vermilion	95.00	85.00

1894, Mar.   Imperfx12½

2	A1 2c vermilion	30.00	75.00
a.	Horiz. pair, imperf between	—	

No. 1 was printed in sheets of 40, with stamps perforated on all sides. No. 2 was printed in sheets of 10 stamps, arranged horizontally and perforated vertically only.

Pagoda and Junk, finer design — A2

Perf. 11½
1894, Dec.   Unwmk.   Litho.

3	A2 2c rose	3.00	6.00
a.	Inverted pair, imperf between	350.00	
4	A2 4c blue	9.00	9.00
5	A2 8c orange	9.00	14.00
a.	Pair, imperf between	450.00	
6	A2 16c mauve	9.00	14.00
a.	Pair, imperf between	—	
b.	Vert. strip of 3, imperf between	525.00	
7	A2 24c green	12.00	17.00

POSTAGE DUE STAMPS
No. 2 handstamped "POSTAGE DUE" in English and Chinese
1895   Unwmk.   Litho.   Perf. 11½

J1	A1 2c vermilion	200.00	200.00

Nos. 3-7 with this handstamp were made after Feb. 2, 1897, and do not appear to have been used. 2c-24c with black overprint, value $175 each. 2c, 16c and 24c, value $325 each.

Nos. 3-7 overprinted

Normal spacing between "POSTAGE" and "DUE" is 17.5mm. Narrow spacing is 16.5mm.

1895

J2	A2 2c rose	32.50	25.00
a.	Narrow spacing	125.00	
b.	Double overprint	125.00	
c.	Inverted overprint	175.00	
J3	A2 4c blue	32.50	27.50
a.	Narrow spacing	125.00	
b.	Inverted overprint	—	
J4	A2 8c orange	32.50	27.50
a.	Narrow spacing	125.00	
b.	Inverted overprint	—	
J5	A2 16c mauve	32.50	27.50
a.	Narrow spacing	125.00	
b.	Inverted overprint	—	
J6	A2 24c green	21.00	37.50
a.	Narrow spacing	125.00	
b.	Inverted overprint	—	

FOOCHOW

A river port on the Min River, Foochow is the capital of Fukien province. It was one of the five original Treaty Ports, opened to foreign trade by the Treaty of Nanking in 1842. Foochow was soon the home of a large foreign community, with a considerable volume of commercial correspondence. By 1863, Shanghai was despatching mail to Foochow and at least as early as 1882 a Shanghai branch agency was operating in the port, using Shanghai stamps.

On Jan. 1, 1895, the Foochow Local Post Office was established, and Shanghai stamps were replaced with a "PAID" handstamp. Distinctive Foochow Local Post stamps were issued on Aug. 1. On Feb. 2, 1897, the Foochow Local Post was merged with the Imperial Chinese Postal Service.

All Foochow issues were lithographed by Waterlow and Sons, London, England, in sheets of 50 (5x10).

Cancellations

The more common cancellation is a circular date stamp inscribed "POSTAL SERVICE FOOCHOW CHINA." Used values are for stamps bearing this cancel. Covers are scarce. Value, $1,000.

Stamps cancelled with "POSTAL SERVICE PAGODA ANCHORAGE" command a $40 premium. Value on cover, $2,500.

Regatta Dragon Boat — A1

Perf. 13½-15
1895, Aug. 1   Unwmk.   Litho.

1	A1 ½c blue	4.00	5.00
2	A1 1c green	4.00	5.00
a.	1c aniline green	24.00	26.00
3	A1 2c orange	14.00	17.50
a.	Imperf	80.00	
4	A1 5c ultramarine	20.00	24.00
a.	Imperf	90.00	
5	A1 6c carmine	20.00	24.00
a.	Imperf	90.00	
6	A1 10c yellow green	24.00	26.00
a.	Imperf	100.00	
7	A1 15c yellow brown	32.50	37.50
8	A1 20c violet	32.50	37.50
9	A1 40c red brown	35.00	47.50

New Colors

1896, July

10	A1 ½c yellow	2.25	3.50
11	A1 1c brown	2.25	3.50

Nos. 1-11 exist with a wide variety of perforations. The following perforations are known:

½c blue: 13½; 13½x14; 14; 14x13½; 14½; 14x14½; 14½x14; 13½x15; 13½x14x14x14.

1c green: 13½; 13½x14; 14; 14x13½; 14½; 14x14½; 15; 14x14½x15; 15x14½; 13½x14x14½14½.

2c orange: 14x14½; 15; 14x15; 15x14½.

5c ultramarine: 14; 14½; 14x14½; 14½; x14; 15; 14x14x14x14½.

6c carmine: 13½; 14; 14x13½; 14x14½.

10c yellow green: 14; 14½; 14½x14; 15; 14½x15; 15x14½; 15x14.

15c yellow brown: 14½; 15.

20c violet: 13½x14; 14; 14x13½; 14½; 14½x14.

40c red brown: 14½; 15.

½c yellow: 13½; 13½x14; 14; 14x13½; 14½; 14x14½; 14½x14; 15; 14½x13½; 14x14.

1c brown: 14; 14½; 15; 14½x15; 15x14½; 13½x14x14½14½.

HANKOW

A river port in Hupeh Province, situated at the junction of the Han and Yangtze Rivers, about 600 miles upriver from Shanghai. An important trading center for tea and other exports, Hankow was served by the Shanghai Local Post as early as 1863, and a Shanghai Agency post office was established in 1878.

The Hankow Municipal Council took over postal operations on Jan. 1, 1893, and the first stamps of the Hankow Local Post were released on May 20. This was the first of the Treaty Port issues. The postal service was absorbed by the Chinese Post Office on Feb. 2, 1897.

Worker Carrying Chests of Tea — A1

Rouletted Horiz. in Color

			Unwmk.	Typo.
1893, May 20				
1	A1	2c violet, *lilac*, surfaced paper	175.00	120.00
2	A1	5c green, *salmon*, surfaced paper	450.00	225.00
a.		Printed on both sides	900.00	
3	A1	10c claret, *dull rose*, unsurfaced paper		525.00	175.00

Printed in vertical strips of 10 stamps, rouletted horizontally. Ten strips were sold in booklets of 100.

On the 2c and 5c values, the upper left Chinese character ("Hank'ow") is composed of two elements, the first being a four-sided box followed by an apostrophe. Only the second element ("Han") appears on the 10c value.

Worker Carrying Chests of Tea — A2

Yellow Stork Tower — A3

Municipal Building — A4

Rouletted Horiz. or Vert. (5c) in Color

1893, May 25-June					
4	A2	2c violet, *lilac*		17.50	14.00
a.		Surface colored paper		20.00	20.00
5	A2	5c green, *salmon*		17.50	14.00
a.		5c green, *flesh*		27.50	27.50
b.		Printed on both sides		35.00	—
6	A2	10c carmine rose, *rose*, surfaced paper		22.50	27.50
a.		Vertically bisected to pay 5c registration		—	
7	A3	20c blue, *buff*		35.00	37.50
8	A4	30c red, *yellow*		35.00	35.00

Nos. 4 and 6-8 were printed in vertical strips of 10, rouletted horizontally. No. 5 was printed in horizontal strips of 10, rouletted vertically.

Issue dates: 20c, 5/25; 30c, 5/26; 5c, 10c, early June; 2c, mid-June.

Faded copies of No. 6 are sometimes mistaken for No. 3. The unsurfaced paper of No. 3 is very rough and porous, while the surfaced paper of No. 6 is smoother and more uniform. Under shortwave ultraviolet light, No. 3 is a dark blue violet, No. 6 a bright red.

Rouletted Horiz. (2c) or Vert. (5c) in Color

			Unwmk.	Litho.
1894, June				
9	A2	2c violet, *buff*	22.50	17.50
a.		2c blue violet, *buff*	22.50	17.50
10	A2	5c green, *pale greenish buff*	27.50	17.50

Worker Carrying Chests of Tea — A5

City Gate & Pagoda — A6

Municipal Building — A7

Watermarked Chinese Characters

				Perf. 15
1894, Sept.				
11	A5	2c green	14.00	20.00
12	A5	5c red brown	18.00	20.00
13	A5	10c blue	22.50	20.00
14	A6	20c orange red	30.00	27.50
15	A7	30c violet	32.50	27.50

Printed by Waterlow and Sons, London, in sheets of 100 (10x10).

Nos. 13-15 surcharged

1896, March-May				
16	A5	ONE CENT on 10c blue	57.50	57.50
a.		Double surcharge, one inverted	1,450.	
17	A6	TWO CENTS on 20c orange red	57.50	57.50
a.		Double surcharge	1,000.	1,000.
b.		"2" with curved foot	150.00	150.00
18	A7	FIVE CENTS on 30c violet	57.50	57.50
a.		Double surcharge	700.00	700.00

Worker Carrying Chests of Tea — A8

City Gate & Pagoda — A9

Municipal Building — A10

			Perf. 11½-12	
			Unwmk.	Litho.
1894, Sept.				
19	A8	2c green	9.00	10.00
20	A8	5c red brown	14.00	10.00
a.		Horizontal pair, imperf vertically	400.00	
21	A8	10c blue	27.50	35.00
a.		10c dark blue	30.00	40.00
b.		Vertical pair, imperf horizontally	425.00	
22	A9	20c orange brown	42.50	35.00
a.		20c yellow orange	45.00	35.00
b.		Aniline ink	50.00	50.00
23	A10	30c violet	22.50	30.00
a.		30c slate violet	22.50	30.00
b.		Short 2nd "L" in "LOCAL"	35.00	35.00
c.		Extra cross bar on "T" of "CENTS"	25.00	25.00
d.		Broken "S" in "CENTS"	27.50	27.50
e.		Horiz. pair, imperf between	425.00	425.00

Nos. 21 and 21a printed on both sides, No. 22 in black, No. 23 in black and No. 23 printed on both sides are proofs.

No. 23 Surcharged

1896, August				
24	A10	ONE CENT on 30c violet, surcharged vertically	225.00	200.00
a.		Pair, one without surcharge	1,750.	
b.		On #23b	275.00	
c.		Vertical pair, imperf horizontally		
d.		Inverted surcharge (reading down)	725.00	
e.		As "a," horiz. pair, imperf between	—	

25	A10	ONE CENT on 30c violet, surcharged horizontally	24.00	24.00
a.		On 30c slate violent (#23a)	24.00	24.00
b.		On #23b	240.00	240.00
c.		On #23c	245.00	
d.		Broken "O" in "ONE"	30.00	30.00
e.		Inverted surcharge	190.00	
f.		Horiz. pair, imperf between	275.00	
g.		Vertical pair, imperf horizontally	325.00	
h.		Double surcharge	245.00	

Nos. 19-23 overprinted "P.P.C."

1897, January				
26	A8	2c green	175.00	—
27	A8	5c red brown	175.00	—
28	A8	10c blue	175.00	—
29	A9	20c orange brown	175.00	—
30	A10	30c violet	175.00	—

In January, 1897, after being ordered to close its offices on Feb. 2, 1897, the Hankow Local Post Office overprinted the stamps it had on hand with the letters "P.P.C." ("Pour Prendre Congee," French for "to take leave"). These stamps were used during the last few days that the post office was in operation. Covers exist and are very rare.

Dangerous forgeries of this overprint exist.

POSTAGE DUE STAMPS
Nos. 6-10 overprinted, Chinese in "Sung" type characters

1894				
J1	A2	2c violet, *buff*	160.00	200.00
J2	A2	5c green, *pale green*	160.00	175.00
J3	A2	10c carmine, *rose*	145.00	200.00
J4	A3	20c blue, *buff*	160.00	200.00
J5	A4	30c red, *yellow*	160.00	200.00

Nos. 6-10 Overprinted, Chinese in ordinary characters, 2mm space between "POSTAGE" and "DUE"

Type 1 — small top character

Type 2 — large top character

Two types of overprint: Type 1, first vertical radical longer, top of left character 2½mm wide; Type 2, first vertical radical shorter, top of left character 3mm wide.

1894-96				
J6	A2	2c violet, *buff*, type 1 ovpt.	22.50	22.50
a.		Inverted overprint	350.00	
b.		Double overprint	325.00	
c.		"E" of "POSTAGE" omitted	225.00	
d.		Type 2 ovpt.	240.00	350.00
J7	A2	5c green, *pale green*, type 1 ovpt.	30.00	30.00
a.		Inverted overprint	325.00	
b.		Double overprint	325.00	
c.		Double overprint, both inverted	450.00	
d.		Type 2 ovpt.	240.00	350.00
J8	A2	10c carmine, *rose* type 1 ovpt.	30.00	30.00
a.		Inverted overprint	400.00	
b.		Double overprint	400.00	
c.		Double overprint, both inverted	725.00	
d.		Type 2 ovpt.	175.00	200.00
J9	A3	20c blue, *buff*, type 1 ovpt.	125.00	115.00
a.		Inverted overprint	525.00	
b.		Double overprint	525.00	
c.		"E" of "POSTAGE" omitted	350.00	
d.		Type 2 ovpt.	150.00	
J10	A4	30c red, *yellow*, type 1 ovpt.	70.00	57.50
a.		Inverted overprint	450.00	
b.		Double overprint	450.00	
c.		Triple overprint	—	
d.		"E" of "POSTAGE" omitted	290.00	275.00
e.		Wide space (4¼mm) between Chinese characters	—	
f.		Type 2 ovpt.	125.00	135.00

Nos. 6, 7, 9 overprinted, 3mm space between "POSTAGE" and "DUE"

1895				
J11	A2	2c violet, *buff*, type 1 ovpt.	575.00	575.00
a.		Type 2 ovpt.	625.00	625.00
J12	A2	10c carmine, *rose* type 1 ovpt.	525.00	525.00
a.		Type 2 ovpt.	625.00	
J13	A3	20c blue, *buff*, type 1 ovpt.	575.00	575.00
a.		Type 2 ovpt.	625.00	625.00

ICHANG

A river port on the north side of the Yangtze River, about 1,100 miles from

---

Shanghai and 400 miles below Hankow. Ichang was the head of steam navigation on the Yangtze and so was the junction point of trade — most importantly, opium, tung oil and silk — between Szechuan and the rest of China.

Ichang was opened as a Treaty Port in 1876, and the first settlement of foreign traders soon followed, in 1878. The Ichang Local Post Office was established in Nov., 1894. Along with the other Treaty Port local posts, it was absorbed into the Chinese Post Office on Feb. 2, 1897.

All Ichang basic issues were lithographed by Tokyo Tsukiji Type Foundry Co., Tokyo, Japan.

Coin-like Design — A1

Brass Cash — A2

Ancient "Ichang" Character — A3

Stylized Pa Kua, "1894" — A4

Modern "Ichang" Character — A5

Pheasant — A6

Otter — A7

Map of the Foreign
Settlement in
Ichang — A8

Narrow Setting
Stamps Printed 3.5-4mm apart
Perf. 10¾-11½

			Unwmk.	Litho.
1894, Dec. 1				
1	A1	½ ca. brown	14.00	18.00
a.		Horiz. pair, imperf between	400.00	
2	A2	1 ca. olive brown	14.00	22.50
a.		Vert. pair, imperf between	575.00	350.00
3	A3	2 ca. red violet	24.00	22.50
4	A4	3 ca. gray	40.00	29.00
5	A5	5 ca. brown rose	20.00	29.00
a.		Horiz. pair, imperf between	790.00	
6	A6	1 m green	72.50	115.00
7	A7	15 ca. blue	70.00	130.00
8	A8	3 m carmine	62.50	85.00
a.		Vert. pair, imperf between	790.00	

Type A   Type B
Wide Setting
Stamps printed 5mm apart

Two types of 1 ca. value: Type A, 2 small
triangles blank, open; Type B, 2 small triangles
shaded closed.

1895				
9	A1	½ ca. red brown	17.50	9.00
10	A2	1 ca. bister brown (Type A)	42.50	35.00
11	A2	1 ca. bister brown (Type B)	22.50	17.50
12	A4	3 ca. gray lilac	35.00	22.50
a.		Horiz. pair, imperf vert.	—	
13	A3	2 ca. red violet	30.00	27.50
14	A8	3 m carmine	57.50	50.00

Handstamped in
Black

1896				
		Surcharged in Violet		
15	A8	2 ca. on 3m carmine (#8)	800.00	800.00
16	A8	2 ca. on 3m carmine (#14)	225.00	145.00
		Surcharged in Black		
17	A8	2 ca. on 3m carmine (#8)	125.00	100.00
18	A8	2 ca. on 3m carmine (#14)	225.00	145.00
a.		Pair, one without surcharge	1,450.	
19	A8	2 ca. on 1 ca. bister brown (#10)	35.00	32.50
20	A8	2 ca. on 1 ca. bister brown (#11)	30.00	22.50
a.		Inverted surcharge	—	—
b.		Double surcharge	—	—

KEWKIANG

A river port in Kiangsi Province, on
the Yangtze River, 458 miles upriver
from Shanghai. Kewkiang was opened
to foreign trade in 1858 and it appears
that at least as early as 1865 an agent
of the Shanghai Local Post was receiving and despatching mails. Shanghai
Local Post stamps were used from Jan.
1, 1893, to June 1, 1894, when the
Kewkiang Local Post took over postal
operations. On Feb. 2, 1897, the Chinese Post Office took over postal services between cities, though the Kewkiang Local Post continued limited local
delivery until late August.

All basic Kewkiang stamps were typographed by Central China Press,
Kewkiang.

Pagoda — A1

Center
Stroke
Omitted

"Kiang" in
Ancient
Characters
A2

"Kiang" in
Modern
Characters
A3

"Kiang" in Modified
Characters — A4

Unwmk.

			Typo.	Perf. 12
1894, June 1				
		On Native Paper		
1	A1	½c black, rose	4.00	4.00
a.		Stroke missing in "Kiang"	100.00	85.00
b.		As "a," corrected by hand	110.00	110.00
c.		Double impression	145.00	
2	A1	½c red, yellow	4.00	4.00
a.		Stroke missing in "Kiang"	97.50	85.00
b.		As "a," corrected by hand	110.00	110.00
c.		Horiz. pair, imperf vert.	—	
3	A2	1c gray black	4.00	4.00
4	A3	2c vermilion	8.00	9.00
a.		2c red, on European paper	12.00	11.00
5	A4	5c slate blue, yellow	10.00	9.00
6	A3	6c yellow	12.00	12.00
a.		6c ocher, on European paper	52.50	42.50
7	A2	10c black, yellow buff	17.00	17.00
		10c black, yellow	17.00	17.00
8	A4	15c red, yellow	17.00	20.00
a.		"1" of "15" omitted	225.00	175.00
9	A4	20c blue, rose	22.50	22.50
10	A3	40c black, red	24.00	27.50

Lu Shan Hills
and Bridge
Over Lung K'ai
Ho
Creek — A5

"Little Orphan
Rock" — A6

1894, June 23				
		On Native Paper		
11	A5	½c black, rose	4.00	9.00
a.		Horiz. pair, imperf between	250.00	
12	A5	½c red, yellow	4.00	9.00
1894, August		**On European Paper**		
13	A6	1c black	5.00	9.00
a.		Horiz. pair, imperf between	325.00	
b.		Double impression	350.00	

Nos. 6, 8, 9
surcharged in black
or blue (#16)

ONE
1
CENT.

1896, August				
14	A4	HALF CENT on 20c	22.50	22.50
a.		Double surcharge	290.00	
b.		"1" of "½" inverted	32.50	32.50
c.		Inverted surcharge	275.00	
d.		Surcharge on reverse	400.00	
15	A4	ONE CENT on 15c	22.50	22.50
a.		Blue surcharge	290.00	110.00
b.		Surcharged on both sides	290.00	
c.		Pair, one without surcharge	750.00	
d.		On #8a	325.00	
e.		Wider space (3mm) between "1" and "CENT"	55.00	

16	A3	TWO CENTS on 6c (BI)	25.00	25.00
a.		Black surcharge	300.00	250.00

POSTAGE DUE STAMPS

Nos. 4a//13
overprinted

Postage
Due

Four types of overprint: type A, narrow setting, overprint slope 20 degrees, "D" larger
(2½mm) and under "os" of "Postage;" type B,
wide setting, overprint slope 20 degrees, "D"
larger (2½mm) and under "st" of "Postage;"
type C, wide setting, overprint slope 30-35
degrees, "D" smaller (2mm) and under "st" of
"Postage;" type D, wide setting, overprint
slope 40-45 degrees, "D" smaller (2mm) and
under "ta" of "Postage."

		Overprinted Type A		
1895, Sept.				
J1		½c black, rose	57.50	70.00
a.		"Postag"	325.00	325.00
J2		½c red, yellow	57.50	70.00
a.		"Postag"	325.00	325.00
b.		Inverted overprint	—	325.00
J3		1c black	52.50	70.00
a.		"Postag"	325.00	325.00
J4		2c red	125.00	225.00
a.		"Postag"	650.00	650.00
b.		Inverted overprint	—	

		Overprinted Type B		
1896				
J5		½c black, rose	30.00	17.00
a.		Inverted overprint	325.00	290.00
J6		½c red, yellow	22.50	17.00
a.		Inverted overprint	325.00	290.00
J7		1c black	20.00	16.00
J8		2c red	22.50	22.00
a.		Inverted overprint	325.00	290.00
J9		5c slate blue, yellow	30.00	20.00
a.		Inverted overprint	325.00	350.00
J10		6c yellow	32.50	22.00
J11		10c black, yellow buff	35.00	28.00
J12		15c red, yellow	40.00	40.00
a.		On #8a	350.00	350.00
J13		20c blue rose	57.50	57.50
J14		40c black, red	57.50	57.50
		Overprinted in Red		
J15		1c black	175.00	175.00
J16		10c black, yellow buff	850.00	850.00

Dangerous forgeries of Nos. J15-J16 exist.

		Overprinted Type C		
J17		½c black, rose	30.00	30.00
J18		½c red, yellow	22.50	17.00
J19		1c black	20.00	16.00
J20		2c red	22.50	22.00
J21		5c slate blue, yellow	30.00	20.00
J22		6c yellow	32.50	22.50
J23		10c black, yellow buff	35.00	27.50
J24		15c red, yellow	40.00	40.00
J25		20c blue rose	57.50	57.50
J26		40c black, red	57.50	57.50

		Overprinted Type D		
J27		½c black, rose	30.00	27.50
J28		½c red, yellow	32.50	27.50
J29		1c black	35.00	22.50
J30		2c red	27.50	27.50
J31		5c slate blue, yellow	30.00	27.50
J32		6c yellow	30.00	27.50
J33		10c black, yellow buff	30.00	30.00
J34		15c red, yellow	32.50	32.50
J35		20c blue rose	42.50	52.50
J36		40c black, red	52.50	62.50

NANKING

A river port on the Yangtze, about 200
miles upriver from Shanghai. An
ancient and historical city, Nanking was
opened to foreign settlement and trade
by the Treaty of Peking in 1860. British
and French settlement began in 1865,
and a European community gradually
developed. Nanking became a center of
European missionary and educational
work, and in 1885 an office of the
Shanghai Agency was established. By
1896 the Nanking Local Post was operating in the city and on Sept. 20, 1896,
the first Nanking local stamps were
issued. Postal operations were taken
over by the Chinese Post Office on Feb.
2, 1897.

All Nanking stamps were lithographed by Tokyo Tsukiji Type Foundry
Co., Tokyo, Japan.

Stone Men
at Approach
to Ming
Tomb — A1

The Drum
Tower — A2

Stone
Elephants at
Approach to
Ming
Tomb — A3

Lotus Lake
Scene — A4

Central Hall
of the
Confucian
Temple — A5

The Great
Bell — A6

"NANKING LOCAL POST" in double-lined Letters
Perf. 11½

			Unwmk.	Litho.
1896, Sept. 20				
1	A1	½c gray	14.00	16.00
a.		Horiz. pair, imperf between	650.00	
b.		Vert. pair, imperf between	650.00	
2	A2	1c rose	14.00	16.00
a.		Horiz. pair, imperf between	875.00	
3	A3	2c gray green	30.00	27.50
a.		Horiz. pair, imperf between	875.00	
4	A4	3c orange yellow	26.00	20.00
a.		3c yellow	26.00	20.00
5	A5	4c claret	30.00	30.00
6	A6	5c violet	32.50	27.50
7	A2	10c yellow green	37.50	27.50
a.		10c deep green	37.50	37.50
8	A2	20c brown	32.50	27.50

Nos. 1-8 were printed in sheets of 25 (5x5).

"NANKING LOCAL POST" in single-lined Letters

1896				
9	A1	½c salmon rose	13.00	14.00

No. 9 was printed in sheets of 25 (5x5).

"NANKING LOCAL POST" in single-lined Letters

1896			**Perf. 12½**	
10	A1	½c lilac brown	16.00	18.00
11	A2	1c rose	27.50	22.50
12	A3	2c green	32.50	27.50
13	A4	3c yellow	35.00	32.50
a.		3c orange yellow		
14	A5	4c brown	37.50	35.00
15	A6	5c blue	37.50	35.00
1897			**Imperf**	
16	A2	1c rose		

Nos. 10-16 were printed in sheets of 100
(10x10).

WEI HAI WEI

A port in Shantung province which,
with adjoining territory, was leased to

Great Britain in 1899. The Cornabe Co. operated a private courier post to Chefoo from Dec. 1898 until Mar. 1899, when a Chinese Imperial Post Office was opened. This was replaced by a British Post Office in Sept., 1899, which provided postal service, using Hong Kong stamps, until the territory was returned to China on Oct. 1, 1930.

Although not one of the Treaty Ports, Wei Hai Wei is generally collected with those issues.

A1   A2

Before regular printed stamps were available, provisional stamps were made by impressing a Cornabe & Co. double circle chop on red native paper in black. The 2c stamp was handstamped once and "2c" was handwritten in the top right and left corners; the letters "C," standing for "Courier" and "P," standing for "Post," were written in the left and right lower corners respectively. The 5c stamps were produced by making two impressions of the Cornabe & Co. double circle chop on red native paper, one of which was inverted. "5c" was handwritten in each of the upper corners, and the words "Courier Post" were written below the stamped impressions. These stamps were signed in continuous horizontal rows on the back of the sheet by G.K. Fergusson, the Honorary Postmaster. 8 sheets of 98 stamps (14x7) or 784 stamps of the 2c denomination and 4 sheets of 98 stamps (14x7) or 392 stamps of the 5c denomination were produced.

1898, Dec. 8   Unwmk.   Imperf

1	A1	2c black, *red*	600.	700.
a.		Vertical signature of G.K. Fergusson	1,200.	1,200.
b.		"P.C." for "C.P."	1,500.	1,500.
c.		Chop inverted	1,500.	
d.		Chop double	1,500.	
2	A2	5c black, *red*	2,500.	1,700.
a.		Vertical signature of G.K. Fergusson	2,100.	2,100.

A3

1899, Jan. 9   Litho.   Perf. 11

3	A3	2c red	175.00	225.00
4	A3	5c olive green	275.00	325.00
a.		Tete-beche pair	—	
b.		Horiz. pair, imperf between	3,000.	3,000.
c.		5c emerald green	350.00	375.00
d.		5c green	350.00	350.00

Nos. 3-4 were lithographed by Kelly & Walsh, Shanghai, in sheets of 64 (8x8) stamps.

Reprints exist on thin paper.

WUHU

A port city on the Yangtze River, 282 miles from the sea. Wuhu was opened up as a Treaty Port in 1876, and a customs house was established in 1877. The Shanghai Local Post was operating in Wuhu by 1888. In June, 1894, the foreign community, composed mostly of Christian missionaries, established a local post, and stamps were issued in Nov. 1894. The Wuhu Local Post was replaced by the Chinese Post Office on Feb. 2, 1897, although it continued to provide service within the city for a short time after.

All basic Wuhu stamps were printed by the Lithographic Society of Shanghai.

Wild Fowl — A1   Rice Field — A2

Pheasants A3   Wuhu Pagoda A4

"Abundance" ("Fu") — A5

First Printing

11¾, 12¼ and compound

1894, Nov. 26   Unwmk.   Litho.

1	A1	½c black	20.00	14.00
a.		Imperf	30.00	20.00
b.		Perf 12	20.00	20.00
2	A2	½c green	14.00	11.00
a.		Perf 11x11¾	50.00	40.00
3	A3	1c brown	19.00	13.00
a.		Perf 12	24.00	24.00
4	A2	2c yellow	16.00	14.00
a.		Imperf	24.00	24.00
5	A4	5c carmine	16.00	19.00
a.		Imperf	24.00	24.00
6	A5	6c blue	22.50	22.50
7	A3	10c brown red	30.00	30.00
8	A4	15c olive green	30.00	30.00
9	A5	20c red	30.00	29.00
10	A1	40c brown	37.50	37.50

Second Printing

1894   Perf. 11

11	A1	½c grayish black	12.00	7.00
a.		Imperf	18.00	12.00
12	A2	½c yellow green	10.00	6.00
a.		½c deep green	10.00	6.00
b.		Imperf	20.00	20.00
13	A3	1c grayish brown	16.00	9.00
a.		Imperf	35.00	
14	A2	2c orange yellow	14.00	13.00
a.		Imperf	35.00	
15	A4	5c red orange	18.00	20.00
a.		Imperf	30.00	30.00
16	A5	6c gray blue	18.00	19.00
a.		Imperf	30.00	30.00
17	A3	10c brown red	32.50	26.00
a.		Imperf	50.00	42.50
18	A4	15c olive green	30.00	26.00
a.		Imperf	40.00	
19	A5	20c orange red	27.50	24.00
a.		Imperf	40.00	
20	A1	40c yellow brown	32.50	32.50
a.		Imperf	50.00	

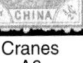

Nos. 1-10 surcharged with denomination in Chinese in black or red (R)

1895   11¾, 12¼ and compound

21	A1	½c black (R)	22.50	19.00
a.		Perf 12¼	30.00	
22	A2	½c green	18.00	16.00
23	A3	1c brown	14.00	11.00
a.		Perf 12	20.00	16.00
24	A2	2c yellow	16.00	14.00
25	A4	5c carmine	22.00	22.00
a.		Inverted surcharge	240.00	
26	A5	6c blue	32.50	32.50
27	A3	10c brown red	35.00	32.50
28	A4	15c olive green	37.50	32.50
29	A5	20c red	47.50	50.00
30	A1	40c brown	70.00	70.00

Nos. 11-20 surcharged with denomination in Chinese

31	A1	½c grayish black (R)	22.00	19.00
a.		Inverted surcharge	240.00	
32	A1	½c grayish black (Black)	160.00	
a.		Inverted surcharge	475.00	
33	A2	½c green	18.00	16.00
a.		Inverted surcharge	240.00	
34	A3	1c brown	14.00	11.00
a.		Inverted surcharge	240.00	
b.		Horiz. pair, imperf between	450.00	
35	A2	2c orange yellow	16.00	14.00
a.		Inverted surcharge	240.00	

36	A4	5c red orange	22.00	22.00
a.		Inverted surcharge	240.00	
37	A5	6c gray blue	32.50	32.50
a.		Inverted surcharge	240.00	
38	A3	10c brown red	35.00	32.50
39	A4	15c olive green	37.50	32.50
40	A5	20c red	47.50	
a.		Inverted surcharge	240.00	
41	A1	40c yellow brown	70.00	70.00
a.		Inverted surcharge	240.00	

Nos. 3//14 surcharged in black or red (R)

1895, Nov.

42	A3	½c on 1c brown, perf 11¾ (R)	26.00	20.00
a.		"2" with straight foot	95.00	65.00
b.		Perf 11	30.00	27.50
c.		As "b," "2" with straight foot	145.00	110.00
d.		Perf 12¼	26.00	20.00
e.		As "d," "2" with straight foot	200.00	
f.		1c yellow brown, perf 11	275.00	275.00
43	A3	½c on 1c brown, perf 12¼ (Black)	375.00	
a.		On 1c yellow brown, perf 11	375.00	
b.		Vert. pair, red and black surcharges setenant, perf 11	500.00	
c.		Vert. pair, red and black surcharges setenant, perf 12¼	500.00	
44	A2	5c on 2c yellow, perf 11	30.00	32.50
a.		Perf 12	32.50	
b.		Double surcharge	725.00	

Other stamps with "5 Cent" surcharges, with and without a bar through the original value, exist but are of speculative nature and had no postal validity.

Cranes A6

Chinese Character ("Fortunate") A7

Chinese Characters ("Wuhu") — A8

Designs: 2c, 10c, owl; 6c, 40c, stag.

1896, Feb.   Perf. 10-10½

45	A6	½c lilac	26.00	19.00
46	A7	½c yellow	19.00	16.00
47	A8	1c blue	16.00	15.00
48	A6	2c green	37.50	32.50
49	A7	5c yellow green	27.50	25.00
50	A6	6c yellow brown	35.00	32.50
51	A6	10c rose	47.50	45.00
52	A6	15c carmine	50.00	42.50
53	A8	20c rose	32.50	35.00
54	A6	40c carmine	45.00	45.00

Surcharged with values in Chinese characters

55	A6	½c lilac	32.50	26.00
56	A7	½c yellow	19.00	19.00
a.		Inverted surcharge	190.00	125.00
57	A8	1c blue	16.00	14.00
a.		Inverted surcharge	160.00	
b.		Vert. pair, one stamp with surcharge omitted	325.00	
58	A6	2c green	47.50	57.50
a.		Inverted surcharge	325.00	225.00
59	A7	5c yellow green	32.50	26.00
a.		Inverted surcharge	325.00	325.00
60	A6	6c yellow brown	32.50	35.00
a.		Inverted surcharge	190.00	190.00
61	A6	10c rose	77.50	65.00
a.		Inverted surcharge	325.00	225.00
62	A6	15c carmine	90.00	65.00
a.		Inverted surcharge	300.00	190.00
63	A8	20c rose	50.00	40.00
a.		Inverted surcharge	190.00	130.00
64	A6	40c carmine	57.50	37.50
a.		Inverted surcharge	190.00	130.00

In Jan. 1897, after being ordered to close its offices on Feb. 2, 1897, the Wuhu Local Post Office overprinted the stamps it had on hand with the letters "P.P.C." ("Pour Prendre Congee," French for "to take leave"). These stamps were used during the last few days that the post office was in operation. Covers exist and are very rare.

Nos. 45-54 overprinted **P.P.C.**

Nos. 45-54 Overprinted in Black

1897, Jan.

65	A6	½c lilac	32.50	37.50
66	A7	½c yellow	32.50	37.50
a.		Double overprint		
67	A8	1c blue	32.50	37.50
68	A6	2c green	45.00	77.50
69	A7	5c yellow green	32.50	57.50
70	A6	6c yellow brown	35.00	47.50
71	A6	10c rose	65.00	77.50
72	A6	15c carmine	45.00	77.50
73	A8	20c rose	30.00	50.00
74	A6	40c carmine	37.50	77.50

Nos. 45-54 Overprinted in Red

75	A6	½c lilac	37.50	37.50
76	A7	½c yellow	35.00	45.00
77	A8	1c blue	32.50	65.00
78	A6	2c green	45.00	77.50
79	A7	5c yellow green	32.50	57.50
80	A6	6c yellow brown	37.50	47.50
81	A6	10c rose	77.50	77.50
82	A6	15c carmine	50.00	77.50
83	A8	20c rose	30.00	50.00
84	A6	40c carmine	77.50	77.50

Nos. 55-64 Overprinted in Black Above Chinese Characters

85	A6	½c lilac	20.00	17.50
86	A7	½c yellow	14.00	20.00
87	A8	1c blue	20.00	19.00
88	A6	2c green	37.50	45.00
89	A7	5c yellow green	19.00	20.00
90	A6	6c yellow brown	26.00	30.00
91	A6	10c rose	65.00	50.00
92	A6	15c carmine	57.50	50.00
93	A8	20c rose	50.00	57.50
94	A6	40c carmine	50.00	57.50

Nos. 55//62 Overprinted in Red Above Chinese Characters

95	A6	½c lilac	30.00	25.00
96	A7	½c yellow	19.00	19.00
97	A8	1c blue	19.00	19.00
98	A6	2c green	57.50	57.50
99	A7	5c yellow green	22.00	24.00
100	A6	6c yellow brown	30.00	32.50
101	A6	15c carmine	70.00	57.50

Nos. 55-64 Overprinted in Black Below Chinese Characters

102	A6	½c lilac	20.00	18.00
103	A7	½c yellow	17.00	22.00
104	A8	1c blue	16.00	26.00
105	A6	2c green	35.00	45.00
106	A7	5c yellow green	19.00	20.00
107	A6	6c yellow brown	24.00	30.00
108	A6	10c rose	65.00	50.00
109	A6	15c carmine	57.50	50.00
110	A8	20c rose	45.00	57.50
111	A6	40c carmine	50.00	57.50

Nos. 55//62 Overprinted in Red Below Chinese Characters

112	A6	½c lilac	30.00	30.00
113	A7	½c yellow	20.00	24.00
114	A8	1c blue	20.00	24.00
115	A6	2c green	57.50	55.00
116	A7	5c yellow green	24.00	24.00
117	A6	6c yellow brown	27.50	32.50
118	A6	15c carmine	70.00	57.50

POSTAGE DUE STAMPS

Regular postage stamps overprinted in black or red (R)

There are three types of overprint: type 1, "P" longer upright, extending to bottom; type 2, "P" short upright, "P" with loops at left; type 3, "P" short upright, "P" without loops at left. All three types exist on Nos. J1-J20, and types 1 and 2 exist on Nos. J28-J37.

Nos. 1-10 Overprinted

J1	A1	½c black (R)	12.00	12.00
a.		Inverted overprint	175.00	

J2	A1	½c black	190.00	
J3	A2	½c green	13.00	12.00
a.		Inverted overprint	175.00	
b.		Perf 11x11¾	60.00	60.00
J4	A3	1c brown	27.50	27.50
a.		Inverted overprint	175.00	
b.		Perf 12¼	27.50	27.50
J5	A2	2c yellow	22.00	16.00
a.		Inverted overprint	175.00	175.00
J6	A4	5c carmine	22.00	20.00
J7	A5	6c blue	27.50	26.00
a.		Inverted overprint	175.00	175.00
J8	A3	10c brown red	37.50	35.00
a.		Inverted overprint	175.00	175.00
J9	A4	15c olive green	37.50	35.00
a.		Inverted overprint	175.00	175.00
J10	A5	20c red	52.50	52.50
a.		Inverted overprint	175.00	175.00
J11	A1	40c brown	65.00	55.00
a.		Inverted overprint	175.00	175.00

Nos. 11-20 Overprinted

J12	A1	½c black (R)	12.00	12.00
a.		Inverted overprint	175.00	
J13	A1	½c black	190.00	
J14	A2	½c green	12.00	12.00
a.		Inverted overprint	175.00	
b.		Perf 11x11¾	60.00	60.00
J15	A3	1c brown	14.00	12.00
a.		Inverted overprint	175.00	
J16	A2	2c orange yellow	22.00	16.00
a.		Inverted overprint	175.00	
J17	A4	5c carmine	19.00	18.00
a.		Inverted overprint	175.00	175.00
J18	A5	6c gray blue	27.50	26.00
a.		Inverted overprint	175.00	175.00
J19	A3	10c brown red	37.50	35.00
a.		Inverted overprint	175.00	175.00
J20	A4	15c olive green	37.50	35.00
a.		Inverted overprint	175.00	175.00
b.		"a" of "Postage" omitted	275.00	
J21	A5	20c red	50.00	50.00
a.		Inverted overprint	175.00	175.00
b.		Vert. overprint, reading down	500.00	500.00
J22	A1	40c brown	65.00	55.00
a.		Inverted overprint	175.00	175.00

Nos. 3//8 Overprinted Type 3

J23	A3	1c brown, perf 11¾	—	—
a.		Perf 12¼	—	—
b.		Imperf, "t" of "Postage" omitted	—	—
J24	A2	2c orange yellow, imperf, "t" of "Postage" omitted	—	—
J25	A4	5c carmine, "t" of "Postage" omitted	—	—
J26	A3	10c brown red	—	—
J27	A4	15c olive green, imperf, overprint inverted	—	—

Nos. 45-54 Overprinted

J28	A6	½c lilac	30.00	26.00
a.		Inverted overprint	190.00	130.00
J29	A7	½c yellow	16.00	16.00
a.		Inverted overprint	130.00	90.00
J30	A8	1c blue	19.00	22.00
J31	A6	2c green	50.00	45.00
a.		Inverted overprint	325.00	240.00
J32	A7	5c yellow green	30.00	26.00
J33	A6	6c yellow brown	37.50	35.00
J34	A6	10c rose	65.00	57.50
a.		Inverted overprint	325.00	240.00
J35	A6	15c carmine	110.00	77.50
a.		"a" of "Postage" omitted	350.00	87.50
J36	A8	20c rose	65.00	60.00
J37	A6	40c carmine	90.00	77.50

Nos. J28-J37 Overprinted

J38	A6	½c lilac	30.00	25.00
a.		Red overprint	60.00	60.00
b.		Overprint reading down	—	
J39	A7	½c yellow	25.00	20.00
a.		Overprint reading down	175.00	150.00
J40	A8	1c blue	25.00	20.00
a.		Red overprint, reading down	175.00	150.00
J41	A6	2c green	45.00	40.00
J42	A7	5c yellow green	30.00	25.00
J43	A6	6c yellow brown	40.00	35.00
J44	A6	10c rose	60.00	50.00
J45	A6	15c carmine	60.00	50.00
J46	A8	20c rose	60.00	50.00
J47	A6	40c carmine	60.00	50.00

CILICIA

sə-'li-sh ̠ē ̠-ə

LOCATION — A territory of Turkey, in Southeastern Asia Minor
AREA — 6,238 sq. mi.
POP. — 383,645
CAPITAL — Adana

British and French forces occupied Cilicia in 1918 and in 1919 its control

was transferred to the French. Eventually part of Cilicia was assigned to the French Mandated Territory of Syria but by the Lausanne Treaty of 1923 which fixed the boundary between Syria and Turkey, Cilicia reverted to Turkey.

40 Paras = 1 Piaster

Issued under French Occupation

Numbers in parentheses are those of basic Turkish or French stamps.

Turkish Stamps of 1913-19 Handstamped

Perf. 11½, 12, 12½, 13½
1919   Unwmk.

On Pictorial Issue of 1913

2	A24	2pa red lilac (254)	9.00	9.00
		Never hinged	16.00	
a.		Inverted overprint	17.50	17.50
		Never hinged	30.00	
b.		Double overprint	20.00	20.00
		Never hinged	30.00	
3	A25	4pa dk brown (255)	7.25	7.25
		Never hinged	14.50	
a.		Inverted overprint	17.50	17.50
		Never hinged	30.00	
b.		Double overprint	20.00	20.00
		Never hinged	30.00	
4	A27	6pa dk blue (257)	27.50	20.00
		Never hinged	52.50	
a.		Inverted overprint	32.50	32.50
		Never hinged	65.00	
b.		Double overprint	32.50	32.50
		Never hinged	65.00	
5	A32	1¾pi slate & red brown (262)	8.75	8.75
		Never hinged	17.50	
a.		Inverted overprint	17.50	17.50
		Never hinged	30.00	
b.		Double overprint	20.00	20.00
		Never hinged	30.00	

On Issue of 1915

6	A17	1pi blue (300)	3.75	3.75
		Never hinged	6.25	
a.		Inverted overprint	8.00	8.00
		Never hinged	16.50	
b.		Double overprint	8.00	8.00
		Never hinged	16.50	
c.		In pair with unovptd. stamp	20.00	20.00
		Never hinged	40.00	
7	A21	20pa carmine rose (318)	13.50	12.00
		Never hinged	27.50	
a.		Inverted overprint	20.00	20.00
		Never hinged	40.00	
b.		Double overprint	25.00	25.00
		Never hinged	40.00	
9	A22	20pa carmine rose (330)	35.00	32.50
		Never hinged	80.00	
a.		Inverted overprint	40.00	40.00
		Never hinged	80.00	
b.		Double overprint	40.00	40.00
		Never hinged	80.00	

On Commemorative Issue of 1916

9A	A41	5pa green (345)	130.00	92.50
		Never hinged	260.00	
10	A41	20pa ultra (347)	7.25	7.25
		Never hinged	12.50	
a.		Double overprint	12.00	12.00
		Never hinged	24.00	
11	A41	1pi violet & black (348)	9.50	9.50
		Never hinged	12.00	
a.		Double overprint	13.50	13.50
		Never hinged	27.50	
b.		Perf 12½	9.50	9.50
		Never hinged	17.50	
c.		In pair with unovptd. stamp	16.00	16.00
		Never hinged	32.50	
12	A41	5pi yel brown & black (349)	4.00	4.00
		Never hinged	6.25	
a.		Inverted overprint	6.50	6.50
		Never hinged	13.50	

On Issue of 1916-18

13	A44	10pa grn (424)	8.75	8.75
		Never hinged	17.50	
a.		Perf 11½ (424a)	8.75	8.75
		Never hinged	17.50	
b.		Double overprint	13.50	3.50
		Never hinged	27.50	

14	A47	50pa ultra (428)	45.00	35.00
		Never hinged	100.00	
a.		Perf 11½ (428a)	45.00	35.00
		Never hinged	100.00	
b.		Double overprint	47.50	45.00
		Never hinged	110.00	
15	A51	25pi carmine, straw (434)	8.75	8.75
		Never hinged	17.50	
16	A52	50pi car (437)	8.75	8.75
		Never hinged	17.50	
17	A52	50pi ind (438)	32.50	32.50
		Never hinged	67.50	

On Issue of 1917

18	A53	5pi on 2pa Prus blue (547)	15.00	15.00
		Never hinged	32.50	
a.		Perf 11½ (547c)	15.00	15.00
		Never hinged	32.50	

On Issue of 1919

19	A47	50pa ultra (555)	40.00	32.50
		Never hinged	87.50	
a.		Perf 11½ (555a)	40.00	32.50
		Never hinged	87.50	
b.		Double overprint	47.50	40.00
		Never hinged	100.00	
20	A48	2pi org brown & indigo (556)	40.00	32.50
		Never hinged	87.50	
21	A49	5pi pale blue & black (557a)	40.00	32.50
		Never hinged	87.50	
a.		Perf 11½ (557)	40.00	32.50
		Never hinged	87.50	
b.		Perf 11½x12½ (557b)	40.00	32.50
		Never hinged	87.50	
c.		Double overprint	47.50	40.00
		Never hinged	100.00	

On Newspaper Stamp of 1916

22	A10	5pa on 10pa gray green (P137)	4.75	4.75
		Never hinged	9.50	
d.		Inverted overprint	11.00	11.00
		Never hinged	24.00	
e.		Double overprint	14.00	14.00
		Never hinged	28.00	

On Semi-Postal Stamps of 1915

22A	A21	20pa carmine rose (B8)	92.50	80.00
		Never hinged	190.00	
22B	A21	1pi ultra (B9)	2,250.	1,700.
		Never hinged	—	
22C	A21	1pi ultra (B13)	1,900.	1,200.

On Semi-Postal Stamps of 1916

23	A17	1pi bl (B19)	10.50	10.50
		Never hinged	21.00	
a.		Inverted overprint	16.00	16.00
		Never hinged	32.50	
b.		Double overprint	16.00	16.00
		Never hinged	32.50	
c.		Perf 13¼	10.50	10.50
		Never hinged	21.00	
24	A21	20pa carmine rose (B28)	3.75	3.75
		Never hinged	6.50	
a.		Inverted overprint	7.50	7.50
		Never hinged	15.50	
b.		Double overprint	7.50	7.50
		Never hinged	15.50	
25	A21	1pi (B29)	8.75	8.75
		Never hinged	17.50	
a.		Inverted overprint	15.00	15.00
		Never hinged	30.00	
b.		Double overprint	15.00	15.00
		Never hinged	30.00	

Turkish Stamps of 1913-18 Handstamped

1919   **On Pictorial Issue of 1913**

31	A24	2pa red lil (254)	4.00	4.00
		Never hinged	6.75	
a.		Inverted overprint	6.50	6.50
		Never hinged	13.50	
b.		Double overprint	6.50	6.50
		Never hinged	13.50	
c.		In pair with unovptd. stamp	16.00	16.00
		Never hinged	32.50	
32	A25	4pa dk brn (255)	15.00	15.00
		Never hinged	32.50	
a.		Inverted overprint	22.00	22.00
		Never hinged	45.00	
b.		Double overprint	22.00	22.00
		Never hinged	45.00	

On Issue of 1915

33	A17	1pi blue (300)	13.50	13.50
		Never hinged	27.50	
a.		Inverted overprint	20.00	20.00
		Never hinged	40.00	

b.		Double overprint	20.00	20.00
		Never hinged	40.00	
34	A22	20pa car rose (330)	5.00	5.00
		Never hinged	9.50	
a.		Inverted overprint	6.00	9.50
		Never hinged	20.00	
b.		Double overprint	9.50	9.50
		Never hinged	20.00	
c.		In pair with unovptd. stamp	20.00	20.00
		Never hinged	40.00	

On Commemorative Issue of 1916

35	A41	20pa ultra (347)	15.00	15.00
		Never hinged	32.50	
a.		Inverted overprint	22.00	22.00
		Never hinged	45.00	
b.		Perf 12½ (347a)	15.00	15.00
		Never hinged	32.50	
36	A41	1pi vio & blk (348)	3.25	3.25
		Never hinged	5.50	
a.		Inverted overprint	6.50	6.50
		Never hinged	13.50	
b.		Perf 12½ (348a)	3.25	3.25
		Never hinged	5.50	

On Issue of 1917

40	A53	5pi on 2pa Prus bl (547)	13.50	13.50
		Never hinged	27.50	
a.		Perf 11½ (547c)	13.50	13.50
		Never hinged	27.50	

On Newspaper Stamp of 1916

41	A10	5pa on 10pa gray grn (P137)	27.50	27.50
		Never hinged	55.00	
a.		Inverted overprint	37.50	37.50
		Never hinged	77.50	
b.		In pair with unovptd. stamp	60.00	60.00
		Never hinged	125.00	

On Semi-Postal Stamp of 1915

41A	A21	20pa car rose (B8)	210.00	150.00
		Never hinged	—	

On Semi-Postal Stamps of 1916

42	A17	1pi blue (B19)	6.50	6.50
		Never hinged	13.50	
a.		Inverted overprint	12.00	12.00
		Never hinged	24.00	
b.		Double overprint	12.00	12.00
		Never hinged	24.00	
c.		Perf 12 (B19a)	8.00	8.00
		Never hinged	16.00	
d.		Perf 12x13½ (B19b)	8.00	8.00
		Never hinged	16.00	
43	A21	20pa car rose (B28)	3.25	3.25
		Never hinged	13.50	
a.		Inverted overprint	8.00	8.00
		Never hinged	16.00	
b.		Double overprint	8.00	8.00
		Never hinged	16.00	
		Nos. 31-43 (11)	316.50	256.50

Turkish Stamps of 1913-19 Handstamped

1919

On Pictorial Issue of 1913

51	A24	2pa red lil (254)	11.00	11.00
		Never hinged	22.50	
a.		Inverted overprint	16.00	16.00
		Never hinged	32.50	
b.		Double overprint	16.00	16.00
		Never hinged	32.50	
c.		In pair with unovptd. stamp	40.00	40.00
		Never hinged	80.00	
52	A25	4pa dk brn (255)	3.75	3.75
		Never hinged	6.50	
a.		Inverted overprint	7.50	7.50
		Never hinged	17.00	
b.		Double overprint	7.50	7.50
		Never hinged	17.00	

On Issue of 1915

53	A17	1pi blue (300)	5.50	5.50
		Never hinged	11.00	
a.		Inverted overprint	11.00	11.00
		Never hinged	23.00	
b.		Double overprint	11.00	11.00
		Never hinged	23.00	
55	A22	5pa ocher (328)	40.00	35.00
		Never hinged	87.50	
a.		Double overprint	47.50	45.00
		Never hinged	100.00	
56	A22	20pa car rose (330)	4.00	4.00
		Never hinged	7.25	
a.		Inverted overprint	8.00	8.00
		Never hinged	16.00	
b.		Double overprint	8.00	8.00
		Never hinged	16.00	
c.		In pair with unovptd. stamp	17.50	17.50
		Never hinged	35.00	

On Commemorative Issue of 1916

57	A41	20pa ultra (347)	4.00	4.00
		Never hinged	7.25	
a.		Inverted overprint	8.00	8.00
		Never hinged	16.00	
b.		Double overprint	8.00	8.00
		Never hinged	16.00	
c.		Double overprint, one inverted	9.50	9.50
		Never hinged	20.00	
d.		In pair with unovptd. stamp	17.50	17.50
		Never hinged	35.00	

58 A41 1pi vio & blk
(348) 3.75 3.75
Never hinged 6.50
a. Inverted overprint 6.50 6.50
Never hinged 13.50
b. Double overprint 6.50 6.50
Never hinged 13.50
59 A41 5pi yel brn & blk
(349) 12.00 12.00
Never hinged 24.00
a. Inverted overprint 16.00 16.00
Never hinged 32.50
b. Double overprint 16.00 16.00
Never hinged 32.50

On Issue of 1916
59A A17 1pi blue (372) — —

On Issue of 1916-18
60 A43 5pa org (421) 45.00 40.00
Never hinged 87.50
a. Inverted overprint 52.50 52.50
Never hinged 110.00
b. Perf 11½ (421a) 45.00 40.00
Never hinged 87.50
61 A46 1pi dl vio (426) 13.50 13.50
Never hinged 27.50
a. Inverted overprint 21.00 21.00
Never hinged 45.00
b. Double overprint 21.00 21.00
Never hinged 45.00
63 A52 50pi green, straw
(439) 35.00 27.50
Never hinged 72.50

On Issue of 1917
64 A53 5pi on 2pa Prus
bl (547) 32.50 27.50
Never hinged 67.50
a. Double overprint 40.00 35.00
Never hinged 80.00
b. Perf 11½ (421a) 32.50 27.50
Never hinged 67.50

On Newspaper Stamp of 1916
65 A10 5pa on 10pa gray
grn (P137) 8.75 8.75
Never hinged 17.50
a. Inverted overprint 13.50 13.50
Never hinged 27.50
b. Double overprint 13.50 13.50
Never hinged 27.50

On Semi-Postal Stamp of 1915
65A A21 20pa car rose (B8) 1,200. 850.00

On Semi-Postal Stamps of 1916
66 A17 1pi blue (B19) 30.00 30.00
Never hinged 67.50
a. Inverted overprint 35.00 35.00
Never hinged 75.00
67 A19 20pa car (B26) 13.50 13.50
Never hinged 27.50
a. Inverted overprint 17.50 17.50
Never hinged 35.00
b. Double overprint 17.50 17.50
Never hinged 35.00
68 A21 20pa car rose
(B28) 180.00 92.50
Never hinged 350.00
69 A21 20pa car rose
(B31) 8.00 8.00
Never hinged 16.00
a. Inverted overprint 15.00 15.00
Never hinged 30.00
b. Double overprint 15.00 15.00
Never hinged 30.00
69C A21 1pi ultra (401) 110.00 80.00
Never hinged 225.00
Nos. 51-69C (20) 1,760. 1,270.

Turkey No. 424
Handstamped

1919
71 A44 10pa green (420) 9.50 9.50
Never hinged 20.00
a. Inverted overprint 15.00 15.00
Never hinged 30.00
b. Double overprint 15.00 15.00
Never hinged 30.00
c. Perf 11½ (420a) 11.00 11.00
Never hinged 23.00

"T.E.O." stands for "Territoires Ennemis Occupés."

Turkish
Stamps of
1913-19
Overprinted in
Black, Red or
Blue

In this setting there are various broken and wrong font letters and the letter "i" is sometimes replaced by a "t."

1919 On Pictorial Issue of 1913
75 A30 1pi blue (R)
(260) 4.75 4.75
Never hinged 9.50
a. Inverted overprint 11.00 11.00
Never hinged 23.00

b. Double overprint 11.00 11.00
Never hinged 23.00
c. Double overprint, one inverted 15.00 15.00
Never hinged 30.00

On Issue of 1915
76 A21 20pa carmine
rose (318) 8.75 8.75
Never hinged 17.50

On Commemorative Issue of 1916
76A A41 5pa grn (345) 200.00 110.00
77 A41 20pa ultra (347) 13.50 13.50
Never hinged 27.50
a. Inverted overprint 20.00 20.00
Never hinged 40.00
b. Double overprint 20.00 20.00
Never hinged 40.00
c. Perf 12½ (347a) 13.50 13.50
Never hinged 27.50
78 A41 1pi violet &
black (348) 24.00 24.00
Never hinged 47.50
a. Inverted overprint 30.00 30.00
Never hinged 60.00
b. Double overprint 30.00 30.00
Never hinged 60.00
c. Double overprint, one inverted 35.00 35.00
Never hinged 70.00

On Issue of 1916-18
79 A43 5pa orange
(Bl) (421) 4.75 4.75
Never hinged 9.50
a. Inverted overprint 9.50 9.50
Never hinged 20.00
b. Double overprint 9.50 9.50
Never hinged 20.00
c. Double overprint, one inverted 11.00 11.00
Never hinged 24.00
d. Perf 11½ (421a) 4.75 4.75
Never hinged 9.50
80 A44 10pa grn (424) 8.75 8.75
Never hinged 17.50
a. Inverted overprint 16.00 16.00
Never hinged 32.50
b. Double overprint 16.00 16.00
Never hinged 32.50
c. Double overprint, one inverted 20.00 20.00
Never hinged 40.00
d. Perf 11½ (424a) 8.75 8.75
Never hinged 17.50
81 A45 20pa dp rose
(Bk) (425) 27.50 27.50
Never hinged 65.00
a. Double overprint 40.00 40.00
Never hinged 80.00
82 A45 20pa dp rose
(Bl) (425) 1.00 1.00
Never hinged 2.00
a. Inverted overprint 5.50 5.50
Never hinged 12.00
b. Double overprint 5.50 5.50
Never hinged 12.00
c. Double overprint, one inverted 7.50 7.50
Never hinged 16.00
83 A48 2pi org brn &
indigo (429) 1.60 1.60
Never hinged 2.40
a. Double overprint 5.50 5.50
Never hinged 12.00
b. Perf 11½ (429a) 1.60 1.60
Never hinged 2.50
83C A49 5pi pale blue
& black (R) (430) 1.60 1.60
Never hinged 3.25
a. Inverted overprint 9.50 9.50
Never hinged 20.00
b. Double overprint 9.50 9.50
Never hinged 20.00
c. Double overprint, one inverted 12.00 12.00
Never hinged 24.00
d. Perf 11½ (430a) 1.60 1.60
Never hinged 3.25
84 A51 25pi carmine,
straw (434) 5.50 5.50
Never hinged 12.00
a. Inverted overprint 12.00 12.00
Never hinged 24.00
b. Double overprint 12.00 12.00
Never hinged 24.00
c. Double overprint, one inverted 13.50 13.50
Never hinged 27.50
85 A52 50pi green,
straw (439) 92.50 87.50
Never hinged 190.00
a. Inverted overprint 130.00 130.00
b. Double overprint 130.00 130.00
c. Double overprint, one inverted 160.00 160.00

On Issue of 1917
85A A53 5pi on 2pa
Prus bl (547) —
86 A53 5pi on 2pa
Prus bl (548) 13.50 13.50
Never hinged 27.50
a. Perf 11½ (548c) 13.50 13.50
Never hinged 27.50

On Newspaper Stamps of 1916-19
87 A10 5pa on 10p
gray green (P137) 2.25 2.25
Never hinged 2.60
a. Inverted overprint 5.50 5.50
Never hinged 12.00

b. Double overprint 5.50 5.50
Never hinged 12.00
c. Double overprint, one inverted 13.50 13.50
Never hinged 27.50
88 A21 5pa on 2pa ol
green (P173) 1.00 1.00
Never hinged 2.00
a. Inverted overprint 5.50 5.50
Never hinged 12.00
b. Double overprint 5.50 5.50
Never hinged 12.00
c. Double overprint, one inverted 6.50 6.50

On Semi-Postal Stamps of 1915-17
90 A21 20pa carmine
rose (B28) 8.75 8.75
Never hinged 17.50
a. Double overprint 16.00 16.00
Never hinged 32.50
91 A41 10pa car (B42) 3.25 3.25
Never hinged 4.75
a. Inverted overprint 7.25 7.25
Never hinged 14.50
b. Double overprint 7.25 7.25
Never hinged 14.50
c. Double overprint, one inverted 12.00 12.00
Never hinged 24.00
d. Perf 12½ (B42b) 3.25 3.25
Never hinged 4.75
92 A11 10pa on 20pa
vio brn (B38) 3.25 3.25
Never hinged 4.75
a. Inverted overprint 9.50 9.50
Never hinged 20.00
b. Double overprint 9.50 9.50
Never hinged 20.00
c. Double overprint, one inverted 13.50 13.50
Never hinged 27.50
93 SP1 10pa red violet (B46) 2.50 2.50
Never hinged 4.00
a. Overprint sideways 8.00 8.00
Never hinged 16.00

It is understood that the newspaper and semi-postal stamps overprinted "Cilicie" were used as ordinary postage stamps.

A1

1920 Blue Surcharge Perf. 11½
98 A1 70pa on 5pa red 2.40 2.40
Never hinged 4.00
a. Double surcharge 40.00 40.00
Never hinged 80.00
b. Triple surcharge 240.00
c. Inverted surcharge 35.00 35.00
Never hinged 72.50
d. Double overprint, one inverted 45.00 45.00
Never hinged 87.50
e. In pair with unovptd. stamp 110.00
Never hinged 190.00
f. "OCCCPATION" for "OCCU-PATION" 17.50 17.50
Never hinged 35.00
g. "OCCUPTTION" for "OCCU-PATION" 17.50 17.50
Never hinged 35.00
99 A1 3½pi on 5pa red 3.00 2.75
Never hinged 4.00
a. Se-tenant with No. 98, horiz. pair 120.00 120.00
Never hinged 225.00
b. As "a," inverted surcharge 240.00 240.00
c. Double surcharge 40.00 40.00
Never hinged 80.00
d. Inverted surcharge 35.00 35.00
Never hinged 72.50
e. Double surcharge, one inverted 45.00 45.00
Never hinged 87.50
f. "OCCCPATION" for "OCCU-PATION" 17.50 17.50
Never hinged 35.00
g. "OCCUPTION" for "OCCU-PATION" 17.50 17.50
Never hinged 35.00
h. "P" of "OCCUPATION" inverted 45.00 45.00
Never hinged 87.50
i. "PIATSRES" for "PIASTERS" 45.00 45.00
Never hinged 87.50

French Offices in Turkey
No. 26 Surcharged

1920 Perf. 14x13½
100 A3 20pa on 10c rose
red (I) 2.00 2.00
Never hinged 2.00
On cover 24.00
a. "PARAS" omitted 72.50 72.50

Never hinged 130.00
b. Second "A" of "PARAS" omitted 72.50 72.50
Never hinged 130.00
c. "S" of "PARAS" inverted 65.00 65.00
Never hinged 110.00
d. Overprint type II 35.00 35.00
Never hinged 65.00
On cover 120.00
e. Overprint type III 35.00 35.00
Never hinged 65.00
On cover 120.00
f. Pair, #100 + #100c 45.00 45.00
Never hinged 80.00
g. Pair, #100 + #100d 45.00 45.00
Never hinged 80.00
h. Strip, #100 + #100c + #100e 110.00 110.00
Never hinged 180.00

Three types of "20" exist on No. 100: I, "2" bold; II "2" faint; III, "0" distinctly taller than "2."

Stamps of France,
1900-17, Surcharged

1920
101 A16 5pa on 2c vio brn 1.60 1.60
Never hinged 2.75
On cover 47.50
102 A22 10pa on 5c green 2.00 2.00
Never hinged 3.25
On cover 47.50
103 A22 20pa on 10c red 4.00 4.00
Never hinged 6.75
On cover 47.50
On cover, single franking 67.50
104 A22 1pi on 25c blue 2.75 2.25
Never hinged 4.00
On cover 32.50
On cover, single franking 52.50
105 A20 2pi on 15c gray
green 12.00 12.00
Never hinged 22.50
On cover 120.00
On cover, single franking 200.00
106 A18 5pi on 40c red &
gray bl 26.00 26.00
Never hinged 47.50
On cover 200.00
On cover, single franking 325.00
107 A18 10pi on 50c bis
brn & lav 32.50 32.50
Never hinged 52.50
On cover 240.00
On cover, single franking 400.00
108 A18 50pi on 1fr claret
& ol grn 180.00 180.00
Never hinged 300.00
On cover 675.00
109 A18 100pi on 5fr dk bl &
buff 900.00 900.00
On cover 2,200.
Nos. 101-109 (9) 1,160. 1,160.

Nos. 106 to 109 surcharged in four lines. "O.M.F." stands for "Occupation Militaire Francaise."

Stamps of France,
1917, Surcharged

1920
110 A16 5pa on 2c vio brn
(109b) 13.00
Never hinged 23.00
a. "S" of "EST" inverted 160.00
111 A22 10pa on 5c grn (110b) 13.00
Never hinged 23.00
a. "S" of "EST" inverted 180.00
b. Double surcharge 75.00
Never hinged 125.00
c. On ordinary paper (110) 19.00
Never hinged 35.00
112 A22 20pa on 10c red (162) 9.75
Never hinged 16.00
a. Inverted surcharge 75.00
Never hinged 125.00
b. Double surcharge 67.50
Never hinged 115.00
c. "S" of "EST" inverted 130.00
113 A22 1pi on 25c bl (168d) 6.00
Never hinged 9.50
a. "S" of "EST" inverted 65.00
Never hinged 115.00
b. On ordinary paper (168) 9.50
Never hinged 16.00
114 A20 2pi on 15c gray grn
(139c) 27.00
Never hinged 47.50
a. "S" of "EST" inverted 240.00
115 A18 5pi on 40c red &
gray bl (121) 50.00
Never hinged 85.00
a. "N" of "SAND." inverted 260.00
116 A18 20pi on 1fr claret & ol
grn (125) 190.00
Never hinged 315.00
a. "O.M.F. Cilicie" omitted 625.00

b. Double surcharge 625.00
c. "N" of "SAND." inverted 525.00
Nos. 110-116 (7) 308.75

On Nos. 115 and 116 "SAND. EST" is placed vertically. "Sand. Est" is an abbreviation of Sandjak de l'Est (Eastern County).

Nos. 110-116 were prepared for use, but never issued.

Stamps of France, 1900-17, Surcharged

First Setting: 1.75-2mm spacing between "Cilicie" and figures of value

1920
117 A16 5pa on 2c vio brn, *grayish (GC)* 1.25 1.25
  Never hinged 1.60
  On cover 32.50
a. Inverted surcharge 32.50 27.50
  Never hinged 47.50
b. "Cilicie" 35.00 35.00
  Never hinged 67.50
c. Surcharge 5pi (error) 60.00 60.00
  Never hinged 110.00
d. "5" omitted from surcharge 35.00 35.00
  Never hinged 67.50
e. As "c," "e" inverted 27.50 27.50
  Never hinged 47.50
f. "S" of "PARAS" inverted 35.00 35.00
  Never hinged 67.50

119 A22 10pa on 5c grn, *grayish (GC)* 1.50 1.50
  Never hinged 1.50
  On cover 22.50
a. Inverted surcharge 30.00 26.00
  Never hinged 50.00
b. Surch. 5pa (error), upright 55.00 55.00
  Never hinged 100.00
c. Surch. 5pa (error), invtd. 75.00 67.50
  Never hinged 140.00
d. "e" in "Cilicie" inverted 32.50 32.50
  Never hinged 52.50
e. "S" in "PARAS" inverted 35.00 35.00
  Never hinged 67.50

121 A22 20pa on 10c red 1.75 1.75
  Never hinged 1.60
  On cover 24.00
  On cover, single franking 32.50
a. Inverted surcharge 32.50 27.50
  Never hinged 52.50
b. Surch. 10pa (error), upright 60.00 60.00
  Never hinged 100.00
c. Surch. 10pa (error), invtd. 80.00 72.50
  Never hinged 150.00
d. "S" in "PARAS" inverted 35.00 35.00
  Never hinged 67.50

122 A22 1pi on 25c bl, *grayish (GC)* 2.00 2.00
  Never hinged 2.40
  On cover 20.00
  On cover, single franking 27.50
a. Double surcharge 72.50 72.50
  Never hinged 120.00
b. Inverted surcharge 55.00 52.50
  Never hinged 92.50
c. First "S" in "PIASTRE" inverted 45.00 45.00
  Never hinged 80.00

123 A20 2pi on 15c gray grn, *grayish (GC)* 2.25 2.25
  Never hinged 4.00
  On cover 40.00
  On cover, single franking 67.50
a. Double surcharge 45.00 45.00
  Never hinged 80.00
b. Inverted surcharge 35.00 32.50
  Never hinged 67.50
c. Double surcharge, one inverted 55.00 55.00
  Never hinged 92.50
d. First "S" in "PIASTRES" inverted 72.50 72.50
  Never hinged 120.00

124 A18 5pi on 40c red & gray bl, *grayish (GC)* 3.50 3.50
  Never hinged 6.50
  On cover 52.50
  On cover, single franking 87.50
a. Double surcharge 65.00 65.00
  Never hinged 110.00
b. Inverted surcharge 45.00 40.00
  Never hinged 72.50
c. First "S" in "PIASTRES" inverted 72.50 72.50
  Never hinged 120.00

125 A18 10pi on 50c bis brn & lavender, *grayish (GC)* 12.50 12.50
  Never hinged 24.00
  On cover 100.00
  On cover, single franking 175.00
a. Double surcharge 60.00 60.00
  Never hinged 110.00
b. Inverted surcharge 55.00 47.50
  Never hinged 62.50
c. First "S" in "PIASTRES" inverted 110.00 110.00
  Never hinged 180.00

---

126 A18 50pi on 1fr claret & ol grn, *grayish (GC)* 17.50 17.50
  Never hinged 35.00
  On cover 140.00
  On cover, single franking 240.00
a. Inverted surcharge 130.00
b. Double surcharge 180.00
c. First "S" in "PIASTRES" inverted 180.00

127 A18 100pi on 5fr dk bl & buff 45.00 45.00
  Never hinged 80.00
  On cover 350.00
  On cover, single franking 800.00
a. Inverted surcharge 180.00
b. First "S" in "PIASTRES" inverted 240.00
Nos. 117-127 (9) 87.25 87.25

Second Setting: 1-1.5mm spacing between "Cilicie" and figures of value

117g A16 5pa on 2c vio brn, *grayish (GC)* .65 .65
  Never hinged 1.20
  On cover 24.00
h. Double surcharge 35.00 35.00
  Never hinged 67.50
i. "Cilicie" omitted 32.50 32.50
  Never hinged 52.50
j. Surch. "O.M.F. / PARAS / 5 / PARAS" 55.00 55.00
  Never hinged 100.00

119f A22 10pa on 5c green, *grayish (GC)* .65 .65
  Never hinged 1.20
  On cover 20.00
g. On ordinary paper 1.60 1.60
  Never hinged 2.40
  On cover 24.00
h. Surch. "O.M.F. / PARAS / 10 / PARAS" 55.00 55.00
  Never hinged 100.00

121e A22 20pa on 10c red .70 .70
  Never hinged 1.20
  On cover 20.00
  On cover, single franking 27.50
f. Double surcharge 35.00 35.00
  Never hinged 65.00
g. Double surcharge, one inverted 47.50 47.50
  Never hinged 80.00

122d A22 1pi on 25c blue, *grayish (GC)* .95 .95
  Never hinged 1.60
  On cover 16.00
  On cover, single franking 24.00
e. Inverted surcharge 35.00 32.50
  Never hinged 07.50
f. On ordinary paper 2.40 2.40
  Never hinged 4.00
  On cover 20.00
  On cover, single franking 27.50

123e A20 2pi on 15c gray grn, *grayish (GC)* 1.00 1.00
  Never hinged 1.60
  On cover 27.50
  On cover, single franking 40.00
f. Second "S" in "PIAS-TRES" omitted 21.00 21.00
  Never hinged 35.00

124d A18 5pi on 40c red & gray bl, *grayish (GC)* 3.25 3.25
  Never hinged 5.50
  On cover 47.50
  On cover, single franking 80.00
e. "PIASRTES" 72.50 72.50
  Never hinged 120.00

125d A18 10pi on 50c bis brn & lavender, *grayish (GC)* 3.25 3.25
  Never hinged 5.50
  On cover 60.00
  On cover, single franking 100.00
e. "PIASRTES" 72.50 72.50
  Never hinged 120.00
f. On ordinary paper 8.00 8.00
  Never hinged 13.50
  On cover 80.00
  On cover, single franking 130.00

126d A18 50pi on 1fr claret & ol grn, *grayish (GC)* 13.50 13.50
  Never hinged 25.00
  On cover 120.00
  On cover, single franking 225.00
e. "PIASRTES" 87.50
  Never hinged 150.00
f. "50" omitted 87.50
  Never hinged 150.00

127c A18 100pi on 5fr dk bl & buff 300.00 300.00
  On cover 1,200.
  On cover, single franking
d. "PIASRTES" 925.00
Nos. 117g-127c (9) 323.95 323.95

This surcharge has "O.M.F." in thicker letters than the preceding issues.

Most of the French stamps overprinted for this issue were from the wartime printings, on poor quality grayish paper (GC, or *Grande Consommation* paper).

For overprints see Nos. C1-C2.

AIR POST STAMPS

Nos. 123 and 124 Handstamped

Perf. 14x13½

1920, July 15   **Unwmk.**
C1 A20 2pi on 15c gray grn 9,250. 9,250.
  On cover 35,000.
C2 A18 5pi on 40c red & gray blue 9,500. 9,500.
  On cover 35,000.
a. "PIASRTES"

A very limited number of Nos. C1 and C2 were used on two air mail flights between Adana and Aleppo. At a later date impressions from a new handstamp were struck "to oblige" on stamps of the regular issue of 1920 (Nos. 123, 124, 125 and 126) that were in stock at the Adana Post Office.

Counterfeits exist.

POSTAGE DUE STAMPS

Turkish Postage Due Stamps of 1914 Handstamped

Handstamped

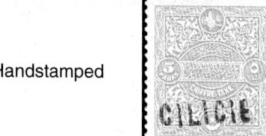

1919   **Unwmk.**   ***Perf. 12***
J1 D1 5pa claret 22.00 22.00
  Never hinged 45.00
a. Inverted overprint 32.50 32.50
  Never hinged 65.00
b. Double surcharge 32.50 32.50
  Never hinged 65.00
J2 D2 20pa red 22.50 22.50
  Never hinged 45.00
a. Inverted overprint 32.50 32.50
  Never hinged 65.00
b. Double surcharge 32.50 32.50
  Never hinged 65.00
J3 D3 1pi dark blue 35.00 35.00
  Never hinged 72.50
a. Inverted overprint 47.50 47.50
  Never hinged 90.00
J4 D4 2pi slate 45.00 45.00
  Never hinged 90.00
a. Inverted overprint 60.00 60.00
  Never hinged 120.00
Nos. J1-J4 (4) 124.50 124.50

Handstamped

J5 D1 5pa claret 26.00 26.00
  Never hinged 52.50
a. Inverted overprint 40.00 40.00
  Never hinged 80.00
b. Double overprint 40.00 40.00
  Never hinged 80.00
J6 D2 20pa red 30.00 30.00
  Never hinged 60.00
a. Inverted overprint 45.00 45.00
  Never hinged 87.50
b. Double overprint 45.00 45.00
  Never hinged 87.50
J7 D3 1pi dark blue 35.00 35.00
  Never hinged 72.50
a. Inverted overprint 47.50 47.50
  Never hinged 95.00
J8 D4 2pi slate 35.00 35.00
  Never hinged 72.50
a. Inverted overprint 47.50 47.50
  Never hinged 95.00
Nos. J5-J8 (4) 126.00 126.00

Handstamped

J9 D1 5pa claret 22.00 22.00
  Never hinged 45.00
a. Inverted overprint 32.50 32.50
  Never hinged 65.00
b. Double overprint 32.50 32.50
  Never hinged 65.00
J10 D2 20pa red 22.50 22.50
  Never hinged 45.00
a. Inverted overprint 32.50 32.50
  Never hinged 65.00
b. Double overprint 35.00 35.00
  Never hinged 65.00
J11 D3 1pi dark blue 35.00 35.00
  Never hinged 67.50
a. Inverted overprint 47.50 47.50
  Never hinged 95.00
J12 D4 2pi slate 22.00 22.00
  Never hinged 45.00
a. Inverted overprint 32.50 32.50
  Never hinged 65.00
Nos. J9-J12 (4) 101.50 101.50

Postage Due Stamps of France Surcharged

1921
J13 D2 1pi on 10c choc 11.00 11.00
  Never hinged 18.00
a. Inverted overprint 130.00
  Never hinged 225.00
b. Period after "O" omitted 35.00
  Never hinged 65.00
c. Period after "M" omitted 35.00
  Never hinged 65.00
J14 D2 2pi on 20c olive grn 11.00 11.00
  Never hinged 18.00
a. Inverted overprint 130.00
  Never hinged 225.00
b. Period after "M" omitted 35.00
  Never hinged 65.00
c. First "S" in "PIASTRES" inverted 32.50
  Never hinged 60.00
J15 D2 3pi on 30c red 11.00 11.00
  Never hinged 17.50
a. Inverted overprint 92.50
  Never hinged 150.00
b. Period after "O" omitted 35.00
  Never hinged 65.00
c. Period after "M" omitted 35.00
  Never hinged 65.00
J16 D2 4pi on 50c vio brn 10.50 10.50
  Never hinged 17.50
a. Inverted overprint 92.50
  Never hinged 150.00
Nos. J13-J16 (4) 43.50 43.50

COCHIN CHINA

'kō-chən 'chī-nə

LOCATION — The southernmost state of French Indo-China in the Cambodian Peninsula.
GOVT. — French Colony
AREA — 26,476 sq. mi.
POP. — 4,615,968
CAPITAL — Saigon

100 Centimes = 1 Franc

Surcharged in Black on Stamps of French Colonies

a

b

c

1886-87		**Unwmk.**	**Perf. 14x13½**	
1	A9(a)	5c on 25c yel, straw	225.00	120.00
		No gum	160.00	
		On cover		2,000.
2	A9(b)	5c on 2c brn, buff	40.00	32.50
		No gum	30.00	
		On cover		1,500.
a.		9¼mm between "5" and "C. CH."	90.00	60.00
3	A9(b)	5c on 25c yel, straw	32.50	27.50
		No gum	26.00	
		On cover		1,200.
a.		Inverted surcharge	275.00	275.00
b.		9¼mm between "5" and "C. CH."	90.00	60.00
4	A9(c)	5c on 25c blk, rose ('87)	60.00	47.50
		No gum	45.00	
		On cover		1,500.
a.		Double surch., one of type b	3,750.	2,750.
b.		Triple surch., two of type b	—	—
c.		Inverted surcharge	375.00	375.00
d.		Double surch., both type "a"	2,750.	3,250.
e.		Triple surch., types "a," "b" and "c"		8,750.
		Nos. 1-4 (4)	357.50	227.50

The space between "5" and "C. CH." on Nos. 2 and 3 is normally 8½mm. The wider spacing occurs in six positions on each pane.
Covers: Values for covers are for commercial items with proper rates.

1888
5	A9	15c on half of 30c brn, bis	72.50
		No gum	55.00

No. 5 was prepared but not issued.
The so-called Postage Due stamps were never issued.
Stamps of Cochin China were superseded by those of Indo-China in 1892.

COLOMBIA

kə-'ləm-bē-ə

LOCATION — On the northwest coast of South America, bordering on the Caribbean Sea and the Pacific Ocean
GOVT. — Republic
AREA — 456,535 sq. mi.
POP. — 28,240,000 (est. 1984)
CAPITAL — Bogota

In 1810 the Spanish Viceroyalty of New Granada gained its independence and with Venezuela and Ecuador formed the State of Greater Colombia. In 1832 this state split into three independent units as Venezuela, Ecuador and the Republic of New Granada. The name of the country has been, successively, Granadine Confederation (1858-61), United States of New Granada (1861), United States of Colombia (1861-65), and the Republic of Colombia (1885 to date).

100 Centavos = 1 Peso

In the earlier days many towns did not have handstamps for canceling and stamps were canceled with pen and ink. Pen cancellations, therefore, do not indicate fiscal use. (Postage stamps were not used for revenue purposes.) Used values for Nos. 1-128 are for stamps with illegible manuscript cancels or handstamp cancels of Bogota or Medellin. Stamps with legible manuscript or other handstamped town-name cancels sell for more.
Fractions of many Colombian stamps of both early and late issues are found canceled, their use to pay postage having been tolerated even though forbidden by the postal laws and regulations. Many are known to have been made for philatelic purposes.

Watermarks

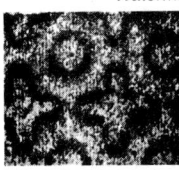

Wmk. 116 — Crosses and Circles

Wmk. 127 — Quatrefoils

Wmk. 194 — Multiple Curvilinear Triangles

Wmk. 229 — Wavy Lines

Wmk. 255 — Wavy Lines and C Multiple

STAMPS OF GREAT BRITAIN USED IN COLOMBIA

Crowned Circle handstamp types and numeral cancellation types A and B are pictured in the Crowned Circle Handstamps and Great Britain Used Abroad section.

Values are for clear cancellations on sound, fault-free stamps, with average to fine centering. In many cases, very fine examples are rare or non-existent.

CARTAGENA

Pre-Stamp Postal Markings

1841
A1	Crowned Circle handstamp Type II, on cover, inscribed "PAID AT CARTHAGENA" in red	1,500.
A2	Crowned Circle handstamp Type I, on cover, inscribed "PAID AT CARTHAGENA" in black	1,100.

Earliest known uses: A1, 1/15/41; A2, 7/1/46.

Stamps of Great Britain, Canceled C56, Type A

1865-84
A3	½p rose red (#58 P 10)	—	
A4	1p rose red (#33, P 78, 87, 100, 111, 113, 117, 119, 125, 172, 189, 217) value from	62.50	
A5	2p blue (#29, P 9)	62.50	
A6	2p blue (#30, P 14)	82.50	
A7	3p rose (#44)	—	
A8	3p rose (#49, P 4, 5)	—	
A9	3p rose (#61, P 12, 17, 18) value from	62.50	
A10	4p vermilion (#43, P 7-14) value from	62.50	
A11	4p vermilion (#69, P 15)	350.00	
A12	4p pale olive green (#70, P 15, 16)	225.00	
A13	6p lilac (#45, P 5, 6)	—	
A14	6p dull violet (#50, P 6)	85.00	
A15	6p violet (#51, P 8)	87.50	
A16	6p gray (#60, P 12)	240.00	
A17	6p gray (#62, P 13-16) value from	62.50	
A18	8p orange (#73)	375.00	
A19	9p straw (#46)	—	
A20	1sh green (#48, P 4)	—	
A21	1sh green (#54, P 4, 5, 7) value from	70.00	
A22	1sh green (#64, P 12, 13) value from	80.00	
	Plates 8-11 value from	80.00	
A23	1sh salmon (#87)	—	
A24	2sh blue (#55)	325.00	
A25	5sh rose (#57, P 1)	650.00	

Stamps of Great Britain, Canceled C65, Type B
A26	½p rose red (#58, P 10)	—	
A27	1p rose red (#33, P 100, 106, 111, 123) value from	85.00	
A28	1½p dull rose (#32)	85.00	
A29	2p blue (#29, P 9)	—	
A30	2p lilac rose (#81)	—	
A31	2½p blue (#68)	—	
A32	3p rose (#49, P 9)	—	
A33	3p rose (#61, P 14, 17, 19, 20)	—	
A34	4p vermilion (#43, P 7-9, 11-14) value from	70.00	
A35	4p vermilion (#69, P 15)	350.00	
A36	4p pale olive green (#70, P 15, 16)	225.00	
A37	6p dull violet (#50, P 6)	105.00	
A38	6p violet (#51, P 8)	105.00	
A39	6p pale buff (#51, P 8)	—	
A40	6p gray (#60, P 12)	240.00	
A41	6p gray (#60, P 13, 15-17) value from	70.00	
A42	8p orange (#73)	450.00	
A43	9p straw (#46)	510.00	
A44	1sh green (#48, P 4)	150.00	
A45	1sh green (#54, P 4-7) value from	75.00	
A46	1sh green (#64, P 12, 13) value from	85.00	
	Plates 8, 11 value from	85.00	
A47	1sh salmon (#87)	—	
A48	2sh blue (#55)	750.00	
A49	2sh brown (#56)	2,750.	
A50	5sh pale rose (#57a, P 1)	575.00	
	Plate 2	725.00	
A51	5sh rose (#57, P 1)	600.00	
	Plate 2	725.00	

The C65 canceler was supplied to the British post office in Cartagena in error. C56 was the obliterator assigned to Cartagena.

CHAGRES

Pre-Stamp Postal Markings
A52	Crowned Circle handstamp, on cover, inscribed "PAID AT CHAGRES" in black	—

Chagres is located in what is now the Republic of Panama. It was the chief Atlantic port of the isthmus from the 18th century and activity reached a zenith during the 1840s-1850s, when it was the Atlantic terminus for the trans-Isthmian route for miners en route to California.
Earliest known use: 9/16/46.

COLON

Pre-Stamp Postal Marking
A53	Crowned Circle handstamp Type VI, on cover, inscribed "PAID AT COLON" in red	5,500.

Colon is located in what is now the Republic of Panama.
Earliest known use: 6/21/54.

Stamps of Great Britain, Canceled E88, Type B

1865-81
A54	1p rose red (#33, see footnote) value from	57.50

#A54 plate numbers 107, 121-123, 125, 127, 130, 131, 133, 136, 142, 150-153, 155-158, 160, 169-171, 174, 176, 178, 179, 184, 187, 188, 194, 195, 201, 209, 213, 214, 217.

A55	1p red brown (#79)	125.00
A56	1½p dull rose (#32, P 3)	125.00
A57	2p blue (#30, P 14, 15) value from	57.50
A58	2p lilac rose (#81)	—
A59	3p rose (#49, P 6, 9)	—
A60	3p rose (#61, P 11, 12, 16, 18-20) value from	65.00
A61	4p vermilion (#43, P 10-14) value from	65.00
A62	4p vermilion (#69, P 15)	—
A63	4p pale olive green (#70, P 15, 16) value from	225.00
A64	4p gray brown (#71, P 17)	375.00
A65	4p gray brown (#84, P 17)	85.00
A66	6p violet (#51, P 6, 8, 9)	—
A67	6p pale buff (#59b, P 11)	—
A68	6p brown (#59, P 11)	75.00
A69	6p gray (#60, P 12)	—
A70	6p gray (#62, P 13-17) value from	62.50
A71	8p orange (#73)	—
A72	9p bister (#52)	260.00
A73	10p red brown (#53)	—
A74	1sh green (#54, P 4-7) value from	57.50
A75	1sh green (#64, P 8-13) value from	75.00
A76	1sh salmon (#65)	425.00
A77	1sh salmon (#87, P 13)	175.00
A78	2sh blue (#55)	175.00
A79	2sh brown (#56)	2,500.
A80	5sh pale rose (#57a, P 1)	575.00
	Plate 2	700.00
A81	5sh rose (#57, P 1)	575.00
	Plate 2	700.00

PANAMA

Pre-Stamp Postal Marking

1846
A82	Crowned Circle handstamp Type I, on cover, inscribed "PAID AT PANAMA" in red	2,200.

Panama is located in what is now the Republic of Panama.
Earliest known use: 8/24/46.

Stamps of Great Britain, Canceled C35, Type A or B

No. A128

1865-81

A83	½p rose red (#58 P 10-15, 19) *value* from	57.50
A84	1p rose red (#33, see footnote) *value* from	37.50

#A84 plate numbers 71, 72, 76, 81, 85, 87-89, 93, 95, 96, 101, 104, 114, 122, 124, 130, 138, 139, 142, 159, 168, 171, 172, 174, 179, 180, 184, 185, 187, 189, 191-193, 196, 197, 200, 203-205, 207-211, 213-215, 218, 224.

A85	1p red brown (#79)	65.00
A86	1½p lake red (#32a, P 3)	75.00
A87	1½p red brown (#80)	—
A88	2p blue (#29, P 9)	42.50
	Plate 12	80.00
A89	2p blue (#30, P 13-15) *value* from	42.50
A90	2p blue (#81)	110.00
A91	2½p claret (#66, P 1)	225.00
A92	2½p claret (#67, P 4, 12, 16)	200.00
A93	2½p blue (#68, P 19)	—
A94	2½p blue (#82, P 22, 23)	—
A95	3p rose (#37)	290.00
A96	3p rose (#44)	—
A97	3p rose (#49, P 4-9) *value* from	57.50
A98	3p rose (#61, P 12, 14-20) *value* from	42.50
A99	3p rose (#83, P 20, 21)	—
A100	4p vermilion (#34a, P4)	125.00
A101	4p vermilion, "hairlines" (#34c, P 4)	—
A102	4p vermilion (#43, P 7-14) *value* from	57.50
A103	4p vermilion (#69, P 15)	350.00
A104	4p pale olive green (#70, P 16)	225.00
	Plate 15	275.00
A105	4p gray brown (#84, P 17, 18) *value* from	57.50
A106	5p deep indigo (#85)	220.00
A107	6p lilac (#39, P 3)	110.00
A108	6p lilac (#39b, P 4)	150.00
A109	6p lilac (#45, P 5)	85.00
	Plate 6	150.00
A110	6p dull violet (#50, P 6)	—
A111	6p violet (#51, P 6, 8, 9) *value* from	80.00
A112	6p pale buff (#59b, P 11)	85.00
	Plate 12	250.00
A113	6p brown (#59, P 11)	57.50
A114	6p gray (#60, P 12)	240.00
A115	6p gray (#62, P 13-17) *value* from	57.50
A116	6p gray (#86, P 17)	80.00
A117	8p orange (#73)	350.00
A118	9p straw (#40)	400.00
A119	9p bister (#52)	290.00
A120	10p red brown (#53)	310.00
A121	1sh green (#48, P 4)	160.00
A122	1sh green (#54, P 4-6) *value* from	52.50
	Plate 7	65.00
A123	1sh green (#64, P 12, 13) *value* from	70.00
	Plates 8-11 *value* from	75.00
A124	1sh salmon (#65, P 13)	450.00
A125	1sh salmon (#87, P 13)	125.00
A126	2sh blue (#55)	150.00
A127	2sh brown (#56)	2,500.
A128	5sh pale rose (#57a, P 1)	550.00
	Plate 2	700.00
A129	5sh rose (#57, P 1)	575.00
	Plate 2	700.00

Later stamps of Great Britain are also known canceled "C35." These originate on mail posted aboard British civilian ships, and on other forms of ship mail which transited through Panama.

SANTA MARTHA

Pre-Stamp Postal Marking

1841

A130	Crowned Circle hand-stamp Type V, on cover, inscribed "PAID AT SANTA MARTHA" in red	2,200.

Earliest known use: 12/15/41.

Stamps of Great Britain, Canceled C62, Type A

1865-81

A131	½p rose red (#58 P 8)	110.00
A132	1p rose red (#33, P 33)	75.00
A133	2p blue (#29, P 9)	110.00
A134	2p blue (#30, P 14)	110.00
A135	4p vermilion (#43, P 7-9, 11-14) *value* from	70.00
A136	4p pale olive green (#70, P 15)	225.00
A137	4p gray brown (#71, P 17)	375.00
A138	4p gray brown (#84, P 17)	85.00
A139	6p lilac (#45, P 5)	115.00
A140	6p gray (#60, P 12)	—
A141	6p gray (#62, P 14)	—
A142	8p orange (#73)	400.00
A143	9p straw (#40)	—
A144	1sh green (#48, P 4)	180.00
A145	1sh green (#54, P 5, 7) *value* from	85.00
A146	1sh green (#64, P 8)	—
A147	2sh blue (#55)	350.00
A148	5sh rose (#57, P 2)	725.00

SAVANILLA (BARRANQUILLA)

Stamps of Great Britain, Canceled F69, Type B

1872-81

A149	½p rose red (#58 P 6)	105.00
A150	1p rose red (#33, P 122, 171) *value* from	75.00
A151	1½p lake red (#32a, P 3)	125.00
A152	3p rose (#49, P 7)	125.00
A153	3p rose (#61, P 20)	115.00
A154	3p rose (#83, P 20)	115.00
A155	4p ver (#43, P 12-14) *value* from	70.00
A156	4p ver (#69, P 15)	350.00
A157	4p pale ol grn (#70, P 16)	260.00
	Plate 15	290.00
A158	4p gray brn (#71, P 17)	425.00
A159	4p gray brn (#84, P 17)	85.00
A160	6p pale buff (#59b, P 11)	—
A161	6p gray (#86, P 16, 17) *value* from	90.00
A162	8p org (#73)	450.00
A163	1sh grn (#54, P 5, 7) *value* from	85.00
A164	1sh grn (#64, P 8, 11-13) *value* from	90.00
A165	1sh salmon (#65, P 13)	450.00
A166	2sh blue (#55)	260.00
A167	5sh rose (#57, P 2)	725.00

ISSUES OF COLOMBIA
Granadine Confederation

A2

Coat of Arms

Type A1 — Asterisks in frame. Wavy lines in background.

Type A2 — Diamond-shaped ornaments in frame. Straight lines in background. Numerals larger.

1859   **Unwmk.   Litho.   *Imperf.***
Wove Paper

1	A1	2½c green	120.00	120.00
a.		2½c yellow green	120.00	120.00
b.		2½c olive green	90.00	90.00
c.		2½c deep green	90.00	90.00
d.		2½c ochre	125.00	125.00
2	A1	5c blue	140.00	87.50
a.		Tête bêche pair	4,500.	7,250.
b.		"50" instead of "5"		7,500.
3	A1	5c violet	375.00	100.00
a.		Tête bêche pair	6,000.	6,000.
b.		"50" instead of "5"		15,000.
c.		50c blue violet	225.00	90.00
d.		50c lilac	225.00	90.00
e.		50c slate	250.00	100.00

4	A1	10c red brown	140.00	80.00
a.		10c buff	140.00	80.00
b.		10c bister brown	100.00	62.50
c.		10c yellow	100.00	62.50
d.		10c orange chestnut	100.00	62.50
e.		10c red orange	125.00	90.00
6	A1	20c blue	120.00	67.50
a.		20c gray blue	120.00	67.50
b.		Se-tenant with 5c	—	—
c.		Tête bêche pair	40,000.	32,500.
d.		20c pale ultramarine	100.00	70.00
7	A1	1p carmine	72.50	120.00
a.		1p rose	110.00	150.00
8	A1	1p rose, *bluish*	350.00	

The 2½c brown and 10c green are essays.
Reprints of No. 7 are in brown rose or brown red. Wavy lines of background are much broken; no dividing lines between stamps.

1860   **Laid Paper**

9	A2	5c lilac	325.00	210.00

Wove Paper

10	A2	5c gray lilac	85.00	65.00
a.		5c lilac	85.00	65.00
11	A2	10c yellow buff	85.00	55.00
a.		Tête bêche pair	7,000.	7,000.
12	A2	20c blue	210.00	140.00

United States of New Granada

Arms of New Granada — A3

1861

13	A3	2½c black	1,450.	400.00
14	A3	5c yellow	400.00	175.00
a.		5c buff	400.00	175.00
16	A3	10c blue	1,250.	175.00
17	A3	20c red	500.00	175.00
18	A3	1p pink	1,250.	375.00

There are 54 varieties of the 5c, 20c, and 1 peso.
Forgeries exist of Nos. 13-18.

United States of Colombia

Coat of Arms
A4   A5   A6

1862

19	A4	10c blue	250.00	125.00
20	A4	20c red	4,500.	725.00
21	A4	50c green	250.00	175.00
22	A4	1p red lilac	600.00	175.00
23	A4	1p red lil, *bluish*	5,500.	1,750.

No. 23 is on a thinner, coarser wove paper than Nos. 19-22.

1863

24	A5	5c orange	100.00	65.00
a.		Star after "Cent"	110.00	72.50
25	A5	10c blue	175.00	24.00
a.		Period after "10"	200.00	30.00
26	A5	20c red	225.00	75.00
a.		Star after "Cent"	250.00	82.50
b.		Transfer of 50c in stone of 20c	18,500.	5,500.

Bluish Paper

28	A5	10c blue	175.00	32.50
a.		Period after "10"	190.00	35.00
29	A5	50c blue	210.00	75.00
a.		Star after "Cent"	210.00	77.50

Ten varieties of each.

1864   **Wove Paper**

30	A6	5c orange	60.00	37.50
a.		Tête bêche pair	475.00	400.00
31	A6	10c blue	55.00	15.00
a.		Period after 10	55.00	15.00
32	A6	20c scarlet	100.00	55.00
33	A6	50c green	85.00	55.00
34	A6	1p red violet	350.00	175.00

Two varieties of each.

Arms of Colombia
A7   A9

A8

1865

35	A7	1c rose	10.00	10.00
a.		bluish pelure paper	30.00	21.00
36	A8	2½c black, *lilac*	21.00	14.00
37	A9	5c yellow	47.50	20.00
a.		5c orange	47.50	20.00
38	A9	10c violet	67.50	4.50
39	A9	20c blue	67.50	20.00
40	A9	50c green	120.00	52.50
41	A9	50c grn (small figures)	120.00	52.50
42	A9	1p vermilion	125.00	18.00
a.		1p rose red	125.00	18.00
b.		Period after "PESO"	150.00	20.00

Ten varieties of each of the 5c, 10c, 20c, and 50c, and six varieties of the 1 peso. No. 36 was used as a carrier stamp.

A10   A11   A12

A13   A14

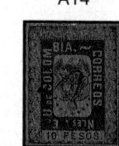

A15   A16

1866   **White Wove Paper**

45	A10	5c orange	72.50	27.50
46	A11	10c lilac	17.00	5.25
a.		Pelure paper	21.00	11.50
47	A12	20c light blue	42.50	21.00
a.		Pelure paper	67.50	52.50
48	A13	50c green	17.00	13.00
49	A14	1p rose red, *bluish*	92.50	32.50
a.		1p vermilion	92.50	32.50
51	A15	5p blk, *green*	500.00	210.00
52	A16	10p blk, *vermilion*	350.00	200.00

There are several varieties of the 1 peso having the letters "U," "N," "S" and "O" smaller.

A17   A18

A19   A20

A21

TEN CENTAVOS:
Type I — "B" of "COLOMBIA" over "V" of "CENTAVOS."
Type II — "B" of "COLOMBIA" over "VO" of "CENTAVOS."
ONE PESO:
Type I — Long thin spear heads. Diagonal lines in lower part of shield.
Type II — Short thick spear heads. Horizontal and a few diagonal lines in lower part of shield.

Type III — Short thick spear heads. Crossed lines in lower part of shield. Ornaments at each side of circle are broken. (See No. 97.)

1868

53	A17	5c orange	67.50	52.50
54	A18	10c lilac (I)	4.25	1.10
a.		10c red violet (I)	4.25	1.10
b.		10c lilac (II)	4.25	1.10
c.		10c red violet (II)	4.25	1.10
d.		Printed on both sides	7.50	2.50
55	A19	20c blue	3.00	1.25
56	A20	50c yellow green	3.50	2.40
57	A21	1p ver (II)	4.25	2.10
a.		Tête bêche pair	140.00	100.00
b.		1p rose red (I)	60.00	27.50
c.		1p rose red (II)	4.00	2.10
		Nos. 53-57 (5)	82.50	59.35

See Nos. 83-84, 96-97.
Counterfeits or reprints.
10c — There is a large white dot at the upper left between the circle enclosing the "X" and the ornament below.
50c — There is a shading of dots instead of dashes below the ribbon with motto. There are crossed lines in the lowest section of the shield instead of diagonal or horizontal ones.
1p — The ornaments in the lettered circle are broken. There are crossed lines in the lowest section of the shield. These counterfeits, or reprints, are on white paper, wove and laid, on colored wove paper and in fancy colors.

A22

Two varieties

1869-70   Wove Paper

59	A22	2½c black, *violet*	4.75	2.50
a.		Laid paper ('70)	325.00	250.00
b.		Laid batonné paper ('70)	30.00	24.00

Nos. 59, 59a, 59b were used as carrier stamps.
Counterfeits, or reprints, are on magenta paper wove or ribbed.

A23   A24

1870   Wove Paper

62	A23	5c orange	2.00	1.25
a.		5c yellow	2.00	1.25
63	A24	25c black, *blue*	16.00	13.00

See No. 89.
In the counterfeits, or reprints, of No. 63, the top of the "2" of "25" does not touch the down stroke. The counterfeits are on paper of various colors.

A25   A26

5 pesos — The ornament at the left of the "C" of "Cinco" cuts into the "C," and the shading of the flag is formed of diagonal lines.
10 pesos — The stars have extra rays between the points, and the central part of the shield has some horizontal lines of shading at each end.

Surface Colored, Chalky Paper

1870

64	A25	5p blk, *green*	100.00	67.50
65	A26	10p blk, *vermilion*	120.00	67.50

See Nos. 77-79, 125-126.

A27   A28

A29

TEN CENTAVOS:
Type I — "S" of "CORREOS" 2½mm high. First "N" of "NACIONALES" small.
Type II — "S" of "CORREOS" 2mm high. First "N" of "NACIONALES" wide.

1871-74   Thin Porous Paper

66	A27	1c green ('72)	3.50	3.50
67	A27	1c rose ('73)	3.50	3.50
a.		1c carmine ('73)	3.50	3.50
68	A28	2c brown	1.60	1.60
a.		2c red brown	1.60	1.60
69	A29	10c vio (I) ('74)	2.50	2.50
a.		10c lilac (I) ('74)	2.50	2.50
b.		10c violet (II) ('74)	2.50	2.50
c.		10c lilac (II) ('74)	2.50	2.50
d.		As #69, laid paper ('72)	140.00	140.00
e.		As "b," laid paper ('72)	140.00	140.00
		Nos. 66-69 (4)	11.10	11.10

Counterfeits or reprints.
1c — The outer frame of the shield is broken near the upper left corner and the "A" of "Colombia" has no cross-bar.
2c — There are scratches across "DOS" and many marks around the letters on the large "2." The counterfeits, or reprints, are on white wove and bluish white laid paper.

Condor — A30

Liberty Head
A31   A32

5 pesos, redrawn — The ornament at the left of the "C" only touches the "C," and the shading of the flag is formed of vertical and diagonal lines.
10 pesos, redrawn — The stars are distinctly five pointed, and there is no shading in the central part of the shield.

1877   Wove Paper

73	A30	5c purple	7.25	2.10
a.		5c lilac	7.25	2.10
74	A31	10c bister brown	3.50	.90
a.		10c red brown	3.50	.90
b.		10c violet brown	3.50	.90
75	A32	20c blue	4.25	1.40
a.		20c violet blue	25.00	3.00
77	A26	10p blk, *rose*	120.00	67.50
78	A25	5p blk, *lt grn,* redrawn	42.50	32.50
79	A26	10p blk, *rose,* redrawn	17.00	2.75
a.		10p blk, *dark rose,* redrawn	17.00	2.75
		Nos. 73-79 (6)	194.50	107.15

Stamps of the issues of 1871-77 are known with private perforations of various gauges, also with sewing machine perforation.
In the counterfeits, or reprints, of the 5 pesos the ornament at the left of the "C" of "Cinco" is separated from the "C" by a black line.
In the counterfeits, or reprints, of the 10 pesos the outer line of the double circle containing "10" is broken at the top, below "OS" of "Unidos," and the vertical lines of shading contained in the double circle are very indistinct. There is a colorless dash below the loop of the "P" of "Pesos."

1876-79   Laid Paper

80	A30	5c lilac	85.00	65.00
81	A31	10c brown	47.50	2.75
82	A32	20c blue	100.00	67.50
83	A20	50c green ('79)	97.50	65.00
84	A21	1p pale red (II) ('79)	62.50	15.00
		Nos. 80-84 (5)	392.50	215.25

1879   Wove Paper

89	A24	25c green	32.50	32.50

1881   Blue Wove Paper

93	A30	5c violet	20.00	13.00
a.		5c lilac	20.00	13.00

94	A31	10c brown	12.00	2.50
95	A32	20c blue	12.00	3.75
96	A20	50c yellow green	12.50	7.50
97	A21	1p ver (III)	17.00	7.50
		Nos. 93-97 (5)	73.50	34.25

For types of 1p, see note over No. 53.

Reprints of the 10c and 20c are much worn. On the 10c the letters "TAVOS" of "CENTA-VOS" often touch. On the 20c the letters "NT" of "VEINTE" touch and the left arm of the "T" is too long. Reprints of the 25c, 50c and 1p have the characteristics previously described. The reprints are on white wove or laid paper, on colored papers, and in fancy colors. Stamps on green paper exist only as reprints.

A34   A35

A36

1 centavo — The period before "UNION" is round and there are rays between the stars and the condors.
2 centavos — The "2's" and "C's" in the corners are placed upright.
5 centavos — The last star at the right almost touches the frame.
10 centavos — The letters of the inscription are thin; there are rays between the stars and the condor.

1881   White Wove Paper   *Imperf.*

103	A34	1c green	5.00	4.00
104	A35	2c vermilion	2.10	1.60
a.		2c rose	2.50	1.60
106	A34	5c blue	5.00	1.60
a.		Printed on both sides		
107	A36	10c violet	4.25	1.25
108	A34	20c black	4.75	2.00
		Nos. 103-108 (5)	21.10	10.45

The stamps of this issue are found with perforations of various gauges, also sewing machine perforation, all of which are unofficial. See Nos. 112, 114-115.

Liberty Head — A37

1881   *Imperf.*

109	A37	1c blk, *green*	3.50	5.00
110	A37	2c blk, *lilac rose*	3.50	5.00
111	A37	5c blk, *lilac*	8.50	1.75
		Nos. 109-111 (3)	15.50	11.75

Nos. 109 to 111 are found with regular or sewing machine perforation, unofficial.
Reprints:
1c — The top line of the stamp and the top frame extend to the left. 2c — There is a curved line over the scroll below the "AV" of "CENTAVOS."
5c — There are scratches across the "5" in the upper left corner. All three values were reprinted on the three colors of paper of the originals.

A37a

Redrawn

1 centavo — The period before "UNION" is square and the rays between the stars and the condor have been wholly or partly erased.
2 centavos — The "2's" and "C's" in the corners are placed diagonally.
5 centavos — The last star at the right touches the wing of the condor.
10 centavos — The letters of the inscription are thick; there are no rays under the stars; the last star at the right touches the wing of the condor and this wing touches the frame.

1883   *Imperf.*

112	A34	1c green	4.75	4.25
113	A37a	2c rose	2.10	1.75
114	A34	5c blue	4.00	1.00
a.		5c ultramarine	4.00	1.00
b.		Printed on both sides, reverse ultra	25.00	20.00
115	A36	10c violet	5.00	1.40
		Nos. 112-115 (4)	15.85	8.40

The stamps of this issue are found with regular or sewing machine perforation, privately applied.

A38   A39

1883   *Perf. 10½, 12, 13½*

116	A38	1c gray grn, *grn*	1.00	1.00
a.		Imperf., pair	5.00	5.00
117	A39	2c red, *rose*	1.00	1.25
a.		2c org red, *rose*	1.00	1.25
b.		2c red, *buff*	12.00	12.00
c.		Imperf., pair (#117 or 117a)	7.75	7.75
d.		"DE LOS" in very small caps	15.00	15.00
118	A38	5c blue, *bluish*	2.50	1.50
a.		5c dk bl, *bluish*	2.50	1.00
b.		5c blue	3.25	2.00
c.		Imperf., pair (#118 or 118a)	7.75	7.75
d.		As "b," imperf., pair	12.00	12.00
119	A39	10c org, *yel*	1.25	1.40
a.		"DE LOS" in large caps	60.00	26.00
b.		Imperf., pair	16.00	16.00
120	A39	20c vio, *lilac*	1.40	1.40
a.		Imperf., pair	16.00	16.00
122	A38	50c brn, *buff*	3.00	3.25
a.		Perf. 12	3.00	3.25
123	A38	1p claret, *bluish*	5.50	1.90
a.		Imperf., pair	16.00	16.00
		Nos. 116-123 (7)	15.65	11.70

Redrawn Types of 1877

1883 (?)   *Perf. 10½, 12*

125	A25	5p orange brown	10.00	6.00
126	A26	10p black, *gray*	10.00	7.25

1886   *Perf. 10½, 11½, 12*

127	A38	5p brown, *straw*	10.00	5.50
a.		Imperf., pair	32.50	32.50
128	A38	10p black, *rose*	10.00	5.50
a.		Imperf., pair	32.50	32.50

Republic of Colombia

A40   Simón Bolívar — A41

Pres. Rafael Núñez — A42

1886   *Perf. 10½ and 13½*

129	A40	1c grn, *grn*	1.75	.70
a.		Imperf., pair	6.75	6.75
130	A41	5c blue, *bl*	1.75	.40
a.		5c ultra, *blue*	1.75	.40
b.		Imperf., pair (#130)	6.75	6.75
131	A42	10c orange	3.50	.70
a.		Imperf., pair	9.25	9.25
b.		Pelure paper	4.50	1.00
		Nos. 129-131 (3)	7.00	1.80

Gen. Antonio Jose de Sucre y Alcala — A43   Gen. Antonio Nariño — A44

1887

133	A43	2c org red, *rose*	2.25	1.00
a.		2c orange red, *yellowish*	6.00	6.00
b.		2c orange red	7.25	7.25
c.		Imperf., pair (#133)	10.00	10.00

134	A44	20c pur, *grysh*	3.00	1.10
a.		Imperf., pair	8.50	8.50
b.		Pelure paper	3.50	2.25

Impressions of No. 134 on white, blue or greenish blue paper were not regularly issued.

Arms — A45

1888

135	A45	50c brn, *buff*	1.75	1.90
a.		Imperf., pair	6.00	6.00
136	A45	1p claret, *bluish*	8.00	2.10
137	A45	1p claret	3.50	1.05
138	A45	5p org brn	8.50	6.50
139	A45	5p black	14.50	9.50
140	A45	10p black, *rose*	21.00	6.75
		Nos. 135-140 (6)	57.25	27.80

See Nos. 155, 158-159.

Nariño — A46

1889

141	A46	20c pur, *grayish*	1.90	1.25
a.		Imperf., pair	9.25	9.25

Impressions on white, blue or greenish blue paper were not regularly issued.

A47   A48

A49   A50

A51

1890-91   **Perf. 10½, 13½, 11**

142	A47	1c grn, *grn*	1.90	1.60
143	A48	2c org red, *rose*	.95	.95
144	A49	5c bl, *grnsh bl*	1.40	.40
a.		5c deep blue, *blue*	1.40	.40
b.		Imperf., pair	5.50	5.50
146	A50	10c brn, *yel*	1.00	.40
a.		10c brown, *buff*	1.00	.40
147	A51	20c vio, pelure paper	3.50	3.50
		Nos. 142-147 (5)	8.75	6.85

A52   A52a

A53   A53a

A54

Perf. 10½, 12, 13½, 14 to 15½

1892-99   **Ordinary Paper**

148	A47	1c red, *yel*	.85	.40
149	A52	2c red, *rose*	42.50	42.50
150	A52	2c green	.50	.30
a.		2c yellow green	.50	.30
151	A49	5c blk, *buff*	13.00	.35
152	A52a	5c org brn, *pale buff*	1.00	.30
a.		5c red brown, *salmon* ('97)	1.00	.30
153	A50	10c bis brn, *rose*	.75	.40
a.		10c brown, *brownish*	2.00	1.60
154	A53	20c brn, *bl*	.75	.40
a.		20c red brown, *blue*	.75	.40
b.		20c yel brn, *grnsh bl* ('97)	5.50	13.00
c.		20c brown, *buff* ('97)	19.00	13.00
155	A45	50c vio, *vio*	1.25	.75
156	A53a	50c red vio, *vio* ('99)	1.75	
157	A54	1p bl, *grnsh*	2.10	.90
a.		1p blue, *buff*	2.10	.90
158	A45	5p red, *pale rose*	8.50	3.25
159	A45	10p blue	16.00	3.25
a.		Thin, pale rose paper	27.50	7.25
		Nos. 148-159 (12)	88.95	
		Nos. 148-155,157-159 (11)		52.80

Type A53a is a redrawing of type A45. The letters of the inscriptions are slightly larger and the numerals "50" slightly smaller than in type A45.

The 20c brown on white paper is believed to be a chemical changeling.

Nos. 148, 150-152a, 153-155, 157, 159 exist imperf. Value per pair, $6-9.

A56

1899

162	A56	1c red, *yellow*	.70	.35
163	A56	5c red brn, *sal*	.70	.35
164	A56	10c brn, *lil rose*	2.00	.95
165	A56	50c blue, *lilac*	1.40	1.25
		Nos. 162-165 (4)	4.80	2.90

Cartagena Issues

A57

1899   **Blue Overprint**   *Imperf.*

167	A57	5c red, *buff*	30.00	30.00
a.		Sewing machine perf.	30.00	30.00
168	A57	10c ultra, *buff*	30.00	30.00
a.		Sewing machine perf.	30.00	30.00

Nos. 167 and 167a differ slightly from the illustration.

Bolivar No. 55 Overprinted with 7 Parallel Wavy Lines and

A58   A59

A60   A61

Perf. 14 (#169), Sewing Machine Perf.

1899   **Purple Overprint**

169	A18	1c black	60.00	60.00
170	A58	1c brn, *buff*	20.00	20.00
171	A59	2c blk, *buff*	20.00	20.00
a.		Altered from 10c	30.00	30.00
172	A60	5c mar, *grnsh bl*	18.00	18.00
a.		Perf. 12	18.00	18.00
b.		Without overprint	10.50	10.50
173	A61	10c red, *sal*	18.00	18.00
a.		Perf. 12	18.00	18.00
		Nos. 169-173 (5)	136.00	136.00

Types A58 and A59 illustrate Nos. 170a and 171a, which were made from altered plates of the 10c (No. 168). Nos. 170 and 171 were made from altered plate of the 5c denomination (No. 167), show part of the top flag of the "5" and differ slightly from the illustrations.

Nos. 170-173 exist imperf. Values about same as perf.

A62

1900   **Purple Overprint**   *Imperf.*

174	A62	5c red	25.00	25.00
a.		Perf. 12	35.00	35.00

A63   A64

"Gobierno Provisorio" at Top

1900   **Litho.**   **Perf. 12 Vertically**

175	A63	1c (ctvo) blk, *bl grn*	47.50	8.00
a.		"cvo."	120.00	14.50
b.		"cvos."	47.50	8.00
c.		"centavo"	55.00	47.50
176	A63	2c black	26.00	6.00
177	A63	5c blk, *pink*	26.00	6.00
a.		Name at side (V)	62.50	9.00
178	A63	10c blk, *pink*	26.00	6.00
a.		Name at side (V)	62.50	9.00
179	A63	20c blk, *yellow*	47.50	8.00
a.		Name at side (G)	92.50	12.00
		Nos. 175-179 (5)	173.00	34.00

"Gobierno Provisional" at Top
Name at Side in Black or Green

180	A64	1c (ctvo.) blk, *bl grn*	47.50	8.00
a.		"centavo"	125.00	47.50
181	A64	2c blk, *bl grn*	30.00	5.00
182	A64	5c blk (G)	30.00	5.00
a.		"ctvos." smaller	47.50	9.00
183	A64	10c blk, *pink*	30.00	5.00
184	A64	20c blk, *yel* (G)	47.50	8.00
		Nos. 180-184 (5)	185.00	31.00

Issues of the rebel provisional government in Cucuta.

A65   A66

Purple Overprint

1901   **Sewing Machine Perf.**

185	A65	1c black	1.00	1.00
a.		Without overprint	2.25	2.25
b.		Double overprint	2.50	2.50
c.		Imperf., pair	2.50	2.50
d.		Inverted overprint	1.25	1.25
186	A66	2c blk, *rose*	1.00	1.00
a.		Imperf., pair	2.50	2.50
b.		Without overprint	2.25	2.25
c.		Double overprint	2.50	2.50

A67   A68

1901   **Rose Overprint**

187	A67	1c blue	1.00	1.00
a.		Imperf., pair	4.00	4.00
188	A68	2c brown	1.00	1.00
a.		Imperf., pair	4.00	4.00
b.		Without overprint	1.00	1.00

A69   A70

Sewing Machine or Regular Perf. 12, 12½

1902   **Magenta Overprint**

189	A69	5c violet	2.25	2.25
a.		Without overprint	2.25	2.25
b.		Double overprint	2.25	2.25
c.		Imperf., pair	4.75	4.75
190	A70	10c yel brn	2.25	2.25
a.		Double overprint	2.25	2.25
b.		Imperf., pair	4.75	4.75
c.		Without overprint	2.25	2.25
d.		Printed on both sides	3.25	3.25

A71   A72

1902   **Magenta Overprint**

191	A71	5c yel brn	2.25	2.25
a.		Without overprint	2.10	2.10
b.		Imperf., pair	6.00	6.00
192	A71	10c black	1.75	1.75
a.		Without overprint	1.50	1.50
b.		Imperf., pair	9.00	9.00
193	A72	20c maroon	5.50	4.50
b.		Imperf., pair	15.00	15.00
		Nos. 191-193 (3)	9.50	8.50

Nos. 191-193 exist tête bêche. Value of 10c and 20c, each $15.

Washed examples of Nos. 167-174, 185-193 are offered as "without overprint."

Barranquilla Issues

Magdalena River — A75

Iron Quay at Sabanilla — A76

La Popa Hill — A77

1902-03   *Imperf.*

194	A75	2c green	1.60	1.60
195	A75	2c dk bl	1.60	1.60
196	A75	2c rouge	22.50	22.50
197	A76	10c scarlet	1.10	1.10
198	A76	10c orange	13.00	13.00
199	A76	10c rose	1.75	1.75
200	A76	10c maroon	1.90	1.90
201	A76	10c claret	1.90	1.90
202	A77	20c violet	3.50	3.50
a.		Laid paper		9.50

203	A77	20c dl bl	9.50	9.50
204	A77	20c dl bl, *pink*	125.00	125.00
205	A77	20c car rose	20.00	20.00
		Nos. 194-205 (12)	203.35	203.35

Sewing Machine Perf. and Perf. 12

194a	A75	2c green	9.50	9.50
195a	A75	2c dark blue	9.50	9.50
196a	A75	2c carmine	47.50	47.50
197a	A76	10c scarlet	4.75	4.75
198a	A76	10c orange	35.00	35.00
199a	A76	10c rose	6.50	6.50
200a	A76	10c maroon	6.50	6.50
201a	A76	10c claret	6.00	6.00
202b	A77	20c purple	.70	.70
c.		20c lilac	.70	.70
203a	A77	20c dull blue	9.50	9.50
204a	A77	20c dull blue, *rose*	150.00	150.00
205b	A77	20c carmine rose	72.50	72.50
		Nos. 194a-205b (12)	357.95	357.95

See Nos. 240-245.

Cruiser
"Cartagena" — A78

Bolívar — A79

General Próspero
Pinzón — A80

A81   A82

1903-04   Imperf.

209	A78	5c blue	2.75	2.75
210	A78	5c bister	4.50	4.50
211	A79	50c yellow	3.75	3.75
212	A79	50c green	4.50	4.50
213	A79	50c scarlet	4.50	4.50
214	A79	50c carmine	4.50	4.50
a.		50c rose	4.50	4.50
215	A79	50c pale brown	4.50	4.50
216	A80	1p yellow brn	1.60	1.60
217	A80	1p rose	2.50	2.50
218	A80	1p blue	2.50	2.50
219	A80	1p violet	25.00	25.00
220	A81	5p claret	5.50	5.50
221	A81	5p pale brown	8.00	8.00
222	A81	5p blue green	7.50	7.50
223	A82	10p pale green	7.75	7.75
224	A82	10p claret	25.00	25.00
		Nos. 209-224 (16)	114.35	114.35

Nos. 216 and 217 measure 20½x26½mm
and No. 218, 18x24mm. Stamps of this issue
exist with forged perforations.

Perf. 12

209a	A78	5c blue	9.50	9.50
210a	A78	5c bister	9.50	9.50
211a	A79	50c yellow	9.50	9.50
b.		50c orange	25.00	25.00
212a	A79	50c green	25.00	25.00
213a	A79	50c scarlet	11.50	11.50
214b	A79	50c rose	11.50	11.50
215a	A79	50c pale brown	11.50	11.50
216a	A80	1p yellow brown	5.25	5.25
217a	A80	1p rose	7.50	7.50
218a	A80	1p blue	9.50	9.50
219a	A80	1p violet	62.50	62.50
220a	A81	5p claret	20.00	20.00
221a	A81	5p pale brown	22.50	22.50
222a	A81	5p blue green	22.50	22.50
223a	A82	10p pale green	30.00	30.00
224a	A82	10p claret	77.50	77.50
		Nos. 209a-224a (16)	345.25	343.25

Laid Paper   Imperf.

240	A76	10c dk bl, *lil*	6.25	6.25
241	A76	10c dk bl, *bluish*	3.75	3.75
242	A76	10c dk bl, *brn*	3.75	3.75
243	A76	10c dk bl, *sal*	9.25	9.25
244	A76	10c dk bl, *grnsh bl*	5.00	5.00
245	A76	10c dk bl, *dp rose*	3.75	3.75
		Nos. 240-245 (6)	31.75	31.75

Perf. 12

240a	A76	10c dk bl, *lilac*	13.50	13.50
241a	A76	10c dk bl, *bluish*	9.25	9.25
242a	A76	10c dk bl, *brn*	9.25	9.25
243a	A76	10c dk bl, *salmon*	72.50	72.50
244a	A76	10c dk bl, *grnsh bl*	20.00	20.00
245a	A76	10c dk bl, *deep rose*	9.25	9.25
		Nos. 240a-245a (6)	133.75	133.75

A82a

Imperf., Sewing Machine Perf.

1902			**Typeset**	
255	A82a	10c black, *rose*	3.50	3.50
256	A82a	20c blk, *orange*	2.50	2.50

This issue was printed in either Cali or
Popayan.

Medellin Issue

A83

1902

257	A83	1c grn, *straw*	.35	.50
258	A83	2c salmon, *rose*	.35	.50
259	A83	5c dp bl, *grnsh*	.35	.50
260	A83	10c pale brn, *straw*	.35	.50
261	A83	20c pur, *rose*	.45	.50
262	A83	50c dl rose, *grnsh*	2.25	3.00
263	A83	1p blk, *yellow*	4.50	6.75
264	A83	5p slate, *blue*	35.00	35.00
265	A83	10p dk brn, *rose*	22.50	22.50
		Nos. 257-265 (9)	66.10	69.75

For overprint see No. L8.

Imperf., Pairs

257a	A83	1c	11.00	11.00
258a	A83	2c	11.00	11.00
259a	A83	5c	11.00	11.00
260a	A83	10c	11.00	11.00
261a	A83	20c	11.00	11.00
262a	A83	50c	11.00	11.00
263a	A83	1p	27.50	27.50
264a	A83	5p	80.00	80.00
265a	A83	10p	50.00	50.00

Regular Issue

A84   A85

A86   A87

A88   A89

A90   A91

A92

1902   Imperf.

266	A84	2c blk, *rose*	.25	.25
267	A85	4c red, *grn*	.25	.25
268	A86	5c grn, *grn*	.25	.25
269	A87	10c blk, *pink*	.25	.25
c.		10c blk, *rose*	1.10	1.10
270	A88	20c brn, *buff*	.25	.25
271	A89	50c dk grn, *rose*	1.40	1.40
272	A90	1p pur, *buff*	.60	.60
273	A91	5p grn, *bl*	4.25	4.25
274	A92	10p grn, *pale grn*	13.00	6.50
		Nos. 266-274 (9)	20.50	14.00

For overprint see No. H4.

Sewing Machine Perf.

266a	A84	2c blk, *rose*	1.90	1.90
267a	A85	4c red, *grn*	1.60	1.60
268a	A86	5c grn, *blue*	1.90	1.90
269a	A87	10c blk, *pink*	1.90	1.90
270a	A88	20c brn, *buff*	3.25	2.50
271a	A89	50c grn, *rose*	6.50	5.25
272a	A90	1p pur, *buff*	7.75	6.50
273a	A91	5p grn, *blue*	35.00	35.00
274a	A92	10p grn, *pale grn*	65.00	65.00
		Nos. 266a-274a (9)	124.80	121.55

1903   Perf. 12

266b	A84	2c blk, *rose*	1.40	1.40
269b	A87	10c blk, *pink*	1.60	1.60
270b	A88	20c brn, *buff*	1.60	1.60
272b	A90	1p pur, *buff*	3.25	3.25
273b	A91	5p grn, *blue*	27.50	27.50
274b	A92	10p grn, *pale grn*	52.50	45.00
		Nos. 266b-274b (6)	87.85	80.80

1903   Imperf.

284	A85	4c blue, *grn*	.35	.35
285	A86	5c blue, *blue*	.35	.35
286	A88	20c blue, *buff*	.35	.35
288	A89	50c blue, *rose*	1.75	1.75
		Nos. 284-288 (4)	2.80	2.80

Sewing Machine Perf.

284a	A85	4c blue, *grn*	2.25	1.75
285a	A86	5c blue, *blue*	2.25	1.75
286a	A88	20c blue, *buff*	3.25	2.50
288a	A89	50c blue, *rose*	6.50	5.75
		Nos. 284a-288a (4)	14.25	11.75

Perf. 12

284b	A85	4c blue, *grn*	2.50	2.50
285b	A86	5c blue, *blue*	2.50	2.50
286b	A88	20c blue, *buff*	3.50	3.50
288b	A89	50c blue, *rose*	9.75	9.75
		Nos. 284b-288b (4)	18.25	18.25

A93

1904   Pelure Paper   Imperf.

303	A93	½c yellow brn	1.10	1.10
304	A90	1c blue green	1.10	1.10
a.		1c yellow green	1.10	1.10
306	A84	2c blue	.90	.65
307	A86	5c carmine	1.00	1.00
308	A87	10c violet	1.10	.90
		Nos. 303-308 (5)	5.20	4.75

For overprint see No. H13.

1904   Perf. 13

303a	A93	½c yellow brown	4.25	4.25
304b	A90	1c blue green	5.50	5.00
c.		1c yellow green	7.50	7.00
306a	A84	2c blue	2.50	2.50

Perf. 12

307a	A86	5c carmine	2.25	2.25
308a	A87	10c violet	2.25	2.25
		Nos. 303a-308a (5)	16.75	16.25

A94   A95

Pres. José Manuel
Marroquín — A96

Imprint: "Lit. J.L.Arango Medellin.
Col."

1904   Wove Paper   Perf. 12

314	A94	½c yellow	.85	.25
315	A94	1c green	.85	.25
316	A94	2c rose	.85	.25
317	A94	5c blue	1.40	.25
318	A94	10c violet	1.75	.25
319	A94	20c black	1.75	.25
320	A95	1p brown	19.00	3.00
321	A96	5p red & blk, *yel*	60.00	60.00
322	A96	10p bl & blk, *grnsh*	60.00	60.00
		Nos. 314-322 (9)	146.45	124.50

Redrawn

314a	A94	½c	.85	.25
315a	A94	1c	.85	.25
316a	A94	2c	.85	.25
317a	A94	5c	1.40	.25
319a	A94	20c	1.75	.25
		Nos. 314a-319a (5)	5.70	1.25

Imperf., Pairs

314b	A94	½c	3.25	3.25
315b	A94	1c	2.50	2.50
316b	A94	2c	3.25	3.25
317b	A94	5c	3.25	3.25
318b	A94	10c	4.25	4.25
319b	A94	20c	7.75	7.75
320a	A95	1p	65.00	65.00
		Nos. 314b-320a (7)	89.25	89.25

On the redrawn types, the imprint is close to
the base of the design instead of being spaced
from it. On the redrawn 2c and 5c, the lower
end of the vertical white line below "OR" of
"CORREOS" forms a hook which turns to the
right instead of to the left as in the originals.
See Nos. 325-330. For surcharges see Nos.
351-354, L1-L7, L9-L13, L15-L25.

A97

100p has different frame.

1903   Imperf.

323	A97	50p org yel, *pale pink*	92.50	92.50
324	A97	100p dk bl, *dk rose*	77.50	77.50

Imprint: "Lit. Nacional"
Perf. 10, 13, 13½ and Compound
1908

325	A94	½c orange	.85	.25
a.		½c yellow	.85	.25
b.		Imperf., pair	2.50	1.90
c.		Without imprint	5.25	5.25
326	A94	1c yel grn	.75	.25
a.		Without imprint	.75	.25
d.		Imperf., pair	4.00	3.25
327	A94	2c red	.75	.25
a.		2c carmine	.75	.25
b.		Imperf., pair	4.00	3.25
328	A94	5c blue	.60	.25
a.		Imperf., pair	4.25	5.25
329	A94	10c violet	50.00	1.00
330	A94	20c gray blk	50.00	1.00
		Nos. 325-330 (6)	102.95	3.00

The above stamps may be easily distinguished from those of 1904 by the perforation, by the height of the design, 24mm instead of
23mm, and by the "Lit. Nacional" imprint.

Camilo Torres
A99

Policarpa
Salavarrieta
A100

Bolívar Demanding
Liberation of
Slaves — A105

Designs: 2c, Nariño. 5c, Bolívar. 10c, Francisco José de Caldas. 20c, Francisco de Paula Santander. 10p, Bolívar Resigning.

1910, Aug.		Engr.		Perf. 12	
331	A99	½c violet & blk		.50	.30
a.		Center inverted		425.00	425.00
332	A100	1c deep green		.40	.25
333	A100	2c scarlet		.40	.25
334	A100	5c deep blue		1.25	.45
335	A100	10c plum		10.00	5.00
336	A100	20c black brn		15.00	5.50
337	A105	1p dk violet		85.00	25.00
338	A105	10p claret		325.00	250.00
		Nos. 331-338 (8)		437.55	286.75

Colombian independence centenary.

Caldas
A107

Monument to
Battle of
Boyacá
A113

View of
Cartagena
A114

Coat of Arms
A118

Designs: 1c, Torres. 2c, Narino. 4c, Santander. 5c, Bolivar. 10c, Jose Maria Cordoba. 1p, Sucre. 2p, Rufino Cuervo. 5p, Antonio Ricaurte y Lozano.

1917		Engr.	Perf. 14	
339	A107	½c bister	.35	.25
340	A107	1c green	.30	.25
341	A107	2c car rose	.30	.25
342	A107	4c violet	.90	.30
343	A107	5c dull blue	3.00	.25
344	A107	10c gray	3.00	.25
345	A113	20c red	1.50	.25
346	A114	50c carmine	1.75	.25
347	A107	1p brt blue	12.00	.40
348	A107	2p orange	13.50	.45
349	A107	5p gray	40.00	11.00
350	A118	10p dk brown	47.50	11.50
		Nos. 339-350 (12)	124.10	26.40

The 1c, 5c, 10c, 50c, 2p, 5p and 10p also exist perf. 11½ and 11½ compounded with 14.
Litho. varieties of Nos. 343, 345 and 346 are counterfeits made to defraud the government. Imperforate examples of Nos. 339-350 are not known to have been regularly issued.
See Nos. 373-374, 400-405. For overprints and surcharges see Nos. 369-370, 377, 409-410, 440, C1, O3, O5-O9.

Nos. 318-319, 329-330
Surcharged in Red

1918		On Issue of 1904		
351	A94	½c on 20c black	1.25	.35
352	A94	3c on 10c violet	3.00	.60
		On Issue of 1908		
353	A94	½c on 20c gray blk	10.00	6.25
354	A94	3c on 10c violet	15.00	5.00
		Nos. 351-354 (4)	29.25	12.20

Nos. 351-354 inclusive exist with surcharge reading up or down. On one stamp in each sheet the letter "S" in "Especie" is omitted. All denominations exist with a small zero before the decimal in the surcharge.

A119

1918		Litho.	Perf. 13½	
358	A119	3c red	.95	.25
a.		Imperf., pair	5.00	5.00

A120

1920		Engr.	Perf. 14	
359	A120	3c red, org	.40	.25
a.		Imperf., pair	3.75	3.75

See No. 371-372. For surcharge see No. 453.

A121

A122

A123

Perf. 10, 13½ and Compound

1920-21			Litho.	
360	A121	½c yellow	1.40	.50
361	A121	1c green	.85	.25
362	A121	2c red	.65	.25
363	A122	3c green	.65	.25
a.		3c yellow green	.65	.25
364	A121	5c blue	1.25	.25
365	A121	10c violet	6.00	1.50
366	A121	20c deep green	6.75	4.00
367	A123	50c dark red	8.50	4.00
		Nos. 360-367 (8)	26.05	11.00

The tablet with "PROVISIONAL" was added separately to each design on the various lithographic stones and its position varies slightly on different stamps in the sheet. For some values there were two or more stones, on which the tablet was placed at various angles.
Nos. 360-366 exist imperf.
See No. 375.

No. 342 Surcharged in Red

a

(15mm wide)
— b

1921				
369	A107	(a) 3c on 4c violet	.95	.25
a.		Double surcharge	15.00	
370	A107	(b) 3c on 4c violet	3.75	2.00

See No. 377.

Types of 1917-21

1923-24		Engr.	Perf. 13½	
371	A120	1½c chocolate	1.25	.60
372	A120	3c blue	.50	.25
373	A107	5c claret ('24)	3.00	.25
374	A107	10c blue	9.25	.50
		Litho.		
375	A121	10c dark blue	12.50	7.25
		Nos. 371-375 (5)	26.50	8.85

No. 342 Surcharged in Red

(18mm wide)

1924				
377	A107	3c on 4c vio	3.75	1.50
a.		Double surcharge	15.00	
b.		Double surch., one invtd.	15.00	
c.		With added surch. "3cs." in red		

A124

1924-25		Litho.	Perf. 10, 10x13½	
379	A124	1c red	.85	.25
380	A124	3c dp blue ('25)	.85	.25

Exist imperf. Value, each pair $6.25.

A125

A126

Black, Red or Green Srch. & Ovpt.
Imprint of Waterlow & Sons

1925			Perf. 14, 14½	
382	A125	1c on 3c bis brn	.70	.25
383	A126	4c violet (R)	.50	.25
a.		Inverted surcharge	8.75	8.75

Imprint of American Bank Note Co.
Perf. 12

384	A125	1c on 3c bis brn	7.50	6.25
a.		Inverted surcharge	19.00	19.00
385	A126	4c violet (G)	.50	.30
a.		Inverted overprint	9.50	9.50
		Nos. 382-385 (4)	9.20	7.05

Correos
Provisional

Revenue stamps of basic types A125 and A126 were handstamped as above in violet or blue by the Cali post office in 1925, but were not authorized by the government. Denominations so overprinted are 1c, 2c, 3c, 4c and 5c.

A127

A128

Perf. 10, 13½x10

1926		Litho.	Wmk. 194	
395	A127	1c gray green	.50	.25
396	A128	4c deep blue	.55	.25

Exist imperf. Value, each pair $5.

Types of 1917 and

Sabana
Station — A129

1926-29		Unwmk. Engr.	Perf. 14	
400	A107	4c deep blue	.50	.25
401	A118	8c dark blue	.60	.25
402	A107	30c olive bister	6.00	.70

403	A129	40c brn & yel brn	9.25	1.25
404	A107	5p violet	9.25	.90
a.		Perf. 11 ('29)	12.00	1.00
405	A118	10p green	15.00	2.50
a.		Perf. 11		
		Nos. 400-405 (6)	40.60	5.85

For surcharges & overprint see Nos. 409-410, O4.

Death of
Bolívar
A130

1930, Dec. 17			Perf. 12½	
408	A130	4c dk blue & blk	.60	.35

Cent. of the death of Simón Bolívar. See Nos. C80-C82.

Nos. 400 and 402
Surcharged in Red or
Dark Blue

1932, Jan. 20			Perf. 14	
409	A107	1c on 4c dp bl (R)	.30	.25
a.		Inverted surcharge	5.25	5.25
410	A107	20c on 30c ol bis	10.00	.70
a.		Inverted surcharge	21.00	
b.		Double surcharge	21.00	

Emerald
Mine — A131

Oil
Wells — A132

Coffee Cultivation
A133

Platinum
Mine — A134

Gold
Mining — A135

Christopher
Columbus — A136

Imprint: "Waterlow & Sons Ltd. Londres"

1932		Wmk. 229	Perf. 12½	
411	A131	1c green	.60	.25
412	A132	2c red	.60	.25
413	A133	5c brown	.70	.25
414	A134	8c blue blk	4.75	.60
415	A135	10c yellow	3.50	.25
416	A136	20c dk blue	10.00	.40
		Nos. 411-416 (6)	20.15	2.00

See Nos. 441-442, 464-466a, 517. For surcharges see Nos. 455, 527, O10-O11, O13, RA30. Post 1940 issues in *Scott Standard Postage Stamp Catalogue*, Vol. 2.

Pedro de
Heredia — A137

Perf. 11½
1934, Jan. 10   Unwmk.   Litho.
417 A137 1c dark green   3.00 .80
418 A137 5c chocolate   3.75 .65
419 A137 8c dark blue   3.00 .80
   Nos. 417-419 (3)   9.75 2.25
Cartagena, 400th anniv. See Nos. C111-C114.

Coffee
Picking — A138

1934, Dec.   Engr.   Perf. 12
420 A138 5c brown   3.00 .25

Soccer — A139   Condor — A145

Allegory of Olympic Games at
Barranquilla — A140

Foot Race
A141

Tennis
A142

Pier at
Puerto
Colombia
A143

View of the
Bay
A144

Designs: 4c, Discus Thrower. 10c, Hurdling.
15c, Athlete in stadium. 18c, Baseball. 24c,
Swimming. 50c, View of Barranquilla. 1p, Post
and Telegraph Building. 2p, Monument to
Flag. 5p, Coat of Arms.

1935, Jan. 26   Litho.   Perf. 11½
421 A139 2c bluish grn &
              buff   1.60 .50
422 A139 4c deep green   1.60 .50

423 A140 5c dk brn & yel   1.60   .50
  a. Horiz. pair, imperf. btwn.   240.00
424 A141 7c dk carmine   3.00 1.75
425 A142 8c blk & pink   2.50 2.50
426 A141 10c brown & bl   3.50 1.75
427 A143 12c indigo   4.25 3.00
428 A141 15c bl & red brn   7.25 5.50
429 A141 18c dk vio & buff   10.00 8.25
430 A144 20c purple & grn   8.50 7.00
431 A144 24c bluish grn &
              ultra   8.50 6.75
432 A144 50c ultra & buff   13.00 10.00
433 A145 1p drab & blue   120.00 62.50
434 A145 2p dull grn &
              gray   140.00 110.00
435 A145 5p pur blk & bl   475.00 500.00
436 A145 10p black & gray   550.00 575.00
   Nos. 421-436 (16)   1,350. 1,295.
3rd Natl. Olympic Games, Barranquilla.
Counterfeits of 10p exist.

Oil
Wells — A155   Gold
                 Mining — A157

Imprint: "American Bank Note Co."
1935, Mar. Unwmk. Engr. Perf. 12
437 A155 2c carmine rose   .45 .25
439 A157 10c deep orange   25.00 .25
  See Nos. 468, 470, 498, 516. For surcharge
and overprints see Nos. 496, 596, O2. Post
1940 issues in Scott Standard Postage Stamp
Catalogue, Vol. 2.

No. 347 Surcharged in
Black

1935, Aug.   Perf. 14
440 A107 12c on 1p brt bl   4.75 1.50

Types of 1932
Imprint: "Lit. Nacional Bogotá"
1935-36   Litho.   Perf. 11, 11½, 12½
441 A131 1c lt green   .25 .25
  a. Imperf., pair   4.25
442 A133 5c brown ('36)   .70 .25
  a. Imperf., pair   4.75 4.00
  For overprint, see No. O1. For surcharge
see No. 527 in Scott Standard Postage Stamp
Catalogue, Vol. 2.

Bolívar
A159   Tequendama
              Falls
              A160

Wmk. Wavy Lines. (229)
1937   Engr.   Perf. 12½
443 A159 1c deep green   .25 .25
  a. Perf. 14   .25 .25
444 A160 12c deep blue   3.25 1.10
  See No. 570. For surcharges and overprints
see Nos. 454, 456, C231, C326, O12. Post
1940 issues in Scott Standard Postage Stamp
Catalogue, Vol. 2.

Soccer Player
A161   Discus
              Thrower
              A162

Runner — A163

1937, Jan. 4   Photo.   Unwmk.
445 A161 3c lt green   1.40 .85
446 A162 10c carmine rose   3.75 1.75
447 A163 1p black   35.00 26.00
   Nos. 445-447 (3)   40.15 28.60
National Olympic Games, Manizales.
For surcharge see No. 452.

Exposition
Palace — A164

Stadium at   Monument to
Barranquilla   the Colors
A165   A166

1937, Jan. 4
448 A164 5c violet brown   2.75 .40
449 A165 15c blue   6.75 4.50
450 A166 50c orange brn   19.00 9.75
   Nos. 448-450 (3)   28.50 14.65
Barranquilla National Exposition.

Stamps of 1926-37
Surcharged in Black

1937-38   Unwmk.   Perf. 12½
452 A161 1c on 3c lt grn   1.00 1.00
  a. Inverted surcharge   2.25 2.25
453 A118 5c on 8c dk bl   .50 .45
  a. Inverted surcharge   2.25 2.25
Wmk. 229
454 A160 2c on 12c dp bl   .50 .40
455 A134 5c on 8c bl blk   .60 .65
  a. Invtd. surcharge   2.00 2.00
456 A160 10c on 12c dp bl
              ('38)   5.50 1.00
  a. Dbl. surcharge   11.00 11.00
   Nos. 452-456 (5)   8.10 3.50

Calle del   Entrance to
Arco — A168   Church of the
                 Rosary — A169

Arms of Bogotá   Gonzálo
A170   Jiménez de
                  Quesada
                  A171

Bochica   Santo Domingo
A172   Convent
                 A173

Mass of the Conquistadors — A174

1938, July 27   Unwmk.   Perf. 12½
457 A168 1c yellow green   .25 .25
458 A169 2c scarlet   .25 .25
459 A170 5c brown blk   .35 .25
460 A171 10c brown   .75 .40
461 A172 15c brt blue   3.75 1.60
462 A173 20c brt red vio   3.75 1.60
463 A174 1p red brown   50.00 29.00
   Nos. 457-463 (7)   59.10 33.35
Bogotá, 400th anniversary.

Types of 1932
Imprint: "Litografia Nacional Bogotá"
1938, Dec. 5   Litho.   Perf. 10½, 11
464 A132 2c rose   1.00 .35
465 A135 10c yellow   2.50 .35
466 A136 20c dull blue   10.00 1.25
  a. 20c dark blue, perf. 12½ ('44) 62.50 6.25
   Nos. 464-466 (3)   13.50 1.95

Types of 1935 and

Bolívar   Coffee Picking
A175   A176

Arms of   Christopher
Colombia   Columbus
A177   A178

Caldas   Sabana Station
A179   A180

Imprint: "American Bank Note Co."
Wmk. 255
1939, Mar. 3   Engr.   Perf. 12
467 A175 1c green   .25 .25
468 A155 2c car rose   .25 .25
469 A176 5c dull brown   .25 .25
470 A157 10c deep orange   .50 .25
471 A177 15c dull blue   1.75 .25
472 A178 20c violet blk   19.00 .25
473 A179 30c olive bister   5.50 .35
474 A180 40c bister brn   17.00 3.75
   Nos. 467-474 (8)   44.50 5.60
  See Nos. 497-499, 515, 518, 574. For
surcharges and overprints see Nos. 506-507,
520-522, 596, RA26, RA47. Post 1940 listings
are in Scott Standard catalogue, Vol. 2.

Gen.
Santander
A181

Allegory
A182

Gen.
Santander
A183

Statue at
Cúcuta
A184

Birthplace of
Santander
A185

Church at
Rosario
A186

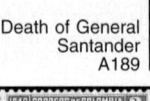

Paya — A187

Bridge at
Boyacá — A188

Death of General
Santander
A189

Invasion of the
Liberators
A190

Perf. 13x13½, 13½x13

1940, May 6   Engr.   Wmk. 229

475	A181	1c olive green	.25	.25
476	A182	2c dk carmine	.50	.35
477	A183	5c sepia	.25	.25
478	A184	8c carmine	1.75	1.75
479	A185	10c orange yel	.80	.60
480	A186	15c dark blue	2.10	1.40
481	A187	20c green	2.75	2.10
482	A188	50c violet	6.50	6.00
483	A189	1p deep rose	20.00	20.00
484	A190	2p orange	65.00	65.00
		Nos. 475-484 (10)	99.90	97.70

Death of General Francisco Santander, cent.

Tobacco Plant
A194

Gen.
Santander
A195

Garcia
Rovira — A196

R.
Galan — A197

Antonio Sucre — A198

1940-43   Engr.   Wmk. 255   Perf. 12

488	A194	8c rose car & grn	1.25	.65
489	A195	15c dp blue ('43)	1.25	.25
490	A196	20c gray blk ('41)	4.75	.50
491	A197	40c brown bis ('41)	2.75	.50
492	A198	1p black	5.00	1.25
		Nos. 488-492 (5)	15.00	3.15

See Nos. 500, 554, RA28 (overprint) in Scott Standard catalogue, Vol. 2.

AIR POST STAMPS

No. 341 Overprinted

1919   Unwmk.   Perf. 14

C1	A107	2c car rose	3,500.	1,700.
a.		Numerals "1" with serifs	7,250.	4,250.

Used for the first experimental flight from Barranquilla to Puerto Colombia, 6/18/19. Values are for faulty stamps.

Issued by Compania Colombiana de Navegacion Aerea

From 1920 to 1932 the internal airmail service of Colombia was handled by the Compania Colombiana de Navegacion Aerea (1920) and the Sociedad Colombo-Alemana de Transportes Aéreos, known familiarly as "SCADTA" (1920-1932).

These organizations, under government contracts, operated and maintained their own post offices and issued stamps which were the only legal franking for airmail service during this period, both in the internal and international mails. All letters had to bear government stamps as well.

Woman and Boy Watching
Plane — AP1

Designs: No. C3, Clouds and small biplane at top. No. C4, Tilted plane viewed close-up from above. No. C5, Flier in plane watching biplane. No. C6, Lighthouse. No. C7, Fuselage and tail of biplane. No. C8, Condor on cliff. No. C9, Plane at rest; pilot foreground. No. C10, Ocean liner.

1920, Feb.   Unwmk.   Litho.   Imperf. Without Gum

C2	AP1	10c multi	3,000.	1,875.
C3	AP1	10c multi	3,800.	1,875.
C4	AP1	10c multi	4,600.	1,875.
C5	AP1	10c multi	3,500.	1,875.
C6	AP1	10c multi	3,000.	1,875.
C7	AP1	10c multi	11,000.	3,800.

C8	AP1	10c multi	6,000.	3,000.
C9	AP1	10c multi	3,500.	1,875.
C10	AP1	10c multi	4,600.	2,750.

Nos. C2-C10 were overprinted on the nine lighter-colored varieties of a set of 18 publicity labels produced for free distribution with packs of cigarettes. These labels were printed setenant, in panes of 18 (3x6). Value for the set of 18 values without overprint: $4,000.

Flier in Plane Watching Biplane — AP2

1920, Mar.

C11	AP2	10c green	60.00	*92.50*

Four other 10c stamps, similar to No. C11, have two designs showing plane, mountains and water. They are printed in deep green or light brown red. Some authorities state that these four were not used regularly.

Issued by Sociedad Colombo-Alemana de Transportes Aereos (SCADTA)

Seaplane over Magdalena
River — AP3

1920-21   Litho.   Perf. 12

C12	AP3	10c yellow ('21)	60.00	47.50
C13	AP3	15c blue ('21)	65.00	52.50
C14	AP3	30c blk, *rose*	30.00	16.00
C15	AP3	30c rose ('21)	60.00	45.00
C16	AP3	50c pale green	60.00	47.50
		Nos. C12-C16 (5)	275.00	208.50

For surcharges see Nos. C17-C24, C36-C37.

No. C16 Handstamp Surcharged in Violet or Black

a

b

c

d

30¢   **30¢**

e

f

g

1921

C17	AP3 (a)	10c on 50c	1,250.	1,200.
C18	AP3 (b)	10c on 50c	1,250.	1,200.
C19	AP3 (c)	10c on 50c	1,250.	1,200.
C20	AP3 (b)	30c on 50c	925.	625.
C21	AP3 (d)	30c on 50c	925.	625.
C22	AP3 (e)	30c on 50c	1,850.	1,450.
C23	AP3 (f)	30c on 50c	1,850.	1,450.
C24	AP3 (g)	30c on 50c	1,850.	1,450.

No. C16 with Typwritten Surcharge in Red

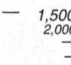

VALOR $0.10

1921

C24A	AP3	10c on 50c	—	*1,500.*
		On cover		*2,000.*
C24B	AP3	30c on 50c		—
		On cover		

Plane over
Magdalena
River — AP4

Plane over
Bogota
Cathedral
AP5

1921   Perf. 11½

C25	AP4	5c orange yellow	4.50	4.00
		On cover, *from*		27.50
C26	AP4	10c slate green	2.10	1.50
		On cover, *from*		27.50
C27	AP4	15c orange brown	2.10	1.60
		On cover, *from*		27.50
C28	AP4	20c red brown	4.50	2.10
		On cover, *from*		27.50
a.		Horiz. pair, imperf. vert.	210.00	

C29	AP4 30c green	2.10	1.10
	On cover, from		25.00
C30	AP4 50c blue	3.25	1.25
	On cover, from		30.00
C31	AP4 60c vermilion	85.00	32.50
	On cover, from		100.00
C32	AP5 1p gray black	22.50	5.00
	On cover, from		80.00
C33	AP5 2p rose	42.50	20.00
	On cover, from		100.00
C34	AP5 3p violet	125.00	72.50
	On cover, from		200.00
C35	AP5 5p olive green	325.00	300.00
	On cover, from		500.00
	Nos. C25-C35 (11)	618.55	441.55

Exist imperf.
For surcharge see No. C52.

Nos. C16 and C12 Handstamp Surcharged

h

i

1921-22 — **Perf. 12**

C36	AP3 (h) 20c on 50c	3,750.	2,500.
C37	AP3 (i) 30c on 10c	850.	575.

Seaplane over Magdalena River — AP6

Plane over Bogota Cathedral AP7

1923-28 **Wmk. 116** **Perf. 14x14½**

C38	AP6 5c orange yellow	1.75	.25
	On cover, from		20.00
C39	AP6 10c green	1.75	.25
	On cover, from		20.00
C40	AP6 15c carmine	1.75	.25
	On cover, from		20.00
C41	AP6 20c gray	1.75	.25
	On cover, from		17.50
C42	AP6 30c blue	1.75	.25
	On cover, from		17.50
C43	AP6 40c purple ('28)	12.50	8.00
	On cover, from		25.00
C44	AP6 50c green	2.10	.25
	On cover, from		20.00
C45	AP6 60c brown	3.25	.25
	On cover, from		22.50
C46	AP6 80c olive grn ('28)	32.50	30.00
	On cover, from		40.00
C47	AP7 1p black	14.50	3.25
	On cover, from		40.00
C48	AP7 2p red orange	21.00	6.00
	On cover, from		80.00
C49	AP7 3p violet	37.50	25.00
	On cover, from		175.00
C50	AP7 5p olive green	67.50	32.50
	On cover, from		250.00
	Nos. C38-C50 (13)	199.60	106.50

For surcharges and overprints see Nos. C51, C53-C54, CF1.

Nos. C41 and C31 Surcharged in Carmine and Dark Blue

No. C51   No. C52

1923

C51	AP6 30c on 20c gray (C)	92.50	57.50
C52	AP4 30c on 60c ver	85.00	37.50
	On cover, from		125.00

Nos. C41-C42 Overprinted in Black

1928 **Wmk. 116** **Perf. 14x14½**

C53	AP6 20c gray	80.00	62.50
C54	AP6 30c blue	80.00	62.50

Goodwill flight of Lt. Benjamin Mendez from New York to Bogota.

Magdalena River and Tolíma Volcano AP8

Columbus' Ship and Plane AP9

1929, June 1 **Wmk. 127** **Perf. 14**

C55	AP8 5c yellow org	1.25	.25
	On cover, from		20.00
C56	AP8 10c red brown	1.25	.25
	On cover, from		20.00
C57	AP8 15c deep green	1.25	.25
	On cover, from		20.00
C58	AP8 20c carmine	1.25	.25
	On cover, from		15.00
C59	AP8 30c gray blue	1.25	.25
	On cover, from		15.00
C60	AP8 40c dull violet	1.25	.25
	On cover, from		30.00
C61	AP8 50c dk olive grn	2.50	.25
	On cover, from		25.00
C62	AP8 60c orange brown	3.75	.25
	On cover, from		25.00
C63	AP8 80c green	11.00	3.25
	On cover, from		40.00
C64	AP9 1p blue	12.00	2.50
	On cover, from		50.00
C65	AP9 2p brown orange	18.00	5.75
	On cover, from		80.00
C66	AP9 3p pale rose vio	42.50	18.00
	On cover, from		175.00
C67	AP9 5p olive green	100.00	37.50
	On cover, from		250.00
	Nos. C55-C67 (13)	197.25	69.00

For surcharges and overprints see Nos. C80-C95, CF2, CF4.

For International Airmail

AP10   AP11

1929, June 1 **Wmk. 127** **Perf. 14**

C68	AP10 5c yellow org	6.25	7.25
	Never hinged	9.50	
C69	AP10 10c red brown	1.25	3.00
	Never hinged	1.80	
C70	AP10 15c deep green	1.25	3.00
	Never hinged	1.80	
C71	AP10 20c carmine	1.25	3.75
	Never hinged	1.80	
C72	AP10 25c violet blue	1.25	.85
	Never hinged	1.80	
C73	AP10 30c gray blue	1.25	.95
	Never hinged	1.80	
C74	AP10 50c dk olive grn	1.25	1.90
	Never hinged	1.80	
C75	AP10 60c brown	2.50	3.00
	Never hinged	3.60	

C76	AP11 1p blue	5.50	7.25
	Never hinged	7.50	
C77	AP11 2p red orange	8.50	10.00
	Never hinged	12.50	
C78	AP11 3p violet	100.00	100.00
	Never hinged	135.00	
C79	AP11 5p olive green	125.00	140.00
	Never hinged	165.00	
	Nos. C68-C79 (12)	255.25	280.95

This issue was sold abroad for use on correspondence to be flown from coastal to interior points of Colombia. Cancellations are those of the country of origin rather than Colombia.
For overprint see No. CF3.

Nos. C63, C66 and C64 Surcharged in Black

m

n

1930, Dec. 15

C80	AP8(m) 10c on 80c	7.25	7.25
C81	AP9(n) 20c on 3p	13.50	13.50
C82	AP9(n) 30c on 1p	17.00	13.50
	Nos. C80-C82 (3)	37.75	34.25

Simon Bolivar (1783-1830).

Colombian Government Issues
Nos. C55-C67 Overprinted in Black

o

p

Wmk. 127

1932, Jan. 1 **Typo.** **Perf. 14**

C83	AP8(o) 5c yellow org	10.00	10.00
	On cover, from		25.00
C84	AP8(o) 10c red brown	2.25	.60
	On cover, from		25.00
C85	AP8(o) 15c deep green	3.75	3.75
	On cover, from		25.00
C86	AP8(o) 20c carmine	1.90	.35
	On cover, from		17.50
C87	AP8(o) 30c gray blue	1.90	.60
	On cover, from		17.50
C88	AP8(o) 40c dull violet	2.50	1.25
	On cover, from		35.00
C89	AP8(o) 50c dk ol grn	5.00	3.75
	On cover, from		30.00
C90	AP8(o) 60c orange brn	4.25	3.75
	On cover, from		30.00
C91	AP8(o) 80c green	17.00	17.00
	On cover, from		50.00
C92	AP9(p) 1p blue	14.50	12.00
	On cover, from		60.00
C93	AP9(p) 2p brown org	37.50	35.00
	On cover, from		100.00
C94	AP9(p) 3p pale rose vio	77.50	65.00
	On cover, from		200.00
C95	AP9(p) 5p olive green	125.00	140.00
	On cover, from		400.00
	Nos. C83-C95 (13)	303.05	293.05

Coffee AP12   Gold AP16

Designs: 10c, 50c, Cattle. 15c, 60c, Petroleum. 20c, 40c, Bananas. 3p, 5p, Emerald.

1932-39 **Wmk. 127** **Photo.** **Perf. 14**

C96	AP12 5c org & blk brn	.90	.25
C97	AP12 10c lake & blk	1.00	.25
C98	AP12 15c bl grn & vio blk	.50	.25
C99	AP12 15c ver & vio blk ('39)	4.00	.25
C100	AP12 20c car & ol blk	.85	.25
C101	AP12 20c turq grn & ol blk ('39)	4.25	.35
C102	AP12 30c dk bl & blk brn	2.40	.25
C103	AP12 40c dk vio & ol bis	1.10	.25
C104	AP12 50c dk grn & brnsh blk	6.75	1.50
C105	AP12 60c dk brn & blk vio	1.40	.25
C106	AP12 80c grn & blk brn	9.50	2.00
C107	AP16 1p dk bl & ol bis	10.00	1.25
C108	AP16 2p org brn & ol bis	16.00	2.75
C109	AP16 3p dk vio & emer	26.00	7.25
C110	AP16 5p gray blk & emer	57.50	21.00
	Nos. C96-C110 (15)	142.15	38.10

For overprint see No. CF5.

Nos. C104, C106-C108 Surcharged

a

b

1934, Jan. 5

C111	AP12(a) 10c on 50c	4.50	4.50
C112	AP12(a) 15c on 80c	6.25	6.25
C113	AP16(b) 20c on 1p	6.50	6.50
C114	AP16(b) 30c on 2p	7.25	7.25
	Nos. C111-C114 (4)	24.50	24.50

400th anniversary of Cartagena.

Nos. C100 and C103 Surcharged in Black or Carmine

1939, Jan. 15

C115	AP12 5c on 20c (Bk)	.35	.35
C116	AP12 5c on 40c (C)	.35	.25
C117	AP12 15c on 20c (Bk)	1.50	.50
a.	Double surcharge	12.00	
b.	Pair, one with dbl. surch.	14.00	
c.	Inverted surcharge	12.00	12.00

No. CF5 Surcharged in Black

C118	AP12 20c on 20c	.70	.70
	Nos. C115-C118 (4)	2.90	1.80

Nos. C102-C103 Surcharged in Black or Red

1940, Oct. 20

C119	AP12 15c on 30c	1.25	.50
a.	Inverted surcharge	12.00	
C120	AP12 15c on 40c (R)	2.00	.75
a.	Double surcharge	12.00	

AIR POST REGISTRATION STAMPS

Issued by Sociedad Colombo-Alemana de Transportes Aereos (SCADTA)

No. C41 Overprinted in Red

1923	**Wmk. 116**		*Perf. 14x14½*	
CF1	AP6	20c gray	4.75	1.10

No. C58 Overprinted in Black

1929	**Wmk. 127**		*Perf. 14*	
CF2	AP8	20c carmine	8.00	7.00
	Never hinged		12.00	

Same Overprint on No. C71

CF3	AP10	20c carmine	6.50	6.00

Colombian Government Issues
Same Overprint on No. C86

1932				
CF4	AP8	20c carmine	6.50	6.00

No. C100 Overprinted

CF5	AP12	20c car & ol blk	6.00	1.25

For surcharge see No. C118.

UNITED STATES DISPATCH FOR EXPEDITED AIRMAIL SERVICE WITHIN COLOMBIA

Colombia (SCADTA) Consular Overprints
Sociedad Colombo-Alemana de Transportes Aereos (S.C.A.D.T.A.)

Establishing an office in New York, the SCADTA Company sold the following two issues, each bearing the agent's signature, "G Mejia" (Gonzalo Mejia), in red ink, to designate use from the United States.

SCADTA — CONSULAR OVERPRINTS

The Sociedad Colombo-Alemana de Transportes Aéreos (SCADTA) was established in Colombia in December 1919 by a group of Colombian and German businessmen, with the aim of organizing efficient and reliable airline service within Colombia. In 1920 the Colombian government granted SCADTA the monopoly for carrying mail within the country and authorized it to establish and maintain its own post offices and to print its own stamps. These stamps represented the company's fees for air service, and all proceeds from their sale were retained by SCADTA. Airmail articles also required regular postage stamps, those of Colombia for domestic mail and, initially, for mail from abroad, or, later, stamps of the country of origin.

In order to encourage foreign airmail to Colombia, SCADTA made its stamps available at Colombian consular offices and trade missions, and through its own agents. For accounting purposes and to prevent speculation due to the frequent currency fluctuations of the period, one or two-letter control overprints were applied denoting the country of origin.

These stamps were superseded by Colombia Nos. C68-C79, which were sold abroad in the equivalent of U.S. gold dollars, thus eliminating the need to identify the various sales offices because of changes in rates of exchange.

NOTE: In order to maintain integrity of presentation, and for the convenience of the collector, the Scott editors have included SCADTA consular overprinted air post registration stamps within the air post sets with which they were issued.

UNITED STATES
Nos. C14, C16 with ms "G Mejia" in red

Quantity printed of each value in parentheses.

1920, November

CLEU1	AP3	30c blk, *rose*		
		(5,000)	100.00	200.00
	Never hinged		150.00	
	On cover			2,000.
CLEU2	AP3	50c green		
		(1,000)	100.00	250.00
	Never hinged		150.00	
	On cover			5,000.
a.	Black signature		—	

Two examples of No. CLEU2 on cover are known. Nos. CLEU1 and CLEU2 exist together on a unique cover.

E.U. or EU - STAMPS FOR USE IN THE UNITED STATES

Colombia Nos. C25-C35 handstamp overprinted in black, letters 6½mm high

1921-23

CLEU3	AP4	5c org yel	15.00	15.00
	Never hinged		20.00	
	On cover			25.00
CLEU4	AP4	10c sl grn	15.00	15.00
	Never hinged		20.00	
	On cover			25.00
CLEU5	AP4	15c org brn	15.00	15.00
	Never hinged		20.00	
	On cover			25.00
CLEU6	AP4	20c red brown	15.00	15.00
	Never hinged		20.00	
	On cover			25.00
CLEU7	AP4	30c green	10.00	10.00
	Never hinged		15.00	
	On cover			150.00
CLEU8	AP4	50c blue	15.00	15.00
	Never hinged		20.00	
	On cover			35.00
CLEU9	AP4	60c vermilion	22.50	25.00
	Never hinged		30.00	
	On cover			175.00
CLEU10	AP5	1p gray black	30.00	30.00
	Never hinged		40.00	
	On cover			100.00
CLEU11	AP5	2p rose	62.50	70.00
	Never hinged		100.00	
	On cover			150.00
CLEU12	AP5	3p violet	87.50	100.00
	Never hinged		125.00	
	On cover			175.00
CLEU13	AP5	5p ol grn	375.00	400.00
	Never hinged		500.00	
	On cover			600.00
Nos. CLEU3-CLEU13 (11)			*662.50*	*710.00*
Nos. CLEU3-CLEU13, never hinged			910.00	

Same overprint in violet on Colombia Nos. C25-C35

1921-23

CLEU14	AP4	5c org yel	15.00	17.50
	Never hinged		20.00	
	On cover			25.00
CLEU15	AP4	10c sl grn	12.50	17.50
	Never hinged		17.50	
	On cover			25.00
CLEU16	AP4	15c org brn	12.50	17.50
	Never hinged		17.50	
	On cover			150.00
CLEU17	AP4	20c red brown	12.50	17.50
	Never hinged		17.50	
	On cover			25.00
CLEU18	AP4	30c green	9.00	12.00
	Never hinged		12.50	
	On cover			125.00
a.	Double overprint		750.00	
b.	Double overprint, vert.		—	
CLEU19	AP4	50c blue	12.50	17.50
	Never hinged		17.50	
	On cover			25.00
CLEU20	AP4	60c vermilion	30.00	25.00
	Never hinged		40.00	
	On cover			50.00
CLEU21	AP5	1p gray black	27.50	37.50
	Never hinged		40.00	
	On cover			100.00
CLEU22	AP5	2p rose	62.50	72.50
	Never hinged		90.00	
	On cover			150.00
CLEU23	AP5	3p violet	112.50	125.00
	Never hinged		165.00	
	On cover			250.00
CLEU24	AP5	5p ol grn	375.00	400.00
	Never hinged		500.00	
	On cover			600.00
Nos. CLEU14-CLEU24 (11)			*681.50*	*759.50*
Nos. CLEU14-CLEU24, never hinged			937.50	

Same overprint in black on Colombia Nos. C38//51, CF1

No. CLEU29

No. CLEU32

1923

CLEU25	AP6	5c org yel	12.50	12.50
	Never hinged		17.50	
	On cover			25.00
CLEU26	AP6	10c green	12.50	12.50
	Never hinged		17.50	
	On cover			30.00
CLEU27	AP6	15c carmine	15.00	15.00
	Never hinged		20.00	
	On cover			30.00
CLEU28	AP6	20c gray	15.00	15.00
	Never hinged		22.50	
	On cover			30.00
CLEU29	AP6	30c blue	5.00	5.00
	Never hinged		7.50	
	On cover			125.00
CLEU30	AP6	50c green	10.00	10.00
	Never hinged		15.00	
	On cover			150.00
CLEU31	AP6	60c brown	10.00	10.00
	Never hinged		15.00	
	On cover			150.00
CLEU32	AP7	1p black	20.00	20.00
	Never hinged		30.00	
	On cover			150.00
CLEU33	AP7	2p red org	27.50	27.50
	Never hinged		37.50	
	On cover			200.00
CLEU34	AP7	3p violet	50.00	50.00
	Never hinged		75.00	
	On cover			200.00
CLEU35	AP7	5p ol grn	87.50	87.50
	Never hinged		125.00	
	On cover			300.00
CFLEU1	AP6	20c gray	37.50	37.50
	Never hinged		125.00	
	On cover			300.00
Nos. CLEU25-CLEU35, CFLEU1 (12)			*302.50*	*302.50*
Nos. CLEU25-CLEU35, CFLEU1, never hinged			432.50	

Same overprint in black on Colombia No. C51

1923

CLEU36	AP6	30c on 20c		
		gray (C)	*1,250.*	*450.00*
	On cover			600.00
a.	"60" instead of "30" at left, on cover		—	

No. CLEU36a is unique.

Same overprint in violet on Colombia Nos. C38//C50, CF1

1923

CLEU37	AP6	5c org yel	12.50	12.50
	Never hinged		17.50	
	On cover			25.00
CLEU38	AP6	10c green	12.50	12.50
	Never hinged		17.50	
	On cover			25.00
CLEU39	AP6	15c carmine	12.50	12.50
	Never hinged		17.50	
	On cover			25.00
CLEU40	AP6	20c gray	12.50	12.50
	Never hinged		17.50	
	On cover			25.00
CLEU41	AP6	30c blue	5.00	5.00
	Never hinged		7.50	
	On cover			125.00
CLEU42	AP6	50c green	10.00	10.00
	Never hinged		15.00	
	On cover			150.00
CLEU43	AP6	60c brown	10.00	10.00
	Never hinged		15.00	
	On cover			150.00
CLEU44	AP7	1p black	20.00	20.00
	Never hinged		30.00	
	On cover			150.00
CLEU45	AP7	2p red org	25.00	25.00
	Never hinged		35.00	
	On cover			175.00
CLEU46	AP7	3p violet	50.00	50.00
	Never hinged		75.00	
	On cover			200.00
CLEU47	AP7	5p ol grn	125.00	87.50
	Never hinged		175.00	
	On cover			300.00
CFLEU2	AP6	20c gray	50.00	50.00
	Never hinged		75.00	
	On cover			125.00
Nos. CLEU37-CLEU47, CFLEU2 (12)			*345.00*	*307.50*
Nos. CLEU37-CLEU47, CFLEU2, never hinged			500.00	

Same overprint in violet on Colombia No. C51

1923

CLEU48	AP6	30c on 20c		
		gray (C)	45.00	22.50
	Never hinged		65.00	
	On cover			100.00

Same overprint in red on Colombia No. C41

1923

CLEU49	AP6	20c gray	60.00	*60.00*
	Never hinged		90.00	
	On cover			200.00

Colombia Nos. C38//C50, CF1 lithograph overprinted in black, letters 10mm high, by the Reichsdruckerei, Berlin, Germany

No. CLEU50

No. CLEU60

Quantity printed of each value in parentheses.

1923, June 4

CLEU50	AP6	5c org yel	(7500)	4.50	4.50
		Never hinged		7.50	
		On cover			75.00
CLEU51	AP6	10c green	(15,000)	2.00	2.00
		Never hinged		3.00	
		On cover			75.00
CLEU52	AP6	15c carmine	(11,600)	3.00	3.00
		Never hinged		4.00	
		On cover			75.00
CLEU53	AP6	20c gray	(45,000)	6.00	6.00
		Never hinged		9.00	
		On cover			75.00
CLEU54	AP6	30c blue	(170,000)	2.00	2.00
		Never hinged		3.00	
		On cover			85.00
CLEU55	AP6	50c green	(5,000)	5.00	5.00
		Never hinged		7.50	
		On cover			
CLEU56	AP6	60c brown	(55,000)	2.75	2.75
		Never hinged		4.00	
		On cover			125.00
CLEU57	AP7	1p black	(8,400)	6.75	6.00
		Never hinged		8.00	
		On cover			150.00
a.		Double impression of basic stamp			1,250.
CLEU58	AP7	2p red org	(3,800)	17.50	17.50
		Never hinged		25.00	
		On cover			175.00
CLEU59	AP7	3p violet	(3,200)	37.50	40.00
		Never hinged		50.00	
		On cover			175.00
CLEU60	AP7	5p ol grn	(3,400)	55.00	55.00
		Never hinged		75.00	
		On cover			250.00

CFLEU3	AP6	20c gray	(2,000)	12.50	12.50
		Never hinged		25.00	
		On cover			180.00
Nos. CLEU50-CLEU60, CFLEU3 (12)				154.50	156.25
Nos. CLEU50-CLEU60, CFLEU3, never hinged				221.00	

Colombia Nos. C40, C42 lithograph overprinted in black, letters 10mm high

1928, Sept. 25

CLEU61	AP6	15c carmine	(1,500)	15.00	15.00
		Never hinged		22.50	
		On cover			75.00
a.		Inverted overprint		300.00	200.00
CLEU62	AP6	30c blue	(49,000)	5.00	5.00
		Never hinged		7.50	
		On cover			35.00
a.		Inverted overprint		450.00	450.00
b.		Double overprint		500.00	500.00

Nos. CLEU61 and CLEU62 were lithograph overprinted in New York in a slightly different font by Fleming & Benedict for the New York agency. There were two printings of the 30c value, the first generally centered toward the

---

top of the stamp, the second toward the bottom.

ARGENTINA & URUGUAY

Nos. C38//C50, CF1 handstamped in black, letters 5mm high

A-U.

1923

CLAU1	AP6	5c org yel	90.00	90.00
CLAU2	AP6	10c green	90.00	90.00
CLAU3	AP6	15c carmine	90.00	90.00
CLAU4	AP6	20c gray	90.00	90.00
CLAU5	AP6	30c blue	75.00	75.00
CLAU6	AP6	50c green	90.00	90.00
CLAU7	AP6	60c brown	90.00	90.00
CLAU8	AP7	1p black	125.00	150.00
CLAU9	AP7	2p red org	175.00	200.00
CLAU10	AP7	3p violet	400.00	450.00
CLAU11	AP7	5p ol grn	450.00	500.00
CFLAU1	AP6	20c gray	175.00	200.00

Nos. C38//C50, CF1 handstamped in black, letters 7½mm high

CLAU12	AP6	5c org yel	90.00	90.00
CLAU13	AP6	10c green	90.00	90.00
CLAU14	AP6	15c carmine	90.00	90.00
CLAU15	AP6	20c gray	90.00	90.00
CLAU16	AP6	30c blue	75.00	75.00
		On cover, from		800.00
CLAU17	AP6	50c green	90.00	90.00
CLAU18	AP6	60c brown	90.00	90.00
CLAU19	AP7	1p black	125.00	150.00
CLAU20	AP7	2p red org	175.00	200.00
CLAU21	AP7	3p violet	400.00	450.00
CLAU22	AP7	5p ol grn	450.00	500.00
CFLAU2	AP6	20c gray	175.00	200.00

BARBADOS

No. C15 with manuscript overprint "G.M. Allayn" in black

1921, November

CLBA1	AP3	30c rose		—
		On cover		

BELGIUM

Nos. C38//50, CF1 overprinted in black, letters 10mm high

1923, Aug. 1

CLB1	AP6	5c org yel	6.00	6.00
CLB2	AP6	10c green	4.00	4.00
CLB3	AP6	15c carmine	6.00	6.00
CLB4	AP6	20c gray	3.50	3.50
CLB5	AP6	30c blue	3.50	3.50
		On cover, from		250.00
CLB6	AP6	50c green	6.00	6.00
CLB7	AP6	60c brown	6.00	6.00
CLB8	AP7	1p black	15.00	16.00
CLB9	AP7	2p red org	20.00	22.50
CLB10	AP7	3p violet	75.00	80.00
CLB11	AP7	5p ol grn	87.50	90.00
CFLB1	AP6	20c gray, "R" 12mm high	100.00	100.00
a.		Overprint "R" 10mm high	37.50	37.50

Nos. CLB1-CFLB1 were lithograph overprinted by the Reichsdruckerei Berlin.

BOLIVIA

Nos. C38//50, CF1 handstamped in black, letters 6½mm high

1923

CLBO1	AP6	5c org yel	15.00	—
CLBO2	AP6	10c green	15.00	—
CLBO3	AP6	15c carmine	15.00	—
CLBO4	AP6	20c gray	15.00	—
CLBO5	AP6	30c blue	10.00	—
CLBO6	AP6	50c green	20.00	—
CLBO7	AP6	60c brown	30.00	—
CLBO8	AP7	1p black	37.50	—
CLBO9	AP7	2p red org	67.50	—
CLBO10	AP7	3p violet	87.50	—
CLBO11	AP7	5p ol grn	140.00	—
CFLBO1	AP6	20c gray	40.00	—

Nos. CLBO1-CFLBO1 were prepared but not issued. All used examples are either canceled by favor or are forgeries.

BRAZIL

Nos. C38//50, CF1 handstamped in black, letters 9½mm high

Br.

1923

CLBR1	AP6	5c org yel	20.00	20.00
CLBR2	AP6	10c green	20.00	20.00
CLBR3	AP6	15c carmine	20.00	20.00
CLBR4	AP6	20c gray	30.00	30.00
CLBR5	AP6	30c blue	20.00	20.00
CLBR6	AP6	50c green	40.00	40.00
CLBR7	AP6	60c brown	50.00	50.00
CLBR8	AP7	1p black	67.50	67.50
CLBR9	AP7	2p red org	100.00	110.00
CLBR10	AP7	3p violet	175.00	190.00
CLBR11	AP7	5p ol grn	375.00	400.00
CFLBR2	AP6	20c gray	67.50	67.50

Nos. C38//50, CF1 handstamped in black, letters 7mm high

1923

CLBR12	AP6	5c org yel	27.50	27.50
CLBR13	AP6	10c green	27.50	27.50
CLBR14	AP6	15c carmine	27.50	27.50
CLBR15	AP6	20c gray	37.50	37.50
CLBR16	AP6	30c blue	22.50	22.50
		On cover, from		800.00
CLBR17	AP6	50c green	40.00	40.00
CLBR18	AP6	60c brown	40.00	40.00
CLBR19	AP7	1p black	50.00	55.00
CLBR20	AP7	2p red org	140.00	150.00
CLBR21	AP7	3p violet	225.00	250.00
CLBR22	AP7	5p ol grn	500.00	550.00
CFLBR3	AP6	20c gray	40.00	45.00

CANADA

Nos. C38//50, CF1 handstamped in black, letters 7mm high

BOLIVIA (continued)

(see above)

1923

CLCA1	AP6	5c org yel	275.00	175.00
		Never hinged	380.00	
		On cover		1,750.
CLCA2	AP6	10c green	275.00	175.00
		Never hinged	380.00	
		On cover		1,750.
a.		Double overprint		750.00
CLCA3	AP6	15c carmine	275.00	150.00
		Never hinged	380.00	
		On cover, from		6,500.
CLCA4	AP6	20c gray	180.00	110.00
		Never hinged	245.00	
		On cover		—
CLCA5	AP6	30c blue	115.00	75.00
		Never hinged	160.00	
		On cover		1,400.
a.		Double overprint		
CLCA6	AP6	50c green	275.00	210.00
		Never hinged	380.00	
		On cover		—
a.		Inverted overprint		
CLCA7	AP6	60c brown	275.00	175.00
		Never hinged	380.00	
		On cover		2,250.
CLCA8	AP7	1p black	275.00	175.00
		Never hinged	380.00	
		On cover		
CLCA9	AP7	2p red org	275.00	175.00
		Never hinged	380.00	
		On cover		
CLCA10	AP7	3p violet	715.00	350.00
		Never hinged	975.00	
		On cover		
CLCA11	AP7	5p ol grn	775.00	450.00
		Never hinged	1,050.	
		On cover		
CFLCA1	AP6	20c gray	900.00	550.00
		Never hinged	1,225.	
		On cover, from		5,500.
a.		With manuscript red "R" overprint		

On No. CFLCA1, the "R" is machine overprinted, while on No. CFLCA1a it is hand-written. The unique example of No. CFLCA1a is on cover.

CANAL ZONE

No. C42 overprinted "P", 10mm (#CLP60), and handstamped "C.Z." in violet, letters 6mm high

1923

CLCZ1	AP6	30c blue	5,000.	5,000.
		On cover		

Five examples of No. CLCZ1 are known, three of them on cover. Forgeries exist.

CHILE

Nos. C38//50, CF1 handstamped in black, letters 7mm high

1923

CLCH1	AP6	5c org yel	20.00	20.00
CLCH2	AP6	10c green	20.00	20.00
CLCH3	AP6	15c carmine	20.00	17.50
CLCH4	AP6	20c gray	20.00	20.00
CLCH5	AP6	30c blue	15.00	12.50
		On cover, from		800.00
CLCH6	AP6	50c green	20.00	20.00
CLCH7	AP6	60c brown	20.00	20.00
CLCH8	AP7	1p black	37.50	37.50
CLCH9	AP7	2p red org	45.00	45.00
CLCH10	AP7	3p violet	87.50	87.50
CLCH11	AP7	5p ol grn	175.00	175.00
CFLCH1	AP6	20c gray	50.00	50.00

COSTA RICA

Nos. C38//50, CF1 handstamped in black, letters 7½mm high

1923

CLCR1	AP6	5c org yel	15.00	15.00
CLCR2	AP6	10c green	15.00	15.00
CLCR3	AP6	15c carmine	20.00	20.00
CLCR4	AP6	20c gray	20.00	20.00
CLCR5	AP6	30c blue	10.00	5.00
		On cover, from		650.00
CLCR6	AP6	50c green	40.00	40.00
CLCR7	AP6	60c brown	60.00	60.00
CLCR8	AP7	1p black	50.00	50.00
CLCR9	AP7	2p red org	75.00	75.00
CLCR10	AP7	3p violet	100.00	100.00
CLCR11	AP7	5p ol grn	175.00	175.00
CFLCR1	AP6	20c gray	50.00	50.00
		On cover, from		1,000.

CUBA

Nos. C38//50, CF1 handstamped in black, letters 7mm high without period, or 8mm high with period

1923

CLC1	AP6	5c org yel	20.00	20.00
CLC2	AP6	10c green	20.00	20.00
a.		Inverted overprint	—	—
CLC3	AP6	15c carmine	20.00	20.00
CLC4	AP6	20c gray	20.00	20.00
CLC5	AP6	30c blue	10.00	10.00
		On cover, from		600.00
CLC6	AP6	50c green	30.00	30.00
CLC7	AP6	60c brown	30.00	30.00
CLC8	AP7	1p black	35.00	35.00
CLC9	AP7	2p red org	45.00	50.00
CLC10	AP7	3p violet	90.00	100.00
CLC11	AP7	5p ol grn	175.00	200.00
CFLC1	AP6	20c gray	40.00	45.00

No. C42 handstamped in violet, 8mm high

CLC12	AP6	30c blue	75.00	75.00

DENMARK, NORWAY & SWEDEN

Nos. C38//50, CF1 handstamped in violet, letters 10½mm high

1923

CLD1	AP6	5c org yel	62.50	62.50
CLD2	AP6	10c green	62.50	62.50
CLD3	AP6	15c carmine	100.00	100.00
CLD4	AP6	20c gray	62.50	62.50
CLD5	AP6	30c blue	30.00	30.00
CLD6	AP6	50c green	50.00	50.00
CLD7	AP6	60c brown	60.00	60.00
CLD8	AP7	1p black	100.00	100.00
CLD9	AP7	2p red org	120.00	120.00
CLD10	AP7	3p violet	275.00	275.00
CLD11	AP7	5p ol grn	375.00	375.00
CFLD1	AP6	20c gray	75.00	75.00

No. C42 handstamped in black, 10½mm high

CLD12	AP6	30c blue	125.00	125.00

Nos. CLD1-CLD12 were overprinted in Copenhagen.

Nos. C38//50, CF1 handstamped in violet, letters 7 or 8mm high

1923

CLD13	AP6	5c org yel	—	—
CLD14	AP6	10c green	—	—
CLD15	AP6	15c carmine	30.00	30.00
CLD16	AP6	20c gray	30.00	30.00
CLD17	AP6	30c blue	32.50	32.50
CLD18	AP6	50c green	62.50	62.50
CLD19	AP6	60c brown	75.00	75.00
CLD20	AP7	1p black	100.00	100.00
CLD21	AP7	2p red org	125.00	140.00
CLD22	AP7	3p violet	210.00	240.00
CLD23	AP7	5p ol grn	250.00	275.00
CFLD2	AP6	20c gray		

Handstamped in Red

CLD24	AP6	5c org yel	30.00	30.00
CLD25	AP6	10c green	40.00	40.00
CLD26	AP6	15c carmine	30.00	30.00
CLD27	AP6	20c gray	40.00	40.00
CLD28	AP6	30c blue	32.50	32.50
CLD29	AP6	50c green	—	—
CLD30	AP6	60c brown	—	—
CLD31	AP7	1p black	—	—
CLD32	AP7	2p red org	—	—
CLD33	AP7	3p violet	—	—
CLD34	AP7	5p ol grn	—	—
CFLD3	AP6	20c gray	82.50	90.00

Nos. CLD13-CFLD3 were overprinted in Barranquilla.

Nos. C38//50, CF1 overprinted in black, letters 10mm high

1927, June 1

CLD35	AP6	5c org yel	6.00	6.00
CLD36	AP6	10c green	6.00	6.00
CLD37	AP6	15c carmine	10.00	10.00
CLD38	AP6	20c gray	10.00	10.00
CLD39	AP6	30c blue	6.00	6.00
		On cover, from		400.00
CLD40	AP6	50c green	6.00	6.00
CLD41	AP6	60c brown	10.00	10.00
CLD42	AP6	10c black	10.00	10.00
CLD43	AP7	2p red org	40.00	40.00
CLD44	AP7	3p violet	50.00	50.00
CLD45	AP7	5p ol grn	87.50	100.00
CFLD4	AP6	20c gray	17.50	17.50

Nos. CLD35-CFLD4 were lithograph overprinted by the Reichsdruckerei Berlin.

FRANCE

Nos. C25-C35 handstamped in black, letters 8mm high

1921-23

CLF1	AP4	5c org yel	20.00	25.00
CLF2	AP4	10c sl grn	20.00	25.00
CLF3	AP4	15c org brn	20.00	25.00
CLF4	AP4	20c red brown	—	—
CLF5	AP4	30c green	17.50	22.50
CLF6	AP4	50c blue	12.50	17.50
CLF7	AP4	60c vermilion	22.50	25.00
CLF8	AP5	1p gray black	75.00	35.00
CLF9	AP5	2p rose	67.50	75.00
CLF10	AP5	3p violet	75.00	85.00
CLF11	AP5	5p ol grn	1,000.	

Nos. C25-C35 handstamped in red, letters 8mm high
With or without period

1923

CLF12	AP4	5c org yel	25.00	25.00
CLF13	AP4	10c sl grn	15.00	15.00
CLF14	AP4	15c org brn	12.50	12.50
CLF15	AP4	20c red brown	25.00	25.00
CLF16	AP4	30c green	30.00	30.00
CLF17	AP4	50c blue	25.00	25.00
CLF18	AP4	60c vermilion	40.00	40.00
CLF19	AP5	1p gray black	20.00	20.00
CLF20	AP5	2p rose	45.00	50.00
CLF21	AP5	3p violet	80.00	90.00
CLF22	AP5	5p ol grn	275.00	300.00

Nos. C25-C35 handstamped in violet, letters 8mm high
With or without period

CLF23	AP4	5c org yel	300.00	300.00
CLF24	AP4	10c sl grn	12.50	12.50
CLF25	AP4	15c org brn	20.00	20.00
CLF26	AP4	20c red brown	150.00	150.00
CLF27	AP4	30c green	15.00	15.00
CLF28	AP4	50c blue	12.50	12.50
CLF29	AP4	60c vermilion	20.00	20.00
CLF30	AP5	1p gray black	30.00	30.00
CLF31	AP5	2p rose	67.50	75.00
CLF32	AP5	3p violet	87.50	100.00

CLF33	AP5	5p ol grn	800.00	1,000.

No. C29 handstamped in blue, letters 8mm high
With period

CLF34	AP4	30c grn	100.00	

Nos. C38//C50, CF1 handstamped in black, letters 6½ or 8mm high
Without period

CLF35	AP6	5c org yel	15.00	15.00
CLF36	AP6	10c green	12.50	12.50
CLF37	AP6	15c carmine	30.00	30.00
CLF38	AP6	20c gray	12.50	12.50
CLF39	AP6	30c blue	10.00	10.00
CLF40	AP6	50c green	12.50	12.50
CLF41	AP6	60c brown	12.50	12.50
CLF42	AP7	1p black	20.00	20.00
CLF43	AP7	2p red org	20.00	25.00
CLF44	AP7	3p violet	50.00	55.00
CLF45	AP7	5p ol grn	75.00	85.00
CFLF1	AP6	20c gray	25.00	27.50

Nos. C38//C50, CF1 handstamped in black, letters 6½ or 8mm high, with period

1923

CLF46	AP6	5c org yel	—	—
CLF47	AP6	10c green	12.50	12.50
CLF48	AP6	15c carmine	30.00	30.00
CLF49	AP6	20c gray	12.50	12.50
CLF50	AP6	30c blue	10.00	10.00
CLF51	AP6	50c green	12.50	12.50
CLF52	AP6	60c brown	15.00	15.00
CLF53	AP7	1p black	—	—
CLF54	AP7	2p red org	30.00	35.00
CLF55	AP7	3p violet	50.00	60.00
CLF56	AP7	5p ol grn	90.00	100.00
CFLF2	AP6	20c gray	25.00	27.50

Nos. C38//C50, CF1 handstamped in violet, letters 6½ or 8mm high, without period

CLF57	AP6	5c org yel	12.00	12.00
CLF58	AP6	10c green	9.00	9.00
CLF59	AP6	15c carmine	12.00	12.00
CLF60	AP6	20c gray	9.00	9.00
CLF61	AP6	30c blue	10.00	10.00
CLF62	AP6	50c green	20.00	20.00
CLF63	AP6	60c brown	20.00	20.00
CLF64	AP7	1p black	20.00	20.00
CLF65	AP7	2p red org	12.00	14.00
CLF66	AP7	3p violet	100.00	110.00
CLF67	AP7	5p ol grn	110.00	120.00
CFLF3	AP6	20c gray	25.00	27.50

Nos. C38//C50, CF1 handstamped in violet, letters 6½ or 8mm high, with period

CLF68	AP6	5c org yel	—	—
CLF69	AP6	10c green	12.00	12.00
CLF70	AP6	15c carmine	12.00	12.00
CLF71	AP6	20c gray	10.00	10.00
CLF72	AP6	30c blue	10.00	10.00
CLF73	AP6	50c green	20.00	20.00
CLF74	AP6	60c brown	20.00	20.00
CLF75	AP7	1p black	—	—
CLF76	AP7	2p red org	27.50	27.50
CLF77	AP7	3p violet	100.00	110.00
CLF78	AP7	5p ol grn	110.00	120.00
CFLF4	AP6	20c gray	25.00	5.00

Nos. C42-C43 handstamped in red, letters 6½ or 8mm high

CLF79	AP6	30c blue	30.00	30.00
CLF80	AP6	50c green	37.50	37.50

Nos. C38//50, CF1 overprinted in black, letters 10mm high

1923, June 4

CLF81	AP6	5c org yel	15.00	17.50
CLF82	AP6	10c green	10.00	10.00
CLF83	AP6	15c carmine	7.50	7.50
CLF84	AP6	20c gray	10.00	10.00
		On cover, from		275.00
a.		On 20c black	190.00	
CLF85	AP6	30c blue	6.50	6.50
CLF86	AP6	50c green	10.00	10.00
CLF87	AP6	60c brown	10.00	10.00
CLF88	AP7	1p black	15.00	15.00
CLF89	AP7	2p red org	30.00	32.50

CLF90	AP7	3p violet	67.50	75.00
CLF91	AP7	5p ol grn	87.50	90.00
CFLF5	AP6	20c gray	30.00	30.00

Nos. CLF81-CFLF5 were lithograph overprinted by the Reichsdruckerei Berlin.

GERMANY, AUSTRIA, CZECHOSLOVAKIA AND, LATER, HUNGARY & YUGOSLAVIA

Nos. C25-C35 handstamped in black or blue-black, letters 20mm high

1921-23

CLA1	AP4	5c org yel	17.00	20.00
CLA2	AP4	10c sl grn	10.00	17.50
a.		Overprint inverted		
CLA3	AP4	15c org brn	17.00	15.00
CLA4	AP4	20c red brown	12.50	17.50
a.		Horizontal pair, imperf vertically	1,000.	
b.		Vertical pair, imperf horizontally		
CLA5	AP4	30c green	12.50	11.00
		On cover, from		350.00
CLA6	AP4	50c blue	15.00	22.50
CLA7	AP4	60c vermilion	45.00	50.00
CLA8	AP5	1p gray black	50.00	55.00
CLA9	AP5	2p rose	55.00	65.00
CLA10	AP5	3p violet	100.00	110.00
CLA11	AP5	5p ol grn	500.00	600.00

No. CLA4 overprinted "R" in red

CFLA1	AP4	20c red brown	1,250.	
		On cover, from	2,500.	

Nos. CLA1-CFLA1 were overprinted in Berlin prior to receipt of overprinted stamps from Barranquilla (Nos. CLA12-CLA22).
Three examples of No. CFLA1 are known. All are used.

Nos. C25-C35 handstamped in violet, letters 6½mm high

1921-23

CLA12	AP4	5c org yel	12.50	—
CLA13	AP4	10c sl grn	9.00	—
CLA14	AP4	15c org brn	20.00	—
CLA15	AP4	20c red brown	12.50	—
CLA16	AP4	30c green	10.00	12.50
CLA17	AP4	50c blue	12.50	17.50
CLA18	AP4	60c vermilion	—	—
CLA19	AP5	1p gray black	—	—
CLA20	AP5	2p rose	70.00	75.00
CLA21	AP5	3p violet	110.00	
CLA22	AP5	5p ol grn	500.00	

Nos. C38//50, CF1 overprinted in black, letters 12mm high

1923, June 4

CLA23	AP6	5c org yel	5.00	5.50
CLA24	AP6	10c green	5.00	5.50
a.		Overprint inverted	300.00	
CLA25	AP6	15c carmine	4.00	4.00
CLA26	AP6	20c gray	4.00	4.00
CLA27	AP6	30c blue	1.50	1.50
		On cover, from		50.00
CLA28	AP6	50c green	5.00	5.00
CLA29	AP6	60c brown	5.00	5.00
CLA30	AP7	1p black	6.00	6.00
CLA31	AP7	2p red org	17.50	18.00
CLA32	AP7	3p violet	37.50	37.50
CLA33	AP7	5p ol grn	67.50	70.00
CFLA2	AP6	20c gray	5.00	5.00
		On cover, from		125.00

Nos. CLA23-CFLA2 were lithograph overprinted by the Reichsdruckerei Berlin.

Nos. C38 overprinted in black, letters 10mm high

1923 (?)

CLA34 AP6 5c org yel — —

No. CLA34 was a proof, printed by the Reichsdruckerei Berlin, that was later put into service when supplies of No. CLA23 were depleted.

GREAT BRITAIN

Nos. C25-C35 handstamped in violet, letters 6½mm high

1921-23

CLGB1	AP4	5c org yel	12.50	16.00
CLGB2	AP4	10c sl grn	10.00	12.50
a.		Pair, one stamp without ovpt.	—	
CLGB3	AP4	15c org brn	10.00	12.50
a.		Double overprint	—	
CLGB4	AP4	20c red brown	12.50	16.00
CLGB5	AP4	30c green	10.00	12.50
		On cover, from		300.00
a.		Imperf	200.00	
CLGB6	AP4	50c blue	25.00	30.00
CLGB7	AP4	60c vermilion	—	
CLGB8	AP5	1p gray black	50.00	55.00
CLGB9	AP5	2p rose	110.00	125.00
CLGB10	AP5	3p violet	150.00	175.00
a.		Double overprint	400.00	450.00
CLGB11	AP5	5p ol grn	400.00	450.00

Handstamped in black

CLGB12	AP4	10c sl grn	20.00	20.00
CLGB13	AP4	60c vermilion	37.50	37.50
CLGB14	AP5	1p gray black	30.00	55.00
CLGB15	AP5	2p rose	175.00	175.00
CLGB16	AP5	3p violet	175.00	175.00

Handstamped in red

CLGB17	AP5	50c blue	45.00	50.00

Nos. C38//50, CF1 handstamped in black, letters 6mm high

1923

CLGB18	AP6	5c org yel	15.00	15.00
CLGB19	AP6	10c green	10.00	10.00
CLGB20	AP6	15c carmine	10.00	10.00
CLGB21	AP6	20c gray	10.00	10.00
CLGB22	AP6	30c blue	5.00	5.00
CLGB23	AP6	50c green	15.00	15.00
CLGB24	AP6	60c brown	15.00	15.00
CLGB25	AP7	1p black	20.00	20.00
CLGB26	AP7	2p red org	50.00	50.00
CLGB27	AP7	3p violet	75.00	75.00
CLGB28	AP7	5p ol grn	125.00	125.00
CFLGB1	AP6	20c gray	25.00	25.00

Handstamped in violet

CLGB29	AP6	5c org yel	15.00	15.00
CLGB30	AP6	10c green	10.00	10.00
CLGB31	AP6	15c carmine	10.00	10.00
CLGB32	AP6	20c gray	10.00	10.00
CLGB33	AP6	30c blue	5.00	5.00
CLGB34	AP6	50c green	15.00	15.00
CLGB35	AP6	60c brown	15.00	15.00
CLGB36	AP7	1p black	17.50	17.50
CLGB37	AP7	2p red org	50.00	50.00
CLGB38	AP7	3p violet	75.00	75.00
CLGB39	AP7	5p ol grn	125.00	140.00
CFLGB2	AP6	20c gray	17.50	20.00

Handstamped in red

CLGB40	AP6	5c org yel	15.00	15.00
CLGB41	AP6	10c green	10.00	10.00
CLGB42	AP6	15c carmine	15.00	15.00
CLGB43	AP6	20c gray	15.00	15.00
CLGB44	AP6	30c blue	10.00	10.00
CLGB45	AP6	50c green	15.00	11.50
CLGB46	AP6	60c brown	20.00	20.00
CLGB47	AP7	1p black	20.00	20.00
CLGB48	AP7	2p red org	50.00	50.00
CLGB49	AP7	3p violet	175.00	190.00
CLGB50	AP7	5p ol grn	250.00	275.00
CFLGB3	AP6	20c gray	25.00	25.00

Nos. C38//50, CF1 overprinted in black, letters 10mm high

1923, June 4

CLGB51	AP6	5c org yel	20.00	22.50
CLGB52	AP6	10c green	15.00	18.00
CLGB53	AP6	15c carmine	15.00	18.00
CLGB54	AP6	20c gray	15.00	18.00
CLGB55	AP6	30c blue	8.00	8.00
		On cover, from		175.00
CLGB56	AP6	50c green	8.00	8.00
CLGB57	AP6	60c brown	8.00	8.00
CLGB58	AP7	1p black	20.00	22.50
a.		Double impression of basic stamp		1,250.
CLGB59	AP7	2p red org	50.00	60.00
CLGB60	AP7	3p violet	100.00	110.00
CLGB61	AP7	5p ol grn	150.00	160.00
CFLGB4	AP6	20c gray	60.00	60.00

Nos. CLGB51–CFLGB4 were lithograph overprinted by the Reichsdruckerei Berlin.

ITALY

Nos. C25-C35 handstamped in red, letter 7½mm high

1921-23

CLIT1	AP4	5c org yel	20.00	20.00
CLIT2	AP4	10c sl grn	15.00	15.00
CLIT3	AP4	15c org brn	15.00	15.00
CLIT4	AP4	20c red brown	20.00	20.00
CLIT5	AP4	30c green	10.00	10.00
CLIT6	AP4	50c blue	40.00	40.00
CLIT7	AP4	60c vermilion	62.50	62.50
CLIT8	AP5	1p gray black	75.00	75.00
CLIT9	AP5	2p rose	110.00	125.00
CLIT10	AP5	3p violet	160.00	175.00
CLIT11	AP5	5p ol grn	750.00	900.00

Handstamped in violet

CLIT12	AP4	5c org yel	17.50	17.50
CLIT13	AP4	10c sl grn	15.00	15.00
CLIT14	AP4	15c org brn	15.00	15.00
CLIT15	AP4	20c red brown	25.00	25.00
CLIT16	AP4	30c green	10.00	10.00
CLIT17	AP4	50c blue	50.00	50.00
CLIT18	AP4	60c vermilion	50.00	50.00
CLIT19	AP5	1p gray black	100.00	100.00
CLIT20	AP5	2p rose	150.00	175.00
CLIT21	AP5	3p violet	300.00	350.00
CLIT22	AP5	5p ol grn	750.00	900.00

Nos. C38//50, CF1 overprinted in black, letter 12mm high

1923, Dec. 11

CLIT23	AP6	5c org yel	11.00	12.50
CLIT24	AP6	10c green	5.00	5.50
CLIT25	AP6	15c carmine	5.00	5.50
CLIT26	AP6	20c gray	5.00	5.50
CLIT27	AP6	30c blue	4.00	5.00
		On cover, from		400.00
a.		Double ovpt., 10mm, 8mm	—	
CLIT28	AP6	50c green	7.50	7.50
CLIT29	AP6	60c brown	7.50	7.50
CLIT30	AP7	1p black	15.00	16.00
CLIT31	AP7	2p red org	20.00	20.00
CLIT32	AP7	3p violet	50.00	50.00
CLIT33	AP7	5p ol grn	67.50	75.00
CFLIT1	AP6	20c gray, "R" 12mm high	17.50	19.00

CFLIT2	AP6	20c gray, "R" 10mm high	30.00	30.00

Nos. C47-C50 overprinted in black, letter 8mm high

CLIT34	AP7	1p black	25.00	30.00
CLIT35	AP7	2p red org	35.00	37.50
CLIT36	AP7	3p violet	75.00	85.00
CLIT37	AP7	5p ol grn	100.00	110.00

Nos. CLIT23-CFLIT37 were lithograph overprinted by the Reichsdruckerei Berlin.

MEXICO

The typewritten overprint "De Mexico" is known on postal stationery and reported on stamps of the 1923 issue.

NETHERLANDS & NETHERLANDS ANTILLES

Nos. C25-C35 handstamped in violet, letters 6mm high
With or without period

1921-23

CLH1	AP4	5c org yel	15.00	16.00
CLH2	AP4	10c sl grn	15.00	16.00
CLH3	AP4	15c org brn	15.00	16.00
CLH4	AP4	20c red brown	20.00	22.50
CLH5	AP4	30c green	10.00	11.00
CLH6	AP4	50c blue	30.00	32.50
CLH7	AP4	60c vermilion, ovpt. with period	37.50	40.00
a.		Overprint without period	—	
CLH8	AP5	1p gray black	110.00	125.00
CLH9	AP5	2p rose	150.00	175.00
CLH10	AP5	3p violet	210.00	240.00
CLH11	AP5	5p ol grn	900.00	

Nos. C38//50, CF1 handstamped in black, letter 6mm high

1923

CLH12	AP6	5c org yel	30.00	30.00
CLH13	AP6	10c green	20.00	20.00
CLH14	AP6	15c carmine	20.00	20.00
CLH15	AP6	20c gray	32.50	32.50
CLH16	AP6	30c blue	25.00	25.00
CLH17	AP6	50c green	25.00	25.00
CLH18	AP6	60c brown	40.00	40.00
CLH19	AP7	1p black	50.00	50.00
CLH20	AP7	2p red org	250.00	275.00
CLH21	AP7	3p violet	150.00	175.00
CLH22	AP7	5p ol grn	300.00	325.00
CFLH1	AP6	20c gray	50.00	50.00

Nos. C38//50, CF1 handstamped in violet, letter 7mm high
Without period

1923

CLH23	AP6	5c org yel	25.00	25.00
CLH24	AP6	10c green	20.00	20.00
CLH25	AP6	15c carmine	20.00	20.00
CLH26	AP6	20c gray	17.50	17.50
CLH27	AP6	30c blue	12.50	12.50
CLH28	AP6	50c green	12.50	12.50
CLH29	AP6	60c brown	20.00	20.00
CLH30	AP7	1p black	30.00	30.00
CLH31	AP7	2p red org	30.00	35.00
CLH32	AP7	3p violet	50.00	55.00
CLH33	AP7	5p ol grn	100.00	125.00
CFLH1A	AP6	20c gray	30.00	32.50

Nos. C42, C47 handstamped in red

CLH34	AP6	30c blue	25.00	25.00
CLH35	AP7	3p violet	100.00	125.00

Nos. C38//50, CF1 handstamped in black, letter 8mm high

1923

CLH36	AP6	5c org yel	25.00	25.00
CLH37	AP6	10c green	20.00	22.50
CLH38	AP6	15c carmine	20.00	22.50
CLH39	AP6	20c gray	20.00	22.00
CLH40	AP6	30c blue	15.00	17.50
CLH41	AP6	50c green	25.00	27.50
CLH42	AP6	60c brown	25.00	27.50
CLH43	AP7	1p black	40.00	45.00
CLH44	AP7	2p red org	60.00	65.00
CLH45	AP7	3p violet	90.00	100.00
CLH46	AP7	5p ol grn	160.00	175.00
CFLH2	AP6	20c gray	40.00	45.00

Nos. C38//50, CF1 overprinted in black, letter 10mm high

1923

CLH47	AP6	5c org yel	15.00	17.50
CLH48	AP6	10c green	6.00	7.00
CLH49	AP6	15c carmine	6.00	7.00
CLH50	AP6	20c gray	6.00	7.00
CLH51	AP6	30c blue	5.00	6.00
		On cover, from		400.00
CLH52	AP6	50c green	6.00	7.00
CLH53	AP6	60c brown	6.00	7.00
CLH54	AP7	1p black	10.00	12.50
CLH55	AP7	2p red org	20.00	22.50
CLH56	AP7	3p violet	45.00	50.00
CLH57	AP7	5p ol grn	75.00	85.00
CFLH3	AP6	20c gray, "R" 12mm high	17.50	20.00
a.		"R" 10mm high	37.50	40.00

Nos. CLH47–CFLH3 were lithograph overprinted by the Reichsdruckerei Berlin.

PANAMA & CANAL ZONE

Nos. C25-C35 handstamped in violet, letters 7½mm high

P.

1921-23

CLP1	AP4	5c org yel	15.00	17.50
CLP2	AP4	10c sl grn	12.50	15.00
CLP3	AP4	15c org brn	12.50	15.00
CLP4	AP4	20c red brown	10.00	12.50
CLP5	AP4	30c green	10.00	12.50
CLP6	AP4	50c blue	17.50	20.00
CLP7	AP4	60c vermilion	22.50	22.50
CLP8	AP5	1p gray black	50.00	55.00
CLP9	AP5	2p rose	110.00	125.00
CLP10	AP5	3p violet	190.00	225.00
CLP11	AP5	5p ol grn	375.00	400.00

Handstamped in black

CLP12	AP4	5c org yel	25.00	27.50
CLP13	AP4	10c sl grn	20.00	22.50
CLP14	AP4	15c org brn	20.00	22.50
CLP15	AP4	20c red brown	35.00	40.00
CLP16	AP4	30c green	30.00	32.50
CLP17	AP4	50c blue	40.00	45.00
CLP18	AP4	60c vermilion	25.00	27.50
CLP19	AP5	1p gray black	80.00	90.00
CLP20	AP5	2p rose	225.00	250.00
CLP21	AP5	3p violet	275.00	300.00
CLP22	AP5	5p ol grn	350.00	400.00

Handstamped in red

CLP23	AP4	5c org yel	15.00	17.50
CLP24	AP4	10c sl grn	20.00	22.50
CLP25	AP4	15c org brn	20.00	22.50
CLP26	AP4	20c red brown	20.00	22.50
CLP27	AP4	30c green	10.00	12.50
CLP28	AP4	50c blue	15.00	17.50
CLP29	AP4	60c vermilion	25.00	27.50
CLP30	AP5	1p gray black	40.00	45.00
CLP31	AP5	2p rose	175.00	190.00
CLP32	AP5	3p violet	275.00	300.00
CLP33	AP5	5p ol grn	575.00	650.00

Nos. C38//50, CF1 handstamped in violet, letter 6½mm high

1923

CLP34	AP6	5c org yel	15.00	17.50
CLP35	AP6	10c green	15.00	17.50
CLP36	AP6	15c carmine	10.00	12.50
CLP37	AP6	20c gray	20.00	20.00
CLP38	AP6	30c blue	15.00	15.00
CLP39	AP6	50c green	15.00	17.50
CLP40	AP6	60c brown	20.00	22.50
CLP41	AP7	1p black	20.00	22.50
CLP42	AP7	2p red org	20.00	22.50
CLP43	AP7	3p violet	50.00	55.00
CLP44	AP7	5p ol grn	100.00	110.00
CFLP1	AP6	20c gray	32.50	35.00

Handstamped in red

CLP45	AP6	5c org yel	25.00	27.50
CLP46	AP6	10c green	20.00	22.50
CLP47	AP6	15c carmine	20.00	22.50
CLP48	AP6	20c gray	20.00	22.50
CLP49	AP6	30c blue	15.00	17.50
CLP50	AP6	50c green	50.00	55.00
CLP51	AP6	60c brown	50.00	55.00
CLP52	AP7	1p black	70.00	80.00
CLP53	AP7	2p red org	100.00	120.00
CLP54	AP7	3p violet	150.00	175.00
CLP55	AP7	5p ol grn	300.00	375.00
CFLP2	AP6	20c gray	110.00	125.00

Nos. C38//50, CF1 overprinted in black, letter 10mm high

1923, June 4

CLP56	AP6	5c org yel	7.50	7.50
CLP57	AP6	10c green	7.50	7.50
CLP58	AP6	15c carmine	7.50	7.50
CLP59	AP6	20c gray	7.50	7.50
CLP60	AP6	30c blue	2.50	2.50
		On cover, from		150.00
		On cover, used in Canal Zone, from		500.00
CLP61	AP6	50c green	12.50	12.50
CLP62	AP6	60c brown	7.50	7.50
CLP63	AP7	1p black	12.50	12.50
CLP64	AP7	2p red org	17.50	19.00
CLP65	AP7	3p violet	30.00	35.00
CLP66	AP7	5p ol grn	55.00	65.00
CFLP3	AP6	20c gray	10.00	12.50

Nos. CLP56--CFLP3 were lithograph overprinted by the Reichsdruckerei Berlin.

PERU

Nos. C38//50, CF1 handstamped in black, letter 7mm high

1923

CLPE1	AP6	5c org yel	15.00	15.00
CLPE2	AP6	10c green	15.00	15.00
CLPE3	AP6	15c carmine	12.00	12.00
CLPE4	AP6	20c gray	12.00	12.00
CLPE5	AP6	30c blue	12.00	12.00
		On philatelic flight cover, from		150.00
CLPE6	AP6	50c green	20.00	20.00
CLPE7	AP6	60c brown	20.00	20.00
CLPE8	AP7	1p black	30.00	32.50
CLPE9	AP7	2p red org	90.00	100.00
CLPE10	AP7	3p violet	90.00	100.00
CLPE11	AP7	5p ol grn	100.00	125.00
CFLPE1	AP6	20c gray	22.50	25.00

Nos. C38//47 handstamped in red, letter 6½mm high

1923

CLPE12	AP6	5c org yel	50.00	55.00
CLPE13	AP6	15c carmine	40.00	45.00
CLPE14	AP6	20c gray	45.00	50.00
CLPE15	AP6	50c green	40.00	45.00
CLPE16	AP6	60c brown	60.00	65.00
CLPE17	AP7	1p black	87.50	95.00

SPAIN

Nos. C25-C35 handstamped in violet, letters 6½mm high
Without period, except for 30c

E

1921-23

CLE1	AP4	5c org yel	14.00	17.50
a.		Pair, one with period, one without	—	
CLE2	AP4	10c sl grn	10.00	12.50
CLE3	AP4	15c org brn	20.00	22.00
CLE4	AP4	20c red brown	12.00	12.00
CLE5	AP4	30c green	12.50	16.00
CLE6	AP4	50c blue	18.00	22.00
CLE7	AP4	60c vermilion	37.50	40.00
CLE8	AP5	1p gray black	50.00	55.00
CLE9	AP5	2p rose	62.50	70.00
CLE10	AP5	3p violet	125.00	150.00
CLE11	AP5	5p ol grn	500.00	600.00

No. CLE1a is unique.

Handstamped in red

CLE12	AP4	5c org yel	25.00	30.00
CLE13	AP4	10c sl grn	25.00	30.00
CLE14	AP4	15c org brn	25.00	30.00
CLE15	AP4	20c red brown	25.00	30.00

CLE16	AP4	30c green	25.00	30.00
CLE17	AP4	50c blue	37.50	45.00
CLE18	AP4	60c vermilion	40.00	50.00
CLE19	AP5	1p gray black	62.50	75.00
CLE20	AP5	2p rose	75.00	85.00
CLE21	AP5	3p violet	125.00	140.00
CLE22	AP5	5p ol grn	870.00	1100.00

Handstamped in black

CLE23	AP4	5c org yel	22.50	25.00

Nos. C38//50, CF1 overprinted in black, letter 10mm high

1923, June 4

CLE24	AP6	5c org yel	15.00	17.50
CLE25	AP6	10c green	10.00	12.50
CLE26	AP6	15c carmine	15.00	17.50
a.		Double overprint	—	
CLE27	AP6	20c gray	15.00	17.50
CLE28	AP6	30c blue	10.00	10.00
		On cover, from		375.00
CLE29	AP6	50c green	12.50	14.00
CLE30	AP6	60c brown	15.00	17.50
CLE31	AP7	1p black	20.00	22.50
CLE32	AP7	2p red org	45.00	55.00
CLE33	AP7	3p violet	62.50	75.00
CLE34	AP7	5p ol grn	80.00	85.00
CFLE1	AP6	20c gray, "R" 12mm high	62.50	75.00
a.		"R" 10mm high	75.00	90.00

Nos. CLE24--CFLE1 were lithograph overprinted by the Reichsdruckerei Berlin.

SWEDEN & NORWAY

Nos. C38//50, CF1 overprinted in black, letter 10mm high

1927, March 10

CLSU1	AP6	5c org yel	10.00	12.00
CLSU2	AP6	10c green	7.50	7.50
CLSU3	AP6	15c carmine	7.50	7.50
CLSU4	AP6	20c gray	10.00	12.00
CLSU5	AP6	30c blue	6.00	6.00
		On cover, from		600.00
CLSU6	AP6	50c green	7.50	7.50
CLSU7	AP6	60c brown	7.50	7.50
CLSU8	AP7	1p black	10.00	12.00
CLSU9	AP7	2p red org	27.50	30.00
CLSU10	AP7	3p violet	50.00	55.00
CLSU11	AP7	5p ol grn	65.00	70.00
CFLSU1	AP6	20c gray	17.50	17.50

Nos. CLSU1--CFLSU1 were lithograph overprinted by the Reichsdruckerei Berlin.

SWITZERLAND & LIECHTENSTEIN

Nos. C25-C35 handstamped in violet, letters 8mm high
Without period, except for 30c

1921-23

CLS1	AP4	5c org yel	15.00	17.50
CLS2	AP4	10c sl grn	15.00	17.50
CLS3	AP4	15c org brn	15.00	17.50
CLS4	AP4	20c red brown	—	
CLS5	AP4	30c green, ovpt. with period	10.00	12.50
CLS6	AP4	50c blue	22.50	22.50
CLS7	AP4	60c vermilion	37.50	42.50
CLS8	AP5	1p gray black	62.50	70.00
CLS9	AP5	2p rose	62.50	70.00
CLS10	AP5	3p violet	325.00	375.00

CLS11	AP5	5p ol grn	450.00	525.00

Handstamped in black

CLS12	AP4	60c vermilion	—	
CLS13	AP5	2p rose	325.00	375.00
CLS14	AP5	3p violet	700.00	750.00
CLS15	AP5	5p ol grn	700.00	750.00

Nos. C38//50, CF1 overprinted in black, letter 10mm high

1924, Jan. 1

CLS16	AP6	5c org yel	10.00	12.00
CLS17	AP6	10c green	6.00	7.50
CLS18	AP6	15c carmine	6.00	7.50
CLS19	AP6	20c gray	6.00	7.50
CLS20	AP6	30c blue	3.00	3.75
		On cover, from		400.00
CLS21	AP6	50c green	7.50	9.00
CLS22	AP6	60c brown	6.00	7.50
CLS23	AP7	1p black	6.00	7.50
CLS24	AP7	2p red org	30.00	32.50
CLS25	AP7	3p violet	40.00	45.00
CLS26	AP7	5p ol grn	55.00	60.00
CFLS1	AP6	20c gray, "R" 12mm high	10.00	12.50
		On cover, from		1,500.
a.		"R" 10mm high	27.50	30.00

Nos. CLS16--CFLS1 were lithograph overprinted by the Reichsdruckerei Berlin.

VENEZUELA

Nos. C25-C35 handstamped in black, letters 8mm high

1921-23

CLV1	AP4	5c org yel	25.00	30.00
CLV2	AP4	10c sl grn	20.00	25.00
CLV3	AP4	15c org brn	20.00	25.00
CLV4	AP4	20c red brown	20.00	25.00
CLV5	AP4	30c green, ovpt. with period	17.50	20.00
CLV6	AP4	50c blue	25.00	30.00
CLV7	AP4	60c vermilion	25.00	30.00
CLV8	AP5	1p gray black	90.00	100.00
CLV9	AP5	2p rose	300.00	350.00
CLV10	AP5	3p violet	450.00	500.00
CLV11	AP5	5p ol grn	1,250.	1,500.

Handstamped in violet

CLV12	AP4	5c org yel	20.00	25.00
CLV13	AP4	10c sl grn	20.00	22.50
CLV14	AP4	15c org brn	20.00	22.50
CLV15	AP4	20c red brown	20.00	22.50
CLV16	AP4	30c green, ovpt. with period	22.50	25.00
CLV17	AP4	50c blue	35.00	35.00
CLV18	AP4	60c vermilion	50.00	50.00
CLV19	AP5	1p gray black	90.00	100.00
CLV20	AP5	2p rose	350.00	400.00
CLV21	AP5	3p violet	450.00	500.00
CLV22	AP5	5p ol grn	800.00	1,000.

Handstamped in red

CLV23	AP4	5c org yel	17.50	25.00
CLV24	AP4	10c sl grn	25.00	27.50
CLV25	AP4	15c org brn	30.00	32.50
CLV26	AP4	20c red brown	30.00	32.50
CLV27	AP4	30c green, ovpt. with period	32.50	35.00
CLV28	AP4	50c blue	35.00	40.00
CLV29	AP4	60c vermilion	60.00	70.00
CLV30	AP5	1p gray black	140.00	150.00
CLV31	AP5	2p rose	400.00	450.00
CLV32	AP5	3p violet	650.00	750.00
CLV33	AP5	5p ol grn	1,000.	1,200.

Nos. C38//50, CF1 handstamped in black, letter 8mm high

1923

CLV34	AP6	5c org yel	22.50	22.50
CLV35	AP6	10c green	17.50	17.50
CLV36	AP6	15c carmine	17.50	17.50
CLV37	AP6	20c gray	17.50	17.50
CLV38	AP6	30c blue	17.50	17.50

CLV39	AP6	50c green	40.00	40.00
CLV40	AP6	60c brown	40.00	40.00
CLV41	AP7	1p black	70.00	70.00
CLV42	AP7	2p red org	300.00	350.00
CLV43	AP7	3p violet	300.00	350.00
CLV44	AP7	5p ol grn	300.00	350.00
CFLV1	AP6	20c gray	30.00	35.00

Nos. C42//C50 handstamped in violet

CLV45	AP6	30c blue	45.00	45.00
CLV46	AP6	50c green	40.00	40.00
CLV47	AP7	1p black	50.00	50.00
CLV48	AP7	2p red org	90.00	100.00
CLV49	AP7	3p violet	100.00	125.00
CLV50	AP7	5p ol grn	125.00	150.00

Nos. C44//C48 handstamped in red

CLV51	AP6	50c green	40.00	45.00
CLV52	AP7	1p black	50.00	55.00
CLV53	AP7	2p red org	90.00	100.00

No. C42 with blue-black locally handstamp overprint, 12mm high

CLV54	AP6	30c blue		200.00

No. CLV54 was used mostly at Puerto Cabello.

Nos. C38//50, CF1 overprinted in black, letter 10mm high

1923, June 4

CLV55	AP6	5c org yel	22.50	22.50
CLV56	AP6	10c green	22.50	22.50
CLV57	AP6	15c carmine	15.00	15.00
CLV58	AP6	20c gray	15.00	15.00
CLV59	AP6	30c blue	15.00	15.00
		On cover, from		500.00
CLV60	AP6	50c green	15.00	15.00
CLV61	AP6	60c brown	15.00	15.00
CLV62	AP7	1p black	22.50	22.50
CLV63	AP7	2p red org	45.00	52.50
CLV64	AP7	3p violet	85.00	100.00
CLV65	AP7	5p ol grn	180.00	225.00
CFLV2	AP6	20c gray	26.00	30.00

Nos. CLV55--CFLV2 were lithograph overprinted by the Reichsdruckerei Berlin.

SPECIAL DELIVERY STAMPS

Special Delivery Messenger — SD1

1917   Unwmk.   Engr.   Perf. 14

E1	SD1	5c dark green	7.00	7.00

REGISTRATION STAMPS

R1

R2

1865   Unwmk.   Litho.   Imperf.

F1	R1	5c black	87.50	47.50
F2	R2	5c black	110.00	50.00

R3   R4

1870
White Paper
Vertical Lines in Background

F3	R3	5c black	3.00	2.50
F4	R4	5c black	3.00	2.50

Horizontal Lines in Background

F5	R3	5c black	10.00	8.50
F6	R4	5c black	3.00	2.50
	Nos. F3-F6 (4)		19.00	16.00

Reprints of Nos. F3 to F6 show either crossed lines or traces of lines in background.

R5

1881   *Imperf.*

F7	R5	10c violet	60.00	52.50
a.	Sewing machine perf.		67.50	60.00
b.	Perf. 11		75.00	62.50

R6

1883   *Perf. 12, 13½*

F8	R6	10c red, *orange*	2.00	2.50

R7

1889-95   *Perf. 12, 13½*

F9	R7	10c red, *grysh*	9.50	4.50
F10	R7	10c red, *yelsh*	9.50	4.50
F11	R7	10c dp brn, *rose buff* ('95)	2.00	1.60
F12	R7	10c yel brn, *lt buff* ('92)	2.00	1.60
	Nos. F9-F12 (4)		23.00	12.20

Nos. F9-F12 exist imperf.

R9

1902   *Imperf.*

F13	R9	20c red brown, *blue*	1.60	1.60
a.	Sewing machine perf.		4.75	4.75
b.	Perf. 12		4.75	4.75

Medellin Issue

R10

1902   **Laid Paper**   *Perf. 12*

F16	R10	10c blk vio	15.00	15.00
a.	Wove paper		21.00	21.00

Regular Issue

1903   *Imperf.*

F17	R9	20c blue, *blue*	1.60	1.60
a.	Sewing machine perf.		4.75	4.75
b.	Perf. 12		4.75	4.75

R11

1904   **Pelure Paper**   *Imperf.*

F19	R11	10c purple	3.75	3.75
a.	Sewing machine perf.		5.00	3.75
b.	Perf. 12		6.25	5.00

R12

Imprint: "J. L. Arango"

1904   **Wove Paper**   *Perf. 12*

F20	R12	10c purple	2.50	.60
a.	Imperf., pair		7.75	7.75

Imprint: "Lit. Nacional"

1909   *Perf. 10, 14, 10x14, 14x10*

F21	R12	10c purple	2.75	.85
a.	Imperf., pair		6.25	6.25

For overprints see Nos. LF1-LF4.

Execution at Cartagena in 1816 — R13

1910, July 20   **Engr.**   *Perf. 12*

F22	R13	10c red & black	21.00	90.00

Centenary of National Independence.

Pier at Puerto Colombia — R14

Tequendama Falls — R15

Perf. 11, 11½, 14, 11½x14
1917, Aug. 25

F23	R14	4c green & ultra	.55	3.50
a.	Center inverted		575.00	575.00
F24	R15	10c deep blue	8.00	.60

R16

1925   **Litho.**   *Perf. 10x13½*

F25	R16	(10c) blue	4.25	1.90
a.	Imperf., pair		15.00	12.50
b.	Perf. 13½x10		7.50	5.00

INSURED LETTER STAMPS ("CUBIERTAS")

The following stamps were affixed to the back of letters which contained valuables (normally, money) and were therefore insured through the post office. The origin and date of dispatch were written in the appropriate lines, and a description of the values enclosed and destination were penned in the appropriate cartouche below. The denomination indicated the payment of insurance and functioned as a receipt.

Often, the recipient signed the stamp and handed it back to the postman, indicating completed delivery. Scott G1 is an exception in that it represented only the payment for registration exclusive of insurance.

Beware of deceiving forgeries which exist for most of the Cubiertas.

ESTADOS UNIDOS DE COLOMBIA

IL1

Unwmk.
1865, July 1   **Litho.**   *Imperf.*
Flag colors handpainted with watercolors

G1	IL1	25c brn, bister, yel, bl & red	25.00 25.00
G2	IL1	50c brn, bister, yel, bl & red	62.50 80.00

IL2

1867   **Litho.**   **Unwmk.**   *Imperf.*
Flag colors handpainted with watercolors

G3	IL2	50c blk, yel, bl & red	25.00 25.00

IL3

"COLOMBIA" AND "CINCUENTA" in White. "CENTAVOS" with White Shading (No. G4)

1870   **Litho.**   *Imperf.*

G4	IL3	50c blk, yel, bl & red	30.00 25.00
G5	IL3	50c As G4, white shading of "CENTAVOS" removed	35.00 30.00

IL4

White Words and Shading Removed. "50" Without Horizontal Shading

1873-77   **Litho.**   *Imperf.*

G6	IL4	50c blk, yel, bl & red	80.00	75.00
a.	blk, yel, pale bl & red		80.00	75.00
b.	blk, yel, very dp bl & red		—	125.00

IL5

"50" With Horizontal Shading. Dateline Ends in "de18".

1880   **Litho.**   **Unwmk.**   *Imperf.*

G7	IL5	50c blk, golden yel, bl & red	100.00	80.00
a.	Wmk. "ESTADO SOBERANO"		—	125.00
b.	Wmk. "ARMS OF CUNDINAMARCA"		—	125.00

IL6

Inscribed "ESTADOS UNIDOS DE COLOMBIA".

1883-86   **Litho.**   *Imperf.*

G8	IL6	50c rose, on white wove paper	20.00	12.50
a.	Deep carmine, white wove paper		20.00	12.50
b.	Red, bluish wove paper		27.50	20.00

REPUBLICA DE COLOMBIA

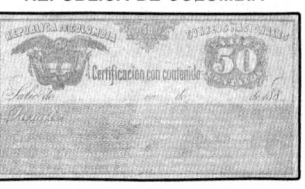

IL7

Inscribed "REPUBLICA DE COLOMBIA".

1887-88   **Litho.**   *Imperf.*

G9	IL7	50c rose, on white wove paper	17.50	12.50
a.	Violet red (shades), bluish wove paper		20.00	20.00

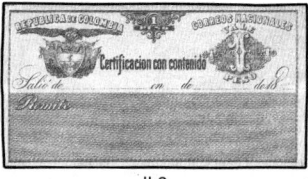

IL8

Dateline ends in "de18".

1890   **Litho.**   *Imperf.*

G10	IL8	10c blue	11.00	16.50
G11	IL8	20c blue	11.00	16.50
G12	IL8	30c blue	11.00	16.50
G13	IL8	40c blue	16.50	22.50
G14	IL8	50c blue	19.00	25.00
G15	IL8	60c blue	19.00	25.00
G16	IL8	70c blue	32.50	35.00
G17	IL8	80c blue	32.50	32.50
G18	IL8	90c blue	37.50	45.00
G19	IL8	1p blue	45.00	55.00

Denominations represent payment of 1% of the declared value of the letter.

IL9

Dateline ends in "de189".

1890   **Litho.**   *Imperf.*
Dateline ends in "de189"

G20	IL9	10c black, *rose*	8.00	12.00
G21	IL9	20c black, *yellow*	8.00	12.00
G22	IL9	30c black, *fawn*	8.00	12.00
G23	IL9	40c black, *blue green*	12.00	16.00
G24	IL9	50c black, *green*	14.00	18.00
G25	IL9	60c orange	14.00	18.00
a.	60c Yellow		35.00	
b.	60c Orange red		15.00	
c.	60c Orange brown		30.00	
G26	IL9	70c blue	16.00	37.50
a.	70c Deep blue		27.50	
G27	IL9	80c dp bluish green	20.00	40.00
a.	80c Deep green		20.00	40.00
b.	80c Yellow green		20.00	40.00

G28 IL9 90c brown	28.00	32.50
G29 IL9 1p bright scarlet		
	vermilion	32.50	55.00
a.	1p Pale red	32.50	50.00
b.	"PESOS" instead of "PESO"		
	in left inscription	32.50	

No. G29b is found in Position 5 in the plate of 10 subjects, and is constant throughout the printing.

IL10

1892-93   **Litho.**   *Imperf.*

G30 IL10 10c black, *rose*	10.00	10.00
a.	10c Black, *pale rose*	10.00	10.00
G31 IL10 20c black, *buff*	10.00	12.50
a.	20c Black, *yellow*	20.00	12.50
b.	20c Black, *very pale buff (almost white)*	25.00	12.50
G32 IL10 30c black, *buff*	10.00	12.50
a.	30c Black, *pale salmon*	10.00	15.00
G33 IL10 40c blk, *pale gray bl*	12.50	15.00
G34 IL10 50c blk, *gray grn*	17.50	15.00
a.	1p Black, *br green*	20.00	20.00
b.	1p Black, *bluish green*	20.00	20.00
c.	1p Black, *buff* (error)	—	20.00

IL11

Two types of condor:
Type I: With wings 38mm long.
Type II: With wings 28mm long.

1905   **Litho.**   *Perf. 13½*

G35 IL11 5c blk, *yel* (II)	8.00	12.00
a.	Type I	16.00	24.00
G36 IL11 10c blk, *bl grn* (II)	12.00	14.00
G37 IL11 15c black, *buff* (II)	14.00	16.00
G38 IL11 20c blk, *bluish gray* (II)	20.00	24.00
G39 IL11 25c blk, *dp dull rose* (II)	28.00	40.00

New Design

Arms at left; large "50" in scrollin center, small "50" in scroll at right. Dateline ends in "DE190".

Two types of "50c":
Type I: "50" at right in circular scroll.
Type II: "50" at right in oblong scroll.

1905   **Litho.**   *Perf. 13½*

G40 50c rod (I)	50.00	50.00
a.	Type II	50.00	50.00
G41 1p pale yellow brown	50.00	75.00
a.	1p Deep yellow brown	50.00	75.00

The editors would like to examine and photograph an example of Nos. G40-G41.

OFFICIAL INSURED LETTER STAMPS

Official Insured Letter Stamps carry no denomination. Used examples often have a manuscript specification of the amount of insurance required.

ILO1

Inscribed "ESTADOS UNIDOS DE COLOMBIA."

1867   *Imperf.*

Size: About 136x85mm

GO1 ILO1 black, *blue batonne paper*	120.00	60.00
a.	Black, *blue* wove ruled paper	120.00	60.00
GO2 ILQ1 black, ... ruled paper	120.00	60.00

ILO2

1870   *Imperf.*

Size: About 142x92mm

GO3 ILO2 black	120.00	65.00
a.	Black, ruled paper	140.00	90.00

ILO3

1874   *Imperf.*

Size: About 141x84mm

GO4 ILO3 black	75.00	50.00
a.	Black, ruled paper		75.00
b.	As "a," vertical ruled lines		

ILO4

1881   *Imperf.*

Size: About 143x96mm

GO5 ILO4 black	60.00	40.00
a.	Black, ruled paper	60.00	40.00
b.	As "a," vertical ruled lines	60.00	40.00
c.	Black, batonne paper	150.00	100.00

ILO5

Special Issue for Cartago

1882   *Imperf.*

GO6 ILO5 black, *yellow*	—	175.00

New Design

Double-lined letters with floral decorations

1884   *Imperf.*

Size: About 140x80mm

GO7 black	—	—
a.	Black, ruled paper	—	—

The editors would like to examine and photograph an example of either Nos. GO7 or GO7a.

ILO7

Dateline ends in "de188".
Two types of inscriptions:
Type I: "SERVICIO DE CORREOS NACIONALES" 83mm long.
Type II: "SERVICIO DE CORREOS NACIONALES" 109mm long.

1884   *Imperf.*

GO8 ILO7 black (I)	75.00	50.00
a.	Black, ruled paper (I)	75.00	50.00
b.	Type II	75.00	50.00
c.	Type II, ruled paper	75.00	50.00
d.	Type II, laid paper	125.00	100.00

ILO8

1884   *Imperf.*

Size: About 105x52mm

GO9 ILO8 black	200.00	150.00
GO10 ILO8 Blk, *lemon yel*	250.00	

ILO9

Dateline reads: "Sale de Bucaramanga en.. de..de 188..".

Special Issue for Bucaramanga

1886   **Unwmk.**   *Imperf.*
Ribbed Paper

GO11 ILO9 blk, red vio & bister	50.00	—
a.	Watermarked	75.00	—

Wove Paper

GO12 ILO9 blk, red vio & bister	—	—
GO13 ILO9 As #GO12, "BUCARAMANGA" omitted from dateline	—	—

ILO10

Dateline reads: "Sale de... en.. de..de 188..". "CERTIFICADO OFICIAL" is narrower than on No. GO13, and is made up of tall, thin letters.

Special Issue for Bucaramanga

1886   **Unwmk.**   *Imperf.*
Ribbed Paper

GO14 ILO10 blk, pink & bister	50.00	—
a.	Watermarked	60.00	—

ILO11

Inscribed "REPÚBLICA DE COLOMBIA."
Dateline reads "Sale de.. en.. de.. de 188..."

1886   *Imperf.*

Size: About 130x84mm

GO15 ILO11 black	—	100.00
a.	Black, ruled paper	—	100.00

ILO12

Dateline reads "Sale de Mompos en.. de.. de 188..."

Special Issue for Mompos

1886   *Imperf.*

GO16 ILO12 black	—	200.00

ILO13

Inscribed "No....ESTADOS UNIDOS DE COLOMBIA"

1887   *Imperf.*

Size: About 135x85mm

GO17 ILO13 black	—	150.00

ILO14

Inscribed "REPUBLICA DE COLOMBIA."

Special Issue for Sagamoso

1887   *Imperf.*

Size: About 108x80mm

GO18 ILO14 black	—	175.00

New Design

As. No. GO14, inscribed "REPUBLICA DE COLOMBIA". Dateline reads: "Sale de... en.. de..de 188..".

Special Issue for Bucaramanga

1886   **Unwmk.**   *Imperf.*
Ribbed Paper

GO19 blk, pink & bister	—	—
a.	Black, pink & bister, on wove paper	—	—

The editors would like to examine and photograph and example of either No. GO19 or GO19a.

ILO16

Inscribed "No. ..." at right. Dateline reads: "Sale de Bucaramanga en.. de..de 188..".

Special Issue for Bucaramanga

1888	Unwmk.		Imperf.	
GO20	ILO16	violet, *buff*	40.00	150.00
a.	"BACARAMANGA" in dateline		—	—
b.	"BUCARAMANGA" removed from dateline		—	—

ILO18

Inscribed "CERTIFICACIÓN OFICIAL." Dateline reads: "Salió de Popayán, en...de....de 18..."

Special Issue for Popayan

1888			Imperf.	
GO22	ILO18	black	200.00	175.00
a.	Black, laid batonne paper		200.00	175.00

New Design

Frame with Simple Arabesque
Inscribed "CERTIFICADO OFFICIAL"
Dateline reads: "Sale de Popayán...de 1888"

Special Issue for Popayan

1888		Imperf.	
	Size: About 132x78mm		
GO23	black, *gray*	—	—
a.	Black, creme laid paper	—	—

The editors would like to examine and photograph an example of either No. GO23 or GO23a.

ILO21

Thick-thin double line border.
Inscribed "CERTIFICADO OFICIAL."
Dateline reads: "Sale de... en..de.. de 18.."

Special Issue for Bogota

1889		Imperf.	
	Size: About 132x85mm		
GO25	ILO21 black		125.00

ILO22

As No. GO25, dateline reads: "Sale de Bogotá... en.. de.. de 18.."

Special Issue for Bogota

1889		Imperf.	
	Size: About 132x85mm		
GO26	ILO22 black		150.00

ILO23

Dateline reads: "Sale de ... en.. de.. de 188.."

Special Issue for Cali

1889		Imperf.	
	Thin, Vertically Ribbed Paper		
GO27	ILO23 black	—	100.00

ILO24

Thick-thin double-line border.
Elaborate ornaments separate lines of text.
Inscribed "VALOR DECLARADO OFICIAL."
Dateline reads: "Sale de... en.. de.. de 189..."

Special Issue for Bogota

1890		Imperf.	
GO28	ILO24 black		200.00

ILO25

Thick-thin double-line border.
Bold, heavy ornaments separate lines of text.
Inscribed "REPUBLICA DE COLOMBIA." in bold, tall letters.

Special Issue for Bogota

1890		Imperf.	
GO29	ILO25 black		200.00

ILO26

Single-line border. Simple typographed text.

Special Issue for Calamar.

1890		Imperf.	
	Vertically Laid Paper		
GO30	ILO26 black	—	250.00

New Design

Heavy border, coiling around bars, with double rectangular frame inside. Eagle and arms at center.
Inscribed at UR: "Servicio Postal Interior", and below: "Certificacion Oficial".

1890		Imperf.	
	Size: About 143x97mm		
GO31	black	—	—

The editors would like to examine and photograph an example of No. GO31.

New Designs

Double-line rectangular frame.
Inscribed "REPUBLICA DE COLOMBIA" in small letters.
Third line of text reads: "SERVICIO DE CORREOS NACIONALES"

1890		Imperf.	
	Size: About 132x85mm		
GO32	black	75.00	75.00
a.	Black, ruled laid paper	75.00	75.00

Letters & Ornaments Frame
Small Ornaments Separate Lines of Text

GO33	black, ruled paper	75.00	75.00
a.	Black, *bluish* ruled paper	72.50	75.00

As No. GO22, Ornaments bolder

GO34	black	75.00	75.00
a.	Black, *bluish* ribbed paper	75.00	75.00

The editors would like to examine and photograph an examples of Nos. GO32-GO34.

Type ILO16 Redrawn

"Numero" at UR.

Special Issue for Bucamaranga

1891		Imperf.	
GO35	ILO16 black	—	—

ILO31

Thin, scalloped frame. "GRAMOS..." added at UR.

1892		Imperf.	
	Size: About 155x94mm		
GO36	ILO31 black	75.00	75.00

New Design

Rope-like frame. Inscriptions same as No. GO36, but "C" of "COLOMBIA" is from a fancy font.

1894		Imperf.	
	Size: About 152x93mm		
GO37	ILO32 black		

The editors would like to examine and photograph an example of No. GO37.

ACKNOWLEDGMENT OF RECEIPT STAMPS

AR1

AR2

1893	Unwmk.	Litho.	Perf. 13½	
H1	AR1 5c ver, *blue*		4.75	4.75

1894			Perf. 12	
H2	AR1 5c vermilion		4.50	5.00

1902-03			Imperf.	
H3	AR2 10c blue, *blue*		3.50	5.00
a.	10c, blue, *greenish blue*		3.50	5.00
b.	Sewing machine perf.		3.50	5.00
c.	Perf. 12		3.50	5.00

The handstamp "AR" in circle is believed to be a postmark.

AR2a

Purple Handstamp

1903		Imperf.	
H4	AR2a 10c black, *pink*	25.00	25.00

AR3

1904	Pelure Paper		Imperf.	
H12	AR3 5c pale blue		10.50	10.50
a.	Perf. 12		10.50	10.50

No. 307 Overprinted in Black, Green or Violet

H13	A86 5c carmine	17.50	17.50

AR4

1904		Perf. 12	
H16	AR4 5c blue	3.25	2.75
a.	Imperf., pair	8.75	8.75

For overprints see Nos. LH1-LH2.

General José Acevedo y Gómez — AR5

1910, July 20		Engr.	
H17	AR5 5c orange & green	7.00	17.50

Centenary of National Independence.

Sabana Station AR6

Map of Colombia AR7

1917		Perf. 14	
H18	AR6 4c bister brown	5.50	6.00
H19	AR7 5c orange brown	5.50	4.50
a.	Imperf., pair	14.00	

LATE FEE STAMPS

LF1

1886   Unwmk.   Litho.   *Perf. 10½*

I1	LF1	2½c blk, *lilac*	4.00	3.25
a.		Imperf., pair	15.00	15.00

LF2

1892   *Perf. 12, 13½*

I2	LF2	2½c dk bl, *rose*	3.50	2.50
a.		Imperf., pair	15.00	
I3	LF2	2½c ultra, *pink*	3.50	2.50

LF3

1902   *Imperf.*

I4	LF3	5c purple, *rose*	1.00	1.00
a.		Perf. 12	2.10	2.10

LF4

1914   *Perf. 10, 13½*

I6	LF4	2c vio brown	5.00	5.00
I7	LF4	5c blue green	5.00	4.25

Overprints illustrated above are unauthorized and of private origin.

POSTAGE DUE STAMPS

These are not, strictly speaking, postage due stamps but were issued to cover an additional fee, "Sobreporte," charged on mail to foreign countries with which Colombia had no postal conventions.

D1   D2

D3

1866   Unwmk.   Litho.   *Imperf.*

J1	D1	25c black, *blue*	80.00	55.00
J2	D2	50c black, *yellow*	55.00	80.00
J3	D3	1p black, *rose*	160.00	125.00
		Nos. J1-J3 (3)	295.00	260.00

DEPARTMENT STAMPS

These stamps are said to be for interior postage, to supersede the separate issues for the various departments.

Regular Issues Handstamped in Black, Violet, Blue or Green — a

On Stamps of 1904

1909   Unwmk.   *Perf. 12*

L1	A94	½c yellow	2.50	2.50
a.		Imperf., pair	7.50	7.50
L2	A94	1c yel grn	3.75	2.50
L3	A94	2c red	5.50	3.75
a.		Imperf., pair	15.00	15.00
L4	A94	5c blue	6.25	4.00
L5	A94	10c violet	8.75	8.75
L6	A94	20c black	14.00	14.00
L7	A95	1p brown	22.50	21.00

On Stamp of 1902

L8	A83	10p dk brn, *rose*	25.00	25.00
		Nos. L1-L8 (8)	88.25	81.50

On Stamps of 1908

Perf. 10, 13, 13½ and Compound

L9	A94	½c orange	2.90	2.90
a.		Imperf., pair	7.50	7.50
L10	A94	1c green	5.00	5.00
a.		Without imprint	6.25	6.25
L11	A94	2c red	5.50	5.50
a.		Imperf., pair	15.00	15.00
L12	A94	5c blue	5.50	5.50
a.		Imperf., pair	15.00	15.00
L13	A94	10c violet	8.75	8.75

On Tolima Stamp of 1888

Perf. 10½

L14	A23	1p red brn	27.50	27.50
		Nos. L9-L14 (6)	55.15	55.15

Regular Issues Handstamped — b

On Stamps of 1904

Perf. 12

L15	A94	½c yellow	2.50	2.50
L16	A94	1c yellow grn	4.25	4.25
L17	A94	2c red	7.50	7.50
L18	A94	5c blue	7.50	7.50
L19	A94	10c violet	10.00	10.00
L20	A94	20c black	14.00	14.00
L21	A94	1p brown	25.00	25.00
		Nos. L15-L21 (7)	70.75	70.75

On Stamps of 1908

Perf. 10, 13, 13½

L22	A94	½c orange	2.75	2.75
L23	A94	1c yellow grn	7.75	7.75
L24	A94	2c red	6.25	6.25
a.		Imperf., pair	15.00	15.00
L25	A94	5c light blue	7.50	7.50
		Nos. L22-L25 (4)	24.25	24.25

The handstamps on Nos. L1-L25 are, as usual, found inverted and double.

DEPARTMENT REGISTRATION STAMPS

Registration Stamps of 1904 Handstamped like Nos. L1-L25

1909   Unwmk.   *Perf. 12*

LF1	R12 (a)	10c purple	30.00	30.00
LF2	R12 (b)	10c purple	30.00	30.00

On Registration Stamp of 1909

Perf. 10, 13

LF3	R12 (a)	10c purple	30.00	30.00
LF4	R12 (b)	10c purple	30.00	30.00
		Nos. LF1-LF4 (4)	120.00	120.00

Minimum total imperf. value per pair, $125.

DEPARTMENT ACKNOWLEDGMENT OF RECEIPT STAMPS

Acknowledgment of Receipt Stamp of 1904 Hstmpd.

1909   Unwmk.   *Perf. 12*

LH1	AR4 (a)	5c blue	30.00	30.00
a.		Imperf., pair	125.00	
LH2	AR4 (b)	5c blue	30.00	30.00
a.		Imperf., pair	125.00	

LOCAL STAMPS FOR THE CITY OF BOGOTA

A1

Pelure Paper

1889   Unwmk.   Litho.   *Perf. 12*

LX1	A1	½c black	1.10	1.10
a.		Imperf., pair	7.25	7.25

Impressions on bright blue and blue-gray paper were not regularly issued.

A2

White Wove Paper

1896   *Perf. 12, 13½*

LX2	A2	½c black	1.10	1.10

A3

1903   *Imperf.*

LX3	A3	10c black, *pink*	7.25	1.40
a.		Perf. 12	7.25	1.40

OFFICIAL STAMPS

Stamps of 1917-1937 Overprinted in Black or Red

a

b

1937   Unwmk.   *Perf. 11, 12, 13½*

O1	A131 (a)	1c green	.25	.25
O2	A157 (a)	10c dp org	.25	.25
O3	A107 (b)	30c olive bis	2.10	1.00
O4	A129 (b)	40c brn & yel brn	1.60	.80
O5	A114 (b)	50c car	1.60	.80
O6	A107 (b)	1p lt bl	13.00	5.50
O7	A107 (b)	2p org	15.00	6.50
O8	A107 (b)	5p gray	47.50	52.50
O9	A118 (b)	10p dk brn	110.00	125.00

Wmk. 229

Perf. 12½

O10	A132 (a)	2c red	.25	.25
O11	A133 (a)	5c brn	.25	.25
O12	A160 (a)	12c dp bl (R)	1.00	.50
O13	A136 (b)	20c dk bl (R)	1.60	.80
		Nos. O1-O13 (13)	194.40	194.40

Tall, wrong font "I's" in OFICIAL exist on all stamps with "a" overprint.

REGISTERED PARCEL STAMPS

PP1

PP2

PP3

PP4

Inscribed "Por Vapor" and "de BARRANQUILLA."

QF1	PP1	black	—	75.00
QF2	PP2	black	—	75.00
QF3	PP3	black	—	75.00

Inscribed "De CALI para", "Por Vapor" removed.

QF4	PP4	black	—	200.00

POSTAL TAX STAMPS

"Greatest
Mother"
PT1

Perf. 11½
1935, May 27   Unwmk.   Litho.
RA1   PT1   5c olive blk & scar   4.00   1.25

Required on all mail during Red Cross Week in 1935 (May 27-June 3) and in 1936.

Mother and Child — PT2

Perf. 10½, 10½x11
1937, May 24   Unwmk.
RA2   PT2   5c red   2.75   .90

Required on all mail during Red Cross Week. The tax was for the Red Cross.

Ministry of Posts and Telegraphs Building
PT3   PT4

1939-45   Litho.   Perf. 10½, 12½
RA3   PT3   ¼c dp bl   .25   .25
RA3A   PT3   ¼c dk vio brn ('45)   .25   .25
RA4   PT3   ½c pink   .25   .25
RA5   PT3   1c violet   .30   .25
RA5A   PT3   1c yel org ('45)   1.75   .70
RA6   PT3   2c pck grn   .55   .25
RA7   PT3   20c lt brn   4.50   1.50
     Nos. RA3-RA7 (7)   7.85   3.45

Obligatory on all mail. The tax was for the construction of the new Communications Building.

The 25c of type PT3 and PT4 were not usable on postal matter.

For overprint see No. 561 in Scott Standard catalogue, Vol. 2.

Perf. 12½x13
1940, Jan. 20   Engr.   Wmk. 229
RA8   PT4   ¼c ultra   .25   .25
RA9   PT4   ½c carmine   .25   .25
RA10   PT4   1c violet   .25   .25
RA11   PT4   2c bl grn   .30   .25
RA12   PT4   20c brown   1.25   .25
     Nos. RA8-RA12 (5)   2.30   1.25

See note after No. RA7. See No. RA18 in Scott Standard catalogue, Vol. 2.

"Protection" — PT5

1940, Apr. 25   Wmk. 255   Perf. 12
RA13   PT5   5c rose carmine   .30   .25
     See No. RA17.

ANTIOQUIA

ant-ē-'ō-kē-ə

Originally a State, now a Department of the Republic of Colombia. Until the revolution of 1885, the separate states making up the United States of Colombia were sovereign governments in their own right. On August 4, 1886, the National Council of Bogotá, composed of two delegates from each state, adopted a new constitution which abolished the sovereign rights of states, which then became departments with governors appointed by the President of the Republic. The nine original states represented at the Bogotá Convention retained some of their previous rights, as management of their own finances, and all issued postage stamps until as late as 1904. For Panama's issues, see Panama Nos. 1-30.

Coat of Arms
A1   A2

A3   A4

Wove Paper
1868   Unwmk.   Litho.   Imperf.
1   A1   2½c blue   1,000.   750.
2   A2   5c green   750.   575.
3   A3   10c lilac   3,000.   1,000.
4   A4   1p red   675.   750.

Reprints of Nos. 1, 3 and 4 are on a bluish white paper and all but No. 3 have scratches across the design.

A5   A6

A7   A8

A9   A10

1869
5   A5   2½c blue   3.75   3.25
6   A6   5c green   5.50   5.00
7   A7   5c green   5.50   5.00
8   A8   10c lilac   7.25   3.50
9   A9   20c brown   7.25   3.50
10   A10   1p rose red   14.50   13.00
a.   1p vermilion   27.50   25.00
     Nos. 5-10 (6)   43.75   33.25

Reprints of Nos. 7, 8 and 10 are on a bluish white paper; reprints of Nos. 5 and 10a on white paper. The 10c blue is believed to be a reprint.

A11   A12

A13   A14

A15   A16

A17   A18

1873
12   A11   1c yellow grn   5.25   4.00
a.   1c green   5.25   4.00
13   A12   5c green   8.75   6.50
14   A13   10c lilac   25.00   21.00
15   A14   20c yellow brn   8.75   7.50
a.   20c dark brown   8.75   7.50
16   A15   50c blue   2.00   1.75
17   A16   1p vermilion   3.75   3.00
18   A17   2p black, yellow   8.75   8.00
19   A18   5p black, rose   65.00   55.00

A19   A20

Liberty Head
A21   A22

Pedro Justo
Berrio — A23

1875-85
20   A19   1c blk, grn, un-
               glazed ('76)   1.60   2.40
a.   Glazed paper   2.60   3.25
b.   1c blk, lt grn, laid paper
               ('85)   3.75   3.50
21   A19   1c black ('76)   1.10   1.00
a.   Laid paper   160.00   110.00
22   A19   1c bl grn ('85)   2.50   4.00
23   A19   1c red lil, laid
               paper ('85)   2.50   4.00
24   A20   2½c blue   2.50   1.90
a.   Pelure paper ('78)   1,500.   1,100.
25   A21   5c green   16.00   14.50
a.   Laid paper   160.00   87.50
26   A22   5c green   16.00   14.50
a.   Laid paper   160.00   87.50
27   A23   10c lilac   25.00   21.00
a.   Laid paper   160.00   125.00
28   A20   10c vio, pelure
               paper ('78)   900.00   675.00

Arms — A24   Liberty — A25

A26   A27

1878-85
29   A24   2½c blue, pelure pa-
               per   2.75   2.50
30   A24   2½c green ('83)   2.50   2.10
a.   Laid paper ('83)   80.00   55.00
31   A24   2½c blk, buff ('85)   7.25   6.50
32   A25   5c green ('83)   4.50   4.00
a.   Pelure paper   32.50   27.50
b.   Laid paper ('82)   40.00   13.00
33   A25   5c violet ('83)   9.50   7.50
     5c blue violet ('83)   9.50   7.50
34   A26   10c vio, laid paper
               ('82)   190.00   65.00
35   A26   10c scar ('83)   2.50   2.10
a.   Tete beche pair   110.00   110.00
36   A27   20c brown ('83)   4.50   4.00
a.   Laid paper ('82)   6.00   5.50

A28   A29

Liberty — A30   Coat of Arms — A31

1883-85
37   A28   5c brown   5.25   3.50
a.   Laid paper   225.00   87.50
38   A28   5c green ('85)   140.00   45.00
a.   Laid paper ('85)   160.00   75.00
39   A28   5c yel, laid paper
               ('85)   5.50   4.50
40   A29   10c bl grn, laid pa-
               per   5.50   4.75
41   A29   10c vio, bl ('85)   5.50   4.50
42   A29   10c lil, laid paper
               ('85)   12.00   7.50
a.   Wove paper ('85)   125.00   80.00
43   A30   20c bl, laid paper
               ('85)   4.50   4.00

1886   Wove Paper
55   A31   1c grn, pink   .65   .55
56   A31   2½c blk, orange   .65   .55
57   A31   5c ultra, buff   2.00   1.75
a.   5c blue, buff   3.75   3.25
58   A31   10c rose, buff   1.75   1.60
a.   Transfer of 50c in stone of
               10c   140.00   140.00
59   A31   20c dk vio, buff   1.75   1.60
61   A31   50c yel brn, buff   3.25   2.75
62   A31   1p yel, grn   5.25   4.50
63   A31   2p green, vio   5.25   4.50
     Nos. 55-63 (8)   20.55   17.80

1887-88
64   A31   1c red, vio   .50   .45
65   A31   2½c lil, pale lil   .50   .60
66   A31   5c car, buff   .65   .65
67   A31   5c red, grn   3.75   1.75
68   A31   10c brn, grn   .65   .80
     Nos. 64-68 (5)   6.05   4.25

Medellin Issue

A32   A33

A34   A35

1888 Typeset

69	A32	2½c blk, *yellow*	16.00	14.50
70	A33	5c blk, *yellow*	8.75	7.50
71	A34	5c red, *yellow*	5.25	4.50
		Nos. 69-71 (3)	30.00	26.50

Two varieties of No. 69, six of No. 70 and ten of No. 71.

1889

72	A35	2½c red	8.00	6.75

Ten varieties including "eentavos."

Regular Issue

Coat of Arms
A36   A37

A38   A39

A40   A41

1889 Litho. Perf. 13½

73	A36	1c blk, *rose*	.25	.25
74	A36	2½c blk, *blue*	.25	.25
75	A36	5c blk, *yellow*	.30	.30
76	A36	10c blk, *green*	.30	.30
		Nos. 73-76 (4)	1.10	1.10

1890

78	A37	20c blue	1.40	1.40
79	A38	50c vio brn	2.50	2.50
a.		Transfer of 20c in stone of 50c	95.00	95.00
80	A38	50c green	2.25	2.25
81	A39	1p red	2.00	2.00
82	A40	2p blk, *mag*	14.50	14.50
83	A41	5p blk, *org red*	22.50	22.50
		Nos. 78-83 (6)	45.15	45.15

Nos. 73-76, 82-83 exist imperf. The so-called "errors" of Nos. 73 to 76, printed on paper of wrong colors, are essays or, possibly, reprints. They exist perforated and imperforate.
See No. 96.

A42   A43

A44   A45

1890 Typeset Perf. 14

84	A42	2½c blk, *buff*	2.25	2.25
85	A43	5c blk, *orange*	2.25	2.25
86	A44	10c blk, *buff*	7.00	7.00
87	A44	10c blk, *rose*	9.00	9.00
88	A45	20c blk, *orange*	9.00	9.00
		Nos. 84-88 (5)	29.50	29.50

20 varieties of the 5c, 10 each of the other values.

A46   A47

1892 Litho. Perf. 13½

89	A46	1c brn, *brnsh*	.40	.40
90	A46	2½c pur, *lil*	.40	.40
92	A46	5c blk, *gray*	1.10	.55
a.		Transfer of 2½c in stone of 5c	200.00	
		Nos. 89-92 (3)	1.90	1.35

1893

93	A46	1c blue	.25	.25
94	A46	2½c green	.40	.40
95	A46	5c vermilion	.25	.25
96	A36	10c pale brown	.25	.25
		Nos. 93-96 (4)	1.15	1.15

1896 Perf. 14

97	A47	2c gray	.25	.25
98	A47	2c lilac rose	.25	.25
99	A47	2½c brown	.25	.25
100	A47	2½c steel blue	.25	.25
101	A47	3c orange	.25	.25
102	A47	3c olive grn	.25	.25
103	A47	5c green	.25	.25
104	A47	5c yellow buff	.30	.30
105	A47	10c brown vio	.55	.55
106	A47	10c violet	.55	.55
107	A47	20c brown org	1.40	1.40
108	A47	20c blue	1.40	1.40
109	A47	50c gray brn	1.40	1.40
110	A47	50c rose	1.40	1.40
111	A47	1p blue & blk	17.50	17.50
112	A47	1p rose red & blk	17.50	17.50
113	A47	2p orange & blk	55.00	55.00
114	A47	2p dk grn & blk	55.00	55.00
115	A47	5p red vio & blk	95.00	95.00
116	A47	5p purple & blk	95.00	95.00
		Nos. 97-116 (20)	343.75	343.75

#115-116 with centers omitted are proofs.

General José María
Córdoba — A48

1899 Perf. 11

117	A48	½c grnsh bl	.25	.25
118	A48	1c slate blue	.25	.25
119	A48	2c slate brown	.25	.25
120	A48	3c red	.25	.25
121	A48	4c bister brown	.25	.25
122	A48	5c green	.25	.25
123	A48	10c scarlet	.25	.25
124	A48	20c gray violet	.25	.25
125	A48	50c olive bister	.25	.25
126	A48	1p greenish blk	.25	.25
127	A48	2p olive gray	.25	.25
		Nos. 117-127 (11)	2.75	2.75

Numerous part-perf. and imperf. varieties of Nos. 117-127 exist.
Used values for Nos. 117-127 are for favor-canceled stamps with oval cancels in violet. Postally used examples are valued at $1.75 each.

A49   A50

A50a

1901 Typeset Perf. 12

128	A49	1c red	.25	.25
129	A50	1c ultra	.65	.65
130	A50	1c bister	.65	.65
130A	A50a	1c dull red	.65	.65
130B	A50a	1c ultra	4.50	4.50
		Nos. 128-130B (5)	6.70	6.70

Eight varieties of No. 128, four varieties of Nos. 129-130B.

A51   A52

Atanasio   Dr. José Félix
Girardot   Restrepo
A53   A54

1902 Litho. Wove Paper

131	A51	1c brt rose	.25	.25
a.		Laid paper	.65	.65
b.		Imperf., pair	2.75	
132	A51	2c blue	.25	.25
a.		Transfer of 3c in stone of 2c	6.00	6.00
133	A51	3c green	.25	.25
a.		Imperf., pair	5.00	
134	A51	4c dull violet	.25	.25
135	A52	5c rose red	.25	.25
136	A53	10c rose lilac	.25	.25
a.		Small head	5.75	5.75
b.		10c rose	.25	.25
137	A53	20c gray green	.25	.25
138	A53	30c brt rose	.25	.25
139	A53	40c blue	.25	.25
140	A53	50c brn, *yel*	.25	.25

Laid Paper

141	A54	1p purple & blk	.80	.80
142	A54	2p rose & blk	.80	.80
143	A54	5p sl bl & blk	1.50	1.50
		Nos. 131-143 (13)	5.60	5.60

1903 Wove Paper

143A	A51	1c blue	.25	.25
144	A51	2c violet	.25	.25
a.		Imperf.	3.00	

A55   A56

A57

Designs: 1p, Francisco Antonio Zea. 2p, Custodio Garcia Rovira. 3p, La Pola (Policarpa Salavarrieta). 4p, J. M. Restrepo. 5p, José Fernández Madrid. 10p, Juan del Corral.

1903-04

145	A55	4c yellow brn	.35	.30
146	A55	5c blue	.35	.30
147	A56	10c yellow	.35	.30
148	A56	20c purple	.35	.30
149	A56	30c brown	.90	.85
150	A56	40c green	.90	.85
151	A56	50c rose	.35	.30
152	A57	1p olive gray	.90	.85
153	A57	2p purple	.90	.85
154	A57	3p dark blue	.90	.85
155	A57	4p dull red	1.50	1.50
156	A57	5p red brown	4.50	2.10
157	A57	10p scarlet	9.25	5.25
		Nos. 145-157 (13)	21.50	14.60

Nos. 145-146, 151, 153-157 exist imperf. Value of pairs, $4 to $5.

Manizales Issue

Stamps of these designs are local private post issues.

OFFICIAL STAMPS Stamps of 1903-04 with overprint "OFICIAL" were never issued.

REGISTRATION STAMPS

R1

1896 Unwmk. Litho. Perf. 14

F1	R1	2½c rose	1.25	1.25
F2	R1	2½c dull blue	1.25	1.25

Córdoba
R2

R3

R4

1899 Perf. 11

F3	R2	2½c dull blue	.25	.25
F4	R3	10c red lilac	.25	.25

1902 Perf. 12

F5	R4	10c purple, *blue*	.30	.30
a.		Imperf.	—	

ACKNOWLEDGMENT OF RECEIPT STAMPS

AR1

1902-03 Unwmk. Litho. Perf. 12

H1	AR1	5c black, *rose*	1.10	1.10
H2	AR1	5c slate ('03)	.35	.35

LATE FEE STAMPS

Córdoba — LF1

1899 Unwmk. Litho. Perf. 11

I1	LF1	2½c dark green	.30	.30
a.		Imperf., pair	3.00	

LF2

LF3

1901   Typeset   Perf. 12
I2   LF2 2½c red violet   .80   .80
a.   2½c purple   .80   .80

1902   Litho.
I3   LF3 2½c violet   .25   .25

City of Medellin

Stamps of the designs shown were not issued by any governmental agency but by the Sociedad de Mejoras Publicas.

BOLIVAR

bə-'lē-ˌvär

Originally a State, now a Department of the Republic of Colombia. (See Antioquia.)

A1

1863-66   Unwmk.   Litho.   Imperf.
1   A1 10c green   1,200. 600.00
a.   Five stars below shield 2,500. 2,400.
2   A1 10c red ('66)   27.50   30.00
a.   Diagonal half used as 5c
        on cover   120.00
b.   Five stars below shield 80.00   72.50
3   A1 1p red   6.75   7.75

Fourteen varieties of each. Counterfeits of Nos. 1 and 1a exist.

Coat of Arms
A2   A3

A4

A5

1873
4   A2   5c blue   7.25   7.25
5   A3   10c violet   7.25   7.25
6   A4   20c yellow green   32.50 32.50
7   A5   80c vermilion   65.00 65.00
     Nos. 4-7 (4)   112.00 112.00

A6

A7

A8

1874-78
8   A6   5c blue   27.50 14.00
9   A7   5c blue ('78)   8.00   7.25
10 A8   10c violet ('77)   4.00   3.75
     Nos. 8-10 (3)   39.50 25.00

Bolívar — A9

Dated "1879"
1879   White Wove Paper   Perf. 12½
11 A9   5c blue   .30   .30
a.   Imperf., pair   .90
12 A9   10c violet   .25   .25
13 A9   20c red   .30   .30
a.   20c green (error)   11.00 11.00

Bluish Laid Paper
15 A9   5c blue   .30   .30
a.   Imperf., pair   2.25
16 A9   10c violet   1.60   1.60
a.   Imperf., pair   4.50
17 A9   20c red   .40   .40
a.   Imperf., pair   2.00
     Nos. 11-17 (6)   3.15   3.15

Stamps of 80c and 1p on white wove paper and 1p on bluish laid paper were prepared but not placed in use.

Dated "1880"
1880   White Wove Paper   Perf. 12½
19 A9   5c blue   .30   .30
a.   Imperf., pair   1.60
20 A9   10c violet   .40   .40
a.   Imperf., pair   1.60
21 A9   20c red   .40   .40
a.   20c green (error)   14.00 14.00
23 A9   80c green   2.50   2.50
24 A9   1p orange   2.75   2.75
a.   Imperf., pair   5.50
     Nos. 19-24 (5)   6.35   6.35

Bluish Laid Paper
25 A9   5c blue   .30   .30
a.   Imperf., pair   1.40
26 A9   10c violet   2.50   2.50
27 A9   20c red   .40   .40
a.   Imperf., pair   3.00
28 A9   1p orange   450.00
a.   Imperf.   475.00

A11

A12

A13

A15

A16

Dated "1882"
White Wove Paper
1882   Perf. 12, 16x12
29 A11 5c blue   .35   .35
30 A12 10c lilac   .25   .25
31 A13 20c red   .35   .35
33 A15 80c green   .65   .65
34 A16 1p orange   .65   .65
     Nos. 29-34 (5)   2.25   2.25

Nos. 29, 30 and 34 are known imperforate. They are printer's waste and were not issued through post offices.

A17

1882   Engr.   Perf. 12
35 A17 5p blue & rose red   .65   .65
a.   Imperf., pair   5.25
b.   Perf. 16   8.00 6.75
c.   Perf. 14   6.75 6.75
36 A17 10p brown & blue   1.75   1.75
a.   Imperf., pair   8.75
b.   Perf. 16   7.25 6.00
c.   Rouletted   8.75 8.75

Dated "1883"
1883   Litho.   Perf. 12, 16x12
37 A11 5c blue   .25   .25
a.   Imperf., pair   1.00
b.   Perf. 12   12.00 2.40
38 A12 10c lilac   .30   .30
39 A13 20c red   .30   .30
41 A15 80c green   .30   .30
42 A16 1p orange   1.60   1.60
a.   Perf. 16x12   2.25   2.25
     Nos. 37-42 (5)   2.75   2.75

1884   Dated "1884"
43 A11 5c blue   .30   .30
a.   Perf. 12   16.00 16.00
44 A12 10c lilac   .25   .25
45 A13 20c red   .25   .25
a.   Perf. 12   8.00   8.00
47 A15 80c green   .30   .35
a.   Perf. 12   4.00   4.00
48 A16 1p orange   .30   .30
     Nos. 43-48 (5)   1.40   1.45

1885   Dated "1885"
49 A11 5c blue   .25   .25
50 A12 10c lilac   .25   .25
51 A13 20c red   .25   .25
53 A15 80c green   .25   .25
54 A16 1p orange   .30   .30
     Nos. 49-54 (5)   1.30   1.30

The note after No. 34 will also apply to imperforate stamps of the 1884-85 issues.

A18

1891   Perf. 14
55 A18 1c black   .30   .30
56 A18 5c orange   .30   .30
a.   Imperf., pair   .90
57 A18 10c carmine   .30   .30
58 A18 20c red   .65   .65
59 A18 50c green   .95   .95
60 A18 1p purple   .95   .95
     Nos. 55-60 (6)   3.45   3.45

For overprint see Colombia No. 169.

Bolívar
A19

José Fernández Madrid
A20

Manuel Rodriguez Torices
A21

José María García de Toledo
A22

1903   Laid Paper   Imperf.
62 A19 50c dk bl, *pink*   .65   .65
a.   Bluish paper   .65   .65
63 A19 50c sl grn, *pink*   .65   .65
a.   Rose paper   2.25   2.25
b.   Greenish blue paper   3.25   3.25
c.   Yellow paper   4.50   4.50
d.   Brown paper   4.50   4.50
e.   Salmon paper   8.00   8.00
64 A19 50c pur, *pink*   2.25   2.25
a.   White paper   4.50   4.50
b.   Brown paper   4.50   4.50
c.   Greenish blue paper   4.50   4.50
d.   Lilac paper   4.50   4.50
e.   Rose paper   4.00   4.00
f.   Yellow paper   4.50   4.50
g.   Salmon paper   6.50   6.50
h.   As "a," wove paper   9.75   9.75
65 A20 1p org, *sal*   .65   .65
a.   Yellow paper   5.00   5.00
b.   Greenish blue paper   16.00 16.00
66 A20 1p gray grn, *lil* 1.60   1.60
a.   Yellow paper   7.00   7.00
b.   Salmon paper   8.00   8.00
c.   Green paper   8.00   8.00
d.   White wove paper   12.00
67 A21 5p car rose, *lil*   .65   .65
a.   Brown paper   1.25   1.25
b.   Yellow paper   1.25   1.25
c.   Greenish blue paper   5.00   5.00
d.   Bluish paper   6.50   6.50
e.   Salmon paper   8.00   8.00
f.   Rose paper   9.75   9.75
68 A22 10p dk bl, *bluish* 1.40   1.40
a.   Greenish blue paper   1.40   1.40
b.   Rose paper   8.00   8.00
c.   Salmon paper   8.00   8.00
d.   Yellow paper   8.00   8.00
e.   Brown paper   9.00   9.00
f.   Lilac paper   12.00 12.00
g.   White paper   9.75   9.75
69 A22 10p pur, *grnsh bl* 3.75   3.75
a.   Bluish paper   8.00   8.00
b.   Rose paper   7.25   7.25
c.   Yellow paper   8.00   8.00
d.   Brown paper   8.00   8.00
     Nos. 62-69 (8)   11.60 11.60

Sewing Machine Perf.
Laid Paper
70 A19 50c dk bl, *pink*   1.10   1.10
a.   Bluish paper   1.10   1.10
71 A19 50c sl grn, *pink* 2.25   2.25
72 A19 50c pur, *grnsh bl* 4.50   4.50
a.   White paper   4.50   4.50
b.   White wove paper   8.00
73 A20 1p org, *sal*   2.25   2.25
a.   Yellow paper   9.75   9.75
74 A20 1p gray grn, *lil* 9.75   9.75
75 A21 5p car rose, *yel* 1.75   1.75
a.   Lilac paper   4.50   4.50
b.   Brown paper   4.50   4.50
c.   Bluish paper   6.00   6.00
d.   White wove paper   9.75
76 A22 10p dk bl, *grnsh bl* 5.00 5.00
a.   Bluish paper   7.50   7.50
b.   Yellow paper   9.75   9.75
c.   As "b," wove paper   12.00
77 A22 10p pur, *grnsh bl* 7.50   7.50
a.   Bluish paper   13.00 13.00
b.   Rose paper   8.50   8.50
c.   Yellow paper   13.00 13.00
     Nos. 70-77 (8)   34.10 34.10

José María del Castillo y Rada — A23

Manuel Anguiano — A24

Pantaleón C.
Ribón — A25

1904   *Sewing Machine Perf.*
89	A23	5c black	.25	.25
90	A24	10c brown	.25	.25
91	A25	20c red	.30	.30
92	A25	20c red brown	.65	.65
		Nos. 89-92 (4)	1.45	1.45

Imperf., pairs
89a	A23	5c black	4.00	4.00
90a	A24	10c brown	3.00	3.00
91a	A25	20c red	7.25	7.25
92a	A25	20c red brown	7.25	7.25

A26

A27

A28

1904   *Imperf.*
93	A26	½c black	.65	.65
a.		Tête bêche pair	3.75	3.75
94	A27	1c blue	1.25	1.25
95	A28	2c purple	1.40	1.40
		Nos. 93-95 (3)	3.30	3.30

REGISTRATION STAMPS

Simón Bolívar
R1   R2
White Wove Paper
Perf. 12½, 16x12

1879   **Unwmk.**   **Litho.**
F1	R1	40c brown	.75	.75

Bluish Laid Paper
F2	R1	40c brown	.75	.75
a.		Imperf., pair	3.50	

Dated "1880"
1880   **White Wove Paper**
F3	R1	40c brown	.35	.35

Bluish Laid Paper
F4	R1	40c brown	.75	.75
a.		Imperf., pair	3.50	

Dated "1882" to "1885"
White Wove Paper
1882-85   *Perf. 16x12*
F5	R2	40c brown (1882)	.35	.35
F6	R2	40c brown (1883)	.30	.30
F7	R2	40c brown (1884)	.30	.30
F8	R2	40c brown (1885)	.30	.30
		Nos. F5-F8 (4)	1.25	1.25

Perf. 12
F5a	R2	40c	19.00	
F6a	R2	40c	16.00	
F7a	R2	40c	16.00	
F8a	R2	40c	16.00	
		Nos. F5a-F8a (4)	67.00	

R3

1903   **Laid Paper**   *Imperf.*
F9	R3	20c orange, *rose*	.65	.65
a.		Salmon paper	1.25	1.25
b.		Greenish blue paper	6.50	6.50

Sewing Machine Perf.
F10	R3	20c orange, *rose*	2.75	2.75
a.		Salmon paper	2.75	2.75
b.		Greenish blue paper	6.50	6.50

R4

1904   **Wove Paper**
F11	R4	5c black	3.25	3.25

ACKNOWLEDGMENT OF RECEIPT STAMPS

AR1

1903   **Unwmk.**   **Litho.**   *Imperf.*
Laid Paper
H1	AR1	20c org, *rose*	2.75	2.75
a.		Yellow paper	1.40	1.40
b.		Greenish blue paper	5.50	5.50
H2	AR1	20c dk bl, *yel*	2.25	2.25
a.		Brown paper	3.75	3.75
b.		Rose paper	2.75	2.75
c.		Salmon paper	7.50	7.50
d.		Greenish blue paper	7.50	7.50

Sewing Machine Perf.
H3	AR1	20c org, *grnsh bl*	6.75	6.75
a.		Yellow paper	7.75	7.75
H4	AR1	20c dk bl, *yel*	7.75	7.75
a.		Lilac paper	7.75	7.75
		Nos. H1-H4 (4)	19.50	19.50

AR2

1904   **Wove Paper**
H5	AR2	2c red	1.25	1.25

LATE FEE STAMPS

LF1

1903   **Unwmk.**   **Litho.**   *Imperf.*
Laid Paper
I1	LF1	20c car rose, *bluish*	.65	.65
I2	LF1	20c pur, *bluish*	.65	.65
a.		Rose paper	2.25	2.25
b.		Brown paper	2.25	2.25
c.		Lilac paper	2.25	2.25
d.		Yellow paper	7.00	7.00

Sewing Machine Perf.
I3	LF1	20c car rose, *bluish*	3.75	3.75
I4	LF1	20c pur, *bluish*	3.75	3.75
a.		Rose paper	6.50	6.50
b.		Lilac paper	6.50	6.50
c.		Yellow paper	12.00	12.00
		Nos. I1-I4 (4)	8.80	8.80

BOYACA

bō-yä-cä

Originally a State, now a Department of the Republic of Colombia. (See Antioquia.)

Diego Mendoza
Pérez — A1

1902   **Unwmk.**   **Litho.**   *Perf. 13½*
Wove Paper
1	A1	5c blue green	.80	.80
a.		Bluish paper	95.00	95.00
b.		Imperf., pair	16.00	16.00

Laid Paper
Perf. 12
2	A1	5c green	110.00	110.00

Coat of Arms
A2   A3

Gen. Próspero   A5
Pinzón — A4

Monument of Battle of Boyacá — A6

President José Manuel Marroquin — A7

1903   **Litho.**   *Imperf.*
4	A2	10c dark gray	.30	.30
5	A3	20c red brown	.35	.35
6	A5	1p red	3.25	3.25
a.		1p claret	3.75	3.75
8	A6	5p black, *rose*	1.25	1.25
a.		5p black, *buff*	12.00	12.00
9	A7	10p black, *buff*	1.25	1.25
a.		10p black, *rose*	12.00	12.00
b.		As "a," tête bêche pair	24.00	
		Nos. 4-9 (5)	6.40	6.40

Perf. 12
10	A2	10c dark gray	.35	.35
11	A3	20c red brown	.40	.40
12	A4	50c green	.35	.35
13	A4	50c dull blue	2.50	2.50
14	A5	1p red	.35	.35
a.		1p claret	3.00	3.00
16	A6	5p black, *rose*	11.00	11.00
a.		5p black, *buff*	9.50	9.50
17	A7	10p black, *buff*	1.10	1.10
a.		10p black, *rose*	11.00	11.00
b.		Tête bêche pair	12.00	12.00
		Nos. 10-17 (7)	16.05	16.05

Statue of Bolívar — A8

1904
18	A8	10c orange	.25	.25
a.		Imperf., pair	3.75	3.75

CAUCA

Stamps of these designs were issued by a provincial post between 1879(?) and 1890.

Stamps of this design are believed to be of private origin and without official sanction.

Items inscribed "No hay estampillas" (No stamps available) and others inscribed "Manuel E. Jiménez" are considered by specialists to be receipt labels, not postage stamps.

CUNDINAMARCA

kün-di-nə-'mär-kə

Originally a State, now a Department of the Republic of Colombia. (See Antioquia.)

Coat of Arms
A1   A2

1870   **Unwmk.**   **Litho.**   *Imperf.*
1	A1	5c blue	5.25	5.25
2	A2	10c red	16.00	16.00

The counterfeits, or reprints, show traces of the cuts made to deface the dies.

A3

A4

A5

A6

1877-82

3	A3	10c red ('82)	3.50	3.50
a.		Laid paper ('77)	4.50	4.50
4	A4	20c green ('82)	7.50	7.50
a.		Laid paper ('77)	12.00	12.00
7	A5	50c purple ('82)	8.25	8.25
8	A6	1p brown ('82)	12.00	12.00
		Nos. 3-8 (4)	31.25	31.25

A7

Redrawn

1884

10	A7	5c blue	.80	.80
11	A7	5c blue (redrawn)	.80	.80
a.		Tête bêche pair	80.00	80.00

The redrawn stamp has no period after "COLOMBIA."

A8

A9

A10

A11

1883 **Typeset**

13	A8	10c black, *yellow*	14.00	14.00
14	A9	50c black, *rose*	14.00	14.00
15	A10	1p black, *brown*	37.50	37.50
16	A11	2r black, *green*		2,200.

Typeset varieties exist: 4 of the 10c, 2 each of 50c and 1p.

Some experts doubt that No. 16 was issued. The variety without signature and watermarked "flowers" is believed to be a proof. Forgeries exist.

A12

1886 **Litho.**

17	A12	5c blue	.80	.80
18	A12	10c red	5.00	5.00
19	A12	10c red, *lilac*	2.75	2.75
20	A12	20c green	4.25	4.25
a.		20c yellow green	5.00	5.00
21	A12	50c purple	5.50	5.50
22	A12	1p orange brown	5.75	5.75
		Nos. 17-22 (6)	24.05	24.05

Nos. 17 to 22 have been reprinted. The colors are aniline and differ from those of the original stamps. The impression is coarse and blurred.

A13

A14

A15

A16

A17

A18

A19

A20

A21

1904 **Perf. 10½, 12**

23	A13	1c orange	.25	.25
24	A14	2c gray blue	.25	.25
25	A15	3c rose	.35	.35
26	A15	5c olive grn	.35	.35
27	A16	10c pale brn	.35	.35
28	A17	15c pink	.35	.35
29	A18	20c blue, *grn*	.35	.35
30	A18	20c blue	.60	.60
31	A19	40c blue	.60	.60
32	A19	40c blue, *buff*	21.00	21.00
33	A20	50c red vio	.60	.60
34	A21	1p gray grn	.60	.60
		Nos. 23-34 (12)	25.65	25.65

Imperf

23a	A13	1c orange	.75	.75
24a	A14	2c blue	.75	.75
b.		2c slate	6.50	6.50
25a	A15	3c rose	.90	.90
26a	A15	5c olive green	1.60	1.60
27a	A16	10c pale brown	2.00	2.00
28a	A17	15c pink	.50	.50
29a	A18	20c blue, *green*	2.00	2.00
30a	A18	20c blue	2.00	2.00
31a	A19	40c blue	.70	.70
32a	A19	40c blue, *buff*	21.00	21.00
33a	A20	50c red violet	.70	.70
34a	A21	1p gray green	.70	.70
		Nos. 23a-34a (12)	33.60	33.60

REGISTRATION STAMPS

R1

1883 **Unwmk.** **Imperf.**

F1	R1	black, *orange*	17.00	17.00

R2

1904 **Perf. 12**

F2	R2	10c bister	.85	.85
a.		Imperf.	3.75	3.75

INSURED LETTER STAMP

IL1

1883 **Imperf.**
Thin Paper with Vertical Mesh

G1	IL1	20c blk, *emerald grn*	80.00	120.00

Magdalena

Items inscribed "No hay estampillas" (No stamps available) are considered by specialists to be not postage stamps but receipt labels.

Panama

Issues of Panama as a state and later Department of Colombia are listed with the Republic of Panama issues (Nos. 1-30).

SANTANDER

săn-ˌtän-ˈde̩ə̩r

Originally a State, now a Department of the Republic of Colombia. (See Antioquia.)

Coat of Arms
A1   A2

1884 **Unwmk.** **Litho.** **Imperf.**

1	A1	1c blue	.30	.30
a.		1c gray blue	.50	.50
2	A2	5c red	.50	.50
3	A2	10c bluish purple	1.90	1.90
a.		Tête bêche pair		
		Nos. 1-3 (3)	2.70	2.70

No. 2 exists unofficially perforated 14.

A3

A4

1886 **Imperf.**

4	A3	1c blue	.90	.90
5	A3	5c red	.30	.30
6	A3	10c red violet	.50	.50
a.		10c deep violet	.50	.50
b.		Inscribed "CINCO CENTAVOS"	26.00	26.00
		Nos. 4-6 (3)	1.70	1.70

The numerals in the upper corners are omitted on No. 5, while on No. 6 there are no numerals in the side panels. No. 6 exists unofficially perforated 12.

1887

7	A4	1c blue	.25	.25
a.		1c ultramarine	1.75	1.75
8	A4	5c red	1.75	1.75
9	A4	10c violet	5.50	5.50
		Nos. 7-9 (3)	7.50	7.50

A5

A6

A7

1889 **Perf. 11½ and 13½**

10	A5	1c blue	.35	.35
11	A6	5c red	1.25	1.25
12	A7	10c purple	.45	.45
a.		Imperf., pair	16.00	20.00
		Nos. 10-12 (3)	2.05	2.05

A8

A9

1892 **Perf. 13½**

13	A8	5c red, *rose buff*	1.00	1.00

1895-96

14	A9	5c brown	.70	.70
15	A9	5c yel grn ('96)	.70	.70

A10

A11

A12

1899 **Perf. 10**

16	A10	1c black, *green*	.35	.35
17	A11	5c black, *pink*	.35	.35

Perf. 13½

18	A12	10c blue	.70	.70
a.		Perf. 12	1.00	1.00
		Nos. 16-18 (3)	1.40	1.40

A13

1903   *Imperf.*

19	A13	50c red	.60	.60
a.		50c rose	.60	.60
b.		"SANTENDER"	2.50	2.50
c.		"Corrcos"	2.50	2.50
d.		"Corceos"	2.50	2.50
e.		Tête bêche pair	4.75	4.75
f.		Pair, one without overprint	2.75	2.75

The overprint "Correos de Departamento Bucaramanga" on the 50c red revenue stamp has been proved to be a cancellation.

A14

A15

Arms
A16

Locomotive
A17

A18

A19

A20

1904   *Imperf.*

22	A14	5c dark green	.25	.25
a.		5c yellow green	.40	.40
24	A15	10c rose	.25	.25
25	A16	20c brown violet	.25	.25
26	A17	50c yellow	.25	.25
27	A18	1p black	.25	.25
28	A19	5p dark blue	.35	.35
29	A20	10p carmine	.40	.40
		Nos. 22-29 (7)	2.00	2.00

1905

30	A14	5c pale blue	.45	.45
31	A15	10c red brown	.45	.45
32	A16	20c yellow green	.45	.45
33	A17	50c red violet	.60	.60
34	A18	1p dark blue	.60	.60
35	A19	5p pink	.60	.60
36	A20	10p red	1.60	1.60
		Nos. 30-36 (7)	4.75	4.75

A21

1907   *Imperf.*

37	A21	½c on 50c rose	.80	*1.60*

City of Cucuta

Stamps of these and similar designs on white and yellow paper, with and without surcharges of ½c, 1c or 2c, are believed to have been produced without government authorization.

TOLIMA

tə-lē-mə

Originally a State, now a Department of the Republic of Colombia.
(See Antioquia.)

A1

1870   Unwmk.   Typeset   *Imperf.*
White Wove Paper

1	A1	5c black	62.50	62.50
2	A1	10c black	75.00	75.00
a.		Vert. se-tenant pair	1,500.	1,500.

Printed from two settings. Setting I, ten types of 5c. Setting II, six types of 5c and four types of 10c.

Blue Laid Batonné Paper

3	A1	5c black	*950.00*

Buff Laid Batonné Paper

4	A1	5c black	150.00	100.00

Blue Wove Paper

5	A1	5c black	70.00	45.00

Blue Vertically Laid Paper

6	A1	5c black	110.00	70.00
a.		Paper with ruled blue vertical lines		

Blue Horizontally Laid Paper

7	A1	5c black	100.00	75.00

Blue Quadrille Paper

8	A1	5c black	150.00	80.00

Ten varieties each of Nos. 3-5 and 7; 20 varieties each of Nos. 6 and 8.
Official imitations were made in 1886 from new settings of the type. There are only 2 varieties of each value. They are printed on blue and white paper, wove, batonné, laid, etc.

A2

A3

A4

A5

Yellowish White Wove Paper

1871   Litho.   *Imperf.*

9	A2	5c deep brown	2.25	2.25
a.		5c red brown	2.25	2.25
b.		Value reads "CINGO"	40.00	40.00
10	A3	10c blue	6.25	6.25
11	A4	50c green	8.00	8.00
12	A5	1p carmine	13.00	13.00
		Nos. 9-12 (4)	29.50	29.50

The 5p stamps, type A2, are bogus varieties made from an altered die of the 5c.
The 10c, 50c and 1 peso stamps have been reprinted on bluish white wove paper. They are from new plates and most copies show traces of fine lines with which the dies had been defaced. Reprints of the 5c have a large cross at the top. The 10c on laid batonné paper is known only as a reprint.

A6

A7

A8

A9

1879
Grayish or White Wove Paper

14	A6	5c yellow brown	.45	.45
a.		5c purple brown	.45	.45
15	A7	10c blue	.50	.50
16	A8	50c green, *bluish*	.50	.50
a.		White paper	1.60	1.60
17	A9	1p vermilion	2.25	2.25
a.		1p carmine rose	9.00	9.00
		Nos. 14-17 (4)	3.70	3.70

A10

Coat of Arms — A12

1883   *Imperf.*

18	A6	5c orange	.45	.45
19	A7	10c vermilion	.95	.95
20	A10	20c violet	1.50	1.50
		Nos. 18-20 (3)	2.90	2.90

1884   *Imperf.*

23	A12	1c gray	.25	.25
24	A12	2c rose lilac	.25	.25
a.		2c slate	.25	.25
25	A12	2½c dull orange	.25	.25
26	A12	5c brown	.25	.25
27	A12	10c blue	.35	.35
a.		10c slate	.25	.25
28	A12	20c lemon	.35	.35
a.		Laid paper	5.00	5.00
29	A12	25c black	.30	.30
30	A12	50c green	.30	.30
31	A12	1p vermilion	.40	.40
32	A12	2p violet	.60	.60
a.		Value omitted	30.00	30.00
33	A12	5p yellow	.40	.40
34	A12	10p lilac rose	1.10	1.10
a.		Laid paper	30.00	30.00
b.		10p gray	*175.00*	
		Nos. 23-34 (12)	4.80	4.80

A13

A14

A15

A16

Condor with Long Wings Touching Flagstaffs

1886   Litho.   *Perf. 10½, 11*
White Paper

36	A13	5c brown	1.40	1.40
a.		5c yellow brown	1.40	1.40
b.		Imperf., pair	17.50	
37	A14	10c blue	3.75	3.75
a.		Imperf., pair	17.50	
38	A15	50c green	3.25	3.25
a.		Imperf., pair	17.50	
39	A16	1p vermilion	2.75	2.75
a.		Imperf., pair	26.00	
		Nos. 36-39 (4)	11.15	11.15

No. 38 has been reprinted in pale gray green, perforated 10½, and No. 39 in bright vermilion, perforated 11½. The impressions show many signs of wear.

Lilac Tinted Paper

36c	A13	5c orange brown	12.50	12.50
37b	A14	10c blue	12.50	12.50
38b	A15	50c green	9.25	9.25
39b	A16	1p vermilion	8.25	8.25
		Nos. 36c-39b (4)	42.50	42.50

Items similar to A15 and A16 but with condor with long wings and upper flag-staffs omitted are forgeries.

A17

A18

Condor with Short Wings
A19   A20

1886   White Paper   *Perf. 12*

44	A19	1c gray	6.25	6.25
45	A17	2c rose lilac	6.50	6.50
46	A18	2½c dull org	19.00	19.00
47	A19	5c brown	8.50	8.00
48	A20	10c blue	8.00	8.00
49	A20	20c lemon	6.50	6.50
a.		Tête bêche pair	275.00	275.00
50	A20	25c black	6.25	6.25
51	A20	50c green	3.75	3.75
52	A20	1p vermilion	5.00	4.25
53	A20	2p violet	7.25	7.25
b.		Tête bêche pair	190.00	190.00
54	A20	5p orange	13.00	13.00
55	A20	10p lilac rose	7.50	7.50
		Nos. 44-55 (12)	97.50	96.25

Imperf., Pairs

44a	A19	1c		17.00
47a	A19	5c		29.00
48a	A20	10c		29.00
52a	A20	1p		21.00
53a	A20	2p		26.00
54a	A20	5p		40.00
55a	A20	10p		17.00

A23

1888   *Perf. 10½*

62	A23	5c red	.25	.25
63	A23	10c green	.30	.30
64	A23	50c blue	.75	.75
65	A23	1p red brown	1.90	1.90
		Nos. 62-65 (4)	3.20	3.20

For overprint see Colombia No. L14.

1895   *Perf. 12, 13½*

66	A23	1c blue, *rose*	.25	.25
67	A23	2c grn, *lt grn*	.25	.25
68	A23	5c red	.25	.25
69	A23	10c green	.50	.50
70	A23	20c blue, *yellow*	.30	.30
71	A23	1p brown	2.10	2.10
		Nos. 66-71 (6)	3.65	3.65

Imperf., Pairs

62a	A23	5c		8.75
63a	A23	10c		12.00
64a	A23	50c		14.50	14.50
65a	A23	1p		21.00
66a	A23	1c		21.00
67a	A23	2c		21.00
70a	A23	20c		24.00

"No Hay Estampillas"
Items inscribed "No hay estampillas" (No stamps available) are considered by specialists to be not postage stamps but receipt labels.

"Honda Issue"
This item seems to be of private origin.

A24

A25

A26

A27

A28

A29

A30

A31

Sewing Machine or Regular Perf. 12

1903-04 **Litho.**

79	A24	4c black, *green*	.25	.25
80	A25	10c dull blue	.25	.25
81	A26	20c orange	.50	.50
82	A27	50c black, *rose*	.25	.25
a.		50c black, *buff*	.25	.25
84	A28	1p brown	.25	.25
85	A29	2p gray	.25	.25
86	A30	5p red	.25	.25
a.		Tête bêche pair	8.00	12.00
87	A31	10p black, *blue*	.25	.25
a.		10p black, *light green*	.25	.25
b.		10p black, *grn, glazed*	3.75	3.75
		Nos. 79-87 (8)	2.25	2.25

Imperf

79a	A24	4c black, *green*	.25	.25
80a	A25	10c dull blue	.25	.25
81a	A26	20c orange	1.25	1.25
82b	A27	50c black, *rose*	1.75	1.75
c.		50c black, *buff*	1.75	1.75
84a	A28	1p brown	.25	.25
85a	A29	2p gray	.25	.25
86b	A30	5p red	.25	.25
c.		Tête bêche pair	12.00	16.00
87c	A31	10p black, *blue*	2.50	2.50
d.		Tête bêche pair		
e.		10p black, *light green*	3.75	3.75
f.		10p black, *green*, glazed	19.00	19.00
		Nos. 79a-87c (8)	6.75	6.75

INSURED LETTER STAMPS

IL1

IL2

Dateline ends with "de...187...".

1879 **Imperf.**

G1	IL1	5c yellow ochre	40.00	40.00
G2	IL2	10c blk, *yel, bl & red*	75.00	75.00
G3	IL2	50c blk, *yel, bl & red*	75.00	100.00

Types of 1879 Redrawn

Dateline ends with "de...18...".

1879, Dec. **Imperf.**

G4	IL1	5c red brown	40.00	40.00
G5	IL2	10c blk, *yel, bl & red*	60.00	60.00
G6	IL2	50c blk, *yel, bl & red*	60.00	90.00

IL3

Dateline ends with "de...188...".

Wmk. With or Without Sheet Watermark "188"

1886 **Imperf.**

G7	IL3	5c blk, *yel, bl & red*	75.00	80.00
G8	IL3	10c blk, *yel, bl & red*	75.00	80.00
G9	IL3	50c blk, *yel, bl & red*	150.00	120.00

1886

White Wove Paper

G10	IL3	5c yellow	20.00	40.00
a.		5c Orange	12.00	25.00
b.		5c Light brown	12.00	25.00
G11	IL3	10c light blue	12.00	25.00
a.		10c Blue	12.00	25.00
b.		10c Ultramarine	12.00	25.00
G12	IL3	50c red	20.00	40.00
a.		50c Brick red	25.00	55.00

IL4

Dateline ends with "de...188...".

1888 **Imperf.**

G13	IL4	5c brown	25.00	40.00
G14	IL4	10c red	25.00	40.00
G15	IL4	50c blue	37.50	60.00

Type of 1888 Redrawn

Dateline ends with "de...18...".

1890 **Imperf.**

G16	IL4	5c brown	35.00	52.50
G17	IL4	10c red	40.00	200.00
G18	IL4	50c blue	100.00	250.00

IL5

Dateline ends with "de...189...".

1896 **Imperf.**

G19	IL5	20c brown	25.00	50.00
G20	IL5	30c blue green	25.00	50.00
a.		30c Olive green	25.00	50.00
G21	IL5	40c brown orange	25.00	50.00
G22	IL5	50c blue	25.00	50.00
G23	IL5	60c black, *yellow*	25.00	50.00
G24	IL5	70c blk, *pale brn*	25.00	55.00
G25	IL5	80c black, *green*	25.00	55.00
G26	IL5	90c black, *pale blue*	25.00	55.00
G27	IL5	1p black, *rose pink*	35.00	55.00

COOK ISLANDS

'kuk 'i-lənds

(Rarotonga)

LOCATION — South Pacific Ocean, northeast of New Zealand
GOVT. — Dependency of New Zealand
AREA — 117 sq. mi.
POP. — 17,754 (1981)
CAPITAL — Rarotonga

Fifteen islands in Northern and Southern groups extend over 850,000 square miles of ocean.

Separate stamp issues used by Aitutaki (1903-32) and Penrhyn Islands (1902-32). Niue is included geographically, but administered separately. It issues separate stamps.

12 Pence = 1 Shilling
20 Shillings = 1 Pound

> **Catalogue values for unused stamps in this country are for Never Hinged items, beginning with Scott 127 in the regular postage section.**

Watermarks

Wmk. 61 —
Single-lined N Z and Star Close Together

Wmk. 62 —
Single-lined N Z and Star Wide Apart

Wmk. 253 —
Multiple N Z and Star

A1

1892 **Unwmk.** **Typo.** **Perf. 12½**
Toned Paper

1	A1	1p black	32.50	30.00
2	A1	1½p violet	47.50	45.00
a.		Imperf, pair	19,000.	
3	A1	2½p blue	47.50	45.00
4	A1	10p carmine	160.00	150.00
		Nos. 1-4 (4)	287.50	270.00

White Paper

5	A1	1p black	32.50	30.00
a.		Vert. pair, imperf. between	11,000.	
6	A1	1½p violet	47.50	45.00
7	A1	2½p blue	47.50	45.00
8	A1	10p carmine	160.00	150.00
		Nos. 5-8 (4)	287.50	270.00

Nos. 1-8 were printed in sheets of 60 (6x10), from a setting of six slightly different cliches.

Queen
Makea
Takau — A2

Wrybill
(Torea) — A3

1893-94 **Wmk. 62** **Perf. 12x11½**

9	A2	1p brown	47.50	52.50
10	A2	1p violet ('94)	13.00	2.50
a.		Perf. 12½ with 12x11½	—	1,900.
11	A2	1½p brt violet	12.00	8.50
12	A2	2½p rose	55.00	27.50
a.		Perf. 12½ with 12x11½	2,750.	—
b.		2½p rose carmine	70.00	55.00
13	A2	5p olive gray	22.50	16.00
14	A2	10p green	85.00	57.50
		Nos. 9-14 (6)	235.00	164.50

Perf. 12½ examples of Nos. 10, 12 are from a part of the normal perf. 12x11½ sheets. They were caused by a partial deviation of the original perforating.

1898-1900 **Perf. 11**

15	A3	½p blue ('00)	6.50	10.00
a.		"d" omitted at upper right	1,750.	
b.		½p steel blue (1st setting)	37.50	52.50
c.		½p steel blue (2nd setting)	23.00	25.00
16	A2	1p brown	22.50	21.00
a.		1p bistre brown ('00)	25.00	25.00
17	A2	1p blue	6.00	5.50
18	A2	1½p violet	13.00	7.50
a.		1½p deep mauve ('00)	11.00	7.50
19	A3	2p chocolate	11.00	8.50
a.		2p brown, thin toned paper	14.00	7.50
20	A2	2½p car rose	24.00	11.00
a.		2½p pale rose	55.00	45.00
21	A2	5p olive gray	27.50	21.00
22	A3	6p red violet	22.50	27.50
a.		6p purple, thin toned paper	29.00	32.50
23	A2	10p green	26.00	57.50
24	A3	1sh car rose	57.50	57.50
a.		1sh red, thin toned paper	70.00	80.00
		Nos. 15-24 (7)	216.50	228.50

The first setting of No. 15 is distinguished by the misplacement of the "½d" in each corner. In the second setting, these values are correctly positioned.

No. 17 Surcharged in Black

1899

25	A2	½p on 1p blue	40.00	50.00
a.		Double surcharge	1,000.	1,200.
b.		Inverted surcharge	1,200.	1,100.

No. 16 Overprinted in Black

1901

26	A2	1p brown	210.00	160.00
a.		Inverted overprint	2,400.	1,900.
c.		Double overprint	1,900.	1,900.

Some single stamps were overprinted by favor. Other varieties could exist.
Forgeries exist.

Types of 1893-98

1902 **Unwmk.**

27	A3	½p green	7.00	7.00
a.		Vert. pair, imperf. horiz.	1,400.	
b.		½p blue green	7.50	8.25
28	A2	1p rose	14.00	17.00
a.		1p rose lake	12.50	7.50
29	A2	2½p dull blue	15.00	25.00
		Nos. 27-29 (3)	36.00	49.00

1902 **Wmk. 61** **Perf. 11**

30	A3	½p green	3.25	3.75
a.		½p gray green	25.00	55.00
31	A2	1p rose	4.75	3.50
32	A2	1½p brt violet	4.75	10.00
33	A3	2p chocolate	6.50	12.00
a.		Figures of value omitted	2,750.	3,600.
b.		Perf. 11x14	2,250.	
34	A2	2½p dull blue	4.50	8.25
35	A2	5p olive gray	42.50	57.50
36	A3	6p purple	37.50	32.50
37	A2	10p blue green	55.00	120.00
38	A3	1sh car rose	55.00	82.50
a.		Perf. 11x14	2,750.	
		Nos. 30-38 (9)	213.75	330.00

1909-19　Perf. 14, 14x14½, 14½x14

39	A3	½p green, perf 14½x14 ('11)	8.00	9.50
a.		½p dp grn, perf 14 ('15)	8.00	17.50
b.		As "a", wmk upright	9.50	18.00
40	A2	1p red, wmk. sideways ('09)	15.00	5.00
a.		1p red, wmk. upright, perf 14	40.00	25.00
b.		1p red, chalky paper, perf 14x14½	6.50	7.00
41	A2	1½p purple, perf 14x15 ('16)	15.00	4.75
a.		1½p purple, perf 14 ('15)	87.50	47.50
42	A3	2p dp brown ('19)	6.00	57.50
43	A2	10p dp green ('18)	27.00	110.00
44	A3	1sh car rose ('19)	32.50	110.00
		Nos. 39-44 (6)	96.00	296.75

Nos. 39-40 are on both ordinary and chalky paper; Nos. 41-44 on chalky paper.

New Zealand Stamps of 1909-19 Surcharged in Dark Blue or Red

1919　Typo.　Perf. 14x15

48	A43	½p yel green (R)	.45	1.25
a.		Pair, one without surcharge		
49	A42	1p carmine	1.25	3.50
50	A47	1½p brown org (R)	.60	.90
51	A43	2p yellow (R)	1.75	2.00
52	A43	3p chocolate	3.25	15.00

Engr.　Perf. 14x14½

53	A44	2½p dull blue (R)	2.75	2.50
a.		Perf 14x13½	2.75	7.50
54	A45	3p violet brown	2.75	2.00
a.		Perf 14x13½	2.25	9.50
55	A45	4p purple	2.25	4.25
a.		Perf 14x13½	2.25	6.50
56	A44	4½p dark green	2.25	9.50
a.		Perf 14x13½	2.25	8.00
57	A45	6p car rose	2.00	5.50
a.		Perf 14x13½	3.50	10.00
58	A44	7½p red brown, perf 14x13½	2.10	6.50
59	A45	9p ol green (R)	3.75	17.50
a.		Perf 14x13½	3.75	17.50
60	A45	1sh vermilion	2.75	22.00
a.		Perf 14x13½	13.00	35.00
		Nos. 48-60 (13)	27.90	92.40

The Polynesian surcharge restates the denomination of the basic stamp.

Vertical Pairs, Perf 14x14½ and 14x13½

53b	#53 + #53a	23.00	52.50
	Block of four, never hinged	65.00	
54b	#54 + #54a	25.00	57.50
	Block of four, never hinged	77.50	
55b	#55 + #55a	23.00	65.00
	Block of four, never hinged	67.50	
56b	#56 + #56a	23.00	75.00
	Block of four, never hinged	67.50	
57b	#57 + #57a	45.00	100.00
	Block of four, never hinged	140.00	
59b	#59 + #59a	45.00	125.00
	Block of four, never hinged	140.00	
60b	#60 + #60a	55.00	140.00
	Block of four, never hinged	175.00	

The Polynesian surcharge restates the denomination of the basic stamp.

Landing of Capt. Cook A4　　Avarua Waterfront A5

Capt. James Cook — A6　　Palm — A7

Houses at Arorangi — A8

Avarua Harbor — A9

1920　Unwmk.　Engr.　Perf. 14

61	A4	½p green & black	4.75	25.00
62	A5	1p car & black	5.50	25.00
a.		Center inverted	700.00	
63	A6	1½p blue & black	10.00	10.00
64	A7	3p red brn & blk	2.50	6.50
65	A8	6p org & red brn	3.75	10.00
66	A9	1sh vio & black	6.50	20.00
		Nos. 61-66 (6)	33.00	96.50

The stamps overprinted or inscribed "Rarotonga" were used throughout the Cook Islands.

For surcharges see Nos. 78, 79.

New Zealand Postal-Fiscal Stamps of 1906-13 Overprinted in Red or Dark Blue — a

Perf. 14, 14½, 14x14½

1921　Typo.　Wmk. 61

67	PF1	2sh blue (R)	32.50	65.00
68	PF1	2sh6p brown	22.50	60.00
69	PF1	5sh green (R)	32.50	77.50
70	PF1	10sh claret	90.00	140.00
71	PF2	£1 rose	140.00	250.00
		Nos. 67-71 (5)	317.50	592.50

Types of 1920 Issue

1924-26　Engr.　Perf. 14

72	A4	½p yel grn & black	5.25	10.00
73	A5	1p carmine & black	7.00	2.50

Issued: ½p, May 13, 1926; 1p, Nov. 10, 1924.

New Zealand Stamps of 1926 Overprinted Type "a" in Red

1926-28　Typo.　Perf. 14, 14½x14

74	A56	2sh blue ('27)	17.50	47.50
a.		2sh dark blue	12.00	47.50
75	A56	3sh violet ('28)	19.00	50.00

Rarotongan Chief (Te Po) — A10

Avarua Harbor — A11

1927, Oct. 15　Engr.　Perf. 14

76	A10	2½p dk bl & red brn	8.00	29.00
77	A11	4p dull vio & bl grn	13.00	20.00

No. 63 Surcharged in Red

1931　Unwmk.

78	A6	2p on 1½p blue & blk	11.00	3.25

Same Surcharge on Type of 1920 Wmk. 61

79	A6	2p on 1½p blue & blk	5.50	13.00

No. 79 was not issued without surcharge.

New Zealand Postal-Fiscal Stamps of 1931-32 Overprinted Type "a" in Blue or Red

1931, Nov. 12　Typo.

80	PF5	2sh6p dp brown (Bl)	12.00	26.00
81	PF5	5sh green (R)	21.00	65.00
82	PF5	10sh dk car (Bl)	45.00	110.00
83	PF5	£1 pink (Bl) ('32)	105.00	190.00
		Nos. 80-83 (4)	183.00	391.00

See Nos. 103-108, 124A-126C.

Landing of Capt. Cook — A12　　Capt. James Cook — A13

Double Canoe — A14　　Islanders Unloading Ship — A15

View of Avarua Harbor — A16　　R.M.S. Monowai — A17

King George V — A18

Unwmk.

1932, Mar. 16　Engr.　Perf. 13

Center in Black

84	A12	½p deep green	4.00	19.00
a.		Perf. 14	32.50	105.00
85	A13	1p brown lake	7.75	5.25
a.		Center inverted	9,500.	9,500.
b.		Perf. 14	17.50	28.00
86	A14	2p brown	3.50	6.50
b.		Perf. 14	10.00	24.00
87	A15	2½p dark ultra	18.00	65.00
b.		Perf. 14	18.00	65.00

Perf. 14

88	A16	4p ultra	12.00	65.00
a.		Perf. 13	25.00	75.00
b.		Perf. 14x13	35.00	130.00
89	A17	6p orange	5.00	17.50
a.		Perf. 13	30.00	57.50
90	A18	1sh deep violet	13.00	26.00
		Nos. 84-90 (7)	63.25	204.25

Nos. 84 to 90 were available for postage in Aitutaki, Penrhyn and Rarotonga and replaced the special issues for those islands.

Inverted centers of the 1p and 2p are from printers waste.

1933-36　Wmk. 61　Perf. 14

91	A12	½p dp green & blk	1.20	5.25
92	A13	1p dk car & black ('35)	1.50	2.40
93	A14	2p brn & blk ('36)	1.75	.60
94	A15	2½p dk ultra & blk	1.75	2.50
95	A16	4p blue & black	1.75	.60
96	A17	6p org & blk ('36)	2.00	2.50
97	A18	1sh dp vio & black ('36)	27.50	42.50
		Nos. 91-97 (7)	37.45	56.35

See Nos. 116-121.

Silver Jubilee Issue

Types of 1932 Overprinted in Black or Red

1935, May 7

98	A13	1p dk car & brn red	.65	2.00
99	A15	2½p dk ultra & bl (R)	1.10	3.50
100	A17	6p dull org & green	5.00	8.50
		Nos. 98-100 (3)	6.75	14.00
		Set, never hinged	19.00	

The vertical spacing of the overprint is wider on No. 100.

New Zealand Stamps of 1935 Overprinted in Black — b

1936, July 15　Typo.　Perf. 14

101	A56	2sh blue	15.00	50.00
102	A56	3sh violet	15.00	80.00

New Zealand Postal-Fiscal Stamps of 1931-35 Overprinted Type "b" in Black or Red

1932-36

103	PF5	2sh6p brown ('36)	35.00	95.00
104	PF5	5sh grn (R) ('36)	40.00	130.00
105	PF5	10sh dk car ('36)	85.00	250.00
106	PF5	£1 pink ('36)	110.00	275.00
107	PF5	£3 lt grn (R)	400.00	650.00
108	PF5	£5 dk blue (R)	225.00	375.00
		Nos. 103-108 (6)	895.00	1,775.

Issue dates: Mar. 1932, July 15, 1936.

New Zealand Stamps of 1937 Overprinted in Black

1937, June 1　Engr.　Perf. 14x13½　Wmk. 253

109	A78	1p rose carmine	.25	.25
110	A78	2½p dark blue	.25	.25
111	A78	6p vermilion	.35	.30
		Nos. 109-111 (3)	.85	.80
		Set, never hinged	2.50	

King George VI A19　　Village and Palms A20

Coastal Scene with Canoe — A21

1938, May 2　Wmk. 61　Perf. 14

112	A19	1sh dp violet & blk	7.00	15.00
113	A20	2sh dk red brn & blk	14.00	19.00
114	A21	3sh yel green & blue	35.00	42.50
		Nos. 112-114 (3)	56.00	76.50
		Set, never hinged	100.00	

See Nos. 122-124.

Mt. Ikurangi behind Avarua — A22

1940, Sept. 2　Engr.　Perf. 13½x14　Wmk. 253

115	A22	3p on 1½p violet & blk	.80	.80

Issued only with surcharge. Stamps without surcharge are from the printer's archives.

Types of 1932-38

1944-46　Engr.　Perf. 14

116	A12	½p dk ol grn & blk ('45)	1.00	4.50
117	A13	1p dk car & blk ('45)	1.50	1.25
118	A14	2p brn & blk ('46)	.90	7.00
119	A15	2½p dk bl & blk ('45)	.60	2.00
120	A16	4p blue & black	2.50	15.00
121	A17	6p org & black	1.00	2.50
122	A19	1sh dp vio & blk	1.00	3.50
123	A20	2sh dk red brn & blk	27.50	50.00
124	A21	3sh yel green & blue ('45)	25.00	40.00
		Nos. 116-124 (9)	61.00	125.75
		Set, never hinged	100.00	

New Zealand Nos. AR76, AR78, AR85 and Type of 1931 Postal-Fiscal Stamps Overprinted Type "b" in Black or Red

1943-50		**Wmk. 253**	**Typo.**	**Perf. 14**
124A	PF5	2sh6p brn ('46)	11.50	22.50
125	PF5	5sh green (R)	7.75	22.50
126	PF5	10sh dp pink ('48)	35.00	90.00
126A	PF5	£1 pink ('47)	40.00	97.50
126B	PF5	£3 lt grn (R) ('46)	47.50	190.00
126C	PF5	£5 dk bl (R) ('50)	175.00	425.00
		Nos. 124A-126C (6)	316.75	847.50
		Set, never hinged	550.00	

For surcharges see Nos. 192-194 in Scott Standard catalogue, Vol. 2.

> **Catalogue values for unused stamps in this section, from this point to the end of the section, are for Never Hinged items.**

Peace Issue
New Zealand Nos. 248, 250, 254 and 255 Overprinted in Black or Blue

c   d

Perf. 13x13½, 13½x13

			Engr.	
1946, June 1				
127	A94 (c)	1p emerald	.40	.25
128	A96 (d)	2p rose vio (Bl)	.40	.40
129	A100(c)	6p org red & red brn	.75	.70
130	A101(c)	8p brn lake & blk (Bl)	.65	.65
		Nos. 127-130 (4)	2.20	2.00

Ngatangiia Channel, Rarotonga A23

Capt. James Cook Statue and Map of Cook Islands — A24

Designs: 1p, Cook and map of Hervey Isls. 2p, Rev. John Williams, his ship Messenger of Peace, and map of Rarotonga. 3p, Aitutaki map and palms. 5p, Mail plane landing at Rarotonga airport. 6p, Tongareva (Penrhyn) scene. 8p, Islander's house, Rarotonga. 2sh, Thatched house, mat weaver. 3sh, Steamer Matua offshore.

Perf. 13½x13, 13x13½

			Engr.	Wmk. 253
1949, Aug.1				
131	A23	½p brown & violet	.25	1.25
132	A23	1p green & orange	4.00	2.50
133	A23	2p carmine & brn	2.50	2.50
134	A23	3p ultra & green	2.25	2.50
135	A23	5p purple & grn	7.00	2.00
136	A23	6p car rose & blk	7.00	3.25
137	A23	8p orange & olive	.75	4.75
138	A24	1sh chocolate & bl	6.50	4.75
139	A24	2sh rose car & brn	4.75	16.00
140	A24	3sh bl grn & lt ultra	12.50	29.00
		Nos. 131-140 (10)	47.50	68.50

For surcharge see No. 147 in Scott Standard catalogue, Vol 2.

CORFU

kor-'fü

LOCATION — An island in the Ionian Sea opposite the Greek-Albanian border
GOVT. — A department of Greece

AREA — 245 sq. mi.
POP. — 114,620 (1938)
CAPITAL — Corfu

In 1923 Italy occupied Corfu (Kerkyra) during a controversy with Greece over the assassination of an Italian official in Epirus.

100 Centesimi = 1 Lira
100 Lepta = 1 Drachma

Watermark

Wmk. 140 — Crown

ISSUED UNDER ITALIAN OCCUPATION

Italian Stamps of 1901-23 Overprinted

1923, Sept. 20		**Wmk. 140**		**Perf. 14**
N1	A48	5c green	9.50	13.00
		Never hinged	24.00	
		On cover		80.00
N2	A48	10c claret	9.50	13.00
		Never hinged	24.00	
		On cover		80.00
N3	A48	15c slate	9.50	13.00
		Never hinged	24.00	
		On cover		90.00
N4	A50	20c brown orange	9.50	13.00
		Never hinged	24.00	
		On cover		90.00
N5	A49	30c orange brown	9.50	13.00
		Never hinged	24.00	
		On cover		125.00
N6	A49	50c violet	9.50	13.00
		Never hinged	24.00	
		On cover		80.00
N7	A49	60c blue	9.50	13.00
		Never hinged	24.00	
		On cover		100.00
a.		Vert. pair, one without overprint	1,600.	
N8	A46	1 l brown & green	9.50	13.00
		Never hinged	24.00	
		On cover		175.00
		Nos. N1-N8 (8)	76.00	104.00
		Set, never hinged	190.00	

Italian Stamps of 1901-23 Surcharged

1923, Sept. 24				
N9	A48	25 l on 10c claret	80.00	45.00
		Never hinged	190.00	
		On cover		140.00
N10	A49	60 l on 25c blue	11.00	
		Never hinged	27.50	
N11	A49	70 l on 30c org brn	11.00	
		Never hinged	27.50	
N12	A49	1.20d on 50c violet	35.00	45.00
		Never hinged	85.00	
		On cover		140.00
N13	A46	2.40d on 1 l brn & grn	35.00	45.00
		Never hinged	85.00	
		On cover		175.00
N14	A46	4.75d on 2 l grn & org	19.00	
		Never hinged	45.00	
		Nos. N9-N14 (6)	191.00	
		Set, never hinged	460.00	
		#N9, N12-N13 on overfranked philatelic cover		600.00

Nos. N10, N11, N14 were not placed in use.

COSTA RICA

ˌkōs-tə-'rē-kə

LOCATION — Central America between Nicaragua and Panama
GOVT. — Republic
AREA — 19,344 sq. mi.
POP. — 2,450,226 (1984)
CAPITAL — San Jose

8 Reales = 100 Centavos = 1 Peso
100 Centimos = 1 Colon (1900)

Watermarks

Wmk. 215 — Small Star in Shield, Multiple

Wmk. 229 — Wavy Lines

Values for unused stamps are for examples with original gum as defined in the catalogue introduction. Very fine examples of Nos. 1-22 will have perforations just clear of the design on one or more sides due to the placement of the stamps on the plates and to imperfect perforating methods.

Coat of Arms — A1

1863		**Unwmk.**	**Engr.**	**Perf. 12**
1	A1	½r blue	.40	1.10
a.		½r light blue	.40	1.10
b.		Pair, imperf. horiz.	6,000.	
2	A1	2r scarlet	1.75	2.25
3	A1	4r green	16.00	16.00
4	A1	1p orange	42.50	42.50
		Nos. 1-4 (4)	60.65	61.85

The ½r was printed from two plates. The second is in light blue with little or no sky over the mountains.
Imperforate stamps of Nos. 1-2 are corner stamps from poorly perforated sheets.

Nos. 1-3 Surcharged in Red or Black

a

b

c   d

e

1881-82		**Red or Black Surcharge**		
7	A1(a)	1c on ½r ('82)	3.00	6.00
a.		On No. 1a	15.00	
8	A1(b)	1c on ½r ('82)	18.00	30.00
9	A1(c)	2c on ½r, #1a	3.00	2.75
a.		On No. 1	8.00	
12	A1(c)	5c on ½r	15.00	
13	A1(d)	5c on ½r ('82)	65.00	
14	A1(d)	10c on 2r (Bk) ('82)	72.50	—
15	A1(e)	20c on 4r ('82)	300.00	—

Overprints with different fonts and "OFICIAL" were never placed in use, and are said to have been surcharged to a dealer's order. The ½r surcharged "DOS CTS" is not a postage stamp. It probably is an essay.
Postally used examples of Nos. 7-15 are rare. Nos. 13-15 exist with a favor cancel having a hyphen between "San" and "Jose." Values same as unused. Fake cancellations exist.
Counterfeits exist of surcharges on Nos. 7-15.

Gen. Prospero Fernández A6   President Bernardo Soto Alfaro A7

1883, Jan. 1				
16	A6	1c green	3.00	1.50
17	A6	2c carmine	3.25	1.50
18	A6	5c blue violet	32.50	2.00
19	A6	10c orange	150.00	12.00
20	A6	40c orange	3.00	3.00
		Nos. 16-20 (5)	191.75	20.00

Unused examples of 40c usually lack gum.
For overprints see Nos. O1-O20, O24, Guanacaste 1-38, 44.

1887				
21	A7	5c blue violet	7.00	.50
22	A7	10c orange	4.00	3.00

Unused examples of 5c usually lack gum.
For overprints see Nos. O22-O23, Guanacaste 42-43, 45.

A8   A9

1889		**Black Overprint**		
23	A8	1c rose	5.00	3.00
24	A9	5c brown	7.00	3.00

Vertical and inverted overprints are fakes.
For overprints see Guanacaste Nos. 47-54.

President Soto Alfaro A10   A11

A12   A13

A14   A15

A16

A17

A18

A19

1889　　　Perf. 14-16 & Compound

25	A10	1c brown		.35	.45
a.		Horiz. pair, imperf. vert	150.00		
b.		Imperf. pair	100.00		
c.		Horiz. or vert. pair, imperf. btwn.	150.00		
26	A11	2c dark green		.35	.45
a.		Imperf., pair	50.00		
b.		Vert. pair, imperf. horiz.	125.00		
c.		Horiz. pair, imperf. btwn.	125.00		
27	A12	5c orange		.45	.35
a.		Imperf., pair	150.00		250.00
b.		Horiz. pair, imperf. btwn.	150.00		
28	A13	10c red brown		.40	.35
a.		Vert. or horiz. pair, imperf. btwn.	150.00		
29	A14	20c yellow green		.30	.35
a.		Vert. pair, imperf. horiz.	200.00		
b.		Horizontal pair, imperf. btwn.	150.00		
30	A15	50c rose red		1.00	
		Telegram cancel			.75
31	A16	1p blue		1.25	
		Telegram cancel			.75
32	A17	2p dull violet		6.00	
a.		2p slate		6.00	
		Telegram cancel			4.00
33	A18	5p olive green		25.00	
		Telegram cancel			10.00
34	A19	10p black		100.00	
		Telegram cancel			45.00
		Nos. 25-34 (10)		135.10	1.95

Nos. 30-34 normally were used on telegrams and most examples were removed from the forms and sold by the government.

Most unused examples of No. 34 have no gum or only part gum. These sell for somewhat less.

For overprints see Nos. O25-O30, Guanacaste 55-67.

Arms of Costa Rica
A20　　　A21

A22　　　A23

A24　　　A25

A26　　　A27

A28

A29

1892　　　Perf. 12-15 & Compound

35	A20	1c grnsh blue	.30	.40
36	A21	2c yellow	.30	.40
37	A22	5c red lilac	.30	.25
a.		5c violet	60.00	.30
38	A23	10c lt green	.80	.35
a.		Horiz. pair, imperf. btwn.		100.00
39	A24	20c scarlet	12.00	.25
a.		Horiz. pair, imperf. btwn.		100.00
40	A25	50c gray blue	4.00	4.25
41	A26	1p green, yel	1.25	1.00
42	A27	2p brown red, lilac	3.00	1.00
a.		2p rose red, pale lil	12.00	1.00
43	A28	5p dk blue, blue	2.00	1.00
44	A29	10p brown, pale buff	35.00	5.00
a.		10p brown, yellow	8.00	
		Nos. 35-44 (10)	58.95	13.90

Imperfs. of Nos. 35-44 are proofs.

Nos. 42-43 unused are normally without gum and are valued thus.

For overprints see Nos. O31-O36.

Statue of Juan Santamaría
A30

Juan Mora Fernández
A31

View of Port Limón — A32

Braulio Carrillo ("Branlio" on stamp) — A33

National Theater — A34

José M. Castro — A35

Birris Bridge — A36

Juan Rafael Mora — A37

Jesús Jiménez — A38

Coat of Arms — A39

1901, Jan.　　　Perf. 12-15½

45	A30	1c green & blk	3.25	.30
a.		Horiz. pair, imperf. btwn.	150.00	
46	A31	2c ver & blk	1.25	.30
47	A32	5c gray blue & blk	3.25	.30
a.		Vert. pair, imperf. btwn.		300.00
48	A33	10c ocher & blk	3.25	.35
49	A34	20c lake & blk	22.50	.25
a.		Vert. pair, imperf. btwn.	1,000.	
50	A35	50c dull lil & dk bl	5.50	1.00
51	A36	1col ol bis & blk	110.00	3.50
52	A37	2col car rose & dk grn	16.00	3.00

53	A38	5col brown & blk	75.00	3.50
54	A39	10col yel grn & brn red	29.00	3.00
		Nos. 45-54 (10)	269.00	15.50

The 2c exists with center inverted. Value, $11,000.

Nos. 45-57 in other colors are private reprints made in 1948. They have little value. For surcharge and overprints see Nos. 58, 78, O37-O44.

Remainders

In 1914 the government sold a large quantity of stamps at very much less than face value. The lot included most regular issues from 1901 to 1911 inclusive, postage due stamps of 1903 and Official stamps of 1901-03. These stamps were canceled with groups of thin parallel bars. The higher valued used stamps, such as Nos. 64, 65-68a, sell for much less than the values quoted, which are for stamps with regular postal cancellations. A few sell for much higher prices.

José M. Cañas — A40

Julián Volio — A41

Eusebio Figueroa Oreamuno — A42

1903　　　Perf. 13½, 14, 15

55	A40	4c red vio & blk	2.00	.70
56	A41	6c olive grn & blk	7.25	4.00
57	A42	25c gray lil & brn	16.00	.30
		Nos. 55-57 (3)	25.25	5.00

See note on private reprints following No. 54.
For overprints see Nos. 81, O45-O47.

No. 49 Surcharged in Black:

1905

58	A34	1c on 20c lake & blk	.60	.60
a.		Inverted surcharge	10.00	10.00
b.		Diagonal surcharge	.60	.60

Examples surcharged in other colors are proofs.

Statue of Juan Santamaria
A43

Juan Mora Fernández
A44

José M. Cañas
A45

Mauro Fernández
A46

Braulio Carrillo — A47

Julián Volio — A48

Eusebio Figueroa Oreamuno
A49

José M. Castro
A50

Jesús Jiménez — A51

Juan Rafael Mora — A52

Perf. 11x14, 14 (1c, 5c, 10c, 25c)

1907　　　Unwmk.

59	A43	1c red brn & ind	8.00	.40
a.		Perf. 11x14	60.00	3.00
b.		Imperf pair	15.00	—
60	A44	2c yel grn & blk	3.00	.30
a.		Perf. 14	3.00	.30
b.		Imperf pair	15.00	—
61	A45	4c car & indigo	12.00	2.50
a.		Perf. 14	500.00	45.00
b.		Imperf pair	15.00	—
62	A46	5c yel & dull bl	3.00	.30
a.		Perf. 11x14	60.00	1.00
b.		Imperf pair	15.00	—
63	A47	10c blue & blk	10.00	.50
a.		Perf. 11x14	20.00	1.00
b.		Imperf pair	30.00	—
64	A48	20c olive grn & blk	25.00	6.00
a.		Perf. 14	25.00	6.00
		Remainder cancel		2.00
b.		Imperf pair	—	—
65	A49	25c gray lil & blk	3.00	3.00
		Remainder cancel		1.00
a.		Perf. 11x14	150.00	50.00
b.		Imperf pair	—	—
66	A50	50c red lil & blue	75.00	25.00
		Remainder cancel		2.00
a.		Perf. 14	175.00	50.00
b.		Imperf pair	100.00	—
67	A51	1col brown & blk	25.00	20.00
		Remainder cancel	25.00	20.00
				2.00
b.		Imperf pair	—	—
68	A52	2col claret & grn	160.00	100.00
		Remainder cancel		3.00
a.		Perf. 14	300.00	150.00
b.		Imperf pair	200.00	
		Nos. 59-68 (10)	324.00	158.00

The remainder cancel value applies to both perforations.

The imperforate varieties of the above set are valued without gum. Ungummed stamps were probably placed on the market in London, while gummed stamps appear to have been sent to Costa Rica and accepted for postal use. There is a small premium for gummed stamps.

The 1c, 2c, 5c, 20c, 50c, 1 col and 2 col exist with center inverted. Value, set $62,500.

Nos. 59-68 exist with papermaker's watermark.

No. 65b with brown vignette is a proof. Value, pair $40. The actual No. 65b (black vignette) is worth much more.

For overprints see Nos. 77, 79-80, 82-84, O48-O55, O60-O64.

Statue of Juan Santamaria
A53

Juan Mora Fernández
A54

José M.
Cañas
A55

Mauro
Fernández
A56

Braulio
Carrillo — A57

Julián
Volio — A58

Eusebio
Figueroa
Oreamuno
A59

Jesús Jiménez
A60

1910   *Perf. 12*

69	A53	1c brown	.25	.25
70	A54	2c dp green	.30	.25
71	A55	4c scarlet	.35	.35
72	A56	5c orange	1.00	.25
73	A57	10c deep blue	.40	.25
74	A58	20c olive grn	.50	.35
75	A59	25c dp violet	17.00	1.50
76	A60	1col dk brown	.50	.50
		Nos. 69-76 (8)	20.30	3.70

For overprints and surcharge see Nos. 111C-111J, B1, C2, O56-O59.

No. 60a Overprinted
in Red

1911   *Perf. 14*

77	A44	2c yel grn & blk	3.00	1.10
a.		Inverted overprint	6.00	5.00
b.		Double overprint, both inverted	45.00	

Stamps of 1901-07
Overprinted in Red or
Black

78	A30	1c grn & blk (R)	3.00	1.00
a.		Black overprint	32.50	18.00
b.		Inverted overprint		
79	A43	1c red brn & ind (Bk)	1.25	.40
a.		Inverted overprint	4.50	3.50
b.		Double overprint	5.50	5.00
80	A44	2c yel grn & blk (Bk)	1.00	.40
a.		Inverted overprint	3.75	3.50
b.		Dbl. ovpt., one as on No. 77	40.00	27.50
c.		Double overprint, one inverted	15.00	15.00
d.		Pair, one stamp No. 77	25.00	18.00
e.		Perf. 11x14	30.00	1.00

No. 55 Overprinted in
Black

81	A40	4c red vio & blk	1.50	.65

Stamps of 1907
Overprinted in Blue,
Black or Rose

Perf. 14, 11x14 (#83, 84)

82	A46	5c yel & bl (Bl)	2.00	.25
a.		"Habilitada"	3.25	2.50
b.		"2911"	5.50	3.25
c.		Roman "I" in "1911"	4.00	2.50
d.		Double overprint	5.50	5.00
e.		Inverted overprint	6.00	3.75
f.		Black overprint	—	2.00
g.		Triple overprint	6.00	
h.		Vert. pair, imperf. horiz.	100.00	
83	A47	10c blue & blk (Bk)	5.00	1.40
a.		As #83, Roman "I" in "1911"	7.00	5.00
c.		As #83, double overprint	20.00	11.50
d.		Perf. 14	45.00	5.25
84	A47	10c blue & blk (R)	15.00	13.50
a.		Roman "I" in "1911"	100.00	100.00
c.		Perf. 14	100.00	100.00
		Nos. 77-84 (8)	31.75	18.70

Many counterfeits of overprint exist.

Telegraph Stamps Surcharged in Rose, Blue or Black

A61

A62

A63

1911   *Perf. 12*

86	A61	1c on 10c bl (R)	.50	.25
a.		"Coereos"	7.75	6.00
b.		Inverted surcharge		
87	A61	1c on 10c bl (Bk)	210.00	87.50
88	A61	1c on 25c vio (Bk)	.50	.25
a.		"Coereos"	8.75	6.00
b.		Pair, one without surcharge	20.00	
c.		Double surcharge	9.00	
e.		Double surch., one inverted	12.50	
89	A61	1c on 50c red brn (Bl)	.55	.40
a.		Inverted surcharge	5.50	5.00
b.		Double surcharge	4.50	
90	A61	1c on 1col brn (R)	.55	.40
91	A61	1c on 5col red (Bl)	1.00	.55
92	A61	1c on 10col dk brn (R)	1.50	.70

Perf. 14

93	A62	2c on 5c brn org (Bk)	3.50	1.90
a.		Inverted surcharge	9.00	3.75
b.		"Correos" inverted	17.50	
c.		Double surcharge	9.00	

Perf. 14x11

94	A62	2c on 10c bl (R)	100.00	100.00
a.		Perf. 14	350.00	350.00
b.		"Correos" inverted	2,000.	
c.		As "b," perf. 14	—	
95	A62	2c on 50c cl (Bk)	1.00	.55
a.		Inverted surcharge	4.50	3.25
b.		Double surcharge	12.50	
c.		Perf. 14	45.00	20.00
96	A62	2c on 1col brn (Bk)	1.25	.70
a.		Inverted surcharge	12.50	
b.		Double surcharge	16.00	
c.		Perf. 14	2.00	.80
97	A62	2c on 2col car (Bk)	1.25	.60
a.		Inverted surcharge	8.00	5.00
b.		"Correos" inverted	10.00	5.50
c.		Double surcharge		
d.		Perf. 14	27.50	16.00
98	A62	2c on 5col grn (Bk)	1.00	.70
a.		Inverted surcharge	10.00	7.00
b.		"Correos" inverted	16.00	4.25
c.		Perf. 14	6.00	3.00
99	A62	2c on 10col mar (Bk)	1.50	.70
a.		"Correos" inverted	400.00	

b.		Perf. 14	6.00	3.00

Perf. 12

100	A63	5c on 5c org (Bl)	.40	.25
a.		Double surcharge	27.50	16.00
b.		Inverted surcharge	27.50	9.50
c.		Pair, one without surcharge	16.00	

Counterfeits exist of Nos. 87, 94 and all minor varieties. Genuine used examples of No. 94 are rare and have a cancel only used on registered mail. Genuine "Coereos" errors do not exist on No. 87. Used examples of No. 94 with target cancels are counterfeits. No. 94c is unique. All examples of Nos. 94b and 94c have stains and are valued thus.

Nos. 93-99 exist with papermaker's watermark.

Coffee Plantation — A64

1921, June 17   Litho.   *Perf. 11½*

103	A64	5c bl & blk	3.00	3.00
a.		Tête bêche pair	15.00	6.50
b.		Imperf., pair	40.00	
c.		As "a," imperf.	150.00	

Centenary of coffee raising in Costa Rica.

Liberty with Torch
of
Freedom — A65

1921   Typo.   *Perf. 11*

104	A65	5c violet	1.00	.40
a.		Imperf, pair	100.00	

Cent. of Central American independence. Beware of trimmed singles that look like No. 104a.
For overprint see No. 111.

Juan Mora and Julio Acosta — A66

1921, Sept. 15   *Perf. 11½*

105	A66	2c orange & blk	1.75	1.75
106	A66	3c green & blk	1.75	1.75
107	A66	6c scarlet & blk	3.00	3.00
108	A66	15c dk blue & blk	5.00	5.00
109	A66	30c orange brn & blk	6.50	6.50
		Nos. 105-109 (5)	18.00	18.00

Centenary of Central American independence. Issue requested by Costa Rican Philatelic Society. Authorized by decree calling for 2,000 of 30c and 5,000 each of other values. Nos. 105-109 imperf were not regularly issued. Inverted centers exist of both perf and imperf. They are rare. Used values are for Independence commemorative cancel.

Each sheet of 20 (4x5) contains 5 tête-bêche pairs. Value, set of 5 pairs $40.

Simón Bolívar — A67

1921   Engr.   *Perf. 12*

110	A67	15c deep violet	.75	.25

For overprint No. 110a see set following No. 111. For surcharge see No. 148.

No. 104
Overprinted

1922   *Perf. 11*

111	A65	5c violet	.75	.40
a.		Inverted overprint	10.00	
b.		Double overprint	15.00	

Stamps of 1910-1921
Overprinted in Blue,
Red, Black or Gold

1922   *Perf. 12*

111C	A53	1c brown (Bl)	.30	.25
111D	A54	2c deep green (R)	.40	.25
111E	A55	4c scarlet	.30	.25
111F	A56	5c orange	2.00	.40
111G	A57	10c deep blue (R)	.75	.40
111H	A67	15c deep violet (G)	4.00	2.00
		Nos. 111C-111H (6)	7.75	3.55

Inverted overprints occur on all values. Value, set $20. Counterfeits predominate.

No. 72 Overprinted

1923

111J	A56	5c orange	3.00	.75
k.		"VD." for "UD."	75.00	75.00

Jesús
Jiménez — A68

1923, June 18   Litho.   *Perf. 11½*

112	A68	2c brown	.40	.40
113	A68	4c green	.40	.40
114	A68	5c blue	.60	.40
115	A68	20c carmine	.85	.50
116	A68	1col violet	1.10	1.25
		Nos. 112-116 (5)	3.35	2.95

Pres. Jesús Jiménez (1823-98). Nos. 112-116, imperf, were not regularly issued. Value, set $5.
For overprints see Nos. O65-O69.

National
Monument
A70

Harvesting
Coffee — A71

Banana
Growing — A73

General Post Office
A74

Columbus Soliciting Aid of Isabella
A75

Christopher Columbus
A76

Columbus at Cariari
A77

Map of Costa Rica — A78

Manuel M. Gutiérrez — A79

1923-26		Engr.	Perf. 12	
117	A70	1c violet	.25	.25
118	A71	2c yellow	.50	.25
119	A73	4c deep green	.75	.30
120	A74	5c light blue	1.50	.25
121	A74	5c yellow grn ('26)	.50	.25
122	A75	10c red brown	3.00	.25
123	A75	10c car rose ('26)	.50	.25
124	A76	12c carmine rose	10.00	3.00
125	A77	20c deep blue	10.00	.65
126	A78	40c orange	11.00	3.00
127	A79	1col olive green	2.40	.80
		Nos. 117-127 (11)	40.40	9.25

See Nos. 151-156. For surcharges & overprints see Nos. 136-140, 147, 189, 218 (in Scott Standard catalogue, Vol. 2), C2.

Rodrigo Arias Maldonado — A80

1924			Perf. 12½	
128	A80	2c dark green	.25	.25
a.		Perf. 14	.50	.25

See No. 162.

Map of Guanacaste
A81

Mission at Nicoya
A82

1924		Litho.	Perf. 12	
129	A81	1c carmine rose	.30	.25
130	A81	2c violet	.40	.25
131	A81	5c green	.40	.25
132	A81	10c orange	2.25	.50
133	A82	15c light blue	1.00	1.00
134	A82	20c gray	2.00	1.00
135	A82	25c light brown	3.00	1.50
		Nos. 129-135 (7)	9.35	4.25

Centenary of annexation of Province of Guanacaste to Costa Rica.
Exist imperf. Value, set, $50.

Stamps of 1923 Surcharged

a

b

1925				
136	A74(a)	3c on 5c lt blue	.30	.25
137	A75(a)	6c on 10c red brn	.40	.25
138	A78(a)	30c on 40c orange	1.50	.40
139	A79(b)	45c on 1col ol grn	1.75	.50
a.		Double surcharge	250.00	
		Nos. 136-139 (4)	3.95	1.40

No. 124 Surcharged

1926				
140	A76	10c on 12c car rose	1.50	.30

College of San Luis, Cartago
A83

Chapui Asylum, San José — A84

Normal School, Heredia
A85

Ruins of Ujarrás
A86

1926		Unwmk. Engr.	Perf. 12½	
143	A83	3c ultra	.55	.25
144	A84	6c dark brown	.55	.25
145	A85	30c deep orange	2.00	.40
146	A86	45c black violet	4.00	1.60
		Nos. 143-146 (4)	7.10	2.50

For surcharges see Nos. 190-190D, 217 (in Scott Standard catalogue, Vol. 2).

No. 124 Surcharged in Black

1928, Jan. 7			Perf. 12	
147	A76	10c on 12c car rose	4.75	4.75

Issued in honor of Col. Charles A. Lindbergh during his Good Will Tour of Central America. The surcharge was privately reprinted using an original die. Reprints can be distinguished by distinct dots under the "10s." All errors and inverted surcharges are reprints.

No. 110 Surcharged

1928				
148	A67	5(c) on 15c dp violet	.25	.25
a.		Inverted surcharge	35.00	

Type I — A88

Type II

Type III

Type IV

Type V

Surcharge Typo. (I-V) & Litho. (V)

1929			Perf. 12½	
149	A88	5c on 2col car (I)	.50	.25
a.-d.		Types II-V	.60	.25
e.		Type V (litho.)	3.00	3.00

Telegraph Stamp Surcharged for Postage as in 1929, Surcharge Lithographed

1929				
150	A88	13c on 40c deep grn	.35	.25
a.		Inverted surcharge	1.00	1.00

Excellent counterfeits exist of No. 150a.

Types of 1923-26 Issues Dated "1929"
Imprint of Waterlow & Sons

1930	Size: 26x21½mm		Perf. 12½	
151	A70	1c dark violet	.70	.25
155	A74	5c green	.70	.25
156	A75	10c carmine rose	.70	.25
		Nos. 151-156 (3)	2.10	.75

Juan Rafael Mora — A89

1931, Jan. 29				
157	A89	13c carmine rose	.60	.25

For surcharge see No. 209 in Scott Standard catalogue, Vol. 2.

Seal of Costa Rica Philatelic Society ("Octubre 12 de 1932") — A90

1932, Oct. 12			Perf. 12	
158	A90	3c orange	.25	.25
159	A90	5c dark green	.40	.25
160	A90	10c carmine rose	.50	.25
161	A90	20c dark blue	.85	.40
		Nos. 158-161 (4)	2.00	1.15

Phil. Exhib., Oct. 12, 1932. See Nos. 179-183.

Maldonado Type of 1924

1934, Aug. 11			Perf. 12½	
162	A80	3c dark green	.25	.25

Red Cross Nurse — A91

1935, May 31			Perf. 12	
163	A91	10c rose carmine	7.50	.25

50th anniv. of the founding of the Costa Rican Red Cross Society.

Air View of Cartago
A92

Miraculous Statuette and View of Cathedral
A93

Vision of 1635 — A94

1935, Aug. 1			Perf. 12½	
164	A92	5c green	.25	.25
165	A93	10c carmine	.25	.25
166	A92	30c orange	.25	.25
167	A94	45c dark violet	1.00	.55
168	A93	50c blue black	1.00	1.00
		Nos. 164-168 (5)	2.75	2.30

Tercentenary of the Patron Saint, Our Lady of the Angels, of Costa Rica.

Map of Cocos Island
A95

1936, Jan. 29   *Perf. 14, 11½ (25c)*
169	A95	4c ocher	.50	.25
170	A95	8c dark violet	.65	.25
171	A95	25c orange	.80	.25
172	A95	35c brown vio	.95	.25
173	A95	40c brown	1.25	.40
174	A95	50c yellow	1.50	.60
175	A95	2col yellow grn	11.00	10.00
176	A95	5col green	30.00	25.00
		Nos. 169-176 (8)	46.65	37.00

Exist imperf. Value, set, $50.
For surcharges see Nos. 196-200 (in Scott Standard catalogue, Vol. 2), C55-C56.

Map of Cocos Island and Ships of Columbus
A96

1936, Dec. 5   *Perf. 12*
177	A96	5c green	.40	.25
178	A96	10c carmine rose	.55	.25

For overprints see Nos. 247 (in Scott Standard catalogue, Vol. 2), O80-O81.

Seal of Costa Rica Philatelic Society ("Diciembre 1937") — A97

1937, Dec. 15
179	A97	2c dark brown	.45	.25
180	A97	3c black	.45	.25
181	A97	5c green	.45	.25
182	A97	10c orange red	.45	.25
		Nos. 179-182 (4)	1.80	1.00

Souvenir Sheet

Imperf
183		Sheet of 4	6.50	4.00
a.	A97	2c dark brown	.25	.25
b.	A97	3c black	.25	.25
c.	A97	5c green	.25	.25
d.	A97	10c orange red	.25	.25

Phil. Exhib., Dec. 1937.

Purple Guaria Orchid, National Flower — A98

Tuna — A99

Native with Donkey Carrying Bananas A101

3c, Cacao pod. 10c, Coffee harvesting.

1937-38   **Wmk. 229**   *Perf. 12½*
184	A98	1c green & vio ('38)	.55	.25
185	A98	3c chocolate ('38)	.55	.25

Unwmk.   *Perf. 12*
186	A99	2c olive gray	.40	.25
187	A101	5c dark green	.55	.25
188	A101	10c carmine rose	.90	.25
		Nos. 184-188 (5)	2.95	1.25

National Exposition.

No. 125 Overprinted in Black

1938, Sept. 23   **Unwmk.**   *Perf. 12*
189	A77	20c deep blue	1.50	.30

No. 146 Surcharged in Red

a

b

c

d

e

1940   *Perf. 12½*
190	A86(a)	15c on 45c blk vio	.60	.30
190A	A86(b)	15c on 45c blk vio	.60	.30
190B	A86(c)	15c on 45c blk vio	.60	.30
190C	A86(d)	15c on 45c blk vio	.60	.30
190D	A86(e)	15c on 45c blk vio	.60	.30
		Nos. 190-190D (5)	3.00	1.50

No. 190D exists with inverted surcharge. Value, $5.

Allegory A103

Black Overprint

1940, Dec. 2   **Engr.**   *Perf. 12*
191	A103	5c green	.25	.25
192	A103	10c rose carmine	.50	.25
193	A103	20c deep blue	1.50	1.00
194	A103	40c brown	4.50	2.75
195	A103	55c orange yellow	11.00	7.50
		Nos. 191-195 (5)	17.75	11.75

Pan-American Health Day. See Nos. C46-C54.
Exist without overprint.

POSTAL-FISCAL STAMPS

From April 1884 through September 1889 revenue stamps were permitted for postal use, when post offices exhausted supplies of regular postage stamps.

Used values are for stamps with postal cancels.

PF1   PF2

1884   **Engr.**   *Perf. 12*
AR1	PF1	1c rose	.50	5.00
AR2	PF1	2c light blue	20.00	5.00

1888
AR3	PF2	5c brown	.50	3.00
AR4	PF2	10c blue	.25	3.00

Nos. AR2-AR4 are normally found without gum.

SEMI-POSTAL STAMPS

No. 72 Surcharged in Red

1922   **Unwmk.**   *Perf. 12*
B1	A56	5c + 5c orange	1.00	.40

Issued for the benefit of the Costa Rican Red Cross Society. In 1928, owing to a temporary shortage of the ordinary 5c stamp, No. B1 was placed on sale as a regular 5c stamp, the surtax being disregarded.

Discus Thrower SP1   Trophy SP2

Parthenon SP3

1924   **Litho.**   *Imperf.*
B2	SP1	5c dark green	1.60	2.00
B3	SP2	10c carmine	1.60	2.00
B4	SP3	20c dark blue	20.00	20.00
a.		Tête bêche pair	60.00	60.00

Perf. 12
B5	SP1	5c dark green	1.60	2.25
B6	SP2	10c carmine	1.60	2.25
B7	SP3	20c dark blue	3.50	4.00
a.		Tête bêche pair	16.00	20.00
		Nos. B2-B7 (6)	29.90	32.50

These stamps were sold at a premium of 10c each, to help defray the expenses of athletic games held at San José in Dec. 1924.

AIR POST STAMPS

Airplane AP1

Perf. 12½

1926, June 4   **Unwmk.**   **Engr.**
C1	AP1	20c ultramarine	3.00	.65

No. 123 Overprinted

1930, Mar. 14   *Perf. 12*
C2	A75	10c carmine rose	2.00	.25

Inverted or double overprints are fakes.

AP3

1930-32   *Perf. 12½*
C3	AP3	5c on 10c dk brn ('32)	.40	.25
C4	AP3	20c on 50c ultra	.50	.25
C5	AP3	40c on 50c ultra	.60	.25
		Nos. C3-C5 (3)	1.50	.75

The existence of genuine inverted or double surcharges of Nos. C3-C5 is in doubt.

Telegraph Stamp Overprinted

1930, Mar. 19
C6	AP3	1col orange	2.00	.50

No. O79 Surcharged in Red

1930, Mar. 11
C7	O7	8c on 1col lilac & blk	.80	.65
C8	O7	20c on 1col lilac & blk	1.25	.70
C9	O7	40c on 1col lilac & blk	2.40	1.50
C10	O7	1col on 1col lilac & blk	3.50	2.00
		Nos. C7-C10 (4)	7.95	4.85

AP6   AP7

Red Surcharge on Revenue Stamps

1931-32   *Perf. 12*
C11	AP6	2col on 2col gray grn	35.00	35.00
C12	AP6	3col on 5col lil brn	35.00	35.00
C13	AP6	5col on 10col gray blk	35.00	35.00
		Nos. C11-C13 (3)	105.00	105.00

There were two printings of this issue which were practically identical in the colors of the stamps and the surcharges.
Nos. C11 and C13 have the date "1929" on the stamp, No. C12 has "1930."

Black Overprint on Telegraph Stamp

1932, Mar. 8   *Perf. 12½*
C14	AP7	40c green	3.00	.30
a.		Inverted overprint	32.50	27.50

Unofficial "proofs," inverts and double overprints were made from a defaced plate.

Mail Plane
about to
Lund
AP8

Allegory of
Flight
AP9

1934, Mar. 14   *Perf. 12*

C15	AP8	5c green	.25	.25
C16	AP8	10c carmine rose	.25	.25
C17	AP8	15c chocolate	.40	.25
C18	AP8	20c deep blue	.40	.25
C19	AP8	25c deep orange	.55	.25
C20	AP8	40c olive blk	1.75	.25
C21	AP8	50c gray blk	.85	.25
C22	AP8	60c orange yel	1.50	.25
C23	AP8	75c dull violet	2.75	.50
C24	AP9	1col deep rose	1.50	.25
C25	AP9	2col lt blue	7.50	.95
C26	AP9	5col black	7.50	4.75
C27	AP9	10col red brown	10.00	8.00
		Nos. C15-C27 (13)	35.20	16.45

Nos. C15-C27 with holes punched through were for use of government officials.
See Nos. C216-C219. For overprints see Nos. C67-C73, C92-C93, C103-C116, CO1-CO13. Post 1940 issues in Scott Standard catalogue, Vol. 2.

Airplane over Poás Volcano — AP10

1937, Feb. 10

C28	AP10	1c black	.45	.35
C29	AP10	2c brown	.45	.35
C30	AP10	3c dk violet	.45	.35
		Nos. C28-C30 (3)	1.35	1.05

First Fair of Costa Rica.

Puntarenas — AP11

Perf. 12, 12½

1937, Dec. 15   Unwmk.

C31	AP11	2c black gray	.25	.25
C32	AP11	5c green	.30	.25
C33	AP11	20c deep blue	.30	.25
C34	AP11	1.40col olive brn	2.50	2.50
		Nos. C31-C34 (4)	3.35	3.25

National
Bank
AP12

1938, Jan. 11   Wmk. 229   *Perf. 12½*

C35	AP12	1c purple	.25	.25
C36	AP12	3c red orange	.25	.25
C37	AP12	10c carmine rose	.30	.25
C38	AP12	75c brown	2.50	2.00
		Nos. C35-C38 (4)	3.30	2.75

Nos. C31-C38 for the Natl. Products Exposition held at San José, Dec. 1937.

Airport Administration Building, La Sabana — AP13

1940, May 2   Engr.   Unwmk.

C39	AP13	5c green	.30	.25
C40	AP13	10c rose pink	.30	.25
C41	AP13	25c lt blue	.40	.25
C42	AP13	35c red brown	.40	.25
C43	AP13	60c red org	.55	.40
C44	AP13	85c violet	1.40	1.00
C45	AP13	2.35col turq grn	6.50	5.50
		Nos. C39-C45 (7)	9.85	7.90

Opening of the Intl. Airport at La Sabana.

Duran
Sanatorium
AP14

Overprinted "Dia Panamericano de la Salud / 2 Diciembre 1940" and Bar in Black

1940, Dec. 2   *Perf. 12*

C46	AP14	10c scarlet	.25	.25
C47	AP14	15c purple	.25	.25
C48	AP14	25c lt blue	.50	.40
C49	AP14	35c bister brn	.70	.65
C50	AP14	60c pck green	1.00	.95
C51	AP14	75c olive	2.75	2.50
C52	AP14	1.35col red org	8.75	8.00
C53	AP14	5col sepia	45.00	40.00
C54	AP14	10col red lilac	140.00	100.00
		Nos. C46-C54 (9)	199.20	153.00

Pan-American Health Day. Nos. C46-C54 exist without overprint. Value, set $5,000.

No. 174
Surcharged in Black or Blue

1940, Dec. 17   *Perf. 14*

C55	A95	15c on 50c yel (Bk)	1.00	1.00
C56	A95	30c on 50c yel (Bl)	1.00	1.00

Pan-American Aviation Day, proclaimed by President F. D. Roosevelt.
The 15c surcharge exists normal and inverted on No. 171, Value, normal $30. Inverted surcharge is worth more.

AIR POST OFFICIAL STAMPS

Air Post
Stamps of
1934
Ovptd. in
Red

1934   Unwmk.   *Perf. 12*

CO1	AP8	5c green	.25	.25
CO2	AP8	10c car rose	.25	.25
CO3	AP8	15c chocolate	.50	.50
CO4	AP8	20c deep blue	.80	.80
CO5	AP8	25c deep org	.80	.80
CO6	AP8	40c olive blk	.80	.80
CO7	AP8	50c gray blk	.80	.80
CO8	AP8	60c org yel	.95	.95
CO9	AP8	75c dull vio	.95	.95
CO10	AP9	1col deep rose	1.60	1.60
CO11	AP9	2col light blue	4.75	4.75
CO12	AP9	5col black	8.00	8.00
CO13	AP9	10col red brown	12.00	12.00
		Nos. CO1-CO13 (13)	32.45	32.45

For overprints see Nos. C103-C116 in Scott Standard catalogue, Vol 2.

POSTAGE DUE STAMPS

D1   D2

1903   Unwmk.   Engr.   *Perf. 14*
Numerals in Black

J1	D1	5c slate blue	6.75	1.25
J2	D1	10c brown orange	6.75	1.25
J3	D1	15c yellow green	3.50	1.75
J4	D1	20c carmine	4.75	1.75
J5	D1	25c slate gray	4.75	2.40
J6	D1	30c brown	6.00	2.50
J7	D1	40c olive bister	6.75	2.50
J8	D1	50c red violet	6.75	2.50
		Nos. J1-J8 (8)	46.00	15.90

1915   Litho.   *Perf. 12*

J9	D2	2c orange	1.25	.55
J10	D2	4c dark blue	1.25	.55
J11	D2	8c gray green	1.25	.55
J12	D2	10c violet	1.25	.55
J13	D2	20c brown	1.25	.55
		Nos. J9-J13 (5)	6.25	2.75

OFFICIAL STAMPS

Values for unused stamps are for examples with original gum as defined in the catalogue introduction. Examples without gum have probably been used and are so regarded.
Very fine examples of Nos. O1-O24 will have perforations just clear of the design on one or more sides.
Nos. O1-O55, to about 1915, normally were not canceled when affixed to official mail. Occasionally they were canceled in a foreign country of destination. Used values are for favor-canceled stamps or for stamps without gum.

Regular Issues Overprinted

Overprinted in Red, Black, Blue or Green

1883-85   Unwmk.   *Perf. 12*

O1	A6	1c green (R)	2.00	1.10
O2	A6	1c green (Bk)	4.00	1.10
O3	A6	2c carmine (Bk)	4.00	1.40
O4	A6	2c carmine (Bl)	2.40	1.60
O5	A6	5c blue vio (R)	7.00	3.00
O6	A6	10c orange (G)	10.00	4.00
O7	A6	40c blue (R)	10.00	4.00
		Nos. O1-O7 (7)	39.40	16.20

Overprinted

1886

O8	A6	1c green (Bk)	3.50	1.10
O9	A6	2c carmine (Bk)	3.50	1.60
O10	A6	5c blue vio (R)	24.00	11.00
O11	A6	10c orange (Bk)	24.00	11.00
		Nos. O8-O11 (4)	55.00	24.70

Overprinted

O12	A6	1c green (Bk)	3.50	1.00
O13	A6	2c carmine (Bk)	3.50	1.40
O14	A6	5c blue vio (R)	24.00	11.00
O15	A6	10c orange (Bk)	24.00	11.00
		Nos. O12-O15 (4)	55.00	24.40

Nos. O8-O11 and O12-O15 exist se-tenant in vertical pairs.

Overprinted in Black

O16	A6	5c blue vio	60.00	35.00
O17	A6	10c orange	—	275.00

Overprinted

1887

O18	A6	1c green	1.25	.55
O19	A6	2c carmine	1.25	.50
O21	A6	10c orange	37.50	24.00
c.		Double overprint	42.50	
O22	A7	5c blue vio	12.00	3.50
O23	A7	10c orange	.90	.50
c.		Double overprint	27.50	
O24	A6	40c blue	1.25	.50
		Nos. O18-O24 (6)	54.15	29.55

Overprinted "OFICAL"

O18a	A6	1c green	14.50	14.50
O19a	A6	2c carmine	14.50	14.50
O22a	A7	5c blue violet	14.50	
O23a	A7	10c orange	14.50	3.50
O24a	A6	40c blue	17.00	17.00
		Nos. O18a-O24a (5)	60.50	

Dangerous counterfeits exist of Nos. O18a-O24a.

Without Period

O18b	A6	1c green	14.50	10.00
O19b	A6	2c carmine	14.50	10.00
O22b	A7	5c blue violet	14.50	10.00
O23b	A7	10c orange	14.50	10.00
		Nos. O18b-O23b (4)	58.00	40.00

Nos. O18b-O23b are from a separate plate without periods. No. O23 exists without period (position 32). These must be collected in pairs.

Issues of 1889-1901
Overprinted

1889   *Perf. 14, 15*

O25	A10	1c brown	.25	.25
O26	A11	2c dk green	.25	.25
O27	A12	5c orange	.25	.25
O28	A13	10c red brown	.25	.25
O29	A14	20c yellow grn	.40	.25
O30	A15	50c rose red	1.40	1.40
		Nos. O25-O30 (6)	2.80	2.65

1892

O31	A20	1c grnsh blue	.25	.25
O32	A21	2c yellow	.25	.25
O33	A22	5c violet	.25	.25
O34	A23	10c lt green	3.50	1.60
O35	A24	20c scarlet	.25	.25
O36	A25	50c gray blue	.65	.55
		Nos. O31-O36 (6)	5.15	3.15

1901-02

O37	A30	1c green & blk	.40	.40
O38	A31	2c ver & blk	.40	.40
O39	A32	5c gray bl & blk	.40	.40
O40	A33	10c ocher & blk	.80	.80
O41	A34	20c lake & blk	1.25	1.25
O42	A35	50c lilac & dk bl	10.00	4.00
O43	A36	1col ol bis & blk	17.50	10.00
		Nos. O37-O43 (7)	30.75	17.25

No. 46 Overprinted in Green

1903
O44	A31	2c ver & blk	3.00	3.00
b.		"PROVISIORO"	10.00	10.00
d.		Inverted overprint	10.00	10.00
f.		As "b," inverted	13.00	10.00

Counterfeit overprints exist.

Regular Issue of 1903 Overprinted Like Nos. O25-O43

1903   *Perf. 14, 12½x14*
O45	A40	4c red vio & blk	1.40	1.40
O46	A41	6c ol grn & blk	1.75	1.75
O47	A42	25c gray lil & brn	9.50	6.00
		Nos. O45-O47 (3)	12.65	9.15

Counterfeit overprints exist.

Regular Issue of 1907 Overprinted

1908   *Perf. 14*
O48	A43	1c red brn & ind	.25	.25
O49	A44	2c yel grn & blk	.25	.25
O50	A45	4c car & ind	.25	.25
O51	A46	5c yel & dull bl	.25	.25
O52	A47	10c blue & blk	.80	.80
O53	A49	25c gray lil & blk	.30	.25
O54	A50	50c red lil & bl	.55	.55
O55	A51	1col brown & blk	1.25	1.25
		Nos. O48-O55 (8)	3.90	3.85

Various varieties of the overprint and basic stamps exist.
Imperf examples of Nos. O48, O49, O53 were found in 1970.

Regular Issue of 1910 Overprinted in Black

1917
O56	A56	5c orange	.40	.40
a.		Inverted overprint	6.00	3.50
O57	A57	10c deep blue	.25	.25
a.		Inverted overprint	3.50	3.50

No. 74 Surcharged

1920   **Red Surcharge**   *Perf. 12*
O58	A58	15c on 20c olive grn	.55	.55

Nos. 72, 61, 59, 65-67 Surcharged or Overprinted

1921   **Black Surcharge**   *Perf. 12*
O59	A56	10c on 5c orange	.50	.50
a.		"10 CTS." inverted	17.50	

              Perf. 14
O60	A45	4c car & indigo	.40	.40
a.		"1291" for "1921"	12.00	
O61	A43	6c on 1c red brn & ind	.55	.55
O62	A49	20c on 25c gray lil & blk	.55	.55

Overprinted like No. O60
O63	A50	50c red lil & bl	2.50	1.75
O64	A51	1col brown & blk	5.00	3.00
		Nos. O59-O64 (6)	9.50	6.75

Nos. O60 to O64 exist with date and new values inverted. These may be printer's waste but probably were deliberately made.

Regular Issue of 1923 Overprinted

1923   *Perf. 11½*
O65	A68	2c brown	.25	.25
O66	A68	4c green	.25	.25
O67	A68	5c blue	.40	.40
O68	A68	20c carmine	.25	.25
O69	A68	1col violet	.50	.50
		Nos. O65-O69 (5)	1.65	1.65

Nos. O65 to O69 exist imperforate but were not regularly issued in that condition.

O7

1926   **Unwmk.**   **Engr.**   *Perf. 12½*
O70	O7	2c ultra & blk	.25	.25
O71	O7	3c mag & blk	.25	.25
O72	O7	4c lt bl & blk	.25	.25
O73	O7	5c grn & blk	.25	.25
O74	O7	6c ocher & blk	.25	.25
O75	O7	10c rose red & blk	.25	.25
O76	O7	20c ol grn & blk	.25	.25
O77	O7	30c red org & blk	.25	.25
O78	O7	45c brown & blk	.25	.25
O79	O7	1col lilac & blk	.50	.50
		Nos. O70-O79 (10)	2.75	2.75

See Nos. O82-O94. For surcharges see Nos. C7-C10.

Regular Issue of 1936 Overprinted in Black

1936   **Unwmk.**   *Perf. 12*
O80	A96	5c green	.25	.25
O81	A96	10c carmine rose	.25	.25

Type of 1926

1937   *Perf. 12½*
O82	O7	2c vio & blk	.25	.25
O83	O7	3c bis brn & blk	.25	.25
O84	O7	4c rose car & blk	.25	.25
O85	O7	5c ol grn & blk	.20	
O86	O7	8c blk brn & blk	.20	
O87	O7	10c rose lake & blk	.20	
O88	O7	20c ind & blk	.25	.25
O89	O7	40c red org & blk	.25	.25
O90	O7	55c dk vio & blk	.25	
O91	O7	1col brn vio & blk	.30	.30
O92	O7	2col gray bl & blk	.70	.70
O93	O7	5col dl yel & blk	3.00	3.00
O94	O7	10col blue & blk	45.00	20.00
		Nos. O82-O94 (13)	51.10	

Nine stamps of this series exist with perforated star (2c, 3c, 4c, 20c, 40c, 1col, 2col, 5col, 10col). These were issued to officials for postal purposes. Unpunched stamps were sold to collectors but had no franking power. Values for unused are for unpunched.

POSTAL TAX STAMPS

The 1927 postal tax stamps covered the 10c per book charge for books sent by mail. The stamps were sold at the post office and applied to any package containing books.

Regular Stamps and Revenue Stamps Overprinted in Black

Nos. RA1B-RA1D Overprinted

1927, Mar. 17
RA1A	A75	10c red brown	25.00	5.00
RA1B		50c brown (overprinted on revenue stamp)	25.00	10.00
RA1C	A79	1col olive green	25.00	10.00
RA1D		2col blue green (overprinted on revenue stamp)	300.00	200.00
		Nos. RA1A-RA1D (4)	375.00	225.00

No. 124 Surcharged in Black

1927, Dec. 23
RA1E	A76	10c on 12c carmine rose	25.00	5.00

GUANACASTE

ˌgwä-nə-ˈkästä

(A province of Costa Rica)

LOCATION — Northwestern coast of Central America
AREA — 4,000 sq. mi. (approx.)
POP. — 69,531 (estimated)
CAPITAL — Liberia

Residents of Guanacaste were allowed to buy Costa Rican stamps, overprinted "Guanacaste," at a discount from face value because of the province's isolation and climate, which made it difficult to keep mint stamps. Use was restricted to the province.
Counterfeits of most Guanacaste overprints are plentiful.

For 1c and 2c stamps between Nos. 1-20, unused values are for examples with or without gum. For 5c stamps between Nos. 5-21, unused examples without gum sell for slightly more than the used value.

Very fine examples of Nos. 1-54 will have perforations just clear of the design on one or more sides.

Dangerous counterfeits exist of Nos. 1-54.

On Issue of 1883

16mm

1885   **Unwmk.**   *Perf. 12*
Overprinted Horizontally in Black
1	A6	1c green	4.00	3.25
2	A6	2c carmine	4.00	3.25
a.		"Gnanacaste"	250.00	
3	A6	10c orange	35.00	21.00
a.		"Gnanacaste"	500.00	

Same Overprint in Red
4	A6	1c green	4.00	3.25
a.		"Gnanacaste"	200.00	
b.		Overprinted in black & red	300.00	
5	A6	5c blue violet	30.00	4.00
a.		"Gnanacaste"	350.00	
6	A6	40c blue	25.00	21.00

17½mm

Overprinted Horizontally in Black
7	A6	1c green	10.00	7.00
8	A6	2c carmine	10.00	7.00
9	A6	5c blue violet	45.00	15.00
10	A6	10c orange	60.00	35.00
11	A6	40c blue	60.00	60.00

Same Overprint in Red
12	A6	5c blue violet	1,000.	200.00
13	A6	40c blue	2,000.	

18½mm — c

Overprinted Horizontally in Black
14	A6	2c carmine	10.00	7.00
15	A6	10c orange	100.00	75.00

Same Overprint in Red
16	A6	1c green	7.00	7.00
a.		Double ovpt., one in blk	250.00	
17	A6	5c blue violet	45.00	15.00
18	A6	40c blue	75.00	75.00

Same Overprint, Vertically in Black
19	A6	1c green	5,000.	
20	A6	2c carmine	4,250.	
21	A6	5c blue violet	700.00	175.00
22	A6	10c orange	150.00	120.00

e   f

g   h

GUANACASTE

Overprinted Type e, Vertically

23	A6	1c green	3,000.	2,000.
24	A6	2c carmine	1,000.	300.00
25	A6	5c blue violet	400.00	75.00
26	A6	10c orange	75.00	75.00

Overprinted Type f, Vertically

27	A6	1c green	3,000.	2,000.
28	A6	2c carmine	1,000.	400.00
29	A6	5c blue violet	400.00	125.00
30	A6	10c orange	100.00	100.00

Overprinted Type g, Vertically

31	A6	1c green	2,500.	2,500.
32	A6	2c carmine	1,000.	300.00
33	A6	5c blue violet	600.00	200.00
34	A6	10c orange	150.00	150.00

Overprinted Type h, Vertically

35	A6	1c green	3,000.	1,500.
36	A6	2c carmine	1,000.	300.00
37	A6	5c blue violet	400.00	75.00
38	A6	10c orange	60.00	60.00

Overprinted Type i, Vertically

39	A6	1c green	—	
39A	A6	2c carmine		275.00
40	A6	5c blue violet		20.00
41	A6	10c orange		200.00

On Issues of 1883-87

Overprinted
Horizontally in Black

1888-89

42	A7	5c blue violet	15.00	3.00

Overprinted
Horizontally in Black

43	A7	5c blue violet	15.00	3.00

Overprinted
Horizontally in Black

44	A6	2c carmine		3.00
45	A7	10c orange		3.00

Inverted overprints are fakes.

On Issue of 1889
Overprinted Like Nos. 7-13,
Horizontally

1889

47	A8	2c blue		20.00

Vertically

48	A8	2c blue (c)		250.00
49	A8	2c blue (e)		75.00
51	A8	2c blue (f)		75.00
52	A8	2c blue (g)		250.00
54	A8	2c blue (h)		75.00

Nos. 47-54 are overprinted "Correos."
Stamps without "Correos" are known postally
used. Unused examples are valued the same
as Nos. 47-54, unused. The 1c without "Correos" is known postally used. The 1c with
"Correos" is counterfeit.

On Nos. 25-33
Overprinted
Horizontally in Black

1889   *Perf. 14 and 15*

55	A10	1c brown	10.00	3.50
56	A11	2c dark green	4.50	1.50
57	A12	5c orange	6.75	2.10
58	A13	10c red brown	6.75	2.10
59	A14	20c yellow green	1.00	.70
60	A15	50c rose red	1.75	1.50
61	A16	1p blue	4.50	4.50

Overprinted Type e, Vertically

62	A17	2p violet	6.75	6.75
63	A18	5p olive green	37.50	37.50
		Nos. 55-63 (9)	79.50	60.15

Nos. 61-63 with remainder cancels sell for
about half the used values shown.

Overprinted "GUAGACASTE"

60a	A15	50c rose red	325.00	325.00
61a	A16	1p blue	325.00	325.00
62a	A17	2p violet	400.00	400.00
63a	A18	5p olive green	600.00	600.00

Values for Nos. 60a-63a used are for examples with remainder cancels.

Overprinted
Horizontally in Black

64	A10	1c brown	2.25	1.50
a.		Vert. pair, imperf. between		
65	A11	2c dark green	2.25	1.50
66	A12	5c orange	2.25	1.50
67	A13	10c red brown	2.25	1.50
		Nos. 64-67 (4)	9.00	6.00

CRETE

'krēt

LOCATION — An island in the Mediter-
ranean Sea south of Greece
GOVT. — A department of Greece
AREA — 3,235 sq. mi.
POP. — 336,150 (1913)
CAPITAL — Canea

Formerly Crete was a province of Turkey. After an extended period of civil
wars, France, Great Britain, Italy and
Russia intervened and declaring Crete
an autonomy, placed it under the
administration of Prince George of
Greece as High Commissioner. In
October, 1908, the Cretan Assembly
voted for union with Greece and in 1913
the union was formally effected.

40 Paras = 1 Piaster
4 Metallik = 1 Grosion (1899)
100 Lepta = 1 Drachma (1900)

AUSTRIAN POST IN CRETE

The Austrian Empire maintained post
offices in three cities in Crete.

Post Office	Open	Close
Candia	1858	1914
Canea	1845	1914
Rettimo	1858	1914

Values in the first column for Nos.
2A1-2A185 are for stamps without
defects tied to piece with legible partial
strikes of town cancellations; values in
the second column are for stamps without defects tied to cover by complete
strikes of town cancellations. Stamps
with legible town cancellations off cover
sell for 25-50% of the on-piece value.

Issue dates refer to dates of stamps'
issue, not necessarily to their usage
with specific Albanian postal markings.

CANDIA

Stamps of Lombardy-Venetia
Canceled in black or red brown with
single circle date stamp with post
office name, month and date,
without year

1863   *Perf. 14*

2A1		2s yellow (#15)	450.00	1,500.
2A2		3s green (#16)	400.00	1,650.
2A3		5s rose (#17)	400.00	1,450.
2A4		10s blue (#18)	350.00	1,200.
2A5		15s yel brn (#19)	425.00	1,300.

1864-65   *Perf. 9½*

2A6		2s yellow (#20)	450.00	1,500.
2A7		3s green (#21)	200.00	850.00
2A8		5s rose (#22)	150.00	700.00

2A9		10s blue (#23)	125.00	500.00
2A10		15s yel brn (#24)	160.00	600.00

**Stamps of Austrian Offices in the
Turkish Empire**
Canceled in black or red brown with
single circle date stamp with post
office name, month and date,
without year

1867-83   *Coarse Print*

2A11		2s yellow (#1)	37.50	450.00
2A12		3s green (#2)	57.50	400.00
2A13		5s red (#3)	27.50	140.00
2A14		10s blue (#4)	20.00	92.50
2A15		15s brown (#5)	24.00	100.00
2A16		25s gray lilac (#6)	50.00	700.00
2A17		50s brown (#7)	57.50	3,750.

Fine Print

2A18		2s yellow (#7C)	1,150.	—
2A19		3s green (#7D)	35.00	275.00
2A20		5s red (#7E)	32.50	150.00
2A21		10s blue (#7F)	20.00	87.50
2A22		15s org brown (#7I)	135.00	775.00
2A23		25s gray lilac (#7J)	250.00	5,000.

**Stamps of Austrian Offices in the
Turkish Empire**
Canceled in blue with single circle
date stamp with post office name,
month and date, without year

1867-83   *Coarse Print*

2A24		2s yellow (#1)	125.00	825.00
2A25		3s green (#2)	150.00	750.00
2A26		5s red (#3)	120.00	500.00
2A27		10s blue (#4)	115.00	450.00
2A28		15s brown (#5)	120.00	475.00
2A29		25s gray lilac (#6)	145.00	1,100.
2A30		50s brown (#7)	150.00	4,250.

Fine Print

2A31		2s yellow (#7C)	1,250.	—
2A32		3s green (#7D)	125.00	625.00
2A33		5s red (#7E)	125.00	525.00
2A34		10s blue (#7F)	115.00	450.00
2A35		15s org brown (#7I)	225.00	1,125.
2A36		25s gray lilac (#7J)	350.00	5,500.

**Stamps of Austrian Offices in the
Turkish Empire**
Canceled in black with circular date
stamp with post office name, month
and date, with year date

1867-83   *Coarse Print*

2A37		2s yellow (#1)	37.50	450.00
2A38		3s green (#2)	57.50	400.00
2A39		5s red (#3)	27.50	140.00
2A40		10s blue (#4)	20.00	92.50
2A41		15s brown (#5)	24.00	100.00
2A42		25s gray lilac (#6)	50.00	700.00
2A43		50s brown (#7)	57.50	3,750.

Fine Print

2A44		2s yellow (#7C)	1,150.	—
2A45		3s green (#7D)	35.00	275.00
2A46		5s red (#7E)	32.50	150.00
2A47		10s blue (#7F)	20.00	87.50
2A48		15s org brown (#7I)	135.00	775.00
2A49		25s gray lilac (#7J)	250.00	5,000.

**Stamps of Austrian Offices in the
Turkish Empire**
Canceled in blue with circular date
stamp with post office name, month
and date, with year date

1867-83   *Coarse Print*

2A50		2s yellow (#1)	300.00	1,325.
2A51		3s green (#2)	325.00	1,250.
2A52		5s red (#3)	285.00	1,000.
2A53		10s blue (#4)	275.00	950.00
2A54		15s brown (#5)	280.00	975.00
2A55		25s gray lilac (#6)	300.00	1,575.
2A56		50s brown (#7)	325.00	4,750.

Fine Print

2A57		2s yellow (#7C)	1,400.	—
2A58		3s green (#7D)	300.00	1,125.
2A59		5s red (#7E)	285.00	1,000.
2A60		10s blue (#7F)	275.00	950.00
2A61		15s org brown (#7I)	385.00	1,625.
2A62		25s gray lilac (#7J)	500.00	6,000.

Candia Agencia del Lloyd Austriaco

Stamps of Lombardy-Venetia
Canceled with with oval postmark
with ornaments in blue

1863   *Perf. 14*

2A63		2s yellow (#15)	—	—
2A64		3s green (#16)	—	—
2A65		5s rose (#17)	3,150.	12,000.
2A66		10s blue (#18)	3,100.	11,050.

2A67		15s yel brn (#19)	3,250.	12,000.

CANEA

Stamps of Lombardy-Venetia
Canceled in black or red brown with
straight-line postmark with name of
post office and date in italic letters

1863   *Perf. 14*

2A68		2s yellow (#15)	350.00	1,250.
2A69		3s green (#16)	300.00	1,350.
2A70		5s rose (#17)	300.00	1,100.
2A71		10s blue (#18)	250.00	850.00
2A72		15s yel brn (#19)	325.00	1,000.

1864-65   *Perf. 9½*

2A73		2s yellow (#20)	375.00	1,100.
2A74		3s green (#21)	110.00	475.00
2A75		5s rose (#22)	60.00	325.00
2A76		10s blue (#23)	32.50	120.00
2A77		15s yel brn (#24)	65.00	240.00

**Stamps of Austrian Offices in the
Turkish Empire**
Canceled in black or red brown with
straight-line postmark with name of
post office and date in italic letters

1867-83   *Coarse Print*

2A78		2s yellow (#1)	30.00	425.00
2A79		3s green (#2)	47.50	350.00
2A80		5s red (#3)	18.75	100.00
2A81		10s blue (#4)	11.50	55.00
2A82		15s brown (#5)	15.00	62.50
2A83		25s gray lilac (#6)	40.00	675.00
2A84		50s brown (#7)	47.50	3,800.

Fine Print

2A85		2s yellow (#7C)	1,150.	—
2A86		3s green (#7D)	27.50	225.00
2A87		5s red (#7E)	22.50	115.00
2A88		10s blue (#7F)	11.00	50.00
2A89		15s org brown (#7I)	125.00	725.00
2A90		25s gray lilac (#7J)	235.00	5,000.

Stamps of Lombardy-Venetia
Canceled in blue with straight-line
postmark with name of post office
and date in italic letters

1863   *Perf. 14*

2A91		2s yellow (#15)	450.00	1,500.
2A92		3s green (#16)	400.00	1,650.
2A93		5s rose (#17)	400.00	1,450.
2A94		10s blue (#18)	350.00	1,200.
2A95		15s yel brn (#19)	425.00	1,300.

1864-65   *Perf. 9½*

2A96		2s yellow (#20)	625.00	1,950.
2A97		3s green (#21)	375.00	1,350.
2A98		5s rose (#22)	325.00	1,200.
2A99		10s blue (#23)	300.00	1,000.
2A100		15s yel brn (#24)	325.00	1,100.

**Stamps of Austrian Offices in the
Turkish Empire**
Canceled in blue with straight-line
postmark with name of post office
and date in italic letters

1867-83   *Coarse Print*

2A101		2s yellow (#1)	130.00	825.00
2A102		3s green (#2)	150.00	750.00
2A103		5s red (#3)	120.00	500.00
2A104		10s blue (#4)	115.00	450.00
2A105		15s brown (#5)	120.00	475.00
2A106		25s gray lilac (#6)	145.00	1,100.
2A107		50s brown (#7)	150.00	4,250.

Fine Print

2A108		2s yellow (#7C)	1,250.	—
2A109		3s green (#7D)	130.00	625.00
2A110		5s red (#7E)	125.00	525.00
2A111		10s blue (#7F)	115.00	450.00
2A112		15s org brown (#7I)	225.00	1,125.
2A113		25s gray lilac (#7J)	340.00	5,500.

**Stamps of Austrian Offices in the
Turkish Empire**
Canceled in black with circular date
stamp with post office name, month
and date, with year date

1867-83   *Coarse Print*

2A114		2s yellow (#1)	30.00	425.00
2A115		3s green (#2)	47.50	350.00
2A116		5s red (#3)	18.75	100.00
2A117		10s blue (#4)	1.50	55.00
2A118		15s brown (#5)	15.00	62.50
2A119		25s gray lilac (#6)	40.00	675.00
2A120		50s brown (#7)	47.50	3,800.

Fine Print

2A121		2s yellow (#7C)	1,150.	—
2A122		3s green (#7D)	27.50	225.00
2A123		5s red (#7E)	22.50	115.00
2A124		10s blue (#7F)	11.00	55.00
2A125		15s org brown (#7I)	125.00	725.00

2A126   25s gray lilac
         (#7J)   235.00 *5,000.*

RETTIMO

Stamps of Lombardy-Venetia

Canceled in black with single circle
date stamp with post office name,
month and date, without year

1863   *Perf. 14*
2A127   2s yellow (#15)   450.00 1,500.
2A128   3s green (#16)   400.00 1,650.
2A129   5s rose (#17)   400.00 1,450.
2A130   10s blue (#18)   350.00 1,200.
2A131   15s yel brn (#19)   425.00 1,300.

1864-65   *Perf. 9½*
2A132   2s yellow (#20)   425.00 1,275.
2A133   3s green (#21)   160.00 675.00
2A134   5s rose (#22)   110.00 525.00
2A135   10s blue (#23)   85.00   325.00
2A136   15s yel brn (#24)   115.00 450.00

Stamps of Austrian Offices in the Turkish Empire

Canceled in black or red brown with
single circle date stamp with post
office name, month and date,
without year

1867-83   *Coarse Print*
2A137   2s yellow (#1)   37.50   450.00
2A138   3s green (#2)   57.50   400.00
2A139   5s red (#3)   27.50   140.00
2A140   10s blue (#4)   20.00   92.50
2A141   15s brown (#5)   24.00   100.00
2A142   25s gray lilac (#6) 50.00   700.00
2A143   50s brown (#7)   57.50   *3,850.*

Fine Print
2A144   2s yellow (#7C)   1,150.
2A145   3s green (#7D)   35.00   275.00
2A146   5s red (#7E)   32.50   150.00
2A147   10s blue (#7F)   20.00   87.50
2A148   15s org brown (#7I) 135.00 775.00
2A149   25s gray lilac (#7J) 250.00 *5,000.*

Stamps of Lombardy-Venetia

Canceled in blue with single circle
date stamp with post office name,
month and date, without year

1863   *Perf. 14*
2A150   2s yellow (#15)   575.00 2,000.
2A151   3s green (#16)   525.00 2,200.
2A152   5s rose (#17)   525.00 2,000.
2A153   10s blue (#18)   500.00 1,750.
2A154   15s yel brn (#19)   575.00 1,850.

1864-65   *Perf. 9½*
2A155   2s yellow (#20)   625.00 1,950.
2A156   3s green (#21)   375.00 1,350.
2A157   5s rose (#22)   325.00 1,200.
2A158   10s blue (#23)   300.00 1,000.
2A159   15s yel brn (#24)   325.00 1,100.

Stamps of Austrian Offices in the Turkish Empire

Canceled in blue with single circle
date stamp with post office name,
month and date, without year

1867-83   *Coarse Print*
2A160   2s yellow (#1)   87.50   650.00
2A161   3s green (#2)   110.00 600.00
2A162   5s red (#3)   77.50   340.00
2A163   10s blue (#4)   70.00   300.00
2A164   15s brown (#5)   75.00   300.00
2A165   25s gray lilac (#6) 100.00 900.00
2A166   50s brown (#7)   110.00 *4,000.*

Fine Print
2A167   2s yellow (#7C)   1,200.
2A168   3s green (#7D)   85.00   475.00
2A169   5s red (#7E)   82.50   350.00
2A170   10s blue (#7F)   70.00   290.00
2A171   15s org brown (#7I) 180.00 975.00
2A172   25s gray lilac (#7J) 300.00 *5,250.*

Stamps of Austrian Offices in the Turkish Empire

Canceled in black with single circle
date stamp with post office name,
month and date, with year

1867-83   *Coarse Print*
2A173   2s yellow (#1)   30.00   425.00
2A174   3s green (#2)   47.50   350.00
2A175   5s red (#3)   18.75   100.00
2A176   10s blue (#4)   11.50   55.00
2A177   15s brown (#5)   15.00   62.50
2A178   25s gray lilac (#6) 40.00   675.00
2A179   50s brown (#7)   45.00   *3,800.*

Fine Print
2A180   2s yellow (#7C)   1,150.
2A181   3s green (#7D)   27.50   225.00
2A182   5s red (#7E)   22.50   115.00
2A183   10s blue (#7F)   11.00   50.00
2A184   15s org brown (#7I) 125.00 725.00
2A185   25s gray lilac (#7J) 235.00 *5,000.*

Issued Under Joint Administration of France, Great Britain, Italy and Russia

British Sphere of Administration District of Heraklion (Candia)

A1

A2

Handstamped

1898   **Unwmk.**   *Imperf.*
1   A1 20pa violet   450.00 250.00
     Never hinged   1,250.

1898   **Litho.**   *Perf. 11½*
2   A2 10pa blue   9.00   3.00
     Never hinged   17.50
  a. Horiz. pair, imperf. btwn.
  b. Imperf., pair   275.00
3   A2 20pa green   15.50   3.00
     Never hinged   24.00
  a. Imperf., pair   275.00

1899
4   A2 10pa brown   9.50   3.00
     Never hinged   18.00
  a. Horiz. pair, imperf. btwn.
  b. Imperf., pair   275.00
5   A2 20pa rose   21.00   3.00
     Never hinged   31.00
  a. Imperf., pair   275.00

Used values for Nos. 2-5 are for stamps
canceled by the straight-line "Heraklion" town
postmark. Stamps canceled with any other
postmark used for postal duty are scarce and
worth much more. Other cancellations, values
from: Ag. Thomas, $65; Ag. Myron, $70;
Arkanais, $90; Episkopi, $170; Kastelli, $175;
Moirais, $175; Xarakas, $190; Chersonissos,
$235; and Moxos.
Counterfeits exist of Nos. 1-5.

Russian Sphere of Administration District of Rethymnon

Coat of Arms
A3   A4

1899   **Handstamped**   *Imperf.*
            Laid paper
            No Gum
10   A3 1m green   12.50   6.00
  a. 2m carmine   340.00 190.00
  b. 2m vermilion
  d. 2m violet   —   525.00
  c. 2m pale grayish rose —   775.00
11   A3 2m black   10.00   6.00
  a. Double impression
12   A3 2m rose   350.00 190.00
  a. 2m carmine   340.00 190.00
  b. 2m vermilion
  c. 2m pale grayish rose —   525.00
  d. 2m violet   —   775.00
13   A4 1m blue   80.00   50.00

Wove paper
10E   A3 1m green   10.50   5.50
  f. 1m blue   —   425.00
  g. 1m violet
11E   A3 2m black   10.50   5.25
  f. 2m Double impression 300.00 300.00
12E   A3 2m rose   150.00 100.00
  f. 2m Very thin paper 650.00 400.00
  g. 2m blue   800.00 525.00
  h. 2m lilac   —   —
  i. 2m violet   —   —
13E   A4 1m blue   95.00   47.50
  f. 1m violet   —   —

Quadrille paper
10J   A3 1m green   325.00
  k. 1m violet   —   *700.00*
  l. 1m blue   —   *700.00*
11J   A3 2m black   325.00 80.00
  k. 2m blue   —   *800.00*
  l. 2m brown   —   *1,575.*
  m. 2m violet   800.00 *700.00*
13J   A4 1m violet

Nos. 10-13 normally have a circular control
mark applied in violet or blue on blocks of four
stamps. They also are known without this control mark (errors) and occasionally with the
small round control marks of the next issue, in
blue or violet (probably proofs). They are
sometimes found with pin-perforations. Other
varieties exist.
Counterfeits exist.

Poseidon's Trident — A5a
A5

1899   **Litho.**   *Perf. 11½*
With Control Mark Overprinted in Violet

Without Stars at Sides

14   A5 1m orange   165.00 100.00
      Never hinged   300.00
15   A5 2m orange   165.00 100.00
      Never hinged   300.00
16   A5 1gr orange   165.00 100.00
      Never hinged   300.00
17   A5 1m green   165.00 100.00
      Never hinged   300.00
18   A5 2m green   165.00 100.00
      Never hinged   300.00
19   A5 1gr green   165.00 100.00
      Never hinged   300.00
20   A5 1m yellow   165.00 100.00
      Never hinged   300.00
21   A5 2m yellow   165.00 100.00
      Never hinged   300.00
22   A5 1gr yellow   165.00 100.00
      Never hinged   300.00
23   A5 1m rose   165.00 100.00
      Never hinged   300.00
24   A5 2m rose   165.00 100.00
      Never hinged   300.00
25   A5 1gr rose   165.00 100.00
      Never hinged   300.00
26   A5 1m violet   165.00 100.00
      Never hinged   300.00
27   A5 2m violet   165.00 100.00
      Never hinged   300.00
28   A5 1gr violet   165.00 100.00
      Never hinged   300.00
29   A5 1m blue   165.00 100.00
      Never hinged   300.00
30   A5 2m blue   165.00 100.00
      Never hinged   300.00
31   A5 1gr blue   165.00 100.00
      Never hinged   300.00
32   A5 1m black   1,100. 1,000.
      Never hinged   2,000.
33   A5 2m black   1,100. 1,000.
      Never hinged   2,000.
34   A5 1gr black   1,100. 1,000.
      Never hinged   2,000.

With Stars at Sides

35   A5a 1m blue   37.50   32.50
      Never hinged   75.00
  a. Imperf., pair   325.00
36   A5a 2m blue   15.00   12.50
      Never hinged   30.00
37   A5a 1gr blue   13.50   9.00
      Never hinged   27.00
38   A5a 1m rose   160.00 75.00
      Never hinged   320.00
39   A5a 2m rose   15.00   12.50
      Never hinged   25.00
40   A5a 1gr rose   12.50   9.00
      Never hinged   27.00
  a. Imperf., pair   325.00
41   A5a 1m green   37.50   32.50
      Never hinged   75.00
  a. Imperf., pair   325.00
42   A5a 2m green   15.00   12.50
      Never hinged   30.00
43   A5a 1gr green   12.50   9.00
      Never hinged   25.00
44   A5a 1m violet   37.50   32.50
      Never hinged   75.00
45   A5a 2m violet   15.00   12.50
      Never hinged   30.00
46   A5a 1gr violet   12.50   10.00
      Never hinged   25.00
  a. Horiz. pair, imperf. btwn. 250.00
  b. Vert. pair, imperf. horiz. 150.00
      Nos. 35-46 (12)   383.50 259.50

Nearly all of Nos. 14 to 46 may be found
without control mark, with double control
marks and in various colors.
Used values for Nos. 10-46 are for stamps
with postmarks of Rethymnon. Thirteen other
post offices existed, and stamps with postmarks
other than Rethymnon are scarce and
command significant premiums: Ag. Galini,
$125; Amari, $90; Anogeia, $525; Garazo,
$160; Damasta, $550; Kastelli, $125; Mar-
garitais, $550; Melampes, $375; Pigi, $125;
Roystika, $70; Xenia, $105; Spili, $105;
Fodede, $550.
Counterfeits exist of Nos. 14-46.

Imperf., Pairs

14a   A5 1m orange   900.00
15a   A5 2m orange   900.00
16a   A5 1gr orange   900.00
17a   A5 1m green   900.00
18a   A5 2m green   900.00
19a   A5 1gr green   900.00
20a   A5 1m yellow   900.00
21a   A5 2m yellow   900.00
22a   A5 1gr yellow   900.00
23a   A5 1m rose   900.00
24a   A5 2m rose   900.00
25a   A5 1gr rose   900.00
26a   A5 1m violet   900.00
27a   A5 2m violet   900.00
28a   A5 1gr violet   900.00

29a   A5 1m blue   900.00
30a   A5 2m blue   900.00
31a   A5 1gr blue   900.00

Issued by the Cretan Government

Hermes — A6

Hera — A7

Prince George of Greece — A8

Talos — A9

Minos — A10

St. George and the Dragon — A11

1900, Mar. 1   **Engr.**   *Perf. 14*
50   A6   1 l violet brown   .50   .30
      Never hinged   1.50
51   A7   5 l green   2.00 .30
      Never hinged   6.00
52   A8   10 l red   1.75 .40
      Never hinged   5.25
53   A7   20 l carmine rose 6.50 1.25
      Never hinged   19.50
      Nos. 50-53 (4)   10.75 2.25

See #64-71. For overprints and surcharges
see #54-63, 72-73, 85, 88, 93, 97-99, 108,
111.

Overprinted

Red Overprint

54   A8   25 l blue   1.10   .85
      Never hinged   3.25
55   A6   50 l lilac   2.25   1.25
      Never hinged   6.75
56   A9   1d gray violet   13.00 12.50
      Never hinged   32.50
57   A10 2d brown   37.50 30.00
      Never hinged   —
58   A11 5d green & blk   190.00 190.00
      Never hinged   575.00
      Nos. 54-58 (5)   243.85 234.60

Black Overprint

59   A8   25 l blue   2.25   .85
      Never hinged   6.75
60   A6   50 l lilac   2.25   1.75
      Never hinged   6.75
61   A9   1d gray violet   10.50 6.50
      Never hinged   32.50
  a. Inverted overprint   450.00 450.00
62   A10 2d brown   27.50 22.50
      Never hinged   82.50
63   A11 5d green & blk   105.00 105.00
      Never hinged   300.00
      Nos. 59-63 (5)   147.50 136.60

1901   **Without Overprint**
64   A6   1 l bister   .90   .90
      Never hinged   2.75
65   A7   20 l orange   4.50   .90
      Never hinged   6.25
66   A8   25 l blue   10.50 .80
      Never hinged   32.50
67   A6   50 l lilac   37.50 26.50
      Never hinged   110.00
68   A6   50 l ultra   13.50 12.50
      Never hinged   25.00
69   A9   1d gray violet   42.50 26.50
      Never hinged   125.00
70   A10 2d brown   13.50 11.00
      Never hinged   42.50

71 A11 5d green & blk 16.50 12.50
Never hinged 52.50
Nos. 64-71 (8) 139.40 91.60

No. 64 is a revenue stamp that was used for postage for short periods in 1901 and 1904. Types A6 to A8 in olive yellow, and types A9 to A11 in olive yellow and black are revenue stamps.

See note following No. 53.

Surcharges with the year "1922" on designs A6, A8, A9, A11, A13, A15-A23 and D1 are listed under Greece.

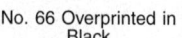

No. 66 Overprinted in Black

1901
72 A8 25 l blue 32.50 1.00
Never hinged 80.00
a. First letter of ovpt. invtd. 500.00 350.00
Never hinged 725.00
b. Inverted overprint 750.00 475.00
Never hinged 1,100.
c. "S" of "PROSORINON" omitted 240.00 100.00
Never hinged 350.00

No. 65 Surcharged in Black

1904, Dec.
73 A7 5 l on 20 l orange 4.50 1.00
Never hinged 6.25
a. Without "5" at right 160.00 160.00

Mycenaean Seal — A12

Britomartis (Cortyna Coin) — A13

Prince George — A14

Kydon and Dog (Cydonia Coin) — A15

Triton (Itanos Coin) — A16

Ariadne (Knossos Coin) — A17

Zeus as Bull Abducting Europa (Cortyna Coin) A18

Palace of Minos Ruins, Knossos A19

Arkadi Monastery and Mt. Ida — A20

1905, Feb. 15
74 A12 2 l dull violet 1.90 .45
Never hinged 4.75
75 A13 5 l yellow grn 2.50 .45
Never hinged 6.25
76 A14 10 l red 2.50 1.00
Never hinged 6.25
77 A15 20 l blue grn 5.75 1.00
Never hinged 17.50
78 A16 25 l ultra 7.25 1.10
Never hinged 22.00
79 A17 50 l yellow brn 8.50 3.50
Never hinged 25.00
80 A18 1d rose car & dp brn 72.50 60.00
Never hinged 220.00
81 A19 3d orange & blk 50.00 40.00
Never hinged 125.00
82 A20 5d ol grn & blk 25.00 21.00
Never hinged 62.50
Nos. 74-82 (9) 175.90 128.50

For overprints see Nos. 86-87, 89, 91-92, 94-95, 104, 106, 109-110, 112-113, 115-120.

The so-called revolutionary stamps of 1905 were issued for sale to collectors and, so far as can be ascertained, were of no postal value.

A. T. A. Zaimis A21

Prince George Landing at Suda A22

1907, Aug. 28
83 A21 25 l blue & blk 42.50 1.25
Never hinged 125.00
84 A22 1d green & blk 12.50 10.00
Never hinged 32.50

Administration under a High Commissioner. For overprints see Nos. 90, 105, 107.

Stamps of 1900-1907 Overprinted in Black

1908, Sept. 21
85 A6 1 l violet brn .65 .50
Never hinged 1.90
86 A12 2 l dull violet .65 .50
Never hinged 1.90
87 A13 5 l yellow grn .65 .50
Never hinged 1.90
88 A8 10 l red 1.25 .85
Never hinged 3.75
89 A15 20 l blue grn 3.25 1.00
Never hinged 9.50
90 A21 25 l blue & blk 8.50 2.50
Never hinged 25.00
91 A17 50 l yellow brn 11.50 4.25
Never hinged 35.00
92 A18 1d rose car & dp brn 95.00 65.00
Never hinged 290.00
93 A10 2d brown 10.50 9.50
Never hinged 32.50
94 A19 3d orange & blk 42.50 35.00
Never hinged 125.00
95 A20 5d ol grn & blk 37.50 32.50
Never hinged 125.00
Nos. 85-95 (11) 211.95 152.10

This overprint exists inverted and double, as well as with incorrect, reversed, misplaced and omitted letters. Similar errors are found on the Postage Due and Official stamps with this overprint.

Hermes by Praxiteles — A23

1908
96 A23 10 l brown red 3.25 .90
a. Pair, one without overprint 200.00 200.00
b. Inverted overprint 85.00 —
c. Double overprint —

Nos. 96 and 114 were not regularly issued without overprint. For overprints see Nos. 103, 114.

No. 53 Surcharged

1909
97 A7 5 l on 20 l car rose 210.00 *210.00*

Forgeries exist of No. 97.

On No. 65
98 A7 5 l on 20 l orange 1.75 1.45
a. Inverted surcharge

Overprinted on Nos. 64, J1

99 A6 1 l bister 4.25 4.25
100 D1 1 l red 1.75 1.75

No. J4 Surcharged

101 D1 2 l on 20 l red 1.75 1.75
b. Inverted surcharge —
c. Second letter of surcharge "D" instead of "P" 50.00 50.00

No. J4 Surcharged

102 D1 2 l on 20 l red 1.60 1.40
a. Double overprint 110.00 110.00

Overprinted in Black

a

b

c

103 A23(a) 10 l brown red 4.00 1.25
Never hinged 9.50
a. Inverted overprint 105.00
Never hinged 270.00
104 A15(a) 20 l blue grn 5.50 1.25
Never hinged 16.00
105 A21(c) 25 l blue & blk 5.75 2.50
Never hinged 16.00
106 A17(a) 50 l yellow brn 9.00 4.50
Never hinged 25.00
107 A22(b) 1d green & blk 13.50 8.00
Never hinged 37.50
108 A10(a) 2d brown 13.50 12.50
Never hinged 37.50
109 A19(b) 3d org & blk 125.00 115.00
Never hinged 375.00
110 A20(b) 5d ol grn & blk 52.50 47.50
Never hinged 160.00
Nos. 103-110 (8) 228.75 192.50

Stamps of 1900-08 Overprinted in Red or Black

1909-10
111 A6 1 l violet brown .45 .25
Never hinged 1.25
112 A12 2 l dull violet .45 .30
Never hinged 1.25
113 A13 5 l yellow green .45 .30
Never hinged 1.25
114 A23 10 l brown red (Bk) .85 .65
Never hinged 1.90
115 A15 20 l blue green 2.00 .70
Never hinged 5.00
116 A16 25 l ultra 3.00 .75
Never hinged 8.25
117 A17 50 l yellow brn 7.00 2.00
Never hinged 19.00
118 A18 1d rose car & dp brn (Bk) 90.00 90.00
Never hinged 270.00
119 A19 3d orange & blk 80.00 80.00
Never hinged 235.00
120 A20 5d ol grn & blk 52.50 52.50
Never hinged 160.00
Nos. 111-120 (10) 236.70 227.45

POSTAGE DUE STAMPS

D1

1901 **Unwmk.** **Litho.** **Perf. 14**
J1 D1 1 l red .30 .30
Never hinged .90
J2 D1 5 l red .60 .40
Never hinged 1.60
J3 D1 10 l red 1.00 .50
Never hinged 2.25
J4 D1 20 l red 1.20 *1.60*
Never hinged 3.25
J5 D1 40 l red 11.00 11.00
Never hinged 32.50
J6 D1 50 l red 11.00 11.00
Never hinged 32.50
J7 D1 1d red 22.50 21.00
Never hinged 62.50
J8 D1 2d red 14.00 12.00
Never hinged 40.00
Nos. J1-J8 (8) 61.60 57.80

For overprints and surcharges see Nos. 100-102, J9-J26.

Surcharged in Black

1901
J9 D1 1d on 1d red 11.00 10.00
Never hinged 32.50

Overprinted in Black

1908

J10	D1	1 l red	.40	.40
		Never hinged	.95	
J11	D1	5 l red	.75	.65
		Never hinged	1.90	
J12	D1	10 l red	.75	.75
		Never hinged	1.90	
J13	D1	20 l red	2.00	2.00
		Never hinged	4.75	
J14	D1	40 l red	8.00	7.50
		Never hinged	22.50	
J15	D1	50 l red	10.00	9.00
		Never hinged	29.00	
J16	D1	1 d red	475.00	475.00
		Never hinged	1,900.	
J17	D1	1 d on 1d red	11.00	11.00
		Never hinged	32.50	
J18	D1	2 d red	18.50	12.00
		Never hinged	50.00	
		Nos. J10-J18 (9)	526.40	518.30

Nos. J10-J18 exist with inverted overprint. See note after No. 95.
Counterfeits of No. J16 exist.

Overprinted in Black

1910

J19	D1	1 l red	.60	.30
		Never hinged	1.25	
J20	D1	5 l red	1.25	.35
		Never hinged	3.25	
J21	D1	10 l red	1.10	.50
		Never hinged	3.25	
J22	D1	20 l red	3.25	1.75
		Never hinged	8.25	
J23	D1	40 l red	10.50	6.00
		Never hinged	32.50	
J24	D1	50 l red	16.00	11.00
		Never hinged	47.50	
J25	D1	1 d red	27.50	27.50
		Never hinged	80.00	
J26	D1	2 d red	27.50	27.50
		Never hinged	80.00	
		Nos. J19-J26 (8)	87.70	74.90

OFFICIAL STAMPS

O1   O2

Unwmk.
1908, Jan. 14   Litho.   Perf. 14

O1	O1	10 l dull claret	21.00	1.25
		Never hinged	62.50	
O2	O2	30 l blue	42.50	1.25
		Never hinged	125.00	

Nos. O1-O2 exist imperf.

Nos. O1-O2
Overprinted

O3	O1	10 l dull claret	16.00	1.25
		Never hinged	47.50	
O4	O2	30 l blue	32.50	1.25
		Never hinged	95.00	

See note after No. 95.

Nos. O1-O2
Overprinted

1910

O5	O1	10 l dull claret	2.25	1.25
		Never hinged	4.25	
O6	O2	30 l blue	2.25	1.25
		Never hinged	4.25	

Nos. O5-O6 remained in use until 1922, nine years after union with Greece.

CUBA
ˈkyü-bə

LOCATION — The largest island of the West Indies; south of Florida
GOVT. — Republic
AREA — 44,206 sq. mi.
POP. — 6,743,000 (est. 1960)
CAPITAL — Havana

Formerly a Spanish possession, Cuba made several unsuccessful attempts to gain her freedom, which finally led to the intervention of the US in 1898. In that year under the Treaty of Paris, Spain relinquished the island to the US in trust for its inhabitants. In 1902 a republic was established and the Cuban Congress took over the government from the military authorities.

8 Reales Plata = 1 Peso
100 Centesimos = 1 Escudo or Peseta (1867)
1000 Milesimas = 100 Centavos = 1 Peso

> **Catalogue values for unused stamps in this country are for Never Hinged items, beginning with Scott RA1 in the postal tax section.**

> Pen cancellations are common on the earlier stamps of Cuba. Stamps so canceled sell for very much less than those with postmark cancellations.

Watermarks

Wmk. 104 —
Loops

Loops from different rows may or may not be directly opposite each other.

Wmk. 105 —   Wmk. 106 —
Crossed Lines   Star

Wmk. 229 —
Wavy Lines

FORERUNNERS

> Crowned Circle handstamp types are pictured in the Crowned Circle Handstamps and Great Britain Used Abroad section.

BRITISH POST OFFICES IN CUBA

Havana

British P.O. opened 1762; stamps supplied 1865; closed May 30, 1877

Pre-Stamp Postal Markings

1841

A1	Crowned Circle handstamp Type II, on cover, inscribed "PAID AT HAVANA"		1,150.
A2	Crowned Circle handstamp Type IV, on cover, inscribed "PAID AT HAVANA" in black		1,150.
A3	Crowned Circle handstamp Type V, on cover, inscribed "PAID AT HAVANA"		950.00

Earliest known uses: A1, 11/13/41; A2, 1848; A3, 7/14/48

Stamps of Great Britain, Canceled C58, or with Circular Date Stamp

1865-77

A4	½p rose red (#58 P 6, 12), value from		85.00
A5	1p rose red (#33, P 86, 90, 93, 115, 120, 123, 144, 146, 171, 174, 208), value from		70.00
A6	2p blue (#29, P 9)		85.00
A7	2p blue (#30, P 14, 15), value from		90.00
A8	3p rose (#49, P 4)		160.00
A9	3p rose (#61, P 18, 19)		—
A10	4p vermilion (#43, P 7, 8, 10-14), value from		75.00
A11	4p vermilion (#69, P 15)		350.00
A12	6p lilac (#45, P 5)		—
A13	6p gray (#62, P 15)		—
A14	8p orange (#73)		—
A15	9p bister (#52)		310.00
A16	10p red brown (#53)		350.00
A17	1sh green (#48, P 4)		185.00
A18	1sh green (#54, P 4, 5), value from		75.00
	Plate 7		125.00
A19	1sh green (#64, P 10, 12, 13), value from		105.00
A20	2sh blue (#55)		275.00
A21	5sh rose (#57, P 1)		600.00
	Plate 2		750.00
a.	5sh pale rose (#57a, P 1)		600.00
	Plate 2		750.00

St. Jago de Cuba

British P.O. opened 1841; stamps supplied 1866; closed May 30, 1877

Pre-Stamp Postal Markings

1841

A22	Crowned Circle handstamp Type III, on cover, inscribed "PAID AT ST JAGO-DE-CUBA" in red	7,000.

Earliest known use: 12/15/41.

Stamps of Great Britain, Canceled C88

1866-77

A23	½p rose red (#58 P 4, 6, 14)		—
A24	1p rose red (#33, P 100, 105, 106, 109, 111, 120, 123, 138, 144, 146-148, 171, 208) value from		175.00
A25	1½p lake red (#32 P 3)		—
A26	2p blue (#29, P 13, 14)		—
A27	2p blue (#30, P 13, 14)		175.00
A28	3p rose (#49, P 5)		175.00
A29	4p vermilion (#43, P 9-14) value from		185.00
A30	4p vermilion (#69, P 15)		625.00
A31	6p violet (#51, P 6, 8, 9) value from		425.00
A32	6p pale buff (#59b, P 11)		—
A33	9p straw (#46)		—
A34	9p bister (#52)		—
A35	10p red brown (#53)		575.00
A36	1sh green (#54, P 4-6) value from		375.00
A37	1sh green (#64, P 9-13)		—
A38	2sh blue (#55)		425.00
A39	5sh rose (#57)		—

Issued under Spanish Dominion

Used also in Puerto Rico: Nos. 1-3, 9-14, 17-21, 32-34, 35A-37, 39-41, 43-45, 47-49, 51-53, 55-57.
Used also in the Philippines: Nos. 2-3.
Identifiable cancellations of those countries will increase the value of the stamps.

Queen Isabella II — A1

Blue Paper

1855   Typo.   Wmk. 104   Imperf.

1	A1	½r p blue green	125.00	6.00
		On cover		27.50
a.		½r p blackish green	125.00	11.00
		On cover		32.50
2	A1	1r p gray green	100.00	4.00
		On cover		25.00
3	A1	2r p carmine	650.00	12.00
		On cover		100.00
4	A1	2r p orange red	1,100.	19.00
		On cover		160.00
a.		2r p vermilion	1,200.	20.00
		On cover		175.00
		Nos. 1-4 (4)	1,975.	41.00

See Nos. 9-14. For surcharges see Nos. 5-8, 15.

> Counterfeit surcharges are plentiful.

Nos. 3-4 Surcharged

1855-56

5	A1	¼r p on 2r p car	1,200.	210.00
		On cover		525.00
a.		Without fraction bar	2,200.	1,200.
6	A1	¼r p on 2r p org red	—	675.00
		On cover		2,200.
a.		Without fraction bar	—	2,200.

Surcharged

7	A1	¼r p on 2r p car	800.00	200.00
		On cover		800.00
a.		Without fraction bar	2,250.	1,250
8	A1	¼r p on 2r p org red	1,200.	375.00
		On cover		1,200.
a.		Without fraction bar	—	2,200.

The "Y ¼" surcharge met the "Ynterior" rate for delivery within the city of Havana.

Rough Yellowish Paper

1856   **Wmk. 105**

9	A1 ½ r p yellow grn	6.75	.85
	On cover		7.50
a.	½ r p greenish blue	6.75	.80
	On cover		9.00
b.	½ r p olive green	6.50	.75
	On cover		9.00
10	A1 1 r p green	1,200.	18.00
	On cover		29.00
a.	1 r p emerald	1,400.	50.00
	On cover		45.00
b.	1 r p olive green	800.00	18.00
	On cover		30.00
11	A1 2 r p orange red	500.00	16.00
	On cover		175.00

White Smooth Paper

1857   **Unwmk.**

12	A1 ½ r p blue	3.50	.80
	On cover		5.00
a.	½ r p ultramarine	8.00	1.25
	On cover		17.50
b.	½ r p dark blue	4.00	1.00
	On cover		10.00
c.	½ r p milky blue (cleaned plate)	5.75	1.00
	On cover		12.50
13	A1 1 r p gray green	3.25	.80
	On cover		8.00
a.	1 r p pale yellow green	3.00	3.25
	On cover		10.00
b.	1 r p dark green	3.25	.70
	On cover		13.50
c.	1 r p pale green (cleaned plate)	6.50	1.25
14	A1 2 r p dull rose	18.50	3.25
	On cover		100.00
a.	2 r p carmine	20.00	3.75
	On cover		125.00
b.	2 r p orange red	18.50	3.25
	On cover		75.00
	Nos. 12-14 (3)	25.25	4.85

Surcharged

1860

15	A1 ¼ r p on 2 r p dl rose	240.00	85.00
	On cover		325.00
a.	1 of ¼ inverted	350.00	150.00
b.	"1 ⅖" instead of "1 ¼"		—

Queen Isabella II
A2   A3

1862-64   *Imperf.*

16	A2 ¼ r p black	16.00	30.00
	On cover		160.00
17	A3 ¼ r p blk, *buff* ('64)	18.00	30.00
	On cover		—
18	A3 ½ r p green ('64)	4.75	.80
	On cover		8.00
19	A3 ½ r p grn, *pale rose* ('64)	11.00	2.00
	On cover		15.00
a.	½ r p grn, *rose lilac*	15.00	2.00
	On cover		15.00
20	A3 1 r p bl, *sal* ('64)	4.75	1.00
	On cover		10.00
a.	Diagonal half used as ½ r p on cover		125.00
21	A3 2 r p ver, *buff* ('64)	25.00	6.00
	On cover		80.00
a.	2 r p red, *buff*	30.00	6.75
	Nos. 16-21 (6)	79.50	69.80

No. 17 Overprinted in Black

1866

22	A3 ¼ r p black, *buff*	80.00	100.00
	On cover		600.00

Exists with handstamped "1866."

A5   A6

1866

23	A5 5c dull violet	57.50	50.00
	On cover		47.50
24	A5 10c blue	6.50	1.00
	On cover		7.50
25	A5 20c green	3.50	1.00
	On cover		11.50
			150.00
26	A5 40c rose	22.50	14.00
	On cover		40.00
a.	40c deep rose	13.50	7.50
	On cover		50.00
	Nos. 23-26 (4)	90.00	66.00

For the Type A5 20c in dull lilac, see Spain No. 87.

Stamps Dated "1867"

1867   *Perf. 14*

27	A5 5c dull violet	55.00	30.00
	On cover		100.00
28	A5 10c blue	29.00	1.40
	On cover		10.00
a.	Imperf., pair	110.00	6.50
b.	Diagonal half used as 5c on cover		140.00
29	A5 20c green	18.00	1.90
	On cover		17.50
a.	Imperf., pair	110.00	70.00
b.	Diag. half used as 10c on cover		150.00
30	A5 40c rose	18.00	15.00
	On cover		—
	Nos. 27-30 (4)	120.00	48.30

1868   **Stamps Dated "1868"**

31	A6 5c dull violet	18.50	9.50
	On cover		30.00
32	A6 10c blue	4.25	1.75
a.	Diagonal half used as 5c on cover		200.00
33	A6 20c green	6.00	3.00
a.	Diag. half used as 10c on cover		200.00
b.	20c yellow green	6.00	3.00
	On cover		18.50
c.	As "b," diag. half used as 10c on cover		140.00
34	A6 40c rose	15.50	8.00
	On cover		80.00
a.	Diag. half used as 20c on cover		240.00
b.	40c carmine rose	16.00	8.25
	On cover		67.50
c.	As "b," diag. half used as 10c on cover		175.00
	Nos. 31-34 (4)	44.25	22.25

Nos. 31-34 Overprinted in Black

1868

35	A6 5c dull violet	75.00	32.50
	On cover		—
35A	A6 10c blue	75.00	32.50
	On cover		—
b.	Diag. half used as 5c on cover		*275.00*
36	A6 20c green	75.00	32.50
	On cover		—
a.	Diag. half used as 10c on cover		—
37	A6 40c rose	75.00	32.50
	Nos. 35-37 (4)	300.00	130.00

1869   **Stamps Dated "1869"**

38	A6 5c rose	67.50	25.00
	On cover		225.00
39	A6 10c red brown	5.00	1.75
	On cover		12.50
a.	Diagonal half used as 5c on cover		140.00
40	A6 20c orange	8.00	2.25
	On cover		20.00
41	A6 40c dull violet	50.00	20.00
	On cover		—
	Nos. 38-41 (4)	130.50	49.00

Nos. 38-41 Ovptd. Like Nos. 35-37

42	A6 5c rose	165.00	42.50
	On cover		200.00
43	A6 10c red brown	52.50	32.50
	On cover		200.00
a.	Diagonal half used as 5c on cover		—
44	A6 20c orange	45.00	32.50
	On cover		200.00
a.	Diag. half used as 10c on cover		—
45	A6 40c dull violet	72.50	32.50
	Nos. 42-45 (4)	335.00	140.00

"Espana"
A8   A9

1870   *Perf. 14*

46	A8 5c blue	300.00	90.00
	On cover		325.00
47	A8 10c green	2.75	.85
	On cover		12.50
a.	Diagonal half used as 5c on cover		200.00
48	A8 20c red brown	2.75	.85
	On cover		20.00
a.	Diag. half used as 10c on cover		240.00
49	A8 40c rose	250.00	50.00
	On cover		350.00

1871

50	A9 12c red lilac	23.00	10.00
	On cover		75.00
51	A9 25c ultra	2.75	.85
a.	Imperf., pair	85.00	85.00
	On cover		12.50
b.	Diagonal half used as 12c on cover		200.00
52	A9 50c gray green	2.75	.85
	On cover		20.00
a.	Imperf., pair	47.50	32.50
b.	Diagonal half used as 25c on cover		200.00
53	A9 1p yel brown	50.00	9.00
	On cover		120.00
a.	Imperf., pair	100.00	100.00
	Nos. 50-53 (4)	78.50	20.70

King Amadeo — A10

1873   *Perf. 14*

54	A10 12½c dark green	35.00	25.00
	On cover		110.00
55	A10 25c gray	2.25	.85
	On cover		12.50
a.	Diagonal half used as 12½c on cover		95.00
b.	25c lilac	6.00	1.10
c.	As "b," half used as 12½c on cover		110.00
56	A10 50c brown	1.60	.80
a.	Imperf., pair	55.00	—
b.	Half used as 25c on cover		90.00
57	A10 1p red brown	350.00	52.50
	On cover		700.00
a.	Diagonal half used as 50c on cover		275.00

"España"   Coat of Arms
A11   A12

1874

58	A11 12½c brown	22.50	18.50
	On cover		65.00
a.	Half used as 5c on cover		140.00
59	A11 25c ultra	.90	.55
	On cover		10.00
a.	Diagonal half used as 12½c on cover		100.00
b.	25c blue	1.75	.75
	On cover		7.50
c.	As "b," diagonal half used as 12½c on cover		100.00
d.	25c blue lilac	1.75	.75
	On cover		12.50
e.	As "d," diagonal half used as 12½c on cover		100.00
60	A11 50c dp violet	1.60	.80
a.	Diagonal half used as 25c on cover		110.00
61	A11 50c gray	1.60	.80
	On cover		17.50
a.	Diagonal half used as 25c on cover		110.00
62	A11 1p carmine	325.00	60.00
a.	Imperf., pair	600.00	210.00
	Nos. 58-62 (5)	351.60	80.65

Examples of Nos. 61, 63-65, 67-87 with fine impressions in slightly different colors are proofs.

1875

63	A12 12½c lt violet	1.25	.90
	On cover		65.00
a.	Imperf., pair	75.00	

64	A12 25c ultra	.65	.30
	On cover		10.00
a.	Imperf., pair	75.00	
b.	Diagonal half used as 12½c on cover		—
65	A12 50c blue green	.75	.35
	On cover		17.50
a.	Imperf., pair	75.00	
b.	Diag. half used as 25c on cover		80.00
66	A12 1p brown	11.50	4.75
b.	Diag. half used as 50c on cover		125.00
	Nos. 63-66 (4)	14.15	6.30

King Alfonso XII
A13   A14

1876

67	A13 12½c green	3.50	1.50
	On cover		45.00
a.	12½c emerald green	3.75	2.00
	On cover		55.00
b.	12½c yellow green	1.50	1.60
	On cover		40.00
68	A13 25c gray	4.00	.35
	On cover		10.00
a.	Diagonal half used as 12½c on cover		90.00
b.	25c pale violet	4.50	.30
	On cover		10.00
d.	25c bluish gray	5.00	.35
	On cover		12.50
69	A13 50c ultra	2.00	.40
	On cover		10.00
a.	Imperf., pair	20.00	16.00
b.	Diag. half used as 25c on cover		75.00
70	A13 1p black	15.00	10.00
a.	Imperf., pair	40.00	40.00
b.	Diag. half used as 50c on cover		125.00
	Nos. 67-70 (4)	24.50	12.25

1877

71	A14 10c lt green	24.00	
72	A14 12½c gray	5.75	2.50
	On cover		17.50
a.	Imperf., pair	32.50	
b.	Diagonal half used on cover		62.50
73	A14 25c dk green	.55	.50
	On cover		10.00
a.	Imperf., pair	32.50	
b.	Diagonal half used as 12½c on cover		62.50
74	A14 50c black	.55	.50
	On cover		10.00
a.	Imperf., pair	32.50	
b.	Half used as 25c on cover		72.50
75	A14 1p brown	24.00	12.00
	On cover		900.00
	Nos. 71-75 (5)	54.85	

No. 71 was not placed in use.

1878   **Stamps Dated "1878"**

76	A14 5c blue	.80	.45
	On cover		20.00
77	A14 10c black	100.00	
78	A14 12½c brown bis	5.00	1.75
	On cover		17.50
a.	12½c olive brown	5.50	1.50
	On cover		22.50
b.	Diagonal half used on cover		65.00
79	A14 25c yel green	.40	.25
	On cover		10.00
b.	No. 79 or 79c, diagonal half used as 12½c on cover		60.00
c.	25c deep green	.40	.25
	On cover		10.00
80	A14 50c dk blue grn	.60	.25
	On cover		10.00
b.	Diagonal half used as 25c on cover		60.00
81	A14 1p carmine	16.00	6.50
b.	1p rose	16.00	6.50
c.	Diagonal half used as 50c on cover		—
	Nos. 76-81 (6)	122.80	9.20

No. 77 was not placed in use.

Imperf., Pairs

76a	A14 5c blue	335.00	35.00
77a	A14 10c black	210.00	
78b	A14 12½c brown bister	35.00	35.00
79a	A14 25c deep green	35.00	35.00
80a	A14 50c dk blue green	160.00	
81a	A14 1p carmine	110.00	

1879   **Stamps Dated "1879"**

82	A14 5c slate black	.60	.25
	On cover		25.00
83	A14 10c orange	150.00	75.00
84	A14 12½c rose	.60	.25
	On cover		20.00
85	A14 25c ultra	.50	.25
	On cover		12.50
a.	Diagonal half used as 12½c on cover		80.00
b.	Imperf., pair	45.00	32.50
86	A14 50c gray	.50	.25
	On cover		12.50
a.	Diag. half used as 25c on cover		80.00
87	A14 1p olive bister	17.00	9.50
	Nos. 82-87 (6)	169.20	85.50

A15 A16

1880

88	A15	5c green	.40	.25
		On cover		17.50
a.		5c dark green	.25	.25
89	A15	10c lake	90.00	
a.		Double impression of frame and lettering	200.00	
90	A15	12½c gray	.40	.25
		On cover		10.00
91	A15	25c gray blue	.40	.25
		On cover		10.00
a.		Diagonal half used as 12½c on cover		75.00
b.		Deformed "5"	7.75	7.50
92	A15	50c brown	.50	.25
		On cover		10.00
a.		Diagonal half used as 25c on cover		65.00
93	A15	1p yellow brn	5.50	2.50
		On cover		90.00
a.		Diagonal half used as 50c on cover		90.00
		Nos. 88-93 (6)	97.20	3.50

No. 89 was not placed in use.

1881

94	A16	1c green	.30	.25
		On cover		10.00
95	A16	2c lake	45.00	
96	A16	2½c olive bister	.50	.30
		On cover		10.00
97	A16	5c gray blue	.30	.25
		On cover		10.00
a.		Diag. half used as 2½c on cover		55.00
98	A16	10c yellow brown	.40	.25
		On cover		10.00
a.		Diagonal half used as 5c on cover		55.00
b.		10c pale brown	.50	.25
		On cover		7.50
c.		As "b," diagonal half used as 5c on cover		55.00
99	A16	20c dark brown	5.00	4.00
		On cover		25.00
		Nos. 94-99 (6)	51.50	5.05

No. 95 was not placed in use.

A17

1882

100	A17	1c green	.50	.35
a.		Diag. half used as ½c on cover		50.00
101	A17	2c lake	2.40	.35
		On cover		25.00
a.		Diag. half used as 1c on cover		50.00
b.		2c rose	4.25	1.10
		On cover		22.50
c.		As "b," diag. half used as 1c on cover		50.00
102	A17	2½c dk brown	5.25	1.75
		On cover		10.00
a.		Diag. half used as 1c on cover		50.00
b.		2½c dk olive brown	4.00	1.75
		On cover		7.50
103	A17	5c gray blue	2.40	.50
		On cover		10.00
a.		Diag. half used as 2½c on cover		55.00
b.		5c dark gray blue	3.50	.90
		On cover		7.50
c.		As "b," diag. half used as 2½c on cover		55.00
104	A17	10c olive bister	.65	.25
		On cover		10.00
a.		Diag. half used as 5c on cover		50.00
105	A17	20c red brown	130.00	27.50
a.		Diag. half used as 10c on cover		110.00
		Nos. 100-105 (6)	141.20	30.70

See Nos. 121-131. For surcharges see Nos. 106-120.

Issue of 1882 Surcharged or Overprinted in Black, Blue or Red

a b

---

c d

e

1883

			Type "a"	
106	A17	5 on 5c (R)	2.50	1.50
		On cover		90.00
a.		Triple surcharge		
b.		Double surcharge	22.50	22.50
c.		Inverted surcharge	29.00	29.00
d.		Without "5" in surcharge	16.50	16.50
e.		Dbl. surch., types "a" & "d"		
107	A17	10 on 10c (Bl)	3.00	1.50
		On cover		140.00
a.		Inverted surcharge	26.00	26.00
b.		Double surcharge	26.00	26.00
108	A17	20 on 20c	40.00	30.00
a.		"10" instead of "20"	75.00	75.00
b.		Double surcharge		

			Type "b"	
109	A17	5 on 5c (R)	2.50	1.50
		On cover		75.00
a.		Inverted surcharge	26.00	26.00
b.		Double surcharge	22.50	22.50
110	A17	10 on 10c (Bl)	9.00	4.00
		On cover		125.00
a.		Inverted surcharge	32.00	32.00
b.		Double surcharge		
111	A17	20 on 20c	100.00	60.00
a.		Double surcharge		
b.		Dbl. surch., types "b" & "c"		

			Type "c"	
112	A17	5 on 5c (R)	2.10	1.40
		On cover		75.00
a.		Inverted surcharge	32.00	32.00
b.		Dbl. surch., types "c" & "d"		
113	A17	10 on 10c (Bl)	9.00	4.00
		On cover		125.00
a.		Inverted surcharge	37.50	37.50
b.		Double surcharge	37.50	37.50
114	A17	20 on 20c	60.00	30.00
a.		"10" instead of "20"	95.00	75.00
b.		Double surcharge	95.00	95.00
c.		Dbl. surch., types "a" & "c"		

			Type "d"	
115	A17	5 on 5c (R)	2.50	1.50
		On cover		75.00
a.		Inverted surcharge	32.00	32.00
b.		Double surcharge	26.00	26.00
116	A17	10 on 10c (Bl)	3.75	2.25
		On cover		125.00
a.		Inverted surcharge	32.00	32.00
b.		Double surcharge	29.00	29.00
117	A17	20 on 20c	80.00	50.00
		On cover		
a.		Dbl. surch., types "a" & "d"		

			Type "e"	
118	A17	5c gray blue (R)	3.00	2.00
		On cover		125.00
a.		Double overprint	35.00	35.00
119	A17	10c olive bis (Bl)	11.00	5.50
		On cover		200.00
a.		Double overprint	37.50	37.50
120	A17	20c red brown	250.00	150.00
a.		Double overprint	300.00	250.00
		Nos. 106-120 (15)	578.35	345.15

Handstamped overprints and surcharges are counterfeits.

Numerous other varieties exist.

Type of 1882

Original 1st retouch 2nd retouch

The differences between the stamps of 1882 and the various retouches are as follows:

Original state: The medallion is surrounded by a heavy line of color of nearly even thickness, touching the horizontal line below the word "Cuba" (or "Filipinas," "Puerto Rico," as the case may be); the opening in the hair above the temple is narrow and pointed.

1st retouch: The line around the medallion is thin, except at the upper right, and does not touch the horizontal line above it; the opening in the hair is slightly wider and a trifle rounded; the lock of hair above the forehead is shaped like a broad "V" and ends in a point; there is a faint white line below it, which is not found on the stamps in the original state. Owing to wear

---

of the plate the shape of the lock of hair and the width of the white line below it vary.

2nd retouch: The opening in the hair forms a semi-circle; the lock above the forehead is nearly straight, having only a slight wave, and the white line is much broader than before.

1883-86

121	A17	1c grn, 2nd retouch	110.00	45.00
122	A17	2½c olive bister	.40	.25
		On cover		10.00
124	A17	2½c violet	.40	.25
		On cover		12.50
a.		2½c red lilac ('85)	.85	.50
		On cover		6.00
b.		2½c ultramarine	95.00	
125	A17	5c gray bl, 1st retouch	2.25	.30
		On cover		6.00
a.		Diag. half used as 2½c on cover		45.00
126	A17	5c gray bl, 2nd retouch	22.50	2.50
		On cover		12.00
a.		Diag. half used as 2½c on cover		50.00
127	A17	10c brn, 1st retouch	2.75	.50
		On cover		10.00
a.		Diagonal half used as 5c on cover		40.00
b.		10c reddish brn, ist retouch	2.50	.45
		On cover		6.00
c.		Imperf, pair	300.00	
128	A17	20c olive bister	13.00	2.75
		On cover		17.50
		Nos. 121-128 (7)	151.30	51.55

1888

129	A17	2½c red brown	1.60	.90
		On cover		10.00
a.		2½c pale brn, 1st retouch	1.40	.80
		On cover		10.00
130	A17	10c blue	1.25	.80
		On cover		10.00
a.		Diagonal half used as 5c on cover		175.00
131	A17	20c brnsh gray	12.00	4.00
		On cover		25.00
		Nos. 129-131 (3)	14.85	5.70

King Alfonso XIII
A18 A19

1890-97

132	A18	1c gray brown	20.00	6.50
		On cover		13.50
133	A18	1c ol gray ('91)	9.50	3.50
		On cover		17.50
134	A18	1c ultra ('94)	4.00	.40
		On cover		12.50
135	A18	1c dk vio ('96)	1.10	.30
		On cover		6.00
136	A18	2c slate blue	8.75	2.50
		On cover		12.50
137	A18	2c lilac brn ('91)	1.75	.55
		On cover		13.50
138	A18	2c rose ('94)	45.00	6.00
		On cover		13.50
139	A18	2c claret ('96)	9.50	.85
		On cover		10.00
140	A18	2½c emerald	12.50	4.50
		On cover		13.50
141	A18	2½c salmon ('91)	57.50	12.00
		On cover		13.50
142	A18	2½c lilac ('94)	3.75	.30
		On cover		12.50
143	A18	2½c rose ('96)	.80	.25
		On cover		10.00
144	A18	5c olive gray	.95	.70
		On cover		12.50
b.		Diagonal half used as 2½c on cover		55.00
145	A18	5c emerald ('91)	1.00	.50
		On cover		12.50
b.		Diagonal half used as 2½c on cover		55.00
146	A18	5c sl blue ('96)	.90	.25
		On cover		5.00
b.		Diagonal half used as 2½c on cover		55.00
147	A18	10c brown violet	12.00	.85
		On cover		
b.		Diagonal half used as 5c on cover		55.00
148	A18	10c claret ('91)	2.25	.50
		On cover		17.50
b.		Diagonal half used as 5c on cover		55.00
149	A18	10c emerald ('96)	2.75	.25
		On cover		12.50
150	A18	20c dk violet	1.00	.65
151	A18	20c ultra ('91)	25.00	8.00
152	A18	20c red brn ('94)	40.00	11.00
		On cover		45.00
153	A18	20c violet ('96)	17.50	5.50
b.		Diagonal half used as 10c on cover		55.00
154	A18	40c orange brn ('97)	37.50	15.00
		On cover		

155	A18	80c lilac brn ('97)	75.00	22.50
		On cover		22.50
		Nos. 132-155 (24)	390.00	101.35

Imperf., Pairs

134a	A18	1c ultramarine	85.00
135a	A18	1c dark violet	90.00
138a	A18	2c rose	85.00
139a	A18	2c claret	90.00
142a	A18	2½c lilac	85.00
143a	A18	2½c rose	95.00
145a	A18	5c emerald	85.00
146a	A18	5c slate blue	85.00
148a	A18	10c claret	80.00
149a	A18	10c emerald	95.00
152a	A18	20c red brown	125.00
153a	A18	20c violet	125.00
154a	A18	40c orange brown	200.00
155a	A18	80c red brown	300.00

1898

156	A19	1m orange brn	.25	.25
157	A19	2m orange brn	.25	.25
158	A19	3m orange brn	.25	.25
159	A19	4m orange brn	5.25	1.60
160	A19	5m orange brn	.30	.25
161	A19	1c black vio	.30	.25
162	A19	2c dk blue grn	.30	.25
163	A19	3c dk brown	.30	.25
164	A19	4c orange	15.50	4.00
165	A19	5c car rose	1.10	.25
166	A19	6c dk blue	.35	.25
167	A19	8c gray brown	1.10	.40
168	A19	10c vermilion	1.10	.40
169	A19	15c slate green	5.25	.40
170	A19	20c maroon	.70	.25
171	A19	40c dark lilac	2.50	.40
172	A19	60c black	2.75	.40
173	A19	80c red brown	16.50	8.00
174	A19	1p yel green	16.50	8.00
175	A19	2p slate blue	32.50	8.00
		Nos. 156-175 (20)	103.05	34.10

Nos. 156-160 were issued for use on newspapers.

Nos. 156-175 exist imperf. Value, unused pairs, $7,500. Only one set of pairs is currently known.

For surcharges see Nos. 176-189C, 196-200.

Issued under Administration of the United States
Puerto Principe Issue
Issues of Cuba of 1898 and 1896 Surcharged

a b

1898-99

176	(a)	1c on 1m org brn	50.00	30.00
177	(b)	1c on 1m org brn	45.00	35.00
a.		Broken figure "1"	75.00	65.00
b.		Inverted surcharge		200.00
d.		As "a," inverted		250.00

c d

178	(c)	2c on 2m org brn	24.00	20.00
a.		Inverted surcharge	250.00	50.00
179	(d)	2c on 2m org brn	40.00	35.00
a.		Inverted surcharge	350.00	100.00

k l

179B	(k)	3c on 1m org brn	300.	175.
c.		Double surcharge	1,500.	750.

An unused example is known with "cents" omitted.

179D	(l)	3c on 1m org brn	1,500.	750.
e.		Double surcharge		

e

f

179F (e) 3c on 2m org brn *1,500.*

Value is for example with minor faults.

179G (f) 3c on 2m org brn — *2,000.*

Value is for example with minor faults.

180 (e) 3c on 3m org brn 30. *30.*
 a. Inverted surcharge *110.*
181 (f) 3c on 3m org brn 75. 75.
 a. Inverted surcharge *200.*

g

h

i

j

182 (g) 5c on 1m org brn 700. 200.
 a. Inverted surcharge *500.*
183 (h) 5c on 1m org brn *1,300.* *500.*
 a. Inverted surcharge *700.*
184 (g) 5c on 2m org brn 750. 275.
185 (h) 5c on 2m org brn 1,500. 500.
186 (g) 5c on 3m org brn 650. 175.
 a. Inverted surcharge 1,200. 700.
187 (h) 5c on 3m org brn 400.
 a. Inverted surcharge 1,000.
188 (g) 5c on 5m org brn 100. 75.
 a. Inverted surcharge 400. 200.
 b. Double surcharge — —
189 (h) 5c on 5m org brn 350. 250.
 a. Inverted surcharge 425.
 b. Double surcharge — —

The 2nd printing of Nos. 188-189 has shiny ink. Values are for the 1st printing.

189C (i) 5c on 5m org brn *7,500.*

Black Surcharge on No. P25

190 (g) 5c on ½m bl grn 250. 75.
 a. Inverted surcharge 500. 150.
 b. Pair, one without surcharge 500.

Value for 190b is for pair with unsurcharged stamp at right. Also exists with unsurcharged stamp at left.

191 (h) 5c on ½m bl grn 300. 90.
 a. Inverted surcharge 200.
192 (i) 5c on ½m bl grn 550. 200.
 a. Dbl. surch., one diagonal *11,500.*
193 (j) 5c on ½m bl grn 800. 300.

Red Surcharge on No. 161

196 (k) 3c on 1c blk vio 65. 35.
 a. Inverted surcharge 325.
197 (l) 3c on 1c blk vio 125. 55.
 a. Inverted surcharge 400.
198 (i) 5c on 1c blk vio 25. 30.
 a. Inverted surcharge 125.
 b. Surcharge vert. reading up *3,500.*
 c. Double surcharge *400.* *600.*
 d. Double invtd. surch. —

Value for No. 198b is for surcharge reading up. One example is known with surcharge reading down.

199 (j) 5c on 1c blk vio 55. 55.
 a. Inverted surcharge 250.
 b. Vertical surcharge *2,000.*
 c. Double surcharge 1,000. 700.

m

200 (m) 10c on 1c blk vio 20. *50.*
 a. Broken figure "1" 40. *100.*

Black Surcharge on Nos. P26-P30

201 (k) 3c on 1m bl grn 350. 350.
 a. Inverted surcharge 450.
 b. "EENTS" 550. 450.
 c. As "b", inverted 850.
202 (l) 3c on 1m bl grn 550. 400.
 a. Inverted surcharge 850.
203 (k) 3c on 2m bl grn 900. 400.
 a. "EENTS" 1,250. 500.
 b. Inverted surcharge 1,150.
 c. As "a," inverted 950.
204 (l) 3c on 2m bl grn 1,250. 600.
 a. Inverted surcharge 750.
205 (k) 3c on 3m bl grn 900. 400.
 a. Inverted surcharge 750.
 b. "EENTS" 1,250. 450.
 c. As "b," inverted 700.
206 (l) 3c on 3m bl grn 1,200. 550.
 a. Inverted surcharge 700.
211 (i) 5c on 1m bl grn 1,800.
 a. "EENTS" — 2,500.
212 (j) 5c on 1m bl grn 2,250.
213 (i) 5c on 2m bl grn 1,800.
 a. "EENTS" — 1,900.
214 (j) 5c on 2m bl grn 1,750.
215 (i) 5c on 3m bl grn 550.
 a. "EENTS" 1,000.
216 (j) 5c on 3m bl grn — 1,000.
217 (i) 5c on 4m bl grn *2,500.* 900.
 a. "EENTS" *3,000.* 1,500.
 b. Inverted surcharge *2,000.*
 c. As "a," inverted 2,000.
218 (j) 5c on 4m bl grn *1,500.*
 a. Inverted surcharge *2,000.*
219 (i) 5c on 8m bl grn *2,500.* 1,250.
 a. Inverted surcharge 1,500.
 b. "EENTS" — 1,800.
 c. As "b," inverted 2,500.
220 (j) 5c on 8m bl grn 2,000.
 a. Inverted surcharge 2,500.

Beware of forgeries of the Puerto Principe issue. Obtaining expert opinions is recommended.

United States Stamps Nos. 279, 267, 267b, 279Bf, 279Bh, 268, 281, 282C and 283 Surcharged in Black

1899 Wmk. 191 *Perf. 12*

221 A87 1c on 1c yel grn 5.00 .40
 Never hinged 12.50
 On cover 15.00
222 A88 2c on 2c reddish car, type III 10.00 .75
 Never hinged 25.00
 On cover 22.50
 b. 2c on 2c vermilion, type III 10.00 .75
222A A88 2c on 2c reddish car, type IV 6.00 .40
 Never hinged 15.00
 On cover 12.50
 c. 2c on 2c vermilion, type IV 6.00 .40
 d. As No. 222A, inverted surcharge *5,500.* *4,000.*
223 A88 2½c on 2c reddish car, type III 5.00 .80
 Never hinged 12.50
 On cover 20.00
 b. 2½c on 2c vermilion, type III 5.00 .80
223A A88 2½c on 2c reddish car, type IV 3.50 .50
 Never hinged 8.75
 On cover 12.50
 c. 2½c on 2c vermilion 3.50 .50
224 A89 3c on 3c pur 12.00 1.75
 Never hinged 30.00
 On cover 25.00
 a. Period between "B" and "A" 40.00 35.00
225 A91 5c on 5c bl 12.50 2.00
 Never hinged [illegible]
 On cover 30.00
226 A94 10c on 10c brn, type I 25.00 6.50
 On cover 110.00
 b. "CUBA" omitted *7,000.* *4,000.*
226A A94 10c on 10c brn, type II *6,000.*
 Nos. 221-226 (8) 79.00 13.10

The 2½c was sold and used as a 2c stamp.

Excellent counterfeits of this and the preceding issue exist, especially inverted and double surcharges.

Issues of the Republic under US Military Rule

Statue of Columbus
A20

Royal Palms
A21

"Cuba"
A22

Ocean Liner
A23

Cane Field — A24

1899 Wmk. US-C (191C) *Perf. 12*

227 A20 1c yel grn 3.50 .25
 Never hinged 8.75
 On cover 2.00
228 A21 2c carmine 3.50 .25
 Never hinged 8.75
 On cover 2.00
 a. scarlet 3.50 .25
 b. Booklet pane of 6 *5,500.*
229 A22 3c purple 3.50 .30
 Never hinged 8.75
 On cover 4.00
230 A23 5c blue 4.50 .30
 Never hinged 11.00
 On cover 4.00
231 A24 10c brown 11.00 .80
 Never hinged 27.50
 On cover 6.50
 Nos. 227-231 (5) 26.00 1.90

No. 228b was issued by the Republic.

See Nos. 233-237. For surcharge see No. 232.

Issues of the Republic

No. 229 Surcharged in Carmine

1902, Sept. 30

232 A22 1c on 3c purple 2.75 .50
 a. Inverted surcharge 150.00 150.00
 b. Surcharge sideways (numeral horizontal) 200.00 200.00
 c. Double surcharge 200.00 200.00

Counterfeits of the errors are plentiful.

Re-engraved

The re-engraved stamps of 1905-07 may be distinguished from the issue of 1899 as follows:

ORIGINAL RE-ENGRAVED

1c — The ends of the label inscribed "Centavo" are rounded instead of square.

2c — The foliate ornaments, inside the oval disks bearing the numerals of value, have been removed.

5c — Two lines forming a right angle have been added in the upper corners of the label bearing the word "Cuba."

10c — A small ball has been added to each of the square ends of the label bearing the word "Cuba."

1905 Unwmk. *Perf. 12*

233 A20 1c green 1.75 .25
234 A21 2c rose 1.20 .25
 a. Booklet pane of 6 150.00
236 A23 5c blue 42.50 1.00
237 A24 10c brown 3.50 .50
 Nos. 233-237 (4) 48.95 2.00

Maj. Gen. Antonio Maceo — A26

1907

238 A26 50c gray bl & blk 1.75 .80

Bartolomé Masó
A27

Máximo Gómez
A28

Julio Sanguily
A29

Ignacio Agramonte
A30

Calixto García
A31

José M. Rodriquez y Rodriquez (Mayia)
A32

Carlos Roloff — A33

1910, Feb. 1
239	A27	1c grn & vio	1.00 .25
a.		Center inverted	260.00 260.00
240	A28	2c car & grn	1.90 .25
a.		Center inverted	575.00 575.00
241	A29	3c vio & bl	1.35 .25
242	A30	5c bl & grn	20.00 .80
243	A31	8c ol & vio	1.35 .30
244	A32	10c brn & bl	8.00 .65
a.		Center inverted	850.00
245	A26	50c vio & blk	1.90 .50
246	A33	1p slate & blk	9.25 4.00
		Nos. 239-246 (8)	44.75 7.00
		Set, never hinged	72.50

1911-13
247	A27	1c green	1.00 .25
248	A28	2c car rose	1.35 .25
a.		Booklet pane of 6 ('13)	82.50
250	A30	5c ultra	3.75 .25
251	A31	8c ol grn & blk	2.00 .60
252	A33	1p black	9.50 2.00
		Nos. 247-252 (5)	17.60 3.35
		Set, never hinged	25.00

Map of Cuba — A34

1914-15
253	A34	1c green	.80 .25
a.		Booklet pane of 6	100.00
254	A34	2c car rose	.95 .25
a.		Booklet pane of 6	100.00
255	A34	2c red ('15)	1.50 .25
a.		Booklet pane of 6	100.00
256	A34	3c violet	4.75 .35
257	A34	5c blue	6.50 .25
258	A34	8c ol grn	5.25 .70
259	A34	10c brown	9.50 .35
260	A34	10c ol grn ('15)	11.50 .55
261	A34	50c orange	75.00 10.00
262	A34	1p gray	110.00 24.00
		Nos. 253-262 (10)	225.75 36.95
		Set, never hinged	400.00

Complete set of eight 1914 stamps, imperf. pairs, value $1,500.

Nos. 253, 254, 256 and E5 exist with "1917 GOB./CONSTITUCIONAL/CAMAGUEY" overprint. These were not authorized.

Gertrudis Gómez de Avellaneda, Cuban Poetess (1814-73) A34a

1914
263	A34a	5c blue	18.00 5.00
		Never hinged	27.50

José Martí A35

Máximo Gómez A36

José de la Luz Caballero A37

Calixto García A38

Ignacio Agramonte A39

Tomás Estrada Palma A40

José A. Saco — A41

Antonio Maceo — A42

Carlos Manuel de Céspedes — A43

1917-18   Unwmk.   Perf. 12
264	A35	1c bl grn	1.00 .25
a.		Booklet pane of 6	40.00
b.		Booklet pane of 30	250.00
265	A36	2c rose	1.05 .25
a.		Booklet pane of 6	50.00
b.		Booklet pane of 30	210.00
266	A36	2c lt red ('18)	.85 .25
a.		Booklet pane of 6	50.00
267	A37	3c violet	1.10 .25
a.		Imperf. pair	275.00
b.		Booklet pane of 6	50.00
268	A38	5c dp bl	1.05 .25
269	A39	8c red brn	5.50 .25
270	A40	10c yel brn	3.25 .25
271	A41	20c gray grn	18.50 1.60
272	A42	50c dl rose	18.50 .70
273	A43	1p black	19.00 .70
		Nos. 264-273 (10)	69.80 4.75
		Set, never hinged	110.00

1925-28   Wmk. 106   Perf. 12
274	A35	1c bl grn	1.10 .25
a.		Booklet pane of 6	350.00
275	A36	2c brt rose	1.20 .25
a.		Booklet pane of 6	75.00
b.		Booklet pane of 30	350.00
276	A38	5c dp bl	2.50 .25
277	A39	8c red brn ('28)	5.75 .65
278	A40	10c yel brn ('27)	7.00 .70
279	A41	20c olive grn	11.00 1.10
		Nos. 274-279 (6)	28.55 3.20
		Set, never hinged	50.00

1926   Imperf.
280	A35	1c blue green	2.75 2.00
281	A36	2c brt rose	2.75 2.00
282	A38	5c deep blue	3.50 2.75
		Nos. 280-282 (3)	9.00 6.75
		Set, never hinged	10.00

See Nos. 304-310. For overprint and surcharge see Nos. 317-318, 644 (in Scott Standard catalogue, Vol. 2).

Arms of Republic A44

1927, May 20   Unwmk.   Perf. 12
283	A44	25c violet	18.00 3.50
		Never hinged	27.50

25th anniversary of the Republic.
For surcharges see Nos. 355, C3.

Tomás Estrada Palma A45

Designs: 2c, Gen. Gerardo Machado. 5c, Morro Castle. 8c, Havana Railway Station. 10c, Presidential Palace. 13c, Tobacco Plantation. 20c, Treasury Building. 30c, Sugar Mill. 50c, Havana Cathedral. 1p, Galician Clubhouse, Havana.

1928, Jan. 2   Wmk. 106
284	A45	1c deep green	.60 .30
285	A45	2c brt rose	.60 .30
286	A45	5c deep blue	1.75 .50
287	A45	8c lt red brn	3.75 1.10
288	A45	10c bister brn	1.50 .80
289	A45	13c orange	2.10 .80
290	A45	20c olive grn	2.50 .95
291	A45	30c dk violet	5.25 .95
292	A45	50c carmine rose	8.00 2.75
293	A45	1p gray black	16.00 6.25
		Nos. 284-293 (10)	42.05 14.50
		Set, never hinged	67.50

Sixth Pan-American Conference.

Capitol, Havana A55

1929, May 18
294	A55	1c green	.50 .35
295	A55	2c carmine rose	.50 .30
296	A55	5c blue	.65 .40
297	A55	10c bister brn	1.35 .50
298	A55	20c violet	4.50 2.75
		Nos. 294-298 (5)	7.50 4.30
		Set, never hinged	12.00

Opening of the Capitol, Havana.

Hurdler — A56

1930, Mar. 15   Engr.
299	A56	1c green	.95 .45
300	A56	2c carmine	.95 .50
301	A56	5c deep blue	1.25 .50
302	A56	10c bister brn	2.50 .95
303	A56	20c violet	15.00 3.25
		Nos. 299-303 (5)	20.65 5.65
		Set, never hinged	32.50

2nd Central American Athletic Games.

Types of 1917 Portrait Issue
Flat Plate Printing

1930-45   Wmk. 106   Engr.   Perf. 10
304	A35	1c blue green	.80 .25
a.		Booklet pane of 6	50.00
b.		Booklet pane of 30	—
305	A36	2c brt rose	75.00 —
a.		Booklet pane of 6	1,200.
305B	A37	3c dk rose vio ('42)	4.00 .75
c.		Booklet pane of 6	42.50
306	A38	5c dk blue	2.75 .25
306A	A39	8c red brn ('45)	2.75 .25
307	A40	10c brown	2.75 .25
a.		10c yellow brown ('35)	3.50 .75
307B	A41	20c olive grn ('41)	4.75 .75
		Nos. 304-307B (7)	92.80 2.50

Nos. 305 and 305B were printed for booklet panes and all examples have straight edges. For surcharge see No. 644.

Rotary Press Printing
308	A35	1c blue grn	1.10 .25
309	A36	2c brt rose	1.10 .25
a.		Booklet pane of 50	
310	A37	3c violet	1.50 .25
a.		3c dull violet ('38)	1.10 .25
b.		3c rose violet ('41)	1.10 .25
c.		Booklet pane of 50	
		Nos. 308-310 (3)	3.70 .75

Flat plate stamps measure 18½x21½mm; rotary press, 19x22mm.

The Mangos of Baragua — A57

War Memorial — A61

Battle of Mal Tiempo A58

Battle of Coliseo A59

Maceo, Gómez and Zayas A60

Wmk. 229
1933, Apr. 23   Photo.   Perf. 12½
312	A57	3c dk brown	2.00 .30
313	A58	5c dk blue	1.75 .40
314	A59	10c emerald	3.50 .40
315	A60	13c red	4.00 1.10
316	A61	20c black	7.75 3.00
		Nos. 312-316 (5)	19.00 5.20
		Set, never hinged	29.00

War of Independence and dedication of the "Soldado Invasor" (the American Army that came to the aid of the revolution against Spain) monument.

Types of 1917 Issues with Carmine or Black Overprint Reading Up or Down

Rotary Press Printing
Wmk. 106
1933, Dec. 23   Engr.   Perf. 10
317	A35	1c blue green (C)	1.50 .25

With Additional Surcharge of New Value and Bars
318	A37	2c on 3c vio (Bk)	1.50 .25

Establishment of a revolutionary junta. Catalogue values for Nos. 317-318 unused are for examples with overprint reading up. Values for overprint reading down, $4.

Dr. Carlos J. Finlay — A62

1934, Dec. 3   Engr.   Perf. 10
319	A62	2c dark carmine	1.35 .50
320	A62	5c dark blue	3.75 1.50
		Set, never hinged	8.00

Cent. of the birth of Dr. Carlos J. Finlay (1833-1915), physician-biologist who found that a mosquito transmitted yellow fever.

Pres. José Miguel Gómez — A63

Gómez Monument A64

1936, May   *Perf. 10*
322 A63 1c green   2.25 .40
323 A64 2c carmine   3.25 .50
   Set, never hinged   8.00

Unveiling of a monument to Gen. José Miguel Gómez, ex-president.

Matanzas Issue

Map of Cuba A65

2c, Map of Free Zone. 4c, S. S. "Rex" in Matanzas Bay. 5c, Ships in Matanzas Bay. 8c, Caves of Bellamar. 10c, Valley of Yumuri. 20c, Yumuri River. 50c, Ships Leaving Port.

Wmk. 229
1936, May 5   **Photo.**   *Perf. 12½*
324 A65 1c blue green   .45 .25
325 A65 2c red   .70 .25
326 A65 4c claret   1.20 .25
327 A65 5c ultra   1.75 .25
328 A65 8c orange brn   3.00 .70
329 A65 10c emerald   3.25 .70
330 A65 20c brown   6.25 2.50
331 A65 50c slate   11.50 3.50
   Nos. 324-331,C18-C21,CE1,E8
     (14)   55.70 21.85
   Set, never hinged   92.50

Exist imperf. Value 20% more.

"Peace and Work" A73

Máximo Gómez Monument — A74

Torch — A75

"Independence" — A76

"Messenger of Peace" — A77

1936, Nov. 18   *Perf. 12½*
332 A73 1c emerald   .75 .25
333 A74 2c crimson   .90 .30
334 A75 4c maroon   1.05 .30
335 A76 5c ultra   4.00 .55
336 A77 8c dk green   6.00 1.20
   Nos. 332-336,C22-C23,E9 (8)   26.55 7.20
   Set, never hinged   48.00

Maj. Gen. Máximo Gómez, birth centenary. Issued both perf and imperf. Values for imperfs are approx. 400% higher.

Sugar Cane — A78

Primitive Sugar Mill — A79

Modern Sugar Mill — A80

Wmk. 106
1937, Oct. 2   **Engr.**   *Perf. 10*
337 A78 1c yellow green   1.75 .40
338 A79 2c red   1.00 .25
339 A80 5c bright blue   2.25 .40
   Nos. 337-339 (3)   5.00 1.05
   Set, never hinged   8.50

Cuban sugar cane industry, 400th anniv.

Argentine Emblem — A81

Mountain Scene (Bolivia) — A82

Arms of Brazil — A83

Canadian Scene — A84

Camilo Henriquez (Chile) A85

Gen, Francisco de Paula Santander (Colombia) A86

Natl. Monument (Costa Rica) — A87

Autograph of José Marti (Cuba) — A88

Columbus Lighthouse (Dominican Rep.) — A89

Juan Montalvo (Ecuador) — A90

Abraham Lincoln (US) A91

Quetzal and Scroll (Guatemala) A92

Arms of Haiti A93

Francisco Morazán (Honduras) A94

Fleet of Columbus — A95

Wmk. 106
1937, Oct. 13   **Engr.**   *Perf. 10*
340 A81 1c deep green   .75 .75
341 A82 1c green   .75 .75
342 A83 2c carmine   .75 .75
343 A84 2c carmine   .75 .75
344 A85 3c violet   1.75 1.75
345 A86 3c violet   1.75 1.75
346 A87 4c bister brown   2.10 2.10
347 A88 4c bister brown   3.75 3.75
348 A89 5c blue   1.90 1.90
349 A90 5c blue   1.90 1.90
350 A91 8c citron   7.00 7.00
351 A92 8c citron   3.25 3.25
352 A93 10c maroon   3.25 3.25
353 A94 10c maroon   3.25 3.25
354 A95 25c rose lilac   35.00 35.00
   Nos. 340-354,C24-C29,E10-
     E11 (23)   132.90 132.90
   Set, never hinged   170.00

Nos. 340-354 were sold by the Cuban PO for 3 days, Oct. 13-15, during which no other stamps were sold. They were postally valid for the full face value. Proceeds from their three-day sale above 30,000 pesos were paid by the Cuban POD to the Assoc. of American Writers and Artists. Remainders were overprinted "SVP" (Without Postal Value).

No. 283 Surcharged in Green

1937, Nov. 19   **Unwmk.**   *Perf. 12*
355 A44 10c on 25c violet   16.00 4.00
   Never hinged   22.50

Centenary of Cuban railroads.

Ciboney Indian and Cigar — A96

Cigar and Globe — A97

Tobacco Plant and Cigars — A98

1939, Aug. 28   **Wmk. 106**   *Perf. 10*
356 A96 1c yellow green   .75 .25
357 A97 2c red   1.00 .25
358 A98 5c brt ultra   1.75 .30
   Nos. 356-358 (3)   3.50 .80
   Set, never hinged   5.25

General Calixto García
A99   A100

1939, Nov. 6   *Perf. 10, Imperf.*
359 A99 2c dark red   .95 .25
360 A100 5c deep blue   1.25 .40
   Set, never hinged   3.50

Birth centenary of General Garcia. Values are for perf examples. Value of imperfs approx. 20% higher.

Gonzalo de Quesada — A101

1940, Apr. 30   **Engr.**   *Perf. 10*
361 A101 2c rose red   1.75 .50
   Never hinged   2.75

Pan American Union, 50th anniversary.

Rotary Club Emblem, Cuban Flag and Tobacco Plant — A102

Lions Emblem, Cuban Flag and Royal Palms — A103

1940, May 18   **Wmk. 106**   *Perf. 10*
362 A102 2c rose red   2.75 .75
   Never hinged   4.00

Rotary Intl. Convention held at Havana.

1940, July 23
363 A103 2c orange vermilion   2.75 .75
   Never hinged   4.00

Lions International Convention, Havana.

Dr. Nicolás J. Gutiérrez
A104

1940, Oct. 28
364	A104 2c orange ver	1.90	.30
365	A104 5c blue	2.50	.30
a.	Sheet of four, imperf., unwmkd.	8.50	3.00
	Never hinged	12.00	
b.	As "a," black overprint ('51)	11.00	4.75
	Never hinged	17.00	
	Set, never hinged	5.50	

100th anniv. of the publication of the 1st Cuban Medical Review, "El Repertorio Medico Habanero."

No. 365a contains 2 each of Nos. 364-365 imperf. and sold for 25c.

For overprint see No. C43A.

In 1951 No. 365a was overprinted in black: "50 Aniversario Descubrimiento Agente Trans-misor de la Flebre Amarilla por el Dr. Carlos J. Finlay Honor a los Martires de la Ciencia 1901 1951." The overprint is illustrated over No. C43A, but does not include the plane and "Correo Aereo."

SEMI-POSTAL STAMPS

Common Design Types pictured following the introduction.

Curie Issue
Common Design Type
Wmk. 106

1938, Nov. 23   Engr.   Perf. 10
B1	CD80 2c + 1c salmon	4.25	1.00
B2	CD80 5c + 1c deep ultra	4.25	1.40
	Set, never hinged	12.00	

40th anniv. of the discovery of radium by Pierre and Marie Curie. Surtax for the benefit of the Intl. Union for the Control of Cancer.

AIR POST STAMPS

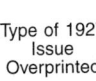
Seaplane over Havana Harbor
AP1

Wmk. 106
1927, Nov. 1   Engr.   Perf. 12
C1	AP1 5c dark blue	8.00	1.00
	Never hinged	13.50	

For overprint see No. C30.

Type of 1927 Issue Overprinted

1928, Feb. 8
C2	AP1 5c carmine rose	6.25	1.60
	Never hinged	9.00	

No. 283 Surcharged in Red

1930, Oct. 27   Unwmk.
C3	A44 10c on 25c violet	5.75	1.60
	Never hinged	8.50	

Airplane and Coast of Cuba — AP3

For Foreign Postage

1931, Feb. 26   Wmk. 106   Perf. 10
C4	AP3 5c green	.45	.25
C5	AP3 10c dk blue	.45	.25
C6	AP3 15c rose	.90	.30
C7	AP3 20c brown	.90	.25
C8	AP3 30c dk violet	1.25	.25
C9	AP3 40c dp orange	4.00	.35
C10	AP3 50c olive grn	6.75	.35
C11	AP3 1p black	10.00	.90
	Nos. C4-C11 (8)	24.70	2.90
	Set, never hinged	37.50	

See No. C40. For surcharges see Nos. C16-C17, C203, C225. Post 1940 issues in Scott Standard catalogue, Vol. 2.

Airplane AP4

For Domestic Postage

1931-46
C12	AP4 5c rose vio ('32)	.40	.25
a.	5c brown violet ('36)	.40	.25
C13	AP4 10c gray blk	.40	.25
C14	AP4 20c car rose	3.25	.90
C14A	AP4 20c rose pink ('46)	1.40	.25
C15	AP4 50c dark blue	5.25	.90
	Nos. C12-C15 (5)	10.70	2.55
	Set, never hinged	17.00	

See No. C130. For overprints see Nos. C31, E29-E30. Post 1940 issues in Scott Standard catalogue, Vol. 2.

Type of 1931 Surcharged in Black

1935, Apr. 24   Perf. 10
C16	AP3 10c + 10c red	15.00	9.50
	Never hinged	20.00	
a.	Double surcharge	110.00	

Imperf
C17	AP3 10c + 10c red	40.00	40.00
	Never hinged	55.00	55.00

Matanzas Issue

Air View of Matanzas AP5

10c, Airship "Macon." 20c, Airplane "The Four Winds." 50c, Air View of Fort San Severino.

Wmk. 229
1936, May 5   Photo.   Perf. 12½
C18	AP5 5c violet	.85	.30
C19	AP5 10c yellow orange	1.00	.50
C20	AP5 20c green	3.75	1.90
C21	AP5 50c greenish slate	9.00	3.75
	Nos. C18-C21 (4)	14.60	6.45
	Set, never hinged	22.50	

Exist imperf. Value 20% more.

"Lightning" AP9

Allegory of Flight AP10

1936, Nov. 18
C22	AP9 5c violet	2.10	1.10
C23	AP10 10c orange brown	2.75	1.50
	Set, never hinged	6.00	

Major Gen. Maximo Gomez, birth cent.

Carlos Antonio López (Paraguay) — AP12

Flat Arch (Panama) — AP11

Inca Gate, Cuzco (Peru) — AP13

Atlacatl (Salvador) AP14

José Enrique Rodó (Uruguay) AP15

Simón Bolívar (Venezuela) AP16

Wmk. 106
1937, Oct. 13   Engr.   Perf. 10
C24	AP11 5c red	7.75	7.75
C25	AP12 5c red	7.75	7.75
C26	AP13 10c blue	7.75	7.75
C27	AP14 10c blue	7.75	7.75
C28	AP15 20c green	10.00	10.00
C29	AP16 20c green	10.00	10.00
	Nos. C24-C29 (6)	47.00	47.00
	Set, never hinged	67.50	

See note after No. 354.

Type of 1927 Overprinted in Black

1938, May   Wmk. 106
C30	AP1 5c dark orange	7.25	1.60
	Never hinged	10.00	

1st airplane flight from Key West to Havana, made by Domingo Rosillo, 1913.

Type of 1931-32 Overprinted

1939, Oct. 15
C31	AP4 10c emerald	32.50	6.50
	Never hinged	55.00	

Issued in connection with an experimental postal rocket flight held at Havana.

Sir Rowland Hill, Map of Cuba and First Stamps of Britain, Spanish Cuba and Republic of Cuba — AP17

1940, Nov. 28   Engr.   Wmk. 106
C32	AP17 10c brown	6.75	2.00
	Never hinged	11.00	

Souvenir Sheet

		Unwmk.	Imperf.
C33		Sheet of 4	22.50	22.50
		Never hinged	35.00	
a.		AP17 10c light brown	5.50	3.50
		Never hinged	8.00	

Cent. of the 1st postage stamp.
Sheet sold for 60c.

No. C33 exists with each of the four stamps overprinted in black: "Exposicion de la ACNU/24 de Octubre de 1951/Dia de las Naciones" and "Historia de la Aviacion" in lower margin. Value, $80.

For overprints see Nos. C39, C211 in Scott Standard catalogue, Vol. 2.

Poet José Heredia and Palms AP18

Heredia and Niagara Falls — AP19

1940, Dec. 30   Wmk. 106
C34	AP18 5c emerald	3.25	1.00
C35	AP19 10c greenish slate	4.00	1.60
	Set, never hinged	11.00	

Death cent. of José Maria Heredia y Campuzano (1803-39), poet and patriot.

AIR POST SPECIAL DELIVERY STAMPS

Matanzas Issue

Matanzas Harbor APSD1

Wmk. 229
1936, May 5   Photo.   Perf. 12½
CE1	ASPD1 15c light blue	5.00	3.50
	Never hinged	8.00	

Exists imperf. Value $6.50 unused, $4.50 used.

SPECIAL DELIVERY STAMPS

Issued under Administration of the United States

US No. E5 Surcharged in Red

1899   Wmk. 191   Perf. 12
E1	SD3 10c blue	130.	100.
	Never hinged	300.	
a.	No period after "CUBA"	575.	400.
b.	Five dots in curved frame above messenger's head (Pl. 882)	2,500.	

Issue of the Republic under US Military Rule

Special
Delivery
Messenger
SD2

Printed by the US Bureau of
Engraving and Printing

1899   **Wmk. US-C (191C)**
Inscribed: "Immediata"

E2	SD2	10c orange	52.50	15.00
		Never hinged	120.00	

Issues of the Republic
Inscribed: "Inmediata"

1902   **Perf. 12**

E3	SD2	10c orange	3.00	1.00

J. B. Zayas
SD3

1910   **Unwmk.**

E4	SD3	10c orange & blue	20.00	3.25
		Never hinged	30.00	
a.		Center inverted	1,250.	

Airplane and
Morro
Castle
SD4

1914, Feb. 24   **Perf. 12**

E5	SD4	10c dark blue	15.00	1.25

Exists imperf. Value, pair $500.

1927   **Wmk. Star (106)**

E6	SD4	10c deep blue	12.00	.50
		Never hinged	18.00	

1935   **Perf. 10**

E7	SD4	10c blue	12.00	.40
		Never hinged	15.00	

Matanzas Issue

Mercury
SD5

Wmk. Wavy Lines (229)
1936, May 5   **Photo.**   **Perf. 12½**

E8	SD5	10c deep claret	8.00	3.50
		Never hinged	9.50	

Exists imperf. Value $7.50 unused, $5 used.

"Triumph of the Revolution" — SD6

1936, Nov. 18

E9	SD6	10c red orange	9.00	2.00
		Never hinged	11.00	

Maj. Gen. Máximo Gómez (1836-1905).

Temple of
Quetzalcoatl
(Mexico)
SD7

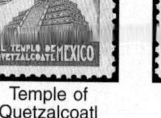

Ruben Dario
(Nicaragua)
SD8

Wmk. 106
1937, Oct. 13   **Engr.**   **Perf. 10**

E10	SD7	10c deep orange	7.00	7.00
E11	SD8	10c deep orange	7.00	7.00
		Set, never hinged	18.00	

Issued for the benefit of the Association of
American Writers and Artists. See note after
No. 354.

POSTAGE DUE STAMPS

Issued under Administration of the United States

Postage Due Stamps of the United
States Nos. J38, J39, J41 and J42
Surcharged in Black Like Nos. 221-
226A

D2

1899   **Wmk. 191**   **Perf. 12**

J1	D2	1c dp claret	45.00	5.25
		Never hinged	110.00	
J2	D2	2c dp claret	45.00	5.25
		Never hinged	110.00	
a.		Inverted surcharge		3,500.
J3	D2	5c dp claret	45.00	5.25
		Never hinged	110.00	
J4	D2	10c dp claret	25.00	2.50
		Never hinged	60.00	
		Nos. J1-J4 (4)	160.00	18.25

Issues of the Republic

D1

1914   **Unwmk.**   **Engr.**   **Perf. 12**

J5	D1	1c carmine rose	8.00	1.25
J6	D1	2c carmine rose	10.00	1.25
J7	D1	5c carmine rose	15.00	2.50
		Nos. J5-J7 (3)	33.00	5.00

1927-28

J8	D1	1c rose red	5.50	.90
J9	D1	2c rose red	8.50	.90
J10	D1	5c rose red	10.00	1.25
		Nos. J8-J10 (3)	24.00	3.05

NEWSPAPER STAMPS

Issued under Spanish Dominion

N1

N2

1888   **Unwmk.**   **Typo.**   **Perf. 14**

P1	N1	½m black	.25	.25
P2	N1	1m black	.25	.30
P3	N1	2m black	.25	.30
P4	N1	3m black	1.60	1.00
P5	N1	4m black	2.10	2.00
P6	N1	8m black	8.00	8.50
		Nos. P1-P6 (6)	12.45	12.35

1890

P7	N2	½m red brown	.55	.65
P8	N2	1m red brown	.55	.65
P9	N2	2m red brown	.90	.95
P10	N2	3m red brown	1.10	1.10
P11	N2	4m red brown	1.00	1.00
P12	N2	8m red brown	8.25	5.50
		Nos. P7-P12 (6)	19.60	14.35

1892

P13	N2	½m violet	.25	.30
P14	N2	1m violet	.25	.30
P15	N2	2m violet	.25	.30
P16	N2	3m violet	1.10	.35
P17	N2	4m violet	4.25	1.90
P18	N2	8m violet	8.75	3.00
		Nos. P13-P18 (6)	14.85	6.15

1894

P19	N2	½m rose	.25	.30
a.		Imperf. pair	40.00	40.00
P20	N2	1m rose	.50	.35
P21	N2	2m rose	.55	.35
P22	N2	3m rose	2.10	1.40
P23	N2	4m rose	3.50	1.60
P24	N2	8m rose	6.00	4.00
		Nos. P19-P24 (6)	12.90	8.00

1896

P25	N2	½m blue green	.25	.30
P26	N2	1m blue green	.25	.30
P27	N2	2m blue green	.25	.30
P28	N2	3m blue green	2.75	1.50
P29	N2	4m blue green	5.75	7.00
P30	N2	8m blue green	10.50	10.00
		Nos. P25-P30 (6)	19.75	19.40

For surcharges see Nos. 190-193, 201-220.

POSTAL TAX STAMPS

Catalogue values for unused
stamps in this section are for
Never Hinged items.

Mother and
Child — PT1

Nurse with
Child — PT2

Wmk. Star. (106)
1938, Dec. 1   **Engr.**   **Perf. 10**

RA1	PT1	1c bright green	.90	.25

The tax benefited the National Council of
Tuberculosis fund for children's hospitals. Obligatory on all mail during December and January. This note applies also to Nos. RA2-RA4,
RA7-RA10, RA12-RA15, RA17-RA21. Post
1940 issues in Scott Standard catalogue, Vol.
2.

1939, Dec. 1

RA2	PT2	1c orange vermilion	.90	.25

"Health" Protecting
Children — PT3

1940, Dec. 1

RA3	PT3	1c deep blue	.90	.25

CYPRUS

'sī-prəs

LOCATION — An island in the Mediter-
ranean Sea off the coast of Turkey
GOVT. — British Colony
AREA — 3,572 sq. mi.
POP. — 645,500 (1982)

CAPITAL — Nicosia

12 Pence = 1 Shilling
40 Paras = 1 Piaster
9 Piasters = 1 Shilling
20 Shillings = 1 Pound

Catalogue values for unused
stamps in this country are for
Never Hinged items, beginning
with Scott 156 in the regular postage section.

STAMPS OF GREAT BRITAIN USED IN CYPRUS

Numeral cancellations on stamps of
Great Britain.

When more than one plate number is
shown, value is for the least expensive.

1878-81

982 (Famagusta)

A1	½p rose (#58, P11, 13), *value from*	800.
A2	1p rose red (#33, P145, 174, 181, 193, 202, 206, 215), *value from*	550.
A3	2p blue (#30, P13-15), *value from*	1,100.
A4	2½p claret (#67, P13, 16), *value from*	1,275.
A5	6p gray (#62, P15)	
A6	1sh green (#64, P12)	3,000.
A7	1sh salmon (#87, P14)	—

974 (Kyrenia)

A8	½p rose (#58, P13)	1,050.
A9	1p rose red (#33, P168, 171, 193, 196, 206, 207, 209, 220), *value from*	675.
A10	2p blue (#30, P13, 15), *value from*	1,150.
A11	2½p claret (#67, P12-15), *value from*	1,150.
A12	4p pale ol grn (#64, P16)	
A13	6p gray (#62, P16)	

942 (Larnaca)

A14	½p rose (#58, P11-15, 19-20), *value from*	300.
A15	1p rose red (#33), *value from*	195.

#A15 plate numbers: 129, 131, 146, 154,
170, 171, 174-179, 181-184, 187, 188, 190-
210, 212-218, 220-222, 225.

A16	1½p lake red (#32, P3)	2,150.
A17	2p blue (#29, P9)	325.
A18	2p blue (#30, P13-15), *value from*	260.
A19	2½p claret (#67, P4-6, 8, 10, 12-17), *value from*	80.
A20	2½p ultra (#68, P17-20), *value from*	575.
A21	2½p ultra (#82, P21)	
A22	4p pale ol grn (#64, P15-16), *value from*	640.
A23	6p gray (#62, P15-17), *value from*	575.
A24	6p pale buff (#59b, P11)	2,900.
A25	8p orange (#73)	6,500.
A26	1sh green (#64, P12-13), *value from*	1,100.
A27	1sh salmon (#87, P14)	
A28	5sh rose (#90, P4)	6,500.

975 (Limassol)

A29	½p rose (#58, P11, 13, 15, 19), *value from*	525.
A30	1p rose red (#33), *value from*	325.

#A30 plate numbers: 160, 171, 173-175,
177, 179, 184, 187, 190, 191, 193, 195-198,
200, 202, 206-210, 213, 215, 216, 218, 220-
222, 225.

A31	1½p lake red (#32, P3)	2,750.
A32	2p blue (#30, P14, 15), *value from*	575.
A33	2½p claret (#67, P11-16), *value from*	275.
A34	2½p ultra (#68, P17, 19, 20), *value from*	1,400.
A35	4p pale ol grn (#64, P16)	950.

969 (Nicosia)

A36	½p rose (#58, P12-15, 20), *value from*	525.
A37	1p rose red (#33), *value from*	325.
A37A	1½p lake red (#32, P3)	3,500.

#A37 plate numbers: 170, 171, 174, 189,
190, 192, 193, 195, 196, 198, 200, 202, 203,
205-207, 210, 212, 214, 215, 218, 221, 222,
225.

A38	2p blue (#30, P14, 15), value from	525.
A39	2½p claret (#67, P10-16), value from	225.
A40	2½p ultra (#68, P20)	850.
A41	4p pale ol grn (#70, P16)	950.
A42	6p gray (#62, P16)	1,100.

981 (Paphos)

A43	½p rose (#58, P13, 15)	
A44	1p rose red (#33, P196, 201, 202, 204, 206, 213, 217), value from	675.
A45	2p blue (#30, P15), value from	1,150.
A46	2½p claret (#67, P13-16), value from	625.

AUSTRIAN OFFICES IN CYPRUS

Values in the first column for Nos. 2A1-2A78 are for stamps without defects tied to piece with legible partial strikes of town cancellations; values in the second column are for stamps without defects tied to cover by complete strikes of town cancellations. Stamps with legible town cancellations off cover sell for 25-50% of the on-piece value.

Issue dates refer to dates of stamps' issue, not necessarily to their usage with specific Cyprian postal markings.

Larnaca

Stamps of Lombardy-Venetia canceled in black with straight-line postmark with name of post office and date, italic lettering

1863			Perf. 14
2A1	2s yellow (#15)	2,100.	7,000.
2A2	3s green (#16)	1,950.	7,200.
2A3	5s rose (#17)	1,950.	7,000.
2A4	10s blue (#18)	1,900.	6,600.
2A5	15s yel brn (#19)	2,000.	6,750.

1864-65			Perf. 9½
2A6	2s yellow (#20)	1,175.	3,650.
2A7	3s green (#21)	775.00	2,850.
2A8	5s rose (#22)	725.00	2,625.
2A9	10s blue (#23)	675.00	2,400.
2A10	15s yel brn (#24)	725.00	2,300.

Stamps of Lombardy-Venetia canceled in blue with straight-line postmark with name of post office and date, italic lettering

1863			Perf. 14
2A11	5s rose (#17)	2,950.	11,500.
2A12	10s blue (#18)	2,900.	11,000.
2A13	15s yel brn (#19)	3,000.	11,500.

1864-65			Perf. 9½
2A14	2s yellow (#20)	1,600.	5,000.
2A15	3s green (#21)	1,200.	4,250.
2A16	5s rose (#22)	1,150.	4,000.
2A17	10s blue (#23)	1,100.	3,800.
2A18	15s yel brn (#24)	1,150.	3,900.

Larnacca di Cipro

Stamps of Lombardy-Venetia canceled in black with single circle date stamp with post office name, month and date, without year

1863			Perf. 14
2A19	2s yellow (#15)	950.00	3,150.
2A20	3s green (#16)	800.00	3,250.
2A21	5s rose (#17)	800.00	3,000.
2A22	10s blue (#18)	750.00	1,600.
2A23	15s yel brn (#19)	850.00	2,800.

1864-65			Perf. 9½
2A24	2s yellow (#20)	900.00	2,800.
2A25	3s green (#21)	525.00	2,000.
2A26	5s rose (#22)	450.00	1,850.
2A27	10s blue (#23)	425.00	1,550.
2A28	15s yel brn (#24)	450.00	1,700.

Stamps of Austrian Offices In the Turkish Empire

Canceled in black or red brown with single circle date stamp with post office name, month and date, without year

1867-83

Coarse Print

2A29	2s yellow (#1)	300.00	1,325.
2A30	3s green (#2)	325.00	1,250.
2A31	5s red (#3)	285.00	1,000.
2A32	10s blue (#4)	275.00	950.
2A33	15s brown (#5)	280.00	975.
2A34	25s gray lilac (#6)	300.00	1,575.
2A35	50s brown (#7)	325.00	4,750.

Fine Print

2A36	2s yellow (#7C)	1,400.	—
2A37	3s green (#7D)	300.00	1,125.
2A38	5s red (#7E)	285.00	1,000.

2A39	10s blue (#7F)	275.00	950.
2A40	15s org brown (#7I)	385.00	1,625.
2A41	25s gray lilac (#7J)	500.00	6,000.

Stamps of Austria

Canceled in black or red brown with single circle date stamp with post office name, month and date, without year

1867-83

Coarse Print

2A42	2kr yellow (#27)	625.00	—
2A43	3kr green (#28)	625.00	—
2A44	5kr red (#29)	625.00	—
2A45	10kr blue (#30)	625.00	2,250.
2A46	15kr brown (#31)	625.00	2,250.
2A47	25kr gray lilac (#32)	625.00	—
2A48	50kr brown (#33)	700.00	—

Fine Print

2A49	2kr yellow (#34)	625.00	—
2A50	3kr green (#35)	625.00	—
2A51	5kr red (#36)	625.00	—
2A52	10kr blue (#37)	625.00	2,250.
2A53	15kr org brown (#38)	625.00	2,250.
2A54	25kr gray (#39)	725.00	—
2A55	50kr brown (#40)	750.00	—

Stamps of Austrian Offices In the Turkish Empire

Canceled in blue with single circle date stamp with post office name, month and date, without year

1867-83

Coarse Print

2A56	2s yellow (#1)	300.00	1,325.
2A57	3s green (#2)	325.00	1,250.
2A58	5s red (#3)	285.00	1,000.
2A59	10s blue (#4)	275.00	950.
2A60	15s brown (#5)	280.00	975.
2A61	25s gray lilac (#6)	300.00	1,575.
2A62	50s brown (#7)	325.00	4,750.

Fine Print

2A63	2s yellow (#7C)	1,400.	—
2A64	3s green (#7D)	300.00	1,125.
2A65	5s red (#7E)	285.00	1,000.
2A66	10s blue (#7F)	275.00	950.
2A67	15s org brown (#7I)	385.00	1,625.
2A68	25s gray lilac (#7J)	500.00	6,000.

1863			Perf. 14
2A69	2s yellow (#15)		—
2A70	3s green (#16)	3,000.	—
2A71	5s rose (#17)	2,950.	11,500.
2A72	10s blue (#18)	2,900.	11,000.
2A73	15s yel brn (#19)	3,000.	11,500.

1864-65			Perf. 9½
2A74	2s yellow (#20)	2,350.	7,500.
2A75	3s green (#21)	1,950.	6,750.
2A76	5s rose (#22)	1,900.	6,750.
2A77	10s blue (#23)	1,850.	6,350.
2A78	15s yel brn (#24)	1,900.	6,500.

BRITISH ADMINISTRATION

Values for unused stamps are for examples with original gum as defined in the catalogue introduction. Very fine examples of Nos. 1, 2 and 7-10 will have perforations touching the design on at least one or more sides due to the narrow spacing of the stamps on the plates and to imperfect perforation methods. Stamps with perfs clear on all four sides are scarce and will command higher prices.

Queen Victoria — A1

A2

A3

A4

A5

A6

A7

Various Watermarks as in Great Britain (#20, 23, 25, 27 & 29)

1880		Typo.		Perf. 14
1	A1	½p rose (P 15)	125.00	115.00
		Plate 12	240.00	300.00
		Plate 19	5,750.	950.00
b.		Double overprint (P 15)		45,000.
2	A2	1p red (P 216)	19.00	55.00
		Plate 217	18.00	60.00
		Plate 174	1,500.	1,500.
		Plate 184	525.00	210.00
		Plate 184	22,000.	3,250.
		Plate 193	840.00	
		Plate 196	725.00	
		Plate 201	22.50	57.50
		Plate 205	90.00	57.50
		Plate 208	135.00	65.00
		Plate 215	18.00	57.50
		Plate 218	26.00	65.00
		Plate 220	550.00	475.00
b.		Double overprint (P 218)	5,400.	
		Double overprint (P 208)	27,500.	
c.		Pair, one without ovpt. (P 208)	27,500.	
3	A3	2½p claret (P 14)	4.50	13.50
		Plate 15	6.00	37.50
4	A4	4p lt ol grn (P 16)	150.00	240.00
5	A5	6p ol gray (P 16)	575.00	750.00
6	A6	1sh green (P 13)	900.00	525.00

Black Surcharge

7	A7	30 paras on 1p red (P 216)	145.00	95.00
		Plate 201	175.00	110.00
		Plate 217	175.00	210.00
		Plate 220	175.00	190.00
b.		Dbl. surch., one invtd. (P 220)	2,000.	1,500.
		Dbl. surch., one invtd. (P 216)	7,750.	

No. 2 Surcharged

18mm Long

1881				
8	A2	½p on 1p (205, 216)	82.50	100.00
		Plate 174	225.00	400.00
		Plate 181	210.00	260.00
		Plate 201	115.00	140.00
		Plate 205	85.00	100.00
		Plate 208	225.00	375.00
		Plate 215	840.00	1,000.
		Plate 217	1,000.	900.00
		Plate 218	550.00	675.00
		Plate 220	325.00	450.00
a.		"HALFPENN" (P216)	3,250.	3,000.

16mm Long

9	A2	½p on 1p (P 201)	140.00	190.00
		Plate 216	400.00	460.00
		Plate 218		17,500.
a.		Double surcharge (P 201, 216)	3,750.	3,000.

13mm Long

10	A2	½p on 1p red (P 215)	52.50	75.00
		Plate 205	425.00	
		Plate 217	175.00	105.00
		Plate 218	90.00	125.00
c.		Double surcharge (P 215)	550.00	700.00
		Double surcharge (P 205)	875.00	
e.		Triple surcharge (P 215)	875.00	
		Triple surcharge (P 205)	4,750.	
		Triple surcharge (P 217)		
		Triple surcharge (P 218)	4,750.	
h.		Quadruple surch. (P 205, 215)	7,500.	
j.		"CYPRUS" double (P 218)	6,000.	

A8

1881, July		Typo.		Wmk. 1
11	A8	½pi emerald green	210.00	52.50
a.		"1/2"pi emerald grn	975.00	550.00
12	A8	1pi rose	425.00	37.50
13	A8	2pi ultramarine	525.00	37.50
a.		2pi ultramarine		1,500.
14	A8	4pi olive green	1,050.	325.00
15	A8	6pi olive gray	1,900.	500.00

Postage and revenue stamps of Cyprus with "J.A.B." (the initials of Postmaster J.A. Bulmer) in manuscript, or with "POSTAL SURCHARGE" (with or without "J. A. B."), were not Postage Due stamps but were employed for accounting purposes between the chief PO at Larnaca and the sub-offices.

See Nos. 19-25, 28-37. For surcharges see Nos. 16-18, 26-27.

A9

A10

1882		Black Surcharge		Wmk. 1
16	A9	½pi on ½pi grn	750.00	92.50
17	A10	30pa on 1pi rose	1,750.	140.00
a.		Double surcharge, one inverted	1,400.	850.00

1884				Wmk. 2
18	A9	½pi on ½pi green	190.00	10.00
a.		Double surcharge		3,200.

See Nos. 26, 27.

1882-94 Die B

For description of Dies A and B see "Dies of British Colonial Stamps" in Table of Contents.

19	A8	½pi green	11.00	2.10
20	A8	30pa violet	8.50	11.50
21	A8	1pi rose	15.50	6.75
22	A8	2pi blue	17.50	2.10
23	A8	4pi pale ol grn	20.00	35.00
b.		4pi olive green	57.50	42.50
24a	A8	6pi	275.00	800.00
25a	A8	12pi	190.00	450.00
		Nos. 19-25a (7)	537.50	1,307.

Die A

19a	A8	½pi	22.50	3.25
b.		½pi emerald	6,000.	525.00
20a	A8	30pa lilac	85.00	27.50
21a	A8	1pi	110.00	4.00
22a	A8	2pi	170.00	4.00
23a	A8	4pi	375.00	35.00
c.		4pi deep olive green ('83)	575.00	47.50
24	A8	6pi olive grn	67.50	21.00
25	A8	12pi brown org	225.00	45.00
		Overprinted "SPECIMEN"	1,200.	
		Nos. 19a-25 (7)	1,055.	139.75

A11

Type I — Figures "½" 8mm apart.
Type II — Figures "½" 6mm apart.
The space between the fraction bars varies from 5½ to 8½mm but is usually 6 or 8mm.

Black Surcharge Type I

1886				Wmk. 2
26	A11	½pi on ½pi grn	525.00	16.00
a.		Type II	325.00	100.00
b.		Double surcharge, type II		

				Wmk. 1
27	A11	½pi on ½pi grn	8,750.	500.00
a.		Type II	24,000.	

No. 27a probably is a proof.

1894-96				Wmk. 2
28	A8	½pi grn & car rose	5.25	1.75
29	A8	30pa violet & green	3.00	3.25
30	A8	1pi rose & ultra	8.50	1.75
31	A8	2pi ultra & mar	11.50	1.75
32	A8	4pi ol green & vio	21.00	11.50
33	A8	6pi ol gray & grn	19.00	35.00
34	A8	9pi brown & rose	25.00	27.50
35	A8	12pi brn org & blk	22.50	67.50

36	A8	18pi slate & brown	60.00 57.50
37	A8	45pi dk vio & ultra	125.00 165.00
		Nos. 28-37 (10)	300.75 372.50
		Set, optd. "SPECIMEN"	375.00

King Edward VII — A12

1903   *Typo.*

38	A12	½pi grn & car rose	11.00 1.40
39	A12	30pa violet & green	22.50 4.25
a.		30pa mauve & green	25.00 9.50
40	A12	1pi carmine rose & ultra	30.00 5.00
41	A12	2pi ultra & mar	90.00 18.00
42	A12	4pi ol green & vio	50.00 22.50
43	A12	6pi ol brown & grn	52.50 145.00
44	A12	9pi brn & car rose	125.00 260.00
45	A12	12pi org brn & blk	21.00 80.00
46	A12	18pi black & brown	100.00 175.00
47	A12	45pi dk vio & ultra	250.00 600.00
		Nos. 38-47 (10)	752.00 1,311.
		Set, optd. "SPECIMEN"	500.00

1904-07   *Wmk. 3*

48	A12	5pa bis & blk ('07)	1.25 2.00
49	A12	10pa org & grn ('07)	6.00 1.90
a.		10pa yellow & green	47.50 6.25
50	A12	½pi grn & car rose	9.00 1.60
51	A12	30pa reddish violet & green	20.00 2.75
a.		30pa violet & green ('10)	22.50 2.90
52	A12	1pi car rose & ultra	12.00 1.10
53	A12	2pi ultra & maroon	16.00 2.00
54	A12	4pi ol grn & red vio	22.00 13.50
55	A12	6pi ol brn & green	24.00 17.00
56	A12	9pi brn & car rose	52.50 9.75
a.		9pi yel brn & carmine rose	57.50 27.50
57	A12	12pi org brn & blk	37.50 57.50
58	A12	18pi black & brown	55.00 15.00
59	A12	45pi dk vio & ultra	120.00 175.00
		Nos. 48-59 (12)	375.25 299.10

King George V — A13

1912

61	A13	10pa orange & green	5.25 2.90
a.		10pa org yel & br green ('15)	2.75 1.60
62	A13	½pi grn & car rose	2.90 .35
a.		½pi yel green & carmine	8.50 2.25
63	A13	30pa violet & green	3.25 2.40
64	A13	1pi car & ultra	5.75 1.90
a.		1pi carmine & blue ('15)	15.00 4.50
65	A13	2pi ultra & maroon	8.50 2.25
66	A13	4pi ol grn & red vio	5.50 5.25
67	A13	6pi ol brn & green	5.75 11.50
68	A13	9pi brn & car rose	42.50 28.00
a.		9pi yellow brown & carmine	45.00 32.50
69	A13	12pi org brn & blk	24.00 57.50
70	A13	18pi black & brown	45.00 50.00
71	A13	45pi dl vio & ultra	130.00 170.00
		Nos. 61-71 (12)	281.15 333.65
		Set, optd. "SPECIMEN"	550.00

1921-23   *Wmk. 4*

72	A13	10pa orange & grn	16.00 13.50
73	A13	10pa gray & yellow	16.00 9.50
74	A13	30pa violet & grn	3.25 2.00
75	A13	30pa green	9.00 1.75
76	A13	1pi rose & ultra	26.00 45.00
77	A13	1pi violet & car	4.00 5.00
78	A13	1½pi orange & blk	12.50 7.25
79	A13	2pi ultra & red vio	35.00 25.00
80	A13	2pi rose & ultra	16.00 27.50
81	A13	2¾pi ultra & red vio	11.00 12.00
82	A13	4pi ol grn & red vio	19.00 26.00
83	A13	6pi ol brn & green	32.50 80.00
84	A13	9pi brn & carmine	42.50 95.00
a.		9pi yel brn & car	125.00 165.00
85	A13	18pi black & brn	90.00 175.00
86	A13	45pi dl vio & ultra	275.00 325.00
		Nos. 72-86 (15)	607.75 849.50
		Set, optd. "SPECIMEN"	700.00

Wmk. 3

87	A13	10sh grn & red, yel	425.00 875.00
88	A13	£1 vio & black, red	1,400. 3,000.
		Nos. 87-88, optd. "SPECIMEN"	625.00

Years of issue: Nos. 73, 75, 77-78, 80-81, 87-88, 1923; others, 1921.

Forged cancellations exist on Nos. 83-88, including a dangerous "LIMASSOL 14 MR 25" fake postmark.

A14

1924-28   **Chalky Paper**   *Wmk. 4*

89	A14	¼pi gray & brn org	2.10 .55
90	A14	½pi gray blk & blk	6.25 14.50
91	A14	½pi grn & dp grn ('25)	2.50 1.10
92	A14	¾pi grn & dp grn	4.25 1.10
93	A14	¾pi gray blk & blk ('25)	4.50 1.10
94	A14	1pi brn vio & org brown	2.40 2.10
95	A14	1½pi org & black	3.50 14.50
96	A14	1½pi carmine ('25)	5.25 1.60
97	A14	2pi car & green	4.25 21.00
98	A14	2pi org & black ('25)	14.50 4.25
99	A14	2½pi ultra ('25)	5.25 1.90
100	A14	2¾pi ultra & dull vio	3.75 5.00
101	A14	4pi ap grn & vio	5.25 5.25
102	A14	4½pi black & yel, *emer*	4.00 5.25
103	A14	6pi grn ol & grn	5.25 9.00
104	A14	9pi brn & dk vio	9.00 5.75
105	A14	12pi org brn & blk	14.50 65.00
106	A14	18pi blk & org	27.50 5.75
		Revenue cancel	1.00
107	A14	45pi gray vio & ultra	65.00 42.50
		Revenue cancel	1.50
108	A14	90pi grn & red, yel	125.00 270.00
		Revenue cancel	3.75
109	A14	£5 blk, yel ('28)	3,750. 8,000.
		On cover (overfranked)	275.00
		Overprinted "SPECIMEN"	1,100.
		Revenue cancel	275.00

Wmk. 3

110	A14	£1 vio & black, red	350.00 900.00
		Revenue cancel	12.50
		Nos. 89-108 (20)	314.00 477.20

Nos. 96 and 99 are on ordinary paper.

Silver Coin of Amathus — A15

Philosopher Zeno — A16

Map of Cyprus — A17

Discovery of Body of St. Barnabas — A18

Cloisters of Bella Paise Monastery — A19

Badge of the Colony — A20

Hospice of Umm Haram at Larnaca — A21

Statue of Richard Coeur de Lion, London — A22

St. Nicholas Cathedral, Famagusta — A23

King George V — A24

Perf. 12

1928, Feb. 1   **Engr.**   *Wmk. 4*

114	A15	¾pi dark violet	3.75 1.60
115	A16	1pi Prus bl & blk	4.00 2.00
116	A17	1½pi red	6.00 2.25
117	A18	2½pi ultramarine	4.75 2.75
118	A19	4pi dp red brown	9.50 9.50
119	A20	6pi dark blue	12.50 32.50
120	A21	9pi violet brown	10.00 17.50
121	A22	18pi dk brn & blk	30.00 35.00
122	A23	45pi dp blue & vio	52.50 62.50
123	A24	£1 ol brn & deep blue	275.00 400.00
		Nos. 114-123 (10)	408.00 565.60
		Set, optd. "SPECIMEN"	750.00

50th year of Cyprus as a British colony.

Ruins of Vouni Palace — A25

Columns at Salamis — A26

Peristerona Church — A27

Soli Theater — A28

Kyrenia Castle and Harbor — A29

Kolossi Castle — A30

St. Sophia Cathedral — A31

Bairakdar Mosque — A32

Queen's Window, St. Hilarion Castle — A33

Buyuk Khan, Nicosia — A34

Forest Scene — A35

1934, Dec. 1   **Engr.**   ***Perf. 12½***

125	A25	¼pi yel brn & ultra	1.40 1.10
		Never hinged	2.10
a.		Vert. pair, imperf. between	52,500. 35,000.
126	A26	½pi green	1.90 1.25
		Never hinged	2.10
a.		Vert. pair, imperf. between	18,000. 20,000.

127	A27	¾pi violet & blk	3.50	.45
		Never hinged	4.50	
a.		Vert. pair, imperf. between	52,500.	
128	A28	1pi brown & blk	3.00	2.50
		Never hinged	4.50	
a.		Vert. pair, imperf. between	26,000.	26,000.
b.		Horiz. pair, imperf. btwn.	19,000.	
129	A29	1½pi rose red	4.00	2.10
		Never hinged	6.00	
130	A30	2½pi dark ultra	5.25	2.40
		Never hinged	7.75	
131	A31	4½pi dk car & blk	5.25	5.00
		Never hinged	14.00	
132	A32	6pi blue & black	12.50	20.00
		Never hinged	26.00	
133	A33	9pi dl vio & blk brown	17.50	8.50
		Never hinged	29.00	
134	A34	18pi ol grn & black	52.50	50.00
		Never hinged	110.00	
135	A35	45pi blk & emer	110.00	85.00
		Never hinged	200.00	
		Nos. 125-135 (11)	216.80	178.30
		Set, never hinged	405.00	
		Set, perf "SPECIMEN"	575.00	

Common Design Types pictured following the introduction.

Silver Jubilee Issue
Common Design Type

1935, May 6 — **Perf. 11x12**

136	CD301	¾pi gray blk & ultra	4.25	1.50
		Never hinged	6.25	
137	CD301	1½pi car & dk bl	6.25	3.00
		Never hinged	9.00	
138	CD301	2½pi ultra & brn	5.25	1.90
		Never hinged	10.00	
139	CD301	9pi brn vio & ind	24.00	28.00
		Never hinged	35.00	
		Nos. 136-139 (4)	39.75	34.40
		Set, never hinged	60.00	
		Set, perf "SPECIMEN"	210.00	

Coronation Issue
Common Design Type

1937, May 12 — **Perf. 11x11½**

140	CD302	¾pi dark gray	1.00	1.00
		Never hinged	2.00	
141	CD302	1½pi dark carmine	1.25	2.50
		Never hinged	2.00	
142	CD302	2½pi deep ultra	1.50	3.00
		Never hinged	3.25	
		Nos. 140-142 (3)	3.75	6.50
		Set, never hinged	7.75	
		Set, perf "SPECIMEN"	140.00	
		Same, never hinged	200.00	

Ruins of Vouni Palace — A36

Columns at Salamis — A37

Peristerona Church — A38

Soli Theater — A39

Kyrenia Castle and Harbor — A40

Kolossi Castle — A41

Map of Cyprus — A42

Bairakdar Mosque — A43

Citadel, Famagusta — A44

Buyuk Khan — A45

King George VI A47

Forest Scene A46

1938-44 — **Wmk. 4** — **Perf. 12½**

143	A36	¼pi yel brn & ultra	.60	.60
		Never hinged	1.75	
144	A37	½pi green	.80	.50
		Never hinged	2.40	
145	A38	¾pi violet & blk	7.25	1.75
		Never hinged	22.00	
146	A39	1pi orange	.90	.40
		Never hinged	2.50	
a.		Perf. 13½x12½ ('44)	375.00	30.00
		Never hinged	575.00	
147	A40	1½pi rose car	3.25	2.00
		Never hinged	6.25	
147A	A40	1½pi lt vio ('43)	.90	.75
		Never hinged	2.50	
147B	A38	2pi carmine & blk ('42)	.90	.45
		Never hinged	2.90	
c.		Perf. 12½x13½ ('44)	2.00	12.50
		Never hinged	3.25	
148	A41	2½pi ultramarine	15.00	4.50
		Never hinged	45.00	
148A	A41	3pi dp ultra ('42)	1.25	.60
		Never hinged	3.50	
149	A42	4½pi gray	.90	.40
		Never hinged	2.50	
150	A43	6pi blue & black	1.25	1.10
		Never hinged	3.75	
151	A44	9pi dk vio & blk	1.00	.80
		Never hinged	2.90	
152	A45	18pi ol grn & blk	5.00	1.75
		Never hinged	14.50	
153	A46	45pi blk & emer	16.00	5.00
		Never hinged	47.50	
154	A47	90pi blk & brt vio	21.00	8.00
		Never hinged	37.50	
155	A47	£1 ind & dl red	45.00	32.50
		Never hinged	67.50	
		Nos. 143-155 (16)	121.00	61.10
		Set, never hinged	275.00	
		Set, perf "SPECIMEN"	450.00	
		Same, never hinged	725.00	

See Nos. 164-166.

Catalogue values for unused stamps in this section, from this point to the end of the section, are for Never Hinged items.

Peace Issue
Common Design Type

1946, Oct. 21 — **Engr.** — **Perf. 13½x14**

156	CD303	1½pi purple	.50	.25
157	CD303	3pi deep blue	.50	.45

Silver Wedding Issue
Common Design Types

1948, Dec. 20 — **Photo.** — **Perf. 14x14½**

158	CD304	1½pi purple	1.00	.55

Engr.; Name Typo. — **Perf. 11½x11**

159	CD305	£1 dark blue	57.50	77.50

UPU Issue
Common Design Types

Perf. 13½, 11x11½

1949, Oct. 10 — **Engr.** — **Wmk. 4**

160	CD306	1½pi violet	.65	1.60
161	CD307	2pi deep carmine	1.75	1.60
162	CD308	3pi indigo	1.10	1.10
163	CD309	9pi rose violet	1.10	4.00
		Nos. 160-163 (4)	4.60	8.30

Types of 1938-43

1951, July 2 — **Engr.** — **Perf. 12½**

164	A37	½pi purple	3.25	.75
165	A40	1½pi deep green	6.25	1.25
166	A41	4pi deep ultra	4.75	1.40
		Nos. 164-166 (3)	14.25	3.40

CYRENAICA

ˌsir-ə-'nā-ə-kə

LOCATION — In northern Africa bordering on the Mediterranean Sea
GOVT. — Italian colony
AREA — 75,340 sq. mi.
POP. — 225,000 (approx. 1934)
CAPITAL — Bengasi (Benghazi)

100 Centesimi = 1 Lira

Used values in italics are for postally used stamps. CTO's sell for about the same as unused, hinged stamps.

Watermark

Wmk. 140 — Crown

Propaganda of the Faith Issue
Italy Nos. 143-146 Overprinted

1923, Oct. 24 — **Wmk. 140** — **Perf. 14**

1	A68	20c ol grn & brn org	11.50	50.00
		Never hinged	29.00	
		On overfranked cover	—	
2	A68	30c claret & brn org	11.50	50.00
		Never hinged	29.00	
		On overfranked cover	—	
a.		Vert. pair, imperf between	1,050.	
b.		Vert. strip of 3, imperf between and at bottom	1,200.	
3	A68	50c violet & brn org	7.50	57.50
		Never hinged	19.00	
		On overfranked cover	—	
4	A68	1 l blue & brown orange	7.50	85.00
		Never hinged	19.00	
		On overfranked cover	—	
a.		Vert. pair, imperf between	1,050.	
b.		Vert. strip of 3, imperf between and at bottom	1,200.	
		Nos. 1-4 (4)	38.00	242.50
		Set, never hinged	90.00	
		Set on overfranked cover	—	

Fascisti Issue

Italy Nos. 159-164 Overprinted in Red or Black

1923, Oct. 29 — **Unwmk.** — **Perf. 14**

5	A69	10c dk grn (R)	11.00	19.00
		Never hinged	27.50	
		On commercial cover		300.00
6	A69	30c dk vio (R)	11.00	19.00
		Never hinged	27.50	
		On commercial cover		300.00
7	A69	50c brn car	11.00	25.00
		Never hinged	27.50	
		On commercial cover		300.00

Wmk. 140

8	A70	1 l blue	11.00	50.00
		Never hinged	27.50	
		On commercial cover		560.00
9	A70	2 l brown	11.00	60.00
		Never hinged	27.50	
		On commercial cover		825.00
10	A71	5 l blk & bl (R)	11.00	90.00
		Never hinged	27.50	
		On commercial cover		—
		Nos. 5-10 (6)	66.00	263.00
		Set, never hinged	150.00	
		Set on overfranked cover		650.00

Manzoni Issue

Italy Nos. 165-170 Ovptd. in Red

1924, Apr. 1 — **Perf. 14**

11	A72	10c brn red & blk	12.00	80.00
		Never hinged	30.00	
12	A72	15c bl grn & blk	12.00	80.00
		Never hinged	30.00	
13	A72	30c blk & slate	12.00	80.00
		Never hinged	30.00	
14	A72	50c org brn & blk	12.00	80.00
		Never hinged	30.00	
15	A72	1 l bl & blk	72.50	475.00
		Never hinged	180.00	
a.		Double overprint	1,200.	
		Never hinged	1,800.	
16	A72	5 l vio & blk	475.00	3,250.
		Never hinged	1,190.	
		Nos. 11-16 (6)	595.50	4,045.
		Set, never hinged	1,500.	
		Set on overfranked cover		—

Vertical overprints on Nos. 11-14 are essays. On Nos. 15-16 the overprint is vertical at the left.
All examples of No. 15a are poorly centered.
Commercial covers of this issue are very rare.

Victor Emmanuel Issue

Italy Nos. 175-177 Overprinted

1925-26 Unwmk. Perf. 11

17	A78	60c brn car	1.60	11.00
		Never hinged	3.00	
		On commercial cover		200.00
18	A78	1 l dark blue	1.60	11.00
		Never hinged	3.00	
		On commercial cover		325.00
19	A78	1.25 l dk bl ('26)	4.75	24.00
		On commercial cover		475.00
a.		Perf. 13½	350.00	1,000.
		Never hinged	900.00	
		Nos. 17-19 (3)	7.95	46.00
		Set, never hinged	20.00	

Issue dates: Nov. 1925, July 1926.

Saint Francis of Assisi Issue

Italian Stamps of 1926 Ovptd.

1926, Apr. 12 Wmk. 140 Perf. 14

20	A79	20c gray green	2.50	14.50
		Never hinged	6.00	
		On commercial cover		125.00
21	A80	40c dark violet	2.50	14.50
		Never hinged	6.00	
		On commercial cover		160.00
22	A81	60c red brown	2.50	26.00
		Never hinged	6.00	
		On commercial cover		160.00

Ovptd. in Red

Unwmk.

23	A82	1.25 l dk bl, perf. 11	2.50	35.00
		Never hinged	6.00	
		On commercial cover		275.00
a.		Pair, one with albino surcharge	1,900.	
		Never hinged	3,500.	
24	A83	5 l + 2.50 l ol grn	8.00	72.50
		Never hinged	16.00	
		On commercial cover		—
a.		Double surcharge, one black, one red	2,400.	
		Never hinged	4,500.	
		Nos. 20-24 (5)	18.00	162.50
		Set, never hinged	40.00	
		Set on overfranked cover		475.00

Volta Issue

Type of Italy 1927, Overprinted

1927, Oct. 10 Wmk. 140 Perf. 14

25	A84	20c purple	6.75	40.00
		Never hinged	17.00	
		On commercial cover		275.00
a.		Overprint omitted	4,250.	
		Never hinged	6,500.	
26	A84	50c dp org	9.50	27.50
		Never hinged	21.00	
		On commercial cover		275.00
a.		Dot omitted after figures of value	55.00	95.00
b.		Double overprint	200.00	
c.		Overprinted "Cirenaica" and "Eritrea" (inverted)	550.00	
27	A84	1.25 l brt bl	14.50	62.50
		Never hinged	35.00	
		On commercial cover		520.00
		Nos. 25-27 (3)	30.75	130.00
		Set, never hinged	72.50	
		Set on overfranked cover		380.00

Monte Cassino Issue

Types of 1929 Issue of Italy, Ovptd. in Red or Blue

1929, Oct. 14

28	A96	20c dk grn (R)	6.50	22.50
		Never hinged	16.00	
		On commercial cover		275.00
29	A96	25c red org (Bl)	6.50	22.50
		Never hinged	16.00	
		On commercial cover		200.00

30	A98	50c + 10c crim (Bl)	6.50	24.00
		Never hinged	16.00	
		On commercial cover		160.00
31	A98	75c + 15c ol brn (R)	6.50	24.00
		Never hinged	16.00	
32	A100	1.25 l + 25c dk vio (R)	14.00	42.50
		On commercial cover		340.00
33	A98	5 l + 1 l saph (R)	14.00	47.50
		Never hinged	35.00	

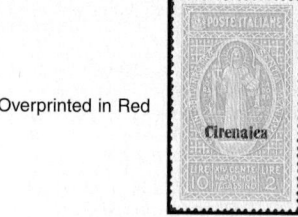

Overprinted in Red

Unwmk.

34	A100	10 l + 2 l gray brn	14.00	72.50
		Never hinged	35.00	
		Nos. 28-34 (7)	68.00	255.50
		Set, never hinged	169.00	
		Set on overfranked cover		475.00

Royal Wedding Issue

Type of Italian Stamps of 1930 Overprinted

1930, Mar. 17 Wmk. 140

35	A101	20c yel grn	3.25	9.50
		Never hinged	8.00	
		On commercial cover		140.00
a.		Without overprint	42,500.	
		Never hinged	65,000.	
36	A101	50c + 10c dp org	2.40	9.50
		Never hinged	6.00	
		On commercial cover		190.00
37	A101	1.25 l + 25c rose red	2.40	19.00
		Never hinged	6.00	
		On commercial cover		300.00
		Nos. 35-37 (3)	8.05	38.00
		Set, never hinged	20.00	
		Set on overfranked cover		180.00

Ferrucci Issue

Types of Italian Stamps of 1930, Ovptd. in Red or Blue

1930, July 26

38	A102	20c violet (R)	6.50	6.50
		Never hinged	16.00	
		On commercial cover		160.00
39	A103	25c dk grn (R)	6.50	6.50
		Never hinged	16.00	
		On commercial cover		190.00
40	A103	50c black (R)	6.50	12.00
		Never hinged	16.00	
		On commercial cover		160.00
41	A103	1.25 l dp bl (R)	6.50	22.50
		Never hinged	16.00	
		On commercial cover		350.00
42	A104	5 l + 2 l dp car	14.50	47.50
		Never hinged	30.00	
		Nos. 38-42 (5)	40.50	95.00
		Set, never hinged	94.00	
		Set on overfranked cover		350.00

Virgil Issue

Italian Stamps of 1930 Ovptd. in Red or Blue

1930, Dec. 4

43	A106	15c vio blk	1.25	12.00
		Never hinged	3.00	
		On commercial cover		175.00
44	A106	20c org brn (Bl)	1.25	4.75
		Never hinged	3.00	
		On commercial cover		100.00
45	A106	25c dk grn	1.25	4.75
		Never hinged	3.00	
		On commercial cover		95.00
46	A106	30c lt brn (Bl)	1.25	4.75
		Never hinged	3.00	
		On commercial cover		100.00

47	A106	50c dl vio	1.25	4.75
		Never hinged	3.00	
		On commercial cover		87.50
48	A106	75c rose red (Bl)	1.25	9.50
		Never hinged	3.00	
		On commercial cover		210.00
49	A106	1.25 l gray bl	1.25	11.00
		Never hinged	3.00	
		On commercial cover		300.00

Unwmk.

50	A106	5 l + 1.50 l dk vio	4.75	47.50
		Never hinged	9.50	
		On commercial cover		—
51	A106	10 l + 2.50 l ol brn (Bl)	4.75	72.50
		Never hinged	9.50	
		Nos. 43-51 (9)	18.25	172.50
		Set, never hinged	40.00	
		Set on overfranked cover		475.00

Saint Anthony of Padua Issue

Italian Stamps of 1931 Ovptd. in Blue or Red

1931, May 7 Wmk. 140

52	A116	20c brown (Bl)	1.60	22.50
		Never hinged	4.00	
		On commercial cover		120.00
53	A116	25c green (R)	1.60	8.00
		Never hinged	4.00	
		On commercial cover		120.00
54	A118	30c gray brn (Bl)	1.60	8.00
		Never hinged	4.00	
		On commercial cover		180.00
55	A118	50c dl vio (Bl)	1.60	8.00
		Never hinged	4.00	
		On commercial cover		120.00
56	A120	1.25 l slate bl (R)	1.60	22.50
		Never hinged	4.00	
		On commercial cover		400.00

Overprinted like Nos. 23-24 in Red or Black
Unwmk.

57	A121	75c black, Opt. Type 1 (R)	1.60	22.50
		Never hinged	4.00	
		On commercial cover		325.00
a.		Overprint Type 2	65.00	100.00
58	A122	5 l + 2.50 l dk brn, Opt. Type 1	11.00	80.00
		Never hinged	27.50	
a.		Overprint Type 2	120.00	260.00
		Nos. 52-58 (7)	20.60	171.50
		Set, never hinged	51.50	
		Set on overfranked cover		540.00

Overprint on Nos. 57-58: Type 1, 14½mm wide; Type 2, 13mm wide.

Carabineer
A1

1934, Oct. 16 Photo. Wmk. 140

59	A1	5c dk ol grn & brn	5.50	22.50
		Never hinged	13.50	
		On commercial cover		350.00
60	A1	10c brn & blk	5.50	22.50
		Never hinged	13.50	
		On commercial cover		300.00
61	A1	20c scar & indigo	5.50	20.00
		Never hinged	13.50	
		On commercial cover		300.00
62	A1	50c pur & brn	5.50	20.00
		Never hinged	13.50	
		On commercial cover		275.00
63	A1	60c org brn & ind	5.50	28.00
		Never hinged	13.50	
		On commercial cover		350.00
64	A1	1.25 l dk bl & grn	5.50	47.50
		Never hinged	13.50	
		On commercial cover		450.00
		Nos. 59-64 (6)	33.00	160.50
		Set, never hinged	81.00	
		Set on overfranked cover		350.00

2nd Colonial Art Exhibition held at Naples. See Nos. C24-C29.

SEMI-POSTAL STAMPS

Many issues of Italy and Italian Colonies include one or more semipostal denominations. To avoid splitting sets,

---

these issues are generally listed as regular postage unless all values carry a surtax.

Holy Year Issue

Italian Semi-Postal Stamps of 1924 Overprinted in Black or Red

1925, June 1 Wmk. 140 Perf. 12

B1	SP4	20c + 10c dk grn & brn	4.00	24.00
		Never hinged	10.00	
		On commercial cover		225.00
B2	SP4	30c + 15c dk brn & brn	4.00	25.00
		Never hinged	10.00	
		On commercial cover		225.00
B3	SP4	50c + 25c vio & brn	4.00	24.00
		Never hinged	10.00	
		On commercial cover		225.00
B4	SP4	60c + 30c dp rose & brn	4.00	32.50
		Never hinged	10.00	
		On commercial cover		300.00
B5	SP8	1 l + 50c dp bl & vio (R)	4.00	47.50
		Never hinged	10.00	
B6	SP8	5 l + 2.50 l org brn & vio (R)	4.00	60.00
		Never hinged	10.00	
		Nos. B1-B6 (6)	24.00	213.00
		Set, never hinged	60.00	
		Set on overfranked cover		500.00

Colonial Institute Issue

"Peace" Substituting Spade for Sword — SP1

1926, June 1 Typo. Perf. 14

B7	SP1	5c + 5c brown	1.20	10.00
		Never hinged	2.50	
		On commercial cover		180.00
B8	SP1	10c + 5c olive grn	1.20	10.00
		Never hinged	2.50	
		On commercial cover		140.00
B9	SP1	20c + 5c blue grn	1.20	10.00
		Never hinged	2.50	
		On commercial cover		110.00
B10	SP1	40c + 5c brown red	1.20	10.00
		Never hinged	2.50	
		On commercial cover		110.00
B11	SP1	60c + 5c orange	1.20	10.00
		Never hinged	3.00	
		On commercial cover		180.00
B12	SP1	1 l + 5c blue	1.20	21.00
		Never hinged	3.00	
		On commercial cover		300.00
		Nos. B7-B12 (6)	7.20	71.00
		Set, never hinged	16.00	
		Set on overfranked cover		260.00

Surtax for Italian Colonial Institute.

Types of Italian Semi-Postal Stamps of 1926 Overprinted like Nos. 17-19

1927, Apr. 21 Unwmk. Perf. 11

B13	SP10	40c + 20c dk brn & blk	4.00	45.00
		Never hinged	10.00	
		On commercial cover		190.00
B14	SP10	60c + 30c brn red & ol brn	4.00	45.00
		Never hinged	10.00	
		On commercial cover		225.00
B15	SP10	1.25 l + 60c dp bl & blk	4.00	65.00
		Never hinged	10.00	
		On commercial cover		400.00
a.		Double overprint	1,750.	
			2,600.	
B16	SP10	5 l + 2.50 l dk grn & blk	6.50	100.00
		Never hinged	13.00	
		Nos. B13-B16 (4)	18.50	255.00
		Set, never hinged	43.00	
		Set on overfranked cover		600.00

The surtax on these stamps was for the charitable work of the Voluntary Militia for Italian National Defense.

Allegory of Fascism
and Victory — SP2

1928, Oct. 15   Wmk. 140   Perf. 14
B17 SP2   20c + 5c bl grn   3.25   14.50
   Never hinged   8.00
   On commercial cover   190.00
B18 SP2   30c + 5c red   3.25   14.50
   Never hinged   8.00
   On commercial cover   190.00
B19 SP2   50c + 10c purple   3.25   24.00
   Never hinged   8.00
   On commercial cover   190.00
B20 SP2   1.25 l + 20c dk bl   4.00   32.50
   Never hinged   10.00
   On commercial cover   525.00
   Nos. B17-B20 (4)   13.75   85.50
   Set, never hinged   34.00
   Set on overfranked cover   325.00

46th anniv. of the Societa Africana d'Italia. The surtax aided that society.

Types of Italian Semi-Postal Stamps of 1926 Overprinted in Red or Black like Nos. 52-56

1929, Mar. 4   Unwmk.   Perf. 11
B21 SP10   30c + 10c red & blk   4.75   27.50
   Never hinged   12.00
   On commercial cover   225.00
B22 SP10   50c + 20c vio & blk   4.75   30.00
   Never hinged   12.00
   On commercial cover   225.00
B23 SP10   1.25 l + 50c brn & bl   7.25   52.50
   Never hinged   18.00
   On commercial cover   475.00
B24 SP10   5 l + 2 l ol grn & blk (Bk)   7.25   100.00
   Never hinged   18.00
   Nos. B21-B24 (4)   24.00   210.00
   Set, never hinged   60.00
   Set on overfranked cover   600.00

Surtax for the charitable work of the Voluntary Militia for Italian Natl. Defense.

Types of Italian Semi-Postal Stamps of 1926 Overprinted in Black or Red like Nos. 52-56

1930, Oct. 20   Perf. 14
B25 SP10   30c + 10c dk grn & bl grn (Bk)   35.00   65.00
   Never hinged   87.50
   On commercial cover   325.00
B26 SP10   50c + 10c dk grn & vio   35.00   100.00
   Never hinged   87.50
   On commercial cover   350.00
B27 SP10   1.25 l + 30c ol brn & red brn   35.00   100.00
   Never hinged   87.50
   On commercial cover   550.00
B28 SP10   5 l + 1.50 l ind & grn   120.00   275.00
   Never hinged   300.00   —
   On commercial cover
   Nos. B25-B28 (4)   225.00   540.00
   Set, never hinged   562.50
   Set on overfranked cover   1,000.

Surtax for the charitable work of the Voluntary Militia for Italian Natl. Defense.

Sower — SP3

1930, Nov. 27   Photo.   Wmk. 140
B29 SP3   50c + 20c ol brn   4.25   26.00
   Never hinged   10.00
   On commercial cover   210.00
B30 SP3   1.25 l + 20c dp bl   4.25   26.00
   Never hinged   10.00
   On commercial cover   300.00
B31 SP3   1.75 l + 20c green   4.25   27.50
   Never hinged   10.00
   On commercial cover   375.00
B32 SP3   2.55 l + 50c purple   9.50   45.00
   Never hinged   21.00
   On commercial cover   600.00

B33 SP3   5 l + 1 l dp car   9.50   67.50
   Never hinged   21.00
   Nos. B29-B33 (5)   31.75   192.00
   Set, never hinged   72.00
   Set on overfranked cover   350.00

25th anniv. of the Italian Colonial Agricultural Institute. The surtax was for the aid of that institution.

AIR POST STAMPS

Air Post Stamps of Tripolitania, 1931, Overprinted in Blue like Nos. 38-42

1932, Jan. 7   Wmk. 140   Perf. 14
C1 AP1   50c rose car   1.60   .40
   Never hinged   4.00
   On commercial cover   20.00
C2 AP1   60c dp org   6.50   14.00
   Never hinged   12.50
   On commercial cover   250.00
C3 AP1   80c dl vio   6.50   22.50
   Never hinged   12.50
   On commercial cover   375.00
   Nos. C1-C3 (3)   14.60   36.90
   Set, never hinged   32.00
   Set on overfranked cover   225.00

Air Post Stamps of Tripolitania, 1931, Overprinted in Blue

1932, May 12
C4 AP1   50c rose car   1.60   2.00
   Never hinged   4.00
   On commercial cover   18.00
C5 AP1   80c dull violet   6.50   27.50
   Never hinged   12.50
   On commercial cover   350.00
   Set, never hinged   16.50
   Set on flight cover   200.00

This overprint was also applied to the 60c, Tripolitania No. C9. The overprinted stamp was never used in Cyrenaica, but was sold at Rome in 1943 by the Postmaster General for the Italian Colonies. Value $10.

Arab on Camel — AP2

Airplane in Flight AP3

1932, Aug. 8   Photo.
C6 AP2   50c purple   14.50   .25
   Never hinged   32.50
   On commercial cover   4.00
C7 AP2   75c brn rose   14.50   16.00
   Never hinged   32.50
   On commercial cover   175.00
C8 AP2   80c deep blue   14.50   30.00
   Never hinged   32.50
   On commercial cover   250.00
C9 AP3   1 l black   5.00   .25
   Never hinged   12.50
   On commercial cover   6.50
C10 AP3   2 l green   5.00   16.00
   Never hinged   12.50
   On commercial cover   475.00
C11 AP3   5 l deep car   10.00   32.50
   Never hinged   25.00
   On commercial cover   800.00
   Nos. C6-C11 (6)   63.50   95.00
   Set, never hinged   140.00
   Set on flight cover   325.00

For surcharges and overprint see Nos. C20-C23.

Graf Zeppelin Issue

Zeppelin and Clouds forming Pegasus AP4

Zeppelin and Ancient Galley AP5

Zeppelin and Giant Bowman AP6

1933, Apr. 15
C12 AP4   3 l dk brn   12.50   125.00
   Never hinged   30.00
   On commercial cover   450.00
C13 AP5   5 l purple   12.50   125.00
   Never hinged   30.00
   On commercial cover   600.00
C14 AP6   10 l dp grn   12.50   240.00
   Never hinged   30.00
   On commercial cover   875.00
C15 AP5   12 l deep blue   12.50   260.00
   Never hinged   30.00
   On commercial cover   1,100.
C16 AP4   15 l carmine   12.50   260.00
   Never hinged   30.00
   On commercial cover   1,100.
C17 AP6   20 l black   12.50   350.00
   Never hinged   30.00
   On commercial cover   1,100.
   Nos. C12-C17 (6)   75.00   1,360.
   Set, never hinged   180.00
   Set on flight cover   4,600.
   Set on 6 flight covers   5,250.

North Atlantic Crossing Issue

Airplane Squadron and Constellations — AP7

1933, June 1
C18 AP7   19.75 l grn & dp bl   21.00   650.00
   Never hinged   52.50
   On commercial cover   2,750.
C19 AP7   44.75 l red & indigo   21.00   650.00
   Never hinged   52.50
   On commercial cover   2,750.
   Set, never hinged   105.00
   Set on flight cover   5,400.

Type of 1932 Ovptd. and Srchd.

1934, Jan. 20
C20 AP3   2 l on 5 l org brn   4.75   95.00
   Never hinged   12.00
   On commercial cover   350.00
C21 AP3   3 l on 5 l yel grn   4.75   95.00
   Never hinged   12.00
   On commercial cover   350.00
C22 AP3   5 l ocher   4.75   110.00
   Never hinged   12.00
   On commercial cover   450.00
C23 AP3   10 l on 5 l rose   6.50   110.00
   Never hinged   16.00
   On commercial cover   600.00
   Nos. C20-C23 (4)   20.75   410.00
   Set, never hinged   52.00
   Set on flight cover   1,800.

For use on mail to be carried on a special flight from Rome to Buenos Aires.

Transport Plane AP8

Venus of Cyrene AP9

1934, Oct. 9
C24 AP8   25c sl bl & org red   5.50   22.50
   Never hinged   13.50
   On commercial cover   350.00
C25 AP8   50c dk grn & ind   5.50   20.00
   Never hinged   13.50
   On commercial cover   225.00
C26 AP8   75c dk brn & org red   5.50   20.00
   Never hinged   13.50
   On commercial cover   300.00
   a.   Imperf.   3,250.
   Never hinged   4,850.
C27 AP9   80c org brn & ol grn   5.50   22.50
   Never hinged   13.50
   On commercial cover   350.00
C28 AP9   1 l scar & ol grn   5.50   27.50
   Never hinged   13.50
   On commercial cover   400.00
C29 AP9   2 l dk bl & brn   5.50   47.50
   Never hinged   13.50
   On commercial cover   550.00
   Nos. C24-C29 (6)   33.00   160.00
   Set, never hinged   81.00
   Set on flight cover   450.00

2nd Colonial Arts Exhib. held at Naples.

AIR POST SEMI-POSTAL STAMPS

King Victor Emmanuel III SPAP1

Wmk. 104
1934, Nov. 5   Photo.   Perf. 14
CB1 SPAP1   25c + 10c gray grn   9.50   27.50
   Never hinged   24.00
   On cover   325.00
CB2 SPAP1   50c + 10c brn   9.50   27.50
   Never hinged   24.00
   On cover   325.00
CB3 SPAP1   75c + 15c rose red   9.50   27.50
   Never hinged   24.00
   On cover   350.00
CB4 SPAP1   80c + 15c brn blk   9.50   27.50
   Never hinged   24.00
   On cover   450.00
CB5 SPAP1   1 l + 20c red brn   9.50   27.50
   Never hinged   24.00
   On cover   475.00
CB6 SPAP1   2 l + 20c brt bl   9.50   27.50
   Never hinged   24.00
CB7 SPAP1   3 l + 25c pur   27.50   130.00
   Never hinged   67.50
CB8 SPAP1   5 l + 25c org   27.50   130.00
   Never hinged   67.50
CB9 SPAP1   10 l + 30c dp vio   27.50   130.00
   Never hinged   67.50

CB10 SPAP1 25 l + 2 l dp
grn 27.50 *130.00*
Never hinged 67.50
Nos. CB1-CB10 (10) 167.00 *685.00*
Set, never hinged 415.00
Set on flown cover 1,900.

65th birthday of King Victor Emmanuel III
and the invasion of Ethiopia.

AIR POST SEMI-POSTAL OFFICIAL STAMP

Type of Air Post Semi-Postal Stamps, 1934, Overprinted Crown and "SERVIZIO DI STATO" in Black
1934, Nov. 5   Wmk. 140   *Perf. 14*
CBO1 SPAP1 25 l + 2 l cop
red 2,600.
Never hinged 5,250.
On flight cover 3,250.

CZECHOSLOVAKIA

,che-kə-slō-'vä-kē-ə

LOCATION — Central Europe
GOVT. — Republic
AREA — 49,355 sq. mi.
POP. — 15,395,970 (1983)
CAPITAL — Prague

The Czechoslovakian Republic consists of Bohemia, Moravia and Silesia, Slovakia and Ruthenia (Carpatho-Ukraine). In March 1939, a German protectorate was established over Bohemia and Moravia, as well as over Slovakia which had meanwhile declared its independence. Ruthenia was incorporated in the territory of Hungary. These territories were returned to the Czechoslovak Republic in 1945, except for Ruthenia, which was ceded to Russia.

100 Haleru = 1 Koruna

> Catalogue values for unused stamps in this country are for Never Hinged items, beginning with Scott 142 in the regular postage section, Scott B144 in the semi-postal section, Scott EX1 in the personal delivery section, and Scott P14 in the newspaper section.

Watermarks

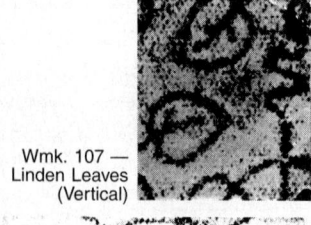

Wmk. 107 — Linden Leaves (Vertical)

Wmk. 135 — Crown in Oval or Circle, Sideways

Wmk. 136   Wmk. 136a

Stamps of Austria overprinted "Ceskoslovenska Republika," lion and "Cesko Slovensky Stat," "Provisorni Ceskoslovenska Vlada" and Arms, and "Ceskoslovenska Statni Posta" and Arms were made privately. A few of them were passed through the post but all have been pronounced unofficial and unauthorized by the Postmaster General.

During the occupation of part of Northern Hungary by the Czechoslovak forces, stamps of Hungary were overprinted "Cesko Slovenska Posta," "Ceskoslovenska Statni Posta" and Arms, and "Slovenska Posta" and Arms. These stamps were never officially issued though examples have passed the post.

Hradcany at Prague — A1

1918-19   Unwmk.   Typo.   *Imperf.*
1 A1 3h red violet .25 .25
2 A1 5h yellow green .25 .25
a. 5h green .95 .60
3 A1 10h rose .25 .25
a. 10h dark red .95 .30
4 A1 20h bluish green .25 .25
5 A1 25h deep blue .25 .25
a. 25h light blue 1.15 .25
b. 25h dark blue .75 .25
c. 25h ultramarine 19.00 12.50
6 A1 30h bister .45 .25
7 A1 40h red orange .45 .25
8 A1 100h brown 1.25 .25
9 A1 200h ultra 2.25 .25
a. 200h violet blue 19.00 25.00
b. 200h blue 11.00 .25
10 A1 400h purple 3.50 .25

On the 3h-40h "Posta Ceskoslovenska" is in white on a colored background; on the higher values the words are in color on a white background.
No. 5c was not valid for postage.
Nos. 1-6 exist as tete-beche gutter pairs.
See Nos. 368, 1554, 1600 in Scott Standard catalogue, Vol. 2. For surcharges see Nos. B130, C1, C4, J15, J19-J20, J22-J23, J30.

Perf. 11½, 13½
13 A1 5h yellow green .80 .25
a. Perf. 11½x10¾ 2.50 .55
14 A1 10h rose .40 .25
15 A1 20h bluish green .40 .25
a. Perf. 11½ .40 .25
16 A1 25h deep blue .60 .25
a. Perf. 11½ 1.50 .65
20 A1 200h ultra 4.25 .25
Nos. 1-10,13-16,20 (15) 15.60 3.75

All values of this issue exist with various private perforations and examples have been used on letters.
The 3h, 30h, 40h, 100h and 400h formerly listed are now known to have been privately perforated.
For overprints see Eastern Silesia Nos. 2, 5, 7-8, 14, 16, 18, 30.

A2

Type II

Type III

Type IV

Type II — Sun behind cathedral. Colorless foliage in foreground.
Type III — Without sun. Shaded foliage in foreground.
Type IV — No foliage in foreground. Positions of buildings changed. Letters redrawn.

1919   *Imperf.*
23 A2 1h dark brown (II) .25 .25
25 A2 5h blue green (IV) .40 .25
a. 5h dark blue green 7.50 —
b. 5h dark green 57.50 —
27 A2 15h red (IV) .85 .25
29 A2 25h dull violet (IV) .65 .25
a. 25h red violet 90.00 5.00
30 A2 50h dull violet (II) .40 .25
31 A2 50h dark blue (IV) .40 .25
32 A2 60h orange (III) 1.60 .25
33 A2 75h slate (IV) 1.20 .25
34 A2 80h olive grn (III) .95 .25
36 A2 120h gray black (IV) 2.50 .35
a. 120h light gray 19.00 .25
b. 120h silver gray 350.00 —
38 A2 300h dark green (III) 8.00 .65
39 A2 500h red brown (IV) 8.50 .50
40 A2 1000h violet (III) 19.00 1.20
a. 1000h bluish violet 42.50 2.40
Nos. 23-40 (13) 44.70 4.95

For overprints see Eastern Silesia Nos. 1, 3-4, 6, 9-13, 15, 17, 20-21.

1919-20   *Perf. 11½, 13¾, 13¾x11½*
41 A2 1h dk brown (II) .25 .25
42 A2 5h blue grn (IV), .25 .25
perf. 13½ .75 .25
a. Perf. 11½ 25.00 4.00
43 A2 10h yellow grn (IV) .40 .25
a. Imperf. 25.00 19.00
b. Perf. 11¾ 13.00 1.25
44 A2 15h brick red (IV) .40 .25
a. Perf. 11½x10¾ 30.00 4.50
b. Perf. 11½x13¾ 85.00 22.50
c. Perf. 13¾x10¾ 125.00 26.00
d. 15h brown red 9.00 10.00
e. 15h red 55.00 52.50
f. 15h carmine — 750.00
g. 15h vermilion red 37.50 —
45 A2 20h rose (IV) .40 .25
a. Imperf. 100.00 95.00
46 A2 25h dull vio (IV), .65 .25
perf. 11½
a. Perf. 11½x10¾ 5.00 1.10
b. Perf. 13¾x10¾ 175.00 40.00
47 A2 30h red violet (IV) .35 .25
a. Imperf. 190.00 190.00
b. Perf. 13¾x13½ 550.00 175.00
c. 30h deep violet .70 .25
d. As "c," perf. 13¾x13½ 625.00 190.00
e. As "c," imperf. 190.00 140.00
50 A2 60h orange (III) .30 .25
a. Perf. 13¾x13½ 25.00 6.25
53 A2 120h gray black (IV) 3.75 .95
Nos. 41-53 (9) 7.25 2.95

Nos. 43a, 45a, 47a and 47e were imperforate by accident and not issued in quantities as were Nos. 23 to 40.
Rouletted stamps of the preceding issues are said to have been made by a postmaster in a branch post office at Prague, or by private firms, but without authority from the Post Office Department.
The 50, 75, 80, 300, 500 and 1000h have been privately perforated.
Unlisted color varieties of types A1 and A2 were not officially released, and some are printer's waste.
For surcharges and overprints see Nos. B131, C2-C3, C5-C6, J16-J18, J21, J24-J29, J31, J42-J43, Eastern Silesia 22-29.

Pres. Thomas Garrigue Masaryk — A4

1920   *Perf. 13½*
61 A4 125h gray blue 1.50 .25
a. 125h ultramarine 40.00 19.00
62 A4 500h slate, *grysh* 4.75 2.50
a. Imperf. 20.00 7.00
63 A4 1000h blk brn, *brnsh* 8.00 5.00
Nos. 61-63 (3) 14.25 7.75

Nos. 61, 61a, 63 imperf. were not regularly issued. Values: unused singles, No. 61 $30; No. 61a $150; No. 62 $30; No. 63 $40.
For surcharge and overprints, see Nos. B131, Eastern Silesia 31-32.

Carrier Pigeon with Letter — A5

Czechoslovakia Breaking Chains to Freedom — A6

Hussite Priest — A7

Agriculture and Science — A8

Type I   Type II

Two types of 40h:
Type I: 9 leaves by woman's hip.
Type II: 10 leaves by woman's hip.

1920   *Perf. 14*
65 A5 5h dark blue .25 .25
a. Perf. 13¾ 325.00 150.00
66 A5 10h blue green .25 .25
a. Perf. 13¾ 225.00 110.00
67 A5 15h red brown .25 .25
68 A6 20h rose .25 .25
69 A6 25h lilac brown .25 .25
70 A6 30h red violet .25 .25
71 A6 40h red brown (I) .60 .25
a. As "b," tête bêche pair 6.75 2.00
b. Perf. 13½ 1.50 .25
c. Type II .25 .25
72 A6 50h carmine .50 .25
73 A6 60h dark blue .50 .25
a. As "b," tête bêche pair 6.00 4.00
b. Perf. 13½ 2.00 .25

Photo.
74 A7 80h purple .25 .25
75 A7 90h black brown .30 .25

Typo.
76 A8 100h dark green 1.00 .25
77 A8 200h violet 1.50 .25
78 A8 300h vermilion 3.50 .25
a. Perf. 13¾x13½ 7.00 .35
79 A8 400h brown 6.00 .45
80 A8 500h deep green 7.00 .45
a. Perf. 13¾x13½ 100.00 5.50
81 A8 600h deep violet 9.00 .45
a. Perf. 13¾x13½ 275.00 7.00
Nos. 65-81 (17) 31.65 4.85

No. 69 has background of horizontal lines.
Imperfs. were not regularly issued.
Nos. 71 and 73 exist as tete-beche gutter pairs.
For surcharges and overprint see Nos. C7-C9, J44-J56.

Type I   Type II

Two types of 20h:

Type I: Base of 2 is long, interior of 0 is angular.

Type II: Base of 2 is short, interior of 0 is an oval.

Type I   Type II

Two types of 25h:

Type I: Top of 2 curves up.

Type II: Top of 2 curves down.

1920-25			*Perf. 14*	
82	A5	5h violet	.25	.25
a.		As "b," tête bêche pair	2.00	1.00
b.		Perf. 13½	1.00	.35
83	A5	10h olive bister	.25	.25
a.		As "b," tête bêche pair	2.25	1.50
b.		Perf. 13½	.80	.25
84	A5	20h deep orange (II)	.25	.25
a.		As "b," tête bêche pair	30.00	14.00
b.		Perf. 13½	6.00	.60
c.		Type I		
85	A5	25h blue green (I)	.25	.25
a.		Type II		.25
86	A5	30h deep violet ('25)	3.00	.25
87	A6	50h yellow green	.25	.25
a.		As "b," tête bêche pair	60.00	27.50
b.		Perf. 13½	12.00	2.00
88	A6	100h dark brown	1.00	.25
a.		Perf. 13½	15.00	.25
89	A6	150h rose	4.50	.50
a.		Perf. 13½	80.00	1.10
90	A6	185h orange	3.00	.25
91	A6	250h dark green	5.00	.25
		Nos. 82-91 (10)	18.50	2.75

Imperfs. were not regularly issued.

Nos. 82-84, 87 exist as tete-beche gutter pairs.

Type of 1920 Issue Redrawn

Type I   Type II   Type III

Type I — Rib of leaf below "O" of POSTA is straight and extends to tip. White triangle above book is entirely at left of twig. "P" has a stubby, abnormal appendage.

Type II — Rib is extremely bent; does not reach tip. Triangle extends at right of twig. "P" like Type I.

Type III — Rib of top left leaf is broken in two. Triangle like Type II. "P" has no appendage.

1923			*Perf. 13¾, 13¾x13½*	
92	A8	100h red, *yellow*, III,		
		perf. 14x13½	1.00	.25
a.		Type I, perf. 13¾	1.25	.25
b.		Type I, perf. 13¾x13½	1.25	.25
c.		Type II, perf. 13¾	1.50	.25
d.		Type II, perf. 13¾x13½	1.50	.25
e.		Type III, perf. 13¾	7.00	.25
93	A8	200h blue, *yellow*, II,		
		perf. 14	5.00	.25
a.		Type I, perf. 13¾x13½	8.50	.25
b.		Type III, perf. 13¾	8.50	.25
c.		Type III, perf. 13¾x13½	52.50	.50
94	A8	300h violet, *yellow*, I,		
		perf. 13¾	3.75	.25
a.		Type II, perf. 13¾	35.00	.25
b.		Type III, perf. 13¾	50.00	.50
c.		Type III, perf. 13¾x13½	7.00	.25
d.		Type III, perf. 13¾	24.00	.35
		Nos. 92-94 (3)	9.75	.75

President Masaryk
A9   A10

1925		*Perf. 13¾x13½, 13¾*		
		Photo.	Wmk. 107	
		Size: 19½x23mm		
95	A9	40h brown orange	.75	.25
96	A9	50h olive green	1.50	.25
97	A9	60h red violet	1.75	.25
		Nos. 95-97 (3)	4.00	.75

Distinctive Marks of the Engravings.

I, II, III — Background of horizontal lines in top and bottom tablets. Inscriptions in Roman letters with serifs.

IV — Crossed horizontal and vertical lines in the tablets. Inscriptions in Antique letters without serifs.

I, II, IV — Shading of crossed diagonal lines on the shoulder at the right.

III — Shading of single lines only.

I — "T" of "Posta" over middle of "V" of "Ceskoslovenska." Three short horizontal lines in lower part of "A" of "Ceskoslovenska."

II — "T" over right arm of "V." One short line in "A."

III — "T" as in II. Blank space in lower part of "A."

IV — "T" over left arm of "V."

Wmk. Horizontally (107)
Engr.
I. First Engraving
Size: 19¾x22½mm

98	A10	1k carmine	.85	.25
99	A10	2k deep blue	2.00	.25
100	A10	3k brown	4.00	.65
101	A10	5k blue green	1.40	.45
		Nos. 98-101 (4)	8.25	1.60

Wmk. Vertically (107)
Size: 19⅛x23mm

101A	A10	1k carmine	100.00	4.00
101B	A10	2k deep blue	100.00	12.50
101C	A10	3k brown	250.00	12.50
101D	A10	5k blue green	5.00	2.00
		Nos. 101A-101D (4)	455.00	31.00

II. Second Engraving
Wmk. Horizontally (107)
Size: 19x21½mm

102	A10	1k carmine	50.00	.50
103	A10	2k deep blue	3.50	.25
104	A10	3k brown	3.50	.50
		Nos. 102-104 (3)	57.00	1.25

III. Third Engraving
Size: 19-19½x21½-22mm
Perf. 10

105	A10	1k carmine rose	1.00	.25
a.		Perf. 14	15.00	.25

IV. Fourth Engraving
Size: 19x22mm

1926			*Perf. 10*	
106	A10	1k carmine rose	1.00	.25

Perf. 14

108	A10	3k brown	4.50	.25

There is a 2nd type of No. 106: with long mustache. Same values. See No. 130, design SP3.

Karlstein Castle — A11

1926, June 1		Engr.	*Perf. 10*	
109	A11	1.20k red violet	.50	.30
110	A11	1.50k car rose	.30	.25
111	A11	2.50k dark blue	3.00	.30
		Nos. 109-111 (3)	3.80	.85

See Nos. 133, 135.

Karlstein   Pernstein
Castle — A12   Castle — A13

Orava Castle   Masaryk
A14   A15

Strahov
Monastery — A16

Hradcany at
Prague
A17

Great
Tatra — A18

Short Mustache   Long, Wavy
                 Mustache

1926-27		Engr.	Wmk. 107	
114	A13	30h gray green	1.25	.25
115	A14	40h red brown	.50	.25
116	A15	50h deep green	.50	.25
117	A15	60h red vio, lil	.85	.25
118	A16	1.20k red violet	4.00	1.50

Perf. 13½

119	A17	2k blue	.75	.25
a.		2k ultramarine	6.00	.75
120	A17	3k deep red	1.50	.25
121	A18	4k brn vio ('27)	4.75	.40
122	A18	5k dk grn ('27)	14.00	2.25
		Nos. 114-122 (9)	28.10	5.65

No. 116 exists in two types. The one with short, straight mustache at left sells for several times as much as that with longer wavy mustache.

See Nos. 137-140.

Coil Stamps
Perf. 10 Vertically

123	A12	20h brick red	.50	.40
a.		Vert. pair, imperf. horiz.	100.00	
124	A13	30h gray green	.35	.25
a.		Vert. pair, imperf. horiz.	100.00	
125	A15	50h deep green	.25	.25
		Nos. 123-125 (3)	1.10	.90

See No. 141.

Short Mustache   Long, Wavy
                 Mustache

1927-31		Unwmk.	*Perf. 10*	
126	A13	30h gray green	.25	.25
127	A14	40h deep brown	.70	.25
128	A15	50h deep green	.25	.25
129	A15	60h red violet	.70	.25
130	A10	1k carmine rose	1.10	.25
131	A15	1k deep red	.75	.25
132	A16	1.20k red violet	.40	.25
133	A11	1.50k carmine ('29)	.55	.25
134	A13	2k dp grn ('29)	.50	.25
135	A11	2.50k dark blue	5.50	.30
136	A14	3k red brown ('31)	.60	.25
		Nos. 126-136 (11)	11.30	2.80

No. 130 exists in two types. The one with longer mustache at right sells for several times as much as the one with the short mustache.

1927-28			*Perf. 13½*	
137	A17	2k ultra	.85	.25
138	A17	3k deep red ('28)	1.90	.65
139	A18	4k brown violet ('28)	6.00	1.00
140	A18	5k dark green ('28)	6.25	.50
		Nos. 137-140 (4)	15.00	2.40

Coil Stamp

1927			*Perf. 10 Vertically*	
141	A12	20h brick red	.50	.25

> **Catalogue values for unused stamps in this section, from this point to the end of the section, are for Never Hinged items.**

Hradec Castle   Brno Cathedral
A19   A25

Masaryk — A27

10th anniv. of Czech. independence: 40h, Town Hall, Levoca. 50h, Telephone exchange, Prague. 60h, Town of Jasina. 1k, Hluboka Castle. 1.20k, Pilgrims' House, Velehrad. 2.50k, Great Tatra. 5k, Old City Square, Prague.

1928, Oct. 22			*Perf. 13½*	
142	A19	30h black	.25	.25
143	A19	40h red brown	.30	.25
144	A19	50h dark green	.35	.35
145	A19	60h orange red	.40	.40
146	A19	1k carmine	.55	.55
147	A19	1.20k brown vio	1.25	1.25
148	A25	2k ultra	1.30	1.30
149	A19	2.50k dark blue	4.00	3.25
150	A27	3k dark brown	2.25	2.25
151	A25	5k deep violet	4.25	4.25
		Nos. 142-151 (10)	14.90	14.10

From one to three sheets each of Nos. 142-148, perf 12½, appeared on the market in the early 1950's.

Coat of Arms — A29

1929-37			*Perf. 10*	
152	A29	5h dark ultra ('31)	.25	.25
153	A29	10h bister brn ('31)	.25	.25
154	A29	20h red	.25	.25
155	A29	25h green	.25	.25
156	A29	30h red violet	.25	.25
157	A29	40h dk brown ('37)	1.50	.25
a.		40h red brown ('29)	4.00	.25
		Nos. 152-157 (6)	2.75	1.50

Coil Stamp
Perf. 10 Vertically

158	A29	20h red	.25	.25

For overprints, see Bohemia and Moravia Nos. 1-5, Slovakia Nos. 2-6.

St. Wenceslas   Founding St.
A30   Vitus' Cathedral
                  A31

Design: 3k, 5k, St. Wenceslas martyred.

1929, May 14 — *Perf. 13½*
159 A30 50h gray green .50 .25
160 A30 60h slate violet .80 .25
161 A31 2k dull blue 1.50 .50
162 A30 3k brown 2.00 .50
163 A30 5k brown violet 7.50 4.00
  Nos. 159-163 (5) 12.30 5.50
Millenary of the death of St. Methodius.

Statue of St. Wenceslas and National Museum, Prague — A33

1929 — *Perf. 10*
164 A33 2.50k deep blue 1.00 .25

Brno Cathedral A34 — Tatra Mountain Scene A35

Design: 5k, Old City Square, Prague.

1929, Oct. 15 — *Perf. 13½*
165 A34 3k red brown 3.00 .25
166 A35 4k indigo 9.50 .55
167 A35 5k gray green 11.00 .50
  Nos. 165-167 (3) 23.50 1.30
See No. 183.

A37

Type I 50 HALÉRŮ
Type II 50 HALÉRŮ

Two types of 50h:
I — A white space exists across the bottom of the vignette between the coat, shirt and tie and the "HALERU" frame panel.
II — An extra frame line has been added just above the "HALERU" panel which finishes off the coat and tie shading evenly.

1930, Jan. 2 — *Perf. 10*
168 A37 50h myrtle green (II) .25 .25
  a. Type I 1.25 .25
169 A37 60h brown violet 1.00 .25
170 A37 1k brown red .40 .25
  Nos. 168-170 (3) 1.65 .75
See No. 234.

Coil Stamp
1931 — *Perf. 10 Vertically*
171 A37 1k brown red 1.25 .65

President Masaryk — A38 — St. Nicholas' Church, Prague — A39

1930, Mar. 1 — *Perf. 13½*
175 A38 2k gray green 2.00 .50
176 A38 3k red brown 3.25 .50
177 A38 8k slate blue 8.00 2.00
178 A38 10k gray black 22.50 5.00
  Nos. 175-178 (4) 35.75 8.00
Fiftieth birthday of President Masaryk.
Nos. 175-178 were each issued in sheets with ornamental tabs at the bottom. Value, set with tabs $65.50.

1931, May 15
183 A39 10k black violet 18.00 3.25

Krivoklat Castle — A40 — Krumlov Castle — A42

Design: 4k, Orlik Castle.

1932, Jan. 2 — *Perf. 10*
184 A40 3.50k violet 4.50 1.50
185 A40 4k deep blue 4.50 .75
186 A42 5k gray green 5.50 .75
  Nos. 184-186 (3) 14.50 3.00

A43 — A44

1932, Mar. 16
187 A43 50h yellow green .75 .25
188 A43 1k brown carmine 2.00 .25
189 A44 2k dark blue 12.00 .60
190 A44 3k red brown 17.50 .60
  Nos. 187-190 (4) 32.25 1.70

Miroslav Tyrs — A45

1933, Feb. 1
191 A45 60h dull violet .30 .25
Miroslav Tyrs (1832-84), founder of the Sokol movement; and the 9th Sokol Congress (Nos. 187-190).

First Christian Church at Nitra
A46 — A47

1933, June 20
192 A46 50h yellow green .60 .30
193 A47 1k carmine rose 9.00 .60
Prince Pribina who introduced Christianity into Slovakia and founded there the 1st Christian church in A.D. 833.
All gutter pairs are vertical. Values unused: No. 192 $350; No. 193 $10,000.

Bedrich Smetana, Czech Composer and Pianist, 50th Death Anniv. — A48

1934, Mar. 26 — *Engr.* — *Perf. 10*
194 A48 50h yellow green .40 .25

Consecration of Legion Colors at Kiev, Sept. 21, 1914 — A49

Ensign Heyduk with Colors A51 — Legionnaires A52

1k, Legion receiving battle flag at Bayonne.

1934, Aug. 15 — *Perf. 10*
195 A49 50h green .75 .25
196 A49 1k rose lake .90 .25
197 A51 2k deep blue 4.00 .60
198 A52 3k red brown 6.75 .75
  Nos. 195-198 (4) 12.40 1.85
20th anniv. of the Czechoslovakian Legion which fought in WWI.

Antonin Dvorák, (1841-1904), Composer — A53

1934, Nov. 22
199 A53 50h green .40 .25

Pastoral Scene — A54

1934, Dec. 17 — *Perf. 10*
200 A54 1k claret .80 .25
  a. Souv. sheet of 15, perf. 13½ 200.00 300.00
  b. As "a," single stamp 10.00 12.50
201 A54 2k blue 2.25 .80
  a. Souv. sheet of 15, perf. 13½ 1,000. 1,000.
  b. As "a," single stamp 42.50 29.00
Centenary of the National Anthem.
Nos. 200-201 were each issued in sheets of 100 stamps and 12 blank labels. Value, set with attached labels: mint $24; used $8.
Nos. 200a & 201a have thick paper, darker shades, no gum. Forgeries exist.

President Masaryk
A55 — A56

1935, Mar. 1
202 A55 50h green, buff .35 .25
203 A55 1k claret, buff .40 .25
204 A56 2k gray blue, buff 2.00 .60
205 A56 3k brown, buff 3.25 .60
  Nos. 202-205 (4) 6.00 1.70
85th birthday of President Masaryk.
Nos. 204-205 were each issued in sheets of 100 stamps and 12 blank labels. Value with attached labels: mint $30; used $10.
See No. 235.

Monument to Czech Heroes at Arras, France — A57

1935, May 4
206 A57 1k rose .85 .25
207 A57 2k dull blue 3.00 .75
20th anniversary of the Battle of Arras.
Nos. 206-207 were each issued in sheets of 100 stamps and 12 blank labels. Value, set with attached labels: mint $22.50; used $22.50.

Gen. Milan Stefánik A58 — Sts. Cyril and Methodius A59

1935, May 18
208 A58 50h green .25 .25

1935, June 22
209 A59 50h green .40 .25
210 A59 1k claret .55 .25
211 A59 2k deep blue 2.00 .50
  Nos. 209-211 (3) 2.95 1.00
Millenary of the arrival in Moravia of the Apostles Cyril and Methodius.

Masaryk — A60

1935, Oct. 20 — *Perf. 12½*
212 A60 1k rose lake .25 .25
No. 212 exists imperforate. See Bohemia and Moravia No. 1A. For overprints see Bohemia and Moravia Nos. 9-10, Slovakia 12.

Statue of Macha, Prague — A61

1936, Apr. 30
213 A61 50h deep green .25 .25
214 A61 1k rose lake .50 .25
Karel Hynek Macha (1810-1836), Bohemian poet.
Nos. 213-214 were each issued in sheets of 100 stamps and 12 blank labels. Value, set with attached labels: mint $2; used 80c.

Jan Amos Komensky (Comenius) — A61a

Pres. Eduard Benes A62 — Gen. Milan Stefánik A63

1936
215 A61a 40h dark blue .25 .25
216 A62 50h dull green .25 .25
217 A63 60h dull violet .25 .25
Nos. 215-217 (3) .75 .75

See no. 252, Slovakia 23A. For overprints see Bohemia and Moravia Nos. 6, 8, Slovakia 7, 9-11.

Castle Palanok near Mukacevo A64

Town of Banska Bystrica A65

Castle at Zvikov — A66

Ruins of Castle at Strecno — A67

Castle at Cesky Raj A68

Palace at Slavkov (Austerlitz) A69

Statue of King George of Podebrad A70

Town Square at Olomouc — A71

Castle Ruins at Bratislava A72

1936, Aug. 1
218 A64 1.20k rose lilac .25 .25
219 A65 1.50k carmine .25 .25
220 A66 2k dark blue green .25 .25
221 A67 2.50k dark blue .40 .25
222 A68 3k brown .40 .25
223 A69 3.50k dark violet 1.60 .55
224 A70 4k dark violet .65 .25
225 A71 5k green .65 .25
226 A72 10k blue 1.10 .55
Nos. 218-226 (9) 5.55 2.85

Nos. 224-226 were each issued in sheets of 100 stamps and 12 blank labels. Value, with attached labels: mint $7; used $2.75.

For overprints and surcharge see Nos. 237-238, 254A, Bohemia and Moravia 11-12, 14-19, Slovakia 13-14, 16-23.

President Benes — A73

Soldiers of the Czech Legion — A74

1937, Apr. 26 Unwmk. Perf. 12½
227 A73 50h deep green .25 .25

For overprints see Nos. 236, Slovakia 8.

1937, June 15
228 A74 50h deep green .25 .25
229 A74 1k rose lake .40 .25

20th anniv. of the Battle of Zborov. Nos. 228-229 were each issued in sheets of 100 stamps and 12 blank labels. Value, set with attached labels: mint $4; used $2.

Cathedral at Prague — A75

Jan Evangelista Purkyne — A76

1937, July 1
230 A75 2k green 1.00 .25
231 A75 2.50k blue 1.50 .80

Founding of the "Little Entente," 16th anniv. Nos. 230-231 were each issued in sheets with blank labels. Value, set with attached labels: mint $22.50; used $11.

1937, Sept. 2
232 A76 50h slate green .25 .25
233 A76 1k dull rose .30 .25

150th anniv. of the birth of Purkyne, Czech physiologist. Nos. 232-233 were printed in sheets of 100 with 12 decorated labels. Value, set with labels, $1.

Masaryk Types of 1930-35
1937, Sept. Perf. 12½
234 A37 50h black .25 .25

With date "14.IX. 1937" in design
235 A56 2k black .30 .25

Death of former President Thomas G. Masaryk on Sept. 14, 1937.
No. 235 was issued in sheets of 100 stamps and 12 inscribed labels. Value, with attached label: mint $1.20; used 60c.

International Labor Bureau Issue
Stamps of 1936-37 Overprinted in Violet or Black

1937, Oct. 6 Perf. 12½
236 A73 50h dp green (Bk) .55 .50
237 A65 1.50k carmine (V) .55 .50
238 A66 2k dp green (V) .95 .60
Nos. 236-238 (3) 2.05 1.60

Bratislava Philatelic Exhibition Issue
Souvenir Sheet

A77

1937, Oct. 24 Perf. 12½
239 A77 Sheet of 2 2.50 3.25
a. 50h dark blue .80 1.20
b. 1k brown carmine .80 1.20

The stamps show a view of Poprad Lake (50h) and the tomb of General Milan Stefanik (1k).
No. 239 overprinted with the Czechoslovak arms and "Czecho-Slovak Participation New York World's Fair 1939, Czecho-Slovak Pavilion" were privately produced to finance Czechoslovak participation in the exhibition. The overprint exists in black, green, red, blue, gold and silver.
No. 239 overprinted "Liberation de la Tchechoslovaquie, 28-X-1945" etc., was sold at a philatelic exhibition in Brussels, Belgium.

St. Barbara's Church, Kutna Hora — A79

Peregrine Falcon, Sokol Emblem — A80

1937, Dec. 4
240 A79 1.60k olive green .25 .25

For overprints see Bohemia and Moravia Nos. 13, Slovakia 15.

1938, Jan. 21
241 A80 50h deep green .25 .25
242 A80 1k rose lake .25 .25

10th Intl. Sokol Games. Nos. 241-242 were each issued in sheets of 100 stamps and 12 inscribed labels. Value, set with attached labels: mint $2; used $1.50.
Imperf. copies of No. 242 are essays.

Legionnaires A81 A82

Legionnaire — A83

1938
243 A81 50h deep green .25 .25
244 A82 50h deep green .25 .25
245 A83 50h deep green .25 .25
Nos. 243-245 (3) .75 .75

20th anniv. of the Battle of Bachmac, Vouziers and Doss Alto. Nos. 243-245 were each issued in sheets of 100 stamps and 12 inscribed labels. Value, with attached labels $1.25, mint or used.

Jindrich Fügner, Co-Founder of Sokol Movement — A84

1938, June 18 Perf. 12½
246 A84 50h deep green .25 .25
247 A84 1k rose lake .25 .25
248 A84 2k slate blue .40 .25
Nos. 246-248 (3) .90 .75

10th Sokol Summer Games. Nos. 246-248 were each issued in sheets of 100 stamps and 12 inscribed labels. Value, with attached labels: mint $2.50; used $2.

View of Pilsen — A85

Cathedral of Kosice — A86

1938, June 24
249 A85 50h deep green .25 .25

Provincial Economic Council meeting, Pilsen. No. 249 was issued in sheets of 150 stamps and 10 labels depicting a flower within a cogwheel. Value, with attached label 40c, mint or used.
For overprint see Bohemia & Moravia No. 7.

1938, July 15 Perf. 12½
250 A86 50h deep green .25 .25

Kosice Cultural Exhibition.

Prague Philatelic Exhibition Issue
Souvenir Sheet

Vysehrad Castle — Hradcany — A87

1938, June 26 Perf. 12½
251 A87 Sheet of 2 5.00 5.00
a. 50h dark blue 1.50 1.50
b. 1k deep carmine 1.50 1.50

See No. 3036 in Scott Standard catalogue, Vol. 2.

Stefánik Type of 1936
1938, Nov. 21
252 A63 50h deep green .25 .25

Allegory of the Republic — A89

1938, Dec. 19 Unwmk.
253 A89 2k lt ultra .30 .25
254 A89 3k pale brown .50 .40

20th anniv. of Independence. Nos. 253-254 were each issued in sheets of 100 stamps and 12 blank labels. Value, set with attached labels $2.50, mint or used.
See No. B153.

"Wir sind frei!"
Stamps of Czechoslovakia, 1918-37, overprinted with a swastika in black or red and "Wir sind frei!" were issued locally and unofficially in 1938 as Czech authorities were evacuating and German authorities arriving. They appeared in the towns of Asch, Karlsbad, Reichenberg-Maffersdorf, Rumburg, etc.
The overprint, sometimes including a surcharge or the town name (as in Karlsbad), exists on many values of postage, air post, semi-postal, postage due and newspaper stamps.

No. 226
Surcharged in
Orange Red

1939, Jan. 18   Unwmk.   Perf. 12½
254A A72 300h on 10k blue   1.60 *2.25*

Opening of the Slovakian Parliament.
No. 254A was issued in sheets of 100
stamps with 12 blank labels. Value, set with
attached labels, mint $4.

View of Jasina —
A89a

Perf. 12½
1939, Mar. 15   Engr.   Unwmk.
254B A89a 3k ultra   25.00 *90.00*

Inauguration of the Carpatho-Ukraine Diet,
Mar. 2, 1939.
Printed for use in the province of Carpatho-
Ukraine but issued in Prague at the same
time.
Used value is for red commemorative
cancel.

The stamps formerly listed as Czechoslovakia Nos. 255, 256 and C18 are
now listed with Bohemia and Moravia
and Slovakia. No. 255 is now Slovakia
23A. No. 256 and C18 are now listed as
Bohemia and Moravia 1A and C1,
respectively.

SEMI-POSTAL STAMPS

Nos. B1-B123 were sold at 1½ times
face value at the Philatelists' Window of
the Prague P.O. for charity benefit.
They were available for ordinary
postage.
Almost all stamps between Nos. B1-
B123 are known with misplaced or
inverted overprints and/or in pairs with
one stamp missing the overprint.
The overprints of Nos. B1-B123 have
been well forged.

Austrian Stamps of
1916-18 Overprinted
in Black or Blue —
a

Two sizes of type A40:
Type I: 25x30mm.
Type II: 26x29mm.

1919   Perf. 12½
B1	A37	3h brt violet	.25	.25
B2	A37	5h lt green	.25	.25
B3	A37	6h dp orange (Bl)	.60	.80
B4	A37	6h dp orange (Bk)	2,000.	2,000.
B5	A37	10h magenta	.80	1.00
B6	A37	12h lt blue	.80	.80
B7	A42	15h dull red	.25	.25
B8	A42	20h dark green	.25	.25
a.		20h green	55.00	40.00
B9	A42	25h blue	.35	.25
B10	A42	30h dull violet	.35	.25
B11	A39	40h olive grn	.40	.40
B12	A39	50h dk green	.40	.40
B13	A39	60h dp blue	.40	.40
B14	A39	80h orange brn	.40	.40
B15	A39	90h red violet	.80	.80
B16	A39	1k car, *yel* (Bl)	.60	.60
B17	A39	1k car, *yel* (Bk)	62.50	62.50
B18	A40	2k light blue (I)	3.25	3.25
a.		2k dark blue (II)	3,000.	2,000.
b.		2k light blue (II)	1.90	1.90
c.		2k dark blue (I)	8,500.	4,000.

B19	A40	3k car rose (I)	37.50	32.50
a.		3k claret (I)	2,500.	900.00
b.		3k carmine rose (II)	2,000.	1,000.
c.		3k claret (II)	5,500.	4,000.
B20	A40	4k yellow grn (I)	20.00	15.00
a.		4k deep green (I)	55.00	45.00
b.		4k yellow green (II)		10.00
B21	A40	10k violet	300.00	160.00
a.		10k deep violet	375.00	275.00
b.		10k black violet	450.00	300.00

The used value of No. B18a is for a stamp
that has only a Czechoslovakian cancellation.
Some examples of Austria No. 160, which
were officially overprinted with type "a" and
sold by the post office, had previously been
used and lightly canceled with Austrian cancellations. These canceled-before-overprinting
stamps, which were postally valid, sell for
about one-fourth as much.

Granite Paper
B22	A40	2k light blue	4.00	2.90
B23	A40	3k carmine rose	10.00	8.25

The 4k and 10k on granite paper with this
overprint were not regularly issued.
Excellent counterfeits of Nos. B1-B23 exist.

Austrian Newspaper
Stamps Overprinted
— b

Imperf
On Stamp of 1908
B26	N8	10h carmine	*3,500.*	*2,000.*

On Stamps of 1916
B27	N9	2h brown	.25	.25
B28	N9	4h green	.40	.40
B29	N9	6h deep blue	.40	.40
B30	N9	10h orange	5.00	5.00
B31	N9	30h claret	1.60	1.60
		Nos. B27-B31 (5)	7.65	7.65

Austrian
Special
Handling
Stamps
Overprinted
in Blue or
Black — c

Perf. 12½
Stamps of 1916 Overprinted
B32	SH1	2h claret, *yel* (Bl)	25.00	25.00
B33	SH1	5h dp grn, *yel* (Bk)	*1,900.*	*825.00*

Stamps of
1917
Overprinted —
d

B34	SH2	2h cl, *yel* (Bl)	.25	.35
a.		Vert. pair, imperf. btwn.	250.00	
B35	SH2	2h cl, *yel* (Bk)	60.00	35.00
B36	SH2	5h grn, *yel* (Bk)	.25	.25

Austrian Air Post Stamps, #C1-C3, Overprinted Type "c" Diagonally
B37	A40	1.50k on 2k lil	175.00	175.00
B38	A40	2.50k on 3k ocher	175.00	175.00
B39	A40	4k gray	1,500.	800.00

1919
Austrian Postage Due Stamps of 1908-13 Overprinted Type "b"
B40	D3	2h carmine	*6,500.*	*2,750.*
B41	D3	4h carmine	25.00	15.00
B42	D3	6h carmine	12.50	8.00
B43	D3	14h carmine	90.00	35.00
B44	D3	25h carmine	45.00	20.00
B45	D3	30h carmine	600.00	300.00
B46	D3	50h carmine	1,200.	825.00

Austria Nos. J49-J56 Overprinted Type "b"
B47	D4	5h rose red	.25	.30
B48	D4	10h rose red	.25	.30
B49	D4	15h rose red	.25	.30
B50	D4	20h rose red	2.00	2.00
B51	D4	25h rose red	2.00	2.00
B52	D4	30h rose red	.65	.65
B53	D4	40h rose red	2.00	2.00
B54	D4	50h rose red	600.00	250.00

Austria Nos. J57-J59 Overprinted Type "a"
B55	D5	1k ultra	12.50	10.00
B56	D5	5k ultra	55.00	35.00
B57	D5	10k ultra		

Austria Nos. J47-J48, J60-J63 Overprinted Type "c" Diagonally
B58	A22	1h gray	32.50	30.00
B59	A23	15h on 2h vio	150.00	110.00
B60	A38	10h on 24h blue	120.00	85.00
B61	A38	15h on 36h vio	1.00	1.00
B62	A38	20h on 54h org	90.00	85.00
B63	A38	50h on 42h choc	1.00	1.00

Hungarian Stamps Ovptd. Type "b"
1919   Wmk. 137   Perf. 15
On Stamps of 1913-16
B64	A4	1f slate	4,000.	1,600.
B65	A4	2f yellow	3.50	2.50
B66	A4	3f orange	45.00	25.00
B67	A4	6f olive green	4.50	4.50
B68	A4	50f lake, *bl*	1.25	1.00
B69	A4	60f grn, *sal*	50.00	20.00
B70	A4	70f red brn, *grn*	4,000.	1,600.

On Stamps of 1916
B71	A8	10f rose	475.00	175.00
B72	A8	15f violet	250.00	100.00

On Stamps of 1916-18
B73	A9	2f brown orange	.25	.25
B74	A9	3f red lilac	.25	.25
B75	A9	5f green	.25	.25
B76	A9	6f grnsh blue	.60	.60
B77	A9	10f rose red	1.40	2.25
B78	A9	15f violet	.25	.25
B79	A9	20f gray brown	14.00	14.00
B80	A9	25f dull blue	1.00	.80
B81	A9	35f brown	10.00	10.00
B82	A9	40f olive green	3.25	2.50

Overprinted Type "d"
B83	A10	50f red vio & lil	1.25	1.60
B84	A10	75f brt bl & pale bl	1.25	1.60
B85	A10	80f yel grn & pale grn	1.25	1.60
B86	A10	1k red brn & cl	2.50	2.00
B87	A10	2k ol brn & bis	10.00	10.00
B88	A10	3k dk vio & ind	37.50	37.50
B89	A10	5k dk brn & lt brn	140.00	90.00
B90	A10	10k vio brn & vio		1,800. 800.00

Overprinted Type "b"
On Stamps of 1918
B91	A11	10f scarlet	.25	.25
B92	A11	20f dark brown	.30	.30
B93	A11	25f deep blue	1.40	1.25
B94	A12	40f olive grn	4.00	3.25
B95	A12	50f lilac	67.50	25.00

On Stamps of 1919
B96	A13	10f red	10.00	8.00
B97	A13	20f dk brn	10,000.	

Same Overprint On Hungarian Newspaper Stamp of 1914
Imperf
B98	N5	(2f) orange	.25	.30

Same Overprint On Hungarian Special Delivery Stamp
Perf. 15
B99	SD1	2f gray grn & red	.25	.35

Same Ovpt. On Hungarian Semi-Postal Stamps
B100	SP3	10f + 2f rose red	.80	.80
B101	SP4	15f + 2f violet	1.25	1.25
B102	SP5	40f + 2f brn car	7.00	3.50
		Nos. B98-B102 (5)	9.55	6.20

Hungarian Postage Due Stamps of 1903-18 Overprinted Type "b"
1919   Wmk. 135   Perf. 11½, 12
B103	D1	50f green & black	525.00	525.00

Wmk. Crown (136, 136a)
Perf. 11½x12, 15
B104	D1	1f green & black	*1,200.*	*1,000.*
B105	D1	2f green & black	*1.000.*	*750.*
B106	D1	12f green & black	*4,250.*	*3,000.*
B107	D1	50f green & black	275.	150.

Wmk. Double Cross (137)
Perf. 15
On Stamps of 1914
B110	D1	1f green & black	*1,250.*	*600.*
B111	D1	2f green & black	700.	550.
B112	D1	5f green & black	*1,325.*	*900.*
B113	D1	12f green & black	*5,250.*	*4,000.*
B114	D1	50f green & black	275.	150.

On Stamps of 1915-18
B115	D1	1f green & red	175.00	140.00
B116	D1	2f green & red	1.00	1.00
B117	D1	6f green & red	12.50	10.00
B118	D1	6f green & red	1.50	1.50
	a.	Pair, one without overprint		
B119	D1	10f green & red	.60	.60
B120	D1	12f green & red	2.00	2.00
B121	D1	15f green & red	7.50	5.00
B122	D1	20f green & red	1.00	1.00
B123	D1	30f green & red	80.00	70.00
		Nos. B115-B123 (9)	281.10	230.90

Excellent counterfeits of Nos. B1-B123 exist.

Bohemian Lion
Breaking its
Chains — SP1

Mother and
Child — SP2

Perf. 11½, 13¾ and Compound
1919   Typo.   Unwmk.
Pinkish Paper
B124	SP1	15h gray green	.25	.25
a.		15h light green	32.50	25.00
B125	SP1	25h dark brown	.25	.25
a.		25h light brown	*5.00*	*4.00*
B126	SP1	50h dark blue	.25	.25

Photo.
Yellowish Paper
B127	SP2	75h slate	.25	.25
B128	SP2	100h brn vio	.25	.25
B129	SP2	120h vio, *yel*	.25	.25
		Nos. B124-B129 (6)	1.50	1.50

Values are for perf 13¾. Other perfs are
valued higher.
Nos. B124-B126 commemorate the 1st
anniv. of Czechoslovak independence. Nos.
B127-B129 were sold for the benefit of Legion-
naires' orphans. Imperforates exist.
See No. 1581 in Scott Standard catalogue,
Vol. 2.

Regular Issues of Czechoslovakia Surcharged in Red

a

b

1920   Perf. 13¾
B130	A1(a)	40h + 20h bister	.75	.90
B131	A2(a)	60h + 20h green	.75	.90
B132	A4(b)	125h + 25h gray bl	3.50	2.75
		Nos. B130-B132 (3)	5.00	4.55

President
Masaryk — SP3

Wmk. Linden Leaves (107)
1923   Engr.   Perf. 13¾x14¾
B133	SP3	50h gray green	.90	.55
B134	SP3	100h carmine	1.10	.90
B135	SP3	200h blue	3.50	3.00
B136	SP3	300h dark brown	3.50	4.25
		Nos. B133-B136 (4)	9.00	8.70

5th anniv. of the Republic.
The gum was applied through a screen and
shows the monogram "CSP" (Ceskoslovenska
Posta). These stamps were sold at double

their face values, the excess being given to the Red Cross and other charitable organizations.

International Olympic Congress Issue

Semi-Postal Stamps of 1923 Overprinted in Blue or Red

1925

B137	SP3	50h gray green	10.00	8.50
B138	SP3	100h carmine	14.50	12.00
B139	SP3	200h blue (R)	72.50	55.00
	Nos. B137-B139 (3)		97.00	75.50
	Set, never hinged		175.00	

These stamps were sold at double their face values, the excess being divided between a fund for post office clerks and the Olympic Games Committee.

Sokol Issue

Semi-Postal Stamps of 1923 Overprinted in Blue or Red

1926

B140	SP3	50h gray green	1.60	4.00
B141	SP3	100h carmine	3.25	4.00
B142	SP3	200h blue (R)	15.00	12.50
a.	Double overprint			
B143	SP3	300h dk brn (R)	20.00	20.00
	Nos. B140-B143 (4)		39.85	40.50
	Set, never hinged		140.00	

These stamps were sold at double their face values, the excess being given to the Congress of Sokols, June, 1926.

> Catalogue values for unused stamps in this section, from this point to the end of the section, are for Never Hinged items.

Midwife Presenting Newborn Child to its Father; after a Painting by Josef Manes
SP4   SP5

1936   Unwmk.   Engr.   Perf. 12½

B144	SP4	50h + 50h green	.75	.75
B145	SP5	1k + 50h claret	1.25	1.25
B146	SP4	2k + 50h blue	2.75	2.75
	Nos. B144-B146 (3)		4.75	4.75

Nos. B144-B146 were each issued in sheets of 100 with 12 labels. Value, set $40.

"Lullaby" by Stanislav Sucharda
SP7

SP6

1937   Perf. 12½

B147	SP6	50h + 50h dull green	.60	.35
B148	SP6	1k + 50h rose lake	1.10	1.10
B149	SP7	2k + 1k dull blue	2.60	1.75
	Nos. B147-B149 (3)		4.30	3.20

Nos. B147-B149 were each issued in sheets of 100 with 12 labels. Value, set $40.

President Masaryk and Little Girl in Native Costume — SP8

1938   Perf. 12½

B150	SP8	50h + 50h deep green	.85	.85
B151	SP8	1k + 50h rose lake	1.25	1.25

Souvenir Sheet

Imperf

B152	SP8	2k + 3k black	6.25	6.25

88th anniv. of the birth of Masaryk (1850-1937).

Nos. B150-B151 were each issued in sheets of 100 stamps and 12 blank labels. Value, set of singles with attached labels: mint $3.75; used $2.50.

Allegory of the Republic Type
Souvenir Sheet

1938   Perf. 12½

B153	A89	2k (+ 8k) dark blue	4.00	4.00

The surtax was devoted to national relief for refugees.

AIR POST STAMPS

Nos. 9, 39-40, 20, and Types of 1919 Srchd. in Red, Blue or Green

1920   Unwmk.   Imperf.

C1	A1	14k on 200h (R)	21.00	18.00
a.	Inverted surcharge		125.00	
C2	A2	24k on 500h (Bl)	50.00	30.00
a.	Inverted surcharge		225.00	
C3	A2	28k on 1000h (G)	32.50	30.00
a.	Inverted surcharge		150.00	
b.	Double surcharge		200.00	
	Nos. C1-C3 (3)		103.50	78.00

Perf. 13¾

C4	A1	14k on 200h (R)	22.50	30.00
a.	Perf. 13¾x13½		95.00	95.00
C5	A2	24k on 500h (Bl)	45.00	70.00
a.	Perf. 13¾x13½		100.00	100.00

Perf. 13¾x13½

C6	A2	28k on 1000h (G)	20.00	27.50
a.	Inverted surcharge		400.00	
b.	Perf. 13¾		475.00	700.00
c.	As "b," invtd. surcharge		350.00	
	Nos. C4-C6 (3)		87.50	127.50
	Nos. C1-C6 (6)		191.00	205.50

Excellent counterfeits of the overprint are known.

Stamps of 1920 Srchd. in Black or Violet

1922, June 15   Perf. 13¾

C7	A8	50h on 100h dl grn	1.50	1.50
a.	Inverted surcharge		150.00	
b.	Double surcharge		160.00	
C8	A8	100h on 200h vio	4.00	3.25
a.	Inverted surcharge		150.00	
C9	A8	250h on 400h brn (V)	6.00	7.50
a.	Inverted surcharge		275.00	
	Nos. C7-C9 (3)		11.50	12.25
	Set, never hinged		20.00	

Fokker Monoplane AP3   Smolik S 19 AP4

Smolik S 19 — AP5

Fokker over Prague AP6

1930, Dec. 16   Engr.   Perf. 13½

C10	AP3	50h deep green	.25	.25
C11	AP3	1k deep red	.30	.45
C12	AP4	2k dark green	.70	1.10
C13	AP4	3k red violet	1.50	1.30
C14	AP5	4k indigo	1.40	1.30
C15	AP5	5k red brown	2.75	4.25
C16	AP5	10k vio blue	5.00	4.25
a.	10k ultra		13.50	12.00
C17	AP6	20k gray violet	5.25	5.25
	Nos. C10-C17 (8)		17.15	18.15

Two types exist of the 50h, 1k and 2k, and three types of the 3k, differing chiefly in the size of the printed area. A "no hill at left" variety of the 3k exists.

Imperf. examples of Nos. C10-C17 are proofs.

See Bohemia and Moravia No. C1.

Perf. 12

C10a	AP3	50h deep green	3.25	5.00
C11a	AP3	1k deep red	18.00	22.50
C12a	AP4	2k dark green	18.00	22.50
C14a	AP5	4k indigo	2.75	3.75
C17a	AP6	20k gray violet	3.50	7.50

Perf. 12x13½, 13½x12

C11b	AP3	1k deep red	6.00	7.50
C12b	AP4	2k dark green	12.00	20.00

Perf. 13¾x12¼

C17b	AP6	20k gray violet	1,750.	

Perf. 12½

C15a	AP5	5k red brown	2,000.	

SPECIAL DELIVERY STAMPS

Doves — SD1

1919-20   Unwmk.   Typo.   Imperf.

E1	SD1	2h red vio, *yel*	.25	.25
E2	SD1	5h yel grn, *yel*	.25	.25
E3	SD1	10h red brn, *yel* ('20)	.80	.80
	Nos. E1-E3 (3)		1.30	1.30

For overprints and surcharge see Nos. P11-P13, Eastern Silesia E1-E2.

1921   White Paper

E1a	SD1	2h red violet	9.50	
E2a	SD1	5h yellow green	6.50	
E3a	SD1	10h red brown	140.00	
	Nos. E1a-E3a (3)		156.00	

It is doubted that Nos. E1a-E3a were regularly issued.

PERSONAL DELIVERY STAMPS

> Catalogue values for unused stamps in this section are for Never Hinged items.

PD1

Design: No. EX2, "D" in each corner.

1937   Unwmk.   Photo.   Perf. 13½

EX1	PD1	50h blue	.25	.25
EX2	PD1	50h carmine	.25	.25

POSTAGE DUE STAMPS

D1

1918-20   Unwmk.   Typo.   Imperf.

J1	D1	5h deep bister	.25	.25
J2	D1	10h deep bister	.25	.25
J3	D1	15h deep bister	.25	.25
J4	D1	20h deep bister	.30	.25
J5	D1	25h deep bister	.45	.25
J6	D1	30h deep bister	.45	.25
J7	D1	40h deep bister	.60	.25
J8	D1	50h deep bister	.75	.25
J9	D1	100h blk brn	1.50	.25
J10	D1	250h orange	11.00	1.40
J11	D1	400h scarlet	15.00	1.40
J12	D1	500h gray grn	7.50	.25
J13	D1	1000h purple	7.50	.25
J14	D1	2000h dark blue	22.50	.60
	Nos. J1-J14 (14)		68.30	6.15

For surcharges and overprints see Nos. J32-J41, J57, Eastern Silesia J1-J11.

Nos. 1, 33-34, 10 Surcharged in Blue

1922

J15	A1	20h on 3h red vio	.30	.25
J16	A1	50h on 75h slate	1.50	.25
J17	A2	60h on 80h olive grn	.80	.25
J18	A2	60h on 80h olive grn	3.00	.25
J19	A1	200h on 400h purple	4.00	.25
	Nos. J15-J19 (5)		9.60	1.25

Same Surcharge on Nos. 1, 10, 30-31, 33-34, 36, 40 in Violet

1923-26

J20	A1	10h on 3h red vio	.25	.25
J21	A1	20h on 3h red vio	.30	.25
J22	A1	30h on 3h red vio	.25	.25
J23	A1	40h on 3h red vio	.25	.25
J24	A2	50h on 75h slate	1.25	.25
J25	A2	60h on 50h dk vio ('26)	4.00	1.25
J26	A2	60h on 50h dk bl ('26)	4.00	1.50
J27	A2	60h on 75h slate	.50	.25
J28	A2	100h on 80h ol grn	27.50	.25
J29	A2	100h on 120h gray blk	1.00	.25
J30	A1	100h on 400h pur ('26)	1.00	.25
J31	A2	100h on 1000h dp vio ('26)	1.60	.25
	Nos. J20-J31 (12)		41.90	5.25

Postage Due Stamp of 1918-20 Surcharged in Violet

1924

J32	D1	50h on 400h scar	.90	.25
J33	D1	60h on 400h scar	3.25	.60
J34	D1	100h on 400h scar	2.00	.25
	Nos. J32-J34 (3)		6.15	1.10

Postage Due Stamps of 1918-20 Surcharged with New Values in Violet as in 1924

1925

J35	D1	10h on 5h bister	.25	.25
J36	D1	20h on 5h bister	.25	.25
J37	D1	30h on 10h bister	.25	.25
J38	D1	40h on 15h bister	.25	.25
J39	D1	50h on 250h org	1.10	.90
J40	D1	60h on 250h org	1.50	.60
J41	D1	100h on 250h org	2.25	.25
		Nos. J35-J41 (7)	5.85	2.10

Stamps of 1918-19 Surcharged with New Values in Violet as in 1922

1926 ---- Perf. 14, 11½

J42	A2	30h on 15h red	.50	.30
J43	A2	40h on 15h red	.50	.30

Surcharged in Violet

1926 ---- Perf. 14

J44	A8	30h on 100h dk grn	.25	.25
J45	A8	40h on 200h violet	.25	.25
J46	A8	40h on 300h ver	.95	.25
a.		Perf. 14x13½		60.00
J47	A8	50h on 500h dp grn	.50	.25
a.		Perf. 14x13½	2.75	
J48	A8	60h on 400h brown	1.00	.25
J49	A8	100h on 600h dp vio	2.50	.35
a.		Perf. 14x13½	30.00	1.25
		Nos. J44-J49 (6)	5.45	1.60

Surcharged in Violet

1927

J50	A6	100h dark brown	.55	.75
a.		Perf. 13½	200.00	10.00

Surcharged in Violet

J51	A6	40h on 185h org	.25	.25
J52	A6	50h on 20h car	.25	.25
a.		50h on 50h carmine (error)		55,000.
J53	A6	50h on 150h rose	.25	.25
a.		Perf. 13½	12.50	2.00
J54	A6	60h on 25h brown	.25	.25
J55	A6	60h on 185h orange	.55	.25
J56	A6	100h on 25h brown	.55	.25
		Nos. J50-J56 (7)	2.65	1.75

No. J52a is known only used.

No. J12 Surcharged in Violet

1927 ---- Imperf.

J57	D1	200h on 500h gray grn	8.00	2.50

Catalogue values for unused stamps in this section, from this point to the end of the section, are for Never Hinged items.

D5

1928 ---- Perf. 14x13½

J58	D5	5h dark red	.25	.25
J59	D5	10h dark red	.25	.25
J60	D5	20h dark red	.25	.25
J61	D5	30h dark red	.25	.25
J62	D5	40h dark red	.25	.25
J63	D5	50h dark red	.25	.25
J64	D5	60h dark red	.25	.25
J65	D5	1k ultra	.25	.25
J66	D5	2k ultra	.50	.25
J67	D5	5k ultra	.75	.25
J68	D5	10k ultra	1.90	.25
J69	D5	20k ultra	3.75	.30
		Nos. J58-J69 (12)	8.90	3.05

LOCAL OFFICIAL STAMPS

Coat of Arms — L1

Typo. & Embossed

1918, Nov. 7 ---- Die Cut Perf 12

OL1	L1	10h blue	12.50	15.00
		Never hinged	20.00	
a.		10h pale blue	42.50	42.50
		Never hinged	60.00	
		On cover		100.00
OL2	L1	20h bright carmine	7.00	7.00
		Never hinged	10.00	
		On cover		42.50

In the first weeks of independence, the Czechoslovak National Council employed the Czech Scouts to maintain a local post in Prague, and Nos. OL1-OL2 were issued for this service. These stamps were in use Nov. 7-25, after which regular postal operations were resumed.

Nos. OL1 and OL2 were printed on grayish paper with yellow gum. A later printing on white paper with white gum was made for sale to collectors. These reprints sell for substantially less than the values above.

The scout delivery service was revived for one day, December 21, 1918, as part of the celebration of Thomas G. Masaryk's arrival in Czechoslovakia. 600 copies of No. OL1 and 1,000 copies of OL2 were overprinted "Prijezd presidenta Masaryka." ("Arrival of President Masaryk") in three lines. Values: overprint on No. OL1, unused $2,250, used $1,100, on cover $4,000; on OL1a, unused $7,500, used $3,500, on cover $10,000; on OL2, unused $2,250, used $900, on cover $3,000.

NEWSPAPER STAMPS

Windhover — N1

1918-20 Unwmk. Typo. Imperf.

P1	N1	2h gray green	.25	.25
P2	N1	5h green ('20)	.25	.25
a.		5h dark green	.40	
P3	N1	6h red	.30	.25
P4	N1	10h dull violet	.25	.25
P5	N1	20h blue	.25	.25
P6	N1	30h gray brown	.25	.25
P7	N1	50h orange ('20)	.30	.25
P8	N1	100h red brown ('20)	.40	.25
		Nos. P1-P8 (8)	2.25	2.00

Nos. P1-P8 exist privately perforated.
For surcharges and overprints see Nos. P9-P10, P14-P16, Eastern Silesia P1-P5.

Stamps of 1918-20 Surcharged in Violet

1925-26

P9	N1	5h on 2h gray green	.50	.40
P10	N1	5h on 6h red ('26)	.25	.40

Special Delivery Stamps of 1918-20 Overprinted in Violet

1926

P11	SD1	5h apple grn, yel	.25	.25
a.		5h dull green, yellow	.50	.40
P12	SD1	10h red brn, yel	.25	.25

With Additional Surcharge of New Value

P13	SD1	5h on 2h red vio, yel	.35	.35
		Nos. P11-P13 (3)	.85	.85

Catalogue values for unused stamps in this section, from this point to the end of the section, are for Never Hinged items.

Newspaper Stamps of 1918-20 Overprinted in Violet

1934

P14	N1	10h dull violet	.25	.25
P15	N1	20h blue	.25	.25
P16	N1	30h gray brown	.25	.25
		Nos. P14-P16 (3)	.75	.75

Overprinted for use by commercial firms only.

Carrier Pigeon — N2

1937 ---- Imperf.

P17	N2	2h bister brown	.25	.25
P18	N2	5h dull blue	.25	.25
P19	N2	7h red orange	.25	.25
P20	N2	9h emerald	.25	.25
P21	N2	10h henna brown	.25	.25
P22	N2	12h ultra	.25	.25
P23	N2	20h dark green	.25	.25
P24	N2	50h dark brown	.25	.25
P25	N2	1k olive gray	.25	.25
		Nos. P17-P25 (9)	2.25	2.25

For overprint see Slovakia Nos. P1-P9.

Bratislava Philatelic Exhibition Issue
Souvenir Sheet

1937 ---- Imperf.

P26	N2	10h henna brn, sheet of 25	4.00	4.00

CZECHOSLOVAK LEGION POST

The Czechoslovak Legion in Siberia issued these stamps for use on its mail and that of local residents. Forgeries exist.

Russia No. 79 Overprinted

1918 ---- Typo. ---- Perf. 14x14½

A1	A15	10k dark blue	2,500.

No. A1 was sold for a few days in Chelyabinsk. It was withdrawn because of a spelling error ("CZESZKJA," instead of "CZESZKAJA").

This overprint was also applied to Russia Nos. 73-78, 80-81, 83-85, 119-121, 123 and 130-131. These were trial printings, never sold to the public, although favor-cancelled covers exist.

Urn and Cathedral at Irkutsk — A1 ---- Armored Railroad Car — A2

Sentinel — A3

1919-20 ---- Litho. ---- Imperf.

1	A1	25k carmine	10.50	—
		Never hinged	21.00	
a.		Perf 11½ ('20)	15.00	—
		Never hinged	30.00	
2	A2	50k yellow green	10.50	—
		Never hinged	21.00	
a.		Perf 11½ ('20)	15.00	—
		Never hinged	30.00	
3	A3	1r red brown	19.00	—
		Never hinged	37.50	
a.		Perf 11½ ('20)	22.50	—
		Never hinged	52.50	

Nos. 1-3 were printed by Makusin & Posochin in Irkutsk and were delivered to the Czech Field Post, imperforate and ungummed, in Dec. 1919. A crackled yellow gum was applied to stamps sold at Field Post offices. In Jan. 1920 a quantity of sheets was perforated 11½.

Nos. 1 and 2 exist in wide horizontal gutter pairs, containing one of each denomination. Value, $700 unused, $1,000 never hinged. No. 3 exists in wide vertical gutter pairs. Value, $1,700 unused, $3,000 never hinged.

Later, ungummed imperforate remainders were sent to Prague, where a smooth white gum was applied. Some of these remainder sheets were perforated 11½ and a large proportion were perforated 13¼. Value, set: $3 unused; $6 never hinged.

Nos. 1-3 and 1a-3a exist overprinted "Balicky do vlasti 50R" ("Packages to the homeland, 50 Rubles") and "Prvi Jugoslavenski puk u Sibiriji" ("First Jugoslav Regiment in Siberia"). Nos. 1-3 also exist overprinted "Vlak cs cerv.krize" ("Train of the Czechoslovak Red Cross"). All are rare.

Lion of Bohemia — A4

Type 1 ---- Type 2

Two types: 1 — 6 points on star-like mace head at right of goblet; large saber handle; measures 20x25¼mm. 2 — 5 points on mace head; small saber handle; measures 19½x25mm.

Perce en Arc in Blue

1920 ---- Embossed

4	A4	(25k) blue & rose, ty 1	3.00	—
		Never hinged	4.00	
a.		Type 2	3.00	—
		Never hinged	4.00	

1st, 2nd ---- 3rd

No. 4 was printed in Prague in 1919 and received in Siberia in 1920. It was overprinted "1920" (No. 5), which was in turn surcharged in various denominations (Nos. 6-14).

There were three printings of No. 4, all of which received the subsequent overprintings. The first printing has a steel blue frame and carmine center. The second printing has a gray-blue frame and red center. The first and second printings were sent to Siberia, apparently in similar quantities, and values for Nos. 4-14 are for examples from these printings.

A third printing was made in Prague in the 1920s to create stamps for sale to collectors. Stamps of the third printing have a deep blue frame and carmine center, with heavy carmine inking at the top of the oval. Values for examples of Nos. 4-14 from this philatelic printing are much lower.

No. 4 Overprinted

1920

5	A4	(25k) bl & rose, type 1	10.00	—
		Never hinged	15.00	
a.		Type 2	10.00	—
		Never hinged	15.00	

Both types of No. 4 received overprint.

No. 5 (type 1) Surcharged with New Values in Green

6	A4	2k bl & rose	35.00
		Never hinged	52.50
7	A4	3k bl & rose	35.00
		Never hinged	52.50
8	A4	5k bl & rose	35.00
		Never hinged	52.50
9	A4	10k bl & rose	35.00
		Never hinged	52.50
10	A4	15k bl & rose	35.00
		Never hinged	52.50
11	A4	25k bl & rose	35.00
		Never hinged	52.50
12	A4	35k bl & rose	35.00
		Never hinged	52.50
13	A4	50k bl & rose	35.00
		Never hinged	52.50
14	A4	1r bl & rose	35.00
		Never hinged	52.50
		Nos. 6-14 (9)	315.00
		Set, never hinged	475.00

Surcharged on No. 5a (type 2)

6a	A4	2k bl & rose	35.00
		Never hinged	52.50
7a	A4	3k bl & rose	35.00
		Never hinged	52.50
8a	A4	5k bl & rose	35.00
		Never hinged	52.50
9a	A4	10k bl & rose	35.00
		Never hinged	52.50
10a	A4	15k bl & rose	35.00
		Never hinged	52.50
11a	A4	25k bl & rose	35.00
		Never hinged	52.50
12a	A4	35k bl & rose	35.00
		Never hinged	52.50
13a	A4	50k bl & rose	35.00
		Never hinged	52.50
14a	A4	1r bl & rose	35.00
		Never hinged	52.50
		Nos. 6a-14a (9)	315.00
		Set, never hinged	475.00

BOHEMIA AND MORAVIA

Catalogue values for unused stamps in this country are for never hinged items, beginning with Scott 20 in the regular postage section, Scott B1 in the semipostal section, Scott J1 in the postage due section, and Scott P1 in the newspaper section.

Masaryk Type of Czechoslovakia with hyphen in "Cesko-Slovensko" A60

1939, Apr. 23

1A	A60	1k rose lake	.25	.25

Prepared by Czechoslovakia prior to the German occupation March 15, 1939. Subsequently issued for use in Bohemia and Moravia.
See No. C1.

German Protectorate

Stamps of Czechoslovakia, 1928-39, Overprinted in Black

Perf. 10, 12½, 12x12½

1939, July 15   **Unwmk.**

1	A29	5h dk ultra	.25	1.25
2	A29	10h brown	.25	1.25
3	A29	20h red	.25	1.25
4	A29	25h green	.25	1.25
5	A29	30h red vio	.25	1.25
6	A61a	40h dk bl	2.50	5.00
7	A85	50h dp grn	.25	1.25
8	A63	60h dl vio	2.50	5.00
9	A60	1k rose lake (212)	.75	1.75
10	A60	1k rose lake (256)	.30	1.25
11	A64	1.20k rose lilac	3.00	5.00
12	A65	1.50k carmine	2.50	5.75
13	A79	1.60k olive grn	5.00	5.75
a.		"Mähnen"	32.50	75.00
14	A66	2k dk bl grn	1.10	4.00
15	A67	2.50k dk bl	3.00	5.00
16	A68	3k brown	3.00	5.75
17	A70	4k dk vio	9.50	6.50
18	A71	5k green	3.50	10.00
19	A72	10k blue	4.75	15.00
		Nos. 1-19 (19)	42.90	83.25
		Set, never hinged	60.00	

The size of the overprint varies, Nos. 1-10 measure 17½x15½mm, Nos. 11-16 19x18mm, Nos. 17 and 19 28x17½mm and No. 18 23½x23mm.

> Catalogue values for unused stamps in this section, from this point to the end of the section, are for never hinged items.

Linden Leaves and Closed Buds — A1

1939-41   **Photo.**   **Perf. 14**

20	A1	5h dark blue	.25	.30
21	A1	10h blk brn	.25	.40
22	A1	20h crimson	.25	.30
23	A1	25h dk bl grn	.25	.30
24	A1	30h dp plum	.25	.30
24A	A1	30h golden brn ('41)	.25	.30
25	A1	40h orange ('40)	.25	.25
26	A1	50h slate grn ('40)	.25	.25
		Nos. 20-26 (8)	2.00	2.40

See Nos. 49-51.

Castle at Zvikov — A2

Karlstein Castle — A3

St. Barbara's Church, Kutna Hora — A4

Cathedral at Prague — A5

Brno Cathedral — A6

Town Square, Olomouc — A7

1939   **Engr.**   **Perf. 12½**

27	A2	40h dark blue	.25	.30
28	A3	50h dk bl grn	.25	.30
29	A4	60h dl vio	.25	.30
30	A5	1k dp rose	.25	.30
31	A6	1.20k rose lilac	.40	.60
32	A6	1.50k rose car	.25	.30
33	A7	2k dk bl grn	.25	.50
34	A7	2.50k dark blue	.25	.30
		Nos. 27-34 (8)	2.15	2.90

No. 31 measures 23½x29½mm, No. 42 measures 18½x23mm.
See nos. 52-53, 53B, 60-61 (overprints) in Scott Standard catalog, Vol. 2.

Zlin — A8

Iron Works at Moravská Ostrava — A9

Prague — A10

1939-40

35	A8	3k dl rose vio	.25	.30
36	A9	4k slate ('40)	.25	.40
37	A10	5k green	.50	.80
38	A10	10k lt ultra	.40	1.00
39	A10	20k yel brn	1.25	2.00
		Nos. 35-39 (5)	2.65	4.50

Types of 1939 and

Neuhaus A11

Pernstein Castle A12

Pardubice Castle — A13

Lainsitz Bridge near Bechyne A14

Samson Fountain, Budweis — A15

Kromeriz A16

Wallenstein Palace, Prague — A17

1940   **Engr.**   **Perf. 12½**

40	A11	50h dk bl grn	.25	.25
41	A12	80h dp bl	.25	.40
42	A6	1.20k vio brn	.40	.25
43	A13	2k gray grn	.25	.25
44	A14	5k dk bl grn	.25	.25
45	A15	6k brn vio	.25	.50
46	A16	8k slate grn	.25	.30
47	A17	10k blue	.45	.30
48	A10	20k sepia	1.10	1.60
		Nos. 40-48 (9)	3.45	4.10

No. 42 measures 18½x23mm; No. 31, 23½x29½mm.

SEMI-POSTAL STAMPS

> Catalogue values for unused stamps in this section are for never hinged items.

Nurse and Wounded Soldier — SP1

Perf. 13½

1940, June 29   **Photo.**   **Unwmk.**

B1	SP1	60h + 40h indigo	.90	1.10
B2	SP1	1.20k + 80h deep plum	.90	1.25

Surtax for German Red Cross.
Labels alternate with stamps in sheets of Nos. B1-B2.

AIR POST STAMP

> Catalogue values for unused stamps in this section are for never hinged items.

Type of Czechoslovakia 1930 with hyphen in "Cesko-Slovensko"

Fokker
Monoplane — AP3

1939, Apr. 22   **Perf. 13½**
C1 AP3 30h rose lilac   .25   .25

Prepared by Czechoslovakia prior to the German occupation March 15, 1939. Subsequently issued for use in Bohemia and Moravia. See No. 1A.

PERSONAL DELIVERY STAMPS

PD1

1939-40 Unwmk. Photo. Perf. 13½
EX1 PD1 50h indigo & blue ('40)   1.25   2.00
EX2 PD1 50h carmine & rose   1.60   2.50

POSTAGE DUE STAMPS

> Catalogue values for unused stamps in this section are for never hinged items.

D1

1939-40 Unwmk. Typo. Perf. 14
J1	D1	5h dark carmine	.25	.30
J2	D1	10h dark carmine	.25	.30
J3	D1	20h dark carmine	.25	.30
J4	D1	30h dark carmine	.25	.30
J5	D1	40h dark carmine	.25	.30
J6	D1	50h dark carmine	.25	.30
J7	D1	60h dark carmine	.25	.30
J8	D1	80h dark carmine	.25	.30
J9	D1	1k bright ultra	.25	.40
J10	D1	1.20k brt ultra ('40)	.30	.40
J11	D1	2k bright ultra	1.00	1.25
J12	D1	5k bright ultra	1.10	1.60
J13	D1	10k bright ultra	1.60	2.00
J14	D1	20k bright ultra	3.25	3.25
		Nos. J1-J14 (14)	9.50	11.30

NEWSPAPER STAMPS

> Catalogue values for unused stamps in this section are for never hinged items.

Carrier Pigeon — N1

1939 Unwmk. Typo. Imperf.
P1	N1	2h ocher	.25	.30
P2	N1	5h ultra	.25	.30
P3	N1	7h red orange	.25	.30
P4	N1	9h emerald	.25	.30
P5	N1	10h henna brown	.25	.30
P6	N1	12h dark ultra	.25	.30
P7	N1	20h dark green	.25	.30
P8	N1	50h red brown	.25	.40
P9	N1	1k greenish gray	.25	.80
		Nos. P1-P9 (9)	2.25	3.30

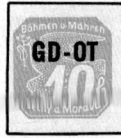

No. P5 Overprinted in Black

1940
P10 N1 10h henna brown   .40   .65
Overprinted for use by commercial firms.

DAHOMEY

də-'hō-mē

LOCATION — West coast of Africa
AREA — 43,483 sq. mi.
POP. — 3,030,000 (est. 1974)
CAPITAL — Porto-Novo

Formerly a native kingdom including Benin, Dahomey was annexed by France in 1894. It became part of the colonial administrative unit of French West Africa in 1895.

100 Centimes = 1 Franc

See French West Africa No. 71 for stamp inscribed "Dahomey" and "Afrique Occidentale Francaise."

Navigation and Commerce — A1

Perf. 14x13½
1899-1905 Typo. Unwmk.
Name of Colony in Blue or Carmine
1	A1	1c black, *lil bl* ('01)	1.60	1.60
		Never hinged	2.75	
		On cover		125.00
2	A1	2c brown, *buff* ('04)	2.40	1.60
		Never hinged	2.75	
		On cover		150.00
3	A1	4c claret, *lav* ('04)	2.40	2.40
		Never hinged	4.50	
		On cover		150.00
4	A1	5c yellow grn ('04)	6.50	4.00
		Never hinged	11.50	
		On cover		87.50
5	A1	10c red ('01)	5.50	3.25
		Never hinged	9.50	
		On cover		80.00
6	A1	15c gray ('01)	5.50	1.60
		Never hinged	9.50	
		On cover		50.00
7	A1	20c red, *grn* ('04)	19.00	15.00
		Never hinged	37.50	
		On cover		140.00
		On cover, single franking		250.00
8	A1	25c black, *rose* ('99)	20.00	20.00
		Never hinged	35.00	
		On cover		425.00
9	A1	25c blue ('01)	21.00	17.00
		Never hinged	35.00	
		On cover		105.00
10	A1	30c brown, *bis* ('04)	24.00	12.00
		Never hinged	42.50	
		On cover		140.00
		On cover, single franking		200.00
11	A1	40c red, *straw* ('04)	24.00	15.00
		Never hinged	45.00	
		On cover		140.00
		On cover, single franking		200.00
12	A1	50c brn, *az* (name in red) ('01)	24.00	22.50
		Never hinged	52.50	
		On cover		190.00
		On cover, single franking		250.00
12A	A1	50c brn, *az* (name in bl) ('05)	32.50	24.00
		Never hinged	55.00	
		On cover		210.00
		On cover, single franking		275.00
13	A1	75c dp vio, *org* ('04)	85.00	55.00
		Never hinged	170.00	
		On cover		475.00
		On cover, single franking		725.00
14	A1	1fr brnz grn, *straw* ('04)	40.00	32.50
		Never hinged	80.00	
		On cover		525.00
		On cover, single franking		775.00
15	A1	2fr violet, *rose* ('04)	110.00	72.50
		Never hinged	225.00	
		On cover		725.00
		On cover, single franking		925.00
16	A1	5fr red lilac, *lav*	135.00	105.00
		Never hinged	280.00	
		On cover		840.00
		On cover, single franking		1,100.
		Nos. 1-16 (17)	558.40	404.95

Perf. 13½x14 stamps are counterfeits.

For surcharges see Nos. 32-41.

Gen. Louis Faidherbe — A2

Oil Palm — A3

Dr. Noel Eugène Ballay — A4

1906-07 Perf. 13½x14
Name of Colony in Red or Blue
17	A2	1c slate	1.60	1.60
		Never hinged	2.75	
		On cover		100.00
18	A2	2c chocolate	2.40	1.60
		Never hinged	4.50	
		On cover		100.00
19	A2	4c choc, *gray bl*	4.00	3.25
		Never hinged	6.75	
		On cover		100.00
20	A2	5c green	9.50	3.25
		Never hinged	19.00	
		On cover		50.00
21	A2	10c carmine (B)	22.50	4.00
		Never hinged	50.00	
		On cover		32.50
22	A3	20c black & red, *azure*	14.50	13.00
		Never hinged	30.00	
		On cover		42.50
23	A3	25c blue, *pnksh*	16.00	13.00
		Never hinged	35.00	
		On cover		55.00
		On cover, single franking		150.00
24	A3	30c choc, *pnksh*	16.00	14.50
		Never hinged	35.00	
		On cover		62.50
		On cover, single franking		110.00
25	A3	35c black, *yellow*	87.50	13.00
		Never hinged	200.00	
		On cover		67.50
		On cover, single franking		105.00
26	A3	45c choc, *grnsh* ('07)	21.00	14.50
		Never hinged	42.50	
		On cover		87.50
		On cover, single franking		140.00
27	A3	50c deep violet	21.00	17.50
		Never hinged	42.50	
		On cover		87.50
		On cover, single franking		190.00
28	A3	75c blue, *orange*	24.00	22.00
		Never hinged	52.50	
		On cover		125.00
		On cover, single franking		260.00
29	A4	1fr black, *azure*	32.00	24.00
		Never hinged	60.00	
		On cover		140.00
		On cover, single franking		275.00
30	A4	2fr blue, *pink*	110.00	110.00
		Never hinged	225.00	
		On cover		340.00
		On cover, single franking		400.00
31	A4	5fr car, *straw* (B)	100.00	105.00
		Never hinged	220.00	
		On cover		340.00
		On cover, single franking		460.00
		Nos. 17-31 (15)	482.00	360.20

Nos. 2-3, 6-7, 9-13 Surcharged in Black or Carmine

Spacing between figures of surcharge 1.5mm (5c), 2mm (10c)

1912 Perf. 14x13½
32	5c on 2c brn, *buff*		2.00	2.40
	Never hinged		3.75	
	On cover			87.50
33	5c on 4c claret, *lav* (C)		1.60	2.00
	Never hinged		2.75	
	On cover			67.50
a.	Double surcharge		275.00	
34	5c on 15c gray (C)		2.00	2.40
	Never hinged		3.75	
	On cover			87.50

35	5c on 20c red, *grn*		2.00	2.40
	Never hinged		3.75	
	On cover			87.50
36	5c on 25c blue (C)		8.00	11.10
	Never hinged		3.75	
	On cover			87.50
a.	Inverted surcharge		220.00	
b.	Pair, one without surcharge		600.00	
37	5c on 30c brown, *bis* (C)		2.00	2.40
	Never hinged		3.75	
	On cover			92.50
38	10c on 40c red, *straw*		2.00	2.40
	Never hinged		3.75	
	On cover			92.50
a.	Inverted surcharge		325.00	
39	10c on 50c brn, *az*, name in bl (C)		2.40	2.75
	Never hinged		4.25	
	On cover			140.00
40	10c on 50c brn, *az*, name in red (C)		1,125.	1,300.
41	10c on 75c violet, *org*		7.25	8.00
	Never hinged		12.50	
	On cover			150.00
a.	Double surcharge		5,500.	
	Nos. 32-39,41 (9)		23.25	27.15

Spacing between figures of surcharge 2.25mm (5c), 2.75mm (10c)
32a	5c on 2c brn, *buff*		12.00	12.00
	Never hinged		20.00	
33b	5c on 4c claret, *lav* (C)		9.50	9.50
	Never hinged		16.00	
c.	Double surcharge, both wider spacing		2,000.	
d.	Double surcharge, one narrow and one wide spacing		5,000.	
34a	5c on 15c gray (C)		12.00	12.00
	Never hinged		20.00	
35a	5c on 20c red, *grn*		12.00	12.00
	Never hinged		20.00	
36c	5c on 25c blue (C)		12.00	12.00
	Never hinged		20.00	
d.	Inverted surcharge		2,200.	
37a	5c on 30c brown, *bis* (C)		12.00	12.00
	Never hinged		20.00	
38b	10c on 40c red, *straw*		80.00	80.00
	Never hinged		145.00	
c.	Inverted surcharge		2,800.	
39a	10c on 50c brn, *az*, name in bl (C)		150.00	150.00
40a	10c on 50c brn, *az*, name in red (C)		11,000.	
41b	10c on 75c violet, *org*		230.00	230.00
	Nos. 32a-39a,41b (9)		529.50	529.50

Man Climbing Oil Palm — A5

1913-39 Perf. 13½x14
42	A5	1c violet & blk	.25	.30
		Never hinged	.40	
		On cover		80.00
a.		Chalky paper	.40	.40
		Never hinged	.70	
		On cover		80.00
43	A5	2c choc & rose	.30	.40
		Never hinged	.55	
		On cover		80.00
44	A5	4c black & brn	.30	.40
		Never hinged	.55	
		On cover		80.00
a.		Chalky paper	.90	.90
		Never hinged	1.40	
		On cover		80.00
45	A5	5c yel grn & bl grn	1.20	.55
		Never hinged	2.10	
		On cover		37.50
a.		Chalky paper	2.75	1.40
		Never hinged	4.75	
		On cover		32.50
46	A5	5c vio brn & vio ('22)	.50	.55
		Never hinged	.75	
		On cover		30.00
47	A5	10c org red & rose	1.60	.80
		Never hinged	2.75	
		On cover		21.00
a.		Half used as 5c on wrapper or printed matter		—
b.		Chalky paper	2.40	1.25
		Never hinged	4.00	
		On cover		25.00
48	A5	10c yel grn & bl grn ('22)	.75	.90
		Never hinged	1.25	
		On cover		55.00
49	A5	10c red & ol ('25)	.40	.40
		Never hinged	.65	
		On cover		21.00
50	A5	15c brn org & dk vio ('17)	.80	.80
		Never hinged	1.30	
		On cover		20.00
a.		Chalky paper	.95	.75
		Never hinged	1.60	
		On cover		20.00
51	A5	20c gray & red brown	.75	.75
		Never hinged	1.20	
		On cover		32.50
a.		Chalky paper	2.00	1.20
		Never hinged	3.25	
		On cover		40.00
b.		20c gray & sepia	1.20	.80
		Never hinged	2.00	

	On cover			32.50
c.	As "b," chalky paper		3.25	1.75
	Never hinged		5.25	
	On cover			40.00
52	A5	20c bluish grn & grn ('26)	.40	.40
	Never hinged		.55	
	On cover			15.00
53	A5	20c mag & blk ('27)	.40	.40
	Never hinged		.55	
	On cover			37.50
54	A5	25c ultra & dp blue	2.00	1.60
	Never hinged		3.50	
	On cover			42.50
	On cover, single franking			100.00
a.	Chalky paper		3.25	2.40
	Never hinged		5.50	
	On cover			50.00
55	A5	25c vio brn & org ('22)	1.20	.95
	Never hinged		1.60	
	On cover			13.50
56	A5	30c choc & vio	2.75	2.40
	Never hinged		4.75	
	On cover			45.00
	On cover, single franking			125.00
a.	Chalky paper		4.00	3.25
	Never hinged		7.25	
	On cover			42.50
57	A5	30c red org & rose ('22)	3.25	3.25
	Never hinged		5.50	
	On cover			42.50
	On cover, single franking			75.00
58	A5	30c yellow & vio ('25)	.40	.40
	Never hinged		.65	
	On cover			12.50
59	A5	30c dl grn & grn ('27)	.40	.40
	Never hinged		.55	
	On cover			37.50
60	A5	35c brown & blk	.80	.80
	Never hinged		1.40	
	On cover			45.00
	On cover, single franking			105.00
a.	Chalky paper		1.25	1.10
	Never hinged		2.00	
	On cover			50.00
61	A5	35c bl grn & grn ('38)	.40	.30
	Never hinged		.55	
	On cover			37.50
62	A5	40c black & red org	.80	.80
	Never hinged		1.20	
	On cover			55.00
	On cover, single franking			125.00
a.	Chalky paper		1.25	1.25
	Never hinged		1.75	
	On cover			62.50
63	A5	45c gray & ultra	.80	.80
	Never hinged		1.25	
	On cover			67.50
	On cover, single franking			140.00
a.	Chalky paper		1.25	1.25
	Never hinged		2.00	
	On cover			62.50
64	A5	50c chocolate & brn	6.50	6.00
	Never hinged		11.00	
	On cover			67.50
	On cover, single franking			150.00
a.	Half used as 25c on cover			500.00
b.	Chalky paper		6.50	6.00
	Never hinged		11.00	
	On cover			67.50
c.	50c dk brown & brn, chalky paper		12.00	9.50
	Never hinged		19.00	
	On cover			80.00
65	A5	50c ultra & bl ('22)	1.60	1.60
	Never hinged		2.40	
	On cover			37.50
	On cover, single franking			67.50
66	A5	50c brn red & bl ('26)	1.20	1.20
	Never hinged		2.00	
	On cover			12.50
67	A5	55c gray grn & choc ('38)	.70	.55
	Never hinged		1.00	
	On cover			12.50
68	A5	60c vio, pnksh ('25)	.40	.40
	Never hinged		.65	
	On cover			30.00
	On cover, single franking			75.00
69	A5	65c yel brn & ol grn ('26)	1.20	1.20
	Never hinged		2.00	
	On cover			19.00
	On cover, single franking			30.00
70	A5	75c blue & violet	1.20	1.20
	Never hinged		1.75	
	On cover			55.00
	On cover, single franking			140.00
a.	Chalky paper		1.60	1.60
	Never hinged		2.40	
	On cover			55.00
71	A5	80c henna brn & ultra ('38)	.40	.40
	Never hinged		.55	
	On cover			62.50
	On cover, single franking			105.00
72	A5	85c dk bl & ver ('26)	1.60	1.60
	Never hinged		2.50	
	On cover			37.50
	On cover, single franking			62.50
73	A5	90c rose & brn red ('30)	.80	.75
	Never hinged		1.25	
	On cover			50.00
	On cover, single franking			92.50
74	A5	90c yel bis & red org ('39)	1.20	.80
	Never hinged		1.60	
	On cover			42.50
	On cover, single franking			92.50

75	A5	1fr blue grn & blk	1.20	1.20
	Never hinged		2.00	
	On cover			75.00
	On cover, single franking			175.00
a.	Chalky paper		2.75	2.00
	Never hinged		4.75	
	On cover			87.50
76	A5	1fr dk bl & ultra ('26)	1.60	1.60
	Never hinged		2.60	
	On cover			25.00
	On cover, single franking			50.00
77	A5	1fr yel brn & lt red ('28)	1.60	1.20
	Never hinged		2.75	
	On cover			27.50
	On cover, single franking			42.50
78	A5	1fr dk red & red org ('38)	1.05	.95
	Never hinged		1.40	
	On cover			37.50
	On cover, single franking			67.50
79	A5	1.10fr vio & bis ('28)	5.50	6.00
	Never hinged		9.25	
	On cover			150.00
	On cover, single franking			340.00
80	A5	1.25fr dp bl & dk brn ('33)	17.50	8.75
	Never hinged		27.50	
	On cover			40.00
	On cover, single franking			105.00
81	A5	1.50fr dk bl & lt bl ('30)	1.30	.80
	Never hinged		2.00	
	On cover			42.50
	On cover, single franking			80.00
82	A5	1.75fr brn & dp buff ('33)	4.00	2.00
	Never hinged		6.50	
	On cover			27.50
	On cover, single franking			42.50
83	A5	1.75fr ind & ultra ('38)	1.45	.95
	Never hinged		2.00	
	On cover			37.50
	On cover, single franking			62.50
84	A5	2fr yel org & choc	1.20	1.60
	Never hinged		2.00	
	On cover			92.50
	On cover, single franking			200.00
a.	Chalky paper		2.40	2.40
	Never hinged		2.75	
	On cover			92.50
85	A5	3fr red violet ('30)	2.75	1.75
	Never hinged		4.50	
	On cover			87.50
	On cover, single franking			190.00
86	A5	5fr violet & dp bl	2.40	2.75
	Never hinged		4.00	
	On cover			110.00
	On cover, single franking			210.00
a.	Chalky paper		3.25	3.25
	Never hinged		5.50	
	On cover			110.00
	Nos. 42-86 (45)		78.80	63.60

The 1c gray and yellow green and 5c dull red and black are Togo Nos. 193a, 196a.

Nos. 47a and 64a were authorized for use in Paouignan during the last part of November 1921. Other values exist as bisects but were not authorized.

For surcharges see Nos. 87-96, B1, B8-B11. Post 1940 issues in Scott Standard catalogue, Vol. 2.

Type of 1913 Surcharged

1922-25

87	A5	60c on 75c vio, pnksh	1.20	1.20
	Never hinged		2.00	
	On cover			27.50
	On cover, single franking			42.50
a.	Double surcharge		200.00	
	Never hinged		320.00	
88	A5	65c on 15c brn org & dk vio ('25)	2.00	2.00
	Never hinged		2.75	
	On cover			75.00
	On cover, single franking			160.00
a.	On #50a		4.75	4.75
	Never hinged		8.00	
	On cover			80.00
89	A5	85c on 15c brn org & dk vio ('25)	2.00	2.00
	Never hinged		2.75	
	On cover			55.00
	On cover, single franking			105.00
	Nos. 87-89 (3)		5.20	5.20

Stamps and Type of 1913-39 Surcharged with New Value and Bars

1924-27

90	A5	25c on 2fr org & choc	1.20	1.20
	Never hinged		2.00	
	On cover			13.50
a.	On #84a		2.40	2.40
	Never hinged		4.00	
	On cover			21.00

91	A5	90c on 75c cer & brn red ('27)	2.00	2.00
	Never hinged		2.75	
	On cover			62.50
	On cover, single franking			100.00
92	A5	1.25fr on 1fr dk bl & ultra (R) ('26)	1.60	1.60
	Never hinged		2.40	
	On cover			62.50
	On cover, single franking			110.00
93	A5	1.50fr on 1fr dk bl & grnsh bl ('27)	2.75	2.75
	Never hinged		4.50	
	On cover			50.00
	On cover, single franking			80.00
94	A5	3fr on 5fr olvn & dp org ('27)	10.50	10.50
	Never hinged		16.00	
	On cover			105.00
	On cover, single franking			210.00
95	A5	10fr on 5fr bl vio & red brn ('27)	8.00	8.00
	Never hinged		13.50	
	On cover			110.00
	On cover, single franking			225.00
96	A5	20fr on 5fr ver & dl grn ('27)	8.75	8.75
	Never hinged		15.00	
	On cover			125.00
	On cover, single franking			250.00
	Nos. 90-96 (7)		34.80	34.80

Common Design Types pictured following the introduction.

Colonial Exposition Issue
Common Design Types

1931		Engr.	Perf. 12½	
		Name of Country in Black		
97	CD70	40c deep green	6.25	6.25
	Never hinged		10.00	
	On cover			110.00
98	CD71	50c violet	6.25	6.25
	Never hinged		10.00	
	On cover			100.00
99	CD72	90c red orange	6.25	6.25
	Never hinged		10.00	
	On cover			165.00
	On cover, single franking			240.00
100	CD73	1.50fr dull blue	6.25	6.25
	Never hinged		10.00	
	On cover			150.00
	On cover, single franking			210.00
	Nos. 97-100 (4)		25.00	25.00

Paris International Exposition Issue
Common Design Types

1937		Engr.	Perf. 13	
101	CD74	20c deep violet	2.00	2.00
	Never hinged		3.25	
	On cover			110.00
102	CD75	30c dark green	2.00	2.00
	Never hinged		3.25	
	On cover			80.00
103	CD76	40c carmine rose	2.00	2.00
	Never hinged		3.25	
	On cover			87.50
104	CD77	50c dark brown	1.60	1.60
	Never hinged		2.75	
	On cover			80.00
105	CD78	90c red	1.60	1.60
	Never hinged		2.75	
	On cover			120.00
	On cover, single franking			200.00
106	CD79	1.50fr ultra	2.00	2.00
	Never hinged		3.25	
	On cover			105.00
	On cover, single franking			190.00
	Nos. 101-106 (6)		11.20	11.20

Souvenir Sheet
Imperf

107	CD77	3fr dp blue & blk	8.75	10.00

Caillié Issue
Common Design Type

1939, Apr. 5		Engr.	Perf. 12½x12	
108	CD81	90c org brn & org	1.00	1.00
	Never hinged		1.60	
	On cover			13.50
109	CD81	2fr brt violet	1.40	1.40
	Never hinged		2.00	
	On cover			32.50
	On cover, single franking			55.00
110	CD81	2.25fr ultra & dk blue	1.50	1.50
	Never hinged		2.00	
	On cover			42.50
	On cover, single franking			67.50
	Nos. 108-110 (3)		3.90	3.90

New York World's Fair Issue
Common Design Type

1939			Engr.	
111	CD82	1.25fr carmine lake	1.20	1.20
	Never hinged		1.75	
	On cover			87.50
	On cover, single franking			175.00
112	CD82	2.25fr ultra	1.20	1.20
	Never hinged		1.75	
	On cover			87.50
	On cover, single franking			150.00

SEMI-POSTAL STAMPS

Regular Issue of 1913 Surcharged in Red

1915		Unwmk.	Perf. 14x13½	
B1	A5	10c + 5c orange red & rose	1.60	1.60
	Never hinged		2.40	
	On cover			60.00

Curie Issue
Common Design Type

1938			Perf. 13	
B2	CD80	1.75fr + 50c brt ultra	9.50	9.50
	Never hinged		15.00	
	On cover			110.00
	On cover, single franking			190.00

French Revolution Issue
Common Design Type

1939			Photo.	
		Name and Value Typo. in Black		
B3	CD83	45c + 25c green	9.50	9.50
	Never hinged		16.00	
	On cover			150.00
B4	CD83	70c + 30c brown	9.50	9.50
	Never hinged		16.00	
	On cover			110.00
B5	CD83	90c + 35c red org	9.50	9.50
	Never hinged		16.00	
	On cover			100.00
B6	CD83	1.25fr + 1fr rose pink	9.50	9.50
	Never hinged		16.00	
	On cover			165.00
	On cover, single franking			250.00
B7	CD83	2.25fr + 2fr blue	9.50	9.50
	Never hinged		16.00	
	On cover			160.00
	On cover, single franking			225.00
	Nos. B3-B7 (5)		47.50	47.50

AIR POST STAMPS

Common Design Type

1940		Unwmk. Engr.	Perf. 12½	
C1	CD85	1.90fr ultra	.40	.40
	Never hinged		.55	
	On cover			50.00
C2	CD85	2.90fr dk red	.55	.55
	Never hinged		.75	
	On cover			50.00
C3	CD85	4.50fr dk gray grn	.80	.80
	Never hinged		1.00	
	On cover			55.00
C4	CD85	4.90fr yel bister	.95	.95
	Never hinged		1.25	
	On cover			67.50
C5	CD85	6.90fr deep org	1.30	1.30
	Never hinged		1.90	
	On cover			87.50
	Nos. C1-C5 (5)		4.00	4.00

POSTAGE DUE STAMPS

Dahomey Natives — D1

D2

1906		Unwmk. Typo.	Perf. 14x13½	
J1	D1	5c grn, grnsh	3.25	3.25
	Never hinged		5.50	
	On cover			105.00
J2	D1	10c red brn	4.00	4.00
	Never hinged		7.25	
	On cover			105.00
J3	D1	15c dark blue	8.00	8.00
	Never hinged		16.00	
	On cover			110.00
J4	D1	20c blk, yellow	5.50	5.50
	Never hinged		12.00	
	On cover			105.00
J5	D1	30c red, straw	8.75	8.75
	Never hinged		18.50	
	On cover			110.00

J6	D1 50c violet	24.00	24.00	
	Never hinged	47.50		
	On cover			150.00
J7	D1 60c blk, *buff*	14.50	14.50	
	Never hinged	29.00		
	On cover			140.00
J8	D1 1fr blk, *pinkish*	45.00	40.00	
	Never hinged	92.50		
	On cover			
	Nos. J1-J8 (8)	113.00	108.00	

1914

J9	D2 5c green	.25	.25
	Never hinged	.40	
	On cover		55.00
J10	D2 10c rose	.55	.55
	Never hinged	.80	
	On cover		55.00
J11	D2 15c gray	.55	.55
	Never hinged	.80	
	On cover		55.00
J12	D2 20c brown	1.10	1.10
	Never hinged	1.60	
	On cover		62.50
J13	D2 30c blue	1.40	1.40
	Never hinged	2.10	
	On cover		62.50
J14	D2 50c black	1.60	1.60
	Never hinged	2.25	
	On cover		67.50
J15	D2 60c orange	2.00	2.00
	Never hinged	2.75	
	On cover		80.00
J16	D2 1fr violet	2.10	2.10
	Never hinged	2.90	
	On cover		105.00
	Nos. J9-J16 (8)	9.55	9.55

Type of 1914 Issue
Surcharged

2F.

1927

J17	D2 2fr on 1fr lilac rose	5.50	5.50
	Never hinged	8.75	
	On cover		140.00
J18	D2 3fr on 1fr org brn	5.50	5.50
	Never hinged	8.75	
	On cover		150.00

DALMATIA

dal-'mă-shē-ə

LOCATION — A promontory in the northwestern part of the Balkan Peninsula, together with several small islands in the Adriatic Sea.
GOVT. — Part of the former Austro-Hungarian crownland of the same name.
AREA — 113 sq. mi.
POP. — 18,719 (1921)
CAPITAL — Zara.

Stamps were issued during Italian occupation. This territory was subsequently annexed by Italy.

100 Centesimi = 1 Corona = 1 Lira

Used values are for postally used stamps.

Issued under Italian Occupation

Italy No. 87 Surcharged

1919, May 1   Wmk. 140   Perf. 14

1	A46 1cor on 1 l brn & grn	4.00	20.00
	Never hinged	10.00	
	On cover		200.00
a.	Pair, one without surcharge	1,050.	1,050.

Italian Stamps of 1906-08 Surcharged — a

1921-22

2	A48 5c on 5c green	4.00	*4.75*
	Never hinged	10.00	
	On cover		*140.00*
3	A48 10c on 10c claret	4.00	*4.75*
	Never hinged	10.00	
	On cover		*140.00*
	[illegible] 675.00 [illegible]		
4	A49 25c on 25c blue ('22)	6.50	*8.00*
	Never hinged	16.00	
	On cover		*80.00*
5	A49 50c on 50c vio ('22)	6.50	*8.00*
	Never hinged	16.00	
	On cover		*160.00*
a.	Double surcharge		*250.00*
b.	Pair, one without surcharge	1,050.	

Italian Stamps of 1901-10 Surcharged — b

6	A46 1cor on 1 l brn & grn ('22)	8.00	*24.00*
	Never hinged	20.00	
	On cover		*360.00*
7	A46 5cor on 5 l bl & rose ('22)	55.00	*150.00*
	Never hinged	135.00	
	On cover		*800.00*
8	A51 10cor on 10 l gray grn & red ('22)	55.00	*150.00*
	Never hinged	135.00	
	On cover		*140.00*
	Nos. 2-8 (7)	139.00	*349.50*

Surcharges similar to these but differing in style or arrangement of type were used in Austria under Italian occupation.

SPECIAL DELIVERY STAMPS

Italian Special Delivery Stamp No. E1 Surcharged type "a"

1921   Wmk. 140   Perf. 14

E1	SD1 25c on 25c rose red	4.75	*20.00*
	Never hinged	12.00	
a.	Double surcharge	400.00	*650.00*

Italian Special Delivery Stamp Surcharged

1922

E2	SD2 1.20 l on 1.20 l	240.00	
	Never hinged	600.00	

No. E2 was not placed in use.

POSTAGE DUE STAMPS

Italian Postage Due Stamps and Type Surcharged types "a" and "b"

1922   Wmk. 140   Perf. 14

J1	D3 (a) 50c on 50c buff & mag	4.00	*9.50*
	Never hinged	10.00	
	On cover		*95.00*
J2	D3 (b) 1cor on 1 l bl & red	9.50	*32.50*
	Never hinged	24.00	
	On cover		*125.00*
J3	D3 (b) 2cor on 2 l bl & red	65.00	*145.00*
	Never hinged	160.00	
	On cover		*450.00*
J4	D3 (b) 5cor on 5 l bl & red	65.00	*145.00*
	Never hinged	160.00	
	Nos. J1-J4 (4)	143.50	*332.00*

DANISH WEST INDIES

'dā-nish 'west 'in-dēs

LOCATION — A group of islands in the West Indies, lying east of Puerto Rico
GOVT. — Danish Colony
AREA — 132 sq. mi.
POP. — 27,086 (1911)

CAPITAL — Charlotte Amalie

The U.S. bought these islands in 1917 and they became the US Virgin Islands, using U.S. stamps and currency. However, for the first six months of U.S. ownership, until September 30, 1917, a postal transition period existed. During this period, either U.S., D.W.I. or mixed frankings could be used. The domestic printed matter or postcard rate was 5 bits or 1 cent, and the foreign printed matter or postcard rate was 10 bits, 2 cents, or 5 bits + 1 cent. The domestic minimum-weight letter rate was 10 bits, 2 cents, or 5 bits + 1 cent, while the foreign minimum letter rate was 25 bits, 5 cents, or any combination of U.S. and D.W.I. stamps that together totaled 25 bits or 5 cents.

Letters posted to foreign destinations during the transition period are rare because of World War I. Values for covers listed here are for the period before the transition. Transition-period covers, including those with mixed franking, sell for much more.

100 Cents = 1 Dollar
100 Bit = 1 Franc (1905)

FORERUNNERS

Crowned Circle handstamp types are pictured in the Crowned Circle Handstamps and Great Britain Used Abroad section.

BRITISH POST OFFICES IN DANISH WEST INDIES

St. Thomas

British P.O. opened Jan., 1809; stamps supplied July 3, 1865; closed to the public Sept. 1, 1877; closed for receiving mail in transit 1879

Pre-Stamp Postal Markings

1849-55

A1	Crowned Circle handstamp Type I, on cover, inscribed "PAID AT ST. THOMAS"	
A2	Crowned Circle handstamp Type IX, on cover, inscribed "PAID AT ST. THOMAS" in black	575. 1,900.

Earliest known uses: A1, 2/20/49; A2, 5/1/55.

Stamps of Great Britain, Canceled C51, or with Circular Date Stamp (Several Types Exist)

No. A32

1865-79

A3	½p rose red (#58 P 5, 6, 8, 10-12), *value from*	42.50	
A4	1p rose red (#20)	—	
A5	1p rose red (#33, P 71, 72, 79, 81, 84-90, 93-102, 105-114, 116-125, 127, 129-131, 133, 134, 136-142, 144-152, 154-167, 169-182, 184-187, 189, 190, 197) *value from*	30.00	
A6	1½p lake red (#32, P1, 3), *value from*	75.00	
A7	2p blue (#29, P 9) Plate 12	35.00 350.00	
A8	2p blue (#30, P 13-15), *value from*	35.00	
A9	3p rose (#44, P 4)	100.00	
A10	3p rose (#49, P 4-10)	50.00	
A11	3p rose (#61, P 11-12, 14-19), *value from*	35.00	

A12	4p vermilion (#34)	85.00	
a.	Hair-lines (#34c)	100.00	
A13	4p vermilion (#43, P 7-14), *value from*	57.50	
A14	4p vermilion (#69, P [illegible])	350.00	
A15	4p pale olive green (#70, P 15, 16)	225.00	
A16	6p lilac (#39c, P 4)	175.00	
A17	6p lilac (#45, P 5) Plate 6	85.00 160.00	
A18	6p dull violet (#50, P 6)	85.00	
A19	6p violet (#51, P 6, 8, 9), *value from*	80.00	
A20	6p brown (#59, P 11)	50.00	
a.	6p pale buff (#59b, P 11) Plate 12	100.00 250.00	
A21	6p gray (#60, P 12)	240.00	
A22	6p gray (#62, P 13-16), *value from*	50.00	
A23	8p orange (#73)	310.00	
A24	9p straw (#40)	325.00	
a.	9p bister (#40a)	350.00	
A25	9p straw (#46)	425.00	
A26	9p bister (#52)	225.00	
A27	10p red brown (#53)	310.00	
A28	1sh green (#48, P 4)	160.00	
A29	1sh green (#54, P 4-7) *value from*	35.00	
A30	1sh green (#64, P 8-13) *value from*	70.00	
A31	2sh blue (#55)	150.00	
A32	5sh rose (#57, P 1) Plate 2	550.00 700.00	

Issued under Danish Dominion Watermarks

Wmk. 111 — Small Crown   Wmk. 112 — Crown

Wmk. 113 — Crown   Wmk. 114 — Multiple Crosses

Coat of Arms — A1

Yellowish Paper
Yellow Wavy-line Burelage, UL to LR

1856   Typo.   Wmk. 111   Imperf.

1	A1 3c dark carmine, brown gum	200.	*275.*
	On cover		*3,000.*
a.	3c dark carmine, yellow gum	225.	*275.*
	On cover		*3,000.*
b.	3c carmine, white gum	4,250.	—

The brown and yellow gums were applied locally.
Reprint: 1981, carmine, back-printed across two stamps ("Reprint by Dansk Post og Telegrafmuseum 1978"), value, pair, $10.

White Paper

1866

Yellow Wavy-line Burelage UR to LL

2	A1 3c rose	40.	*75.*
	On cover		*3,000.*

No. 2 reprints, unwatermarked: 1930, carmine, value $100. 1942, rose carmine, back-printed across each row ("Nytryk 1942 G. A. Hagemann Danmark og Dansk Vestindiens Frimærker Bind 2"), value $50.

1872   Perf. 12½

3	A1 3c rose	100.	*275.*
	On cover		*7,500.*

1873   **Without Burelage**
4   A1   4c dull blue   250.   475.
       On cover   —
 a.   Imperf., pair   775.
 b.   Horiz. pair, imperf. vert.   575.

The 1930 reprint of No. 4 is ultramarine, unwatermarked and imperf., value $100.
The 1942 4c reprint is blue, unwatermarked, imperf. and has printing on back (see note below No. 2), value $60.

A2

Normal Frame   **Inverted Frame**

The arabesques in the corners have a main stem and a branch. When the frame is in normal position, in the upper left corner the branch leaves the main stem half way between two little leaflets. In the lower right corner the branch starts at the foot of the second leaflet. When the frame is inverted the corner designs are, of course, transposed.

White Wove Paper
Varying from Thin to Thick
1874-79   Wmk. 112   Perf. 14x13½

Values for inverted frames, covers and blocks are for the cheapest variety.

5   A2   1c green & brown
           red   22.50   30.00
       On cover   250.00
 a.   1c green & rose lilac, thin
       paper   80.00   125.00
 b.   1c green & red violet, me-
       dium paper   45.00   65.00
 c.   1c green & claret, thick pa-
       per   20.00   30.00
 e.   As "c," inverted frame   25.00   32.50
 f.   As "a," inverted frame   475.00

No. 5 exists with "b" surcharge, "10 CENTS 1895." See note below No. 15.

6   A2   3c blue & carmine   27.50   20.00
       On cover   225.00
 a.   3c light blue & rose car-
       mine, thin paper   65.00   50.00
 b.   3c deep blue & dark car-
       mine, medium paper   40.00   17.00
 c.   3c greenish blue & lake,
       thick paper   32.50   17.00
 d.   Imperf., pair   375.00   —
 e.   Inverted frame, thick paper   30.00   20.00
 f.   As "a," inverted frame   350.00
7   A2   4c brown & dull
           blue   16.00   19.00
       On cover   225.00
 b.   4c brown & ultramarine,
       thin paper   225.00   225.00
 c.   Diagonal half used as 2c
       on cover   140.00
 d.   As "b," inverted frame   900.00   1,400.
8   A2   5c grn & gray
           ('76)   30.00   25.00
       On cover   250.00
 a.   5c yellow green & dark
       gray, thin paper   55.00   37.50
 b.   5c greenish blue, thick paper   30.00   25.00
9   A2   7c lilac & orange   35.00   95.00
       On cover   1,100.
 a.   7c lilac & yellow   90.00   100.00
 b.   Inverted frame   65.00   150.00
10   A2   10c blue & brn
           ('76)   30.00   30.00
       On cover   300.00
 a.   10c dark blue & black
       brown, thin paper   70.00   45.00
 b.   Period between "t" & "s" of
       "cents"   35.00   30.00
 c.   Inverted frame   27.50   32.50
11   A2   12c red lil & yel grn
           ('77)   42.50   175.00
       On cover   1,750.
 a.   12c lilac & deep green   160.00   200.00
12   A2   14c lilac & green   650.00   1,250.
       On cover   —
13   A2   50c vio, thin paper   190.00   300.00
       On cover   2,500.
 a.   50c gray violet, thick paper   250.00   375.00
       Nos. 5-13 (9)   1,043.   1,944.

The central element in the fan-shaped scrollwork at the outside of the lower left corner of Nos. 5a and 7b looks like an elongated diamond.
    See Nos. 16-20. For surcharges see Nos. 14-15, 23-28, 40.

Nos. 9 and 13 Surcharged in Black

   a   b

1887
14   A2 (a) 1c on 7c lilac &
             orange   100.00   200.00
       On cover   3,000.
 a.   1c on 7c lilac & yellow   120.00   225.00
 b.   Double surcharge   250.00   500.00
 c.   Inverted frame   110.00   350.00

1895
15   A2 (b) 10c on 50c violet,
             thin paper   42.50   67.50
       On cover   275.00

The "b" surcharge also exists on No. 5, with "10" found in two sizes. These are essays.

Type of 1873
1896-1901   Perf. 13
16   A2   1c green & red vi-
           olet, inverted
           frame ('98)   15.00   22.50
       On cover   150.00
 a.   Normal frame   300.00   450.00
17   A2   3c blue & lake, inverted
           frame ('98)   12.00   17.50
       On cover   150.00
 a.   Normal frame   250.00   425.00
18   A2   4c bister & dull
           blue ('01)   17.50   15.00
       On cover   150.00
 a.   Diagonal half used as 2c
       on cover   100.00
 b.   Inverted frame   60.00   85.00
       On cover   250.00
 c.   As "b," diagonal half used
       as 2c on cover   350.00
19   A2   5c green & gray,
           inverted frame   35.00   35.00
       On cover   325.00
 a.   Normal frame   800.00   1,200.
20   A2   10c blue & brown
           ('01)   80.00   150.00
       On cover   1,150.
 a.   Inverted frame   1,000.   2,000.
 b.   Period between "t" and "s"
       of "cents"   170.00   160.00
       Nos. 16-20 (5)   159.50   240.00

Arms — A5

1900
21   A5   1c light green   3.00   3.00
       On cover   80.00
       On cover, single franking   300.00
22   A5   5c light blue   17.50   25.00
       On cover   300.00

See Nos. 29-30. For surcharges see Nos. 41-42.

Nos. 6, 17, 20 Surcharged

   c

Surcharge "c" in Black
1902   Perf. 14x13½
23   A2   2c on 3c blue &
           carmine, in-
           verted frame   700.00   900.00
       On cover   4,000.
 a.   "2" in date with straight tail   750.00   950.00
 b.   Normal frame   —
24   A2   2c on 3c blue &
           lake, inverted
           frame   10.00   27.50
       On cover   160.00
 a.   "2" in date with straight tail   12.00   32.50
 b.   Dated "1901"   750.00   750.00
 c.   Normal frame   175.00   300.00
 d.   Dark green surcharge   2,750.
 e.   As "d" & "a"   —   —
 f.   As "d" & "c"   —   —

Only one example of No. 24f can exist.

25   A2   8c on 10c blue &
           brown   25.00   42.50
       On cover   225.00
 a.   "2" with straight tail   30.00   45.00
 b.   On No. 20b   32.50   45.00
 c.   Inverted frame   250.00   425.00

   d

Surcharge "d" in Black
1902   Perf. 13
27   A2   2c on 3c blue &
           lake, inverted
           frame   12.00   32.50
       On cover   500.00
 a.   Normal frame   240.00   425.00
28   A2   8c on 10c blue &
           brown   12.00   14.00
       On cover   175.00
 a.   On No. 20b   18.50   25.00
 b.   Inverted frame   225.00   400.00
       Nos. 23-28 (5)   759.00   1,016.

1903   Wmk. 113
29   A5   2c carmine   8.00   22.50
       On cover   125.00
30   A5   8c brown   27.50   35.00
       On cover   250.00

King   St. Thomas
Christian   Harbor — A9
IX — A8

1905   Typo.
31   A8   5b green   3.75   3.25
       On cover   35.00
32   A8   10b red   3.75   3.25
       On cover   35.00
33   A8   20b green & blue   8.75   8.25
       On cover   150.00
34   A8   25b ultramarine   8.75   10.50
       On cover   85.00
35   A8   40b red & gray   8.25   8.25
       On cover   225.00
36   A8   50b yellow & gray   10.00   12.00
       On cover   250.00

Perf. 12
Wmk. Two Crowns (113)
Frame Typographed, Center Engraved
37   A9   1fr green & blue   17.50   45.00
       On cover   625.00
38   A9   2fr orange red &
           brown   30.00   60.00
       On cover   1,100.
39   A9   5fr yellow & brown   77.50   275.00
       On cover   1,750.
       Nos. 31-39 (9)   168.25   425.50

On cover values are for commercial usages, usually parcel address cards. Philatelic covers are valued at approximately 25% of these values.

Nos. 18, 22 and 30 Surcharged in Black

1905   Wmk. 112
40   A2   5b on 4c bister & dull
           blue   16.00   50.00
       On cover   250.00
 a.   Inverted frame   45.00   90.00
41   A5   5b on 5c light blue   12.50   47.50
       On cover   250.00

                                      Wmk. 113
42   A5   5b on 8c brown   14.00   50.00
       On cover   250.00
       Nos. 40-42 (3)   42.50   147.50

Favor cancels exist on Nos. 40-42. Value 25% less.

Frederik VIII — A10

Frame Typographed, Center Engraved
1908   Wmk. 113   Perf. 13
43   A10 5b green   1.90   1.90
       On cover   22.50

44   A10 10b red   1.90   1.90
       On cover   22.50
45   A10 15b violet & brown   3.75   4.50
       On cover   125.00
46   A10 20b green & blue   30.00   27.50
       On cover   110.00
47   A10 25b blue & dark
           blue   1.90   2.50
       On cover   35.00
48   A10 30b claret & slate   50.00   52.50
       On cover   350.00
49   A10 40b vermilion &
           gray   5.75   9.50
       On cover   210.00
50   A10 50b yellow & brown   5.75   14.00
       On cover   210.00
       Nos. 43-50 (8)   100.95   114.30

Christian X — A11

1915   Wmk. 114   Perf. 14x14½
51   A11 5b yellow green   4.00   5.50
       On cover   45.00
52   A11 10b red   4.00   55.00
       On cover   110.00
53   A11 15b lilac & red brown   4.00   55.00
       On cover   300.00
54   A11 20b green & blue   4.00   55.00
       On cover   350.00
55   A11 25b blue & dark blue   4.00   17.50
       On cover   110.00
56   A11 30b claret & black   4.00   100.00
       On cover   900.00
57   A11 40b orange & black   4.00   100.00
       On cover   550.00
58   A11 50b yellow & brown   3.75   100.00
       On cover   650.00
       Nos. 51-58 (8)   31.75   488.00

Forged and favor cancellations exist.

POSTAGE DUE STAMPS

Royal Cipher,
"Christian 9 Rex"
D1

1902   Litho.   Unwmk.   Perf. 11½
J1   D1   1c dark blue   5.00   17.50
       On cover   400.00
J2   D1   4c dark blue   12.50   22.50
       On cover   350.00
J3   D1   6c dark blue   22.50   60.00
       On cover   450.00
J4   D1   10c dark blue   20.00   65.00
       On cover   400.00
       Nos. J1-J4 (4)   60.00   165.00

There are five types of each value. On the 4c they may be distinguished by differences in the figure "4"; on the other values differences are minute.
    Used values of Nos. J1-J8 are for canceled stamps. Uncanceled stamps without gum have probably been used. Value 60% of unused. On cover values are for stamps tied by cancellation.
    Excellent counterfeits of Nos. J1-J4 exist.

Numeral of value — D2

1905-13   Perf. 13
J5   D2   5b red & gray   4.50   6.75
       On cover   450.00
J6   D2   20b red & gray   7.50   14.00
       On cover   450.00
J7   D2   30b red & gray   6.75   14.00
       On cover   450.00
J8   D2   50b red & gray   6.00   35.00
       On cover   900.00
 a.   Perf. 14x14½ ('13)   37.50   140.00
 b.   Perf. 11½   325.00

All values of this issue are known imperforate, but were not regularly issued.
    Used values of Nos. J5-J8 are for canceled stamps. Uncanceled examples without gum have probably been used. Value 60% of unused.
    On cover values are for stamps tied by cancellation.
    Counterfeits of Nos. J5-J8 exist.
    Danish West Indies stamps were replaced by those of the U.S. in 1917, after the U.S. bought the islands.

DANZIG

'dant̪-sig

LOCATION — In northern Europe bordering on the Baltic Sea.
AREA — 754 sq. mi.
POP. — 407,000 (approx. 1939)
CAPITAL — Danzig

Established as a "Free City and State" under the protection of the League of Nations in 1920, Danzig was seized by Germany in 1939.

100 Pfennig = 1 Gulden (1923)
100 Pfennig = 1 Mark

Watermarks

Wmk. 108 — Honeycomb   Wmk. 109 — Webbing

Wmk. 110 — Octagons

Wmk. 125 — Lozenges   Wmk. 237 — Swastikas

Used Values of 1920-23 are for favor-canceled stamps unless otherwise noted. Postally used examples bring much higher prices.

German Stamps of 1906-20 Overprinted in Black

Perf. 14, 14½, 15x14½

1920   **Wmk. 125**

1	A16	5pf green	.30 / .50
	Never hinged	1.75	
	Postally used		2.00
	On cover		5.00
a.	Pair, one without overprint	85.00	
	Never hinged	240.00	
b.	Double overprint	—	
2	A16	10pf car rose	.30 / .30
	Never hinged	1.25	
	Postally used		2.00
	On cover		5.00
a.	10pf deep carmine	34.00 / 30.00	
	Never hinged	120.00	
	Postally used		150.00
	On cover		200.00
3	A22	15pf violet brown	.30 / .30
	Never hinged	1.75	
	Postally used		3.75
	On cover		6.25
4	A16	20pf blue violet	.30 / 1.10
	Never hinged	1.25	
	Postally used		3.75
	On cover		8.50
5	A16	30pf org & blk, buff	.30 / .30
	Never hinged	1.25	
	Postally used		2.50
	On cover		8.50

a.	Pair, one without overprint	— / —	
6	A16	40pf car rose	.30 / .30
	Never hinged	1.25	
	Postally used		1.75
	On cover		8.50
7	A16	50pf pur & blk, buff	1.10 / 1.00
	Never hinged	1.40	
	Postally used		3.90
	On cover		8.50
a.	Pair, one without overprint	150.00	
	Never hinged	425.00	
8	A17	1m red	.50 / .60
	Never hinged	2.50	
	Postally used		4.50
	On cover		10.00
a.	Pair, one without overprint	85.00	
	Never hinged	250.00	
9	A17	1.25m green	.50 / .60
	Never hinged	2.50	
	Postally used		4.50
	On cover		10.00
a.	1.25m deep bluish green	60.00 / 34.00	
	Never hinged	210.00	
	Postally used		190.00
	On cover		225.00
10	A17	1.50m yellow brn	.90 / 1.60
	Never hinged	4.25	
	Postally used		6.00
	On cover		14.50
11	A21	2m blue	3.25 / 7.25
	Never hinged	14.50	
	Postally used		26.00
	On cover		50.00
a.	Double overprint	375.00	
	Never hinged	825.00	
b.	2m blue black	125.00 / 125.00	
	Never hinged	375.00	
	Postally used		1,250.
	On cover		1,600.
12	A21	2.50m lilac rose	3.00 / 4.50
	Never hinged	11.25	
	Postally used		12.50
	On cover		25.00
a.	2.50m deep lilac rose	3.00 / 6.00	
	Never hinged	17.00	
	Postally used		17.00
	On cover		37.50
b.	2.50m lake rose	100.00 / 110.00	
	Never hinged	300.00	
	Postally used		850.00
	On cover		1,100.
13	A19	3m black violet	7.50 / 10.50
	Never hinged	40.00	
	Postally used		110.00
	On cover		375.00
a.	3m blackish slate-violet	67.50 / 135.00	
	Never hinged	220.00	
	Postally used		1,000.
	On cover		1,250.
14	A16	4m black & rose	4.75 / 6.00
	Never hinged	27.50	
	Postally used		37.50
	On cover		92.50
15	A20	5m slate & car (25x17 holes)	2.50 / 3.75
	Never hinged	10.00	
	Postally used		37.50
	On cover		85.00
a.	Center & "Danzig" invtd.	15,000.	
	Never hinged	—	
b.	Inverted overprint		20,000.
c.	5m slate & car (26x17 holes)	2,500.	
	Never hinged	7,250.	

Nos. 1-15 (15)   25.20 / 37.90
Set, never hinged   122.50

The 5pf brown, 10pf orange and 40pf lake and black with this overprint were not regularly issued. Value for trio, $450.
For surcharges see Nos. 19-23, C1-C3.
Issued: 40pf, 9/13; 1.50m, 3m 7/20; 4m, 12/21; others 6/14.

Nos. 5, 4 Surcharged in Various Sizes

1920

19	A16	5pf on 30pf (V)	.25 / .25
	Never hinged	1.00	
	Postally used		2.10
	On cover		4.25
20	A16	10pf on 20pf (R)	.25 / .25
	Never hinged	1.40	
	Postally used		2.00
	On cover		4.25
a.	Double surcharge	110.00	
	Never hinged	250.00	
21	A16	25pf on 30pf (G)	.25 / .25
	Never hinged	1.40	
	Postally used		2.00
	On cover		6.25
a.	Inverted surcharge	85.00	
	Never hinged	250.00	
22	A16	60pf on 30pf (Br)	.70 / 1.00
	Never hinged	4.00	
	Postally used		5.00
	On cover		10.00
a.	Double surcharge	85.00 / 290.00	
	Never hinged	250.00	

23	A16	80pf on 30pf (V)	.70 / 1.00
	Never hinged	4.00	
	Postally used		5.00
	On cover		10.00

Issued: No. 21, 8/10. No. 20, 8/17. Nos. 19, 22-23, 11/1

German Stamps Surcharged in Various Styles

No. 25   No. 27

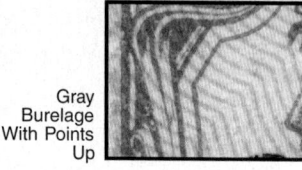

No. 30

Gray Burelage With Points Up

Gray Burelage with Points Up

25	A16	1m on 30pf org & blk, buff (Bk)	.85 / 1.50
	Never hinged	4.25	
	Postally used		4.25
	On cover		17.00
a.	Pair, one without surcharge		
e.	Double burlage, both pointing up	75.00 / 150.00	
	Never hinged	250.00	
	Postally used		850.00
26	A16	1¼m on 3pf brn (R)	1.00 / 1.50
	Never hinged	4.50	
	Postally used		5.00
	On cover		18.00
e.	Double burlage, both pointing up	75.00 / 150.00	
	Never hinged	250.00	
	Postally used		500.00
27	A22	2m on 35pf red brn (Bl)	1.50 / 1.50
	Never hinged	6.75	
	Postally used		5.00
	On cover		17.00
d.	Surcharge omitted	70.00 / —	
	Never hinged	260.00	
e.	Double burlage, both pointing up	110.00 / 170.00	
	Never hinged	340.00	
	Postally used		675.00
28	A22	3m on 7½pf org (G)	1.00 / 1.50
	Never hinged	4.50	
	Postally used		8.50
	On cover		21.00
d.	Double surcharge	170.00	
	Never hinged	425.00	
e.	Double burlage, both pointing up	67.50 / 125.00	
	Never hinged	200.00	
	Postally used		500.00
29	A22	5m on 2pf gray (R)	1.00 / 2.00
	Never hinged	4.50	
	Postally used		10.00
	On cover		25.00
30	A22	10m on 7½pf org (Bk)	3.00 / 7.00
	Never hinged	27.50	
	Postally used		22.00
	On cover		135.00
d.	Double surcharge	42.50	
	Never hinged	250.00	
e.	Double burlage, both pointing up	75.00 / 125.00	
	Never hinged	210.00	
	Postally used		600.00

Nos. 19-30 (11)   10.50 / 17.75
Set, never hinged   64.00

Gray Burelage with Points Down

26a	A16	1¼m on 3pf brown	36.00 / 42.50
	Never hinged	115.00	
	Postally used		100.00
	On cover		150.00
f.	Double burlage, both pointing down	42.50 / 160.00	
	Never hinged	300.00	
	Postally used		675.00
27a	A22	2m on 35pf red brn	400.00 / 325.00
	Never hinged	1,650.	
	Postally used		750.00
	On cover		1,000.
28a	A22	3m on 7½pf orange	25.00 / 17.00
	Never hinged	140.00	
	Postally used		50.00
	On cover		85.00
29a	A22	5m on 2pf gray	25.00 / 40.00
	Never hinged	140.00	
	Postally used		140.00
	On cover		210.00
30a	A22	10m on 7½pf orange	5.75 / 11.00
	Never hinged	32.50	
	Postally used		45.00
	On cover		150.00

Nos. 26a-30a (5)
Set, never hinged   2,100.

Violet Burelage with Points Up

25b	A16	1m on 30pf org & blk, buff	85.00 / 30.00
	Never hinged	350.00	
	Postally used		75.00
	On cover		170.00
26b	A16	1¼m on 3pf brown	4.50 / 6.50
	Never hinged	17.50	
	Postally used		21.00
	On cover		50.00
g.	Double burlage, both pointing up	210.00 / 250.00	
	Never hinged	850.00	
27b	A22	2m on 35pf red brn	11.50 / 37.50
	Never hinged	45.00	
	Postally used		140.00
	On cover		210.00
f.	Double burlage, both pointing up	210.00 / 250.00	
	Never hinged	850.00	
28b	A22	3m on 7½pf orange	2.50 / 2.50
	Never hinged	11.50	
	Postally used		10.00
	On cover		42.50
f.	Double burlage, both pointing up	210.00 / 250.00	
	Never hinged	850.00	
29b	A22	5m on 2pf gray	1.25 / 2.50
	Never hinged	4.25	
	Postally used		12.50
	On cover		42.50
30b	A22	10m on 7½pf orange	1.25 / 2.50
	Never hinged	4.25	
	Postally used		13.50
	On cover		42.50
g.	Double burlage, both pointing up	210.00 / 250.00	
	Never hinged	850.00	

Nos. 25b-30b (6)   106.00 / 81.50
Set, never hinged   430.00

Violet Burelage With Points Down

Violet Burelage with Points Down

25c	A16	1m on 30pf org & blk, buff	1.25 / 2.50
	Never hinged	4.25	
	Postally used		15.50
	On cover		24.00
d.	Double burlage, both pointing down	210.00 / 250.00	
	Never hinged	850.00	
26c	A16	1¼m on 3pf brown	6.50 / 11.00
	Never hinged	30.00	
	Postally used		45.00
	On cover		82.50
d.	Double burlage, both pointing down	210.00 / 250.00	
	Never hinged	850.00	
27c	A22	2m on 35pf red brn	30.00 / 50.00
	Never hinged	95.00	
	Postally used		275.00
	On cover		340.00
g.	Double burlage, both pointing down	210.00 / 250.00	
	Never hinged	850.00	
28c	A22	3m on 7½pf orange	40.00 / 85.00
	Never hinged	175.00	
	Postally used		340.00
	On cover		425.00
g.	Double burlage, both pointing down	210.00 / 250.00	
	Never hinged	850.00	
29c	A22	5m on 2pf gray	6.50 / 8.50
	Never hinged	22.50	
	Postally used		37.50
	On cover		500.00
e.	Double burlage, both pointing down	210.00 / 250.00	
	Never hinged	850.00	
30c	A22	10m on 7½pf orange	13.50 / 29.00
	Never hinged	55.00	
	Postally used		110.00
	On cover		150.00
h.	Double burlage, both pointing down	210.00 / 250.00	
	Never hinged	850.00	
i.	Double burlage, one pointing up, one down	210.00 / 250.00	
	Never hinged	850.00	

Nos. 25c-30c (6)   97.75 / 186.00
Set, never hinged   380.00

Burelage Omitted

25f	A16	1m on 30pf org & blk, buff	3.25 / 6.00
	Never hinged	12.50	
	Postally used		21.00
	On cover		50.00
26h	A16	1¼m on 3pf brown	110.00 / 175.00
	Never hinged	340.00	
	Postally used		750.00
	On cover		1,000.
27h	A22	2m on 35pf red brn	135.00 / 175.00
	Never hinged	425.00	
	Postally used		925.00
	On cover		1,500.
28h	A22	3m on 7½pf orange	240.00 / 375.00
	Never hinged	850.00	
	Postally used		1,350.
29f	A22	5m on 2pf gray	240.00 / 375.00
	Never hinged	850.00	
	Postally used		850.00
	On cover		1,350.

30j	A22	10m on 7½pf orange	9.25	21.00
		Never hinged	21.00	
		Postally used		100.00
		On cover		135.00

Excellent counterfeits of the surcharges are known.

German Stamps of 1906-20 Overprinted in Blue

1920

31	A22	2pf gray	110.00	200.00
		Never hinged	375.00	
		Postally used		450.00
		On cover		2,100.
32	A22	2½pf gray	150.00	300.00
		Never hinged	550.00	
		Postally used		600.00
		On cover		3,400.
33	A16	3pf brown	11.00	17.00
		Never hinged	37.50	
		Postally used		50.00
		On cover		125.00
a.		Double overprint	75.00	—
		Never hinged	180.00	
34	A16	5pf green	.55	.65
		Never hinged	2.25	
		Postally used		2.50
		On cover		7.50
a.		Double overprint	85.00	
		Never hinged	200.00	
35	A22	7½pf orange	40.00	57.50
		Never hinged	150.00	
		Postally used		150.00
		On cover		300.00
36	A16	10pf carmine	3.75	7.00
		Never hinged	15.00	
		Postally used		30.00
		On cover		67.50
a.		10pf dark rose red	22.50	37.50
		Never hinged	85.00	
		Postally used		175.00
		On cover		250.00
b.		Double overprint	—	
37	A22	15pf dk violet	.60	.65
		Never hinged	2.90	
		Postally used		5.25
		On cover		9.00
a.		15pf deep brownish violet	55.00	67.50
		Never hinged	225.00	
		Postally used		225.00
		On cover		260.00
b.		Double overprint	85.00	
		Never hinged	200.00	
38	A16	20pf blue violet	.55	.65
		Never hinged	2.90	
		Postally used		2.90
		On cover		8.50

Overprinted in Carmine or Blue

39	A16	25pf org & blk, yel	.55	.65
		Never hinged	2.90	
		Postally used		2.60
		On cover		8.50
40	A16	30pf org & blk, buff	50.00	92.50
		Never hinged	160.00	
		Postally used		200.00
		On cover		425.00
42	A16	40pf lake & blk	2.25	2.50
		Never hinged	7.50	
		Postally used		18.50
		On cover		67.50
a.		Inverted overprint	210.00	
b.		Double overprint	425.00	
c.		40pf red & black	19.00	30.00
		Never hinged	100.00	
		Postally used		110.00
		On cover		150.00
43	A16	50pf pur & blk, buff	175.00	300.00
		Never hinged	550.00	
		Postally used		850.00
		On cover		3,000.
44	A16	60pf mag (Bl)	1,250.	2,100.
		Never hinged	2,500.	
		Postally used		3,400.
45	A16	75pf green & blk	.55	.60
		Never hinged	2.75	
		Postally used		5.00
		On cover		11.00
46	A16	80pf lake & blk, rose	2.40	4.25
		Never hinged	8.50	
		Postally used		37.50
		On cover		125.00
47	A17	1m carmine	1,200.	2,100.
		Never hinged	2,500.	
		On cover		3,400.
a.		Double overprint	4,250.	

Overprinted in Carmine

48	A21	2m gray blue	1,200.	2,100.
		Never hinged	2,500.	
		On cover		3,400.

Counterfeit overprints of Nos. 31-48 exist.

Nos. 44, 47 and 48 were issued in small quantities and usually affixed directly to the mail by the postal clerk.
For surcharge see No. 62.
Issued: 5pf, 15pf, 20pf, 25pf, 75pf, 8/20. Others, 8/30.

A8

Hanseatic Trading Ship — A9

Serrate Roulette 13½

1921, Jan. 31		Typo.	Wmk. 108	
49	A8	5pf brown & violet	.25	.25
		Never hinged	1.50	
		Postally used		1.90
		On cover		3.40
50	A8	10pf orange & dk vio	.25	.25
		Never hinged	1.50	
		Postally used		1.90
		On cover		4.25
51	A8	25pf green & car rose	.50	.65
		Never hinged	2.25	
		Postally used		1.90
		On cover		4.25
52	A8	40pf carmine rose	3.75	3.25
		Never hinged	15.00	
		Postally used		6.00
		On cover		12.50
53	A8	80pf ultra	.50	.50
		Never hinged	2.25	
		Postally used		7.00
		On cover		12.50
54	A9	1m car rose & blk	1.60	1.60
		Never hinged	7.50	
		Postally used		6.75
		On cover		17.00
55	A9	2m dk blue & dk grn	5.00	4.75
		Never hinged	21.00	
		Postally used		21.00
		On cover		37.50
56	A9	3m blk & grnsh bl	1.75	2.25
		Never hinged	8.25	
		Postally used		9.75
		On cover		17.00
57	A9	5m indigo & rose red	1.75	2.25
		Never hinged	8.25	
		Postally used		9.25
		On cover		21.00
58	A9	10m dk grn & brn org	2.50	4.50
		Never hinged	15.00	
		Postally used		34.00
		On cover		50.00
		Nos. 49-58 (10)	17.85	20.25
		Set, never hinged	82.50	

Issued in honor of the Constitution.
Nos. 49 and 50 with center in red instead of violet and Nos. 49-51, 54-58 with center inverted are probably proofs. All values of this issue exist imperforate but are not known to have been regularly issued in that condition.

1921, Mar. 11			Perf. 14	
59	A8	25pf green & car rose	.50	.85
		Never hinged	4.00	
		Postally used		1.75
		On cover		9.25
60	A8	40pf carmine rose	.50	.85
		Never hinged	4.00	
		Postally used		2.60
		On cover		9.25
61	A8	80pf ultra	5.00	10.00
		Never hinged	26.00	
		Postally used		23.00
		On cover		37.50
		Nos. 59-61 (3)	6.00	11.70
		Set, never hinged	34.00	

No. 45 Surcharged in Black

1921, May 6			Wmk. 125	
62	A16	60pf on 75pf	.95	.90
		Never hinged	5.50	
		Postally used		4.25
		On cover		9.50
a.		Double surcharge	100.00	110.00
		Never hinged	250.00	
		On cover		600.00
b.		Pair, one stamp without "Danzig" overprint	42.50	175.00
		Never hinged	125.00	
		Postally used		—

c.		Double surcharge, one inverted	85.00	75.00
		Never hinged	210.00	
		Postally used		300.00
d.		Surcharge "60" in center of design	17.00	42.50
		Never hinged	60.00	
		Postally used		85.00
		On cover		175.00

Surcharge on No. 62 normally appears at top of design.

Arms — A11

Coat of Arms — A12

Wmk. 108 (Upright or Sideways)

1921-22			Perf. 14	
63	A11	5(pf) orange	.25	.25
		Never hinged	.90	
		Postally used		3.50
		On cover		5.00
64	A11	10(pf) dark brown	.25	.25
		Never hinged	.70	
		Postally used		2.00
		On cover		5.00
65	A11	15(pf) green	.25	.25
		Never hinged	.70	
		Postally used		1.60
		On cover		4.25
66	A11	20(pf) slate	.25	.25
		Never hinged	.70	
		Postally used		1.60
		On cover		4.25
67	A11	25(pf) dark green	.25	.25
		Never hinged	.70	
		Postally used		1.60
		On cover		4.25
68	A11	30(pf) blue & car	.25	.25
		Never hinged	.85	
		Postally used		1.60
		On cover		4.25
a.		Center inverted	67.50	150.00
		Never hinged	160.00	
69	A11	40pf green & car	.25	.25
		Never hinged	.85	
		Postally used		1.60
		On cover		3.40
a.		Center inverted	50.00	150.00
		Never hinged	160.00	
70	A11	50pf dk grn & car	.25	.25
		Never hinged	.85	
		Postally used		1.60
		On cover		3.50
71	A11	60pf carmine	.45	.45
		Never hinged	1.50	
		Postally used		3.00
		On cover		6.25
72	A11	80pf black & car	.35	.45
		Never hinged	.85	
		Postally used		3.40
		On cover		7.50

Paper With Faint Gray Network

73	A11	1m org & car	.50	.40
		Never hinged	1.40	
		Postally used		2.10
		On cover		4.25
a.		Center inverted	67.50	150.00
		Never hinged	210.00	
b.		Background omitted	5.75	30.00
		Never hinged	15.00	
		On cover		75.00
74	A11	1.20m blue violet	1.25	1.25
		Never hinged	6.75	
		Postally used		3.75
		On cover		12.50
a.		Background omitted	7.50	30.00
		Never hinged	24.00	
		On cover		110.00
75	A11	2m gray & car	3.25	4.25
		Never hinged	11.00	
		Postally used		7.50
		On cover		15.00
a.		Background omitted	15.00	45.00
		Never hinged	45.00	
		On cover		125.00
76	A11	3m violet & car	9.00	10.00
		Never hinged	32.50	
		Postally used		29.00
		On cover		50.00

Serrate Roulette 13½
Wmk. 108 Upright

77	A12	5m grn, red & blk	1.25	3.00
		Never hinged	6.00	
		Postally used		17.00
		On cover		34.00
78	A12	9m rose, red & org ('22)	3.00	8.50
		Never hinged	14.50	
		Postally used		150.00
		On cover		210.00
a.		Background omitted	42.50	
		Never hinged	125.00	
79	A12	10m ultra, red & blk	1.25	3.00
		Never hinged	6.00	
		Postally used		25.00
		On cover		42.50
a.		Background omitted	67.50	3.00
		Never hinged	200.00	
80	A12	20m red & black	1.25	3.00
		Never hinged	6.00	
		Postally used		50.00
		On cover		85.00
a.		Background omitted	67.50	
		Never hinged	200.00	
		Nos. 63-80 (18)	23.55	36.30
		Set, never hinged	85.00	

Wmk. 108 Sideways

77a	A12	5m grn, red & blk	1.25	2.75
		Never hinged	6.00	
		Postally used		67.50
		On cover		80.00
78b	A12	9m rose, red & org	2.75	8.00
		Never hinged	14.50	
		Postally used		175.00
		On cover		240.00
79b	A12	10m ultra, red & blk	1.25	2.75
		Never hinged	5.50	
		Postally used		72.50
		On cover		105.00
80b	A12	20m red & blk	1.25	2.75
		Never hinged	6.00	
		Postally used		140.00
		On cover		190.00

In this and succeeding issues the mark values usually have the face of the paper covered with a gray network. This network is often very faint and occasionally is omitted.

Nos. 64-76 exist imperf. Value, each $16-$50 unused, $50-$150 never hinged.

See Nos. 81-93, 99-105. For surcharges and overprints see Nos. 96-98, O1-O33.

Issued: Nos. 63-76, 6/3/21. Nos. 77, 79-80, 8/1/21. No. 78, 2/1/22. Nos. 77a-80a, 3/1922.

Type of 1921 and

A13

Coat of Arms — A13a

1922		Wmk. 108 Upright	Perf. 14	
81	A11	75(pf) deep vio	.25	.25
		Never hinged	.75	
		Postally used		1.60
		On cover		4.00
82	A11	80(pf) green	.25	.25
		Never hinged	.75	
		Postally used		32.50
		On cover		60.00
83	A11	1.25m vio & car	.25	.25
		Never hinged	.75	
		Postally used		2.00
		On cover		4.00
84	A11	1.50m slate gray	.25	.40
		Never hinged	.75	
		Postally used		2.00
		On cover		4.00
85	A11	2m car rose	.25	.25
		Never hinged	.75	
		Postally used		1.60
		On cover		4.00
86	A11	2.40m dk brn & car	1.00	2.00
		Never hinged	5.25	
		Postally used		32.50
		On cover		65.00
87	A11	3m car lake	.25	.40
		Never hinged	.75	
		Postally used		2.00
		On cover		4.00
a.		dark carmine red	64.00	67.50
		Never hinged	240.00	
		Postally used		525.00
		On cover		600.00
88	A11	4m dark blue	1.00	2.00
		Never hinged	5.50	
		Postally used		9.00
		On cover		13.50
89	A11	5m deep grn	.25	.35
		Never hinged	.75	
		Postally used		1.60
		On cover		4.00
a.		Wmk. sideways	16.00	55.00
		Never hinged	65.00	
		Postally used		275.00
		On cover		475.00
90	A11	6m car lake	.25	.35
		Never hinged	.75	
		Postally used		1.60
		On cover		4.00
a.		6m car rose, wmk. 109 sideways	1,800.	
		Never hinged	3,900.	
91	A11	8m light blue	.45	1.60
		Never hinged	2.25	
		Postally used		20.00
		On cover		27.50
92	A11	10m orange	.25	.35
		Never hinged	.75	
		Postally used		4.00
		On cover		4.00
93	A11	20m org brn	.25	.35
		Never hinged	.75	
		Postally used		4.00
		On cover		4.00
94	A13	50m gold & car	2.00	6.50
		Never hinged	9.00	
		Postally used		175.00
		On cover		210.00
a.		50m gold & red	57.50	120.00
		Never hinged	220.00	
		Postally used		525.00
		On cover		725.00

95 A13a 100m metallic grn & red ... 3.25 / 6.00
Never hinged 14.00
Postally used ... 2,400.
On cover ... 3,500.
Nos. 81-95 (15) 10.20 / 21.30
Set, never hinged 42.50

Wmk. 109 Sideways

94b A13 50m gold & car ... 2.00 / 12.00
Never hinged 9.00
Postally used ... 175.00
On cover ... 240.00
c. As "a" 7.25 / 12.50
Never hinged 26.00
Postally used ... 175.00
On cover ... 210.00
95b A13a 100m metallic grn & red ... 3.00 / 5.00
Never hinged 10.50
Postally used ... 210.00
On cover ... 350.00

No. 95 has buff instead of gray network.
Nos. 81-83, 85-86, 88 exist imperf. Value, each $12.50.
Nos. 94-95 exist imperf. Value, each $50
Issued: 75pf, 80pf, 1.25m, 2m, 2.40m, 4m, 2/1. 50m, 100m, 3/10. 1.50m, 3m, 8m, 7/29. 6m, 20m, 10/30. 5m, 10m, 11/9.

Nos. 87, 88 and 91 Surcharged in Black or Carmine

1922

96 A11 6m on 3m car lake ... .25 / .60
Never hinged 1.40
Postally used ... 2.50
On cover ... 4.00
a. Double surcharge
97 A11 8m on 4m dk blue ... .30 / .85
Never hinged 1.20
Postally used ... 16.00
On cover ... 24.00
a. Double surcharge 60.00 / 145.00
Never hinged 140.00
b. Pair, one without surcharge 120.00
Never hinged 325.00
98 A11 20m on 8m lt bl (C) ... .30 / .60
Never hinged 1.75
Postally used ... 15.00
On cover ... 24.00
Nos. 96-98 (3) .85 / 2.05
Set, never hinged 4.00

Issued: No. 97, 5/15. Nos. 96, 98, 10/2.

Wmk. 109 Sideways

1922-23   *Perf. 14*

99 A11 4m dark blue ... .25 / .40
Never hinged .90
Postally used ... 2.40
On cover ... 8.00
100 A11 5m dark green ... .25 / .40
Never hinged .90
Postally used ... 1.90
On cover ... 4.00
a. Wmk. 110 2,750.
Never hinged 4,000.
b. Wmk. 109 upright .45 / .80
Never hinged 2.10
Postally used ... 4.75
On cover ... 8.00
102 A11 10m orange ... .25 / .40
Never hinged .90
Postally used ... 1.60
On cover ... 4.00
b. Wmk. 109 upright .45 / .80
Never hinged 1.90
On cover ... 4.00 / 8.00
103 A11 20m orange brn ... .25 / .40
Never hinged .90
Postally used ... 2.00
On cover ... 4.00
b. Wmk. 109 upright .45 / .80
Never hinged 1.90
On cover ... 3.50 / 8.50

Paper Without Network
Wmk. 109 Upright

104 A11 40m pale blue ... .25 / .60
Never hinged .90
Postally used ... 10.00
On cover ... 20.00

---

105 A11 80m red ... .25 / .60
Never hinged .90
Postally used ... 52.50
On cover ... 80.00
Nos. 99-105 (6) 1.50 / 2.80
Set, never hinged 5.40

Nos. 100, 102 and 103 also exist with watermark vertical. Values slightly higher.

Nos. 104-105 exist imperf. Value, each $12.50 unused, $32.50 never hinged.
Issued: No. 99, 12/16/22. Nos. 104-105, 5/15/1923. Others, 1/1923.

A15   A15a

Coat of Arms
A16

1922-23   **Wmk. 109 Upright**   *Perf. 14*
Paper With Gray Network

106 A15 50m pale bl & red ... .25 / .40
Never hinged .90
Postally used ... 1.75
On cover ... 4.00
a. Wmk. sideways .45 / .80
Never hinged 1.75
Postally used ... 4.00
On cover ... 8.00
107 A15a 100m dk grn & red ... .25 / .40
Never hinged .90
Postally used ... 1.75
On cover ... 4.00
a. Wmk. sideways .75 / .80
Never hinged 3.75
Postally used ... 4.75
On cover ... 10.00
108 A15a 150m violet & red ... .25 / .40
Never hinged .90
Postally used ... 3.25
On cover ... 8.00
109 A16 250m violet & red ... .35 / .40
Never hinged 2.25
Postally used ... 80.00
On cover ... 105.00
110 A16 500m gray blk & red ... .35 / .40
Never hinged 2.25
Postally used ... 32.50
On cover ... 65.00
111 A16 1000m brn & red ... .35 / .40
Never hinged 2.25
Postally used ... 21.00
On cover ... 40.00
112 A16 5000m silver & red ... 1.50 / 6.00
Never hinged 7.50
Postally used ... 65.00
On cover ... 105.00

Paper Without Network

113 A15 50m pale blue ... .40 / .60
Never hinged .90
Postally used ... 140.00
On cover ... 190.00
114 A15a 100m deep green ... .40 / .60
Never hinged .90
Postally used ... 4.75
On cover ... 9.50
115 A15 200m orange ... .40 / .60
Never hinged .90
Postally used ... 2.25
On cover ... 6.00
Nos. 106-115 (10) 4.50 / 10.20
Set, never hinged 19.00

Nos. 108-112 exist imperf. Value, each $50 unused, $125 never hinged.
Nos. 113-115 exist imperf. Value, each $35 unused, $92.50 never hinged.
See Nos. 123-125. For surcharges and overprints see Nos. 126, 137-140, 143, 156-167, O35-O38.
Issued: No. 106, 11/21/22. No. 107, 12/14/22. 150m, 250m, 500m, 1000m, 1/24/23. 5000m, 2/27/23. No. 113, 200m, 7/20/23. No. 114, 4/27/23.

A17

1923   *Perf. 14*
Paper With Gray Network

117 A17 250m violet & red ... .25 / .50
Never hinged .75
Postally used ... 12.00
On cover ... 24.00

---

118 A17 300m bl grn & red ... .25 / .50
Never hinged .65
Postally used ... 2.75
On cover ... 6.00
119 A17 500m gray & red ... .25 / .50
Never hinged .70
Postally used ... 2.50
On cover ... 6.00
120 A17 1000m brown & red ... .25 / .50
Never hinged .75
Postally used ... 2.50
On cover ... 6.00
121 A17 3000m violet & red ... .25 / .50
Never hinged .75
Postally used ... 14.00
On cover ... 24.00
123 A16 10,000m orange & red ... .60 / .60
Never hinged 3.00
Postally used ... 14.50
On cover ... 20.00
124 A16 20,000m pale bl & red ... .60 / 1.00
Never hinged 3.00
Postally used ... 25.00
On cover ... 32.50
125 A16 50,000m green & red ... .60 / 1.00
Never hinged 3.00
Postally used ... 21.00
On cover ... 27.50
Nos. 117-125 (8) 3.05 / 5.10
Set, never hinged 12.50

Nos. 117, 119-121 exist imperf. Value, each $19 unused, $45 never hinged; Nos. 123-125 also exist imperf. Values each, $25 unused, $85 never hinged.
See Nos. 127-135. For surcharges & overprints see Nos. 141-142, 144-155, O39-O41.
Issued: 300m, 3/22. 250m, 5/15. 500m, 6/29. 1000m, 7/29. 3000m, 8/3. 10,000m, 8/8. 20,000m, 8/13. 50,000m, 8/20.

Network Omitted

117a A17 250m 19.00 / 16.50
Never hinged 45.00
Postally used ... 90.00
118a A17 300m 19.00 / 16.50
Never hinged 45.00
Postally used ... 90.00
119a A17 500m 19.00 / 16.50
Never hinged 45.00
Postally used ... 90.00
120a A17 1000m 19.00 / 16.50
Never hinged 45.00
Postally used ... 90.00
121a A17 3000m 19.00 / 16.50
Never hinged 45.00
Postally used ... 90.00
123a A16 10,000m 22.50 / 22.50
Never hinged 75.00
Postally used ... 150.00
124a A16 20,000m 22.50 / 27.50
Never hinged 75.00
Postally used ... 240.00
125a A16 50,000m 22.50 / 27.50
Never hinged 75.00
Postally used ... 240.00

Nos. 117a, 119a-121a exist imperf. Value each, $19 unused, $45 never hinged.

No. 124 Surcharged in Red

1923, Aug. 14
126 A16 100,000m on #124 ... 1.25 / 6.00
Never hinged 4.50
Postally used ... 110.00
On cover ... 140.00
a. On #124a 6.00 / 16.00
Never hinged 16.00
Postally used ... 325.00
On cover ...

No. 126 exists imperf. Value $50 unused, $125 never hinged.

1923   *Perf. 14*
Paper Without Network

127 A17 1000m brown ... .25 / .40
Never hinged .70
Postally used ... 4.00
On cover ... 9.50
129 A17 5000m rose ... .25 / .40
Never hinged .70
Postally used ... 1.75
On cover ... 6.00
131 A17 20,000m pale blue ... .25 / .40
Never hinged .70
Postally used ... 1.75
On cover ... 6.00
132 A17 50,000m green ... .25 / .40
Never hinged .70
Postally used ... 1.75
On cover ...
a. Wmk. 110 —
b. Wmk. two vert. interlaced ribbons 4,000.

Never hinged *7,500.*

Paper With Gray Network
133 A17 100,000m deep blue ... .25 / .40
Never hinged .70
Postally used ... 2.10
On cover ... 8.00
a. Network omitted 8.00 / 16.00
Never hinged 24.00
Postally used ... 55.00
134 A17 250,000m violet ... .25 / .40
Never hinged .70
Postally used ... 2.10
On cover ... 10.00
a. Network omitted 8.00 / 16.00
Never hinged 24.00
Postally used ... 55.00
135 A17 500,000m slate ... .25 / .40
Never hinged .70
Postally used ... 2.10
On cover ... 6.00
a. Network omitted 8.00 / 16.00
Never hinged 24.00
Postally used ... 55.00
Nos. 127-135 (7) 1.75 / 2.80
Set, never hinged 5.00

Nos. 127, 129, 131-135 exist imperf. Value each, $40 unused, $100 never hinged.
Issued: No. 127, 7/24. Nos. 129, 131, 8/25. No. 132, 9/1. No. 133, 9/11. No. 135, 9/16.

Abbreviations:
th=(tausend) thousand
mil=million

Nos. 115, 114, 132, and Type of 1923 Surcharged

1923   *Perf. 14*
Paper Without Network

137 A15 40th m on 200m ... .85 / 2.00
Never hinged 5.25
Postally used ... 190.00
On cover ... 240.00
a. Double surcharge 85.00
Never hinged 160.00
b. Pair, one without surch. —
138 A15 100th m on 200m ... .85 / 2.00
Never hinged 4.75
Postally used ... 26.00
On cover ... 47.50
139 A15 250th m on 200m ... 6.25 / 13.00
Never hinged 30.00
Postally used ... 250.00
On cover ... 350.00
140 A15a 400th m on 100m ... .60 / .40
Never hinged 3.00
Postally used ... 12.00
On cover ... 16.00
a. Pair, one without surch. —
141 A17 500th m on #132 ... .40 / .40
Never hinged 2.10
Postally used ... 5.25
On cover ... 8.00

On 10,000m

142 A17 1mil m org ... 3.75 / 6.25
Never hinged 15.00
Postally used ... 440.00
On cover ... 550.00

The surcharges on Nos. 140-142 differ in details from those on Nos. 137-139.

Type of 1923 Surcharged

Paper With Gray Network
On 1,000,000m

143 A16 10mil m org ... .40 / 1.25
Never hinged 3.00
Postally used ... 95.00
On cover ... 125.00
a. Network omitted 24.00 / 20.00
Never hinged 65.00
Postally used ... 475.00
Nos. 137-143 (7) 13.10 / 25.30
Set, never hinged 55.00

Nos. 142-143 exist imperf. Values: No. 142 unused $50, never hinged $125; No. 143 unused $25, never hinged $85.
Issued: Nos. 137-139, 9/1. No. 141, 9/8. No. 142, 9/13. No. 143, 10/1.

Type of 1923 Surcharged

Wmk. 109 Upright
Perf. 14
10,000m rose on paper without Network

144	A17	1mil m on 10,000m	.25	.40
	Never hinged		1.00	
	Postally used			1.90
	On cover			6.00
145	A17	2mil m on 10,000m	.25	.40
	Never hinged		1.00	
	Postally used			2.25
	On cover			6.00
146	A17	3mil m on 10,000m	.25	.40
	Never hinged		1.00	
	Postally used			2.25
	On cover			6.00
147	A17	5mil m on 10,000m	.35	.40
	Never hinged		1.50	
	Postally used			1.90
	On cover			6.00
b.	Double surcharge		85.00	
	Never hinged		160.00	

10,000m gray lilac on paper without Network

148	A17	10mil m on 10,000m	.40	.75
	Never hinged		1.60	
	Postally used			7.25
	On cover			16.00
149	A17	20mil m on 10,000m	.40	.75
	Never hinged		1.60	
	Postally used			8.75
	On cover			20.00
150	A17	25mil m on 10,000m	.25	.75
	Never hinged		1.40	
	Postally used			32.50
	On cover			47.50
151	A17	40mil m on 10,000m	.25	.75
	Never hinged		1.40	
	Postally used			32.50
	On cover			47.50
a.	Double surcharge		52.50	
	Never hinged		160.00	
152	A17	50mil m on 10,000m	.25	.75
	Never hinged		1.40	
	Postally used			11.00
	On cover			20.00

Type of 1923
Surcharged in Red

10,000m gray lilac on paper without Network

153	A17	100mil m on 10,000m	.25	.75
	Never hinged		1.40	
	Postally used			4.00
	On cover			8.00
154	A17	300mil m on 10,000m	.25	.75
	Never hinged		1.40	
	Postally used			12.00
	On cover			20.00
155	A17	500mil m on 10,000m	.25	.75
	Never hinged		1.40	
	Postally used			2.75
	On cover			8.00
	Nos. 144-155 (12)		3.40	7.60
	Set, never hinged		15.00	

Nos. 144-147 exist imperf. Value, each $25 unused, $85 never hinged. Nos. 148-155 exist imperf. Value, each $32.50 unused, $85 never hinged.

Issued: Nos. 148-150, 152, 10/15. No. 153, 10/22. Nos. 151, 154-155, 10/23.

Types of 1923
Surcharged

1923, Oct. 31   Wmk. 110   *Perf. 14*

156	A15	5pf on 50m	.40	.40
	Never hinged		2.25	
	Postally used			2.00
	On cover			4.00
157	A15	10pf on 50m	.40	.40
	Never hinged		2.25	
	Postally used			2.00
	On cover			4.00
158	A15a	20pf on 100m	.40	.40
	Never hinged		2.25	
	Postally used			2.00
	On cover			4.00
159	A15	25pf on 50m	3.50	9.00
	Never hinged		16.00	
	Postally used			32.50
	On cover			52.50
160	A15	30pf on 50m	3.50	2.00
	Never hinged		16.00	
	Postally used			5.25
	On cover			12.00
161	A15a	40pf on 100m	2.00	2.00
	Never hinged		11.00	
	Postally used			8.75
	On cover			16.00
162	A15a	50pf on 100m	2.00	3.00
	Never hinged		13.50	
	Postally used			12.00
	On cover			20.00
163	A15a	75pf on 100m	8.00	16.00
	Never hinged		30.00	
	Postally used			55.00
	On cover			80.00

Type of 1923 Surcharged

1923, Nov. 5

164	A16	1g on 1mil m rose	4.50	6.25
	Never hinged		24.00	
	Postally used			14.50
	On cover			47.50
165	A16	2g on 1mil m rose	12.00	17.50
	Never hinged		35.00	
	Postally used			60.00
	On cover			160.00
166	A16	3g on 1mil m rose	20.00	62.50
	Never hinged		110.00	
	Postally used			160.00
	On cover			350.00
167	A16	5g on 1mil m rose	25.00	67.50
	Never hinged		125.00	
	Postally used			550.00
	On cover			800.00
	Nos. 156-167 (12)		81.70	186.95
	Set, never hinged		385.00	

Issued: Nos. 156-163, 10/31. Nos. 164-167, 11/5.

Coat of Arms — A19

1924-37   Wmk. 109   *Perf. 14*

168	A19	3pf brn, *yelsh*	1.25	1.50
	Never hinged		4.75	
	On cover			6.00
a.	3pf dp brn, *white*		2.10	1.90
	Never hinged		7.25	
	On cover			6.00
170	A19	5pf org, *yelsh*	3.25	.55
	Never hinged		6.50	
	On cover			4.00
a.	White paper		8.50	2.00
	Never hinged		45.00	
	On cover			4.00
c.	Tête bêche pair		375.00	
	Never hinged		725.00	
d.	Syncopated perf., #170		10.50	9.25
	Never hinged		30.00	
	On cover			27.50
e.	Syncopated perf., #170a		210.00	22.50
	Never hinged		110.00	
	On cover			27.50
171	A19	7pf yel grn	1.60	3.00
	Never hinged		4.25	
	On cover			10.50
172	A19	8pf yel grn	1.60	6.00
	Never hinged		6.50	
	On cover			17.50
173	A19	10pf grn, *yelsh*	5.50	.50
	Never hinged		15.50	
	On cover			4.00
a.	White paper		8.50	2.50
	Never hinged		32.50	
	On cover			4.00
c.	10pf blue grn, *yellowish*		5.00	1.10
	Never hinged		13.00	
	On cover			4.00
d.	Tête bêche pair		325.00	
	Never hinged		750.00	
e.	Syncopated perf., #173		18.00	11.00
	Never hinged		55.00	
	On cover			40.00
f.	Syncopated perf., #173a		27.50	13.00
	Never hinged		100.00	
	On cover			40.00
g.	Syncopated perf., #173c		11.00	14.50
	Never hinged		37.50	
	On cover			—
175	A19	15pf gray	3.75	.65
	Never hinged		21.00	
	On cover			4.00
a.	15pf dark greenish gray		12.00	4.50
	Never hinged		52.50	
	On cover			8.00
176	A19	15pf red, *yelsh*	2.10	1.10
	Never hinged		9.50	
	On cover			4.00
a.	White paper		4.50	1.10
	Never hinged		25.00	
	On cover			4.00
177	A19	20pf carmine & red	13.50	.65
	Never hinged		34.50	
	On cover			4.00
a.	20pf dp lilac red & rose red		32.50	12.00
	Never hinged		130.00	
	On cover			27.50
178	A19	20pf gray	1.75	2.50
	Never hinged		5.50	
	On cover			9.50
179	A19	25pf slate & red	22.50	3.75
	Never hinged		100.00	
	On cover			12.00
180	A19	25pf carmine	17.00	1.60
	Never hinged		52.50	
	On cover			6.00
181	A19	30pf green & red	12.50	.85
	Never hinged		47.50	
	On cover			7.00
a.	30pf dk grn & dk rose red		32.50	12.50
	Never hinged		160.00	
	On cover			55.00
182	A19	30pf dk violet	1.60	4.25
	Never hinged		5.25	
	On cover			12.00

183	A19	35pf ultra	4.50	1.50
	Never hinged		11.00	
	On cover			10.00
a.	35pf greyish ultra		14.50	5.50
	Never hinged		40.00	
	On cover			12.00
184	A19	40pf dk blue & blue	12.00	1.00
	Never hinged		27.50	
	On cover			12.00
185	A19	40pf yel brn & red	6.50	12.50
	Never hinged		30.00	
	On cover			40.00
186	A19	40pf dk blue	1.60	3.75
	Never hinged		5.50	
	On cover			18.00
a.	Imperf.		60.00	
	Never hinged		170.00	
187	A19	50pf blue & red	16.00	8.50
	Never hinged		67.50	
	On cover			24.00
a.	Yellowish paper		25.00	11.50
	Never hinged		57.50	
	On cover			80.00
b.	50pf dk ultra & dk rose red		24.00	11.00
	Never hinged		110.00	
	On cover			40.00
188	A19	55pf plum & scar	5.00	14.50
	Never hinged		17.50	
	On cover			67.50
189	A19	60pf dk grn & red	6.25	19.00
	Never hinged		30.00	
	On cover			47.50
190	A19	70pf yel grn & red	2.10	7.50
	Never hinged		10.50	
	On cover			47.50
191	A19	75pf violet & red, *yellowish*	7.50	29.00
	Never hinged		17.50	
	On cover			120.00
a.	White paper		10.00	8.50
	Never hinged		32.50	
	On cover			40.00
b.	75pf dk pur & dk rose red		16.00	16.00
	Never hinged		55.00	
	On cover			40.00
192	A19	80pf dk org brn & red	2.10	7.50
	Never hinged		10.50	
	On cover			47.50
	Nos. 168-192 (23)		151.45	131.65
	Set, never hinged		625.00	

The 5pf and 10pf with syncopated perforations (Netherlands type C) are coils.

See Nos. 225-232. For overprints and surcharges see Nos. 200-209, 211-215, 241-252, B9-B11, O42-O52.

Issued: No. 168, 10/1935. No. 168a, 2/19/27. No. 170, 2/1935. Nos. 170a, 173a, 175a, 1/19/24. Nos. 170d, 173e, 173g, 1937. Nos. 170e, 173f, 1932. No. 171, 4/27/33. No. 172, 8/14/37. No. 173, 3/1935. No. 173c, 6/24/37. No. 175, 3/1924. No. 176, 1936. No. 176a, 8/20/25. No. 177, 1/26/24. No. 178, 186, 6/20/35. No. 179, 181, 187, 191a, 3/12/24. No. 180, 6/5/25. No. 181a, 9/1930. No. 182, 8/21/35. No. 183, 1925. No. 183a, 1930. No. 184, 2/14/24. Nos. 185, 189, 4/15/35. No. 187a, 3/1938. No. 187b, 2/1930. No. 188, 4/17/37. No. 190, 192, 9/5/35. No. 191, 2/1937. No. 191b, 4/1932.

Oliva Castle
and Cathedral
A20

St. Mary's
Church
A23

Council
Chamber on the
Langenmarkt
A24

2g, Mottlau River & Krantor. 3g, View of Zoppot.

1924-32   Engr.   Wmk. 125

193	A20	1g yel grn & blk	21.00	45.00
	Never hinged		105.00	
	On cover			120.00
	Parcel post cancel			20.00
194	A20	1g org & gray blk	17.00	3.75
	Never hinged		67.50	
	On cover			12.00
	Parcel post cancel			1.00
a.	1g red orange & blk		17.00	11.00
	Never hinged		67.50	
	On cover			60.00
	Parcel post cancel			40.00
195	A20	2g red vio & blk	45.00	110.00
	Never hinged		205.00	
	On cover			240.00
	Parcel post cancel			40.00
196	A20	2g rose & blk	3.75	8.00
	Never hinged		14.50	
	On cover			21.00
	Parcel post cancel			1.75

197	A20	3g dk blue & blk	4.25	5.00
	Never hinged		24.00	
	On cover			40.00
	Parcel post cancel			2.25
198	A23	5g brn red & blk	4.25	8.50
	Never hinged		24.00	
	On cover			72.50
	Parcel post cancel			1.90
199	A24	10g dk brn & blk	21.00	110.00
	Never hinged		110.00	
	On cover			600.00
	Parcel post cancel			18.00
	Nos. 193-199 (7)		116.25	290.25
	Set, never hinged		550.00	

See No. 233. For overprints and surcharges see Nos. 210, 253-254, C31-C35.

Issued: Nos. 193, 195, 9/22/24. Nos. 194, 196, 11/28/24. No. 194a, 5/1932.

Stamps of 1924-25
Overprinted in Black,
Violet or Red

1930, Nov. 15   Typo.   Wmk. 109

200	A19	5pf orange	2.50	3.75
	Never hinged		9.50	
	On cover			10.00
201	A19	10pf yellow grn (V)	3.50	4.50
	Never hinged		14.00	
	On cover			10.00
202	A19	15pf red	6.00	11.00
	Never hinged		19.00	
	On cover			24.00
203	A19	20pf carmine & red	3.00	6.00
	Never hinged		9.50	
	On cover			10.00
204	A19	25pf slate & red	4.25	11.00
	Never hinged		24.00	
	On cover			24.00
205	A19	30pf green & red	8.50	25.00
	Never hinged		34.00	
	On cover			47.50
206	A19	35pf ultra (R)	32.50	100.00
	Never hinged		145.00	
	On cover			225.00
207	A19	40pf dk bl & bl (R)	11.50	45.00
	Never hinged		42.50	
	On cover			60.00
208	A19	50pf dp blue & red	32.50	85.00
	Never hinged		125.00	
	On cover			160.00
209	A19	75pf violet & red	32.50	92.50
	Never hinged		130.00	
	On cover			160.00

Engr.   Wmk. (125)

210	A20	1g orange & blk (R)	32.50	85.00
	Never hinged		125.00	
	On cover			160.00
	Nos. 200-210 (11)		169.25	468.75
	Set, never hinged		675.00	

10th anniv. of the Free State. Counterfeits exist.

Nos. 171 and 183 Surcharged in Red, Blue or Green

Nos. 211-214   No. 215

1934-36

211	A19	6pf on 7pf (R)	.85	1.60
	Never hinged		3.75	
	On cover			6.00
212	A19	8pf on 7pf (Bl)	2.10	2.40
	Never hinged		7.75	
	On cover			9.50
213	A19	8pf on 7pf (R)	1.25	2.50
	Never hinged		5.75	
	On cover			9.50
214	A19	8pf on 7pf (G)	.85	2.50
	Never hinged		4.50	
	On cover			9.50
215	A19	30pf on 35pf (Bl)	12.00	25.00
	Never hinged		40.00	
	On cover			40.00
a.	on #183a		24.00	72.50
	Never hinged		90.00	
	On cover			100.00
	Nos. 211-215 (5)		17.05	34.00
	Set, never hinged		60.00	

Issued: Nos. 211, 215-216, 215a, 12/28/34. No. 212, 6/5/35. No. 213, 7/13/36. No. 214, 12/23/36.

Bathing
Beach,
Brösen
A25

View of
Brösen
Beach
A26

War Memorial at
Brösen — A27

1936, June 23   Typo.   Wmk. 109

216	A25 10pf deep green		.70	.70
	Never hinged		3.00	
	On commercial cover			12.00
a.	10pf dark opal green		12.00	32.50
	Never hinged		60.00	
	On commercial cover			65.00
	On first day cover			80.00
217	A26 25pf rose red		1.25	2.40
	Never hinged		3.00	
	On commercial cover			12.00
	On first day cover			40.00
218	A27 40pf bright blue		2.25	4.50
	Never hinged		7.50	
	On commercial cover			20.00
	On first day cover			40.00
	Nos. 216-218 (3)		4.20	7.60
	Set, never hinged		15.00	

Village of Brösen, 125th anniversary.
Exist imperf. Value each, $40 unused, $110
never hinged.

Skyline of
Danzig — A28

1937, Mar. 27

219	A28 10pf dark blue		.50	1.40
	Never hinged		2.25	
	On cover			4.75
220	A28 15pf violet brown		1.60	2.00
	Never hinged		6.00	
	On cover			8.00
	Set, never hinged		11.25	
	Set of 2, #219-220 on one			
	1st day cover			20.00

Air Defense League.

Danzig Philatelic Exhibition Issue
Souvenir Sheet

St. Mary's Church — A29

1937, June 6   Wmk. 109   Perf. 14

221	A29 50pf dark opal green		3.25	21.00
	Never hinged		11.00	
	On commercial cover			80.00
	With Exhibition cancel			20.00
a.	10pf blackish green		16.00	42.50
	Never hinged		40.00	
	On commercial cover			160.00
	With Exhibition cancel			47.50
	On first day cover			120.00

Danzig Philatelic Exhib., June 6-8, 1937.
No. 221a is the first printing (June 6); No.
221 is the second printing (October).

Arthur Schopenhauer
A30   A31

Design: 40pf, Full-face portrait, white hair.

Unwmk.

1938, Feb. 22   Photo.   Perf. 14

222	A30 15pf dull blue		1.45	2.40
	Never hinged		4.00	
	On cover			8.00
223	A31 25pf sepia		3.50	8.00
	Never hinged		12.00	
	On cover			16.00
224	A31 40pf orange ver		1.50	3.25
	Never hinged		4.00	
	On commercial cover			12.00
	Nos. 222-224 (3)		6.45	13.65
	Set, never hinged		20.00	
	Set of 3, #222-224 on one			
	1st day cover			37.50

150th anniv. of the birth of Schopenhauer.

Type of 1924-35

1938-39   Typo.   Wmk. 237   Perf. 14

225	A19 3pf brown		.90	7.50
	Never hinged		2.75	
	On cover			16.00
226	A19 5pf orange		.90	2.10
	Never hinged		2.75	
	On cover			16.00
b.	Syncopated perf.		1.40	7.50
	Never hinged		5.50	
	On cover			13.00
227	A19 8pf yellow grn		4.00	35.00
	Never hinged		16.50	
	On cover			47.50
228	A19 10pf blue green		.90	2.10
	Never hinged		2.75	
	On cover			4.00
b.	Syncopated perf.		3.00	10.00
	Never hinged		14.00	
	On cover			20.00
229	A19 15pf scarlet		1.60	8.50
	Never hinged		5.50	
	On cover			20.00
230	A19 25pf carmine		2.10	12.50
	Never hinged		10.00	
	On cover			24.00
231	A19 40pf dark blue		2.10	29.00
	Never hinged		10.00	
	On cover			55.00
232	A19 50pf brt bl & red		2.10	135.00
	Never hinged		10.00	
	On cover			200.00

Engr.

233	A20 1g red org & blk		6.75	120.00
	Never hinged		25.00	
	On cover			200.00
	Nos. 225-233 (9)		21.35	351.70
	Set, never hinged		90.00	

Sizes: No. 233, 32½x21¼mm; No. 194,
31x21mm.

Nos. 226b and 228b are coils with Netherlands type C perforation.

Issued: 3pf, 7/1938. 5pf, 25pf, 7/23/38. 8pf,
9/1938. 10pf, 15pf, 1g, 10/1938. 40pf, 7/19/38.
50pf, 6/1939. No. 226b, 8/24/38. No. 228b,
7/18/38.

Knights in
Tournament,
1500 — A33

French Leaving
Danzig,
1814 — A35

Stamp Day: 10pf, Signing of Danzig-Swe-
den neutrality treaty, 1630. 25pf, Battle of
Weichselmünde, 1577.

Unwmk.

1939, Jan. 7   Photo.   Perf. 14

234	A33 5pf dark green		.40	2.10
	Never hinged		2.00	
	On commercial cover			8.00
235	A33 10pf copper brown		.85	2.50
	Never hinged		2.90	
	On commercial cover			8.00
236	A35 15pf slate black		1.25	3.00
	Never hinged		3.75	
	On commercial cover			9.50
237	A35 25pf brown violet		1.60	4.25
	Never hinged		4.50	
	On commercial cover			17.50
	Nos. 234-237 (4)		4.10	11.85

Set, never hinged		13.00
Set of 4, #234-237 on one		
1st day cover		30.00

Gregor
Mendel — A37

15pf, Dr. Robert Koch. 25pf, Wilhelm
Roentgen.

1939, Apr. 29   Photo.   Perf. 13x14

238	A37 10pf copper brown		.65	.85
	Never hinged		1.60	
	On commercial cover			6.00
239	A37 15pf indigo		.65	2.75
	Never hinged		2.75	
	On commercial cover			6.00
240	A37 25pf dark olive green		1.25	2.75
	Never hinged		2.75	
	On cover			9.50
	Nos. 238-240 (3)		2.55	6.35
	Set, never hinged		7.25	
	Set of 3, #238-240 on one 1st day			
	cover			20.00

Issued in honor of the achievements of Mendel, Koch and Roentgen.

**Issued under German
Administration**
Stamps of Danzig, 1925-39,
Surcharged in Black

a   b

c

1939   Wmk. 109   Perf. 14

241	A19(b) 4rpf on 35pf ultra		.75	2.50
	Never hinged		2.00	
	On cover			4.75
242	A19(b) 12rpf on 7pf yel grn		1.50	2.25
	Never hinged		4.50	
	On cover			4.75
243	A19(a) 20rpf gray		3.00	8.50
	Never hinged		9.00	
	On cover			12.00

Wmk. 237

244	A19(a) 3rpf brown		.75	2.40
	Never hinged		2.25	
	On cover			4.75
245	A19(a) 5rpf orange		.65	3.00
	Never hinged		2.00	
	On cover			4.75
246	A19(a) 8rpf yellow grn		1.10	4.25
	Never hinged		3.50	
	On cover			8.00
247	A19(a) 10rpf blue grn		2.25	4.25
	Never hinged		7.00	
	On cover			8.00
248	A19(a) 15rpf scarlet		6.00	12.00
	Never hinged		19.00	
	On cover			17.50
249	A19(a) 25rpf carmine		4.50	11.00
	Never hinged		14.50	
	On cover			16.00
250	A19(a) 30rpf dk violet		2.00	4.50
	Never hinged		6.00	
	On cover			8.75
251	A19(a) 40rpf dk blue		2.75	6.00
	Never hinged		7.50	
	On cover			12.00
252	A19(a) 50rpf brt bl & red		4.00	7.00
	Never hinged		12.00	
	On cover			13.50

Thick Paper

253	A20(c) 1rm on 1g red org & blk		14.00	60.00
	Never hinged		45.00	
	On cover			80.00
a.	Thin white paper		42.50	160.00
	Never hinged		160.00	
	On cover			225.00

Wmk. 125
Thin White Paper

254	A20(c) 2rm on 2g rose & blk		20.00	65.00
	Never hinged		55.00	
	On cover			95.00
a.	Thick paper		18.00	67.50
	Never hinged		60.00	
	On cover			95.00
b.	As "a," "Deutsches Reich" omitted from			
	surcharge		1,000.	—
	Never hinged		1,750.	
c.	As "a," "2 Reichmark" omitted from			
	surcharge		1,000.	1,750.
	Never hinged		1,750.	
	Nos. 241-254 (14)		63.25	192.65
	Set, never hinged		190.00	

Nos. 241-254 were valid throughout
Germany.

SEMI-POSTAL STAMPS

St. George and
Dragon — SP1

Wmk. 108

1921, Oct. 16   Typo.   Perf. 14
Size: 19x22mm

B1	SP1 30pf + 30pf grn & org		.45	.85
	Never hinged		1.50	
	Postally used			110.00
	On cover			160.00
B2	SP1 60pf + 60pf rose & org		1.25	1.60
	Never hinged		5.25	
	Postally used			110.00
	On cover			160.00

Size: 25x30mm
Serrate Roulette 13½

B3	SP1 1.20m + 1.20m dk bl & org		2.00	2.25
	Never hinged		8.25	
	Postally used			110.00
	On cover			160.00
	Nos. B1-B3 (3)		3.70	4.70
	Set, never hinged		15.00	

Nos. B1-B3 exist imperf. Value each, $45
unused, $125 never hinged.

Aged
Pensioner
SP2

1923, Mar.   Wmk. 109   Perf. 14
Paper With Gray Network

B4	SP2 50m + 20m lake		.25	.60
	Never hinged		1.10	
	Postally used			42.50
	On cover			100.00
B5	SP2 100m + 30m red vio		.25	.60
	Never hinged		1.10	
	Postally used			42.50
	On cover			100.00
	Set, never hinged		2.20	

Nos. B4-B5 exist imperf. Value each, $50
unused, $210 never hinged.

Philatelic Exhibition Issue

Neptune
Fountain — SP3

Various Frames.

1929, July 7   Engr.   Unwmk.

B6	SP3 10pf yel grn & gray		2.40	1.60
	Never hinged		8.25	
	Exhibition cancellation			6.00
	On cover			24.00

B7	SP3 15pf car & gray	2.40	1.60
	Never hinged	8.25	
	Exhibition cancellation		6.00
	On cover		35.00
B8	SP3 25pf ultra & gray	8.50	13.00
	Never hinged	27.50	
	Exhibition cancellation		47.50
	On cover		65.00
a.	25pf violet blue & black	25.00	62.50
	Never hinged	92.50	
	On cover		110.00
b.	25pf deep gray bl & blk	47.50	225.00
	Never hinged	175.00	
	On cover		275.00
	Nos. B6-B8 (3)	13.30	16.20
	Set, never hinged	45.00	
	Set of 3, #B6-B8 on one 1st day cover		200.00

These stamps were sold exclusively at the Danzig Philatelic Exhibition, June 7-14, 1929, at double their face values, the excess being for the aid of the exhibition.

Regular Issue of 1924-25 Surcharged in Black

1934, Jan. 15 — Wmk. 109

B9	A19 5pf + 5pf orange	8.50	21.00
	Never hinged	42.50	
	On cover		60.00
B10	A19 10pf + 5pf yel grn	21.00	50.00
	Never hinged	100.00	
	On cover		110.00
B11	A19 15pf + 5pf carmine	12.50	37.50
	Never hinged	77.50	
	On cover		80.00
	Nos. B9-B11 (3)	42.00	108.50
	Set, never hinged	220.00	

Surtax for winter welfare. Counterfeits exist.

Stock Tower — SP4   George Hall — SP6

City Gate, 16th Century SP5

1935, Dec. 16   Typo.   Perf. 14

B12	SP4 5pf + 5pf orange	.60	1.60
	Never hinged	2.10	
	On cover		5.50
B13	SP5 10pf + 5pf green	1.10	2.50
	Never hinged	3.25	
	On cover		9.50
B14	SP6 15pf + 10pf scarlet	2.50	3.75
	Never hinged	9.00	
	On cover		16.00
	Nos. B12-B14 (3)	4.20	7.85
	Set, never hinged	14.00	
	Set of 3, #B12-B14 on one 1st day cover		40.00

Surtax for winter welfare.

Milk Can Tower SP7   Frauentor SP8

Krantor — SP9

Langgarter Gate — SP10

High Gate SP11

1936, Nov. 25

B15	SP7 10pf + 5pf dk bl	1.50	4.50
	Never hinged	11.00	
	On cover		16.00
a.	Imperf.	75.00	
	Never hinged	180.00	
B16	SP8 15pf + 5pf dull grn	1.50	6.00
	Never hinged	11.00	
	On cover		16.00
B17	SP9 25pf + 10pf red brn	2.25	9.00
	Never hinged	14.50	
	On cover		24.00
B18	SP10 40pf + 20pf brn & red brn	3.00	11.00
	Never hinged	17.50	
	On cover		27.50
B19	SP11 50pf + 20pf bl & dk bl	5.00	17.00
	Never hinged	21.00	
	On cover		40.00
	Nos. B15-B19 (5)	13.25	47.50
	Set, never hinged	75.00	

Surtax for winter welfare.

SP12   SP13

1937, Oct. 30   Wmk. 109 Sideways

B20	SP12 25pf + 25pf dk car	2.50	5.25
	Never hinged	14.00	
	On cover		47.50
a.	Wmk. upright	10.50	40.00
	Never hinged	35.00	
	On cover		95.00

Wmk. 109 Upright

B21	SP13 40pf + 40pf blue & red	2.50	5.25
	Never hinged	13.00	
	On cover		45.00
a.	Souvenir sheet of 2, #B20a-B21	60.00	100.00
	Never hinged	110.00	
	Exposition cancellation		90.00
	On cover		275.00
	Set, never hinged	27.50	

Founding of Danzig community at Magdeburg.

Madonna SP14   Mercury SP15

Weather Vane, Town Hall SP16   Neptune Fountain SP17

St. George and Dragon — SP18

1937, Dec. 13

B23	SP14 5pf + 5pf brt violet	2.50	7.50
	Never hinged	7.50	
	On cover		15.00
B24	SP15 10pf + 10pf dk brn	2.50	6.25
	Never hinged	7.50	
	On cover		12.00
B25	SP16 15pf + 5pf bl & yel brn	2.50	8.25
	Never hinged	7.50	
	On cover		15.00
B26	SP17 25pf + 10pf bl grn & grn	3.25	11.00
	Never hinged	11.00	
	On cover		20.00
B27	SP18 40pf + 25pf brt car & bl	5.75	17.50
	Never hinged	21.00	
	On cover		40.00
	Nos. B23-B27 (5)	16.50	50.50
	Set, never hinged	55.00	
	Set of 5, #B23-B27 on one 1st day cover		100.00

Surtax for winter welfare. Designs are from frieze of the Artushof.

"Peter von Danzig" Yacht Race — SP19

Ships: 10pf+5pf, Dredger Fu Shing. 15pf+10pf, S. S. Columbus. 25pf+10pf, S. S. City of Danzig. 40pf+15pf, Peter von Danzig, 1472.

1938, Nov. 28   Photo.   Unwmk.

B28	SP19 5pf + 5pf dk bl grn	1.10	1.60
	Never hinged	6.00	
	On cover		16.00
B29	SP19 10pf + 5pf gldn brn	1.40	3.00
	Never hinged	6.00	
	On cover		16.00
B30	SP19 15pf + 10pf ol grn	1.60	3.00
	Never hinged	7.50	
	On cover		12.00
B31	SP19 25pf + 10pf indigo	2.50	4.25
	Never hinged	9.00	
	On cover		13.50
B32	SP19 40pf + 15pf vio brn	3.00	7.25
	Never hinged	12.50	
	On cover		20.00
	Nos. B28-B32 (5)	9.60	19.10
	Set, never hinged	40.00	
	Set of 5, #B28-B32 on one 1st day cover		60.00

Surtax for winter welfare.

AIR POST STAMPS

No. 6 Surcharged in Blue or Carmine

1920, Sept. 29   Wmk. 125   Perf. 14

C1	A16 40pf on 40pf	1.10	2.90
	Never hinged	4.50	
	Postally used		10.50
	On flight cover		24.00
	On commercial flown cover		45.00
a.	Double surcharge	125.00	250.00
	Never hinged	340.00	
C2	A16 60pf on 40pf (C)	1.10	2.90
	Never hinged	4.50	
	Postally used		11.00
	On flight cover		120.00
	On commercial flown cover		225.00
a.	Double surcharge	125.00	250.00
	Never hinged	340.00	
C3	A16 1m on 40pf	1.10	2.90
	Never hinged	4.50	
	Postally used		14.50
	On flight cover		27.50
	On commercial flown cover		55.00
	Nos. C1-C3 (3)	3.30	8.70
	Set, never hinged	13.50	

Plane faces left on No. C2.

AP3

Plane over Danzig AP4

Wmk. (108) Upright

1921-22   Typo.   Perf. 14

C4	AP3 40(pf) blue green	.25	.45
	Never hinged	1.20	
	Postally used		5.50
	On commercial flown cover		27.50
C5	AP3 60(pf) dk violet	.25	.45
	Never hinged	1.20	
	Postally used		4.75
	On commercial flown cover		9.50
C6	AP3 1m carmine	.25	.45
	Never hinged	1.20	
	Postally used		4.75
	On commercial flown cover		12.00
C7	AP3 2m org brn	.25	.45
	Never hinged	1.20	
	Postally used		4.75
	On commercial flown cover		12.00

Serrate Roulette 13½

Size: 34½x23mm

C8	AP4 5m violet blue	1.25	2.25
	Never hinged	4.75	
	Postally used		9.50
	On commercial flown cover		20.00
C9	AP4 10m dp grn	2.00	4.50
	Never hinged	8.00	
	Postally used		40.00
	On commercial flown cover		65.00
	Nos. C4-C9 (6)	4.25	8.55
	Set, never hinged	18.00	

Nos. C4-C9 exist imperf. Value, each $32.50 unused, $125 never hinged.
Issued: Nos. C4-C5, C7-C8, 5/3/21. No. C6, 4/3/21. No. C9, 5/15/22.

Wmk. 108 Sideways

C4a	AP3 40(pf)	25.00	8.00
	Never hinged	55.00	
C5a	AP3 60(pf)	65.00	80.00
	Never hinged	190.00	
C6a	AP3 1m		—
C7a	AP3 2m	80.00	175.00
	Never hinged	200.00	
C8a	AP4 5m	1,400.	2,400.
	Never hinged	2,800.	
b.	imperf	2,000.	3,250.
	Never hinged	4,000.	
	Postally used		
C9a	AP4 10m	24.00	80.00
	Never hinged	60.00	

Issued: Nos. C4a-C5a, C7a-C8a, 5/3/21. No. C6a, 4/3/21. No. C9a, 5/15/22.

1923 Wmk. (109) Upright — Perf. 14

C10 AP3 40(pf) blue green .40 2.10
Never hinged 2.60
Postally used 240.00
On commercial flown cover 350.00
C11 AP3 60(pf) dk violet .40 2.10
Never hinged 2.60
Postally used 250.00
On commercial flown cover 350.00
a. Double impression —
C12 AP3 1m carmine .40 2.10
Never hinged 2.60
Postally used 140.00
On commercial flown cover 240.00
C13 AP3 2m org brown .40 2.10
Never hinged 2.60
Postally used 120.00
On commercial flown cover 160.00
C14 AP3 25m pale blue .30 .60
Never hinged 2.25
Postally used 4.25
On commercial flown cover 10.00

Serrate Roulette 13½
Size: 34½x23mm

C15 AP4 5m violet blue .40 1.00
Never hinged 2.75
Postally used 120.00
On commercial flown cover 200.00
C16 AP4 10m deep green .40 1.00
Never hinged 2.75
Postally used 120.00
On commercial flown cover 120.00

Paper With Gray Network

C17 AP4 20m org brn .40 1.00
Never hinged 2.75
Postally used 27.50
On commercial flown cover 60.00

Size: 40x23mm

C18 AP4 50m orange .30 .60
Never hinged 2.25
Postally used 24.00
On commercial flown cover 40.00
C19 AP4 100m red .30 .60
Never hinged 2.25
Postally used 3.25
On commercial flown cover 8.00
C20 AP4 250m dark brown .30 .60
Never hinged 2.25
Postally used 32.50
On commercial flown cover 60.00
C21 AP4 500m car rose .30 .60
Never hinged 2.25
Postally used 24.00
On commercial flown cover 40.00
Nos. C10-C21 (12) 4.30 14.40
Set, never hinged 30.00

Nos. C11, C12, C14-C21 exist imperf. Value, Nos. C11, C12, C15-C17, each $8.50 unused; $32.50 never hinged. Value, Nos. C14, C18-C21, each $40 unused, $125 never hinged.
Issued: Nos. C10, C13, C15-C16, 1/3/23. Nos. C14, C18, C20-C21, 4/27/23. Nos. C17, 1/10/23. No. C19, 2/5/23.
Nos. C18, C19 and C21 exist with wmk. sideways, both perf. and imperf. Value each, $60 unused and $160 never hinged.

Network Omitted

C18a AP4 50m 20.00 16.00
Never hinged 55.00
Postally used 120.00
C19a AP4 100m 8.75 24.00
Never hinged 24.00
Postally used 120.00
C20a AP4 250m 8.75 24.00
Never hinged 24.00
Postally used 200.00
C21a AP4 500m 14.00 16.00
Never hinged 40.00
Postally used 160.00

Issued: Nos. C18a, C20a-C21a, 4/27/23. No. C19a, 2/5/23.

Post Horn and Airplanes — AP5

1923, Oct. 18 — Perf. 14
Paper Without Network

C22 AP5 250,000m scarlet .25 1.25
Never hinged 1.10
Postally used 350.00
On commercial flown cover 400.00
C23 AP5 500,000m scarlet .25 1.25
Never hinged 1.10
Postally used 350.00
On commercial flown cover 400.00

Exist imperf. Value, each: $50 unused; $125 never hinged.

Surcharged

On 100,000m

C24 AP5 2mil m scarlet .25 1.25
Never hinged 1.10
Postally used 350.00
On commercial flown cover 400.00

On 50,000m

C25 AP5 5mil m scarlet .25 1.25
Never hinged 1.10
Postally used 350.00
On commercial flown cover 400.00
b. Cliché of 10,000m in sheet of 50,000m 32.50 160.00
Never hinged 110.00
Postally used 4,000.
c. As "b," surcharge omitted 6,250.
Never hinged 10,500.

Exist imperf. Value, each $125 unused, $290 never hinged.
Nos. C24 and C25 were not regularly issued without surcharge, although examples have been passed through the post. Values: C24 unused $8.50, never hinged $32.50; C25 unused $12, never hinged $21.

Plane over Danzig
AP6 AP7

1924

C26 AP6 10(pf) vermilion 22.50 3.75
Never hinged 85.00
On commercial flown cover 13.50
C27 AP6 20(pf) carmine rose 2.10 1.50
Never hinged 6.50
On commercial flown cover 9.50
C28 AP6 40(pf) olive brown 3.00 1.75
Never hinged 9.25
On commercial flown cover 11.50
C29 AP6 1g deep green 3.00 3.00
Never hinged 9.25
On commercial flown cover 16.00
C30 AP7 2½g violet brown 17.50 35.00
Never hinged 65.00
On commercial flown cover 95.00
Nos. C26-C30 (5) 48.10 45.00
Set, never hinged 175.00

Exist imperf. Value Nos. C26, C30, $85 unused, $200 never hinged; others, each $40 unused, $110 never hinged.
Issued: Nos. C26-C27, C29, 6/6. No. C28, 6/4. No. C30, 6/7.

Nos. 193, 195, 197-199 Srchd. in Various Colors

1932 — Wmk. 125

C31 A20 10pf on 1g (G) 8.50 23.00
Never hinged 40.00
On commercial flown cover 60.00
C32 A20 15pf on 2g (V) 8.50 23.00
Never hinged 40.00
On commercial flown cover 60.00
C33 A20 20pf on 3g (Bl) 8.50 23.00
Never hinged 40.00
On commercial flown cover 60.00
C34 A23 25pf on 5g (R) 8.50 23.00
Never hinged 40.00
On commercial flown cover 60.00
C35 A24 30pf on 10g (Br) 8.50 23.00
Never hinged 40.00
On commercial flown cover 60.00
Nos. C31-C35 (5) 42.50 115.00
Set, never hinged 200.00

Intl. Air Post Exhib. of 1932. The surcharges were variously arranged to suit the shapes and designs of the stamps. The stamps were sold at double their surcharged values, the excess being donated to the exhibition funds.
No. C31 exists with inverted surcharge and with double surcharge. Value each, $85 unused, $210 never hinged.

Airplane
AP8 AP9

1935, Oct. 24 — Wmk. 109

C36 AP8 10pf scarlet 1.60 .85
Never hinged 7.50
On commercial flown cover 2.90
C37 AP8 15pf yellow 1.60 1.25
Never hinged 7.50
On commercial flown cover 6.00
C38 AP8 25pf dark green 1.60 1.60
Never hinged 7.50
On commercial flown cover 9.50
C39 AP8 50pf gray blue 0.00 10.00
Never hinged 22.50
On commercial flown cover 32.50
C40 AP9 1g magenta 3.25 13.50
Never hinged 16.00
On commercial flown cover 32.50
Nos. C36-C40 (5) 16.05 27.20
Set, never hinged 59.50
Set of 5, #C36-C40 on one 1st day cover 60.00

Nos. C36 and C40 exist imperf. Values: C36 unused $20, never hinged $62.50; C40 unused $29, never hinged $85.
See Nos. C42-C45.

Souvenir Sheet

DAPOSTA 1937

St. Mary's Church — AP10

1937, June 6 — Perf. 14

C41 AP10 50pf dark grayish blue 3.50 21.00
Never hinged 10.50
On commerical cover 80.00
Exhibition cancellation 26.00
a. 50pf dark ultramarine 16.00 140.00
Never hinged 40.00
On commercial cover 150.00
Exhibition cancellation 57.50
On first day cover 115.00

C41a is the first printing (June 6); C41 is the second printing (October).

Danzig Phil. Exhib., June 6-8, 1937.

Type of 1935
1938-39 — Wmk. 237

C42 AP8 10pf scarlet 1.25 4.25
Never hinged 5.25
On commercial flown cover 12.00
C43 AP8 15pf yellow ('39) 2.25 13.00
Never hinged 13.00
On commercial flown cover 40.00
C44 AP8 25pf dark green 1.60 7.25
Never hinged 7.75
On commercial flown cover 32.50
C45 AP8 50pf gray blue ('39) 4.25 62.50
Never hinged 19.00
On commercial flown cover 95.00
Nos. C42-C45 (4) 9.35 87.00
Set, never hinged 45.00

Issued: Nos. C42, C44, 7/1938. No. C43, 7/8/38. No. C44, 2/13/39.

POSTAGE DUE STAMPS

Danzig Coat of Arms — D1

1921-22 Typo. Wmk. (108) — Perf. 14
Paper Without Network

J1 D1 10(pf) deep violet .25 .50
Never hinged .90
Postally used 9.50
On cover 47.50
J2 D1 20(pf) deep violet .25 .50
Never hinged .90
Postally used 9.50
On cover 47.50
J3 D1 40(pf) deep violet .25 .50
Never hinged .90
Postally used 12.50
On cover 47.50
J4 D1 60(pf) deep violet .25 .50
Never hinged .90
Postally used 12.50
On cover 47.50
J5 D1 75(pf) dp violet ('22) .25 .50
Never hinged .90
Postally used 24.00
On cover 95.00
J6 D1 80(pf) deep violet .25 .50
Never hinged .90
Postally used 12.00
On cover 47.50
J7 D1 120(pf) deep violet .25 .50
Never hinged .90
Postally used 16.00
On cover 47.50
J8 D1 200(pf) dp violet ('22) .85 1.10
Never hinged 3.25
Postally used 32.50
On cover 80.00
J9 D1 240(pf) deep violet .25 1.10
Never hinged 1.00
Postally used 24.00
On cover 60.00
J10 D1 300(pf) dp violet ('22) .85 1.10
Never hinged 3.25
Postally used 21.00
On cover 80.00
J11 D1 400(pf) deep violet .85 1.10
Never hinged 3.25
Postally used 21.00
On cover 95.00
J12 D1 500(pf) deep violet .85 1.10
Never hinged 3.25
Postally used 21.00
On cover 40.00
J13 D1 800(pf) deep violet ('22) .85 1.10
Never hinged 3.25
Postally used 55.00
On cover 105.00
J14 D1 20m dp violet ('22) .85 1.10
Never hinged 3.25
Postally used 45.00
On cover 95.00
Nos. J1-J14 (14) 7.10 11.20
Set, never hinged 27.50

Nos. J1-J14 exist imperf. Value, each $30 unused, $75 never hinged.

1923 — Wmk. 109 Sideways

J15 D1 100(pf) deep violet .65 .85
Never hinged 2.25
Postally used 725.00
On cover 800.00
J16 D1 200(pf) deep violet 2.50 4.25
Never hinged 7.50
Postally used 1,050.
On cover 1,200.
J17 D1 300(pf) deep violet .65 .85
Never hinged 2.25
Postally used 1,050.
On cover 1,200.
J18 D1 400(pf) deep violet .65 .85
Never hinged 2.25
Postally used 1,050.
On cover 1,200.
J19 D1 500(pf) deep violet .65 .85
Never hinged 2.00
Postally used 240.00
On cover 350.00
a. Wmk. Upright .65 1.10
Never hinged 2.25
Postally used 175.00
On cover 250.00
J20 D1 800(pf) deep violet 1.40 4.25
Never hinged 7.50
Postally used 1,750.
On cover 2,000.
J21 D1 10m deep violet .65 1.10
Never hinged 2.25
Postally used 24.00
On cover 60.00
a. Wmk. Upright .65 1.10
Never hinged 2.25
Postally used 160.00
On cover 200.00
J22 D1 20m deep violet .65 .85
Never hinged 2.25
Postally used 65.00
On cover 110.00
J23 D1 50m deep violet .65 .85
Never hinged 2.25
Postally used 16.00
On cover 80.00

Paper With Gray Network

J24 D1 100m deep violet .65 1.10
Never hinged 2.25
Postally used 24.00
On cover 80.00
J25 D1 500m deep violet .65 1.10
Never hinged 2.25
Postally used 16.00
On cover 80.00
Nos. J15-J25 (11) 9.75 16.90
Set, never hinged 35.00

Nos. J15, J17, J22-J25 exist imperf. Value each, $12.50 unused, $40 never hinged.
Issued: Nos. J15, J21, J23, 1/10. Nos. J16-J20, J22, 1/1923. Nos. J19a, J21a, J24-J25, 4/3.

Nos. J22-J23 and Type of 1923 Surcharged

1923, Oct. 1
Paper without Network

J26 D1 5000m on 50m .40 .85
Never hinged 2.00
Postally used 1,250.
On cover —
J27 D1 10,000m on 20m .40 .85
Never hinged 2.00
Postally used 1,250.
On cover —
J28 D1 50,000m on 500m .40 .85
Never hinged 2.00
Postally used 1,250.
On cover —

J29	D1 100,000m on 20m		.85	1.25
	Never hinged	2.00		
	Postally used			1,300.
	On cover			—
	Nos. J26-J29 (4)		2.05	3.80
	Set, never hinged	8.00		

On No. J26 the numerals of the surcharge are all of the larger size.

A 1000(m) on 100m deep violet was prepared but not issued. Value, $145, never hinged $350.

Nos. J26-J28 exist imperf. Value each, $18 unused, $45 never hinged.

Danzig Coat of Arms — D2

1923-28   Wmk. 110

J30	D2 5(pf) blue & blk		.85	.85
	Never hinged	2.50		
	On cover			35.00
J31	D2 10(pf) blue & blk		.40	.85
	Never hinged	2.50		
	On cover			24.00
J32	D2 15(pf) blue & blk		1.25	1.25
	Never hinged	5.25		
	On cover			60.00
J33	D2 20(pf) blue & blk		1.25	2.10
	Never hinged	4.00		
	On cover			72.50
J34	D2 30(pf) blue & blk		8.50	2.10
	Never hinged	21.00		
	On cover			72.50
J35	D2 40(pf) blue & blk		2.10	3.25
	Never hinged	6.00		
	On cover			120.00
J36	D2 50(pf) blue & blk		2.10	2.50
	Never hinged	6.00		
	On cover			65.00
J37	D2 60(pf) blue & blk		13.00	20.00
	Never hinged	37.50		
	On cover			240.00
J38	D2 100(pf) blue & blk		16.50	11.00
	Never hinged	55.00		
	On cover			140.00
J39	D2 3g blue & car		7.50	45.00
	Never hinged	40.00		
	On cover			350.00
a.	"Guldeu" instead of "Gulden"		325.00	1,050.
	Never hinged	1,050.		
	Nos. J30-J39 (10)		53.45	88.90
	Set, never hinged	180.00		

Used values of Nos. J30-J39 are for postally used stamps.

See Nos. J43-J47.

Postage Due Stamps of 1923 Issue Surcharged in Red

1932, Dec. 20

J40	D2 5pf on 40(pf)		2.50	7.50
	Never hinged	11.00		
	On cover			175.00
J41	D2 10pf on 60(pf)		30.00	10.00
	Never hinged	110.00		
	On cover			160.00
J42	D2 20pf on 100(pf)		2.50	7.50
	Never hinged	11.00		
	On cover			175.00
	Nos. J40-J42 (3)		35.00	25.00
	Set, never hinged	133.00		

Type of 1923

1938-39   Wmk. 237   *Perf. 14*

J43	D2 10(pf) bl & blk ('39)		1.25	62.50
	Never hinged	5.50		
	On cover			325.00
J44	D2 30(pf) bl & blk		2.10	50.00
	Never hinged	8.00		
	On cover			325.00
J45	D2 40(pf) bl & blk ('39)		6.25	100.00
	Never hinged	27.50		
	On cover			600.00
J46	D2 60(pf) bl & blk ('39)		6.25	100.00
	Never hinged	40.00		
	On cover			600.00
J47	D2 100(pf) bl & blk		10.00	72.50
	Never hinged	40.00		
	On cover			725.00
	Nos. J43-J47 (5)		25.85	385.00
	Set, never hinged	120.00		

OFFICIAL STAMPS

Regular Issues of 1921-22 Overprinted — a

1921-22   Wmk. 108   *Perf. 14x14½*

O1	A11 5(pf) orange		.25	.25
	Never hinged	.60		
	Postally used			27.50
	On cover			110.00
O2	A11 10(pf) dark brown		.25	.25
	Never hinged	.60		
	Postally used			6.50
	On cover			72.50
a.	Inverted overprint	60.00		
	Never hinged	170.00		
O3	A11 15(pf) green		.25	.25
	Never hinged	.60		
	Postally used			6.50
	On cover			72.50
O4	A11 20(pf) slate		.25	.25
	Never hinged	.60		
	Postally used			6.00
	On cover			80.00
O5	A11 25(pf) dark green		.25	.25
	Never hinged	.60		
	Postally used			6.00
	On cover			72.50
O6	A11 30(pf) blue & car		.60	.60
	Never hinged	1.35		
	Postally used			6.00
	On cover			72.50
O7	A11 40(pf) grn & car		.25	.25
	Never hinged	.60		
	Postally used			12.00
	On cover			72.50
O8	A11 50(pf) dk grn & car		.25	.25
	Never hinged	.60		
	Postally used			5.25
	On cover			55.00
O9	A11 60(pf) carmine		.25	.25
	Never hinged	.60		
	Postally used			4.75
	On cover			52.50
O10	A11 75(pf) dp vio		.25	.40
	Never hinged	.75		
	Postally used			2.75
	On cover			40.00
O11	A11 80(pf) black & car		.85	.85
	Never hinged	2.90		
	Postally used			16.00
	On cover			72.50
O12	A11 80(pf) green		.25	2.50
	Never hinged	.75		
	Postally used			210.00
	On cover			325.00

Paper With Faint Gray Network

O14	A11 1m org & car		.25	.25
	Never hinged	.75		
	Postally used			3.25
	On cover			40.00
O15	A11 1.20m blue violet		1.25	1.25
	Never hinged	4.00		
	Postally used			24.00
	On cover			95.00
O16	A11 1.25m vio & car		.25	.40
	Never hinged	.75		
	Postally used			80.00
	On cover			—
O17	A11 1.50m slate gray		.25	.40
	Never hinged	.90		
	Postally used			7.25
	On cover			40.00
O18	A11 2m gray & car		14.00	12.00
	Never hinged	62.50		
	Postally used			60.00
	On cover			120.00
a.	Inverted overprint	110.00		
	Never hinged	250.00		
O19	A11 2m car rose		.25	.40
	Never hinged	.75		
	Postally used			3.25
	On cover			47.50
O20	A11 2.40m dk brn & car		1.25	2.50
	Never hinged	9.00		
	Postally used			65.00
	On cover			120.00
O21	A11 3m violet & car		8.50	12.00
	Never hinged	37.50		
	Postally used			55.00
	On cover			110.00
O22	A11 3m car lake		.25	.40
	Never hinged	.90		
	Postally used			12.00
	On cover			47.50
O23	A11 4m dk blue		1.25	.85
	Never hinged	9.00		
	Postally used			75.00
	On cover			120.00
O24	A11 5m dp grn		.25	.40
	Never hinged	.90		
	Postally used			32.50
	On cover			80.00
O25	A11 6m car lake		.25	.40
	Never hinged	.90		
	Postally used			14.50
	On cover			72.50
O26	A11 10m orange		.25	.40
	Never hinged	.90		
	Postally used			10.50
	On cover			60.00
O27	A11 20m org brn		.25	.40
	Never hinged	.90		
	Postally used			20.00
	On cover			80.00
	Nos. O1-O27 (26)		32.45	38.40
	Set, never hinged	140.00		

Double overprints exist on Nos. O1-O2, O5-O7, O10 and O12.

Issued: Nos. O10, O12, O16-O17, O19-O20, O22-O27, 1922.

Same Overprint on No. 96

O28	A11 6m on 3m		.25	.75
	Never hinged	.90		
	Postally used			14.50
	On cover			72.50
a.	Inverted overprint	30.00		
	Never hinged	85.00		

No. 77 Overprinted

Serrate Roulette 13½

1922   Wmk. 108 Sideways

O29	A12 5m grn, red & blk		4.00	11.00
	Never hinged	18.00		
	Postally used			105.00
	On cover			160.00
a.	Wmk. upright	4.25	10.50	
	Never hinged	20.00		
	Postally used			95.00
	On cover			140.00

Nos. 99-103, 106-107 Overprinted Type "a"

1922-23   Wmk. 109   *Perf. 14*

O30	A11 4m dark blue		.25	.50
	Never hinged	1.40		
	Postally used			35.00
	On cover			120.00
O31	A11 5m dark green		.25	.50
	Never hinged	1.40		
	Postally used			42.50
	On cover			100.00
O32	A11 10m orange		.25	.50
	Never hinged	1.40		
	Postally used			8.00
	On cover			60.00
O33	A11 20m orange brn		.25	.50
	Never hinged	1.40		
	Postally used			8.00
	On cover			87.50
O34	A15 50m pale blue & red		.25	.50
	Never hinged	1.40		
	Postally used			7.25
	On cover			32.50
O35	A15a 100m dk grn & red		.25	.50
	Never hinged	1.40		
	Postally used			12.50
	On cover			60.00

Nos. 113-115, 118-120 Overprinted Type "a"

O36	A15 50m pale blue		.25	.50
	Never hinged	1.40		
	Postally used			1,350.
	On cover			1,600.
a.	Inverted overprint	25.00		
	Never hinged	62.50		
O37	A15a 100m dark green		.25	.50
	Never hinged	1.40		
	Postally used			350.00
	On cover			525.00
O38	A15 200m orange		.25	.50
	Never hinged	1.40		
	Postally used			32.50
	On cover			200.00
a.	Inverted overprint	25.00		
	Never hinged	62.50		

Paper With Gray Network

O39	A17 300m bl grn & red		.25	.50
	Never hinged	1.40		
	Postally used			325.00
	On cover			475.00
O40	A17 500m gray & red		.25	.50
	Never hinged	1.40		
	Postally used			450.00
	On cover			800.00
a.	Network omitted	14.00	5.75	
	Never hinged	37.50		
O41	A17 1000m brn & red		.25	.50
	Never hinged	1.40		
	Postally used			95.00
	On cover			240.00
a.	Network omitted	14.50	8.00	
	Never hinged	40.00		
	Nos. O30-O41 (12)		3.00	6.00
	Set, never hinged	16.80		

Issued: No. O30, 12/16/22. Nos. O31-O34, 1/10/23. Nos. O36-O40, 7/20/23. No. O41, 7/29/23.

Regular Issue of 1924-25 Overprinted

1924-25   *Perf. 14x14½*

O42	A19 5pf red orange		2.10	3.25
	Never hinged	6.75		
	On cover			24.00
a.	5pf orange	15.00	9.50	

	Never hinged	52.50		
	On cover			40.00
O43	A19 10pf green		6.00	9.00
	Never hinged	22.50		
	On cover			22.50
a.	10pf dark green	2.00	3.00	
	Never hinged	6.25		
	On cover			13.50
O44	A19 15pf gray		2.10	3.25
	Never hinged	7.00		
	On cover			16.00
a.	15pf dk greenish gray	5.25	4.25	
	Never hinged	17.50		
	On cover			27.50
O45	A19 15pf red		18.00	10.00
	Never hinged	60.00		
	On cover			20.00
O46	A19 20pf car & red		2.10	2.10
	Never hinged	7.00		
	On cover			20.00
O47	A19 25pf slate & red		18.00	27.50
	Never hinged	55.00		
	On cover			120.00
O48	A19 30pf green & red		3.00	3.75
	Never hinged	8.50		
	On cover			24.00
a.	30pf dk grn & rose red	27.50	11.00	
	Never hinged	110.00		
	On cover			60.00
O49	A19 35pf ultra		42.50	50.00
	Never hinged	175.00		
	On cover			105.00
O50	A19 40pf dk bl & dull bl		6.50	8.50
	Never hinged	19.00		
	On cover			72.50
O51	A19 50pf dp blue & red		21.00	42.50
	Never hinged	65.00		
	On cover			275.00
O52	A19 75pf violet & red		32.50	120.00
	Never hinged	150.00		
	On cover			325.00
	Nos. O42-O52 (11)		153.80	279.85
	Set, never hinged	575.00		

Double overprints exist on Nos. O42-O44, O47, O50-O52.

Issued: Nos. O42-O43, O44a, O46, O50, 3/1/24. Nos. O42a, O45, O49, 1925. Nos. O48, O51-O52, 3/12/24.

DENMARK

'den-,märk

LOCATION — Northern part of a peninsula which separates the North and Baltic Seas, and includes the surrounding islands
GOVT. — Kingdom
AREA — 16,631 sq. mi.
POP. — 5,112,130 (1984)
CAPITAL — Copenhagen

96 Skilling = 1 Rigsbank Daler
100 Ore = 1 Krone (1875)

Values for unused stamps are for examples with original gum as defined in the catalogue introduction. Very fine examples of Nos. 9-37 and O1-O9 will have perforations clear of the framelines but with the design noticeably off center. Well centered stamps are quite scarce and will command substantial premiums.

Watermarks

Wmk. 111 —
Small Crown

Wmk. 112 —
Crown

Wmk. 113 —
Crown

Wmk. 114 —
Multiple Crosses

Royal Emblems — A2

1851   Typo.   Wmk. 111   Imperf.
With Yellow Burelage

1	A1	2rs blue	3,500.	1,000.
		On cover		2,200.
a.		First printing	8,250.	2,400.
		On cover		7,250.
2	A2	4rs brown	600.00	40.00
		On cover		120.00
a.		First printing	600.00	40.00
		On cover		160.00
b.		4rs yellow brown	875.00	55.00
		On cover		125.00
c.		4rs chestnut (4th printing)	2,400.	250.00
		On cover		500.00

Full margins = 1mm.

The first printing of Nos. 1 and 2 had the burelage printed from a copper plate, giving a clear impression with the lines in slight relief. The subsequent impressions had the burelage typographed, with the lines fainter and not rising above the surface of the paper.

Nos. 1-2 were reprinted in 1885 and 1901 on heavy yellowish paper, unwatermarked and imperforate, with a brown burelage. No. 1 was also reprinted without burelage, on both yellowish and white paper. Value for least costly reprint of No. 1, $50.

No. 2 was reprinted in 1951 in 10 shades with "Colour Specimen 1951" printed on the back. It was also reprinted in 1961 in 2 shades without burelage and with "Farve Nytryk 1961" printed on the back. Value for least costly reprint of No. 2, $8.50.

Numeral Postmarks on No. 2

Values in the left column are for very fine used stamps with clear, legible numeral cancels. Values in the right column are for very fine stamps with clear, legible numeral cancels on complete covers.

1	Kjøbenhavn	40.00	120.00
2	Hamburg	350.00	—
3	Lübeck	500.00	—
4	Aalborg	40.00	145.00
5	Aarhus	40.00	120.00
6	Aabenraa	52.50	150.00
7	Assens	52.50	150.00
8	Bogense	52.50	145.00
9	Bredstedt	95.00	375.00
10	Burg	62.50	200.00
11	Cappeln	62.50	200.00
12	Christiansfeld	52.50	200.00
13	Ebeltoft	52.50	135.00
14	Eckernförde	52.50	150.00
15	Faaborg	52.50	150.00
16	Flensburg	52.50	135.00
17	Fredericia	52.50	135.00
18	Frederiksborg	52.50	135.00
19	Frederikshavn	52.50	135.00
20	Frederikssund	52.50	135.00
21	Friedrichstad	62.50	135.00
22	Grenaae	50.00	135.00
23	Haderslev	50.00	135.00
24	Helsingor	40.00	145.00
25	Horsholm	52.50	135.00
26	Hjoring	52.50	135.00
27	Hobroe	52.50	135.00
28	Holbek	52.50	135.00
29	Holstebro	52.50	135.00
30	Horsens	52.50	135.00
31	Husum	62.50	225.00
32	Kallundborg	52.50	150.00
33	Kjerteminde	52.50	150.00
34	Kbhvns. jernb. postkontor	40.00	150.00
35	Kjoge	52.50	145.00
36	Kolding	52.50	145.00
37	Korsoer	52.50	145.00
38	Lemvig	52.50	150.00
39	Lyngbye	100.00	160.00
40	Logstoer	52.50	140.00
41	Mariboe	52.50	140.00
42	Middelfart	52.50	140.00
43	Nakskov	52.50	140.00
44	Nestved	52.50	150.00
45	Nibe	52.50	140.00
46	Nyborg	52.50	140.00
47	Nykjobing, Falster	52.50	140.00
48	Nykjobing, Jylland	62.50	200.00
49	Nykjobing, Sjaelland	52.50	150.00
50	Nysted	52.50	125.00
51	Odense	40.00	125.00
52	Praestoe	52.50	190.00
53	Randers	52.50	140.00
54	Rendsburg	52.50	190.00
55	Ribe	52.50	175.00
56	Ringkjobing	52.50	140.00
57	Ringsted	52.50	140.00
58	Roeskilde	40.00	135.00
59	Rudkjobing	52.50	140.00
60	Rodby	52.50	160.00
61	Ronne	52.50	210.00
62	Saxkjobing	52.50	160.00
63	Skanderborg	52.50	140.00
64	Skive	52.50	140.00
65	Slagelse	52.50	140.00
66	Schleswig	52.50	150.00
67	Soro	52.50	140.00
68	Stege	52.50	140.00
69	Stubbekjobing	52.50	130.00
70	Svendborg	52.50	150.00
71	Sonderborg	62.50	150.00
72	Thisted	52.50	140.00
73	Tonder	52.50	260.00
74	Tonning	62.50	260.00
75	Varde	52.50	175.00
76	Vejle	52.50	130.00
77	Viborg	52.50	125.00
78	Vordingborg	52.50	125.00
79	Wyck	95.00	300.00
80	Aeroeskjobing	95.00	750.00
81	Aarosund	750.00	—
82	Frederiksvaerk	62.50	130.00
83	Garding	72.50	275.00
84	Herning	52.50	130.00
85	Hojer	150.00	550.00
86	Leck	100.00	375.00
87	Logumkloster	62.50	260.00
88	Mariager	52.50	150.00
89	Marstal	125.00	475.00
90	Ronnede	52.50	150.00
91	Silkeborg	52.50	140.00
92	Skjelskjor	52.50	125.00
93	Storehedinge	52.50	150.00
94	Taastrup	92.50	450.00
95	Aakirkeby	190.00	1,500.
96	Allinge	190.00	1,000.
97	Augustenborg	140.00	1,200.
98	Fjerritslev	52.50	125.00
99	Fredensborg	52.50	150.00
100	Gaabense	95.00	125.00
101	Graasten	75.00	225.00
102	Gudhjem	2,000.	—
103	Hasle	260.00	—
104	Nexo	160.00	450.00
105	Nordborg	250.00	550.00
106	Skagen	52.50	150.00
107	Skjernbro	52.50	160.00
108	Skodborghuus	—	—
109	Snoghoi	—	—
110	Stokkemarke	100.00	825.00
111	Svaneke	125.00	1,000.
112	Saeby	52.50	175.00
113	Altona	52.50	130.00
114	Elmshorn	625.00	—
115	Eutin	100.00	375.00
116	Glückstadt	52.50	260.00
117	Heide	62.50	325.00
118	Heiligenhafen	52.50	375.00
119	Itzehoe	52.50	160.00
120	Kellinghusen	95.00	475.00
121	Kiel	52.50	130.00
122	Lütjenburg	95.00	525.00
123	Meldorf	95.00	425.00
124	Neumünster	62.50	160.00
125	Neustadt	150.00	425.00
126	Nortoft	160.00	—
127	Oldenburg	62.50	275.00
128	Oldesloe	75.00	375.00
129	Pinneberg	75.00	275.00
130	Plön	75.00	275.00
131	Preetz	62.50	225.00
132	Remmels	250.00	550.00
133	Segeberg	62.50	175.00
134	Uetersen	75.00	175.00
135	Ahrensbock	160.00	350.00
136	Ahrensburg	325.00	1,100.
137	Barmstedt	125.00	875.00
138	Bornhöved	72.50	450.00
139	Bramstedt	100.00	300.00
140	Brunsbüttel	100.00	300.00
141	Crempe	425.00	—
142	Elmshorn	175.00	750.00
143	Lunden	175.00	325.00
144	Reinbeck	225.00	325.00
145	Schwartau	175.00	300.00
146	Wandsbeck	125.00	275.00
147	Wilster	75.00	175.00
148	Lauenburg	75.00	375.00
149	Mölln	175.00	400.00
150	Ratzeburg	190.00	275.00
151	Büchen	525.00	1,300.
152	Schwarzenbeck	425.00	900.00
153	Friedrichsruhe	950.00	1,275.
154	L.P. No. 5 Blankenese (Blankenese-Altona)	325.00	1,275.
155	Bordesholm	190.00	1,275.
156	L.P. No. 2 (Hanerau-Itzehoe)	325.00	1,100.
157	L.P. No. 4 (Kaltenkirchen-Bramstedt)	525.00	1,100.
158	Lensahn	525.00	1,100.
159	L.P. No. 3 (Schonfeld-Itzehoe)	—	1,150.
160	L.P. Schönwalde	950.00	1,275.
161	Bahnhof Rendsburg	95.00	350.00
162	Altona Bahnhof	95.00	200.00
163	Bandholm	95.00	175.00
164	Vedbaeck	—	—
165	Slangerup	—	—
166	Humlebaek	275.00	750.00
167	Rungsted	—	—
168	Holstenske Jb. postkontor	—	—
169	Holstenske Jb. postkontor	—	—
170	Holstenske Jb. postkontor	275.00	925.00
171	Gettorf	525.00	1,550.
172	Marne	325.00	650.00
173	Trittau	325.00	1,750.

The initials "L.P." are short for "Land Postrute," which means a rural post route.

Dotting in Spandrels
A3

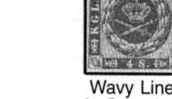

Wavy Lines in Spandrels
A4

1854-57

3	A3	2s blue ('55)	75.00	60.00
		Never hinged	150.00	
		On cover		210.00
4	A3	4s brown	325.00	15.00
		Never hinged	650.00	
		On cover		30.00
a.		4s yellow brown	350.00	15.00
		Never hinged	700.00	
		On cover		30.00
5	A3	8s green ('57)	300.00	67.50
		Never hinged	600.00	
		On cover		300.00
		On cover, single franking		350.00
a.		8s yellow green	300.00	80.00
		Never hinged	600.00	
		On cover		300.00
		On cover, single franking		350.00
6	A3	16s gray lilac ('57)	525.00	190.00
		Never hinged	1,100.	
		On cover		900.00
		On cover, single franking		1,000.
		Nos. 3-6 (4)	1,225.	332.50

Full margins = 1mm.

See No. 10. For denominations in cents see Danish West Indies Nos. 1-4.

1858-62

7	A4	4s yellow brown	65.00	8.50
		Never hinged	140.00	
		On cover		24.00
a.		4s brown	67.50	8.00
		Never hinged	150.00	
		On cover		24.00
b.		Wmk. 112 ('62)	62.50	9.00
		Never hinged	140.00	
		On cover		27.50
8	A4	8s green	800.00	82.50
		Never hinged	2,000.	
		On cover		475.00
		On cover, single franking		540.00

Full margins = 1mm.

Nos. 2 to 8 inclusive are known with unofficial perforation 12 or 13, and Nos. 4, 5, 7 and 8 with unofficial roulette 9½.

Nos. 3, 6-8 were reprinted in 1885 on heavy yellowish paper, unwatermarked, imperforate and without burelage. Nos. 4-5 were reprinted in 1924 on white paper, unwatermarked, imperforate, gummed and without burelage. Value for No. 3, $15; Nos. 4-5, each $110; No. 6, $20; Nos. 7-8, each $15.

1863   Wmk. 112   Rouletted 11

9	A4	4s brown	100.00	15.00
		Never hinged	175.00	
		On cover		35.00
a.		4s deep brown	100.00	15.00
		Never hinged	175.00	
		On cover		35.00
b.		4s red brown	100.00	15.00
		Never hinged	175.00	
		On cover		35.00
10	A3	16s violet	1,400.	650.00
		On cover		4,750.
		On cover, single franking		5,400.

Royal Emblems — A5

1864-68   Perf. 13

11	A5	2s blue ('65)	65.00	35.00
		Never hinged	210.00	
		On cover		72.50
12	A5	3s red vio ('65)	80.00	75.00
		Never hinged	260.00	
		On cover		350.00
		On cover, single franking		725.00
13	A5	4s red	40.00	8.00
		Never hinged	85.00	
		On cover		18.00
14	A5	8s bister ('68)	275.00	95.00
		Never hinged	725.00	
		On cover		350.00
15	A5	16s olive green	475.00	175.00
		Never hinged	1,200.	
		On cover		350.00
		On cover, single franking		540.00
		Nos. 11-15 (5)	935.00	388.00

Nos. 11-15 were reprinted in 1886 on heavy yellowish paper, unwatermarked, imperforate and without gum. The reprints of all values except the 4s were printed in two vertical rows of six, inverted with respect to each other, so that horizontal pairs are always tête bêche. Value $12 each.

Nos. 13 and 15 were reprinted in 1942 with printing on the back across each horizontal row: "Nytryk 1942. G. A. Hagemann: Danmarks og Vestindiens Frimaerker, Bind 2." Value, $70 each.

Imperf, single

11a	A5	2s blue	95.00	95.00
		As "a," pair	240.00	240.00
12a	A5	3s red violet	140.00	
		As "a," pair	475.00	
13a	A5	4s red	77.50	90.00
		On cover		2,000.
		As "a," pair	240.00	
14a	A5	8s bister	375.00	
		As "a," pair	900.00	
15a	A5	16s olive green	450.00	
		As "a," pair	975.00	

1870   Perf. 12½

11b	A5	2s blue	275.00	350.00
		Never hinged	600.00	
		On cover		500.00
12b	A5	3s red violet	475.00	650.00
		Never hinged	950.00	
		On cover		1,200.
14b	A5	8s bister	475.00	475.00
		Never hinged	1,300.	
		On cover		1,100.
15b	A5	16s olive green	725.00	1,450.
		Never hinged	1,450.	
		On cover		3,600.
		Nos. 11b-15b (4)	1,950.	2,925.

A6

Normal Frame   Inverted Frame

The arabesques in the corners have a main stem and a branch. When the frame is in normal position, in the upper left corner the branch leaves the main stem half way between two little leaflets. In the lower right corner the branch starts at the foot of the second leaflet. When the frame is inverted the corner designs are, of course, transposed.

1870-71   Wmk. 112   Perf. 14x13½
Paper Varying from Thin to Thick

16	A6	2s gray & ultra ('71)	70.00	27.50
		Never hinged	180.00	
		On cover		72.50
a.		2s gray & blue	70.00	27.50
		Never hinged	180.00	
		On cover		72.50
17	A6	3s gray & brt lil ('71)	100.00	110.00
		Never hinged	240.00	
		On cover		200.00
18	A6	4s gray & car	40.00	10.00
		Never hinged	180.00	
		On cover		21.00
19	A6	8s gray & brn ('71)	200.00	75.00
		Never hinged	725.00	
		On cover		240.00

```
20  A6  16s gray & grn ('71)      275.00  175.00
        Never hinged              850.00
        On cover                          725.00
        On cover, single franking         900.00
```

Perf. 12½

```
21  A6  2s gray & bl ('71)      2,000.  3,250.
        Never hinged            6,000.
        On cover                        6,500.
        On cover, single franking       7,000.
22  A6  4s gray & car            150.00  125.00
        Never hinged             450.00
        On cover                         150.00
24  A6  48s brn & lilac          450.00  275.00
        Never hinged           1,300.
        On cover                        2,400.
        On cover, single franking       2,600.
```

Nos. 16-20, 24 were reprinted in 1886 on thin white paper, unwatermarked, imperforate and without gum. These were printed in sheets of 10 in which 1 stamp has the normal frame (value $32.50 each) and 9 the inverted (value $11 each).

Imperf, single

```
16b  A6   2s    250.
17a  A6   3s    240.
18a  A6   4s    200.
19a  A6   8s    250.
20a  A6  16s    400.
24a  A6  48s    425.  —
```

Inverted Frame

```
16c  A6   2s   1,000.    775.
17b  A6   3s   2,500.  2,000.
18b  A6   4s     775.   87.50
         On cover                250.
19b  A6   8s   1,750.    900.
20b  A6  16s   2,000.  1,750.
24b  A6  48s   2,750.  1,900.
```

1875-79   Perf. 14x13½

```
25  A6  3o gray blue &
            gray            18.00   15.00
        Never hinged        36.00
        On cover                    37.50
        On cover, single franking   75.00
    a.  1st "A" of "DANMARK" miss-
            ing             60.00  150.00
        Never hinged       190.00
    b.  Imperf            750.00
    c.  Inverted frame     18.00   16.00
        Never hinged        36.00
        On cover                    50.00
26  A6  4o slate & blue    25.00    .50
        Never hinged        85.00
        On cover                     3.75
    a.  4o gray & blue      25.00   1.10
        Never hinged        95.00
        On cover                     3.75
    b.  4o slate & ultra    90.00   17.00
        Never hinged       425.00
        On cover                    40.00
    c.  4o gray & ultra     75.00   16.00
        Never hinged       425.00
        On cover                    40.00
    d.  Imperf             75.00
        On cover                     —
        Pair               —
    e.  As #26, inverted frame  25.00  .50
        Never hinged        85.00
        On cover                     3.50
    f.  As "b," inverted frame  400.00  240.00
27  A6  5o rose & blue
            ('79)          30.00   72.50
        Never hinged        60.00
        On cover                   725.00
        On cover, single franking  900.00
    a.  Ball of lower curve of large
            "5" missing    125.00  300.00
        Never hinged       300.00
    b.  Inverted frame    1,000.  2,250.
        Never hinged      2,100.
28  A6  8o slate & car     22.50    .50
        Never hinged       105.00
        On cover                     2.75
    a.  8o gray & carmine   75.00   5.00
        Never hinged       260.00
        On cover                    16.00
    b.  Imperf            150.00
        On cover                     —
        Pair               —
    c.  Inverted frame     22.50    .50
        Never hinged        95.00
        On cover                     2.75
    d.  8o gray & aniline red ('86)  72.50  9.50
        Never hinged       260.00
        On cover                    25.00
    e.  As "d," imperf    150.00
        On cover                     —
    f.  As "d," inverted frame (pos.
            69)            750.00  190.00
29  A6  12o sl & dull lake  10.00   4.00
        Never hinged        20.00
        On cover                    55.00
        On cover, single franking   72.50
    a.  12o gray & bright lilac  65.00  8.00
        Never hinged       180.00
        On cover                    72.50
    b.  12o gray & dull magenta  72.50  10.00
        Never hinged       180.00
        On cover                    95.00
    c.  Inverted frame     14.00    4.00
        Never hinged        35.00
        On cover                    42.50
30  A6  16o slate & brn    77.50    6.50
        Never hinged       220.00
        On cover                    47.50
        On cover, single franking   77.50
    a.  16o light gray & brown  77.50  17.00
        Never hinged       220.00
        On cover                    52.50
        On cover, single franking   85.00
    b.  Inverted frame     52.50    4.50
        Never hinged       145.00
        On cover                    52.50
    c.  As "a," inverted frame  120.00  45.00
        Never hinged       250.00
        On cover                   120.00
31  A6  20o rose & gray    90.00   32.50
        Never hinged       425.00
        On cover                   175.00
    a.  20o carmine & gray  90.00   32.50
        Never hinged       350.00
        On cover                   130.00
```

```
    b.  Inverted frame     90.00   32.50
        Never hinged       350.00
        On cover                   130.00
32  A6  25o gray & green   65.00   40.00
        Never hinged       140.00
        On cover                   260.00
        On parcel post receipt card  240.00
    a.  Inverted frame     77.50   62.50
        Never hinged       325.00
        On cover                   450.00
33  A6  50o brown & vio    70.00   37.50
        Never hinged       225.00
        On cover                   240.00
        On parcel post receipt card  190.00
    a.  50o brown & blue violet  400.00  175.00
        Never hinged     1,000.
        On cover                 1,200.
    b.  Inverted frame     70.00   32.50
        Never hinged       240.00
        On cover                   225.00
34  A6  100o gray & org
            ('77)         110.00   60.00
        Never hinged       350.00
        On cover                   300.00
        On parcel post receipt card  300.00
    a.  Imperf, single    375.00
    b.  Inverted frame    150.00   60.00
        Never hinged       425.00
        On cover                   275.00
    c.  100o greenish gray & or-
            ange yellow ('87)  130.00  60.00
        Never hinged       350.00
        On cover                   290.00
    d.  100o bluish gray & orange
            yellow ('91)  130.00   60.00
        Never hinged       350.00
        On cover                   350.00
        Nos. 25-34 (10)   518.00  269.00
    Set, never hinged   1,625.
```

The stamps of this issue on thin semi-transparent paper are far scarcer than those on thicker paper.
See Nos. 41-42, 44, 46-47, 50-52. For surcharges see Nos. 55, 79-80, 136.

Arms — A7

Two types of numerals in corners

Small Numerals

Large Numerals

1882

Small Corner Numerals

```
35  A7  5o green         240.00  100.00
        Never hinged       725.00
        On cover                   950.00
        On cover, single franking 1,100.
37  A7  20o blue         190.00   70.00
        Never hinged       650.00
        On cover                   160.00
```

1884-88

Larger Corner Numerals

```
38  A7  5o green          15.00    3.50
        Never hinged        75.00
        On cover                    18.00
    a.  Imperf              —
39  A7  10o carmine ('85)  16.00    2.50
        Never hinged        95.00
        On cover                    18.00
    a.  Small numerals in corners
            ('88)          550.00  725.00
        Never hinged     1,200.
        On cover                 3,000.
    b.  Imperf, single    175.00
    c.  Pair, Nos. 39, 39a  600.00  875.00
        Never hinged     1,200.
40  A7  20o blue          30.00    5.00
        Never hinged       110.00
        On cover                    24.00
    a.  Pair, Nos. 37, 40  400.00  875.00
        Never hinged       825.00
        On cover                 2,750.
    b.  Imperf              —
        Nos. 38-40 (3)     61.00   11.00
    Set, never hinged    285.00
```

Stamps with large corner numerals have white line around crown and lower oval touches frame.
The plate for No. 39, was damaged and 3 clichés in the bottom row were replaced by clichés for post cards, which had small numerals in the corners.
Two clichés with small numerals were inserted in the plate of No. 40.
See Nos. 43, 45, 48-49, 53-54. For surcharge see No. 56.

1895-1901   Wmk. 112   Perf. 13

```
41  A6  3o blue & gray     10.00    7.25
        Never hinged        21.00
        On cover                    24.00
42  A6  4o slate & bl ('96)  4.50    .40
        Never hinged        10.50
        On cover                     2.40
43  A7  5o green           12.00     .75
        Never hinged        35.00
        On cover                     3.00
```

```
44  A6  8o slate & car      4.50     .45
        Never hinged        12.00
        On cover                     2.40
45  A7  10o rose car       24.00     .65
        Never hinged        60.00
        On cover                     4.00
46  A6  12o sl & dull lake   7.00    4.00
        Never hinged        15.00
        On cover                    47.50
47  A6  16o slate & brown   19.00    4.50
        Never hinged        35.00
        On cover                    47.50
48  A7  20o blue           30.00    2.40
        Never hinged        85.00
        On cover                    12.00
49  A7  24o brown ('01)     7.00    6.00
        Never hinged        18.00
        On cover                   120.00
        On cover, single franking  240.00
50  A6  25o gray & grn
            ('98)          110.00   19.50
        Never hinged       240.00
        On cover                   150.00
51  A6  50o brown & vio
            ('97)           60.00   24.00
        Never hinged       150.00
        On cover                   140.00
        On cover, single franking  300.00
52  A6  100o slate & org   90.00   35.00
        Never hinged       200.00
        On cover                   140.00
        On cover, single franking  300.00
        Nos. 41-52 (12)   378.00  104.90
    Set, never hinged     875.00
```

Inverted Frame

```
41b  A6   3o              12.00    7.00
         Never hinged      24.00
         On cover                  19.00
42a  A6   4o               4.50     .45
         Never hinged      10.50
         On cover                   2.40
44a  A6   8o               4.50     .40
         Never hinged      12.00
         On cover                   2.40
46a  A6  12o              14.00    4.50
         Never hinged      24.00
         On cover                  47.50
47a  A6  16o              30.00    5.00
         Never hinged      47.50
         On cover                  65.00
50a  A6  25o              60.00   27.50
         Never hinged     120.00
         On cover                 160.00
51a  A6  50o              95.00   32.50
         Never hinged     200.00
         On cover                 160.00
52a  A6  100o             90.00   57.50
         Never hinged     200.00
         On cover                 160.00
         Nos. 41b-52a (8)  310.00  134.95
    Set, never hinged     635.00
```

1902-04   Wmk. 113

```
41c  A6   3o blue & gray   2.75    3.00
         Never hinged       6.00
         On cover                  18.00
42b  A6   4o slate & blue  17.00   20.00
         Never hinged      35.00
         On cover                  42.50
43a  A7   5o green         2.00     .25
         Never hinged       6.00
         On cover                   2.75
44d  A6   8o slate & carmine  525.00  425.00
         Never hinged    1,050.
45a  A7  10o rose carmine  3.00     .25
         Never hinged       9.00
         On cover                   3.00
48a  A7  20o blue         20.00    4.75
         Never hinged      47.50
         On cover                  18.00
50b  A6  25o gray & green  10.50   4.50
         Never hinged      26.00
         On cover                 105.00
51b  A6  50o brown & violet  27.50  20.00
         Never hinged      72.50
         On cover                 130.00
         On cover, single franking 260.00
52b  A6  100o slate & orange  30.00  15.00
         Never hinged      72.50
         On cover                 130.00
         On cover, single franking 300.00
         Nos. 41c-52b (9)  637.75  492.75
    Set, never hinged   1,325.
```

Inverted Frame

```
41d  A6   3o              75.00  130.00
         Never hinged     240.00
         On cover                 180.00
42c  A6   4o             140.00  130.00
         Never hinged     425.00
         On cover                 180.00
50c  A6  25o             210.00   60.00
         Never hinged     540.00
         On cover                 140.00
51c  A6  50o             260.00  240.00
         Never hinged     650.00
         On cover                 175.00
52c  A6  100o            225.00  240.00
         Never hinged     650.00
         On cover                 300.00
         Nos. 41d-52c (5)  910.00  800.00
    Set, never hinged   2,500.
```

1902   Wmk. 113

```
53  A7  1o orange           .75     .65
        Never hinged        1.20
        On cover                     3.50
    a.  Imperf              —        —
54  A7  15o lilac          11.00     .75
        Never hinged        30.00
        On cover                    21.00
    a.  Imperf, single    4,250.
```

Nos. 44d, 44, 49 Surcharged

a   b

1904-12   Wmk. 113

```
55  A6(a)  4o on 8o sl & car  3.50   4.00
        Never hinged         6.00
        On cover                    24.00
    a.  Wmk. 112 ('12)      21.00   60.00
        Never hinged        42.50
        On cover                   140.00
    b.  As "a," inverted frame  —  6,000.
        Never hinged
```

Wmk. 112

```
56  A7(b)  15o on 24o brown  5.75   17.50
        Never hinged         6.00
        On cover                    42.50
    a.  Short "15" at right  27.50  105.00
        Never hinged        60.00
    Set, never hinged      16.00
```

A10

1905-17   Wmk. 113   Perf. 13

```
57  A10  1o orange ('06)    2.00     .90
        Never hinged         6.50
        On cover                     2.40
58  A10  2o carmine         4.00     .65
        Never hinged        14.00
        On cover                     4.75
    a.  Perf. 14x14½ ('17)   3.25   16.00
        Never hinged         6.50
        On cover                    35.00
59  A10  3o gray            7.75     .65
        Never hinged        20.00
        On cover                     1.75
60  A10  4o dull blue      10.00    1.00
        Never hinged        24.00
        On cover                     4.25
    a.  Perf. 14x14½ ('17)   9.75   37.50
        Never hinged        20.00
        On cover                    60.00
61  A10  5o dp green ('12)   4.00    .50
        Never hinged         9.75
        On cover                     1.20
62  A10  10o dp rose ('12)   5.25    .30
        Never hinged        16.00
        On cover                     1.75
63  A10  15o lilac         19.00    2.50
        Never hinged        52.50
        On cover                    12.00
64  A10  20o dk blue ('12)  35.00    .90
        Never hinged        97.50
        On cover                    12.00
        Nos. 57-64 (8)      87.00    7.40
    Set, never hinged     240.00
```

The three wavy lines in design A10 are symbolical of the three waters which separate the principal Danish islands.
See Nos. 85-96, 1338-1342A, 1468-1473. For surcharges and overprints see Nos. 163, 181, J1, J38, Q1-Q2.

King Christian IX A11   King Frederik VIII A12

1904-05   Engr.

```
65  A11  10o scarlet        2.75     .65
        Never hinged         7.00
        On cover                     2.40
66  A11  20o blue          20.00    2.50
        Never hinged        45.00
        On cover                    15.00
67  A11  25o brown ('05)   24.00    7.00
        Never hinged        97.50
        On cover                    52.50
        On cover, single franking   60.00
68  A11  50o dull vio ('05)  100.00  120.00
        Never hinged       260.00
        On cover                   300.00
        On cover, single franking  350.00
69  A11  100o ocher ('05)  13.00   60.00
        Never hinged        26.00
        On cover                   300.00
        On cover, single franking  425.00
        Nos. 65-69 (5)    159.75  190.15
    Set, never hinged     435.00
```

1905-06   Re-engraved

```
70  A11  5o green           4.00     .50
        Never hinged         7.50
```

71 A11 10o scarlet ('06) 14.00 .55
Never hinged 32.50
Set, never hinged 44.00

The re-engraved stamps are much clearer than the originals, and the decoration on the king's left breast has been removed.

1907-12

72 A12 5o green 1.25 .40
Never hinged 2.50
a. Imperf. —
73 A12 10o red 3.25 .30
Never hinged 5.25
a. Imperf. —
74 A12 20o indigo 14.00 .65
Never hinged 29.00
a. 20o bright blue ('11) 14.00 2.50
Never hinged 27.50
75 A12 25o olive brn 27.50 1.25
Never hinged 65.00
76 A12 35o dp org ('12) 6.00 7.00
Never hinged 8.50
77 A12 50o claret 32.50 6.75
Never hinged 65.00
78 A12 100o bister brn 90.00 5.00
Never hinged 275.00
Nos. 72-78 (7) 174.50 21.35
Set, never hinged 450.00

Nos. 47, 31 and O9 Surcharged

c d

Dark Blue Surcharge

1912 Wmk. 112 Perf. 13
79 A6(c) 35o on 16o 14.00 65.00
Never hinged 27.50
a. Inverted frame 250.00 500.00
Never hinged 400.00

Perf. 14x13½
80 A6(c) 35o on 20o 30.00 80.00
Never hinged 60.00
a. Inverted frame 115.00 275.00
Never hinged 190.00

Black Surcharge

81 O1(d) 35o on 32o 42.50 120.00
Never hinged 90.00
Nos. 79-81 (3) 86.50 265.00
Set, never hinged 180.00

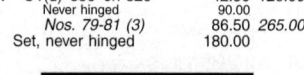

General Post Office,
Copenhagen — A15

1912 Engr. Wmk. 113 Perf. 13
82 A15 5k dark red 425.00 175.00
Never hinged 1,300.

See Nos. 135, 843 (in Scott Standard Catalogue Vol. 2).

Perf. 14x14½
1913-30 Typo. Wmk. 114
85 A10 1o dp orange ('14) .30 .25
Never hinged .60
a. Bklt. pane, 2 ea #85, 91 + 2 labels 20.00
86 A10 2o car ('13) 3.25 .50
Never hinged 7.25
a. Imperf 125.00 250.00
b. Booklet pane, 4 + 2 labels 27.50
87 A10 3o gray ('13) 5.25 .50
Never hinged 11.00
88 A10 4o blue ('13) 6.50 .65
Never hinged 15.00
a. Half used as 2o on cover 1,250.
89 A10 5o dk brown ('21) .65 .50
Never hinged 1.80
a. Imperf 175.00
b. Booklet pane, 4 + 2 labels 14.00
90 A10 5o lt green ('30) 1.40 .50
Never hinged 5.00
a. Booklet pane, 4 + 2 labels 16.00
b. Booklet pane of 50
91 A10 7o apple grn ('26) 5.00 7.75
Never hinged 10.50
a. Booklet pane, 4 + 2 labels 20.00
92 A10 7o dk violet ('30) 7.00 6.50
Never hinged 37.50
93 A10 8o gray ('21) 7.00 3.25
Never hinged 9.50
94 A10 10o green ('21) .85 .50
Never hinged 2.40
a. Imperf 200.00
b. Booklet pane, 4 + 2 labels 37.50
95 A10 10o bister brn ('30) 2.00 .50
Never hinged 7.25
a. Booklet pane, 4 + 2 labels 16.00
b. Booklet pane of 50

96 A10 12o violet ('26) 22.50 9.75
Never hinged 52.50
Nos. 85-96 (12) 68.70 31.15
Set, never hinged 160.00

No. 88a was used with No. 97 in Faroe Islands, Jan. 3-23, 1919.

Surcharge and surcharge following No. 64.

King Christian X
A16 A17

1913-28 Typo. Perf. 14x14½
97 A16 5o green 1.10 .50
Never hinged 3.00
a. Bklt. pane of 4, with P# 400.00
98 A16 7o orange ('18) 2.25 2.50
Never hinged 7.25
99 A16 8o dk gray ('20) 9.75 6.50
Never hinged 24.00
100 A16 10o red 1.50 .25
Never hinged 3.50
a. Imperf 200.00
b. Bklt. pane of 4, with P# 500.00
101 A16 12o gray grn ('18) 6.50 10.00
Never hinged 10.50
102 A16 15o violet 2.00 .30
Never hinged 4.25
103 A16 20o dp blue 11.50 .50
Never hinged 35.00
104 A16 20o brown ('21) 1.00 .25
Never hinged 1.75
105 A16 20o red ('26) 1.25 .50
Never hinged 2.40
106 A16 25o dk brown 11.50 .50
Never hinged 47.50
107 A16 25o brn & blk ('20) 75.00 8.00
Never hinged 150.00
108 A16 25o red ('22) 3.25 2.00
Never hinged 4.75
109 A16 25o yel grn ('25) 3.00 .50
Never hinged 4.75
110 A16 27o ver & blk ('18) 27.50 65.00
Never hinged 60.00
111 A16 30o green & blk ('18) 35.00 3.25
Never hinged 90.00
112 A16 30o orange ('21) 2.50 2.50
Never hinged 4.75
113 A16 30o dk blue ('25) 1.50 1.00
Never hinged 2.40
114 A16 35o orange 20.00 7.00
Never hinged 60.00
115 A16 35o yel & blk ('19) 7.50 7.25
Never hinged 12.00
116 A16 40o vio & blk ('18) 15.00 4.50
Never hinged 60.00
117 A16 40o gray bl & blk ('20) 32.50 8.50
Never hinged 95.00
118 A16 40o dk blue ('22) 4.50 1.60
Never hinged 8.50
119 A16 40o orange ('25) 1.50 2.00
Never hinged 3.00
120 A16 50o claret 32.50 5.75
Never hinged 90.00
121 A16 50o claret & blk ('19) 57.50 2.00
Never hinged 160.00
122 A16 50o lt gray ('22) 7.75 .50
Never hinged 30.00
a. 50o olive gray ('21) 65.00 7.75
Never hinged 175.00
123 A16 60o brn & bl ('19) 52.50 6.50
Never hinged 180.00
a. 60o brown & ultra ('19) 190.00 19.00
Never hinged 650.00
124 A16 60o grn bl ('21) 8.00 1.00
Never hinged 30.00
125 A16 70o brn & grn ('20) 20.00 4.50
Never hinged 72.50
126 A16 80o bl grn ('15) 40.00 20.00
Never hinged 90.00
127 A16 90o brn & red ('20) 15.00 5.25
Never hinged 32.50
128 A16 1k brn & bl ('22) 45.00 2.50
Never hinged 90.00
129 A16 2k gray & cl ('25) 57.50 26.00
Never hinged 110.00
130 A16 5k vio & brn ('27) 5.25 7.75
Never hinged 7.50
131 A16 10k ver & yel grn ('28) 250.00 55.00
Never hinged 775.00
Nos. 97-131 (35) 868.10 271.65
Set, never hinged 2,350.

No. 97 surcharged "2 ORE" is Faroe Islands No. 1. Two of the 14 printings of No. 97a have no P# in the selvage. These sell for more.

Nos. 87 and 98, 89 and 94, 89 and 104, 90 and 95, 97 and 103, 100 and 102 exist se-tenant in coils for use in vending machines.

For surcharges and overprints see Nos. 161-162, 176-177, 182-184, J2-J8, M1-M2, Q3-Q10.

1913-20 Engr.
132 A17 1k yellow brown 77.50 1.25
Never hinged 325.00
133 A17 2k gray 110.00 7.00
Never hinged 450.00

134 A17 5k purple ('20) 13.00 10.00
Never hinged 32.50
Nos. 132-134 (3) 200.50 18.25
Set, never hinged 807.50

For overprint see No, Q11.

G.P.O. Type of 1912
Perf. 14x14½
1915 Wmk. 114 Engr.
135 A15 5k dark red ('15) 425.00 175.00
Never hinged 1,300.

Nos. 46 and O10 Surcharged in Black type "c" and

e

1915 Wmk. 112 Typo. Perf. 13
136 A6 (c) 80o on 12o 42.50 125.00
Never hinged 65.00
a. Inverted frame 525.00 975.00
Never hinged 725.00
137 O1 (e) 80o on 8o 32.50 140.00
Never hinged 75.00
a. "POSTERIM" 52.50 275.00
Never hinged 97.50
Set, never hinged 140.00

Newspaper Stamps Surcharged

On Issue of 1907
1918 Wmk. 113 Perf. 13
138 N1 27o on 1o olive 90.00 250.00
Never hinged 180.00
139 N1 27o on 5o blue 90.00 250.00
Never hinged 180.00
140 N1 27o on 7o car 90.00 250.00
Never hinged 180.00
141 N1 27o on 10o dp lil 90.00 250.00
Never hinged 180.00
142 N1 27o on 68o yel brn 7.00 35.00
Never hinged 10.50
143 N1 27o on 5k rose & yel grn 5.75 22.50
Never hinged 9.50
144 N1 27o on 10k bis & bl 7.00 30.00
Never hinged 12.00
Nos. 138-144 (7) 379.75 1,087.
Set, never hinged 750.00

On Issue of 1914-15
Wmk. Multiple Crosses (114)
Perf. 14x14½
145 N1 27o on 1o ol gray 3.25 14.50
Never hinged 4.75
146 N1 27o on 5o blue 8.00 26.00
Never hinged 12.00
147 N1 27o on 7o rose 3.25 9.75
Never hinged 4.75
148 N1 27o on 8o green 5.00 15.50
Never hinged 4.75
149 N1 27o on 10o dp lil 3.25 12.00
Never hinged 4.75
150 N1 27o on 20o green 4.50 13.00
Never hinged 8.50
151 N1 27o on 29o org yel 3.25 12.00
Never hinged 4.75
152 N1 27o on 38o orange 32.50 97.50
Never hinged 45.00
153 N1 27o on 41o yel brn 8.00 50.00
Never hinged 12.00
154 N1 27o on 1k bl grn & mar 3.25 13.00
Never hinged 4.75
Nos. 145-154 (10) 74.25 263.25
Set, never hinged 110.00

Kronborg
Castle — A20

Sonderborg
Castle — A21

Roskilde
Cathedral — A22

Perf. 14½x14, 14x14½
1920, Oct. 5 Typo.
156 A20 10o red 3.75 .35
Never hinged 7.50

157 A21 20o slate 3.00 .50
Never hinged 6.00
158 A22 40o dark brown 12.50 4.50
Never hinged 21.00
Nos. 156-158 (3) 19.25 5.35
Set, never hinged 40.00

Reunion of Northern Schleswig with Denmark.
See Nos. 159-160. For surcharges see Nos. B1-B2.

1921
159 A20 10o green 7.75 .50
Never hinged 19.00
160 A22 40o dark blue 57.50 13.00
Never hinged 135.00
Set, never hinged 155.00

Stamps of 1918
Surcharged in Blue

1921-22
161 A16 8o on 7o org ('22) 2.00 5.00
Never hinged 6.50
162 A16 8o on 12o gray grn 2.00 15.00
Never hinged 7.00
Set, never hinged 13.50

No. 87 Surcharged

1921
163 A10 8o on 3o gray 3.75 5.25
Never hinged 7.50

Christian X
A23

Christian IV
A24

A25

A26

1924, Dec. 1 Perf. 14x14½
164 A23 10o green 7.00 7.75
Never hinged 14.00
165 A24 10o green 7.00 7.75
Never hinged 14.00
166 A25 10o green 7.00 7.75
Never hinged 14.00
167 A26 10o green 7.00 7.75
Never hinged 14.00
a. Block of 4, #164-167 37.50 60.00
Never hinged 75.00
168 A23 15o violet 7.00 7.75
Never hinged 14.00
169 A24 15o violet 7.00 7.75
Never hinged 14.00
170 A25 15o violet 7.00 7.75
Never hinged 14.00
171 A26 15o violet 7.00 7.75
Never hinged 14.00
a. Block of 4, #168-171 37.50 60.00
Never hinged 75.00
172 A23 20o dark brown 7.00 7.75
Never hinged 14.00
173 A24 20o dark brown 7.00 7.75
Never hinged 14.00
174 A25 20o dark brown 7.00 7.75
Never hinged 14.00
175 A26 20o dark brown 7.00 7.75
Never hinged 14.00
a. Block of 4, #172-175 37.50 60.00
Never hinged 75.00
Nos. 164-175 (12) 84.00 93.00
Set, never hinged 168.00
#167a, 171a, 175a, never hinged 225.00

300th anniv. of the Danish postal service.

Stamps of 1921-22 Surcharged

k l

1926

176	A16 (k) 20o on 30o org	4.75	*16.00*
	Never hinged	9.50	
177	A16 (l) 20o on 40o dk bl	7.50	*18.00*
		15.00	
	Set, never hinged	22.50	

A27

A28

1926, Mar. 11　　　Perf. 14x14½

178	A27 10o dull green	1.10	.45
	Never hinged	2.25	
179	A28 20o dark red	1.50	.45
	Never hinged	3.00	
180	A28 30o dark blue	7.00	2.00
	Never hinged	14.00	
	Nos. 178-180 (3)	9.60	2.90
	Set, never hinged	19.00	

75th anniv. of the introduction of postage stamps in Denmark.

Stamps of 1913-26 Surcharged in Blue or Black

No. 181

Nos. 182-184

1926-27　　　Perf. 14x14½

181	A10 7o on 8o gray (Bl)	1.40	*5.75*
	Never hinged	3.00	
182	A16 7o on 27o ver & blk	4.25	*15.00*
	Never hinged	8.50	
183	A16 7o on 20o red ('27)	.65	*2.00*
	Never hinged	1.20	
184	A16 12o on 15o violet	2.75	*7.75*
	Never hinged	4.25	

Surcharged on Official Stamps of 1914-23

185	O1 (e) 7o on 1o org	4.00	*16.00*
	Never hinged	6.00	
186	O1 (e) 7o on 3o gray	7.75	*29.00*
	Never hinged	12.00	
187	O1 (e) 7o on 4o blue	3.25	*14.00*
	Never hinged	5.00	
188	O1 (e) 7o on 5o grn	52.50	*125.00*
	Never hinged	90.00	
189	O1 (e) 7o on 10o grn	4.00	*15.50*
	Never hinged	6.50	
190	O1 (e) 7o on 15o vio	4.00	*15.50*
	Never hinged	6.50	
191	O1 (e) 7o on 20o ind	19.00	*77.50*
	Never hinged	30.00	
a.	Double surcharge	650.00	*850.00*
		725.00	
	Nos. 181-191 (11)	103.55	*323.00*
	Set, never hinged	155.00	

Caravel
A30

Christian X
A31

1927　　　Typo.　　　Perf. 14x14½

192	A30 15o red	5.75	.30
	Never hinged	12.00	
193	A30 20o gray	10.50	2.25
	Never hinged	24.00	
194	A30 25o light blue	1.10	.40
	Never hinged	2.40	
195	A30 30o ocher	1.25	.40
	Never hinged	3.00	
196	A30 35o red brown	20.00	1.50
	Never hinged	55.00	
197	A30 40o yel green	19.00	.40
	Never hinged	47.50	
	Nos. 192-197 (6)	57.60	5.25
	Set, never hinged	170.00	

See Nos. 232-238J. For surcharges & overprints see Nos. 244-245, 269-272, Q12-Q14, Q19-Q25.

1930, Sept. 26

210	A31 5o apple grn	2.25	.25
	Never hinged	3.75	
a.	Booklet pane, 4 + 2 labels	18.00	
211	A31 7o violet	6.50	4.00
	Never hinged	16.00	
212	A31 8o dk gray	22.50	32.50
	Never hinged	67.50	
213	A31 10o yel brn	4.25	.25
	Never hinged	7.00	
a.	Booklet pane, 4 + 2 labels	29.00	
214	A31 15o red	9.50	.25
	Never hinged	40.00	

215	A31 20o lt gray	25.00	9.75
	Never hinged	57.50	
216	A31 25o lt blue	8.25	1.25
	Never hinged	20.00	
217	A31 30o yel buff	8.75	1.75
	Never hinged	21.00	
218	A31 35o red brown	11.00	4.50
	Never hinged	25.00	
219	A31 40o dp green	9.50	1.25
	Never hinged	25.00	
	Nos. 210-219 (10)	107.50	55.75
	Set, never hinged	280.00	

60th birthday of King Christian X.

Wavy Lines and Numeral of Value — A32

Type A10 Redrawn

1933-40　Unwmk.　Engr.　Perf. 13

220	A32 1o gray blk	.25	.25
	Never hinged	.20	
221	A32 2o scarlet	.25	.25
	Never hinged	.20	
222	A32 4o blue	.30	.25
	Never hinged	.50	
223	A32 5o yel grn	1.00	.25
	Never hinged	1.75	
a.	5o gray green	32.50	65.00
	Never hinged	42.50	
b.	Tête bêche gutter pair	8.00	15.50
	Never hinged	24.00	
c.	Booklet pane of 4	11.00	
d.	Bklt. pane, 1 #223a, 3 #B6	37.50	
e.	As "b," without gutter	13.00	26.00
	Never hinged	17.50	
224	A32 5o rose lake ('38)	.25	.25
	Never hinged	.20	
a.	Booklet pane of 4	.40	
b.	Booklet pane of 10	.90	
224C	A32 6o orange ('40)	.30	.25
		.35	
225	A32 7o violet	2.00	.50
	Never hinged	2.40	
226	A32 7o yel grn ('38)	1.10	.75
	Never hinged	1.40	
226A	A32 7o lt brown ('40)	.25	.50
		.35	
227	A32 8o gray	.45	.50
		.60	
227A	A32 8o yellow grn ('40)	.25	.50
	Never hinged	.35	
228	A32 10o yellow org	10.00	.25
	Never hinged	18.00	
a.	Tête bêche gutter pair	35.00	52.50
	Never hinged	95.00	
b.	Booklet pane of 4	110.00	
c.	As "a," without gutter	40.00	65.00
	Never hinged	100.00	
229	A32 10o lt brown ('37)	9.50	.50
	Never hinged	24.00	
a.	Booklet pane of 4	100.00	
b.	Booklet pane of 4, 1 #229, 3 #B7	32.50	
230	A32 10o violet ('38)	.60	.25
	Never hinged	1.20	
a.	Booklet pane of 4	2.75	
b.	Bklt. pane, 2 #230, 2 #B10	4.50	
	Nos. 220-230 (14)	26.50	5.25
	Set, never hinged	50.00	

Design A10 was typographed. They had a solid background with groups of small hearts below the heraldic lions in the upper corners and below "DA" and "RK" of "DANMARK." The numerals of value were enclosed in single-lined ovals.

Design A32 is line-engraved and has a background of crossed lines. The hearts have been removed and the numerals of value are now in double-lined ovals. Two types exist of some values.

The 1o, No. 220, was issued on fluorescent paper in 1969.

No. 230 with wide margins is from booklet pane No. 230b.

Surcharges of 20, 50 & 60öre on #220, 224 and 224C are listed as Faroe Islands #2-3, 5-6.

See Nos. 318, 333, 382, 416, 437-437A, 493-498, 629, 631, 688-695, 793-795, 883-886, 1111-1113, 1116, 1295B. For overprints and surcharges see Nos. 257, 263, 267-268, 355-356, Q15-Q17, Q31, Q43. Post 1940 issues in Scott Standard catalogue, Vol. 2.

Certain Tête-Bêche pairs of 1938-55 issues which reached the market in 1971, and were not regularly issued, are not listed. This group comprises 24 different major-number vertical pairs of types A32, A47, A61 and SP3 (13 with gutters, 11 without), and pairs of some minor numbers and shades. They were removed from booklet pane sheets.

Type of 1927 Issue

Type I

Type I — Two columns of squares between sail and left frame line.

1933-34　　　Engr.　　　Perf. 13

232	A30 20o gray	13.50	.50
	Never hinged	24.00	
233	A30 25o blue	77.50	29.00
	Never hinged	180.00	
234	A30 25o brown ('34)	20.00	.25
	Never hinged	47.50	
235	A30 30o orange yel	1.25	1.60
	Never hinged	2.40	
236	A30 30o blue ('34)	1.00	.50
	Never hinged	1.90	
237	A30 35o violet	.50	.50
	Never hinged	.70	
238	A30 40o yellow grn	5.00	.25
	Never hinged	8.50	
	Nos. 232-238 (7)	118.75	32.60
	Set, never hinged	265.00	

Type II

Type II — One column of squares between sail and left frame line.

1933-40

238A	A30 15o deep red	2.50	.50
	Never hinged	4.75	
k.	Booklet pane of 4	26.00	
l.	Bklt. pane, 1 #238A, 3 #B8	42.50	
238B	A30 15o yel red ('40)	7.75	.25
	Never hinged	9.50	
238C	A30 20o gray blk ('39)	4.50	.65
	Never hinged	8.50	
238D	A30 20o red ('40)	.50	.25
	Never hinged	.95	
238E	A30 25o dp brown ('39)	.80	.50
	Never hinged	1.20	
238F	A30 30o blue ('39)	2.00	.65
	Never hinged	4.25	
238G	A30 30o orange ('40)	.50	.50
	Never hinged	.75	
238H	A30 35o violet ('40)	.90	.75
	Never hinged	1.80	
238I	A30 40o yel grn ('39)	13.00	.50
	Never hinged	30.00	
238J	A30 40o blue ('40)	1.00	.25
	Never hinged	1.40	
	Nos. 238A-238J (10)	33.45	4.80
	Set, never hinged	62.50	

Nos. 232-238J, engraved, have crosshatched background. Nos. 192-197, typographed, have solid background.

For No. 238A surcharged 20 ore see Denmark No. 271, Faroe Islands No. 4.

See note on surcharges and overprints following No. 197.

King Christian X — A33

1934-41　　　Perf. 13

239	A33 50o gray	1.00	.25
	Never hinged	2.40	
240	A33 60o blue grn	2.10	.50
	Never hinged	6.50	
240A	A33 75o dk blue ('41)	.45	.50
	Never hinged	.60	
241	A33 1k lt brown	3.25	.25
	Never hinged	10.50	
242	A33 2k dull red	6.00	1.00
	Never hinged	12.50	
243	A33 5k violet	8.00	3.25
	Never hinged	27.50	
	Nos. 239-243 (6)	20.80	5.75
	Set, never hinged	60.00	

For overprints see Nos. Q26-Q27.

Nos. 233, 235 Surcharged in Black

1934, June 9

244	A30 4o on 25o blue	.50	.50
	Never hinged	.95	
245	A30 10o on 30o org yel	2.00	3.25
	Never hinged	4.75	
	Set, never hinged	6.25	

"The Ugly Duckling"
A34

Andersen
A35

"The Little Mermaid" — A36

1935, Oct. 1　　　Perf. 13

246	A34 5o lt green	4.00	.25
	Never hinged	9.00	
a.	Tête bêche gutter pair	10.00	*15.00*
		36.00	
b.	Booklet pane of 4	40.00	
c.	As "a," without gutter	15.00	*20.00*
	Never hinged	45.00	
247	A35 7o dull vio	2.50	*4.00*
		6.50	
248	A36 10o orange	6.50	.25
		16.00	
a.	Tête bêche gutter pair	13.00	*29.00*
		48.00	
b.	Booklet pane of 4	65.00	
c.	As "a," without gutter	20.00	*40.00*
	Never hinged	65.00	
249	A35 15o red	16.00	.25
		42.50	
a.	Tête bêche gutter pair	32.50	*45.00*
		95.00	
b.	Booklet pane of 4	160.00	
c.	As "a," without gutter	40.00	*65.00*
		110.00	
250	A35 20o gray	16.00	1.25
		45.00	
251	A35 30o dl bl	2.50	.50
		5.00	
	Nos. 246-251 (6)	47.50	*6.50*
	Set, never hinged	124.00	

Centenary of the publication of the earliest installment of Hans Christian Andersen's "Fairy Tales."

Nikolai Church
A37

Hans Tausen
A38

Ribe Cathedral — A39

1936　　　Perf. 13

252	A37 5o green	1.10	.25
	Never hinged	3.25	
a.	Booklet pane of 4	21.00	
253	A37 7o violet	1.25	*5.25*
	Never hinged	2.50	
254	A38 10o lt brown	1.60	.25
	Never hinged	4.75	
a.	Booklet pane of 4	25.00	
255	A38 15o dull rose	2.50	.25
	Never hinged	7.00	
256	A39 30o blue	16.00	1.25
	Never hinged	42.50	
	Nos. 252-256 (5)	22.45	7.25
	Set, never hinged	60.00	

Church Reformation in Denmark, 400th anniv.

No. 229 Overprinted in Blue

1937, Sept. 17

257	A32 10o lt brown	1.40	*2.50*
	Never hinged	2.00	

Jubilee Exhib. held by the Copenhagen Phil. Club on their 50th anniv. The stamps were on sale at the Exhib. only, each holder of a ticket of admission (1k) being entitled to purchase 20 stamps at face value; of a season ticket (5k), 100 stamps.

| Yacht and Summer Palace, Marselisborg A40 | Christian X in Streets of Copenhagen A41 |

Equestrian Statue of Frederik V and Amalienborg Palace — A42

1937, May 15 *Perf. 13*
258	A40	5o green	1.10	.25
		Never hinged	2.50	
a.		Booklet pane of 4	15.00	
259	A41	10o brown	1.10	.25
		Never hinged	2.50	
a.		Booklet pane of 4	15.00	
260	A42	15o scarlet	1.10	.25
		Never hinged	2.50	
a.		Booklet pane of 4	17.00	
261	A41	30o blue	19.00	2.75
		Never hinged	42.50	
		Nos. 258-261 (4)	22.30	3.50
		Set, never hinged	50.00	

25th anniv. of the accession to the throne of King Christian X.

Emancipation Column, Copenhagen — A43

1938, June 20 *Perf. 13*
262	A43	15o scarlet	.50	.50
		Never hinged	1.25	

Abolition of serfdom in Denmark, 150th anniv.

No. 223 Overprinted in Red on Alternate Stamps

1938, Sept. 2
263	A32	5o yellow grn, pair	3.25	13.00
		Never hinged	5.25	

10th Danish Philatelic Exhibition.

| Bertel Thorvaldsen A44 | Statue of Jason A45 |

1938, Nov. 17 *Engr.* *Perf. 13*
264	A44	5o rose lake	.35	.35
		Never hinged	.60	
265	A45	10o purple	.50	.25
		Never hinged	.90	
266	A44	30o dark blue	1.40	.50
		Never hinged	3.00	
		Nos. 264-266 (3)	2.25	1.10
		Set, never hinged	5.25	

The return to Denmark in 1838 of Bertel Thorvaldsen, Danish sculptor.

Stamps of 1933-39 Surcharged with New Values in Black

a

b

c

1940
267	A32 (a)	6o on 7o yel grn	.30	.50
			.40	
268	A32 (a)	6o on 8o gray	.30	.50
			.40	
269	A30 (b)	15o on 40o #238	.90	5.25
			2.00	
270	A30 (b)	15o on 40o #238I	.90	1.60
			1.60	
271	A30 (c)	20o on 15o dp red	1.10	.25
			1.60	
272	A30 (b)	40o on 30o #238F	.90	.25
			1.60	
		Nos. 267-272 (6)	4.40	8.35
		Set, never hinged	8.00	

SEMI-POSTAL STAMPS

Nos. 159, 157 Surcharged in Red

Wmk. Multiple Crosses (114)
1921, June 17 *Perf. 14½x14*
B1	A20	10o + 5o green	15.00	65.00
		Never hinged	40.00	
		On cover		85.00
B2	A21	20o + 10o slate	19.00	77.50
		Never hinged	57.50	
		On cover		85.00
		Set, never hinged	97.50	

| Crown and Staff of Aesculapius SP1 | Dybbol Mill SP2 |

1929, Aug. 1 *Engr.*
B3	SP1	10o yellow green	4.25	7.75
		Never hinged	7.25	
		On cover		13.00
a.		Booklet pane of 2	27.50	
B4	SP1	15o brick red	6.25	15.00
		Never hinged	15.00	
		On cover		16.00
a.		Booklet pane of 2	32.50	
B5	SP1	25o deep blue	26.50	57.50
		Never hinged	52.50	
		On cover		65.00
a.		Booklet pane of 2	135.00	
		Nos. B3-B5 (3)	37.00	80.25
		Set, never hinged	75.00	

These stamps were sold at a premium of 5 öre each for benefit of the Danish Cancer Committee.

1937, Jan. 20 *Unwmk.* *Perf. 13*
B6	SP2	5o + 5o green	.55	1.25
		Never hinged	1.25	
B7	SP2	10o + 5o lt brown	3.25	9.00
		Never hinged	6.50	
B8	SP2	15o + 5o carmine	3.25	9.00
		Never hinged	6.50	
		Nos. B6-B8 (3)	7.05	19.25
		Set, never hinged	14.00	

The surtax was for a fund in memory of H. P. Hanssen, statesman.

Nos. 223 and B6, Nos. 229 and B7, Nos. 238A and B8 are found se-tenant in booklets. For booklet panes, see Nos. 223d, 229b and 238AI.

Queen Alexandrine — SP3

1939-40 *Perf. 13*
B9	SP3	5o + 3o rose lake & red ('40)	.25	.25
		Never hinged	.40	
a.		Booklet pane of 4	2.00	2.00
B10	SP3	10o + 5o dk violet & red	.25	.25
		Never hinged	.50	
B11	SP3	15o + 5o scarlet & red	.30	.75
		Never hinged	.75	
		Nos. B9-B11 (3)	.80	1.25
		Set, never hinged	1.65	

The surtax was for the Danish Red Cross. Nos. 230 and B10 have been issued se-tenant in booklets. See No. 230b. In this pane No. 230 measures 23½x31mm from perf. to perf.

AIR POST STAMPS

| Airplane and Plowman AP1 | Towers of Copenhagen AP2 |

Wmk. Multiple Crosses (114)
1925-29 *Typo.* *Perf. 12x12½*
C1	AP1	10o yellow green	26.00	45.00
		Never hinged	65.00	
C2	AP1	15o violet ('26)	52.50	90.00
		Never hinged	130.00	
C3	AP1	25o scarlet	40.00	72.50
		Never hinged	90.00	
C4	AP1	50o lt gray ('29)	100.00	300.00
		Never hinged	275.00	
C5	AP1	1k choc ('29)	90.00	275.00
		Never hinged	225.00	
		Nos. C1-C5 (5)	308.50	782.50
		Set, never hinged	785.00	

Unwmk.
1934, June 9 *Engr.* *Perf. 13*
C6	AP2	10o orange	.70	1.40
		Never hinged	1.25	
C7	AP2	15o red	3.25	6.50
		Never hinged	6.50	
C8	AP2	20o Prus blue	3.25	6.50
		Never hinged	6.50	
C9	AP2	50o olive black	3.25	6.50
		Never hinged	6.50	
C10	AP2	1k brown	16.00	26.00
		Never hinged	24.00	
		Nos. C6-C10 (5)	26.45	46.90
		Set, never hinged	47.00	

LATE FEE STAMPS

| LF1 | Coat of Arms — LF2 |

Perf. 14x14½
1923 *Typo.* *Wmk. 114*
I1	LF1	10o green	13.00	5.25
		Never hinged	40.00	
a.		Double overprint	2,600.	

No. I1 was, at first, not a postage stamp but represented a tax for the services of the post office clerks in filling out postal forms and writing addresses. In 1923 it was put into use as a Late Fee stamp.

1926-31
I2	LF2	10o green	9.00	1.25
		Never hinged	26.00	

I3	LF2	10o brown ('31)	8.25	.50
		Never hinged	20.00	
		Set, never hinged	45.00	

1934 *Unwmk.* *Engr.* *Perf. 13*
I4	LF2	5o green	.25	.25
		Never hinged	.35	
I5	LF2	10o orange	.25	.25
		Never hinged	.20	
		Set, never hinged	1.00	

POSTAGE DUE STAMPS

Regular Issues of 1913-20 Overprinted

Perf. 14x14½
1921, May 1 *Wmk. 114*
J1	A10	1o deep orange	2.00	5.25
		Never hinged	6.00	
J2	A16	5o green	5.25	5.25
		Never hinged	16.00	
J3	A16	7o orange	4.00	6.50
		Never hinged	9.50	
J4	A16	10o red	26.00	16.00
		Never hinged	65.00	
J5	A16	20o deep blue	19.00	11.50
		Never hinged	52.50	
J6	A16	25o brown & blk	26.00	7.75
		Never hinged	85.00	
J7	A16	50o claret & blk	10.00	6.50
		Never hinged	26.00	
		Nos. J1-J7 (7)	92.25	58.75
		Set, never hinged	260.00	

Same Overprint in Dark Blue On Military Stamp of 1917
1921, Nov. 23
J8	A16	10o red	10.00	16.00
		Never hinged	35.00	
a.		"S" inverted	160.00	210.00
		Never hinged	300.00	

Numeral of Value — D1

Typographed (Solid Panel)
1921-30 *Perf. 14x14½*
J9	D1	1o orange ('22)	1.25	2.50
		Never hinged	4.00	
J10	D1	4o blue ('25)	2.50	3.25
		Never hinged	7.00	
J11	D1	5o brown ('22)	2.75	2.50
		Never hinged	7.00	
J12	D1	5o lt green ('30)	2.50	2.50
		Never hinged	6.50	
J13	D1	7o apple grn ('27)	15.00	26.00
		Never hinged	45.00	
J14	D1	7o dk violet ('30)	40.00	52.50
		Never hinged	97.50	
J15	D1	10o yellow grn ('22)	3.25	2.50
		Never hinged	10.00	
J16	D1	10o lt brown ('30)	1.90	2.50
		Never hinged	5.75	
J17	D1	20o grnsh blue ('21)	1.60	2.50
		Never hinged	5.25	
a.		Double impression	2,500.	
J18	D1	20o gray ('30)	3.25	4.50
		Never hinged	8.50	
J19	D1	25o scarlet ('23)	4.00	5.25
		Never hinged	17.00	
J20	D1	25o violet ('26)	3.25	5.25
		Never hinged	9.00	
J21	D1	25o lt blue ('30)	5.25	7.75
		Never hinged	14.00	
J22	D1	1k dk blue ('21)	77.50	15.00
		Never hinged	220.00	
J23	D1	1k brn & dk bl ('25)	9.00	13.00
		Never hinged	26.00	
J24	D1	5k purple ('25)	20.00	13.00
		Never hinged	52.50	
		Nos. J9-J24 (16)	193.00	160.50
		Set, never hinged	535.00	

Engraved (Lined Panel)
1934-55 *Unwmk.* *Perf. 13*
J25	D1	1o slate	.25	.25
		Never hinged	.35	
J26	D1	2o carmine	.25	.50
		Never hinged	.35	
J27	D1	5o yellow green	.25	.50
		Never hinged	.40	
J28	D1	6o dk olive ('41)	.40	.65
		Never hinged	.90	
J29	D1	8o magenta ('50)	2.00	4.00
		Never hinged	3.25	
J30	D1	10o orange	.25	.25
		Never hinged	.40	
J31	D1	12o dp ultra ('55)	.40	1.25
		Never hinged	.90	
J32	D1	15o lt violet ('54)	.50	.65
		Never hinged	.90	

J33	D1	20o gray	.35	.25
		Never hinged	.60	
J34	D1	25o blue	.50	.65
		Never hinged	.65	
J35	D1	30o green ('53)	.50	.65
		Never hinged	.65	
J36	D1	40o claret ('49)	.50	.65
		Never hinged	1.00	
J37	D1	1k brown	.50	.65
		Never hinged	1.00	
		Nos. J25-J37 (13)	6.65	10.90
		Set, never hinged	11.00	

No. 96 Surcharged in Black

1934 Wmk. 114 Perf. 14x14½

J38	A10	15o on 12o violet	5.25	6.50
		Never hinged	19.00	

MILITARY STAMPS

Nos. 97 and 100 Overprinted in Blue

1917 Wmk. 114 Perf. 14x14½

M1	A16	5o green	16.00	52.50
		Never hinged	37.50	
a.		"S" inverted	250.00	350.00
		Never hinged	450.00	
M2	A16	10o red	16.00	26.00
		Never hinged	42.50	
a.		"S" inverted	250.00	400.00
		Never hinged	400.00	
		Set, never hinged	75.00	
		#M1a, M2a, never hinged	850.00	

The letters "S F" are the initials of "Soldater Frimaerke" (Soldier's Stamp).
For overprint see No. J8.

OFFICIAL STAMPS

Small State Seal — O1

Wmk. Crown (112)
1871 Typo. Perf. 14x13½

O1	O1	2s blue	190.00	160.00
		Never hinged	650.00	
		On cover		180.00
a.		2s ultra	190.00	160.00
		Never hinged	650.00	
		On cover		180.00
b.		Imperf	400.00	
		As "b," pair	1,050.	
O2	O1	4s carmine	77.50	32.50
		Never hinged	250.00	
		On cover		30.00
a.		Imperf	400.00	
		As "a," pair	1,100.	
O3	O1	16s green	450.00	325.00
		Never hinged	1,200.	
		On cover		1,750.
a.		Imperf	450.00	
		As "a," pair	1,250.	

Perf. 12½

O4	O1	4s carmine	5,750.	575.00
		On cover		600.00
O5	O1	16s green	400.00	550.00
		Never hinged	1,000.	
		On cover		1,900.
		#O1-O3, O5, never hinged	3,200.	

Nos. O4-O5 values are for stamps with defective perfs.
Nos. O1-O3 were reprinted in 1886 upon white wove paper, unwatermarked and imperforate. Value $10 each.

1875 Perf. 14x13½

O6	O1	3o violet	13.00	40.00
		Never hinged	50.00	
		On cover		120.00
O7	O1	4o grnsh blue	12.00	9.00
		Never hinged	40.00	
		On cover		18.00
O8	O1	8o carmine	12.00	2.50
		Never hinged	40.00	
		On cover		9.00
a.		Imperf	—	

O9	O1	32o green	29.00	32.50
		Never hinged	70.00	
		On cover		180.00
		Nos. O6-O9 (4)	66.00	84.00
		Set, never hinged	200.00	

For surcharge see No. 81.

1899-02 Perf. 13

O9A	O1	3o red lilac ('02)	4.00	13.00
		Never hinged	10.00	
		On cover		30.00
c.		Imperf	350.00	
		As "c," pair	950.00	
O9B	O1	4o blue	3.25	4.00
		Never hinged	10.00	
		On cover		15.00
O10	O1	8o carmine	20.00	26.00
		Never hinged	65.00	
		On cover		72.50
		Nos. O9A-O10 (3)	27.25	43.00
		Set, never hinged	85.00	

For surcharge see No. 137.

1902-06 Wmk. 113

O11	O1	1o orange	1.75	4.00
		Never hinged	4.00	
		On cover		15.00
O12	O1	3o red lilac ('06)	1.25	1.60
		Never hinged	4.00	
		On cover		15.00
O13	O1	4o blue ('03)	2.50	5.75
		Never hinged	6.50	
		On cover		24.00
O14	O1	5o green	2.50	.65
		Never hinged	6.50	
		On cover		8.50
O15	O1	10o carmine	4.00	2.50
		Never hinged	9.00	
		On cover		14.50
		Nos. O11-O15 (5)	12.00	14.50
		Set, never hinged	30.00	

1914-23 Wmk. 114 Perf. 14x14½

O16	O1	1o orange	1.40	2.50
		Never hinged	2.50	
		On cover		20.00
O17	O1	3o gray ('18)	4.00	17.00
		Never hinged	10.00	
		On cover		65.00
O18	O1	4o blue ('16)	30.00	65.00
		Never hinged	57.50	
		On cover		125.00
O19	O1	5o green ('15)	2.50	1.90
		Never hinged	6.50	
		On cover		10.00
O20	O1	5o choc ('23)	5.25	26.00
		Never hinged	13.00	
		Postally used		17.00
		On cover		
O21	O1	10o red ('17)	13.00	7.00
		Never hinged	32.50	
		On cover		25.00
O22	O1	10o green ('21)	4.50	7.75
		Never hinged	13.00	
		On cover		25.00
O23	O1	15o violet ('19)	14.00	40.00
		Never hinged	32.50	
		On cover		100.00
O24	O1	20o indigo ('20)	20.00	17.00
		Never hinged	52.50	
		On cover		57.50
		Nos. O16-O24 (9)	94.65	184.15
		Set, never hinged	220.00	

For surcharges see Nos. 185-191.
No. O20 is valued CTO.
Official stamps were discontinued Apr. 1, 1924.

NEWSPAPER STAMPS

Postal documents as listed below were official Post Office forms supplied to publishers. Newspaper stamps were affixed to the forms to pay postage for the delivery of bundles of papers.

Numeral of Value — N1

1907 Typo. Wmk. 113 Perf. 13

P1	N1	1o olive	13.00	4.00
		Never hinged	40.00	
		On postal document		325.00
P2	N1	5o blue	26.00	13.00
		Never hinged	95.00	
		On postal document		325.00
P3	N1	7o carmine	15.00	2.50
		Never hinged	55.00	
		On postal document		250.00
P4	N1	10o deep lilac	45.00	4.50
		Never hinged	145.00	
		On postal document		325.00
P5	N1	20o green	40.00	2.50
		Never hinged	130.00	
		On postal document		325.00
P6	N1	38o orange	45.00	2.00
		Never hinged	160.00	
		On postal document		400.00
P7	N1	68o yellow brown	110.00	40.00
		Never hinged	400.00	
		On postal document		450.00

P8	N1	1k bl grn & claret	32.50	4.50
		Never hinged	130.00	
		On postal document		325.00
P9	N1	5k rose & yel grn	190.00	45.00
		Never hinged	725.00	
		On postal document		525.00
P10	N1	10k bister & blue	190.00	45.00
		Never hinged	725.00	
		On postal document		525.00
		Nos. P1-P10 (10)	706.50	163.00
		Set, never hinged	2,650.	

For surcharges see Nos. 138-144.

1914-15 Wmk. 114 Perf. 14x14½

P11	N1	1o olive gray	15.00	3.25
		Never hinged	80.00	
		On postal document		325.00
P12	N1	5o blue	40.00	13.00
		Never hinged	145.00	
		On postal document		325.00
P13	N1	7o rose	40.00	4.50
		Never hinged	145.00	
		On postal document		275.00
P14	N1	8o green ('15)	40.00	4.50
		Never hinged	145.00	
		On postal document		325.00
P15	N1	10o deep lilac	65.00	4.50
		Never hinged	260.00	
		On postal document		325.00
P16	N1	20o green	260.00	5.25
		Never hinged	725.00	
		On postal document		325.00
a.		Imperf., pair	1,100.	
P17	N1	29o orange yel ('15)	65.00	5.75
		Never hinged	315.00	
		On postal document		325.00
P18	N1	38o orange	2,000.	175.00
		Never hinged	3,250.	
		On postal document		—
P19	N1	41o yellow brn ('15)	85.00	4.50
		Never hinged	400.00	
		On postal document		325.00
P20	N1	1k blue grn & mar	110.00	5.25
		Never hinged	600.00	
		On postal document		275.00
		Nos. P11-P17,P19-P20 (9)	720.00	50.50
		Set, never hinged	2,825.	

For surcharges see Nos. 145-154.

PARCEL POST STAMPS

These stamps were for use on postal packets sent by the Esbjerg-Fano Ferry Service.

Regular Issues of 1913-30 Overprinted

1919-41 Wmk. 114 Perf. 14x14½

Q1	A10	10o green ('22)	20.00	20.00
		Never hinged	65.00	
Q2	A10	10o bister brn ('30)	24.00	13.00
		Never hinged	72.50	
Q3	A16	10o red	45.00	90.00
		Never hinged	110.00	
a.		"POSFFAERGE"	200.00	450.00
		Never hinged	400.00	
Q4	A16	15o violet	20.00	40.00
		Never hinged	52.50	
a.		"POSFFAERGE"	240.00	525.00
		Never hinged	450.00	
Q5	A16	30o orange ('22)	20.00	40.00
		Never hinged	52.50	
Q6	A16	30o dk blue ('26)	4.00	7.00
		Never hinged	7.75	
Q7	A16	50o cl & blk ('20)	260.00	325.00
		Never hinged	525.00	
Q8	A16	50o lt gray ('22)	26.00	26.00
		Never hinged	77.50	
a.		50o olive gray ('22)	200.00	400.00
		Never hinged	525.00	
Q9	A16	1k brn & bl ('24)	52.50	26.00
		Never hinged	200.00	
Q9A	A16	5k vio & brn ('41)	1.75	2.75
		Never hinged	3.25	
Q10	A16	10k ver & grn ('30)	72.50	110.00
		Never hinged	110.00	

Engr.

Q11	A17	1k yellow brn	100.00	190.00
		Never hinged	260.00	
a.		"POSFFAERGE"	1,300.	2,350.
		Never hinged	1,950.	
		Nos. Q1-Q11 (12)	645.75	889.75
		Set, never hinged	1,540.	

1927-30

Q12	A30	15o red ('27)	20.00	14.00
		Never hinged	40.00	
Q13	A30	30o ocher ('27)	13.00	24.00
		Never hinged	40.00	

Q14	A30	40o yel grn ('30)	24.00	14.00
		Never hinged	72.50	
		Nos. Q12-Q14 (3)	57.00	52.00
		Set, never hinged	152.50	

Overprinted on Regular Issues of 1933-40

1936-42 Unwmk. Perf. 13

Q15	A32	5o rose lake ('42)	.30	.30
		Never hinged	.40	
Q16	A32	10o yellow org	20.00	20.00
		Never hinged	52.50	
Q17	A32	10o lt brown ('38)	1.40	1.90
		Never hinged	2.50	
Q18	A32	10o purple ('39)	.30	.30
		Never hinged	.40	
Q19	A30	15o deep red	.75	1.50
		Never hinged	1.00	
Q20	A30	30o blue, I	4.50	6.00
		Never hinged	7.75	
Q21	A30	30o blue, II ('40)	12.00	29.00
		Never hinged	26.00	
Q22	A30	30o org, II ('42)	.50	.75
		Never hinged	.95	
Q23	A30	40o yel grn, I	4.50	7.75
		Never hinged	10.00	
Q24	A30	40o yel grn, II ('40)	13.00	29.00
		Never hinged	26.00	
Q25	A30	40o blue, II ('42)	.75	1.50
		Never hinged	1.00	
Q26	A33	50o gray	1.00	1.50
		Never hinged	2.00	
Q27	A33	1k lt brown	1.00	1.50
		Never hinged	2.00	
		Nos. Q15-Q27 (13)	60.00	101.00
		Set, never hinged	132.50	

DIEGO-SUAREZ

dē-ˌā-gō ˈswär-əs

LOCATION — A town at the northern end of Madagascar

GOVT. — French Colony

POP. — 12,237

From 1885 to 1896 Diego-Suarez, (Antsirane), a French naval base, was a separate colony and issued its own stamps. These were succeeded by stamps of Madagascar.

100 Centimes = 1 Franc

Values for unused stamps are for examples with original gum as defined in the catalogue introduction except for Nos. 6-10 and J1-J2 which are valued without gum.

Stamps of French Colonies Handstamp Surcharged in Violet

1890 **Unwmk.**   **Perf. 14x13½**

1	A9	15c on 1c blk, *bl*	300.00	100.00
		On cover		625.00
2	A9	15c on 5c grn, *grnsh*	650.00	100.00
		On cover		650.00
3	A9	15c on 10c blk, *lav*	300.00	92.50
		On cover		625.00
4	A9	15c on 20c red, *grn*	650.00	80.00
		On cover		550.00
5	A9	15c on 25c blk, *rose*	130.00	52.50
		On cover		250.00

Inverted Surcharge

1a	A9	15c on 1c blk, *bl*	475.00	225.00
2a	A9	15c on 5c grn, *grnsh*	1,200.	325.00
3a	A9	15c on 10c blk, *lav*	1,200.	450.00
4a	A9	15c on 20c red, *grn*	1,200.	325.00
5a	A9	15c on 25c blk, *rose*	550.00	250.00

Double Surcharge

1b	A9	15c on 1c blk, *bl*	750.00	375.00
2b	A9	15c on 5c grn, *grnsh*	3,000.	3,000.
3b	A9	15c on 10c blk, *lav*	1,400.	475.00
4b	A9	15c on 20c red, *grn*	1,400.	475.00
c.		Dble. surch., both inverted		950.00
5b	A9	15c on 25c blk, *rose*	475.00	250.00

Counterfeits exist.

Ship Flying French Flag — A2   France — A5

Symbolical of Union of France and Madagascar
A3   A4

1890   **Litho.**   **Imperf.**

6	A2	1c black	1,150.	240.00
		On cover		1,050.
7	A3	5c black	1,100.	200.00
		On cover		875.00
8	A4	15c black	210.00	95.00
		On cover		300.00
9	A5	25c black	225.00	110.00
		On cover		375.00

Counterfeits exist of Nos. 6-9.

A6

1891

10	A6	5c black	350.00	100.00
		On cover		1,050.

Excellent counterfeits exist of No. 10.

Stamps of French Colonies Surcharged in Red or Black

No. 11   No. 12

1892   **Perf. 14x13½**

11	A9	5c on 10c blk, *lav* (R)	210.00	105.00
		On cover		1,100.
a.		Inverted surcharge	475.00	400.00
12	A9	5c on 20c red, *grn*	190.00	72.50
		On cover		1,000.
a.		Inverted surcharge	450.00	400.00

Stamps of French Colonies Overprinted in Black or Red

1892

13	A9	1c blue (R)	32.50	20.00
		Never hinged	55.00	
		On cover		190.00
14	A9	2c brown, *buff*	32.50	20.00
		Never hinged	55.00	
		On cover		190.00
15	A9	4c claret, *lav*	55.00	45.00
		Never hinged	105.00	
		On cover		225.00
16	A9	5c green, *grnsh*	120.00	80.00
		Never hinged	225.00	
		On cover		275.00
17	A9	10c black, *lavender*	40.00	32.50
		Never hinged	75.00	
		On cover		100.00
b.		Double overprint	240.00	180.00
18	A9	15c blue, *pale blue*	32.50	20.00
		Never hinged	52.50	
		On cover		80.00
19	A9	20c red, *grn*	40.00	32.50
		Never hinged	80.00	
		On cover		150.00
20	A9	25c black, *rose*	36.00	20.00
		Never hinged	52.50	
		On cover		75.00
21	A9	30c brown, *bis* (R)	1,300.	925.00
22	A9	35c black, *yellow*	1,300.	925.00
23	A9	75c carmine, *rose*	72.50	52.50
		Never hinged	145.00	
		On cover		425.00
a.		Double overprint		400.00
24	A9	1fr brnz grn, *straw* (R)	80.00	52.50
		Never hinged	175.00	
		On cover		550.00
a.		Double overprint	240.00	210.00

Inverted Overprint

13a	A9	1c	225.00	190.00
14a	A9	2c	225.00	190.00
15a	A9	4c		325.00
16a	A9	5c	240.00	200.00
17a	A9	10c	240.00	200.00
20a	A9	25c	240.00	200.00
21a	A9	30c		1,700.
22a	A9	35c		1,700.

Navigation and Commerce
A10   A11

1892   **Typo.**   **Perf. 14x13½**
Name of Colony in Blue or Carmine

25	A10	1c black, *blue*	2.00	2.00
		Never hinged	3.25	
		On cover		125.00
26	A10	2c brown, *buff*	2.75	2.75
		Never hinged	5.00	
		On cover		125.00
27	A10	4c claret, *lav*	3.25	3.25
		Never hinged	5.75	
		On cover		125.00
28	A10	5c green, *grnsh*	6.50	6.50
		Never hinged	11.00	
		On cover		67.50
29	A10	10c black, *lavender*	8.75	7.25
		Never hinged	16.00	
		On cover		62.50
30	A10	15c bl, quadrille paper	16.50	11.00
		Never hinged	30.00	
		On cover		62.50
31	A10	20c red, *green*	22.50	17.50
		Never hinged	45.00	
		On cover		110.00
		On cover, single franking		200.00
32	A10	25c black, *rose*	20.00	16.00
		Never hinged	32.50	
		On cover		62.50
33	A10	30c brown, *bister*	24.00	17.50
		Never hinged	45.00	
		On cover		100.00
		On cover, single franking		150.00
34	A10	40c red, *straw*	30.00	22.50
		Never hinged	55.00	
		On cover		105.00
		On cover, single franking		150.00
35	A10	50c carmine, *rose*	47.50	36.00
		Never hinged	92.50	
		On cover		150.00
		On cover, single franking		210.00
36	A10	75c violet, *org*	55.00	45.00
		Never hinged	110.00	
		On cover		250.00
		On cover, single franking		425.00
37	A10	1fr brnz grn, *straw*	77.50	60.00
		Never hinged	150.00	
		On cover		375.00
		On cover, single franking		625.00
		Nos. 25-37 (13)	316.25	247.25

Perf. 13½x14 stamps are counterfeits.

1894   **Perf. 14x13½**

38	A11	1c black, *blue*	2.00	2.00
		Never hinged	3.25	
		On cover		92.50
39	A11	2c brown, *buff*	2.75	2.40
		Never hinged	4.75	
		On cover		92.50
40	A11	4c claret, *lav*	3.25	2.75
		Never hinged	5.50	
		On cover		92.50
41	A11	5c green, *grnsh*	5.50	4.75
		Never hinged	10.00	
		On cover		50.00
42	A11	10c black, *lavender*	7.25	7.25
		Never hinged	12.50	
		On cover		37.50
43	A11	15c blue, quadrille paper	13.50	6.50
		Never hinged	24.00	
		On cover		37.50
44	A11	20c red, *grn*	22.50	14.00
		Never hinged	40.00	
		On cover		105.00
		On cover, single franking		160.00
45	A11	25c black, *rose*	13.50	9.50
		Never hinged	24.00	
		On cover		50.00
46	A11	30c brown, *bister*	14.00	6.50
		Never hinged	27.50	
		On cover		92.50
		On cover, single franking		120.00
47	A11	40c red, *straw*	14.00	6.50
		Never hinged	27.50	
		On cover		92.50
		On cover, single franking		120.00
48	A11	50c carmine, *rose*	25.00	13.50
		Never hinged	40.00	
		On cover		110.00
		On cover, single franking		150.00
49	A11	75c violet, *org*	13.50	9.00
		Never hinged	24.00	
		On cover		150.00
		On cover, single franking		250.00
50	A11	1fr brnz grn, *straw*	30.00	24.00
		Never hinged	60.00	
		On cover		275.00
		On cover, single franking		400.00
		Nos. 38-50 (13)	166.75	108.65

Bisected stamps of type A11 are mentioned in note after Madagascar No. 62. For surcharges see Madagascar Nos. 56-57, 61-62.

Perf. 13½x14 stamps are counterfeits.

POSTAGE DUE STAMPS

D1   D2

1891 **Unwmk.** **Litho.** **Imperf.**

J1	D1	5c violet	300.00	87.50
		On cover		775.00
J2	D2	50c black	250.00	110.00
		On cover		775.00

Excellent counterfeits exist of Nos. J1-J2.

Postage Due Stamps of French Colonies Ovptd. Like Nos. 13-24

1892

J3	D1	1c black	130.00	72.50
		On cover		525.00
J4	D1	2c black	130.00	65.00
		On cover		475.00
a.		Inverted overprint	450.00	300.00
J5	D1	3c black	130.00	65.00
		On cover		475.00
J6	D1	4c black	130.00	60.00
		On cover		475.00
J7	D1	5c black	130.00	72.50
		On cover		525.00
J8	D1	10c black	36.00	32.50
		Never hinged	67.50	
		On cover		190.00
a.		Inverted overprint	450.00	450.00
J9	D1	15c black	36.00	32.50
		Never hinged	67.50	
		On cover		190.00
a.		Double overprint	575.00	500.00
J10	D1	20c black	200.00	135.00
		On cover		725.00
a.		Double overprint	600.00	500.00
J11	D1	30c black	120.00	60.00
		On cover		475.00
a.		Inverted overprint	450.00	300.00
J12	D1	60c black	1,200.	775.00
J13	D1	1fr brown	2,800.	1,500.

DOMINICA

ˌdä-mə-ˈnē-kə

LOCATION — The largest island of the Windward group in the West Indies. Southeast of Puerto Rico.
AREA — 290 sq. mi.
POP. — 74,859 (1981)
CAPITAL — Roseau

Formerly a Presidency of the Leeward Islands, Dominica became a separate colony under the governor of the Windward Islands on January 1, 1940.

12 Pence = 1 Shilling
20 Shillings = 1 Pound
100 Cents = 1 Dollar (1949)

Catalogue values for unused stamps in this country are for Never Hinged items, beginning with Scott 112.

PRE-STAMP POSTAL MARKINGS

Crowned Circle handstamp type I is pictured in the Crowned Circle Handstamps and Great Britain Used Abroad section.

1845
A1 I "Dominica" crowned circle handstamp in red, on cover ... 625.00

This marking was used in black as a cancel from 1874 to 1883.

STAMPS OF GREAT BRITAIN USED IN DOMINICA

Numeral cancellation type A is pictured in the Crowned Circle Handstamps and Great Britain Used Abroad section.

1858-60   **A07 (Roseau)**
A2	A	1p rose red (#20)	320.00
A3	A	2p blue (#29, P7)	900.00
A4	A	4p rose (#26)	375.00
A5	A	6p lilac (#27)	350.00
A6	A	1sh green (#28)	1,800.

Queen Victoria — A1

Perf. 12½
1874, May 4   Typo.   Wmk. 1
1	A1	1p violet	170.00	55.00
a.	Vertical half used as ½p on cover			9,000.
2	A1	6p green	625.00	115.00
3	A1	1sh deep lilac rose	375.00	80.00
		Nos. 1-3 (3)	1,170.	250.00

During 1875-87 some issues were manuscript dated with village names. These are considered postally used. Stamps with entire village names sell for much more, starting at $100.

1877-79   **Perf. 14**
4	A1	½p bister ('79)	16.00	62.50
5	A1	1p violet	13.00	3.25
a.	Diagonal or vertical half used as ½p on cover			2,600.
6	A1	2½p red brown ('79)	260.00	40.00
7	A1	4p blue ('79)	130.00	44.00
8	A1	6p green	170.00	22.50
9	A1	1sh dp lilac rose	140.00	57.50
		Nos. 4-9 (6)	729.00	189.75

For surcharges see Nos. 10-15.

No. 5 Bisected and Surcharged in Black or Red

a   b   c

1882
10	A1(a)	½p on half of 1p	240.00	57.50
a.	Inverted surcharge		1,150.	900.00
b.	Surcharge tete beche pair		2,600.	2,000.
11	A1(b)	½p on half of 1p	72.50	32.50
a.	Surch. reading downward		72.50	32.50
b.	Double surcharge		900.00	
12	A1(c)	½p on half of 1p (R)	35.00	20.00
a.	Inverted surcharge		1,150.	550.00
b.	Double surcharge		1,850.	750.00
		Nos. 10-12 (3)	347.50	110.00

The existence of genuine examples of No. 10b has been questioned.

Nos. 8 and 9 Surcharged in Black

1886
13	A1	½p on 6p green	8.00	9.00
14	A1	1p on 6p green	45,000.	12,500.
15	A1	1p on 1sh	19.00	21.00
a.	Double surcharge		11,500.	4,250.

All examples of No. 14 may have small pin marks which may have been part of the surcharging process.

1883-89   **Wmk. 2**
16	A1	½p bister ('83)	4.75	11.50
17	A1	½p green ('86)	3.75	6.25
18	A1	1p violet ('86)	47.50	16.00
a.	Half used as ½p on cover			2,350.
19	A1	1p dp carmine ('89)	3.75	10.50
a.	1p rose ('87)		19.00	22.00
b.	Vert. half used as ½p on cover			2,100.
20	A1	2½p red brn ('84)	160.00	3.00
21	A1	2½p ultra ('88)	4.25	6.00
22	A1	4p gray ('86)	5.50	7.75
23	A1	6p orange ('88)	19.00	85.00
24	A1	1sh dp lil rose ('88)	200.00	450.00
		Nos. 16-24 (9)	448.50	596.00

Roseau, Capital of Dominica — A6

King Edward VII — A7

1903   **Wmk. 1**   **Perf. 14**
Ordinary Paper
25	A6	½p gray green	5.25	3.50
26	A6	1p car & black	10.50	1.00
27	A6	2p brn & gray grn	3.25	5.75
28	A6	2½p ultra & blk	8.00	5.25
29	A6	3p black & vio	10.50	4.50
30	A6	6p org brn & blk	9.50	22.50
31	A6	1sh gray grn & red vio	35.00	52.50
32	A6	2sh red vio & blk	32.50	30.00
33	A6	2sh6p ocher & gray	23.00	92.50
34	A7	5sh brown & blk	125.00	175.00
		Nos. 25-34 (9)	137.50	222.50
		Set, ovptd "SPECIMEN"	180.00	

1906-07   **Chalky Paper**
25a		½p gray green	19.00	21.00
26a		1p car & black	40.00	7.25
27a		2p brn & gray grn	47.50	47.50
28a		2½p ultra & blk ('07)	28.00	62.50
29a		3p black & vio	52.50	35.00
31a		1sh gray grn & red vio	85.00	175.00

1907-20   **Chalky Paper**   **Wmk. 3**
35	A6	½p gray green	11.00	7.50
36	A6	1p car & black	2.50	.55
37	A6	2p brn & gray grn	11.00	20.00
38	A6	2½p ultra & black	5.50	27.50
39	A6	3p black & vio	5.00	17.00
40	A6	3p vio, yel, chalky paper ('09)	3.75	5.25
a.	3p vio, yel, ordinary paper ('12)		3.50	5.00
b.	3p vio, pale yel, ordinary paper ('20)		9.75	19.00
41	A6	6p org brn & blk ('08)	65.00	100.00
42	A6	6p vio & dl vio, chalky paper ('09)	12.50	19.00
a.	6p vio & dl vio, ordinary paper ('15)		4.00	20.00
43	A6	1sh gray grn & red vio	4.75	67.50
44	A6	1sh blk, green, chalky paper ('10)	3.75	3.50
a.	1sh blk, green, ordinary paper ('15)		4.25	4.50
45	A6	2sh red vio & blk ('08)	30.00	40.00
46	A6	2sh ultra & vio, bl ('19)	32.50	110.00
47	A6	2sh6p ocher & gray grn ('08)	27.50	75.00
48	A6	2sh6p red & blk, bl ('20)	32.50	125.00
49	A7	5sh brn & blk ('08)	75.00	75.00
		Nos. 35-49 (15)	322.25	692.80

For type surcharged see No. 55.

1908-09   **Ordinary Paper**
50	A6	½p green	9.50	6.25
a.	½p deep green		3.75	6.50
51	A6	1p scarlet	2.00	.75
a.	1p carmine		4.50	.45
52	A6	2p gray ('09)	4.50	17.50
53	A6	2½p ultramarine	9.50	9.75
a.	2½p bright blue ('18)		5.75	10.50
		Nos. 50-53 (4)	25.50	34.25

King George V — A8

1914   **Chalky Paper**   **Perf. 14**
54	A8	5sh grn & scar, yel	70.00	100.00

Type of 1903 Surcharged

1920
55	A6	1½p on 2½p orange	6.25	4.75

1921   **Ordinary Paper**   **Wmk. 4**
56	A6	½p green	3.50	21.00
57	A6	1p rose red	2.75	4.00
58	A6	1½p orange	4.75	17.00
59	A6	2p gray	4.25	4.00
60	A6	2½p ultra	2.75	12.50
61	A6	6p vio & dl vio	3.50	45.00
62	A6	2sh ultra & vio, bl	50.00	125.00
63	A6	2sh6p red & blk, bl	45.00	140.00
		Nos. 56-63 (8)	116.50	368.50

No. 61 is on chalky paper.

Seal of Colony and George V — A9

1923-33   **Chalky Paper**   **Wmk. 4**
65	A9	½p green & blk	2.50	.85
66	A9	1p violet & blk	5.00	2.25
67	A9	1p scar & black	17.00	1.40
68	A9	1½p car & black	6.00	.90
69	A9	1½p dp brn & blk	15.50	.95
70	A9	2p gray & black	3.75	.65
71	A9	2½p org & black	3.25	10.00
72	A9	2½p ultra & black	7.75	2.25
73	A9	3p ultra & black	3.25	16.00
74	A9	3p red & blk, yel	3.50	1.40
75	A9	4p brown & blk	4.00	7.25
76	A9	6p red vio & blk	4.75	9.00
77	A9	1sh blk, emerald	3.00	3.75
78	A9	2sh ultra & blk, bl	16.00	27.50
79	A9	2sh6p red & blk, bl	22.50	27.50
80	A9	3sh vio & blk, yel	4.50	15.00
81	A9	4sh red & blk, emer	20.00	30.00
82	A9	5sh grn & blk, yel	30.00	62.50
		Nos. 65-82 (18)	172.25	219.15

Issue years: Nos. 80, 82, 1927; Nos. 72, 74, 1928; Nos. 67, 69, 1933; others, 1923.

1923   **Wmk. 3**
83	A9	3sh vio & blk, yel	5.75	72.50
84	A9	5sh grn & blk, yel	10.00	65.00
85	A9	£1 vio & blk, red	260.00	375.00
		Nos. 83-85 (3)	275.75	512.50

Common Design Types pictured following the introduction.

Silver Jubilee Issue
Common Design Type
Perf. 13½x14
1935, May 6   Wmk. 4   Engr.
90	CD301	1p car & blue	1.60	.35
91	CD301	1½p gray blk & ultra	5.75	3.25
92	CD301	2½p blue & brn	5.75	4.75
93	CD301	1sh brt vio & ind	5.75	11.50
		Nos. 90-93 (4)	18.85	19.85
		Set, never hinged	27.50	

Coronation Issue
Common Design Type
1937, May 12   Perf. 11x11½
94	CD302	1p dark carmine	.25	.25
95	CD302	1½p brown	.25	.25
96	CD302	2½p deep ultra	.35	1.90
		Nos. 94-96 (3)	.85	2.40
		Set, never hinged	1.50	

Fresh-Water Lake — A10

Layou River — A11

Picking Limes — A12

Boiling Lake — A13

1938-47   **Wmk. 4**   **Perf. 12½**
97	A10	½p grn & red brn	.25	.25
98	A11	1p car & gray	.25	.25
99	A12	1½p rose vio & grn	.25	.75
100	A13	2p brn blk & dp rose	.35	2.25
101	A12	2½p ultra & rose vio	2.75	1.90
102	A11	3p red brn & ol	.25	.60
103	A12	3½p red vio & brt ultra	1.00	2.10
104	A10	6p vio & yel grn	.50	1.60
105	A11	7p org brn & grn	1.00	1.60
106	A13	1sh olive & vio	1.50	1.60
107	A11	2sh red vio & blk	3.50	12.50
108	A10	2sh6p scar ver & blk	7.50	5.75

109	A11	5sh dk brn & bl	4.00	*12.00*
110	A13	10sh dl org & blk	8.50	*12.00*
		Nos. 97-110 (14)	31.60	*55.15*
		Set, never hinged	75.00	

Issued: 3½p, 7p, 2sh, 10sh, 10/15/47; others, 8/15/38.

King George VI — A14

1940, Apr. 15   Photo.   Perf. 14½x14

111	A14	¼p brown violet	1.00	*.25*

> Catalogue values for unused stamps in this section, from this point to the end of the section, are for Never Hinged items.

Peace Issue
Common Design Type

1946, Oct. 14   Engr.   Perf. 13½x14

112	CD303	1p carmine	.25	.25
113	CD303	3½p deep blue	.25	.25

Silver Wedding Issue
Common Design Types

1948, Dec. 1   Photo.   Perf. 14x14½

114	CD304	1p scarlet	.25	.25

Engraved; Name Typographed
Perf. 11½x11

115	CD305	10sh orange brn	25.00	*32.50*

UPU Issue
Common Design Types
Engr.: Name Typo. on 6c and 12c

1949, Oct. 10   Perf. 13½, 11x11½

116	CD306	5c blue	.25	.25
117	CD307	6c chocolate	1.25	*3.00*
118	CD308	12c rose violet	.50	*2.10*
119	CD309	24c olive	.30	.30
		Nos. 116-119 (4)	2.30	5.65

University Issue
Common Design Types

1951, Feb. 16   Engr.   Perf. 14x14½

120	CD310	3c purple & green	.60	*1.25*
121	CD311	12c dp car & dk bl grn	.80	.50

George VI   Drying Cocoa
A15   A16

Picking
Oranges — A17

Designs: 2c and 60c, Carib Baskets. 3c and 48c, Lime Plantation. 4c, Picking Oranges. 5c, Bananas. 6c, Botanical Gardens. 8c, Drying Vanilla Beans. 12c and $1.20, Fresh Water Lake. 14c, Layou River. 24c, Boiling Lake.

Perf. 14½x14

1951, July 1   Photo.   Wmk. 4

122	A15	½c brown	.25	.25

Perf. 13x13½
Engr.

123	A16	1c red org & blk	.25	.30
124	A16	2c dp grn & red brn	.25	.25
125	A16	3c red vio & bl grn	.25	*3.50*
126	A16	4c dk brn & brn org	.75	*3.75*
127	A16	5c rose red & blk	1.10	.30
128	A16	6c org brn & ol grn	1.10	.30
129	A16	8c dp bl & dp grn	3.00	1.50
130	A16	12c emer & gray	.75	*2.00*
131	A16	14c pur & blue	1.25	*3.50*
132	A16	24c rose car & red vio	1.00	.40

133	A16	48c red org & bl grn	4.50	*13.50*
134	A16	60c gray & car	4.00	*9.25*
135	A16	$1.20 gray & emer	7.75	*7.25*

Perf. 13½x13

136	A17	$2.40 gray & org	30.00	*57.50*
		Nos. 122-136 (15)	56.20	*103.55*

Nos. 125, 127, 129 and 131 Overprinted in Black or Carmine

1951, Oct. 15   Perf. 13x13½

137	A16	3c red vio & bl green	.25	.75
138	A16	5c rose red & black	.30	*1.75*
139	A16	8c dp blue & dp grn (C)	.40	.25
140	A16	14c purple & blue (C)	1.75	.45
		Nos. 137-140 (4)	2.70	3.20

Adoption of a new constitution for the Windward Islands, 1951.

WAR TAX STAMPS

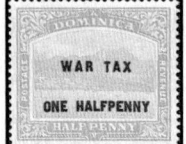

No. 50 Surcharged in Red

1916   Wmk. 3   Perf. 14

MR1	A6	½p on ½p green	3.00	.85

No. 50 Overprinted in Black

1918

MR2	A6	½p green	5.00	*6.25*

Nos. 50, 40 in Black or Red

1918

MR3	A6	½p green	.25	.30
MR4	A6	3p violet, *yel* (R)	4.00	*4.50*

Type of 1908-09 Surcharged in Red

1919

MR5	A6	1½p on 2½p orange	.25	*.60*

DOMINICAN REPUBLIC

də-'mi-ni-kən ri-'pə-blik

LOCATION — Comprises about two-thirds of the island of Hispaniola in the West Indies.
GOVT. — Republic
AREA — 18,700 sq. mi.
POP. — 5,982,000 (est. 1983)

CAPITAL — Santo Domingo

8 Reales = 1 Peso
100 Centavos = 1 Peso (1880)
100 Centimos = 1 Franco (1883)
100 Centavos = 1 Peso (1885)

Watermarks

Wmk. 115 —
Diamonds

Wmk. 116 —
Crosses and
Circles

FORERUNNERS

BRITISH POST OFFICES IN DOMINICAN REPUBLIC
Puerto Plata

British P.O. opened by 1867; closed 1871; reopened 1876; closed 1881

Stamps of Great Britain, Canceled C86, or with Circular Date Stamp

1876-81

A1	½p rose red (#58, P 10, 12, 14), *value from*	85.00
A2	1p rose red (#33, P 123, 130, 136, 146, 151, 178, 199, 200, 205, 217) *value from*	70.00
A3	1½p lake red (#32, P 3)	125.00
A4	2p blue (#30, P 13, 14), *value from*	85.00
A5	2½p claret (#67, P 13, 14), *value from*	250.00
A6	3p rose (#61, P 18)	105.00
A7	4p vermilion (#43, P 14)	105.00
A8	4p vermilion (#69, P 15)	375.00
A9	4p pale olive green (#70, P 15)	290.00
A10	6p violet (#51, P 8)	—
A11	6p gray (#62, P 15)	85.00
A12	8p orange (#73)	450.00
A13	1sh green (#54, P 4, 7) *value from*	75.00
A14	1sh green (#64, P 11-13) *value from*	85.00
A15	2sh blue (#55)	310.00
A16	5sh rose (#57, P 2)	—

Santo Domingo

British P.O. opened by 1867; closed 1871; reopened 1876; closed 1881

Stamps of Great Britain, Canceled C87, or with Circular Date Stamp

1876-81

A17	½p rose red (#58, P 5, 6, 8, 10, 11, 13), *value from*	105.00
A18	1p rose red (#33, P 146, 154, 171, 173, 174, 176, 178, 186, 190, 197, 220) *value from*	80.00
A19	1½p lake red (#32, P 3)	125.00
A20	2p blue (#30, P 13, 14), *value from*	110.00
A21	3p rose (#61, P 18)	—
A22	4p vermilion (#43, P 11, 12, 14)	110.00
A23	4p vermilion (#69, P 15)	510.00
A24	4p pale olive green (#70, P 15)	310.00
A25	6p gray (#62, P 15)	—
A26	8p orange (#73)	—
A27	9p bister (#52)	—
A28	1sh green (#54, P 4)	—
A29	1sh green (#64, P 10-13) *value from*	110.00
A30	2sh blue (#55)	—

Dominican Republic

Coat of Arms
A1   A2

1865   Unwmk.   Typo.   Imperf.
Wove Paper

1	A1	½r black, *rose*	700.	650.
2	A1	1r black, *dp green*	1,100.	1,000.

Twelve varieties of each.

Laid Paper

3	A2	½r black, *pale green*	550.	475.
4	A2	1r black, *straw*	1,800.	1,200.

Twelve varieties of the ½r, ten of the 1r.

A3   A4

1866   Laid Paper   Unwmk.

5	A3	½r black, *straw*	200.00	160.00
6	A3	1r black, *pale green*	2,500.	2,000.
7	A4	1r black, *pale green*	175.00	125.00

Nos. 5-8 have 21 varieties (sheets of 21).

Wmk. 115

8	A3	1r black, *pale green*	13,000.	13,000.
a.	"CORREOS" and "Un Real" doubled		21,000.	

The unique example of No. 8a is centered in the grade of fine, has a shallow thin spot and pinhole.

1866-67   Wove Paper   Unwmk.

9	A3	½r black, *rose* ('67)	60.00	60.00
10	A3	1r blk, *pale green*	85.00	75.00
a.	Inscription dbl., top & bottom		400.00	400.00
11	A3	1r black, *blue* ('67)	60.00	37.50
a.	1r black, *light blue* ('67)	50.00	30.00
b.	No space btwn. "Un" and "real"		600.00	500.00
c.	Without inscription at top & bottom		1,500.	1,000.
d.	Inscription invtd., top & bottom		—	
		Nos. 9-11 (3)	205.00	172.50

1867-71   Pelure Paper

13	A3	½r black, *rose*	150.00	75.00
15	A3	½r black, *lav* ('68)	250.00	210.00
a.	Without inscription at top and bottom		525.00	
b.	Dbl. inscriptions, one invtd.		425.00	
16	A3	½r black, *grnsh gray* ('68)	260.00	225.00
17	A3	½r black, *yellow* ('68)	12,000.	
18	A3	½r black, *ol* ('69)	3,000.	5,500.
22	A3	1r black, *blue*	4,000.	
23	A3	1r black, *lavender*	225.00	200.00
24	A4	1r black, *rose* ('68)	225.00	225.00
25	A4	1r black, *mag* ('69)	2,250.	1,300.
26	A4	1r black, *sal* ('71)	300.00	225.00

Value for No. 17 is for an example with very fine centering and small faults. Value for No. 22 is for a faulty example with very fine centering and appearance.

1870-73   Ordinary Paper

27	A3	½r black, *magenta*	2,500.	4,750.
28	A3	½r blue, *rose* (blk inscription) ('71)	50.00	42.50
a.	Blue inscription	500.00	500.00
b.	Without inscription at top and bottom		—	
29	A3	½r black, *yel* ('73)	30.00	21.00
a.	Without inscription at top and bottom		700.00	700.00

30	A4	1r black, *vio* ('73)	30.00	21.00
a.		Without inscription at top and bottom	700.00	700.00
31	A4	1r black, *dk grn*	60.00	50.00

Nos. 9-31 have 21 varieties (sheets of 21). Nos. 29 and 30 are known pin-perforated, unofficially.

Bisects are known of several of the early 1r stamps.

A5

A6

1879 — Perf. 12½x13

32	A5	½r violet	3.00	2.10
a.		Imperf., pair	9.00	9.00
b.		Horiz. pair, imperf. vert.	17.00	
33	A5	½r violet, *bluish*	2.50	1.80
a.		Imperf., pair	9.00	7.50
34	A5	1r carmine	4.50	2.10
a.		Imperf., pair	11.50	9.00
b.		Perf. 13	11.50	7.50
c.		Perf. 13x12½	11.50	7.50
35	A5	1r carmine, *sal*	2.50	1.50
a.		Imperf., pair	8.25	8.25
		Nos. 32-35 (4)	12.50	7.50

In 1891 15 stamps of 1879-83 were surcharged "U P U," new values and crossed diagonal lines.

1880 — Typo. — Rouletted in Color

36	A6	1c green	1.40	.90
a.		Laid paper	50.00	50.00
37	A6	2c red	1.00	.75
a.		Pelure paper	40.00	40.00
b.		Laid paper	40.00	40.00
38	A6	5c blue	1.50	.70
39	A6	10c rose	3.25	.90
40	A6	20c brown	2.00	.85
41	A6	25c violet	2.25	1.25
42	A6	50c orange	3.00	1.75
43	A6	75c ultra	5.75	3.00
a.		Laid paper	40.00	40.00
44	A6	1p gold	7.50	4.50
a.		Laid paper	50.00	50.00
b.		Double impression	42.50	42.50
		Nos. 36-44 (9)	27.65	14.60

1881 — Network Covering Stamp

45	A6	1c green	.90	.50
46	A6	2c red	.90	.50
47	A6	5c blue	1.25	.50
48	A6	10c rose	1.50	.65
49	A6	20c brown	1.50	.90
50	A6	25c violet	1.75	1.00
51	A6	50c orange	2.00	1.40
52	A6	75c ultra	6.00	4.50
53	A6	1p gold	8.00	7.00
		Nos. 45-53 (9)	23.80	16.95

Preceding Issues (Type A6) Srch. with Value in New Currency

a   b

c   d

e   f

g

h

i

1883 — Without Network

54	(a)	5c on 1c green	1.50	1.60
b.		Inverted surcharge	21.00	21.00
c.		Surcharged "25 céntimos"	50.00	50.00
d.		Surcharged "10 céntimos"	27.50	27.50
55	(b)	5c on 1c green	25.00	9.00
b.		Double surcharge	100.00	
c.		Inverted surcharge	65.00	65.00
56	(c)	5c on 1c green	17.00	9.50
b.		Surcharged "10 céntimos"	35.00	35.00
c.		Surcharged "25 céntimos"	37.50	37.50
57	(a)	10c on 2c red	5.00	3.00
b.		Inverted surcharge	27.50	27.50
d.		Surcharged "5 céntimos"	52.50	52.50
e.		Surcharged "25 céntimos"	75.00	75.00
58	(c)	10c on 2c red	4.50	3.50
a.		"Céntimo"		
b.		Inverted surcharge	37.50	37.50
c.		Surcharged "25 céntimos"	60.00	60.00
d.		"10" omitted	60.00	60.00
59	(a)	25c on 5c blue	7.00	4.50
a.		Surcharged "5 céntimos"	52.50	
b.		Surcharged "10 céntimos"	52.50	52.50
c.		Surcharged "50 céntimos"	75.00	75.00
d.		Inverted surcharge	50.00	50.00
60	(c)	25c on 5c blue	7.50	3.50
a.		Inverted surcharge	45.00	37.50
b.		Surcharged "10 céntimos"	45.00	37.50
e.		"25" omitted	75.00	
f.		Surcharged on back		75.00
61	(a)	50c on 10c rose	27.50	12.50
a.		Inverted surcharge	50.00	45.00
62	(c)	50c on 10c rose	35.00	17.50
a.		Inverted surcharge	52.50	52.50
63	(d)	1fr on 20c brown	15.00	9.75
64	(e)	1fr on 20c brown	17.50	9.75
a.		Comma after "Franco,"	27.50	27.50
65	(f)	1fr on 20c brown	25.00	17.50
a.		Inverted surcharge		75.00
66	(g)	1fr25c on 25c violet	21.00	15.00
a.		Inverted surcharge	65.00	65.00
67	(g)	2fr50c on 50c orange	16.00	12.00
a.		Inverted surcharge	35.00	27.50
68	(g)	3fr75c on 75c ultra	27.50	25.00
b.		Inverted surcharge	60.00	60.00
c.		Laid paper	75.00	75.00
70	(i)	5fr on 1p gold	550.00	500.00
a.		"s" of "francos" inverted	700.00	700.00

With Network

71	(a)	5c on 1c green	3.00	2.50
b.		Inverted surcharge	22.50	22.50
c.		Double surcharge	22.50	22.50
d.		Surcharged "25 céntimos"	42.50	42.50
e.		"5" omitted	75.00	75.00
72	(b)	5c on 1c green	21.00	9.00
b.		Inverted surcharge	60.00	60.00
73	(c)	5c on 1c green	27.50	11.50
b.		Surcharged "10 céntimos"	50.00	42.50
c.		Surcharged "25 céntimos"	60.00	
74	(a)	10c on 2c red	3.75	2.25
a.		Surcharged "5 céntimos"	52.50	45.00
b.		Surcharged "25 céntimos"	67.50	67.50
c.		"10" omitted	57.50	
75	(c)	10c on 2c red	3.00	2.00
a.		Inverted surcharge	30.00	17.00
76	(a)	25c on 5c blue	7.50	3.50
a.		Surcharged "10 céntimos"	75.00	
b.		Surcharged "5 céntimos"	60.00	
c.		Surcharged "50 céntimos"	67.50	
77	(c)	25c on 5c blue	60.00	30.00
a.		Inverted surcharge		
b.		Surcharged on back		
78	(a)	50c on 10c rose	25.00	7.50
a.		Inverted surcharge	50.00	30.00
b.		Surcharged "25 céntimos"	60.00	
79	(c)	50c on 10c rose	30.00	9.50
a.		Inverted surcharge	60.00	
80	(d)	1fr on 20c brown	12.00	9.75
81	(e)	1fr on 20c brown	14.50	12.50
a.		Comma after "Franco"	35.00	35.00
b.		Inverted surcharge	75.00	
82	(f)	1fr on 20c brown	25.00	20.00
83	(g)	1fr25c on 25c violet	45.00	30.00
a.		Inverted surcharge	75.00	
84	(g)	2fr50c on 50c orange	19.00	12.50
a.		Inverted surcharge	35.00	27.50
85	(g)	3fr75c on 75c ultra	45.00	42.50
86	(h)	5fr on 1p gold	140.00	140.00
a.		Inverted surcharge		
87	(i)	5fr on 1p gold	190.00	190.00

Many minor varieties exist in Nos. 54-87: accent on "i" of "centimos"; "5" with straight top; "1" with straight serif.

A7

A7a

1885-91 — Engr. — Perf. 12

88	A7	1c green	1.00	.50
89	A7	2c vermilion	1.00	.50
90	A7	5c blue	1.40	.50
91	A7a	10c orange	2.25	.65
92	A7a	20c dark brown	2.25	.80
93	A7a	50c violet ('91)	7.50	6.50
94	A7	1p carmine ('91)	20.00	13.50
95	A7	2p red brown ('91)	25.00	16.00
		Nos. 88-95 (8)	60.40	38.95

Nos. 93, 94, 95 were issued without gum. Imperf. varieties are proofs.
For surcharges see Nos. 166-168.

Coat of Arms — A8

1895 — Perf. 12½x14

96	A8	1c green	1.25	.50
97	A8	2c orange red	1.25	.50
98	A8	5c blue	1.40	.50
99	A8	10c orange	3.25	1.60
		Nos. 96-99 (4)	7.15	3.10

Exist imperforate but were not issued.

1897 — Perf. 14

96a	A8	1c green	1.40	.50
97a	A8	2c orange red	8.00	.75
98a	A8	5c blue	1.40	.75
99a	A8	10c orange	2.75	1.50
		Nos. 96a-99a (4)	13.55	3.50

Voyage of Diego Méndez from Jamaica — A9

Enriquillo's Revolt — A10

Sarcophagus of Columbus A11

"Española" Guarding Remains of Columbus A12

Toscanelli Replying to Columbus A13

Bartolomé de las Casas Defending Indians — A14

Columbus at Salamanca A15

Columbus' Mausoleum A16

1899, Feb. 27 — Litho. — Perf. 11½

100	A9	1c brown violet	7.25	5.25
102	A10	2c rose red	1.75	.70
103	A11	5c blue	2.00	.70
104	A12	10c orange	5.00	1.60
a.		Tête bêche pair	42.50	42.50
105	A13	20c brown	10.00	8.25
106	A14	50c yellow green	11.50	9.75
a.		Tête bêche pair	60.00	60.00
107	A15	1p black, *gray bl*	27.00	22.00
108	A16	2p bister brown	45.00	47.50

1900, Jan.

109	A11	¼c black	.75	1.60
110	A15	½c black	.75	1.60
110A	A9	1c gray green	.75	.65
		Nos. 100-110A (11)	111.75	99.60

Nos. 100-110A were issued to raise funds for a Columbus mausoleum.

Imperf., Pairs

100a	A9	1c brown violet	16.50	16.50
102a	A10	2c rose red	5.00	
103a	A11	5c blue	5.75	
104b	A12	10c orange	8.75	
105a	A13	20c brown	15.00	
106b	A14	50c yellow green	17.50	
c.		As "b," tête bêche pair	125.00	
107a	A15	1p black, *gray blue*	42.50	
108a	A16	2p bister brown	70.00	
109a	A11	¼c black	3.75	4.25
110b	A15	½c black	3.75	4.25
110c	A9	1c gray green	3.50	

Map of Hispaniola A17

1900, Oct. 21 — Unwmk. — Perf. 14

111	A17	¼c dark blue	.75	.40
112	A17	½c rose	.75	.40
113	A17	1c olive green	.75	.40
114	A17	2c deep green	.75	.40
115	A17	5c red brown	.75	.40
a.		Vertical pair, imperf. between	17.50	

Perf. 12

116	A17	10c orange	.75	.40
117	A17	50c lilac	3.00	2.50
a.		20c rose (error)	6.00	6.00
118	A17	50c black	2.75	2.50
119	A17	1p brown	3.00	2.50
		Nos. 111-119 (9)	13.25	9.90

Several varieties in design are known in this issue. They were deliberately made. Counterfeits of Nos. 111-119 abound.

A18

1901-06 — Typo. — Perf. 14

120	A18	½c carmine & vio	.70	.40
121	A18	½c blk & org ('05)	1.80	.95
122	A18	½c grn & blk ('06)	.85	.30
123	A18	1c ol grn & vio	.70	.25
124	A18	1c blk & ultra ('05)	1.80	.85
125	A18	1c car & blk ('06)	1.00	.45
126	A18	2c dp grn & vio	.80	.25
127	A18	2c blk & vio ('05)	2.25	.70
128	A18	2c org brn & blk ('06)	1.40	.25
129	A18	5c org brn & vio	.80	.25
130	A18	5c black & cl ('05)	2.50	1.25
131	A18	5c blue & blk ('06)	1.25	.30
132	A18	10c orange & vio	1.40	.45
133	A18	10c blk & grn ('05)	4.25	2.25
134	A18	10c red vio & blk ('06)	1.40	.40
135	A18	20c brn vio & vio	2.50	.95
136	A18	20c blk & ol ('05)	13.50	8.75
137	A18	20c ol grn & blk ('06)	3.25	
138	A18	50c gray blk & vio	8.00	5.50
139	A18	50c blk & red brn ('05)	47.50	34.00

140	A18	50c brn & blk		
		('06)	8.75	7.75
141	A18	1p brn & vio	18.00	10.00
142	A18	1p blk & gray		
		('05)	200.00	225.00
143	A18	1p violet & blk		
		('06)	21.00	13.50
		Nos. 120-143 (24)	348.00 318.00

Issued: 11/15/01; 5/11/05; 8/17/06.
See Nos. 172-176. For surcharges see Nos.151-156.

Francisco Sánchez — A19

Juan Pablo Duarte — A20

Ramón Mella — A21

Ft. Santo Domingo — A22

1902, Feb. 25 Engr. Perf. 12

144	A19	1c dk green & blk	.35	.35
145	A20	2c scarlet & blk	.35	.35
146	A20	5c blue & blk	.35	.35
147	A19	10c orange & blk	.35	.35
148	A21	12c purple & blk	.35	.35
149	A21	20c rose & blk	.60	.60
150	A22	50c brown & blk	.90	.90
		Nos. 144-150 (7)	3.25	3.25

Center Inverted

144a	A19	1c	6.00	3.50
145a	A20	2c	6.00	3.50
146a	A20	5c	6.00	3.50
148a	A21	12c	6.00	3.50
149a	A21	20c	6.00	3.50
150a	A22	50c	6.00	3.50
		Nos. 144a-150a (6)	36.00 21.00

400th anniversary of Santo Domingo. Imperforate varieties of Nos. 144 to 150 were never sold to the public.

Nos. 138, 141 Surcharged in Black

1904, Aug.

151	A18	2c on 50c	9.25	7.25
152	A18	2c on 1p	13.50	9.25
b.		"2" omitted	50.00	50.00
153	A18	5c on 50c	4.25	2.25
154	A18	5c on 1p	5.25	4.00
155	A18	10c on 50c	8.25	6.75
156	A18	10c on 1p	8.75	6.75
		Nos. 151-156 (6)	49.25 36.25

Inverted Surcharge

151a	A18	2c on 50c	15.00	15.00
152a	A18	2c on 1p	15.00	15.00
c.		As "a," "2" omitted	85.00	85.00
153a	A18	5c on 50c	5.50	5.50
154a	A18	5c on 1p	7.00	6.50
155a	A18	10c on 50c	14.00	14.00
156a	A18	10c on 1p	10.00	10.00
		Nos. 151a-156a (6)	66.50 66.00

Official Stamps of 1902 Overprinted

1904, Aug. 16 Red Overprint

157	O1	5c dk blue & blk	5.75	3.00
a.		Inverted overprint	7.25	5.75

Black Overprint

158	O1	2c scarlet & blk	17.00	5.25
a.		Inverted overprint	20.00	6.50
159	O1	5c blue & blk	5,500.	3,500.
160	O1	10c yellow grn & blk	10.50	10.50
a.		Inverted overprint	14.00	14.00

Official Stamps of 1902 Surcharged

161	O1	1c on 20c yellow & blk	4.75	3.00
a.		Inverted surcharge	7.25	5.50

Nos. J1-J2 Surcharged or Overprinted in Black

1904-05 Surcharged "CENTAVOS"

162	D1	1c on 2c olive gray	250.00 200.00
a.		"entavos"		
b.		"Dominican"	350.00 300.00
c.		"Centavo"	350.00 300.00

Carmine Surcharge or Overprint

163	D1	1c on 2c olive gray	3.50	1.10
a.		Inverted surcharge	4.75	2.50
b.		"Domihicana"	15.00	15.00
c.		As "b," inverted	40.00	40.00
d.		"Dominican"	10.50	10.50
e.		"Centavos" omitted	30.00	30.00
g.		"entavos"	30.00	
163F	D1	1c on 4c olive gray	35.00	7.00
164	D1	2c olive gray	.95	.60
a.		"Domihicana"	11.00	11.00
b.		Inverted overprint	1.90	1.90
c.		As "a," inverted	25.00	25.00
d.		"Dominican"	5.75	5.75
e.		"Centavo" omitted	12.50	10.00
f.		"entavos"	12.50	12.50
g.		As "f," inverted	40.00	40.00
h.		As "d," inverted	40.00	40.00

Surcharged "CENTAVO"

165	D1	1c on 4c olive gray	.95	.70
a.		"Domihicana"	10.00	10.00
c.		Inverted surcharge	1.75	1.75
d.		"1" omitted	3.50	3.50
e.		As "a," inverted	32.50	32.50
f.		As "d," inverted	40.00	40.00
g.		Double surcharge	30.00	30.00

No. 92 Surcharged in Red

1905, Apr. 4

166	A7a	2c on 20c dk brown	8.75	7.25
a.		Inverted surcharge	15.00	15.00
167	A7a	5c on 20c dk brown	4.75	2.50
a.		Inverted surcharge	16.00	16.00
b.		Double surcharge	25.00	25.00
168	A7a	10c on 20c dk brown	8.75	7.25
		Nos. 166-168 (3)	22.25 17.00

Nos. 166-168 exist with inverted "A" for "V" in "CENTAVOS" in surcharge.

No. J2 Surcharged in Red

1906, Jan. 16 Perf. 14

169	D1	1c on 4c olive gray	.95	.50
a.		Inverted surcharge	10.50	10.50
b.		Double surcharge	25.00	

Nos. J4, J3 Surcharged in Black

1906, May 1

170	D1	1c on 10c olive gray	1.10	.40
a.		Inverted surcharge	10.50	10.50
b.		Double surcharge	14.00	14.00

c.		"OMINICANA"	20.00	20.00
d.		As "c," inverted	150.00	
171	D1	2c on 5c olive gray	1.10	.40
a.		Inverted surcharge	10.50	10.50
b.		Double surcharge	35.00	

The varieties small "C" or small "A" in "REPUBLICA" are found on Nos. 170, 171.

Arms Type of 1901-06

1907-10 Wmk. 116

172	A18	½c grn & blk ('08)	.85	.25
173	A18	1c orange & blk	.85	.25
174	A18	2c orange brn & blk	.85	.25
175	A18	5c blue & blk	.85	.25
176	A18	10c red vio & blk ('10)	8.00	1.00
		Nos. 172-176 (5)	11.40	2.00

No. O6 Overprinted in Red

1911, July 11 Perf. 13½x14, 13½x13

177	O2	2c scarlet & black	1.60	.60
a.		"HABILITAOO"	8.75	6.00
b.		Inverted overprint	21.00	
c.		Double overprint	21.00	

A23   Juan Pablo Duarte — A24

1911-13 Center in Black Perf. 14

178	A23	½c orange ('13)	.25	.25
179	A23	1c green	.25	.25
180	A23	2c carmine	.25	.25
181	A23	5c gray blue ('13)	.80	.25
182	A23	10c red violet	1.60	.45
183	A23	20c olive green	11.50	11.50
184	A23	50c yellow brn ('12)	3.75	3.75
185	A23	1p violet ('12)	5.75	4.25
		Nos. 178-185 (8)	24.15 20.95

See Nos. 230-232.

1914, Apr. 13 Perf. 13x14
Background Red, White and Blue

186	A24	½c orange & blk	.60	.30
187	A24	1c green & blk	.60	.30
188	A24	2c rose & blk	.60	.30
189	A24	5c slate & blk	.60	.40
190	A24	10c magenta & blk	1.40	.70
191	A24	20c olive grn & blk	2.50	1.90
192	A24	50c brown & blk	3.50	2.75
193	A24	1p dull lilac & blk	5.50	4.00
		Nos. 186-193 (8)	15.30 10.65

Cent. of the birth of Juan Pablo Duarte (1813-1876), patriot and revolutionary.

Official Stamps of 1909-12 Surcharged in Violet or Overprinted in Red

a

b

1915, Feb. Perf. 13½x13, 13½x14

194	O2 (a)	½c on 20c orange & blk	.35	.35
a.		Inverted surcharge	6.00	6.00
b.		Double surcharge	8.75	8.75
c.		"Habilitado" omitted	5.25	5.25
195	O2 (b)	1c blue grn & blk	.80	.25
a.		Inverted overprint	6.00	6.00
b.		Double overprint	7.00	
c.		Overprinted "1915" only	12.50	
196	O2 (b)	2c scarlet & blk	1.25	.25
a.		Inverted overprint	5.25	5.25
b.		Double overprint	7.75	7.75
c.		Overprinted "1915" only	8.75	
d.		"1915" double		

197	O2 (b)	5c dk blue & blk	1.00	.25
a.		Inverted overprint	7.00	7.00
b.		Double overprint	8.75	8.75
c.		Double ovpt., one invtd.	27.50	
d.		Overprinted "1915" only	8.50	
198	O2 (b)	10c yel grn & blk	2.75	2.50
a.		Inverted overprint	10.00	
199	O2 (b)	20c orange & blk	9.25	7.25
a.		"Habilitado" omitted	15.55 10.85
		Nos. 194-199 (6)		

Nos. 194, 196-198 are known with both perforations. Nos. 195, 199 are only perf. 13½x13.

The variety capital "I" for "1" in "Habilitado" occurs once in each sheet in all denominations.

A25

Type of 1911-13 Redrawn Overprinted "1915" in Red

TWO CENTAVOS:
Type I — "DOS" in small letters.
Type II — "DOS" in larger letters with white dot at each end of the word.

1915 Unwmk. Litho. Perf. 11½

200	A25	½c violet & blk	.85	.25
a.		Imperf., pair	5.75	
201	A25	1c yel brn & blk	.85	.25
a.		Imperf., pair	6.50	
b.		Vert. pair, imperf. horiz.	10.50	
c.		Horiz. pair, imperf. vert.	10.50	
202	A25	2c ol grn & blk (I)	3.75	.25
a.		Imperf., pair	10.00	
203	A25	2c ol grn & blk (II)	6.00	.25
a.		Center omitted	87.50	
b.		Frame omitted	87.50	
c.		Imperf., pair	15.00	
d.		Horiz. pair, imperf. vert.	15.00	
204	A25	5c magenta & blk	3.75	.25
a.		Pair, one without overprint	65.00	
b.		Imperf., pair	6.50	
205	A25	10c gray blue & blk	3.75	.50
a.		Imperf., pair	7.75	
b.		Horiz. pair, imperf. vert.	35.00	
206	A25	20c rose red & blk	8.25	1.40
a.		Imperf., pair	12.50	
207	A25	50c green & blk	10.50	4.00
a.		Imperf., pair	25.00	
208	A25	1p orange & blk	21.00	7.00
a.		Imperf., pair	52.50	
		Nos. 200-208 (9)	58.70 14.15

Type of 1915 Overprinted "1916" in Red

1916

209	A25	½c violet & blk	2.25	.25
a.		Imperf., pair	21.00	
210	A25	1c green & blk	3.25	.25
a.		Imperf., pair	21.00	

Type of 1915 Overprinted "1917" in Red

1917-19

213	A25	½c red lilac & blk	3.50	.30
a.		Horiz. pair, imperf. btwn.	47.50 47.50
214	A25	1c yellow grn & blk	1.60	.25
a.		Vert. pair, imperf. btwn.	50.00	
215	A25	2c olive grn & blk	2.25	.25
a.		Imperf., pair	35.00	
216	A25	5c magenta & blk	23.00	.85
		Nos. 213-216 (4)	30.35	1.65

Type of 1915 Overprinted "1919" in Red

1919

219	A25	2c olive grn & blk	17.00	.25

Type of 1915 Overprinted "1920" in Red

1920-27

220	A25	½c lilac rose & blk	.60	.25
a.		Horiz. pair, imperf. btwn.	25.00 25.00
b.		Inverted overprint		
c.		Double overprint		
d.		Double overprint, one invtd.		
221	A25	1c yellow grn & blk	.75	.25
a.		Overprint omitted	70.00	
b.		Horiz. pair, imperf. btwn.	40.00	
222	A25	2c olive grn & blk	.75	.25
a.		Vertical pair, imperf. between	27.50	
223	A25	5c dp rose & blk	9.00	.50
224	A25	10c blue & black	5.75	.25
225	A25	20c rose red & blk		
		('27)	7.75	.50
226	A25	50c green & blk ('27)	65.00 21.00
		Nos. 220-226 (7)	89.60 23.00

Type of 1915 Overprinted "1921" in Red

1921

227	A25	1c yellow grn & blk	5.25	.30
a.		Horiz. pair, imperf. btwn.	45.00 45.00
b.		Imperf., pair	45.00 45.00
228	A25	2c olive grn & blk	5.75	.40
a.		Vert. pair, imperf. btwn.	45.00	

Redrawn Design of 1915 without Overprint
1922
230	A25	1c green	3.75	.25
231	A25	2c carmine (II)	3.75	.25
232	A25	5c blue	5.75	.25
		Nos. 230-232 (3)	13.25	.75

Nos. 230-232 exist imperf.

A26 A27

Second Redrawing

TEN CENTAVOS:
Type I — Numerals 2mm high. "DIEZ" in thick letters with large white dot at each end.
Type II — Numerals 3mm high. "DIEZ" in thin letters with white dot with colored center at each end.

1924-27
233	A26	1c green	1.60	.25
a.		Vert. pair, imperf. btwn.	35.00	35.00
234	A26	2c red	.85	.25
235	A26	5c blue	2.25	.25
236	A26	10c pale bl & blk (I) ('26)	12.00	3.00
236A	A26	10c pale bl & blk (II)	22.50	1.10
236B	A26	50c gray grn & blk ('26)	60.00	33.00
237	A26	1p orange & blk ('27)	19.00	12.50
		Nos. 233-237 (7)	118.20	50.35

In the second redrawing the shield has a flat top and the design differs in many details from the stamps of 1911-13 and 1915-22.

1927
238	A27	½c lilac rose & blk	.30	.25

Exhibition Pavilion — A28

1927   Unwmk.   Perf. 12
239	A28	2c carmine	1.10	.50
240	A28	5c ultra	2.10	.50

Natl. and West Indian Exhib. at Santiago de los Caballeros.

Ruins of Columbus' Fortress A29

1928
241	A29	½c lilac rose	.95	.35
242	A29	1c deep green	.70	.25
a.		Horiz. pair, imperf. btwn.	25.00	
243	A29	2c red	.95	.25
244	A29	5c dark blue	2.75	.35
245	A29	10c light blue	2.75	.30
246	A29	20c rose	4.75	.40
247	A29	50c yellow green	13.50	8.25
248	A29	1p orange yellow	35.00	27.00
		Nos. 241-248 (8)	61.35	37.15

Reprints exist of 1c, 2c and 10c.
Issued: 1c, 2c, 10c, Oct. 1; others, Dec.

Horacio Vasquez — A30   Convent of San Ignacio de Loyola — A31

1929, May-June
249	A30	½c dull rose	.60	.30
250	A30	1c gray green	.60	.25
251	A30	2c red	.70	.25
252	A30	5c dark ultra	1.40	.35
253	A30	10c pale blue	2.10	.50
		Nos. 249-253 (5)	5.40	1.65

Signing of the "Frontier" treaty with Haiti.
Issue dates: 2c, May; others, June.

Imperf., Pairs
249a	A30	½c	12.50
250a	A30	1c	12.50
251a	A30	2c	12.50
252a	A30	5c	14.00

1930, May 1   Perf. 11½
254	A31	½c red brown	.70	.45
a.		Imperf., pair	55.00	55.00
255	A31	1c deep green	.65	.25
256	A31	2c vermilion	.65	.25
a.		Imperf., pair	60.00	
257	A31	5c deep blue	2.10	.35
258	A31	10c light blue	4.25	1.25
		Nos. 254-258 (5)	8.35	2.55

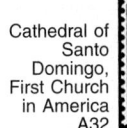

Cathedral of Santo Domingo, First Church in America A32

1931   Perf. 12
260	A32	1c deep green	.85	.25
a.		Imperf., pair	50.00	
261	A32	2c scarlet	.60	.25
a.		Imperf., pair	50.00	
262	A32	3c violet	.85	.25
263	A32	7c dark blue	2.50	.25
264	A32	8c bister	3.00	.85
265	A32	10c light blue	5.75	1.25
a.		Imperf., pair	35.00	
		Nos. 260-265 (6)	13.55	3.10

Issued: 3c-7c, Aug. 1; others, July 11.
For overprint see No. RAC8.

A33

Overprinted or Surcharged in Black
1932, Dec. 20   Perf. 12
Cross in Red
265B	A33	1c yellow green	.55	.50
265C	A33	3c on 2c violet	.80	.60
265D	A33	5c blue	4.50	4.75
265E	A33	7c on 10c turq bl	6.00	6.25
		Nos. 265B-265E (4)	11.85	12.10

Proceeds of sale given to Red Cross. Valid Dec. 20 to Jan. 5, 1933.
Inverted and pairs, one without surcharge or overprint, exist on Nos. 265B-265D, as well as missing letters.

Fernando Arturo de Merino (1833-1906) as President — A35

Cathedral of Santo Domingo A36

Designs: ½c, 5c, 8c, Tomb of Merino. 1c, 3c, 10c, as Archbishop.

1933, Feb. 27   Engr.   Perf. 14
266	A35	½c lt violet	.45	.35
267	A35	1c yellow green	.60	.25
268	A35	2c lt red	1.00	.75
269	A35	3c deep violet	.70	.30
270	A35	5c dark blue	.80	.35
271	A35	7c ultra	1.40	.50
272	A35	8c dark green	1.75	1.00
273	A35	10c orange yel	1.50	.60
274	A35	20c carmine rose	3.00	1.75
275	A36	50c lemon	11.25	7.75
276	A36	1p dark brown	26.00	19.00
		Nos. 266-276 (11)	48.45	32.60

For surcharges see Nos. G1-G7.

Tower of Homage, Ozama Fortress — A37

1932   Litho.   Perf. 12
278	A37	1c green	1.75	.25
279	A37	3c violet	1.10	.25

Issue dates: 1c, July 2; 3c, June 22.

"CORREOS" added at left
1933, May 28
283	A37	1c dark green	.50	.25

President Rafael L. Trujillo
A38   A39

1933, Aug. 16   Engr.   Perf. 14
286	A38	1c yellow grn & blk	.75	.35
287	A39	3c dp violet & blk	.90	.35
288	A38	7c ultra & blk	2.00	.75
		Nos. 286-288 (3)	3.65	1.45

42nd birthday of President Rafael Leonidas Trujillo Molina.

San Rafael Bridge — A40

1934   Litho.   Perf. 12
289	A40	½c dull violet	.70	.40
290	A40	1c dark green	1.00	.25
291	A40	3c violet	1.75	.25
		Nos. 289-291 (3)	3.45	.90

Opening of San Rafael Bridge.
Issue dates: ½c, 3c, Mar. 3; 1c, Feb. 17.

Trujillo Bridge A41

1934
292	A41	½c red brown	.70	.25
293	A41	1c green	1.00	.25
294	A41	3c purple	1.40	.25
		Nos. 292-294 (3)	3.10	.75

Opening of the General Trujillo Bridge near Ciudad Trujillo.
Issue dates: 1c, Aug. 24. Others, Sept. 7.

Ramfis Bridge A42

1935, Apr. 6
295	A42	1c green	.70	.25
296	A42	3c yellow brown	.70	.25
297	A42	5c brown violet	2.10	1.00
298	A42	10c rose	4.25	1.40
		Nos. 295-298 (4)	7.75	2.90

Opening of the Ramfis Bridge over the Higuamo River.

President Trujillo — A43

A44

A45

1935   Perf. 11
299	A43	3c yellow & brown	.30	.25
300	A44	5c org red, bl, red & bis	.40	.25
301	A45	7c ultra, bl, red & brn	.60	.25
302	A44	10c red vio, bl, red & bis	1.00	.25
		Nos. 299-302 (4)	2.30	1.00

Ratification of a treaty setting the frontier between Dominican Republic and Haiti.
Issued: 3c, 10/29; 5c, 10c, 11/25; 7c, 11/8.

National Palace A46

1935, Apr. 1   Perf. 11½
303	A46	25c yellow orange	3.75	.30

Obligatory for all mail addressed to the president and cabinet ministers.

Post Office, Santiago A47

1936
304	A47	½c bright violet	.30	.35
305	A47	1c green	.30	.25

Issue dates: ½c, Jan. 14; 1c, Jan. 4.

George Washington Ave., Ciudad Trujillo — A48

1936, Feb. 22
306	A48	½c brn & vio brn	.40	.45
a.		Imperf., pair	52.50	
307	A48	2c carmine & brn	.40	.30
308	A48	3c yellow org & red brn	.70	.25
309	A48	7c ultra, blue & brn	1.60	1.25
a.		Imperf., pair	52.50	
		Nos. 306-309 (4)	3.10	2.25

Dedication of George Washington Avenue, Ciudad Trujillo.

José Nuñez de   Felix M. del
Cáceres — A49   Monte — A55

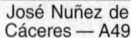

Proposed National Library — A56

1c, Gen. Gregorio Luperon. 2c, Emiliano Tejera. 3c, Pres. Trujillo. 5c, Jose Reyes. 7c, Gen. Antonio Duverge. 25c, Francisco J. Peynado. 30c, Salome Urena. 50c, Gen. Jose M. Cabral. 1p, Manuel de Jesus Galvan. 2p, Gaston F. Deligne.

1936 Unwmk. Engr. Perf. 13½, 14
310	A49	½c dull violet	.40	.25
311	A49	1c dark green	.30	.25
312	A49	2c carmine	.30	.25
313	A49	3c violet	.40	.25
314	A49	5c deep ultra	.70	.30
315	A49	7c slate blue	1.25	.60
316	A55	10c orange	1.25	.30
317	A56	20c olive green	5.75	3.00
318	A55	25c gray violet	6.75	8.75
319	A55	30c scarlet	8.25	11.50
320	A55	50c black brown	9.75	6.25
321	A55	1p black	27.50	35.00
322	A55	2p yellow brown	80.00	90.00
		Nos. 310-322 (13)	142.60	156.70

The funds derived from the sale of these stamps were returned to the National Treasury Fund for the erection of a building for the National Library and Archives.
Issued: 3c, 7c, Mar. 18; others, May 22.

President Trujillo and Obelisk — A62

1937, Jan. 11 Litho. Perf. 11½
323	A62	1c green	.30	.25
324	A62	3c violet	.40	.25
325	A62	7c blue & turq blue	1.10	1.10
		Nos. 323-325 (3)	1.80	1.60

1st anniv. of naming Ciudad Trujillo.

Discus Thrower and Flag — A63

Flag in Red and Blue
1937, Aug. 14
326	A63	1c dark green	11.50	1.00
327	A63	3c violet	14.50	1.00
328	A63	7c dark blue	26.00	5.25
		Nos. 326-328 (3)	52.00	7.25

1st Natl. Olympic Games, Aug. 16, 1937.

Symbolical of Peace, Labor and Progress — A64

1937, Sept. 18 Perf. 12
329	A64	3c purple	.50	.25

"8th Year of the Benefactor."

Monument to Father Francisco Xavier Billini (1837-90) — A65

1937, Dec. 29
330	A65	½c deep orange	.25	.25
331	A65	5c purple	.60	.25

Globe and Torch of Liberty — A66

1938, Feb. 22 Perf. 11½
332	A66	1c green	.50	.25
333	A66	3c purple	.70	.25
334	A66	10c orange	1.40	.25
		Nos. 332-334 (3)	2.60	.75

150th anniv. of the Constitution of the US.

Pledge of Trinitarians, City Gate and National Flag — A67

1938, July 16 Perf. 12
335	A67	1c green, red & dk bl	.50	.25
336	A67	3c purple, red & bl	.60	.25
337	A67	10c orange, red & bl	1.25	.40
		Nos. 335-337 (3)	2.35	.90

Trinitarians and patriots, Francisco Del Rosario Sanchez, Matías Ramón Mella and Juan Pablo Duarte, who helped free their country from foreign domination.

Seal of the University of Santo Domingo — A68

1938, Oct. 28
338	A68	½c orange	.40	.25
339	A68	1c dp green & lt green	.40	.25
340	A68	3c purple & pale vio	.50	.25
341	A68	7c dp blue & lt blue	1.00	.50
		Nos. 338-341 (4)	2.30	1.25

Founding of the University of Santo Domingo, on Oct. 28, 1538.

Trylon and Perisphere, Flag and Proposed Columbus Lighthouse — A69

Flag in Blue and Red
1939, Apr. 30 Litho. Perf. 12
342	A69	½c red org & org	.35	.25
343	A69	1c green & lt green	.40	.25
344	A69	3c purple & pale vio	.40	.25
345	A69	10c orange & yellow	1.40	.65
		Nos. 342-345, C33 (5)	4.55	2.25

New York World's Fair.

A70   A71

1939, Sept. Typo.
346	A70	½c black & pale gray	.40	.25
347	A70	1c black & yel grn	.50	.25
348	A70	3c black & yel brn	.50	.25
349	A70	7c black & dp ultra	1.10	.90
350	A70	10c black & brt red vio	2.10	.40
		Nos. 346-350 (5)	4.60	2.05

José Trujillo Valdez (1863-1935), father of President Trujillo Molina.

Flags in National Colors
Map of the Americas and flags of 21 American republics.

1940, Apr. 14 Litho. Perf. 11½
351	A71	1c deep green	.35	.25
352	A71	2c carmine	.45	.25
353	A71	3c red violet	.60	.25
354	A71	10c orange	1.25	.25
355	A71	1p chestnut	18.00	13.50
		Nos. 351-355 (5)	20.65	14.50

Pan American Union, 50th anniv.

Sir Rowland Hill — A72

1940, May 6 Perf. 12
356	A72	3c brt red vio & rose lil	3.25	.40
357	A72	7c dk blue & lt blue	6.75	1.75

Centenary of first postage stamp.

Julia Molina Trujillo A73

1940, May 26
358	A73	1c grn, lt grn & dk grn	.40	.25
359	A73	2c brt red, buff & dp rose	.40	.25
360	A73	3c org, dl org & brn org	.55	.25
361	A73	7c bl, pale bl & dk bl	1.10	.35
		Nos. 358-361 (4)	2.45	1.10

Issued in commemoration of Mother's Day.

Map of Caribbean A74

1940, June 6 Perf. 11½
362	A74	3c brt car & pale rose	.50	.25
363	A74	7c dk blue & lt blue	1.00	.25
364	A74	1p yel grn & pale grn	10.00	9.00
		Nos. 362-364 (3)	11.50	9.50

2nd Inter-American Caribbean Conf. held at Ciudad Trujillo, May 31 to June 6.

Marion Military Hospital — A75

1940, Dec. 24
365	A75	½c chestnut & fawn	.25	.25

AIR POST STAMPS

Map of Hispaniola — AP1

Perf. 11½
1928, May 31 Litho. Unwmk.
C1	AP1	10c deep ultra	5.25	2.50

1930
C2	AP1	10c ocher	3.50	3.00
a.		Vert. pair, imperf. btwn.	600.00	
C3	AP1	15c scarlet	6.75	4.00
C4	AP1	20c dull green	3.25	.85
C5	AP1	30c violet	6.75	4.50
		Nos. C2-C5 (4)	20.25	12.35

Nos. C2-C5 have only "CENTAVOS" in lower panel. Issued: 10c, 20c, 1/24; 15c, 30c, 2/14.

1930
C6	AP1	10c light blue	1.75	.60
C7	AP1	15c blue green	3.25	1.00
C8	AP1	20c yellow brown	3.50	.85
a.		Horiz. pair, imperf. vert.	450.00	450.00
C9	AP1	30c chocolate	6.25	1.75
		Nos. C6-C9 (4)	14.75	4.20

Issue dates: 10c, 15c, 20c, Sept.; 30c, Oct.

Batwing Sundial Erected in 1753 — AP2

1931-33 Perf. 12
C10	AP2	10c carmine	3.50	.50
C11	AP2	10c light blue	1.75	.50
C12	AP2	10c dark green	6.25	2.75
C13	AP2	15c rose lilac	2.75	.50
C14	AP2	20c dark blue	6.25	2.25
a.		Numerals reading up at left and down at right	5.75	2.75
b.		Imperf., pair	250.00	
C15	AP2	30c green	2.50	.25
C16	AP2	50c red brown	6.25	.50
C17	AP2	1p deep orange	10.00	2.75
		Nos. C10-C17 (8)	39.25	10.00

Issued: No. C11, 7/2/32; No. C12, 5/28/33; others 8/16.

Airplane and Ozama Fortress AP3

1933, Nov. 20
C18 AP3 10c dark blue   3.50 .60

Airplane and Trujillo Bridge AP4

1934, Sept. 20
C19 AP4 10c dark blue   3.00 .50

Symbolic of Flight AP5

1935, Apr. 29
C20 AP5 10c lt blue & dk blue   1.60 .50

AP6

1936, Feb. 11   **Perf. 11½**
C21 AP6 10c dk bl & turq bl   2.50 .50

Allegory of Flight AP7

1936, Oct. 17
C22 AP7 10c dk bl, bl & turq bl   2.25 .40

Macoris Airport AP8

1937, Oct. 22
C23 AP8 10c green   1.00 .25

Fleet of Columbus AP9

Air Fleet AP10

Proposed Columbus Lighthouse — AP11

1937, Nov. 9   **Perf. 12**
C24 AP9 10c rose red   1.75 1.40
C25 AP10 15c purple   1.40 .95
C26 AP11 20c dk bl & lt bl   1.40 1.25
C27 AP10 25c red violet   2.00 1.25
C28 AP11 30c yellow green   1.75 1.25
C29 AP10 50c brown   3.50 1.75
C30 AP11 75c dk olive grn   10.50 10.50
C31 AP9 1p orange   6.25 2.50
    Nos. C24-C31 (8)   28.55 20.85

Goodwill flight to all American countries by the planes "Colon," "Pinta," "Nina" and "Santa Maria."

No. C30 was reproduced imperf. on No. 1019.

Pan American Clipper AP12

1938, July 30
C32 AP12 10c green   1.25 .25

Trylon and Perisphere, Plane and Proposed Columbus Lighthouse — AP13

1939, Apr. 30
C33 AP13 10c green & lt green   2.00 .85
    New York World's Fair.

Airplane AP14

1939, Oct. 18
C34 AP14 10c green & dp green   1.60 .25
a.   Pair, imperf. btwn.   450.00

Proposed Columbus Lighthouse, Plane and Caravels — AP15

Christopher Columbus and Proposed Lighthouse — AP16

Proposed Lighthouse — AP17

Christopher Columbus — AP18

Caravel — AP19

1940, Oct. 12
C35 AP15 10c sapphire & lt bl   1.10 .60
C36 AP16 15c org brn & brn   1.60 1.00
C37 AP17 20c rose red & red   1.60 1.00
C38 AP18 25c brt red lil & red vio   1.60 .50
C39 AP19 50c green & lt green   3.00 1.75
    Nos. C35-C39 (5)   8.90 4.85

Discovery of America by Columbus and proposed Columbus memorial lighthouse in Dominican Republic.

AIR POST OFFICIAL STAMPS

Nos. O13-O14 Overprinted in Blue

    Unwmk.
1930, Dec. 3   **Typo.**   **Perf. 12**
CO1 O3 10c light blue   15.00 17.50
a.   Pair, one without ovpt.   900.00
CO2 O3 20c orange   15.00 17.50

SPECIAL DELIVERY STAMPS

Biplane SD1

    Perf. 11½
1920, Apr.   **Unwmk.**   **Litho.**
E1 SD1 10c deep ultra   6.75 1.40
a.   Imperf., pair

Special Delivery Messenger — SD2

1925
E2 SD2 10c dark blue   21.00 5.75

SD3

1927
E3 SD3 10c red brown   6.75 1.40
a.   "E EXPRESO" at top   55.00 55.00

INSURED LETTER STAMPS

Merino Issue of 1933 Surcharged in Red or Black

1935, Feb. 1   **Unwmk.**   **Perf. 14**
G1 A35 8c on 7c ultra   .60 .25
a.   Inverted surcharge   18.00
G2 A35 15c on 10c org yel   .65 .25
a.   Inverted surcharge   18.00
G3 A35 30c on 8c dk green   2.25 .90
G4 A35 45c on 20c car rose (Bk)   3.25 1.10
G5 A36 70c on 50c lemon   7.75 1.75
    Nos. G1-G5 (5)   14.50 4.25

Merino Issue of 1933 Surcharged in Red

1940
G6 A35 8c on ½c lt vio   2.75 2.75
G7 A35 8c on 7c ultra   3.25 3.25

Coat of Arms — IL1

1940-45   **Litho.**   **Perf. 11½**
    Arms in Black
G8 IL1 8c brown red   .85 .25
a.   8c dk red, no shading on inner frame   1.10 .25
G9 IL1 15c dp orange ('45)   1.75 .25
G10 IL1 30c dk green ('41)   2.00 .25
a.   30c yellow green   2.00 .25
G11 IL1 45c ultra ('44)   2.25 .30
G12 IL1 70c olive brn ('44)   2.10 .30
    Nos. G8-G12 (5)   8.95 1.35

See Nos. G13-G16, G24-G27 in Scott Standard catalogue, Vol. 2.

POSTAGE DUE STAMPS

D1

1901   **Unwmk.**   **Typo.**   **Perf. 14**
J1 D1 2c olive gray   .90 .25
J2 D1 4c olive gray   1.10 .25
J3 D1 5c olive gray   1.90 .30
J4 D1 10c olive gray   3.25 .95
    Nos. J1-J4 (4)   7.15 1.75

For surcharges and overprint see Nos. 162-165, 169-171.

1909   **Wmk. 116**
J5 D1 2c olive gray   1.50 .50
J6 D1 4c olive gray   1.50 .50
J7 D1 6c olive gray   2.00 .75
J8 D1 10c olive gray   4.00 2.50
    Nos. J5-J8 (4)   9.00 4.25

1913

J9	D1	2c olive green	.60	.30
J10	D1	4c olive green	.70	.40
J11	D1	6c olive green	1.10	.50
J12	D1	10c olive green	1.25	.60
		Nos. J9-J12 (4)	3.65	1.80

1922   Unwmk.   Litho.   Perf. 11½

J13	D1	1c olive green	.70	.70

OFFICIAL STAMPS

Bastion of February 27
O1

Unwmk.

1902, Feb. 25   Perf. 12

O1	O1	2c scarlet & blk	.65	.30
O2	O1	5c dk blue & blk	.85	.25
O3	O1	10c yel org & blk	1.00	.55
O4	O1	20c yellow & blk	1.25	.55
a.		Imperf., pair	11.00	
		Nos. O1-O4 (4)	3.75	1.65

For overprints and surcharge see Nos. 157-161.

Bastion of Feb. 27
O2

Columbus Lighthouse
O3

Perf. 13½x13, 13½x14

1909-12   Wmk. 116   Typo.

O5	O2	1c blue grn & blk	.40	.25
O6	O2	2c scarlet & blk	.50	.30
O7	O2	5c dk blue & blk	1.00	.40
O8	O2	10c yel grn & blk ('12)	1.60	.95
O9	O2	20c orange & blk ('12)	2.75	2.25
		Nos. O5-O9 (5)	6.25	4.15

The 2c, 5c are found in both perforations; 1c, 20c perf. 13½x13; 10c perf. 13½x14.
For overprints and surcharge see Nos. 177, 194-199.

1928   Unwmk.   Perf. 12

O10	O3	1c green	.25	.25
O11	O3	2c red	.25	.25
O12	O3	5c ultramarine	.30	.30
O13	O3	10c light blue	.40	.40
O14	O3	20c orange	.60	.60
		Nos. O10-O14 (5)	1.80	1.80

For overprints see Nos. CO1-CO2.

Proposed Columbus Lighthouse
O4

1937   Litho.   Perf. 11½

O15	O4	3c dark purple	1.10	.30
O16	O4	7c indigo & blue	1.20	.40
O17	O4	10c orange yellow	1.30	.60
		Nos. O15-O17 (3)	3.60	1.30

Proposed Columbus Lighthouse
O5

1939-41

O18	O5	1c dp grn & lt grn	.50	.25
O19	O5	2c crim & pale pink	.50	.25
O20	O5	3c purple & lt vio	.50	.25
O21	O5	5c dk bl & lt bl ('40)	.85	.40
O21A	O5	5c lt blue ('41)	1.50	1.00
O22	O5	7c brt bl & lt bl ('41)	1.40	.25
O23	O5	10c yel org & pale org ('41)	1.40	.35
O24	O5	20c brn org & buff ('41)	4.25	.70
O25	O5	50c brt red lil & pale lil ('41)	5.00	.10
		Nos. O18-O25 (9)	15.90	5.55

POSTAL TAX STAMPS

Santo Domingo after Hurricane
PT1

Hurricane's Effect on Capital
PT2

1930, Dec. Unwmk. Litho. Perf. 12

RA1	PT1	1c green & rose	.25	.25
RA2	PT1	2c red rose	.25	.25
RA3	PT2	5c ultra & rose	.30	.25
RA4	PT2	10c yellow & rose	.40	.30

Imperf

RA5	PT1	1c green & rose	.40	.30
RA6	PT1	2c red & rose	.50	.30
RA7	PT2	5c ultra & rose	.60	.50
RA8	PT2	10c yellow & rose	.90	.75
		Nos. RA1-RA8 (8)	3.60	2.90

For surcharges see Nos. RAC1-RAC7.

Tête bêche Pairs

RA1a	PT1	1c green & rose	1.75	1.75
RA2a	PT1	2c red rose	1.75	1.50
RA3a	PT1	5c ultra & rose	1.75	2.10
RA4a	PT1	10c yellow & rose	2.10	2.10
RA5a	PT1	1c green & rose	1.75	1.75
RA6a	PT1	2c red & rose	1.75	1.75
RA7a	PT1	5c ultra & rose	2.10	2.10
RA8a	PT1	10c yellow & rose	2.10	2.10
		Nos. RA1a-RA8a (8)	15.05	15.15

POSTAL TAX AIR POST STAMPS

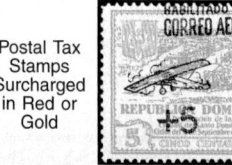

Postal Tax Stamps Surcharged in Red or Gold

1930, Dec. 3   Unwmk.   Perf. 12

RAC1	PT2	5c + 5c blk & rose (R)	27.00	31.00
a.		Tête bêche pair	125.00	
b.		"Habilitado Para" missing	52.50	
RAC2	PT2	10c + 10c blk & rose (R)	27.00	31.00
a.		Tête bêche pair	125.00	
b.		"Habilitado Para" missing	52.50	
c.		Gold surcharge	95.00	95.00
d.		As "c," tête bêche pair	450.00	
e.		As "c" and "b"	250.00	

Nos. RAC1-RAC2 were on sale one day.

RAC4	PT2	5c + 5c ultra & rose (R)	6.75	6.75
a.		Tête bêche pair	45.00	
b.		Inverted surcharge	42.50	
c.		Tête bêche pair, inverted surcharge	600.00	
d.		Pair, one without surcharge	190.00	
e.		"Habilitado Para" missing	15.00	
RAC5	PT2	10c + 10c yel & rose (G)	5.25	5.25
a.		Tête bêche pair	42.50	
b.		"Habilitado Para" missing	18.00	

Imperf

RAC6	PT2	5c + 5c ultra & rose (R)	6.75	6.75
a.		Tête bêche pair	52.50	
b.		"Habilitado Para" missing	18.00	
RAC7	PT2	10c + 10c yel & rose (G)	6.75	6.75
a.		Tête bêche pair	52.50	
b.		"Habilitado Para" missing	18.00	
		Nos. RAC1-RAC7 (6)	79.50	87.50

It was obligatory to use Nos. RA1-RA8 and RAC1-RAC7 on all postal matter, in amounts equal to the ordinary postage.

This surtax was for the aid of sufferers from the hurricane of Sept. 3, 1930.

No. 261 Overprinted in Green

1933, Oct. 11

RAC8	A32	2c scarlet	.50	.40
a.		Double overprint	9.00	
b.		Pair, one without overprint	375.00	

By official decree this stamp, in addition to the regular postage, had to be used on every letter, etc., sent by the internal air post service.

EAST AFRICA & UGANDA PROTECTORATES

ˈēst ˈa-fri-kə and ü-ˈgan-də prə-ˈtek-t̬ə-ˌrəts

LOCATION — Central East Africa, bordering on the Indian Ocean
GOVT. — Former British Protectorate
AREA — 350,000 sq. mi. (approx.)
POP. — 6,503,507 (approx.)
CAPITAL — Mombasa

This territory, formerly administered by the British East Africa Colony, was divided between Kenya Colony and the Uganda Protectorate. See Kenya, Uganda and Tanzania.

16 Annas = 1 Rupee
100 Cents = 1 Rupee (1907)

King Edward VII

A1   A2

1903   Typo.   Wmk. 2   Perf. 14

1	A1	½a gray green	5.00	17.00
2	A1	1a car & black	2.25	1.50
3	A1	2a vio & dull vio	10.50	3.00
4	A1	2½a ultramarine	14.50	60.00
5	A1	3a gray grn & brn	25.00	67.50
6	A1	4a blk & gray grn	13.50	27.50
7	A1	5a org brn & blk	22.50	60.00
8	A1	8a pale blue & blk	26.00	50.00

Wmk. 1

9	A2	1r gray green	22.50	60.00
a.		On chalky paper	72.50	100.00
10	A2	2r vio & dull vio	87.50	100.00
11	A2	3r blk & gray grn	140.00	250.00
12	A2	4r lt green & blk	150.00	275.00
13	A2	5r car & black	150.00	275.00
14	A2	10r ultra & black	400.00	550.00
a.		On chalky paper	375.00	450.00
15	A2	20r ol gray & blk	675.00	1,600.
		Overprinted "SPECIMEN"	150.00	
16	A2	50r org brn & blk	1,900.	3,750.
		Overprinted "SPECIMEN"	350.00	
		Nos. 1-14 (14)	1,069.	1,796.
		Set, ovptd "SPECIMEN"	500.00	

1904-07   Wmk. 3   Chalky Paper

17	A1	½a gray green	10.50	3.75
18	A1	1a car & black	11.50	2.00
19	A1	2a vio & dull vio	3.50	3.25
21	A1	3a gray grn & brn	4.75	35.00
22	A1	4a blk & gray grn	9.25	22.50
23	A1	5a org brn & blk	8.00	18.50
24	A1	8a pale blue & blk	8.75	21.00
25	A2	1r gray green	35.00	75.00
26	A2	2r vio & dl vio	47.50	67.50
27	A2	3r blk & gray grn	70.00	125.00
28	A2	4r lt green & blk	100.00	180.00
29	A2	5r car & black	120.00	150.00
29A	A2	10r ultra & black	275.00	325.00
30	A2	20r ol gray & black	675.00	1,250.
30A	A2	50r org brn & blk	2,100.	3,750.
		Nos. 17-29 (12)	428.75	703.50

Ordinary Paper

17a		½a gray green	9.75	3.50
18a	A1	1a car & black	4.50	1.00
19a		2a vio & dull vio	3.75	3.00
20	A1	2½a blue	10.00	37.50
a.		2½a blue & ultramarine	9.50	21.00
21a		3a gray grn & brn	4.25	35.00
22a		4a blk & gray grn	8.50	20.00
23a		5a org brn & blk	9.25	17.50
24a	A1	8a pale blue & blk	8.75	10.50

1907-08

31	A1	1c brown ('08)	3.00	.25
32	A1	3c gray green	17.50	.80
a.		3c blue green	19.00	3.50
33	A1	6c carmine	3.25	.25
a.		6c carmine, single plate ('10)	17.50	.35
34	A1	10c citron & violet	11.00	10.00
35	A1	12c red vio & dl vio	12.00	3.50
36	A1	15c ultramarine	30.00	11.00
37	A1	25c blue green	14.50	8.50
38	A1	50c org brn & green	14.50	14.50
39	A1	75c pale bl & gray blk ('08)	5.50	40.00
		Nos. 31-39 (9)	111.25	88.80
		Set, ovptd "SPECIMEN"	210.00	

Nos. 31-33, 36 are on ordinary paper.
On No. 33a, there is a distinct white line separating the lower tablets from the rest of the design. This is not present on No. 33. The word "PROTECTORATE" is in taller letters on No. 33a.

King George V

A3   A4

1912-18   Ordinary Paper   Wmk. 3

40	A3	1c black	.40	2.10
41	A3	3c green	2.50	.75
a.		Booklet pane of 6		
b.		3c deep blue green ('17)	5.00	1.75
42	A3	6c carmine	1.50	.70
a.		Booklet pane of 6		
b.		6c scarlet ('17)	20.00	3.00
43	A3	10c yel orange	2.50	.65
a.		10c orange ('21)	11.50	4.00
44	A3	12c gray	3.25	.65
45	A3	15c ultramarine	3.25	1.00

Chalky Paper

46	A3	25c scar & blk, yel	.65	1.60
a.		25c scar & blk, lemon ('16)	12.50	12.50
		Overprinted "SPECIMEN"	40.00	
b.		25c scar & blk, org buff ('21)	50.00	19.00
c.		25c scar & blk, pale yel ('21)	11.50	5.75
47	A3	50c violet & black	1.90	1.60
48	A3	75c black, green	1.90	21.00
a.		75c blk, emerald	13.50	65.00
b.		75c blk, bl grn, olive back	7.25	9.25
c.		75c blk, emer, olive back	50.00	175.00
49	A4	1r black, green	2.25	5.25
a.		1r black, emerald	6.00	60.00
50	A4	2r blk & red, bl	24.50	45.00
51	A4	3r gray grn & vio	24.50	110.00
52	A4	4r grn & red, yel	55.00	125.00
a.		4r grn & red, pale yellow	110.00	190.00
53	A4	5r dl vio & ultra	60.00	175.00
54	A4	10r grn & red, grn	180.00	275.00
55	A4	20r vio & blk, red	425.00	425.00
56	A4	20r bl & violet, blue ('18)	500.00	550.00
57	A4	50r gray grn & rose red	900.00	975.00
		Overprinted "SPECIMEN"	175.00	
a.		50r dull green & dull rose, ordinary paper	925.00	975.00
58	A4	100r blk & vio, red	6,000.	3,000.
		Overprinted "SPECIMEN"	400.00	

59	A4	500r red & grn, grn	25,000.	
		Overprinted "SPECIMEN"	850.00	
		Nos. 40-54 (15)	364.10	765.30
		Nos. 40-54 (15), ovptd "SPECIMEN"	1,000.	

1914   Surface-colored Paper

60	A3	25c scarlet & blk, yel	.65	5.50
61	A3	75c black, green	1.25	19.50
		Nos. 60-61, ovptd "SPECIMEN"	75.00	

Stamps of types A3 and A4 with watermark 4 are listed under Kenya, Uganda and Tanzania.

The 1r through 50r with revenue cancellations sell for minimal prices. The 100r and 500r were available for postage but were nearly always used fiscally.

For surcharge see No. 62.

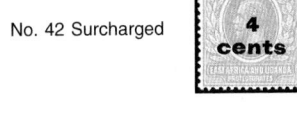

No. 42 Surcharged

1919

62	A3	4c on 6c carmine	1.50	.25
		Handstamped "SPECIMEN"	70.00	
a.	Double surcharge		150.00	240.00
b.	Without squares over old value		50.00	85.00
c.	Pair, one without surcharge		2,000.	2,250.
d.	Inverted surcharge		325.00	475.00
e.	Surcharged on back		400.00	

For later issues see Kenya, Uganda and Tanzania.

For stamps of East Africa and Uganda overprinted "G. E. A." see German East Africa.

EASTERN RUMELIA

ˈē-stərn rü-ˈmēl-yə

(South Bulgaria)

LOCATION — In southern Bulgaria
GOVT. — An autonomous unit of the Turkish Empire.
CAPITAL — Philippopolis (Plovdiv)

In 1885 the province of Eastern Rumelia revolted against Turkish rule and united with Bulgaria, adopting the new name of South Bulgaria. This union was assured by the Treaty of Bucharest in 1886, following the war between Serbia and Bulgaria.

40 Paras = 1 Piaster

Counterfeits of all overprints are plentiful.

Stamps of Turkey, 1876-84, Overprinted in Blue

No. 1

A2   A3

1880   Unwmk.   Perf. 13½

1	A5	½pi on 20pa yel	67.50	57.50
a.	Horiz. pair, one without overprint			400.00
3	A2	10pa blk & rose	55.00	
4	A2	20pa vio & grn	87.50	67.50

6	A2	2pi blk & buff	115.00	100.00
7	A2	5pi red & bl	450.00	500.00
8	A3	10pa blk & red lil	57.50	

Nos. 3 & 8 were not placed in use.
Inverted and double overprints of all values exist.

Same, with Extra Overprint "R. O."

9	A3	10pa blk & red lil	97.50	95.00

Crescent and Turkish Inscriptions of Value — A4

1881   Typo.   Perf. 13½

10	A4	5pa blk & olive	17.00	1.35
11	A4	10pa blk & green	65.00	1.35
12	A4	20pa blk & rose	1.75	1.25
b.	Cliché of 10pa in plate of 20pa		625.00	
		In pair with No. 12	1,000.	
13	A4	1pi blk & blue	5.75	4.50
14	A4	5pi rose & blue	57.50	82.50

Tête bêche pairs and imperforates were not placed in use, and were found only in the remainder stock. This is true also of No. 12b, and of a cliché of Turkey No. 63 in the 1pi plate.

Perf. 11½

10a	A4	5pa blk & olive	30.00	
11a	A4	10pa blk & green	30.00	
12a	A4	20pa blk & rose	30.00	
13a	A4	1pi blk & blue	30.00	
14a	A4	5pi rose & blue	45.00	

Nos. 10a-14a were not placed in use, and were found only in the remainder stock.

1884   Perf. 11½

15	A4	5pa lil & pale lil	.55	.45
16	A4	10pa grn & pale grn	.25	.45
17	A4	20pa car & pale rose	.55	
18	A4	1pi bl & pale bl	1.15	
19	A4	5pi brn & pale brn	400.00	

Nos. 17-19 were not placed in use, and were found only in the remainder stock.
Nos. 15-19 imperf. are from remainders.
For overprints see Turkey Nos. 542-545.

Perf. 13½

15a	A4	5pa lil & pale lil	1.15	3.50
16a	A4	10pa grn & pale grn	17.50	17.00
17a	A4	20pa car & pale rose	20.00	
18a	A4	1pi bl & pale bl	20.00	
19a	A4	5pi brn & pale brn	475.00	

Nos. 17a-19a were not placed in use, and were found only in the remainder stock.

South Bulgaria

Counterfeits of all overprints are plentiful.

Nos. 10-14 Overprinted in Two Types

a   b

Type a — Four toes on each foot.
Type b — Three toes on each foot.

Blue Overprint

1885   Unwmk.   Perf. 13½

20	A4 (a)	5pa blk & olive	325.00	375.00
21	A4 (a)	10pa blk & grn	875.00	825.00
22	A4 (a)	20pa blk & rose	325.00	—
a.	Type "b"		325.00	
b.	Type "a", perf. 11½		325.00	375.00
c.	Type "b", perf. 11½		225.00	
23	A4 (a)	1pi blk & blue	37.50	72.50
a.	Type "b"		82.50	97.50
24	A4 (b)	5pi rose & blue	1,100.	
a.	Type "a"		725.00	

Black Overprint

24B	A4 (a)	20pa blk & rose	275.00	—
25	A4 (a)	1pi blk & bl	55.00	115.00
a.	Type "b"		65.00	82.50
26	A4 (b)	5pi rose & bl	675.00	

Same Overprint on Nos. 15-17

Blue Overprint

Perf. 11½

27	A4 (b)	5pa lil & pale lil, type "b"	22.50	57.50
a.	Type "a"		35.00	82.50
b.	Perf. 13½, type "b"		87.50	97.50
c.	Perf. 13½, type "a"		225.00	250.00
28	A4 (b)	10pa grn & pale grn	40.00	75.00
a.	Type "a"		57.50	115.00

29	A4 (b)	20pa car & pale rose	275.00	375.00
a.	Type "a"		325.00	375.00

Black Overprint

Perf. 13½

30	A4 (b)	5pa lil & pale lil	40.00	67.50
a.	Type "a"		40.00	67.50
b.	Type "b", perf. 11½		55.00	65.00

Perf. 11½

31	A4 (a)	10pa grn & pale grn	42.50	85.00
a.	Type "b"		65.00	—
b.	Type "a", perf. 13½		60.00	115.00
32	A4 (b)	20pa car & pale rose	55.00	65.00
a.	Type "a"		55.00	82.50

Nos. 10-17 Handstamped in Black in Two Types

a   b

Type a — First letter at top circular.
Type b — First letter at top oval.

1885   Perf. 13½

33	A4 (b)	5pa blk & olive	300.00	250.00
a.	Type "a"		250.00	
34	A4 (b)	10pa blk & grn	225.00	250.00
a.	Type "a"		300.00	
35	A4 (b)	20pa blk & rose	72.50	85.00
a.	Type "a"		135.00	170.00
36	A4 (a)	1pi blk & bl	87.50	115.00
a.	Type "b"		90.00	125.00
37	A4 (a)	5pi rose & blue, type "a"	2,500.	—
a.	Type "b"			

Perf. 13½

38	A4 (a)	5pa blk & pale lil	26.00	44.00
a.	Type "b"		32.50	44.00
b.	Perf. 11½, type "a"		225.00	275.00
c.	Perf. 11½, type "b"		225.00	275.00

Perf. 11½

39	A4 (a)	10pa grn & pale grn	29.00	35.00
a.	Type "b"		57.50	57.50
40	A4 (a)	20pa car & pale rose	29.00	50.00
a.	Type "b"		57.50	28.00

Nos. 20-40 exist with inverted and double handstamps. Overprints in unlisted colors are proofs.

The stamps of South Bulgaria were superseded in 1886 by those of Bulgaria.

EASTERN SILESIA

ˈē-stərn sī-ˈlē-zhē-ə

LOCATION — In central Europe
GOVT. — Former Austrian crownland
AREA — 1,987 sq. mi.
POP. — 680,422 (estimated 1920)
CAPITAL — Troppau

After World War I, this territory was occupied by Czechoslovakia and eventually was divided between Poland and Czechoslovakia, the dividing line running through Teschen.

100 Heller = 1 Krone
100 Fennigi = 1 Marka

Plebiscite Issues

Stamps of Czechoslovakia 1918-20, Overprinted in Black, Blue, Violet or Red

1920   Unwmk.   Imperf.

1	A2	1h dark brown	.25	.30
2	A1	3h red violet	.25	.30
3	A2	5h blue green	23.50	22.50
4	A2	15h red	11.50	11.00
5	A1	20h blue green	.25	.25
6	A2	25h dull violet	.75	.75
7	A1	30h bister (R)	.25	.25
8	A1	40h red orange	.30	.30
9	A2	50h dull violet	.60	.45

10	A2	50h dark blue	2.60	1.50
11	A2	60h orange (Bl)	.75	.75
12	A2	75h slate (R)	.50	.75
13	A2	80h olive grn (R)	.50	.75
14	A1	100h brown	1.10	1.10
15	A2	120h gray blk (R)	1.60	2.25
16	A1	200h ultra (R)	1.60	2.00
17	A2	300h green (R)	6.25	7.50
18	A1	400h purple (R)	2.60	3.00
19	A2	500h red brn (Bl)	5.25	6.00
a.	Black overprint		6.25	9.00
20	A1	1000h violet (Bl)	13.00	13.50
a.	Black overprint		62.50	75.00
21	A2	1000h violet (Bl)	13.00	13.50
a.	Black overprint		62.50	75.00
		Nos. 1-21 (20)	73.40	75.15

Perf. 11½, 13¾

22	A2	1h dark brown	.25	.25
23	A2	5h bister green	.30	.25
24	A2	10h yellow green	.30	.25
a.	Imperf.		260.00	210.00
25	A2	15h red	.50	.25
26	A2	20h rose	.50	.35
a.	Imperf.		300.00	250.00
27	A2	30h dull violet	.50	.35
28	A2	30h red violet (Bl)	.35	.35
29	A2	60h orange (Bl)	.50	.50
30	A1	200h ultra (R)	3.00	3.00
		Nos. 22-30 (9)	6.20	5.55

The letters "S. O." are the initials of "Silésie Orientale."
Forged cancellations are found on Nos. 1-30.

Overprinted in Carmine or Violet

31	A4	500h sl, grysh (C)	40.00	
32	A4	1000h blk brn, brnsh	40.00	

Excellent counterfeits of this overprint exist.

Stamps of Poland, 1919, Overprinted

1920   Perf. 11½

41	A10	5f green	.25	.25
42	A10	10f red brown	.25	.25
43	A10	15f light red	.25	.25
44	A11	25f olive green	.25	.25
45	A11	50f blue green	.25	.25

Overprinted

46	A12	1k deep green	.25	.25
47	A12	1.50k brown	.25	.25
48	A12	2k dark blue	.25	.25
49	A13	2.50k dull violet	.30	.25
50	A14	5k slate blue	.50	.25
		Nos. 41-50 (10)	2.80	2.50

SPECIAL DELIVERY STAMPS

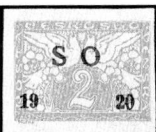

Czechoslovakia Special Delivery Stamps Ovptd. in Blue

1920   Unwmk.   Imperf.

E1	SD1	2h red violet, yel	.25	.25
a.	Black overprint		4.75	.80
E2	SD1	5h yellow green, yel	.25	.25
a.	Black overprint		8.00	5.00

Nos. E1-E2a exist on white paper.

POSTAGE DUE STAMPS

Czechoslovakia Postage Due Stamps Overprinted In Blue or Red

1920   Unwmk.   Imperf.

J1	D1	5h deep bis (Bl)	.25	.25
a.		Black overprint	72.50	62.50
J2	D1	10h deep bister	.25	.25
J3	D1	15h deep bister	.25	.25
J4	D1	20h deep bister	.25	.25
J5	D1	25h deep bister	.25	.25
J6	D1	30h deep bister	.25	.25
J7	D1	40h deep bister	.50	.25
J8	D1	50h deep bister	2.60	3.00
J9	D1	100h blk brn (R)	2.60	3.00
J10	D1	500h gray grn (R)	5.75	4.50
J11	D1	1000h purple (R)	8.50	11.50
		Nos. J1-J11 (11)	21.45	23.75

Forged cancellations exist.

NEWSPAPER STAMPS

Czechoslovakia Newspaper Stamps Overprinted in Black like Nos. 1-30

1920   Unwmk.   Imperf.

P1	N1	2h gray green	.30	.30
P2	N1	6h red	.25	.25
P3	N1	10h dull violet	.40	.25
P4	N1	20h blue	.65	.25
P5	N1	30h gray brown	.65	.25
		Nos. P1-P5 (5)	2.25	1.30

ECUADOR

'e-kwə-ˌdor

LOCATION — Northwest coast of South America, bordering on the Pacific Ocean
GOVT. — Republic
AREA — 116,270 sq. mi.
POP. — 8,420,000 (est. 1984)
CAPITAL — Quito

The Republic of Ecuador was so constituted on May 11, 1830, after the Civil War that separated the original members of the Republic of Colombia, founded by Simon Bolivar by uniting the Presidency of Quito with the Viceroyalty of New Grenada and the Captaincy of Venezuela. The Presidency of Quito became the Republic of Ecuador.

8 Reales = 1 Peso
100 Centavos = 1 Sucre (1881)

Watermarks

Wmk. 117 — Liberty Cap

Wmk. 127 — Quatrefoils

Wmk. 233 — "Harrison & Sons, London" in Script Letters

STAMPS OF GREAT BRITAIN USED IN ECUADOR
Guayaquil

Stamps of Great Britain cancelled Type A "C41"

1865-80

A1	½p rose red, plates 5, 6 (#58), value from		70.00
A2	1p rose red ('57) (#20)		—
A3	1p rose red, plates 74, 78, 85, 92, 94, 105, 110, 115, 133, 140, 145, 166, 174, 180, 216 (#33), value from		50.00
A4	1½p lake red, plate 3 (#32)		100.00
A5	2p blue, plate 9 (#29)		55.00
A6	2p blue, plates 13, 14 (#30), value from		50.00
A7	3p rose ('62) (#37)		290.00
A8	3p rose ('65) (#44)		140.00
A9	3p rose ('67-'73), plates 6, 7, 9, 10 (#49), value from		57.50
A10	3p rose ('73-'80), plates 11, 12, 15-20 (#61), value from		57.50
A11	4p vermilion ('62), plate 4 (#34a)		140.00
A12	4p vermilion ('62), "hair lines" (#34c)		140.00
A13	4p vermilion ('65-'73), plates 7-14 (#43), value from		57.50
A14	4p vermilion ('76), plate 15 (#69)		350.00
A15	4p pale olive green, plate 15 (#70)		225.00
A16	4p pale olive green, plate 16 (#70)		225.00
A17	6p lilac, plate 4 (#39b)		175.00
A18	6p lilac ('65-'67), plate 5 (#45)		85.00
A19	6p lilac ('65-'67), plate 6 (#45)		85.00
A20	6p dull violet ('67), plate 6 (#50)		—
A21	6p violet ('67-'70), plates 6, 8, 9 (#51), value from		80.00
A22	6p pale buff ('72-'73), plate 11 (#59b)		92.50
A23	6p pale buff ('72-'73), plate 12 (#59b)		225.00
A24	6p brown ('72), plates 11, 12 (#59)		—
A25	6p gray ('73), plate 12 (#60)		—
A26	6p gray ('73), plates 13-16 (#60), value from		57.50
A27	8p orange ('76) (373)		375.00
A28	9p straw ('62) (#40)		310.00
A29	9p bister ('67) (#52)		225.00
A30	10p red brown ('67) (#53)		350.00
A31	1sh green ('65) (#48)		185.00
A32	1sh green ('67-'73), plates 4-6 (#54), value from		50.00
A33	1sh green ('67-'73), plate 7 (#54)		85.00
A34	1sh green ('73-'77), plates 8-11 (#64), value from		90.00
A35	1sh green ('73-'77), plates 12, 13 (#64), value from		85.00
A36	2sh blue ('67) (#55)		175.00
A37	2sh brown ('80) (#56)		2,600.
A38	5sh rose ('67-'74), plate 1 (#57)		550.00
A39	5sh rose ('67-'74), plate 2 (#57)		700.00

Issues of the Republic

Coat of Arms
A1   A2

1865-72   Unwmk.   Typo.   Imperf.
Quadrille Paper

1	A1	1r yellow ('72)	60.00	55.00
		On wrapper		150.00
		On cover		—

Wove Paper

2	A1	½r ultra	40.00	20.00
		On wrapper		125.00
		On cover		250.00
a.		½r gray blue ('67)	40.00	15.00
		On wrapper		125.00
		On cover		125.00
b.		Batonne paper ('70)	50.00	25.00
c.		Blue paper ('72)	250.00	100.00
d.		Embossed arms	—	400.00
e.		Watermarked		1,000.
3	A1	1r buff	25.00	18.00
		On wrapper		150.00
		On cover		300.00
a.		1r orange buff	30.00	20.00
		On wrapper		175.00
		On cover		325.00
4	A1	1r yellow	25.00	15.00
		On wrapper		125.00
		On cover		250.00
a.		1r olive yellow ('66)	32.50	22.50
		On wrapper		175.00
		On cover		400.00
b.		Laid paper	175.00	110.00
c.		Half used as ½r on cover		900.00
d.		Batonne paper	40.00	30.00
e.		Embossed arms	—	500.00
f.		Watermarked		1,000.
5	A1	1r green	300.00	55.00
		On wrapper		150.00
		On cover		300.00
a.		Half used as ½r on cover		900.00
b.		Embossed arms	—	700.00
c.		Watermarked		1,000.
6	A2	4r red ('66)	500.00	200.00
		On wrapper		700.00
		On cover		1,000.
a.		4r red brown ('66)	700.00	200.00
		On wrapper		700.00
		On cover		1,100.
b.		Arms in circle	500.00	250.00
c.		Printed on both sides	550.00	
d.		Half used as 2r on cover		1,600.
e.		Embossed arms	—	900.00
f.		Watermarked	—	2,000.
		Nos. 1-6 (6)	950.00	363.00

Letter paper embossed with arms of Ecuador was used in printing a number of sheets of Nos. 2, 4-6.
Papermakers' watermarks on No. 2e, 4f, 5c and 6f reads "Rolland Freres".
On the 4r the oval holding the coat of arms is usually 13½-14mm wide, but on about one-fifth of the stamps in the sheet it is 15-15½mm wide, almost a circle.
The 2r, 8r and 12r, type A1, are bogus.
Proofs of the ½r, type A1, are known in black and green.
An essay of type A2 shows the condor's head facing right.

1871-72   Blue-surface Paper

7	A1	½r ultra	50.00	25.00
		On wrapper		175.00
		On cover		350.00
8	A1	1r yellow	300.00	100.00
		On wrapper		750.00
		On cover		—

Unofficial reprints of types A1-A2 differ in color, have a different sheet makeup and lack gum. Type A1 reprints usually have a double frameline at left. All stamps on blue paper with horiz. blue lines are reprints.

A3   A4

1872   White Paper   Litho.   Perf. 11

9	A3	½r blue	30.00	5.00
10	A4	1r orange	40.00	7.00
11	A3	1p rose	5.00	25.00
		Nos. 9-11 (3)	75.00	37.00

The 1r surcharged 4c is fraudulent.

A5   A6

A7   A8

A9   A10

1881, Nov. 1   Engr.   Perf. 12

12	A5	1c yellow brn	.40	.25
13	A6	2c lake	.40	.25
14	A7	5c blue	10.00	.50
15	A8	10c orange	.40	.25
16	A9	20c gray violet	.40	.25
17	A10	50c blue green	2.00	3.00
		Nos. 12-17 (6)	13.60	4.50

The 1c surcharged 3c, and 20c surcharged 5c are fraudulent.
For overprints see Nos. O1-O6.

No. 17 Surcharged in Black

1883, Apr.

18	A10	10c on 50c blue grn	50.00	30.00
a.		Double surcharge		

Dangerous forgeries exist.

A12   A13

A14   A15

1887

19	A12	1c blue green	.50	.40
20	A13	2c vermilion	1.00	.40
21	A14	5c blue	3.00	.50
22	A15	80c olive green	6.00	15.00
		Nos. 19-22 (4)	10.50	16.30

For overprints see Nos. O7-O10.

President Juan Flores — A16

1892

23	A16	1c orange	.30	1.00
24	A16	2c dk brown	.30	1.00
25	A16	5c vermilion	.30	1.00
26	A16	10c green	.30	1.00
27	A16	20c red brown	.30	1.00
28	A16	50c maroon	.30	2.00
29	A16	1s blue	.30	4.00
30	A16	5s purple	1.00	8.00
		Nos. 23-30 (8)	3.10	19.00

The issues of 1892, 1894, 1895 and 1896 were printed by the Hamilton Bank Note Co., New York, to the order of N. F. Seebeck, who held a contract for stamps with the government of Ecuador.
No. 30 in green is said to be an essay or color trial.
For surcharges and overprints see Nos. 31-37, O11-O17.

Nos. 29 and 30 Surcharged in Black

1893

Surcharge Measures 25½x2½mm

31	A16	5c on 1s blue	6.00	6.00
32	A16	5c on 5s purple	10.00	9.00
a.		Double surcharge		

Surcharge Measures 24x2¼mm

33	A16	5c on 1s blue	3.00	3.00
a.		Double surcharge, one inverted		
34	A16	5c on 5s purple	12.00	10.00
a.		Double surcharge, one invtd.		

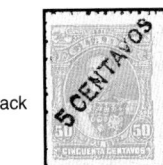

Nos. 28-30
Surcharged in Black

35	A16	5c on 50c maroon	2.00	2.00
a.		Inverted surcharge		5.00
36	A16	5c on 1s blue	2.50	2.00
37	A16	5c on 5s purple	10.00	10.00
		Nos. 31-37 (7)	45.50	42.00

Pres. Juan
Flores — A19

38	A19	5c on 5s lake	4.00	4.00

It is stated that No. 38 was used exclusively
as a postage stamp and not for telegrams.

Pres. Vicente
Rocafuerte — A20

Dated "1894"

1894	**Various Frames**		**Perf. 12**	
39	A20	1c blue	.40	.40
40	A20	2c yellow brn	.40	.40
41	A20	5c green	.40	.40
b.		Perf. 14	6.00	2.00
42	A20	10c vermilion	.70	.60
43	A20	20c black	1.10	.70
44	A20	50c orange	6.00	2.00
45	A20	1s carmine	9.50	4.00
46	A20	5s dark blue	12.00	6.00
		Nos. 39-46 (8)	30.50	14.50

1895		**Same, Dated "1895"**		
47	A20	1c blue	.90	.70
48	A20	2c yellow brn	.90	.70
49	A20	5c green	.70	.50
50	A20	10c vermilion	.70	.40
51	A20	20c black	1.00	1.00
52	A20	50c orange	3.50	2.25
53	A20	1s carmine	21.00	8.00
54	A20	5s dark blue	8.50	4.00
		Nos. 47-54 (8)	37.20	17.55

Reprints of the 2c, 10c, 50c, 1s and 5s of
the 1894-95 issues are generally on thick
paper. Original issues are on thin to medium
thick paper. To distinguish reprints from originals, a comparison of paper thickness, paper
color, gum, printing clarity and direction of
paper weave is necessary. Value 20 cents
each.

For overprints see Nos. 77-112, O20-O33,
O50-O91.

A21 A22

A23 A24

A25 A26

A27 A28

1896			**Wmk. 117**	
55	A21	1c dk green	.70	.60
56	A22	2c red	.70	.40
57	A23	5c blue	.70	.40
58	A24	10c bister brn	.60	.90
59	A25	20c orange	1.40	2.00
60	A26	50c dark blue	5.00	3.00
61	A27	1s yellow brn	4.00	4.00
62	A28	5s violet	14.00	5.50
		Nos. 55-62 (8)	27.10	16.80

		Unwmk.		
62A	A21	1c dk green	1.00	.40
62B	A22	2c red	1.10	.40
62C	A23	5c blue	1.10	.70
62D	A24	10c bister brn	.70	1.40
62E	A25	20c orange	6.00	5.50
62F	A26	50c dark blue	2.00	2.75
62G	A27	1s yellow brn	6.00	8.00
62H	A28	5s violet	15.00	6.00
		Nos. 62A-62H (8)	32.90	25.15

Reprints of Nos. 55-62H are on very thick
paper, with paper weave direction vertical.
Value 20 cents each.

For surcharges and overprints see Nos. 74,
76, 113-114, O34-O49.

Vicente Roca,
Diego Noboa and
José
Olmedo — A28a

General Juan
Francisco
Elizalde — A28b

Perf. 11½

1896, Oct. 9		**Unwmk.**	**Litho.**	
63	A28a	1c rose	.55	.55
64	A28b	2c blue	.55	.55
65	A28a	5c green	.75	.55
66	A28b	10c ocher	.75	.75
67	A28a	20c red	1.10	3.25
68	A28b	50c violet	1.75	4.75
69	A28a	1s orange	3.25	8.00
		Nos. 63-69 (7)	8.70	18.60

Success of the Liberal Party in 1845 & 1895.
For overprints see Nos. 115-125.

A29

Black Surcharge

1896, Nov.			**Perf. 12**	
70	A29	1c on 1c ver, "1893-1894"	1.00	.60
a.		Inverted surcharge	2.50	2.00
b.		Double surcharge	8.00	7.00
71	A29	2c on 2c bl, "1893-1894"	2.00	1.75
a.		Inverted surcharge	4.00	3.50
72	A29	5c on 10c org, "1887-1888"	2.00	.60
a.		Inverted surcharge	4.00	1.75
b.		Double surcharge	7.00	4.00
c.		Surcharged "2cts"	1.00	.80
d.		"1893-1894"	6.00	5.00
73	A29	10c on 4c brn, "1887-1888"	2.00	1.10
a.		Inverted surcharge	4.00	1.75
b.		Double surcharge	6.00	3.50

c.		Double surcharge, one inverted		
d.		Surcharged "1 cto"	2.00	2.75
e.		"1891-1892"	17.00	13.50
		Nos. 70-73 (4)	7.00	4.05

Similar surcharges of type A29 include:
Dated "1887-1888" — 1c on 1c blue green, 1c
on 2c red, 1c on 4c brown, 1c on 10c yellow;
2c on 2c red, 2c on 10c yellow; 10c on 1c
green.
Dated "1891-1892" — 1c on 1c blue green,
1c on 4c brown.
Dated "1893-1894" — 2c on 10c yellow; 10c
on 1c vermilion, 10c on 10s black.
For overprints see Nos. O18-O19.

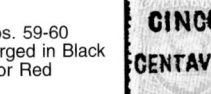

Nos. 59-60
Surcharged in Black
or Red

1896, Oct.			**Wmk. 117**	
74	A25	5c on 20c orange	40.00	40.00
76	A26	10c on 50c dk bl (R)	50.00	50.00
a.		Double surcharge		

The surcharge is diag., horiz. or vert.

Nos. 39-54
Overprinted

On Issue of 1894

1897		**Unwmk.**		
77	A20	1c blue	2.25	2.25
78	A20	2c yellow brn	1.90	1.30
79	A20	5c green	.90	.90
80	A20	10c vermilion	2.75	2.25
81	A20	20c black	3.00	2.75
82	A20	50c orange	6.50	3.25
83	A20	1s carmine	19.00	6.50
84	A20	5s dark blue	110.00	90.00
		Nos. 77-84 (8)	146.30	109.20

On Issue of 1895

85	A20	1c blue	6.00	5.50
86	A20	2c yellow brn	2.25	2.25
87	A20	5c green	1.90	1.60
88	A20	10c vermilion	7.00	6.00
89	A20	20c black	1.90	1.75
90	A20	50c orange	32.50	13.00
91	A20	1s carmine	14.50	7.50
92	A20	5s dark blue	14.50	14.50
		Nos. 85-92 (8)	80.55	52.10

Nos. 39-54
Overprinted

On Issue of 1894

1897				
93	A20	1c blue	1.40	.90
94	A20	2c yellow brn	1.20	.75
95	A20	5c green	.60	.50
96	A20	10c vermilion	3.50	1.75
97	A20	20c black	3.75	2.50
98	A20	50c orange	7.00	2.75
99	A20	1s carmine	13.00	8.50
100	A20	5s dark blue	115.00	85.00
		Nos. 93-100 (8)	145.45	102.65

On Issue of 1895

101	A20	1c blue	3.25	1.60
102	A20	2c yellow brn	1.60	1.60
103	A20	5c green	1.75	1.00
104	A20	10c vermilion	5.50	4.50
105	A20	20c black	5.00	1.20
106	A20	50c orange	1.75	1.75
107	A20	1s carmine	8.00	7.00
108	A20	5s dark blue	9.50	9.50
		Nos. 101-108 (8)	36.35	28.15

Overprints on Nos. 77-108 are to be found
reading upward from left to right and downward from left to right, as well as inverted.

Overprinted

1897		**On Issue of 1894**		
109	A20	10c vermilion	—	—

On Issue of 1895

110	A20	2c yellow brn	—	—
111	A20	1s carmine	—	—
112	A20	5s dark blue	—	—

Nos. 56, 59 Overprinted like Nos. 93-108

1897, June			**Wmk. 117**	
113	A22	2c red	—	—
114	A25	20c orange	—	—

Many forged overprints on Nos. 77-114
exist, made on original stamps and reprints.

Stamps or Types
of 1896
Overprinted in
Black

1897		**Unwmk.**	**Perf. 11½**	
115	A28a	1c rose	3.75	3.75
116	A28b	2c blue	3.00	3.00
117	A28b	10c ocher	3.00	3.00
118	A28a	1s yellow	15.00	15.00
		Nos. 115-118 (4)	24.75	24.75

No. 63
Overprinted in
Black

1897				
119	A28a	1c rose	.60	.50

Nos. 63-66
Overprinted in
Black

1897				
122	A28a	1c rose	4.50	4.00
123	A28b	2c blue	4.50	4.00
124	A28a	5c green	4.50	4.00
125	A28b	10c ocher	4.50	4.00
a.		Double overprint	10.50	9.50
		Nos. 122-125 (4)	18.00	16.00

The 20c, 50c and 1s with this overprint in
black and all values of the issue overprinted in
blue are reprints.

Overprint Inverted

122a	A28a	1c	6.00	5.50
123a	A28b	2c	6.00	5.50
124a	A28a	5c	6.00	5.50
125b	A28b	10c	6.00	5.50

Coat of Arms — A33

1897, June 23		**Engr.**	**Perf. 14-16**	
127	A33	1c dk yellow grn	.35	.25
128	A33	2c orange red	.35	.25
129	A33	5c lake	.35	.25
130	A33	10c dk brown	.35	.25
131	A33	20c black	.45	.40
132	A33	50c dull blue	.45	.25
133	A33	1s gray	.90	1.25
134	A33	5s dark lilac	4.00	5.00
		Nos. 127-134 (8)	7.20	8.30

No. 135

No. 136

1899, May
135	A33	1c on 2c orange red	3.00	1.50
136	A33	5c on 10c brown	2.50	1.00
	a.	Double surcharge		

Luis Vargas Torres A36

Abdón Calderón A37

Juan Montalvo A38

José Mejia A39

Santa Cruz y Espejo — A40

Pedro Carbo — A41

José Joaquin Olmedo A42

Pedro Moncayo A43

1899   *Perf. 12½-16*
137	A36	1c gray blue & blk	.40	.25
	a.	Horiz. pair, imperf. vert.		
138	A37	2c brown lil & blk	.40	.25
139	A38	5c lake & blk	.70	.25
140	A39	10c violet & blk	.70	.25
141	A40	20c green & blk	.70	.25
142	A41	50c lil rose & blk	1.75	.55
143	A42	1s ocher & blk	8.00	2.75
144	A43	5s lilac & blk	14.50	7.50
		Nos. 137-144 (8)	27.15	12.05

1901   *Perf. 12*
145	A36	1c scarlet & blk	.45	.25
146	A37	2c green & blk	.45	.25
147	A38	5c brown lil & blk	.45	.25
148	A39	10c dp blue & blk	.50	.25
149	A40	20c gray & blk	.50	.25
150	A41	50c lt blue & blk	1.75	.95
151	A42	1s brown & blk	6.00	2.75
152	A43	5s gray blk & blk	9.00	5.75
		Nos. 145-152 (8)	19.10	10.70

In July, 1902, following the theft of a quantity of stamps during a fire at Guayaquil, the Government authorized the governors of the provinces to handstamp their stocks. Many varieties of these handstamps exist.

Other control marks were used in 1907.

For overprints see Nos. O103-O106, O167.

A44

Surcharged on Revenue Stamp Dated 1901-1902

1903-06   *Perf. 14, 15*
153	A44	1c on 5c gray lil ('06)	.75	.40
154	A44	1c on 20c gray ('06)	10.00	4.50
155	A44	1c on 25c yellow	1.50	.40
	a.	Double surcharge		
156	A44	1c on 1s bl ('06)	77.50	50.00
157	A44	3c on 5c gray lil ('06)	10.00	4.00
158	A44	3c on 20c gray ('06)	25.00	15.00
159	A44	3c on 25c yel ('06)	24.00	15.00
159A	A44	3c on 1s blue ('06)	3.75	2.25
		Nos. 153-159A (8)	152.50	91.55

Counterfeits are plentiful.
See Nos. 191-197.

Capt. Abdón Calderón
A45   A46

1904, July 31   *Perf. 12*
160	A45	1c red & blk	.45	.30
161	A45	2c blue & blk	.50	.35
162	A46	5c yellow & blk	1.90	1.00
163	A45	10c red & blk	6.00	2.00
164	A46	20c blue & blk	10.00	8.00
165	A46	50c yellow & blk	85.00	*120.00*
		Nos. 160-165 (6)	103.85	131.65

Centenary of the birth of Calderón.

Presidents

Vicente Roca — A47

Diego Noboa — A48

Francisco Robles — A49

José M. Urvina — A50

García Moreno — A51

Jerónimo Carrión — A52

Javier Espinoza A53

Antonio Borrero A54

1907, July   *Perf. 14, 15*
166	A47	1c red & blk	1.00	.25
167	A48	2c pale blue & blk	2.00	.25
168	A49	3c orange & blk	3.00	.25
169	A50	5c lilac rose & blk	3.75	.25
170	A51	10c dp blue & blk	7.50	.25
171	A52	20c yellow grn & blk	10.00	.35
172	A53	50c violet & blk	22.50	.70
173	A54	1s green & blk	30.00	2.00
		Nos. 166-173 (8)	79.75	4.30

The stamps of the 1907 issue frequently have control marks similar to those found on

the 1899 and 1901 issues. These marks were applied to distinguish the stamps issued in the various provinces and to serve as a check on local officials.

Locomotive — A55

García Moreno — A56

Gen. Eloy Alfaro — A57

Abelardo Moncayo — A58

Archer Harman — A59

James Sivewright — A60

Mt. Chimborazo A61

1908, June 25
174	A55	1c red brown	1.10	*2.10*
175	A56	2c blue & blk	1.30	*2.25*
176	A57	5c claret & blk	2.75	*5.25*
177	A58	10c ocher & blk	1.75	*2.75*
178	A59	20c green & blk	1.75	*3.75*
179	A60	50c gray & blk	1.75	*3.75*
180	A61	1s black	3.50	*8.00*
		Nos. 174-180 (7)	13.90	27.85

Opening of the Guayaquil-Quito Railway.

José Mejía Vallejo — A62

Principal Exposition Building — A70

Designs: 2c, Francisco J. E. Santa Cruz y Espejo. 3c, Francisco Ascásubi. 5c, Juan Salinas. 10c, Juan Pio de Montúfar, el Marques de Selva Alegre. 20c, Carlos de Montúfar. 50c, Juan de Dios Morales. 1s, Manuel R. de Quiroga.

1909, Aug. 10   *Perf. 12*
181	A62	1c green	.35	.65
182	A62	2c blue	.35	.65
183	A62	3c orange	.35	.75
184	A62	5c claret	.05	.75
185	A62	10c yellow brn	.45	.75
186	A62	20c gray	.45	1.10
187	A62	50c vermilion	.45	1.10
188	A62	1s olive grn	.45	1.40
189	A70	5s violet	1.25	2.75
		Nos. 181-189 (9)	4.45	9.90

National Exposition of 1909.

No. 187 Surcharged

1909
| 190 | A62 | 5c on 50c vermilion | .90 | .75 |

Revenue Stamps Surcharged as in 1903

1910   *Perf. 14, 15*
Stamps Dated 1905-1906
191	A44	1c on 5c green	2.25	1.75
192	A44	5c on 20c blue	9.50	2.00
193	A44	5c on 25c violet	18.00	3.50

Stamps Dated 1907-1908
194	A44	1c on 5c green	.40	.40
195	A44	5c on 20c blue	14.00	9.50
196	A44	5c on 25c violet	1.20	.40

Stamp Dated 1909-1910
| 197 | A44 | 5c on 20c blue | 80.00 | 60.00 |
| | | *Nos. 191-197 (7)* | 125.35 | 77.55 |

Presidents

Roca — A71

Noboa — A72

Robles — A73

Urvina — A74

Moreno — A75

Borrero — A76

1911-28   *Perf. 12*
198	A71	1c scarlet & blk	.80	.25
199	A71	1c orange ('16)	.80	.25
200	A71	1c lt blue ('25)	.40	.25
201	A72	2c blue & blk	1.10	.25
202	A72	2c green ('16)	1.10	.25
203	A72	2c dk violet ('25)	1.10	.25
204	A73	3c orange & blk ('13)	2.25	.30
205	A73	3c black ('15)	1.50	.25
206	A74	5c scarlet & blk	1.90	.25
207	A74	5c violet ('15)	1.90	.25
208	A74	5c rose ('25)	.70	.25
209	A74	5c dk brown ('28)	.70	.25
210	A75	10c dp blue & blk	2.25	.25
211	A75	10c dp blue ('15)	2.25	.25
212	A75	10c yellow grn ('25)	.70	.25
213	A75	10c black ('28)	1.60	.25
214	A76	1s green & blk	12.00	1.50
215	A76	1s orange & blk ('27)	8.00	.25
		Nos. 198-215 (18)	41.05	5.80

For overprints see Nos. 260-262, O107-O122, O124-O134, O156-O157, O160-O162, O164-O166, O168-O173, O175-O178, O183-O184, O189, RA1.

A77

1912   *Perf. 14, 15*
216 A77 1c on 1s green   1.00   1.00
217 A77 2c on 2s carmine   2.50   1.50
218 A77 2c on 5s dull blue   1.50   1.50
219 A77 2c on 10s yellow   5.00   5.00
   a.   Inverted surcharge   16.00   12.00
     Nos. 216-219 (4)   10.00   9.00

No. 216 exists with narrow "V" and small "U" in "UN" and Nos. 217, 218 and 219 with "D" with serifs or small "O" in "DOS."

Enrique Váldez — A78

Jerónimo Carrión — A79

Javier Espinoza — A80

1915-17   *Perf. 12*
220 A78 4c red & blk   .40   .25
221 A79 20c green & blk ('17)   3.50   .25
222 A80 50c dp violet & blk   6.00   .45
     Nos. 220-222 (3)   9.90   .95

For overprints see Nos. O123, O135, O163, O174.

Olmedo — A86

Monument to "Fathers of the Country" — A95

Laurel Wreath and Star — A104

Designs: 2c, Rafael Ximena. 3c, Roca. 4c, Luis F. Vivero. 5c, Luis Febres Cordero. 6c, Francisco Lavayen. 7c, Jorge Antonio de Elizalde. 8c, Baltazar Garcia. 9c, Jose de Antepara. 15c, Luis Urdaneta. 20c, Jose M. Villamil. 30c, Miguel Letamendi. 50c, Gen. Antonio Jose de Sucre. 60c, Juan Illingworth. 70c, Roca. 80c, Rocafuerte. 1s, Simon Bolivar.

1920
223 A86 1c yellow grn   .35   .25
224 A86 2c carmine   .35   .25
225 A86 3c yellow brn   .35   .25
226 A86 4c myrtle green   .55   .25
227 A86 5c pale blue   .55   .25
228 A86 6c red orange   .90   .30
229 A86 7c brown   2.25   .75
230 A86 8c apple green   1.25   .35
231 A86 9c lake   4.25   1.50
232 A95 10c lt blue   1.50   .25
233 A86 15c dk gray   2.25   .35
234 A86 20c dk violet   2.25   .25
235 A86 30c brt violet   4.25   1.40
236 A86 40c dk brown   7.50   2.10
237 A86 50c dk green   5.25   .55
238 A86 60c dk blue   9.50   2.10
239 A86 70c gray   16.00   4.75
240 A86 80c orange yel   16.50   4.75

241 A104 90c green   17.00   4.75
242 A86 1s pale blue   24.00   8.50
     Nos. 223-242 (20)   116.80   33.90

Cent. of the independence of Guayaquil. For overprints and surcharges see Nos. 263, 274-292, O136-O155, O179-O182, O185-O188.

Postal Tax Stamp of 1924 Overprinted

1925
259 PT6 20c bister brown   4.00   1.50

Stamps of 1915-25 Overprinted in Black or Red Upright (1c, 3c, 5c) or Inverted (2c, 4c, 10c)

1926
260 A71 1c lt blue   12.50   10.50
261 A72 2c dk violet   12.50   10.50
262 A73 3c black (R)   12.50   10.50
263 A86 4c myrtle green   12.50   10.50
264 A74 5c rose   17.50   10.50
265 A75 10c yellow grn   17.50   10.50
     Nos. 260-265 (6)   85.00   63.00

Quito-Esmeraldas railway opening. Upright overprints on 2c, 4c, 10c and inverted overprints on 1c, 3c, 5c sell for more.

Postal Tax Stamps of 1920-24 Overprinted

1927
266 PT6 1c olive green   .50   .25
   a.   "POSTAI"   1.40   .85
   b.   Double overprint   2.00   .85
   c.   Inverted overprint   2.00   .85
267 PT6 2c deep green   .50   .25
   a.   "POSTAI"   1.40   .85
   b.   Double overprint   2.00   .85
268 PT6 20c bister brown   1.00   .25
   a.   "POSTAI"   8.50   5.00
     Nos. 266-268 (3)   2.00   .75

Quito Post Office — A109

1927, June
269 A109 5c orange   .50   .25
270 A109 10c dark green   .70   .25
271 A109 20c violet   .80   .25
     Nos. 269-271 (3)   2.00   .75

Opening of new Quito P.O. For overprint see No. O190.

Postal Tax Stamp of 1924 Overprinted in Dark Blue

1928
273 PT6 20c bister brown   .50   .25
   a.   Double overprint, one inverted   2.00   .70

See No. 339 for 10c with same overprint.

Nos. 235, 239-240 Ovptd. in Red Brown and Srchd. in Dark Blue

1928, July 8
274 A86 10c on 30c violet   16.00   16.00
275 A86 50c on 70c gray   20.00   20.00
276 A86 1s on 80c org yel   22.50   22.50
     Nos. 274-276 (3)   58.50   58.50

Quito-Cayambe railway opening.

Stamps of 1920 Surcharged

1928, Oct. 9
277 A86 1c on 1c yel grn   15.00   15.00
278 A86 1c on 2c car   .30   .30
279 A86 2c on 3c yel brn   2.25   2.25
   a.   Dbl. surch., one reading up   30.00   30.00
280 A86 2c on 4c myr grn   1.50   1.50
281 A86 2c on 5c lt blue   .60   .45
   a.   Dbl. surch., one reading up   30.00   30.00
282 A86 2c on 7c brown   75.00   75.00
283 A86 5c on 6c red org   .40   .30
   a.   "5 ctvos." omitted   37.50   37.50
284 A86 10c on 7c brown   1.25   1.25
285 A86 20c on 8c apple grn   .35   .30
   a.   Double surcharge
286 A95 40c on 10c blue   4.25   4.25
287 A86 40c on 15c dk gray   1.25   1.25
288 A86 50c on 20c dk vio   13.25   13.25
289 A86 1s on 40c dk brown   4.50   4.50
290 A86 5s on 30c dk green   5.25   5.25
291 A86 10s on 60c dk blue   19.50   19.50

With Additional Surcharge in Red

292 A86 10c on 2c on 7c brn   .55   .55
   a.   Red surcharge double   30.00   30.00
     Nos. 277-292 (16)   145.20   144.90

National Assembly of 1928. Counterfeit overprints exist of Nos. 277-291.

A111

Surcharged in Various Colors
1928, Oct. 31   *Perf. 14*
293 A111 5c on 20c gray lil (Bk)   3.00   1.75
294 A111 10c on 20c gray lil (R)   3.00   1.75
295 A111 20c on 1s grn (O)   3.00   1.75
296 A111 50c on 1s grn (Bl)   3.75   1.40
297 A111 1s on 1s grn (V)   4.75   1.75
298 A111 5s on 2s red (G)   15.00   9.00
299 A111 10s on 2s red (Br)   18.00   12.00
   a.   Black surcharge   15.00   10.00
     Nos. 293-299 (7)   50.50   29.40

Quito-Otavalo railway opening. See Nos. 586-587 in Scott Standard catalogue, Vol. 2.

Postal Tax Stamp of 1924 Overprinted in Red

1929   *Perf. 12*
302 PT6 2c deep green   .50   .25

There are two types of overprint on No. 302 differing slightly.

A112

1929   **Red Overprint**
303 A112 1c dark blue   .50   .25
   a.   Overprint reading down   .75   .50

See Nos. 586-587 in Scott Standard catalogue, Vol. 2.

Plowing — A113

Cultivating Cacao — A114

Cacao Pod — A115

Growing Tobacco — A116

Exportation of Fruits — A117

Landscape — A118

Loading Sugar Cane — A119

Scene in Quito A120

Scene in Quito A121

Olmedo — A122

Monument to Simón Bolívar — A125

Designs: 2s, Sucre. 5s, Bolivar.

1930, Aug. 1   **Perf. 12½**
304	A113	1c yellow & car	.30	.25
305	A114	2c yellow & grn	.30	.25
306	A115	5c dp grn & vio brn	.35	.25
307	A116	6c yellow & red	.45	.25
308	A117	10c orange & ol grn	.45	.25
309	A118	16c red & yel grn	.55	.25
310	A119	20c ultra & yel	.90	.25
311	A120	40c orange & sepia	1.10	.35
312	A121	50c orange & sepia	1.10	.40
313	A122	1s dp green & blk	4.25	.45
314	A122	2s dk blue & blk	6.50	2.00
315	A122	5s dk violet & blk	11.50	3.00
316	A125	10s car rose & blk	40.00	6.50
		Nos. 304-316 (13)	67.75	14.45

Centenary of founding of republic.
For surcharges and overprints see Nos. 319-320, 331-338, RA25, RA33, RA43.

A126   A127

1933   **Red Overprint**   **Perf. 15**
317	A126	10c olive brown	1.15	.25

Blue Overprint
318	A127	10c olive brown	.70	.25
a.		Inverted overprint	5.00	5.00

For overprint see No. 339.

Nos. 307, 309 Surcharged in Black

1933   **Perf. 12½**
319	A116	5c on 6c yellow & red	1.00	.25
320	A118	10c on 16c red & yel grn	2.00	.25
a.		Inverted overprint	4.00	4.00

Landscape A128   Mt. Chimborazo A129

1934-45   **Perf. 12**
321	A128	5c violet	1.40	.55
322	A128	5c blue	1.40	.55
323	A128	5c dark brown	1.40	.55
323A	A128	5c slate blk ('45)	1.40	.55
324	A128	10c rose	1.40	.55
325	A128	10c dark green	1.40	.55
326	A128	10c brown	1.40	.55
327	A128	10c orange	1.40	.55
328	A128	10c olive green	1.40	.55
329	A128	10c gray blk ('35)	1.40	.55
329A	A128	10c red lilac ('44)	1.40	.55

Perf. 14
330	A129	1s carmine rose	1.60	.55
		Nos. 321-330 (12)	17.00	6.60

Stamps of 1930 Srchd. or Ovptd. in various colors

INAUGURACION MONUMENTO A BOLIVAR
5 ctvs.
QUITO, 24 DE JULIO DE 1935.

1935   **Perf. 12½**
331	A116	5c on 6c (Bl)	.90	.35
332	A116	10c on 6c (G)	1.25	.35
333	A119	20c (R)	1.75	.35
334	A120	40c (G)	2.50	.35
335	A121	50c (G)	3.00	.45
336	A122	1s on 5s (Gold)	7.00	1.25
337	A122	2s on 5s (Gold)	9.50	1.75
338	A125	5s on 10s (Bl)	12.00	5.00
		Nos. 331-338,C35-C38 (12)	87.90	29.85

Unveiling of a monument to Bolivar at Quito, July 24, 1935.

A129a

1935, Oct. 13 Photo.   **Perf. 11½x11**
338A	A129a	5c ultra & black	.25	.25
338B	A129a	10c orange & blue	.25	.25
338C	A129a	40c dk carmine & red	.20	.30
338D	A129a	1S blue green & red	.30	.70
338E	A129a	2S violet & red	.55	1.20
		Nos. 338A-338E,C38A-C38E (10)	4.30	7.60

Columbus Day. Nos. 338A-338E and C38A-C38E were prepared by the Sociedad Colombista Panamericana and were sold by the Ecuadorian post office through Oct. 30.

Telegraph Stamp Overprinted Diagonally in Red like No. 273

1935   **Perf. 14½**
339	A126	10c olive brown	.75	.25

Map of Galápagos Islands A130   Galapagos Land Iguana A131

Galápagos Tortoise — A132

Charles R. Darwin — A133

Columbus A134

Island Scene A135

1936   **Perf. 14**
340	A130	2c black	1.00	.25
341	A131	5c olive grn	1.25	.25
342	A132	10c brown	2.40	.30
343	A133	20c dk violet	2.75	.45
344	A134	1s dk carmine	5.00	.85
345	A135	2s dark blue	7.75	1.40
		Nos. 340-345 (6)	20.15	3.50

Cent. of the visit of Charles Darwin to the Galápagos Islands, Sept. 17, 1835.
For overprints see Nos. O191-O195.

Tobacco Stamp Overprinted in Black

1936   **Rouletted 7**
346	PT7	1c rose red	.50	.25
a.		Horiz. pair, imperf. vert.		
b.		Double surcharge		

No. 346 is similar to type PT7 but does not include "CASA CORREOS."

Louis Godin, Charles M. de la Condamine and Pierre Bouguer A136

Portraits: 5c, 20c, Antonio Ulloa, La Condamine and Jorge Juan.

1936   **Engr.**   **Perf. 12½**
347	A136	2c deep blue	.50	.30
348	A136	5c dark green	.50	.30
349	A136	10c deep orange	.50	.30
350	A136	20c violet	.80	.30
351	A136	50c dark red	1.25	.30
		Nos. 347-351,C39-C42 (9)	6.60	2.60

Bicentenary of Geodesical Mission to Quito.

Independence Monument — A137

1936   **Perf. 13½x14**
352	A137	2c green	2.25	1.25
353	A137	5c dark violet	2.25	1.25
354	A137	10c carmine rose	2.25	1.25
355	A137	20c black	2.25	1.25
356	A137	50c blue	3.25	2.10
357	A137	1s dark red	3.75	3.25
		Nos. 352-357,C43-C50 (14)	50.50	41.35

1st Intl. Philatelic Exhibition at Quito.

Coat of Arms — A138

Overprint in Black or Red

1937   **Perf. 12½**
359	A138	5c olive green	2.00	.30
360	A138	10c dark blue (R)	2.00	.25

For overprint see No. 562.

Andean Landscape A139   Atahualpa, the Last Inca A140

Hat Weavers — A141

Coast Landscape A142   Gold Washing A143

1937, Aug. 19   **Perf. 11½**
361	A139	2c green	.50	.25
362	A140	5c deep rose	.50	.25
363	A141	10c blue	.50	.25
364	A142	20c deep rose	1.50	.30
365	A143	1s olive green	2.00	.35
		Nos. 361-365 (5)	5.00	1.40

For overprints see Nos. O196-O200.

"Liberty" Carrying Flag of Ecuador — A144

Engraved and Lithographed
1938, Feb. 22   **Perf. 12**
Center Multicolored
366	A144	2c blue	.25	.25
367	A144	5c violet	.35	.25
368	A144	10c black	.55	.25
369	A144	20c brown	.65	.25
370	A144	50c black	1.10	.25
371	A144	1s olive blk	1.75	.30
372	A144	2s dk brn	3.25	.55
		Nos. 366-372,C57-C63 (14)	22.40	4.50

US Constitution, 150th anniversary.
For overprints and surcharges see Nos. 413-415, 444-446, RA46, RA52. Post 1940 issues in Scott Standard catalogue, Vol. 2.

A145   A146

A147   A148

Designs: 10c, Winged figure holding globe. 50c, Cactus, winged wheel. 1s, "Communications." 2s, "Construction."

Perf. 13, 13x13½

1938, Oct. 30   **Engr.**
373 A145 10c bright ultra .40 .25
374 A146 50c deep red violet .40 .25
375 A147 1s copper red .70 .25
376 A148 2s dark green 1.10 .25
   Nos. 373-376 (4) 2.60 1.00

Progress of Ecuador Exhibition.
For overprints see Nos. C105-C113 in Scott Standard catalogue, Vol. 2.

Parade of Athletes — A149

Runner — A150   Basketball — A151

Wrestlers A152   Diver A153

1939, Mar.   **Perf. 12**
377 A149 5c carmine rose 3.00 .55
378 A150 10c deep blue 3.50 .65
379 A151 50c gray olive 5.75 .85
380 A152 1s dull violet 7.75 .85
381 A153 2s dull olive green 12.50 .95
   Nos. 377-381,C65-C69 (10) 78.35 6.15

First Bolivarian Games (1938), Bogota.

Dolores Mission A154   Trylon and Perisphere A155

1939, June 16   **Perf. 12½x13**
382 A154 2c blue green .50 .25
383 A154 5c rose red .50 .25
384 A154 10c ultra .50 .25
385 A154 50c yellow brown 1.20 .25
386 A154 1s black 1.90 .25
387 A154 2s purple 1.25 .40
   Nos. 382-387,C73-C79 (13) 11.25 3.40

Golden Gate International Exposition.

For surcharges see Nos. 429, 436 in Scott Standard catalogue, Vol. 2.

1939, June 30
388 A155 2c lt olive green .80 .35
389 A155 5c red orange .80 .35
390 A155 10c ultra .80 .35
391 A155 50c slate gray 1.10 .35
392 A155 1s rose carmine 1.90 .35
393 A155 2s black brown 2.25 .40
   Nos. 388-393,C80-C86 (13) 16.55 4.15

New York World's Fair.
For surcharge see No. 437.

Flags of the 21 American Republics — A156

1940   **Perf. 12**
394 A156 5c dp rose & blk 1.00 .25
395 A156 10c dk blue & blk .40 .25
396 A156 50c Prus green & blk .60 .25
397 A156 1s dp violet & blk 1.00 .30
   Nos. 394-397,C87-C90 (8) 8.30 2.75

Pan American Union, 50th anniversary.

AIR POST STAMPS

In 1928-30, the internal airmail service of Ecuador was handled by the Sociedad Colombo-Alemana de Transportes Aereos ("SCADTA") under government sanction. During this period SCADTA issued stamps which were the only legal franking for airmail service except that handled under contract with Pan American-Grace Airways. SCADTA issues are Nos. C1-C6, C16-C25, CF1-CF2.

Colombia Air Post Stamps of 1923 Surcharged in Carmine

"Provisional" at 45 degree Angle
Perf. 14x14½
1928, Aug. 28   **Wmk. 116**
C1 AP6 50c on 10c green 110.00 70.00
C2 AP6 75c on 15c car 210.00 160.00
C3 AP6 1s on 20c gray 70.00 42.50
C4 AP6 1½s on 30c blue 45.00 35.00
C5 AP6 3s on 60c brown 85.00 52.50
   Nos. C1-C5 (5) 520.00 360.00

"Provisional" at 41 degree Angle
1929, Mar. 20
C1a AP6 50c on 10c green 125.00 110.00
C2a AP6 75c on 15c carmine 225.00 175.00
C3a AP6 1s on 20c gray 225.00 175.00
   Nos. C1a-C3a (3) 575.00 460.00

C6 AP6 50c on 10c green 700.00 1,700.
A 75c on 15c carmine with "Cts." between the surcharged numerals exists. There is no evidence that it was regularly issued or used.
For overprints see Nos. CF1-CF1a.

Plane over River Guayas — AP1

Unwmk.
1929, May 5   **Engr.**   **Perf. 12**
C8 AP1 2c black .40 .25
C9 AP1 5c carmine rose .40 .25
C10 AP1 10c deep brown .40 .25
C11 AP1 20c dark violet .90 .25
C12 AP1 50c deep green 1.60 .45
C13 AP1 1s dark blue 6.00 2.75
C14 AP1 5s orange yellow 25.00 11.00
C15 AP1 10s orange red 135.00 57.50
   Nos. C8-C15 (8) 169.70 72.70

Establishment of commercial air service in Ecuador. The stamps were available for all forms of postal service and were largely used for franking ordinary letters.
Nos. C13-C15 show numerals in color on white background. Counterfeits of No. C15 exist.
See Nos. C26-C31. For overprints and surcharge see Nos. C32-C38, C287 (in Scott Standard catalogue, Vol. 2), CO1-CO12.

Jesuit Church La Compania AP2   Mount Chimborazo AP3

Wmk. 127
1929, Apr. 1   **Litho.**   **Perf. 14**
C16 AP2 50c red brown 4.50 2.25
C17 AP2 75c green 4.50 2.25
C18 AP2 1s rose 7.00 2.25
C19 AP2 1⅕s gray blue 7.00 2.25
C20 AP2 2s violet 11.50 4.50
C21 AP2 3s brown 11.50 4.50
C22 AP3 5s lt blue 40.00 14.00
C23 AP3 10s lt red 85.00 30.00
C24 AP3 15s violet 140.00 60.00
C25 AP3 25s olive green 190.00 70.00
   Nos. C16-C25 (10) 501.00 192.00

For overprint see No. CF2.

Plane Type of 1929
1930-44   **Unwmk.**   **Engr.**   **Perf. 12**
C26 AP1 1s carmine lake 6.50 .55
C27 AP1 1s green ('44) 1.00 .25
C28 AP1 5s olive green 10.00 3.75
C29 AP1 5s purple ('44) 2.00 .25
C30 AP1 10s black 30.00 5.50
C31 AP1 10s brt ultra ('44) 4.50 .30
   Nos. C26-C31 (6) 54.00 10.60

Nos. C26-C31 show numerals in color on white background.
For surcharge see No. C287 in Scott Standard catalogue, Vol. 2.

Type of 1929 Overprinted in Various Colors

AP4

1930, June 4
C32 AP4 1s car lake (Bk) 22.50 22.50
   a. Double ovpt. (R Br + Bk) 75.00
C33 AP4 5s olive grn (Bl) 22.50 22.50
C34 AP4 10s black (R Br) 22.50 22.50
   Nos. C32-C34 (3) 67.50 67.50

Flight of Capt. Benjamin Mendez from Bogota to Quito, bearing a crown of flowers for the tomb of Grand Marshal Sucre.

Air Post Official Stamps of 1929-30 Ovptd. in Various Colors or Srchd. Similarly in Upper & Lower Case

1935, July 24
C35 AP1 50c deep green (Bl) 12.50 5.00
C36 AP1 50c olive brn (R) 12.50 5.00
C37 AP1 1s on 5s ol grn (Bk) 12.50 5.00
   a. Double surcharge 95.00
C38 AP1 2s on 10s black (R) 12.50 5.00
   Nos. C35-C38 (4) 50.00 20.00

Unveiling of a monument to Bolívar at Quito, July 24th, 1935.

AP5

1935, Oct. 13   **Photo.**   **Perf. 11½x11**
C38A AP5 5c ultra & red .25 .30
C38B AP5 10c brown & black .25 .50
C38C AP5 50c green & red .25 .50
C38D AP5 1S carmine & blue .80 1.20
C38E AP5 5S gray grn & red 1.20 2.40
   Nos. C38A-C38E (5) 2.75 4.90

Columbus Day. Nos. 338A-338E and C38A-C38E were prepared by the Sociedad Colombista Panamericana and were sold by the Ecuadorian post office through Oct. 30. Nos. C38B-C38E exist imperf.

Geodesical Mission Issue
Nos. 349-351 Overprinted in Blue or Black and Type of Regular issue

1936, July 3   **Perf. 12½**
C39 A136 10c deep orange (Bl) .60 .25
C40 A136 20c violet (Bk) .60 .25
C41 A136 50c dark red (Bl) .60 .25
C42 A136 70c black 1.25 .35
   Nos. C39-C42 (4) 3.05 1.10

For surcharge see No. RA42.

Philatelic Exhibition Issue
Type of Regular Issue Overprinted "AEREA"

1936, Oct. 20   **Perf. 13½x14**
C43 A137 2c rose 5.00 5.00
C44 A137 5c brown orange 5.00 5.00
C45 A137 10c brown 5.00 5.00
C46 A137 20c ultra 5.00 5.00
C47 A137 50c red violet 5.00 5.00
C48 A137 1s green 5.00 5.00
   Nos. C43-C48 (6) 30.00 30.00

Condor and Plane — AP6

Perf. 13½
C49 AP6 70c orange brown 2.25 .50
C50 AP6 1s dull violet 2.25 .50

Nos. C43-C50 were issued for the 1st Intl. Phil. Exhib. at Quito.

Condor over "El Altar" — AP7

1937-46   **Perf. 11½, 12**
C51 AP7 10c chestnut 5.00 .25
C52 AP7 20c olive black 6.50 .25
C53 AP7 40c rose car ('46) 6.50 .25
C54 AP7 70c black brown 9.00 .25
C55 AP7 1s gray black 14.00 .25
C56 AP7 2s dark violet 24.00 .65
   Nos. C51-C56 (6) 65.00 1.90

Issue dates: 40c, Oct. 7; others, Aug. 19.
For overprints see Nos. 463-464 (in Scott Standard catalogue, Vol. 2), CO13-CO17.

Portrait of Washington, American Eagle and Flags — AP8

Engraved and Lithographed
1938, Feb. 9   Perf. 12
Center Multicolored

C57	AP8	2c brown	.40	.25
C58	AP8	5c black	.40	.25
C59	AP8	10c brown	.40	.25
C60	AP8	20c dark blue	.80	.25
C61	AP8	50c violet	1.75	.25
C62	AP8	1s black	3.25	.25
C63	AP8	2s violet	7.50	.90
		Nos. C57-C63 (7)	14.50	2.40

150th anniv. of the US Constitution.
In 1947, Nos. C61-C63 were overprinted in dark blue: "Primero la Patria!" and plane. These revolutionary propaganda stamps were later renounced by decree. Value $20.
For overprints see Nos. C102-C104, C139-C141 in Scott Standard catalogue, Vol. 2.

No. RA35 Surcharged in Red

1938, Nov. 16   Perf. 13½
C64	PT12	65c on 3c ultra	.40	.25

A national airmail concession was given to the Sociedad Ecuatoriano de Transportes Aereos (SEDTA) in July, 1938. No. RA35 was surcharged for SEDTA postal requirements. SEDTA operated through 1940.

Army Horseman — AP9   Woman Runner — AP10

Tennis — AP11   Boxing — AP12

Olympic Fire — AP13

1939, Mar.   Engr.   Perf. 12
C65	AP9	5c lt green	1.60	.25
C66	AP10	10c salmon	2.25	.25
C67	AP11	50c redsh brown	11.50	.25
C68	AP12	1s black brown	13.50	.45
C69	AP13	2s rose carmine	17.00	1.10
		Nos. C65-C69 (5)	45.85	2.30

First Bolivarian Games (1938).

Plane over Chimborazo AP14

1939, May 1   Perf. 13x12½
C70	AP14	1s yellow brown	.40	.25
C71	AP14	2s rose violet	.70	.25
C72	AP14	5s black	1.90	.25
		Nos. C70-C72 (3)	3.00	.75

Golden Gate Bridge and Mountain Peak — AP15   Empire State Building and Mountain Peak — AP16

1939   Perf. 12½x13
C73	AP15	2c black	.40	.25
C74	AP15	5c rose red	.40	.25
C75	AP15	10c indigo	.40	.25
C76	AP15	50c rose violet	.40	.25
C77	AP15	1s chocolate	.80	.25
C78	AP15	2s yellow brown	1.00	.25
C79	AP15	5s emerald	2.00	.25
		Nos. C73-C79 (7)	5.40	1.75

Golden Gate International Exposition.
For surcharge & overprint see Nos. 434 (in Scott Standard catalogue, Vol. 2), CO18.

1939
C80	AP16	2c brown orange	.65	.30
C81	AP16	5c dark carmine	.65	.20
C82	AP16	10c indigo	.65	.30
C83	AP16	50c slate green	.65	.30
C84	AP16	1s deep orange	1.30	.30
C85	AP16	2s dk red violet	1.50	.30
C86	AP16	5s dark gray	3.50	.30
		Nos. C80-C86 (7)	8.90	2.00

New York World's Fair.
For surcharge see No. 435 in Scott Standard catalogue, Vol. 2.

Map of the Americas and Airplane — AP17

1940, July 9
C87	AP17	10c red org & blue	.45	.25
C88	AP17	70c sepia & blue	.45	.25
C89	AP17	1s copper brn & blue	.90	.25
C90	AP17	10s black & blue	3.50	.95
		Nos. C87-C90 (4)	5.30	1.70

Pan American Union, 50th anniversary.

AIR POST REGISTRATION STAMPS

Issued by Sociedad Colombo-Alemana de Transportes Aereos (SCADTA)

Nos. C3 and C3a Overprinted in Carmine

1928-29   Wmk. 116   Perf. 14x14½
CF1	AP6	1s on 20c (#C3)	110.00	100.00
a.		1s on 20c (#C3a) ('29)	140.00	110.00

No. C18 Overprinted in Black

1929, Apr. 1   Wmk. 127   Perf. 14
CF2	AP2	1s rose	85.00	55.00

AIR POST OFFICIAL STAMPS

Nos. C8-C15 Overprinted in Red or Black

1929, May   Unwmk.   Perf. 12
CO1	AP1	2c black (R)	1.00	.50
CO2	AP1	5c carmine rose	1.00	.50
CO3	AP1	10c deep brown	1.00	.50
CO4	AP1	20c dark violet	1.00	.50
CO5	AP1	50c deep green	4.00	2.00
CO6	AP1	1s dark blue	4.00	2.00
a.		Inverted overprint	240.00	
CO7	AP1	5s orange yellow	18.00	7.75
CO8	AP1	10s orange red	210.00	75.00
		Nos. CO1-CO8 (8)	240.00	88.75

Establishment of commercial air service in Ecuador.
Counterfeits of No. CO8 exist.
See Nos. CO9-CO12. For overprints and surcharges see Nos. C35-C38.

1930, Jan. 9
CO9	AP1	50c olive brown	3.50	1.75
CO10	AP1	1s carmine lake	4.50	2.25
CO11	AP1	5s olive green	11.00	5.50
CO12	AP1	10s black	21.00	10.50
		Nos. CO9-CO12 (4)	40.00	20.00

For surcharges and overprint see Nos. C36-C38.

Air Post Stamps of 1937 Overprinted in Black

1937, Aug. 19
CO13	AP7	10c chestnut	.50	.25
CO14	AP7	20c olive black	.50	.25
CO15	AP7	70c black brown	.60	.25
CO16	AP7	1s gray black	.70	.25
CO17	AP7	2s dark violet	.70	.30
		Nos. CO13-CO17 (5)	3.00	1.30

For overprints see Nos. 463-464 in Scott Standard catalogue, Vol. 2.

No. C79 Overprinted in Black

1940, Aug. 1   Perf. 12½x13
CO18	AP15	5s emerald	2.00	.60

SPECIAL DELIVERY STAMPS

Numeral — SD1

1928   Unwmk.   Perf. 12
E1	SD1	2c on 2c blue	8.00	9.00
E2	SD1	5c on 2c blue	7.00	9.00
E3	SD1	10c on 2c blue	7.00	6.00
a.		"10 CTVOS" inverted	21.00	25.00
E4	SD1	20c on 2c blue	10.00	9.00
E5	SD1	50c on 2c blue	12.00	9.00
		Nos. E1-E5 (5)	44.00	42.00

POSTAGE DUE STAMPS

Numeral — D1

1896   Engr.   Wmk. 117   Perf. 12
J1	D1	1c blue green	6.00	6.50
J2	D1	2c blue green	6.00	6.50
J3	D1	5c blue green	6.00	6.50
J4	D1	10c blue green	6.00	6.50
J5	D1	20c blue green	6.00	8.50
J6	D1	50c blue green	6.00	13.00
J7	D1	100c blue green	6.00	17.00
		Nos. J1-J7 (7)	42.00	64.50

Reprints are on very thick paper with distinct watermark and vertical paper-weave direction. Value 15c each.

Unwmk.
J8	D1	1c blue green	5.00	6.00
J9	D1	2c blue green	5.00	6.00
J10	D1	5c blue green	5.00	6.00
J11	D1	10c blue green	5.00	6.00
J12	D1	20c blue green	5.00	7.50
J13	D1	50c blue green	5.00	10.50
J14	D1	100c blue green	5.00	15.00
		Nos. J8-J14 (7)	35.00	57.00

Coat of Arms — D2

1929
J15	D2	5c deep blue	.40	.40
J16	D2	10c orange yellow	.40	.40
J17	D2	20c red	.60	.60
		Nos. J15-J17 (3)	1.40	1.40

OFFICIAL STAMPS

Regular Issues of 1881 and 1887 Handstamped in Black

1886   Unwmk.   Perf. 12
O1	A5	1c yellow brown	2.50	2.50
O2	A6	2c lake	3.00	3.00
O3	A7	5c blue	6.75	8.75
O4	A8	10c orange	5.25	3.25
O5	A9	20c gray violet	5.25	5.25
O6	A10	50c blue green	15.00	11.50
		Nos. O1-O6 (6)	37.75	34.25

1887
O7	A12	1c green	3.25	2.50
O8	A13	2c vermilion	3.25	3.25
O9	A14	5c blue	5.25	2.50
O10	A15	80c olive green	17.50	10.00
		Nos. O7-O10 (4)	29.25	18.25

Nos. O1-O10 are known with red handstamp but these are believed to be speculative.
The overprint on the 1886-87 issues is handstamped and is found in various positions.

Flores — O1   Arms — O1a

1892   Carmine Overprint
O11	O1	1c ultramarine	.25	.40
O12	O1	2c ultramarine	.25	.40
O13	O1	5c ultramarine	.25	.40
O14	O1	10c ultramarine	.25	.60
O15	O1	20c ultramarine	.25	.90
O16	O1	50c ultramarine	.25	.90
O17	O1	1s ultramarine	.35	1.00
		Nos. O11-O17 (7)	1.85	4.60

1894
O18	O1a	1c slate green (R)	15.00	
O19	O1a	2c lake (Bk)	20.00	

Nos. O18 and O19 were not placed in use.

Rocafuerte — O2

Dated "1894"

1894   **Carmine Overprint**
O20	O2	1c gray black	.60	1.00
O21	O2	2c gray black	.60	.60
O22	O2	5c gray black	.60	.60
O23	O2	10c gray black	.75	1.00
O24	O2	20c gray black	1.00	1.00
O25	O2	50c gray black	3.75	3.75
O26	O2	1s gray black	6.00	6.00
	Nos. O20-O26 (7)		*13.30*	*13.95*

Dated "1895"

1895   **Carmine Overprint**
O27	O2	1c gray black	5.25	5.25
O28	O2	2c gray black	7.50	7.50
O29	O2	5c gray black	1.50	1.50
O30	O2	10c gray black	7.50	7.50
O31	O2	20c gray black	11.00	10.50
O32	O2	50c gray black	75.00	75.00
O33	O2	1s gray black	3.75	3.75
	Nos. O27-O33 (7)		*111.50*	*111.00*

Reprints of 1894-95 issues are on very thick paper with paper weave found both horizontal and vertical for all denominations. Generally they are blacker than originals.
For overprints see Nos. O50-O91.

Types of 1896 Overprinted in Carmine

1896   **Wmk. 117**
O34	A21	1c olive bister	1.00	1.00
O35	A22	2c olive bister	1.00	1.00
O36	A23	5c olive bister	1.00	1.00
O37	A24	10c olive bister	1.00	1.00
O38	A25	20c olive bister	1.00	1.00
O39	A26	50c olive bister	1.00	1.00
O40	A27	1s olive bister	3.00	3.00
O41	A28	5s olive bister	6.00	6.00
	Nos. O34-O41 (8)		*15.00*	*15.00*

Reprints of Nos. O34-O41 are on thick paper with vertical paper weave direction.

Unwmk.
O42	A21	1c olive bister	3.00	3.00
O43	A22	2c olive bister	3.00	3.00
O44	A23	5c olive bister	3.00	3.00
O45	A24	10c olive bister	3.00	3.00
O46	A25	20c olive bister	3.00	3.00
O47	A26	50c olive bister	3.00	3.00
O48	A27	1s olive bister	7.50	7.50
O49	A28	5s olive bister	10.50	10.50
	Nos. O42-O49 (8)		*36.00*	*36.00*

Reprints of Nos. O42-O49 all have overprint in black. Value 20 cents each.

Nos. O20-O26 Overprinted

1897-98
O50	O2	1c gray black	20.00	20.00
O51	O2	2c gray black	35.00	35.00
O52	O2	5c gray black	200.00	200.00
O53	O2	10c gray black	30.00	30.00
O54	O2	20c gray black	20.00	20.00
O55	O2	50c gray black	35.00	35.00
O56	O2	1s gray black	55.00	55.00
	Nos. O50-O56 (7)		*395.00*	*395.00*

Nos. O20-O26 Overprinted

O57	O2	1c gray black	4.00	4.00
O58	O2	2c gray black	9.00	9.00
O59	O2	5c gray black	90.00	90.00
O60	O2	10c gray black	100.00	100.00
O61	O2	20c gray black	25.00	25.00

O62	O2	50c gray black	15.00	15.00
O63	O2	1s gray black	165.00	165.00
	Nos. O57-O63 (7)		*408.00*	*408.00*

Nos. O20-O26 Overprinted

O64	O2	1c gray black	40.00	40.00
O65	O2	2c gray black	40.00	40.00
O66	O2	5c gray black	40.00	40.00
O67	O2	10c gray black	40.00	40.00
O68	O2	20c gray black	40.00	40.00
O69	O2	50c gray black	40.00	40.00
O70	O2	1s gray black	40.00	40.00
	Nos. O64-O70 (7)		*280.00*	*280.00*

Nos. O27-O33 Overprinted in Black like Nos. O50-O56
O71	O2	1c gray black	20.00	20.00
O72	O2	2c gray black	20.00	20.00
O73	O2	5c gray black	20.00	20.00
O74	O2	10c gray black	20.00	20.00
O75	O2	20c gray black	30.00	30.00
O76	O2	50c gray black	275.00	275.00
O77	O2	1s gray black	100.00	100.00
	Nos. O71-O77 (7)		*485.00*	*485.00*

Nos. O27-O33 Overprinted

O78	O2	1c gray black	35.00	35.00
O79	O2	2c gray black	30.00	30.00
O80	O2	5c gray black	30.00	30.00
O81	O2	10c gray black	32.50	32.50
O82	O2	20c gray black	42.50	42.50
O83	O2	50c gray black	30.00	30.00
O84	O2	1s gray black	30.00	30.00
	Nos. O78-O84 (7)		*230.00*	*230.00*

Nos. O27-O33 Overprinted like #O64-O70
O85	O2	1c gray black	90.00	90.00
O86	O2	2c gray black	20.00	20.00
O87	O2	5c gray black	80.00	80.00
O88	O2	10c gray black	80.00	80.00
O89	O2	20c gray black	140.00	140.00
O90	O2	50c gray black	85.00	85.00
O91	O2	1s gray black	165.00	165.00
	Nos. O85-O91 (7)		*660.00*	*660.00*

Many forged overprints of Nos. O50-O91 exist, made on the original stamps and reprints.

O3

1898-99   **Perf. 15, 16**

Black Surcharge
O92	O3	5c on 50c lilac	10.00	10.00
a.	Inverted surcharge		25.00	25.00
O93	O3	10c on 20s org	15.00	15.00
a.	Double surcharge		40.00	30.00
O94	O3	10c on 50c lilac	140.00	140.00
O95	O3	20c on 50c lilac	30.00	30.00
O96	O3	20c on 50s green	30.00	30.00
	Nos. O92-O96 (5)		*225.00*	*225.00*

Green Surcharge
O97	O3	5c on 50c lilac	10.00	10.00
a.	Double surcharge			5.00
b.	Double surcharge, blk and grn			12.00
c.	Same as "b," blk surch. invtd.			5.00

1899   **Red Surcharge**
O98	O3	5c on 50c lilac	10.00	10.00
a.	Double surcharge			20.00
b.	Dbl. surch., blk and red			25.00
O99	O3	20c on 50s green	15.00	15.00
a.	Inverted surcharge			40.00
b.	Dbl. surch., red and blk			60.00

Similar Surcharge in Black Value in Words in Two Lines
O100	O3	1c on 5c blue		650.00

Red Surcharge
O101	O3	2c on 5c blue		1,150.
O102	O3	4c on 20c blue		800.00

Types of Regular Issue of 1899 Ovptd. in Black

1899   **Perf. 14, 15**
O103	A37	2c orange & blk	.70	1.60
O104	A39	10c orange & blk	.70	1.60
O105	A40	20c orange & blk	.50	2.50
O106	A41	50c orange & blk	.50	3.25
	Nos. O103-O106 (4)		*2.40*	*8.95*

For overprint see No. O167.

The above overprint was applied to remainders of the postage stamps of 1904 with the idea of increasing their salability. They were never regularly in use as official stamps.

Regular Issue of 1911-13 Overprinted in Black

1913   **Perf. 12**
O107	A71	1c scarlet & blk	3.50	3.50
O108	A72	2c blue & blk	3.50	3.50
O109	A73	3c orange & blk	2.25	2.25
O110	A74	5c scarlet & blk	4.50	4.50
O111	A75	10c blue & blk	4.50	4.50
	Nos. O107-O111 (5)		*18.25*	*18.25*

Regular Issue of 1911-13 Overprinted

1916-17   **Overprint 22x3½mm**
O112	A72	2c blue & blk	25.00	18.00
O113	A74	5c scarlet & blk	25.00	18.00
O114	A75	10c blue & blk	15.00	12.00
	Nos. O112-O114 (3)		*65.00*	*48.00*

Overprint 25x4mm
O115	A71	1c scarlet & blk	1.10	1.10
O116	A72	2c blue & blk	1.60	1.60
a.	Inverted overprint		5.00	5.00
O117	A73	3c orange & blk	1.00	1.00
O118	A74	5c scarlet & blk	1.60	1.60
O119	A75	10c blue & blk	1.60	1.60
	Nos. O115-O119 (5)		*6.90*	*6.90*

Same Overprint On Regular Issue of 1915-17
O120	A71	1c orange	1.40	1.40
O121	A72	2c green	1.40	1.40
O122	A73	3c black	2.25	2.25
O123	A78	4c red & blk	2.25	2.25
a.	Inverted overprint			15.00
O124	A74	5c violet	1.40	1.40
O125	A75	10c blue	2.75	2.75
O126	A79	20c green & blk	15.00	15.00
	Nos. O120-O126 (7)		*26.45*	*26.45*

Regular Issues of 1911-17 Overprinted in Black or Red

O127	A71	1c orange	.90	.90
O128	A72	2c green	.70	.70
O129	A73	3c black (Bk)	.90	.90

O130	A73	3c black (R)	.90	.70
a.	Inverted overprint			
O131	A78	4c red & blk	.90	.90
O132	A74	5c violet	1.75	.90
O133	A75	10c blue & blk	4.50	1.75
O134	A75	10c blue	.90	.90
O135	A79	20c green & blk	4.50	1.75
	Nos. O127-O135 (9)		*15.95*	*9.40*

Regular Issue of 1920 Overprinted

1920
O136	A86	1c green	1.25	1.25
a.	Inverted overprint		17.00	
O137	A86	2c carmine	1.00	1.00
O138	A86	3c yellow brn	1.25	1.25
O139	A86	4c dark green	2.00	2.00
a.	Inverted overprint		17.00	—
O140	A86	5c blue	2.00	2.00
O141	A86	6c orange	1.25	1.25
O142	A86	7c brown	2.00	2.00
O143	A86	8c yellow green	2.50	2.50
O144	A86	9c red	3.25	3.25
O145	A95	10c blue	2.00	2.00
O146	A86	15c gray	11.00	11.00
O147	A86	20c deep violet	14.50	14.50
O148	A86	30c violet	17.00	17.00
O149	A86	40c dark brown	21.00	21.00
O150	A86	50c dark green	14.50	14.50
O151	A86	60c dark blue	17.00	17.00
O152	A86	70c gray	17.00	17.00
O153	A86	80c yellow	21.00	21.00
O154	A104	90c green	21.00	21.00
O155	A86	1s blue	45.00	45.00
	Nos. O136-O155 (20)		*217.50*	*217.50*

Cent. of the independence of Guayaquil.

Stamps of 1911 Overprinted

1922
O156	A71	1c scarlet & blk	9.00	9.00
O157	A72	2c blue & blk	4.50	4.50

Revenue Stamps of 1919-1920 Overprinted like Nos. O156 and O157

1924
O158	PT3	1c dark blue	2.00	2.00
O159	PT3	2c green	12.50	12.50

Regular Issues of 1911-17 Overprinted

1924
O160	A71	1c orange	7.00	7.00
a.	Inverted overprint		15.00	

Overprinted in Black or Red

O161	A72	2c green	.60	.60
O162	A73	3c black (R)	.80	.80
O163	A78	4c red & blk	1.25	1.25
O164	A74	5c violet	1.25	1.25
O165	A75	10c deep blue	1.25	1.25
O166	A76	1s green & blk	7.00	7.00
	Nos. O160-O166 (7)		*19.15*	*19.15*

No. O106 with Additional Overprint

1924   *Perf. 14, 15*
O167 A41 50c orange & blk   2.25 2.25

Nos. O160-O167 exist with inverted overprint.

No. 199 Overprinted

1924   *Perf. 12*
O168 A71 1c orange   5.50 5.50

Regular Issues of 1911-25 Overprinted

1925
O169	A71	1c scarlet & blk	10.00 4.25
a.	Inverted overprint		15.00
O170	A71	1c orange	.60 .60
a.	Inverted overprint		4.00
O171	A72	2c green	.60 .60
a.	Inverted overprint		4.00
O172	A73	3c black (Bk)	.60 .60
O173	A73	3c black (R)	1.10 1.10
O174	A78	4c red & blk	.60 .60
O175	A74	5c violet	.80 .80
O176	A74	5c rose	.80 .80
O177	A75	10c deep blue	.60 .60
	Nos. O169-O177 (9)		15.70 9.95

Regular Issues of 1916-25 Ovptd. Vertically Up or Down

1927, Oct.
O178	A71	1c orange	2.00 2.00
O179	A86	2c carmine	2.00 2.00
O180	A86	3c yellow brown	2.00 2.00
O181	A86	4c myrtle green	2.00 2.00
O182	A86	5c pale blue	2.00 2.00
O183	A75	10c yellow green	2.00 2.00
	Nos. O178-O183 (6)		12.00 12.00

Regular Issues of 1920-27 Overprinted

1928
O184	A71	1c lt blue	1.25 1.25
O185	A86	2c carmine	1.25 1.25
O186	A86	3c yellow brown	1.25 1.25
a.	Inverted overprint		5.00
O187	A86	4c myrtle green	1.25 1.25
O188	A86	5c lt blue	1.25 1.25
O189	A75	10c yellow green	1.25 1.25
O190	A109	20c violet	11.00 11.00
a.	Overprint reading up		3.50 2.25
	Nos. O184-O190 (7)		18.50 10.00

The overprint is placed vertically reading down on No. O190.

Regular Issue of 1936 Overprinted in Black

1936   *Perf. 14*
O191	A131	5c olive green	1.50 1.50
O192	A132	10c brown	1.50 1.50
O193	A133	20c dark violet	1.90 .70
O194	A134	1s dark carmine	2.25 1.10
O195	A135	2s dark blue	2.50 1.75
	Nos. O191-O195 (5)		9.65 6.55

Regular Postage Stamps of 1937 Overprinted in Black

1937   *Perf. 11½*
O196	A139	2c green	.40 .40
O197	A140	5c deep rose	.40 .40
O198	A141	10c blue	.40 .40
O199	A142	20c deep rose	.40 .40
O200	A143	1s olive green	.40 .40
	Nos. O196-O200 (5)		2.00 2.00

POSTAL TAX STAMPS

Roca — PT1

1920   Unwmk.   *Perf. 12*
RA1 PT1 1c orange   .75 .30

PT2   PT3

RA2	PT2	1c red & blue	1.10 .25
a.	"de" inverted		10.50 5.25
b.	Double overprint		10.00 .60
c.	Inverted overprint		10.00 .60
RA3	PT3	1c deep blue	1.25 .25
a.	Inverted overprint		6.00 1.00
b.	Double overprint		6.00 1.00

For overprints see Nos. O158-O159.

PT4   PT5

Red or Black Surcharge or Overprint
Stamp Dated 1911-1912
RA4 PT4 20c deep blue   — 30.00
Stamp Dated 1913-1914
RA5 PT4 20c deep blue (R)   2.25 .35
Stamp Dated 1917-1918
RA6	PT4	20c olive green (R)	6.50 .55
a.	Dated 1919-20		25.00
RA7	PT5	1c on 2c green	.90 .25

Stamp Dated 1911-1912
RA8	PT5	1c on 5c green	.90 .25
a.	Double surcharge		

Stamp Dated 1913-1914
RA9	PT5	1c on 5c green	8.00 .55
a.	Double surcharge		12.00 4.00

On Nos. RA7, RA8 and RA9 the surcharge is found reading upward or downward. For surcharges see Nos. RA15-RA16.

Post Office — PT6

1920-24   Engr.
RA10	PT6	1c olive green	.40 .25
RA11	PT6	2c deep green	.40 .25
RA12	PT6	20c bister brn ('24)	1.75 .25
RA13	PT6	2s violet	11.50 3.25
RA14	PT6	5s blue	20.00 5.75
	Nos. RA10-RA14 (5)		34.05 9.75

For overprints and surcharge see Nos. 259, 266-268, 273, 302, RA17.

Revenue Stamps of 1917-18 Srchd. Vertically in Red reading up or down

1921-22
RA15	PT5	20c on 1c dk blue	55.00 6.50
RA16	PT5	20c on 2c green	55.00 6.50

No. RA12 Surcharged in Green

1924
RA17	PT6	2c on 20c bis brn	.60 .25
a.	Inverted surcharge		14.00 5.00
b.	Double surcharge		4.00 2.00

PT7

1924   *Rouletted 7*
RA18	PT7	1c rose red	.90 .25
a.	Inverted overprint		3.50

Similar Design, Eagle at left
Perf. 12
RA19	PT7	2c blue	.90 .25
a.	Inverted overprint		3.50 1.75

For overprints and surcharges see Nos. 346, O201, RA32, RA34, RA37, RA44-RA45, RA47.

PT8

Inscribed "Timbre Fiscal"
1924
RA20	PT8	1c yellow	4.50 .85
RA21	PT8	2c dark blue	1.40 .35

Inscribed "Region Oriental"
RA22	PT8	1c yellow	.70 .30
RA23	PT8	2c dark blue	1.40 .35
	Nos. RA20-RA23 (4)		8.00 1.85

Overprint on No. RA22 reads down or up.

Revenue Stamp Overprinted in Blue

1934
RA24		2c green	.50 .25
a.	Blue overprint inverted		3.50 1.75
b.	Blue ovpt. dbl., one invtd.		4.00 1.25

Postage Stamp of 1930 Overprinted in Red
Perf. 12½
RA25 A119 20c ultra & yel   .50 .25

Telegraph Stamp Overprinted in Red, like No. RA24, and Surcharged diagonally in Black

1934   *Perf. 14*
RA26		2c on 10c olive brn	.70 .25
a.	Double surcharge		5.50

Overprint Blue, Surcharge Red
RA27   2c on 10c olive brn   .70 .25

PT9   PT10

1934-36   *Perf. 12*
RA28	PT9	2c green	.60 .25
a.	Both overprints in red ('36)		.60 .25

Postal Tax stamp of 1920-24, overprinted in red "POSTAL" has been again overprinted "CASA de Correos y Teleg. de Guayaquil" in black.

Perf. 14½x14
1934   Photo.   Wmk. 233
RA29 PT10 2c yellow green   .50 .25

For the rebuilding of the GPO at Guayaquil. For surcharge see No. RA31.

Symbols of Post and Telegraph Service PT11

1935
RA30 PT11 20c claret   .50 .25

For the rebuilding of the GPO at Guayaquil.

No. RA29 Surcharged in Red and Overprinted in Black

1935
RA31	PT10	3c on 2c yel grn	.40 .25
a.	Double surcharge		

Social and Rural Workers' Insurance Fund.

Tobacco Stamp Surcharged in Black

Seguro Social	3
del Campesino	*ctvs.*

1936   Unwmk.   Rouletted 7
RA32 PT7 3c on 1c rose red   .60   .25
a.   Lines of words reversed   2.00   .25
b.   Horiz. pair, imperf. vert.

Issued for the Social and Rural Workers' Insurance Fund.

No. 310
Overprinted in Black

1936   Perf. 12½
RA33 A119 20c ultra & yel   .60   .25
a.   Double overprint

Tobacco Stamp Surcharged in Black

1936   Rouletted 7
RA34 PT7 3c on 1c rose red   .60   .25
Social and Rural Workers' Insurance Fund.

Worker — PT12

1936   Engr.   Perf. 13½
RA35 PT12 3c ultra   .40   .25
Social and Rural Workers' Insurance Fund.
For surcharges see Nos. C64, RA36, RA53-RA54 (in Scott Standard catalogue, Vol. 2).

Surcharged in Black

1936
RA36 PT13 5c on 3c ultra   .60   .25
This combines the 2c for the rebuilding of the post office with the 3c for the Social and Rural Workers' Insurance Fund.

National Defense Issue
Tobacco Stamp Surcharged in Black

TIMBRE PATRIOTICO
DIEZ CENTAVOS

1936   Rouletted 7
RA37 PT7 10c on 1c rose   .90   .25
a.   Double surcharge

Symbolical of
Defense — PT14

1937-42   Perf. 12½
RA38 PT14 10c deep blue   .90   .25
A 1s violet and 2s green exist in type PT14.
For surcharge see No. RA40.

Overprinted or Surcharged in Black

PT15

1937   Engr. & Typo.   Perf. 13½
RA39 PT15 5c lt brn & red   2.00   .25
d.   Inverted overprint   20.00

No. RA38 Surcharged in Red

1937   Engr.   Perf. 12½
RA40 PT14 5c on 10c dp blue   1.10   .25

Map of Ecuador — PT16

1938   Perf. 14x13½
RA41 PT16 5c carmine rose   .70   .25
Social and Rural Workers' Insurance Fund.

No. C42 Surcharged in Red

1938   Perf. 12½
RA42 AP5 20c on 70c black   1.10   .25

No. 307
Surcharged in Red

CAMPAÑA
CONTRA
EL CANCER

1938
RA43 A116 5c on 6c yel & red   .40   .25
This stamp was obligatory on all mail from Nov. 23rd to 30th, 1938. The tax was for the Intl. Union for the Control of Cancer.

Tobacco Stamp Surcharged in Black

POSTAL ADICIONAL
CINCO CENTAVOS

1939   Rouletted
RA44 PT7 5c on 1c rose   .70   .25
a.   Double surcharge
b.   Triple surcharge

Tobacco Stamp Surcharged in Blue

CASAS DE CORREOS
Y TELEGRAFOS
CINCO CENTAVOS

1940
RA45 PT7 5c on 1c rose red   1.00   .25
a.   Double surcharge   3.50   3.50

No. 370 Surcharged in Carmine

1940   Perf. 11½
RA46 A144 20c on 50c blk & multi   .50   .25
a.   Double surcharge, one inverted

Tobacco Stamp Surcharged in Black

1940   Rouletted
RA47 PT7 20c on 1c rose red   6.00   .50

Farmer
Plowing — PT17

1940   Perf. 13x13½
RA48 PT17 5c carmine rose   .70   .25

Communication Symbols — PT18

1940-43   Perf. 12
RA49 PT18 5c copper brown   .70   .25
RA49A PT18 5c green ('43)   .70   .25
For overprint and surcharges see #534, E6, I1 in Scott Standard catalogue, Vol. 2.

EGYPT

'ē-jəpt

LOCATION — Northern Africa, bordering on the Mediterranean and the Red Sea
GOVT. — Monarchy
AREA — 386,900 sq. mi.
POP. — 46,000,000 (est. 1984)
CAPITAL — Cairo

Modern Egypt was a part of Turkey until 1914 when a British protectorate was declared over the country and the Khedive was deposed in favor of Hussein Kamil under the title of sultan. In 1922 the protectorate ended and the reigning sultan was declared king of the new monarchy.

40 Paras = 1 Piaster
1000 Milliemes = 100 Piasters = 1 Pound (1888)

Catalogue values for unused stamps in this country are for Never Hinged items, beginning with Scott B1 in the semi-postal section.

Watermarks

Wmk. 118 —
Pyramid and Star

Wmk. 119 —
Crescent and Star

Wmk. 120 —
Triple Crescent and Star

Wmk. 195 —
Multiple Crown and Arabic F

"F" in watermark stands for Fuad.

GREAT BRITAIN POST OFFICES IN EGYPT

PRE-STAMP POSTAL MARKINGS
Crowned Circle handstamps types I, II and VII are pictured in the Crowned Circle Handstamps and Great Britain Used Abroad section.

Alexandria
1843, May 13
A1 II "Alexandria" crowned circle handstamp in red, on cover   3,500.

Cairo
1859, Mar. 23
A2 VII "Cairo" crowned circle handstamp in red, on cover   5,000.
A3 VII "Cairo" crowned circle handstamp in black, on cover   5,000.

Suez
1847, July 16
A4 I "Suez" crowned circle handstamp in red, on cover   5,750.
A5 I "Suez" crowned circle handstamp in black, on cover   5,750.

STAMPS OF GREAT BRITAIN USED IN EGYPT ALEXANDRIA / CAIRO

Stamps of Great Britain Cancelled with barred oval "BO1" obliterator

1859-78
A6 ½p rose (#58, P5, 6, 8, 10, 13-15, 19-20), from   23.00
A7 1p rose red (#20)   8.00
a.   1p red brown (#20b)   —
A8 1p rose red (#33, see footnote), from   11.50
A9 2p blue (#29, P7-9), from   12.50
A10 2p blue (#30, P13-15), from   12.50

A11	2½p claret (#66, P1-3)	40.00
a.	Bluish paper (#66a, P1)	70.00
	As "a," P2	*1,500.*
b.	Lettered "LH-FL" (#66b)	*1,675.*
A12	2½p claret (#67, P3-9), *from*	29.00
A13	3p rose (#37)	140.00
A14	3p rose (#44)	70.00
A15	3p rose (#49, P4-9), *from*	30.00
A16	3p rose (#61, P11-12, 14-16, 18, 19), *from*	30.00
A17	4p rose (#26)	47.50
A18	4p vermilion (#34)	47.50
a.	Hairlines (#34b)	47.50
A19	4p vermilion (#43, P7-14), *from*	32.50
A20	4p vermilion (#69, P15)	225.00
A21	4p pale ol grn (#70, P15)	150.00
A22	6p lilac (#27)	55.00
A23	6p lilac (#39, P3)	47.50
a.	Hairlines (#39b)	90.00
A24	6p lilac (#45, P5)	37.50
	Plate 6	90.00
A25	6p dull violet (#50, P6)	47.50
A26	6p violet (#51, P8-9)	45.00
a.	Imperf. (#51b, P8)	5,000.
A27	6p brown (#59, P11)	32.00
a.	6p pale buff (#59b, P11)	80.00
	As "a," plate 12	225.00
A28	6p gray (#60)	100.00
A29	6p gray (#62, P13-15), *from*	27.50
A30	9p straw (#40)	300.00
a.	9p bister (#40a)	—
A31	9p straw (#46)	—
A32	9p bister (#52)	—
A33	10p red brown (#53)	275.00
A34	1sh green (#28)	140.00
A35	1sh green (#42)	85.00
A36	1sh green (#48)	40.00
A37	1sh green (#54, P4-6)	17.50
	Plate 7	50.00
A38	1sh green (#64, P12-13)	32.00
	Plates 8-11	45.00
A39	2sh blue (#55)	150.00
a.	2sh pale blue (#55a)	200.00
A40	5sh rose (#57, P1)	550.00
	Plate 2	700.00

When more than one plate number is shown, value is for the least expensive.

A8 plate numbers: 71-74, 76, 78-99, 101-104, 106-115, 117-125, 127, 129-131, 133, 134, 136-140, 142-150, 152, 154, 156, 157, 159, 160, 162, 163, 165, 168-172, 174, 175, 177, 179-183, 185, 188, 190, 198, 200, 203, 206, 210, 220.

SUEZ
Stamps of Great Britain
Cancelled with "BO2" Type A or B obliterator or with circular date stamp
1859-78

A41	½p rose (#58, P6, 10-14), *from*	35.00
A42	1p rose red (#20)	12.00
A43	1p rose red (#33, see footnote)	13.50
A44	2p blue (#29, P9)	17.00
	Plate 8	25.00
A45	2p blue (#30, P13)	17.00
	Plates 14-15	25.00
A46	2½p claret (#66, P1-2)	40.00
	Plate 3	50.00
a.	Bluish paper (#66a, P1)	75.00
	Plates 2-3	—
b.	Lettered "LH-FL" (#66b)	2,000.
A47	2½p claret (#67, P3-9), *from*	30.00
	Plate 10	35.00
A48	3p rose (#37)	160.00
A49	3p rose (#44)	85.00
A50	3p rose (#49, P5-8, 10), *from*	30.00
A51	3p rose (#61, P12, 16)	30.00
A52	4p vermilion (#26)	62.50
A53	4p vermilion (#34)	55.00
a.	Hairlines (#34b)	60.00
A54	4p vermilion (#43, P7-14), *from*	32.50
A55	4p vermilion (#69, P15)	—
A56	4p pale ol grn (#70, P15)	225.00
A57	6p lilac (#27)	62.50
A58	6p lilac (#39, P3)	50.00
a.	Hairlines (#39b)	90.00
A59	6p lilac (#45, P5)	42.50
	Plate 6	100.00
A60	6p dull violet (#50, P6)	55.00
A61	6p violet (#51, P8-9)	42.50
A62	6p brown (#59, P11)	37.50
a.	6p pale buff (#59b, P11)	80.00
	As "a," plate 12	3,250.
A63	6p gray (#60)	110.00
A64	6p gray (#62, P15-16)	32.50
	Plates 13-14	32.50
A65	8p orange (#73)	—
A66	9p straw (#40)	300.00
a.	9p bister (#40a)	—
A67	9p bister (#52)	—
A68	10p red brown (#53)	275.00
A69	1sh green (#28)	175.00
A70	1sh green (#42)	97.50
A71	1sh green (#48)	55.00
A72	1sh green (#54, P4-6)	24.00
	Plate 7	45.00
A73	1sh green (#64, P12)	35.00
	Plates 8-11	40.00
A74	2sh blue (#55)	180.00
a.	2sh pale blue (#55a)	225.00
A75	5sh rose (#57, P1)	550.00
	Plate 2	700.00

When more than one plate number is shown, value is for the least expensive.

A8 plate numbers: 70-74, 76, 79-81, 83-87, 90-91, 93-94, 96-97, 100-101, 106-108, 110, 113, 118-125, 129-131, 134, 136-138, 140, 142-145, 147-154, 156, 158-168, 170, 174, 176-182, 184-187, 189-190, 198, 205.

Values for unused stamps are for examples with original gum as defined in the catalogue introduction. Very fine examples of Nos. 1-15 will have perforations that are clear of the framelines but with the design noticeably off center. Well centered stamps are extremely scarce and will command substantial premiums.

Turkish Numerals

١	٢	٣	٤	٥
1	2	3	4	5
٦	٧	٨	٩	٠
6	7	8	9	0

Turkish Suzerainty

A1   A2

A3   A4

A5   A6

A7

Surcharged in Black
Wmk. 118
1866, Jan. 1   Litho.   Perf. 12½

1	A1	5pa greenish gray	57.50	37.50
		Never hinged	115.00	
a.		Imperf., pair	250.00	
b.		Pair, imperf. between	400.00	
c.		Perf. 12½x13	77.50	57.50
d.		Perf. 13	325.00	365.00
e.		5pa gray	50.00	30.00
2	A2	10pa brown	75.00	37.50
		Never hinged	150.00	
a.		Imperf., pair	210.00	
b.		Pair, imperf. between	450.00	
c.		Perf. 13	240.00	260.00
d.		Perf. 12½x13	325.00	350.00
e.		Perf. 12½x15	100.00	57.50
3	A3	20pa blue	105.00	40.00
		Never hinged	210.00	
a.		Imperf., pair	300.00	
b.		Pair, imperf. between	500.00	
c.		Perf. 12½x13	125.00	95.00
d.		Perf. 13	500.00	325.00
e.		20pa greenish blue	105.00	35.00
4	A4	2pi yellow	125.00	52.50
		Never hinged	210.00	
a.		Imperf.	150.00	125.00
b.		Imperf. vert. or horiz., pair	500.00	425.00
c.		Perf. 12½x15	190.00	
d.		Diagonal half used as 1pi on cover		3,000.
e.		Perf. 12½x13, 13x12½	165.00	67.50
5	A5	5pi rose	325.00	250.00
		Never hinged	650.00	
a.		Imperf.	425.00	375.00
b.		Imperf. vert. or horiz., pair	1,250.	
d.		Inscription of 10pi, imperf.	950.00	850.00
e.		Perf. 12½x13, 13x12½	350.00	275.00
		As "d," perf. 12½x15	1,050.	1,000.
g.		Perf. 13	650.00	
6	A6	10pi slate bl	375.00	325.00
		Never hinged	750.00	
a.		Imperf.	550.00	450.00
b.		Pair, imperf. between	2,500.	
c.		Perf. 12½x13, 13x12½	550.00	550.00
d.		Perf. 13	1,000.	

Unwmk.
Typo.

7	A7	1pi rose lilac	80.00	5.50
		Never hinged	160.00	
a.		Imperf.	125.00	
b.		Horiz. pair, imperf. vert.	500.00	
c.		Perf. 12½x13, 13x12½	110.00	25.00
d.		Perf. 13	400.00	250.00
e.		Perf. 12½x15	350.00	
		Nos. 1-7 (7)	1,142.	748.00

Single imperforates of types A1-A10 are sometimes simulated by trimming wide-margined examples of perforated stamps.

No. 4d must be dated between July 16 and July 31, 1867.

Proofs of Nos. 1-7 are on smooth white paper, unwatermarked and imperforate. Proofs of No. 7 are on thinner paper than No. 7a.

Sphinx and Pyramid — A8

Perf. 15x12½
1867   Litho.   Wmk. 119

8	A8	5pa orange	42.50	11.00
		Never hinged	65.00	
a.		Imperf.	250.00	—
b.		Horiz. pair, imperf between	190.00	
c.		Vert. pair, imperf between	—	
9	A8	10pa lilac ('69)	70.00	11.00
		Never hinged	100.00	
a.		10pa violet	95.00	14.00
b.		Half used as 5pa on newspaper piece		850.00
11	A8	20pa yellow green ('69)	135.00	14.00
		Never hinged	210.00	
a.		20pa deep green	135.00	17.00
13	A8	1pi rose red	27.50	1.10
		Never hinged	42.50	
a.		Imperf, pair	150.00	
d.		Pair, imperf. between	300.00	
d.		Rouletted	70.00	
e.		1pi lake red	175.00	32.50
14	A8	2pi blue	150.00	18.00
		Never hinged	225.00	
a.		Imperf.	325.00	
b.		Horiz. pair, imperf. vert.	500.00	
d.		Perf. 12½	275.00	
15	A8	5pi brown	375.00	200.00
		Never hinged	575.00	
		Nos. 8-15 (6)	800.00	255.10

There are 4 types of each value, so placed that any block of 4 contains all types.

A9   A10

Clear Impressions
Thick Opaque Paper
Typographed by the Government at Boulac
Perf. 12½x13½ Clean-cut
1872   Wmk. 119

19	A9	5pa brown	10.00	5.50
		Never hinged	15.00	
20	A9	10pa lilac	9.00	3.75
		Never hinged	13.50	
21	A9	20pa blue	67.50	4.75
		Never hinged	105.00	
22	A9	1pi rose red	72.50	2.25
		Never hinged	110.00	
h.		Half used as 20pa on cover		750.00
23	A9	2pi dull yellow	100.00	15.00
		Never hinged	150.00	
j.		Half used as 1p on cover		1,200.
24	A9	2½pi dull violet	95.00	25.00
		Never hinged	145.00	
25	A9	5pi green	325.00	42.50
		Never hinged	500.00	
i.		Tête bêche pair	8,000.	
		Nos. 19-25 (7)	679.00	98.75

Perf. 13½ Clean-cut

19a	A9	5pa brown	27.50	10.00
20a	A9	10pa dull lilac	7.00	3.50
22a	A9	20pa blue	90.00	22.00
21a	A9	1pi rose red	95.00	4.00
23a	A9	2pi dull yellow	20.00	4.50
24a	A9	2½pi dull violet	800.00	225.00
25a	A9	5pi green	325.00	62.50

Litho.

21m	A9	20pa blue, perf. 12½x13½	160.00	80.00
21n	A9	20pa blue, perf. 13½	250.00	65.00
21p	A9	20pa blue, imperf.	—	
21q	A9	20pa blue, pair, imperf. between	—	2,000.
22m	A9	1pi rose red, perf. 12½x13½	550.00	20.00
22n	A9	1pi rose red, perf. 13½	875.00	50.00

Typographed
Blurred Impressions
Thinner Paper
Perf. 12½ Rough
1874-75   Wmk. 119

26	A10	5pa brown ('75)	22.50	3.75
		Never hinged	35.00	
e.		Imperf.	200.00	200.00
f.		Vert. pair, imperf. horiz.	1,000.	
g.		Tête bêche pair	45.00	45.00
20b	A9	10pa gray lilac	16.00	3.75
g.		Tête bêche pair	225.00	225.00
21b	A9	20pa gray blue	105.00	4.00
k.		Half used as 10pa on cover	—	
22b	A9	1pi vermilion	12.00	1.75
f.		Imperf.	—	150.00
g.		Tête bêche pair	150.00	125.00
23b	A9	2pi yellow	90.00	5.75
e.		Imperf.	600.00	600.00
24b	A9	2½pi deep violet	9.25	6.25
f.		Imperf.	—	
g.		Tête bêche pair	600.00	600.00
25b	A9	5pi yellow green	65.00	22.50
e.		Imperf.	400.00	

No. 26f normally occurs tête-bêche.

Perf. 13½x12½ Rough

26c	A10	5pa brown	24.00	4.50
i.		Tête bêche pair	62.50	62.50
20c	A9	10pa gray lilac	37.50	3.50
i.		Tête bêche pair	225.00	225.00
21c	A9	20pa gray blue	11.00	3.75
h.		Pair, imperf. between	350.00	
22c	A9	1pi vermilion	90.00	3.25
i.		Tête bêche pair	500.00	500.00
23c	A9	2pi yellow	10.00	6.25
g.		Tête bêche pair	500.00	500.00
k.		Half used as 1pi on cover		4,000.

Perf. 12½x13½ Rough

23d	A9	2pi yellow ('75)	80.00	17.00
h.		Tête bêche pair	1,250.	
24d	A9	2½pi dp violet ('75)	80.00	20.00
i.		Tête bêche pair	1,150.	800.00
25d	A9	5pi yel green ('75)	375.00	300.00

Nos. 24b, 24d Surcharged in Black

1879, Jan. 1   Perf. 12½ Rough

27	A9	5pa on 2½pi dull vio	10.00	9.00
		Never hinged	15.00	
a.		Imperf.	450.00	450.00
b.		Tête bêche pair	7,500.	
c.		Inverted surcharge	125.00	75.00
d.		Perf. 12½x13½ rough	12.00	12.00
e.		As "d," tête bêche pair	7,500.	
f.		As "d," inverted surcharge	150.00	150.00
28	A9	10pa on 2½pi dull vio	12.50	12.50
		Never hinged	20.00	
a.		Imperf.	400.00	400.00
b.		Tête bêche pair	2,500.	
c.		Inverted surcharge	125.00	82.50
d.		Perf. 12½x13½ rough	17.00	17.00
e.		As "d," tête bêche pair	3,000.	
f.		As "d," inverted surcharge	150.00	125.00

A11   A12

A13   A14

A15   A16

1879-1902   Typo.   Perf. 14x13½
Ordinary Paper

29	A11	5pa green	4.25	1.25
30	A12	10pa violet	57.50	5.00
31	A12	10pa lilac rose ('81)	70.00	10.00
32	A12	10pa blue ('82)	8.00	1.75
33	A12	10pa green ('84)	2.50	2.00
34	A13	20pa ultra	67.50	1.25
35	A13	20pa rose ('84)	22.00	1.25
36	A14	1pi rose	42.50	.30

37	A14	1pi ultra ('84)	5.75	.30
38	A15	2pi orange yel	42.50	1.50
39	A15	2pi orange brn	27.50	.50
40	A16	5pi green	77.50	11.50
41	A16	5pi gray ('84)	25.00	.50
		Nos. 29-41 (13)	452.50	38.10

Chalky Paper

37a	A14	1pi ultra ('02)	3.50	.25
39a	A15	2pi orange brn ('02)	13.50	.25
41a	A16	5pi gray ('02)	18.00	.25

Nos. 29-31, 35-41 imperf are proofs.
For overprints see Nos. 42, O6-O7.

A17

1884, Feb. 1

42	A17	20pa on 5pi green	14.00	2.25
a.		Inverted surcharge	70.00	62.50
b.		Double surcharge	—	

A18

A19

A20   A21

A22   A23

1888-1906   **Ordinary Paper**

43	A18	1m brown	3.50	.25
44	A19	2m green	3.00	.25
45	A20	3m maroon ('92)	8.00	2.25
46	A20	3m orange ('93)	5.75	.25
48	A22	5m carmine rose	6.50	.25
a.		5m rose, aniline ink	5.00	
49	A23	10p purple ('89)	35.00	1.00
a.		10m purple, aniline ink	20.00	.85
		Nos. 43-49 (6)	61.75	4.25

Chalky Paper

43a	A18	1m pale brown ('02)	4.00	.25
44a	A19	2m green ('02)	1.25	.25
46a	A20	3m yel org ('02)	3.00	.25
47	A21	4m brown red ('06)	4.75	.25
a.		Half used as 2m on cover	—	
48b	A22	5m rose ('02)	3.00	.25
49b	A23	10p mauve ('02)	22.50	.55

Nos. 43-44, 47-48 imperf are proofs.
For overprints see Nos. O2-O5, O8-O10, O14-O15.

Boats on Nile   Cleopatra
A24   A25

Ras-el-Tin Palace   Giza Pyramids
A26   A27

Sphinx   Colossi of
A28   Thebes
           A29

Pylon of Karnak   Citadel at
and Temple of   Cairo — A31
Khonsu — A30

Rock Temple of   Aswan
Abu   Dam — A33
Simbel — A32

Perf. 13½x14

1914, Jan. 8   **Wmk. 119**
Chalk-surfaced Paper

50	A24	1m olive brown	1.25	.80
51	A25	2m dp green	3.75	.25
52	A26	3m orange	3.50	.50
53	A27	4m red	4.50	.75
54	A28	5m lake	4.25	.25
a.		Booklet pane of 6	250.00	
55	A29	10m dk blue	7.50	.40

Perf. 14

56	A30	20m olive grn	8.00	.70
57	A31	50m red violet	24.00	1.10
58	A32	100m black	25.00	1.40
59	A33	200m plum	42.50	4.00
		Nos. 50-59 (10)	124.25	10.15

All values of this issue exist imperforate on both watermarked and unwatermarked paper but are not known to have been issued in that condition.
See Nos. 61-69, 72-74. For overprints and surcharge see Nos. 60, 78-91, O11-O13, O16-O27, O30.

British Protectorate

No. 52 Surcharged

2 Milliemes

1915, Oct. 15

60	A26	2m on 3m orange	1.25	2.25
a.		Inverted surcharge	250.00	250.00

Scenic Types of 1914 and

Statue of Ramses II
A34   A35

1921-22   **Wmk. 120**   **Perf. 13½x14**
Chalk-surfaced Paper

61	A24	1m olive brown	1.50	3.00
62	A25	2m dp green	9.00	4.75
63	A25	2m red ('22)	6.00	2.50
64	A26	3m orange	9.00	6.00
65	A27	4m green ('22)	8.00	6.50
66	A28	5m lake	7.00	1.75
67	A28	5m pink	14.00	.25
68	A29	10m dp blue	12.00	.70
69	A29	10m lake ('22)	3.50	.70
70	A34	15m indigo ('22)	10.00	.30
71	A35	15m indigo ('22)	40.00	5.00

Perf. 14

72	A30	20m olive green	12.50	.40
73	A31	50m maroon	10.00	1.25
74	A32	100m black	95.00	7.50
		Nos. 61-74 (14)	237.50	40.60

For overprints see Nos. O28-O29.

Independent Kingdom

Stamps of 1921-22 Overprinted

1922, Oct. 10

78	A24	1m olive brown	1.50	1.10
a.		Inverted overprint	475.00	450.00
b.		Double overprint	225.00	
79	A25	2m red	1.10	.65
a.		Double overprint	225.00	
80	A26	3m orange	2.25	1.10
81	A27	4m green	1.50	1.00
b.		Inverted overprint	225.00	
82	A28	5m pink	2.75	.25
83	A29	10m lake	2.75	.25
84	A34	15m indigo	5.75	1.10
85	A35	15m indigo	4.50	1.10

Perf. 14

86	A30	20m olive green	6.00	1.10
a.		Inverted overprint	200.00	—
b.		Double overprint	300.00	—
87	A31	50m maroon	9.00	1.10
a.		Inverted overprint	400.00	500.00
88	A32	100m black	22.50	1.25
a.		Inverted overprint	500.00	160.00
b.		Double overprint	400.00	150.00
		Nos. 78-88 (11)	59.60	10.00

Same Overprint on Nos. 58-59
Wmk. Crescent and Star (119)

90	A32	100m black	90.00	50.00
91	A33	200m plum	30.00	1.60

Proclamation of the Egyptian monarchy.
The overprint signifies "The Egyptian Kingdom, March 15, 1922." It exists in four types, one lithographed and three typographed on Nos. 78-87, but lithographed only on Nos. 88-91.

King Fuad
A36   A37

1923-24   **Photo.**   **Wmk. 120**   **Perf. 13½**
Size 18x22½mm

92	A36	1m orange	.35	.25
93	A36	2m black	1.10	.25
94	A36	3m brown	1.00	.65
a.		Imperf., pair	225.00	
95	A36	4m yellow grn	.90	.50
96	A36	5m orange brn	.45	.25
a.		Imperf., pair	50.00	
97	A36	10m rose	2.00	.25
98	A36	15m ultra	3.25	.25

Perf. 14
Size: 22x28mm

99	A36	20m dk green	6.25	.25
100	A36	50m myrtle grn	10.00	.25
101	A36	100m red violet	25.00	.55
102	A36	200m violet ('24)	45.00	2.00
a.		Imperf., pair	325.00	
103	A37	£1 ultra & dk vio ('24)	175.00	27.50
a.		Imperf., pair	1,750.	
		Nos. 92-103 (12)	270.30	32.95

For overprints & surcharge see Nos. 167, O31-O38.

Thoth Carving Name of King Fuad — A38

1925, Apr.   **Litho.**   **Perf. 11**

105	A38	5m brown	11.00	6.00
		Never hinged	13.50	
106	A38	10m rose	22.50	12.50
		Never hinged	27.00	
107	A38	15m ultra	22.50	14.00
		Never hinged	30.00	
		Nos. 105-107 (3)	56.00	32.50

International Geographical Congress, Cairo.
Nos. 106-107 exist with both white and yellowish gum.

Oxen Plowing
A39

1926   **Wmk. 195**   **Perf. 13x13½**

108	A39	5m lt brown	3.00	2.00
		Never hinged	4.50	
109	A39	10m brt rose	2.75	2.00
		Never hinged	4.00	
110	A39	15m dp blue	3.00	2.00
		Never hinged	4.50	
111	A39	50m Prus green	14.00	5.00
		Never hinged	20.00	
112	A39	100m brown vio	22.50	8.00
		Never hinged	30.00	
113	A39	200m brt violet	32.50	17.50
		Never hinged	45.00	
		Nos. 108-113 (6)	77.75	36.50

12th Agricultural and Industrial Exhibition at Gezira.
For surcharges see Nos. 115-117.

King Fuad — A40

Perf. 14x14½
1926, Apr. 2   **Photo.**   **Wmk. 120**

114	A40	50p brn vio & red vio	140.00	22.50
		Never hinged	210.00	

58th birthday of King Fuad.
For overprint and surcharge see Nos. 124, 166.

Nos. 111-113 Surcharged

10 MILLIEMES

Perf. 13x13½
1926, Aug. 24   **Wmk. 195**

115	A39	5m on 50m Prus green	2.50	2.50
		Never hinged	3.50	
116	A39	10m on 100m brown vio	2.50	2.50
		Never hinged	3.50	

117 A39 15m on 200m brt vio-
　let　　　　　　　2.50　2.50
　　Never hinged　　　　8.50
　a.　Double surcharge　300.00
　　Nos. 115-117 (3)　　7.50　7.50

Ship of Hatshepsut — A41

1926, Dec. 9　Litho.　Perf. 13x13½
118 A41　5m brown & blk　3.00　1.40
　　Never hinged　　　　3.25
119 A41　10m dp red & blk　3.50　1.50
　　Never hinged　　　　4.50
120 A41　15m dp blue & blk　4.00　1.50
　　Never hinged　　　　4.75
　　Nos. 118-120 (3)　10.50　4.40

International Navigation Congress, Cairo.
For overprints see Nos. 121-123.

Nos. 118-120, 114 Overprinted — a

No. 114
Overprinted — b

1926, Dec. 21
121 A41 (a)　5m　　275.00　150.00
122 A41 (a)　10m　　275.00　150.00
123 A41 (a)　15m　　275.00　150.00
　　Perf. 14x14½
　　Wmk. 120
124 A40 (b)　50p　1,600. 875.00

Inauguration of Port Fuad opposite Port Said.
Nos. 121-123 have a block over "Le Caire"
at lower left.
Forgeries of Nos. 121-124 exist.

Branch of
Cotton
A42

Perf. 13x13½
1927, Jan. 25　　　　Wmk. 195
125 A42　5m dk brown & sl grn　1.75　.80
　　Never hinged　　　　2.75
126 A42　10m dp red & slate grn　2.75　1.50
　　Never hinged　　　　3.50
127 A42　15m dp blue & slate grn　3.50　1.50
　　Never hinged　　　　5.25
　　Nos. 125-127 (3)　　8.00　3.80

International Cotton Congress, Cairo.

King Fuad
A43　　　A44

A45

A46

Type I　　Type II

Early printings of the seven values indicated
were printed from plates with screens of vertical dots in the vignettes (type I). All values
were printed later from plates with screens of
diagonal dots (type II).

Perf. 13x13½
1927-37　　Wmk. 195　　Photo.
Type II
128 A43　1m orange　　.35　.25
　a.　Type I　　　　3.00　.50
129 A43　2m black　　.35　.25
　a.　Type I　　　　10.00　5.00
130 A43　3m olive brn　.35　.55
　a.　Type I　　　　2.00　.75
131 A43　3m dp green ('30)　.65　.25
132 A43　4m yellow grn　1.25　1.10
　a.　Type I　　　　60.00　10.00
133 A43　4m brown ('30)　1.10　.55
134 A43　4m dp green ('34)　.85　.40
135 A43　5m dk red brn
　　　　　('29)　　.95　.40
　a.　Type I　　　　3.00　.75
136 A43　10m dk red ('29)　1.40　.25
　a.　10m orange red, type I　2.00　.30
137 A43　10m purple ('34)　3.75　.25
138 A43　13m car rose ('32)　1.50　.40
139 A43　15m ultra　　2.50　.25
　a.　Type I　　　　10.00　.50
140 A43　15m dk violet ('34)　5.25　.25
141 A43　20m ultra ('34)　9.25　.30

Perf. 13½x14
142 A44　20m olive grn　3.25　.40
143 A44　20m ultra ('32)　7.50　.25
144 A44　40m olive brn ('32)　4.25　.25
145 A44　50m Prus green　3.50　.25
　a.　50m greenish blue　5.50　.25
146 A44　100m brown vio　10.00　.35
　a.　100m claret　　12.00　.35
147 A44　200m deep violet　9.00　1.25

Printings of Nos. 142, 145 and 146, made in
1929 and later, were from new plates with
stronger impressions and darker colors.

Lithographed; Center Photogravure
Perf. 13x13½
148 A45　500m choc & Prus
　　　　　bl, entirely
　　　　　photo ('32)　100.00　25.00
　a.　Frame litho, vignette photo　125.00　11.50
149 A46　£1 dk grn & org
　　　　　brn, entirely
　　　　　photo ('37)　125.00　8.25
　a.　Frame litho, vignette photo　140.00　7.00
　　Nos. 128-149 (22)　292.00　41.45

Statue of Amenhotep,
Son of Hapu — A47

1927, Dec. 29　Photo.　Perf. 13½x13
150 A47　5m orange brown　1.50　1.00
151 A47　10m copper red　2.00　1.00
152 A47　15m deep blue　3.25　1.00
　　Nos. 150-152 (3)　6.75　3.00

Statistical Congress, Cairo.

Imhotep — A48　　Mohammed Ali
　　　　　　　　Pasha — A49

1928, Dec. 15
153 A48　5m orange brown　1.10　.65
154 A49　10m copper red　1.25　.65

Intl. Congress of Medicine at Cairo and the
cent. of the Faculty of Medicine at Cairo.

Prince
Farouk — A50

1929, Feb. 11　　　　Litho.
155 A50　5m choc & gray　2.00　1.40
156 A50　10m dull red & gray　3.00　1.50
157 A50　15m ultra & gray　3.00　1.50
158 A50　20m Prus blue & gray　3.50　1.50
　　Nos. 155-158 (4)　11.50　5.90

Ninth birthday of Prince Farouk.
Nos. 155-158 with black or brown centers
are trial color proofs. They were sent to the
UPU, but were never placed on sale to the
public, although some are known used.

Tomb Fresco at El-Bersheh — A51

1931, Feb. 15　　　Perf. 13x13½
163 A51　5m brown　　1.50　1.00
164 A51　10m copper red　2.50　1.75
165 A51　15m dark blue　3.50　2.00
　　Nos. 163-165 (3)　7.50　4.75

14th Agricultural & Industrial Exhib., Cairo.

**Nos. 114 and 103 Surcharged in
Black**

1932　Wmk. 120　Perf. 14x14½
166 A40　50m on 50p　20.00　2.75
Perf. 14
167 A37　100m on £1　250.00　190.00

Locomotive of 1852 — A52

Perf. 13x13½
1933, Jan. 19　Litho.　Wmk. 195
168 A52　5m shown　14.00　7.00
169 A52　13m 1859　21.00　12.00
170 A52　15m 1862　21.00　12.00
171 A52　20m 1932　21.00　12.00
　　Nos. 168-171 (4)　77.00　43.00

International Railroad Congress, Heliopolis.

Commercial Passenger
Airplane — A56

Dornier
Do-X
A57

Graf
Zeppelin
A58

1933, Dec. 20　　　　Photo.
172 A56　5m brown　　6.50　3.00
173 A56　10m brt violet　15.00　12.00
174 A57　13m brown car　18.00　15.00
175 A57　15m violet　　18.00　13.00
176 A58　20m blue　　24.00　20.00
　　Nos. 172-176 (5)　81.50　63.00

International Aviation Congress, Cairo.

A59　　　Khedive Ismail
　　　　　Pasha — A60

1934, Feb. 1　　　　Perf. 13½
177 A59　1m dp orange　.60　1.10
178 A59　2m black　　.60　1.10
179 A59　3m brown　　.75　1.25
180 A59　4m blue green　1.25　.40
181 A59　5m red brown　1.40　.25
182 A59　10m violet　　2.50　.35
183 A59　13m copper red　4.00　2.25
184 A59　15m dull violet　4.50　1.75
185 A59　20m ultra　　3.00　.40
186 A59　50m Prus blue　9.50　.65
187 A59　100m olive grn　9.50　1.25
188 A59　200m dp violet　75.00　7.25
Perf. 13½x13
189 A60　50p brown　225.00　90.00
190 A60　£1 Prus blue　400.00　150.00
　　Nos. 177-190 (14)　737.60　258.00

10th Congress of UPU, Cairo.

King Fuad — A61

1936-37   Perf. 13½

191	A61	1m dull orange	.55	.90
		Never hinged	.85	
192	A61	2m black	1.75	.25
		Never hinged	2.60	
193	A61	4m dk green	2.00	.25
		Never hinged	3.00	
194	A61	5m chestnut	1.40	.55
		Never hinged	2.10	
195	A61	10m purple ('37)	2.50	.35
		Never hinged	3.75	
196	A61	15m brown violet	2.75	.50
		Never hinged	4.00	
197	A61	20m sapphire	3.25	.35
		Never hinged	5.00	
		Nos. 191-197 (7)	14.20	3.15

Entrance to Agricultural Building — A62

Agricultural Building — A63

Design: 15m, 20m, Industrial Building.

1936, Feb. 15   Perf. 13½x13

198	A62	5m brown	1.75	1.00
		Never hinged	2.75	

Perf. 13x13½

199	A63	10m violet	2.00	1.10
		Never hinged	3.00	
200	A63	13m copper red	3.25	2.25
		Never hinged	5.00	
201	A63	15m dark violet	1.75	1.25
		Never hinged	2.75	
202	A63	20m blue	3.75	2.25
		Never hinged	5.50	
		Nos. 198-202 (5)	12.50	7.85

15th Agricultural & Industrial Exhib., Cairo.

Signing of Treaty — A65

1936, Dec. 22   Perf. 11

203	A65	5m brown	.80	.80
		Never hinged	1.45	
204	A65	15m dk violet	1.00	1.00
		Never hinged	1.50	
205	A65	20m sapphire	1.75	1.75
		Never hinged	2.75	
		Nos. 203-205 (3)	3.55	3.55

Signing of Anglo-Egyptian Treaty, Aug. 26, 1936.

King Farouk — A66

Medal for Montreux Conf. — A67

1937-44   Wmk. 195   Perf. 13x13½

206	A66	1m brown org	.30	.25
		Never hinged	.40	
207	A66	2m vermilion	.30	.25
		Never hinged	.40	
208	A66	3m brown	.30	.25
		Never hinged	.40	
209	A66	4m green	.30	.25
		Never hinged	.40	
210	A66	5m red brown	.50	.25
		Never hinged	.65	
211	A66	6m lt yel grn ('40)	.60	.25
		Never hinged	.75	

212	A66	10m purple	.30	.25
		Never hinged	.40	
213	A66	13m rose car	.60	.35
		Never hinged	.75	
214	A66	15m dk vio brn	.50	.25
		Never hinged	.65	
215	A66	20m blue	.75	.35
		Never hinged	.95	
216	A66	20m lil gray ('44)	.75	.25
		Never hinged	.95	
		Nos. 206-216 (11)	5.20	2.95

For overprints see Nos. 301, 303, 345, 348, 360E, N3, N6, N8, N22, N25, N27 in Scott Standard catalogue, Vol. 2.

1937, Oct. 15   Perf. 13½x13

217	A67	5m red brown	.75	.55
		Never hinged	1.50	
218	A67	15m dk violet	1.25	1.10
		Never hinged	2.25	
219	A67	20m sapphire	1.50	1.25
		Never hinged	2.25	
		Nos. 217-219 (3)	3.50	2.90

Intl. Treaty signed at Montreux, Switzerland, under which foreign privileges in Egypt were to end in 1949.

Eye of Ré — A68

1937, Dec. 8   Perf. 13x13½

220	A68	5m brown	.90	.80
		Never hinged	1.60	
221	A68	15m dk violet	1.00	.90
		Never hinged	1.90	
222	A68	20m sapphire	1.25	1.00
		Never hinged	1.90	
		Nos. 220-222 (3)	3.15	2.70

15th Ophthalmological Congress, Cairo, December, 1937.

King Farouk, Queen Farida — A69

1938, Jan. 20   Perf. 11

223	A69	5m red brown	6.50	5.00
		Never hinged	10.00	

Royal wedding of King Farouk and Farida Zulficar.

Inscribed: "11 Fevrier 1938"
1938, Feb. 11

224	A69	£1 green & sepia	200.00	150.00

King Farouk's 18th birthday.

Cotton Picker — A70

1938, Jan. 26   Perf. 13½x13

225	A70	5m red brown	.75	.75
226	A70	15m dk violet	2.25	1.50
227	A70	20m sapphire	2.00	1.75
		Nos. 225-227 (3)	5.00	4.00

18th International Cotton Congress at Cairo.

Pyramids of Giza and Colossus of Thebes A71

1938, Feb. 1   Perf. 13x13½

228	A71	5m red brown	1.40	1.00
229	A71	15m dk violet	2.00	1.25
230	A71	20m sapphire	2.25	1.25
		Nos. 228-230 (3)	5.65	3.50

Intl. Telecommunication Conf., Cairo.

Branch of Hydnocarpus — A72

1938, Mar. 21   Perf. 13x13½

231	A72	5m red brown	1.25	1.25
232	A72	15m dk violet	1.75	1.25
233	A72	20m sapphire	1.75	1.25
		Nos. 231-233 (3)	4.75	3.75

International Leprosy Congress, Cairo.

King Farouk and Pyramids — A73

King Farouk
A74   A75

Backgrounds: 40m, Hussan Mosque. 50m, Cairo Citadel. 100m, Aswan Dam. 200m, Cairo University.

1939-46   Photo.   Perf. 14x13½

234	A73	30m gray	.75	.25
a.		30m slate gray	.75	
234B	A73	30m ol grn ('46)	.80	.25
235	A73	40m dk brown	.85	.25
236	A73	50m Prus green	1.00	.25
237	A73	100m brown vio	1.40	.25
238	A73	200m dk violet	5.00	.25

Perf. 13½x13

239	A74	50p green & sep	11.00	3.25
240	A75	£1 dp bl & dk brn	26.00	6.00
		Nos. 234-240 (8)	46.80	10.75

For £1 with A77 portrait, see No. 269D. See Nos. 267-269D.
For overprints see Nos. 310-314, 316, 355-358, 360, 363-364, N13-N19, N32-N38. These issues in Scott Standard catalogue, Vol. 2.

SEMI-POSTAL STAMPS

> Catalogue values for unused stamps in this section are for Never Hinged items.

Princess Ferial — SP1

Perf. 13½x14
1940, May 17   Photo.   Wmk. 195

B1	SP1	5m + 5m copper brown	4.50	1.25

AIR POST STAMPS

Mail Plane in Flight AP1

Perf. 13x13½
1926, Mar. 10   Wmk. 195   Photo.

C1	AP1	27m deep violet	30.00	30.00

1929, July 17

C2	AP1	27m orange brown	9.00	2.25

Zeppelin Issue
No. C2 Surcharged in Blue or Violet

1931, Apr. 6

C3	AP1	50m on 27m (Bl)	85.00	75.00
a.		"1951" instead of "1931"	110.00	100.00
C4	AP1	100m on 27m (V)	85.00	80.00

Airplane over Giza Pyramids AP2

1933-38   Litho.   Perf. 13x13½

C5	AP2	1m orange & blk	.30	.50
C6	AP2	2m gray & blk	.80	1.50
C7	AP2	2m org red & blk ('38)	2.75	2.00
C8	AP2	3m ol brn & blk	.60	.35
C9	AP2	4m green & blk	.90	.90
C10	AP2	5m dp brown & blk	.75	.25
C11	AP2	6m dk green & blk	1.50	1.25
C12	AP2	7m dk blue & blk	1.25	1.00
C13	AP2	8m violet & blk	.80	.25
C14	AP2	9m dp red & blk	2.00	1.50
C15	AP2	10m violet & brn	.75	.70
C16	AP2	20m dk green & brn	.60	.25
C17	AP2	30m dull blue & brn	.75	.25
C18	AP2	40m dp red & brn	15.00	.60
C19	AP2	50m orange & brn	13.00	.25
C20	AP2	60m gray & brn	6.00	1.10
C21	AP2	70m dk blue & bl grn	3.50	1.00
C22	AP2	80m ol brn & bl grn	3.50	1.00
C23	AP2	90m org & bl grn	4.00	1.00
C24	AP2	100m vio & bl grn	9.00	.80
C25	AP2	200m dp red & bl grn	12.00	1.75
		Nos. C5-C25 (21)	79.75	18.20

See Nos. C34-C37. For overprint see No. C38. These issues in Scott Standard catalogue, Vol. 2.

SPECIAL DELIVERY STAMPS

Motorcycle Postman — SD1

Perf. 13x13½
1926, Nov. 28   Photo.   Wmk. 195

E1	SD1	20m dark green	35.00	9.50

1929, Sept.

E2	SD1	20m brown red & black	6.75	1.75

POSTAGE DUE STAMPS

D1   D2

Wmk. Crescent and Star (119)

1884, Jan. 1   Litho.   Perf. 10½

J1	D1	10pa red	57.50	9.50
a.		Horiz. pair, imperf. vert.	150.00	
J2	D1	20pa red	175.00	50.00
J3	D1	1pi red	145.00	52.50
J4	D1	2pi red	240.00	12.50
J5	D1	5pi red	20.00	60.00
		Nos. J1-J5 (5)	637.50	184.50

1886, Aug. 1   Unwmk.

J6	D1	10pa red	75.00	17.50
a.		Horiz. pair, imperf. vert.	135.00	
J7	D1	20pa red	260.00	50.00
J8	D1	1pi red	37.50	10.00
a.		Pair, imperf. between	200.00	135.00
J9	D1	2pi red	37.50	5.00
a.		Pair, imperf. between	175.00	
		Nos. J6-J9 (4)	410.00	82.50

1888, Jan. 1   Perf. 11½

J10	D2	2m green	22.50	27.50
a.		Horiz. pair, imperf. between	225.00	200.00
J11	D2	5m rose red	45.00	27.50
J12	D2	1pi blue	145.00	40.00
a.		Pair, imperf. between	300.00	
J13	D2	2pi yellow	155.00	20.00
J14	D2	5pi gray	240.00	210.00
a.		Period after "PIASTRES"	325.00	250.00
		Nos. J10-J14 (5)	607.50	325.00

Excellent counterfeits of #J1-J14 are plentiful.

There are 4 types of each of Nos. J1-J14, so placed that any block of 4 contains all types.

D3

Perf. 14x13½

1889   Wmk. 119   Typo.

J15	D3	2m green	10.00	.70
a.		Half used as 1m on cover		350.00
J16	D3	4m maroon	3.75	.70
J17	D3	1pi ultra	7.75	.70
J18	D3	2pi orange	7.50	1.00
a.		Half used as 1p on cover		—
		Nos. J15-J18 (4)	29.00	3.10

Nos. J15-J18 exist on both ordinary and chalky paper. Imperf. examples of Nos. J15-J17 are proofs.

Black Surcharge

Type I — D4   Type II

Type I: the spacing between the last two Arabic characters at the right is 2mm. Type II: spacing is 3mm, and there is an added sign on top of the second character from the right.

1898

J19	D4	3m on 2pi orange		
		(I)	2.10	6.25
a.		Inverted surcharge	65.00	82.50
b.		Pair, one without surcharge	—	
c.		Arabic "3" over "2"	125.00	
d.		3m on 2pi orange (II)	5.50	18.00
e.		As "d," inverted surcharge	57.50	70.00
f.		As "d," double surcharge	225.00	

D5   D6

1921   Wmk. 120   Perf. 14x13½

J20	D5	2m green	3.75	6.75
J21	D5	4m vermilion	7.50	19.00
J22	D6	10m deep blue	12.50	25.00
		Nos. J20-J22 (3)	23.75	50.75

1921-22

J23	D5	2m vermilion	1.00	2.25
J24	D5	4m green	6.00	2.00
J25	D6	10m lake ('22)	6.50	1.50
		Nos. J23-J25 (3)	13.50	5.75

Nos. J18, J23-J25 Overprinted

1922, Oct. 10   Wmk. 119

J26	D3	2pi orange	7.50	10.50
a.		Overprint right side up	30.00	30.00

Wmk. 120

J27	D5	2m vermilion	1.00	3.00
J28	D5	4m green	1.60	3.00
J29	D6	10m lake	2.50	1.90
		Nos. J26-J29 (4)	12.60	18.40

Overprint on Nos. J26-J29 is inverted.

Arabic Numeral — D7

Perf. 13x13½

1927-56   Litho.   Wmk. 195
Size: 18x22½mm

J30	D7	2m slate	.85	.50
J31	D7	2m orange ('38)	1.00	1.10
J32	D7	4m green	.85	.55
J33	D7	4m ol brn ('32)	8.00	5.25
J34	D7	5m brown	4.25	1.10
J35	D7	6m gray grn ('41)	2.75	2.10
J36	D7	8m brn vio	1.60	.65
J37	D7	10m brick red ('29)	1.25	.35
a.		10m deep red	1.90	1.00
J38	D7	12m rose lake ('41)	1.90	3.75
J38A	D7	20m dk red ('56)	2.50	2.50

Perf. 13½x14
Size: 22x28mm

J39	D7	30m purple	5.25	3.75
		Nos. J30-J39 (11)	30.20	21.60

See Nos. J47-J59, Nos. J40-J46 and NJ1-NJ7 (overprints) in Scott Standard catalogue, Vol. 2.

LOCAL STAMPS

SUEZ CANAL COMPANY

Steamship — L1

1868, July 8   Litho.   Imperf.

L1	L1	1c black	275.00	1,150.
		On cover		22,500.
L2	L1	5c green	100.00	575.00
		On cover		11,500.
L3	L1	20c blue	90.00	575.00
		On cover		11,500.
L4	L1	40c pink	150.00	850.00
		On cover		17,000.

Nos. L1-L4 were issued by the Suez Canal Co. for use on letters and printed matter carried between canal ports. Items addressed to further destinations required additional French or Egyptian postage.

These issues were recognized officially by the French Consulate Offices at Port Said and Suez but not by the Egyptian Post Office, which suppressed their use at the end of August 1868.

Nos. L1-L4 exist with portions of the papermaker's watermark, "LA + F" (La Croix Freres).

Many forgeries exist of the stamps of the Suez Canal Co., including excellent counterfeits created from the genuine plate of the 40c value, stolen from the company's archives.

MILITARY STAMPS

The "British Forces" and "Army post" stamps were special issues provided at a reduced rate for the purchase and use by the British military forces in Egypt and their families for ordinary letters sent to Great Britain and Ireland by a concessionary arrangement made with the Egyptian government. From Nov. 1, 1932 to Feb. 29, 1936, in order to take advantage of the concessionary rate, it was mandatory to use #M1-M11 by affixing them to the backs of envelopes. An "Egypt Postage Prepaid" handstamp was applied to the face of the envelopes. Envelopes bearing these stamps were to be posted only at British military post boxes. Envelopes bearing the 1936-39 "Army Post" stamps (#M12-M15, issued by the Egyptian Postal Administration) also were sold at the concessionary rate and also were to be posted only at British military post boxes. The "Army Post" stamps were withdrawn in 1941, but the concession continued without the use of special stamps. The concession was finally canceled in 1951.

Imperf examples of Nos. M1-M4, M6, M9 (without overprint) and M10 are proofs.

M1

Unwmk.

1932, Nov. 1   Typo.   Perf. 11

M1	M1	1pi red & deep blue	100.00	4.50

For similar design see No. M3.

M2

1932, Nov. 26   Typo.   Perf. 11½

M2	M2	3m blk, sage grn	57.50	80.00

See Nos. M4, M6, M10.

M3

1933, Aug.   Typo.   Perf. 11

M3	M3	1pi red & deep blue	47.50	1.10

Camel Type of 1932

1933, Nov. 13   Typo.   Perf. 11½

M4	M2	3m brown lake	8.75	57.50

M4

1934, June 1   Photo.   Perf. 14½x14

M5	M4	1pi bright carmine	55.00	1.25

See Nos. M7-M8. For overprint and surcharge see Nos. M9, M11.

Camel Type of 1932

1934, Nov. 17   Typo.   Perf. 11½

M6	M2	3m deep blue	8.25	30.00

Type of 1934

1934, Dec. 5   Photo.   Perf. 14½x14

M7	M4	1pi green	6.00	6.00

Type of 1934

1935, Apr. 24   Perf. 13½x14

M8	M4	1pi bright carmine	2.90	3.75

Type of 1934 Overprinted in Red

1935, May 6   Perf. 14

M9	M4	1pi ultramarine	350.00	275.00

Camel Type of 1932

1935, Nov. 23   Typo.   Perf. 11½

M10	M2	3m vermilion	2.25	45.00

No. M8 Surcharged

1935, Dec. 16   Photo.   Perf. 13½x14

M11	M4	3m on 1pi brt car	25.00	100.00

Fuad Type of 1927
Inscribed "Army Post"

M5

1936, Mar. 1   Wmk. 195

M12	M5	3m green	2.50	2.50
M13	M5	10m carmine	7.00	.25

King Farouk — M6

1939, Dec. 16   Perf. 13x13½

M14	M6	3m green	6.00	12.00
M15	M6	10m carmine rose	8.00	.25

OFFICIAL STAMPS

O1

Wmk. Crescent and Star (119)

1893, Jan. 1   Typo.   Perf. 14x13½

O1	O1	orange brown	3.75	.25

No. O1 exists on ordinary and chalky paper. Imperf. examples of No. O1 are proofs.

Regular Issues of 1884-93 Overprinted

1907

O2	A18	1m brown	2.40	.35
O3	A19	2m green	4.25	.25
O4	A20	3m orange	4.75	1.25
O5	A22	5m car rose	7.75	.25
O6	A14	1pi ultra	4.75	.25
O7	A16	5pi gray	17.00	6.00
		Nos. O2-O7 (6)	40.90	8.35

Nos. O2-O3, O5-O7 imperf. are proofs.

No. 48 Overprinted   **O.H.H.S.**

1913

O8	A22	5m carmine rose	9.50	.70
a.		Inverted overprint		90.00
b.		No period after "S"	65.00	19.00

Regular Issues Overprinted

1914-15   On Issues of 1888-1906

O9	A19	2m green	5.00	10.00
a.		Inverted overprint	42.50	42.50
b.		Double overprint	450.00	
c.		No period after "S"	16.00	16.00
O10	A21	4m brown red	7.50	5.50
a.		Inverted overprint	225.00	160.00

On Issue of 1914

O11	A24	1m olive brown	2.50	5.00
a.		No period after "S"	14.00	30.00
O12	A26	3m orange	3.75	6.00
a.		No period after "S"	16.00	30.00
O13	A28	5m lake	4.75	2.75
a.		No period after "S"	17.50	26.00
b.		Two periods after "S"	17.50	26.00
		Nos. O9-O13 (5)	23.50	29.25

Regular Issues Overprinted

1915, Oct.   On Issues of 1888-1906

O14	A19	2m green	5.50	5.00
a.		Inverted overprint	24.00	24.00
b.		Double overprint	30.00	
O15	A21	4m brown red	11.00	11.00

On Issue of 1914

O16	A28	5m lake	15.00	1.75
a.		Pair, one without overprint	325.00	
		Nos. O14-O16 (3)	31.50	17.75

Nos. 50, 63, 52, 67 Overprinted

1922   Wmk. 120

O17	A24	1m olive brown	4.25	16.00
O18	A25	2m red	10.00	24.00
O19	A26	3m orange	77.50	150.00
O20	A28	5m pink	21.00	6.00
		Nos. O17-O20 (4)	112.75	196.00

Regular Issues of 1921-22 Overprinted

1922

O21	A24	1m olive brn	1.50	3.25
O22	A25	2m red	2.00	4.50
O23	A26	3m orange	3.25	5.00
O24	A27	4m green	7.00	9.00
a.		Two periods after "H" none after "S"	175.00	175.00
O25	A28	5m pink	4.00	1.00
a.		Two periods after "H" none after "S"	75.00	75.00
O26	A29	10m deep blue	7.00	8.00
O27	A29	10m lake ('23)	10.00	4.00
a.		Two periods after "H" none after "S"	100.00	100.00
O28	A34	15m indigo	8.00	7.00
O29	A35	15m indigo	160.00	160.00
a.		Two periods after "H" none after "S"	250.00	250.00
O30	A31	50m maroon	20.00	18.00

Regular Issue of 1923 Overprinted in Black or Red

1924   Perf. 13½x14

O31	A36	1m orange	2.10	2.25
O32	A36	2m gray (R)	2.75	3.50
O33	A36	3m brown	6.75	6.75
O34	A36	4m yellow green	8.50	8.50
O35	A36	5m orange brown	2.00	1.05
O36	A36	10m rose	5.50	4.00
O37	A36	15m ultra	9.25	6.75

Perf. 14

O38	A36	50m myrtle green	25.00	13.50
		Nos. O31-O38 (8)	61.85	46.30

O2

Perf. 13x13½

1926-35   Litho.   Wmk. 195
Size: 18½x22mm

O39	O2	1m lt orange	1.05	.55
O40	O2	2m black	.70	.40
O41	O2	3m olive brn	2.00	1.35
O42	O2	4m lt green	1.75	1.60
O43	O2	5m brown	2.10	.55
O44	O2	10m dull red	5.25	.55
O45	O2	10m brt vio ('34)	3.00	.60
O46	O2	15m dp blue	5.25	1.25
O47	O2	15m brown vio ('34)	5.25	1.10
O48	O2	20m dp blue ('35)	5.50	1.60

Perf. 13½
Size: 22½x27½mm

O49	O2	20m olive green	7.50	2.75
O50	O2	50m myrtle green	10.00	2.00
		Nos. O39-O50 (12)	49.35	14.30

O3

1938, Dec.   Size: 22½x19mm

O51	O3	1m orange	.35	.35
O52	O3	2m red	.35	.35
O53	O3	3m olive brown	1.60	1.60
O54	O3	4m yel green	1.00	1.00
O55	O3	5m brown	.50	.50
O56	O3	10m brt violet	.60	.60
O57	O3	15m rose violet	1.60	1.60
O58	O3	20m blue	1.60	1.60

Perf. 14x13½
Size: 26½x22mm

O59	O3	50m myrtle green	3.75	3.00
		Nos. O51-O59 (9)	11.35	10.60

ELOBEY, ANNOBON & CORISCO

ˌel-ə-ˈbā, ˌan-ə-ˈbän and kə-ˈris-ˌkō

LOCATION — A group of islands near the Guinea Coast of western Africa.
GOVT. — Spanish colonial possessions administered as part of the Continental Guinea District. A second district under the same governor-general included Fernando Po.
AREA — 13¾ sq. mi.
POP. — 2,950 (estimated 1910)
CAPITAL — Santa Isabel

100 Centimos = 1 Peseta

King Alfonso XIII — A1

1903   Unwmk.   Typo.   *Perf. 14*
Control Numbers on Back

1	A1	¼c carmine	.80	.55
2	A1	½c dk violet	.80	.55
3	A1	1c black	.80	.55
4	A1	2c red	.80	.55
5	A1	3c dk green	.80	.55
6	A1	4c dk blue grn	.80	.55
7	A1	5c violet	.80	.55
8	A1	10c rose lake	1.60	1.60
9	A1	15c orange buff	4.75	1.75
10	A1	25c dark blue	8.25	6.00
11	A1	50c red brown	10.00	10.50
12	A1	75c black brn	10.00	14.50
13	A1	1p orange red	16.00	20.00
14	A1	2p chocolate	44.00	60.00
15	A1	3p dp olive grn	65.00	75.00
16	A1	4p claret	150.00	100.00
17	A1	5p blue green	175.00	110.00
18	A1	10p dull blue	325.00	165.00
		Nos. 1-18 (18)	815.20	568.20
		Set, never hinged	1,500.	

Dated "1905"
1905   Control Numbers on Back

19	A1	1c carmine	1.40	.70
20	A1	2c dp violet	5.25	.70
21	A1	3c black	1.40	.70
22	A1	4c dull red	1.40	.70
23	A1	5c dp green	1.40	.70
24	A1	10c blue grn	4.75	.90
25	A1	15c violet	5.25	4.75
26	A1	25c rose lake	5.25	4.75
27	A1	50c orange buff	9.50	7.25
28	A1	75c dark blue	9.50	7.25
29	A1	1p red brown	19.50	16.00
30	A1	2p black brn	21.00	22.50
31	A1	3p orange red	21.00	23.00
32	A1	4p dk brown	160.00	72.50
33	A1	5p bronze grn	170.00	80.00
34	A1	10p claret	375.00	225.00
		Nos. 19-34 (16)	811.60	467.40
		Set, never hinged	1,500.	

Nos. 19-22 Surcharged in Black or Red

1906

35	A1	10c on 1c rose (Bk)	11.50	6.50
a.		Inverted surcharge	11.50	6.50
b.		Value omitted	30.00	16.00
c.		Frame omitted	16.00	7.50
d.		Double surcharge	11.50	6.50
e.		Surcharged "15 cents"	30.00	16.00
f.		Surcharged "25 cents"	52.50	22.50
g.		Surcharged "50 cents"	37.50	22.50
h.		"1906" omitted	17.50	7.50
36	A1	15c on 2c dp vio (R)	11.50	6.50
a.		Frame omitted	12.50	6.50
b.		Surcharged "25 cents"	16.00	9.00
c.		Inverted surcharge	11.50	6.50
d.		Double surcharge	11.50	6.50
37	A1	25c on 3c blk (R)	11.50	6.50
a.		Inverted surcharge	11.50	6.50
b.		Double surcharge	11.50	6.50
c.		Surcharged "15 cents"	16.00	6.50
d.		Surcharged "50 cents"	25.00	11.00
38	A1	50c on 4c red (Bk)	11.50	6.50
a.		Inverted surcharge	11.50	6.50
b.		Value omitted	35.00	17.50
c.		Frame omitted	17.50	8.00
d.		Double surcharge	11.50	8.00
f.		"1906" omitted	17.50	8.00

g.		Surcharged "10 cents"	32.50	16.00
h.		Surcharged "25 cents"	32.50	16.00
		Nos. 35-38 (4)	46.00	26.00

Eight other surcharges were prepared but not issued: 10c on 50c, 75c, 1p, 2p and 3p; 15c on 50c and 5p; 50c on 5c.
Exist with surcharges in different colors: #35 in blue, #35 in violet, #36 in black or violet, #37 in black or violet, #38 in blue, violet or red. Value, set of 10, $135.

King Alfonso XIII — A2

1907   Control Numbers on Back

39	A2	1c dk violet	.60	.45
40	A2	2c black	.60	.45
41	A2	3c red orange	.60	.45
42	A2	4c dk green	.60	.45
43	A2	5c blue green	.60	.45
44	A2	10c violet	6.00	5.50
45	A2	15c carmine	2.00	1.75
46	A2	25c orange	2.00	1.75
47	A2	50c blue	2.00	1.75
48	A2	75c brown	6.25	2.75
49	A2	1p black brn	10.50	4.75
50	A2	2p orange red	14.50	7.50
51	A2	3p dk brown	14.00	8.25
52	A2	4p bronze grn	14.50	7.75
53	A2	5p claret	21.00	8.25
54	A2	10p rose	52.50	25.00
		Nos. 39-54 (16)	148.25	77.25
		Set, never hinged	275.00	

Stamps of 1907 Surcharged

1908-09   Black Surcharge

55	A2	5c on 3c red org ('09)	2.25	1.25
56	A2	5c on 4c dk grn ('09)	2.25	1.25
57	A2	5c on 10c violet	4.50	5.00
58	A2	25c on 10c violet	22.50	15.00
		Nos. 55-58 (4)	31.50	22.50

1910   Red Surcharge

59	A2	5c on 1c dark violet	1.75	.90
60	A2	5c on 2c black	1.75	.90

Nos. 55-60 exist with surcharge inverted (value set, $125 unused or used); with double surcharge, one black, one red (value set, $300 unused or used); with "PARA" omitted (value set, $150.00 unused or used).
The same 5c surcharge was also applied to Nos. 45-54, but these were not issued (value set, $250).
In 1909, stamps of Spanish Guinea replaced those of Elobey, Annobon and Corisco.

Revenue stamps surcharged as above were unauthorized although some were postally used.

EPIRUS

i-ˈpī-rəs

LOCATION — A region of southeastern Europe, now divided between Greece and Albania.

During the First Balkan War (1912-13), this territory was occupied by the Greek army, and the local Greek majority wished to be united with Greece. Italy and Austria-Hungary favored its inclusion in the newly created Albania, however, which both powers expected to dominate. Greek forces were withdrawn subsequently in early 1914. The local population resisted inclusion in Albania and established the Autonomous Republic of Northern Epirus on Feb. 28, 1914. Resistance to Albanian control continued until October, when Greece reoccupied the country. Northern Epirus was administered as an integral part of Greece, and it was expected that Greece's annexation of the territory would become official following World War I. Instead, in 1916, Italian pressure and its own military reverses in Anatolia caused Greece to withdraw from Epirus and to formally cede the territory to Albania.

100 Lepta = 1 Drachma

Chimarra Issue

Double-headed Eagle, Skull and Crossbones — A1

Handstamped
1914, Feb. 10   Unwmk.   *Imperf.*
Control Mark in Blue
Without Gum

1	A1	1 l black & blue	475.00	240.00
a.		Tête-bêche pair		3,000.
2	A1	5 l blue & red	475.00	240.00
3	A1	10 l red & blk	475.00	240.00
4	A1	25 l blue & red	475.00	240.00
		Nos. 1-4 (4)	1,900.	960.00
		Set, on over-franked cover or postcard		1,750.

All values exist without control mark. This mark is a solid blue oval, about 12x8mm, containing the colorless Greek letters "SP," the first two letters of Spiromilios, the Chimarra commander.
All four exist with denomination inverted and the 1 l, 5 l and 10 l with denomination double. The values above are for the first printing on somewhat transparent shiny, white, thin, wove paper, which is sometimes known as "rice paper."
A second printing was made from original handstamps, on similar thin wove paper, but not transluscent, known as "Spetsiotis Reprints." Value, unused or canceled to order, each $55. Later printings were made from original handstamps on other papers, generally thicker and whiter, sometimes surfaced. Value, unused or canceled to order, each $45.
Values above are for genuine stamps expertized by knowledgeable authorities. Most of the stamps offered as Nos. 1-4 in the marketplace are forgeries. Most resemble the stamps from the second reprinting, but the designs differ in details of the lettering, monogram and skull. Such forgeries have only nominal commercial value.
Some experts question the official character of this issue.

Argyrokastro Issues
Stamps of Turkey surcharged "AUTONOMOUS EPIRUS" and new denominations in several formats in Greek currency.

On Turkish stamps of 1908

    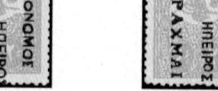

No. 4A   No. 4B

1914, Mar. 2

4A	A19	1d on 2½pi (#137)	9.50	10.00
		Never hinged	19.00	
4B	A19	2d on 2½pi (#137)	9.50	10.00
		Never hinged	19.00	
a.		Horiz. pair, #4A, 4B	29.00	

No. 4C   No. 4D

4C	A19	5d on 25pi (#140)	75.00	80.00
		Never hinged	150.00	
4D	A19	5d on 50pi (#141)	115.00	120.00
		Never hinged	225.00	

On Turkish stamps of 1909-10

4E	A21	5 l on 5pa (#151)	75.00	—
		Never hinged	150.00	

No. 4F   No. 4G

4F	A21	5 l on 10pa (#152)	3.00	3.00
		Never hinged	6.00	
4G	A21	10 l (oval "O") on 20pa (#153)	2.00	2.00
		Never hinged	4.00	
a.		Double surcharge	75.00	

No. 4H   No. 4I

4H	A21	10 l (round "O") on 20pa (#153)	2.00	2.00
		Never hinged	4.00	
a.		Double surcharge	75.00	
b.		Horiz. pair (#4G, 4H)	14.50	
c.		Horiz. pair (#4Ga, 4Ha)	375.00	
4I	A21	20 l on 1pi (#154)	2.00	2.00
		Never hinged	4.00	
a.		Double surcharge	75.00	

No. 4J   No. 4K

4J	A21	25 l on 1pi (#154)	2.00	2.00
		Never hinged	4.00	
a.		Double surcharge	75.00	
b.		Horiz. pair (#4I, 4J)	14.50	
c.		Horiz. pair (#4Ia, 4Ja)	375.00	
4K	A21	40 l on 2pi (#155)	3.00	3.00
		Never hinged	6.00	

No. 4L   No. 4M

4L	A21	80 l on 2pi (#155)	3.00	3.00
		Never hinged	6.00	
a.		Horiz. pair (#4K, 4L)	17.00	
4M	A21	1d on 5pi (#157)	12.00	12.00
		Never hinged	24.00	

No. 4N   No. 4O

4N	A21	2d on 5pi (#157)	12.00	12.00
		Never hinged	24.00	
a.		Horiz. pair (#4M, 4N)	37.50	
4O	A21	5d on 10pi (#158)	75.00	*80.00*
		Never hinged	150.00	
a.		Double surcharge		
4P	A21	5d on 10pa (#152)	125.00	*150.00*
		Never hinged	250.00	
4Q	A21	5d on 20pa (#153)	125.00	*150.00*
		Never hinged	250.00	

4R	A21	5d on 1pi (#154)	125.00	*150.00*
		Never hinged	250.00	
4S	A21	5d on 50pi (#160)	125.00	*150.00*
		Never hinged	250.00	

On Turkish stamps of 1909-11 (with "Béhié")

4T	A21	5 l on 10pa (#161)	75.00	
		Never hinged	150.00	
4U	A21	10 l (oval "O") on 20pa (#162)	75.00	
		Never hinged	150.00	
4V	A21	10 l (round "O") on 20pa (#162)	75.00	
		Never hinged	150.00	
a.		Horiz. pair (#4U, 4V)	400.00	
4W	A21	20 l on 1pi (#163)	75.00	
		Never hinged	150.00	
4X	A21	25 l on 1pi (#163)	75.00	
		Never hinged	150.00	
a.		Horiz. pair (#4W, 4X)	400.00	
4Y	A21	40 l on 2pi (#164)	75.00	
		Never hinged	150.00	
4Z	A21	80 l on 2pi (#164)	75.00	
		Never hinged	150.00	
a.		Horiz. pair (#4Y, 4Z)	400.00	
4AA	A21	5d on 10pa (#161)	125.00	
		Never hinged	150.00	
4BB	A21	5d on 20pa (#162)	125.00	
		Never hinged	250.00	
4CC	A21	5d on 1pi (#163)	125.00	
		Never hinged	250.00	

On Turkish Newspaper Stamps of 1910-11

 No. 4DD

 No. 4EE

4DD	A21	30 l on 2pa on 5pa (#P67)	80.00	
		Never hinged	160.00	
4EE	A21	50 l on 2pa on 5pa (#P67)	80.00	
		Never hinged	160.00	
a.		Horiz. pair (#4DD, 4EE)	150.00	

 No. 4FF

4FF	A21	30 l on 2pa (#P68)	2.00	2.00
		Never hinged	4.00	
4GG	A21	50 l on 2pa (#P68)	2.00	2.00
		Never hinged	4.00	
a.		Horiz. pair (#4FF, 4GG)	15.00	

Covers exist, starting at $50 for the most common (Nos. 4G, 4H, 4I, 4J).

Provisional Government Issues

Infantryman with Rifle
A2 A3

Serrate Roulette 13½

1914, Mar. Litho.

5	A2	1 l orange	.50	.95
		Never hinged	1.00	
6	A2	5 l green	.50	.95
		Never hinged	1.00	
7	A3	10 l carmine	.50	.95
		Never hinged	1.00	
8	A3	25 l deep blue	.50	.95
		Never hinged	1.00	
		on registered cover		*175.00*
9	A2	50 l brown	1.50	1.40
		Never hinged	3.00	
		On overfranked cover		*50.00*
10	A2	1d violet	2.40	2.40
		Never hinged	4.75	
		On overfranked cover		*50.00*
11	A2	2d blue	13.25	13.00
		Never hinged	26.50	
		on overfranked cover		*100.00*
12	A2	5d gray green	17.00	17.00
		Never hinged	35.00	
		On overfranked cover		*100.00*
		Nos. 5-12 (8)	36.15	*37.60*
		Set on philatelic cover		*200.00*

Issue dates: 10 l, 25 l, Mar. 5; balance of set, Mar. 26.

 Flag of Epirus — A5

1914, Aug. 28

15	A5	1 l brown & blue	.55	.65
		Never hinged	.70	
16	A5	5 l green & blue	.55	.65
		Never hinged	.70	
17	A5	10 l rose red & blue	.60	.70
		Never hinged	1.20	
18	A5	25 l dk blue & blue	1.10	1.10
		Never hinged	2.75	
19	A5	50 l violet & blue	1.10	1.10
		Never hinged	2.75	
20	A5	1d carmine & blue	5.75	7.00
		Never hinged	14.50	
21	A5	2d orange & blue	1.50	2.00
		Never hinged	3.50	
22	A5	5d dk green & blue	9.50	9.50
		Never hinged	24.00	
		Nos. 15-22 (8)	20.65	*22.70*

Koritsa Issue

 A7

1914, Sept. 25

26	A7	25 l dk blue & blue	5.00	4.75
		Never hinged	10.00	
27	A7	50 l violet & blue	11.00	11.00
		Never hinged	22.50	

Nos. 26 and 27 were issued at Koritsa (Korce) to commemorate that city's occupation by Epirot forces.

Chimarra Issues

 King Constantine I — A8

1914, Oct.

28	A8	1 l yellow green	125.00	75.00
		Never hinged	300.00	
29	A8	2 l red	110.00	40.00
		Never hinged	275.00	
30	A8	5 l dark blue	110.00	75.00
		Never hinged	275.00	
31	A8	10 l orange brown	75.00	25.00
		Never hinged	175.00	
a.		10 l red brown (Nov.)	140.00	110.00
		Never hinged	350.00	
32	A8	20 l carmine	160.00	80.00
		Never hinged	400.00	
a.		20 l rose carmine	140.00	
		Never hinged	350.00	
33	A8	25 l gray blue	110.00	75.00
		Never hinged	275.00	
33A	A8	50 l yellow green	160.00	80.00
		Never hinged	400.00	
33B	A8	1d carmine	160.00	80.00
		Never hinged	400.00	
a.		1d rose carmine	225.00	
		Never hinged	500.00	
33C	A8	2d pale yellow green	225.00	110.00
		Never hinged	550.00	
33D	A8	5d orange brown	400.00	275.00
		Never hinged	1,000.	
		Nos. 28-33D (10)	1,635.	*915.00*

Nos. 28-33D were printed by Papachrysanthou, Athens. The papermaker's watermark "PARCHIMINE JOHANNOT" appears on some stamps in the set.

1911-23 Issues of Greece Overprinted

1914, Aug. 24 Perf. Perf. 11½

34	A24	1 l green	60.00	60.00
		Never hinged	150.00	
35	A25	2 l carmine	50.00	50.00
		Never hinged	130.00	
36	A24	3 l vermilion	50.00	50.00
		Never hinged	130.00	
37	A26	5 l green	60.00	60.00
		Never hinged	150.00	

38	A24	10 l carmine	60.00	60.00
		Never hinged	150.00	
39	A25	20 l slate	85.00	85.00
		Never hinged	210.00	
40	A25	25 l blue	170.00	170.00
		Never hinged	425.00	
41	A26	50 l violet brn	100.00	100.00
		Never hinged	180.00	
		Nos. 34-41 (8)	635.00	*635.00*

The 2 l and 3 l are engraved stamps of the 1911-21 issue; the others are lithographed stamps of the 1912-23 issue.
Overprint reads: "Greek Chimarra 1914."
Stamps of this issue are with or without a black monogram (S.S., for S. Spiromilios) in manuscript. Counterfeits are plentiful.

Moschopolis Issue

A9 Arms

A10 Ancient Epirot Coins/Medals

1914, Sept. Engr. Perf. 14½

42	A9	1 l yellow brown	1.00	*3.00*
		Never hinged	2.00	
a.		Imperf., pair	40.00	
		Never hinged	60.00	
b.		1 l yellow	25.00	20.00
		Never hinged	40.00	
43	A9	2 l black	1.00	*3.00*
		Never hinged	2.00	
a.		Imperf., pair	40.00	
		Never hinged	60.00	
b.		2 l blue black	25.00	20.00
		Never hinged	40.00	
44	A9	3 l yellow	1.00	*3.00*
		Never hinged	2.00	
a.		Imperf., pair	40.00	
		Never hinged	60.00	
b.		3 l yellow brown	25.00	20.00
		Never hinged	40.00	
c.		3 l brown	25.00	20.00
		Never hinged	40.00	
45	A9	5 l green	1.00	*3.00*
		Never hinged	2.00	
a.		Imperf., pair	40.00	
		Never hinged	60.00	
46	A9	10 l red	1.00	*3.00*
		Never hinged	2.00	
a.		Imperf., pair	40.00	
		Never hinged	60.00	
47	A9	25 l deep blue	1.00	*3.00*
		Never hinged	2.00	
a.		Imperf., pair	40.00	
		Never hinged	60.00	
b.		25 l blue green	25.00	20.00
		Never hinged	40.00	
48	A9	30 l violet	1.00	*3.00*
		Never hinged	2.00	
a.		Imperf., pair	40.00	
		Never hinged	60.00	
b.		30 l deep violet	25.00	20.00
		Never hinged	40.00	
c.		30 l green	35.00	
		Never hinged	50.00	
49	A9	40 l olive gray	1.00	*3.00*
		Never hinged	2.00	
a.		Imperf., pair	40.00	
		Never hinged	60.00	
b.		40 l gray brown	25.00	20.00
		Never hinged	40.00	
c.		40 l blue green	35.00	
		Never hinged	50.00	
d.		40 l deep brown	35.00	
		Never hinged	50.00	
50	A9	50 l violet black	1.00	*3.00*
		Never hinged	2.00	
a.		Imperf., pair	40.00	
		Never hinged	60.00	
b.		50 l brown black	25.00	20.00
		Never hinged	40.00	
51	A10	1d yellow brown & olive	5.00	*10.00*
		Never hinged	10.00	
a.		Imperf., pair	80.00	
		Never hinged	120.00	
b.		1d olive green & rose	25.00	
		Never hinged	37.50	
52	A10	2d carmine & gray	4.00	*10.00*
		Never hinged	8.00	
a.		Imperf., pair	80.00	
		Never hinged	120.00	
b.		2d orange & blue	25.00	
53	A10	3d gray green & red brown	4.50	*10.00*
		Never hinged	9.00	
a.		Imperf., pair	80.00	
		Never hinged	120.00	
b.		3d blue gray & brownish red	25.00	
54	A10	5d olive & yellow brown	4.00	*10.00*
		Never hinged	8.00	
a.		Imperf., pair	80.00	
		Never hinged	120.00	
b.		5d blue gray & yellow brown	25.00	
55	A10	10d orange & blue	4.50	*12.50*
		Never hinged	9.00	
a.		Imperf., pair	80.00	
		Never hinged	120.00	
b.		10d red & blue	25.00	
		Never hinged	37.50	
56	A10	25d violet & black	4.50	*17.50*
		Never hinged	9.00	
a.		Imperf., pair	80.00	
		Never hinged	120.00	
b.		25d brown violet & black	25.00	25.00
		Never hinged	45.00	

c.		25d green & red brown	25.00	
		Never hinged	45.00	
		Nos. 42-56 (15)	35.50	*97.00*

Nos. 42-56 were privately printed in early 1914. In June 1914, the Epirots occupied Moschopolis (Voskopoje), and these stamps were authorized for use by the local military commander in Sept. After the occupation of Moschopolis by Greek forces in Nov., remaining stocks of this issue were sent to Athens, where they were destroyed in 1931.

The 1d exists with center omitted. Value $100. The 1d, 2d, 10d and 25d exist with center inverted. Values, each $65.

Stamps of the following designs were locals, privately produced. Issued primarily for propaganda and for philatelic purposes, their postal use is in dispute. The 1920 design is a fantasy item, created long after Epirus was annexed by Albania.

From 1914: 1st design, 3 varieties. 2nd design, 6 varieties. 3rd design, 7 varieties.

From 1920: 4th design, 4 varieties.

OCCUPATION STAMPS

Issued under Greek Occupation

Greek Occupation Stamps of 1913 Overprinted Horizontally

Serrate Roulette 13½

1914-15 Black Overprint Unwmk.

N1	O1	1 l brown	.80	.80
		Never hinged	2.75	
b.		Inverted overprint	24.00	19.00
		Never hinged	35.00	
c.		Double overprint	24.00	19.00
		Never hinged	35.00	
d.		Double overprint, one inverted	25.00	20.00
		Never hinged	37.50	
N2	O2	2 l red	.80	.80
		Never hinged	2.75	
b.		2 l rose	1.25	1.25
		Never hinged	4.00	
c.		As #N2, inverted overprint	24.00	19.00

	Never hinged	35.00	
d.	As "b", inverted overprint	28.00	22.50
	Never hinged	42.50	
e.	As #N2, double overprint	24.00	19.00
	Never hinged	35.00	
f.	As "b", double overprint	28.00	22.50
	Never hinged	42.50	
g.	As #N2, double overprint, one inverted	25.00	25.00
	Never hinged	37.50	
N4	O2 3 l orange	.80	.80
	Never hinged	2.75	
b.	Inverted overprint	19.00	15.00
	Never hinged	29.00	
c.	Double overprint	19.00	15.00
	Never hinged	29.00	
d.	Double overprint, one inverted	25.00	20.00
	Never hinged	37.50	
N5	O1 5 l green	2.00	2.00
	Never hinged	4.50	
b.	Inverted overprint	33.00	26.50
	Never hinged	50.00	
N6	O1 10 l rose red	2.75	2.75
	Never hinged	10.00	
a.	Inverted overprint	47.50	37.50
	Never hinged	70.00	
b.	Double overprint	47.50	37.50
	Never hinged	70.00	
N7	O1 20 l violet	7.50	7.50
	Never hinged	16.50	
a.	Inverted overprint	47.50	37.50
	Never hinged	72.50	
b.	Double overprint	80.00	65.00
	Never hinged	120.00	
N8	O2 25 l pale blue	2.75	2.75
	Never hinged	10.00	
N9	O1 30 l gray green	14.00	14.00
	Never hinged	50.00	
N10	O2 40 l indigo	19.00	19.00
	Never hinged	65.00	
N11	O1 50 l dark blue	21.00	21.00
	Never hinged	72.50	
N12	O2 1d violet brown	135.00	135.00
	Never hinged	465.00	
a.	Inverted overprint	300.00	225.00
	Never hinged	450.00	
b.	Double overprint	360.00	300.00
	Never hinged	550.00	
	Nos. N1-N12 (11)	206.40	206.40

Red Overprint

N1a	O1 1 l brown	5.75	
	Never hinged	11.50	
N2a	O2 2 l red	5.75	
	Never hinged	11.50	
N4a	O2 3 l orange	5.75	
	Never hinged	11.50	
N5a	O1 5 l green	5.75	
	Never hinged	11.50	

Nos. N1a-N5a were not issued. Exist canceled.

Regular Issues of Greece, 1911-23, Ovptd. Reading Up

On Issue of 1911-21

1916   **Engr.**

N17	A24 3 l vermilion	11.50	11.50
	Never hinged	22.50	
a.	Overprint reading down	14.50	
	Never hinged	29.00	
N18	A26 30 l carmine rose	40.00	40.00
	Never hinged	55.00	
a.	Overprint reading down	225.00	
	Never hinged	450.00	
N19	A27 1d ultra	85.00	85.00
	Never hinged	170.00	
N20	A27 2d vermilion	95.00	95.00
	Never hinged	190.00	
N21	A27 3d carmine rose	122.50	122.50
	Never hinged	250.00	
N22	A27 5d ultra	—	—
	Never hinged		
a.	Double overprint	950.00	950.00
	Never hinged	1,900.	
b.	Overprint reading down	675.00	
	Never hinged	1,375.	
	Nos. N17-N22 (6)	354.00	354.00

On Issue of 1912-23

1916   **Litho.**

N23	A24 1 l green	2.75	2.75
	Never hinged	5.50	
a.	Overprint reading down	9.50	
	Never hinged	19.00	
b.	As #N23, "I" omitted	20.00	
	Never hinged	30.00	
c.	As #N23, inverted "L" in place of "E" in "Epirus"	20.00	
	Never hinged	30.00	
N24	A25 2 l carmine	2.75	2.75
	Never hinged	5.50	
a.	Overprint reading down	9.50	
	Never hinged	19.00	
b.	As #N24, "I" omitted	20.00	
	Never hinged	30.00	
c.	As #N24, inverted "L" in place of "E" in "Epirus"	20.00	
	Never hinged	30.00	
N25	A24 3 l vermilion	2.75	2.75
	Never hinged	5.50	
a.	Overprint reading down	14.00	
	Never hinged	28.00	
b.	As #N25, "I" omitted	20.00	
	Never hinged	30.00	
c.	As #N25, inverted "L" in place of "E" in "Epirus"	20.00	
	Never hinged	30.00	
N26	A26 5 l green	2.75	2.75
	Never hinged	5.50	
a.	Overprint reading down	14.00	

	Never hinged	28.00	
b.	As #N26, "I" omitted	24.00	
	Never hinged	35.00	
c.	As #N27, inverted "L" in place of "E" in "Epirus"	24.00	
	Never hinged	35.00	
N27	A24 10 l carmine	2.75	2.75
	Never hinged	5.50	
a.	Overprint reading down	?	?
	Never hinged	55.00	
b.	As #N27, "I" omitted	27.50	
	Never hinged	42.50	
c.	As #N27, inverted "L" in place of "E" in "Epirus"	27.50	
	Never hinged	42.50	
N28	A25 20 l slate	2.75	2.75
	Never hinged	5.50	
a.	As #N28, "I" omitted	35.00	
	Never hinged	50.00	
b.	As #N28, inverted "L" in place of "E" in "Epirus"	35.00	
	Never hinged	50.00	
N29	A25 25 l blue	3.75	3.75
	Never hinged	7.50	
a.	As #N29, "I" omitted	35.00	
	Never hinged	50.00	
b.	As #N29, inverted "L" in place of "E" in "Epirus"	35.00	
	Never hinged	50.00	
N30	A26 30 l rose	21.00	21.00
	Never hinged	42.00	
a.	Overprint reading down	225.00	
	Never hinged	450.00	
b.	As #N30, "I" omitted	95.00	
	Never hinged	145.00	
c.	As #N30, inverted "L" in place of "E" in "Epirus"	95.00	
	Never hinged	145.00	
N31	A25 40 l indigo	14.00	14.00
	Never hinged	28.00	
a.	Overprint reading down	225.00	
	Never hinged	450.00	
b.	As #N31, "I" omitted	95.00	
	Never hinged	145.00	
c.	As #N31, inverted "L" in place of "E" in "Epirus"	95.00	
	Never hinged	145.00	
N32	A26 50 l violet brown	24.00	9.50
	Never hinged	50.00	
a.	As #N32, "I" omitted	110.00	
	Never hinged	160.00	
b.	As #N32, inverted "L" in place of "E" in "Epirus"	110.00	
	Never hinged	160.00	
	Nos. N23-N32 (10)	79.25	64.75

In each sheet, there are two varieties in the overprint: the "I" in "Epirus" omitted and an inverted "L" in place of the first letter of the word.

Counterfeits exist of Nos. N1-N32.

Postage stamps issued in 1940-41, during Greek occupation, are listed under Greece.

ERITREA

ˌer-ə-ˈtrē-ə

LOCATION — In northeast Africa, bordering on the Red Sea
GOVT. — Italian Colony
AREA — 15,754 sq. mi. (1936)
POP. — 600,573 (1931)
CAPITAL — Asmara

Eritrea was incorporated as a State of Italian East Africa in 1936.

100 Centesimi = 1 Lira

All used values to about 1916 are for postally used stamps. From 1916, used values in italics are for postally used stamps. CTO's, for stamps valued postally used, sell for about the same as unused, hinged stamps.

Watermark

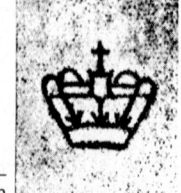

Wmk. 140 — Crown

Stamps of Italy Overprinted

a   b

1892   **Wmk. 140**   *Perf. 14*

Overprinted Type "a" in Black

1	A6 1c bronze grn	10.00	10.00
	Never hinged	24.00	
	No gum	2.50	
	On cover		120.00
a.	Inverted overprint	675.00	675.00
	Never hinged	—	
b.	Double overprint	1,900.	
	Never hinged	2,400.	
c.	Vert. pair, one without overprint	4,500.	
	Never hinged	5,750.	
2	A7 2c org brn	5.00	5.00
	Never hinged	12.00	
	No gum	1.40	
	On cover		95.00
a.	Inverted overprint	600.00	600.00
	Never hinged	—	
b.	Double overprint	1,900.	
	Never hinged	2,400.	
3	A33 5c green	160.00	17.50
	Never hinged	400.00	
	No gum	40.00	
	On cover		87.50
a.	Inverted overprint	8,000.	4,500.
	Never hinged	10,000.	

Overprinted Type "b" in Black

4	A17 10c claret	210.00	17.50
	Never hinged	525.00	
	No gum	40.00	
	On cover		87.50
5	A17 20c orange	375.00	12.00
	Never hinged	950.00	
	No gum	75.00	
	On cover		60.00
6	A17 25c blue	1,450.	55.00
	Never hinged	3,500.	
	No gum	325.00	
	On cover		400.00
7	A25 40c brown	13.50	*32.50*
	Never hinged	32.50	
	No gum	3.25	
	On cover		325.00
8	A26 45c slate grn	13.50	*32.50*
	Never hinged	32.50	
	No gum	3.25	
	On cover		350.00
9	A27 60c violet	13.50	72.50
	Never hinged	40.00	
	No gum	3.25	
	On cover		725.00
10	A28 1 l brn & yel	65.00	*80.00*
	Never hinged	160.00	
	No gum	9.00	
	On cover		950.00
11	A38 5 l bl & rose	650.00	550.00
	Never hinged	1,625.	
	No gum	140.00	
	On cover		8,400.
	Nos. 1-11 (11)	2,965.	884.50
	Set, never hinged	7,300.	

1895-99

Overprinted type "a" in Black

12	A39 1c brown ('99)	22.50	12.00
	Never hinged	55.00	
	No gum	3.25	
	On cover		120.00
13	A40 2c org brn ('99)	4.75	2.40
	Never hinged	12.00	
	No gum	.60	
	On cover		95.00
14	A41 5c green	4.75	2.40
	Never hinged	12.00	
	No gum	.60	
	On cover		47.50
a.	Inverted overprint	525.00	*4,250.*

Overprinted type "b" in Black

15	A34 10c claret ('98)	4.75	2.40
	Never hinged	12.00	
	No gum	.60	
	On cover		72.50
16	A35 20c orange	4.75	3.25
	Never hinged	12.00	
	No gum	.80	
	On cover		55.00
17	A36 25c blue	4.75	4.75
	Never hinged	12.00	
	No gum	.80	
	On cover		240.00
18	A37 45c olive grn	37.50	*27.50*
	Never hinged	100.00	
	No gum	6.50	
	On cover		550.00
	Nos. 12-18 (7)	83.75	*54.70*
	Set, never hinged	215.00	

1903-28

Overprinted type "a" in Black

19	A42 1c brown	1.60	*1.25*
	Never hinged	4.00	
	On cover		16.00
a.	Inverted overprint	125.00	125.00
20	A43 2c orange brn	1.60	.60
	Never hinged	4.00	
	On cover		16.00
21	A44 5c blue green	120.00	.60
	Never hinged	300.00	
	On cover		9.50
22	A45 10c claret	140.00	.60
	Never hinged	350.00	
	On cover		9.50
23	A45 20c orange	6.50	1.25
	Never hinged	16.00	
	On cover		14.50
24	A45 25c blue	1,200.	18.00
	Never hinged	3,000.	
	On cover		140.00
a.	Double overprint	1,100.	
25	A45 40c brown	1,300.	30.00
	Never hinged	3,300.	
	On cover		325.00
26	A45 45c olive grn	8.00	*10.00*
	Never hinged	20.00	
	On cover		200.00

27	A45 50c violet	475.00	32.50
	Never hinged	1,200.	
	On cover		475.00
28	A46 75c dk red & rose ('??)	90.00	20.00
	Never hinged	200.00	
	On cover		120.00
29	A46 1 l brown & grn	8.00	.85
	Never hinged	20.00	
	On cover		110.00
30	A46 1.25 l bl & ultra ('28)	40.00	20.00
	Never hinged	100.00	
	On cover		275.00
31	A46 2 l dk grn & org ('25)	87.50	*100.00*
	Never hinged	210.00	
	On cover		475.00
32	A46 2.50 l dk grn & org ('28)	175.00	72.50
	Never hinged	425.00	
	On cover		725.00
33	A46 5 l blue & rose	55.00	45.00
	Never hinged	140.00	
	On cover		4,000.
	Nos. 19-33 (15)	3,698.	353.15
	Set, never hinged	9,250.	

Surcharged in Black

1905

34	A45 15c on 20c orange	80.00	20.00
	Never hinged	200.00	
	On cover		100.00

1908-28

Overprinted type "a" in Black

35	A48 5c green	1.20	1.00
	Never hinged	3.50	
	On cover		8.00
36	A48 10c claret ('09)	1.20	1.00
	Never hinged	3.50	
	On cover		14.50
37	A48 15c slate ('20)	22.50	14.50
	Never hinged	55.00	
	On cover		80.00
38	A49 20c green ('25)	16.00	11.00
	Never hinged	40.00	
	On cover		65.00
39	A49 20c lilac brn ('28)	8.00	3.25
	Never hinged	20.00	
	On cover		87.50
40	A49 25c blue ('09)	6.50	2.25
	Never hinged	15.00	
	On cover		35.00
41	A49 30c gray ('25)	16.00	14.50
	Never hinged	40.00	
	On cover		120.00
42	A49 40c brown ('16)	55.00	40.00
	Never hinged	140.00	
	On cover		125.00
43	A49 50c violet ('16)	16.00	2.10
	Never hinged	40.00	
	On cover		160.00
44	A49 60c brown car ('18)	27.50	*28.00*
	Never hinged	70.00	
	On cover		120.00
a.	Printed on both sides		*1,750.*
45	A49 60c brown org ('28)	110.00	*225.00*
	Never hinged	275.00	
	On cover		600.00
46	A51 10 l gray grn & red ('16)	425.00	*775.00*
	Never hinged	1,050.	
	Nos. 35-46 (12)	704.90	*1,117.*
	Set, never hinged	1,750.	

See No. 53.

A1

Government Building at Massaua — A2

1910-29   **Unwmk.**   **Engr.**   *Perf. 13½*

47	A1 15c slate	390.00	30.00
	Never hinged	975.00	
	On cover		175.00
a.	Perf. 11 ('29)	40.00	*55.00*
	Never hinged	100.00	
	On cover		600.00
48	A2 25c dark blue	7.25	*17.50*
	Never hinged	18.00	
	On cover		250.00
a.	Perf. 12	875.00	875.00

For surcharges see Nos. 51-52.

Farmer
Plowing — A4

1914-28

49	A3	5c green	1.20	*2.50*
		Never hinged	2.00	
		On cover		65.00
a.		Perf. 11 ('28)	210.00	75.00
		Never hinged	525.00	
		On cover		525.00
50	A4	10c carmine	4.75	*4.25*
		Never hinged	12.00	
		On cover		80.00
a.		Perf. 11 ('28)	12.00	47.50
		Never hinged	30.00	
		On cover		450.00
b.		Perf. 13½x14	62.50	62.50
		Never hinged	140.00	
		On cover		*450.00*

No. 47 Surcharged in Red or Black

1916

51	A1	5c on 15c slate (R)	8.75	*15.00*
		Never hinged	22.00	
		On cover		240.00
52	A1	20c on 15c slate	4.00	*4.25*
		Never hinged	10.00	
		On cover		120.00
a.		"CEN" for "CENT"	47.50	47.50
		Never hinged	120.00	
b.		"CENT" omitted	190.00	190.00
		Never hinged	450.00	
c.		"ENT"	47.50	47.50
		Never hinged	120.00	
		Set, never hinged	32.00	

Italy No. 113
Overprinted in Black —
f

1921 Wmk. 140 Perf. 14

53	A50	20c brown orange	4.75	*15.00*
		Never hinged	12.00	
		On cover		52.50

Victory Issue
Italian Victory Stamps of 1921
Overprinted type "f" 13mm long

1922

54	A64	5c olive green	2.00	*7.25*
		Never hinged	5.00	
		On cover		125.00
55	A64	10c red	2.00	*7.25*
		Never hinged	5.00	
		On cover		240.00
56	A64	15c slate green	2.00	*11.00*
		Never hinged	5.00	
		On cover		250.00
57	A64	25c ultra	2.00	*11.00*
		Never hinged	5.00	
		On cover		300.00
		Nos. 54-57 (4)	8.00	36.50
		Set, never hinged	20.00	
		Set on overfranked, philatelic cover		180.00

Somalia Nos. 10-16
Overprinted In Black
g

1922 Wmk. 140

58	A1	2c on 1b brn	4.75	*17.50*
		Never hinged	12.00	
		On cover		120.00
a.		Pair, one missing "ERI-TREA"	2,250.	
		Never hinged	3,000.	
59	A1	5c on 2b bl grn	4.75	*13.00*
		Never hinged	12.00	
		On cover		80.00
60	A2	10c on 1a claret	4.75	*2.40*
		Never hinged	12.00	
		On cover		80.00
61	A2	15c on 2a brn org	4.75	*2.40*
		Never hinged	12.00	
		On cover		80.00
62	A2	25c on 2½a blue	4.75	*2.40*
		Never hinged	12.00	
		On cover		120.00
63	A2	50c on 5a yellow	22.50	*13.50*
		Never hinged	55.00	
		On cover		250.00
a.		"ERITREA" double		*1,600.*
64	A2	1 l on 10a lilac	22.50	*22.50*
		Never hinged	55.00	
		On cover		450.00
a.		"ERITREA" double	1,600.	1,600.
		Never hinged	2,000.	
b.		Pair, one missing "ERI-TREA"	3,000.	
		Never hinged	4,000.	
		Nos. 58-64 (7)	68.75	73.70
		Set, never hinged	170.00	

See Nos. 81-87.

Propagation of the Faith Issue
Italy Nos. 143-146 Overprinted

1923

65	A68	20c ol grn & brn org	12.00	*52.50*
		Never hinged	30.00	
66	A68	30c claret & brn org	12.00	*52.50*
		Never hinged	30.00	
67	A68	50c vio & brn org	8.00	*60.00*
		Never hinged	20.00	
68	A68	1 l bl & brn org	8.00	*92.50*
		Never hinged	20.00	
		Nos. 65-68 (4)	40.00	257.50
		Set, never hinged	100.00	

Fascisti Issue

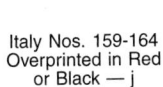

Italy Nos. 159-164
Overprinted in Red
or Black — j

1923 Unwmk. Perf. 14

69	A69	10c dk green (R)	11.00	*20.00*
		Never hinged	27.50	
		On cover		325.00
70	A69	30c dk violet (R)	11.00	*20.00*
		Never hinged	27.50	
		On cover		325.00
71	A69	50c brown carmine	11.00	*27.50*
		Never hinged	27.50	
		On cover		325.00

Wmk. 140

72	A70	1 l blue	11.00	*52.50*
		Never hinged	27.50	
		On cover		600.00
73	A70	2 l brown	11.00	*65.00*
		Never hinged	27.50	
		On cover		875.00
74	A71	5 l black & blue (R)	11.00	*95.00*
		Never hinged	27.50	
		Nos. 69-74 (6)	66.00	280.00
		Set, never hinged	165.00	
		Set on overfranked, philatelic cover		775.00

Manzoni Issue
Italy Nos. 165-170 Overprinted in Red

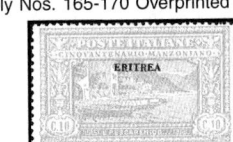

1924 Perf. 14

75	A72	10c brown red & blk	12.00	*80.00*
		Never hinged	30.00	
76	A72	15c blue grn & blk	12.00	*80.00*
		Never hinged	30.00	
77	A72	30c black & slate	12.00	*80.00*
		Never hinged	30.00	
78	A72	50c org brn & blk	12.00	*80.00*
		Never hinged	30.00	
79	A72	1 l blue & blk	72.50	*475.00*
		Never hinged	180.00	
80	A72	5 l violet & blk	475.00	*3,250.*
		Never hinged	1,200.	
		Nos. 75-80 (6)	595.50	4,045.
		Set, never hinged	1,500.	

On Nos. 79 and 80 the overprint is placed
vertically at the left side.

Somalia Nos. 10-16 Overprinted
type "g" in Blue or Red

1924

Bars over Original Values

81	A1	2c on 1b brn	17.50	*27.50*
		Never hinged	45.00	
		On cover		175.00
a.		Pair, one without "ERI-TREA"	2,400.	
		Never hinged	2,750.	
82	A1	5c on 2b bl grn (R)	17.50	*17.50*
		Never hinged	45.00	
		On cover		110.00
83	A2	10c on 1a rose red	9.50	*16.00*
		Never hinged	24.00	
		On cover		87.50
84	A2	15c on 2a brn org	9.50	*16.00*
		Never hinged	24.00	
		On cover		110.00
a.		Pair, one without "ERI-TREA"	2,400.	
		Never hinged	3,000.	
b.		"ERITREA" inverted	1,750.	1,750.
		Never hinged	2,250.	
85	A2	25c on 2½a bl (R)	9.50	*11.00*
		Never hinged	24.00	
		On cover		140.00
a.		Double surcharge	1,200.	
		Never hinged	1,500.	
86	A2	50c on 5a yellow	9.50	*20.00*
		Never hinged	24.00	
		On cover		240.00
87	A2	1 l on 10a lil (R)	9.50	*27.50*
		Never hinged	24.00	
		On cover		475.00
		Nos. 81-87 (7)	82.50	135.50
		Set, never hinged	200.00	

Stamps of Italy, 1901-08 Overprinted
type "j" in Black

1924

88	A42	1c brown	9.50	*9.50*
		Never hinged	23.00	
		On cover		72.50
a.		Inverted overprint	325.00	
b.		Vertical pair, one without ovpt.	1,750.	
		Never hinged	2,400.	
89	A43	2c orange brown	6.50	*8.00*
		Never hinged	14.00	
		On cover		72.50
b.		Vertical pair, one without ovpt.	1,750.	
		Never hinged	2,400.	
90	A48	5c green	9.50	*8.75*
		Never hinged	23.00	
		On cover		47.50
		Nos. 88-90 (3)	25.50	26.25
		Set, never hinged	60.00	

Victor Emmanuel Issue

Italy Nos. 175-177
Overprinted — k

1925-26 Unwmk. Perf. 11

91	A78	60c brown car	2.40	*9.50*
		Never hinged	6.00	
		On cover		140.00
a.		Perf. 13½	13.00	40.00
		Never hinged	32.50	
		On cover		450.00

92	A78	1 l dark blue	2.40	*14.50*
		Never hinged	6.00	
		On cover		260.00
a.		Perf. 13½	24,000.	9,500.
		Never hinged	36,000.	

Perf. 13½

93	A78	1.25 l dk blue ('26)	4.00	*32.50*
		Never hinged	10.00	
		On cover		600.00
a.		Perf. 11	8.00	40.00
		Never hinged	20.00	
		On cover		525.00
		Nos. 91-93 (3)	8.80	56.50
		Set, never hinged	22.00	

Saint Francis of Assisi Issue
Italian Stamps of 1926 Overprinted

1926 Wmk. 140 Perf. 14

94	A79	20c gray green	2.40	*14.00*
		Never hinged	6.00	
		On cover		125.00
95	A80	40c dark violet	2.40	*14.00*
		Never hinged	6.00	
		On cover		160.00
96	A81	60c red violet	2.40	*26.00*
		Never hinged	6.00	
		On cover		160.00

Overprinted in Red

Unwmk. Perf. 11

97	A82	1.25 l dark blue	2.40	*36.00*
		Never hinged	6.00	
		On cover		275.00

Perf. 14

98	A83	5 l + 2.50 l ol grn	8.00	*72.50*
		Never hinged	20.00	
		Nos. 94-98 (5)	17.60	162.50
		Set, never hinged	44.00	
		Set on overfranked philatelic cover		475.00

Italian Stamps of 1926 Overprinted
type "f" in Black

1926 Wmk. 140 Perf. 14

99	A46	75c dk red & rose	80.00	*20.00*
		Never hinged	200.00	
		On cover		120.00
a.		Double overprint	450.00	
100	A46	1.25 l blue & ultra	40.00	*20.00*
		Never hinged	100.00	
		On cover		275.00
101	A46	2.50 l dk green & org	175.00	*72.50*
		Never hinged	425.00	
		On cover		725.00
		Nos. 99-101 (3)	295.00	112.50
		Set, never hinged	725.00	

Volta Issue

Type of Italy, 1927,
Overprinted — o

1927

102	A84	20c purple	6.50	*40.00*
		Never hinged	16.00	
		On cover		275.00
103	A84	50c deep orange	9.50	*27.50*
		Never hinged	24.00	
		On cover		275.00
a.		Double overprint	200.00	
		Never hinged	320.00	
104	A84	1.25 l brt blue	14.00	*65.00*
		Never hinged	35.00	
		On cover		525.00
		Nos. 102-104 (3)	30.00	132.50
		Set, never hinged	75.00	

Italian Stamps of 1925-28
Overprinted type "a" in Black

1928-29

105	A86	7½c lt brown ('29)	24.00	*72.50*
		Never hinged	60.00	
		On cover		325.00

106	A86	50c brt violet		87.50	65.00
		Never hinged	210.00		
		On cover			160.00
		Set, never hinged	270.00		

Italian Stamps of 1927-28 Overprinted type "f"

1928-29

107	A86	50c brt violet		72.50	60.00
		Never hinged	175.00		
		On cover			140.00

Unwmk. Perf. 11

107A	A85	1.75 l deep brown		95.00	52.50
		Never hinged	240.00		
		On cover			190.00

Italy No. 192 Overprinted type "o"

1928 Wmk. 140 Perf. 14

108	A85	50c brown & slate		24.00	12.00
		Never hinged	60.00		
		On cover			65.00

Monte Cassino Issue

Types of 1929 Issue of Italy Overprinted in Red or Blue

1929 Perf. 14

109	A96	20c dk green (R)		6.50	22.50
		Never hinged	16.00		
		On cover			275.00
110	A96	25c red orange (Bl)		6.50	22.50
		Never hinged	16.00		
		On cover			200.00
111	A98	50c + 10c crim (Bl)		6.50	24.00
		Never hinged	16.00		
		On cover			160.00
112	A98	75c + 15c ol brn (R)		6.50	24.00
		Never hinged	16.00		
		On cover			275.00
113	A96	1.25 l + 25c dl vio (R)		14.50	45.00
		Never hinged	35.00		
		On cover			340.00
114	A98	5 l + 1 l saph (R)		14.50	47.50
		Never hinged	35.00		

Overprinted in Red

Unwmk.

115	A100	10 l + 2 l gray brn		14.50	72.50
		Never hinged	35.00		
		Nos. 109-115 (7)		69.50	258.00
		Set, never hinged	170.00		
		Set on overfranked philatelic cover			475.00

Royal Wedding Issue

Type of Italian Stamps of 1930 Overprinted

1930 Wmk. 140

116	A101	20c yellow green		3.25	9.50
		Never hinged	8.00		
		On cover			140.00
117	A101	50c + 10c dp orange		2.40	9.50
		Never hinged	6.00		
		On cover			190.00
118	A101	1.25 l + 25c rose red		2.40	19.00
		Never hinged	6.00		
		On cover			300.00
		Nos. 116-118 (3)		8.05	38.00
		Set, never hinged	20.00		
		Set on overfranked, philatelic cover			175.00

Lancer — A5

Scene in Massaua A6

2c, 35c, Lancer. 5c, 10c, Postman. 15c, Lineman. 25c, Askari (infantryman). 2 l, Railroad viaduct. 5 l, Asmara Deghe Selam. 10 l, Camels.

1930 Wmk. 140 Litho. Perf. 14

119	A5	2c brt bl & blk		4.75	20.00
		Never hinged	11.00		
		On cover			160.00
120	A5	5c dk vio & blk		8.00	2.40
		Never hinged	20.00		
		On cover			87.50
121	A5	10c yel brn & blk		8.00	1.25
		Never hinged	20.00		
		On cover			47.50
122	A5	15c dk grn & blk		8.00	1.60
		Never hinged	20.00		
		On cover			87.50
123	A5	25c gray grn & blk		8.00	1.25
		Never hinged	20.00		
		On cover			55.00
124	A5	35c red brn & blk		12.50	35.00
		Never hinged	30.00		
		On cover			200.00
125	A6	1 l dk bl & blk		8.00	1.25
		Never hinged	20.00		
		On cover			55.00
126	A6	2 l choc & blk		12.50	40.00
		Never hinged	30.00		
		On cover			375.00
127	A6	5 l ol grn & blk		24.00	52.50
		Never hinged	60.00		
		On cover			1,100.
128	A6	10 l dl bl & blk		32.50	100.00
		Never hinged	80.00		
		Nos. 119-128 (10)		126.25	255.25
		Set, never hinged	310.00		
		Set on overfranked philatelic cover			475.00

Ferrucci Issue

Types of Italian Stamps of 1930 Overprinted type "f" in Red or Blue

1930

129	A102	20c violet (R)		6.50	6.50
		Never hinged	16.00		
		On cover			160.00
130	A103	25c dk green (R)		6.50	6.50
		Never hinged	16.00		
		On cover			190.00
131	A103	50c black (R)		6.50	12.00
		Never hinged	16.00		
		On cover			160.00
132	A103	1.25 l dp blue (R)		6.50	22.50
		Never hinged	16.00		
		On cover			350.00
133	A104	5 l + 2 l dp car (Bl)		14.50	47.50
		Never hinged	30.00		
		Nos. 129-133 (5)		40.50	95.00
		Set, never hinged	99.00		
		Set on overfranked philatelic cover			350.00

Virgil Issue

Types of Italian Stamps of 1930 Overprinted in Red or Blue

1930 Photo.

134	A106	15c violet black		1.25	12.00
		Never hinged	3.25		
		On cover			175.00
135	A106	20c orange brown		1.25	4.75
		Never hinged	3.25		
		On cover			100.00
136	A106	25c dark green		1.25	4.75
		Never hinged	3.25		
		On cover			95.00
137	A106	30c lt brown		1.25	4.75
		Never hinged	3.25		
		On cover			100.00
138	A106	50c dull violet		1.25	4.75
		Never hinged	3.25		
		On cover			87.50

139	A106	75c rose red		1.25	9.50
		Never hinged	3.25		
		On cover			210.00
140	A106	1.25 l gray blue		1.25	12.00
		Never hinged	3.25		
		On cover			300.00

Unwmk. Engr.

141	A106	5 l + 1.50 l dk vio		4.75	47.50
		Never hinged	11.00		
142	A106	10 l + 2.50 l ol brn		4.75	72.50
		Never hinged	11.00		
		Nos. 134-142 (9)		18.25	172.50
		Set, never hinged	44.00		
		Set on overfranked philatelic cover			475.00

Saint Anthony of Padua Issue

Types of Italian Stamps of 1931 Overprinted type "f" in Blue, Red or Black

1931 Photo. Wmk. 140

143	A116	20c brown (Bl)		1.60	22.50
		Never hinged	4.50		
		On cover			120.00
144	A116	25c green (R)		1.60	8.00
		Never hinged	4.50		
		On cover			120.00
145	A118	30c gray brn (Bl)		1.60	8.00
		Never hinged	4.50		
		On cover			120.00
146	A118	50c dl violet (Bl)		1.60	8.00
		Never hinged	4.50		
		On cover			180.00
147	A120	1.25 l slate bl (R)		1.60	40.00
		Never hinged	5.00		
		On cover			400.00

Unwmk. Engr.

148	A121	75c black (R)		1.60	22.50
		Never hinged	5.00		
		On cover			325.00
149	A122	5 l + 2.50 l dk brn (Bk)		11.00	80.00
		Never hinged	27.50		
		Nos. 143-149 (7)		20.60	189.00
		Set, never hinged	55.00		
		Set on overfranked philatelic cover			540.00

Victor Emmanuel III — A13

1931 Photo. Wmk. 140

150	A13	7½c olive brown		1.60	6.50
		Never hinged	4.00		
		On cover			80.00
151	A13	20c slate bl & car		1.60	.25
		Never hinged	4.00		
		On cover			2.50
152	A13	30c ol grn & brn vio		1.60	.25
		Never hinged	4.00		
		On cover			2.50
153	A13	40c bl & yel grn		2.40	.25
		Never hinged	6.00		
		On cover			14.50
154	A13	50c bis brn & ol		1.60	.25
		Never hinged	4.00		
		On cover			2.50
155	A13	75c carmine rose		4.75	.25
		Never hinged	12.00		
		On cover			14.50
156	A13	1.25 l violet & indigo		6.50	6.50
		Never hinged	16.00		
		On cover			14.50
157	A13	2.50 l dull green		6.50	14.50
		Never hinged	16.00		
		On cover			225.00
		Nos. 150-157 (8)		26.55	28.75
		Set, never hinged	65.00		
		Set on overfranked philatelic cover			140.00

Camel A14

Temple Ruins — A18

Designs: 2c, 10c, Camel. 5c, 15c, Shark fishery. 25c, Baobab tree. 35c, Pastoral scene. 2 l, African elephant. 5 l, Eritrean man. 10 l, Eritrean woman.

1934 Photo. Wmk. 140

158	A14	2c deep blue		2.40	4.75
		Never hinged	6.00		
		On cover			35.00
159	A14	5c black		4.00	.10
		Never hinged	10.00		
		On cover			3.25
160	A14	10c brown		4.00	.35
		Never hinged	10.00		
		On cover			3.25
161	A14	15c orange brn		4..75	1.60
		Never hinged	12.00		
		On cover			32.50
162	A14	25c gray green		4.00	.35
		Never hinged	10.00		
		On cover			3.25
163	A14	35c purple		12.50	9.50
		Never hinged	30.00		
		On cover			52.50
164	A18	1 l dk blue gray		.80	.35
		Never hinged	2.00		
		On cover			3.25
165	A14	2 l olive black		35.00	3.25
		Never hinged	87.50		
		On cover			20.00
166	A18	5 l carmine rose		19.00	6.50
		Never hinged	47.50		
		On cover			260.00
167	A18	10 l red orange		27.50	22.50
		Never hinged	67.50		
		On cover			525.00
		Nos. 158-167 (10)		109.20	49.55
		Set, never hinged	275.00		
		Set on overfranked philatelic cover			275.00

Abruzzi Issue

Types of 1934 Issue Overprinted in Black or Red

1934

168	A14	10c dull blue (R)		22.50	32.50
		Never hinged	55.00		
		On cover			400.00
169	A14	15c blue		16.00	32.50
		Never hinged	40.00		
		On cover			400.00
170	A14	35c green (R)		9.50	32.50
		Never hinged	24.00		
		On cover			450.00
171	A18	1 l copper red		9.50	32.50
		Never hinged	24.00		
		On cover			450.00
172	A14	2 l rose red		27.50	32.50
		Never hinged	67.50		
		On cover			450.00
173	A18	5 l purple (R)		19.00	55.00
		Never hinged	47.50		
174	A18	10 l olive grn (R)		19.00	72.50
		Never hinged	47.50		
		Nos. 168-174 (7)		123.00	290.00
		Set, never hinged	300.00		
		Set on overfranked philatelic cover			550.00

Grant's Gazelle A22

1934 Photo.

175	A22	5c ol grn & brn		5.50	22.50
		Never hinged	13.50		
		On cover			350.00
176	A22	10c yel brn & blk		5.50	22.50
		Never hinged	13.50		
		On cover			300.00
177	A22	20c scar & indigo		5.50	20.00
		Never hinged	13.50		
		On cover			300.00
178	A22	50c dk vio & brn		5.50	20.00
		Never hinged	13.50		
		On cover			275.00
179	A22	60c org brn & ind		5.50	27.50
		Never hinged	13.50		
		On cover			350.00
180	A22	1.25 l dk bl & grn		5.50	47.50
		Never hinged	13.50		
		On cover			450.00
		Nos. 175-180 (6)		33.00	160.00
		Set, never hinged	80.00		
		Set on overfranked philatelic cover			350.00

Second Colonial Arts Exhibition, Naples. See Nos. C1-C6.

SEMI-POSTAL STAMPS

Many issues of Italy and Italian Colonies include one or more semipostal denominations. To avoid splitting sets, these issues are generally listed as regular postage, airmail, etc., unless all values carry a surtax.

Italy Nos. B1-B3 Overprinted type "f"

				Wmk. 140	Perf. 14

1915-16   **Wmk. 140**   *Perf. 14*

B1 SP1 10c + 5c rose — 4.00 / 16.00
  Never hinged 10.00
  On cover — 120.00
  a. "EPITREA" 32.50 / 45.00
  b. Inverted overprint 800.00 / 800.00
B2 SP2 15c + 5c slate 32.50 / 27.50
  Never hinged 80.00
  On cover — 225.00
B3 SP2 20c + 5c orange 4.75 / 35.00
  Never hinged 12.00
  On cover — 325.00
  a. "EPITREA" 80.00 / 110.00
  b. Inverted overprint 800.00 / 800.00
  c. Pair, one without ovpt. — 4,500.
  Nos. B1-B3 (3) 41.25 / 78.50
  Set, never hinged 102.00

No. B2 Surcharged

1916

B4 SP2 20c on 15c+5c slate 32.50 / 35.00
  Never hinged 80.00
  On cover — 325.00
  a. "EPITREA" 80.00 / 110.00
  b. Pair, one without overprint 2,000.
    Never hinged 2,500.
  Nos. B1-B4 on overfranked philatelic cover — 275.00

Counterfeits exist of the minor varieties of Nos. B1, B3-B4.

Holy Year Issue
Italy Nos. B20-B25 Overprinted in Black or Red

1925   *Perf. 12*

B5 SP4 20c + 10c dk grn & brn 4.00 / 24.00
  Never hinged 10.00
  On cover — 225.00
B6 SP4 30c + 15c dk brn & brn 4.00 / 27.50
  Never hinged 10.00
  On cover — 225.00
  a. Double overprint
B7 SP4 50c + 25c vio & brn 4.00 / 24.00
  Never hinged 10.00
  On cover — 225.00
B8 SP4 60c + 30c dp rose & brn 4.00 / 32.50
  Never hinged 10.00
  On cover — 300.00
  a. Inverted overprint
B9 SP8 1 l + 50c dp bl & vio (R) 4.00 / 40.00
  Never hinged 10.00
B10 SP8 5 l + 2.50 l org brn & vio (R) 4.00 / 60.00
  Never hinged 10.00
  Nos. B5-B10 (6) 24.00 / 208.00
  Set, never hinged 60.00
  Set on overfranked philatelic cover — 500.00

Colonial Institute Issue

"Peace" Substituting Spade for Sword — SP1

1926   **Typo.**   *Perf. 14*

B11 SP1 5c + 5c brown 1.20 / 9.50
  Never hinged 3.00
  On cover — 180.00
B12 SP1 10c + 5c olive grn 1.20 / 9.50
  Never hinged 3.00
  On cover — 140.00

B13 SP1 20c + 5c blue grn 1.20 / 9.50
  Never hinged 3.00
  On cover — 110.00
B14 SP1 40c + 5c brown red 1.20 / 9.50
  Never hinged 3.00
  On cover — 110.00
B15 SP1 60c + 5c orange 1.20 / 9.50
  Never hinged 3.00
  On cover — 180.00
B16 SP1 1 l + 5c blue 1.20 / 20.00
  Never hinged 3.00
  On cover — 300.00
  Nos. B11-B16 (6) 7.20 / 67.50
  Set, never hinged 18.00
  Set on overfranked philatelic cover — 260.00

The surtax of 5c on each stamp was for the Italian Colonial Institute.

Italian Semi-Postal Stamps of 1926 Overprinted

1927   **Unwmk.**   *Perf. 11½*

B17 SP10 40c + 20c dk brn & blk 4.00 / 45.00
  Never hinged 10.00
  On cover — 190.00
B18 SP10 60c + 30c brn red & ol brn 4.00 / 45.00
  Never hinged 10.00
  On cover — 225.00
B19 SP10 1.25 l + 60c dp bl & blk 4.00 / 65.00
  Never hinged 10.00
  On cover — 400.00
B20 SP10 5 l + 2.50 l dk grn & blk 6.50 / 100.00
  Never hinged 16.00
  Nos. B17-B20 (4) 18.50 / 255.00
  Set, never hinged 46.00
  Set on overfranked philatelic cover — 600.00

The surtax on these stamps was for the charitable work of the Voluntary Militia for Italian National Defense.

Fascism and Victory — SP2

1928   **Wmk. 140**   **Typo.**   *Perf. 14*

B21 SP2 20c + 5c blue grn 3.25 / 14.00
  Never hinged 8.00
  On cover — 190.00
B22 SP2 30c + 5c red 3.25 / 14.00
  Never hinged 8.00
  On cover — 190.00
B23 SP2 50c + 10c purple 3.25 / 24.00
  Never hinged 8.00
  On cover — 190.00
B24 SP2 1.25 l + 20c dk blue 4.00 / 32.50
  Never hinged 10.00
  On cover — 525.00
  Nos. B21-B24 (4) 13.75 / 84.50
  Set, never hinged 34.00
  Set on overfranked philatelic cover — 325.00

The surtax was for the Society Africana d'Italia, whose 46th anniv. was commemorated by the issue.

Types of Italian Semi-Postal Stamps of 1928 Overprinted type "f"

1929   **Unwmk.**   *Perf. 11*

B25 SP10 30c + 10c red & blk 4.75 / 27.50
  Never hinged 12.00
  On cover — 225.00
B26 SP10 50c + 20c vio & blk 4.75 / 30.00
  Never hinged 12.00
  On cover — 225.00
B27 SP10 1.25 l + 50c brn & bl 7.25 / 52.50
  Never hinged 18.00
  On cover — 475.00
B28 SP10 5 l + 2 l olive grn & blk 7.25 / 100.00
  Never hinged 18.00
  Nos. B25-B28 (4) 24.00 / 210.00
  Set, never hinged 60.00
  Set on overfranked philatelic cover — 600.00

Surtax for the charitable work of the Voluntary Militia for Italian Natl. Defense.

Types of Italian Semi-Postal Stamps of 1930 Overprinted type "f" in Black or Red

1930   *Perf. 14*

B29 SP10 30c + 10c dk grn & bl grn (Bk) 35.00 / 65.00
  Never hinged 87.50
  On cover — 325.00
B30 SP10 50c + 10c dk grn & vio 35.00 / 100.00
  Never hinged 87.50
  On cover — 360.00
B31 SP10 1.25 l + 30c ol brn & red brn 35.00 / 100.00
  Never hinged 87.50
  On cover — 550.00
B32 SP10 5 l + 1.50 l ind & grn 120.00 / 275.00
  Never hinged 300.00
  Nos. B29-B32 (4) 225.00 / 540.00
  Set, never hinged 560.00
  Set on overfranked philatelic cover — 1,050.

Surtax for the charitable work of the Voluntary Militia for Italian Natl. Defense.

Agriculture — SP3

1930   **Photo.**   **Wmk. 140**

B33 SP3 50c + 20c ol brn 4.00 / 25.00
  Never hinged 10.00
  On cover — 210.00
B34 SP3 1.25 l + 20c dp bl 4.00 / 25.00
  Never hinged 10.00
  On cover — 300.00
B35 SP3 1.75 l + 20c green 4.00 / 27.50
  Never hinged 10.00
  On cover — 375.00
B36 SP3 2.55 l + 50c purple 9.50 / 45.00
  Never hinged 23.00
  On cover — 600.00
B37 SP3 5 l + 1 l dp car 9.50 / 67.50
  Never hinged 23.00
  Nos. B33-B37 (5) 31.00 / 190.00
  Set, never hinged 76.00
  Set on overfranked philatelic cover — 350.00

Italian Colonial Agricultural Institute, 25th anniv. The surtax aided that institution.

AIR POST STAMPS

Plowing AP3

Plane and Cacti AP6

Designs: 25c, 1.50 l, Plowing. 50c, 2 l, Plane over mountain pass. 60c, 5 l, Plane and trees. 75c, 10 l, Plane and cacti. 1 l, 3 l, Bridge.

1936   **Photo.**

C7 AP3 25c deep green 4.75 / 4.75
  Never hinged 12.00
  On cover — 72.50
C8 AP3 50c dark brown 3.25 / .35
  Never hinged 8.00
  On cover — 2.50
C9 AP3 60c brown orange 6.50 / 16.00
  Never hinged 16.00
  On cover — 240.00
C10 AP6 75c orange brown 4.75 / 1.60
  Never hinged 12.00
  On cover — 20.00
C11 AP3 1 l deep blue 1.60 / .35
  Never hinged 4.00
  On cover — 2.50
C12 AP3 1.50 l purple 6.50 / .85
  Never hinged 16.00
  On cover — 40.00
C13 AP3 2 l gray blue 6.50 / 3.25
  Never hinged 16.00
  On cover — 120.00
C14 AP3 3 l copper red 25.00 / 27.50
  Never hinged 62.50
  On cover — 250.00
C15 AP3 5 l green 19.00 / 8.00
  Never hinged 47.50
  On cover — 550.00
C16 AP6 10 l rose red 45.00 / 27.50
  Never hinged 110.00
  On cover — 1,050.
  Nos. C7-C16 (10) 122.85 / 90.15
  Set, never hinged 300.00
  Set on overfranked philatelic cover — 450.00

AIR POST SEMI-POSTAL STAMPS

King Victor Emmanuel III — SPAP1

1934   **Wmk. 140**   **Photo.**   *Perf. 14*

CB1 SPAP1 25c + 10c 9.50 / 27.50
  Never hinged 24.00
  On cover — 325.00
CB2 SPAP1 50c + 10c 9.50 / 27.50
  Never hinged 24.00
  On cover — 325.00
CB3 SPAP1 75c + 15c 9.50 / 27.50
  Never hinged 24.00
  On cover — 350.00
CB4 SPAP1 80c + 15c 9.50 / 27.50
  Never hinged 24.00
  On cover — 450.00
CB5 SPAP1 1 l + 20c 9.50 / 27.50
  Never hinged 24.00
  On cover — 475.00
CB6 SPAP1 2 l + 20c 9.50 / 27.50
  Never hinged 24.00
CB7 SPAP1 3 l + 25c 27.50 / 125.00
  Never hinged 67.50
CB8 SPAP1 5 l + 25c 27.50 / 125.00
  Never hinged 67.50
CB9 SPAP1 10 l + 30c 27.50 / 125.00
  Never hinged 67.50
CB10 SPAP1 25 l + 2 l 27.50 / 125.00
  Never hinged 67.50
  Nos. CB1-CB10 (10) 167.00 / 665.00
  Set, never hinged 410.00
  Set on overfranked philatelic flown cover — 1,900.

65th birthday of King Victor Emmanuel III and the nonstop flight from Rome to Mogadiscio. Used values are for stamps canceled to order.

Italian Semi-Postal Stamps of 1926 Overprinted

AIR POST STAMPS

Desert Scene AP1

Design: 80c, 1 l, 2 l, Plane and globe.

Wmk. Crowns (140)

1934, Oct. 17   **Photo.**   *Perf. 14*

C1 AP1 25c sl bl & org red 5.50 / 22.50
  Never hinged 13.50
  On cover — 350.00
C2 AP1 50c grn & indigo 5.50 / 20.00
  Never hinged 13.50
  On cover — 225.00
C3 AP1 75c brn & org red 5.50 / 20.00
  Never hinged 13.50
  On cover — 300.00
C4 AP1 80c org brn & ol grn 5.50 / 22.50
  Never hinged 13.50
  On cover — 350.00
C5 AP1 1 l scar & ol grn 5.50 / 27.50
  Never hinged 13.50
  On cover — 400.00
C6 AP1 2 l dk bl & brn 5.50 / 47.50
  Never hinged 13.50
  On cover — 550.00
  Nos. C1-C6 (6) 33.00 / 160.00
  Set, never hinged 81.00
  Set on overfranked philatelic cover — 450.00

Second Colonial Arts Exhibition, Naples.

AIR POST SEMI-POSTAL OFFICIAL STAMP

Type of Air Post Semi-Postal Stamps, 1934, Overprinted in Black

1934	Wmk. 140	Perf. 14
CBO1 SPAP1 25 l + 2 l cop red	2,800.	
Never hinged	5,500.	
On flight cover		3,250.

SPECIAL DELIVERY STAMPS

Special Delivery Stamps of Italy, Overprinted type "a"

1907	Wmk. 140	Perf. 14
E1 SD1 25c rose red	24.00	20.00
Never hinged	60.00	
On cover		180.00
a. Double overprint	—	

1909

E2 SD2 30c blue & rose	145.00	240.00
Never hinged	375.00	
On cover		675.00

1920

E3 SD1 50c dull red	4.00	24.00
Never hinged	10.00	
On cover		275.00

"Italia"
SD1

1924	Engr.	Unwmk.
E4 SD1 60c dk red & brn	6.50	24.00
Never hinged	16.00	
On cover		180.00
a. Perf. 13½	14.00	40.00
Never hinged	35.00	
On cover		—
E5 SD1 2 l dk blue & red	17.50	27.50
Never hinged	42.50	
On cover		525.00
Set, never hinged	59.00	

For surcharges see Nos. E6-E8.

Nos. E4 and E5 Surcharged in Dark Blue or Red

v

w

1926

E6 SD1 70c on 60c (Bl)	6.50	16.00
Never hinged	17.50	
On cover		180.00
E7 SD1 2.50 l on 2 l (R)	17.50	27.50
Never hinged	42.50	
On cover		600.00
Set, never hinged	60.00	

Type of 1924 Surcharged in Blue or Black

1927-35		Perf. 11
E8 SD1 1.25 l on 60c dk red & brn (Bl)	16.00	4.00
Never hinged	40.00	
On cover		12.00
a. Perf. 14 (Bl) ('35)	110.00	24.00
Never hinged	275.00	
On cover		200.00
b. Perf. 11 (Bk) ('35)	9,500.	1,250.
Never hinged	14,500.	
On cover		4,750.
c. Perf. 14 (Bk) ('35)	400.00	65.00
Never hinged	1,000.	
On cover		450.00

AUTHORIZED DELIVERY STAMP

Authorized Delivery Stamp of Italy, No. EY2, Overprinted Type "f" in Black

1939-41	Wmk. 140	Perf. 14
EY1 AD2 10c dk brown ('41)	.80	
Never hinged	2.00	
a. 10c reddish brown	27.50	47.50
Never hinged	72.50	
On cover		475.00

On No. EY1a, which was used in Italian East Africa, the overprint hits the figures "10." On No. EY1, which was sold in Rome, the overprint falls above the 10's.

POSTAGE DUE STAMPS

Postage Due Stamps of Italy Overprinted type "a" at Top

1903	Wmk. 140	Perf. 14
J1 D3 5c buff & mag	24.00	47.50
Never hinged	47.50	
On cover		550.00
a. Double overprint	550.00	
J2 D3 10c buff & mag	16.00	47.50
Never hinged	32.50	
On cover		325.00
J3 D3 20c buff & mag	16.00	32.50
Never hinged	32.50	
On cover		325.00
J4 D3 30c buff & mag	24.00	35.00
Never hinged	47.50	
On cover		475.00
J5 D3 40c buff & mag	80.00	72.50
Never hinged	160.00	
On cover		475.00
J6 D3 50c buff & mag	87.50	72.50
Never hinged	175.00	
On cover		325.00
J7 D3 60c buff & mag	24.00	72.50
Never hinged	47.50	
On cover		725.00
J8 D3 1 l buff & mag	16.00	40.00
Never hinged	32.50	
On cover		550.00
J9 D3 2 l buff & mag	200.00	180.00
Never hinged	400.00	
On cover		1,250.
J10 D3 5 l buff & mag	325.00	340.00
Never hinged	650.00	
J11 D3 10 l buff & mag	3,600.	875.00
Never hinged	7,200.	
Set, #J1-J10, never hinged	1,600.	

Same with Overprint at Bottom

1920-22

J1b D3 5c buff & magenta	4.75	16.00
Never hinged	9.50	
On cover		540.00
c. Numeral and ovpt. inverted	550.00	550.00
Never hinged	—	
J2a D3 10c buff & magenta	8.00	16.00
Never hinged	16.00	
On cover		260.00
J3a D3 20c buff & magenta	950.00	475.00
Never hinged	1,900.	
On cover		3,000.
J4a D3 30c buff & magenta	65.00	65.00
Never hinged	130.00	
On cover		460.00
J5a D3 40c buff & magenta	47.50	52.50
Never hinged	95.00	
On cover		525.00
J6a D3 50c buff & magenta	24.00	47.50
Never hinged	47.50	
On cover		260.00
J7a D3 60c buff & magenta	24.00	47.50
Never hinged	47.50	
On cover		650.00
J8a D3 1 l blue & magenta	40.00	47.50
Never hinged	80.00	
On cover		525.00
J9a D3 2 l blue & magenta	1,900.	1,450.
Never hinged	3,750.	
On cover		11,000.
J10a D3 5 l blue & magenta	475.00	350.00
Never hinged	950.00	
J11a D3 10 l blue & magenta	47.50	100.00
Never hinged	95.00	
Set, never hinged	7,125.	

1903		Wmk. 140
J12 D4 50 l yellow	875.00	300.00
Never hinged	1,750.	
J13 D4 100 l blue	475.00	180.00
Never hinged	950.00	
Set, never hinged	2,700.	

1927

J14 D3 60c buff & brown	160.00	240.00
Never hinged	325.00	
On cover		725.00

Postage Due Stamps of Italy, 1934, Overprinted type "j" in Black

1934

J15 D6 5c brown	.80	16.00
Never hinged	2.00	
On cover		550.00
J16 D6 10c blue	.80	3.25
Never hinged	2.00	
On cover		275.00
J17 D6 20c rose red	4.00	4.75
Never hinged	10.00	
a. Inverted overprint	—	260.00
J18 D6 25c green	4.00	6.50
Never hinged	10.00	
On cover		260.00
J19 D6 30c red orange	4.00	16.00
Never hinged	10.00	
On cover		400.00
J20 D6 40c black brown	4.00	16.00
Never hinged	10.00	
On cover		475.00
J21 D6 50c violet	4.00	2.40
Never hinged	10.00	
On cover		200.00
J22 D6 60c black	8.00	24.00
Never hinged	20.00	
On cover		550.00
J23 D7 1 l red orange	4.00	3.25
Never hinged	10.00	
On cover		400.00
a. Inverted overprint	550.00	
Never hinged	800.00	
J24 D7 2 l green	16.00	47.50
Never hinged	40.00	
On cover		550.00
J25 D7 5 l violet	28.00	55.00
Never hinged	70.00	
J26 D7 10 l blue	32.50	65.00
Never hinged	82.50	
J27 D7 20 l carmine rose	40.00	72.50
Never hinged	100.00	
a. Inverted overprint	550.00	—
Nos. J15-J27 (13)	150.10	332.15
Set, never hinged	375.00	

PARCEL POST STAMPS

These stamps were used by affixing them to the way bill so that one half remained on it following the parcel, the other half staying on the receipt given the sender. Most used halves are right halves. Complete stamps were obtainable canceled, probably to order. Both unused and used values are for complete stamps.

Parcel Post Stamps of Italy, 1914-17, Overprinted type "j" in Black on Each Half

1916	Wmk. 140	Perf. 13½
Q1 PP2 5c brown	145.00	225.00
Never hinged	290.00	
Q2 PP2 10c deep blue	2,600.	4,250.
Never hinged	5,250.	
Q3 PP2 25c red	290.00	350.00
Never hinged	575.00	
Q4 PP2 50c orange	72.50	225.00
Never hinged	145.00	
Q5 PP1 1 l violet	145.00	225.00
Never hinged	290.00	
Q6 PP2 2 l green	110.00	225.00
Never hinged	225.00	
Q7 PP2 3 l bister	875.00	625.00
Never hinged	1,750.	
Q8 PP2 4 l slate	875.00	625.00
Never hinged	1,750.	
Set #Q1, Q3-Q8, never hinged	5,200.	

Halves Used, Each

Q1	4.25
Q2	85.00
Q3	5.50
Q4	3.00
Q5	3.00
Q6	8.50
Q7	19.00
Q8	19.00

Overprinted type "f" on Each Half

1917-24

Q9 PP2 5c brown	3.25	8.00
Never hinged	6.50	
On parcel post receipt card		250.00
Q10 PP2 10c deep blue	3.25	8.00
Never hinged	6.50	
Q11 PP2 20c black	3.25	8.00
Never hinged	6.50	
Q12 PP2 25c red	3.25	8.00
Never hinged	6.50	
On parcel post receipt card		120.00

Q13 PP2 50c orange	6.50	12.00
Never hinged	13.00	
On parcel post receipt card		120.00
Q14 PP2 1 l violet	6.50	12.00
Never hinged	13.00	
On parcel post receipt card		160.00
Q15 PP2 2 l green	6.50	12.00
Never hinged	13.00	
Q16 PP2 3 l bister	6.50	12.00
Never hinged	13.00	
Q17 PP2 4 l slate	6.50	20.00
Never hinged	13.00	
Q18 PP2 10 l rose lil ('24)	87.50	190.00
Never hinged	175.00	
Q19 PP2 12 l red brn ('24)	240.00	375.00
Never hinged	475.00	
Q20 PP2 15 l olive grn ('24)	240.00	375.00
Never hinged	475.00	
Q21 PP2 20 l brn vio ('24)	325.00	525.00
Never hinged	650.00	
Nos. Q9-Q21 (13)	938.00	1,565.
Set, never hinged	1,860.	

Halves Used, Each

Q9	1.20
Q10	1.20
Q11	1.20
Q12	1.20
Q13	1.20
Q14	1.20
Q15	1.60
Q16	4.25
Q17	4.25
Q18	8.50
Q19	12.50
Q20	12.50
Q21	17.00

Parcel Post Stamps of Italy, 1927-39, Overprinted type "f" on Each Half

1927-37

Q21A PP3 10c dp blue ('37)	8,750.	1,250.
Never hinged	13,500.	
Q22 PP3 25c red ('37)	550.00	72.50
Never hinged	1,100.	
Q23 PP3 30c ultra ('29)	4.00	24.00
Never hinged	8.00	
On parcel post receipt card		200.00
Q24 PP3 50c orange ('36)	725.00	47.50
Never hinged	1,450.	
Q25 PP3 60c red ('29)	4.00	24.00
Never hinged	8.00	
On parcel post receipt card		200.00
Q26 PP3 1 l brown vio ('36)	325.00	47.50
Never hinged	650.00	
a. 1 l lilac	400.00	47.50
Never hinged	800.00	
On parcel post receipt card		125.00
Q27 PP3 2 l green ('36)	325.00	47.50
Never hinged	650.00	
On parcel post receipt card		150.00
Q28 PP3 3 l bister	9.50	40.00
Never hinged	19.00	
Q29 PP3 4 l gray	9.50	40.00
Never hinged	19.00	
Q30 PP3 10 l rose lilac ('36)	525.00	800.00
Never hinged	1,050.	
Q31 PP3 20 l lilac brn ('36)	525.00	800.00
Never hinged	1,050.	
Nos. Q22-Q31 (10)	3,002.	
Set, never hinged	6,000.	
Nos. Q21A-Q31 (11)		3,193.

Halves Used, Each

Q21A	27.50
Q22	1.20
Q23	.65
Q24	1.70
Q25	.85
Q26	1.25
Q26a	1.25
Q27	1.25
Q28	1.25
Q29	1.25
Q30	37.50
Q31	37.50

ESTONIA

e-ˈstō-nē-ə

LOCATION — Northern Europe, bordering on the Baltic Sea and the Gulf of Finland
GOVT. — Republic
AREA — 18,353 sq. mi.
POP. — 1,542,000 (1986)
CAPITAL — Tallinn

Formerly a part of Russia, Estonia declared its independence in 1918. In 1940 it was incorporated in the Union of Soviet Socialist Republics.

100 Kopecks = 1 Ruble (1918)
100 Penni = 1 Mark (1919)
100 Sents = 1 Kroon (1928)

Watermark

Wmk. 207 — Arms of Finland in the Sheet

Watermark covers a large part of sheet.

A1   A2

1918-19	Unwmk.	Litho.	Imperf.	
1	A1	5k pale red	1.00	.85
2	A1	15k bright blue	1.00	.85
3	A2	35p brown ('19)	1.00	.90
a.		Printed on both sides	200.00	
b.		35p olive	80.00	80.00
4	A2	70p olive grn ('19)	1.60	2.10
		Nos. 1-4 (4)	4.60	4.70

Nos. 1-4 exist privately perforated.

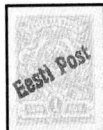

Russian Stamps of 1909-17 Handstamped in Violet or Black

1919, May 7	Perf. 14, 14½x15, 13½		
8	A14	1k orange	5,500.	5,500.
9	A14	2k green	45.00	45.00
10	A14	3k red	52.50	52.50
11	A14	5k claret	45.00	45.00
12	A15	10k dk bl (Bk)	85.00	85.00
13	A15	10k dk bl	500.00	500.00
14	A14	10k on 7k lt bl	1,500.	1,500.
15	A11	15k red brn & bl	67.50	67.50
16	A11	25k grn & vio	77.50	77.50
17	A11	35k red brn & grn	5,500.	5,500.
18	A8	50k vio & grn	190.00	190.00
19	A9	1r pale brn, brn & org	325.00	325.00
20	A13	10r scar, yel & gray	9,500.	9,500.

Imperf				
21	A14	1k orange	62.50	62.50
22	A14	2k green	950.00	950.00
23	A14	3k red	85.00	85.00
24	A9	1r pale brn, brn & red org	425.00	425.00

| 25 | A12 | 3½r maroon & grn | 1,200. | 1,200. |
| 26 | A13 | 5r dk bl, grn & pale bl | 1,500. | 1,500. |

Provisionally issued at Tallinn. This overprint has been extensively counterfeited. Values are for genuine examples competently expertized. No. 20 is always creased.

Gulls — A3

1919, May 13		Imperf.	
27	A3	5p yellow	2.50	5.50

A4   A5   A6

A7   Viking Ship — A8

1919-20		Perf. 11½	
28	A4	10p green	.45	.80

Imperf				
29	A4	5p orange	.25	.25
30	A4	10p green	.25	.25
31	A5	15p rose	.25	.30
32	A6	35p blue	.25	.30
33	A7	70p dl vio ('20)	.25	.30
34	A8	1m bl & blk brn	4.25	1.60
a.		Gray granite paper ('20)	1.60	.80
35	A8	5m yel & blk	6.25	4.75
a.		Gray granite paper ('20)	3.25	1.25
36	A8	15m yel grn & vio ('20)	3.50	2.40
37	A8	25m ultra & blk brn ('20)	6.50	5.50
		Nos. 28-37 (10)	22.20	16.45
		Set, never hinged	32.50	

The 5m exists with inverted center. Not a postal item.
See Nos. 76-77. For surcharges see Nos. 55, 57.

Skyline of Tallinn — A9

1920-24	Pelure Paper	Imperf.	
39	A9	25p green	.35	.40
40	A9	25p yellow ('24)	.35	.30
41	A9	35p rose	.40	.40
42	A9	50p green ('21)	.40	.25
43	A9	1m vermilion	1.25	.80
44	A9	2m blue	.80	.40
45	A9	2m ultramarine	1.00	1.25
46	A9	2.50m blue	1.25	.80
		Nos. 39-46 (8)	5.80	4.60
		Set, never hinged	16.50	

Nos. 39-46 with sewing machine perforation are unofficial.
For surcharge see No. 56.

Stamps of 1919-20 Surcharged

1920		Imperf.	
55	A5	1m on 15p rose	.50	.50
56	A9	1m on 35p rose	.70	.50
57	A7	2m on 70p dl vio	.85	.60
		Nos. 55-57 (3)	2.05	1.60
		Set, never hinged	4.25	

Weaver A10   Blacksmith A11

1922-23		Typo.	Imperf.	
58	A10	½m orange ('23)	2.75	8.00
59	A10	1m brown ('23)	4.75	11.00
60	A10	2m yellow green	4.75	8.00
61	A10	2½m claret	5.50	8.00
62	A11	5m rose	8.00	8.00
63	A11	9m red ('23)	12.00	24.00
64	A11	10m deep blue	6.00	16.00
		Set, never hinged (7)	43.75	83.00
		Set, never hinged	105.00	

1922-25		Perf. 14	
65	A10	½m orange ('23)	1.25	.80
66	A10	1m brown ('23)	2.40	.80
67	A10	2m yellow green	2.40	.40
68	A10	2½m claret	4.75	.80
69	A10	3m blue green ('24)	2.00	.40
70	A11	5m rose	2.75	.40
71	A11	9m red ('23)	4.75	1.60
72	A11	10m deep blue	6.00	.40
73	A11	12m red ('25)	6.00	1.75
74	A11	15m plum ('25)	8.00	1.40
75	A11	20m ultra ('25)	20.00	.80
		Nos. 65-75 (11)	60.30	9.55
		Set, never hinged	130.00	

See No. 89. For surcharges see Nos. 84-88.

Viking Ship Type of 1920

1922, June 8		Perf. 14x13½	
76	A8	15m yel grn & vio	8.00	.80
77	A8	25m ultra & blk brn	10.00	3.25
		Set, never hinged	35.00	

Map of Estonia — A13

1923-24	Paper with Lilac Network		
78	A13	100m ol grn & bl	20.00	3.50

Paper with Buff Network			
79	A13	300m brn & bl ('24)	72.50	17.50
		Set, never hinged	210.00	

For surcharges see Nos. 106-107.

National Theater, Tallinn — A14

Paper with Blue Network			
1924, Dec. 9		Perf. 14x13½	
81	A14	30m violet & blk	10.00	4.00

Paper with Rose Network			
82	A14	70m car rose & blk	15.00	8.00
		Set, never hinged	50.00	

For surcharge see No. 105.

Vanemuine Theater, Tartu — A15

Paper with Lilac Network			
1927, Oct. 25			
83	A15	40m dp bl & ol brn	10.00	3.50
		Never hinged	20.00	

Stamps of 1922-25 Surcharged in New Currency in Red or Black

1928		Perf. 14	
84	A10	2s yellow green	1.50	1.25
85	A11	5s rose red (B)	1.50	1.25
86	A11	10s deep blue	2.40	1.25
a.		Imperf., pair	1,300.	
87	A11	15s plum (B)	6.50	1.25
88	A11	20s ultra	4.50	1.25
		Nos. 84-88 (5)	16.40	6.25
		Set, never hinged	35.00	

10th anniversary of independence.

3rd Philatelic Exhibition Issue
Blacksmith Type of 1922-23

1928, July 6			
89	A11	10m gray	4.50	7.50
		Never hinged	9.00	

Sold only at Tallinn Philatelic Exhibition. Exists imperf. Value $1,000.

Arms — A16

Paper with Network in Parenthesis

1928-40		Perf. 14, 14½x14	
90	A16	1s dk gray (bl)	.50	.25
a.		Thick gray-toned laid paper ('40)	10.00	27.50
91	A16	2s yel grn (org)	.60	.25
92	A16	4s grn (brn) ('29)	1.25	.25
93	A16	5s red (grn)	.35	.25
a.		5 feet on lowest lion	45.00	32.50
94	A16	8s vio (buff) ('29)	3.00	.25
95	A16	10s lt bl (lilac)	3.00	.25
96	A16	12s crimson (grn)	2.25	.25
97	A16	15s yel (blue)	3.00	.25
98	A16	15s car (gray) ('35)	14.50	1.75
99	A16	20s slate bl (red)	4.25	.25
100	A16	25s red vio (grn) ('29)	10.50	.25
101	A16	25s bl (brn) ('35)	12.00	1.75
102	A16	40s red org (bl) ('29)	11.00	.60
103	A16	60s gray (brn) ('29)	15.00	.60
104	A16	80s brn (bl) ('29)	15.00	.60
		Nos. 90-104 (15)	96.20	7.80
		Set, never hinged	175.00	

Types of 1924 Issues Surcharged

1930, Sept. 1		Perf. 14x13½	
Paper with Green Network			
105	A14	1k on 70m car & blk	12.00	5.50
Paper with Rose Network			
106	A13	2k on 300m brn & bl	30.00	16.00
Paper with Blue Network			
107	A13	3k on 300m brn & bl	60.00	27.50
		Nos. 105-107 (3)	102.00	49.00
		Set, never hinged	210.00	

University
Observatory
A17

University of
Tartu
A18

**Paper with Network as in
Parenthesis**

1932, June 1   *Perf. 14*
108	A17	5s red (yellow)	5.25	.80
109	A18	10s light bl (lilac)	2.40	.80
110	A17	12s car (blue)	8.25	4.00
111	A18	20s dk bl (green)	6.00	1.60
		Nos. 108-111 (4)	21.90	7.20
		Set, never hinged	55.00	

University of Tartu tercentenary.

Narva
Falls — A19

1933, Apr. 1   Photo.   *Perf. 14x13½*
112	A19	1k gray black	7.00	3.00
		Never hinged	15.00	

See No. 149.

Ancient Bard Playing
Harp — A20

**Paper with Network as in
Parenthesis**

1933, May 29   Typo.   *Perf. 14*
113	A20	2s green (orange)	1.60	.30
114	A20	5s red (green)	2.75	.30
115	A20	10s blue (lilac)	3.50	.30
		Nos. 113-115 (3)	7.85	.90
		Set, never hinged	17.00	

Tenth National Song Festival.
Nos. 113-115 exist imperf. Value $125.

Woman
Harvester — A21

1935, Mar. 1   Engr.   *Perf. 13½*
116	A21	3k black brown	.80	6.50
		Never hinged	1.60	

Pres. Konstantin
Päts — A22

1936-40   Typo.   *Perf. 14*
117	A22	1s chocolate	.80	.25
118	A22	2s yellow green	.80	.25
119	A22	3s dp org ('40)	8.00	6.00
120	A22	4s rose vio	1.25	.80
121	A22	5s lt blue grn	1.50	.30
122	A22	6s rose lake	1.25	.25
123	A22	6s dp green ('40)	27.50	42.00
124	A22	10s greenish blue	1.50	.25
125	A22	15s crim rose ('37)	1.90	.40
126	A22	15s dp bl ('40)	3.25	2.50
127	A22	18s dp car ('39)	20.00	7.00
128	A22	20s brt vio	3.00	.35
129	A22	25s dk bl ('38)	8.00	1.25
130	A22	30s bister ('38)	14.00	1.25
131	A22	30s ultra ('39)	16.00	5.00
132	A22	50s org brn	7.00	1.00
133	A22	60s brt pink	16.00	4.50
		Nos. 117-133 (17)	131.75	73.35
		Set, never hinged	255.00	

St. Brigitta
Convent
Entrance
A23

Ruins of
Convent, Pirita
River
A24

Front View of
Convent — A25

Seal of
Convent — A26

**Paper with Network as in
Parenthesis**

1936, June 10   *Perf. 13½*
134	A23	5s green (buff)	.40	.40
135	A24	10s blue (lil)	.40	.40
136	A25	15s red (org)	1.25	4.00
137	A26	25s ultra (brn)	1.60	5.50
		Nos. 134-137 (4)	3.65	10.30
		Set, never hinged	8.00	

St. Brigitta Convent, 500th anniversary.

Harbor at
Tallinn — A27

1938, Apr. 11   Engr.   *Perf. 14*
138	A27	2k blue	1.00	8.00
		Never hinged	1.75	

Friedrich R.
Faehlmann
A28

Friedrich R.
Kreutzwald
A29

1938, June 15   Typo.   *Perf. 13½*
139	A28	5s dark green	.70	.50
140	A29	10s deep brown	.70	.50
141	A29	15s dark carmine	1.00	.90
142	A28	25s dark carmine	1.60	1.40
a.		Sheet of 4, #139-142	10.00	80.00
		Nos. 139-142 (4)	4.00	3.30
		Set, never hinged	10.00	

Society of Estonian Scholars centenary.

Hospital at
Pärnu — A30

Beach
Hotel — A31

1939, June 20   Typo.   *Perf. 14x13½*
144	A30	5s dark green	1.60	1.60
145	A31	10s deep red violet	.80	1.60
146	A30	18s dark carmine	1.60	5.50
147	A31	30s deep blue	1.75	7.25
a.		Sheet of 4, #144-147	15.00	87.50
		Nos. 144-147 (4)	5.65	15.95
		Set, never hinged	11.00	

Cent. of health resort and baths at Pärnu.

Narva Falls Type of 1933
1940, Apr. 15   Engr.
149	A19	1k slate green	1.40	12.00
		Never hinged	2.50	

The sky consists of heavy horizontal lines
and the background consists of horizontal and
vertical lines.

Carrier Pigeon
and Plane — A32

1940, July 30   Typo.
150	A32	3s red orange	.25	.25
151	A32	10s purple	.25	.25
152	A32	15s rose brown	.25	.25
153	A32	30s dark blue	1.60	1.25
		Nos. 150-153 (4)	2.35	2.00
		Set, never hinged	5.00	

Assisting
Wounded
Soldier — SP1

Offering Aid to
Wounded
Hero — SP2

1920, June   Unwmk.   Litho.   *Imperf.*
B1	SP1	35p + 10p red & ol grn	.75	2.00
B2	SP2	70p + 15p dp bl & brn	.75	2.00

Surcharged

1920
B3	SP1	1m on No. B1	.50	.30
B4	SP2	2m on No. B2	.50	.30

Nurse and Wounded
Soldier — SP3

1921, Aug. 1   *Imperf.*
B5	SP3	2½ (3½)m org, brn & car	2.00	7.25
B6	SP3	5 (7)m ultra, brn & car	2.00	7.25

1922, Apr. 26   *Perf. 13½x14*
B7	SP3	2½ (3½)m org, brn & car	2.00	7.25
a.		Vert. pair, imperf. horiz.	30.00	80.00
B8	SP3	5 (7)m ultra, brn & car	2.00	7.25
a.		Vert. pair, imperf. horiz.	30.00	80.00

Nos. B5-B8
Overprinted

1923, Oct. 8   *Imperf.*
B9	SP3	2½ (3½)m	60.00	160.00
B10	SP3	5 (7)m	60.00	160.00

                 Perf. 13½x14
B11	SP3	2½ (3½)m	60.00	160.00
a.		Vert. pair, imperf. horiz.	200.00	800.00
B12	SP3	5 (7)m	60.00	160.00
a.		Vert. pair, imperf. horiz.	200.00	800.00
		Nos. B9-B12 (4)	240.00	640.00

Excellent forgeries are plentiful.

Nos. B7 and B8
Surcharged

1926, June 15
B13	SP3	5 (6)m on #B7	3.75	8.00
a.		Vert. pair, imperf. horiz.	24.00	120.00
B14	SP3	10 (12)m on #B8	4.50	8.00
a.		Vert. pair, imperf. horiz.	24.00	120.00

Nos. B5-B14 had the franking value of the
lower figure. They were sold for the higher figure, the excess going to the Red Cross
Society.

Kuressaare
Castle
SP4

Tartu
Cathedral
SP5

Tallinn
Castle
SP6

Narva Fortress
SP7

View of
Tallinn — SP8

Laid Paper
Perf. 14½x14
1927, Nov. 19   Typo.   Wmk. 207
B15	SP4	5m + 5m bl grn & ol, *grysh*	.90	8.00
B16	SP5	10m + 10m dp bl & brn, *cream*	.90	8.00
B17	SP6	12m + 12m rose red & ol grn, *bluish*	.90	8.00

Perf. 14x13½
B18	SP7	20m + 20m bl & choc, *gray*	1.75	8.00
B19	SP8	40m + 40m org brn & slate, *buff*	1.75	8.00
		Nos. B15-B19 (5)	6.20	40.00

The money derived from the surtax was
donated to the Committee for the commemoration of War for Liberation.

Red Cross Issue

Symbolical of
Succor to
Injured — SP9

Symbolical of
"Light of
Hope" — SP10

1931, Aug. 1   Unwmk.   *Perf. 13½*
B20	SP9	2s + 3s grn & car	8.00	8.00
B21	SP10	5s + 3s red & car	8.00	8.00
B22	SP10	10s + 3s lt bl & car	8.00	8.00
B23	SP9	20s + 3s dk bl & car	12.00	20.00
		Nos. B20-B23 (4)	36.00	44.00
		Set, never hinged	75.00	

Nurse and
Child
SP11

Taagepera
Sanatorium
SP12

Lorraine Cross and
Flower — SP13

Paper with Network as in Parenthesis

1933, Oct. 1   *Perf. 14, 14½*

B24	SP11	5s + 3s ver (grn)	6.00 8.00
B25	SP12	10s + 3s lt bl & red (vio)	6.00 8.00
B26	SP13	12s + 3s rose & red (grn)	8.00 12.00
B27	SP12	20s + 3s dk bl & red (org)	10.00 16.00
		Nos. B24-B27 (4)	30.00 44.00
		Set, never hinged	72.50

The surtax was for a fund to combat tuberculosis.

Coats of Arms

Narva — SP14

Pärnu — SP15

Tartu — SP16

Tallinn — SP17

Paper with Network as in Parenthesis

1936, Feb. 1   *Perf. 13½*

B28	SP14	10s + 10s grn & ultra (gray)	3.50 8.00
B29	SP15	15s + 15s car & bl (gray)	3.50 12.00
B30	SP16	25s + 25s gray bl & red (brn)	4.50 16.00
B31	SP17	50s + 50s blk & dl org (ol)	17.00 52.50
		Nos. B28-B31 (4)	28.50 88.50
		Set, never hinged	52.50

Paide
SP18

Rakvere
SP19

Valga
SP20

Viljandi
SP21

Paper with Network as in Parenthesis

1937, Jan. 2   *Perf. 13½x14*

B32	SP18	10s + 10s grn (gray)	3.00 6.50
B33	SP19	15s + 15s red brn (gray)	3.00 6.50
B34	SP20	25s + 25s dk bl (lil)	5.00 9.50

B35	SP21	50s + 50s dk vio (gray)	9.00 24.00
		Nos. B32-B35 (4)	20.00 46.50
		Set, never hinged	40.00

Baltiski — SP22

Võru — SP23

Haapsalu
SP24

Kuressaare
SP25

Designs are the armorial bearings of various cities

1938, Jan. 21
Paper with Gray Network

B36	SP22	10s + 10s dk brn	3.00 8.00
B37	SP23	15s + 15s car & grn	3.50 12.00
B38	SP24	25s + 25s dk bl & car	5.00 20.00
B39	SP25	50s + 50s blk & org yel	8.00 40.00
a.		Sheet of 4, #B36-B39	35.00 80.00
		Nos. B36-B39 (4)	19.50 80.00
		Set, never hinged	40.00

Annual charity ball, Tallinn, Jan. 2, 1938.

Viljandimaa
SP27

Pärnumaa
SP28

Tartumaa
SP29

Harjumaa
SP30

Designs are the armorial bearings of various cities

1939, Jan. 10   *Perf. 13½*
Paper with Gray Network

B41	SP27	10s + 10s dk bl grn	3.50 8.00
B42	SP28	15s + 15s carmine	4.00 8.00
B43	SP29	25s + 25s dk blue	5.50 20.00
B44	SP30	50s + 50s brn lake	14.00 47.50
a.		Sheet of 4, #B41-B44	45.00 175.00
		Nos. B41-B44 (4)	27.00 83.50
		Set, never hinged	47.50

Võrumaa
SP32

Järvamaa
SP33

Läänemaa
SP34

Saaremaa
SP35

Designs are the armorial bearings of various cities

1940, Jan. 2   **Typo.**   *Perf. 13½*
Paper with Gray Network

B46	SP32	10s + 10s dp grn & ultra	2.50 12.00
B47	SP33	15s + 15s dk car & ultra	2.50 16.00
B48	SP34	25s + 25s dk bl & scar	3.00 24.00
B49	SP35	50s + 50s ocher & ultra	8.00 32.50
		Nos. B46-B49 (4)	16.00 84.50
		Set, never hinged	30.00

AIR POST STAMPS

Airplane
AP1

Unwmk.

1920, Mar. 13   **Typo.**   *Imperf.*

C1	AP1	5m yel, blk & lt grn	3.00 5.50
		Never hinged	7.00

No. C1 Overprinted "1923" in Red

1923, Oct. 1

C2	AP1	5m multicolored	8.00 32.50
		Never hinged	15.00

No. C1 Surcharged in Red

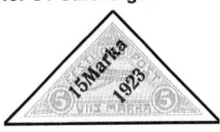

1923, Oct. 1

C3	AP1	15m on 5m multi	16.00 47.50
		Never hinged	30.00

Pairs of No. C1
Surcharged in
Black or Red

1923, Oct.

C4	AP1	10m on 5m+5m (B)	10.00 35.00
C5	AP1	20m on 5m+5m	20.00 55.00
C6	AP1	45m on 5m+5m	80.00 200.00

Rough Perf. 11½

C7	AP1	10m on 5m+5m (B)	550.00 1,200.
C8	AP1	20m on 5m+5m	200.00 525.00
		Nos. C4-C8 (5)	860.00 2,015.
		Set, never hinged	1,700.

The pairs comprising Nos. C7 and C8 are imperforate between. Forged surcharges and perforations abound. Authentication is required.

Monoplane in Flight — AP2

Designs: Various views of planes in flight.

1924, Feb. 12   *Imperf.*

C9	AP2	5m yellow & blk	2.00 8.00
C10	AP2	10m blue & blk	2.00 8.00
C11	AP2	15m red & blk	2.00 8.00
C12	AP2	20m green & blk	2.00 8.00
C13	AP2	45m violet & blk	2.00 16.00
		Nos. C9-C13 (5)	10.00 48.00
		Set, never hinged	15.00

The paper is covered with a faint network in pale shades of the frame colors. There are four varieties of the frames and five of the pictures.

1925, July 15   *Perf. 13½*

C14	AP2	5m yellow & blk	1.50 8.00
C15	AP2	10m blue & blk	1.50 8.00
C16	AP2	15m red & blk	1.50 8.00
C17	AP2	20m green & blk	1.50 8.00
C18	AP2	45m violet & blk	1.50 16.00
		Nos. C14-C18 (5)	7.50 48.00
		Set, never hinged	11.00

Counterfeits of Nos. C1-C18 are plentiful.

OCCUPATION STAMPS

Issued under German Occupation
For Use in Tartu (Dorpat)

Russian Stamps of 1909-
12 Surcharged

1918   **Unwmk.**   *Perf. 14x14½*

N1	A15	20pf on 10k dk bl	35.00 80.00
a.		20pf on 10k light blue	225.00
N2	A8	40pf on 20k bl & car	35.00 80.00
		Set, Never Hinged	130.00

Forged overprints exist.

ETHIOPIA

,e-the-'o-pe-ə

(Abyssinia)

LOCATION — Northeastern Africa
GOVT. — Monarchy
AREA — 471,800 sq. mi.
POP. — 40,000,000 (est. 1984)
CAPITAL — Addis Ababa

During the Italian occupation (1936-1941) Nos. N1-N7 were used, also stamps of Italian East Africa, Eritrea and Somalia.

16 Guerche = 1 Menelik Dollar or 1 Maria Theresa Dollar

100 Centimes = 1 Franc (1905)

40 Paras = 1 Piaster (1908)

16 Mehalek = 1 Thaler or Talari (1928)

100 Centimes = 1 Thaler (1936)

Watermarks

Wmk. 140 — Crown

Wmk. 282 — Ethiopian Star and Amharic Characters, Multiple

Excellent forgeries of Nos. 1-86 exist.

Very Fine examples of Nos. 1-86 and J1-J42 will have perforations touching the design on one or more sides due to the narrow spacing of the stamps on the plates and imperfect perforating methods. Stamps with margins clear on all sides are scarce and command high premiums.

On March 9, 1894 Menelik II awarded Alfred Ilg a concession to develop a railway, including postal service. Ilg's stamps, Nos. 1-79, were valid locally and to Djibouti. Mail to other countries had to bear stamps of Obock, Somali Coast, etc.

Ethiopia joined the UPU Nov. 1, 1908.

Menelik II
A1

Lion of Judah
A2

Amharic numeral "8"

Perf. 14x13½

		1895, Jan.	Unwmk.	Typo.
1	A1	¼g green	4.00	2.00
2	A1	½g red	4.00	2.00
3	A1	1g blue	4.00	2.00
4	A1	2g dark brown	4.00	2.00
5	A2	4g lilac brown	4.00	2.00
6	A2	8g violet	4.00	2.00
7	A2	16g black	4.00	2.00
		Nos. 1-7 (7)	28.00	14.00

For 4g, 8g and 16g stamps of type A1, see Nos. 3a, J4a and J7a.

Earliest reported use is Jan. 29, 1895.

Forged cancellations are plentiful.

For overprints see Nos. 8-86, J8-J28, J36-J42. For surcharges see Nos. 94-100, J29-J35.

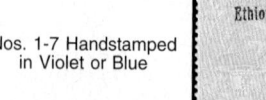

Nos. 1-7 Handstamped in Violet or Blue

Overprint 9¼x2½mm, Serifs on "E"

		1901, July 18		
8	A1	¼g green	27.50	27.50
9	A1	½g red	27.50	27.50
10	A1	1g blue	27.50	27.50
11	A1	2g dark brown	27.50	27.50
12	A2	4g lilac brown	32.50	32.50
13	A2	8g violet	47.50	47.50
14	A2	16g black	60.00	60.00
		Nos. 8-14 (7)	250.00	250.00

Violet overprints were issued July 18, 1901, for postal use, while the blue overprints were issued in Jan. 1902 for philatelic purposes. The blue overprints were not used in the mails. Values for unused stamps are for examples with blue overprints. Unused stamps with violet overprints are worth much more.

Overprints 8¼mm wide are unofficial reproductions.

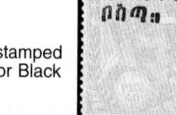

Nos. 1-7 Handstamped in Violet, Blue or Black

Overprint 11x3mm, Low Colons

		1902, Apr. 1		
15	A1	¼g green	6.00	6.00
16	A1	½g red	9.00	7.00
17	A1	1g blue	10.00	10.00
18	A1	2g dark brown	14.00	14.00
19	A2	4g lilac brown	24.00	24.00
20	A2	8g violet	30.00	30.00
21	A2	16g black	55.00	55.00
		Nos. 15-21 (7)	148.00	146.00

The handstamp reads "Bosta" (Post). Overprints 10¾mm and 11mm wide with raised colons are unofficial reproductions.

Nos. 1-7 Handstamped in Black

		1903, Apr. 15	Overprint 16x3¾mm	
22	A1	¼g green	7.50	7.50
23	A1	½g red	12.00	12.00
24	A1	1g blue	15.00	15.00
25	A1	2g dark brown	19.00	19.00
26	A2	4g lilac brown	27.50	27.50
27	A2	8g violet	37.50	37.50
28	A2	16g black	57.50	57.50
		Nos. 22-28 (7)	176.00	176.00

The handstamp reads "Malekt." (Also "Melekt," message). Original stamps have blurred colons. Unofficial reproductions have clean colons. Nos. 22-28 have black overprints only. All other colors are fakes.

Nos. 1-7 Handstamped in Violet or Blue

Overprint 18¼mm Wide

		1904, Dec.		
36	A1	¼g green	15.00	15.00
37	A1	½g red	20.00	
38	A1	1g blue	25.00	
39	A1	2g dark brown	27.50	
40	A2	4g lilac brown	35.00	
41	A2	8g violet	57.50	
42	A2	16g black	75.00	
		Nos. 36-42 (7)	255.00	

The handstamp reads "Malekathe" (message). This set was never issued.

Preceding Issues Surcharged with New Values in French Currency in Blue, Violet, Rose or Black

a

b

On Nos. 1-7

		1905, Jan. 1	Overprint 3mm High	
43	A1 (a)	5c on ¼g	10.00	10.00
44	A1 (a)	10c on ½g	10.00	10.00
45	A1 (a)	20c on 1g	10.00	10.00
46	A1 (a)	40c on 2g	11.00	11.00
47	A2 (a)	80c on 4g	21.00	21.00
48	A2 (b)	1.60fr on 8g	22.50	22.50
49	A2 (b)	3.20fr on 16g	40.00	40.00
		Nos. 43-49 (7)	124.50	124.50

Nos. 48-49 exist with period or comma.

On No. 8, "Ethiopie" in Blue

50	A1 (a)	5c on ¼g	120.00	100.00

On No. 15, "Bosta" in Black

51	A1 (a)	5c on ¼g	40.00	40.00

On No. 22, "Malekt" in Black

52	A1 (a)	5c on ¼g	140.00	75.00

Unofficial reproductions exist of Nos. 50, 51, 52. The 5c on No. 36, 10c, 20c, 40c, 80c, and 1.60fr surcharges exist as unofficial reproductions only.

c

d

		1905		On No. 2
54	A1 (c)	5c on half of ½g	10.00	10.00

On No. 21, "Bosta" in Black

55	A2 (d)	5c on 16g blk	200.00	100.00

On No. 55, "Bosta" is in black.

On No. 28, "Malekt" in Black

56	A2 (d)	5c on 16g blk	250.00	250.00
		Nos. 54-56 (3)	460.00	360.00

Nos. 55-56 issued Mar. 30.

The overprints and surcharges on Nos. 8 to 56 inclusive were handstamped, the work being very roughly done.

As is usual with handstamped overprints and surcharges there are many inverted and double, but most of them are fakes or unofficial reproductions.

Surcharged with New Values in Various Colors and in Violet

Overprint 14¾x3½mm

		1906, Jan. 1		
57	A1	5c on ¼g green	10.00	10.00
58	A1	10c on ½g red	12.00	12.00
59	A1	20c on 1g blue	12.00	12.00
60	A1	40c on 2g dk brn	12.00	12.00
61	A2	80c on 4g lilac brn	12.00	12.00
62	A2	1.60fr on 8g violet	27.50	27.50
63	A2	3.20fr on 16g black	45.00	45.00
		Nos. 57-63 (7)	136.50	136.50

Two types of the 4-character overprint ("Menelik"): 14x¾x3½mm and 16x4mm.

Surcharged in Violet Brown

		1906, July 1	Overprint 16x4¼mm	
64	A1	5c on ¼g grn	9.25	9.25
a.		Surcharged "20"	75.00	75.00
65	A1	10c on ½g red	11.00	11.00
66	A1	20c on 1g blue	17.50	17.50
67	A1	40c on 2g dk brn	17.50	17.50
68	A2	80c on 4g lil brn	25.00	25.00
69	A2	1.60fr on 8g vio	25.00	25.00
70	A2	3.20fr on 16g blk	60.00	60.00
		Nos. 64-70 (7)	165.25	165.25

The control overprint reads "Menelik."

Surcharged in Violet

e

f

		1907, June 21		
71	A1 (e)	¼ on ¼g grn	8.75	8.75
72	A1 (e)	½ on ½g red	8.75	8.75
73	A1 (f)	1 on 1g blue	11.00	11.00
74	A1 (f)	2 on 2g dk brn	12.00	12.00
a.		Surcharged "40"	65.00	
75	A2 (f)	4 on 4g lil brn	13.00	13.00
a.		Surcharged "80"	57.50	
76	A2 (f)	8 on 8g vio	30.00	30.00
77	A2 (f)	16 on 16g blk	37.50	37.50
		Nos. 71-77 (7)	121.00	121.00

Nos. 71-72 are also found with stars farther away from figures.

The control overprint reads "Dagmawi" ("Second"), meaning Emperor Menelik II.

On stamps with "1" in surcharge, genuine examples have straight serifs, forgeries have curved serifs.

Nos. 2, 23 Surcharged in Bluish Green

		1908, Aug. 14		
78	A1	1pi on ½g red (#2)	15.00	15.00
79	A1	1pi on ½g red (#23)	850.00	

Official reproductions exist. Value, set $25.
Forgeries exist.

The surcharges on Nos. 57-78 are handstamped and are found double, inverted, etc.

Surcharged in Black

		1908, Nov. 1		
80	A1	¼p on ¼g grn	1.50	1.50
81	A1	½p on ½g red	1.50	1.50
82	A1	1p on 1g blue	2.25	2.25
83	A1	2p on 2g dk brn	3.75	3.75
84	A2	4p on 4g lil brn	5.25	5.25
85	A2	8p on 8g vio	12.50	12.50
86	A2	16p on 16g blk	18.00	18.00
		Nos. 80-86 (7)	44.75	44.75

Surcharges on Nos. 80-85 are found double, inverted, etc. Forgeries exist.

These are the 1st stamps valid for international mail.

King Solomon's Throne — A3

Menelik in Native Costume — A4

Menelik in Royal
Dress — A5

1909, Jan. 29   *Perf. 11½*

87	A3	¼g blue green	1.10	.85
88	A3	½g rose	1.25	.85
89	A4	1g green & org	6.25	2.50
90	A4	2g blue	4.75	3.00
91	A4	4g green & car	7.00	5.50
92	A5	8g ver & dp grn	15.00	10.00
93	A5	16g ver & car	22.50	16.50
		Nos. 87-93 (7)	57.85	39.20

For overprints see Nos. 101-115, J43-J49, J55-J56. For surcharges see Nos. 116-119.

Nos. 1-7 Handstamped
and Surcharged in ms.

1911, Oct. 1   *Perf. 14x13½*

94	A1	¼g on ¼g grn	50.00	
95	A1	½g on ½g red	50.00	
96	A1	1g on 1g blue	50.00	
97	A1	2g on 2g dk brn	50.00	
98	A2	4g on 4g lil brn	50.00	
99	A2	8g on 8g violet	50.00	
100	A2	16g on 16g black	50.00	
		Nos. 94-100 (7)	350.00	

Nos. 94-100 were produced as a philatelic speculation by the postmaster at Dire-Dawa. The overprint is abbreviated from "Affranchissement Exceptionnel Faute Timbres" (Special Franking Lacking Stamps). The overprints and surcharges were applied to stamps on cover and then canceled. These covers were then sold to dealers in Europe. No. 98 is known postally used on a small number of commercial covers.

Nos. 94-100 without surcharge are forgeries.

Stamps of 1909 Handstamped in Violet or Black

Nos. 101-102   Nos. 104-107

1917, Mar. 30   *Perf. 11½*

101	A3	¼g blue grn (V)	7.50	6.75
102	A3	½g rose (V)	7.50	6.75
104	A4	2g blue (Bk)	10.00	8.25
105	A4	4g grn & car (Bk)	15.00	17.00
106	A5	8g ver & dp grn (Bk)	25.00	22.50
107	A5	16g ver & car (Bk)	40.00	35.00
		Nos. 101-107 (6)	105.00	96.25

Coronation of Empress Zauditu and appointment of Prince Tafari as Regent and Heir to the throne.

Exist with overprint inverted and double.

Stamps of 1909 Overprinted in Blue, Black or Red

Nos. 108-111   Nos. 112-115

1917, Apr. 5-Oct. 1

108	A3	¼g blue grn (Bl)	1.25	1.25
109	A3	½g rose (Bl)	1.25	1.25
110	A3	1g grn & org (Bl)	2.25	2.25

111	A4	2g blue (R)	82.50	87.25
112	A4	2g blue (Bk)	1.25	1.25
113	A4	4g grn & car (Bl)	1.25	1.25
a.		Black overprint	11.00	11.00
114	A5	8g ver & dp grn (Bl)	1.25	1.25
115	A5	16g ver & car (Bl)	2.25	2.25
		Nos. 108-115 (8)	93.25	98.00

Coronation of Empress Zauditu.
Nos. 108-115 all exist with double overprint, inverted overprint, double overprint, one inverted, and various combinations.

Nos. 114-115 with Additional Surcharge

k   l

m   n

1917, May 28

116	A5 (k)	¼g on 8g	5.00	4.00
117	A5 (l)	½g on 8g	5.00	4.00
118	A5 (m)	1g on 16g	11.00	8.00
119	A5 (n)	2g on 16g	12.00	9.00
		Nos. 116-119 (4)	33.00	25.00

Nos. 116-119 all exist with the numerals double and inverted and No. 116 with the Amharic surcharge missing.

Sommering's
Gazelle — A6

Prince
Tafari — A9

Cathedral
of St.
George
A12

Empress Waizeri
Zauditu — A18

¼g, Giraffes. ½g, Leopard. 2g, Prince Tafari, diff. 4g, Prince Tafari, diff. 8g, White rhinoceros. 12g, Somali ostriches. 1t, African elephant. 2t, Water buffalo. 3t, Lions. 5t, 10t, Empress Zauditu.

1919, June 16   *Typo.*   *Perf. 11½*

120	A6	⅛g violet & brn	.25	.25
121	A6	¼g bl grn & drab	.25	.25
122	A6	½g scar & ol grn	.25	.25
123	A9	1g rose lil & gray grn		.25
124	A9	2g dp ultra & fawn		.25
125	A9	4g turq bl & org	.25	2.50
126	A12	6g lt blue & org	.25	.25

127	A12	8g ol grn & blk brn	.35	.25
128	A12	12g red vio & gray	.50	.30
129	A12	1t rose & gray blk	.90	.40
130	A12	2t black & brown	2.50	
131	A12	3t grn & dp org	2.50	1.90
132	A18	4t brn & lil rose	3.00	2.50
133	A18	5t carmine & gray	4.00	4.00
134	A18	10t gray grn & bis	8.00	5.25
		Nos. 120-134 (15)	23.50	
		Nos. 120-129,131-134 (14)		18.25

No. 130 was not issued.
For overprints see Nos. J50-J54. For surcharges see Nos. 135-154.

Reprints have brownish gum that is cracked diagonally. Originals have smooth, white gum. Reprints exist imperf. and some values with inverted centers. Value for set, unused or canceled, $5.

No. 132 Surcharged
in Blue

1919, Oct.

135	A18	4g on 4t brn & lil rose	3.50	3.50

Nos. 135-154
The Amharic surcharge indicates the new value and, therefore, varies on Nos. 135-154. There are numerous defective letters and figures, several types of the "2" of "½," the errors "guerhce," "gnerche," etc.

Many varieties of surcharge, such as double, inverted, lines transposed or omitted, and inverted "2" in "½," exist.

There are many irregularly produced settings in imitation of Nos. 136-154 which differ slightly from the originals. These may be essays or proofs.

Stamps of 1919
Surcharged

1921-22

136	A6	½g on ⅛g vio & brn ('22)	1.00	1.00
137	A6	1g on ½g grn & db	2.50	1.00
138	A9	2g on 1g lil brn & gray grn ('22)	1.00	1.50
139	A18	2g on 4t brn & lil rose ('22)	35.00	15.00
140	A6	2½g on ½g scar & ol grn	1.00	1.50
141	A9	4g on 2g ultra & fawn ('22)	1.00	1.25
		Nos. 136-141 (6)	41.50	21.25

No. 139 has been forged.

Stamps and Type of
1919 Surcharged

1925-28

142	A12	½g on 1t rose & gray blk ('26)	1.00	1.00
a.		Without colon ('28)	12.50	12.50
143	A18	½g on 5t car & gray ('26)	2.00	1.00
144	A12	1g on 6g bl & org	1.00	1.00

145	A12	1g on 12g lil & gray	400.00	400.00
146	A12	1g on 3t grn & org ('26)	22.50	16.00
147	A18	1g on 10t gray grn & bis ('26)	1.00	*1.00*
		Nos. 142-147 (6)	427.50	420.00

On No. 142 the surcharge is at the left side of the stamp, reading upward. On No. 142a it is at the right, reading downward. The two surcharges are from different, though similar, settings. On No. 146 the surcharge is at the right, reading upward. See note following No. 154.

Type of
1919
Srchd.

1926
147A	A12	1g on 12g lil & gray	400.00	

Forgeries exist.

Nos. 126-
128 Srchd.

1926
148	A12	½g on 8g	3.00	1.25
149	A12	1g on 6g	80.00	50.00
150	A12	1g on 12g	350.00	
		Nos. 148-150 (3)	433.00	51.25

The Amharic line has 7 (½g) or 6 characters (1g).

Nos. 126-
128, 131
Srchd.

1927
151	A12	½g on 8g	1.50	1.50
152	A12	1g on 6g	60.00	40.00
153	A12	1g on 12g	5.00	1.50
154	A12	1g on 3t	400.00	
		Nos. 151-154 (4)	466.50	43.00

The Amharic line has 7 (½g) or 4 characters (1g). No. 152 has the lines closer together than do the others.

Forgeries of No. 154 exist.

Prince
Tafari — A22

Empress
Zauditu — A23

1928, Sept. 5   *Typo.*   *Perf. 13½x14*

155	A22	⅛m org & lt bl	1.50	1.40
156	A23	¼m ind & red org	.90	*1.40*
157	A22	½m gray grn & blk	1.50	*1.40*
158	A23	1m dk car & blk	.90	*1.40*
159	A22	2m dk bl & blk	.90	*1.40*
160	A23	4m yel & olive	.90	*1.40*
161	A22	8m vio & olive	2.40	1.40
162	A23	1t org brn & vio	2.75	1.40
163	A22	2t grn & bister	4.25	3.75
164	A23	3t choc & grn	6.75	3.75
		Nos. 155-164 (10)	22.75	18.20

For overprints and surcharges see Nos. 165-209, 217-230, C1-C10.

Preceding Issue
Overprinted in Black,
Violet or Red

1928, Sept. 1
165	A22	⅛m (Bk)	3.25	3.25
166	A23	¼m (V)	3.25	3.25
167	A22	½m (V)	3.25	3.25
168	A22	1m (V)	3.25	3.25
169	A22	2m (R)	3.25	3.25
170	A22	4m (Bk)	3.25	3.25
171	A22	8m (R)	3.25	3.25
172	A23	1t (Bk)	4.50	4.50
173	A22	2t (R)	6.00	6.00
174	A23	3t (R)	6.00	6.00
		Nos. 165-174 (10)	39.25	39.25

Opening of General Post Office, Addis
Ababa.
Exist with overprint inverted, double, double,
one inverted, etc.

Nos. 155, 157, 159,
161, 163
Handstamped in
Violet, Red or Black

1928, Oct. 7
175	A22	⅛m (V)	4.25	4.25
176	A22	½m (R)	4.25	4.25
177	A22	2m (R)	4.25	4.25
178	A22	8m (Bk)	4.25	4.25
179	A22	2t (V)	4.25	4.25
		Nos. 175-179 (5)	21.25	21.25

Crowning of Prince Tafari as king (Negus)
on Oct. 7, 1928.
Nos. 175-177 exist with overprint vertical,
inverted, double, etc.
Forgeries exist.

Nos. 155-164
Overprinted in Red
or Green

1930, Apr. 3
180	A22	⅛m org & lt bl (R)	1.40	1.40
181	A23	¼m ind & red org (G)	1.40	1.40
182	A22	½m gray grn & blk (R)	1.40	1.40
183	A22	1m dk car & blk (G)	1.40	1.40
184	A22	2m dk bl & blk (R)	1.40	1.40
185	A23	4m yel & ol (R)	2.10	2.10
186	A22	8m vio & ol (R)	3.00	3.00
187	A23	1t org brn & vio (R)	5.00	5.00
188	A22	2t grn & bis (R)	6.00	6.00
189	A23	3t choc & grn (R)	8.00	8.00
		Nos. 180-189 (10)	31.10	31.10

Proclamation of King Tafari as King of Kings
of Abyssinia under the name "Haile Selassie."
A similar overprint, set in four vertical lines,
was printed on all denominations of the 1928
issue. It was not considered satisfactory and
was rejected. The trial impressions were not
placed on sale to the public, but some stamps
reached private hands and have been passed
through the post.

Nos. 155-164
Overprinted in Red
or Olive Brown

1930, Apr. 3
190	A22	⅛m orange & lt bl	1.40	1.40
191	A23	¼m ind & red org (OB)	1.40	1.40
192	A22	½m gray grn & blk	1.40	1.40
193	A22	1m dk car & blk (OB)	1.40	1.40
194	A22	2m dk blue & blk	1.40	1.40
195	A23	4m yellow & ol	2.10	2.10
196	A22	8m violet & ol	3.00	3.00
197	A23	1t org brn & vio	5.00	5.00
198	A22	2t green & bister	6.00	6.00
199	A23	3t chocolate & grn	8.00	8.00
		Nos. 190-199 (10)	31.10	31.10

Proclamation of King Tafari as Emperor
Haile Selassie.
All stamps of this series exist with "H" of
"HAILE" omitted and with many other varieties.

Nos. 155-164
Handstamped in
Violet or Red

1930, Nov. 2
200	A22	⅛m (V)	1.10	1.10
201	A23	¼m (V)	1.10	1.10
202	A22	½m (R)	1.10	1.10
203	A23	1m (V)	1.10	1.10
204	A22	2m (R)	1.10	1.10
205	A23	4m (V)	1.10	1.10
206	A22	8m (V or R)	1.90	1.90
207	A23	1t (R)	3.00	3.00
208	A22	2t (V or R)	4.50	4.50
209	A23	3t (V or R)	6.50	6.50
		Nos. 200-209 (10)	22.50	22.50

Coronation of Emperor Haile Selassie, Nov.
2, 1930.

Haile Selassie
Coronation
Monument, Symbols
of Empire — A24

1930, Nov.   **Engr.**   **Perf. 12½**
210	A24	1g orange	1.00	1.00
211	A24	2g ultra	1.00	1.00
212	A24	4g violet	1.00	1.00
213	A24	8g dull green	1.00	1.00
214	A24	1t brown	1.25	1.25
215	A24	3t green	2.00	2.00
216	A24	5t red brown	2.00	2.00
		Nos. 210-216 (7)	9.25	9.25

Coronation of Emperor Haile Selassie.
Issued: 4g, 11/2; others, 11/23.
Reprints of Nos. 210 to 216 exist. Colors are
more yellow and the ink is thicker and slightly
glossy. Ink on the originals is dull and granular. Value 35c each.

**Nos. 158-160, 164 Surcharged in
Green, Red or Blue**

1/8 Mehalek

1/2 Mehalek	1/2 Mehalek
Type I	Type II

1931   **Perf. 13½x14**
217	A23	⅛m on 1m	.80	.80
218	A22	⅛m on 2m (R)	.80	.80
219	A23	⅛m on 4m	.80	.80
220	A23	¼m on 1m (Bl)	.80	.80
221	A23	¼m on 2m (R)	1.50	1.50
222	A23	¼m on 4m	1.50	1.50
225	A23	½m on 1m (Bl)	1.50	1.50
226	A23	½m on 2m (R)	1.50	1.50
227	A23	½m on 4m, type II	1.50	1.50
a.		½m on 4m, type I	10.00	10.00
228	A23	½m on 3t (R)	12.00	12.00
230	A22	1m on 2m (R)	3.00	3.00
		Nos. 217-230 (11)	25.70	25.70

The ½m on ⅛m orange & light blue and ½m
on ¼m indigo & red orange were clandestinely
printed and never sold at the post office.
No. 230 with double surcharge in red and
blue is a color trial.
Many varieties exist.
Issued: 1m, Apr.; others, 3/20.

Prince Makonnen A25	Empress Menen A27

View of
Hawash
River and
Railroad
Bridge
A26

Designs: 2g, 8g, Haile Selassie (profile). 4g,
1t, Statue of Menelik II. 3t, Empress Menen
(full face). 5t, Haile Selassie (full face).

Perf. 12½, 12x12½, 12½x12
1931, June 27   **Engr.**
232	A25	⅛g red	.40	.40
233	A26	¼g olive green	1.10	1.10
234	A25	½g dark violet	1.10	1.10
235	A25	1g red orange	1.10	1.10
236	A27	2g ultra	1.10	1.10
237	A25	4g violet	1.25	1.25
238	A27	8g blue green	2.00	2.00
239	A25	1t chocolate	24.00	10.00
240	A27	3t yellow green	7.00	3.00
241	A27	5t red brown	12.00	5.50
		Nos. 232-241 (10)	51.05	26.55

For overprints see Nos. B1-B5. For
surcharges see Nos. 242-246.
Reprints of Nos. 232-236, 238-240 are on
thinner and whiter paper than the originals. On
originals the ink is dull and granular. On
reprints, heavy, caked and shiny. Value 20c
each.

**Nos. 232-236 Surcharged in Blue or
Carmine**

2 c

1936, Jan. 29   **Perf. 12x12½, 12½x12**
242	A25	1c on ⅛g red	2.00	1.00
243	A26	2c on ¼g ol grn (C)	2.00	1.00
244	A25	3c on ½g dk vio	2.00	1.10
245	A27	5c on 1g red org	2.50	1.50
246	A27	10c on 2g ultra (C)	3.25	1.90
		Nos. 242-246 (5)	11.75	6.50

SEMI-POSTAL STAMPS

Types of 1931,
Overprinted in Red
at Upper Left

Perf. 12x12½, 12½x12
1936, Feb. 24   **Unwmk.**
B1	A27	1g light green	.60	.60
B2	A27	2g rose	.60	.60
B3	A25	4g blue	.60	.60
B4	A27	8g brown	.85	.85
B5	A25	1t purple	.85	.85
		Nos. B1-B5 (5)	3.50	3.50

Nos. B1-B5 were sold at twice face value,
the surtax going to the Red Cross.

AIR POST STAMPS

Regular Issue of
1928 Handstamped in
Violet, Red, Black or
Green

Perf. 13½x14
1929, Aug. 17   **Unwmk.**
C1	A22	⅛m orange & lt bl	.90	1.00
C2	A23	¼m ind & red org	.90	1.00
C3	A22	½m gray grn & blk	.90	1.00
C4	A23	1m dk car & blk	.90	1.00
C5	A22	2m dk blue & blk	1.00	1.25
C6	A23	4m yellow & olive	1.00	1.25
C7	A22	8m violet & olive	1.00	1.25
C8	A23	1t org brn & vio	1.25	1.25
C9	A22	2t green & bister	1.60	2.00
C10	A23	3t choc & grn	1.75	2.00
		Nos. C1-C10 (10)	11.20	13.00

The overprint signifies "17 August 1929-Air-
plane of the Ethiopian Government." The
stamps commemorate the arrival at Addis
Ababa of the 1st airplane of the Ethiopian
Government.
There are 3 types of the overprint: (I)
19 ½mm high; "colon" at right of bottom word.
(II) 20mm high; same "colon." (III) 19 ½mm
high; no "colon." Many errors exist.

Symbols of Empire,
Airplane and
Map — AP1

1931, June 17   **Engr.**   **Perf. 12½**
C11	AP1	1g orange red	.25	.25
C12	AP1	2g ultra	.25	.30
C13	AP1	4g violet	.25	.40
C14	AP1	8g blue green	.50	.80
C15	AP1	1t olive brown	1.25	1.00
C16	AP1	2t carmine	2.25	3.75
C17	AP1	3t yellow green	3.25	5.00
		Nos. C11-C17 (7)	8.00	11.50

Nos. C11 to C17 exist imperforate.
Reprints of C11 to C17 exist. Paper is thinner and gum whiter than the originals and the
ink is heavy and shiny. Originals have ink that
is dull and granular. Reprints usually sell at
about one-tenth of above values.

POSTAGE DUE STAMPS

Very Fine examples of Nos. J1-J42 will have perforations touching the design on one or more sides.

Nos. 1-4 and unissued values Overprinted

Perf. 14x13½

1896, June 10   Unwmk.

Black Overprint

J1	A1	¼g green	1.45
J2	A1	½g red	1.45
J3	A1	4g lilac brown	1.00
J4	A1	8g violet	1.00
a.	Without overprint		1.00

Red Overprint

J5	A1	1g blue	1.45
J6	A1	2g dark brown	1.45
J7	A1	16g black	1.00
a.	Without overprint		1.00
		Nos. J1-J7 (7)	8.80

Nos. J1-J7 were not issued. Forgeries exist.

Nos. 1-7 Handstamped in Various Colors

a   b

1905, Jan. 1

J8	A1 (a)	¼g green	55.00	55.00
J9	A1 (a)	½g red	55.00	55.00
J10	A1 (a)	1g blue	55.00	55.00
J11	A1 (a)	2g dk brown	55.00	55.00
J12	A2 (a)	4g lilac brown	55.00	55.00
J13	A2 (a)	8g violet	55.00	55.00
J14	A2 (a)	16g black	55.00	55.00
		Nos. J8-J14 (7)	385.00	385.00

1905, June 1

J15	A1 (b)	¼g green	55.00	55.00
J16	A1 (b)	½g red	55.00	55.00
J17	A1 (b)	1g blue	55.00	55.00
J18	A1 (b)	2g dark brown	55.00	55.00
J19	A2 (b)	4g lilac brown	55.00	55.00
J20	A2 (b)	8g violet	55.00	55.00
J21	A2 (b)	16g black	55.00	55.00
		Nos. J15-J21 (7)	385.00	385.00

Excellent forgeries of Nos. J8-J42 exist.

Nos. 1-7 Handstamped in Blue or Violet

1906, July 1

J22	A1	¼g green	14.50	14.50
J23	A1	½g red	14.50	14.50
J24	A1	1g blue	14.50	14.50
J25	A1	2g dark brown	14.50	14.50
J26	A2	4g lilac brown	14.50	14.50
J27	A2	8g violet	21.00	21.00
J28	A2	16g black	25.00	25.00
		Nos. J22-J28 (7)	118.50	118.50

Nos. J22-J27 exist with inverted overprint, also No. J22 with double overprint. Forgeries exist.

With Additional Surcharge of Value Handstamped as on Nos. 71-77

1907, July 1

J29	A1 (e)	¼ on ¼g grn	14.00	14.00
J30	A1 (e)	½ on ½g red	14.00	14.00
J31	A1 (f)	1 on 1g blue	14.00	14.00
J32	A1 (f)	2 on 2g dk brown	8.00	
J33	A2 (f)	4 on 4g lilac brn	14.00	14.00
J34	A2 (f)	8 on 8g violet	14.00	14.00
J35	A2 (f)	16 on 16g blk	22.50	22.50
		Nos. J29-J35 (7)	106.50	106.50

Nos. J30-J35 exist with inverted surcharge. Nos. J30, J33-J35 exist with double surcharge.

Nos. 1-7 Handstamped in Black

1908, Dec. 1

J36	A1	¼g green	1.40	1.25
J37	A1	½g red	1.40	1.25
J38	A1	1g blue	1.40	1.25
J39	A1	2g dark brown	1.75	1.50
J40	A2	4g lilac brown	2.50	2.50
J41	A2	8g violet	5.50	6.25
J42	A2	16g black	17.50	20.00
		Nos. J36-J42 (7)	31.45	34.00

Nos. J36 to J42 exist with inverted overprint and Nos. J36, J37, J38 and J40 with double overprint.
Forgeries of Nos. J36-J56 exist.

Same Handstamp on Nos. 87-93

1912, Dec. 1   Perf. 11½

J43	A3	¼g blue green	1.75	1.25
J44	A3	½g rose	1.75	1.50

1913, July 1

J45	A3	1g green & org	6.00	4.25
J46	A4	2g blue	7.00	6.00
J47	A4	4g green & car	11.00	7.00
J48	A5	8g ver & dp grn	14.00	11.00
J49	A5	16g ver & car	35.00	27.50
		Nos. J43-J49 (7)	76.50	58.50

Nos. J43-J49, all exist with inverted, double and double, one inverted overprint.

Same Handstamp on Nos. 120-124 in Blue Black

1925-27   Perf. 11½

J50	A6	⅛g violet & brn	18.00	18.00
J51	A6	¼g bl grn & db	18.00	18.00
J52	A6	½g scar & ol grn	20.00	20.00
J53	A9	1g rose lil & gray grn	20.00	20.00
J54	A9	2g dp ultra & fawn	20.00	20.00
		Nos. J50-J54 (5)	96.00	96.00

Same Handstamp on Nos. 110, 112

1930 (?)

J55	A3 (i)	1g green & org	30.00	30.00
J56	A4 (j)	2g blue	30.00	30.00

The status of Nos. J55-J56 is questioned.

OCCUPATION STAMPS

Issued under Italian Occupation
100 Centesimi = 1 Lira

OS1

Emperor Victor Emmanuel III — OS2

1936   Wmk. 140   Perf. 14

N1	OS1	10c org brn	16.00	9.50
		Never hinged	35.00	
		On cover		140.00
N2	OS1	20c purple	14.50	4.00
		Never hinged	30.00	
		On cover		125.00
N3	OS2	25c dark green	9.50	.80
		Never hinged	20.00	
		On cover		40.00
N4	OS2	30c dark brown	9.50	1.60
		Never hinged	20.00	
		On cover		40.00
N5	OS2	50c rose car	4.00	.40
		Never hinged	8.00	
		On cover		32.50
N6	OS1	75c deep orange	36.00	8.00
		Never hinged	67.50	
		On cover		225.00
N7	OS1	1.25 l deep blue	36.00	12.00
		Never hinged	67.50	
		On cover		300.00
		Nos. N1-N7 (7)	125.50	36.30
		Set, never hinged	300.00	

Issued: Nos. N3-N5, May 22; others Dec. 5.
For later issues see Italian East Africa.

FALKLAND ISLANDS

ˈfȯl-klənd ˈī-ləndz

LOCATION — A group of islands about 300 miles east of the Straits of Magellan at the southern limit of South America
GOVT. — British Crown Colony
AREA — 4,700 sq. mi.
POP. — 1,813 (1980)
CAPITAL — Stanley

12 Pence = 1 Shilling
20 Shillings = 1 Pound

> Catalogue values for unused stamps in this country are for Never Hinged items, beginning with Scott 97 in the regular postage section, Scott 1L1 in Falkland Island Dependencies regular issues, and Scott 2L1, 3L1, 4L1, 5L1 in the Issues for Separate Islands.

Values for unused stamps are for examples with original gum as defined in the catalogue introduction.
Nos. 1-4, 7-8, and some printings of Nos. 5-6, exist with straight edges on one or two sides, being the imperforate margins of the sheets. This occurs in 24 out of 60 stamps. Catalogue values are for stamps with perforations on all sides.

Queen Victoria — A1

1878-79   Unwmk.   Engr.   *Perf. 14*

1	A1	1p claret	850.00	500.00
2	A1	4p dark gray ('79)	1,400.	200.00
3	A1	6p green	110.00	85.00
4	A1	1sh bister brown	85.00	80.00

No. 2 is known with paper maker's watermark "TURNER, CHAFFORD MILLS," in double-lined capital letters. Values, unused $2,500, used $475.

1883-95   Wmk. 2

5	A1	1p brt claret ('94)	130.00	95.00
a.	1p claret		425.00	190.00
b.	Horiz. pair, imperf. vert.		80,000.	
c.	1p red brown ('91)		300.00	95.00
d.	Diag. half of #5c used as ½p on cover			4,250.
6	A1	4p olive gray ('95)	14.00	27.50
a.	4p gray black		575.00	100.00
b.	4p olive gray black ('89)		200.00	65.00
c.	4p brownish black ('94)		900.00	400.00

No. 6c has watermark reversed.
For surcharge see No. 19E.

1886   Wmk. 2 Sideways

7	A1	1p claret	95.00	65.00
a.	1p brownish claret		125.00	60.00
b.	Diagonal half of #7a used as ½p on cover			3,750.
8	A1	4p olive gray	525.00	60.00
a.	4p pale gray black		840.00	90.00

For surcharge see No. 19.

1891-1902 — Wmk. 2

No.	Type	Description	Unused	Used
9	A1	½p green ('92)	19.00	18.00
a.		½p blue green	27.50	32.50
10	A1	½p yel green ('99)	2.25	3.50
11	A1	1p orange brown	100.00	80.00
a.		Diagonal half used as ½p on cover		4,250.
11B	A1	1p pale red ('99)	9.00	3.50
12	A1	1p org red ('02)	16.00	4.75
13	A1	2p magenta ('96)	7.00	14.00
14	A1	2½p deep blue ('94)	275.00	160.00
15	A1	2½p ultra ('94)	50.00	14.00
a.		2½p pale ultra ('98)	50.00	20.00
b.		2½p dull blue	350.00	32.50
c.		2½p deep ultra ('01)	50.00	42.50
d.		2½p pale chalky ultra	240.00	60.00
16	A1	6p yellow ('96)	52.50	55.00
a.		6p orange ('92)	250.00	190.00
17	A1	9p ver ('95)	55.00	65.00
a.		9p salmon ('96)	60.00	70.00
18	A1	1sh gray brn ('95)	80.00	65.00
a.		1sh bis brn ('96)	75.00	55.00
		Nos. 9-18 (11)	665.75	482.75

Nos. 7 and 5a Surcharged in Black

1891 — Wmk. 2 Sideways

No.	Type	Description	Unused	Used
19	A1	½p on half of 1p, #7	725.00	360.00
d.		Unsevered pair	3,750.	1,350.

Wmk. 2

No.	Type	Description	Unused	Used
19E	A1	½p on half of 1p, #5a	825.00	325.00
f.		Unsevered pair	4,500.	1,800.

Genuine used bisects should be canceled with a segmented circular cork cancel. Any other cancel must be linked by date to known mail ship departures. This surcharge exists on "souvenir" bisects, including examples of No. 11, and can be found inverted, double and sideways.

A3   A4

1898 — Wmk. 1

No.	Type	Description	Unused	Used
20	A3	2sh6p dark blue	290.00	290.00
21	A4	5sh brown red	260.00	260.00
		Set of two, ovptd. "SPECIMEN"	525.00	

A5   A6

King Edward VII
1904-07 — Wmk. 3 — Perf. 14

No.	Type	Description	Unused	Used
22	A5	½p yellow green	7.00	1.75
23	A5	1p red, wmk. sideways ('07)	1.50	4.25
a.		Wmk. upright ('04)	16.00	1.75
b.		Thick paper ('08)	22.50	2.00
24	A5	2p dull vio ('04)	24.00	32.50
a.		2p reddish pur ('12)	260.00	310.00
25	A5	2½p ultramarine	35.00	10.00
a.		2½p deep blue	300.00	200.00
26	A5	6p orange ('05)	50.00	57.50
27	A5	1sh bis brn ('05)	50.00	40.00
28	A5	5sh dark gray green	175.00	160.00
a.		3sh green	160.00	140.00
29	A6	5sh dull red ('05)	240.00	160.00
		Nos. 22-29 (8)	582.50	466.00
		Nos. 22-29 (8), ovptd. "SPECIMEN"	700.00	

A7   A8

King George V
1912-14

No.	Type	Description	Unused	Used
30	A7	½p yel grn	3.00	3.75
31	A7	1p red	5.50	2.75
32	A7	2p brn vio	27.50	24.00
33	A7	2½p deep ultra	24.00	25.00
34	A7	6p orange	17.50	22.50
35	A7	1sh bis brn	40.00	37.50
36	A8	3sh dark green	100.00	95.00
37	A8	5sh brown red	115.00	120.00
38	A8	5sh plum ('14)	260.00	260.00
39	A8	10sh red, green	200.00	260.00
40	A8	£1 black, red	525.00	600.00
		Nos. 30-40 (11)	1,317.	1,450.

For overprints see Nos. MR1-MR3.

1921-29 — Wmk. 4

No.	Type	Description	Unused	Used
41	A7	½p yellow green	3.50	4.50
42	A7	1p red ('24)	6.00	2.10
43	A7	2p brown vio ('23)	22.00	8.50
44	A7	2½p dark blue	22.00	20.00
a.		2½p Prussian blue ('29)	375.00	550.00
45	A7	2½p vio, yel ('23)	6.00	42.50
46	A7	6p orange ('25)	10.00	45.00
47	A7	1sh bister brown	21.00	57.50
48	A8	3sh dk green ('23)	100.00	190.00
		Nos. 41-48 (8)	190.50	370.10

No. 43 Surcharged   [2½D]

1928

No.	Type	Description	Unused	Used
52	A7	2½p on 2p brn vio	1,300.	1,400.
a.		Double surcharge	45,000.	

Beware of forged surcharges.

King George V — A9

1929-31 — Perf. 14

No.	Type	Description	Unused	Used
54	A9	½p green	1.40	3.25
55	A9	1p scarlet	4.00	.90
56	A9	2p gray	4.00	3.25
57	A9	2½p blue	4.50	2.50
58	A9	4p deep orange	22.00	15.00
59	A9	6p brown violet	22.00	15.00
60	A9	1sh black, green	25.00	37.50
a.		1sh black, emerald	25.00	37.50
61	A9	2sh6p red, blue	67.50	67.50
62	A9	5sh green, yel	105.00	120.00
63	A9	10sh red, green	225.00	260.00

Wmk. 3

No.	Type	Description	Unused	Used
64	A9	£1 black, red	350.00	425.00
		Nos. 54-64 (11)	830.40	949.90

Issue dates: 4p, 1931, others, Sept. 2.

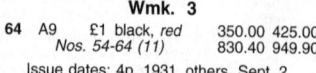

Romney Marsh Ram — A10

Iceberg A11

Whaling Ship — A12

A13 — "Port Louis"

Map of the Islands A14

South Georgia A15

Blue Whale A16

Government House A17   King Penguin — A19

Battle Memorial — A18   Coat of Arms — A20   King George V — A21

1933, Jan. 2 — Wmk. 4 — Perf. 12

No.	Type	Description	Unused	Used
65	A10	½p green & blk	3.75	10.00
66	A11	1p dl red & blk	3.75	2.50
67	A12	1½p lt bl & blk	20.00	23.00
68	A13	2p ol brn & blk	15.00	25.00
69	A14	3p dl vio & blk	24.00	30.00
70	A15	4p orange & blk	25.00	25.00
71	A16	6p gray & black	65.00	85.00
72	A17	1sh ol grn & blk	70.00	100.00
73	A18	2sh6p dp vio & blk	225.00	340.00
74	A19	5sh yellow & blk	900.00	1,250.
a.		5sh yellow orange & black	2,750.	2,900.
75	A20	10sh lt brn & blk	800.00	1,350.
76	A21	£1 rose & black	2,400.	3,000.
		Nos. 65-76 (12)	4,551.	6,240.

Cent. of the permanent occupation of the islands as a British colony.

Common Design Types pictured following the introduction.

Silver Jubilee Issue
Common Design Type
1935, May 7 — Perf. 11x12

No.	Type	Description	Unused	Used
77	CD301	1p carmine & ...	...	...
78	CD301	2½p ultra & brown	12.50	2.10
79	CD301	4p indigo & grn	19.00	6.75
80	CD301	1sh brn vio & ind	15.00	4.00
		Nos. 77-80 (4)	50.00	13.35
		Set, never hinged	75.00	

Coronation Issue
Common Design Type
1937, May 12 — Perf. 11x11½

No.	Type	Description	Unused	Used
81	CD302	½p deep green	.25	.25
82	CD302	1p dark carmine	.75	.55
83	CD302	2½p deep ultra	1.90	1.50
		Nos. 81-83 (3)	2.90	2.30
		Set, never hinged	4.00	

Whale Jawbones (Centennial Monument) — A22

Nos. 85, 86A, Black-necked swan. Nos. 85B, 86, Battle memorial. 2½p, 3p, Flock of sheep. 4p, Upland goose. 6p, R.R.S. "Discovery II." 9p, R.R.S. "William Scoresby." 1sh, Mt. Sugar Top. 1sh3p, Turkey vultures. 2sh6p, Gentoo penguins. 5sh, Sea lions. 10sh, Deception Island. £1, Arms of Colony.

1938-46 — Perf. 12

No.	Type	Description	Unused	Used
84	A22	½p green & blk	.25	.75
85	A22	1p red & black	2.50	1.00
a.		1p rose carmine & black	22.50	1.00
85B	A22	1p dk vio & blk	2.00	2.00
86	A22	2p dk vio & blk	1.30	1.00
86A	A22	2p rose car & black	1.40	4.00
87	A22	2½p deep bl & black	1.00	.50
87A	A22	3p deep bl & black	5.50	6.50
88	A22	4p rose vio & black	2.75	1.75
89	A22	6p brown & blk	7.50	4.25
90	A22	9p sl bl & blk	17.50	4.25
91	A22	1sh dull blue	25.00	5.00
92	A22	1sh3p carmine & blk	2.00	1.50
93	A22	2sh6p gray black	40.00	22.50
94	A22	5sh org brown & ultra	100.00	90.00
a.		5sh yel brown & indigo	625.00	150.00
95	A22	10sh org blk & blk	90.00	62.50
96	A22	£1 dk vio & blk	90.00	75.00
		Nos. 84-96 (16)	388.70	282.50
		Set, never hinged	600.00	

Issued: Nos. 85B, 86A, 3p, 7/14/41; 1sh3p, 12/10/46; No. 94a, 1942; others, 1/3/38. See Nos. 101-102. For overprints see Nos. 2L1-2L8, 3L1-3L8, 4L1-4L8.

> **Catalogue values for unused stamps in this section, from this point to the end of the section, are for Never Hinged items.**

Peace Issue
Common Design Type
Perf. 13½x14
1946, Oct. 7 — Engr. — Wmk. 4

No.	Type	Description	Unused	Used
97	CD303	1p purple	.35	.80
98	CD303	3p deep blue	.55	.55

Silver Wedding Issue
Common Design Types
1948, Nov. 1 — Photo. — Perf. 14x14½

No.	Type	Description	Unused	Used
99	CD304	2½p bright ultra	2.10	1.10

Engr.; Name Typo.
Perf. 11½x11

No.	Type	Description	Unused	Used
100	CD305	£1 purple	110.00	82.50

Types of 1938-46
2½p, Upland goose. 6p, R.R.S. "Discovery II."

Perf. 12
1949, June 15 — Engr. — Wmk. 4

No.	Type	Description	Unused	Used
101	A22	2½p dp blue & black	6.75	8.50
102	A22	6p gray black	6.75	4.50

UPU Issue
Common Design Types
Engr.; Name Typo. on 3p, 1sh3p
1949, Oct. 10   *Perf. 13½, 11x11½*

103	CD306	1p violet	1.90	1.10
104	CD307	3p indigo	5.25	4.00
105	CD308	1sh3p green	4.00	3.50
106	CD309	2sh blue	4.50	9.50
	Nos. 103-106 (4)		15.65	18.10

Sheep
A35

Arms of the
Colony — A36

Designs: 1p, R.M.S. Fitzroy. 2p Upland goose. 2½p, Map. 4p, Auster plane. 6p, M.S.S. John Biscoe. 9p, "Two Sisters" peaks. 1sh, Gentoo penguins. 1sh 3p, Kelp goose and gander. 2sh 6p, Sheep shearing. 5sh, Battle memorial. 10sh, Sea lion and clapmatch. £1, Hulk of "Great Britain."

Perf. 13½x13, 13x13½

1952, Jan. 2   **Engr.**   **Wmk. 4**

107	A35	½p green	1.30	1.10
108	A35	1p red	2.60	.55
109	A35	2p violet	4.75	3.25
110	A35	2½p ultra & blk	2.10	.70
111	A36	3p deep ultra	2.40	1.30
112	A35	4p claret	12.50	2.00
113	A35	6p yellow brn	14.00	1.30
114	A35	9p orange yel	12.50	2.60
115	A36	1sh black	29.00	1.10
116	A35	1sh3p red orange	19.00	7.00
117	A36	2sh6p olive	22.50	13.50
118	A36	5sh red violet	20.00	11.00
119	A35	10sh gray	30.00	19.00
120	A35	£1 black	37.50	25.00
	Nos. 107-120 (14)		210.15	89.40

WAR TAX STAMPS

Regular Issue of 1912-14 Overprinted

1918, Oct. 7   **Wmk. 3**   *Perf. 14*

MR1	A7	½p yellow green	.55	7.25
MR2	A7	1p red	.55	4.00
a.		Double overprint	3,500.	
MR3	A7	1sh bister brown	6.50	52.50
a.		Pair, one without overprint	16,500.	
	Nos. MR1-MR3 (3)		7.60	63.75

No. MR3a probably is caused by a foldover and is not constant.

FALKLAND ISLANDS DEPENDENCIES

> Catalogue values for unused stamps in this section are for Never Hinged items.

Map of Falkland Islands — A1

Engr., Center Litho. in Black
1946, Feb. 1   **Wmk. 4**   *Perf. 12*

1L1	A1	½p yellow green	1.10	3.50
1L2	A1	1p blue violet	1.30	1.90
1L3	A1	2p deep carmine	1.30	2.60
1L4	A1	3p ultramarine	1.90	5.25
1L5	A1	4p deep plum	2.40	5.00
1L6	A1	6p orange yellow	3.75	5.25
1L7	A1	9p brown	2.25	4.00
1L8	A1	1sh rose violet	3.00	5.00
	Nos. 1L1-1L8 (8)		17.00	32.50

Nos. 1L1-1L8 were reissued in 1948, printed on more opaque paper with the lines of the map finer and clearer. Value for set, unused or used $120.
See No. 1L13.

Common Design Types pictured following the introduction.

Peace Issue
Common Design Type
1946, Oct. 4   *Perf. 13½x14*

1L9	CD303	1p purple	.50	.50
1L10	CD303	3p deep blue	.90	.50

Silver Wedding Issue
Common Design Types
1948, Dec. 6   **Photo.**   *Perf. 14x14½*

1L11	CD304	2½p brt ultra	1.75	3.25

Perf. 11½x11
Engr.

1L12	CD305	1sh blue violet	2.50	2.75

Type of 1946
1949, Mar. 6   *Perf. 12*
Center Litho. in Black

1L13	A1	2½p deep blue	8.00	4.25

UPU Issue
Common Design Types
Engr.; Name Typo. on 2p, 3p
1949, Oct. 10   *Perf. 13½, 11x11½*

1L14	CD306	1p violet	1.25	3.00
1L15	CD307	2p deep carmine	5.25	4.00
1L16	CD308	3p indigo	4.00	2.25
1L17	CD309	6p red orange	5.00	4.25
	Nos. 1L14-1L17 (4)		15.50	14.00

ISSUES FOR THE SEPARATE ISLANDS

Graham Land

Nos. 84, 85B, 86A, 87A, 88-91
Overprinted in Red

1944, Feb. 12   **Wmk. 4**   *Perf. 12*

2L1	A22	½p green & black	.50	2.10
2L2	A22	1p dk vio & black	.50	1.10
2L3	A22	2p rose car & blk	.60	1.10
2L4	A22	3p deep bl & blk	.60	1.10
2L5	A22	4p rose vio & blk	2.10	1.90
2L6	A22	6p brown & black	22.50	2.75
2L7	A22	9p slate bl & blk	1.50	2.00
2L8	A22	1sh dull blue	1.50	2.00
	Nos. 2L1-2L8 (8)		29.80	14.05

South Georgia

1944, Apr. 3   **Wmk. 4**   *Perf. 12*

3L1	A22	½p green & black	.40	2.25
3L2	A22	1p dark vio & blk	.40	1.10
3L3	A22	2p rose car & blk	.60	1.10
3L4	A22	3p deep bl & blk	.60	1.10
3L5	A22	4p rose vio & blk	2.25	2.00

3L6	A22	6p brown & black	22.50	2.50
3L7	A22	9p slate bl & blk	1.50	2.00
3L8	A22	1sh dull blue	1.50	2.00
	Nos. 3L1-3L8 (8)		29.75	14.05

South Orkneys

1944, Feb. 21   **Wmk. 4**   *Perf. 12*

4L1	A22	½p green & black	.50	2.10
4L2	A22	1p dark vio & blk	.50	1.10
4L3	A22	2p rose car & blk	.80	1.10
4L4	A22	3p deep bl & blk	.80	1.10
4L5	A22	4p rose vio & blk	2.25	2.00
4L6	A22	6p brown & black	22.50	2.50
4L7	A22	9p slate bl & blk	1.50	2.00
4L8	A22	1sh dull blue	1.50	1.75
	Nos. 4L1-4L8 (8)		30.35	13.65

South Shetlands

1944   **Wmk. 4**   *Perf. 12*

5L1	A22	½p green & black	.50	2.10
5L2	A22	1p dark vio & blk	.50	1.10
5L3	A22	2p rose car & blk	.60	1.10
5L4	A22	3p deep bl & blk	.60	1.10
5L5	A22	4p rose vio & blk	2.25	2.00
5L6	A22	6p brown & black	22.50	2.50
5L7	A22	9p slate bl & blk	1.50	2.00
5L8	A22	1sh dull blue	1.50	2.00
	Nos. 5L1-5L8 (8)		29.95	13.90

FAR EASTERN REPUBLIC

'fär 'ē-stərn ri-'pə-blik

LOCATION — In Siberia east of Lake Baikal
GOVT. — Republic
AREA — 900,745 sq. mi.
POP. — 1,560,000 (approx. 1920)
CAPITAL — Chita

A short-lived independent government was established here in 1920.

100 Kopecks = 1 Ruble

Watermark

Wmk. 171 — Diamonds

Vladivostok Issue
Russian Stamps Surcharged or Overprinted

a

b

---

c

On Stamps of 1909-17
Perf. 14, 14½x15, 13½
1920   **Unwmk.**

2	A14(a)	2k green	10.00	10.00
3	A14(a)	3k red	10.00	10.00
4	A11(b)	3k on 35k red brn & grn	40.00	50.00
5	A15(a)	4k carmine	10.00	12.00
6	A11(b)	4k on 70k brn & org	10.00	12.00
8	A11(b)	7k on 15k red brn & bl	2.00	2.00
a.		Inverted surcharge	100.00	
b.		Pair, one ovptd. "DBP" only	100.00	
9	A15(a)	10k dark blue	75.00	55.00
a.		Overprint on back	90.00	
10	A12(c)	10k on 3½r mar & lt grn	25.00	25.00
11	A11(a)	14k blue & rose	45.00	35.00
12	A11(a)	15k red brn & bl	30.00	25.00
13	A8(a)	20k blue & car	125.00	100.00
14	A11(b)	20k on 14k bl & rose	10.00	8.00
a.		Surcharge on back	30.00	
15	A11(a)	25k green & vio	25.00	15.00
16	A11(a)	35k red brn & org	50.00	35.00
17	A8(a)	50k brn vio & org	10.00	12.00
18	A9(a)	1r pale brn, dk brn & org	750.00	750.00

On Stamps of 1917
Imperf

21	A14(a)	1k orange	15.00	10.00
22	A14(a)	2k gray grn	15.00	10.00
23	A14(a)	3k red	15.00	10.00
25	A11(b)	7k on 15k red brn & dp bl	2.00	5.00
a.		Pair, one ovptd. "DBP" only	100.00	
b.		Pair, one ovptd "DBP" only	100.00	
26	A12(c)	10k on 3½r mar & lt grn	15.00	15.00
27	A9(a)	1r pale brn, brn & red org	20.00	20.00

On Stamps of Siberia 1919
Perf. 14, 14½x15

30	A14(a)	35k on 2k green	5.00	8.00
a.		"DBP" on back	25.00	50.00

Imperf

31	A14(a)	35k on 2k green	30.00	25.00
32	A14(a)	70k on 1k orange	7.50	10.00

Counterfeit surcharges and overprints abound, including digital forgeries.

On Russia Nos. AR2, AR3

A1

Perf. 14½x15
Wmk. 171

35	A1(b)	1k on 5k green, buff	20.00	15.00
36	A1(b)	2k on 10k brown, buff	30.00	30.00

The letters on these stamps resembling "DBP," are the Russian initials of "Dalne Vostochnaya Respublika" (Far Eastern Republic).

Chita Issue

A2   A2a

1921   **Unwmk.**   **Typo.**   *Imperf.*

38	A2	2k gray green	1.50	1.50
39	A2a	4k rose	3.00	3.00
40	A2	5k claret	3.00	3.00
41	A2a	10k blue	2.50	2.50
	Nos. 38-41 (4)		10.00	10.00

For overprints see Nos. 62-65.

Blagoveshchensk Issue

A3

1921   Litho.   Imperf.
42	A3	2r red	2.75	2.00
43	A3	3r dark green	2.75	2.00
44	A3	5r dark blue	2.75	2.00
a.		Tête bêche pair	45.00	30.00
45	A3	15r dark brown	2.75	2.00
46	A3	30r dark violet	2.75	2.00
a.		Tête bêche pair	35.00	30.00
		Nos. 42-46 (5)	13.75	10.00

Remainders of Nos. 42-46 were canceled in colored crayon or by typographed bars. These sell for half of foregoing values.

Chita Issue

A4   A5

1922   Litho.   Imperf.
49	A4	1k orange	.75	.85
50	A4	3k dull red	.40	.45
51	A5	4k dp rose & buff	.40	.45
52	A4	5k orange brown	.80	.45
53	A4	7k light blue	1.50	1.50
a.		Perf. 11½	2.00	2.50
b.		Rouletted 9	3.00	3.00
c.		Perf. 11½x rouletted	6.50	6.50
54	A5	10k dk blue & red	.60	.65
55	A4	15k dull rose	.80	1.10
56	A5	20k blue & red	.80	1.10
57	A5	30k green & red org	1.00	1.10
58	A5	50k black & red org	2.25	2.25
		Nos. 49-58 (10)	9.30	9.90

The 4k exists with "4" omitted. Value $100.

Vladivostok Issue

Stamps of 1921
Overprinted in Red

1922   Imperf.
62	A2	2k gray green	35.00	25.00
a.		Inverted overprint	250.00	
63	A2a	4k rose	35.00	25.00
a.		Inverted overprint	250.00	
b.		Double overprint	250.00	
64	A2	5k claret	35.00	35.00
a.		Inverted overprint	100.00	
b.		Double overprint	350.00	
65	A2a	10k blue	35.00	35.00
a.		Inverted overprint	100.00	
		Nos. 62-65 (4)	140.00	120.00

Russian revolution of Nov. 1917, 5th anniv. Once in the setting the figures "22" of 1922 have the bottom stroke curved instead of straight. Value, each $75.

Vladivostok Issue

Russian Stamps of
1922-23 Surcharged in
Black or Red

1923   Imperf.
66	A50	1k on 100r red	.40	1.00
a.		Inverted surcharge	60.00	
67	A50	2k on 70r violet	.40	.75
68	A49	5k on 10r blue (R)	.40	.75
69	A50	10k on 50r brown	.90	1.25
a.		Inverted surcharge	250.00	

Perf. 14½x15
70	A50	1k on 100r red	.90	1.25
		Nos. 66-70 (5)	3.00	5.00

OCCUPATION STAMPS

Issued under Occupation of General Semenov

Chita Issue

Russian Stamps of 1909-18
Surcharged

a   b

c

1920   Unwmk.   Perf. 14, 14x15½
N1	A15 (a)	1r on 4k car	150.00	100.00
N2	A8 (b)	2r50k on 20k bl & car	40.00	30.00
N3	A14 (c)	5r on 5k claret	25.00	40.00
a.		Double surcharge	65.00	
N4	A11 (a)	10r on 70k brn & org	20.00	25.00
		Nos. N1-N4 (4)	235.00	195.00

FAROE ISLANDS

'far-ü 'i-lənds

(The Faroes)

LOCATION — North Atlantic Ocean
GOVT. — Part of the Kingdom of Denmark
AREA — 540 sq. mi.
POP. — 52,347 (1984)
CAPITAL — Thorshavn

100 Ore = 1 Krone

Denmark No. 97
Handstamp Surcharged

1919, Jan.   Typo.   Perf. 14x14½
1	A16	2o on 5o green	1,400.	475.00
		Never hinged	3,650.	

Counterfeits of surcharge exist. Denmark No. 88a, the bisect, was used with Denmark No. 97 in Faroe Islands Jan. 3-23, 1919.

Denmark Nos. 220, 224, 238A, 224C Surcharged in Blue or Black

Nos. 2, 5-6   No. 3

No. 4

1940-41   Engr.   Perf. 13
2	A32	20o on 1o ('41)	45.00	110.00
3	A32	20o on 5o ('41)	45.00	35.00
4	A30	20o on 15o (Bk)	60.00	22.50
5	A32	20o on 5o (Bk)	300.00	90.00
6	A32	60o on 6o (Bk)	125.00	250.00
		Nos. 2-6 (5)	575.00	507.50
		Set, never hinged	1,150.	

Issued during British administration.

FERNANDO PO

fər-'nan-‚dō 'pō

LOCATION — An island in the Gulf of Guinea off west Africa.
GOVT. — Spanish Colony
AREA — 800 sq. mi.
POP. — 62,612 (1960)
CAPITAL — Santa Isabel

Together with the islands of Elobey, Annobon and Corisco, Fernando Po came under the administration of Spanish Guinea. Postage stamps of Spanish Guinea were used until 1960.

100 Centimos = 1 Escudo = 2.50 Pesetas
100 Centimos = 1 Peseta
1000 Milesimas = 100 Centavos = 1 Peso (1882)

FORERUNNERS

Crowned Circle handstamp type VII and Numeral Cancellation type B are pictured in the Crowned Circle Handstamps and Great Britain Used Abroad section.

P.O. at St. Thomas opened Apr. 1, 1858; canceler supplied 1874; closed in 1877

1859
A1	I	Crowned circle handstamp Type VII inscribed "FERNANDO-P" in red, on cover	6,250.

Earliest known use: 2/19/59.

STAMPS OF GREAT BRITAIN USED IN FERNANDO PO
Canceled "247"

1874-77
A2	4p vermilion (#43, P 13, 14)	—
A3	4p vermilion (#69, P 15)	—
A4	6p gray (#62, P 13-16)	—

Issued under Spanish Dominion

Isabella   Alfonso
II — A1   XII — A2

1868   Unwmk.   Typo.   Perf. 14
1	A1	20c brown	450.00	140.00
a.		20c red brown	525.00	140.00

No. 1 is valued in the grade of fine, as illustrated. Examples with very fine centering are uncommon and sell for more. Forgeries exist.

1879
Centimos de Peseta
2	A2	5c green	57.50	15.00
3	A2	10c rose	42.50	15.00
4	A2	50c blue	100.00	15.00
		Nos. 2-4 (3)	200.00	45.00

1882-89
Centavos de Peso
5	A2	1c green	9.50	5.50
6	A2	2c rose	18.00	8.75
7	A2	5c gray blue	60.00	12.00
8	A2	10c dk brown ('89)	82.50	6.75
		Nos. 5-8 (4)	170.00	33.00

Nos. 5-7 Handstamp
Surcharged in Blue,
Black or Violet — a

1884-95
9	A2	50c on 1c green ('95)	120.00	19.00
11	A2	50c on 2c rose	32.00	6.00
12	A2	50c on 5c blue ('87)	150.00	25.00
		Nos. 9-12 (3)	302.00	50.00

Values above are for examples surcharged in black. Stamps surcharged in violet or blue are worth about 25% more.
Inverted and double surcharges exist. No. 12 exists overprinted in carmine. Value $100.

King Alfonso XIII — A4

1894-97   Perf. 14
13	A4	⅛c slate ('96)	22.00	3.00
14	A4	2c rose ('96)	15.50	2.50
15	A4	5c blue grn ('97)	16.00	2.50
16	A4	6c dk violet ('96)	13.00	3.00
17	A4	10c blk vio ('94)	450.00	115.00
18	A4	10c lake ('95)	50.00	8.75
19	A4	10c brn ('96)	10.50	2.50
20	A4	12½c dk brown ('96)	11.50	3.00
21	A4	20c slate bl ('96)	11.50	3.00
22	A4	25c claret ('96)	23.00	3.00
		Nos. 13-22 (10)	623.00	146.25

Stamps of 1894-97 Handstamped in Blue, Black or Red

b   c

Type "b" Surcharge
1896-98
22A	A4	5c on ⅛c slate (Bl)	100.00	27.50
23	A4	5c on 2c rose (Bl)	50.00	16.50
23A	A4	5c on 6c dk vio (Bl)	150.00	45.00
24	A4	5c on 10c brn vio (Bl)	150.00	45.00
24A	A4	5c on 10c org brn (Bl)	150.00	45.00
24B	A4	5c on 10c dk brn (Bk)	67.50	27.50
25	A4	5c on 12½c brn (Bl)	37.50	13.00
a.		Black surcharge	37.50	13.00
25B	A4	5c on 20c sl bl (R)	150.00	45.00
25C	A4	5c on 25c claret (Bk)	150.00	35.00
		Nos. 22A-25C (9)	1,005.	299.50

Type "c" Surcharge
26	A4	5c on ⅛c slate (Bk)	32.50	6.75
27	A4	5c on 2c rose (Bl)	32.50	6.75
a.		Black surcharge	32.50	6.75
28	A4	5c on 5c green (R)	160.00	22.00
29	A4	5c on 6c dk vio (R)	23.00	14.00
a.		Violet surcharge	24.00	15.50
30	A4	5c on 10c org brn (Bk)	210.00	27.50
30A	A4	5c on 10c dk brn (Bk)	160.00	26.00
30B	A4	5c on 10c lake (Bl)	400.00	110.00
31	A4	5c on 12½c brn (Bl)	70.00	11.00
32	A4	5c on 20c sl bl (R)	40.00	10.50
33	A4	5c on 25c claret (Bk)	37.50	11.00
a.		Blue surcharge	37.50	13.50
		Nos. 26-33 (10)	1,165.	245.50

Exist surcharged in other colors.

Type "a" Srch. in Blue or Black
1898-99
34	A4	50c on 2c rose	92.50	11.50
35	A4	50c on 10c brn vio	220.00	33.00
36	A4	50c on 10c lake	230.00	33.00
37	A4	50c on 10c org brn	220.00	33.00
38	A4	50c on 12½c brn (Bk)	190.00	22.00

The "a" surch. also exists on ⅛c, 5c & 25c. Values, $325, $225 and $210, respectively.

Revenue Stamps Privately Handstamped in Blue

Arms

A5   A6

1897-98   *Imperf.*
39	A5	5c on 10c rose	28.00	12.50
40	A6	10c rose	24.00	11.00

Revenue Stamps Handstamped in Black or Red

A7

A8

A9

Arms — A9a

1899   *Imperf.*
41	A7	15c on 10c green	45.00	23.00
a.		Blue surcharge, vertical	39.00	21.00
42	A8	10c on 25c green	120.00	65.00
43	A9	15c on 25c green	190.00	120.00
43A	A9a	15c on 25c green (R)	1,800.	1,100.
b.		Black surcharge	1,800.	1,100.

Surcharge on No. 41 is either horizontal, inverted or vertical.
On No. 42 "CORREOS" is ovptd. in red.
On Nos. 43A and 43Ab, the signature is always in black.

King Alfonso XIII — A10

Double-lined shaded letters at sides.

1899   *Perf. 14*
44	A10	1m orange brn	2.40	.45
45	A10	2m orange brn	2.40	.45
46	A10	3m orange brn	2.40	.45
47	A10	4m orange brn	2.40	.45
48	A10	5m orange brn	2.40	.45
49	A10	1c black vio	2.40	.45
50	A10	2c dk blue grn	2.40	.45
51	A10	3c dk brown	2.40	.45
52	A10	4c orange	13.00	1.10
53	A10	5c carmine rose	2.50	.45
54	A10	6c dark blue	2.50	.45
55	A10	8c gray brn	8.00	.45
56	A10	10c vermilion	5.25	.45
57	A10	15c slate grn	5.25	.45
58	A10	20c maroon	14.50	1.10
59	A10	40c violet	100.00	19.00
60	A10	60c black	100.00	19.00
61	A10	80c red brown	100.00	19.00
62	A10	1p yellow grn	325.00	92.50
63	A10	2p slate blue	325.00	95.00
		Nos. 44-63 (20)	1,020.	252.55

Nos. 44-63 exist imperf. Value for set, $1,650.
See Nos. 66-85. For surcharges see Nos. 64-65, 88-88B.

1900   Surcharged type "a"
64	A10	50c on 20c maroon	16.00	2.50
a.		Blue surcharge	32.00	4.75

Surcharged type "b"
64B	A10	5c on 20c maroon	300.00	40.00

Surcharged type "c"
65	A10	5c on 20c maroon	9.50	2.40
		Nos. 64-65 (3)	325.50	44.90

1900   Dated "1900"

Solid letters at sides.
66	A10	1m black	3.00	.50
67	A10	2m black	3.00	.50
68	A10	3m black	3.00	.50
69	A10	4m black	3.00	.50
70	A10	5m black	3.00	.50
71	A10	1c green	3.00	.50
72	A10	2c violet	3.00	.50
73	A10	3c rose	3.00	.50
74	A10	4c black brn	3.00	.50
75	A10	5c blue	3.00	.50
76	A10	6c orange	3.00	.50
77	A10	8c bronze grn	3.00	.50
78	A10	10c claret	3.00	.50
79	A10	15c dk violet	3.00	.50
80	A10	20c olive brn	3.00	.50
81	A10	40c brown	7.75	2.25
82	A10	60c green	16.50	2.50
83	A10	80c dark blue	17.50	3.75
84	A10	1p red brown	110.00	30.00
85	A10	2p orange	190.00	62.50
		Nos. 66-85 (20)	386.75	108.50
		Set, never hinged	750.00	

Nos. 66-85 exist imperf. Value, set $2,500.

Revenue Stamps Overprinted or Surcharged with Handstamp in Red or Black

A11

A12

1900   *Imperf.*
86	A11	10c blue (R)	37.50	17.50
87	A12	5c on 10c blue	100.00	40.00
		Set, never hinged	175.00	

Nos. 52 and 80 Surcharged type "a" in Violet or Black

1900
88	A10	50c on 4c orange (V)	14.00	4.00
a.		Green surcharge	22.50	12.00
88B	A10	50c on 20c ol brn	14.00	3.50
		Set, never hinged	37.50	

A13

A14

1901   *Perf. 14*
89	A13	1c black	2.75	.90
90	A13	2c orange brn	2.75	.90
91	A13	3c dk violet	2.75	.90
92	A13	4c lt violet	2.75	.90
93	A13	5c orange red	1.75	.90
94	A13	10c violet brn	1.75	.90
95	A13	25c dp blue	1.75	.90
96	A13	50c claret	2.75	.90
97	A13	75c dk brown	2.00	.90
98	A13	1p blue grn	62.50	6.00
99	A13	2p red brown	39.00	9.00
100	A13	3p olive grn	39.00	12.00
101	A13	4p dull red	38.00	12.00
102	A13	5p dk green	47.50	12.00
103	A13	10p buff	105.00	35.00
		Nos. 89-103 (15)	352.00	94.10
		Set, never hinged	650.00	

Dated "1902"

1902   Control Numbers on Back
104	A13	5c dk green	2.60	.45
105	A13	10c slate	2.90	.50
106	A13	25c claret	6.25	1.00
107	A13	50c violet brn	15.00	3.25
108	A13	75c lt violet	15.00	3.25
109	A13	1p car rose	18.50	4.00
110	A13	2p olive grn	40.00	9.50
111	A13	5p orange red	57.50	20.00
		Nos. 104-111 (8)	157.75	41.95
		Set, never hinged	250.00	

Exist imperf. Value for set, $1,500.

Dated "1903"

1903   *Perf. 14*

Control Numbers on Back
112	A14	¼c dk violet	.45	.25
113	A14	½c black	.45	.25
114	A14	1c scarlet	.45	.25
115	A14	3c dk green	.45	.30
116	A14	4c blue grn	.45	.30
117	A14	4c violet	.45	.30
118	A14	5c rose lake	.50	.30
119	A14	10c orange buff	.60	.45
120	A14	15c blue green	2.50	1.00
121	A14	25c red brown	2.75	1.25
122	A14	50c black brn	4.50	2.00
123	A14	75c carmine	16.50	3.50
124	A14	1p dk brown	25.00	6.00
125	A14	2p dk olive grn	32.50	7.50
126	A14	3p claret	32.50	7.50
127	A14	4p dark blue	40.00	12.50
128	A14	5p dp dull blue	60.00	16.00
129	A14	10p dull red	130.00	27.50
		Nos. 112-129 (18)	350.05	87.15
		Set, never hinged	600.00	

Dated "1905"

1905   Control Numbers on Back
136	A14	1c dp violet	.40	.30
137	A14	2c black	.40	.30
138	A14	3c vermilion	.40	.30
139	A14	4c dp green	.40	.30
140	A14	5c blue grn	.45	.35
141	A14	10c violet	1.60	.75
142	A14	15c car lake	1.60	.75
143	A14	25c orange buff	12.50	2.25
144	A14	50c green	8.00	2.75
145	A14	75c red brown	11.00	7.50
146	A14	1p dp gray brn	12.50	7.50
147	A14	2p carmine	20.00	12.50
148	A14	3p deep brown	32.50	14.00
149	A14	4p bronze grn	40.00	18.00
150	A14	5p claret	62.50	25.00
151	A14	10p deep blue	90.00	35.00
		Nos. 136-151 (16)	294.25	127.55
		Set, never hinged	525.00	

King Alfonso XIII — A15

1907   Control Numbers on Back
152	A15	1c blue black	.30	.25
153	A15	2c car rose	.30	.25
154	A15	3c dp violet	.30	.25
155	A15	4c black	.30	.25
156	A15	5c orange buff	.35	.25
157	A15	10c maroon	2.00	.80
158	A15	15c bronze grn	.55	.35
159	A15	25c dk brown	30.00	10.50
160	A15	50c blue green	.35	.30
161	A15	75c vermilion	.45	.30
162	A15	1p dull blue	3.00	.60
163	A15	2p brown	11.00	3.50
164	A15	3p lake	11.00	3.50
165	A15	4p violet	11.00	3.50
166	A15	5p black brn	11.00	3.50
167	A15	10p orange brn	11.00	3.50
		Nos. 152-167 (16)	92.90	31.60
		Set, never hinged	250.00	

No. 157 Handstamp Surcharged in Black, Blue or Red

1908
168	A15	5c on 10c mar (Bk)	2.75	2.00
a.		Blue surcharge	10.00	5.50
b.		Red surcharge	30.00	10.00
169	A15	25c on 10c mar (Bk)	60.00	20.00
		Set, never hinged	77.50	

The surcharge on Nos. 168-169 exist inverted, double, etc. The surcharge also exists on other stamps.

Seville-Barcelona Issue of Spain, 1929, Overprinted in Blue or Red

1929   *Perf. 11*
170	A52	5c rose lake	.25	.25
171	A53	10c green (R)	.25	.25
a.		Perf. 14	.65	.65
172	A50	15c Prus bl (R)	.25	.25
173	A51	20c purple (R)	.25	.25
174	A50	25c brt rose	.25	.25
175	A52	30c black brn	.25	.25
176	A53	40c dk blue (R)	.70	.70
177	A51	50c dp orange	1.50	1.50
178	A52	1p blue blk (R)	5.75	5.75
179	A53	4p deep rose	27.50	27.50
180	A53	10p brown	35.00	35.00
		Nos. 170-180 (11)	71.95	71.95
		Set, never hinged	135.00	

FIJI

'fē-ˌjē

LOCATION — Group of 332 islands (106 inhabited) in the South Pacific Ocean east of New Hebrides
GOVT. — British Colony
AREA — 7,078 sq. mi.
POP. — 646,561 (1981)
CAPITAL — Suva

12 Pence = 1 Shilling
20 Shillings = 1 Pound
100 Cents = 1 Dollar (1872-74)

Catalogue values for unused stamps in this country are for Never Hinged items, beginning with Scott 137 in the regular postage section and Scott B1 in the semi-postal section.

Values for unused stamps are for examples with original gum as defined in the catalogue introduction except for Nos. 1-10 which are valued without gum. Additionally, Nos. 1-10 are valued with roulettes showing on two or more sides, but expect small faults that do not detract from the appearance of the stamps. Very few examples of Nos. 1-10 will be found free of faults, and these will command substantial premiums.

Watermark

Wmk. 17 — FIJI POSTAGE Across Center Row of Sheet

A1

1870 Unwmk. Typeset *Rouletted*
Thin Quadrille Paper

1	A1	1p black, *pink*	4,250.	4,500.
2	A1	3p black, *pink*	5,000.	4,750.
a.	Comma after "EXPRESS"		7,500.	7,500.
3	A1	6p black, *pink*	2,600.	2,750.
5	A1	1sh black, *pink*	2,100.	2,400.

1871   Thin Vertically Laid Paper

6	A1	1p black, *pink*	1,150.	2,100.
7	A1	3p black, *pink*	1,900.	3,400.
8	A1	6p black, *pink*	1,600.	2,100.
9	A1	9p black, *pink*	3,400.	4,000.
a.	Comma after "EXPRESS"		4,250.	
10	A1	1sh black, *pink*	1,900.	1,900.

This service was established by the *Fiji Times*, a weekly newspaper, for the delivery of the newspaper. Since there was no postal service to the other islands, delivery of letters to agents of the newspaper on the islands was offered to the public.

Nos. 1-5 were printed in the same sheet, one horizontal row of 6 of each (6p, 1sh, 1p, 3p). Nos. 6-10 were printed from the same plate with three 9p replacing three 3p.

The rose tint of the paper is somewhat fugitive and is partially or totally lost on most surviving examples.

A vertical se-tenant strip of four of No. 5 on yellow paper is in the Royal Collection and is considered to be a proof or specimen, ex-Ferrari, and is unique.

A vertical se-tenant strip of four of Nos. 6, 8, 9, 10 exists. Value about $45,000.

A single 1p stamp of the 1871 setting on white wove ordinary paper is in the Royal Collection.

Most used examples have pen cancels.

Covers: Covers bearing Nos. 1-5 are very rare, values starting at about $30,000. Covers bearing Nos 6-10 are very rare, values starting at about $27,500.

As with most 19th-century laid papers, there are perpendicular lines widely spaced apart, which represent the supports in the papermaking grid. These lines are clearly visible and only occasionally are entirely missing on one stamp.

Up to three sets of imitations exist. One on pink laid paper, pin-perforated, measuring

22½x16mm. Originals measure 22½x18½mm. A later printing was made on pink wove paper. Forgeries also exist plus fake cancellations.

Crown and "CR" (Cakobau Rex)
A2   A3

A4

1871 Typo. Wmk. 17 *Perf. 12½*
Wove Paper

15	A2	1p blue	62.50	140.00
16	A3	3p green	125.00	400.00
17	A4	6p rose	170.00	325.00
		Nos. 15-17 (3)	357.50	865.00

Sheets of 50 (10x5).
For overprints and surcharges see Nos. 18-39.

Stamps of 1871 Surcharged in Black

1872, Jan. 13

18	A2	2c on 1p blue	60.00	65.00
a.	2c on 1p pale blue		62.50	75.00
19	A3	6c on 3p green	90.00	90.00
20	A4	12c on 6p rose	125.00	90.00
		Nos. 18-20 (3)	275.00	245.00

Nos. 18-20 with Additional Overprint in Black

b   c

1874, Oct. 10

21	A2(b)	2c on 1p blue	1,250.	315.00
a.	No period after "R"		3,250.	1,150.
22	A2(c)	2c on 1p blue	1,150.	300.00
a.	Invtd. "A" instead of "V"		3,250.	1,500.
b.	Period after "R" is a Maltese Cross		3,250.	1,500.
c.	No period after "R"		3,250.	1,500.
d.	Round raised period after "V"		3,250.	1,500.
e.	Round raised period after "V" and "R"		3,250.	1,500.
23	A3(b)	6c on 3p green	3,250.	1,000.
a.	No period after "R"		5,250.	2,000.
24	A3(c)	6c on 3p green	2,750.	750.00
a.	Inverted "A"		2,100.	1,900.
b.	Period after "R" is a Maltese Cross		5,250.	2,000.
c.	No period after "R"		5,500.	2,000.
d.	Round raised period after "V"		5,500.	2,000.
e.	Round raised period after "V" and "R"		5,500.	2,000.
25	A4(b)	12c on 6p rose	1,050.	260.00
a.	"V.R." inverted		7,500.	
b.	No period after "R"		3,000.	1,150.
26	A4(c)	12c on 6p rose	1,000.	250.00
a.	Inverted "A"		2,900.	1,350.
b.	Period after "R" is a Maltese Cross		3,000.	1,350.
c.	"V.R." inverted		—	7,000.
d.	No period after "R"		3,000.	1,350.
e.	Round raised period after "V"		3,000.	1,350.
f.	Round raised period after "V" and "R"		3,000.	1,350.

Types "b" and "c" were in the same sheet.

Nos. 23-26 with Additional Surcharge in Black or Red

1875

27	A3(b)	2p on 6c on 3p	2,750.	800.00
a.	Period btwn. "2" and "d"		4,500.	1,600.
b.	"V.R." double		5,000.	4,500.
c.	No period after "R"		4,500.	1,600.
28	A3(b)	2p on 6c on 3p (R)	900.00	325.00
a.	Period btwn. "2" and "d"		2,250.	850.00
b.	No period after "R"		2,250.	900.00
29	A3(c)	2p on 6c on 3p	1,900.	600.00
a.	Inverted "A"		4,500.	1,600.
b.	Period after "R" is a Maltese Cross		4,500.	1,600.
c.	No period after "2d"		4,500.	1,600.
d.	No period after "R"		2,250.	900.00
e.	Round raised period after "V"		4,500.	1,600.
f.	Round raised period after "V" and "R"		4,500.	1,600.
30	A3(c)	2p on 6c on 3p (R)	750.00	250.00
a.	Inverted "A"		2,100.	850.00
b.	Period after "R" is a Maltese Cross		2,250.	875.00
c.	No period after "2d"		2,250.	875.00
d.	No period after "R"		2,250.	875.00
e.	Round raised period after "V"		2,250.	875.00
f.	Round raised period after "V" and "R"		2,250.	875.00
31	A4(b)	2p on 12c on 6p	3,250.	1,000.
a.	Period btwn. "2" and "d"			
b.	No period after "2d"			
c.	"2d, VR" double			5,500.
32	A4(c)	2p on 12c on 6p	3,000.	900.00
a.	Inverted "A"		4,500.	1,400.
b.	No period after "2d"			
c.	"2d, VR" double			5,500.
d.	Round raised period after "R"		—	1,200.
e.	Round raised period after "R"		—	1,200.
f.	As "a," with raised period after "V"		3,000.	1,000.
g.	As "a," with raised period after "V" and "R"		4,500.	1,500.

Types of 1871 Overprinted or Surcharged in Black

e   f

1876, Jan. 31   Unwmk.
Wove Paper

33	A2(e)	1p ultramarine	60.00	60.00
a.	Inverted surcharge			
b.	Dbl. impression of stamp		1,000.	
c.	Horiz. pair, imperf vert.		1,000.	
34	A3(e+f)	2p on 3p dk grn	60.00	65.00
a.	Dbl. surch. "Two Pence"			
b.	2p on 3p pale green		70.00	65.00
35	A4(e)	6p rose	70.00	65.00
a.	6p carmine rose		70.00	65.00
b.	Surcharge inverted			
c.	Dbl. impression of stamp		2,850.	
		Nos. 33-35 (3)	190.00	190.00

1877   Laid Paper

36	A2(e)	1p ultramarine	30.00	50.00
a.	Horiz. pair, imperf. vert.		1,100.	
b.	1p deep blue		30.00	50.00
37	A3(e+f)	2p on 3p dk grn	80.00	85.00
		2p on 3p yellow green	80.00	80.00
b.	Perf 10		400.00	
c.	Perf 11		375.00	
d.	Horiz. pair, imperf. vert.		1,100.	
e.	Horiz. pair, imperf. between		1,000.	
38	A3(e+f)	4p on 3p lilac	110.00	27.50
a.	Horiz. pair, imperf. vert.		1,000.	
39	A4(e)	6p rose	60.00	37.50
a.	Horiz. pair, imperf. vert.		800.00	
b.	6p carmine rose		60.00	45.00
		Nos. 36-39 (4)	280.00	200.00

Many of the preceding stamps are known imperforate. They are printer's waste and were never issued.

A12   A13

Queen Victoria
A14   A15

Perf. 10-13½ & Compound
1878-90 Wove Paper Typo.

40	A12	1p ultra ('79)	16.00	16.00
a.	1p blue		65.00	6.50
41	A12	2p green	32.50	1.75
b.	2p ultramarine (error)		40,000.	
42	A12	4p brt vio ('90)	14.00	9.00
a.	4p mauve		27.50	12.00
43	A13	6p brt rose ('80)	14.00	4.75
a.	Printed on both sides		2,500.	2,000.
44	A14	1sh yel brn ('81)	60.00	12.50
a.	1sh deep brown		100.00	32.50

Litho. & Typo.

45	A15	5sh blk & red brn ('82)	75.00	50.00
		Nos. 40-45 (6)	211.50	94.00

No. 41b was not put on sale. All examples were supposed to be destroyed.

A quantity of No. 45 was sold as remainders, canceled-to-order with the following Suva dates: 15.DEC.00; 22.DE.1900; 28.DEC.1900; 12.DEC.01; 15.DEC.01; 16.DE.1901; 21.JUN.02; 15.DEC.02; 15. DE. 1902; and 21.DE.1902. Examples so canceled are worth less than postally used examples. No. 45 imperf was sold only as a remainder, canceled "Suva, 15.DEC.00."

A late printing of the 5sh, made from an electrotyped plate, exists in gray black and red orange, perf 12, differing from No. 45 in many details. It was also sold only as a remainder, canceled "Suva, 15.DEC.00." It is scarce.

For surcharges see Nos. 46-52.

1881-90   *Perf. 10*

40d	A12	1p ultramarine	27.50	3.50

Surcharged type "f" in Black
1878-90   Typo.

46	A12	2p on 3p green	12.00	35.00
47	A12	4p on 1p vio ('90)	75.00	60.00
48	A12	4p on 2p lilac ('83)	100.00	16.00
		Nos. 46-48 (3)	187.00	111.00

Nos. 40-43 Surcharged in Black

g   h

j   k

1891-92   *Perf. 10*

49	A12(g)	½p on 1p ('92)	62.50	80.00
50	A12(h)	2½p on 2p	52.50	55.00
a.	Wider space (2mm) between "2" and "½"		150.00	150.00
51	A12(j)	5p on 4p ('92)	62.50	80.00
52	A13(k)	5p on 6p ('92)	67.50	75.00
a.	"FIVE" and "PENCE" 3mm apart		75.00	85.00
		Nos. 49-52 (4)	245.00	290.00

A18   A20

Fijian Canoe — A19

1891-96   Perf. 10-12 & Compound
53	A18	½p grnsh blk ('92)	2.75	7.00
a.		½p gray	3.75	7.00
54	A19	1p black ('93)	14.00	7.50
55	A19	1p lilac rose ('96)	16.00	1.10
56	A19	2p green ('93)	9.00	.85
57	A20	2½ red brown	6.50	5.50
58	A19	5p ultra ('93)	20.00	8.00
		Nos. 53-58 (6)	68.25	29.95

Edward VII — A22

1903, Feb. 1   Wmk. 2   Perf. 14
59	A22	½p gray grn & pale grn	2.50	2.25
60	A22	1p vio & blk, red	17.00	.65
61	A22	2p vio & orange	4.50	1.40
62	A22	2½p vio & ultra, bl	15.00	3.50
63	A22	3p vio & red vio	1.60	4.00
64	A22	4p violet & blk	1.60	2.75
65	A22	5p vio & green	1.60	2.75
66	A22	6p vio & car rose	1.60	2.00
67	A22	1sh grn & car rose	15.00	77.50
68	A22	5sh green & blk	85.00	170.00
69	A22	£1 gray & ultra	400.00	475.00
		Revenue cancel		75.00
		Nos. 59-68 (10)	145.40	266.80

Numerals of 2p, 4p, 6p and 5sh of type A22 are in color on plain tablet.

1904-12   Ordinary Paper   Wmk. 3
70	A22	½p grn & pale grn ('04)	16.50	3.25
70A	A22	½p green ('08)	15.00	3.50
71	A22	1p vio & black, red ('04)	32.50	.25
72	A22	1p carmine ('06)	16.50	.25
73	A22	2½p ultra ('10)	6.75	7.75

Chalky Paper
74	A22	6p violet ('10)	25.00	40.00
75	A22	1sh grn & car rose ('09)	32.50	42.50
76	A22	1sh black, green ('11)	8.50	11.50
77	A22	5sh grn & scarlet, yel ('11)	72.50	105.00
78	A22	£1 vio & black, red ('12)	360.00	300.00
		Nos. 70-77 (9)	225.75	214.00

George V — A23

Die I

For description of Dies I and II see "Dies of British Colonial Stamps" in Table of Contents.

1912-23   Ordinary Paper
79	A23	¼p brown ('16)	2.75	.40
80	A23	½p green	2.75	1.10
81	A23	1p scarlet	2.75	.50
a.		1p carmine ('16)	2.25	.25
82	A23	2p gray ('14)	2.00	.25
83	A23	2½p ultra ('14)	3.50	3.75
84	A23	3p violet, yel	4.50	9.00
a.		Die II ('21)	3.25	32.00
85	A23	4p black & red, yel ('14)	24.00	22.50
a.		Die II ('23)	3.25	35.00

Chalky Paper
86	A23	5p dl vio & ol grn ('14)	5.50	12.50
87	A23	6p dl vio & red vio ('14)	2.40	6.00
88	A23	1sh black, green ('14)	1.30	14.50
a.		1sh black, blue green, ol back	5.50	67.50
b.		1sh black, emerald ('21)	5.50	67.50
c.		Die II ('22)	3.25	37.50
89	A23	2sh 6p black & red, blue	37.50	35.00
90	A23	5sh grn & scar, yellow	37.50	45.00
91	A23	£1 vio & black, red	300.00	325.00
a.		Die II ('21)	300.00	325.00

		Revenue cancel		52.50

Surface-colored Paper
92	A23	1sh black, green	1.25	14.50
		Nos. 79-90,92 (13)	127.70	165.00

Numerals of ¼p, 1½p, 2p, 4p, 6p, 2sh, 2sh6p and 5sh of type A23 are in color on plain tablet.
For overprints see Nos. MR1-MR2.

Die II

1922-27   Wmk. 4   Ordinary Paper
93	A23	¼p dark brown	3.25	27.50
94	A23	½p green	.85	1.50
95	A23	1p rose red	4.00	1.00
96	A23	1p violet ('27)	1.40	.25
97	A23	1½p rose red ('27)	4.50	1.50
98	A23	2p gray	1.40	.25
a.		"2d" and value tablet omitted		28,000.
99	A23	3p ultra ('23)	3.00	1.20
100	A23	4p blk & red, yel	12.00	7.00
101	A23	5p dl vio & ol green	1.75	2.25
102	A23	6p dl vio & red violet	2.40	1.50

Chalky Paper
103	A23	1sh blk, emerald	9.00	4.00
104	A23	2sh vio & ultra, bl ('27)	30.00	72.50
105	A23	2sh6p blk & red, bl	12.50	35.00
106	A23	5sh vio & scar, yellow	47.50	90.00
		Nos. 93-106 (14)	133.55	245.45

The only known example of No. 98a is the center stamp of an unused block of nine.

Common Design Types pictured following the introduction.

Silver Jubilee Issue
Common Design Type

1935, May 6   Perf. 13½x14
110	CD301	1½p carmine & blue	1.00	9.00
111	CD301	2p gray blk & ultra	1.50	.50
112	CD301	3p blue & brown	2.75	4.50
113	CD301	1sh brt vio & indigo	10.00	15.00
		Nos. 110-113 (4)	15.25	29.00
		Set, never hinged	24.00	

Coronation Issue
Common Design Type

1937, May 12   Perf. 11x11½
114	CD302	1p dark violet	.45	1.25
115	CD302	2p gray black	.45	2.25
116	CD302	3p indigo	.45	2.25
		Nos. 114-116 (3)	1.35	5.75
		Set, never hinged	2.00	

Outrigger Canoe — A24

Fijian Village — A25

Outrigger Canoe A26

Map of Fiji Islands A27

Canoe and Arms of Fiji — A28

Sugar Cane — A29   Spear Fishing at Night — A30

Arms of Fiji — A31

Suva Harbor — A32

River Scene — A33

Fijian House — A34

Papaya Tree — A35   Bugler — A36

Designs: No. 121, Government buildings. 8p, 1sh5p, 1sh6p, Arms of Fiji.

Perf. 13½, 12½ (1p)

		1938-55 Engr. Wmk. 4		
117	A24	½p green	.25	1.00
		Never hinged	.25	
c.		Perf. 14 ('41)	16.00	4.75
		Never hinged	21.00	
d.		Perf. 12 ('48)	.80	4.00
		Never hinged	1.30	
118	A25	1p blue & brn	.40	.25
		Never hinged	.55	
119	A26	1½p rose car (empty canoe)	12.00	.50
		Never hinged	16.00	
120	A27	2p grn & org brn (no "180 degree")	30.00	.50
		Never hinged	42.50	
121	A27	2p mag & grn	.45	.80
		Never hinged	.55	
a.		Perf. 12 ('46)	1.25	.90
		Never hinged	2.10	

Perf. 12½, 13x12 (6p), 14 (8p)
122	A28	3p dp ultra	.80	.40
		Never hinged	1.60	
123	A29	5p rose red & blue	32.50	13.00
		Never hinged	45.00	
124	A29	5p rose red & yel grn	.25	.40
		Never hinged	.25	
125	A27	6p blk (no "180 degree")	45.00	16.00
		Never hinged	62.50	
126	A31	8p rose car	1.40	3.00
		Never hinged	2.75	
a.		Perf. 13 ('50)	.55	3.50
		Never hinged	.75	
127	A30	1sh black & yel	.75	.90
		Never hinged	1.90	

Perf. 14
128	A31	1sh5p car & black	.25	.25
		Never hinged	.30	

128A	A31	1sh6p ultra	2.75	3.50
		Never hinged	3.75	
b.		Perf. 13 ('55)	1.10	20.00
		Never hinged	1.30	

Perf. 12½
129	A32	2sh vio & org	2.00	.55
		Never hinged	2.75	
130	A33	2sh6p brn & grn	2.75	2.00
		Never hinged	5.25	
131	A34	5sh dk vio & grn	2.75	2.25
		Never hinged	5.25	
131A	A35	10sh emer & brn org	27.50	52.50
		Never hinged	45.00	
131B	A36	£1 car & ultra	37.50	65.00
		Never hinged	52.50	
		Nos. 117-131B (18)	199.30	162.80

Issued: 1sh5p, 6/13/40; 5p, 10/1/40; No. 121, 5/19/42; 8p, 11/15/48; 10sh, £1, 3/13/50; 1sh6p, 8/1/50; others, 4/5/38.

Types of 1938-40 Redrawn
Perf. 13½ (1½p, 2p, 6p), 14 (2½p)
		1940-49 Wmk. 4		
132	A26	1½p rose car (man in canoe)	1.00	3.00
a.		Perf. 12 ('49)	.80	1.60
b.		Perf. 14 ('42)	14.50	22.50
133	A27	2p grn & org brn ("180 degree")	12.50	17.50
134	A27	2½p grn & org brn	.50	1.25
a.		Perf. 12 ('48)	.80	.60
b.		Perf. 14 ('42)	.55	1.00
135	A27	6p blk ("180 degree")	2.50	2.40
a.		Perf. 12 ('47)	1.40	1.75
		Nos. 132-135 (4)	16.50	24.15

No. 132, type A26, has a man sitting in the canoe.
Nos. 133-135, type A27, have 180 degree added to the lower right hand corner of the design.
Issued: 2½p, Jan. 6, 1942; others Oct. 1, 1940.

No. 133 Surcharged in Black

1941, Feb. 10   Perf. 13½
136	A27	2½p on 2p grn & org brn	1.50	1.00
		Never hinged	2.50	

Catalogue values for unused stamps in this section, from this point to the end of the section, are for Never Hinged items.

Peace Issue
Common Design Type
1946, Aug. 17   Perf. 13½
137	CD303	2½p bright green	.25	1.50
138	CD303	3p deep blue	.25	.25

Silver Wedding Issue
Common Design Types
1948, Dec. 17   Photo.   Perf. 14x14½
139	CD304	2½p dark green	.70	1.75

Engr.; Name Typo.
Perf. 11½x11
140	CD305	5sh blue violet	17.50	9.00

UPU Issue
Common Design Types
Engr.; Name Typo. on 3p, 8p
Perf. 13½, 11x11½
		1949, Oct. 10 Wmk. 4		
141	CD306	2p red violet	.35	.75
142	CD307	3p indigo	2.25	5.75
143	CD308	8p dp carmine	.35	4.50
144	CD309	1sh6p blue	.40	3.00
		Nos. 141-144 (4)	3.35	14.00

SEMI-POSTAL STAMPS

Catalogue values for unused stamps in this section are for Never Hinged items.

Children at Play — SP1

Rugby Player — SP2

Perf. 13x13½
1951, Sept. 17   Engr.   Wmk. 4
B1	SP1	1p + 1p brown	.30	1.60
B2	SP2	2p + 1p deep green	.45	1.10

POSTAGE DUE STAMPS

D1

D2

D3

1917   Unwmk.   Typeset   Perf. 11
Laid Papers; Without Gum
J1	D1	½p black	1,300.	500.00
J2	D2	½p black	550.00	300.00
J3	D3	1p black	500.00	140.00
a.	Narrow setting		375.00	
J4	D3	2p black	350.00	80.00
a.	Narrow setting		1,250.	
J5	D3	3p black	525.00	120.00
J6	D3	4p black	1,250.	550.00
a.	Strip of 8, 3 #J3, 1 ea. #J1 and #J6, and 3 #J5		19,000.	
	Nos. J1-J6 (6)		4,475.	1,690.

There were two printings of this issue. In the first printing, the 2d was printed in sheets of 84 (7x12), and the other four values were printed together in sheets of 96 (8x12), with each row consisting of three 1p, one ½p, one 4p and three 3p values. Setenant multiples exist. Sheets were not perforated on the margins, so that marginal stamps were not perforated on the outer edge. Examples from the first printing are 25mm wide (including margins).

In the second printing, the ½p, 1p and 2p were printed in separate sheets of 84 (7x12). The clichés were set a little closer, so that examples of this printing are 23mm wide.

D4

D5

Perf. 14
1918, June 1   Typo.   Wmk. 3
J7	D4	½p black	3.25	30.00
	On cover			500.00
J8	D4	1p black	3.75	5.50
	On cover			150.00
J9	D4	2p black	3.50	8.00
	On cover			150.00
J10	D4	3p black	3.50	52.50
	On cover			2,000.
J11	D4	4p black	6.50	30.00
	On cover			750.00
	Nos. J7-J11 (5)		20.50	126.00

Cover values for Nos. J7-J11 are for properly franked commercial items. Philatelic usages also exist and sell for less.

1940   Wmk. 4   Perf. 12½
J12	D5	1p bright green	5.00	72.50
	On cover			600.00
J13	D5	2p bright green	10.00	72.50
	On cover			600.00
J14	D5	3p bright green	11.00	80.00
	On cover			600.00
J15	D5	4p bright green	12.00	85.00
	On cover			650.00
J16	D5	5p bright green	14.00	90.00
	On cover			850.00
J17	D5	6p bright green	15.00	90.00
	On cover			750.00
J18	D5	1sh dk carmine	15.00	115.00
	On cover			750.00
J19	D5	1sh6p dk carmine	15.00	175.00
	On cover			750.00
	Nos. J12-J19 (8)		97.00	780.00
	Set, never hinged		140.00	

Virtually all covers with Nos. J12-J19 are overfranked and of philatelic origin. The values above are for such covers.

WAR TAX STAMPS

Regular Issue of 1912-16 Overprinted

WAR STAMP

Die I
1916   Wmk. 3   Perf. 14
MR1	A23	½p green	1.90	9.00
a.	Inverted overprint		700.00	
b.	Double overprint			
MR2	A23	1p scarlet	3.50	.80
a.	1p carmine		37.50	26.00
b.	Pair, one without ovpt.		8,000.	
c.	Inverted overprint		800.00	

Most examples of #MR2b are within horiz. strips of 12.

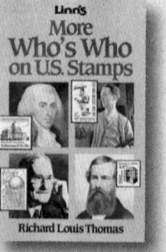

FINLAND

'fin-lənd

(Suomi)

LOCATION — Northern Europe bordering on the Gulfs of Bothnia and Finland
GOVT. — Republic
AREA — 130,119 sq. mi.
POP. — 4,869,858 (1984)
CAPITAL — Helsinki

Finland was a Grand Duchy of the Russian Empire from 1809 until December 1917, when it declared its independence.

100 Kopecks = 1 Ruble
100 Pennia = 1 Markka (1866)

Catalogue values for unused stamps in this country are for Never Hinged items, beginning with Scott B39 in the semi-postal section.

Unused stamps are valued with original gum as defined in the catalogue introduction except for Nos. 1-3B which are valued without gum. Used values for Nos. 1-3B are for pen-canceled examples.

Very fine examples of the serpentine rouletted issues, Nos. 4-13c, will have roulettes cutting the design slightly on one or more sides and will have all "teeth" complete and intact. Stamps with roulettes clear of the design on all four sides are extremely scarce and sell for substantial premiums.

Watermarks

Wmk. 121 — Multiple Swastika   Wmk. 208 — Post Horn

Wmk. 168 — Wavy Lines and Letters

Issues under Russian Empire

Coat of Arms — A1

1856-58 Unwmk. Typo. *Imperf.*
Small Pearls in Post Horns
Wove Paper

1	A1	5k blue	6,750.	1,600.
		On cover, pen cancellation		5,750.
		Pen and town cancellation		1,900.
		On cover		8,000.
		Town cancellation		3,250.
		On cover		10,000.
a.		Tête bêche pair	80,000.	80,000.
		Pen and town cancellation		75,000.
		Town cancellation		120,000.
2	A1	10k rose	8,750.	400.
		On cover, pen cancellation		975.
		Pen and town cancellation		575.
		On cover		1,850.
		Town cancellation		925.
		On cover		2,850.
a.		Tête bêche pair	80,000.	65,000.
		Pen and town cancellation		75,000.
		Town cancellation		120,000.
e.		10k carmine	8,750.	450.
		Pen and town cancellation		650.
		Town cancellation		900.
f.		10k dark carmine	9,250.	500.
		Pen and town cancellation		725.
		Town cancellation		950.
g.		10k lilac red	—	725.
		Pen and town cancellation		1,200.
		Town cancellation		1,800.

Cut to shape

1	A1	5k blue		150.
		On cover, pen cancellation		1,000.
		Pen and town cancellation		200.
		On cover		1,200.
		Town cancellation		250.
		On cover		1,750.
2	A1	10k rose		65.
		On cover, pen cancellation		550.
		Pen and town cancellation		90.
		On cover		600.
		Town cancellation		100.
		On cover		700.

Wide Vertically Laid Paper

2C	A1	10k rose ('58)	—	1,400.
		Pen and town cancellation		1,800.
		Town cancellation		2,500.
d.		Tête bêche pair		—

Cut to shape

2C	A1	10k rose		200.
		Pen and town cancellation		250.
		Town cancellation		300.

Narrow Vertically Laid Paper

2C	A1	10k carmine		625.
		Pen and town cancellation		800.
		Town cancellation		1,100.

Full margins = 1½mm.

The wide vertically laid paper has 13-14 distinct lines per 2 centimeters. The narrow laid paper has lines that sometimes are indistinct.

A 5k blue with small pearls exists on narrow vertically laid paper. It is rare.

Stamps on diagonally laid paper are envelope cut squares. Envelope cut squares also exist on unwatermarked wove paper.

Large Pearls in Post Horns
1858   Wove Paper

3	A1	5k blue	11,000.	1,800.
		On cover, pen cancellation		4,000.
		Pen and town cancellation		1,550.
		On cover		7,250.
		Town cancellation		2,500.
		On cover		8,500.
a.		Tête bêche pair	60,000.	
		Pen and town cancellation		65,000.

Cut to shape

3	A1	5k blue		125.
		On cover, pen cancellation		750.
		Pen and town cancellation		150.
		On cover		1,250.
		Town cancellation		200.
		On cover		1,750.

Full margins = 1½mm.

1859   Wide Vertically Laid Paper

3B	A1	5k blue	—	18,000.
		Pen and town cancellation		25,000.

Cut to shape

3B	A1	5k blue		2,000.
		Pen and town cancellation		2,500.

Reprints of Nos. 2 and 3, made in 1862, are on brownish paper, on vertically laid paper, and in tête bêche pairs on normal and vertically laid paper. Reprints of 1871, 1881 and 1893 are on yellowish or white paper. Value for least costly of each, $85.

In 1956, Nos. 2 and 3 were reprinted for the Centenary with post horn watermark and gum. Value, $85 each.

Coat of Arms — A2

I — Depth 1-1¼mm

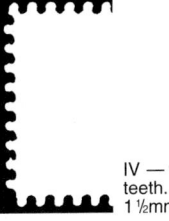

II — Depth 1½-1¾mm   III — Depth 2-2¼mm

IV — Shovel-shaped teeth. Depth 1¼-1½mm

Wove Paper

1860		**Serpentine Roulette 7½, 8**		
4	A2	5k blue, *bluish,* I	850.00	200.00
		On cover		1,200.
a.		Roulette II	800.00	225.00
		On cover		1,600.
b.		Perf. vert.		
5	A2	10k rose, *pale rose,* I	575.00	57.50
		On cover		260.00
a.		Roulette II	1,150.	160.00
		On cover		850.00

Four types of indentation are noted:

A3   A4

1866-74   *Serpentine Roulette*

6	A3	5p pur brn, *lil,* I ('73)	375.00	170.00
		On cover		1,250.
a.		Roulette II		4,000.
		On cover		
b.		5p red brn, *lil,* III ('71)	350.00	180.00
		On cover		1,300.
7	A3	8p blk, *grn,* III ('67)	275.00	170.00
		On cover		2,850.
a.		Ribbed paper, III ('72)	1,150.	925.00
		On cover		—
b.		Roulette II ('74)	340.00	275.00
		On cover		2,850.
c.		As "b," ribbed paper ('74)	340.00	225.00
		On cover		2,300.
d.		Roulette I ('73)	525.00	325.00
		On cover		2,850.
e.		As "d," ribbed paper	1,050.	400.00
		On cover		—
f.		Serpentine roulette 10½ ('67)		13,500.
8	A3	10p blk, *yel,* III ('70)	675.00	350.00
		On cover		2,000.
a.		10p blk, *buff,* II	800.00	450.00
		On cover		2,000.
b.		10p blk, *buff,* I ('73)	750.00	375.00
		On cover		2,300.
9	A3	20p bl, *bl,* III	575.00	57.50
		On cover		190.00
a.		Roulette II	575.00	90.00
		On cover		290.00
b.		Roulette I ('73)	675.00	115.00
		On cover		225.00
c.		Roulette IV ('74)	—	1,150.
		On cover		
d.		Perf. horiz.		—
e.		Printed on both sides (40p blue on back)		—
10	A3	40p rose, *lil rose,* III	525.00	67.50
		On cover		260.00
a.		Ribbed paper, III ('73)	675.00	200.00
		On cover		525.00
b.		Roulette II	525.00	85.00

		On cover		260.00
c.		As "b," ribbed paper ('73)	675.00	170.00
		On cover		450.00
d.		Roulette I	750.00	170.00
		On cover		525.00
e.		As "d," ribbed paper	675.00	115.00
		On cover		400.00
f.		Roulette IV	—	2,275.
g.		As "f," ribbed paper		—
h.		Serpentine roulette 10½		—
11	A4	1m yel brn, III ('67)	2,250.	850.00
		On cover		15,000.
a.		Roulette II	2,850.	1,700.
		On cover		

Nos. 7f and 10h are private roulettes and are also known in compound serpentine roulette 10½ and 7½.

Nos. 4-11 were reprinted in 1893 on thick wove paper. Colors differ from originals. Roulette type IV. Value for Nos. 4-5, each $40, Nos. 6-10, each $50. Value for No. 11, $55.

Thin or Thick Laid Paper

12	A3	5p red brn, *lil,* III	290.00	160.00
		On cover		900.00
a.		Roulette II	300.00	300.00
		On cover		1,750.
b.		Roulette I	290.00	300.00
		On cover		1,750.
d.		5p blk, *buff,* roul. III (error)		20,000.
e.		Tête bêche pair		
		On cover		300,000.
13	A3	10p black, *buff,* III	675.00	290.00
		On cover		1,900.
a.		10p black, *yel,* II	850.00	290.00
		On cover		1,900.
b.		10p black, *yel,* I	1,150.	750.00
		On cover		2,850.
c.		10p red brown, *lil,* III (error)	8,000.	7,000.

Forgeries of Nos. 11 and 13c exist.

Cover values for Nos. 6-13 are for covers bearing stamps with full teeth.

Nos. 6-13 with Short Teeth

Values below are for used stamps with one or two short roulettes. Stamps with teeth entirely missing or with several short roulettes are worth much less.

6	62.50
6a	2,100.
6b	50.00
7	50.00
7a	300.00
7b	80.00
7c	45.00
7d	90.00
7e	180.00
7f	14,000.
8	80.00
8a	115.00
8b	125.00
9	19.00
9a	32.50
9b	40.00
9c	525.00
10	21.00
10a	110.00
10b	21.00
10c	85.00
10d	45.00
10e	45.00
10f	1,000.
10g	1,400.
11	225.00
11a	600.00
12	45.00
12a	70.00
12b	70.00
12d	15,000.
13	80.00
13a	85.00
13b	160.00
13c	3,500.

A5

1875		**Perf. 14x13½**		
16	A5	32p lake	2,400.	425.00
		On cover		15,500.

Forgeries exist of No. 16 that have been created by perforating cut squares.

1875-82		**Perf. 11**		
17	A5	2p gray	50.00	50.00
		Never hinged	120.00	
		On cover		800.00
		On cover, single franking		575.00
		On postal stationery		625.00
18	A5	5p orange	100.00	12.00
		Never hinged	300.00	
		On cover		170.00
		On cover, single franking		200.00
a.		5p yellow org	125.00	11.50
		Never hinged	300.00	
		On cover		170.00
		On cover, single franking		200.00

19 A5 8p blue green 200.00 57.50
  Never hinged 450.00
  On cover — 4,000.
  On newsprint, single franking — 7,000.
a. 8p yellow green 200.00 85.00
  Never hinged 450.00
  On cover — 4,000.
  On newsprint, single franking — 7,000.
20 ... ('81) 400.00 57.50
  On cover — 2,100.
  On cover, single franking — 3,750.
21 A5 20p ultra 100.00 3.50
  Never hinged 300.00
  On cover — 42.50
a. 20p blue 100.00 4.00
  Never hinged 300.00
  On cover — 45.00
b. 20p Prussian blue 300.00 30.00
  On cover — 350.00
c. Tête bêche pair — 3,500.
22 A5 25p carmine ('79) 250.00 13.50
  Never hinged 600.00
  On cover — 300.00
a. 25p rose ('82) 400.00 57.50
  On cover — 600.00
23 A5 32p carmine 400.00 175.00
  On cover — 600.00
a. 32p rose 350.00 62.50
  Never hinged 775.00
  On cover — 575.00
24 A5 1m violet ('77) 625.00 125.00
  On cover — 13,000.
  Nos. 17-24 (8) 2,125. 494.00

A souvenir card issued in 1974 for NORDIA 1975 reproduced a block of four of the unissued "1 MARKKAA" design.
Nos. 19, 23 were reprinted in 1892-93, perf. 12½. Value $25.00 each. They exist imperf.

1881-83   Perf. 12½
25 A5 2p gray 10.00 12.00
  Never hinged 35.00
  On cover — 425.00
a. Imperf., pair 575.00 575.00
26 A5 5p orange 50.00 6.00
  Never hinged 92.50
a. Tête bêche pair 7,000. 4,500.
b. Imperf. vert., pair — 145.00
c. Imperf. horiz., pair —
27 A5 10p brown 70.00 15.00
  Never hinged 180.00
  On cover — 1,450.
  On cover, single franking — 2,850.
28 A5 20p ultra 50.00 2.00
  Never hinged 95.00
  On cover — 29.00
a. 20p blue 50.00 30.00
  Never hinged 95.00
  On cover — 30.00
b. Tête bêche pair 3,000. 2,500.
c. Imperf., pair —
29 A5 25p rose ('82) 40.00 40.00
  Never hinged 90.00
  On cover — 300.00
a. 25p carmine 35.00 8.00
  Never hinged 100.00
  On cover — 300.00
b. Tête bêche pair 15,000. 300.00
30 A5 1m violet ('82) 350.00 40.00
  Never hinged 600.00
  On cover — 11,000.
  Nos. 25-30 (6) 570.00 115.00

Nos. 27-29 were reprinted in 1893 in deeper shades, perf. 12½. Value $35 each.
Most examples of No. 28c are from printer's waste.

1881   Perf. 11x12½
26d A5 5p orange 450.00 90.00
  On cover — 1,700.
27a A5 10p brown 925.00 225.00
  On cover — 5,750.
28d A5 20p ultra 575.00 42.50
  On cover — 1,900.
28e A5 20p blue 575.00 42.50
  On cover — 1,700.
29c A5 25p rose 675.00 190.00
  On cover —
29d A5 25p carmine 650.00 125.00
  On cover —
30a A5 1m violet — 1,450.
  On cover —

1881   Perf. 12½x11
26e A5 5p orange 450.00 90.00
  On cover — 1,800.
27b A5 10p brown — 325.00
  On cover —
28f A5 20p ultra 575.00 45.00
  On cover — 1,800.
28g A5 20p blue 575.00 45.00
  On cover — 1,800.
29e A5 25p rose — 290.00
  On cover —
29f A5 25p carmine 575.00 115.00
  On cover —

1885   Perf. 12½
31 A5 5p emerald 15.00 1.00
  Never hinged 35.00
  On cover — 24.00
a. 5p yellow green 15.00 1.00
  Never hinged 42.50
  On cover — 30.00
b. Tête bêche pair 12,000. 10,000.
32 A5 10p carmine 22.50 2.25
  Never hinged 45.00
  On cover — 75.00
a. 10p rose 22.50 2.25
  Never hinged 45.00
  On cover — 75.00
33 A5 20p orange 22.50 .50
  Never hinged 57.50
  On cover — 15.00

a. 20p yellow 29.00 .65
  Never hinged 60.00
  On cover — 17.50
b. Tête bêche pair — 3,500.
34 A5 25p ultra 45.00 2.90
  Never hinged 90.00
  On cover — 100.00
a. 25p blue 45.00 2.90
  Never hinged 90.00
  On cover — 100.00
35 A5 1m gray & rose 30.00 17.00
  Never hinged 55.00
  On cover — 3,750.
36 A5 5m green & rose 375.00 375.00
  Never hinged 1,100.
  On cover —
37 A5 10m brown & rose 600.00 600.00
  Never hinged 1,200.
  On cover —

Denomination on No. 35 is spelled "MARKKA". Denomination on Nos. 36-37 is spelled "MARKKAA",

 A6

1889-92   Perf. 12½
38 A6 2p slate ('90) .75 1.25
  Never hinged 1.40
  On cover — 60.00
39 A6 5p green ('90) 24.00 .50
  Never hinged 65.00
  On cover — 8.50
40 A6 10p carmine ('90) 45.00 .50
  Never hinged 120.00
  On cover — 10.00
a. 10p rose ('90) 60.00 .60
  Never hinged 130.00
  On cover — 18.00
b. Imperf. 100.00
  Never hinged 145.00
41 A6 20p orange ('92) 55.00 .50
  Never hinged 120.00
  On cover — 6.00
a. 20p yellow ('89) 60.00 1.25
  Never hinged 140.00
  On cover — 30.00
42 A6 25p ultra ('91) 60.00 .85
  Never hinged 130.00
  On cover — 27.50
a. 25p blue 65.00 1.15
  Never hinged 140.00
  On cover — 27.50
43 A6 1m slate & rose ('92) 3.50 2.75
  Never hinged 9.50
  On cover — 120.00
a. 1m brnsh gray & rose ('90) 19.00 2.75
  Never hinged 40.00
  On cover — 120.00
44 A6 5m green & rose ('90) 20.00 60.00
  Never hinged 47.50
  On cover — 11,000.
45 A6 10m brown & rose ('90) 28.00 80.00
  Never hinged 65.00
  On cover — 6,000.
  Nos. 38-45 (8) 236.25 146.35

The 2p slate, perf. 14x13, is believed to be an essay.
See Nos. 60-63.

See Russia for types similar to A7-A18.
Finnish stamps have "dot in circle" devices or are inscribed "Markka," "Markkaa," "Pen." or "Pennia."

Imperial Arms of Russia
A7   A8   A9

A10   A11

Laid Paper

  On cover — 60.00
1891-92   Wmk. 168   Perf. 14½x15
46 A7 1k orange yel 4.75 10.50
  Never hinged 9.50
  On cover — 150.00
47 A7 2k green 5.75 10.50
  Never hinged ...
  On cover — 85.00
48 A7 3k carmine 10.50 16.00
  Never hinged 18.00
  On cover — 75.00
49 A8 4k rose 12.50 15.00
  Never hinged 20.00
  On cover — 55.00
50 A7 7k dark blue 5.75 2.25
  Never hinged 14.50
  On cover — 30.00
51 A8 10k dark blue 14.00 14.00
  Never hinged 32.50
  On cover — 150.00
52 A9 14k blue & rose 18.50 26.00
  Never hinged 35.00
  On cover — 650.00
53 A8 20k blue & car 17.50 20.00
  Never hinged 27.50
  On cover — 425.00
54 A9 35k violet & grn 23.00 52.50
  Never hinged 40.00
  On cover — 2,100.
55 A8 50k violet & grn 29.00 37.50
  Never hinged 62.50
  On cover — 1,500.

Perf. 13½
56 A10 1r brown & org 80.00 80.00
  Never hinged 140.00
  On cover — 2,400.
57 A11 3½r black & gray 275.00 475.00
  Never hinged 475.00
  On cover — 9,000.
a. 3½r black & yellow (error) 14,000. 17,000.
58 A11 7r black & yellow 210.00 300.00
  Never hinged 375.00
  On cover — 15,000.
  Nos. 46-58 (13) 706.25 1,059.

Forgeries of Nos. 57, 57a, 58 exist.

Type of 1889-90
Wove Paper
1895-96   Unwmk.   Perf. 14x13
60 A6 5p green .50 .50
  Never hinged 2.25
  On cover — 4.25
61 A6 10p carmine .70 .50
  Never hinged 2.25
  On cover — 9.00
a. 10p rose 60.00 5.00
  Never hinged 140.00
  On cover — 22.00
62 A6 20p orange .70 .50
  Never hinged 2.25
  On cover — 6.00
a. 20p yellow .70 .45
  Never hinged 2.75
  On cover — 5.00
b. Imperf. 150.00
  Never hinged 190.00
63 A6 25p ultra .65 .65
  Never hinged 2.25
  On cover — 12.00
a. 25p blue .75 .65
  Never hinged 3.50
  On cover — 7.50
b. Imperf. 105.00
  Never hinged 140.00
  Nos. 60-63 (4) 2.55 2.15

A12   A13

A14   A15

1901   Litho.   Perf. 14½x15
Chalky Paper
64 A12 2p yellow 5.25 7.00
  Never hinged 13.00
  On cover — 15.00
65 A12 5p green 10.50 1.40
  Never hinged 26.00
  On cover — 4.25
66 A13 10p carmine 24.00 2.25
  Never hinged 47.50
  On cover — 4.00
67 A12 20p dark blue 57.50 1.25
  Never hinged 100.00
  On cover — 3.00
68 A14 1m violet & grn 325.00 9.25
  Never hinged 575.00

  On cover — 60.00
Perf. 13½
69 A15 10m black & gray 300.00 300.00
  Never hinged 625.00
  Nos. 47-69 (6) 722.25 321.15

Imperf sheets of 10p and 20p, stolen during production, were privately perforated 11½ to defraud the P.O. Uncanceled imperfs. of Nos. 65-68 are believed to be proofs.
See Nos. 70-75, 82.

Types of 1901 Redrawn

 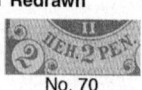
No. 64   No. 70

2p. On No. 64, the "2" below "II" is shifted slightly leftward. On No. 70, the "2" is centered below "II."

No. 65   No. 71

5p. On No. 65, the frame lines are very close. On No. 71, a clear white space separates them.

Nos. 66, 67   Nos. 72, 73

10p, 20p. On Nos. 66-67, the horizontal central background lines are faint and broken. On Nos. 72-73, they are clear and solid, though still thin.

20p. On No. 67, "H" close to "2" with period midway. On No. 73 they are slightly separated with period close to "H."

No. 68   Nos. 74, 74a

1m. On No. 68, the "1" following "MARKKA" lacks serif at base. On Nos. 74-74a, this "1" has serif.

No. 69   No. 75

10m. On No. 69, the serifs of "M" and "A" in top and bottom panels do not touch. On No. 75, the serifs join.

Perf. 14¼x14¾, 14¼x14
1901-14   Typo.   Ordinary Paper
70 A12 2p orange .60 1.40
  Never hinged 1.40
  On cover — 7.00
71 A12 5p green 1.75 .75
  Never hinged 4.00
  On cover — 2.00
a. Perf 14¼x14 ('06) 1.75 .75
  Never hinged 3.50
  On cover — 3.00
72 A13 10p carmine 9.25 .60
  Never hinged 21.00
  On cover — 2.00
a. Perf 14¼x14 ('07) 55.00 .50
  Never hinged 120.00
  On cover — 2.00
b. Background inverted, perf 14¼x14¾ 15.00 2.25
  Never hinged 35.00
c. Background inverted, perf 14¼x14 80.00 2.25
  Never hinged 140.00
73 A12 20p dark blue 6.00 .60
  Never hinged 15.00
  On cover — 2.00
a. Perf 14¼x14 ('06) 70.00 .65
  Never hinged 120.00
  On cover — 4.25
74 A14 1m lil & grn, perf. 14¼x14 ('14) 1.40 .75
  Never hinged 3.50
  On cover — 12.00
a. 1m violet & blue green, perf. 14¼x14¾ ('02) 9.00 .90

Never hinged	21.00		
On cover			12.00
Nos. 70-74 (5)	19.00	4.10	

Perf. 13½

75	A15	10m blk & drab ('03)	140.00	55.00
	Never hinged		275.00	
	On cover			725.00

Imperf Pairs

70a	A12	2p	325.00	475.00
	Never hinged		400.00	
71b	A12	5p	85.00	175.00
	Never hinged		100.00	
72d	A13	10p	100.00	210.00
	Never hinged		120.00	
73b	A12	20p	175.00	210.00
	Never hinged		210.00	
74b	A14	1m	160.00	185.00
	Never hinged		190.00	
	Nos. 70a-74b (5)		845.00	1,255.

A16   A17   A18

1911-16   Perf. 14, 14¼x14¾

77	A16	2p orange	.30	1.00
	Never hinged		.70	
	On cover			4.00
78	A16	5p green	.35	.45
	Never hinged		.70	
	On cover			1.75
a.	Imperf.		—	
	Never hinged		—	
b.	Perf. 14¼x14¾		400.00	350.00
	Never hinged		750.00	
	On cover			1,750.
79	A17	10p rose ('15)	.30	.55
	Never hinged		.60	
	On cover			1.75
a.	Imperf.		85.00	175.00
	Never hinged		110.00	
	On cover			475.00
b.	Perf. 14¼x14¾ ('16)		4.00	6.00
	Never hinged		6.00	
	On cover			8.50
80	A16	20p deep blue	.30	.55
	Never hinged		.50	
	On cover			2.00
a.	Imperf.		180.00	135.00
	On cover			200.00
b.	Perf. 14¼x14¾		14.00	4.00
	Never hinged		35.00	
	On cover			4.00
81	A18	40p violet & blue	.30	.45
	Never hinged		.50	
	On cover			4.50
a.	Perf. 14¼x14¾		3,600.	3,600.
	Nos. 77-81 (5)		1.55	3.00

There are three minor types of No. 79. Values are for the least expensive type.

Perf. 14½

82	A15	10m blk & grnsh gray ('16)	135.00	190.00
	Never hinged		275.00	
	On cover			1,100.
a.	Horiz. pair, imperf. vert.		3,500.	

**Republic
Helsinki Issue**

Arms of the Republic
A19   A20

Type I

Type II

Two types of the 40p.
Type I — Thin figures of value.
Type II — Thick figures of value.

Perf. 14, 14¼x14¾

1917-30   Unwmk.

83	A19	5p green	.25	.25
	Never hinged		.30	
	On cover			1.60
84	A19	5p gray ('19)	.25	.25
	Never hinged		.30	
	On cover			1.60
85	A19	10p rose	.30	.50
	Never hinged		.50	
	On cover			1.60
a.	Imperf., pair		225.00	400.00
	Never hinged		290.00	
86	A19	10p green ('19)	1.50	.75
	Never hinged		2.75	
	On cover			2.50
a.	Perf. 14¼x14¾			2,750.
87	A19	10p brt blue ('21)	.40	.50
	Never hinged		.50	
	On cover			2.50
a.	10p grysh ultra		.40	.50
	Never hinged		.50	
	On cover			2.50
88	A19	20p buff	.30	.50
	Never hinged		.50	
	On cover			2.50
89	A19	20p rose ('20)	.30	.50
	Never hinged		1.00	
	On cover			2.50
90	A19	20p brown ('24)	.65	.90
	Never hinged		2.10	
	On cover			5.25
a.	Perf. 14¼x14¾		.60	25.00
	Never hinged		1.40	
	On cover			700.00
91	A19	25p blue	.25	.50
	Never hinged		.50	
	On cover			5.25
92	A19	25p lt brown ('19)	.25	.25
	Never hinged		.30	
	On cover			2.50
93	A19	30p green ('23)	.30	.65
	Never hinged		.80	
	On cover			2.50
94	A19	40p violet (I)	.25	.25
	Never hinged		.50	
a.	Perf. 14¼x14¾		400.00	26.00
	Never hinged		750.00	
	On cover			52.50
95	A19	40p bl grn (II) ('29)	.50	3.00
	Never hinged		.70	
	On cover			4.00
a.	Type I ('24)		12.00	5.25
	Never hinged		25.00	
	On cover			13.00
b.	Perf. 14¼x14¾		1.25	21.00
	Never hinged		2.25	
	On cover			35.00
96	A19	50p orange brn	.25	.50
	Never hinged		.80	
	On cover			5.25
97	A19	50p dp blue ('19)	3.50	.25
	Never hinged		7.00	
	On cover			4.50
a.	Perf. 14¼x14¾			2,000.
98	A19	50p green ('21)	4.00	.50
	Never hinged		16.00	
	On cover			2.50
a.	Perf. 14¼x14¾		.30	1.50
	Never hinged		.50	
	On cover			4.00
99	A19	60p red vio ('21)	.50	.50
	Never hinged		2.25	
	On cover			1.60
a.	Imperf., pair		—	—
100	A19	75p yellow ('21)	.25	.70
	Never hinged		.30	
	On cover			9.75
101	A19	1m dull rose & blk	12.00	.25
	Never hinged		26.00	
	On cover			1.50
102	A19	1m red org ('25)	7.50	24.00
	Never hinged		21.00	
	On cover			45.00
a.	Perf. 14 ('30)		.25	550.00
	Never hinged		.45	
	On cover			1,500.
103	A19	1½m bl grn & red vio ('29)	.25	2.50
	Never hinged		.65	
a.	Perf. 14¼x14¾		.25	1.60
	Never hinged		.50	
	On cover			4.00
104	A19	2m green & blk ('21)	2.40	.70
	Never hinged		6.00	
	On cover			7.00
105	A19	2m dk blue & ind ('22)	2.40	.50
	Never hinged		6.00	
	On cover			7.25
a.	Perf. 14¼x14¾		.65	4.00
	Never hinged		1.75	
	On cover			47.50
106	A19	3m blue & blk ('21)	60.00	.65
	Never hinged		105.00	
	On cover			7.00
107	A19	5m red vio & blk	14.50	.50
	Never hinged		32.50	
	On cover			7.50
108	A19	10m brn & gray blk, perf. 14	1.00	1.25
	Never hinged		2.10	
	On cover			775.00
a.	10m light brown & black, perf. 14¼x14¾ ('29)		3.50	400.00
	Never hinged		6.50	
	On cover			1,750.
110	A19	25m dull red & yel ('21)	.90	26.00
	Never hinged		1.25	
	On cover			325.00
	Nos. 83-108,110 (27)		114.95	67.60

Examples of a 2½p gray of this type exist. They are proofs from the original die which were distributed through the UPU. No plate was made for this denomination.

See Nos. 127-140, 143-152. For surcharge and overprints see Nos. 119-126, 153-154.

Vasa Issue

1918   Litho.   Perf. 11½

111	A20	5p green	.50	1.25
	Never hinged		.90	
	On cover			8.50
112	A20	10p red	.50	1.25
	Never hinged		.90	
	On cover			8.50
113	A20	30p slate	.80	3.00
	Never hinged		1.40	
	On cover			57.50
114	A20	40p brown vio	.30	1.25
	Never hinged		.65	
	On cover			13.00
115	A20	50p orange brn	.50	4.50
	Never hinged		.90	
	On cover			80.00
116	A20	70p gray brown	2.25	21.00
	Never hinged		3.50	
	On cover			115.00
117	A20	1m red & gray	.50	1.60
	Never hinged		.90	
	On cover			35.00
118	A20	5m red violet & gray	40.00	100.00
	Never hinged		85.00	
	On cover			1,450.
	Nos. 111-118 (8)		45.35	133.85

Nos. 111-118 exist imperforate but were not regularly issued in that condition.
Sheet margin examples, perf. on 3 sides, imperf. on margin side, were sold by post office.

Stamps and Type of
1917-29 Surcharged

1919   Perf. 14

119	A19	10p on 5p green	.50	.55
	Never hinged		1.00	
	On cover			3.50
120	A19	20p on 10p rose	.50	.55
	Never hinged		1.00	
	On cover			3.50
121	A19	50p on 25p blue	1.00	.65
	Never hinged		2.50	
	On cover			8.00
122	A19	75p on 20p orange	.50	.80
	Never hinged		1.00	
	On cover			9.00
	Nos. 119-122 (4)		2.50	2.55

**Stamps and Type of 1917-29
Surcharged**

Nos. 123-125   No. 126

1921

123	A19	30p on 10p green	.65	.90
	Never hinged		1.40	
	On cover			3.50
124	A19	60p on 40p red violet	3.50	1.20
	Never hinged		7.00	
	On cover			4.50
125	A19	90p on 10p rose	.25	.50
	Never hinged		.45	
	On cover			10.50
126	A19	1½m on 50p blue	1.25	.50
	Never hinged		4.00	
	On cover			9.50
a.	Thin "2" in "½"		11.00	7.00
	Never hinged		24.00	
b.	Imperf., pair		240.00	425.00
	Never hinged		350.00	
	Nos. 123-126 (4)		5.65	3.10

Arms Type of 1917-29
Perf. 14, 14¼x14¾

1925-29   Wmk. 121

127	A19	10p ultra ('27)	.50	2.50
	Never hinged		.70	
	On cover			7.00
128	A19	20p brown	.50	2.00
	Never hinged		.70	
	On cover			5.25
129	A19	25p brn org ('29)	.80	90.00
	Never hinged		1.75	
	On cover			350.00
130	A19	30p yel green	.25	.90
	Never hinged		.25	
	On cover			4.00
a.	Perf. 14¼x14¾		3.00	7.00
	Never hinged		5.75	
131	A19	40p blue grn (I) ('26)	3.00	.90
	Never hinged		8.00	
	On cover			1.75
a.	Perf. 14¼x14¾ ('26)		4.50	1.20
	Never hinged		14.00	
	On cover			2.25
b.	Type II ('28)		120.00	70.00
	Never hinged		275.00	
	On cover			85.00
c.	As "b," perf. 14¼x14¾ ('28)		4.00	1.25

	Never hinged	14.00	
	On cover		2.25
132	A19	50p gray grn ('26)	1.10	.70
	Never hinged		2.25	
	On cover			2.25
a.	Perf. 14¼x14¾ ('26)		.40	.50
	Never hinged		1.35	
	On cover			2.25
133	A19	60p red violet	.25	.90
	Never hinged		.25	
	On cover			2.25
134	A19	1m dp orange	4.75	.50
	Never hinged		10.50	
	On cover			2.25
a.	Perf. 14¼x14¾		100.00	.80
	Never hinged		225.00	
	On cover			3.50

Perf. 14¼x14¾

135	A19	1½m blue green & red violet ('26)	4.75	.50
	Never hinged		14.00	
	On cover			2.00
a.	Perf. 14 ('26)		47.50	.50
	Never hinged		85.00	
	On cover			1.50
136	A19	2m dk blue & indigo ('27)	.65	.50
	Never hinged		1.35	
	On cover			3.50
a.	Perf. 14		.90	.50
	Never hinged		2.25	
	On cover			3.00
137	A19	3m chlky blue & blk ('26)	.90	.50
	Never hinged		2.00	
	On cover			4.00
138	A19	5m red violet & blk ('27)	.50	.50
	Never hinged		1.15	
	On cover			6.25
a.	Perf. 14		1.25	.50
	Never hinged		2.75	
	On cover			4.00
139	A19	10m lt brn & blk ('27)	3.50	32.50
	Never hinged		5.75	
	On cover			200.00
140	A19	25m dp org & yel ('27)	18.00	325.00
	Never hinged		35.00	
	Nos. 127-140 (14)		39.45	457.90

No. 130a is not known cancelled during the period in which it was valid for postal use.

A21

Wmk. 208

1927, Dec. 6   Typo.   Perf. 14

141	A21	1½m deep violet	.25	.50
	Never hinged		.25	
	On cover			7.50
142	A21	2m deep blue	.25	1.75
	Never hinged		.25	
	On cover			16.00

10th anniv. of Finnish independence.

Arms Type of 1917-29
Perf. 14, 14¼x14¾

1927-29   Wmk. 208

143	A19	20p lt brown ('29)	1.60	22.50
	Never hinged		2.50	
	On cover			32.50
144	A19	40p bl grn (II) ('28)	.25	.55
	Never hinged		.25	
	On cover			1.25
145	A19	50p gray grn ('28)	.25	.50
	Never hinged		.55	
	On cover			3.00
146	A19	1m dp orange	.25	1.00
	Never hinged		.45	
	On cover			1.75
a.	Imperf., pair		115.00	200.00
	Never hinged		175.00	
	On cover			675.00
b.	Perf. 14		1.10	1.10
	Never hinged		2.00	
	On cover			2.25
147	A19	1½m bl grn & red vio ('28)	2.50	.65
	Never hinged		2.25	
	On cover			5.25
a.	Perf. 14		1,000.	26.00
	Never hinged		1,750.	
	On cover			32.50
148	A19	2m dk bl & ind ('28)	.25	.65
	Never hinged		.55	
	On cover			3.50
149	A19	3m chlky bl & blk ('28)	.25	.90
	Never hinged		.65	
	On cover			3.25
a.	Perf. 14		1.50	4.50
	Never hinged		2.75	
	On cover			11.50
150	A19	5m red vio & blk ('28)	.25	.60
	Never hinged		.65	
	On cover			11.50
151	A19	10m lt brown & blk ('28)	1.25	40.00
	Never hinged		2.50	
	On cover			350.00

152 A19   25m brown org & yel   1.50   190.00
   Never hinged   2.50
   On cover   1,150.
   Nos. 143-152 (10)   8.35   *257.35*

Nos. 146-147
Overprinted

1928, Nov. 10   Litho.   Wmk. 208
153 A19   1m deep orange   7.00   21.00
   Never hinged   14.00
   On cover   40.00
154 A19   1½m bl grn & red vio   7.00   21.00
   Never hinged   14.00
   On cover   40.00
   Set, never hinged   28.00

Nos. 153 and 154 were sold exclusively at the Helsinki Philatelic Exhibition, Nov. 10-18, 1928, and were valid only during that period.

S. S. "Bore" Leaving Turku — A23

Turku Cathedral — A24

Turku Castle — A25

Wmk. 208
1929, May 22   Typo.   Perf. 14
155 A23   1m olive green   1.35   *5.25*
   Never hinged   4.00
   On cover   11.50
156 A24   1½m chocolate   2.25   *4.00*
   Never hinged   7.25
   On cover   10.50
157 A25   2m dark gray   .45   *4.50*
   Never hinged   1.25
   On cover   16.00
   Nos. 155-157 (3)   4.05   *13.75*
   Set, never hinged   12.50

Founding of the city of Turku (Abo), 700th anniv.

A26

1930-46   Unwmk.   Perf. 14
158 A26   5p chocolate   .25   *.50*
   Never hinged   .25
   On cover   3.50
159 A26   10p dull violet   .25   .25
   Never hinged   .25
   On cover   3.50
160 A26   20p yel grn   .30   *.50*
   Never hinged   .65
   On cover   8.50
161 A26   25p yel brn   .25   .25
   Never hinged   .25
   On cover   1.75
162 A26   40p blue grn   1.75   .25
   Never hinged   5.25
   On cover   3.50
163 A26   50p yellow   .50   .35
   Never hinged   1.35
   On cover   3.50
164 A26   50p blue grn ('32)   .25   .25
   Never hinged   .25
   On cover   1.00
   b. Imperf., pair   125.00   *175.00*
   Never hinged   175.00
165 A26   60p dark gray   .50   .65
   Never hinged   .80
   On cover   8.50
165A A26   75p dp org ('42)   .25   *.50*
   Never hinged   .90
   On cover   1.35

166 A26   1m red org   .50   .25
   Never hinged   .90
   On cover   1.35
166B A26   1m yel grn ('42)   .25   .25
   Never hinged   .35
   On cover   1.00
167 A26   1.20m crimson   .65
   On cover   11.50
168 A26   1.25m yel ('32)   .25   .25
   Never hinged   .55
   On cover   1.50
169 A26   1½m red vio   1.90   .25
   Never hinged   5.75
   On cover   1.35
170 A26   1½m car ('32)   .25   .25
   Never hinged   .55
   On cover   2.25
170A A26   1½m sl ('40)   .25   .25
   Never hinged   .55
   On cover   2.25
170B A26   1.75m org yel ('40)   .55   .55
   Never hinged   1.35
   On cover   2.25
171 A26   2m indigo   .30   .25
   Never hinged   .55
   On cover   4.00
172 A26   2m dp vio ('32)   5.25   .25
   Never hinged   12.50
   On cover   .80
173 A26   2m car ('36)   .25   .25
   Never hinged   .55
   On cover   1.35
   Complete booklet, panes of 4 #161, 164, 166, 168, 173   5.75
173B A26   2m yel org ('42)   .30   .25
   Never hinged   .25
   On cover   .80
173C A26   2m blue grn ('45)   .25   .25
   Never hinged   .45
   On cover   4.50
174 A26   2½m brt blue ('32)   2.75   .50
   Never hinged   7.00
   On cover   5.75
174A A26   2½m car ('42)   .25   .25
   Never hinged   .45
   On cover   2.75
174B A26   2.75m rose vio ('40)   .25   .25
   Never hinged   .25
   On cover   .80
175 A26   3m olive blk   24.00   .50
   Never hinged   57.50
   On cover   4.00
175B A26   3m car ('45)   .25   .25
   Never hinged   .55
   On cover   2.25
175C A26   3m yel ('45)   .35   *.80*
   Never hinged   .65
   On cover   17.50
176 A26   3½m brt bl ('36)   8.00   .25
   Never hinged   21.00
   On cover   4.50
176A A26   3½m olive ('42)   .25   .25
   Never hinged   .25
   On cover   .80
176B A26   4m olive ('45)   .50   .25
   Never hinged   1.00
   On cover   2.25
176C A26   4½m saph ('42)   .25   .25
   Never hinged   .25
   On cover   7.00
176D A26   5m saph ('45)   .50   .25
   Never hinged   1.35
   On cover   2.25
176E A26   5m pur ('45)   .50   .50
   Never hinged   1.35
   On cover   4.50
   j. Imperf., pair   135.00   *180.00*
   Never hinged   185.00
176F A26   5m yel ('46)   .70   .25
   Never hinged   1.75
   On cover   .80
   k. Imperf., pair   135.00   *175.00*
   Never hinged   185.00
176G A26   6m car ('45)   .50   .50
   Never hinged   1.15
   On cover   1.75
   m. Imperf., pair   175.00   *225.00*
   Never hinged   225.00
176H A26   8m pur ('46)   .25   .25
   Never hinged   .45
   On cover   .90
176I A26   10m saph ('45)   .90   .25
   Never hinged   2.50
   On cover   3.50
   Nos. 158-176I (38)   55.15   *13.75*

See Nos. 257-262, 270-274, 291-296, 302-304. For surcharges and overprints see Nos. 195-196, 212, 221-222, 243, 250, 275, M2-M3. Post 1940 issues in Scott Standard catalogue, Vol. 2.

Stamps of types A26-A29 overprinted "ITA KARJALA" are listed under Karelia, Nos. N1-N15 in Scott Standard catalogue, Vol. 2.

Castle in Savonlinna A27

Lake Saima — A28

Woodchopper A29

1930   Engr.
177 A27   5m blue   .25   *.50*
   Never hinged   .45
   On cover   3.50
178 A28   10m gray lilac   45.00   4.50
   Never hinged   125.00
   On cover   135.00
179 A29   25m black brown   .75   .50
   Never hinged   2.25
   On cover   3.50
   Nos. 177-179 (3)   46.00   5.50
   Set, never hinged   130.00

See Nos. 205, 305 (in Scott Standard catalogue, Vol. 2). For overprint see No. C1.

Elias Lönnrot — A30

Seal of Finnish Literary Society — A31

1931, Jan. 1   Typo.
180 A30   1m olive brown   2.50   *5.75*
   Never hinged   5.25
   On cover   8.00
181 A31   1½m dull blue   11.50   5.75
   Never hinged   35.00
   On cover   11.50

Centenary of Finnish Literary Society.

A32

1931, Feb. 28
182 A32   1½m red   2.75   9.50
   Never hinged   6.00
   On cover   12.50
183 A32   2m blue   2.75   11.50
   Never hinged   6.00
   On cover   20.00

1st use of postage stamps in Finland, 75th anniv.

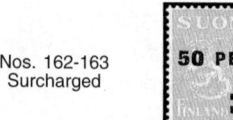
Nos. 162-163 Surcharged

1931, Dec.
195 A26   50p on 40p blue grn   1.25   .70
   Never hinged   4.00
   On cover   3.50
196 A26   1.25m on 50p yellow   3.75   2.10
   Never hinged   12.00
   On cover   5.75

Svinhufvud — A33

1931, Dec. 15
197 A33   2m gray blue & blk   1.35   *4.00*
   Never hinged   3.75
   On cover   8.00

Pres. Pehr Eyvind Svinhufvud, 70th birthday.

Lake Saima Type of 1930
1932-43   Re-engraved
205 A28   10m red violet ('43)   .50   .50
   Never hinged   1.25
   On cover   5.00
   a.   10m dark violet   19.00   .70
   Never hinged   37.50
   On cover   25.00

On Nos. 205 and 205a the lines of the islands, the clouds and the foliage are much deeper and stronger than on No. 178.

Alexis Kivi — A34

1934, Oct. 10   Typo.
206 A34   2m red violet   1.50   *4.50*
   Never hinged   5.00
   On cover   7.50

Alexis Kivi, Finnish poet (1834-1872).

Bards Reciting the "Kalevala" A35

Goddess Louhi, As Eagle Seizing Magic Mill — A36

Kullervo — A37

1935, Feb. 28   Engr.
207 A35   1¼m brown lake   1.15   *1.80*
   Never hinged   3.50
   On cover   6.00
208 A36   2m black   3.00   1.50
   Never hinged   8.00
   On cover   5.00
209 A37   2½m blue   2.75   2.25
   Never hinged   6.25
   On cover   11.50
   Nos. 207-209 (3)   6.90   5.55
   Set, never hinged   18.00

Cent. of the publication of the "Kalevala" (Finnish National Epic).

No. 170 Surcharged in Black

1937, Feb.
212 A26   2m on 1½m car   4.75   .90
   Never hinged   12.50
   On cover   5.00

Gustaf
Mannerheim — A38

1937, June 4   Photo.   Perf. 14
213 A38 2m ultra   .65 *1.45*
   Never hinged   1.75
   On cover   3.50

70th birthday of Field Marshal Baron Carl Gustaf Mannerheim, June 4th, 1937.

Swede-Finn
Co-operation in
Colonization
A39

1938, June 1
214 A39 3½m dark brown   1.00 *3.00*
   Never hinged   3.00
   On cover   7.50

Tercentenary of the colonization of Delaware by Swedes and Finns.

Early Post
Office — A40

Designs: 1¼m, Mail delivery in 1700. 2m, Modern mail plane. 3½m, Helsinki post office.

1938, Sept. 6   Photo.   Perf. 14
215 A40 50p green   .25   .75
   Never hinged   .60
   On cover   3.00
216 A40 1¼m dk blue   1.15 *4.00*
   Never hinged   2.75
   On cover   5.75
217 A40 2m scarlet   1.15 *1.25*
   Never hinged   5.75
   On cover   3.50
218 A40 3½m slate black   3.50 *10.50*
   Never hinged   8.00
   On cover   12.50
   Nos. 215-218 (4)   6.05 *16.50*
Set, never hinged   17.00

300th anniv. of the Finnish Postal System. Margin strips of each denomination (3 of No. 215, 2 each of Nos. 216, 217, 218) were pasted on to advertising sheets and stapled into a booklet. Value, $120.

Post Office,
Helsinki — A44

1939-42   Photo.
219 A44 4m brown black   .25   *.50*
   Never hinged   .45
   On cover   3.50

           Engr.
219A A44 7m black brn ('42)   .45   *.50*
   Never hinged   .90
   On cover   7.50
219B A44 9m rose lake ('42)   .50   *.50*
   Never hinged   1.15
   On cover   7.50
   Nos. 219-219B (3)   1.20 *1.50*
Set, never hinged   2.50

See No. 248 in Scott Standard catalogue, Vol. 2.

> **Catalogue values for unused stamps in this section, from this point to the end of the section, are for Never Hinged items.**

University of
Helsinki — A45

1940, May 1   Photo.
220 A45 2m dp blue & blue   .80 *1.00*
   On cover   5.00

300th anniv. of the founding of the University of Helsinki.

Nos. 168 and 173
Surcharged in Black

1940, June 16   Typo.
221 A26 1.75m on 1.25m yel   3.00 *4.00*
   On cover   7.50
222 A26 2.75m on 2m carmine   7.25   .70
   On cover   6.00

SEMI-POSTAL STAMPS

Arms — SP1

      Unwmk.
1922, May 15   Typo.   Perf. 14
B1 SP1 1m + 50p gray & red   1.10 *11.00*
   Never hinged   2.25
a. Perf. 13x13½   11.00
   Never hinged   22.50

Red Cross   Symbolic
Standard   SP3
SP2

Ship of Mercy — SP4

1930, Feb. 6
B2 SP2 1m + 10p red org &
         red   1.75 *12.00*
   Never hinged   4.00
   On cover   24.00
B3 SP3 1½m + 15p grysh grn
         & red   1.35 *12.00*
   Never hinged   2.75
   On cover   24.00
B4 SP4 2m + 20p dk bl &
         red   3.25 *52.50*
   Never hinged   5.75
   On cover   80.00
   Nos. B2-B4 (3)   6.35 *76.50*
Set, never hinged   12.50

The surtax on this and subsequent similar issues was for the benefit of the Red Cross Society of Finland.

Church in   SP8
Hattula — SP5

Designs: 1½m+15p, Castle of Hameenlinna. 2m+20p, Fortress of Viipuri.

1931, Jan. 1   Cross in Red   Engr.
B5 SP5 1m + 10p gray grn   1.75 *12.50*
   Never hinged   3.50
   On cover   20.00
B6 SP5 1½m + 15p lil brn   11.00 *15.00*
   Never hinged   29.00
   On cover   20.00

B7 SP5 2m + 20p dull bl   1.75 *32.50*
   Never hinged   2.75
   On cover   75.00
   Nos. B5-B7 (3)   14.50 *60.00*
Set, never hinged   35.00

1931, Oct. 15   Typo.   Rouletted 4, 5
B8 SP8 1m + 4m black   12.50 *52.50*
   Never hinged   20.00
   On cover   85.00

The surtax was to assist the Postal Museum of Finland in purchasing the Richard Granberg collection of entire envelopes.

Helsinki University   Nikolai Church
Library   at Helsinki
SP9   SP10

2½m+25p, Parliament Building, Helsinki.

1932, Jan. 1   Perf. 14
B9 SP9 1¼m + 10p ol bis &
        red   1.75 *15.00*
   Never hinged   4.50
   On cover   18.00
B10 SP10 2m + 20p dp vio &
        red   .45 *7.50*
   Never hinged   .90
   On cover   12.50
B11 SP9 2½m + 25p lt blue &
        red   1.15 *28.00*
   Never hinged   2.25
   On cover   57.50
   Nos. B9-B11 (3)   3.35 *50.50*
Set, never hinged   8.00

Bishop   Michael
Magnus   Agricola
Tawast   SP13
SP12

Design: 2½m+25p, Isacus Rothovius.

1933, Jan. 20   Engr.
B12 SP12 1¼m + 10p blk brn
        & red   3.00 *11.00*
   Never hinged   8.00
   On cover   24.00
B13 SP13 2m + 20p brn vio
        & red   .90 *2.75*
   Never hinged   1.75
   On cover   5.75
B14 SP13 2½m + 25p indigo &
        red   .80 *5.75*
   Never hinged   1.75
   On cover   17.50
   Nos. B12-B14 (3)   4.70 *19.50*
Set, never hinged   10.50

Evert
Horn — SP15

Designs: 2m+20p, Torsten Stalhandske. 2½m+25p, Jakob (Lazy Jake) de la Gardie.

1934, Jan.   Cross in Red
B15 SP15 1¼m + 10p brown   .70 *3.00*
   Never hinged   1.75
   On cover   12.00
B16 SP15 2m + 20p gray lil   1.35 *5.25*
   Never hinged   7.00
   On cover   11.00
B17 SP15 2½m + 25p gray   .70 *2.75*
   Never hinged   1.75
   On cover   16.00
   Nos. B15-B17 (3)   2.75 *11.00*
Set, never hinged   10.50

Mathias   Robert Henrik
Calonius   Rehbinder
SP18   SP21

Designs: 2m+20p, Henrik C. Porthan. 2½m+25p, Anders Chydenius.

1935, Jan. 1   Cross in Red
B18 SP18 1¼m + 15p brown   .90 *2.75*
   Never hinged   1.75
   On cover   12.00
B19 SP18 2m + 20p gray lil   1.75 *5.25*
   Never hinged   4.75
   On cover   12.00
B20 SP18 2½m + 25p gray bl   .70 *2.75*
   Never hinged   1.35
   On cover   20.00
   Nos. B18-B20 (3)   3.35 *10.75*
Set, never hinged   8.00

1936, Jan. 1   Cross in Red
2m+20p, Count Gustaf Mauritz Armfelt. 2½m+25p, Count Arvid Bernard Horn.
B21 SP21 1¼m + 15p dk brn   .75 *2.25*
   Never hinged   1.35
   On cover   12.00
B22 SP21 2m + 20p vio brn   2.75 *7.00*
   Never hinged   7.50
   On cover   12.00
B23 SP21 2½m + 25p blue   .65 *3.50*
   Never hinged   1.35
   On cover   20.00
   Nos. B21-B23 (3)   4.15 *12.75*
Set, never hinged   10.00

Type "Uusimaa"   Type
SP24   "Turunmaa"
             SP25

Design: 3½m+35p, Type "Hameenmaa."

1937, Jan. 1   Cross in Red
B24 SP24 1¼m + 15p brown   .70 *2.75*
   Never hinged   1.75
   On cover   12.00
B25 SP25 2m + 20p brn lake   12.50 *9.00*
   Never hinged   42.50
   On cover   12.00
B26 SP24 3½m + 35p indigo   .90 *3.50*
   Never hinged   2.25
   On cover   24.00
   Nos. B24-B26 (3)   14.10 *15.25*
Set, never hinged   47.50

Aukuste   Skiing
Makipeska   SP31
SP27

Designs: 1¼m+15p, Robert Isidor Orn. 2m+20p, Edward Bergenheim. 3½m+35p, Johan Mauritz Nordenstam.

1938, Jan. 5   Cross in Red   Engr.
B27 SP27 50p + 5p dk grn   .50 *1.35*
   Never hinged   .90
   On cover   6.00
B28 SP27 1¼m + 15p dk brn   .80 *2.25*
   Never hinged   1.75
   On cover   12.00
B29 SP27 2m + 20p rose
         lake   7.00 *7.50*
   Never hinged   14.00
   On cover   10.00
B30 SP27 3½m + 35p dk blue   .55 *3.50*
   Never hinged   1.15
   On cover   15.00
   Nos. B27-B30 (4)   8.85 *14.60*
Set, never hinged   18.00

1938, Jan. 18

Designs: 2m+1m, Ski jumper. 3.50m+1.50m, Skier.

B31	SP31	1.25m + 75p sl grn	3.00	13.00
		Never hinged	7.00	
		On cover		20.00
B32	SP31	2m + 1m dk grn	3.00	13.00
		On cover		20.00
B33	SP31	3.50m + 1.50m dk blue	3.00	13.00
		Never hinged	7.00	
		On cover		20.00
		Nos. B31-B33 (3)	9.00	39.00
		Set, never hinged	21.00	

Ski championships held at Lahti.

Soldier SP34

Battlefield at Solferino SP35

1938, May 16

B34	SP34	2m + ½m blue	1.40	5.00
		Never hinged	4.00	
		On cover		8.00

Victory of the White Army over the Red Guards. The surtax was for the benefit of the members of the Union of the Finnish Front.

1939, Jan. 2   Cross in Scarlet

B35	SP35	50p + 5p dk grn	.70	1.75
		Never hinged	1.20	
		On cover		8.50
B36	SP35	1¼m + 15p dk brn	.80	2.25
		Never hinged	1.20	
		On cover		8.50
B37	SP35	2m + 20p lake	11.50	14.50
		Never hinged	29.00	
		On cover		17.50
B38	SP35	3½m + 35p dk bl	.70	2.75
		Never hinged	1.20	
		On cover		17.50
		Nos. B35-B38 (4)	13.70	21.25
		Set, never hinged	32.50	

Intl. Red Cross Soc., 75th anniv.

Catalogue values for unused stamps in this section, from this point to the end of the section, are for Never Hinged items.

Soldiers with Crossbows SP36

Arms of Finland SP40

1¼m+15p, Cavalryman. 2m+20p, Soldier of Charles XII of Sweden. 3½m+35p, Officer and soldier of War with Russia, 1808-1809.

1940, Jan. 3   Cross in Red

B39	SP36	50p + 5p dk grn	1.25	1.75
		On cover		6.00
B40	SP36	1¼m + 15p dk brn	3.25	2.75
		On cover		7.00
B41	SP36	2m + 20p lake	5.25	3.50
		On cover		8.00
B42	SP36	3½m + 35p dp ultra	3.25	4.00
		On cover		12.00
		Nos. B39-B42 (4)	13.00	12.00

The surtax aided the Finnish Red Cross.

1940, Feb. 15   Litho.

B43	SP40	2m + 2m indigo	.50	1.75
		On cover		6.00

The surtax was given to a fund for the preservation of neutrality.

AIR POST STAMPS

No. 170 Overprinted in Red

1930, Sept. 24   Unwmk.   Perf. 14

C1	A28	10m gray lilac	125.00	275.00
		Never hinged	225.00	
		On cover		300.00
a.		1830 for 1930	2,500.	10,000.
		Never hinged	3,250.	
		On cover		16,500.

Overprinted expressly for use on mail carried in "Graf Zeppelin" on return flight from Finland to Germany on Sept. 24, 1930, after which trip the stamps ceased to be valid for postage. Forgeries are almost always on No. 205, rather than No. 178.

FIUME

ˈfyü-ˌmā

LOCATION — A city and surrounding territory on the Adriatic Sea
AREA — 8 sq. mi.
POP. — 44,956 (estimated 1924)

Fiume was under Hapsburg rule after 1466 and was transferred to Hungarian control after 1870. Of mixed Italian and Croatian population and strategically important, it was Hungary's only international seaport. Following World War I, Fiume was disputed between Italy and the newly created Kingdom of the Serbs, Croats and Slovenes (later Yugoslavia). A force of Allied troops occupied the city in Nov. 1918, while its future status was negotiated at the Paris Peace Conference.

In Sept. 1919, the Italian nationalist poet Gabriele d'Annunzio organized his legionnaires and seized Fiume, together with the islands of Arbe, Carnaro and Veglia, in the name of Italy. D'Annunzio established an autonomous administration, which soon came into conflict with the Italian government. There followed several years of instability, with three Italian interventions after 1920. In Jan. 1924, the Treaty of Rome between Italy and Yugoslavia established formal Italian sovereignty over Fiume, and Fiume stamps were replaced by those of Italy after March 31, 1924.

100 Filler = 1 Korona
100 Centesimi = 1 Corona (1919)
100 Centesimi = 1 Lira

The overprints on Nos. 1-23a have been extensively forged. Even the inexpensive values are difficult to find with genuine overprints. Forgeries of many later issues also exist, most created for the packet trade in the 1920s. Values are for genuine stamps. Collectors should be aware that stamps sold "as is" are likely to be forgeries, and unexpertized collections should be assumed to consist of mostly forged stamps. Education plus working with knowledgeable dealers is mandatory in this collecting area. More valuable stamps should be expertized.

Hungarian Stamps of 1916-18 Typograph Overprinted

1918, Dec. 2   Wmk. 137   Perf. 15
On Stamps of 1916
White Numerals

1	A8	10f rose	—	—
		Never hinged	100.00	11.00
		On cover	200.00	
2	A8	15f violet	47.50	40.00
		Never hinged	120.00	
		On cover		100.00

No. 1 with typographed overprint is unique.

Typographed Overprint
On Stamps of 1916-18
Colored Numerals

3	A9	2f brown orange	4.75	2.40
		Never hinged	8.75	
		On cover		45.00
4	A9	3f red violet	4.75	2.40
		Never hinged	8.75	
		On cover		45.00
5	A9	5f green	4.75	2.40
		Never hinged	8.75	
		On cover		45.00
6	A9	6f grnsh blue	4.75	2.40
		Never hinged	8.75	
		On cover		45.00
7	A9	10f rose red, inverted ovpt.	24,000.	11,000.
		Never hinged	36,000.	
		On cover		—
8	A9	15f violet	4.75	2.40
		Never hinged	8.75	
		On cover		45.00
9	A9	20f gray brown	4.75	2.40
		Never hinged	8.75	
		On cover		45.00
10	A9	25f deep blue	16.00	3.25
		Never hinged	32.50	
		On cover		75.00
11	A9	35f brown	9.50	4.75
		Never hinged	16.00	
		On cover		100.00
12	A9	40f olive green	95.00	40.00
		Never hinged	225.00	
		On cover		200.00

White Numerals

13	A10	50f red vio & lil	6.50	4.00
		Never hinged	10.50	
		On cover		50.00
14	A10	75f brt bl & pale bl	13.00	4.75
		Never hinged	25.00	
		On cover		50.00
15	A10	80f grn & pale grn	13.00	4.00
		Never hinged	25.00	
		On cover		50.00
16	A10	1k red brn & claret	40.00	9.50
		Never hinged	85.00	
		On cover		120.00
17	A10	2k ol brn & bis	6.50	4.50
		Never hinged	10.50	
		On cover		200.00
18	A10	3k dk vio & ind	55.00	27.50
		Never hinged	110.00	
		On cover		350.00
19	A10	5k dk brn & lt brn	145.00	27.50
		Never hinged	275.00	
		On cover		500.00
20	A10	10k vio brn & vio	8,750.	3,250.
		Never hinged	12,500.	
		On cover		—

Handstamped Overprint

3a	A9	2f brown orange	24.00	24.00
		Never hinged	47.50	
4a	A9	3f red violet	24.00	24.00
		Never hinged	47.50	
5a	A9	5f green	24.00	24.00
		Never hinged	47.50	
6a	A9	6f grnsh blue	35.00	24.00
		Never hinged	70.00	
7a	A9	10f rose red	72.50	27.50
		Never hinged	100.00	
8a	A9	15f violet	45.00	27.50
		Never hinged	90.00	
9a	A9	20f gray brown	300.00	120.00
		Never hinged	600.00	
10a	A9	25f deep blue	72.50	24.00
		Never hinged	160.00	
11a	A9	35f brown	72.50	24.00
		Never hinged	150.00	
12a	A9	40f olive green	45.00	24.00
		Never hinged	85.00	

White Numerals

13a	A10	50f red vio & lil	24.00	24.00
		Never hinged	50.00	
14a	A10	75f brt bl & pale bl	105.00	24.00
		Never hinged	210.00	
15a	A10	80f grn & pale grn	105.00	24.00
		Never hinged	210.00	
16a	A10	1k red brn & claret	47.50	24.00
		Never hinged	85.00	
17a	A10	2k ol brn & bis	80.00	32.50
		Never hinged	160.00	
18a	A10	3k dk vio & ind	1,050.	95.00
		Never hinged	2,000.	
19a	A10	5k dk brn & lt brn	950.00	95.00
		Never hinged	1,800.	
20a	A10	10k vio brn & vio	475.00	240.00
		Never hinged	900.00	

Inverted or double overprints exist on most of Nos. 4-15. No. 7 only exists with inverted overprint.

Typographed Overprint
On Stamps of 1918

21	A11	10f scarlet	4.00	4.00
		Never hinged	8.25	
		On cover		30.00
22	A11	20f dark brown	3.25	2.40
		Never hinged	6.25	
		On cover		35.00
23	A12	40f olive green	27.50	11.00
		Never hinged	67.50	
		On cover		50.00

Handstamped Overprint
On Stamps of 1918

21a	A11	10f scarlet	24.00	24.00
		Never hinged	55.00	
22a	A11	20f dark brown	27.50	24.00
		Never hinged	55.00	
23a	A12	40f olive green	37.50	20.00
		Never hinged	75.00	

The overprint on Nos. 3-23a was applied by 2 printing plates and 6 handstamps. Values are for the less costly. All genuine printed overprints on No. 7 are inverted and are extremely scarce.

Postage Due Stamps of Hungary, 1915-20 Ovptd. & Surcharged in Black

1919, Jan.

24	D1	45f on 6f green & red	20.00	16.00
		Never hinged	60.00	
		On cover		75.00
a.		Pair, one with inverted surcharge	1,450.	
25	D1	45f on 20f green & red	60.00	16.00
		Never hinged	140.00	
		On cover		87.50
		Set, never hinged	200.00	

Hungarian Savings Bank Stamp Surcharged in Black — A2

1919, Jan. 29

26	A2	15f on 10f dk violet	24.00	20.00
		Never hinged	60.00	
		On cover		60.00

Overprints on Nos. 24-26 are typographed.

"Italy" — A3

Italian Flag on Clock-Tower in Fiume — A4

"Revolution" A5

Sailor Raising Italian Flag at Fiume (1918) A6

Nos. 30-43 exist on three types of paper: (A) grayish, porous paper, printed in sheets of 70 stamps (Jan, Feb. printings); (B) translucent or semi-translucent good quality white paper, printed in sheets of 70 stamps (March printing); and (C) good quality medium white paper, plain and opaque, sometimes grayish or yellowish, printed in sheets of 100 (April printing).

Perf. 11½
1919, April   Unwmk.   Litho.
Good Quality Medium White Paper (C)

27	A3	2c dull blue	2.40	2.40
		Never hinged	5.00	
		On cover		35.00
28	A3	3c gray brown	2.40	2.40
		Never hinged	5.00	
		On cover		40.00
a.		Perf 10½	1,000.	
		Never hinged	2,000.	
29	A3	5c yellow green	2.40	2.40
		Never hinged	5.00	
		On cover		35.00
30	A4	10c rose	40.00	27.50
		Never hinged	100.00	
31	A4	15c violet	2.40	2.40
		Never hinged	4.25	
		On cover		35.00

32	A4	20c green	95.00	*140.00*
		Never hinged	240.00	
		On cover		*600.00*
33	A5	25c dark blue	3.25	2.40
		Never hinged	6.25	
		On cover		35.00
34	A6	30c deep violet	3.25	2.40
		Never hinged	6.25	
		On cover		35.00
a.		Perf 10½	*1,000.*	
		Never hinged	*2,000.*	
35	A5	40c brown	3.25	2.40
		Never hinged	6.25	
		On cover		35.00
36	A5	45c orange	3.25	2.40
		Never hinged	6.25	
		On cover		35.00
37	A6	50c yellow green	3.25	2.40
		Never hinged	6.25	
		On cover	—	35.00
a.		Perf 10½		
38	A6	60c claret	3.25	2.40
		Never hinged	6.25	
		On cover		35.00
39	A6	1cor brown orange	4.75	2.40
		Never hinged	10.50	
		On cover		35.00
40	A6	2cor brt blue	4.75	2.40
		Never hinged	10.50	
		On cover		45.00
a.		Perf 10½	*1,000.*	
		Never hinged	*2,000.*	
41	A6	3cor orange red	6.50	2.40
		Never hinged	12.50	
		On cover		60.00
a.		Perf 10½	*2,400.*	
		Never hinged	*4,800.*	
42	A6	5cor deep brown	40.00	40.00
		Never hinged	85.00	
		On cover	—	90.00
a.		Perf 10½	*4,800.*	
43	A6	10cor olive green	135.00	90.00
		Never hinged	340.00	
		On cover		*600.00*
		Nos. 27-43 (17)	355.10	328.70

1919, Jan.-Feb.
Poor Quality Grayish Paper (A)

30a	A4	10c rose	25.00	16.00
		Never hinged	62.50	
		On cover		45.00
31a	A4	15c violet	32.50	*40.00*
		Never hinged	80.00	
		On cover		50.00
32a	A4	20c emerald green	4.00	*4.00*
		Never hinged	10.00	
		On cover		45.00
33a	A5	25c light blue	16.00	2.40
		Never hinged	40.00	
		On cover		45.00
36a	A5	45c bister orange	4.00	4.00
		Never hinged	10.00	
		On cover		45.00
b.		Perf 10½	—	*1,600.*
38a	A6	60c claret	32.50	20.00
		Never hinged	80.00	
		On cover		45.00
39a	A6	1cor brown orange	8.00	4.00
		Never hinged	20.00	
b.		Perf 10½	—	—
40b	A6	2cor cobalt blue	—	—
		Never hinged	—	
42b	A6	5cor deep brown	—	—
		Never hinged	—	
43a	A6	10cor olive green	47.50	*80.00*
		Never hinged	120.00	
		On cover		*175.00*

1919, Mar.
Good Quality Translucent White Paper (B)

27a	A3	2c dull blue	2.40	*4.00*
		Never hinged	6.00	
		On cover		25.00
28b	A3	3c gray brown	2.40	*4.00*
		Never hinged	6.00	
		On cover		25.00
29a	A3	5c yellow green	2.40	*4.00*
		Never hinged	6.00	
		On cover		25.00
30b	A4	10c car rose	—	—
31b	A4	15c violet	3.25	16.00
		Never hinged	8.00	
		On cover		35.00
33b	A5	25c blue	3.25	6.50
		Never hinged	8.00	
		On cover		35.00
35a	A5	40c brown	3.25	*4.00*
		Never hinged	8.00	
		On cover		30.00
36c	A5	45c orange	200.00	*240.00*
		Never hinged	500.00	
		On cover		*500.00*
40c	A6	2cor cobalt blue	12.00	*16.00*
		Never hinged	30.00	
		On cover		*550.00*
d.		Perf 10½	*1,200.*	
		Never hinged	*1,800.*	
41b	A6	3cor org vermilion	12.00	*16.00*
		Never hinged	30.00	
		On cover		*550.00*
c.		Perf 10½		
42c	A6	5cor choc brown	100.00	100.00
		Never hinged	250.00	
43b	A6	10cor olive green	110.00	*80.00*
		Never hinged	275.00	
		On cover		*550.00*

Part-perf. examples of most of this series are known.

For surcharges see Nos. 58, 60, 64, 66-69.

A7 A8

A9

A10

1919, July 28 — Perf. 11½

46	A7	5c yellow green	2.40	1.60
		Never hinged	4.50	
		On cover		*45.00*
47	A8	10c rose	2.40	1.60
		Never hinged	4.50	
		On cover		35.00
48	A9	30c violet	11.00	4.00
		Never hinged	26.00	
		On cover		*45.00*
49	A10	40c yellow brown	2.40	*2.40*
		Never hinged	26.00	
		On cover		*40.00*
50	A10	45c orange	11.00	8.00
		Never hinged	26.00	
		On cover		*40.00*
51	A9	50c yellow green	11.00	8.00
		Never hinged	26.00	
		On cover		*40.00*
52	A9	60c claret	11.00	8.00
		Never hinged	27.00	
		On cover		*90.00*
a.		Perf. 13x12½	190.00	
		Never hinged	475.00	
b.		Perf. 10½	350.00	
		Never hinged	875.00	
53	A9	10cor olive green	11.00	22.50
		Never hinged	27.00	
		On cover		*450.00*
a.		Perf. 13x12½	65.00	105.00
		Never hinged	160.00	
		On cover		*600.00*
b.		Perf. 10½	350.00	375.00
		Never hinged	875.00	
		On cover		*750.00*
		Nos. 46-53 (8)	62.20	56.10
		Set, never hinged	145.00	

Five other denominations (25c, 1cor, 2cor, 3cor and 5cor) were not officially issued. Some examples of the 25c are known canceled, a few examples having been sold at post offices along with full sets of Nos. 46-53. Values: 25c blue, $1,050 unused, $1,875 never hinged, $3,000 used; 1cor brown orange, perf 11½, $160 unused, $400 never hinged; 1cor brown orange, perf 12½-13, unused $30, never hinged $75; 2cor blue, perf 11½, unused $72.50, never hinged $180; 2cor blue, perf 12½-13, unused $30, never hinged $75; 3cor vermilion, perf 11½, unused $55, never hinged $140; 3cor vermilion, perf 12½-13, unused $105, never hinged $260; 5cor brown, perf 11½, unused $160, never hinged $400; 5cor brown, perf 12½-13, unused $190, never hinged $460.

For surcharges see Nos. 59, 61-63, 65, 70.

Stamps of 1919 Handstamp Surcharged

1919-20

58	A4	5c on 20c grn ('20)	2.40	2.40
		Never hinged	4.50	
59	A10	5c on 25c blue	2.40	2.40
		Never hinged	4.50	
60	A5	10c on 45c orange	2.40	2.40
		Never hinged	4.50	
61	A9	15c on 30c vio ('20)	2.40	2.40
		Never hinged	4.50	
62	A10	15c on 45c orange	2.40	2.40
		Never hinged	4.50	
63	A9	15c on 60c cl ('20)	2.40	2.40
		Never hinged	4.50	

64	A6	25c on 50c yel grn ('20)	20.00	*35.00*
		Never hinged	47.50	
65	A9	25c on 50c yel grn ('20)	2.40	2.40
		Never hinged	4.50	
66	A6	55c on 1cor brn org	40.00	40.00
		Never hinged	100.00	
67	A6	55c on 2cor brt bl	6.50	*9.50*
		Never hinged	13.00	
68	A6	55c on 3cor org red	6.50	8.00
69	A6	55c on 5cor dp brn	6.50	8.00
70	A9	55c on 10cor ol grn	32.50	35.00
		Never hinged	82.50	
		Nos. 58-70 (13)	128.80	152.30
		Set, never hinged	300.00	

Semi-Postal Stamps of 1919 Surcharged

a

b

1919-20

73	SP6(a)	5c on 5c green	2.40	2.40
		Never hinged	5.00	
74	SP6(a)	10c on 10c rose	2.40	2.40
		Never hinged	5.00	
75	SP6(a)	15c on 15c gray	2.40	2.40
		Never hinged	5.00	
76	SP6(a)	20c on 20c org	2.40	2.40
		Never hinged	5.00	
77	SP9(a)	25c on 25c bl ('20)	2.40	2.40
		Never hinged	5.00	
78	SP7(b)	45c on 45c ol grn	4.00	4.00
		Never hinged	7.50	
79	SP7(b)	60c on 60c rose	4.00	4.00
		Never hinged	7.50	
80	SP7(b)	80c on 80c vio-let	2.40	2.40
		Never hinged	5.00	
81	SP7(b)	1cor on 1cor sl	4.00	4.00
		Never hinged	7.50	
82	SP8(a)	2cor on 2cor red brn	6.50	6.50
		Never hinged	13.00	
83	SP8(a)	3cor on 3cor blk brn	8.00	8.00
		Never hinged	22.00	
84	SP8(a)	5cor on 5cor yel brn	9.50	9.50
		Never hinged	25.00	
85	SP8(a)	10cor on 10cor dk vio ('20)	4.00	4.00
		Never hinged	7.50	
		Nos. 73-85 (13)	54.40	54.40
		Set, never hinged	120.00	

Double or inverted surcharges, or imperf. varieties, exist on most of Nos. 73-85.

There are three settings of the surcharges on Nos. 73-85 except No. 77 which is known only with one setting.

Gabriele d'Annunzio — A11 | Severing the Gordian Knot — A12

1920, Sept. 12 — Typo. — Perf. 11½
Pale Buff Background

86	A11	5c green	2.40	2.40
		Never hinged	5.00	
87	A11	10c carmine	2.40	2.40
		Never hinged	5.00	
88	A11	15c dark gray	2.40	2.40
		Never hinged	5.00	
89	A11	20c orange	2.40	2.40
		Never hinged	5.00	

90	A11	25c dark blue	3.25	3.25
		Never hinged	7.00	
91	A11	30c red brown	3.25	3.25
		Never hinged	7.00	
92	A11	45c olive gray	4.75	4.75
		Never hinged	10.00	
93	A11	50c lilac	4.75	4.75
		Never hinged	10.00	
94	A11	55c bister	4.75	4.75
		Never hinged	10.00	
95	A11	1 l black	20.00	*27.50*
		Never hinged	47.50	
96	A11	2 l red violet	20.00	*27.50*
		Never hinged	47.50	
97	A11	3 l dark green	20.00	*27.50*
		Never hinged	47.50	
98	A11	5 l brown	80.00	55.00
		Never hinged	200.00	
99	A11	10 l gray violet	20.00	*27.50*
		Never hinged	47.50	
		Nos. 86-99 (14)	190.35	195.35
		Set, never hinged	450.00	

Counterfeits of Nos. 86 to 99 are plentiful. For overprints see Nos. 134-148.

1920, Sept. 12

Designs: 10c, Ancient emblem of Fiume. 20c, Head of "Fiume." 25c, Hands holding daggers.

100	A12	5c green	57.50	35.00
		Never hinged	135.00	
101	A12	10c deep rose	35.00	27.50
		Never hinged	85.00	
102	A12	20c brown orange	57.50	27.50
		Never hinged	135.00	
103	A12	25c indigo	35.00	*65.00*
		Never hinged	85.00	
a.		25c blue	130.00	130.00
		Never hinged	325.00	
		Nos. 100-103 (4)	185.00	155.00
		Set, never hinged	440.00	

Anniv. of the occupation of Fiume by d'Annunzio. They were available for franking the correspondence of the legionnaires on the day of issue only, Sept. 12, 1920.

Counterfeits of Nos. 100-103 are plentiful. For overprints and surcharges see Nos. 104-133, E4-E9.

Nos. 100-103 Overprinted or Surcharged in Black or Red

1920, Nov. 20

104	A12	1c on 5c green	2.40	2.40
		Never hinged	5.00	
a.		Inverted overprint	55.00	55.00
b.		Double overprint	200.00	
105	A12	2c on 25c indigo (R)	2.40	2.40
		Never hinged	5.00	
a.		Inverted overprint	55.00	55.00
b.		Double overprint	72.50	72.50
c.		2c on 25c blue (R)	80.00	80.00
		Never hinged	200.00	
106	A12	5c green	20.00	2.40
		Never hinged	57.50	
a.		Inverted overprint	47.50	47.50
b.		Double overprint	72.50	72.50
107	A12	10c rose	20.00	2.40
		Never hinged	57.50	
a.		Inverted overprint	55.00	55.00
b.		Double overprint	72.50	72.50
108	A12	15c on 10c rose	2.40	2.40
		Never hinged	5.00	
a.		Inverted overprint	65.00	65.00
b.		Double overprint	72.50	72.50
109	A12	15c on 20c brn org	2.40	*2.40*
		Never hinged	5.00	
a.		Inverted overprint	65.00	65.00
b.		Double overprint	72.50	72.50
110	A12	15c on 25c indigo (R)	2.40	*2.40*
		Never hinged	5.00	
a.		Inverted overprint	65.00	65.00
b.		Double overprint	72.50	72.50
c.		15c on 25c blue (R)	225.00	225.00
		Never hinged	550.00	
d.		As "c," inverted overprint	475.00	475.00
e.		As "c," double overprint	475.00	
111	A12	20c brown orange	2.40	2.40
		Never hinged	5.00	
a.		Inverted overprint	27.50	27.50
b.		Double overprint	125.00	125.00
112	A12	25c indigo (R)	2.40	2.40
		Never hinged	5.00	
a.		Inverted overprint	24.00	24.00
b.		25c blue (R)	8.00	8.00
		Never hinged	19.00	
113	A12	25c indigo (Bk)	175.00	175.00
		Never hinged	500.00	
a.		Inverted overprint	450.00	450.00
b.		25c blue (Bk)	240.00	240.00
		Never hinged	560.00	
c.		As "b," inverted over-print	725.00	
114	A12	25c on 10c rose	2.40	4.75
		Never hinged	5.00	
a.		Double overprint	72.50	72.50

115 A12 50c on 20c brn
    org   5.00   2.40
    Never hinged   14.00
  a.   Double overprint   72.50   72.50
116 A12 55c on 5c green   21.00   4.75
    Never hinged   57.50
  a.   Inverted overprint   95.00   95.00
  b.   Double overprint   72.50   72.50
117 A12   1 l on 10c rose   47.50   40.00
    Never hinged   120.00
  a.   Inverted overprint   275.00   275.00
  b.   Double overprint   275.00
118 A12   1 l on 25c indi-
    go (R)   100.00   100.00
    Never hinged   290.00
  a.   1 l on 25c blue (R)   600.00   600.00
    Never hinged   1,500.
  b.   As "a," inverted overprint   875.00   725.00
119 A12   2 l on 5c green   47.50   40.00
    Never hinged   120.00
  a.   Inverted overprint   325.00
  b.   Double overprint   200.00
120 A12   5 l on 10c rose   225.00   240.00
    Never hinged   600.00
  a.   Inverted overprint   725.00   725.00
  b.   Double overprint   725.00
121 A12   10 l on 20c brn
    org   700.00   550.00
    Never hinged   2,000.
  a.   Inverted overprint   1,600.   800.00
  b.   Double overprint   1,600.   800.00
    Nos. 104-121 (18)   1,380.   1,178.
    Set, never hinged   3,850.

The Fiume Legionnaires of d'Annunzio occupied the islands of Arbe and Veglia in the Gulf of Carnaro Nov. 13, 1920-Jan. 5, 1921.
Varieties of overprint or surcharge exist for most of Nos. 104-121.
Nos. 113, 117-121, 125, 131 have a backprint.

Nos. 106-107, 111,
113, 115-116
Overprinted or
Surcharged at top

1920, Nov. 28
"ARBE" 11mm wide

122 A12 5c green   35.00   24.00
    Never hinged   82.50
123 A12 10c rose   45.00   *52.50*
    Never hinged   105.00
124 A12 20c brown org   87.50   52.50
    Never hinged   215.00
125 A12 25c deep blue   52.50   *52.50*
    Never hinged   115.00
126 A12 50c on 20c brn
    org   95.00   52.50
    Never hinged   240.00
127 A12 55c on 5c green   95.00   52.50
    Never hinged   240.00
    Nos. 122-127 (6)   410.00   286.50
    Set, never hinged   1,000.

The overprint on Nos. 122-125 comes in two widths: 11mm and 14mm. Values are for the 11mm width.

"ARBE" 14mm wide

122a A12 5c green   400.00   225.00
    Never hinged   900.00
123a A12 10c rose   400.00   225.00
    Never hinged   925.00
124a A12 20c brown org   400.00   225.00
    Never hinged   925.00
125a A12 25c deep blue   900.00   445.00
    Never hinged   2,050.
    Nos. 122a-125a (4)   2,100.   1,120.
    Set, never hinged   4,800.

Nos. 122a-125a issued Nov. 13.

Nos. 106-107, 111,
113, 115-116
Overprinted or
Surcharged at top

1920, Nov. 28
"VEGLIA" 17mm wide

128 A12 5c green   35.00   24.00
    Never hinged   85.00
129 A12 10c rose   45.00   *52.50*
    Never hinged   105.00
130 A12 20c brown orange   87.50   52.50
    Never hinged   210.00
131 A12 25c deep blue   52.50   *52.50*
    Never hinged   120.00
132 A12 50c on 20c brn org   95.00   52.50
    Never hinged   240.00
133 A12 55c on 5c green   95.00   52.50
    Never hinged   240.00
    Nos. 128-133 (6)   410.00   286.50
    Set, never hinged   1,000.

"VEGLIA" 19mm wide

128a A12 5c green   400.00   225.00
    Never hinged   900.00
129a A12 10c rose   400.00   225.00
    Never hinged   900.00
130a A12 20c brown org   400.00   225.00
    Never hinged   900.00
131a A12 25c deep blue   800.00   450.00
    Never hinged   2,100.
    Nos. 128a-131a (4)   2,075.   1,125.
    Set, never hinged   4,800.

Nos. 122a-125a issued Nov. 13.

Nos. 122-133 exist with double and inverted overprints.
Counterfeits of these overprints exist.

Nos. 86-99
Overprinted

1921, Feb. 2
"Provvisorio" 20mm wide
Space between lines 3mm
Pale Buff Background

134 A11 5c green   2.40   2.40
    Never hinged   5.50
    On cover   32.50
  a.   Inverted overprint   27.50   27.50
    Never hinged   40.00
  b.   Double overprint   52.50   52.50
135 A11 10c carmine   2.40   2.40
    Never hinged   5.50
    On cover   32.50
  a.   Inverted overprint   27.50   27.50
    Never hinged   40.00
  b.   Double overprint   52.50   52.50
136 A11 15c dark gray   2.40   *2.40*
    Never hinged   5.50
    On cover   37.50
  a.   Inverted overprint   27.50   27.50
    Never hinged   40.00
  b.   Double overprint   52.50   52.50
137 A11 20c orange   4.00   4.00
    Never hinged   9.00
    On cover   37.50
  a.   Inverted overprint   27.50   27.50
    Never hinged   40.00
  b.   Double overprint   27.50   27.50
138 A11 25c dark blue   4.00   4.00
    Never hinged   9.00
    On cover   40.00
  a.   Inverted overprint   27.50   27.50
    Never hinged   40.00
  b.   Double overprint   52.50   52.50
139 A11 30c red brown   4.00   4.00
    Never hinged   9.00
    On cover   35.00
  a.   Inverted overprint   27.50   27.50
    Never hinged   40.00
  b.   Double overprint   27.50   27.50
140 A11 45c olive gray   2.40   2.40
    Never hinged   5.50
    On cover   37.50
  a.   Inverted overprint   55.00   55.00
    Never hinged   82.50
  b.   Double overprint   40.00   40.00
141 A11 50c lilac   4.00   4.00
    Never hinged   9.00
    On cover   37.50
  a.   Inverted overprint   27.50   27.50
    Never hinged   40.00
142 A11 55c bister   4.00   4.00
    Never hinged   9.00
    On cover   55.00
  a.   Inverted overprint   16.00   16.00
    Never hinged   24.00
143 A11   1 l black   145.00   *180.00*
    Never hinged   325.00
    On cover   850.00
  a.   Inverted overprint   350.00   350.00
    Never hinged   500.00
144 A11   2 l red violet   95.00   95.00
    Never hinged   215.00
    On cover   225.00
145 A11   3 l dark green   95.00   95.00
    Never hinged   225.00
    On cover   375.00
146 A11   5 l brown   95.00   95.00
    Never hinged   215.00
    On cover   600.00
147 A11   10 l gray violet   95.00   95.00
    Never hinged   240.00
    On cover   675.00

With Additional
Surcharge

148 A11   1 l on 30c red
    brown   2.50   2.50
    Never hinged   4.50
  a.   Inverted overprint   27.50   27.50

    Never hinged   42.50
  b.   Double overprint   55.00   55.00
    Nos. 134-148 (15)   557.10   592.10
    Set, never hinged   1,400.

See Nos. F10-F11

Second Printing, Milan
"Provvisorio" 21mm wide
Space between overprint lines 4mm
1921, Dec. 18

148A A11 5c yellow green   50.00   *57.50*
    Never hinged   125.00
    On cover   300.00
148B A11 10c carmine   135.00   40.00
    Never hinged   340.00
    On cover   300.00
  c.   Vert. pair, imperf. be-
    tween   650.00

First Constituent Assembly

Nos. B4-B15
Overprinted

1921, Apr. 24

149 SP6 5c blue green   6.50   4.75
    Never hinged   12.50
150 SP6 10c rose   6.50   4.75
    Never hinged   12.50
  a.   Inverted overprint   65.00   65.00
151 SP6 15c gray   6.50   4.75
    Never hinged   12.50
152 SP6 20c orange   6.50   4.75
    Never hinged   12.50
153 SP7 45c olive green   17.50   12.00
    Never hinged   37.50
154 SP7 60c car rose   17.50   12.00
    Never hinged   37.50
  a.   Inverted overprint   47.50   47.50
155 SP7 80c brt violet   27.50   24.00
    Never hinged   62.50

With Additional Overprint "L"

156 SP7   1 l on 1cor dk
    slate   32.50   *35.00*
    Never hinged   85.00
  a.   Inverted overprint   80.00   80.00
157 SP8   2 l on 2cor red
    brn   120.00   4.25
    Never hinged   300.00
  a.   Inverted overprint   325.00   160.00
158 SP8   3 l on 3cor
    black brn   120.00   *130.00*
    Never hinged   300.00
159 SP8   5 l on 5cor yel
    brn   120.00   4.25
    Never hinged   300.00
160 SP8   10 l on 10cor dk
    vio   175.00   175.00
    Never hinged   450.00
  a.   Inverted overprint   475.00   400.00
    Nos. 149-160 (12)   656.00   415.50
    Set, never hinged   1,625.

The overprint exists inverted on several denominations.

Second Constituent Assembly
"Constitution" Issue of 1921 With
Additional Overprint "1922"

1922

161 SP6 5c blue green   4.75   3.25
    Never hinged   11.00
  a.   Inverted overprint   24.00   24.00
162 SP6 10c rose   2.40   *2.40*
    Never hinged   4.50
  a.   Inverted overprint   24.00   24.00
  b.   Double overprint, one invert-
    ed   40.00   40.00
163 SP6 15c gray   20.00   12.00
    Never hinged   50.00
164 SP6 20c orange   2.40   2.40
    Never hinged   4.50
  a.   Inverted overprint   32.50   32.50
  b.   Double overprint   40.00   40.00
  c.   Double overprint, one invert-
    ed   —   —
165 SP7 45c olive grn   13.00   12.00
    Never hinged   30.00
  a.   Inverted overprint   40.00   40.00
166 SP7 60c car rose   2.40   *3.25*
    Never hinged   4.50
167 SP7 80c brt violet   2.40   *3.25*
    Never hinged   4.50
168 SP7   1 l on 1cor dk slate   2.40   *2.40*
    Never hinged   4.50
  a.   Inverted overprint   55.00   55.00
  b.   Double overprint   40.00   40.00
169 SP8   2 l on 2cor red brn   20.00   16.00
    Never hinged   47.50
170 SP8   3 l on 3cor blk brn   2.50   *3.25*
    Never hinged   4.50
171 SP8   5 l on 5cor yel brn   2.50   *3.25*
    Never hinged   4.50
    Nos. 161-171 (11)   74.75   63.45
    Set, never hinged   170.00

Nos. 161-171 have the overprint in heavier type than Nos. 149-160 and "IV" in Roman instead of sans-serif numerals.

Venetian   Roman
Ship — A16   Arch — A17

St. Vitus — A18   Rostral
                  Column — A19

1923, Mar. 23   *Perf. 11½*
Pale Buff Background

172 A16 5c blue green   2.40   2.40
    Never hinged   4.25
173 A16 10c violet   2.40   2.40
    Never hinged   4.25
174 A16 15c brown   2.40   2.40
    Never hinged   4.25
175 A17 20c orange red   2.40   2.40
    Never hinged   4.25
176 A17 25c dark gray   2.40   2.40
    Never hinged   4.25
177 A17 30c dark green   2.40   2.40
    Never hinged   4.25
178 A18 50c dull blue   2.40   2.40
    Never hinged   4.25
179 A18 60c rose   4.00   *4.00*
    Never hinged   6.25
180 A18   1 l dark blue   4.00   *4.00*
    Never hinged   6.25
181 A19   2 l violet brown   65.00   20.00
    Never hinged   175.00
182 A19   3 l olive bister   55.00   45.00
    Never hinged   125.00
183 A19   5 l yellow brown   55.00   52.50
    Never hinged   125.00
    Nos. 172-183 (12)   199.80   142.30
    Set, never hinged   465.00

Nos. 172-183
Overprinted

1924, Feb. 22
Pale Buff Background

184 A16 5c blue green   2.40   *12.00*
    Never hinged   4.25
  a.   Inverted overprint   20.00   *40.00*
  b.   Double overprint   130.00
185 A16 10c violet   2.40   *12.00*
    Never hinged   4.25
  a.   Inverted overprint   16.00   *40.00*
186 A16 15c brown   2.40   *12.00*
    Never hinged   4.25
  a.   Inverted overprint   17.00   *40.00*
187 A17 20c orange red   2.40   *12.00*
    Never hinged   4.25
  a.   Inverted overprint   21.00   *40.00*
  b.   Double overprint   260.00
188 A17 25c dk gray   2.40   *12.00*
    Never hinged   4.25
189 A17 30c dk green   2.40   *12.00*
    Never hinged   4.25
  a.   Inverted overprint   42.50
190 A18 50c dull blue   2.40   *12.00*
    Never hinged   4.25
  a.   Inverted overprint   42.50   42.50
191 A18 60c red   2.40   *12.00*
    Never hinged   4.25
  a.   Inverted overprint   87.50
192 A18   1 l dark blue   2.40   *12.00*
    Never hinged   4.25
  a.   Inverted overprint   21.00   *40.00*
193 A19   2 l violet brown   4.00   *32.50*
    Never hinged   8.75
  a.   Inverted overprint   130.00   *160.00*
194 A19   3 l olive   6.00   *40.00*
    Never hinged   17.00
195 A19   5 l yellow brown   6.00   *40.00*
    Never hinged   17.00
    Nos. 184-195 (12)   37.60   220.50
    Set, never hinged   80.00

The overprint exists inverted on almost all values.

Nos. 172-183
Overprinted

1924, Mar. 1
Pale Buff Background

196	A16	5c blue green	2.40	20.00
		Never hinged	4.25	
197	A16	10c violet	2.40	20.00
		Never hinged	4.25	
198	A16	15c brown	2.40	20.00
		Never hinged	4.25	
199	A17	20c orange red	2.40	20.00
		Never hinged	4.25	
200	A17	25c dark gray	2.40	20.00
		Never hinged	4.25	
201	A17	30c dark gray	2.40	20.00
		Never hinged	4.25	
202	A18	50c dull blue	2.40	20.00
		Never hinged	4.25	
203	A18	60c red	2.40	20.00
		Never hinged	4.50	
204	A18	1 l dark blue	2.40	20.00
		Never hinged	4.50	
205	A19	2 l violet brown	4.00	27.50
		Never hinged	7.25	
206	A19	3 l olive	4.00	27.50
		Never hinged	8.00	
207	A19	5 l yellow brown	4.00	27.50
		Never hinged	8.00	
		Nos. 196-207 (12)	*33.60*	*262.50*
		Set, never hinged	62.50	

Postage stamps of Fiume were superseded by stamps of Italy.

SEMI-POSTAL STAMPS

Semi-Postal Stamps of
Hungary, 1916-17
Overprinted

1918, Dec. 2   Wmk. 137   Perf. 15
Typographed Overprint

B1	SP3	10f + 2f rose	8.00	8.00
		Never hinged	17.50	
a.		Inverted overprint	72.50	40.00
b.		Double overprint	240.00	120.00
B2	SP4	15f + 2f dl vio	8.00	8.00
		Never hinged	17.50	
a.		Inverted overprint	145.00	40.00
b.		Double overprint	145.00	47.50
B3	SP5	40f + 2f brn car	14.50	8.00
		Never hinged	37.50	
a.		Inverted overprint	87.50	37.50
		Nos. B1-B3 (3)	*30.50*	*24.00*
		Set, never hinged	72.50	

Handstamped Overprint

B1c	SP3	10f + 2f rose	125.00	80.00
		Never hinged	250.00	
B2c	SP4	15f + 2f dl vio	90.00	60.00
		Never hinged	180.00	
B3c	SP5	40f + 2f brn car	27.50	27.50
		Never hinged	45.00	
		Nos. B1c-B3c (3)	*242.50*	*167.50*
		Set, never hinged	525.00	

Statue of Romulus
and Remus Being
Suckled by
Wolf — SP6

Venetian
Galley — SP7

Church of St.
Mark's,
Venice — SP8

Perf. 11½
1919, May 18   Unwmk.   Typo.

B4	SP6	5c +5 l bl grn	47.50	32.50
		Never hinged	120.00	
B5	SP6	10c +5 l rose	47.50	32.50
		Never hinged	120.00	
B6	SP6	15c +5 l dk gray	47.50	32.50
		Never hinged	120.00	
B7	SP6	20c +5 l orange	47.50	32.50
		Never hinged	120.00	
B8	SP7	45c +5 l ol grn	47.50	32.50
		Never hinged	120.00	
B9	SP7	60c +5 l car rose	47.50	32.50
		Never hinged	120.00	
B10	SP7	80c +5 l lilac	47.50	32.50
		Never hinged	120.00	
B11	SP7	1cor +5 l slate	47.50	32.50
		Never hinged	120.00	
B12	SP8	2cor +5 l red brn	47.50	32.50
		Never hinged	120.00	
B13	SP8	3cor +5 l blk brn	47.50	32.50
		Never hinged	120.00	
B14	SP8	5cor +5 l yel brn	47.50	32.50
		Never hinged	120.00	
B15	SP8	10cor +5 l dk vio	47.50	32.50
		Never hinged	120.00	
		Nos. B4-B15 (12)	*570.00*	*390.00*
		Set, never hinged	1,450.	

200th day of peace. The surtax aided Fiume students in Italy. "Posta di Fiume" is printed on the back of Nos. B4-B16.
The surtax is shown on the stamps as "LIRE 5" but actually was 5cor.
For surcharges and overprints see Nos. 73-85, 149-171, J15-J26.

Dr. Antonio
Grossich — SP9

1919, Sept. 20

B16	SP9	25c + 2 l blue	3.25	3.25
		Never hinged	8.00	

Surtax for the Dr. Grossich Foundation.
For overprint and surcharge, see No. 77.

SPECIAL DELIVERY STAMPS

1916 Special Delivery
Stamp of Hungary
Overprinted

1918, Dec. 2   Wmk. 137   Perf. 15
Typographed Overprint

E1	SD1	2f gray green & red	4.75	4.75
		Never hinged	12.00	
a.		Double overprint	190.00	175.00

Handstamped overprints sell for more.

Handstamped Overprint

E1c	SD1	2f gray green & red	85.00	27.50
		Never hinged	170.00	

SD3

Perf. 11½
1920, Sept. 12   Unwmk.   Typo.

E2	SD3	30c slate blue	25.00	25.00
		Never hinged	62.50	

E3	SD3	50c rose	25.00	25.00
		Never hinged	62.50	
		Set, never hinged	125.00	

For overprints see Nos. E10-E11.

Nos. 102 and 100
Surcharged

1920, Nov.

E4	A12	30c on 20c brn org	190.00	175.00
		Never hinged	500.00	
a.		Inverted overprint	625.00	
b.		Double overprint	625.00	
E5	A12	50c on 5c green	290.00	125.00
		Never hinged	700.00	
a.		Inverted overprint	1,000.	
b.		Double overprint	1,000.	
c.		Double overprint, one inverted	1,100.	

Nos. E4-E5 have a backprint.

Same Surcharge as on Nos. 124, 122

E6	A12	30c on 20c brn org	275.00	180.00
		Never hinged	560.00	
E7	A12	50c on 5c green	210.00	180.00
		Never hinged	425.00	
a.		Double overprint	950.00	

Overprint on Nos. E6-E7 is 11mm wide.

Same Surcharge as on Nos. 130, 128

E8	A12	30c on 20c brn org	275.00	180.00
		Never hinged	560.00	
E9	A12	50c on 5c green	210.00	180.00
		Never hinged	425.00	
a.		Double overprint	950.00	950.00
		Nos. E4-E9 (6)	*1,450.*	*1,020.*
		Set, never hinged	2,900.	

Overprint on Nos. E8-E9 is 17mm wide.

Nos. E2 and E3 Overprinted

1921, Feb. 2

E10	SD3	30c slate blue	11.00	12.00
		Never hinged	25.00	
a.		Inverted overprint	120.00	120.00
b.		Double overprint	40.00	40.00
E11	SD3	50c rose	15.00	12.00
		Never hinged	37.50	
a.		Inverted overprint	27.50	27.50
b.		Double overprint	105.00	105.00
		Set, never hinged	62.50	

Fiume in
16th
Century
SD4

1923, Mar. 23   Perf. 11, 11½

E12	SD4	60c rose & buff	24.00	24.00
		Never hinged	60.00	
E13	SD4	2 l dk bl & buff	24.00	24.00
		Never hinged	60.00	
		Set, never hinged	120.00	

Nos. E12-E13 Overprinted

1924, Feb. 22

E14	SD4	60c car & buff	3.25	20.00
		Never hinged	8.00	

E15	SD4	2 l dk bl & buff	3.25	20.00
		Never hinged	8.00	
a.		Inverted overprint	130.00	160.00
		Set, never hinged	16.00	

Nos. E12-E13 Overprinted

1924, Mar. 1

E16	SD4	60c car & buff	4.00	80.00
		Never hinged	10.00	
E17	SD4	2 l dk bl & buff	4.00	80.00
		Never hinged	10.00	
		Set, never hinged	20.00	

POSTAGE DUE STAMPS

Postage Due
Stamps of Hungary,
1915-1916,
Overprinted

1918, Dec.   Wmk. 137   Perf. 15
Typographed Overprint

J1	D1	6f green & black	525.00	175.00
		Never hinged	1,100.	
a.		Inverted overprint	1,050.	
J2	D1	12f green & black	800.00	400.00
		Never hinged	1,600.	
a.		Double overprint	950.00	
J3	D1	50f green & black	225.00	125.00
		Never hinged	450.00	
a.		Double overprint	950.00	
		Set, never hinged	3,150.	

Handstamped Overprint

J1c	D1	6f green & black	190.00	105.00
		Never hinged	380.00	
d.		Double overprint	—	1,450.
J2c	D1	12f green & black	180.00	72.50
		Never hinged	360.00	
d.		Double overprint	—	1,450.
J3c	D1	50c green & black	65.00	35.00
		Never hinged	130.00	
d.		Double overprint	—	1,450.
		Set, never hinged	870.00	

Typographed Overprint

J4	D1	1f green & red	175.00	240.00
		Never hinged	350.00	
J5	D1	2f green & red	6.50	6.50
		Never hinged	13.00	
a.		Inverted overprint	52.50	45.00
b.		Double overprint	175.00	
J6	D1	5f green & red	72.50	72.50
		Never hinged	145.00	
a.		Inverted overprint	175.00	130.00
J7	D1	6f green & red	6.50	6.50
		Never hinged	13.00	
a.		Inverted overprint	25.00	25.00
b.		Double overprint	27.50	
J8	D1	10f green & red	90.00	27.50
		Never hinged	180.00	
a.		Inverted overprint	440.00	
J9	D1	12f green & red	6.50	6.50
		Never hinged	13.00	
J10	D1	15f green & red	650.00	550.00
		Never hinged	1,300.	
J11	D1	20f green & red	6.50	6.50
		Never hinged	13.00	
a.		Inverted overprint	45.00	32.50
J12	D1	30f green & red	1,600.	1,300.
		Never hinged	3,200.	
		Nos. J4-J12 (9)	*2,613.*	*2,216.*
		Set, never hinged	5,225.	

Handstamped Overprint

J4c	D1	1f green & red	40.00	24.00
		Never hinged	77.50	
d.		Inverted overprint		425.00
e.		Double overprint	525.00	190.00
J5c	D1	2f green & red	120.00	72.50
		Never hinged	300.00	
d.		Inverted overprint	440.00	
e.		Double overprint		
J6c	D1	5f green & red	40.00	47.50
		Never hinged	80.00	
d.		Inverted overprint	320.00	440.00
e.		Double overprint	525.00	525.00
J7c	D1	6f green & red	77.50	72.50
		Never hinged	155.00	
d.		Inverted overprint		440.00
e.		Double overprint	—	950.00
J8c	D1	10f green & red	32.50	32.50
		Never hinged	65.00	
d.		Inverted overprint	475.00	475.00
J9c	D1	12f green & red	77.50	72.50
		Never hinged	160.00	
d.		Inverted overprint		800.00
J10c	D1	15f green & red	32.50	32.50
		Never hinged	65.00	
d.		Inverted overprint		800.00
e.		Double overprint	440.00	440.00
J11c	D1	20f green & red	725.00	145.00
		Never hinged	1,450.	
d.		Inverted overprint	1,275.	550.00

J12c	D1	30f green & red	32.50	32.50
		Never hinged	65.00	
d.		Inverted overprint		900.00
e.		Double overprint	950.00	950.00
		Nos. j4c-j12c (9)	1,177.	531.50
		Set, never hinged	2,350.	

Six minor varieties of the handstamp exist. Some are sought by specialists at much higher values. Forgeries of No. J10 exist.

Eagle — D2

Perf. 11½

1919, July 28   Unwmk.   Typo.

J13	D2	2c brown	2.40	2.40
		Never hinged	6.00	
J14	D2	5c brown	2.40	2.40
		Never hinged	6.00	
		Set, never hinged	12.00	

Semi-Postal Stamps of 1919 Overprinted and Surcharged

1921, Mar. 21

J15	SP6	2c on 15c gray	6.50	6.50
		Never hinged	14.50	
J16	SP6	4c on 10c rose	4.75	4.75
		Never hinged	12.00	
J17	SP9	5c on 25c blue	4.75	4.75
		Never hinged	12.00	
J18	SP6	6c on 20c orange	4.75	4.75
		Never hinged	12.00	
J19	SP6	10c on 20c orange	6.50	6.50
		Never hinged	14.50	

Nos. B8-B11 Surcharged

J20	SP7	20c on 45c olive grn	2.40	4.75
		Never hinged	5.75	
J21	SP7	30c on 1cor dk slate	12.00	12.00
		Never hinged	24.00	
J22	SP7	40c on 80c violet	4.75	6.50
		Never hinged	12.00	
J23	SP7	50c on 60c carmine	4.75	6.50
		Never hinged	12.00	
J24	SP7	60c on 45c olive grn	2.40	4.75
		Never hinged	5.75	
J25	SP7	80c on 45c olive grn	2.40	4.75
		Never hinged	5.75	

Surcharged like Nos. J15-J19

J26	SP8	1 l on 2cor red brown	24.00	24.00
		Never hinged	60.00	
		Nos. J15-J26 (12)	79.95	90.50
		Set, never hinged	190.00	

See note below No. 85 regarding settings of "Valore Globale" overprint.

NEWSPAPER STAMPS

Newspaper Stamp of Hungary, 1914, Overprinted like Nos. 1-23

1918, Dec. 2   Wmk. 137   *Imperf.*
Typographed Overprint

P1	N5	(2f) orange	4.75	3.25
		Never hinged	15.00	
a.		Inverted overprint	55.00	52.50
b.		Double overprint	210.00	190.00

Handstamped Overprint

P1c	N5	(2f) orange	72.50	27.50
		Never hinged	145.00	
d.		Double overprint	875.00	875.00

Handstamped overprints sell for more.

Eagle
N1

1919   Unwmk.   *Perf. 11½*

P2	N1	2c deep buff	9.50	14.50
		Never hinged	24.00	

Re-engraved

P3	N1	2c deep buff	9.50	14.50
		Never hinged	24.00	
		Set, never hinged	48.00	

In the re-engraved stamp the top of the "2" is rounder and broader, the feet of the eagle show clearly and the diamond at bottom has six lines instead of five.

Steamer — N2

1920, Sept. 12

P4	N2	1c gray green	4.00	3.25
		Never hinged	10.00	
a.		Imperf	24.00	24.00

FRANCE

'fran̬ts

LOCATION — Western Europe
GOVT. — Republic
AREA — 210,033 sq. mi.
POP. — 54,539,000 (est. 1984)
CAPITAL — Paris

100 Centimes = 1 Franc

Catalogue values for unused stamps in this country are for Never Hinged items, beginning with Scott 299 in the regular postage section, Scott B42 in the semi-postal section, Scott S1 for franchise stamps, and Scott N27 for occupation stamps.

Watermarks

Wmk. 407

Ceres — A1

FORTY CENTIMES

Type I   Type II

1849-50   Typo.   Unwmk.   *Imperf.*

1	A1	10c bis, *yelsh* ('50)	2,000.	275.00
		On cover, single franking		625.00
a.		10c dark bister, *yelsh*	2,300.	350.00
		On cover, single franking		725.00
b.		10c greenish bister	2,750.	425.00
		On cover, single franking		1,250.

c.		10c deep greenish bister	4,000.	750.00
		On cover, single franking		1,650.
d.		As #1, tête beche pair	(4,100.)	(6,250.)
		On cover		42,500.
e.		As #1a, tête beche pair	132,500.	18,500.
		On cover		37,000.
f.		As #1b, tête beche pair	132,500.	18,500.
		On cover		37,500.
2	A1	15c green, *grnsh*	23,000.	900.00
		On cover, single franking		1,650.
a.		15c yellow green, *grnsh* ('50)	22,500.	900.00
		On cover, single franking		1,650.
b.		15c dark green	24,750.	1,100.
		On cover, single franking		1,850.
c.		Tête bêche pair	—	
		On cover front		310,000.
3	A1	20c blk, *yelsh*	400.00	45.00
		On cover, single franking		95.00
a.		20c black	475.00	55.00
		On cover, single franking		130.00
b.		20c black, *buff*	1,400.	225.00
		On cover, single franking		340.00
c.		Tête bêche pair	10,000.	6,600.
		On cover		14,500.
4	A1	20c dark blue	2,850.	
a.		20c blue, *bluish*	2,200.	
b.		20c blue, *yelsh*	3,500.	
c.		Tête bêche pair	70,000.	
e.		As "a," tête bêche pair	62,500.	
f.		As "b," tête bêche pair	100,000.	
6	A1	25c lt bl, *bluish*	6,750.	40.00
		On cover, single franking		65.00
a.		25c blue, *bluish* ('50)	6,750.	40.00
		On cover, single franking		65.00
b.		25c blue, *yelsh*	6,400.	50.00
		On cover, single franking		100.00
c.		Tête bêche pair	200,000.	16,000.
		On cover		30,000.
7	A1	40c org, *yelsh* (I) ('50)	3,750.	475.00
		With dark brownish gum	2,250.	
		On cover, single franking		725.00
a.		40c org ver, *yelsh* (I)	4,250.	525.00
		On cover, single franking		950.00
b.		40c orange, *yelsh* (II)	25,000.	6,750.
		On cover, single franking		12,750.
c.		Pair, types I and II	40,000.	13,250.
		On cover		20,000.
f.		Pair, type II	105,000.	52,500.
		On cover		77,500.
g.		Vertical half used as 20c on cover		215,000.
8	A1	1fr vermilion, *yelsh*	90,000.	15,500.
		On cover, single franking		27,000.
a.		1fr dull orange red	90,000.	19,500.
		On cover, single franking		29,000.
b.		Tête bêche pair, no gum	95,000.	172,500.
		On cover		315,000.
c.		1fr pale ver ("Vervelle")	26,500.	
d.		As "c," tête bêche pair	550,000.	

A cover bearing a single franking with 1fr vermilion, No. 8, realized the equivalent of U.S. $36,350 at a Geneva auction in 2004.

A Tête-bêche pair, No. 8b, in a used horizontal strip of three sold at a Paris auction in 2003 for the equivalent of U.S. $287,500.

9	A1	1fr light carmine	12,000.	875.00
		On cover, single franking		2,000.
a.		Tête bêche pair	235,000.	23,500.
		On cover		50,000.
b.		1fr brown carmine	13,250.	1,100.
		On cover, single franking		1,300.
c.		1fr dark carmine, *yelsh*	11,500.	825.00
		On cover, single franking		1,050.
e.		1fr red brown	16,000.	2,000.
		On cover, single franking, *from*		2,500.

Full margins = ¾mm.

No. 4 was printed but not yet gummed when the rate change to 25c made them unnecessary. An essay with a red "25" surcharge on No. 4 was rejected.

An ungummed sheet of No. 8c was found in 1895 among the effects of Anatole A. Hulot, the printer. It was sold to Ernest Vervelle, a Parisian dealer, by whose name the stamps are known.

No. 9e exists used from the beginning of 1849. On-cover values: January to March dates, $6,000; April and May dates, $5,500; June and later dates, $3,000.

See Nos. 329-329e, 612-613, 624. Post 1940 issues in Scott Standard catalogue, Vol. 2.

Values for stamps without gum

1	A1	10c bis, *yelsh*	1,000.
a.		10c dark bister, *yelsh*	1,100.
b.		10c greenish bister	775.
c.		10c deep greenish bister	1,900.
d.		As #1, tête bêche pair	57,500.
2	A1	15c green, *grnsh*	11,500.
a.		15c yellow green, *grnsh*	11,000.
b.		15c dark green	12,250.
3	A1	20c blk, *yelsh*	190.
a.		20c black	240.
b.		20c black, *buff*	525.
4	A1	20c dark blue	2,850.
a.		20c blue, *bluish*	2,200.
b.		20c blue, *yellowish*	3,500.
6	A1	25c lt bl, *bluish*	3,400.
a.		25c blue, *bluish* ('50)	3,400.
b.		25c blue, *yelsh*	3,200.
7	A1	40c org, *yelsh* (I)	1,900.
a.		40c org ver, *yelsh* (I)	2,100.
b.		40c orange, *yelsh* (II)	7,750.
c.		Pair, types I and II	12,250.
f.		Pair, type II	33,000.
8	A1	1fr vermilion, *yelsh*	60,000.
a.		1fr dull orange red	50,000.
c.		1fr pale ver ("Vervelle")	26,500.
9	A1	1fr light carmine	5,500.
b.		1fr brown carmine, *yelsh*	6,600.
c.		1fr dark carmine, *yelsh*	5,750.
e.		1fr red brown	7,200.

Values for blocks of 4

1	A1	10c bis, *yelsh*	11,000.	12,000.
		On cover		17,000.
b.		10c greenish bister	15,500.	13,250.
		On cover		19,000.
2	A1	15c green, *grnsh*	120,000.	62,000.
		On cover		100,000.
b.		15c dark green	130,000.	75,000.
		On cover		125,000.
3	A1	20c blk, *yelsh*	2,000.	4,800.
		On cover		11,000.
a.		20c black	2,500.	5,250.
		On cover		11,000.
4	A1	20c dark blue	14,000.	
a.		20c blue, *bluish*	14,000.	
b.		20c blue, *yelsh*	16,500.	
6	A1	25c lt bl, *bluish*	35,000.	5,250.
		On cover		9,250.
a.		25c blue, *bluish* ('50)	35,000.	5,250.
		On cover		9,250.
7	A1	40c org, *yelsh* (I)	24,000.	18,000.
		On cover		27,500.
8	A1	1fr vermilion, *yelsh*	500,000.	120,000.
a.		1fr dull orange red	500,000.	145,000.
c.		1fr pale ver ("Vervelle")	175,000.	
9b	A1	1fr brown carmine, *yelsh*	65,000.	13,750.
		On cover		26,000.
c.		1fr dark carmine, *yelsh*	75,000.	18,000.
		On cover		29,000.
d.		1fr red brown	280,000.	

Values for used pairs

1	A1	10c bis, *yelsh*	875.
a.		10c dark bister, *yelsh*	800.
b.		10c greenish bister	1,100.
c.		10c deep greenish bister	2,400.
2	A1	15c green, *grnsh*	2,300.
a.		15c yellow green, *grnsh*	2,300.
b.		15c dark green	2,750.
3	A1	20c blk, *yelsh*	120.
a.		20c black	140.
b.		20c black, *buff*	675.
6	A1	25c lt bl, *bluish*	100.
b.		25c blue, *bluish* ('50)	100.
			150.
7	A1	40c org, *yelsh* (I)	1,100.
a.		40c org ver, *yelsh* (I)	1,300.
c.		Pair, types I and II	14,000.
c.		Pair, type II	55,000.
8	A1	1fr vermilion, *yelsh*	60,000.
a.		1fr dull orange red	60,000.
9	A1	1fr light carmine	1,850.
b.		1fr brown carmine	2,750.
c.		1fr dark carmine, *yelsh*	2,100.
e.		1fr red brown	5,500.

Values for pairs on cover

1	A1	10c bis, *yelsh*	1,400.
a.		10c dark bister, *yelsh*	1,500.
b.		10c greenish bister	1,850.
c.		10c deep greenish bister	3,250.
2	A1	15c green, *grnsh*	39,000.
a.		15c yellow green, *grnsh*	36,500.
b.		15c dark green	40,000.
3	A1	20c blk, *yelsh*	250.
a.		20c black	260.
b.		20c black, *buff*	800.
6	A1	25c lt bl, *bluish*	240.
a.		25c blue, *bluish* ('50)	240.
b.		25c blue, *bluish*	260.
7	A1	40c org, *yelsh*	1,400.
a.		40c org ver, *yelsh* (I)	1,500.
c.		Pair, types I and II	22,000.
f.		Pair, type II	85,000.
8	A1	1fr vermilion, *yelsh*	87,500.
a.		1fr dull orange red	100,000.
9	A1	1fr light carmine	3,250.
b.		1fr brown carmine	3,750.
c.		1fr dark carmine, *yelsh*	5,250.

Nos. 1, 4a, 6a, 7 and 13 are of similar designs and colors to French Colonies Nos. 9, 11, 12, 14, and 8. There are numerous shades of each. Identification by those who are not experts can be difficult, though cancellations can be used as a guide for used stamps.

Because of the date of issue the Colonies stamps are similar in shades and papers to the perforated French stamps, Nos. 23a, 54, 57-59, and are not as clearly printed. Except for No. 13, unused, the French Colonies stamps sell for much less than the values shown here for properly identified French versions.

Expertization of these stamps is recommended.

1862   Re-issue

1g	A1	10c bister	550.
		No gum	315.
2d	A1	15c yellow green	700.
		No gum	325.
3d	A1	20c black, *yellowish*	450.
		No gum	200.
4d	A1	20c blue	450.
		No gum	200.
6d	A1	25c blue	500.
		No gum	250.
7d	A1	40c orange (I)	700.
		No gum	325.
7e	A1	40c orange (II)	11,500.
		No gum	3,750.
h.		Pair, types I and II	16,500.
		No gum	5,500.
i.		Pair, type II	28,500.
		No gum	11,000.
9d	A1	1fr pale lake	750.
		No gum	375.

The re-issues are fine impressions in lighter colors and on whiter paper than the originals. An official imitation of the essay, 25c on 20c blue, also in a lighter shade and on whiter paper, was made at the same time as the re-issues.

Values for blocks of 4

1d	A1	10c bister	3,000.
2d	A1	15c yellow green	4,000.
3d	A1	20c black, *yellowish*	2,500.
4d	A1	20c blue	2,500.
6d	A1	25c blue	2,900.
7d	A1	40c orange (I)	3,750.
9d	A1	1fr pale lake	4,250.

President Louis Napoleon — A2

1852

10	A2	10c pale bister, *yelsh*	39,000.	575.00
		On cover, single franking		1,000.
a.		10c dark bister, *yelsh*	40,000.	650.00
		On cover, single franking		1,100.
c.		10c dark brownish bister	42,500.	1,100.
		On cover, single franking		1,650.
11	A2	25c blue, *bluish*	3,100.	40.00
		On cover, single franking		75.00
b.		25c dark blue, *bluish*	3,700.	70.00
		On cover, single franking		125.00
c.		25c greenish blue	3,150.	52.50
		On cover, single franking		100.00

Full margins = ¾mm.

Values for stamps without gum

10	A2	10c pale bister, *yelsh*	15,000.
a.		10c dark bister, *yelsh*	16,000.
c.		10c dark brownish bister	20,000.
11	A2	25c blue, *bluish*	1,750.
b.		25c dark blue, *bluish*	2,100.
c.		25c greenish blue	1,900.

Values for used pairs

10	A2	10c pale bister, *yelsh*	1,400.
11	A2	25c blue, *bluish*	110.

A sheet margin pair of 10 centimes, No. 10, realized the equivalent of U.S. $20,000 at a Geneva auction in 2004.

Values for pairs on cover

10	A2	10c pale bister, *yelsh*	2,300.
a.		10c dark bister, *yelsh*	2,900.
c.		10c dark brownish bister	3,750.
11	A2	25c blue, *bluish*	325.
b.		25c dark blue, *bluish*	375.
c.		25c greenish blue	260.

Values for used strips of 3

10	A2	10c pale bister, *yelsh*	3,300.
11	A2	25c blue, *bluish*	275.

Values for used strips of 4

10	A2	10c pale bister, *yelsh*	5,300.
11	A2	25c blue, *bluish*	650.

Values for used strips of 5

10	A2	10c pale bister, *yelsh*	11,000.
11	A2	25c blue, *bluish*	1,500.

Values for blocks of 4

10	A2	10c pale bister, *yelsh*	220,000.	55,000.00
		On cover		87,500.00
11	A2	25c blue, *bluish*	16,500.	2,400.00
		On cover		4,000.00

1862   Re-issue

10b	A2	10c bister	700.00
11a	A2	25c blue	450.00

The re-issues are in lighter colors and on whiter paper than the originals.

Values for blocks of 4

10b	A2	10c bister	3,300.
11a	A2	25c blue	2,500.

Emperor Napoleon III — A3

Die I. The curl above the forehead directly below "R" of "EMPIRE" is made up of two lines very close together, often appearing to form a single thick line. There is no shading across the neck.

Die II. The curl is made of two distinct, more widely separated lines. There are lines of shading across the upper neck.

1853-60   Imperf.

12	A3	1c ol grn, *pale bl* ('60)	200.00	80.00
		On cover		200.00
		On cover, single franking		350.00
a.		1c bronze grn, *pale bluish*	200.00	95.00
		On cover		210.00
		On cover, single franking		375.00
13	A3	5c grn, *grnsh* (I) ('54)	800.00	85.00
		On cover		175.00
		On cover, single franking		250.00
a.		5c dark green	1,250.	160.00
		On cover		350.00

		On cover, single franking		500.00
14	A3	10c bis, *yelsh* (I)	450.00	9.00
		On cover, single franking		13.00
a.		10c yellow, *yelsh* (I)	1,500.	37.50
		On cover, single franking		52.50
b.		10c bister brn, *yelsh* (I)	550.00	25.00
		On cover, single franking		37.50
c.		10c bister, *yelsh* (II) ('60)	550.00	22.50
		On cover, single franking		35.00
d.		Half used as 5c on cover		135,000.
15	A3	20c bl, *bluish* (I) ('54)	190.00	1.50
		On cover, single franking		3.25
a.		20c dark bl, *bluish* (I)	275.00	2.00
		On cover, single franking		3.50
b.		20c milky blue (I)	275.00	12.50
		On cover, single franking		25.00
c.		20c blue, *lilac* (I)	5,500.	82.50
		On cover		130.00
d.		20c blue, *bluish* (II) ('60)	325.00	4.75
		On cover		7.00
e.		Half used as 10c on cover		18,500.
f.		Tête bêche pair	190,000.	
16	A3	20c bl, *grnsh* (II)	6,500.	190.00
		On cover, single franking		290.00
a.		20c blue, *greenish* (I)	5,000.	125.00
		On cover		225.00
17	A3	25c bl, *bluish* (I)	2,500.	250.00
		On cover, single franking		425.00
a.		25c milky blue (I)	2,000.	190.00
		On cover, single franking		440.00
18	A3	40c org, *yelsh* (I)	2,500.	12.50
		On cover, single franking		20.00
a.		40c org ver, *yellowish*	2,750.	20.00
b.		Half used as 20c on cover		32.50
				145,000.
19	A3	80c lake, *yelsh* (I) ('54)	3,600.	82.50
		On cover		175.00
a.		Tête bêche pair	400,000.	28,000.00
b.		Half used as 40c on cover		42,500.
				40,000.00
20	A3	80c rose, *pnksh* (I) ('60)	2,400.	47.50
		On cover, single franking		90.00
a.		Tête-bêche pair	64,000.	23,000.00
		On cover, single franking		22,500.00
b.		80c bright rose	2,800.	75.00
		On cover, single franking		140.00
d.		80c pale rose	2,600.	47.50
		On cover, single franking		90.00
e.		80c bright gooseberry red ("groseille")	5,200.	250.00
		On cover, single franking		400.00
21	A3	1fr lake, *yelsh* (I)	9,500.	3,250.00
		On cover		5,250.
		On cover, single franking		7,500.
a.		Tête bêche pair	375,000.	170,000.00
		On cover		210,000.00

Full margins = ¾mm.

Most values of the 1853-60 issue are known privately rouletted, pin-perf., perf. 7 and percé en scie.

A vertical mint pair of No. 19a was sold at a Paris auction in 2003 for the equivalent of $345,000.

A vertical pair of No. 19a on cover, addressed to Peru, was sold at a Paris auction in 2003 for the equivalent of $57,500.

A horizontal mint pair of No. 20a was sold at a Paris auction in 2003 for the equivalent of $46,000.

A horizontal pair of No. 20a on cover, addressed to Tuscany, was sold at a Paris auction in 2003 for the equivalent of $17,250.

An example of No. 21a, tête bêche pair within a mint block of 6, was sold at a Paris auction in 2003 for the equivalent of $431,250.

Values for bisected stamps on cover

14d	A3	10c Nangis, 5/7/55		160,000.
15e	A3	20c Bordeaux, Feb. '56		18,500.
15e	A3	20c Marines, Sep. '56		24,000.
15e	A3	20c Meru, Sep. '56		24,000.
15e	A3	20c Sainte-Sigolene, Feb. '56		25,000.
15e	A3	20c Vebron, June '61-Jan '62		26,000.
15e	A3	20c Villars-de-Lans, Jan '58		25,000.
18b	A3	40c Mostaganem, May '60		140,000.
19b	A3	80c Givors		60,000.

Nos. 14d and 18b are unique.

Values for stamps without gum

12	A3	1c ol grn, *pale bl*	100.00
a.		1c bronze grn, *pale bluish*	100.00
13	A3	5c grn, *grnsh* (I)	400.00
a.		5c dark green	950.00
14	A3	10c bis, *yelsh* (I)	225.00
a.		10c yellow, *yelsh* (I)	675.00
b.		10c bister brn, *yelsh* (I)	225.00
c.		10c bister, *yelsh* (II)	225.00
15	A3	20c bl, *bluish*	95.00
a.		20c dark bl, *bluish* (I)	140.00
b.		20c milky blue (I)	125.00
c.		20c blue, *lilac* (I)	2,700.
d.		20c blue, *bluish* (II)	130.00
16	A3	20c bl, *grnsh* (II)	3,250.
a.		20c blue, *greenish*	3,000.
17	A3	25c bl, *bluish*	1,250.
a.		25c milky blue (I)	1,250.
18	A3	40c org, *yelsh* (I)	1,250.
a.		40c org ver, *yellowish*	1,750.
19	A3	80c lake, *yelsh* (I)	1,800.
20	A3	80c rose, *pnksh* (I)	1,900.
b.		80c bright rose	1,150.
20d	A3	80c pale rose	950.00
20e	A3	80c bright gooseberry red ("groseille")	2,600.
21	A3	1fr lake, *yelsh* (I)	3,600.

Values for pairs

12	A3	1c ol grn, *pale bl*	450.00	195.00
a.		1c bronze grn, *pale bluish*	450.00	200.00
13	A3	5c grn, *grnsh* (I)	1,750.	195.00
a.		5c dark green	4,250.	500.00
14	A3	10c bis, *yelsh* (I)	950.00	22.50
a.		10c yellow, *yelsh* (I)	4,000.	130.00

b.		10c bister brn, *yelsh* (I)		3,250.	87.50
c.		10c bister brn, *yelsh* (II)		950.00	47.50
15	A3	20c bl, *bluish* (I)		400.00	5.25
a.		20c dark bl, *bluish* (I)		625.00	4.75
b.		20c milky blue (I)		625.00	32.50
c.		20c blue, *lilac* (I)		11,000.	210.00
d.		20c blue, *bluish* (I)		875.00	14.50
16	A3	20c bl, *grnsh* (II)		12,500.	475.00
a.		20c blue, *greenish* (I)		10,000.	310.00
17	A3	25c bl, *bluish* (I)		5,000.	600.00
a.		25c milky blue (I)		5,000.	600.00
18	A3	40c org, *yelsh* (I)		5,000.	32.50
a.		40c org ver, *yellowish* (I)		7,400.	47.50
19	A3	80c lake, *yelsh* (I)		10,000.	300.00
20	A3	80c rose, *pnksh* (I)		5,000.	130.00
21	A3	1fr lake, *yelsh* (I)		20,000.	7,600.

Values for pairs on cover

12	A3	1c ol grn, *pale bl,* on cover, paying 2c rate		500.00
a.		1c bronze grn, *pale bluish,* on cover, paying 2c rate		550.00
13	A3	5c grn, *grnsh* (I) on cover, paying 10c rate		275.00
a.		5c dark green, on cover, paying 10c rate		575.00
14	A3	10c bis, *yelsh* (I)		26.00
a.		10c yellow, *yelsh*		120.00
b.		10c bister brn, *yelsh* (I)		97.50
c.		10c bister, *yelsh* (II)		90.00
15	A3	20c bl, *bluish* (I)		7.00
a.		20c dark bl, *bluish* (I)		7.75
b.		20c milky blue (I)		67.50
c.		20c blue, *lilac* (I)		325.00
d.		20c blue, *bluish* (I)		15.00
16	A3	20c bl, *grnsh* (II)		725.00
a.		20c blue, *greenish* (I)		550.00
17	A3	25c bl, *bluish* (I)		1,100.
a.		25c milky blue (I)		1,200.
18	A3	40c org, *yelsh* (I)		52.50
a.		40c org ver, *yellowish* (I)		80.00
19	A3	80c lake, *yelsh* (I)		450.00
20	A3	80c rose, *pnksh* (I)		250.00
		Strip of 3 on cover		325.00
		Strip of 4 on cover		450.00
		Strip of 5 on cover		725.00
21	A3	1fr lake, *yelsh* (I)		22,000.

Blocks of 4

12	A3	1c ol grn, *pale bl,*		950.00	1,150.
		On cover			2,250.
13	A3	5c grn, *grnsh*		3,750.	1,200.
		On cover			2,300.
a.		5c dark green		9,200.	2,400.
		On cover			4,000.
14	A3	10c bister, *yellowish* (I)		2,100.	300.00
		On cover			525.00
c.		10c bister, *yellowish* (II)		2,750.	475.00
		On cover			725.00
15	A3	20c blue, *bluish* (I)		875.00	95.00
		On cover			200.00
a.		20c dark blue, *bluish* (I)		1,450.	130.00
		On cover			225.00
d.		20c blue, *bluish* (II)		1,850.	475.00
		On cover			700.00
16	A3	20c blue, *greenish* (II)		3,000.	
		On cover			4,750.
a.		20c blue, *greenish* (I)		1,750.	
		On cover			2,800.
17	A3	25c bl, *bluish* (I)		12,000.	2,700.
		On cover			4,300.
18	A3	40c orange, *yellowish* (I)		12,000.	800.00
		On cover			1,450.
19	A3	80c lake, *yellowish* (I)		18,000.	1,000.
		On cover			1,850.
20	A3	80c rose, *pinkish* (I)		12,000.	600.00
		On cover			1,100.
21	A3	1fr lake, *yellowish* (I)		64,000.	35,000.
					55,000.

1862   **Re-issue**

17c	A3	25c blue (I)	525.
19c	A3	80c lake (I)	2,200.
21c	A3	1fr lake (I)	1,800.
d.		Tête bêche pair	32,000.

Blocks of 4

17c	A3	25c lake (I)	2,400.
19c	A3	80c lake (I)	10,500.
21c	A3	1fr lake (I)	9,500.
d.		Tête bêche pair in block	40,000.

The re-issues are in lighter colors and on whiter paper than the originals.

1862-71   **Perf. 14x13½**

22	A3	1c ol grn, *pale bl* (II)		160.00	40.00
		On cover			87.50
		On cover, single franking			150.00
a.		1c bronze grn, *pale bl* (II)		100.00	32.50
		On cover, single franking			150.00
b.		1c bronze gold ("mordore")		350.00	
23	A3	5c yel grn, *grnsh* (I)		375.00	20.00
		On cover			45.00
		On cover, single franking			125.00
a.		5c deep green, *grnsh* (I)		250.00	16.00
		On cover			37.50
		On cover, single franking			100.00
24	A3	5c grn, *pale bl* ('71) (I)		1,950.	100.00
		On cover			160.00
		On cover, single franking			310.00
25	A3	10c bis, *yelsh* (II)		1,600.	4.25
		On cover, single franking			6.50
a.		10c yel brn, *yelsh* (I)		2,000.	10.50
		On cover, single franking			17.00
26	A3	20c bl, *bluish* (II)		225.00	1.60
		On cover			2.25
a.		Tête bêche pair (II)		5,000.	1,300.
		On cover			2,500.
b.		20c dark blue		275.00	2.75
		On cover, single franking			3.25
c.		20c pale blue		250.00	2.50
		On cover, single franking			5.00
d.		20c blue, *azure*		375.00	1.75
		On cover, single franking			3.25
27	A3	40c org, *yelsh* (I)		1,400.	7.50
		On cover, single franking			11.50
a.		40c pale orange		1,300.	7.50
		On cover, single franking			11.50
b.		40c yellow orange		1,500.	8.25
		On cover, single franking			11.50
c.		40c bright orange		1,850.	10.75
		On cover, single franking			15.00
28	A3	80c rose, *pnksh* (I)		1,300.	37.50
		On cover			52.50
		On cover, single franking			70.00
a.		80c bright rose, *pinkish* (I)		1,500.	57.50
		On cover			85.00
		On cover, single franking			95.00
b.		80c carmine rose (I)		2,100.	85.00
		On cover			140.00
		On cover, single franking			150.00
c.		Tête bêche pair (I)		20,500.	8,250.
		On cover			20,500.

No. 26a imperf is from a trial printing.

Values for stamps without gum

22	A3	1c ol grn, *pale bl* (II)		65.00
a.		1c bronze grn, *pale bl* (II)		65.00
b.		1c bronze gold ("mordore")		125.00
23	A3	5c yel grn, *grnsh* (I)		87.50
a.		5c deep green, *grnsh*		105.00
24	A3	5c green, *pale bl* (I)		525.00
25	A3	10c bis, *yelsh* (II)		375.00
a.		10c yel brn, *yelsh* (II)		525.00
26	A3	20c bl, *bluish* (II)		80.00
b.		20c dark blue		120.00
c.		20c pale blue		110.00
d.		20c blue, *azure*		140.00
27	A3	40c org, *yelsh* (I)		440.00
a.		40c pale orange		450.00
b.		40c yellow orange		460.00
c.		40c bright orange		650.00
28	A3	80c rose, *pnksh* (I)		440.00
a.		80c bright rose, *pinkish* (I)		450.00
b.		80c carmine rose (I)		650.00

Values for used pairs

22	A3	1c ol grn, *pale bl* (II)		90.00
a.		1c bronze grn, *pale bl* (II)		92.50
23	A3	5c yel grn, *grnsh* (I)		45.00
a.		5c deep green, *grnsh*		32.50
24	A3	5c green, *pale bl* (I)		250.00
25	A3	10c bis, *yelsh* (II)		10.50
a.		10c yel brn, *yelsh* (II)		22.50
26	A3	20c bl, *bluish* (II)		3.25
b.		20c dark blue		4.00
c.		20c pale blue		6.75
d.		20c blue, *azure*		4.75
27	A3	40c org, *yelsh* (I)		20.00
a.		40c pale orange		20.00
b.		40c yellow orange		21.00
c.		40c bright orange		24.00
28	A3	80c rose, *pnksh* (I)		95.00
a.		80c bright rose, *pinkish* (I)		180.00

b.		80c carmine rose (I)			200.00

Values for pairs on cover

22	A3	1c ol grn, *pale bl* (II)			700.00
a.		1c bronze grn, *pale bl* (II)			400.00
23	A3	5c yel grn, *grnsh* (II)			60.00
a.		5c deep green, *grnsh* (I)			47.50
24	A3	5c green, *pale bl* (I)			425.00
25	A3	10c bis, *yelsh* (II)			12.50
a.		10c yel brn, *yelsh* (II)			30.00
26	A3	20c bl, *bluish* (II)			4.75
b.		20c dark blue			4.75
c.		20c pale blue			8.00
d.		20c blue, *azure*			5.50
27	A3	40c org, *yelsh* (I)			30.00
a.		40c pale orange			30.00
b.		40c yellow orange			32.50
c.		40c bright orange			35.00
28	A3	80c rose, *pnksh*			130.00
a.		80c bright rose, *pinkish* (I)			225.00
b.		80c carmine rose (I)			325.00

Values for strips of 3

22	A3	1c ol grn, *pale bl* (II)			140.00
		On cover			525.00
23	A3	5c yel grn, *grnsh* (I)			80.00
		On cover			120.00
24	A3	5c green, *pale bl* (I)			450.00
		On cover			850.00
25	A3	10c bis, *yelsh* (II)			30.00
		On cover			47.50
26	A3	20c bl, *bluish* (I)			5.50
		On cover			27.50
27	A3	40c org, *yelsh* (I)			65.00
		On cover			100.00
28	A3	80c rose, *pnksh* (I)			180.00
		On cover			275.00
		Strip of 4			350.00
		On cover			675.00
		Strip of 5			540.00
		On cover			1,000.

Values for blocks of 4

22	A3	1c ol grn, *pale bl* (II)		750.00	400.00
		On cover			675.00
23	A3	5c yel grn, *grnsh* (I)		900.00	250.00
		On cover			425.00
24	A3	5c green, *pale bl* (I)		10,000.	1,050.
		On cover			1,650.
25	A3	10c bis, *yelsh* (II)		6,750.	150.00
		On cover			325.00
26	A3	20c bl, *bluish* (II)		1,000.	110.00
		On cover			210.00
27	A3	40c org, *yelsh* (I)		6,250.	300.00
		On cover			550.00
28	A3	80c rose, *pnksh* (I)		6,000.	450.00
		On cover			750.00

A4   A5

Napoleon III — A6

1863-70   **Perf. 14x13½**

29	A4	1c brnz grn, *pale bl* ('70)		45.00	20.00
		On cover			32.50
		On cover, single franking			70.00
a.		1c olive green, *pale blue*		45.00	20.00
		On cover			32.50
		On cover, single franking			70.00
30	A4	2c red brn, *yelsh*		120.00	25.00
		On cover			50.00
		On cover, single franking			75.00
b.		Half used as 1c on cover			64,000.
31	A4	4c gray		250.00	52.50
		On cover			105.00
		On cover, single franking			300.00
a.		Tete beche pair		22,000.	13,250.
		On cover			37,500.
d.		Half used as 2c on cover			60,000.
32	A5	10c bis, *yelsh* ('67)		325.00	6.00
		On cover, single franking			10.00
c.		Half used as 5c on cover with other stamps			3,750.
d.		Half used as 5c on cover, single franking			28,500.
33	A5	20c bl, *bluish* ('67)		225.00	1.60
		On cover, single franking			2.40
c.		Half used as 10c on cover			52,500.
34	A5	30c brn, *yelsh* ('67)		750.00	17.00
		On cover			24.00
		On cover, single franking			30.00
a.		30c dk brn, *yellowish*		1,300.	37.50
		On cover			45.00
		On cover, single franking			52.50
b.		30c pale brn		750.00	17.50
		On cover			25.00
		On cover, single franking			30.00

35	A5	40c pale org, *yellowish*		800.00	10.00
		On cover, single franking			14.00
a.		40c org, *yelsh* ('68)		1,200.	13.50
		On cover, single franking			14.00
c.		Half used as 20c on cover			42,500.
36	A5	80c rose, *pnksh*		1,500.	24.00
		On cover			35.00
		On cover, single franking			40.00
a.		80c carmine, *yellowish*		1,400.	40.00
		On cover			60.00
		On cover, single franking			75.00
d.		Half used as 40c on cover			50,000.
e.		Quarter used as 20c on cover			57,500.
37	A6	5fr gray lil, *lav* ('69)		6,000.	825.00
		On cover			1,450.
		On cover, single franking			20,000.
a.		"5" and "F" omitted			112,500.
c.		5fr bluish gray, *lavender*		6,500.	1,000.
		On cover			1,525.
		On cover, single franking			20,000.
d.		As #37, "5" and "F" in light blue		8,000.	1,100.

No. 33 exists in two types, differing in the size of the dots at either side of POSTES.

On No. 37, the "5" and "F" vary in height from 3¾mm to 4 ½mm. These figures normally appear in gray but exist in blue or black.

All known examples of No. 37a are more or less damaged.

No. 29 was reprinted in 1887 by authority of Granet, Minister of Posts. The reprints show a yellowish shade under the ultraviolet lamp. Value $850.

For surcharge see No. 49.

Values for stamps without gum

29	A4	1c bronze green, *pale blue*		20.00
a.		1c olive green, *pale blue*		24.00
30	A4	2c red brown, *yellowish*		60.00
31	A4	4c gray		120.00
32	A5	10c bistre, *yellowish*		120.00
33	A5	20c blue, *bluish*		120.00
34	A5	30c brown, *yellowish*		250.00
a.		30c dark brown, *yellowish*		475.00
35	A5	40c orange, *yellowish*		250.00
a.		40c pale orange, *yellowish*		250.00
36	A5	80c rose, *pinkish*		275.00
a.		80c carmine, *yellowish*		525.00
37	A6	5fr gray lilac, *lavender*		2,100.
c.		5fr bluish gray, *lavender*		2,200.

Original Issue Imperfs

31c	A4	4c gray		400.	175.
32b	A5	10c bis, *yelsh*		450.	175.
33b	A5	20c bl, *bluish*		375.	160.
					19,000.
36c	A5	80c rose, *pnksh*		—	9,000.
37b	A6	5fr gray lil, *lav*		10,000.	
		No gum		3,000.	
		Block of 4		45,000.	

Imperfs, "Rothschild" Re-issue
Paper Colors are the Same

29b	A4	1c olive green		1,200.
		No gum		550.00
30a	A4	2c pale red brown		190.00
		No gum		90.00
31b	A4	4c pale gray		160.00
		No gum		70.00
32a	A5	10c pale bister		160.00
		No gum		70.00
33a	A5	20c pale blue		275.00
		No gum		125.00
34c	A5	30c pale brown		200.00
		No gum		70.00
35b	A5	40c pale orange		240.00
		No gum		85.00
36b	A5	80c rose		475.00
		No gum		200.00

The re-issues constitute the "Rothschild Issue." These stamps were authorized exclusively for the banker to use on his correspondence. Used examples exist.

The listings for Ballons Montes covers that appeared following Scott 41 have been moved. They now appear after the Semi-Postal stamp listings.

Ceres

A7   A8

A9

A10

A11

Bordeaux Issue

On the lithographed stamps, except for type I of the 20c, the shading on the cheek and neck is in lines or dashes, not in dots. On the typographed stamps the shading is in dots. The 2c, 5c, 10c and 20c (types II and III) occur in two or more types. The most easily distinguishable are:

2c — Type A. To the left of and within the top of the left "2" are lines of shading composed of dots.

2c — Type B. These lines of dots are replaced by solid lines.

5c — Type A. The head and hairline merge with the background of the medallion, without a distinct separation.

5c — Type B. A white line separates the contour of the head and hairline from the background of the medallion.

10c — Type A. The inner frame lines are of the same thickness as all other frame lines.

10c — Type B. The inner frame lines are much thicker than the others.

Three Types of the 20c.

A9 — The inscriptions in the upper and lower labels are small and there is quite a space between the upper label and the circle containing the head. There is also very little shading under the eye and in the neck.

A10 — The inscriptions in the labels are similar to those of the first type, the shading under the eye and in the neck is heavier and the upper label and circle almost touch.

A11 — The inscriptions in the labels are much larger than those of the two preceding types, and are similar to those of the other values of the same type in the set.

1870-71 Litho. Imperf.

38	A7	1c ol grn, *pale bl*	160.00	115.00
		On cover		180.00
		On cover, single franking		1,000.
a.		1c bronze green, *pale blue*	200.00	150.00
		On cover		250.00
		On cover, single franking		1,250.
39	A7	2c red brn, *yelsh (B)*	275.00	250.00
		On cover		400.00
		On cover, single franking		2,000.
a.		2c brick red, *yelsh (B)*	925.00	800.00
		On cover		900.00
		On cover, single franking		2,750.
b.		2c chestnut, *yelsh (B)*	1,500.	850.00
		On cover		1,300.
		On cover, single franking		2,100.
c.		2c chocolate, *yelsh (A)*	925.00	800.00
		On cover		1,250.
		On cover, single franking		2,600.
40	A7	4c gray	300.00	250.00
		On cover		650.00
		On cover, single franking		14,750.
41	A8	5c yel green, *greenish (B)*	275.00	200.00
		On cover		750.00
		On cover, single franking		3,750.
a.		5c grn, *grnsh (B)*	350.00	175.00
		On cover		750.00
		On cover, single franking		3,750.
b.		5c emerald, *greenish (B)*	5,000.	1,250.
		On cover		2,500.
		On cover, single franking		8,250.
c.		5c yellowish green, *greenish (A)*	2,250.	3,000.
		On cover		27,500.
42	A8	10c bis, *yelsh (A)*	1,000.	60.00
		On cover		90.00
		On cover, single franking		110.00
a.		10c bister, *yellowish (B)*	1,000.	100.00
		On cover		130.00
		On cover, single franking		160.00
43	A9	20c bl, *bluish*	26,000.	650.00
		On cover		900.00
		20c dark blue, *bluish*	26,000.	650.00
		On cover, single franking		1,300.
44	A10	20c bl, *bluish*	1,150.	55.00
		On cover		60.00
		20c dark blue, *bluish*	1,250.	100.00
		On cover, single franking		150.00
b.		20c ultra, *bluish*	24,000.	3,800.
		On cover		4,750.
45	A11	20c bl, *bluish ('71)*	1,000.	20.00
		On cover		27.50
a.		20c ultra, *bluish*	2,750.	1,250.
		On cover		1,650.
46	A8	30c brn, *yelsh*	375.00	225.00
		On cover		350.00
		On cover, single franking		375.00
a.		30c blk brn, *yelsh*	2,000.	825.00
		On cover		1,300.
		On cover, single franking		1,350.
47	A8	40c org, *yelsh*	475.00	115.00
		On cover		160.00
a.		40c yel orange, *yelsh*	1,450.	250.00
		On cover		375.00
b.		40c red orange, *yelsh*	725.00	190.00
		On cover, single franking		300.00

---

c.		40c scarlet, *yelsh*	3,200.	775.00
		On cover, single franking		1,350.
d.		40c lemon yellow	10,000.	2,000.
		On cover, single franking		2,100.
e.		40c ochre	7,500.	1,750.
		On cover, single franking		2,750.
f.		40c orange vermilion	1,350.	325.00
		On cover, single franking		450.00
g.		40c pale red	1,350.	725.00
		On cover, single franking		1,400.
48	A8	80c rose, *pinkish*	750.00	250.00
		On cover		525.00
		On cover, single franking		575.00
a.		80c dull rose, *pinkish*	1,000.	275.00
		On cover		575.00
		On cover, single franking		600.00
b.		80c bright rose	900.00	300.00
		On cover		650.00
		On cover, single franking		675.00
c.		80c carmine rose	1,050.	350.00
		On cover		725.00
		On cover, single franking		750.00
d.		80c deep carmine rose	1,050.	350.00
		On cover		725.00
		On cover, single franking		950.00
e.		80c salmon	4,500.	1,900.
		On cover		3,300.
		On cover, single franking		3,500.
f.		80c reddish crimson	2,500.	1,900.
		On cover		1,750.
		On cover, single franking		3,300.

All values of the 1870 issue are known privately rouletted, pin-perf and perf. 14. See Nos. 50-53.

Values for stamps without gum

38	A7	1c olive green, *pale bl*	100.00
a.		1c bronze green, *pale blue*	125.00
39	A7	2c red brown, *yellowish (B)*	175.00
a.		2c brick red, *yellowish (B)*	500.00
b.		2c chestnut, *yellowish (B)*	925.00
c.		2c chocolate, *yellowish (A)*	500.00
40	A7	4c gray	175.00
41	A8	5c yellow green, *greenish (B)*	110.00
a.		5c green, *grnsh (B)*	140.00
b.		5c emerald, *greenish (B)*	400.00
c.		5c yellowish green, *greenish (A)*	1,200.
42	A8	10c bister, *yellowish (A)*	600.00
a.		10c bister, *yellowish (B)*	600.00
43	A9	20c dark blue, *bluish*	13,500.
44	A10	20c dark blue, *bluish*	575.00
a.		20c ultramarine, *bluish*	13,500.
45	A11	20c blue, *bluish ('71)*	575.00
a.		20c ultramarine, *bluish*	1,600.
46	A8	30c brown, *yellowish*	240.00
a.		30c black brown, *yellowish*	1,250.
47	A8	40c orange, *yellowish*	290.00
a.		40c yellow orange, *yellowish*	875.00
b.		40c red orange, *yellowish*	450.00
c.		40c scarlet, *yellowish*	875.00
d.		40c lemon yellow	6,250.
e.		40c ochre	4,500.
f.		40c orange vermilion	825.00
g.		40c pale red	825.00
48	A8	80c rose, *pinkish*	325.00
a.		80c dull rose, *pinkish*	600.00
b.		80c bright rose	550.00
c.		80c carmine rose	650.00
d.		80c deep carmine rose	650.00
e.		80c salmon	2,750.
f.		80c reddish crimson	1,500.

A12

Dark Blue Surcharge

1871 Typo. Perf. 14x13½

49	A12	10c on 10c bister		1,900.
		Without gum		950.00
		Block of 4, with gum		9,500.
a.		Pale blue surcharge		1,900.
		Without gum		1,050.
		Block of 4, with gum		10,500.

No. 49 was never placed in use. Counterfeits exist.

A13

Two types of the 40c as in the 1849-50 issue.

1870-73 Typo. Perf. 14x13½

50	A7	1c ol grn, *pale bl*	60.00	24.00
		On cover		40.00
		On cover, single franking		90.00
a.		1c bronze grn, *pale bl ('72)*	65.00	15.00
		On cover		50.00
		On cover, single franking		125.00
51	A7	2c red brn, *yelsh ('70)*	120.00	15.00
		On cover		45.00
		On cover, single franking		90.00

52	A7	4c gray ('70)	300.00	45.00
		On cover		150.00
		On cover, single franking		300.00
53	A7	5c yel grn, *pale bl ('72)*	190.00	8.25
		On cover		20.00
		On cover, single franking		29.00
a.		5c green	190.00	8.25
		On cover		20.00
		On cover, single franking		29.00
54	A13	10c bis, *yelsh*	650.00	72.50
		On cover		140.00
		On cover, single franking		200.00
a.		Tête beche pair	6,500.	2,600.
		On cover		5,500.
b.		Half used as 5c on cover		5,000.
55	A13	10c bis, *rose ('73)*	300.00	10.50
		On cover		16.50
		On cover, single franking		20.00
a.		Tête bêche pair	4,800.	2,100.
		On cover		3,500.
56	A13	15c bis, *yelsh ('71)*	425.00	5.00
		On cover		8.25
a.		Tête bêche pair	55,000.	18,000.
		On cover		30,000.
57	A13	20c dl bl, *bluish*	275.00	7.50
		On cover		10.50
a.		20c bright blue, *bluish*	400.00	9.00
		On cover		14.00
b.		Tête bêche pair	4,500.	1,650.
		On cover		4,000.
c.		Half used as 10c on cover		62,500.
d.		Quarter used as 5c on cover		57,500.
58	A13	25c bl, *bluish ('71)*	145.00	1.60
		On cover		1.75
a.		25c dk bl, *bluish*	175.00	1.60
		On cover		1.75
b.		Tête bêche pair	9,500.	4,000.
		On cover		10,750.
59	A13	40c org, *yelsh (I)*	600.00	7.00
		On cover		11.50
a.		40c orange yel, *yelsh (I)*	650.00	10.00
		On cover		150.00
b.		40c orange, *yelsh (II)*	3,500.	150.00
		On cover		300.00
c.		40c orange yel, *yelsh (II)*	3,500.	150.00
		On cover		300.00
d.		Pair, types I and II	7,250.	575.00
		On cover		1,100.
e.		Pair, both type II	17,500.	2,150.
		On cover		4,100.
f.		Half used as 20c on circular		25,000.
g.		Half used as 20c on cover		50,000.

No. 58 exists in three main plate varieties, differing in one or another of the flower-like corner ornaments.

Margins on this issue are extremely small. Nos. 54, 57 and 58 were reprinted imperf. in 1887. See note after No. 37.

Values for stamps without gum

50	A7	1c olive green, *pale bl*	16.00
a.		1c bronze green, *pale blue ('72)*	20.00
51	A7	2c red brown, *yellowish ('70)*	55.00
52	A7	4c gray	150.00
53	A7	5c yellow green, *pale blue*	95.00
a.		5c green	95.00
54	A13	10c bister, *yellowish*	225.00
55	A13	10c bister, *rose*	250.00
56	A13	15c bister, *yellowish*	225.00
57	A13	20c dull blue, *bluish*	120.00
a.		20c bright blue, *bluish*	120.00
58	A13	25c blue, *bluish*	72.50
a.		25c dark blue, *bluish*	87.50
59	A13	40c orange, *yellowish (I)*	240.00
a.		40c orange yellow, *yellowish (I)*	300.00
b.		40c orange, *yellowish (II)*	1,100.
c.		40c orange yellow, *yellowish (II)*	1,100.
d.		Pair, types I and II	2,100.
e.		Pair, both type II	6,250.

Imperf.

50b	A7	1c	325.00
		No gum	150.00
51a	A7	2c	400.00
		No gum	200.00
52a	A7	4c	675.00
		No gum	325.00
53b	A7	5c yel grn, *pale bl*	325.00
		No gum	160.00
55b	A13	10c	525.00
		No gum	260.00
56b	A13	15c	450.00
		No gum	225.00

A14

1872-75 Perf. 14x13½

Larger Numerals

60	A14	10c bis, *rose ('75)*	450.00	17.50
		On cover		20.00
		On cover, single franking		24.00
a.		Cliché of 15c in plate of 10c	4,250.	4,750.
		On cover		25,000.
b.		Pair, #60, 60a	7,500.	9,500.
		On cover		52,000.
61	A14	15c bister ('73)	375.00	4.00
		On cover		8.00
		On cover, single franking		12.00
62	A14	30c brn, *yelsh*	800.00	6.50
		On cover		12.00
		On cover, single franking		15.00
63	A14	80c rose, *pnksh*	1,200.	13.50
		On cover		29.00
b.		80c carmine rose	875.00	13.50
		On cover		29.00

		On cover, single franking		40.00
c.		80c bright carmine	1,100.	26.00
		On cover		40.00
		On cover, single franking		57.50

Values for stamps without gum

60	A14	10c bister, *rose ('75)*	225.00
61	A14	15c bister	225.00
62	A14	30c brown, *yellowish*	375.00
63	A14	80c rose, *pinkish*	450.00
b.		80c carmine rose	450.00
c.		80c bright carmine	550.00

Imperf.

62a	A14	30c	600.00
		No gum	290.00
63a	A14	80c	850.00
		No gum	290.00

Values for Nos. 64-240 are for stamps with all perforations clear of the framelines. Stamps with perforations touching the framelines on one or two sides are worth about 35% less than the values quoted. Values for stamps on cover are for average stamps on very fine, clean, complete covers.

Peace and Commerce ("Type Sage") — A15

Type I. The "N" of "INV" is under the "B" of "REPUBLIQUE."

Type II. The "N" of "INV" is under the "U" of "REPUBLIQUE."

Type I

1876-78 Perf. 14x13½

64	A15	1c grn, *grnsh*	140.00	70.00
		Never hinged	225.00	
		On cover		240.00
		On cover, single franking		700.00
65	A15	2c grn, *grnsh*	1,450.	250.00
		Never hinged	2,250.	
		On cover		375.00
		On cover, single franking		625.00
66	A15	4c grn, *grnsh*	160.00	55.00
		Never hinged	240.00	
		On cover		225.00
		On cover, single franking		675.00
67	A15	5c grn, *grnsh*	700.00	45.00
		Never hinged	1,150.	
		On cover		62.50
		On cover, single franking		90.00
68	A15	10c grn, *grnsh*	825.00	22.50
		Never hinged	1,400.	
		On cover		32.50
		On cover, single franking		45.00
69	A15	15c gray lil, *grysh*	825.00	18.00
		Never hinged	1,400.	
		On cover		25.00
		On cover, single franking		45.00
70	A15	20c red brn, *straw*	600.00	18.00
		Never hinged	925.00	
		On cover		32.50
		On cover, single franking		82.50
71	A15	20c bl, *bluish*	40,000.	
		Ovptd. "SPECIMEN," no gum	12,500.	
72	A15	25c ultra, *bluish*	7,750.	57.50
		Never hinged	12,000.	
		On cover		75.00
		On cover, single franking		82.50
73	A15	30c brn, *yelsh*	425.00	8.25
		Never hinged	650.00	
		On cover		10.00
		On cover, single franking		11.50
74	A15	40c red, *straw ('78)*	600.00	35.00
		Never hinged	950.00	
		On cover		50.00
		On cover, single franking		55.00
75	A15	75c car, *rose*	950.00	13.50
		Never hinged	1,500.	
		On cover		21.00
		On cover, single franking		37.50
76	A15	1fr brnz grn, *straw*	925.00	11.00
		Never hinged	1,450.	
		On cover		37.50
		On cover, single franking		100.00

No. 71 was never put into use. The reprints of No. 71 are type II. They are imperforate or with forged perforation.

For overprints and surcharges see Offices in China Nos. 1-17, J7-J10, J20-J22, Offices in Egypt, Alexandria 1-15, Port Said 1-17, Offices in Turkish Empire 1-7, Cavalle 1-8, Dedeagh 1-8, Port Lagos 1-5, Vathy 1-9, Offices in Zanzibar 1-33, 50-54, Offices in Morocco 1-8, and Madagascar 14-27.

Values for stamps without gum

64	A15	1c grn, *greenish*	50.00
65	A15	2c green, *greenish*	375.00
66	A15	4c grn, *greenish*	50.00
67	A15	5c grn, *greenish*	240.00
68	A15	10c green, *greenish*	260.00
69	A15	15c gray lilac, *grayish*	275.00
70	A15	20c red brown, *straw*	160.00
71	A15	20c blue, *bluish*	22,750.
72	A15	25c ultramarine, *bluish*	2,500.
73	A15	30c brown, *yellowish*	160.00
74	A15	40c red, *straw*	160.00
75	A15	75c carmine, *rose*	290.00
76	A15	1fr bronze green, *straw*	275.00

Values for blocks of 4

64 A15 1c grn, *grnsh* 725.00 375.00
Never hinged 1,050.
On cover 950.00
65 A15 2c grn, *grnsh* 7,000. 2,400.
Never hinged 11,000.
On cover 3,500.
66 A15 4c grn, *grnsh* 750.00 450.00
Never hinged 1,100.
On cover 1,050.
67 A15 5c grn, *grnsh* 3,300. 375.00
Never hinged 5,000.
On cover 625.00
68 A15 10c grn, *grnsh* 4,100. 375.00
Never hinged 6,250.
On cover 575.00
69 A15 15c gray lil, *grnsh* 4,100. 350.00
Never hinged 6,250.
On cover 575.00
70 A15 20c red brn, *straw* 2,750. 360.00
Never hinged 4,400.
On cover 700.00
72 A15 25c ultra, *bluish* 45,000. 2,200.
Never hinged 55,000.
On cover 3,250.
73 A15 30c brn, *yelsh* 1,900. 140.00
Never hinged 2,900.
On cover 310.00
74 A15 40c red, *straw* ('78) 2,900. 275.00
Never hinged 4,500.
On cover 440.00
75 A15 75c car, *rose* 4,500. 175.00
Never hinged 7,250.
On cover 300.00
76 A15 1fr brnz grn, *straw* 4,500. 160.00
Never hinged 7,000.
On cover 400.00

Imperf.

64a A15 1c 175.00
Never hinged 275.00
65a A15 2c 1,100.
Never hinged 1,650.
66a A15 4c 190.00
Never hinged 275.00
67a A15 5c 575.00
Never hinged 1,000.
68a A15 10c 650.00
Never hinged 1,000.
69a A15 15c 650.00
Never hinged 1,000.
70a A15 20c 425.00
Never hinged 675.00
73a A15 30c 300.00
Never hinged 475.00
74a A15 40c 275.00
Never hinged 440.00
75a A15 75c 600.00
Never hinged 1,000.
76a A15 1fr 450.00
Never hinged 700.00

Beware of French Colonies Nos. 24-29.

Type II

1876-77   *Perf. 14x13½*
77 A15 2c grn, *grnsh* 115.00 19.00
Never hinged 175.00
On cover 42.50
On cover, single franking 90.00
78 A15 5c grn, *grnsh* 25.00 .60
Never hinged 37.50
On cover 1.00
a. Imperf. 175.00
Never hinged 275.00
79 A15 10c grn, *grnsh* 1,100. 240.00
Never hinged 1,600.
On cover 290.00
On cover, single franking 390.00
80 A15 15c gray lil, *grysh* 675.00 1.90
Never hinged 1,050.
On cover 2.50
On cover, single franking 2.75
81 A15 25c ultra, *bluish* 425.00 1.00
Never hinged 750.00
On cover 1.35
On cover, single franking 1.65
a. 25c blue, *bluish* 475.00 1.50
Never hinged 725.00
On cover 2.00
On cover, single franking 2.50
b. Pair, types I & II 65,000. 17,500.
No gum 20,000.
On cover 52,500.
c. Imperf. 325.00
Never hinged 525.00
d. 25c ultramarine, *pale greenish* 675.00
On cover 1,100.
On cover, single franking 1,350.
82 A15 30c yel brn, *yelsh* 82.50 1.40
Never hinged 140.00
On cover 2.25
On cover, single franking 5.00
a. 30c brown, *yellowish* 90.00 1.40
Never hinged 140.00
On cover 2.25
On cover, single franking 5.00
b. Imperf. 525.00
Never hinged 800.00
83 A15 75c car, *rose* ('77) 1,775. 110.00
Never hinged 2,750.
On cover 225.00
On cover, single franking 500.00
84 A15 1fr brnz grn, *straw* ('77) 150.00 7.50
Never hinged 225.00
On cover 32.50
On cover, single franking 105.00
a. Imperf. 1,100.
Never hinged 1,650.
b. 1fr deep olive green, *straw* 150.00 10.00
Never hinged 250.00
On cover 45.00
On cover, single franking 115.00

Beware of French Colonies Nos. 31, 35.

1877-80
86 A15 1c blk, *lil bl* 3.75 1.75
Never hinged 5.75
On cover 2.90
On cover, single franking 4.25
a. 1c black, *gray blue* 3.75 1.75
Never hinged 5.75
On cover, single franking 2.90 4.25
b. Imperf. 75.00
Never hinged 115.00
87 A15 1c blk, *Prus bl* ('80) 12,500. 5,500.
Never hinged 16,000.
No gum 4,250.
On cover
On cover, single franking 18,750.

Values for No. 87 are for examples with the perfs touching the design on at least one side.

88 A15 2c brn, *straw* 4.50 1.90
Never hinged 7.50
On cover 3.00
On cover, single franking 7.00
a. 2c brown, *yellow* 4.50 1.90
Never hinged 7.50
On cover 3.00
On cover, single franking 7.00
b. Imperf. 275.00
Never hinged 290.00
89 A15 3c blk, *straw* ('78) 250.00 47.50
Never hinged 310.00
On cover 425.00
On cover, single franking 900.00
a. Imperf. 150.00
Never hinged 225.00
90 A15 4c claret, *lav* 5.00 1.90
Never hinged 7.50
On cover 11.50
On cover, single franking 110.00
a. 4c vio brown, *lavender* 8.25 4.50
Never hinged 12.50
On cover 15.00
On cover, single franking 140.00
b. Imperf. 60.00
Never hinged 95.00
91 A15 10c blk, *lavender* 35.00 1.00
Never hinged 52.50
On cover 1.60
On cover, single franking 2.10
a. 10c black, *rose lilac* 37.50 1.00
Never hinged 57.50
On cover 2.10
On cover, single franking 2.10
b. 10c black, *lilac* 37.50 1.00
Never hinged 57.50
On cover 2.10
On cover, single franking 2.10
c. Imperf. 70.00
Never hinged 115.00
92 A15 15c blue ('78) 27.50 .80
Never hinged 32.50
On cover .85
On cover, single franking 1.00
a. Imperf. 100.00
Never hinged 150.00
b. 15c blue, *bluish* 450.00 15.00
Never hinged 650.00
On cover 16.50
On cover, single franking 25.00
93 A15 25c blk, *red* ('78) 1,075. 25.00
Never hinged 1,650.
No gum 310.00
On cover 40.00
On cover, single franking 45.00
a. Imperf. 675.00
Never hinged 1,100.
94 A15 35c blk, *yel* ('78) 525.00 35.00
Never hinged 825.00
On cover 75.00
On cover, single franking 140.00
a. 35c blk, *yel org* 525.00 35.00
Never hinged 825.00
On cover 77.50
On cover, single franking 140.00
b. Imperf. 250.00
Never hinged 400.00
95 A15 40c red, *straw* ('80) 90.00 2.10
Never hinged 150.00
On cover 6.25
On cover, single franking 7.50
a. As #95, imperf. 250.00
Never hinged 360.00
b. 40c pale orange red, *straw* 90.00 2.10
Never hinged 150.00
On cover 7.00
On cover, single franking 7.50
96 A15 5fr vio, *lav* 450.00 70.00
Never hinged 700.00
On cover 400.00
On cover, single franking 3,500.
a. As #96, imperf. 750.00
Never hinged 1,250.
b. 5fr red lilac, *lavender* 650.00 90.00
Never hinged 950.00
On cover 475.00
On cover, single franking 4,000.
c. 5fr bright violet, *lavender* 650.00 100.00
Never hinged 950.00
On cover 500.00
On cover, single franking 4,000.

Beware of French Colonies Nos. 38-40, 42, 44.

1879-90
97 A15 3c gray, *grysh* ('80) 4.00 1.75
Never hinged 5.00
On cover 11.00
On cover, single franking 82.50
a. Imperf. 65.00
Never hinged 100.00
98 A15 20c red, *yel grn* 37.50 4.25
Never hinged 57.50
On cover 27.50
On cover, single franking 140.00
a. 20c red, *deep green* ('84) 70.00 5.75
Never hinged 110.00
On cover 32.50
On cover, single franking 150.00
b. Imperf. 100.00
Never hinged 150.00
99 A15 25c yel, *straw* 325.00 5.00
Never hinged 525.00
On cover 11.50
On cover, single franking 12.50
a. Imperf. 300.00
Never hinged 400.00
100 A15 25c blk, *pale rose* ('86) 70.00 1.60
Never hinged 115.00
On cover 2.60
On cover, single franking 3.60
a. Imperf. 150.00
Never hinged 240.00
101 A15 50c rose, *rose* ('00) 200.00 3.25
Never hinged 325.00
On cover 11.50
On cover, single franking 29.00
a. 50c carmine, *rose* 225.00 3.25
Never hinged 350.00
On cover 12.50
On cover, single franking 30.00
102 A15 75c dp vio, *org* ('90) 200.00 32.50
Never hinged 350.00
On cover 105.00
On cover, single franking 250.00
a. 75c deep violet, *yellow* 275.00 45.00
Never hinged 400.00
On cover 115.00
On cover, single franking 290.00
Nos. 97-102 (6) 836.50 48.35

Beware of French Colonies No. 43.

1892   **Quadrille Paper**
103 A15 15c blue 17.00 .80
Never hinged 18.00
On cover 1.40
On cover, single franking 4.50
a. Imperf. 175.00
Never hinged 260.00

1898-1900   **Ordinary Paper**
104 A15 5c yel grn 16.00 1.25
Never hinged 25.00
On cover 2.00
On cover, single franking 4.75
a. Imperf. 82.50
Never hinged 140.00

Type I
105 A15 5c yel grn 14.00 1.25
Never hinged 21.00
On cover 2.00
On cover, single franking 2.25
a. Imperf. 550.00
Never hinged 900.00
No gum 190.00
106 A15 10c blk, *lavender* 25.00 3.00
Never hinged 40.00
On cover 3.75
On cover, single franking 4.25
a. Imperf. 250.00
Never hinged 400.00
No gum 82.50
107 A15 50c car, *rose* 250.00 40.00
Never hinged 390.00
On cover 65.00
On cover, single franking 105.00
108 A15 2fr brn, *azure* ('00) 140.00 50.00
Never hinged 200.00
On cover 440.00
On cover, single franking 4,500.
b. Imperf. 2,400.
Never hinged 3,550.
No gum 835.00
Nos. 104-108 (5) 445.00 95.50

See No. 226.
Reprints of A15, type II, were made in 1887 and left imperf. See note after No. 37. Value for set of 27, $4,000.

Liberty, Equality, Fraternity
A16

"The Rights of Man"
A17

Liberty and Peace
A18

1900-29   *Perf. 14x13½*
109 A16 1c gray .55 .40
Never hinged .90
On cover .85
On cover, single franking 2.10
b. Grayish paper (GC) ('16) .65 .55
Never hinged 1.10
On cover 1.20
110 A16 2c violet brn .70 .25
Never hinged 1.40
On cover 1.00
On cover, single franking 4.25
b. Grayish (GC) paper ('17) 1.60 .25
Never hinged 3.00
On cover 1.00
111 A16 3c orange .45 .10
Never hinged .90
On cover 2.50
On cover, single franking 8.25
a. 3c red 19.00 7.50
Never hinged 32.50
b. Imperf. 11.50
Never hinged 11.50
c. Grayish (GC) paper ('17) .55 .55
Never hinged 1.00
On cover 2.75

112 A16 4c yellow brn 3.25 1.60
Never hinged 5.25
On cover 3.25
On cover, single franking 55.00
113 A16 5c green 2.00 .35
Never hinged 4.25
On cover .70
b. Booklet pane of 10 350.00
114 A16 7½c lilac ('26) .60 .40
Never hinged 1.25
115 A16 10c lilac ('29) 4.00 .60
Never hinged 6.25
On cover 6.75
On cover, single franking 57.50
116 A17 10c carmine 25.00 1.50
Never hinged 75.00
On cover 10.00
On cover, single franking 15.00
a. Numerals printed separately 24.00 10.00
Never hinged 65.00
On cover 15.00
On cover, single franking 18.00
117 A17 15c orange 8.00 .60
Never hinged 20.00
On cover .70
On cover, single franking .85
118 A17 20c brown vio 55.00 9.00
Never hinged 150.00
On cover 17.50
On cover, single franking 42.50
119 A17 25c blue 125.00 1.75
Never hinged 325.00
On cover 4.50
On cover, single franking 9.00
a. Numerals printed separately 115.00 9.00
Never hinged 325.00
On cover 12.50
On cover, single franking 20.00
120 A17 30c violet 70.00 5.75
Never hinged 210.00
On cover 17.50
On cover, single franking 42.50
121 A18 40c red & pale bl 15.00 .85
Never hinged 52.50
On cover 1.60
On cover, single franking 2.10
b. Grayish (GC) paper ('16) 25.00 1.20
Never hinged 67.50
On cover 2.75
122 A18 45c green & bl ('06) 29.00 2.10
Never hinged 105.00
On cover 7.00
b. Grayish (GC) paper ('16) 45.00 4.00
Never hinged 110.00
On cover 8.75
123 A18 50c bis brn & gray 100.00 1.65
Never hinged 325.00
On cover 3.25
On cover, single franking 3.75
b. Grayish paper (GC) ('16) 200.00 2.00
Never hinged 375.00
On cover 4.50
124 A18 60c vio & ultra ('20) 1.00 1.25
Never hinged 1.90
On cover 5.00
125 A18 1fr claret & ol grn 26.50 .85
Never hinged 90.00
On cover 2.90
On cover, single franking 4.50
b. Grayish paper (GC) ('16) 52.50 .95
Never hinged 130.00
On cover 4.50
126 A18 2fr gray vio & yel 750.00 75.00
Never hinged 2,000.
On cover 260.00
On cover, single franking 1,600.
127 A18 2fr org & pale bl ('20) 42.50 .60
Never hinged 140.00
On cover 9.00
On cover, single franking 29.00
128 A18 3fr vio & bl ('25) 26.50 7.50
Never hinged 52.50
On cover 20.00
On cover, single franking 57.50
129 A18 3fr brt vio & rose ('27) 55.00 2.75
Never hinged 125.00
On cover 26.00
On cover, single franking 50.00
130 A18 5fr dk bl & buff 82.50 5.00
Never hinged 275.00
On cover 35.00
On cover, single franking 140.00
131 A18 10fr grn & red ('26) 125.00 16.50
Never hinged 300.00
On cover 37.50
On cover, single franking 100.00
132 A18 20fr mag & grn ('26) 200.00 37.50
Never hinged 475.00
On cover 140.00
On cover, single franking 390.00
Nos. 109-132 (24) 1,747. 174.20

In the 10c and 25c values, the first printings show the numerals to have been impressed by a second operation, whereas, in later printings, the numerals were inserted in the plates. Two operations were used for all 20c and 30c, and one operation for the 15c.

No. 114 was issued precanceled only. Values for precanceled stamps in first column are for those which have not been through the post and have original gum. Values in the second column are for postally used, gumless stamps.

See Offices in China Nos. 34, 40-44, Offices in Crete 1-5, 10-15, Offices in Egypt, Alexandria 16-20, 26-30, 77, 84-86, Port Said 18-22, 28-32, 83, 90-92, Offices in Turkish Empire 21-26, 31-33, Cavalle 9, Dedeagh 9.

For overprints and surcharge see Nos. 197, 246, C1-C2, M1, P7. Offices in China 57, 62-65, 71, 73, 75, 83-85, J14, J27, Offices in Crete 17-20, Offices in Egypt, Alexandria 31-32, 34-35, 40-48, 57-64, 66, 71-73, Port Said

33, 35-40, 43, 46-57, 59, 65-71, 73, 78-80, Offices in Turkish Empire 35-38, 47-49, Cavalle 13-15, Dedeagh 16-18, Offices in Zanzibar 39, 45-49, 55, Offices in Morocco 11-15, 20-22, 26-29, 35-41, 49-54, 72-76, 84-85, 87-89, B6.

Imperf.

109a	A16	1c	62.50	
	Never hinged		95.00	
110a	A16	2c	75.00	60.00
	Never hinged		110.00	
	Without gum		55.00	
111b	A16	3c	62.50	
	Never hinged		95.00	
112a	A16	4c	160.00	
	Never hinged		240.00	
	Without gum		140.00	
113a	A16	5c	82.50	
	Never hinged		125.00	
	Without gum		65.00	
116b	A17	10c #116 or 116a	275.00	140.00
	Never hinged		400.00	
	Without gum		150.00	
117a	A17	15c	200.00	175.00
	Never hinged		310.00	
	Without gum		140.00	
119b	A17	25c #119 or 119a	550.00	
	Never hinged		825.00	
	Without gum		325.00	
121a	A18	40c	225.00	160.00
	Never hinged		350.00	
	Without gum		140.00	
122a	A18	45c	300.00	
	Never hinged		425.00	
	Without gum		190.00	
123a	A18	50c	425.00	375.00
	Never hinged		675.00	
	Without gum		325.00	
124a	A18	60c	575.00	
	Never hinged		1,000.	
	Without gum		425.00	
125a	A18	1fr	275.00	225.00
	Never hinged		375.00	
	Without gum		200.00	
126a	A18	2fr Without gum	1,450.	
127a	A18	2fr	525.00	
	Never hinged		950.00	
	Without gum		400.00	
128a	A18	3fr	800.00	500.00
	Never hinged		1,250.	
129a	A18	3fr	475.00	
	Never hinged		700.00	
130a	A18	5fr	1,050.	
	Never hinged		1,500.	
	Without gum		475.00	

Flat Plate & Rotary Press

The following stamps were printed by both flat plate and rotary press: Nos. 109-113, 144-146, 163, 166, 168, 170, 177-178, 185, 192 and P7.

"Rights of Man" A19   Sower A20

1902

133	A19	10c rose red	32.50	.90
	Never hinged		150.00	
	On cover			1.40
	On cover, single franking			3.00
134	A19	15c pale red	11.00	.60
	Never hinged		37.50	
	On cover			.65
	On cover, single franking			.85
135	A19	20c brown violet	82.50	14.00
	Never hinged		225.00	
	On cover			22.50
	On cover, single franking			62.50
136	A19	25c blue	100.00	2.25
	Never hinged		390.00	
	On cover			5.50
	On cover, single franking			10.00
137	A19	30c lilac	250.00	14.50
	Never hinged		575.00	
	On cover			22.50
	On cover, single franking			50.00
	Nos. 133-137 (5)		476.00	32.25

Imperf.

133a	A19	10c rose red	450.00	275.00
	Never hinged		650.00	
	Without gum		200.00	
134a	A19	15c pale red	450.00	325.00
	Never hinged		650.00	
	Without gum		250.00	
135a	A19	20c brown violet	800.00	475.00
	Never hinged		1,250.	
	Without gum		350.00	
136a	A19	25c blue	950.00	625.00
	Never hinged		1,450.	
137a	A19	30c lilac	1,100.	675.00
	Never hinged		1,475.	

See Offices in China Nos. 35-39, Offices in Crete 6-10, Offices in Egypt, Alexandria 21-25, 81-82, Port Said 23-27, 87-88, Offices in Turkish Empire 26-30, Cavalle 10-11, Dedeagh 10-11.

For overprints and surcharges see Nos. M2, Offices in China 45, 58-61, 66-70, 76-82, J15-J16, J28-J30, Offices in Crete 16, Offices in Egypt, Alexandria 33, 36-39, 49-50, 52-56, 65, 67-70, B1-B4, Port Said 34, 41-42, 44-45, 57, 60-64, 77, 74-77, B1-B4, Offices in Turkish Empire 34, 39, Cavalle 12, Dedeagh 15, Offices in Zanzibar 40-44, 56-59, Offices in

Morocco 16-19, 30-34, 42-48, 77-83, 86, B1-B5, B7, B9.

1903-38

138	A20	10c rose	8.00	.40
	Never hinged		18.00	
	On cover			.85
139	A20	15c slate grn	4.00	.25
	Never hinged		9.00	
	On cover			.75
b.	Booklet pane of 10		450.00	
c.	Grayish (GC) paper ('16)		4.50	.25
	Never hinged		9.50	
	On cover			.75
140	A20	20c violet brn	67.50	1.90
	Never hinged		150.00	
	On cover			9.00
	On cover, single franking			40.00
141	A20	25c dull blue	75.00	1.40
	Never hinged		160.00	
	On cover			4.25
	On cover, single franking			6.50
142	A20	30c violet	175.00	5.25
	Never hinged		375.00	
	On cover			13.00
	On cover, single franking			30.00
143	A20	45c lt violet ('26)	6.00	1.90
	Never hinged		11.50	
	On cover			7.00
	On cover, single franking			45.00
144	A20	50c dull blue ('21)	27.50	1.40
	Never hinged		62.50	
	On cover			7.00
	On cover, single franking			10.00
145	A20	50c gray grn ('26)	6.25	1.25
	Never hinged		11.50	
	On cover			3.00
	On cover, single franking			22.50
146	A20	50c vermilion ('26)	1.25	.25
	Never hinged		2.25	
	On cover			.50
	On cover, single franking			.50
a.	Booklet pane of 10		40.00	
147	A20	50c grnsh bl ('38)	1.00	.35
	Never hinged		1.90	
	On cover			2.10
	On cover, single franking			5.75
148	A20	60c lt vio ('24)	6.25	2.10
	Never hinged		13.00	
	On cover			7.50
	On cover, single franking			16.50
149	A20	65c rose ('24)	3.00	1.75
	Never hinged		5.25	
	On cover			5.75
	On cover, single franking			42.50
150	A20	65c gray grn ('27)	6.50	2.10
	Never hinged		14.00	
	On cover			10.00
	On cover, single franking			55.00
151	A20	75c rose lil ('26)	5.25	.60
	Never hinged		10.00	
	On cover			2.50
	On cover, single franking			4.50
152	A20	80c ver ('25)	26.50	9.50
	Never hinged		52.50	
	On cover			14.00
	On cover, single franking			50.00
153	A20	85c ver ('24)	13.50	3.25
	Never hinged		27.00	
	On cover			5.75
	On cover, single franking			10.00
154	A20	1fr dull blue ('26)	6.00	.75
	Never hinged		13.00	
	On cover			4.25
	On cover, single franking			18.00
	Nos. 138-154 (17)		438.50	34.40
	Set, never hinged		940.00	

See Nos. 941, 942A. For surcharges and overprints see Nos. 229-230, 232-233, 236, 256, B25, B29, B32, B36, B40, M3-M4, M6, Offices in Turkish Empire 46, 54.

Imperf.

138a	A20	10c	175.00	
	Never hinged		275.00	
	Without gum		105.00	
139a	A20	15c	140.00	55.00
	Never hinged		200.00	
	Without gum		82.50	
140a	A20	20c	300.00	160.00
	Never hinged		460.00	
	Without gum		115.00	
141a	A20	25c	350.00	
	Never hinged		525.00	
	Without gum		110.00	
142a	A20	30c	625.00	
	Never hinged		925.00	
	Without gum		225.00	
144a	A20	50c	140.00	
	Never hinged		200.00	
145a	A20	50c	125.00	
	Never hinged		190.00	
146b	A20	50c Without gum	70.00	
147a	A20	50c	67.50	
	Never hinged		110.00	
149a	A20	65c	300.00	
	Never hinged		500.00	
151a	A20	75c	450.00	
	Never hinged		650.00	
154a	A20	1fr	1,000.	
	Never hinged		1,400.	

Ground A21   No Ground A22

1906, Apr. 13
With Ground Under Feet of Figure

155	A21	10c red	2.50	1.75
	Never hinged		4.25	
	On cover			5.00

	On cover, single franking			5.50
a.	Imperf, pair, without gum	275.00	225.00	
	As "a," with gum	450.00		
	Never hinged		775.00	

1906-37

TEN AND THIRTY-FIVE CENTIMES
Type I — Numerals and letters of the inscriptions thin.
Type II — Numerals and letters thicker.

No Ground Under the Feet

156	A22	1c olive bis ('33)	.25	.30
	Never hinged		.40	
	On cover			3.25
	On cover, single franking			50.00
a.	1c bistre brown ('36)		.25	.25
	Never hinged		.40	
	On cover			3.25
	On cover, single franking			40.00
157	A22	2c dk green ('33)	.25	.30
	Never hinged		.40	
	On cover			2.50
	On cover, single franking			45.00
158	A22	3c ver ('33)	.25	.30
	Never hinged		.40	
	On cover			18.00
	On cover, single franking			82.50
159	A22	5c green ('07)	1.50	.25
	Never hinged		2.75	
	On cover			.55
	On cover, single franking			.65
a.	Imperf., pair		40.00	30.00
	Never hinged		60.00	
	Without gum		18.00	
b.	Booklet pane of 10		100.00	
c.	Grayish (GC) paper ('16)		2.75	.35
	Never hinged		30.00	
	On cover			.80
160	A22	5c orange ('21)	1.25	.30
	Never hinged		2.50	
	On cover			1.00
	On cover, single franking			3.00
a.	Booklet pane of 10		72.50	
161	A22	5c cerise ('34)	.25	.25
	Never hinged		.40	
	On cover			4.00
	On cover, single franking			120.00
162	A22	10c red (II) ('07)	1.50	.25
	Never hinged		2.75	
	On cover			.60
	On cover, single franking			.65
a.	Imperf., pair		37.50	115.00
	Never hinged		65.00	
	No gum			13.50
b.	10c red (I) ('06)		8.25	1.00
	Never hinged		29.00	
	On cover			2.75
	On cover, single franking			3.00
c.	As #162b, imperf., pair		37.50	115.00
d.	Booklet pane of 10 (I)		125.00	
e.	Booklet pane of 10 (II)		75.00	
f.	Booklet pane of 6 (II)		240.00	
g.	Grayish (GC) paper ('16)		12.00	2.10
	Never hinged		19.00	
	On cover			3.50
163	A22	10c grn (II) ('21)	1.00	.55
	Never hinged		1.60	
	On cover			.60
	On cover, single franking			1.00
a.	10c green (I) ('27)		32.50	37.50
	Never hinged		45.00	
	On cover			75.00
	On cover, single franking			175.00
b.	Booklet pane of 10 (II, "Phena")		350.00	
c.	Booklet pane of 10 (I, "Mineraline")		3,200.	
164	A22	10c ultra ('32)	1.40	.25
	Never hinged		2.40	
	On cover			1.60
	On cover, single franking			20.00
165	A22	15c red brn ('26)	.25	.25
	Never hinged		.50	
	On cover			.40
	On cover, single franking			.40
a.	Booklet pane of 10		27.50	
166	A22	20c brown	3.00	.65
	Never hinged		7.00	
	On cover			2.00
	On cover, single franking			2.50
a.	Imperf., pair		82.50	100.00
	Never hinged		105.00	
	Without gum		27.50	
b.	20c black brown		6.00	2.00
	Never hinged		13.00	
	On cover			3.75
	On cover, single franking			4.00
c.	Grayish (GC) paper ('17)		6.50	.80
	Never hinged		12.00	
	On cover			3.25
167	A22	20c red vio ('26)	.25	.25
	Never hinged		.50	
	On cover			.50
	On cover, single franking			.65
a.	Booklet pane of 10		7.50	
168	A22	25c blue	2.40	.25
	Never hinged		4.50	
	On cover			.50
	On cover, single franking			.65
a.	Booklet pane of 10		37.50	
b.	Imperf, pair (dark blue)		45.00	60.00
	Never hinged		75.00	
c.	Imperf, pair (pale blue)		180.00	120.00
	Never hinged		290.00	
d.	Grayish (GC) paper ('17)		4.00	1.20
	Never hinged		6.75	
	On cover			2.40
169	A22	25c yel brown ('27)	.25	.25
	Never hinged		.40	
	On cover			.65
	On cover, single franking			1.00
a.	25c red brown		.30	.25
	Never hinged		.65	
	On cover			.80
170	A22	30c orange	13.50	1.40
	Never hinged		30.00	
	On cover			2.50
	On cover, single franking			6.25
a.	Imperf, pair		200.00	175.00
	Never hinged		300.00	
	Without gum		80.00	
b.	Grayish (GC) paper ('16)		15.00	1.75

	Never hinged		32.50	
171	A22	30c red ('21)	6.50	2.25
	Never hinged		15.00	
	On cover			7.00
	On cover, single franking			10.00
172	A22	30c cerise ('25)	1.25	.80
	Never hinged		2.10	
	On cover			3.50
	On cover, single franking			9.00
a.	Booklet pane of 10		13.50	
b.	Imperf, pair		575.00	
	Never hinged		900.00	
173	A22	30c lt blue ('25)	3.75	.60
	Never hinged		5.75	
	On cover			2.50
	On cover, single franking			9.00
a.	Booklet pane of 10		35.00	
b.	Imperf, pair		2,200.	
174	A22	30c cop red ('37)	.25	.30
	Never hinged		.65	
	On cover			1.00
	On cover, single franking			2.00
a.	Booklet pane of 10		9.00	
175	A22	35c vio (II) ('26)	8.25	.90
	Never hinged		15.00	
	On cover			2.00
	On cover, single franking			2.50
a.	Imperf, pair		150.00	120.00
	Never hinged		225.00	
	Without gum		72.50	
b.	35c violet (I) ('06)		150.00	7.50
	Never hinged		310.00	
	On cover			22.00
	On cover, single franking			26.00
c.	As "b," Imperf, pair, without gum		575.00	
176	A22	35c grn ('37)	.50	.55
	Never hinged		1.00	
	On cover			3.00
	On cover, single franking			6.00
a.	Imperf, pair		750.00	
	Never hinged		1,050.	
177	A22	40c olive ('25)	1.40	.55
	Never hinged		3.25	
	On cover			2.50
	On cover, single franking			5.00
b.	Booklet pane of 10		30.00	
178	A22	40c ver ('26)	2.50	.80
	Never hinged		4.50	
	On cover			2.50
	On cover, single franking			3.50
a.	Booklet pane of 10		25.00	
179	A22	40c violet ('27)	2.00	.90
	Never hinged		3.50	
	On cover			1.60
	On cover, single franking			2.00
180	A22	40c lt ultra ('28)	1.25	.50
	Never hinged		2.25	
	On cover			1.50
	On cover, single franking			1.60
a.	40c gray blue		1.60	.85
	Never hinged		2.90	
	On cover			2.00
181	A22	1.05fr ver ('25)	9.50	5.25
	Never hinged		18.50	
	On cover			13.00
	On cover, single franking			50.00
182	A22	1.10fr cerise ('27)	11.50	2.50
	Never hinged		22.00	
	On cover			9.00
	On cover, single franking			32.50
a.	1.10fr bright rose		16.50	4.00
	Never hinged		29.00	
	On cover			11.50
183	A22	1.40fr cerise ('26)	20.00	22.50
	Never hinged		37.50	
	On cover			120.00
	On cover, single franking			750.00
a.	1.40fr bright rose		25.00	25.00
	Never hinged		45.00	
184	A22	2fr Prus grn ('31)	14.00	1.75
	Never hinged		24.00	
	On cover			16.50
	On cover, single franking			62.50
a.	2fr blackish green		18.00	3.00
	Never hinged		31.00	
	On cover			20.00
	Nos. 156-184 (29)		109.95	45.95
	Set, never hinged		225.00	

The 10c and 35c, type I, were slightly retouched by adding thin white outlines to the sack of grain, the underside of the right arm and the back of the skirt. It is difficult to distinguish the retouches except on clearly-printed stamps. The white outlines were made stronger on the stamps of type II.

Stamps of types A16, A18, A20 and A22 were printed in 1916-20 on paper of poor quality, usually grayish and containing bits of fiber. This is called G. C. (Grande Consommation) paper. These wartime printings are noted (GC) in the descriptions above.

Nos. 160, 162b, 163, 175b and 176 also exist imperf.

See Nos. 241-241b. For surcharges and overprint see Nos. 227-228, 234, 238, 240, 400, B1, B24, B28, B31, B35, B37, B39, B41, M5, P8, Offices in Turkish Empire 40-45, 52, 55.

Louis Pasteur — A23

1923-26

185	A23	10c green	.55	.30
	Never hinged		1.25	
	On cover			1.00
	On cover, single franking			1.60
a.	Booklet pane of 10		15.00	

186	A23	15c green ('24)	1.40	.30
		Never hinged	3.00	
		On cover		1.00
		On cover, single franking		3.75
187	A23	20c green ('26)	2.75	.90
		Never hinged	4.50	
		On cover		4.25
		On cover, single franking		5.75
188	A23	30c red	.90	1.50
		Never hinged	1.60	
		On cover		3.75
		On cover, single franking		6.50
189	A23	30c green ('26)	.55	.50
		Never hinged	1.25	
		On cover		3.25
		On cover, single franking		6.50
190	A23	45c red ('24)	1.90	2.10
		Never hinged	3.50	
		On cover		4.50
		On cover, single franking		9.00
191	A23	50c blue	4.50	.50
		Never hinged	7.75	
		On cover		4.50
		On cover, single franking		14.00
192	A23	75c blue ('24)	3.75	1.00
		Never hinged	6.00	
		On cover		3.25
		On cover, single franking		6.50
a.		Imperf., pair	250.00	
		Never hinged	410.00	
		Without gum	250.00	
193	A23	90c red ('26)	11.00	3.50
		Never hinged	20.00	
		On cover		5.25
		On cover, single franking		9.00
194	A23	1fr blue ('25)	21.00	.50
		Never hinged	40.00	
		On cover		4.50
		On cover, single franking		29.00
195	A23	1.25fr blue ('26)	25.00	8.00
		Never hinged	41.00	
		On cover		22.00
		On cover, single franking		52.50
196	A23	1.50fr blue ('26)	5.25	.50
		Never hinged	15.00	
		On cover		2.00
		On cover, single franking		4.00
		Nos. 185-196 (12)	78.55	19.60
		Set, never hinged	150.00	

Nos. 185, 188 and 191 were issued to commemorate the cent. of the birth of Pasteur.
For surcharges and overprint see Nos. 231, 235, 257, B26, B30, B33, C4.

No. 125
Overprinted
in Blue

1923, June 15

197	A18	1fr claret & ol grn	440.00	500.00
		Never hinged	825.00	
		On cover		650.00
		On cover, single franking		650.00

Allegory of Olympic Games at Paris A24

The Trophy A25

Milo of Crotona — A26   Victorious Athlete — A27

1924, Apr. 1   Perf. 14x13½, 13½x14

198	A24	10c gray grn & yel grn	2.25	1.25
		Never hinged	6.25	
		On cover		2.90
		On cover, single franking		5.75
199	A25	25c rose & dk rose	3.00	.80
		Never hinged	7.50	
		On cover		2.90
		On cover, single franking		5.75
200	A26	30c brn red & blk	9.50	11.00
		Never hinged	21.00	
		On cover		29.00
		On cover, single franking		60.00

201	A27	50c ultra & dk bl	26.00	5.75
		Never hinged	90.00	
		On cover		37.50
		On cover, single franking		100.00
		Nos. 198-201 (4)	40.75	18.80
		Set, never hinged	125.00	

Imperf Singles

198a	A24	10c	1,500.	
		Never hinged	1,500.	
199a	A25	25c	1,000.	725.
		Never hinged	1,500.	
200a	A26	30c	1,000.	
		Never hinged	1,500.	
201a	A27	50c	1,000.	1,000.
		Never hinged	1,500.	
		On cover		6,500.

8th Olympic Games, Paris.

Pierre de Ronsard (1524-85), Poet — A28

1924, Oct. 6   Perf. 14x13½

219	A28	75c blue, bluish	1.90	1.40
		Never hinged	2.75	
		On cover		10.50
		On cover, single franking		20.00

"Light and Liberty" Allegory A29

Majolica Vase — A30

Potter Decorating Vase — A31

Terrace of Château A32

1924-25   Perf. 14x13½, 13½x14

220	A29	10c dk grn & yel ('25)	.55	.75
		Never hinged	1.25	
		On cover		2.00
		On cover, single franking		5.00
221	A30	15c ind & grn ('25)	.55	.85
		Never hinged	1.25	
		On cover		2.00
		On cover, single franking		5.00
a.		Imperf.	400.00	
		Never hinged	640.00	
b.		As "a," setenant with normal	500.00	
		Never hinged	775.00	
222	A31	25c vio brn & garnet	.80	.50
		Never hinged	1.80	
		On cover		2.50
		On cover, single franking		6.25
a.		Imperf, se-tenant with normal	2,050.	
		Never hinged	2,750.	
223	A32	25c gray bl & vio ('25)	1.60	.65
		Never hinged	2.25	
		On cover		2.50
		On cover, single franking		6.25
a.		Imperf.	450.00	150.00
		Never hinged	700.00	
b.		As "a," setenant with normal	575.00	
		Never hinged	900.00	
224	A31	75c indigo & ultra	3.50	2.25
		Never hinged	6.50	
		On cover		6.50
		On cover, single franking		16.50
a.		Imperf, no gum	150.00	
225	A29	75c dk bl & lt bl ('25)	18.00	6.50
		Never hinged	37.50	
		On cover		19.00
		On cover, single franking		32.50
a.		Imperf.	375.00	
		Never hinged	650.00	

b.		As "a," setenant with normal	550.00	
		Never hinged	1,000.	
		Nos. 220-225 (6)	25.00	11.50
		Set, never hinged	52.50	

Intl. Exhibition of Decorative Modern Arts at Paris, 1925.

Philatelic Exhibition Issue
Souvenir Sheet

A32a

1925, May 2   Perf. 14x13½

226	A32a	Sheet of 4, A15 II	1,100.	1,100.
		Never hinged	3,750.	
		On cover		2,000.
a.		Imperf. sheet	5,000.	1,750.
		Never hinged	7,750.	
b.		5fr carmine, perf.	125.00	140.00
		Never hinged	225.00	
		On cover		250.00
		On cover, single franking		250.00
c.		5fr carmine, imperf.	900.00	
		Never hinged	1,325.	

These were on sale only at the Intl. Phil. Exhib., Paris, May, 1925. Size: 140x220mm.

Nos. 148-149, 152-153, 173, 175, 181, 183, 192, 195 Surcharged

1926-27

227	A22	25c on 30c lt bl	.25	.50
		Never hinged	.50	
		On cover		3.25
		On cover, single franking		5.75
a.		Pair, one without surcharge	1,050.	925.00
		Never hinged	1,500.	
228	A22	25c on 35c violet	.25	.50
		Never hinged	.50	
		On cover		3.75
		On cover, single franking		6.50
a.		Double surcharge	525.00	350.00
		Never hinged	750.00	
b.		Pair, one without surcharge	550.00	925.00
		Never hinged	825.00	
229	A20	50c on 60c lt vio ('27)	1.40	1.10
		Never hinged	2.50	
		On cover		4.25
		On cover, single franking		6.00
a.		Pair, one without surcharge	525.00	925.00
		Never hinged	750.00	
230	A20	50c on 65c rose ('27)	.75	.55
		Never hinged	1.50	
		On cover		3.75
		On cover, single franking		8.25
a.		Inverted surcharge	1,225.	1,400.
		Never hinged	1,850.	
b.		Pair, one without surcharge	675.00	925.00
		Never hinged	1,100.	
231	A23	50c on 75c blue	3.25	1.50
		Never hinged	5.25	
		On cover		4.00
		On cover, single franking		8.25
232	A20	50c on 80c ver ('27)	1.25	1.10
		Never hinged	2.25	
		On cover		5.25
		On cover, single franking		27.50
a.		Pair, one without surcharge	475.00	925.00
		Never hinged	675.00	

233	A20	50c on 85c ver ('27)	2.25	1.00
		Never hinged	5.00	
		On cover		4.25
		On cover, single franking		10.00
234	A22	50c on 1.05fr ver	1.25	.75
		Never hinged	2.25	
		On cover		4.25
		On cover, single franking		8.25
a.		Pair, one without surcharge	475.00	925.00
		Never hinged	700.00	
235	A23	50c on 1.25fr blue	2.75	2.25
		Never hinged	5.25	
		On cover		5.00
		On cover, single franking		12.50
a.		Pair, one without surcharge	525.00	925.00
		Never hinged	750.00	
236	A20	55c on 60c lt vio	125.00	52.50
		Never hinged	240.00	
		On cover		160.00
		On cover, single franking		160.00
238	A22	90c on 1.05fr ver ('27)	2.25	2.75
		Never hinged	3.75	
		On cover		5.00
		On cover, single franking		11.00
a.		Pair, one without surcharge	1,000.	925.00
		Never hinged	1,500.	
240	A22	1.10fr on 1.40fr cer	1.00	1.10
		Never hinged	1.90	
		On cover		7.50
		On cover, single franking		45.00
a.		Pair, one without surcharge	575.00	925.00
		Never hinged	825.00	
		Nos. 227-240 (12)	141.65	65.60
		Set, never hinged	275.00	

Issue dates: Nos. 229-230, 232-234, 1927.
No. 236 is known only precanceled. See second note after No. 132.
Nos. 229, 230, 234, 238 and 240 have three bars instead of two. The 55c surcharge has thinner, larger numerals and a rounded "c." Width, including bars, is 17mm, instead of 13mm.
The 55c was used only precanceled at the Magasins du Louvre department store in Paris, August 1926.

Strasbourg Exhibition Issue
Souvenir Sheet

A32b

1927, June 4

241	A32b	Sheet of 2	1,000.	1,000.
		Never hinged	2,300.	
		On cover		1,400.
a.		5fr light ultra (A22)	250.00	250.00
		Never hinged	400.00	
		On cover		300.00
b.		10fr carmine rose (A22)	250.00	250.00
		Never hinged	400.00	
		On cover		300.00
		In pair with #241a and label	500.00	540.00
		Never hinged	800.00	

Sold at the Strasbourg Philatelic Exhibition as souvenirs. Size: 111x140mm.

Marcelin Berthelot (1827-1907), Chemist and Statesman — A33

1927, Sept. 7

242	A33	90c dull rose	1.90	.60
		Never hinged	3.00	
		On cover		3.00
		On cover, single franking		4.25

For surcharge see No. C3.

Lafayette, Washington, S. S. Paris and Airplane "Spirit of St. Louis" — A34

1927, Sept. 15
243 A34 90c dull red 1.25 1.75
  Never hinged 2.50
  On cover 5.75
  On cover, single franking 9.00
  a. Value omitted 2,000. 1,725.
    Never hinged 2,600.
    On cover 2,200.
244 A34 1.50fr deep blue 4.00 2.50
  Never hinged 7.50
  On cover 5.75
  On cover, single franking 9.00
  a. Value omitted 1,450.
    Never hinged 1,850.
  Set, never hinged 10.00

Visit of American Legionnaires to France, September, 1927. Exist imperf.

Joan of Arc — A35

1929, Mar.
245 A35 50c dull blue 1.90 .25
  Never hinged 2.75
  On cover .85
  On cover, single franking 2.00
  a. Booklet pane of 10 50.00
    Never hinged 160.00
  b. Imperf. 140.00
    Never hinged 210.00

500th anniv. of the relief of Orleans by the French forces led by Joan of Arc.

No. 127 Overprinted in Blue

1929, May 18
246 A18 2fr org & pale bl 600.00 600.00
  Never hinged 1,325.
  On cover 750.00
  On cover, single franking 750.00

Sold exclusively at the Intl. Phil. Exhib., Le Havre, May, 1929, for 7fr, which included a 5fr admission ticket.
Excellent counterfeits of No. 246 exist.

Reims Cathedral — A37

Die I, II, III   Die IV

Die I   Die II   Die III

Die I — The window of the 1st turret on the left is made of 2 lines. The horizontal line of the frame surrounding 3F is not continuous.
Die II — Same as Die I but the line under 3F is continuous.
Die III — Same as Die II but there is a deeply cut line separating 3 and F.
Die IV — Same as Die III but the window of the first turret on the left is made of three lines.

Mont-Saint-Michel — A38

Die I   Die II

Die I — The line at the top of the spire is broken.
Die II — The line is unbroken.

Port of La Rochelle A39

Dies I & II   Die III

Die I — The top of the "E" of "POSTES" has a serif. The oval of shading inside the "0" of "10 fr" and the outer oval are broken at their bases.
Die II — The same top has no serif. Interior and exterior of "0" broken as in Die I.
Die III — Top of "E" has no serif. Interior and exterior of "0" complete.

Pont du Gard, Nimes A40

Dies I & II

Die III

Die I — Shading of the first complete arch in the left middle tier is made of horizontal lines. Size 36x20¾mm. Perf. 13½.
Die II — Same, size 35½x21mm. Perf. 11.
Die III — Shading of same arch is made of three diagonal lines. Thin paper. Perf. 13.

1929-33 Engr. Perf. 11, 13, 13½
247 A37 3fr dk gray ('30) (I) 62.50 2.40
  Never hinged 115.00
  On cover 6.25
  On cover, single franking 25.00
247A A37 3fr dk gray ('30) (II) 125.00 3.50
  Never hinged 200.00
  On cover 10.00
  On cover, single franking 37.50
247B A37 3fr dk gray ('30) (III) 375.00 24.00
  Never hinged 600.00
  On cover 45.00
  On cover, single franking 70.00
248 A37 3fr bluish sl ('31) (IV) 60.00 2.40
  Never hinged 115.00
  On cover 6.25
  On cover, single franking 25.00
249 A38 5fr brn ('30) (I) 24.00 4.25
  Never hinged 40.00
  On cover 6.50
  On cover, single franking 22.00
250 A38 5fr brn ('31) (II) 21.00 .75
  Never hinged 32.50
  On cover 5.75
  On cover, single franking 19.00

251 A39 10fr lt ultra (I) 95.00 15.00
  Never hinged 160.00
  On cover 25.00
  On cover, single franking 45.00
251A A39 10fr ultra (II) 140.00 26.00
  Never hinged 225.00
  On cover 40.00
  On cover, single franking 60.00
252 A39 10fr dk ultra ('31) (III) 70.00 6.50
  Never hinged 140.00
  On cover 19.00
  On cover, single franking 40.00
253 A40 20fr red brown (I) 275.00 40.00
  Never hinged 500.00
  On cover 100.00
  On cover, single franking 300.00
  a. 20fr pale red brown (I) 1,250. 350.00
    Never hinged 2,000.
254 A40 20fr brt red brn ('30) (II) 1,000. 350.00
  Never hinged 1,650.
  On cover 750.00
  On cover, single franking 1,350.
254A A40 20fr org brn ('31) (III) 250.00 35.00
  Never hinged 450.00
  On cover 82.50
  On cover, single franking 275.00
  b. 20fr pale orange brown (III) 240.00 30.00
    Never hinged 475.00
  Nos. 247-254A (12) 2,497. 509.80

View of Algiers A41

1929, Jan. 1 Typo.
255 A41 50c blue & rose red 2.40 .50
  Never hinged 5.50
  On cover 1.40
  On cover, single franking 4.50
  a. Imperf 210.00 130.00
    Never hinged 310.00

Cent. of the 1st French settlement in Algeria.

Nos. 146 and 196 Overprinted

CONGRÈS DU B. I. T. 1930

1930, Apr. 23 Perf. 14x13½
256 A20 50c vermilion 3.00 3.25
  Never hinged 6.50
  On cover 8.25
  On cover, single franking 18.00
257 A23 1.50fr blue 20.00 14.50
  Never hinged 40.00
  On cover 29.00
  On cover, single franking 37.50
  Set, never hinged 47.50

Intl. Labor Bureau, 48th Congress, Paris.

Colonial Exposition Issue

Fachi Woman — A42

French Colonials A43

1930-31 Typo. Perf. 14x13½
258 A42 15c gray black 1.10 .30
  Never hinged 2.25
  On cover 1.00
  On cover, single franking 3.25
259 A42 40c dark brown 2.40 .30
  Never hinged 4.75
  On cover 1.00
  On cover, single franking 2.00
260 A42 50c dark red .65 .25
  Never hinged 1.10
  On cover 1.00
  a. Booklet pane of 10 12.50
261 A42 1.50fr deep blue 9.00 .65
  Never hinged 21.00
  On cover 2.75
  On cover, single franking 4.50

Perf. 13½
Photo.
262 A43 1.50fr dp blue ('31) 45.00 2.75
  Never hinged 95.00
  On cover 4.00
  On cover, single franking 6.50
  Nos. 258-262 (5) 58.15 4.25
  Set, never hinged 125.00

No. 260 has two types: type 1 shows four short downward hairlines near top of head, type 2 has no lines. Booklet stamps are type 2.

Arc de Triomphe A44

1931 Engr. Perf. 13
263 A44 2fr red brown 40.00 1.25
  Never hinged 80.00
  On cover 5.00
  On cover, single franking 11.00

Peace with Olive Branch — A45

1932-39 Typo. Perf. 14x13½
264 A45 30c dp green 1.00 .55
  Never hinged 2.00
  On cover 2.00
  On cover, single franking 5.75
265 A45 40c brt violet .30 .30
  Never hinged .55
  On cover 1.40
  On cover, single franking 2.50
266 A45 45c yellow brown 1.75 1.00
  Never hinged 3.75
  On cover 10.00
  On cover, single franking 40.00
267 A45 50c rose red .25 .25
  Never hinged .30
  On cover .40
  On cover, single franking .40
  a. Imperf., pair 140.00
    Never hinged 210.00
  b. Booklet pane of 10 5.50
    Never hinged 10.00
268 A45 55c dull vio ('37) .60 .25
  Never hinged 1.25
  On cover 1.00
  On cover, single franking 2.75
269 A45 60c ocher ('37) .30 .25
  Never hinged .50
  On cover 4.50
  On cover, single franking 26.00
270 A45 65c violet brown .50 .50
  Never hinged 1.00
  On cover .80
  On cover, single franking 4.50
271 A45 65c brt ultra ('37) .25 .25
  Never hinged .50
  On cover .80
  On cover, single franking .90
  a. Booklet pane of 10 7.00
    Never hinged 10.00
272 A45 75c olive green .25 .30
  Never hinged .30
  On cover .85
  On cover, single franking 3.75
273 A45 80c orange ('38) .25 .25
  Never hinged .30
  On cover 1.00
  On cover, single franking 4.50
274 A45 90c dk red 32.50 2.00
  Never hinged 62.50
  On cover 5.25
  On cover, single franking 10.00
275 A45 90c brt green ('38) .25 .25
  Never hinged .30
  On cover 1.25
  On cover, single franking 5.25
276 A45 90c ultra ('38) .90 .25
  Never hinged 1.50
  On cover .50
  On cover, single franking 1.00
  a. Booklet pane of 10 8.50
    Never hinged 12.00
  b. Imperf 260.00
    Never hinged 450.00
277 A45 1fr orange 3.25 .25
  Never hinged 6.25
  On cover 2.00
  On cover, single franking 6.50
278 A45 1fr rose pink ('38) 3.25 .50
  Never hinged 5.75
  On cover 1.40
  On cover, single franking 4.50
279 A45 1.25fr brown ol 75.00 4.75
  Never hinged 160.00
  On cover 6.25
  On cover, single franking 32.50
280 A45 1.25fr rose car ('39) 1.90 2.25
  Never hinged 3.50
  On cover 3.00
  On cover, single franking 10.00
281 A45 1.40fr brt red vio ('39) 5.75 5.25
  Never hinged 11.00
  On cover 13.00
  On cover, single franking 60.00
282 A45 1.50fr deep blue .30 .30
  Never hinged .55
  On cover 1.00
  On cover, single franking 4.00

283 A45 1.75fr magenta ... 4.00 .50
  Never hinged ... 9.50
  On cover ... 1.00
  On cover, single franking ... 4.00
  Nos. 264-283 (20) ... 132.55 20.20
  Set, never hinged ... 275.00

The 50c is found in 4 types, differing in the lines below belt and size of C.
For surcharges and overprints see Nos. 298, 333, 401-403, 405-409, M7-M9, S1.

Le Puy-en-Velay — A46

1933   **Engr.**   **Perf. 13**
290 A46 90c rose ... 3.00 1.10
  Never hinged ... 5.75
  On cover ... 2.00
  On cover, single franking ... 4.00

Aristide Briand A47   Paul Doumer A48

Victor Hugo — A49

1933, Dec. 11   **Typo.**   **Perf. 14x13½**
291 A47 30c blue green ... 17.00 8.00
  Never hinged ... 32.50
  On cover ... 11.00
  On cover, single franking ... 16.50
292 A48 75c red violet ... 27.50 1.90
  Never hinged ... 62.50
  On cover ... 2.75
  On cover, single franking ... 8.25
  a. Imperf ... 825.00
293 A49 1.25fr claret ... 6.00 2.25
  Never hinged ... 11.00
  On cover ... 5.75
  On cover, single franking ... 27.50
  Nos. 291-293 (3) ... 50.50 12.15
  Set, never hinged ... 110.00

Dove and Olive Branch A50   Joseph Marie Jacquard A51

1934, Feb. 20
294 A50 1.50fr ultra ... 50.00 15.00
  Never hinged ... 95.00
  On cover ... 29.00
  On cover, single franking ... 50.00

1934, Mar. 14   **Engr.**   **Perf. 14x13**
295 A51 40c blue ... 3.00 1.10
  Never hinged ... 4.50
  On cover ... 1.60
  On cover, single franking ... 3.25

Jacquard (1752-1834), inventor of an improved loom for figured weaving.

Jacques Cartier A52

1934, July 18   **Perf. 13**
296 A52 75c rose lilac ... 30.00 2.25
  Never hinged ... 87.50
  On cover ... 5.00
  On cover, single franking ... 16.50

297 A52 1.50fr blue ... 50.00 4.25
  Never hinged ... 130.00
  On cover ... 5.25
  On cover, single franking ... 13.00
  Set, never hinged ... 210.00
Cartier's discovery of Canada, 400th anniv.

No. 279 Surcharged

1934, Nov.   **Perf. 14x13½**
298 A45 50c on 1.25fr brn ol ... 3.75 .65
  Never hinged ... 7.00
  On cover ... 2.75
  On cover, single franking ... 13.00

> **Catalogue values for unused stamps in this section, from this point to the end of the section, are for Never Hinged items.**

Breton River Scene A53

1935, Feb.   **Engr.**   **Perf. 13**
299 A53 2fr blue green ... 70.00 1.00
  Hinged ... 32.50
  On cover ... 4.50
  On cover, single franking ... 16.50

S. S. Normandie A54

1935, Apr.
300 A54 1.50fr dark blue ... 29.00 2.00
  Hinged ... 14.00
  On cover ... 5.00
  On cover, single franking ... 8.25
  a. 1.50fr pale blue ('36) ... 145.00 19.00
    Hinged ... 55.00
    On cover ... 40.00
    On cover, single franking ... 65.00
  b. 1.50fr blue green ('36) ... 30,000. 12,500.
    Hinged ... 19,000.
  c. 1.50fr turquoise ('36) ... 400.00 40.00
    Hinged ... 275.00
    On cover ... 90.00
    On cover, single franking ... 140.00
  d. As #300, imperf ... 300.00
    Hinged ... 200.00

Maiden voyage of the transatlantic steamship, the "Normandie."

Benjamin Delessert A55

1935, May 20
301 A55 75c blue green ... 47.50 1.75
  Hinged ... 17.50
  On cover ... 4.00
  On cover, single franking ... 12.50

Opening of the International Savings Bank Congress, May 20, 1935.

View of St. Trophime at Arles A56   Victor Hugo (1802-85) A57

1935, May 3
302 A56 3.50fr dark brown ... 70.00 4.25
  Hinged ... 27.50
  On cover ... 9.00
  On cover, single franking ... 25.00

1935, May 30   **Perf. 14x13**
303 A57 1.25fr magenta ... 8.25 2.00
  Hinged ... 4.00
  On cover ... 5.75
  On cover, single franking ... 29.00

Cardinal Richelieu — A58   Jacques Callot — A59

1935, June 12   **Perf. 13**
304 A58 1.50fr deep rose ... 70.00 1.75
  Hinged ... 20.00
  On cover ... 3.25
  On cover, single franking ... 6.50

Tercentenary of the founding of the French Academy by Cardinal Richelieu.

1935, Nov.   **Perf. 14x13**
305 A59 75c red ... 19.00 .75
  Hinged ... 10.00
  On cover ... 2.50
  On cover, single franking ... 6.50

300th anniv. of the death of Jacques Callot, engraver.

André Marie Ampère (1775-1836), Scientist, by Louis Boilly — A60

1936, Feb. 27   **Perf. 13**
306 A60 75c brown ... 37.50 2.00
  Hinged ... 17.50
  On cover ... 3.25
  On cover, single franking ... 8.25

Windmill at Fontvielle, Immortalized by Daudet — A61

1936, Apr. 27
307 A61 2fr ultra ... 5.75 .40
  Hinged ... 3.00
  On cover ... 3.25
  On cover, single franking ... 9.00

Publication, in 1866, of Alphonse Daudet's "Lettres de mon Moulin," 75th anniv.

Pilâtre de Rozier and his Balloon A62

1936, June 4
308 A62 75c Prus blue ... 37.50 2.75
  Hinged ... 19.00
  On cover ... 5.75
  On cover, single franking ... 14.00

150th anniversary of the death of Jean Francois Pilâtre de Rozier, balloonist.

Rouget de Lisle — A63

"La Marseillaise" — A64

1936, June 27
309 A63 20c Prus green ... 5.75 2.00
  Hinged ... 3.25
  On cover ... 3.25
  On cover, single franking ... 5.00
310 A64 40c dark brown ... 11.50 3.25
  Hinged ... 5.50
  On cover ... 5.00
  On cover, single franking ... 5.75

Cent. of the death of Claude Joseph Rouget de Lisle, composer of "La Marseillaise."

Canadian War Memorial at Vimy Ridge A65

1936, July 26
311 A65 75c henna brown ... 25.00 2.00
  Hinged ... 9.50
  On cover, single franking ... 5.75
312 A65 1.50fr dull blue ... 32.50 9.50
  Hinged ... 16.00
  On cover ... 16.50
  On cover, single franking ... 29.00

Unveiling of the Canadian War Memorial at Vimy Ridge, July 26, 1936.

A66

Jean Léon Jaurès A67

1936, July 30
313 A66 40c red brown ... 5.75 1.40
  Hinged ... 4.00
  On cover ... 2.00
  On cover, single franking ... 5.00
314 A67 1.50fr ultra ... 32.50 3.75
  Hinged ... 13.00
  On cover ... 5.00
  On cover, single franking ... 10.00

Assassination of Jean Léon Jaurès (1859-1914), socialist and politician.

Herald — A68

Allegory of Exposition A69

1936, Sept. 15   Typo.   Perf. 14x13½

315	A68	20c brt violet	1.00	.50
		Hinged	.30	
		On cover		2.00
		On cover, single franking		7.75
316	A68	30c Prus green	4.00	1.75
		Hinged	2.40	
		On cover		2.75
		On cover, single franking		28.00
317	A68	40c ultra	2.50	.50
		Hinged	1.00	
		On cover		1.60
		On cover, single franking		5.00
318	A68	50c red orange	2.25	.25
		Hinged	1.00	
		On cover		.85
		On cover, single franking		1.00
319	A69	90c carmine	25.00	7.50
		Hinged	11.00	
		On cover		15.00
		On cover, single franking		29.00
320	A69	1.50fr ultra	67.50	4.00
		Hinged	30.00	
		On cover		7.50
		On cover, single franking		25.00
		Nos. 315-320 (6)	*102.25*	*14.50*

Publicity for the 1937 Paris Exposition.

"Peace" A70

1936, Oct. 1   Engr.   Perf. 13

321	A70	1.50fr blue	27.50	4.00
		Hinged	12.50	
		On cover		7.50
		On cover, single franking		18.00

Skiing A71

1937, Jan. 18

322	A71	1.50fr dark blue	14.00	1.75
		Hinged	7.00	
		On cover		4.00
		On cover, single franking		8.25

Intl. Ski Meet at Chamonix-Mont Blanc.

Pierre Corneille, Portrait by Charles Le Brun — A72

1937, Feb. 15

323	A72	75c brown carmine	3.75	1.40
		Hinged	1.90	
		On cover		2.75
		On cover, single franking		6.50

300th anniv. of the publication of "Le Cid."

Paris Exposition Issue

Exposition Allegory A73

1937, Mar. 15

324	A73	1.50fr turq blue	4.00	1.25
		Hinged	2.25	
		On cover		2.75
		On cover, single franking		6.50

Jean Mermoz (1901-36), Aviator A74

Memorial to Mermoz — A75

1937, Apr. 22

325	A74	30c dk slate green	1.00	.55
		Hinged	.50	
		On cover		2.75
		On cover, single franking		8.25
326	A75	3fr dark violet	13.50	3.75
		Hinged	6.25	
		On cover		12.50
		On cover, single franking		32.50
a.		3fr violet	15.00	4.50
		Hinged	6.75	
		On cover		13.00
b.		3fr gray violet (non-Fluorescent)	325.00	100.00
		Hinged	200.00	

Electric Train A76

Streamlined Locomotive A77

1937, May 31

327	A76	30c dk green	1.40	1.75
		Hinged	1.00	
		On cover		3.25
		On cover, single franking		5.75
328	A77	1.50fr dk ultra	15.00	8.25
		Hinged	7.25	
		On cover		14.00
		On cover, single franking		37.50

13th International Railroad Congress.

Intl. Philatelic Exhibition Issue
Souvenir Sheet

Ceres Type A1 of 1849-50 — A77a

1937, June 18   Typo.   Perf. 14x13½

329	A77a	Sheet of 4	700.00	300.00
		Lightly hinged in margins	360.00	
		On cover		*475.00*
a.		5c ultra & dark brown	90.00	47.50

		Lightly hinged	40.00	
		On cover		*160.00*
b.		15c red & rose red	90.00	47.50
		Lightly hinged	40.00	
		On cover		*160.00*
c.		30c ultra & rose red	90.00	47.50
		Lightly hinged	40.00	
		On cover		*160.00*
d.		50c red & dark brown	90.00	47.50
		Lightly hinged	40.00	
		On cover		*160.00*
e.		Sheet of 4, imperf.	3,000.	
		Lightly hinged in margins	2,350.	

Issued in sheets measuring 150x220mm. The sheets were sold only at the exhibition in Paris, a ticket of admission being required for each sheet purchased.

René Descartes, by Frans Hals — A78

1937, June   Engr.   Perf. 13
Inscribed "Discours sur la Méthode"

330	A78	90c copper red	3.25	1.40
		Hinged	1.90	
		On cover		3.25
		On cover, single franking		10.00

Inscribed "Discours de la Méthode"

331	A78	90c copper red	11.00	1.75
		Hinged	5.50	
		On cover		3.25
		On cover, single franking		12.50

3rd centenary of the publication of "Discours de la Méthode" by René Descartes.

France Congratulating USA — A79

1937, Sept. 17

332	A79	1.75fr ultra	4.50	2.00
		Hinged	2.50	
		On cover		3.25
		On cover, single franking		5.00

150th anniv. of the US Constitution.

No. 277 Surcharged in Red

1937, Oct.   Perf. 14x13½

333	A45	80c on 1fr orange	1.90	.85
		Hinged	.80	
		On cover		13.00
		On cover, single franking		65.00
a.		Inverted surcharge	*1,225.*	
		Hinged	*825.00*	

Mountain Road at Iseran A80

1937, Oct. 4   Engr.   Perf. 13

334	A80	90c dark green	3.75	.30
		Hinged	1.90	
		On cover		1.25
		On cover, single franking		4.50

Issued in commemoration of the opening of the mountain road at Iseran, Savoy.

Ceres — A81

1938-40   Typo.   Perf. 14x13½

335	A81	1.75fr dk ultra	1.40	.55
		Hinged	.55	
		On cover		1.00
		On cover, single franking		5.25

336	A81	2fr car rose ('39)	.30	.30
		Hinged	.20	
		On cover		1.10
		On cover, single franking		13.00
337	A81	2.25fr ultra ('39)	15.00	1.10
		Hinged	8.00	
		On cover		1.25
		On cover, single franking		5.25
338	A81	2.50fr green ('39)	3.00	.50
		Hinged	1.25	
		On cover		1.25
		On cover, single franking		5.25
339	A81	2.50fr vio blue ('40)	1.25	.75
		Hinged	.65	
		On cover		1.25
		On cover, single franking		6.25
340	A81	3fr rose lilac ('39)	1.25	.50
		Hinged	.55	
		On cover		1.25
		On cover, single franking		4.50
		Nos. 335-340 (6)	*22.20*	*3.70*

For surcharges see Nos. 397-399.

Léon Gambetta (1838-82), Lawyer and Statesman — A82

1938, Apr. 2   Engr.   Perf. 13

341	A82	55c dark violet	.55	.40
		Hinged	.35	
		On cover		1.40
		On cover, single franking		4.50

Arc de Triomphe of Orange A82a

Miners A83

Keep and Gate of Vincennes A86

Palace of the Popes, Avignon A84

Medieval Walls of Carcassonne — A85

Port of St. Malo — A87

1938

342	A82a	2fr brown black	1.75	1.25
		Hinged	.55	
		On cover		3.75
		On cover, single franking		16.50
343	A83	2.15fr violet brn	9.50	1.00
		Hinged	4.75	
		On cover		1.60
		On cover, single franking		5.00
344	A84	3fr car brown	26.50	5.00
		Hinged	12.50	
		On cover		11.00
		On cover, single franking		40.00
345	A85	5fr deep ultra	1.50	.40
		Hinged	.75	
		On cover		2.90
		On cover, single franking		18.00

346 A86 10fr brown, *blue* 3.25 1.90
　Hinged 1.50
　On cover 4.00
　On cover, single franking 45.00
347 A87 20fr dk blue green 80.00 19.00
　Hinged 37.50
　On cover 30.00
　On cover, single franking 61.00
　Nos. 342-347 (6) 122.50 28.55

For surcharges see Nos. 410-413.

Clément Ader, Air Pioneer A88

1938, June 16
348 A88 50fr ultra (thin paper) 150.00 65.00
　Hinged 95.00
　On cover 200.00
　On cover, single franking 450.00
a. 50fr dark ultra (thick paper) 175.00 77.50
　Hinged 100.00
　On cover 200.00
　On cover, single franking 450.00

For surcharge, see No. 414.

Soccer Players A89

1938, June 1
349 A89 1.75fr dark ultra 29.00 13.50
　Hinged 13.50
　On cover 26.00
　On cover, single franking 60.00

World Cup Soccer Championship.

Costume of Champagne Region — A90　Jean de La Fontaine — A91

1938, June 13
350 A90 1.75fr dark ultra 7.50 4.50
　Hinged 3.75
　On cover 6.50
　On cover, single franking 12.50

Tercentenary of the birth of Dom Pierre Pérignon, discoverer of the champagne process.

1938, July 8
351 A91 55c dk blue green 1.00 .80
　Hinged .65
　On cover 1.40
　On cover, single franking 2.75

Jean de La Fontaine (1621-1695) the fabulist.

Seal of Friendship and Peace, Victoria Tower and Arc de Triomphe A92

1938, July 19
352 A92 1.75fr ultra 1.25 .80
　Hinged .65
　On cover 2.90
　On cover, single franking 5.25

Visit of King George VI and Queen Elizabeth of Great Britain to France.

Mercury — A93

1938-42　Typo.　Perf. 14x13½
353 A93 1c dark brown ('39) .25 .25
　Hinged .25
　On cover 11.00
　On cover, single franking 90.00
354 A93 2c slate grn ('39) .25 .25
　Hinged .25
　On cover 26.00
　On cover, single franking 130.00
355 A93 5c rose .25 .25
　Hinged .25
　On cover 11.00
　On cover, single franking 60.00
356 A93 10c ultra .25 .25
　Hinged .25
　On cover 2.75
　On cover, single franking 30.00
357 A93 15c red orange .25 .25
　Hinged .25
　On cover 2.75
　On cover, single franking 57.50
358 A93 15c orange brn ('39) 1.00 .50
　Hinged .55
　On cover 3.75
　On cover, single franking 57.50
359 A93 20c red violet .25 .25
　Hinged .25
　On cover 3.75
　On cover, single franking 26.00
360 A93 25c blue green .25 .25
　Hinged .25
　On cover 7.00
　On cover, single franking 30.00
361 A93 30c rose red ('39) .25 .25
　Hinged .25
　On cover 1.10
　On cover, single franking 3.75
362 A93 40c dk violet ('39) .25 .25
　Hinged .25
　On cover 1.00
　On cover, single franking 2.75
363 A93 45c lt green ('39) .80 .50
　Hinged .50
　On cover 7.75
　On cover, single franking 13.00
364 A93 50c deep blue ('39) 4.00 .40
　Hinged 2.25
　On cover 3.75
　On cover, single franking 20.00
365 A93 50c dk green ('41) .55 .35
　Hinged .30
　On cover 3.75
　On cover, single franking 25.00
366 A93 50c grnsh blue ('42) .25 .25
　Hinged .25
　On cover 1.00
　On cover, single franking 4.50
367 A93 60c red orange ('39) .25 .25
　Hinged .25
　On cover 3.25
　On cover, single franking 15.00
368 A93 70c magenta ('39) .25 .25
　Hinged .25
　On cover 1.00
　On cover, single franking 2.75
369 A93 75c dk org brn ('39) 7.50 2.50
　Hinged 3.75
　On cover 32.50
　On cover, single franking 130.00
　Nos. 353-369 (17) 16.85 7.25

No. 366 exists imperforate. See Nos. 455-458. For overprints and surcharge see Nos. 404, 499-502. Post 1940 issues in Scott Standard catalogue, Vol. 2.

Self-portrait — A95

1939, Mar. 15　Engr.　Perf. 13
370 A95 2.25fr Prussian blue 8.25 3.50
　Hinged 3.50
　On cover 5.00
　On cover, single franking 9.00

Paul Cézanne (1839-1906), painter.

Georges Clemenceau and Battleship Clemenceau — A96

1939, Apr. 18
371 A96 90c ultra 1.00 .75
　Hinged .50
　On cover 2.00
　On cover, single franking 4.50

Laying of the keel of the warship "Clemen-

Statue of Liberty, French Pavilion, Trylon and Perisphere A97

1939-40
372 A97 2.25fr ultra 17.00 6.50
　Hinged 8.00
　On cover 10.00
　On cover, single franking 16.50
373 A97 2.50fr ultra ('40) 22.50 9.50
　Hinged 8.50
　On cover 14.50
　On cover, single franking 20.00

New York World's Fair.

Joseph Nicéphore Niepce and Louis Jacques Mandé Daguerre A98

1939, Apr. 24
374 A98 2.25fr dark blue 16.00 7.00
　Hinged 7.00
　On cover 10.00
　On cover, single franking 16.50

Centenary of photography.

Iris — A99

1939-44　Typo.　Perf. 14x13½
375 A99 80c red brown ('40) .25 .25
　Hinged .25
　On cover .65
　On cover, single franking 8.25
376 A99 80c yellow grn ('44) .25 .25
　Hinged .25
　On cover 3.00
　On cover, single franking 12.00
377 A99 1fr green 1.00 .25
　Hinged .55
　On cover .65
　On cover, single franking 1.25
378 A99 1fr crimson ('40) .40 .35
　Hinged .25
　On cover .65
　On cover, single franking 1.25
　a. Booklet pane of 10 7.50
379 A99 1fr grnsh blue ('44) .25 .25
　Hinged .25
　On cover 2.00
　On cover, single franking 7.50
380 A99 1.20fr violet ('44) .25 .25
　Hinged .25
　On cover 1.25
　On cover, single franking 2.50
381 A99 1.30fr ultra ('40) .25 .25
　Hinged .25
　On cover 3.75
　On cover, single franking 16.50
382 A99 1.50fr red org ('41) .25 .25
　Hinged .25
　On cover 1.25
　On cover, single franking 12.50
383 A99 1.50fr henna brn ('44) .25 .25
　Hinged .25
　On cover 1.25
　On cover, single franking 5.75
384 A99 2fr violet brn ('44) .25 .25
　Hinged .25
　On cover 1.25
　On cover, single franking 5.25
385 A99 2.40fr car rose ('44) .25 .25
　Hinged .25
　On cover 3.00
　On cover, single franking 140.00
386 A99 3fr orange ('44) .25 .25
　Hinged .25
　On cover 2.00
　On cover, single franking 10.00
387 A99 4fr ultra ('44) .25 .25
　Hinged .25
　On cover 3.00
　On cover, single franking 15.00
　Nos. 375-387 (13) 4.15 3.35

Pumping Station at Marly A100

1939　Engr.　Perf. 13
388 A100 2.25fr brt ultra 25.00 5.00
　Hinged 11.00
　On cover 7.50
　On cover, single franking 16.50

France's participation in the International Water Exposition at Liège.

St. Gregory of Tours — A101

1939, June 10
389 A101 90c red .90 .55
　Hinged .50
　On cover 1.60
　On cover, single franking 3.75

14th centenary of the birth of St. Gregory of Tours, historian and bishop.

"The Oath of the Tennis Court" by Jacques David A102

1939, June 20
390 A102 90c deep slate green 3.50 1.90
　Hinged 1.90
　On cover 2.50
　On cover, single franking 4.00

150th anniversary of French Revolution.

Cathedral of Strasbourg — A103

1939, June 23
391 A103 70c brown carmine 1.50 1.00
　Hinged .75
　On cover 1.60
　On cover, single franking 4.00

500th anniv. of the completion of Strasbourg Cathedral.

Porte Chaussée, Verdun A104

1939, June 23
392 A104 90c black brown 1.00 .80
　Hinged .80
　On cover 1.60
　On cover, single franking 3.75

23rd anniv. of the Battle of Verdun.

View of Pau A105

1939, Aug. 25
393	A105	90c brt rose, *gray bl*	1.25	1.25
	Hinged		.80	
	On cover			3.75
	On cover, single franking			10.00

Maid of Languedoc A106

Bridge at Lyons A107

1939
394	A106	70c black, *blue*	.50	.40
	Hinged		.40	
	On cover			3.75
	On cover, single franking			25.00
395	A107	90c dull brown vio	1.00	*1.25*
	Hinged		.90	
	On cover			4.50
	On cover, single franking			25.00

Imperforates
Nearly all French stamps issued from 1940 onward exist imperforate. Officially 20 sheets, ranging from 25 to 100 subjects, were left imperforate.

Georges Guynemer (1894-1917), World War I Ace — A108

1940, Nov. 7
396	A108	50fr ultra	16.00	9.00
	Hinged		8.00	
	On cover			77.50
	On cover, single franking			240.00

Stamps of 1938-39 Surcharged in Carmine

1940-41   *Perf. 14x13½*
397	A81	1fr on 1.75fr dk ultra	.30	.30
	Hinged		.25	
	On cover			1.25
	On cover, single franking			4.00
398	A81	1fr on 2.25fr ultra ('41)	.30	.30
	Hinged		.25	
	On cover			1.25
	On cover, single franking			4.50
399	A81	1fr on 2.50fr grn ('41)	1.40	1.40
	Hinged		.65	
	On cover			1.60
	On cover, single franking			4.50
	Nos. 397-399 (3)		2.00	2.00

Stamps of 1932-39 Surcharged in Carmine, Red (#408) or Black (#407)

1940-41   *Perf. 13, 14x13½*
400	A22	30c on 35c grn ('41)	.30	.30
	Hinged		.25	
	On cover			2.00
	On cover, single franking			12.50
401	A45	50c on 55c dl vio ('41)	.30	.30
	Hinged		.25	
	On cover			1.25
	On cover, single franking			18.00
a.	Inverted surcharge		*1,000.*	
	Lightly hinged		*575.00*	
402	A45	50c on 65c brt ultra ('41)	.30	.30
	Hinged		.25	
	On cover			1.25
	On cover, single franking			18.00

403	A45	50c on 75c ol grn ('41)	.30	.30
	Hinged		.25	
	On cover			1.25
	On cover, single franking			18.00
404	A93	50c on 75c dk org brn ('41)	.30	.30
	Hinged		.25	
	On cover			1.25
	On cover, single franking			37.50
405	A45	50c on 80c org ('41)	.30	.30
	Hinged		.25	
	On cover			1.25
	On cover, single franking			20.00
406	A45	50c on 90c ultra ('41)	.30	.30
	Hinged		.25	
	On cover			1.25
	On cover, single franking			18.00
a.	Inverted surcharge		*550.00*	
	Lightly hinged		*375.00*	
b.	"05" instead of "50"		*9,000.*	6,400.
	Lightly hinged		*6,400.*	
407	A45	1fr on 1.25fr rose car (Bk) ('41)	.30	.30
	Hinged		.25	
	On cover			1.25
	On cover, single franking			4.00
408	A45	1fr on 1.40fr brt red vio (R) ('41)	.40	.40
	Hinged		.25	
	On cover			1.25
	On cover, single franking			5.00
a.	Double surcharge		*1,600.*	
	Lightly hinged		*1,150.*	
409	A45	1fr on 1.50fr dk bl ('41)	1.40	1.40
	Hinged		.25	
	On cover			1.25
	On cover, single franking			4.00
410	A83	1fr on 2.15fr vio brn	.40	.40
	Hinged		.25	
	On cover			1.25
	On cover, single franking			3.75
a.	Inverted surcharge		*12,000.*	5,250.
	On cover			10,000.
411	A85	2.50fr on 5fr dp ultra ('41)	.40	.40
	Hinged		.25	
	On cover			5.25
	On cover, single franking			25.00
a.	Double surcharge		*350.00*	190.00
	Lightly hinged		*240.00*	
412	A86	5fr on 10fr brn, *bl* ('41)	1.90	1.90
	Hinged		1.00	
	On cover			6.00
	On cover, single franking			52.50
413	A87	10fr on 20fr dk bl grn ('41)	1.60	1.60
	Hinged		1.00	
	On cover			77.50
	On cover, single franking			210.00
414	A88	20fr on 50fr dk ultra (#348a) ('41)	70.00	37.50
	Hinged		29.00	
	On cover			110.00
	On cover, single franking			325.00
a.	20fr on 50fr ultra, thin paper (#348)		*75.00*	50.00
	On cover			125.00
	On cover, single franking			325.00
	Nos. 400-414 (15)		78.50	46.00

Issued: No. 410, 1940; others, 1941.

SEMI-POSTAL STAMPS

No. 162 Surcharged in Red

and

SP2

1914   Unwmk.   Typo.   *Perf. 14x13½*
B1	A22	10c + 5c red	5.00	4.25
	Never hinged		7.00	
	On cover			9.50
	On cover, single franking			17.50
B2	SP2	10c + 5c red	32.50	3.25
	Never hinged		90.00	
	On cover			10.50
	On cover, single franking			17.00
a.	Booklet pane of 10		*600.00*	
	Never hinged		*800.00*	

Issue dates: No. B1, Aug. 11; No. B2, Sept. 10.
For overprint see Offices in Morocco No. B8.

Widow at Grave SP3   War Orphans SP4

Woman Plowing — SP5

"Trench of Bayonets" SP6

Lion of Belfort SP7

"La Marseillaise" — SP8

1917-19
B3	SP3	2c + 3c vio brn	4.50	5.00
	Never hinged		10.00	
	On cover			7.50
B4	SP4	5c + 5c grn ('19)	21.00	9.50
	Never hinged		60.00	
	On cover			13.50
B5	SP5	15c + 10c gray green	30.00	27.50
	Never hinged		85.00	
	On cover			35.00
B6	SP5	25c + 15c dp bl	80.00	57.50
	Never hinged		175.00	
	On cover			87.50
B7	SP6	35c + 25c slate & vio	135.00	125.00
	Never hinged		350.00	
	On cover			200.00
B8	SP7	50c + 50c pale brn & dk brn	225.00	180.00
	Never hinged		650.00	
	On cover			300.00
B9	SP8	1fr + 1fr cl & mar	425.00	400.00
	Never hinged		1,100.	
	On cover			550.00
B10	SP8	5fr + 5fr dp bl & blk	1,600.	1,550.
	Never hinged		4,000.	
	On cover			*2,000.*
	Nos. B3-B10 (8)		2,520.	2,354.

See No. B20-B23. For surcharges see No. B12-B19.

Hospital Ship and Field Hospital SP9

1918, Aug.
B11	SP9	15c + 5c sl & red	125.00	60.00
	Never hinged		250.00	
	On cover			95.00

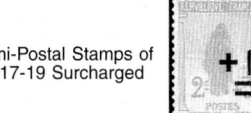

Semi-Postal Stamps of 1917-19 Surcharged

1922, Sept. 1
B12	SP3	2c + 1c violet brn	.50	*.80*
	Never hinged		1.00	
	On cover			2.75
B13	SP4	5c + 2½c green	.80	*1.25*
	Never hinged		1.50	
	On cover			2.75
B14	SP5	15c + 5c gray grn	1.25	*1.60*
	Never hinged		2.60	
	On cover			4.00

B15	SP5	25c + 5c deep bl	2.30	*2.50*
	Never hinged		4.75	
	On cover			5.50
B16	SP6	35c + 5c slate & vio	13.00	*15.00*
	Never hinged		30.00	
	On cover			27.50
B17	SP7	50c + 10c pale brn & dk brn	19.00	*24.00*
	Never hinged		39.00	
	On cover			40.00
a.	Pair, one without surcharge			
B18	SP8	1fr + 25c cl & mar	32.50	*37.50*
	Never hinged		60.00	
	On cover			110.00
B19	SP8	5fr + 1fr bl & blk	150.00	*155.00*
	Never hinged		275.00	
	On cover			*300.00*
	Nos. B12-B19 (8)		219.35	237.65
	Set, never hinged		415.00	

Style and arrangement of surcharge differs for each denomination.

Types of 1917-19
1926-27
B20	SP3	2c + 1c violet brn	1.50	1.40
	Never hinged		4.00	
	On cover			4.50
B21	SP7	50c + 10c ol brn & dk brn	20.00	12.50
	Never hinged		72.50	
	On cover			27.50
B22	SP8	1fr + 25c dp rose & red brn	55.00	42.50
	Never hinged		150.00	
	On cover			100.00
B23	SP8	5fr + 1fr sl bl & blk	105.00	93.00
	Never hinged		240.00	
	On cover			*300.00*
	Nos. B20-B23 (4)		181.50	156.40

Sinking Fund Issues

Types of Regular Issues of 1903-07 Surcharged in Red or Blue

1927, Sept. 26
B24	A22	40c + 10c lt blue (R)	5.75	5.75
	Never hinged		10.50	
	On cover			20.00
a.	Missing first "e" in "Amortissement"		*150.00*	160.00
	Never hinged		240.00	
B25	A20	50c + 25c green (Bl)	8.25	*9.00*
	Never hinged		14.00	
	On cover			27.50
a.	Missing dot on "i" of "Caisse"		*85.00*	92.50
	Never hinged		125.00	

Surcharge on No. B25 differs from illustration.

Type of Regular Issue of 1923 Surcharged in Black

B26	A23	1.50fr + 50c orange	14.50	14.00
	Never hinged		37.50	
	On cover			*40.00*
a.	Pair, one without surcharge		*2,000.*	
	Never hinged		2,700.	
	Nos. B24-B26 (3)		28.50	28.75

See Nos. B28-B33, B35-B37, B39-B41.

Industry and Agriculture SP10

1928, May   Engr.   *Perf. 13½*
B27	SP10	1.50fr + 8.50fr dull blue	140.00	*150.00*
	Never hinged		225.00	
	On cover			225.00
	On cover, single franking			300.00
a.	Blue green		*500.00*	550.00
	Never hinged		725.00	

Types of 1903-23 Issues Surcharged like Nos. B24-B26
1928, Oct. 1   *Perf. 14x13½*
B28	A22	40c + 10c gray lilac (R)	13.00	*14.00*
	Never hinged		32.50	
	On cover			25.00
a.	Missing first "e" in "Amortissement"		*160.00*	180.00
	Never hinged		275.00	

B29 A20   50c + 25c or-
ange brn
(Bl)   32.50   29.00
  Never hinged   60.00
  On cover   55.00
a. Missing dot on "i" of
  "Caisse"   110.00 120.00
  Never hinged   175.00

~~B30 A21 1.50fr + 50c~~
lilac (Bk)   52.50   42.50
  Never hinged   100.00
  On cover   72.50
  Nos. B28-B30 (3)   98.00   85.50

Types of 1903-23 Issues Surcharged like Nos. B24-B26

1929, Oct. 1

B31 A22   40c + 10c green   18.00   *19.00*
  Never hinged   37.50
  On cover   30.00
a. Missing first "e" in "Amor-
  tissement"   175.00 *200.00*
  Never hinged   300.00
b. Missing dot on "i" of
  "Caisse"   72.50   80.00
  Never hinged   120.00
B32 A20   50c + 25c lilac
rose   30.00   30.00
  Never hinged   60.00
  On cover   52.50
a. Missing dot on "i" of
  "Caisse"   130.00 140.00
  Never hinged   180.00
B33 A23 1.50fr + 50c chest-
nut   60.00   *65.00*
  Never hinged   130.00
  On cover   *110.00*
  Nos. B31-B33 (3)   108.00 114.00

"The Smile of Reims" SP11

1930, Mar. 15   Engr.   Perf. 13

B34 SP11 1.50fr + 3.50fr
red vio   80.00   *82.50*
  Never hinged   130.00
  On cover   125.00
  On cover, single franking   225.00
a. Booklet pane of 4   300.00
  Never hinged   525.00
b. Booklet pane of 8   600.00
  Never hinged   1,050.
  Complete booklet, #B34b 1,100.

Booklets containing No. B34 have two panes of 4 (No. B34a) connected by a gutter, the complete piece constituting #B34b, which is stapled into the booklet through the gutter.

Types of 1903-07 Issues Surcharged like Nos. B24-B25

1930 Oct. 1   Perf. 14x13½

B35 A22   40c + 10c cerise   20.00   *21.00*
  Never hinged   70.00
  On cover   32.50
a. Missing dot on "i" of
  "Caisse"   72.50   75.00
  Never hinged   110.00
B36 A20   50c + 25c gray
brown   37.50   *42.50*
  Never hinged   120.00
  On cover   67.50
a. Missing dot on "i" of
  "Caisse"   120.00 120.00
  Never hinged   175.00
b. Missing dot on "i" of "Amor-
  tissement"   120.00 120.00
  Never hinged   175.00
B37 A22 1.50fr + 50c violet   65.00   70.00
  Never hinged   190.00
  On cover   100.00
a. "C" below "t" of "Amortisse-
  ment"   200.00 *200.00*
  Never hinged   260.00
  Nos. B35-B37 (3)   122.50 133.50

Allegory, French Provinces SP12

1931, Mar. 1   Perf. 13

B38 SP12 1.50fr + 3.50fr
green   125.00 *140.00*
  Never hinged   300.00
  On cover   240.00
  On cover, single franking   325.00

Types of 1903-07 Issues Surcharged like Nos. B24-B25

1931, Oct. 1   Perf. 14x13½

B39 A22   40c + 10c ol grn   40.00   *45.00*
  Never hinged   100.00
  On cover   75.00
a. Missing dot on "i" of
  "Caisse"   110.00 92.50
  Never hinged   160.00

B40 A20   50c + 25c gray
vio   100.00 *110.00*
  Never hinged   235.00
  On cover   *175.00*
a. Missing first "e" in "Amor-
  tissement"   190.00 210.00
  Never hinged   300.00
B41 A22 1.50fr + 50c deep
~~red~~   180.00 *110.00*
  Never hinged   200.00
  On cover   *160.00*
a. "C" below "t" of "Amortisse-
  ment"   230.00 *230.00*
  Never hinged   310.00
  Nos. B39-B41 (3)   240.00 265.00

> Catalogue values for unused stamps in this section, from this point to the end of the section, are for Never Hinged items.

"France" Giving Aid to an Intellectual SP13

Symbolic of Music SP14

1935, Dec. 9   Engr.   Perf. 13

B42 SP13 50c + 10c ultra   4.00   2.50
  Hinged   2.50
  On cover   4.75
  On cover, single franking   8.75
B43 SP14 50c + 2fr dull red 125.00 45.00
  Hinged   55.00
  On cover   65.00
  On cover, single franking   110.00

The surtax was for the aid of distressed and exiled intellectuals.
For surcharge see No. B47.

Statue of Liberty SP15   Children of the Unemployed SP16

1936-37

B44 SP15 50c + 25c dk blue
('37)   7.50   5.00
  Hinged   4.00
  On cover   8.75
  On cover, single franking   17.50
B45 SP15 75c + 50c violet   20.00   10.00
  Hinged   9.50
  On cover   16.00
  On cover, single franking   27.50

Surtax for the aid of political refugees.
For surcharge see No. B47.

1936, May

B46 SP16 50c + 10c copper
red   7.50   5.00
  Hinged   4.50
  On cover   8.75
  On cover, single franking   13.50

The surtax was for the aid of children of the unemployed.

No. B43 Surcharged in Black

1936, Nov.

B47 SP14 20c on 50c + 2fr dull
red   4.75   3.50
  Hinged   3.25
  On cover   5.50
  On cover, single franking   9.50

Jacques Callot SP17

Anatole France (Jacques Anatole Thibault) — SP18

Hector Berlioz SP19

Victor Hugo SP20

Auguste Rodin SP21

Louis Pasteur SP22

1936-37   Engr.

B48 SP17 20c + 10c brown
car   4.50   2.50
  Hinged   2.25
  On cover   6.50
  On cover, single franking   14.50
B49 SP18 30c + 10c emer
('37)   5.00   2.75
  Hinged   2.25
  On cover   5.50
  On cover, single franking   9.50
B50 SP19 40c + 10c emer   4.50   2.75
  Hinged   2.25
  On cover   6.75
  On cover, single franking   11.00
B51 SP20 50c + 10c copper
red   8.75   3.75
  Hinged   3.75
  On cover   6.75
  On cover, single franking   8.75
B52 SP21 90c + 10c rose
red ('37)   13.00 6.50
  Hinged   6.00
  On cover   10.50
  On cover, single franking   16.00
B53 SP22 1.50fr + 50c deep
ultra   40.00 20.00
  Hinged   20.00
  On cover   30.00
  On cover, single franking   52.50
  Nos. B48-B53 (6)   75.75 38.25

The surtax was used for relief of unemployed intellectuals.

1938

B54 SP18 30c + 10c brown
car   3.00   1.75
  Hinged   1.75
  On cover   5.25
  On cover, single franking   11.00
B55 SP17 35c + 10c dull
green   3.50   2.40
  Hinged   2.40
  On cover   5.25
  On cover, single franking   10.50
B56 SP19 55c + 10c dull vio 10.00 4.00
  Hinged   6.00
  On cover   6.50
  On cover, single franking   10.50
B57 SP20 65c + 10c ultra   11.50 4.00
  Hinged   6.00
  On cover   6.50
  On cover, single franking   10.50

B58 SP21   1fr + 10c car
lake   8.50   4.50
  Hinged   4.75
  On cover   6.75
  On cover, single franking   14.50
B59 SP22 1.75fr + 25c dp blue 35.00 17.00
  Hinged   17.00
  ~~Vf none~~   *85.00* 40.00
  On cover, single franking
  Nos. B54-B59 (6)   71.50 33.65

Tug of War SP23

Foot Race SP24

Hiking — SP25

1937, June 16

B60 SP23 20c + 10c brown   3.00   2.25
  Hinged   1.60
  On cover   4.50
  On cover, single franking   11.00
B61 SP24 40c + 10c red
brown   3.00   2.25
  Hinged   1.60
  On cover   4.50
  On cover, single franking   10.50
B62 SP25 50c + 10c black brn 3.00 2.25
  Hinged   1.60
  On cover   4.50
  On cover, single franking   10.50
  Nos. B60-B62 (3)   9.00   6.75

The surtax was for the Recreation Fund of the employees of the Post, Telephone and Telegraph.

Pierre Loti (Louis Marie Julien Viaud) SP26

1937, Aug.

B63 SP26 50c + 20c rose car 7.50   5.00
  Hinged   3.75
  On cover   10.50
  On cover, single franking   27.50

The surtax was for the Pierre Loti Monument Fund.

"France" and Infant SP27

1937-39

B64 SP27 65c + 25c brown vio 5.25   2.75
  Hinged   3.25
  On cover   5.25
  On cover, single franking   7.50
B65 SP27 90c + 30c pck bl ('39) 3.50 2.75
  Hinged   2.10
  On cover   6.50
  On cover, single franking   16.00

The surtax was used for public health work.

Winged Victory
of Samothrace
SP28

Jean Baptiste
Charcot
SP29

1937, Aug.
B66 SP28 30c blue green 175.00 40.00
  Hinged 65.00
  On cover 67.50
  On cover, single franking 110.00
B67 SP28 55c red 175.00 40.00
  Hinged 65.00
  On cover 67.50
  On cover, single franking 110.00

On sale at the Louvre for 2.50fr. The surtax of 1.65fr was for the benefit of the Louvre Museum.

1938-39
B68 SP29 65c + 35c dk bl grn 3.00 3.00
  Hinged 1.60
  On cover 5.25
  On cover, single franking 8.75
B69 SP29 90c + 35c brt red vio ('39) 30.00 13.50
  Hinged 11.00
  On cover 17.50
  On cover, single franking 40.00

Surtax for the benefit of French seamen.

Palace of
Versailles
SP30

1938, May 9
B70 SP30 1.75fr + 75c dp bl 37.50 19.00
  Hinged 19.00
  On cover 30.00
  On cover, single franking 47.50

Natl. Exposition of Painting and Sculpture at Versailles.
The surtax was for the benefit of the Versailles Concert Society.

French Soldier
SP31

Monument
SP32

1938, May 16
B71 SP31 55c + 70c brown vio 8.50 5.25
  Hinged 4.75
  On cover 9.50
  On cover, single franking 27.50
B72 SP31 65c + 1.10fr pck bl 8.50 5.25
  Hinged 4.75
  On cover 9.50
  On cover, single franking 27.50

The surtax was for a fund to erect a monument to the glory of the French Infantrymen.

1938, May 25
B73 SP32 55c + 45c vermilion 22.50 12.50
  Hinged 10.00
  On cover 25.00
  On cover, single franking 52.50

The surtax was for a fund to erect a monument in honor of the Army Medical Corps.

Reims Cathedral
SP33

"France"
Welcoming Her
Sons
SP34

1938, July 10
B74 SP33 65c + 35c ultra 17.50 10.50
  Hinged 8.50
  On cover 19.00
  On cover, single franking 29.00

Completion of the reconstruction of Reims Cathedral, July 10, 1938.

1938, Aug. 8
B75 SP34 65c + 60c rose car 8.50 5.75
  Hinged 4.00
  On cover 10.50
  On cover, single franking 24.00

The surtax was for the benefit of French volunteers repatriated from Spain.

Curie Issue
Common Design Type
1938, Sept. 1
B76 CD80 1.75fr + 50c dp ultra 21.00 12.50
  Hinged 8.75
  On cover 21.00
  On cover, single franking 32.50

Victory
Parade
Passing Arc
de
Triomphe
SP36

1938, Oct. 8
B77 SP36 65c + 35c brown car 5.75 4.50
  Hinged 3.25
  On cover 8.75
  On cover, single franking 20.00

20th anniversary of the Armistice.

Student and
Nurse — SP37

1938, Dec. 1
B78 SP37 65c + 60c pck blue 15.00 8.25
  Hinged 8.00
  On cover 14.50
  On cover, single franking 27.50

The surtax was for Student Relief.

Blind Man
and Radio
SP38

1938, Dec.
B79 SP38 90c + 25c brown vio 15.00 9.00
  Hinged 8.00
  On cover 14.50
  On cover, single franking 20.00

The surtax was used to help provide radios for the blind.

Civilian Facing
Firing
Squad — SP39

Red Cross
Nurse — SP40

1939, Feb. 1
B80 SP39 90c + 35c black brn 17.00 10.50
  Hinged 8.75
  On cover 17.00
  On cover, single franking 22.50

The surtax was used to erect a monument to civilian victims of World War I.

1939, Mar. 24
B81 SP40 90c + 35c dk sl grn, turq bl & red 13.00 8.25
  Hinged 6.75
  On cover 12.50
  On cover, single franking 17.50

75th anniv. of the Intl. Red Cross Soc.

Army
Engineer
SP41

1939, Apr. 3
B82 SP41 70c + 50c vermilion 12.50 8.25
  Hinged 6.00
  On cover 12.50
  On cover, single franking 52.50

Army Engineering Corps. The surtax was used to erect a monument to those members who died in World War I.

Ministry of
Post,
Telegraph
and
Telephone
SP42

1939, Apr. 8
B83 SP42 90c + 35c turq blue 37.50 20.00
  Hinged 19.00
  On cover 30.00
  On cover, single franking 47.50

The surtax was used to aid orphans of employees of the postal system. Opening of the new building for the Ministry of Post, Telegraph and Telephones.

Mother and
Child — SP43

Eiffel
Tower — SP44

1939, Apr. 24
B84 SP43 90c + 35c red 3.75 2.50
  Hinged 2.40
  On cover 5.25
  On cover, single franking 8.75

The surtax was used to aid children of the unemployed.

1939, May 5
B85 SP44 90c + 50c red violet 15.00 9.00
  Hinged 8.75
  On cover 12.50
  On cover, single franking 20.00

50th anniv. of the Eiffel Tower. The surtax was used for celebration festivities.

Puvis de
Chavannes — SP45

Claude
Debussy
SP46

Honoré de
Balzac
SP47

Claude
Bernard
SP48

1939-40
B86 SP45 40c + 10c ver 1.75 1.00
  Hinged .80
  On cover 4.00
  On cover, single franking 9.50
B87 SP46 70c + 10c brn vio 8.25 2.50
  Hinged 3.50
  On cover 5.25
  On cover, single franking 11.00
B87A SP46 80c + 10c brn vio ('40) 9.00 7.50
  Hinged 4.25
  On cover 12.00
  On cover, single franking 16.00
B88 SP47 90c + 10c brt red vio 7.25 2.50
  Hinged 3.25
  On cover 5.25
  On cover, single franking 10.50
B88A SP47 1fr + 10c brt red vio ('40) 9.00 7.50
  Hinged 4.25
  On cover 12.00
  On cover, single franking 16.00
B89 SP48 2.25fr + 25c brt ultra 28.00 11.50
  Hinged 14.50
  On cover 19.00
  On cover, single franking 27.50
B89A SP48 2.50fr + 25c brt ultra ('40) 9.00 7.50
  Hinged 4.25
  On cover 13.50
  On cover, single franking 21.00
Nos. B86-B89A (7) 72.25 40.00

The surtax was used to aid unemployed intellectuals.

Mothers and Children
SP49   SP50

1939, June 15
B90 SP49 70c + 80c bl, grn & vio 5.25 4.50
  Hinged 3.25
  On cover 8.75
  On cover, single franking 16.00
B91 SP50 90c + 60c dk brn, dl vio & brn 8.50 5.25
  Hinged 4.75
  On cover 8.75
  On cover, single franking 16.00

The surtax was used to aid France's repopulation campaign.

"The Letter" by Jean Honoré Fragonard SP51   Statue of Widow and Children SP52

1939, July 6
B92 SP51 40c + 60c multi   4.25   2.75
    Hinged   2.40
    On cover   5.25
    On cover, single franking   8.00

The surtax was used for the Postal Museum.

1939, July 20
B93 SP52 70c + 30c brown vio   25.00   12.00
    Hinged   12.00
    On cover   18.00
    On cover, single franking   32.50

Surtax for the benefit of French seamen.

French Soldier SP53

Colonial Trooper SP54

1940, Feb. 15
B94 SP53 40c + 60c sepia   3.75   2.75
    Hinged   2.00
    On cover   7.25
    On cover, single franking   14.50
B95 SP54 1fr + 50c turq blue   3.75   2.75
    Hinged   2.00
    On cover   7.25
    On cover, single franking   14.50

The surtax was used to assist the families of mobilized men.

World Map Showing French Possessions — SP55

1940, Apr. 15
B96 SP55 1fr + 25c scarlet   2.75   2.75
    Hinged   2.00
    On cover   5.25
    On cover, single franking   8.00

Marshal Joseph J. C. Joffre SP56

Marshal Ferdinand Foch — SP57

Gen. Joseph S. Galliéni SP58

Woman Plowing SP59

1940, May 1
B97 SP56 80c + 45c choc   8.25   6.00
    Hinged   3.50
    On cover   10.50
    On cover, single franking   20.00
B98 SP57 1fr + 50c dk vio   7.50   6.00
    Hinged   3.25
    On cover   10.50
    On cover, single franking   20.00
B99 SP58 1.50fr + 50c brown red   7.50   4.00
    Hinged   3.25
    On cover   10.50
    On cover, single franking   17.50
B100 SP59 2.50fr + 50c indigo & dl bl   15.00   11.50
    Hinged   7.50
    On cover   18.00
    On cover, single franking   47.50
    Nos. B97-B100 (4)   38.25   27.50

The surtax was used for war charities.

Doctor, Nurse, Soldier and Family SP60

Nurse and Wounded Soldier SP61

1940, May 12
B101 SP60 80c + 1fr dk grn & red   8.25   6.00
    Hinged   4.00
    On cover   12.50
    On cover, single franking   72.50
B102 SP61 1fr + 2fr sep & red   11.50   6.50
    Hinged   5.25
    On cover   11.00
    On cover, single franking   21.00

The surtax was used for the Red Cross.

Nurse with Injured Children — SP62

1940, Nov. 12
B103 SP62 1fr + 2fr sepia   1.25   .80
    Hinged   .80
    On cover   3.25
    On cover, single franking   8.75

The surtax was used for victims of the war.

Wheat Harvest SP63

Sowing SP64

Grapes SP65

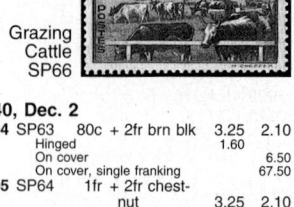

Grazing Cattle SP66

1940, Dec. 2
B104 SP63 80c + 2fr brn blk   3.25   2.10
    Hinged   1.60
    On cover   6.50
    On cover, single franking   67.50
B105 SP64 1fr + 2fr chestnut   3.25   2.10
    Hinged   1.60
    On cover   6.50
    On cover, single franking   21.00
B106 SP65 1.50fr + 2fr brt vio   3.25   2.10
    Hinged   1.60
    On cover   6.50
    On cover, single franking   52.50
B107 SP66 2.50fr + 2fr dp grn   4.00   2.25
    Hinged   2.00
    On cover   6.50
    On cover, single franking   52.50
    Nos. B104-B107 (4)   13.75   8.55

The surtax was for national relief.

BALLONS MONTES

"Ballons Montes" are letters which left Paris between Sept. 23, 1870, and Jan. 28, 1871, toward the end of the Franco-Prussian War. Placed under siege by the German army, the French capital was isolated from the rest of the world. With all other means of communication severed, Parisians took to the air, inaugurating what many consider to be the world's first air mail. Of the 67 balloons that were launched from Paris, 56 carried mail that passed through the Paris Post Office, including private letters, newspapers and official documents. While some balloons were unmanned, most carried at least a single person in addition to the 225-275 pounds of mail.

Ballons Montes can usually be identified by examination of the dates of posting, transit and arrival postmarks. Carried by capricious winds, each balloon landed in a different and unexpected location. Some crashed, some fell into the English Channel and many came down in German-controlled territory. When balloons landed in French territory or countries friendly to France, postal authorities enthusiastically aided the Parisians by sending the recovered mail by the most direct and efficient route to its destination. This use of a bewildering variety of postal routes is reflected in the unusual postal markings found on most Ballon Montes. While mail that fell into German hands was usually confiscated, on some occasions, German authorities actually helped deliver the mail to its intended destination. Mail confiscated by the Germans was posted following the conclusion of hostilities.

Ballon Montes are valued according to five criteria, three of which are reflected in the listings that follow. The base value is determined by the balloon that carried the cover. Values for the destination and the franking used to pay the postage are then added to the base value as premiums. Not reflected in the listings are premiums for the nature and contents of the cover and any postmarks applied to the cover prior to its departure on the balloon. **Covers are valued in Very Fine condition.**

Balloon Name & Base Value
Sept. 23 Departure 08:00 a.m.
BM1   *Neptune*   10,500.

Sept. 25 Departure 11:00 a.m.
BM2   *Ville de Florence*   700.

Sept. 29 Departure 10:30 a.m.
BM3   *Etats-Unis*   550.
   a. With transit pmk: *Gare de Mantes* Sept. 29   3,250.

Sept. 30 Departure 09:30 a.m.
BM4   *Celeste*   425.

Sept. 30 Departure noon
BM5   Unnamed #1   325.

Oct. 7 Departure 11:10 a.m.
BM6   *Armand-Barbes*   275.

Oct. 7 Departure 11:10 a.m.
BM7   *George-Sand*   4,000.

Oct. 7 Departure 02:15 p.m.
BM8   Unnamed #2   350.

Shortly after take-off, No. BM8 crashed inside the French defensive lines and within sight of the encircling German forces. The mail carried by No. BM8 was salvaged and returned to Paris where it was re-posted on subsequent balloons.

Oct. 12 Departure 08:00 a.m.
BM9   *Washington*   275.
   a. With transit pmk: *Douai* Oct. 13   2,750.

Oct. 12 Departure 09:00 a.m.
BM10   *Louis-Blanc*   275.
   a. With Traveling Post Office pmk: *Lille a Paris* Oct. 12   1,850.

Oct. 14 Departure 10:00 a.m.
BM11   *Godefroy-Caraignac*   325.
   a. With transit pmk: *Chaumont* Oct. 16   2,500.

Oct. 14 Departure 01:15 p.m.
BM12   *Jean-Bart #1*   440.

Oct. 16 Departure 07:30 a.m.
BM13   *Jules-Favre #1*   250.

Oct. 16 Departure 09:50 a.m.
BM14   *Jean-Bart #2*   250.

Oct. 18 Departure 11:45 a.m.
BM15   *Victor Hugo*   325.

Oct. 19 Departure 09:15 a.m.
BM16   *Republique Universelle*   350.
   a. With transit pmk: *Renwez*   3,200.
   b. With transit pmk: *Rocroi* Oct. 16   3,200.

No. BM16 was also named *La Lafayette.*

Oct. 22 Departure 11:30 a.m.
BM17   *Garibaldi*   325.

Oct. 25 Departure 08:30 a.m.
BM18   *Montgolfier*   2,400.

Oct. 27 Departure 09:00 a.m.
BM19   *Vauban*   325.
   a. With transit pmk: *Bar-le-Duc*   2,750.

Oct. 27 Departure 02:10 p.m.
BM20   *Bretagne*   16,000.

No. BM20 was also named *le Normandie* (A).

Oct. 29 Departure noon
BM21   *Colonel Charras*   300.

Nov. 2 Departure 08:45 a.m.
BM22   *Fulton*   325.

Nov. 4 Departure 09:30 a.m.
BM23   *Ferdinand Flocon*   275.
   a. With transit pmk: *Nantes*   675.

Nov. 4 Departure 02:00 p.m.
BM24   *Galilee*   425.

Nov. 6 Departure 09:45 a.m.
BM25   *Ville de Chateaudun*   275.

Nov. 7 Departure 10:00 a.m.
BM26   Unnamed #3   10,500.

Nov. 8 Departure 08:20 a.m.
BM27   *Gironde*   350.

Nov. 12 Departure 09:00 a.m.
BM28   *Daguerre*   325.

Nov. 12 Departure 09:15 a.m.
BM29   *Niepce*   6,250.

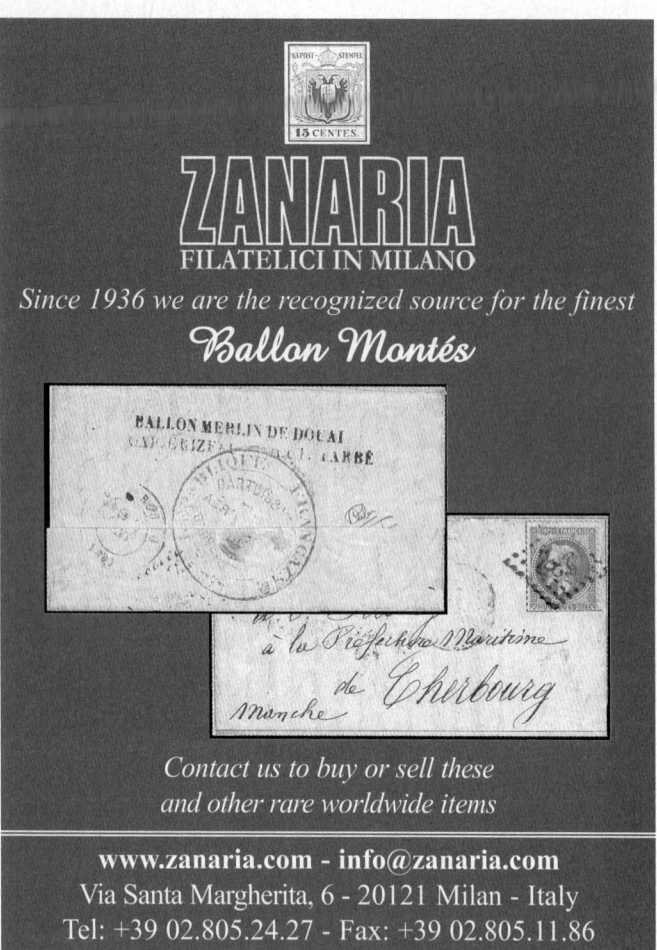
Nov. 18 Departure 11:15 p.m.
BM30 *General Ulrich*   275.
  a. With transit pmk: *Luzarches*   1,500.

Nov. 21 Departure 00:45 a.m.
BM31 *Archimede*   325.

Nov. 24 Departure 11:30 a.m.
BM32 *Egalite*   7,750.

Nov. 24 Departure 11:30 a.m.
BM33 *Ville d'Orleans*   500.
  a. Re-posted from Norway   1,000.
  b. With transit pmk: *London Dec.*
    2/Dec. 4   1,350.

Nov. 28 Departure 11:00 p.m.
BM34 *Jacquard*   2,250.
  a. With transit pmk: *Falmouth*   7,000.
  b. Re-posted from La Rochelle Dec. 21 6,000.

Nov. 30 Departure 11:30 p.m.
BM35 *Jules-Favre #2*   300.

Dec. 1 Departure 05:15 a.m.
BM36 *Bataille de Paris*   5,500.

Dec. 2 Departure 08:00 a.m.
BM37 *Volta*   55,000.
  No mail is known from No. BM37.

Dec. 5 Departure 01:00 p.m.
BM38 *Franklin*   350.
  a. With transit pmk: *Nantes*   1,800.

Dec. 5 Departure 06:00 a.m.
BM39 *Armee de Bretagne*   4,500.

Dec. 7 Departure 01:00 a.m.
BM40 *Denis-Papin*   400.

Dec. 11 Departure 02:15 a.m.
BM41 *General Renault*   350.
  a. With transit pmk: *Foucarmont*   3,250.

Dec. 15 Departure 04:45 a.m.
BM42 *Ville de Paris*   450.
  a. Re-posted at Paris, July 1871   1,100.

Dec. 17 Departure 01:15 a.m.
BM43 *Parmentier*   325.

Dec. 17 Departure 01:25 a.m.
BM44 *Gutenberg*   4,000.

Dec. 18 Departure 05:00 a.m.
BM45 *Davy*   500.
  a. With transit pmk: *Beaune*   2,750.

Dec. 20 Departure 02:00 a.m.
BM46 *General Chanzy*   975.

Dec. 22 Departure 02:30 a.m.
BM47 *Lavoisier*   325.

Dec. 23 Departure 04:30 a.m.
BM48 *Delivrance*   350.
  a. With transit pmk: *Roche-sur-Yon* 475.

Dec. 24
BM49 *Rouget-de-L'isle*   5,500.

Dec. 27 Departure 04:00 a.m.
BM50 *Tourville*   325.

Dec. 27 Departure 04:00 a.m.
BM51 *Merlin de Douai*   40,000.

Dec. 29 Departure 04:00 a.m.
BM52 *Bayard*   350.

Dec. 31 Departure 05:00 a.m.
BM53 *Armee de la Loire*   350.

Jan. 4 Departure 01:00 a.m.
BM54 *Newton*   325.

Jan. 9 Departure 03:00 a.m.
BM55 *Duquesne*   285.

Jan. 10 Departure 04:15 a.m.
BM56 *Gambetta*   350.

Jan. 11 Departure 03:00 a.m.
BM57 *Kepler*   350.
  a. With transit pmk: *Paris a Brest* 475.

Jan. 13 Departure 06:00 a.m.
BM58 *Monge*   27,500.

Jan. 13 Departure 03:30 a.m.
BM59 *General Faidherbe*   350.
  a. With transit pmk: *Ste Foy*   925.

Jan. 15 Departure 03:00 a.m.
BM60 *Vaucanson*   350.

Jan. 16 Departure 07:00 a.m.
BM61 *Steenackers*   42,500.

  Nos. BM20, BM26, BM29, BM32, BM36,
BM44, BM46, BM49, BM58 and BM61 only
carried "Plis Conflies," which did not pass
through the Paris Post Office, but were delivered to either the balloon, the balloon company or the balloon's pilot directly. These covers normally carry postage and were canceled
on transit or arrival.

Jan. 18 Departure 03:00 a.m.
BM62 *Poste de Paris*   375.

Jan. 20 Departure 05:15 a.m.
BM63 *General Bourbaki*   350.

Jan. 22 Departure 04:00 a.m.
BM64 *General Daumesnil*   325.

Jan. 24 Departure 03:00 a.m.
BM65 *Torricelli*   425.

Jan. 27 Departure 03:30 a.m.
BM66 *Richard Wallace*   2,600.

Jan. 28 Departure 05:45 a.m.
BM667 *General Cambronne*   1,100.

Destinations of Mail Carried by Ballons Montes

The Premium Value listed by destination is
combined with the premium for the stamp
used (shown in the following listings) and
added to the base value for each Ballon Montes listed above.

French Area
Rate, Destination & Premium

D1	20c	French Occupied Terri-	
		tory (without arrival	
		pmk.)	+225.
	a. With French arrival pmk.		+1,150.
	b. With German arrival pmk.		+3,250.
D2	20c	Island of Corsica	+1,750.
D3	20c	Algeria	+1,250.
D4	70c	West Indies	+9,000.
D5	80c	Gabon	+35,000.
D6	50c	Guadeloupe	+16,000.
D7	50c	Martinique	+14,000.
D8	20c	Monaco	+8,500.
D9	70c	New Caledonia	+17,000.
D10	50c	Reunion	+25,000.
D11	50c	Senegal	+25,000.
D12	40c	Tunisia	+22,500.

Europe

D13	60c	Austria	+2,500.
D14	30c	Baden	+3,250.
D15	40c	Bavaria	+2,400.
D16	30c	Belgium	+200.
D17	50c	Bremen	+3,500.
D18	50c	Brunswick	+3,500.
D19	50c	Bulgaria	+18,500.
D20	40c	Canary Islands	+14,000.
	a. 80c Via England		+10,500.
D21	40c	Cyprus	+15,500.
D22	50c	Denmark	+8,250.
	a. 70c Via Thurn & Taxis		+10,500.
D23	40c, 50c	Germany	3,250.
	a. With arrival pmk		+3,500.
D24	40c	Gibraltar	+17,500.
D25	30c	Great Britain	+200.
D26	60c	Greece (Sea post)	+27,500.
D27	30c	Isle of Wight	+1,750.
D28	30c	Ireland	+2,400.
D29	40c	Italy	+1,250.
D30	30c	Jersey	+875.
D31	60c	Liechtenstein	+21,000.
D32	25c	Luxembourg	+8,250.
D33	80c	Madeira	+12,000.
D34	40c	Malta	+15,500.
D35	60c	Montenegro	+16,500.
D36	40c	Netherlands	+750.
D37	70c	Norway	+13,750.
	a. 1fr Via Denmark		+17,500.
D38	80c	Poland	+17,500.
D39	40c	Portugal	+3,500.
D40	40c	Prussia	+2,750.
D41	40c	Rhodes	+17,500.
D42	50c	Roman States	+2,750.

D43	40c	Romania	+19,000.
	a. 80c By land post		+24,000.
D44	80c	Russia (without arrival pmk.)	+13,750.
D45	1fr	South Russia (without arrival pmk.)	+2,750.
	a. With arrival pmk.		+21,000.
D46	50c	Saxony	+2,750.
D47	30c	Scotland	+2,500.
D48	40c	Spain	+3,500.
D49	60c	Sweden (via Denmark)	+10,500.
	a. 70 Via Thurn & Taxis		+12,000.
D50	30c	Switzerland	+150.
D51	40c	Turkey (sea post)	+4,250.
	a. 80 Land post		+5,500.
D52	50c	Walachia	+18,500.

Other Areas

D53	80c	Argentina	+13,750.
D54	80c	Australia	+45,000.
D55	1fr	Bolivia	+25,000.
D56	80c	Brazil	+17,500.
D57	80c	Canada (via England)	+14,000.
	a. Canada		+45,000.
D58	80c	Cape of Good Hope	+35,000.
D59	80c	Ceylon	+21,000.
D60	80c	Chile	+16,500.
D61	80c	China	+55,000.
D62	80c	Cuba	+17,500.
D63	40c	Egypt	+5,000.
D64	80c	Haiti	+22,500.
D65	80c	Hong Kong	+55,000.
D66	80c	India	+14,500.
D67	80c	Jamaica	+21,000.
D68	80c	Japan	+45,000.
D69	80c	Malaysia	+22,500.
D70	80c	Mauritius	+25,000.
D71	80c	Mexico	+16,000.
	a. 1fr Via Panama		+17,500.
D72	80c	Newfoundland	+22,500.
D73	80c	Panama	+17,500.
D74	80c	Paraguay	+17,500.
D75	1fr	Peru	+25,000.
D76	80c	Philippines	+20,000.
D77	80c	Puerto Rico	+22,500.
D78	40c	Tangier	+12,500.
D79	70c, 80c	United States	+5,250.
	a. 1fr Interior		+9,500.
D80	80c	Uruguay	+17,500.
D81	80c	Venezuela	+21,500.
D82	70c	West Indies	+17,500.

Franking used on Mail Carried by Ballons Montes

The Premium Value shown for the stamp
used is combined with the premium value of
the destination and then added to the base
value for each of the Ballon Montes listed
above. Stamps shown without a value attach
no premium to the base value of the cover.

1853-1860
France Scott Number & Premium

15	20c blue, *bluish*		+6,000.
18	40c org, *yelsh*		+7,000.

1862-71

22	1c ol grn, *pale bl*		+3,250.
23	5c yel grn, *grnish*		+975.
25	10c bis, *yelsh*		+700.
26	20c bl, *bluish*		+350.
27	40c org, *yelsh*		+1,250.
28	80c rose, *pinkish*		+2,800.

1863-70

29	1c bronze grn, *pale bl*		+2,600.
30	2c red brn, *yelsh*		+3,000.
31	4c grey		+3,000.
32	10c bis, *yelsh*		+75.
33	20c bl, *bluish*		no premium
34	30c brn, *yelsh*		no premium
35	40c org, *yelsh*		+150.
36	80c rose, *pinkish*		+475.

1870

54	10c bis, *yelsh*		+200
	a. tete beche pair		+11,000.
57	20c bl, *bluish*		no premium
	b. tete beche pair		+11,000.

AIR POST STAMPS

Nos. 127,
130
Overprinted
in Dark
Blue or
Black

Perf. 14x13½

1927, June 25   **Unwmk.**
C1 A18 2fr org & bl (DB)   200.00 225.00
  Never hinged   400.00
  On cover, stamp very fine   525.00

C2 A18 5fr dk bl & buff 200.00 225.00
　　Never hinged 400.00
　　On cover, stamp very fine 525.00

On sale only at the Intl. Aviation Exhib. at Marseilles, June, 1927. One set could be purchased by each holder of an admission ticket. Excellent counterfeits exist.

Stamps centered in the grade of fine sell for about 30 percent less.

Nos. 242, 196
Surcharged

1928, Aug. 23
C3 A33 10fr on 90c 2,400. 1,800.
　　Never hinged 3,500.
　　On cover 2,200.
　　a. Inverted surcharge 16,500. 16,500.
　　　Never hinged 25,000.
　　　On cover 19,000.
　　b. Space between "10" and
　　　bars 6½mm 3,100. 3,100.
　　　Never hinged 5,100.
　　　On cover 3,900.
C4 A23 10fr on 1.50fr 10,000. 8,250.
　　Never hinged 14,000.
　　On cover 10,500.
　　a. Space between "10" and
　　　bars 6½mm 13,000. 13,000.
　　　Never hinged 20,000.
　　　On cover 12,500.

Nos. C3-C4 received their surcharge in New York by order of the French consul general. They were for use in paying the 10fr fee for letters leaving the liner Ile de France on a catapulted hydroplane when the ship was one day off the coast of France on its eastward voyage.

The normal space between "10" and bars is 4½mm, but on 10 stamps in each pane of 50 the space is 6½mm. Counterfeits exist.

View of Marseille, Church of Notre Dame at Left — AP1

1930-31 Engr. Perf. 13
C5 AP1 1.50fr dp carmine 21.00 4.00
　　Never hinged 40.00
　　On cover 5.50
　　On cover, single franking 16.00
　　a. With perf. initials
　　　"E.I.P.A.30" 2,750. 3,750.
　　　Never hinged 3,600.
　　b. Pair, C5, C5a 3,400.
　　　Never hinged 5,500.
C6 AP1 1.50fr dk bl ('31) 19.00 2.25
　　Never hinged 35.00
　　On cover 4.75
　　On cover, single franking 6.50
　　a. 1.50fr ultramarine 50.00 21.00
　　　Never hinged 90.00
　　　On cover, single franking 32.50
　　b. As "a," with perf. initials 47.50
　　　"E.I.P.A.30" 450.00 350.00
　　　Never hinged 700.00
　　　On cover 450.00
　　c. Pair, C6a, C6b 600.00
　　　Never hinged 1,100.
　　d. 1.50fr bright ultra 290.00 175.00
　　　Never hinged 450.00

Nos. C5a, C6a were sold at the Intl. Air Post Exhib., Paris, Nov. 6-20, 1930, at face value plus 5fr, the price of admission.

Forgeries abound of Nos. C5a and C6b. Certificates from recognized authorities are recommended.

Blériot's Monoplane AP2

1934, Sept. 1 Perf. 13
C7 AP2 2.25fr violet 24.00 6.00
　　Never hinged 32.50
　　On cover 12.00
　　On cover, single franking 24.00

1st flight across the English Channel, by Louis Blériot.

Plane over Paris AP3

1936
C8 AP3 85c deep green 2.25 2.25
　　Never hinged 6.50
　　On cover 5.50
　　On cover, single franking 16.00
　　a. 85c green 14.00 4.00
　　　Never hinged 20.00
C9 AP3 1.50fr blue 10.50 5.50
　　Never hinged 18.00
　　On cover 8.75
　　On cover, single franking 14.50
C10 AP3 2.25fr violet 18.00 7.00
　　Never hinged 35.00
　　On cover 10.00
　　On cover, single franking 17.50
C11 AP3 2.50fr rose 32.50 8.25
　　Never hinged 45.00
　　On cover 12.00
　　On cover, single franking 21.00
C12 AP3 3fr ultra 26.00 2.50
　　Never hinged 37.50
　　On cover 5.50
　　On cover, single franking 20.00
C13 AP3 3.50fr orange brn 62.50 24.00
　　Never hinged 105.00
　　On cover 32.50
　　On cover, single franking 60.00
C14 AP3 50fr emerald 825.00 325.00
　　Never hinged 1,450.
　　On cover 525.00
　　On cover, single franking 1,200.
　　a. 50fr deep green 1,000. 525.00
　　　Never hinged 1,650.
　　b. 50fr green 850.00 350.00
　　　Never hinged 1,500.
　　Nos. C8-C14 (7) 976.75 374.50

Monoplane over Paris — AP4

Paper with Red Network Overprint

1936, July 10 Perf. 12½
C15 AP4 50fr ultra 625.00 310.00
　　Never hinged 1,700.
　　On cover 525.00
　　On cover, single franking 1,200.
　　a. Red network inverted 800.00 375.00
　　　Never hinged 1,300.

Airplane and Galleon — AP5

Airplane and Globe AP6

1936, Aug. 17 Perf. 13
C16 AP5 1.50fr dk ultra 17.50 5.25
　　Never hinged 35.00
　　On cover 7.50
　　On cover, single franking 21.00
C17 AP6 10fr Prus green 290.00 130.00
　　Never hinged 700.00
　　On cover 175.00
　　On cover, single franking 240.00

100th air mail flight across the South Atlantic.

POSTAGE DUE STAMPS

D1

1859-70 Unwmk. Litho. Imperf.
J1 D1 10c black 30,500. 240.00
　　No gum 7,250.
　　On cover 625.00
J2 D1 15c black ('70) 140.00 250.00
　　No gum 40.00
　　On cover 1,300.

Full margins = 1mm.

In the lithographed stamps the central bar of the "E" of "CENTIMES" is very short, and the accent on "a" slants at an angle of 30 degree, for the 10c and 17 degree for the 15c, while on the typographed the central bar of the "E" is almost as wide as the top and bottom bars and the accent on the "a" slants at an angle of 47 degree.

No. J2 is known rouletted unofficially.

1859-78 Typo.
J3 D1 10c black 30.00 17.50
　　No gum 8.75
　　On cover 32.50
J4 D1 15c black ('63) 35.00 15.00
　　No gum 9.50
　　On cover 32.50
J5 D1 20c black ('77) 4,100.
　　No gum 3,250.
J6 D1 25c black ('71) 150.00 50.00
　　No gum 47.50
　　On cover 110.00
　　a. Double impression 6,000.
J7 D1 30c black ('78) 225.00 125.00
　　No gum 72.50
　　On cover 250.00
J8 D1 40c blue ('71) 325.00 425.00
　　No gum 105.00
　　On cover 2,350.
　　a. 40c ultramarine 6,500. 5,700.
　　　No gum 3,250.
　　　On cover 24,000.
　　b. 40c Prussian blue 2,600.
　　　No gum 1,300.
J9 D1 60c bister ('71) 475.00 1,050.
　　No gum 225.00
　　On cover 9,500.
J10 D1 60c blue ('78) 60.00 110.00
　　No gum 20.00
　　On cover 1,350.
　　a. 60c dark blue 600.00 725.00
　　　No gum 225.00
　　　On cover 2,250.
J10B D1 60c black 2,700.
　　No gum 1,600.

Full margins = 1 ¼mm.

The 20c & 60c black were not put into use. Nos. J3, J4, J6, J8 and J9 are known rouletted unofficially and Nos. J4, J6, J7 and J10 pin-perf. unofficially.

D2

1882-92 Perf. 14x13½
J11 D2 1c black 2.50 2.50
　　On cover 20.00
J12 D2 2c black 30.00 26.00
　　On cover 450.00
J13 D2 3c black 30.00 25.00
　　On cover 550.00
J14 D2 4c black 60.00 40.00
　　On cover 525.00
J15 D2 5c black 130.00 32.50
　　On cover 60.00
J16 D2 10c black 110.00 2.50
　　On cover 25.00
J17 D2 15c black 77.50 10.50
　　On cover 35.00
J18 D2 20c black 350.00 140.00
　　On cover 400.00
J19 D2 30c black 210.00 2.50
　　On cover 30.00
J20 D2 40c black 140.00 60.00
　　On cover 160.00
J21 D2 50c blk ('92) 600.00 175.00
　　On cover 425.00
J22 D2 60c blk ('84) 600.00 57.50
　　On cover 290.00
J23 D2 1fr black 750.00 350.00
　　On cover 3,400.
J24 D2 2fr blk ('84) 1,400. 825.00
　　On cover 8,000.
J25 D2 5fr blk ('84) 3,000. 1,600.
　　On cover —

Excellent counterfeits exist of Nos. J23-J25.
See Nos. J26-J45A. For overprints and surcharges see Offices in China Nos. J1-J6, J33-J40, Offices in Egypt, Alexandria J1-J5, Port Said J1-J8, Offices in Zanzibar 60-62, J1-J5, Offices in Morocco 9-10, 24-25, J1-J5, J10-J12, J17-J22, J35-J41.

1884
J26 D2 1fr brown 400.00 90.00
　　On cover 1,700.
J27 D2 2fr brown 190.00 130.00
　　On cover 7,000.
J28 D2 5fr brown 450.00 325.00
　　On cover —

1893-1941
J29 D2 5c blue ('94) .25 .30
　　Never hinged .55
　　On cover .80
J30 D2 10c brown .25 .30
　　Never hinged .55
　　On cover .80
J31 D2 15c lt grn ('94) 28.00 1.40
　　Never hinged 50.00
　　On cover 3.50
J32 D2 20c ol grn ('06) 6.50 .65
　　Never hinged 11.00
　　On cover 2.00
J33 D2 25c rose ('23) 6.50 3.75
　　Never hinged 11.00
　　On cover 6.75
J34 D2 30c red ('94) .25 .25
　　Never hinged .55
　　On cover .80
J35 D2 30c org red ('94) 475.00 85.00
　　Never hinged 875.00
J36 D2 40c rose ('25) 11.50 4.50
　　Never hinged 21.00
　　On cover 7.25
J37 D2 45c grn ('24) 9.00 5.25
　　Never hinged 19.00
　　On cover 8.75
J38 D2 50c brn vio ('95) .50 .30
　　Never hinged .85
　　On cover 1.20
　　a. 50c lilac .50 .30
　　　Never hinged .85
　　　On cover 1.20
J39 D2 60c bl grn ('25) 1.00 .55
　　Never hinged 1.60
　　On cover 1.20
J40 D2 1fr rose, straw
　　　('96) 475.00 375.00
　　Never hinged 875.00
　　On cover 550.00
J41 D2 1fr red brn, straw
　　　('20) 9.50 .30
　　Never hinged 19.00
　　On cover 1.20
J42 D2 1fr red brn ('35) 1.25 .40
　　Never hinged 2.25
　　On cover 1.20
J43 D2 2fr red org ('10) 225.00 65.00
　　Never hinged 425.00
　　On cover 150.00
J44 D2 2fr brt vio ('26) .65 .75
　　Never hinged 1.20
　　On cover 4.00
J45 D2 3fr magenta ('26) .65 .75
　　Never hinged 1.20
　　On cover 4.75
J45A D2 5fr red org ('41) 1.40 2.25
　　Never hinged 2.50
　　On cover 9.50

D3

1908-25
J46 D3 1c olive grn 1.00 1.25
　　Never hinged 2.10
　　On cover 9.50
J47 D3 10c violet 1.10 .30
　　Never hinged 2.60
　　On cover 5.50
　　a. Imperf., pair 175.00
　　　Never hinged 275.00
J48 D3 20c bister ('19) 40.00 1.25
　　Never hinged 75.00
　　On cover 8.75
J49 D3 30c bister ('09) 14.00 .40
　　Never hinged 27.50
　　On cover 4.75
J50 D3 50c red ('09) 275.00 60.00
　　Never hinged 550.00
　　On cover 200.00
J51 D3 60c red ('25) 2.75 3.75
　　Never hinged 5.00
　　On cover 16.00
　　Nos. J46-J51 (6) 333.85 66.95

"Recouvrements" stamps were used to recover charges due on undelivered or refused mail which was returned to the sender.

For surcharges see Offices in Morocco Nos. J6-J9, J13-J16, J23-J26, J42-J45.

Nos. J49-J50
Surcharged

1917
J52 D3 20c on 30c bister 20.00 4.00
　　Never hinged 40.00
　　On cover 12.50
J53 D3 40c on 50c red 10.50 4.00
　　Never hinged 22.50
　　On cover 12.50
　　a. Double surcharge 475.00
　　　Never hinged 600.00

In Jan. 1917 several values of the current issue of postage stamps were handstamped "T" in a triangle and used as postage due stamps.

Recouvrements Stamps of 1908-25 Surcharged

1926

J54	D3 50c on 10c lilac	3.50	3.25
	Never hinged	6.75	
	On cover		12.50
J55	D3 60c on 1c ol grn	7.00	5.00
	Never hinged	12.50	
	On cover		16.00
J56	D3 1fr on 60c red	18.00	10.00
	Never hinged	35.00	
	On cover		32.50
J57	D3 2fr on 60c red	18.00	10.50
	Never hinged	35.00	
	On cover		32.50
	Nos. J54-J57 (4)	46.50	28.75

D4

1927-31

J58	D4 1c olive grn ('28)	1.00	1.00
	Never hinged	1.90	
	On cover		8.00
J59	D4 10c rose ('31)	1.90	1.40
	Never hinged	3.75	
	On cover		9.50
J60	D4 30c bister	4.50	.50
	Never hinged	10.50	
	On cover		5.50
J61	D4 60c red	4.50	.50
	Never hinged	10.50	
	On cover		4.75
J62	D4 1fr violet	14.00	3.25
	Never hinged	27.50	
	On cover		16.00
J63	D4 1fr Prus grn ('31)	17.00	.55
	Never hinged	35.00	
	On cover		7.25
J64	D4 2fr blue	80.00	42.50
	Never hinged	175.00	
	On cover		110.00
J65	D4 2fr olive brn ('31)	150.00	26.00
	Never hinged	275.00	
	On cover		92.50
	Nos. J58-J65 (8)	272.90	75.70

Nos. J62 to J65 have the numerals of value double-lined.

Nos. J64, J62
Surcharged in Red or Black

1929

J66	D4 1.20fr on 2fr blue	42.50	11.00
	Never hinged	105.00	
	On cover		40.00
J67	D4 5fr on 1fr vio (Bk)	65.00	15.00
	Never hinged	140.00	
	On cover		47.50

No. J61 Surcharged

1931

J68	D4 1fr on 60c red	30.00	2.75
	Never hinged	60.00	
	On cover		12.50

MILITARY STAMPS

Regular Issue Overprinted in Black or Red

1901-39	**Unwmk.**	**Perf. 14x13½**	
M1	A17 15c orange ('01)	65.00	6.00
	Never hinged	160.00	
	On cover		20.00
a.	Inverted overprint	300.00	150.00
b.	Imperf., pair	425.00	
M2	A19 15c pale red ('03)	65.00	6.00
	Never hinged	200.00	
	On cover		16.00

M3	A20 15c slate grn ('04)	52.50	6.00
	Never hinged	130.00	
	On cover		16.00
a.	No period after "M"	110.00	57.50
	Never hinged	190.00	
b.	Imperf., pair	290.00	
	Never hinged	400.00	
M4	A20 10c grn ('06)		
	Never hinged	80.00	
	On cover		17.50
a.	No period after "M"	82.50	45.00
	Never hinged	150.00	
b.	Imperf., pair	350.00	
	Never hinged	475.00	
M5	A22 10c red ('07)	1.75	1.00
	Never hinged	2.75	
	On cover		4.75
a.	Inverted overprint	105.00	65.00
	Never hinged	140.00	
b.	Imperf., pair	190.00	
	Never hinged	275.00	
M6	A20 50c vermilion ('29)	4.75	1.00
	Never hinged	9.25	
	On cover		4.75
a.	No period after "M"	32.50	18.00
	Never hinged	55.00	
b.	Period in front of F	32.50	18.00
	Never hinged	55.00	
M7	A45 50c rose red ('34)	2.75	.55
	Never hinged	7.25	
	On cover		4.00
a.	No period after "M"	29.00	16.00
b.	Inverted overprint	150.00	110.00
	Never hinged	210.00	
M8	A45 65c brt ultra (R) ('38)	.30	.30
	Never hinged	.70	
	On cover		3.25
a.	No period after "M"	29.00	16.00
	Never hinged	45.00	
M9	A45 90c ultra (R) ('39)	.40	.35
	Never hinged	.70	
	On cover		12.00
	Nos. M1-M9 (9)	222.45	29.45

"F. M." are initials of Franchise Militaire (Military Frank). See No. S1.

NEWSPAPER STAMPS

Coat of Arms — N1

		Unwmk.	**Typo.**	**Imperf.**
1868				
P1	N1 2c lilac	300.00		65.00
	No gum	150.00		
	On newspaper			240.00
P2	N1 2c (+ 2c) blue	600.00		275.00
	No gum	275.00		
	On newspaper			1,050.

			Perf. 12½	
P3	N1 2c lilac	52.50		25.00
	No gum	20.00		
	On newspaper			72.50
P4	N1 2c (+ 4c) rose	250.00		100.00
	No gum	72.50		
	On newspaper			425.00
P5	N1 2c (+ 2c) blue	75.00		35.00
	No gum	27.50		
	On newspaper			110.00
P6	N1 5c lilac	1,250.		550.00
	No gum	400.00		
	On newspaper			3,500.

Nos. P2, P4, and P5 were sold for face plus an added fiscal charge indicated in parenthesis. Nos. P1, P3 and P6 were used simply as fiscals.

The 2c rose and 5c lilac imperforate and the 5c rose and 5c blue, both imperforate and perforated, were never put to use.

Nos. P1-P6 were reprinted for the 1913 Ghent Exhibition and the 1937 Paris Exhibition (PEXIP).

No. 109 Surcharged in Red

1919		**Perf. 14x13½**	
P7	A16 ½c on 1c gray	.30	.30
	Never hinged	.65	
	On cover		35.00
	On printed matter, single franking		600.00
a.	Inverted surcharge	1,200.	1,150.
	Never hinged	1,900.	
b.	Double surcharge		7,500.

No. 156 Surcharged

1933			
P8	A22 ½c on 1c olive bister	.30	.30
	Never hinged	.65	
	½c on 1c brown bister	.55	.80
	Never hinged	1.00	

PARCEL POST STAMPS

Inscribed "I APPORT A LA GARE" — PP1

Perfs As Noted

		Unwmk.	**Typo.**
1892			
Q1	PP1 25c brown, *yel*, perf 13½	825.00	290.00
	Never hinged	1,500.	
Q2	PP1 25c brown, *yel*, perf 11	30.00	24.00
	Never hinged	45.00	—
a.	On postal document	400.00	
	Printed on both sides	650.00	

Inscribed "II VALEUR DECLAREE" — PP2

Q3	PP2 10c red, perf 13½	1,000.	275.00
	Never hinged	1,750.	
	On postal document		1,000.
Q4	PP2 10c red, perf 10x13½	875.00	325.00
	Never hinged	1,600.	
Q5	PP2 10c org red, perf 11	30.00	14.00
	Never hinged	42.50	
	On postal document		115.00
Q6	PP2 10c red, imperf	22.50	16.50
	Never hinged	32.50	
	On postal document		140.00

Inscribed "III LIVRAISON PAR EXPRESS" — PP3

Q7	PP3 25c green, perf 13½	57.50	32.50
	On postal document	115.00	180.00
Q8	PP3 25c red, perf 11	45.00	24.00
	Never hinged	70.00	
	On postal document		140.00

See Nos. Q22-Q26.

Locomotive — PP4

A set of six stamps, in the design above, was prepared in 1901 as postal tax stamps for expedited parcels but were not issued. All are perf 14x13½. Values: 5c gray, $3, never hinged $4; 10c gray, $3, never hinged $5; 20c rose, $20, never hinged $29; 50c blue, $7, never hinged $11.50; 1fr brown, $8, never hinged $12; 2fr brown red, $37.50, never hinged $57.50.

PP5

1918		**Perf. 11**	

Type I: Large Trefoil Under "N" of "MAJORATION"

Q9	PP5 5c black	1.25	.85
	Never hinged	2.00	
	On postal document		42.50
Q10	PP5 15c brn lilac	1.25	.85
	Never hinged	2.00	
	On postal document		42.50

Imperforate

Q11	PP5 5c black	3.25	2.50
	Never hinged	6.25	
	On postal document		42.50
Q12	PP5 15c brn lilac	9.00	4.25
	Never hinged	14.00	
	On postal document		45.00
	Nos. Q9-Q12 (4)	14.75	8.45

40c values, perforated 11 and imperf, in orange, were prepared but not issued. Value, perf or imperf, $375.

Type II: Small Trefoil Under "O" of "MAJORATION"

		Perf. 11	
Q13	PP5 5c black	140.00	45.00
	Never hinged	275.00	
	On postal document		325.00
Q14	PP5 35c red	3.75	2.50
	Never hinged	5.00	
	On postal document		37.50
Q15	PP5 50c vio blue	4.50	1.60
	Never hinged	7.00	
	On postal document		50.00
Q16	PP5 1fr yellow	4.25	1.60
	Never hinged	7.00	
	On postal document		50.00

Imperforate

Q17	PP5 5c black	130.00	45.00
	Never hinged	260.00	
	On postal document		350.00
Q18	PP5 15c brn lilac	30.00	16.50
	Never hinged	50.00	
	On postal document		90.00
Q19	PP5 35c red	3.25	2.50
	Never hinged	6.75	
	On postal document		42.50
Q20	PP5 50c vio blue	24.00	14.00
	Never hinged	40.00	
	On postal document		75.00
Q21	PP5 1fr yellow	18.50	12.50
	Never hinged	30.00	
	On postal document		75.00
	Nos. Q13-Q21 (9)	358.25	141.20

See Nos. Q41-Q44, Q143-Q145.
For surcharges, see Nos. Q28-Q40.

Type of 1892

		Perf. 10½x11	
1918-23			
Q22	PP1 30c brn, *yel*	37.50	16.50
	Never hinged	55.00	
	On postal document		140.00
a.	Imperf	200.00	
	Never hinged	290.00	
Q23	PP1 60c brn, *straw* ('23)	47.50	30.00
	Never hinged	70.00	
	On postal document		180.00
a.	Imperf	190.00	
	Never hinged	275.00	
Q24	PP2 15c vermilion ('22)	16.00	11.00
	Never hinged	23.00	
	On postal document		65.00
Q25	PP3 30c green	40.00	21.00
	Never hinged	57.50	
	On postal document		140.00
a.	Imperf	240.00	
	Never hinged	325.00	
Q26	PP3 60c green ('23)	75.00	50.00
	Never hinged	110.00	
	On postal document		325.00
	Nos. Q22-Q26 (5)	216.00	128.50

PP6

1924, Oct.		**Perf. 14**	
Q27	PP6 15c rose & blue	4.00	3.75
	Never hinged	5.00	
a.	Imperf	550.00	
	Never hinged	750.00	

No. Q27 is a postal tax stamp, issued to show the collection of a new 15c excise fee on rail parcels. On July 3, 1925, its use was extended to all fiscal categories.

Surcharged in Black or Red (R) on Nos. Q9//Q16 and Types of 1918

1926 — *Perf. 13*

Q28	PP5	20c on 2fr rose	1.90	1.10
		Never hinged	2.75	
		On postal document		42.50
Q29	PP5	30c on 2fr yellow	1.90	1.10
		Never hinged	2.75	
		On postal document		42.50
a.		"0f30" omitted	190.00	
		Never hinged	250.00	
Q30	PP5	40c on 3fr gray	1.90	1.40
		Never hinged	2.75	
		On postal document		42.50
Q31	PP5	45c on 3fr orange	1.90	1.40
		Never hinged	2.75	
		On postal document		42.50
a.		Period after "f" omitted	19.00	19.00
		Never hinged	30.00	
Q32	PP5	95c on 1fr yel	8.00	2.75
		Never hinged	12.50	
		On postal document		70.00
a.		Imperf	90.00	
		Never hinged	150.00	
Q33	PP5	1.35fr on 3fr vio	10.50	4.50
		Never hinged	14.00	
		On postal document		70.00
a.		Imperf	150.00	
		Never hinged	225.00	
Q34	PP5	1.45fr on 5fr black (R)	1.90	1.00
		Never hinged	2.75	
		On postal document		45.00
Q35	PP5	1.75fr on 2fr blue	10.50	4.50
		Never hinged	14.00	
		On postal document		75.00
Q36	PP5	1.85fr on 10c orange	1.90	1.20
		Never hinged	2.75	
		On postal document		50.00
Q37	PP5	1.95fr on 15c lilac ben	2.50	1.75
		Never hinged	3.50	
		On postal document		50.00
a.		Imperf	110.00	
		Never hinged	175.00	
Q38	PP5	2.35fr on 25c green	1.90	1.00
		Never hinged	2.75	
		On postal document		50.00
a.		Imperf	110.00	
		Never hinged	175.00	
Q39	PP5	2.90fr on 35c red	2.50	1.00
		Never hinged	3.50	
		On postal document		50.00
a.		Dots before and after "f"	140.00	
		Never hinged	200.00	
b.		Imperf	125.00	
		Never hinged	190.00	
Q40	PP5	3.30fr on 50c blue violet (R)	2.50	1.25
		Never hinged	3.50	
		On postal document		50.00
a.		Double surcharge	250.00	
		Never hinged	375.00	
b.		Imperf	90.00	
		Never hinged	140.00	
		Nos. Q28-Q40 (13)	49.80	23.95

Type of 1918

1926 — *Perf. 11*

Q41	PP5	10c orange	2.00	1.25
		Never hinged	3.75	
		On postal document		42.50
a.		Imperf	4.00	
		Never hinged	6.50	
Q42	PP5	25c pale green	2.00	1.25
		Never hinged	3.75	
		On postal document		42.50
a.		Imperf	4.00	
		Never hinged	6.50	
Q43	PP5	2fr pale blue	25.00	14.50
		Never hinged	42.50	
		On postal document		130.00
a.		Imperf	50.00	
		Never hinged	80.00	
Q44	PP5	3fr violet	110.00	67.50
		Never hinged	190.00	
		On postal document		325.00
a.		Imperf	225.00	
		Never hinged	360.00	
		Nos. Q41-Q44 (4)	139.00	84.50

Inscribed "APPORT A LA GARE" — PP7

1926

Q45	PP7	1fr on 60c brn, yel	13.50	10.50
		Never hinged	24.00	
		On postal document		75.00
a.		Imperf	190.00	
		Never hinged	300.00	
Q46	PP7	1fr brn, yel	17.50	13.00
		Never hinged	30.00	
		On postal document		75.00

Q47	PP7	1.30fr on 1fr brn, yel	17.50	12.50
		Never hinged	30.00	
		On postal document		80.00
Q48	PP7	1.50fr brn, yel	20.00	11.50
		Never hinged	32.50	
		On postal document		75.00
Q49	PP7	1.65fr brn, yel	15.00	12.50
		Never hinged	24.00	
		On postal document		75.00
Q50	PP7	1.90fr on 1fr brn, yel	17.50	12.50
		Never hinged	30.00	
		On postal document		80.00
Q51	PP7	2.10fr on 1.65fr brn, yel	17.50	12.50
		Never hinged	30.00	
		On postal document		80.00
		Nos. Q45-Q51 (7)	118.50	85.00

See Nos. Q91-Q95, footnote following No. Q102, Q143-Q145.

For overprints and surcharges, see Nos. Q76-Q78, Q83-Q86, Q91-Q92, boxed note following Q95, Q96-Q99, Q107-QQ109, boxed note following Q159.

PP8

Type I — Type II — Type III

1926-38

Q52	PP8	15c brown, yel, type I	7.50	3.00
		Never hinged	11.00	
		On postal document		55.00
a.		Imperf	180.00	
		Never hinged	275.00	
Q53	PP8	15c brown, yel, type II ('32)	8.00	4.25
		Never hinged	11.50	
		On postal document		70.00
a.		Type III ('38)	210.00	
		Never hinged	275.00	
b.		As "a," imperf	240.00	
		Never hinged	300.00	

Nos. Q52-Q53a were issued for use in Paris only. No. Q53a was prepared but not issued.

Inscribed "VALEUR DECLAREE" — PP9

The additional numerals overprinted on Nos. Q56-Q63 and on Nos. Q72-Q75 indicate the weight category of the parcels being sent.

1926

Q54	PP9	50c on 15c red	3.00	1.60
		Never hinged	5.00	
		On postal document		45.00
a.		Imperf	180.00	
		Never hinged	275.00	
Q55	PP9	50c red	750.00	750.00
		Never hinged	1,200.	
		On postal document	1,200.	
a.		Imperf	1,650.	
Q56	PP9	50c red, ovptd. "1"	4.50	2.00
		Never hinged	7.00	
		On postal document		45.00
a.		Imperf	200.00	
		Never hinged	300.00	
b.		Double overprint "1"	300.00	
		Never hinged	400.00	
Q57	PP9	55c on 15c red, ovptd. "1"	6.75	5.00
		Never hinged	11.50	
		On postal document		50.00
a.		Imperf	190.00	—
Q58	PP9	55c on 50c red, ovptd. "1"	6.75	5.00
		Never hinged	11.50	
		On postal document		50.00
Q59	PP9	65c on 50c red	2.50	2.50
		Never hinged	4.25	
		On postal document		40.00
Q60	PP9	65c on 50c red, ovptd. "1"	15.00	8.25
		Never hinged	27.50	
		On postal document		45.00
Q61	PP9	1.50fr on 50c red, ovptd. "3"	7.00	5.00
		Never hinged	12.00	
		On postal document		50.00
a.		Imperf	275.00	
		Never hinged	375.00	

Q62	PP9	2.00fr on 50c red, ovptd. "4"	8.25	3.75
		Never hinged	14.00	
		On postal document		55.00
Q63	PP9	2.50fr on 50c red, ovptd. "5"	15.00	8.25
		Never hinged	26.50	
		On postal document		75.00
		Nos. Q54-Q63 (10)	818.75	791.35

See Nos. Q79, Q93, Q150-Q152.

For overprints and surcharges, see No. Q87, boxed note following No. Q95, Q100, Q110, Q123-Q124, Q138.

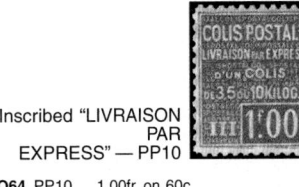

Inscribed "LIVRAISON PAR EXPRESS" — PP10

Q64	PP10	1.00fr on 60c grn	13.50	10.50
		Never hinged	24.00	
		On postal document		75.00
a.		Imperf	225.00	
		Never hinged	325.00	
Q65	PP10	1.00fr green	125.00	75.00
		Never hinged	250.00	—
Q66	PP10	1.30fr on 1fr grn	16.50	12.50
		Never hinged	29.00	
		On postal document		85.00
Q67	PP10	1.50fr green	16.50	15.00
		Never hinged	32.50	
		On postal document		70.00
Q68	PP10	1.65fr green	16.50	15.00
		Never hinged	32.50	
		On postal document		70.00
Q69	PP10	1.90fr on 1.50fr grn	16.50	12.50
		Never hinged	30.00	
		On postal document		85.00
Q70	PP10	2.10fr on 1.65fr grn	30.00	14.00
		Never hinged	50.00	
		On postal document		85.00
		Nos. Q64-Q70 (7)	234.50	154.50

For overprints and surcharges, see Nos. Q80-Q82, Q88-Q90, Q94, boxed note following Q95, Q101-Q105, Q111-Q113, Q125-Q132, Q139-Q141, Q146-Q149.

Inscribed "INTERETS A LA LIVRAISON" — PP11

Q71	PP11	50c lilac	3.00	1.60
		Never hinged	5.00	
		On postal document		50.00
a.		Imperf	225.00	190.00
		Never hinged	325.00	
Q72	PP11	50c lil, ovptd. "1"	6.75	4.25
		Never hinged	10.00	
		On postal document		55.00
a.		Imperf	200.00	
		Never hinged	300.00	
Q73	PP11	1.50fr on 50c lil, ovptd. "3"	7.50	5.00
		Never hinged	11.50	
		On postal document		55.00
a.		Imperf	200.00	
		Never hinged	300.00	
Q74	PP11	2.00fr on 50c lil ovptd. "4"	10.00	7.00
		Never hinged	16.00	
		On postal document		75.00
Q75	PP11	2.50fr on 50c lil ovptd. "5"	10.00	7.00
		Never hinged	16.50	
		On postal document		80.00
a.		Imperf	210.00	
		Never hinged	310.00	
		Nos. Q71-Q75 (5)	37.25	24.85

1926 Issues Overprinted

1928

Inscribed "APPORT A LA GARE"

Q76	PP7	1.00fr brn, yel	16.50	14.00
		Never hinged	25.00	
		On postal document		80.00
a.		Imperf	190.00	190.00
		Never hinged	300.00	
Q77	PP7	1.50fr brn, yel	16.50	13.00
		Never hinged	25.00	
		On postal document		80.00
Q78	PP7	1.65fr brn, yel	16.50	13.00
		Never hinged	25.00	

		On postal document		80.00

Inscribed "VALEUR DECLAREE"

Q79	PP9	50c red	5.75	4.25
		Never hinged	8.25	
		On postal document		45.00
a.		Imperf	190.00	190.00
		Never hinged	300.00	
b.		Inverted overprint	210.00	
		Never hinged	310.00	

Inscribed "LIVRAISON PAR EXPRESS"

Q80	PP10	1.00fr green	17.00	13.50
		Never hinged	26.00	
		On postal document		80.00
Q81	PP10	1.50fr green	17.00	13.50
		Never hinged	26.00	
		On postal document		80.00
Q82	PP10	1.65fr green	17.00	13.50
		Never hinged	27.50	
		On postal document		80.00
		Nos. Q76-Q82 (7)	106.25	84.75

1926 Issues Surcharged

1928

Inscribed "APPORT A LA GARE"

Q83	PP7	1.45fr on 60c brn, yel	7.00	6.75
		Never hinged	10.00	
		On postal document		55.00
Q84	PP7	1.45fr on 1fr brn, yel	40.00	32.50
		Never hinged	70.00	
		On postal document		125.00
Q85	PP7	2.15fr on 1.50fr brn, yel	62.50	42.50
		Never hinged	105.00	
		On postal document		200.00
Q86	PP7	2.35fr on 1.65fr brn, yel	62.50	42.50
		Never hinged	105.00	
		On postal document		180.00

Inscribed "VALEUR DECLAREE"

Q87	PP9	75c on 50c red	2.10	1.60
		Never hinged	3.25	
		On postal document		40.00
a.		Imperf	210.00	
		Never hinged	400.00	

Inscribed "LIVRAISON PAR EXPRESS"

Q88	PP10	1.45fr on 1fr green	62.50	42.50
		Never hinged	105.00	
		On postal document		200.00
Q89	PP10	2.15fr on 1.50fr green	62.50	42.50
		Never hinged	105.00	
		On postal document		200.00
Q90	PP10	2.35fr on 1.65fr green	62.50	42.50
		Never hinged	105.00	
		On postal document		200.00
		Nos. Q83-Q90 (8)	361.60	253.35

Types of 1926 and

PP12

1933-34

Inscribed "APPORT A LA GARE"

Q91	PP7	1.45fr brn, yel	55.00	25.00
		Never hinged	82.50	
		On postal document		100.00
Q92	PP7	2.35fr brn, yel	1,400.	
		Never hinged	1,900.	

A 2.15fr value, brown on yellow paper, was prepared but not issued without overprint or surcharge.

For overprints and surcharges, see Nos. Q96, Q98, Q99, Q107-Q109, Q115, Q116, Q118, Q120-Q122, Q135-Q137.

Inscribed "VALEUR DECLAREE"

Q93	PP9	75c red	18.00	3.25
		Never hinged	22.50	
		On postal document		15.00
a.		Imperf		180.00

For overprints and surcharges on No. Q93, see Nos. Q110, Q123, Q124, Q138.

A 1.15fr black in this design, imperf, was prepared but not issued. Value, $400.

Inscribed "LIVRAISON PAR EXPRESS"

Q94	PP10	1.45fr yel grn	450.00	300.00
	Never hinged		675.00	

Two other values, 2.15fr and 2.35fr were prepared but not issued without overprint or surcharge.

For overprints and surcharges, see Nos. Q101, Q103, Q105, Q111-Q113, Q125, Q126, Q128, Q130-Q132. Q139-Q141.

Inscribed "COLIS ENCOMBRANT"

Q95	PP12	2fr blue ('34)	45.00	21.00
	Never hinged		70.00	
	On postal document		115.00	

For overprints and surcharges, see Nos. Q106, Q114, Q133, Q134, Q142.

Nos. Q46, Q48, Q49, Q55, Q65, Q67 and Q68 overprinted "B" were not issued. Values: 1fr (No. Q46), $95; never hinged $130; 1.50fr (No. Q48), $95, never hinged $130; 1.65fr (No. Q49), $95, never hinged $130; 50c (No. Q55), $95, never hinged $130; 1fr (No. Q65), $92.50, never hinged $140; 1.50fr (No. Q67), $92.50, never hinged $140; 1.65fr (No. Q68), $92.50, never hinged $140.

Stamps and Types of 1926-34 Overprinted

1937

Inscribed "APPORT A LA GARE"

Q96	PP7	1.45fr brn, yel	6.75	6.75
	Never hinged		10.00	
	On postal document		65.00	
Q97	PP7	2.15fr on 1.50fr brn, yel	37.50	31.00
	Never hinged		57.50	
	On postal document		150.00	
Q98	PP7	2.15fr brn, yel	25.00	19.00
	Never hinged		37.50	
	On postal document		125.00	
Q99	PP7	2.35fr brn, yel	25.00	19.00
	Never hinged		37.50	
	On postal document		125.00	

Inscribed "VALEUR DECLAREE"

Q100	PP9	75c red	17.50	16.50
	Never hinged		25.00	
	On postal document		95.00	
a.	Imperf		225.00	
	Never hinged		325.00	

Inscribed "LIVRAISON PAR EXPRESS"

Q101	PP10	1.45fr green	17.50	16.50
	Never hinged		25.00	
	On postal document		100.00	
Q102	PP10	2.15fr on 1.50fr grn	17.50	16.50
	Never hinged		25.00	
	On postal document		100.00	
Q103	PP10	2.15fr green	42.50	30.00
	Never hinged		67.50	
	On postal document		150.00	
a.	Imperf		210.00	
	Never hinged		315.00	
Q104	PP10	2.35fr on 1.65fr grn	250.00	110.00
	Never hinged		350.00	—
Q105	PP10	2.35fr green	17.50	12.50
	Never hinged		26.00	
	On postal document		100.00	

Inscribed "COLIS ENCOMBRANT"

Q106	PP12	2fr blue	37.50	35.00
	Never hinged		57.50	
	On postal document		180.00	
	Nos. Q96-Q106 (11)		494.25	312.75

For overprints and surcharges, see Nos. Q146-Q149.

Types of 1933-34 Surcharged

1937

Inscribed "APPORT A LA GARE"

Q107	PP7	1.85fr on 1.45fr brn, yel	15.00	12.50
	Never hinged		26.00	
	On postal document		57.50	
Q108	PP7	2.75fr on 2.15fr brn, yel	26.00	17.50
	Never hinged		45.00	
	On postal document		125.00	
Q109	PP7	3.05fr on 2.55fr brn, yel	50.00	26.00
	Never hinged		90.00	
	On postal document		140.00	

Inscribed "VALEUR DECLAREE"

Q110	PP9	.95c on 75c red	42.50	25.00
	Never hinged		67.50	
	On postal document		125.00	

Inscribed "LIVRAISON PAR EXPRESS"

Q111	PP10	1.85fr on 1.45fr grn	70.00	45.00
	Never hinged		120.00	
	On postal document		210.00	
Q112	PP10	2.75fr on 2.15fr grn	70.00	45.00
	Never hinged		120.00	
	On postal document		210.00	
Q113	PP10	3.05fr on 2.35fr grn	70.00	45.00
	Never hinged		120.00	
	On postal document		210.00	

Inscribed "COLIS ENCOMBRANT"

Q114	PP12	2.60fr on 2fr bl	17.50	17.50
	Never hinged		26.00	
	On postal document		85.00	
	Nos. Q107-Q114 (8)		361.00	233.50

Stamps and Types of 1926-34 Overprinted

1937

Inscribed "APPORT A LA GARE"

Q115	PP7	1.45fr brn, yel	3.00	2.50
	Never hinged		4.50	
	On postal document		45.00	
Q116	PP7	1.85fr on 1.45fr brn, yel	3.00	2.50
	Never hinged		4.50	
	On postal document		45.00	
Q117	PP7	2.15fr on 1.50fr brn, yel	2.50	2.50
	Never hinged		4.25	
	On postal document		45.00	
Q118	PP7	2.15fr brn, yel	42.50	35.00
	Never hinged		62.50	
	On postal document		140.00	
Q119	PP7	2.35fr on 1.65fr brn, yel	575.00	475.00
	Never hinged		800.00	—
Q120	PP7	2.35fr brn, yel	3.00	2.50
	Never hinged		4.50	
	On postal document		45.00	
Q121	PP7	2.75fr on 2.15fr brn, yel	3.25	2.50
	Never hinged		5.75	
	On postal document		45.00	
Q122	PP7	3.05fr on 2.35fr brn, yel	6.50	6.25
	Never hinged		10.00	
	On postal document		50.00	

Inscribed "VALEUR DECLAREE"

Q123	PP9	75c red	3.75	3.50
	Never hinged		5.50	
	On postal document		45.00	
a.	Pair, one without overprint		225.00	
	Never hinged		350.00	
Q124	PP9	95c on 75c red	3.00	3.00
	Never hinged		3.75	
	On postal document		45.00	

Inscribed "LIVRAISON PAR EXPRESS"

Q125	PP10	1.45fr green	4.25	3.25
	Never hinged		6.25	
	On postal document		42.50	
Q126	PP10	1.85fr on 1.45fr brn, yel	5.75	4.25
	Never hinged		8.25	
	On postal document		50.00	
Q127	PP10	2.15fr on 1.50fr grn	375.00	325.00
	Never hinged		500.00	
Q128	PP10	2.15fr green	18.50	16.50
	Never hinged		27.50	
	On postal document		95.00	

Q129	PP10	2.35fr on 1.65fr grn	675.00	725.00
	Never hinged		775.00	
Q130	PP10	2.35fr green	11.00	10.50
	Never hinged		15.00	
	On postal document		44.00	
Q131	PP10	2.75fr on 2.15fr grn	35.00	45.00
	Never hinged		55.00	
	On postal document		115.00	
Q132	PP10	3.05fr on 2.35fr grn	35.00	45.00
	Never hinged		55.00	
	On postal document		115.00	

Inscribed "COLIS ENCOMBRANT"

Q133	PP12	2fr blue	3.00	2.10
	Never hinged		4.50	
	On postal document		50.00	
a.	Pair, imperf between		130.00	
	Never hinged		210.00	
Q134	PP12	2.60fr on 2fr bl	3.25	2.50
	Never hinged		5.50	
	On postal document		50.00	
	Nos. Q115-Q134 (20)		1,811.	1,714.

For additional surcharges, see Nos. Q146-Q149.

Stamps and Types of 1933-34 Surcharged

1938

Inscribed "APPORT A LA GARE"

Q135	PP7	2.30fr on 1.45fr brn, yel	3.75	3.00
	Never hinged		5.50	
	On postal document		42.50	
Q136	PP7	3.45fr on 2.15fr brn, yel	3.75	3.00
	Never hinged		5.50	
	On postal document		42.50	
Q137	PP7	3.85fr on 1.45fr brn, yel	3.75	3.00
	Never hinged		5.50	
	On postal document		42.50	

Inscribed "VALEUR DECLAREE"

Q138	PP9	1.15fr on 75c red	1.60	1.60
	Never hinged		2.50	
	On postal document		42.50	

Inscribed "LIVRAISON PAR EXPRESS"

Q139	PP10	2.30fr on 1.45fr grn	3.75	3.00
	Never hinged		5.50	
	On postal document		45.00	
Q140	PP10	3.45fr on 2.15fr grn	3.75	3.00
	Never hinged		5.50	
	On postal document		45.00	
Q141	PP10	3.85fr on 2.35fr grn	3.75	3.00
	Never hinged		5.50	
	On postal document		45.00	

Inscribed "COLIS ENCOMBRANT"

Q142	PP12	3.25fr on 2fr bl	1.60	1.60
	Never hinged		2.50	
	On postal document		50.00	
	Nos. Q135-Q142 (8)		25.70	21.20

For Nos. Q135-Q138, Q140-Q142 overprinted "E," see editor's note following No. Q159.

Type of 1918

1938 — 11, Imperf (#Q161)

Q143	PP5	10c gray black	17.50	16.00
	Never hinged		26.00	
	On postal document		350.00	
a.	Imperf		26.00	
	Never hinged		42.50	
Q144	PP5	20c brown lilac	17.50	16.00
	Never hinged		26.00	
	On postal document		400.00	
a.	Imperf		42.50	
	Never hinged		62.50	
Q145	PP5	25c green, imperf	50.00	20.00
	Never hinged		80.00	
	Nos. Q143-Q145 (3)		85.00	52.00

Two additional values, a 10c rose lilac and a 15c ultramarine, were prepared with this set but not issued. Values, each stamp: $90, never hinged $150. Both stamps also exist imperf. Values, each: $82.50; never hinged $150.

Nos. Q103, Q105, Q112, Q113 Overprinted

1938 — Perf. 11

Q146	PP10	2.30fr on 2.15fr green	62.50	62.50
	Never hinged		80.00	
	On postal document		250.00	
Q147	PP10	2.30fr on 2.35fr green	62.50	62.50
	Never hinged		80.00	
	On postal document		250.00	

Q148	PP10	2.30fr on 2.75fr on 2.15fr green	125.00	100.00
	Never hinged		175.00	
	On postal document		350.00	
Q149	PP10	2.30fr on 3.05fr on 2.35fr green	125.00	100.00
	Never hinged		175.00	
	On postal document		350.00	
	Nos. Q146-Q149 (4)		375.00	325.00

Types of 1926 and

PP13   PP14

PP15   PP16

1938-39

Inscribed "VALEUR DECLAREE"

Q150	PP9	1fr red ('39)	2.50	2.50
	Never hinged		4.00	
	On postal document		35.00	
Q151	PP9	1.15fr red	1.25	1.25
	Never hinged		2.10	
	On postal document		40.00	
	Imperf		140.00	
	Never hinged		225.00	
Q152	PP9	5fr red ('39)	2.50	2.75
	Never hinged		4.00	
	On postal document		40.00	

Inscribed "AU DESSUS DE 10"

Q153	PP13	2.40fr brown, yellow	2.50	2.75
	Never hinged		4.00	
	On postal document		37.50	
Q154	PP13	3.50fr brown, yellow	2.50	2.75
	Never hinged		4.00	
	On postal document		37.50	
Q155	PP13	3.80fr brown, yelloe	2.50	2.75
	Never hinged		4.00	
	On postal document		37.50	
	Imperf		125.00	
	Never hinged		190.00	

Inscribed "REMBOURSEMENT"

Q156	PP14	2.50fr yel grn ('39)	2.50	2.25
	Never hinged		4.00	
	On postal document		35.00	
Q157	PP14	7.50fr yel grn ('39)	2.75	2.50
	Never hinged		4.25	
	On postal document		35.00	

Inscribed "INTERET A LA LIVRAISON"

Q158	PP15	1fr lilac ('39)	9.50	6.75
	Never hinged		14.00	
	On postal document		50.00	

Inscribed "ENCOMBRANT"

Q159	PP16	3.20fr blue	11.00	7.50
	Never hinged		16.00	
	On postal document		55.00	
	Nos. Q150-Q159 (10)		39.50	33.75

Two additional values, 3.45fr and 3.85fr, type PP7, brown on yellow paper, imperforate, were prepared but not issued. Values, each: $140; never hinged, $225.

Nos. Nos. Q135-Q138, Q140-Q142 were overprinted "E" in 1939, in anticipation of new rates to take effect April 1, but were not issued. Values: 2.30fr on 1.45fr, $675, never hinged $1,000; 3.45fr on 2.15fr, $875, never hinged $1,300; 3.85fr on 2.35fr, $875, never hinged $1,300; 1.15fr on 75c, $300, never hinged $450; 3.45fr on 2.15fr, $2,800, never hinged $4,000; 3.85fr on 2.35fr, $2,800, never hinged $4,000;

3.25fr on 2fr, $675, never hinged $1,000.

FRANCHISE STAMPS

No. 276 Overprinted "F"

			1939 Unwmk. Perf. 14x13½		
S1	A45	90c ultramarine		1.90	2.50
	Never hinged			2.75	
	On cover				16.00
a.	Period following "F"			30.00	30.00
	Never hinged			50.00	

No. S1 was for the use of Spanish refugees in France. "F" stands for "Franchise."

OCCUPATION STAMPS

FRANCO-PRUSSIAN WAR
Issued under German Occupation
(Alsace and Lorraine)

OS1

1870   Typo.   Unwmk.   Perf. 13½x14
Network with Points Up

N1	OS1	1c bronze green	75.00	100.00
	Never hinged		110.00	
	On cover, single franking			215.00
a.	1c olive grn		75.00	100.00
	Never hinged		110.00	
	On cover, single franking			215.00
N2	OS1	2c dark brown	125.00	175.00
	Never hinged		180.00	
	On cover			315.00
	On cover, single franking			950.00
a.	2c red brown		115.00	175.00
	Never hinged		170.00	
	On cover			315.00
	On cover, single franking			950.00
N3	OS1	4c gray	135.00	100.00
	Never hinged		190.00	
	On cover			215.00
	On cover, single franking			650.00
N4	OS1	5c yel grn	125.00	14.00
	Never hinged		180.00	
	On cover			82.50
	On cover, single franking			150.00
a.	5c deep green		130.00	15.00
	Never hinged		190.00	
	On cover			87.50
	On cover, single franking			160.00
N5	OS1	10c bistre brn	110.00	5.75
	Never hinged		160.00	
	On cover			40.00
	On cover, single franking			45.00
a.	10c yellow brown		110.00	6.50
	Never hinged		160.00	
	On cover			45.00
	On cover, single franking			50.00
b.	Network lemon yellow		135.00	10.00
	Never hinged		200.00	
	On cover			90.00
	On cover, single franking			100.00
N6	OS1	20c ultra	115.00	16.50
	Never hinged		170.00	
	On cover			65.00
	On cover, single franking			77.50
a.	20c milky blue		115.00	15.00
	Never hinged		170.00	
	On cover			70.00
	On cover, single franking			82.50
N7	OS1	25c brown	150.00	100.00
	Never hinged		215.00	
	On cover			275.00
	On cover, single franking			325.00
a.	25c black brown		145.00	100.00
	Never hinged		210.00	
	On cover			275.00
	On cover, single franking			325.00

There are three varieties of the 4c and two of the 10c, differing in the position of the figures of value, and several other setting varieties.

Network with Points Down

N8	OS1	1c olive grn	350.00	625.00
	Never hinged		550.00	
	On cover			1,600.
N9	OS1	2c red brn	150.00	550.00
	Never hinged		250.00	
	On cover			1,100.
	On cover, single franking			2,000.
N10	OS1	4c gray	150.00	200.00
	Never hinged		250.00	
	On cover			350.00
	On cover, single franking			825.00
N11	OS1	5c yel grn	6,500.	650.00
	Never hinged			
	On cover			1,750.
	On cover, single franking			2,600.
N12	OS1	10c bister	150.00	21.50
	Never hinged		250.00	
	On cover			100.00
	On cover, single franking			115.00
a.	Network lemon yellow		225.00	50.00
	Never hinged		300.00	
	On cover			200.00
	On cover, single franking			250.00

N13	OS1	20c ultra	225.00	90.00
	Never hinged		300.00	
	On cover			250.00
	On cover, single franking			275.00
N14	OS1	25c brown	450.00	300.00
	Never hinged		650.00	
	On cover			650.00
	On cover, single franking			825.00

Official imitations have the network with points downward. The "P" of "Postes" is 2½mm from the border in the imitations and 3mm in the originals.

The word "Postes" measures 12¾ to 13mm on the imitations, and from 11 to 12½mm on the originals.

The imitations are perf. 13½x14½; originals, perf. 13½x14¼.

The stamps for Alsace and Lorraine were replaced by stamps of the German Empire on Jan. 1, 1872.

WORLD WAR I
German Stamps of 1905-16
Surcharged

1916   Wmk. 125   Perf. 14, 14½

N15	A16	3c on 3pf brown	1.25	1.25
	Never hinged		2.90	
	On cover			100.00
N16	A16	5c on 5pf green	1.25	1.25
	Never hinged		2.90	
	On cover			100.00
N17	A22	8c on 7½pf org	2.00	2.00
	Never hinged		3.75	
	On cover			105.00
N18	A16	10c on 10pf car	2.00	2.00
	Never hinged		3.75	
	On cover			100.00
N19	A22	15c on 15pf yel brn	1.25	1.25
	Never hinged		2.90	
	On cover			100.00
N20	A16	25c on 20pf blue	1.25	1.25
	Never hinged		2.90	
	On cover			100.00
a.	25c on 20pf ultramarine		2.00	2.00
	Never hinged		5.25	
	On cover			160.00
N21	A16	40c on 30pf org & blk, *buff*	2.90	2.75
	Never hinged		6.00	
	On cover			180.00
N22	A16	50c on 40pf lake & blk	2.90	2.75
	Never hinged		7.00	
	On cover			250.00
N23	A16	75c on 60pf mag	12.50	12.50
	Never hinged		35.00	
	On cover			600.00
N24	A16	1fr on 80pf lake & blk, *rose*	12.50	12.50
	Never hinged		35.00	
	On cover			600.00

N25	A17	1fr25c on 1m car	47.50	47.50
	Never hinged		150.00	
a.	Double surcharge		—	
N26	A21	2fr50c on 2m gray bl	47.50	47.50
	Never hinged		150.00	
a.	Double surcharge		—	
	Nos. N15-N26 (12)		134.80	134.50

These stamps were also used in parts of Belgium occupied by the German forces.

> **Catalogue values for unused stamps in this section, from this point to the end of the section, are for Never Hinged items.**

WORLD WAR II
Alsace
Issued under German Occupation

> Values for unused copies of N27-N58 are for never hinged stamps.

Stamps of Germany 1933-36 Overprinted in Black

1940   Wmk. 237   Perf. 14

N27	A64	3pf olive bister	.80	.55
	On cover			4.00
	On cover, single franking			12.50
N28	A64	4pf dull blue	.80	.55
	On cover			4.00
	On cover, single franking			20.00
N29	A64	5pf brt green	.80	.55
	On cover			3.25
	On cover, single franking			20.00
N30	A64	6pf dark green	.80	.55
	On cover, single franking			2.75
N31	A64	8pf vermilion	.80	.55
	On cover			.40
	On cover, single franking			12.50
a.	Inverted overprint		1,500.	
N32	A64	10pf chocolate	.80	.55
	On cover			5.00
	On cover, single franking			82.50
a.	Inverted overprint		4,000.	
N33	A64	12pf dp carmine	1.00	.55
	On cover			3.75
N34	A64	15pf maroon	1.00	.55
	On cover			8.25
	On cover, single franking			77.50
N35	A64	20pf brt blue	1.65	.75
	On cover			11.50
	On cover, single franking			50.00
N36	A64	25pf ultra	1.65	.75
	On cover			11.50
	On cover, single franking			40.00
N37	A64	30pf olive grn	1.65	.75
	On cover			12.50
	On cover, single franking			82.50
N38	A64	40pf red violet	2.90	1.00
	On cover			16.50
	On cover, single franking			40.00
N39	A64	50pf dk grn & blk	7.00	3.25
	On cover			29.00
	On cover, single franking			50.00
N40	A64	60pf claret & blk	7.00	3.25
	On cover			29.00
	On cover, single franking			50.00
N41	A64	80pf dk blue & blk	17.50	7.00
	On cover			52.50
	On cover, single franking			65.00
N42	A64	100pf orange & blk	17.50	7.00
	On cover			62.50
	On cover, single franking			125.00
	Nos. N27-N42 (16)		63.65	28.15

Lorraine
Issued under German Occupation

Stamps of Germany 1933-36 Overprinted in Black

1940   Wmk. 237   Perf. 14

N43	A64	3pf olive bister	1.00	.75
	On cover			5.00
	On cover, single franking			14.00
N44	A64	4pf dull blue	1.00	.75
	On cover			5.00
	On cover, single franking			22.00
N45	A64	5pf brt green	1.00	4.00
	On cover			22.50
	On cover, single franking			—
N46	A64	6pf dark green	1.00	.75
	On cover			3.75
N47	A64	8pf vermilion	1.00	.75
	On cover			5.00
	On cover, single franking			14.00
N48	A64	10pf chocolate	1.50	.85
	On cover			6.00
	On cover, single franking			90.00
N49	A64	12pf deep carmine	1.50	.85
	On cover			3.75
N50	A64	15pf maroon	1.50	.75
	On cover			10.00
	On cover, single franking			90.00
a.	Inverted surcharge		—	
N51	A64	20pf brt blue	1.65	1.00
	On cover			12.50
	On cover, single franking			52.50
N52	A64	25pf ultra	1.40	1.00
	On cover			12.50
	On cover, single franking			45.00
N53	A64	30pf olive grn	2.10	1.00
	On cover			14.00
	On cover, single franking			90.00
N54	A64	40pf red violet	2.50	1.25
	On cover			18.00
	On cover, single franking			45.00
N55	A64	50pf dk grn & blk	6.00	3.00
	On cover			27.50
	On cover, single franking			52.50

N56	A64	60pf claret & blk	6.00	3.00
	On cover			27.50
	On cover, single franking			52.50
N57	A64	80pf dk blue & blk	18.00	7.50
	On cover			60.00
	On cover, single franking			75.00
N58	A64	100pf orange & blk	18.00	7.50
	On cover			65.00
	On cover, single franking			125.00
	Nos. N43-N58 (16)		65.15	34.70

Besetztes Gebiet Nordfrankreich

These three words, in a rectangular frame covering two stamps, were hand-stamped in black on Nos. 267, 367 and 369 and used in the Dunkerque region in July-August, 1940. The German political officer of Dunkerque authorized the overprint. The prevalence of forgeries and later favor overprints make expertization mandatory.

FRANCE OFFICES ABROAD

OFFICES IN CHINA

Prior to 1923 several of the world powers maintained their own post offices in China for the purpose of sending and receiving overseas mail. French offices were maintained in Canton, Hoi Hao (Hoihow), Kwangchowan (Kouang-tchéou-wan), Mongtseu (Mong-tseu), Packhoi (Paknoi), Tong King (Tchongking), Yunnan Fou (Yunnanfu).

100 Centimes = 1 Franc
100 Cents = 1 Piaster
100 Cents = 1 Dollar

Peace and Commerce Stamps of France Ovptd. in Red, Carmine or Black

1894-1900	**Unwmk.**	**Perf. 14x13½**	
1	A15	5c green, *greenish* (R)	3.25	3.00
	Never hinged	7.25	
	On cover		50.00
a.	5c green, *greenish* (C)	1.25	1.10
	Never hinged	5.75	
	On cover		50.00
2	A15	5c yel grn, I (R) ('00)	4.25	3.00
	Never hinged	7.50	
	On cover		50.00
a.	Type II	47.50	32.50
	Never hinged	105.00	
	On cover		350.00
3	A15	10c blk, *lav*, I (R)	9.25	3.00
	Never hinged	17.00	
	On cover		32.50
a.	Type II	27.50	17.50
	On cover		190.00
b.	Type II (C)	17.50	11.00
	On cover		140.00
4	A15	15c bl (R)	12.50	4.25
	Never hinged	26.00	
	On cover		32.50
a.	Black overprint	—	
b.	Carmine overprint	12.50	4.00
	Never hinged	26.00	
	On cover		32.50
5	A15	20c red, *grn*	7.50	5.00
	Never hinged	15.00	
	On cover		60.00
	On cover, single franking		160.00
6	A15	25c blk, *rose* (C)	9.25	2.50
	Never hinged	17.50	
	On cover		52.50
	On cover, single franking		70.00
a.	Double overprint	225.00	
b.	Pair, one without overprint	550.00	
c.	Red overprint	17.50	3.25
	Never hinged	40.00	
d.	Imperf	120.00	45.00
	Never hinged	260.00	
7	A15	30c brn, *bis*	9.25	6.25
	Never hinged	18.00	
	On cover		72.50
	On cover, single franking		90.00
8	A15	40c red, *straw*	9.25	7.50
	Never hinged	18.00	
	On cover		85.00
	On cover, single franking		175.00
9	A15	50c car, *rose*, I	26.00	17.50
	Never hinged	52.50	
	On cover		150.00
	On cover, single franking		200.00
a.	Carmine overprint	62.50	
	Never hinged	115.00	
b.	Type II (Bk)	25.00	16.00
	Never hinged	60.00	
	On cover		200.00
	On cover, single franking		325.00
10	A15	75c dp vio, *org* (R)	80.00	60.00
	Never hinged	160.00	
	On cover		525.00
	On cover, single franking		900.00
a.	Carmine overprint	80.00	60.00
	Never hinged	160.00	
	On cover		525.00
	On cover, single franking		900.00
11	A15	1fr brnz grn, *straw*	17.00	8.50
	Never hinged	37.50	
	On cover		200.00
	On cover, single franking		275.00
a.	Double overprint	425.00	450.00
12	A15	2fr brn, *az* ('00)	30.00	29.00
	Never hinged	65.00	
	On cover		400.00
	On cover, single franking		650.00
12A	A15	5fr red lil, *lav*	75.00	60.00
	Never hinged	160.00	
	On cover		650.00
	On cover, single franking		1,050.
b.	Red overprint	525.00	
	Never hinged	—	
	Nos. 1-12A (13)	292.50	209.50

For surcharges and overprints see Nos. 13-17, J7-J10, J20-J23.

No. 11 Surcharged in Black

13	A15	25c on 1fr brnz grn, *straw*	125.00	75.00
	On cover		625.00
	On cover, single franking		1,050.

No. 6 Surcharged in Red

1901

14	A15	2c on 25c blk, *rose*	1,100.	340.00
	On cover		1,900.
15	A15	4c on 25c blk, *rose*	1,350.	450.00
	On cover		2,250.
16	A15	6c on 25c blk, *rose*	1,100.	375.00
	On cover		1,900.
17	A15	16c on 25c blk, *rose*	325.00	200.00
	On cover		1,250.
a.	Black surcharge		7,250.
	Nos. 14-17 (4)	3,875.	1,365.

Stamps of Indo-China Surcharged in Black

Two types of Nos. 18-33: type I, 13mmx3mm, "C" and "H" wide, "E" with fine serifs; type II, 12½mmx2¾mm, "C" and "H" narrower, "E" with heavy serifs.

1902-04

Type I ('02)

18	A3	1c blk, *lil bl*	4.00	4.00
	Never hinged	8.00	
	On cover		110.00
19	A3	2c brn, *buff*	4.25	4.25
	Never hinged	8.00	
	On cover		110.00
20	A3	4c claret, *lav*	5.50	5.50
	Never hinged	12.00	
	On cover		110.00
21	A3	5c yellow grn	6.50	5.50
	Never hinged	14.00	
	On cover		85.00
22	A3	10c red	6.75	6.00
	Never hinged	14.00	
	On cover		75.00
23	A3	15c gray	7.50	6.75
	Never hinged	16.00	
	On cover		70.00
24	A3	20c red, *grn*	18.00	16.00
	Never hinged	42.50	
	On cover		210.00
	On cover, single franking		375.00
25	A3	25c blk, *rose*	16.00	12.50
	Never hinged	37.50	
	On cover		160.00
	On cover, single franking		225.00
27	A3	30c brn, *bis*	27.50	27.50
	Never hinged	70.00	
	On cover		325.00
	On cover, single franking		450.00
28	A3	40c red, *straw*	60.00	50.00
	Never hinged	150.00	
	On cover		700.00
	On cover, single franking		1,000.
29	A3	50c car, *rose*	67.50	67.50
	Never hinged	160.00	
	On cover		1,000.
	On cover, single franking		1,250.
31	A3	75c vio, *org*	60.00	60.00
	Never hinged	150.00	
	On cover		1,100.
	On cover, single franking		1,600.
32	A3	1fr brnz grn, *straw*	87.50	87.50
	Never hinged	210.00	
	On cover		1,200.
	On cover, single franking		2,000.
33	A3	5fr red lil, *lavender*	110.00	110.00
	Never hinged	260.00	
	On cover		1,300.
	On cover, single franking		2,400.
	Nos. 18-33 (14)	481.00	463.00

Type II ('04)

18a	A3	1c blk, *lil bl*	2.50	2.50
	Never hinged	4.75	
	On cover		62.50
19a	A3	2c brn, *buff*	8.25	7.25
	Never hinged	17.50	
	On cover		100.00
20a	A3	4c claret, *lav*	4.25	3.40
	Never hinged	8.00	
	On cover		65.00
21a	A3	5c yellow grn	5.00	3.40
	Never hinged	8.50	
	On cover		50.00

22a	A3	10c red	8.50	8.00
	Never hinged	17.50	
	On cover		65.00
24a	A3	20c red, *grn*	9.25	8.50
	Never hinged	17.50	
	On cover		65.00
25a	A3	25c blk, *rose*	13.50	12.50
	Never hinged	22.50	
	On cover		100.00
	On cover, single franking		150.00
26	A3	25c blue	10.00	8.50
	Never hinged	20.00	
	On cover		75.00
	On cover, single franking		110.00
27a	A3	30c brn, *bis*	9.25	8.50
	Never hinged	17.50	
	On cover		75.00
	On cover, single franking		100.00
28a	A3	40c red, *straw*	25.00	21.00
	Never hinged	47.50	
	On cover		110.00
	On cover, single franking		160.00
30	A3	50c brn, *azure*	10.00	9.25
	Never hinged	20.00	
	On cover		125.00
	On cover, single franking		210.00
31a	A3	75c vio, *org*	40.00	37.50
	Never hinged	75.00	
	On cover		325.00
	On cover, single franking		525.00
32a	A3	1fr brnz grn, *straw*	45.00	42.50
	Never hinged	85.00	
	On cover		475.00
	On cover, single franking		625.00
33a	A3	5fr red lil, *lavender*	97.50	90.00
	Never hinged	180.00	
	On cover		625.00
	On cover, single franking		1,200.
	Nos. 18a-33a (14)	287.00	262.80

The Chinese characters surcharged on Nos. 18-33 are the Chinese equivalents of the French values and therefore differ on each denomination. Many varieties of surcharge exist.

Liberty, Equality and Fraternity
A3

"Rights of Man"
A4

A5

1902-03   **Typo.**

34	A3	5c green	6.00	3.75
	Never hinged	9.50	
	On cover		65.00
35	A4	10c rose red ('03)	3.00	2.10
	Never hinged	5.50	
	On cover		40.00
36	A4	15c pale red	3.00	2.10
	Never hinged	5.50	
	On cover		32.50
37	A4	20c brn vio ('03)	8.50	7.25
	Never hinged	16.00	
	On cover		100.00
	On cover, single franking		150.00
38	A4	25c blue ('03)	6.75	3.40
	Never hinged	13.50	
	On cover		50.00
	On cover, single franking		70.00
39	A4	30c lilac ('03)	9.25	7.50
	Never hinged	16.00	
	On cover		50.00
	On cover, single franking		150.00
40	A5	40c red & pale bl	19.00	16.00
	Never hinged	35.00	
	On cover		110.00
	On cover, single franking		150.00
41	A5	50c bis brn & lav	23.00	19.00
	Never hinged	47.50	
	On cover		125.00
	On cover, single franking		200.00
42	A5	1fr claret & ol grn	30.00	19.00
	Never hinged	60.00	
	On cover		150.00
	On cover, single franking		325.00
43	A5	2fr gray vio & yel	62.50	45.00
	Never hinged	125.00	
	On cover		325.00
	On cover, single franking		475.00
44	A5	5fr dk bl & buff	92.50	72.50
	Never hinged	175.00	
	On cover		400.00
	On cover, single franking		625.00
	Nos. 34-44 (11)	263.50	197.60

For surcharges and overprints see Nos. 45, 57-85, J14-J16, J27-J30.

Surcharged in Black

1903

45	A4	5c on 15c pale red	17.50	12.00
	Never hinged	32.50	
	On cover		90.00
a.	Inverted surcharge	125.00	75.00
	Never hinged	250.00	

Stamps of Indo-China, 1904-06, Surcharged as Nos. 18-33 in Black

Two types of overprint on 15c: type I, "China" above Chinese characters (2nd printing); type II, "China" below Chinese characters (1st printing).

1904-05

46	A4	1c olive grn	2.10	2.10
	Never hinged	3.25	
	On cover		70.00
47	A4	2c vio brn, *buff*	2.10	2.10
	Never hinged	3.25	
	On cover		70.00
47A	A4	4c cl, *bluish*	975.00	800.00
	On cover		2,250.
48	A4	5c deep grn	2.10	2.10
	Never hinged	3.25	
	On cover		30.00
49	A4	10c carmine	3.00	3.00
	Never hinged	4.75	
	On cover		40.00
50	A4	15c org brn, *bl* (I)	3.00	3.00
	Never hinged	4.50	
	On cover		50.00
a.	Type II	4.00	2.90
	Never hinged	7.25	
	On cover		55.00
51	A4	20c red, *grn*	11.50	11.00
	Never hinged	19.00	
	On cover		80.00
	On cover, single franking		125.00
52	A4	25c deep blue	10.00	6.00
	Never hinged	17.50	
	On cover		50.00
	On cover, single franking		80.00
53	A4	40c blk, *bluish*	8.50	6.00
	Never hinged	15.00	
	On cover		50.00
	On cover, single franking		80.00
54	A4	1fr pale grn	360.00	300.00
	On cover		1,100.
	On cover, single franking		1,750.
55	A4	2fr brn, *org*	42.50	37.50
	Never hinged	75.00	
	On cover		325.00
	On cover, single franking		750.00
56	A4	10fr org brn, *grn*	165.00	155.00
	Never hinged	300.00	
	On cover		900.00
	On cover, single franking		1,750.
	Nos. 46-56 (12)	1,584.	1,327.

Many varieties of the surcharge exist.

Stamps of 1902-03 Surcharged in Black

1907

57	A3	2c on 5c green	2.50	1.60
	Never hinged	4.00	
	On cover		30.00
a.	Perf 11	160.00	
	Never hinged	260.00	
58	A4	4c on 10c rose red	2.50	1.75
	Never hinged	4.00	
	On cover		30.00
a.	Pair, one without surcharge	—	
b.	Perf 11	160.00	
	Never hinged	260.00	
59	A4	6c on 15c pale red	3.40	2.50
	Never hinged	5.25	
	On cover		40.00
60	A4	8c on 20c brn vio	6.00	6.00
	Never hinged	11.00	
	On cover		80.00
a.	"8" inverted	75.00	75.00
	Never hinged	150.00	
61	A4	10c on 25c blue	2.10	1.25
	Never hinged	3.50	
	On cover		30.00
62	A5	20c on 50c bis brn & lav	6.25	3.75
	Never hinged	12.00	
	On cover		50.00
a.	Double surcharge		
b.	Triple surcharge	440.00	440.00
63	A5	40c on 1fr claret & ol grn	22.00	13.50
	Never hinged	40.00	
	On cover		100.00
64	A5	2pi on 5fr dk bl & buff	23.00	13.50
	Never hinged	40.00	
	On cover		125.00
a.	Double surcharge	2,300.	1,900.
	Nos. 57-64 (8)	67.75	43.85

Stamps of 1902-03 Surcharged in Black

1911-22

65	A3	2c on 5c green	2.10	1.50
		Never hinged	3.50	
		On cover		30.00
66	A4	4c on 10c rose red	2.50	1.75
		Never hinged	4.75	
		On cover		30.00
67	A4	6c on 15c org	5.00	2.10
		Never hinged	8.50	
		On cover		40.00
68	A4	8c on 20c brn vio	2.10	1.80
		Never hinged	3.50	
		On cover		70.00
69	A4	10c on 25c bl ('21)	4.25	2.10
		Never hinged	8.50	
		On cover		30.00
70	A4	20c on 50c bl ('22)	55.00	55.00
		Never hinged	100.00	
		On cover		500.00
71	A5	40c on 1fr cl & ol grn	7.50	6.00
		Never hinged	13.50	
		On cover		80.00

No. 44
Surcharged

73	A5	$2 on 5fr bl & buff ('22)	175.00	200.00
		Never hinged	300.00	
		On cover		850.00
		Nos. 65-73 (8)	253.45	270.25

Types of 1902-03 Surcharged like Nos. 65-71

1922

75	A3	1c on 5c org	6.00	6.75
		Never hinged	10.50	
		On cover		100.00
		On cover, single franking		225.00
76	A4	2c on 10c grn	6.75	7.50
		Never hinged	12.00	
		On cover		110.00
		On cover, single franking		225.00
77	A4	3c on 15c org	9.25	11.00
		Never hinged	16.00	
		On cover		125.00
		On cover, single franking		225.00
78	A4	4c on 20c red brn	11.00	13.50
		Never hinged	20.00	
		On cover		200.00
		On cover, single franking		225.00
79	A4	5c on 25c dk vio	6.00	6.00
		Never hinged	10.50	
		On cover		62.50
		On cover, single franking		225.00
80	A4	6c on 30c red	12.00	11.00
		Never hinged	23.00	
		On cover		100.00
		On cover, single franking		225.00
82	A4	10c on 50c blue	14.50	12.00
		Never hinged	26.00	
		On cover		125.00
		On cover, single franking		225.00
83	A5	20c on 1fr claret & ol grn	35.00	40.00
		Never hinged	700.00	
		On cover		400.00
		On cover, single franking		500.00
84	A5	40c on 2fr org & pale bl	45.00	55.00
		Never hinged	80.00	
		On cover		700.00
		On cover, single franking		800.00
85	A5	$1 on 5fr dk bl & buff	150.00	160.00
		Never hinged	250.00	
		On cover		850.00
		On cover, single franking		—
		Nos. 75-85 (10)	295.50	322.75

POSTAGE DUE STAMPS

Postage Due Stamps of
France Handstamped in
Red or Black

1901-07   Unwmk.   Perf. 14x13½

J1	D2	5c lt bl (R)	7.50	4.25
		Never hinged	16.00	
		On cover		100.00
a.		Double overprint	160.00	
		Never hinged	300.00	
J2	D2	10c choc (R)	11.00	6.00
		Never hinged	21.00	
		On cover		650.00
a.		Double overprint	160.00	
		Never hinged	300.00	
J3	D2	15c lt grn (R)	11.00	7.50
		Never hinged	21.00	
		On cover		250.00
a.		Pair, one stamp without ovpt.	275.00	
b.		Imperf, single	160.00	
J4	D2	20c ol grn (R) ('07)	12.50	11.00
		Never hinged	22.50	
		On cover		650.00
J5	D2	30c carmine	17.00	12.00
		Never hinged	35.00	
		On cover		650.00
a.		Double overprint	160.00	
J6	D2	50c lilac	17.00	12.50
		Never hinged	35.00	
		On cover		650.00
a.		Triple overprint	160.00	

---

b.		Pair, one stamp without over-print	275.00	
		Nos. J1-J6 (6)	76.00	53.25

Stamps of 1894-1900
Handstamped in
Carmine

1903

J7	A15	5c yel grn	—	2,250.
a.		Purple handstamp	—	
b.		5c green, greenish	—	
J8	A15	10c blk, lavender	—	
a.		Purple handstamp	—	
J9	A15	15c blue	2,750.	1,250.
a.		Purple handstamp	—	
J10	A15	30c brn, bister	1,500.	350.00
		On cover		3,250.
a.		Purple handstamp	—	

Same Handstamp on Stamps of 1902-03 in Carmine

1903

J14	A3	5c green	—	2,000.
a.		Purple handstamp	—	
J15	A4	10c rose red	750.	425.00
		On cover		3,500.
a.		Purple handstamp	—	
J16	A4	15c pale red	750.	325.00
a.		Purple handstamp	—	

Stamps of 1894-1900
Handstamped in
Carmine

1903

J20	A1	5c yellow green	—	1,100.
		On cover		3,500.
a.		Purple handstamp	—	
b.		5c green, greenish	—	
J21	A1	10c blk, lavender	—	
a.		Purple handstamp	—	
J22	A1	15c blue	1,250.	350.
a.		Purple handstamp	—	
J23	A1	30c brn, bister	600.	325.
		On cover		3,250.
a.		Purple handstamp	—	

Same Handstamp on Stamps of 1902-03 in Carmine or Purple

1903

J27	A3	5c green (C)	—	1,750.
a.		Purple handstamp	—	
J28	A4	10c rose red (C)	340.	225.
		On cover		3,500.
a.		Purple handstamp	—	
J29	A4	15c pale red (C)	675.	225.
a.		Purple handstamp	—	
J30	A4	30c lilac (P)		

The handstamps on Nos. J7-J30 are found inverted, double, etc.

The cancellations on these stamps should have dates between Sept. 1, and Nov. 30, 1903, to be genuine.

Postage Due Stamps of France, 1893-1910 Surcharged like Nos. 65-71

1911

J33	D2	2c on 5c blue	3.00	2.50
		Never hinged	5.25	
		On cover		625.00
a.		Double surcharge	140.00	—
		Never hinged	240.00	
J34	D2	4c on 10c choc	3.00	2.50
		Never hinged	5.25	
		On cover		625.00
a.		Double surcharge	140.00	
		Never hinged	240.00	
J35	D2	8c on 20c ol grn	3.40	3.00
		Never hinged	6.50	
		On cover		625.00
a.		Double surcharge	140.00	
		Never hinged	240.00	
J36	D2	20c on 50c lilac	3.40	3.00
		Never hinged	6.50	
		On cover		625.00
		Nos. J33-J36 (4)	12.80	11.00

1922

J37	D2	1c on 5c blue	82.50	95.00
		Never hinged	145.00	
J38	D2	2c on 10c brn	145.00	165.00
		Never hinged	250.00	
J39	D2	4c on 20c ol grn	145.00	165.00
		Never hinged	250.00	
J40	D2	10c on 50c brn vio	125.00	185.00
		Never hinged	225.00	
		Nos. J37-J40 (4)	497.50	610.00

CANTON

Stamps of Indo-China,
1892-1900, Overprinted
in Red

1901   Unwmk.   Perf. 14x13½

1	A3	1c blk, lil bl	2.10	2.10
		Never hinged	4.50	
		On cover		100.00
1A	A3	2c brn, buff	2.50	2.50
		Never hinged	5.00	
		On cover		100.00
2	A3	4c claret, lav	4.25	4.25
		Never hinged	8.50	
		On cover		100.00
2A	A3	5c grn, grnsh	600.00	600.00
		Never hinged	1,100.	
		On cover		2,000.
3	A3	5c yel grn	3.40	3.40
		Never hinged	7.25	
		On cover		65.00
4	A3	10c blk, lavender	7.25	7.25
		Never hinged	13.50	
		On cover		85.00
5	A3	15c blue, quadrille paper	6.75	6.75
		Never hinged	14.00	
		On cover		70.00
6	A3	15c gray	7.50	7.50
		Never hinged	16.00	
		On cover		85.00
a.		Double overprint	19.00	
7	A3	20c red, grn	22.50	22.50
		Never hinged	45.00	
		On cover		300.00
		On cover, single franking		600.00
8	A3	25c blk, rose	13.50	13.50
		Never hinged	27.50	
		On cover		160.00
		On cover, single franking		225.00
9	A3	30c brn, bister	32.50	32.50
		Never hinged	65.00	
		On cover		325.00
		On cover, single franking		450.00
10	A3	40c red, straw	32.50	32.50
		Never hinged	65.00	
		On cover		325.00
		On cover, single franking		450.00
11	A3	50c car, rose	35.00	35.00
		Never hinged	75.00	
		On cover		600.00
		On cover, single franking		900.00
12	A3	75c dp vio, org	35.00	35.00
		Never hinged	75.00	
		On cover		600.00
		On cover, single franking		900.00
13	A3	1fr brnz grn, straw	45.00	45.00
		Never hinged	95.00	
		On cover		700.00
		On cover, single franking		1,100.
14	A3	5fr red lil, lav	250.00	250.00
		On cover		1,600.
		On cover, single franking		2,600.
		Nos. 1-14 (16)	1,099.	1,099.

The Chinese characters in the overprint on Nos. 1-14 read "Canton." On Nos. 15-64, they restate the denomination of the basic stamp.

Surcharged in Black

1903-04

15	A3	1c blk, lil bl	4.25	4.25
		Never hinged	8.50	
		On cover		120.00
16	A3	2c brn, buff	4.50	4.25
		Never hinged	9.50	
		On cover		120.00
17	A3	4c claret, lav	4.50	4.25
		Never hinged	9.50	
		On cover		120.00
18	A3	5c yellow green	4.25	4.25
		Never hinged	8.50	
		On cover		85.00
19	A3	10c rose red	4.50	4.25
		Never hinged	9.50	
		On cover		70.00
20	A3	15c gray	4.50	4.25
		Never hinged	9.50	
		On cover		65.00
21	A3	20c red, grn	21.00	17.50
		Never hinged	45.00	
		On cover		225.00
		On cover, single franking		475.00
22	A3	25c blue	7.50	7.50
		Never hinged	16.00	
		On cover		85.00
		On cover, single franking		110.00
23	A3	25c blk, rose ('04)	10.00	8.50
		Never hinged	21.00	
		On cover		85.00
		On cover, single franking		110.00
24	A3	30c brn, bister	27.50	21.00
		Never hinged	57.50	
		On cover		110.00
		On cover, single franking		140.00
25	A3	40c red, straw	67.50	55.00
		Never hinged	140.00	
		On cover		400.00
		On cover, single franking		525.00

26	A3	50c car, rose	340.00	310.00
		On cover		975.00
		On cover, single franking		1,300.
27	A3	50c brn, az ('04)	85.00	72.50
		On cover		525.00
		On cover, single franking		800.00
28	A3	75c dp vio, org	67.50	67.50
		On cover		575.00
		On cover, single franking		900.00
a.		"INDO-CHINE" inverted	55,000.	
29	A3	1fr brnz grn, straw	67.50	67.50
		On cover		625.00
		On cover, single franking		1,100.
30	A3	5fr red lil, lav	67.50	67.50
		On cover		800.00
		On cover, single franking		1,300.
		Nos. 15-30 (16)	787.50	720.00

Many varieties of the surcharge exist on Nos. 15-30.

Stamps of Indo-China,
1892-1906, Surcharged
in Red or Black

A second printing of the 1906 surcharges of Canton, Hoi Hao, Kwangchowan, Mongtseu, Packhoi, Tong King and Yunnan Fou was made in 1908. The inks are grayish instead of full black and vermilion instead of carmine. Values are for the cheaper variety which usually is the second printing.

The 4c and 50c of the 1892 issue of Indo-China are known with this surcharge and similarly surcharged for other cities in China. The surcharges on these two stamps are always inverted. It is stated that they were irregularly produced and never issued.

1906

31	A4	1c ol grn (R)	2.50	2.50
		Never hinged	4.50	
		On cover		50.00
32	A4	2c vio brn, buff	2.50	2.50
		Never hinged	4.50	
		On cover		50.00
33	A4	4c cl, bluish (R)	2.50	2.50
		Never hinged	4.50	
		On cover		50.00
34	A4	5c dp grn (R)	2.10	2.10
		Never hinged	3.50	
		On cover		37.50
35	A4	10c carmine	3.00	3.00
		Never hinged	5.25	
		On cover		37.50
36	A4	15c org brn, bl	22.50	22.50
		Never hinged	50.00	
		On cover		200.00
37	A4	20c red, grn	12.50	12.50
		Never hinged	26.00	
		On cover		210.00
		On cover, single franking		260.00
38	A4	25c deep blue	5.00	5.00
		Never hinged	8.75	
		On cover		65.00
		On cover, single franking		110.00
39	A4	30c pale brn	17.00	17.00
		Never hinged	35.00	
		On cover		240.00
		On cover, single franking		300.00
40	A4	35c blk, yel (R)	12.50	12.50
		Never hinged	26.00	
		On cover		100.00
		On cover, single franking		130.00
41	A4	40c blk, bluish (R)	21.00	21.00
		Never hinged	45.00	
		On cover		325.00
		On cover, single franking		450.00
42	A4	50c bister brn	14.50	14.50
		Never hinged	32.50	
		On cover		200.00
		On cover, single franking		325.00
43	A3	75c dp vio, org (R)	67.50	67.50
		On cover		65.00
		On cover, single franking		800.00
44	A4	1fr pale grn	30.00	30.00
		Never hinged	60.00	
		On cover		650.00
		On cover, single franking		850.00
45	A4	2fr brn, org (R)	42.50	42.50
		Never hinged	87.50	
		On cover		725.00
		On cover, single franking		900.00
46	A3	5fr red lil, lav	92.50	92.50
		On cover		850.00
		On cover, single franking		1,300.
47	A4	10fr org brn, grn	85.00	85.00
		On cover		900.00
		On cover, single franking		2,000.
		Nos. 31-47 (17)	435.10	435.10

Surcharge exists inverted on 1c, 25c & 1fr.

Stamps of Indo-China,
1907, Srchd. in Red or
Blue

Chinese Characters

1908

48	A5	1c ol brn & blk	1.25	1.25
		Never hinged	2.40	
		On cover		32.50

#	Type	Description	Un	Used
49	A5	2c brn & blk	1.25	1.25
		Never hinged	2.40	
		On cover		32.50
50	A5	4c bl & blk	2.50	1.25
		Never hinged	4.50	
		On cover		32.50
51	A5	5c grn & blk	2.50	2.10
		Never hinged	4.50	
		On cover		20.00
52	A5	10c red & blk (Bl)	3.40	2.50
		Never hinged	6.50	
		On cover		20.00
53	A5	15c vio & blk	4.25	3.40
		Never hinged	8.00	
		On cover		20.00
54	A6	20c vio & blk	5.00	5.00
		Never hinged	9.50	
		On cover		22.50
55	A6	25c bl & blk	5.00	4.25
		Never hinged	9.50	
		On cover		32.50
		On cover, single franking		52.50
56	A6	30c brn & blk	8.50	8.50
		Never hinged	16.00	
		On cover		60.00
		On cover, single franking		100.00
57	A6	35c ol grn & blk	8.50	8.50
		Never hinged	16.00	
		On cover		52.50
		On cover, single franking		72.50
58	A6	40c brn & blk	11.00	8.50
		Never hinged	22.50	
		On cover		65.00
		On cover, single franking		110.00
59	A6	50c car & blk (Bl)	11.00	8.50
		Never hinged	22.50	
		On cover		72.50
		On cover, single franking		120.00
60	A7	75c ver & blk (Bl)	11.00	10.00
		Never hinged	22.50	
		On cover		80.00
		On cover, single franking		130.00
61	A8	1fr car & blk (Bl)	18.00	15.00
		Never hinged	35.00	
		On cover		150.00
		On cover, single franking		300.00
62	A9	2fr grn & blk	45.00	37.50
		Never hinged	87.50	
		On cover		175.00
		On cover, single franking		350.00
63	A10	5fr bl & blk	62.50	55.00
		Never hinged	120.00	
		On cover		260.00
		On cover, single franking		525.00
64	A11	10fr pur & blk	92.50	92.50
		Never hinged	175.00	
		On cover		425.00
		On cover, single franking		800.00
		Nos. 48-64 (17)	293.15	265.00

Nos. 48-64 Surcharged with New Values in Cents or Piasters in Black, Red or Blue

1919

#	Type	Description	Un	Used
65	A5	⅖c on 1c	1.25	1.25
		Never hinged	2.40	
		On cover		32.50
66	A5	⅘c on 2c	1.25	1.25
		Never hinged	2.40	
		On cover		32.50
67	A5	1⅘c on 4c (R)	1.25	1.25
		Never hinged	2.40	
		On cover		32.50
68	A5	2c on 5c	1.60	1.60
		Never hinged	3.25	
		On cover		20.00
69	A5	4c on 10c (Bl)	2.10	1.60
		Never hinged	3.50	
		On cover		20.00
a.		Chinese "2" instead of "4"	42.50	42.50
70	A5	6c on 15c	2.50	2.10
		Never hinged	4.50	
		On cover		16.00
71	A6	8c on 20c	4.25	2.10
		Never hinged	7.25	
		On cover		22.50
72	A6	10c on 25c	5.00	1.60
		Never hinged	8.75	
		On cover		27.50
a.		Double surcharge	140.00	140.00
		Never hinged	240.00	
73	A6	12c on 30c	2.10	2.10
		Never hinged	3.50	
		On cover		29.00
74	A6	14c on 35c	2.10	1.60
		Never hinged	3.50	
		On cover		29.00
a.		Closed "4"	10.00	10.00
		Never hinged	17.50	
		On cover		65.00
75	A6	16c on 40c	2.50	1.60
		Never hinged	4.75	
		On cover		45.00
76	A6	20c on 50c (Bl)	2.50	2.10
		Never hinged	4.75	
		On cover		45.00
77	A7	30c on 75c (Bl)	2.50	2.10
		Never hinged	4.75	
		On cover		52.50
a.		Double surcharge	750.00	750.00
78	A8	40c on 1fr (Bl)	12.50	7.50
		Never hinged	22.50	
		On cover		52.50
79	A9	80c on 2fr (R)	19.00	12.00
		Never hinged	32.50	
		On cover		95.00
80	A10	2pi on 5fr (R)	32.50	32.50
		Never hinged	65.00	
		On cover		525.00
81	A11	4pi on 10fr (R)	32.50	32.50
		Never hinged	65.00	
		On cover		600.00
		Nos. 65-81 (17)	127.40	106.75

HOI HAO

Stamps of Indo-China Overprinted in Red

1901   Unwmk.   Perf. 14x13½

#	Type	Description	Un	Used
1	A3	1c blk, lil bl	3.40	3.40
		Never hinged	6.50	
		On cover		120.00
2	A3	2c brn, buff	4.25	4.25
		Never hinged	8.00	
		On cover		120.00
3	A3	4c claret, lav	4.25	4.25
		Never hinged	8.00	
		On cover		120.00
4	A3	5c yel grn	5.00	5.00
		Never hinged	8.75	
		On cover		85.00
5	A3	10c blk, lavender	13.50	12.00
		Never hinged	32.50	
		On cover		100.00
6	A3	15c blue	1,850.	800.00
		On cover		2,000.
7	A3	15c gray	7.50	5.00
		Never hinged	15.00	
		On cover		72.50
8	A3	20c red, grn	32.50	25.00
		Never hinged	75.00	
		On cover		300.00
		On cover, single franking		600.00
9	A3	25c blk, rose	17.00	12.50
		Never hinged	35.00	
		On cover		160.00
		On cover, single franking		225.00
10	A3	30c brn, bister	67.50	67.50
		On cover		650.00
		On cover, single franking		900.00
11	A3	40c red, straw	67.50	67.50
		On cover		650.00
		On cover, single franking		900.00
12	A3	50c car, rose	67.50	67.50
		On cover		800.00
		On cover, single franking		1,200.
13	A3	75c dp vio, org	250.00	225.00
		On cover		1,000.
		On cover, single franking		1,500.
14	A3	1fr brnz grn, straw	800.00	740.00
		On cover		2,750.
		On cover, single franking		4,500.
15	A3	5fr red lil, lav	800.00	675.00
		On cover		2,750.
		On cover, single franking		5,250.
		Nos. 1-15 (15)	3,989.	2,713.

The Chinese characters in the overprint on Nos. 1-15 read "Hoi Hao." On Nos. 16-66, they restate the denomination of the basic stamp.

Surcharged in Black

1903-04

#	Type	Description	Un	Used
16	A3	1c blk, lil bl	2.50	2.50
		Never hinged	4.50	
		On cover		100.00
17	A3	2c brn, buff	2.50	2.50
		Never hinged	4.50	
		On cover		100.00
18	A3	4c claret, lav	4.25	4.25
		Never hinged	7.25	
		On cover		100.00
19	A3	5c yel grn	4.25	4.25
		Never hinged	7.25	
		On cover		80.00
20	A3	10c red	4.25	4.25
		Never hinged	7.25	
		On cover		65.00
21	A3	15c gray	5.00	5.00
		Never hinged	8.75	
		On cover		65.00
22	A3	20c red, grn	7.50	7.50
		Never hinged	15.00	
		On cover		11.00
		On cover, single franking		200.00
23	A3	25c blue	5.00	5.00
		Never hinged	8.75	
		On cover		85.00
		On cover, single franking		110.00
24	A3	25c blk, rose ('04)	8.50	8.50
		Never hinged	16.00	
		On cover		85.00
		On cover, single franking		110.00
25	A3	30c brn, bister	6.75	6.75
		Never hinged	14.00	
		On cover		100.00
		On cover, single franking		140.00
26	A3	40c red, straw	32.50	32.50
		Never hinged	72.50	
		On cover		160.00
		On cover, single franking		240.00
27	A3	50c car, rose	30.00	30.00
		Never hinged	60.00	
		On cover		175.00
		On cover, single franking		275.00
28	A3	50c brn, az ('04)	170.00	170.00
		On cover		725.00
		On cover, single franking		1,050.
29	A3	75c dp vio, org	50.00	50.00
		Never hinged	105.00	
		On cover		600.00
		On cover, single franking		900.00
a.		"INDO-CHINE" inverted	45,000.	

#	Type	Description	Un	Used
30	A3	1fr brnz grn, straw	67.50	67.50
		Never hinged	130.00	
		On cover		650.00
		On cover, single franking		1,100.
01	A3	5fr red lil, lav	225.00	225.00
		On cover		1,100.
		On cover, single franking		1,600.
		Nos. 16-31 (16)	625.50	625.50

Many varieties of the surcharge exist on Nos. 1-31.

Stamps of Indo-China, 1892-1906, Surcharged in Red or Black

1906

#	Type	Description	Un	Used
32	A4	1c ol grn (R)	8.50	8.50
		Never hinged	17.50	
		On cover		130.00
33	A4	2c vio brn, buff	8.50	8.50
		Never hinged	17.50	
		On cover		130.00
34	A4	4c cl, bluish (R)	8.50	8.50
		Never hinged	17.50	
		On cover		130.00
35	A4	5c dp grn (R)	8.50	8.50
		Never hinged	17.50	
		On cover		100.00
36	A4	10c carmine	8.50	8.50
		Never hinged	17.50	
		On cover		100.00
37	A4	15c org brn, bl	32.50	32.50
		Never hinged	75.00	
		On cover		260.00
38	A4	20c red, grn	13.50	13.50
		Never hinged	27.50	
		On cover		200.00
		On cover, single franking		260.00
39	A4	25c deep blue	11.00	11.00
		Never hinged	24.00	
		On cover		150.00
		On cover, single franking		225.00
40	A4	30c pale brn	13.50	13.50
		Never hinged	27.50	
		On cover		240.00
		On cover, single franking		300.00
41	A4	35c blk, yel (R)	21.00	21.00
		Never hinged	45.00	
		On cover		260.00
		On cover, single franking		350.00
42	A4	40c blk, bluish (R)	21.00	21.00
		Never hinged	45.00	
		On cover		325.00
		On cover, single franking		450.00
43	A4	50c gray brn	21.00	21.00
		Never hinged	45.00	
		On cover		350.00
		On cover, single franking		525.00
44	A3	75c dp vio, org (R)	62.50	62.50
		On cover		650.00
		On cover, single franking		800.00
45	A4	1fr pale grn	62.50	62.50
		On cover		650.00
		On cover, single franking		900.00
46	A4	2fr brn, org (R)	62.50	62.50
		On cover		725.00
		On cover, single franking		1,100.
47	A3	5fr red lil, lav	135.00	135.00
		On cover		850.00
		On cover, single franking		1,300.
48	A4	10fr org brn, grn	150.00	150.00
		On cover		900.00
		On cover, single franking		1,500.
		Nos. 32-48 (17)	648.50	648.50

Stamps of Indo-China, 1907, Srchd. in Red or Blue

Chinese Characters

1908

#	Type	Description	Un	Used
49	A5	1c ol brn & blk	1.70	1.70
		Never hinged	3.25	
		On cover		32.50
50	A5	2c brn & blk	1.70	1.70
		Never hinged	3.25	
		On cover		32.50
51	A5	4c bl & blk	1.70	1.70
		Never hinged	5.25	
		On cover		20.00
52	A5	5c grn & blk	3.00	3.00
		Never hinged	5.25	
		On cover		20.00
53	A5	10c red & blk (Bl)	3.00	3.00
		Never hinged	5.25	
		On cover		20.00
54	A5	15c vio & blk	6.75	6.75
		Never hinged	15.00	
		On cover		27.50
55	A6	20c vio & blk	7.50	7.50
		Never hinged	15.00	
		On cover		32.50
56	A6	25c bl & blk	7.50	7.50
		Never hinged	15.00	
		On cover		47.50
		On cover, single franking		65.00
57	A6	30c brn & blk	7.50	7.50
		Never hinged	15.00	
		On cover		65.00
		On cover, single franking		110.00
58	A6	35c ol grn & blk	7.50	7.50
		Never hinged	15.00	
		On cover		60.00
		On cover, single franking		85.00

#	Type	Description	Un	Used
59	A6	40c brn & blk	8.50	8.50
		Never hinged	17.00	
		On cover		65.00
		On cover, single franking		110.00
61	A6	50c car & blk (Bl)	10.00	10.00
		Never hinged	17.50	
		On cover		22.50
		On cover, single franking		130.00
62	A7	75c ver & blk (Bl)	10.00	10.00
		Never hinged	17.50	
		On cover		85.00
		On cover, single franking		140.00
63	A8	1fr car & blk (Bl)	29.00	29.00
		Never hinged	55.00	
		On cover		165.00
		On cover, single franking		325.00
64	A9	2fr grn & blk	42.50	42.50
		Never hinged	75.00	
		On cover		200.00
		On cover, single franking		400.00
65	A10	5fr bl & blk	75.00	75.00
		Never hinged	150.00	
		On cover		300.00
		On cover, single franking		600.00
66	A11	10fr pur & blk	110.00	110.00
		Never hinged	200.00	
		On cover		475.00
		On cover, single franking		850.00
		Nos. 49-66 (17)	332.85	332.85

Nos. 49-66 Surcharged with New Values in Cents or Piasters in Black, Red or Blue

1919

#	Type	Description	Un	Used
67	A5	⅖c on 1c	1.25	1.25
		Never hinged	2.40	
		On cover		32.50
68	A5	⅘c on 2c	1.25	1.25
		Never hinged	2.40	
		On cover		32.50
69	A5	1⅘c on 4c (R)	2.10	2.10
		Never hinged	3.50	
		On cover		32.50
70	A5	2c on 5c	2.50	2.50
		Never hinged	4.50	
		On cover		20.00
71	A5	4c on 10c (Bl)	3.00	3.00
		Never hinged	5.25	
		On cover		16.00
72	A5	6c on 15c	2.50	2.50
		Never hinged	4.50	
		On cover		16.00
73	A6	8c on 20c	4.25	4.25
		Never hinged	8.00	
		On cover		27.50
a.		"S" of "CENTS" omitted	170.00	170.00
		Never hinged	260.00	
74	A6	10c on 25c	6.75	6.75
		Never hinged	13.50	
		On cover		32.50
75	A6	12c on 30c	4.25	4.25
		Never hinged	8.00	
		On cover		40.00
76	A6	14c on 35c	3.40	3.40
		Never hinged	6.50	
		On cover		40.00
a.		Closed "4"	42.50	42.50
		Never hinged	80.00	
77	A6	16c on 40c	4.25	4.25
		Never hinged	8.00	
		On cover		45.00
79	A6	20c on 50c (Bl)	3.40	3.40
		Never hinged	6.50	
		On cover		52.50
80	A7	30c on 75c (Bl)	11.00	11.00
		Never hinged	19.00	
		On cover		100.00
81	A8	40c on 1fr (Bl)	22.00	22.00
		Never hinged	45.00	
		On cover		130.00
82	A9	80c on 2fr (R)	62.50	62.50
		Never hinged	110.00	
		On cover		325.00
83	A10	2pi on 5fr (R)	92.50	92.50
		Never hinged	160.00	
		On cover		675.00
a.		Triple surch. of new value	750.00	750.00
84	A11	4pi on 10fr (R)	225.00	225.00
		Never hinged	425.00	
		On cover		850.00
		Nos. 67-84 (17)	451.90	451.90

KWANGCHOWAN

A Chinese Territory leased to France, 1898 to 1945.

Stamps of Indo-China, 1892-1906, Surcharged in Red or Black

1906   Unwmk.   Perf. 14x13½

#	Type	Description	Un	Used
1	A4	1c ol grn (R)	8.50	8.50
		Never hinged	17.50	
		On cover		110.00
2	A4	2c vio brn, buff	8.50	8.50
		Never hinged	17.50	
		On cover		110.00
3	A4	4c cl, bluish (R)	8.50	8.50
		Never hinged	17.50	
		On cover		110.00
4	A4	5c dp grn (R)	8.50	8.50
		Never hinged	17.50	
		On cover		80.00
5	A4	10c carmine	8.50	8.50
		Never hinged	17.50	
		On cover		80.00

6	A4	15c org brn, *bl*	32.50	32.50
		Never hinged	75.00	
		On cover		275.00
7	A4	20c red, *grn*	13.50	13.50
		Never hinged	27.50	
		On cover		200.00
		On cover, single franking		225.00
8	A4	25c deep blue	11.00	11.00
		Never hinged	24.00	
		On cover		150.00
		On cover, single franking		210.00
9	A4	30c pale brn	13.50	13.50
		Never hinged	27.50	
		On cover		240.00
		On cover, single franking		300.00
10	A4	35c blk, *yel* (R)	21.00	21.00
		Never hinged	45.00	
		On cover		275.00
		On cover, single franking		360.00
11	A4	40c blk, *bluish* (R)	21.00	21.00
		Never hinged	45.00	
		On cover		325.00
		On cover, single franking		450.00
12	A4	50c bister brn	25.00	25.00
		Never hinged	52.50	
		On cover		360.00
		On cover, single franking		525.00
13	A3	75c dp vio, *org* (R)	67.50	67.50
		On cover		650.00
		On cover, single franking		800.00
14	A4	1fr pale grn	42.50	42.50
		On cover		650.00
		On cover, single franking		900.00
15	A4	2fr brn, *org* (R)	55.00	55.00
		On cover		725.00
		On cover, single franking		1,050.
16	A3	5fr red lil, *lav*	225.00	225.00
		On cover		850.00
		On cover, single franking		1,300.
17	A4	10fr org brn, *grn*	275.00	275.00
		On cover		1,000.
		On cover, single franking		2,000.
		Nos. 1-17 (17)	845.00	845.00

Various varieties of the surcharge exist on Nos. 2-10.

Stamps of Indo-China, 1907, Srchd. in Red or Blue

Value in Chinese

1908

18	A5	1c ol brn & blk	1.70	1.70
		Never hinged	3.25	
		On cover		32.50
19	A5	2c brn & blk	1.70	1.70
		Never hinged	3.25	
		On cover		32.50
20	A5	4c bl & blk	1.70	1.70
		Never hinged	3.25	
		On cover		32.50
21	A5	5c grn & blk	1.70	1.70
		Never hinged	3.25	
		On cover		20.00
22	A5	10c red & blk (Bl)	1.70	1.70
		Never hinged	3.25	
		On cover		20.00
23	A5	15c vio & blk	4.25	4.25
		Never hinged	8.00	
		On cover		27.50
24	A6	20c vio & blk	6.75	6.75
		Never hinged	12.00	
		On cover		32.50
25	A6	25c bl & blk	6.75	6.75
		Never hinged	12.00	
		On cover		40.00
		On cover, single franking		65.00
26	A6	30c brn & blk	10.00	10.00
		Never hinged	18.00	
		On cover		65.00
		On cover, single franking		105.00
27	A6	35c ol grn & blk	14.50	14.50
		Never hinged	27.50	
		On cover		80.00
		On cover, single franking		120.00
28	A6	40c brn & blk	14.50	14.50
		Never hinged	27.50	
		On cover		85.00
		On cover, single franking		135.00
30	A6	50c car & blk (Bl)	17.00	17.00
		Never hinged	32.50	
		On cover		90.00
		On cover, single franking		150.00
31	A7	75c ver & blk (Bl)	17.00	17.00
		Never hinged	32.50	
		On cover		105.00
		On cover, single franking		175.00
32	A8	1fr car & blk (Bl)	24.00	24.00
		Never hinged	35.00	
		On cover		130.00
		On cover, single franking		215.00
33	A9	2fr grn & blk	32.50	32.50
		Never hinged	65.00	
		On cover		160.00
		On cover, single franking		240.00
34	A10	5fr bl & blk	75.00	75.00
		Never hinged	140.00	
		On cover		275.00
		On cover, single franking		450.00
35	A11	10fr pur & blk	105.00	105.00
		Never hinged	200.00	
		On cover		360.00
		On cover, single franking		600.00
a.		Double surcharge	1,050.	
b.		Triple surcharge	1,050.	
		Nos. 18-35 (17)	335.75	335.75

The Chinese characters overprinted on Nos. 1 to 35 repeat the denomination of the basic stamp.

Nos. 18-35 Srchd. in Cents or Piasters in Black, Red or Blue

1919

36	A5	²⁄₅c on 1c	1.25	.85
		Never hinged	2.40	
		On cover		27.50
37	A5	⅘c on 2c	1.25	.85
		Never hinged	2.40	
		On cover		27.50
38	A5	1⅗c on 4c (R)	1.25	.85·
		Never hinged	2.40	
		On cover		27.50
39	A5	2c on 5c	2.10	1.25
		Never hinged	3.50	
		On cover		20.00
a.		"2 CENTS" inverted	97.50	
		Never hinged	160.00	
40	A5	4c on 10c (Bl)	3.75	3.40
		Never hinged	7.25	
		On cover		20.00
41	A5	6c on 15c	2.10	2.10
		Never hinged	3.50	
		On cover		20.00
42	A6	8c on 20c	4.25	4.25
		Never hinged	8.00	
		On cover		32.50
43	A6	10c on 25c	14.50	13.50
		Never hinged	26.00	
		On cover		40.00
44	A6	12c on 30c	3.40	3.40
		Never hinged	6.50	
		On cover		47.50
45	A6	14c on 35c	3.40	3.40
		Never hinged	6.50	
		On cover		60.00
a.		Closed "4"	45.00	37.50
		Never hinged	80.00	
46	A6	16c on 40c	2.10	2.10
		Never hinged	3.50	
		On cover		65.00
48	A6	20c on 50c (Bl)	2.10	2.10
		Never hinged	3.50	
		On cover		72.50
49	A7	30c on 75c (Bl)	11.00	11.00
		Never hinged	19.00	
		On cover		85.00
50	A8	40c on 1fr (Bl)	12.00	12.00
		Never hinged	22.50	
		On cover		100.00
a.		"40 CENTS" inverted		
51	A9	80c on 2fr (R)	20.00	20.00
		Never hinged	35.00	
		On cover		110.00
52	A10	2pi on 5fr (R)	175.00	175.00
		Never hinged	350.00	
		On cover		600.00
53	A11	4pi on 10fr (R)	32.50	32.50
		Never hinged	65.00	
		On cover		225.00
		Nos. 36-53 (17)	291.95	288.55

Stamps of Indo-China, 1922-23, Overprinted in Black, Red or Blue

1923

54	A12	¹⁄₁₀c blk & sal (Bl)	.35	.35
		Never hinged	.55	
		On cover		27.50
a.		Accent omitted on "TCHÉOU"	.45	.45
		Never hinged	.80	
55	A12	⅕c dp bl & blk (R)	.35	.35
		Never hinged	.55	
		On cover		27.50
a.		Black overprint	135.00	
		Never hinged	225.00	
b.		Accent omitted on "TCHÉOU"	.45	.45
		Never hinged	.80	
56	A12	⅖c ol brn & blk (R)	.40	.40
		Never hinged	.65	
		On cover		27.50
a.		Accent omitted on "TCHÉOU"	.55	.55
		Never hinged	.90	
57	A12	⅘c brt rose & blk	.60	.60
		Never hinged	.80	
		On cover		17.00
a.		Accent omitted on "TCHÉOU"	.80	.80
		Never hinged	1.40	
58	A12	1c yel brn & blk (Bl)	.60	.60
		Never hinged	.80	
		On cover		12.00
a.		Accent omitted on "TCHÉOU"	.80	.80
		Never hinged	1.40	
59	A12	2c gray grn & blk (R)	.95	.95
		Never hinged	1.60	
		On cover		12.00
a.		Accent omitted on "TCHÉOU"	1.40	1.40
		Never hinged	2.25	
60	A12	3c vio & blk (R)	1.00	1.00
		Never hinged	1.90	
		On cover		8.00
a.		Accent omitted on "TCHÉOU"	1.40	1.40
		Never hinged	2.40	
61	A12	4c org & blk	1.25	1.25
		Never hinged	2.40	
		On cover		8.00
a.		Accent omitted on "TCHÉOU"	1.60	1.60
		Never hinged	3.25	

62	A12	5c car & blk	1.25	1.25
		Never hinged	2.40	
		On cover		8.00
a.		Accent omitted on "TCHÉOU"	1.60	1.60
		Never hinged	3.25	
63	A13	6c dl red & blk	1.25	1.25
		Never hinged	1.90	
		On cover		8.00
a.		Accent omitted on "TCHÉOU"	1.60	1.60
		Never hinged	3.25	
64	A13	7c ol grn & blk	1.70	1.70
		Never hinged	2.75	
		On cover		10.00
a.		Accent omitted on "TCHÉOU"	2.40	2.40
		Never hinged	4.00	
65	A13	8c black (R)	2.50	2.50
		Never hinged	4.00	
		On cover		16.00
a.		Accent omitted on "TCHÉOU"	3.25	3.25
		Never hinged	5.25	
66	A13	9c yel & blk	2.50	2.50
		Never hinged	4.00	
		On cover		16.00
a.		Accent omitted on "TCHÉOU"	3.25	3.25
		Never hinged	5.25	
67	A13	10c bl & blk	2.10	2.10
		Never hinged	3.25	
		On cover		16.00
a.		Accent omitted on "TCHÉOU"	2.75	2.75
		Never hinged	4.75	
68	A13	11c vio & blk	2.10	2.10
		Never hinged	3.25	
		On cover		20.00
a.		Accent omitted on "TCHÉOU"	2.75	2.75
		Never hinged	4.75	
69	A13	12c brn & blk	2.10	2.10
		Never hinged	3.25	
		On cover		24.00
a.		Accent omitted on "TCHÉOU"	2.75	2.75
		Never hinged	4.75	
70	A13	15c org & blk	3.00	3.00
		Never hinged	4.50	
		On cover		29.00
a.		Accent omitted on "TCHÉOU"	4.00	4.00
		Never hinged	6.50	
71	A13	20c bl & blk, *straw* (R)	3.00	3.00
		Never hinged	4.50	
		On cover		32.50
a.		Accent omitted on "TCHÉOU"	4.00	4.00
		Never hinged	6.50	
72	A13	40c ver & blk, *bluish* (Bl)	3.40	3.40
		Never hinged	5.50	
		On cover		40.00
a.		Accent omitted on "TCHÉOU"	4.75	4.75
73	A13	1pi bl grn & blk, *grnsh*	7.50	7.50
		Never hinged	12.00	
		On cover		65.00
a.		Accent omitted on "TCHÉOU"	11.00	11.00
		Never hinged	20.00	
74	A13	2pi vio brn & blk, *pnksh* (Bl)	17.00	17.00
		Never hinged	27.50	
		On cover		85.00
a.		Accent omitted on "TCHÉOU"	24.00	24.00
		Never hinged	40.00	
		Nos. 54-74 (21)	54.90	54.90

Indo-China Stamps of 1927 Overprinted in Black or Red

1927

75	A14	¹⁄₁₀c lt ol grn (R)	.35	.35
		Never hinged	.55	
		On cover		26.00
a.		Accent omitted on "TCHÉOU"	.50	.50
		Never hinged	.85	
76	A14	⅕c yellow	.35	.35
		Never hinged	.55	
		On cover		26.00
a.		Accent omitted on "TCHÉOU"	.50	.50
		Never hinged	.85	
77	A14	⅖c lt blue (R)	.50	.50
		Never hinged	.80	
		On cover		26.00
a.		Accent omitted on "TCHÉOU"	.75	.75
		Never hinged	1.10	
78	A14	⅘c dp brown	.50	.50
		Never hinged	.80	
		On cover		17.50
a.		Accent omitted on "TCHÉOU"	.75	.75
		Never hinged	1.10	
79	A14	1c orange	.85	.85
		Never hinged	1.25	
		On cover		12.00
a.		Accent omitted on "TCHÉOU"	1.20	1.20
		Never hinged	2.40	
80	A14	2c blue grn (R)	1.25	1.25
		Never hinged	2.50	
		On cover		12.00
a.		Accent omitted on "TCHÉOU"	1.60	1.60
		Never hinged	2.75	
81	A14	3c indigo (R)	1.25	1.25
		Never hinged	2.50	
		On cover		8.00
a.		Accent omitted on "TCHÉOU"	1.60	1.60
		Never hinged	3.25	

82	A14	4c lilac rose	1.25	1.25
		Never hinged	2.50	
		On cover		9.00
a.		Accent omitted on "TCHÉOU"	1.60	1.60
		Never hinged	2.75	
83	A14	5c deep violet	1.25	1.25
		Never hinged	2.50	
		On cover		8.00
a.		Accent omitted on "TCHÉOU"	1.60	1.60
		Never hinged	2.75	
84	A15	6c deep red	1.25	1.25
		Never hinged	2.50	
		On cover		8.00
a.		Accent omitted on "TCHÉOU"	1.60	1.60
		Never hinged	2.75	
85	A15	7c lt brown	1.25	1.25
		Never hinged	2.50	
		On cover		11.00
a.		Accent omitted on "TCHÉOU"	1.60	1.60
		Never hinged	2.75	
86	A15	8c gray grn (R)	1.25	1.25
		Never hinged	2.50	
		On cover		16.00
a.		Accent omitted on "TCHÉOU"	1.60	1.60
		Never hinged	2.75	
87	A15	9c red violet	1.70	1.70
		Never hinged	2.75	
		On cover		16.00
a.		Accent omitted on "TCHÉOU"	2.40	2.40
		Never hinged	4.00	
88	A15	10c lt bl (R)	1.70	1.70
		Never hinged	2.75	
		On cover		16.00
a.		Accent omitted on "TCHÉOU"	2.40	2.40
		Never hinged	4.00	
89	A15	11c orange	1.70	1.70
		Never hinged	2.75	
		On cover		20.00
a.		Accent omitted on "TCHÉOU"	2.40	2.40
		Never hinged	4.00	
90	A15	12c myr grn (R)	1.70	1.70
		Never hinged	2.75	
		On cover		24.00
a.		Accent omitted on "TCHÉOU"	2.40	2.40
		Never hinged	4.00	
91	A16	15c dl rose & ol brn	3.00	3.00
		Never hinged	5.25	
		On cover		30.00
92	A16	20c vio & sl (R)	2.50	2.50
		Never hinged	4.50	
		On cover		32.50
93	A17	25c org brn & lil rose	2.50	2.50
		Never hinged	4.50	
		On cover		40.00
94	A17	30c dp bl & ol gray (R)	1.70	1.70
		Never hinged	2.75	
		On cover		47.50
95	A18	40c ver & lt bl	1.70	1.70
		Never hinged	2.75	
		On cover		47.50
96	A18	50c lt grn & sl (R)	2.50	2.50
		Never hinged	4.50	
		On cover		52.50
97	A19	1pi dk bl, blk & yel (R)	4.25	4.25
		Never hinged	7.25	
		On cover		72.50
98	A19	2pi red, dp bl & org (R)	6.00	6.00
		Never hinged	9.50	
		On cover		85.00
a.		Double overprint	160.00	
		Nos. 75-98 (24)	42.25	42.25

Stamps of Indo-China, 1931-41, Overprinted in Black or Red

1937-41   **Perf. 13, 13½**

99	A20	¹⁄₁₀c Prus blue (R)	.25	.25
		Never hinged	.40	
		On cover		20.00
a.		Accent omitted on "TCHÉOU"	.40	.40
		Never hinged	.65	
100	A20	⅕c lake	.25	.25
		Never hinged	.40	
		On cover		20.00
a.		Accent omitted on "TCHÉOU"	.40	.40
		Never hinged	.65	
101	A20	⅖c orange red	.40	.40
		Never hinged	.65	
		On cover		20.00
a.		Accent omitted on "TCHÉOU"	.55	.55
		Never hinged	.85	
102	A20	½c red brown	.35	.35
		Never hinged	.55	
		On cover		20.00
a.		Accent omitted on "TCHÉOU"	.50	.50
		Never hinged	.80	
103	A20	⅘c dk violet	.35	.35
		Never hinged	.55	
		On cover		16.00
a.		Accent omitted on "TCHÉOU"	.50	.50
		Never hinged	.80	
104	A20	1c black brown	.35	.35
		Never hinged	.55	
		On cover		12.00
a.		Accent omitted on "TCHÉOU"	.50	.50
		Never hinged	.80	
105	A20	2c dk green	.35	.35
		Never hinged	.55	
		On cover		11.00
a.		Inverted overprint	140.00	
		Never hinged	225.00	

b.	Accent omitted on "TCHÉOU"		.50	.50
	Never hinged		.80	
106	A21 3c dk green		.75	.75
	Never hinged		1.10	
	On cover			8.00
a.	Accent omitted on "TCHÉOU"		1.10	1.10
	Never hinged		1.75	
107	A21 3c yel brn ('41)		.??	.??
	Never hinged		.55	
	On cover			16.00
a.	Accent omitted on "TCHÉOU"		.50	.50
	Never hinged		.80	
108	A21 4c dk blue (R)		1.00	1.00
	Never hinged		1.60	
	On cover			8.00
a.	Accent omitted on "TCHÉOU"		1.40	1.40
	Never hinged		2.40	
109	A21 4c dk green ('41)		.35	.35
	Never hinged		.55	
	On cover			16.00
a.	Accent omitted on "TCHÉOU"		.50	.50
	Never hinged		.80	
110	A21 4c yel org ('41)		2.75	2.75
	Never hinged		4.50	
	On cover			32.50
a.	Accent omitted on "TCHÉOU"		4.00	3.25
	Never hinged		6.75	
111	A21 5c dp violet		.95	.95
	Never hinged		1.40	
	On cover			8.00
a.	Accent omitted on "TCHÉOU"		1.40	1.40
	Never hinged		2.40	
112	A21 5c dp green ('41)		.50	.50
	Never hinged		.75	
	On cover			13.00
a.	Accent omitted on "TCHÉOU"		.75	.75
	Never hinged		1.00	
113	A21 6c orange red		.65	.65
	Never hinged		.85	
	On cover			8.00
a.	Accent omitted on "TCHÉOU"		.95	.95
	Never hinged		1.40	
114	A21 7c black (R) ('41)		.65	.65
	Never hinged		.85	
	On cover			13.00
a.	Accent omitted on "TCHÉOU"		.95	.95
	Never hinged		1.40	
115	A21 8c rose lake ('41)		.75	.75
	Never hinged		1.10	
	On cover			1.00
	Never hinged		1.50	
116	A21 9c blk, yel (R) ('41)		1.00	1.00
	Never hinged		1.50	
a.	Accent omitted on "TCHÉOU"		2.25	2.25
	Never hinged		3.50	
d.	Black overprint		9.25	9.25
	Never hinged		14.00	
117	A22 10c dk blue (R)		1.10	1.10
	Never hinged		1.75	
	On cover			9.00
a.	Accent omitted on "TCHÉOU"		1.60	1.60
	Never hinged		2.75	
118	A22 10c ultra, pink (R) ('41)		.85	.85
	Never hinged		1.25	
a.	Accent omitted on "TCHÉOU"		1.25	1.25
	Never hinged		1.75	
119	A22 15c dk bl (R)		.75	.75
	Never hinged		1.20	
	On cover			10.50
a.	Accent omitted on "TCHÉOU"		1.10	1.10
	Never hinged		1.75	
120	A22 18c bl (R) ('41)		.65	.65
	Never hinged		.85	
	On cover			20.00
a.	Accent omitted on "TCHÉOU"		.95	.95
	Never hinged		1.40	
121	A22 20c rose		.75	.75
	Never hinged		1.20	
	On cover			10.50
a.	Accent omitted on "TCHÉOU"		1.10	1.10
	Never hinged		1.60	
122	A22 21c olive grn		.75	.75
	Never hinged		1.20	
	On cover			15.00
a.	Accent omitted on "TCHÉOU"		1.10	1.10
	Never hinged		1.75	
123	A22 22c green ('41)		.60	.60
	Never hinged		.80	
a.	Accent omitted on "TCHÉOU"		1.00	1.00
	Never hinged		1.50	
124	A22 25c dp violet		3.00	3.00
	Never hinged		4.75	
	On cover			20.00
a.	Accent omitted on "TCHÉOU"		4.00	4.00
	Never hinged		7.25	
125	A22 25c dk bl (R) ('41)		.85	.85
	Never hinged		1.25	
126	A22 30c orange brn		.85	.85
	Never hinged		1.20	
	On cover			22.50
a.	Accent omitted on "TCHÉOU"		1.20	1.20
	Never hinged		2.00	
127	A23 50c dk brown		1.10	1.10
	Never hinged		1.60	
	On cover			22.50
128	A23 60c dl violet		1.10	1.10
	Never hinged		1.60	
	On cover			29.00
129	A23 70c lt bl ('41)		.85	.85
	Never hinged		1.20	
	On cover			32.50
130	A23 1pi yel green		2.10	2.10
	Never hinged		3.25	
131	A23 2pi red		2.25	2.25
	Never hinged		3.50	
	On cover			47.50
	Nos. 99-131 (33)		29.55	29.55

Common Design Types pictured following the introduction.

Colonial Arts Exhibition Issue
Common Design Type
Souvenir Sheet

			Engr.	Imperf.
1937				
132	CD79 30c grn & sepia		9.25	11.00
	Never hinged		15.00	
	On cover			105.00
	On cover, single franking			160.00

New York World's Fair Issue
Common Design Type

1939	**Unwmk.**		**Perf. 12½x12**	
133	CD82 13c car lake		1.??	1.??
	Never hinged		2.40	
	On cover			60.00
	On cover, single franking			110.00
134	CD82 23c ultra		1.25	1.25
	Never hinged		2.40	
	On cover			60.00
	On cover, single franking			110.00

SEMI-POSTAL STAMPS

French Revolution Issue
Common Design Type

1939	**Unwmk.**	**Photo.**	**Perf. 13**	

Name and Value typo. in Black

B1	CD83 6c + 2c green		9.25	9.25
	Never hinged		15.00	
	On cover			120.00
B2	CD83 7c + 3c brown		9.25	9.25
	Never hinged		15.00	
	On cover			85.00
B3	CD83 9c + 4c red org		9.25	9.25
	Never hinged		15.00	
	On cover			72.50
B4	CD83 13c + 10c rose pink		9.25	9.25
	Never hinged		15.00	
	On cover			120.00
	On cover, single franking			175.00
B5	CD83 23c + 20c blue		9.25	9.25
	Never hinged		15.00	
	On cover			120.00
	On cover, single franking			175.00
	Nos. B1-B5 (5)		46.25	46.25

MONGTSEU (MENGTSZ)

Stamps of Indo-China Surcharged in Black

1903-04	**Unwmk.**		**Perf. 14x13½**	
1	A3 1c blk, lil bl		7.50	7.50
	Never hinged		15.00	
	On cover			130.00
2	A3 2c brn, buff		6.75	6.75
	Never hinged		13.00	
	On cover			130.00
3	A3 4c claret, lav		8.50	8.50
	Never hinged		16.00	
	On cover			130.00
4	A3 5c yel grn		6.00	6.00
	Never hinged		10.50	
	On cover			100.00
5	A3 10c red		9.25	9.25
	Never hinged		17.50	
	On cover			90.00
6	A3 15c gray		10.00	10.00
	Never hinged		19.00	
	On cover			85.00
7	A3 20c red, grn		12.50	12.50
	Never hinged		24.00	
	On cover			160.00
	On cover, single franking			300.00
7C	A3 25c blk, rose		725.00	725.00
	On cover			2,000.
	On cover, single franking			2,750.
8	A3 25c blue		12.50	12.50
	Never hinged		24.00	
	On cover			130.00
	On cover, single franking			175.00
9	A3 30c brn, bister		11.00	11.00
	Never hinged		21.00	
	On cover			150.00
	On cover, single franking			200.00
10	A3 40c red, straw		75.00	75.00
	Never hinged		140.00	
	On cover			525.00
	On cover, single franking			725.00
11	A3 50c car, rose		440.00	440.00
	On cover			1,600.
	On cover, single franking			2,400.
12	A3 50c brn, az ('04)		150.00	150.00
	On cover			600.00
	On cover, single franking			850.00
13	A3 75c dp vio, org		120.00	120.00
	On cover			625.00
	On cover, single franking			900.00
a.	"INDO-CHINE" inverted		67,500.	
14	A3 1fr brnz grn, straw		110.00	110.00
	On cover			725.00
	On cover, single franking			1,100.
15	A3 5fr red lil, lav		110.00	110.00
	On cover			800.00
	On cover, single franking			1,300.
	Nos. 1-15 (16)		1,814.	1,814.

Many surcharge varieties exist on Nos. 1-15.

Stamps of Indo-China, 1892-1906, Surcharged in Red or Black

1906				
16	A4 1c ol grn (R)		5.00	5.00
	Never hinged		9.00	
	On cover			110.00
17	A4 3c ?? brn (R)		5.00	5.00
	Never hinged		9.00	
	On cover, single franking			110.00
18	A4 4c cl, bluish (R)		5.00	5.00
	Never hinged		9.00	
	On cover			110.00
19	A4 5c dp grn (R)		6.00	6.00
	Never hinged		10.50	
	On cover			85.00
20	A4 10c carmine		5.00	5.00
	Never hinged		9.00	
	On cover			85.00
21	A4 15c org brn, bl		35.00	35.00
	Never hinged		75.00	
	On cover			260.00
22	A4 20c red, grn		13.50	13.50
	Never hinged		28.00	
	On cover			200.00
	On cover, single franking			260.00
23	A4 25c deep blue		10.00	10.00
	Never hinged		22.50	
	On cover			150.00
	On cover, single franking			215.00
24	A4 30c pale brn		13.50	13.50
	Never hinged		28.00	
	On cover			240.00
	On cover, single franking			300.00
25	A4 35c blk, yel (R)		12.50	12.50
	Never hinged		28.00	
	On cover			260.00
	On cover, single franking			350.00
26	A4 40c blk, bluish (R)		20.00	20.00
	Never hinged		35.00	
	On cover			325.00
	On cover, single franking			475.00
27	A4 50c bister brn		21.00	21.00
	Never hinged		45.00	
	On cover			350.00
	On cover, single franking			525.00
28	A3 75c dp vio, org (R)		67.50	67.50
	Never hinged		65.00	
	On cover			650.00
	On cover, single franking			800.00
a.	"INDO-CHINE" inverted		67,500.	
29	A4 1fr pale grn		42.50	42.50
	Never hinged		90.00	
	On cover			625.00
	On cover, single franking			900.00
30	A4 2fr brn, org (R)		55.00	55.00
	Never hinged		125.00	
	On cover			825.00
	On cover, single franking			1,050.
31	A3 5fr red lil, lav		140.00	140.00
	On cover			850.00
	On cover, single franking			1,300.
32	A4 10fr org brn, grn		150.00	150.00
	On cover			1,000.
	On cover, single franking			2,000.
a.	Chinese characters inverted		1,750.	2,100.
	Nos. 16-32 (17)		606.50	606.50

Inverted varieties of the surcharge exist on Nos. 19, 22 and 32.

Stamps of Indo-China, 1907, Srchd. in Red or Blue

Value in Chinese

1908				
33	A5 1c ol brn & blk		1.25	1.25
	Never hinged		2.40	
	On cover			32.50
34	A5 2c brn & blk		1.25	1.25
	Never hinged		2.40	
	On cover			32.50
35	A5 4c bl & blk		1.25	1.25
	Never hinged		2.40	
	On cover			32.50
36	A5 5c grn & blk		1.25	1.25
	Never hinged		2.40	
	On cover			20.00
37	A5 10c red & blk (Bl)		3.00	3.00
	Never hinged		5.25	
	On cover			20.00
38	A5 15c vio & blk		3.00	3.00
	Never hinged		5.25	
	On cover			26.00
39	A6 20c vio & blk		6.00	6.00
	Never hinged		10.50	
	On cover			32.50
40	A6 25c bl & blk		15.00	15.00
	Never hinged		27.50	
	On cover			100.00
	On cover, single franking			160.00
41	A6 30c brn & blk		6.75	6.75
	Never hinged		13.50	
	On cover			65.00
	On cover, single franking			110.00
42	A6 35c ol grn & blk		7.50	7.50
	Never hinged		16.00	
	On cover			60.00
	On cover, single franking			87.50
43	A6 40c brn & blk		5.00	5.00
	Never hinged		9.00	
	On cover			65.00
	On cover, single franking			110.00
45	A6 50c car & blk (Bl)		6.75	6.75
	Never hinged		13.50	
	On cover			80.00
	On cover, single franking			130.00
46	A7 75c ver & blk (Bl)		14.50	14.50
	Never hinged		27.50	
	On cover			90.00
	On cover, single franking			160.00
47	A8 1fr car & blk (Bl)		13.50	13.50
	Never hinged		24.00	
	On cover			160.00
	On cover, single franking			325.00

48	A9 2fr grn & blk		19.00	19.00
	Never hinged		32.50	
	On cover			350.00
49	A10 5fr bl & blk		105.00	105.00
	Never hinged		210.00	
	On cover			600.00
50	A11 10fr pur & blk		125.00	125.00
	Never hinged		240.00	
	On cover			725.00
	Nos. 33-50 (17)		335.00	335.00

The Chinese characters overprinted on Nos. 1 to 50 repeat the denomination of the basic stamp.

Nos. 33-50 Srchd. in Cents or Piasters in Black, Red or Blue

1919				
51	A5 ⅖c on 1c		1.70	1.70
	Never hinged		2.40	
	On cover			32.50
52	A5 ⅘c on 2c		1.70	1.70
	Never hinged		2.40	
	On cover			32.50
53	A5 1³⁄₅c on 4c		1.70	1.70
	Never hinged		2.40	
	On cover			32.50
54	A5 2c on 5c		1.70	1.70
	Never hinged		2.40	
	On cover			20.00
55	A5 4c on 10c (Bl)		3.00	3.00
	Never hinged		5.25	
	On cover			16.00
56	A5 6c on 15c		3.00	3.00
	Never hinged		5.25	
	On cover			16.00
57	A6 8c on 20c		6.75	6.75
	Never hinged		12.00	
	On cover			26.00
58	A6 10c on 25c		5.00	5.00
	Never hinged		9.00	
	On cover			40.00
59	A6 12c on 30c		5.00	5.00
	Never hinged		9.00	
	On cover			40.00
60	A6 14c on 35c		3.40	3.40
	Never hinged		35.00	
a.	Closed "4"		21.00	21.00
	Never hinged		8.00	
61	A6 16c on 40c		4.25	4.25
	Never hinged		8.00	
	On cover			47.50
63	A6 20c on 50c (Bl)		5.00	5.00
	Never hinged		9.00	
	On cover			60.00
64	A7 30c on 75c (Bl)		9.25	9.25
	Never hinged		16.00	
	On cover			72.50
65	A8 40c on 1fr (Bl)		10.00	10.00
	Never hinged		17.50	
	On cover			90.00
66	A9 80c on 2fr (R)		10.00	10.00
	Never hinged		17.50	
	On cover			105.00
a.	Triple surch., one inverted		550.00	550.00
67	A10 2pi on 5fr (R)		200.00	200.00
	Never hinged		375.00	
	On cover			650.00
a.	Triple surch., one inverted		625.00	625.00
b.	Double surcharge		925.00	925.00
68	A11 4pi on 10fr (R)		30.00	30.00
	Never hinged		65.00	
	On cover			200.00
	Nos. 51-68 (17)		301.45	301.45

PAKHOI

Stamps of Indo-China Surcharged in Black

1903-04	**Unwmk.**		**Perf. 14x13½**	
1	A3 1c blk, lil bl		6.75	6.75
	Never hinged		12.00	
	On cover			120.00
2	A3 2c brn, buff		6.75	6.75
	Never hinged		12.00	
	On cover			120.00
3	A3 4c claret, lav		6.75	6.75
	Never hinged		12.00	
	On cover			120.00
4	A3 5c yel grn		5.00	5.00
	Never hinged		9.50	
	On cover			85.00
5	A3 10c red		5.00	5.00
	Never hinged		9.50	
	On cover			80.00
6	A3 15c gray		5.00	5.00
	Never hinged		9.50	
	On cover			72.50
7	A3 20c red, grn		11.00	11.00
	Never hinged		20.00	
	On cover			110.00
	On cover, single franking			175.00
8	A3 25c blue		9.25	9.25
	Never hinged		15.00	
	On cover			100.00
	On cover, single franking			120.00

9 A3 25c blk, *rose*('04) 6.75 6.75
  Never hinged 11.00
  On cover 100.00
  On cover, single franking 120.00
10 A3 30c brn, *bister* 8.50 8.50
  Never hinged 15.00
  On cover 120.00
  On cover, single franking 160.00
11 A3 40c red, *straw* 57.50 57.50
  Never hinged 110.00
  On cover 200.00
  On cover, single franking 260.00
12 A3 50c car, *rose* 340.00 340.00
  Never hinged
  On cover 1,100.
  On cover, single franking 1,300.
13 A3 50c brn, *az* ('04) 47.50 47.50
  Never hinged 90.00
  On cover 260.00
  On cover, single franking 450.00
14 A3 75c dp vio, *org* 67.50 67.50
  Never hinged
  On cover 600.00
  On cover, single franking 850.00
  a. "INDO-CHINE" inverted 47,500.
15 A3 1fr brnz grn, *straw* 67.50 67.50
  On cover 650.00
  On cover, single franking 1,100.
16 A3 5fr red lil, *lav* 135.00 135.00
  On cover 800.00
  On cover, single franking 1,300.
  Nos. 1-16 (16) 785.75 785.75

Many varieties of the surcharge exist.

Stamps of Indo-China 1892-1906, Surcharged in Red or Black

1906
17 A4 1c ol grn (R) 8.50 8.50
  Never hinged 17.50
  On cover 130.00
18 A4 2c vio brn, *buff* 8.50 8.50
  Never hinged 17.50
  On cover 130.00
19 A4 4c cl, *bluish* (R) 8.50 8.50
  Never hinged 17.50
  On cover 130.00
20 A4 5c dp grn (R) 8.50 8.50
  Never hinged 17.50
  On cover 100.00
21 A4 10c carmine 8.50 8.50
  Never hinged 17.50
  On cover 100.00
22 A4 15c org brn, *bl* 32.50 32.50
  Never hinged 75.00
  On cover 260.00
23 A4 20c red, *grn* 13.50 13.50
  Never hinged 27.50
  On cover 200.00
  On cover, single franking 260.00
24 A4 25c deep blue 11.00 11.00
  Never hinged 22.50
  On cover 150.00
  On cover, single franking 260.00
25 A4 30c pale brn 13.50 13.50
  Never hinged 27.50
  On cover 250.00
  On cover, single franking 300.00
26 A4 35c blk, *yel* (R) 21.00 21.00
  Never hinged 45.00
  On cover 260.00
  On cover, single franking 360.00
27 A4 40c blk, *bluish*(R) 21.00 21.00
  Never hinged 45.00
  On cover 325.00
  On cover, single franking 475.00
28 A4 50c bister brn 21.00 21.00
  Never hinged 45.00
  On cover 360.00
  On cover, single franking 525.00
29 A3 75c dp vio, *org* (R) 67.50 67.50
30 A4 1fr pale grn 42.50 42.50
31 A4 2fr brn, *org*(R) 55.00 55.00
32 A3 5fr red lil, *lav* 140.00 140.00
33 A4 10fr org brn, *grn* 150.00 150.00
  Nos. 17-33 (17) 631.00 631.00

Various surcharge varieties exist on Nos. 17-24.

Stamps of Indo-China, 1907, Surcharged "PAKHOI" and Value in Chinese in Red or Blue

1908
34 A5 1c ol brn & blk 1.25 1.25
  Never hinged 2.40
  On cover 32.50
35 A5 2c brn & blk 1.25 1.25
  Never hinged 2.40
  On cover 32.50
36 A5 4c bl & blk 1.25 1.25
  Never hinged 2.40
  On cover 32.50
37 A5 5c grn & blk 1.70 1.70
  Never hinged 3.25
  On cover 20.00
38 A5 10c red & blk (Bl) 1.70 1.70
  Never hinged 3.25
  On cover 20.00
39 A5 15c vio & blk 2.10 2.10
  Never hinged 4.00
  On cover 26.00
40 A6 20c vio & blk 2.50 2.50
  Never hinged 4.75
  On cover 32.50
41 A6 25c bl & blk 3.00 3.00
  Never hinged 5.50
  On cover 40.00
  On cover, single franking 65.00

42 A6 30c brn & blk 3.40 3.40
  Never hinged 6.00
  On cover 65.00
  On cover, single franking 105.00
43 A6 35c ol grn & blk 3.40 3.40
  Never hinged 6.00
  On cover 60.00
  On cover, single franking 87.50
44 A6 40c brn & blk 3.40 3.40
  Never hinged 6.00
  On cover 65.00
  On cover, single franking 110.00
46 A6 50c car & blk (Bl) 3.40 3.40
  Never hinged 6.00
  On cover 80.00
  On cover, single franking 130.00
47 A7 75c ver & blk (Bl) 7.25 7.25
  Never hinged 12.00
  On cover 95.00
  On cover, single franking 150.00
48 A8 1fr car & blk (Bl) 7.50 7.50
  Never hinged 15.00
  On cover 160.00
  On cover, single franking 325.00
49 A9 2fr grn & blk 16.00 16.00
  Never hinged 35.00
  On cover 200.00
  On cover, single franking 360.00
50 A10 5fr bl & blk 85.00 85.00
  Never hinged 150.00
  On cover 325.00
  On cover, single franking 525.00
51 A11 10fr pur & blk 150.00 150.00
  Never hinged 275.00
  On cover 450.00
  On cover, single franking 800.00
  Nos. 34-51 (17) 294.10 294.10

The Chinese characters overprinted on Nos. 1 to 51 repeat the denomination of the basic stamps.

Nos. 34-51 Surcharged with New Values in Cents or Piasters in Black, Red or Blue

1919
52 A5 $\frac{2}{5}$c on 1c 1.25 1.25
  Never hinged 2.40
  On cover 32.50
  a. "PAK-HOI" and Chinese double 170.00
  Never hinged 300.00
53 A5 $\frac{4}{5}$c on 2c 1.25 1.25
  Never hinged 2.40
  On cover 32.50
54 A5 1$\frac{3}{5}$c on 4c (R) 1.25 1.25
  Never hinged 2.40
  On cover 32.50
55 A5 2c on 5c 2.50 2.50
  Never hinged 4.50
  On cover 20.00
  a. "S" omitted from "CENTS" 72.50 70.00
  Never hinged 140.00
56 A5 4c on 10c (Bl) 3.40 3.40
  Never hinged 6.50
  On cover 20.00
57 A5 6c on 15c 1.70 1.70
  Never hinged 3.25
  On cover 27.50
58 A6 8c on 20c 3.40 3.40
  Never hinged 6.50
  On cover 27.50
59 A6 10c on 25c 5.00 5.00
  Never hinged 8.50
  On cover 40.00
60 A6 12c on 30c 1.70 1.70
  Never hinged 3.25
  On cover 40.00
  a. "12 CENTS" double 675.00
  Never hinged 350.00
61 A6 14c on 35c 1.25 1.25
  Never hinged 2.40
  On cover 40.00
  a. Closed "4" 14.50 14.50
  Never hinged 26.00
62 A6 16c on 40c 3.00 3.00
  Never hinged 5.25
  On cover 47.50
64 A6 20c on 50c (Bl) 2.10 2.10
  Never hinged 4.00
  On cover 60.00
65 A7 30c on 75c (Bl) 9.25 9.25
  Never hinged 17.50
  On cover 75.00
66 A8 40c on 1fr (Bl) 12.50 12.50
  Never hinged 22.50
  On cover 95.00
67 A9 80c on 2fr (R) 10.00 10.00
  Never hinged 17.50
  On cover 105.00
68 A10 2pi on 5fr (R) 16.00 16.00
  Never hinged 32.50
  On cover 130.00
69 A11 4pi on 10fr (R) 35.00 35.00
  Never hinged 70.00
  On cover 200.00
  Nos. 52-69 (17) 110.55 110.55

TCHONGKING (CHUNGKING)

Stamps of Indo-China Surcharged in Black

1903-04 Unwmk. Perf. 14x13½
1 A3 1c blk, *lil bl* 5.00 5.00
  Never hinged 9.50
  On cover 120.00

2 A3 2c brn, *buff* 5.00 5.00
  Never hinged 9.50
  On cover 120.00
3 A3 4c claret, *lav* 6.00 6.00
  Never hinged 10.50
  On cover 120.00
4 A3 5c yel grn 6.00 6.00
  Never hinged 10.50
  On cover 87.50
5 A3 10c red 6.00 6.00
  Never hinged 10.50
  On cover 80.00
6 A3 15c gray 6.00 6.00
  Never hinged 10.50
  On cover 75.00
7 A3 20c red, *grn* 8.50 8.50
  Never hinged 16.00
  On cover 110.00
  On cover, single franking 180.00
8 A3 25c blue 55.00 55.00
  Never hinged 110.00
  On cover 300.00
  On cover, single franking 400.00
9 A3 25c blk, *rose* ('04) 10.00 10.00
  Never hinged 19.00
  On cover 100.00
  On cover, single franking 120.00
10 A3 30c brn, *bister* 15.00 15.00
  Never hinged 32.50
  On cover 200.00
  On cover, single franking 450.00
11 A3 40c red, *straw* 62.50 62.50
  Never hinged 120.00
  On cover 400.00
  On cover, single franking 525.00
12 A3 50c car, *rose* 225.00 225.00
  On cover 800.00
  On cover, single franking 1,100.
13 A3 50c brn, *az* ('04) 140.00 140.00
  On cover 650.00
  On cover, single franking 900.00
14 A3 75c vio, *org* 45.00 45.00
  Never hinged 95.00
  On cover 525.00
  On cover, single franking 850.00
15 A3 1fr brnz grn, *straw* 60.00 60.00
  On cover 650.00
  On cover, single franking 1,100.
16 A3 5fr red lil, *lav* 105.00 105.00
  On cover 800.00
  On cover, single franking 1,300.
  Nos. 1-16 (16) 760.00 760.00

Many surcharge varieties exist on Nos. 1-14.
Stamps of Indo-China and French China, issued in 1902 with similar overprint, but without Chinese characters, were not officially authorized.

Stamps of Indo-China, 1892-1906, Surcharged in Red or Black

1906
17 A4 1c ol grn (R) 8.50 8.50
  Never hinged 12.50
  On cover 130.00
  a. "T" omitted from "TCH'ONG" 160.00 160.00
18 A4 2c vio brn, *buff* 8.50 8.50
  Never hinged 12.50
  On cover 130.00
  a. "T" omitted from "TCH'ONG" 160.00 160.00
19 A4 4c cl, *bluish* (R) 8.50 8.50
  Never hinged 12.50
  On cover 130.00
  a. "T" omitted from "TCH'ONG" 140.00 140.00
20 A4 5c dp grn (R) 8.50 8.50
  Never hinged 12.50
  On cover 100.00
  a. "T" omitted from "TCH'ONG" 160.00 160.00
21 A4 10c carmine 8.50 8.50
  Never hinged 12.50
  On cover 100.00
  a. "T" omitted from "TCH'ONG" 160.00 160.00
22 A4 15c org brn, *bl* 32.50 32.50
  Never hinged 80.00
  On cover 260.00
  a. "T" omitted from "TCH'ONG" 400.00 400.00
23 A4 20c red, *grn* 13.50 13.50
  Never hinged 27.50
  On cover 200.00
  On cover, single franking 260.00
  a. "T" omitted from "TCH'ONG" 240.00 240.00
24 A4 25c deep blue 11.00 11.00
  Never hinged 24.00
  On cover 150.00
  On cover, single franking 225.00
  a. "T" omitted from "TCH'ONG" 240.00 240.00
25 A4 30c pale brn 13.50 13.50
  Never hinged 27.50
  On cover 250.00
  On cover, single franking 325.00
  a. "T" omitted from "TCH'ONG" 240.00 240.00
26 A4 35c blk, *yellow* (R) 21.00 21.00
  Never hinged 45.00
  On cover 275.00
  On cover, single franking 375.00
  a. "T" omitted from "TCH'ONG" 240.00 240.00
27 A4 40c blk, *bluish* (R) 21.00 21.00
  Never hinged 45.00
  On cover 325.00
  On cover, single franking 475.00
  a. "T" omitted from "TCH'ONG" 240.00 240.00
28 A4 50c bis brn 25.00 25.00
  Never hinged 52.50
  On cover 375.00
  On cover, single franking 525.00
  a. "T" omitted from "TCH'ONG" 275.00 275.00
29 A3 75c dp vio, *org* (R) 67.50 67.50
  On cover 650.00
  On cover, single franking 800.00
  a. "T" omitted from "TCH'ONG" 675.00 675.00
30 A4 1fr pale grn 42.50 42.50
  Never hinged 90.00
  On cover 650.00

  a. "T" omitted from "TCH'ONG" 475.00 475.00
  On cover 900.00
31 A4 2fr brn, *org* (R) 55.00 55.00
  Never hinged 120.00
  On cover 750.00
  a. "T" omitted from "TCH'ONG" 550.00 550.00
32 A3 5fr red lil, *lav* 140.00 140.00
  On cover 850.00
  a. "T" omitted from "TCH'ONG" 1,000. 1,000.
33 A4 10fr org brn, *grn* 150.00 150.00
  On cover 1,300.
  a. "T" omitted from "TCH'ONG" 2,000. 2,000.
  Nos. 17-33 (17) 635.00 635.00

Other surcharge varieties exist. Inverted surcharge on 1c and 2c are of private origin.

Stamps of Indo-China, 1907, Surcharged "TCHONGKING" and Value in Chinese in Red or Blue

1908
34 A5 1c ol brn & blk .85 .85
  Never hinged 1.60
  On cover 32.50
35 A5 2c brn & blk .85 .85
  Never hinged 1.60
  On cover 32.50
36 A5 4c bl & blk 1.25 1.25
  Never hinged 2.40
  On cover 32.50
37 A5 5c grn & blk 2.10 2.10
  Never hinged 3.75
  On cover 20.00
38 A5 10c red & blk (Bl) 2.10 2.10
  Never hinged 3.75
  On cover 20.00
39 A5 15c vio & blk 3.00 3.00
  Never hinged 5.25
  On cover 27.50
40 A6 20c vio & blk 3.00 3.00
  Never hinged 5.25
  On cover 32.50
41 A6 25c bl & blk 5.50 5.50
  Never hinged 11.00
  On cover 47.50
  On cover, single franking 65.00
42 A6 30c brn & blk 3.40 3.40
  Never hinged 6.50
  On cover 65.00
  On cover, single franking 110.00
43 A6 35c ol grn & blk 7.50 7.50
  Never hinged 14.00
  On cover 60.00
  On cover, single franking 85.00
44 A6 40c brn & blk 15.00 15.00
  Never hinged 27.50
  On cover 65.00
  On cover, single franking 110.00
45 A6 50c car & blk (Bl) 12.00 12.00
  Never hinged 20.00
  On cover 80.00
  On cover, single franking 130.00
46 A7 75c ver & blk (Bl) 10.00 10.00
  Never hinged 17.50
  On cover 85.00
  On cover, single franking 140.00
47 A8 1fr car & blk (Bl) 13.50 13.50
  Never hinged 26.00
  On cover 160.00
  On cover, single franking 325.00
48 A9 2fr grn & blk 85.00 85.00
  Never hinged 160.00
  On cover 325.00
  On cover, single franking 525.00
49 A10 5fr bl & blk 37.50 37.50
  Never hinged 72.50
  On cover 240.00
  On cover, single franking 475.00
50 A11 10fr pur & blk 225.00 225.00
  Never hinged 400.00
  On cover 600.00
  On cover, single franking 800.00
  Nos. 34-50 (17) 427.55 427.55

The Chinese characters overprinted on Nos. 1 to 50 repeat the denomination of the basic stamp.

Nos. 34-50 Surcharged with New Values in Cents or Piasters in Black, Red or Blue

1919
51 A5 $\frac{2}{5}$c on 1c 1.25 1.25
  Never hinged 2.40
  On cover 32.50
52 A5 $\frac{4}{5}$c on 2c 1.25 1.25
  Never hinged 2.40
  On cover 32.50
53 A5 1$\frac{3}{5}$c on 4c (R) 1.25 1.25
  Never hinged 2.40
  On cover 32.50
54 A5 2c on 5c 1.70 1.70
  Never hinged 3.25
  On cover 20.00
55 A5 4c on 10c (Bl) 1.25 1.25
  Never hinged 2.40
  On cover 16.00
56 A5 6c on 15c 1.70 1.70
  Never hinged 3.25
  On cover 16.00
57 A6 8c on 20c 3.00 1.25
  Never hinged 5.25
  On cover 27.50
58 A6 10c on 25c 8.50 8.50
  Never hinged 16.00
  On cover 40.00
59 A6 12c on 30c 3.00 1.25
  Never hinged 5.25
  On cover 40.00
60 A6 14c on 35c 2.10 1.70
  Never hinged 3.75
  On cover 40.00
  a. Closed "4" 35.00 35.00
  Never hinged 62.50

61	A6	16c on 40c	2.10	1.70
		Never hinged	5.50	
		On cover		47.50
a.		"16 CENTS" double	125.00	125.00
		Never hinged	225.00	
62	A6	20c on 50c (Bl)	11.00	10.00
		Never hinged	19.00	
63	A7	30c on 75c (Bl)	9.25	6.75
		Never hinged	17.50	
		On cover		75.00
64	A8	40c on 1fr (Bl)	9.25	6.75
		Never hinged	17.50	
		On cover		95.00
65	A9	80c on 2fr (R)	9.25	6.75
		Never hinged	17.50	
		On cover		110.00
66	A10	2pi on 5fr (R)	9.25	9.25
		Never hinged	17.50	
		On cover		120.00
67	A11	4pi on 10fr (R)	17.50	17.50
		Never hinged	32.50	
		On cover		200.00
		Nos. 51-67 (17)	92.60	79.80

YUNNAN FOU

(Formerly Yunnan Sen, later known as Kunming)

Stamps of Indo-China Surcharged in Black

				1903-04 Unwmk. Perf. 14x13½
1	A3	1c blk, *lil bl*	6.75	6.75
		Never hinged	12.00	
		On cover		110.00
2	A3	2c brn, *buff*	6.75	6.75
		Never hinged	12.00	
		On cover		110.00
3	A3	4c claret, *lav*	7.50	7.50
		Never hinged	15.00	
		On cover		110.00
4	A3	5c yel green	6.75	6.75
		Never hinged	12.00	
		On cover		75.00
5	A3	10c red	7.50	7.50
		Never hinged	15.00	
		On cover		65.00
6	A3	15c gray	7.50	7.50
		Never hinged	15.00	
		On cover		65.00
7	A3	20c red, *grn*	12.50	12.50
		Never hinged	24.00	
		On cover		100.00
		On cover, single franking		175.00
8	A3	25c blue	7.50	7.50
		Never hinged	15.00	
		On cover		90.00
		On cover, single franking		120.00
9	A3	30c brn, *bister*	12.50	12.50
		Never hinged	25.00	
		On cover		110.00
		On cover, single franking		160.00
10	A3	40c red, *straw*	75.00	60.00
		On cover		160.00
		On cover, single franking		240.00
11	A3	50c car, *rose*	350.00	350.00
		On cover		900.00
		On cover, single franking		1,200.
12	A3	50c brn, *az* ('04)	180.00	180.00
		On cover		500.00
		On cover, single franking		800.00
13	A3	75c dp vio, *org*	67.50	62.50
		On cover		500.00
		On cover, single franking		1,000.
a.		"INDO-CHINE" inverted	47,500.	
14	A3	1fr brnz grn, *straw*	67.50	62.50
		On cover		600.00
		On cover, single franking		1,000.
15	A3	5fr red lil, *lav*	125.00	125.00
		On cover		650.00
		On cover, single franking		1,200.
		Nos. 1-15 (15)	940.25	915.25

The Chinese characters overprinted on Nos. 1 to 15 repeat the denomination of the basic stamp.
Many varieties of the surcharge exist.

Stamps of Indo-China, 1892-1906, Surcharged in Red or Black

				1906 Unwmk. Perf. 14x13½
17	A4	1c ol grn (R)	5.00	5.00
		Never hinged	9.00	
		On cover		100.00
18	A4	2c vio brn, *buff*	5.00	5.00
		Never hinged	9.00	
		On cover		100.00
19	A4	4c cl, *bluish* (R)	5.00	5.00
		Never hinged	9.00	
		On cover		100.00
20	A4	5c dp grn (R)	5.00	5.00
		Never hinged	9.00	
		On cover		75.00
21	A4	10c carmine	5.00	5.00
		Never hinged	9.00	
		On cover		75.00

22	A4	15c org brn, *bl*	35.00	35.00
		Never hinged	75.00	
		On cover		240.00
23	A4	20c red, *grn*	13.50	13.50
		Never hinged	27.50	
		On cover		160.00
		On cover, single franking		240.00
24	A4	25c deep blue	11.00	11.00
		Never hinged	24.00	
		On cover		130.00
		On cover, single franking		200.00
25	A4	30c pale brn	13.50	13.50
		Never hinged	27.50	
		On cover		200.00
		On cover, single franking		275.00
26	A4	35c blk, *yel* (R)	17.00	17.00
		Never hinged	35.00	
		On cover		240.00
		On cover, single franking		325.00
27	A4	40c blk, *bluish* (R)	17.00	17.00
		Never hinged	35.00	
		On cover		300.00
		On cover, single franking		400.00
28	A4	50c bister brn	21.00	21.00
		Never hinged	45.00	
		On cover		325.00
		On cover, single franking		475.00
29	A3	75c dp vio, *org* (R)	67.50	67.50
		On cover		525.00
		On cover, single franking		750.00
30	A4	1fr pale grn	42.50	42.50
		On cover		525.00
		On cover, single franking		800.00
31	A4	2fr brn, *org* (R)	55.00	55.00
		On cover		600.00
		On cover, single franking		900.00
32	A3	5fr red lil, *lav*	140.00	140.00
		On cover		1,200.
33	A4	10fr org brn, *grn*	150.00	150.00
		On cover		875.00
		On cover, single franking		1,800.
		Nos. 17-33 (17)	608.00	608.00

Various varieties of the surcharge exist on Nos. 18, 20, 21 and 27.

Stamps of Indo-China, 1907, Surcharged "YUNNANFOU," and Value in Chinese in Red or Blue

				1908
34	A5	1c ol brn & blk	1.25	1.25
		Never hinged	2.40	
		On cover		32.50
35	A5	2c brn & blk	1.25	1.25
		Never hinged	2.40	
		On cover		32.50
36	A5	4c bl & blk	2.10	2.10
		Never hinged	4.00	
		On cover		32.50
37	A5	5c grn & blk	3.00	3.00
		Never hinged	5.25	
		On cover		20.00
38	A5	10c red & blk (Bl)	3.00	3.00
		Never hinged	5.25	
		On cover		20.00
39	A5	15c vio & blk	6.75	6.75
		Never hinged	12.00	
		On cover		22.50
40	A6	20c vio & blk	6.25	6.25
		Never hinged	11.00	
		On cover		32.50
41	A6	25c bl & blk	9.25	9.25
		Never hinged	17.50	
		On cover		40.00
		On cover, single franking		65.00
42	A6	30c brn & blk	7.50	7.50
		Never hinged	15.00	
		On cover		65.00
		On cover, single franking		110.00
43	A6	35c ol grn & blk	7.50	7.50
		Never hinged	15.00	
		On cover		55.00
		On cover, single franking		80.00
44	A6	40c brn & blk	8.50	8.50
		Never hinged	16.00	
		On cover		60.00
		On cover, single franking		110.00
45	A6	50c car & blk (Bl)	9.25	9.25
		Never hinged	17.50	
		On cover		65.00
		On cover, single franking		120.00
46	A7	75c ver & blk (Bl)	11.00	11.00
		Never hinged	22.50	
		On cover		80.00
		On cover, single franking		130.00
47	A8	1fr car & blk (Bl)	17.00	17.00
		Never hinged	32.50	
		On cover		130.00
		On cover, single franking		250.00
48	A9	2fr grn & blk	29.00	29.00
		Never hinged	47.50	
		On cover		160.00
		On cover, single franking		325.00
a.		"YUNANNFOU"	2,500.	2,500.
b.		Pair, #48, #48a	3,000.	
49	A10	5fr bl & blk	60.00	60.00
		Never hinged	110.00	
		On cover		250.00
		On cover, single franking		400.00
a.		"YUNANNFOU"	2,500.	2,500.
b.		Pair, #49, #49a	3,000.	
50	A11	10fr pur & blk	120.00	120.00
		Never hinged	200.00	
		On cover		400.00
		On cover, single franking		650.00
a.		"YUNANNFOU"	2,500.	2,500.
b.		Pair, #50, #50a	3,000.	
		Nos. 34-50 (17)	302.60	302.60

The Chinese characters overprinted on Nos. 17-50 repeat the denomination of the basic stamp.

Nos. 34-50 Surcharged with New Values in Cents or Piasters in Black, Red or Blue

				1910
51	A5	½c on 1c	1.25	1.25
		Never hinged	2.40	
		On cover		32.50
a.		New value double	140.00	
		Never hinged	350.00	
52	A5	½c on 2c	1.25	1.25
		Never hinged	2.40	
		On cover		32.50
53	A5	1½c on 4c (R)	1.25	1.25
		Never hinged	2.40	
		On cover		32.50
54	A5	2c on 5c	2.10	2.10
		Never hinged	3.50	
		On cover		20.00
a.		Triple surcharge	210.00	
55	A5	4c on 10c (Bl)	1.70	1.70
		Never hinged	3.25	
		On cover		20.00
56	A5	6c on 15c	3.00	3.00
		Never hinged	5.25	
		On cover		20.00
57	A6	8c on 20c	2.10	2.10
		Never hinged	3.50	
		On cover		27.50
58	A6	10c on 25c	3.75	3.75
		Never hinged	7.25	
		On cover		40.00
59	A6	12c on 30c	9.25	9.25
		Never hinged	27.50	
		On cover		47.50
60	A6	14c on 35c	14.50	14.50
		Never hinged	40.00	
		On cover		60.00
a.		Closed "4"	140.00	140.00
		Never hinged	240.00	
61	A6	16c on 40c	9.25	9.25
		Never hinged	17.50	
		On cover		65.00
62	A6	20c on 50c (Bl)	3.00	3.00
		Never hinged	5.25	
		On cover		65.00
63	A7	30c on 75c (Bl)	9.25	9.25
		Never hinged	17.50	
		On cover		65.00
64	A8	40c on 1fr (Bl)	35.00	35.00
		Never hinged	72.50	
		On cover		130.00
65	A9	80c on 2fr (R)	14.50	14.50
		Never hinged	27.50	
		On cover		90.00
a.		Triple surch., one inverted	250.00	
66	A10	2pi on 5fr (R)	67.50	67.50
		Never hinged	130.00	
		On cover		250.00
67	A11	4pi on 10fr (R)	35.00	35.00
		Never hinged	72.50	
		On cover		190.00
		Nos. 51-67 (17)	213.65	213.65

OFFICES IN CRETE

Austria, France, Italy and Great Britain maintained their own post offices in Crete during the period when that country was an autonomous state.

100 Centimes = 1 Franc

Liberty, Equality and Fraternity A1

"Rights of Man" A2

Liberty and Peace (Symbolized by Olive Branch) — A3

				Perf. 14x13½
				1902-03 Unwmk. Typo.
1	A1	1c dark gray	2.50	2.50
		Never hinged	4.50	
		On cover		100.00
a.		A1 1c light gray	2.50	2.50
		Never hinged	4.50	
		On cover		100.00
2	A1	2c violet brown	2.50	2.50
		Never hinged	4.50	
		On cover		100.00
3	A1	3c red orange	2.50	2.50
		Never hinged	4.50	
		On cover		100.00
4	A1	4c yellow brown	2.50	2.50
		Never hinged	4.50	
		On cover		100.00
5	A1	5c green	2.50	2.50
		Never hinged	4.50	
		On cover		65.00
6	A2	10c rose red	3.00	2.50
		Never hinged	5.25	
		On cover		65.00
7	A2	15c pale red ('03)	4.25	3.00
		Never hinged	7.25	
		On cover		65.00

8	A2	20c brown vio ('03)	5.00	3.75
		Never hinged	8.00	
		On cover		100.00
		On cover, single franking		175.00
9	A2	25c blue ('03)	6.75	4.25
		Never hinged	11.00	
		On cover		80.00
		On cover, single franking		110.00
10	A2	30c lilac ('03)	6.25	4.25
		Never hinged	10.00	
		On cover		80.00
		On cover, single franking		100.00
11	A3	40c red & pale bl	12.50	11.00
		Never hinged	19.00	
		On cover		90.00
		On cover, single franking		110.00
12	A3	50c bis brn & lav	17.00	12.50
		Never hinged	27.50	
		On cover		150.00
		On cover, single franking		240.00
13	A3	1fr claret & ol grn	24.00	22.00
		Never hinged	35.00	
		On cover		275.00
		On cover, single franking		475.00
14	A3	2fr gray vio & yel	37.50	35.00
		Never hinged	65.00	
		On cover		525.00
		On cover, single franking		625.00
15	A3	5fr dk blue & buff	62.50	55.00
		Never hinged	100.00	
		On cover		600.00
		On cover, single franking		875.00
		Nos. 1-15 (15)	191.25	165.75

A4   A5

				1903 Black Surcharge
16	A4	1pi on 25c blue	55.00	45.00
		Never hinged	92.50	
		On cover		275.00
		On cover, single franking		400.00
a.		Ovptd. "PIASRTE"	225.00	225.00
17	A5	2pi on 50c bis brn & lav	72.50	55.00
		Never hinged	120.00	
		On cover		300.00
		On cover, single franking		475.00
18	A5	4pi on 1fr claret & ol grn	110.00	97.50
		Never hinged	160.00	
		On cover		475.00
		On cover, single franking		725.00
19	A5	8pi on 2fr gray vio & yel	135.00	135.00
		Never hinged	225.00	
		On cover		525.00
		On cover, single franking		875.00
20	A5	20pi on 5fr dk bl & buff	225.00	215.00
		On cover		875.00
		On cover, single franking		1,300.
		Nos. 16-20 (5)	597.50	547.50

OFFICES IN EGYPT

French post offices formerly maintained in Alexandria and Port Said.

100 Centimes = 1 Franc

ALEXANDRIA

Stamps of France Ovptd. in Red, Blue or Black

				1899-1900 Unwmk. Perf. 14x13½
1	A15	1c blk, *lil bl* (R)	2.10	2.10
		On cover	4.00	
		On cover		65.00
a.		Double overprint	150.00	
b.		Triple overprint	180.00	
2	A15	2c brn, *buff* (Bl)	3.25	2.50
		Never hinged	6.00	
		On cover		65.00
3	A15	3c gray, *grysh* (Bl)	3.25	2.50
		Never hinged	6.00	
		On cover		65.00
4	A15	4c cl, *lav* (Bl)	4.25	3.25
		Never hinged	7.25	
		On cover		65.00
5	A15	5c yel grn, (I) (R)	6.00	3.25
		Never hinged	11.50	
		On commercial cover		65.00
a.		Type II (R)	160.00	97.50
		Never hinged	325.00	
		On cover		525.00
6	A15	10c blk, *lav,* (I) (R)	9.25	7.50
		Never hinged	20.00	
		On cover		47.50
		On cover		75.00
a.		Type II (R)	62.50	37.50
		Never hinged	140.00	
		On cover		275.00
7	A15	15c blue (R)	9.25	4.25
		Never hinged	17.00	
		On cover		20.00
		On commercial cover		75.00

8	A15	20c red, *grn*	14.50	7.50
		Never hinged	27.50	
		On cover		55.00
		On cover, single franking		100.00
9	A15	25c blk, *rose* (R)	7.50	4.25
		Never hinged	14.00	
		On cover		32.50
		On cover, single franking		50.00
		On commercial cover		75.00
a.		Inverted overprint	97.50	
b.		Double ovpt., one invtd.	160.00	
10	A15	30c brn, *bis*	15.00	12.00
		Never hinged	29.00	
		On cover		50.00
		On cover, single franking		75.00
11	A15	40c red, *straw*	13.50	13.50
		Never hinged	26.00	
		On cover		55.00
		On cover, single franking		75.00
12	A15	50c car, *rose* (II)	35.00	17.50
		Never hinged	70.00	
		On cover		90.00
		On cover, single franking		120.00
a.		Type I	150.00	27.50
		Never hinged	325.00	
		On cover		110.00
		On cover, single franking		150.00
13	A15	1fr brnz grn, *straw*	32.50	22.50
		Never hinged	67.50	
		On cover		110.00
		On cover, single franking		220.00
		On commercial cover		750.00
14	A15	2fr brn, *az* ('00)	82.50	80.00
		Never hinged	175.00	
		On cover		325.00
		On cover, single franking		525.00
15	A15	5fr red lil, *lav*	120.00	110.00
		Never hinged	250.00	
		On cover		400.00
		On cover, single franking		650.00
		Nos. 1-15 (15)	357.85	292.60

Covers: Values for commercial covers are for covers with correct postage rates. Postcards sell for somewhat less than covers.

A2   A3

A4

1902-13

16	A2	1c pale gray	.80	.65
		Never hinged	1.40	
		On cover		45.00
a.		1c gray ('13)	.80	.80
		Never hinged	1.60	
		On cover		45.00
b.		1c slate ('20)	1.60	1.20
		Never hinged	2.75	
		On cover		52.50
c.		Grayish paper (GC) ('18)	1.20	.80
		Never hinged	2.00	
		On cover		52.50
17	A2	2c violet brn	.75	.75
		Never hinged	1.40	
		On cover		50.00
18	A2	3c red orange	.75	.75
		Never hinged	1.40	
		On cover		50.00
19	A2	4c yellow brn	1.00	.85
		Never hinged	1.75	
		On cover		52.50
20	A2	5c green	5.00	4.25
		Never hinged	8.75	
		On cover		13.00
		On commercial cover		40.00
21	A3	10c rose red	1.50	.75
		Never hinged	2.75	
		On cover		10.00
		On commercial cover		40.00
22	A3	15c orange ('13)	1.75	1.25
		Never hinged	3.25	
		On cover		13.00
		On commercial cover		35.00
a.		15c pale red ('03)	4.75	1.60
		Never hinged	8.00	
		On cover		16.00
		On commercial cover		37.50
23	A3	20c brn vio ('03)	3.00	1.50
		Never hinged	5.25	
		On cover		20.00
		On cover, single franking		26.00
		On commercial cover		52.50
24	A3	25c blue ('03)	1.75	.75
		Never hinged	3.25	
		On cover		16.00
		On cover, single franking		26.00
		On commercial cover		35.00
a.		25c dark blue	1.50	.50
		On cover		16.00
		On commercial cover		52.50
25	A3	30c violet ('03)	7.50	4.25
		Never hinged	15.00	
		On cover		16.00
		On cover, single franking		21.00
a.		30c lilac ('13)	11.00	6.75
		Never hinged	19.00	
		On cover		16.00
		On cover, single franking		20.00
b.		Grayish paper (GC) ('18)	9.50	5.25
		Never hinged	17.00	
		On cover		20.00
26	A4	40c red & pale bl	5.00	2.50
		Never hinged	8.75	
		On cover		20.00
		On cover, single franking		27.50

27	A4	50c bis brn & lav	11.00	3.00
		Never hinged	22.50	
		On cover		27.50
		On cover, single franking		50.00
a.		Grayish paper (GC)	13.00	4.50
		Never hinged	25.00	
		On cover		27.50
28	A4	1fr cl & ol grn	10.00	4.25
		Never hinged	19.00	
		On cover		40.00
		On cover, single franking		100.00
29	A4	2fr gray vio & yel	24.00	12.00
a.		2fr deep violet & yellow	—	—
30	A4	5fr dk bl & buff	29.00	17.00
		Never hinged	62.50	
		On cover		85.00
		On cover, single franking		175.00
		Nos. 16-30 (15)	102.80	54.50

The 2c, 5c, 10c, 20c and 25c exist imperf. Value, each: $55 unused, $100 never hinged. See Nos. 77-86. For surcharges see Nos. 31-73, B1-B4.

Covers: Values for commercial covers are for covers with correct postage rates. Postcards sell for somewhat less than covers.

Stamps of 1902-03 Surcharged Locally in Black

1921

31	A2	2m on 5c green	7.50	5.00
		Never hinged	14.00	
		On cover		65.00
32	A2	3m on 3c red org	14.50	12.00
		Never hinged	26.00	
		On cover		65.00
a.		Larger numeral	140.00	125.00
		Never hinged	250.00	
		On cover		525.00
33	A3	4m on 10c rose	6.75	6.00
		Never hinged	11.00	
		On cover		65.00
34	A2	5m on 1c gray	14.50	12.00
		Never hinged	26.00	
		On cover		95.00
a.		On #16b (GC)	62.50	130.00
35	A2	5m on 4c yel brn	19.00	13.50
		Never hinged	35.00	
		On cover		110.00
36	A3	6m on 15c orange	6.75	6.00
		Never hinged	11.50	
		On cover		52.50
a.		Larger numeral	110.00	110.00
		Never hinged	210.00	
		On cover		475.00
37	A3	8m on 20c brn vio	7.50	6.00
		Never hinged	14.00	
		On cover		65.00
a.		Larger numeral	80.00	60.00
		Never hinged	140.00	
		On cover		275.00
38	A3	10m on 25c blue	4.25	4.25
		Never hinged	6.25	
		On cover		27.50
a.		Inverted surcharge	45.00	45.00
		Never hinged	80.00	
b.		Double surcharge	45.00	45.00
		Never hinged	80.00	
39	A3	12m on 30c vio	17.50	17.50
		Never hinged	32.50	
		On cover		120.00
a.		Grayish paper (GC)	21.00	22.50
		Never hinged	35.00	
40	A2	15m on 2c vio brn	14.50	14.50
		Never hinged	26.00	
		On cover		110.00

Nos. 26-30 Surcharged

41	A4	15m on 40c	25.00	19.00
		Never hinged	40.00	
		On cover		130.00
42	A4	15m on 50c (#27a)	12.00	12.00
		Never hinged	22.50	
		On cover		100.00
a.		White paper (#29)	37.50	40.00
		Never hinged	70.00	
43	A4	30m on 1fr	175.00	175.00
		Never hinged	290.00	
		On cover		800.00
44	A4	60m on 2fr	250.00	250.00
		On cover		1,200.
a.		Larger numeral	1,050.	1,050.
		On cover		2,600.
45	A4	150m on 5fr	350.00	350.00
		On cover		1,450.

Port Said Nos. 20 and 19 Surcharged like Nos. 32 and 40

45A	A2	3m on 3c red org	150.00	150.00
		Never hinged	240.00	
46	A2	15m on 2c vio brn	150.00	150.00
		Never hinged	260.00	
		Nos. 31-46 (17)	1,224.	1,202.

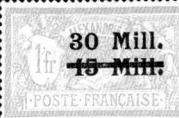

Alexandria No. 28 Srchd.

1921

46A	A4	30m on 15m on 1fr	1,200.	*1,350.*

The surcharge "15 Mill." was made in error and is canceled by a bar.

The surcharges were lithographed on Nos. 31, 33, 38, 39 and 42 and typographed on the other stamps of the 1921 issue. Nos. 34, 36 and 37 were surcharged by both methods.

Alexandria Stamps of 1902-03 Surcharged in Paris

1921-23

47	A2	1m on 1c slate	3.25	2.50
		Never hinged	5.25	
		On cover		40.00
48	A2	2m on 5c green	2.25	1.90
		Never hinged	5.50	
		On cover		40.00
49	A3	4m on 10c rose	2.75	2.50
		Never hinged	4.50	
		On cover		32.50
50	A3	4m on 10c green ('23)	2.50	2.50
		Never hinged	4.75	
		On cover		32.50
51	A2	5m on 3c red org ('23)	6.75	5.00
		Never hinged	10.50	
		On cover		52.50
52	A3	6m on 15c orange	2.25	1.90
		Never hinged	3.50	
		On cover		27.50
53	A3	8m on 20c brn vio	2.25	1.25
		Never hinged	3.50	
		On cover		24.00
54	A3	10m on 25c blue	1.40	1.25
		Never hinged	2.40	
		On cover		20.00
55	A3	10m on 30c vio	4.25	3.25
		Never hinged	6.50	
		On cover		32.50
56	A3	15m on 50c bl ('23)	3.25	3.00
		Never hinged	5.25	
		On cover		32.50

Nos. 27-30 and Type of 1902 Surcharged

57	A4	15m on 50c	5.00	3.25
		Never hinged	7.50	
		On cover		32.50
a.		Grayish paper (GC)	6.50	5.50
		Never hinged	11.50	
		On cover		47.50
58	A4	30m on 1fr	4.25	3.00
		Never hinged	6.75	
		On cover		40.00
59	A4	60m on 2fr	2,250.	*2,400.*
60	A4	60m on 2fr org & pale bl ('23)	13.50	13.00
		Never hinged	21.00	
		On cover		52.50
61	A4	150m on 5fr	13.50	8.50
		Never hinged	21.00	
		On cover		62.50
		Nos. 47-58,60-61 (14)	67.15	52.80

Stamps and Types of 1902-03 Surcharged with New Values and Bars in Black

1925

62	A2	1m on 1c slate	1.25	1.25
		Never hinged	2.40	
		On cover		47.50
63	A2	2m on 5c orange	1.25	1.25
		Never hinged	2.40	
		On cover		47.50
64	A2	2m on 5c green	1.75	1.75
		Never hinged	2.00	
		On cover		40.00
65	A3	4m on 10c green	1.10	.85
		Never hinged	2.00	
		On cover		40.00
66	A2	5m on 3c red org	1.50	1.25
		Never hinged	2.75	
		On cover		32.50
67	A3	6m on 15c orange	1.40	1.25
		Never hinged	2.00	
		On cover		32.50
68	A3	8m on 20c brn vio	1.75	1.40
		Never hinged	2.75	
		On cover		32.50
69	A3	10m on 25c blue	1.10	1.00
		Never hinged	2.00	
		On cover		27.50
70	A3	15m on 50c blue	2.40	1.40
		Never hinged	3.50	
		On cover		27.50

71	A4	30m on 1fr cl & ol grn	3.50	2.90
		Never hinged	6.50	
		On cover		32.50
72	A4	60m on 2fr org & pale bl	4.25	3.50
		Never hinged	7.50	
		On cover		47.50
73	A4	150m on 5fr dk bl & buff	6.00	5.00
		Never hinged	9.50	
		On cover		52.50
		Nos. 62-73 (12)	27.25	22.80

Types of 1902-03 Issue

1927-28

77	A2	3m orange ('28)	2.50	2.10
		Never hinged	3.50	
		On cover		47.50
81	A3	15m slate blue	2.50	2.10
		Never hinged	3.50	
		On cover		27.50
82	A3	20m rose lil ('28)	6.75	5.00
		Never hinged	11.50	
		On cover		40.00
84	A4	50m org & blue	11.00	9.35
		Never hinged	19.00	
		On cover		52.50
85	A4	100m sl bl & buff	15.00	12.00
		Never hinged	25.00	
		On cover		65.00
86	A4	250m gray grn & red	25.00	16.00
		Never hinged	45.00	
		On cover		90.00
		Nos. 77-86 (6)	62.75	46.55

SEMI-POSTAL STAMPS

Regular Issue of 1902-03 Surcharged in Carmine

1915		**Unwmk.**	***Perf. 14x13½***	
B1	A3	10c + 5c rose	1.25	1.25
		Never hinged	2.25	
		On cover		15.00

Sinking Fund Issue

Type of 1902-03 Issue Surcharged in Blue or Black

1927-30				
B2	A3	15m + 5m deep org	6.00	6.00
		Never hinged	10.50	
		On cover		52.50
B3	A3	15m + 5m red vio ('28)	9.25	9.25
		Never hinged	16.00	
		On cover		65.00
a.		15m + 5m violet ('30)	15.00	15.00
		Never hinged	25.00	
		On cover		90.00

Type of 1902-03 Issue Surcharged as in 1927-28

1929				
B4	A3	15m + 5m fawn	12.00	12.00
		Never hinged	19.00	
		On cover		75.00

POSTAGE DUE STAMPS

Postage Due Stamps of France, 1893-1920, Surcharged in Paris in Black

1922		**Unwmk.**	***Perf. 14x13½***	
J1	D2	2m on 5c blue	2.50	2.50
		Never hinged	4.50	
		On cover		52.50
J2	D2	4m on 10c brown	2.50	2.50
		Never hinged	4.50	
		On cover		52.50
J3	D2	10m on 30c rose red	3.00	3.00
		Never hinged	5.50	
		On cover		52.50
J4	D2	15m on 50c brn vio	3.25	3.25
		Never hinged	6.50	
		On cover		60.00
J5	D2	30m on 1fr red brn, *straw*	4.50	4.50
		Never hinged	8.00	
		On cover		75.00
		Nos. J1-J5 (5)	15.75	15.75

D3

1928   Typo.

J6	D3	1m slate	1.60	1.60
	Never hinged		2.75	
	On cover			47.50
J7	D3	2m light blue	1.25	1.25
	Never hinged		2.40	
	On cover			47.50
J8	D3	4m lilac rose	1.75	1.75
	Never hinged		3.25	
	On cover			32.50
J9	D3	5m gray green	2.00	2.00
	Never hinged		4.00	
	On cover			27.50
J10	D3	10m light red	2.50	2.50
	Never hinged		4.00	
	On cover			27.50
J11	D3	20m violet brn	2.25	2.25
	Never hinged		3.00	
	On cover			27.50
J12	D3	30m green	5.00	5.00
	Never hinged		7.50	
	On cover			47.50
J13	D3	40m lt violet	6.25	6.25
	Never hinged		9.50	
	On cover			65.00
	Nos. J6-J13 (8)		22.60	22.60

Nos. J6-J13 were also available for use in Port Said.

PORT SAID

Stamps of France Overprinted in Red, Blue or Black

1899-1900   Unwmk.   Perf. 14x13½

1	A15	1c blk, *lil bl* (R)	2.10	1.70
	Never hinged		3.50	
	On cover			62.50
2	A15	2c brn, *buff* (bl)	2.10	1.70
	Never hinged		3.50	
	On cover			62.50
3	A15	3c gray, *grysh* (Bl)	2.10	2.10
	Never hinged		3.50	
	On cover			62.50
4	A15	4c claret, *lav* (Bl)	1.75	*2.10*
	Never hinged		3.50	
	On cover			62.50
5	A15	5c yel grn (I) (R)	11.00	5.00
	Never hinged		17.50	
	On cover			32.50
	On cover, single franking			110.00
a.	Type II (R)		55.00	25.00
	Never hinged		100.00	
	On cover			100.00
6	A15	10c blk, *lav* (I) (R)	14.00	12.50
	Never hinged		25.00	
	On cover			47.50
	On cover, single franking			110.00
a.	Type II (R)		72.50	55.00
	Never hinged		130.00	
	On cover			325.00
7	A15	15c blue (R)	14.00	8.50
	Never hinged		25.00	
	On cover			40.00
	On cover, single franking			110.00
8	A15	20c red, *grn*	17.00	11.00
	Never hinged		30.00	
	On cover			65.00
	On cover, single franking			110.00
9	A15	25c blk, *rose* (R)	14.00	5.00
	Never hinged		26.00	
	On cover			32.50
	On cover, single franking			47.50
	On commercial cover			110.00
a.	Double overprint		300.00	
b.	Inverted overprint		300.00	
10	A15	30c brn, *bister*	17.00	14.00
	Never hinged		32.50	
	On cover			47.50
	On cover, single franking			60.00
a.	Inverted overprint		325.00	
11	A15	40c red, *straw*	14.00	14.00
	Never hinged		26.00	
	On cover			52.50
	On cover, single franking			75.00
12	A15	50c car, *rose* (II)	20.00	14.00
	Never hinged		35.00	
	On cover			75.00
	On cover, single franking			100.00
a.	Type I		300.00	100.00
b.	Double overprint (II)		425.00	
13	A15	1fr brnz grn, *straw*	30.00	17.50
	Never hinged		57.50	
	On cover			100.00
	On cover, single franking			160.00
	On commercial cover			725.00
14	A15	2fr brn, *az* ('00)	75.00	65.00
	Never hinged		140.00	
	On cover			325.00
	On cover, single franking			525.00

15	A15	5fr red lil, *lav*	120.00	92.50
	Never hinged		225.00	
	On cover			400.00
	On cover, single franking			650.00
	Nos. 1-15 (15)		354.05	266.60

Covers: Values for commercial covers are for covers with correct postage rates. Postcards sell for somewhat less than covers.

Regular Issue Surcharged in Red

PORT-SAID VINGT-CINQ

1899

16	A15	25c on 10c blk, *lav*	130.00	32.50
	Never hinged		325.00	
	On cover			260.00
a.	Inverted surcharge			250.00

With Additional Surcharge "25" in Red

17	A15	25c on 10c blk, *lav*	475.00	160.00
	Never hinged		1,000.	
a.	"25" inverted		1,500.	1,400.
b.	"25" in black			2,600.
c.	As "b," "VINGT CINQ" inverted			3,400.
d.	As "b," "25" vertical			3,400.
e.	As "c" and "d"			3,400.

A2

A3

A4

1902-03   Typo.

18	A2	1c pale gray ('16)	.65	.65
	Never hinged		1.60	
	On cover			47.50
a.	1c gray ('02)		.80	.80
	Never hinged		1.60	
	On cover			47.50
b.	1c slate ('20)		.80	.80
	Never hinged		1.60	
	On cover			47.50
19	A2	2c violet brn	.75	.75
	Never hinged		1.60	
	On cover			47.50
a.	Grayish paper (GC) ('18)		1.20	1.20
	Never hinged		2.40	
	On cover			52.50
20	A2	3c red orange	.85	.75
	Never hinged		1.60	
	On cover			47.50
21	A2	4c yellow brown	1.10	.90
	Never hinged		2.00	
	On cover			52.50
22	A2	5c blue green ('04)	1.20	.85
	Never hinged		2.00	
	On cover			13.00
	On commercial cover			50.00
a.	5c yellow green		5.00	3.00
	Never hinged		8.75	
	On cover			13.00
	On commercial cover			50.00
23	A3	10c rose red	1.60	1.10
	Never hinged		3.25	
	On cover			11.00
	On commercial cover			50.00
24	A3	15c pale red ('03)	3.25	2.25
	Never hinged		6.50	
	On cover			11.00
	On commercial cover			40.00
a.	15c orange		5.00	3.00
	Never hinged		8.75	
	On cover			16.00
	On commercial cover			40.00
25	A3	20c brn vio ('03)	3.25	2.25
	Never hinged		6.50	
	On cover			24.00
	On cover, single franking			47.50
	On commercial cover			50.00
26	A3	25c blue ('03)	2.50	1.60
	Never hinged		4.50	
	On cover			16.00
	On cover, single franking			26.00
	On cover, single franking			45.00
a.	25c dark blue		4.25	3.50
	Never hinged		11.50	
27	A3	30c gray violet ('03)	6.75	5.00
	Never hinged		11.50	
	On cover			21.00
	On cover, single franking			26.00
a.	30c red violet ('09)		6.75	5.00
	Never hinged		11.50	
	On cover			16.00
	On cover, single franking			21.00
28	A4	40c red & pale bl	6.00	4.25
	Never hinged		11.00	
	On cover			27.50
	On cover, single franking			35.00
29	A4	50c bis brn & lav	9.25	6.75
	Never hinged		17.50	
	On cover			47.50
	On cover, single franking			65.00
30	A4	1fr claret & ol grn	12.00	9.25
	Never hinged		22.50	
	On cover			60.00
	On cover, single franking			95.00

31	A4	2fr gray vio & yel	15.00	15.00
	Never hinged		35.00	
	On cover			75.00
	On cover, single franking			111.11
	2fr dull & yellow		9.75	
32	A4	5fr dk bl & buff	35.00	32.50
	Never hinged		80.00	
	On cover			120.00
	On cover, single franking			240.00
	Nos. 18-32 (15)		99.15	83.85

See Nos. 83-92. For surcharges see Nos. 33-80, B1-B4.

2 Millièmes

Stamps of 1902-03 Surcharged Locally

1921

33	A2	2m on 5c green	10.00	10.00
	Never hinged		22.50	
	On cover			100.00
a.	Inverted surcharge		50.00	50.00
	Never hinged		90.00	
34	A3	4m on 10c rose	9.25	9.25
	Never hinged		19.00	
	On cover			85.00
a.	Inverted surcharge		50.00	50.00
	Never hinged		90.00	
35	A2	5m on 1c slate	14.00	14.00
	Never hinged		26.00	
	On cover			100.00
a.	Inverted surcharge		92.50	92.50
	Never hinged		175.00	
b.	5m on 1c light gray		26.00	26.00
	Never hinged		45.00	
	On cover			110.00
c.	Surcharged "2 Milliemes" on #35		67.50	67.50
	Never hinged		130.00	
d.	As "c," surcharge inverted		175.00	175.00
	Never hinged		300.00	
36	A2	5m on 2c	24.00	24.00
	Never hinged		40.00	
	On cover			110.00
a.	Surcharged "2 Milliemes"		75.00	75.00
	Never hinged		150.00	
b.	As "a," inverted		160.00	160.00
	Never hinged		190.00	
37	A2	5m on 3c	15.00	15.00
	Never hinged		32.50	
	On cover			100.00
a.	Inverted surcharge		62.50	62.50
b.	On Alexandria #18		400.00	400.00
38	A2	5m on 4c	11.00	11.00
	Never hinged		25.00	
	On cover			75.00
a.	Inverted surcharge		80.00	80.00
	Never hinged		160.00	
39	A2	10m on 2c	25.00	25.00
	Never hinged		45.00	
	On cover			110.00
40	A2	10m on 4c	35.00	35.00
	Never hinged		75.00	
	On cover			160.00
a.	Inverted surcharge		85.00	85.00
	Never hinged		225.00	
b.	Double surcharge		100.00	105.00
	Never hinged		200.00	
41	A3	10m on 25c	9.25	9.25
	Never hinged		22.50	
	On cover			60.00
a.	Inverted surcharge		85.00	85.00
	Never hinged		160.00	
42	A3	12m on 30c	42.50	42.50
	Never hinged		90.00	
	On cover			60.00
43	A2	15m on 4c	10.00	10.00
	Never hinged		22.50	
	On cover			75.00
a.	Inverted surcharge		85.00	85.00
	Never hinged		160.00	
b.	Double surcharge		92.50	97.50
	Never hinged		175.00	
44	A3	15m on 15c pale red	67.50	67.50
	Never hinged		130.00	
	On cover			250.00
a.	Inverted surcharge		160.00	160.00
	Never hinged		310.00	
45	A3	15m on 20c	67.50	67.50
	Never hinged		130.00	
	On cover			250.00
a.	Inverted surcharge		160.00	160.00
	Never hinged		310.00	
46	A4	30m on 50c	300.00	300.00
	On cover			1,000.
47	A4	60m on 50c	350.00	350.00
	On cover			1,100.
48	A4	150m on 50c	400.00	400.00
	On cover			1,300.

Nos. 46, 47 and 48 have a bar between the numerals and "Millièmes," which is in capital letters.

Same Surcharge on Stamps of French Offices in Turkey, 1902-03

49	A2	2m on 2c vio brn	160.00	160.00
	Never hinged		30.00	
50	A2	5m on 1c gray	150.00	150.00
	Never hinged		260.00	
a.	"5" inverted		7,250.	
	Nos. 33-50 (18)		1,700.	1,700.

---

15 MILLIEMES

Nos. 28-32 Surcharged

51	A4	15m on 40c	60.00	60.00
	Never hinged		130.00	
	On cover			260.00
52	A4	15m on 50c	85.00	85.00
	Never hinged		175.00	
	On cover			360.00
b.	Bar below 15		50.00	50.00
	Never hinged		105.00	
	On cover			240.00
53	A4	30m on 1fr	300.00	300.00
				1,000.
54	A4	60m on 2fr	85.00	*92.50*
			260.00	
	On cover			300.00
55	A4	150m on 5fr	250.00	*275.00*
	Never hinged		575.00	
	On cover			1,200.
	Nos. 51-55 (5)		780.00	812.50

Overprinted "MILLtEMES"

51a	A4	15m on 40c	425.00	425.00
	Never hinged		800.00	
52a	A4	15m on 50c	500.00	500.00
	Never hinged		950.00	
53a	A4	30m on 1fr	1,400.	1,400.
	Never hinged		2,600.	
54a	A4	60m on 2fr	400.00	400.00
	Never hinged		750.00	
55a	A4	150m on 5fr	1,050.	1,050.
	Never hinged		2,000.	
	Nos. 51a-55a (5)		3,775.	3,775.

2 MILLIEMES

Stamps of 1902-03 Surcharged in Paris

1921-23

56	A2	1m on 1c slate	1.60	1.60
	Never hinged		2.50	
	On cover			27.50
57	A2	2m on 5c green	1.60	1.60
	Never hinged		2.75	
	On cover			27.50
58	A3	4m on 10c rose	2.50	2.50
	Never hinged		4.50	
	On cover			27.50
59	A2	5m on 3c red org	9.25	9.25
	Never hinged		16.00	
	On cover			75.00
60	A3	6m on 15c orange	3.25	3.25
	Never hinged		6.50	
	On cover			40.00
a.	6m on 15c pale red		14.00	14.00
	Never hinged		26.00	
	On cover			80.00
61	A3	8m on 20c brn vio	5.00	5.00
	Never hinged		8.75	
	On cover			40.00
62	A3	10m on 25c blue	2.50	2.50
	Never hinged		4.75	
	On cover			20.00
63	A3	10m on 30c violet	7.50	7.50
	Never hinged		14.00	
	On cover			65.00
64	A3	15m on 50c blue	6.75	6.75
	Never hinged		11.00	
	On cover			47.50

15 MILLIEMES

Nos. 29-32 and Type of 1902 Surcharged

65	A4	15m on 50c	6.00	6.00
	Never hinged		9.50	
	On cover			20.00
66	A4	30m on 1fr	9.25	9.25
	Never hinged		17.50	
	On cover			65.00
67	A4	60m on 2fr	130.00	130.00
	Never hinged		240.00	
	On cover			475.00
68	A4	60m on 2fr org & pale blue	12.50	12.50
	Never hinged		24.00	
	On cover			60.00
69	A4	150m on 5fr	20.00	20.00
	Never hinged		35.00	
	On cover			130.00
	Nos. 56-69 (14)		217.70	217.70

1 MILLIEME

Stamps and Types of 1902-03 Surcharged

1925

70	A2	1m on 1c light gray	.75	.75
	Never hinged		1.20	
	On cover			47.50
a.	1m on 1c slate		2.00	2.00
	Never hinged		3.25	

71	A2	2m on 5c green	1.10	1.10
		Never hinged	2.00	
		On cover		47.50
72	A3	4m on 10c rose red	.90	.90
		Never hinged	1.60	
		On cover		40.00
73	A2	5m on 3c red org	1.10	1.10
		Never hinged	2.00	
		On cover		32.50
74	A3	6m on 15c orange	1.10	1.10
		Never hinged	2.00	
		On cover		32.50
75	A3	8m on 20c brn vio	1.00	1.00
		Never hinged	1.60	
		On cover		30.00
76	A3	10m on 25c blue	1.40	1.40
		Never hinged	1.75	
		On cover		27.50
77	A3	15m on 50c blue	1.60	1.60
		Never hinged	2.75	
		On cover		30.00
78	A4	30m on 1fr cl & ol grn	2.75	2.75
		Never hinged	4.50	
		On cover		32.50
79	A4	60m on 2fr org & pale blue	2.50	2.50
		Never hinged	4.50	
		On cover		32.50
80	A4	150m on 5fr dk bl & buff	4.25	4.25
		Never hinged	7.50	
		On cover		32.50
		Nos. 70-80 (11)	18.45	18.45

Type of 1902-03 Issue and

1927-28

83	A5	3m orange ('28)	2.10	2.10
		Never hinged	3.25	
		On cover		47.50
87	A3	15m slate bl	2.50	2.50
		Never hinged	3.50	
		On cover		27.50
88	A3	20m rose lil ('28)	2.50	2.50
		Never hinged	3.50	
		On cover		32.50
90	A4	50m org & blue	4.50	4.50
		Never hinged	8.00	
		On cover		47.50
91	A4	100m slate bl & buff	6.00	6.00
		Never hinged	9.50	
		On cover		52.50
92	A4	250m gray grn & red	9.25	9.25
		Never hinged	16.00	
		On cover		65.00
		Nos. 83-92 (6)	26.85	26.85

SEMI-POSTAL STAMPS

A5 Regular Issue of 1902-03 Surcharged in Carmine

1915   Unwmk.   Perf. 14x13½

B1	A3	10c + 5c rose	1.60	1.60
		Never hinged	2.75	
		On cover		15.00

Sinking Fund Issue

Type of 1902-03 Issue Surcharged like Alexandria Nos. B2-B3 in Blue or Black

1927-30

B2	A3	15m + 5m dp org (Bl)	5.00	5.00
		Never hinged	8.75	
		On cover		52.50
a.		Dot omitted from "i" in "Caisse"	95.00	100.00
		Never hinged	160.00	
B3	A3	15m + 5m red vio ('28)	8.50	8.50
		Never hinged	14.50	
		On cover		65.00
a.		Dot omitted from "i" in "Caisse"	105.00	110.00
		Never hinged	175.00	
b.		15m + 5m violet ('30)	14.00	14.00
		Never hinged	26.00	
		On cover		90.00
c.		As "b," dot omitted from "i" in "Caisse"	150.00	160.00
		Never hinged	225.00	
B4	A3	15m + 5m fawn ('29)	10.00	10.00
		Never hinged	17.50	
		On cover		75.00
a.		Dot omitted from "i" in "Caisse"	120.00	125.00
		Never hinged	225.00	
		Nos. B2-B4 (3)	23.50	23.50

POSTAGE DUE STAMPS

Postage Due Stamps of France, 1893-1906, Srchd. Locally in Black

---

1921   Unwmk.   Perf. 14x13½

J1	D2	12m on 10c brown	62.50	67.50
		Never hinged	150.00	
		On cover		325.00
J2	D2	15m on 5c blue	92.50	105.00
		Never hinged	225.00	
		On cover		600.00
J3	D2	30m on 20c ol grn	92.50	105.00
		Never hinged	225.00	
		On cover		600.00
a.		Inverted surcharge	1,100.	1,100.
J4	D2	30m on 50c red vio	3,000.	3,400.

Same Surcharged in Red or Blue

1921

J5	D2	2m on 5c bl (R)	55.00	60.00
		Never hinged	120.00	
		On cover		300.00
a.		Blue surcharge	190.00	300.00
b.		Accent omitted from "è" of "Millièmes"	190.00	200.00
c.		Second "m" of "Millièmes" inverted	190.00	200.00
d.		"S" of "Millièmes" omitted	190.00	225.00
J6	D2	4m on 10c brn (Bl)	55.00	62.50
		Never hinged	120.00	
		On cover		300.00
a.		Surcharged "15 Millièmes"	725.00	725.00
b.		Accent omitted from "è" of "MILLIèMES"	190.00	200.00
c.		Second "m" of "Millièmes" inverted	190.00	200.00
d.		"S" of "Millièmes" omitted	190.00	225.00
J7	D2	10m on 30c red (Bl)	55.00	60.00
		Never hinged	120.00	
		On cover		300.00
a.		Inverted surcharge	160.00	160.00
b.		Accent omitted from "è" of "Millièmes"	190.00	190.00
c.		Second "M" of "Millièmes" inverted	190.00	190.00
d.		"S" of "Millièmes" omitted	190.00	225.00
e.		"Q" for "0" in surcharge (1Qm)	1,450.	1,500.
J8	D2	15m on 50c brn vio (Bl)	67.50	72.50
		Never hinged	140.00	
		On cover		360.00
a.		Inverted surcharge	160.00	160.00
b.		Accent omitted from "è" of "Millièmes"	190.00	190.00
c.		Second "m" of "Millièmes" inverted	190.00	190.00
d.		"S" of "Millièmes" omitted	210.00	240.00
e.		As "a," accent omitted from è of "Millièmes"	425.00	
		Never hinged	675.00	
		Nos. J5-J8 (4)	232.50	255.00

Alexandria Nos. J6-J13 were also available for use in Port Said.

OFFICES IN TURKEY (LEVANT)

Various powers maintained post offices in the Turkish Empire before World War I by authority of treaties which ended with the signing of the Treaty of Lausanne in 1923. The foreign post offices were closed Oct. 27, 1923.

100 Centimes = 1 Franc
25 Centimes = 40 Paras = 1 Piaster

Stamps of France Surcharged in Black or Red

1885-1901   Unwmk.   Perf. 14x13½

1	A15	1pi on 25c yel, *straw*	550.00	16.00
		On cover		75.00
		On cover, single franking		110.00
a.		Inverted surcharge	2,500.	2,400.
2	A15	1pi on 25c blk, *rose* (R) ('86)	4.25	1.25
		Never hinged	8.00	
		On cover		13.00
		On cover, single franking		20.00
a.		Inverted surcharge	400.00	325.00
3	A15	2pi on 50c car, *rose* (II) ('90)	18.00	3.00
		Never hinged	35.00	
		On cover		32.50
		On cover, single franking		52.50
a.		Type I ('01)	375.00	50.00
		Never hinged	725.00	
		On cover		525.00
		On cover, single franking		875.00

4	A15	3pi on 75c car, *rose*	30.00	15.00
		Never hinged	60.00	
		On cover		85.00
		On cover, single franking		120.00
5	A15	4pi on 1fr brnz grn, *straw*	30.00	15.00
		Never hinged	60.00	
		On cover		100.00
		On cover, single franking		160.00
6	A15	8pi on 2fr brn, *az* ('00)	37.50	25.00
		Never hinged	67.50	
		On cover		200.00
		On cover, single franking		325.00
7	A15	20pi on 5fr red lil, *lav* ('90)	110.00	60.00
		Never hinged	225.00	
		On cover		650.00
		On cover, single franking		1,050.
		Nos. 1-7 (7)	779.75	135.25

A2   A3

A4

A5

A6

1902-07   Typo.   Perf. 14x13½

21	A2	1c gray	.65	.65
		Never hinged	1.25	
		On cover		47.50
a.		1c pale gray ('11)	.65	.65
		Never hinged	1.25	
		On cover		47.50
b.		1c slate ('20)	.80	.80
		Never hinged	1.50	
		On cover		47.50
c.		Grayish paper (GC) ('18)	1.25	1.00
		Never hinged	2.00	
		On cover		52.50
22	A2	2c vio brn	.65	.65
		Never hinged	1.25	
		On cover		47.50
a.		Grayish paper (GC) ('18)	1.25	1.00
		Never hinged	2.00	
		On cover		52.50
23	A2	3c red org	.65	.65
		Never hinged	1.25	
		On cover		47.50
a.		Grayish paper (GC) ('18)	1.25	1.00
		Never hinged	2.00	
		On cover		52.50
24	A2	4c yel brn	3.00	1.10
		Never hinged	4.75	
		On cover		65.00
a.		Imperf., pair	90.00	
25	A2	5c grn ('06)	1.00	.65
		Never hinged	1.60	
		On cover		13.00
26	A2	10c rose red	1.00	.65
		Never hinged	1.60	
		On cover		10.00
27	A3	15c pale red ('03)	3.00	1.25
		Never hinged	4.75	
		On cover		11.00
28	A3	20c brn vio ('03)	3.25	2.00
		Never hinged	6.00	
		On cover		27.50
29	A3	25c blue ('07)	45.00	60.00
		Never hinged	80.00	
		On cover		37.50
a.		Imperf., pair	425.00	
30	A3	30c lilac ('03)	6.00	3.00
		Never hinged	9.50	
		On cover		13.00
		On cover, single franking		20.00
31	A4	40c red & pale bl	6.00	3.25
		Never hinged	9.50	
		On cover		20.00
		On cover, single franking		27.50
32	A4	50c bis brn & lav ('07)	190.00	225.00
		On cover		5,000.
a.		Imperf., pair	925.00	
33	A4	1fr claret & ol grn ('07)	425.00	450.00
		On cover		6,000.
a.		Imperf., pair	1,100.	

Black Surcharge

34	A5	1pi on 25c bl ('03)	1.20	.65
		Never hinged	2.00	
		On cover		16.00
		On cover, single franking		27.50

---

a.		Second "I" omitted	32.50	25.00
		Never hinged	55.00	
b.		Double surcharge	72.50	60.00
		Never hinged	130.00	
35	A6	2pi on 50c bis brn & lavender	4.25	1.60
		Never hinged	7.25	
		On cover		27.50
		On cover, single franking		47.50
36	A6	4pi on 1fr cl & ol grn	5.00	2.10
		Never hinged	9.00	
		On cover		32.50
		On cover, single franking		65.00
a.		Imperf., pair	750.00	
37	A6	8pi on 2fr gray vio & yel	20.00	15.00
		Never hinged	35.00	
		On cover		65.00
		On cover, single franking		110.00
38	A6	20pi on 5fr dk bl & buff	10.00	6.00
		Never hinged	16.00	
		On cover		55.00
		On cover, single franking		125.00
		Nos. 21-38 (18)	725.65	774.20

Nos. 29, 32-33 were used during the early part of 1907 in the French Offices at Harar and Diredawa, Ethiopia. Djibouti and Port Said stamps were also used.

No. 27 Surcharged in Green

1905

39	A3	1pi on 15c pale red	2,100.	325.
		On cover		1,750.
a.		"Piastte"	6,500.	1,450.
b.		Se-tenant pair, #39, #39a	11,000.	2,600.
		Never hinged	16.00	
		On cover		55.00

Stamps of France 1900-21 Surcharged

On A22   On A20

On A18

1921-22

40	A22	30pa on 5c grn	1.00	1.00
		Never hinged	1.60	
		On cover		16.00
41	A22	30pa on 5c org	1.00	.85
		Never hinged	1.60	
		On cover		16.00
42	A22	1pi20pa on 10c red	1.10	1.10
		Never hinged	1.60	
		On cover		13.00
43	A22	1pi20pa on 10c grn	1.10	.85
		Never hinged	1.60	
		On cover		16.00
44	A22	3pi30pa on 25c bl	1.60	1.00
		Never hinged	2.40	
		On cover		11.00
45	A22	4pi20pa on 30c org	1.60	1.10
		Never hinged	2.40	
		On cover		16.00
a.		"4" omitted	1,050.	
46	A20	7pi20pa on 50c bl	1.60	1.25
		Never hinged	2.40	
		On cover		20.00
		On cover, single franking		27.50
47	A18	15pi on 1fr car & ol grn	3.00	2.10
		Never hinged	4.00	
		On cover		27.50
		On cover, single franking		40.00
48	A18	30pi on 2fr org & pale bl	12.50	10.00
		Never hinged	20.00	
		On cover		47.50
		On cover, single franking		75.00
49	A18	75pi on 5fr dk bl & buff	11.00	7.50
		Never hinged	17.50	
		On cover		52.50
		On cover, single franking		100.00
		Nos. 40-49 (10)	35.50	26.75

Stamps of France, 1903-07, Handstamped

1923

52	A22	1pi20pa on 10c red	62.50	60.00
		Never hinged	110.00	
		On cover		275.00
54	A20	3pi30pa on 15c gray grn (GC)	25.00	25.00
		Never hinged	50.00	
		On cover		120.00
a.		On normal paper	52.50	52.50
		Never hinged	87.50	
55	A22	7pi20pa on 35c vio	30.00	30.00
		Never hinged	47.50	
		On cover		130.00
a.		Grayish paper (GC)	47.50	47.50
		Never hinged	80.00	
b.		1pi20pa on 35c violet	1,400.	1,400.
c.		Se-tenant pair, #55, #55b	2,600.	
		Nos. 52-55 (3)	117.50	115.00

CAVALLE (CAVALLA)

Stamps of France Ovptd. or Srchd. in Red, Blue or Black

1893-1900   Unwmk.   Perf. 14x13½

1	A15	5c grn, grnsh (R)	25.00	21.00
		Never hinged	47.50	
		On cover		160.00
2	A15	5c yel grn (I) ('00) (R)	21.00	20.00
		Never hinged	35.00	
		On cover		150.00
3	A15	10c blk, lav (II)	25.00	24.00
		Never hinged	47.50	
		On cover		165.00
a.		10c black, lavender (I)	160.00	130.00
		On cover		525.00
4	A15	15c blue (R)	45.00	27.50
		Never hinged	75.00	
		On cover		150.00
5	A15	1pi on 25c blk, rose	27.50	19.00
		Never hinged	47.50	
		On cover		275.00
		On cover, single franking		400.00
6	A15	2pi on 50c car, rose	87.50	60.00
		Never hinged	175.00	
		On cover		800.00
		On cover, single franking		1,000.
7	A15	4pi on 1fr brnz grn, straw (R)	87.50	80.00
		Never hinged	175.00	
		On cover		1,000.
		On cover, single franking		1,200.
8	A15	8pi on 2fr brn, az ('00) (Bk)	110.00	110.00
		On cover		1,100.
		On cover, single franking		1,500.
		Nos. 1-8 (8)	428.50	361.50

A3   A4

A5

A6

1902-03

9	A3	5c green	2.00	1.60
		Never hinged	3.50	
		On cover		100.00
10	A4	10c rose red ('03)	2.00	1.60
		Never hinged	3.50	
		On cover		100.00
11	A4	15c orange	2.40	1.60
		Never hinged	4.00	
		On cover		100.00
a.		15c pale red ('03)	11.00	11.00
		Never hinged	21.00	
		On cover		165.00

Surcharged in Black

12	A5	1pi on 25c bl	4.25	2.40
		Never hinged	7.25	
		On cover		130.00
		On cover, single franking		180.00
13	A6	2pi on 50c bis brn & lav	12.00	6.75
		Never hinged	19.00	
		On cover		160.00
		On cover, single franking		225.00

14	A6	4pi on 1fr cl & ol grn	15.00	12.00
		Never hinged	24.00	
		On cover		200.00
		On cover, single franking		300.00
15	A6	8pi on 2fr gray vio & yel	10.00	10.00
		Never hinged	32.50	
		On cover		240.00
		On cover, single franking		425.00
		Nos. 9-15 (7)	57.65	43.95

DEDEAGH (DEDEAGATCH)

Stamps of France Ovptd. or Srchd. in Red, Blue or Black

1893-1900   Unwmk.   Perf. 14x13½

1	A15	5c grn, grnsh (II) (R)	16.00	14.00
		Never hinged	27.50	
		On cover		130.00
2	A15	5c yel grn (I) ('00) (R)	14.00	14.00
		Never hinged	24.00	
		On cover		130.00
3	A15	10c blk, lav (II)	25.00	19.00
		Never hinged	45.00	
		On cover		130.00
a.		Type I	42.50	29.00
		Never hinged	75.00	
		On cover		165.00
4	A15	15c blue (R)	32.50	29.00
		Never hinged	60.00	
		On cover		120.00
5	A15	1pi on 25c blk, rose	37.50	32.50
		Never hinged	67.50	
		On cover		325.00
		On cover, single franking		475.00
a.		Dot omitted from "i" in "Piastre"	110.00	110.00
6	A15	2pi on 50c car, rose	62.50	45.00
		Never hinged	110.00	
		On cover		525.00
		On cover, single franking		875.00
a.		Dot omitted from "i" in "Piastres"	160.00	160.00
7	A15	4pi on 1fr brnz grn, straw (R)	75.00	67.50
		Never hinged	150.00	
		On cover		875.00
		On cover, single franking		1,100.
a.		Dot omitted from "i" in "Piastres"	210.00	210.00
8	A15	8pi on 2fr brn, az ('00) (Bk)	110.00	92.50
		Never hinged	200.00	
		On cover		1,000.
		On cover, single franking		1,500.
a.		Dot omitted from "i" in "Piastres"	325.00	325.00
		Nos. 1-8 (8)	372.50	313.50

A3   A4

A5

A6

1902-03

9	A3	5c green	3.00	2.50
		Never hinged	4.75	
		On cover		100.00
10	A4	10c rose red ('03)	3.00	2.50
		Never hinged	4.75	
		On cover		100.00
11	A4	15c orange	6.00	5.00

Black Surcharge

		Never hinged	11.00	
		On cover		130.00
15	A5	1pi on 25c bl ('03)	3.25	2.50
		Never hinged	5.50	
		On cover		130.00
		On cover, single franking		180.00
16	A6	2pi on 50c bis brn & lav	11.00	9.25
		Never hinged	19.00	
		On cover		175.00
		On cover, single franking		260.00
a.		Double surcharge	275.00	

17	A6	4pi on 1fr cl & ol grn	20.00	16.00
		Never hinged	32.50	
		On cover, single franking		360.00
18	A6	8pi on 2fr gray vio & yel	30.00	30.00
		Never hinged	32.50	
		On cover		225.00
		On cover, single franking		360.00
		Never hinged	52.50	
		On cover		300.00
		On cover, single franking		500.00
		Nos. 9-18 (7)	76.25	62.75

PORT LAGOS

Stamps of France Ovptd. or Srchd. in Red or Blue

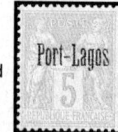

1893   Unwmk.   Perf. 14x13½

1	A15	5c grn, grnsh (R)	30.00	30.00
		Never hinged	55.00	
		On cover		325.00
2	A15	10c blk, lav	60.00	45.00
		Never hinged	110.00	
		On cover		525.00
3	A15	15c blue (R)	85.00	67.50
		Never hinged	160.00	
		On cover		600.00
4	A15	1pi on 25c blk, rose	70.00	55.00
		Never hinged	140.00	
		On cover		85.00
		On cover, single franking		1,200.
a.		Dot omitted from "i" in "Piastres"	200.00	200.00
5	A15	2pi on 50c car, rose	175.00	92.50
		On cover		1,100.
		On cover, single franking		1,750.
a.		Dot omitted from "i" in "Piastres"	500.00	425.00
6	A15	4pi on 1fr brnz grn, straw (R)	110.00	92.50
		On cover		1,500.
		On cover, single franking		2,300.
a.		Dot omitted from "i" in "Piastres"	325.00	325.00
		Nos. 1-6 (6)	530.00	382.50

VATHY (SAMOS)

Stamps of France Ovptd. or Srchd. in Red, Blue or Black

Vathy

1894-1900   Unwmk.   Perf. 14x13½

1	A15	5c grn, grnsh (R)	8.50	7.50
		Never hinged	14.50	
		On cover		110.00
2	A15	5c yel grn (I) ('00) (R)	8.50	7.50
		Never hinged	16.00	
		On cover		110.00
a.		Type II	80.00	80.00
		Never hinged	150.00	
		On cover		675.00
b.		Se-tenant pair, #2, #2a	1,200.	
3	A15	10c blk, lav (I)	16.00	13.00
		Never hinged	32.50	
		On cover		110.00
a.		Type II	50.00	42.50
		Never hinged	95.00	
		On cover		525.00
4	A15	15c blue (R)	16.00	15.00
		Never hinged	30.00	
5	A15	1pi on 25c blk, rose	16.00	11.00
		Never hinged	22.50	
		On cover		100.00
		On cover, single franking		130.00
a.		Dot omitted from "i" in "Piastres"	52.50	52.50
		Never hinged	425.00	
6	A15	2pi on 50c car, rose	29.00	25.00
		Never hinged	55.00	
		On cover		300.00
		On cover, single franking		475.00
a.		Dot omitted from "i" in "Piastres"	80.00	80.00
		Never hinged	275.00	
7	A15	4pi on 1fr brnz grn, straw (R)	37.50	32.50
		Never hinged	67.50	
		On cover		525.00
		On cover, single franking		725.00
a.		Dot omitted from "i" in "Piastres"	110.00	110.00
		Never hinged	275.00	
8	A15	8pi on 2fr brn, az ('00) (Bk)	70.00	70.00
		Never hinged	140.00	
		On cover		1,000.
		On cover, single franking		1,500.
a.		Dot omitted from "i" in "Piastres"	210.00	210.00
		Never hinged	275.00	

9	A15	20pi on 5fr lil, lav ('00) (Bk)	100.00	100.00
		Never hinged		
		On cover		1,100.
		On cover, single franking		1,600.
a.		Dot omitted from "i" in "Piastres"	275.00	275.00
		Never hinged	550.00	
		Nos. 1-9 (9)	301.50	281.50

OFFICES IN ZANZIBAR

Until 1906 France maintained post offices in the Sultanate of Zanzibar, but in that year Great Britain assumed direct control over this protectorate and the French withdrew their postal system.

16 Annas = 1 Rupee

Stamps of France Surcharged in Red, Carmine, Blue or Black

1894-96   Unwmk.   Perf. 14x13½

1	A15	½a on 5c grn, grnsh	10.00	7.50
2	A15	1a on 10c blk, lav (Bl)	15.00	12.50
3	A15	1½a on 15c bl ('96)	22.50	21.00
a.		"ANNAS"	100.00	92.50
b.		Carmine surcharge	19.00	15.00
4	A15	2a on 20c red, grn ('96) (Bk)	19.00	15.00
a.		"ANNA"	2,300.	2,300.
5	A15	2½a on 25c blk, rose (Bl)	12.50	9.25
a.		Double surcharge	250.00	250.00
6	A15	3a on 30c brn, bis ('96) (Bk)	21.00	18.00
7	A15	4a on 40c red, straw ('96) (Bk)	29.00	25.00
8	A15	5a on 50c car, rose (Bl)	37.50	32.50
9	A15	7½a on 75c vio, org ('96)	500.00	400.00
10	A15	10a on 1fr brnz grn, straw	67.50	55.00
a.		Carmine surcharge	50.00	
11	A15	50a on 5fr red lil, lav ('96) (Bk)	325.00	260.00
		Nos. 1-11 (11)	1,059.	855.75

1894

12	A15	½a & 5c on 1c blk, lil bl (R)	200.00	220.00
13	A15	1a & 10c on 3c gray, grysh (R)	180.00	200.00
14	A15	2½a & 25c on 4c cl, lav (Bk)	230.00	275.00
15	A15	5a & 50c on 20c red, grn (Bk)	250.00	275.00
16	A15	10a & 1fr on 40c red, straw (Bk)	475.00	525.00
		Nos. 12-16 (5)	1,335.	1,495.

There are two distinct types of the figures 5c, four of the 25c and three of each of the others of this series.

Stamps of France Srchd. in Red, Carmine, Blue or Black

1896-1900

17	A15	½a on 5c grn, grnsh (R)	11.00	8.50
a.		Carmine surcharge	11.00	8.50
18	A15	½a on 5c yel grn (I) (R)	7.50	6.75
a.		Type II	9.25	7.50
19	A15	1a on 10c blk, lav (II) (Bl)	9.25	7.50
a.		Type I	22.50	19.00
20	A15	1½a on 15c bl (R)	11.00	9.25
21	A15	2a on 20c red, grn	9.25	9.25
a.		"ZANZIBAR" double	210.00	210.00
b.		"ZANZIBAR" triple	210.00	210.00

22	A15	2½a on 25c blk, rose (Bl)	11.00	9.25
a.		Inverted surcharge	275.00	210.00
23	A15	3a on 30c brn, bis	11.00	9.25
24	A15	4a on 40c red, straw	13.50	10.00
25	A15	5a on 50c rose, rose (II) (Bl)	45.00	32.50
a.		Type I	125.00	100.00
26	A15	10a on 1fr brnz grn, straw (R)	29.00	25.00
a.		Carmine surcharge	12.50	11.50
27	A15	20a on 2fr brn, az	35.00	29.00
a.		"ZANZIBAS"	675.00	750.00
b.		"ZANZIBAR" triple		1,600.
28	A15	50a on 5fr lil, lav	67.50	62.50
a.		"ZANZIBAS"	9,250.	
		Nos. 17-28 (12)	260.00	218.75

For surcharges see Nos. 50-54.

A4

A5

1897

29	A4	2½a & 25c on ½a on 5c grn, grnsh	1,300.	240.
30	A4	2½a & 25c on 1a on 10c lav	4,500.	1,100.
31	A4	2½a & 25c on 1½a on 15c blue	4,400.	950.
32	A5	5a & 50c on 3a on 30c brn, bis	4,400.	950.
33	A5	5a & 50c on 4a on 40c red, straw	4,500.	1,300.

Printed on the Margins of Sheets of French Stamps

A6

A7

Perf. 14x13½ on one or more sides

1897

34	A6	2½a & 25c grn, grnsh		1,300.
35	A6	2½a & 25c blk, lav		4,000.
36	A6	2½a & 25c blue		3,000.
37	A7	5a & 50c brn, bis		2,900.
38	A7	5a & 50c red, straw		4,000.

There are 5 varieties of figures in the above surcharges.

Surcharged in Red or Black

A8

A9

A10

1902-03   *Perf. 14x13½*

39	A8	½a on 5c grn (R)	6.75	6.00
40	A9	1a on 10c rose red ('03)	7.50	7.50
41	A9	1½a on 15c pale red ('03)	15.00	14.00
42	A9	2a on 20c brn vio ('03)	18.00	15.00
43	A9	2½a on 25c bl ('03)	18.00	15.00
44	A9	3a on 30c lil ('03)	13.00	13.00
a.		5a on 30c (error)	325.00	375.00
45	A10	4a on 40c red & pale bl	30.00	25.00
46	A10	5a on 50c bis brn & lav	25.00	21.00
47	A10	10a on 1fr cl & ol grn	32.50	29.00

48	A10	20a on 2fr gray vio & yel	85.00	75.00
49	A10	50a on 5fr dk bl & buff	100.00	92.50
		Nos. 39-49 (11)	350.75	313.00

For see Reunion Nos. 55-59.

Nos. 23-24 Surcharged in Black

a

b

c

1904

50	A15 (a)	25c & 2½a on 4a on 40c	1,000.	
51	A15 (b)	50c & 5a on 3a on 30c	1,200.	
52	A15 (b)	50c & 5a on 4a on 40c	6,500.	1,200.
53	A15 (c)	1fr & 10a on 3a on 30c	2,000.	
54	A15 (c)	1fr & 10a on 4a on 40c	2,000.	

Nos. 39-40, 44 Surcharged in Red or Black

d

e

f

g

55	A8 (d)	25c & 2a on ½a on 5c (R)	3,100.	140.00
56	A9 (e)	25c & 2½a on 1a on 10c	6,500.	150.00
a.		Inverted surcharge		1,500.
57	A9 (e)	25c & 2½a on 3a on 30c		2,400.
a.		Inverted surcharge		4,100.
b.		Double surch., both invtd.		2,600.
58	A9 (f)	50c & 5a on 3a on 30c		1,250.
59	A9 (g)	1fr & 10a on 3a on 30c		2,000.

No. J1-J3 With Various Surcharges Overprinted: "Timbre" in Red

60	D1	½a on 5c blue	450.00

Overprinted "Affrancht" in Black

61	D1	1a on 10c brown	450.00

With Red Bars Across "CHIFFRE" and "TAXE"

62	D1	1½a on 15c green	1,000.

The illustrations are not exact reproductions of the new surcharges but are merely intended to show their relative positions and general styles.

POSTAGE DUE STAMPS

Postage Due Stamps of France Srchd. in Red, Blue or Black Like Nos. 17-28

1897   Unwmk.   Perf. 14x13½

J1	D2	½a on 5c blue (R)	21.00	12.50
J2	D2	1a on 10c brn (Bl)	21.00	12.50
a.		Inverted surcharge	160.00	190.00
J3	D2	1½a on 15c grn (R)	32.50	12.50
J4	D2	3a on 30c car (Bk)	29.00	21.00
J5	D2	5a on 50c lil (Bl)	32.50	25.00
a.		2½a on 50c lilac (Bl)	1,400.	1,300.
		Nos. J1-J5 (5)	136.00	83.50

For overprints see Nos. 60-62.

FRENCH COLONIES

'french 'kä-lə-nēz

From 1859 to 1906 and in 1944 and 1945 special stamps were issued for use in all French Colonies which did not have stamps of their own.

100 Centimes = 1 Franc

Perforations: Nos. 1-45 are known variously perforated privately.

Gum: Many of Nos. 1-45 were issued without gum. Some were gummed locally.

Reprints: Nos. 1-7, 9-12, 24, 26-42, 44 and 45 were reprinted officially in 1887. These reprints are ungummed and the colors of both design and paper are deeper or brighter than the originals. Value for Nos. 1-6, $20 each.

Eagle and Crown — A1

1859-65   Unwmk.   Typo.   Imperf.

1	A1	1c ol grn, pale bl ('62)	24.00	27.50
		On cover		275.00
2	A1	5c yel grn, grnsh ('62)	24.00	16.00
		On cover		110.00
3	A1	10c bister, yel	32.50	8.00
		On cover		35.00
a.		Pair, one sideways	1,000.	525.00
		On cover		1,600.
4	A1	20c bl, bluish ('65)	35.00	13.50
		On cover		42.50
5	A1	40c org, yelsh	27.50	13.50
		On cover		52.50
6	A1	80c car rose, pnksh ('65)	110.00	60.00
		On cover		250.00
		Nos. 1-6 (6)	253.00	138.50

Values for stamps on cover are for covers paying ordinary rates and emanating from the most populated colonies such as Martinique and Guadeloupe. Covers originating from more remote areas command premiums.

Values for blocks of 4

1	A1	1c ol grn, pale bl	140.00	250.00
2	A1	5c yel grn, grnsh	120.00	200.00
3	A1	10c bister, yel	160.00	60.00
a.		Block, one sideways		
4	A1	20c bl, bluish	175.00	175.00
5	A1	40c org, yelsh	140.00	130.00
6	A1	80c car rose, pnksh	540.00	600.00

Napoleon III
A2   A3

Ceres
A4

Napoleon III
A5

1871-72   Imperf.

7	A2	1c ol grn, pale bl ('72)	80.00	80.00
		On cover		290.00
8	A3	5c yel grn, grnsh ('72)	1,000.	400.00
		On cover		1,650.
9	A4	10c bis, yelsh	375.00	130.00
		On cover		350.00
a.		Tête bêche pair	55,000.	22,500.
		On cover		60,000.

10	A4	15c bis, yelsh ('72)	325.00	13.00
		On cover		57.50
11	A4	20c blue, bluish	525.00	125.00
		On cover		450.00
a.		Tête bêche pair	—	18,000.
		On cover		40,000.
12	A4	25c bl, bluish ('72)	175.00	13.00
		On cover		110.00
13	A5	30c brn, yelsh	175.00	60.00
		On cover		140.00
14	A4	40c org, yelsh (I)	250.00	13.00
		On cover		52.50
a.		Type II	3,500.	650.00
		On cover		1,400.
b.		Pair, types I & II	7,250.	1,750.
		On cover		3,900.
c.		Type II, pair	22,000.	7,250.
		On cover		27,000.
15	A5	80c rose, pnksh	1,100.	115.00
		On cover		450.00
		Nos. 7-15 (9)	4,005.	949.00

For 40c types I-II see illustrations over France #1.

See note after France No. 9 for additional information on Nos. 8-9, 11-12, 14.

Values for blocks of 4

7	A2	1c ol grn, pale bl	400.00	650.00
8	A3	5c yel grn, grnsh	7,750.	8,750.
9	A4	10c bis, yelsh	1,850.	1,700.
a.		Tête bêche pair		
10	A4	15c bis, yelsh	1,600.	140.00
11	A4	20c blue, bluish	2,600.	1,500.
a.		Tête bêche pair		
12	A4	25c bl, bluish	900.00	130.00
13	A5	30c brn, yelsh	940.00	400.00
14	A4	40c org, yelsh (I)	1,800.	525.00
a.		Type II	—	—
b.		Block, 1 type II	—	—
c.		Block, 2 type II	—	—
15	A5	80c rose, pnksh	5,400.	2,900.

Ceres
A6   A7

1872-77   Imperf.

16	A6	1c ol grn, pale bl ('73)	13.00	14.50
		Never hinged	25.00	
		On cover		260.00
17	A6	2c red brn, yelsh ('76)	475.00	750.00
		On cover		10,750.
18	A6	4c gray ('76)	11,000.	475.00
		On cover		16,000.
19	A6	5c grn, pale bl	17.50	9.50
		Never hinged	35.00	
		On cover		175.00
20	A7	10c bis, rose ('76)	240.00	13.00
		On cover		35.00
21	A7	15c bister ('77)	525.00	100.00
		On cover		600.00
22	A7	30c brn, yelsh	130.00	21.00
		On cover		57.50
23	A7	80c rose, pnksh ('73)	625.00	140.00
		On cover		650.00

No. 17 was used only in Cochin China, 1876-77. Excellent forgeries of Nos. 17 and 18 exist.

With reference to the stamps of France and French Colonies in the same designs and colors see the note after France No. 9.

Values for blocks of 4

16	A6	1c ol grn, pale bl	65.	100.
		Never hinged	130.	
17	A6	2c red brn, yelsh	2,500.	
18	A6	4c gray	—	
19	A6	5c grn, pale bl	100.	100.
		Never hinged	200.	
20	A7	10c bis, rose	1,250.	225.
21	A7	15c bister	2,500.	1,250.
22	A7	30c brn, yelsh	625.	200.
23	A7	80c rose, pnksh	3,100.	1,100.

Peace and Commerce — A8

1877-78   Type I   Imperf.

24	A8	1c grn, grnsh	35.00	45.00
		Never hinged	70.00	
		On cover		350.00
25	A8	4c grn, grnsh	24.00	14.50
		Never hinged	47.50	
		On cover		350.00
26	A8	30c brn, yelsh ('78)	52.50	52.50
		Never hinged	105.00	
		On cover		175.00
27	A8	40c ver, straw	35.00	21.00
		Never hinged	70.00	
		On cover		80.00
28	A8	75c rose, rose ('78)	75.00	100.00
		On cover		290.00
a.		75c carmine, rose	110.00	95.00
		On cover		525.00

29	A8	1fr brnz grn, *straw*		60.00	67.50
		Never hinged		120.00	
		On cover			100.00
		Nos. 24-29 (6)		281.50	300.50

Type II

30	A8	2c grn, *grnsh*		17.50	11.00
		Never hinged		35.00	
		On cover			250.00
31	A8	5c grn, *grnsh*		24.00	5.50
		Never hinged		47.50	
		On cover			87.50
32	A8	10c grn, *grnsh*		125.00	24.00
		Never hinged		250.00	
		On cover			175.00
33	A8	15c gray, *grnsh*		250.00	72.50
		On cover			290.00
34	A8	20c red brn, *straw*		52.50	9.50
		Never hinged		105.00	
		On cover			92.50
35	A8	25c ultra *bluish*		52.50	8.75
		Never hinged		105.00	
		On cover			87.50
a.		25c blue, *bluish* ('78)		4,250.	175.00
		On cover			450.00
36	A8	35c vio blk, *org* ('78)		67.50	32.50
		On cover			175.00
		Nos. 30-36 (7)		589.00	163.75
		Nos. 24-36 (13)		870.50	464.25

Values for blocks of 4

24	A8	1c grn, *grnsh*		225.00	260.00
25	A8	4c grn, *grnsh*		125.00	130.00
26	A8	30c brn, *yelsh*		150.00	210.00
		Never hinged		500.00	
27	A8	40c ver, *straw*		90.00	175.00
28	A8	75c rose, *rose*		290.00	375.00
a.		75c carmine, *rose*		625.00	600.00
29	A8	1fr brnz grn, *straw*		175.00	190.00

Type II

30	A8	2c grn, *grnsh*		87.50	65.00
		Never hinged		180.00	
31	A8	5c grn, *grnsh*		120.00	75.00
		Never hinged		240.00	
32	A8	10c grn, *grnsh*		575.00	160.00
33	A8	15c gray, *grnsh*		1,450.	1,300.
34	A8	20c red brn, *straw*		250.00	240.00
35	A8	25c ultra, *bluish*		250.00	100.00
a.		25c blue, *bluish*		—	3,250.
36	A8	35c vio blk, *org*		340.00	275.00

Type II

1878-80

38	A8	1c blk, *lil bl*		21.00	21.00
		Never hinged		42.50	
		On cover			175.00
39	A8	2c brn, *buff*		21.00	24.00
		Never hinged		42.50	
		On cover			175.00
40	A8	4c claret, *lav*		32.50	45.00
		Never hinged		65.00	
		On cover			175.00
41	A8	10c blk, *lav* ('79)		120.00	27.50
		Never hinged		240.00	
		On cover			130.00
42	A8	15c blue ('79)		35.00	17.50
		Never hinged		70.00	
		On cover			67.50
43	A8	20c red, *grn* ('79)		87.50	17.50
		Never hinged		175.00	
		On cover			87.50
44	A8	25c blk, *red* ('79)		600.00	275.00
		On cover			1,200.
45	A8	25c yel, *straw* ('80)		725.00	32.50
		On cover			100.00
		Nos. 38-45 (8)		1,642.	460.00

No. 44 was used only in Mayotte, Nossi-Be and New Caledonia. Forgeries exist.

The 3c yellow, 3c gray, 15c yellow, 20c blue, 25c rose and 5fr lilac were printed together with the reprints, and were never issued.

Values for blocks of 4

38	A8	1c blk, *lil bl*		110.00	180.00
39	A8	2c brn, *buff*		87.50	125.00
40	A8	4c claret, *lav*		160.00	240.00
		Never hinged		325.00	
41	A8	10c blk, *lav*		600.00	240.00
42	A8	15c blue		190.00	200.00
43	A8	20c red, *grn*		450.00	200.00
44	A8	25c blk, *red*		3,100.	—
45	A8	25c yel, *straw*		3,500.	425.00

Commerce — A9

1881-86   *Perf. 14x13½*

46	A9	1c blk, *lil bl*		5.50	4.75
		Never hinged		11.00	
		On cover			60.00
47	A9	2c brn, *buff*		5.50	4.75
		Never hinged		11.00	
		On cover			60.00
48	A9	4c claret, *lav*		5.50	5.50
		Never hinged		11.00	
		On cover			60.00
49	A9	5c grn, *grnsh*		6.50	3.25
		Never hinged		13.00	
		On cover			40.00
50	A9	10c blk, *lavender*		11.00	4.75
		Never hinged		22.50	
		On cover			52.50
51	A9	15c blue		16.00	3.25
		Never hinged		32.50	
		On cover			32.50
52	A9	20c red, *yel grn*		52.50	18.00
		Never hinged		105.00	
		On cover			110.00

53	A9	25c yel, *straw*		17.50	5.50
		Never hinged		35.00	
		On cover			52.50
54	A9	25c blk, *rose* ('86)		24.00	3.25
		Never hinged		47.50	
		On cover			32.50
55	A9	30c brn, *bis*		45.00	21.00
		Never hinged		90.00	
		On cover			110.00
56	A9	35c vio blk, *yel org*		40.00	30.00
		Never hinged		80.00	
		On cover			160.00
a.		35c violet black, *yellow*		100.00	52.50
		On cover			200.00
57	A9	40c ver, *straw*		45.00	27.50
		Never hinged		90.00	
		On cover			160.00
58	A9	75c car, *rose*		120.00	60.00
		Never hinged		240.00	
		On cover			275.00
59	A9	1fr brnz grn, *straw*		80.00	45.00
		Never hinged		160.00	
		On cover			275.00
		Nos. 46-59 (14)		474.00	236.50

Nos. 46-59 exist imperforate. They are proofs and were not used for postage, except the 10c.

For stamps of type A9 surcharged with numerals see: Cochin China, Diego Suarez, Gabon, Malagasy (Madagascar), Nossi-Be, New Caledonia, Reunion, Senegal, Tahiti.

Values for blocks of 4

46	A9	1c blk, *lil bl*		32.50	87.50
		Never hinged		47.50	
47	A9	2c brn, *buff*		32.50	87.50
		Never hinged		47.50	
48	A9	4c claret, *lav*		32.50	87.50
		Never hinged		47.50	
49	A9	5c grn, *grnsh*		35.00	52.50
		Never hinged		72.50	
50	A9	10c blk, *lavender*		60.00	87.50
		Never hinged		120.00	
51	A9	15c blue		87.50	87.50
		Never hinged		175.00	
52	A9	20c red, *yel grn*		240.00	240.00
		Never hinged		475.00	
53	A9	25c yel, *straw*		87.50	87.50
		Never hinged		175.00	
54	A9	25c blk, *rose*		120.00	87.50
		Never hinged		240.00	
55	A9	30c brn, *bis*		200.00	210.00
56	A9	35c vio blk, *yel org*		200.00	250.00
a.		35c violet black, *yellow*		475.00	475.00
57	A9	40c ver, *straw*		225.00	240.00
58	A9	75c car, *rose*		600.00	925.00
59	A9	1fr brnz grn, *straw*		400.00	400.00

POSTAGE DUE STAMPS

D1

1884-85   Unwmk.   Typo.   *Imperf.*

			Typo.	*Imperf.*
J1	D1	1c black	4.00	4.00
		Never hinged	8.00	
J2	D1	2c black	4.00	4.00
		Never hinged	8.00	
J3	D1	3c black	4.00	4.00
		Never hinged	8.00	
J4	D1	4c black	4.75	4.00
		Never hinged	9.50	
J5	D1	5c black	6.50	3.25
		Never hinged	12.50	
J6	D1	10c black	8.75	6.50
		Never hinged	17.50	
J7	D1	15c black	13.00	10.50
		Never hinged	25.00	
J8	D1	20c black	16.00	10.50
		Never hinged	32.50	
J9	D1	30c black	17.50	8.75
		Never hinged	35.00	
J10	D1	40c black	21.00	8.75
		Never hinged	42.50	
J11	D1	60c black	27.50	16.00
		Never hinged	55.00	
J12	D1	1fr brown	35.00	27.50
		Never hinged	72.50	
a.		1fr black	300.00	
J13	D1	2fr brown	35.00	27.50
		Never hinged	72.50	
a.		2fr black	300.00	*325.00*
J14	D1	5fr brown	110.00	67.50
a.		5fr black	425.00	*450.00*

Values for blocks of 4

				Imperf.
J1	D1	1c black	24.00	*72.50*
		Never hinged	47.50	
J2	D1	2c black	24.00	*72.50*
		Never hinged	47.50	
J3	D1	3c black	24.00	*72.50*
		Never hinged	47.50	
J4	D1	4c black	25.00	*75.00*
		Never hinged	52.50	
J5	D1	5c black	35.00	*45.00*
		Never hinged	72.50	
J6	D1	10c black	47.50	*65.00*
		Never hinged	95.00	
J7	D1	15c black	65.00	*100.00*
		Never hinged	130.00	
J8	D1	20c black	80.00	*100.00*
		Never hinged	160.00	
J9	D1	30c black	87.50	*92.50*
		Never hinged	175.00	
J10	D1	40c black	100.00	*120.00*
		Never hinged	200.00	
J11	D1	60c black	130.00	*160.00*
		Never hinged	275.00	

J12	D1	1fr brown		180.00	*200.00*
		Never hinged		360.00	
a.		1fr black		190.00	*200.00*
J13	D1	2fr brown		360.00	
		Never hinged		360.00	
a.		2fr black		300.00	*325.00*
J14	D1	5fr brown		540.00	*750.00*
a.		5fr black		425.00	*450.00*

Nos. J12a, J13a and J14a were not regularly issued.

1894-1906

J15	D1	5c pale blue		1.60	1.60
		Never hinged		2.75	
J16	D1	10c gray brown		1.60	1.60
		Never hinged		2.75	
J17	D1	15c pale green		1.60	1.60
		Never hinged		2.75	
J18	D1	20c olive grn ('06)		1.60	1.60
		Never hinged		2.75	
J19	D1	30c carmine		2.75	1.60
		Never hinged		4.75	
J20	D1	50c lilac		2.75	1.60
		Never hinged		4.75	
J21	D1	60c brown, *buff*		4.50	2.75
		Never hinged		8.00	
a.		60c dark violet, *buff*		4.75	2.75
		Never hinged		9.50	
J22	D1	1fr red, *buff*		7.50	4.50
		Never hinged		11.00	
a.		1fr rose, *buff*		27.50	19.00
		Never hinged		47.50	
		Nos. J15-J22 (8)		23.90	16.85

Values for blocks of 4

J15	D1	5c pale blue		8.00	22.50
		Never hinged		14.00	
J16	D1	10c gray brown		8.00	22.50
		Never hinged		14.00	
J17	D1	15c pale green		8.00	22.50
		Never hinged		14.00	
J18	D1	20c olive grn ('06)		8.00	22.50
		Never hinged		14.00	
J19	D1	30c carmine		12.00	25.00
		Never hinged		22.50	
J20	D1	50c lilac		12.00	25.00
		Never hinged		22.50	
J21	D1	60c brown, *buff*		20.00	40.00
		Never hinged		40.00	
a.		60c dark violet, *buff*		24.00	40.00
		Never hinged		47.50	
J22	D1	1fr red, *buff*		35.00	65.00
		Never hinged		55.00	
a.		1fr rose, *buff*		140.00	*160.00*
		Never hinged		240.00	

For overprints see New Caledonia Nos. J1-J8.

FRENCH CONGO

'french 'kän̪_d͡ʒgō

LOCATION — Central Africa
GOVT. — French possession

French Congo was originally a separate colony, but was joined in 1888 to Gabon and placed under one commissioner-general with a lieutenant-governor presiding in Gabon and another in French Congo. In 1894 the military holdings in Ubangi were attached to French Congo, and in 1900 the Chad military protectorate was added. Postal service was not established in Ubangi or Chad, however, at that time. In 1906 Gabon and Middle Congo were separated and French Congo ceased to exist as such. Chad and Ubangi remained attached to Middle Congo as the joint dependency of "Ubangi-Chari-Chad," and Middle Congo stamps were used there.

100 Centimes = 1 Franc

Watermarks

Wmk. 122
Thistle Branch

Wmk. 123 —
Rose Branch

Wmk. 124
Olive Branch

Stamps of French Colonies Surcharged Horizontally in Red or Black

1891   Unwmk.   *Perf. 14x13½*

1	A9	5c on 1c blk, *lil bl* (R)		6,500.	4,750.
		On cover			7,500.
a.		Double surcharge		20,000.	
2	A9	5c on 1c blk, *lil bl*		210.00	110.00
		On cover			500.00
a.		Double surcharge		650.00	425.00
3	A9	5c on 15c blue		350.00	190.00
		On cover			600.00
a.		Double surcharge		725.00	375.00
5	A9	5c on 25c blk, *rose*		130.00	57.50
		On cover			425.00
a.		Inverted surcharge			
b.		Surcharge vertical		275.00	115.00
c.		Surcharge horiz.		675.00	650.00

The error, No. 3a, occurred when paper meant for printing No. 6 was inadvertently placed in the stack intended for printing No. 3.

First "O" of "Congo" is a Capital, "Francais" with Capital "F"

1891-92

6	A9	5c on 20c red, *grn*		1,300.	425.00
		On cover			1,750.
7	A9	5c on 25c blk, *rose*		200.00	110.00
		On cover			450.00
a.		Surcharge vertical		250.00	105.00
8	A9	10c on 25c blk, *rose*		250.00	85.00
		On cover			450.00
a.		Inverted surcharge		400.00	175.00
		On cover			1,000.
b.		Surcharge vertical		275.00	100.00
		On cover			400.00
d.		Double surcharge		425.00	225.00
		On cover			400.00
9	A9	10c on 40c red, *straw*		2,750.	400.00
		On cover			1,650.
10	A9	15c on 25c blk, *rose*		225.00	57.50
		On cover			450.00
a.		Surcharge vertical		275.00	100.00
		On cover			550.00
c.		Double surcharge		425.00	200.00

First "O" of Congo small Surcharge Vert., Down or Up No Period

11	A9	5c on 25c blk, *rose*		300.00	135.00
		On cover			350.00
12	A9	10c on 25c blk, *rose*			—
13	A9	10c on 25c blk, *rose*		425.00	190.00
		On cover			950.00

The listings Nos. 5a and 12 are being re-evaluated. The Catalogue Editors would appreciate any information on these stamps.

Postage Due Stamps of French Colonies Surcharged in Red or Black Reading Down or Up

1892   *Imperf.*

14	D1	5c on 5c blk (R)		175.00	140.00
		On cover			675.00
a.		Double surcharge		1,450.	—
		On cover			
15	D1	5c on 20c blk (R)		175.00	135.00
		On cover			675.00
16	D1	5c on 30c blk (R)		225.00	165.00
		On cover			675.00
17	D1	10c on 1fr brown		175.00	130.00
		On cover			675.00
a.		Double surcharge		4,100.	
b.		Surcharge horiz.			*2,350.*
c.		"Congo" omitted			*500.00*
		Nos. 14-17 (4)		750.00	570.00

Excellent counterfeits of Nos. 1-17 exist.

Navigation and
Commerce — A3

1892-1900 Typo. Perf. 14x13½
Colony Name in Blue or Carmine

18	A3	1c blk, *lil bl*	1.60	1.60
		Never hinged	2.75	
		On cover		140.00
a.		Name double	225.00	165.00
19	A3	2c brn, *buff*	3.00	3.00
		Never hinged	5.25	
		On cover		140.00
a.		Name double	225.00	175.00
20	A3	4c claret, *lav*	3.25	3.25
		Never hinged	6.00	
		On cover		140.00
a.		Name in blk and in blue	225.00	175.00
21	A3	5c grn, *grnsh*	6.25	6.00
		Never hinged	10.50	
		On cover		87.50
22	A3	10c blk, *lavender*	22.50	20.00
		Never hinged	42.50	
		On cover		125.00
a.		Name double	850.00	600.00
23	A3	10c red ('00)	3.00	2.25
		Never hinged	5.25	
		On cover		45.00
24	A3	15c blue, quadrille		
		paper	55.00	25.50
		Never hinged	115.00	
		On cover		125.00
25	A3	15c gray ('00)	9.25	6.75
		Never hinged	15.00	
		On cover		67.50
26	A3	20c red, *grn*	25.00	18.50
		Never hinged	42.50	
		On cover		150.00
		On cover, single franking		150.00
27	A3	25c blk, *rose*	25.00	18.00
		Never hinged	47.50	
		On cover		92.50
28	A3	25c blue ('00)	11.00	11.00
		Never hinged	22.50	
		On cover		100.00
29	A3	30c brn, *bis*	32.50	21.00
		Never hinged	62.50	
		On cover		250.00
		On cover, single franking		340.00
30	A3	40c red, *straw*	57.50	32.50
		Never hinged	115.00	
		On cover		260.00
		On cover, single franking		375.00
31	A3	50c car, *rose*	50.00	32.50
		Never hinged	105.00	
		On cover		210.00
		On cover, single franking		310.00
32	A3	50c brn, *az* ('00)	15.00	14.00
		Never hinged	26.00	
		On cover		150.00
		On cover, single franking		200.00
a.		Name double	775.00	775.00
33	A3	75c dp vio, *org*	45.00	35.00
		Never hinged	90.00	
		On cover		310.00
		On cover, single franking		500.00
34	A3	1fr brnz grn, *straw*	57.50	32.50
		Never hinged	120.00	
		On cover		375.00
		On cover, single franking		625.00
		Nos. 18-34 (17)	422.35	283.35

Perf. 13½x14 stamps are counterfeits.
For surcharges see Nos. 50-51.
No. 21 exists in yellow green on pale green.
The stamp was prepared but not issued.

Leopard — A4

Type 1 Type 2

Bakalois Coconut
Woman — A5 Grove — A6

Design A4 exists in two types. Type 1: end
of left tusk extends behind and above right
tusk. Type 2: end of left tusk does not appear
behind right tusk. Type 2 of design A4 appears
in position 91 of each pane of 100.

1900-04 Wmk. 122 Perf. 11
Thick Paper

35	A4	1c brn vio & gray li-lac (1)	.80	.80
		Never hinged	1.40	
		On cover		75.00
a.		Background inverted	72.50	72.50
		Never hinged	130.00	
b.		Value doubled	45.00	45.00
		Never hinged	82.50	
c.		Type 2	47.50	47.50
		Never hinged	75.00	
d.		Pair, types 1 and 2	52.50	52.50
		Never hinged	82.50	
e.		Thin paper, perf 11½ ('04)	1.50	1.50
		Never hinged	2.60	
36	A4	2c brn & org (1)	.80	.80
		Never hinged	1.40	
		On cover		75.00
a.		Imperf., pair	75.00	75.00
		Never hinged	120.00	
b.		Pair, imperf between	92.50	105.00
		Never hinged	82.50	
c.		Type 2	48.00	48.00
		Never hinged	75.00	
d.		Pair, types 1 and 2	52.50	52.50
		Never hinged	82.50	
e.		Thin paper, perf 11½ ('04)	1.50	1.50
		Never hinged	2.60	
f.		2c dark red & red (1) (error)	167.50	250.00
g.		As "f," type 2	750.00	
h.		As "f," imperf single	925.00	
37	A4	4c scar & gray bl	1.60	1.20
		Never hinged	2.90	
		On cover		75.00
a.		Background inverted	90.00	75.00
		Never hinged	160.00	
b.		Type 2	52.50	52.50
		Never hinged	82.50	
c.		Pair, types 1 and 2	60.00	55.00
		Never hinged	92.50	
d.		Thin paper, perf 11½ ('04)	3.00	2.75
		Never hinged	5.25	
e.		4c dark red & red (1) (error)	700.00	
f.		As "e," type 2	2,250.	
38	A4	5c grn & gray grn (1)	2.75	1.50
		Never hinged	4.50	
		On cover		60.00
a.		Imperf., pair	140.00	140.00
		Never hinged	240.00	
b.		Pair, imperf between	82.50	
		Never hinged	140.00	
c.		Type 2	52.50	52.50
		Never hinged	82.50	
d.		Pair, types 1 and 2	60.00	60.00
		Never hinged	92.50	
e.		Thin paper, perf 11½ ('04)	6.00	3.75
		Never hinged	11.00	
39	A4	10c dk red & red (1)	7.50	3.00
		Never hinged	13.00	
		On cover		105.00
a.		Imperf., pair	140.00	140.00
		Never hinged	240.00	
b.		Type 2	120.00	120.00
		Never hinged	180.00	
c.		Pair, types 1 and 2	140.00	140.00
		Never hinged	200.00	
d.		Thin paper, perf 11½ ('04)	8.25	3.75
		Never hinged	13.50	
40	A4	15c dl vio & ol grn (1)	2.40	1.20
		Never hinged	4.00	
		On cover		95.00
a.		Imperf. pair	120.00	
		Never hinged	200.00	
b.		Type 2	75.00	75.00
		Never hinged	110.00	
c.		Pair, types 1 and 2	80.00	80.00
		Never hinged	110.00	
d.		Thin paper, perf 11½ ('04)	3.00	1.50
		Never hinged	5.25	

Wmk. 123

41	A5	20c yel grn & org	2.40	2.00
		Never hinged	4.75	
		On cover		105.00
		On cover, single franking		175.00
a.		Center double	140.00	
		Never hinged	225.00	
b.		Thin paper, perf 11½ ('04)	4.50	4.00
		Never hinged	7.50	
42	A5	25c bl & pale bl	3.75	2.25
		Never hinged	5.50	
		On cover		80.00
a.		Thin paper, perf 11½ ('04)	4.50	4.00
		Never hinged	8.00	
43	A5	30c car rose & org	4.75	2.40
		Never hinged	8.00	
		On cover		140.00
		On cover, single franking		225.00
a.		Thin paper, perf 11½ ('04)	8.25	4.50
		Never hinged	15.00	
44	A5	40c org brn & brt grn	5.75	2.60
		Never hinged	10.00	
		On cover		150.00
		On cover, single franking		225.00
a.		Imperf., pair	115.00	115.00
		Never hinged	200.00	
b.		Center and value inverted	190.00	160.00
c.		Thin paper, perf 11½ ('04)	6.75	3.75
		Never hinged	13.00	
45	A5	50c gray vio & lil	7.25	6.00
		Never hinged	15.00	
		On cover		110.00
		On cover, single franking		150.00
a.		Thin paper, perf 11½ ('04)	12.00	10.50
		Never hinged	22.50	
46	A5	75c red vio & org	17.00	12.00
		Never hinged	32.50	
		On cover		190.00
		On cover, single franking		310.00
a.		Imperf., pair	120.00	120.00
		Never hinged	210.00	
b.		Pair, imperf between	130.00	
		Never hinged	225.00	
c.		Thin paper, perf 11½ ('04)	30.00	18.50
		Never hinged	52.50	

Wmk. 124

47	A6	1fr gray lil & ol	26.00	18.50
		Never hinged	47.50	
		On cover		250.00
		On cover, single franking		440.00
a.		Center and value inverted	275.00	275.00
b.		Imperf., pair	140.00	140.00
		Never hinged	240.00	
48	A6	2fr car & brn	50.00	30.00
		Never hinged	110.00	
		On cover, single franking		310.00
				550.00
a.		Imperf., pair	300.00	300.00
		Never hinged	550.00	
b.		Frame double		240.00
49	A6	5fr brn org & gray	85.00	75.00
		Never hinged	175.00	
		On cover		225.00
		On cover, single franking		375.00
a.		5fr ocher & gray	750.00	950.00
b.		Center and value inverted	425.00	425.00
c.		Wmk. 123	500.00	500.00
d.		Imperf., pair	800.00	800.00
e.		Center and value double	375.00	375.00
		Nos. 35-49 (15)	217.75	159.25

For surcharges see Nos. 52-53.

Nos. 26 and 29
Surcharged in Black

1900 Unwmk. Perf. 14x13½

50	A3	5c on 20c red, *grn* 26,000.	6,000.	
a.		Double surcharge		18,000.
51	A3	15c on 30c brn, *bis* 20,000.	2,600.	
		On cover		7,500.
a.		Double surcharge		6,000.

Nos. 43 and 48 Surcharged in Black

a

b

1903 Wmk. 123 Perf. 11

52	A5	5c on 30c	300.00	150.00
		On cover		550.00
a.		Inverted surcharge		2,750.
b.		Ovptd. "SPECIMEN" in violet		550.00

Wmk. 124

53	A6	10c on 2fr	375.00	150.00
		On cover		550.00
a.		Inverted surcharge		2,750.
b.		Double surcharge		3,100.

Counterfeits of the preceding surcharges
are known.

FRENCH EQUATORIAL AFRICA

ˈfrench ˌē-kwə-ˈtōr-ē-əl ˈa-fri-kə

LOCATION — North of Belgian Congo
and south of Libya.
GOVT. — French Colony
AREA — 959,256 square miles
POP. — 4,491,785
CAPITAL — Brazzaville

In 1910 Gabon and Middle Congo,
with its military dependencies, were
politically united as French Equatorial
Africa. The component colonies were
granted administrative autonomy. In
1915 Ubangi-Chari-Chad was made an
autonomous civilian colony and in 1920
Chad was made a civil colony. In 1934

---

the four colonies were administratively
united as one colony, but this federation
was not completed until 1936. Each colony had its own postal administration
until 1936. The postal issues of the former colonial subdivisions are listed
under the names of those colonies.

100 Centimes = 1 Franc

**Stamps of Gabon, 1932, Overprinted
"Afrique Equatoriale Francaise" and
Bars Similar to "a" and "b" in Black**
Perf. 13x13½, 13½x13

1936 Unwmk.

1	A16	1c brown violet	.30	.50
		Never hinged	.50	
		On cover		24.00
2	A16	2c black, *rose*	.70	.80
		Never hinged	1.00	
		On cover		24.00
3	A16	4c green	1.25	1.60
		Never hinged	1.90	
		On cover		24.00
4	A16	5c grnsh blue	1.60	1.60
		Never hinged	2.40	
		On cover		17.50
5	A16	10c red, *yel*	1.40	1.50
		Never hinged	2.00	
		On cover		17.50
6	A17	40c brown violet	3.50	2.75
		Never hinged	5.25	
		On cover		8.00
7	A17	50c red brown	4.00	2.00
		Never hinged	6.50	
		On cover		5.50
8	A17	1fr yel grn, *bl*	32.50	13.50
		Never hinged	55.00	
		On cover		32.50
		On cover, single franking		47.50
9	A18	1.50fr dull blue	9.00	2.75
		Never hinged	14.00	
		On cover		14.50
		On cover, single franking		32.50
10	A18	2fr brown red	19.00	13.00
		Never hinged	32.50	
		On cover		25.00
		On cover, single franking		35.00
		Nos. 1-10 (10)	73.25	40.00

**Stamps of Middle Congo, 1933
Overprinted in Black**

a

b

c

1936

11	A4 (b)	1c lt brown	.30	.50
		Never hinged	.50	
		On cover		24.00
12	A4 (b)	2c dull blue	.30	.50
		Never hinged	.50	
		On cover		24.00
13	A4 (b)	4c olive green	1.60	1.60
		Never hinged	2.40	
		On cover		24.00
14	A4 (b)	5c red violet	1.00	1.00
		Never hinged	1.50	
		On cover		17.50
15	A4 (b)	10c slate	1.75	1.25
		Never hinged	2.75	
		On cover		13.50
16	A4 (b)	15c dk violet	2.10	1.60
		Never hinged	3.00	
		On cover		13.50
17	A4 (b)	20c red, *pink*	2.10	1.60
		Never hinged	3.00	
		On cover		16.00
18	A4 (b)	25c orange	3.50	2.40
		Never hinged	4.75	
		On cover		12.00
19	A5 (a)	40c orange brn	4.25	2.75
		Never hinged	6.75	
		On cover		8.00
20	A5 (c)	50c black violet	4.25	2.40
		Never hinged	6.75	
		On cover		4.75
21	A5 (c)	75c black, *pink*	6.00	4.75
		Never hinged	9.50	
		On cover		8.00
22	A5 (a)	90c carmine	6.00	4.00
		Never hinged	9.50	
		On cover		22.50
		On cover, single franking		47.50

23	A5 (c)	1.50fr dark blue	3.75	2.00
	Never hinged		5.25	
	On cover			14.50
	On cover, single franking			32.50
24	A6 (a)	5fr slate blue	57.50	35.00
	Never hinged		85.00	
	On cover			87.50
	On cover, single franking			150.00
25	A6 (a)	10fr bister	65.00	50.00
	Never hinged		52.50	
	On cover			87.50
	On cover, single franking			32.50
26	A6 (a)	20fr dark brown	40.00	32.50
	Never hinged		60.00	
	On cover			110.00
	On cover, single franking			35.00
	Nos. 11-26 (16)		169.40	123.85

Other overprints inscribed "Afrique Equitoriale Francaise" in a different type font on earlier Middle Congo stamps are listed under Middle Congo.

Common Design Types pictured following the introduction.

Paris International Exposition Issue
Common Design Types

1937, Apr. 15		Engr.	*Perf. 13*	
27	CD74	20c dark violet	2.40	2.40
	Never hinged		3.50	
	On cover			60.00
28	CD75	30c dark green	2.40	2.40
	Never hinged		3.50	
	On cover			47.50
29	CD76	40c carmine rose	2.40	2.40
	Never hinged		3.50	
	On cover			45.00
30	CD77	50c dk brn & bl	2.40	2.40
	Never hinged		3.50	
	On cover			40.00
31	CD78	90c red	2.50	2.50
	Never hinged		3.75	
	On cover			60.00
	On cover, single franking			100.00
32	CD79	1.50fr ultra	2.50	2.50
	Never hinged		3.75	
	On cover			52.50
	On cover, single franking			92.50
	Nos. 27-32 (6)		14.60	14.60

Logging on Loéme River — A1

People of Chad — A2

Pierre Savorgnan de Brazza A3

Emile Gentil — A4

Paul Crampel A5

Governor Victor Liotard A6

Two types of 25c:
Type I — Wide numerals (4mm).
Type II — Narrow numerals (3½mm).

1937-40		Photo.	*Perf. 13½x13*	
33	A1	1c brown & yel	.25	.25
	Never hinged		.40	
	On cover			17.50
34	A1	2c violet & grn	.25	.25
	Never hinged		.40	
	On cover			17.50

35	A1	3c blue & yel ('40)	.25	.30
	Never hinged		.40	
	On cover			16.00
36	A1	4c magenta & bl	.30	.30
	Never hinged		.50	
	On cover			17.50
37	A1	5c dk & lt green	.50	.30
	Never hinged		.65	
	On cover			14.50
38	A2	10c magenta & blue	.30	.30
	Never hinged		.50	
	On cover			14.50
39	A2	15c blue & buff	.30	.30
	Never hinged		.50	
	On cover			17.50
40	A2	20c brown & yellow	.30	.30
	Never hinged		.50	
	On cover			12.00
41	A2	25c cop red & bl (I)	.75	.30
	Never hinged		1.00	
	On cover			8.00
a.	Type II		2.75	2.00
	Never hinged		3.75	
	On cover			17.50
42	A3	30c gray grn & grn	.80	.55
	Never hinged		1.10	
	On cover			8.00
43	A3	30c chlky bl, ind & buff ('40)	.40	.50
	Never hinged		.55	
	On cover			8.00
44	A2	35c dp grn & yel ('38)	1.00	.80
	Never hinged		1.35	
	On cover			17.50
45	A3	40c cop red & bl	.40	.30
	Never hinged		.55	
	On cover			6.50
46	A3	45c dk bl & lt grn	5.00	3.50
	Never hinged		6.00	
	On cover			25.00
47	A3	45c dp grn & yel grn ('40)	.55	.65
	Never hinged		.75	
	On cover			16.00
48	A3	50c brown & yellow	.40	.25
	Never hinged		.65	
	On cover			10.50
49	A3	55c pur & bl ('38)	.85	.75
	Never hinged		1.20	
	On cover			4.75
50	A3	60c mar & gray bl ('40)	.65	.75
	Never hinged		.90	
	On cover			13.50
51	A4	65c dk bl & lt grn	.80	.40
	Never hinged		1.10	
	On cover			4.00
52	A4	70c dp vio & buff ('40)	.75	.80
	Never hinged		.95	
	On cover			16.00
53	A4	75c ol blk & dl yel	6.25	4.25
	Never hinged		9.00	
	On cover			14.50
54	A4	80c brn & yel ('38)	.55	.55
	Never hinged		.80	
	On cover			30.00
	On cover, single franking			52.50
55	A4	90c copper red & buff	.55	.40
	Never hinged		.80	
	On cover			8.00
	On cover, single franking			12.00
56	A4	1fr dk vio & lt grn	2.25	1.10
	Never hinged		3.00	
	On cover			22.50
	On cover, single franking			40.00
57	A3	1fr cer & dl org ('38)	3.25	1.25
	Never hinged		4.25	
	On cover			22.50
	On cover, single franking			40.00
58	A4	1fr bl grn & sl grn ('40)	.55	.55
	Never hinged		.75	
	On cover			4.00
59	A5	1.25fr cop red & buff	1.25	.90
	Never hinged		2.00	
	On cover			24.00
	On cover, single franking			65.00
60	A5	1.40fr dk brn & pale grn ('40)	1.00	1.25
	Never hinged		1.50	
	On cover			24.00
	On cover, single franking			52.50
61	A5	1.50fr dk & lt blue	1.50	.75
	Never hinged		2.10	
	On cover			20.00
	On cover, single franking			45.00
62	A5	1.60fr dp vio & buff ('40)	1.00	1.25
	Never hinged		1.50	
	On cover			24.00
	On cover, single franking			60.00
63	A5	1.75fr brn & yel	1.75	.90
	Never hinged		2.40	
	On cover			16.00
	On cover, single franking			27.50
64	A4	1.75fr bl & lt bl ('38)	.75	.65
	Never hinged		.80	
	On cover			30.00
	On cover, single franking			52.50
65	A5	2fr dk & lt green	.95	.75
	Never hinged		1.25	
	On cover			16.00
	On cover, single franking			32.50
66	A6	2.15fr brn, vio & yel ('38)	1.00	.80
	Never hinged		1.40	
	On cover			20.00
	On cover, single franking			27.50
67	A6	2.25fr bl & lt bl ('39)	1.60	1.60
	Never hinged		2.00	
	On cover			35.00
	On cover, single franking			72.50
68	A6	2.50fr rose lake & buff ('40)	1.25	1.25
	Never hinged		1.75	
	On cover			20.00
	On cover, single franking			40.00

69	A6	3fr dk blue & buff	.80	.40
	Never hinged		1.30	
	On cover			24.00
70	A6	5fr dk & lt green	1.40	1.00
	Never hinged		2.10	
	On cover			24.00
	On cover, single franking			52.50
71	A6	10fr dk violet & bl	3.75	2.50
	Never hinged		5.25	
	On cover			27.50
	On cover, single franking			60.00
72	A6	20fr ol blk & dl yel	4.25	3.50
	Never hinged		5.75	
	On cover			32.50
	On cover, single franking			72.50
	Nos. 33-72 (40)		50.45	37.45

For overprints and surcharges see Nos. 80-127, 129-141, B2-B3, B10-B13, B22-B23. Post 1940 issues in Scott Standard catalogue, Vol. 2.

Colonial Arts Exhibition Issue
Souvenir Sheet
Common Design Type

1937				*Imperf.*
73	CD79	3fr red brown	11.00	12.00
	Never hinged		15.00	
	On cover			72.50
	On cover, single franking			110.00

Count Louis Edouard Bouet-Willaumez and His Ship "La Malouine" — A7

1938, Dec. 5			*Perf. 13½*	
74	A7	65c gray brown	1.25	1.25
	Never hinged		3.50	
	On cover			45.00
75	A7	1fr deep rose	1.25	1.25
	Never hinged		2.25	
	On cover			40.00
76	A7	1.75fr blue	1.60	1.60
	Never hinged		3.25	
	On cover			60.00
	On cover, single franking			100.00
77	A7	2fr dull violet	2.40	2.40
	Never hinged		3.25	
	On cover			52.50
	On cover, single franking			92.50
	Nos. 74-77 (4)		6.50	6.50
	Set, never hinged		12.00	

Centenary of Gabon.

New York World's Fair Issue
Common Design Type

1939, May 10		Engr.	*Perf. 12½x12*	
78	CD82	1.25fr carmine lake	1.75	1.75
	Never hinged		2.25	
	On cover			45.00
	On cover, single franking			100.00
79	CD82	2.25fr ultra	1.90	1.90
	Never hinged		2.75	
	On cover			45.00
	On cover, single franking			92.50
	Set, never hinged		5.00	

Stamps of 1936-40, Overprinted in Carmine or Black

Nos. 80-82, 84-88, 93

Nos. 83, 89-92, 94-125

1940-41			*Perf. 13½x13*	
80	A1	1c brn & yel (C)	2.40	2.40
	Never hinged		3.25	
	On cover			80.00
81	A1	2c vio & grn (C)	2.40	2.40
	Never hinged		3.25	
	On cover			80.00
82	A1	3c blue & yel (C)	2.40	2.40
	Never hinged		3.25	
	On cover			80.00
83	A4	4c ol grn (No. 13)	16.00	13.00
	Never hinged		27.50	
	On cover			200.00
b.	Inverted overprint		120.00	150.00
	Never hinged		190.00	
84	A1	5c dk grn & lt grn (C)	2.40	2.40
	Never hinged		3.25	
	On cover			80.00
85	A2	10c magenta & bl	2.40	2.40
	Never hinged		5.00	
	On cover			100.00

86	A2	15c blue & buff (C)	2.40	2.40
	Never hinged		3.25	
	On cover			100.00
87	A2	20c brn & yel (C)	2.40	2.40
	Never hinged		3.25	
	On cover			100.00
88	A2	25c cop red & bl	9.50	9.50
	Never hinged		14.50	
	On cover			130.00
89	A3	30c gray grn & grn (C)	20.00	13.50
	Never hinged		34.00	
	On cover			175.00
90	A3	30c gray grn & grn ('41)	3.25	3.25
	Never hinged		5.50	
	On cover			120.00
91	A3	30c chlky bl, ind & buff (C) ('41)	10.50	8.75
	Never hinged		16.00	
	On cover			120.00
92	A3	30c chlky bl, ind & buff ('41)	14.50	13.00
	Never hinged		27.50	
	On cover			150.00
93	A2	35c dp grn & yel (C)	2.40	2.40
	Never hinged		4.00	
	On cover			100.00
94	A3	40c cop red & bl	1.60	1.60
	Never hinged		2.75	
b.	Inverted overprint			100.00
95	A3	45c dp grn & yel grn (C)	1.60	1.20
	Never hinged		2.75	
	On cover			80.00
96	A3	45c dp grn & yel grn ('41)	2.00	2.00
	Never hinged		3.25	
	On cover			120.00
97	A3	50c brn & yel (C)	8.00	6.50
	Never hinged		12.50	
	On cover			120.00
98	A3	50c brn & yel ('41)	7.25	7.25
	Never hinged		11.50	
	On cover			120.00
99	A3	55c pur & bl (C)	1.60	1.20
	Never hinged		2.75	
	On cover			80.00
100	A3	55c pur & bl ('41)	2.00	2.00
	Never hinged		3.25	
	On cover			130.00
101	A3	60c mar & gray bl	1.60	1.60
	Never hinged		2.75	
	On cover			80.00
102	A4	65c dk bl & lt grn	1.60	1.60
	Never hinged		2.75	
	On cover			80.00
103	A4	70c dp vio & buff	1.60	1.60
	Never hinged		2.75	
	On cover			80.00
104	A4	75c ol blk & dl yel	67.50	67.50
	Never hinged		150.00	
	On cover			300.00
105	A4	80c brown & yellow	1.60	1.60
	Never hinged		2.75	
	On cover			80.00
106	A4	90c cop red & buff	1.60	1.60
	Never hinged		2.75	
	On cover			80.00
107	A4	1fr bl grn & sl grn	11.00	9.50
	Never hinged		21.00	
	On cover			130.00
108	A4	1fr bl grn & sl grn (C) ('41)	9.50	8.00
	Never hinged		20.00	
	On cover			165.00
109	A3	1fr cer & dl org	2.40	2.40
	Never hinged		4.00	
	On cover			80.00
110	A5	1.40fr dk brn & pale grn	1.60	1.60
	Never hinged		2.75	
	On cover			80.00
111	A5	1.50fr dk bl & lt bl	1.60	1.60
	Never hinged		2.75	
	On cover			80.00
112	A5	1.60fr dp vio & buff	1.60	1.60
	Never hinged		2.75	
	On cover			80.00
113	A5	1.75fr brown & yel	2.00	2.00
	Never hinged		3.25	
	On cover			100.00
114	A6	2.15fr brn, vio & yel	2.00	2.00
	Never hinged		3.25	
	On cover			100.00
115	A6	2.25fr bl & lt bl (C)	1.60	1.60
	Never hinged		2.75	
	On cover			80.00
116	A6	2.25fr bl & lt bl ('41)	4.00	4.00
	Never hinged		6.50	
	On cover			140.00
117	A6	2.50fr rose lake & buff	1.60	1.60
	Never hinged		2.75	
	On cover			100.00
118	A6	3fr dk bl & buff (C)	1.60	1.60
	Never hinged		2.75	
	On cover			80.00
119	A6	3fr dk bl & buff ('41)	4.00	4.00
	Never hinged		6.50	
	On cover			130.00
120	A6	5fr dk grn & lt grn (C)	4.00	4.00
	Never hinged		6.00	
	On cover			100.00
121	A6	5fr dk grn & lt grn ('41)	125.00	67.50
	Never hinged		225.00	
	On cover			240.00
122	A6	10fr dk vio & bl (C)	3.25	3.25
	Never hinged		5.50	
	On cover			100.00
123	A6	10fr dk vio & bl ('41)	110.00	67.50
	Never hinged		200.00	
	On cover			260.00

124	A6	20fr ol blk & dl yel (C)	2.40	2.40
		Never hinged	4.00	
		On cover		100.00
125	A6	20fr ol blk & dl yel ('41)	18.00	16.00
		Never hinged	30.00	
		On cover		180.00
		Nos. 80-125 (46)	499.65	379.60

For overprints and surcharges see Nos. 129-132, B12-B13, B22-B23.

For types of Nos. 38/61 without "RF," see Nos. 155A-155B in the *Scott Standard Postage Stamp Catalogue,* Vol. 2.

Double Overprint

80a	A1	1c	325.00	225.00
		Never hinged	690.00	
81a	A1	2c	35.00	
		Never hinged	62.50	
82a	A1	3c	35.00	
		Never hinged	62.50	
83a	A4	4c	75.00	
		Never hinged	125.00	
84a	A1	5c	35.00	
		Never hinged	62.50	
85a	A2	10c	35.00	40.00
		Never hinged	62.50	
86a	A2	15c	35.00	
		Never hinged	62.50	
87a	A2	20c	35.00	
		Never hinged	62.50	
88a	A2	25c	55.00	
		Never hinged	125.00	
89a	A3	30c	110.00	120.00
		Never hinged	200.00	
		On cover		225.00
90a	A3	30c		55.00
91a	A3	30c	47.50	47.50
		Never hinged	85.00	
93a	A2	35c	250.00	
		Never hinged	360.00	
94a	A3	40c	45.00	
		Never hinged	75.00	
96a	A3	45c	47.50	65.00
		Never hinged	85.00	
98a	A3	50c	47.50	
		Never hinged	85.00	
100a	A3	55c	45.00	
		Never hinged	82.50	
102a	A4	65c	47.50	
		Never hinged	85.00	
103a	A4	70c	47.50	
		Never hinged	85.00	
105a	A4	80c	47.50	
		Never hinged	85.00	
106a	A4	90c	45.00	
		Never hinged	82.50	
b.		one inverted	120.00	
		Never hinged	190.00	
109a	A4	1fr One inverted	120.00	
		Never hinged	190.00	
110a	A5	1.40fr	47.50	
		Never hinged	85.00	
111a	A5	1.50fr	47.50	
		Never hinged	85.00	
114a	A6	2.15fr	40.00	
		Never hinged	67.50	
115a	A6	2.25fr	60.00	
		Never hinged	100.00	
116a	A6	2.25fr	45.00	
		Never hinged	82.50	
117a	A6	2.50fr	47.50	
		Never hinged	85.00	
119a	A6	3fr	45.00	
		Never hinged	82.50	
123a	A6	10fr	60.00	67.50
		Never hinged	100.00	
124a	A6	20fr	60.00	
		Never hinged	100.00	
		Nos. 96a-124a (17)	900.00	

Nos. 48, 51 Surcharged in Black or Carmine

1940

126	A3	75c on 50c	.75	.75
		Never hinged	1.10	
		On cover		32.50
a.		Double surcharge	40.00	
		Never hinged	60.00	
127	A4	1fr on 65c (C)	.90	.90
		Never hinged	1.25	
		On cover		4.00
a.		Double surcharge	32.50	
		Never hinged	40.00	
		Set, never hinged	2.35	

Middle Congo No. 67 Overprinted in Carmine like No. 80
Perf. 13½

128	A4	4c olive green	65.00	60.00
		Never hinged	100.00	
		On cover		200.00

Stamps of 1940 With Additional Overprint in Black

1940
Perf. 13½x13

129	A4	80c brown & yel	17.50	13.50
		On card		92.50
a.		Overprint without "2"	150.00	
130	A4	1fr bl grn & sl grn	22.50	18.00
		On card		110.00

131	A3	1fr cer & dull org	19.00	14.50
		On card		120.00
132	A5	1.50fr dk bl & lt bl	17.00	13.50
		On card		120.00
		Nos. 129-132 (4)	76.00	59.50
		Set, never hinged	85.00	

Arrival of General de Gaulle in Brazzaville, capital of Free France, Oct. 24, 1940.

These stamps were sold affixed to post cards and at a slight increase over face value to cover the cost of the cards. Values for unused stamps are for examples without gum.

For surcharges see Nos. B12-B13, B22-B23 in Scott Standard catalogue, Vol. 2.

SEMI-POSTAL STAMPS

Common Design Type

1938, Oct. 24			**Engr.**	
B1	CD80	1.75fr + 50c brt ul-tra	24.00	24.00
		Never hinged	37.50	
		On cover		67.50
		On cover, single franking		120.00

Nos. 51, 64 Surcharged in Black or Red

1938, Nov. 7			*Perf. 13x13½*	
B2	A4	65c + 35c dk bl & lt grn (R)	2.50	2.50
		Never hinged	3.50	
		On cover		35.00
		On cover, single franking		80.00
B3	A4	1.75fr + 50c bl & lt bl	2.50	2.50
		Never hinged	7.75	
		On cover		35.00
		On cover, single franking		120.00
		Set, never hinged	11.00	

The surtax was for welfare.

French Revolution Issue
Common Design Type
Name and Value Typo. in Black

1939, July 5			**Photo.**	
B4	CD83	45c + 25c green	14.50	14.50
		Never hinged	24.00	
		On cover		75.00
B5	CD83	70c + 30c brown	14.50	14.50
		Never hinged	24.00	
		On cover		55.00
B6	CD83	90c + 35c red org	14.50	14.50
		Never hinged	24.00	
		On cover		47.50
B7	CD83	1.25fr + 1fr rose pink	14.50	14.50
		Never hinged	24.00	
		On cover		87.50
		On cover, single franking		140.00
B8	CD83	2.25fr + 2fr blue	14.50	14.50
		Never hinged	24.00	
		On cover		80.00
		On cover, single franking		120.00
		Nos. B4-B8 (5)	72.50	72.50
		Set, never hinged	120.00	

Surtax used for the defense of the colonies.

AIR POST STAMPS

Hydroplane over Pointe-Noire — AP1

Trimotor over Stanley Pool — AP2

1937		**Unwmk.**	**Photo.**	*Perf. 13½*	
C1	AP1	1.50fr ol blk & yel	.40	.40	
		Never hinged	.65		
		On cover		22.50	
C2	AP1	2fr mag & blue	.60	.60	
		Never hinged	.75		
		On cover		17.50	
C3	AP1	2.50fr grn & buff	.60	.60	
		Never hinged	.75		
		On cover		25.00	
C4	AP1	3.75fr brn & lt grn	.90	.90	
		Never hinged	1.20		
		On cover		30.00	

C5	AP2	4.50fr cop red & bl	.90	.90
		Never hinged	1.20	
		On cover		32.50
C6	AP2	6.50fr bl & lt grn	1.60	1.60
		Never hinged	2.40	
		On cover		32.50
C7	AP2	8.50fr red brn & yel	1.75	1.75
		Never hinged	2.60	
		On cover		35.00
C8	AP2	10.75frvio & lt grn	1.75	1.75
		Never hinged	2.60	
		On cover		40.00
		Nos. C1-C8 (8)	8.50	8.50

For overprints and surcharges see Nos. C9-C16, CB2 (in Scott Standard catalog, Vol. 2).

Nos. C1, C3-C7 Overprinted in Black like Nos. 133-141

1940-41				
C9	AP1	1.50fr ('41)	250.00	250.00
		On cover	475.00	
		On cover		450.00
C10	AP1	2.50fr	2.50	2.50
		Never hinged	4.25	
		On cover		80.00
a.		Double overprint	300.00	300.00
		Never hinged	425.00	
b.		Inverted overprint	300.00	300.00
		Never hinged	425.00	
C11	AP1	3.75fr ('41)	250.00	250.00
		On cover	475.00	
		On cover		450.00
C12	AP2	4.50fr	3.50	3.50
		Never hinged	5.75	
		On cover		100.00
a.		Double overprint	300.00	300.00
		Never hinged	425.00	
C13	AP2	6.50fr	4.25	4.25
		Never hinged	7.25	
		On cover		100.00
a.		Double overprint	130.00	130.00
		Never hinged	200.00	
C14	AP2	8.50fr	3.25	3.25
		Never hinged	5.50	
		On cover		100.00

No. C8 Surcharged in Carmine

C15	AP2	50fr on 10.75fr	12.00	12.00
		Never hinged	20.00	
		On cover		130.00

No. C3 Surcharged in Black

C16	AP1	10fr on 2.50fr ('41)	97.50	97.50
		Never hinged	155.00	
		On cover		225.00
		Nos. C9-C16 (8)	623.00	623.00

Counterfeits of Nos. C9 and C11 exist.

See note following No. 141 in Scott Standard catalogue, Vol. 2.

AIR POST SEMI-POSTAL STAMP

French Revolution Issue
Common Design Type

1939	**Unwmk.**	**Photo.**	*Perf. 13*	
Name and Value Typo. in Orange				
CB1	CD83	4.50fr + 4fr brn blk	35.00	35.00

POSTAGE DUE STAMPS

Numeral of Value on Equatorial Butterfly — D1

1937		**Unwmk.**	**Photo.**	*Perf. 13*	
J1	D1	5c redsh pur & lt bl	.25	.40	
		Never hinged	.40		
		On cover		20.00	
J2	D1	10c cop red & buff	.25	.40	
		Never hinged	.40		
		On cover		20.00	
J3	D1	20c dk grn & grn	.30	.50	
		Never hinged	.50		
		On cover		20.00	
J4	D1	25c red brn & buff	.30	.50	
		Never hinged	.50		
		On cover		20.00	
J5	D1	30c cop red & lt bl	.50	.55	
		Never hinged	.55		
		On cover		20.00	

J6	D1	45c mag & yel grn	.75	.80
		Never hinged	.95	
		On cover		24.00
J7	D1	50c dk ol grn & buff	.80	.95
		Never hinged	1.10	
		On cover		24.00
J8	D1	60c redsh pur & yel	.95	1.10
		Never hinged	1.25	
		On cover		27.50
J9	D1	1fr brown & yel	1.00	1.20
		Never hinged	1.40	
		On cover		27.50
J10	D1	2fr dk bl & buff	1.40	1.50
		Never hinged	1.75	
		On cover		35.00
J11	D1	3fr red brn & lt grn	1.75	1.75
		Never hinged	2.25	
		On cover		45.00
		Nos. J1-J11 (11)	8.25	9.65
		Set, never hinged	11.00	

FRENCH GUIANA

'french gē-'a-nə

LOCATION — On the northeast coast of South America bordering on the Atlantic Ocean.
GOVT. — French colony
AREA — 34,740 sq. mi.
POP. — 28,537 (1946)
CAPITAL — Cayenne

100 Centimes = 1 Franc

Stamps of French Colonies Surcharged in Black

1886, Dec.   **Unwmk.**   **Imperf.**

1	A8	5c on 2c grn, *grnsh*, srchg 12mm high	750.00 675.00
a.		Double surcharge	1,900. 1,900.
b.		Surcharge 10½mm high	900.00 825.00
c.		No "f" after "O"	950.00 850.00

Perf. 14x13½

2	A9	5c on 2c brn, *buff*, srchg 12mm high	650.00 600.00
a.		No "f" after "O"	525.00 450.00
b.		As "a," double surcharge	1,700. 1,700.

Nos. 1-2 unused are valued without gum.

Stamps of French Colonies Overprinted in Black

"Av" of Date Line Inverted-Reversed
1887, Apr.   **Imperf.**

4	A8	20c on 35c blk, *org*	70.00 57.50
		On cover	1,500.
a.		Double surcharge	225.00 225.00
b.		No "f" after "O"	150.00 150.00

Date Line Reads "Avril 1887"

5	A8	5c on 2c grn, *grnsh*	175.00 125.00
a.		Double surcharge	900.00 900.00
b.		No "f" after "O"	375.00 375.00
c.		Pair, one stamp without surcharge	1,500.
6	A8	20c on 35c blk, *org*	375.00 375.00
a.		Double surcharge	1,250. 1,250.
b.		No "f" after "O"	850.00 850.00
c.		Vertical pair, #6 + #4	2,200.
7	A7	25c on 30c brn, *yelsh*	55.00 47.50
		On cover	2,500.
a.		Double surcharge	900.00 900.00
b.		No "f" after "O"	275.00 275.00

Nos. 4-7 unused are valued without gum.

French Colonies Nos. 22 and 26 Surcharged

8	A7	5c on 30c brn, *yelsh*	155.00 140.00
		On cover	3,000.
a.		Double surcharge	800.00 800.00
b.		Inverted surcharge	1,200. 1,200.
c.		Pair, one without surcharge	1,600.
9	A8	5c on 30c brn, *yelsh*	1,500. 1,500.

Nos. 8-9 unused are valued without gum.

French Colonies Nos. 22 and 28 Surcharged

1888

10	A7	5c on 30c brn, *yelsh*	155.00 140.00
		On cover	3,750.
b.		Double surcharge	500.00 500.00
c.		Inverted surcharge	600.00 600.00
11	A8	10c on 75c car, *rose*	400.00 290.00
		No gum	290.00
a.		Double surcharge	1,100. 1,100.
b.		Pair, one stamp without surcharge	2,500.

No. 10 unused is valued without gum.

Stamps of French Colonies Overprinted in Black

1892, Feb. 20   **Imperf.**

12	A8	2c grn, *grnsh*	850.00 975.00
		On cover	2,250.
a.		Inverted overprint	3,500.
13	A7	30c brn, *yelsh*	155.00 155.00
		On cover	625.00
a.		Inverted overprint	575.00 575.00
14	A8	35c blk, *orange*	2,850. 3,000.
15	A8	40c red, *straw*	175.00 140.00
		No gum	130.00
		On cover	675.00
16	A8	75c car, *rose*	180.00 140.00
		No gum	140.00
		On cover	1,050.
a.		Inverted overprint	625.00 550.00
		No gum	500.00
17	A8	1fr brnz grn, *straw*	210.00 160.00
		On cover	180.00
a.		Inverted overprint	800.00 800.00
b.		Double overprint	800.00 800.00
c.		Triple overprint	1,800. 1,800.

Nos. 12-14 unused are valued without gum.

1892   **Perf. 14x13½**

18	A9	1c blk, *lil bl*	47.50 35.00
		Never hinged	100.00
		On cover	600.00
19	A9	2c brn, *buff*	45.00 37.50
		Never hinged	95.00
		On cover	600.00
20	A9	4c claret, *lav*	42.50 37.50
		Never hinged	105.00
		On cover	725.00
21	A9	5c grn, *grnsh*	47.50 35.00
		Never hinged	100.00
		On cover	375.00
a.		Inverted overprint	150.00 150.00
b.		Double overprint	150.00 150.00
22	A9	10c blk, *lavender*	67.50 40.00
		Never hinged	160.00
		On cover	350.00
a.		Inverted overprint	200.00 200.00
b.		Double overprint	275.00 275.00
23	A9	15c blue	67.50 45.00
		Never hinged	160.00
		On cover	350.00
a.		Double overprint	275.00 200.00
24	A9	20c red, *grn*	55.00 42.50
		Never hinged	125.00
		On cover	375.00
a.		Inverted overprint	225.00 225.00
25	A9	25c blk, *rose*	75.00 35.00
		On cover	475.00
a.		Double overprint	275.00 275.00
b.		Triple overprint	300.00 300.00
26	A9	30c brn, *bis*	47.50 40.00
		Never hinged	100.00
		On cover	475.00
27	A9	35c blk, *orange*	225.00 225.00
		On cover	1,500.
a.		Inverted overprint	575.00 575.00
28	A9	40c red, *straw*	135.00 135.00
		On cover	675.00
a.		Inverted overprint	300.00 300.00
29	A9	75c car, *rose*	145.00 125.00
		On cover	925.00
30	A9	1fr brnz grn, *straw*	250.00 220.00
		On cover	1,150.
a.		Double overprint	375.00
		Nos. 18-30 (13)	1,250. 1,052.

French Colonies No. 51 Surcharged

1892, Dec.

31	A9	5c on 15c blue	70.00 47.50
		On cover	325.00
		On cover, single franking	1,500.
a.		Double surcharge	300.00 275.00
b.		No "f" after "O"	160.00 135.00
c.		Pair, one stamp without surcharge	1,700. 1,700.

Navigation and Commerce — A12

1892-1904   **Typo.**   **Perf. 14x13½**
Name of Colony in Blue or Carmine

32	A12	1c blk, *lil bl*	2.00 1.75
		Never hinged	3.00
		On cover	160.00
33	A12	2c brn, *buff*	1.45 1.45
		Never hinged	1.90
		On cover	160.00
34	A12	4c claret, *lav*	2.00 1.90
		Never hinged	3.00
		On cover	125.00
a.		"GUYANE" double	275.00
35	A12	5c grn, *grnsh*	12.50 11.00
		Never hinged	20.00
		On cover	62.50
36	A12	5c yel grn ('04)	2.40 1.60
		Never hinged	3.75
		On cover	40.00
37	A12	10c blk, *lavender*	13.50 8.25
		Never hinged	20.00
		On cover	50.00
38	A12	10c red ('00)	4.75 1.60
		Never hinged	8.00
		On cover	45.00
39	A12	15c blue, quadrille paper	42.50 4.00
		Never hinged	77.50
		On cover	35.00
40	A12	15c gray, *lt gray* ('00)	122.50 110.00
		Never hinged	245.00
		On cover	625.00
41	A12	20c red, *grn*	25.00 18.00
		Never hinged	47.50
		On cover	85.00
		On cover, single franking	175.00
42	A12	25c blk, *rose*	20.00 5.50
		Never hinged	40.00
		On cover	42.50
		On cover, single franking	97.50
43	A12	25c blue ('00)	22.50 22.50
		Never hinged	37.50
		On cover	240.00
		On cover, single franking	325.00
44	A12	30c brn, *bis*	24.00 18.00
		Never hinged	45.00
		On cover	42.50
		On cover, single franking	72.50
45	A12	40c red, *straw*	24.00 16.00
		Never hinged	45.00
		On cover	85.00
		On cover, single franking	175.00
46	A12	50c car, *rose*	35.00 18.00
		Never hinged	65.00
		On cover	175.00
		On cover, single franking	300.00
47	A12	50c brn, *az* ('00)	26.00 26.00
		Never hinged	45.00
		On cover	275.00
		On cover, single franking	425.00
48	A12	75c dp vio, *org*	37.50 27.50
		Never hinged	75.00
		On cover	175.00
		On cover, single franking	325.00
49	A12	1fr brn grn, *straw*	18.00 14.00
		Never hinged	37.50
		On cover	190.00
		On cover, single franking	350.00
50	A12	2fr vio, *rose* ('02)	180.00 16.00
		Never hinged	375.00
		On cover	400.00
		On cover, single franking	850.00
		Nos. 32-50 (19)	615.60 323.05

Perf. 13½x14 stamps are counterfeits.
For surcharges see Nos. 87-93.

Great Anteater — A13   Washing Gold — A14

Palm Grove at Cayenne A15

1905-28

51	A13	1c black	.40 .40
		Never hinged	.65
		On cover	45.00
		On cover, single franking	160.00
52	A13	2c blue	.40 .40
		Never hinged	.65
		On cover	40.00
		On cover, single franking	140.00
a.		Imperf	57.50
		Never hinged	105.00
53	A13	4c red brn	.40 .40
		Never hinged	.65
		On cover	40.00
		On cover, single franking	120.00
54	A13	5c green	1.25 1.10
		Never hinged	1.75
		On cover	32.50
55	A13	5c org ('22)	.40 .45
		Never hinged	.65
		On cover	40.00
		On cover, single franking	100.00
56	A13	10c rose	1.50 1.10
		Never hinged	2.10
		On cover	32.50
57	A13	10c grn ('22)	.65 .40
		Never hinged	1.10
		On cover	32.50

58	A13	10c red, *bluish* ('25)	.45 .45
		Never hinged	.70
		On cover	27.50
59	A13	15c violet	1.15 1.25
		Never hinged	2.40
		On cover	40.00
60	A14	20c red brn	.65 .65
		Never hinged	.95
		On cover	32.50
61	A14	25c blue	3.00 1.60
		Never hinged	4.75
		On cover	47.50
		On cover, single franking	120.00
62	A14	25c vio ('22)	.60 .50
		Never hinged	1.10
		On cover	27.50
63	A14	30c black	2.50 1.00
		Never hinged	4.00
		On cover	40.00
		On cover, single franking	120.00
64	A14	30c rose ('22)	.50 .60
		Never hinged	1.00
		On cover	40.00
65	A14	30c red org ('25)	.45 .45
		Never hinged	.70
		On cover	24.00
66	A14	30c dk grn, *grnsh* ('28)	1.35 1.35
		Never hinged	2.00
		On cover	47.50
67	A14	35c blk, *yel* ('06)	.65 .65
		Never hinged	1.00
		On cover	40.00
		On cover, single franking	150.00
68	A14	40c rose	1.50 .85
		Never hinged	2.50
		On cover	40.00
		On cover, single franking	92.50
69	A14	40c black ('22)	.40 .45
		Never hinged	.65
		On cover	32.50
		On cover, single franking	100.00
70	A14	45c olive ('07)	1.00 .95
		Never hinged	1.50
		On cover	40.00
		On cover	80.00
71	A14	50c violet	4.25 3.50
		Never hinged	6.50
		On cover	40.00
		On cover, single franking	120.00
72	A14	50c blue ('22)	.55 .65
		Never hinged	1.00
		On cover	40.00
		On cover, single franking	100.00
73	A14	50c gray ('25)	.80 .80
		Never hinged	1.20
		On cover	47.50
		On cover, single franking	110.00
74	A14	60c lil, *rose* ('25)	.65 .65
		Never hinged	.95
		On cover	45.00
		On cover, single franking	100.00
75	A14	65c myr grn ('26)	.85 .80
		Never hinged	1.20
		On cover	60.00
		On cover, single franking	110.00
76	A14	75c green	1.60 1.40
		Never hinged	2.40
		On cover	55.00
		On cover, single franking	180.00
77	A14	85c magenta ('26)	.85 .80
		Never hinged	1.30
		On cover	67.50
		On cover, single franking	120.00
78	A15	1fr rose	.90 .85
		Never hinged	1.50
		On cover	47.50
		On cover, single franking	100.00
a.		Imperf	82.50
		Never hinged	135.00
79	A15	1fr bl, *bluish* ('25)	.85 .80
		Never hinged	1.30
		On cover	55.00
		On cover, single franking	120.00
80	A15	1fr bl, *yel grn* ('28)	2.75 2.75
		Never hinged	4.00
		On cover	52.50
		On cover, single franking	80.00
81	A15	1.10fr lt red ('28)	1.50 1.50
		Never hinged	2.25
		On cover	60.00
		On cover, single franking	110.00
82	A15	2fr blue	1.35 1.35
		Never hinged	2.50
		On cover	60.00
		On cover, single franking	120.00
83	A15	2fr org red, *yel* ('26)	2.75 2.40
		Never hinged	4.50
		On cover	67.50
		On cover, single franking	140.00
84	A15	5fr black	8.50 6.50
		Never hinged	15.00
		On cover	80.00
		On cover, single franking	180.00
a.		Imperf	82.50
		Never hinged	140.00
85	A15	10fr grn, *yel* ('24)	14.00 14.50
		Never hinged	22.00
		On cover	80.00
		On cover, single franking	180.00
a.		Printed on both sides	140.00
		Never hinged	240.00
b.		Chalky paper	14.50 16.00
		Never hinged	24.00
86	A15	20fr brn lake ('24)	17.50 17.50
		Never hinged	24.00
		On cover	110.00
		On cover, single franking	225.00
a.		Chalky paper	21.00 19.00
		Never hinged	32.50
		Nos. 51-86 (36)	79.45 71.75

For surcharges see Nos. 94-108, B1-B2.

Issue of 1892 Surcharged in Black or Carmine

1912
Spacing between figures of surcharge 1.5mm (5c), 2mm (10c)

No.	Type	Description		
87	A12	5c on 2c brn, *buff*	1.60	2.00
		Never hinged	2.75	
		On cover		90.00
88	A12	5c on 4c cl, *lav* (C)	1.20	1.60
b.		Chalky paper	14.50	16.00
		Never hinged	2.10	
		On cover		90.00
89	A12	5c on 20c red, *grn*	1.75	1.90
		Never hinged	3.00	
		On cover		90.00
90	A12	5c on 25c blk, *rose* (C)	4.00	4.75
		Never hinged	6.50	
		On cover		120.00
91	A12	5c on 30c brn, *bis* (C)	1.75	1.90
		Never hinged	3.00	
		On cover		90.00
92	A12	10c on 40c red, *straw*	1.40	1.90
		Never hinged	2.40	
		On cover		90.00
a.		Pair, one stamp without surcharge	1,250.	
93	A12	10c on 50c car, *rose*	4.25	5.25
		Never hinged	7.00	
		On cover		120.00
a.		Double surcharge	550.00	
		Nos. 87-93 (7)	15.95	19.30

Spacing between figures of surcharge 2.25mm (5c), 2.75mm (10c)

No.	Type	Description		
87a	A12	5c on 2c brn, *buff*	21.00	21.00
		Never hinged	45.00	
88a	A12	5c on 4c cl, *lav* (C)	12.50	12.50
		Never hinged	24.00	
89a	A12	5c on 20c red, *grn*	21.00	21.00
		Never hinged	40.00	
90a	A12	5c on 25c blk, *rose* (C)	35.00	35.00
		Never hinged	67.50	
91a	A12	5c on 30c brn, *bis* (C)	21.00	21.00
		Never hinged	40.00	
92b	A12	10c on 40c red, *straw*	140.00	140.00
		Never hinged	275.00	
93b	A12	10c on 50c car, *rose*	300.00	300.00
		Never hinged	550.00	
		Nos. 87a-93b (7)	550.50	550.50

No. 59 Surcharged in Various Colors

1922

No.	Type	Description		
94	A13	1c on 15c vio (Bk)	.65	.75
		Never hinged	.95	
		On cover		60.00
		On cover, single franking		160.00
a.		Double surcharge	90.00	
		Never hinged	135.00	
95	A13	2c on 15c vio (Bl)	.65	.75
		Never hinged	.95	
		On cover		60.00
		On cover, single franking		150.00
a.		Inverted surcharge	97.50	
		Never hinged	155.00	
b.		In pair with unovptd. stamp	250.00	
		Never hinged	425.00	
c.		No. 95a, in pair with unovptd. stamp	850.00	
		Never hinged	1,275.	
96	A13	4c on 15c vio (G)	.65	.75
		Never hinged	.95	
		On cover		52.50
		On cover, single franking		140.00
a.		Double surcharge	90.00	
		Never hinged	135.00	
b.		In pair with unovptd. stamp	275.00	
		Never hinged	475.00	
97	A13	5c on 15c vio (R)	.65	.75
		Never hinged	.95	
		On cover		45.00
		On cover, single franking		100.00
a.		In pair with unovptd. stamp	275.00	
		Never hinged	475.00	
		Nos. 94-97 (4)	2.60	3.00

Type of 1905-28 Srchd. in Blue

1923

No.	Type	Description		
98	A15	10fr on 1fr grn, *yel*	22.50	24.00
		Never hinged	32.50	
		On cover		100.00
		On cover, single franking		225.00
99	A15	20fr on 5fr lilac, *rose*	22.50	24.00
		Never hinged	32.50	
		On cover		125.00
		On cover, single franking		260.00

Stamps and Types of 1905-28 Srchd. in Black or Red

1924-27

No.	Type	Description		
100	A13	25c on 15c vio ('25)	.85	.85
		Never hinged	1.20	
		On cover		32.50
a.		Triple surcharge	130.00	130.00
		Never hinged	205.00	
b.		In pair with unovptd. stamp	260.00	
		Never hinged	425.00	
101	A15	25c on 2fr bl ('24)	.90	.95
		Never hinged	1.60	
		On cover		32.50
a.		Double surcharge	140.00	
		Never hinged	225.00	
b.		Triple surcharge	150.00	
		Never hinged	240.00	
102	A14	65c on 45c ol (R) ('25)	1.75	1.90
		Never hinged	2.75	
		On cover		60.00
		On cover, single franking		130.00
103	A14	85c on 45c ol (R) ('25)	1.75	1.90
		Never hinged	2.75	
		On cover		67.50
		On cover, single franking		140.00
104	A14	90c on 75c red ('27)	1.50	1.50
		Never hinged	2.50	
		On cover		65.00
		On cover, single franking		140.00
105	A15	1.05fr on 2fr lt yel brn ('27)	1.50	1.50
		Never hinged	2.50	
		On cover		72.50
		On cover, single franking		160.00
106	A15	1.25fr on 1fr ultra (R) ('26)	1.60	1.75
		Never hinged	2.75	
		On cover		45.00
		On cover, single franking		80.00
107	A15	1.50fr on 1fr lt bl ('27)	1.60	1.75
		Never hinged	2.75	
		On cover		47.50
		On cover, single franking		120.00
108	A15	3fr on 5fr vio ('27)	1.75	2.00
		Never hinged	3.00	
		On cover		55.00
		On cover, single franking		130.00
a.		No period after "F"	12.00	12.00
		Never hinged	20.00	
		Nos. 100-108 (9)	13.20	14.10

Carib Archer — A16

Shooting Rapids, Maroni River A17

Government Building, Cayenne — A18

1929-40   Perf. 13½x14

No.	Type	Description		
109	A16	1c gray lil & grnsh bl	.25	.25
		Never hinged	.40	
		On cover		55.00
a.		Imperf	35.00	
		Never hinged	50.00	
110	A16	2c dk red & bl grn	.25	.25
		Never hinged	.40	
		On cover		52.50
a.		Imperf	35.00	
		Never hinged	50.00	
111	A16	3c gray lil & grnsh bl ('40)	.30	.30
		Never hinged	.50	
		On cover		52.50
112	A16	4c ol brn & red vio	.30	.30
		Never hinged	.55	
		On cover		52.50
113	A16	5c Prus bl & red org	.30	.30
		Never hinged	.55	
		On cover		47.50
114	A16	10c mag & brn	.30	.30
		Never hinged	.55	
		On cover		45.00
115	A16	15c yel brn & red org	.30	.30
		Never hinged	.55	
		On cover		40.00
a.		Imperf	35.00	
		Never hinged	50.00	
116	A16	20c dk bl & ol grn	.30	.30
		Never hinged	.55	
		On cover		32.50
117	A16	25c dk red & dk brn	.50	.50
		Never hinged	.75	
		On cover		27.50

Perf. 14x13½

No.	Type	Description		
118	A17	30c dl & lt grn	.70	.70
		Never hinged	1.00	
		On cover		32.50
119	A17	30c grn & brn ('40)	.50	.50
		Never hinged	.70	
		On cover		472.50
120	A17	35c Prus grn & ol grn ('38)	1.10	1.10
		Never hinged	1.40	
		On cover		32.50
121	A17	40c org brn & ol gray	.30	.30
		Never hinged	.55	
		On cover		32.50
122	A17	45c grn & dk brn	1.20	1.20
		Never hinged	1.60	
		On cover		32.50
123	A17	45c ol grn & lt grn ('40)	.70	.70
		Never hinged	1.00	
		On cover		45.00
124	A17	50c dk bl & ol gray	.40	.40
		Never hinged	.55	
		On cover		27.50
a.		Imperf	35.00	
		Never hinged	50.00	
125	A17	55c vio bl & car ('38)	1.50	1.50
		Never hinged	2.00	
		On cover		35.00
126	A17	60c sal & grn ('40)	.75	.75
		Never hinged	1.05	
		On cover		40.00
a.		Imperf	47.50	
		Never hinged	67.50	
127	A17	65c sal & grn	1.10	1.10
		Never hinged	1.40	
		On cover		40.00
128	A17	70c ind & sl bl ('40)	1.30	1.30
		Never hinged	1.90	
		On cover		32.50
129	A17	75c ind & sl bl	1.15	1.15
		Never hinged	1.75	
		On cover		35.00
130	A17	80c blk & vio bl ('38)	.80	.80
		Never hinged	1.00	
		On cover		35.00
131	A17	90c dk red & ver	1.10	1.10
		Never hinged	1.50	
		On cover		40.00
		On cover, single franking		80.00
132	A17	90c red vio & brn ('39)	1.30	1.30
		Never hinged	1.60	
		On cover		32.50
133	A17	1fr lt vio & brn	.70	.70
		Never hinged	1.00	
		On cover		40.00
		On cover, single franking		72.50
134	A17	1fr car & lt red ('38)	2.10	2.10
		Never hinged	3.00	
		On cover		47.50
		On cover, single franking		80.00
135	A17	1fr blk & vio bl ('40)	.80	.80
		Never hinged	1.00	
		On cover		32.50
136	A18	1.05fr ver & olivine	6.25	6.25
		Never hinged	9.75	
		On cover		60.00
		On cover, single franking		110.00
137	A18	1.10fr ol brn & red vio	7.25	5.75
		Never hinged	11.50	
		On cover		67.50
		On cover, single franking		140.00
138	A18	1.25fr blk brn & bl grn ('33)	.80	.80
		Never hinged	1.20	
		On cover		40.00
		On cover, single franking		67.50
139	A18	1.25fr rose & lt red ('39)	1.10	1.10
		Never hinged	1.40	
		On cover		72.50
		On cover, single franking		110.00
140	A18	1.40fr ol brn & red vio ('40)	1.30	1.30
		Never hinged	1.75	
		On cover		52.50
		On cover, single franking		80.00
141	A18	1.50fr dk bl & lt bl	.40	.40
		Never hinged	.65	
		On cover		47.50
		On cover, single franking		100.00
142	A18	1.60fr ol brn & bl grn ('40)	1.30	1.30
		Never hinged	1.75	
		On cover		52.50
		On cover, single franking		110.00
143	A18	1.75fr brn red & blk brn ('33)	2.25	2.25
		Never hinged	3.00	
		On cover		55.00
		On cover, single franking		110.00
144	A18	1.75fr vio bl ('38)	1.75	1.75
		Never hinged	2.40	
		On cover		47.50
		On cover, single franking		80.00
145	A18	2fr dk grn & rose red	.65	.65
		Never hinged	1.00	
		On cover		67.50
		On cover, single franking		110.00
146	A18	2.25fr vio bl ('39)	1.30	1.30
		Never hinged	1.60	
		On cover		65.00
		On cover, single franking		100.00
147	A18	2.50fr cop red & brn ('40)	1.30	1.30
		Never hinged	1.75	
		On cover		65.00
		On cover, single franking		100.00
148	A18	3fr brn red & red vio	.75	.75
		Never hinged	1.20	
		On cover		55.00
		On cover, single franking		110.00
149	A18	5fr dl vio & yel grn	1.25	1.25
		Never hinged	2.00	
		On cover		65.00
		On cover, single franking		110.00
150	A18	10fr ol gray & dp ultra	1.50	1.50
		Never hinged	2.10	
		On cover		87.50
		On cover, single franking		160.00
151	A18	20fr indigo & ver	2.50	2.50
		Never hinged	3.50	
		On cover		95.00
		On cover, single franking		180.00
		Nos. 109-151 (43)	51.95	50.45

For types A16-A18 without "RF," see Nos. 170C-170E.

Common Design Types pictured following the introduction.

Colonial Exposition Issue
Common Design Types

1931   Engr.   Perf. 12½
Name of Country in Black

No.	Type	Description		
152	CD70	40c dp green	5.50	5.50
		Never hinged	7.50	
		On cover		65.00
153	CD71	50c violet	5.50	5.50
		Never hinged	7.50	
		On cover		47.50
154	CD72	90c red orange	5.50	5.50
		Never hinged	7.50	
		On cover, single franking		120.00
155	CD73	1.50fr dull blue	5.50	5.50
		Never hinged	7.50	
		On cover		72.50
		On cover, single franking		110.00
		Nos. 152-155 (4)	22.00	22.00

Recapture of Cayenne by d'Estrées, 1676 — A19

Products of French Guiana A20

1935, Oct. 21   Perf. 13

No.	Type	Description		
156	A19	40c gray brn	5.75	5.75
		Never hinged	8.00	
		On cover		65.00
157	A19	50c dull red	10.00	8.00
		Never hinged	14.00	
		On cover		47.50
158	A19	1.50fr ultra	5.75	5.75
		Never hinged	8.00	
		On cover		72.50
		On cover, single franking		110.00
159	A20	1.75fr lilac rose	12.50	11.50
		Never hinged	19.00	
		On cover		65.00
		On cover, single franking		92.50
160	A20	5fr brown	10.00	9.00
		Never hinged	14.00	
		On cover		65.00
		On cover, single franking		92.50
161	A20	10fr blue green	10.50	10.00
		Never hinged	16.00	
		On cover		140.00
		On cover, single franking		180.00
		Nos. 156-161 (6)	54.50	50.00

Tercentenary of the founding of French possessions in the West Indies.

Paris International Exposition Issue
Common Design Types

1937, Apr. 15

162	CD74	20c deep violet	1.75	1.75
		Never hinged	2.50	
		On cover		60.00
163	CD75	30c dark green	1.75	1.75
		Never hinged	2.50	
		On cover		47.50
164	CD76	40c carmine rose	1.75	1.75
		Never hinged	2.50	
		On cover		45.00
165	CD77	50c dark brown	1.75	1.75
		Never hinged	2.50	
		On cover		40.00
166	CD78	90c red	1.75	1.75
		Never hinged	2.75	
		On cover		80.00
		On cover, single franking		140.00
167	CD79	1.50fr ultra	2.25	2.25
		Never hinged	3.50	
		On cover		72.50
		On cover, single franking		120.00
		Nos. 162-167 (6)	11.00	11.00

Colonial Arts Exhibition Issue
Souvenir Sheet
Common Design Type

1937   *Imperf.*

168	CD75	3fr violet	11.50	13.50
		Never hinged	16.00	
		On cover		100.00
		On cover, single franking		150.00
a.		Marginal inscription inverted	2,600.	
		Never hinged	3,400.	

New York World's Fair Issue
Common Design Type

1939, May 10   **Engr.**   *Perf. 12½x12*

169	CD82	1.25fr car lake	1.30	1.30
		Never hinged	1.75	
		On cover		80.00
		On cover, single franking		130.00
170	CD82	2.25fr ultra	1.30	1.30
		Never hinged	1.75	
		On cover		72.50
		On cover, single franking		110.00

SEMI-POSTAL STAMPS

Regular Issue of 1905-28 Surcharged in Red

1915   **Unwmk.**   *Perf. 13½x14*

B1	A13	10c + 5c rose	17.50	18.00
		Never hinged	29.00	
		On cover		175.00
a.		Inverted surcharge	250.00	250.00
b.		Double surcharge	250.00	250.00

Regular Issue of 1905-28 Surcharged in Rose

B2	A13	10c + 5c rose	1.60	1.60
		Never hinged	2.40	
		On cover		25.00

Curie Issue
Common Design Type

1938   *Perf. 13*

B3	CD80	1.75fr + 50c brt ultra	13.50	13.50
		Never hinged	19.50	

French Revolution Issue
Common Design Type

1939   **Photo.**
Name and Value in Black

B4	CD83	45c + 25c green	11.50	11.50
		Never hinged	17.00	
		On cover		92.50
B5	CD83	70c + 30c brown	11.50	11.50
		Never hinged	17.00	
		On cover		67.50
B6	CD83	90c + 35c red org	11.50	11.50
		Never hinged	17.00	
		On cover		65.00
B7	CD83	1.25fr + 1fr rose pink	11.50	11.50
		Never hinged	17.00	
		On cover		110.00
		On cover, single franking		160.00
B8	CD83	2.25fr + 2fr blue	11.50	11.50
		Never hinged	17.00	
		On cover		100.00
		On cover, single franking		140.00
		Nos. B4-B8 (5)	57.50	57.50

AIR POST STAMPS

Cayenne — AP1

Perf. 13½

1933, Nov. 20   **Unwmk.**   **Photo.**

C1	AP1	50c orange brn	.30	.30
		Never hinged	.50	
		On cover		52.50
C2	AP1	1fr yellow grn	.50	.50
		Never hinged	.90	
		On cover		35.00
C3	AP1	1.50fr dk blue	.70	.70
		Never hinged	1.05	
		On cover		55.00
		On cover, single franking		110.00
C4	AP1	2fr orange	.70	.70
		Never hinged	1.05	
		On cover		55.00
		On cover, single franking		110.00
C5	AP1	3fr black	.85	.85
		Never hinged	1.10	
		On cover		65.00
		On cover, single franking		110.00
C6	AP1	5fr violet	.85	.85
		Never hinged	1.10	
		On cover		72.50
		On cover, single franking		120.00
C7	AP1	10fr olive grn	.85	.85
		Never hinged	1.10	
		On cover		92.50
		On cover, single franking		160.00
C8	AP1	20fr scarlet	1.25	1.25
		Never hinged	2.00	
		On cover		100.00
		On cover, single franking		160.00
		Nos. C1-C8 (8)	6.00	6.00

For No. C1 without "RF," see No. C8A.
A 20fr violet exists, but was not regularly issued. Value, $175.

AIR POST SEMI-POSTAL STAMP

French Revolution Issue
Common Design Type
Unwmk.

1939, July 5   **Photo.**   *Perf. 13*
Name & Value Typo. in Orange

CB1	CD83	5fr + 4fr brn blk	22.00	22.00
a.		Never hinged	35.00	
		On cover		47.50
		On cover, single franking		100.00

SOCIETE DE TRANSPORTS AERIENS GUYANAIS

During 1920-22, a pioneering airline, *La Société des Transports Aériens Guyanais*, maintained service between Cayenne, Saint Laurent du Maroni and Inini, with less regular flights to Paramaribo, Surinam. During July-Oct. 1921, T.A.G. produced stamps to prepay the 75c internal airmail fee, under contract with the postal authorities. After October, these stamps were replaced by regular French Guiana issues.

Nos CL1-CL15 were issued without gum.

APSO1

1921, July 8   *Imperf.*

CL1	APSO1	75c red vio, bluish	1,600.	1,750.
		On cover		3,750.
		Block of 4	7,000.	7,750.

1921, July 9   *Pin-Perf*

CL2	APSO1	75c red vio, org brn	2,600.	2,300.
		On cover		5,000.
		Block of 4	10,500.	10,500.

Nos CL1-CL2 were for use on the St. Laurent du Maroni-Cayenne Route. Used examples were usually cancelled by a manuscript signature in red ink.

All stamps were overprinted in red violet with a large oval inscribed "Societe Des Transports Aeriens Guyanais" on the front, and by a similar overprint, inscribed "St. Laurent du Maroni" on the reverse. Because the overprint covers four stamps, each individual stamp shows approximately one-fourth of the oval.

APSO2

1921, July 8   *Imperf.*

CL3	APSO2	75c blk, *grayish*	1,200.	750.00
		On cover		1,500.
		Tête-bêche pair	12,000.	12,000.
CL4	APSO2	75c blk, *bluish*	1,250.	800.00
		On cover		1,550.
		Tête-bêche pair	12,000.	12,000.
CL5	APSO2	75c blk, *sal*	1,350.	850.00
		On cover		1,750.

For flights from Cayene, St. Laurent du Maroni and return. Flown letters bearing Nos. CL3-CL15 were cancelled "Avion"

Because the letters "T.A.G." and the denomination "0.75" were printed separately from the rest of the design, their position on the stamp varies.

APSO3

Two Die Types:
Type I, lower part of right frame line straight.
Type II, lower part of right frame line curved outward.
There are many minor differences between the two dies, but the angle of the frame line is sufficient for identification.

1921, Sept.

CL6	APSO3	75c blk, *gray* (I)	1,350.	975.00
		On cover		2,100.
		Tête-bêche pair	12,000.	12,000.
CL7	APSO3	75c blk, *bluish* (I)	1,400.	1,050.
		On cover		2,100.
		Tête-bêche pair	12,000.	12,000.
CL8	APSO3	75c blk, *sal* (I)	15,000.	
CL9	APSO3	75c blk, *rose* (II)	1,700.	1,250.
		On cover		2,400.

For flights from Cayenne to St. Laurent du Maroni and return and from St. Laurent du Maroni to Inini and return.

APSO4

1921, Sept.

CL10	APSO4	75c blk, *gray*	2,900.	2,750.
		On cover		5,500.
CL11	APSO4	75c blk, *bluish*	3,000.	
CL12	APSO4	75c blk, *sal*	1,400.	1,200.
		On cover		2,400.
CL13	APSO4	75c blk, *rose*	1,800.	1,500.
		On cover		3,000.
CL14	APSO4	75c blk, *yel*	1,900.	1,800.
		On cover		3,600.
CL15	APSO4	75c blk, *straw*	1,900.	1,800.
		On cover		3,600.

Nos. CL10-CL15 were for use on all T.A.G. flights.

POSTAGE DUE STAMPS

Postage Due Stamps of France, 1893-1926, Overprinted

1925-27   **Unwmk.**   *Perf. 14x13½*

J1	D2	5c light blue	.70	.75
		Never hinged	1.30	
		On cover. *from*		200.00
a.		In pair with unovptd. stamp	375.00	
J2	D2	10c brown	1.00	1.10
		Never hinged	1.75	
		On cover. *from*		200.00
J3	D2	20c olive green	1.10	1.25
		Never hinged	2.10	
		On cover. *from*		200.00
J4	D2	50c violet brown	1.50	1.60
		Never hinged	2.60	
		On cover. *from*		200.00
J5	D2	3fr magenta ('27)	11.00	12.50
		Never hinged	27.00	
		On cover. *from*		200.00

Surcharged in Black

J6	D2	15c on 20c ol grn	1.00	1.10
		Never hinged	1.75	
		On cover. *from*		200.00
a.		Blue surcharge	67.50	
		Never hinged	105.00	
J7	D2	25c on 5c lt bl	1.30	1.40
		Never hinged	2.50	
		On cover. *from*		200.00
a.		In pair with unovptd. stamp	375.00	
J8	D2	30c on 20c ol grn	1.50	1.60
		Never hinged	2.60	
		On cover. *from*		200.00
J9	D2	45c on 10c brn	1.50	1.60
		Never hinged	2.60	
		On cover. *from*		200.00
J10	D2	60c on 5c lt bl	1.50	1.60
		Never hinged	2.60	
		On cover. *from*		200.00
J11	D2	1fr on 20c ol grn	2.25	2.40
		Never hinged	3.75	
		On cover. *from*		250.00
J12	D2	2fr on 50c vio brn	2.25	2.40
		Never hinged	3.75	
		On cover. *from*		250.00
		Nos. J1-J12 (12)	26.60	29.30

Royal Palms — D3   Guiana Girl — D4

1929, Oct. 14   **Typo.**   *Perf. 13½x14*

J13	D3	5c indigo & Prus bl	.45	.50
		Never hinged	.60	
		On cover. *from*		300.00
J14	D3	10c bis brn & Prus grn	.45	.50
		Never hinged	.60	
		On cover. *from*		300.00
J15	D3	20c grn & rose red	.45	.50
		Never hinged	.60	
		On cover. *from*		300.00
J16	D3	30c ol brn & rose red	.45	.50
		Never hinged	.60	
		On cover. *from*		300.00
J17	D3	50c vio & ol brn	.95	1.00
		Never hinged	1.25	
		On cover. *from*		300.00
J18	D3	60c brn red & ol brn	1.30	1.40
		Never hinged	2.00	
		On cover. *from*		300.00
J19	D4	1fr dp bl & org brn	1.75	1.90
		Never hinged	2.60	
		On cover. *from*		300.00
J20	D4	2fr brn red & bluish grn	2.00	2.10
		Never hinged	3.00	
		On cover. *from*		300.00
J21	D4	3fr violet & blk	4.25	4.50
		Never hinged	5.75	
		On cover. *from*		300.00
		Nos. J13-J21 (9)	12.05	12.90

FRENCH GUINEA

'french 'gi-nē

LOCATION — On the coast of West Africa, between Portuguese Guinea and Sierra Leone.
GOVT. — Former French colony
AREA — 89,436 sq. mi.
POP. — 2,058,442 (est. 1941)
CAPITAL — Conakry

French Guinea stamps were replaced by those of French West Africa around 1944-45. French Guinea became the Republic of Guinea Oct. 2, 1958.

100 Centimes = 1 Franc

Navigation and Commerce
A1

Fulah Shepherd
A2

Perf. 14x13½

1892-1900   Typo.   Unwmk.
Name of Colony in Blue or Carmine

1	A1	1c black, *lilac bl*	1.75	1.60
		Never hinged	2.50	
		On cover		100.00
2	A1	2c brown, *buff*	2.25	2.00
		Never hinged	3.25	
		On cover		100.00
3	A1	4c claret, *lav*	3.00	2.10
		Never hinged	4.75	
		On cover		87.50
4	A1	5c green, *grnsh*	9.50	5.00
		Never hinged	17.50	
		On cover		52.50
5	A1	10c blk, *lavender*	8.25	5.00
		Never hinged	14.50	
		On cover		47.50
6	A1	10c red ('00)	45.00	40.00
		Never hinged	85.00	
		On cover		120.00
7	A1	15c blue, quadrille paper	15.50	7.50
		Never hinged	27.50	
		On cover		55.00
8	A1	15c gray, *lt gray* ('00)	110.00	100.00
		Never hinged	225.00	
		On cover		240.00
9	A1	20c red, *grn*	22.00	13.50
		Never hinged	40.00	
		On cover		87.50
		On cover, single franking		150.00
10	A1	25c black, *rose*	15.50	8.25
		Never hinged	27.50	
		On cover		45.00
11	A1	25c blue ('00)	25.00	25.00
		Never hinged	42.50	
		On cover		120.00
12	A1	30c brown, *bis*	40.00	35.00
		Never hinged	77.50	
		On cover		92.50
		On cover, single franking		140.00
13	A1	40c red, *straw*	40.00	35.00
		Never hinged	77.50	
		On cover		92.50
		On cover, single franking		140.00
a.		"GUINEE FRANCAISE" double	500.00	500.00
14	A1	50c car, *rose*	42.50	35.00
		Never hinged	85.00	
		On cover		120.00
		On cover, single franking		160.00
15	A1	50c brown, *az* ('00)	40.00	40.00
		Never hinged	67.50	
		On cover		200.00
		On cover, single franking		260.00
16	A1	75c dp vio, *org*	57.50	47.50
		Never hinged	115.00	
		On cover		225.00
		On cover, single franking		340.00
17	A1	1fr brnz grn, *straw*	50.00	40.00
		Never hinged	100.00	
		On cover		240.00
		On cover, single franking		400.00
		Nos. 1-17 (17)	527.75	442.45

Perf. 13½x14 stamps are counterfeits.
For surcharges see Nos. 48-54.

1904

18	A2	1c black, *yel grn*	1.20	1.20
		Never hinged	2.10	
		On cover		72.50
19	A2	2c vio brn, *buff*	1.20	1.20
		Never hinged	2.10	
		On cover		72.50
20	A2	4c carmine, *bl*	1.60	1.60
		Never hinged	2.75	
		On cover		67.50
21	A2	5c green, *grnsh*	1.75	1.60
		Never hinged	3.00	
		On cover		40.00
22	A2	10c carmine	3.50	2.00
		Never hinged	6.00	
		On cover		32.50

23	A2	15c violet, *rose*	10.00	5.25
		Never hinged	16.50	
		On cover		35.00
24	A2	20c carmine, *grn*	14.50	13.50
		Never hinged	25.00	
		On cover		67.50
		On cover, single franking		130.00
25	A2	25c blue	17.00	10.50
		Never hinged	35.00	
		On cover		32.50
26	A2	30c brown	22.50	16.00
		Never hinged	42.50	
		On cover		65.00
		On cover, single franking		87.50
27	A2	40c red, *straw*	32.50	23.00
		Never hinged	65.00	
		On cover		65.00
		On cover, single franking		87.50
28	A2	50c brown, *az*	32.50	24.00
		Never hinged	65.00	
		On cover		60.00
		On cover, single franking		80.00
29	A2	75c green, *org*	32.50	27.50
		Never hinged	65.00	
		On cover		110.00
		On cover, single franking		150.00
30	A2	1fr brnz grn, *straw*	47.50	45.00
		Never hinged	97.50	
		On cover		160.00
		On cover, single franking		275.00
31	A2	2fr red, *org*	90.00	90.00
		Never hinged	190.00	
		On cover		400.00
32	A2	5fr green, *yel grn*	110.00	110.00
		Never hinged	235.00	
		On cover		325.00
		On cover, single franking		525.00
		Nos. 18-32 (15)	418.25	372.35

For surcharges see Nos. 55-62.

Gen. Louis Faidherbé
A3

Oil Palm — A4

Dr. Noel Eugène Ballay
A5

1906-07
Name of Colony in Red or Blue

33	A3	1c gray	.80	.80
		Never hinged	1.40	
		On cover		55.00
34	A3	2c brown	1.25	1.25
		Never hinged	2.25	
		On cover		55.00
35	A3	4c brown, *bl*	1.60	1.60
		Never hinged	2.75	
		On cover		55.00
36	A3	5c green	3.50	2.00
		Never hinged	6.25	
		On cover		25.00
37	A3	10c carmine (B)	26.00	1.75
		Never hinged	52.50	
		On cover		13.00
38	A4	20c black, *blue*	6.50	4.00
		Never hinged	12.00	
		On cover		20.00
39	A4	25c blue, *pnksh*	7.25	6.50
		Never hinged	13.00	
		On cover		32.50
		On cover, single franking		87.50
40	A4	30c brown, *pnksh*	8.50	4.25
		Never hinged	15.50	
		On cover		32.50
		On cover, single franking		55.00
41	A4	35c black, *yellow*	5.00	2.40
		Never hinged	9.00	
		On cover		32.50
		On cover, single franking		45.00
42	A4	45c choc, *grnsh gray*	6.75	4.00
		Never hinged	12.50	
		On cover		35.00
		On cover, single franking		55.00
43	A4	50c dp violet	14.00	10.50
		Never hinged	27.50	
		On cover		45.00
		On cover, single franking		80.00
44	A4	75c blue, *org*	8.75	4.00
		Never hinged	14.00	
		On cover		65.00
		On cover, single franking		125.00
45	A5	1fr black, *az*	22.50	22.50
		Never hinged	42.50	
		On cover		75.00
		On cover, single franking		150.00
46	A5	2fr blue, *pink*	42.50	45.00
		Never hinged	90.00	
		On cover		120.00
		On cover, single franking		225.00

47	A5	5fr car, *straw* (B)	60.00	65.00
		Never hinged	125.00	
		On cover		130.00
		On cover, single franking		250.00
		Nos. 33-47 (15)	214.90	175.55

Regular Issues Surcharged in Black or Carmine

1912
Spacing between figures of surcharge 1.5mm (5c), 2mm (10c)
On Issue of 1892-1900

48	A1	5c on 2c brown, *buff*	1.60	2.00
		Never hinged	2.75	
		On cover		52.50
49	A1	5c on 4c cl, *lav* (C)	1.25	1.60
		Never hinged	2.00	
		On cover		35.00
50	A1	5c on 15c blue (C)	1.25	1.60
		Never hinged	2.00	
		On cover		40.00
51	A1	5c on 20c red, *grn*	4.25	5.25
		Never hinged	6.50	
		On cover		67.50
52	A1	5c on 30c brn, *bis* (C)	5.75	6.50
		Never hinged	9.75	
		On cover		75.00
53	A1	10c on 40c red, *straw*	2.40	3.25
		Never hinged	3.75	
		On cover		55.00
54	A1	10c on 75c dp vio, *org*	8.00	9.50
		Never hinged	14.00	
		On cover		75.00
a.		Double surcharge, inverted	325.00	

On Issue of 1904

55	A2	5c on 2c vio brn, *buff*	1.10	1.20
		Never hinged	1.75	
		On cover		32.50
a.		Pair, one without surcharge	650.00	
b.		Inverted surcharge	210.00	
56	A2	5c on 4c car, *blue*	1.25	1.25
		Never hinged	2.10	
		On cover		35.00
57	A2	5c on 15c violet, *rose*	1.25	1.25
		Never hinged	2.10	
		On cover		35.00
58	A2	5c on 20c car, *grn*	1.60	1.60
		Never hinged	2.40	
		On cover		45.00
59	A2	5c on 25c blue (C)	1.60	2.00
		Never hinged	2.40	
		On cover		47.50
60	A2	5c on 30c brown (C)	2.25	2.40
		Never hinged	3.75	
		On cover		52.50
61	A2	10c on 40c red, *straw*	2.00	2.40
		Never hinged	3.25	
		On cover		55.00
62	A2	10c on 50c brn, *az* (C)	5.25	5.50
		Never hinged	8.75	
		On cover		67.50
		Nos. 48-62 (15)	40.80	47.30

Spacing between figures of surcharge 2.25mm (5c), 2.75mm (10c)

48a	A1	5c on 2c brown, *buff*	97.50	97.50
		Never hinged	160.00	
49a	A1	5c on 4c cl, *lav* (C)	42.50	42.50
		Never hinged	65.00	
50a	A1	5c on 15c blue (C)	50.00	50.00
		Never hinged	80.00	
51a	A1	5c on 20c red, *grn*	225.00	225.00
52a	A1	5c on 30c brn, *bis* (C)	625.00	625.00
53a	A1	10c on 40c red, *straw*	50.00	50.00
		Never hinged	80.00	
54b	A1	10c on 75c dp vio, *org*	200.00	200.00
c.		Double surcharge, inverted	3,800.	

On Issue of 1904

55c	A2	5c on 2c vio brn, *buff*	35.00	35.00
		Never hinged	52.50	
56a	A2	5c on 4c car, *blue*	35.00	35.00
		Never hinged	52.50	
57a	A2	5c on 15c violet, *rose*	35.00	35.00
		Never hinged	52.50	
58a	A2	5c on 20c car, *grn*	50.00	50.00
		Never hinged	80.00	
59a	A2	5c on 25c blue (C)	125.00	125.00
		Never hinged	190.00	
60a	A2	5c on 30c brown (C)	160.00	160.00
		Never hinged	225.00	
61a	A2	10c on 40c red, *straw*	50.00	50.00
		Never hinged	80.00	
62a	A2	10c on 50c brn, *az* (C)	67.50	67.50
		Never hinged	100.00	
		Nos. 48a-62a (15)	1,847.	1,847.

Ford at Kitim — A6

1913-33   Perf. 13½x14

63	A6	1c violet & bl	.25	.25
		Never hinged	.40	
		On cover		45.00
a.		Imperf.	70.00	
64	A6	2c brn & vio brn	.25	.25
		Never hinged	.40	
		On cover		45.00
a.		Double impression of vio brn	175.00	
65	A6	4c gray & black	.25	.25
		Never hinged	.40	
		On cover		45.00
66	A6	5c yel grn & bl grn	1.30	.40
		Never hinged	2.10	
		On cover		17.50
a.		Booklet pane of 4	—	
		Complete booklet, 10 #66a	200.00	
b.		Chalky paper	1.20	.40
		Never hinged	1.90	
		On cover		17.50
67	A6	5c brn vio & grn ('22)	.25	.25
		Never hinged	.40	
		On cover		14.00
68	A6	10c red org & rose	1.10	.40
		Never hinged	1.60	
		On cover		10.00
a.		Booklet pane of 4	—	
		Complete booklet, 10 #68a	400.00	
b.		Chalky paper	1.00	.40
		Never hinged	1.40	
		On cover		10.00
69	A6	10c yel grn & bl grn ('22)	.50	.25
		Never hinged	.85	
		On cover		25.00
70	A6	10c vio & ver ('25)	.70	.30
		Never hinged	1.25	
		On cover		30.00
a.		Imperf.	45.00	
71	A6	15c vio brn & rose, chalky paper ('16)	.80	.40
		Never hinged	1.25	
		On cover		10.00
a.		Booklet pane of 4	—	
		Complete booklet, 10 #71a	1,000.	
72	A6	15c gray grn & yel grn ('25)	.40	.25
		Never hinged	.65	
		On cover		10.00
73	A6	15c red brn & rose lil ('27)	.40	.30
		Never hinged	.65	
		On cover		17.50
74	A6	20c brown & violet	.40	.40
		Never hinged	.75	
		On cover		17.50
75	A6	20c grn & bl grn ('26)	.80	.80
		Never hinged	1.20	
		On cover		8.75
76	A6	20c brn red & brn ('27)	.80	.50
		Never hinged	1.10	
		On cover		21.00
77	A6	25c ultra & blue	3.25	1.60
		Never hinged	5.25	
		On cover		17.50
		On cover, single franking		45.00
a.		Chalky paper	4.50	2.75
		Never hinged	8.25	
		On cover		20.00
78	A6	25c black & vio ('22)	.80	.80
		Never hinged	1.25	
		On cover		5.50
79	A6	30c vio brn & grn	1.75	1.20
		Never hinged	3.00	
		On cover		30.00
		On cover, single franking		55.00
80	A6	30c red org & rose ('22)	1.20	1.00
		Never hinged	1.90	
		On cover		21.00
		On cover, single franking		40.00
81	A6	30c rose red & grn ('25)	.30	.30
		Never hinged	.50	
		On cover		8.75
82	A6	30c dl grn & bl grn ('28)	1.60	1.20
		Never hinged	2.75	
		On cover		25.00
83	A6	35c blue & rose	.55	.55
		Never hinged	.95	
		On cover		25.00
		On cover, single franking		55.00
84	A6	40c green & gray	1.10	.90
		Never hinged	1.75	
		On cover		30.00
		On cover, single franking		65.00
85	A6	45c brown & red	1.25	1.10
		Never hinged	2.00	
		On cover		35.00
		On cover, single franking		80.00
86	A6	50c ultra & black	7.25	4.75
		Never hinged	12.50	
		On cover		40.00
		On cover, single franking		87.50

87 A6 50c ultra & bl ('22) — 1.25 .80
Never hinged — 2.00
On cover — 20.00
On cover, single franking — 40.00
88 A6 50c yel brn & ol ('25) — .80 .65
Never hinged — 1.25
On cover — 30.00
On cover, single franking — 55.00
89 A6 60c vio, *pnksh* ('25) — .65 .65
Never hinged — .95
On cover — 17.50
On cover, single franking — 52.50
90 A6 65c yel brn & sl bl ('26) — 2.00 1.30
Never hinged — 3.25
On cover — 10.00
On cover, single franking — 17.50
91 A6 75c red & ultra — 1.40 1.40
Never hinged — 2.25
On cover — 30.00
On cover, single franking — 75.00
92 A6 75c indigo & dl bl ('25) — 1.25 1.10
Never hinged — 2.00
On cover — 17.50
On cover, single franking — 40.00
93 A6 75c mag & yel grn ('27) — 1.60 1.20
Never hinged — 2.75
On cover — 12.50
94 A6 85c ol grn & red brn ('26) — 1.20 1.20
Never hinged — 2.00
On cover — 21.00
On cover, single franking — 80.00
95 A6 90c brn red & rose ('30) — 6.25 5.00
Never hinged — 10.00
On cover — 35.00
On cover, single franking — 87.50
96 A6 1fr violet & black — 1.60 1.60
Never hinged — 2.75
On cover — 45.00
On cover, single franking — 95.00
97 A6 1.10fr vio & ol brn ('28) — 6.50 7.50
Never hinged — 8.00
On cover — 80.00
On cover, single franking — 200.00
98 A6 1.25fr vio & yel brn ('33) — 2.40 1.60
Never hinged — 3.25
On cover — 17.50
On cover, single franking — 55.00
99 A6 1.50fr dk bl & lt bl ('30) — 6.00 2.50
Never hinged — 9.25
On cover — 32.50
On cover, single franking — 80.00
100 A6 1.75fr ol brn & vio ('33) — 1.70 1.60
Never hinged — 2.60
On cover — 13.00
On cover, single franking — 17.50
101 A6 2fr orange & vio brn — 3.50 2.40
Never hinged — 5.75
On cover — 52.50
On cover, single franking — 110.00
102 A6 3fr red violet ('30) — 8.25 5.75
Never hinged — 14.00
On cover — 60.00
On cover, single franking — 110.00
103 A6 5fr black & vio — 15.00 14.50
Never hinged — 25.00
On cover — 67.50
On cover, single franking — 130.00
104 A6 5fr dl bl & blk ('22) — 2.50 2.50
Never hinged — 3.75
On cover — 45.00
On cover, single franking — 80.00
Nos. 63-104 (42) — 91.10 71.65

For surcharges see Nos. 105-115, B1.
Nos. 66, 68 and 77 pasted on colored cardboard and overprinted "VALEUR D'ECHANGE" were used as emergency currency in 1920.

Type of 1913-33 Surcharged

1922
105 A6 60c on 75c violet, *pnksh* — .70 .70
Never hinged — 1.00
On cover — 12.50
On cover, single franking — 21.00

Stamps and Type of 1913-33 Surcharged

1924-27
106 A6 25c on 2fr org & brn (R) — .50 .50
Never hinged — .75
On cover — 6.50
107 A6 25c on 5fr dull bl & blk — .50 .50
Never hinged — .75
On cover — 6.50
108 A6 65c on 75c rose & ultra ('25) — 1.40 1.40
Never hinged — 2.00
On cover — 40.00
On cover, single franking — 87.50
109 A6 85c on 75c rose & ultra ('25) — 2.10 2.10
Never hinged — 3.25
On cover — 30.00
On cover, single franking — 55.00
110 A6 90c on 75c brn red & cer ('27) — 2.40 2.40
Never hinged — 3.50
On cover — 32.50
On cover, single franking — 55.00
111 A6 1.25fr on 1fr dk bl & ultra ('26) — 1.25 1.25
Never hinged — 1.90
On cover — 35.00
On cover, single franking — 67.50
112 A6 1.50fr on 1fr dp bl & lt bl ('27) — 2.00 2.00
Never hinged — 3.00
On cover — 25.00
On cover, single franking — 45.00
113 A6 3fr on 5fr mag & sl ('27) — 4.25 4.25
Never hinged — 7.00
On cover — 52.50
On cover, single franking — 110.00
114 A6 10fr on 5fr bl & bl grn, *bluish* ('27) — 9.00 9.00
Never hinged — 14.00
On cover — 65.00
On cover, single franking — 130.00
115 A6 20fr on 5fr rose lil & brn ol, *pnksh* ('27) — 21.00 21.00
Never hinged — 32.50
On cover — 100.00
On cover, single franking — 190.00
Nos. 106-115 (10) — 44.40 44.40

Common Design Types pictured following the introduction.

Colonial Exposition Issue
Common Design Types
1931 Engr. *Perf. 12½*
Name of Country in Black
116 CD70 40c deep green — 5.00 5.00
Never hinged — 8.00
On cover — 65.00
a. "GUINEE FRANCAISE" omitted — 60.00 70.00
Never hinged — 92.50
On cover — 160.00
117 CD71 50c violet — 5.00 5.00
Never hinged — 8.00
On cover — 52.50
118 CD72 90c red orange — 5.00 5.00
Never hinged — 8.00
On cover — 80.00
On cover, single franking — .130
a. "GUINEE FRANCAISE" omitted — 60.00 70.00
Never hinged — 92.50
On cover — 160.00
119 CD73 1.50fr dull blue — 5.00 5.00
Never hinged — 8.50
On cover — 72.50
On cover, single franking — 110.00
a. "GUINEE FRANCAISE" omitted — 60.00 70.00
Never hinged — 92.50
On cover — 160.00
Nos. 116-119 (4) — 20.00 20.00
Set, never hinged — 32.50

Paris International Exposition Issue
Common Design Types
1937 *Perf. 13*
120 CD74 20c deep violet — 2.10 2.10
Never hinged — 3.25
On cover — 65.00
121 CD75 30c dark green — 2.10 2.10
Never hinged — 3.25
On cover — 55.00
122 CD76 40c carmine rose — 2.10 2.10
Never hinged — 3.25
On cover — 47.50
123 CD77 50c dark brown — 2.00 2.00
Never hinged — 3.25
On cover — 45.00
124 CD78 90c red — 2.00 2.00
Never hinged — 3.25
On cover — 65.00
On cover, single franking — 110.00

125 CD79 1.50fr ultra — 2.25 2.25
Never hinged — 3.50
On cover — 55.00
On cover, single franking — 100.00
Nos. 120-125 (6) — 12.55 12.55
Set, never hinged — 20.00

Colonial Arts Exhibition Issue
Souvenir Sheet
Common Design Type
1937 *Imperf.*
126 CD76 3fr Prussian green — 10.00 11.00
Never hinged — 15.50
On cover — 72.50
On cover, single franking — 110.00

Guinea Village A7

Hausa Basket Workers A8

Forest Waterfall A9

Guinea Women — A10

1938-40 *Perf. 13*
128 A7 2c vermilion — .25 .25
Never hinged — .40
On cover — 21.00
129 A7 3c ultra — .25 .25
Never hinged — .40
On cover — 21.00
130 A7 4c green — .25 .25
Never hinged — .40
On cover — 21.00
131 A7 5c rose car — .25 .25
Never hinged — .40
On cover — 17.50
132 A7 10c peacock blue — .25 .25
Never hinged — .40
On cover — 17.50
133 A7 15c violet brown — .25 .25
Never hinged — .40
On cover — 14.00
134 A8 20c dk carmine — .30 .25
Never hinged — .50
On cover — 9.50
135 A8 25c pck blue — .40 .25
Never hinged — .65
On cover — 12.50
136 A8 30c ultra — .40 .25
Never hinged — .65
On cover — 8.00
137 A8 35c green — .55 .50
Never hinged — .80
On cover — 21.00
138 A8 40c blk brn ('40) — .30 .30
Never hinged — .50
On cover — 8.75
139 A8 45c dk green ('40) — .30 .30
Never hinged — .50
On cover — 20.00
140 A8 50c red brown — .55 .50
Never hinged — .80
On cover — 10.00
141 A9 55c dk ultra — 1.25 .80
Never hinged — 1.75
On cover — 5.50
142 A9 60c dk ultra ('40) — 1.25 .80
Never hinged — 1.75
On cover — 16.00
143 A9 65c green — 1.40 .80
Never hinged — 1.90
On cover — 4.00
144 A9 70c green ('40) — 1.40 1.40
Never hinged — 1.90
On cover — 20.00
145 A9 80c rose violet — .75 .55
Never hinged — 1.00
On cover — 35.00
On cover, single franking — 65.00
146 A9 90c rose vio ('39) — 1.40 1.25
Never hinged — 1.90
On cover — 27.50
On cover, single franking — 60.00
147 A9 1fr orange red — 2.75 2.00
Never hinged — 3.50
On cover — 27.50
On cover, single franking — 52.50

148 A9 1fr brn blk ('40) — .50 .50
Never hinged — .65
On cover — 4.75
149 A9 1.25fr org red ('40) — 1.40 1.40
Never hinged — 1.90
On cover — 40.00
On cover, single franking — 80.00
150 A9 1.40fr brown ('40) — 1.40 1.25
Never hinged — 1.90
On cover — 27.50
On cover, single franking — 60.00
151 A9 1.50fr violet — 2.50 2.00
Never hinged — 3.50
On cover — 16.00
On cover, single franking — 32.50
152 A10 1.60fr org red ('40) — 1.40 1.40
Never hinged — 1.75
On cover — 27.50
On cover, single franking — 67.50
153 A10 1.75fr ultra — .90 .80
Never hinged — 1.25
On cover — 21.00
On cover, single franking — 45.00
154 A10 2fr magenta — 1.00 .70
Never hinged — 1.30
On cover — 12.50
On cover, single franking — 21.00
155 A10 2.25fr brt ultra ('39) — 1.75 1.75
Never hinged — 2.25
On cover — 35.00
On cover, single franking — 72.50
156 A10 2.50fr brn blk ('40) — 1.40 1.40
Never hinged — 1.75
On cover — 24.00
On cover, single franking — 47.50
157 A10 3fr peacock blue — 1.00 .40
Never hinged — 1.35
On cover — 32.50
On cover, single franking — 55.00
158 A10 5fr rose violet — 1.00 .80
Never hinged — 1.35
On cover — 32.50
On cover, single franking — 55.00
159 A10 10fr slate green — 1.50 1.25
Never hinged — 2.25
On cover — 35.00
On cover, single franking — 65.00
160 A10 20fr chocolate — 2.75 2.00
Never hinged — 3.50
On cover — 45.00
On cover, single franking — 75.00
Nos. 128-160 (33) — 33.00 27.10

For surcharges see Nos. B8-B11 in Scott Standard catalogue, Vol. 2.

Caillié Issue
Common Design Type
1939 Engr. *Perf. 12½x12*
161 CD81 90c org brn & org — .90 .90
Never hinged — 1.10
On cover — 5.50
162 CD81 2fr brt violet — 1.10 1.10
Never hinged — 1.50
On cover — 17.50
On cover, single franking — 32.50
163 CD81 2.25fr ultra & dk bl — 1.20 1.20
Never hinged — 1.75
On cover — 21.00
On cover, single franking — 35.00
Nos. 161-163 (3) — 3.20 3.20

René Caillié, French explorer, death cent.

New York World's Fair Issue
Common Design Type
1939
164 CD82 1.25fr carmine lake — 1.40 1.40
Never hinged — 2.40
On cover — 47.50
On cover, single franking — 100.00
165 CD82 2.25fr ultra — 1.40 1.40
Never hinged — 2.40
On cover — 47.50
On cover, single franking — 92.50

SEMI-POSTAL STAMPS

Regular Issue of 1913 Surcharged in Red

1915 Unwmk. *Perf. 13½x14*
B1 A6 10c + 5c org & rose — 1.60 1.60
Never hinged — 2.40
On cover — 35.00
a. Chalky paper — 2.00 1.60
Never hinged — 3.25
On cover — 35.00

Exists on both ordinary and chalky paper.

Curie Issue
Common Design Type
1938 Engr. *Perf. 13*
B2 CD80 1.75fr + 50c brt ultra — 9.00 9.00
Never hinged — 14.00
On cover — 65.00
On cover, single franking — 110.00

French Revolution Issue
Common Design Type

1939   Photo.
Name and Value Typo. in Black

B3	CD83 45c + 25c green	9.75	9.75
	Never hinged	16.00	
	On cover		92.50
B4	CD83 70c + 30c brown	9.75	9.75
	Never hinged	16.00	
	On cover		67.50
B5	CD83 90c + 35c red org	9.75	9.75
	Never hinged	16.00	
	On cover		60.00
B6	CD83 1.25fr + 1fr rose pink	9.75	9.75
	Never hinged	16.00	
	On cover		100.00
	On cover, single franking		150.00
B7	CD83 2.25fr + 2fr blue	9.75	9.75
	Never hinged	16.00	
	On cover		92.50
	On cover, single franking		140.00
	Nos. B3-B7 (5)	48.75	48.75
	Set, never hinged	80.00	

AIR POST STAMPS

Common Design Type

1940   Unwmk.   Engr.   *Perf. 12½x12*

C1	CD85 1.90fr ultra	.70	.70
	Never hinged	.95	
	On cover		25.00
C2	CD85 2.90fr dark red	.80	.80
	Never hinged	1.15	
	On cover		25.00
C3	CD85 4.50fr dk gray grn	.95	.95
	Never hinged	1.25	
	On cover		32.50
C4	CD85 4.90fr yellow bis	.95	.95
	Never hinged	1.25	
	On cover		35.00
C5	CD85 6.90fr dp orange	1.50	1.50
	Never hinged	2.10	
	On cover		45.00
	Nos. C1-C5 (5)	4.90	4.90

POSTAGE DUE STAMPS

Fulah Woman — D1   Heads and Coast — D2

1905   Unwmk.   Typo.   *Perf. 14x13½*

J1	D1 5c blue	2.40	3.25
	Never hinged	4.25	
	On cover		72.50
J2	D1 10c brown	2.40	3.25
	Never hinged	3.75	
	On cover		72.50
J3	D1 15c green	6.50	6.50
	Never hinged	11.00	
	On cover		87.50
J4	D1 30c rose	6.50	6.50
	Never hinged	11.00	
	On cover		87.50
J5	D1 50c black	10.00	13.00
	Never hinged	17.50	
	On cover		110.00
J6	D1 60c dull orange	14.00	16.00
	Never hinged	27.00	
	On cover		110.00
J7	D1 1fr violet	42.50	47.50
	Never hinged	80.00	
	Nos. J1-J7 (7)	84.30	96.00

1906-08

J8	D2 5c grn, *grnsh* ('08)	21.00	13.00
	Never hinged	42.50	
	On cover		87.50
J9	D2 10c violet brn ('08)	6.00	5.50
	Never hinged	11.00	
	On cover		72.50
J10	D2 15c dk blue ('08)	6.00	5.50
	Never hinged	11.00	
	On cover		72.50
J11	D2 20c blk, *yellow*	6.00	5.50
	Never hinged	11.00	
	On cover		75.00
J12	D2 30c red, *straw* ('08)	28.00	26.00
	Never hinged	62.50	
	On cover		130.00
J13	D2 50c violet ('08)	25.00	26.00
	Never hinged	55.00	
	On cover		130.00
J14	D2 60c blk, *buff* ('08)	23.00	22.50
	Never hinged	45.00	
	On cover		110.00
J15	D2 1fr blk, *pnksh* ('08)	14.00	13.50
	Never hinged	27.00	
	On cover		100.00
	Nos. J8-J15 (8)	129.00	117.50

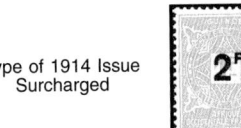

D3

1914

J16	D3 5c green	.40	*.55*
	Never hinged	.65	
	On cover		32.50
J17	D3 10c rose	.40	*.65*
	Never hinged	.65	
	On cover		32.50
J18	D3 15c gray	.55	*.90*
	Never hinged	.80	
	On cover		32.50
J19	D3 20c brown	.80	.80
	Never hinged	1.00	
	On cover		35.00
J20	D3 30c blue	.80	.80
	Never hinged	1.00	
	On cover		35.00
J21	D3 50c black	1.00	*1.25*
	Never hinged	1.45	
	On cover		40.00
J22	D3 60c orange	2.25	*2.40*
	Never hinged	2.75	
	On cover		45.00
J23	D3 1fr violet	2.25	*2.40*
	Never hinged	2.75	
	On cover		55.00
	Nos. J16-J23 (8)	8.45	9.75

Type of 1914 Issue Surcharged

1927

J24	D3 2fr on 1fr lil rose	8.00	*8.50*
	Never hinged	10.50	
	On cover		72.50
a.	No period after "F"	30.00	*32.50*
	Never hinged	40.00	
J25	D3 3fr on 1fr org brn	8.00	*8.50*
	Never hinged	10.50	
	On cover		80.00

D4

1938   Engr.

J26	D4 5c dk violet	.25	.30
	Never hinged	.40	
	On cover		27.50
J27	D4 10c carmine	.25	.30
	Never hinged	.40	
	On cover		27.50
J28	D4 15c green	.25	.30
	Never hinged	.40	
	On cover		27.50
J29	D4 20c red brown	.30	.40
	Never hinged	.40	
	On cover		27.50
J30	D4 30c rose violet	.30	.40
	Never hinged	.40	
	On cover		27.50
J31	D4 50c chocolate	.65	.70
	Never hinged	.80	
	On cover		32.50
J32	D4 60c peacock blue	1.10	1.10
	Never hinged	1.25	
	On cover		35.00
J33	D4 1fr vermilion	1.10	1.10
	Never hinged	1.25	
	On cover		35.00
J34	D4 2fr ultra	1.10	1.10
	Never hinged	1.25	
	On cover		45.00
J35	D4 3fr black	1.75	1.75
	Never hinged	2.25	
	On cover		55.00
	Nos. J26-J35 (10)	7.05	7.45

A 10c of type D4 without "RF" was issued in 1944 by the Vichy Government. See Scott No. J36 in Vol. 2 of the *Scott Standard Postage Stamp Catalogue.*

FRENCH INDIA

'french 'in-dē-ə

LOCATION — East coast of India bordering on Bay of Bengal.
GOVT. — French Territory
AREA — 196 sq. mi.
POP. — 323,295 (1941)
CAPITAL — Pondichéry

French India was an administrative unit comprising the five settlements of

---

Chandernagor, Karikal, Mahé, Pondichéry and Yanaon.

100 Centimes = 1 Franc
24 Caches = 1 Fanon (1923)
8 Fanons = 1 Rupie

Navigation and Commerce — A1

Perf. 14x13½

1892-1907   Typo.   Unwmk.
Colony Name in Blue or Carmine

1	A1 1c blk, *lil bl*	1.40	1.00
	Never hinged	2.40	
	On cover		60.00
2	A1 2c brn, *buff*	2.40	1.50
	Never hinged	3.75	
	On cover		60.00
3	A1 4c claret, *lav*	3.00	2.50
	Never hinged	5.25	
	On cover		60.00
4	A1 5c grn, *grnsh*	6.00	3.75
	Never hinged	10.00	
	On cover		32.50
5	A1 10c blk, *lavender*	13.50	2.75
	Never hinged	23.00	
	On cover		20.00
6	A1 10c red ('00)	5.00	2.40
	Never hinged	8.75	
	On cover		14.00
7	A1 15c blue, quadrille paper	16.00	5.50
	Never hinged	28.00	
	On cover		24.00
8	A1 15c gray, *lt gray* ('00)	30.00	30.00
	Never hinged	55.00	
	On cover		80.00
9	A1 20c red, *grn*	8.00	5.50
	Never hinged	13.00	
	On cover		40.00
	On cover, single franking		67.50
10	A1 25c blk, *rose*	5.25	2.75
	Never hinged	8.75	
	On cover		35.00
	On cover, single franking		60.00
11	A1 25c blue ('00)	19.00	16.00
	Never hinged	35.00	
	On cover		100.00
	On cover, single franking		160.00
12	A1 30c brn, *bis*	57.50	50.00
	Never hinged	110.00	
	On cover		180.00
	On cover, single franking		240.00
13	A1 35c blk, *yel* ('06)	19.00	9.00
	Never hinged	32.50	
	On cover		40.00
	On cover, single franking		52.50
14	A1 40c red, *straw*	7.50	7.25
	Never hinged	13.00	
	On cover		40.00
	On cover, single franking		55.00
15	A1 45c blk, *gray grn* ('07)	5.25	*6.00*
	Never hinged	8.75	
	On cover		45.00
	On cover, single franking		65.00
16	A1 50c car, *rose*	7.25	7.25
	Never hinged	11.00	
	On cover		52.50
	On cover, single franking		80.00
17	A1 50c brn, *az* ('00)	16.00	*17.50*
	Never hinged	30.00	
	On cover		150.00
	On cover, single franking		240.00
18	A1 75c dp vio, *org*	9.75	*9.50*
	Never hinged	17.50	
	On cover		92.50
	On cover, single franking		160.00
19	A1 1fr brnz grn, *straw*	14.00	*14.50*
	Never hinged	23.00	
	On cover		140.00
	On cover, single franking		240.00
	Nos. 1-19 (19)	245.80	194.65

Perf. 13½x14 stamps are counterfeits.

Nos. 10 and 16 Surcharged in Carmine or Black

1903

20	A1 5c on 25c blk, *rose*	400.00	240.00
	On cover		350.00
21	A1 10c on 25c blk, *rose*	375.00	225.00
	On cover		340.00
22	A1 15c on 25c blk, *rose*	125.00	115.00
	On cover		160.00
23	A1 40c on 50c car, *rose* (Bk)	525.00	425.00
	On cover		550.00
	On cover, single franking		675.00
	Nos. 20-23 (4)	1,425.	1,005.

Counterfeits of Nos. 20-23 abound.

A2

Revenue Stamp Surcharged in Black

1903

24	A2 5c gray blue	30.00	30.00
	Never hinged	52.50	
	On cover		80.00

The bottom of the revenue stamps were cut off.

Brahma — A5

Kali Temple near Pondichéry — A6

1914-22   *Perf. 13½x14, 14x13½*

25	A5 1c gray & blk	.30	.30
	Never hinged	.55	
	On cover		32.50
a.	1c light gray & black	.55	.55
	Never hinged	.95	
	On cover		32.50
26	A5 2c brn vio & blk	.30	.30
	Never hinged	.55	
	On cover		32.50
27	A5 2c grn & brn vio ('22)	.45	.45
	Never hinged	.70	
	On cover		27.50
28	A5 3c brown & blk	.40	.40
	Never hinged	.65	
	On cover		32.50
29	A5 4c orange & blk	.40	.40
	Never hinged	.65	
	On cover		32.50
30	A5 5c bl grn & blk	.70	.70
	Never hinged	1.20	
	On cover		14.50
31	A5 5c vio brn & blk ('22)	.60	.60
	Never hinged	.70	
	On cover		12.00
32	A5 10c dp rose & blk	1.25	1.25
	Never hinged	2.10	
	On cover		8.00
33	A5 10c grn & blk ('22)	.90	.90
	Never hinged	1.40	
	On cover		20.00
34	A5 15c vio & blk	1.10	1.10
	Never hinged	1.90	
	On cover		8.00
35	A5 20c org red & blk	2.00	2.00
	Never hinged	3.50	
	On cover		11.00
36	A5 25c blue & blk	2.00	2.00
	Never hinged	3.50	
	On cover		8.00
	On cover, single franking		9.50
37	A5 25c ultra & fawn ('22)	1.60	1.60
	Never hinged	2.25	
	On cover		6.50
38	A5 30c ultra & blk	4.00	4.00
	Never hinged	6.00	
	On cover		20.00
	On cover, single franking		45.00
39	A5 30c rose & blk ('22)	1.75	1.75
	Never hinged	2.90	
	On cover		16.00
	On cover, single franking		27.50
40	A6 35c choc & blk	2.25	2.25
	Never hinged	4.00	
	On cover		9.50
	On cover, single franking		16.00
41	A6 40c org red & blk	2.25	2.25
	Never hinged	4.00	
	On cover		12.00
	On cover, single franking		20.00
42	A6 45c bl grn & blk	2.25	2.25
	Never hinged	4.00	
	On cover		27.50
	On cover, single franking		65.00
43	A6 50c dp rose & blk	2.25	2.25
	Never hinged	4.00	
	On cover		32.50
	On cover, single franking		72.50
44	A6 50c ultra & bl ('22)	3.00	3.00
	Never hinged	4.75	
	On cover		14.50
	On cover, single franking		27.50
45	A6 75c blue & blk	4.50	4.50
	Never hinged	7.75	
	On cover		24.00
	On cover, single franking		45.00
46	A6 1fr yellow & blk	4.50	4.50
	Never hinged	7.75	
	On cover		32.50
	On cover, single franking		80.00

47	A6	2fr violet & blk	6.75	6.75
		Never hinged	11.00	
		On cover		45.00
		On cover, single franking		87.50
48	A6	5fr ultra & blk	3.50	3.50
		Never hinged	5.75	
		On cover		47.50
		On cover, single franking		9?.50
49	A6	5fr [illegible]	9.50	9.50
		Never hinged	8.00	
		On cover		45.00
		On cover, single franking		80.00
		Nos. 25-49 (25)	54.50	54.50

For surcharges see Nos. 50-79, 113-116, 156A, B1-B5. Post 1940 issues in Scott Standard catalogue, Vol. 2.

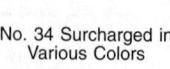

No. 34 Surcharged in Various Colors

1922

50	A5	1c on 15c (Bk)	.80	.80
		Never hinged	1.25	
		On cover		40.00
51	A5	2c on 15c (Bl)	.80	.80
		Never hinged	1.40	
		On cover		40.00
53	A5	5c on 15c (R)	.80	.80
		Never hinged	1.40	
		On cover		40.00
		Nos. 50-53 (3)	2.40	2.40

Stamps and Types of 1914-22 Surcharged with New Values in Caches, Fanons and Rupies in Black, Red or Blue

No. 55

No. 69

No. 78

1923-28

54	A5	1ca on 1c gray & blk (R)	.30	.30
		Never hinged	.55	
		On cover		27.50
a.		Imperf.	50.00	50.00
55	A5	2ca on 5c vio brn & blk	.50	.50
		Never hinged	.70	
		On cover		20.00
a.		Horizontal pair, imperf. between	—	
b.		Imperf.	45.00	45.00
56	A5	3ca on 3c brn & blk	.55	.55
		Never hinged	.85	
		On cover		20.00
57	A5	4ca on 4c org & blk	.80	.80
		Never hinged	1.40	
		On cover		16.00
58	A5	6ca on 10c grn & blk	.95	.95
		Never hinged	1.50	
		On cover		12.00
a.		Double surcharge	175.00	
59	A6	6ca on 45c bl grn & blk (R)	.95	.95
		Never hinged	1.50	
		On cover		12.00
60	A5	10ca on 20c dp red & bl grn ('28)	2.50	2.50
		Never hinged	4.00	
		On cover		20.00
61	A5	12ca on 15c vio & blk	.95	.95
		Never hinged	1.50	
		On cover		12.00

62	A5	15ca on 20c org & blk	1.50	1.50
		Never hinged	2.25	
		On cover		9.50
63	A6	16ca on 35c lt bl & yel brn ('28)	2.60	2.60
		Never hinged		
		On cover		20.00
64	A5	18ca on 30c rose & blk	2.40	2.40
		Never hinged	4.00	
		On cover		13.50
65	A6	20ca on 45c grn & dl red ('28)	2.00	1.50
		Never hinged	3.00	
		On cover		13.50
66	A5	1fa on 25c dp grn & rose red ('28)	3.50	3.50
		Never hinged	6.00	
		On cover		24.00
67	A6	1fa3ca on 35c choc & blk (Bl)	1.10	1.10
		Never hinged	1.75	
		On cover		9.50
68	A6	1fa6ca on 40c org & blk (R)	1.50	1.25
		Never hinged	2.40	
		On cover		12.00
69	A6	1fa12ca on 50c ultra & bl (Bl)	1.75	1.50
		Never hinged	2.90	
		On cover		14.50
70	A6	1fa12ca on 75c bl & blk (Bl)	1.25	1.25
		Never hinged	4.75	
		On cover		24.00
a.		Double surcharge	145.00	
		Never hinged	250.00	
71	A6	1fa16ca on 75c brn red & grn ('28)	3.50	3.00
		Never hinged	6.00	
		On cover		20.00
72	A5	2fa9ca on 25c ultra & fawn (Bl)	1.50	1.20
		Never hinged	2.40	
		On cover		13.50
73	A6	2fa12ca on 1fr vio & dk brn ('28)	3.00	3.00
		Never hinged	5.25	
		On cover		24.00
74	A6	3fa3ca on 1fr yel & blk (R)	1.75	1.45
		Never hinged	2.90	
		On cover		16.00
a.		Double surcharge	145.00	
		Never hinged	250.00	
75	A6	6fa6ca on 2fr vio & blk (Bl)	5.25	4.50
		Never hinged	8.75	
		On cover		40.00
76	A6	1r on 1fr grn & dp bl (R) ('26)	9.50	7.75
		Never hinged	17.50	
		On cover		47.50
77	A6	2r on 5fr rose & blk (R)	7.50	7.00
		Never hinged	15.00	
		On cover		24.00
a.		Double surcharge	145.00	
		Never hinged	250.00	
78	A6	3r on 2fr gray & bl vio (R) ('26)	21.00	19.00
		Never hinged	37.50	
		On cover		52.50
79	A6	5r on 5fr rose & blk, grnsh ('26)	27.50	24.00
		Never hinged	45.00	
		On cover		80.00
		Nos. 54-79 (26)	105.60	95.00

Nos. 60, 63, 66 and 73 have the original value obliterated by bars.

A7

A8

1929

80	A7	1ca dk gray & blk	.25	.25
		Never hinged	.40	
		On cover		20.00
81	A7	2ca vio brn & blk	.25	.25
		Never hinged	.40	
		On cover		16.00
82	A7	3ca brn & blk	.25	.25
		Never hinged	.40	
		On cover		16.00
83	A7	4ca org & blk	.30	.30
		Never hinged	.45	
		On cover		12.00

84	A7	6ca gray grn & grn	.30	.30
		Never hinged	.45	
		On cover		9.50
85	A7	10ca brn, red & grn	.30	.30
		Never hinged	.45	
		On cover		8.00
86	A8	12ca grn & lt grn	.75	.70
		Never hinged	1.20	
		On cover		8.00
87	A7	16ca brt bl & blk	.95	.95
		Never hinged	1.35	
		On cover		7.25
88	A7	18ca brn red & ver	.95	.95
		Never hinged	1.35	
		On cover		6.50
89	A7	20ca dk bl & grn, bluish	.75	.75
		Never hinged	1.20	
		On cover		6.50
90	A8	1fa gray grn & rose red	.75	.70
		Never hinged	1.20	
		On cover		8.00
91	A8	1fa6ca red org & blk	.75	.70
		Never hinged	1.20	
		On cover		8.00
92	A8	1fa12ca dp bl & ultra	.75	.70
		Never hinged	1.20	
		On cover		9.50
93	A8	1fa16ca rose red & grn	.95	.95
		Never hinged	1.35	
		On cover		11.00
94	A8	2fa12ca brt vio & brn	1.20	1.00
		Never hinged	2.00	
		On cover		12.00
95	A8	6fa6ca dl vio & blk	1.20	1.00
		Never hinged	2.00	
		On cover		14.50
a.		Imperf.	50.00	
96	A8	1r gray grn & dp bl	1.10	1.00
		Never hinged	1.80	
		On cover		16.00
a.		Imperf.	50.00	
97	A8	2r rose & blk	1.60	1.20
		Never hinged	2.00	
		On cover		20.00
a.		Imperf.	50.00	
98	A8	3r lt gray & gray lil	3.00	2.25
		Never hinged	4.75	
		On cover		27.50
99	A8	5r rose & blk, grnsh	3.00	2.40
		Never hinged	5.00	
		On cover		32.50
		Nos. 80-99 (20)	19.35	16.90

For overprints and surcharges see Nos. 117-134, 157-176, 184-209G in the *Scott Standard Postage Stamp Catalogue*, Vol. 2.

Common Design Types pictured following the introduction.

Colonial Exposition Issue
Common Design Types

1931		**Engr.**	**Perf. 12½**	
100	CD70	10ca deep green	4.50	4.50
		Never hinged	6.00	
		On cover		52.50
101	CD71	12ca violet	4.50	4.50
		Never hinged	6.75	
		On cover		45.00
102	CD72	18ca red orange	4.50	4.50
		Never hinged	6.75	
		On cover		72.50
		On cover, single franking		105.00
103	CD73	1fa12ca dull blue	4.50	4.50
		Never hinged	6.75	
		On cover		65.00
		On cover, single franking		92.50
		Nos. 100-103 (4)	18.00	18.00

Paris International Exposition Issue
Common Design Types

1937			**Perf. 13**	
104	CD74	8ca dp violet	2.00	2.00
		Never hinged	3.00	
		On cover		60.00
105	CD75	12ca dk green	2.25	2.25
		Never hinged	3.25	
		On cover		52.50
106	CD76	16ca car rose	2.25	2.25
		Never hinged	3.25	
		On cover		45.00
107	CD77	20ca dk brown	1.40	1.40
		Never hinged	2.25	
		On cover		40.00
108	CD78	1fa12ca red	1.75	1.75
		Never hinged	2.60	
		On cover		65.00
		On cover, single franking		100.00
109	CD79	2fa12ca ultra	2.25	2.25
		Never hinged	3.25	
		On cover		55.00
		On cover, single franking		92.50
		Nos. 104-109 (6)	11.90	11.90

For overprints see Nos. 135-139, 177-181 in the *Scott Standard Postage Stamp Catalogue*, Vol. 2.

Colonial Arts Exhibition Issue
Souvenir Sheet
Common Design Type

1937			**Imperf.**	
110	CD79	5fa red violet	9.25	12.50
		Never hinged	14.50	
		On cover		72.50
		On cover, single franking		105.00

For overprint see No. 140 in the *Scott Standard Postage Stamp Catalogue*, Vol. 2.

New York World's Fair Issue
Common Design Type

1939		**Engr.**		
111	CD82	1fa12ca car lake	1.25	1.25
		Never hinged	2.00	
		On cover		40.00
		On cover, single franking		80.00
112	CD82	2fa12ca ultra	1.75	1.75
		Never hinged	2.40	
		On cover		40.00
		On cover, single franking		72.50

For overprints see Nos. 141-142, 182-183 in the *Scott Standard Postage Stamp Catalogue*, Vol. 2.

SEMI-POSTAL STAMPS

Regular Issue of 1914 Surcharged in Red

Two printings: 1st, surcharge at bottom of stamp; 2nd, surcharge centered toward top.

1915		**Unwmk.**	**Perf. 14x13½**	
B1	A5	10c + 5c rose & blk (1st)	2.10	2.10
		Never hinged	4.00	
		On cover		20.00
a.		Second printing	2.00	2.00
		Never hinged	3.50	
		On cover		20.00
b.		As "a," inverted surcharge	210.00	210.00

Issued: No. B1, 6/15/15; No. B1a, 11/15.

Regular Issue of 1914 Surcharged in Red

1916

B2	A5	10c + 5c rose & blk	21.00	21.00
		Never hinged	40.00	
		On cover		67.50
a.		Inverted surcharge	210.00	210.00
b.		Double surcharge	210.00	210.00

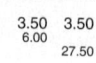

No. 32 Surcharged

B3	A5	10c + 5c rose & blk	3.50	3.50
		Never hinged	6.00	
		On cover		27.50

No. 32 Surcharged

B4	A5	10c + 5c rose & blk	1.60	1.60
		Never hinged	2.75	
		On cover		16.00

No. 32 Surcharged

B5 A5 10c + 5c rose & blk   2.25   2.25
Never hinged   3.50
On cover   20.00

Curie Issue
Common Design Type

1938   **Engr.**   **Perf. 13**
B6 CD80 2fa12ca + 20ca brt
ultra   10.00   10.00
Never hinged   13.50
On cover   47.50
On cover, single franking   80.00

French Revolution Issue
Common Design Type

1939   **Photo.**
Name and Value Typo. in Black

B7 CD83 18ca + 10ca
grn   9.00   9.00
Never hinged   14.50
On cover   72.50
B8 CD83 1fa6ca + 12ca
brn   9.00   9.00
Never hinged   14.50
On cover   55.00
B9 CD83 1fa12ca + 16ca
red org   9.00   9.00
Never hinged   14.50
On cover   47.50
B10 CD83 1fa16ca + 1fa16ca
rose pink   9.00   9.00
Never hinged   14.50
On cover   80.00
On cover, single franking   125.00
B11 CD83 2fa12ca + 3fa blue   9.00   9.00
Never hinged   14.50
On cover   80.00
On cover, single franking   110.00
Nos. B7-B11 (5)   45.00   45.00

POSTAGE DUE STAMPS

Postage Due Stamps of France Surcharged like Nos. 54-75 in Black, Blue or Red

1923   **Unwmk.**   **Perf. 14x13½**
J1 D2   6ca on 10c brn   1.25   1.25
Never hinged   2.00
On cover   60.00
J2 D2   12ca on 25c rose
(Bk)   1.25   1.25
Never hinged   2.00
On cover   60.00
J3 D2   15ca on 20c ol grn
(R)   1.60   1.60
Never hinged   2.75
On cover   60.00
J4 D2   1fa6ca on 30c red   1.60   1.60
Never hinged   2.75
On cover   65.00
J5 D2   1fa12a on 50c brn vio   2.75   2.75
Never hinged   4.75
On cover   67.50
J6 D2   1fa15ca on 5c bl (Bk)   3.00   3.00
Never hinged   4.75
On cover   72.50
J7 D2   3fa3ca on 1fr red brn,
straw   3.25   3.25
Never hinged   5.50
On cover   80.00
Nos. J1-J7 (7)   14.70   14.70

Types of Postage Due Stamps of French Colonies, 1884-85, Surcharged with New Values as in 1923 in Red or Black Bars over Original Values

1928
J8 D1   4ca on 20c gray lil   1.60   1.60
Never hinged   2.40
On cover   52.50
J9 D1   1fa on 30c orange   3.25   3.25
Never hinged   4.75
On cover   60.00
J10 D1 1fa16ca on 5c bl blk
(R)   3.25   3.25
Never hinged   4.75
On cover   65.00
J11 D1   3fa on 1fr lt grn   3.75   3.75
Never hinged   6.50
On cover   72.50
Nos. J8-J11 (4)   11.85   11.85

D3

1929   **Typo.**
J12 D3   4ca deep red   .50   .50
Never hinged   .80
On cover   20.00
J13 D3   6ca blue   .65   .65
Never hinged   1.00
On cover   20.00
J14 D3   12ca green   .65   .65
Never hinged   1.00
On cover   20.00
J15 D3   1fa brown   1.25   1.25
Never hinged   1.90
On cover   24.00
J16 D3 1fa12ca lilac gray   1.25   1.25
Never hinged   1.90
On cover   24.00
J17 D3 1fa16ca buff   1.75   1.75
Never hinged   2.75
On cover   27.50
J18 D3   3fa lilac   2.10   2.10
Never hinged   3.25
On cover   32.50
Nos. J12-J18 (7)   8.15   8.15

FRENCH MOROCCO

'french mə-'rä-ₖkō

LOCATION — Northwest coast of Africa
GOVT. — French Protectorate
AREA — 153,870 sq. mi.
POP. — 8,340,000 (estimated 1954)
CAPITAL — Rabat

100 Centimos = 1 Peseta
100 Centimes = 1 franc (1917)

French Offices in Morocco

A1   A2

Stamps of France Surcharged in Red or Black

1891-1900   **Unwmk.**   **Perf. 14x13½**
1 A1   5c on 5c grn,
grnsh (R)   13.00   4.00
Never hinged   22.50
On cover   42.50
a.   Imperf., pair   175.00
Never hinged   320.00
2 A1   5c on 5c yel grn
(II) (R) ('99)   35.00   27.50
Never hinged   65.00
On cover   240.00
a.   Type I   32.50   30.00
Never hinged   60.00
On cover   225.00
3 A1 10c on 10c blk, lav
(II) (R)   32.50   3.25
Never hinged   60.00
On cover   50.00
a.   Type I   45.00   20.00
Never hinged   87.50
On cover   175.00
b.   10c on 25c black, rose   1,100.   1,200.
On cover   1,200.
4 A1 20c on 20c red, grn   37.50   27.50
Never hinged   75.00
On cover   210.00
On cover, single franking   260.00
5 A1 25c on 25c blk,
rose (R)   32.50   4.00
Never hinged   60.00
On cover   97.50
On cover, single franking   120.00
a.   Double surcharge   250.00
b.   Imperf., pair   175.00
On cover   315.00
6 A1 50c on 50c car,
rose (II)   100.00   45.00
Never hinged   170.00
On cover   275.00
On cover, single franking   400.00
a.   Type I   400.00   260.00
On cover   675.00
On cover, single franking   800.00
7 A1   1p on 1fr brnz
grn, straw   110.00   80.00
Never hinged   220.00
On cover   325.00
On cover, single franking   350.00
8 A1   2p on 2fr brn, az
(Bk) ('00)   240.00   240.00
Never hinged   475.00
On cover   625.00
On cover, single franking   725.00
Nos. 1-8 (8)   600.50   431.25

No. 3b was never sent to Morocco.

France Nos. J15-J16 Overprinted in Carmine

1893
9 A2   5c black   3,250.   1,200.
On cover   1,700.
10 A2 10c black   2,900.   800.
On cover   1,050.

Counterfeits exist.

Surcharged in Red or Black

A3   A4

A5

1902-10
11 A3   1c on 1c gray (R)
('08)   2.40   1.20
Never hinged   3.50
On cover   24.00
12 A3   2c on 2c vio brn
('08)   2.40   1.20
Never hinged   3.50
On cover   24.00
13 A3   3c on 3c red org
('08)   3.25   1.60
Never hinged   5.50
On cover   24.00
14 A3   4c on 4c yel brn
('08)   13.00   8.00
Never hinged   23.00
On cover   35.00
15 A3   5c on 5c grn (R)   9.00   4.00
Never hinged   15.50
On cover   40.00
a.   Double surcharge   340.00
16 A4 10c on 10c rose red
('03)   7.25   3.25
Never hinged   11.00
On cover   27.50
a.   Surcharge omitted   225.00
Never hinged   390.00
17 A4 20c on 20c brn vio
('03)   32.50   22.50
Never hinged   52.50
On cover   80.00
On cover, single franking   120.00
18 A4 25c on 25c bl ('03)   32.50   3.25
Never hinged   52.50
On cover   45.00
On cover, single franking   60.00
19 A4 35c on 35c vio ('10)   40.00   24.00
Never hinged   19.00
On cover   35.00
20 A5 50c on 50c bis brn &
lav ('03)   62.50   14.50
Never hinged   105.00
On cover   80.00
21 A5   1p on 1fr cl & ol grn
('03)   110.00   75.00
Never hinged   180.00
On cover   180.00
On cover, single franking   225.00
22 A5   2p on 2fr gray vio &
yel ('03)   140.00   100.00
Never hinged   240.00
On cover   225.00
On cover, single franking   275.00
Nos. 11-22 (12)   454.80   258.50

Nos. 11-14 exist spelled CFNTIMOS or GENTIMOS.
The 25c on 25c with surcharge omitted is listed as No. 81a.
For overprints and surcharges see Nos. 26-37, 72-79, B1, B3.

Postage Due Stamps
Nos. J1-J2
Handstamped

1903
24 D2   5c on 5c light blue   1,500.   1,400.
On postcard   3,000.
25 D2 10c on 10c chocolate   2,800.   2,600.
On postcard   4,000.

Nos. 24 and 25 were used only on Oct. 10, 1903. Used stamps were not canceled, the overprint serving as a cancellation.
Numerous counterfeits exist.

Types of 1902-10 Issue Surcharged in Red or Blue

1911-17
26 A3   1c on 1c gray (R)   .90   .90
Never hinged   1.35
On cover   16.00
27 A3   2c on 2c vio brn   .95   .95
Never hinged   1.40
On cover   16.00
28 A3   3c on 3c orange   .95   .95
Never hinged   1.40
On cover   16.00
29 A3   5c on 5c green (R)   .95   .55
Never hinged   1.40
On cover   8.00
30 A4 10c on 10c rose   1.00   .65
Never hinged   1.45
On cover   5.50
a.   Imperf., pair   275.00
Never hinged   375.00
31 A4 15c on 15c org ('17)   3.50   2.40
Never hinged   4.75
On cover   6.50
32 A4 20c on 20c brn vio   5.00   3.25
Never hinged   7.50
On cover   12.00
33 A4 25c on 25c blue (R)   2.40   1.60
Never hinged   4.00
On cover   16.00
On cover, single franking   24.00
34 A4 35c on 35c violet (R)   9.50   4.75
Never hinged   14.50
On cover   16.00
On cover, single franking   20.00
35 A5 40c on 40c red &
pale bl ('17)   8.75   5.50
Never hinged   13.00
On cover   20.00
On cover, single franking   24.00
36 A5 50c on 50c bis brn &
lav (R)   27.00   14.50
Never hinged   42.50
On cover   32.50
On cover, single franking   60.00
37 A5   1p on 1fr cl & ol
grn   21.00   8.00
Never hinged   35.00
On cover   27.50
On cover, single franking   80.00
Nos. 26-37 (12)   81.90   44.00

For surcharges see Nos. B1, B3.

The Administration Cherifinne des Postes, Telegraphes et Telephones was formed in 1911 under French guidance, and stamps of this design were issued by the Cherifien posts in 1912-13. See listings under "Morocco."

French Protectorate
Issue of 1911-17 Overprinted "Protectorat Francais"

A6   A7

A8

1914-21
38 A6   1c on 1c lt gray   .65   .50
Never hinged   .95
On cover   8.00
a.   1c dk gray ('22)   .65   .50
Never hinged   .95
On cover   8.00
39 A6   2c on 2c vio brn   .65   .65
Never hinged   .95
On cover   8.00
40 A6   3c on 3c orange   1.00   .65
Never hinged   1.50
On cover   8.00
41 A6   5c on 5c green   .95   .50
Never hinged   1.40
On cover   4.75
a.   New value omitted   275.00   275.00
Never hinged   410.00

42	A7	10c on 10c rose	.80	.30
		Never hinged	1.00	
		On cover		3.25
a.		New value omitted	550.00	550.00
43	A7	15c on 15c org ('17)	.80	.80
		Never hinged	1.15	
		On cover		3.25
a.		New value omitted	120.00	120.00
		Never hinged	100.00	
44	A7	20c on 20c brn vio	4.75	3.50
		Never hinged	7.00	
		On cover		8.00
a.		"Protectorat Francais" double	300.00	300.00
		Never hinged	425.00	
45	A7	25c on 25c blue	2.40	.80
		Never hinged	4.25	
		On cover		9.50
		On cover, single franking		13.50
a.		New value omitted	350.00	350.00
		Never hinged	525.00	
46	A7	25c on 25c violet ('21)	1.25	.40
		Never hinged	1.75	
		On cover		2.40
a.		"Protectorat Francais" omitted	80.00	80.00
		Never hinged	120.00	
b.		"Protectorat Francais" double	175.00	175.00
		Never hinged	250.00	
c.		"Protectorat Francais" dbl. (R + Bk)	175.00	175.00
		Never hinged	250.00	
47	A7	30c on 30c vio ('21)	20.00	9.00
		Never hinged	31.00	
		On cover		24.00
		On cover, single franking		40.00
48	A7	35c on 35c violet	5.25	1.60
		Never hinged	7.75	
		On cover		9.50
		On cover, single franking		13.50
49	A8	40c on 40c red & pale bl	20.00	8.75
		Never hinged	30.00	
		On cover		27.50
		On cover, single franking		35.00
a.		New value omitted	375.00	375.00
		Never hinged	540.00	
50	A8	45c on 45c grn & bl ('21)	50.00	40.00
		Never hinged	70.00	
		On cover		67.50
		On cover, single franking		92.50
51	A8	50c on 50c bis brn & lav	1.60	.80
		Never hinged	2.40	
		On cover		12.00
		On cover, single franking		20.00
a.		"Protectorat Francais" invtd.	200.00	200.00
		Never hinged	290.00	
b.		"Protectorat Francais" double	450.00	450.00
		Never hinged	650.00	
52	A8	1p on 1fr cl & ol grn	3.25	.80
		Never hinged	5.00	
		On cover		9.50
		On cover, single franking		27.50
a.		"Protectorat Francais" invtd.	350.00	350.00
		Never hinged	525.00	
b.		New value double	200.00	200.00
		Never hinged	260.00	
c.		New value dbl., one invtd.	210.00	210.00
		Never hinged	300.00	
53	A8	2p on 2fr gray vio & yel	6.00	1.60
		Never hinged	9.25	
		On cover		13.50
		On cover, single franking		40.00
a.		New value omitted	175.00	175.00
		Never hinged	260.00	
b.		"Protectorat Francais" omitted	110.00	110.00
		Never hinged	160.00	
c.		New value double		225.00
d.		New value dbl., one invtd.	210.00	210.00
54	A8	5p on 5fr dk bl & buff	15.00	4.75
		Never hinged	22.50	
		On cover		16.00
		On cover, single franking		52.50
		Nos. 38-54 (17)	134.35	75.25

For surcharges see Nos. B2, B4-B5.

Tower of Hassan, Rabat — A9

Mosque of the Andalusians, Fez — A10

City Gate Chella A11

Koutoubiah, Marrakesh A12

Bab Mansour, Meknes A13

Roman Ruins, Volubilis A14

1917   Engr.   Perf. 13½x14, 14x13½

55	A9	1c grnsh gray	.50	.50
		Never hinged	.65	
		On cover		10.00
56	A9	2c brown lilac	.65	.50
		Never hinged	.90	
		On cover		8.75
57	A9	3c orange brn	.70	.55
		Never hinged	.95	
		On cover		9.50
a.		Imperf., pair	87.50	
		Never hinged	140.00	
58	A10	5c yellow grn	.70	.40
		Never hinged	.95	
		On cover		6.50
59	A10	10c rose red	.70	.40
		Never hinged	.95	
		On cover		4.00
60	A10	15c dark gray	.70	.50
		Never hinged	.95	
		On cover		2.40
a.		Imperf., pair	65.00	
		Never hinged	95.00	
61	A11	20c red brown	3.25	2.40
		Never hinged	4.75	
		On cover		5.50
62	A11	25c dull blue	3.50	1.25
		Never hinged	5.75	
		On cover		4.75
		On cover, single franking		16.00
63	A11	30c gray violet	4.50	2.75
		Never hinged	6.75	
		On cover		6.00
		On cover, single franking		12.00
64	A12	35c orange	4.50	2.75
		Never hinged	6.75	
		On cover		8.75
		On cover, single franking		16.00
65	A12	40c ultra	1.60	1.25
		Never hinged	2.40	
		On cover		6.50
		On cover, single franking		11.00
66	A12	45c gray green	29.00	13.00
		Never hinged	47.50	
		On cover		27.50
		On cover, single franking		45.00
67	A13	50c dk brown	5.25	2.75
		Never hinged	8.50	
		On cover		8.00
		On cover, single franking		12.00
a.		Imperf., pair	65.00	
		Never hinged	95.00	
68	A13	1fr slate	13.00	4.00
		Never hinged	19.50	
		On cover		10.00
		On cover, single franking		18.00
a.		Imperf., pair	65.00	
		Never hinged	95.00	
69	A14	2fr black brown	160.00	92.50
		Never hinged	250.00	
		On cover		225.00
70	A14	5fr dk gray grn	45.00	37.50
		Never hinged	72.50	
		On cover		87.50
		On cover, single franking		180.00
71	A14	10fr black	45.00	37.50
		Never hinged	72.50	
		On cover		87.50
		On cover, single franking		180.00
		Nos. 55-71 (17)	318.55	200.50

See note following No. 115. See Nos. 93-105. For surcharges see Nos. 120-121.

Types of the 1902-10 Issue Overprinted

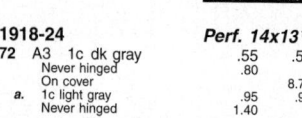
TANGER

1918-24   Perf. 14x13½

72	A3	1c dk gray	.55	.55
		Never hinged	.80	
		On cover		8.75
a.		1c light gray	.95	.95
		Never hinged	1.40	

		On cover		9.50
b.		Grayish paper ('18)	1.40	1.40
		Never hinged	2.00	
		On cover		11.00
73	A3	2c violet brn	.65	.65
		Never hinged	.95	
		On cover		8.75
74	A3	3c red orange	.95	.95
		Never hinged	1.30	
		On cover		8.75
a.		Grayish paper ('19)	1.60	1.60
		Never hinged	2.40	
75	A3	5c green	1.00	1.00
		Never hinged	1.40	
		On cover		9.50
76	A3	5c orange ('23)	2.00	2.00
		Never hinged	2.50	
		On cover		7.25
77	A4	10c rose	2.00	1.60
		Never hinged	2.50	
		On cover		1.60
78	A4	10c green ('24)	2.00	1.60
		Never hinged	2.50	
		On cover		4.75
79	A4	15c orange	1.60	1.20
		Never hinged	2.60	
		On cover		4.75
80	A4	20c violet brn	2.40	2.00
		Never hinged	3.60	
		On cover		3.25
81	A4	25c blue	2.40	2.00
		Never hinged	3.50	
		On cover		8.75
a.		"TANGER" omitted	400.00	400.00
		On cover		6.50
82	A4	30c red org ('24)	3.25	2.75
		Never hinged	4.50	
		On cover		8.75
		On cover, single franking		17.50
83	A4	35c violet	3.25	2.40
		Never hinged	5.50	
		On cover		8.00
		On cover, single franking		12.00
84	A5	40c red & pale bl	3.25	2.40
		Never hinged	5.00	
		On cover		8.00
85	A5	50c bis brn & lav	27.50	16.00
		Never hinged	37.50	
		On cover		30.00
		On cover, single franking		40.00
86	A4	50c blue ('24)	21.00	13.50
		Never hinged	32.50	
		On cover		17.50
		On cover, single franking		27.50
87	A5	1fr claret & ol grn	15.00	6.75
		Never hinged	22.50	
		On cover		17.50
		On cover, single franking		55.00
88	A5	2fr org & pale bl ('24)	85.00	77.50
		Never hinged	130.00	
		On cover		125.00
		On cover, single franking		175.00
89	A5	5fr dk bl & buff ('24)	70.00	70.00
		Never hinged	110.00	
		On cover		125.00
		On cover, single franking		200.00
		Nos. 72-89 (18)	243.80	204.85

Types of 1917 and

Tower of Hassan, Rabat — A15

Bab Mansour, Meknes A16

Roman Ruins, Volubilis A17

1923-27   Photo.   Perf. 13½

90	A15	1c olive green	.25	.25
		Never hinged	.40	
		On cover		8.75
91	A15	2c brown vio	.25	.25
		Never hinged	.40	
		On cover		8.75
92	A15	3c yellow brn	.25	.25
		Never hinged	.40	
		On cover		8.75
93	A10	5c orange	.25	.25
		Never hinged	.40	
		On cover		6.50
94	A10	10c yellow grn	.25	.25
		Never hinged	.40	
		On cover		7.25
95	A10	15c dk gray	.25	.25
		Never hinged	.40	
		On cover		4.00
96	A11	20c red brown	.25	.25
		Never hinged	.40	
		On cover		3.25

97	A11	20c red vio ('27)	.50	.50
		Never hinged	.65	
		On cover		8.00
98	A11	25c ultra	.30	.30
		Never hinged	.00	
		On cover		2.40
99	A11	30c deep red	.30	.30
		Never hinged	.50	
		On cover		2.40
100	A11	30c turq bl ('27)	1.10	.75
		Never hinged	1.60	
		On cover		8.00
101	A12	35c violet	1.00	.85
		Never hinged	1.35	
		On cover		8.00
		On cover, single franking		13.50
102	A12	40c orange red	.25	.25
		Never hinged	.40	
		On cover		5.50
103	A12	45c deep green	.30	.30
		Never hinged	.50	
		On cover		8.00
		On cover, single franking		13.50
104	A16	50c dull turq	.50	.30
		Never hinged	.65	
		On cover		8.00
		On cover, single franking		20.00
105	A12	50c olive grn ('27)	.65	.30
		Never hinged	.90	
		On cover		2.40
106	A16	60c lilac	.95	.50
		Never hinged	1.25	
		On cover		6.50
		On cover, single franking		12.00
107	A16	75c red vio ('27)	.70	.50
		Never hinged	.90	
		On cover		4.00
		On cover, single franking		5.50
108	A16	1fr deep brown	.70	.55
		Never hinged	.95	
		On cover		8.75
		On cover, single franking		21.00
109	A16	1.05fr red brn ('27)	1.50	.85
		Never hinged	2.25	
		On cover		12.00
		On cover, single franking		27.50
110	A16	1.40fr dull rose ('27)	1.00	.75
		Never hinged	1.20	
		On cover		8.75
		On cover, single franking		14.50
111	A16	1.50fr turq bl ('27)	1.40	.30
		Never hinged	1.90	
		On cover		10.00
		On cover, single franking		21.00
112	A17	2fr olive brn	1.40	1.00
		Never hinged	1.90	
		On cover		17.50
		On cover, single franking		87.50
113	A17	3fr dp red ('27)	1.75	1.00
		Never hinged	2.40	
		On cover		14.50
		On cover, single franking		27.50
114	A17	5fr dk gray grn	3.50	2.50
		Never hinged	4.75	
		On cover		32.50
		On cover, single franking		110.00
115	A17	10fr black	11.00	4.75
		Never hinged	17.50	
		On cover		45.00
		On cover, single franking		160.00
		Nos. 90-115 (26)	30.55	18.30

Nos. 90-110, 112-115 exist imperf. The stamps of 1917 were line engraved. Those of 1923-27 were printed by photogravure and have in the margin at lower right the imprint "Helio Vaugirard."

See No. B36 in Scott Standard catalogue, Vol. 2. For surcharges see Nos. 122-123.

No. 102 Surcharged in Black

1930

120	A12	15c on 40c orange red	1.60	1.60
		Never hinged	2.25	
		On cover		3.25
a.		Surcharge bars omitted	72.50	72.50
		Never hinged	115.00	
b.		Pair, one with surcharge omitted	325.00	
		Never hinged	500.00	

Nos. 100, 106 and 110 Surcharged in Blue Similarly to No. 176

1931

121	A11	25c on 30c turq blue	2.50	2.10
		Never hinged	3.25	
		On cover		4.75
a.		Inverted surcharge	140.00	140.00
		Never hinged	200.00	
122	A16	50c on 60c lilac	1.00	.40
		Never hinged	1.30	
		On cover		2.40
a.		Inverted surcharge	150.00	150.00
		Never hinged	210.00	
b.		Double surcharge	150.00	150.00
		Never hinged	210.00	
c.		Surcharge bars omitted	90.00	
		Never hinged	140.00	
123	A16	1fr on 1.40fr rose	3.75	1.60
		Never hinged	4.50	
		On cover		4.75
		On cover, single franking		8.00

a.	Inverted surcharge	150.00	150.00	
	Never hinged	225.00		
b.	Surcharge bars omitted	90.00		
	Never hinged	140.00		
	Nos. 121-123 (3)	7.25	4.10	

Old Treasure House and Tribunal, Tangier A18

Roadstead at Agadir A19

Post Office at Casablanca A20

Moulay Idriss of the Zehroun A21

Kasbah of the Oudayas, Rabat A22

Court of the Medersa el Attarine at Fez A23
Saadiens' Tombs at Marrakesh A25

Kasbah of Si Madani el Glaoui at Ouarzazat A24

1933-34   Engr.   Perf. 13

124	A18	1c olive blk	.25	.25
	Never hinged	.40		
	On cover		5.50	
125	A18	2c red violet	.25	.25
	Never hinged	.40		
	On cover		5.50	
126	A19	3c dark brown	.25	.25
	Never hinged	.40		
	On cover		5.50	
127	A19	5c brown red	.25	.25
	Never hinged	.40		
	On cover		4.75	
128	A20	10c blue green	.30	.30
	Never hinged	.50		
	On cover		4.00	
129	A20	15c black	.30	.30
	Never hinged	.50		
	On cover		4.00	
130	A20	20c red brown	.30	.30
	Never hinged	.50		
	On cover		4.00	
131	A21	25c dark blue	.30	.30
	Never hinged	.50		
	On cover		4.00	
132	A21	30c emerald	.50	.30
	Never hinged	.65		
	On cover		4.75	
133	A21	40c black brn	.50	.30
	Never hinged	.65		
	On cover		2.40	
134	A22	45c brown vio	.80	.70
	Never hinged	1.00		
	On cover		5.25	
135	A22	50c dk blue grn	.80	.30
	Never hinged	1.00		
	On cover		1.60	

a.	Booklet pane of 10	—		
b.	Booklet pane of 20	—		
	Complete booklet, #135b	1,500.		
136	A22	65c brown red	.30	.30
	Never hinged	.50		
	On cover		6.75	
a.	Booklet pane of 10	—		
b.	Booklet pane of 20	—		
	Complete booklet, #136b	60.00		
137	A23	75c red violet	.80	.30
	Never hinged	1.00		
	On cover		2.40	
138	A23	90c orange red	.50	.30
	Never hinged	.65		
	On cover		4.75	
	On cover, single franking		12.00	
139	A23	1fr deep brown	1.10	.50
	Never hinged	1.50		
	On cover		3.25	
	On cover, single franking		4.00	
140	A23	1.25fr black ('34)	1.50	1.25
	Never hinged	2.10		
	On cover		3.25	
	On cover, single franking		10.00	
141	A24	1.50fr ultra	.50	.30
	Never hinged	.65		
	On cover		4.75	
	On cover, single franking		9.50	
142	A24	1.75fr myr grn ('34)	.80	.30
	Never hinged	1.00		
	On cover		3.25	
	On cover, single franking		7.25	
143	A24	2fr yellow brn	4.75	.80
	Never hinged	5.75		
	On cover		8.75	
	On cover, single franking		17.50	
144	A24	3fr car rose	60.00	7.00
	Never hinged	85.00		
	On cover		13.50	
	On cover, single franking		27.50	
145	A25	5fr red brown	12.00	2.50
	Never hinged	19.00		
	On cover		8.75	
	On cover, single franking		27.50	
146	A25	10fr black	9.00	7.25
	Never hinged	13.00		
	On cover		13.50	
	On cover, single franking		27.50	
147	A25	20fr bluish gray	8.25	7.25
	Never hinged	12.50		
	On cover		13.50	
	On cover, single franking		32.50	
	Nos. 124-147 (24)	104.30	31.85	

Booklets containing Nos. 135 and 136 each have two panes of 10 (Nos. 135a, 136a) connected by a gutter, the complete piece constituting No. 135b or 136b, which is stapled into the booklet through the gutter.

For surcharges see Nos. 148, 176, B13-B20.

No. 135 Srchd. in Red

1939
148	A22	40c on 50c dk bl grn	.95	.50

Mosque of Salé — A26
Sefrou — A27

Cedars — A28

Goatherd A29

Ramparts of Salé — A30

Scimitar-horned Oryxes — A31
Fez — A33

Valley of Draa A32

1939-42
149	A26	1c rose violet	.25	.25
	Never hinged	.30		
	On cover		4.75	
150	A27	2c emerald	.25	.25
	Never hinged	.30		
	On cover		4.75	
151	A27	3c ultra	.25	.25
	Never hinged	.30		
	On cover		4.75	
152	A26	5c dk bl grn	.25	.25
	Never hinged	.30		
	On cover		4.00	
153	A27	10c brt red vio	.25	.25
	Never hinged	.30		
	On cover		4.00	
154	A28	15c dk green	.25	.25
	Never hinged	.30		
	On cover		4.00	
155	A28	20c black grn	.25	.25
	Never hinged	.30		
	On cover		4.00	
156	A29	30c deep blue	.25	.25
	Never hinged	.30		
	On cover		3.25	
157	A29	40c chocolate	.25	.25
	Never hinged	.30		
	On cover		1.60	
158	A29	45c Prus green	.55	.55
	Never hinged	.65		
	On cover		6.50	
159	A30	50c rose red	1.50	.90
	Never hinged	1.60		
	On cover		7.25	
159A	A30	50c Prus grn ('40)	.30	.25
	Never hinged	.40		
	On cover		5.50	
160	A30	60c turq blue	1.25	.75
	Never hinged	1.50		
	On cover		5.50	
160A	A30	60c choc ('40)	.30	.25
	Never hinged	.40		
	On cover		4.00	
161	A31	70c dk violet	.25	.25
	Never hinged	.30		
	On cover		1.60	
162	A32	75c grnsh blk	.50	.50
	Never hinged	.65		
	On cover		4.50	
163	A32	80c pck bl ('40)	.30	.25
	Never hinged	.40		
	On cover		1.60	
163A	A32	80c dk grn ('42)	.30	.25
	Never hinged	.40		
	On cover		4.75	
164	A30	90c ultra	.30	.25
	Never hinged	.40		
	On cover		1.60	
165	A28	1fr chocolate	.30	.25
	Never hinged	.40		
	On cover		1.60	
165A	A32	1.20fr rose vio ('42)	.70	.30
	Never hinged	.85		
	On cover		1.60	
166	A32	1.25fr henna brn	1.25	.70
	Never hinged	1.60		
	On cover		13.50	
167	A32	1.40fr rose violet	.70	.30
	Never hinged	.85		
	On cover		6.00	
	On cover, single franking		13.50	
168	A30	1.50fr cop red ('40)	.30	.25
	Never hinged	.35		
	On cover		13.50	
	On cover, single franking		13.50	
168A	A30	1.50fr rose ('42)	.25	.25
	Never hinged	.30		
	On cover		1.60	
169	A33	2fr Prus green	.25	.25
	Never hinged	.30		
	On cover		4.00	
	On cover, single franking		8.75	
170	A33	2.25fr dark blue	.70	.50
	Never hinged	.85		
	On cover		4.75	
	On cover, single franking		9.50	
170A	A26	2.40fr red ('42)	.30	.30
	Never hinged	.40		
	On cover		8.00	
	On cover, single franking		24.00	

171	A26	2.50fr scarlet	1.00	.70
	Never hinged	1.10		
	On cover		3.25	
	On cover, single franking		5.50	
171A	A26	2.50fr dp blue ('40)	1.10	.70
	Never hinged	1.40		
	On cover		4.75	
	On cover, single franking		9.50	
172	A33	3fr black brown	.50	.30
	Never hinged	.65		
	On cover		3.25	
	On cover, single franking		5.50	
172A	A26	4fr dp ultra ('42)	.30	.30
	Never hinged	.40		
	On cover		3.25	
	On cover, single franking		16.00	
172B	A32	4.50fr grnsh blk ('42)	.70	.55
	Never hinged	.85		
	On cover		3.25	
	On cover, single franking		5.50	
173	A31	5fr dark blue	.70	.50
	Never hinged	.85		
	On cover		3.25	
	On cover, single franking		8.00	
174	A31	10fr red	1.25	.90
	Never hinged	1.60		
	On cover		6.50	
	On cover, single franking		13.50	
174A	A31	15fr Prus grn ('42)	4.75	4.00
	Never hinged	6.00		
	On cover		8.00	
	On cover, single franking		20.00	
175	A31	20fr dk vio brn	2.25	1.75
	Never hinged	2.75		
	On cover		8.00	
	On cover, single franking		17.50	
	Nos. 149-175 (37)	25.10	19.25	
	Set, never hinged	32.00		

See Nos. 197-219 in Scott Standard catalogue, Vol. 2. For surcharges see Nos. 244, 261-262, B21-B24, B26, B28, B32 in Scott Standard catalogue, Vol. 2.

No. 136 Srchd. in Black

1940
176	A22	35c on 65c brown red	1.75	.95
	Never hinged	2.10		
	On cover		4.00	
a.	Pair, one without surcharge	3.25	2.40	
	Never hinged	4.00		
	On cover		4.75	

The surcharge was applied on alternate rows in the sheet, making No. 176a. This was done to make a pair equal 1fr, the new rate.

SEMI-POSTAL STAMPS

French Protectorate

No. 30 Surcharged in Red ➗ **5c**

1914   Unwmk.   Perf. 14x13½
B1	A4	10c + 5c on 10c	24,000.	28,000.

Known only with inverted red surcharge.

No. 42 Surcharged in Red

B2	A7	10c + 5c on 10c rose	6.50	6.50
	Never hinged	9.50		
	On cover		13.50	
a.	Double surcharge	175.00	175.00	
	Never hinged	260.00		
b.	Inverted surcharge	225.00	225.00	
	Never hinged	325.00		
c.	"c" omitted	110.00	110.00	
	Never hinged	160.00		

On Nos. B1 and B2 the cross is set up from pieces of metal (quads), the horizontal bar being made from two long pieces, the vertical bar from two short pieces. Each cross in the setting of twenty-five differs from the others.

No. 30 Handstamp Surcharged in Red

B3	A4	10c + 5c on 10c rose	*1,650.*	*1,300.*
	On cover		*2,250.*	

No. B3 was issued at Oujda. The surcharge ink is water-soluble.

No. 42 Surcharged in Vermilion or Carmine

B4	A7	10c + 5c on 10c			
		(V)	25.00	25.00	
	Never hinged		37.50		
	On cover			35.00	
a.	Double surcharge		240.00	240.00	
	Never hinged		350.00		
b.	Inverted surcharge		240.00	240.00	
	Never hinged		350.00		
c.	Double surch., one invtd.		200.00	200.00	
	Never hinged		350.00		
B5	A7	10c +5c on 10c			
		(C)	475.00	525.00	
a.	Inverted surcharge		1,600.	1,600.	

On Nos. B4-B5 the horizontal bar of the cross is single and not as thick as on Nos. B1-B2.

No. B5 was sold largely at Casablanca.

Carmine Surcharge SP1

Black Overprint SP2

1915

B6	SP1	5c + 5c green	3.25	2.40
	Never hinged		4.50	
	On cover			5.50
a.	Inverted surcharge		300.00	300.00
	Never hinged		450.00	
B7	SP2	10c + 5c rose	4.75	4.75
	Never hinged		7.00	
	On cover			8.75

No. B6 was not issued without the Red Cross surcharge. No. B7 was used in Tangier.

France No. B2 Overprinted in Black — SP3

B8	SP3	10c + 5c red	7.50	7.50
	Never hinged		10.50	
	On cover			13.50

No. 30 Surcharged in Carmine — SP4

1917

B9	SP4	10c + 5c on 10c rose	3.50	3.50
	Never hinged		5.00	
	On cover			5.50

On No. B9 the horizontal bar of the cross is made from a single, thick piece of metal.

Marshal Hubert Lyautey — SP5

1935, May 15   Photo.   Perf. 13x13½

B10	SP5	50c + 50c red	10.00	10.00
	Never hinged		15.00	
	On cover			16.00
B11	SP5	1fr + 1fr dk grn	11.00	11.00
	Never hinged		17.00	
	On cover			20.00
B12	SP5	5fr + 5fr blk brn	45.00	45.00
	Never hinged		67.50	
	On cover			125.00
	Nos. B10-B12 (3)		66.00	66.00
	Set, never hinged		98.50	

Stamps of 1933-34 Surcharged in Blue or Red

1938   **Perf. 13**

B13	A18	2c + 2c red vio	4.75	4.75
	Never hinged		7.25	
	On cover			12.50
B14	A19	3c + 3c dk brn	4.75	4.75
	Never hinged		7.25	
	On cover			12.50
B15	A20	20c + 20c red brn	4.75	4.75
	Never hinged		7.25	
	On cover			12.50
B16	A21	40c + 40c blk brn	4.75	4.75
		(R)		
	Never hinged		7.25	
	On cover			8.75
B17	A22	65c + 65c brn red	5.25	5.25
	Never hinged		7.50	
	On cover			8.75
B18	A23	1.25fr + 1.25fr blk (R)	5.25	5.25
	Never hinged		7.50	
	On cover			20.00
B19	A24	2fr + 2fr yel brn	5.25	5.25
	Never hinged		8.00	
	On cover			16.00
B20	A25	5fr + 5fr red brn	5.25	5.25
	Never hinged		8.00	
	On cover			27.50
	Nos. B13-B20 (8)		40.00	40.00
	Set, never hinged		60.00	

AIR POST STAMPS

French Protectorate

Biplane over Casablanca AP1

1922-27   Photo.   Unwmk.   Perf. 13½

C1	AP1	5c dp orange ('27)	.50	.50
	Never hinged		.80	
	On cover			5.50
C2	AP1	25c dp ultra	1.10	.95
	Never hinged		1.75	
	On cover			2.40
C3	AP1	50c grnsh blue	1.25	.90
	Never hinged		.90	
	On cover			8.00
C4	AP1	75c dp blue	85.00	13.50
	Never hinged		135.00	
	On cover			27.50
C5	AP1	75c dp green	1.00	.50
	Never hinged		1.10	
	On cover			7.25
C6	AP1	80c vio brn ('27)	1.75	.55
	Never hinged		2.75	
	On cover			5.50
C7	AP1	1fr vermilion	1.00	.50
	Never hinged		1.75	
	On cover			8.00
C8	AP1	1.40fr brn lake ('27)	2.40	1.25
	Never hinged		3.75	
	On cover			4.00
C9	AP1	1.90fr dp blue ('27)	2.50	1.60
	Never hinged		3.75	
	On cover			5.50
C10	AP1	2fr black vio	2.25	1.10
	Never hinged		3.40	
	On cover			17.50
a.	2fr deep violet		2.25	1.40
	Never hinged		3.40	
	On cover			16.00
C11	AP1	3fr gray blk	2.50	1.60
	Never hinged		3.40	
	On cover			13.50
	Nos. C1-C11 (11)		101.25	22.95

The 25c, 50c, 75c deep green and 1fr each were printed in two of three types, differing in frameline thickness, or hyphen in "Helio-Vaugirard" imprint.

Imperf., Pairs

C1a	AP1	5c	65.00	65.00
	Never hinged		210.00	
C2a	AP1	25c	72.50	72.50
	Never hinged		105.00	
C3a	AP1	50c	72.50	72.50
	Never hinged		115.00	
C4a	AP1	75c	600.00	600.00
	Never hinged		825.00	
C5a	AP1	75c	72.50	72.50
	Never hinged		105.00	
C6a	AP1	80c	72.50	72.50
	Never hinged		125.00	
C7a	AP1	1fr	90.00	90.00
	Never hinged		260.00	
C10b	AP1	2fr	225.00	225.00
	Never hinged		350.00	

Nos. C8-C9 Srchd. in Blue or Black

1931, Apr. 10

C12	AP1	1fr on 1.40fr		
		(B)	1.90	1.90
	Never hinged		2.75	
	On cover			5.25
a.	Inverted surcharge		325.00	325.00
	Never hinged		650.00	
C13	AP1	1.50fr on 1.90fr		
		(Bk)	2.10	2.10
	Never hinged		3.00	
	On cover			4.50

Rabat and Tower of Hassan AP2

Casablanca AP3

1933, Jan.   **Engr.**

C14	AP2	50c dark blue	.85	.80
	Never hinged		1.20	
	On cover			2.00
C15	AP2	80c orange brn	.85	.65
	Never hinged		1.20	
	On cover			2.75
C16	AP2	1.50fr brown red	.85	.80
	Never hinged		1.20	
	On cover			5.50
C17	AP3	2.50fr carmine rose	6.75	1.25
	Never hinged		9.25	
	On cover			4.75
C18	AP3	5fr violet	3.50	2.00
	Never hinged		4.75	
	On cover			4.75
C19	AP3	10fr blue green	1.50	1.25
	Never hinged		2.10	
	On cover			5.50
	Nos. C14-C19 (6)		14.30	6.75

For surcharges see Nos. CB22-CB23.

Storks and Minaret, Chella — AP4

Plane and Map of Morocco AP5

1939-40   **Perf. 13**

C20	AP4	80c Prus green	.25	.25
	Never hinged		.30	
	On cover			2.40
C21	AP4	1fr dk red	.25	.25
	Never hinged		.30	
	On cover			2.00
C22	AP5	1.90fr ultra	.40	.30
	Never hinged		.50	
	On cover			4.00
C23	AP5	2fr red vio ('40)	.40	.30
	Never hinged		.50	
	On cover			9.50
C24	AP5	3fr chocolate	.50	.25
	Never hinged		.60	
	On cover			2.75
C25	AP4	5fr violet	1.40	.80
	Never hinged		2.00	
	On cover			7.25
C26	AP5	10fr turq blue	1.25	.55
	Never hinged		1.60	
	On cover			13.50
	Nos. C20-C26 (7)		4.45	2.70

AIR POST SEMI-POSTAL STAMPS

French Protectorate

Moorish Tribesmen SPAP1

Designs: 25c, Moor plowing with camel and burro. 50c, Caravan nearing Saffi. 75c, Walls, Marrakesh. 80c, Sheep grazing at Azrou. 1fr, Gate at Fez. 1.50fr, Aerial view of Tangier. 2fr, Aerial view of Casablanca. 3fr, Storks on old wall, Rabat. 5fr, Moorish fete.

Perf. 13½

1928, July 26   Photo.   Unwmk.

			Unwmk.	
CB1	SPAP1	5c dp blue	5.50	5.50
	Never hinged		9.25	
	On cover			12.50
CB2	SPAP1	25c brn org	5.50	5.50
	Never hinged		9.25	
	On cover			8.75
CB3	SPAP1	50c red	5.50	5.50
	Never hinged		9.25	
	On cover			12.50
CB4	SPAP1	75c org brn	5.50	5.50
	Never hinged		9.25	
	On cover			9.50
CB5	SPAP1	80c olive grn	5.50	5.50
	Never hinged		9.25	
	On cover			13.50
CB6	SPAP1	1fr orange	5.50	5.50
	Never hinged		9.25	
	On cover			12.00
CB7	SPAP1	1.50fr Prus bl	5.50	5.50
	Never hinged		9.25	
	On cover			18.00
CB8	SPAP1	2fr dp brown	5.50	5.50
	Never hinged		9.25	
	On cover			13.50
CB9	SPAP1	3fr dp violet	5.50	5.50
	Never hinged		9.25	
	On cover			25.00
CB10	SPAP1	5fr brown blk	5.50	5.50
	Never hinged		9.25	
	On cover			35.00
	Nos. CB1-CB10 (10)		55.00	55.00

These stamps were sold in sets only and at double their face value. The money received for the surtax was divided among charitable and social organizations. The stamps were not sold at post offices but solely by subscription to the Moroccan Postal Administration.

Overprinted in Red or Blue (25c, 50c, 75c, 1fr)

1929, Feb. 1

CB11	SPAP1	5c dp blue	5.50	5.50
	Never hinged		9.25	
	On cover			12.50
CB12	SPAP1	25c brown org	5.50	5.50
	Never hinged		9.25	
	On cover			8.75
CB13	SPAP1	50c red	5.50	5.50
	Never hinged		9.25	
	On cover			8.75
CB14	SPAP1	75c org brn	5.50	5.50
	Never hinged		9.25	
	On cover			9.50
CB15	SPAP1	80c olive grn	5.50	5.50
	Never hinged		9.25	
	On cover			12.50
CB16	SPAP1	1fr orange	5.50	5.50
	Never hinged		9.25	
	On cover			12.00
CB17	SPAP1	1.50fr Prus bl	5.50	5.50
	Never hinged		9.25	
	On cover			18.00
CB18	SPAP1	2fr dp brown	5.50	5.50
	Never hinged		9.25	
	On cover			13.50
CB19	SPAP1	3fr dp violet	5.50	5.50
	Never hinged		9.25	
	On cover			25.00
CB20	SPAP1	5fr brown blk	5.50	5.50
	Never hinged		9.25	
	On cover			37.50
	Nos. CB11-CB20 (10)		55.00	55.00

These stamps were sold at double their face values and only in Tangier. The surtax benefited various charities.

Marshal Hubert Lyautey SPAP10

1935, May 15   *Perf. 13½*
CB21	SPAP10 1.50fr + 1.50fr blue	21.00	21.00
	Never hinged	34.00	
	On cover		52.50

Nos. C14, C19 Surcharged in Red

1938   *Perf. 13*
CB22	AP2 50c + 50c dk bl	6.50	6.50
	Never hinged	10.00	
	On cover		13.50
CB23	AP3 10fr + 10fr bl grn	6.50	6.50
	Never hinged	10.00	
	On cover		20.00

POSTAGE DUE STAMPS

French Offices in Morocco

Postage Due Stamps and Types of France Surcharged in Red or Black

1896   Unwmk.   *Perf. 14x13½*
On Stamps of 1891-93
J1	D2 5c on 5c lt bl (R)	8.75	5.50
	Never hinged	15.00	
	On cover		67.50
J2	D2 10c on 10c choc (R)	13.00	5.50
	Never hinged	25.00	
	On cover		67.50
J3	D2 30c on 30c car	32.50	25.00
	Never hinged	62.50	
	On cover		225.00
a.	Pair, one without surcharge		
J4	D2 50c on 50c lilac	32.50	25.00
	Never hinged	62.50	
	On cover		225.00
a.	"S" of "CENTIMOS" omitted	340.00	250.00
J5	D2 1p on 1fr lil brn	340.00	325.00
	On cover		750.00

1909-10   **On Stamps of 1908-10**
J6	D3 1c on 1c ol grn (R)	3.25	3.25
	Never hinged	5.50	
	On cover		32.50
J7	D3 10c on 10c violet	40.00	35.00
	Never hinged	80.00	
	On cover		300.00
J8	D3 30c on 30c bister	47.50	40.00
	Never hinged	90.00	
	On cover		325.00
J9	D3 50c on 50c red	72.50	72.50
	Never hinged	125.00	
	On cover		400.00
	Nos. J6-J9 (4)	163.25	150.75

Postage Due Stamps of France Surcharged in Red or Blue

1911   **On Stamps of 1893-96**
J10	D2 5c on 5c blue (R)	4.75	4.75
	Never hinged	7.75	
	On cover		24.00
J11	D2 10c on 10c choc (R)	16.00	16.00
	Never hinged	26.00	
	On cover		45.00
a.	Double surcharge	225.00	260.00
		325.00	
J12	D2 50c on 50c lil (Bl)	20.00	20.00
	Never hinged	40.00	
	On cover		55.00

On Stamps of 1908-10
J13	D3 1c on 1c ol grn (R)	3.25	3.25
	Never hinged	4.75	
	On cover		20.00
J14	D3 10c on 10c vio (R)	8.50	8.50
	Never hinged	14.50	
	On cover		32.50
J15	D3 30c on 30c bis (R)	10.00	10.00
	Never hinged	18.50	
	On cover		35.00
J16	D3 50c on 50c red (Bl)	16.00	16.00
	Never hinged	28.00	
	On cover		47.50
	Nos. J10-J16 (7)	78.50	78.50

For surcharges see Nos. J23-J26.

French Protectorate

Type of 1911 Issue Overprinted "Protectorat Francais" — D4

1915-17
J17	D4 1c on 1c black	.55	.55
	Never hinged	.80	
	On cover		20.00
a.	New value double	175.00	
		260.00	
J18	D4 5c on 5c blue	2.75	2.00
	Never hinged	4.00	
	On cover		24.00
a.	Grayish paper ('17)	2.75	2.75
	Never hinged	4.25	
J19	D4 10c on 10c choc	3.25	2.00
	Never hinged	5.00	
	On cover		24.00
J20	D4 20c on 20c ol grn	3.25	2.00
	Never hinged	5.00	
	On cover		24.00
J21	D4 30c on 30c rose red, grayish	7.25	5.50
	Never hinged	11.50	
	On cover		32.50
J22	D4 50c on 50c vio brn	11.00	6.50
	Never hinged	19.00	
	On cover		35.00
	Nos. J17-J22 (6)	28.05	18.55

Nos. J13 to J16 With Additional Overprint "Protectorat Francais"

1915
J23	D3 1c on 1c ol grn	1.60	1.60
	Never hinged	2.50	
	On cover		20.00
J24	D3 10c on 10c violet	3.25	2.75
	Never hinged	4.50	
	On cover		24.00
J25	D3 30c on 30c bister	3.25	2.75
	Never hinged	5.25	
	On cover		24.00
J26	D3 50c on 50c red	3.25	3.25
	Never hinged	5.50	
	On cover		24.00
	Nos. J23-J26 (4)	11.35	10.35

D5

1917-26   Typo.
J27	D5 1c black	.25	.25
	Never hinged	.40	
	On cover		13.50
a.	Grayish paper ('17)	.50	.50
	Never hinged	.80	
			16.00
J28	D5 5c deep blue	.30	.25
	Never hinged	.50	
	On cover		13.50
a.	Grayish paper ('17)	.80	.65
	Never hinged	1.20	
J29	D5 10c brown	.55	.30
	Never hinged	.80	
	On cover		13.50
J30	D5 20c olive green	2.50	1.40
	Never hinged	3.50	
	On cover		17.50
J31	D5 30c rose	.30	.30
	Never hinged	.50	
	On cover		13.50
a.	Grayish paper ('17)	1.00	1.00
	Never hinged	1.60	
			17.50
J32	D5 50c lilac brown	.55	.25
	Never hinged	.80	
	On cover		12.00
J33	D5 1fr red brn, straw ('26)	1.00	.70
	Never hinged	1.60	
	On cover		13.50
J34	D5 2fr violet ('26)	2.00	1.25
	Never hinged	3.00	
	On cover		17.50
	Nos. J27-J34 (8)	7.45	4.70

See #J49-J56, Morocco #J1-J4 in Scott Standard catalogue, Vol. 2. For surcharges see #J46-J48 in Scott Standard catalogue, Vol. 2.

Postage Due Stamps of France, 1882-1906 Overprinted

1918
J35	D2 1c black	1.25	1.25
	Never hinged	1.90	
	On cover		13.50
J36	D2 5c blue	2.00	2.00
	Never hinged	3.00	
	On cover		17.50
a.	Grayish paper ('17)	3.50	3.50
	Never hinged	5.50	
	On cover		27.50

J37	D2 10c chocolate	2.00	2.00
	Never hinged	3.00	
	On cover		17.50
a.	Grayish paper ('17)	5.00	5.00
	Never hinged	7.50	
	On cover		27.50
J38	D2 15c green	4.50	4.50
	Never hinged	7.75	
	On cover		27.50
J39	D2 20c olive green	6.50	6.50
	Never hinged	9.00	
	On cover		27.50
J40	D2 30c rose red, grayish	14.50	14.50
	Never hinged	25.00	
	On cover		47.50
J41	D2 50c violet brown	21.00	21.00
	Never hinged	35.00	
	On cover		60.00
	Nos. J35-J41 (7)	51.75	51.75

Postage Due Stamps of France, 1908-19 Overprinted

1918
J42	D3 1c olive green	1.25	1.25
	Never hinged	1.90	
	On cover		13.50
a.	Grayish paper	2.25	2.25
	Never hinged	3.25	
	On cover		17.50
J43	D3 10c violet	2.75	2.75
	Never hinged	4.00	
	On cover		17.50
a.	Grayish paper ('17)	2.25	2.25
	Never hinged	3.75	
			16.00
J44	D3 20c bister, grayish	8.00	8.00
	Never hinged	12.00	
	On cover		32.50
J45	D3 40c red	20.00	20.00
	Never hinged	30.00	
	On cover		55.00
	Nos. J42-J45 (4)	32.00	32.00

PARCEL POST STAMPS

French Protectorate

PP1

1917   Unwmk.   *Perf. 13½x14*
Q1	PP1 5c green	1.00	.65
	Never hinged	1.70	
Q2	PP1 10c carmine	1.00	.65
	Never hinged	1.70	
Q3	PP1 20c lilac brown	1.10	.80
	Never hinged	1.70	
Q4	PP1 25c blue	1.75	.80
	Never hinged	3.00	
Q5	PP1 40c dark brown	2.75	1.20
	Never hinged	4.00	
Q6	PP1 50c red orange	3.75	.80
	Never hinged	5.25	
Q7	PP1 75c pale slate	4.50	2.40
	Never hinged	7.25	
Q8	PP1 1fr ultra	6.25	.80
	Never hinged	10.50	
Q9	PP1 2fr gray	9.00	1.50
	Never hinged	14.50	
Q10	PP1 5fr violet	14.00	1.60
	Never hinged	23.00	
Q11	PP1 10fr black	23.00	1.60
	Never hinged	40.00	
	Nos. Q1-Q11 (11)	68.10	12.80

FRENCH OCEANIA

ˈfrench ˌpä-lə-ˈnē-zhə

(French Polynesia)

LOCATION — South Pacific Ocean
GOVT. — French Overseas Territory
AREA — 1,522 sq. mi.
POP. — 172,000 (est. 1984)
CAPITAL — Papeete

In 1903 various French Establishments in the South Pacific were united to form a single colony. Most important of the island groups are the Society Islands, Marquesas Islands, the Tuamotu group and the Gambier, Austral, and Rapa Islands. Tahiti, largest of the Society group, ranks first in importance.

100 Centimes = 1 Franc

Navigation and Commerce — A1

Perf. 14x13½
1892-1907   Typo.   Unwmk.
Name of Colony in Blue or Carmine
1	A1 1c black, lil bl	1.60	1.60
	Never hinged	2.40	
	On cover or postcard, in combination		115.00
2	A1 2c brown, buff	2.75	2.75
	Never hinged	4.50	
	On cover or postcard, in combination		115.00
3	A1 4c claret, lav	4.50	4.00
	Never hinged	8.25	
	On cover or postcard, in combination		115.00
4	A1 5c green, grnsh	13.50	9.50
	Never hinged	20.00	
	On cover		80.00
	On commercial cover		150.00
5	A1 5c yellow grn ('06)	5.00	2.40
	Never hinged	9.00	
	On cover		100.00
	On commercial cover		135.00
6	A1 10c blk, lavender	30.00	12.50
	Never hinged	57.50	
	On cover		100.00
	On commercial cover		200.00
7	A1 10c red ('00)	5.00	2.40
	Never hinged	9.00	
	On cover		60.00
	On commercial cover		175.00
8	A1 15c blue, quadrille paper	35.00	12.00
	Never hinged	65.00	
	On cover		80.00
	On commercial cover		200.00
9	A1 15c gray, lt gray ('00)	10.00	7.25
	Never hinged	22.00	
	On cover		67.50
	On commercial cover		300.00
10	A1 20c red, grn	17.50	16.00
	Never hinged	35.00	
	On cover		80.00
	On cover, single franking		140.00
	On commercial cover		400.00
11	A1 25c black, rose	60.00	30.00
	Never hinged	120.00	
	On cover		160.00
	On cover, single franking		240.00
12	A1 25c blue ('00)	32.50	16.00
	Never hinged	65.00	
	On cover		130.00
	On cover, single franking		160.00
	On commercial cover		290.00
13	A1 30c brown, bis	16.00	14.50
	Never hinged	32.50	
	On cover		92.50
	On cover, single franking		120.00
	On commercial cover		600.00
14	A1 35c black, yel ('06)	11.00	9.50
	Never hinged	22.00	
	On cover		120.00
	On cover, single franking		160.00
	On commercial cover		600.00
15	A1 40c red, straw	132.50	80.00
	Never hinged	275.00	
	On cover		360.00
	On cover, single franking		525.00
	On commercial cover		800.00
16	A1 45c blk, gray grn ('07)	6.75	6.75
	Never hinged	13.00	
	On cover		105.00
	On cover, single franking		150.00
	On commercial cover		900.00
17	A1 50c car, pale rose	10.00	10.00
	Never hinged	19.50	
	On cover		240.00
	On cover, single franking		350.00
a.	50c rose, pale rose	10.00	9.00
	Never hinged	19.50	
	On cover		225.00
	On cover, single franking		350.00
18	A1 50c brown, az ('00)	275.00	250.00
	On cover		600.00
	On cover, single franking		725.00
	On commercial cover		2,250.
19	A1 75c dp vio, org	12.00	12.00
	Never hinged	26.00	
	On cover		260.00
	On cover, single franking		400.00
	On commercial cover		625.00
20	A1 1fr brnz grn, straw	13.50	13.50
	Never hinged	27.50	
	On cover		260.00
	On cover, single franking		400.00
	Nos. 1-20 (20)	694.10	512.65

Perf. 13½x14 stamps are counterfeits.
For overprint and surcharge see Nos. 55, B1.

Tahitian Girl — A2

Kanakas — A3

Fautaua Valley — A4

1913-30

21	A2	1c violet & brn	.25	.25
		Never hinged	.40	
		On cover		60.00
22	A2	2c brown & blk	.25	.25
		Never hinged	.40	
		On cover		60.00
23	A2	4c orange & bl	.35	.35
		Never hinged	.45	
		On cover		52.50
24	A2	5c grn & yel grn	1.60	.90
		Never hinged	3.00	
a.		Double impression of yel grn	500.00	
		On cover		30.00
25	A2	5c bl & blk ('22)	.50	.50
		Never hinged	.65	
		On cover		45.00
		On commercial cover		55.00
26	A2	10c rose & org	2.25	2.25
		Never hinged	3.75	
		On cover		32.50
		On commercial cover		55.00
27	A2	10c bl grn & yel grn ('22)	1.25	1.25
		Never hinged	1.60	
		On cover		40.00
		On commercial cover		55.00
28	A2	10c org red & brn red, bluish ('26)	1.40	1.40
		Never hinged	2.10	
		On cover		47.50
		On commercial cover		60.00
29	A2	15c org & blk ('15)	.85	.65
		Never hinged	1.30	
		On cover		27.50
		On commercial cover		60.00
a.		Imperf., pair	175.00	
		Never hinged, pair	275.00	
		Single on cover		92.50
30	A2	20c black & vio	1.10	1.00
		Never hinged	1.90	
		On cover		27.50
		On commercial cover		60.00
a.		Imperf., pair	175.00	
		Never hinged	350.00	
31	A2	20c grn & bl grn ('26)	1.00	1.00
		Never hinged	1.60	
		On cover		40.00
		On commercial cover		62.50
32	A2	20c brn red & dk brn ('27)	1.60	1.60
		Never hinged	1.80	
		On cover		40.00
		On commercial cover		65.00
33	A3	25c ultra & blue	1.50	1.25
		Never hinged	2.50	
		On cover		40.00
		On cover, single franking		60.00
34	A3	25c vio & rose ('22)	.75	.75
		Never hinged	1.20	
		On cover		27.50
		On commercial cover		55.00
35	A3	30c gray & brown	5.00	4.00
		Never hinged	8.00	
		On cover		55.00
		On cover, single franking		80.00
a.		Imperf., pair	325.00	
		Never hinged	525.00	
36	A3	30c rose & red org ('22)	3.25	3.25
		Never hinged	5.25	
		On cover		60.00
		On cover, single franking		75.00
37	A3	30c blk & red org ('26)	.75	.75
		Never hinged	1.050	
		On cover		27.50
		On cover, single franking		60.00
38	A3	30c slate bl & bl grn ('27)	1.75	1.75
		Never hinged	2.50	
		On cover		40.00
		On cover, single franking		65.00
39	A3	35c green & rose	1.25	1.25
		Never hinged	2.10	
		On cover		40.00
		On cover, single franking		75.00
40	A3	40c black & green	1.10	1.10
		Never hinged	1.80	
		On cover		40.00
		On cover, single franking		60.00
41	A3	45c orange & red	1.10	1.10
		Never hinged	1.90	
		On cover		47.50
		On cover, single franking		67.50
42	A3	50c dk brown & blk	17.50	13.50
		Never hinged	29.00	
		On cover		52.50
		On cover, single franking		75.00

43	A3	50c ultra & bl ('22)	1.25	1.25
		Never hinged	1.65	
		On cover		52.50
		On cover, single franking		75.00
44	A3	50c gray & bl vio ('26)	1.10	1.10
		Never hinged	1.50	
		On cover		35.00
		On cover, single franking		60.00
45	A3	60c green & blk ('25)	1.25	1.25
		Never hinged	2.00	
		On cover		60.00
		On cover, single franking		75.00
46	A3	65c ol brn & red vio ('27)	3.25	3.25
		Never hinged	5.00	
		On cover		47.50
		On cover, single franking		75.00
47	A3	75c vio brn & vio	2.50	2.50
		Never hinged	4.00	
		On cover		40.00
		On cover, single franking		60.00
48	A3	90c brn red & rose ('30)	16.50	16.50
		Never hinged	22.50	
		On cover		67.50
		On cover, single franking		100.00
a.		Imperf., pair	225.00	
49	A4	1fr rose & black	6.25	4.25
		Never hinged	10.50	
		On cover		40.00
		On cover, single franking		60.00
50	A4	1.10fr vio & dk brn ('28)	1.60	1.60
		Never hinged	2.40	
		On cover		60.00
		On cover, single franking		160.00
51	A4	1.40fr bis brn & vio ('29)	4.00	4.00
		Never hinged	6.50	
		On cover		47.50
		On cover, single franking		67.50
52	A4	1.50fr ind & bl ('30)	16.50	16.50
		Never hinged	23.00	
		On cover		47.50
		On cover, single franking		60.00
53	A4	2fr dk brown & grn	6.25	4.25
		Never hinged	10.50	
		On cover		60.00
		On cover, single franking		80.00
54	A4	5fr violet & bl	11.00	11.00
		Never hinged	18.50	
		On cover		80.00
		On cover, single franking		120.00
a.		Imperf., pair	225.00	
		Nos. 21-54 (34)	117.80	107.55

For surcharges see Nos. 56-71, B2-B4.

No. 7 Overprinted

1915

55	A1	10c red	6.75	6.75
		Never hinged	11.50	
		On cover		120.00
a.		Inverted overprint	225.00	225.00
		Never hinged	365.00	

For surcharge see No. B1.

No. 29 Surcharged

1916

56	A2	10c on 15c org & blk	3.50	3.50
		Never hinged	5.25	
		On cover		40.00

Nos. 22, 41 and 29 Surcharged

1921

57	A2	5c on 2c brn & blk	36.00	36.00
		Never hinged	55.00	
		On cover		120.00
58	A3	10c on 45c org & red	36.00	36.00
		Never hinged	55.00	
		On cover		120.00

59	A2	25c on 15c org & blk	9.00	9.00
		Never hinged	15.00	
		On cover		52.50
		Nos. 57-59 (3)	81.00	81.00

On No. 58 the new value and date are set wide apart and without bar.

Types of 1913-30 Issue Surcharged in Black or Red

1923-27

60	A3	60c on 75c bl & brn	.75	.75
		Never hinged	1.10	
		On cover		60.00
		On cover, single franking		80.00
61	A4	65c on 1fr dk bl & ol (R) ('25)	2.25	2.25
		Never hinged	3.00	
		On cover		60.00
		On cover, single franking		80.00
62	A4	85c on 1fr dk bl & ol (R) ('25)	2.25	2.25
		Never hinged	3.00	
		On cover		60.00
		On cover, single franking		80.00
63	A3	90c on 75c brn red & cer ('27)	3.00	3.00
		Never hinged	4.50	
		On cover		67.50
		On cover, single franking		92.50
		Nos. 60-63 (4)	8.25	8.25

No. 26 Surcharged

1924

64	A2	45c on 10c rose & org	3.00	3.00
		Never hinged	5.00	
		On cover		40.00
a.		Inverted surcharge	2,400.	2,400.

Stamps and Type of 1913-30 Surcharged with New Value and Bars in Black or Red

1924-27

65	A4	25c on 2fr dk brn & grn	1.10	1.10
		Never hinged	1.60	
		On cover		40.00
66	A4	25c on 5fr vio & bl	1.10	1.10
		Never hinged	1.60	
		On cover		40.00
67	A4	1.25fr on 1fr dk bl & ultra (R) ('26)	1.20	1.20
		Never hinged	1.75	
		On cover		67.50
		On cover, single franking		80.00
68	A4	1.50fr on 1fr dk bl & lt bl ('27)	4.00	4.00
		Never hinged	6.00	
		On cover		80.00
		On cover, single franking		120.00
69	A4	20fr on 5fr org & brt vio ('27)	32.50	26.00
		Never hinged	47.50	
		On cover		130.00
		On cover, single franking		190.00
		Nos. 65-69 (5)	39.90	33.40

Surcharged in Black or Red

1926

70	A4	3fr on 5fr gray & blue	3.25	2.50
		Never hinged	5.00	
		On cover		72.50
		On cover, single franking		110.00
71	A4	10fr on 5fr grn & blk (R)	7.25	7.25
		Never hinged	11.00	
		On cover		100.00
		On cover, single franking		160.00

Papetoai Bay, Moorea A5

1929, Mar. 25

72	A5	3fr green & dk brn	8.00	8.00
		Never hinged	12.00	
		On cover		40.00
		On cover, single franking		52.50
73	A5	5fr lt blue & dk brn	15.00	15.00
		Never hinged	22.00	
		On cover		60.00
		On cover, single franking		80.00
74	A5	10fr lt red & dk brn	45.00	45.00
		Never hinged	70.00	
		On cover		100.00
		On cover, single franking		160.00
75	A5	20fr lilac & dk brn	57.50	57.50
		Never hinged	87.50	
		On cover		125.00
		On cover, single franking		180.00
		Nos. 72-75 (4)	125.50	125.50

For overprints see Nos. 128, 130, 132, 134 in Scott Standard catalogue, Vol. 2.

Common Design Types pictured following the introduction.

Colonial Exposition Issue
Common Design Types
1931, Apr. 13   Engr.   Perf. 12½
Name of Country Printed in Black

76	CD70	40c deep green	7.50	7.50
		Never hinged	12.50	
		On cover		40.00
77	CD71	50c violet	7.50	7.50
		Never hinged	12.50	
		On cover		32.50
78	CD72	90c red orange	7.50	7.50
		Never hinged	12.50	
		On cover		60.00
		On cover, single franking		87.50
79	CD73	1.50fr dull blue	7.50	7.50
		Never hinged	12.50	
		On cover		52.50
		On cover, single franking		80.00
		Nos. 76-79 (4)	30.00	30.00

Spear Fishing A12

Tahitian Girl — A13

Idols A14

1934-40   Photo.   Perf. 13½, 13½x13

80	A12	1c gray black	.25	.25
		Never hinged	.40	
		On cover		60.00
81	A12	2c claret	.35	.35
		Never hinged	.55	
		On cover		60.00
82	A12	3c lt blue ('40)	.35	.35
		Never hinged	.55	
		On cover		52.50
83	A12	4c orange	.60	.60
		Never hinged	.75	
		On cover		52.50
84	A12	5c violet	.90	.90
		Never hinged	1.25	
		On cover		40.00
85	A12	10c dark brown	.40	.40
		Never hinged	.60	
		On cover		40.00
86	A12	15c green	.60	.60
		Never hinged	.80	
		On cover		32.50
87	A12	20c red	.60	.60
		Never hinged	.80	
		On cover		24.00
88	A13	25c gray blue	.90	.90
		Never hinged	1.25	
		On cover		35.00
89	A13	30c yellow green	1.20	1.20
		Never hinged	1.75	
		On cover		35.00
90	A13	30c orange brn ('40)	.80	.80
		Never hinged	1.10	
		On cover		24.00
91	A14	35c dp green ('38)	4.00	4.00
		Never hinged	6.00	
		On cover		52.50

92	A13 40c red violet	.60	.60
	Never hinged	.80	
	On cover		20.00
93	A13 45c brown orange	9.00	9.00
	Never hinged	13.00	
	On cover		60.00
94	A13 45c dk green ('39)	1.60	1.60
	Never hinged	2.25	
	On cover		32.50
95	A13 50c violet	.60	.60
	Never hinged	.80	
	On cover		20.00
96	A13 55c blue ('38)	6.75	6.75
	Never hinged	9.00	
	On cover		47.50
97	A13 60c black ('39)	.75	.75
	Never hinged	1.05	
	On cover		32.50
98	A13 65c brown	3.25	3.25
	Never hinged	4.25	
99	A13 70c brt pink ('39)	1.40	1.40
	Never hinged	1.80	
	On cover		20.00
100	A13 75c olive green	9.00	9.00
	Never hinged	12.50	
	On cover		45.00
101	A13 80c violet brn ('38)	2.00	2.00
	Never hinged	2.75	
	On cover		35.00
102	A13 90c rose red	.90	.90
	Never hinged	1.25	
	On cover		32.50
	On cover, single franking		60.00
103	A14 1fr red brown	.90	.90
	Never hinged	1.25	
	On cover		27.50
	On cover, single franking		52.50
104	A14 1.25fr brown violet	8.25	8.25
	Never hinged	12.00	
	On cover		52.50
	On cover, single franking		67.50
105	A14 1.25fr rose red ('39)	1.25	1.25
	Never hinged	1.60	
	On cover		32.50
	On cover, single franking		60.00
106	A14 1.40fr orange yel ('39)	1.25	1.25
	Never hinged	1.75	
	On cover		32.50
	On cover, single franking		60.00
107	A14 1.50fr blue	.90	.90
	Never hinged	1.25	
	On cover		32.50
	On cover, single franking		52.50
108	A14 1.60fr dull vio ('39)	1.40	1.40
	Never hinged	2.00	
	On cover		32.50
	On cover, single franking		60.00
109	A14 1.75fr olive	6.75	6.75
	Never hinged	9.00	
	On cover		60.00
	On cover, single franking		80.00
110	A14 2fr red	1.10	1.10
	Never hinged	1.40	
	On cover		45.00
	On cover, single franking		60.00
111	A14 2.25fr deep blue ('39)	1.25	1.25
	Never hinged	1.60	
	On cover		32.50
	On cover, single franking		52.50
112	A14 2.50fr black ('39)	1.25	1.25
	Never hinged	1.60	
	On cover		32.50
	On cover, single franking		60.00
113	A14 3fr brown org ('39)	1.50	1.50
	Never hinged	2.00	
	On cover		40.00
	On cover, single franking		67.50
114	A14 5fr red violet ('39)	1.00	1.00
	Never hinged	1.20	
	On cover		47.50
	On cover, single franking		80.00
115	A14 10fr dark green ('39)	3.00	3.00
	Never hinged	4.00	
	On cover		55.00
	On cover, single franking		92.50
116	A14 20fr dark brown ('39)	3.50	3.50
	Never hinged	4.75	
	On cover		65.00
	On cover, single franking		120.00
	Nos. 80-116 (37)	80.10	80.10

For overprints see Nos. 126-127, 129, 131, 133, 135 in Scott Standard catalogue, Vol. 2.

Paris International Exposition Issue
Common Design Types
1937   Engr.   Perf. 13

117	CD74 20c deep violet	3.50	3.50
	Never hinged	5.00	
	On cover		52.50
118	CD75 30c dark green	3.50	3.50
	Never hinged	5.00	
	On cover		52.50
119	CD76 40c carmine rose	3.50	3.50
	Never hinged	5.00	
	On cover		52.50
120	CD77 50c dk brown & blue	4.25	4.25
	Never hinged	6.50	
	On cover		60.00
121	CD78 90c red	4.25	4.25
	Never hinged	6.50	
	On cover		60.00
	On cover, single franking		80.00
122	CD79 1.50fr ultra	5.00	5.00
	Never hinged	7.75	
	On cover		52.50
	On cover, single franking		72.50
	Nos. 117-122 (6)	24.00	24.00

Colonial Arts Exhibition Issue
Souvenir Sheet
Common Design Type
1937   Imperf.

123	CD78 3fr emerald	36.00	52.50
	Never hinged	55.00	
	On cover		120.00
	On cover, single franking		160.00

New York World's Fair Issue
Common Design Type
1939, May 10   Engr.   Perf. 12½x12

124	CD82 1.25fr carmine lake	2.40	2.40
	Never hinged	4.00	
	On cover		52.50
	On cover, single franking		72.50
125	CD82 2.25fr ultra	2.40	2.40
	Never hinged	4.00	
	On cover		52.50
	On cover, single franking		72.50
	Set, never hinged	8.00	

SEMI-POSTAL STAMPS

Nos. 55 and 26
Surcharged in Red

1915   Unwmk.   Perf. 14x13½

B1	A1 10c + 5c red	32.50	32.50
	Never hinged	55.00	
	On cover		80.00
a.	"e" instead of "c"	87.50	87.50
	Never hinged	140.00	
b.	Inverted surcharge	225.00	225.00
	Never hinged	350.00	
c.	Double surcharge	525.00	525.00
B2	A2 10c + 5c rose & org	12.50	12.50
	Never hinged	21.00	
	On cover		72.50
a.	"e" instead of "c"	65.00	65.00
	Never hinged	110.00	
b.	"c" inverted	65.00	65.00
	Never hinged	110.00	
c.	Inverted surcharge	300.00	300.00
	Never hinged	475.00	
d.	As "a," inverted surcharge	400.00	
e.	As "b," inverted surcharge	400.00	

Surcharged in Carmine

B3	A2 10c + 5c rose & org	5.50	5.50
	Never hinged	9.50	
	On cover		52.50
a.	"e" instead of "c"	45.00	45.00
	Never hinged	72.50	
b.	Inverted surcharge	200.00	200.00
	Never hinged	340.00	
c.	Double surcharge	200.00	200.00
	Never hinged	340.00	
d.	As "a," inverted surcharge	325.00	

Surcharged in Carmine

1916

B4	A2 10c + 5c rose & org	5.50	5.50

Curie Issue
Common Design Type
1938   Engr.   Perf. 13

B5	CD80 1.75fr + 50c brt ultra	20.00	20.00
	Never hinged	32.50	
	On cover		60.00
	On cover, single franking		92.50

French Revolution Issue
Common Design Type
1939   Photo.
Name and Value Typo. in Black

B6	CD83 45c + 25c grn	17.50	17.50
	Never hinged	29.00	
	On cover		80.00

B7	CD83 70c + 30c brn	17.50	17.50
	Never hinged	29.00	
	On cover		67.50
B8	CD83 90c + 35c red org	17.50	17.50
	Never hinged	29.00	
	On cover		60.00
B9	CD83 1.25fr + 1fr rose pink	17.50	17.50
	Never hinged	29.00	
	On cover		80.00
	On cover, single franking		120.00
B10	CD83 2.25fr + 2fr blue	17.50	17.50
	Never hinged	29.00	
	On cover		72.50
	On cover, single franking		110.00
	Nos. B6-B10 (5)	87.50	87.50
	Set, never hinged	145.00	

AIR POST STAMP

Seaplane in Flight AP1

Perf. 13½
1934, Nov. 5   Unwmk.   Photo.

C1	AP1 5fr green	1.25	1.25
	Never hinged	1.60	
	On cover		47.50

For overprint see No. C2 in Scott Standard catalogue, Vol. 2.
For Type AP1 without "RF," see Nos. C1A-C1D in Scott Standard catalogue, Vol. 2.

AIR POST SEMI-POSTAL STAMP

French Revolution Issue
Common Design Type
Unwmk.
1939, July 5   Photo.   Perf. 13
Name and Value Typo. in Orange

CB1	CD83 5fr + 4fr brn blk	35.00	35.00
	Never hinged	60.00	
	On cover		87.50
	On cover, single franking		125.00

POSTAGE DUE STAMPS

Postage Due Stamps of French Colonies, 1894-1906, Overprinted

1926-27   Unwmk.   Perf. 14x13½

J1	D1 5c light blue	.95	.95
	Never hinged	1.60	
	On cover		60.00
J2	D1 10c brown	.95	.95
	Never hinged	1.60	
	On cover		55.00
J3	D1 20c olive green	1.40	1.40
	Never hinged	2.40	
	On cover		55.00
J4	D1 30c dull red	1.60	1.60
	Never hinged	2.75	
	On cover		60.00
J5	D1 40c rose	3.50	3.50
	Never hinged	6.50	
	On cover		60.00
J6	D1 60c blue green	3.50	3.50
	Never hinged	6.50	
	On cover		60.00
J7	D1 1fr red brown, *straw*	3.75	3.75
	Never hinged	7.00	
	On cover		60.00
J8	D1 3fr magenta ('27)	15.00	15.00
	Never hinged	29.00	
	On cover		80.00

With Additional Surcharge of New Value

J9	D1 2fr on 1fr orange red	4.00	4.75
	Never hinged	7.25	
	On cover		65.00
	Nos. J1-J9 (9)	34.65	35.40

Fautaua Falls, Tahiti — D2   Tahitian Youth — D3

1929   Typo.   Perf. 13½x14

J10	D2 5c lt blue & dk brn	.75	.75
	Never hinged	1.20	
	On cover		60.00
J11	D2 10c vermilion & grn	.75	.75
	Never hinged	1.20	
	On cover		60.00
J12	D2 30c dk brn & dk red	1.75	1.75
	Never hinged	2.60	
	On cover		52.50
J13	D2 50c yel grn & dk brn	1.40	1.40
	Never hinged	2.00	
	On cover		52.50
J14	D2 60c dl vio & yel grn	4.00	4.00
	Never hinged	6.00	
	On cover		60.00
J15	D3 1fr Prus bl & red vio	3.50	3.50
	Never hinged	5.25	
	On cover		60.00
J16	D3 2fr brn red & dk brn	2.00	2.10
	Never hinged	3.25	
	On cover		67.50
J17	D3 3fr bl vio & bl grn	2.10	2.40
	Never hinged	3.25	
	On cover		80.00
	Nos. J10-J17 (8)	16.25	16.65

FRENCH SUDAN

'french sü-'dan

LOCATION — In northwest Africa, north of French Guinea and Ivory Coast
GOVT. — French Colony
AREA — 590,966 sq. mi.
POP. — 3,794,270 (1941)
CAPITAL — Bamako

In 1899 French Sudan was abolished as a separate colony and was divided among Dahomey, French Guinea, Ivory Coast, Senegal and Senegambia and Niger. Issues for French Sudan were resumed in 1921.

From 1906 to 1921 a part of this territory was known as Upper Senegal and Niger. A part of Upper Volta was added in 1933.

100 Centimes = 1 Franc

French Colonies Nos. 58-59 Srchd. in Black

Perf. 14x13½

1894, Apr. 12　　　　　　**Unwmk.**
1　A9　15c on 75c car, *rose*　4,600. 2,300.
　　　On cover　　　　　　　　　　　　4,600.
2　A9　25c on 1fr brnz grn, *straw*　5,000. 1,700.
　　　On cover　　　　　　　　　　　　3,500.

The imperforate stamp like No. 1 was made privately in Paris from a fragment of the lithographic stone which had been used in the Colony for surcharging No. 1.
Counterfeit surcharges exist.

Navigation and Commerce — A2

1894-1900　　Typo.　　Perf. 14x13½
Name of colony in Blue or Carmine
3　A2　1c blk, *lil bl*　　　1.75　1.75
　　Never hinged　　　　　3.00
　　On cover　　　　　　　　　　140.00
4　A2　2c brn, *buff*　　　2.50　2.50
　　Never hinged　　　　　4.25
　　On cover　　　　　　　　　　140.00
5　A2　4c claret, *lav*　　6.00　6.00
　　Never hinged　　　　　11.00
　　On cover　　　　　　　　　　140.00
6　A2　5c grn, *grnsh*　　9.50　9.50
　　Never hinged　　　　　16.00
　　On cover　　　　　　　　　　67.50
7　A2　10c blk, *lav*　　21.00　21.00
　　Never hinged　　　　　37.50
　　On cover　　　　　　　　　　60.00
8　A2　10c red ('00)　　　7.25　7.25
　　Never hinged　　　　　12.00
　　On cover　　　　　　　　　　52.50
9　A2　15c blue, quadrille paper　6.50　6.50
　　Never hinged　　　　　12.00
　　On cover　　　　　　　　　　65.00
10　A2　15c gray, *lt gray* ('00)　7.50　7.50
　　Never hinged　　　　　13.50
　　On cover　　　　　　　　　　52.50
11　A2　20c red, *grn*　　32.50　32.50
　　Never hinged　　　　　62.50
　　On cover　　　　　　　　　　120.00
　　On cover, single franking　　225.00
12　A2　25c blk, *rose*　27.50　27.50
　　Never hinged　　　　　52.50
　　On cover　　　　　　　　　　72.50
13　A2　25c blue ('00)　　8.50　8.50
　　Never hinged　　　　　14.50
　　On cover　　　　　　　　　　55.00
14　A2　30c brn, *bister*　40.00　40.00
　　Never hinged　　　　　80.00
　　On cover　　　　　　　　　　90.00
　　On cover, single franking　　125.00
15　A2　40c red, *straw*　35.00　35.00
　　Never hinged　　　　　70.00
　　On cover　　　　　　　　　　92.50
　　On cover, single franking　　125.00
16　A2　50c car, *rose*　57.50　57.50
　　Never hinged　　　　　115.00
　　On cover　　　　　　　　　　150.00
　　On cover, single franking　　180.00
17　A2　50c brn, *az* ('00)　15.00　15.00
　　Never hinged　　　　　32.50
　　On cover　　　　　　　　　　100.00
　　On cover, single franking　　140.00
18　A2　75c dp vio, *org*　52.50　52.50
　　Never hinged　　　　　110.00
　　On cover　　　　　　　　　　225.00
　　On cover, single franking　　350.00

19　A2　1fr brnz grn, *straw*　11.00　11.00
　　Never hinged　　　　　18.50
　　On cover　　　　　　　　　　240.00
　　On cover, single franking　　400.00
　　Nos. 3-19 (17)　　341.50 341.50

Perf. 13½x14 stamps are counterfeits.
Nos. 8, 10, 13, 17 were issued in error. They were accepted for use in the other colonies.
Covers: Values are for commercial with correct frankings. Philatelic covers sell for less.

Camel and Rider — A3

Stamps of Upper Senegal and Niger Overprinted in Black

1921-30　　　　　Perf. 13½x14
21　A3　1c brn vio & vio　　.25　.40
　　Never hinged　　　　　
　　On cover　　　　　　　　　　52.50
22　A3　2c dk gray & dl vio　.30　.50
　　Never hinged　　　　　.50
　　On cover　　　　　　　　　　52.50
23　A3　4c blk & blue　　.30　.50
　　Never hinged　　　　　.50
　　On cover　　　　　　　　　　52.50
24　A3　5c ol brn & dk brn　.30　.40
　　Never hinged　　　　　.50
　　On cover　　　　　　　　　　27.50
25　A3　10c yel grn & bl grn　1.00　.55
　　Never hinged　　　　　1.50
　　On cover　　　　　　　　　　55.00
26　A3　10c red vio & bl ('25)　.40　.50
　　Never hinged　　　　　.65
　　On cover　　　　　　　　　　17.50
27　A3　15c red brn & org　.50　.55
　　Never hinged　　　　　.85
　　On cover　　　　　　　　　　32.50
28　A3　15c yel grn & dp grn ('25)　.40　.40
　　Never hinged　　　　　.65
　　On cover　　　　　　　　　　12.00
29　A3　15c org brn & vio ('27)　1.60　1.60
　　Never hinged　　　　　2.40
　　On cover　　　　　　　　　　17.50
30　A3　20c brn vio & blk　.50　.55
　　Never hinged　　　　　.85
　　On cover　　　　　　　　　　27.50
31　A3　25c blk & bl grn　1.25　.80
　　Never hinged　　　　　1.90
　　On cover　　　　　　　　　　24.00
a.　Booklet pane of 4　　　—
　　Complete booklet, 5 #31a　575.00
32　A3　30c red org & rose　1.60　1.60
　　Never hinged　　　　　2.60
　　On cover　　　　　　　　　　40.00
　　On cover, single franking　　80.00
33　A3　30c bl grn & blk ('26)　.80　.70
　　Never hinged　　　　　1.15
　　On cover　　　　　　　　　　9.50
34　A3　30c dl grn & bl grn ('28)　2.00　2.00
　　Never hinged　　　　　3.00
　　On cover　　　　　　　　　　27.50
35　A3　35c rose & vio　.40　.55
　　Never hinged　　　　　.55
　　On cover　　　　　　　　　　35.00
　　On cover, single franking　　47.50
36　A3　40c gray & rose　1.25　1.25
　　Never hinged　　　　　2.40
　　On cover　　　　　　　　　　27.50
　　On cover, single franking　　40.00
37　A3　45c bl & ol brn　1.25　1.25
　　Never hinged　　　　　1.90
　　On cover　　　　　　　　　　47.50
　　On cover, single franking　　80.00
38　A3　50c ultra & bl　1.60　1.25
　　Never hinged　　　　　2.60
　　On cover　　　　　　　　　　32.50
　　On cover, single franking　　80.00
39　A3　50c red org & bl ('26)　1.25　1.25
　　Never hinged　　　　　2.00
　　On cover　　　　　　　　　　10.50
40　A3　60c vio, *pnksh* ('26)　1.25　1.25
　　Never hinged　　　　　2.00
　　On cover　　　　　　　　　　27.50
　　On cover, single franking　　72.50
41　A3　65c bis & pale bl ('28)　1.60　1.60
　　Never hinged　　　　　2.40
　　On cover　　　　　　　　　　32.50
　　On cover, single franking　　55.00
42　A3　75c org & ol brn　1.60　2.00
　　Never hinged　　　　　2.40
　　On cover　　　　　　　　　　35.00
　　On cover, single franking　　87.50
43　A3　90c brn red & pink ('30)　5.50　5.50
　　Never hinged　　　　　7.25
　　On cover　　　　　　　　　　35.00
　　On cover, single franking　　72.50
44　A3　1fr dk brn & dl vio　1.60　2.00
　　Never hinged　　　　　2.50
　　On cover　　　　　　　　　　47.50
　　On cover, single franking　　110.00
45　A3　1.10fr gray lil & red vio ('28)　2.75　3.50
　　Never hinged　　　　　6.75
　　On cover　　　　　　　　　　130.00
　　On cover, single franking　　260.00

46　A3　1.50fr dp bl & bl ('30)　5.50　5.50
　　Never hinged　　　　　8.75
　　On cover　　　　　　　　　　32.50
　　On cover, single franking　　85.00
47　A3　2fr grn & bl　　2.40　2.75
　　Never hinged　　　　　4.00
　　On cover　　　　　　　　　　60.00
　　On cover, single franking　　120.00
48　A3　3fr red vio ('30)　12.00　12.00
　　Never hinged　　　　　19.00
　　On cover　　　　　　　　　　67.50
　　On cover, single franking　　120.00
a.　Double overprint　　190.00
　　Never hinged　　　　　275.00
49　A3　5fr vio & blk　　6.75　6.75
　　Never hinged　　　　　12.50
　　On cover　　　　　　　　　　72.50
　　On cover, single franking　　140.00
　　Nos. 21-49 (29)　　57.90　59.45

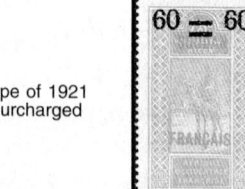

Type of 1921 Surcharged

1922, Sept. 28
50　A3　60c on 75c vio, *pnksh*　.80　.80
　　Never hinged　　　　　1.50
　　On cover　　　　　　　　　　27.50
　　On cover, single franking　　40.00

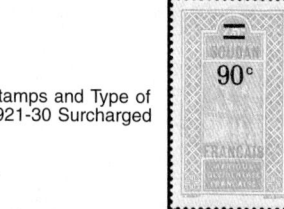

Stamps and Type of 1921-30 Surcharged

1925-27
51　A3　25c on 45c　　.80　.80
　　Never hinged　　　　　1.15
　　On cover　　　　　　　　　　12.50
52　A3　65c on 75c　　2.00　2.40
　　Never hinged　　　　　3.00
　　On cover　　　　　　　　　　55.00
　　On cover, single franking　　110.00
53　A3　85c on 2fr　　2.00　2.40
　　Never hinged　　　　　3.00
　　On cover　　　　　　　　　　47.50
　　On cover, single franking　　87.50
54　A3　85c on 5fr　　2.00　2.40
　　Never hinged　　　　　3.00
　　On cover　　　　　　　　　　47.50
　　On cover, single franking　　87.50
55　A3　90c on 75c brn red & sal pink ('27)　2.40　2.75
　　Never hinged　　　　　3.75
　　On cover　　　　　　　　　　52.50
　　On cover, single franking　　92.50
56　A3　1.25fr on 1fr dp bl & lt bl (R) ('26)　1.25　1.60
　　Never hinged　　　　　2.10
　　On cover　　　　　　　　　　52.50
　　On cover, single franking　　87.50
57　A3　1.50fr on 1fr dp bl & ultra ('27)　1.60　2.00
　　Never hinged　　　　　2.60
　　On cover　　　　　　　　　　40.00
　　On cover, single franking　　72.50
58　A3　3fr on 5fr dl red & brn org ('27)　6.50　5.50
　　Never hinged　　　　　11.00
　　On cover　　　　　　　　　　72.50
　　On cover, single franking　　150.00
59　A3　10fr on 5fr brn red & bl grn ('27)　24.00　21.00
　　Never hinged　　　　　37.50
　　On cover　　　　　　　　　　80.00
　　On cover, single franking　　160.00
60　A3　20fr on 5fr vio & ver ('27)　29.00　29.00
　　Never hinged　　　　　45.00
　　On cover　　　　　　　　　　87.50
　　On cover, single franking　　175.00
　　Nos. 51-60 (10)　　71.55　69.85

Sudanese Woman — A4

Entrance to the Residency at Djenné — A5

Sudanese Boatman — A6

1931-40　　Typo.　　Perf. 13x14
61　A4　1c dk red & blk　.25　.25
　　Never hinged　　　　　.40
　　On cover　　　　　　　　　　45.00
62　A4　2c dp blue & org　.25　.25
　　Never hinged　　　　　.40
　　On cover　　　　　　　　　　45.00
63　A4　3c dk red & blk ('40)　.25　.25
　　Never hinged　　　　　.40
　　On cover　　　　　　　　　　24.00
64　A4　4c gray lil & rose　.25　.25
　　Never hinged　　　　　.40
　　On cover　　　　　　　　　　45.00
65　A4　5c indigo & grn　.25　.25
　　Never hinged　　　　　.40
　　On cover　　　　　　　　　　45.00
66　A4　10c ol grn & rose　.25　.25
　　Never hinged　　　　　.40
　　On cover　　　　　　　　　　21.00
67　A4　15c blk & brt vio　.30　.30
　　Never hinged　　　　　.50
　　On cover　　　　　　　　　　16.00
68　A4　20c hn brn & lt bl　.30　.30
　　Never hinged　　　　　.50
　　On cover　　　　　　　　　　17.50
69　A4　25c red vio & lt red　.30　.30
　　Never hinged　　　　　.50
　　On cover　　　　　　　　　　17.50
70　A5　30c grn & lt grn　.75　.50
　　Never hinged　　　　　.95
　　On cover　　　　　　　　　　24.00
71　A5　30c dk bl & red org ('40)　.30　.30
　　Never hinged　　　　　.40
　　On cover　　　　　　　　　　12.00
72　A5　35c ol grn & grn ('38)　.50　.50
　　Never hinged　　　　　.75
　　On cover　　　　　　　　　　24.00
73　A5　40c ol grn & pink　.30　.30
　　Never hinged　　　　　.50
　　On cover　　　　　　　　　　8.75
74　A5　45c dk bl & red org　.95　.65
　　Never hinged　　　　　1.40
　　On cover　　　　　　　　　　21.00
75　A5　45c ol grn & grn ('40)　.50　.50
　　Never hinged　　　　　.65
　　On cover　　　　　　　　　　16.00
76　A5　50c red & black　.30　.30
　　Never hinged　　　　　.50
　　On cover　　　　　　　　　　8.75
77　A5　55c ultra & car ('38)　.55　.55
　　Never hinged　　　　　.80
　　On cover　　　　　　　　　　8.00
78　A5　60c brt bl & brn ('40)　1.20　1.20
　　Never hinged　　　　　1.65
　　On cover　　　　　　　　　　16.00
79　A5　65c brt vio & blk　.65　.55
　　Never hinged　　　　　.90
　　On cover　　　　　　　　　　32.50
80　A5　70c vio bl & car rose ('40)　.80　.80
　　Never hinged　　　　　1.20
　　On cover　　　　　　　　　　20.00
81　A5　75c brt bl & ol brn　2.40　2.00
　　Never hinged　　　　　3.25
　　On cover　　　　　　　　　　14.50
82　A5　80c car & brn ('38)　.55　.55
　　Never hinged　　　　　.80
　　On cover　　　　　　　　　　40.00
　　On cover, single franking　　67.50
83　A5　90c dp red & red org　1.60　.80
　　Never hinged　　　　　2.10
　　On cover　　　　　　　　　　24.00
　　On cover, single franking　　55.00
84　A5　90c brt vio & sl blk ('39)　.90　1.00
　　Never hinged　　　　　1.25
　　On cover　　　　　　　　　　27.50
　　On cover, single franking　　65.00
85　A5　1fr indigo & grn　8.00　2.40
　　Never hinged　　　　　21.00
　　On cover　　　　　　　　　　18.00
86　A5　1fr rose red ('38)　4.75　2.40
　　Never hinged　　　　　6.75
　　On cover　　　　　　　　　　24.00
　　On cover, single franking　　45.00
87　A5　1fr car & brn ('40)　.80　.80
　　Never hinged　　　　　1.40
　　On cover　　　　　　　　　　5.50
88　A6　1.25fr vio & dl vio ('33)　.80　.80
　　Never hinged　　　　　1.00
　　On cover　　　　　　　　　　16.00
　　On cover, single franking　　45.00
89　A6　1.25fr red ('39)　.90　1.00
　　Never hinged　　　　　1.25
　　On cover　　　　　　　　　　40.00
　　On cover, single franking　　80.00
90　A6　1.40fr brt vio & blk ('40)　.90　.90
　　Never hinged　　　　　1.25
　　On cover　　　　　　　　　　27.50
　　On cover, single franking　　60.00
91　A6　1.50fr dk bl & ultra　.65　.55
　　Never hinged　　　　　.90
　　On cover　　　　　　　　　　24.00
　　On cover, single franking　　47.50

92	A6	1.60fr brn & dp bl ('40)	.90	.90
		Never hinged	1.25	
		On cover		27.50
		On cover, single franking		60.00
93	A6	1.75fr dk brn & dp bl ('33)	.80	.80
		Never hinged	1.00	
		On cover		12.00
		On cover, single franking		17.50
94	A6	1.75fr vio bl ('38)	.80	.80
		Never hinged	1.05	
		On cover		24.00
		On cover, single franking		40.00
95	A6	2fr org brn & grn	.75	.55
		Never hinged	.95	
		On cover		21.00
		On cover, single franking		40.00
96	A6	2.25fr vio bl & ultra ('39)	1.00	1.10
		Never hinged	1.30	
		On cover		35.00
		On cover, single franking		72.50
97	A6	2.50fr lt brown ('40)	1.60	1.60
		Never hinged	2.25	
		On cover		20.00
		On cover, single franking		35.00
98	A6	3fr Prus grn & brn	.75	.40
		Never hinged	.95	
		On cover		27.50
		On cover, single franking		67.50
99	A6	5fr red & blk	2.00	1.20
		Never hinged	2.75	
		On cover		32.50
		On cover, single franking		65.00
100	A6	10fr dull bl & grn	2.00	2.00
		Never hinged	2.75	
		On cover		35.00
		On cover, single franking		67.50
101	A6	20fr red vio & brn	2.40	2.40
		Never hinged	4.00	
		On cover		45.00
		On cover, single franking		75.00
		Nos. 61-101 (41)	44.45	33.50

For surcharges see Nos. B7-B10 in Scott Standard catalogue, Vol. 2.
For 10c and 30c, without "RF," see Nos. 120-121 in Scott Standard catalogue, Vol. 2.

Common Design Types pictured following the introduction.

Colonial Exposition Issue
Common Design Types

1931, Apr. 13   Engr.   Perf. 12½
Name of Country Printed in Black

102	CD70	40c deep green	4.75	4.75
		Never hinged	8.00	
		On cover		67.50
103	CD71	50c violet	4.75	4.75
		Never hinged	8.00	
		On cover		55.00
104	CD72	90c red orange	4.75	4.75
		Never hinged	8.00	
		On cover		100.00
		On cover, single franking		140.00
105	CD73	1.50fr dull blue	4.75	4.75
		Never hinged	8.00	
		On cover		87.50
		On cover, single franking		120.00
		Nos. 102-105 (4)	19.00	19.00

Paris International Exposition Issue
Common Design Types

1937, Apr. 15   Perf. 13

106	CD74	20c deep violet	2.00	2.00
		Never hinged	3.00	
		On cover		75.00
107	CD75	30c dark green	2.00	2.00
		Never hinged	3.00	
		On cover		55.00
108	CD76	40c carmine rose	2.00	2.00
		Never hinged	3.00	
		On cover		55.00
109	CD77	50c dark brown	1.60	1.60
		Never hinged	2.75	
		On cover		52.50
110	CD78	90c red	1.60	1.60
		Never hinged	2.75	
		On cover		75.00
		On cover, single franking		140.00
111	CD79	1.50fr ultra	2.00	2.00
		Never hinged	3.00	
		On cover		87.50
		On cover, single franking		110.00
		Nos. 106-111 (6)	11.20	11.20

Colonial Arts Exhibition Issue
Souvenir Sheet
Common Design Type

1937   Engr.   Imperf.

112	CD77	3fr magenta & blk	8.75	10.50
		Never hinged	13.00	
		On cover		92.50
		On cover, single franking		140.00

Caillie Issue
Common Design Type

1939, Apr. 5   Perf. 12½x12

113	CD81	90c org brn & org	.95	.95
		Never hinged	1.15	
		On cover		8.75
114	CD81	2fr brt violet	1.10	1.10
		Never hinged	1.40	
		On cover		21.00
		On cover, single franking		35.00

115	CD81	2.25fr ultra & dk bl	1.10	1.10
		Never hinged	1.40	
		On cover		25.00
		On cover, single franking		45.00
		Nos. 113-115 (3)	3.15	3.15

New York World's Fair Issue
Common Design Type

1939, May 10

116	CD82	1.25fr car lake	1.20	1.20
		Never hinged	1.75	
		On cover		55.00
		On cover, single franking		110.00
117	CD82	2.25fr ultra	1.20	1.20
		Never hinged	1.75	
		On cover		55.00
		On cover, single franking		100.00

SEMI-POSTAL STAMPS

Curie Issue
Common Design Type
Unwmk.

1938, Oct. 24   Engr.   Perf. 13

B1	CD80	1.75fr + 50c brt ultra	12.50	12.50
		Never hinged	21.00	
		On cover		72.50
		On cover, single franking		125.00

French Revolution Issue
Common Design Type

1939, July 5   Photo.
Name and Value Typo. in Black

B2	CD83	45c + 25c green	10.00	10.00
		Never hinged	17.50	
		On cover		100.00
B3	CD83	70c + 30c brown	10.00	10.00
		Never hinged	17.50	
		On cover		75.00
B4	CD83	90c + 35c red org	10.00	10.00
		Never hinged	17.50	
		On cover		67.50
B5	CD83	1.25fr + 1fr rose pink	10.00	10.00
		Never hinged	17.50	
		On cover		110.00
		On cover, single franking		160.00
B6	CD83	2.25fr + 2fr blue	10.00	10.00
		Never hinged	17.50	
		On cover		100.00
		On cover, single franking		150.00
		Nos. B2-B6 (5)	50.00	50.00

AIR POST STAMPS

Common Design Type
Perf. 12½x12

1940, Feb. 8   Unwmk.   Engr.

C1	CD85	1.90fr ultra	.40	.40
		Never hinged	.55	
		On cover		27.50
C2	CD85	2.90fr dark red	.55	.55
		Never hinged	.75	
		On cover		27.50
C3	CD85	4.50fr dk gray green	.95	.95
		Never hinged	1.20	
		On cover		32.50
C4	CD85	4.90fr yellow bister	.95	.95
		Never hinged	1.20	
		On cover		40.00
C5	CD85	6.90fr deep orange	1.10	1.10
		Never hinged	1.50	
		On cover		47.50
		Nos. C1-C5 (5)	3.95	3.95

POSTAGE DUE STAMPS

Postage Due Stamps of Upper Senegal and Niger Overprinted — D1

Perf. 14x13½

1921, Dec.   Unwmk.   Typo.

J1	D1	5c green	.50	.65
		Never hinged	.80	
		On cover		40.00
J2	D1	10c rose	.65	.80
		Never hinged	1.00	
		On cover		40.00
J3	D1	15c gray	.80	.95
		Never hinged	1.25	
		On cover		40.00
J4	D1	20c brown	1.10	1.25
		Never hinged	1.75	
		On cover		45.00
J5	D1	30c blue	1.10	1.25
		Never hinged	1.75	
		On cover		45.00
J6	D1	50c black	1.90	2.10
		Never hinged	2.75	
		On cover		47.50

J7	D1	60c orange	2.00	2.25
		Never hinged	3.00	
		On cover		55.00
J8	D1	1fr violet	2.40	2.60
		Never hinged	3.50	
		On cover		67.50
		Nos. J1-J8 (8)	10.45	11.85

Type of 1921 Issue Surcharged

1927, Oct. 10

J9	D1	2fr on 1fr lilac rose	7.25	8.00
J10	D1	3fr on 1fr org brown	7.25	8.00

D2

1931, Mar. 9

J11	D2	5c green	.25	.30
		Never hinged	.40	
		On cover		32.50
J12	D2	10c rose	.25	.30
		Never hinged	.40	
		On cover		32.50
J13	D2	15c gray	.30	.50
		Never hinged	.50	
		On cover		32.50
J14	D2	20c dark brown	.30	.50
		Never hinged	.50	
		On cover		35.00
J15	D2	30c dark blue	.50	.55
		Never hinged	.65	
		On cover		35.00
J16	D2	50c black	.55	.65
		Never hinged	.80	
		On cover		40.00
J17	D2	60c deep orange	.70	.80
		Never hinged	.95	
		On cover		45.00
J18	D2	1fr violet	1.10	1.20
		Never hinged	1.40	
		On cover		52.50
J19	D2	2fr lilac rose	1.60	1.60
		Never hinged	1.90	
		On cover		65.00
J20	D2	3fr red brown	1.60	1.60
		Never hinged	1.90	
		On cover		72.50
		Nos. J11-J20 (10)	7.15	8.00

FUNCHAL

fün-'shäl

LOCATION — A city and administrative district in the Madeira island group in the Atlantic Ocean northwest of Africa

GOVT. — A part of the Republic of Portugal

POP. — 150,574 (1900)

Postage stamps of Funchal were superseded by those of Portugal.

1000 Reis = 1 Milreis

STAMPS OF PORTUGAL USED IN FUNCHAL

Barred Numeral "51"

Queen Maria II

1853

A1	5r orange brown (#1)	1,425.	
A2	25r blue (#2)	92.50	
A3	50r deep yellow green (#3)	1,400.	
a.	50r blue green (#3a)		
A4	100r lilac (#4)	3,000.	

1855   King Pedro V (Straight Hair)

A5	5r red brown (#5)	1,425.	
A6	25r blue, type II (#6)	72.50	
a.	Type I (#6a)	67.50	
A7	50r green (#7)	110.00	
A8	100r lilac (#8)	115.00	

1856-58   King Pedro V (Curled Hair)

A9	5r brown (#9)	175.00	
A10	25r blue, type II (#10)	110.00	
a.	Type I (#10a)	110.00	
A11	25r rose, type II (#11) ('58)	36.00	

1862-64   King Luiz

A12	5r brown (#12)	110.00	
A13	10r orange (#13)	115.00	
A14	25r rose (#14)	40.00	
A15	50r yellow green (#15)	110.00	
A16	100r lilac (#16) ('64)	100.00	

1866-67   King Luiz
Imperf.

A17	5r black (#17)	115.00	
A18	10r yellow (#18)	175.00	
A19	20r bister (#19)	175.00	
A20	25r rose (#20) ('67)	132.50	
A21	50r green (#21)	175.00	
A22	80r orange (#22)	175.00	
A23	100r dark lilac (#23) ('67)	225.00	
A24	120r blue (#24)	115.00	

Perf. 12½

A28	25r rose (#28)	95.00	

King Carlos

A1   A2

1892-93   Typo.   Unwmk.
Enamel Surfaced Paper,
Perf. 12½

1	A1	5r yellow	3.00	2.00
		Never hinged	4.25	
a.		Half used as 2½r on entire newspaper		17.50
2	A1	10r red violet	2.50	2.00
		Never hinged	3.50	
3	A1	15r chocolate	3.50	2.50
		Never hinged	5.00	
4	A1	20r lavender	4.50	2.50
		Never hinged	5.00	
a.		Perf. 13½	9.00	7.50
5	A1	25r dark green	6.00	1.35
		Never hinged	10.00	
6	A1	50r ultramarine	7.00	2.50
		Never hinged	14.50	
7	A1	75r carmine	8.50	6.00
		Never hinged	11.00	
8	A1	80r yellow green	14.00	11.00
		Never hinged	20.00	
9	A1	100r brn, yel ('93)	10.00	5.00
		Never hinged	12.50	
a.		Diagonal half used as 50r on cover		50.00
11	A1	200r dk bl, bl ('93)	65.00	45.00
		Never hinged	82.50	
12	A1	300r dk bl, sal ('93)	70.00	55.00
		Never hinged	110.00	
		Nos. 1-12 (11)	193.00	134.85

Enamel Surfaced Paper,
Perf. 13½

1c	A1	5r yellow	3.00	1.50
		Never hinged	4.00	
2a	A1	10r red violet	3.25	2.10
		Never hinged	4.75	
3a	A1	15r chocolate	4.50	2.10
		Never hinged	6.25	
4b	A1	20r lavender	8.75	6.25
		Never hinged	12.50	
6a	A1	50r ultramarine	8.75	5.50
		Never hinged	12.50	
7a	A1	75r carmine	8.75	5.50
		Never hinged	12.50	
8a	A1	80r yellow green	17.50	12.00
		Never hinged	20.00	
10	A1	150r car, rose ('93)	60.00	30.00
		Never hinged	72.50	

Enamel Surfaced Paper,
Perf. 11½

1b	A1	5r yellow	4.00	2.75
5a	A1	25r dark green	6.00	1.00
6b	A1	50r ultramarine	4.75	2.10

Chalky Paper,
Perf. 12½

3b	A1	15r chocolate	14.00	10.00
		Never hinged	20.00	
8b	A1	80r yellow green	16.00	11.00
		Never hinged	22.50	

Chalky Paper,
Perf. 13½

6c	A1	50r ultramarine	12.50	7.25
		Never hinged	19.00	

Nos. 1-12 were issued on two types of paper: enamel surfaced, which is white, with a uniform low gloss; and chalky, which bears a low-gloss application in a pattern of tiny lozenges, producing a somewhat duller appearance.

The reprints of this issue have shiny white gum and clean-cut perforation 13½. The shades differ from those of the originals and the uncolored paper is thin.

1897-1905   Perf. 11¾
Name and Value in Black except Nos. 25 and 34

13	A2	2½r gray	.50	.35
		Never hinged	.60	
14	A2	5r orange	[..]	[..]
		Never hinged	.60	
15	A2	10r light green	.50	.35
		Never hinged	.60	
16	A2	15r brown	5.50	5.00
		Never hinged	8.00	
17	A2	15r gray grn ('99)	3.75	2.75
		Never hinged	5.25	
18	A2	20r gray vio	1.40	.75
		Never hinged	1.75	
19	A2	25r sea green	2.75	.75
		Never hinged	3.75	
20	A2	25r car rose ('99)	1.40	.55
		Never hinged	1.75	
a.		Booklet pane of 6		
21	A2	50r dark blue	8.00	5.00
		Never hinged	9.75	
a.		Perf. 12½	21.00	9.00
		Never hinged	18.00	
22	A2	50r ultra ('05)	1.50	.90
		Never hinged	1.75	
23	A2	65r slate blue ('98)	1.25	.90
		Never hinged	1.50	
24	A2	75r rose	2.00	.95
		Never hinged	2.75	
25	A2	75r brn & red, *yel* ('05)	4.00	1.40
		Never hinged	4.75	
26	A2	80r violet	1.40	1.10
		Never hinged	2.00	
27	A2	100r dark blue, *blue*	1.40	1.10
		Never hinged	2.00	
a.		Diagonal half used as 50r on cover		75.00
28	A2	115r org brn, *pink* ('98)	4.00	1.40
		Never hinged	5.25	
29	A2	130r gray brown, *buff* ('98)	5.00	1.40
		Never hinged	6.50	
30	A2	150r lt brn, *buff*	5.00	1.25
		Never hinged	6.50	
31	A2	180r sl, *pnksh* ('98)	5.00	1.40
		Never hinged	6.50	
32	A2	200r red vio, *pale lil*	5.00	2.10
		Never hinged	6.50	
33	A2	300r blue, *rose*	5.00	2.10
		Never hinged	6.50	
34	A2	500r blk & red, *bl*	8.00	2.40
		Never hinged	10.50	
a.		Perf. 12½	15.00	7.75
		Never hinged	17.50	
		Nos. 13-34 (22)	72.85	34.25

Yellowish Paper

13a	A2	2½r gray	.50	.35
		Never hinged	.60	
14a	A2	5r orange	.50	.35
		Never hinged	.60	
15a	A2	10r lightt green	.50	.35
		Never hinged	.60	
17a	A2	15r gray grn ('99)	3.25	2.25
		Never hinged	4.75	
18a	A2	20r gray vio	1.40	.75
		Never hinged	1.75	
20b	A2	25r car rose ('99)	1.40	.55
		Never hinged	1.75	
23a	A2	65r slate blue ('98)	1.25	.90
		Never hinged	1.50	
24a	A2	75r rose	1.40	.95
		Never hinged	2.00	

GABON
ga-'bōⁿ

LOCATION — West coast of Africa, at the equator
GOVT. — French colony
AREA — 102,089 sq. mi.
POP. — 1,367,000 (est. 1984)
CAPITAL — Libreville

Gabon originally was under the control of French West Africa. In 1886, it was united with French Congo. In 1904, Gabon was granted a certain degree of colonial autonomy which prevailed until 1934, when it merged with French Equatorial Africa.

100 Centimes = 1 Franc

Stamps of French Colonies of 1881-86 Handstamp Surcharged in Black

a   b

1886   Unwmk.   Perf. 14x13½

1	A9 (a)	5c on 20c red, *grn*	575.00	625.00
		On cover		2,500.
a.		"5" double	3,850.	
2	A9 (b)	10c on 20c red, *grn*	550.00	575.00
		On cover		2,500.
a.		"0" double	1,400.	1,250.
b.		"10" double	1,400.	1,250.
3	A9 (b)	25c on 20c red, *grn*	100.00	75.00
		Never hinged	215.00	
		On cover		260.00
a.		"25" double	750.00	525.00
b.		"25" omitted	1,200.	1,200.
c.		"GAB" inverted	1,100.	925.00
d.		"GAB" double	550.00	450.00
e.		56-dot diamond grid around "GAB"	6,750.	1,900.
				10,000.
4	A9 (b)	50c on 15c bl	1,500.	2,100.
		On cover		6,750.
a.		"GAB" omitted	3,200.	
5	A9 (b)	75c on 15c bl	1,900.	2,300.
		On cover		7,750.
a.		"75" double	5,000.	

On Nos. 3 and 5 the surcharge slants down; on No. 4 it slants up. The number of dots varies.
Counterfeits of Nos. 1-15 exist.
Covers: Values are for commercial covers with correct frankings.

Handstamp Surcharged in Black — c

1888-89

6	A9	15c on 10c blk, *lav*	6,000.	1,500.
		On cover		5,250.
7	A9	15c on 1fr brnz grn, *straw*	2,400.	1,200.
		On cover		3,500.
8	A9	25c on 5c grn, *grnsh*	1,500.	325.00
		On cover		1,050.
a.		Double surcharge	4,000.	4,000.
9	A9	25c on 10c blk, *lav*	6,000.	1,900.
		On cover		6,250.
10	A9	25c on 75c car, *rose*	4,000.	2,100.
		On cover		5,000.

Official reprints exist.

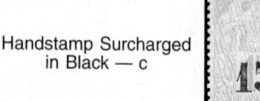

Postage Due Stamps of French Colonies Handstamp Surcharged in Black — d

1889   Imperf.

11	D1	15c on 5c black	325.00	275.00
		On cover		1,100.
a.		"TIMBRE" omitted	1,000.	675.00
b.		"TIMBRE" double	650.00	
c.		"15" omitted	1,000.	625.00
d.		"15" double	650.00	
e.		"GABON" double	650.00	
12	D1	15c on 30c black	5,000.	3,800.
		On cover		8,400.
a.		"GABON" omitted	6,500.	
b.		"15" omitted	6,500.	
13	D1	25c on 20c black	150.00	120.00
		On cover		425.00
a.		"25" double	325.00	325.00
b.		"GABON" double	325.00	
c.		"TIMBRE" double	325.00	

A8

1889   Typeset

14	A8	15c blk, *rose*	1,900.	1,200.
		On cover		4,000.
a.		"GAB" omitted	8,500.	
b.		"GAB" double	3,250.	
15	A8	25c blk, *green*	1,200.	950.
		On cover		2,750.
a.		"GAB" omitted	5,750.	
b.		"GAB" inverted	2,850.	
c.		"GAB" double	2,850.	

Ten varieties of each. Nos. 14-15 exist with small "f" in "Francaise."

Navigation and Commerce — A9

Name of Colony in Blue or Carmine

1904-07   Typo.   Perf. 14x13½

16	A9	1c blk, *lil bl*	1.20	1.20
		Never hinged	2.00	
		On cover		190.00
17	A9	2c brn, *buff*	1.60	1.60
		Never hinged	3.00	
		On cover		190.00
a.		"GABON" double	600.00	180.00
		On cover		250.00
18	A9	4c claret, *lav*	2.75	2.00
		Never hinged	5.50	
		On cover		190.00
19	A9	5c yellow green	3.25	2.40
		Never hinged	6.50	
		On cover		75.00
20	A9	10c rose	10.50	7.50
		Never hinged	17.00	
		On cover		92.50
21	A9	15c gray	11.00	7.50
		Never hinged	18.50	
		On cover		92.50
22	A9	20c red, *grn*	15.00	14.00
		Never hinged	25.00	
		On cover		190.00
		On cover, single franking		210.00
23	A9	25c blue	14.00	7.50
		Never hinged	27.00	
		On cover		80.00
24	A9	30c yel brn	16.00	15.00
		Never hinged	30.00	
		On cover		250.00
		On cover, single franking		350.00
25	A9	35c blk, *yel* ('06)	24.00	24.00
		Never hinged	45.00	
		On cover		225.00
		On cover, single franking		310.00
26	A9	40c red, *straw*	25.00	20.00
		Never hinged	40.00	
		On cover		250.00
		On cover, single franking		340.00
27	A9	45c blk, *gray grn* ('07)	37.50	32.50
		Never hinged	80.00	
		On cover		310.00
		On cover, single franking		400.00
28	A9	50c brn, *az*	16.00	14.00
		Never hinged	35.00	
		On cover		190.00
		On cover, single franking		250.00
29	A9	75c dp vio, *org*	25.00	25.00
		Never hinged	40.00	
		On cover		340.00
		On cover, single franking		550.00
30	A9	1fr brnz grn, *straw*	40.00	40.00
		Never hinged	80.00	
		On cover		400.00
		On cover, single franking		690.00
31	A9	2fr vio, *rose*	80.00	80.00
		Never hinged	135.00	
		On cover		625.00
		On cover, single franking		900.00
32	A9	5fr lil, *lav*	127.50	127.50
		Never hinged	210.00	
		On cover		800.00
		On cover, single franking		1,125.
		Nos. 16-32 (17)	450.30	421.70

Perf. 13½x14 stamps are counterfeits.
For surcharges see Nos. 72-84.
Covers: Values are for commercial covers with correct frankings. Philatelic covers sell for less.

Fang Warrior — A10   Fang Woman — A12

Libreville A11

Inscribed: "Congo Français"

1910   Perf. 13½x14

33	A10	1c choc & org	2.00	2.00
		Never hinged	5.00	
		On cover		110.00
34	A10	2c black & choc	2.75	2.75
		Never hinged	3.75	
		On cover		110.00
35	A10	4c vio & dp bl	2.50	2.50
		Never hinged	3.50	
		On cover		110.00
36	A10	5c ol gray & grn	4.00	4.00
		Never hinged	5.50	
		On cover		50.00
37	A10	10c red & car	5.75	5.75
		Never hinged	7.25	
		On cover		37.50
38	A10	20c choc & dk vio	8.00	8.00
		Never hinged	14.00	
		On cover		80.00
39	A11	25c dp bl & choc	8.00	8.00
		Never hinged	14.00	
		On cover		80.00
		On cover, single franking		190.00
40	A11	30c gray blk & red	40.00	40.00
		Never hinged	80.00	
		On cover		175.00
		On cover, single franking		250.00
41	A11	35c dk vio & grn	24.00	24.00
		Never hinged	45.00	
		On cover		140.00
		On cover, single franking		200.00
42	A11	40c choc & ultra	32.50	32.50
		Never hinged	57.50	
		On cover		190.00
		On cover, single franking		275.00
43	A11	45c carmine & vio	52.50	52.50
		Never hinged	90.00	
		On cover		200.00
		On cover, single franking		340.00
44	A11	50c bl grn & gray	75.00	75.00
		Never hinged	135.00	
		On cover		275.00
		On cover, single franking		475.00
45	A11	75c org & choc	130.00	130.00
		Never hinged	260.00	
		On cover		400.00
		On cover, single franking		600.00
46	A12	1fr dk brn & bis	130.00	130.00
		Never hinged	260.00	
		On cover		400.00
		On cover, single franking		625.00
47	A12	2fr carmine & brn	325.00	325.00
		On cover		650.00
		On cover, single franking		925.00
48	A12	5fr blue & choc	325.00	325.00
		On cover		690.00
		On cover, single franking		950.00
		Nos. 33-48 (16)	1,167.	1,167.

Inscribed: "Afrique Equatoriale"

1910-22   Dull Cream Paper

49	A10	1c choc & org	.30	.40
		Never hinged	.45	
		On cover		87.50
a.		White paper	1.00	1.20
		Never hinged	1.75	
		On cover		87.50
b.		Center double	130.00	
		Never hinged	225.00	
c.		1c gray brown & orange	.30	.30
		Never hinged	.45	
		On cover		87.50
50	A10	2c black & choc	.30	.40
		Never hinged	.45	
		On cover		87.50
a.		White paper	1.00	1.20
		Never hinged	1.75	
		On cover		87.50
b.		2c gray black & deep olive	.65	.80
		Never hinged	1.00	
		On cover		87.50
51	A10	4c vio & dp bl	.50	.55
		Never hinged	.85	
		On cover		87.50
a.		White paper	1.00	1.20
		Never hinged	1.75	
		On cover		87.50
b.		4c violet & blue black	.90	1.00
		Never hinged	1.75	
		On cover		87.50
52	A10	5c ol gray & grn	.95	.55
		Never hinged	1.60	
		On cover		32.50
53	A10	5c gray blk & ocher ('22)	1.25	1.25
		Never hinged	2.00	
		On cover		30.00
54	A10	10c red & car	1.40	1.00
		Never hinged	2.40	
		On cover		21.00
a.		White paper	3.25	2.75
		Never hinged	5.25	
		On cover		25.00
b.		10c vermilion & carmine	3.50	3.25
		Never hinged	6.00	
		On cover		25.00
55	A10	10c yel grn & bl grn ('22)	1.25	1.25
		Never hinged	2.00	
		On cover		50.00
56	A10	15c brn vio & rose ('18)	1.25	.80
		Never hinged	1.90	
		On cover		19.00
57	A10	20c ol brn & dk vio	6.50	5.50
		Never hinged	11.00	
		On cover		42.50
a.		20c brown & dk vio	17.00	13.50
		Never hinged	30.00	
		On cover		75.00
58	A11	25c dp bl & choc	1.40	1.00
		Never hinged	2.50	
		On cover		40.00
		On cover, single franking		105.00
59	A11	25c Prus bl & blk ('22)	1.60	1.60
		Never hinged	2.25	
		On cover		15.00
60	A11	30c gray blk & red	1.60	1.60
		Never hinged	2.60	
		On cover		50.00
		On cover, single franking		125.00
61	A11	30c rose & red ('22)	2.00	2.40
		Never hinged	3.00	
		On cover		80.00
62	A11	35c dk vio & grn	1.25	1.25
		Never hinged	1.75	
		On cover		45.00
		On cover, single franking		67.50
a.		White paper	1.25	
		Never hinged	2.00	
		On cover		45.00
63	A11	40c choc & ultra	1.60	1.60
		Never hinged	2.60	
		On cover		55.00
		On cover, single franking		80.00
64	A11	45c carmine & vio	1.60	1.60
		Never hinged	2.40	
		On cover, single franking		67.50
		On cover		80.00
a.		White paper	4.00	3.50
		Never hinged	7.50	
		On cover		80.00

65	A11 45c blk & red ('22)	2.75	3.25
	Never hinged	4.00	
	On cover		55.00
	On cover, single franking		92.50
66	A11 50c bl grn & gray	2.00	2.00
	Never hinged	3.00	
	On cover		67.50
	On cover, single franking		150.00
a.	White paper	3.50	3.50
	Never hinged	6.00	
	On cover		80.00
67	A11 50c dk bl & bl ('22)	1.60	1.60
	Never hinged	2.75	
	On cover		32.50
	On cover, single franking		62.50
68	A11 75c org & choc	6.75	6.75
	Never hinged	11.00	
	On cover		80.00
	On cover, single franking		140.00
69	A12 1fr dk brn & bis	3.25	3.25
	Never hinged	5.25	
	On cover		87.50
	On cover, single franking		165.00
70	A12 2fr car & brn	6.75	7.25
	Never hinged	11.00	
	On cover		92.50
	On cover, single franking		200.00
71	A12 5fr blue & choc	10.00	10.00
	Never hinged	15.00	
	On cover		110.00
	On cover, single franking		210.00
	Nos. 49-71 (23)	57.85	56.85

For overprints & surcharges see Nos. 85-119, B1-B3.

Stamps of 1904-07 Surcharged in Black or Carmine

Spacing between figures of surcharge 1.5mm (5c), 2mm (10c)

1912

72	A9 5c on 2c brn, buff	1.60	2.00
	Never hinged	2.50	
	On cover		92.50
73	A9 5c on 4c cl, lav (C)	1.60	2.00
	Never hinged	2.50	
	On cover		92.50
74	A9 5c on 15c gray (C)	1.25	1.25
	Never hinged	1.60	
	On cover		55.00
75	A9 5c on 20c red, grn	1.25	1.60
	Never hinged	2.00	
	On cover		75.00
76	A9 5c on 25c bl (C)	1.25	1.60
	Never hinged	2.00	
	On cover		67.50
77	A9 5c on 30c pale brn (C)	1.60	2.00
	Never hinged	2.50	
	On cover		100.00
78	A9 10c on 40c red, straw	1.25	1.60
	Never hinged	1.75	
	On cover		62.50
a.	Double surcharge	2,400.	
79	A9 10c on 45c blk, gray grn (C)	1.25	1.60
	Never hinged	1.75	
	On cover		62.50
80	A9 10c on 50c brn, az (C)	1.60	2.00
	Never hinged	2.40	
	On cover		92.50
81	A9 10c on 75c dp vio, org	1.60	2.00
	Never hinged	2.40	
	On cover		100.00
82	A9 10c on 1fr brnz grn, straw	1.60	2.00
	Never hinged	2.40	
	On cover		92.50
83	A9 10c on 2fr vio, rose	1.60	2.00
	Never hinged	2.40	
	On cover		92.50
a.	Inverted surcharge	340.00	340.00
	Never hinged	500.00	
84	A9 10c on 5fr lil, lav	5.50	5.50
	Never hinged	6.50	
	On cover		120.00
	Nos. 72-84 (13)	22.95	27.15

Spacing between figures of surcharge 2.25mm (5c), 2.75mm (10c)

72a	A9 5c on 2c brn, buff	9.50	9.50
	Never hinged	16.00	
73a	A9 5c on 4c cl, lav (C)	9.50	9.50
	Never hinged	16.00	
74a	A9 5c on 15c gray (C)	8.00	8.00
	Never hinged	13.50	
75a	A9 5c on 20c red, grn	8.75	8.75
	Never hinged	14.50	
76a	A9 5c on 25c bl (C)	8.75	8.75
	Never hinged	14.50	
77a	A9 5c on 30c pale brn (C)	12.00	12.00
	Never hinged	20.00	
78a	A9 10c on 40c red, straw	32.50	32.50
	Never hinged	52.50	
79a	A9 10c on 45c blk, gray grn (C)	35.00	35.00
	Never hinged	60.00	
80a	A9 10c on 50c brn, az (C)	50.00	50.00
	Never hinged	60.00	
81a	A9 10c on 75c dp vio, org	70.00	70.00
	Never hinged	120.00	
82a	A9 10c on 1fr brnz grn, straw	70.00	70.00
	Never hinged	120.00	

83b	A9 10c on 2fr vio, rose	70.00	70.00
	Never hinged	120.00	
c.	Inverted surcharge	4,000.	4,000.
84a	A9 10c on 5fr lil, lav	160.00	160.00
	Nos. 72a-84a (13)	544.00	544.00

Se-tenant pairs
Se-tenant Pairs, Both Ovpt. Settings

72b	A9 5c on 2c, #72 + #72a	12.00	12.00
	Never hinged	20.00	
73b	A9 5c on 4c, #73 + #73a	12.00	12.00
	Never hinged	20.00	
74b	A9 5c on 15c, #74 + #74a	10.00	10.00
	Never hinged	17.50	
75b	A9 5c on 20c, #75 + #75a	11.00	11.00
	Never hinged	19.00	
76b	A9 5c on 25c, #76 + #76a	11.00	11.00
	Never hinged	19.00	
77b	A9 5c on 30c, #77 + #77a	16.00	16.00
	Never hinged	27.50	
78b	A9 10c on 40c, #78 + #78a	32.50	32.50
	Never hinged	52.50	
79b	A9 10c on 45c, #79 + #79a	35.00	35.00
	Never hinged	60.00	
80b	A9 10c on 50c, #80 + #80a	50.00	50.00
	Never hinged	70.00	
81b	A9 10c on 75c, #81 + #81a	75.00	75.00
	Never hinged	135.00	
82b	A9 10c on 1fr, #82 + #82a	75.00	75.00
	Never hinged	135.00	
83d	A9 10c on 2fr, #83 + #83b	75.00	75.00
	Never hinged	135.00	
84b	A9 10c on 5fr, #84 + #84a	180.00	180.00
	Nos. 72b-84b (13)	594.50	594.50

Stamps of 1910-22 Overprinted in Black, Blue or Carmine

On A10, A12

On A11

1924-31

85	A10 1c brown & org	.30	.40
	Never hinged	.45	
	On cover		67.50
a.	White paper (#49a)	.80	.80
	Never hinged	1.20	
	On cover		67.50
86	A10 2c blk & choc (Bl)	.50	.60
	Never hinged	.70	
	On cover		67.50
a.	White paper (#50a)	1.05	1.05
	Never hinged	1.60	
	On cover		67.50
87	A10 4c violet & ind	.30	.40
	Never hinged	.45	
	On cover		67.50
a.	White paper (#51a)	.80	.80
	Never hinged	1.20	
	On cover		67.50
88	A10 5c gray blk & ocher	.45	.55
	Never hinged	.70	
	On cover		30.00
89	A10 10c yel grn & bl grn	1.00	1.00
	Never hinged	1.40	
	On cover		22.50
a.	Double overprint (Bk & Bl)	175.00	
	Never hinged	260.00	
90	A10 10c dk bl & brn ('26) (C)	.40	.40
	Never hinged	.65	
	On cover		30.00
a.	Overprint omitted	350.00	350.00
	Never hinged	550.00	
b.	Double overprint		475.00
91	A10 15c brn vio & rose (Bl)	1.00	1.00
	Never hinged	1.40	
	On cover		20.00
92	A10 15c rose & brn vio ('31) (Bl)	1.25	1.25
	Never hinged	1.60	
	On cover		12.50
a.	Overprint omitted	250.00	
	Never hinged	325.00	
93	A10 20c ol brn & dk vio (C)	1.00	1.00
	Never hinged	1.40	
	On cover		30.00
a.	Inverted overprint	180.00	180.00
	Never hinged	260.00	
b.	Double overprint		400.00
c.	Double overprint, both inverted	525.00	
		800.00	
94	A11 25c Prus bl & blk (C)	.95	.95
	Never hinged	1.40	
	On cover		13.50

95	A11 30c rose & red (Bl)	.90	1.00
	Never hinged	1.35	
	On cover		40.00
	On cover, single franking		92.50
96	A11 30c blk & org ('26)	1.00	1.00
	Never hinged	1.40	
	On cover		16.00
a.	Overprint omitted	10,000.	
97	A11 30c dk grn & bl grn ('28)	1.25	1.25
	Never hinged	1.75	
	On cover		42.50
a.	Overprint omitted	1,800.	
98	A11 35c dk vio & grn (Bl)	.80	.95
	Never hinged	1.10	
	On cover		50.00
	On cover, single franking		87.50
a.	White paper (#62a)	1.60	1.60
	Never hinged	2.75	
99	A11 40c choc & ultra (C)	.75	.90
	Never hinged	1.05	
	On cover		55.00
	On cover, single franking		92.50
a.	In pair with unovptd. stamp (#63)	3,600.	
100	A11 45c blk & red (Bl)	1.50	1.50
	Never hinged	1.40	
	On cover		20.00
	On cover, single franking		30.00
101	A11 50c dk bl & bl (C)	1.00	1.00
	Never hinged	1.40	
	On cover		16.00
	On cover, single franking		30.00
a.	White paper (#67a)	2.00	2.00
	Never hinged	3.25	
102	A11 50c car & grn ('26)	1.10	1.10
	Never hinged	1.60	
	On cover		16.00
103	A11 65c dp bl & red org ('27)	4.50	4.00
	Never hinged	6.00	
	On cover		32.50
	On cover, single franking		75.00
104	A11 75c org & brn (Bl)	2.25	2.25
	Never hinged	3.25	
	On cover		40.00
	On cover, single franking		87.50
105	A11 90c brn red & rose ('30)	2.75	2.75
	Never hinged	4.50	
	On cover		62.50
	On cover, single franking		110.00
106	A12 1fr dk brn & bis	1.90	1.90
	Never hinged	2.60	
	On cover		40.00
	On cover, single franking		87.50
107	A12 1.10fr dl grn & rose red ('28)	6.00	7.50
	Never hinged	8.50	
	On cover		165.00
	On cover, single franking		375.00
108	A12 1.50fr pale bl & dk bl ('30)	1.25	1.25
	Never hinged	2.00	
	On cover		55.00
	On cover, single franking		100.00
a.	Overprint omitted	290.00	
	Never hinged	475.00	
109	A12 2fr rose & brn	2.25	2.50
	Never hinged	3.25	
	On cover		67.50
	On cover, single franking		140.00
110	A12 3fr red vio ('30)	10.50	9.25
	Never hinged	2.00	
	On cover		92.50
	On cover, single franking		190.00
a.	Overprint omitted	275.00	
	Never hinged	450.00	
111	A12 5fr dp bl & choc	5.50	6.50
	Never hinged	9.25	
	On cover		75.00
	On cover, single franking		150.00
	Nos. 85-111 (27)	52.35	54.15

Types of 1924-31 Issues Surcharged with New Values in Black or Carmine

1925-28

112	A12 65c on 1fr ol grn & brn	1.25	1.25
	Never hinged	2.00	
	On cover		80.00
	On cover, single franking		190.00
113	A12 85c on 1fr ol grn & brn	1.25	1.25
	Never hinged	1.90	
	On cover		67.50
	On cover, single franking		140.00
114	A11 90c on 75c brn red & cer ('27)	1.75	1.75
	Never hinged	2.60	
	On cover		67.50
	On cover, single franking		125.00
a.	"90" omitted	240.00	
	Never hinged	375.00	
115	A12 1.25fr on 1fr dk bl & ultra (C)	1.25	1.25
	Never hinged	1.90	
	On cover		75.00
	On cover, single franking		150.00
116	A12 1.50fr on 1fr lt bl & dk bl ('27)	2.00	2.00
	Never hinged	3.25	
	On cover		62.50
	On cover, single franking		110.00

117	A12 3fr on 5fr mag & ol brn	9.25	9.00
	Never hinged	12.00	
	On cover		110.00
	On cover, single franking		225.00
a.	Period after "F" omitted	32.50	32.50
	Never hinged	55.00	
118	A12 10fr on 5fr org brn & grn ('27)	14.50	14.50
	Never hinged	17.50	
	On cover		140.00
	On cover, single franking		275.00
a.	Period after "F" omitted	40.00	40.00
	Never hinged	67.50	
119	A12 20fr on 5fr red vio & org red ('27)	16.00	17.50
	Never hinged	21.00	
	On cover		140.00
	On cover, single franking		310.00
a.	Period after "F" omitted	45.00	45.00
	Never hinged	67.50	
	Nos. 112-119 (8)	47.25	48.50

Bars cover the old denominations on Nos. 114-119.

Common Design Types pictured following the introduction.

Colonial Exposition Issue
Common Design Types

1931   *Perf. 12½*
Name of Country in Black

120	CD70 40c dp green	4.00	4.00
	Never hinged	5.50	
	On cover		110.00
121	CD71 50c violet	4.00	4.00
	Never hinged	5.50	
	On cover		92.50
122	CD72 90c red orange	4.00	4.00
	Never hinged	5.50	
	On cover		165.00
	On cover, single franking		240.00
123	CD73 1.50fr dull blue	5.50	5.50
	Never hinged	7.25	
	On cover		150.00
	On cover, single franking		200.00
	Nos. 120-123 (4)	17.50	17.50

Timber Raft on Ogowe River A16

Count Savorgnan de Brazza — A17

Village of Setta Kemma A18

1932-33   Photo.   *Perf. 13x13½*

124	A16 1c brown violet	.25	.25
	Never hinged	.40	
			27.50
125	A16 2c blk, rose	.25	.25
	Never hinged	.40	
			27.50
126	A16 4c green	.30	.30
	Never hinged	.45	
			27.50
127	A16 5c grnsh blue	.55	.55
	Never hinged	.80	
			20.00
128	A16 10c red, yel	.55	.55
	Never hinged	.80	
			16.00
129	A16 15c red, grn	.70	.65
	Never hinged	1.00	
			20.00
130	A16 20c deep red	.70	.65
	Never hinged	1.00	
			16.00
131	A16 25c brown red	.70	.50
	Never hinged	1.00	
			30.00
132	A17 30c yellow grn	2.00	1.60
	Never hinged	3.25	
			42.50
133	A17 40c brown vio	2.25	1.10
	Never hinged	3.00	
			13.50
134	A17 45c blk, dl grn	3.25	2.40
	Never hinged	4.75	
			50.00
135	A17 50c red brown	1.60	1.25
	Never hinged	2.00	
			9.50

136	A17	65c Prus blue	6.50	6.50
		Never hinged	11.00	
		On cover		80.00
137	A17	75c blk, *red org*	4.00	3.25
		Never hinged	5.75	
		On cover		16.00
138	A17	90c rose red	4.00	3.25
		Never hinged	5.75	
		On cover		42.50
		On cover, single franking		
139	A17	1fr yel grn, *bl*	27.50	24.00
		Never hinged	50.00	
		On cover		80.00
		On cover, single franking		110.00
140	A18	1.25fr dp vio ('33)	2.25	2.00
		Never hinged	3.00	
		On cover		32.50
		On cover, single franking		92.50
141	A18	1.50fr dull blue	11.00	7.25
		Never hinged	18.50	
		On cover		67.50
		On cover, single franking		190.00
142	A18	1.75fr dp green ('33)	2.50	2.00
		Never hinged	3.50	
		On cover		32.50
		On cover, single franking		50.00
143	A18	2fr brn red	52.50	45.00
		Never hinged	110.00	
		On cover		200.00
		On cover, single franking		275.00
144	A18	3fr yel grn, *bl*	6.00	4.50
		Never hinged	9.50	
		On cover		67.50
		On cover, single franking		125.00
145	A18	5fr red brown	15.00	13.50
		Never hinged	25.00	
		On cover		80.00
		On cover, single franking		140.00
146	A18	10fr blk, *red org*	32.50	27.50
		Never hinged	60.00	
		On cover		165.00
		On cover, single franking		275.00
147	A18	20fr dk violet	47.50	40.00
		Never hinged	87.50	
		On cover		190.00
		On cover, single franking		325.00
		Nos. 124-147 (24)	224.35	188.80

SEMI-POSTAL STAMPS

No. 37 Surcharged in Red

1916   Unwmk.   Perf. 13½x14

B1	A10	10c + 5c red & car	30.00	30.00
		Never hinged	60.00	
		On cover		140.00
a.		Double surcharge	200.00	225.00
		Never hinged	300.00	
b.		"5" omitted	80.00	80.00
		Never hinged	140.00	
c.		Cross omitted	260.00	
d.		In pair with unsurcharged stamp	550.00	

Same Surcharge on No. 54 in Red

B2	A10	10c + 5c red & car	37.50	37.50
		Never hinged	85.00	
		On cover		165.00
a.		Double surcharge	200.00	225.00
		Never hinged	340.00	
b.		Inverted surcharge	175.00	
		Never hinged	340.00	
c.		Double surcharge, one inverted	175.00	200.00
		Never hinged	340.00	
d.		In pair with unsurcharged stamp	550.00	

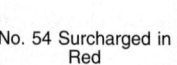

No. 54 Surcharged in Red

1917

B3	A10	10c + 5c red & car	2.40	2.40
		Never hinged	3.25	
		On cover		67.50

POSTAGE DUE STAMPS

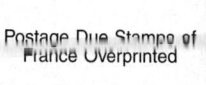

Postage Due Stamps of France Overprinted A. E. F.

1928   Unwmk.   Perf. 14x13½

J1	D2	5c light blue	.40	.55
		Never hinged	.60	
		On cover		92.50
J2	D2	10c gray brown	.40	.65
		Never hinged	.60	
		On cover		92.50
J3	D2	20c olive green	1.25	1.60
		Never hinged	2.25	
		On cover		92.50
J4	D2	25c bright rose	1.25	1.60
		Never hinged	2.10	
		On cover		100.00
J5	D2	30c light red	1.60	2.00
		Never hinged	2.50	
		On cover		100.00
J6	D2	45c blue green	2.00	2.40
		Never hinged	3.00	
		On cover		105.00
J7	D2	50c brown violet	3.00	3.25
		Never hinged	4.25	
		On cover		110.00
a.		Period omitted after "F"	17.50	17.50
		Never hinged	32.50	
J8	D2	60c yellow brown	3.00	3.25
		Never hinged	4.25	
		On cover		120.00
J9	D2	1fr red brown	3.00	3.25
		Never hinged	4.25	
		On cover		125.00
J10	D2	2fr orange red	4.75	4.75
		Never hinged	6.50	
		On cover		140.00
J11	D2	3fr bright violet	5.50	5.50
		Never hinged	7.50	
		On cover		150.00
		Nos. J1-J11 (11)	26.15	28.80

Chief Makoko, de Brazza's Aide — D3

Count Savorgnan de Brazza — D4

1930   Typo.   Perf. 13½x14

J12	D3	5c dk bl & olive	1.25	1.25
		Never hinged	1.80	
		On cover		42.50
J13	D3	10c dk red & brn	1.40	1.40
		Never hinged	2.00	
		On cover		42.50
J14	D3	20c green & brn	1.90	1.90
		Never hinged	3.00	
		On cover		42.50
J15	D3	25c lt bl & brn	1.90	1.90
		Never hinged	3.00	
		On cover		50.00
J16	D3	30c bis brn & Prus bl	2.75	2.75
		Never hinged	4.50	
		On cover		50.00
J17	D3	45c Prus bl & ol	4.50	4.50
		Never hinged	7.00	
		On cover		55.00
J18	D3	50c red vio & brn	4.75	4.75
		Never hinged	6.50	
		On cover		55.00
J19	D3	60c gray lil & bl blk	9.00	9.00
		Never hinged	12.00	
		On cover		62.50
J20	D4	1fr bis brn & bl blk	12.50	12.50
		Never hinged	17.50	
		On cover		80.00
J21	D4	2fr violet & brn	16.00	16.00
		Never hinged	22.50	
		On cover		92.50
J22	D4	3fr dp red & brn	18.00	18.00
		Never hinged	30.00	
		On cover		105.00
		Nos. J12-J22 (11)	73.95	73.95

Fang Woman — D5

1932   Photo.   Perf. 13x13½

J23	D5	5c dk bl, *bl*	1.10	1.10
		Never hinged	1.75	
		On cover		42.50
J24	D5	10c red brown	1.25	1.25
		Never hinged	2.25	
		On cover		42.50
J25	D5	20c orange	2.00	2.00
		Never hinged	3.00	
		On cover		42.50
J26	D5	25c yel grn, *bl*	2.00	2.00
		Never hinged	3.00	
		On cover		42.50
J27	D5	30c car rose	2.10	2.10
		Never hinged	3.10	
		On cover		50.00
J28	D5	45c red org, *yel*	7.75	7.75
		Never hinged	10.00	
		On cover		75.00
J29	D5	50c dk violet	2.50	2.50
		Never hinged	4.00	
		On cover		55.00
J30	D5	60c dull blue	3.75	3.75
		Never hinged	5.50	
		On cover		55.00
J31	D5	1fr blk, *red org*	9.50	9.50
		Never hinged	13.50	
		On cover		92.50
J32	D5	2fr dark green	11.00	11.00
		Never hinged	16.00	
		On cover		92.50
J33	D5	3fr rose lake	11.50	11.50
		Never hinged	13.50	
		On cover		100.00
		Nos. J23-J33 (11)	54.45	54.45

GAMBIA

ˈgam-bē-ə

LOCATION — Extending inland from the mouth of the Gambia River on the west coast of Africa
GOVT. — Republic in British Commonwealth
AREA — 4,068 sq. mi.
POP. — 695,886 (1983)
CAPITAL — Banjul

The British Crown Colony and Protectorate of Gambia became independent in 1965 and a republic in 1970.

12 Pence = 1 Shilling

> **Catalogue values for unused stamps in this country are for Never Hinged items, beginning with Scott 144.**

Queen Victoria
A1   A2

Typographed and Embossed

			Unwmk.	Imperf.
1869, Jan.				
1	A1	4p pale brown	550.00	240.00
		No gum	400.00	
a.		4p brown	650.00	240.00
		No gum	475.00	
2	A1	6p blue	625.00	240.00
		No gum	450.00	
a.		6p deep blue	650.00	240.00
		No gum	475.00	
b.		6p pale blue	3,250.	1,250.
		No gum	2,500.	

				Wmk. 1
1874, Aug.				
3	A1	4p brown	450.00	240.00
		No gum	300.00	
a.		4p pale brown	450.00	250.00
		No gum	300.00	
4	A1	6p blue	400.00	240.00
		No gum	290.00	
a.		6p deep blue	400.00	250.00
		No gum	290.00	
b.		Panel sloping down from left to right	950.00	525.00
		No gum	650.00	

Nos. 1-4 are often seen with flat embossing. Unused values for are for fine-very fine examples with sharp, detailed embossing. Values for unused stamps without gum and used stamps are for examples with average embossing.
The name panel sloping down variety, No. 4b, is from a top right corner position. A top left corner position exists with a less noticeable sloping of the panel down from right to left; it is worth less. **Covers:** Nos. 1-4 on cover are rare. Values start at about $7,500.

1880, June   Perf. 14

5	A1	½p orange	15.50	22.50
6	A1	1p maroon	8.50	7.00
7	A1	2p rose	50.00	12.50
8	A1	3p ultra	72.50	37.50
9	A1	4p pale brown	350.00	22.50
10	A1	6p blue	140.00	52.50
a.		Panel sloping down from left to right	375.00	175.00
11	A1	1sh green	300.00	165.00
a.		1sh deep green	375.00	180.00
		Nos. 5-11 (7)	936.50	319.50

The watermark on Nos. 5-11 exists both upright and sideways.
See footnote following No. 4.

1886-93   Wmk. 2 Sideways

12	A1	½p gray grn	5.25	3.50
a.		½p deep green ('87)	4.50	2.25
13	A1	1p rose car ('87)	10.50	12.50
b.		1p aniline car	8.50	14.00
c.		1p pale carmine	7.00	14.00
14		2p deep orange	4.00	10.50
b.		2p orange	15.00	5.75
15	A1	2½p dp br blue	11.00	1.40
a.		2½ ultramarine ('87)	9.50	2.25
16	A1	3p gray	10.00	17.00
a.		3p slate gray ('86)	10.00	16.00
17	A1	4p dp brown	14.00	2.25
a.		4p brown ('87)	13.00	2.25
18	A1	6p slate green ('93)	19.00	67.50
a.		6p pale olive green ('86)	100.00	60.00
b.		6p bronze green ('89)	45.00	72.50
c.		As "a," panel sloping down from left to right	325.00	125.00
d.		As "b," panel sloping down from left to right	95.00	180.00
e.		6p olive green ('87)	80.00	70.00
f.		As "e," panel sloping down from left to right	250.00	175.00
g.		6p dp bronze grn ('89)	42.50	70.00
h.		As "g," panel sloping down from left to right	90.00	170.00
19	A1	1sh violet	9.00	24.00
a.		1sh purple	8.00	22.50
b.		1sh aniline violet	1,250.	
		Nos. 12-19 (8)	82.75	138.65

See footnote following No. 4.

1898, Jan.   Typo.   Wmk. 2

20	A2	½p gray green	3.25	2.00
21	A2	1p carmine rose	2.75	.85
22	A2	2p brn org & pur	7.00	4.00
23	A2	2½p ultramarine	3.50	2.75
24	A2	3p red vio & ultra	42.50	14.00
25	A2	4p brown & ultra	16.00	37.50
26	A2	6p ol grn & car rose	15.00	45.00
27	A2	1sh vio & green	40.00	85.00
		Nos. 20-27 (8)	130.00	191.10
		Set, ovptd. "SPECIMEN"	180.00	

King Edward VII — A3

1902-05   Perf. 14

28	A3	½p green	5.00	2.75
29	A3	1p car rose	11.50	1.10
30	A3	2p org & pur	3.75	2.25
31	A3	2½p ultramarine	42.50	20.00
32	A3	3p red vio & ultra	16.00	4.00
33	A3	4p brn & ultra	6.25	37.50
34	A3	6p ol grn & rose	12.50	14.00
35	A3	1sh bluish vio & green	47.50	92.50
36	A3	1sh6p grn & red, *yel*	10.00	25.00
37	A3	2sh black & org	55.00	72.50
38	A3	2sh6p pur & brn, *yel*	17.50	75.00
39	A3	3sh red & grn, *yel*	22.50	72.50
		Nos. 28-39 (12)	250.00	419.10
		Set, ovptd. "SPECIMEN"	180.00	

Numerals of 5p, 7½p, 10p, 1sh6p, 2sh, 2sh6p and 3sh of type A3 are in color on plain tablet.
Issue dates: 1p, Mar. 13. ½p, 3p, Apr. 19. 2p, 2½p, 4p, 6p, 1sh, 2sh, June 14. 1sh6p, 2sh6p, 3sh, Apr. 6, 1905.
For surcharges, see Nos. 65-66.

1904-09   Wmk. 3

41	A3	½p green	5.25	.35
42	A3	1p car rose	5.25	.25
a.		1p carmine ('09)	16.00	.25
43	A3	2p org & pur ('06)	14.00	2.50
44	A3	2p gray ('09)	2.25	12.50
45	A3	2½p br blue ('05)	10.50	5.50
a.		2½ ultra & br blue	21.00	29.00
46	A3	3p red vio & ultra	14.50	2.25
47	A3	3p vio ('09)	6.25	1.10
a.		3p violet, *lemon yellow*	6.25	2.00
48	A3	4p brn & ultra ('06)	21.00	45.00
49	A3	4p blk & red, *yel* ('09)	2.75	.75
50	A3	5p gray & black	16.00	30.00
51	A3	5p org & vio ('09)	2.75	1.40

52	A3	6p ol grn & rose ('06)	22.00	75.00
53	A3	6p dull vio ('09)	2.75	2.50
54	A3	7½p blue grn & red	17.00	65.00
55	A3	7½p brn & ultra ('09)	4.00	2.75
56	A3	10p ol bis & red	27.50	52.50
57	A3	10p ol grn & car rose ('09)	5.25	8.00
58	A3	1sh violet & grn	37.50	62.50
59	A3	1sh blk, grn ('09)	5.25	20.00
60	A3	1sh 6p vio & grn ('09)	27.50	80.00
61	A3	2sh black & org	100.00	125.00
62	A3	2sh vio & bl, bl ('09)	16.00	22.50
63	A3	2sh 6p blk & red, bl ('09)	24.00	22.50
64	A3	3sh yel & grn ('09)	40.00	55.00
		Nos. 41-64 (24)	429.25	694.85

Nos. 38-39 Surcharged in Black

a   b

Type a (I) — The word "PENNY" is 5mm from the horizontal bars.
Type a (II) — "PENNY" is 4mm from the bars.

1906, Apr.   Wmk. 2

65	A3	½p on 2sh6p, type I	57.50	70.00
a.		Type II	62.50	75.00
66	A3	1p on 3sh	62.50	35.00
a.		Double surcharge	2,150.	5,750.

King George V — A4

1912-22   Wmk. 3

70	A4	½p dp green	3.00	1.75
a.		½p green	3.25	1.75
b.		½p pale green ('16)	5.50	3.75
71	A4	1p carmine	2.75	1.75
a.		1p scarlet ('16)	7.25	1.00
b.		1p rose red	3.75	.35
72	A4	1½p ol brn & grn	.60	.35
73	A4	2p gray	.60	3.25
74	A4	2½p dp br blue	5.00	3.50
a.		2½p bright blue	5.00	2.75
75	A4	3p violet, yel	1.10	.35
a.		3p violet, lemon ('17)	16.00	20.00
b.		3p violet, org buff ('20)	11.50	9.50
c.		3p violet, pale yellow	1.40	1.10
76	A4	4p blk & red, yel	1.10	11.50
a.		4p blk & red, lemon ('17)	3.00	8.50
b.		4p blk & red, org buff ('20)	9.00	12.50
c.		4p blk & red, pale yellow	1.75	10.00
77	A4	5p orange & vio	1.10	2.25
78	A4	6p dl vio & red violet	2.00	2.75
79	A4	7½p brn & ultra	4.25	12.00
80	A4	10p ol grn & car rose	5.00	20.00
a.		10p dp ol grn & car rose	4.25	17.50
81	A4	1sh blk, green	3.25	1.10
a.		1sh black, emerald	2.50	24.00
82	A4	1sh6p blk & green	18.00	11.50
83	A4	2sh vio & bl, bl	6.75	7.00
84	A4	2sh6p blk & red, bl	7.00	16.00
85	A4	3sh vel & green	13.50	45.00
86	A4	5sh grn & red, yel ('22)	125.00	200.00
		Nos. 70-86 (17)	200.00	340.05
		Set, ovptd. "SPECIMEN"	400.00	

Numerals of 1½p, 5p, 7½p, 10p, 1sh6p, 2sh, 2sh6p, 3sh, 4sh and 5sh of type A3 are in color on colorless tablet. No. 86 is on chalky paper.

1921-22   Wmk. 4

87	A4	½p green	.35	22.50
88	A4	1p carmine	1.60	9.50
89	A4	1½p ol grn & bl grn	2.00	19.00
90	A4	2p gray	1.10	2.75
91	A4	2½p ultramarine	.60	10.50
92	A4	5p org & violet	2.00	22.50
93	A4	6p dl vio & red vio	2.25	20.00
94	A4	7½p brn & ultra	2.25	47.50
95	A4	10p yel grn & car rose	8.00	25.00
96	A4	4sh gray & red ('22)	105.00	210.00
		Nos. 87-96 (10)	125.15	389.25
		Set, ovptd. "SPECIMEN"	225.00	

No. 96 is on chalky paper.

George V and Elephant — A5   George V — A6

1922-27   Engr.   Wmk. 4
Head and Shield in Black

102	A5	½p green	.65	.65
a.		½p deep green ('25)	6.50	1.75
103	A5	1p brown	1.10	.30
104	A5	1½p carmine	1.10	.30
105	A5	2p gray	1.10	4.75
106	A5	2½p orange	2.40	15.00
107	A5	3p ultramarine	1.10	.25
108	A5	4p car, org ('27)	21.00	30.00
109	A5	5p yellow green	4.25	16.00
110	A5	6p claret	1.50	.35
111	A5	7½p vio, yel ('27)	21.00	95.00
112	A5	10p blue	5.75	20.00
113	A5	1sh vio, org ('24)	3.75	2.50
a.		1sh dk violet, yel buff ('29)	55.00	50.00
114	A6	1sh6p blue	21.00	19.00
115	A6	2sh vio, blue	12.50	8.00
116	A6	2sh6p dark green	12.50	11.00
117	A6	3sh aniline vio	26.00	90.00
a.		3sh black purple	275.00	475.00
118	A6	4sh brown	24.00	24.00
119	A6	5sh dk grn, yel ('26)	37.50	67.50
120	A6	10sh yellow green	85.00	145.00
		Nos. 102-120 (19)	283.20	549.60
		Set, ovptd. "SPECIMEN"	450.00	

1922, Sept. 1   Wmk. 3
Head & Shield in Black

121	A5	4p carmine, yel	5.00	6.00
122	A5	7½p violet, yel	7.50	9.50
123	A6	1sh violet, orange	32.50	42.50
124	A6	5sh dk green, yel	62.50	215.00
		Nos. 121-124 (4)	107.50	273.00
		Set, ovptd. "SPECIMEN"	160.00	

The Specimen overprint on No. 124 is handstamped.

Common Design Types pictured following the introduction.

Silver Jubilee Issue
Common Design Type

1935, May 6   Wmk. 4   Perf. 11x12

125	CD301	1½p carmine & bl	.85	2.75
		Never hinged	1.25	
126	CD301	3p ultra & brn	1.50	2.50
		Never hinged	2.25	
127	CD301	6p ol grn & lt bl	3.25	7.50
		Never hinged	4.50	
128	CD301	1sh brn vio & ind	14.00	16.00
		Never hinged	20.00	
		Nos. 125-128 (4)	19.60	28.75
		Set, never hinged	29.00	
		Set, perf "SPECIMEN"	110.00	

Coronation Issue
Common Design Type

1937, May 12   Perf. 11x11½

129	CD302	1p brown	.25	1.30
		Never hinged	.35	
130	CD302	1½p dark carmine	.25	1.30
		Never hinged	.35	
131	CD302	3p deep ultra	.50	2.10
		Never hinged	.75	
		Nos. 129-131 (3)	1.00	4.70
		Set, never hinged	1.45	
		Set, perf "SPECIMEN"	110.00	

King George VI and Elephant Badge of Gambia — A7

1938-46   Perf. 12

132	A7	½p bl grn & blk	.25	.80
		Never hinged	.25	
133	A7	1p brn & red vio	.25	.55
		Never hinged	.25	
134	A7	1½p rose red & brn lake	.25	2.25
		Never hinged	.25	
b.		1½ scarlet & brn lake	4.00	5.75
c.		1½ br car & brn lake	175.00	14.00
		Never hinged	210.00	
134A	A7	1½p gray black & ultra ('44)	.25	1.75
		Never hinged	.30	
135	A7	2p gray black & ultra	3.00	3.75
		Never hinged	15.00	

135A	A7	2p rose red & brn lake ('43)	.65	2.50
		Never hinged	1.30	
136	A7	3p blue & brt bl	.30	.25
		Never hinged	.40	
136A	A7	5p dk vio brn & olive ('41)	.45	.60
		Never hinged	.55	
137	A7	6p plum & ol grn	1.25	.40
		Never hinged	3.25	
138	A7	1sh vio & sl blk	1.60	.25
		Never hinged	5.00	
138A	A7	1sh3p bl & choc ('46)	2.00	2.75
		Never hinged	4.25	
139	A7	2sh bl & dp rose	5.00	3.75
		Never hinged	11.50	
140	A7	2sh6p sl grn & sep	10.00	2.75
		Never hinged	16.00	
141	A7	4sh dk vio & red orange	17.50	2.75
		Never hinged	35.00	
142	A7	5sh org red & dk blue	17.50	4.50
		Never hinged	35.00	
143	A7	10sh blk & yel org	20.00	8.00
		Never hinged	37.50	
		Nos. 132-143 (16)	80.25	37.60
		Set, never hinged	165.00	
		Set, perf "SPECIMEN"	450.00	

Issued: 5p, 3/13; No. 135A, 10/1; No. 134A, 1/22; 1sh3p, 11/28; others, 4/1.

> Catalogue values for unused stamps in this section, from this point to the end of the section, are for Never Hinged items.

Peace Issue
Common Design Type

1946, Aug. 6   Engr.   Perf. 13½

144	CD303	1½p black	.25	.50
145	CD303	3p deep blue	.25	.45
		Set, perf "SPECIMEN"	95.00	

Silver Wedding Issue
Common Design Types

1948, Dec. 24   Photo.   Perf. 14x14½

146	CD304	1½p black	.25	.25

Perf. 11½x11
Engr.; Name Typo.

147	CD305	£1 purple	25.00	26.00

UPU Issue
Common Design Types
Engr.; Name Typo. on 3p, 6p
Perf. 13½, 11x11½

1949, Oct. 10   Wmk. 4

148	CD306	1½p slate	.40	1.60
149	CD307	3p indigo	1.75	2.10
150	CD308	6p red lilac	.80	3.50
151	CD309	1sh violet	.55	.65
		Nos. 148-151 (4)	3.50	7.85

GEORGIA
ˈjor-jə

LOCATION — In the southern part of Russia, bordering on the Black Sea and occupying the entire western part of Trans-Caucasia
GOVT. — A Soviet Socialist Republic
AREA — 25,760 sq. mi. (1920)
POP. — 2,372,403 (1920)
CAPITAL — Tbilisi (Tiflis)

Georgia was formerly a province of the Russian Empire and later a part of the Transcaucasian Federation of Soviet Republics. Stamps of Georgia were replaced in 1923 by those of Transcaucasian Federated Republics.

100 Kopecks = 1 Ruble

Tiflis
A 6k local stamp, imperforate and embossed without color on white paper, was issued in November, 1857, at Tiflis by authority of the viceroy. The square design shows a coat of arms.

National Republic

St. George

A1   A2

1919   Litho.   Unwmk.   Perf. 11½

1	A1	10k blue	.80	.80
2	A1	40k red orange	.80	.80
a.		Tête bêche pair	50.00	50.00
3	A1	50k emerald	.80	.80
4	A1	60k red	.80	.80
5	A1	70k claret	.80	.80
6	A2	1r orange brown	.80	.80
		Nos. 1-6 (6)	4.80	4.80

Imperf

7	A1	10k blue	.80	.80
8	A1	40k red orange	.80	.80
a.		Tête bêche pair	50.00	50.00
9	A1	50k emerald	.80	.80
10	A1	60k red	.80	.80
11	A1	70k claret	.80	.80
12	A2	1r orange brown	.80	.80
		Nos. 7-12 (6)	4.80	4.80

Queen Thamar — A3

1920   Perf. 11½

13	A3	2r red brown	.65	1.00
14	A3	3r gray blue	.65	1.00
15	A3	5r orange	.65	1.00
		Nos. 13-15 (3)	1.95	3.00

Imperf

16	A3	2r red brown	.65	1.00
17	A3	3r gray blue	.65	1.00
18	A3	5r orange	.65	1.00
		Nos. 16-18 (3)	1.95	3.00

Nos. 1-18 with parts of design inverted, sideways or omitted are fraudulent varieties.

Overprints meaning "Day of the National Guard, 12, 12, 1920" (5 lines) and "Recognition of Independence, 27, 1, 1921" (4 lines) were applied, probably in Italy, to remainders taken by government officials who fled when Russian forces occupied Georgia.

"Constantinople" and new values were unofficially surcharged on stamps of 1919-20 by a consul in Turkey.

Soviet Socialist Republic

Soldier with Flag — A5   Peasant Sowing Grain — A6

Industry and Agriculture — A7

1922   Unwmk.   Perf. 11½

26	A5	500r rose	8.00	3.25
27	A6	1000r bister brown	8.00	3.25
28	A7	2000r slate	11.50	6.00
29	A7	3000r brown	11.50	6.00
30	A7	5000r green	11.50	6.00
		Nos. 26-30 (5)	50.50	24.50

Forgeries exist of Nos. 26-30.
Nos. 26 to 30 exist imperforate but were not so issued. Value for set, $100.

Nos. 26-30 Handstamped with New Values in Violet

1923

36	A6	10,000r on 1000r	6.50	6.50
a.		Black surcharge	20.00	25.00
b.		20,000r on 1000r	200.00	
37	A7	15,000r on 2000r, blk surch.	7.75	8.00
a.		Black surcharge	30.00	30.00
38	A5	20,000r on 500r	7.75	8.50
a.		Black surcharge	15.00	7.50
39	A7	40,000r on 5000r	5.50	5.50
a.		Black surcharge	15.00	15.00
40	A7	80,000r on 3000r	7.75	8.50
a.		Black surcharge	15.00	17.50
		Nos. 36-40 (5)	35.25	37.50

There were two types of the handstamped surcharges, with the numerals 5½mm and 6½mm high. The impressions are often too indistinct to measure or even to distinguish the numerals.

Double and inverted surcharges exist, as is usual with handstamps.

Surcharged in Black

43	A6	10,000r on 1000r	7.50	7.50
44	A7	15,000r on 2000r	5.00	5.00
45	A5	20,000r on 500r	2.50	2.50
46	A7	40,000r on 5000r	5.00	5.00
47	A7	80,000r on 3000r	5.00	5.00
		Nos. 43-47 (5)	25.00	25.00

Nos. 43, 45, 46 and 47 exist imperforate but were not so issued. Value $25 each.

Russian Stamps of 1909-18 Handstamp Surcharged

Type I — Surcharge 20x5½mm.
Type II — Surcharge 22x7¼mm.

1923 Perf. 14½x15

48	A14	10,000r on 7k lt bl	150.00	150.00
49	A11	15,000r on 15k red brn & bl (I)	15.00	15.00
a.		Type II	10.00	10.00

Type I Surcharge Handstamped on Armenia No. 141

50	A11	15,000r on 5r on 15k red brn & bl	200.00	500.00
a.		Type II		
		Nos. 48-50 (3)	365.00	665.00

Russian Stamps and Types of 1909-18 Surcharged in Dark Blue or Black

1923 Perf. 11½, 14½x15

51	A14	75,000r on 1k org	3.00	4.25
a.		Imperf.	150.00	150.00
52	A14	200,000r on 5k cl	4.00	5.00
53	A8	300,000r on 20k bl & car (Bk)	4.00	5.00
a.		Dark blue surcharge	70.00	100.00
54	A14	350,000r on 3k red	7.00	8.00
a.		Imperf.	7.00	7.25

Imperf

55	A14	700,000r on 2k grn	7.00	10.00
a.		Perf. 14½x15	27.50	32.50
		Nos. 51-55 (5)	25.00	32.25

SEMI-POSTAL STAMPS

Surcharge in Red or Black

SP1 SP2

SP3 SP4

1922 Unwmk. Perf. 11½

B1	SP1	1000r on 50r vio (R)	.75	3.00
B2	SP2	3000r on 100r brn red	.75	3.00
B3	SP3	5000r on 250r gray grn	.75	3.00
B4	SP4	10,000r on 25r blue (R)	.75	3.00
		Nos. B1-B4 (4)	3.00	12.00

Nos. B1-B4 exist imperf but were not so issued. Value slightly more than perforated examples.

GERMAN EAST AFRICA

ˈjər-mən ˈēst ˈa-fri-kə

LOCATION — In East Africa, bordering on the Indian Ocean
GOVT. — German Colony
AREA — 384,180 sq. mi.
POP. — 7,680,132 (1913)
CAPITAL — Dar-es Salaam

Following World War I, the greater part of this German Colonial possession was mandated to Great Britain. The British ceded to the Belgians the provinces of Ruanda and Urundi. The Kionga triangle was awarded to the Portuguese and became part of the Mozambique Colony. The remaining area became the British Mandated Territory of Tanganyika.

64 Pesa = 1 Rupee
100 Heller = 1 Rupee (1905)
100 Centimes = 1 Franc (1916)

Stamps of Germany surcharged in Black

Nos. 1-5 Nos. 6-10

1893 Unwmk. Perf. 13½x14½
Surcharge 15¼mm long

1	A9	2pes on 3pf brown	35.00	47.50
		Never hinged	160.00	
		On cover		340.00
a.		Surcharge 16¾mm long	—	
2	A9	3pes on 5pf green	45.00	47.50
		Never hinged	225.00	
		On cover		340.00
a.		Surcharge 14¼mm long	850.00	
		Never hinged	2,000.	
b.		Surcharge 16¼mm long	1,100.	
		Never hinged	2,200.	
3	A10	5pes on 10pf car	35.00	27.50
		Never hinged	190.00	
		On cover		175.00
a.		Surcharge 14¼mm long	2,100.	
		Never hinged	6,000.	
b.		Surcharge 16¼mm long	2,100.	
		Never hinged	6,000.	

Surcharge 16¼mm long

4	A10	10pes on 20pf ultra	27.50	14.00
		Never hinged	120.00	
		On cover		80.00

Surcharge 16¾mm long

5	A10	25pes on 50pf red brn	35.00	27.50
		Never hinged	125.00	
		On cover		140.00
a.		Surcharge 17½mm long	100.00	42.50
		On cover		300.00
		On cover		150.00
		Nos. 1-5 (5)	177.50	164.00

Covers: Value for No. 5 is for overfranked complete covers, usually philatelic.

1896

6	A9	2pes on 3pf dk brn	2.10	37.50
		Never hinged	6.75	
		On cover		175.00
a.		2pes on 3pf light brown	28.00	45.00
		Never hinged	100.00	
		On cover		210.00
b.		2pes on 3pf grayish brown	11.50	11.50
		Never hinged	35.00	
		On cover		67.50
c.		2pes on 3pf reddish brown	110.00	200.00
		Never hinged	450.00	
		On cover		750.00
7	A9	3pes on 5pf green	2.50	4.50
		Never hinged	6.00	
		On cover		35.00
8	A10	5pes on 10pf car	4.75	4.50
		Never hinged	12.50	
		On cover		35.00
9	A10	10pes on 20pf ultra	5.25	5.25
		Never hinged	15.00	
		On cover		42.50
10	A10	25pes on 50pf red brn	23.00	28.00
		Never hinged	92.50	
		On cover		85.00
		Nos. 6-10 (5)	37.60	79.75

Covers: Value for No. 10 is for overfranked complete covers, usually philatelic.

A5

Kaiser's Yacht "Hohenzollern" — A6

1900 Typo. Perf. 14

11	A5	2p brown	2.75	1.60
		Never hinged	7.50	
		On cover		67.50
12	A5	3p green	2.75	2.00
		Never hinged	7.50	
		On cover		30.00
13	A5	5p carmine	3.25	2.50
		Never hinged	11.00	
		On cover		35.00
14	A5	10p ultra	5.25	4.75
		Never hinged	17.00	
		On cover		60.00
15	A5	15p org & blk, sal	5.25	6.50
		Never hinged	19.00	
		On cover		85.00
16	A5	20p lake & blk	7.25	14.00
		Never hinged	27.50	
		On cover		85.00
17	A5	25p pur & blk, sal	7.25	14.00
		Never hinged	24.00	
		On cover		42.50
18	A5	40p lake & blk, rose	8.75	22.50
		Never hinged	27.50	
		On cover		72.50

Engr.
Perf. 14½x14

19	A6	1r claret	19.00	47.50
		Never hinged	60.00	
		On cover		120.00
20	A6	2r yel green	9.50	80.00
		Never hinged	27.50	
		On cover		240.00
21	A6	3r car & slate	200.00	300.00
		Never hinged	450.00	
		On cover		500.00
a.		red & slate	120.00	180.00
		Never hinged	300.00	
		On cover		425.00
		Nos. 11-21 (11)	271.00	495.35

Covers: Values for Nos. 17-21 are for overfranked complete covers, usually philatelic.

Value in Heller

1905 Typo. Perf. 14

22	A5	2½h brown	4.00	1.75
		Never hinged	13.50	
		On cover		21.00
23	A5	4h dk olive green	14.00	5.50
		Never hinged	45.00	
		On cover		21.00
a.		4h green	14.00	1.60
		Never hinged	35.00	
		On cover		55.00
b.		4h dark yellowish green	27.50	20.00
		Never hinged	100.00	
		On cover		45.00
24	A5	7½h carmine	14.00	1.60
		Never hinged	35.00	
		On cover		17.00
25	A5	15h ultra	24.00	6.00
		Never hinged		25.00
a.		15h violet blue	47.50	16.00
		Never hinged	150.00	
		On cover		45.00
26	A5	20h org & blk, yel	14.00	16.00
		Never hinged	35.00	
		On cover		45.00
27	A5	30h lake & blk	14.00	6.00
		Never hinged	35.00	
		On cover		19.00
28	A5	45h pur & blk	27.50	35.00
		Never hinged	60.00	
		On cover		85.00
29	A5	60h lake & blk, rose	35.00	95.00
		Never hinged	120.00	
		On cover		275.00
		Nos. 22-29 (8)	146.50	166.85

Covers: Values for Nos. 27-29 are for overfranked complete covers, usually philatelic.

1905-16 Wmk. Lozenges (125)

31	A5	2½h brn ('06)	.95	.95
		Never hinged	3.00	
		On cover		25.00
32	A5	4h grn ('06)	.95	.65
		Never hinged	3.25	
		On cover		17.00
b.		Booklet pane of 4 + 2 labels	45.00	
		Never hinged	100.00	
c.		Booklet pane of 5 + label	400.00	
		Never hinged	700.00	
33	A5	7½h car ('06)	1.10	1.60
		Never hinged	4.75	
		On cover		17.00
b.		Booklet pane of 4 + 2 labels	45.00	
		Never hinged	100.00	
c.		Booklet pane of 5 + label	400.00	
		Never hinged	700.00	
34	A5	15h dk blue ('08)	2.25	1.50
		Never hinged	10.00	
		On cover		21.00
a.		15h ultramarine ('06)	10.00	11.00
		Never hinged	25.00	
		On cover		42.50
35	A5	20h org & blk, yel ('11)	2.50	20.00
		Never hinged	9.25	
		On cover		67.50
36	A5	30h lake & blk ('09)	2.60	8.00
		Never hinged	9.25	
		On cover		50.00
37	A5	45h pur & blk ('06)	5.50	55.00
		Never hinged	20.00	
		On cover		300.00
38	A5	60h lake & blk, rose	30.00	190.00
		Never hinged	75.00	
		On cover		425.00

Engr.
Perf. 14½x14

39	A6	1r red ('16)	12.00	25,000.
		Never hinged	85.00	
		On cover		55,000.
40	A6	2r yel grn	47.50	
		Never hinged	110.00	
41	A6	3r car & sl ('08)	47.50	240.00
		Never hinged	140.00	
		On cover		500.00
a.		3r red & blackish green ('08)	160.00	400.00
		Never hinged	475.00	
		On cover		675.00
		Nos. 31-41 (11)	152.85	25,517.

No. 40 was never placed in use.

The frame of No. 41a fluoresces bright orange under ultra-violet light.

Booklet panes of 6 made from sheet stamps exist of the 4h and 7½h.

Forged cancellations are found on Nos. 35-39, 41.

Covers: Values for Nos. 37-38, 41 are for overfranked complete covers, usually philatelic.

In early 1916, German East African authorities ordered supplies of provisional stamps, printed by the press of the Evangelical Mission in Wuga. Three values in denominations most urgently needed were produced in March, but before they could be issued, new stocks of regular stamps were received from Germany. To prevent their capture by the British, the provisionals were buried until 1922, when they were retrieved by the German government and sold at auction. Because of their long storage in the tropical climate, 90-95% of the stamps were destroyed and those surviving are usually brittle and somewhat faded.

Values: 2½h violet brown, $55; 7½h, carmine, $25; 1r pink, $1,400.

OCCUPATION STAMPS

Issued Under Belgian Occupation
Stamps of Belgian Congo, 1915, Handstamped "RUANDA" in Black, Blue or Red Violet

			1916	Unwmk.	Perf. 13½ to 15
N1	A29	5c green & blk			65.00
N2	A30	10c carmine & blk			65.00
N3	A21	15c blue grn & blk			125.00
N4	A31	25c blue & blk			65.00
N5	A23	40c brown red & blk			65.00
N6	A24	50c brown lake & blk			75.00
N7	A25	1fr olive bis & blk			250.00
N8	A27	5fr ocher & blk			3,000.
		Nos. N1-N7 (7)			710.00

Stamps of Belgian Congo, 1915, Handstamped "URUNDI" in Black, Blue or Red Violet

N9	A29	5c green & blk	65.00
N10	A30	10c carmine & blk	65.00
N11	A21	15c bl grn & blk	125.00
N12	A31	25c blue & blk	65.00
N13	A23	40c brn red & blk	65.00
N14	A24	50c brn lake & blk	75.00
N15	A25	1fr ol bis & blk	250.00
N16	A27	5fr ocher & blk	3,000.
		Nos. N9-N15 (7)	710.00

Stamps of Belgian Congo overprinted "Karema," "Kigoma" and "Tabora" were not officially authorized.
Nos. N1-N16 exist with forged overprint.

Stamps of Belgian Congo, 1915, Ovptd. in Dark Blue

			1916		Perf. 12½ to 15
N17	A29	5c green & blk			1.00 .30
		On cover			—
b.		Inverted overprint			200.00 —
N18	A30	10c carmine & blk			1.25 .50
		On cover			32.50
N19	A21	15c bl grn & blk			1.00 .30
		On cover			27.50
N20	A31	25c blue & blk			6.50 1.75
		On cover			37.50
N21	A23	40c brn red & blk			14.00 6.00
		On cover			70.00
N22	A24	50c brn lake & blk			17.50 6.00
		On cover			45.00
N23	A25	1fr olive bis & blk			3.00 .75
N24	A27	5fr ocher & blk			3.50 1.75
		Nos. N17-N24 (8)			47.75 17.35

Nos. N17-N18, N20-N22 Surcharged in Black or Red

			1922		
N25	A24	5c on 50c brn lake & blk			.75 .45
		Never hinged			1.50
		On cover			—
N26	A29	10c on 5c grn & blk (R)			.75 .40
		Never hinged			1.50
		On cover			22.50
N27	A23	25c on 40c brn red & blk (R)			3.75 2.00
		Never hinged			16.50
		On cover			27.50
N28	A30	30c on 10c car & blk			.75 .30
		Never hinged			1.50
		On cover			27.50
N29	A31	50c on 25c bl & blk (R)			.75 .30
		Never hinged			1.50
		On cover			27.50
		Nos. N25-N29 (5)			6.75 3.45

No. N25 has the surcharge at each side.

ISSUED UNDER BRITISH OCCUPATION

Stamps of Nyasaland Protectorate, 1913-15 Overprinted

			1916	Wmk. 3	Perf. 14
N101	A3	½p green			1.75 9.50
a.		Double overprint (R & Bk)			
N102	A3	1p carmine			1.75 3.75
N103	A3	3p violet, yel			18.00 18.00
a.		Double overprint			26,000.
N104	A3	4p scar & blk, yel			42.00 42.00
N105	A3	1sh black, green			55.00 60.00
		Nos. N101-N105 (5)			118.50 133.25
		Set, ovptd. "SPECIMEN"			190.00

"N.F." stands for "Nyasaland Force."

Stamps of East Africa and Uganda, 1912-14, Overprinted in Black or Red

			1917		
N106	A3	1c black (R)			.25 .95
N107	A3	3c blue green			.25 .25
N108	A3	6c carmine			.25 .25
N109	A3	10c brown orange			.60 .70
N110	A3	12c gray			.60 2.50
N111	A3	15c ultramarine			1.50 3.50
N112	A3	25c scar & blk, yel			.90 4.00
N113	A3	50c violet & blk			1.50 3.75
N114	A3	75c blk, bl grn, olive back (R)			1.20 5.25
a.		75c black, emerald (R)			3.75 52.50

Overprinted

N115	A4	1r blk, green(R)	4.25 8.00
a.		1r black, emerald (R)	9.50 65.00
N116	A4	2r blk & red, bl	13.00 55.00
N117	A4	3r gray grn & vio	15.00 95.00
N118	A4	4r grn & red, yel	22.50 105.00
N119	A4	5r dl vio & ultra	45.00 110.00
N120	A4	10r grn & red, grn	120.00 375.00
a.		10r grn & red, emerald	130.00 450.00
N121	A3	20r vio & blk, red	250.00 500.00
N122	A3	50r gray grn & red	600.00 950.00
		Nos. N106-N120 (15)	226.80 769.15

See Tanganyika for "G.E.A." overprints on stamps inscribed "East Africa and Uganda Protectorates" with watermark 4.

SEMI-POSTAL STAMPS

Issued under Belgian Occupation

Semi-Postal Stamps of Belgian Congo, 1918, Overprinted

			1918	Unwmk.	Perf. 14, 15
NB1	A29	5c + 10c grn & bl			.50 .50
		Never hinged			1.25
NB2	A30	10c + 15c car & bl			.80 .50
		Never hinged			1.60
NB3	A21	15c + 20c bl grn & bl			1.00 .50
		Never hinged			2.00
NB4	A31	25c + 25c dp & pale bl			1.50 .50
		Never hinged			3.00
NB5	A23	40c + 40c brn red & bl			1.00 .75
		Never hinged			3.75
NB6	A24	50c + 50c brn lake & bl			1.50 1.00
		Never hinged			3.75
NB7	A25	1fr + 1fr ol bis & bl			2.75 2.75
		Never hinged			4.25
NB8	A27	5fr + 5fr ocher & bl			9.50 8.50
		Never hinged			17.00

NB9	A28	10fr + 10fr grn & bl	70.00 70.00
		Never hinged	200.00
		Nos. NB1-NB9 (9)	88.55 85.00

The letters "A.O." are the initials of "Afrique Orientale" (East Africa).

MAFIA ISLAND

Mafia is a small island on the Indian Ocean coast of German East Africa, near the mouth of the Rufiji River. It was captured by the British in December, 1914, and in January, 1915, the military authorities began to overprint stamps for the use of civilian personnel on the island. Overprinted stamps were used, until the island's transfer to Tanganyikan administration in 1918.

Stamps of German East Africa with Manuscript Overprint "G R Mafia J D M."

			1915		
NL1	A5	2½h brown			3,750.
NL2	A5	4h green			3,750.
a.		Mss. "JDM GR Mafia"			4,250.
NL3	A5	7½h carmine			3,750.
a.		Mss. "JDM GR Mafia"			
NL4	A5	15h ultra			3,750.
NL5	A5	20h org & blk, yel			
NL6	A5	30h lake & blk			—
NL7	A5	45h pur & blk			—
NL8	A6	2r yel grn			—

Initials are those of Lt. Col. J.D. Mackay, Military Governor.

German East Africa #31//41, Zanzibar #141//146 Handstamped

Black Overprint

			1915, Jan.		
NL9	A5	2½h brown			1,200.
NL10	A5	4h green			1,050.
NL11	A5	7½h carmine			625.00
a.		Pair, one without ovpt.			8,250.
NL12	A5	15h ultra			675.00
NL13	A5	20h org & blk, yel			975.00
NL14	A5	30h lake & blk			1,100.
a.		Pair, one without ovpt.			9,000.
NL15	A5	45h pur & blk			1,100.
a.		Pair, one without ovpt.			9,000.
NL16	A6	1r red			16,500.
NL17	A6	2r yellow green			18,000.
NL18	A6	3r car & slate			19,500.

Deep Purple Overprint

NL19	A5	4h green	1,350.
NL20	A5	7½h carmine	825.00
NL21	A5	15h ultra	1,050.
NL22	A5	20h org & blk, yel	1,200.
a.		Pair, one without ovpt.	7,500.
b.		Double ovpt.	
NL23	A5	30h lake & blk	1,650.
a.		Double ovpt.	
NL24	A5	45h pur & blk	1,650.

Reddish Violet Overprint

NL25	A5	2½h brown	300.00
a.		Pair, one without ovpt.	4,850.
b.		Initialled "JDM"	2,250.
NL26	A5	4h green	450.00
a.		Pair, one without ovpt.	4,850.
b.		Initialled "JDM"	2,250.
NL27	A5	7½h carmine	150.00
a.		Pair, one without ovpt.	3,750.
b.		Initialled "JDM"	2,250.
NL28	A5	15h ultramarine	250.00
a.		Pair, one without ovpt.	4,250.
b.		Initialled "JDM"	2,250.

NL29	A5	20h org & blk, yel	500.00
a.		Pair, one without ovpt.	5,000.
b.		Initialled "JDM"	2,000.
NL30	A5	30h lake & blk	550.00
a.		Pair, one without ovpt.	5,000.
b.		Initialled "JDM"	2,500.
NL31	A5	45h pur & blk	675.00
a.		Pair, one without ovpt.	5,500.
b.		Initialled "JDM"	2,500.
NL32	A6	1r red	11,000.
NL33	A6	2r yellow green	12,500.
NL34	A6	3r car & slate	14,500.

The reddish violet overprint is often under-inked and may be faint.

On Zanzibar 1915 Issue
Surcharge in Black

NL35	1c gray (#141)	—
NL36	3c yellow green (#142)	—
NL37	6c carmine (#143)	1,650. 1,500.
NL38	15c ultramarine (#146)	—

German East Africa #13//41, Zanzibar #141, 143 with same handstamped overprint and surcharged with new values

#NL44

#NL49

			1915, May		
		On 1900 Issue			
NL39	A5	6c on 5p carmine			—
NL40	A5	6c on 20p lake & black			—
NL41	A5	6c on 40p carmine			—

On 1905-16 Issues
Surcharge in Green, Violet or Black

NL42	A5	6c on 2½h brown	2,400. 2,550.
a.		Pair, one without surcharge	9,750.
b.		Inverted surcharge	
c.		Double surcharge	
NL43	A5	6c on 4h green	2,550. 2,750.
a.		Pair, one without surcharge	9,750.
b.		Inverted surcharge	
c.		Double surcharge	
NL44	A5	6c on 7½h carmine	2,450. 2,750.
a.		Pair, one without surcharge	
b.		Inverted surcharge	
c.		Double surcharge	
NL45	A5	6c on 15h ultramarine	2,250. 2,750.
a.		Double surcharge	
b.		Triple surcharge	
c.		Inverted surcharge	
NL46	A5	6c on 20h org & blk, yel	3,350. 3,400.
a.		Inverted surcharge	
NL47	A5	6c on 30h lake & blk	4,100. 4,500.
a.		Inverted surcharge	
NL48	A5	6c on 45h purple & black	4,100. 4,100.
a.		Pair, one without surcharge	
b.		Inverted surcharge	
NL49	A6	6c on 1r red	57,500.
a.		Double surcharge	
NL50	A6	6c on 2r yellow green	62,500.
a.		Double surcharge	
NL51	A6	6c on 3r carmine & slate	72,500.

On Zanzibar 1914 Issue
Surcharge in Black

NL52	6c on 1c gray (#141)	—
NL53	6c on 6c carmine (#143)	—

German East Africa Fiscal Stamps Handstamped in Bluish Green or Violet

#NL60

1915, Sept.
Inscribed "Statistik Des Waaren-Verkhers"

NL54	24p vermilion, *buff,*	1,100.	1,650.
NL55	12½p brown	1,200.	1,800.
a.	Pair, one without over-print	15,000.	
NL56	25h dull green	1,200.	1,800.
NL57	50h slate	1,200.	1,800.
a.	Pair, one without over-print	15,000.	
NL58	1r lilac	1,200.	1,800.

#NL59

Inscribed "Ubersetzungs Gebuhren"

NL59	25h gray	1,200.	1,800.

Handstamped in three lines, serifed type

1915, Sept.
On Nos. NL55-60

NL60	24p vermilion, buff, (#55)	1,650.	
NL61	12½p brown (#56)	1,800.	
a.	"G.R. POST MAFIA" inverted		
NL62	25h dull green (#57)	1,800.	
NL63	50h slate (#58)	1,800.	
NL64	1r lilac (#59)	1,800.	
NL65	25h gray (#60)	1,800.	
a.	Pair, one without overprint	11,250.	

#NL67

On unoverprinted Fiscal Stamps

NL66	24p vermilion, *buff*	—	
NL67	12½p brown	—	
NL68	25h dull green	—	
NL69	50h slate	—	
NL70	1r lilac	—	
NL71	25h gray	—	
a.	Inverted ovpt.		

On German East African Stamps in Green, Violet or Black

NL72	A5 7½h carmine	—	
NL73	A5 20h org & blk, *yel*	—	
NL74	A5 30h lake & blk	—	

On Zanzibar Stamps in Green, Violet or Black

NL75	1c gray (#141)	—	
NL76	3c yellow green (#142)	—	
NL77	6c carmine (#143)	—	
NL78	15c ultramarine (#146)	—	

On Indian Expeditionary Force Stamps (India #M34-M43) in Green, Greenish Black or Blue

NL79	3p gray (#M34)	55.00	125.00
a.	Pair, one without overprint		2,750.
NL80	½a violet (#M35)	82.50	135.00
a.	Pair, one without overprint	3,500.	2,750.
NL81	1a carmine rose (#M36)	90.00	135.00
NL82	2a violet (#M37)	125.00	225.00
NL83	2½a ultramarine (#M38)	180.00	275.00
NL84	3a orange brown (#M39)	195.00	275.00
a.	Pair, one without overprint		4,500.
NL85	4a olive green (#M40)	225.00	375.00
NL86	8a purple (#M41)	410.00	600.00
a.	Pair, one without overprint		5,000.
NL87	12a dull claret (#M42)	475.00	750.00
NL88	1r green & red brown (#M43)	550.00	825.00
a.	Double overprint, one inverted		2,750.

Handstamp exists inverted, double and sideways.

Handstamped in three lines, sans-serif italic type, in green, greenish black or blue

On Indian Expeditionary Force Stamps (India #M34-M43)

1916, Oct.

NL89	3p gray (#M34)	250.00	250.00
NL90	½a green (#M35)	275.00	275.00
NL91	1a carmine rose (#M36)	225.00	250.00
NL92	2a violet (#M37)	300.00	300.00
NL93	2½a ultramarine (#M38)	300.00	350.00
NL94	3a orange brown (#M39)	325.00	500.00
NL95	4a olive green (#M40)	500.00	500.00
NL96	8a purple (#M41)	600.00	675.00
NL97	12a dull claret (#M42)	700.00	800.00
NL98	1r green & red brown (#M43)	1,000.	1,000.

Some values exist with handstamp inverted.

GERMAN NEW GUINEA

ˈjər-mən ˈnü ˈgi-nē

LOCATION — A group of islands in the west Pacific Ocean, including a part of New Guinea and adjacent islands of the Bismarck Archipelago.
GOVT. — German Protectorate
AREA — 93,000 sq. mi.
POP. — 601,427 (1913)
CAPITAL — Herbertshohe (later Kokopo)

The islands were occupied by Australian troops during World War I and renamed "New Britain." By covenant of the League of Nations they were made a mandated territory of Australia in 1920. The old name of "New Guinea" has since been restored. Postage stamps were issued under all regimes. For other listings see New Britain (1914-15), North West Pacific Islands (1915-22) and New Guinea.

100 Pfennig = 1 Mark

Stamps of Germany Overprinted in Black

			Perf. 13½x14½
1897-99		**Unwmk.**	
1	A9 3pf brown	8.00	8.00
	Never hinged	20.00	
	On cover		85.00
a.	3pf reddish brown ('99)	135.00	240.00
	Never hinged	500.00	
	On cover		600.00
b.	3pf yellow brown ('99)	31.00	57.50
	Never hinged	92.50	
	On cover		125.00
2	A9 5pf green	4.00	5.00
	Never hinged	7.50	
	On cover		75.00
3	A10 10pf carmine	6.50	8.00
	Never hinged	13.50	
	On cover		100.00
4	A10 20pf ultra	9.00	12.00
	Never hinged	22.00	
	On cover		175.00
5	A10 25pf orange ('98)	29.00	52.50
	Never hinged	67.50	
	On cover		175.00
a.	Inverted overprint	2,250.	
	Never hinged	4,500.	
6	A10 50pf red brown	32.50	50.00
	Never hinged	85.00	
	On cover		100.00
	Nos. 1-6 (6)	89.00	135.50

Covers: Value for No. 6 is for overfranked complete cover, usually philatelic.

Kaiser's Yacht "Hohenzollern"
A3   A4

		Typo.	**Perf. 14**
1901			
7	A3 3pf brown	1.25	1.25
	Never hinged	2.50	
	On cover		102.00
8	A3 5pf green	6.50	1.25
	Never hinged	17.00	
	On cover		42.50
9	A3 10pf carmine	20.00	3.00
	Never hinged	67.50	
	On cover		50.00
10	A3 20pf ultra	1.60	3.00
	Never hinged	4.25	
	On cover		85.00
11	A3 25pf org & blk, *yel*	1.75	16.00
	Never hinged	4.25	
	On cover		175.00
12	A3 30pf org & blk, *sal*	1.75	20.00
	Never hinged	4.25	
	On cover		175.00
13	A3 40pf lake & blk	1.75	23.00
	Never hinged	4.25	
	On cover		175.00
14	A3 50pf pur & blk, *sal*	2.00	20.00
	Never hinged	4.25	
	On cover		60.00
15	A3 80pf lake & blk, *rose*	3.75	27.50
	Never hinged	6.75	
	On cover		85.00
	Engr.		
	Perf. 14½x14		
16	A4 1m carmine	8.00	52.50
	Never hinged	25.00	
	On cover		100.00
17	A4 2m blue	8.00	77.50
	Never hinged	25.00	
	On cover		140.00
18	A4 3m blk vio	11.00	150.00
	Never hinged	35.00	
	On cover		210.00
19	A4 5m slate & car	160.00	500.00
	Never hinged	425.00	
	On cover		800.00
	Nos. 7-19 (13)	227.25	895.00

Fake cancellations exist on Nos. 10-19.
Covers: Values for Nos. 14-19 are for overfranked complete cover, usually philatelic.

A5

A6

Wmk. Lozenges (125)

		Typo.	**Perf. 14**
1914-19			
20	A3 3pf brown ('19)		.80
	Never hinged		1.75
21	A5 5pf green		1.60
	Never hinged		3.50
22	A5 10pf carmine		1.60
	Never hinged		3.50
	Engr.		
	Perf. 14½x14		
23	A6 5m slate & carmine		32.50
	Never hinged		120.00
	Nos. 20-23 (4)		36.50

Nos. 20-23 were never placed in use.
Nos. 21-23 have "NEUGUINEA" as one word without a hyphen.

GERMAN SOUTH WEST AFRICA

'jər-mən 'sauth 'west 'a-fri-kə

LOCATION — In southwest Africa, bordering on the South Atlantic.
GOVT. — German Colony
AREA — 322,450 sq. mi. (1913)
POP. — 94,372 (1913)
CAPITAL — Windhoek

The Colony was occupied by South African troops during World War I and in 1920 was mandated to the Union of South Africa by the League of Nations. See South-West Africa.

100 Pfennig = 1 Mark

Stamps of Germany
Overprinted

1897   **Unwmk.**   **Perf. 13½x14½**

1	A9	3pf dark brown	8.25	12.00
		Never hinged	30.00	
		On cover		75.00
a.		3pf yellow brown	50.00	2,800.
		Never hinged	160.00	—
b.		3pf olive brown	60.00	
		Never hinged	190.00	
c.		3pf reddish brown	—	2,500.
		Never hinged	—	
2	A9	5pf green	4.50	4.75
		Never hinged	12.50	
		On cover		30.00
3	A10	10pf carmine	21.00	15.00
		Never hinged	62.50	
		On cover		85.00
4	A10	20pf ultra	5.75	5.25
		Never hinged	25.00	
		On cover		35.00
5	A10	25pf orange	225.00	29,000.
		Never hinged	640.00	
6	A10	50pf red brown	225.00	29,000.
		Never hinged	640.00	
		Nos. 1-4 (4)	39.50	37.00

Nos. 5 and 6 were prepared for issue but were not sent to the Colony.

Overprinted in Black on
2 lines

1899

7	A9	3pf dark brown	4.00	12.00
		Never hinged	17.00	
		On cover		110.00
a.		3pf reddish brown	52.50	160.00
		Never hinged	190.00	
b.		3pf yellow brown	7.00	12.00
		Never hinged	22.50	
		On cover		55.00
8	A9	5pf green	3.25	3.25
		Never hinged	11.00	
		On cover		21.00
9	A10	10pf carmine	3.25	4.00
		Never hinged	11.00	
		On cover		21.00
10	A10	20pf ultra	11.50	15.00
		Never hinged	47.50	
		On cover		50.00
11	A10	25pf orange	350.00	400.00
		Never hinged	1,000.	
		On cover		850.00
12	A10	50pf red brown	12.00	12.00
		Never hinged	50.00	
		On cover		50.00

Covers: Value for No. 12 is for overfranked complete covers, usually philatelic.

Kaiser's Yacht "Hohenzollern"
   A3   A4

1900   **Typo.**   **Perf. 14**

13	A3	3pf brown	4.00	1.60
		Never hinged	10.00	
		On cover		67.50
14	A3	5pf green	20.00	1.60
		Never hinged	50.00	
		On cover		17.00

15	A3	10pf carmine	14.00	.80
		Never hinged	50.00	
		On cover		17.00
16	A3	20pf ultra	30.00	1.50
		Never hinged	80.00	
		On cover		17.00
17	A3	25pf org & blk, *yel*	1.50	5.50
		Never hinged	6.00	
		On cover		25.00
18	A3	30pf org & blk, *sal*	72.50	2.75
		Never hinged	225.00	
		On cover		17.00
19	A3	40pf lake & blk	1.75	3.25
		Never hinged	6.00	
		On cover		17.00
20	A3	50pf pur & blk, *sal*	2.10	2.10
		Never hinged	6.75	
		On cover		17.00
21	A3	80pf lake & blk, *rose*	2.10	9.00
		Never hinged	6.75	
		On cover		37.50

Engr.
Perf. 14½x14

22	A4	1m carmine	110.00	30.00
		Never hinged	375.00	
		On cover		67.50
23	A4	2m blue	30.00	37.50
		Never hinged	100.00	
		On cover		75.00
24	A4	3m blk vio	32.50	50.00
		Never hinged	125.00	
		On cover		92.50
25	A4	5m slate & car	200.00	160.00
		Never hinged	400.00	
		On cover		375.00
		Nos. 13-25 (13)	520.45	305.60

Covers: Values for Nos. 20-25 are for overfranked complete covers, usually philatelic.

Wmk. Lozenges (125)

1906-19   **Typo.**   **Perf. 14**

26	A3	3pf dk brn ('07)	.80	3.75
		Never hinged	2.10	
		On cover		50.00
a.		3pf yellow brown ('13)	.80	2.90
		Never hinged	2.00	
		On cover		32.50
27	A3	5pf green	.80	1.40
		Never hinged	2.10	
		On cover		21.00
b.		Bklt. pane of 6 (2 #27, 4 #28)	40.00	
		Never hinged	75.00	
c.		Booklet pane of 5 + label	160.00	
		Never hinged	390.00	
28	A3	10pf lt rose	1.00	1.40
		Never hinged	4.50	
		On cover		17.00
a.		10pf red ('13)	3.50	17.00
		Never hinged	12.50	
		On cover		100.00
b.		Booklet pane of 5 + label	400.00	
		Never hinged	800.00	
29	A3	20pf ultra ('11)	1.00	3.75
		Never hinged	4.25	
		On cover		25.00
30	A3	30pf org & blk, *pale yellow* ('11)	16.00	52.50
		Never hinged	60.00	
		On cover		1,000.
a.		30pf orange & black, *pale orange* ('13)	6.50	—
		On cover	17.00	

Engr.
Perf. 14½x14

31	A4	1m carmine ('12)	12.50	75.00
		Never hinged	55.00	
		On cover		300.00
32	A4	2m blue ('11)	12.50	75.00
		Never hinged	55.00	
		On cover		300.00
33	A4	3m blk vio ('19)	14.00	
		Never hinged	47.50	
a.		3m gray violet	40.00	
		Never hinged	150.00	
34	A4	5m slate & car	36.00	300.00
		Never hinged	125.00	
		On cover		850.00
a.		5m slate & rose red	100.00	
		Never hinged	290.00	
		Nos. 26-34 (9)	94.60	512.80

Nos. 33, 33a, 34a were never placed in use.
Booklet panes of 6 made from sheet stamps exist of the 5pf and 10pf.
Forged cancellations are found on Nos. 30-32, 34.
Covers: Values for Nos. 31-34 are for overfranked complete covers, usually philatelic.

GERMAN STATES

'jər-mən 'stāts

Watermarks

Wmk. 92 —
17mm wide

Wmk. 93 —
14mm wide

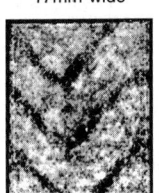

Wmk. 94 — Horiz.
WavyLines Wide
Apart

Wmk. 95v —
Vert. Wavy
Lines Close
Together

Wmk. 95h —
Horiz. Wavy Lines
Close Together

Wmk. 102 — Post
Horn

Wmk. 116 —
Crosses and Circles

Wmk. 128 — Wavy Lines

Wmk. 130 —
Wreath of Oak
Leaves

Wmk. 148 —
Small Flowers

Wmk. 162 —
Laurel Wreath

Wmk. 192 —
Circles

BADEN

LOCATION — In southwestern Germany
GOVT. — Former Grand Duchy
AREA — 5,817 sq. mi.
POP. — 1,432,000 (1864)
CAPITAL — Karlsruhe (Principal city)

Baden was a member of the German Confederation. In 1870 it became part of the German Empire.

60 Kreuzer = 1 Gulden

Values for unused stamps are for examples with original gum as defined in the catalogue introduction except for Nos. 1-9 which are valued without gum. Very fine examples of Nos. 1-9 will have one or two margins touching the framelines due to the very narrow spacing of the stamps on the plates. Stamps with margins clear of the framelines on all four sides are scarce and sell for considerably more.

A1

1851-52　Unwmk.　Typo.　*Imperf.*

1	A1	1kr blk, *dk buff*	290.00	250.00
	With gum		500.00	
	On cover			600.00
2	A1	3kr blk, *yellow*	140.00	16.00
	With gum		240.00	
	On cover			40.00
3	A1	6kr blk, *yel grn*	440.00	45.00
	With gum		800.00	
	On cover			125.00
4	A1	9kr blk, *lil rose*	90.00	25.00
	With gum		200.00	
	On cover			95.00
	Nos. 1-4 (4)		960.00	336.00

Thin Paper (First Printing, 1851)

1a	A1	1kr black, *buff*	2,000.	800.00
	With gum		3,600.	
	On cover			1,750.
2a	A1	3kr black, *or-ange*	675.00	35.00
	With gum		1,600.	
	On cover			95.00
3a	A1	6kr black, *blue green*	2,250.	90.00
	With gum		3,600.	
	On cover			250.00
4a	A1	9kr black, *deep rose*	2,800.	160.00
	With gum		4,500.	
	On cover			475.00

No. 4b

4b	A1	9kr black, *bl grn (error)*	1,300,000.	
	On cover			2,000,000.

Values for pairs

1	A1	1kr blk, *dk buff*	1,600.	550.00
	With gum		3,200.	
	On cover			1,500.
2	A1	3kr blk, *yellow*	360.00	52.50
	With gum		875.00	
	On cover			95.00
	Gutter pair (10)			8,000.
				40,000.
3	A1	6kr blk, *yel grn*	1,200.	160.00
	With gum		2,750.	
	On cover			275.00
	Gutter pair (2)			30,000.
4	A1	9kr blk, *lil rose*	240.00	145.00
	With gum		600.00	
	On cover			650.00

Thin Paper

1a	A1	1kr black, *buff*	—	2,000.
	On cover			2,550.
	Gutter pair (1)			115,000.
2a	A1	3kr black, *or-ange*	2,400.	160.00
	With gum		4,800.	
	On cover			200.00
3a	A1	6kr black, *blue green*	—	325.00
	With gum		9,500.	
	On cover			800.00
4a	A1	9kr black, *deep rose*	—	1,600.
	With gum		10,400.	

Values for strips of 3

1	A1	1kr blk, *dk buff*	960.00	
	On cover			1,600.
2	A1	3kr blk, *yellow*	960.00	180.00
	With gum		1,750.	
	On cover			400.00
3	A1	6kr blk, *yel grn*	600.00	
	On cover			1,300.
4	A1	9kr blk, *lil rose*	400.00	400.00
	With gum		960.00	
	On cover			800.00

Thin Paper

1a	A1	1kr black, *buff*		2,900.
	On cover			4,000.
2a	A1	3kr black, *or-ange*	3,200.	550.00
	With gum		6,800.	
	On cover			800.00
3a	A1	6kr black, *blue green*		1,450.
	On cover			2,600.
4a	A1	9kr black, *deep rose*		4,800.

Values for blocks of 4

1	A1	1kr blk, *dk buff*	—	4,000.
2	A1	3kr blk, *yellow*	—	1,450.
	With gum		5,200.	
3	A1	6kr blk, *yel grn*	—	4,000.
	With gum		8,000.	
4	A1	9kr blk, *lil rose*	600.00	3,000.
	With gum		2,000.	

Thin Paper

1a	A1	1kr black, *buff*		4,000.
2a	A1	3kr black, *or-ange*	—	2,550.
	With gum		9,600.	
3a	A1	6kr black, *blue green*	—	—
	With gum		24,000.	
4a	A1	9kr black, *deep rose*	—	—
	With gum		24,000.	

1853-58

6	A1	1kr black	175.00	27.50
	With gum		480.00	
	On cover			110.00
a.	Tête bêche gutter pair			40,000.
7	A1	3kr black, *green*	160.00	8.00
	With gum		320.00	
	On cover			24.00
8	A1	3kr black, *bl ('58)*	675.00	30.00
	With gum		1,450.	
	On cover			110.00
a.	Printed on both sides			
9	A1	6kr black, *yellow*	250.00	27.50
	With gum		550.00	
	On cover			67.50
	Nos. 6-9 (4)		1,260.	93.00

Values for pairs

6	A1	1kr black	600.00	120.00
	With gum		1,750.	
	On cover			225.00
7	A1	3kr blk, *green*		32.50
	With gum		2,000.	
	On cover			47.50
8	A1	3kr blk, *blue, (58)*	1,600.	145.00
	With gum		3,200.	
	On cover			200.00
9	A1	6kr blk, *yellow*		240.00
	With gum		2,000.	

Values for used strips of 3

6	A1	1kr black		175.00
	On cover			290.00
7	A1	3kr blk, *green*		95.00
	On cover			120.00
8	A1	3kr blk, *blue, (58)*		360.00
	On cover			600.00
9	A1	6kr blk, *yellow*		800.00

Values for blocks of 4

6	A1	1kr black		*1,450.*
	With gum		4,800.	
7	A1	3kr blk, *green*		*2,250.*
	With gum		4,800.	
	On cover			*3,200.*
8	A1	3kr blk, *blue, (58)*		*2,400.*
	With gum		8,000.	
9	A1	6kr blk, *yellow*		*8,900.*
	With gum		7,200.	

Full margins of Nos. 1-4, 6-9 = ½mm.

Reissues (1865) of Nos. 1, 2, 3, 6, 7 and 8 exist on thick paper and No. 9 on thin paper; the color of the last is brighter than that of the original.

Covers: Values for Nos. 1-9 on cover are for covers bearing stamps with one or more margins touching, but not into the design. Covers bearing stamps with full clear margins are rare and command substantial premiums.

5-Ring Numeral Postmarks

Values are for neat and clearly legible numeral cancellations in five concentric circles struck on the imperforate issues of Baden (#1-9).

The left column is for fairly complete strikes on sound single stamps. The right column is for complete covers.

All values are premiums to be added to the value of the stamps or stamps on covers, upon which the cancels are struck.

1 Aach	+40.00	+100.00
1 Aach (red)	+1,100.	+4,000.
2 Achem	+5.00	+20.00
3 Adelsheim	+20.00	+50.00
3 Adelsheim (blue)	+220.00	+60.00
4 Aglasterhausen	+25.00	+60.00
4 Aglasterhausen (blue)	+180.00	+500.00
5 Allensbach	+200.00	+500.00
5 Allensbach (red)	+1,100.	+3,750.
6 Altbreisach	+5.00	+10.00
7 Appenweier	+25.00	+80.00
8 Baden	0.00	0.00
8 Baden (red)	+800.00	+800.00
9 Beroldzheim	+300.00	+1,000.
9 Beroldzheim (red)	+1,500.	+4,250.
10 Beuggen (blue)	+400.00	+1,200.
Rheinfelden	+40.00	+80.00
11 Biberach	+50.00	+120.00
11 Biberach (blue)	+300.00	+1,000.
12 Bischofsheim a. Rh.	+10.00	+30.00
12 bischofsheim a. Rh. (blue)	+250.00	+800.00
13 Bischofsheim a. T.	+10.00	+20.00
13 Bischofsheim a. T. (blue)	+180.00	+500.00
14 Blumberg	+80.00	+250.00
14 Blumberg (red)	+900.00	+3,500.
15 Blumenfeld	+50.00	+200.00
15 Blumenfeld (blue)	+200.00	+750.00
16 Bonndorf	+5.00	+15.00
16 Bonndorf (red)	+750.00	+2,500.
16 Bonndorf (blue)	+250.00	+600.00
17 Boxberg	+10.00	+30.00
17 Boxberg (red)	+500.00	+1,500.
17 Boxberg (blue)	+120.00	+350.00
18 Bretten	+5.00	+10.00
19 Bruchsal	0.00	0.00
19 Bruchsal (red)	+400.00	+1,000.
20 Buchen	+5.00	+20.00
20 Buchen (blue)	+150.00	+500.00
21 Buehl	+5.00	+10.00
21 Buehl (blue)	+200.00	+500.00
22 Burg	+200.00	+450.00
22 Burg (blue)	+1,100.	+3,750.
23 Burkheim	+100.00	+250.00
23 Burkheim (red)	+1,000.	+3,500.
24 Carlsruhe	0.00	0.00
24 Carlsruhe (red)	+1,000.	+4,500.
25 Constanza	0.00	0.00
25 Constanz (red)	+400.00	+1,000.
26 Dinglingen	+15.00	+50.00
27 Donaueschingen	0.00	0.00
28 Durlach	0.00	0.00
28 Durlach (blue)	+50.00	+150.00
29 Durmersheim	+250.00	+1,350.
29 Durmersheim (red)	+1,100.	+3,750.
30 Dürrheim	+80.00	+250.00
31 Eberbach	+5.00	+10.00
31 Eberbach (red)	+450.00	+1,200.
32 Efringen	+40.00	+100.00
32 Efringen (red)	+400.00	+1,000.
32 Efringen (blue)	+400.00	+1,000.
33 Eichtersheim	+25.00	+80.00
33 Eichtersheim (blue)	+400.00	+1,000.
34 Eigeltingen	+50.00	+120.00
34 Eigeltingen (red)	+300.00	+750.00
35 Elzach		+750.00
35 Elzach (blue)	+450.00	+1,200.
36 Emmendingen	0.00	0.00
36 Emmendingen (blue)	+200.00	+500.00
37 Endingen	+10.00	+40.00
37 Endingen (blue)	+250.00	+600.00
38 Engen	+5.00	+20.00
38 Engen (blue)	+200.00	+500.00
39 Eppingen	+10.00	+30.00
39 Eppingen (red)	+1,000.	+3,000.
39 Eppingen (blue)	+80.00	+250.00
40 Ernstthal	+300.00	+750.00
40 Ernstthal (blue)	+1,000.	+2,500.
41 Ettenheim	+5.00	+10.00
41 Ettenheim (blue)	+250.00	+600.00
42 Ettlingen	0.00	0.00
42 Ettlingen (blue)	+400.00	+1,200.
43 Freiburg	0.00	0.00
43 Freiburg (red)	+800.00	+2,500.
44 Freudenberg	+150.00	+400.00
44 Freudenberg (blue)	+500.00	+1,800.00
45 Furtwangen	+15.00	+40.00
45 Furtwangen (blue)	+600.00	+2,000.
46 Gaggenau	+80.00	+150.00
47 Geisingen	+30.00	+80.00
47 Geisingen (blue)	+1,500.	+3,500.
48 Gengenbach	+25.00	+60.00
48 Gengenbach (red)	+300.00	+1,200.
49 Gerlachsheim	+15.00	+40.00
50 Gernsbach	+10.00	+30.00
51 Graben	+500.00	+1,500.
51 Graben (red)	+1,500.	+10,000.
51 Neckaretz		
52 Griesbach	+80.00	+250.00
52 Greisbach (red)	+700.00	+2,500.
53 Haltingen	+30.00	+60.00
53 Haltingen (red)	+700.00	+2,000.
54 Hardheim	+80.00	+250.00
54 Hardheim (red)	+800.00	+2,500.
55 Haslach	+15.00	+40.00
55 Haslach (blue)	+250.00	+600.00
56 Hausach	+15.00	+40.00
57 Heidelberg	0.00	0.00
58 Heilgenberg	+40.00	+80.00
58 Heilgenberg (red)	+350.00	+1,200.
59 Heitersheim	+30.00	+60.00
60 Hilzingen	+40.00	+100.00
60 Hilzingen (blue)	+300.00	+800.00
61 Höllsteig	+60.00	+200.00
61 Höllsteig (red)	+800.00	+3,000.
61 Höllsteig (blue)	+800.00	+2,500.
62 Holzberg	+15.00	+40.00
62 Hornberg (blue)	+150.00	+400.00
63 Hüfingen	+10.00	+30.00
63 Hüfingen (red)	+400.00	+1,200.
63 Hüfingen (blue)	+500.00	+1,200.
64 Hundheim	+700.00	+4,500.
64 Hernsbach		+4,500.
65 Ichenheim	+700.00	+3,000.
65 Ichenheim (blue)	+1,500.	+4,500.
66 Jestetten	+30.00	+80.00
66 Jestetten (blue)	+40.00	+100.00
67 Kandern	+30.00	+80.00
68 Kehl	+5.00	+10.00
68 Kehl (red)	+400.00	+1,000.
69 Kenzingen	+5.00	+10.00
69 Kenzingen (red)	+700.00	+2,500.
70 Kippenheim	+10.00	+20.00
71 Kleinlaufenburg	+25.00	+50.00
71 Kleinlaufenburg (blue)	+120.00	+300.00
72 Kork	+20.00	+30.00
72 Kork (blue)	+400.00	+1,000.
73 Krauheim	+25.00	+50.00
73 Krauheim (red)	+600.00	+1,250.
74 Krotzingen	+40.00	+150.00
74 Krotzingen (blue)	+60.00	+150.00
75 Königschaffhausen	+30.00	+80.00
76 Königshofen	+120.00	+400.00
77 Külsheim	+180.00	+500.00
77 Meckesheim	—	—
78 Ladenburg	+20.00	+50.00
78 Ladenburg (red)	+1,000.	+3,000.
79 Lahr	0.00	0.00
80 Langenbrücken	+30.00	+80.00
81 Langendenzlingen	+25.00	+60.00
82 Lenzkirch	+10.00	+30.00
82 Lenzkirch (red)	+600.00	+1,500.
82 Lenzkirch (blue)	+150.00	+400.00
83 Löffingen	+15.00	+40.00
83 Löffingen (blue)	+150.00	+350.00
84 Lörrach	0.00	0.00
84 Lörrach (red)	+120.00	+350.00
85 Ludwigshafen	+25.00	+50.00
85 Ludwigshafen (blue)	+400.00	+1,200.
86 Malsch	+60.00	+250.00
86 Malsch (blue)	+400.00	+1,200.
87 Mannheim	0.00	0.00
88 Markdorf	+25.00	+70.00
88 Markdorf (red)	+700.00	+2,000.
89 Meersburg	+20.00	+50.00
90 Merchingen	+25.00	+60.00
90 Merchingen (blue)	+400.00	+1,000.
91 Moehringen	+30.00	+60.00
91 Moehringen (blue)	+400.00	+1,000.
92 Möskirch	+5.00	+10.00
92 Möskirch (red)	+200.00	+500.00
92 Möskirch (blue)	+60.00	+150.00
92 Möskirch (green)	—	—
93 Mosbach	+5.00	+20.00
93 Mosbach (red)	+200.00	+600.00
93 Mosbach (blue)	+300.00	+700.00
94 Mühlburg	+30.00	+80.00
95 Müllheim	0.00	0.00
95 Müllheim (red)	+700.00	+2,000.
96 Muggensturm	+120.00	+400.00
96 Muggensturm (blue)	+1,000.	+5,000.
97 Munzingen	+150.00	+400.00
97 Munzingen (red)	+500.00	+1,500.
97 Munzingen (blue)	+200.00	+600.00
98 Neckarbischofsheim	+20.00	+40.00
98 Neckarbischofsheim (blue)	+500.00	+1,500.
99 Neckargemünd	+20.00	+40.00
99 Neckargemünd (red)	+700.00	+2,000.
99 Neckargemünd (blue)	+250.00	+600.00
100 Neustadt	+5.00	+10.00
100 Neustadt (red)	+400.00	+1,200.
100 Neustadt (blue)	+150.00	+350.00
101 Oberkirch	+10.00	+40.00
101 Oberkirch (red)	+300.00	+800.00
102 Oberlauchringen	+40.00	+150.00
103 Oberschefflenz	+40.00	+150.00
103 Oberschefflenz (blue)		
104 Offenburg	+500.00	+1,500.
104 Offenburg (red)	0.00	0.00
104 Offenburg (blue)	+150.00	+350.00
105 Oppenau	+20.00	+40.00
106 Orschweier	+30.00	+100.00
107 Osterburken	+60.00	+150.00
107 Osterburken (red)	+700.00	+2,500.
107 Osterburken (blue)	+500.00	+1,500.
108 Petersthal	+60.00	
108 Petersthal (blue)	+600.00	+1,500.
109 Pforzheim	0.00	0.00
109 Pforzheim (red)	+1,200.	+3,500.
109 Pforzheim (blue)	+1,500.	+4,500.
110 Pfullendorf	+20.00	+60.00
110 Pfullendorf (red)	+500.00	+1,500.
110 Pfullendorf (blue)	+80.00	+200.00
111 Philippsburg	+30.00	+100.00
111 Philippsburg (blue)	+300.00	+800.00
112 Radolfzell	+5.00	+20.00
112 Radolfzell (red)	+1,500.	+8,000.
113 Randegg	+50.00	+150.00
113 Randegg (red)	+800.00	+3,000.
113 Randegg (blue)	+160.00	+500.00
113 Gailingen		
114 Rappenau	+40.00	+100.00
114 Rappenau (blue)	+250.00	+800.00
115 Rastatt	0.00	0.00
115 Rastatt (red)	+50.00	+100.00
115 Rastatt (blue)	+300.00	+800.00
116 Renchen	+20.00	+40.00
116 Renchen (blue)	+400.00	+1,000.
117 Riedern	+350.00	+1,200.
117 Riedern (blue)	+200.00	+400.00
117 Gottmadingen		
117 Gottmadingen (blue)		
118 Riegel	+10.00	+30.00
118 Riegel (red)	+400.00	+1,000.
118 Riegel (blue)	+400.00	+1,000.
119 Rippoldsau	+150.00	+300.00
119 Rippoldsau (red)	+400.00	+1,000.
119 Rippoldsau (blue)	+300.00	+600.00
120 Rothenfels	+200.00	+500.00
120 Rothenfels (red)	+500.00	+1,500.
121 Sackingen	0.00	0.00
121 Sackingen (red)	+300.00	+700.00
121 Sackingen (blue)	+400.00	+1,000.
122 Salem	+20.00	+40.00
122 Salem (red)	+500.00	+1,500.
122 Salem (blue)	+350.00	+1,000.
123 St. Blasien	+15.00	+40.00
123 St. Blasien (red)	+1,000.	+6,000.
123 St. Blasien (blue)	+500.00	+1,200.
124 St. Georgen	+25.00	+60.00
125 Schallstadt	+80.00	+200.00
125 Schallstadt (blue)	+150.00	+300.00
126 Schappach	+2,000.	+7,500.
126 Schappach (blue)	+400.00	+1,500.
127 Schiltach	+15.00	+40.00
127 Schiltach (red)	+400.00	+1,200.
128 Schleingen	+15.00	+50.00
128 Schleingen (red)	+500.00	+1,500.
128 Schleingen (blue)	+500.00	+1,500.
129 Schönau	+20.00	+50.00
130 Schopfheim	+15.00	+40.00
130 Schopfheim (red)	+1,000.	+7,000.
130 Schopfheim (blue)	+100.00	+250.00
131 Schwetzingen	+5.00	+10.00
131 Schwetzingen (blue)	+300.00	+700.00
132 Singen	+10.00	+30.00
132 Singen (red)	+700.00	+2,000.
133 Sinsheim	+5.00	+10.00
133 Sinsheim (red)	+600.00	+1,900.
134 Stadel		+50,000.
134 Brennet	+40.00	+150.00
135 Staufen	+5.00	+10.00
136 Steinen	+30.00	+60.00
136 Steinen (red)	+1,000.	+3,000.
136 Steinen (blue)	+1,000.	+3,000.
137 Steißlingen	+1,200.	+5,000.
137 Steißlingen (red)	+2,500.	+10,000.
138 Stetten A.K.M.	+60.00	+180.00
138 Stetten A.K.M. (blue)	+400.00	+1,200.
139 Stockach	0.00	0.00
139 Stockach (red)	+500.00	+2,000.
140 Stollhofen	+250.00	+1,200.
140 Lichtenau	+50.00	+150.00
141 Stühlingen	+15.00	+80.00
141 Stühlingen (red)	+600.00	+2,000.
141 Stühlingen (blue)	+400.00	+1,200.
142 Sulzburg	+15.00	+50.00
142 Sulzburg (blue)	+400.00	+1,200.
143 Todtnau	+25.00	+100.00
143 Todtnau (red)	+500.00	+2,500.
144 Thiengen	+15.00	+50.00
144 Thiengen (blue)	+150.00	+300.00
145 Triberg	+10.00	+20.00
145 Triberg (red)	+600.00	+2,000.
145 Triberg (blue)	+400.00	+1,200.
146 Überlingen	+5.00	+10.00
146 Überlingen (red)	+500.00	+1,500.
147 Uihlingen	+500.00	+2,500.
147 Uihlingen (red)	+1,500.	+5,500.
147 Albbruck	—	—
148 Villingen	0.00	0.00
149 Vöhrenbach	+20.00	+50.00
149 Vöhrenbach (red)	+700.00	+2,500.
150 Waghäusel	+20.00	+50.00
150 Waghäusel (red)	+100.00	+350.00
151 Waibstadt	+25.00	+80.00
151 Waibstadt (blue)	—	—
152 Waldkirch	+10.00	+30.00
153 Waldshut	0.00	0.00
153 Waldshut (red)	+100.00	+300.00
154 Walldürn	+20.00	+50.00
154 Walldürn (red)	+500.00	+2,000.
155 Weingarten	+50.00	+150.00
155 Weingarten (red)	+500.00	+2,000.
156 Weinheim	+5.00	+10.00
157 Wertheim	+5.00	+10.00
157 Wertheim (blue)	+100.00	+300.00
158 Wiesenbach	+500.00	+1,500.
158 Wiesenbach (red)	+1,500.	+6,000.
158 Wiesenbach (blue)	+1,200.	+3,500.
159 Wiesloch	+5.00	+10.00
159 Wiesloch (red)	+500.00	+2,500.
160 Wilferdingen	+100.00	+250.00
161 Wolfach	+10.00	+30.00
161 Wolfach (blue)	+400.00	+1,200.
162 Zell a.H.	+10.00	+40.00
162 Zell a.H. (blue)	+60.00	+150.00
163 Zell i.W.	+10.00	+20.00
163 Zell i.W. (red)	+300.00	+700.00
164 Bahnpost	+250.00	+3,000.
165 Rittersbach	+1,200.	+5,000.
165 Rittersbach (red)	+4,000.	+15,000.
166 Gondelsheim	+150.00	+400.00
167 Heidelsheim	+80.00	+400.00
167 Heidelsheim (red)	+600.00	+2,500.
168 Dertingen	+8,000.	+50,000.
169 Werbach	+600.00	+3,000.
170 Basel, Bad, Bahnhof	+1,200.	+4,750.
171 Badenweiler	+80.00	+200.00
171 Badenweiler (blue)	+1,200.	+4,000.
172 Weiterdingen	+2,000.	+10,000.
172 Weiterdingen (blue)	+4,000.	+15,000.
173 Steinbach	+120.00	+300.00

174 Mannheim Bhf.	+40.00	+150.00
175 Baden Bhf.	+50.00	+100.00
176 Bronnbach	+1,500.	+10,000.
177 Karlsruhe Stadtpost	+10.00	+40.00

Coat of Arms
A2   A3

1860-62   *Perf. 13½*

```
10 A2 1kr black                90.00   30.00
     No gum           32.50
     Never hinged     340.00
     On cover                         80.00
     On cover, single franking       110.00
12 A2 3kr ultra ('61)          90.00   24.00
     No gum           32.50
     Never hinged     250.00
     On cover                         60.00
 a.  3kr Prussian blue         300.00  80.00
     No gum           110.00
     Never hinged     825.00
     On cover                         200.00
 b.  3kr violet ultramarine    400.00  190.00
     No gum           160.00
     On cover                         475.00
13 A2 6kr red org ('61)        100.00  80.00
     No gum           40.00
     Never hinged     575.00
     On cover                         200.00
 a.  6kr yellow orange ('62)   200.00  90.00
     No gum           100.00
     Never hinged     750.00
     On cover                         225.00
14 A2 9kr rose ('61)           250.00  175.00
     No gum           95.00
     Never hinged     1,000.
     On cover                         475.00
     Nos. 10-14 (4)            530.00  309.00
```

Examples of Nos. 10-14 and 18 with all perforations intact sell for considerably more.

Values for pairs

```
10 A2 1kr black                160.00  55.00
     No gum           72.50
     On cover                         120.00
12 A2 3kr ultra                320.00  55.00
     No gum           120.00
     On cover                         145.00
 a.  3kr Prussian blue         1,200.  240.00
     No gum           320.00
     On cover                         400.00
 b.  3kr violet ultramarine    1,200.  575.00
     No gum           360.00
     On cover                         960.00
13 A2 6kr red org              320.00  175.00
     No gum           120.00
     On cover                         400.00
 a.  6kr yellow orange         520.00  240.00
     No gum           200.00
     On cover                         440.00
14 A2 9kr rose                 600.00  475.00
     No gum           240.00
     On cover                         875.00
```

Values for strips of 3

```
10 A2 1kr black                250.00  110.00
     No gum           110.00
     On cover                         160.00
12 A2 3kr ultra                475.00  120.00
     No gum           175.00
     On cover                         175.00
 a.  3kr Prussian blue         2,000.  640.00
     No gum           800.00
     On cover                         800.00
 b.  3kr violet ultramarine    1,200.
     On cover                         1,750.
13 A2 6kr red org              550.00  400.00
     No gum           200.00
     On cover                         720.00
 a.  6kr yellow orange         720.00  440.00
     No gum           275.00
     On cover                         720.00
14 A2 9kr rose                 960.00  1,100.
     No gum           400.00
     On cover                         1,600.
```

Values for blocks of 4

```
10 A2 1kr black                400.00  960.00
     No gum           160.00
12 A2 3kr ultra                600.00  800.00
     No gum           240.00
 a.  3kr Prussian blue         3,600.  2,400.
     No gum           960.00
 b.  3kr violet ultramarine     —
13 A2 6kr red org              800.00  1,750.
     No gum           320.00
 a.  6kr yellow orange         960.00  2,250.
     No gum           400.00
14 A2 9kr rose                 2,000.  2,800.
     No gum           800.00
```

1862   *Perf. 10*

```
15 A2 1kr black                65.00   85.00
     Never hinged     200.00
     On cover                         190.00
     On cover, single franking       360.00
 a.  1kr silver gray           7,000.  7,000.
     On cover                         17,000.
 b.  1kr gray black            800.00  875.00
     On cover                         2,000.
16 A2 6kr Prus bl ('62)        140.00  72.50
     Never hinged     500.00
     On cover                         150.00
 a.  6kr blue ('63)            160.00  100.00
     Never hinged     600.00
     On cover                         210.00
17 A2 9kr brown                90.00   72.50
     Never hinged     500.00
     On cover                         140.00
 a.  9kr dark brown            350.00  275.00
     Never hinged     1,200.
     On cover                         600.00
 b.  9kr bister                140.00  250.00
     Never hinged     700.00
```

```
     On cover                         340.00
```

Perf. 13½

```
18 A3 3kr rose                 2,500.  300.00
     No gum           800.00
     On cover                         675.00
```

Values for pairs

```
15 A2 1kr black                150.00  200.00
     No gum           47.50
     On cover                         300.00
 a.  1kr silver gray                   20,000.
 b.  1kr gray black                    2,000.
     On cover                         2,800.
16 A2 6kr Prus bl              320.00  260.00
     No gum           125.00
     On cover                         325.00
 a.  6kr blue                  360.00  300.00
     No gum           145.00
     On cover                         400.00
17 A2 9kr brown                300.00  200.00
     No gum           110.00
     On cover                         320.00
 a.  9kr dark brown            1,000.  800.00
     No gum           400.00
     On cover                         960.00
 b.  9kr bister                375.00  650.00
     No gum           160.00
     On cover                         720.00
18 A3 3kr rose                 6,000.  960.00
     No gum           2,000.
     On cover                         1,300.
```

Values for strips of 3

```
15 A2 1kr black                225.00  400.00
     No gum           80.00
     On cover                         550.00
 a.  1kr silver gray                   4,400.
 b.  1kr gray black                    5,600.
16 A2 6kr Prus bl              450.00  400.00
     No gum           160.00
     On cover                         675.00
 a.  6kr blue                  520.00  475.00
     No gum           200.00
     On cover                         800.00
17 A2 9kr brown                450.00  450.00
     No gum           160.00
     On cover                         800.00
 a.  9kr dark brown            1,500.  1,300.
     No gum           550.00
     On cover                         1,900.
 b.  9kr bister
     No gum           275.00
     On cover                         1,900.
18 A3 3kr rose                         1,500.
     On cover                         2,800.
```

Values for blocks of 4

```
15 A2 1kr black                300.00  1,450.
     No gum           110.00
 a.  1kr silver gray            —       —
 b.  1kr gray black             —       —
16 A2 6kr Prus bl              1,450.  1,450.
     No gum           240.00
 a.  6kr blue                  1,600.  1,600.
     No gum           300.00
17 A2 9kr brown                2,800.  3,200.
     No gum           400.00
 a.  9kr dark brown            3,200.  3,200.
     No gum           800.00
 b.  9kr bister                2,800.  3,200.
     No gum           275.00
18 A3 3kr rose                  —      2,400.
     strip of 4
```

1862-65   *Perf. 10*

```
19 A3 1kr black ('64)          47.50   15.00
     No gum           16.00
     Never hinged     120.00
     On cover                         32.50
     On cover, single franking       140.00
 a.  1kr silver gray           2,250.
     On cover                         4,000.
 b.  1kr gray black            440.00  300.00
     On cover                         560.00
20 A3 3kr rose                 62.50   4.00
     No gum           16.00
     Never hinged     150.00
     On cover                         8.00
 a.  Imperf.                   40,000. 40,000.
     On cover                         100,000.
22 A3 6kr ultra ('65)          11.00   27.50
     No gum           4.00
     Never hinged     30.00
     On cover                         60.00
 a.  6kr Prussian blue ('64)   575.00  70.00
     No gum           175.00
     Never hinged     2,000.
     On cover                         175.00
23 A3 9kr brn ('64)            16.00   30.00
     No gum           6.00
     Never hinged     35.00
     On cover                         72.50
 a.  9kr bister                375.00  90.00
     No gum           110.00
     Never hinged     800.00
     On cover                         175.00
 b.  Printed on both sides             6,500.
 c.  9kr dark brown            500.00  440.00
     No gum           175.00
     Never hinged     1,500.
     On cover                         1,400.
24 A3 18kr green               400.00  575.00
     No gum           125.00
     Never hinged     1,200.
     On cover                         2,400.
     On cover, single franking       2,900.
 a.  18kr dark green           1,400.  1,600.
     No gum           360.00
     Never hinged     4,000.
     On cover                         8,800.
25 A3 30kr deep orange         32.50   2,250.
     No gum           12.00
     Never hinged     72.50
     On cover                         7,200.
     On cover, single franking       19,000.
 a.  30kr yellow orange        140.00  2,400.
     No gum           52.50
     Never hinged     600.00
```

```
     On cover                         8,250.
     On cover, single franking       9,000.
```

Forged cancellations are known on No. 25.

Values for pairs

```
19 A3 1kr black                140.00  40.00
     On cover                         55.00
 a.  1kr silver gray           5,200.
     On cover                         6,400.
 b.  1kr gray black            800.00
     On cover                         1,200.
20 A3 3kr rose                 125.00  8.00
     On cover                         15.00
22 A3 6kr ultra                24.00   72.50
     On cover                         95.00
 a.  6kr Prussian blue         1,750.  175.00
     On cover                         360.00
23 A3 9kr brown                40.00   80.00
     On cover                         160.00
 a.  9kr bister                960.00  240.00
     On cover                         475.00
 c.  9kr dark brown            1,400.  1,100.
     On cover                         2,000.
24 A3 18kr green               1,600.  1,600.
     On cover                         6,400.
 a.  18kr dark green           4,000.  3,600.
     On cover                         21,000.
25 A3 30kr deep orange         80.00   5,200.
     On cover                         14,500.
 a.  30kr yellow orange        400.00  6,000.
     On cover                         22,500.
```

Values for strips of 3

```
19 A3 1kr black                200.00  72.50
     On cover                         90.00
 a.  1kr silver gray           8,000.
     On cover                         9,500.
 b.  1kr gray black            1,400.
     On cover                         2,000.
20 A3 3kr rose                 175.00  22.50
     On cover                         40.00
22 A3 6kr ultra                35.00   240.00
     On cover                         360.00
 a.  6kr Prussian blue         2,500.  675.00
     On cover                         1,200.
23 A3 9kr brown                60.00   225.00
     On cover                         400.00
 a.  9kr bister                        400.00
     On cover                         640.00
 c.  9kr dark brown            2,200.  1,800.
     On cover                         3,000.
24 A3 18kr green               4,400.
 a.  18kr dark green            —
25 A3 30kr deep orange         125.00  7,500.
 a.  30kr yellow orange        600.00
```

Values for blocks of 4

```
19 A3 1kr black                300.00  800.00
     Never hinged     640.00
20 A3 3kr rose                 260.00  800.00
     Never hinged     600.00
22 A3 6kr ultra                52.50   1,600.
     Never hinged     95.00
 a.  6kr Prussian blue         3,600.  2,000.
     Never hinged      —
23 A3 9kr brown                80.00   1,400.
     Never hinged     160.00
 c.  9kr dark brown            3,200.   —
     Never hinged     6,400.
24 A3 18kr green               4,400.   —
     Never hinged      —
25 A3 30kr deep orange         160.00   —
     Never hinged     325.00
 a.  30kr yellow orange        960.00   —
     Never hinged     2,800.
```

A4

1868

```
26 A4 1kr green                4.00    9.00
     Never hinged     9.50
     On cover                         16.00
     On wrapper, single franking     70.00
27 A4 3kr rose                 2.75    4.50
     Never hinged     5.25
     On cover                         8.00
28 A4 7kr dull blue            20.00   35.00
     Never hinged     47.50
     On cover                         100.00
 a.  7kr sky blue              42.50   100.00
     Never hinged     90.00
     On cover                         300.00
     On cover, single franking       700.00
     Nos. 26-28 (3)            26.75   48.50
```

Forged cancellations are known on No. 28a.

Values for pairs

```
26 A4 1kr green                9.50    20.00
     On cover                         32.50
27 A4 3kr rose                 4.75    9.50
     On cover                         20.00
28 A4 7kr dull blue            45.00   100.00
     On cover                         200.00
 a.  7kr sky blue              100.00  400.00
     On cover                         1,300.
```

Values for strips of 3

```
26 A4 1kr green                14.50   27.50
     On cover                         40.00
27 A4 3kr rose                 8.00    40.00
     On cover                         60.00
28 A4 7kr dull blue            65.00   325.00
     On cover                         475.00
 a.  7kr sky blue              160.00  1,200.
     On cover                         2,200.
```

Values for blocks of 4

```
26 A4 1kr green                17.50   400.00
     Never hinged     45.00
27 A4 3kr rose                 9.50    1,800.
     Never hinged     20.00
```

```
28 A4 7kr dull blue            90.00   3,000.
     Never hinged     200.00
 a.  7kr sky blue              225.00   —
     Never hinged      —
```

The postage stamps of Baden were superseded by those of the German Empire on Jan. 1, 1872, but Official stamps were used during the year 1905.

RURAL POSTAGE DUE STAMPS

RU1

1862   Unwmk.   *Perf. 10*
Thin Paper

```
LJ1 RU1 1kr blk, yellow        5.00    325.00
      Never hinged    8.00
      On cover                        575.00
 a.   Thick paper             140.00  600.00
      Never hinged    275.00
      On cover                        1,400.
LJ2 RU1 3kr blk, yellow        2.75    125.00
      Never hinged    5.50
      On cover                        240.00
 a.   Thick paper             120.00  400.00
      Never hinged    225.00
      On cover                        960.00
LJ3 RU1 12kr blk, yellow       35.00   13,500.
      Never hinged    72.50
      On cover                        32,500.
 a.   Half used as 6kr on cover       25,000.
 b.   Quarter used as 3kr on cover     —
      Nos. LJ1-LJ3 (3)        42.75   13,950.
```

On No. LJ3, "LAND-POST" is a straight line.
Paper of #LJ1a, LJ2a is darker yellow.
Forged cancellations abound on Nos. LJ1-LJ3.

Values for pairs

```
LJ1 RU1 1kr blk, yellow        11.00   800.00
      On cover                        960.00
 a.   Thick paper             300.00  1,400.
      On cover                        2,100.
LJ2 RU1 3kr blk, yellow        6.00    275.00
      On cover                        440.00
 a.   Thick paper             240.00  960.00
      On cover                        1,800.
LJ3 RU1 12kr blk, yellow       110.00  32,000.
      On cover                        60,000.
```

Values for strips of 3

```
LJ1 RU1 1kr blk, yellow        16.00   1,200.
      On cover                        1,600.
 a.   Thick paper             475.00  2,200.
      On cover                        3,000.
LJ2 RU1 3kr blk, yellow        9.50    475.00
      On cover                        525.00
 a.   Thick paper             400.00  1,600.
      On cover                        2,200.
LJ3 RU1 12kr blk, yellow       160.00
```

Values for blocks of 4

```
LJ1 RU1 1kr blk, yellow        24.00   2,000.
      Never hinged    40.00
 a.   Thick paper             640.00  3,200.
      Never hinged    1,300.
LJ2 RU1 3kr blk, yellow        12.00   1,600.
      Never hinged    24.00
 a.   Thick paper             525.00  2,800.
      Never hinged    1,100.
LJ3 RU1 12kr blk, yellow       210.00
      Never hinged    400.00
```

> *A used single of the 12kr stamp (Scott No. LJ3) tied to a small piece by a neat c.d.s., sold for the equivalent of U.S. $24,400 at a German auction in 2003.*

OFFICIAL STAMPS
See Germany Nos. OL16-OL21.

BAVARIA

LOCATION — In southern Germany
GOVT. — Kingdom
AREA — 30,562 sq. mi. (1920)
POP. — 7,150,146 (1919)
CAPITAL — Munich

Bavaria was a member of the German Confederation and became part of the German Empire in 1870. After World War I, it declared itself a republic.

It lost its postal autonomy on Mar. 31, 1920.

60 Kreuzer = 1 Gulden
100 Pfennig = 1 Mark (1874)

Values for unused stamps are for examples with original gum as defined in the catalogue introduction. Unused examples of the 1849-78 issues without gum sell for about 50-60% of the figures quoted.

A1   Broken Circle — A1a

Two plates used for No. 1:
Plate I: Rough impression, framelines around figure "1" broken or incomplete.
Plate II: Fine impression, framelines around "1" complete.

1849   Unwmk.   Typo.   Imperf.

No.	Type	Description	Unused	Used
1	A1	1kr black (I)	1,000.	2,250.
		Pen & postmark cancels		1,400.
		Pen cancel		1,400.
		On cover, postmark cancel		4,750.
		On cover, pen cancel		5,500.
		On cover, pen & postmark cancels		4,000.
		On printed matter, single franking		7,250.
		On printed matter, pair		13,000.
		Pair with gutter between	19,000.	90,000.
a.		1kr deep black (I)	2,800.	3,000.
		Pen cancel		1,900.
		Pen & postmark cancels		2,000.
		On cover, pen & postmark cancels		5,800.
b.		Tête bêche pair	125,000.	
c.		1kr black (II)	2,800.	2,600.
		Pen cancel		2,000.
		Pen & postmark cancels		1,600.
		On cover, pen & postmark cancels		4,800.
		On cover, pen cancel		6,500.
		On cover, postmark cancel		6,600.
		On printed matter, single franking		8,000.
d.		1kr deep black (II)	4,800.	4,000.
		On cover, pen & postmark cancels		8,000.

Full margins = 1mm.
There are dividing lines between stamps.

With Silk Thread

No.	Type	Description	Unused	Used
2	A1a	3kr blue	60.00	3.50
		On cover		12.00
		On printed matter, single franking		225.00
		Pair with gutter between	2,750.	12,000.
		On cover		26,000.
a.		3kr greenish blue	60.00	3.50
		On cover		12.00
b.		3kr deep blue	60.00	3.50
		On cover		12.00
3	A1a	6kr brown	7,000.	240.00
		Pen cancel		240.00
		Pen & postmark cancels		160.00
		On cover		500.00
		Pair with gutter between	—	30,000.

Full margins = 1mm.
There are dividing lines between stamps.

No. 1 exists with silk thread, from a single proof sheet, value about $4,000.

Values for pairs

No.	Type	Description	Unused	Used
1	A1	1kr black (I)	2,200.	5,200.
		Pen & postmark cancels		4,000.
		On cover		14,500.
a.		1kr deep black (I)	6,400.	8,000.
		Pen & postmark cancels		6,400.
		On cover		16,000.
c.		1kr black (II)		5,600.
d.		1kr deep black (II)		9,600.
2	A1a	3kr blue	140.00	16.00
		On cover		40.00
a.		3kr greenish blue	140.00	16.00
		On cover		40.00
b.		3kr deep blue	140.00	16.00
		On cover		40.00
3	A1a	6kr brown	20,000.	1,200.
		On cover		2,400.

Values for strips of 3

No.	Type	Description	Unused	Used
1	A1	1kr black (I)	3,600.	8,800.
		Pen & postmark cancels		7,200.
		On cover		20,800.
a.		1kr deep black (I)	8,800.	13,600.
		Pen & postmark cancels		10,400.
		On cover		22,400.
c.		1kr black (II)		10,400.
		On cover		20,800.
d.		1kr deep black (II)		14,400.
2	A1a	3kr blue	200.00	72.50
				140.00
a.		3kr greenish blue	200.00	72.50
				140.00
b.		3kr deep blue	225.00	82.50
				160.00
3	A1a	6kr brown		—

Values for blocks of 4

No.	Type	Description	Unused	Used
1	A1	1kr black (I)	4,800.	58,000.
a.		1kr deep black	—	
2	A1a	3kr blue	325.00	1,450.
a.		3kr greenish blue	325.00	1,450.
b.		3kr deep blue	325.00	1,450.
3	A1a	6kr brown	—	—

Complete circle — A2

1850-58   With Silk Thread

No.	Type	Description	Unused	Used
4	A2	1kr pink	95.00	22.50
		Never hinged	160.00	
		On cover		72.50
		On wrapper, single franking		160.00
		On cover, single franking, local delivery		300.00
		Pair with gutter between	2,500.	25,000.
		On cover		52,000.
a.		1kr lilac rose	400.00	50.00
		Never hinged	640.00	
		On cover		95.00
5	A2	6kr brown	50.00	6.50
		Never hinged	90.00	
		On cover		27.50
		Pair with gutter between	4,000.	16,000.
		On cover		36,000.
a.		Half used as 3kr on cover		16,000.
6	A2	9kr yellow green	70.00	16.00
		Never hinged	130.00	
		On cover		45.00
		Pair with gutter between	2,600.	16,000.
		On cover		48,000.
a.		9kr blue green ('53)	11,000.	150.00
		On cover		500.00
		Pair with gutter between	—	
b.		9kr pale blue green	6,500.	140.00
		On cover		21,750.
		Pair with gutter between	—	
		On cover		47,500.
7	A2	12kr red ('58)	150.00	140.00
		Never hinged	275.00	
		On cover		600.00
		On cover, single franking		700.00
		Pair with gutter between	4,000.	26,000.
8	A2	18kr yel ('54)	140.00	190.00
		Never hinged	325.00	
		On cover		960.00
		On cover, single franking		1,200.
		Pair with gutter between	2,500.	26,000.
		Nos. 4-8 (5)	505.00	375.00

Full margins = 1mm.
There are dividing lines between stamps.

Values for pairs

No.	Type	Description	Unused	Used
4	A2	1kr pink	240.00	125.00
		On cover		325.00
a.		1kr lilac rose	—	200.00
		On cover		400.00
5	A2	6kr brown	125.00	47.50
		On cover		80.00
6	A2	9kr yel grn	160.00	160.00
		On cover		300.00
a.		9kr blue green	—	800.00
		On cover		1,400.
b.		9kr pale blue green	—	275.00
		On cover		525.00
7	A2	12kr red	360.00	875.00
		On cover		1,400.
8	A2	18kr yellow	300.00	960.00
		On cover		1,600.

Values for strips of 3

No.	Type	Description	Unused	Used
4	A2	1kr pink	350.00	175.00
		On cover		425.00
a.		1kr lilac rose	—	250.00
		On cover		500.00
5	A2	6kr brown	175.00	475.00
		On cover		675.00
6	A2	9kr yel grn	300.00	350.00
		On cover		625.00
a.		9kr blue green	—	1,600.
		On cover		2,800.
b.		9kr pale blue green	—	550.00
		On cover		950.00
7	A2	12kr red	500.00	2,200.
		On cover		3,200.
8	A2	18kr yellow	475.00	2,200.
		On cover		2,400.

Values for blocks or strips of 4

No.	Type	Description	Unused	Used
4	A2	1kr pink	500.00	2,400.
a.		1kr lilac rose		3,200.
5	A2	6kr brown	275.00	2,800.
6	A2	9kr yel grn	400.00	3,200.
a.		9kr blue green		9,600.
b.		9kr pale blue green		7,200.
7	A2	12kr red	800.00	8,000.
8	A2	18kr yellow	875.00	6,000.

1862

No.	Type	Description	Unused	Used
9	A2	1kr yellow	80.00	20.00
		Never hinged	110.00	
		On cover		95.00
		On wrapper, single franking		190.00
		On cover, single franking, local delivery		410.00
		Pair with gutter between	3,000.	25,000.
10	A1a	3kr rose	140.00	4.00
		Never hinged	260.00	
		On cover		12.00
		On printed matter, single franking		225.00
		On wrapper, single franking		300.00
a.		3kr carmine	52.50	6.00
		Never hinged	95.00	
		On cover		14.50
		Pair with gutter between	2,400.	13,000.
		On cover		30,000.
11	A2	6kr blue	70.00	12.00
		Never hinged	110.00	
		On cover		15.00
		Pair with gutter between	2,400.	16,000.
		On cover		48,000.
a.		6kr ultra	2,400.	9,000.
b.		Half used as 3kr on cover		10,000.
12	A2	9kr bister	110.00	16.00
		Never hinged	200.00	
		On cover		55.00
		Pair with gutter between	3,000.	21,000.
13	A2	12kr yel grn	95.00	70.00
		Never hinged	175.00	
		On cover		260.00
		On cover, single franking		400.00
		Pair with gutter between	3,000.	
a.		Half used as 6kr on cover		32,000.
14	A2	18kr ver red	900.00	140.00
		Never hinged	1,650.	
		On cover		1,200.
		On cover, single franking		2,400.
a.		18kr pale red	190.00	450.00
		On cover		2,000.
		On cover, single franking		4,800.
		Pair with gutter between	3,000.	
		Nos. 9-14 (6)	1,395.	262.00

Full margins = 1mm.
There are dividing lines between stamps.

No. 11a was not put in use.

Values for pairs

No.	Type	Description	Unused	Used
9	A2	1kr yellow	200.00	110.00
		On cover		325.00
10	A1a	3kr rose	640.00	16.00
		On cover		35.00
a.		3kr carmine	125.00	24.00
		On cover		40.00
11	A2	6kr blue	160.00	160.00
		On cover		360.00
12	A2	9kr bister	260.00	160.00
		On cover		360.00
13	A2	12kr yel grn	210.00	400.00
		On cover		875.00
14	A2	18kr ver red	2,800.	600.00
		On cover		2,000.
a.		18kr pale red	475.00	1,400.
		On cover		3,600.

Values for strips of 3

No.	Type	Description	Unused	Used
9	A2	1kr yellow	300.00	200.00
		On cover		525.00
10	A1a	3kr rose	960.00	47.50
		On cover		80.00
a.		3kr carmine	175.00	55.00
		On cover		90.00
11	A2	6kr blue	550.00	400.00
		On cover		675.00
12	A2	9kr bister	400.00	800.00
		On cover		1,400.
13	A2	12kr yel grn	325.00	960.00
		On cover		1,750.
14	A2	18kr ver red		2,400.
		On cover		4,000.
a.		18kr pale red	725.00	

Values for blocks or strips of 4

No.	Type	Description	Unused	Used
9	A2	1kr yellow	400.00	2,400.
10	A1a	3kr rose	1,200.	960.00
a.		3kr carmine	240.00	1,400.
11	A2	6kr blue	400.00	2,000.
12	A2	9kr bister	525.00	8,000.
13	A2	12kr yel grn	440.00	—
14	A2	18kr ver red	—	6,000.
a.		18kr pale red	875.00	

Coat of Arms — A3

1867-68   Embossed

No.	Type	Description	Unused	Used
15	A3	1kr yel grn	65.00	12.00
		Never hinged	100.00	
		On cover		40.00
		On wrapper, single franking		125.00
		On cover, single franking, local delivery		200.00
		Pair with gutter between	2,600.	13,000.
a.		1kr dark blue green	300.00	52.50
		Never hinged	525.00	
		On cover		175.00
		Pair with gutter between		14,000.
16	A3	3kr rose	70.00	2.40
		Never hinged	110.00	
		On cover		8.00
		Pair with gutter between	3,000.	12,000.
a.		Printed on both sides		200.00
17	A3	6kr ultra	45.00	19.00
		Never hinged	72.50	
		On cover		125.00
		Pair with gutter between		1,600.
a.		Half used as 3kr on cover		75,000.
18	A3	6kr bis ('68)	80.00	50.00
		Never hinged	140.00	
		On cover		300.00
		On cover, single franking		4,000.
		Pair with gutter between		3,400.
a.		Half used as 3kr on cover		32,000.
19	A3	7kr ultra ('68)	400.00	16.00
		Never hinged	800.00	
		On cover		60.00
		Pair with gutter between		8,000.
a.		7kr Prus bl ('69)	3,300.	800.00
		On cover		2,400.
b.		7kr royal bl ('69)	2,000.	525.00
		Never hinged	2,400.	
		On cover		1,400.
20	A3	9kr bister	45.00	35.00
		Never hinged	72.50	
		On cover		175.00
		Pair with gutter between		1,900.
21	A3	12kr lilac	350.00	95.00
		Never hinged	960.00	
		Pair with gutter between	8,000.	
		On cover		450.00
22	A3	18kr red	140.00	175.00
		Never hinged	240.00	
		On cover		2,600.
		On cover, single franking		3,600.
		Pair with gutter between	2,400.	
		Nos. 15-22 (8)	1,195.	404.40

Full margins = 1 ¼mm.

The paper of the 1867-68 issues often shows ribbed or laid lines.

Values for pairs

No.	Type	Description	Unused	Used
15	A3	1kr yellow green	140.00	32.50
		On cover		160.00
a.		1kr dk blue green	640.00	160.00
		On cover		340.00
16	A3	3kr rose	140.00	14.50
		On cover		47.50
17	A3	6kr ultra	95.00	160.00
		On cover		360.00
18	A3	6kr bister	175.00	300.00
		On cover		640.00
19	A3	7kr ultra	1,200.	240.00
		On cover		360.00
a.		7kr Prussian blue		2,700.
b.		7kr royal blue		1,800.
		On cover		2,200.
20	A3	9kr bister	95.00	275.00
		On cover		600.00
21	A3	12kr lilac	800.00	525.00
		On cover		960.00
22	A3	18kr red	290.00	960.00
		On cover		4,000.

Values for strips of 3

No.	Type	Description	Unused	Used
15	A3	1kr yellow green	225.00	55.00
		On cover		125.00
a.		1kr dk blue green	960.00	250.00
		On cover		440.00
16	A3	3kr rose	225.00	80.00
		On cover		160.00
17	A3	6kr ultra	175.00	725.00
		On cover		1,200.
18	A3	6kr bister	275.00	960.00
		On cover		1,600.
19	A3	7kr ultra	2,000.	800.00
		On cover		1,450.
20	A3	9kr bister	175.00	1,200.
		On cover		2,000.
21	A3	12kr lilac	1,450.	1,750.
		On cover		3,200.
22	A3	18kr red	450.00	2,400.
		On cover		6,000.

Values for blocks of 4

No.	Type	Description	Unused	Used
15	A3	1kr yellow green	400.00	1,600.
16	A3	3kr rose	600.00	800.00
				2,000.
17	A3	6kr ultra	250.00	3,600.
18	A3	6kr bister	400.00	4,500.
19	A3	7kr ultra	3,400.	2,400.
20	A3	9kr bister	250.00	
21	A3	12kr lilac	4,800.	5,600.
22	A3	18kr red	640.00	

1870-72   Wmk. 92   Perf. 11½
Without Silk Thread

No.	Type	Description	Unused	Used
23	A3	1kr green	12.00	1.60
		Never hinged	22.00	
		On cover		8.00
		Pair with gutter between	325.00	
		Never hinged	475.00	
b.		Unwmk.	240.00	95.00
		Never hinged	440.00	
c.		1kr deep yellow green	32.50	4.75
		Never hinged	55.00	
		On cover		16.00
		Pair with gutter between	400.00	
		Never hinged	640.00	
24	A3	3kr rose	24.00	1.60
		Never hinged	45.00	
		On cover		6.40
		Pair with gutter between	300.00	
		Never hinged	440.00	
b.		Unwmk.	150.00	65.00
		Never hinged	200.00	
25	A3	6kr bister	30.00	30.00
		Never hinged	65.00	
		On cover		125.00
		On cover, single franking		1,350.
		Pair with gutter between	600.00	
		Never hinged	960.00	
b.		Unwmk.	160.00	125.00
		Never hinged	275.00	
26	A3	7kr ultra	3.50	4.50
		Never hinged	7.25	
		On cover		24.00
		Pair with gutter between	325.00	
		Never hinged	560.00	
a.		7kr Prussian blue	20.00	14.00
		Never hinged	34.00	
		On cover		50.00
c.		7kr dk ultra	640.00	175.00
		On cover		725.00
d.		7kr ultra, unwmk.	160.00	125.00
		Never hinged	275.00	
27	A3	9kr pale brn ('72)	5.50	4.00
		Never hinged	11.50	
		On cover		175.00
		On parcel post receipt card, single franking		350.00
		Pair with gutter between	525.00	
		Never hinged	875.00	
28	A3	10kr yellow	6.50	15.00
		Never hinged	13.00	
		On cover		150.00
		On parcel post receipt card, single franking		325.00
		On parcel post receipt card, two singles		325.00
		On cover, two singles		440.00
		Pair with gutter between	440.00	
		Never hinged	575.00	
b.		10kr yellowish orange	15.00	42.50
		Never hinged	30.00	
		On cover		250.00

			On parcel post receipt card, single franking		350.00
			On parcel post receipt card, two singles		400.00
			On cover, two singles		625.00
			Pair with gutter between	525.00	
			Never hinged	800.00	
29	A3	12kr lilac		1,200.	4,800.
			Never hinged	2,000.	
			Pair with gutter between	7,200.	
			Never hinged	9,000.	
30	A3	18kr dull brick red		16.00	16.00
			Never hinged	32.00	
			On cover		875.00
			On parcel post receipt card		
			Pair with gutter between	560.00	
			Never hinged	800.00	
b.		18kr dark brick red		120.00	70.00
			Never hinged	325.00	
			On cover		—
			On parcel post receipt card		1,100.

The paper of the 1870-75 issues frequently appears to be laid with the lines either close or wide apart.
See Nos. 33-37.
Reprints exist.

Values for blocks of 4

23	A3	1kr green	65.00	275.00
		Never hinged	130.00	
b.		1kr deep yellow green	190.00	400.00
		Never hinged	360.00	
24	A3	3kr rose	140.00	200.00
		Never hinged	260.00	
25	A3	6kr bister	175.00	875.00
		Never hinged	300.00	
26	A3	7kr ultra	20.00	640.00
		Never hinged	35.00	
a.		7kr Prussian blue	125.00	7,000.
		Never hinged	240.00	
27	A3	9kr pale brown	50.00	600.00
		Never hinged	80.00	
28	A3	10kr yellow	32.50	800.00
		Never hinged	60.00	
b.		10kr yellowish orange	110.00	
		Never hinged	200.00	
29	A3	12kr	6,000.	25,000.
		Never hinged		
30	A3	18kr dull brick red	65.00	475.00
		Never hinged	125.00	
b.		18kr dark brick red	675.00	

Imperf

23d	A3	1kr		1,600.
24c	A3	3kr	1,600.	1,600.
25c	A3	6kr		2,400.
26e	A3	7kr		2,400.
30d	A3	18kr		2,400.

Wmk. 93

23a	A3	1kr green	100.00	9.50
		Never hinged	190.00	
		On cover		27.50
e.		1kr deep yellow green	160.00	35.00
		Never hinged	290.00	
		On cover		80.00
24a	A3	3kr rose	95.00	2.40
		Never hinged	160.00	
		On cover		12.00
25a	A3	6kr bister	175.00	70.00
		Never hinged	325.00	
		On cover		260.00
		On cover, single franking		1,750.
26b	A3	7kr ultra	140.00	35.00
		Never hinged	260.00	
		On cover		125.00
g.		7kr dk ultra		300.00
		On cover		1,200.
27a	A3	9kr pale brown	290.00	475.00
		Never hinged	525.00	
		On parcel post receipt card		1,100.
		On cover, single franking		2,200.
28a	A3	10kr yellow	240.00	360.00
		Never hinged	440.00	
		On parcel post receipt card		875.00
		On cover, single franking		1,400.
		On parcel post receipt card, two singles		1,400.
		On cover, two singles		2,000.
c.		10kr yellowish orange	325.00	400.00
		Never hinged	600.00	
		On parcel post receipt card		900.00
		On cover, single franking		1,300.
		On parcel post receipt card, two singles		1,600.
29a	A3	12kr lilac	360.00	1,125.
		Never hinged	640.00	
		On cover		3,600.
		On cover, single franking		7,200.
		Pair with gutter between		
30a	A3	18kr dull brick red	300.00	190.00
		Never hinged	625.00	
		On cover		—
		On parcel post receipt card		1,250.
c.		18kr dark brick red	400.00	225.00
		Never hinged	675.00	
		On cover		—
		On parcel post receipt card		1,400.

Values for blocks of 4

23a	A3	1kr green	640.00	475.00
e.		1kr deep yellow green		1,200.
24a	A3	3kr rose	560.00	450.00
25a	A3	6kr bister	1,000.	
26b	A3	7kr ultra	950.00	
27a	A3	9kr pale brown	2,200.	
28a	A3	10kr yellow	1,450.	
c.		10kr yelsh org	2,800.	
29a	A3	12kr lilac, wmk. 92	1,750.	26,000.
30c	A3	18kr dull brick red	1,900.	

Imperf

23f	A3	1kr		1,800.
24d	A3	3kr		1,800.
26f	A3	7kr		2,800.
30e	A3	18kr		2,800.

A4

1874-75   Wmk. 92   *Imperf.*

31	A4	1m violet	675.00	85.00
		Never hinged	1,000.	
		On cover, single franking		7,250.
		On parcel post receipt card		1,400.
a.		1m deep violet	2,000.	200.00
		Never hinged	3,200.	
		On cover		8,750.
		On parcel post receipt card		1,750.

Perf. 11½

32	A4	1m violet ('75)	200.00	55.00
		Never hinged	350.00	
		On cover, single franking		2,850.
		On parcel post receipt card		950.00
a.		1m deep violet	475.00	125.00
		Never hinged	800.00	
		On cover, single franking		3,200.
		On parcel post receipt card		1,600.

Values for blocks of 4

31	A4	1m violet	8,000.	1,400.
31a		1m deep violet	8,750.	1,800.
32	A4	1m violet	1,600.	950.00
32a		1m deep violet	2,800.	

See Nos. 46-47, 54-57, 73-76.

1875   Wmk. 94

33	A3	1kr green	.80	24.00
		Never hinged	1.60	
		On cover		125.00
		Pair with gutter between	12.00	
		Never hinged	22.50	
34	A3	3kr rose	.80	8.00
		Never hinged	1.50	
		On cover		40.00
		Pair with gutter between	9.50	
		Never hinged	17.50	
35	A3	7kr ultra	5.25	275.00
		Never hinged	10.00	
		On cover		1,400.
		Pair with gutter between	95.00	
		Never hinged	175.00	
36	A3	10kr yellow	30.00	250.00
		Never hinged	70.00	
		On cover		1,600.
		Two singles on cover		3,250.
		Pair with gutter between	475.00	
		Never hinged	800.00	
37	A3	18kr red	24.00	60.00
		Never hinged	47.50	
		On cover		27,500.
		On parcel post receipt card		22,000.
		Pair with gutter between	325.00	
		Never hinged	600.00	
		Nos. 33-37 (5)	60.85	617.00

Values for blocks of 4

33	A3	1kr green	3.50	1,300.
		Never hinged	7.25	
34	A3	3kr rose	4.00	400.00
		Never hinged	7.25	
35	A3	7kr ultra	27.50	4,800.
		Never hinged	52.50	
36	A3	10kr yel	200.00	4,800.
		Never hinged	400.00	
37	A3	18kr red	160.00	2,600.
		Never hinged	300.00	

False cancellations exist on Nos. 29, 29a, 33-37.

A5

1876-78   Embossed   *Perf. 11½*

38	A5	3pf lt grn	35.00	1.60
		Never hinged	90.00	
		On cover		16.00
a.		3pf lt yel grn	80.00	24.00
		Never hinged	175.00	
		On cover		60.00
39	A5	5pf dk grn	90.00	16.00
		Never hinged	225.00	
		On cover		40.00
		On cover, single franking		100.00
a.		5pf dk bluish grn	325.00	20.00
		Never hinged	1,200.	
		On cover		55.00
40	A5	5pf lilac ('78)	160.00	20.00
		Never hinged	375.00	
		On cover		95.00
a.		5pf lt reddish vio	275.00	52.50
		Never hinged	560.00	
		On cover		140.00
41	A5	10pf rose	190.00	1.25
		Never hinged	640.00	
		On cover		9.50
a.		10pf dk magenta	360.00	160.00
		Never hinged	875.00	
		On cover		325.00
42	A5	20pf ultra	190.00	3.25
		Never hinged	600.00	
		On cover		25.00
		On postcard, single franking		160.00
a.		20pf gray blue	450.00	80.00
		Never hinged	950.00	
		On cover		120.00
43	A5	25pf yel brn	175.00	6.50
		Never hinged	450.00	
		On cover		725.00
		On postcard, single franking		725.00
		On cover, single franking		750.00
44	A5	50pf scarlet	55.00	7.25
		Never hinged	125.00	
		On cover		1,500.
		On parcel post receipt card		1,100.
45	A5	50pf brn ('78)	800.00	27.50
		Never hinged	2,000.	
		On cover		1,500.
		On parcel post receipt card		700.00

46	A4	1m violet	1,900.	90.00
		Never hinged	3,600.	
		On cover		3,500.
		On parcel post receipt card		675.00
47	A4	2m orange	24.00	12.00
		Never hinged	52.50	
		On cover		2,200.
		On parcel post receipt card		275.00

The paper of the 1876-78 issue often shows ribbed lines.
See Nos. 48-53, 58-72. For overprints and surcharge see Nos. 237, O1-O5.

Values for blocks of 4

38	A5	3pf green	160.00	125.00
		Never hinged	325.00	
		On cover		325.00
a.		3pf lt yel grn	360.00	
		Never hinged	800.00	
39	A5	5pf dk green	360.00	160.00
		Never hinged	1,000.	
		On cover		1,200.
a.		5pf dk bluish green	1,400.	200.00
		On cover		1,200.
40	A5	5pf lilac	800.00	600.00
		Never hinged	1,900.	
		On cover		2,000.
a.		5pf lt reddish violet	1,400.	800.00
		Never hinged	2,800.	
		On cover		2,800.
41	A5	10pf rose	800.00	200.00
		On cover		1,200.
42	A5	20pf ultramarine		160.00
a.		20pf gray blue		600.00
43	A5	25pf yel brn		325.00
44	A5	50pf scarlet	275.00	525.00
			550.00	
45	A5	50pf brown		6,000.
46	A4	1m violet	9,600.	6,000.
47	A4	2m orange	125.00	60.00
		Never hinged	275.00	

1881-1911   Wmk. 95v   *Perf. 11½*

48	A5	3pf green	12.00	.80
		Never hinged	28.00	
		On cover		12.00
49	A5	5pf lilac	17.50	1.25
		Never hinged	35.00	
		On cover		16.00
50	A5	10pf carmine	12.50	.65
		Never hinged	27.50	
		On cover		4.00
b.		10pf magenta	24.00	4.00
		Never hinged	60.00	
		On cover		25.00
51	A5	20pf ultramarine	14.00	.80
		Never hinged	30.00	
		On cover		9.50
52	A5	25pf yellow brown	125.00	3.50
		Never hinged	240.00	
		On cover		400.00
		On postal card, single franking		500.00
		On cover, single franking, local delivery		740.00
		On parcel post receipt card		290.00
53	A5	50pf deep brown	145.00	3.25
		Never hinged	275.00	
		On cover		300.00
		Two singles on cover		775.00
		On parcel post receipt card		275.00
		On cover, single franking		500.00
54	A4	1m rose lil ('00)	225.00	1.40
		Never hinged	500.00	
		On cover		350.00
		On parcel post receipt card		70.00
		Two singles on parcel post receipt card		425.00
a.		1m brownish lilac, toned paper	62.50	3.00
		Never hinged	140.00	
		On cover		350.00
		On cover, single franking		1,100.
		On parcel post receipt card		140.00
b.		1m brownish pur, toned paper	1,100.	110.00
		Never hinged	2,500.	
		On cover		1,400.
		On cover, single franking		2,500.
		On parcel post receipt card		875.00
c.		1m brownish lilac, white paper	45.00	50.00
		Never hinged	87.50	
		On cover		600.00
		On cover, single franking		175.00
		On parcel post receipt card		175.00
55	A4	2m orange ('01)	5.50	8.00
		Never hinged	13.00	
		On cover		875.00
		On cover, single franking		1,400.
		Two singles on cover		2,300.
		On parcel post receipt card		175.00
a.		Toned paper ('90)	90.00	14.00
		Never hinged	190.00	
		On cover		1,300.
		On cover, single franking		1,800.
		Two singles on cover		2,900.
		On parcel post receipt card		325.00
56	A4	3m olive gray ('00)	24.00	30.00
		Never hinged	47.50	
		On cover		2,200.
		On cover, single franking		2,200.
		On parcel post receipt card		600.00
a.		White paper ('06)	175.00	400.00
		Never hinged	300.00	
		On cover		2,900.
		On cover, single franking		3,600.
		On parcel post receipt card		1,300.
b.		Yellowish translucent paper ('11)	110.00	550.00
		Never hinged	175.00	
		On cover		2,200.
		On cover, single franking		2,500.
		On parcel post receipt card		875.00
57	A4	5m yellow green ('00)	24.00	30.00
		Never hinged	47.50	
		On cover		2,200.
		On cover, single franking		2,200.
		On parcel post receipt card		800.00
a.		White paper ('06)	150.00	350.00
		Never hinged	275.00	
		On cover		2,900.
		On cover, single franking		3,600.
		On parcel post receipt card		1,400.
b.		Yellowish translucent paper ('11)	80.00	150.00

		Never hinged	125.00	
		On cover, single franking		2,200.
		On cover, single franking		2,500.
		On parcel post receipt card		950.00
		Nos. 48-57 (10)	604.50	79.65

Nos. 54-55 are on white paper. Nos. 56-57 are on toned paper. A 2m lilac was not regularly issued.

Values for blocks of 4

48	A5	3pf green	72.50	60.00
		Never hinged	150.00	
		On cover		125.00
49	A5	5pf lilac	87.50	40.00
		Never hinged	175.00	
		On cover		125.00
50	A5	10pf carmine	60.00	40.00
		Never hinged	140.00	
		On cover		60.00
b.		10pf magenta	160.00	60.00
		Never hinged	400.00	
51	A5	20pf ultramarine	70.00	55.00
		Never hinged	140.00	
52	A5	25pf yellow brown	600.00	95.00
		Never hinged	1,200.	
53	A5	50pf deep brown	640.00	125.00
		Never hinged	1,300.	
54	A4	1m rose	22.50	40.00
		Never hinged	47.50	
a.		1m brownish lilac, toned paper	325.00	80.00
		Never hinged	800.00	
e.		1m brownish lilac, white paper	250.00	—
		Never hinged	550.00	
55	A4	2m orange	18.00	37.50
		Never hinged	35.00	
a.		Toned paper	475.00	80.00
		Never hinged	1,000.	

Imperf.

48a	A5	3pf	400.00	2,000.
		Never hinged	800.00	
49a	A5	5pf	2,000.	
		Never hinged	3,200.	
50a	A5	10pf	400.00	2,000.
		Never hinged	800.00	
		On cover		2,500.
51a	A5	20pf	1,600.	
		Never hinged	3,600.	
52a	A5	25pf	1,600.	
		Never hinged	3,600.	
53a	A5	50pf	1,600.	
		Never hinged	3,600.	
54d	A4	1m rose	140.00	
		Never hinged	275.00	
e.		As "a."	4,000.	
		Never hinged	6,400.	
55b	A4	2m org	75.00	
		Never hinged	150.00	
56c	A4	3m As "a."	300.00	
		Never hinged	600.00	
57c	A4	5m As "a."	300.00	
		Never hinged	600.00	

1888-1900   Wmk. 95h   *Perf. 14½*
 White Paper

58	A5	2pf gray ('00)	2.40	.55
		Never hinged	5.50	
		On cover		7.25
60	A5	3pf brown ('00)	.30	.65
		Never hinged	.80	
		On cover		2.40
b.		3pf black brown	9.75	8.00
		Never hinged	25.00	
		On cover		25.00
62	A5	5pf dk grn ('00)	.30	.65
		Never hinged	.80	
		On cover		2.00
63	A5	10pf carmine	.40	.80
		Never hinged	.80	
		On cover		2.00
64	A5	20pf ultra	.40	.80
		Never hinged	.80	
		On cover		3.25
		On postal card, single franking		28.00
b.		20pf grayish blue	.65	1.60
		Never hinged	1.25	
		On cover		8.00
66	A5	25pf orange ('00)	.60	1.10
		Never hinged	.95	
		On cover		22.50
		On cover, single franking		67.50
67	A5	30pf ol grn ('00)	.80	1.40
		Never hinged	2.00	
		On cover		24.00
		On postal card, single franking		75.00
68	A5	40pf yellow ('00)	.80	1.10
		Never hinged	2.00	
		On cover		35.00
70	A5	50pf maroon ('00)	.50	1.60
		Never hinged	.95	
		On cover		35.00
		On cover, single franking		47.50
		On parcel post receipt card		20.00
71	A5	80pf lilac ('00)	3.25	4.00
		Never hinged	7.25	
		On cover		175.00
		On cover, single franking		275.00
		On parcel post receipt card		55.00
		Nos. 58-71 (10)	9.75	12.65

Nos. 59, 61, 65, 69 and 70 are on toned paper; Nos. 67-68 on white.

Values for blocks of 4

58	A5	2pf gray	65.00	80.00
		Never hinged	175.00	
		On cover		125.00
63	A5	10pf carmine	2.00	3.25
		Never hinged	3.50	
		On cover		9.50
64	A5	20pf ultra	2.00	6.50
		Never hinged	3.50	
		On cover		9.50
b.		20pf grayish blue	3.50	16.00
		Never hinged	8.00	

	On cover			32.50

Imperf

58b	A5	2pf	72.50	
	Never hinged		175.00	
60c	A5	3pf	72.50	
	Never hinged		160.00	
62b	A5	5pf	75.00	
	Never hinged		160.00	
63c	A5	10pf	72.50	
	Never hinged		100.00	
64c	A5	20pf	75.00	
	Never hinged		160.00	
66b	A5	25pf	75.00	
	Never hinged		200.00	
70b	A5	50pf	130.00	
	Never hinged		260.00	

1888-99   Toned Paper

58a	A5	2pf gray ('99)	12.00	5.25
	Never hinged		35.00	
	On cover			16.00
59	A5	3pf green	9.25	2.10
	Never hinged		35.00	
	On cover			12.00
60a	A5	3pf dk ocher brn ('90)	9.25	.40
	Never hinged		23.00	
	On cover			3.25
d.	3pf yel brn		26.00	6.75
	Never hinged		65.00	
	On cover			13.50
61	A5	5pf lilac	24.00	5.50
	Never hinged		67.50	
	On cover			20.00
a.	5pf brownish violet		20.00	7.50
	Never hinged			
	On cover			30.00
62a	A5	5pf dk green ('90)	10.00	.65
	Never hinged		25.00	
	On cover			3.25
d.	Imperf		600.00	1,200.
	On cover			3,200.
63a	A5	10pf car red	6.75	.80
	Never hinged		17.50	
	On cover			3.25
b.	Imperf.		72.50	175.00
	Never hinged		225.00	
	On cover			525.00
d.	10pf lilac red		20.00	8.00
	Never hinged		60.00	
	On cover			20.00
64a	A5	20pf ultra	10.00	1.25
	Never hinged		30.00	
	On cover			5.50
d.	20pf grayish blue		14.00	4.00
	Never hinged		40.00	
	On cover			12.00
65	A5	25pf yel brn	32.50	6.75
	Never hinged		90.00	
	On cover			190.00
	On cover, single franking			250.00
	On parcel post receipt card			90.00
66a	A5	25pf org ('90)	16.50	1.60
	Never hinged		55.00	
	On cover			22.50
69	A5	50pf dp brn	60.00	6.75
	Never hinged		160.00	
	On cover			160.00
	On cover, single franking			190.00
	On parcel post receipt card			82.50
70a	A5	50pf mar ('90)	47.50	2.40
	Never hinged		95.00	
	On cover			65.00
	On parcel post receipt card			24.00
71a	A5	80pf lilac ('99)	32.50	12.00
	Never hinged		95.00	
	On cover			275.00
	On cover, single franking			375.00
	On parcel post receipt card			80.00

Values for blocks of 4

58a	A5	2pf gray	55.00	70.00
	On cover			110.00
59	A5	3pf green	50.00	15.00
	Never hinged		150.00	
60a	A5	3pf dk ocher brn ('90)	70.00	7.00
	Never hinged		150.00	
	On cover			21.00
d.	3pf yel brn		160.00	62.50
	Never hinged		375.00	
61	A5	5pf lilac	125.00	37.50
	Never hinged		325.00	
	On cover			125.00
a.	5pf brownish violet		125.00	95.00
	Never hinged		325.00	
	On cover			190.00
62a	A5	5pf dk green	80.00	8.00
	Never hinged		175.00	
	On cover			24.00
63a	A5	10pf car red	30.00	8.00
	Never hinged		90.00	
	On cover			16.00
d.	10pf lilac red		125.00	95.00
	Never hinged		325.00	
	On cover			200.00
64a	A5	20pf ultra	55.00	20.00
	Never hinged		160.00	
	On cover			60.00
d.	20pf grayish blue		80.00	47.50
	Never hinged		240.00	
	On cover			95.00
65	A5	25pf yel brn	160.00	47.50
	Never hinged		440.00	
66a	A5	25pf org ('90)	95.00	15.00
	Never hinged		300.00	
	On cover			77.50
69	A5	50pf dp brn	275.00	60.00
	Never hinged		800.00	
70a	A5	50pf mar ('90)	275.00	35.00
	Never hinged		540.00	
	On parcel post receipt card			130.00
71a	A5	80pf lilac	175.00	125.00
	Never hinged		450.00	

1911, Jan. 23   Wmk. 95v

72	A5	5pf dark green	.65	13.50
	Never hinged		1.50	
	On cover			20.00
	On registered cover			60.00
	On first day cover			40.00

1911, Jan.   Wmk. 95h   Perf. 11½

73	A4	1m rose lilac	4.00	27.50
	Never hinged		7.00	
	On cover			350.00
	On parcel post receipt card			425.00

74	A4	2m orange	17.00	37.50
	Never hinged		20.00	
	On cover			1,400.
	On parcel post receipt card			875.00
75	A4	3m olive gray	17.00	57.50
	Never hinged		22.00	
	On cover			2,900.
	On parcel post receipt card			1,300.
76	A4	5m pale yel grn	17.00	57.50
	Never hinged		22.00	
	On cover			2,900.
	On parcel post receipt card			1,300.
	Nos. 73-76 (4)		55.00	180.00

See note after No. 91 concerning used values.

Values for canceled to order and on philatelic covers

73	A4	1m rose lilac		92.50
	On overfranked cover			65.00
74	A4	2m orange		14.00
	On overfranked cover			82.50
75	A4	3m olive gray		22.00
	On overfranked cover			140.00
76	A4	5m pale yellow green		22.00
	On overfranked cover			210.00

See note after No. 91 concerning used values.

A6

A7

A8

Prince Regent Luitpold
Perf. 14x14½

1911   Wmk. 95h   Litho.

77	A6	3pf brn, *gray brn*	.30	.30
	Never hinged		1.25	
	On cover			1.25
a.	"911" for "1911"		325.00	325.00
	Never hinged		525.00	
78	A6	5pf dk grn, *grn*	.30	.30
	Never hinged		1.25	
	On cover			1.25
a.	Tête bêche pair		4.50	10.50
b.	Booklet pane of 4 + 2 labels		100.00	150.00
c.	Bklt. pane of 5 + label		225.00	375.00
d.	Bklt. pane of 6		35.00	
79	A6	10pf scar, *buff*	.30	.30
	Never hinged		.80	
	On cover			1.25
a.	Tête bêche pair		5.75	62.50
b.	"911" for "1911"		15.00	15.00
	Never hinged		25.00	
d.	Booklet pane of 5 + label		65.00	30.00
80	A6	20pf dp bl, *bl*	2.00	.75
	Never hinged		9.00	
	On cover			3.75
81	A6	25pf vio brn, *buff*	3.25	1.25
	On cover			14.00
	Never hinged		12.00	

Perf. 11½
Wmk. 95v

82	A7	30pf org buff, *buff*	2.25	1.25
	Never hinged		7.50	
	On cover			14.00
83	A7	40pf ol grn, *buff*	4.00	1.25
	Never hinged		13.50	
	On cover			14.00
84	A7	50pf cl, *gray brn*	3.25	3.25
	Never hinged		11.00	
	On cover			25.00
84A	A7	60pf dk grn, *buff*	3.25	3.25
	Never hinged		11.00	
	On cover			27.50
85	A7	80pf vio, *gray brn*	9.00	11.00
	Never hinged		29.00	
	On cover			80.00
86	A8	1m brn, *gray brn*	3.25	4.00
	Never hinged		11.00	
	On parcel post receipt card			27.50
87	A8	2m dk grn, *grn*	4.75	12.00
	Never hinged		14.00	
	On parcel post receipt card			40.00
88	A8	3m lake, *buff*	13.00	65.00
	Never hinged		28.00	
	On parcel post receipt card			160.00
89	A8	5m dk bl, *buff*	13.00	45.00
	Never hinged		32.50	
	On parcel post receipt card			300.00
90	A8	10m org, *yel*	22.50	65.00
	Never hinged		47.50	
	On parcel post receipt card			400.00
91	A8	20m blk brn, *yel*	25.00	32.50
	Never hinged		50.00	
	On parcel post receipt card			475.00
	Nos. 77-91 (16)		109.40	246.40

90th birthday of Prince Regent Luitpold.
All values exist in 2 types except No. 84A.
Used values: Nos. 73-76 and 77-91 often were canceled en masse for accounting purposes. These cancels are perfectly clear, and

used values are for stamps canceled thus. Postally used examples are worth about twice as much.

Imperf

77b	A6	3pf	32.50	
	Never hinged		50.00	
78e	A6	5pf	12.50	
	Never hinged		24.00	
79e	A6	10pf	27.50	
	Never hinged		47.50	
80a	A6	20pf	27.50	
	Never hinged		47.50	
81a	A6	25pf	30.00	
	Never hinged		50.00	
82a	A7	30pf	30.00	
	Never hinged		50.00	
83a	A7	40pf	60.00	
	Never hinged			
84b	A7	50pf	32.50	95.00
	Never hinged		47.50	
85a	A7	80pf	50.00	120.00
	Never hinged		65.00	
86a	A8	1m	275.00	
	Never hinged		450.00	
87a	A8	2m	960.00	
	Never hinged		1,400.	
88a	A8	3m		600.00
89a	A8	5m	400.00	
	Never hinged		600.00	
90a	A8	10m	400.00	
	Never hinged		600.00	
91a	A8	20m	400.00	
	Never hinged		600.00	

Prince Regent Luitpold — A9

1911, June 10   Unwmk.

92	A9	5pf grn, yel & blk	.80	1.40
	Never hinged		1.40	
	On cover			4.00
b.	Horiz. pair, imperf. btwn.		140.00	225.00
93	A9	10pf rose, yel & blk	1.25	2.40
	Never hinged		2.40	
	On cover			6.50
b.	Pair, imperf. between		140.00	225.00

Silver Jubilee of Prince Regent Luitpold.

Used values of Nos. 94-275, B1-B3 are for postally used stamps. Canceled-to-order stamps, which abound, sell for same prices as unused.

A10   A11

King Ludwig III
A12   A13

Perf. 14x14½

1914-20   Wmk. 95h   Photo.
Wartime & Later Printings ('16-'20)
Coarse Impressions, Dull Colors

94	A10	2pf gray ('18)	.25	2.00
	Never hinged		.65	
	On cover			2.40
95	A10	3pf brown	.25	2.00
	Never hinged		.65	
	On cover			2.40
96	A10	5pf yellow grn	1.10	2.00
	Never hinged		3.25	
	On cover			2.40
a.	5pf dark green		1.10	2.00
	Never hinged		3.25	
b.	Tête bêche pair		3.50	16.50
c.	Booklet pane of 5 + 1 label		16.00	60.00
97	A10	7½pf dp green ('16)	.25	2.00
	On cover			2.40
a.	Tête bêche pair		2.40	11.00
b.	Booklet pane of 6		16.00	
98	A10	10pf vermilion	1.40	2.00
	On cover			2.40
a.	Tête bêche pair		3.50	16.50
b.	Booklet pane of 5 + 1 label		16.00	60.00

99	A10	10pf car rose ('16)	.25	2.00
	Never hinged		.65	
	On cover			2.40
100	A10	15pf ver ('16)	.25	2.00
	Never hinged		.65	
	On cover			2.40
b.	Booklet pane of 5 + 1 label		6.75	24.00
101	A10	15pf car ('20)	1.50	27.50
	Never hinged		3.50	
	On cover			47.50
102	A10	20pf blue	.25	2.00
	Never hinged		.65	
	On cover			2.40
103	A10	25pf gray	.25	2.00
	Never hinged		.65	
	On cover			2.40
104	A10	30pf orange	1.25	2.00
	Never hinged		2.75	
	On cover			2.75
105	A10	40pf olive grn	.25	2.00
	Never hinged		.65	
	On cover			2.40
106	A10	50pf red brn	.25	2.00
	Never hinged		.65	
	On cover			2.40
107	A10	60pf blue grn	.80	2.00
	Never hinged		2.75	
	On cover			3.50
108	A10	80pf violet	.25	2.00
	Never hinged		.65	
	On cover			5.50

Perf. 11½
Wmk. 95v

109	A11	1m brown	.25	2.00
	Never hinged		.70	
	On cover			9.50
110	A11	2m violet	.30	2.75
	Never hinged		.80	
	On cover			14.50
111	A11	3m scarlet	.40	5.50
	Never hinged		.95	
	On cover			27.50

Wmk. 95h

112	A12	5m deep blue	.55	20.00
	Never hinged		1.25	
	On cover			35.00
113	A12	10m yellow grn	1.75	55.00
	Never hinged		4.00	
	On cover			125.00
114	A12	20m brown	3.25	80.00
	Never hinged		6.50	
	On cover			190.00
	Nos. 94-114 (21)		15.05	220.75

Pre-war Printings ('14-'15)
Clear Impressions, Bright Colors

Values for used stamps, covers and parcel post receipt cards with dated cancellations between Mar. 30, 1914, and Dec. 31, 1915.

95c	A10	3pf brown		1.40
	On cover			2.10
96d	A10	5pf yellow grn		1.50
	On cover			2.10
96e	A10	5pf dark green		1.50
	On cover			1.90
98c	A10	10pf vermilion		1.50
	On cover			2.10
102a	A10	20pf blue		2.25
	On cover			5.50
103a	A10	25pf gray		8.50
	On cover			24.00
104a	A10	30pf orange		5.00
	On cover			20.00
105a	A10	40pf olive grn		8.50
	On cover			20.00
106a	A10	50pf red brn		8.50
	On cover			20.00
107a	A10	60pf blue grn		11.00
	On cover			20.00
108a	A10	80pf violet		11.00
	On cover			32.50
109a	A11	1m brown		7.00
	On cover			27.50
110a	A11	2m violet		14.00
	On parcel post receipt card			65.00
111a	A11	3m scarlet		5.50
	On parcel post receipt card			27.50
112a	A12	5m deep blue		77.50
	On parcel post receipt card			275.00
113a	A12	10m yellow grn		275.00
	On parcel post receipt card			625.00
114a	A12	20m brown		250.00
	On parcel post receipt card			625.00
	Nos. 95c-114a (17)			689.65

See Nos. 117-135. For overprints and surcharges see Nos. 115, 136-175, 193-236, B1-B3.

No. 94 Surcharged

1916   Wmk. 95h   Perf. 14x14½

115	A13	2½pf on 2pf gray	.25	2.00
a.	Double surcharge			

Ludwig III Types of 1914-20

1916-20   Imperf.

117	A10	2pf gray	.25	14.50
118	A10	3pf brown	.25	14.50
119	A10	5pf pale yel grn	.25	14.50
120	A10	7½pf dp green	.25	14.50
a.	Tête bêche pair		3.25	25.00
121	A10	10pf car rose	.25	14.50
122	A10	15pf vermilion	.25	14.50
a.	Tête bêche pair		3.25	25.00
123	A10	20pf blue	.25	14.50
124	A10	25pf gray	.25	14.50
125	A10	30pf orange	.25	14.50
126	A10	40pf olive grn	.25	14.50
127	A10	50pf red brown	.25	14.50
128	A10	60pf dark green	.25	16.00

129	A10	80pf violet	.25	16.00
130	A11	1m brown	.35	16.00
131	A11	2m violet	.35	20.00
132	A11	3m scarlet	.50	27.50
133	A12	5m deep blue	.95	45.00
134	A12	10m yellow green	1.60	65.00
135	A12	20m brown	2.25	110.00
		Nos. 117-135 (19)	*9.25*	*475.00*

Stamps and Type of 1914-20 Overprinted

a   b

Wmk. 95h or 95v

1919   **Perf. 14x14½**

Overprint "a"

136	A10	3pf brown	.25	2.00
137	A10	5pf yellow grn	.25	2.00
138	A10	7½pf deep green	.25	2.00
139	A10	10pf car rose	.25	2.00
140	A10	15pf vermilion	.25	2.00
141	A10	20pf blue	.25	2.00
142	A10	25pf gray	.25	2.00
143	A10	30pf orange	.25	2.00
144	A10	35pf orange	.25	2.50
a.		Without overprint	100.00	
145	A10	40pf olive grn	.25	2.00
146	A10	50pf red brown	.25	2.00
147	A10	60pf dark green	.25	2.00
148	A10	75pf red brown	.25	2.00
a.		Without overprint	22.50	225.00
149	A10	80pf violet	.25	2.00

Perf. 11½

Overprint "a"

150	A11	1m brown	.25	2.00
151	A11	2m violet	.25	2.00
152	A11	3m scarlet	.45	4.75

Overprint "b"

153	A12	5m deep blue	.90	12.00
154	A12	10m yellow green	1.40	50.00
155	A12	20m dk brown	2.50	80.00
		Nos. 136-155 (20)	*9.25*	*149.25*

Inverted overprints exist on Nos. 137-143, 145-147, 149. Value, each $15.
Double overprints exist on Nos. 137, 139, 143, 145, 150. Values, $30-$75.

Imperf

Overprint "a"

156	A10	3pf brown	.25	20.00
157	A10	5pf pale yel grn	.25	20.00
158	A10	7½pf dp green	.25	20.00
159	A10	10pf car rose	.25	20.00
160	A10	15pf vermilion	.25	20.00
161	A10	20pf blue	.25	20.00
162	A10	25pf gray	.25	20.00
163	A10	30pf orange	.25	20.00
164	A10	35pf orange	.25	20.00
a.		Without overprint	13.00	
165	A10	40pf olive grn	.25	20.00
166	A10	50pf red brown	.25	20.00
167	A10	60pf dk green	.25	20.00
168	A10	75pf red brown	.25	20.00
a.		Without overprint	190.00	
169	A10	80pf violet	.25	20.00
170	A11	1m brown	.25	24.00
171	A11	2m violet	.50	27.50
172	A11	3m scarlet	.70	45.00

Overprint "b"

173	A12	5m deep blue	.95	55.00
174	A12	10m yellow grn	1.40	80.00
175	A12	20m brown	2.75	80.00
		Nos. 156-175 (20)	*10.05*	*591.50*

Stamps of Germany 1906-19 Overprinted

1919   **Wmk. 125**   **Perf. 14, 14½**

176	A22	2½pf gray	.25	2.00
177	A16	3pf brown	.25	2.00
178	A16	5pf green	.25	2.00
179	A22	7½pf orange	.25	2.00
180	A16	10pf carmine	.25	2.00
181	A22	15pf dk violet	.25	2.00
a.		Double overprint	375.00	1,050.
182	A16	20pf ultra	.25	2.00
183	A16	25pf org & blk, yel	.25	2.00
184	A22	35pf red brown	.25	2.00
185	A16	40pf lake & blk	.40	2.00
186	A16	75pf green & blk	.55	2.40

187	A16	80pf lake & blk, rose	.55	3.25
188	A17	1m car rose	1.25	4.75
189	A21	2m dull blue	1.60	11.00
190	A19	3m gray violet	1.60	13.00
191	A20	5m slate & car	1.60	13.00
a.		Inverted overprint	3,575.	
		Nos. 176-191 (16)	*9.80*	*67.40*

Bavarian Stamps of 1914-16 Overprinted

c   d

Wmk. 95h or 95v

1919-20   **Perf. 14x14½**

Overprint "c"

193	A10	3pf brown	.25	2.00
194	A10	5pf yellow grn	.25	2.00
195	A10	7½pf dp green	.25	16.00
196	A10	10pf car rose	.25	2.00
197	A10	15pf vermilion	.25	2.00
198	A10	20pf blue	.25	2.00
199	A10	25pf gray	.25	2.00
200	A10	30pf orange	.25	2.00
201	A10	40pf olive grn	.25	14.50
202	A10	50pf red brown	.25	2.00
203	A10	60pf dk green	.25	14.50
204	A10	75pf olive bister	.40	14.50
205	A10	80pf violet	.25	3.50

Perf. 11½

Overprint "c"

206	A11	1m brown	.25	3.50
207	A11	2m violet	.25	4.25
208	A11	3m scarlet	.35	6.00

Overprint "d"

209	A12	5m deep blue	1.10	17.50
210	A12	10m yellow grn	2.00	35.00
211	A12	20m dk brown	2.40	60.00
		Nos. 193-211 (19)	*9.75*	*205.25*

Imperf

Overprint "c"

212	A10	3pf brown	.25	12.00
213	A10	5pf pale yel grn	.25	12.00
214	A10	7½pf deep green	.25	22.50
215	A10	10pf car rose	.25	12.00
216	A10	15pf vermilion	.25	12.00
217	A10	20pf blue	.25	12.00
a.		Double overprint	50.00	
218	A10	25pf gray	.25	12.00
219	A10	30pf orange	.25	13.50
220	A10	40pf olive grn	.25	14.50
221	A10	50pf red brn	.25	14.50
222	A10	60pf dk green	.25	14.50
223	A10	75pf olive bis	.25	35.00
a.		Without overprint	5.00	
224	A10	80pf violet	.25	14.50
225	A11	1m brown	.25	22.50
226	A11	2m violet	.25	22.50
227	A11	3m scarlet	.65	27.50

Overprint "d"

228	A12	5m deep blue	1.10	40.00
229	A12	10m yellow grn	2.00	70.00
230	A12	20m brown	2.40	110.00
		Nos. 212-230 (19)	*9.90*	*493.50*

Ludwig Type of 1914, Printed in Various Colors and Surcharged

1919   **Perf. 11½**

231	A11	1.25m on 1m yel grn	.25	2.40
232	A11	1.50m on 1m orange	.25	3.25
233	A11	2.50m on 1m gray	.45	6.50
		Nos. 231-233 (3)	*.95*	*12.15*

1920   **Imperf.**

234	A11	1.25m on 1m yel grn	.30	35.00
a.		Without surcharge	400.00	
235	A11	1.50m on 1m org	.30	35.00
a.		Without surcharge	8.00	
236	A11	2.50m on 1m gray	.65	35.00
a.		Without surcharge	8.00	
		Nos. 234-236 (3)	*1.25*	*105.00*

No. 60 Surcharged in Dark Blue

1920   **Perf. 14½**

237	A5	20pf on 3pf brown	.25	2.00
a.		Inverted surcharge	9.00	30.00
b.		Double surcharge	95.00	225.00

Plowman A14

"Electricity" Harnessing Light to a Water Wheel A15

Sower — A16

Madonna and Child — A17

von Kaulbach's "Genius" — A18

TWENTY PFENNIG
Type I — Foot of "2" turns downward.
Type II — Foot of "2" turns upward.

Perf. 14x14½

1920		**Wmk. 95h**		**Typo.**
238	A14	5pf yellow grn	.25	2.40
239	A14	10pf orange	.25	2.40
240	A14	15pf carmine	.25	2.40
241	A14	20pf violet (I)	.25	2.40
a.		20pf violet (II)	10.00	1,400.
242	A15	30pf dp blue	.25	3.25
243	A15	40pf brown	.25	2.40
244	A16	50pf vermilion	.25	2.40
245	A16	60pf blue green	.25	2.40
246	A16	75pf lilac rose	.25	2.40

Perf. 12x11½

		Wmk. 95v		
247	A17	1m car & gray	.35	2.40
248	A17	1¼m ultra & ol bis	.25	2.40
249	A17	1½m dk grn & gray	.25	3.25
250	A17	2½m blk & gray	.25	32.50

Perf. 11½x12

		Wmk. 95h		
251	A18	3m pale blue	.55	14.50
252	A18	5m orange	.55	14.50
253	A18	10m deep green	.95	25.00
254	A18	20m black	1.40	32.50
		Nos. 238-254 (17)	*6.80*	*149.50*

Imperf. Pairs

238a	A14	5pf yellow grn	65.00	450.00
239a	A14	10pf orange	160.00	
241b	A15	20pf violet (I)	65.00	
243a	A15	40pf brown	140.00	
244a	A16	50pf vermilion	80.00	
245a	A16	60pf blue green	47.50	
246a	A16	75pf lilac rose	47.50	
247a	A17	1m car & gray	8.00	32.50
248a	A17	1¼m ultra & ol bis	8.00	32.50
249a	A17	1½m dk grn & gray	8.00	32.50
250a	A17	2½m blk & gray	18.00	160.00
251a	A18	3m pale blue	14.00	80.00
252a	A18	5m orange	14.00	80.00
253a	A18	10m deep green	14.00	95.00
254a	A18	20m black	14.00	125.00

Perf. 12x11½

1920		**Litho.**		**Wmk. 95v**
255	A17	2½m black & gray	.50	65.00

On No. 255 the background dots are small, hazy and irregularly spaced. On No. 250 they are large, clear, round, white and regularly spaced in rows. The backs of the typo. stamps

usually show a raised impression of parts of the design.

Stamps and Types of Preceding Issue Overprinted

1920

256	A14	5pf yellow green	.25	1.60
a.		Inverted overprint	30.00	
b.		Imperf., pair	37.50	375.00
257	A14	10pf orange	.25	1.60
a.		Imperf., pair	37.50	375.00
b.		Inverted overprint	30.00	600.00
258	A14	15pf carmine	.25	1.60
a.		Inverted overprint	30.00	
259	A15	20pf violet	.25	1.60
a.		Inverted overprint	30.00	750.00
b.		Double overprint	13.00	
c.		Imperf., pair	50.00	
260	A15	30pf deep blue	.25	1.60
a.		Inverted overprint	30.00	
b.		Imperf., pair	50.00	375.00
261	A15	40pf brown	.25	1.60
a.		Inverted overprint	30.00	750.00
b.		Imperf., pair	50.00	
262	A16	50pf vermilion	.25	2.40
a.		Inverted overprint	30.00	900.00
263	A16	60pf blue green	.50	1.40
264	A16	75pf lilac rose	.40	5.25
a.		Inverted overprint	30.00	
265	A16	80pf dark blue	.40	2.75
a.		Without overprint	100.00	
b.		Imperf., pair	50.00	

Overprinted in Black or Red

266	A17	1m car & gray	.50	2.75
a.		Imperf., pair	50.00	375.00
b.		Inverted overprint	52.50	
267	A17	1¼m ultra & ol bis	.50	2.75
a.		Imperf., pair	47.50	
268	A17	1½m dk grn & gray	.50	3.50
a.		Imperf., pair	47.50	
269	A17	2m vio & ol bis	.80	4.00
a.		Without overprint	32.50	
b.		Imperf., pair	50.00	
270	A17	2½m (#250) (R)	.25	2.75
c.		Imperf., pair	50.00	
270A	A17	2½m (#255) (R)	.95	95.00
b.		Imperf., pair	50.00	

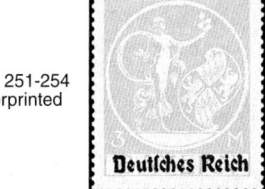

Nos. 251-254 Overprinted

271	A18	3m pale blue	3.25	9.50
272	A18	4m dull red	3.25	10.00
a.		Without overprint	47.50	
273	A18	5m orange	3.25	9.50
274	A18	10m dp green	5.25	16.00
275	A18	20m black	6.00	13.00
		Nos. 256-275 (21)	*27.55*	*190.15*

Nos. 256-275 were available for postage through all Germany, but were used almost exclusively in Bavaria.

SEMI-POSTAL STAMPS

Regular Issue of 1914-20 Surcharged in Black

1919   **Wmk. 95h**   **Perf. 14x14½**

B1	A10	10pf + 5pf car rose	.40	2.00
a.		Inverted surcharge	26.00	65.00
b.		Surcharge on back	50.00	
c.		Imperf., pair	325.00	
B2	A10	15pf + 5pf ver	.40	2.00
a.		Inverted surcharge	26.00	65.00
b.		Imperf., pair	190.00	

B3   A10   20pf + 5pf blue   .40   2.40
   a.   Inverted surcharge   26.00   65.00
   b.   Imperf., pair   375.00
     Nos. B1-B3 (3)   1.20   6.40

Surtax was for wounded war veterans.

AIR POST SEMI-OFFICIAL STAMPS

Symbol of
Bavarian Air
Club — CL1

1912, October   Unwmk.   Perf. 11½
CL1   APL1   25pf deep Prus-
      sian blue   150.00   300.00
   Never hinged   300.00
   On flight cover, *canceled*
     Munich   375.00
   On flight cover, *canceled*
     Nurnberg   750.00

No. CL1 was issued under the auspices of
the Aero Club of Bavaria for its inaugural flight.
The stamp paid the airmail fee, but postal regulations required that Bavarian stamps also be
affixed to covers and postcards to pay regular
Bavarian postage.
Forgeries exist.

POSTAGE DUE STAMPS

    D1   D2

With Silk Thread

1862   Typeset   Unwmk.   Imperf.
J1   D1   3kr black   125.00   325.00
   Never hinged   175.00
   No gum   57.50
   Pen cancel   87.50
   On cover   875.00
   On cover, pen cancel   275.00
   Pair with gutter between   1,300.
   Never hinged   2,000.
   No gum   700.00
   a.   "Empfange"   375.00   1,000.
     Never hinged   600.00
     On cover   2,200.

Values for Multiples

J1   D1   3kr Pair   275.00   1,200.
   Never hinged   475.00
   On cover   1,600.
J1   D1   3kr Strip of 3   440.00   2,400.
   Never hinged   725.00
   On cover   3,200.
J1   D1   3kr Block or strip of
     4   725.00   4,800.
   Never hinged   1,100.

Full margins = 1¼mm at sides, ¾mm at top
and bottom. There are vertical dividing lines
between stamps.

Without Silk Thread

1870   Typo.   Wmk. 93   Perf. 11½
J2   D1   1kr black   12.00   800.00
   Never hinged   20.00
   On cover   1,600.
   Pair with gutter between   95.00
   Never hinged   200.00
   a.   Wmk. 92   55.00   1,750.
     Never hinged   110.00
     On cover   2,800.
     Pair with gutter between   225.00
     Never hinged   400.00
J3   D1   3kr black   12.00   475.00
   Never hinged   20.00
   On cover   960.00
   Pair with gutter between   125.00
   Never hinged   225.00
   a.   Wmk. 92   55.00   960.00
     Never hinged   110.00
     On cover   1,900.
     Pair with gutter between   240.00
     Never hinged   425.00

Type of 1876 Regular Issue
Overprinted in Red "Vom
Empfänger zahlbar"

1876   Wmk. 94
J4   D2   3pf gray   16.00   40.00
   Never hinged   45.00
   On cover   95.00
   Pair with gutter between   200.00

J5   D2   5pf gray   10.00   17.00
   Never hinged   40.00
   On cover   72.50
   Pair with gutter between   175.00
J6   D2   10pf gray   3.25   1.25
   Never hinged   16.00
   On cover   16.00
   Pair with gutter between   95.00
   a.   Vert. half used as 5pf on cov-
     er   2,800.
     Nos. J4-J6 (3)   29.25   58.25

1883   Wmk. 95v
J7   D2   3pf gray   90.00   100.00
   Never hinged   200.00
   On cover   400.00
   Pair with gutter between   600.00
J8   D2   5pf gray   55.00   70.00
   Never hinged   110.00
   On cover   200.00
   Pair with gutter between   400.00
J9   D2   10pf gray   2.40   .80
   Never hinged   8.00
   On cover   8.00
   Pair with gutter between   160.00
   a.   "Empfaner"   140.00   140.00
     Never hinged   275.00
     On cover   275.00
   b.   "zahlbar"   80.00   80.00
     Never hinged   200.00
     On cover   200.00
   c.   Imperf.   95.00
     Never hinged   160.00
     Nos. J7-J9 (3)   147.40   170.80

1895-1903   Wmk. 95h   Perf. 14½
J10   D2   2pf gray   .80   2.40
   Never hinged   1.60
   On cover   12.00
   Pair with gutter between   8.00   40.00
   Never hinged   16.00
J11   D2   3pf gray ('03)   .80   2.50
   Never hinged   1.60
   On cover   16.00
   Pair with gutter between   12.00   40.00
   Never hinged   20.00
J12   D2   5pf gray ('03)   1.00   1.75
   Never hinged   2.10
   On cover   13.50
   Pair with gutter between   7.00   37.50
   Never hinged   14.00
J13   D2   10pf gray ('03)   .60   .90
   Never hinged   1.25
   On cover   10.00
   Pair with gutter between   7.00   37.50
   Never hinged   10.50
     Nos. J10-J13 (4)   3.20   7.55

Imperf

J10b   D2   2pf   60.00
   Never hinged   95.00
   Pair with gutter between   300.00
   Never hinged   475.00
J11c   D2   3pf   60.00
   Never hinged   95.00
   Pair with gutter between   300.00
   Never hinged   475.00
J12b   D2   5pf   60.00
   Never hinged   95.00
   Pair with gutter between   300.00
   Never hinged   475.00
J13c   D2   10pf   60.00
   Never hinged   95.00
   Pair with gutter between   300.00
   Never hinged   475.00

1888   Rose-toned Paper
J10a   D2   2pf gray   2.00   4.75
   Never hinged   4.50
   On cover   14.00
   Pair with gutter between   16.00   47.50
   Never hinged   32.50
J11a   D2   3pf gray   2.60   2.40
   Never hinged   6.50
   On cover   13.50
   Pair with gutter between   70.00
   b.   Inverted overprint   2,200.
     On cover   3,500.
J12a   D2   5pf gray   2.60   2.60
   Never hinged   6.50
   On cover   13.50
   Pair with gutter between   72.50
J13a   D2   10pf gray   2.60   1.25
   Never hinged   6.50
   On cover   9.00
   Pair with gutter between   90.00
   b.   As "a," double overprint   2,200.
     On cover   3,500.
     Nos. J10a-J13a (4)   9.80   11.00

No. J13b was used at Pirmasens.

Surcharged in Red in Each Corner

1895
J14   D2   2pf on 3pf gray   150,000.

Six used examples of No. J14 exist, all used
in Aichach. There are two covers (each bearing two examples) and two loose stamps.

OFFICIAL STAMPS

Nos. 77-81, 84, 95-96, 98-99, 102
perforated with a large E were issued
for official use in 1912-16.

Regular Issue of 1888-
1900 Overprinted

1908   Wmk. 95h   Perf. 14½
O1   A5   3pf dk brown (R)   .75   4.50
O2   A5   5pf dk green (R)   .25   .40
O3   A5   10pf carmine (G)   .25   .40
O4   A5   20pf ultra (R)   .50   .80
O5   A5   50pf maroon   4.50   8.00
     Nos. O1-O5 (5)   6.25   14.10

Nos. O1-O5 were issued for the use of railway officials. "E" stands for "Eisenbahn."

Coat of
Arms — O1

1916-17   Typo.   Perf. 11½
O6   O1   3pf bister brn   .25   .80
O7   O1   5pf yellow grn   .25   .80
O8   O1   7½pf grn, *grn*   .25   .50
O9   O1   7½pf grn ('17)   .25   1.20
O10   O1   10pf deep rose   .25   1.20
O11   O1   15pf red, *buff*   .30   1.20
O12   O1   15pf red ('17)   .25   1.20
O13   O1   20pf dp bl, *bl*   2.00   2.25
O14   O1   20pf dp blue ('17)   .25   1.20
O15   O1   25pf red   .25   .65
O16   O1   30pf orange   .25   .65
O17   O1   60pf dark green   .25   1.25
O18   O1   1m dl vio, *gray*   .95   3.25
O19   O1   1m maroon ('17)   2.75   475.00
     Nos. O6-O19 (14)   8.50   491.15

Used values of Nos. O6-O69 are for
postally used stamps. Canceled-to-
order stamps, which abound, sell for
same prices as unused.

Official Stamps
and Type of 1916-
17 Overprinted

1918
O20   O1   3pf bister brn   .25   13.50
O21   O1   5pf yellow green   .25   2.00
O22   O1   7½pf gray green   .25   13.00
O23   O1   10pf deep rose   .25   2.25
O24   O1   15pf red   .25   2.25
O25   O1   20pf blue   .25   2.25
O26   O1   25pf gray   .25   2.25
O27   O1   30pf orange   .25   2.25
O28   O1   35pf orange   .25   2.25
O29   O1   50pf olive gray   .25   2.50
O30   O1   60pf dark green   .30   13.50
O31   O1   75pf red brown   .35   3.50
O32   O1   1m dl vio, *gray*   1.10   14.50
O33   O1   1m maroon   4.00   375.00
     Nos. O20-O33 (14)   8.25   451.00

    O2   O3

     O4

1920   Typo.   Perf. 14x14½
O34   O2   5pf yellow grn   .25   6.50
O35   O2   10pf orange   .25   6.50
O36   O2   15pf carmine   .25   6.50
O37   O2   20pf violet   .25   6.50
O38   O2   30pf dark blue   .25   7.25
O39   O2   40pf bister   .25   7.25

Perf. 14½x14
Wmk. 95v
O40   O3   50pf vermilion   .25   22.50
O41   O3   60pf blue green   .25   9.50
O42   O3   70pf dk violet   .25   27.50
   a.   Imperf., pair   26.00

O43   O3   75pf deep rose   .25   35.00
O44   O3   80pf dull blue   .25   35.00
O45   O3   90pf olive green   .25   55.00
O46   O4   1m dark brown   .25   50.00
   a.   Imperf., pair   72.50
O47   O4   1¼m green   .25   65.00
O48   O4   1½m vermilion   .25   65.00
   a.   Imperf. pair   25.00
O49   O4   2½m deep blue   .25   70.00
   a.   Imperf. pair   72.50
O50   O4   3m dark red   .25   100.00
   a.   Imperf. pair   20.00
O51   O4   5m black   1.50   125.00
   a.   Imperf. pair   72.50
     Nos. O34-O51 (18)   5.75   700.00

Stamps of Preceding
Issue Overprinted

1920, Apr. 1
O52   O2   5pf yellow green   .25   3.25
   a.   Imperf., pair   26.00
O53   O2   10pf orange   .25   1.90
O54   O2   15pf carmine   .25   2.00
O55   O2   20pf violet   .25   1.60
O56   O2   30pf dark blue   .25   1.60
O57   O2   40pf bister   .25   1.60
O58   O3   50pf vermilion   .25   2.00
   a.   Imperf., pair   26.00
O59   O3   60pf blue green   .25   1.60
O60   O3   70pf dark violet   2.00   2.75
O61   O3   75pf deep rose   .35   1.40
O62   O3   80pf dull blue   .25   1.40
O63   O3   90pf olive green   1.60   3.50

Similar Ovpt., Words 8mm apart
O64   O4   1m dark brown   .25   2.00
   a.   Imperf., pair   26.00
O65   O4   1¼m green   .25   2.00
O66   O4   1½m vermilion   .25   2.00
O67   O4   2½m deep blue   .25   2.00
   a.   Imperf., pair   37.50
O68   O4   3m dark red   .25   2.00
O69   O4   5m black   8.75   25.00
     Nos. O52-O69 (18)   16.20   59.60

Nos. O52-O69 could be used in all parts of
Germany, but were almost exclusively used in
Bavaria.

BERGEDORF

LOCATION — A town in northern
  Germany.
POP. — 2,989 (1861)

Originally Bergedorf belonged jointly
to the Free City of Hamburg and the
Free City of Lübeck. In 1867 it was
purchased by Hamburg.

     16 Schillings = 1 Mark

Values for unused stamps are for
examples with original gum as defined
in the catalogue introduction. Copies
without gum sell for about 40% of the
figures quoted. Values for used stamps
are for examples canceled with parallel
bars. Copies bearing dated town postmarks sell for more.

Combined Arms of Lübeck and
Hamburg
    A1   A2   A3

    A4   A5

1861-67   Unwmk.   Litho.   Imperf.
1   A1   ½s blk, *pale bl*   45.00   725.00
   Never hinged   90.00
   No gum   16.00
   On cover   3,600.
   Pair with gutter between   225.00
   Never hinged   325.00
   No gum   87.50
   a.   ½s black, *blue* ('67)   125.00   4,750.
     Never hinged   240.00
     No gum   47.50

	On cover			26,000.
	Pair with gutter between	500.00	
	Never hinged	875.00	
	No gum	225.00	
2	A3 1s blk, *white*	45.00	375.00
	Never hinged	80.00	
	No gum	16.00	
	On cover		2,600.
	Pair with gutter between	160.00	
	Never hinged	300.00	
	No gum	65.00	
a.	Tête bêche pair, vert.	225.00	
	Never hinged	340.00	
	No gum	87.50	
b.	Tête bêche pair, horiz.	300.00	
	Never hinged	550.00	
	No gum	120.00	
3	A4 1½s blk, *yellow*	20.00	1,600.
	Never hinged	40.00	
	No gum	8.00	
	On cover		5,200.
	Pair with gutter between	175.00	
	Never hinged	300.00	
	No gum	72.50	
a.	Tête bêche pair	125.00	
	Never hinged	225.00	
	No gum	55.00	
	Pair with gutter between	300.00	
	Never hinged	550.00	
	No gum	125.00	
4	A2 3s blue, *pink*	25.00	2,000.
	Never hinged	45.00	
	No gum	8.00	
	On cover		12,000.
	Pair with gutter between	175.00	
	Never hinged	325.00	
	No gum	80.00	
5	A5 4s blk, *brown*	25.00	2,250.
	Never hinged	45.00	
	No gum	8.00	
	On cover		23,500.
	Pair with gutter between	175.00	
	Never hinged	325.00	
	No gum	80.00	
	Nos. 1-5 (5)	160.00	6,950.

Full margins Nos. 1-3 = 1½mm; No. 4 = ¾mm; No. 5 = 1mm. There are vertical dividing lines between stamps.

Values for pairs

1	A1 ½s blk, *pale bl*	95.00	1,800.
	Never hinged	190.00	
a.	½s black, *blue*	300.00	14,500.
	Never hinged	575.00	
2	A3 1s blk, *white*	95.00	1,600.
	Never hinged	175.00	
3	A4 1½s blk, *yellow*	47.50	3,500.
	Never hinged	95.00	
4	A2 3s blue, *pink*	52.50	—
	Never hinged	95.00	
5	A5 4s blk, *brown*	52.50	15,000.
	Never hinged	95.00	

Values for strips of 3

1	A1 ½s blk, *pale bl*	150.00	10,000.
	Never hinged	275.00	
a.	½s black, *blue*	500.00	—
	Never hinged	875.00	
2	A3 1s blk, *white*	150.00	8,000.
	Never hinged	275.00	
3	A4 1½s blk, *yellow*	72.50	—
	Never hinged	140.00	
4	A2 3s blue, *pink*	80.00	—
	Never hinged	140.00	
5	A5 4s blk, *brown*	80.00	—
	Never hinged	140.00	

Values for blocks or strips of 4

1	A1 ½s blk, *pale bl*	210.00	16,000.
	Never hinged	360.00	
a.	½s black, *blue*	650.00	—
	Never hinged	1,200.	
2	A3 1s blk, *white*	200.00	12,000.
	Never hinged	360.00	
3	A4 1½s blk, *yellow*	95.00	—
	Never hinged	190.00	
4	A2 3s blue, *pink*	110.00	—
	Never hinged	200.00	
5	A5 4s blk, *brown*	110.00	—
	Never hinged	200.00	

Counterfeit cancellations are plentiful.

No. 3 exists in a tête bêche gutter pair. Value, unused $310.

The ½s on violet and 3s on rose, listed previously, as well as a 1s and 1½s on thick paper and 4s on light rose brown, come from proof sheets and were never placed in use. A 1½ "SCHILLINGE" (instead of SCHILLING) also exists only as a proof.

REPRINTS
½ SCHILLING
There is a dot in the upper part of the right branch of "N" of "EIN." The upper part of the shield is blank or almost blank. The horizontal bar of "H" in "HALBER" is generally defective.
1 SCHILLING
The "1" in the corners is generally with foot. The central horizontal bar of the "E" of "EIN" is separated from the vertical branch by a black line. The "A" of "POSTMARKE" has the horizontal bar incomplete or missing. The horizontal bar of the "H" of "SCHILLING" is separated from the vertical branches by a dark line at each side, sometimes the bar is missing.
1½ SCHILLINGE
There is a small triangle under the right side of the tower, exactly over the "R" of "POSTMARKE."
3 SCHILLINGE
The head of the eagle is not shaded. The horizontal bar of the second "E" of "BERGEDORF" is separated from the vertical branch by a thin line. There is generally a colored dot in the lower half of the "S" of "POSTMARKE."
4 SCHILLINGE
The upper part of the shield is blank or has two or three small dashes. In most of the reprints there is a diagonal dash across the

wavy lines of the groundwork at the right of "I" and "E" of "VIER."
Reprints, value $1 each.

These stamps were superseded by those of the North German Confederation in 1868.

BREMEN

LOCATION — In   northwestern
Germany
AREA — 99 sq. mi.
POP. — 122,402 (1871)

Bremen was a Free City and member of the German Confederation. In 1870 it became part of the German Empire.

22 Grote = 10 Silbergroschen.

Values for unused stamps are for examples with original gum as defined in the catalogue introduction.

Coat of Arms — A1

I

II

III

Type I. The central part of the scroll below the word Bremen is crossed by one vertical line.
Type II. The center of the scroll is crossed by two vertical lines.
Type III. The center of the scroll is crossed by three vertical lines.

1855	Unwmk. Litho. *Imperf.*		

Horizontally Laid Paper

1	A1 3gr black, *blue*	200.00	290.00
	Never hinged	400.00	
	No gum	110.00	
	On cover		2,000.

Vertically Laid Paper

1A	A1 3gr black, *blue*	450.00	600.00
	Never hinged	950.00	
	No gum	150.00	
	On cover		2,500.

Full margins = 1½mm.

No. 1 can be found with parts of a papermaker's watermark, consisting of lilies. Value: unused $700; unused, no gum, $400; used $1,000; on cover $4,000.
See Nos. 9-10.

Values for pairs

1	A1 3gr black, *blue*	500.00	—
	Never hinged	875.00	
	No gum	300.00	
1A	A1 3gr black, *blue*	1,500.	—
	Never hinged	2,500.	
	No gum	1,000.	

Values for strips of 3

1	A1 3gr black, *blue*	950.00	—
	Never hinged	500.00	
	Types I, II and III	—	—
1A	A1 3gr black, *blue*	2,500.	—
	Types I, II and III	1,000.	—

Values for blocks of 4

1	A1 3gr black, *blue*	1,450.	—
	Never hinged	2,250.	
	No gum	800.00	
1A	A1 3gr black, *blue*	—	—

A2

A3

FIVE GROTE

Type I. The shading at the left of the ribbon containing "funf Grote" runs downward from the shield.
Type II. The shading at the left of the ribbon containing "funf Grote" runs upward.

1856-60			Wove Paper	
2	A2 5gr blk, *rose*	150.00	300.00
	Never hinged	325.00	
	No gum	80.00	
	On cover		3,200.
a.	Printed on both sides		4,000.
b.	"Marken" (not issued)	12.00	
	Never hinged	20.00	
	No gum	8.00	
3	A2 7gr blk, *yel* ('60)	240.00	725.00
	Never hinged	475.00	
	No gum	95.00	
	On cover		4,500.
a.	Thin paper	560.00	900.00
	Never hinged	—	
	No gum	240.00	
	On cover		4,800.
4	A3 5sgr green ('59)	500.00	300.00
	Never hinged	500.00	
	No gum	150.00	
	On cover		2,500.
a.	Chalky paper	60.00	2,000.
	Never hinged	95.00	
	No gum	30.00	
b.	5sgr yellow green	160.00	300.00
	Never hinged	225.00	
	No gum	65.00	
	On cover		2,600.

Full margins: No. 2 = 1¼mm; No. 3 = 1½mm; No. 5 = 1mm. There are vertical dividing lines between stamps.

See Nos. 6, 8, 12-13, 15.

Values for pairs

2	A2 5gr black, *rose*	400.00	2,000.
	Never hinged	725.00	
	No gum	225.00	
3	A2 7gr black, *yel*	575.00	—
	Never hinged	1,100.	
	No gum	300.00	
4	A3 5sgr green	600.00	—
	Never hinged	1,200.	
	No gum	400.00	
a.	Chalky paper	130.00	—
	Never hinged	225.00	
	No gum	72.50	
b.	5sgr yellow green	325.00	1,500.
	Never hinged	575.00	
	No gum	175.00	

Values for strips of 3

2	A2 5gr black, *rose*	640.00	—
	Never hinged	1,200.	
	No gum	325.00	
3	A2 7gr black, *yel*	1,100.	—
	Never hinged	1,800.	
	No gum	500.00	
4	A3 5sgr green	1,200.	—
	Never hinged	2,000.	
	No gum	600.00	
a.	Chalky paper	225.00	—
	Never hinged	375.00	
	No gum	110.00	
b.	5sgr yellow green	575.00	—
	Never hinged	1,100.	
	No gum	325.00	

Values for blocks of 4

2	A2 5gr blk, *rose*	875.00	—
	Never hinged	1,700.	
	No gum	575.00	
3	A2 7gr blk, *yel*	1,450.	—
	Never hinged	2,600.	
	No gum	650.00	
4	A3 5sgr green	1,750.	—
	Never hinged	—	
	No gum	900.00	
a.	Chalky paper	300.00	—
	Never hinged	500.00	
	No gum	175.00	
b.	5sgr yellow green	800.00	—
	Never hinged	1,450.	
	No gum	450.00	

A4

A5

1861-63			*Serpentine Roulette*	
5	A4 2gr orange ('63)	400.00	2,000.
	No gum	240.00	
	On cover		5,750.
a.	2gr red orange	800.00	3,500.
	No gum	400.00	
	On cover		8,500.
b.	Chalky paper	350.00	3,250.
	No gum	210.00	
	On cover		7,000.
c.	as "a," chalky paper	800.00	3,500.
	No gum	400.00	
	On cover		12,000.
6	A2 5gr blk, *rose* ('62)	350.00	225.00
	No gum	110.00	
	On cover		900.00
	Two singles on cover		2,500.
a.	Horiz. pair, imperf between	—	
b.	Double impression	—	
7	A5 10gr black	700.00	950.00
	No gum	350.00	
	On cover		2,800.
	Two singles on cover		7,000.
8	A3 5sgr yellow green ('63)	1,100.	200.00
	No gum	625.00	
	On cover		900.00
a.	Chalky paper	600.00	450.00
	No gum	325.00	
	On cover		1,400.

b.	5sgr green	925.00	225.00
	No gum	550.00	
	On cover		1,000.

Full margins of No. 5 = 1mm. There are dividing lines between stamps.

See Nos. 11, 14.

Values for pairs

5	A4 2gr orange	1,000.	5,200.
	No gum	550.00	
a.	2gr red orange	2,000.	—
	No gum	1,000.	
b.	Chalky paper	2,000.	—
	No gum	1,000.	
c.	as "a," chalky paper	1,800.	—
	No gum	1,100.	
6	A2 5gr blk, *rose*	1,000.	1,000.
	No gum	600.00	
7	A5 10gr black	2,500.	2,450.
	No gum	1,250.	
8	A3 5sgr green	—	—
a.	Chalky paper	—	
b.	5sgr yellow green	—	

Values for strips of 3

5	A4 2gr orange	1,150.	
	No gum	900.00	
a.	2gr red orange	—	
	No gum	—	
b.	Chalky paper	—	
	No gum	—	
c.	as "a," chalky paper	3,000.	
	No gum	2,000.	
6	A2 5gr blk, *rose*	—	
7	A5 10gr black	5,000.	
8	A3 5sgr green	—	
a.	Chalky paper	—	
b.	5sgr yellow green	—	

Values for blocks of 4

5	A4 2gr orange	2,100.	
	No gum	1,250.	
a.	2gr red orange	—	
	No gum	—	
b.	Chalky paper	—	
	No gum	—	
c.	as "a," chalky paper	4,500.	
	No gum	3,000.	
6	A2 5gr blk, *rose*	—	
7	A5 10gr black	—	11,000.
8	A3 5sgr green	—	
a.	Chalky paper	—	
b.	5sgr yellow green	—	

1863
Horizontally (H) or Vertically (V) Laid Paper

9	A1 3gr blk, *blue* (V)	650.00	725.00
	No gum	400.00	
	On cover		2,400.
a.	3gr black, *blue* (H)	2,250.	4,000.
	No gum	1,250.	
	On cover		12,500.

Values for pairs

9	A1 3gr blk, *blue* (V)	1,500.	2,500.
	No gum	850.00	
a.	3gr black, *blue* (H)	—	

1866-67   *Perf. 13*

10	A1 3gr black, *blue*	80.00	325.00
	Never hinged	125.00	
	No gum	35.00	
	On cover		1,400.

Wove Paper

11	A4 2gr orange	95.00	325.00
	Never hinged	175.00	
	No gum	47.50	
	On cover		1,200.
	Pair with gutter between	3,250.	
	Never hinged	5,000.	
	No gum	2,000.	
a.	2gr red orange	450.00	800.00
	Never hinged	650.00	
	No gum	125.00	
	On cover		1,900.
b.	Horiz. pair, imperf. btwn.	3,250.	
12	A2 5gr blk, *rose*	125.00	325.00
	Never hinged	225.00	
	No gum	65.00	
	On cover		3,250.
a.	Horiz. pair, imperf. btwn.	1,250.	
	No gum	700.00	
13	A2 7gr blk, *yel* ('67)	150.00	4,500.
	Never hinged	240.00	
	No gum	80.00	
	On cover		16,000.
14	A5 10gr black ('67)	190.00	1,125.
	Never hinged	360.00	
	No gum	110.00	
	On cover		4,000.
15	A3 5sgr green	140.00	3,750.
	Never hinged	360.00	
	No gum	72.50	
	On cover		40,000.
a.	5sgr yellow green	450.00	175.00
	Never hinged	700.00	
	No gum	250.00	
	On cover		1,250.
b.	As "a," chalky paper	450.00	275.00
	Never hinged	800.00	
	No gum	250.00	
	On cover		3,250.

Values for pairs

10	A1 3gr black, *blue*	225.00	—
	Never hinged	400.00	
	No gum	125.00	
11	A4 2gr orange	225.00	1,250.
	Never hinged	400.00	
	No gum	125.00	
a.	2gr red orange	—	
12	A2 5gr blk, *rose*	325.00	1,200.
	Never hinged	560.00	
	No gum	160.00	
13	A2 7gr blk, *yel* ('67)	525.00	—
	Never hinged	960.00	
	No gum	275.00	
14	A5 10gr black ('67)	475.00	3,200.
	Never hinged	800.00	
	No gum	275.00	

15 A3 5sgr green   650.00   —
        Never hinged   1,200.
        No gum   400.00
a. 5sgr yellow green   —
b. As "a," chalky paper   —

Values for Blocks of 4

10 A3 3gr black, blue   800.00
        Never hinged   1,400.
        No gum   475.00
11 A4 2gr orange   525.00
        Never hinged   960.00
        No gum   275.00
12 A2 5gr blk, rose   800.00
        Never hinged   960.00
        No gum   400.00
13 A2 7gr blk, yel ('67)   1,100.
        Never hinged   2,100.
        No gum   725.00
14 A5 10gr black ('67)   1,000.
        Never hinged   1,800.
        No gum   640.00
15 A3 5sgr green   1,900.
        Never hinged   3,000.
        No gum   1,100.

The stamps of Bremen were superseded by those of the North German Confederation on Jan. 1, 1868.

BRUNSWICK

LOCATION — In northern Germany
GOVT. — Former duchy
AREA — 1,417 sq. mi.
POP. — 349,367 (1880)
CAPITAL — Brunswick

Brunswick was a member of the German Confederation and, in 1870 became part of the German Empire.

12 Pfennigs = 1 Gutegroschen

30 Silbergroschen (Groschen) = 24 Gutegroschen = 1 Thaler

Values for unused stamps are for examples with original gum as defined in the catalogue introduction except for Nos. 1-3 which are valued without gum. Nos. 1-3 with original gum sell for much higher prices.

The "Leaping Saxon Horse" — A1

The ½gr has white denomination and "Gr" in right oval.

1852 **Unwmk.** **Typo.** **Imperf.**
1 A1 1sgr rose   2,200. 300.00
        On cover   1,200.
2 A1 2sgr blue   1,450. 250.00
        On cover   960.00
a. Half used as 1sgr on cover   —
3 A1 3sgr vermilion   1,450. 250.00
        On cover   900.00

Full margins = 1¼mm.

Values for used pairs
1 A1 1sgr rose   1,400.
        On cover   3,000.
2 A1 2sgr blue   2,800.
3 A1 3sgr vermilion   2,800.

Values for used strip of 3
1 A1 1sgr   6,000.
        On cover   9,600.

See Nos. 4-11, 13-22.

1853-63   **Wmk. 102**
4 A1 ¼ggr blk, brn ('56) 800.00 250.00
        No gum   400.00
        On cover   960.00
        On cover, single franking, local post 13,000.
5 A1 ⅓sgr black ('56)   140.00 325.00
        No gum   60.00
        On cover   2,600.
        On cover, single franking, local post 7,250.
6 A1 ½gr blk, grn ('63)   25.00 240.00
        Never hinged   50.00
        No gum   9.50
        On cover   725.00
        On cover, single franking 1,100.
a. Thin paper (.065mm)   40.00 400.00
        Never hinged   80.00
        No gum   20.00
                                   650.00
7 A1 1sgr blk, orange   55.00
        No gum   240.00
                                   150.00
a. 1sgr black, orange buff 400.00 65.00
        No gum   260.00
                                   175.00
8 A1 1sgr blk, yel ('61) 400.00 50.00
        No gum   240.00
                                   125.00
a. Diagonal half used as ½sgr on cover 18,000.

9 A1 2sgr blk, blue   325.00 65.00
        No gum   200.00
        On cover   175.00
a. Diagonal half used as 1sgr on cover 9,600.
b. Vertical half used as 1sgr on cover 18,000.
c. 2sgr black, pale blue   — 160.00
        On cover   440.00
d. As "c," half used as 1sgr on cover 14,000.
e. Thick paper (.13mm)   — 225.00
        On cover   475.00
f. Wmk. inverted   3,600. 1,450.
10 A1 3sgr blk, rose   475.00 80.00
        No gum   325.00
        On cover   240.00
11 A1 3sgr rose ('62)   600.00 200.00
        No gum   325.00
        On cover   475.00
a. 3sgr carmine   — 275.00
        On cover   560.00

Full margins = 1mm.

Values for pairs
4 A1 ¼ggr blk, brn   2,000. 725.00
        On cover   1,400.
5 A1 ⅓sgr black   600.00 1,200.
        On cover   8,000.
6 A1 ½gr blk, grn   60.00 675.00
        No gum   24.00
        Never hinged   125.00
        On cover   1,000.
7 A1 1sgr blk, orange   200.00
        On cover   325.00
a. 1sgr black, orange buff 1,600. 200.00
        On cover   325.00
8 A1 1sgr blk, yel   210.00
        On cover   360.00
9 A1 2sgr blk, blue   800.00 400.00
        On cover   800.00
c. 2sgr black, pale blue   —
e. Thick paper (.13mm)   —
10 A1 3sgr blk, rose   — 360.00
        On cover   800.00
11 A1 3sgr rose   1,600. 725.00
        No gum   960.00
        On cover   1,200.
a. 3sgr carmine   800.00
        On cover   1,600.

Values for strips of 3
4 A1 ¼ggr blk, brn   — 1,200.
        On cover   1,800.
5 A1 ⅓sgr black   1,600. 2,200.
        On cover   4,000.
6 A1 ½gr blk, grn   90.00 1,300.
        No gum   40.00
7 A1 1sgr blk, orange   — 360.00
        On cover   960.00
a. 1sgr black, orange buff   — 360.00
        On cover   960.00
8 A1 1sgr blk, yel   — 1,200.
9 A1 2sgr blk, blue   — 1,200.
10 A1 3sgr blk, rose   — 1,200.
11 A1 3sgr rose   — 1,200.
a. 3sgr carmine   — 1,200.

Values for blocks or strips of 4
4 A1 ¼ggr blk, brn   — 2,000.
        On cover   2,800.
6 A1 ½gr blk, grn   125.00 2,400.
        Never hinged   240.00
        No gum   60.00
7 A1 1sgr blk, orange   — 3,000.
8 A1 1sgr blk, yel   3,600. 3,200.
        No gum   2,000.
9 A1 2sgr blk, blue   2,000.
        On cover   6,000.
10 A1 3sgr blk, rose   — 2,400.
11 A1 3sgr rose   — 4,000.
a. 3sgr carmine   6,000.

A3   A4

1857
12 A3 Four ¼ggr blk, brn ('57)   40.00 95.00
        No gum   16.00
        Single on cover   150.00
        Two ¼ggr on cover   110.00
        Three ¼ggr on cover   150.00
        Four ¼ggr on cover   240.00
        Five ¼ggr on cover   310.00
        Ten ¼ggr on cover   1,400.
a. Four ¼ggr blk, yel brown   — 210.00
        On cover   440.00

Full margins = 1mm.

Values for pairs
12 A3 Four ¼ggr blk, brn   95.00 325.00
        Never hinged   240.00
        No gum   40.00
        On cover   800.00
a. Four ¼ggr blk, yel brown   640.00

Values for strips of 3
12 A3 Four ¼ggr blk, brn   160.00
        Never hinged   400.00
        No gum   125.00

Values for blocks of 4
12 A3 Four ¼ggr blk, brn   300.00
        No gum   125.00

Covers: Each multiple corresponds to a rate based on distance and destination. Values are for covers correctly franked.
The bister on white paper was not issued. Value $6.

1864   *Serpentine Roulette 16*
13 A1 ⅓sgr black   475.00 2,250.
        No gum   275.00
        On cover   4,800.
14 A1 ½gr blk, green   190.00 3,000.
        No gum   110.00
        On cover   11,000.
15 A1 1sgr blk, yellow   2,850. 1,425.
        No gum   1,800.
        On cover   7,250.
16 A1 1sgr yellow   400.00 145.00
        No gum   240.00
        On cover   325.00
17 A1 2sgr blk, blue   400.00 340.00
        No gum   240.00
        On cover   960.00
a. Half used as 1sgr on cover 12,000.
e. Thick paper (.13mm)   — 800.00
        On cover   —
18 A1 3sgr rose   800.00 525.00
        No gum   475.00
        On cover   1,000.

Rouletted 12
20 A1 1sgr, yellow   11,000.
21 A1 1sgr yellow   600.00 325.00
        On cover   875.00
22 A1 3sgr rose   — 2,500.

Nos. 13, 16, 18, 21-22 are on white paper. Faked roulettes of Nos. 13-22 exist.

Values for pairs
13 A1 ⅓sgr black   5,600.
16 A1 1sgr yellow   475.00
        On cover   800.00
17 A1 2sgr blk, blue   960.00 1,400.
        No gum   560.00
18 A1 3sgr rose   2,400. 1,600.
        No gum   1,600.
21 A1 1sgr yellow   700.00
        On cover   1,500.

Values for strips of 3
13 A1 ⅓sgr black   8,000.
16 A1 1sgr yellow   14,500.
17 A1 2sgr blk, blue   1,600. 800.00
        No gum   960.00
18 A1 3sgr rose   4,000.
21 A1 1sgr yellow   1,100.

Values for blocks or strips of 4
13 A1 ⅓sgr black   3,200.
        No gum   2,400.
17 A1 2sgr blk, blue   3,200.
18 A1 3sgr rose   4,000.

Serpentine Roulette
1865 **Embossed**   **Unwmk.**
23 A4 ½gr black   27.50 350.00
        Never hinged   55.00
        On cover   1,600.
        On wrapper or newsprint, single franking 3,200.
24 A4 1gr carmine   3.00 50.00
        Never hinged   4.75
        On cover   140.00
25 A4 2gr ultra   8.75 125.00
        Never hinged   16.00
        On cover   360.00
a. 2gr gray blue   8.75 125.00
        Never hinged   16.00
        On cover   360.00
c. Half used as 1sgr on cover 20,000.
26 A4 3gr brown   8.00 160.00
        Never hinged   16.00
        On cover   475.00
        Nos. 23-26 (4)   47.25 685.00

Faked cancellations of Nos. 5-26 exist.

Values for pairs
23 A4 ½gr black   65.00 960.00
        Never hinged   140.00
24 A4 1gr carmine   5.50 175.00
        Never hinged   9.50
25 A4 2gr ultra   19.00 400.00
        Never hinged   35.00
a. 2gr gray blue   19.00 400.00
        Never hinged   35.00
26 A4 3gr brown   20.00 475.00
        Never hinged   32.50

Values for strips of 3
23 A4 ½gr black   95.00 1,600.
        Never hinged   200.00
24 A4 1gr carmine   8.75 360.00
        Never hinged   16.00
25 A4 2gr ultra   27.50 640.00
        Never hinged   52.50
a. 2gr gray blue   27.50 640.00
        Never hinged   52.50
26 A4 3gr brown   27.50 875.00
        Never hinged   47.50

Values for blocks or strips of 4
23 A4 ½gr black   140.00 4,000.
        Never hinged   275.00
24 A4 1gr carmine   12.00
        Never hinged   22.50
25 A4 2gr ultra   47.50
        Never hinged   72.50
a. 2gr gray blue   47.50
        Never hinged   72.50
26 A4 3gr brown   40.00
        Never hinged   65.00

Imperf., Pairs
23a A4 ½gr   110.00
        Never hinged   150.00
24a A4 1gr   32.50
        Never hinged   47.50
25b A4 2gr   92.50
        Never hinged   150.00
26a A4 3gr   110.00
        Never hinged   150.00

Stamps of Brunswick were superseded by those of the North German Confederation on Jan. 1, 1868.

Numeral Postmarks

These values are premiums to be added to the used value of the stamp. The left column has the premium for Nos. 1-22, the right column has the premium to be added for Nos. 23-26.

1 Badenhausen +120.00 +225.00
2 Bahrdorf +700.00
3 Bevern +225.00 +310.00
4 Blankenburg +22.50 +310.00
5 Bodenburg +120.00 +82.50
6 Boerssum +92.50 +125.00
7 Braunlage +67.50 +92.50
7 Braunlage (red) +5,400.
8 Braunschweig +9.25
9 Braunschweig, Small 9 ('52-'63) —
9 Braunschweig, Large 9 ('63-'67) +14.00
10 Calvoerde +92.50 +120.00
11 Delligsen +140.00 +190.00
12 Eschershausen +47.50 +70.00
13 Fuerstenberg +250.00 +375.00
14 Gandersheim +37.50 +62.50
15 Gittelde +92.50 +110.00
16 Greene (to 10/10/65) +225.00
16 Naensen (after 10/10/65) +340.00
17 Gross-Winnigstedt +250.00 +310.00
18 Halle am der Weser +150.00 +190.00
19 Harzburg +55.00 +110.00
20 Hasselfelde +70.00 +100.00
21 Helmstedt +22.50 +2,000.
22 Hessen +140.00 +225.00
23 Hohengeiss +190.00 +225.00
24 Holzminden +28.00 +82.50
25 Jerxheim +55.00 +82.50
26 Immendorf (to 12/31/60) +475.00
26 Hehlen (from 11/1/62) +340.00 +460.00
27 Kleine Rheuden (to Oct. '64) +200.00
27 Bornum b. Seesen (after Oct. '64) +225.00 +290.00
28 Koenigslutter +37.50 +47.50
29 Kreinensen +55.00 +82.50
30 Langelsheim +92.50 +125.00
31 Lehre +190.00 +225.00
32 Lutter a Bge. +82.50 +110.00
33 Oker +92.50 +150.00
34 Ottenstein +225.00 +460.00
35 Ruebeland +460.00 +625.00
36 Salder, thick lines +150.00
36 Salder, thin lines +92.50 +110.00
37 Schoeningen +22.50 +55.00
38 Schoeppenstedt +47.50 +92.50
39 Seesen +32.50 +47.50
40 Stadtoldendorf +47.50 +70.00
41 Tanne +625.00 +825.00
42 Thedinghausen +140.00 +250.00
43 Vechelde +70.00 +92.50
44 Velpke +225.00 +140.00
45 Vorsfelde +82.50 +110.00
46 Walkenreid +700.00
47 Wolfenbuettel +19.00
48 Zorge +775.00 +1,100.
49 Mainzholzen (to 10/10/65) +1,400.
49 Vorwohle (from 10/10/65) +1,800.
50 Braunschweig +8,750.

Stamps of Brunswick were superseded by those of the North German Confederation on Jan. 1, 1868.

HAMBURG

LOCATION — Northern Germany
GOVT. — A former Free City
AREA — 160 sq. mi.
POP. — 453,869 (1880)
CAPITAL — Hamburg

Hamburg was a member of the German Confederation and became part of the German Empire in 1870.

16 Schillings = 1 Mark

Values for unused stamps are for examples with original gum as defined in the catalogue introduction.

Value Numeral on Arms — A1

1859 **Typo.** **Wmk. 128** **Imperf.**
1 A1 ½s black   100.00 600.00
        No gum   45.00
        On cover, single franking 6,400. 10,300.
2 A1 1s brown   100.00 95.00
        No gum   45.00
        On cover   900.00
a. Period betweenn "M" and "B" 240.00 475.00
        No gum   140.00
3 A1 2s red   100.00 100.00
        No gum   45.00
        On cover   800.00
4 A1 3s blue   100.00 125.00
        No gum   45.00
        On cover   1,100.

5	A1	4s yellow green	80.00	1,450.
		No gum	47.50	
		On cover		16,000.
a.		4s green	125.00	1,300.
		No gum	80.00	
		On cover		14,500.
b.		Double impression		
6	A1	7s orange	100.00	47.50
		No gum	55.00	
		On cover		325.00
7	A1	9s yellow	200.00	2,000.
		No gum	125.00	
		On cover		14,500.

Full margins = 1¾mm at sides, ¾mm at top and bottom. There are vertical dividing lines between stamps.

See Nos. 13-21.

Values for pairs

1	A1	½s black	450.00	2,000.
2	A1	1s brown	960.00	325.00
		On cover		1,100.
3	A1	2s red	450.00	725.00
		On cover		1,600.
4	A1	3s blue	960.00	800.00
		On cover		2,400.
5	A1	4s yellow green	200.00	7,200.
a.		4s green	725.00	7,200.
6	A1	7s orange	400.00	200.00
		On cover		1,300.
7	A1	9s yellow	725.00	8,000.

Values for strips of 3

1	A1	½s black	600.00	
2	A1	1s brown	1,500.	800.00
3	A1	2s red	600.00	3,200.
4	A1	3s blue	1,500.	4,000.
5	A1	4s yellow green	325.00	—
a.		4s green	1,000.	
6	A1	7s orange	960.00	640.00
7	A1	9s yellow	1,100.	11,500.

Values for blocks of 4, Unused without gum and used

1	A1	½s black	400.00	
2	A1	1s brown	900.00	
3	A1	2s red	400.00	
4	A1	3s blue	900.00	
5	A1	4s yellow green	240.00	
a.		4s green	640.00	
6	A1	7s orange	400.00	
7	A1	9s yellow	760.00	18,000.

A2   A3

1864   Litho.

9	A2	1¼s gray	90.00	80.00
		No gum	52.50	
		On cover		325.00
a.		1¼s lilac	150.00	85.00
		No gum	90.00	
		On cover		360.00
b.		1¼s red lilac	125.00	72.50
		No gum	72.50	
		On cover		360.00
c.		1¼s blue	425.00	850.00
		No gum	310.00	
		On cover		3,600.
d.		1¼s greenish gray	110.00	200.00
		No gum	72.50	
		On cover		360.00
e.		1¼s mauve(1st printing)	475.00	850.00
		No gum	290.00	
		On cover		2,400.
12	A3	2½s green	140.00	140.00
		No gum	82.50	
		On cover		560.00

Full margins = 1¼mm.

See Nos. 22-23.

The 1¼s and 2½s have been reprinted on watermarked and unwatermarked paper.

Values for pairs

9	A2	1¼s gray	1,350.	250.00
		On cover		525.00
a.		1¼s lilac	1,350.	390.00
b.		1¼s red lilac	1,350.	250.00
		On cover		475.00
c.		1¼s blue	1,500.	—
d.		1¼s greenish gray	475.00	360.00
e.		1¼s mauve(1st printing)	1,500.	2,400.
12	A3	2½s green	560.00	450.00

Values for strips of 3

9	A2	1¼s gray	2,000.	810.00
a.		1¼s lilac	2,000.	
b.		1¼s red lilac	2,000.	775.00
c.		1¼s blue	—	—
d.		1¼s greenish gray	725.00	1,200.
e.		1¼s mauve(1st printing)	2,500.	4,750.
12	A3	2½s green	950.00	1,100.

Values for unused blocks of 4

9	A2	1¼s gray	2,600.	
		No gum	1,250.	
a.		1¼s lilac	2,600.	
		No gum	1,250.	
b.		1¼s red lilac	2,600.	
		No gum	1,250.	
c.		1¼s blue	—	
d.		1¼s greenish gray	1,050.	
		No gum	475.00	
e.		1¼s mauve(1st printing)	4,050.	
		No gum	2,000.	
12	A3	2½s green	1,600.	
		No gum	725.00	

1864-65   Typo.   Perf. 13½

13	A1	½s black	8.00	12.00
		No gum	4.00	
		On cover		72.50
a.		Horiz. pair, imperf between	72.50	
		No gum	35.00	
14	A1	1s brown	13.00	17.50
		No gum	6.50	
		On cover		60.00
a.		Half used as ½s on cover		16,000.
b.		Horiz. pair, imperf between	450.00	650.00
15	A1	2s red	16.00	20.00
		No gum	8.00	
		On cover		95.00
17	A1	3s ultra	40.00	40.00
		No gum	24.00	
		On cover		160.00
a.		Imperf., pair	140.00	
		No gum	70.00	
b.		Horiz. pair, imperf. vert.		
c.		3s blue	42.50	29.00
		No gum	22.50	
		On cover		140.00
d.		3s Prussian blue	140.00	110.00
		No gum	55.00	
		On cover		540.00
18	A1	4s green	12.00	20.00
		No gum	7.75	
		On cover		190.00
a.		4s blue green	210.00	40.00
		No gum	110.00	
		On cover		190.00
19	A1	7s orange	160.00	125.00
		No gum	90.00	
		On cover		560.00
20	A1	7s vio ('65)	11.50	16.00
		No gum	5.50	
		On cover		95.00
a.		Imperf, pair	275.00	
		No gum	140.00	
21	A1	9s yellow	25.00	2,000.
		No gum	13.50	
		On cover		20,000.
a.		Vert. pair, imperf btwn.	400.00	

Litho.

22	A2	1¼s lilac	95.00	12.00
		No gum	55.00	
		On cover		30.00
a.		1¼s red lilac	95.00	12.00
		No gum	55.00	
		On cover		30.00
b.		1¼s violet	95.00	12.00
		No gum	55.00	
		On cover		32.50
c.		As "a," imperf, pair	140.00	
		No gum	110.00	
23	A3	2½s yel grn, blurred printing	125.00	35.00
		No gum	60.00	
		On cover		80.00
a.		2½s blue green, blurred printing	125.00	35.00
		No gum	60.00	
		On cover		80.00
b.		2½s green, fine printing	125.00	30.00
		No gum	80.00	
		On cover		100.00

The 1¼s has been reprinted on watermarked and unwatermarked paper; the 2½s on unwatermarked paper.

Values for used pairs

13	A1	½s black	42.50
14	A1	1s brown	45.00
15	A1	2s red	72.50
17	A1	3s ultra	115.00
c.		3s blue	125.00
d.		3s Prussian blue	510.00
18	A1	4s green	72.50
a.		4s blue green	125.00
19	A1	7s orange	300.00
20	A1	7s violet	60.00
21	A1	9s yellow	7,500.
22	A2	1¼s lilac	32.50
a.		1¼s red lilac	32.50
b.		1¼s violet	30.00
23	A3	2½s yel grn	100.00
a.		2½s blue green	125.00
b.		2½s green	140.00

Values for used strips of 3

13	A1	½s black	100.00
14	A1	1s brown	125.00
15	A1	2s red	160.00
17	A1	3s ultra	260.00
d.		3s Prussian blue	990.00
18	A1	4s green	210.00
a.		4s blue green	425.00
19	A1	7s orange	
20	A1	7s violet	160.00
21	A1	9s yellow	10,800.
22	A2	1¼s lilac	160.00
b.		1¼s violet	160.00
23	A3	2½s yel grn	260.00

Values for Blocks of 4, unused without gum

13	A1	½s black	17.50	990.00
14	A1	1s brown	42.50	1,800.
15	A1	2s red	27.50	1,600.
17	A1	3s ultra	110.00	
c.		3s blue	100.00	
d.		3s Prussian blue	500.00	
18	A1	4s green	22.50	
19	A1	7s orange	625.00	
20	A1	7s violet	25.00	
21	A1	9s yellow	57.50	20,000.
22	A2	1¼s lilac	390.00	1,700.
b.		1¼s violet	425.00	
23	A3	2½s yel grn	325.00	
b.		2½s green	350.00	1,700.

A4   A5

1866   Rouletted 10
1866   Unwmk.   Embossed

24	A4	1¼s violet	40.00	35.00
		No gum	21.00	
a.		1¼s red violet	72.50	72.50
		No gum	40.00	
		On cover		140.00
25	A5	1½s rose	12.50	125.00
		No gum	6.25	
		On cover		600.00

Values for used pairs

24	A4	1¼s violet		100.00
a.		1¼s red violet		175.00
25	A5	1½s rose		340.00

Values for used strips of 3

24	A4	1¼s violet		325.00
a.		1¼s red violet		475.00
25	A5	1½s rose		725.00

Values for unused blocks of 4, without gum

24	A4	1¼s violet		110.00
a.		1¼s red violet		225.00
25	A5	1½s rose		22.50

REPRINTS

1¼s: The rosettes between the words of the inscription have a well-defined open circle in the center of the originals, while in the reprints this circle is filled up.

In the upper part of the top of the "g" of "Schilling", there is a thin vertical line which is missing in the reprints.

The two lower lines of the triangle in the upper left corner are of different thicknesses in the originals, while in the reprints they are of equal thickness.

The labels at the right and left containing the inscriptions are 2¾mm in width in the originals while they are 2½mm in reprints.

1½s: The originals are printed on thinner paper than the reprints. This is easily seen by turning the stamps over, when on the originals the color and impression will clearly show through, which is not the case in the reprints.

The vertical stroke of the upper part of the "g" in Schilling is very short on the originals, scarcely crossing the top line, while in the reprints it almost touches the center of the "g."

The lower part of the "g" of Schilling on the originals, barely touches the inner line of the frame, in some stamps it does not touch it at all, while in the reprints the whole stroke runs into the inner line of the frame.

A6

1867   Typo.   Wmk. 128   Perf. 13½

26	A6	2½s dull green	12.50	80.00
		No gum	6.50	
		On cover		175.00
a.		2½s dark green	65.00	100.00
		No gum	32.50	
		On cover		250.00
b.		Imperf., pair	225.00	
		No gum	87.50	
c.		Horiz. pair, imperf between	92.50	
		No gum	44.00	

Values for used pairs

26	A6	2½s dull green		200.00
a.		2½s dark green		260.00

Values for used strips of 3

26	A6	2½s dull green		375.00
a.		2½s dark green		440.00

Values for unused blocks of 4, without gum

26	A6	2½s dull green		27.50
a.		2½s dark green		160.00

Forged cancellations exist on almost all stamps of Hamburg, especially on Nos. 4, 7, 21 and 25.

Nos. 1-23 and 26 exist without watermark, but they come from the same sheets as the watermarked stamps.

The stamps of Hamburg were superseded by those of the North German Confederation on Jan. 1, 1868.

HANOVER

LOCATION — Northern Germany
GOVT. — A former Kingdom
AREA — 14,893 sq. mi.
POP. — 3,191,000
CAPITAL — Hanover

Hanover was a member of the German Confederation and became in 1866 a province of Prussia.

10 Pfennigs = 1 Groschen
24 Gute Groschen = 1 Thaler
30 Silbergroschen = 1 Thaler (1858)

Values for unused stamps are for examples with original gum as defined in the catalogue introduction. Examples without gum sell for about 50-60% of the figures quoted.

Coat of Arms
A1   A2

Wmk. Square Frame
1850   Rose Gum   Typo.   Imperf.

1	A1	1g g blk, gray bl	3,250.	50.00
		On cover, single franking		160.00
		On cover, multiple franking		400.00

Full margins = 1mm.

See Nos. 2, 11.
The reprints have white gum and no watermark.

Values for multiples

1	A1	1g g horiz. pair		190.00
1	A1	1g g vert. pair	4,000.	160.00
		On cover		475.00
1	A1	1g g horiz. strip of 3		800.00
1	A1	1g g vert. strip of 3	1,450.	800.00
		On cover		2,000.
1	A1	1g g vert. strip of 4		4,500.
1	A1	1g g horiz.. strip of 4		
		On cover		10,000.
1	A1	1g g block of 4		8,000.
		On cover		32,000.

Horizontal multiples are particularly scarce as the stamps were dispensed to the public in vertical strips

The off-cover vert. strip of 4 is unique.

1851-55   Wmk. 130

2	A1	1g g blk, gray grn	80.00	9.00
		No gum	40.00	
		On cover, single franking		20.00
		On cover, multiple franking		30.00
		On cover with #3		3,250.
		On cover with #3a		3,300.
a.		1g g black, yellow green	950.00	32.50
		No gum	325.00	
		On cover, single franking		95.00
		On cover, multiple franking		125.00
b.		Wmk. inverted	500.00	240.00
		On cover		475.00
c.		As "a," wmk inverted		600.00
		On cover		1,600.
3	A2	1/10th blk, salmon	95.00	50.00
		No gum	55.00	
		On cover, single franking		120.00
		On cover, multiple franking		240.00
		On cover with other stamps		600.00
a.		1/10th black, crimson ('55)	95.00	50.00
		No gum	55.00	
		On cover, single franking		95.00
		On cover, multiple franking		240.00
		On cover with other stamps		600.00
b.		Bisect on cover		—
c.		Wmk. inverted		1,600.
d.		As "a," wmk. inverted	460.00	240.00
		On cover		600.00
5	A2	1/15th blk, gray bl	160.00	80.00
		No gum	80.00	
		On cover, single franking		200.00
		On cover, multiple franking		475.00
		On cover with other stamps		590.00
a.		Bisect on cover		—
b.		Wmk inverted		1,000.
		On cover		2,800.
6	A2	1/10th blk, yellow	240.00	60.00
		No gum	125.00	
		On cover, single franking		125.00
		On cover, multiple franking		610.00
		On cover with other stamps		775.00
a.		1/10th black, orange	240.00	60.00
		No gum	125.00	
		On cover, single franking		125.00
		On cover, multiple franking		610.00
		On cover with other stamps		775.00
b.		Wmk. inverted		1,600.
c.		As "a," wmk. inverted		1,600.
		Nos. 2-6 (4)	575.00	199.00

Full margins = 1mm.

Bisects Nos. 3b, 5a, 12a and 13a were used for ½g.
See Nos. 8, 12-13.
The 1/10th has been reprinted on unwatermarked paper, with white gum.

Values for horizontal pairs

2	A1	1g g black, gray grn	475.00	27.50
		On cover		57.50
		On registered cover		175.00
a.		1g g black, yellow green	150.00	
		On cover		390.00

On first telegraph form ('52)		20,000.	
On telegraph form ('56)		5,750.	
3	A2	⅒oth black, *salmon*	475.00	27.50
No gum	300.00	
On cover		775.00
a.	⅒oth black, *crimson*	475.00	150.00
No gum	300.00	
On cover		325.00
5	A2	⅒oth black, *gray bl*	725.00	450.00
No gum	300.00	
On cover		1,400.
6	A2	⅒oth black, *yellow*	990.00	360.00
No gum	300.00	
On cover		1,400.
a.	⅒oth black, *orange*	990.00	360.00
No gum	300.00	
On cover		1,200.

Values for vertical pairs

2	A1	1g g black, *gray grn*	400.00	24.00
On cover		47.50
a.	1g g black, *yellow green*	125.00
On cover		325.00
3	A2	⅒oth black, *salmon*	400.00	200.00
No gum	240.00	
On cover		650.00
a.	⅒oth black, *crimson*	400.00	125.00
No gum	240.00	
On cover		275.00
5	A2	⅒sth black, *gray bl*	600.00	375.00
No gum	240.00	
On cover		1,200.
6	A2	⅒oth black, *yellow*	825.00	300.00
No gum	240.00	
On cover		1,000.
a.	⅒oth black, *orange*	825.00	300.00
No gum	240.00	
On cover		1,000.

Values for horizontal strips of 3

2	A1	1g g black, *gray grn*	760.00	125.00
On cover		290.00
a.	1g g black, *yellow green*	675.00	675.00
On cover		1,200.
3	A2	⅒oth black, *salmon*	900.00	900.00
On cover		2,400.
a.	⅒oth black, *crimson*	390.00	875.00
On cover		875.00
5	A2	⅒sth black, *gray bl*	3,000.	2,900.
On cover		7,200.
6	A2	⅒oth black, *yellow*	2,000.	2,000.
On cover		3,900.
a.	⅒oth black, *orange*	2,100.	1,950.
On cover		3,900.

Values for vertical strips of 3

2	A1	1g g black, *gray grn*	640.00	100.00
On cover		240.00
a.	1g g black, *yellow green*	560.00	560.00
On cover		1,000.
3	A2	⅒oth black, *salmon*	750.00	725.00
On cover		2,000.
a.	⅒oth black, *crimson*	325.00	350.00
On cover		825.00
5	A2	⅒sth black, *gray bl*	2,500.	2,450.
On cover		6,000.
6	A2	⅒oth black, *gray bl*	1,650.	1,650.
On cover		3,250.
a.	⅒oth black, *orange*	1,725.	1,625.
On cover		3,250.

Values for vertical strips of 4

2	A1	1g g black, *gray grn*	850.00	500.00
On cover		1,300.
6	A2	⅒oth black, *yellow*	4,000.

Values for vertical strips of 5

2	A1	1g g black, *gray grn*	—	1,150.

Values for blocks of 4

2	A1	1g g black, *gray grn*	1,600.	2,000.
On cover		8,000.
a.	1g g black, *yellow green*	5,000.
3	A2	⅒oth black, *salmon*	2,400.
a.	⅒oth black, *crimson*	2,125.
5	A2	⅒sth black, *gray bl*	3,200.
6	A2	⅒oth black, *yellow*	1,750.
a.	⅒oth black, *orange*	1,750.

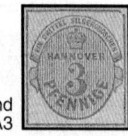

Crown and
Numeral — A3

1853   **Wmk. 130**

7	A3 3pf rose	400.00	300.00
No gum	250.00	
On cover		800.00
a.	3pf dark lilac rose	2,000.	960.00
No gum	875.00	
On cover		2,250.

Full margins = 1mm.

See Nos. 9, 16-17, 25.
The reprints of No. 7 have white gum.

Values for horizontal pairs

7	A3 3pf rose	1,200.	800.00
On cover		1,600.
a.	3pf dark lilac rose	—	2,800.
On cover		4,800.

Values for used vertical pairs

7	A3 3pf rose		1,600.
a.	3pf dark lilac rose		3,000.

Values for used horizontal strips of 3

7	A3 3pf rose		1,900.
a.	3pf dark lilac rose		3,600.

Values for blocks of 4

7	A3 3pf rose		4,000.
a.	3pf dark lilac rose		8,000.

Fine Network in Second Color

1855   **Unwmk.**

8	A2	⅒oth blk & org	200.00	160.00
No gum	140.00	
On cover		400.00
a.	⅒oth black & yellow	400.00	275.00
No gum	240.00	
On cover		725.00

Full margins = 1mm.

No. 8 with olive yellow network and other values with fine network are essays.

Values for horizontal pairs

8	A2	⅒oth blk & org	800.00	600.00
No gum	475.00	
On cover		1,600.
a.	⅒oth black & yellow		800.00

Values for vertical pairs

8	A2	⅒oth blk & org		640.00
a.	⅒oth black & yellow		—

Values for strips of 3

8	A2	⅒oth blk & org		1,300.
a.	⅒oth black & yellow		1,625.

Large Network in Second Color

1856-57

9	A3	3pf rose & blk	275.00	275.00
No gum	85.00	
On cover		525.00
a.	3pf rose & gray	400.00	350.00
No gum	130.00	
On cover		800.00
11	A1	1g g blk & grn	55.00	12.00
No gum	19.00	
On cover		32.50
12	A2	⅒oth blk & rose	125.00	32.50
No gum	45.00	
On cover		80.00
a.	Bisect on cover		13,500.
b.	⅒oth black & carmine	950.00	475.00
No gum	350.00	
On cover		950.00
13	A2	⅒sth blk & bl	95.00	72.50
No gum	30.00	
On cover		200.00
a.	Bisect on cover		12,000.
14	A2	⅒oth blk & org ('57)	725.00	55.00
No gum	320.00	
On cover		160.00

Full margins = 1mm.

The reprints have white gum, and the network does not cover all the outer margin.

Values for pairs

9	A3	3pf rose & blk	950.00	650.00
On cover		1,350.
a.	3pf rose & gray	1,600.	800.00
On cover		1,600.
11	A1	1g g blk & grn	250.00	47.50
On cover		125.00
12	A2	⅒oth blk & rose	400.00	100.00
On cover		200.00
b.	⅒oth black & carmine		1,400.
13	A2	⅒sth blk & bl	275.00	325.00
On cover		1,200.
14	A2	⅒oth blk & org		275.00
On cover		1,000.

Values for horizontal strips of 3

9	A3	3pf rose & blk		1,600.
a.	3pf rose & gray		1,400.
11	A1	1g g blk & grn	400.00	250.00
On cover		600.00
12	A2	⅒oth blk & rose	950.00	250.00
On cover		600.00
b.	⅒oth black & carmine		—
13	A2	⅒sth blk & bl	475.00	1,600.
14	A2	⅒oth blk & org		1,600.

Values for blocks of 4

9	A3	3pf rose & blk	1,600.	1,600.
On cover		4,000.
a.	3pf rose & gray	2,000.	2,000.
On cover		4,800.
11	A1	1g g blk & grn	950.00	2,000.
12	A2	⅒oth blk & rose	1,100.	1,500.
b.	⅒oth black & carmine		—
13	A2	⅒sth blk & bl	1,400.	—
14	A2	⅒oth blk & org		—

1859-63   **Without Network**

16	A3 3pf pink	140.00	100.00
Never hinged	250.00	
No gum	65.00	
On cover		400.00
a.	3pf carmine rose	80.00	90.00
Never hinged	160.00	
No gum	32.50	
On cover		250.00
17	A3 3pf grn (Drei Zehntel) ('63)	400.00	950.00
Never hinged	800.00	
On cover		3,200.
On cover, single franking, local delivery		4,000.

Full margins = 1mm.

Values for pairs

16	A3	3pf pink	325.00	475.00
16a	A3	3pf carmine rose	175.00	250.00
17	A3	3pf green	950.00	2,400.

Values for horizontal strips of 3

16	A3	3pf pink	475.00	800.00
16a	A3	3pf carmine rose	400.00	475.00
On cover		1,600.
17	A3	3pf green	1,600.	4,000.
On cover		8,000.

Values for blocks of 4

16	A3	3pf pink	650.00	1,200.
16a	A3	3pf carmine rose	400.00	950.00
On cover		6,000.
17	A3	3pf green	3,200.	7,500.

Examples of No. 25 with rouletting trimmed off are sometimes offered as No. 17. Minimum size of No. 17 acknowledged as genuine: 21½x24½mm.

The reprints of No. 16 have pink gum instead of red; the extremities of the banderol point downward instead of outward.

Crown and
Post
Horn — A7

King George
V — A8

1859-61   **Imperf.**

18	A7	½g black ('60)	120.00	200.00
Never hinged	325.00	
On cover		600.00
a.	Rose gum	400.00	325.00
Never hinged	800.00	
On cover		900.00
19	A8	1g rose	4.00	4.50
Never hinged	9.50	
On cover		8.00
a.	1g vio rose	20.00	20.00
Never hinged	32.50	
On cover		47.50
b.	1g carmine	80.00	32.50
Never hinged	140.00	
On cover		80.00
c.	Half used as ½g on cover		12,000.
20	A8	2g ultra	16.00	40.00
Never hinged	26.00	
On cover		95.00
a.	Half used as 1g on cover		8,000.
b.	2g dark blue	16.00	45.00
Never hinged	26.00	
On cover		125.00
22	A8	3g yellow	260.00	60.00
Never hinged	450.00	
On cover		160.00
a.	3g orange yellow	160.00	95.00
Never hinged	275.00	
On cover		250.00
23	A8	3g brown ('61)	27.50	50.00
Never hinged	52.50	
On cover		125.00
a.	One third used as 1g on cover		—
b.	3g gray brown ('61)	80.00	250.00
Never hinged	140.00	
On cover		475.00
c.	3g black brown ('61)	400.00	400.00
Never hinged	800.00	
On cover		800.00
24	A8	10g green ('61)	275.00	875.00
Never hinged	400.00	
On cover		4,800.
On cover, single franking		6,000.

Full margins = 1mm.

Reprints of ½g are on thick toned paper with yellowish gum. Originals are on white paper with rose or white gum. Reprints exist tête bêche.

Reprints of 3g yellow and 3g brown have white or pinkish gum. Originals have rose or orange gum.

Values for pairs

18	A7	½g black	400.00	475.00
On cover		1,300.
a.	Rose gum	1,000.	800.00
On cover		2,250.
19	A8	1g rose	9.50	11.00
On cover		32.50
a.	1g vio rose	45.00	47.50
On cover		125.00
b.	1g carmine	200.00	80.00
On cover		250.00
20	A8	2g ultra	45.00	110.00
On cover		325.00
b.	2g dark blue	35.00	140.00
On cover		400.00
22	A8	3g yellow	550.00	140.00
On cover		480.00
a.	3g orange yellow	400.00	200.00
On cover		600.00
23	A8	3g brown	60.00	250.00
On cover		725.00
b.	3g gray brown	200.00	600.00
On cover		1,400.
c.	3g black brown	950.00	950.00
24	A8	10g green	525.00	2,800.
On cover		12,000.

Values for horizontal strips of 3

18	A7	½g black	1,000.	2,400.
a.	Rose gum	1,600.	
19	A8	1g rose	13.50	47.50
On cover		100.00
a.	1g vio rose	72.50	140.00
On cover		325.00
b.	1g carmine		140.00
On cover		400.00
20	A8	2g ultra	72.50	475.00
b.	2g dark blue	55.00	800.00
22	A8	3g yellow	900.00	250.00
a.	3g orange yellow	725.00	350.00

23	A8	3g brown	95.00	900.00
b.	3g gray brown	325.00	700.00
			2,000.
c.	3g black brown		
24	A8	10g green		800.00	—

Values for blocks of 4

18	A7	½g black	3,200.	6,400.
a.	Rose gum	2,200.	3,500.
19	A8	1g rose	22.50	2,000.
a.	1g vio rose	125.00	
b.	1g carmine	110.00	1,050.
20	A8	2g ultra	130.00	2,400.
b.	2g dark blue	90.00	
22	A8	3g yellow	1,600.	400.00
a.	3g orange yellow	1,200.	460.00
23	A8	3g brown	125.00	3,200.
b.	3g gray brown	475.00	
c.	3g black brown		
24	A8	10g green	1,200.	7,200.

1864   **White Gum**   *Perce en Arc 16*

25	A3	3pf grn (Drei Zehntel)	30.00	60.00
On cover		65.00	
			150.00
26	A7	½g black	275.00	275.00
Never hinged	475.00	
On cover		600.00
27	A8	1g rose	12.00	8.00
Never hinged	25.00	
On cover		12.00
28	A8	2g ultra	125.00	60.00
Never hinged	240.00	
On cover		160.00
a.	Half used as 1g on cover		16,000.
29	A8	3g brown	70.00	70.00
Never hinged	125.00	
On cover		175.00
	Nos. 25-29 (5)	512.00	473.00

Reprints of 3g are percé en arc 13½.

Rose Gum

25a	A3	3pf green	80.00	80.00
Never hinged	140.00	
On cover		200.00
26a	A7	½g black	475.00	450.00
On cover		1,000.
27a	A8	1g rose	40.00	25.00
Never hinged	60.00	
On cover		47.50
29a	A8	3g brown	1,200.	1,200.
On cover		2,400.

Used examples of Nos. 25a-29a retain the rose color on the reverse after the gum has been removed.

Values for pairs

25	A3	3pf green	80.00	200.00
On cover		400.00
26	A7	½g black	725.00	600.00
On cover		1,200.
27	A8	1g rose	25.00	25.00
On cover		47.50
28	A8	2g ultra	325.00	160.00
On cover		400.00
29	A8	3g brown	160.00	200.00
On cover		400.00

Rose Gum

25a	A3	3pf green	250.00	250.00
On cover		550.00
26a	A7	½g black	1,200.	1,000.
On cover		2,000.
27a	A8	1g rose	95.00	60.00
On cover		125.00
29a	A8	3g brown	3,200.	4,050.

Values for horizontal strips of 3

25	A3	3pf green	125.00	325.00
26	A7	½g black	1,000.	1,000.
27	A8	1g rose	47.50	80.00
On cover		200.00
28	A8	2g ultra	600.00	1,000.
On cover		1,600.
29	A8	3g brown	250.00	600.00

Rose Gum

25a	A3	3pf green	350.00	400.00
26a	A7	½g black	1,750.	1,750.
27a	A8	1g rose	200.00	140.00
On cover		325.00
29a	A8	3g brown		

Values for blocks of 4

25	A3	3pf green	150.00	950.00
On cover		2,000.
26	A7	½g black	1,750.	2,700.
27	A8	1g rose	90.00	1,200.
28	A8	2g ultra	800.00	1,150.
29	A8	3g brown	340.00	2,000.

Rose Gum

25a	A3	3pf green	800.00	950.00
On cover		2,000.
26a	A7	½g black	3,200.	3,400.
27a	A8	1g rose	350.00	1,600.
29a	A8	3g brown		6,000.

The stamps of Prussia superseded those of Hanover on Oct. 1, 1866.

LUBECK

LOCATION — Situated on an arm of the Baltic Sea between the former German States of Holstein and Mecklenburg.

GOVT. — Former Free City and State

AREA — 115 sq. mi.

POP. — 136,413

CAPITAL — Lubeck

Lubeck was a member of the German Confederation and became part of the German Empire in 1870.

16 Schillings = 1 Mark

Values for Nos. 1-7 unused are for stamps without gum. Nos. 6 and 7 with gum sell for about twice the figures quoted. Values for Nos. 8-14 unused are for examples with original gum as defined in the catalogue introduction. Nos. 8-14 without gum sell for about 50-60% of the figures quoted.

Coat of Arms — A1

1859   Litho.   Wmk. 148   Imperf.

1	A1	½g gray lilac	475.00	2,000.
	With original gum		2,200.	
	On cover			6,400.
	On cover, single franking			9,500.
2	A1	1s orange	475.00	2,000.
	With original gum		2,400.	
	On cover			4,000.
3	A1	2s brown	27.50	240.00
	With original gum		120.00	
	On cover			800.00
a.	Value in words reads "ZWEI EIN HALB"		400.00	7,200.
	On cover			56,000.
4	A1	2½s rose	50.00	800.00
	With original gum		200.00	
	On cover			2,000.
5	A1	4s green	27.50	600.00
	With original gum		100.00	
	On cover			1,400.
a.	4s yellow green		32.50	

Full margins = ¾mm.

The 1872 reprints of the 1859 issue are unwatermarked and printed in bright colors. Values: unused, $240 each; never hinged, $550 each.

Values for pairs

1	A1	½g gray lilac	1,600.	—
2	A1	1s orange	1,600.	5,600.
	On cover			6,500.
3	A1	2s brown	52.50	1,200.
	On cover			2,800.
a.	Value in words reads "ZWEI EIN HALB"		950.00	—
4	A1	2½s rose	125.00	4,800.
	On cover			6,900.
5	A1	4s green	52.50	—
	On cover			5,000.
a.	4s yellow green		80.00	

Values for blocks of 4

1	A1	½g gray lilac	—
2	A1	1s orange	—
3	A1	2s brown	90.00
a.	Value in words reads "ZWEI EIN HALB"		—
4	A1	2½s rose	325.00
5	A1	4s green	110.00
5a	A1	4s yel grn	190.00

1862   Unwmk.

6	A1	½s lilac	17.50	1,600.
	With original gum		40.00	
	On cover			4,000.
	On cover, single franking			7,700.
7	A1	1s yellow orange	30.00	1,600.
	With original gum		90.00	
	On cover			4,000.

Full margins = ¾mm.

Values for pairs

6	A1	½s lilac	35.00	4,800.
7	A1	1s yellow orange	72.50	4,800.

Values for strips of 3

6	A1	½s lilac	55.00
7	A1	1s yellow orange	100.00

Values for blocks of 4

6	A1	½s lilac	80.00
7	A1	1s yellow orange	140.00

A2   A3

1863   Rouletted 11½
Eagle embossed

8	A2	½s green	50.00	72.50
	Never hinged		95.00	
	No gum		16.00	
	On cover			400.00
	On cover, single franking			400.00

9	A2	1s orange	125.00	160.00
	Never hinged		275.00	
	No gum		52.50	
	On cover			350.00
a.	Rouletted 10		200.00	475.00
	Never hinged		475.00	
	No gum		80.00	
	On cover			3,200.
10	A2	2s rose	27.50	65.00
	Never hinged		65.00	
	No gum		12.00	
	On cover			240.00
11	A2	2½s ultra	125.00	400.00
	Never hinged		240.00	
	No gum		65.00	
	On cover			1,200.
12	A2	4s bister	55.00	100.00
	Never hinged		100.00	
	No gum		27.50	
	On cover			325.00
	Nos. 8-12 (5)		382.50	797.50

The 1872 reprints are imperforate and without embossing. Values: unused, $120 each; never hinged, $225 each.

Values for pairs

8	A2	½s green	85.00	200.00
	Never hinged		260.00	
9	A2	1s orange	260.00	275.00
	Never hinged		725.00	
a.	Rouletted 10		650.00	2,750.
10	A2	2s rose	55.00	150.00
	Never hinged		140.00	
11	A2	2½s ultra	300.00	1,200.
	Never hinged		650.00	
12	A2	4s bister	110.00	325.00
	Never hinged		250.00	

Values for strips of 3

8	A2	½s green	150.00	250.00
	Never hinged		400.00	
9	A2	1s orange	600.00	450.00
	Never hinged		1,400.	
a.	Rouletted 10		1,000.	10,000.
10	A2	2s rose	90.00	800.00
	Never hinged		200.00	
11	A2	2½s ultra	475.00	1,800.
	Never hinged		1,350.	
12	A2	4s bister	240.00	950.00
	Never hinged		375.00	

Values for blocks of 4

8	A2	½s green	225.00	800.00
	Never hinged		550.00	
9	A2	1s orange	800.00	2,400.
a.	Rouletted 10		1,350.	
10	A2	2s rose	125.00	
	Never hinged		275.00	
11	A2	2½s ultra	600.00	
12	A2	4s bister	225.00	
	Never hinged		550.00	

1864   Litho.   Imperf.

13	A3	1¼s dark brown	45.00	55.00
	Never hinged		110.00	
	No gum		20.00	
	On cover			200.00
a.	1¼s reddish brown		32.50	125.00
	Never hinged		55.00	
	No gum		14.50	
	On cover			360.00

Values for pairs

13	A3	1¼s dark brown	125.00	240.00
	Never hinged		250.00	
	No gum		47.50	
a.	1¼s reddish brown		80.00	400.00
	Never hinged		150.00	
	No gum		32.50	

Values for used strips of 3

13	A3	1¼s dark brown	175.00	800.00
	Never hinged		375.00	
	No gum		72.50	
a.	1¼s reddish brown		150.00	1,200.
	Never hinged		325.00	
	No gum		52.50	

Values for blocks of 4

13	A3	1¼s dark brown	250.00
	No gum		100.00
a.	1¼s reddish brown		200.00
	No gum		72.50

A4

1865   Rouletted 11½
Eagle embossed

14	A4	1½s red lilac	30.00	85.00
	Never hinged		55.00	
	No gum		14.50	
	On cover			225.00

Value for pair

14	A4	1½s red lilac	72.50	290.00
	Never hinged		140.00	
	No gum		32.50	

Value for strip of 3

14	A4	1½s red lilac	100.00	950.00
	Never hinged		200.00	

	No gum	47.50

Value for block of 4

14	A4	1½s red lilac	140.00	
	Never hinged		300.00	
	No gum		72.50	

The 1872 reprints are imperforate and without embossing. Values: unused, $120; never hinged, $225.

Counterfeit cancellations are found on Nos. 1-14.

The stamps of Lübeck were superseded by those of the North German Confederation on Jan. 1, 1868.

MECKLENBURG-SCHWERIN

LOCATION — In northern Germany, bordering on the Baltic Sea.
GOVT. — Grand Duchy
AREA — 5,065 sq. mi. (approx.)
POP. — 674,000 (approx.)
CAPITAL — Schwerin

Mecklenburg-Schwerin was a member of the German Confederation and became part of the German Empire in 1870.

48 Schillings = 1 Thaler

Values for unused stamps are for examples with original gum as defined in the catalogue introduction. Examples without gum sell for about 70% of the figures quoted.

Coat of Arms

A1   A2

1856   Unwmk.   Typo.   Imperf.

1	A1	Four ¼s red	150.00	125.00
	Never hinged		260.00	
	No gum		95.00	
	On cover			250.00
a.	¼s red		14.50	12.00
	No gum		8.00	
	Single on cover			225.00
	Two ¼s on cover			160.00
	Two ¼s on postal envelope			200.00
	Three ¼s on cover			260.00
	Five ¼s on cover			390.00
	Six ¼s on cover			—
	Seven ¼s on cover			—
2	A2	3s yellow	95.00	55.00
	Never hinged		160.00	
	No gum		55.00	
	On cover			200.00
	3s orange		80.00	55.00
	Never hinged		160.00	
	No gum		65.00	
	On cover			200.00
3	A2	5s blue	225.00	275.00
	Never hinged		400.00	
	No gum		150.00	
	On cover			1,000.
	Nos. 1-3 (3)		470.00	455.00

Full margins: No. 1 = ¾mm; Nos. 2-3 = 1¼mm.

Covers: Each multiple of No. 1a corresponds to a rate based on distance and destination. Values are for covers correctly franked. See Nos. 4, 6-8.

Values for pairs

1	A1	Four ¼s red	800.00	400.00
	No gum		475.00	
	On cover			800.00
a.	¼s red		32.50	24.00
	No gum		20.00	
	On cover			160.00
2	A2	3s yellow	325.00	300.00
	No gum		190.00	
	On cover			800.00
a.	3s orange		325.00	300.00
	No gum		190.00	
	On cover			800.00
3	A2	5s blue	1,400.	1,750.
	No gum		900.00	
	On cover			4,000.

A3

1864-67   Rouletted 11½

4	A1	Four ¼s red	2,800.	1,900.
	No gum		1,900.	
	Four ¼s on cover			4,800.
a.	¼s red		175.00	240.00

	No gum	47.50

Value for block of 4

(continued)

	No gum		125.00	
	Single on cover			1,350.
b.	Pair of ¼s red		600.00	
	On cover			2,000.
	On postal stationery			2,400.
5	A3	Four ¼s red	70.00	60.00
	Never hinged		120.00	
	No gum		37.50	
	Four ¼s on cover			160.00
	¼s red		9.50	9.50
	Never hinged		16.00	
	No gum		4.00	
	¼s on cover or postal stationery			120.00
	Two ¼s on cover			125.00
6	A2	2s gray lil ('67)	140.00	1,600.
	Never hinged		260.00	
	No gum		67.50	
	On cover			11,200.
a.	2s red violet ('66)		240.00	240.00
	Never hinged		400.00	
	No gum		110.00	
	On cover			1,100.
7	A2	3s org yel, wide margin ('67)	45.00	300.00
	Never hinged		72.50	
	No gum		22.50	
	On cover			950.00
a.	Narrow margin ('65)		160.00	125.00
	Never hinged		275.00	
	No gum		80.00	
	Single on cover			800.00
8	A2	5s bister brn	160.00	240.00
	Never hinged		225.00	
	No gum		72.50	
	On cover			1,200.
a.	Thick paper		240.00	340.00
	Never hinged		400.00	
	No gum		125.00	
	On cover			1,450.
b.	Ribbed paper		250.00	250.00
	Never hinged		475.00	
	No gum		160.00	
	On cover			1,350.

The overall size of No. 7, including margin, is 24½x24½mm. That of No. 7a is 23½x23mm.

Covers: Each multiple of Nos. 4-5 corresponds to a rate based on distance and destination. Values are for covers correctly franked.

The bister on white paper was not issued. Value $12.

Values for pairs

4	A1	Four ¼s red		5,500.
	On cover			16,000.
5	A3	Four ¼s red	140.00	125.00
	Never hinged		260.00	
	On cover			230.00
6	A2	2s gray lil ('67)	350.00	—
	No gum		160.00	
a.	2s red violet ('66)		650.00	1,450.
	No gum		300.00	
	On cover			4,000.
7	A2	3s org yel, wide margin ('67)	140.00	1,350.
	No gum		52.50	
	On cover			3,600.
a.	Narrow margin ('65)		725.00	350.00
	No gum		340.00	
	On cover			1,450.
8	A2	5s bister brn	350.00	1,100.
	No gum		175.00	
	On cover			1,600.
a.	Thick paper		650.00	1,350.
	No gum		325.00	
	On cover			1,750.
b.	Ribbed paper			—

Counterfeit cancellations exist on those stamps valued higher used than unused.

These stamps were superseded by those of the North German Confederation on Jan. 1, 1868.

MECKLENBURG-STRELITZ

LOCATION — In northern Germany, divided by Mecklenburg-Schwerin
GOVT. — Grand Duchy
AREA — 1,131 sq. mi.
POP. — 106,347
CAPITAL — Neustrelitz

Mecklenburg-Strelitz was a member of the German Confederation and became part of the German Empire in 1870.

30 Silbergroschen = 48 Schillings = 1 Thaler

Values for unused stamps are for examples with original gum as defined in the catalogue introduction. Examples without gum sell for about 50% of the figures quoted.

Coat of Arms

A1   A2

Rouletted 11½
1864 Unwmk. Embossed

1	A1 ¼sg orange	175.00	2,400.
	Never hinged	275.00	
	No gum	80.00	
	On cover		80,000.
a.	¼sg yellow orange	340.00	4,000.
	Never hinged	600.00	
	No gum		
	On cover		
2	A1 ⅓sg green	80.00	1,350.
	Never hinged	140.00	
	No gum	32.50	
	On cover		10,500.
a.	⅓sg dark green	140.00	2,400.
	Never hinged	300.00	
	No gum	72.50	
	On cover		13,500.
3	A1 1sch violet	290.00	3,200.
	Never hinged	550.00	
	No gum	130.00	
	On cover		9,600.
4	A2 1sg rose	140.00	190.00
	Never hinged	275.00	
	No gum	65.00	
	On cover		525.00
5	A2 2sg ultra	40.00	800.00
	Never hinged	95.00	
	No gum	13.50	
	On cover		2,000.
6	A2 3sg bister	40.00	1,275.
	Never hinged	90.00	
	No gum	16.50	
	On cover		4,800.

Counterfeit cancellations abound.

Values for pairs

1	A1 ¼sg orange	375.00	5,600.
	No gum	175.00	
a.	¼sg yellow orange	1,000.	—
	No gum	475.00	
2	A1 ⅓sg green	175.00	2,800.
	No gum	80.00	
			11,000.
a.	⅓sg dark green	350.00	5,500.
	No gum	175.00	
			14,500.
3	A1 1sch violet	650.00	—
	No gum	325.00	
4	A2 1sg rose	325.00	525.00
	No gum	140.00	
	On cover		1,000.
5	A2 2sg ultra	95.00	2,000.
	Never hinged	200.00	
	No gum	40.00	
6	A2 3sg bister	72.50	3,600.
	No gum	32.50	
	On cover		20,000.

These stamps were superseded by those of the North German Confederation in 1868.

OLDENBURG

LOCATION — In northwestern Germany, bordering on the North Sea.
GOVT. — Grand Duchy
AREA — 2,482 sq. mi.
POP. — 483,042 (1910)
CAPITAL — Oldenburg

Oldenburg was a member of the German Confederation and became part of the German Empire in 1870.

30 Silbergroschen = 1 Thaler
30 Groschen = 1 Thaler

Values for unused stamps are for examples with original gum as defined in the catalogue introduction. Examples without gum sell for about 50% of the figures quoted.

A1   A2

1852-55 Unwmk. Litho. Imperf.

1	A1 ⅟₃₀th blk, blue	350.00	27.50
	No gum	190.00	
	On cover		80.00
2	A1 ⅟₁₅th blk, rose	800.00	80.00
	No gum	475.00	
	On cover		200.00
3	A1 ⅟₁₀th blk, yellow	800.00	95.00
	No gum	475.00	
	On cover		200.00
4	A2 ⅓sg blk, grn ('55)	1,275.	1,100.
	No gum	675.00	
	On newspaper or circular		2,400.
	On cover		5,500.

Full margins = 1mm.

There are three types of Nos. 1 and 2.

Values for pairs

1	A1 ⅟₃₀th black, blue	1,200.	400.00
	No gum	650.00	
	On cover		950.00

2	A1 ⅟₁₅th black, rose	8,000.	550.00
	No gum	4,500.	
	On cover		2,200.
	A1 ⅟₁₀th black, yellow	8,000.	1,300.
	On cover		2,400.
4	A2 ⅓sgr black, grn	6,000.	2,800.
	No gum	3,200.	

Values for strips of 3

1	A1 ⅟₃₀th black, blue	2,400.	640.00
	No gum	1,600.	
	On cover		1,600.
2	A1 ⅟₁₅th black, rose		2,800.
3	A1 ⅟₁₀th black, yellow		2,400.
4	A2 ⅓sgr black, grn	12,000.	8,000.
	No gum	7,200.	
	On cover		16,000.

Values for blocks of 4

1	A1 ⅟₃₀th blk, blue	3,600.	—
	No gum	2,000.	
2	A1 ⅟₁₅th black, rose	—	40,000.
	On cover		
3	A1 ⅟₁₀th black, yellow	—	40,000.
	On cover		
4	A2 ⅓sgr black, grn	21,500.	
	No gum	12,000.	

A3   A4

1859

5	A3 ⅓g blk, green	2,600.	2,900.
	On cover		31,500.
	On newspaper or circular		20,000.
6	A3 1g blk, blue	725.00	45.00
	On cover		95.00
7	A3 2g blk, rose	1,050.	600.00
	On cover		2,500.
8	A3 3g blk, yellow	1,050.	600.00
	On cover		2,400.
a.	"OLBENBURG"	1,600.	1,200.
	On cover		4,000.

Full margins = 1½mm.

See Nos. 10, 13-15.

Values for pairs

5	A3 ⅓g black, green		12,000.
6	A3 1g black, blue		160.00
7	A3 2g black, rose		2,800.
8	A3 3g black, yellow		4,000.

Values for strips of 3

5	A3 ⅓g black, green		26,000.
6	A3 1g black, blue		550.00
7	A3 2g black, rose		16,000.
8	A3 3g black, yellow		16,500.

1861

9	A4 ¼g orange	300.00	4,000.
	On cover		28,000.
10	A3 ⅓g green	475.00	875.00
	On cover		8,000.
	On cover, single franking		15,000.
a.	⅓g bluish green	475.00	875.00
	On cover		8,000.
	On cover, single franking		15,000.
b.	⅓g moss green	1,600.	2,800.
	On cover		14,000.
	On cover, single franking		20,000.
c.	"OLDEIBURG"	875.00	1,450.
d.	"Dritto"	875.00	1,450.
e.	"Drittd"	875.00	1,450.
f.	Printed on both sides		5,000.
12	A4 ½g redsh brn	450.00	525.00
	On cover		2,400.
a.	½g dark brown	450.00	525.00
	On cover		2,400.
13	A3 1g blue	240.00	160.00
	On cover		350.00
a.	1g gray blue	475.00	250.00
	On cover		600.00
b.	Printed on both sides		3,750.
14	A3 2g red	450.00	450.00
	On cover		1,750.
15	A3 3g yellow	450.00	450.00
	On cover		2,200.
a.	"OLDEIBURG"	800.00	875.00
b.	Printed on both sides		5,000.

Full margins = 1mm.

Forged cancellations are found on Nos. 9, 10, 12 and their minor varieties.

Coat of Arms — A5

1862 Embossed Rouletted 11½

16	A5 ⅓g green	200.00	190.00
	On cover		950.00
17	A5 ½g orange	200.00	110.00
	On cover		250.00
a.	½g orange red	250.00	160.00
	On cover		400.00
18	A5 1g rose	110.00	16.00
	On cover		40.00

19	A5 2g ultra	200.00	50.00
	On cover		125.00
20	A5 3g bister	210.00	52.50
	On cover		125.00

1867 Rouletted 10

21	A5 ⅓g green	32.50	725.00
	On cover		4,800.
22	A5 ½g orange	40.00	360.00
	On cover		1,600.
23	A5 1g rose	20.00	55.00
	On cover		140.00
a.	Half used as ½g on cover		
24	A5 2g ultra	20.00	475.00
	On cover		4,800.
25	A5 3g bister	45.00	400.00
	On cover		4,400.
	Nos. 21-25 (5)	157.50	2,015.

Forged cancellations are found on Nos. 21-25.

The stamps of Oldenburg were replaced by those of the North German Confederation on Jan. 1, 1868.

PRUSSIA

LOCATION — The greater part of northern Germany.
GOVT. — Independent Kingdom
AREA — 134,650 sq. mi.
POP. — 40,165,219 (1910)
CAPITAL — Berlin

Prussia was a member of the German Confederation and became part of the German Empire in 1870.

12 Pfennigs = 1 Silbergroschen
60 Kreuzer = 1 Gulden (1867)

Values for unused stamps are for examples with original gum as defined in the catalogue introduction. Examples without gum sell for about 50% of the figures quoted.

King Frederick William IV
A1   A2

1850-56 Engr. Wmk. 162 Imperf.
Background of Crossed Lines

1	A1 4pf yel grn ('56)	110.00	72.50
	On cover		225.00
a.	4pf dark green	160.00	125.00
	On cover		300.00
2	A1 6pf (½sg) red org	90.00	52.50
	On cover		200.00
3	A2 1sg black, rose	80.00	14.00
	On cover		20.00
a.	1sg black, bright red	20,000.	450.00
	On cover		1,400.
4	A2 2sg black, blue	110.00	16.00
a.	Half used as 1sg on cover		57.50
5	A2 3sg black, yellow	110.00	16.00
	On cover		32.50
a.	3sg black, orange buff	325.00	37.50
	On cover		95.00
	Nos. 1-5 (5)	500.00	171.00

Full margins = ½mm.

See Nos. 10-13.

Values for pairs

1	A1 4pf yellow green	240.00	150.00
	On cover		550.00
1a	A1 4pf dark green	475.00	275.00
	On cover		725.00
2	A1 6pf (½ sgr) red orange	240.00	125.00
	On cover		450.00
3	A1 1sg black, rose	200.00	25.00
	On cover		47.50
a.	1sg black, bright red		1,000.
	On cover		2,500.
4	A2 2sg black, blue	250.00	90.00
	On cover		175.00
5	A2 3sg black, yellow	250.00	57.50
	On cover		125.00
a.	3sg black, orange buff		125.00
	On cover		475.00

Reprints exist on watermarked and unwatermarked paper.

A3   A4

Solid Background
1857 Typo. Unwmk

6	A3 1sg rose	325.00	35.00
	On cover		72.50
a.	1sg carmine rose	360.00	50.00
	On cover		110.00
7	A3 2sg blue	1,280.	90.00
	On cover		250.00
a.	2sg dark blue	1,750.	125.00
	On cover		400.00
b.	Half used as 1sg on cover		
8	A3 3sg orange	160.00	40.00
	On cover		125.00
a.	3sg yellow	1,600.	95.00
	On cover		350.00
b.	3sg deep orange	800.00	120.00
	On cover		400.00
	Nos. 6-8 (3)	1,765.	165.00

Full margins = 1¾mm.

The reprints of Nos. 6-8 have a period instead of a colon after "SILBERGR."

Thin translucent paper

6b	A3 1sg rose	650.00	110.00
6c	A3 1sg carmine rose	600.00	125.00
7c	A3 2sg blue		110.00
7d	A3 2sg dark blue	2,000.	110.00
8c	A3 3sg orange	325.00	47.50
8d	A3 3sg yellow		250.00
8e	A3 3sg deep orange		600.00

Values for pairs

6	A3 1sg rose	800.00	80.00
	On cover		200.00
a.	1sg carmine rose	950.00	110.00
	On cover		250.00
7	A3 2sg blue		250.00
	On cover		800.00
a.	2sg dark blue		475.00
	On cover		800.00
8	A3 3sg orange	475.00	125.00
	On cover		350.00
a.	3sg yellow		400.00
	On cover		725.00
b.	3sg deep orange		325.00
	On cover		800.00

Background of Crossed Lines
1858-60 Typo.

9	A4 4pf green	80.00	32.50
	On cover		140.00

Engr.

10	A1 6pf (½sg) org ('59)	190.00	160.00
	On cover		550.00
a.	6pf (½sg) brick red	275.00	225.00
	On cover		800.00

Typo.

11	A2 1sg rose	32.50	4.00
	On cover		11.50
12	A2 2sg blue	110.00	17.50
	On cover		80.00
a.	2sg dark blue	160.00	42.50
	On cover		140.00
b.	Half used as 1sg on cover		
13	A2 3sg orange	95.00	16.00
	On cover		55.00
a.	3sg yellow	140.00	20.00
	On cover		65.00
	Nos. 9-13 (5)	507.50	230.00

Full margins: Nos. 9, 11-13 = ¾mm; No. 10 = ½mm.

Values for pairs

9	A4 4pf green	200.00	90.00
	On cover		250.00
10	A1 6pf (½sgr) orange	475.00	350.00
	On cover		800.00
a.	6pf (½sgr) brick red	650.00	475.00
	On cover		1,000.
11	A2 1sg rose	80.00	9.50
	On cover		25.00
12	A2 2sg blue	275.00	60.00
	On cover		140.00
a.	2sg dark blue	400.00	125.00
	On cover		325.00
13	A2 3sg orange	225.00	40.00
	On cover		100.00
a.	3sg yellow	350.00	55.00
	On cover		110.00

Coat of Arms
A6   A7

1861-67 Embossed Rouletted 11½

14	A6 3pf red lilac ('67)	27.50	45.00
	On cover		160.00
a.	3pf red violet ('65)	325.00	275.00
	On cover		725.00
15	A6 4pf yellow green	12.00	12.00
	On cover		52.50
a.	4pf green	42.50	55.00
	On cover		140.00
16	A6 6pf orange	12.00	14.50
	On cover		55.00
a.	6pf vermilion	125.00	65.00
	On cover		150.00
17	A7 1sg rose	3.50	1.60
	On cover		3.50
18	A7 2sg ultra	12.00	1.60
	On cover		8.50
a.	2sg blue	400.00	27.50
	On cover		125.00

20	A7	3sg bister	8.75	2.00
		On cover		8.00
a.		3sg gray brown ('65)	—	29.00
		On cover		125.00
		Nos. 14-20 (6)	75.75	76.70

Values for pairs

14	A6	3pf red lilac	60.00	125.00
		On cover		290.00
a.		3pf red violet	675.00	800.00
		On cover		2,100.
15	A6	4pf yellow green	27.50	27.50
		On cover		200.00
a.		4pf green	100.00	140.00
		On cover		400.00
16	A6	6pf orange	27.50	35.00
		On cover		80.00
a.		6pf vermilion	300.00	175.00
		On cover		325.00
17	A7	1sg rose	9.50	4.00
		On cover		9.50
18	A7	2sg ultramarine	25.00	4.75
		On cover		45.00
a.		2sg blue	950.00	125.00
		On cover		450.00
20	A7	3sg bistre	25.00	8.00
		On cover		32.50
a.		3sg gray brown	—	95.00
		On cover		200.00

A8   A9

Typographed in Reverse on Paper Resembling Goldbeater's Skin

1866				**Rouletted 10**
21	A8	10sg rose	95.00	105.00
		Never hinged	250.00	
		On cover		650.00
		On cover, single franking		1,400.
		On parcel post receipt card		650.00
22	A9	30sg blue	110.00	225.00
		Never hinged	250.00	
		On cover		1,600.
		On parcel post receipt card		2,500.

Values for pairs

21	A8	10sg rose	200.00	225.00
		Never hinged	525.00	
		On parcel post receipt card		4,800.
22	A9	30sg blue	250.00	475.00
		Never hinged	550.00	
		On parcel post receipt card		4,600.

Values for blocks of 4

21	A8	10sg rose	475.00	1,300.
		Never hinged	1,100.	
22	A9	30sg blue	600.00	1,600.
		Never hinged	1,200.	

Perfect examples of Nos. 21-22 are extremely rare.

Covers: Values for Nos. 21-22 on covers and parcel post receipt cards are for stamps used in 1866-1867. Later items are worth considerably less. Covers bearing stamps in perfect condition are extremely rare and are worth much more than the value stated.

See Nos. 4, 6-8.

A10

1867		**Embossed**		**Rouletted 16**
23	A10	1kr green	30.00	45.00
		Never hinged	95.00	
		On cover		200.00
24	A10	2kr orange	45.00	95.00
		Never hinged	140.00	
		On cover		475.00
25	A10	3kr rose	24.00	27.50
		Never hinged	65.00	
		On cover		80.00
26	A10	6kr ultra	24.00	45.00
		Never hinged	87.50	
		On cover		160.00
27	A10	9kr bister brown	27.50	47.50
		Never hinged	72.50	
		On cover		160.00
		Nos. 23-27 (5)	150.50	260.00

Values for pairs

23	A10	1kr green	60.00	95.00
		On cover		325.00
24	A10	2kr orange	95.00	225.00
		On cover		1,000.
25	A10	3kr rose	55.00	125.00
		On cover		400.00
26	A10	6kr ultramarine	55.00	125.00
		On cover		450.00
27	A10	9kr bister brown	80.00	125.00
		On cover		475.00

Imperforate stamps of the above sets are proofs.

The stamps of Prussia were superseded by those of the North German Confederation on Jan. 1, 1868.

OFFICIAL STAMPS

See Germany Nos. OL1-OL15.

SAXONY

LOCATION — In central Germany
GOVT. — Kingdom
AREA — 5,787 sq. mi.
POP. — 2,500,000 (approx.)
CAPITAL — Dresden

Saxony was a member of the German Confederation and became a part of the German Empire in 1870.

10 Pfennings = 1 Neu-Groschen
30 Neu-Groschen = 1 Thaler

Values for unused stamps are for examples with original gum as defined in the catalogue introduction. Examples without gum sell for about 50-60% of the figures quoted.

A1

1850		**Unwmk.**	**Typo.**	**Imperf.**
1	A1	3pf brick red	8,000.	6,500.
		No gum	4,000.	
		On cover or wrapper		20,000.
a.		3pf cherry red	12,000.	13,600.
		No gum	6,850.	
		On cover or wrapper		32,000.
b.		3pf brown red	12,000.	10,500.
		No gum	6,850.	
		On cover or wrapper		28,000.

Full margins = 1mm.

There are vertical dividing lines between stamps.

Values for pairs

1	A1	3pf brick red	20,000.	22,400.
		No gum	11,000.	
		On cover or wrapper		36,000.
1a	A1	3pf cherry red	30,500.	48,000.
		No gum	21,000.	
		On cover or wrapper		80,000.
1b	A1	3pf brown red	30,500.	40,000.
		No gum	21,000.	
		On cover or wrapper		71,000.

Values for strips of 3

1	A1	3pf brick red	48,000.	52,000.

Values for strips of 4 or blocks of 4

1	A1	3pf brick red	145,000.	200,000.
1b	A1	3pf brown red	175,000.	

Cancellations and usages

1	A1	3pf brick red, pen cancelled		6,800.
		On cover, wrapper or circular		28,000.
1	A1	3pf brick red, with mute canceller		7,200.
		On cover, wrapper or circular		28,000.
1	A1	3pf brick red, with numeral cancellation, from		9,000.
		On cover, wrapper or circular		—
1	A1	3pf brick red, pair or two singles on local delivery cover		40,000.

Coat of Arms — A2   Frederick Augustus II — A3

1851				
2	A2	3pf green	125.00	95.00
		No gum	65.00	
		On cover		190.00
		On local cover, single franking		600.00
		On cover, pen canceled (railway)		240.00
a.		3pf yellow green	1,750.	800.00
		No gum	975.00	
		On cover		1,350.

Nos. 2 and 2a are valued with the margin just touching the design in one or two places. Stamps with margins all around sell for considerably more.

Stamps with very fine impressions, from the first printing, command substantial premiums.

1851-52				**Engr.**
3	A3	½ng black, gray	72.50	12.00
		No gum	25.00	
		On cover		35.00
a.		½ng black, pale blue (error)	20,000.	
5	A3	1ng black, rose	95.00	12.00
		No gum	40.00	
		On cover		27.50
6	A3	2ng black, pale bl	250.00	70.00
		No gum	100.00	
		On cover		160.00
7	A3	2ng blk, dk bl ('52)	725.00	55.00
		No gum	400.00	
		On cover		125.00
8	A3	3ng black, yellow	160.00	25.00
		No gum	72.50	
		On cover		60.00
		Nos. 3-8 (5)	1,302.	174.00

Full margins = ¾mm.

The error No. 3a occurred when paper meant for printing No. 6 was inadvertently placed in the stack of paper for printing No. 3.

King John I — A4

1855-60				
9	A4	½ng black, gray	16.00	8.00
		No gum	6.50	
		On cover		9.50
a.		"1½" at left or right	—	
		On cover		1,300.
10	A4	1ng black, rose	16.00	8.00
		No gum	6.50	
		On cover		9.50
11	A4	2ng black, dark blue	24.00	20.00
		No gum	9.50	
		On cover		40.00
a.		2ng black, blue	72.50	47.50
		No gum	32.50	
		On cover		95.00
12	A4	3ng black, yellow	24.00	16.00
		No gum	7.50	
		On cover		27.50
13	A4	5ng ver ('56)	90.00	65.00
		No gum	32.50	
		On cover		160.00
a.		5ng orange brown ('60)	325.00	325.00
		No gum	115.00	
		On cover		950.00
b.		5ng deep brown ('57)	725.00	175.00
		No gum	260.00	
		On cover		625.00
14	A4	10ng milky blue ('56)	225.00	225.00
		No gum	95.00	
		On cover		1,100.
		On cover, single franking		2,200.
a.		10ng dk blue ('59)	275.00	300.00
		No gum	125.00	
		On cover		1,450.
		On cover, single franking		3,200.

Full margins = ¾mm.

The ½ng is found in 3 types, the 1ng in 2. In 1861 the 5ng and 10ng were printed on hard, brittle, translucent paper.

A5   A6

Typo.; Arms Embossed

1863				**Perf. 13**
15	A5	3pf blue green	4.00	40.00
		No gum	1.60	
		On cover		95.00
a.		3pf yellow green	95.00	125.00
		No gum	22.50	
		On cover		240.00
16	A5	½ng orange	4.00	2.75
		No gum	1.60	
		On cover		8.00
a.		½ng red orange	24.00	6.00
		No gum	9.25	
		On cover		11.00
17	A6	1ng rose	1.60	2.40
		No gum	.50	
		On cover		8.00
a.		Vert. pair, imperf. between	225.00	
b.		Horiz. pair, imperf. between	375.00	
18	A6	2ng blue	2.75	8.00
		No gum	.75	
		On cover		19.00
a.		2ng dark blue	12.00	32.50
		No gum	4.75	
		On cover		80.00
19	A6	3ng red brown	4.50	12.00
		No gum	1.75	
		On cover		25.00
a.		3ng bister brown	24.00	9.50
		No gum	9.25	
		On cover		19.00
20	A6	5ng dull violet	30.00	47.50
		No gum	12.00	
		On cover		130.00
a.		5ng gray violet	16.00	450.00
		No gum	6.00	
		On cover		875.00

b.		5ng gray blue	30.00	72.50
		No gum	11.00	
		On cover		225.00
c.		5ng slate	22.50	250.00
		No gum	11.00	
		On cover		550.00

The stamps of Saxony were superseded on Jan. 1, 1868, by those of the North German Confederation.

SCHLESWIG-HOLSTEIN

LOCATION — In northern Germany.
GOVT. — Duchies
AREA — 7,338 sq. mi.
POP. — 1,519,000 (approx.)
CAPITAL — Schleswig

Schleswig-Holstein was an autonomous territory from 1848 to 1851 when it came under Danish rule. In 1864, it was occupied by Prussia and Austria, and in 1866 it became a province of Prussia.

16 Schillings = 1 Mark

Values for unused stamps are for examples with original gum as defined in the catalogue introduction. Stamps without gum sell for about 50% of the figures quoted.

Coat of Arms — A1

Typographed; Arms Embossed

1850		**Unwmk.**		**Imperf.**
		With Silk Threads		
1	A1	1s dl bl & grnsh bl	325.00	5,600.
		No gum	175.00	
		On cover		9,600.
a.		1s Prussian blue	725.00	
		No gum	400.00	
b.		Double silk thread	1,200.	
		No gum	800.00	
2	A1	2s rose & pink	560.00	7,200.
		No gum	325.00	
		On cover		20,000.
		On cover, #1 and 2		55,000.
a.		2s deep pink & rose	725.00	
		No gum	350.00	
b.		Double embossing	3,100.	
		No gum	1,600.	

Full margins = ½mm.

Values for stamps with legible town postmarks

1	A1	1s dull blue & greenish blue, from		14,500.
		On cover		24,000.
2	A1	2s rose & pink, from		16,000.

Values for stamps with legible town cancellations start at the figure above.

Values for pairs

1	A1	1s dull blue & greenish blue	875.00	13,500.
		No gum	525.00	
1a	A1	1s prussian blue	1,750.	
		No gum	950.00	
2	A1	2s rose & pink	1,350.	30,500.
		No gum	800.00	
2a	A1	2s deep pink & rose	1,900.	
		No gum	1,100.	

Values for strips of 3

1	A1	1s dull blue & greenish blue	1,450.	
		No gum	800.00	
1a	A1	1s prussian blue	2,550.	
		No gum	1,600.	
2	A1	2s rose & pink	2,000.	
		No gum	1,300.	
2a	A1	2s deep pink & rose	2,800.	
		No gum	1,750.	

Values for blocks or strips of 4

1	A1	1s dull blue & greenish blue	1,750.	
		No gum	1,100.	
1a	A1	1s prussian blue	3,350.	
		No gum	1,750.	
2	A1	2s rose & pink	2,800.	
		No gum	1,750.	
2a	A1	2s deep pink & rose	4,000.	
		No gum	2,400.	

Forged cancellations are found on Nos. 1-2, 5-7, 9, 16 and 19.

A2　　　　　A3

1865　　　　Typo.　　Rouletted 11½

3	A2	½s rose	40.00	45.00
		On cover		225.00
		On cover, single franking		240.00
4	A2	1¼s green	20.00	20.00
		On cover		35.00
5	A3	1⅓s red lilac	45.00	125.00
		On cover		600.00
		On cover, single franking		12,000.
6	A2	2s ultra	50.00	240.00
		On cover		600.00
7	A3	4s bister	65.00	1,300.
		On cover		6,000.
		Nos. 3-7 (5)	220.00	1,730.

Schleswig

A4　　　　　A5

1864　　　　Typo.　　Rouletted 11½

8	A4	1¼s green	45.00	20.00
		On cover		32.50
9	A4	4s carmine	95.00	450.00
		On cover		800.00

1865　　　　　　　Rouletted 10, 11½

10	A4	½s green	32.50	55.00
		On cover		225.00
		On cover, single franking		240.00
11	A4	1¼s red lilac	55.00	25.00
		On cover		32.50
a.		1¼s gray lilac ('67)	255.00	47.50
		On cover		95.00
b.		Half of #11a used as ½s on cover		32,000.
12	A5	1⅓s rose	27.50	60.00
		On cover		300.00
		On cover, single franking		1,900.
13	A4	2s ultra	27.50	60.00
		On cover		90.00
14	A4	4s bister	32.50	80.00
		On cover		160.00
		Nos. 10-14 (5)	175.00	280.00

Holstein

A6

Type I — Small lettering in frame. Wavy lines in spandrels close together.
Type II — Small lettering in frame. Wavy lines wider apart.
Type III — Larger lettering in frame and no periods after "H R Z G." Wavy lines as II.

1864　　　　Litho.　　　Imperf.

15	A6	1¼s bl & gray, I	52.50	55.00
		On cover		160.00
a.		Half used as ⅝s on cover		9,500.
16	A6	1¼s bl & gray, II	800.00	2,400.
		On cover		32,000.
a.		Half used as ⅝s on cover		24,000.
17	A6	1¼s bl & gray, III	45.00	55.00
		On cover		110.00
		With town datestamp		200.00
		On cover, with town datestamp		400.00
a.		Half used as ⅝s on cover		8,000.

Full margins = ¾mm.

A7

1864　　　　Typo.　　　Rouletted 8

18	A7	1¼s blue & rose	45.00	20.00
		On cover		40.00
a.		Half used as ½s on cover		2,000.

A8

1865　　　　　　　　　Rouletted 8

19	A8	½s green	65.00	95.00
		On cover		325.00
		On cover, single franking		340.00
20	A8	1¼s red lilac	47.50	25.00
		On cover		35.00
21	A8	2s blue	52.50	17.00
		On cover		120.00
		Nos. 19-21 (3)	165.00	167.50

A9　　　　　A10

1865-66　　　　　　Rouletted 7 and 8

22	A9	1¼s red lilac ('66)	72.50	25.00
		On cover		35.00
a.		Half used as ⅝s on cover		24,000.
23	A10	1⅓s carmine	60.00	45.00
		On cover		300.00
		On cover, single franking		2,000.
24	A9	2s blue ('66)	145.00	160.00
		On cover		335.00
25	A10	4s bister	65.00	80.00
		On cover		160.00
		Nos. 22-25 (4)	342.50	310.00

These stamps were superseded by those of North German Confederation on Jan. 1, 1868.

THURN AND TAXIS

A princely house which, prior to the formation of the German Empire, enjoyed the privilege of a postal monopoly. These stamps were superseded on July 1, 1867, by those of Prussia, followed by those of the North German Postal District on Jan. 1, 1868, and later by stamps of the German Empire on Jan. 1, 1872.

Values are for stamps with four complete margins just clear of the framelines. Stamps with margins just touching the framelines on one or two sides are worth approximately 60% of the values quoted. Stamps with four large margins are rare and command premiums of up to 500% over the values quoted.

Values for unused stamps are for examples with original gum as defined in the catalogue introduction. Stamps without gum sell for about 50% of the figures quoted.

NORTHERN DISTRICT
30 Silbergroschen or Groschen = 1 Thaler

A1　　　　　A2

1852-58　　Unwmk.　Typo.　Imperf.

1	A1	¼sgr blk, red brn ('54)	265.00	60.00
		No gum	175.00	
		On cover		160.00
		On cover tied by town datestamp		550.00
		On cover, single franking		690.00
		On news wrapper, single franking		1,000.
2	A1	½sgr blk, buff ('58)	125.00	250.00
		No gum	80.00	
		On cover		690.00
		On cover tied by town datestamp		1,350.
3	A1	½sgr blk, green	725.00	40.00
		No gum	500.00	
		On cover		160.00
		On newspaper wrapper		690.00
a.		½sgr black, olive green	650.00	27.50
		No gum	575.00	
		On cover		125.00
		On newspaper wrapper		675.00
4	A1	1sgr blk, dk bl	1,325.	140.00
		No gum		
		On cover		325.00
5	A1	1sgr blk, lt bl ('53)	800.00	22.50
		No gum	525.00	
		On cover		82.50
6	A1	2sgr blk, rose	850.00	32.50
		No gum	575.00	
		On cover		100.00
a.		Half used as 1sgr on cover		10,000.

7	A1	3sgr blk, brownish yellow	1,000.	30.00
		No gum	675.00	
		On cover		60.00
a.		3sgr blk, pale orange yellow	1,000.	80.00
		No gum	675.00	
		On cover		175.00

Full margins = ¼mm.

Reprints of Nos. 1-12, 15-20, 23-24, were made in 1910. They have "ND" in script on the back. Value, $6.50 each.

1859-60

8	A1	¼sgr red ('60)	67.50	67.50
		Never hinged	140.00	
		No gum	42.50	
		On cover		160.00
		On cover, single franking		400.00
9	A1	½gr green	300.00	95.00
		Never hinged	525.00	
		No gum	200.00	
		On cover		300.00
		On cover, four clear margins		550.00
10	A1	1sgr blue	300.00	45.00
		Never hinged	525.00	
		No gum	200.00	
		On cover		100.00
		On cover, four clear margins		160.00
11	A1	2sgr rose ('60)	145.00	80.00
		Never hinged	240.00	
		No gum	95.00	
		On cover		210.00
		On cover, four clear margins		410.00
12	A1	3sgr red brn ('60)	145.00	110.00
		Never hinged	240.00	
		No gum	95.00	
		On cover		325.00
		On cover, four clear margins		625.00
13	A2	5sgr lilac	2.75	400.00
		Never hinged	4.00	
		No gum	1.75	
		On cover		1,000.
		On cover, four clear margins		2,200.
14	A2	10sgr orange	2.75	875.00
		Never hinged	4.00	
		No gum	1.75	
		On cover		4,750.
		On cover, four clear margins		10,250.
		On cover, single franking		18,500.

Full margins = ¼mm.

Excellent forged cancellations exist on Nos. 13 and 14. For reprints, see note after No. 7.

1862-63

15	A1	¼sgr black ('63)	35.00	75.00
		Never hinged	57.50	
		No gum	25.00	
		On cover		200.00
		On cover, four clear margins		300.00
		On cover, single franking		600.00
		Single franking on newspaper		700.00
16	A1	½sgr green ('63)	50.00	250.00
		Never hinged	82.50	
		No gum	30.00	
		On cover		550.00
		On cover, four clear margins		1,100.
		On newsprint, single franking		1,100.
17	A1	½sgr org yel	100.00	47.50
		Never hinged	175.00	
		No gum	65.00	
		On cover		210.00
		On cover, four clear margins		210.00
18	A1	1sgr rose ('63)	67.50	27.50
		Never hinged	110.00	
		No gum	42.50	
		On cover		160.00
		On cover, four clear margins		160.00
19	A1	2sgr blue ('63)	60.00	100.00
		Never hinged	100.00	
		No gum	18.00	
		On cover		250.00
		On cover, four clear margins		500.00
20	A1	3sgr bister ('63)	27.50	55.00
		Never hinged	55.00	
		No gum	18.00	
		On cover		190.00
		On cover, four clear margins		190.00
		Nos. 15-20 (6)	340.00	555.00

Full margins = ¼mm.

For reprints, see note after No. 7.

1865　　　　　　　　　Rouletted

21	A1	¼sgr black	7.50	400.00
		Never hinged	13.00	
		On cover		825.00
		On cover, single franking		2,200.
22	A1	½sgr green	11.00	240.00
		Never hinged	22.50	
		On cover		875.00
		On cover, single franking		1,350.
23	A1	½sgr yellow	22.50	37.50
		Never hinged	40.00	
		On cover		92.50
24	A1	1sgr rose	25.00	25.00
		Never hinged	40.00	
		On cover		62.50
25	A1	2sgr blue	1.50	67.50
		Never hinged	2.75	
		On cover		140.00

26	A1	3sgr bister	2.75	27.50
		Never hinged	4.50	
		On cover		82.50
		Nos. 21-26 (6)	70.25	797.50

For reprints, see note after No. 7.

1866　　　　Rouletted in Colored Lines

27	A1	¼sgr black	2.00	1,250.
		Never hinged	3.00	
		On cover		3,250.
		On cover, single franking		7,500.
28	A1	½sgr green	2.00	600.00
		Never hinged	3.00	
		On cover		2,250.
29	A1	½sgr yellow	2.00	120.00
		Never hinged	3.00	
		On cover		275.00
30	A1	1sgr rose	1.50	60.00
		Never hinged	2.75	
		On cover		140.00
a.		Horizontal pair without rouletting between	150.00	1,500.
b.		Half used as ½sgr on cover		52,500.
31	A1	2sgr blue	1.50	600.00
		Never hinged	2.75	
		On cover		1,300.
32	A1	3sgr bister	1.50	150.00
		Never hinged	2.75	
		On cover		375.00
		Nos. 27-32 (6)	10.50	2,780.

Forged cancellations on Nos. 2, 13-14, 15-16, 21-22, 25-32 are plentiful.

SOUTHERN DISTRICT
60 Kreuzer = 1 Gulden

A1　　　　　A2

1852-53　　Unwmk.　　　Imperf.

42	A1	1kr blk, lt grn	240.00	15.00
		No gum	160.00	
		On cover		60.00
		On cover, four clear margins		115.00
		On cover, single franking		140.00
		On newsprint, single franking		175.00
a.		9kr black, dull bluish green	500.00	40.00
		No gum	500.00	
		On cover		300.00
		On cover, four clear margins		325.00
		On cover, single franking		300.00
43	A1	3kr blk, dk bl	925.00	50.00
		No gum	575.00	
		On cover		125.00
		On cover, four clear margins		275.00
44	A1	3kr blk, bl ('53)	800.00	20.00
		No gum	525.00	
		On cover		75.00
		On cover, four clear margins		140.00
45	A1	6kr blk, rose	800.00	11.00
		No gum	525.00	
		On cover		60.00
		On cover, four clear margins		110.00
46	A1	9kr blk, brnish yell	875.00	17.50
		No gum	550.00	
		On cover		60.00
		On cover, four clear margins		120.00
a.		9kr blk, pale orange yellow	750.00	45.00
		No gum	500.00	
		On cover		90.00
		On cover, four clear margins		160.00

Full margins = ¼mm.

Reprints of Nos. 42-50, 53-56 were made in 1910. Each has "ND" in script on the back. Value, each $6.50.

1859

47	A1	1kr green	25.00	10.00
		Never hinged	37.50	
		No gum	16.00	
		On cover		35.00
		On cover, four clear margins		70.00
		On cover, single franking		120.00
		Single franking, printed matter		135.00
48	A1	3kr blue	560.00	25.00
		Never hinged	1,100.	
		On cover		80.00
		On cover, four clear margins		160.00
49	A1	6kr rose	560.00	67.50
		Never hinged	1,100.	
		On cover		185.00
		On cover, four clear margins		375.00
50	A1	9kr yellow	560.00	67.50
		Never hinged	1,150.	
		On cover		350.00
		On cover, four clear margins		700.00
51	A2	15kr lilac	2.75	175.00
		Never hinged	4.00	
		On cover		525.00
		On cover, four clear margins		1,150.

52 A2 30kr orange 2.75 475.00
Never hinged 4.00
No gum 1.90
On cover 1,500.
On cover, four clear margins 3,400.
On cover, single franking 13,500.

Forged cancellations exist on Nos. 51 and 52. For reprints, see note after No. 46.

1862
53 A1 3kr rose 13.50 30.00
Never hinged 27.50
On cover 75.00
On cover, four clear margins 160.00
54 A1 6kr blue 13.50 30.00
Never hinged 27.50
On cover 80.00
On cover, four clear margins 160.00
55 A1 9kr bister 13.50 35.00
Never hinged 27.50
On cover 115.00
On cover, four clear margins 190.00
Nos. 53-55 (3) 40.50 95.00

For reprints, see note after No. 46.

1865 Rouletted
56 A1 1kr green 12.50 13.50
Never hinged 22.50
On cover 35.00
On cover, single franking 140.00
Single franking on printed matter 140.00
57 A1 3kr rose 18.50 7.50
Never hinged 30.00
On cover 27.50
58 A1 6kr blue 1.50 20.00
Never hinged 2.50
On cover 50.00
59 A1 9kr bister 2.25 22.50
Never hinged 3.75
On cover 60.00
Nos. 56-59 (4) 34.75 63.50

For reprint of No. 56, see note after No. 46.

1866 Rouletted in Colored Lines
60 A1 1kr green 1.50 22.50
Never hinged 2.50
On cover 65.00
On cover, single franking 200.00
61 A1 3kr rose 1.50 20.00
Never hinged 2.50
On cover 65.00
62 A1 6kr blue 1.50 37.50
Never hinged 2.50
On cover 77.50
63 A1 9kr bister 1.50 32.50
Never hinged 2.50
On cover 100.00
Nos. 60-63 (4) 6.00 112.50

Forged cancellations exist on Nos. 51-52, 58-63.
The Thurn & Taxis Stamps, Northern and Southern Districts, were replaced on July 1, 1867, by those of Prussia.

WURTTEMBERG

LOCATION — In southern Germany
GOVT. — Kingdom
AREA — 7,530 sq. mi.
POP. — 2,580,000 (approx.)
CAPITAL — Stuttgart

Württemberg was a member of the German Confederation and became a part of the German Empire in 1870. It gave up its postal autonomy on March 31, 1902, but official stamps were issued until 1923.

16 Kreuzer = 1 Gulden
100 Pfennigs = 1 Mark (1875)

Values for unused stamps are for examples with original gum as defined in the catalogue introduction. Unused stamps without gum of Nos. 1-46 sell for about 60-70% of the figures quoted. Unused stamps without gum of Nos. 47-54 sell for about 50% of the figures quoted.

A1   A1a

1851-52 Unwmk. Typo. Imperf.
1 A1 1kr blk, buff 1,125. 95.00
On cover 375.00
a. 1kr black, straw 3,500. 500.00
On cover 950.00

---

2 A1 3kr blk, yellow 275.00 7.25
On cover 19.00
a. 3kr black, orange 3,000. 300.00
On cover 750.00
4 A1 6kr blk, yel grn 1,450. 32.50
On cover 90.00
a. 6kr black, blue green 2,600. 50.00
On cover 130.00
5 A1 9kr blk, rose 4,800. 95.00
On cover 90.00
6 A1a 18kr blk, dl vio ('52) 1,750. 725.00
On cover 1,750.
On cover, single franking 3,200.

Values for Pairs
1 A1 1kr blk, buff 400.00
1a A1 1kr blk, straw 1,750.
2 A1 3kr blk, yellow 60.00
2a A1 3kr blk, orange 2,200.
4 A1 6kr blk, yel grn 475.00
4a A1 6kr blk, yel grn 500.00
5 A1 9kr blk, rose 675.00
6 A1a 18kr blk, dl vio ('52) 2,400.

Values for Strips of 3
1 A1 1kr blk, buff 1,200.
1a A1 1kr blk, straw 3,250.
2 A1 3kr blk, yellow 275.00
2a A1 3kr blk, orange
4 A1 6kr blk, yel grn 2,800.
4a A1 6kr blk, yel grn 2,800.
5 A1 9kr blk, rose 3,000.
6 A1a 18kr blk, dl vio ('52) 6,000.

Full margins = 1mm.

On the "reprints" the letters of "Württemberg" are smaller, especially the first "e"; the right branch of the "r's" of Württemberg runs upward in the reprints and downward in the originals.

Coat of Arms — A2

With Orange Silk Threads
Typographed and Embossed
1857
7 A2 1kr yel brn 800.00 80.00
On cover 250.00
a. 1kr dark brown 1,100. 225.00
On cover 350.00
9 A2 3kr yel org 400.00 14.00
On cover 27.50
10 A2 6kr green 800.00 65.00
On cover 175.00
11 A2 9kr car rose 1,925. 70.00
On cover 175.00
a. 9kr dk lilac red 950.00
On cover 2,400.
12 A2 18kr blue 3,350. 1,350.
On cover 3,200.
On cover, single franking 6,000.

Values for Pairs
7 A2 1kr yellow brown 250.00
On traveled printed matter 800.00
a. 1kr dark brown 500.00
9 A2 3kr yellow orange 45.00
10 A2 6kr green 325.00
11 A2 9kr carmine rose 650.00
a. 9kr dk lilac red 4,500.
12 A2 18kr blue 4,500.

Full margins = 1/4mm.

Very fine examples of Nos. 7-12 with have one or two margins touching, but not cutting, the frameline.
See Nos. 13-46, 53.
The reprints have red or yellow silk threads and are printed 2mm apart, while the originals are 3/4mm apart.

1859 Without Silk Threads
13 A2 1kr brown 650.00 100.00
On cover 325.00
a. 1kr dark brown 2,000. 725.00
On cover 1,600.
15 A2 3kr yel org 275.00 14.00
On cover 25.00
16 A2 6kr green 9,600. 125.00
On cover 250.00
17 A2 9kr car rose 1,275. 80.00
On cover 140.00
a. 9kr dk reddish lilac 1,000.
On cover 2,000.
18 A2 18kr dark blue 3,000. 1,450.
On cover 5,000.
On cover, single franking 9,500.

Values for Pairs
13 A2 1kr brown 325.00
On traveled printed matter 900.00
a. 1kr dark brown 1,750.
15 A2 3kr yellow org 55.00
16 A2 6kr green 800.00
17 A2 9kr car rose 600.00
18 A2 18kr dark blue 4,800.

Full margins = 3/4mm.

The colors of the reprints are brighter; they are also printed 2mm apart instead of 1 1/4mm.

1860 Perf. 13½
19 A2 1kr brown 1,125. 125.00
On cover 475.00
20 A2 3kr yel org 325.00 9.50
On cover 25.00
21 A2 6kr green 3,000. 100.00
On cover 250.00
22 A2 9kr carmine 1,200. 120.00
On cover 450.00
a. 9kr dk lake red 2,000.
On cover 4,000.

Values for Pairs
19 A2 1kr brown 450.00
On traveled printed matter 900.00
20 A2 3kr yellow org 72.50
21 A2 6kr green 325.00
22 A2 9kr carmine 600.00
a. 9kr dk lake red 6,000.

1861 Thin Paper
23 A2 1kr brown 950.00 275.00
On cover 600.00
a. 1kr black brown 1,000. 250.00
On cover 600.00
25 A2 3kr yel org 200.00 65.00
On cover 140.00
26 A2 6kr green 400.00 110.00
On cover 225.00
27 A2 9kr rose 1,275. 275.00
On cover 600.00
a. 9kr claret 1,500. 350.00
On cover 725.00
29 A2 18kr dark blue 3,000. 2,250.
On cover 4,000.
On cover, single franking 6,000.

Values for Pairs
23 A2 1kr brown 600.00
On traveled printed matter 1,000.
a. 1kr black brown 650.00
25 A2 3kr yellow org 160.00
26 A2 6kr green 325.00
27 A2 9kr rose 1,200.
a. 9kr claret 1,750.
29 A2 18kr dark blue 4,600.

Examples of Nos. 23-29 with all perforations intact sell for considerably more.

1862 Perf. 10
30 A2 1kr blk brn 650.00 440.00
On cover 1,200.
31 A2 3kr yel org 800.00 47.50
On cover 200.00
32 A2 6kr green 525.00 160.00
On cover 360.00
33 A2 9kr claret 4,000. 800.00
On cover 2,200.

Values for Pairs
30 A2 1kr black brown 1,450.
On traveled printed matter 1,850.
31 A2 3kr yellow orange 200.00
32 A2 6kr green 525.00
33 A2 9kr claret 3,600.

1863
34 A2 1kr yel grn 45.00 13.50
On cover 25.00
a. 1kr green 400.00 95.00
On cover 250.00
36 A2 3kr rose 325.00 5.50
On cover 9.50
a. 3kr dark claret 1,600. 275.00
On cover 600.00
37 A2 6kr blue 160.00 55.00
On cover 145.00
39 A2 9kr yel brn 750.00 175.00
On cover 475.00
a. 9kr red brown 260.00 52.50
On cover 240.00
b. 9kr black brown 1,200. 190.00
On cover 600.00
40 A2 18kr orange 1,200. 400.00
On cover 950.00
On cover, single franking 1,750.

Values for Pairs
34 A2 1kr yellow grn 27.50
On traveled printed matter 125.00
a. 1kr green 275.00
36 A2 3kr rose 9.00
a. 3kr dark claret 950.00
37 A2 6kr blue 175.00
39 A2 9kr yellow brn 600.00
a. 9kr red brown 250.00
b. 9kr black brown 600.00
40 A2 18kr orange 1,200.

1865-68 Rouletted 10
41 A2 1kr yel grn 45.00 12.00
On cover 25.00
a. 1kr dark green 575.00 275.00
On cover 800.00
42 A2 3kr rose 45.00 3.25
On cover 7.00
a. 3kr claret 1,900. 2,250.
On cover 4,000.
43 A2 6kr blue 275.00 52.50
On cover 140.00
44 A2 7kr slate bl ('68) 960.00 125.00
On cover 325.00
45 A2 9kr bis brn 1,500. 120.00
On cover 200.00
a. 9kr red brown 1,150. 80.00
On cover 150.00
46 A2 18kr orange ('67) 1,800. 950.00
On cover 2,750.
On cover, single franking 4,000.

Values for Pairs
41 A2 1kr yellow grn 32.50
On traveled printed matter 140.00
a. 1kr dark green 725.00

---

42 A2 3kr rose 12.00
a. 3kr claret 6,000.
43 A2 6kr blue 175.00
44 A2 7kr slate bl ('68) 400.00
45 A2 9kr bister brn ('66) 360.00
a. 9kr red brown 240.00
46 A2 18kr orange ('67) 2,500.

A3

1869-73 Typo. & Embossed
47 A3 1kr yel grn 32.50 2.40
On cover 8.00
a. 1kr bl grn 225.00 72.50
On cover 200.00
48 A3 2kr orange 175.00 140.00
On cover 400.00
49 A3 3kr rose 16.00 1.60
On cover 4.00
50 A3 7kr blue 67.50 17.50
On cover 40.00
51 A3 9kr lt brn ('73) 80.00 40.00
On cover 240.00
a. 9kr org brn 240.00 225.00
On cover 600.00
52 A3 14kr orange 88.00 45.00
On cover 325.00
On cover, single franking 700.00
a. 14kr lemon yellow 1,500. 1,500.
On cover 4,000.
On cover, single franking 4,800.
b. 14kr dp yel org 240.00 125.00
On cover 675.00
On cover, single franking 1,000.
Nos. 47-52 (6) 459.00 246.50

Values for Pairs
47 A3 1kr yellow grn 8.00
On cover 32.50
On traveled printed matter 80.00
On traveled printed matter abroad, from, 90.00
a. 1kr bl grn 240.00
48 A3 2kr orange 350.00
On cover 675.00
49 A3 3kr rose 4.00
On cover 20.00
50 A3 7kr blue 60.00
On cover 140.00
51 A3 9kr lt brn ('73) 125.00
On cover 600.00
a. 9kr org brn 140.00
52 A3 14kr orange 140.00
a. 14kr lemon yellow 4,000.
b. 14kr dp yel org 400.00

See No. 54.

1873 Imperf.
53 A2 70kr red violet 1,750. 4,000.
On parcel post receipt card 50,000.
a. 70kr violet 2,900. 5,250.
On parcel post receipt card 52,000.

Values for Pairs
53 A2 70kr red violet 11,000.
a. 70kr violet 12,000.

Nos. 53 and 53a have single or double lines of fine black dots printed in the gutters between the stamps.

1874 Perf. 11½x11
54 A3 1kr yellow green 110.00 40.00
On cover 125.00
Pair 125.00

A4   A5

1875-1900 Typo.
55 A4 2pf sl gray ('93) 2.00 .95
Never hinged 4.00
On cover 8.00
56 A4 3pf green 20.00 1.60
Never hinged 47.50
On cover 16.00
57 A4 3pf brn ('90) .80 .55
Never hinged 1.75
On cover 2.00
a. Imperf., pair 160.00
Never hinged 330.00
58 A4 5pf violet 9.50 .80
Never hinged 19.00
On cover 2.40
59 A4 5pf grn ('90) 1.60 .55
Never hinged 3.25
On cover 2.00
a. 5pf blue green 300.00 24.00
Never hinged 600.00
On cover 80.00
b. Imperf., pair 175.00
Never hinged 315.00
60 A4 10pf carmine 1.60 .80
Never hinged 3.00
On cover 2.40
a. 10pf rose 85.00 1.25
Never hinged 185.00
On cover 6.50
b. Imperf., pair 80.00
Never hinged 160.00

61	A4 20pf ultra		1.60	1.60
	Never hinged	4.00		
	On cover			4.00
a.	20pf dull blue		1.60	1.60
	Never hinged	4.00		
b.	Imperf. pair			3.75
		175.00		
62	A4 25pf red brn		125.00	12.00
	Never hinged	250.00		
	On cover			55.00
63	A4 25pf org ('90)		2.75	1.60
	Never hinged	5.50		
	On cover			20.00
a.	Imperf., pair	175.00		
		350.00		
64	A5 30pf org & blk ('00)		4.00	5.50
	Never hinged	9.00		
	On cover			40.00
65	A5 40pf dp rose & blk ('00)		4.00	6.50
	Never hinged	8.00		
	On cover			95.00
66	A4 50pf gray		725.00	40.00
	Never hinged	1,450.		
	On cover			725.00
	On parcel post receipt card			395.00
67	A4 50pf gray grn		65.00	6.50
	Never hinged	135.00		
	On cover			80.00
	On parcel post receipt car			25.00
68	A4 50pf pur brn ('90)		3.25	.95
	Never hinged	8.50		
	On cover			80.00
a.	50pf red brown		640.00	65.00
	Never hinged	1,200.		
	On cover			800.00
	On parcel post receipt card			275.00
b.	As #68, imperf., pair	175.00		
		350.00		
69	A4 2m yellow		800.00	260.00
	Never hinged	1,400.		
	On cover			3,250.
	On parcel post receipt card			2,000.
70	A4 2m ver, buff ('79)		2,800.	125.00
	Never hinged	—		
	On cover			3,250.
	On parcel post receipt card			2,000.
71	A5 2m org & blk ('86)		8.00	12.00
	Never hinged	15.00		
	Telegraph cancel			4.50
	On cover			325.00
	On parcel post receipt card			65.00
a.	2m yellow & black		450.00	72.50
	Never hinged	800.00		
	On cover			500.00
	On parcel post receipt card			150.00
b.	Imperf., pair	125.00		
	Never hinged	325.00		
72	A5 5m bl & blk ('81)		45.00	160.00
	Never hinged	65.00		
	Telegraph cancel			72.50
	On cover			—
	On parcel post receipt card			6,000.
a.	Double impression of figure of value	200.00		

No. 70 has "Unverkäuflich" (not for sale) printed on its back to remind postal clerks that it, like No. 69, was for their use and not to be sold to the public.

The regular postage stamps of Württemberg were superseded by those of the German Empire in 1902. Official stamps were in use until 1923.

WURTTEMBERG OFFICIAL STAMPS

For the Communal Authorities

O1

Perf. 11½x11

1875-1900	Typo.		Unwmk.	
O1	O1 2pf sl gray ('00)		3.00	1.60
	Never hinged	6.75		
	On cover			3.25
O2	O1 3pf brn ('96)		3.00	1.60
	Never hinged	6.75		
	On cover			4.50
O3	O1 5pf violet		45.00	2.40
	Never hinged	95.00		
	On cover			12.00
a.	Imperf., pair			4,000.
O4	O1 5pf bl grn ('90)		1.60	1.45
	Never hinged	4.00		
	On cover			3.25
a.	Imperf., pair	55.00		
		105.00		
O5	O1 10pf rose		9.50	2.25
	Never hinged	20.00		
	On cover			4.75
a.	Imperf., pair	95.00		
		180.00		

O6	O1 25pf org ('00)		25.00	8.00
	Never hinged	65.00		
	On cover			12.00
	Nos. O1-O6 (6)		87.10	17.30

See Nos. O12-O32. For overprints and surcharges see Nos. O7-O11, O40-O93.

Used Values
When italicized, used values for Nos. O7-O183 are for favor-canceled stamps. Postally used stamps command a premium.

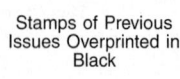

Stamps of Previous Issues Overprinted in Black

1906, Jan. 30

O7	O1 2pf slate gray		45.00	80.00
	Never hinged	80.00		
	On cover			120.00
O8	O1 3pf dk brown		14.00	12.00
	Never hinged	27.50		
	On cover			20.00
O9	O1 5pf green		6.50	4.75
	Never hinged	13.00		
	On cover			8.00
O10	O1 10pf deep rose		6.50	4.75
	Never hinged	13.00		
	On cover			8.00
O11	O1 25pf orange		47.50	72.50
	Never hinged	87.50		
	On cover			140.00
	Nos. O7-O11 (5)		119.50	174.00
	Set, C.T.O.			40.00

Centenary of Kingdom of Württemberg. Nos. O7-O11 also exist imperf but it is doubtful if they were ever issued in that condition.

1906-21			Wmk. 116	
O12	O1 2pf slate gray		4.00	.40
	Never hinged	8.00		
	On cover			16.00
O13	O1 2½pf gray blk ('16)		.80	.25
	Never hinged	1.60		
	On cover			3.50
O14	O1 3pf dk brown		.95	.40
	Never hinged	2.00		
	On cover			2.75
O15	O1 5pf green		.80	.40
	Never hinged	1.60		
	On cover			2.40
O16	O1 7½pf orange ('16)		.80	.25
	Never hinged	1.60		
	On cover			3.50
O17	O1 10pf dp rose		.80	.40
	Never hinged	1.60		
	On cover			2.00
O18	O1 10pf orange ('21)		.30	.30
	Never hinged	.55		
	On cover			2.40
O19	O1 15pf yellow brn ('16)		2.40	.25
	Never hinged	4.75		
	On cover			4.00
O20	O1 15pf purple ('17)		1.25	.25
	Never hinged	2.40		
	On cover			5.50
a.	15pf blackish violet ('21)		.30	1.40
	Never hinged	.55		
	On cover			2.40
O21	O1 20pf dp ultra ('11)		1.60	.40
	Never hinged	3.25		
	On cover			4.00
O22	O1 20pf dp green ('21)		.30	.30
	Never hinged	.55		
	On cover			2.60
O23	O1 25pf orange		.95	.40
	Never hinged	2.40		
	On cover			4.00
O24	O1 25pf brn & blk ('17)		1.25	.25
	Never hinged	2.40		
	On cover			8.00
O25	O1 35pf brown ('19)		1.60	.95
	Never hinged	3.25		
	On cover			95.00
O26	O1 40pf rose red ('21)		.30	.30
	Never hinged	.55		
	On cover			2.40
O27	O1 50pf rose lake ('11)		14.50	.40
	Never hinged	25.00		
	On cover			47.50
O28	O1 50pf vio brn ('21)		.30	.30
	Never hinged	.80		
	On cover			2.50
O29	O1 60pf olive grn ('21)		.50	.30
	Never hinged	1.25		
	On cover			3.25
O30	O1 1.25m emerald ('21)		.30	.30
	Never hinged	.80		
	On cover			2.60
O31	O1 2m gray ('21)		.30	.30
	Never hinged	.80		
	On cover			2.60
O32	O1 3m brown ('21)		.50	.30
	Never hinged	.80		
	On cover			2.60
	Nos. O12-O32 (21)		34.50	7.40

No. O24 contains solid black numerals.
Nos. O12-O32 exist imperf. Value, each pair, $6.50-$17.50.

O3

Perf. 14½x14

1916, Oct. 6	Typo.	Unwmk.	
O33	O3 2½pf slate	1.60	*1.60*
O34	O3 7½pf orange	1.60	*1.60*
O35	O3 10pf car rose	1.60	*1.60*
O36	O3 15pf yellow brn	1.60	*1.60*
O37	O3 20pf blue	1.60	*1.60*
O38	O3 25pf gray blk	4.00	*1.60*
O39	O3 50pf red brown	8.00	*1.60*
	Nos. O33-O39 (7)	20.00	*11.20*

25th year of the reign of King Wilhelm II.

Stamps of 1900-06 Surcharged

Perf. 11½x11

1916, Sept. 10		Wmk. 116	
O40	O1 25pf on 25pf orange	4.00	*.95*
a.	Without wmk.	40.00	

No. O13 Surcharged in Blue

1919		Wmk. 116	
O42	O1 2pf on 2½pf gray blk	.80	*.50*

Official Stamps of 1906-19 Overprinted

1919			
O43	O1 2½pf gray blk	.40	*.60*
O44	O1 3pf dk brown	12.00	*.60*
O45	O1 5pf green	.30	*.60*
O46	O1 7½pf orange	1.00	*.60*
O47	O1 10pf rose	.30	*.60*
O48	O1 15pf purple	.30	*.60*
O49	O1 20pf ultra	.40	*.60*
O50	O1 25pf brown & blk	.40	*.60*
O51	O1 35pf brown	4.00	*.60*
O52	O1 50pf red brown	5.50	*.60*
	Nos. O43-O52 (10)	24.60	*6.00*

Stag — O4

		Wmk. 192		
1920, Mar. 19	Litho.		*Perf. 14½*	
O53	O4 10pf maroon	1.45	*1.60*	
O54	O4 15pf brown	1.45	*1.60*	
O55	O4 20pf indigo	1.45	*1.60*	
O56	O4 30pf deep green	1.45	*1.60*	
O57	O4 50pf yellow	3.25	*1.60*	
O58	O4 75pf bister	3.25	*1.60*	
	Nos. O53-O58 (6)	12.30	*9.60*	

Official Stamps of 1906-19 Overprinted

Perf. 11½x11

1920, Apr. 1		Wmk. 116	
O59	O1 5pf green	4.00	10.00
O60	O1 10pf deep rose	2.40	4.75
O61	O1 15pf dp violet	2.40	5.25

O62	O1 20pf ultra		4.00	8.75
a.	Wmk. 192		4.75	8.75
O63	O1 50pf red brown		6.50	20.00
	Nos. O59-O63 (5)		19.30	48.75

Nos. O59 to O88 were available for postage throughout all Germany but were used almost exclusively in Württemberg.

Stamps of 1917-21 Surcharged in Black, Red or Blue

1923

O64	O1 5m on 10pf orange	.25	*.50*
O65	O1 10m on 15pf dp violet	.25	*.50*
O66	O1 12m on 40pf rose red	.25	*.50*
O67	O1 20m on 10pf orange	.80	*.50*
O68	O1 25m on 20pf green	.25	*.50*
O69	O1 40m on 20pf green	.25	*.50*
O70	O1 50m on 60pf olive grn	.25	*.50*

Surcharged

O71	O1 60m on 1.25m emerald	.25	*.50*
O72	O1 100m on 40pf rose red	.25	*.50*
O73	O1 200m on 2m gray (R)	.25	*.50*
O74	O1 300m on 50pf red brn (Bl)	.25	*.50*
O75	O1 400m on 3m brn (Bl)	.25	*.50*
O76	O1 1000m on 60pf ol grn	.25	*.50*
O77	O1 2000m on 1.25m emerald	.25	*.50*
	Nos. O64-O77 (14)	4.05	*7.00*

Abbreviations:
Th = (Tausend) Thousand
Mil = (Million) Million
Mlrd = (Milliarde) Billion

Surcharged

1923

O78	O1 5th m on 10pf orange	.25	*.50*
O79	O1 20th m on 40pf rose red	.25	*.50*
O80	O1 50th m on 15pf violet	.80	*.50*
O81	O1 75th m on 2m gray	1.60	*.50*
O82	O1 100th m on 20pf green	.25	*.50*
O83	O1 250th m on 3m brown	.25	*.50*

Surcharged

O84	O1 1mil m on 60pf ol grn	1.25	*.50*
O85	O1 2mil m on 50pf red brn	.25	*.50*
O86	O1 5mil m on 1.25m emer	.25	*.50*

Surcharged

O87	O1 4 mlrd m on 50pf red brn	4.00	*.50*
O88	O1 10 mlrd m on 3m brn	3.25	*.50*
	Nos. O78-O88 (11)	12.40	5.50

No. O23 Surcharged in Rentenpfennig as

1923, Dec.

O89	O1 3pf on 25pf orange	.50	*.40*
O90	O1 5pf on 25pf orange	.40	*.40*
O91	O1 10pf on 25pf orange	.40	*.40*

O92	O1	20pf on 25pf orange	.50	.40
O93	O1	50pf on 25pf orange	.40	.40
		Nos. O89-O93 (5)	2.20	2.00

For the State Authorities

O6

Perf. 11½x11

		1881-1902	Typo.	Unwmk.
O94	O6	2pf sl gray ('96)	1.60	1.60
O95	O6	3pf green	25.00	4.50
O96	O6	3pf dk brown ('90)	1.60	.80
O97	O6	5pf violet	8.00	1.90
O98	O6	5pf green ('90)	2.40	.80
O99	O6	10pf rose	8.00	1.90
O100	O6	20pf ultra	1.00	2.40
O101	O6	25pf brown	35.00	6.50
O102	O6	25pf orange ('90)	5.25	1.40
O103	O6	30pf org & blk ('02)	2.00	3.25
O104	O6	40pf dp rose & blk ('02)	2.00	3.25
O105	O6	50pf gray grn	6.50	8.75
O106	O6	50pf maroon ('91)	1.60	4.00
a.		50pf red brown ('90)	240.00	1,750.
O107	O6	1m yellow	72.50	175.00
O108	O6	1m violet ('90)	5.50	16.00
		Nos. O94-O108 (15)	177.95	232.05

See #O119-O135. For overprints & surcharges see #O109-O118, O146-O164, O176-O183.

Overprinted in Black

1906

O109	O6	2pf slate gray	27.50	6.00
O110	O6	3pf dk brown	5.50	6.00
O111	O6	5pf green	4.75	6.00
O112	O6	10pf dp rose	4.50	6.00
O113	O6	20pf ultra	4.75	6.00
O114	O6	25pf orange	11.00	6.00
O115	O6	30pf org & blk	9.50	6.00
O116	O6	40pf dp rose & blk	32.50	6.00
O117	O6	50pf red brown	32.50	6.00
O118	O6	1m purple	65.00	6.00
		Nos. O109-O118 (10)	197.50	60.00

Cent. of the kingdom of Württemberg.
Nos. O109 to O118 are also found imperforate, but it is doubtful if they were ever issued in that condition. Value, each: unused $45; never hinged $90.

		1906-19		Wmk. 116
O119	O6	2pf slate gray	.50	.40
O120	O6	2½pf gray blk ('16)	.55	.40
O121	O6	3pf dk brown	.50	.40
O122	O6	5pf green	.50	.40
O123	O6	7½pf orange ('16)	.55	.40
O124	O6	10pf deep rose	.50	.40
O125	O6	15pf yel brn ('16)	.65	.40
O126	O6	15pf purple ('17)	1.25	.40
O127	O6	20pf ultra	.65	.40
O128	O6	25pf orange	.50	.40
O129	O6	25pf brn & blk ('17)	.50	.40
O130	O6	30pf org & blk	.50	.40
O131	O6	35pf brown ('19)	1.60	2.40
O132	O6	40pf dp rose & blk	.50	.40
O133	O6	50pf red brown	.65	.40
O134	O6	1m purple	2.40	.40
O135	O6	1m sl & blk ('17)	2.40	.80
		Nos. O119-O135 (17)	14.70	9.20

King Wilhelm II — O8

		1916	Unwmk. Typo.	Perf. 14
O136	O8	2½pf slate	.80	.45
O137	O8	7½pf orange	.80	.45
O138	O8	10pf carmine	.80	.45
O139	O8	15pf yellow brn	.80	.45
O140	O8	20pf blue	.80	.45
O141	O8	25pf gray blk	1.60	.65
O142	O8	30pf green	1.60	.65
O143	O8	40pf claret	2.40	1.25
O144	O8	50pf red brn	3.25	1.60
O145	O8	1m violet	3.25	1.60
		Nos. O136-O145 (10)	16.10	8.00

25th year of the reign of King Wilhelm II.

Stamps of 1890-1906 Surcharged

		1916-19	Wmk. 116	Perf. 11½x11
O146	O6	25pf on 25pf orange	2.75	.80
a.		Without watermark	35.00	14,400.
O147	O6	50pf on 50pf red brn	1.60	1.10
a.		Inverted surcharge	32.50	

Beware of fake cancels on No. O146a.

No. O120 Surcharged in Blue

		1919		Wmk. 116
O149	O6	2pf on 2½pf gray blk	1.60	1.60

Official Stamps of 1890-1919 Overprinted

1919

O150	O6	2½pf gray blk	.55	.40
O151	O6	3pf dk brown	7.25	.80
a.		Without watermark	52.50	
O152	O6	5pf green	.40	.40
O153	O6	7½pf orange	.40	.40
O154	O6	10pf rose	.40	.40
O155	O6	15pf purple	.40	.40
O156	O6	20pf ultra	.40	.40
O157	O6	25pf brn & blk	.40	.40
a.		Inverted overprint	95.00	240.00
O158	O6	30pf org & blk	.80	.40
a.		Inverted overprint	475.00	—
O159	O6	35pf brown	.55	.40
O160	O6	40pf rose & blk	.55	.40
O161	O6	50pf claret	.80	.65
O162	O6	1m slate & blk	.80	.80
		Nos. O150-O162 (13)	13.70	6.25

Nos. O151, O151a Surcharged in Carmine

		1920		Wmk. 116
O164	O6	75pf on 3pf dk brn	1.25	1.25
a.		Without watermark	80.00	20.00

View of Stuttgart O9

10pf, 50pf, 2.50m, 3m, View of Stuttgart. 15pf, 75pf, View of Ulm. 20pf, 1m, View of Tubingen. 30pf, 1.25m, View of Ellwangen.

		Wmk. 192		
		1920, Mar. 25	Typo.	Perf. 14½
O166	O9	10pf maroon	.55	1.20
O167	O9	15pf brown	.55	1.20
O168	O9	20pf indigo	.55	1.20
O169	O9	30pf blue grn	.55	1.20
O170	O9	50pf yellow	.55	1.20
O171	O9	75pf bister	.55	1.20
O172	O9	1m orange red	.80	1.20
O173	O9	1.25m dp violet	.80	1.20
O174	O9	2.50m dark ultra	2.00	1.20
O175	O9	3m yellow grn	2.40	1.20
		Nos. O166-O175 (10)	9.30	12.00

Official Stamps of 1906-19 Overprinted

		1920	Wmk. 116	Perf. 11½x11
O176	O6	5pf green	2.40	4.00
O177	O6	10pf deep rose	1.60	3.25
O178	O6	15pf purple	1.60	3.25
O179	O6	20pf ultra	1.60	1.60
a.		Wmk. 192	125.00	325.00
O180	O6	30pf orange & blk	1.60	4.00
O181	O6	40pf dp rose & blk	1.60	3.25
O182	O6	50pf red brown	1.60	4.00
O183	O6	1m slate & blk	2.40	8.00
		Nos. O176-O183 (8)	14.40	31.35

The note after No. O63 will also apply to Nos. O176-O183.

NORTH GERMAN CONFEDERATION

Northern District
30 Groschen = 1 Thaler
Southern District
60 Kreuzer = 1 Gulden
Hamburg
16 Schillings = 1 Mark

Values for unused stamps are for examples with original gum as defined in the catalogue introduction. Stamps without gum sell for about 50% of the figures quoted.

A1   A2

Rouletted 8½ to 10, 11 to 12½ and Compound

		1868	Typo.	Unwmk.
1	A1	¼gr violet	15.00	15.00
		Never hinged	50.00	
		On cover		55.00
		On cover, single franking		150.00
b.		¼gr red lilac	35.00	22.00
		On cover		57.50
		On cover, single franking		150.00
c.		¼gr gray violet	65.00	37.50
		On cover		160.00
		On cover, single franking		550.00
2	A1	½gr green	30.00	4.00
		Never hinged	65.00	
		On cover		16.00
3	A1	½gr orange	30.00	2.50
		Never hinged	65.00	
		On cover		8.00
4	A1	1gr rose	20.00	1.60
		Never hinged	40.00	
		On cover		4.25
b.		Half used as ½gr on cover		
5	A1	2gr ultra	80.00	3.25
		Never hinged	125.00	
		On cover		8.00
6	A1	5gr bister	80.00	9.50
		Never hinged	125.00	
		On cover		65.00
7	A2	1kr green	35.00	8.00
		Never hinged	60.00	
		On cover		25.00
8	A2	2kr orange	55.00	55.00
		Never hinged	90.00	
		On cover		140.00
9	A2	3kr rose	35.00	3.25
		Never hinged	60.00	
		On cover		8.00
10	A2	7kr ultra	160.00	11.00
		Never hinged	260.00	
		On cover		47.50
11	A2	18kr bister	35.00	65.00
		Never hinged	65.00	
		On cover		200.00
		Nos. 1-11 (11)	575.00	178.10

See Nos. 13-23.

Imperf

1a	A1	¼gr red lilac	200.00	—
2a	A1	½gr green	95.00	—
3a	A1	½gr orange	140.00	—
4a	A1	1gr rose	80.00	—
5a	A1	2gr ultra	275.00	—
6a	A1	5gr bister	275.00	—
7a	A2	1kr green	72.50	125.00
8a	A2	2kr orange	200.00	95.00
9a	A2	3kr rose	80.00	100.00
10a	A2	7kr ultra	350.00	675.00
11a	A2	18kr bister	350.00	675.00

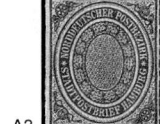

A3

1868

12	A3 (½s)	lilac brown	110.00	55.00
		Never hinged	200.00	
		On cover		125.00
a.		½gr reddish brown	110.00	55.00
		Never hinged	200.00	
		On cover		125.00
b.		½gr dark carmine brown	140.00	140.00
		On cover		325.00
c.		½gr violet brown	200.00	200.00
		On cover		360.00
d.		Imperf	200.00	
		Never hinged	350.00	

See No. 24.

		1869		Perf. 13½x14
13	A1	¼gr lilac	14.50	16.00
		Never hinged	35.00	
		On cover		40.00
a.		¼gr red violet	25.00	20.00
		Never hinged	40.00	
		On cover		52.50
14	A1	½gr green	5.25	2.75
		Never hinged	10.00	
		On cover		8.00
15	A1	½gr orange	5.25	3.50
		Never hinged	10.00	
		On cover		6.50
16	A1	1gr rose	4.00	1.60
		Never hinged	7.25	
		On cover		4.00
17	A1	2gr ultra	7.25	2.00
		Never hinged	16.00	
		On cover		6.50
18	A1	5gr bister	8.75	10.00
		Never hinged	19.00	
		On cover		40.00
19	A2	1kr green	12.75	10.00
		Never hinged	25.00	
		On cover		16.00
20	A2	2kr orange	40.00	110.00
		Never hinged	95.00	
		On cover		250.00
21	A2	3kr rose	7.25	3.25
		Never hinged	14.50	
		On cover		6.50
22	A2	7kr ultra	11.00	12.00
		Never hinged	17.50	
		On cover		27.50
23	A2	18kr bister	150.00	1,750.
		Never hinged	250.00	
		On cover		6,000.
		On cover, single franking		8,000.
		Pair on cover		10,500.
		Nos. 13-23 (11)	266.00	1,921.

Counterfeit cancels exist on No. 23.

1869

24	A3 (½s)	dull violet brown	4.75	8.75
		Never hinged	8.00	
		On cover		32.50
a.		½s dark red brown	9.25	19.00
		Never hinged	25.00	
		On cover		60.00
b.		½s dark brown	80.00	55.00
		Never hinged	180.00	
		On cover		125.00

A4   A5

			Perf. 14x13½	
25	A4	10gr gray	325.00	400.00
		Never hinged	550.00	
		Pen cancellation		65.00
		On cover with postmark		2,000.
		On cover with pen cancellation		200.00
		On cover with pen cancellation and postmark		400.00
26	A5	30gr blue	240.00	960.00
		Never hinged	450.00	
		Pen cancellation		140.00
		On cover with postmark		6,000.
		On cover with pen cancellation		475.00
		On cover with pen cancellation and postmark		1,450.

Counterfeit cancels exist on No. 26.
See Germany designs A2, A3 and A8 for similar stamps.

OFFICIAL STAMPS

O1

		1870	Unwmk. Typo.	Perf. 14½x14
O1	O1	¼gr black & buff	27.50	45.00
		Never hinged	65.00	
		On cover		140.00
O2	O1	½gr black & buff	9.50	20.00
		Never hinged	20.00	
		On cover		80.00
O3	O1	½gr black & buff	2.75	4.00
		Never hinged	5.50	
		On cover		15.00

O4	O1	1gr black & buff	2.75	2.00
		Never hinged	5.50	
		On cover		4.00
O5	O1	2gr black & buff	7.25	4.75
		Never hinged	13.00	
		On cover		15.00
O6	O1	1kr black & gray	7.50	900.00
		Never hinged	65.00	
		On cover		700.00
O7	O1	2kr black & gray	80.00	875.00
		Never hinged	160.00	
		On cover		2,400.
O8	O1	3kr black & gray	25.00	47.50
		Never hinged	57.50	
		On cover		200.00
O9	O1	7kr black & gray	45.00	275.00
		Never hinged	80.00	
		On cover		700.00
		Nos. O1-O9 (9)	232.25	1,523.

Counterfeit cancels exist on Nos. O6-O9.
The stamps of the North German Confederation were replaced by those of the German Empire on Jan. 1, 1872.

GERMANY

ˈjər-mə-nē

LOCATION — In northern Europe bordering on the Baltic and North Seas
AREA — 182,104 sq. mi. (until 1945)
POP. — 67,032,242 (1946)
CAPITAL — Berlin

30 Silbergroschen or Groschen = 1 Thaler
60 Kreuzer = 1 Gulden
100 Pfennigs = 1 Mark (1875)

Watermarks

Wmk. 48 —
Diagonal
Zigzag Lines

Wmk. 116 —
Crosses and
Circles

Wmk. 125 —
Lozenges

Wmk. 126 —
Network

Wmk. 127 —
Quatrefoils

Wmk. 192 —
Circles

Wmk. 223 —
Eagle

Wmk. 237 —
Swastikas

Wmk. 241 —
Cross

Empire

Values for unused stamps are for examples with original gum as defined in the catalogue introduction. Any exceptions are specifically mentioned.

Imperial Eagle — A1

Typographed, Center Embossed
1872   Unwmk.   Perf. 13½x14½
Eagle with small shield

1	A1	¼gr violet	225.00	95.00
		Never hinged	1,350.	
		On cover		400.00
2	A1	⅓gr green	525.00	40.00
		Never hinged	4,000.	
a.		Imperf.		65.00
b.		⅓gr dk gray grn	1,300.	135.00
		Never hinged	12,000.	
		On cover		275.00
3	A1	½gr red orange	1,050.	45.00
		Never hinged	6,000.	
		On cover		65.00
a.		½gr orange yellow	1,250.	52.50
		Never hinged	12,000.	
		On cover		65.00
4	A1	1gr rose	325.00	8.00
		Never hinged	1,600.	
		On cover		16.00
a.		Imperf.		
b.		Half used as ½gr on cover		55,000.
5	A1	2gr ultra	1,700.	15.00
		Never hinged	11,000.	
		On cover		32.50
a.		Imperf.		9,500.
6	A1	5gr bister	900.00	95.00
		Never hinged	7,250.	
		On cover		250.00
a.		Imperf.		11,000.
7	A1	1kr green	725.00	55.00
		Never hinged	5,250.	
		On cover		110.00
8	A1	2kr orange	40.00	175.00
		Never hinged	145.00	
		On cover		325.00
a.		2kr red orange	650.00	325.00
		Never hinged	5,250.	
		On cover		400.00
9	A1	3kr rose	1,900.	16.00
		Never hinged	13,000.	
		On cover		24.00
10	A1	7kr ultra	2,600.	95.00
		Never hinged	14,500.	
		On cover		145.00
11	A1	18kr bister	525.00	400.00
		Never hinged	3,500.	
		On cover		1,800.

Values for imperforates are for copies postmarked at Leipzig (⅓gr), Coblenz (1gr), Hoengen (2gr) and Leutersdorf (5gr).

A2

A3

1872   Typo.   Perf. 14½x13½

12	A2	10gr gray	55.00	1,450.
		Never hinged	130.00	
		Pen cancellation		175.00
		Pen cancellation and postmark		240.00
		On cover with postmark		4,000.
		On cover with pen cancellation		525.00
		On cover with pen cancellation and postmark		650.00
13	A3	30gr blue	110.00	2,750.
		Never hinged	240.00	
		Pen cancellation		600.00
		Pen cancellation and postmark		875.00
		On cover with postmark		11,250.
		On cover with pen cancellation		1,300.
		On cover with pen cancellation and postmark		1,500.

For similar designs see A8, North German Confederation A4, A5.

A4

A5

Center Embossed
1872   Perf. 13½x14½
Eagle with large shield

14	A4	¼gr violet	75.00	130.00
		Never hinged	225.00	
		On cover		375.00
15	A4	⅓gr yellow green	35.00	15.00
		Never hinged	140.00	
		On cover		37.50
a.		⅓gr blue green	130.00	120.00
		Never hinged	450.00	
		On cover		300.00
16	A4	½gr orange	37.50	9.00
		Never hinged	140.00	
		On cover		15.00
a.		Imperf.		
17	A4	1gr rose	75.00	6.00
		Never hinged	225.00	
		On cover		12.00
a.		Imperf.		16,500.
		On cover		75,000.
b.		Half used as ½gr on cover		67,500.
18	A4	2gr ultra	22.50	6.75
		Never hinged	75.00	
		On cover		15.00
19	A4	2½gr orange brn	2,000.	75.00
		Never hinged	18,750.	
		On cover		210.00
a.		2½gr lilac brown	5,250.	600.00
		Never hinged	23,000.	
		On cover		900.00
20	A4	5gr bister	30.00	30.00
		Never hinged	140.00	
		On cover		140.00
a.		Imperf.		8,250.
		On cover		150,000.
21	A4	1kr yel grn	37.50	35.00
		Never hinged	140.00	
		On cover		60.00
a.		1kr blue green	300.00	525.00
		Never hinged	1,400.	
		On cover		900.00
22	A4	2kr orange	500.00	2,400.
		Never hinged	2,400.	
		On cover		3,500.
23	A4	3kr rose	22.50	7.00
		Never hinged	87.50	
		On cover		15.00
24	A4	7kr ultra	32.50	67.50
		Never hinged	140.00	
		On cover		120.00
25	A4	9kr red brown	450.00	410.00
		Never hinged	1,900.	
		On cover		575.00
a.		9kr lilac brown	1,500.	500.00
		Never hinged	11,500.	
		On cover		900.00

26	A4	18kr bister	35.00	2,100.
		Never hinged	110.00	
		On cover		13,000.

Values for Nos. 17a and 20a are for copies postmarked at Potsdam (1gr), Damgarten or Anklam (5gr).

Nos. 14-26 with embossing inverted are fraudulent.

1874   Brown Surcharge

27	A5	2½gr on 2½gr brn	37.50	42.50
		Never hinged	92.50	
		On cover		170.00
28	A5	9kr on 9kr brown	82.50	450.00
		Never hinged	170.00	
		On cover		825.00

A6

A7

"Pfennige"

1875-77   Typo.

29	A6	3pf blue green	57.50	5.25
		Never hinged	450.00	
		On cover		10.00
a.		yellow green	100.00	9.25
		Never hinged	875.00	
		On cover		19.00
30	A6	5pf violet	97.50	3.75
		Never hinged	925.00	
		On cover		5.75

Center Embossed

31	A7	10pf rose	42.50	1.50
		Never hinged	300.00	
		On cover		4.00
a.		reddish brown ('75)	1,350.	190.00
		Never hinged	—	
		On cover		260.00
32	A7	20pf ultra	450.00	1.90
		Never hinged	2,700.	
		On cover		7.50
a.		blue	525.00	30.00
		Never hinged	3,850.	
		On cover		45.00
33	A7	25pf red brown	500.00	18.00
		Never hinged	4,500.	
		On cover		60.00
		On cover, single franking		550.00
a.		yellow brown	2,300.	100.00
		Never hinged	19,000.	
		On cover		210.00
b.		deep brown ('78)	2,750.	225.00
		Never hinged	21,500.	
		On cover		300.00
		On cover, single franking		750.00
34	A7	50pf gray	1,650.	11.00
		Never hinged	7,500.	
		On cover		57.50
		On cover, single franking		85.00
a.		gray black	3,400.	340.00
		Never hinged		
		On cover		450.00
		On cover, single franking		600.00
35	A7	50pf ol gray ('77)	1,900.	14.00
		Never hinged	11,500.	
		On cover		70.00
a.		dk ol green	3,750.	325.00
		Never hinged	17,500.	
		On cover		450.00
		Nos. 29-35 (7)	*4,697.*	*55.40*

See Nos. 37-42. For surcharges see Offices in Turkey Nos. 1-6.

Values for used blocks of 4

29	A6	3pf blue green	425.00
a.		3pf yellow green	450.00
30	A6	5pf violet	30.00
31	A7	10pf rose	22.50
a.		10pf reddish brown	—
32	A7	20pf ultramarine	190.00
a.		20pf blue	300.00
33	A7	25pf red brown	350.00
a.		25pf yellow brown	800.00
b.		25pf deep brown	—
34	A7	50pf gray	150.00
a.		50pf gray black	1,500.
35	A7	50pf olive gray	190.00
a.		50pf dark olive green	1,100.

**Half of No. 54 Handstamp
Surcharged in Violet**

3PF

1901   *Perf. 14*

65B	A11 3pf on half of 5pf	9,750.	7,500.
	Never hinged	26,500.	
	On newsprint wrapper		16,500.

This provisional was produced aboard the German cruiser Vineta. The purser, with the ship commander's approval, surcharged and bisected 300 5pf stamps so the ship's post office could meet the need for a 3pf (printed matter rate). The crew wanted to send home U.S. newspapers reporting celebrations of the Kaiser's birthday.

Forgeries exist and improper usages as well.

A16

1902   **Typo.**

65C	A16 2pf gray	1.50	.60
	Never hinged	6.75	
	On cover		2.50
66	A16 3pf brown	.75	1.00
	Never hinged	2.60	
	On cover		3.00
a.	"DFUTSCHES"	9.75	42.50
	Never hinged	30.00	
	On cover		145.00
b.	3pf yellow brown	240.00	45.00
	Never hinged	675.00	
	On cover		75.00
67	A16 5pf green	4.00	1.00
	Never hinged	15.00	
	On cover		2.25
a.	5pf deep blue green	325.00	9.50
	Never hinged	950.00	
	On cover		24.00
68	A16 10pf carmine	9.00	1.00
	Never hinged	37.50	
	On cover		2.25
69	A16 20pf ultra	30.00	1.00
	Never hinged	120.00	
	On cover		4.50
a.	20pf violet blue	600.00	75.00
	Never hinged	2,250.	
	On cover		160.00
b.	20pf gray blue	900.00	1,150.
	Never hinged	6,750.	
70	A16 25pf org & blk, *yel*	45.00	2.10
	Never hinged	180.00	
	On cover		19.00
71	A16 30pf org & blk, *sal*	60.00	.60
	Never hinged	225.00	
	On cover		19.00
72	A16 40pf lake & blk	90.00	1.00
	Never hinged	300.00	
	On cover		19.00
73	A16 50pf pur & blk, *buff*	70.00	1.10
	Never hinged	275.00	
	On cover		27.50
74	A16 80pf lake & blk, *rose*	200.00	3.00
	Never hinged	800.00	
	On cover		47.50
	Nos. 65C-74 (10)	510.25	12.40
	Set, never hinged	1,965.	

Nos. 65C-74 exist imperf. Value, set: unused $1,600; never hinged $3,750.

See Nos. 80-91, 118-119, 121-132, 169, 174, 210. For surcharges see Nos. 133-136, B1, Offices in China 37-42, 47-52, Offices in Morocco 20-28, 33-41, 45-53, Offices in Turkey 31-38, 43-50, 55-59.

A17

A18

A19

A20

**Perf. 14¼-14½ (26x17 holes)
Engr.**

75	A17 1m carmine rose	240.00	2.75
	Never hinged	1,400.	
	On parcel post receipt card		27.50
	On registered letter		52.50
a.	Imperf.	900.00	11,500.
	Never hinged	3,000.	
76	A18 2m gray blue	82.50	97.50
	Never hinged	260.00	
	On parcel post receipt card		300.00
	On registered letter		600.00
77	A19 3m black violet	225.00	19.00
	Never hinged	1,350.	
	On parcel post receipt card		315.00
	On registered letter		625.00
a.	Imperf.	900.00	11,500.
	Never hinged	3,000.	
78	A20 5m slate & car	210.00	19.00
	Never hinged	675.00	
	On parcel post receipt card		325.00
	On registered letter		650.00
a.	Imperf.	900.00	11,500.
	Never hinged	2,750.	

See Nos. 92, 94-95, 102, 111-113. For surcharges see Nos. 115-116, Offices in China 43, 45-46, 53, 55-56, Offices in Morocco 29, 31-32, 42, 44, 54, 56-57, Offices in Turkey 39, 41-42, 51, 53-54.

A21

79	A21 2m gray blue	120.00	5.00
	Never hinged	375.00	
	On parcel post receipt card		110.00
	On registered letter		225.00
a.	Imperf.	900.00	11,500.
	Never hinged	2,600.	
	Nos. 75-79 (5)	877.50	143.25
	Set, never hinged	3,125.	

See Nos. 93, 114. For surcharges see Nos. 117, Offices in China 44, 54, Offices in Morocco 30, 43, 55, Offices in Turkey 40, 52.

Perf. 14 (25x16 holes)

75b	A17 1m carmine red	600.00	26.00
	Never hinged	1,900.	
	On parcel post receipt card		125.00
	On registered letter		250.00
77b	A19 3m black violet	75.00	26.00
	Never hinged	275.00	
	On parcel post receipt card		450.00
	On registered letter		900.00
78b	A20 5m slate & car	26,000.	4,500.
	Never hinged	37,500.	
	On parcel post receipt card		6,750.
	On registered letter		13,500.
79b	A18 2m gray blue	975.00	30.00
	Never hinged	2,800.	
	On parcel post receipt card		210.00
	On registered letter		425.00

**1905-19 Typo. Wmk. 125 Perf. 14
Wartime Printing
Stamps with dark colors, indistinct impressions, yellow gum**

81	A16 3pf brown ('15)	.60	1.50
	Never hinged	1.40	
	On cover		1.90
a.	3pf dark brown	22.50	105.00
	Never hinged	52.50	
	On cover		135.00
82	A16 5pf green (shades)	.60	1.50
	Never hinged	1.40	
	On cover		1.90
b.	Bklt. pane of 5 + label ('11)	250.00	500.00
	Never hinged	500.00	
c.	Bklt. pane of 4 + 2 labels ('10)	400.00	800.00
	Never hinged	800.00	
d.	Bklt. pane of 2 + 4 labels ('12)	250.00	500.00
	Never hinged	500.00	
e.	Bklt. pane, #82 + 5 #83 ('17)	75.00	190.00
	Never hinged	190.00	

f.	Bklt. pane, 2 #82 + 4 #83 ('20)	21.00	50.00
	Never hinged	50.00	
g.	Bklt. pane, 4 #82 + 2 #83 ('19)	21.00	50.00
	Never hinged	50.00	
83	A16 10pf red	.90	1.60
	Never hinged	1.40	
	On cover		1.90
b.	Bklt. pane of 5 + label ('10)	325.00	650.00
	Never hinged	650.00	
c.	Bklt. pane of 4 + 2 labels ('12)	300.00	625.00
	Never hinged	625.00	
d.	10pf carmine red	2.00	1.50
	Never hinged	5.25	
e.	10pf orange red	75.00	160.00
	Never hinged	225.00	
			230.00
f.	10pf lilac red	260.00	82.50
	Never hinged	900.00	
	On cover		150.00
84	A16 20pf blue vio ('18)	.75	1.50
	Never hinged	2.10	
			1.50
a.	20pf light blue	13.00	3.75
	Never hinged	52.50	
	On cover		8.25
b.	20pf ultramarine	8.00	1.50
	Never hinged	42.50	
			2.25
c.	Imperf.	625.00	2,750.
	Never hinged	1,750.	
d.	Half used as 10pf on cover		700.00

No. 84d was used at Field Post Office No. 107 in 1915, and at Field Post Office No. 766 during 1917.

85	A16 25pf org & blk, *yel*	.60	1.50
	Never hinged	1.40	
	On cover		1.90
86	A16 30pf org & blk, *buff*	.75	1.50
	Never hinged	1.40	
	On cover		1.90
a.	30pf org & blk, *cr*	26.00	90.00
	Never hinged	82.50	
	On cover		150.00
87	A16 40pf lake & black	1.10	1.50
	Never hinged	3.25	
	On cover		1.90
88	A16 50pf pur & blk, *buff*	.75	1.50
	Never hinged	1.40	
	On cover		1.90
a.	50pf pur & blk, *yel org*	19.00	75.00
	Never hinged	47.50	
	On cover		110.00
89	A16 60pf magenta	1.50	1.50
	Never hinged	4.50	
	On cover		1.90
a.	60pf red violet	22.50	13.50
	Never hinged	67.50	
	On cover		60.00
90	A16 75pf green & blk ('19)	.25	2.25
	Never hinged	.75	
	On cover		3.75
a.	75pf dk bluish grn & greenish blk	1.10	3.00
	Never hinged	3.75	
	On cover		4.50
91	A16 80pf lake & blk, *rose*	1.10	1.90
	Never hinged	3.25	
	On cover		5.00

**Perf. 14½ (25x17 holes)
Engr.**

92	A17 1m car rose	2.60	2.25
	Never hinged	7.50	
	On cover		3.75
93	A21 2m brt blue	5.25	4.75
	Never hinged	14.00	
	On cover		9.75
a.	2m gray blue ('16)	42.50	52.50
	Never hinged	140.00	
	On cover		90.00
94	A19 3m violet gray	3.00	4.25
	Never hinged	9.00	
	On cover		19.00
b.	3m blk violet	11.50	26.00
	Never hinged	26.00	
	On cover		55.00
95	A20 5m slate & car	3.00	4.75
	Never hinged	7.50	
	On cover		27.50
a.	Center inverted	45,000.	65,000.
	Never hinged		67,500.
	Nos. 80-95 (15)	22.45	33.65
	Set, Never Hinged	67.00	

Perf. 14¼-14¾ (26x17 holes)

92a	A17 1m car red	140.00	110.00
	Never hinged	500.00	
			150.00
93b	A21 2m bright blue	105.00	47.50
	Never hinged	325.00	
			82.50
94c	A19 3m violet gray	225.00	500.00
	Never hinged	675.00	
			975.00
95b	A20 5m slate & car	65.00	97.50
	Never hinged	150.00	
			375.00
	Nos. 92a-95b (4)	535.00	755.00

Labels in No. 82c contain an "X." The version with advertising is worth 3 times as much. No. 82f has three 10pf stamps in the top row. The version with 3 on the bottom row is worth 4 times as much.

**Pre-War Printing
Stamps with bright colors,
sharp impressions, high quality
(often surfaced) paper, white gum**

80	A16 2pf gray ('05)	1.60	2.60
	Never hinged	4.50	
	On cover		9.00
81b	A16 3pf dk yellowish brn ('05)	2.25	1.50
	Never hinged	5.25	
			1.90
82h	A16 5pf dk bluish grn	1.60	1.40
	Never hinged	6.00	
			1.90
82i	A16 5pf yel grn ('05)	35.00	14.00
	Never hinged	140.00	
			37.50
83g	A16 10pf red	.90	1.40
	Never hinged	10.50	
			1.90
83h	A16 10pf rose red ('05)	10.50	1.40
	Never hinged	45.00	
			1.90
83i	A16 10pf carmine	225.00	150.00
	Never hinged	900.00	
			375.00
83j	A16 10pf orange red	180.00	3,750.
	Never hinged	525.00	
	On cover (late '13-14)		5,250.
84e	A16 20pf ultra	11.50	1.50
	Never hinged	57.50	
			2.25
84f	A16 20pf light bl ('06)	250.00	4.50
	Never hinged	900.00	
			11.50
84g	A16 20pf vio bl ('06)	190.00	5.25
	Never hinged	750.00	
			11.50
85a	A16 25pf org & blk, *yel* ('06)	37.50	2.75
	Never hinged	145.00	
			7.50
86b	A16 30pf org & blk, *pale yel* ('05)	35.00	1.75
	Never hinged	135.00	
			6.50
86c	A16 30pf org & blk, *yel org*	750.00	82.50
	Never hinged	2,500.	
			180.00
87a	A16 40pf lake & blk ('06)	37.50	2.10
	Never hinged	150.00	
			11.50
88b	A16 50pf pur & blk, *pale yel* ('06)	60.00	2.10
	Never hinged	180.00	
			11.50
88c	A16 50pf pur & blk, *yel org*	900.00	75.00
	Never hinged	3,600.	
			150.00
89b	A16 60pf magenta ('11)	190.00	13.50
	Never hinged	675.00	
			75.00
89c	A16 60pf violet	—	900.00
	Never hinged		
			—
91a	A16 80pf lake & blk, *rose* ('06)	19.00	3.00
	Never hinged	75.00	
			11.50

**Engr.
Perf. 14¼-14¾ (26x17 holes)**

92b	A17 1m car red ('06)	67.50	2.25
	Never hinged	315.00	
			22.50
93c	A21 2m brt blue ('06)	65.00	3.00
	Never hinged	275.00	
			22.50
94a	A19 3m brnsh vio ('11)	52.50	26.00
	Never hinged	190.00	
			110.00
95c	A20 5m slate & car ('06)	45.00	21.00
	Never hinged	90.00	
			135.00

Surcharged and overprinted stamps of designs A16-A22 are listed under Allenstein, Belgium, Danzig, France, Latvia, Lithuania, Marienwerder, Memel, Poland, Romania, Saar and Upper Silesia.

A22

1916-19   **Typo.**

96	A22 2pf lt gray ('18)	.30	3.75
	Never hinged	.75	
	On cover		7.75
97	A22 2½pf lt gray	.25	1.90
	Never hinged	.60	
	On cover		2.50
98	A22 7½pf red orange	.50	2.25
	Never hinged	1.75	
	On cover		2.60
b.	Bklt. pane, 4 #98 + 2 #100	110.00	275.00
	Never hinged	275.00	
c.	Bklt. pane, 2 #98 + 4 #99	125.00	300.00
	Never hinged	300.00	
d.	Bklt. pane, 2 #98 + 4 #100	110.00	275.00
	Never hinged	275.00	
e.	Bklt. pane, 2 #82 + 4 #98	37.50	90.00
	Never hinged	90.00	
f.	7½pf yellow orange	3.50	2.25
	Never hinged	13.50	
			3.00
99	A22 15pf yellow brown	3.00	2.25
	Never hinged	13.50	
	On cover		3.50
a.	15pf olive brown	19.00	21.00
	Never hinged	60.00	
			42.50

100 A22 15pf dk violet ('17) .25 *1.90*
Never hinged 1.00
On cover *2.25*
a. 15pf blue violet 75.00 75.00
Never hinged 190.00
On cover 190.00
b. Bklt. pane, 4 #82 + 2 #100 110.00 275.00
Never hinged 275.00
c. Bklt. pane, 2 #83 + 4 #100 82.50 210.00
Never hinged 210.00
d. 15pf blackish violet 3.00 *3.50*
Never hinged 9.00
On cover 4.50
101 A22 35pf red brown ('19) .30 *2.25*
Never hinged .75
On cover *3.75*
a. 35pf dk lake brown 21.00 18.00
Never hinged 60.00
On cover 52.50
Nos. 96-101 (6) 4.60 *14.30*
Set, never hinged 17.00

See No. 120. For surcharge see No. B2.
Nos. 98e and 100c have the 2 stamps first in the bottom row.

Type of 1902

1920 Engr. Wmk. 192 Perf. 14½
102 A19 3m black violet 1,875. *3,750.*
Never hinged 4,500.

Republic
National Assembly Issue

A23

A24

Rebuilding Germany — A25

Designs: A23, Live Stump of Tree Symbolizing that Germany will Survive her Difficulties. A24, New Shoots from Oak Stump Symbolical of New Government.

Perf. 13x13½
1919-20 Unwmk. Typo.
105 A23 10pf carmine rose .25 *1.50*
Never hinged .75
On cover *2.60*
106 A24 15pf choc & blue .25 *1.50*
Never hinged .75
On cover *2.60*
107 A25 25pf green & red .25 *1.50*
Never hinged .75
On cover *2.60*
a. "1019" instead of "1919" 97.50 *300.00*
Never hinged 225.00
On cover *425.00*
108 A25 30pf red vio & red ('20) .25 *2.25*
Never hinged 1.25
On cover *2.60*
a. A25 30pf pale lilac & brownish red 4.50 *15.00*
Never hinged 19.00
On cover *27.50*
b. "1019" instead of "1919" 45.00 *150.00*
Never hinged 105.00
On cover *225.00*
Nos. 105-108 (4) 1.00 *6.75*
Set, never hinged 3.50

Types of 1902
Perf. 15x14½
1920 Wmk. 125 Offset
111 A17 1m red 3.75 *2.40*
Never hinged 15.00
On cover *3.25*
a. Double impression 120.00 *600.00*
Never hinged 350.00
b. 1m brown lilac 35.00 27.50
Never hinged 100.00
On cover *47.50*
c. As "b," double impression *800.00*
112 A17 1.25m green 3.75 *1.90*
Never hinged 7.50
On cover *2.50*
a. Double impression 900.00
113 A17 1.50m yellow brown .50 *1.90*
Never hinged 1.25
On cover *2.50*
a. 1.50m dark brown 15.00 *90.00*
Never hinged 45.00
On cover *190.00*
b. 1.50m red brown 19.00 15.00
Never hinged 80.00
On cover *25.00*
c. As "a," double impression 100.00 *725.00*
Never hinged 275.00
d. As "b," double impression *875.00*
114 A21 2.50m lilac rose .50 *2.50*
Never hinged 1.50
On cover *3.00*
a. 2.50m magenta 1.50 2.25
Never hinged 6.00

Types of 1902 Surcharged

b. 2.50m brown lilac .75 *2.75*
Never hinged 1.90
On cover *3.75*
c. Double impression 100.00 *725.00*
Never hinged 275.00
d. As "a," double impression *650.00*
e. As "b," double impression *650.00*
Nos. 111-114 (4) 8.50 *8.70*
Set, never hinged 25.00

Nos. 111, 112 and 113 differ from the illustration in many minor respects. The numerals of Nos. 75 and 92 are outlined, with shaded background. Those of No. 111 are plain, with solid background and flags have been added to the top of the building, at right and left.

1920 Engr. Perf. 14½
115 A17 1.25m on 1m green .40 *6.00*
Never hinged 1.50
On cover *13.00*
116 A17 1.50m on 1m org brn .40 *7.25*
Never hinged 1.50
On cover *13.50*
117 A21 2.50m on 2m lilac rose 8.75 *200.00*
Never hinged 26.00
On cover *300.00*
Nos. 115-117 (3) 9.55 *213.25*
Set, never hinged 29.00

Germania Types of 1902-16
1920 Typo. Perf. 14, 14½
118 A16 5pf brown .25 *2.00*
Never hinged .70
On cover *2.60*
a. 5pf dark brown 1.60 6.00
Never hinged 4.25
On cover *11.50*
119 A16 10pf orange .25 *1.50*
Never hinged .55
On cover *1.90*
a. Tête bêche pair 1.75 *7.00*
Never hinged 3.00
d. Bklt. pane, 4 #119 + 2 #123 8.25 13.50
Never hinged 13.50
120 A22 15pf violet brn .25 *1.90*
Never hinged .70
On cover *2.60*
a. Imperf. 67.50
Never hinged 190.00
b. 15pf pale lake brn 1.50 *6.00*
Never hinged 4.25
On cover *10.50*
c. Bklt. pane, 4 #84 + 2 #120 22.50 30.00
Never hinged 40.00
121 A16 20pf green .25 *2.25*
Never hinged .90
On cover *2.60*
a. Imperf. *1,200.*
b. 20pf yellow green 1.10 *3.00*
Never hinged 3.00
On cover *7.50*
c. 20pf blue green 37.50 *100.00*
Never hinged 120.00
On cover *140.00*
123 A16 30pf dull blue .25 *1.50*
Never hinged .60
On cover *1.90*
a. Tête bêche pair 3.50 13.50
Never hinged 6.00
d. Bklt. pane, 2 #123 + 4 #124 8.25 15.00
Never hinged 15.00
124 A16 40pf carmine rose .25 *1.90*
Never hinged .60
On cover *2.25*
a. Tête bêche pair 1.90 *7.00*
Never hinged 3.00
b. Imperf. 150.00 *900.00*
Never hinged 375.00
d. Bklt. pane, 2 #124 + 4 #126 12.00 75.00
Never hinged 20.00
125 A16 50pf red lilac .60 *2.25*
Never hinged 1.60
On cover *3.00*
126 A16 60pf olive green .25 *1.60*
Never hinged .55
On cover *1.90*
a. Tête bêche pair 2.75 20.00
Never hinged 4.50
c. Imperf. 160.00
Never hinged 425.00
127 A16 75pf red violet .60 *1.90*
Never hinged 1.90
On cover *3.00*
128 A16 80pf blue violet .25 *2.25*
Never hinged .75
On cover *3.00*
a. Imperf. 190.00
Never hinged 450.00
b. 80pf grayish ultra 22.50 *75.00*
Never hinged 75.00
On cover *105.00*
129 A16 1m violet & grn .25 *2.25*
Never hinged .55
On cover *3.00*
a. Imperf. 77.50
Never hinged 190.00
130 A16 1¼m ver & mag .25 *1.90*
Never hinged .55
On cover *2.25*
131 A16 2m carmine & bl .60 *1.50*
Never hinged 2.25
On cover *3.00*

132 A16 4m black & rose .25 *2.25*
Never hinged .55
On cover *3.75*
Nos. 118-132 (14) 4.55 *26.95*
Set, never hinged 12.50

Stamps of 1920 Surcharged

No. 133

No. 135

Nos. 134, 136

1921, Aug.
133 A16 1.60m on 5pf .25 *2.25*
Never hinged 1.00
On cover *3.00*
a. On #118a 75.00 *425.00*
Never hinged 190.00
On cover *500.00*
134 A16 3m on 1¼m .25 *2.60*
Never hinged 1.00
On cover *3.50*
135 A16 5m on 75pf (G) .25 *2.25*
Never hinged 1.15
On cover *3.00*
136 A16 10m on 75pf .40 *2.25*
Never hinged 1.35
On cover *3.50*
Nos. 133-136 (4) 1.15 *9.35*
Set, never hinged 4.50

In 1920 the current stamps of Bavaria were overprinted "Deutsches Reich". These stamps were available for postage throughout Germany, but because they were used almost exclusively in Bavaria, they are listed among the issues of that state.

A26

Iron Workers A27
Miners A28

Farmers A29
Post Horn A30

Numeral of Value — A31

Plowing A32

Wmk. Lozenges (125)
1921 Typo. Perf. 14
137 A26 5pf claret .25 *2.00*
Never hinged .45
On cover *4.50*

138 A26 10pf olive green .25 *2.00*
Never hinged .75
On cover *2.60*
a. Tête bêche pair 5.50 37.50
Never hinged 9.00
b. Bklt. pane, 5 #138 + 1 #141 12.00 —
Never hinged 20.00
c. 10pf blackish olive 52.50 *275.00*
Never hinged 150.00
On cover *375.00*
139 A26 15pf grnsh blue .25 *1.60*
Never hinged .45
On cover *3.00*
140 A26 25pf dark brown .25 *1.60*
Never hinged .45
On cover *2.25*
141 A26 30pf blue green .25 *1.60*
Never hinged .45
On cover *2.25*
a. Tête bêche pair 5.50 37.50
Never hinged 9.00
b. Bklt. pane, 2 #124 + 4 #141 12.00 75.00
Never hinged 20.00
142 A26 40pf red orange .25 *1.60*
Never hinged .45
On cover *1.90*
143 A26 50pf violet .30 *1.60*
Never hinged 1.15
On cover *2.60*
144 A27 60pf red violet .25 *1.60*
Never hinged .45
On cover *1.90*
145 A27 80pf carmine rose .25 *5.25*
Never hinged .45
On cover *15.00*
146 A28 100pf yellow grn .30 *2.00*
Never hinged 1.05
On cover *5.75*
147 A28 120pf ultra .25 *1.60*
Never hinged .45
On cover *3.75*
148 A29 150pf orange .25 *2.00*
Never hinged .90
On cover *3.75*
149 A29 160pf slate grn .25 *8.50*
Never hinged .45
On cover *19.00*
150 A30 2m dp vio & rose .40 *3.50*
Never hinged 1.50
On cover *7.50*
151 A30 3m red & yel .40 *15.00*
Never hinged 1.50
On cover *30.00*
152 A30 4m dp grn & yel grn .25 *3.50*
Never hinged 1.00
On cover *6.00*

Engr.
153 A31 5m orange .30 *2.25*
Never hinged 1.00
On cover *3.25*
a. 5m brown orange 15.00 25.00
Never hinged 55.00
On cover *45.00*
b. 5m red orange 75.00 *200.00*
Never hinged 200.00
On cover *260.00*
154 A31 10m carmine rose .50 *3.00*
Never hinged 1.90
On cover *5.25*
155 A32 20m indigo & grn 3.00 *2.75*
Never hinged 7.50
On cover *5.25*
a. Green background inverted 190.00 *1,050.*
Never hinged 675.00
On cover *1,150.*
b. 20m blk bl & dull grn 30.00 72.50
Never hinged 75.00
On cover *130.00*
Nos. 137-155 (19) 8.20 *62.95*
Set, never hinged 20.00

See Nos. 156-209, 211, 222-223, 225, 227. For surcharges and overprints see Nos. 241-245, 247-248, 261-262, 273-276, B6-B7, O24.

1922 Litho. Perf. 14½x14
156 A31 100m brown vio, *buff* .25 *1.40*
Never hinged .75
On cover *3.00*
157 A31 200m rose, *buff* .25 *1.40*
Never hinged .55
On cover *3.00*
158 A31 300m green, *buff* .25 *1.40*
Never hinged .55
On cover *2.25*
159 A31 400m bis brn, *buff* .55 *2.25*
Never hinged 1.50
On cover *7.50*
a. 400m ol brn, *buff* 7.50 *90.00*
Never hinged 22.50
On cover *190.00*
b. 400m red brn, *buff* 15.00 *140.00*
Never hinged 50.00
On cover *190.00*
c. 400m pale brn, *buff* 26.00 *225.00*
Never hinged 72.50
On cover *300.00*
160 A31 500m orange, *buff* .25 *1.40*
Never hinged .35
On cover *3.00*
Nos. 156-160 (5) 1.55 *7.85*
Set, never hinged 3.00

Postally Used vs. CTO
Values quoted for canceled stamps of the 1921-1923 issues are for postally used stamps. These bring higher prices than the plentiful canceled-to-order stamps made by applying genuine handstamps to remainders. C.T.O. examples sell for about the same price as unused stamps. Certification of postal usage by competent authorities is necessary.

Perf. 14, 14½
1921-22   Typo.   Wmk. 126

161 A26 5pf claret .75 200.00
  Never hinged 2.25
  On cover   375.00
162 A26 10pf olive grn 7.00 190.00
  Never hinged 20.50
  On cover   350.00
163 A26 15pf grnsh blue .55 225.00
  Never hinged 1.50
  On cover   375.00
164 A26 25pf dark brown .25 3.75
  Never hinged .45
  On cover   9.00
165 A26 30pf blue green .85 325.00
  Never hinged 2.60
  On cover   675.00
166 A26 40pf red orange .25 3.75
  Never hinged .45
  On cover   9.00
167 A26 50pf violet ('21) .25 1.50
  Never hinged 1.00
168 A27 60pf red violet .25 20.00
  Never hinged .45
  On cover   34.00
169 A16 75pf red violet .40 2.75
  Never hinged 1.35
a. 75pf rose lilac 115.00 135.00
  Never hinged 360.00
  On cover   200.00
170 A26 75pf deep ultra .25 3.00
  Never hinged .45
171 A27 80pf car rose .40 57.50
  Never hinged 1.20
  On cover   90.00
172 A28 100pf olive green .25 1.50
  Never hinged 1.00
  On cover   2.25
a. Imperf. 60.00 1,500.
  Never hinged 150.00
b. 100pf bluish green 6.00 30.00
  Never hinged 16.50
  On cover   52.50
c. 100pf blackish green 7.50 22.50
  Never hinged 22.50
  On cover   30.00
173 A28 120pf ultra .70 110.00
  Never hinged 2.00
  On cover   190.00
174 A16 1¼m ver & mag .25 1.50
  Never hinged .60
  On cover   3.00
175 A29 150pf orange .25 1.50
  Never hinged .45
a. Imperf. 37.50
  Never hinged 110.00   1.90
176 A29 160pf slate green .70 175.00
  Never hinged 2.00
  On cover   260.00
177 A30 2m violet & rose .25 1.50
  Never hinged .45
  On cover   1.90
178 A30 3m red & yel ('21) .25 1.50
  Never hinged .45
  On cover   2.25
a. Imperf. 37.50 375.00
  Never hinged 110.00
179 A30 4m dp grn & yel grn .25 1.50
  Never hinged .45
  On cover   2.60
180 A30 5m org & yel .30 2.00
  Never hinged 1.15
  On cover   2.60
a. Imperf. 130.00
  Never hinged 300.00 3,000.
181 A30 10m car & pale rose .30 2.25
  Never hinged 1.10
  On cover   4.50
a. Pale rose (background) omitted 45.00 975.00
  Never hinged 150.00
182 A30 20m violet & org .25 3.00
  Never hinged .55
  On cover   5.50
183 A30 30m brown & yel .25 1.50
  Never hinged .65
  On cover   1.90
184 A30 50m dk grn & vio .25 1.50
  Never hinged .65
  On cover   2.60
  Nos. 161-184 (24) 15.45 1,336.
  Set, never hinged 37.50

1922-23

SIX MARKS:
Type I — Numerals upright.
Type II — Numerals leaning toward the right and slightly thinner.

EIGHT MARKS:
Type I — Numerals 2½mm wide with thick strokes.
Type II — Numerals 2mm wide with thinner strokes.

185 A30 2m blue violet .25 1.50
  Never hinged .75
  On cover   1.90
a. Imperf. 100.00
  Never hinged 190.00
b. 2m deep reddish vio 2.25 6.75
  Never hinged 6.50
  On cover   15.00
c. 2m deep violet 19.00 82.50
  Never hinged 45.00
  On cover   135.00
186 A30 3m red .25 1.50
  Never hinged .55
  On cover   1.90
187 A30 4m dark green .25 1.50
  Never hinged .75
  On cover   1.90
a. Imperf. 30.00
  Never hinged 75.00
b. 4m deep blue green 1.50 5.25

  Never hinged 4.00
  On cover   9.00
188 A30 5m orange .25 1.50
  Never hinged .75
  On cover   1.90
a. Imperf. 80.00
  Never hinged 160.00
189 A30 8m dark blue (II) .25 1.50
  Never hinged .75
  On cover   1.90
a. Type I .25 1.90
  Never hinged 1.10
  On cover   2.60
b. Imperf. 80.00
  Never hinged 160.00
190 A30 8m olive green (I) .25 1.50
  Never hinged .75
  On cover   2.60
a. Type II .40 37.50
  Never hinged 1.20
  On cover   50.00
191 A30 20m dk violet ('23) .25 1.50
  Never hinged .75
  On cover   2.25
192 A30 30m pur brn ('23) .25 7.50
  Never hinged .75
  On cover   13.50
a. 30m deep brown 1.25 35.00
  Never hinged 4.25
  On cover   65.00
193 A30 40m lt green .25 2.25
  Never hinged .90
  On cover   3.00

Engr.
194 A31 5m orange .25 1.50
  Never hinged 1.10
  On cover   2.60
a. Imperf. 140.00 2,100.
  Never hinged 225.00
b. 5m red orange 26.00 67.50
  Never hinged 75.00
  On cover   97.50
c. 5m brown orange 75.00 27.50
  Never hinged 375.00
  On cover   55.00
195 A31 10m carmine rose .55 2.25
  Never hinged 1.50
  On cover   4.50
196 A32 20m indigo & grn .25 3.50
  Never hinged .65
  On cover   5.50
a. Imperf. 175.00 2,100.
  Never hinged 225.00
b. Green background inverted 32.50 675.00
  Never hinged 75.00
c. Green background double 750.00 3,750.
  Never hinged 2,600.
  Nos. 185-196 (12) 3.30 27.50
  Set, never hinged 8.85

1922-23   Litho.   Perf. 14½x14
198 A31 50m indigo .25 1.50
  Never hinged .75
  On cover   2.60
199 A31 100m brn vio, *buff* ('23) .25 1.40
  Never hinged .55
  On cover   2.60
200 A31 200m rose, *buff* ('23) .25 1.90
  Never hinged .75
  On cover   2.60
a. 200m pale red, *buff* 3.00 26.00
  Never hinged 10.00
  On cover   40.00
b. 200m reddish lilac, *buff* 22.50 75.00
  Never hinged 72.50
  On cover   110.00
201 A31 300m grn, *buff* ('23) .25 1.50
  Never hinged .40
  On cover   1.90
202 A31 400m bis brn, *buff* ('23) .25 1.50
  Never hinged .40
  On cover   1.90
203 A31 500m org, *buff* ('23) .25 1.50
  Never hinged .40
  On cover   1.90
204 A31 1000m gray ('23) .25 1.50
  Never hinged .40
  On cover   1.90
205 A31 2000m bl ('23) .35 1.90
  Never hinged .50
  On cover   1.90
a. 2000m dark blue .75 6.00
  Never hinged 2.60
  On cover   12.50
206 A31 3000m brn ('23) .25 2.75
  Never hinged .75
  On cover   3.75
a. 3000m deep yel brn .75 3.25
  Never hinged 2.60
  On cover   5.25
b. 3000m dk gray brn .85 4.75
  Never hinged 2.75
  On cover   9.00
c. 3000m blk brn 67.50 300.00
  Never hinged 160.00
  On cover   450.00
207 A31 4000m vio ('23) .25 1.50
  Never hinged .55
  On cover   3.75
a. Imperf. 37.50 190.00
  Never hinged 110.00
208 A31 5000m gray grn ('23) .30 1.50
  Never hinged 1.00
  On cover   4.50
a. Imperf. 52.50 225.00
  Never hinged 150.00
b. 5000m dp bl grn 1.40 37.50
  Never hinged 4.00
  On cover   60.00
c. 5000m blk grn 6.75 150.00
  Never hinged 25.00
  On cover   260.00

209 A31 100,000m ver ('23) .25 1.40
  Never hinged .55
  On cover   3.00
a. Imperf. 52.50 225.00
  Never hinged 150.00
  Nos. 198-209 (12) 0.15 17.35
  Set, never hinged 6.50

1920-22   Wmk. 127   Typo.
210 A16 1¼m ver & mag 450.00 975.00
  Never hinged 1,350.
  On cover   1,350.
211 A30 50m grn & vio ('22) 2.25 825.00
  Never hinged 5.25
  On cover   1,500.

Wmk. 127 was intended for use only in printing revenue stamps.

Arms of Munich — A33

Wmk. Network (126)
1922, Apr. 22   Typo.   Perf. 13x13½
212 A33 1¼m claret .25 1.90
  Never hinged .75
  On cover   3.00
a. 1¼m brn car 2.60 7.50
  Never hinged 7.50
  On cover   15.00
b. 1¼m pale lilac rose 30.00 300.00
  Never hinged 82.50
  On cover   450.00
213 A33 2m dark violet .25 1.90
  Never hinged .75
  On cover   3.00
a. 2m dk red vio 20.00 130.00
  Never hinged 65.00
  On cover   165.00
214 A33 3m vermilion .25 1.90
  Never hinged .55
  On cover   3.00
215 A33 4m deep blue .25 1.90
  Never hinged .55
  On cover   3.00

Wmk. Lozenges (125)
216 A33 10m brown, *buff* .60 2.75
  Never hinged 2.40
  On cover   7.50
a. 10m vio brn, *buff* 26.00 90.00
  Never hinged 97.50
  On cover   120.00
217 A33 20m lilac rose, *pink* 3.75 11.50
  Never hinged 12.00
  On cover   26.00
a. 20m red, *pink* 12.00 52.50
  Never hinged 37.50
  On cover   90.00
  Nos. 212-217 (6) 5.35 21.85
  Set, never hinged 17.00

Munich Industrial Fair.

Type of 1921 and

Miners — A34   A35

1922-23   Wmk. 126   Perf. 14
221 A34 5m orange .25 13.00
  Never hinged .30
  On cover   30.00
222 A29 10m dull blue ('22) .25 1.50
  Never hinged .30
  On cover   1.90
223 A29 12m vermilion ('22) .25 1.50
  Never hinged .30
  On cover   3.75
224 A34 20m red lilac .25 1.50
  Never hinged .55
  On cover   1.90
a. Wmk. sideways .75 60.00
  Never hinged 2.60
  On cover   115.00
225 A29 25m olive brown .25 1.50
  Never hinged .30
  On cover   2.75
226 A34 30m olive green .25 2.25
  Never hinged .65
  On cover   7.50
a. 30m blk ol grn .75 37.50
  Never hinged 2.25
  On cover   67.50
227 A29 40m green .25 1.50
  Never hinged .90
  On cover   2.25
228 A34 50m grnsh blue .40 125.00
  Never hinged 1.20
  On cover   190.00
229 A35 100m violet .25 1.50
  Never hinged .75
  On cover   2.60
a. 100m purple violet .30 1.50
  Never hinged .75
  On cover   3.00
230 A35 200m carmine rose .25 1.50
  Never hinged .45
  On cover   3.75

231 A35 300m green .25 1.40
  Never hinged .35
  On cover   3.00
232 A35 400m dark brown .25 5.75
  Never hinged 1.00
  On cover   11.00
233 A35 500m red orange .25 6.50
  Never hinged .35
  On cover   11.00
234 A35 1000m slate .25 1.40
  Never hinged .35
  On cover   3.75
  Nos. 221-234 (14) 3.65 165.80
  Set, never hinged 7.00

The 50m was issued only in vertical coils. Nos. 222-223 exist imperf.
For surcharges and overprints see Nos. 246, 249-260, 263-271, 277, 310, B5, O22-O23, O25-O28.

Wartburg Castle — A36

Cathedral of Cologne — A37

1923   Engr.
237 A36 5000m deep blue .30 3.25
  Never hinged .90
  On cover   5.75
a. Imperf. 300.00 1,200.
  Never hinged 750.00
b. 5000m dk grn bl 6.00 75.00
  Never hinged 16.50
  On cover   115.00
238 A37 10,000m brn ol .30 4.00
  Never hinged 1.10
  On cover   11.50
a. 10,000m ol grn .75 12.00
  Never hinged 2.50
  Set, never hinged 2.00   19.00

Abbreviations:
Th = (Tausend) Thousand
Mil = (Million) Million
Mlrd = (Milliarde) Billion

A38

1923   Typo.
238A A38 5th m grnsh blue .25 17.00
  Never hinged .40
  On cover   37.50
b. Imperf. 90.00
  Never hinged 240.00
239 A38 50th m bister .25 1.50
  Never hinged .40
  On cover   2.25
a. Imperf. 22.50 3,750.
  Never hinged 60.00
240 A38 75th m dark violet .25 11.00
  Never hinged .40
  On cover   19.00
  Nos. 238A-240 (3) .75 29.50
  Set, never hinged 1.20

For surcharges see Nos. 272, 278.

Stamps and Types of 1922-23
Surcharged in Black, Blue, Green or Brown

No. 241

No. 243

No. 246

No. 253

No. 269

Wmk. Lozenges (125)

1923				Perf. 14	
241	A26	8th m on 30pf		.25	1.75
		Never hinged		.40	
		On cover			2.60
a.		"8" inverted		21.00	325.00
		Never hinged		60.00	

Wmk. Network (126)

242	A26	5th m on 40pf	.25	1.60
		Never hinged	.40	
		On cover		2.60
242A	A26	8th m on 30pf	24.00	6,000.
		Never hinged	60.00	
		On cover		9,000.
243	A29	15th m on 40m	.25	2.00
		Never hinged	.75	
		On cover		2.25
244	A29	20th m on 12m	.25	1.50
		Never hinged	.40	
		On cover		3.00
a.		Inverted surcharge	120.00	1,100.
245	A29	20th m on 25m	.25	2.25
		Never hinged	.40	
		On cover		4.25
246	A35	20th m on 200m	.25	2.25
		Never hinged	.75	
		On cover		2.25
a.		Inverted surcharge	57.50	750.00
		Never hinged	150.00	
247	A29	25th m on 25m	.25	14.50
		Never hinged	.40	
		On cover		35.00
248	A29	30th m on 10m dp bl	.25	1.50
		Never hinged	.40	
		On cover		3.00
a.		Inverted surcharge	70.00	
		Never hinged	180.00	
249	A35	30th m on 200m pale bl (Bl)	.25	1.50
		Never hinged	.40	
		On cover		3.00
a.		Without surcharge	115.00	
		Never hinged	225.00	
250	A35	75th m on 300m yel grn	.25	14.50
		Never hinged	.40	
		On cover		32.50
a.		Imperf.	45.00	
		Never hinged	125.00	
251	A35	75th m on 400m yel grn	.25	1.50
		Never hinged	.75	
		On cover		2.25
252	A35	75th m on 1000m yel grn	.25	1.90
		Never hinged	.75	
		On cover		2.60
a.		Without surcharge	115.00	
		Never hinged	225.00	
253	A35	100th m on 100m	.25	2.25
		Never hinged	.75	
		On cover		3.75
a.		Double surcharge	37.50	450.00
		Never hinged	97.50	
b.		Inverted surcharge	14.50	
		Never hinged	37.50	600.00
254	A35	100th m on 400m bluish grn (G)	.25	1.50
		Never hinged	.40	
		On cover		1.90
a.		Imperf.	50.00	750.00
		Never hinged	115.00	
b.		Without surcharge	115.00	
		Never hinged	225.00	
255	A35	125th m on 1000m sal	.25	1.90
		Never hinged	.60	
		On cover		3.00
256	A35	250th m on 200m	.25	5.25
		Never hinged	.40	
		On cover		13.00
a.		Inverted surcharge	35.00	
		Never hinged	90.00	
b.		Double surcharge	52.50	
		Never hinged	140.00	

257	A35	250th m on 300m dp grn	.25	17.00
		Never hinged	.40	
		On cover		30.00
a.		Inverted surcharge	35.00	
		Never hinged	90.00	
258	A35	250th m on 400m	.25	19.00
		Never hinged	.40	
		On cover		30.00
a.		Inverted surcharge	26.00	
		Never hinged	75.00	
259	A35	250th m on 500m pink	.25	1.50
		Never hinged	.40	
		On cover		1.90
a.		Imperf.	52.50	675.00
		Never hinged	125.00	
260	A35	250th m on 500m red org	.25	19.00
		Never hinged	.40	
		On cover		30.00
a.		Double surcharge	30.00	975.00
		Never hinged	75.00	
b.		Inverted surcharge	30.00	
		Never hinged	82.50	
261	A26	800th m on 5pf lt grn (G)	.25	4.25
		Never hinged	.40	
		On cover		9.00
a.		Imperf.	35.00	150.00
		Never hinged	90.00	
262	A26	800th m on 10pf lt grn (G)	.25	5.00
		Never hinged	.40	
		On cover		9.00
a.		Imperf.	30.00	
		Never hinged	90.00	
263	A35	800th m on 200m	.25	75.00
		Never hinged	.55	
		On cover		190.00
a.		Double surcharge	75.00	975.00
		Never hinged	190.00	
b.		Inverted surcharge	37.50	
		Never hinged	110.00	
264	A35	800th m on 300m lt grn (G)	.25	5.00
		Never hinged	.40	
		On cover		7.50
a.		Black surcharge	47.50	
		Never hinged	75.00	
265	A35	800th m on 400m dk brn	.25	14.50
		Never hinged	.40	
		On cover		40.00
a.		Inverted surcharge	42.50	
		Never hinged	110.00	
b.		Double surcharge	75.00	
		Never hinged	190.00	
266	A35	800th m on 400m lt grn (G)	.25	3.75
		Never hinged	.40	
		On cover		7.50
267	A35	800th m on 500m lt grn (G)	.25	1,500.
		Never hinged	.40	
		On cover		1,900.
a.		800th m on 500m red org (Bk)	37.50	
		Never hinged	67.50	
268	A35	800th m on 1000m lt grn (G)	.25	1.50
		Never hinged	.70	
		On cover		3.00
269	A35	2mil m on 200m rose red	.25	2.25
		Never hinged	.75	
		On cover		4.50
b.		2mil m on 200m car rose (#230)	1,500.	
		Never hinged	3,400.	
c.		As "b," wmk sideways	3.00	325.00
		Never hinged	7.50	
		On cover		525.00
270	A35	2mil m on 300m dp grn	.25	2.25
		Never hinged	.50	
		On cover		3.75
a.		Inverted surcharge	42.50	
		Never hinged	110.00	
b.		Double surcharge	75.00	
		Never hinged	190.00	
271	A35	2mil m on 500m dl rose	.25	6.50
		Never hinged	.40	
		On cover		11.50
272	A38	2mil m on 5th m dl rose	.25	1.50
		Never hinged	.90	
		On cover		2.25
b.		Imperf.	42.50	125.00
		Never hinged	85.00	

Nos. 264a, 267a were not put in use.

Serrate Roulette 13½

273	A26	400th m on 15pf bis (Br)	.25	4.50
		Never hinged	.40	
		On cover		7.50
a.		Imperf.	52.50	275.00
		Never hinged	125.00	
274	A26	400th m on 25pf bis (Br)	.25	4.50
		Never hinged	.40	
		On cover		7.50
a.		Imperf.	90.00	275.00
		Never hinged	225.00	

275	A26	400th m on 30pf bis (Br)	.25	4.50
		Never hinged	.40	
		On cover		7.50
a.		Imperf.	45.00	
		Never hinged	110.00	
b.		Double surcharge	90.00	
		Never hinged	175.00	
276	A26	400th m on 40pf bis (Br)	.25	4.50
		Never hinged	.40	
		On cover		7.50
a.		Imperf.	45.00	
		Never hinged	110.00	
b.		Double surcharge	90.00	
		Never hinged	175.00	
277	A35	2mil m on 200m rose red	.45	150.00
		Never hinged	.65	
		On cover		210.00
278	A38	2mil m on 5th m dull rose	.25	9.00
		Never hinged	.40	
		On cover		16.50

Nos. 241-278 (39) 33.70 7,912.
Set, never hinged 51.00

Surcharge Omitted

272c	A38	2mil m on 5th m	150.00
		Never hinged	375.00
273b	A26	400th m on 15pf	150.00
		Never hinged	375.00
274b	A26	400th m on 25pf	150.00
		Never hinged	375.00
275c	A26	400th m on 30pf	150.00
		Never hinged	375.00
276c	A26	400th m on 40pf	150.00
		Never hinged	375.00

A39

A39a

The stamps of types A39 and A39a usually have the value darker than the rest of the design.

1923		Wmk. 126		Perf. 14	
280	A39	500th m brown		.25	2.75
		Never hinged		.40	
		On cover			7.50
281	A39	1mil m grnsh bl		.25	1.60
		Never hinged		.70	
		On cover			2.25
a.		Imperf.		52.50	1,500.
		Never hinged		115.00	
b.		1mil m grnsh bl (rotary press)		.25	2.10
282	A39	2mil m dull vio		.25	20.00
		Never hinged		.75	
		On cover			37.50
a.		2mil m deep pur		22.50	7,500.
		Never hinged		75.00	
		On cover			9,000.
284	A39	4mil m yel grn		.25	1.50
		Never hinged		.75	
		On cover			2.60
a.		Value double		57.50	
		Never hinged		140.00	
b.		Imperf.		42.50	
		Never hinged		97.50	
c.		4mil m yel grn (rotary press)		.55	34.00
285	A39	5mil m rose		.25	1.50
		Never hinged		.70	
		On cover			1.90
a.		5mil m rose (rotary press)		.25	2.60
286	A39	10mil m red		.25	1.50
		Never hinged		.40	
		On cover			1.90
a.		Value double		50.00	3,750.
		Never hinged		125.00	
287	A39	20mil m ultra		.25	1.90
		Never hinged		.65	
		On cover			2.60
a.		20mil m blk bl (rotary press)		12.00	1,500.
		Never hinged		30.00	
		On cover			2,100.
288	A39	30mil m red brn		.25	9.25
		Never hinged		.40	
		On cover			19.00
289	A39	50mil m dull ol grn		.25	1.90
		Never hinged		.75	
		On cover			2.75
a.		Imperf.		52.50	350.00
		Never hinged		125.00	
b.		Value inverted		45.00	
		Never hinged		120.00	
c.		50mil m bl grn (rotary press)		1.90	50.00
		Never hinged		5.00	
		On cover			115.00
290	A39	100mil m gray		.25	1.50
		Never hinged		.40	
		On cover			2.60
291	A39	200mil m bis brn		.25	1.50
		Never hinged		.65	
		On cover			2.60
a.		Imperf.		42.50	
		Never hinged		97.50	
b.		200mil m bis brn (rotary press)		.30	1.10
293	A39	500mil m ol grn		.25	1.40
		Never hinged		.40	
		On cover			2.25
294	A39a	1mlrd m choc		.30	1.90
		Never hinged		.90	
		On cover			2.60
a.		1mird m blk brn (flat press)		500.00	6,750.
		Never hinged		1,200.	
		On cover			11,000.

b.		1mird m blk brn (rotary press)	7.75	90.00
		Never hinged	24.00	
		On cover		120.00
295	A39a	2mlrd m pale brn & grn	.25	1.90
		Never hinged	.70	
		On cover		2.60
a.		2mlrd m pale brn & grn (rotary press)	.45	1.60
296	A39a	5mlrd m yellow & brn	.25	1.50
		Never hinged	.70	
		On cover		2.60
a.		5mlrd m yellow & brn (rotary press)	.25	1.50
297	A39a	10mlrd m ap grn & grn	.25	1.50
		Never hinged	.70	
		On cover		3.00
a.		Imperf.	45.00	275.00
		Never hinged	115.00	
b.		10mlrd m ap grn & grn (rotary press)	.30	1.10
298	A39a	20mlrd m bluish grn & brn	.25	1.90
		Never hinged	.70	
		On cover		3.00
a.		20mlrd m bluish grn & brn (rotary press)	.30	1.50
299	A39a	50mlrd m bl & dp bl	.25	35.00
		Never hinged	.90	
		On cover		75.00

Nos. 280-299 (18) 4.55 90.00
Set, never hinged 11.50

Nos. 294, 294a are 21.5x17.7mm. Nos. 287a, 289c, 294b are 22x18mm. Nos. 287, 289 exist from both flat and rotary press printings.
See Nos. 301-309. For surcharges and overprints see Nos. 311-321, O40-O46.

Value Omitted

280a	A39	500th m	92.50	360.00
		Never hinged	190.00	
281b	A39	1mil m	55.00	
		Never hinged	150.00	
284c	A39	4mil m	72.50	
		Never hinged	150.00	
285a	A39	5mil m	72.50	375.00
		Never hinged	150.00	
286b	A39	10mil m	100.00	375.00
		Never hinged	190.00	
287b	A39	20mil m	37.50	
		Never hinged	75.00	
290a	A39	100mil m	50.00	
		Never hinged	97.50	
291b	A39	200mil m	72.50	
		Never hinged	120.00	
293a	A39	500mil m	50.00	
		Never hinged	97.50	
294c	A39	1mird m	50.00	150.00
		Never hinged	97.50	
296a	A39	5mird m	50.00	
		Never hinged	97.50	
298a	A39	20mird m	62.50	
		Never hinged	125.00	
299a	A39	50mird m	62.50	
		Never hinged	125.00	

Serrate Roulette 13½

301	A39	10mil m red	.55	45.00
		Never hinged	1.60	
		On cover		75.00
302	A39	20mil m ultra	.55	300.00
		Never hinged	1.50	
		On cover		425.00
303	A39	50mil m dull grn	.55	6.00
		Never hinged	1.50	
		On cover		13.00
304	A39	200mil m bis brn	.55	11.50
		Never hinged	1.50	
		On cover		19.00
305	A39a	1mlrd m choc	.55	7.50
		Never hinged	1.50	
		On cover		12.50
306	A39a	2mlrd m pale brn & grn	.55	3.50
		Never hinged	1.50	
		On cover		7.50
307	A39a	5mlrd m yel & brn	.75	2.25
		Never hinged	1.90	
		On cover		6.75
308	A39a	20mlrd m bluish grn & brn	.75	11.50
		Never hinged	2.10	
		On cover		19.00
309	A39a	50mlrd m bl & dp bl	1.90	675.00
		Never hinged	5.25	
		On cover		1,500.

Nos. 301-309 (9) 6.70 1,062.
Set, never hinged 18.50

Stamps and Types of 1923 Surcharged with New Values

1923				Perf. 14	
		Design Type A35			
310		1mlrd m on 100m vio		.25	29.00
		Never hinged		1.25	
		On cover			57.50
a.		Inverted surcharge		115.00	
		Never hinged		300.00	
b.		Deep reddish purple		60.00	3,600.
		Never hinged		150.00	
		On cover (Munich)			5,250.
		Design Type A39			
311		5mlrd m on 2mil m		.25	140.00
		Never hinged		.90	
		On cover			190.00
a.		Inverted surcharge		19.00	
		Never hinged		57.50	
b.		Double surcharge		45.00	
		Never hinged		110.00	
c.		Deep purple		52.50	9,750.
		Never hinged		150.00	
312		5mlrd m on 4mil m		.25	22.50
		Never hinged		.65	
		On cover			37.50
a.		Inverted surcharge		37.50	1,200.

	Never hinged		110.00	
b.	Double surcharge		37.50	
	Never hinged		97.50	
313	5mlrd m on 10mil m		.25	2.75
	Never hinged		.55	
	On cover			5.50
a.	Inverted surcharge		19.00	1,100.
	Never hinged		57.50	
b.	Double surcharge		77.00	
	Never hinged		97.50	
314	10mlrd m on 20mil m		.25	4.50
	Never hinged		.75	
	On cover			6.75
a.	Double surcharge		45.00	
	Never hinged		125.00	
b.	Inverted surcharge		26.00	
	Never hinged		75.00	
c.	Triple surcharge		525.00	
d.	On #287a		32.50	1,650.
	Never hinged		92.50	
	On cover			2,750.
315	10mlrd m on 50mil m		.25	4.50
	Never hinged		.65	
	On cover			7.50
a.	Inverted surcharge		19.00	900.00
	Never hinged		57.50	
b.	Double surcharge		45.00	
	Never hinged		125.00	
c.	On #289c		135.00	1,500.
	Never hinged		400.00	
	On cover			2,750.
316	10mlrd m on 100mil m		.25	7.50
	Never hinged		.55	
	On cover			13.00
a.	Inverted surcharge		26.00	1,500.
	Never hinged		75.00	
b.	Double surcharge		45.00	
	Never hinged		125.00	
	Nos. 310-316 (7)		1.75	210.75
	Set, never hinged		5.25	

No. 310b was issued in Bavaria only and is known as the Hitler provisional. Excellent forgeries exist.

Serrate Roulette 13½
Design Type A39

319	5mlrd m on 10mil m		1.90	190.00
	Never hinged		6.00	
	On cover			325.00
a.	Inverted surcharge		26.00	1,100.
	Never hinged		67.50	
b.	Double surcharge		45.00	
	Never hinged		110.00	
320	10mlrd m on 20mil m		5.00	110.00
	Never hinged		10.50	
	On cover			160.00
321	10mlrd m on 50mil m		1.90	37.50
	Never hinged		6.00	
	On cover			105.00
a.	Inverted surcharge		26.00	1,100.
	Never hinged		67.50	
	Nos. 319-321 (3)		8.80	337.50
	Set, never hinged		22.50	

A40

German Eagle — A41

1923   Perf. 14

323	A40	3pf brown	.40	.25
	Never hinged		2.25	
	On cover			.85
324	A40	5pf dark green	.40	.25
	Never hinged		2.25	
	On cover			.85
325	A40	10pf carmine	.40	.25
	Never hinged		2.25	
	On cover			.85
326	A40	20pf deep ultra	1.20	.40
	Never hinged		5.25	
	On cover			1.10
327	A40	50pf orange	2.75	1.00
	Never hinged		19.00	
	On cover			5.25
328	A40	100pf brn vio	8.50	1.20
	Never hinged		52.50	
	On cover			11.00
	Nos. 323-328 (6)		13.65	3.35
	Set, never hinged		85.00	

For overprints see Nos. O47-O52.

Imperf

323a	A40	3pf	125.00	275.00
	Never hinged		300.00	
324a	A40	5pf	110.00	—
	Never hinged		260.00	
325a	A40	10pf	140.00	260.00
	Never hinged		350.00	
326a	A40	20pf	140.00	260.00
	Never hinged		350.00	
327a	A40	50pf	800.00	—
	Never hinged		2,250.	
328a	A40	100pf	175.00	—
	Never hinged		525.00	
	Nos. 323a-328a (6)		1,490.	795.00
	Set, never hinged		3,650.	

Value Omitted

323b	A40	3pf	180.00	300.00
	Never hinged		525.00	
324b	A40	5pf	160.00	300.00
	Never hinged		375.00	
325b	A40	10pf	160.00	300.00
	Never hinged		450.00	
326b	A40	20pf	165.00	300.00
	Never hinged		525.00	
327b	A40	50pf	160.00	
	Never hinged		375.00	

328b	A40	100pf	160.00	
	Never hinged		375.00	
	Nos. 323b-328b (6)		985.00	
	Set, never hinged		2,475.	

1924   Wmk. 126

330	A41	3pf lt brown	.30	.40
	Never hinged		1.50	
	On cover			1.10
331	A41	5pf lt green	.30	.40
	Never hinged		2.00	
	On cover			.75
332	A41	10pf vermilion	.40	.40
	Never hinged		2.60	
	On cover			.75
333	A41	20pf dull blue	1.90	.40
	Never hinged		26.00	
	On cover			2.25
334	A41	30pf rose lilac	1.90	.45
	Never hinged		26.00	
	On cover			3.75
335	A41	40pf olive green	13.00	.75
	Never hinged		90.00	
	On cover			5.75
336	A41	50pf orange	15.00	1.15
	Never hinged		130.00	
	On cover			6.00
	Nos. 330-336 (7)		32.80	3.95
	Set, never hinged		277.50	

The values above 5pf have "Pf" in the upper right corner.
For overprints see Nos. O53-O61.

Imperf.

330a	A41	3pf	140.00	375.00
	Never hinged		350.00	
331a	A41	5pf	175.00	375.00
	Never hinged		425.00	
332a	A41	10pf	225.00	
	Never hinged		525.00	
333a	A41	20pf	160.00	
	Never hinged		375.00	
334a	A41	30pf	160.00	
	Never hinged		375.00	
335a	A41	40pf	190.00	
	Never hinged		450.00	
	Nos. 330a-335a (6)		1,050.	
	Set, never hinged		2,500.	

Watermark Sideways

330b	A41	3pf	125.00	37.50
	Never hinged		300.00	
331b	A41	5pf		5,000.
	Never hinged		10,000.	
332b	A41	10pf	25.00	12.00
	Never hinged		90.00	

Rheinstein Castle — A43

View of Cologne A44

Marienburg Castle — A45

1924   Engr.   Wmk. 126

337	A43	1m green	13.00	3.50
	Never hinged		40.00	
	On cover			9.00
a.	Watermark sideways ('27)		35.00	12.00
	Never hinged		97.50	
				42.50
338	A44	2m blue	18.00	3.50
	Never hinged		50.00	
				30.00
339	A45	3m claret	25.00	6.50
	Never hinged		70.00	
				60.00
	Nos. 337-339 (3)		56.00	13.50
	Set, never hinged		160.00	

See No. 387.

Dr. Heinrich von Stephan   A46   A47

1924-28   Typo.

340	A46	10pf dark green	.55	.30
	Never hinged		1.90	
				1.50
a.	Imperf		325.00	

341	A46	20pf dark blue	1.50	.75
	Never hinged		5.75	
				2.25
342	A47	60pf red brown	3.75	.75
	Never hinged		19.00	
	On cover			6.00
	On laid paper (LG)		22.50	13.50
	Never hinged		105.00	
				45.00
343	A47	80pf slate	10.00	1.50
	Never hinged		52.50	
				35.00
	Nos. 340-343 (4)		15.80	3.30
	Set, never hinged		79.00	

Universal Postal Union, 50th anniversary.

Traffic Wheel — A48

German Eagle Watching Rhine Valley — A49

1925, May 30   Perf. 13½x13

345	A48	5pf deep green	4.25	5.50
	Never hinged		21.00	
	On cover			19.00
346	A48	10pf vermilion	4.25	10.50
	Never hinged		21.00	
	On cover			22.50
	Set, never hinged		42.00	

German Traffic Exhibition, Munich, May 30-Oct. 11, 1925.

1925   Perf. 14

347	A49	5pf green	.45	.40
	Never hinged		2.25	
	On cover			.75
348	A49	10pf vermilion	.70	.40
	Never hinged		3.75	
	On cover			.75
349	A49	20pf deep blue	5.25	1.10
	Never hinged		29.00	
	On cover			4.25
	Nos. 347-349 (3)		6.40	1.90
	Set, never hinged		35.00	

1000 years' union of the Rhineland with Germany.

Speyer Cathedral A50

1925, Sept. 11   Engr.

350	A50	5m dull green	37.50	16.00
	Never hinged		135.00	
	On cover			65.00

Johann Wolfgang von Goethe — A51

Designs: 3pf, 25pf, Goethe. 5pf, Friedrich von Schiller. 8pf, 20pf, Ludwig van Beethoven. 10pf, Frederick the Great. 15pf, Immanuel Kant. 30pf, Gotthold Ephraim Lessing. 40pf, Gottfried Wilhelm Leibnitz. 50pf, Johann Sebastian Bach. 80pf, Albrecht Durer.

1926-27   Typo.   Perf. 14

351	A51	3pf olive brown	1.25	.40
	Never hinged		4.75	
	On cover			1.10
352	A51	3pf bister ('27)	1.25	.40
	Never hinged		8.00	
	On cover			1.10
353	A51	5pf dark green	1.25	.40
	Never hinged		9.50	
	On cover			.75
b.	5pf light green ('27)		1.50	.40
	Never hinged		8.00	
				1.25
354	A51	8pf blue grn ('27)	1.60	.40
	Never hinged		8.75	
				1.25
355	A51	10pf carmine	1.60	.40
	Never hinged		8.75	
				1.10
356	A51	15pf vermilion	2.40	.40
	Never hinged		13.50	
				.75
a.	Booklet pane of 8 + 2 labels		1,100.	
	Never hinged		1,800.	
357	A51	20pf myrtle grn	11.00	1.20
	Never hinged		125.00	
				5.50

a.	Wmk. sideways		2,250.	375.00
	Never hinged		11,250.	
358	A51	25pf blue	3.50	.90
	Never hinged		29.50	
359	A51	30pf olive grn	6.50	.65
	Never hinged		45.00	
				4.00
360	A51	40pf dp violet	12.00	.65
	Never hinged		120.00	
				6.50
361	A51	50pf brown	15.00	8.00
	Never hinged		120.00	
				27.50
362	A51	80pf chocolate	30.00	5.00
	Never hinged		375.00	
				57.50
	Nos. 351-362 (12)		87.35	18.80
	Set, never hinged		875.00	

Imperf

351a	A51	3pf Never hinged	525.	
352a	A51	3pf Never hinged	525.	
353a	A51	5pf Never hinged	525.	
354a	A51	8pf Never hinged	525.	
356b	A51	15pf Never hinged	525.	
357b	A51	20pf Never hinged	2,000.	

I.A.A.
10.-15.10.1927

Nos. 354, 356 and 358 Overprinted

1927, Oct. 10

363	A51	8pf blue green	17.50	67.50
	Never hinged		62.50	
	On cover			110.00
364	A51	15pf vermilion	17.50	67.50
	Never hinged		62.50	
	On cover			110.00
365	A51	25pf blue	17.50	67.50
	Never hinged		62.50	
	On cover			140.00
	Nos. 363-365 (3)		52.50	202.50
	Set, never hinged		187.50	

"I.A.A." stands for "Internationales Arbeitsamt," (Intl. Labor Bureau), an agency of the League of Nations. Issued in connection with a meeting of the I.A.A. in Berlin, Oct. 10-15, 1927, they were on sale to the public.

Pres. Friedrich Ebert A60

Pres. Paul von Hindenburg A61

1928-32   Typo.   Perf. 14

366	A60	3pf bister	.25	.65
	Never hinged		2.25	
	On cover			1.10
367	A61	4pf lt blue ('31)	.90	1.25
	Never hinged		4.75	
				1.50
a.	Tête bêche pair		22.50	40.00
	Never hinged		37.50	
b.	Bklt. pane of 9 + label		100.00	190.00
	Never hinged		165.00	
368	A61	5pf lt green	.40	.65
	Never hinged		1.60	
	On cover			1.00
a.	Tête bêche pair		18.00	30.00
	Never hinged		30.00	
b.	Imperf.		125.00	
	Never hinged		250.00	
c.	Bklt. pane of 6 + 4 labels		82.50	120.00
	Never hinged		140.00	
d.	Bklt. pane, 4 #368 + 6 #369		100.00	180.00
	Never hinged		165.00	
369	A60	6pf lt olive grn ('32)	.75	.70
	Never hinged		4.75	
				1.00
a.	Bklt. pane, 2 #369 + 8 #373		100.00	180.00
	Never hinged		165.00	
370	A60	8pf dark green	.25	.65
	Never hinged		1.60	
	On cover			1.00
a.	Tête bêche pair		18.00	30.00
	Never hinged		30.00	
b.	Watermark sideways		65.00	145.00
	Never hinged		160.00	
	On cover			—
371	A60	10pf vermilion	2.00	2.40
	Never hinged		13.50	
				5.50
372	A60	10pf red violet ('30)	.85	.80
	Never hinged		8.00	
				1.25
373	A61	12pf orange ('32)	1.60	.70
	Never hinged		9.50	
				1.00
a.	Tête bêche pair		22.50	37.50
	Never hinged		37.50	
374	A61	15pf car rose	.65	.65
	Never hinged		3.50	
				1.00
a.	Tête bêche pair		18.00	30.00
	Never hinged		30.00	
b.	Bklt. pane 6 + 4 labels		82.50	120.00

```
              Never hinged        140.00
  c.  Imperf                      350.00
375 A60  20pf Prus green    6.25          4.75
         Never hinged       40.00
         On cover                         7.25
  a.  Imperf.               300.00
      Never hinged          650.00
376 A60  20pf gray ('30)    6.25          .80
         Never hinged       47.50
         On cover                         2.50
377 A61  25pf blue          8.00          .95
         Never hinged       47.50
         On cover                         2.00
378 A60  30pf olive green   5.50          .95
         Never hinged       35.00
         On cover                         2.00
379 A61  40pf violet        16.00         .95
         Never hinged       175.00
         On cover                         4.00
380 A60  45pf orange        9.50          3.25
         Never hinged       72.50
         On cover                         6.50
381 A61  50pf brown         10.50         2.75
         Never hinged       115.00
         On cover                         8.00
382 A60  60pf orange brn    12.00         3.25
         Never hinged       115.00
         On cover                         8.00
383 A61  80pf chocolate     24.00         7.25
         Never hinged       275.00
         On cover                         40.00
384 A61  80pf yel bis ('30) 9.25          2.40
         Never hinged       70.00
         On cover                         32.50
     Nos. 366-384 (19)      114.90        35.75
     Set, never hinged      1,025.
```

Stamps of 1928
Overprinted

1930, June 30
```
385 A60  8pf dark green     1.60          .95
         Never hinged       7.00
         On cover                         1.40
386 A61  15pf carmine rose  2.00          .95
         Never hinged       9.00
         On cover                         1.40
     Set, never hinged      16.00
```

Issued in commemoration of the final evacuation of the Rhineland by the Allied forces.

View of Cologne
A63

1930   Engr.   Wmk. 126
Inscribed: "Reichsmark"
```
387 A63  2m dark blue       27.50         15.00
         Never hinged       110.00
         On cover                         95.00
```

A type of design A43 in green exists with "Reichsmark" instead of "Mark." It was not issued, though some examples are known in private hands. Value $15,000.

Pres. von Hindenburg
A64

Frederick the Great
A65

1932, Oct. 1   Typo.   Wmk. 126
```
391 A64  4pf blue           .55           .60
         Never hinged       2.00
         On cover                         2.50
392 A64  5pf brt green      .90           .60
         Never hinged       3.25
         On cover                         2.75
393 A64  12pf dp orange     5.00          .60
         Never hinged       18.50
         On cover                         2.50
394 A64  15pf dk red        3.00          10.00
         Never hinged       11.00
         On cover                         55.00
395 A64  25pf ultra         2.50          .75
         Never hinged       9.00
         On cover                         8.00
396 A64  40pf violet        21.00         1.60
         Never hinged       77.50
         On cover                         20.00
397 A64  50pf dk brown      4.00          11.00
         Never hinged       14.00
         On cover                         55.00
     Nos. 391-397 (7)       36.95         25.15
     Set, never hinged      135.00
```

85th birthday of von Hindenburg.
See Nos. 401-431, 436-441. For surcharges and overprints see France N27-N58, Luxembourg N1-N16 and Poland N17-N29.

1933, Apr. 12   Photo.
```
398 A65  6pf dk green       .80           .95
         Never hinged       4.75
         On cover                         1.90
  a.  Tête bêche pair       18.00         30.00
      Never hinged          30.00
399 A65  12pf carmine       1.20          .95
         Never hinged       7.25
         On cover                         1.90
  a.  Tête bêche pair       18.00         30.00
      Never hinged          30.00
  b.  Bklt. pane of 5 + label 75.00       65.00
      Never hinged          120.00
400 A65  25pf ultra         42.50         22.50
         Never hinged       250.00
         On cover                         37.50
     Nos. 398-400 (3)       44.50         24.40
     Set, never hinged      260.00
```

Celebration of Potsdam Day.

Hindenburg Type of 1932

1933   Typo.
```
401 A64  3pf olive bister   17.50         .80
         Never hinged       95.00
         On cover                         2.75
402 A64  4pf dull blue      4.00          .80
         Never hinged       17.50
         On cover                         1.50
403 A64  6pf dk green       2.00          .80
         Never hinged       7.50
         On cover                         2.40
404 A64  8pf dp orange      6.50          .80
         Never hinged       15.00
         On cover                         2.40
  a.  Bklt. pane, 3 #404 + 5 #406  110.00  180.00
      Never hinged          190.00
  b.  Open "D"              20.00         4.00
      Never hinged          52.50
405 A64  10pf chocolate     4.00          .80
         Never hinged       22.50
         On cover                         8.00
406 A64  12pf dp carmine    2.40          .80
         Never hinged       15.00
         On cover                         2.40
  a.  Bklt. pane, 4 #392 + 4 #406  82.50   150.00
      Never hinged          120.00
407 A64  15pf maroon        5.50          27.50
         Never hinged       22.50
         On cover                         55.00
408 A64  20pf brt blue      7.25          1.60
         Never hinged       55.00
         On cover                         20.00
409 A64  30pf olive grn     7.25          1.40
         Never hinged       19.00
         On cover                         20.00
410 A64  40pf red violet    29.00         2.75
         Never hinged       220.00
         On cover                         35.00
411 A64  50pf dk grn & blk  16.00         2.40
         Never hinged       110.00
         On cover                         65.00
412 A64  60pf claret & blk  29.00         1.00
         Never hinged       200.00
         On cover                         60.00
413 A64  80pf dk blue & blk 9.50          1.20
         Never hinged       24.00
         On cover                         87.50
414 A64  100pf orange & blk 25.00         13.50
         Never hinged       140.00
         On cover                         120.00
     Nos. 401-414 (14)      164.90        56.15
     Set, never hinged      950.00
```

Hindenburg Type of 1932

1933-36   Wmk. 237   Perf. 14
```
415 A64  1pf black          .25           .40
         Never hinged       .40
         On cover                         .65
  a.  Bklt. pane, 4 #415, 3 #417, label  15.00  17.00
      Never hinged          26.00
  b.  Bklt. pane, 3 #415, 3 #416 + 2 #418  21.00  37.50
      Never hinged          35.00
  c.  Bklt. pane, 2 #415, 5 #420, label  22.50  42.50
      Never hinged          37.50
  d.  Bklt. pane, 4 #415 + 4 #422  21.00  37.50
      Never hinged          35.00
416 A64  3pf olive bis ('34) .25          .40
         Never hinged       .40
         On cover                         .65
  a.  Bklt. pane, 4 #416 + 4 #418  22.50  42.50
      Never hinged          37.50
  b.  Bklt. pane, 4 #416 + 4 #419  21.00  37.50
      Never hinged          35.00
  c.  Bklt. pane, 6 #416, 1 #422, label  12.00  17.00
      Never hinged          19.00
417 A64  4pf dull blue ('34) .25          .40
         Never hinged       .40
         On cover                         .65
  a.  Bklt. pane, 3 #417, 4 #422, label  21.00  37.50
      Never hinged          35.00
418 A64  5pf brt green ('34) .25          .40
         Never hinged       .40
         On cover                         .65
  a.  Bklt. pane, 2 #418, 5 #419, label  15.00  17.00
      Never hinged          19.00
  b.  Bklt. pane, 2 #418, 3 #419 + 3 #420  21.00  37.50
      Never hinged          35.00
  c.  Bklt. pane, 4 #418 + 4 #420  40.00  75.00
      Never hinged          67.50
419 A64  6pf dk green ('34)  .25          .40
         Never hinged       .40
         On cover                         .65
  b.  Bklt. pane of 7 + label  9.00       17.00
      Never hinged          15.00
  c.  Bklt. pane, 1 #419, 6 #422, label  67.50  105.00
      Never hinged          120.00
420 A64  8pf dp orange ('34) .25          .40
         Never hinged       .40
         On cover                         .65
  a.  Bklt. pane, 3 #420, 4 #422, label  15.00  17.00
      Never hinged          27.50
  b.  Open "D"              4.50          4.00
      Never hinged          13.00
```

```
421 A64  10pf choc ('34)    .25           .40
         Never hinged                     .75
422 A64  12pf dp car ('34)  .25           .40
         On cover           .40
                                          .75
  a.  Bklt. pane of 7 + label  22.50      42.50
      Never hinged          37.50
423 A64  15pf maroon ('34)  .30           .40
         Never hinged       1.60
         On cover                         .75
424 A64  20pf brt blue ('34) .45          .40
         Never hinged       3.50
         On cover                         .75
425 A64  25pf ultra ('34)   .45           .40
         Never hinged       3.50
         On cover                         .75
426 A64  30pf olive grn ('34) .75         .40
         Never hinged       7.25
         On cover                         .75
427 A64  40pf red violet ('34) 1.60       .40
         Never hinged       10.50
         On cover                         1.60
428 A64  50pf dk grn & blk ('34) 3.25     .40
         Never hinged       15.00
         On cover                         1.90
429 A64  60pf claret & blk ('34) .75      .40
         Never hinged       6.50
         On cover                         1.90
430 A64  80pf dk bl & blk ('36) 2.40      1.25
         Never hinged       6.75
         On cover                         3.75
431 A64  100pf orange & blk ('34) 3.25    1.20
         Never hinged       8.75
         On cover                         5.50
     Nos. 415-431 (17)      15.20         8.45
     Set, never hinged      65.00
```

Karl Peters — A66

Designs: 3pf, Franz Adolf E. Lüderitz. 6pf, Dr. Gustav Nachtigal. 12pf, Karl Peters. 25pf, Hermann von Wissmann.

1934, June 30   Perf. 13x13½
```
432 A66  3pf brown & choc   2.50          6.50
         Never hinged       25.00
         On cover                         20.00
433 A66  6pf dk grn & choc  .95           1.60
         Never hinged       9.00
         On cover                         4.75
434 A66  12pf dk car & choc 2.75          1.60
         Never hinged       27.50
         On cover                         4.75
435 A66  25pf brt blue & choc 9.50        20.00
         Never hinged       92.50
         On cover                         47.50
     Nos. 432-435 (4)       15.70         29.70
     Set, never hinged      154.00
```

Issued in remembrance of the lost colonies of Germany.

Hindenburg Memorial Issue
Type of 1932
With Black Border

1934, Sept. 4   Perf. 14
```
436 A64  3pf olive bister   .50           .45
         Never hinged       4.00
         On cover                         1.60
437 A64  5pf brt green      .50           .55
         Never hinged       4.00
         On cover                         2.00
438 A64  6pf dk green       1.00          .45
         Never hinged       9.00
         On cover                         1.00
439 A64  8pf vermilion      2.40          .45
         Never hinged       20.00
         On cover                         1.60
440 A64  12pf deep carmine  3.00          .45
         Never hinged       25.00
         On cover                         1.00
441 A64  25pf ultra         7.50          8.75
         Never hinged       65.00
         On cover                         20.00
     Nos. 436-441 (6)       14.90         11.10
     Set, never hinged      127.00
```

Swastika, Sun and Nuremberg Castle — A70

1934, Sept. 1   Photo.
```
442 A70  6pf dark green     3.00          .60
         Never hinged       28.00
         On cover                         1.50
  a.  Imperf, never hinged  750.00
443 A70  12pf dark carmine  4.00          .60
         Never hinged       40.00
         On cover                         1.50
  a.  Imperf, never hinged  750.00
     Set, never hinged      68.00
```

Nazi Congress at Nuremberg.

Allegory "Saar Belongs to Germany" A71

German Eagle A72

1934, Aug. 26   Typo.   Wmk. 237
```
444 A71  6pf dark green     3.25          .60
         Never hinged       32.50
         On cover                         1.25
445 A72  12pf dark carmine  4.00          .60
         Never hinged       40.00
         On cover                         1.25
     Set, never hinged      72.50
```

Issued to mark the Saar Plebiscite.

Friedrich von Schiller A73

Germania Welcoming Home the Saar A74

1934, Nov. 5
```
446 A73  6pf green          2.25          .60
         Never hinged       27.50
         On cover                         1.00
447 A73  12pf carmine       5.00          .60
         Never hinged       60.00
         On cover                         1.00
     Set, never hinged      87.50
```

175th anniv. of the birth of von Schiller.

1935, Jan. 16   Photo.
```
448 A74  3pf brown          .25           1.20
         Never hinged       3.25
         On cover                         2.40
449 A74  6pf dark green     .25           .75
         Never hinged       3.25
         On cover                         .80
450 A74  12pf lake          2.00          .75
         Never hinged       20.00
         On cover                         1.00
451 A74  25pf dark blue     7.25          8.50
         Never hinged       70.00
         On cover                         20.00
     Nos. 448-451 (4)       9.75          11.20
     Set, never hinged      96.50
```

Return of the Saar to Germany.

German Soldier A75

Wreath and Swastika A76

1935, Mar. 15
```
452 A75  6pf dark green     1.60          1.60
         Never hinged       8.00
         On cover                         2.75
453 A75  12pf copper red    1.75          1.60
         Never hinged       9.00
         On cover                         2.75
     Set, never hinged      17.00
```

Issued to commemorate War Heroes' Day.

1935, Apr. 26   Unwmk.
```
454 A76  6pf dark green     1.10          1.40
         Never hinged       8.00
         On cover                         3.50
455 A76  12pf crimson       1.75          1.40
         Never hinged       12.00
         On cover                         3.50
     Set, never hinged      20.00
```

Young Workers' Professional Competitions.

Heinrich
Schütz — A77

"The
Eagle" — A80

Wmk. Swastikas (237)
1935, June 21   Engr.   Perf. 14
456 A77 6pf shown   .85   .80
     Never hinged   5.50
     On cover   1.60
457 A77 12pf Bach   1.20   .80
     Never hinged   8.00
     On cover   1.60
458 A77 25pf Handel   1.75   .90
     Never hinged   12.00
     On cover   5.50
     Nos. 456-458 (3)   3.80 2.50
     Set, never hinged   25.50

Schütz-Bach-Handel celebration.

1935, July 10   Perf. 14
Designs: 12pf, Modern express train. 25pf,
"The Hamburg Flyer." 40pf, Streamlined
locomotive.
459 A80 6pf dark green   .95   .80
     Never hinged   6.50
     On cover   3.25
  a.   Imperf   475.00
460 A80 12pf copper red   .95   .80
     Never hinged   6.50
     On cover   3.25
  a.   Imperf   475.00
461 A80 25pf ultra   5.50 1.90
     Never hinged   35.00
     On cover   22.50
  a.   Imperf   475.00
462 A80 40pf red violet   9.00 1.90
     Never hinged   60.00
     On cover   24.00
  a.   Imperf   475.00
     Nos. 459-462 (4)   16.40 5.40
     Set, never hinged   108.00

Centenary of railroad in Germany.
Values for never hinged examples of Nos.
459a-462a are 3x the hinged values.

Bugler of Hitler
Youth Movement
A84

Eagle and
Swastika over
Nuremberg
A85

1935, July 25   Photo.
463 A84 6pf deep green   1.25 2.40
     Never hinged   7.25
     On cover   5.50
464 A84 15pf brown lake   2.50 3.25
     Never hinged   16.00
     On cover   7.25
     Set, never hinged   23.00

Hitler Youth Meeting.

1935, Aug. 30   Engr.
465 A85 6pf gray green   1.25   .55
     Never hinged   5.50
     On cover   1.25
466 A85 12pf dark carmine   2.25   .55
     Never hinged   10.50
     On cover   1.25
     Set, never hinged   16.00

1935 Nazi Congress at Nuremberg.

Nazi Flag
Bearer and
Feldherrnhalle
at
Munich — A86

1935, Nov. 5   Photo.   Perf. 13½
467 A86 3pf brown   .25   .70
     Never hinged   3.25
     On cover   1.25

---

468 A86 12pf dark carmine   .60   .70
     Never hinged   9.50
     On cover   1.25
     Set, never hinged   12.75

12th anniv. of the 1st Hitler "Putsch" at
Munich, Nov. 9, 1923.

1936, Jan. 6
469 A87 40pf sapphire   6.40 3.25
     Never hinged   45.00
     On cover   16.00

10th anniv. of the Lufthansa air service.

Gottlieb
Daimler — A88

Carl
Benz — A89

1936, Feb. 15   Perf. 14
470 A88 6pf dark green   .70 1.00
     Never hinged   5.50
     On cover   1.00
471 A89 12pf copper red   .90 1.00
     Never hinged   7.25
     On cover   1.25
     Set, never hinged   12.75

The 50th anniv. of the automobile; Intl. Automobile and Motorcycle Show, Berlin.

Otto von
Guericke
A90

Symbolical of
Municipalities
A91

1936, May 4
472 A90 6pf dark green   .30 1.25
     Never hinged   1.30
     On cover   .80

250th anniv. of the death of the German
inventor, Otto von Guericke, May 11, 1686.

1936, June 3
473 A91 3pf dark brown   .50   .30
     Never hinged   2.00
     On cover   1.60
474 A91 5pf deep green   .70   .30
     Never hinged   2.75
     On cover   1.60
475 A91 12pf lake   .90   .60
     Never hinged   3.75
     On cover   1.60
476 A91 25pf dark ultra   1.90 1.10
     Never hinged   7.50
     On cover   6.00
     Nos. 473-476 (4)   4.00 2.30
     Set, never hinged   16.00

6th Intl. Cong. of Municipalities, June 7-13.

Allegory of
Recreation
Congress
A92

Salute to
Swastika
A93

1936, June 30
477 A92 6pf dark green   .65   .55
     Never hinged   4.75
     On cover   2.50
478 A92 15pf deep claret   1.25 1.00
     Never hinged   9.50
     On cover   3.25
     Set, never hinged   14.25

World Congress for Vacation and Recreation held at Hamburg.

1936, Sept. 3   Perf. 14
479 A93 6pf deep green   .60   .60
     Never hinged   4.50
     On cover   1.40
480 A93 12pf copper red   1.00   .60
     Never hinged   6.75
     On cover   1.40
     Set, never hinged   11.25

The 1936 Nazi Congress.

Shield
Bearer — A94

German and
Austrian
Carrying Nazi
Flag — A95

1937, Mar. 3   Engr.   Unwmk.
481 A94 3pf brown   .50   .40
     Never hinged   2.40
     On cover   .80
482 A94 6pf green   .65   .40
     Never hinged   3.25
     On cover   .80
483 A94 12pf carmine   1.25   .75
     Never hinged   6.50
     On cover   .80
     Nos. 481-483 (3)   2.40 1.55
     Set, never hinged   12.00

The Reich's Air Protection League.

Wmk. Swastikas (237)
1938, Apr. 8   Photo.   Perf. 14x13½
              Size: 23x28mm
484 A95 6pf dark green   .80   .65
     Never hinged   2.00
     On cover   .80

Unwmk.   Perf. 12½
           Size: 21½x26mm
485 A95 6pf deep green   .80 1.40
     Never hinged   2.00
     On cover   1.60

Union of Austria and Germany.

Cathedral
Island
A96

Hermann
Goering
Stadium
A97

Town Hall,
Breslau — A98

Centennial
Hall,
Breslau — A99

1938, June 21   Engr.   Perf. 14
486 A96 3pf dark brown   .30   .55
     Never hinged   1.25
     On cover   2.00
487 A97 6pf deep green   .30   .55
     Never hinged   1.25
     On cover   1.40
488 A98 12pf copper red   .75   .55
     Never hinged   3.25
     On cover   1.40
489 A99 15pf violet brown   1.75   .80
     Never hinged   7.25
     On cover   4.00
     Nos. 486-489 (4)   3.10 2.45
     Set, never hinged   13.00

16th German Gymnastic and Sports Festival held at Breslau, July 23-31, 1938.

Nazi Emblem — A100

1939, Apr. 4   Photo.   Wmk. 237
490 A100 6pf dark green   1.90 4.00
     Never hinged   9.00
     On cover   7.25
491 A100 12pf deep carmine 2.50 4.00
     Never hinged   11.00
     On cover   7.25
     Set, never hinged   20.00

Young Workers' Professional Competitions.

St. Mary's
Church — A101

The Krantor,
Danzig — A102

1939, Sept. 18
492 A101 6pf dark green   .45   .80
     Never hinged   1.60
     On cover   1.60
493 A102 12pf orange red   .65   .80
     Never hinged   2.40
     On cover   1.60
     Set, never hinged   4.00

Unification of Danzig with the Reich.

Johannes
Gutenberg and
Library at
Leipzig — A103

Designs: 6pf, "High House," Leipzig. 12pf,
Old Town Hall, Leipzig. 25pf, View of Leipzig
Fair.

Inscribed "Leipziger Messe"
              Perf. 10½
1940, Mar. 3   Photo.   Unwmk.
494 A103 3pf dark brown   .45   .50
     Never hinged   1.60
     On cover   1.60
495 A103 6pf dk gray green   .45   .50
     Never hinged   1.60
     On cover   1.25
496 A103 12pf henna brown   .45   .50
     Never hinged   1.60
     On cover   1.25
497 A103 25pf ultra   1.10 1.25
     Never hinged   3.25
     On cover   4.75
     Nos. 494-497 (4)   2.45 2.75
     Set, never hinged   8.00

Leipzig Fair.

SEMI-POSTAL STAMPS

Issues of the Republic

Nos. 83, 83d, 100,
100a, 100d Surcharged

1919, May 1   Wmk. 125   Perf. 14
B1 A16 10pf + 5pf on #83d   .45 4.50
     Never hinged   1.60
     On cover   9.00
  a.   On #83   5.25 140.00
     Never hinged   14.50
     On cover   240.00
B2 A22 15pf + 5pf on #100   .45 4.75
     Never hinged   1.60
     On cover   9.00
  a.   On #100a   12.00 250.00
     Never hinged   32.50
     On cover   275.00
  b.   On #100d   15.00 350.00
     Never hinged   47.50
     On cover   650.00
     Set, never hinged   3.25

The surtax was for the war wounded.

"Planting
Charity" — SP1

Feeding the
Hungry — SP2

1922, Dec. 11   Litho.   Wmk. 126
B3 SP1 6m + 4m ultra & brn   .25 24.00
     Never hinged   1.00
     On cover   40.00

B4 SP1 12m + 8m red org & bl
gray .25 *24.00*
Never hinged 1.00
On cover *40.00*
Set, never hinged 2.00

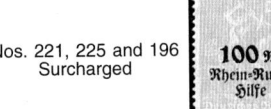

Nos. 221, 225 and 196
Surcharged

1923, Feb. 19
B5 A34 5m + 100m .25 *9.00*
Never hinged .65
On cover *20.00*
B6 A29 25m + 500m .25 *22.50*
Never hinged .65
On cover *47.50*
a. Inverted surcharge 75.00
Never hinged 200.00
B7 A32 20m + 1000m 2.10 *87.50*
Never hinged 4.50
On cover *150.00*
a. Inverted surcharge 1,000. *3,750.*
Never hinged 2,200.
b. Green background invert-
ed 325.00 *1,750.*
Never hinged 800.00
Nos. B5-B7 (3) 2.60 *119.00*
Set, never hinged 6.50

Note following No. 160 applies to Nos. B1-B7.

1924, Feb. 25   Typo.   Perf. 14½x15
Designs: 10pf+30pf, Giving drink to the thirsty. 20pf+60pf, Clothing the naked. 50pf+1.50m, Healing the sick.
B8 SP2 5pf + 15pf dk grn 1.75 *3.50*
Never hinged 7.00
On cover *9.50*
B9 SP2 10pf + 30pf ver 1.75 *3.50*
Never hinged 7.00
On cover *12.00*
B10 SP2 20pf + 60pf dk blue 6.00 *8.50*
Never hinged 24.00
On cover *24.00*
B11 SP2 50pf + 1.50m red
brn 24.00 *67.50*
Never hinged 92.50
On cover *120.00*
Nos. B8-B11 (4) 33.50 *83.00*
Set, never hinged 130.00

The surtax was used for emergency aid. See No. B58.

Prussia — SP6

1925, Dec. 15   Perf. 14
Inscribed: "1925"
B12 SP6 5pf + 5pf shown .60 *2.00*
Never hinged 2.00
On cover *8.00*
B13 SP6 10pf + 10pf Bavaria 2.00 *6.00*
Never hinged 6.00
On cover *12.00*
B14 SP6 20pf + 20pf Saxony 9.00 *14.50*
Never hinged 28.00
On cover *35.00*
a. Bklt. pane of 2 + 2 labels 375.00 *1,100.*
Never hinged 600.00
Nos. B12-B14 (3) 11.60 *22.50*
Set, never hinged 36.00

1926, Dec. 1   Inscribed: "1926"
B15 SP6 5pf + 5pf Wurt-
temberg 1.00 *2.25*
Never hinged 3.25
On cover *4.75*
B16 SP6 10pf + 10pf Baden 1.75 *3.00*
Never hinged 5.25
On cover *6.00*
a. Bklt. pane of 6 + 2 labels 275.00 *675.00*
Never hinged 450.00
B17 SP6 25pf + 25pf Thurin-
gia 9.50 *20.00*
Never hinged 30.00
On cover *42.50*
B18 SP6 50pf + 50pf Hesse 45.00 *105.00*
Never hinged 140.00
On cover *140.00*
Nos. B15-B18 (4) 57.25 *130.25*
Set, never hinged 178.50

Nos. B15-B16 are usually found with sideways watermarks. Both exist with an upright watermark, which is very scarce. No. B18 is usually found with an upright watermark. Examples of No. B18 with a sideways watermark are scarce.
See Nos. B23-B32.

Pres. Paul von
Hindenburg — SP13

1927, Sept. 26   Photo.
B19 SP13 8pf dark green .75 *1.50*
Never hinged 2.50
On cover *6.00*
a. Bklt. pane, 4 #B19, 3 #B20
+ label 110.00 *190.00*
Never hinged 175.00
B20 SP13 15pf scarlet 1.40 *2.40*
Never hinged 4.00
On cover *8.00*
B21 SP13 25pf deep blue 10.50 *22.50*
Never hinged 35.00
On cover *45.00*
B22 SP13 50pf bister brown 13.00 *25.00*
Never hinged 45.00
On cover *50.00*
Nos. B19-B22 (4) 25.65 *51.40*
Set, never hinged 86.50

80th birthday of Pres. Hindenburg. The stamps were sold at double face value. The surtax was given to a fund for War Invalids.

Arms Type of 1925
Design: 8pf+7pf, Mecklenburg-Schwerin.

1928, Nov. 15   Typo.
Design Type SP6
Inscribed: "1928"
B23 SP6 5pf + 5pf Hamburg .60 *4.00*
Never hinged 2.00
On cover *6.00*
B24 SP6 8pf + 7pf multi .50 *4.00*
Never hinged 2.00
On cover *6.00*
a. Bklt. pane, 4 #B24, 3 #B25 +
label 225.00 *450.00*
Never hinged 400.00
B25 SP6 15pf + 15pf Oldenburg .75 *4.00*
Never hinged 2.50
On cover *8.00*
B26 SP6 25pf + 25pf Brunswick 17.00 *52.50*
Never hinged 52.50
On cover *80.00*
B27 SP6 50pf + 50pf Anhalt 40.00 *95.00*
Never hinged 135.00
On cover *130.00*
Nos. B23-B27 (5) 58.85 *159.50*
Set, never hinged 194.00

Nos. B23-B26 are valued with sideways watermark. All exist with upright watermark, which is scarce to very rare.

1929, Nov. 4   Inscribed: "1929"
Coats of Arms: 8pf+4pf, Lippe-Detmold. 25pf+10pf, Mecklenburg-Strelitz. 50pf+40pf, Schaumburg-Lippe.
B28 SP6 5pf + 2pf Bremen .75 *2.00*
Never hinged 2.50
On cover *4.00*
a. Bklt. pane of 6 + 2 labels 90.00 *140.00*
Never hinged 150.00
B29 SP6 8pf + 4pf multi .85 *2.00*
Never hinged 3.00
On cover *4.00*
a. Bklt. pane, 4 #B29, 3 #B30
+ label 120.00 *140.00*
Never hinged 190.00
B30 SP6 15pf + 5pf Lubeck 1.20 *1.50*
Never hinged 4.00
On cover *5.50*
B31 SP6 25pf + 10pf multi 17.00 *52.50*
Never hinged 55.00
On cover *55.00*
B32 SP6 50pf + 40pf choc,
ocher & red 42.50 *95.00*
Never hinged 127.50
On cover *120.00*
a. "PE" for "PF" 150.00 *400.00*
Never hinged 475.00
Nos. B28-B32 (5) 62.30 *153.00*
Set, never hinged 192.00

Cathedral of
Aachen — SP24

Brandenburg
Gate,
Berlin — SP25

Castle of
Marienwerder
SP26

Statue of St.
Kilian and
Marienburg
Fortress at
Würzburg
SP27

Souvenir Sheet
Wmk. 223
1930, Sept. 12   Engr.   Perf. 14
B33 Sheet of 4 440.00 *1,600.*
Never hinged 1,250.
On cover *1,800.*
a. SP24 8pf + 4pf dark green 30.00 *90.00*
Never hinged 85.00
b. SP25 15pf + 5pf carmine 30.00 *90.00*
Never hinged 85.00
c. SP26 25pf + 10p dark blue 30.00 *90.00*
Never hinged 85.00
d. SP27 50pf + 40pf dark
brown 30.00 *90.00*
Never hinged 85.00
Any single, never hinged 50.00
Any single, on cover *200.00*

Intl. Phil. Exhib., Berlin, Sept. 12-21, 1930. No. B33 is watermarked Eagle on each stamp and "IPOSTA"-"1930" in the margins. Size: approximately 105x150. Each holder of an admission ticket was entitled to purchase one sheet. The ticket cost 1m and the sheet 1.70m (face value 98pf, charity 59pf, special paper 13pf).
The margin of the souvenir sheet is ungummed.

**Types of International Philatelic
Exhibition Issue**
1930, Nov. 1   Wmk. 126
B34 SP24 8 + 4pf dp green .50 *.95*
Never hinged 3.00
On cover *4.00*
a. Bklt. pane of 7 + label 90.00 *175.00*
Never hinged 150.00
b. Bklt. pane, 3 #B34, 4
#B35 + label 120.00 *190.00*
Never hinged 190.00
B35 SP25 15 + 5pf car .60 *1.25*
Never hinged 4.00
On cover *6.50*
B36 SP26 25 + 10pf dk blue 9.00 *22.50*
Never hinged 29.00
On cover *35.00*
B37 SP27 50 + 40pf dp brn 24.00 *85.00*
Never hinged 80.00
On cover *120.00*
Nos. B34-B37 (4) 34.10 *109.70*
Set, never hinged 116.00

The surtax was for charity.

The Zwinger
at Dresden
SP28

Breslau City
Hall
SP29

Heidelberg
Castle
SP30

Holsten Gate,
Lübeck
SP31

1931, Nov. 1
B38 SP28 8 + 4pf dk grn .45 *1.20*
Never hinged 2.75
On cover *5.50*
a. Bklt. pane of 7 + label 90.00 *175.00*
Never hinged 150.00
b. Bklt. pane, 3 #B38, 4
#B39 + label 100.00 *190.00*
Never hinged 175.00
B39 SP29 15 + 5pf carmine .45 *1.20*
Never hinged 2.75
On cover *6.50*
B40 SP30 25 + 10pf dk blue 14.00 *32.50*
Never hinged 47.50
On cover *47.50*
B41 SP31 50 + 40pf dp
brown 40.00 *80.00*
Never hinged 135.00
On cover *120.00*
Nos. B38-B41 (4) 54.90 *114.90*
Set, never hinged 188.00

The surtax was for charity.

Nos. B38-B39
Surcharged

1932, Feb. 2
B42 SP28 6 + 4pf on 8+4pf 4.50 *9.75*
Never hinged 20.00
On cover *16.00*

B43 SP29 12 + 3pf on 15+5pf 5.25 *12.00*
Never hinged 25.00
On cover *24.00*
Set, never hinged 45.00

Wartburg
Castle — SP32

Stolzenfels
Castle — SP33

Nuremberg
Castle — SP34

Lichtenstein
Castle — SP35

Marburg
Castle — SP36

1932, Nov. 1   Engr.
B44 SP32 4 + 2pf lt blue .60 *1.20*
Never hinged 3.50
On cover *5.50*
a. Bklt. pane, 5 #B44, 5 #B45 45.00 *85.00*
Never hinged 75.00
B45 SP33 6 + 4pf olive grn .90 *1.20*
Never hinged 4.00
On cover *4.75*
B46 SP34 12 + 3pf lt red .60 *1.20*
Never hinged 3.50
On cover *6.50*
b. Bklt. pane of 8 + 2 labels 45.00 *85.00*
Never hinged 75.00
B47 SP35 25 + 10pf dp blue 9.50 *19.00*
Never hinged 32.50
On cover *32.50*
B48 SP36 40 + 40pf brn vio 32.50 *65.00*
Never hinged 110.00
On cover *95.00*
Nos. B44-B48 (5) 44.10 *87.60*
Set, never hinged 153.00

The surtax was for charity.

"Tannhäuser"
SP37

Designs: 4pf+2pf, "Der Fliegende Holländer." 5pf+2pf, "Das Rheingold." 6pf+4pf, "Die Meistersinger." 8pf+4pf, "Die Walküre." 12pf+3pf, "Siegfried." 20pf+10pf, "Tristan und Isolde." 25pf+15pf, "Lohengrin." 40pf+35pf, "Parsifal."

Wmk. Swastikas (237)
1933, Nov. 1   Perf. 13½x13
B49 SP37 3 + 2pf bis brn 4.25 *6.00*
Never hinged 25.00
On cover *9.50*
B50 SP37 4 + 2pf dk blue 2.75 *2.40*
Never hinged 15.00
On cover *4.00*
b. Bklt. pane, 5 #B50, 5
#B52 140.00 *260.00*
Never hinged 225.00
B51 SP37 5 + 2pf brt grn 6.75 *7.25*
Never hinged 40.00
On cover *13.00*
B52 SP37 6 + 4pf gray
grn 2.75 *2.40*
Never hinged 15.00
On cover *4.00*
B53 SP37 8 + 4pf dp org 4.00 *4.00*
Never hinged 22.50
On cover *8.00*
b. Bklt. pane, 5 #B53, 4
#B54 + label 140.00 *260.00*
Never hinged 225.00
B54 SP37 12 + 3pf brn red 4.00 *2.75*
Never hinged 22.50
On cover *7.50*
B55 SP37 20 + 10pf blue 200.00 *200.00*
Never hinged 1,200.
On cover *360.00*
B56 SP37 25 + 15pf ultra 47.50 *40.00*
Never hinged 270.00
On cover *72.50*
B57 SP37 40 + 35pf mag 125.00 *125.00*
Never hinged 750.00
On cover *200.00*
Nos. B49-B57 (9) 397.00 *389.80*
Set, never hinged 2,360.

Perf. 13½x14
B50a SP37 4 + 2pf dark blue 2.75 *3.00*
Never hinged 16.00
On cover *4.50*
B52a SP37 6 + 4pf gray grn 2.75 *4.75*
Never hinged 16.00
On cover *8.00*

B53a	SP37	8 + 4pf dp org	3.50	4.50
		Never hinged	20.00	
		On cover		8.00
B54a	SP37	12 + 3pf brn red	3.50	6.75
		Never hinged	20.00	
		On cover		10.50
B55a	SP37	20 + 10pf blue	125.00	100.00
		Never hinged	750.00	
		Nos. B53a-B55a (5)	137.50	119.00
		Set, never hinged	822.00	

Types of Semi-Postal Stamps of 1924 Issue Overprinted Souvenir Sheet

1933, Nov. 29   Typo.   Perf. 14½

B58		Sheet of 4	1,450.	10,500.
		Never hinged	5,600.	
		On cover		12,000.
a.	SP2	5 + 15pf dark green	90.00	400.00
b.	SP2	10 + 30pf vermilion	90.00	400.00
c.	SP2	20 + 60pf dark green	90.00	400.00
d.	SP2	50pf + 1.50m dk brown	90.00	400.00
		Any single, never hinged	240.00	
		Any single, on cover		650.00

The Swastika watermark covers the four stamps and above them appears a further watermark "10 Jahre Deutsche Nothilfe" and "1923-1933" below. Sheet size: 208x148mm. The margin of the souvenir sheet is ungummed.

Businessman SP46   Judge SP54

Designs: 4pf+2pf, Blacksmith. 5pf+2pf, Mason. 6pf+4f, Miner. 8pf+4pf, Architect. 12pf+3pf, Farmer. 20pf+10pf, Agricultural Chemist. 25pf+15pf, Sculptor.

1934, Nov. 5   Engr.   Perf. 13x13½

B59	SP46	3 + 2pf brown	1.25	1.50
		Never hinged	7.25	
		On cover		4.50
B60	SP46	4 + 2pf black	.90	1.50
		Never hinged	4.75	
		On cover		4.00
a.		Bklt. pane, 5 #B60, 5 #B62	52.50	105.00
		Never hinged	90.00	
B61	SP46	5 + 2pf green	6.50	8.00
		Never hinged	35.00	
		On cover		20.00
B62	SP46	6 + 4pf dull grn	.75	.65
		Never hinged	4.00	
		On cover		4.00
B63	SP46	8 + 4pf org brn	1.25	2.00
		Never hinged	7.25	
		On cover		4.50
a.		Bklt. pane, 5 #B63, 4 #B64 + label	82.50	150.00
		Never hinged	140.00	
B64	SP46	12 + 3pf hn brn	.55	.65
		Never hinged	3.25	
B65	SP46	20 + 10pf Prus bl	16.00	22.50
		Never hinged	90.00	
		On cover		40.00
B66	SP46	25 + 15pf ultra	17.50	22.50
		Never hinged	95.00	
		On cover		40.00
B67	SP54	40 + 35pf plum	37.50	70.00
		Never hinged	200.00	
		On cover		110.00
		Nos. B59-B67 (9)	82.20	129.30
		Set, never hinged	450.00	

Souvenir Sheet

SP55

1935, June 23   Wmk. 241   Perf. 14

B68	SP55	Sheet of 4	875.00	700.00
		On cover		800.00
a.		3pf red brown	35.00	40.00
b.		6pf dark green	35.00	40.00
c.		12pf dark carmine	35.00	40.00
d.		25pf dark blue	35.00	40.00
		Any single, on cover		110.00

Watermarked cross on each stamp and "OSTROPA 1935" in the margins of the sheet. Size: 148x104mm. 1.70m was the price of a ticket of admission to the Intl. Exhib., Königsberg, June 23-July 3, 1935.

Because the gum on No. B68 contains sulphuric acid and tends to damage the sheet, most collectors prefer to remove it. **Catalogue unused values are for sheet and singles without gum.**

East Prussia SP59   Skating SP69

Designs (Costumes of Various Sections of Germany): 4pf+3pf, Silesia. 5pf+3pf, Rhineland. 6pf+4pf, Lower Saxony. 8pf+4pf, Brandenburg. 12pf+6pf, Black Forest. 15pf+10pf, Hesse. 25pf+15pf, Upper Bavaria. 30pf+20pf, Friesland. 40pf+35pf, Franconia.

Wmk. Swastikas (237)

1935, Oct. 4   Perf. 14x13½

B69	SP59	3 + 2pf dk brown	.30	.40
		Never hinged	1.60	
		On cover		2.25
a.		Bklt. pane, 4 #B69, 5 #B74 + label	40.00	75.00
		Never hinged	70.00	
B70	SP59	4 + 3pf gray	1.20	1.50
		Never hinged	6.50	
		On cover		3.00
B71	SP59	5 + 3pf emerald	.30	1.00
		Never hinged	1.60	
		On cover		2.00
a.		Bklt. pane, 5 #B71, 5 #B72	27.50	50.00
		Never hinged	45.00	
B72	SP59	6 + 4pf dk green	.25	.40
		Never hinged	.80	
		On cover		1.60
B73	SP59	8 + 4pf yel brn	1.90	1.50
		Never hinged	9.50	
		On cover		5.50
B74	SP59	12 + 6pf dk car	.25	.40
		Never hinged	1.00	
		On cover		1.00
B75	SP59	15 + 10pf red brn	4.50	6.00
		Never hinged	22.50	
		On cover		21.00
B76	SP59	25 + 15pf ultra	8.00	6.50
		Never hinged	40.00	
		On cover		20.00
B77	SP59	30 + 20pf olive brn	9.50	20.00
		Never hinged	47.50	
		On cover		32.50
B78	SP59	40 + 35p plum	8.50	14.00
		Never hinged	45.00	
		On cover		32.50
		Nos. B69-B78 (10)	34.70	51.70
		Set, never hinged	160.00	

1935, Nov. 25   Perf. 13½

12+6pf, Ski jump. 25+15pf, Bobsledding.

B79	SP69	6 + 4pf green	.95	1.40
		Never hinged	5.00	
		On cover		3.25
B80	SP69	12 + 6pf carmine	1.90	1.20
		Never hinged	10.00	
		On cover		4.75
B81	SP69	25 + 15pf ultra	8.00	8.00
		Never hinged	40.00	
		On cover		16.00
		Nos. B79-B81 (3)	10.85	10.60
		Set, never hinged	55.00	

Winter Olympic Games held in Bavaria, Feb. 6-16, 1936.

1936, May 8

Designs: 3pf+2pf, Horizontal bar. 4pf+3pf, Diving. 6pf+4pf, Soccer. 8pf+4pf, Throwing javelin. 12pf+6pf, Torch runner. 15pf+10pf,

Fencing. 25pf+15pf, Sculling. 40pf+35pf, Equestrian.

B82	SP69	3 + 2pf brown	.30	.45
		Never hinged	2.00	
		On cover		1.60
a.		Bklt. pane, 5 #B82, 5 #B86	27.50	50.00
		Never hinged	45.00	
B83	SP69	4 + 3pf indigo	1.00	.75
		Never hinged	1.80	
		On cover		2.25
a.		Bklt. pane, 5 #B83, 5 #B84	27.50	50.00
		Never hinged	45.00	
B84	SP69	6 + 4pf green	.25	.45
		Never hinged	1.60	
		On cover		2.00
B85	SP69	8 + 4pf red org	3.00	1.25
		Never hinged	20.00	
		On cover		3.00
B86	SP69	12 + 6pf carmine	.35	.45
		Never hinged	2.25	
		On cover		1.60
B87	SP69	15 + 10pf brn vio	5.50	3.00
		Never hinged	35.00	
		On cover		12.00
B88	SP69	25 + 15pf ultra	3.00	4.00
		Never hinged	20.00	
		On cover		12.00
B89	SP69	40 + 35pf violet	5.50	8.00
		Never hinged	35.00	
		On cover		17.50
		Nos. B82-B89 (8)	18.15	18.35
		Set, never hinged		

Summer Olympic Games, Berlin, 8/1-16/36. See Nos. B91-B92.

Souvenir Sheet

Horse Race — SP80

1936, June 22   Wmk. 237   Perf. 14

B90	SP80	42pf brown	12.50	14.50
		Never hinged	25.00	
		On cover		40.00

A surtax of 1.08m was to provide a 100,000m sweepstakes prize. Wmk. 237 appears on the stamp, with "Munchen Riem 1936" watermarked on sheet margin.
For overprint see No. B105.

Types of 1936 Souvenir Sheets

1936, Aug. 1   Perf. 14x13½

B91	SP69	Sheet of 4	40.00	50.00
		Never hinged	110.00	
		On cover		200.00
B92	SP69	Sheet of 4	40.00	50.00
		Never hinged	110.00	
		On cover		200.00
		Set, never hinged	220.00	

11th Olympic Games, Berlin. No. B91 contains Nos. B82-B84, B89. No. B92 contains Nos. B85-B88.
Wmk. 237 appears on each stamp with "XI Olympische Spiele-Berlin 1936" watermarked on sheet margin. Sold for 1m each.

Frontier Highway, Munich — SP81

Designs: 4pf+3pf, Ministry of Aviation. 5pf+3pf, Nuremberg Memorial. 6pf+4pf, Bridge over the Saale, Saxony. 8pf+4pf, Germany Hall, Berlin. 12pf+6pf, German Alpine highway. 15pf+10pf, Fuhrer House, Munich. 25pf+15pf, Bridge over the Mangfall. 40pf+35pf, Museum of German Art, Munich.

Perf. 13½x14

1936, Sept. 21   Unwmk.

B93	SP81	3pf + 2pf blk brn	.25	.40
		Never hinged	1.00	
		On cover		1.20
a.		Bklt. pane, 4 #B93 + 5 #B98 + label	27.50	55.00
		Never hinged	45.00	
B94	SP81	4pf + 3pf black	.25	.50
		Never hinged	1.20	
		On cover		2.00
B95	SP81	5pf + 3pf brt grn	.25	.40
		Never hinged	1.20	
		On cover		1.20
a.		Bklt. pane, 5 #B95, 5 #B96	14.00	26.00
		Never hinged	22.50	
B96	SP81	6pf + 4pf dk grn	.25	.40
		Never hinged	1.00	
		On cover		.80
B97	SP81	8pf + 4pf brown	.95	1.40
		Never hinged	5.50	
		On cover		2.40
B98	SP81	12pf + 6pf brn car	.25	.40
		Never hinged	1.00	
		On cover		1.40

B99	SP81	15pf + 10pf vio brn	3.50	3.50
		Never hinged	20.00	
		On cover		7.50
B100	SP81	25pf + 15pf indigo	2.40	7.00
		Never hinged	13.50	
		On cover		12.00
B101	SP81	40pf + 35pf rose		
		Never hinged		
		On cover		16.00
		Nos. B93-B101 (9)	12.10	20.00
		Set, never hinged	66.00	

Souvenir Sheets

Adolf Hitler — SP90

Wmk. 237

1937, Apr. 5   Photo.   Perf. 14

B102	SP90	Sheet of 4	19.00	12.50
		Never hinged	55.00	
		On cover		75.00
a.		6pf dark green	1.20	1.60
		Never hinged	4.50	
		On cover		5.50

48th birthday of Adolf Hitler. Sold for 1m. See Nos. B103-B104. For overprint see No. B106.

1937, Apr. 16   Imperf.

B103	SP90	Sheet of 4	40.00	24.00
		Never hinged	175.00	
		On cover		50.00
a.		6pf dark green	4.00	3.00
		Never hinged	12.50	
		On cover		12.00

German Natl. Phil. Exhib., Berlin, June 16-18, 1937 and the Phil. Exhib. of the Stamp Collectors Group of the Strength Through Joy Organization at Hamburg, Apr. 17-20, 1937. Sold at the Exhib. post offices for 1.50m.

No. B102 with Marginal Inscriptions

Perf. 14 and Rouletted

1937, June 10   Wmk. 237

B104	SP90	Sheet of 4	40.00	70.00
		Never hinged	250.00	
		On cover		200.00
a.		6pf dark grn + 25pf label	4.00	7.00
		Never hinged	16.00	
		On cover		20.00

No. B104 inscribed in the margin beside each stamp "25 Rpf. einschliesslich Kulturspende" in three lines.
The sheets were rouletted to allow for separation of each stamp with its component label. Sold at the post office as individual stamps with labels attached or in complete sheets.

Souvenir Sheet No. B90 Overprinted in Red

1937, Aug. 1   Perf. 14

B105	SP80	42pf brown	65.00	105.00
		Never hinged	150.00	
		On cover		550.00
a.		Inverted overprint	14,500.	27,500.

4th running of the "Brown Ribbon" horse race at the Munich-Riem Race Course, Aug. 1, 1937.

Souvenir Sheet No. B104 Overprinted in Black on Each Stamp

Perf. 14 and Rouletted

1937, Sept. 3   **Wmk. 237**
B106 SP90   Sheet of 4   75.00   45.00
    Never hinged   260.00
                       80.00
  a.   6pf dark grn + 25pf label   4.50   6.00
    Never hinged   14.00
    On cover   19.00

1937 Nazi Congress at Nuremburg.

Lifeboat — SP91

Designs: 4pf+3pf, Lightship "Elbe I." 5pf+3pf, Fishing smacks. 6pf+4pf, Steamer. 8pf+4pf, Sailing vessel. 12pf+6pf, The "Tannenberg." 15pf+10pf, Sea-Train "Schwerin." 25pf+15pf, S. S. Hamburg. 40pf+35pf, S. S. Bremen.

Perf. 13½

1937, Nov. 4   **Engr.**   **Unwmk.**
B107 SP91   3pf + 2pf dk brwn   .25   .40
    Never hinged   .40
    On cover   1.25
  a.   Bklt. pane, 4 #B107 + 5
        #B112 + label   27.50   50.00
    Never hinged   47.50
B108 SP91   4pf + 3pf black   1.00   1.20
    Never hinged   8.00
    On cover   2.75
B109 SP91   5pf + 3pf yel grn   .25   .40
    Never hinged   .40
    On cover   1.75
  a.   Bklt. pane, 5 #B109, 5
        #B110   14.00   27.50
    Never hinged   24.00
B110 SP91   6pf + 4pf bl grn   .25   .40
    Never hinged   .40
    On cover   1.25
B111 SP91   8pf + 4pf orange   .60   1.25
    Never hinged   4.75
    On cover   2.75
B112 SP91   12pf + 6pf car lake   .25   .40
    Never hinged   .80
    On cover   1.25
B113 SP91   15pf + 10pf vio brn   1.25   4.00
    Never hinged   10.00
    On cover   12.00
B114 SP91   25pf + 15pf ultra   3.00   4.00
    Never hinged   24.00
    On cover   9.50
B115 SP91   40pf + 35pf red vio   5.00   8.00
    Never hinged   40.00
    On cover   20.00
    Nos. B107-B115 (9)   11.85   20.05
    Set, never hinged   88.75

No. B115 actually pictures the S.S. Europa.

Youth Carrying Torch and Laurel — SP100

Adolf Hitler — SP101

Wmk. 237

1938, Jan. 28   **Photo.**   **Perf. 14**
B116 SP100   6 + 4pf dk green   1.20   2.00
    Never hinged   8.00
    On cover   3.25
B117 SP100   12 + 8pf brt car   1.20   2.00
    Never hinged   8.00
    On cover   4.00
    Set, never hinged   16.00

Assumption of power by the Nazis, 5th anniv.

1938, Apr. 13   **Engr.**   **Unwmk.**
B118 SP101   12 + 38pf copper
             red   2.00   2.75
    Never hinged   10.00
    On cover   5.50

Hitler's 49th birthday.

Horsewoman SP102

1938, July 20
B119 SP102   42 + 108pf dp
             brn   22.50   45.00
    Never hinged   125.00
    On cover   67.50

5th "Brown Ribbon" at Munich.

Adolf Hitler SP103

Theater at Saarbrücken SP104

1938, Sept. 1
B120 SP103   6 + 19pf deep grn   2.25   4.00
    Never hinged   16.00
    On cover   6.50

1938 Nazi Congress at Nuremberg. The surtax was for Hitler's National Culture Fund.

1938, Oct. 9   **Photo.**   **Wmk. 237**
B121 SP104   6 + 4pf blue grn   1.50   2.00
    Never hinged   9.50
    On cover   5.50
B122 SP104   12 + 8pf dk car   1.90   2.75
    Never hinged   12.00
    On cover   8.00
    Set, never hinged   21.50

Inauguration of the theater of the District of Saarpfalz at Saarbrücken. The surtax was for Hitler's National Culture Fund.

Castle of Forchtenstein SP105

Designs (scenes in Austria and various flowers): 4pf+3pf, Flexenstrasse in Vorarlberg. 5pf+3pf, Zell am See, Salzburg. 6pf+4pf, Grossglockner. 8pf+4pf, Ruins of Aggstein. 12pf+6pf, Prince Eugene Monument, Vienna. 15pf+10pf, Erzberg. 25pf+15pf, Hall, Tyrol. 40pf+35pf, Braunau.

Unwmk.

1938, Nov. 18   **Engr.**   **Perf. 14**
B123 SP105   3 + 2pf olive
            brn   .25   .45
    Never hinged   .65
    On cover   1.60
  a.   Bklt. pane, 4 #B123, 5
        #B128 + label   27.50   50.00
    Never hinged   47.50
B124 SP105   4 + 3pf indi-
            go   1.75   1.25
    Never hinged   8.75
    On cover   3.25
B125 SP105   5 + 3pf em-
            erald   .25   .45
    Never hinged   .50
    On cover   2.00
  a.   Bklt. pane, 5 #B125, 5
        #B126   12.50   27.50
    Never hinged   24.00
B126 SP105   6 + 4pf dk
            grn   .25   .40
    Never hinged   .50
    On cover   1.25
B127 SP105   8 + 4pf red
            org   1.75   1.25
    Never hinged   8.75
    On cover   3.25
B128 SP105   12 + 6pf dk
            car   .25   .45
    Never hinged   .55
    On cover   1.25
B129 SP105   15 + 10pf dp
            cl   3.00   4.50
    Never hinged   16.00
    On cover   12.00
B130 SP105   25 + 15pf dk
            blue   2.75   4.50
    Never hinged   13.50
    On cover   8.00
B131 SP105   40 + 35pf
            plum   6.25   8.00
    Never hinged   32.50
    On cover   16.00
    Nos. B123-B131 (9)   16.50   21.25
    Set, never hinged   81.00

The surtax was for "Winter Help."

Sudeten Couple — SP114

1938, Dec. 2   **Photo.**   **Wmk. 237**
B132 SP114   6 + 4pf blue grn   1.60   3.25
    Never hinged   13.50
    On cover   6.50
B133 SP114   12 + 8pf dk car   2.40   3.25
    Never hinged   19.00
    On cover   8.00
    Set, never hinged   32.50

Annexation of the Sudeten Territory. The surtax was for Hitler's National Culture Fund.

Early Types of Automobiles SP115

Designs: 12pf+8pf, Racing cars. 25pf+10pf, Modern automobile.

1939
B134 SP115   6 + 4pf dk grn   3.75   3.50
    Never hinged   24.00
    On cover   8.00
B135 SP115   12 + 8pf brt car   3.75   3.50
    Never hinged   24.00
    On cover   9.50
B136 SP115   25 + 10pf dp blue   6.25   6.50
    Never hinged   40.00
    On cover   14.50
    Nos. B134-B136 (3)   13.75   13.50
    Set, never hinged   88.00

Berlin Automobile and Motorcycle Exhibition. The surtax was for Hitler's National Culture Fund. For overprints see Nos. B141-B143.

Adolf Hitler SP118

Exhibition Building SP119

Unwmk.

1939, Apr. 13   **Engr.**   **Perf. 14**
B137 SP118   12 + 38pf carmine   1.50   4.50
    Never hinged   9.00
    On cover   9.50

Hitler's 50th birthday. The surtax was for Hitler's National Culture Fund.

1939, Apr. 22   **Photo.**   **Perf. 12½**
B138 SP119   6 + 4pf dk green   1.25   3.00
    Never hinged   6.50
    On cover   7.25
B139 SP119   15 + 5pf dp plum   1.90   4.00
    Never hinged   9.50
    On cover   8.00
    Set, never hinged   16.00

Horticultural Exhib. held at Stuttgart. Surtax for Hitler's National Culture Fund.

Adolf Hitler — SP120

Perf. 14x13½

1939, Apr. 28   **Wmk. 237**
B140 SP120   6 + 19pf black brn   4.00   5.00
    Never hinged   12.50
    On cover   9.50

Day of National Labor. The surtax was for Hitler's National Culture Fund. See No. B147.

Nos. B134-B136 Overprinted in Black

1939, May 18   **Perf. 14**
B141 SP115   6 + 4pf dk
            green   19.00   27.50
    Never hinged   75.00
    On cover   60.00
B142 SP115   12 + 8pf brt car   19.00   27.50
    Never hinged   75.00
    On cover   60.00
B143 SP115   25 + 10pf dp
            blue   19.00   27.50
    Never hinged   75.00
    On cover   60.00
    Nos. B141-B143 (3)   57.00   82.50
    Set, never hinged   225.00

Nurburgring Auto Races, 5/21, 7/23/39.

Racehorse "Investment" and Jockey SP121

1939, June 18   **Engr.**   **Unwmk.**
B144 SP121   25 + 50pf ultra   15.00   15.00
    Never hinged   65.00
    On cover   28.00

70th anniv. of the German Derby. The surtax was divided between Hitler's National Culture Fund and the race promoters.

Man Holding Rearing Horse — SP122

1939, July 12
B145 SP122   42 + 108pf dp
            brown   15.00   24.00
    Never hinged   62.50
    On cover   40.00

6th "Brown Ribbon" at Munich.

"Venetian Woman" by Albrecht Dürer — SP123

1939, July 12   **Photo.**   **Wmk. 237**
B146 SP123   6 + 19pf dk grn   5.25   10.00
    Never hinged   27.50
    On cover   16.00

Day of German Art. The surtax was used for Hitler's National Culture Fund.

Hitler Type of 1939
Inscribed "Reichsparteitag 1939"

1939, Aug. 25   **Perf. 14x13½**
B147 SP120   6 + 19pf blk brn   4.50   9.50
    Never hinged   19.00
    On cover   14.50

1939 Nazi Congress at Nuremberg.

Meeting in German Hall, Berlin SP124

Designs: 4pf+3pf, Meeting of postal and telegraph employees. 5pf+3pf, Professional competitions. 6pf+4pf, 6pf+9pf, Professional camp. 8pf+4pf, 8pf+12pf, Gold flag competitions. 10pf+5pf, Awarding prizes. 12&f+6pf, 12pf+18pf, Automobile race. 15pf+10pf, Sports. 16pf+10pf, 16pf+24pf, Postal police. 20pf+10pf, 20pf+30pf, Glider workshops.

24pf+10pf, 24pf+36pf, Mail coach. 25pf+15pf, Convalescent home, Konigstein.

Perf. 13½x14

1939-41	Unwmk.		Photo.
B148	3 + 2pf bister brn	2.25	5.25
	Never hinged	13.00	
	On cover		
B149	4 + 3pf slate blue	2.00	5.25
	Never hinged	11.00	
	On cover		12.00
B150	5 + 3pf brt bl grn	.60	1.50
	Never hinged	3.25	
	On cover		4.75
B151	6 + 4pf myrtle grn	.75	1.50
	Never hinged	4.00	
	On cover		4.00
B151A	6 + 9pf dk grn ('41)	.75	2.25
	Never hinged	4.00	
	On cover		3.25
B152	8 + 4pf dp org	.75	1.50
	Never hinged	4.00	
	On cover		4.00
B152A	8 + 12pf hn brn ('41)	.90	1.50
	Never hinged	6.00	
	On cover		4.00
B153	10 + 5pf dk brown	.75	2.00
	Never hinged	4.00	
	On cover		4.00
B154	12 + 6pf rose brown	.90	2.00
	Never hinged	4.75	
	On cover		4.00
B154A	12 + 18pf dk car rose ('41)	1.10	2.00
	Never hinged	6.00	
	On cover		2.75
B155	15 + 10pf dp red lilac	.75	2.25
	Never hinged	4.00	
	On cover		8.00
B156	16 + 10pf slate grn	.75	2.25
	Never hinged	4.00	
	On cover		9.50
B156A	16 + 24pf black ('41)	1.10	4.00
	Never hinged	6.00	
	On cover		8.75
B157	20 + 10pf ultra	.75	2.25
	Never hinged	4.00	
	On cover		12.00
B157A	20 + 30pf ultra ('41)	1.50	4.00
	Never hinged	8.00	
	On cover		12.00
B158	24 + 10pf ol grn	2.00	4.00
	Never hinged	10.00	
	On cover		12.00
B158A	24 + 36pf pur ('41)	3.75	12.00
	Never hinged	20.00	
	On cover		20.00
B159	25 + 15pf dk blue	1.90	3.25
	Never hinged	10.00	
	On cover		13.50
	Nos. B148-B159 (18)	23.25	58.75
	Set, never hinged	125.00	

The surtax was used for Hitler's National Culture Fund and the Postal Employees' Fund. See Nos. B273, B275-B277 in Scott Standard catalogue, Vol. 3.

Elbogen Castle — SP136

Buildings: 4pf+3pf, Drachenfels on the Rhine. 5pf+3pf, Kaiserpfalz at Goslar. 6pf+4pf, Clocktower at Graz. 8pf+4pf, Town Hall, Frankfurt. 12pf+6pf, Guild House, Klagenfurt. 15pf+10pf, Ruins of Schreckenstein Castle. 25pf+15pf, Fortress of Salzburg. 40pf+35pf, Castle of Hohentwiel.

1939	Unwmk.	Engr.	Perf. 14
B160	SP136 3 + 2pf dk brn	.25	.45
	Never hinged	1.00	
	On cover		1.40
a.	Bklt. pane, 4 #B160, 5 #B165 + label	27.50	50.00
	Never hinged	47.50	
B161	SP136 4 + 3pf gray blk	1.60	2.00
	Never hinged	7.25	
	On cover		4.00
B162	SP136 5 + 3pf emerald	.35	.55
	Never hinged	1.60	
	On cover		1.25
a.	Bklt. pane, 5 #B162, 5 #B163	13.00	26.00
	Never hinged	24.00	
B163	SP136 6 + 4pf slate grn	.25	.40
	Never hinged	1.00	
	On cover		1.25
B164	SP136 8 + 4pf red org	1.60	1.75
	Never hinged	7.25	
	On cover		2.75
B165	SP136 12 + 6pf dk car	.35	.80
	Never hinged	3.25	
	On cover		2.25
B166	SP136 15 + 10pf brn vio	2.40	4.75
	Never hinged	11.00	
	On cover		9.50
B167	SP136 25 + 15pf ultra	1.90	4.75
	Never hinged	8.75	
	On cover		9.50
B168	SP136 40 + 35pf rose vio	2.50	6.50
	Never hinged	12.00	
	On cover		12.50
	Nos. B160-B168 (9)	11.20	21.95
	Set, never hinged	53.00	

Hall of Honor at Chancellery, Berlin — SP145

1940, Mar. 28

B169	SP145 24 + 76pf dk grn	6.00	17.00
	Never hinged	28.00	
	On cover		24.00

2nd National Stamp Exposition, Berlin.

Child Greeting Hitler — SP146

Perf. 14x13½

1940, Apr. 10		Photo.	Wmk. 237
B170	SP146 12 + 38pf cop red	1.50	6.00
	Never hinged	14.00	
	On cover		12.00

51st birthday of Adolf Hitler.

Armed Warrior SP147   Horseman SP148

1940, Apr. 30   Unwmk.   **Perf. 14**

B171	SP147 6 + 4pf sl grn & lt grn	.30	1.25
	Never hinged	1.40	
	On cover		2.75

Issued to commemorate May Day.

Perf. 14x13½

1940, June 22			Wmk. 237
B172	SP148 25 + 100pf dp ultra	4.25	11.00
	Never hinged	21.00	
	On cover		16.00

Blue Ribbon race, Hamburg, June 30, 1940. Surtax for Hitler's National Culture Fund.

Chariot SP149

Unwmk.

1940, July 20   Engr.   **Perf. 14**

B173	SP149 42 + 108pf brown	22.50	26.00
	Never hinged	90.00	
	On cover		40.00

7th "Brown Ribbon" at Munich. The surtax was for Hitler's National Culture Fund and the promoters of the race.

View of Malmedy SP150

Design: 12pf+8pf, View of Eupen.

Perf. 14x13½

1940, July 25		Photo.	Wmk. 237
B174	SP150 6 + 4pf dk green	1.20	3.00
	Never hinged	5.00	
	On cover		4.00

B175	SP150 12 + 8pf org red	1.20	3.00
	Never hinged	5.00	
	On cover		4.00
	Set, never hinged	10.00	

Issued on the occasion of the reunion of Eupen-Malmedy with the Reich.

Rocky Cliffs of Heligoland SP152

1940, Aug. 9   **Unwmk.**

B176	SP152 6 + 94pf brt grn & red org	6.00	12.00
	Never hinged	24.00	
	On cover		16.00

Heligoland's 50th year as part of Germany.

Artushof in Danzig — SP153

Buildings: 4pf+3pf, Town Hall, Thorn. 5pf+3pf, Castle at Kaub. 6pf+4pf, City Theater, Poznan. 8pf+4pf, Castle at Heidelberg. 12pf+6pf, Porta Nigra Trier. 15pf+10pf, New German Theater, Prague. 25pf+15pf, Town Hall, Bremen. 40pf+35pf, Town Hall, Munster.

1940, Nov. 5		Engr.	Perf. 14
B177	SP153 3 + 2pf dk brn	.30	.45
	Never hinged	1.00	
	On cover		2.00
a.	Bklt. pane, 4 #B177 + 5 #B182 + label	27.50	47.50
	Never hinged	45.00	
B178	SP153 4 + 3pf bluish blk	1.00	.80
	Never hinged	3.25	
	On cover		3.25
B179	SP153 5 + 3pf yel grn	.30	.45
	Never hinged	1.00	
	On cover		1.40
a.	Bklt. pane, 5 #B179, 5 #B180	14.00	27.50
	Never hinged	24.00	
B180	SP153 6 + 4pf dk grn	.35	.45
	Never hinged	1.10	
	On cover		1.00
B181	SP153 8 + 4pf dp org	1.50	.85
	Never hinged	4.75	
	On cover		3.25
B182	SP153 12 + 6pf carmine	.35	.45
	Never hinged	1.25	
	On cover		1.45
B183	SP153 15 + 10pf dk vio brn	1.50	2.75
	Never hinged	5.25	
	On cover		5.50
B184	SP153 25 + 15pf dp ultra	2.00	2.75
	Never hinged	6.75	
	On cover		6.00
B185	SP153 40 + 35pf red lil	4.00	6.50
	Never hinged	13.50	
	On cover		12.00
	Nos. B177-B185 (9)	11.30	15.45
	Set, never hinged	37.50	

von Behring — SP162

1940, Nov. 26   **Photo.**

B186	SP162 3 + 4pf dp green	1.25	2.25
	Never hinged	4.75	
	On cover		3.25
B187	SP162 25 + 10pf brt ultra	1.90	2.25
	Never hinged	7.25	
	On cover		4.00
	Set, never hinged	12.00	

Dr. Emil von Behring (1854-1917), bacteriologist.

AIR POST STAMPS

Issues of the Republic

Post Horn with Wings — AP1

Biplane AP2

Perf. 15x14½

1919, Nov. 10		Typo.	Unwmk.
C1	AP1 10pf orange	.25	2.75
	Never hinged	.70	
	On cover		8.00
C2	AP2 40pf dark green	.25	3.25
	Never hinged	.70	
	On cover		8.00
a.	Imperf.	2,000.	
	Set, never hinged	1.40	

No. C2a is ungummed.

Carrier Pigeon — AP3

1922-23	Wmk. 126	Perf. 14, 14½	
	Size: 19x23mm		
C3	AP3 25(pf) chocolate	.45	18.00
	Never hinged	2.00	
	On cover		32.50
C4	AP3 40(pf) orange	.35	24.00
	Never hinged	2.00	
	On cover		40.00
C5	AP3 50(pf) violet	.25	8.25
	Never hinged	.75	
	On cover		20.00
C6	AP3 60(pf) carmine	.50	20.00
	Never hinged	2.00	
	On cover		30.00
C7	AP3 80(pf) blue grn	.35	20.00
	Never hinged	1.50	
	On cover		30.00

	Perf. 13x13½		
	Size: 22x28mm		
C8	AP3 1m dk grn & pale grn	.25	3.75
	Never hinged	.25	
	On cover		9.00
C9	AP3 2m lake & gray	.25	3.75
	Never hinged	.50	
	On cover		9.00
C10	AP3 3m dk blue & gray	.25	4.50
	Never hinged	.80	
	On cover		9.00
C11	AP3 5m red org & yel	.25	3.75
	Never hinged	.50	
	On cover		9.00
C12	AP3 10m vio & rose ('23)	.25	10.50
	Never hinged	.50	
	On cover		19.00
C13	AP3 25m brn & yel ('23)	.25	8.50
	Never hinged	.50	
	On cover		16.50
C14	AP3 100m ol grn & rose ('23)	.25	7.25
	Never hinged	.50	
	On cover		16.50
	Nos. C3-C14 (12)	3.65	132.25
	Set, never hinged	11.50	

1923

C15	AP3 5m vermilion	.25	45.00
	Never hinged	.45	
	On cover		75.00
C16	AP3 10m violet	.25	10.50
	Never hinged	.45	
	On cover		21.00
C17	AP3 25m dark brown	.25	10.50
	Never hinged	.40	
	On cover		19.00
C18	AP3 100m olive grn	.25	11.00
	Never hinged	.40	
	On cover		16.50
C19	AP3 200m deep blue	.25	32.50
	Never hinged	.40	
	On cover		67.50
a.	Imperf.	60.00	
	Never hinged	150.00	
	Nos. C15-C19 (5)	1.25	109.50
	Set, never hinged	2.25	

Issued: Nos. C15-C18, 6/1. No. C19, 7/25. Note following No. 160 applies to Nos. C1-C19.

1924, Jan. 11   Perf. 14
Size: 19x23mm

C20	AP3	5(pf) yellow grn	1.25	2.25
		Never hinged	4.25	
		On cover		4.50
C21	AP3	10(pf) carmine	1.25	1.90
		Never hinged	4.25	
		On cover		6.00
C22	AP3	20(pf) violet blue	6.75	5.25
		Never hinged	21.00	
		On cover		10.00
C23	AP3	50(pf) orange	11.00	24.00
		Never hinged	110.00	
		On cover		37.50
C24	AP3	100(pf) dull violet	30.00	55.00
		Never hinged	200.00	
		On cover		75.00
C25	AP3	200(pf) grnsh blue	55.00	75.00
		Never hinged	260.00	
		On cover		300.00
C26	AP3	300(pf) gray	97.50	100.00
		Never hinged	575.00	
		On cover		450.00
a.		Imperf.	900.00	
		Never hinged	1,650.	
		Nos. C20-C26 (7)	202.75	263.40
		Set, never hinged	1,130.	

German Eagle — AP4

1926-27

C27	AP4	5pf green	1.20	1.20
		Never hinged	3.00	
		On cover		2.25
C28	AP4	10pf rose red	2.00	1.20
		Never hinged	5.50	
		On cover		2.00
b.		Tête bêche pair	160.00	275.00
		Never hinged	275.00	
d.		Bklt. pane 10 (6 No. C28 + 4 No. C29)	225.00	350.00
		Never hinged	375.00	
C29	AP4	15pf lilac rose ('27)	2.00	2.00
		Never hinged	17.00	
		On cover		3.75
a.		Double impression	1,375.	
C30	AP4	20pf dull blue	2.00	2.00
		Never hinged	17.00	
		On cover		4.50
a.		Tête bêche pair	160.00	275.00
		Never hinged	275.00	
b.		Bklt. pane 4 (4 No. C30 + 6 labels)	225.00	350.00
		Never hinged	375.00	
c.		Bklt. pane 5 (5 No. C30 + 5 labels)	450.00	1,000.
		Never hinged	900.00	
C31	AP4	50pf brown org	18.00	5.25
		Never hinged	225.00	
		On cover		17.50
C32	AP4	1m black & salmon	18.00	6.00
		Never hinged	115.00	
		On cover		20.00
C33	AP4	2m black & blue	18.00	22.50
		Never hinged	160.00	
		On cover		47.50
C34	AP4	3m black & ol grn	55.00	95.00
		Never hinged	425.00	
		On cover		160.00
		Nos. C27-C34 (8)	116.20	135.15
		Set, never hinged	967.50	

"Graf Zeppelin" Crossing Ocean — AP5

1928-31   Photo.

C35	AP5	1m carmine ('31)	25.00	35.00
		Never hinged	80.00	
		On cover		65.00
C36	AP5	2m ultra	45.00	52.50
		Never hinged	240.00	
		On cover		100.00
C37	AP5	4m black brown	27.50	35.00
		Never hinged	100.00	
		On cover		100.00
		Nos. C35-C37 (3)	97.50	122.50
		Set, never hinged	420.00	

Issued: 2m, 4m, Sept. 20. 1m, May 8.
For overprints see Nos. C40-C45.

AP6

1930, Apr. 19   Wmk. 126

C38	AP6	2m ultra	250.00	400.00
		Never hinged	1,350.	
		On cover		425.00
C39	AP6	4m black brown	250.00	400.00
		Never hinged	1,400.	
		On cover		425.00
		Set, never hinged	2,750.	

First flight of Graf Zeppelin to South America. No. C38 is value with horizontal watermark. No. C39 is valued with vertical watermark. No. C38 with vertical watermark and No. C39 with horizontal watermark are worth 10%-20% more.
Counterfeits exist of Nos. C38-C45.

Nos. C35-C37 Overprinted in Brown

1931, July 15

C40	AP5	1m carmine	120.00	110.00
		Never hinged	450.00	
		On cover		200.00
a.		Hyphen in ovpt. omitted	475.00	1,200.
		Never hinged	2,000.	
		On cover		1,750.
C41	AP5	2m ultra	175.00	200.00
		Never hinged	1,000.	
		On cover		350.00
a.		Hyphen in ovpt. omitted	525.00	1,200.
		Never hinged	2,200.	
		On cover		1,750.
C42	AP5	4m black brown	450.00	675.00
		Never hinged	1,750.	
		On cover		875.00
a.		Hyphen in ovpt. omitted		12,000.
		Nos. C40-C42 (3)	745.00	985.00
		Set, never hinged	3,200.	

Polar flight of Graf Zeppelin.

Nos. C35-C37 Overprinted

1933, Sept. 25

C43	AP5	1m carmine	800.00	400.00
		Never hinged	2,700.	
		On cover		450.00
C44	AP5	2m ultra	75.00	200.00
		Never hinged	250.00	
		On cover		275.00
C45	AP5	4m black brown	75.00	200.00
		Never hinged	250.00	
		On cover		650.00
		Nos. C43-C45 (3)	950.00	800.00
		Set, never hinged	3,200.	

Graf Zeppelin flight to Century of Progress International Exhibition, Chicago.

Swastika Sun, Globe and Eagle — AP7

Otto Lilienthal — AP8

Design: 3m, Count Ferdinand von Zeppelin.

Perf. 14, 13½x13
1934, Jan. 21   Typo.   Wmk. 237

C46	AP7	5(pf) brt green	1.10	.90
		Never hinged	4.75	
		On cover		2.00
C47	AP7	10(pf) brt carmine	1.10	.90
		Never hinged	4.75	
		On cover		2.40
C48	AP7	15(pf) ultra	1.90	1.25
		Never hinged	6.50	
		On cover		2.40
C49	AP7	20(pf) dull blue	3.50	1.75
		Never hinged	12.50	
		On cover		3.25
C50	AP7	25(pf) brown	4.75	2.00
		Never hinged	40.00	
		On cover		3.25
C51	AP7	40(pf) red violet	7.00	1.20
		Never hinged	65.00	
		On cover		3.25
C52	AP7	50(pf) dk green	12.50	.90
		Never hinged	95.00	
		On cover		6.00
C53	AP7	80(pf) orange yel	4.00	4.00
		Never hinged	50.00	
		On cover		27.50
C54	AP7	100(pf) black	8.00	2.75
		Never hinged	65.00	
		On cover		27.50

C55	AP8	2m green & blk	17.50	20.00
		Never hinged	60.00	
		On cover		60.00
C56	AP8	3m blue & blk	32.50	45.00
		Never hinged	160.00	
		On cover		80.00
		Nos. C46-C56 (11)	93.85	80.65
		Set, never hinged	600.00	

"Hindenburg" — AP10

Perf. 14, 14½x14
1936, Mar. 16   Engr.

C57	AP10	50pf dark blue	19.00	1.00
		Never hinged		8.00
C58	AP10	75pf dull green	20.00	1.25
		On cover		10.00

The note concerning gum after No. B68 also applies to Nos. C57-C58.
Unused values are for stamps without gum.

Count Zeppelin — AP11

Airship Gondola — AP12

1938, July 5   Unwmk.   Perf. 13½

C59	AP11	25pf dull blue	2.90	1.50
		Never hinged	17.50	
		On cover		9.50
C60	AP12	50pf green	4.50	1.50
		Never hinged	27.50	
		On cover		9.50
		Set, never hinged	45.00	

Count Ferdinand von Zeppelin (1838-1917), airship inventor and builder.

AIR POST SEMI-OFFICIAL STAMPS

Pigeon holding letter — CL1

Perf. 11½
1912, June 10   Typo.   Unwmk.

CL1	APL1	10pf deep red orange, pale gray	6.50	24.00
		Never hinged	24.00	
		On cover		35.00
CL2	APL1	20pf deep red orange, pale gray	16.00	65.00
		Never hinged	55.00	
		On cover		80.00
CL3	APL1	30pf Deep green, pale gray	35.00	95.00
		Never hinged	100.00	
		On cover		325.00

Nos. CL1-CL3 were issued for the first Rhine-Main airmail flights in Germany. The flights raised money for charities under the patronage of the Grand Duke of Hesse, in conjunction with postal authorities who authorized the stamps. Mail was carried between Darmstadt and Frankfurt am Main by the airship "Schwaben" or the airplane "Gelber Hund". Postage was prepared with regularly issued stamps in addition to the semi-official air post stamps.

Nos. CL1-CL3 Surcharged in Dark Blue

1912, June 10

CL4	APL1	1m on 10pf deep red orange, pale gray	500.00	160.00
		Never hinged	2,000.	
		On cover		225.00
a.		Inverted overprint	5,500.	14,500.
		Never hinged	12,000.	
		On cover		16,000.
b.		"Huna" instead of "Hund"	1,200.	290.00
		Never hinged	4,000.	
		On cover		400.00

Approximately 10,000 semi-official air post stamps on covers were surcharged and carried as souvenirs on the airplane "Gelber Hund".

Nos. CL1, CL2 Overprinted

1912, June 22

CL5	APL1	10pf deep red orange, pale gray	725.00	2,400.
		Never hinged	1,750.	
		On cover		2,750.
CL6	APL1	20pf deep red orange, pale gray	100.00	1,400.
		Never hinged	350.00	
		On cover		1,750.

OFFICIAL STAMPS

Issues of the Republic

In 1920 the Official Stamps of Bavaria and Wurttemberg then current were overprinted "Deutsches Reich" and made available for official use in all parts of Germany. They were, however, used almost exclusively in the two states where they originated and we have listed them among the issues of those states.

O1

O2

O3

O4

O5

O6

O7

O8

O9   O10

O11   O12

1920-21 Typo. Wmk. 125 Perf. 14

O1	O1	5pf deep green	.90	14.00
		Never hinged	4.00	
		On cover		20.00
O2	O2	10pf car rose	.25	1.75
		Never hinged	.50	
		On cover		2.25
O3	O2	10pf orange ('21)	.60	450.00
		Never hinged	2.50	
		On cover		600.00
O4	O3	15pf violet brn	.25	2.25
		Never hinged	.50	
		On cover		3.00
a.		Imperf. ('21)	750.00	750.00
O5	O4	20pf deep ultra	.25	2.00
		Never hinged	.50	
		On cover		2.25
O6	O5	30pf org, buff	.25	2.00
		Never hinged	.50	
		On cover		2.25
O7	O6	40pf carmine	.25	2.00
		Never hinged	.50	
		On cover		2.25
O8	O7	50pf violet, buff	.25	2.00
		Never hinged	.50	
		On cover		2.25
O9	O8	60pf red brown ('21)	.25	2.00
		Never hinged	1.20	
		On cover		2.00
O10	O9	1m red, buff	.25	2.00
		Never hinged	.50	
		On cover		2.25
O11	O10	1.25m dk bl, yel	.25	2.25
		Never hinged	.50	
		On cover		4.75
O12	O11	2m dark blue	4.25	4.00
		Never hinged	24.00	
		On cover		8.00
O13	O12	5m brown, yel	.25	3.00
		Never hinged	.50	
		On cover		3.75
		Nos. O1-O13 (13)	8.25	489.25
		Set, never hinged	36.50	

The value of No. O4a is for a stamp postmarked at Bautzen.
See No. O15. For surcharges see Nos. O29-O33, O35-O36, O38.

Postally Used vs. CTO

Values quoted for canceled examples of Nos. O1-O46 are for postally used stamps. See note after No. 160.

O13   O14

O15

Wmk. 126, 125 (#O16-O17)
1922-23

O14	O13	75pf dark blue	.25	8.00
		Never hinged	.80	
		On cover		16.00
O15	O11	2m dark blue	.25	1.50
		Never hinged	.50	
		On cover		2.00
a.		Imperf.	97.50	
		Never hinged	300.00	
O16	O14	3m brown, rose	.25	1.50
		Never hinged	.50	
		On cover		4.00
O17	O15	10m dk grn, rose	.25	1.50
		Never hinged	.80	
		On cover		2.00
O18	O15	10m dk grn, rose	.25	9.00
		Never hinged	.80	
		On cover		16.00
O19	O15	20m dk bl, rose	.25	1.50
		Never hinged	.50	
		On cover		2.00

O20	O15	50m vio, rose	.25	1.50
		Never hinged	.50	
		On cover		2.00
a.		Imperf	100.00	
		Never hinged	325.00	
O21	O15	100m rose red, rose	.25	1.50
		Never hinged	.60	
		On cover		2.00
a.		Imperf	110.00	775.00
		Never hinged	325.00	
		Nos. O14-O21 (8)	2.00	26.00
		Set, never hinged	5.00	

Issue date: Nos. O18-O21, 1923.
Nos. O20-O21 exist imperf.
For surcharges see Nos. O34, O37, O39.

Regular Issue of 1923 Overprinted — a

1923

O22	A34	20m red lilac	.30	7.50
		Never hinged	1.10	
		On cover		16.00
O23	A34	30m olive grn	.25	35.00
		Never hinged	.50	
		On cover		55.00
O24	A29	40m green	.25	3.00
		Never hinged	1.10	
		On cover		6.25
O25	A35	200m car rose	.25	1.50
		Never hinged	.50	
		On cover		2.00
O26	A35	300m green	.25	1.50
		Never hinged	.50	
		On cover		2.00
O27	A35	400m dk brn	.25	1.50
		Never hinged	.50	
		On cover		2.00
O28	A35	500m red orange	.25	1.50
		Never hinged	.50	
		On cover		2.00
		Nos. O22-O28 (7)	1.80	51.50
		Set, never hinged	4.50	

Official Stamps of 1920-23 Surcharged with New Values
Abbreviations:
Th=(Tausend) Thousand
Mil=(Million) Million
Mlrd=(Milliarde) Billion

1923   Wmk. 125

O29	O12	5th m on 5m	.25	3.00
		Never hinged	.30	
		On cover		8.00
a.		Inverted surcharge	50.00	
		Never hinged	115.00	
O30	O5	20th m on 30pf	.25	3.00
		Never hinged	.30	
		On cover		8.00
a.		Inverted surcharge	55.00	
		Never hinged	130.00	
b.		Imperf.	60.00	
		Never hinged	150.00	
O31	O3	100th m on 15pf	.25	3.00
		Never hinged	.30	
		On cover		8.00
a.		Imperf.	60.00	
		Never hinged	150.00	
b.		Inverted surcharge	50.00	
		Never hinged	115.00	
O32	O2	250th m on 10pf car rose	.25	3.00
		Never hinged	.30	
		On cover		8.00
a.		Double surcharge	50.00	
		Never hinged	115.00	
O33	O5	800th m on 30pf	.60	300.00
		Never hinged	1.60	
				400.00

Official Stamps and Types of 1920-23 Surcharged with New Values
Wmk. 126

O34	O15	75th m on 50m	.25	3.00
		Never hinged	.30	
		On cover		8.00
a.		Inverted surcharge	50.00	
		Never hinged	115.00	
O35	O3	400th m on 15pf brn	.25	27.50
		Never hinged	.30	
		On cover		45.00
O36	O5	800th m on 30pf org, buff	.30	4.50
		Never hinged	1.10	
		On cover		12.00
O37	O13	1 mil m on 75pf	.25	37.50
		Never hinged	.30	
		On cover		95.00
O38	O2	2 mil m on 10pf car rose	.30	3.75
		Never hinged	1.10	
		On cover		8.00
a.		Imperf.	95.00	
		Never hinged	225.00	
O39	O15	5 mil m on 100m	.25	5.75
		Never hinged	.30	
		On cover		12.50
		Nos. O29-O39 (11)	3.20	394.00
		Set, never hinged	6.00	

The 10, 15 and 30 pfennig are not known with this watermark and without surcharge.

Nos. 290-291, 295-299 Overprinted Type "a"
1923

O40	A39	100 mil m	.25	150.00
		Never hinged	.60	
				350.00
O41	A39	200 mil m	.30	150.00
		Never hinged	1.10	
				350.00
O42	A39a	2 mlrd m	.25	115.00
		Never hinged	.90	
				350.00
O43	A39a	5 mlrd m	.25	90.00
		Never hinged	1.50	
				350.00
O44	A39a	10 mlrd m	3.75	140.00
		Never hinged	10.00	
				350.00
O45	A39a	20 mlrd m	3.75	150.00
		Never hinged	13.50	
				350.00
O46	A39a	50 mlrd m	2.00	200.00
		Never hinged	5.75	
				425.00
		Nos. O40-O46 (7)	10.55	995.00
		Set, never hinged	34.50	

Same Overprint on Nos. 323-328, Values in Rentenpfennig
1923

O47	A40	3pf brown	.25	.75
		Never hinged	1.50	
		On cover		2.25
O48	A40	5pf dk green	.25	.75
		Never hinged	1.50	
		On cover		1.50
a.		Inverted overprint	115.00	300.00
		Never hinged	300.00	
O49	A40	10pf carmine	.25	.75
		Never hinged	1.50	
		On cover		1.50
a.		Inverted overprint	80.00	175.00
		Never hinged	150.00	
b.		Imperf.	60.00	
		Never hinged	150.00	
O50	A40	20pf dp ultra	.60	1.10
		Never hinged	2.75	
		On cover		2.00
O51	A40	50pf orange	.60	1.50
		Never hinged	3.50	
		On cover		15.00
O52	A40	100pf brown vio	3.75	7.50
		Never hinged	15.00	
		On cover		125.00
		Nos. O47-O52 (6)	5.70	12.35
		Set, never hinged	25.75	

Same Overprint On Issues of 1924
1924

O53	A41	3pf lt brown	.35	2.25
		Never hinged	2.25	
		On cover		3.50
a.		Inverted overprint	60.00	300.00
		Never hinged	300.00	
O54	A41	5pf lt green	.25	.75
		Never hinged	1.50	
		On cover		1.10
a.		Imperf.	75.00	
		Never hinged	225.00	
b.		Inverted overprint	110.00	
		Never hinged	300.00	
O55	A41	10pf vermilion	.25	.75
		Never hinged	1.00	
		On cover		1.10
O56	A41	20pf blue	.25	.75
		Never hinged	1.10	
		On cover		2.75
O57	A41	30pf rose lilac	.75	.75
		Never hinged	4.00	
		On cover		2.75
O58	A41	40pf olive green	.75	.75
		Never hinged	4.00	
		On cover		6.00
O59	A41	50pf orange	6.75	3.75
		Never hinged	20.00	
		On cover		10.00
O60	A47	60pf red brown	1.50	3.75
		Never hinged	8.00	
		On cover		24.00
O61	A47	80pf slate	6.75	35.00
		Never hinged	21.00	
		On cover		350.00
		Nos. O53-O61 (9)	17.60	48.50
		Set, never hinged	62.50	

O16

1927-33   Perf. 14

O62	O16	3pf bister	.30	.75
		Never hinged	1.15	
		On cover		1.50
O63	O16	4pf lt bl ('31)	.50	.90
		Never hinged	1.50	
		On cover		2.25
O64	O16	4pf blue ('33)	6.75	13.50
		Never hinged	57.50	
		On cover		26.00
O65	O16	5pf green	.25	.75
		Never hinged	.60	
		On cover		1.50
O66	O16	6pf pale ol grn ('32)	.75	.90
		Never hinged	2.60	
		On cover		2.25
O67	O16	8pf dk grn	.30	.75
		Never hinged	1.10	
		On cover		1.50

O68	O16	10pf carmine	7.50	6.00
		Never hinged	27.00	
		On cover		22.50
O69	O16	10pf ver ('29), wmk. upright	15.00	19.00
		Never hinged	70.00	
		On cover		67.50
a.		Wmk. sideways	15.00	20.00
		Never hinged	60.00	
				45.00
O70	O16	10pf red vio ('30)	.45	.90
		Never hinged	1.50	
		On cover		1.90
a.		Imperf.	150.00	
		Never hinged	400.00	
O71	O16	10pf choc ('33)	3.00	9.00
		Never hinged	27.50	
				15.00
O72	O16	12pf org ('32)	.50	.90
		Never hinged	1.50	
				2.25
O73	O16	15pf vermilion	1.75	.90
		Never hinged	6.00	
				3.00
O74	O16	15pf car ('29)	.45	.90
		Never hinged	1.40	
				2.25
O75	O16	20pf Prus grn, wmk. upright	7.50	3.00
		Never hinged	26.00	
				9.00
a.		Wmk. sideways	20.00	75.00
		Never hinged	85.00	
				120.00
O76	O16	20pf gray ('30), wmk. upright	2.25	1.10
		Never hinged	6.75	
				1.90
a.		Wmk. sideways	675.00	450.00
		Never hinged	5,000.	
O77	O16	30pf olive grn	.90	.90
		Never hinged	3.25	
				1.50
O78	O16	40pf violet, wmk upright	.75	.90
		Never hinged	3.75	
		On cover		3.25
a.		Wmk sideways	8.25	30.00
		Never hinged	32.50	
				80.00
O79	O16	60pf red brn ('28)	1.10	1.90
		Never hinged	5.00	
				8.00
		Nos. O62-O79 (18)	50.00	62.95
		Set, never hinged	275.00	

Swastika — O17

1934, Jan. 18   Wmk. 237

O80	O17	3pf bister	.75	1.10
		Never hinged	3.25	
				2.40
O81	O17	4pf dull blue	.30	.90
		Never hinged	1.00	
				2.00
O82	O17	5pf brt green	.25	1.10
		Never hinged	.60	
				9.50
O83	O17	6pf dk green	.25	.90
		Never hinged	.60	
				1.60
a.		Imperf.	150.00	
		Never hinged	400.00	
O84	O17	8pf vermilion	2.25	.90
		Never hinged	7.25	
				2.00
O85	O17	10pf chocolate	.30	7.50
		Never hinged	1.40	
				12.00
O86	O17	12pf brt carmine	2.25	1.50
		Never hinged	12.00	
				2.25
a.		Unwmkd.	5.00	7.00
		Never hinged	12.00	
O87	O17	15pf claret	.90	9.00
		Never hinged	4.75	
				16.00
O88	O17	20pf light blue	.45	1.50
		Never hinged	1.60	
				2.25
O89	O17	30pf olive grn	.90	1.50
		Never hinged	2.75	
				3.75
O90	O17	40pf red violet	.90	1.50
		Never hinged	2.75	
				8.00
O91	O17	50pf orange yel	1.40	3.75
		Never hinged	4.75	
				17.50
		Nos. O80-O91 (12)	10.90	31.15
		Set, never hinged	42.50	

LOCAL OFFICIAL STAMPS
For Use in Prussia

("Nr. 21" refers to the district of Prussia) — LO1

1903 Unwmk. Typo. Perf. 14, 14½

OL1	LO1	2pf slate	1.20	4.50
		Never hinged	2.25	
		On cover		24.00
OL2	LO1	3pf bister brn	1.20	4.50
		Never hinged	2.25	
		On cover		21.00
OL3	LO1	5pf green	.30	.50
		Never hinged	.80	
		On cover		13.50
OL4	LO1	10pf carmine	.30	.50
		Never hinged	.80	
		On cover		8.00
OL5	LO1	20pf ultra	.30	.50
		Never hinged	.80	
		On cover		8.00
OL6	LO1	25pf org & blk, yel	.75	1.75
		Never hinged	1.50	
		On cover		21.00
OL7	LO1	40pf lake & blk	.75	2.00
		Never hinged	1.50	
		On cover		27.50
OL8	LO1	50pf pur & blk, sal	.90	2.00
		Never hinged	2.00	
		On cover		40.00
		Nos. OL1-OL8 (8)	5.70	16.25
		Set, never hinged	11.90	

LO2

LO3

LO4

LO5

LO6

LO7

LO8

1920 Typo. Wmk. 125 Perf. 14

OL9	LO2	5pf green	.25	3.00
		Never hinged	1.10	
		On cover		6.00
OL10	LO3	10pf carmine	.70	1.50
		Never hinged	3.25	
		On cover		3.25
OL11	LO4	15pf vio brn	.25	1.50
		Never hinged	.55	
		On cover		2.75
OL12	LO5	20pf dp ultra	.25	1.40
		Never hinged	.50	
		On cover		2.75
OL13	LO6	30pf org, buff	.25	1.40
		Never hinged	.50	
		On cover		2.75
OL14	LO7	50pf brn lil, buff	.30	1.50
		Never hinged	1.60	
		On cover		2.75
OL15	LO8	1m red, buff	8.25	3.75
		Never hinged	32.50	
		On cover		12.00
		Nos. OL9-OL15 (7)	10.25	14.05
		Set, never hinged	40.00	

For Use in Baden

LO9

1905 Unwmk. Typo. Perf. 14, 14½

OL16	LO9	2pf gray blue	52.50	75.00
		Never hinged	600.00	
		On cover		145.00
OL17	LO9	3pf brown	6.00	10.50
		Never hinged	27.50	
		On cover		40.00
OL18	LO9	5pf green	4.25	7.50
		Never hinged	19.00	
		On cover		20.00
OL19	LO9	10pf rose	.75	2.10
		Never hinged	3.25	
		On cover		17.50

OL20	LO9	20pf blue	1.50	3.00
		Never hinged	12.00	
		On cover		20.00
OL21	LO9	25pf org & blk, yel	35.00	52.50
		Never hinged	240.00	
		On cover		130.00
		Nos. OL16-OL21 (6)	100.00	150.60
		Set, never hinged	900.00	

NEWSPAPER STAMPS

Newsboy and Globe — N1

Wmk. Swastikas (237)

1939, Nov. 1 Photo. Perf. 14

P1	N1	5pf green	.60	5.25
		Never hinged	2.50	
		On wrapper or address label		200.00
P2	N1	10pf red brown	.60	5.25
		Never hinged	2.50	
		On wrapper or address label		200.00
		Set, never hinged	5.00	

FRANCHISE STAMPS

For use by the National Socialist German Workers' Party

Party Emblem — F1

1938 Typo. Wmk. 237 Perf. 14

S1	F1	1pf black	.70	3.00
		Never hinged	6.00	
		On cover		8.00
S2	F1	3pf bister	.70	1.90
		Never hinged	6.00	
		On cover		6.50
S3	F1	4pf dull blue	.70	1.50
		Never hinged	7.25	
		On cover		4.00
S4	F1	5pf brt green	.40	1.50
		Never hinged	2.75	
		On cover		8.00
S5	F1	6pf dk green	.40	1.50
		Never hinged	2.75	
		On cover		4.00
S6	F1	8pf vermilion	2.75	1.50
		Never hinged	24.00	
		On cover		4.00
S7	F1	12pf brt car	4.50	1.50
		Never hinged	42.50	
		On cover		4.00
S8	F1	16pf gray	.65	9.00
		Never hinged	6.00	
		On cover		32.50
S9	F1	24pf citron	1.00	4.75
		Never hinged	11.00	
		On cover		24.00
S10	F1	30pf olive	1.00	7.50
		Never hinged	8.75	
		On cover		24.00
S11	F1	40pf red violet	1.00	11.00
		Never hinged	10.00	
		On cover		32.50
		Nos. S1-S11 (11)	13.80	44.65
		Set, never hinged	127.00	

GERMAN OCCUPATION STAMPS

100 Centimes = 1 Franc
100 Pfennig = 1 Mark

Issued under Belgian Occupation

Belgian Stamps of 1915-1920 Overprinted

Perf. 11½, 14, 14½

1919-21 Unwmk.

1N1	A46	1c orange	.30	.60
		Never hinged	1.10	
		On parcel post receipt card		67.50
1N2	A46	2c chocolate	.30	.60
		Never hinged	1.10	
		On parcel post receipt card		67.50
1N3	A46	3c gray blk ('21)	.30	1.90
		Never hinged	1.50	
		On parcel post receipt card		100.00
1N4	A46	5c green	.60	1.10
		Never hinged	1.50	
		On parcel post receipt card		67.50
1N5	A46	10c carmine	1.25	1.90
		Never hinged	5.25	
		On parcel post receipt card		67.50
1N6	A46	15c purple	.60	1.10
		Never hinged	2.25	
		On parcel post receipt card		67.50
1N7	A46	20c red violet	.90	1.25
		Never hinged	3.00	
		On parcel post receipt card		67.50
1N8	A46	25c blue	1.10	1.50
		Never hinged	4.50	
		On parcel post receipt card		67.50
1N9	A54	25c dp blue ('21)	3.75	11.00
		Never hinged	12.50	
		On parcel post receipt card		100.00

Belgian Stamps of 1915-1920 Overprinted

1N10	A47	35c brn org & blk	1.10	1.25
		Never hinged	4.50	
		On parcel post receipt card		85.00
1N11	A48	40c green & blk	1.10	2.25
		Never hinged	5.25	
		On parcel post receipt card		85.00
1N12	A49	50c car rose & blk	5.50	10.00
		Never hinged	19.00	
		On parcel post ereceipt card		85.00
1N13	A56	65c cl & blk ('21)	3.00	11.00
		Never hinged	9.00	
		On cover		—
1N14	A50	1fr violet	21.00	19.00
		Never hinged	60.00	
		On cover		—
1N15	A51	2fr slate	35.00	45.00
		Never hinged	135.00	
		On cover		—
1N16	A52	5fr deep blue	8.25	11.00
		Never hinged	34.00	
		On cover		—
1N17	A53	10fr brown	55.00	60.00
		Never hinged	150.00	
		On cover		—
		Nos. 1N1-1N17 (17)	139.05	180.45
		Set, never hinged	450.00	

Nos. 1N1-1N17 were valid for postage until April 30, 1931, nearly one year after the Belgians and other occupation forces evacuated the Rhineland. Mixed frankings with Belgian stamps were permitted. The values for used stamps are for stamps with cancels from the Belgian military post offices in occupied Germany.

Nos. 1N14-1N17 exist with two overprint types: spacing between "Allemagne" and "Duitshland" 2mm (1919) and 1mm (1920).

Belgian Stamps of 1915 Surcharged

Nos. 1N18-1N22   Nos. 1N23-1N24

Black Surcharge

1920

1N18	A46	5pf on 5c green	.40	.35
		Never hinged	1.10	
		On cover		14.00
		On cover, single franking		45.00
1N19	A46	10pf on 10c car	.50	.45
		Never hinged	1.40	
		On cover		14.00
		On cover, single franking		37.50
1N20	A46	15pf on 15c pur	.70	.70
		Never hinged	1.60	
		On cover		14.00
1N21	A46	20pf on 20c red vio	.70	1.00
		Never hinged	1.60	
		On cover		14.00
		On cover, single franking		37.50

1N22	A46	30pf on 25c blue	1.10	1.25
		Never hinged	2.75	
		On cover		14.00
		On cover, single franking		37.50

Red Surcharge

1N23	A49	75pf on 50c car rose & blk	15.00	19.00
		Never hinged	40.00	
		On cover		65.00
1N24	A50	1m25pf on 1fr violet	21.00	21.00
		Never hinged	60.00	
		Nos. 1N18-1N24 (7)	39.40	43.75
		Set, never hinged	135.00	

EUPEN ISSUE
Belgian Stamps of 1915-20 Overprinted

Eupen

Eupen

Nos. 1N25-1N36   Nos. 1N37-1N41

1920-21 Perf. 11½, 14, 14½

1N25	A46	1c orange	.30	.40
		Never hinged	.75	
		On cover		8.75
1N26	A46	2c chocolate	.30	.40
		Never hinged	.75	
		On cover		8.75
1N27	A46	3c gray blk ('21)	.45	1.40
		Never hinged	1.10	
		On cover		50.00
1N28	A46	5c green	.45	.90
		Never hinged	1.10	
		On cover		8.75
		On cover, single franking		45.00
1N29	A46	10c carmine	.75	1.25
		Never hinged	1.90	
		On cover		8.75
		On cover, single franking		32.50
1N30	A46	15c purple	1.10	1.25
		Never hinged	2.60	
		On cover		8.75
1N31	A46	20c red violet	1.25	1.40
		Never hinged	3.00	
		On cover		8.75
		On cover, single franking		50.00
1N32	A46	25c blue	1.10	1.90
		Never hinged	2.60	
		On cover		10.00
		On cover, single franking		27.50
1N33	A54	25c dp blue ('21)	3.50	9.50
		Never hinged	9.00	
		On cover		45.00
		On cover, single franking		50.00
1N34	A47	35c brn org & blk	1.40	1.90
		Never hinged	3.75	
		On cover		32.50
1N35	A48	40c green & blk	1.75	2.25
		Never hinged	4.50	
		On cover		32.50
1N36	49	50c car rose & blk	5.00	7.25
		Never hinged	12.50	
		On cover		32.50
		On cover, single franking		110.00
1N37	A56	65c cl & blk ('21)	2.75	11.00
		Never hinged	6.75	
		On cover		65.00
1N38	A50	1fr violet	20.00	19.00
		Never hinged	47.50	
		On cover		65.00
1N39	A51	2fr slate	32.50	30.00
		Never hinged	82.50	
		On cover		120.00
1N40	A52	5fr deep blue	10.50	11.00
		Never hinged	26.00	
1N41	A53	10fr brown	45.00	50.00
		Never hinged	120.00	
		Nos. 1N25-1N41 (17)	128.10	150.80
		Set, never hinged	325.00	

MALMEDY ISSUE
Belgian Stamps of 1915-20 Overprinted

Malmédy

Nos. 1N42-1N50   Nos. 1N51-1N53

Malmédy

Nos. 1N54-1N58

1920-21

1N42	A46	1c orange	.25	.40
		Never hinged	.50	
		On cover		8.75
1N43	A46	2c chocolate	.25	.40
		Never hinged	.50	
		On cover		8.75
1N44	A46	3c gray blk ('21)	.35	1.60
		Never hinged	.90	
		On cover		50.00
1N45	A46	5c green	.45	.90
		Never hinged	1.25	
		On cover		8.75
		On cover, single franking		45.00
1N46	A46	10c carmine	.70	1.25
		Never hinged	1.90	
		On cover		8.75
1N47	A46	15c purple	1.10	1.40
		Never hinged	3.00	
		On cover		8.75
1N48	A46	20c red violet	1.50	1.90
		Never hinged	3.75	
		On cover		8.75
		On cover		50.00
1N49	A46	25c blue	1.25	1.90
		Never hinged	3.00	
		On cover		11.00
		On cover, single franking		27.50
1N50	A54	25c dp blue ('21)	3.50	8.75
		Never hinged	9.00	
		On cover		45.00
		On cover, single franking		50.00
1N51	A47	35c brn org & blk	1.25	2.25
		Never hinged	3.75	
		On cover		32.50
1N52	A48	40c green & blk	1.50	2.25
		Never hinged	3.75	
		On cover		32.50
1N53	A49	50c car rose & blk	6.00	7.25
		Never hinged	15.00	
		On cover		30.00
		On cover, single franking		35.00
1N54	A56	65c cl & blk ('21)	2.75	11.00
		Never hinged	6.75	
		On cover		65.00
1N55	A50	1fr violet	20.00	17.00
		Never hinged	47.50	
		On cover		65.00
		On cover, single franking		100.00
1N56	A51	2fr slate	32.50	30.00
		Never hinged	82.50	
		On cover		125.00
		On cover, single franking		325.00
1N57	A52	5fr deep blue	10.50	17.00
		Never hinged	26.00	
		On cover		—
1N58	A53	10fr brown	45.00	55.00
		Never hinged	110.00	
		On cover		—
		Nos. 1N42-1N58 (17)	128.85	160.25
		Set, never hinged	325.00	

OCCUPATION POSTAGE DUE STAMPS

Belgian Postage Due Stamps of 1919-20, Overprinted

1920   Unwmk.   Perf. 14½

1NJ1	D3	5c green	.75	1.10
		Never hinged	1.90	
		On cover		50.00
		On cover, single franking		65.00
1NJ2	D3	10c carmine	1.50	1.90
		Never hinged	3.75	
		On cover		50.00
1NJ3	D3	20c gray green	3.00	4.50
		Never hinged	7.50	
		On cover		65.00
1NJ4	D3	30c bright blue	3.00	4.50
		Never hinged	7.50	
		On cover		65.00
		On cover, single franking		100.00
1NJ5	D3	50c gray	15.00	15.00
		Never hinged	37.50	
		Nos. 1NJ1-1NJ5 (5)	23.25	27.00
		Set, never hinged	57.50	

Belgian Postage Due Stamps of 1919-20, Overprinted

Unwmk.

1NJ6	D3	5c green	1.50	1.10
		Never hinged	3.75	
		On cover		65.00
		On cover, single franking		100.00
1NJ7	D3	10c carmine	3.00	1.90
		Never hinged	7.50	
		On cover		65.00
a.		Inverted overprint	100.00	90.00
		Never hinged		82.50
1NJ8	D3	20c gray green	10.50	11.50
		Never hinged	26.00	
		On cover		82.50
1NJ9	D3	30c bright blue	6.00	8.50
		Never hinged	15.00	
		On cover		100.00

1NJ10	D3	50c gray	12.00	11.00
		Never hinged	30.00	
		On cover		140.00
		Nos. 1NJ6-1NJ10 (5)	33.00	34.00
		Set, never hinged	82.50	

Nos. 1NJ1-1NJ10 were valid for postage until April 30, 1931, nearly one year after the Belgians and other occupation forces evacuated the Rhineland. Mixed frankings with Belgian stamps were permitted. The values for used stamps are for stamps with cancels from the Belgian military post offices in occupied Germany.

GERMANY OFFICES ABROAD

OFFICES IN CHINA

100 Pfennings = 1 Mark
100 Cents = 1 Dollar (1905)

Stamps of Germany, 1889-90, Overprinted in Black at 56 degree Angle

1898   Unwmk.   Perf. 13½x14½

1	A9	3pf dark brown	5.25	5.00
		Never hinged	19.00	
		On cover		27.50
a.		3pf yellow brown	12.00	12.00
		Never hinged	42.50	
		On cover		92.50
b.		3pf reddish ocher	37.50	125.00
		Never hinged	190.00	
		On cover		300.00
2	A9	5pf green	2.75	2.25
		Never hinged	10.00	
		On cover		19.00
3	A10	10pf carmine	5.75	6.25
		Never hinged	19.00	
		On cover		17.00
4	A10	20pf ultramarine	17.00	16.50
		Never hinged	42.50	
		On cover		37.50
5	A10	25pf orange	32.50	30.00
		Never hinged	75.00	
		On cover		92.50
6	A10	50pf red brown	16.00	12.50
		Never hinged	37.50	
		Nos. 1-6 (6)	79.25	72.50

Overprinted at 45 degree Angle

1c	A9	3pf yellow brown	135.00	23,000.
		Never hinged	400.00	
		On cover		37,500.
1d	A9	3pf reddish ocher	375.00	
		Never hinged	1,000.	
e.		3pf gray brown	1,850.	
		Never hinged	3,000.	
2a	A9	5pf green	11.50	12.50
		Never hinged	30.00	
		On cover		35.00
3a	A10	10pf carmine	30.00	10.50
		Never hinged	92.50	
		On cover		27.50
4a	A10	20pf ultramarine	14.00	10.50
		Never hinged	40.00	
		On cover		27.50
5a	A10	25pf orange	50.00	60.00
		Never hinged	190.00	
		On cover		160.00
6a	A10	50pf red brown	20.00	16.50
		Never hinged	75.00	
		On cover		57.50

Value for No. 1c used is for a stamp with small 1898 Shanghai cancel. Examples with other cancellations or later Shanghai cancels sell for about half the value quoted.

Covers: Values for Nos. 6, 6a are for overfranked complete covers, usually philatelic.

Foochow Issue

Nos. 3 and 3a Handstamp Surcharged

1900

16	A10	5pf on 10pf, #3	600.00	850.00
		Never hinged	1,350.	
		On cover		2,000.
a.		On No. 3a	550.00	900.00
		Never hinged	1,100.	
		On cover		2,000.

For similar 5pf surcharges on 10pf carmine, see Tsingtau Issue, Kiauchau.

Tientsin Issue

German Stamps of 1000 Issue Handstamped

1900

17	A11	3pf brown	575.00	750.00
		Never hinged	2,100.	
		On cover		1,350.
18	A11	5pf green	375.00	350.00
		Never hinged	1,350.	
		On cover		1,500.
a.		Double overprint	2,000.	
		Never hinged	2,500.	
19	A11	10pf carmine	900.00	850.00
		Never hinged	4,250.	
		On cover		2,250.
a.		Double overprint	4,250.	
		Never hinged	4,500.	
20	A11	20pf ultra	750.00	900.00
		Never hinged	2,300.	
		On cover		2,600.
a.		Double overprint	4,250.	
		Never hinged	6,000.	
21	A11	30pf org & blk, sal	4,750.	4,750.
		Never hinged	13,750.	
		On cover		11,500.
a.		Double overprint	12,500.	
		Never hinged	15,000.	
22	A11	50pf pur & blk, sal	29,000.	15,000.
		Never hinged	52,500.	
		On cover		27,500.
a.		Double overprint	—	
		Never hinged	15,000.	
23	A11	80pf lake & blk, rose	4,750.	4,500.
		Never hinged	13,500.	
		On cover		11,500.
a.		Double overprint	12,500.	
		Never hinged	15,000.	

This handstamp is known inverted and double on most values.
Excellent faked handstamps are plentiful.
Unissued denominations include 25pf black and orange, *yellow* (value unused, $37,500); 40pf carmine and black (value unused, $37,500); 2m deep blue; and 3m violet black. Used examples are favor canceled.

Covers: Values for Nos. 22-23 are for overfranked complete covers, usually philatelic.

Regular Issue

German Stamps of 1900 Overprinted

A14

A15

1901   Perf. 14, 14½
Overprinted Horizontally in Black

24	A11	3pf brown	1.50	1.90
		Never hinged	5.25	
		On cover		75.00
a.		3pf light red brown	105.00	45.00
		Never hinged	375.00	
		On cover		190.00
25	A11	5pf green	1.50	1.50
		Never hinged	5.25	
		On cover		15.00
26	A11	10pf carmine	2.50	1.10
		Never hinged	7.00	
		On cover		15.00
27	A11	20pf ultra	3.25	1.50
		Never hinged	10.00	
		On cover		15.00
28	A11	25pf blk & blk, yel	9.00	16.00
		Never hinged	27.50	
		On cover		35.00
29	A11	30pf org & blk, sal	9.00	13.00
		Never hinged	27.50	
		On cover		27.50
30	A11	40pf lake & blk	9.00	9.00
		Never hinged	27.50	
		On cover		27.50
31	A11	50pf pur & blk, sal	9.00	9.00
		Never hinged	27.50	
		On cover		19.00
32	A11	80pf lake & blk, rose	11.00	11.00
		Never hinged	30.00	

		On cover		27.50

Overprinted in Black or Red

33	A12	1m car rose	27.50	32.50
		Never hinged	97.50	
34	A13	2m gray blue	27.50	30.00
		Never hinged	85.00	
		On cover		70.00
35	A14	3m blk vio (R)	45.00	65.00
		Never hinged	150.00	
		On cover		130.00
36	A15	5m slate & car, I	1,275.	2,250.
		Never hinged	2,750.	
		On cover		—
b.		Red and/or white retouched	210.00	300.00
		Never hinged	525.00	
		On cover		600.00
36A	A15	5m slate & car, II	210.00	300.00
		Never hinged	525.00	
		On cover		600.00
		Nos. 24-36A (14)	1,640.	2,741.

See note after Germany No. 65A for information on retouches on No. 36. For description of the 5m Type I and Type II, see note above Germany No. 62.

Surcharged on German Stamps of 1902 in Black or Red

a

b

c

1905   Unwmk.

37	A16(a)	1c on 3pf	2.90	3.50
		Never hinged	7.50	
		On cover		22.50
38	A16(a)	2c on 5pf	2.90	1.60
		Never hinged	12.00	
		On cover		15.00
39	A16(a)	4c on 10pf	5.25	1.60
		Never hinged	21.00	
		On cover		15.00
40	A16(a)	10c on 20pf	2.90	1.75
		Never hinged	11.00	
		On cover		15.00
41	A16(a)	20c on 40pf	20.00	7.50
		Never hinged	60.00	
		On cover		30.00
42	A16(a)	40c on 80pf	32.50	13.00
		Never hinged	115.00	
		On cover		30.00
43	A17(b)	½d on 1m (26x17 perf. holes)	16.00	20.00
		Never hinged	72.50	
		On cover		45.00
a.		½d on 1m, 25x16 perf. holes	67.50	65.00
		Never hinged	210.00	
		On cover		175.00
44	A21(b)	1d on 2m	17.50	21.00
		Never hinged	52.50	
		On cover		45.00
45	A19(c)	1½d on 3m (R) (26x17 perf. holes)	255.00	115.00
		Never hinged	900.00	
		On cover		150.00
a.		1½d on 3m, 25x16 perf. holes	16.00	45.00
		Never hinged	55.00	
		On cover		85.00
46	A20(b)	2½d on 5m	110.00	300.00
		Never hinged	350.00	
		On cover		650.00
		Nos. 37-46 (10)	464.95	484.95

Surcharged on German Stamps of 1905 in Black or Red

1906-13   Wmk. 125

47	A16(a)	1c on 3pf	.40	1.25
		Never hinged	.75	
		On cover		15.00
48	A16(a)	2c on 5pf	.40	1.25
		Never hinged	.75	
		On cover		15.00
49	A16(a)	4c on 10pf	.40	1.50
		Never hinged	.75	
		On cover		15.00
50	A16(a)	10c on 20pf	.85	6.50
		Never hinged	1.75	
		On cover		15.00

51 A16(a) 20c on 40pf .90 *3.50*
  Never hinged 1.75
  On cover 9.00
52 A16(a) 40c on 80pf 1.10 *50.00*
  Never hinged 1.75
  On cover 150.00
53 A17(b) ½d on 1m 6.00 *37.50*
  Never hinged 19.00
  On cover 110.00
54 A21(b) 1d on 2m 9.00 *37.50*
  Never hinged 52.50
  On cover 85.00
55 A19(c) 1½d on 3m (R) 7.50 *110.00*
  Never hinged 57.50
  On cover 240.00
56 A20(b) 2½d on 5m (26x17 perf. holes) 29.00 *70.00*
  Never hinged 110.00
  On cover 190.00
a. 2½d on 5m, 25x17 perf. holes 30.00
  Never hinged 150.00
  On cover 85.00
  Nos. 47-56 (10) 55.55 *319.00*

Forged cancellations exist.

OFFICES IN MOROCCO

100 Centimos = 1 Peseta

German Stamps of Germany
Surcharged in Black

1899 **Unwmk.** **Perf. 13½x14½**
1 A9 3c on 3pf dk brn 3.25 2.10
  Never hinged 7.50
  On cover 30.00
2 A9 5c on 5pf green 3.25 2.40
  Never hinged 7.50
  On cover 22.50
3 A10 10c on 10pf car 9.00 7.50
  Never hinged 19.00
  On cover 35.00
4 A10 25c on 20pf ultra 18.00 15.00
  Never hinged 37.50
  On cover 60.00
5 A10 30c on 25pf orange 27.50 *32.50*
  Never hinged 75.00
  On cover 140.00
6 A10 60c on 50pf red brn 24.00 *37.50*
  Never hinged 65.00
  On cover 92.50
  Nos. 1-6 (6) 85.00 *97.00*

Covers: Value for No. 6 is for overfranked complete covers, usually philatelic.
Before Nos. 1-6 were issued, the same six basic stamps of Germany's 1889-1900 issue were overprinted "Marocco" diagonally without the currency-changing surcharge line, but were not issued. Value set, $775 hinged, $1,800. never hinged.

German Stamps of
1900 Surcharged

A12

A13

A14

A15

Black or Red Surcharge
1900 **Perf. 14, 14½**
7 A11 3c on 3pf brn 1.25 *2.25*
  Never hinged 2.75
  On cover 11.50
8 A11 5c on 5pf grn 1.50 1.50
  Never hinged 5.00
  On cover 15.00
9 A11 10c on 10pf car 2.00 1.50
  Never hinged 7.00
  On cover 15.00
10 A11 25c on 20pf ultra 3.00 2.75
  Never hinged 9.00
  On cover 27.50
11 A11 30c on 25pf org & blk, *yel* 9.00 *15.00*
  Never hinged 35.00
  On cover 35.00
12 A11 35c on 30pf org & blk, *sal* 6.75 6.25
  Never hinged 22.50
  On cover 30.00
13 A11 50c on 40pf lake & blk 6.75 6.25
  Never hinged 22.50
  On cover 30.00
14 A11 60c on 50pf pur & blk, *sal* 14.00 *32.50*
  Never hinged 50.00
  On cover 60.00
15 A11 1p on 80pf lake & blk, *rose* 12.00 11.00
  Never hinged 42.50
  On cover 45.00
16 A12 1p25c on 1m car rose 32.50 *45.00*
  Never hinged 100.00
  On cover 100.00
17 A13 2p50c on 2m gray bl 37.50 *57.50*
  Never hinged 100.00
  On cover 110.00
18 A14 3p75c on 3m blk vio (R) 45.00 *65.00*
  Never hinged 170.00
  On cover 150.00
19 A15 6p25c on 5m sl & car, type I 975.00 *1,325.*
  Never hinged 1,950.
  On cover —
b. Red and/or white retouched 200.00 *325.00*
  Never hinged 550.00
  On cover 600.00
c. White only retouched 200.00 *325.00*
  Never hinged 525.00
  On cover 900.00
19A A15 6p25c on 5m sl & car, type II 1,500.
  Never hinged 3,000.
  On cover —
  Nos. 7-19A (14) 2,646. *1,571.*

See note after Germany No. 65A for information on retouches on No. 19. For description of the 5m Type I and Type II, see note above Germany No. 62.

New Surcharge Plates
1903
8D A11 5c on 5pf grn 70.00 11.00
  Never hinged 190.00
  On cover 75.00
16D A12 1p25c on 1m car rose 350.00 190.00
  Never hinged 1,050.
  On cover 450.00
17D A13 2p50c on 2m gray bl 500.00 110.00
  never hinged 2,100.
  On cover 300.00
18D A14 3p75c on 3m blk vio (R) 1,300. 240.00
  Never hinged 4,500.
  On cover 575.00
19D A15 6p25c on 5m sl & car, type II 210.00 270.00
  Never hinged 475.00
  On cover 750.00

The 1903 printing Nos. 8D, 16D-18D, 19D differs from Nos. 8, 16-18 and 19A in the "M" and "t" of the surcharge.

German Stamps of 1902 Surcharged in Black or Red

a

b

c

1905 **Unwmk.**
20 A16(a) 3c on 3pf 2.75 2.75
  Never hinged 7.00
  On cover 22.50
21 A16(a) 5c on 5pf 4.75 1.10
  Never hinged 11.00
  On cover 15.00
22 A16(a) 10c on 10pf 8.25 1.10
  Never hinged 27.50
  On cover 15.00
23 A16(a) 25c on 20pf 19.00 3.00
  Never hinged 45.00
  On cover 27.50
24 A16(a) 30c on 25pf 6.75 5.50
  Never hinged 19.00
  On cover 45.00
25 A16(a) 35c on 30pf 10.00 5.50
  Never hinged 30.00
  On cover 45.00
26 A16(a) 50c on 40pf 9.50 7.75
  Never hinged 27.50
  On cover 45.00
27 A16(a) 60c on 50pf 21.00 *24.00*
  Never hinged 52.50
  On cover 50.00
28 A16(a) 1p on 80pf 21.00 19.00
  Never hinged 52.50
  On cover 45.00
29 A17(b) 1p25c on 1m 52.50 37.50
  Never hinged 200.00
  On cover 67.50
30 A21(b) 2p50c on 2m 95.00 *150.00*
  Never hinged 270.00
  On cover 260.00
31 A19(c) 3p75c on 3m (R) 42.50 *55.00*
  Never hinged 120.00
  On cover 370.00
32 A20(b) 6p25c on 5m 150.00 *210.00*
  Never hinged 325.00
  Nos. 20-32 (13) 443.00 *522.20*

Surcharged on Germany No. 54
32A A11(a) 5c on 5pf 8.00 *24.00*
  Never hinged 18.00
  On cover 1,900.

German Stamps of 1905 Surcharged
1906-11 **Wmk. 125**
33 A16(a) 3c on 3pf 8.75 2.10
  Never hinged 18.00
  On cover 22.50
34 A16(a) 5c on 5pf 6.50 1.10
  Never hinged 13.50
  On cover 15.00
35 A16(a) 10c on 10pf 6.50 1.10
  Never hinged 13.50
  On cover 15.00
36 A16(a) 25c on 20pf 16.00 7.50
  Never hinged 42.50
  On cover 30.00
37 A16(a) 30c on 25pf 19.00 11.50
  Never hinged 45.00
  On cover 45.00
38 A16(a) 35c on 30pf 16.00 9.75
  Never hinged 32.50
  On cover 45.00
39 A16(a) 50c on 40pf 32.50 *150.00*
  Never hinged 70.00
  On cover 275.00
40 A16(a) 60c on 50pf 25.00 17.00
  Never hinged 65.00
  On cover 35.00
41 A16(a) 1p on 80pf 125.00 *275.00*
  Never hinged 325.00
  On cover 525.00
42 A17(b) 1p25c on 1m 62.50 *175.00*
  Never hinged 160.00
  On cover 300.00
43 A21(b) 2p50c on 2m 62.50 *175.00*
  Never hinged 160.00
  On cover 300.00
44 A20(b) 6p25c on 5m 125.00 *325.00*
  Never hinged 325.00
  On cover 600.00
  Nos. 33-44 (12) 505.25 *1,150.*

Excellent forgeries exist of No. 41.

Surcharge Spelled "Marokko" in Black or Red
1911
45 A16(a) 3c on 3pf .55 *.75*
  Never hinged 1.00
  On cover 19.00
46 A16(a) 5c on 5pf .55 *1.00*
  Never hinged 1.00
  On cover 15.00
47 A16(a) 10c on 10pf .55 *1.10*
  Never hinged 1.10
  On cover 15.00
48 A16(a) 25c on 20pf .65 *1.40*
  Never hinged 1.10
  On cover 22.50
49 A16(a) 30c on 25pf 1.50 *16.00*
  Never hinged 3.50
  On cover 35.00
50 A16(a) 35c on 30pf 1.50 *8.75*
  Never hinged 3.50
  On cover 35.00
51 A16(a) 50c on 40pf 1.25 *5.25*
  Never hinged 2.75
  On cover 22.50
52 A16(a) 60c on 50pf 2.40 *37.50*
  Never hinged 5.50
  On cover 75.00

53 A16(a) 1p on 80pf 1.60 *24.00*
  Never hinged 4.50
  On cover 57.50
54 A17(b) 1p25c on 1m 4.50 *65.00*
  Never hinged 11.50
  On cover 110.00
55 A21(b) 2p50c on 2m 6.00 *47.50*
  Never hinged 13.50
  On cover 100.00
56 A19(c) 3p75c on 3m (R) 10.50 *225.00*
  Never hinged 24.00
  On cover 425.00
57 A20(b) 6p25c on 5m 19.00 *325.00*
  Never hinged 45.00
  On cover 575.00
  Nos. 45-57 (13) 50.55 *758.25*

Forged cancellations exist.

OFFICES IN THE TURKISH EMPIRE

Unused values for Nos. 1-6 are for stamps with original gum. Stamps without gum sell for about one-third of the figures quoted.

40 Paras = 1 Piaster

A1

A2

German Stamps of 1880-83 Surcharged in Black or Blue
1884 **Unwmk.** **Perf. 13½x14½**
1 A1 10pa on 5pf dull vio 55.00 *32.50*
  Never hinged 725.00
  On cover 375.00
2 A2 20pa on 10pf rose 80.00 *80.00*
  Never hinged 1,050.
  On cover 300.00
3 A2 1pi on 20pf ultra (Bk) 65.00 8.00
  Never hinged 300.00
  On cover 92.50
4 A2 1pi on 20pf ultra (Bl) 2,250. 72.50
  Never hinged 6,750.
  On cover 375.00
5 A2 1¼pi on 25pf brn 190.00 *250.00*
  Never hinged 1,700.
  On cover 925.00
a. 1¼ on 25pf choc brn ('91) 175.00 *250.00*
  Never hinged 1,650.
6 A2 2½pi on 50pf gray grn 100.00 80.00
  Never hinged 1,100.
  On cover 925.00
a. 2½pi on 50pf deep olive grn 275.00 *210.00*
  Never hinged 2,300.
  On cover 1,100.
  Nos. 1-6 (6) 2,740. *523.00*

There are two types of the surcharge on the 1¼pi and 2½pi stamps, the difference being in the spacing between the figures and the word "PIASTER."
Covers: Values for Nos. 6, 6a are for overfranked complete covers, usually philatelic.
There are re-issues of these stamps which vary only slightly from the originals in overprint measurements.

German Stamps of 1889-1900 Surchargd in Black

A3

A4

A5

1889
8 A3 10pa on 5pf grn 3.75 4.00
  Never hinged 23.00
  On cover 27.50
9 A4 20pa on 10pf car 8.00 2.75
  Never hinged 50.00
  On cover 23.00
10 A4 1pi on 20pf ultra 5.50 2.40
  Never hinged 35.00
  On cover 27.50
11 A5 1¼pi on 25pf org 27.50 20.00
  Never hinged 135.00
  On cover 100.00

12	A5	2½pi on 50pf choc	37.50	24.00
		Never hinged	260.00	
		On cover		150.00
a.		2½pi on 50pf copper brown	200.00	125.00
		Never hinged	1,450.	
		On cover		450.00
		Nos. 8-12 (5)	82.25	53.15

Covers: Values for Nos. 12, 12a are for overfranked complete covers, usually philatelic.

German Stamps of 1900 Surcharged

| | A11 | | A12 | |

A13

A14

A15

1900				Perf. 14, 14½
		Black or Red Surcharge		
13	A11	10pa on 5pf grn	1.75	1.75
		Never hinged	5.25	
		On cover		15.00
14	A11	20pa on 10pf car	2.75	2.25
		Never hinged	6.00	
		On cover		15.00
15	A11	1pi on 20pf ultra	4.75	1.90
		Never hinged	11.50	
		On cover		15.00
16	A11	1¼pi on 25pf org & blk, yel	6.50	4.75
		Never hinged	22.50	
		On cover		19.00
17	A11	1½pi on 30pf org & blk, sal	6.50	4.75
		Never hinged	22.50	
		On cover		19.00
18	A11	2pi on 40pf lake & blk	6.50	4.75
		Never hinged	22.50	
		On cover		19.00
19	A11	2½pi on 50pf pur & blk, sal	12.50	13.50
		Never hinged	35.00	
		On cover		35.00
20	A11	4pi on 80pf lake & blk, rose	14.00	13.50
		Never hinged	45.00	
		On cover		35.00
21	A12	5pi on 1m car rose	40.00	40.00
		Never hinged	110.00	
		On cover		100.00
22	A13	10pi on 2m gray bl	35.00	45.00
		Never hinged	110.00	
		On cover		92.50
23	A14	15pi on 3m blk vio (R)	50.00	110.00
		Never hinged	160.00	
		On cover		275.00
24	A15	25pi on 5m sl & car, type I	640.00	1,250.
		Never hinged	1,750.	
		On cover		750.00
a.		Double surcharge		11,000.
d.		Red and/or white re-touched	175.00	250.00
		Never hinged	500.00	
		On cover		675.00
e.		White only retouched	290.00	500.00
		Never hinged	700.00	
		On cover		200.00
24B	A15	25pi on 5m sl & car, type II	290.00	500.00
		Never hinged	700.00	
		On cover		750.00
c.		Double surcharge	9,750.	—
		Never hinged	9,800.	
		Nos. 13-24B (13)	1,110.	1,992.

See note after Germany No. 65A for information on retouches on No. 24. For description of the 5m Type I and Type II, see note above Germany No. 62.

Covers: Values for Nos. 19-24B are for overfranked complete covers, usually philatelic.

German Stamps of 1900 Surcharged in Black

1903-05				
25	A11	10pa on 5pf green	9.50	13.50
		Never hinged	32.50	
		On cover		75.00
26	A11	20pa on 10pf car	30.00	19.00
		Never hinged	75.00	
		On cover		100.00
27	A11	1pi on 20pf ultra	8.75	7.25
		Never hinged	30.00	
		On cover		60.00

German Stamps of 1900, 1905 Surcharged in Black

28	A12	5pi on 1m car rose	140.00	95.00
		Never hinged	375.00	
		On cover		290.00
29	A13	10pi on 2m bl ('05)	160.00	275.00
		Never hinged	450.00	
		On cover		525.00
30	A15	25pi on 5m sl & car	190.00	550.00
		Never hinged	650.00	
		On cover		850.00
a.		Double surcharge	7,500.	
		Never hinged	9,250.	
		Nos. 25-30 (6)	538.25	959.75

The 1903-05 surcharges may be easily distinguished from those of 1900 by the added bar at the top of the letter "A."

German Stamps of 1902 Surcharged in Black or Red

a

b

1905				Unwmk.
31	A16(a)	10pa on 5pf	3.50	2.50
		Never hinged	5.75	
		On cover		15.00
32	A16(a)	20pa on 10pf	9.00	3.25
		Never hinged	19.00	
		On cover		15.00
33	A16(a)	1pi on 20pf	19.00	2.00
		Never hinged	50.00	
		On cover		15.00
34	A16(a)	1¼pi on 25pf	9.50	8.00
		Never hinged	22.50	
		On cover		26.00
35	A16(a)	1½pi on 30pf	14.00	16.00
		Never hinged	70.00	
		On cover		45.00
36	A16(a)	2pi on 40pf	22.50	16.00
		Never hinged	57.50	
		On cover		45.00
37	A16(a)	2½pi on 50pf	9.50	22.50
		Never hinged	15.00	
		On cover		57.50
38	A16(a)	4pi on 80pf	27.50	17.50
		Never hinged	70.00	
		On cover		42.50
39	A17(b)	5pi on 1m	47.50	45.00
		Never hinged	140.00	
		On cover		75.00
40	A21(b)	10pi on 2m	40.00	47.50
		Never hinged	85.00	
		On cover		110.00
41	A19(b)	15pi on 3m (R)	47.50	55.00
		Never hinged	170.00	
		On cover		130.00
42	A20(b)	25pi on 5m	240.00	550.00
		Never hinged	500.00	
		On cover		1,000.
		Nos. 31-42 (12)	489.50	785.25

German Stamps of 1905 Surcharged in Black or Red

1906-12				Wmk. 125
43	A16(a)	10pa on 5pf	2.40	.90
		Never hinged	5.25	
		On cover		15.00
44	A16(a)	20pa on 10pf	4.75	.90
		Never hinged	5.75	
		On cover		15.00
45	A16(a)	1pi on 20pf	6.50	.90
		Never hinged	19.00	
		On cover		15.00
46	A16(a)	1¼pi on 25pf	13.00	13.00
		Never hinged	42.50	
		On cover		37.50

47	A16(a)	1½pi on 30pf	13.00	10.00
		Never hinged	42.50	
		On cover		27.50
48	A16(a)	2pi on 40pf	6.00	1.90
		Never hinged	17.00	
		On cover		19.00
49	A16(a)	2½pi on 50pf	9.50	17.00
		Never hinged	37.50	
		On cover		30.00
50	A16(a)	4pi on 80pf	15.00	22.50
		Never hinged	52.50	
		On cover		42.50
51	A17(b)	5pi on 1m	35.00	32.50
		Never hinged	100.00	
		On cover		85.00
52	A21(b)	10pi on 2m	35.00	47.50
		Never hinged	110.00	
		On cover		110.00
53	A19(b)	15pi on 3m (R)	60.00	475.00
		Never hinged	275.00	
		On cover		1,500.
54	A20(b)	25pi on 5m	32.50	80.00
		Never hinged	75.00	
		On cover		240.00
		Nos. 43-54 (12)	232.65	702.60

German Stamps of 1905 Surcharged Diagonally in Black

1908				
55	A16	5c on 5pf	1.60	2.75
		Never hinged	3.75	
		On cover		15.00
56	A16	10c on 10pf	2.75	4.75
		Never hinged	6.00	
		On cover		22.50
57	A16	25c on 20pf	6.50	25.00
		Never hinged	17.00	
		On cover		75.00
58	A16	50c on 40pf	27.50	60.00
		Never hinged	85.00	
		On cover		150.00
59	A16	100c on 80pf	50.00	65.00
		Never hinged	140.00	
		On cover		210.00
		Nos. 55-59 (5)	88.35	157.50

Forged cancellations exist on Nos. 37, 53-54, 57-59.

GIBRALTAR

jə-ˈbrol-tər

LOCATION — A fortified promontory, including the Rock, extending from Spain's southeast coast at the entrance to the Mediterranean Sea
GOVT. — British Crown Colony
AREA — 2.5 sq. mi.
POP. — 31,183 (1982)
CAPITAL — Gibraltar

12 Pence = 1 Shilling
20 Shillings = 1 Pound
100 Centimos = 1 Peseta (1889-95)

> Catalogue values for unused stamps in this country are for Never Hinged items, beginning with Scott 119 in the regular postage section.

STAMPS OF GREAT BRITAIN USED IN GIBRALTAR

British Post Office opened Jan. 1, 1857. Transferred to Colonial authority Jan. 1, 1886.

> Values are for clear cancellations on sound, fault-free stamps, with average to fine centering. In many cases, very fine examples are rare or non-existent.

Canceled with barred "G" obliterator

1857-59				
A1	1p red brown, Die I (#8)			425.00
A2	1p red brown, Die II (#9)			750.00
A3	1p red brown, Die II (#12)			375.00

A4	1p red brown, Die II (#16)		95.00
A5	1p rose red (#20)		25.00
A6	2p blue (#13)		475.00
A7	2p blue (#19)		400.00
A8	2p blue (#?)		80.00
A9	2p blue, Plate 7 (#29)		350.00
A10	4p rose (#26)		65.00
a.	Thick glazed paper		
A11	6p lilac (#27)		45.00
a.	Blued paper (#27c)		900.00
A12	1sh green (#28)		125.00
a.	Thick glazed paper (#28d)		
b.	Blued paper (#28c)		1,600.

Canceled with barred oval "A26" obliterator

1859-85			
A13	½p rose red, plates 4-6, 8, 10-15, 19, 20 (#58), value from		37.50
A14	1p red brown (#3), value from		2,000.
A15	1p red brown, Die II (#16)		210.00
A16	1p rose red (#20)		15.00
A17	1p rose red, plates 71-74, 76, 78-125, 127, 129-225 (#33)		24.00
A18	1½p lake red, plates 1, 3 (#32), value from		700.00
A19	2p blue (#17)		160.00
A20	2p blue, plates 7, 8, 9, 12 (#29), value from		25.00
A21	2p blue, plates 13, 14, 15 (#30), value from		25.00
A22	2½p claret, plates 1, 2, 3 (#66), value from		30.00
a.	Bluish paper, plates 1, 2 (#66a), value from		110.00
b.	Lettered "LH-FL" (#66b)		2,750.
A23	2½p claret, plates 3-17 (#67), value from		22.50
A24	2½p blue plates 17-20 (#68), value from		14.50
A25	2½p blue plates 21-23 (#82), value from		12.00
A26	3p rose (#37)		275.00
A27	3p rose (#44)		80.00
A28	3p rose, plates 4-10 (#49), value from		52.50
A29	3p rose, plates 11, 12, 14-20 (#61), value from		65.00
A30	3p rose, plates 20, 21 (#83)		—
A31	3p on 3d violet (#94)		200.00
A32	4p rose (#26)		95.00
a.	Thick glazed paper (#26b)		—
A33	4p vermilion, plate 3 (#34)		52.50
a.	Hair lines (#34c)		60.00
A34	4p vermilion, plates 7-14 (#43), value from		32.50
A35	4p vermilion, plate 15 (#69)		325.00
A36	4p pale olive green, plate 15 (#70)		175.00
	Plate 16 (#70)		160.00
A37	4p gray brown, plate 17 (#71)		375.00
A38	4p gray brown, plates 17, 18 (#84), value from		70.00
A39	6p lilac (#27)		45.00
A40	6p lilac, plate 3 (#39)		40.00
a.	Hairlines, plate 4 (#39d)		100.00
A41	6p lilac, plate 5 (#45)		45.00
	Plate 6 (#45)		100.00
A42	6p dull violet, plate 6 (#50)		50.00
A43	6p violet, plates 6, 8, 9 (#51)		35.00
A44	6p brown plate 11		37.50
a.	6p pale buff, plate 11 (#59b)		160.00
	Plate 12 (#59b)		175.00
A45	6p gray, plate 12 (#60)		110.00
A46	6p gray, plates 13-17 (#62), value from		37.50
A47	6p gray, plates 17, 18 (#86), value from		350.00
A48	6p on 6p violet (#95)		125.00
A49	8p orange (#73)		700.00
A50	9p straw (#40)		750.00
a.	9p bister (#40a)		400.00
A51	9p straw (#46)		700.00
A52	9p bister (#52)		350.00
A53	10p red brown (#53)		160.00
A54	1sh green (#28)		125.00
A55	1sh green (#42)		80.00
A56	1sh green (#45)		65.00
A57	1sh green, plates 4-7 (#54), value from		32.50
A58	1sh green, plates 8-13 (#64), value from		75.00
A59	1sh salmon, plate 13 (#65)		450.00

A60	1sh salmon, plates 13, 14 (#87), value from	120.00	
A61	2sh blue (#55)	300.00	
A62	5sh rose, plate 1 (#57)	1,000.	

1880

A63	½p deep green (#78)	30.00	
a.	½p green (#78c)	30.00	
A64	1p red brown (#79)	30.00	
A65	1½p red brown (#80)	350.00	
A66	2p lilac rose (#81)	75.00	
a.	2p deep lilac rose (#81a)	75.00	
A67	5p indigo (#85)	150.00	

1881

| A68 | 1p lilac, 14 dots (#88) | 37.50 | |
| A69 | 1p lilac, 16 dots (#89) | 11.00 | |

1883-84

A70	½p slate blue (#98)	30.00	
A71	2p lilac (#100)	120.00	
A72	2½p lilac (#101)	20.00	—
A73	3p lilac (#102)		—
A74	4p dull green (#103)	200.00	
A75	6p dull green (#105)		—

POSTAL FISCAL STAMPS
Canceled with barred oval "A26" obliterator

1878-81

| AAR1 | 1p purple, wmk. 28 ('78) | | 750.00 |
| AAR2 | 1p purple, wmk. 29 ('81) | | 1,200. |

Types of Bermuda Overprinted in Black

1886, Jan. 1   Wmk. 2   Perf. 14

1	A6	½p green	20.00	10.00
2	A1	1p rose	85.00	5.50
3	A2	2p violet brown	140.00	92.50
4	A8	2½p ultra	200.00	4.25
5	A7	4p orange brn	190.00	110.00
6	A4	6p violet	300.00	225.00
7	A5	1sh bister brn	500.00	400.00
		Nos. 1-7 (7)	1,435.	847.25

Forged overprints of No. 7 are plentiful.

Victoria
A6   A7

A8   A9

1886-98   Typo.

8	A6	½p dull green ('87)	16.00	4.50
9	A6	½p gray grn ('98)	13.00	2.00
10	A7	1p rose ('87)	50.00	5.00
11	A7	1p car rose ('98)	13.00	.55
12	A8	2p brn violet	35.00	29.00
13	A8	2p brn vio & ultra ('98)	27.50	2.00
14	A9	2½p brt ultra ('98)	40.00	.80
a.		2½p ultramarine	95.00	3.25
16	A8	4p orange brn	90.00	90.00
17	A8	4p org brn & grn ('98)	21.00	7.50
18	A8	6p violet	140.00	130.00
19	A8	6p vio & car rose ('98)	47.50	25.00
20	A8	1sh bister	275.00	225.00
21	A8	1sh bis & car rose ('98)	47.50	18.00
		Nos. 8-14,16-21 (13)	815.50	539.35

Stamps of 1886 Issue Surcharged in Black

10 CENTIMOS

1889, July

22	A6	5c on ½p green	9.00	30.00
23	A7	10c on 1p rose	14.50	17.50
24	A8	25c on 2p brn vio	6.00	11.00
a.		Small "I" in "CENTIMOS"	140.00	190.00
b.		Broken "N"	140.00	190.00
25	A9	25c on 2½p ultra	26.00	2.75
a.		Small "I" in "CENTIMOS"	400.00	125.00
b.		Broken "N"	400.00	125.00
26	A8	40c on 4p org brn	62.50	87.50
27	A8	50c on 6p violet	67.50	87.50
28	A8	75c on 1sh bister	67.50	82.50
		Nos. 22-28 (7)	253.00	318.75
		Set, ovptd. "SPECIMEN"	375.00	

There are two varieties of the figure "5" in the 5c, 25c, 50c and 75c.

A11

1889-95

29	A11	5c green	6.00	1.00
30	A11	10c rose	5.50	.60
a.		Value omitted	6,500.	
31	A11	20c ol green ('95)	15.00	100.00
31A	A11	20c on grn & brn ('95)	50.00	24.00
32	A11	25c ultra	25.00	.90
a.		25c deep ultramarine	35.00	.90
33	A11	40c orange brn	4.75	4.25
34	A11	50c violet	4.25	2.50
35	A11	75c olive green	42.50	42.50
36	A11	1p bister	92.50	25.00
36A	A11	1p bis & bl ('95)	6.00	8.50
37	A11	2p blk & car rose ('95)	13.00	37.50
38	A11	5p steel blue	52.50	125.00
		Nos. 29-38 (12)	317.00	371.75

King Edward VII
A12   A13

1903, May 1

39	A12	½p grn & bl grn	12.00	11.00
40	A12	1p violet, red	37.50	.70
41	A12	2p grn & car rose	26.00	37.50
42	A12	2½p vio & blk, bl	8.50	.70
43	A12	6p violet & pur	32.50	26.00
44	A12	1sh blk & car rose	32.50	42.50
45	A13	2sh green & ultra	175.00	275.00
46	A13	4sh vio & green	140.00	200.00
47	A13	8sh vio & blk, bl	160.00	190.00
48	A13	£1 vio & blk, red	600.00	700.00
		Nos. 39-48 (10)	1,224.	1,483.
		Set, ovptd. "SPECIMEN"	575.00	

1904-12   Wmk. 3   Ordinary Paper

49A	A12	½p dull grn & br grn	16.00	3.00
50	A12	1p violet, red	15.00	.60
a.		Bisected, used as ½p on card		1,800.
51	A12	1p car ('07)	6.50	.70
52	A12	2p grn & car rose ('05)	18.00	7.50
53	A12	2p gray ('10)	10.00	13.00
55	A12	2½p ultra ('07)	6.25	1.90
56	A12	6p vio & pur ('06)	47.50	27.50
a.		6p vio & red violet ('12)	160.00	450.00
57	A12	1sh blk & car rose ('05)	65.00	20.00
59	A13	2sh grn & ultra ('05)	97.50	125.00

Chalky Paper

49	A12	½p blue green ('07)	12.00	2.00
49Ab	A12	½p dull grn & br grn ('04)	14.00	8.00
50b	A12	1p violet, red ('05)	8.00	1.00
52a	A12	2p grn & car rose ('07)	10.00	11.00
54	A12	2½p vio & blk, bl ('07)	45.00	110.00
56b	A12	6p vio & pur ('08)	35.00	18.00
57a	A12	1sh blk & car rose ('06)	572.50	17.50
58	A12	1sh blk, grn ('10)	27.50	25.00
59a	A13	2sh grn & ultra ('07)	97.50	120.00

60	A13	2sh vio & bl, bl ('10)	60.00	57.50
61	A13	4sh vio & grn	325.00	400.00
62	A13	4sh blk & red ('10)	150.00	175.00
63	A13	8sh vio & grn ('11)	225.00	250.00
64	A12	£1 vio & blk, red	600.00	650.00
		Nos. 49-64 (14)	2,181.	1,845.

No. 56a, used, must have a 1912 cancellation. Stamps used later sell for about the same as unused.

A14

King George V — A15

1912, July 17   Ordinary Paper

66	A14	½p green	4.00	.80
a.		½p yellow green ('17)	5.75	2.00
67	A14	1p carmine	4.00	.90
a.		1p scarlet ('16)	7.00	1.60
68	A14	2p gray	17.50	1.75
69	A14	2½p ultra	10.00	2.50
a.		2½p pale ultramarine ('17)	8.00	2.25

Chalky Paper

70	A14	6p dl vio & red vio	11.00	19.00
71	A14	1sh black, green	14.00	4.25
a.		1sh black, emerald ('24)	28.00	110.00
b.		1sh blk, bl grn, ol back ('19)	23.00	80.00
c.		1sh blk, emer, ol back ('23)	30.00	82.50
72	A15	2sh vio & ultra, bl	30.00	4.00
73	A15	4sh black & scar	37.50	65.00
74	A15	8sh vio & green	95.00	120.00
75	A15	£1 vio & blk, red	160.00	250.00
		Nos. 66-75 (10)	383.00	468.20
		Set, ovptd. "SPECIMEN"	575.00	

1921-32   Ordinary Paper   Wmk. 4

76	A14	½p green ('26)	1.60	1.90
77	A14	1p rose red	2.25	1.40
78	A14	1½p red brown ('22)	2.25	.60
a.		1½p pale red brown ('24)	2.25	.40
79	A14	2p gray	1.60	1.60
80	A14	2½p ultra	22.50	60.00
81	A14	3p ultra	2.75	1.75
a.		3p br blue ('22)	3.50	4.75

Chalky Paper

82	A14	6p dl vio & red vio ('26)	1.75	4.00
a.		6p gray lilac & red violet ('23)	7.00	5.50
83	A14	1sh black, emer	12.00	24.00
84	A14	1sh ol grn & blk	17.50	27.50
a.		1sh brn olive & black ('32)	17.50	18.00
85	A15	2sh gray vio & ultra, blue	21.00	80.00
a.		2sh red vio & ultra, blue ('25)	8.25	47.50
86	A15	2sh red brn & black	11.00	37.50
87	A15	2sh6p green & blk	11.00	25.00
88	A15	4sh black & scar	75.00	130.00
89	A15	5sh car & black	17.50	75.00
90	A15	8sh vio & green	300.00	500.00
91	A15	10sh ultra & black	37.50	80.00
92	A15	£1 org & black	180.00	275.00
93	A15	£5 dl vio & blk	1,750.	5,500.
		Ovptd. "SPECIMEN"	800.00	
		Nos. 76-92 (17)	717.20	1,325.
		Nos. 76-92, ovptd. "SPECIMEN"	1,200.	

Years issued: Nos. 83, 85, 4sh, 8sh, 1924. 2sh6p, 5sh, 10sh, £5, 1925. £1, 1927. Nos. 84, 86, 1929.

**Type of 1912 Issue Inscribed:
"THREE PENCE"**

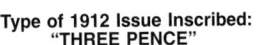

1930, Apr. 12   Ordinary Paper

| 94 | A14 | 3p ultramarine | 9.50 | 2.25 |
| | | Perf "SPECIMEN" | 80.00 | |

Rock of Gibraltar A16

1931-33   Engr.   Perf. 14

96	A16	1p red	2.50	3.50
a.		Perf. 13½x14	18.50	7.50
97	A16	1½p red brown	2.75	3.25
a.		Perf. 13½x14	15.00	5.00
98	A16	2p gray ('32)	8.75	2.25
a.		Perf. 13½x14	20.00	4.00
99	A16	3p dk blue ('33)	8.00	4.25
a.		Perf. 13½x14	35.00	42.50
		Nos. 96-99 (4)	22.00	13.25
		Set, never hinged	45.00	
		Set, perf "SPECIMEN"	190.00	
		Nos. 96a-99a (4)	88.50	59.00
		Set, never hinged	160.00	

Common Design Types pictured following the introduction.

Silver Jubilee Issue
Common Design Type

1935, May 6   Perf. 11x12

100	CD301	2p black & ultra	1.40	2.50
101	CD301	3p ultra & brown	3.50	4.00
102	CD301	6p indigo & green	13.00	18.50
103	CD301	1sh brown vio & ind	15.00	22.50
		Nos. 100-103 (4)	32.90	47.50
		Set, never hinged	57.50	
		Set, perf "SPECIMEN"	225.00	

Coronation Issue
Common Design Type

1937, May 12   Perf. 11x11½

104	CD302	½p deep green	.25	.45
105	CD302	2p gray black	.85	3.00
106	CD302	3p deep ultra	1.50	3.00
		Nos. 104-106 (3)	2.60	6.45
		Set, never hinged	5.00	
		Set, perf "SPECIMEN"	180.00	

George VI — A17

Rock of Gibraltar A18

Designs: 2p, Rock from north side. 3p, 5p, Europa Point. 6p, Moorish Castle. 1sh, South-port Gate. 2sh, Eliott Memorial. 5sh, Government House. 10sh, Catalan Bay.

Perf. 13, 13½x14 (½p, No. 118), 14 (1½p)

1938-49   Engr.   Wmk. 4

107	A17	½p gray green	.25	.40
108	A18	1p red brn ('42)	.35	.55
a.		1p chestnut, perf. 14	27.50	2.75
b.		1p chestnut, perf. 13½	27.50	2.50
c.		Perf. 13½, wmk. sideways ('41)	6.75	8.25
109	A18	1½p carmine rose	30.00	.90
b.		Perf. 13½	275.00	45.00
109A	A18	1½p gray vio ('43)	.25	1.60
110	A18	2p dk gray ('42)	.35	1.40
a.		Perf. 14	27.50	.55
c.		Perf. 13½	1.75	.45
d.		Perf. 13½, wmk. sideways ('41)	650.00	52.50
110B	A18	2p car rose ('44)	.30	.55
111	A18	3p blue ('42)	.35	.35
a.		Perf. 14	140.00	6.00
b.		Perf. 13½	22.50	1.10
112	A18	5p red org ('47)	1.00	1.25
113	A18	6p dl vio & car rose	3.75	1.90
a.		Perf. 14	125.00	1.60
b.		Perf. 13½	50.00	4.00
114	A18	1sh grn & blk ('42)	3.00	4.50
a.		Perf. 14	45.00	27.50
b.		Perf. 13½	70.00	8.25
115	A18	2sh org brn & blk ('42)	4.00	6.50
a.		Perf. 14	70.00	30.00
b.		Perf. 13½	140.00	42.50

116	A18	5sh dk car & blk ('44)	12.50	21.00
a.		Perf 14 ('38)	100.00	175.00
b.		Perf. 13½	40.00	22.50
117	A18	10sh bl & blk ('43)	27.50	27.50
a.		Perf. 14	70.00	150.00
118	A17	£1 orange	37.50	47.50
		Nos. 107-118 (14)	121.10	115.00
		Set, never hinged	190.00	
		Set, perf "SPECIMEN"	800.00	

Nos. 108c and 110d were issued in coils. No. 108 (1p, perf. 13) exists with watermark both normal and sideways. Nos. 110 and 110B (both 2p, perf. 13) have watermark sideways. For overprints see Nos. 127-130.

> Catalogue values for unused stamps in this section, from this point to the end of the section, are for Never Hinged items.

Peace Issue
Common Design Type
1946, Oct. 12   *Perf. 13½x14*

119	CD303	½p bright green	.30	.50
120	CD303	3p bright ultra	.45	.50
		Set, perf "SPECIMEN"	140.00	

Silver Wedding Issue
Common Design Types
1948, Dec. 1 Photo.   *Perf. 14x14½*

121	CD304	½p dark green	1.00	3.00

Engr.; Name Typo.
Perf. 11½x11

122	CD305	£1 brown orange	70.00	87.50
		Set, hinged	55.00	

UPU Issue
Common Design Types
Engr.; Name Typo. on 3p, 6p
Perf. 13½, 11x11½
1949, Oct. 10   Wmk. 4

123	CD306	2p rose carmine	1.00	1.25
124	CD307	3p indigo	2.50	1.50
125	CD308	6p rose violet	2.00	2.50
126	CD309	1sh blue green	1.25	4.25
		Nos. 123-126 (4)	6.75	9.50

Nos. 110B, 111, 113-114 overprinted in Black or Carmine

1950, Aug. 1   *Perf. 13x12½*

127	A18	2p carmine rose	.40	1.50
128	A18	3p blue	1.00	1.25
129	A18	6p dl vio & car rose	1.25	2.00
a.		Double overprint	1,000.	1,300.
130	A18	1sh grn & blk (C)	1.25	2.00
		Nos. 127-130 (4)	3.90	6.75

Adoption of Constitution of 1950.

WAR TAX STAMP

No. 66 Overprinted

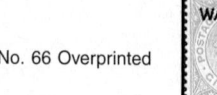

1918, Apr.   Wmk. 3   *Perf. 14*

MR1	A14	½p green	1.75	2.40
a.		Double overprint	900.00	

GILBERT & ELLICE ISLANDS

'gil-bərt ən,d,'e-ləs 'ī-lənds

LOCATION — Groups of islands in the Pacific Ocean northeast of Australia
GOVT. — British Crown Colony
AREA — 375 sq. mi.
POP. — 57,816 (est. 1973)

CAPITAL — Tarawa

The Gilbert group of which Butaritari, Tarawa and Tamana are the more important, is on the Equator. Ellice Islands, Phoenix Islands, Line Islands (Fanning, Washington and Christmas), and Ocean Island are included in the Colony. The islands were annexed by Great Britain in 1892 and formed into the Gilbert and Ellice Islands Colony in 1915 on request of the native governments.
The colony divided into the Gilbert Islands and Tuvalu, Jan. 1, 1976.

12 Pence = 1 Shilling
20 Shillings = 1 Pound

> Catalogue values for unused stamps in this country are for Never Hinged items, beginning with Scott 52.

Stamps and Type of Fiji Overprinted in Black or Red

1911, Jan. 1   Wmk. 3   *Perf. 14*
Ordinary Paper

1	A22	½p green	7.50	50.00
2	A22	1p carmine	50.00	30.00
a.		Pair, one without overprint		
3	A22	2p gray	17.50	17.50
4	A22	2½p ultramarine	18.00	45.00

Chalky Paper

5	A22	5p violet & ol grn	65.00	95.00
6	A22	6p violet	25.00	50.00
7	A22	1sh black, *green*	26.00	70.00
		Nos. 1-7 (7)	209.00	357.50
		Set, ovptd. "SPECIMEN"	350.00	

Nos. 1-7 are known with a forged Ocean Island postmark dated "JY 15 11."

Pandanus — A2

1911, Mar.   Engr.   Ordinary Paper

8	A2	½p green	5.00	22.50
9	A2	1p carmine	2.75	10.00
10	A2	2p gray	1.50	7.50
11	A2	2½p ultramarine	8.50	14.00
		Nos. 8-11 (4)	17.75	54.00
		Set, ovptd. "SPECIMEN"	160.00	

King George V — A3

For description of Dies I and II, see front section of the Catalogue.

1912-24   Die I

				Typo.
14	A3	½p deep green	.60	6.00
a.		½p yellow green ('14)	5.00	12.50
15	A3	1p carmine	2.50	9.00
a.		1p scarlet ('15)	4.25	15.00
16	A3	2p gray ('16)	16.00	26.00
17	A3	2½p ultra ('16)	2.00	11.00

Chalky Paper

18	A3	3p vio, *yel* ('19)	2.75	10.00
19	A3	4p blk & red, *yel*	.90	6.50
20	A3	5p vio & ol grn	1.00	6.25
21	A3	6p vio & red vio	1.50	6.75
22	A3	1sh black, *green*	1.50	5.25
23	A3	2sh vio & ultra, *bl*	15.00	30.00
24	A3	2sh6p blk & red, *bl*	18.00	25.00
25	A3	5sh grn & red, *yel*	37.50	65.00

Die II

26	A3	£1 vio & blk, *red* ('24)	600.00	1,500.
		Nos. 14-26 (13)	700.25	1,706.
		Set, ovptd. "SPECIMEN"	700.00	

1921-27   Die II   Wmk. 4   Ordinary Paper

27	A3	½p green	3.25	3.25
28	A3	1p deep vio ('27)	5.00	7.50
29	A3	1½p scarlet ('24)	5.00	3.00
30	A3	2p gray	8.00	40.00

Chalky Paper

31	A3	10sh green & red, *emer* ('24)	160.00	375.00
		Nos. 27-31 (5)	181.25	428.75
		Set, ovptd. "SPECIMEN"	300.00	

Most of Nos. 14-31 are known with the forged cancellation described in the note following Nos. 1-7.

Common Design Types pictured following the introduction.

Silver Jubilee Issue
Common Design Type
1935, May 6   Engr.   *Perf. 11x12*

33	CD301	1p black & ultra	2.25	12.00
34	CD301	1½p car & blue	1.75	4.00
35	CD301	3p ultra & brn	5.50	17.50
36	CD301	1sh brn vio & indigo	30.00	20.00
		Nos. 33-36 (4)	39.50	53.50
		Set, never hinged	65.00	
		Set, perf "SPECIMEN"	170.00	

Coronation Issue
Common Design Type
1937, May 12   *Perf. 13½x14*

37	CD302	1p dark purple	.25	.65
38	CD302	1½p carmine	.25	.65
39	CD302	3p bright ultra	.45	.70
		Nos. 37-39 (3)	.95	2.00
		Set, never hinged	1.25	
		Set, perf "SPECIMEN"	140.00	

Great Frigate Bird — A4

Pandanus — A5

Designs: 1½p, Canoe crossing reef. 2p, Canoe and boat house. 2½p, Islander's house. 3p, Seascape. 5p, Ellice Islands canoe. 6p, Coconut trees. 1sh, Phosphate loading jetty, Ocean Island. 2sh, Cutter "Nimanoa." 2sh6p, Gilbert Islands canoe. 5sh, Coat of arms of colony.

Perf. 11½x11 (Nos. 40, 43, 50), 12½ (Type A5), 13½ (Nos. 42, 44, 45, 48)
1939, Jan. 14   Engr.   Wmk. 4

40	A4	½p dk grn & sl bl	.40	1.00
41	A5	1p dk vio & brt bl green	.25	1.50
42	A4	1½p car & black	.25	1.25
43	A4	2p black & brn	.40	1.00
44	A4	2½p dp olive & blk	.30	1.00
a.		2½ olive grn & black ('43)	3.00	5.50
45	A4	3p ultra & black	.30	1.00
a.		Perf. 12 ('55)	.40	2.25
46	A5	5p dk brn & dp ultra	3.50	2.50
a.		5p dp brn & ultra ('43)	3.75	10.00
b.		5p blackish brn & ultra ('44)	3.50	6.00
47	A5	6p dl vio & olive	.45	.60
48	A4	1sh gray bl & blk	5.50	3.75
a.		1sh turq blue & blk ('43)	5.50	3.75
b.		Perf. 12 ('51)	2.00	16.00
49	A5	2sh red org & ultra	7.00	10.00
50	A4	2sh6p brt bl grn & bl	7.00	11.00
51	A5	5sh dp blue & red	8.50	16.00
		Nos. 40-51 (12)	33.85	50.60
		Set, never hinged	70.00	
		Set, perf "SPECIMEN"	450.00	

> Catalogue values for unused stamps in this section, from this point to the end of the section, are for Never Hinged items.

Peace Issue
Common Design Type
1946, Dec. 16   *Perf. 13½x14*

52	CD303	1p deep magenta	.25	.25
53	CD303	3p deep blue	.25	.25
		Set, perf "SPECIMEN"	110.00	

Silver Wedding Issue
Common Design Types
1949, Aug. 29 Photo.   *Perf. 14x14½*

54	CD304	1p violet	.25	.25

Engraved; Name Typographed
Perf. 11½x11

55	CD305	£1 red	15.00	24.00

UPU Issue
Common Design Types
Engr.; Name Typo. on 2p, 3p
1949, Oct. 1   *Perf. 13½, 11x11½*

56	CD306	1p rose violet	.75	1.25
57	CD307	2p gray black	2.50	2.75
58	CD308	3p indigo	.80	2.75
59	CD309	1sh blue	.80	2.00
		Nos. 56-59 (4)	4.85	8.75

POSTAGE DUE STAMPS

D1

1940, Aug.   Typo.   Wmk. 4   *Perf. 12*

J1	D1	1p emerald	5.50	24.00
J2	D1	2p dark red	6.00	24.00
J3	D1	3p chocolate	8.25	25.00
J4	D1	4p deep blue	10.00	35.00
J5	D1	5p deep green	13.00	35.00
J6	D1	6p brt red vio	13.00	35.00
J7	D1	1sh dull violet	22.50	50.00
J8	D1	1sh6p turq green	32.50	90.00
		Nos. J1-J8 (8)	110.75	318.00
		Set, never hinged	175.00	
		Set, perf "SPECIMEN"	225.00	

WAR TAX STAMP

No. 15a Overprinted

1918   Wmk. 3   *Perf. 14*

MR1	A3	1p scarlet	.70	6.50
		Overprinted "SPECIMEN"	75.00	

GOLD COAST

'gōld 'kōst

LOCATION — West Africa between Dahomey and Ivory Coast
GOVT. — Former British Crown Colony
AREA — 91,843 sq. mi.
POP. — 3,089,000 (1952)
CAPITAL — Accra

Attached to the colony were Ashanti and Northern Territories (protectorate). Togoland, under British mandate, was also included for administrative purposes.

12 Pence = 1 Shilling
20 Shillings = 1 Pound

> **Catalogue values for unused stamps in this country are for Never Hinged items, beginning with Scott 128.**

Queen Victoria — A1

Perf. 12½

1875, July	Typo.		Wmk. 1	
1	A1	1p blue	550.00	95.00
2	A1	4p red violet	525.00	140.00
3	A1	6p orange	825.00	75.00
	Nos. 1-3 (3)		1,900.	310.00

1876-79			Perf. 14	
4	A1	½p bister ('79)	90.00	32.50
5	A1	1p blue	30.00	8.00
a.	Half used as ½p on cover			4,500.
6	A1	2p green ('79)	125.00	11.50
a.	Half used as 1p on cover			4,250.
b.	Quarter used as ½p on cover			7,500.
7	A1	4p red violet	250.00	7.25
a.	Quarter used as 1p on cover			10,000.
b.	Half used as 2p on cover			7,750.
8	A1	6p orange	250.00	25.00
a.	One sixth used as 1p on cover			13,000.
b.	Half used as 3p on cover			10,000.
	Nos. 4-8 (5)		745.00	84.25

Handstamp Surcharged "1D" in Black

1883, May

9   A1 1p on 4p red violet

Some experts question the status of No. 9. One canceled example is in the British Museum. Another is supposed to exist (Ferrari).

1883-91			Wmk. 2	
10	A1	½p bister ('83)	225.00	80.00
11	A1	½p green ('84)	4.25	1.50
a.	½p dull green		4.25	1.10
12	A1	1p blue ('83)	1,000.	85.00
13	A1	1p rose ('84)	4.75	.60
a.	Half used as ½p on cover			5,000.
b.	1p carmine		4.75	
14	A1	2p gray ('84)	35.00	6.50
a.	2p slate		8.00	6.00
b.	Half used as 1p on cover			5,000.
15	A1	2½p blue ('91)	11.00	.85
16	A1	3p ol green ('89)	22.50	11.00
a.	3p olive bister		22.50	10.00
17	A1	4p dull vio ('84)	22.50	3.50
a.	4p claret		27.50	6.00
b.	Half used as 2p on cover			—
18	A1	6p orange ('89)	22.50	6.00
a.	One sixth used as 1p on cover			—
b.	6p orange brown		17.00	6.00
19	A1	1sh purple ('88)	12.00	2.50
a.	1sh violet		40.00	15.00
20	A1	2sh brown ('84)	60.00	17.50
a.	2sh yellow brown ('88)		95.00	42.50

No. 18 Surcharged in Black

1889, Mar.

21	A1	1p on 6p orange	140.00	60.00
a.	Double surcharge			4,500.

The surcharge exists in two spacings between "PENNY" and bar: 7mm (normal) and 8mm.

No. 21a does not exist unused.

Queen Victoria — A3

1889

22	A3	5sh lilac & ultra	75.00	23.00
23	A3	10sh lilac & red	110.00	17.50
a.	10sh lilac & carmine		800.00	290.00
24	A3	20sh green & red	3,250.	

1894

25	A3	20sh vio & blk, *red*	190.00	40.00
	Nos. 22-25, ovptd. "SPEC-IMEN"		450.00	

1898-1902				
26	A3	½p lilac & green	6.00	1.25
27	A3	1p lil & car rose	6.50	.60
28	A3	2p lil & red ('02)	60.00	175.00
29	A3	2½p lilac & ultra	9.50	9.50
30	A3	3p lilac & yel	9.50	3.50
31	A3	6p lilac & purple	11.00	3.25
32	A3	1sh gray grn & blk	18.00	35.00
33	A3	2sh gray grn & car rose	30.00	35.00
34	A3	5sh grn & lil ('00)	85.00	50.00
35	A3	10sh grn & brn ('00)	180.00	65.00
	Nos. 26-35 (10)		415.50	378.10
	Set, ovptd. "SPECIMEN"		225.00	

Numerals of 2p, 3p and 6p of type A3 are in color on colorless tablet.

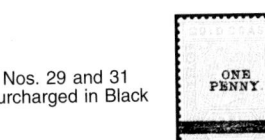

Nos. 29 and 31 Surcharged in Black

1901, Oct. 6

36	A3	1p on 2½p lil & ultra	8.50	6.00
a.	"ONE" omitted		1,200.	
37	A3	1p on 6p lilac & pur	8.50	4.25
a.	"ONE" omitted		325.00	650.00

Beware of copies offered as No. 37a that have part of "ONE" showing.

King Edward VII — A5

1902			Wmk. 2	
38	A5	½p violet & green	1.75	.50
39	A5	1p vio & car rose	1.75	.25
40	A5	2p vio & red org	35.00	8.50
41	A5	2½p vio & ultra	5.50	11.00
42	A5	3p vio & orange	5.50	2.50
43	A5	6p violet & pur	6.00	2.75
44	A5	1sh green & blk	19.00	4.00
45	A5	2sh grn & car rose	20.00	30.00
46	A5	5sh green & violet	60.00	110.00
47	A5	10sh green & brn	80.00	150.00
48	A5	20sh vio & blk, *red*	180.00	225.00
	Nos. 38-48 (11)		414.50	544.50
	Set, ovptd. "SPECIMEN"		225.00	

Numerals of 2p, 3p, 6p and 2sh6p of type A5 are in color on colorless tablet.

1904-07		Wmk. 3	Ordinary Paper	
49	A5	½p vio & grn ('07)	3.00	8.50
50	A5	1p vio & car rose	15.00	1.00
a.	Chalky paper ('06)		11.50	2.25
51	A5	2p vio & red org	11.00	1.75
a.	Chalky paper ('06)		30.00	2.75
52	A5	2½p vio & ultra ('06)	65.00	75.00
53	A5	3p vio & org ('05)	70.00	7.00
a.	Chalky paper ('06)		24.00	1.00
54	A5	6p vio & pur ('06)	90.00	4.50
a.	Chalky paper ('06)		45.00	2.00
55	A5	2sh6p grn & yel ('06), chalky paper	35.00	130.00
	Nos. 49-55 (7)		289.00	227.75

1907-13		Ordinary Paper		
56	A5	½p green	11.00	.40
a.	½p blue green ('09)		15.00	2.25
57	A5	1p carmine	16.00	.50
58	A5	2p gray ('09)	2.75	.55
59	A5	2½p ultramarine	17.50	4.50

		Chalky Paper		
60	A5	3p violet, *yel* ('09)	9.50	.65
61	A5	6p dull violet ('08)	32.50	1.50
a.	6p dull violet & red violet		7.00	5.50
62	A5	1sh blk, *grn* ('09)	23.00	.65
63	A5	2sh violet & bl, *bl* ('10)	18.00	16.00
a.	Ordinary paper		9.50	19.00
64	A5	2sh6p blk & red, *blue* ('11)	40.00	105.00
65	A5	5sh grn & red, *yel* ('13)	65.00	225.00
	Nos. 56-65 (10)		235.25	354.75
	Set, ovptd. "SPECIMEN"		325.00	

No. 63 is on both ordinary and chalky paper.

King Edward VII — A6

1908, Nov.		Ordinary Paper		
66	A6	1p carmine	7.50	.25
	Ovptd. "SPECIMEN"		50.00	

King George V
A7   A8

For description of Dies I and II, see front section of the Catalogue.

Die I

1913-21		Ordinary Paper		
69	A7	½p green	3.00	2.25
70	A8	1p carmine	1.50	.25
a.	1p scarlet		3.75	.60
71	A7	2p gray	10.00	3.00
72	A7	2½p ultramarine	13.00	2.00

		Chalky Paper		
73	A7	3p vio, *yel* ('15)	3.75	1.00
a.	Die II ('19)		65.00	6.00
74	A7	6p dull vio & red vio	9.50	2.75
75	A7	1sh black, *green*	5.50	1.75
a.	1sh black, *emerald*		2.75	2.50
b.	1sh black, *bl grn*, ol back		11.00	.95
c.	Die II ('21)		1.75	.60
76	A7	2sh vio & bl, *bl*	11.00	4.50
a.	Die II ('21)		190.00	77.50
77	A7	2sh6p blk & red, *bl*	12.00	16.00
a.	Die II ('21)		32.50	50.00
78	A7	5sh grn & red, *yel*	25.00	70.00
a.	Die II ('21)		42.50	180.00
79	A7	10sh grn & blk, *grn* ('16)	70.00	120.00
a.	10sh grn & red, *emer*		50.00	200.00
b.	10sh grn & red, *bl grn*, ol back		35.00	95.00
80	A7	20sh vio & blk, *red*	160.00	120.00

	Surface-colored Paper			
81	A7	3p violet, *yel*	2.10	1.00
82	A7	5sh grn & red, *yel*	25.00	72.50
	Nos. 69-82 (14)		351.35	417.00

Numerals of 2p, 3p, 6p and 2sh6p of type A7 are in color on plain tablet.

Die II

1921-25		Ordinary Paper	Wmk. 4	
83	A7	½p green ('22)	1.00	.60
84	A8	1p brown ('22)	.90	.25
85	A7	1½p carmine ('22)	2.10	.25
86	A7	2p gray	2.25	.40
87	A7	2½p orange ('23)	2.50	12.00
88	A7	3p ultra ('22)	2.10	1.25

		Chalky Paper		
89	A7	6p dl vio & red vio ('22)	3.75	3.50
90	A7	1sh blk, *emer* ('25)	7.00	4.00
91	A7	2sh vio & bl, *bl* ('24)	4.00	4.00
92	A7	2sh6p blk & red, *bl* ('25)	10.00	40.00
93	A7	5sh grn & red, *yel* ('25)	24.00	80.00

		Die I		
94	A7	15sh dl vio & grn ('21)	190.00	500.00
a.	Die II ('25)		140.00	500.00
95	A7	£2 grn & org	500.00	1,500.
	Nos. 83-95 (13)		749.60	2,146.

Christiansborg Castle — A9

1928, Aug. 1	Photo.	Perf. 13½x14½		
98	A9	½p green	1.20	.50
99	A9	1p red brown	1.00	.25
100	A9	1½p scarlet	3.50	1.75
101	A9	2p slate	3.50	.25
102	A9	2½p yellow	3.75	4.25
103	A9	3p ultramarine	3.50	.50
104	A9	6p dull vio & blk	4.25	.50
105	A9	1sh red org & blk	5.50	1.25
106	A9	2sh purple & black	30.00	6.00
107	A9	5sh ol green & car	72.50	52.50
	Nos. 98-107 (10)		128.70	67.75
	Set, ovptd. "SPECIMEN"		225.00	

Common Design Types pictured following the introduction.

Silver Jubilee Issue
Common Design Type

1935, May 6	Engr.	Perf. 11x12		
108	CD301	1p black & ultra	1.00	.60
109	CD301	3p ultra & brown	3.25	7.25
110	CD301	6p indigo & green	17.00	22.50
111	CD301	1sh brn vio & indigo	5.50	32.50
	Nos. 108-111 (4)		26.75	62.85
	Set, never hinged		40.00	
	Set, perf "SPECIMEN"		125.00	

Coronation Issue
Common Design Type

1937, May 12		Perf. 11x11½		
112	CD302	1p brown	.85	2.50
113	CD302	2p dark gray	1.00	4.75
114	CD302	3p deep ultra	1.25	2.75
	Nos. 112-114 (3)		3.10	10.00
	Set, never hinged		6.00	
	Set, perf "SPECIMEN"		100.00	

A10

George VI and Christiansborg Castle — A11

1938-41		Wmk. 4	Perf. 12	
115	A10	½p green	.35	.50
116	A10	1p red brown	.35	.25
117	A10	1½p rose red	.35	.50
118	A10	2p gray black	.35	.25
119	A10	3p ultramarine	.35	.35
120	A10	4p rose lilac	.70	1.25
121	A10	6p rose violet	.70	.25
122	A10	9p red orange	1.10	.55
123	A11	1sh gray grn & blk	1.40	.65
124	A11	1sh3p turq grn & red brown	1.75	.50
125	A11	2sh dk vio & dp bl	4.75	19.00
126	A11	5sh rose car & ol green	9.25	22.00
127	A11	10sh purple & black	6.50	29.00
	Nos. 115-127 (13)		27.90	75.05
	Set, never hinged		40.00	
	Set, perf "SPECIMEN"		325.00	

Issued: 10sh, July, 1940; 1sh3p, Apr. 12, 1941; others, Apr. 1.

> **Catalogue values for unused stamps in this section, from this point to the end of the section, are for Never Hinged items.**

Peace Issue
Common Design Type
1946, Oct. 14   **Perf. 13½**
128 CD303 2p purple   .25   .25
  a.   Perf. 13½x14   19.00   3.00
129 CD303 4p deep red violet   1.60   3.50
  a.   Perf. 13½x14   3.50   .75
    ...port OF(L)CIMEN   90.00

A12

A13

½p, Mounted Constable. 1p, Christiansborg Castle. 1½p, Emblem of Joint Provincial Council. 2p, Talking Drums. 2½p, Map. 3p, Manganese mine. 4p, Lake Bosumtwi. 6p, Cacao farmer. 1sh, Breaking cacao pods. 2sh, Trooping the colors. 5sh, Surfboats. 10sh, Forest.

1948, July 1   Engr.   Perf. 12
130 A12   ½p emerald   .25   .40
131 A13   1p deep blue   .25   .25
132 A13   1½p red   1.50   1.00
133 A12   2p chocolate   .65   .25
134 A13   2½p lt brown & red   2.50   4.50
135 A13   3p blue   5.00   1.00
136 A13   4p dk car rose   4.25   4.00
137 A12   6p org & black   .40   .40
138 A13   1sh red org & blk   2.25   .25
139 A13   2sh rose car & ol
            brn   6.50   4.00
140 A12   5sh gray & red vio   35.00 11.00
141 A12   10sh ol grn & black   16.00 11.00
    Nos. 130-141 (12)   74.55 38.20
    Set, perf "SPECIMEN"   325.00

Silver Wedding Issue
Common Design Types
1948, Dec. 20   Photo.   Perf. 14x14½
142 CD304 1½p scarlet   .25   .25
Engraved; Name Typographed
Perf. 11½x11
143 CD305 10sh dk brn olive   35.00 37.50

UPU Issue
Common Design Types
Engr.; Name Typo. on 2½p and 3p
1949, Oct. 10   Perf. 13½, 11x11½
144 CD306   2p red brown   .25   .25
145 CD307   2½p deep orange   1.90   4.50
146 CD308   3p indigo   .45   1.75
147 CD309   1sh blue green   .45   .45
    Nos. 144-147 (4)   3.05   6.95

POSTAGE DUE STAMPS

D1

1923   Typo.   Wmk. 4   Perf. 14
Yellowish Toned Paper
J1 D1 ½p black   19.00 125.00
J2 D1 1p black   .95   1.50
J3 D1 2p black   13.00   3.50
J4 D1 3p black   22.50   3.50
    Nos. J1-J4 (4)   55.45 133.00
    Set, ovptd. "SPECIMEN" 85.00

1951-52   Typo.   Wmk. 4   Perf. 14
Chalk-Surfaced Paper
J5 D1 2p black   3.75   27.50
  a. Wmk. 4a (error)   600.00
  b. Wmk. 4, crown missing (error)   1,100.
J6 D1 3p black   3.25   26.00
  a. Wmk. 4a (error)   550.00
  b. Wmk. 4, crown missing (error)   1,100.
J7 D1 6p black ('52) 2.10 13.00
  a. Wmk. 4a (error)   1,000.
  b. Wmk. 4, crown missing (error)   1,600.

J8 D1 1sh black ('52) 2.10 80.00
  a. Wmk. 4a (error)   1,200.
    Nos. J5-J8 (4)   11.20 146.50
    Issued: Nos. J7-J8, 10/1.

WAR TAX STAMP

Regular Issue of 1913
Surcharged

1918, June   Wmk. 3   Perf. 14
MR1 A8 1p on 1p scarlet 3.25 1.00
    Ovptd. "SPECIMEN"   57.50

GRAND COMORO
'grand 'kä-mə-ˌrō

LOCATION — One of the Comoro Islands in the Mozambique Channel between Madagascar and Mozambique.
GOVT. — French Colony
AREA — 385 sq. mi. (approx.)
POP. — 50,000 (approx.)
CAPITAL — Moroni
    See Comoro Islands

100 Centimes = 1 Franc

Navigation and Commerce — A1

Perf. 14x13½
1897-1907   Typo.   Unwmk.
Name of Colony in Blue or Carmine
1   A1 1c blk, lil bl   1.25   1.25
      Never hinged   2.00
      On cover   310.00
2   A1 2c brn, buff   2.00   2.00
      Never hinged   3.10
      On cover   350.00
3   A1 4c claret, lav   2.50   2.50
      Never hinged   3.75
      On cover   375.00
4   A1 5c grn, grnsh   4.50   4.50
      Never hinged   7.25
      On cover   250.00
5   A1 10c blk, lavender 10.00   6.50
      Never hinged   18.00
      On cover   290.00
6   A1 10c red ('00)   11.00 11.00
      Never hinged   17.50
      On cover   225.00
7   A1 15c blue, quadrille
            paper   22.00 14.50
      Never hinged   45.00
      On cover   275.00
8   A1 15c gray, lt gray
            ('00)   11.00 11.00
      Never hinged   18.00
      On cover   225.00
9   A1 20c red, grn   12.50 12.50
      Never hinged   24.00
      On cover   310.00
      On cover, single franking 425.00
10 A1 25c blk, rose   18.50 17.00
      Never hinged   32.50
      On cover   340.00
      On cover, single franking 500.00
11 A1 25c blue ('00)   22.00 21.50
      Never hinged   45.00
      On cover   250.00
      On cover, single franking 440.00
12 A1 30c brn, bister   23.00 20.00
      Never hinged   45.00
      On cover   275.00
      On cover, single franking 500.00
13 A1 35c blk, yel ('06) 22.00 20.00
      Never hinged   45.00
      On cover   275.00
      On cover, single franking 500.00
14 A1 40c red, straw   23.00 20.00
      Never hinged   45.00
      On cover   310.00
      On cover, single franking 425.00
15 A1 45c blk, gray grn
            ('07)   85.00 70.00
      Never hinged   170.00
      On cover   625.00
      On cover, single franking 875.00
16 A1 50c car, rose   45.00 24.00
      Never hinged   87.50
      On cover   425.00
      On cover, single franking 550.00

17 A1 50c brn, bluish ('00) 47.50 45.00
      Never hinged   100.00
      On cover   375.00
      On cover, single franking 550.00
18 A1 75c dp vio, org   60.00 40.00
      Never hinged   120.00
      On cover   800.00
      On cover, single franking 625.00
19 A1 1fr brnz grn, straw 42.50 36.00
      Never hinged   92.50
      On cover   550.00
      On cover, single franking 625.00
    Nos. 1-19 (19)   465.25 379.25
Perf. 13½x14 stamps are counterfeits.

Issues of 1897-1907 Surcharged in Black or Carmine

05   10

1912
Spacing between figures of surcharge 1.5mm (5c), 2mm (10c)
20 A1   5c on 2c brn,
            buff   1.50   1.50
      Never hinged   2.50
      On cover   77.50
  a. Inverted surcharge   260.00
  b. Pair, one without
        surcharge   1,700.
  e. As "a," one without
        surcharge   2,400.
21 A1   5c on 4c cl, lav
            (C)   1.60   1.60
      Never hinged   2.75
      On cover   72.50
  a. Pair, one without
        surcharge   1,000.
22 A1   5c on 15c blue
            (C)   1.50   1.50
      Never hinged   2.50
      On cover   77.50
23 A1   5c on 20c red,
            grn   1.75   1.75
      Never hinged   2.90
      On cover   100.00
24 A1   5c on 25c blk,
            rose (C)   1.60   1.60
      Never hinged   2.75
      On cover   87.50
25 A1   5c on 30c brn,
            bis (C)   1.75   1.75
      Never hinged   3.10
      On cover   87.50
26 A1 10c on 40c red,
            straw   2.00   2.00
      Never hinged   3.50
      On cover   100.00
27 A1 10c on 45c blk,
            gray grn (C) 2.75   2.75
      Never hinged   5.00
      On cover   92.50
28 A1 10c on 50c car,
            rose   2.50   2.50
      Never hinged   4.25
      On cover   92.50
29 A1 10c on 75c dp vio,
            org   3.00   3.00
      Never hinged   6.00
      On cover   140.00
    Nos. 20-29 (10)   19.95 19.95
Spacing between figures of surcharge 2.25mm (5c), 2.75mm (10c)
20c A1   5c on 2c brn, buff 7.50   7.50
      Never hinged   14.00
21b A1   5c on 4c cl, lav (C) 8.50 8.50
      Never hinged   18.00
22a A1   5c on 15c blue (C) 11.00 11.00
      Never hinged   21.00
23a A1   5c on 20c red, grn 12.50 12.50
      Never hinged   25.00
24a A1   5c on 25c blk, rose
            (C)   12.00 12.00
      Never hinged   21.00
25a A1   5c on 30c brn, bis 13.50 13.50
      Never hinged   25.00
26a A1 10c on 40c red,
            straw   92.50 92.50
      Never hinged   190.00
27a A1 10c on 45c blk, gray
            grn (C)   92.50 92.50
      Never hinged   190.00
28a A1 10c on 50c car, rose 92.50 92.50
      Never hinged   190.00
29a A1 10 on 75c dp vio,
            org   150.00 150.00
      Never hinged   240.00
    Nos. 20c-29a (10) 492.50 492.50
Se-tenant Pairs, Both Ovpt. Settings
20d A1   5c on 2c, #20 +
            #20c   10.00 10.00
      Never hinged   19.00
21c A1   5c on 4c, #21 +
            #21b   9.50   9.50
      Never hinged   18.00
22b A1   5c on 15c, #22 +
            #22a   12.00 12.00
      Never hinged   21.00
23b A1   5c on 20c, #23 +
            #23a   14.00 14.00
      Never hinged   21.00
24b A1   5c on 25c, #24 +
            #24a   12.00 12.00
      Never hinged   21.00
25b A1   5c on 30c, #25 +
            #25a   14.00 14.00
      Never hinged   25.00

26b A1 10c on 40c, #26 +
            #26a   95.00 95.00
      Never hinged   190.00
27b A1 10c on 45c, #27 +
            #27a   100.00 100.00
      Never hinged   190.00
28b A1 10c on 50c, #28 +
            #28a   100.00 100.00
      Never hinged   190.00
29b A1 10c on 75c, #29 +
            #29a   160.00 160.00
      Never hinged   240.00
    Nos. 20d-29b (10) 526.50 526.50

Nos. 20-29 were available for use in Madagascar and the entire Comoro archipelago.
Stamps of Grand Comoro were superseded by those of Madagascar, and in 1950 by those of Comoro Islands.

GREAT BRITAIN
'grāt 'bri-t°n

(United Kingdom)

LOCATION — Northwest of the continent of Europe and separated from it by the English Channel
GOVT. — Constitutional monarchy
AREA — 94,511 sq. mi.
POP. — 55,767,387 (1981)
CAPITAL — London

12 Pence = 1 Shilling
20 Shillings = 1 Pound

The letters in the corners of the early postage issues indicate position in the horizontal and vertical rows in which that particular specimen was placed.

In the case of illustration A1, this stamp came from the first horizontal row (A) and was the 11th stamp (K) from the left in that row. The left corner refers to the horizontal row and the right corner to the vertical row. Thus no two stamps on the plate bore the same combination of letters.

When four corner letters are used (starting in 1858), the lower ones indicate the stamp's position in the sheet and the top ones are the same letters reversed.

> **Catalogue values for unused stamps in this country are for Never Hinged items, beginning with Scott 264 in the regular postage section, Scott J34 in the postage due section, Scott 10 in British Offices — East Africa Forces, and Scott 93, Scott 246 and Scott 523 in British Offices in Morocco. All of the listings in British Offices — for Use in Eritrea and for Use in Tripolitania are valued as never-hinged.**

Watermarks

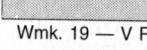

Wmk. 18 —   Wmk. 19 — V R
Small Crown

Wmk. 20 —   Wmk. 21 —
Large Crown   Small Garter

Wmk. 22 — Medium Garter

Wmk. 23 — Large Garter

Wmk. 24 — Heraldic Emblems

Wmk. 25 — Spray of Rose

Wmk. 26 — Maltese Cross

Wmk. 27 — "Half Penny" in Script

Wmk. 28 — Anchor

Wmk. 29 — Orb

Wmk. 30 — Imperial Crown

Wmk. 31 — Anchor

Wmk. 32 — Crown and GvR Multiple

Wmk. 33 — Crown and GvR

Wmk. 33 — In the normal watermark (sometimes termed the "repeated" watermark) the letters "GvR" are extended. The royal cyphers are placed one above the other and usually two appear on each stamp. In the multiple watermark the letters "GvR" are condensed, the cyphers are smaller and are so placed that those in each succeeding row are below the spaces between the cyphers in the row above.

Wmk. 34 — Large Crown and GvR

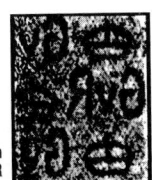

Wmk. 35 — Crown and Block GvR Multiple

Wmk. 219 — Large Crown and GvR

Wmk. 250 — Crown and E8R Multiple

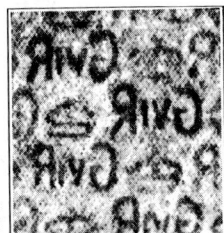

Wmk. 251 — Crown and GviR Multiple

Wmk. 259 — Crown and Large G VI R

Values for mint stamps of Great Britain are for stamps with original gum as defined in the catalogue introduction.

Values for unused and used stamps in this country are for examples with fresh color and all the attributes of fine-to-very fine condition (unless specified otherwise) through 1900 (Scott 126). All other stamps are for examples in the condition of very fine. Expect perforations to touch the design on one or two sides on all engraved stamps (Scott Nos. 8-21, 29-33 and 58) and early small format typographed stamps (Nos. 22-28, 34-56, 59-73, 78-89 and 94-95) because of the very narrow spacing between the stamps in the setting of the plates. Examples with margins clear of the design on all four sides range from scarce to very rare and command substantial premiums.

Cancellations on stamps from the 1847 issue to the 1900 issues are, in many cases beyond, are usually heavy. Values quoted are for stamps with better than average cancellations. **Poorly centered stamps and heavily canceled stamps may sell for 10 to 20 percent of the values listed here.**

Stamps with circular datestamps (especially those with a steel cds) range from scarce to very rare and command much higher prices. Premiums to be applied for fresh mint stamps with original gum and for used stamps that have both fine to very fine centering and circular datestamps can be found in footnotes for stamps from Scott 8 through Scott 126, including Official stamps for this period. For stamps that have both fine to very fine centering and circular datestamps, add the premiums together. Apply these premiums to covers, taking into account the overall condition of the cover and the stamps.

Queen Victoria — A1

1840, May   Wmk. 18   Engr.   *Imperf.*
White Paper

1	A1	1p black	11,000.	320.00
		On cover		640.00
a.		1p intense black	15,000.	325.00
		On cover		600.00
b.		1p gray black (worn plate)	14,000.	360.00
		On cover		500.00
c.		Watermark inverted	45,000.	2,500.
d.		On blued paper (Plates 1-8), *from*	65,000.	675.00
2	A1	2p blue	35,000.	700.00
		On cover		2,250.
a.		2p pale blue	45,000.	900.00
		On cover		2,350.
b.		2p deep bright blue	42,500.	1,000.
		On cover		2,350.
c.		Watermark inverted	82,500.	6,000.

Full margins = ½mm.

No. 1 was printed from 11 plates; No. 2 from 2 plates. The 1p plates 1, 2, 5, 6, 8 and 9 can be found in two or more states. Stamp and on cover values are for the most common plates.
Issue dates: 1p, May 6; 2p, May 7.
See Nos. 3, 8-9, 11-12, 14, 16, 18, 20, O1.
Compare designs A1-A2 with A8, A10.

Values for pairs
1	A1	1p black, *from*	55,000.	1,250.
		On cover, *from*		1,500.

2	A1	2p blue, *from*	110,000.	2,100.
		On cover, *from*		2,500.

Values for strips of 3
1	A1	1p black	75,000.	1,875.
		On cover		—
2	A1	2p blue	150,000.	3,250.
		On cover		—

Values for blocks of 4
1	A1	1p black	145,000.	25,000.
		On cover		—
2	A1	2p blue	275,000.	40,000.
		On cover		—

Values for Certified Plated Examples

Stamps from each plate used for Nos. 1-2 can be plated with certainty by experts. Certificates are recommended. Values are for the most common shades of each plate.

1		1p black		
		Plate 1, 1st state	18,500.	350.
		Plate 1, 2nd state	12,500.	325.
		Plate 2	12,500.	325.
		Plate 3	20,000.	425.
		Plate 4	12,500.	325.
		Plate 5	12,500.	325.
		Plate 6	13,500.	325.
		Plate 7	13,500.	350.
		Plate 8	16,500.	475.
		Plate 9	20,000.	625.
		Plate 10	25,000.	850.
		Plate 11	22,500.	4,500.
2		2p blue		
		Plate 1	35,000.	750.
		Plate 2	45,000.	1,000.

Values for cancellations
No. 1, Left Column
No. 2, Right Column

Maltese Cross, red	390.	925.
Maltese Cross, black	360.	875.
Maltese Cross, blue	12,500.	15,000.
Maltese Cross, magenta	3,100.	12,500.
Maltese Cross, yellow		
"Penny Post" straight line, black	5,500.	15,000.
Town postmark, black, *from*	17,000.	9,000.
Town postmark, red, *from*	18,500.	
Town postmark, yellow, *from*	60,000.	
Numeral postmark, 1844 onwards, *from*	1,800.	2,500.

Maltese Crosses with Numerals in Center, black
No. 1	17,500.	17,500.
No. 2	17,500.	17,500.
No. 3	17,500.	17,500.
No. 4	17,500.	17,500.
No. 5	17,500.	17,500.
No. 6	17,500.	17,500.
No. 7	17,500.	17,500.
No. 8	17,500.	17,500.
No. 9	17,500.	17,500.
No. 10	17,500.	17,500.
No. 11	17,500.	17,500.
No. 12	17,500.	17,500.

Early Dates on Cover
May 6	165,000.	—
May 7	20,500.	—
May 8	9,250.	16,500.
May 9	5,000.	75,000.
May 10 (Sunday)	65,000.	180,000.
May 11-16	3,600.	18,000.
May 17 (Sunday)	15,500.	52,000.
May 18-23	2,900.	18,000.
May 24 (Sunday)	14,500.	52,000.
May 25-30	2,050.	18,000.
May 31 (Sunday)	13,500.	52,000.

Used in Combination with Mulready Envelopes & Letter Sheets
1d black on U1	15,500.
1p black on U2	39,000.
1p black on U3	15,500.
1p black on U4	39,500.
2p blue on U1	50,000.
2p blue on U2	43,500.
2p blue on U3	50,000.
2p blue on U4	43,500.

A1a

A2

1841   Bluish Paper
3	A1a	1p red brown	625.00	9.00
		On cover		27.50
a.		1p orange brown	1,350.	55.00

	On cover		125.00
b.	1p lake red	5,500.	825.00
	On cover		1,650.
c.	Rouletted 12	26,000.	
d.	"A" missing in lower right corner (position BA, P77)	—	25,000.
e.	Watermark inverted	4,000.	360.00
f.	On deep blue paper	725.00	24.00
4	A2　2p blue	1,500.	88.00
	On cover		190.00
a.	2p pale blue	6,000.	50.00
	On cover		190.00
b.	2p deep bright blue	5,000.	55.00
	On cover		165.00
c.	2p violet blue	15,000.	1,000.
	On cover		165.00
d.	Watermark inverted	6,750.	100.00
e.	"Ivory Head"	6,500.	90.00

Full margins = ½mm.

No. 3 exists on silk thread paper, but was not regularly issued.

No. 4 was printed from two plates. See Nos. 10, 13, 15, 17, 19, 21.

Values for pairs

3	A1a　1p red brown	1,200.	52.50
	On cover		65.00
4	A2　2p blue	15,000.	275.00
	On cover		625.00

Values for strips of 3

3	A1a　1p red brown	2,000.	92.50
	On cover		300.00
4	A2　2p blue	15,000.	275.00
	On cover		925.00

Values for blocks of 4

3	A1a　1p red brown	3,250.	350.00
	On cover		1,100.
	With Maltese Cross postmarks		900.00
			1,350.
4	A2　2p blue	42,500.	1,750.
	On cover		
	With Maltese Cross postmarks		6,250.

Values for cancellations
No. 3, Left Column
No. 4, Right Column

Maltese Cross, red	5,250.	22,750.
Maltese Cross, black	57.50	275.00
Maltese Cross, blue	675.00	5,250.
"Penny Post" straight line, black	1,150.	
Town postmark, black (from)	825.00	3,650.
Town postmark, red (from)	15,500.	
Town postmark, yellow (from)	—	—
Town postmark, blue (from)	2,600.	4,650.
Town postmark, green (from)	5,250.	—
Numeral postmark, black (from)	24.00	85.00
Numeral postmark, blue (from)	250.00	1,000.
Numeral postmark, red (from)	10,000.	29,500.
Numeral postmark, green (from)	3,100.	8,250.
Numeral postmark, violet (from)	4,250.	

Maltese Crosses with Numerals in Center, black

No. 1	185.00	725.00
No. 2	185.00	725.00
No. 3	235.00	725.00
No. 4	625.00	725.00
No. 5	185.00	785.00
No. 6	165.00	725.00
No. 7	165.00	1,250.
No. 8	165.00	1,050.
No. 9	185.00	1,250.
No. 10	325.00	1,550.
No. 11	350.00	875.00
No. 12	350.00	575.00

Used in Combination with Mulready Envelopes & Letter Sheets

1d red brown on U1	15,000.
1p red brown on U2	42,500.
1p red brown on U3	15,000.
1p red brown on U4	47,500.
2p blue on U1	42,500.
2p blue on U2	47,500.
2p blue on U3	42,500.
2p blue on U4	42,500.

During the reigns of Victoria and Edward VII, many color trials were produced on perfed, gummed and watermarked papers.

Nos. 5-7 were printed one stamp at a time on the sheet. Space between the stamps usually is very small. Impressions that touch, or even overlap, are numerous.

Stamps with margins ½mm beyond the outer frame are considered as having full margins. Values for mint or used single embossed stamps are for full-margin examples.

Cover values are for average stamps with complete design but clear, white margins on one or two sides only. On-cover examples with four full margins sell for much more.

A3	A3a

With Vertical Silk Threads

1847	Embossed		Unwmk.
5	A3　1sh pale green	20,000.	900.00
	Block of 4	145,000.	
	On cover		1,275.
	Pair on cover		2,400.
	Cut to shape		15.00
a.	1sh green	20,000.	925.00
	On cover		1,350.
	Pair on cover		2,400.
	Cut to shape		15.00
b.	1sh deep green	25,000.	1,050.
	On cover		1,400.
	Pair on cover		2,500.
	Cut to shape		22.50

Die numbers (on base of bust): 1 and 2.

1848			
6	A3a　10p red brown	11,500.	1,500.
	Block of 4	92,500.	14,500.
	On cover		3,000.
	Pair on cover		4,500.
	Cut to shape	500.00	20.00

Die numbers (on base of bust): 1, 2, 3, 4; also without die number.

A4

1854			Wmk. 19
7	A4　6p red violet	18,000.	1,000.
	Block of 4	145,000.	
	On cover		1,900.
	Pair on cover		3,250.
a.	6p dull violet	18,000.	1,000.
	On cover		1,900.
	Pair on cover		32,500.
b.	6p deep violet	26,000.	4,250.
	On cover		4,250.
c.	6p mauve	18,500.	1,000.
	On cover		2,000.
	Pair on cover		3,250.
	Cut to shape		10.00
d.	Watermark inverted	18,000.	1,000.
e.	Watermark inverted and reversed		1,000.
f.	Watermark upright		1,900.

The normal watermark 19 appears reversed when viewed from the front and as 'VR' when viewed from the back. This should be taken into consideration when determing whether the watermark is inverted or reversed.

1854-55	Wmk. 18　Engr.　Perf. 16
	Bluish Paper

8	A1　1p red brown	325.00	30.00
	Block of 4	2,500.	400.00
	On cover		57.50
	Pair on cover		100.00
a.	1p yellow brown	375.00	45.00
	On cover		85.00
9	A1　1p red brown, re-engraved ('55)	425.00	60.00
	Block of 4	3,600.	625.00
	On cover		115.00
	Pair on cover		225.00
a.	Imperf.		—
b.	Watermark inverted	1,250.	250.00
10	A2　2p blue	4,000.	90.00
	Block of 4	20,000.	1,850.
	On cover		200.00
a.	2p pale blue	4,500.	100.00
	On cover		200.00
b.	2p blue, plate 5	8,000.	300.00
	On cover		500.00

In the re-engraved 1p stamps, the lines of the features are deeper and stronger, the fillet behind the ear more distinct, the shading about the eye heavier, the line of the nostril is turned downward at right and an indentation of color appears between lower lip and chin.

Perf. 14

11	A1　1p red brown ('55)	625.00	80.00
	Block of 4	5,250.	725.00
	On cover		145.00
a.	Imperf.		—
b.	Watermark inverted		300.00
12	A1　1p red brown, re-engraved ('55)	600.00	67.50
	Block of 4	4,400.	675.00
	On cover		115.00
	Pair on cover		195.00
a.	1p org brn, re-engraved	1,700.	150.00
	On cover		250.00
b.	As #12, watermark inverted	1,675.	350.00

13	A2　2p blue ('55)	10,000.	210.00
	Block of 4		2,500.
	On cover		375.00
	Plate 5	10,500.	375.00
	Block of 4		3,250.
	On cover		500.00
a.	Imperf. (P5)		10,000.
b.	As b, Plate 5		975.00

Wmk. 20 exists in two types. The first includes two vertical prongs, rising from the top of the crown's headband and extending into each of the two balancing midsections. The second type (illustrated), introduced in 1861, omits these prongs.

1855	Wmk. 20		Perf. 16
	Bluish Paper		
14	A1　1p red brown, re-engraved	2,000.	110.00
	Block of 4	9,250.	1,200.
	On cover		225.00
	Pair on cover		400.00
a.	Watermark inverted		425.00
15	A2　2p blue	14,000.	450.00
	Block of 4		3,600.
	On cover		575.00
a.	Imperf. (P5)		11,000.
b.	Watermark inverted		1,000.

Some specialists regard No. 15a as a proof.

1855	Bluish Paper		Perf. 14
16	A1　1p red brown, re-engraved	225.00	21.00
	Block of 4	2,000.	300.00
	On cover		40.00
	Pair on cover		70.00
a.	1p orange brn, re-engraved	650.00	62.50
	On cover		95.00
b.	1p brown rose, re-engraved	325.00	50.00
	On cover		90.00
c.	Imperf.	4,000.	3,500.
17	A2　2p blue	2,500.	72.50
	Block of 4	16,500.	1,000.
	On cover		180.00
a.	Watermark inverted		325.00

1856-58	White Paper		Perf. 16
18	A1　1p rose red, re-engraved ('57)	2,400.	72.50
	Block of 4	12,500.	575.00
	On cover		160.00
	Pair on cover		320.00
a.	Watermark inverted		475.00
19	A2　2p blue, thin lines ('58)	12,500.	375.00
	Block of 4		3,250.
	On cover		550.00
a.	Watermark inverted		1,000.

Perf. 14

20	A1　1p rose red, re-engraved ('57)	55.00	11.50
	Block of 4	325.00	100.00
	On cover		22.50
a.	Imperf.	4,500.	3,500.
b.	1p red brown, re-engraved	2,000.	375.00
	On cover		1,100.
c.	As #20, watermark inverted	150.00	75.00
d.	Double perf.	500.00	90.00
21	A2　2p blue, thin lines ('57)	3,000.	70.00
	Block of 4	17,500.	1,150.
	On cover		180.00
a.	Imperf.		11,000.
b.	Vertical pair, imperf horiz.		20,000.
c.	Watermark inverted		325.00
d.	Double perf.		180.00

For examples of Nos. 8-21 with margins clear of the design on all four sides, add a 50 percent premium to the value listed. For stamps with clear circular datestamps, apply a 75 percent premium. Add the two premiums together for covers with stamps having these attributes.

Nos. 18, 20-21, 24-29, etc., used abroad.

See Antigua, Argentina, Bahamas, Bolivia, Brazil, British Guiana, British Honduras, Chile, Colombia, Cuba, Cyprus, Danish West Indies, Dominica, Dominican Republic, Ecuador, Egypt, Gibraltar, Grenada, Haiti, Jamaica, Malta, Mexico, Montserrat, Nevis, Nicaragua, Offices in the Turkish Empire, Peru, Puerto Rico, St. Christopher, St. Lucia, St. Vincent, Tobago, Uruguay, Venezuela, and Virgin Islands for listings of numeral cancels numbered A01-A15, A18, A26-A37, A39-A49, A51-A62, A64-A78, B01-B02, B32, C, C28, C30, C35-C43, C51, C56, C57-C63, C65, C81-C83, C86-C88, D22, D74, D87, E53, E88, F69, F83-F85, F87-F88, G, S, G06, 124, 582, 942, 969, 974, 975, 981, 982.

See Ascension for local cancellations used on Great Britain stamps.

Queen Victoria — A5

1855	Typo.		Wmk. 21
22	A5　4p rose, *bluish*	8,750.	440.00
	Block of 4	62,500.	
	On cover		775.00
a.	Watermark inverted		1,250.
23	A5　4p rose, *white*	—	1,150.
	On cover		

Compare design A5 with A11, A16, A31.

1856			Wmk. 22
24	A5　4p rose, *bluish*	11,250.	540.
	Block of 4	62,500.	3,600.
	On cover		775.
a.	Watermark inverted		1,250.
b.	White glazed paper	9,250.	
25	A5　4p rose, *white*	8,800.	400.
	Block of 4	55,000.	
	On cover		675.

1857			Wmk. 23
26	A5　4p rose, *white*	1,750.	125.00
	Block of 4	12,500.	800.00
	On cover		215.00
a.	4p carmine rose, *white*	2,000.	125.00
	On cover		215.00
b.	Thick glazed paper	6,750.	360.00
	On cover		—
c.	Watermark inverted (as #26)		360.00

A6	A7

1856			Wmk. 24
27	A6　6p lilac	1,400.	100.00
	Block of four	8,000.	725.00
	On cover		200.00
a.	6p deep lilac	1,850.	140.00
	On cover		225.00
b.	Wmk. 3 roses and shamrock		—
c.	6p lilac, blued paper	8,250.	950.00
d.	6p lilac, thick paper	4,200.	400.00
e.	Watermark inverted	3,150.	360.00
f.	Watermark inverted & reversed	5,200.	
28	A7　1sh green	3,000.	300.00
	Block of four	16,000.	2,100.
	On cover		425.00
a.	1sh pale green	3,000.	300.00
	On cover		425.00
b.	1sh deep green	5,750.	450.00
	On cover		575.00
c.	1sh green, blued paper		2,000.
d.	1sh green, thick paper		365.00
e.	Imperf		—
f.	Watermark inverted		625.00
f.	Watermark inverted & reversed		1,350.

Compare design A6 with A13, A18, A22. Compare A7 with A15, A21, A29.

For examples of Nos. 22-28 with margins clear of the design on all four sides, add a 50 percent premium to the value listed. For stamps with clear circular datestamps, apply a 75 percent premium. Add the two premiums together for covers with stamps having these attributes.

Forgeries of No. 27c and 28c exist.

A8	A9

1858-69	Engr.　Wmk. 20　Perf. 14

29	A8　2p deep blue (P9)	350.00	12.50
	On cover		50.00
a.	2p blue	350.00	12.50
	Plate 7	1,600.	55.00
	Block of four	10,000.	1,150.
	On cover		200.00
	Watermark inverted		750.00
	Plate 8	1,450.	40.00
	Block of four	9,250.	775.00
	On cover		160.00
	Watermark inverted		275.00
	Plate 9	350.00	12.50
	Block of four	2,150.	155.00
	On cover		50.00
	Watermark inverted		235.00
	Plate 12	3,000.	135.00
	Block of four	14,000.	875.00
	On cover		300.00
	Watermark inverted		440.00
b.	Imperf. (P9)		12,500.
c.	Watermark inverted		235.00

Plate numbers are contained in the scroll work at the sides of the stamp.

Lines Above and Below Head Thinner

30	A8 2p blue ('69)		
	(P13)	350.00	32.50
	Block of four	2,500.	300.00
	On cover		75.00
	Plate 14	475.00	35.00
	Block of four	3,150.	400.00
	On cover		70.00
	Watermark inverted		335.00
	Plate 15	500.00	35.00
	Block of four	3,400.	525.00
	Watermark inverted		475.00
	On cover		70.00
a.	Imperf. (P13)	10,500.	
b.	Watermark inverted, *from*		310.00

1860-70

31	A9 1½p lilac rose, *bluish* (P1)		
	('60)	8,750.	11,000.
32	A9 1½p dull rose		
	('70) (P3)	500.00	65.00
	Block of four	2,500.	600.00
	On cover		275.00
a.	1½p lake red	600.00	65.00
	On cover, #32 or 32a		275.00
	Plate 1	725.00	90.00
	On cover		325.00
c.	Imperf (P13)	9,500.	
d.	Lettered "OP-PC"	—	
e.	Watermark inverted (P3)		450.00
f.	Imperf (P3)	9,250.	

The 1½p stamps from Plate 1 carry no plate number. The Plate 3 number is in the border at each side above the lower corner letters.

No. 31 was prepared but not issued.

Queen Victoria — A10

1864

33	A10 1p rose red	25.00	2.75
a.	1p brick red	25.00	2.75
b.	1p lake red	25.00	2.75
	Block of four, *from*	125.00	30.00
	On cover, #33, 33a or 33b		8.50
c.	Imperf. (P116, see footnote)	8,750.	4,500.

Plate numbers are contained in the scroll work at the sides of the stamp.

No. 33 was printed from 1864 to 1879.

Thirty-nine plate numbers besides Plate 116 (No. 33c) are also known imperforate and used. Values for used examples start at $450.

Stamps from plate 177 have been altered and offered as plate 77.

For examples of Nos. 29-33 with margins clear of the design on all four sides, add a 50 percent premium to the value listed. For stamps with clear circular datestamps, apply a 75 percent premium. Add the two premiums together for covers with stamps having these attributes.

Plate Numbers

Plate 71	52.50	4.00
On cover		5.75
Plate 72	57.50	5.00
Plate 73	57.50	4.00
Plate 74	57.50	3.00
Plate 76	52.50	3.00
Plate 77	—	500.00.
Plate 78	125.00	3.00
Plate 79	45.00	3.00
Plate 80	62.50	3.00
Plate 81	62.50	3.00
Plate 82	125.00	5.00
Plate 83	150.00	9.00
Plate 84	77.50	3.00
Plate 85	57.50	4.00
Plate 86	67.50	5.00
Plate 87	45.00	3.00
Plate 88	180.00	10.00
Plate 89	57.50	3.00
Plate 90	57.50	3.00
Plate 91	72.50	7.25
Plate 92	52.50	3.00
Plate 93	67.50	3.00
Plate 94	62.50	6.00
Plate 95	57.50	3.00
Plate 96	62.50	3.00
Plate 97	57.50	4.50
Plate 98	67.50	7.00
Plate 99	72.50	6.00
Plate 100	77.50	3.00
Plate 101	77.50	11.50
Plate 102	62.50	3.00
Plate 103	67.50	5.00
Plate 104	100.00	6.25
Plate 105	125.00	9.50
Plate 106	72.50	3.00
Plate 107	77.50	9.00
Plate 108	105.00	3.00
Plate 109	115.00	4.50
Plate 110	77.50	11.50
Plate 111	67.50	3.00
Plate 112	87.50	3.00
Plate 113	67.50	16.00
Plate 114	325.00	16.00
Plate 115	125.00	3.00
Plate 116	100.00	11.50
Plate 117	62.50	3.00
Plate 118	67.50	3.00
Plate 119	62.50	3.00
Plate 120	26.00	3.00
Plate 121	57.50	11.50
Plate 122	26.00	3.00
Plate 123	57.50	3.00
Plate 124	42.50	3.00
Plate 125	57.50	3.00

Plate 127	72.50	3.00
Plate 129	57.50	11.00
Plate 130	72.50	3.00
Plate 131	82.50	21.00
Plate 132	180.00	28.00
Plate 133	155.00	11.50
Plate 134	26.00	3.00
Plate 135	125.00	30.00
Plate 136	125.00	25.00
Plate 137	42.50	3.00
Plate 138	32.50	3.00
Plate 139	77.50	21.00
Plate 140	32.50	3.00
Plate 141	155.00	11.50
Plate 142	92.50	30.00
Plate 143	77.50	17.50
Plate 144	125.00	26.00
Plate 145	47.50	3.00
Plate 146	57.50	7.00
Plate 147	67.50	4.00
Plate 148	57.50	4.00
Plate 149	57.50	7.00
Plate 150	26.00	3.00
Plate 151	77.50	11.50
Plate 152	77.50	7.50
Plate 153	135.00	11.50
Plate 154	67.50	3.00
Plate 155	67.50	3.00
Plate 156	62.50	3.00
Plate 157	67.50	3.00
Plate 158	47.50	3.00
Plate 159	47.50	3.00
Plate 160	47.50	3.00
Plate 161	77.50	9.00
Plate 162	67.50	9.00
Plate 163	67.50	9.00
Plate 164	67.50	9.00
Plate 165	62.50	3.00
Plate 166	62.50	7.25
Plate 167	62.50	3.00
Plate 168	67.50	11.00
Plate 169	77.50	9.25
Plate 170	52.50	3.00
Plate 171	26.00	3.00
Plate 172	47.50	3.00
Plate 173	92.50	11.50
Plate 174	47.50	3.00
Plate 175	77.50	3.00
Plate 176	77.50	3.00
Plate 177	57.50	3.00
Plate 178	77.50	4.50
Plate 179	67.50	3.00
Plate 180	77.50	6.75
Plate 181	62.50	3.00
Plate 182	125.00	6.75
Plate 183	72.50	4.00
Plate 184	47.50	3.00
Plate 185	67.50	4.00
Plate 186	87.50	3.00
Plate 187	67.50	3.00
Plate 188	92.50	12.50
Plate 189	92.50	12.50
Plate 190	67.50	7.50
Plate 191	47.50	9.25
Plate 192	67.50	3.00
Plate 193	47.50	3.00
Plates 194-195	67.50	11.00
Plate 196	67.50	11.00
Plate 197	67.50	11.50
Plate 198	57.50	7.25
Plate 199	72.50	7.25
Plate 200	77.50	3.00
Plate 201	47.50	6.25
Plate 202	77.50	11.00
Plate 203	47.50	21.00
Plate 204	72.50	3.00
Plate 205	72.50	4.00
Plate 206	72.50	11.50
Plate 207	72.50	11.50
Plate 208	72.50	18.50
Plate 209	62.50	10.50
Plate 210	87.50	16.00
Plate 211	92.50	26.00
Plate 212	77.50	13.50
Plate 213	77.50	13.50
Plate 214	87.50	24.00
Plate 215	87.50	24.00
Plate 216	92.50	24.00
Plate 217	92.50	9.25
Plate 218	87.50	11.00
Plate 219	125.00	87.50
Plate 220	57.50	9.25
Plate 221	92.50	21.00
Plate 222	105.00	52.50
Plate 223	125.00	77.50
Plate 224	155.00	57.50
Plate 225	3,300.	825.00

Plate Numbers On Cover

Plate 71	8.50
Plate 72	10.00
Plate 73	8.50
Plates 73-76, 78-81	8.50
Plate 77	—
Plate 82	24.00
Plate 83	35.00
Plate 84	8.00
Plate 85	12.00
Plate 86	9.50
Plate 87	8.50
Plate 88	47.50
Plate 89	8.50
Plate 90	12.00
Plate 91	14.00
Plate 92	8.50
Plate 93	8.50
Plate 94	12.00
Plates 95-96	8.50
Plate 97	8.50
Plate 98	15.00
Plate 99	12.00
Plate 100	35.00
Plate 101	23.00
Plate 102	8.50
Plate 103	12.00
Plate 104	35.00
Plate 105	27.50
Plate 106	8.50
Plate 107	18.00
Plate 108	27.50
Plate 109	24.00
Plate 110	24.00
Plate 111	8.50
Plate 112	20.00
Plate 113	30.00
Plate 114	30.00
Plate 115	24.00
Plate 116	24.00
Plates 117-120	8.50
Plate 121	24.00
Plates 122-125, 127	8.50
Plate 129	21.00

Plate 130	8.50
Plate 131	42.50
Plate 132	57.50
Plate 133	47.50
Plate 134	8.50
Plate 135	60.00
Plate 136	50.00
Plates 137, 138	8.50
Plate 139	42.50
Plate 140	8.50
Plate 141	35.00
Plate 142	60.00
Plate 143	35.00
Plate 144	52.50
Plate 145	8.50
Plate 146	14.00
Plate 147	10.00
Plate 148	8.50
Plate 149	14.00
Plate 150	8.50
Plate 151	24.00
Plate 152	15.00
Plate 153	60.00
Plates 154-160	8.50
Plate 161	27.50
Plate 162	17.50
Plate 163	9.00
Plate 164	14.00
Plate 165	8.50
Plate 166	15.00
Plate 167	8.50
Plate 168	21.00
Plate 169	24.00
Plates 170-172	8.50
Plate 173	24.00
Plate 174	8.50
Plates 175-176	14.00
Plate 177	8.50
Plate 178	24.00
Plate 179	9.00
Plate 180	35.00
Plate 181	8.50
Plate 182	32.50
Plate 183	9.00
Plate 184	20.00
Plate 185	24.00
Plate 186	20.00
Plate 187	9.00
Plate 188	25.00
Plates 189-190	32.50
Plate 191	20.00
Plate 192	8.50
Plate 193	14.00
Plates 194-195	21.00
Plate 196	14.00
Plate 197	24.00
Plates 198-199	15.00
Plate 200	13.00
Plate 201	24.00
Plate 202	30.00
Plate 203	24.00
Plate 204	24.00
Plates 205-207	32.50
Plate 208	37.50
Plate 209	37.50
Plate 210	32.50
Plate 211	120.00
Plates 212-217	72.50
Plate 218	120.00
Plate 219	180.00
Plate 220	72.50
Plate 221	100.00
Plate 222	120.00
Plate 223	155.00
Plate 224	130.00
Plate 225	1,600.

A11

1862 Typo. Wmk. 23

34	A11 4p vermilion	1,900.	75.00
	Block of four	11,000.	750.00
	On cover		140.00
a.	4p bright red	2,100.	92.50
	On cover		160.00
b.	Hair lines (P4)	2,150.	65.00
	On cover		165.00
c.	As "a," hair lines (P4)	2,150.	75.00
	On cover		175.00
d.	Imperf. (P4)	3,800.	
e.	Watermark inverted		315.00

Hair lines on No. 34b, 34c and 34d are fine colorless lines drawn diagonally across the corners of the stamp.

A12

A13

A14

A15

1862 Wmk. 24

37	A12 3p pale rose	2,500.	300.00
	Block of four	14,000.	3,250.
	On cover		550.00
a.	3p deep rose	5,000.	525.00
	On cover		800.00

b.	With white dots under side ornaments	40,000.	16,000.
d.	As "b," imperf.	6,750.	
e.	Thick paper		465.00
39	A13 6p lilac (P3)	2,250.	105.00
	Block of four	12,500.	750.00
	On cover		210.00
a.	6p lilac, blued paper		1,400.
b.	6p lilac, thick paper		375.00
c.	6p lilac, wmk. 3 roses & thistle		8,000.
d.	6p lilac, hair lines (P4) ('64)	2,900.	210.00
	On cover		240.00
e.	As "d," imperf.	4,500.	
f.	As "d," thick paper	4,000.	260.00
g.	Wmk. missing shamrock		
h.	6p deep lilac (P3)	2,600.	120.00
	On cover		275.00
40	A14 9p straw (p2)	3,900.	400.00
	Block of four	24,000.	
	On cover		900.00
a.	9p straw, blued paper		
b.	9p straw, thick paper	6,000.	525.00
c.	9p straw, wmk. 3 roses & thistle		—
d.	9p bister (P2)	5,500.	525.00
	On cover		925.00
e.	9p bister, hair lines (P3)	35,000.	14,000.
42	A15 1sh green	3,100.	260.00
	Block of four	16,500.	1,500.
	On cover		450.00
a.	1sh deep green (P1)	4,750.	450.00
	On cover		600.00
c.	1sh deep green, with hair lines (P2)	35,000.	
d.	Thick paper		340.00
e.	As "c," imperf	7,500.	

Hair lines on Nos. 39d, 39e, 39f, 39g, 40e and 42c are fine colorless lines drawn diagonally across the corners of the stamp.

Compare design A14 with A19.

For examples of Nos. 34-42 with margins clear of the design on all four sides, add a 50 percent premium to the value listed. For stamps with clear circular datestamps, apply a 75 percent premium. Add the two premiums together for covers with stamps having these attributes.

Forgeries exist of Nos. 39a and 40a.
Stamps from plate 2 are unissued.

A16

1865 Wmk. 23

43	A16 4p vermilion (P12)	600.00	62.50
	Block of four	3,500.	650.00
	On cover		145.00
	Plate 9	625.00	72.50
	Plate 10	850.00	150.00
	On cover		225.00
	Plate 11	650.00	72.50
	On cover		175.00
	Plate 13	375.00	47.50
	Plate 14	800.00	92.50
	On cover		200.00
a.	4p dull vermilion (P8)	550.00	90.00
	Block of four	3,300.	550.00
	On cover		200.00
	Plate 7	600.00	100.00
	Block of four	3,300.	550.00
	On cover		200.00
	Plate 8	625.00	72.50
	Block of four	3,300.	550.00
	On cover		200.00
	Plates 9	625.00	72.50
	Block of four	3,300.	550.00
	On cover		175.00
	Plate 10	850.00	150.00
	Block of four	4,250.	725.00
	On cover		225.00
	Plate 11	650.00	72.50
	Block of four	3,300.	550.00
	On cover		175.00
	Plate 12	600.00	62.50
	Block of four	3,250.	525.00
	On cover		175.00
	Plate 14	800.00	92.50
	Block of four	3,900.	625.00
	On cover		200.00
	Plate 13	375.00	47.50
	Block of four	3,600.	550.00
	On cover		175.00
b.	Imperf. (P11,12)	7,750.	

A17

(Hyphen after SIX) — A18

A19

A20

1865 — Wmk. 24

44	A17 3p rose (P4)	2,350.	215.00
	Block of four	12,500.	1,600.
	On cover		400.00
a.	Wmk. error, 3 roses & shamrock	6,250.	1,250.
b.	Thick paper	3,500.	260.00
c.	Watermark inverted		500.00
45	A18 6p lilac (P5)	1,125.	100.00
	Block of four	6,250.	650.00
	On cover		190.00
a.	6p deep lilac	1,875.	180.00
	On cover		190.00
	Plate 6	3,700.	190.00
	On cover		350.00
b.	Double impression (P6)		16,500.
c.	Wmk. error, 3 roses & shamrock (P5)		1,400.
	As "c," Plate 6		2,400.
d.	Thick paper	1,500.	140.00
e.	Watermark inverted (P6)	1,875.	215.00
f.	Watermark inverted (P6)	6,250.	450.00
46	A19 9p straw (P4)	4,500.	575.00
	On cover		1,150.
	Plate 5	20,000.	
a.	Wmk. error, 3 roses & shamrock (P4)	—	2,250.
b.	Thick paper (P4)	5,250.	800.00
c.	Watermark inverted		1,150.
47	A20 10p red brn (P1)		55,000.
48	A21 1sh green (P4)	2,500.	225.00
	Block of four	14,000.	1,350.
	On cover		400.00
a.	Thick paper	3,250.	350.00
b.	Wmk. error, 3 roses & shamrock		1,500.
c.	Vert. pair, imperf. btwn.		16,500.
d.	Watermark inverted		625.00

No. 46, plate 5 is from a proof sheet.
See Nos. 49-50, 52-54. Compare design A17 with A27.

For examples of Nos. 43-48 with margins clear of the design on all four sides, add a 40 percent premium to the value listed. For stamps with clear circular datestamps, apply a 60 percent premium. Add the two premiums together for covers with stamps having these attributes.

(No hyphen after SIX) — A22

A23

1867-80 — Wmk. 25

49	A17 3p rose (P5)	525.00	62.50
	On cover		110.00
a.	3p deep rose	825.00	92.50
	On cover		120.00
	Plate 4	1,850.	300.00
	On cover		425.00
	Plate 6	550.00	62.50
	On cover		95.00
	Plate 7	400.00	67.50
	On cover		105.00
	Plate 8	600.00	62.50
	On cover		100.00
	Plate 9	600.00	67.50
	On cover		110.00
	Plate 10	900.00	145.00
	On cover		225.00
b.	Imperf. (P5,6,8,9)	10,000.	
50	A18 6p dull violet (P6)	1,850.	92.50
	On cover		175.00
a.	6p bright violet (P6)	1,750.	100.00
	On cover		175.00
b.	Imperf. (P6)		5,000.
51	A22 6p red violet ('69) (P9)	650.00	90.00
	On cover		145.00
a.	6p violet (P9)	675.00	92.50
	On cover		155.00
	Plate 8	675.00	135.00
	On cover		200.00
	Plate 10		35,000.
b.	Imperf. (P8, 9)	10,000.	4,500.
52	A19 9p bister (P4) ('67)	2,400.	300.00
	On cover		525.00
a.	Imperf. (P4)	15,000.	
53	A20 10p red brown (P1)	3,500.	350.00
	On cover		800.00
	Plate 2	50,000.	15,000.
a.	10p deep red brown	5,000.	600.00
	On cover		900.00
b.	Imperf. (P1)	12,000.	
54	A21 1sh green (P4)	1,200.	40.00
	On cover		100.00
	Plate 5	825.00	40.00
	On cover		92.50
	Plate 6	1,200.	40.00
	On cover		80.00

	Plate 7	1,400.	82.50
	On cover		135.00
a.	1sh deep green	1,250.	70.00
	On cover		95.00
b.	Imperf. (P4)	8,750.	5,500.
55	A23 2sh blue (P1)	3,750.	200.00
	On cover		750.00
a.	2sh pale blue	4,750.	800.00
	Plate 3		14,000.
b.	Imperf. (P1)	20,000.	
c.	2sh cobalt blue (P1)	22,000.	2,900.
d.	2sh milky blue (P1)	20,000.	1,850.
56	A23 2sh pale brn (P1) ('80)	27,500.	3,750.
	On cover		9,250.
a.	Imperf.		27,500.

No. 51, plate 10 and No. 53, plate 2, are from proof sheets.

For examples of Nos. 49-56 with margins clear of the design on all four sides, add a 35 percent premium to the value listed. For stamps with clear circular datestamps, apply a 40 percent premium. Add the two premiums together for covers with stamps having these attributes.

A24

1867 — Wmk. 26 — Perf. 15½x15

57	A24 5sh rose (P1)	11,000.	600.00
	Plate 2	17,500.	1,200.
a.	5sh pale rose	11,000.	600.00
	Plate 2	17,500.	1,200.
b.	Imperf. (P1)	19,000.	19,000.

See No. 90. Compare design A24 with A51.

For examples of No. 57 with margins clear of the design on all four sides, add a 50 percent premium to the value listed. For stamps with clear circular datestamps, apply a 50 percent premium. Add the two premiums together for covers with stamps having these attributes.

A25

1870 — Engr. — Wmk. 27 — Perf. 14

58	A25 ½p rose (P5)	110.00	22.00
	Block of four	575.00	210.00
	On cover		65.00
	Plate 1	325.00	90.00
	Block of four	1,500.	800.00
	On cover		240.00
	Plate 3	225.00	50.00
	Block of four	1,000.	800.00
	On cover		130.00
	Plate 4	150.00	37.50
	Block of four	750.00	375.00
	On cover		95.00
	Plate 5	110.00	22.50
	Block of four	575.00	210.00
	On cover		40.00
	Plate 6	125.00	22.00
	Block of four	575.00	210.00
	On cover		65.00
	Plate 8	575.00	210.00
	Block of four		300.00
	On cover		850.00
	Plate 9	6,000.	850.00
	Block of four	25,000.	7,500.
	On cover		1,650.
	Plate 10	125.00	22.00
	Block of four	575.00	210.00
	On cover		72.50
	Plate 11, 13	125.00	22.00
	Block of four	575.00	210.00
	On cover		72.50
	Plate 12, 14	125.00	22.00
	Block of four	600.00	210.00
	On cover		72.50
	Plate 15	180.00	40.00
	Block of four	900.00	400.00
	On cover		130.00
	Plate 19	300.00	60.00
	Block of four	1,500.	600.00
	On cover		160.00
	Plate 20	350.00	80.00
	Block of four	1,750.	800.00
	On cover		240.00
a.	Imperf (see footnote)	—	—
b.	Watermark inverted & reversed	310.00	100.00

Plates 1, 4-6, 8, 13 and 14 are known imperf. Values: from $3,750 unused, $3,250 used.

For examples of No. 58 with margins clear of the design on all four sides, add a 125 percent premium to the value listed. For stamps with clear circular datestamps, apply a 75 percent premium. Add the two premiums together for covers with stamps having these attributes.

A26

A27

A28

A29

Type A28 has a lined background.

1872-73 — Wmk. 25 — Typo.

59	A26 6p brown (P11)	800.00	55.00
	On cover		140.00
	Plate 12		4,000.
a.	6p deep brown (P11)	1,300.	110.00
	On cover		210.00
	Plate 12		3,500.
b.	6p pale buff (P11)	1,000.	100.00
	On cover		275.00
	Plate 12	3,300.	300.00
	On cover		525.00
60	A26 6p gray (P12) ('73)	1,900.	250.00
	On cover		325.00
a.	Imperf.		10,000.

For examples of Nos. 59-60 with margins clear of the design on all four sides, add a 25 percent premium to the value listed. For stamps with clear circular datestamps, apply a 25 percent premium. Add the two premiums together for covers with stamps having these attributes.

1873-80

61	A27 3p rose (shades) (P11)	400.00	50.00
	On cover		70.00
	Plates 12	500.00	50.00
	On cover		70.00
	Plate 14	525.00	50.00
	On cover		70.00
	Plates 15-16	400.00	50.00
	On cover		70.00
	Plates 17-18	500.00	50.00
	On cover		70.00
	Plate 19	425.00	50.00
	On cover		70.00
	Plate 20	800.00	110.00
	On cover		130.00
62	A28 6p gray (P13-16)	500.00	70.00
	On cover		115.00
	Plate 17	1,000.	165.00
	On cover		250.00
63	A28 6p buff (P13)		25,000.
64	A29 1sh pale green (P12, 13)	600.00	120.00
	On cover		240.00
	Plate 10	750.00	160.00
	On cover		275.00
	Plate 11	750.00	140.00
	On cover		260.00
	Plate 14		40,000.
a.	1sh deep green (P8, 9)	1,000.	180.00
	On cover		290.00
65	A29 1sh sal (P13) ('80)	4,750.	700.00
	On cover		1,500.

No. 63, plate 13, and No. 64, plate 14, are from proof sheets.

See Nos. 83, 86-87. For surcharges see Nos. 94-95. For overprints see Nos. O6, O30.

For examples of Nos. 61-65 with margins clear of the design on all four sides, add a 40 percent premium to the value listed. For stamps with clear circular datestamps, apply a 60 percent premium. Add the two premiums together for covers with stamps having these attributes.

A30

1875 — Wmk. 28

66	A30 2½p claret (P1, 2)	600.00	90.00
	On cover		160.00
	Plate 3	900.00	135.00
	On cover		195.00
a.	Bluish paper (P1)	900.00	140.00
	On cover		205.00
	Plate 2	8,250.	1,500.
	Plate 3		2,000.
	Plate 3		5,500.
	On cover		7,750.
b.	Lettered "LH-FL"	29,000.	2,500.
	On cover		—

Forgeries exist of 66a.

1876-80 — Wmk. 29

67	A30 2½p claret (P4-9, 11-16)	500.00	60.00
	On cover		105.00
	Plate 3	1,300.	125.00
	Plate 10		100.00
	On cover	550.00	75.00
	On cover		115.00
	Plate 17	1,750.	275.00
	On cover		525.00
68	A30 2½p ultra ('80) (P19, 20)	550.00	65.00
	On cover		110.00
	Plate 17	550.00	65.00
	On cover		110.00
	Plate 18	550.00	45.00
	On cover		75.00

A31

A32

1876-80 — Wmk. 23

69	A31 4p vermilion (P15)	2,750.	500.00
	On cover		1,000.
	Plate 16		35,000.
70	A31 4p pale ol grn ('77) (P16)	1,350.	325.00
	On cover		575.00
	Plate 15	1,350.	325.00
	On cover		650.00
	Plate 17		20,000.
a.	Imperf (P15)		1,400.
71	A31 4p gray brn (P17) ('80)	2,750.	500.00
	On cover		1,500.
72	A32 8p brn lilac (P1) ('76)	11,750.	
73	A32 8p org (P1) ('76)	1,750.	350.00
	On cover		600.00

Some specialists consider No. 70a a proof.
No. 72 was never placed in use.
No. 69, plate 16, is from proof sheets.

For examples of Nos. 66-73 with margins clear of the design on all four sides, add a 50 percent premium to the value listed. For stamps with clear circular datestamps, apply a 50 percent premium. Add the two premiums together for covers with stamps having these attributes.

A33

A34

1878 — Wmk. 26 — Perf. 15½x15

74	A33 10sh slate (P1)	60,000.	3,250.
75	A34 £1 brn lilac (P1)	90,000.	4,500.

See Nos. 91-92. Compare design A34 with A52.

For examples of Nos. 74-75 with margins clear of the design on all four sides, add a 40 percent premium to the value listed. For stamps with clear circular datestamps, apply a 60 percent premium. Add the two premiums together for covers with stamps having these attributes.

A35

A36

A38

A39

A40

A37

1880-81   Wmk. 30   Perf. 14

78	A35	½p deep green	50.00	13.50
		On cover		27.50
a.		Imperf.	4,400.	
b.		No watermark	9,000.	
c.		½p green	50.00	20.00
		On cover		37.50
79	A36	1p red brown	27.50	12.50
		On cover		30.00
a.		Imperf.	5,000.	
b.		Wmk. 29, error		25,000.
80	A37	1½p red brown	240.00	50.00
		On cover		150.00
81	A38	2p lilac rose	300.00	100.00
a.		2p deep rose	350.00	100.00
82	A30	2½p ultra ('81) (P23)	425.00	32.50
		On cover		55.00
		Plate 21	475.00	40.00
		On cover		55.00
		Plate 22	425.00	40.00
		On cover		55.00
a.		Imperf. (P23)	750.00	
83	A27	3p rose ('81) (P21)	500.00	90.00
		On cover		175.00
		Plate 20	900.00	155.00
		On cover		225.00
84	A31	4p gray brown (P17, 18)	440.00	67.50
		On cover		180.00
85	A39	5p dp indigo ('81)	725.00	125.00
		On cover		275.00
a.		Imperf.	6,750.	4,500.
86	A28	6p gray (P18)	375.00	72.50
		On cover		125.00
		Plate 17	440.00	72.50
		On cover		125.00
87	A29	1sh salmon (P14) ('81)	700.00	165.00
		On cover		525.00
		Plate 13	700.00	165.00
		On cover		525.00
		Nos. 78-87 (10)	3,782.	728.50

Some specialists consider No. 82a a proof. The 1sh in purple was not issued. Value, unused, $8,750.

See No. 98. For overprints, see Nos. O2-O3.

Compare design A35 with A54.

For examples of Nos. 78-87 with margins clear of the design on all four sides, add a 50 percent premium to the value listed. For stamps with clear circular datestamps, apply a 25 percent premium. Add the two premiums together for covers with stamps having these attributes.

Die I   Die II

1881

88	A40	1p lilac (14 dots in each angle)	225.00	32.50
		On cover		52.50
89	A40	1p lilac (16 dots in each angle)	2.75	2.00
		On cover		4.00
a.		Printed on both sides	900.	
b.		Imperf., pair	7,250.	
c.		Unwmkd.	7,750.	
d.		Bluish paper	4,750.	
e.		Printed on the gummed side	925.	
f.		As "a," reverse impression inverted	1,000.	

For overprints, see Nos. O4, O37, O45 and O55.

For examples of Nos. 88-89 with margins clear of the design on all four sides, add a 25 percent premium to the value listed. For stamps with clear circular datestamps, apply a 25 percent premium. Add the two premiums together for covers with stamps having these attributes.

1882-83   Wmk. 31

90	A24	5sh rose, bluish (P4)	35,000.	5,000.
a.		White paper	32,500.	5,000.
91	A33	10sh slate, bluish (P1)	135,000.	5,000.
a.		White paper	155,000.	4,750.
92	A34	£1 brown lilac, bluish (P1)	155,000.	10,000.
a.		White paper	180,000.	9,250.

A41

1882   Wmk. Two Anchors (31)

93	A41	£5 brt orange (P1)	14,000.	5,000.
a.		£5 pale dull orange, bluish	72,500.	15,500.
b.		£5 bright orange, bluish	72,500.	15,500.

The paper of No. 93b is less bluish than that of No. 93a, and it is a later printing.

For examples of Nos. 90-93 with margins clear of the design on all four sides, add a 25 percent premium to the value listed. For stamps with clear circular datestamps, apply a 50 percent premium. Add the two premiums together for covers with stamps having these attributes.

Types of 1873-80 Surcharged in Carmine

1883   Wmk. 30

94	A27	3p on 3p violet	625.00	150.00
		On cover		440.00
95	A28	6p on 6p violet	675.00	150.00
		On cover		440.00
a.		Double surcharge		12,500.

For examples of Nos. 94-95 with margins clear of the design on all four sides, add a 40 percent premium to the value listed. For stamps with clear circular datestamps, apply a 50 percent premium. Add the two premiums together for covers with stamps having these attributes.

A44

1883   Wmk. 31

96	A44	2sh6p lilac	625.00	165.00
a.		Bluish paper	9,250.	3,750.

For examples of No. 96 with margins clear of the design on all four sides, add a 25 percent premium to the value listed. For stamps with clear circular datestamps, apply a 25 percent premium. Add the two premiums together for covers with stamps having these attributes.

See British Offices Abroad for overprints on types A44-A133.

These overprints include "M.E.F.," "B.A.," "B.M.A.," "E.A.F.," "CHINA," "Morocco Agencies," "TANGIER," "LEVANT," "PARAS," and "PIASTRE(S)."

A45

A46

A47

A48

A49

A50

1883-84   Wmk. 30

98	A35	½p slate blue ('84)	29.00	9.00
		On cover		18.50
99	A45	1½p lilac ('84)	120.00	42.50
		On cover		125.00
100	A46	2p lilac ('84)	225.00	77.50
		On cover		155.00
101	A47	2½p lilac ('84)	90.00	18.00
		On cover		30.00
102	A48	3p lilac ('84)	275.00	100.00
		On cover		190.00
103	A49	4p green ('84)	575.00	210.00
		On cover		360.00
104	A45	5p green ('84)	575.00	210.00
		On cover		360.00
105	A46	6p green ('84)	600.00	240.00
		On cover		400.00
106	A50	9p green	1,250.	475.00
		On cover		2,500.
107	A48	1sh green ('84)	1,450.	300.00
		On cover		625.00
		Nos. 98-107 (10)	5,189.	1,682.

For examples of Nos. 98-107 with margins clear of the design on all four sides, add a 50 percent premium to the value listed. For stamps with clear circular datestamps, apply a 50 percent premium. Add the two premiums together for covers with stamps having these attributes.

Imperforate Singles

98a	A35	½p	3,750.
99a	A45	1½p	3,750.
100a	A46	2p	4,750.
101a	A47	2½p	4,750.
102a	A48	3p	4,750.
103a	A49	4p	4,750.
104a	A45	5p	5,500.
105a	A46	6p	5,500.
107a	A48	1sh	8,250.

Nos. 99-107 were printed by De La Rue in a newly invented doubly fugitive ink that was only available in lilac and green. The stamps were unpopular with the public and postal clerks because they were unattractive and the different denominations were difficult to distinguish from one another.

Values are for stamps of good color. Faded stamps sell for much less. Soaking stamps will cause the color to run.

No. 104 with line instead of period under "d" was not regularly issued. Value, $27,500.

For overprints see Nos. O5, O7, O27-O29.

A51

A52

1884   Wmk. 31

108	A51	5sh carmine rose	1,100.	250.00
a.		Bluish paper	18,750.	4,000.
b.		5sh deep crimson	1,000.	250.00
109	A52	10sh ultra	2,250.	550.00
a.		10sh cobalt	40,000.	8,500.
b.		Bluish paper	40,000.	8,500.
c.		As "a," bluish paper	65,000.	14,000.

For overprints see Nos. O8-O9.

For examples of Nos. 108-109 with margins clear of the design on all four sides, add a 25 percent premium to the value listed. For stamps with clear circular datestamps, apply a 25 percent premium. Add the two premiums together for covers with stamps having these attributes.

A53

1884   Wmk. 30

110	A53	£1 brown violet	32,500.	3,000.
a.		Frame broken, position JC or TA	62,500.	5,250.

See Nos. 123-124. For overprints see Nos. O10, O13, O15.

For examples of No. 110 with margins clear of the design on all four sides, add a 25 percent premium to the value listed. For stamps with clear circular datestamps, apply a 25 percent premium. Add the two premiums together for covers with stamps having these attributes.

Queen Victoria Jubilee Issue

A54

A55

A56

A57

A58

A59

A60

A61

A62

A63

A64

A65

Two types of 5p:
I — Squarish dots beside "d."
II — Tiny vertical dashes beside "d."

1887-92   Wmk. 30

111	A54	½p vermilion	1.80	1.10
		On cover		7.00
a.		Printed on both sides		
b.		Double impression	29,000.	
c.		Imperf.	4,400.	
d.		Printed on gummed side	3,300.	—
112	A55	1½p violet & grn	18.00	8.25
		On cover		25.00
a.		Double impression of violet		9,250.
113	A56	2p grn & car rose	35.00	13.50
		On cover		27.50
a.		2p green & vermilion	440.00	250.00
		On cover		750.00
114	A57	2½p violet, blue	25.00	3.50
		On cover		8.00
a.		Imperf.	10,500.	
b.		Printed on gummed side	13,500.	
115	A58	3p violet, yellow	25.00	3.50
		On cover		37.50
a.		3p violet, orange	825.00	175.00
		On cover		750.00
b.		Imperf.	10,500.	
116	A59	4p brown & grn	40.00	15.00
		On cover		42.50
117	A60	4½p car rose & grn ('92)	11.00	45.00
		On cover		92.50
118	A61	5p lilac & bl, II	42.50	12.50
		On cover		50.00
a.		Type I	825.00	125.00
		On cover		215.00
119	A62	6p violet, rose	40.00	12.50
		On cover		90.00
120	A63	9p blue & lilac	77.50	45.00
		On cover		250.00
121	A64	10p car rose & lilac ('90)	62.50	42.50
		On cover		275.00
a.		Imperf.	16,500.	
b.		10p scarlet & lilac	97.50	62.50
		On cover		265.00
c.		10p dp carmine & red lilac	625.00	250.00
122	A65	1sh green	275.00	72.50
		On cover		195.00
		Nos. 111-122 (12)	653.30	274.85

The unpopular green and lilac issue (Nos. 98-107) were replaced by these stamps in colored inks and papers that made it easier to distinguish the different denominations.

Soaking these stamps will cause the color to run.

See Nos. 125-126. For overprints see Nos. O11-O12, O14, O16-O18, O31-O36, O38, O44, O46-O48, O54, O56-O58, O65-O66.

1888   **Wmk. Three Orbs (29)**

123	A53	£1 brown violet	75,000.	4,400.
a.		Frame broken, position JC or TA	135,000.	9,250.

1891   **Wmk. 30**

124	A53	£1 green	4,000.	800.00
a.		Frame broken, position JC or TA	8,750.	2,000.

1900   **Wmk. 30**

125	A54	½p blue green	2.00	2.25
		On cover		6.50
a.		Imperf	7,250.	
b.		Printed on gum side		
126	A65	1sh car rose & green	67.50	145.00
		On cover		1,000.

No. 125 in bright blue is a color changeling.

For examples of Nos. 111-126 with margins clear of the design on all four sides, add a 25 percent premium to the value listed. For stamps with clear circular datestamps, apply a 25 percent premium. Add the two premiums together for covers with stamps having these attributes.

King Edward VII
A66   A67

A68   A69

A70   A71

A72   A73

A74   A75

A76   A77

A78

The stamps of King Edward VII were printed by three printers. De La Rue (DLR) held the contract from Jan. 1, 1902, through Dec. 31, 1910. De La Rue was replaced by Harrison & Sons (H) on Jan. 1, 1911. From July 1911, the bi-colored issues were produced by Somerset House (S), while Harrison continued to produce most of the monocolor stamps.

De La Rue printings were made on both ordinary and chalky papers and tend to be more finely printed than those of either of its successors. Soaking the green De La Rue stamps will cause the color to run.

The Harrison printings are only on ordinary paper. The stamps perforated 15x14 were only printed by Harrison & Sons and can serve as a comparison to identify printings.

The Somerset House printings are all on ordinary paper, except the 6p dull purple on Dickinson Coated paper (#135f) and the 6p bright magenta on chalky paper (#135j).

1902-11   **Wmk. 30**   *Perf. 14*
Ordinary Paper

127	A66	½p gray green (DLR)	2.00	1.75
		Never hinged	3.25	
		On cover		2.90
a.		½p blue green (DLR)	2.00	1.75
		Never hinged	3.25	
		On cover		2.90
b.		½p deep bluish green '11 (H)	12.50	6.50
		Never hinged	18.00	
		On cover		7.50
c.		½p very pale bluish grn ('11) (H)	45.00	45.00
		Never hinged	70.00	
		On cover		65.00
d.		½p bright green (fine impression; '11) (H)	275.00	175.00
		Never hinged	425.00	
		On cover		—
128	A66	1p scarlet (DLR)	2.25	1.60
		Never hinged	3.25	
		On cover		2.90
a.		1p rose red ('11) (H)	9.25	14.00
		Never hinged	13.50	
		On cover		20.00
b.		1p rose carmine ('11) (H)	62.50	35.00
		Never hinged	95.00	
		On cover		50.00
c.		1p aniline rose ('11) (H)	225.00	145.00
		Never hinged	325.00	
		On cover		—
d.		1p aniline pink ('11) (H)	650.00	360.00
		Never hinged	1,000.	
		On cover		—
e.		Booklet pane of 6	110.00	
f.		No watermark ('11) (H)	47.50	90.00
		Never hinged	65.00	
g.		Imperf., pair (DLR)	29,000.	
h.		1p rose carmine (02) (DLR)	30.00	20.00
		Never hinged	42.50	
129	A67	1½p vio & green (DLR)	45.00	22.50
		Never hinged	65.00	
		On cover		35.00
a.		1½p slate purple & green	50.00	22.50
		Never hinged	75.00	
		On cover		35.00
b.		1½p reddish pur & bright grn ('11) (S)	50.00	40.00
		Never hinged	80.00	
		On cover		57.50
c.		1½p dull purple & green ('12) (S)	35.00	32.50
		Never hinged	50.00	
		On cover		60.00
130	A68	2p yel grn & car (DLR)	52.50	22.50
		Never hinged	82.50	
		On cover		35.00
a.		2p gray grn & car red '04 (DLR)	60.00	32.50
		Never hinged	85.00	
		On cover		40.00
b.		2p deep grn & red ('11) (S)	27.50	20.00
		Never hinged	47.50	
		On cover		55.00
c.		2p deep grn & car ('11-'12) (S)	30.00	22.50
		Never hinged	45.00	
		On cover		55.00
131	A66	2½p ultra (DLR)	22.50	11.50
		Never hinged	32.50	
		On cover		22.50
a.		2½p pale ultra (DLR)	22.50	11.50
		Never hinged	32.50	
		On cover		22.50
b.		2½p bright blue ('11) (H)	62.50	35.00
		Never hinged	110.00	
		On cover		57.50
132	A69	3p dull pur, org yel (DLR)	45.00	19.00
		Never hinged	80.00	
		On cover		35.00
a.		3p deep pur, org yel (DLR)	45.00	19.00
		Never hinged	80.00	
		On cover		35.00
b.		3p purple, lemon ('11) (H)	92.50	235.00
		Never hinged	150.00	
		On cover		625.00
c.		3p gray, lemon ('11) (H)	4,500.	
		Never hinged	6,750.	
133	A70	4p gray brn & grn (DLR)	57.50	35.00
		Never hinged	110.00	
		On cover		50.00
a.		4p choc brn & green ('11) (H)	57.50	35.00
		Never hinged	100.00	
		On cover		45.00

134	A71	5p dull pur & ultra (DLR)	67.50	22.50
		Never hinged	87.50	
		On cover		57.50
a.		5p dull reddish pur & brt blue ('11) (S)	35.00	22.50
		Never hinged	55.00	
		On cover		75.00
b.		5p deep reddish pur & brt blue ('11) (S)	35.00	22.50
		Never hinged	55.00	
		On cover		75.00
135	A66	6p pale dull vio (DLR)	45.00	22.50
		Never hinged	55.00	
		On cover		55.00
a.		6p slate purple (DLR)	45.00	22.50
		Never hinged	55.00	
		On cover		55.00
b.		6p red violet ('11) (S)	45.00	26.00
		Never hinged	62.50	
		On cover		60.00
c.		6p dark violet ('12) (S)	45.00	30.00
		Never hinged	62.50	
		On cover		65.00
d.		6p deep plum ('13) (S)	32.50	80.00
		Never hinged	45.00	
		On cover		140.00
e.		6p royal purple ('11) (S)	57.50	100.00
		Never hinged	95.00	
		On cover		195.00
f.		6p dull purple, "Dickinson" coated paper ('13) (S)	250.00	190.00
		Never hinged	500.00	
g.		No cross on crown (S), from	1,000.	
		Never hinged	1,500.	
136	A72	9p ultra & dull vio (DLR)	100.00	70.00
		Never hinged	190.00	
		On cover		210.00
a.		9p ultra & slate vio ('11) (S)	100.00	70.00
		Never hinged	190.00	
		On cover		210.00
b.		9p lt bl & reddish pur ('11) (S)	92.50	85.00
		Never hinged	160.00	
		On cover		210.00
c.		9p deep brt bl & deep dull reddish pur ('11) (S)	92.50	85.00
		Never hinged	160.00	
		On cover		200.00
d.		9p blue & dull reddish pur ('11) (S)	70.00	70.00
		Never hinged	125.00	
		On cover		200.00
e.		9p blue & deep plum ('13) (S)	70.00	70.00
		Never hinged	125.00	
		On cover		200.00
f.		9p cobalt bl & slate vio ('11) (S)	140.00	115.00
		Never hinged	210.00	
		On cover		200.00
137	A73	10p car & dull pur (DLR)	100.00	70.00
		Never hinged	175.00	
		On cover		240.00
a.		10p scarlet & dull pur (S)	92.50	85.00
		Never hinged	125.00	
		On cover		240.00
b.		10p aniline pink & dull reddish pur ('11) (S)	290.00	260.00
		Never hinged	450.00	
		On cover		375.00
c.		10p car & dull reddish pur ('12) (S)	92.50	70.00
		Never hinged	150.00	
		On cover		260.00
d.		As No. 137, no cross on crown, from	400.00	260.00
		Never hinged	600.00	
138	A74	1sh car & dull grn (DLR)	92.50	40.00
		Never hinged	150.00	
		On cover		155.00
a.		1sh scar & dark green ('11) (S)	125.00	70.00
		Never hinged	190.00	
		On cover		160.00
b.		1sh scar & deep dark grn ('11) (S)	80.00	40.00
		Never hinged	120.00	
		On cover		125.00
c.		1sh car & lt green ('12) (S)	62.50	40.00
		Never hinged	100.00	
		On cover		180.00

Wmk. 31

139	A75	2sh6p lilac (DLR)	260.00	150.00
		Never hinged	575.00	
		On cover		800.00
a.		2sh6p dark violet ('11) (S)	300.00	200.00
		Never hinged	600.00	
		On cover		600.00
b.		2sh6p dull grayish pur ('11) (S)	850.00	475.00
		Never hinged	1,500.	
		On cover		—
c.		2sh6p dull reddish pur ('11) (S)	275.00	190.00
		Never hinged	625.00	
		On cover		1,100.
140	A76	5sh car rose (DLR)	400.00	225.00
		Never hinged	600.00	
		On cover		1,000.
a.		5sh deep brt carmine (DLR)	400.00	225.00
		Never hinged	600.00	
		On cover		1,000.
b.		5sh carmine (S)	425.00	225.00
		Never hinged	650.00	
		On cover		1,100.
141	A77	10sh ultra (DLR)	875.00	525.00
		Never hinged	1,600.	
		On cover		—
a.		10sh bright blue ('12) (S)	1,000.	625.00
		Never hinged	1,750.	
		On cover		—

Wmk. Three Imperial Crowns (30)

142	A78	£1 blue green (DLR)	2,000.	825.00
		Never hinged	3,250.	
		On cover		—
b.		£1 deep green ('11) (S)	2,000.	800.00

		Never hinged	3,250.	—
		Nos. 127-138 (12)	631.75	338.85

CHALKY PAPER

129d	A67	1½p pale pur & green ('05) (DLR)	45.00	22.50
		Never hinged	65.00	
		On cover		32.50
e.		1½p slate pur & bl grn (DLR)	45.00	20.00
		Never hinged	65.00	
		On cover		35.00
130d	A68	2p pale gray grn & car red ('06) (DLR)	55.00	32.50
		Never hinged	80.00	
		On cover		54.00
e.		2p pale gray grn & scar ('09) (DLR)	45.00	30.00
		Never hinged	90.00	
		On cover		50.00
f.		2p dull bl grn & car ('07) (DLR)	80.00	57.50
		Never hinged	160.00	
		On cover		110.00
132d	A69	3p dull pur, org yel ('06) (DLR)	200.00	80.00
		Never hinged	300.00	
		On cover		100.00
e.		3p pale reddish pur, org yel ('06) (DLR)	200.00	80.00
		Never hinged	300.00	
		On cover		100.00
f.		3p dull reddish pur, yel, lemon back ('06) (DLR)	200.00	92.50
		Never hinged	300.00	
		On cover		—
g.		3p pale pur, lemon (DLR)	45.00	20.00
		Never hinged	65.00	
		On cover		40.00
h.		3p purple, lemon (DLR)	45.00	20.00
		Never hinged	65.00	
		On cover		40.00
133b	A70	4p choc brn & grn (DLR)	57.50	35.00
		Never hinged	85.00	
		On cover		85.00
c.		4p choc brn & deep green ('06) (DLR)	45.00	21.00
		Never hinged	65.00	
		On cover		45.00
134c	A71	5p dull pur & ultra ('06) (DLR)	62.50	22.50
		Never hinged	92.50	
		On cover		55.00
d.		5p slate pur & ultra ('06) (DLR)	57.50	22.50
		Never hinged	85.00	
		On cover		52.50
135h	A66	6p pale dull pur ('06) (DLR)	45.00	22.50
		Never hinged	60.00	
		On cover		55.00
i.		6p dull purple ('06) (DLR)	45.00	22.50
		Never hinged	60.00	
		On cover		55.00
j.		6p bright magenta ('11) (S)	12,500.	
			17,500.	
136g	A72	9p ultra & dull vio ('05) (DLR)	100.00	70.00
		Never hinged	190.00	
		On cover		200.00
h.		9p ultra & slate vio ('05) (DLR)	100.00	70.00
		Never hinged	190.00	
		On cover		210.00
137e	A73	10p car & dull pur ('06) (DLR)	100.00	70.00
		Never hinged	175.00	
		On cover		210.00
f.		10p car & slate vio ('06) (DLR)	100.00	70.00
		Never hinged	175.00	
		On cover		210.00
g.		10p scar & dull pur ('10) (DLR)	110.00	70.00
		Never hinged	175.00	
		On cover		210.00
h.		Chalky paper, no cross on crown (DLR), from	450.00	275.00
		Never hinged	750.00	
138d	A74	1sh car & dull grn ('05) (DLR)	92.50	40.00
		Never hinged	150.00	
		On cover		140.00
e.		1sh scar & dull green ('10) (DLR)	92.50	57.50
		Never hinged	150.00	
		On cover		140.00

Wmk. 31

139d	A75	2sh6p pale dull pur ('05) (DLR)	290.00	175.00
		Never hinged	525.00	
		On cover		925.00
e.		2sh6p deep dull pur (DLR)	260.00	175.00
		Never hinged	500.00	
		On cover		925.00

See Nos. 143, 144, 146-150. For overprints see Nos. O19-O26, O39-O43, O49-O53, O59-O64, O67-O83.

See British Offices Abroad for overprints on types A44-A133.

These overprints include "M.E.F.," "B.A.," "B.M.A.," "E.A.F.," "CHINA," "Morocco Agencies," "TANGIER," "LEVANT," "PARAS," and "PIASTRE(S)."

1904   **Wmk. 30**

143	A66	½p pale yel grn (DLR)	2.00	1.75
		Never hinged	3.00	
		On cover		3.00
a.		½p yellow green (DLR)	2.00	1.75
		Never hinged	3.00	
		On cover		3.00
b.		Booklet pane of 5 + label (DLR, H)	525.00	

c.	Booklet pane of 6 (DLR, H)	190.00	
d.	Double impression (DLR)	29,000.	
e.	Imperf., pair (H)	37,500.	

Edward VII — A79

1909-10

144	A70	4p pale orange (DLR)	20.00	16.00
		Never hinged	30.00	
		On cover		40.00
a.		4p orange red (DLR)	22.50	17.50
		Never hinged	32.50	
		On cover		40.00
b.		4p brown orange (DLR)	190.00	150.00
		Never hinged	250.00	
		On cover		—
c.		4p bright orange ('11) (H)	100.00	62.50
		Never hinged	175.00	
		On cover		190.00
145	A79	7p gray ('10) (DLR)	42.50	22.50
		Never hinged	80.00	
		On cover		225.00
a.		7p deep gray blk ('10) (DLR)	125.00	110.00
		Never hinged	160.00	
		On cover		300.00
b.		7p slate gray ('12) (S)	17.50	25.00
		Never hinged	25.00	
		On cover		300.00

1911   **Perf. 15x14**

146	A66	½p dull yel green (H)	45.00	50.00
		Never hinged	65.00	
		On cover		110.00
a.		½p deep dull green (H)	45.00	50.00
		Never hinged	65.00	
		On cover		110.00
147	A66	1p carmine rose (H)	17.50	17.50
		Never hinged	30.00	
		On cover		35.00
a.		1p pale car rose (H)	25.00	17.50
		Never hinged	37.50	
		On cover		35.00
b.		1p rose red (H)	47.50	30.00
		Never hinged	70.00	
		On cover		47.50
148	A66	2½p brt ultra (H)	25.00	17.50
		Never hinged	55.00	
		On cover		37.50
a.		2½p dull blue (H)	25.00	17.50
		Never hinged	55.00	
		On cover		32.50
149	A69	3p violet, lemon (H)	52.50	17.50
		Never hinged	85.00	
		On cover		45.00
a.		3p gray, lemon (H)	3,400.	
		Never hinged	5,000.	
150	A70	4p orange (H)	35.00	17.50
		Never hinged	55.00	
		On cover		75.00
		Nos. 146-150 (5)	175.00	120.00

King George V
A80   A81
Original Die, Type 1

½p: on the right-hand dolphin, the three uppermost scales form a complete triangle.
1p: the ribbon on the wreath at the right of the crown is crossed by two complete lines from top to bottom.

Perf. 15x14

1911, June 22   **Wmk. 30**

151	A80	½p yellow green	5.75	4.50
		Never hinged	8.25	
a.		Booklet pane of 6	175.00	
b.		Perf. 14 (error)	18,500.	1,050.
		Never hinged	—	
c.		½p bluish green	400.00	210.00
		Never hinged	550.00	
152	A81	1p carmine	5.25	3.00
		Never hinged	7.50	
a.		Booklet pane of 6	175.00	
b.		Perf. 14 (error)	—	
		Never hinged	—	
c.		1p pale carmine	16.00	3.50
		Never hinged	25.00	
d.		As "c," booklet pane of 6	125.00	
e.		As "c," no cross on crown	875.00	525.00
		Never hinged	1,275.	

Original Die, Type 2

½p: on the right-hand dolphin, the three uppermost scales do not complete the triangle, with the line on the left side of the top scale missing entirely.
1p: the ribbon on the wreath at the right of the crown is crossed by one complete line from top to bottom, the other being interrupted.

151d	A80	½p bright green	9.00	1.75
		Never hinged	17.50	
f.		½p yellow green	13.50	1.75
		Never hinged	27.50	
g.		½p bluish green	190.00	110.00
		Never hinged	300.00	
152g	A81	1p carmine	10.00	3.50
		Never hinged	16.50	
h.		1p pale carmine	11.50	4.50
		Never hinged	18.00	
i.		As "h," no cross on crown	825.00	525.00
		Never hinged		
j.		1p rose pink	140.00	50.00
		Never hinged	200.00	
k.		1p scarlet	50.00	21.00
		Never hinged	100.00	
l.		1p aniline scarlet	235.00	125.00
		Never hinged	390.00	

1912, Jan. 1   **Re-engraved**

153	A80	½p yellow green	10.00	4.50
		Never hinged	15.00	
a.		No cross on crown	110.00	57.50
		Never hinged	175.00	
b.		½p green	10.00	4.50
		Never hinged	15.00	
c.		½p deep green	17.50	9.25
		Never hinged	21.00	
154	A81	1p scarlet	7.50	3.50
		Never hinged	11.00	
a.		No cross on crown	92.50	57.50
		Never hinged	150.00	
b.		1p aniline scarlet	180.00	100.00
		Never hinged	250.00	
c.		As "b," no cross on crown	1,450.	

In the re-engraved stamps the lines of the hair and beard are clearer. The re-engraved ½p has 3 lines of shading instead of 4 between the point of neck and frame; in the 1p the body of the lion is nearly covered by lines of shading.

1912, Aug.   Wmk. 33   Perf. 15x14
Die I (Before Re-engraving)

155	A80	½p yellow green	45.00	45.00
		Never hinged	90.00	
a.		Booklet pane of 6	270.00	
		Never hinged	525.00	
156	A81	1p scarlet	30.00	30.00
		Never hinged	50.00	
a.		Booklet pane of 6	210.00	
		Never hinged	375.00	

Die II (Re-engraved)

157	A80	½p yellow green	8.00	3.50
		Never hinged	17.50	
a.		No cross on crown	210.00	130.00
		Never hinged	325.00	
158	A81	1p scarlet	9.25	4.75
		Never hinged	15.00	
a.		No cross on crown	110.00	57.50
		Never hinged	160.00	

1912, Sept.-Oct.   **Wmk. 32**

158A	A80	½p yellow green	15.50	9.25
		Never hinged	25.00	
d.		½p green	14.00	9.25
		Never hinged	21.00	
e.		Imperf., pair	300.00	
		Never hinged	400.00	
f.		No cross on crown	180.00	130.00
		Never hinged	290.00	
158B	A81	1p scarlet	20.00	11.50
		Never hinged	30.00	
e.		Imperf., pair	300.00	
		Never hinged	400.00	
f.		No cross on crown	155.00	62.50
		Never hinged	225.00	

A82   **A83**

A84   **A85**

A86   **A87**

A88   **A89**

King George V — A90

TWO PENCE:

Die I — Four horizontal lines above the head. Heavy colored lines above and below the bottom tablet. The inner frame line is closer to the central design than it is to the outer frame line.

Die II — Three lines above the head. Thinner lines above and below the bottom tablet. The inner frame line is midway between the central design and the outer frame line.

1912-13   Wmk. 33   Perf. 15x14

159	A82	½p green ('13)	1.10	1.10
		Never hinged	1.60	
a.		Double impression	26,000.	
b.		Booklet pane of 6	90.00	
		Never hinged	135.00	
c.		½p deep green	5.50	2.25
		Never hinged	9.00	
d.		½p yellow green	6.50	3.50
		Never hinged	10.00	
e.		½p blue green	45.00	29.00
		Never hinged	57.50	
f.		½p very yellow green ('14)	8,500.	
		Never hinged	12,750.	
160	A83	1p scarlet	1.10	1.10
		Never hinged	1.90	
a.		Booklet pane of 6	100.00	
		Never hinged	140.00	
b.		Tete beche pair	77,500.	
c.		1p vermilion	5.75	2.90
		Never hinged	8.50	
d.		1p pale rose red	21.00	5.25
		Never hinged	24.00	
e.		1p carmine red	12.50	5.75
		Never hinged	20.00	
f.		1p scarlet vermilion	140.00	57.50
		Never hinged	175.00	
161	A84	1½p red brown	4.50	1.75
		Never hinged	7.00	
a.		"PENCF"	350.00	260.00
		Never hinged	325.00	
b.		1½p orange brown	21.00	17.50
		Never hinged	32.50	
c.		1½p chestnut	5.75	1.10
		Never hinged	9.75	
d.		As "c," "PENCF"	130.00	115.00
		Never hinged	190.00	
e.		1½p chocolate brown	11.50	2.25
		Never hinged	17.50	
f.		As "e," Unwmkd.	235.00	235.00
		Never hinged	350.00	
g.		Booklet pane of 6	125.00	
		Never hinged	275.00	
h.		Booklet pane of 4 + 2 labels	675.00	
162	A85	2p deep org (I)	5.00	3.50
		Never hinged	6.50	
a.		2p deep orange (II) ('21)	5.75	4.25
		Never hinged	9.50	
b.		Booklet pane of 6 (I)	200.00	
		Booklet pane of 6 (II)	300.00	
		Never hinged	350.00	
			475.00	
d.		2p bright orange (I)	5.75	3.50
		Never hinged	9.50	
e.		2p orange yellow (I)	9.00	3.50
		Never hinged	15.00	
163	A86	2½p ultramarine	14.00	4.50
		Never hinged	24.00	
a.		2½ cobalt blue	14.00	4.50
		Never hinged	24.00	
b.		2½ bright blue ('14)	14.00	4.50
		Never hinged	24.00	
c.		2½ indigo blue ('20)	3,650.	2,600.
		Never hinged	5,000.	
d.		2½ Prussian blue	1,050.	825.00
		Never hinged	1,550.	
164	A87	3p bluish violet ('13)	9.25	3.25
		Never hinged	15.00	
a.		3p violet	8.50	3.50
		Never hinged	15.00	
b.		3p reddish violet	14.00	3.25
		Never hinged	21.00	
165	A88	4p slate green	17.50	2.25
		Never hinged	26.00	
a.		4p pale gray green	29.00	5.75
		Never hinged	40.00	
b.		4p deep gray green ('13)	45.00	26.00
		Never hinged	67.50	
166	A89	5p yellow brown	17.50	5.75
		Never hinged	26.00	
a.		Unwmkd.	1,250.	
		Never hinged	1,750.	
b.		5p brown ('13)	17.50	5.75
		Never hinged	26.00	
c.		5p bister brown	145.00	67.50
		Never hinged	215.00	
167	A89	6p rose lilac	17.50	8.00
		Never hinged	30.00	
a.		6p dull violet ('13)	30.00	11.50
		Never hinged	35.00	
b.		Perf. 14	92.50	115.00
		Never hinged	130.00	
c.		6p reddish purple	30.00	5.75
		Never hinged	40.00	
d.		6p dp reddish purple	40.00	7.00
		Never hinged	60.00	
168	A89	7p ol grn ('13)	22.50	10.50
		Never hinged	32.50	
a.		7p bronze green ('15)	72.50	29.00
		Never hinged	115.00	

b.		7p sage green ('17)	72.50	19.00
		Never hinged	115.00	
169	A89	8p black, yellow ('13)	37.50	12.50
		Never hinged	65.00	
a.		8p black, buff, granite ('17)	45.00	17.50
		Never hinged	62.50	
170	A90	9p black brown ('13)	22.50	6.75
		Never hinged	32.50	
171	A90	10p light blue ('13)	25.00	22.50
		Never hinged	42.50	
a.		10p bright blue	92.50	32.50
		Never hinged	145.00	
172	A90	1sh bister ('13)	24.00	4.50
		Never hinged	35.00	
a.		1sh bister brown	40.00	14.00
		Never hinged	65.00	
		Nos. 159-172 (14)	218.95	87.95

No. 167 is on chalky paper.

The distinctive yellow green ink used in printing No. 159f, also called "Cyprus" green, is fluorescent under UV light, unlike the inks used in printing other ½p varieties.

See Nos. 177-178, 183, 187-200, 210, 212-220.

Compare design A82 with A97.

See British Offices Abroad for overprints on types A44-A133.
These overprints include "M.E.F.," "B.A.," "B.M.A.," "E.A.F.," "CHINA," "Morocco Agencies," "TANGIER," "LEVANT," "PARAS," and "PIASTRE(S)."

Waterlow Brothers & Layton Printing (1913)

"Britannia Rule the Waves" A91

Measure 22mm vertically. Perforation holes are larger and evenly spaced.

1913   Engr.   Wmk. 34   Perf. 11x12

173	A91	2sh6p dark brown	275.00	180.00
		Never hinged	390.00	
b.		2sh6p black brown	290.00	190.00
		Never hinged	425.00	
174	A91	5sh rose car	525.00	375.00
		Never hinged	1,050.	
175	A91	10sh indigo blue	1,000.	475.00
		Never hinged	2,000.	
176	A91	£1 green	3,250.	1,550.
		Never hinged	4,900.	
a.		£1 dull blue green	3,250.	1,800.
		Never hinged	5,000.	
		Nos. 173-176 (4)	5,050.	2,580.

De La Rue & Co. Printing (1915)

Measure 22mm vertically. Gum tends to be yellowish and patchy. The top right and top left perf teeth are wider than the others. Perforation holes are smaller.

1915   Engr.   Wmk. 34   Perf. 11x12

173a	A91	2sh6p lt brn (worn plate)	360.00	290.00
		Never hinged	600.00	
173c	A91	2sh6p dp yel brn	350.00	250.00
		Never hinged	600.00	
173d	A91	2sh6p yel brn	300.00	225.00
		Never hinged	525.00	
173e	A91	2sh6p sepia brn	290.00	260.00
		Never hinged	450.00	
174a	A91	5sh br carmine	475.00	375.00
		Never hinged	575.00	
174b	A91	5sh carmine	450.00	360.00
		Never hinged	625.00	
174c	A91	5sh pale carmine (worn plate)	625.00	460.00
		Never hinged	900.00	
175a	A91	10sh light blue	3,000.	825.00
		Never hinged	4,500.	
175b	A91	10sh blue	2,600.	825.00
		Never hinged	3,900.	
175c	A91	10sh deep blue	3,150.	1,000.
		Never hinged	4,750.	

See Nos. 179-181, 222-224.

1913   Wmk. 32   Typo.   Perf. 15x14
Coil Stamps

177	A82	½p green	175.00	210.00
		Never hinged	250.00	
178	A83	1p scarlet	260.00	260.00
		Never hinged	375.00	

Bradbury, Wilkinson & Co. Printing (1918-19)
Seahorses Types of 1913-15 Retouched

Measure 22.5-23mm vertically. Most examples have a small dot of color at top center, outside of frameline. Perforation holes are larger and usually are evenly spaced.

1919   Engr.   Wmk. 34   Perf. 11x12

179	A91	2sh6p olive brown	125.00	75.00
		Never hinged	225.00	
a.		2sh6p gray brown	125.00	75.00
		Never hinged	225.00	
b.		2sh6p chocolate brown	140.00	80.00
		Never hinged	260.00	
c.		2sh6p reddish brown	140.00	80.00
		Never hinged	260.00	
180	A91	5sh car rose	300.00	125.00
		Never hinged	325.00	
181	A91	10sh blue	425.00	160.00
		Never hinged	500.00	
		Nos. 179-181 (3)	850.00	360.00

Type of 1912-13

1922   Typo.   Wmk. 33   Perf. 15x14

183	A90	9p olive green	120.00	35.00
		Never hinged	250.00	

British Empire Exhibition Issue

British Lion and George V
A92

Wmk. 35
1924, Apr. 23   Engr.   Perf. 14

185	A92	1p vermilion	11.50	12.50
		Never hinged	17.50	
186	A92	1½p dark brown	17.50	17.50
		Never hinged	26.00	

See Nos. 203-204.

Types of 1912-13 Issue

1924   Typo.   Perf. 15x14

187	A82	½p green	1.10	1.10
		Never hinged	1.50	
a.		Wmk. sideways	10.00	4.00
		Never hinged	20.00	
b.		Booklet pane of 6	90.00	
		Never hinged	140.00	
c.		Double impression	11,500.	
188	A83	1p scarlet	1.10	1.10
		Never hinged	1.40	
a.		Wmk. sideways	22.50	17.50
		Never hinged	45.00	
b.		Booklet pane of 6	90.00	
		Never hinged	140.00	
189	A84	1½p red brown	1.10	1.10
		Never hinged	1.40	
a.		Tête bêche pair	550.00	875.00
		Never hinged	775.00	
b.		Wmk. sideways	20.00	4.00
		Never hinged	40.00	
c.		Booklet pane of 6	50.00	
		Never hinged	75.00	
d.		Bklt. pane of 4 + 2 labels	235.00	
		Never hinged	375.00	
e.		Double impression	19,000.	
190	A85	2p dp orange (II)	2.90	2.90
		Never hinged	3.75	
a.		Wmk. sideways	110.00	110.00
		Never hinged	200.00	
b.		Unwatermarked	1,000.	
		Never hinged	1,500.	
191	A86	2½p ultra	5.75	3.50
		Never hinged	10.00	
a.		Unwatermarked	2,100.	
		Never hinged	3,250.	
192	A87	3p violet	11.50	2.75
		Never hinged	19.00	
193	A88	4p slate green	15.00	2.75
		Never hinged	29.00	
a.		Printed on gummed side	3,900.	
194	A89	5p yel brown	22.50	4.00
		Never hinged	47.50	
195	A89	6p dull violet	3.50	1.75
		Never hinged	5.00	
a.		6p purple, chalky paper	14.00	2.90
		Never hinged	25.00	
198	A90	9p olive green	13.50	4.00
		Never hinged	27.50	
199	A90	10p dull blue	45.00	45.00
		Never hinged	110.00	
200	A90	1sh bister	25.00	3.50
		Never hinged	55.00	
		Nos. 187-200 (12)	147.95	73.45

Nos. 187a, 188a, 189b, 190a issued in coils.
Inverted watermarks on the three lowest values are usually from booklet panes.
Nos. 188-189 were issued also on experimental paper with variety of Wmk. 35: closer spacing; letters shorter, rounder.

British Empire Exhibition Issue
Type of 1924, Dated "1925"

1925, May 9   Engr.   Perf. 14

203	A92	1p vermilion	17.00	32.50
		Never hinged	25.00	
204	A92	1½p brown	45.00	80.00
		Never hinged	67.50	

A93

A94

A95

St. George Slaying the Dragon A96

1929, May 10   Typo.   Perf. 15x14

205	A93	½p green	2.50	2.50
		Never hinged	3.75	
a.		Wmk. sideways	45.00	45.00
		Never hinged	120.00	
b.		Booklet pane of 6	150.00	
206	A94	1p scarlet	2.50	2.50
		Never hinged	3.75	
a.		Wmk. sideways	82.50	82.50
		Never hinged	120.00	
b.		Booklet pane of 6	150.00	
207	A94	1½p dark brown	2.50	2.00
		Never hinged	4.00	
a.		Wmk. sideways	45.00	45.00
		Never hinged	90.00	
b.		Booklet pane of 6	60.00	
c.		Booklet pane of 4 + 2 labels	400.00	
208	A95	2½p deep blue	11.50	11.50
		Never hinged	24.00	
		Nos. 205-208 (4)	19.00	18.50

Inverted watermarks on the three lowest values are usually from booklet panes.
Nos. 205a, 206a and 207a were issued in coils.

Wmk. 219
Engr.   Perf. 12

209	A96	£1 black	800.00	800.00
		Never hinged	1,500.	

Universal Postal Union, 9th Congress.

A97

Type A97 designs are re-engraved versions of the types of the 1912-13 issue, with the most obvious difference being the solid appearance of the central field. The backgrounds appear to be solid, although the photoengraving screen can be seen under magnification.

Perf. 14½x14
1934-36   Photo.   Wmk. 35

210	A97	½p dark green	.45	.45
		Never hinged	.90	
a.		Wmk. sideways	8.00	3.25
		Never hinged	17.50	
b.		Booklet pane of 6	85.00	
211	A97	1p carmine	.45	.45
		Never hinged	.90	
a.		Wmk. sideways	15.00	15.00
		Never hinged	40.00	
b.		Booklet pane of 6	85.00	
c.		Imperf., pair	5,000.	
d.		Pair, imperf. btwn.	7,000.	
e.		Printed on gummed side	575.00	
212	A97	1½p red brown	.45	.45
		Never hinged	.90	
a.		Imperf., pair	1,100.	
b.		Wmk. sideways	6.00	2.00
		Never hinged	18.00	
c.		Booklet pane of 6	30.00	
d.		Booklet pane of 4 + 2 labels	160.00	
213	A97	2p red org ('35)	.55	.55
		Never hinged	1.60	
a.		Imperf., pair	5,000.	
b.		Wmk. sideways	90.00	70.00
		Never hinged	275.00	
214	A97	2½p ultra ('35)	.90	.75
		Never hinged	3.00	
215	A97	3p dk violet ('35)	.90	1.00
		Never hinged	3.00	
216	A97	4p dk sl grn ('35)	1.75	1.00
		Never hinged	4.00	
217	A97	5p yel brown ('36)	6.00	1.50
		Never hinged	19.00	

218	A97	9p dk ol grn ('35)	9.00	2.75
		Never hinged	19.00	
219	A97	10p Prus blue ('36)	15.00	11.00
		Never hinged	32.50	
220	A97	1sh bister brn ('36)	15.00	1.25
		Never hinged	40.00	
		Nos. 210-220 (11)	50.45	21.15

The designs in this set are slightly smaller than the 1912-13 issue.
Inverted watermarks on the three lowest values are usually from booklet panes.
Nos. 210a, 211a, 212b and 213b were issued in coils.

Britannia Type of 1913-19 Reengraved

1934   Engr.   Wmk. 34   Perf. 11x12

222	A91	2sh6p brown	80.00	25.00
		Never hinged	150.00	
223	A91	5sh carmine	175.00	60.00
		Never hinged	375.00	
224	A91	10sh dark blue	375.00	65.00
		Never hinged	750.00	
		Nos. 222-224 (3)	630.00	150.00

Printed by Waterlow & Sons. Can be distinguished by the crossed lines in background of portrait. Previous issues have horizontal lines only.

Silver Jubilee Issue

A98

Perf. 14½x14
1935, May 7   Photo.   Wmk. 35

226	A98	½p dark green	1.00	.60
		Never hinged	1.40	
a.		Booklet pane of 4	40.00	
227	A98	1p carmine	1.25	1.75
		Never hinged	2.00	
a.		Booklet pane of 4	40.00	
228	A98	1½p red brown	1.00	.60
		Never hinged	1.40	
a.		Booklet pane of 4	17.50	
229	A98	2½p ultra	4.00	4.50
		Never hinged	6.50	
a.		2½p Prussian blue	9,500.	11,000.
		Never hinged	11,000.	
		Nos. 226-229 (4)	7.25	7.45

25th anniv. of the reign of George V. Device at right differs on 1½p and 2½p.
Inverted watermarks on the three lowest values are usually from booklet panes.

Edward VIII — A99

1936   Wmk. 250

230	A99	½p dark green	.25	.25
		Never hinged	.40	
a.		Booklet pane of 6	2.00	
		Never hinged	2.75	
231	A99	1p crimson	.50	.50
		Never hinged	.70	
a.		Booklet pane of 6	17.50	
		Never hinged	25.00	
232	A99	1½p red brown	.25	.35
		Never hinged	.40	
a.		Booklet pane of 6	11.00	
		Never hinged	15.00	
b.		Booklet pane of 4 + 2 labels	62.50	
		Never hinged	85.00	
c.		Booklet pane of 2	20.00	
		Never hinged	30.00	
233	A99	2½p bright ultra	.25	1.00
		Never hinged	40	
		Nos. 230-233 (4)	1.25	2.10

Inverted watermarks on the three lowest values are usually from booklet panes.

King George VI and Queen Elizabeth A100

Perf. 14½x14
1937, May 13   Wmk. 251

234	A100	1½p purple brown	.25	.25
		Never hinged	.35	

Coronation of George VI and Elizabeth.

See British Offices Abroad for overprints on types A44-A133.
These overprints include "M.E.F.," "B.A.," "B.M.A.," "E.A.F.," "CHINA," "Morocco Agencies," "TANGIER," "LEVANT," "PARAS," and "PIASTRE(S)."

A101

A102

King George VI — A103

Nos. 235-240 show face and neck highlighted, background solid.

1937-39

235	A101	½p deep green	.25	.25
		Never hinged	.30	
a.		Wmk. sideways	.40	.45
		Never hinged	.55	
b.		Booklet pane of 6	32.50	
		Never hinged	45.00	
c.		Booklet pane of 4	60.00	32.50
		Never hinged	85.00	
d.		Booklet pane of 2	70.00	
		Never hinged	100.00	
236	A101	1p scarlet	.25	.25
		Never hinged	.30	
a.		Wmk. sideways	8.50	7.50
		Never hinged	22.50	
b.		Booklet pane of 6	40.00	
		Never hinged	55.00	
c.		Booklet pane of 4	100.00	100.00
		Never hinged	150.00	
d.		Booklet pane of 2	70.00	
		Never hinged	100.00	
237	A101	1½p red brown	.25	.25
		Never hinged	.40	
a.		Wmk. sideways	.65	1.25
		Never hinged	1.40	
b.		Booklet pane of 6	35.00	
		Never hinged	50.00	
c.		Booklet pane of 4 + 2 labels	85.00	
		Never hinged	120.00	
d.		Booklet pane of 2	20.00	
		Never hinged	30.00	
238	A101	2p orange ('38)	.60	.50
		Never hinged	1.00	
a.		Wmk. sideways	30.00	32.50
		Never hinged	80.00	
b.		Booklet pane of 6	100.00	
		Never hinged	150.00	
239	A101	2½p bright ultra	.25	.25
		Never hinged	.35	
a.		Wmk. sideways	45.00	32.50
		Never hinged	90.00	
b.		Booklet pane of 6	85.00	
		Never hinged	120.00	
c.		Tête bêche pair	22,000.	
240	A101	3p dk purple ('38)	3.00	.95
		Never hinged	5.00	
241	A102	4p gray green ('38)	.45	.75
		Never hinged	.70	
a.		Imperf., pair	7,000.	
		Never hinged	8,500.	
b.		Horiz. pair, imperf. on 3 sides	7,500.	
		Never hinged	9,000.	
242	A102	5p lt brown ('38)	1.10	.80
		Never hinged	3.00	
a.		Imperf., pair	6,000.	
		Never hinged	8,000.	
b.		Horiz. pair, imperf. on 3 sides	7,000.	
		Never hinged	8,500.	
243	A102	6p rose lilac ('39)	.80	.60
		Never hinged	1.50	
244	A103	7p emerald ('39)	2.00	.60
		Never hinged	6.00	
a.		Horiz. pair, imperf. on 3 sides	6,500.	
		Never hinged	8,500.	
245	A103	8p brt rose ('39)	3.25	.80
		Never hinged	7.00	
246	A103	9p dp ol green ('39)	3.25	.80
		Never hinged	6.50	
247	A103	10p royal bl ('39)	3.25	.80
		Never hinged	6.50	
a.		Imperf., pair	5,700.	
		Never hinged	7,000.	
248	A103	1sh brown ('39)	3.25	1.00
		Nos. 235-248 (14)	21.95	8.60
		Set, never hinged	47.00	

Nos. 235a, 236a, 237a, 238a and 239a were issued in coils.
Nos. 235c and 236c are watermarked sideways.

The ½p, 1p, 1½p, 2p and 2½p with watermark inverted are from booklet panes.
No. 238 bisects were used in Guernsey from 12/27/40 to 2/24/41. Value, on cover $32.50.
See Nos. 258-263, 266, 280-285.

Oman Surcharges

Various definitive and commemorative stamps between Nos. 243 and 372 were surcharged in annas (a), new paisa (np) and rupees (r) for use in Oman. The surcharges do not indicate where the stamps were used.

King George VI and Royal Arms — A104

King George VI — A105

1939-42   Engr.   Wmk. 259   Perf. 14
249	A104	2sh6p chestnut	42.50	6.00
		Never hinged	110.00	
249A	A104	2sh6p yel green ('42)	8.00	1.50
		Never hinged	16.00	
250	A104	5sh dull red	10.00	2.00
		Never hinged	25.00	
251	A105	10sh indigo	150.00	24.00
		Never hinged	325.00	
251A	A105	10sh ultra ('42)	17.50	5.00
		Never hinged	45.00	
		Nos. 249-251A (5)	228.00	38.50

See No. 275.

Victoria and George VI A106

Perf. 14½x14
1940, May 6   Photo.   Wmk. 251
252	A106	½p deep green	.25	.25
		Never hinged	.30	
253	A106	1p scarlet	1.00	.40
		Never hinged	1.10	
254	A106	1½p red brown	.25	.75
		Never hinged	.55	
255	A106	2p orange	.50	.75
		Never hinged	1.00	
256	A106	2½p brt ultra	1.00	.55
		Never hinged	2.25	
257	A106	3p dark purple	1.75	3.50
		Never hinged	3.00	
		Nos. 252-257 (6)	4.75	6.20

Centenary of the postage stamp.
No. 255 bisects were used in Guernsey from 12/27/40 to 2/24/41. Value, on cover, $40.

Type of 1937-39, with Background Lightened

1941-42
258	A101	½p green	.25	.25
		Never hinged	.30	
a.		Booklet pane of 6	14.00	
		Never hinged	20.00	
b.		Booklet pane of 2	7.00	
		Never hinged	10.00	
c.		Imperf., pair	6,500.	
		Never hinged	8,500.	
d.		Tete beche pair	8,000.	
		Never hinged	17,500.	
e.		Booklet pane of 4		
259	A101	1p vermilion	.25	.25
		Never hinged	.30	
a.		Wmk. sideways ('42)	3.00	5.75
		Never hinged	5.00	
b.		Booklet pane of 2	35.00	
		Never hinged	50.00	
c.		Imperf., pair	6,000.	
		Never hinged	8,000.	
d.		Booklet pane of 4		
e.		Horiz. pair, imperf on 3 sides	6,000.	
		Never hinged	8,500.	
260	A101	1½p lt red brn ('42)	.30	.85
		Never hinged	.60	
a.		Booklet pane of 2	7.00	

b.		Never hinged	10.00	
261	A101	2p light orange	.25	.50
		Never hinged	.50	
a.		Wmk. sideways ('42)	16.50	21.00
		Never hinged	32.50	
b.		Booklet pane of 6	17.50	
		Never hinged	25.00	
c.		Imperf., pair	5,500.	
		Never hinged	7,500.	
d.		Tete beche pair	11,500.	
		Never hinged	17,500.	
262	A101	2½p ultra	.25	.40
		Never hinged	.35	
a.		Wmk. sideways ('42)	9.00	11.00
		Never hinged	17.50	
b.		Booklet pane of 6	11.00	
		Never hinged	15.00	
c.		Imperf., pair	3,350.	
		Never hinged	4,750.	
d.		Tete beche pair	11,500.	
		Never hinged	17,500.	
263	A101	3p violet	1.40	1.10
		Never hinged	5.00	
		Nos. 258-263 (6)	2.70	3.35

The ½p, 2p and 2½p with inverted watermarks are from booklets.
Nos. 259a, 261a and 262a were issued in coils.
Nos. 258b, 258e, 259b, 259d, 260a-260b are made from sheets.

> Catalogue values for unused stamps in this section, from this point to the end of the section, are for Never Hinged items.

Peace Issue

A107

King George VI and Symbols of Peace and Industry A108

Perf. 14½x14
1946, June 11   Photo.   Wmk. 251
264	A107	2½p bright ultra	.25	.25
265	A108	3p violet	.25	.45

Return to peace at the close of WW II.

George VI Type of 1939
1947, Dec. 29
266	A103	11p violet brown	2.50 2.00

A109

King George VI and Queen Elizabeth A110

1948, Apr. 26   Perf. 14½x14, 14x14½
267	A109	2½p brt ultra	.40	.25
268	A110	£1 dp chalky blue	40.00	40.00

25th anniv. of the marriage of King George VI and Queen Elizabeth.

A111

Vraicking (Gathering Seaweed) A112

1948, May 10   Perf. 14½x14
269	A111	1p red	.25	.25
270	A112	2½p bright ultra	.25	.25

3rd anniversary of the liberation of the Channel Islands from German occupation.
Sold at post offices in the Channel Islands and at major philatelic windows in the United Kingdom, and valid for postage throughout Great Britain.

A113

A114

A115

A116

1948, July 29
271	A113	2½p bright ultra	.40	.25
272	A114	3p deep violet	.65	.50
273	A115	6p red violet	2.75	.75
274	A116	1sh dark brown	4.25	1.75
		Nos. 271-274 (4)	8.05	3.25

1948 Olympic Games held at Wembley during July and August.

George VI Type of 1939
Wmk. 259
1948, Oct. 1   Engr.   Perf. 14
275	A105	£1 red brown	25.00	20.00

A117

A118

A119

A120

Perf. 14½x14
1949, Oct. 10   Photo.   Wmk. 251
276	A117	2½p bright ultra	.25	.25
277	A118	3p brt violet	.25	.50
278	A119	6p red violet	.45	.55
279	A120	1sh brown	.90	1.10
		Nos. 276-279 (4)	1.85	2.40

UPU, 75th anniversary.

Types of 1937
1950-51   Wmk. 251   Perf. 14½x14
280	A101	½p light orange	.25	.25
a.		Booklet pane of 2	10.00	
b.		Booklet pane of 4	15.00	
c.		Booklet pane of 6	10.00	
d.		Imperf., pair	6,000.	
e.		Tete beche pair	18,000.	
281	A101	1p ultramarine	.25	.25
a.		Wmk. sideways	.50	.90
b.		Booklet pane of 2	10.00	
c.		Booklet pane of 4	20.00	
d.		Booklet pane of 6	35.00	
e.		Booklet pane of 3 + 3 labels	20.00	
f.		Imperf., pair	5,000.	
g.		Horiz. pair, imperf on 3 sides	6,500.	
282	A101	1½p green	.50	.50
a.		Wmk. sideways	2.00	3.00
b.		Booklet pane of 2	10.00	
c.		Booklet pane of 4	15.00	
d.		Booklet pane of 6	25.00	
283	A101	2p lt red brown	.60	.45
a.		Wmk. sideways	1.50	1.25
b.		Booklet pane of 6	25.00	
c.		Tete beche pair	18,000.	
d.		Horiz. pair, imperf on 3 sides	8,000.	
284	A101	2½p vermilion	.50	.45
a.		Wmk. sideways	1.00	1.00
b.		Booklet pane of 6	8.00	
c.		Tete beche pair		
285	A102	4p ultra ('50)	1.50	1.50
a.		Double impression	8,250.	
		Nos. 280-285 (6)	3.60	3.40

Inverted watermarks on Nos. 280-284 are usually from booklets.
Nos. 281a, 282a, 283a and 284a were issued in coils.

H.M.S. Victory A121

St. George Slaying the Dragon A122

Royal Arms A123

Design: 5sh, White Cliffs, Dover.

Perf. 11x12
1951, May 3   Engr.   Wmk. 259
286	A121	2sh6p green	9.00	1.10
287	A121	5sh dull red	30.00	1.75
288	A122	10sh ultra	32.50	9.75
289	A123	£1 lt red brown	35.00	18.00
		Nos. 286-289 (4)	106.50	30.60

Britannia, Symbols of Commerce and Prosperity, King George VI — A124

Festival Symbol A125

Perf. 14½x14

1951, May 3   Photo.   Wmk. 251
290 A124 2½p scarlet   .25   .25
291 A125 4p bright ultra   .35   .75

Festival of Britain, 1951.

Complete Booklets
can be found following the Letter
Sheets section.

POSTAGE DUE STAMPS

D1   D2

Perf. 14x14½

1914-24   Typo.   Wmk. 33
J1	D1	½p emerald	.50	.30
		Never hinged	2.00	
J2	D1	1p rose	.50	.30
		Never hinged	2.00	
a.		1p pale carmine	.85	.55
		Never hinged	1.75	
b.		1p carmine, thick chalky paper ('24)	2.60	4.00
		Never hinged	4.90	
J3	D1	1½p red brown ('22)	47.50	20.00
		Never hinged	160.00	
J4	D1	2p brown black	.50	.30
		Never hinged	2.00	
J5	D1	3p violet ('18)	6.50	.85
		Never hinged	30.00	
a.		3p bluish violet ('18)	7.00	3.00
		Never hinged	12.50	
J6	D1	4p gray green ('21)	47.50	5.75
		Never hinged	150.00	
J7	D1	5p org brown	8.00	4.00
		Never hinged	22.50	
J8	D1	1sh blue ('15)	45.00	5.50
		Never hinged	170.00	
a.		1sh deep bright blue	45.00	5.75
		Never hinged	150.00	
		Nos. J1-J8 (8)	156.00	37.00

1924-30   Wmk. 35
J9	D1	½p emerald	1.10	.85
		Never hinged	3.00	
J10	D1	1p car rose	.65	.30
		Never hinged	3.00	
J11	D1	1½p red brown	52.50	22.50
		Never hinged	175.00	
J12	D1	2p black brown	1.60	.30
		Never hinged	10.50	
J13	D1	3p violet	2.25	.30
		Never hinged	11.50	
a.		Experimental wmk.	75.00	55.00
		Never hinged	110.00	
b.		Printed on the gummed side	125.00	
		Never hinged	160.00	
J14	D1	4p deep green	17.50	4.00
		Never hinged	67.50	
J15	D1	5p org brown ('30)	65.00	45.00
		Never hinged	165.00	
J16	D1	1sh blue	11.50	1.10
		Never hinged	45.00	
J17	D2	2sh6p brown, *yellow*	85.00	2.25
		Never hinged	250.00	
		Nos. J9-J17 (9)	237.10	76.60

The experimental watermark of No. J13a
resembles Wmk. 35 but is spaced more
closely, with letters short and rounded, crown
with flat arch and sides high, lines thicker.

1936-37   Wmk. 250
J18	D1	½p emerald ('37)	7.50	10.00
		Never hinged	13.50	
J19	D1	1p car rose ('37)	1.50	1.75
		Never hinged	2.50	
J20	D1	2p blk brown ('37)	10.00	12.50
		Never hinged	17.50	
J21	D1	3p violet ('37)	1.50	2.00
		Never hinged	2.25	
J22	D1	4p slate green	24.00	32.50
		Never hinged	50.00	
J23	D1	5p bister ('37)	20.00	26.00
		Never hinged	30.00	
a.		5p orange brown	35.00	30.00
		Never hinged	75.00	
J24	D1	1sh blue ('36)	7.50	8.50
		Never hinged	16.00	
J25	D2	2sh6p brn, *yel* ('37)	140.00	12.50
		Never hinged	350.00	
		Nos. J18-J25 (8)	212.00	105.75

1938-39   Wmk. 251
J26	D1	½p emerald	8.50	5.75
		Never hinged	13.00	
J27	D1	1p carmine rose	1.40	.85
		Never hinged	3.50	
J28	D1	2p black brown	1.50	.85
		Never hinged	3.00	
J29	D1	3p violet	7.00	1.10
		Never hinged	14.00	
J30	D1	4p slate green	40.00	10.00
		Never hinged	110.00	
J31	D1	5p bister ('39)	6.75	.85
		Never hinged	16.00	

J32	D1	1sh blue	25.00	2.25
		Never hinged	80.00	
J33	D2	2sh6p brown, *yel* ('39)	40.00	3.00
		Never hinged	95.00	
		Nos. J26-J33 (8)	130.15	24.65

> **Catalogue values for unused stamps in this section, from this point to the end of the section, are for Never Hinged items.**

1951-52
J34	D1	½p orange	3.50	3.50
J35	D1	1p violet blue	1.50	.75
J36	D1	1½p green ('52)	2.00	2.50
J37	D1	4p bright blue	50.00	24.00
J38	D1	1sh olive bister	32.50	10.00
		Nos. J34-J38 (5)	89.50	40.75

OFFICIAL STAMPS

Type of Regular Issue of 1840 "V R" in Upper Corners

O1

1840   Wmk. 18   Imperf.
O1 O1 1p black   35,000. 35,000.
    On cover   —

No. O1 was never placed in use but examples are known used and on covers that passed through the mails by oversight. The stamp also was used experimentally to test cancellations.

Postage stamps perforated with a crown and initials "H.M.O.W.," "O.W.," "B.T." or "S.O.," or with only the initials "H.M.S.O." or "D.S.I.R.," were used for official purposes.

Counterfeits exist of Nos. O2-O83.

Inland Revenue
Regular Issues Overprinted in Black

a

b

Type "a" is overprinted on the stamps of ½ penny to 1 shilling inclusive, type "b" on the higher values.

1882-85   Wmk. 30   Perf. 14
O2	A35	½p pale green	135.00	52.50
		On cover		115.00
a.		½p green	110.00	37.50
O3	A35	½p slate bl ('85)	87.50	30.00
		On cover		140.00
O4	A40	1p lilac	7.75	5.25
		On cover		30.00
a.		"OFFICIAL" omitted		10,000.
b.		Ovpt. lines transposed		
O5	A47	2½p lilac ('85)	520.00	190.00
		On cover		1,500.
O6	A28	6p gray	600.00	140.00
		On cover		
O7	A48	1sh green ('85)	6,250.	1,900.
		On cover		

Wmk. 31
O8	A51	5sh car rose ('85)	10,000.	2,500.
a.		Bluish paper ('85)	17,500.	6,250.
b.		Raised period after "R"	10,500.	3,150.
O9	A52	10sh ultra	11,500.	3,600.
a.		10sh cobalt	37,500.	10,000.
b.		Bluish paper	24,000.	7,250.
c.		Raised period after "R"	12,500.	4,500.

Wmk. Three Imperial Crowns (30)
O10	A53	£1 brown vio	80,000.	31,500.
a.		Frame broken (JC or TA)		
			90,000.	

1888-89   Wmk. 30
O11	A54	½p vermilion	12.50	5.25
		On cover		100.00
a.		"I.R." omitted	5,750.	
O12	A65	1sh green ('89)	950.00	350.00
		On cover		3,650.

1890   Wmk. Three Orbs (29)
O13	A53	£1 brown vio	100,000.	42,500.
a.		Frame broken (JC or TA)	125,000.	

1891   Wmk. 30
O14	A57	2½p violet, *blue*	150.00	21.00
		On cover		450.00

Wmk. Three Imperial Crowns (30)

1892
O15	A53	£1 green	12,500.	2,600.
a.		No period after "R"	—	4,250.
b.		Frame broken (JC or TA)	21,000.	5,500.

For examples of Nos. O2-O15 with margins clear of the design on all four sides, add a 20 percent premium to the value listed. For stamps with clear circular datestamps, apply a 20 percent premium. Add the two premiums together for covers with stamps having these attributes.

1901   Wmk. 30
O16	A54	½p blue green	19.00	12.50
		On cover		350.00
O17	A62	6p violet, *rose*	400.00	115.00
		On cover		
O18	A65	1sh car rose & green	4,400.	1,900.
		On cover		

1902-04
O19	A66	½p gray green	32.50	3.25
		On cover		125.00
O20	A66	1p carmine	21.00	2.50
		On cover		82.50
O21	A66	2½p ultra	950.00	260.00
O22	A66	6p dull vio ('04)	400,000.	190,000.
O23	A74	1sh car rose & green	3,750.	725.00

Wmk. 31
O24	A76	5sh car rose	36,500.	10,500.
a.		Raised period after "R"	42,500.	12,500.
O25	A77	10sh ultra	110,000.	47,500.
a.		Raised period after "R"	125,000.	47,500.

Wmk. Three Imperial Crowns (30)
O26	A78	£1 green	62,500.	25,000.

Nos. O4, O8, O9 and O13 also exist with overprint in blue black.

Government Parcels

Overprinted

1883-86   Wmk. 30
O27	A45	1½p lilac ('86)	400.00	92.50
O28	A46	6p green ('86)	3,150.	1,250.
O29	A50	9p green	2,600.	1,050.
O30	A29	1sh salmon (P13)	1,675.	290.00
		Plate 14	3,500.	525.00
		Nos. O27-O30 (4)	7,825.	2,682.

1887-92
O31	A55	1½p violet & green	145.00	18.50
O32	A56	2p green & car rose ('91)	235.00	40.00
O33	A60	4½p car rose & grn ('92)	375.00	260.00
O34	A62	6p violet, *rose*	260.00	62.50
O35	A63	9p blue & lil ('88)	400.00	92.50
O36	A65	1sh green	675.00	260.00
		Nos. O31-O36 (6)	2,090.	733.50

1897
O37	A40	1p lilac	92.50	22.50
a.		Inverted overprint	7,250.	3,400.

1900
O38	A65	1sh car rose & grn	625.00	260.00
a.		Inverted overprint		17,500.

For examples of Nos. O27-38 with margins clear of the design on all four sides, add a 25 percent premium to the value listed. For stamps with clear circular datestamps, apply a 100 percent premium. Add the two premiums together for covers with stamps having these attributes.

1902
O39	A66	1p carmine	32.50	14.00
O40	A68	2p green & car	160.00	40.00
O41	A66	6p dull violet	260.00	40.00
a.		Double overprint, one albino	7,500.	
O42	A72	9p ultra & violet	625.00	175.00
O43	A74	1sh car rose & grn	1,350.	300.00
		Nos. O39-O43 (5)	2,427.	569.00

Office of Works

Overprinted

1896
O44	A54	½p vermilion	300.00	135.00
		On cover		800.00
O45	A40	1p lilac	500.00	135.00
		On cover		950.00

For examples of Nos. O44-O45 with margins clear of the design on all four sides, add a 20 percent premium to the value listed. For stamps with clear circular datestamps, apply a 15 percent premium. Add the two premiums together for covers with stamps having these attributes.

1901-02
O46	A54	½p blue green	450.00	200.00
O47	A61	5p lilac & ultra	3,650.	1,250.
		On cover		
O48	A64	10p car rose & lil	6,250.	2,100.
		On cover		

1902
O49	A66	½p gray green	575.00	160.00
		On cover		1,900.
O50	A66	1p carmine	575.00	160.00
		On cover		425.00
O51	A68	2p green & car	2,000.	425.00
		On cover		3,250.
O52	A66	2½p ultramarine	3,400.	625.00
		On cover		4,250.
O53	A73	10p car rose & vio	40,000.	7,000.
		On cover		

Army
Overprinted

a   b

1896
O54	A54(a)	½p vermilion	6.25	2.75
		On cover		62.50
a.		"OFFICIAL"	290.00	125.00
b.		Lines of ovpt. transposed	4,500.	
O55	A40(a)	1p lilac	6.25	6.00
		On cover		100.00
a.		"OFFICIAI"	225.00	140.00
O56	A57(b)	2½p violet, *blue*	45.00	30.00
		On cover		725.00
		Nos. O54-O56 (3)	57.50	38.75

1900
O57	A54(a)	½p blue green	6.25	12.50
		On cover		125.00

For examples of Nos. O54-O57 with margins clear of the design on all four sides, add a 20 percent premium to the value listed. For stamps with clear circular datestamps, apply a 15 percent premium. Add the two premiums together for covers with stamps having these attributes.

1901
O58	A62(b)	6p violet, *rose*	100.00	52.50
		On cover		1,650.

1902
O59	A66(a)	½p gray green	6.00	2.40
		On cover		110.00

O60	A66(a)	1p carmine	6.00	2.40
		On cover		110.00
a.		"ARMY" omitted		
O61	A66(a)	6p dull violet	175.00	80.00
		On cover		
		Nos. O59-O61 (3)	187.00	84.80

Overprinted

1903

| O62 | A66 | 6p dull violet | 3,250. | 1,550. |

Royal Household

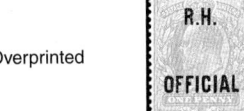

Overprinted

1902

O63	A66	½p gray green	400.00	220.00
		On cover		1,200.
O64	A66	1p carmine	350.00	190.00
		On cover		1,100.

Board of Education

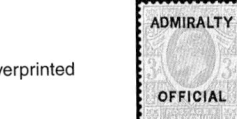

Overprinted

1902

| O65 | A61 | 5p lilac & ultra | 4,650. | 1,150. |
| O66 | A65 | 1sh car rose & grn | 10,500. | 5,750. |

1902-04

O67	A66	½p gray green	160.00	40.00
		On cover		400.00
O68	A66	1p carmine	160.00	40.00
		On cover		425.00
O69	A66	2½p ultramarine	5,000.	410.00
O70	A71	5p lilac & ultra ('04)	31,500.	10,000.
		On cover		—
O71	A74	1sh car rose & grn	180,000.	—

Admiralty

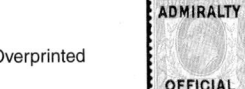

Overprinted

1903

O72	A66	½p gray green	28.00	13.50
		On cover		—
O73	A66	1p carmine	17.00	6.75
		On cover		325.00
O74	A67	1½p vio & green	310.00	145.00
		On cover		—
O75	A68	2p green & car	340.00	160.00
		On cover		—
O76	A66	2½p ultra	475.00	145.00
		On cover		—
O77	A69	3p violet, yel	425.00	160.00
		Nos. O72-O77 (6)	1,595.	630.25

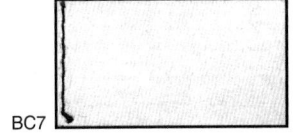

Overprinted

1903

O78	A66	½p gray green	57.50	22.50
		On cover		525.00
O79	A66	1p carmine	57.50	22.50
		On cover		145.00
O80	A67	1½p vio & green	1,150.	625.00
		On cover		—
O81	A68	2p green & car	2,750.	840.00
		On cover		—

O82	A66	2½p ultramarine	2,850.	890.00
		On cover		—
O83	A69	3p violet, yel	2,500.	375.00
		On cover		—

The two types of the "Admiralty Official" overprint differ principally in the shape of the letter "M."

ENVELOPES

Britannia Sending Letters to World (William Mulready, Designer) — E1

1840

| U1 | E1 | 1p black | 360.00 | *525.00* |
| U2 | E1 | 2p blue | 450.00 | *2,000.* |

LETTER SHEETS

| U3 | E1 | 1p black | 335.00 | *500.00* |
| U4 | E1 | 2p blue | 440.00 | *2,000.* |

BOOKLETS

Booklets are listed in denomination sequence by reign. Numbers in parenthesis following each listing reflect the number of cover varieties or edition numbers that apply to each cover style. Values shown for complete booklets are for examples containing most panes having full perforations on two edges of the pane only. Booklets containing most or all panes with very fine, full perforations on all sides are scarce and will sell for more. Also, in booklets where most of the value is contained in only one pane of several, it is assumed that this pane has full perforations on two sides only. If this pane is very fine, the booklet will be worth a considerable premium over the value given.

Sterling Currency

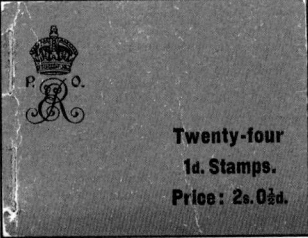

BC1

1904

| BK1 | BC1 | 2sh½p *red*, 4 #128e | 350.00 |

1906-11

| BK2 | BC1 | 2sh *red*, 2 #128e, 3 #143c, #143b | 950.00 |
| BK3 | BC1 | 2sh *red*, 3 #128e, 1 each #143b-143c (4) | 1,150. |

Cover inscription on Nos. BK2-BK3 revised to reflect changed contents.

1911

| BK4 | BC1 | 2sh *red*, 2#151a, 3 #152a | 750.00 |

BC2

1912-13

| BK5 | BC2 | 2sh *red*, 2 #151a, 3 #152a | 1,050. |
| BK6 | BC2 | 2sh *red*, 2 #155a, 3 #156a (4) | 1,000. |

Cover inscription on Nos. BK5-BK6 shows only Inland Postage Rates.

1913

| BK7 | BC2 | 2sh *red*, 2 #159b, 3 #160a (35) | 500.00 |
| BK8 | BC2 | 2sh *org*, 2 #159b,3 #160a (20) | 525.00 |

BC3

1917

| BK9 | BC3 | 2sh *org*, 2 #159b, 3 #160a (17) | 500.00 |

BC4

1924-34

| BK10 | BC4 | 2sh *blue*, #159b, 160a, 161d-161e (2) | 1,250. |
| BK11 | BC4 | 2sh *blue*, #187b, 188b, 189c-189d (277) | 475.00 |

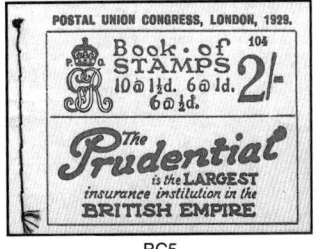

BC5

1929

| BK12 | BC5 | 2sh blue, *buff*, #205b-207b, 207c | 550.00 |

1935

| BK13 | BC4 | 2sh *blue*, #210b-211b, 212c-212d (58) | 550.00 |

BC6

1935

| BK14 | BC6 | 2sh blue, *buff*, #226a-227a, 3 #228a | 100.00 |

1918-19

| BK15 | BC4 | 3sh *org*, 2 each #159b, 160a, 161d (11) | 650.00 |
| BK16 | BC4 | 3sh *org*, #159b, 160a, 3 #161d (15) | 650.00 |

Cover used for Nos. BK15-BK16 does not have inscription above top line.

1921

| BK17 | BC4 | 3sh *blue*, 3 #162b (3) | 850.00 |
| BK18 | BC4 | 3sh *blue*, 3 #162c (3) | 900.00 |

1922

| BK19 | BC4 | 3sh *scar*, #159b, 160a, 3 #161d (33) | 850.00 |
| BK20 | BC4 | 3sh *blue*, 4 #161d (2) | 900.00 |

1924-34

| BK21 | BC4 | 3sh *scar*, #187b-188b, 3 #189c (237) | 375.00 |

1929

| BK22 | BC5 | 3sh blue, *buff*, #205b-206b, 3 #207b (5) | 450.00 |

1935

| BK23 | BC4 | 3sh *scar*, #210b-211b, 3 #212c (27) | 375.00 |
| BK24 | BC6 | 3sh red, *buff*, #226a-227a, 5 #228a (4) | 100.00 |

1920

| BK25 | BC4 | 3sh6p *org*, #160a, 3 #162b (6) | 850.00 |

Cover used for No. BK25 does not have inscription above top line.

1921

| BK26 | BC4 | 3sh6p *org red*, #159b, 160a, 161d, 2 #162b (7) | 900.00 |
| BK27 | BC4 | 3sh6p *org red*, #159b, 160a, 161d, 2 #162c (13) | 900.00 |

1931-35

BK28	BC4	5sh *grn*, #187b-188b, 189d, 5 #189c	4,000.
BK29	BC4	5sh *buff*, #187b-188b, 189d, 5 #189c (7)	1,250.
BK30	BC4	5sh *buff*, #210b-211b, 212d, 5 #212c (7)	450.00

BC7

1936

| BK31 | BC7 | 6p *buff*, 2 #232c | 70.00 |

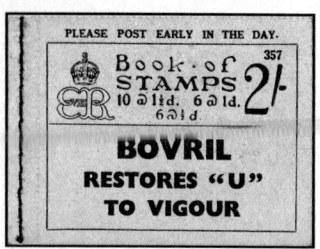

BC8

BK32 BC8	2sh *blue*, #230a-231a, #232a-232b (31)	140.00
BK33 BC8	3sh *scar*, #230a-231a, 3 #232a (12)	110.00
BK34 BC8	5sh *buff*, #230a-231a, 6 #232a (2)	250.00

1938-40

BK35 BC7	6p *buff*, 2 #237d	70.00
BK36 BC7	6p *pink*, #235d-237d	325.00
BK37 BC7	6p *pale grn*, #235c-236c	150.00

No. BK37 is 53x41mm.

1947-51

BK38 BC7	1sh *buff*, 2 each #258b-259b, 260a	27.50
BK39 BC7	1sh *buff*, 2 each #280a, 281b-282b	27.50
BK40 BC7	1sh *buff*, #258e, 259d, 260b	6,000.
BK41 BC7	1sh *buff*, #280b-282b	32.50

Nos. BK40-BK41 are 53x41mm.

Round GPO Emblem — BC9

1952-53

| BK42 BC9 | 1sh *buff*, #280b, 281c-282c | 22.50 |
| *a.* | Inland postage rate corrected in ink on inside booklet cover | 25.00 |

Oval GPO Emblem — BC10

1954

| BK43 BC10 | 1sh *buff*, #280b, 281c-282c | 32.50 |

1937

| BK44 BC8 | 2sh *blue*, #235b-236b, #237b-237c (26) | 450.00 |

BC11

1938

| BK45 BC11 | 2sh *blue*, #235b-236b, #237b-237c (95) | 450.00 |

1940-42   2sh6p Booklets

| BK46 BC11 | *scar*, #235b, #238b-239b (7) | 1,050. |
| BK47 BC11 | *blue*, #235b, #238b-239b (6) | 1,050. |

Denomination part of cover of Nos. BK46-BK47 is printed in white on black background.

| BK48 BC11 | *grn*, #235b, #238b-239b (80) | 550.00 |
| BK49 BC11 | *grn*, #258a, #261b-262b (120) | 550.00 |

BC12

1943

| BK50 BC12 | *grn*, #258a, #261b-262b (90) | 65.00 |

With booklets issued in August and September 1943, commercial advertising on British booklets was discontinued. Covers and interleaving were used for Post Office slogans. Booklets were no longer numbered, but carried the month and year of issue.

1951-52

| BK51 BC12 | *grn*, #280c, #283b-284b (10) | 42.50 |
| BK52 BC12 | *grn*, #280c, 281e, #282d, 284b (15) | 40.00 |

1937-38   3sh Booklets

| BK53 BC8 | *scar*, #235a-236a, 3 #237b (10) | 850.00 |
| BK54 BC11 | *scar*, #235a-236a, 3 #237b (34) | 850.00 |

1937-43   5sh Booklets

BK55 BC8	*buff*, #235b-236b, 237c, 5 #237b (3)	1,000.
BK56 BC11	*buff*, #235b-236b, 237c, 5 #237b (9)	950.00
BK57 BC11	*buff*, #235b, 238b, 3 #239b (16)	975.00
BK58 BC11	*buff*, #258a, 261b, 3 #262b (20)	950.00

1943-53

| BK59 BC12 | *tan*, #258a, 261b, 3 #262b (49) | 110.00 |
| BK60 BC12 | *tan*, #258a, 261b, 3 #262b (20) | 1,250. |

Cover on No. BK60 has thick horizontal lines separating the GPO emblem and the various inscriptions.

BK61 BC12	*tan*, #280a, 283b, 3 #284b (5)	62.50
BK62 BC12	*tan*, #280c, 281e, 282d, 3 #284b (5)	62.50
BK63 BC12	*tan*, #280c, 281d-282d, 283b, 2 #284b (2)	62.50

BC13

1953-54   2sh6p Booklets

BK64 BC12	*grn*, #280c, 281e, 294c, #296a (6)	29.00
BK65 BC13	*grn*, #280c, 281e, 294c, 296a (7)	32.50
BK66 BC13	*grn*, #281e, 292c, 294c, 296a	500.00

5sh Booklets

BK67 BC12	*brn*, #280c, 281d, 283b, 294c, 2 #296a (3)	40.00
BK68 BC13	*brn*, #280c, 281d, 283b, 294c, 2 #296a (2)	45.00
BK69 BC13	*brn*, #281d, 283b, 292c, 294c, 2 #296a	300.00
BK70 BC13	*brn*, #283b, 292c-294c, 2 #296a	160.00

GUERNSEY OCCUPATION STAMPS

Issued Under German Occupation

> Bisects of Great Britain Nos. 238 and 255 were used in Guernsey from 12/27/40 to 2./24/41. Values, on cover or postcard: No. 238, $45; No. 255, $40.

OS1

Rouletted 14x7

1941-44	Typo.		Unwmk.
N1 OS1	½p light green	3.50	3.50
	Never hinged	6.00	
a.	½p dull green	2.50	2.00
	Never hinged	4.00	
b.	½p pale yellow green	2.50	3.00
	Never hinged	4.00	
c.	½p emerald green	3.50	2.00
	Never hinged	6.00	
d.	½p bluish green	20.00	13.00
	Never hinged	32.00	
e.	½p bright green	13.00	10.00
	Never hinged	22.00	
f.	½p olive green	27.50	25.00
	Never hinged	45.00	
g.	Imperf, pair	140.00	
	Never hinged	225.00	
h.	Horiz. pair, imperf between	450.00	
	Never hinged	750.00	
i.	Vert. pair, imperf between	525.00	
	Never hinged	875.00	
N2 OS1	1p red	3.00	2.00
	Never hinged	3.50	
a.	Printed double	65.00	
	Never hinged	110.00	
b.	1p pale vermilion	3.00	*2.00*
	Never hinged	5.00	
c.	1p carmine red	2.10	*2.00*
	Never hinged	3.50	
d.	Imperf, pair	125.00	90.00
	Never hinged	175.00	
e.	Horiz. pair, imperf between	550.00	
	Never hinged	800.00	
f.	Vert. pair, imperf between	750.00	
	Never hinged	950.00	
N3 OS1	2½p ultramarine	8.00	12.00
	Never hinged	13.00	
a.	2½p pale ultramarine	6.00	*7.00*
	Never hinged	10.00	
	Nos. N1-N3 (3)	14.50	17.50

Issued: No. N1b, 4/7/41; No. N1c, 6/41; No. N1d, 11/41; No. N1e, 2/42; No. N1a, 9/42; No. N1f, 2/43; No. N1, from 7/43; No. N2, 2/18/41; No. N2a, 7/43; No. N2b, 1943; No. N3, 4/12/44; No. N3a, 7/44.

Additional shades and papers exist. The rouletting is very crude and may not be measurable. This is not a defect.

Bluish French Bank Note Paper

Wmk. 396 Chain Link Fence

			Rouletted 14x7
N4 OS1	½p green	27.50	27.50
	Never hinged	30.00	
N5 OS1	1p red	14.50	*21.00*
	Never hinged	16.00	

Issue dates: ½p, Mar. 11; 1p, Apr. 9. Nos. N1-N5 remained valid until 4/13/46.

JERSEY OCCUPATION STAMPS

Issued Under German Occupation

OS1

1941-42   Typo.   Unwmk.   *Perf. 11*

N1 OS1	½p bright green	5.00	6.00
	Never hinged	8.00	
a.	Imperf, pair	500.00	
	Never hinged	650.00	
b.	Vert. pair, imperf between	450.00	
	Never hinged	750.00	
c.	Horiz. pair, imperf between	600.00	
	Never hinged	800.00	
d.	On grayish paper	7.25	12.00
	Never hinged	12.00	
N2 OS1	1p vermilion	5.00	5.00
	Never hinged	8.00	
a.	Imperf, pair	240.00	
	Never hinged	325.00	
b.	Vert. pair, imperf between	765.00	
	Never hinged	850.00	
c.	Horiz. pair, imperf between	675.00	
	Never hinged	750.00	
d.	On chalk-surfaced paper	32.50	50.00
	Never hinged	55.00	
e.	On grayish paper	8.50	*14.00*
	Never hinged	14.00	

Issue dates: No. N1, 1/29/42; No. N1d, 1/43; No. N2, 4/1/41; No. N2e, 1/43.

Jersey Views — OS2

Designs: ½p, Old Jersey farm; 1p, Portelet Bay; 1½p, Corbiere Lighthouse; 2p, Elizabeth Castle; 2½, Mont Orgueil Castle; 3p, Gathering seaweed.

1943-44   Perf. 13½

N3 OS2	½p dark green	7.25	12.00
	Never hinged	12.00	
a.	On rough, gray paper	9.00	14.00
	Never hinged	15.00	
N4 OS2	1p scarlet	1.75	.80
	Never hinged	3.00	
a.	On newsprint	2.10	1.50
	Never hinged	3.50	
N5 OS2	1½p brown	7.25	5.75
	Never hinged	8.00	
N6 OS2	2p orange	6.75	2.00
	Never hinged	7.50	
N7 OS2	2½p blue	2.00	1.40
	Never hinged	3.00	
a.	On newsprint	.90	1.75
	Never hinged	1.25	
b.	On pelure paper	160.00	
	Never hinged	275.00	
N8 OS2	3p red violet	2.00	2.75
	Never hinged	3.00	
	Nos. N3-N8 (6)	27.00	24.70

Issued: ½p, 1p, 6/1/43; 1½p, 2p, 6/8/43; 2½p, 3p, 6/29/43; No. N4a, 2/28/44; No. N7a, 2/25/44.

Nos. N1-N8 remained valid until 4/13/46.

GREAT BRITAIN OFFICES ABROAD

OFFICES IN AFRICA

Catalogue values for unused stamps in this section are for Never Hinged items, except for Nos. 1a-5c, which are for hinged stamps with original gum, except as noted.

MIDDLE EAST FORCES

For use in Ethiopia, Cyrenaica, Eritrea, the Dodecanese and Somalia

Stamps of Great Britain, 1937-42 Overprinted in Black or Blue Black

London Printing — ovpt. 14mm long, square dots

1942-43		**Wmk. 251**	**Perf. 14½x14**	
1	A101	1p scarlet	2.00	3.00
2	A101	2p orange	1.50	4.50
3	A101	2½p bright ultra	1.10	1.40
4	A101	3p dark purple	.90	.35
a.		Double overprint		4,750.
5	A102	5p lt brn (Blk)	.80	.35
a.		Blue black overprint ('43)	4.25	.25
6	A102	6p rose lilac ('43)	.45	.25
7	A103	9p dp olive grn ('43)	1.00	.25
8	A103	1sh brown ('43)	.55	.25
		Wmk. 259		
		Perf. 14		
9	A104	2sh6p yel green ('43)	8.00	1.10
		Nos. 1-9 (9)	16.30	11.45

Cairo Printing — ovpt. 13.5mm long, square dots

1a	A101	1p scarlet	40.00	17.50
		Never hinged	62.50	
2a	A101	2p orange	65.00	120.00
		Never hinged	85.00	
3a	A101	2½p bright ultramarine	45.00	8.50
		Never hinged	65.00	
4b	A101	3p dark purple	105.00	45.00
		Never hinged	140.00	
5b	A102	5p light brown	350.00	100.00
		Never hinged	450.00	

Cairo Printing — ovpt. 13.5mm long, round dots

1b	A101	1p scarlet	32.50	12.00
		Never hinged	50.00	
2b	A101	2p orange	45.00	110.00
		Never hinged	75.00	
3b	A101	2½p bright ultramarine	37.50	8.50
		Never hinged	60.00	
4c	A101	3p dark purple	85.00	45.00
		Never hinged	130.00	
5c	A102	5p light brown	250.00	95.00
		Never hinged	440.00	

Vertical pairs, square and round dots

1c	A101	1p #1a + #1b	150.00	160.00
		Never hinged	225.00	
2c	A101	2p #2a + #2b	300.00	700.00
		Never hinged	450.00	
3c	A101	2½p #3a + 3b	200.00	80.00
		Never hinged	325.00	
4d	A101	3p #4b + #4c	400.00	350.00
		Never hinged	650.00	
5d	A101	5p #5b + #5c	1,200.	975.00
		Never hinged	1,825.	

The Cairo printing was made on panes of 60 (6x10), with rows 2, 3 and 7 overprinted with square dots, and the other seven rows printed with rounds dots.

Same Overprint in Blue Black on Nos. 259, 261, 262 and 263

1943, Jan. 1			**Wmk. 251**	
10	A101	1p vermilion	1.75	.25
11	A101	2p light orange	1.75	1.40
12	A101	2½p ultramarine	.55	.25
13	A101	3p violet	1.75	.25
		Nos. 10-13 (4)	5.80	2.15

There were two printings of Nos. 1-5, both issued Mar. 2, 1942, and both black. Nos. 5a and 6-13 compose a third printing, also made in London. On these stamps, issued Jan. 1, 1943, the overprint is 13½mm wide. The 2sh6p overprint is black, the others blue black.

Same Ovpt. in Black on #250, 251A

1947		**Wmk. 259**	**Perf. 14**	
14	A104	5sh dull red	15.00	20.00
15	A105	10sh ultramarine	17.50	11.50

In 1950 Nos. 1-15 were declared valid for use in Great Britain. Used values are for

---

stamps postmarked in territory of issue. Others sell for about 25 percent less.

POSTAGE DUE STAMPS

Catalogue values for unused stamps in this section are for Never Hinged items.

Postage Due Stamps of Great Britain Overprinted in Blue

1942		**Wmk. 251**	**Perf. 14x14½**	
J1	D1	½p emerald	.35	14.00
J2	D1	1p carmine rose	.35	2.00
J3	D1	2p black brown	1.40	1.40
J4	D1	3p violet	.55	4.75
J5	D1	1sh blue	4.25	14.00
		Nos. J1-J5 (5)	6.90	36.15

No. J1-J5 were used in Eritrea.

FOR USE IN ERITREA

Catalogue values for unused stamps in this section are for Never Hinged items.

100 Cents = 1 Shilling

Stamps of Great Britain 1937-42 Surcharged — a

		Perf. 14½x14		
1948, June -49			**Wmk. 251**	
1	A101	5c on ½p green (II)	1.60	.75
		On commercial cover		75.00
2	A101	10c on 1p vermilion (II)	1.60	2.75
		On commercial cover		75.00
3	A101	20c on 2p light org (II)	1.10	2.50
		On commercial cover		75.00
4	A101	25c on 2½p ultra (II)	1.35	.70
		On commercial cover		75.00
5	A101	30c on 3p violet (II)	1.60	5.00
		On commercial cover		75.00
6	A101	40c on 5p light brown	1.10	4.75
		On commercial cover		75.00
7	A101	50c on 6p rose lilac	.70	1.10
		On commercial cover		150.00
8	A103	75c on 9p deep ol grn	1.35	.85
		On commercial cover		75.00
9	A103	1sh on 1sh brown	1.35	.55
		On commercial cover		375.00

Great Britain Nos. 249A, 250 and 251A Surcharged

		Wmk. 259		
		Perf. 14		
10	A104	2sh50c on 2sh6p yel grn	9.25	11.50
		On commercial cover		950.00
11	A104	5sh on 5sh dl red	9.25	18.00
		On commercial cover		7,500.
12	A105	10sh on 10sh ultra	25.00	26.00
		On commercial cover		16,500.

Great Britain No. 245 Surcharged Type "a"

		Wmk. 251		
		Perf. 14½x14		
13	A103	65c on 8p brt rose ('49)	8.00	2.25
		Nos. 1-13 (13)	63.25	75.70

"B. M. A." stands for British Military Administration.

Stamps of Great Britain 1937-42 Surcharged — c

1950, Feb. 6				
14	A101	5c on ½p green (II)	1.60	9.25
		On commercial cover		150.00
15	A101	10c on 1p ver (II)	.45	3.50
		On commercial cover		75.00
16	A101	20c on 2p lt orange (II)	.55	.90
		On commercial cover		62.50
17	A101	25c on 2½p ultra (II)	.55	.70
		On commercial cover		325.00
18	A101	30c on 3p violet (II)	.45	2.50
		On commercial cover		75.00
19	A102	40c on 5p light brown	.80	2.00
		On commercial cover		225.00
20	A102	50c on 6p rose lilac	.45	.25
		On commercial cover		75.00
21	A103	65c on 8p bright rose	3.25	1.75
		On commercial cover		75.00
22	A103	75c on 9p dp ol grn	.65	.30
		On commercial cover		125.00
23	A103	1sh on 1sh brown	.45	.25
		On commercial cover		75.00

Great Britain Nos. 249A, 250, 251A Surcharged

		Wmk. 259	**Perf. 14**	
24	A104	2sh50c on 2sh6p yel grn	8.00	5.50
		On commercial cover		1,100.
		On parcel post receipt		1,100.
		On telegram form		600.00
25	A104	5sh on 5sh dl red	8.00	14.00
		On commercial cover		4,500.
		On parcel post receipt		2,250.
		On telegram form		750.00
26	A105	10sh on 10sh ultra	70.00	62.50
		On commercial cover		7,500.
		On parcel post receipt		15,000.
		On telegram form		85,000.
		Nos. 14-26 (13)	95.20	103.40

Great Britain Nos. 280, 281, 283 and 284 Surcharged Type "c"

		Perf. 14½x14		
1951, May 3			**Wmk. 251**	
27	A101	5c on ½p lt orange	.55	.95
28	A101	10c on 1p ultra	.55	.85
29	A101	20c on 2p lt red brown	.55	.35
30	A101	25c on 2½p vermilion	.55	.35

Great Britain Nos. 286-288 Surcharged

		Perf. 11x12		
1951, May 31			**Wmk. 259**	
31	A121	2sh50c on 2sh6p grn	11.50	26.00
32	A121	5sh on 5sh dl red	24.00	26.00
33	A122	10sh on 10sh ultra	25.00	26.00
		Nos. 27-33 (7)	62.70	80.50

Surcharge arranged to fit the design on No. 33.

POSTAGE DUE STAMPS

Catalogue values for unused stamps in this section are for Never Hinged items.

Great Britain Nos. J26-J29, J32 Surcharged

1948		**Wmk. 251**	**Perf. 14x14½**	
J1	D1	5c on ½p emer	11.00	25.00
J2	D1	10c on 1p car rose	11.00	27.50
J3	D1	20c on 2p blk brn	12.00	18.00
J4	D1	30c on 3p violet	11.00	18.00
J5	D1	1sh on 1sh blue	20.00	35.00
		Nos. J1-J5 (5)	65.00	123.50

Great Britain Nos. J26 to J29 and J32 Surcharged

1950, Feb. 6				
J6	D1	5c on ½p emer	13.00	55.00
J7	D1	10c on 1p car rose	13.00	18.50
a.		"C" of CENTS omitted		2,750.
		Lightly hinged		1,850.
J8	D1	20c on 2p blk brn	13.00	20.00
J9	D1	30c on 3p violet	17.50	28.00
J10	D1	1sh on 1sh blue	17.50	28.00
a.		Period after "A" omitted		450.00
		Lightly hinged		300.00
		Nos. J6-J10 (5)	74.00	149.50

EAST AFRICAN FORCES

FOR USE IN SOMALIA (ITALIAN SOMALILAND)

Catalogue values for unused stamps in this section are for Never Hinged items.

12 Pence = 1 Shilling
100 Cents = 1 Shilling

Stamps of Great Britain 1938-42 Overprinted in Blue

		Perf. 14½x14		
1943, Jan. 15			**Wmk. 251**	
1	A101	1p vermilion	.80	.65
2	A101	2p light orange	1.75	1.40
3	A101	2½p ultramarine	.80	3.75
4	A101	3p violet	1.10	.25
5	A101	5p light brown	1.90	.45
6	A101	6p rose lilac	1.10	1.40
7	A103	9p dp olive green	1.60	2.40
8	A103	1sh brown	3.00	.25

On Great Britain No. 249A

1946		**Wmk. 259**	**Perf. 14**	
9	A104	2sh6p yellow green	16.00	8.00
		Nos. 1-9 (9)	28.05	18.55

Stamps of Great Britain, 1937-42 Surcharged

		Perf. 14½x14		
1948, May 27			**Wmk. 251**	
10	A101	5c on ½p grn (II)	1.40	2.10
11	A101	15c on 1½p lt red brn (II)	2.00	17.50
12	A101	20c on 2p lt org (II)	3.50	5.00
13	A101	25c on 2½p ultra (II)	2.50	5.00
14	A101	30c on 3p vio (II)	2.50	10.50
15	A102	40c on 5p lt brown	1.40	.25
16	A102	50c on 6p rose lilac	.55	2.25
17	A103	75c on 9p dp ol grn	2.25	21.00
18	A103	1sh on 1sh brown	1.40	.25

Great Britain Nos. 249A and 250 Surcharged

	Wmk. 259		**Perf. 14**
19	A104 2sh50c on 2sh6p yel grn	5.00	29.00
20	A104 5sh on 5sh dl red	11.00	45.00
	Nos. 10-20 (11)	33.50	137.85

Stamps of Great Britain 1937-42 Surcharged

Perf. 14½x14

		1950, Jan. 2	**Wmk. 251**	
21	A101	5c on ½p grn (II)	.25	3.50
22	A101	15c on 1½p lt red brn (II)	.85	19.00
23	A101	20c on 2p lt org (II)	.85	8.50
24	A101	25c on 2½p ultra (II)	.55	8.50
25	A101	30c on 3p violet (II)	1.40	5.00
26	A102	40c on 5p light brn	.65	1.10
27	A102	50c on 6p rose lilac	.55	1.10
28	A103	75c on 9p deep ol grn	2.25	8.00
29	A103	1sh on 1sh brown	.70	1.75

Great Britain Nos. 249A and 250 Surcharged

		Wmk. 259	**Perf. 14**	
30	A104	2sh50c on 2sh 6p yel grn	4.50	27.50
31	A104	5sh on 5sh dull red	12.50	35.00
		Nos. 21-31 (11)	25.05	118.95

FOR USE IN TRIPOLITANIA

Catalogue values for unused stamps in this section are for Never Hinged items.

Stamps of Great Britain, 1937-42, Surcharged

M.A.L. = Military Authority Lire

Perf. 14½x14

		1948, July 1	**Wmk. 251**	
1	A101	1 l on ½p green (II)	1.00	1.75
2	A101	2 l on 1p ver (II)	.35	.25
3	A101	3 l on 1½p lt red brn (II)	.35	.55
4	A101	4 l on 2p lt org (II)	.35	.80
5	A101	5 l on 2½p ultra (II)	.35	.25
6	A101	6 l on 3p violet (II)	.35	.45
7	A102	10 l on 5p lt brown	.35	.25
8	A102	12 l on 6p rose lilac	.35	.25
9	A103	18 l on 9p dp ol grn	.90	.75
10	A103	24 l on 1sh brown	.80	1.75

Great Britain Nos. 249A, 250 and 251A Surcharged

		Wmk. 259	**Perf. 14**	
11	A104	60 l on 2sh6p yel grn	4.00	9.75
12	A104	120 l on 5sh dl red	17.50	21.00
13	A105	240 l on 10sh ultra	25.00	110.00
		Nos. 1-13 (13)	51.65	147.80

Stamps of Great Britain 1937-42 Surcharged

Perf. 14½x14

		1950, Feb. 6	**Wmk. 251**	
14	A101	1 l on ½p green (II)	3.00	14.00
15	A101	2 l on 1p ver (II)	2.75	.45
16	A101	3 l on 1½p lt red brn (II)	1.10	14.00
17	A101	4 l on 2p lt org (II)	1.10	5.00
18	A101	5 l on 2½p ultra (II)	.80	.80
19	A101	6 l on 3p violet (II)	2.00	3.75
20	A102	10 l on 5p lt brown	.55	4.50
21	A102	12 l on 6p rose lilac	2.25	.55
22	A103	18 l on 9p dp ol grn	2.50	2.75
23	A103	24 l on 1sh brown	2.75	4.25

Great Britain Nos. 249A, 250 and 251A Surcharged

		Wmk. 259	**Perf. 14**	
24	A104	60 l on 2sh6p yel grn	7.50	14.00
25	A104	120 l on 5sh dl red	22.50	25.00
26	A105	240 l on 10sh ultra	42.50	57.50
		Nos. 14-26 (13)	91.30	146.55

Great Britain Nos. 280-284 Surcharged like Nos. 14-23

Perf. 14½x14

		1951, May 3	**Wmk. 251**	
27	A101	1 l on ½p lt org	.25	7.00
28	A101	2 l on 1p ultra	.25	1.10
29	A101	3 l on 1½p green	.35	9.25
30	A101	4 l on 2p lt red brown	.25	1.40
31	A101	5 l on 2½p ver	.30	8.50

Great Britain Nos. 286-288 Surcharged

		1951, May 3	**Wmk. 259**	**Perf. 11x12**	
32	A121	60 l on 2sh6p grn		6.25	25.00
33	A121	120 l on 5sh dl red		10.00	30.00
34	A122	240 l on 10sh ultra		42.50	57.50
		Nos. 27-34 (8)		60.15	139.75

Surcharge arranged to fit the design on No. 34.

POSTAGE DUE STAMPS

Catalogue values for unused stamps in this section are for Never Hinged items.

Great Britain Nos. J26-J29, J32 Surcharged

		1948	**Wmk. 251**	**Perf. 14x14½**	
J1	D1	1 l on ½p emer		6.25	57.50
J2	D1	2 l on 1p car rose		2.75	30.00
J3	D1	4 l on 2p blk brn		8.50	37.50
J4	D1	6 l on 3p violet		8.50	24.00
J5	D1	24 l on 1sh blue		32.50	110.00
		Nos. J1-J5 (5)		58.50	259.00

Great Britain Nos. J26-J29, J32 Surcharged

		1950, Feb. 6		
J6	D1	1 l on ½p emer	14.00	92.50
J7	D1	2 l on 1p car rose	3.00	30.00
J8	D1	4 l on 2p blk brn	4.50	40.00
J9	D1	6 l on 3p violet	21.00	70.00
J10	D1	24 l on 1sh blue	55.00	160.00
		Nos. J6-J10 (5)	97.50	392.50

CHINA

100 Cents = 1 Dollar

Stamps of Hong Kong, 1912-14, Overprinted

		1917	**Wmk. 3**	**Perf. 14**	
		Ordinary Paper			
1	A11	1c brown		4.50	3.00
2	A11	2c deep green		8.00	.35
3	A12	4c scarlet		6.25	.35
4	A13	6c orange		6.25	.70
5	A12	8c gray		14.00	1.40
6	A11	10c ultramarine		14.00	.35
		Chalky Paper			
7	A14	12c violet, *yel*		12.50	5.00
8	A14	20c olive grn & vio		14.00	.70
9	A15	25c red vio & dl vio (on #117)		9.25	17.50
10	A13	30c orange & violet		40.00	6.25
11	A14	50c black, *emerald*		40.00	6.50
a.		50c blk, *blue green*, ol back		75.00	1.75
b.		50c blk, *emerald*, ol back		50.00	9.75
12	A11	$1 blue & vio, *bl*		80.00	2.90
13	A14	$2 black & red		260.00	62.50
14	A13	$3 violet & grn		625.00	210.00
15	A14	$5 red & grn, *bl grn*, ol back		400.00	290.00
16	A13	$10 blk & vio, *red*		1,000.	550.00
		Nos. 1-16 (16)		2,533.	1,157.

Stamps of Hong Kong, 1921-26, Overprinted

		1922-27	**Wmk. 4**	
		Ordinary Paper		
17	A11	1c brown	2.60	4.25
18	A11	2c green	4.00	2.60
19	A12	4c scarlet	7.00	2.60
20	A13	6c orange	5.00	4.75
21	A12	8c gray	9.25	17.50
22	A11	10c ultramarine	10.00	4.00
		Chalky Paper		
23	A14	20c ol grn & vio	16.00	5.75
24	A15	25c red violet & dull vio	26.00	80.00
25	A14	50c blk, *emerald* ('27)	70.00	210.00
26	A11	$1 ultra & vio, *bl*	85.00	70.00
27	A14	$2 black & red	225.00	290.00
		Nos. 17-27 (11)	459.85	691.45

MOROCCO

100 Centimos = 1 Peseta
12 Pence = 1 Shilling
20 Shillings = 1 Pound
100 Centimes = 1 Franc

These stamps were issued for various purposes:
a — For general use at the British Post Offices throughout Morocco.
b — For use in the Spanish Zone of Northern Morocco.
c — For use in the French Zone of Southern Morocco.
d — For use in the International Zone of Tangier.
For convenience these stamps are listed in four groups according to the coinage expressed or surcharged on the stamps, namely:
1 — Value expressed in Spanish currency.
2 — Value in British currency.
3 — Value in French currency.
4 — Stamps overprinted "Tangier."

Spanish Currency

Gibraltar Stamps of 1889-95 Overprinted

		1898	**Wmk. 2**	**Perf. 14**	
		Black Overprint			
1	A11	5c green		3.00	3.00
		On cover			25.00
2	A11	10c carmine rose		5.00	.85
		On cover			50.00
b.		Double overprint		625.00	
3	A11	20c olive green		11.00	6.25
		On cover			400.00
4	A11	25c ultramarine		4.50	.70
		On cover			300.00
5	A11	40c orange brown		7.00	3.75
		On cover			500.00
6	A11	50c violet		20.00	26.00
		On cover			500.00
7	A11	1pe bister & blue		20.00	30.00
		On cover			300.00
8	A11	2pe blk & car rose		25.00	30.00
		On cover			300.00
		Nos. 1-8 (8)		95.50	100.55

Covers: Values for Nos. 1-6 are for covers bearing stamps paying thr correct rates. Values for Nos. 7-8 are for overfranked covers, usually philatelic.

		Dark Blue Overprint		
9	A11	40c orange brown	50.00	35.00
		On cover		500.00
10	A11	50c violet	14.00	14.00
		On cover		500.00
11	A11	1pe bister & blue	175.00	210.00
		On cover		

		Inverted "V" for "A"		
1a	A11	5c	40.00	50.00
2a	A11	10c	260.00	310.00
3a	A11	20c	85.00	95.00
4a	A11	25c	140.00	150.00
5a	A11	40c	190.00	210.00
6a	A11	50c	290.00	375.00
7a	A11	1pe	275.00	400.00
8a	A11	2pe	350.00	400.00

Overprinted in Black

(Narrower "M," ear of "g" horiz.)

		1899		
12	A11	5c green	.55	1.10
		On cover		15.00
13	A11	10c carmine rose	2.90	.35
		On cover		25.00
14	A11	20c olive green	8.00	.80
		On cover		150.00
15	A11	25c ultramarine	12.50	1.00
		On cover		100.00
16	A11	40c orange brown	47.50	35.00
		On cover		350.00
17	A11	50c violet	11.00	4.00
		On cover		350.00
18	A11	1pe bister & blue	32.50	50.00
		On cover		250.00
19	A11	2pe blk & car rose	62.50	55.00
		On cover		300.00
		Nos. 12-19 (8)	177.45	147.25

Covers: Values for Nos. 18-19 are for overfranked covers, usually philatelic.

		"M" with long serif		
12a	A11	5c	10.00	15.00
13a	A11	10c	11.50	13.50
14a	A11	20c	40.00	42.50
15a	A11	25c	50.00	55.00
16a	A11	40c	260.00	290.00
17a	A11	50c	125.00	140.00
18a	A11	1pe	175.00	290.00
19a	A11	2pe	375.00	400.00

Type of Gibraltar, 1903, with Value in Spanish Currency, Overprinted

		1903-05		
20	A12	5c gray grn & bl grn	11.00	4.00
21	A12	10c violet, *red*	9.75	.45
22	A12	20c gray grn & car rose ('04)	20.00	52.50
23	A12	25c vio & blk, *bl*	9.25	.35
24	A12	50c violet	100.00	190.00
25	A12	1pe blk & car rose	47.50	175.00
26	A12	2pe black & ultra	57.50	140.00
		Nos. 20-26 (7)	255.00	562.30

		"M" with long serif		
20a	A12	5c	57.50	62.50
21a	A12	10c	50.00	45.00
22a	A12	20c	110.00	210.00
23a	A12	25c	57.50	50.00
24a	A12	50c	400.00	700.00
25a	A12	1pe	260.00	575.00
26a	A12	2pe	300.00	550.00

1905-06　Wmk. 3　Chalky Paper

27	A12	5c gray grn & bl grn	11.00	3.50
28	A12	10c violet, *red*	12.50	2.25
29	A12	20c gray grn & car rose ('06)	6.25	35.00
30	A12	25c violet & blk, *bl* ('06)	45.00	9.75
31	A12	50c violet	8.50	50.00
32	A12	1pe blk & car rose	32.50	92.50
33	A12	2pe black & ultra	18.00	40.00
		Nos. 27-33 (7)	133.75	233.00

No. 29 is on ordinary paper. Nos. 27 and 28 are on both ordinary and chalky paper.

"M" with long serif

27a	A12	5c	62.50	50.00
28a	A12	10c	62.50	42.50
29a	A12	20c	57.50	175.00
30a	A12	25c	350.00	175.00
31a	A12	50c	175.00	290.00
32a	A12	1pe	225.00	375.00
33a	A12	2pe	210.00	290.00

Numerous other minor overprint varieties exist of Nos. 1-33.

British Stamps of 1902-10 Surcharged in Spanish Currency

a　　　　　b

1907-10　Wmk. 30

34(a)	A66	5c on ½p pale grn	9.25	.25
35(a)	A66	10c on 1p car	13.50	.25
36(a)	A67	15c on 1½p vio & grn	3.50	.25
a.		"1" of "15" omitted	5,400.	
37(a)	A68	20c on 2p grn & car	3.00	.25
38(a)	A66	25c on 2½p ultra	2.00	.25
39(a)	A70	40c on 4p brn & grn	1.40	3.50
40(a)	A70	40c on 4p org ('10)	1.10	.70
41(a)	A71	50c on 5p lil & ultra	2.25	3.75
42(a)	A73	1pe on 10p car rose & vio	25.00	14.00

Wmk. 31

43(b)	A75	3pe on 2sh6p vio	24.00	29.00
44(b)	A76	6pe on 5sh car rose	40.00	52.50
45(b)	A77	12pe on 10sh ultra	85.00	85.00
		Nos. 34-45 (12)	210.00	189.70

Nos. 36-37, 39-43 are on chalky paper.

Great Britain Nos. 153, 154 and 148 Surcharged

1912　Wmk. 30　Perf. 15x14

46(a)	A80	5c on ½p yel grn	3.50	.25
47(a)	A81	10c on 1p scarlet	1.10	.25
48(a)	A66	25c on 2½p ultra	42.50	30.00
		Nos. 46-48 (3)	47.10	30.50

British Stamps of 1912-18 Surcharged in Black or Carmine

c　　　　　d

e

1914-18　Wmk. 33

49	A82(a)	5c on ½p grn	.85	.25
50	A83(d)	10c on 1p scar	1.75	.25
51	A84(c)	15c on 1½p red brn('15)	1.10	.25
52	A85(d)	20c on 2p org (I)	1.10	.25
53	A86(d)	25c on 2½p ultra	2.00	.25
54	A90(d)	1pe on 10p lt bl	4.00	8.00

Wmk. 34

Perf. 11x12

55	A91(e)	3pe on 2sh6p lt brn	35.00	160.00
a.		3pe on 2sh6p dark brown	45.00	125.00
56	A91(e)	6pe on 5sh scar	32.50	55.00
a.		6pe on 5sh light carmine	150.00	210.00
57	A91(e)	12pe on 10sh dk bl(C)	110.00	190.00
a.		12pe on 10sh blue	100.00	190.00
		Nos. 49-57 (9)	188.30	414.25

Great Britain Nos. 159, 165 Surcharged in Spanish Currency

f　　　　　g

1917-23　Wmk. 33　Perf. 15x14

58	A82(f)	3c on ½p green	1.40	5.00
59	A88(g)	40c on 4p sl green	3.50	4.50

Great Britain Nos. 189, 191, 179 Surcharged in Spanish Currency

1926　Wmk. 35

60	A84(c)	15c on 1½p red brn	8.50	26.00
61	A86(d)	25c on 2½p ultra	2.90	2.90

Wmk. 34

Perf. 11x12

62	A91(e)	3pe on 2sh6p brn	26.00	85.00
		Nos. 60-62 (3)	37.40	113.90

British Stamps of 1924 Surcharged in Spanish Currency

1929-31　Wmk. 35　Perf. 15x14

63	A82(a)	5c on ½p grn('31)	3.00	17.50
64	A83(d)	10c on 1p scar	21.00	30.00
65	A85(d)	20c on 2p org (II) ('31)	3.50	10.00
66	A88(g)	40c on 4p sl grn ('30)	2.90	2.90
		Nos. 63-66 (4)	30.40	60.40

Silver Jubilee Issue

Great Britain Nos. 226-229 Srchd. in Blue or Red

1935, May 8　Perf. 14½x14

67	A98	5c on ½p dk grn	1.10	1.10
68	A98	10c on 1p car	3.00	2.50
a.		Pair, one reading "CEN-TIMES"	1,600.	1,800.
69	A98	15c on 1½p red brn	6.25	20.00
70	A98	25c on 2½p ultra (R)	4.00	2.50
		Nos. 67-70 (4)	14.35	26.10

25th anniv. of the reign of King George V.

> **Catalogue values for unused stamps in this section, from this point to the end of the section, are for Never Hinged items.**

Great Britain Nos. 210-214, 216, 219 Surcharged in Spanish Currency

1935-37　Photo.

71	A97(a)	5c on ½p dk grn('36)	1.25	21.00
72	A97(d)	10c on 1p car	3.25	11.00
73	A97(c)	15c on 1½p red brn	7.00	3.75
74	A97(d)	20c on 2p red org ('36)	.75	.30
75	A97(d)	25c on 2½p ultra('36)	1.75	5.00
76	A97(d)	40c on 4p dk sl grn ('37)	.75	3.50
77	A97(d)	1pe on 10p Prus bl ('37)	7.00	.35
		Nos. 71-77 (7)	21.75	44.90

Great Britain Nos. 230-233 Surcharged

"MOROCCO" 14mm

1936　Wmk. 250

78	A99	5c on ½p dk green	.25	.25
79	A99	10c on 1p crimson	.55	2.25
a.		"Morocco" 15mm long	4.00	16.00
80	A99	15c on 1½p red brown	.25	.25
81	A99	25c on 2½p brt ultra	.25	.25
		Nos. 78-81 (4)	1.30	3.00

Great Britain #234 Surcharged in Blue

Perf. 14½x14

1937, May 13　Wmk. 251

82	A100	15c on 1½p purple brn	.80	.80

Coronation of George VI and Elizabeth.

Great Britain Nos. 235-237, 239, 241, 244 Surcharged in Blue or Black

h

1937-40

83	A101	5c on ½p dp grn (Bl)	1.40	.35
84	A101	10c on 1p scarlet	1.10	.25
85	A101	15c on 1½p red brown (Bl)	1.40	.30
86	A101	25c on 2½p brt ultra	2.25	1.40
87	A102	40c on 4p gray green ('40)	35.00	15.00
88	A103	70c on 7p emer ('40)	2.00	16.00
		Nos. 83-88 (6)	43.15	33.30

Great Britain Nos. 252-254, 256 Surcharged in Blue or Black

1940, May 6

89	A106	5c on ½p deep grn (Bl)	.35	3.00
90	A106	10c on 1p scarlet	4.25	2.90
91	A106	15c on 1½p red brn (Bl)	.80	2.90
92	A106	25c on 2½p brt ultra	.90	1.10
		Nos. 89-92 (4)	6.30	9.90

Centenary of the postage stamp.

Great Britain Nos. 267 and 268 Surcharged in Black

i

j

Perf. 14½x14, 14x14½

1948, Apr. 26　Wmk. 251

93	A109(i)	25c on 2½p	1.10	.35
94	A110(j)	45pe on £1	19.00	25.00

25th anniv. of the marriage of King George VI and Queen Elizabeth.

Great Britain Nos. 271-274 Surcharged "MOROCCO AGENCIES" and New Value

1948, July 29　Perf. 14½x14

95	A113	25c on 2½p brt ultra	.55	1.40
96	A114	30c on 3p dp vio	.55	1.40
97	A115	60c on 6p red vio	.55	1.40
98	A116	1.20pe on 1sh dk brn	.70	1.40
a.		Double surcharge	925.00	
		Nos. 95-98 (4)	2.35	5.60

1948 Olympic Games, Wembley, July-Aug. A square of dots obliterates the original denomination on No. 98.

Great Britain Nos. 280-282, 284-285, 247 Surcharged Type "h"

1951-52　Wmk. 251　Perf. 14½x14

99	A101	5c on ½p lt orange	2.25	5.00
100	A101	10c on 1p ultra	3.75	8.50
101	A101	15c on 1½p green	2.00	19.00
102	A101	25c on 2½p ver	2.00	11.00
103	A102	40c on 4p ultra ('52)	.70	11.50
104	A103	1pe on 10p ryl bl ('52)	2.50	4.00
		Nos. 99-104 (6)	13.20	59.00

BRITISH CURRENCY

Stamps of Morocco Agencies were accepted for postage in Great Britain, starting in mid-1950. Examples with contemporaneous Morocco cancellations sell for more.

British Stamps of 1902-11 Overprinted

a　　　　　b

Overprint "a" 14½mm long

1907-12　Wmk. 30　Perf. 14

Ordinary Paper

201	A66	½p pale yel grn	2.50	9.75
202	A66	1p carmine	11.00	6.25

Chalky Paper

203	A68	2p green & car	11.50	6.25
204	A70	4p brown & grn	4.25	4.50
205	A70	4p orange ('12)	11.50	12.50
a.		Perf. 15x14	25.00	27.50
206	A66	6p dull vio	17.00	21.00
207	A74	1sh car rose & grn	30.00	19.00

Overprinted Type "b"

Wmk. 31

208	A75	2sh6p violet	92.50	140.00
		Nos. 201-208 (8)	180.25	219.25

British Stamps of 1912-18 Overprinted Type "a"

Perf. 14½x14, 15x14

1914-21　Wmk. 33

209	A82	½p green ('18)	4.00	.55
210	A83	1p scarlet ('17)	1.00	.25
211	A84	1½p red brn ('21)	3.75	14.00
212	A85	2p orange ('18)	4.50	.70
213	A87	3p violet ('21)	1.40	.40
214	A88	4p slate grn ('21)	3.75	1.40
215	A89	6p dull vio ('21)	5.50	17.50
216	A90	1sh bister ('17)	6.25	1.40

c

Wmk. 34　Perf. 11x12

217	A91	2sh6p lt brown	42.50	57.50
a.		2sh6p brown	55.00	35.00
b.		2sh6p black brown	52.50	62.50
c.		Double overprint	1,900.	1,350.
		Nos. 209-217 (9)	72.65	93.70

Same Overprint on Great Britain Nos. 179-180

1925-31
218	A91	2sh6p gray brown	42.50	29.00
219	A91	5sh car rose ('31)	62.50	100.00

British Stamps of 1924 Overprinted Type "a" (14½mm long)

1925-31   **Wmk. 35**   **Perf. 15x14**
220	A82	½p green	2.25	.55
221	A84	1½p red brn ('31)	13.50	15.00
222	A85	2p dp org (Die II)	2.50	1.10
223	A86	2½p ultra	2.50	5.75
224	A89	6p red vio ('31)	2.25	9.50
225	A90	1sh bister	19.00	5.75
		Nos. 220-225 (6)	42.00	37.65

Silver Jubilee Issue
Great Britain Nos. 226-229
Overprinted in Blue or Red

1935, May 8   **Perf. 14½x14**
226	A98	½p dark green (Bl)	1.40	7.50
227	A98	1p carmine (Bl)	1.40	7.50
228	A98	1½p red brown (Bl)	2.50	11.00
229	A98	2½p ultramarine (R)	2.90	2.90
		Nos. 226-229 (4)	8.20	28.90

25th anniversary of the reign of King George V.

British Stamps of 1924 Overprinted Type "a" (15½mm long)

1935-36
230	A82	½p green	9.50	45.00
231	A86	2½p ultra	110.00	35.00
232	A88	4p slate green	8.00	40.00
233	A89	6p red violet	1.10	.70
234	A90	1sh bister	62.50	57.50
		Nos. 230-234 (5)	191.10	178.20

British Stamps of 1934-36 Overprinted "MOROCCO AGENCIES"

1935-36
235	A97	1p carmine	3.50	16.00
236	A97	1½p red brn ('36)	3.50	19.00
237	A97	2p red org ('36)	1.40	9.00
238	A97	2½p ultra ('36)	2.00	4.75
239	A97	3p dk violet ('36)	.55	.35
240	A97	4p dk slate grn ('36)	.55	.35
241	A97	1sh bis brn ('36)	.90	4.00

Overprinted Type "c"
Wmk. 34
Perf. 11x12
242	A91	2sh6p brown	45.00	70.00
243	A91	5sh carmine ('37)	27.50	110.00
		Nos. 235-243 (9)	84.90	233.45

> Catalogue values for unused stamps in this section, from this point to the end of the section, are for Never Hinged items.

Great Britain Nos. 231, 233 Overprinted

"MOROCCO" 14mm

1936   **Wmk. 250**   **Perf. 14½x14**
244	A99	1p crimson	.25	.25
a.		"Morocco" 15mm long	7.00	19.00
245	A99	2½p bright ultra	.25	.25
a.		"Morocco" 15mm long	1.10	4.75

Great Britain Nos. 258-263, 241-248, 266, 249A-250 Overprinted "MOROCCO AGENCIES" (14½mm long)

1949, Aug. 16   **Wmk. 251**
246	A101	½p green	2.00	8.00
247	A101	1p vermilion	3.00	10.00
248	A101	1½p lt red brown	3.00	9.50
249	A101	2p lt orange	3.50	10.00
250	A101	2½p ultra	3.75	11.50
251	A101	3p violet	1.75	2.00
252	A102	4p gray green	.55	1.40

253	A102	5p lt brown	3.50	17.00
254	A102	6p rose lilac	1.75	1.75
255	A103	7p emerald	.55	18.00
256	A103	8p brt rose	3.50	7.50
257	A103	9p dp olive grn	.55	12.50
258	A103	10p royal blue	.55	7.50
259	A103	11n violet brn	.00	0.50
260	A103	1sh brown	3.00	7.00

"MOROCCO AGENCIES"
17½mm long
Wmk. 259
Perf. 14
261	A104	2sh6p yellow grn	18.00	40.00
262	A104	5sh dull red	32.50	70.00
		Nos. 246-262 (17)	82.25	242.15

Great Britain Nos. 280-284, 286-287 Overprinted "MOROCCO AGENCIES" (14½mm long)

Perf. 14½x14
1951, May 3   **Wmk. 251**
263	A101	½p lt orange	2.25	1.10
264	A101	1p ultra	2.25	1.60
265	A101	1½p green	2.25	3.00
266	A101	2p lt red brown	2.50	4.50
267	A101	2½p vermilion	2.25	4.75

"MOROCCO AGENCIES"
17½mm long
Wmk. 259
Perf. 11x12
268	A121	2sh6p green	15.00	24.00
269	A121	5sh dull red	15.00	26.00
		Nos. 263-269 (7)	41.50	64.95

French Currency
British Stamps of 1912-22 Surcharged in French Currency in Red or Black

h   i

Perf. 14½x14, 15x14
1917-24   **Wmk. 33**
401	A82(h)	3c on ½p green (R)	1.10	2.90
402	A82(h)	5c on ½p green	.45	1.75
403	A83(h)	10c on 1p scarlet	3.75	.45
404	A84(h)	15c on 1½p red brn	2.90	.25
405	A86(h)	25c on 2½p ultra	2.25	.25
406	A88(h)	40c on 4p slate grn	2.90	1.75
407	A89(h)	50c on 5p yel brn ('23)	.90	3.00
408	A90(h)	75c on 9p ol grn ('24)	1.10	.85
409	A90(i)	1fr on 10p lt blue	8.00	3.50
		Nos. 401-409 (9)	23.35	14.70

Great Britain No. 179 Surcharged

k

1924   **Wmk. 34**   **Perf. 11x12**
410	A91(k)	3fr on 2sh6p brn	8.50	1.75

British Stamps of 1924 Surcharged in French Currency as in 1917-24

1925-26   **Wmk. 35**   **Perf. 15x14**
411	A82(h)	5c on ½p green	.35	7.50
412	A83(h)	10c on 1p scarlet	.35	2.25
413	A84(h)	15c on 1½p red brn	1.10	2.00
414	A86(h)	25c on 2½p ultra	1.75	.55
415	A88(h)	40c on 4p sl green	.70	.90
416	A89(h)	50c on 5p yel brown	1.75	.25
417	A90(h)	75c on 9p ol green	4.00	.25
418	A90(i)	1fr on 10p dl blue	1.40	.25
		Nos. 411-418 (8)	11.40	13.95

Great Britain Nos. 180, 198 and 200 Surcharged type "k"

1932   **Wmk. 34**   **Perf. 11x12**
419	A91	6fr on 5sh car rose	42.50	47.50

1934   **Wmk. 35**   **Perf. 14½x14**
420	A90	90c on 9p ol green	18.00	8.50
421	A90	1.50fr on 1sh bister	11.50	2.50

Silver Jubilee Issue
Great Britain Nos. 226-229
Surcharged in Blue or Red

1935, May 8   **Perf. 14½x14**
422	A98	5c on ½p dk green	.25	.25
423	A98	10c on 1p carmine	3.00	.85
424	A98	15c on 1½p red brn	.40	.55
425	A98	25c on 2½p ultra (R)	.25	.35
		Nos. 422-425 (4)	3.90	2.00

25th anniv. of the reign of King George V.

British Stamps of 1934-36 Surcharged Types "h" or "k"
Perf. 14½x14
1935-37   **Photo.**   **Wmk. 35**
426	A97(h)	5c on ½p dk grn	.55	5.75
427	A97(h)	10c on 1p car ('36)	.40	.35
428	A97(h)	15c on 1½p red brn	5.50	6.25
429	A97(h)	25c on 2½p ultra	.35	.25
430	A97(h)	40c on 4p dk sl grn	.35	.25
431	A97(h)	50c on 5p yel brn	.35	.25
432	A97(h)	90c on 9p dk ol grn	.40	2.00
433	A97(k)	1fr on 10p Prus bl	.35	.35
434	A97(h)	1.50fr on 1sh bister brn ('37)	.85	3.75

Waterlow Printing
Wmk. 34   Perf. 11x12
435	A91(k)	3fr on 2sh6p brn	5.50	14.00
436	A91(k)	6fr on 5sh car ('36)	7.00	24.00
		Nos. 426-436 (11)	21.60	57.20

Great Britain Nos. 230, 232 Surcharged

1936   **Wmk. 250**   **Perf. 14½x14**
437	A99	5c on ½p dark green	.25	.25
438	A99	15c on 1½p red brown	.25	.25

Great Britain No. 234 Surcharged in Blue

1937, May 13   **Wmk. 251**
439	A100	15c on 1½p purple brn	.35	.25

Coronation of George VI and Elizabeth.

Great Britain No. 235 Surcharged in Blue

1937
440	A101	5c on ½p deep green	2.50	2.90

For Use in the International Zone of Tangier

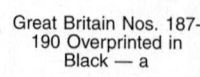

Great Britain Nos. 187-190 Overprinted in Black — a

1927   **Wmk. 35**   **Perf. 15x14**
501	A82	½p green	3.50	.25
502	A83	1p scarlet	3.50	.30
503	A84	1½p red brown	7.00	4.25
504	A85	2p orange (II)	3.75	.25
		Nos. 501-504 (4)	17.75	5.05

Same Overprint on Great Britain Nos. 210-212

1934-35   **Photo.**   **Perf. 14½x14**
505	A97	½p dark green	1.40	1.75
506	A97	1p carmine	4.75	2.75
507	A97	1½p red brown	.55	.25
		Nos. 505-507 (3)	6.70	4.75

Silver Jubilee Issue
Great Britain Nos. 226-228
Overprinted in Blue

b

1935, May 8
508	A98	½p dark green	1.40	5.75
509	A98	1p carmine	16.00	17.00
510	A98	1½p red brown	1.40	1.10
		Nos. 508-510 (3)	18.80	23.85

25th anniv. of the reign of King George V.

Great Britain Nos. 230-232 Overprinted Type "a"

1936   **Wmk. 250**
511	A99	½p dark green	.25	.25
512	A99	1p crimson	.25	.25
513	A99	1½p red brown	.25	.25
		Nos. 511-513 (3)	.75	.75

Great Britain No. 234 Overprinted Type "b" in Blue

1937, May 13   **Wmk. 251**
514	A100	1½p purple brown	.55	.55

Coronation of George VI and Elizabeth.

Great Britain Nos. 235-237 Overprinted in Blue or Black — c

1937   **Perf. 14½x14**
515	A101	½p deep green (Bl)	2.75	1.75
516	A101	1p scarlet (Bk)	8.00	1.75
517	A101	1½p red brown (Bl)	2.75	.30
		Nos. 515-517 (3)	13.50	3.80

Great Britain Nos. 252-254 Ovptd. Type "a" in Blue or Black

1940, May 6
518	A106	½p deep green (Bl)	.35	5.50
519	A106	1p scarlet (Bk)	.50	.60
520	A106	1½p red brown (Bl)	2.25	5.75
		Nos. 518-520 (3)	3.10	11.85

Centenary of the postage stamp.

Great Britain Nos. 258 and 259 Overprinted Type "c" in Blue or Black

1944-45
521	A101	½p green (Bl)	12.50	5.00
522	A101	1p ver (Bk) ('45)	12.50	3.50

> Catalogue values for unused stamps in this section, from this point to the end of the section, are for Never Hinged items.

Great Britain Nos. 264-265 Overprinted

d

e

1946, June 11

523	A107(d)	2½p bright ultra	.75 .75
524	A108(e)	3p violet	.75 2.25

Return to peace at close of World War II.

Great Britain Nos. 267 and 268 Overprinted Type "a"

1948, Apr. 26   Perf. 14½x14, 14x14½

525	A109	2½p bright ultra	.60 .25
a.	Pair, one without overprint		5,400.
526	A110	£1 dp chalky bl	22.50 29.00

25th anniv. of the marriage of King George VI and Queen Elizabeth.

Great Britain Nos. 271 to 274 Overprinted Type "a"

1948, July 29   Perf. 14½x14

527	A113	2½p bright ultra	1.10 2.25
528	A114	3p deep violet	1.10 2.25
529	A115	6p red violet	1.10 2.25
530	A116	1sh dark brown	1.10 1.40
	Nos. 527-530 (4)		4.40 8.15

1948 Olympic Games, Wembley, July-Aug.

Stamps of Great Britain, 1937-47, and Nos. 249A, 250 and 251A Overprinted Type "c"

1949, Jan. 1

531	A101	2p lt org (II)	5.75 7.00
532	A101	2½p ultra (II)	2.00 7.00
533	A101	3p violet (II)	.80 1.40
534	A102	4p gray green	12.50 11.50
535	A102	5p light brown	4.25 22.50
536	A102	6p rose lilac	.80 .35
537	A103	7p emerald	1.40 15.00
538	A103	8p bright rose	4.25 12.50
539	A103	9p deep ol grn	1.40 13.50
540	A103	10p royal blue	1.40 15.00
541	A103	11p violet brn	1.75 12.50
542	A103	1sh brown	1.40 3.00

Wmk. 259

Perf. 14

543	A104	2sh6p yellow grn	5.00 13.50
544	A104	5sh dull red	15.00 42.50
545	A105	10sh ultra	50.00 110.00
	Nos. 531-545 (15)		107.70 287.25

Great Britain Nos. 276 to 279 Overprinted Type "a"

Perf. 14½x14

1949, Oct. 10   Wmk. 251

546	A117	2½p bright ultra	.80 3.00
547	A118	3p bright violet	.80 2.00
548	A119	6p red violet	.80 1.40
549	A120	1sh brown	.80 3.75
	Nos. 546-549 (4)		3.20 10.15

Great Britain Nos. 280-288 Overprinted Type "c" or "a" (Shilling Values)

1950-51

550	A101	½p lt orange	1.00 1.75
551	A101	1p ultra	1.10 3.50
552	A101	1½p green	1.10 16.00
553	A101	2p lt red brn	1.10 2.90
554	A101	2½p vermilion	1.10 5.75
555	A102	4p ultra ('50)	3.50 3.50

Wmk. 259

Perf. 11x12

556	A121	2sh6p green	11.00 5.75
557	A121	5sh dull red	17.50 19.00
558	A122	10sh ultra	22.50 19.00
	Nos. 550-558 (9)		59.90 77.15

TURKISH EMPIRE

STAMPS OF GREAT BRITAIN USED IN THE TURKISH EMPIRE

Values are for clear cancellations on sound, fault-free stamps, with average to fine centering. In many cases, very fine stamps are rare or non-existent.

BEIRUT

British P.O. opened 1873; closed Sept. 30, 1914

No. A22

Stamps of Great Britain, Canceled with barred oval "G06" or circular date stamp "BEYROUT"

1873-80

A1	½p rose red (#58, P 12-14)	52.50
	Plate 19	110.00
	Plate 20	150.00
A2	1p rose red (#33, P107, 118, 130, 140, 145, 148, 155, 157, 162, 167, 177, 179, 180, 184-187, 195, 198, 200, 203, 204, 211, 213, 215, 218, 220, 222) *value from*	22.50
A3	1½p lake red (#32, P 3)	350.00
A4	2p blue (#30, P 13-15), *value from*	30.00
A5	2½p claret (#66, P 1-3), *value from*	37.50
a.	Bluish paper (#66a, P 1)	87.50
A6	2½p claret (#67, P 3-17), *value from*	30.00
A7	2½p blue (#68, P 17-20), *value from*	19.00
A8	2½p blue (#82, P 21-23), *value from*	13.50
	On cover, *value from*	75.00
A9	3p rose (#49, P 10)	—
A10	3p rose (#61, P 12, 15, 16, 18-20), *value from*	52.50
A11	3p rose (#83, P 20, 21)	—
A12	4p vermilion (#43, P 11-14), *value from*	45.00
A13	4p vermilion (#69, P 15)	375.00
A14	4p pale olive green (#70, P 15)	250.00
	Plate 16	225.00
A15	4p gray brown (#71, P 17)	—
A16	4p gray brown (#84, P17, 18), *value from*	60.00
A17	6p violet (#52, P 8, 9)	—
A18	6p brown (#59, P 11)	50.00
a.	6p pale buff (#59b, P 11)	100.00
	Plate 12	250.00
A19	6p gray (#60, P 12)	—
A20	6p gray (#62, P 13-17), *value from*	35.00
A21	8p orange (#73)	500.00
A22	10p red brown (#53)	325.00
A23	1sh green (#54, P 6, 7) *value from*	37.50
A24	1sh green (#64, P 8-10, 12, 13) *value from*	52.50
A25	1sh salmon (#65, P 13)	—
A26	1sh salmon (#87, P 13, 14)	80.00
A27	2sh blue (#55)	175.00
A28	5sh rose (#57, P 1)	775.00
	Plate 2	925.00

1880

A29	½p deep green (#78)	13.50
a.	½p green (#78c)	14.50
A30	1p red brown (#79)	19.00
A31	1½p red brown (#80)	210.00
A32	2p lilac rose (#81)	72.50
a.	2p deep lilac rose (#81a)	72.50
A33	5p indigo (#85)	110.00

1881

A34	1p lilac, 14 dots (#88)	—
A35	1p lilac, 16 dots (#88)	8.00

1883-84

A36	½p slate blue (#98)	21.00
A37	1½p lilac (#99)	105.00
A38	2p lilac (#100)	87.50
A39	2½p lilac (#101)	13.50
	On cover	75.00
A41	4p dull green (#103)	225.00
A42	5p dull green (#104)	130.00
A45	1sh dull green (#107)	375.00

1887-92

A46	½p vermilion	10.00
A53	6p violet, *rose*	27.50
A56	1sh dull green	175.00

1900

A57	½p blue green	13.50
A58	1sh car rose & grn	210.00

1902-04

A59	½p blue green	5.75
A60	½p yellow green	6.00
A61	1p scarlet	5.50
A65	1sh car & dull grn	37.50

CONSTANTINOPLE

British P.O. opened Sept. 1, 1857; closed Sept. 30, 1914; reopened Feb. 4, 1919; closed Sept. 27, 1923

No. A124

Stamps of Great Britain, Canceled with barred oval "C" or circular date stamp "CONSTANTINOPLE"

1857-83

A75	½p rose red (#58, P 5, 6, 10-15, 20), *value from*	30.00
A76	1p red brown (#8)	—
A77	1p red brown (#12)	—
A78	1p red brown (#16)	22.50
A79	1p rose red (#20)	8.50
A80	1p rose red (#33, P 71-74, 76, 78-81, 83, 85, 87, 89, 90, 92-97, 99, 101, 102, 105, 106, 108-110, 113, 116, 118-125, 127, 129-131, 134-138, 140, 141, 143-152, 155-167, 170-184, 186-198, 200, 201, 203-208, 210, 212, 214-216, 220, 222, 224) *value from*	10.00
A81	1½p lake red (#32a, P 1)	250.00
A82	2p blue (#17)	—
A83	2p blue (#29, P 7)	65.00
	Plate 8	55.00
	Plate 9	14.00
	Plate 12	200.00
	Plate 13	27.50
	Plate 14	37.50
	Plate 15	37.50
A84	2½p claret (#66, P 1-3), *value from*	35.00
a.	Bluish paper (#66a, P 1, 2)	65.00
b.	Lettered "LH-FL" (#66b)	—
A85	2½p claret (#67, P 3-17), *value from*	27.50
A86	2½p blue (#68, P 17-20), *value from*	13.50
A87	2½p blue (#82, P 21-23), *value from*	9.00
A88	3p rose (#37)	160.00
A89	3p rose (#44)	87.50
A90	3p rose (#49, P 4-10), *value from*	82.50
A91	3p rose (#61, P 11, 12, 15-18, 19), *value from*	30.00
A92	3p rose (#83, P 21)	—
A93	3p on 3p violet (#94)	—
A94	4p (#26)	55.00
a.	4p carmine rose (#26a)	—
A95	4p vermilion (#34, P 3)	45.00
a.	Hairlines (#34c)	60.00
A96	4p vermilion (#43, P 7-14), *value from*	30.00
A97	4p vermilion (#69, P 15)	375.00
A98	4p pale olive green (#70, P 15)	250.00
	Plate 16	225.00
A99	4p gray brown (#71, P 17)	—
A100	4p gray brown (#84, P17, 18), *value from*	47.50
A101	6p lilac (#27)	70.00
A102	6p lilac (#39, P 3)	75.00
a.	6p lilac, thick paper (#39b, P 4)	200.00
A103	6p lilac (#45, P 5)	42.50
	Plate 6	175.00
A104	6p dull violet (#50, P 6)	50.00
A105	6p violet (#51, 6, 8, 9), *value from*	37.50
A106	6p brown (#59, P 11)	35.00
a.	6p pale buff (#59b, P 11)	80.00
	Plate 12	225.00
A107	6p gray (#60, P 12)	90.00
A108	6p gray (#62, P 13-16), *value from*	30.00
A109	6p gray (#86, P 17, 18), *value from*	30.00
A110	6p on 6p violet (#95)	100.00
A111	8p orange (#73)	375.00
A112	10p red brown (#47)	32,500.
A113	10p red brown (#53)	190.00
A114	1sh green (#28)	275.00
a.	1sh green, thick paper (#28d)	275.00
A115	1sh green (#42)	70.00
A116	1sh green (#48, P 4)	75.00
A117	1sh green (#54, P 4-7), *value from*	20.00
A118	1sh green (#64, P 8-13), *value from*	32.50
A119	1sh salmon (#65, P 13)	240.00
A120	1sh salmon (#87, P 13, 14), *value from*	55.00
A121	2sh blue (#55)	150.00
A122	5sh rose (#57, P 1)	575.00
	Plate 2	850.00
A123	5sh rose, *blue* (#90)	1,600.
a.	White paper (#90a)	1,000.

1880

A124	½p deep green (#78)	9.00
a.	½p green (#78c)	11.00

A125	1p red brown (#79)	12.50
A126	2p lilac rose (#81)	50.00
a.	2p deep rose (#81a)	50.00
A127	5p indigo (#85)	—

1881

A128	1p lilac, 14 dots (#88)	—
A129	1p lilac, 16 dots (#88)	4.00

1883-84

A130	½p slate blue (#98)	9.00
A131	1½p lilac (#99)	—
A132	2p lilac (#100)	75.00
A133	2½p lilac (#101)	10.00
A134	3p lilac (#102)	—
A135	4p dull green (#103)	—
A136	5p dull green (#104)	130.00
A137	6p dull green (#105)	—
A138	9p dull green (#106)	—
A139	1sh dull green (#107)	300.00
A140	2sh6p lilac, *bluish* (#90)	775.00
a.	White paper (#90a)	100.00
A141	5sh rose (#108)	—
a.	Bluish paper (#108a)	—

1887-92

A142	½p vermilion	4.00
A150	6p violet, *rose*	13.50
A153	1sh dull green	100.00

1900

A154	½p blue green	6.50
A155	1sh car rose & grn	175.00

1902-04

A156	½p blue green	4.50
A157	½p yellow green	5.00
A158	1p scarlet	4.00
A165	6p purple	13.00
A168	1sh car & dull grn	27.50
A169	2sh6p lilac	—
A170	5sh carmine	—

Postal Fiscal stamps of Great Britain are found used in Constantinople. They are rare.

SALONICA

British P.O. opened May 1, 1900; closed October, 1914

Stamps of Great Britain, Canceled with circular date stamp "SALONICA," with single or double circle

1887-92

A197	½p vermilion	22.50
A198	1p lilac	25.00
A199	6p violet, *rose*	35.00
A200	5sh rose (#90a)	1,050.

1900

A201	½p blue green	25.00
A202	1sh car rose & grn	225.00

1902-04

A203	½p blue green	27.50
A204	½p yellow green	22.50
A205	1p scarlet	22.50
A206	6p purple	—
A207	1sh car & dull grn	60.00

SMYRNA

British P.O. opened 1872; closed Sept. 30, 1914; reopened Mar. 1, 1919; closed Sept., 1922

Stamps of Great Britain, Canceled with barred numeral "F87" or with circular date stamps (various types)

1872-83

A229	½p rose red (#58, P 11-15), *value from*	35.00
A230	1p rose red (#33, P 120, 124, 134, 137-140, 142, 143, 145, 146, 148-153, 155-164, 166-178, 183-188, 193, 195, 196, 198, 200, 201, 204, 210, 212, 215, 217, 218), *value from*	16.00
A231	1½p lake red (#32a, P 1, 3), *value from*	275.00
A232	2p blue (#15)	—
A233	2p blue (#30, P 13-15), *value from*	19.00
A234	2½p claret (#66, P 1-3), *value from*	32.50
a.	Bluish paper (#66a, P 1, 2)	70.00
b.	Lettered "LH-FL" (#66b)	—
A235	2½p claret (#67, P 3-17), *value from*	26.00
A236	2½p blue (#68, P 17-20), *value from*	22.50
A237	2½p blue (#82, P 21-23), *value from*	11.00

A238	3p rose (#49, P 5, 7, 9, 10), value from	47.50
A239	3p rose (#61, P 14, 15)	—
A240	4p vermilion (#43, P 12-14), value from	30.00
A241	4p vermilion (#69, P 15)	375.00
A242	4p pale olive green (#70, P 15)	250.00
	Plate 16	225.00
A243	4p gray brown (#71, P 17)	—
A244	4p gray brown (#84, P17, 18), value from	42.50
A245	6p brown (#59, P 11), value from	—
a.	6p pale buff (#59b, P 11)	100.00
	Plate 12	225.00
A246	6p gray (#60, P 12)	95.00
A247	6p gray (#62, P 13-17), value from	30.00
A248	6p gray (#86, P 17, 18), value from	60.00
A249	6p on 6p violet (#95)	125.00
A250	8p orange (#73)	—
A251	9p bister (#52)	400.00
A252	10p red brown (#53)	275.00
A253	1sh green (#54, P 6, 7), value from	—
A254	1sh green (#64, P 8-13), value from	35.00
A255	1sh salmon (#65, P 13)	250.00
A256	1sh salmon (#87, P 13, 14), value from	60.00
A257	5sh rose (#57, P 2)	—

1880

A258	½p deep green (#78)	10.00
a.	½p green (#78c)	10.00
A259	1p red brown (#79)	15.00
A260	1½p red brown (#80)	140.00
A261	2p lilac rose (#81)	52.50
a.	2p deep rose (#81a)	52.50
A262	5p indigo (#85)	82.50

1881

A263	1p lilac, 16 dots (#88)	6.00

1883-84

A264	½p slate blue (#98)	17.50
A266	2p lilac (#100)	82.50
A267	2½p lilac (#101)	12.00
A269	4p dull green (#103)	—
A270	5p dull green (#104)	140.00
A273	1sh dull green (#107)	350.00

1887-92

A275	½p vermilion	6.00
A282	6p violet, rose	22.50
A283	1sh dull green	140.00

1900

A285	½p blue green	8.75
A286	1sh car rose & grn	—

1902-04

A287	½p blue green	5.50
A288	½p yellow green	6.00
A289	1p scarlet	5.50
A296	6p purple	16.00
A299	1sh car & dull grn	30.00
A300	2sh6p lilac	—
A301	5sh carmine	—

STAMBOUL

British P.O. opened Apr. 1, 1884; closed Aug. 25, 1896; reopened Feb. 10, 1908; closed Sept. 30, 1914.

Stamps of Great Britain, Canceled with barred "S" or circular date stamps "BRITISH POST OFFICE CONSTANTINOPLE S" or "BRITISH POST OFFICE STAMBOUL"

1883-84

A323	½p slate blue (#98)	27.50
A324	2p lilac (#99)	13.50
A325	2p lilac (#100)	—
A326	2½p lilac (#101)	16.00
A327	5p dull green (#104)	160.00

1887-92

A330	½p vermilion	16.00
A338	6p violet, rose	37.50
A341	1sh dull green	—

BRITISH STAMPS OVERPRINTED
40 Paras = 1 Piaster
12 Pence = 1 Shilling (1905)

a

b

c

d

Surcharged on Great Britain Nos. 101, 104, 96

			1885, Apr. 1	**Wmk. 30**	**Perf. 14**
1	A47(a)	40pa on 2½p lil		110.00	1.50
		On cover			10.00
2	A45(b)	80pa on 5p grn		210.00	12.50
		On cover			80.00

Wmk. 31

3	A44(c)	12pi on 2sh6p lilac	52.50	27.50
		On cover		250.00
a.		Bluish paper	400.00	260.00
		On cover		1,600.
		Nos. 1-3 (3)	372.50	41.50

Great Britain Nos. 114, 118 Surcharged

			1887		**Wmk. 30**
4	A57(a)	40pa on 2½p vio, bl		4.75	.25
		On cover			5.00
a.		Double surcharge		2,250.	2,900.
5	A61(b)	80pa on 5p lil & bl		17.50	.35
		On cover			5.00
a.		Small "0" in "80"		225.00	100.00
		On cover			375.00

Great Britain No. 111 Handstamp Surcharged

1893, Feb. 25

6	A54(d)	40pa on ½p ver	500.00	125.00
		On cover		375.00

No. 6 was a provisional, made and used at Constantinople for five days. Excellent forgeries are known.

Great Britain No. 121
Surcharged — e

1896

7	A64(e)	4pi on 10p car rose & lil	47.50	9.25
		On cover		50.00

British Stamps of 1902 Surcharged

			1902-05		**Wmk. 30**
8	A66(a)	40pa on 2½p ultra		17.50	.25
9	A71(b)	80pa on 5p lil & bl		6.50	2.90
a.		Small "0" in "80"		250.00	210.00
10	A73(e)	4pi on 10p car rose & vio		13.50	4.50

Wmk. 31

11	A75(c)	12pi on 2sh6p vio ('03)	40.00	40.00
12	A76(c)	24pi on 5sh car rose ('05)	35.00	47.50
		Nos. 8-12 (5)	115.00	95.15

Great Britain Nos. 131, 134 Surcharged — f

			1906		**Wmk. 30**
13	A66(f)	1pi on 2½p ultra		17.50	.25
14	A71(f)	2pi on 5p lil & ultra		32.50	2.75

Nos. 10, 11, 14 are on both ordinary and chalky paper.

Great Britain Nos. 127-135, 138 Overprinted — g

1905

15	A66	½p pale green	10.00	.25
16	A66	1p carmine	9.50	.25
17	A67	1½p violet & grn	6.25	2.00
18	A68	2p green & car	3.50	8.00
19	A66	2½p ultra	10.00	22.50

20	A69	3p violet, yel	7.25	13.50
21	A70	4p brown & grn	10.00	50.00
22	A71	5p lilac & ultra	19.00	32.50
23	A66	6p dull violet	15.00	29.00
24	A74	1sh car rose & grn	42.50	57.50
		Nos. 15-24 (10)	133.00	215.50

Nos. 17, 18 and 24 are on both ordinary and chalky paper.

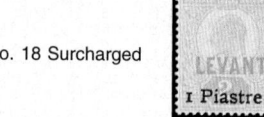

No. 18 Surcharged

1906, July 2

25	A68	1pi on 2p grn & car	1,500.	700.00

British Stamps of 1902-09 Surcharged

j

k

1909

26	A67	30pa on 1½p vio & grn	11.50	1.40
27	A69	1pi10pa on 3p vio, yel	13.50	40.00
28	A70	1pi30pa on 4p brn & grn	5.75	19.00
29	A70	1pi30pa on 4p org	20.00	70.00
30	A66	2pi20pa on 6p dl violet	22.50	70.00
31	A74	5pi on 1sh car rose & grn	5.00	11.00
		Nos. 26-31 (6)	78.25	211.40

No. 29 is on ordinary paper, the others are on chalky paper.

Great Britain Nos. 132, 144, 135 Surcharged

m

n

1910

32	A69(m)	1¼pi on 3p vio, yel	.60	1.25
33	A70(m)	1¾pi on 4p orange	.60	.75
34	A66(n)	2½pi on 6p dl vio	1.60	.80
		Nos. 32-34 (3)	2.80	2.80

There are three different varieties of "4" in the fraction of the 1¾ piastre.

Great Britain Nos. 151-154 Overprinted Type g

			1911-12		**Perf. 15x14**
35	A80	½p yellow green		2.25	1.75
36	A81	1p carmine		.55	7.00

Re-engraved

37	A80	½p yel grn ('12)	.90	.25
38	A81	1p scarlet ('12)	.90	1.75

Great Britain No. 148
Surcharged — o

39	A66(o)	1pi on 2½p ultra	15.00	3.00
		Nos. 35-39 (5)	19.60	13.75

The surcharge on No. 39 exists in two types with the letters 2½ and 3mm high respectively. The stamp also differs from No. 13 in the perforation.

British Stamps of 1912-13 Surcharged with New Values

			1913-14		**Wmk. 33**
40	A84(j)	30pa on 1½p red brown		4.00	16.00
41	A86(o)	1pi on 2½p ultra		8.50	.25
42	A87(m)	1¼pi on 3p vio		5.50	4.75
43	A88(n)	1¾pi on 4p sl grn		3.50	7.00

44	A90(o)	4pi on 10p lt bl	9.00	22.50
45	A90(o)	5pi on 1sh bis	45.00	70.00
		Nos. 40-45 (6)	75.50	120.50

British Stamps of 1912-19 Overprinted Type "g"

1913-21

46	A82	½p green	.45	1.40
47	A83	1p scarlet	.35	5.75
48	A85	2p orange ('21)	1.40	32.50
49	A87	3p violet ('21)	8.50	11.50
50	A88	4p sl grn ('21)	5.75	16.00
51	A89	5p yel brn ('21)	13.50	32.50
52	A89	6p dl vio ('21)	30.00	10.00
53	A90	1sh bister ('21)	15.00	10.00

Wmk. 34

Perf. 11x12

54	A91	2sh6p brn ('21)	42.50	100.00
		Nos. 46-54 (9)	117.45	219.65

British Stamps of 1912-19 Surcharged as in 1909-10 and

p

q

1921   **Wmk. 33**   **Perf. 14½x14**

55	A82(j)	30pa on ½p grn	.90	13.50
a.		Inverted surcharge	100.00	
56	A83(n)	1½pi on 1p scar	1.75	1.40
57	A86(p)	3¾pi on 2½p ultra	1.50	.35
58	A87(p)	4½pi on 3p vio	2.25	4.25
59	A89(p)	7½pi on 5p yel brn	.60	.25
60	A90(p)	15pi on 10p lt bl	.85	.25
61	A90(p)	18¾pi on 1sh bis	5.00	5.00

Wmk. 34

Perf. 11x12

62	A91(q)	45pi on 2sh6p brown	22.50	52.50
63	A91(q)	90pi on 5sh car rose	30.00	35.00
64	A91(q)	180pi on 10sh blue	52.50	45.00
		Nos. 55-64 (10)	117.85	157.50

GREECE

'grēs

(Hellas)

LOCATION — Southern part of the Balkan Peninsula in southeastern Europe, bordering on the Ionian, Aegean and Mediterranean Seas
GOVT. — Republic
AREA — 50,949 sq. mi.
POP. — 9,740,417 (1981)
CAPITAL — Athens

In 1923 the reigning king was forced to abdicate and the following year Greece was declared a republic. In 1935, the king was recalled by a "plebiscite" of the people. Greece became a republic in June 1973. The country today includes the Aegean Islands of Chios, Mytilene (Lesbos), Samos, Icaria (Nicaria) and Lemnos, the Ionian Islands (Corfu, etc.) Crete, Macedonia, Western Thrace and part of Eastern Thrace, the Mount Athos District, Epirus and the Dodecanese Islands.

100 Lepta = 1 Drachma

Values for unused stamps are for examples with original gum as defined in the catalogue introduction. Any exceptions will be noted.

Values for Large Hermes Head stamps with double control numbers on the back, Nos. 20e, 21c, 27a, et al, are for examples with two distinct and separate impressions, not for blurred or "slide doubles" caused by paper slippage on the press.

Watermarks

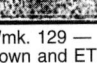

Wmk. 129 — Crown and ET

Wmk. 252 — Crowns

Paris Print

Hermes (Mercury) — A1

Paris Print, Fine Impression

The enlarged illustrations show the head in various states of the plates. The differences are best seen in the shading lines on the cheek and neck.

1861 Unwmk. Typo. *Imperf.*
Without Figures on Back

1	A1	1 l choc, *brnish*	600.00	550.00
		No gum	200.00	
		On cover, single franking		1,150.
		Single franking on newspaper		*1,350.*
a.		1 l red brown, *brnish*	725.00	600.00
		No gum	240.00	

		On cover, single franking		1,200.
		Single franking on newspaper		*1,350.*
b.		1 l brown	575.00	475.00
		No gum	200.00	
		On cover, single franking		1,150.
		Single franking on newspaper		*1,350.*
2	A1	2 l ol bis, *straw*	67.50	87.50
		No gum	40.00	
		On cover, with other stamps		*2,000.*
		On cover, single franking		*2,250.*
a.		2 l brown buff, *buff*	55.00	75.00
		No gum	40.00	
		On cover, with other stamps		*2,000.*
		On cover, single franking		*2,250.*
b.		2 l yellowish bister	55.00	75.00
		No gum	22.50	
		On cover, single franking		*2,000.*
3	A1	5 l yel grn, *grnsh*	700.00	150.00
		No gum	240.00	
		On cover		475.00
a.		5 l emerald green	875.00	175.00
		No gum	180.00	
		On cover		325.00
4	A1	20 l bl, *bluish*	1,150.	95.00
		No gum	275.00	
		On cover		240.00
a.		20 l deep blue, *bluish*	1,100.	340.00
		No gum	475.00	
		On cover		600.00
b.		On pelure paper	1,350.	*275.00*
		On cover		600.00
5	A1	40 l vio, *bl*	325.00	130.00
		On cover		600.00
6	A1	80 l rose, *pink*	250.00	120.00
		No gum	110.00	
		On cover		550.00
a.		80 l carmine, *pink*	250.00	120.00
		No gum	110.00	
		On cover		550.00

Large Figures, 8mm high, on Back

7	A1	10 l red org, *bl*	1,040.	500.00
		No gum	450.00	
		On cover		1,650.
a.		"10" on back inverted	—	
c.		"0" of "10" invtd. on back	—	*1,850.*
d.		"1" of "10" invtd. on back	—	*2,750.*

Full margins = ¾mm.

No. 7 without "10" on back is a proof.
Trial impressions of Paris prints exist in many shades, some being close to those of the issued stamps. The gum used was thin and smooth instead of thick, brownish and crackly as on the issued stamps.

See Nos. 8-58. For surcharges see Nos. 130, 132-133, 137-139, 141-143, 147-149, 153-154, 157-158.

Values for stamps in pairs

1	A1	1 l choc, *brnish*	1,375.	*1,650.*
a.		1 l red brown, *brnish*	1,500.	*1,850.*
2	A1	2 l ol bis, *straw*	110.00	*300.00*
a.		2 l brown buff, *buff*	165.00	*300.00*
3	A1	5 l yel grn, *grnsh*	1,500.	450.00
4	A1	20 l bl, *bluish*	2,400.	290.00
a.		20 l deep blue, *bluish*		1,000.
5	A1	40 l vio, *bl*	620.00	650.00
6	A1	80 l rose, *pink*	550.00	615.00
a.		80 l carmine, *pink*	675.00	410.00
7	A1	10 l red org, *bl*	2,000.	1,550.

Values for stamps in strips of 3

1	A1	1 l choc, *brnish*	3,000.	600.00
2	A1	2 l ol bis, *straw*	180.00	600.00
3	A1	5 l yel grn, *grnsh*	—	900.00
4	A1	20 l bl, *bluish*	—	800.00
5	A1	40 l vio, *bl*	1,600.	
6	A1	80 l rose, *pink*	1,100.	1,250.
7	A1	10 l red org, *bl*	—	3,250.

Values for stamps in blocks of 4

1	A1	1 l choc, *brnish*	13,500.	12,750.
		No gum	3,000.	
2	A1	2 l ol bis, *straw*	400.00	1,000.
		No gum	275.00	
3	A1	5 l yel grn, *grnsh*	9,250.	—
		No gum	3,500.	
4	A1	20 l bl, *bluish*	10,500.	
		No gum	3,500.	
5	A1	40 l vio, *bl*	4,250.	
		No gum	2,000.	
6	A1	80 l rose, *pink*	1,750.	
		No gum	1,000.	
7	A1	10 l red org, *bl*	13,000.	
		No gum	4,500.	

Faint quadrille, horizontal or vertical lines are visible in the background of some Athens print large Hermes head stamps.

Nos. 16, 16a, 16b are the only 1 l stamps that have these lines.

Athens Prints

Athens Print, Typical Fine Impression

Athens Print, Typical Coarse Impression

Figures on Back
5 l:

#11   #18-45

Fine Printing (F)
Fine Printing (F, '62) see footnote
Coarse Printing (C)
1861-62   Without Figures on Back

8	A1	1 l choc, *brnish* (F, '62)	490.00	*490.00*
		No gum	350.00	
		On cover		2,750.
a.		1 l dk chocolate, *brnish* (F)	1,300.	1,325.
		No gum	700.00	
		On cover		4,250.
b.		1 l chocolate, *brnish*	590.00	590.00
		No gum	460.00	
		On cover		2,750.
9	A1	2 l bis brn, *bister* (F)	75.00	*110.00*
		No gum	40.00	
		On cover		1,500.
a.		2 l dark brown, *straw*, (C)	6,750.	—
		On cover		—
b.		2 l bister brown, *bister* (C)	90.00	*135.00*
		On cover		1,750.
c.		2 l bister brown, *bister* (F, '62)	90.00	*135.00*
		On cover		1,750.
10	A1	20 l dk bl, *bluish* (C)	15,000.	—
		On cover		75,000.

With Figures on Back

11	A1	5 l grn, *grnsh* (F)	300.00	135.00
		No gum	175.00	
		On cover		1,500.
a.		5 l green, *greenish* (C)	375.00	190.00
		On cover		—
b.		As "a," double "5" on back (F, C)		*2,850.*
c.		5 l green, *greenish,* bl grn figures on back (F, '62)	350.00	135.00
		On cover		—
12	A1	10 l org, *grnsh* (F, '62)	600.00	90.00
		No gum	325.00	
		On cover		—
a.		10 l orange, *greenish* (C)	1,950.	300.00
		On cover		—
c.		10 l orange, *greenish* (F)	600.00	135.00
		On cover		—
13	A1	20 l blue, *bluish* (F, '62)	475.00	57.50
		On cover		125.00
a.		20 l dull blue, *bluish* (C)	6,750.	245.00
		On cover		625.00
b.		20 l dark blue, *bluish,* (F)	3,500.	110.00
		On cover		490.00
14	A1	40 l red vio, *pale bl* (F, '62)	5,250.	475.00
		On cover		1,250.
a.		40 l red violet, *blue* (C)	10,000.	600.00
		On cover		1,500.
b.		40 l red violet, *blue,* (F)	5,250.	475.00
		On cover		1,250.
15	A1	80 l carmine, *pink* (F, '62)	1,200.	165.00
		On cover		475.00
a.		80 l carmine, *pink* (F)	1,200.	165.00
		On cover		475.00
b.		80 l dl rose, *pink* (F, '62)	1,200.	165.00
		On cover		475.00

Full margins = ¾mm.

Nos. 8-15 are known as the "Athens Provisionals." The first printings were not very successful, producing the "coarse printings." Later printings used an altered printing method that gave better results (the "fine printings"). All these were issued in the normal manner by the Post Office.

Nos. 8, 9c, 11c, 12, 13, 14, 15 have uninterrupted and even shading lines that do not taper off at the ends. They were produced in May 1862 (F, '62). Other fine printing stamps were produced in Feb.-Apr. 1862 (F).

The numerals on the back are strongly shaded in the right lines with the corresponding left lines being quite thin. The colors of the numerals are generally strong and often show clumps of ink.

Nos. 15a and 15b have vermilion figures on the back, while those of all later printings are carmine.

Athens Print, Consecutive Print

With Figures on Back
Except 1 l, 2 l

1862-67

16	A1	1 l brn, *brnish* (poor print)	60.00	60.00
		No gum	35.00	
		On cover		350.00
a.		1 l red brn, *brnish* (poor print)	150.00	150.00
		No gum	85.00	
		On cover		850.00
b.		1 l choc, *brnish*	67.50	67.50
		No gum	35.00	
		On cover		350.00
17	A1	2 l bister, *bister*	55.00	60.00
		No gum	30.00	
		On cover		825.00
a.		2 l brnsh bis, *bister*	13.00	24.00
		No gum	7.50	
		On cover		550.00
18	A1	5 l grn, *grnsh*	250.00	24.00
		No gum	125.00	
		On cover		80.00
a.		5 l yellowish green, *grnsh*	250.00	12.00
		No gum	125.00	
		On cover		80.00
19	A1	10 l org, *blue* ('64)	400.00	47.50
		No gum	225.00	
		On cover		95.00
a.		10 l yel org, *bluish*	650.00	60.00
		No gum	350.00	
		On cover		150.00
b.		As "b," "10" inverted on front of stamp		*23,500.*
c.		10 l red org, *bl* (Dec. '65)	650.00	27.50
		No gum	350.00	
		On cover		75.00
d.		"01" on back	9,000.	*175.00*
20	A1	20 l bl, *bluish*	250.00	24.00
		No gum	115.00	
		On cover		17.50
a.		20 l lt bl, *bluish* (fine print)	375.00	24.00
		No gum	200.00	
		On cover		275.00
b.		20 l dark blue, *bluish*	2,000.	67.50
		No gum	1,200.	
		On cover, single franking		275.00
c.		20 l blue, *greenish*	1,700.	37.50
		No gum	950.00	
		On cover, single franking		275.00
d.		"80" on back		*2,450.*
e.		Double "20" on back		*1,500.*
f.		Without "20" on back		*5,500.*
21	A1	40 l lilac, *bl*	550.00	37.50
		No gum	300.00	
		On cover		275.00
a.		40 l grayish lilac, *blue*	1,750.	37.50
		On cover		275.00
b.		40 l lilac brown, *lil gray*	1,500.	47.50
		On cover		275.00
c.		Double "40" on back		1,600.
22	A1	80 l car, *pale rose*	80.00	24.00
		No gum	37.50	
		On cover		325.00
a.		80 l rose, *pale rose*	80.00	24.00
		No gum	37.50	
		On cover		325.00
b.		"8" on back inverted	—	550.00
c.		"80" on back inverted		—
d.		"8" only on back		700.00
e.		"0" only on back		700.00

Nos. 16-22 represent a series of printings for each value, from 1862 through 1867, until a major cleaning of the plates was done in 1868. Impressions range from very fine and clear to coarse and blotchy.

Some printings of Nos. 16, 16a, 16b show faint vertical, horizontal or quadrilled lines in the background. Later 1 l stamps do not show these lines.

Many stamps of this and succeeding issues which are normally imperforate are known privately rouletted, pin-perforated, percé en scie, etc.

With Figures on Back, Except 1 l, 2 l

1868   From Cleaned Plates

23	A1	1 l gray brn, *brnish*	67.50	75.00
		No gum	37.50	
		On cover, single franking		475.00
a.		1 l brown, *brownish*	67.50	82.50
		No gum	37.50	
		On cover, single franking		475.00
b.		1 l chocolate brown	67.50	82.50
		No gum	37.50	
		On cover, single franking		150.00
c.		1 l chocolate brown	67.50	82.50
		No gum	37.50	
		On cover, single franking		150.00
24	A1	2 l gray bis, *bister*	32.50	47.50
		No gum	19.00	
		On cover, single franking		550.00
25	A1	5 l grn, *grnsh*	6,500.	150.00
		No gum	3,750.	
		On cover, with other stamps		300.00
		On cover, single franking		—
a.		5 l yellow green, *grnsh*	6,500.	50.00
		No gum	3,750.	
		On cover, with other stamps		300.00
		On cover, single franking		—
26	A1	10 l pale org, *bluish*	1,650.	40.00
		No gum	900.00	
		On cover, with other stamps		80.00
		On cover, single franking		—
a.		"01" on back	—	—
b.		10 l red orange, *bluish*	1,650.	40.00
		No gum	900.00	
		On cover, with other stamps		80.00
		On cover, single franking		—
c.		10 l red orange, *very blue*	—	175.00
d.		10 l salmon, *bluish*	—	650.00
27	A1	20 l pale bl, *bluish*	1,500.	24.00
		No gum	825.00	
		On cover		47.50
a.		Double "20" on back	—	1,450.
28	A1	40 l rose vio, *bl*	325.00	37.50
		On cover		275.00
a.		"20" on back, corrected to "40"	—	2,750.
29	A1	80 l rose car, *pale rose*	190.00	250.00
		On cover		750.00

The "0" on the back of No. 29 is printed more heavily than the "8."

With Figures on Back, Except 1 l

1870

30	A1	1 l deep reddish brn, *brnish*	175.00	200.00
		On cover, single franking		900.00
a.		1 l redsh brn, *brnish*	200.00	240.00
		On cover, single franking		950.00
31	A1	20 l lt bl, *bluish*	1,900.	24.00
		On cover		67.50
a.		20 l blue, *bluish*	2,000.	35.00
		On cover		75.00
b.		"02" on back		1,225.
c.		"20" on back inverted		675.00

Nos. 30 and 30a have short lines of shading on cheek. The spandrels of No. 31 are very pale with the lines often broken or missing.

This was an Athens Printing made under supervision of German workmen.

Medium to Thin Paper
With Figures on Back, Except 1 l, 2 l

1870   Without Mesh

32	A1	1 l brn, *brnish*	325.00	325.00
		On cover		500.00
a.		1 l purple brown, *brnish*	325.00	325.00
		On cover		500.00
33	A1	2 l sal bis, *bister*	19.00	45.00
		On cover		475.00
34	A1	5 l grn, *grnsh*	6,000.	120.00
		On cover		250.00
35	A1	10 l lt red org, *grnsh*	—	240.00
		On cover		500.00
a.		"01" on back	—	—
b.		"10" on back inverted	—	—
36	A1	20 l bl, *bluish*	1,400.	24.00
		On cover		60.00
a.		"02" on back	—	600.00
b.		Double "20" on back	—	1,375.
37	A1	40 l sal, *grnsh*	825.00	82.50
		On cover		400.00
a.		40 l lilac, *greenish*		75,000.

The stamps of this issue have rather coarse figures on back.

No. 37a is printed in the exact shade of the numerals on the back of No. 37.

Thin Transparent Paper
With Figures on Back, Except 1 l

1872   Showing Mesh

38	A1	1 l grayish brown, *straw*	55.00	75.00
		On cover		150.00
a.		1 l red brn, *yelsh*	82.50	115.00
		On cover		225.00
39	A1	5 l grn, *greenish*	675.00	30.00
		On cover		60.00
a.		5 l dark green, *grnsh*	725.00	40.00
		On cover		60.00
b.		Double "5" on back		225.00

40	A1	10 l red org, *grnsh*	1,050.	37.50
		On cover		80.00
a.		10 l red orange, *pale lilac*	7,750.	150.00
		On cover		300.00
b.		As #40, "10" on back inverted	—	90.00
c.		Double "10" on back	—	1,125.
d.		"0" on back	—	525.00
e.		"01" on back	—	2,100.
41	A1	20 l dp bl, *bluish*	1,375.	30.00
		On cover		67.50
a.		20 l blue, *bluish*	1,375.	32.50
		On cover		67.50
b.		20 l dark blue, *blue*	2,500.	55.00
		On cover		140.00
42	A1	40 l brn, *bl*	45.00	*67.50*
		On cover		200.00
a.		40 l olive brown, *blue*	45.00	70.00
		On cover		200.00
b.		40 l red violet, *blue*	1,000.	95.00
		On cover		300.00
c.		40 l gray violet, *blue*	825.00	75.00
		On cover		240.00
d.		Figures on back bister (#42b, 42c)	1,100.	95.00

The mesh is not apparent on Nos. 38, 38a.

On Cream Paper Unless Otherwise Stated
With Figures on Back, Except 1 l, 2 l

1875

43	A1	1 l gray brn	15.00	12.00
		On cover		40.00
a.		1 l Deep red brown	35.00	20.00
		On cover		100.00
b.		1 l black brown, *yellowish*	175.00	*160.00*
		On cover		—
c.		1 l red brown	45.00	60.00
		On cover		82.50
d.		1 l dark red brown	75.00	*87.50*
		On cover		110.00
e.		1 l purple brown	75.00	*87.50*
		On cover		110.00
44	A1	2 l bister	30.00	*32.50*
		On cover		72.50
45	A1	5 l pale yellow green	200.00	30.00
		On cover		45.00
a.		5 l dk yel grn	275.00	40.00
		On cover		45.00
46	A1	10 l orange	425.00	45.00
		On cover		65.00
a.		10 l orange, *yellow*	240.00	25.00
		On cover		50.00
b.		"00" on back	925.00	200.00
c.		"0" on back	—	260.00
d.		"1" on back	—	260.00
e.		"0" on back	—	225.00
f.		"01" on back	—	535.00
g.		Double "10" on back	—	800.00
		On cover		—
47	A1	20 l ultra	160.00	24.00
		On cover		67.50
a.		20 l blue	290.00	24.00
		On cover		67.50
b.		20 l deep Prussian blue	1,600.	60.00
		On cover		200.00
c.		"02" on back	—	475.00
d.		"20" on back inverted	—	11,000.
e.		"2" instead of "20," inverted	—	*3,000.*
f.		Double "20" on back	—	*1,350.*
g.		"20" inverted, on front of stamp		210,000.
48	A1	40 l salmon	30.00	*90.00*
		On cover		1,000.

The back figures are found in many varieties, including "1" and "0" inverted in "10."

Value for No. 47e is for example with "2" of "02" broken (deformed). Also known with unbroken "2"; value used about $600.

Paris Print, Clear Impression

1876   Without Figures on Back

49	A1	30 l ol brn, *yelsh*	290.00	60.00
		On cover		525.00
a.		30 l brown, *yellowish*	500.00	135.00
		On cover		950.00
50	A1	60 l grn, *grnsh*	40.00	115.00
		On cover		3,000.

Athens Print, Coarse Impression, Yellowish Paper

51	A1	30 l dark brown	75.00	13.50
		On cover		40.00
		30 l black brown	75.00	13.50
		On cover		40.00
52	A1	60 l green	625.00	67.50
		On cover		3,000.

Without Figures on Back

1880-82   Cream Paper

53	A1	5 l green	30.00	9.50
		On cover, single franking		275.00
54	A1	10 l orange	27.50	9.50
		On cover		140.00
a.		10 l yellow	27.50	9.50
		On cover, single franking		140.00
b.		10 l red orange	8,250.	75.00
		On cover		—
55	A1	20 l ultra	450.00	190.00
		On cover, single franking		550.00
56	A1	20 l pale rose (aniline ink) ('82)	8.25	8.25
		On cover		35.00
a.		20 l rose (aniline ink) ('82)	8.25	8.25
		On cover		35.00
b.		20 l deep carmine	275.00	160.00
		On cover		—
57	A1	30 l ultra ('82)	225.00	17.50
		On cover, single franking		175.00
a.		30 l slate blue	230.00	17.50
		On cover, single franking		175.00

58	A1	40 l lilac	67.50	15.00
		On cover, single franking		375.00
a.		40 l violet	67.50	24.00
		On cover, single franking		375.00

Stamps of type A1 were not regularly issued with perf. 11½ but were freely used on mail.

Hermes — A2

Lepta denominations have white numeral tablets.

Belgian Print, Clear Impression

1886-88   *Imperf.*

64	A2	1 l brown ('88)	4.00	4.00
65	A2	2 l bister ('88)	9.50	225.00
66	A2	5 l yel grn ('88)	12.00	2.75
67	A2	10 l yellow ('88)	16.00	2.40
68	A2	20 l car rose ('88)	45.00	4.00
69	A2	25 l blue	160.00	2.75
70	A2	40 l violet ('88)	105.00	30.00
71	A2	50 l gray grn	8.25	2.75
72	A2	1d gray	120.00	4.00
		Nos. 64-72 (9)	*479.75*	*277.65*

See Nos. 81-116. For surcharges see Nos. 129, 134, 140, 144, 150, 151-152, 155-156.

1891   *Perf. 11½*

81	A2	1 l brown	8.25	3.50
82	A2	2 l bister	13.50	
83	A2	5 l yel grn	27.50	13.00
84	A2	10 l yellow	40.00	13.00
85	A2	20 l car rose	55.00	18.00
86	A2	25 l blue	275.00	25.00
87	A2	40 l violet	190.00	190.00
88	A2	50 l gray grn	22.50	6.50
89	A2	1d gray	200.00	8.25
		Nos. 81-89 (9)	*831.75*	*277.25*

The Belgian Printings perf. 13½ and most of the values perf. 11½ (Nos. 82-86) were perforated on request of philatelists at the main post office in Athens. While not regularly issued they were freely used for postage.

Athens Print, Poor Impression
Wmk. Greek Words in Some Sheets

1889-95   *Imperf.*

90	A2	1 l black brn	6.75	2.75
a.		1 l brown	6.75	4.00
91	A2	2 l pale bister	1.75	1.60
a.		2 l buff	2.75	*2.75*
92	A2	5 l green	11.00	1.60
a.		Double impression	200.00	
b.		5 l deep green	40.00	9.50
93	A2	10 l yellow	125.00	5.50
a.		10 l orange	47.50	4.00
b.		10 l dull yellow	125.00	5.50
94	A2	20 l carmine	11.00	8.25
a.		20 l rose	75.00	40.00
95	A2	25 l dull blue	125.00	9.50
a.		25 l indigo	150.00	6.75
b.		25 l ultra	125.00	6.75
c.		25 l brt blue	135.00	9.50
96	A2	25 l lilac	13.50	2.75
a.		25 l red vio ('93)	20.00	4.00
97	A2	40 l red vio ('91)	125.00	27.50
98	A2	40 l blue ('93)	9.50	2.75
99	A2	1d gray ('95)	475.00	8.25

Perf. 13½

100	A2	1 l brown	80.00	—
101	A2	2 l buff	2.00	1.60
104	A2	20 l carmine	67.50	5.25
a.		20 l rose	80.00	6.25
105	A2	40 l red violet	130.00	47.50

Other denominations of type A2 were not officially issued with perf. 13½.

Perf. 11½

107	A2	1 l brown	3.00	1.60
a.		1 l black brown	7.25	5.75
108	A2	2 l pale bister	2.50	2.00
a.		2 l buff	2.75	2.75
109	A2	5 l pale green	13.50	2.00
a.		5 l deep green	55.00	3.00
110	A2	10 l yellow	95.00	1.25
a.		10 l dull yellow	165.00	2.50
b.		10 l orange	300.00	5.75
111	A2	20 l carmine	55.00	.75
a.		20 l rose	160.00	1.60
112	A2	25 l dull blue	110.00	3.75
a.		25 l indigo	300.00	21.00
b.		25 l ultra	110.00	52.50
c.		25 l bright blue	160.00	9.00
113	A2	25 l lilac	6.75	1.60
a.		25 l red violet	20.00	2.75
114	A2	40 l red violet	160.00	37.50
115	A2	40 l blue	16.50	2.75
116	A2	1d gray	600.00	10.50

Partly-perforated varieties sell for about twice as much as normal stamps.

The watermark on Nos. 90-116 consists of three Greek words meaning Paper for Public Service. It is in double-lined capitals, measures 270x35mm, and extends across three panes.

Boxers — A3

Discobolus by Myron — A4

Vase Depicting Pallas Athene (Minerva) — A5

Chariot Driving A6

Stadium and Acropolis A7

Statue of Hermes by Praxiteles — A8

Statue of Victory by Paeonius — A9

Acropolis and Parthenon A10

Perf. 14x13½, 13½x14

1896   Unwmk.

117	A3	1 l ocher	4.00	3.00
118	A3	2 l rose	3.00	3.00
a.		Without engraver's name	30.00	21.00
119	A4	5 l lilac	12.50	5.25
120	A4	10 l slate gray	12.50	7.25
121	A5	20 l red brn	25.00	8.25
122	A6	25 l red	30.00	10.50
123	A5	40 l violet	14.50	9.50
124	A6	60 l black	42.50	21.00
125	A7	1d blue	115.00	26.00
126	A8	2d bister	325.00	105.00
a.		Horiz. pair, imperf. btwn.		
127	A9	5d green	575.00	500.00
128	A10	10d brown	625.00	500.00
		Nos. 117-128 (12)	*1,784.*	*1,248.*

1st intl. Olympic Games of the modern era, held at Athens. Counterfeits of Nos. 123-124 and 126-128 exist.

For surcharges see Nos. 159-164.

Preceding Issues Surcharged

1900   *Imperf.*

129	A2	20 l on 25 l dl bl, #95c	3.00	1.60
a.		20 l on 25 l indigo, #95a	67.50	47.50
b.		20 l on 25 l ultra, #95b	70.00	55.00
c.		Double surcharge	57.50	57.50
d.		Triple surcharge	85.00	85.00
e.		Inverted surcharge	60.00	57.50
f.		"20" above word	110.00	105.00
g.		Pair, one without surcharge	250.00	250.00
h.		"20" without word	165.00	165.00

130	A1	30 l on 40 l vio, *cr*, #58a	6.50	6.25
a.		30 l on 40 l lilac, #58	15.50	15.50
b.		Broad "0" in "30"	10.50	8.25
c.		First letter of word is "A"	135.00	135.00
d.		Double surcharge	625.00	625.00
132	A1	40 l on 2 l bis, *cr*, #44	8.50	8.25
a.		Broad "0" in "40"	12.50	12.50
b.		First letter of word is "A"	165.00	165.00
133	A1	50 l on 40 l sal, *cr*, #48	6.25	6.25
a.		Broad "0" in "50"	10.00	8.25
b.		First letter of word is "A"	135.00	135.00
c.		"50" without word	200.00	175.00
d.		"50" above word	200.00	175.00
134	A2	1d on 40 l red vio (No. 97)	15.50	6.25
137	A1	3d on 10 l org, *cr*, #54	52.50	52.50
a.		3d on 10 l yellow, #54a	52.50	52.50
138	A1	5d on 40 l red vio, *bl*, #21	150.00	150.00
a.		5d on 40 l red vio, *bl*, #28	190.00	190.00
b.		"20" on back corrected to "40"	1,400.	
139	A1	5d on 40 l red vio, *bl*, #42b	575.00	

Perf. 11½

140	A2	20 l on 25 l dl bl, #112	3.25	3.25
a.		20 l on 25 l indigo, #112a	100.00	90.00
b.		20 l on 25 l ultra, #112b	80.00	77.50
c.		Double surcharge	67.50	70.00
d.		Triple surcharge	95.00	95.00
e.		Inverted surcharge	67.50	67.50
f.		"20" above word	150.00	150.00
141	A1	30 l on 40 l vio, *cr*, #58a	10.50	10.50
a.		30 l on 40 l lilac, #58	17.50	17.50
b.		Broad "0" in "30"	12.50	12.50
c.		First letter of word is "A"	150.00	150.00
d.		Double surcharge		
142	A1	40 l on 2 l bis, *cr*, #44	15.50	15.50
a.		Broad "0" in "40"	15.50	15.50
b.		First letter of word is "A"	165.00	165.00
143	A1	50 l on 40 l sal, *cr*, #48	10.50	10.50
a.		Broad "0" in "50"	12.50	12.50
b.		First letter of word is "A"	135.00	135.00
c.		"50" without word	200.00	175.00
144	A2	1d on 40 l red vio, #114	145.00	160.00
147	A1	3d on 10 l yel, *cream,* #54a	57.50	57.50
a.		3d on 10 l org, *cr*, #54	60.00	65.00
148	A1	5d on 40 l red vio, *bl*, #21	150.00	175.00
a.		5d on 40 l red vio, *bl*, #28	175.00	225.00
149	A1	5d on 40 l red vio, *bl*, #42b	625.00	

Perf. 13½

150	A2	2d on 40 l red vio, #105	12.00	12.50

The 1d on 40 l perf. 13½ and the 2d on 40 l, both imperf. and perf. 13½, were not officially issued.

Surcharge Including "A M"

"A M" = "Axia Metalliki" or "Value in Metal (gold)."

1900			***Imperf.***	
151	A2	25 l on 40 l vio, #70	6.00	10.50
152	A2	50 l on 25 l bl, #69	26.50	24.00
153	A1	1d on 40 l brn, *bl*, #42b	125.00	*150.00*
154	A1	2d on 5 l grn, *cr*, #53	16.00	*21.00*

Perf. 11½

155	A2	25 l on 40 l vio, #87	12.00	15.50
156	A2	50 l on 25 l bl, #86	52.50	62.50
157	A1	1d on 40 l brn, *bl*, #42b	160.00	160.00
158	A1	2d on 5 l grn, *cr*, #53	20.00	26.00
		Nos. 151-158 (8)	418.00	469.50

Partly-perforated varieties of Nos. 129-158 sell for about two to three times as much as normal stamps.

Surcharge in Red

1900-01			***Perf. 14x13½***	
159	A7	5 l on 1d blue	15.00	9.50
a.		Wrong font "M" with serifs	75.00	*80.00*
b.		Double surcharge	225.00	200.00
160	A5	25 l on 40 l vio	70.00	67.50
a.		Double surcharge	900.00	
161	A8	50 l on 2d bister	80.00	62.50
a.		Broad "0" in "50"	80.00	62.50
162	A9	1d on 5d grn ('01)	250.00	200.00
a.		Greek "Δ" instead of "A" as 3rd letter	650.00	700.00

163	A10	2d on 10d brn ('01)	70.00	*100.00*
a.		Greek "Δ" instead of "A" as 3rd letter	275.00	250.00
		Nos. 159-163 (5)	485.00	439.50

Black Surcharge on No. 160

164	A5	50 l on 25 l on 40 l vio (R + Bk)	500.00	475.00
a.		Broad "0" in "50"	475.00	575.00

Nos. 151-164 and 179-183, gold currency stamps, were generally used for parcel post and foreign money orders. They were also available for use on letters, but cost about 20 per cent more than the regular stamps of the same denomination.

Counterfeit surcharges exist of Nos. 159-164.

Giovanni da Bologna's Hermes

A11   A12

A13

Type I   Type II

FIVE LEPTA.

Type I — Letters of "ΕΛΛΑΣ" not outlined at top and left. Only a few faint horizontal lines between the outer vertical lines at sides.

Type II — Letters of "ΕΛΛΑΣ" fully outlined. Heavy horizontal lines between the vertical frame lines.

Perf. 11½, 12½, 13½

1901		**Engr.**		**Wmk. 129**	
165	A11	1 l yellow brn		.40	.25
166	A11	2 l gray		.60	.25
167	A11	3 l orange		.65	.30
168	A12	5 l grn, type I		.80	.25
a.		5 l yellow green, type I		.60	.25
b.		5 l yellow green, type II		.60	.25
169	A12	10 l rose		3.25	.25
170	A11	20 l red lilac		6.50	.25
171	A12	25 l ultra		6.50	.25
172	A11	30 l dl vio		12.00	2.00
173	A11	40 l dk brn		25.00	3.00
174	A11	50 l brn lake		20.00	1.50

Perf. 12½, 14 and Compound

175	A13	1d black	47.50	3.00
a.		Horiz. pair, imperf. btwn.	325.00	
c.		Horiz. pair, imperf. vert.	300.00	
d.		Vert. pair, imperf. horiz.	300.00	

Litho.
Perf. 12½

176	A13	2d bronze	11.00	8.00
177	A13	3d silver	11.00	*12.00*
178	A13	5d gold	13.00	*15.00*
		Nos. 165-178 (14)	158.20	46.30
		Set, never hinged	325.00	

All values 1 l through 1d issued on both thick and thin paper. Nos. 173-174 are values for thin paper — values for thick paper are higher.

For overprints and surcharges see Nos. RA3-RA13, N16, N109.

Imperf., Pairs

165a	A11	1 l	12.00
166a	A11	2 l	15.00
167a	A11	3 l	15.00
168c	A12	5 l	12.00
169a	A12	10 l	19.00
170a	A11	20 l	15.00
171a	A12	25 l	15.00
172a	A11	30 l	250.00
173a	A11	40 l	300.00
174a	A11	50 l	70.00
175b	A13	1d	250.00

Nos. 165a-175a were issued on both thick and thin paper. Values are for the less expensive thin paper.

Hermes — A14

1902, Jan. 1		**Engr.**	***Perf. 13½***	
179	A14	5 l deep orange	2.00	1.10
a.		Imperf., pair	82.50	
180	A14	25 l emerald	30.00	3.00
a.		Imperf., pair	550.00	
181	A14	50 l ultra	30.00	3.75
182	A14	1d rose red	30.00	8.25
183	A14	2d orange brn	52.50	50.00
		Nos. 179-183 (5)	144.50	66.10
		Set, never hinged	375.00	

See note after No. 164. In 1913 remainders of Nos. 179-183 were used as postage dues.

Apollo Throwing Discus
A15

Jumper, with Jumping Weights
A16

Victory — A17

Atlas and Hercules
A18

Struggle of Hercules and Antaeus
A19

Wrestlers
A20

Daemon of the Games
A21

Foot Race
A22

Nike, Priest and Athletes in Pre-Games Offering to Zeus
A23

Wmk. Crown and ET (129)

1906, Mar.		**Engr.**	**Perf. 13½, 14**	
184	A15	1 l brown	.55	.40
a.		Imperf., pair	300.00	
185	A15	2 l gray	.55	.40
a.		Imperf., pair	300.00	
186	A15	3 l orange	.55	.40
a.		Imperf., pair	300.00	
187	A15	5 l green	1.25	.40
a.		Imperf., pair	110.00	
188	A17	10 l rose red	3.00	.60
a.		Imperf., pair	300.00	
189	A18	20 l magenta	5.00	.60
a.		Imperf., pair	575.00	
190	A19	25 l ultra	6.00	.85
a.		Imperf., pair	575.00	
191	A20	30 l dl pur	5.00	2.75
a.		Double impression	1,100.	
192	A21	40 l dk brown	5.00	2.75
193	A18	50 l brn lake	10.00	3.25
194	A22	1d gray blk	65.00	13.00
a.		Imperf., pair	1,100.	
195	A22	2d rose	100.00	35.00
196	A22	3d olive yel	155.00	125.00
197	A23	5d dull blue	160.00	140.00
		Nos. 184-197 (14)	516.90	325.40
		Set, never hinged	1,500.	

Greek Special Olympic Games of 1906 at Athens, celebrating the 10th anniv. of the modern Olympic Games.

Surcharged stamps of this issue are revenues.

A24

Iris Holding Caduceus
A25

Hermes Donning Sandals
A26

Hermes Carrying Infant Arcas — A27

Hermes, from Old Cretan Coin — A28

Designs A24 to A28 are from Cretan and Arcadian coins of the 4th Century, B.C.

Serrate Roulette 13½

1911-21		**Engr.**	**Unwmk.**	
198	A24	1 l green	.65	.30
199	A25	2 l car rose	.65	.30
200	A24	3 l vermilion	.95	.30
201	A26	5 l green	2.00	.30
202	A24	10 l car rose	9.50	.30
203	A25	20 l gray lilac	3.00	.80
204	A25	25 l ultra	15.00	.80
a.		Rouletted in black	190.00	140.00
205	A26	30 l car rose	4.50	1.60
206	A25	40 l deep blue	10.00	4.00
207	A26	50 l dl vio	15.00	3.00
208	A27	1d ultra	20.00	.80
209	A27	2d vermilion	27.50	.95
210	A27	3d car rose	27.50	1.40
a.		Size 20¼x25½mm ('21)	100.00	50.00
211	A27	5d ultra	35.00	4.00
a.		Size 20¼x25½mm ('21)	200.00	25.00

212	A27	10d dp bl ('21)	140.00	70.00
a.		Size 20x26½mm ('11)	300.00	125.00
213	A28	25d deep blue	87.50	55.00
		Nos. 198-213 (16)	398.75	143.85
		Set, never hinged	750.00	

The 1921 reissues of the 3d, 5d and 10d ... 20x26½mm instead of 20x26½mm.
See Nos. 214-231. For overprints see Nos. 233-248B, N1, N10-N15, N17-N52A, N110-N148, Thrace 22-30, N26-N75.

Imperf., Pairs

198a	A24	1 l	90.00	90.00
200a	A24	3 l	240.00	240.00
201a	A26	5 l	30.00	30.00
202a	A24	10 l	52.50	52.50
203a	A25	20 l	225.00	225.00
204b	A25	25 l	300.00	300.00
206a	A25	40 l	350.00	
207a	A26	50 l	350.00	
208a	A27	1d	350.00	
209a	A27	2d	350.00	
210b	A27	3d	350.00	
211b	A27	5d	240.00	
212b	A27	10d As "a"	1,600.	
213a	A28	25d	2,250.	

Serrate Roulette 10½x13½, 13½
1913-23   Litho.

214	A24	1 l green	.25	.25
a.		Without period after "ΕΛ–ΛΑΣ"	77.50	—
215	A25	2 l rose	.25	.25
216	A24	3 l vermilion	.25	.25
217	A26	5 l green	.25	.25
218	A24	10 l carmine	.25	.25
219	A25	15 l dl bl ('18)	.35	.25
220	A25	20 l slate	.35	.25
221	A25	25 l ultra	4.00	.50
a.		25 l blue		.20
c.		Double impression		—
222	A26	30 l rose ('14)	.95	.40
223	A25	40 l indigo ('14)	2.10	.70
224	A26	50 l vio brn ('14)	4.25	.35
225	A26	80 l vio brn ('23)	5.25	1.40
226	A27	1d ultra ('19)	7.00	.70
227	A27	2d ver ('19)	6.50	.70
228	A27	3d car rose ('20)	8.50	.80
229	A27	5d ultra ('22)	12.00	1.00
230	A27	10d dp bl ('22)	12.00	1.25
231	A28	25d indigo ('22)	16.00	4.75
		Nos. 214-231 (18)	80.50	14.30
		Set, never hinged	225.00	

Nos. 221, 223 and 226 were re-issued in 1926, printed in Vienna from new plates. There are slight differences in minor details.
The 10 lepta brown, on thick paper, type A28, is not a postage stamp. It was issued in 1922 to replace coins of this denomination during a shortage of copper.

Imperf., Pairs

214b	A24	1 l	65.00	
215a	A25	2 l	110.00	
216a	A24	3 l	175.00	
217a	A26	5 l	65.00	
218a	A24	10 l	82.50	
220a	A25	20 l	82.50	
221b	A25	25 l	175.00	
222a	A26	30 l	175.00	
223a	A25	40 l	175.00	
224a	A26	50 l	300.00	
225b	A26	80 l	92.50	
226a	A27	1d		250.00
227a	A27	2d	100.00	
228b	A27	3d	300.00	
229a	A27	5d	360.00	

Raising Greek Flag at Suda Bay, Crete — A29

1913, Dec. 1   Engr.   Perf. 14½

232	A29	25 l blue & black	8.00	5.00
		Never hinged	16.00	
a.		Imperf., pair	1,400.	

Union of Crete with Greece. Used only in Crete.

Stamps of 1911-14 Overprinted in Red or Black

Serrate Roulette 13½
1916, Nov. 1   Litho.

233	A24	1 l green (R)	.25	.25
234	A25	2 l rose	.25	.25
235	A24	3 l vermilion	.25	.25
236	A26	5 l green (R)	.50	.40
237	A24	10 l carmine	.75	.40
238	A25	20 l slate (R)	1.50	.40
239	A25	25 l blue (R)	1.50	.40
a.		25 l ultra	140.00	26.00
240	A26	30 l rose	1.50	.90
a.		Pair, one without ovpt.		

241	A25	40 l indigo (R)	11.00	3.00
242	A26	50 l vio brn (R)	37.50	2.50

Engr.

243	A24	3 l vermilion	.50	.50
244	A26	30 l car rose	1.25	1.25
245	A27	1d ultra (R)	40.00	4.00
a.		Rouletted in black	325.00	225.00
246	A27	2d vermilion	24.00	3.50
247	A27	3d car rose	14.00	3.50
248	A27	5d ultra (R)	95.00	15.00
248A	A27	10d dp bl (R)	24.00	22.50
		Nos. 233-248B (17)	253.75	55.80
		Set, never hinged	500.00	

Most of Nos. 233-248B exist with overprint double, inverted, etc. Minimum value of errors $18. Excellent counterfeits of the overprint varieties exist.

Issued by the Venizelist Provisional Government

Iris — A32

1917, Feb. 5   Litho.   Perf. 14

249	A32	1 l dp green	.40	.25
250	A32	5 l yel grn	.40	.25
251	A32	10 l rose	.80	.35
252	A32	25 l lt blue	1.10	.35
253	A32	50 l gray vio	9.00	2.50
254	A32	1d ultra	2.25	.75
255	A32	2d lt red	4.50	1.50
256	A32	3d claret	25.00	7.75
257	A32	5d gray bl	5.75	3.00
258	A32	10d dk blue	70.00	20.00
259	A32	25d slate	125.00	160.00
		Nos. 249-259 (11)	244.20	196.70
		Set, never hinged	500.00	

The 4d was used only as a revenue stamp.

Imperf., Pairs

249a	A32	1 l	9.50	
250a	A32	5 l	9.50	
251a	A32	10 l	9.50	
252a	A32	25 l	17.50	
253a	A32	50 l	25.00	
254a	A32	1d	22.50	
255a	A32	2d	30.00	
256a	A32	3d	65.00	
257a	A32	5d	65.00	
258a	A32	10d	110.00	
259a	A32	25d	125.00	

Stamps of 1917 Surcharged

1923

260	A32	5 l on 10 l rose	.25	.25
a.		Inverted surcharge	24.00	35.00
261	A32	50 l on 50 l gray vio	.25	.25
262	A32	1d on 1d ultra	.25	.25
a.		1d on 1d gray	.25	.25
263	A32	2d on 2d lt red	.55	.55
264	A32	3d on 3d claret	1.60	1.60
265	A32	5d on 5d dk bl	2.00	2.00
266	A32	25d on 25d slate	27.50	27.50
		Nos. 260-266 (7)	32.40	32.40
		Set, never hinged	125.00	

Same Surcharge on Occupation of Turkey Stamps, 1913
Perf. 13½

267	O2	5 l on 3 l org	.25	.25
a.		Inverted surcharge	19.00	
268	O1	10 l on 20 l vio	1.50	1.50
a.		Inverted surcharge	82.50	
269	O2	10 l on 25 l pale bl	.25	.25
a.		Inverted surcharge	60.00	35.00
270	O1	10 l on 30 l gray grn	.25	.25
271	O2	10 l on 40 l ind	1.25	1.25
272	O1	50 l on 50 l dk bl	.25	.25
a.		Inverted surcharge	72.50	37.50
273	O1	2d on 2d gray brn	60.00	60.00
274	O2	3d on 3d dl bl	4.50	6.00
a.		Imperf., pair	500.00	
275	O1	5d on 5d gray	4.00	7.00
276	O2	10d on 1d vio brn	15.00	22.50
276A	O2	10d on 10d car	800.00	
		Nos. 267-276 (10)	87.25	99.25
		Set, never hinged	150.00	

Dangerous counterfeits of No. 276A exist.

Same Surcharge on Stamps of Crete
Perf. 14
On Crete Nos. 50, 52, 59

276B	A6	5 l on 1 l red brn	27.50	27.50
277	A8	10 l on 10 l red	.25	.25
277B	A8	10 l on 25 l bl	110.00	110.00

On Crete Nos. 66-69, 71

278	A8	10 l on 25 l blue	.25	.25
279	A6	50 l on 50 l lilac	.45	.70
279A	A6	50 l on 50 l ultra	8.50	14.00
280	A9	50 l on 1d gray vio	3.00	4.00
280A	A11	50 l on 5d grn & blk	27.50	27.50

On Crete Nos. 77-82

281	A15	10 l on 20 l bl grn	125.00	125.00
282	A16	10 l on 25 l ultra	.45	.45
a.		Double surcharge	50.00	50.00
283	A17	50 l on 50 l yel brn	.25	.35
284	A18	50 l on 1d rose car & brn	2.00	1.75
a.		Imperf., pair	425.00	
285	A19	3d on 3d org & blk	14.00	14.00
286	A20	5d on 5d ol grn & blk	9.00	9.00

On Crete Nos. 83-84

287	A21	10 l on 25 l bl & blk	3.25	1.75
a.		Imperf., pair		
287B	A22	50 l on 1d grn & blk	8.00	4.50

On Crete No. 96

288	A23	10 l on 10 l brn red	.25	.25
a.		Inverted surcharge	45.00	40.00

On Crete No. 91

288B	A17	50 l on 50 l yel brn	800.00	

Dangerous counterfeits of the overprint on No. 288B are plentiful.

On Crete No. 109

289	A19	3d on 3d org & blk	17.50	17.50

On Crete Nos. 111, 113-120

290	A6	5 l on 1 l vio brn	.25	.25
a.		Inverted surcharge	25.00	
291	A13	10 l on 5 l grn	.25	.25
a.		Inverted surcharge	47.50	
292	A23	10 l on 10 l brn red	.25	.25
a.		Inverted surcharge	47.50	
293	A15	10 l on 20 l bl grn	.30	.30
a.		Inverted surcharge	47.50	
294	A16	10 l on 25 l ultra	.35	.35
a.		Inverted surcharge	47.50	
295	A17	50 l on 50 l yel brn	.40	.40
296	A18	50 l on 1d rose car & brn	5.25	5.25
a.		Inverted surcharge		
b.		Double surcharge	225.00	
c.		Double surch., one invtd.		
d.		Imperf., pair		
297	A19	3d on 3d org & blk	16.00	16.00
298	A20	5d on 5d ol grn & blk	200.00	200.00

Dangerous counterfeits of No. 298 exist.

Crete Nos. J2-J9

299	D1	5 l on 5 l red	.25	.25
a.		Inverted surcharge	45.00	6.75
300	D1	5 l on 10 l red	.30	.30
301	D1	5 l on 20 l red	12.00	12.00
a.		Inverted surcharge		
302	D1	5 l on 40 l red	.30	.30
303	D1	50 l on 50 l red	.30	.55
304	D1	50 l on 1d red	.30	.50
a.		Double surcharge		
305	D1	50 l on 1d on 1d red	9.50	9.50
306	D1	2d on 2d red	1.25	1.25

On Crete Nos. J11-J13

307	D1	5 l on 5 l red	6.00	6.00
308	D1	5 l on 10 l red	1.50	1.50
a.		"ΕΛΛΑΣ" inverted	6.50	
309	D1	10 l on 20 l red	55.00	55.00

On Crete Nos. J20-J22, J24-J26

310	D1	5 l on 5 l red	.25	.25
311	D1	5 l on 10 l red	.25	.25
a.		Inverted surcharge	12.00	
312	D1	10 l on 20 l red	.25	.25
313	D1	50 l on 50 l red	.55	.55
314	D1	50 l on 1d red	4.00	4.00
315	D1	2d on 2d red	7.00	7.00

These surcharged Postage Due stamps were intended for the payment of ordinary postage.
Nos. 260 to 315 were surcharged in commemoration of the revolution of 1922.
Nos. 59, 91, 109, 111, 113-120, J20-J22, J24-J26 are on stamps previously overprinted by Crete.

Issues of the Republic

Lord Byron — A33

Byron at Missolonghi — A34

1924, Apr. 16   Engr.   Perf. 12

316	A33	80 l dark blue	.55	.25
317	A34	2d dk vio & blk	1.25	.65
		Set, never hinged	3.25	

Death of Lord Byron (1788-1824) at Missolonghi.

Tomb of Markos Botsaris — A35

Serrate Roulette 13½
1926, Apr. 24   Litho.

318	A35	25 l lilac	.85	.50
		Never hinged	1.75	

Centenary of the defense of Missolonghi against the Turks.

Corinth Canal A36

Dodecanese Costume A37

Macedonian Costume A38

Monastery of Simon Peter on Mt. Athos A39

White Tower of Salonika A40

Temple of Hephaestus A41

The Acropolis — A42

Cruiser "Georgios Averoff" — A43

Academy of Sciences, Athens — A44

Temple of
Hephaestus
A45

Acropolis
A46

Perf. 12½x13, 13, 13x12½, 13½, 13½x13

1927, Apr. 1   **Engr.**

321	A36	5 l dark green	.25	.25
a.		Vert. pair, imperf. horiz.	140.00	92.50
322	A37	10 l orange red	.30	.25
a.		Horiz. pair, imperf. between	140.00	92.50
c.		Double impression	77.50	
323	A38	20 l violet	.30	.25
324	A39	25 l slate blue	.50	.25
a.		Imperf., pair	140.00	140.00
b.		Vert. pair, imperf. between	150.00	110.00
325	A40	40 l slate blue	.50	.25
326	A36	50 l violet	1.10	.25
327	A36	80 l dk bl & blk	.95	.25
a.			825.00	
328	A41	1 d dk bl & bis brn (I)	1.10	.25
a.		Imperf., pair	150.00	125.00
b.		Center inverted		6,500.
c.		Double impression of center	325.00	225.00
d.		Double impression of frame	325.00	225.00
329	A42	2 d dk green & blk	6.50	.30
a.		Imperf., pair	600.00	800.00
330	A43	3 d dp violet & blk	6.00	.30
a.		Double impression of center	225.00	275.00
b.		Center inverted		8,000.
331	A44	5 d yellow & blk	15.00	2.00
a.		Imperf., pair	925.00	925.00
b.		Center inverted	10,000.	4,500.
c.		5d yellow & green	110.00	37.50
332	A45	10 d brn car & blk	45.00	11.00
333	A44	15 d brt yel grn & blk	57.50	16.00
334	A46	25 d green & blk	110.00	18.00
a.		Double impression of center	—	
		Nos. 321-334 (14)	245.00	49.60
		Set, never hinged	700.00	

See Nos. 364-371 and notes preceding No. 364. For overprints see Nos. RA55, RA57, RA60; and RA66, RA70-RA71 in Scott Standard catalogue, Vol. 3.

This series as prepared, included a 1 lepton dark brown, type A37, but that value was never issued. Most stamps were burned. Value $300.

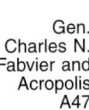

Gen. Charles N. Fabvier and Acropolis A47

1927, Aug. 1   **Perf. 12**

335	A47	1 d red	.30	.25
336	A47	3 d dark blue	2.00	.60
337	A47	6 d green	12.00	9.00
		Nos. 335-337 (3)	14.30	9.85
		Set, never hinged	42.50	

Cent. of the liberation of Athens from the Turks in 1826.
For surcharges see Nos. 376-377.

Bay of Navarino and Pylos A48

Battle of Navarino A49

"Edward" omitted — A50

"Edward" added — A51

Admiral de Rigny — A52

Admiral van der Heyden — A53

Designs: Nos. 340-341, Sir Edward Codrington.

Perf. 13½x12½, 12½x13½, 13x12½, 12½x13

1927-28   **Litho.**

338	A48	1.50d gray green	1.60	.35
a.		Imperf., pair	275.00	
b.		Horiz. pair, imperf. btwn.	875.00	
c.		Horiz. pair, imperf. vert.	250.00	
339	A49	4 d dk gray bl ('28)	7.00	1.50
340	A50	5 d dk brn & gray	5.50	4.75
a.		5d blk brn & blk ('28)	13.00	6.50
341	A51	5 d dk brn & blk ('28)	35.00	12.00
342	A52	5 d vio bl & blk ('28)	35.00	12.00
343	A53	5 d lake & blk ('28)	20.00	9.50
		Nos. 338-343 (6)	104.10	40.10
		Set, never hinged	275.00	

Centenary of the naval battle of Navarino.
For surcharges see Nos. 372-375.

Admiral Lascarina Bouboulina A54

Athanasios Diakos A55

Map of Greece in 1830 and 1930 — A56

Sortie from Missolonghi A58

Patriots Declaring Independence — A57

Portraits: 10 l, Constantine Rhigas Ferreos. 20 l, Gregorios V. 40 l, Prince Alexandros Ypsilantis. No. 345, Bouboulina. No. 355, Diakos. No. 346, Theodoros Kolokotronis. No. 356, Konstantinos Kanaris. No.347, Georgios Karaiskakis. No. 357, Markos Botsaris. 2d, Andreas Miaoulis. 3d, Lazaros Koundouriotis. 5d, Count John Capo d'Istria (Capodistria), statesman and doctor. 10d, Petros Mavromichalis. 15d, Dionysios Solomos. 20d, Adamantios Korais.

Various Frames

1930, Apr. 1   **Engr.**   **Perf. 13½, 14**
Imprint of Perkins, Bacon & Co.

344	A55	10 l brown	.25	.25
345	A54	50 l red	.25	.25
346	A54	1 d car rose	.30	.30
347	A55	1.50d lt blue	.40	.40
348	A55	2 d orange	.45	.45
349	A55	5 d purple	1.50	1.50
350	A54	10 d gray blk	6.50	6.50
351	A55	15 d yellow grn	12.00	12.00
352	A55	20 d blue blk	17.50	17.50

Imprint of Bradbury, Wilkinson & Co.
Perf. 12

353	A55	20 l black	.25	.25
354	A55	40 l blue grn	.25	.25
355	A55	50 l brt blue	.25	.25
356	A55	1 d brown org	.30	.30
357	A55	1.50d dk red	.40	.40
358	A55	3 d dk brown	.65	.65
359	A54	4 d dk blue	3.00	3.00
360	A57	25 d black	17.50	17.50
361	A58	50 d red brn	45.00	45.00
		Nos. 344-361 (18)	106.75	106.75
		Set, never hinged	275.00	

Greek independence, cent. Some exist imperf.

Arcadi Monastery and Abbot Gabriel (Mt. Ida in Background) A60

1930, Nov. 8   **Perf. 12**

363	A60	8 d deep violet	13.00	1.10
		Never hinged	55.00	

Issue of 1927 Re-engraved

50 l, Design is clearer, especially "50" and the 10 letters.

Type I

Type II

1d. Type I — Greek letters "Λ," "A," "Δ" have sharp pointed tops; numerals "1" are 1½mm wide at the foot, and have a straight slanting serif at top.

1d. Type II — Greek letters "Λ," "A," "Δ" have flat tops; numerals "1" are 2mm wide at foot and the serif at top is slightly curved. Perf. 14. There are many minor differences in the lines of the two designs.

1d. Type III — The "1" in lower left corner has no serif at left of foot. Lines of temple have been deepened, so details stand out more clearly.

2d. On 1927 stamp the Parthenon is indistinct and blurred. On 1933 stamp it is strongly outlined and clear. Between the two pillars at lower right are four blocks of marble. These blocks are clear and distinct on the 1933 stamp but run together on the 1927 issue.

3d. Design is clearer, especially vertical lines of shading in smoke stacks and reflections in the water. Two or more sides perf. 11½.

10d. Background and shading of entire stamp have been lightened. Detail of frame is clearer and more distinct.

15d. Many more lines of shading in sky and foreground. Engraving is sharp and clear, particularly in frame. Two or more sides perf. 11½.

25d. Background has been lightened and foreground reduced until base of larger upright column is removed and fallen column appears nearly submerged.

Sizes in millimeters:
50 l, 1927, 18x24¾. 1933, 18½x24½.
1d, 1927, 24¾x17¾. 1931, 24¾x17¼. 1933, 24½x18¼.
2d, 1927, 24½x17¾. 1933, 24½x18½.

Perf. 11½, 11½x12½, 12½x10, 13, 13x12½, 14

1931-35

364	A36	50 l dk vio ('33)	4.00	1.00
365	A41	1 d dk bl & org brn, type II	10.00	1.00
366	A41	1 d dk bl & org brn, type III ('33)	5.75	.25
367	A42	2 d dk grn & blk ('33)	2.75	.50
368	A43	3 d red vio & blk ('34)	3.25	.25
369	A45	10 d brn car & blk	47.50	1.50
a.		Imperf., pair	1,100.	
370	A44	15 d pale yel grn & blk ('34)	82.50	17.50
371	A46	25 d dk grn & blk ('35)	25.00	17.00
		Nos. 364-371 (8)	180.75	39.00
		Set, never hinged	600.00	

Nos. 336-337, 340-343 Surcharged in Red

1932   **Perf. 12½x13½, 12½x13**

372	A52	1.50d on 5d	2.00	.25
373	A53	1.50d on 5d	2.00	.25
a.		Double surcharge	110.00	
374	A50	2 d on 5d	5.00	.25
375	A51	2 d on 5d	9.00	.25

Perf. 12

376	A47	2 d on 3d	2.25	.25
a.		Double surcharge	125.00	
377	A47	4 d on 6d	2.50	1.10
		Nos. 372-377 (6)	22.75	2.35
		Set, never hinged	50.00	

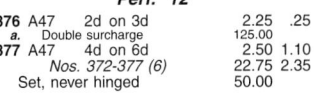

Adm. Pavlos Koundouriotis and Cruiser "Averoff" — A61

Pallas Athene — A62

Youth of Marathon — A63

1933   **Perf. 13½x13, 13x13½**

378	A61	50 d black & ind	50.00	1.60
a.		Imperf., pair	2,250.	
379	A62	75 d blk & vio brn	110.00	175.00
a.		Imperf., pair	825.00	
		Never hinged	1,700.	
380	A63	100 d brn & dull grn	625.00	29.00
a.		Imperf., pair	2,750.	
		Nos. 378-380 (3)	785.00	205.60
		Set, never hinged	1,800.	

The imperf pairs are without gum.
For surcharges see Nos. 386-387.

Approach to Athens Stadium A64

Perf. 11½, 11½x10, 13½x11½

1934, Dec. 10

381	A64	8 d blue	65.00	2.25
		Never hinged	200.00	

Perforations on No. 381 range from 10½ to 13, including compounds.

Church of Pantanassa, Mistra — A65

1935, Nov. 1   *Perf. 13x12½*
382	A65	4d brown	17.00	1.60
		Never hinged	47.50	
a.		Horiz. pair, imperf. between	725.00	
b.		Imperf., pair	725.00	

Issues of the Monarchy
J71, J76, J82, 380, 379 Surcharged in Red or Blue

Nos. 383-385   Nos. 386-387

Serrate Roulette 13½
1935, Nov. 24   *Litho.*
383	D3	50 l on 40 l indigo (R)	.25	.25
a.		Double surcharge		27.50
384	D3	3d on 3d car (Bl)	.55	.40

Perf. 13
385	D3	3d on 3d rose red (Bl)	2.75	2.00

Perf. 13x13½
386	A63	5d on 100d (R)	2.25	2.00
387	A62	15d on 75d (Bl)	6.50	6.00
		Nos. 383-387 (5)	12.30	10.65
		Set, never hinged	30.00	

King Constantine — A66

Center Engr., Frame Litho.
Perf. 12x13½
1936, Nov. 18   *Wmk. 252*
389	A66	3d black & brown	.55	.40
a.		Pair, printer's name in Greek	22.50	
b.		Pair, printer's name in English	22.50	
390	A66	8d black & blue	1.10	.90
a.		Pair, printer's name in Greek	22.50	
b.		Pair, printer's name in English	22.50	
		Set, never hinged	3.25	

Re-burial of the remains of King Constantine and Queen Sophia.

Two printings exist, the first containing varieties "a" and "b" with gray border; second with black border.

King George II — A67   Pallas Athene — A68

1937, Jan. 24   *Engr.*   *Perf. 12½x12*
391	A67	1d green	.25	.25
392	A67	3d red brown	.25	.25
393	A67	8d dp blue	.90	.40
394	A67	100d carmine lake	12.00	12.00
		Nos. 391-394 (4)	13.40	12.90
		Set, never hinged	30.00	

For surcharges see Nos. 484-487, 498-500, RA86-RA87, N241-N242 in Scott Standard catalogue, Vol. 3.

1937, Apr. 17   *Unwmk.*   *Perf. 11½*
395	A68	3d yellow brown	.55	.25
		Never hinged	1.10	

Centenary of the University of Athens.

Contest with Bull — A69

Lady of Tiryns — A70   Zeus of Dodona — A71

Coin of Amphictyonic League A72

Diagoras of Rhodes, Victor at Olympics A73

Venus of Melos — A74

Battle of Salamis A75

Chariot of Panathenaic Festival A76

Alexander the Great at Battle of Issos — A77

St. Paul Preaching to Athenians A78

St. Demetrius' Church at Salonika A79

Leo III Victory over Arabs — A80

Allegorical Figure of Glory — A81

Perf. 13½x12, 12x13½
1937, Nov. 1   *Litho.*   *Wmk. 252*
396	A69	5 l brn red & bl	.25	.25
a.		Double impression of frame	60.00	
397	A70	10 l bl & brn red	.25	.25
a.		Double impression of frame	60.00	
398	A71	20 l black & grn	.25	.25
399	A72	40 l green & blk	.25	.25
a.		Green impression doubled	60.00	
400	A73	50 l brown & blk	.25	.25
401	A74	80 l ind & yel brn	.25	.25

Engr.
402	A75	2d ultra	.25	.25
403	A76	5d red	.25	.25
a.		Printer's name omitted	5.50	
404	A77	6d olive brn	.25	.25
405	A78	7d dk brown	.55	.50
406	A79	10d red brown	.25	.25
407	A80	15d green	.25	.25
408	A81	25d dk blue	.25	.25
		Nos. 396-408 (13)	3.55	3.50
		Set, never hinged	4.00	

See Nos. 413, 459-466. For overprints and surcharges see Nos. 455-458, 476-477, RA75-RA78, RA83-RA85, N202-N217, N246-N247. Post 1940 issues in Scott Standard catalogue, Vol. 3.

Cerigo, Paxos, Lefkas
Greek stamps with Italian overprints for the islands of Cerigo (Kithyra), Paxos and Lefkas (Santa Maura) are fraudulent.

Royal Wedding Issue

Princess Frederika-Louise and Crown Prince Paul — A82

1938   *Wmk. 252*   *Perf. 13½x12*
409	A82	1d green	.25	.25
410	A82	3d orange brn	.30	.25
411	A82	8d dark blue	.55	.65
		Nos. 409-411 (3)	1.10	1.15
		Set, never hinged	2.75	

Arms of Greece, Romania, Yugoslavia and Turkey — A83

Perf. 12x12½
1938, Feb. 8   *Litho.*   *Unwmk.*
412	A83	6d blue	5.50	1.75
		Never hinged	14.00	

Balkan Entente.

Tiryns Lady Type of 1937
Corrected Inscription
1938   *Wmk. 252*   *Perf. 12x13½*
413	A70	10 l blue & brn red	.50	.70
		Never hinged	.85	

The first four letters of the third word of the inscription read "TIPY" instead of "TYPI."

Statue of King Constantine — A84

Perf. 12x13½
1938, Oct. 8   *Engr.*   *Unwmk.*
414	A84	1.50d green	.45	.25
415	A84	30d orange brn	2.25	3.25
		Set, never hinged	5.50	

For overprint see No. N218.

Coats of Arms of Ionian Islands — A85

Fort at Corfu — A86

King George I of Greece and Queen Victoria of England A87

Perf. 12½x12, 13½x12
1939, May 21   *Engr.*   *Unwmk.*
416	A85	1d dk blue	.85	.25
417	A86	4d green	2.90	1.00
418	A87	20d yellow org	17.00	17.00
419	A87	20d dull blue	17.00	17.00
420	A87	20d car lake	17.00	17.00
		Nos. 416-420 (5)	54.75	52.25
		Set, never hinged	125.00	

75th anniv. of the union of the Ionian Islands with Greece.

Runner with Shield — A88

10th Pan-Balkan Games: 3d, Javelin thrower. 6d, Discus thrower. 8d, Jumper.

Perf. 12x13½
1939, Oct. 1   *Litho.*   *Unwmk.*
421	A88	50 l slate grn & grn	.25	.25
422	A88	3d henna brn & dl rose	1.25	.55
423	A88	6d cop brn & dl org	3.00	2.25
424	A88	8d ultra & gray	3.00	2.50
		Nos. 421-424 (4)	7.50	5.55
		Set, never hinged	18.00	

Arms of Greece, Romania, Turkey and Yugoslavia — A92

Perf. 13x12½
1940, May 27   *Wmk. 252*
425	A92	6d blue	10.00	2.25
426	A92	8d blue gray	7.00	2.25
		Set, never hinged	45.00	

Balkan Entente.

Emblem of Youth Organization A93

Boy Member — A94

Designs: 3d, 100d, Emblem of Greek Youth Organization. 10d, Girl member. 15d, Javelin Thrower. 20d, Column of members. 25d, Flag bearers and buglers. 30d, Three youths. 50d, Line formation. 75d, Coat of arms.

Perf. 12½, 13½x12½

			1940, Aug. 3	Litho.	Wmk. 252
427	A93	3d sil, dp ultra & red		.85	1.25
428	A94	5d dk bl & blk		6.50	7.50
429	A94	10d red org & blk		7.50	10.00
430	A94	15d dk grn & blk		30.00	32.50
431	A94	20d lake & blk		25.00	25.00
432	A94	25d dk bl & blk		25.00	25.00
433	A94	30d rose vio & blk		25.00	25.00
434	A94	50d lake & blk		30.00	30.00
435	A94	75d dk bl, brn & gold		30.00	32.50
436	A93	100d sil, dp ultra & red		50.00	37.50
		Nos. 427-436,C38-C47 (20)		555.70	529.00
		Set, never hinged		1,000.	

4th anniv. of the founding of the Greek Youth Organization. The stamps were good for postal duty Aug. 3-5, 1940, only. They remained on sale until Feb. 3, 1941.
For overprints see Nos. N219-N238.

AIR POST STAMPS

Italy-Greece-Turkey-Rhodes Service

Flying Boat off Phaleron Bay — AP1

Flying Boat over Acropolis — AP2

Flying Boat over Map of Southern Europe — AP3

Flying Boat Seen through Colonnade — AP4

Perf. 11½

			1926, Oct. 20	Unwmk.	Litho.
C1	AP1	2d multicolored		1.60	1.25
a.		Horiz. pair, imperf. vert.		725.00	

C2	AP2	3d multicolored		12.00	11.00
C3	AP3	5d multicolored		1.60	1.25
C4	AP4	10d multicolored		12.00	12.00
		Nos. C1-C4 (4)		27.20	25.50
		Set, never hinged		80.00	

Graf Zeppelin Issue

Zeppelin over Acropolis AP5

1933, May 2   *Perf. 13½x12½*

C5	AP5	30d rose red		13.00	13.00
C6	AP5	100d deep blue		52.50	52.50
C7	AP5	120d dark brown		52.50	52.50
		Nos. C5-C7 (3)		118.00	118.00
		Set, never hinged		325.00	

Propeller and Pilot's Head AP6

Temple of Apollo, Corinth AP7

Plane over Hermoupolis, Syros — AP8

Allegory of Flight
AP9   AP12

Map of Italy-Greece-Turkey-Rhodes Airmail Route — AP10

Head of Hermes and Airplane — AP11

1933, Oct. 10   **Engr.**   *Perf. 12*

C8	AP6	50d green & org		.25	.25
C9	AP7	1d bl & brn org		.30	.25
C10	AP8	3d dk vio & org brn		.50	.50
C11	AP9	5d brn org & dk bl		7.25	4.50
C12	AP10	10d dp red & blk		1.50	1.40
C13	AP11	20d black & grn		7.25	4.00
C14	AP12	50d dp brn & dp bl		50.00	55.00
		Nos. C8-C14 (7)		67.05	65.90
		Set, never hinged		200.00	

By error the 1d stamp is inscribed in the plural "ΔΡΑΧΜΑΙ" instead of the singular "ΔΡΑΧΜΗ." This stamp exists bisected, used as a 50 lepta denomination.

All values of this set exist imperforate but were not regularly issued.

For General Air Post Service

Airplane over Map of Greece — AP13   Airplane over Map of Icarian Sea — AP14

Airplane over Acropolis AP15

Perf. 13x13½, 13x12½, 13½x13, 12½x13

1933, Nov. 2

C15	AP13	50d green		.25	.25
C16	AP13	1d red brown		.30	.55
C17	AP14	2d lt violet		.60	.85
C18	AP15	5d ultra		3.50	3.50
a.		Imperf., pair		650.00	550.00
b.		Horiz. pair, imperf. vert.		650.00	
C19	AP14	10d car rose		6.50	7.75
C20	AP13	25d dark blue		30.00	20.00
C21	AP15	50d dark brown		30.00	42.50
a.		Imperf., pair		775.00	650.00
		Nos. C15-C21 (7)		71.15	75.40
		Set, never hinged		225.00	

Helios Driving the Sun Chariot AP16

Iris — AP17

Daedalus Preparing Icarus for Flying — AP18

Pallas Athene Holding Pegasus — AP19

Hermes AP20   Zeus Carrying off Ganymede AP21

Triptolemos, King of Eleusis AP22

Bellerophon and Pegasus — AP23

Phrixos and Helle on the Ram Flying over the Hellespont AP24

Perf. 13x12½, 12½x13

1935, Nov. 10   **Engr.**

Grayish Paper

Size: 34x23½mm, 23½x34mm

C22	AP16	1d deep red		1.50	1.50
C23	AP17	2d dull blue		1.50	1.50
C24	AP18	5d dk violet		17.50	4.00
C25	AP19	7d blue violet		25.00	7.25
C26	AP20	10d bister brown		5.00	5.00
C27	AP21	25d rose		6.00	5.75
C28	AP22	30d dark green		2.00	2.00
C29	AP23	50d violet		8.00	6.00
C30	AP24	100d brown		2.50	2.25
		Nos. C22-C30 (9)		69.00	35.25
		Set, never hinged		150.00	

Re-engraved

Size: 34¼x24mm, 24x34¼mm

1937-39   **White Paper**

C31	AP16	1d red		.30	.25
C32	AP17	2d gray blue		.30	.25
C33	AP18	5d violet		.30	.25
C34	AP19	7d dp ultra		.30	.25
C35	AP20	10d brn org		2.40	3.50
		Nos. C31-C35 (5)		3.60	4.50
		Set, never hinged		7.00	

Issued: #C35, 3/1/39; others 8/3/37.

Postage Due Stamp, 1913, Overprinted in Red

Serrate Roulette 13½

1938, Aug. 8   **Litho.**   **Unwmk.**

C36	D3	50d violet brown		.25	.25
		Never hinged		.25	
a.		"O" for "P" in word at foot		30.00	30.00

Same Overprint on No. J79 in Red

1939, June 26   *Perf. 13½x12½*

C37	D3	50d dark brown		.25	.25
		Never hinged		.25	

Meteora Monasteries, near Trikkala — AP25

Designs: 4d, Simon Peter Monastery. 6d, View of Santorin. 8d, Church of Pantanassa. 16d, Santorin view. 32d, Ponticonissi, Corfu. 45d, Acropolis, Athens. 55d, Erechtheum. 65d, Temple of Nike Apteros. 100d, Temple of the Olympian Zeus, Athens.

Wmk. Crowns (252)

1940, Aug. 3   **Litho.**   *Perf. 12½*

C38	AP25	2d red org & blk		.85	1.25
C39	AP25	4d dk grn & blk		4.00	3.50
C40	AP25	6d lake & blk		7.25	6.50
C41	AP25	8d dk bl & blk		18.75	16.50
C42	AP25	16d rose vio & blk		30.00	25.00
C43	AP25	32d red org & blk		40.00	47.50
C44	AP25	45d dk grn & blk		52.50	47.50
C45	AP25	55d lake & blk		52.50	47.50
C46	AP25	65d dk bl & blk		52.50	47.50

C47 AP25 100d rose vio & blk   67.50   60.00
Nos. C38-C47 (10)   325.85   302.75
Set, never hinged   800.00

4th anniv. of the founding of the Greek Youth Organization. The stamps were good for postal duty on Aug. 3-5, 1940 (sic). They remained on sale until Feb. 3, 1941.

For overprints see Nos. N229-N238.

POSTAGE DUE STAMPS

D1   D2

Perf. 9, 9½, and 10, 10½ and Compound

1875		Litho.		Unwmk.	
J1	D1	1 l	green & black	1.50	1.50
J2	D1	2 l	green & black	1.50	1.50
J3	D1	5 l	green & black	1.75	1.25
J4	D1	10 l	green & black	1.75	1.25
J5	D1	20 l	green & black	42.50	30.00
J6	D1	40 l	green & black	8.25	5.50
J7	D1	60 l	green & black	42.50	30.00
J8	D1	70 l	green & black	8.25	5.50
J9	D1	80 l	green & black	17.50	14.50
J10	D1	90 l	green & black	11.00	11.00
J11	D1	1 d	green & black	12.00	11.00
J12	D1	2 d	green & black	13.00	11.00
	Nos. J1-J12 (12)			161.50	124.00

Imperforate and part perforated, double and inverted center varieties of Nos. J1-J12 are believed to be printers' waste.

Perf. 12, 13 and 10½x13

J13	D1	1 l	green & black	1.60	1.60
J14	D1	2 l	green & black	22.50	22.50
J15	D1	5 l	green & black	2.75	2.75
J16	D1	10 l	green & black	3.25	3.25
J17	D1	20 l	green & black	40.00	27.50
J18	D1	40 l	green & black	10.00	7.75
J19	D1	60 l	green & black	42.50	27.50
J20	D1	70 l	green & black	7.75	7.75
J21	D1	80 l	green & black	12.00	12.00
J22	D1	90 l	green & black	17.50	12.00
J23	D1	1 d	green & black	27.50	17.50
J24	D1	2 d	green & black	22.50	17.50
	Nos. J13-J24 (12)			209.85	159.60

Redrawn
"Lepton" or "Lepta" in Larger Greek Letters

1876		*Perf. 9, 9½, and 10, 10½*			
J25	D2	1 l	green & black	4.50	4.50
J26	D2	2 l	dk grn & blk	6.00	5.75
J27	D2	5 l	dk grn & blk	360.00	275.00
J28	D2	10 l	green & black	3.00	2.10
J29	D2	20 l	green & black	4.00	3.00
J30	D2	40 l	green & black	32.50	25.00
J31	D2	60 l	green & black	27.50	15.00
J32	D2	70 l	green & black	22.50	25.00
J33	D2	80 l	green & black	17.50	15.00
J34	D2	90 l	green & black	17.50	16.00
J35	D2	100 l	green & black	22.50	15.00
J36	D2	200 l	green & black	22.50	15.00
	Nos. J25-J36 (12)			540.00	416.35

Perf. 11½ to 13

J37	D2	1 l	yel grn & blk	1.75	.95
J38	D2	2 l	yel grn & blk	1.75	.95
J39	D2	5 l	yel grn & blk	4.75	1.25
J40	D2	10 l	yel grn & blk	2.75	2.00
a.		Perf. 10-10½x11 ½-13		4.00	
J41	D2	20 l	yel grn & blk	2.75	2.00
J42	D2	40 l	yel grn & blk	15.00	11.00
J43	D2	60 l	yel grn & blk	9.50	9.50
J47	D2	100 l	yel grn & blk	12.00	12.00
J48	D2	200 l	yel grn & blk	13.50	11.00
	Nos. J37-J48 (9)			63.75	50.65

Footnote below #J12 applies also to #J25-J48.

D3

1902		Engr. Wmk. 129 Perf. 13½			
J49	D3	1 l	chocolate	.30	.25
J50	D3	2 l	gray	.30	.25
J51	D3	3 l	orange	.30	.25
J52	D3	5 l	yel grn	.30	.25
J53	D3	10 l	scarlet	.30	.25

J54	D3	20 l	lilac	.45	.25
J55	D3	25 l	ultra	8.00	4.00
J56	D3	30 l	dp vio	.50	.25
J57	D3	40 l	dk brn	.60	.50
J58	D3	50 l	red brn	.60	.40
J59	D3	1 d	black	1.50	.90

Litho.

J60	D3	2 d	bronze	2.00	1.25
J61	D3	3 d	silver	3.00	3.00
J62	D3	5 d	gold	6.50	9.00
	Nos. J49-J62 (14)			24.65	20.85

See Nos. J63-J88, J90-J93. For overprints and surcharges see Nos. 383-385, J89, RA56, RA58-RA59, NJ1-NJ31. Post 1940 issues in Scott Standard catalogue, Vol. 3.

Imperf., Pairs

J50a	D3	2 l	90.00
J51a	D3	3 l	90.00
J52a	D3	5 l	90.00
J55a	D3	25 l	150.00
J56a	D3	30 l	150.00
J58a	D3	50 l	150.00
J59a	D3	1 d	150.00

Serrate Roulette 13½

1913-26				Unwmk.	
J63	D3	1 l	green	.25	.25
J64	D3	2 l	carmine	.25	.25
J65	D3	3 l	vermilion	.25	.25
J66	D3	5 l	green	.25	.25
a.		Imperf., pair		150.00	
b.		Double impression		60.00	
c.		"o" for "p" in lowest word		5.00	5.00
J67	D3	10 l	carmine	.25	.25
J68	D3	20 l	slate	.25	.25
J69	D3	25 l	ultra	.25	.25
J70	D3	30 l	carmine	.25	.25
J71	D3	40 l	indigo	.25	.25
J72	D3	50 l	vio brn	.30	.25
a.		"o" for "p" in lowest word		25.00	20.00
J73	D3	80 l	lil brn ('24)	.40	.25
J74	D3	1 d	blue	8.00	1.25
a.		1d ultramarine		12.00	5.00
J75	D3	2 d	vermilion	8.00	1.50
J76	D3	3 d	carmine	8.00	1.50
J77	D3	5 d	ultra	30.00	12.00
J78	D3	5 d	gray bl ('26)	8.00	4.00
	Nos. J63-J78 (16)			64.95	20.00

In 1922-23 and 1941-42 some postage due stamps were used for ordinary postage.

In 1916 Nos. J52, and J63 to J75 were surcharged for the Mount Athos District (see note after No. N166) but were never issued there. By error some of them were put in use as ordinary postage due stamps in Dec., 1924. In 1932 the balance of them was burned.

Type of 1902 Issue
Perf. 13, 13½x12½, 13½x13

1930				Litho.	
J79	D3	50 l	dk brown	.30	.30
J80	D3	1 d	lt blue	.30	.30
J81	D3	2 d	lt red	.30	.30
J82	D3	3 d	rose red	27.50	25.00
J83	D3	5 d	gray blue	.30	.30
J84	D3	10 d	gray green	.30	.30
J85	D3	15 d	red brown	.30	.30
J86	D3	25 d	light red	.70	.65
	Nos. J79-J86 (8)			30.00	27.45

Type of 1902 Issue

1935		Engr. Perf. 12½x13			
J87	D3	50 d	orange	.30	.30
J88	D3	100 d	slate green	.30	.30

POSTAL TAX STAMPS

"The Tragedy of War" — PT1

Serrate Roulette 13½

1914			Litho.	Unwmk.	
RA1	PT1	2 l	red ('18)	.30	.25
a.		2 l carmine		.35	.25
b.		Imperf., pair		200.00	
RA2	PT1	5 l	blue	.50	.75
a.		Imperf., pair		250.00	

Red Cross, Nurse, Wounded and Bearers — PT1a

1915		*Serrate Roulette 13*		
RA2B	PT1a	(5 l)	dk bl & red	10.00	2.00

The tax was for the Red Cross.

Women's Patriotic League Badge — PT1b

1915, Nov.			*Perf. 11½*	
RA2C	PT1b	(5 l)	dk bl & car	1.25	1.00
d.		Horiz. pair, imperf. btwn.		55.00	

The tax was for the Greek Women's Patriotic League.

Nos. 165, 167, 170, 172-175
Surcharged in Black or Brown

a   b

In type "b" the letters, especially those in the first line, are thinner than in type "a," making them appear taller.

Perf. 11½, 12½, 13½ and Compound

1917		Engr.		Wmk. 129	
RA3	A11(a)	1 l on 1 l		1.50	1.50
a.		Double surcharge		7.00	
RA4	A11(a)	1 l on 1 l (Br)		22.50	22.50
RA5	A11(a)	1 l on 3 l		.30	.30
RA6	A11(b)	1 l on 3 l		.30	.30
a.		Triple surcharge		5.00	
b.		Dbl. surch., one invtd.		5.00	
c.		"K.M." for "K.Π."		20.00	
RA7	A11(a)	5 l on 1 l		2.00	2.00
a.		Double surcharge		10.00	
b.		Dbl. surch., one invtd.		10.00	
c.		Inverted surcharge		12.00	
RA8	A11(a)	5 l on 20 l		.65	.65
a.		Double surcharge		12.00	
b.		Dbl. surch., one invtd.		12.00	
RA9	A11(a)	5 l on 40 l		.65	.65
a.		Imperf.			
RA10	A11(b)	5 l on 50 l		.65	.65
a.		Double surcharge		25.00	
b.		Dbl. surch., one invtd.		25.00	
RA11	A13(b)	5 l on 1d		2.25	2.25
a.		Imperf.			
b.		Inverted surcharge		50.00	
RA12	A11(a)	10 l on 30 l		.80	.80
a.		Imperf.			
b.		Double surcharge		20.00	
RA13	A11(a)	30 l on 30 l		.90	.90
a.		Double surcharge		20.00	
	Nos. RA3-RA13 (11)			32.50	32.50

Same Surcharge On Occupation Stamps of 1912
Serrate Roulette 13½

1917			Litho.	Unwmk.	
RA14	O2 (b)	5 l on 25 l pale bl		.55	.55
a.		Triple surch., one invtd.		15.00	
b.		Double surcharge		8.00	
RA15	O2 (b)	5 l on 40 l indigo		.55	.55
a.		Double surch., one invtd.		8.00	
b.		Double surcharge		8.00	
RA16	O1 (b)	5 l on 50 l dk bl		.55	.55
a.		Double surcharge		10.00	
b.		Inverted surcharge		10.00	
	Nos. RA14-RA16 (3)			1.65	1.65

There are many wrong font, omitted and misplaced letters and punctuation marks and similar varieties in the surcharges on Nos. RA3 to RA16.

Revenue Stamps Surcharged in Brown

"Victory"

1917					
RA17	R1	1 l on 10 l blue		.70	.70
RA18	R1	1 l on 80 l blue		.70	.70
RA19	R1	5 l on 10 l blue		15.00	20.00
RA20	R1	5 l on 60 l blue		4.00	4.00
a.		Perf. vert. through middle		6.00	10.00
RA21	R1	5 l on 80 l blue		3.00	3.00
a.		Perf. vert. through middle		8.00	6.00
b.		Inverted surcharge			
RA22	R1	10 l on 70 l blue		16.00	12.00
a.		Perf. vert. through middle		6.00	8.00
RA23	R1	10 l on 90 l blue		12.00	8.00
a.		Perf. vert. through middle		20.00	25.00
RA24	R1	20 l on 20 l blue		725.00	525.00
RA25	R1	20 l on 30 l blue		4.00	4.00
RA26	R1	20 l on 40 l blue		12.00	10.00
RA27	R1	20 l on 50 l blue		8.00	6.00
RA28	R1	20 l on 60 l blue		400.00	250.00
RA29	R1	20 l on 80 l blue		40.00	32.50
RA30	R1	20 l on 90 l blue		4.00	6.00
a.		Inverted surcharge		70.00	
	Nos. RA17-RA30 (14)			1,244.	881.90

No. RA19 is known only with vertical perforation through the middle.

Counterfeits exist of Nos. RA17-RA43, used.

Surcharged in Brown or Black

RA31	R1	1 l on 50 l vio (Bk)		.80	1.25
RA32	R1	5 l on 10 l bl (Br)		.80	1.25
a.		Inverted surcharge		80.00	
b.		Left "5" invert.		80.00	
RA33	R1	5 l on 10 l vio (Br)		.80	1.25
RA34	R1	10 l on 50 l vio (Br)		5.50	10.00
RA35	R1	10 l on 50 l vio (Bk)		22.50	20.00
RA36	R1	20 l on 2d bl (Bk)		8.00	8.00
a.		Surcharged "20 lept. 30"		65.00	65.00
b.		Horiz. pair, imperf. btwn.			
	Nos. RA31-RA36 (6)			38.40	41.75

The "T," fourth Greek letter of the denomination in the surcharge ("ΛΕΠΤ."), is normally omitted on Nos. RA31, RA34-RA36.

Corfu Issue

Surcharged in Black

1917					
RA37	R1	1 l on 10 l blue		2.00	2.00
RA38	R1	5 l on 50 l blue		75.00	75.00
RA39	R1	10 l on 50 l blue		675.00	575.00
RA40	R1	20 l on 50 l blue		2,850.	1,075.

Surcharged in Black

RA41	R1	10 l on 50 l blue		12.00	9.00
RA42	R1	20 l on 50 l blue		26.00	17.50
RA43	R1	30 l on 50 l blue		17.50	12.00

Surcharged in Black

RA44 R1 5 l on 10 l vio & red 8.00 12.00
  a. "K" with serifs 12.00 20.00

Counterfeits exist of Nos. RA17-RA44. Similar stamps with denominations higher than 30 lepta were for revenue use.

Wounded Soldier — PT2

1918 *Serrate Roulette 13½, 11½*
RA45 PT2 5 l bl, yel & red 8.00 2.00

Overprinted

RA46 PT2 5 l blue, yel & red 9.50 2.00

The letters are the initials of Greek words equivalent to "Patriotic Relief Institution." The proceeds were given to the Patriotic League, for the aid of disabled soldiers.
Counterfeits exist of Nos. RA45-RA46.

PT3

Surcharge in Red
1922 *Litho.* *Perf. 11½*
Dark Blue & Red
RA46A PT3 5 l on 10 l *300.00* 14.00
RA46B PT3 5 l on 20 l 95.00 50.00
RA46C PT3 5 l on 30 l 275.00 240.00
RA46D PT3 5 l on 1d 9.50 *60.00*

Counterfeit surcharges exist. Examples of Nos. RA46A-RA46C without surcharge, each 50 cents.

Red Cross Help to Soldier and Family PT3a

St. Demetrius PT4

1924 *Perf. 11½, 13½ x 12½*
RA47 PT3a 10 l blue, buff & red .70 .25
  a. Imperf., pair 40.00
  b. Horiz. pair, imperf. btwn. 40.00

Proceeds were given to the Red Cross.

1934 *Perf. 11½*
RA48 PT4 20 l brown .40 .25
  a. Horizontal pair, imperf. between 10.00
  b. Vertical pair, imperf. between 15.00
  c. Imperf., pair 20.00

No. RA48 was obligatory as a tax on all interior mail, including air post, mailed from Salonika.

For surcharge see No. RA69 in Scott Standard catalogue, Vol. 3.

PT5 PT6

"Health"
1934, Dec. 28 *Perf. 13, 13x13½*
RA49 PT5 10 l bl grn, org & buff .25 .25
  a. Vert. pair, imperf. horiz.
RA50 PT5 20 l ultra, org & buff .55 .25
RA51 PT5 50 l grn, org & buff 2.00 .50
  Nos. RA49-RA51 (3) 2.80 1.00

For surcharge see No. RA67 in Scott Standard catalogue, Vol. 3.

1935
RA52 PT6 10 l yel grn, org & buff .40 .25
RA53 PT6 20 l ultra, org & buff .40 .25
RA54 PT6 50 l grn, org & buff 1.25 .65
  Nos. RA52-RA54 (3) 2.05 1.15

The use of #RA49-RA54 was obligatory on all mail during 4 weeks each year including Christmas, the New Year and Easter, and on parcel post packages at all times. For the benefit of the tubercular clerks and officials of the Post, Telephone and Telegraph Service.
See No. RA64. For surcharge see No. RA68 in Scott Standard catalogue, Vol. 3.

No. 364 Overprinted in Red

1937, Jan. 20 **Engr.** *Perf. 13x12½*
RA55 A36 50 l violet 1.40 .25
  a. Inverted overprint .75 .25

No. RA55a first appeared as an error, then was issued deliberately in quantity to avoid speculation.

Same Overprint in Blue on No. J67
Litho.
Serrate Roulette 13½
RA56 D3 10 l carmine .80 .25
  a. Inverted overprint 50.00

No. RA56 with blue overprint double exists only with additional black overprint of Ionian Islands No. NRA1a.

Same Overprint in Green on No. 364
1937 **Engr.** *Perf. 13x12½*
RA57 A36 50 l violet .75 .25

Nos. J66, J68 and 323 Surcharged in Blue or Black

Serrate Roulette 13½
1938 *Litho.* **Unwmk.**
RA58 D3 50 l on 5 l grn 2.40 .80
  a. "O" for "P" in lowest word 25.00 25.00
  b. Vert. pair, imperf. horiz. 55.00
RA59 D3 50 l on 20 l slate 2.40 .80

Engr. *Perf. 13x12½*
RA60 A38 50 l on 20 l vio (Bk) .75 .25
  Nos. RA58-RA60 (3) 5.55 1.85

Surcharge on No. RA60 is 14½x16½mm.

Queens Olga and Sophia PT7

1939, Feb. 1 **Litho.** *Perf. 13½x12*
RA61 PT7 10 l brt rose, *pale rose* .25 .25
RA62 PT7 50 l gray grn, *pale grn* .25 .25
RA63 PT7 1d dl bl, *lt bl* .25 .25
  Nos. RA61-RA63 (3) .75 .75

For overprints and surcharges see Nos. RA65, RA79-RA81A (in Scott Standard catalogue, Vol. 3), NRA1-NRA3.

"Health" Type of 1935
1939 *Perf. 12½*
RA64 PT6 50 l brn & buff .55 .30

No. RA62 Overprinted in Red

1940 *Perf. 13½x12*
RA65 PT7 50 l gray grn, *pale grn* .25 .25
  a. Inverted overprint 35.00
  b. Pair, one without surcharge 20.00

Proceeds of #RA64-RA65 were used for the benefit of the tubercular clerks and officials of the Post, Telephone and Telegraph Service. #RA65 was used in Albania during the Greek occupation, 1940-41 without additional overprint.

OCCUPATION AND ANNEXATION STAMPS

During the Balkan wars, 1912-13, Greece occupied certain of the Aegean Islands and part of Western Turkey. She subsequently acquired these territories and they were known as the New Greece.
Most of the special issues for the Aegean Islands were made by order of the military commanders.

For Use in the Aegean Islands Occupied by Greece

CHIOS

Greece No. 221 Overprinted in Red

Serrate Roulette 13½
1913 **Litho.** **Unwmk.**
N1 A25 25 l ultramarine 60.00 *75.00*
  Never hinged 120.00
  a. Inverted overprint 225.00 175.00
  Never hinged 450.00
  b. "Λ" for "Δ" in overprint 225.00 175.00
  Never hinged 450.00
  c. As "b," overprint inverted 550.00 550.00
  Never hinged 1,100.

ICARIA (NICARIA)

Penelope — I1

1912 **Unwmk.** **Litho.** *Perf. 11½*
N2 I1 2 l orange 1.60 2.40
  Never hinged 3.25
N3 I1 5 l blue green 1.60 2.40
  Never hinged 3.25
N4 I1 10 l rose 1.60 2.40
  Never hinged 3.25
N5 I1 25 l ultra 1.60 2.40
  Never hinged 3.25
N6 I1 50 l gray lilac 2.40 3.25
  Never hinged 4.75
N7 I1 1d dark brown 3.25 *9.00*
  Never hinged 6.50
N8 I1 2d claret 4.00 *15.00*
  Never hinged 8.00

N9 I1 5d slate 5.50 *22.50*
  Never hinged 11.00
  Nos. N2-N9 (8) 21.55 *59.35*

Counterfeits of Nos. N1-N15 are plentiful.

Stamps of Greece, 1911-23, Overprinted Reading Up

1913 **Engr.**
On Issue of 1911-21
N10 A25 2 l car rose 55.00 40.00
  Never hinged 110.00
N11 A24 3 l vermilion 55.00 40.00
  Never hinged 110.00

Litho.
On Issue of 1912-23
N12 A24 1 l green 55.00 40.00
  Never hinged 110.00
N13 A24 3 l vermilion 55.00 40.00
  Never hinged 110.00
N14 A26 5 l green 55.00 40.00
  Never hinged 110.00
N15 A24 10 l carmine 55.00 40.00
  Never hinged 110.00
  Nos. N10-N15 (6) 330.00 240.00

LEMNOS

Regular Issues of Greece Overprinted in Black

On Issue of 1901
1912 **Wmk. 129** **Engr.** *Perf. 13½*
N16 A11 20 l red lilac 2.00 2.00
  Never hinged 3.00
  a. Inverted overprint 25.00
  Never hinged 37.50
  b. Double overprint 25.00
  Never hinged 37.50

On Issue of 1911-21
Unwmk.
Serrate Roulette 13½
N17 A24 1 l green .60 .60
  Never hinged .90
  a. Inverted overprint 15.00
  Never hinged 22.50
  b. Double overprint 15.00
  Never hinged 22.50
N18 A25 2 l carmine rose .70 .70
  Never hinged 1.00
  a. Inverted overprint 15.00
  Never hinged 22.50
  b. Double overprint 15.00
  Never hinged 22.50
N19 A24 3 l vermilion .70 .70
  Never hinged 1.00
  a. Inverted overprint 17.50
  Never hinged 26.00
  b. Double overprint 17.50
  Never hinged 26.00
  c. Double ovpt., one inverted 25.00
  Never hinged 37.50
  d. Triple overprint 85.00
  Never hinged 125.00
  e. Triple ovpt., one inverted 85.00
  Never hinged 125.00
  f. Inverted ovpt. on face, upright ovpt. on reverse 110.00
  Never hinged 160.00
N20 A26 5 l green .70 .70
  Never hinged 1.00
  a. Inverted overprint 17.50
  Never hinged 26.00
  b. Double overprint 17.50
  Never hinged 26.00
N21 A24 10 l car rose 1.00 1.00
  Never hinged 1.50
  a. Inverted overprint 17.50
  Never hinged 26.00
  b. Double overprint 17.50
  Never hinged 26.00
N22 A25 20 l gray lilac 1.50 1.50
  Never hinged 2.25
  a. Inverted overprint 15.00
  Never hinged 22.50
  b. Double overprint 25.00
  Never hinged 37.50
N23 A25 25 l ultra 1.75 1.75
  Never hinged 2.75
  a. Inverted overprint 25.00
  Never hinged 37.50
  b. Double overprint 25.00
  Never hinged 37.50
N24 A26 30 l car rose 3.00 3.00
  Never hinged 4.50
  a. Inverted overprint 55.00
  Never hinged 82.50
  b. Double overprint 55.00
  Never hinged 82.50
N25 A25 40 l deep blue 4.50 4.50
  Never hinged 6.75
  a. Inverted overprint 65.00
  Never hinged 87.50

N26	A26	50 l dl violet	4.50	4.50
		Never hinged	6.75	
N27	A27	1d ultra	6.00	6.00
		Never hinged	9.00	
a.		Inverted overprint	60.00	
		Never hinged	90.00	
N28	A27	2d vermilion	20.00	20.00
N29	A27	5d car rose	22.50	22.50
		Never hinged	45.00	
N30	A27	5d ultra	26.00	26.00
		Never hinged	52.50	
a.		Double overprint	80.00	
		Never hinged	120.00	
N31	A27	10d deep blue	80.00	80.00
		Never hinged	160.00	
N32	A28	25d deep blue	150.00	150.00
		Never hinged	300.00	
		Nos. N17-N32 (16)	323.45	323.45

"Α" for "Λ" in "ΛΗΜΝΟΣ"

N17g	A24	1 l green	6.00	6.00
		Never hinged	9.00	
N18g	A25	2 l carmine rose	6.00	6.00
		Never hinged	9.00	
N19g	A24	3 l vermilion	6.00	6.00
		Never hinged	9.00	
N20g	A26	5 l green	10.00	10.00
		Never hinged	15.00	
N21g	A24	10 l carmine rose	10.00	10.00
		Never hinged	15.00	
N22g	A25	20 l gray lilac	10.00	10.00
		Never hinged	15.00	
N23g	A25	25 l ultramarine	10.00	10.00
		Never hinged	15.00	
N24g	A26	30 l carmine rose	12.00	12.00
		Never hinged	18.00	
N25g	A25	40 l deep blue	15.00	15.00
		Never hinged	22.50	
N26g	A26	50 l dull violet	15.00	15.00
		Never hinged	22.50	
N27g	A27	1d ultramarine	20.00	20.00
		Never hinged	30.00	
N28g	A27	2d vermilion	120.00	120.00
		Never hinged	180.00	
N29g	A27	3d carmine rose	120.00	120.00
		Never hinged	180.00	
N30g	A27	5d ultramarine	150.00	150.00
		Never hinged	225.00	
N31g	A27	10d deep blue	600.00	600.00
		Never hinged	900.00	

Large "Σ" for "Λ" in "ΛΗΜΝΟΣ"

N17h	A24	1 l green	6.00	6.00
		Never hinged	9.00	
N18h	A25	2 l carmine rose	6.00	6.00
		Never hinged	9.00	
N19h	A24	3 l vermilion	6.00	6.00
		Never hinged	9.00	
N20h	A26	5 l green	10.00	10.00
		Never hinged	15.00	
N21h	A24	10 l carmine rose	10.00	10.00
		Never hinged	15.00	
N22h	A25	20 l gray lilac	10.00	10.00
		Never hinged	15.00	
N23h	A25	25 l ultramarine	10.00	10.00
		Never hinged	15.00	
N24h	A26	30 l carmine rose	12.00	12.00
		Never hinged	18.00	
N25h	A25	40 l deep blue	15.00	15.00
		Never hinged	22.50	
N26h	A26	50 l dull violet	15.00	15.00
		Never hinged	22.50	
N27h	A27	1d ultramarine	20.00	20.00
		Never hinged	30.00	
N28h	A27	2d vermilion	120.00	120.00
		Never hinged	180.00	
N29h	A27	3d carmine rose	120.00	120.00
		Never hinged	180.00	
N30h	A27	5d ultramarine	150.00	150.00
		Never hinged	225.00	
N31h	A27	10d deep blue	600.00	600.00
		Never hinged	900.00	

Round "O" for "Λ" in "ΛΗΜΝΟΣ"

N17i	A24	1 l green	4.00	4.00
		Never hinged	6.00	
N18i	A25	2 l carmine rose	4.00	4.00
		Never hinged	6.00	
N19i	A24	3 l vermilion	4.00	4.00
		Never hinged	6.00	
N20i	A26	5 l green	6.00	6.00
		Never hinged	9.00	
N21i	A24	10 l carmine rose	6.00	6.00
		Never hinged	9.00	
N22i	A25	20 l gray lilac	6.00	6.00
		Never hinged	9.00	
N23i	A25	25 l ultramarine	7.00	7.00
		Never hinged	10.50	
N24i	A26	30 l carmine rose	8.00	8.00
		Never hinged	12.00	
N25i	A25	40 l deep blue	9.00	9.00
		Never hinged	13.50	
N26i	A26	50 l dull violet	9.00	9.00
		Never hinged	13.50	
N27i	A27	1d ultramarine	16.00	16.00
		Never hinged	24.00	
N28i	A27	2d vermilion	75.00	75.00
		Never hinged	110.00	
N29i	A27	3d carmine rose	75.00	75.00
		Never hinged	110.00	
N30i	A27	5d ultramarine	110.00	110.00
		Never hinged	160.00	
N31i	A27	10d deep blue	390.00	390.00
		Never hinged	575.00	
N32i	A28	25d deep blue	700.00	700.00
		Never hinged	1,050.	

"Δ" for "Λ" in "ΛΗΜΝΟΣ"

N17j	A24	1 l green	4.00	4.00
		Never hinged	6.00	
N18j	A25	2 l carmine rose	4.00	4.00
		Never hinged	6.00	
N19j	A24	3 l vermilion	4.00	4.00
		Never hinged	6.00	
N20j	A26	5 l green	6.00	6.00
		Never hinged	9.00	
N21j	A24	10 l carmine rose	6.00	6.00
		Never hinged	9.00	
N22j	A25	20 l gray lilac	6.00	6.00
		Never hinged	9.00	
N23j	A25	25 l ultramarine	6.00	6.00
		Never hinged	9.00	
N24j	A26	30 l carmine rose	8.00	8.00
		Never hinged	12.00	
N25j	A25	40 l deep blue	8.00	8.00
		Never hinged	12.00	
N26j	A26	50 l dull violet	9.00	9.00
		Never hinged	13.50	

N27j	A27	1d ultramarine	16.00	16.00
		Never hinged	24.00	
N28j	A27	2d vermilion	75.00	75.00
		Never hinged	110.00	
N29j	A27	3d carmine rose	75.00	75.00
		Never hinged	110.00	
N30j	A27	5d ultramarine	95.00	95.00
		Never hinged	140.00	
N31j	A27	10d deep blue	350.00	350.00
		Never hinged	525.00	

On Issue of 1912-23
Litho.

N33	A24	1 l green	.60	.60
		Never hinged	.90	
a.		Inverted overprint	15.00	
		Never hinged	22.50	
b.		Double overprint	15.00	
		Never hinged	22.50	
c.		Double overprint, one inverted	25.00	
		Never hinged	37.50	
d.		Double overprint, both inverted	25.00	
		Never hinged	37.50	
e.		Inverted overprint on face, upright overprint on reverse	110.00	
		Never hinged	160.00	
f.		Without period after "ΕΛ–ΛΑΣ" (on #214a)	275.00	275.00
		Never hinged	400.00	
N34	A26	5 l green	.70	.70
		Never hinged	1.00	
a.		Inverted overprint	12.00	
		Never hinged	18.00	
b.		Double overprint	12.00	
		Never hinged	18.00	
N35	A24	10 l carmine	.70	.70
a.		Inverted overprint		150.00
b.		Double overprint	17.50	
		Never hinged	26.00	
N36	A25	25 l ultra	3.00	3.00
		Never hinged	4.50	
a.		Inverted overprint	25.00	
		Never hinged	37.50	
b.		Double overprint	15.00	
		Never hinged	22.50	
		Nos. N33-N36 (4)	5.00	5.00

Red Overprint
On Issue of 1911-23
Engr.

N37	A25	40 l deep blue	2.00	2.00
		Never hinged	3.00	
N38	A26	50 l dull violet	2.00	2.00
		Never hinged	3.00	
N39	A27	1d ultramarine	3.00	3.00
		Never hinged	4.50	
N40	A27	3d car rose	15.00	15.00
		Never hinged	30.00	
N41	A27	5d gray blue	400.00	300.00
		Never hinged	800.00	
N42	A27	10d deep blue	120.00	100.00
		Never hinged	240.00	
N43	A28	25d deep blue	180.00	150.00
		Never hinged	275.00	
a.		Round "O" in "ΛΗΜΝΟΣ"	650.00	
		Never hinged	975.00	

Litho.

N44	A24	5 l green	1.00	1.00
		Never hinged	15.00	
a.		Inverted overprint	—	
		Never hinged	—	
b.		Double overprint	—	
		Never hinged	—	
N45	A25	25 l ultramarine	2.00	2.00
		Never hinged	3.00	
a.		Double overprint, one oblique		30.00
		Nos. N37-N45 (9)	725.00	575.00

"Δ" for "Λ" in "ΛΗΜΝΟΣ"

N37d	A25	40 l deep blue	22.50	22.50
		Never hinged	32.50	
N38d	A26	50 l dull violet	22.50	22.50
		Never hinged	32.50	
N39d	A27	1d ultramarine	22.50	22.50
		Never hinged	32.50	
N40d	A27	3d carmine rose	75.00	75.00
		Never hinged	110.00	
N41d	A27	5d ultramarine	425.00	425.00
		Never hinged	625.00	

Carmine Overprint
Engr.

N46	A25	2 l carmine	3.00	3.00
		Never hinged	4.50	
N47	A24	3 l vermilion	3.00	3.00
		Never hinged	4.50	
N48	A25	20 l gray blue	12.00	12.00
		Never hinged	18.00	
N49	A26	30 l carmine rose	6.00	6.00
		Never hinged	9.00	
N50	A27	2d vermilion	360.00	360.00
		Never hinged	725.00	
N51	A27	3d carmine rose	130.00	110.00
		Never hinged	260.00	
N51A	A27	5d ultramarine	65.00	65.00
		Never hinged	130.00	
N51B	A28	25d deep blue	1,300.	450.00
		Never hinged	2,600.	

Litho.

N51C	A24	1 l green	2.00	2.00
		Never hinged	3.00	
a.		Without period after "ΕΛ–ΛΑΣ" (on #214a)	375.00	375.00
		Never hinged	575.00	
b.		As "a.," double overprint	—	—
N52	A24	10 l carmine	4.00	4.00
		Never hinged	6.00	
		Nos. N46-N52 (10)	1,885.	1,015.

"Δ" for "Λ" in "ΛΗΜΝΟΣ"

N46d	A25	2 l carmine rose	10.00	10.00
		Never hinged	15.00	
N47d	A24	3 l vermilion	15.00	15.00
		Never hinged	22.50	

N48d	A25	20 l gray blue	50.00	50.00
		Never hinged	75.00	
N49d	A26	30 l carmine rose	15.00	15.00
		Never hinged	22.50	
N50d	A27	2d vermilion	500.00	500.00
		Never hinged	750.00	
N51d	A27	3d carmine rose	225.00	225.00
		Never hinged	325.00	
N51Ad	A27	5d ultramarine	200.00	200.00
		Never hinged	300.00	
N51Cd	A24	1 l green	10.00	10.00

No. N33 with Added "Greek Administration" Overprint, as on Nos. N109-N148, in Black

1913

N52A	A24	1 l green	25.00	25.00
		Never hinged	50.00	
b.		Period omitted after "ΕΛ–ΛΑΣ" (on #N33f)	450.00	
		Never hinged	675.00	
c.		Inverted "ΛΗΜΝΟΣ" overprint (on No. N33a)	120.00	
		Never hinged	240.00	
d.		Double"ΛΗΜΝΟΣ" overprint (on No. N33a)	120.00	
		Never hinged	240.00	

Counterfeits of Nos. N16-N52A are plentiful.

MYTILENE (LESBOS)

Turkey Nos. 162, 158
Overprinted in Blue

Perf. 12, 13½ and Compound

1912			Typo.	Unwmk.
N53	A21	20pa rose	35.00	35.00
		Never hinged	52.50	
N54	A21	10pi dull red	140.00	140.00
		Never hinged	210.00	

On Turkey Nos. P68, 151-155, 137, 157-158 in Black

N55	A21	2pa olive green	4.00	4.00
		Never hinged	6.00	
N56	A21	5pa ocher	4.00	4.00
		Never hinged	6.00	
N57	A21	10pa blue green	4.00	4.00
		Never hinged	6.00	
N58	A21	20pa rose	4.00	4.00
		Never hinged	6.00	
N59	A21	1pi ultra	8.00	8.00
		Never hinged	12.00	
N60	A21	2pi blue black	30.00	30.00
		Never hinged	45.00	
N61	A19	2½pi dk brown	14.00	14.00
		Never hinged	21.00	
N62	A21	5pi dk violet	30.00	30.00
		Never hinged	45.00	
N63	A21	10pi dull red	140.00	140.00
		Never hinged	210.00	
		Nos. N55-N63 (9)	238.00	238.00

On Turkey Nos. 161-163, 145 in Black

N64	A21	10pa blue green	12.00	12.00
		Never hinged	18.00	
a.		Double overprint	75.00	75.00
		Never hinged	110.00	
N65	A21	20pa rose	12.00	12.00
		Never hinged	18.00	
N66	A21	1pi ultra	12.00	12.00
		Never hinged	18.00	
N67	A19	2pi blue black	80.00	80.00
		Never hinged	120.00	

Nos. N55, N58, N65, N59 Surcharged in Blue or Black

N68	A21	25 l on 2pa	16.00	16.00
		Never hinged	24.00	
a.		New value inverted	60.00	60.00
		Never hinged	90.00	
b.		25 "ΛΕΠΤΑ"	35.00	35.00
		Never hinged	52.50	
N69	A21	50 l on 20pa	16.00	16.00
		Never hinged	24.00	
a.		New value inverted	60.00	60.00
		Never hinged	90.00	
N70	A21	1d on 20pa (N65) (Bk)	60.00	60.00
		Never hinged	90.00	
a.		New value inverted	120.00	120.00
		Never hinged	180.00	
b.		"ΔΙΔΡΑΧΜΗ" for "ΔΡΑΧΜΗ"	135.00	135.00
		Never hinged	200.00	
N71	A21	2d on 1pi (Bk)	22.50	22.50
a.		New value inverted		
b.		"ΔΙΔΡΑΧΜΗ" instead of "ΔΙΔΡΑΧΜΩΝ"	120.00	120.00
		Never hinged	180.00	

Same Overprint on Turkey No. J49

N72	A19	1pi blk, *dp rose*	65.00	65.00
		Never hinged	97.50	

The overprint is found on all values reading up or down with inverted "i" in the first word and inverted "e" in the third word.
No. N72 was only used for postage.
Counterfeits of Nos. N53-N72 are plentiful.

SAMOS
Issues of the Provisional Government

Map of Samos
OS1

1912		Unwmk.	Typo.	*Imperf.*
N73	OS1	5 l gray green	30.00	10.00
		Never hinged	75.00	
a.		5 l red (error)	330.00	330.00
		Never hinged	825.00	
b.		5 l blue (error)	330.00	330.00
		Never hinged	825.00	
c.		Tête bêche pair	575.00	450.00
		Never hinged	1,450.	
N74	OS1	10 l red	25.00	10.00
		Never hinged	62.50	
a.		10 l pale green (error)	330.00	330.00
		Never hinged	825.00	
b.		10 l blue (error)	330.00	330.00
		Never hinged	825.00	
c.		Tête bêche pair	575.00	450.00
		Never hinged	1,450.	
N75	OS1	25 l blue	60.00	20.00
		Never hinged	150.00	
a.		25 l pale green (error)	575.00	—
		Never hinged	1,450.	
b.		25 l red (error)	575.00	—
		Never hinged	1,450.	
c.		25 l violet (error)	4,000.	
d.		Tête bêche pair	3,000.	2,000.
		Never hinged	7,500.	
		Nos. N73-N75 (3)	40.00	40.00

Only one example of No. N75c is known.
Counterfeits exist of Nos. N73 to N75.

Hermes — OS2

1912		Litho.	*Perf. 11½*	

Without Overprint

N76	OS2	1 l gray	2.00	1.50
		Never hinged	4.00	
N77	OS2	5 l lt green	2.00	1.50
		Never hinged	4.00	
N78	OS2	10 l rose	3.00	1.80
		Never hinged	6.00	
b.		Half used as 5 l on cover		200.00
N79	OS2	25 l lt blue	8.00	2.00
		Never hinged	16.00	
N80	OS2	50 l violet brn	18.00	6.00
		Never hinged	35.00	

With Overprint

N81	OS2	1 l gray	1.00	1.10
		Never hinged	2.00	
N82	OS2	5 l blue grn	1.00	1.10
		Never hinged	2.00	
N83	OS2	10 l rose	1.00	1.00
		Never hinged	2.00	
b.		Half used as 5 l on cover		200.00
N84	OS2	25 l blue	2.00	1.50
		Never hinged	4.00	
N85	OS2	50 l violet brn	10.00	7.00
		Never hinged	20.00	
N86	OS2	1d orange	15.00	13.00
		Never hinged	30.00	
		Nos. N76-N86 (11)	63.00	37.50

For overprints and surcharge see Nos. N92-N103.

Imperf., Pairs
Without Overprint

N76a	OS2	1 l	40.00	30.00
		Never hinged	60.00	
N77a	OS2	5 l	40.00	30.00
		Never hinged	60.00	
N78a	OS2	10 l	40.00	30.00
		Never hinged	60.00	
N79a	OS2	25 l	40.00	30.00
		Never hinged	60.00	
N80a	OS2	50 l	40.00	30.00
		Never hinged	60.00	

With Overprint

N81a	OS2	1 l	100.00	40.00
		Never hinged	150.00	
N82a	OS2	5 l	100.00	40.00
		Never hinged	150.00	
N83a	OS2	10 l	100.00	40.00
		Never hinged	150.00	
N84a	OS2	25 l	100.00	40.00
		Never hinged	150.00	
N85a	OS2	50 l	100.00	40.00
		Never hinged	150.00	

Church in Savior's Name and Fort Ruins OS3

Manuscript Initials in Red or Black

1913

N87	OS3	1d brown (R)	25.00	12.00
		Never hinged	50.00	
N88	OS3	2d deep blue (R)	25.00	12.00
		Never hinged	50.00	
N89	OS3	5d gray grn (R)	45.00	20.00
		Never hinged	90.00	
N90	OS3	10d yellow grn (R)	150.00	150.00
		Never hinged	300.00	
N91	OS3	25d red (Bk)	120.00	150.00
		Never hinged	240.00	
b.		Horiz. pair, imperf. vert.	1,450.	
		Never hinged	2,200.	
		Nos. N87-N91 (5)	365.00	344.00

Victory of the Greek fleet in 1824 and the union with Greece of Samos in 1912. The manuscript initials are those of Pres. Themistokles Sofulis.

Values the same for stamps without initials. Exist imperf. Counterfeits of Nos. N87-N91 are plentiful.

For overprints see Nos. N104-N108.

Imperf., Pairs

N87a	OS3	1 d	300.00
		Never hinged	450.00
N88a	OS3	2 d	300.00
		Never hinged	450.00
N89a	OS3	5 d	440.00
		Never hinged	660.00
N90a	OS3	10 d	1,800.
		Never hinged	2,700.
N91a	OS3	25 d	1,800.
		Never hinged	2,700.

Nos. N76 to N80 Overprinted

ΕΛΛΑΣ

1914

N92	OS2	1 l gray	8.00	6.00
		Never hinged	16.00	
a.		Inverted overprint	200.00	160.00
		Never hinged	400.00	
N93	OS2	5 l lt green	8.00	6.00
		Never hinged	16.00	
a.		Inverted overprint	200.00	160.00
		Never hinged	400.00	
N94	OS2	10 l rose	8.00	6.00
		Never hinged	16.00	
a.		Double overprint	60.00	
		Never hinged	120.00	
b.		Inverted overprint	230.00	175.00
		Never hinged	450.00	
N95	OS2	25 l lt blue	8.00	6.00
		Never hinged	16.00	
b.		Inverted overprint	230.00	175.00
		Never hinged	450.00	
N96	OS2	50 l violet brn	8.00	6.00
		Never hinged	16.00	
a.		Double overprint	130.00	100.00
		Never hinged	260.00	
b.		Inverted overprint	170.00	135.00
		Never hinged	340.00	
		Nos. N92-N96 (5)	40.00	30.00

Charity Issues of Greek Administration

Nos. N81 to N86 Overprinted in Red or Black

ΕΛΛΑΣ

1915

N97	OS2	1 l gray (R)	18.00	22.00
		Never hinged	35.00	
a.		Black overprint	190.00	190.00
		Never hinged	375.00	
N98	OS2	5 l blue grn (Bk)	2.00	2.50
		Never hinged	4.00	
a.		Red overprint	160.00	160.00
		Never hinged	325.00	
b.		Double overprint	220.00	220.00
		Never hinged	450.00	
N99	OS2	10 l rose (Bk)	2.00	2.50
		Never hinged	4.00	
a.		Red overprint	160.00	160.00
		Never hinged	325.00	
b.		Inverted overprint	150.00	150.00
		Never hinged	300.00	
N100	OS2	25 l blue (Bk)	2.00	2.00
		Never hinged	4.00	
a.		Red overprint	160.00	160.00
		Never hinged	325.00	

N101	OS2	50 l violet brn (Bk)	2.00	2.00
		Never hinged	60.00	
a.		Red overprint	160.00	160.00
		Never hinged	325.00	
N102	OS2	1d orange (R)	3.00	3.00
		Never hinged	6.00	
a.		Inverted overprint	220.00	220.00
		Never hinged	325.00	
b.		Black overprint	190.00	190.00
		Never hinged	375.00	
c.		Double black overprint	220.00	220.00
		Never hinged	325.00	

No. N102 With Additional Surcharge in Black

N103	OS2	1 l on 1d orange	20.00	20.00
		Never hinged	40.00	
a.		Black surcharge double	325.00	325.00
		Never hinged	650.00	
b.		Black surcharge inverted	160.00	
		Nos. N97-N103 (7)	49.00	54.00

Issue of 1913 Overprinted in Red or Black

Without Sofoulis' Initials Above Overprint

1915

N104	OS3	1d brown (R)	30.00	25.00
		Never hinged	60.00	
N105	OS3	2d dp blue (R)	35.00	35.00
		Never hinged	70.00	
a.		Double overprint		
N106	OS3	5d gray grn (R)	30.00	25.00
		Never hinged	60.00	
N107	OS3	10d yellow grn (Bk)	90.00	70.00
		Never hinged	175.00	
a.		Inverted overprint	1,450.	1,450.
		Never hinged	2,900.	
N108	OS3	25d red (Bk)	825.00	725.00
		Never hinged	1,650.	
		Nos. N104-N108 (5)	1,010.	880.00

Nos. N97 to N108 inclusive have an embossed control mark, consisting of a cross encircled by a Greek inscription.

Most examples of Nos. N104-N108 lack the initials. Stamps with initials range in value from $80 to $1,050 unused.

Counterfeits of Nos. N104-N108 are plentiful.

FOR USE IN PARTS OF TURKEY OCCUPIED BY GREECE (NEW GREECE)

Regular Issues of Greece Overprinted

Black Overprint Meaning "Greek Administration"
On Issue of 1901
Overprint Reading Up

1912	**Wmk. 129**	**Engr.**	**Perf. 13½**	
N109	A11	20 l red lilac	3.00	3.00
		Never hinged	6.00	
a.		Double overprint	175.00	175.00
		Never hinged	350.00	

On Issue of 1911-21
Unwmk.
Serrate Roulette 13½

N110	A24	1 l green	1.00	1.00
		Never hinged	2.00	
a.		Double overprint	6.00	6.00
		Never hinged	12.00	
N111	A25	2 l car rose	1.00	1.00
		Never hinged	2.00	
a.		Double overprint	6.00	6.00
		Never hinged	12.00	
N112	A24	3 l vermilion	1.00	1.00
		Never hinged	2.00	
a.		Double overprint	6.00	6.00
		Never hinged	12.00	

N113	A26	5 l green	1.00	1.00
		Never hinged	2.00	
a.		Double overprint	14.00	14.00
		Never hinged	28.00	
N114	A24	10 l car rose	2.00	2.00
		Never hinged	4.00	
a.		Double overprint	15.00	15.00
		Never hinged	30.00	
N115	A25	20 l gray lilac	3.00	3.00
		Never hinged	6.00	
a.		Double overprint	25.00	25.00
		Never hinged	50.00	
b.		Double ovpt., one inverted	110.00	110.00
		Never hinged	160.00	
c.		Triple overprint	140.00	—
		Never hinged	275.00	
N116	A25	25 l ultra	3.00	3.00
		Never hinged	6.00	
a.		Double overprint	27.50	27.50
		Never hinged	55.00	
N117	A26	30 l car rose	3.00	3.00
		Never hinged	6.00	
a.		Double overprint	35.00	35.00
		Never hinged	70.00	
N118	A25	40 l deep blue	5.00	5.00
		Never hinged	10.00	
a.		Double overprint	35.00	35.00
		Never hinged	70.00	
N119	A26	50 l dl violet	5.00	5.00
		Never hinged	10.00	
a.		Double overprint	35.00	35.00
		Never hinged	70.00	
N120	A27	1d ultra	12.00	12.00
		Never hinged	24.00	
a.		1d gray ultramarine (on #208a)	150.00	150.00
		Never hinged	300.00	
b.		Double overprint	100.00	100.00
		Never hinged	200.00	
c.		Double ovpt., one inverted	2,500.	
N121	A27	2d vermilion	50.00	25.00
		Never hinged	100.00	
a.		Double overprint	200.00	200.00
		Never hinged	400.00	
N122	A27	3d car rose	60.00	35.00
		Never hinged	120.00	
N123	A27	5d ultra	25.00	35.00
		Never hinged	50.00	
a.		Double overprint	50.00	50.00
		Never hinged	100.00	
N124	A27	10d deep blue	275.00	275.00
		Never hinged	550.00	
a.		Double overprint	550.00	
		Never hinged	1,900.	
N125	A28	25d dp bl, ovpt. horiz.	340.00	340.00
		Never hinged	675.00	
a.		Last "Σ" of "ΔΙΟΙΚΗΣΙΣ" inverted	2,750.	

On Issue of 1913-23
Litho.

N126	A24	1 l green	1.00	1.00
		Never hinged	2.00	
a.		Double overprint	6.00	6.00
		Never hinged	12.00	
b.		Double ovpt., one inverted	85.00	85.00
		Never hinged	175.00	
c.		Period omitted after "ΕΛ–ΛΑΣ" (on #214a)	150.00	
		Never hinged	300.00	
N127	A26	5 l green	1.00	1.00
		Never hinged	2.00	
a.		Double overprint	6.00	6.00
		Never hinged	12.00	
N128	A24	10 l carmine	3.00	3.00
		Never hinged	6.00	
a.		Double overprint	6.00	6.00
		Never hinged	12.00	
b.		Double overprint, one inverted	140.00	140.00
		Never hinged	275.00	
N129	A25	25 l blue	5.00	5.00
		Never hinged	10.00	
a.		Double overprint	35.00	35.00
		Never hinged	70.00	
b.		Triple overprint	225.00	
		Never hinged	450.00	
		Nos. N109-N129 (21)	800.00	760.00

Overprinted Reading Down (Inverted)

N109d	A11	20 l red lilac	10.00	10.00
		Never hinged	20.00	
N110d	A24	1 l green	50.00	50.00
		Never hinged	150.00	
N111d	A25	2 l carmine rose	2.00	2.00
		Never hinged	4.00	
e.		Double overprint	120.00	
		Never hinged	240.00	
N112d	A24	3 l carmine rose	3.00	3.00
		Never hinged	6.00	
N113d	A25	5 l green	4.00	4.00
		Never hinged	8.00	
N114d	A24	10 l carmine rose	175.00	175.00
		Never hinged	525.00	
N115d	A25	20 l gray lilac	9.00	9.00
		Never hinged	18.00	
e.		Double overprint	225.00	225.00
		Never hinged	450.00	
f.		Pair, one without ovpt.	160.00	
		Never hinged	320.00	
N116d	A25	25 l ultramarine	140.00	140.00
		Never hinged	425.00	
N117d	A26	30 l carmine rose	450.00	450.00
		Never hinged	1,350.	
N118d	A26	40 l deep blue	300.00	275.00
		Never hinged	900.00	
N119d	A26	40 l dull violet	550.00	500.00
		Never hinged	1,650.	
N120d	A27	1d ultra	110.00	100.00
		Never hinged	275.00	
e.		1d gray ultra (on #208a)	90.00	90.00
		Never hinged	275.00	
N121d	A27	2d vermilion	175.00	175.00
		Never hinged	525.00	
N122d	A27	3d carmine rose	150.00	150.00
		Never hinged	450.00	
N123d	A27	5d ultramarine	725.00	725.00
		Never hinged	2,200.	
N126d	A24	1 l green	12.00	12.00
		Never hinged	24.00	
e.		Double overprint	120.00	120.00
		Never hinged	240.00	

N127d	A26	5 l green	4.00	4.00
		Never hinged	8.00	
e.		Double overprint	225.00	225.00
		Never hinged	450.00	
N128d	A24	10 l carmine	4.00	4.00
		Never hinged	8.00	
N129d	A25	25 l carmine	95.00	95.00
		Never hinged	300.00	
e.		Double overprint	100.00	100.00
		Never hinged	300.00	

Red Overprint, Reading Up
On Issues of 1911-21
Engr.

N130	A24	1 l green	1.00	1.00
		Never hinged	2.00	
N131	A26	5 l green	1.00	1.00
		Never hinged	2.00	
N132	A25	20 l gray lilac	5.00	5.00
		Never hinged	10.00	
a.		Inverted overprint (reading down)		3,000.
N133	A25	40 l deep blue	2.00	3.00
		Never hinged	4.00	
a.		Double overprint	325.00	325.00
		Never hinged	650.00	
b.		Pair, one stamp without overprint	125.00	
		Never hinged	250.00	
N134	A26	50 l dull violet	3.00	3.00
		Never hinged	6.00	
a.		Double overprint, one black, one red	1,250.	
		Never hinged	2,500.	
N135	A27	1d ultramarine	20.00	15.00
		Never hinged	40.00	
N136	A27	2d vermilion	95.00	100.00
		Never hinged	190.00	
N137	A27	3d carmine rose	40.00	50.00
		Never hinged	80.00	
N138	A27	5d ultramarine	550.00	400.00
		Never hinged	1,600.	
N139	A27	10 deep blue d	60.00	60.00
		Never hinged	120.00	
a.		Double overprint	725.00	725.00
		Never hinged	1,450.	
b.		Double ovpt., one inverted	725.00	725.00
		Never hinged	1,450.	
c.		Double ovpt., one black, one red	1,250.	
		Never hinged	2,500.	
N140	A28	25d deep blue, ovpt. horiz.	800.00	800.00
		Never hinged	2,400.	
a.		Double overprint	1,800.	
		Never hinged	5,400.	
b.		Inverted overprint (reading down)	650.00	650.00
		Never hinged	1,300.	

Litho.

N141	A26	5 l green	2.00	1.00
		Never hinged	4.00	
a.		Inverted overprint (reading down)		3,000.
N142	A25	25 l ultra, ovpt. horiz.	3.00	2.00
		Never hinged	6.00	
a.		Inverted overprint (reading down)	275.00	
		Never hinged	550.00	
		Nos. N130-N142 (13)	1,582.	1,441.

Carmine Overprint, Reading Up
Engr.

N143	A25	2 l carmine rose	15.00	13.00
		Never hinged	37.50	
a.		Double overprint	75.00	75.00
		Never hinged	190.00	
b.		Inverted overprint (reading down)	—	—
N144	A24	3 l vermilion	15.00	15.00
		Never hinged	37.50	
N145	A25	20 l gray lilac	65.00	65.00
		Never hinged	37.50	
a.		Double overprint	140.00	
		Never hinged	350.00	
N146	A25	25 l ultramarine	100.00	95.00
		Never hinged	250.00	
N147	A26	30 l carmine rose	110.00	110.00
		Never hinged	275.00	
a.		Double overprint	325.00	
		Never hinged	800.00	
N148	A27	2d vermilion	260.00	260.00
		Never hinged	650.00	
a.		Double overprint	375.00	
		Never hinged	950.00	
N149	A27	5d ultramarine	540.00	
		Never hinged	1,350.	
a.		Double overprint	700.00	
		Never hinged	2,100.	

Litho.

N150	A24	1 l green	10.00	12.00
		Never hinged	25.00	
b.		Period omitted after "ΕΛ–ΛΑΣ" (on #214a)	450.00	
		Never hinged	1,100.	
N151	A24	10 l carmine rose	90.00	80.00
		Never hinged	240.00	
		Nos. N143-N151 (9)	1,205.	650.00

There are numerous broken, missing and wrong font letters with a Greek "Λ" instead of "Δ" as the first letter of the second word.
Counterfeits exist of Nos. N109-N151.

Cross of	Eagle of Zeus
Constantine	O2
O1	

1912   Litho.

N150A	O1	1 l brown, *gray-ish*	.25	.25
		Never hinged	.50	
c.		1 l brown, *yellowish*	.50	.50
		Never hinged	1.00	
N152	O2	2 l red, *yellow-ish*	.50	.50
		Never hinged	1.00	
a.		2 l rose	1.25	1.25
		Never hinged	2.50	
N153	O2	3 l orange, *grayish*	.30	.25
		Never hinged	.60	
a.		3 l orange, *yellowish*	.50	.50
		Never hinged	1.00	
N154	O1	5 l green, *gray-ish*	.25	.25
		Never hinged	.50	
a.		5 l green, *yellowish*	1.25	.70
		Never hinged	2.50	
N155	O1	10 l rose red, *grayish*	.25	.25
		Never hinged	.50	
a.		10 l rose red, *yellowish*	9.00	.50
		Never hinged	18.00	
N156	O1	20 l violet, *gray-ish*	25.00	5.00
		Never hinged	50.00	
N157	O2	25 l pale blue, *yellowish*	3.00	1.25
		Never hinged	6.00	
N158	O1	30 l gray green, *yellowish*	80.00	3.25
		Never hinged	160.00	
N159	O2	40 l indigo, *gray-ish*	.25	.25
		Never hinged	.50	
a.		40 l indigo, *yellowish*	15.00	5.00
		Never hinged	30.00	
b.		Double impression	—	
N160	O1	50 l dark blue, *yellowish*	5.00	3.00
		Never hinged	25.00	
N161	O2	1 d violet brn, *grayish*	25.00	5.00
		Never hinged	50.00	
N162	O1	2 d gray brown, *grayish*	60.00	8.00
		Never hinged	120.00	
N163	O2	3 d dull blue, *yellowish*	225.00	40.00
		Never hinged	1,800.	
a.		3 d dull blue, *grayish*	875.00	140.00
N164	O1	5 d gray, *yellow-ish*	225.00	45.00
		Never hinged	1,800.	
N165	O2	10 d carmine, *grayish*	250.00	350.00
		Never hinged	500.00	
N166	O1	25 d gray blk, *yellowish*	250.00	350.00
		Never hinged	500.00	
		Nos. N150A-N166 (16)	1,149.	812.25

Occupation of Macedonia, Epirus and some of the Aegean Islands.

Sold only in New Greece.

Dangerous forgeries of Nos. N165-N166 exist.

In 1916 some stamps of this issue were overprinted in Greek: "I (era) Koinotis Ag (iou) Orous" for the Mount Athos Monastery District. They were never placed in use and most of them were destroyed.

For surcharges and overprints see Nos. 267-276A, RA14-RA16, Thrace 31-33.

Imperf., Pairs
Without Overprint

N150d	O1	1 l (as #N150c)	600.00	
		Never hinged	900.00	
N151b	O2	2 l	600.00	
		Never hinged	900.00	
N153b	O2	3 l (as #153a)	500.00	
		Never hinged	750.00	
N154b	O1	5 l (as #154a)	200.00	
		Never hinged	300.00	
N155b	O1	10 l (as #155a)	220.00	
		Never hinged	325.00	
N156b	O1	20 l	1,900.	
		Never hinged	2,850.	
N157b	O2	25 l	2,400.	
		Never hinged	3,600.	
N158b	O1	30 l	2,400.	
		Never hinged	3,600.	
N159b	O2	40 l	2,400.	
		Never hinged	3,600.	
N163b	O2	3 d	3,600.	
		Never hinged	3,600.	

CAVALLA

Bulgaria Nos. 89-97
Surcharged in Red

1913   Unwmk.   Engr.   *Perf. 12*

N167	A20	5 l on 1s myrtle green	30.00	30.00
		Never hinged	45.00	
N168	A25	10 l on 10s red & black	600.00	500.00
		Never hinged	900.00	
N169	A25	10 l on 15s brown bister	85.00	85.00
		Never hinged	125.00	
N170	A26	10 l on 25s ul-tramarine & black	50.00	40.00
		Never hinged	75.00	
N171	A21	15 l on 2s car-mine & black	85.00	65.00
		Never hinged	75.00	
N172	A22	20 l on 3s lake & black	85.00	65.00
		Never hinged	125.00	
N173	A23	25 l on 5s green & black	25.00	15.00
		Never hinged	37.50	
N174	A24	50 l on 10s red & black	50.00	30.00
		Never hinged	75.00	
N175	A25	1 d on 15s brown bister	300.00	250.00
		Never hinged	450.00	
N176	A27	1 d on 30s blue & black	120.00	120.00
		Never hinged	180.00	
N177	A28	1 d on 50s ocher & black	180.00	180.00
		Never hinged	270.00	

Blue Surcharge

N178	A24	50 l on 10s red & black	25.00	25.00
		Never hinged	37.50	
		Nos. N167-N178 (11)	1,035.	905.00

The counterfeits and reprints of Nos. N167-N178 are difficult to distinguish from originals. Many overprint varieties exist.

Some specialists question the status of Nos. N167-N178.

DEDEAGATCH

(Alexandroupolis)

D1-(10 lepta)

1913   Unwmk.   Typeset   *Perf. 11½*
Control Mark in Red

N179	D1	5 l black	65.00	40.00
N180	D1	10 l black	10.00	6.00
N181	D1	25 l black	10.00	9.00
a.		Sheet of 8	130.00	130.00
		Nos. N179-N181 (3)	85.00	55.00

Nos. N179-N181 issued without gum in sheets of 8, consisting of one 5 l, three 10 l normal, one 10 l inverted, three 25 l and one blank. The sheet yields se-tenant pairs of 5 l & 10 l, 10 l & 25 l; tete beche pairs of 5 l & 10 l, 10 l & 25 l and 10 l & 10 l.

Also issued imperf., value $200 unused, $150 canceled.

The 5 l reads "PENTE LEPTA" in Greek letters; the 10 l is illustrated; the 25 l carries the numeral "25."

Bulgaria Nos. 89-90,
92-93, 95 Surcharged

Red Surcharge

1913   *Perf. 12*

N182	A20	5 l on 1s myr grn	90.00	50.00
a.		"ΔΙΟΙΚΗΣΙΣ" instead of "ΔΕΔΕΑΓΤΣ"	100.00	
			200.00	140.00
N183	A26	1 d on 25s ultra & blk	130.00	75.00
		Never hinged	260.00	

Blue Surcharge

N184	A24	10 l on 10s red & blk	40.00	25.00
		Never hinged	80.00	
a.		"ΔΕΔΕΑΓΤΕ" instead of "ΔΕΔΕΑΓΤΕ"	200.00	140.00
b.		Double surcharge	1,650.	
c.		As "b," "ΔΕΔΕΑΓΤΕ" instead of "ΔΕΔΕΑΓΤΕ"	4,400.	
N185	A23	25 l on 5s grn & blk	50.00	35.00
		Never hinged	100.00	
a.		"ΔΕΔΕΑΓΤΕ" instead of "ΔΕΔΕΑΓΤΕ"	50.00	35.00
N187	A21	50 l on 2s car & blk	90.00	60.00
		Never hinged	180.00	
a.		"ΔΕΔΕΑΓΤΕ" instead of "ΔΕΔΕΑΓΤΕ"	225.00	150.00
		Nos. N182-N185,N187 (5)	400.00	245.00

The surcharges on Nos. N182 to N187 are printed from a setting of eight, which was used for all, with the necessary changes of value. No. 6 in the setting has a Greek "L" instead of "D" for the third letter of the third word of the surcharge.

The 25 l surcharge also exists on 8 examples of the 25s, Bulgaria No. 95.

D2

D3

1913, Sept. 15   Typeset   *Perf. 11½*
Control Mark in Blue

N188	D2	1 l blue	325.00	100.00
N189	D2	2 l blue	325.00	100.00
N190	D2	3 l blue	325.00	100.00
N191	D2	5 l blue	325.00	100.00
N192	D2	10 l blue	325.00	100.00
N193	D2	25 l blue	325.00	100.00
N194	D2	40 l blue	325.00	100.00
N195	D2	50 l blue	325.00	100.00
		Nos. N188-N195 (8)	2,600.	800.00

Issued without gum in sheets of 8 containing all values.

Counterfeits of Nos. N188-N195 exist.

1913, Sept. 25   Typeset
Control Mark in Blue

N196	D3	1 l blue, *gray blue*	250.00	80.00
N197	D3	5 l blue, *gray blue*	250.00	80.00
N198	D3	10 l blue, *gray blue*	250.00	80.00
N199	D3	25 l blue, *gray blue*	250.00	80.00
N200	D3	30 l blue, *gray blue*	250.00	80.00
N201	D3	50 l blue, *gray blue*	250.00	80.00
		Nos. N196-N201 (6)	1,500.	480.00

Nos. N196 to N201 were issued without gum in sheets of six containing all values.

Counterfeits of Nos. N182-N201 are plentiful.

FOR USE IN NORTH EPIRUS
(ALBANIA)

Greek
Stamps of
1937-38
Overprinted
in Black

Perf. 13½x12, 12x13½

1940   Litho.   Wmk. 252

N202	A69	5 l brn red & bl	.25	.25
		Never hinged	.99.00	
N203	A70	10 l bl & brn red (No. 413)	.25	.25
		Never hinged	.30	
a.		Double impression of frame	160.00	
N204	A71	20 l blk & grn	.25	.25
		Never hinged	.30	
a.		Inverted overprint	55.00	
N205	A72	40 l grn & blk	.25	.25
		Never hinged	.30	
a.		Inverted overprint	55.00	
N206	A73	50 l brn & blk	.25	.25
		Never hinged	.30	
N207	A74	80 l ind & yel brn	.40	.40
		Never hinged	.60	
N208	A67	1 d green	.40	.40
		Never hinged	.60	
a.		Inverted overprint	100.00	
b.		"ΔΙΟΙΚΗΕΙΕ" instead of "ΔΙΟΙΚΗΕΙΕ"	22.50	
		Never hinged	45.00	
N209	A75	2 d ultra	.40	.40
		Never hinged	.60	
N210	A67	3 d red brn	.40	.40
		Never hinged	.60	
a.		"ΔΙΟΙΚΗΕΙΕ" instead of "ΔΙΟΙΚΗΕΙΕ"	22.50	
		Never hinged	45.00	
N211	A76	5 d red	.60	.60
		Never hinged	1.20	
N212	A77	6 d ol brn	.80	.80
		Never hinged	1.75	
N213	A78	7 d dk brn	.80	.80
		Never hinged	1.75	
N214	A67	8 d deep blue	.80	.80
		Never hinged	1.75	
a.		"ΔΙΟΙΚΗΕΙΕ" instead of "ΔΙΟΙΚΗΕΙΕ"	22.50	
		Never hinged	45.00	
N215	A79	10 d red brn	2.00	2.00
		Never hinged	45.00	
N216	A80	15 d green	2.00	2.00
		Never hinged	3.00	
N217	A81	25 d dark blue	4.75	4.00
		Never hinged	7.25	
a.		Inverted overprint	90.00	
		Never hinged	160.00	

Engr.
Unwmk.

N218	A84	30 d org brn	5.00	8.00
		Never hinged	14.00	
		Nos. N202-N218 (17)	19.60	21.85

Same Overprinted in Carmine on National Youth Issue

1941   Litho.   *Perf. 12½, 13½x12½*

N219	A93	3 d sil, dp ultra & red	.70	1.00
		Never hinged	1.00	
N220	A94	5 d dk bl & blk	3.75	3.75
		Never hinged	5.00	
N221	A94	10 d red org & blk	5.00	5.00
		Never hinged	7.00	
N222	A94	15 d dk grn & blk	18.00	17.00
		Never hinged	24.00	
N223	A94	20 d lake & blk	15.00	17.00
		Never hinged	20.00	
N224	A94	25 d dk bl & blk	15.00	17.00
		Never hinged	20.00	
N225	A94	30 d rose vio & blk	15.00	17.00
		Never hinged	20.00	
N226	A94	50 d lake & blk	15.00	17.00
		Never hinged	20.00	
N227	A94	75 d dk bl, brn & gold	17.50	17.00
		Never hinged	20.00	
N228	A93	100 d sil, dp ultra & red	20.00	22.50
		Never hinged	27.50	
a.		Inverted overprint	850.00	
		Never hinged	1,200.	
		Nos. N219-N228 (10)	124.95	134.25

Same Overprint in Carmine on National Youth Air Post Stamps

N229	AP25	2 d red org & blk	.75	1.10
		Never hinged	1.10	
a.		Inverted overprint	175.00	
		Never hinged	250.00	
N230	AP25	4 d dk grn & blk	3.50	4.00
		Never hinged	5.00	
a.		Inverted overprint	175.00	
		Never hinged	250.00	
N231	AP25	6 d lake & blk	5.00	5.00
a.		Inverted overprint	175.00	
		Never hinged	250.00	
N232	AP25	8 d dk bl & blk	7.00	8.00
		Never hinged	10.00	
N233	AP25	16 d rose vio & blk	13.50	15.00
		Never hinged	19.00	
N234	AP25	32 d red org & blk	16.00	18.00
		Never hinged	22.00	
N235	AP25	45 d dk grn & blk	16.00	18.00
		Never hinged	22.00	
N236	AP25	55 d lake & blk	16.00	18.00
		Never hinged	22.00	
N237	AP25	65 d dk bl & blk	16.00	18.00
		Never hinged	22.00	

N238	AP25	100d rose vio & blk	27.50	30.00
		Never hinged	40.00	
a.		Inverted overprint	850.00	
		Never hinged	1,200.	
		Nos. N229-N238 (10)	121.25	135.10

Some specialists have questioned the status of Nos. N230a and N231a.

For other stamps issued by Greece for use in occupied parts of Epirus and Thrace, see the catalogue listings of those countries.

POSTAGE DUE STAMPS

FOR USE IN PARTS OF TURKEY OCCUPIED BY GREECE (NEW GREECE)

Postage Due Stamps of Greece, 1902, Overprinted

1912　Wmk. 129　Engr.　*Perf. 13½*
Black Overprint, Reading Up

NJ1	D3	1 l chocolate	.60	.60
		Never hinged	1.20	
a.		Double overprint	22.50	
		Never hinged	45.00	
b.		Double overprint, one inverted	50.00	
		Never hinged	100.00	
c.		Double overprint, one on reverse	75.00	
		Never hinged	150.00	
d.		Inverted overprint (reading down)	50.00	70.00
		Never hinged	100.00	
NJ2	D3	2 l gray	.60	.60
		Never hinged	1.20	
a.		Double overprint	20.00	
		Never hinged	40.00	
b.		Double overprint, one inverted	40.00	
		Never hinged	80.00	
c.		Double overprint, one on reverse reading down	350.00	
		Never hinged	700.00	
d.		Inverted overprint (reading down)	50.00	70.00
		Never hinged	100.00	
NJ3	D3	3 l orange	.60	.60
		Never hinged	1.20	
a.		Double overprint	15.00	
		Never hinged	30.00	
b.		Double overprint, one inverted	60.00	
		Never hinged	120.00	
c.		Double overprint, both inverted	100.00	
		Never hinged	200.00	
NJ4	D3	5 l yel grn	1.00	1.00
		Never hinged	2.00	
a.		Double overprint	35.00	
		Never hinged	70.00	
NJ5	D3	10 l scarlet	1.50	1.50
		Never hinged	3.00	
a.		Double overprint	25.00	
		Never hinged	50.00	
NJ6	D3	20 l lilac	1.50	1.50
		Never hinged	3.00	
NJ7	D3	30 l dp vio	3.00	3.00
		Never hinged	6.00	
a.		Double overprint	120.00	
		Never hinged	240.00	
b.		Double overprint, one on reverse	260.00	
		Never hinged	525.00	
NJ8	D3	40 l dk brn	5.00	5.00
		Never hinged	10.00	
a.		Double overprint	190.00	
		Never hinged	375.00	
NJ9	D3	50 l red brn	8.00	8.00
		Never hinged	16.00	
NJ10	D3	1d black	45.00	45.00
		Never hinged	90.00	
NJ11	D3	2d bronze (overprint reading down)	70.00	80.00
		Never hinged	175.00	
NJ12	D3	3d silver (overprint reading down)	140.00	120.00
		Never hinged	350.00	
NJ13	D3	5d gold (overprint reading down)	225.00	250.00
		Never hinged	560.00	
		Nos. NJ1-NJ13 (13)	501.80	516.80

Red Overprint, Reading Up

NJ14	D3	1 l chocolate	1.00	1.00
		Never hinged	2.00	
NJ15	D3	2 l gray	1.00	1.00
		Never hinged	2.00	
a.		Double overprint	125.00	
		Never hinged	250.00	
NJ16	D3	5 l yellow green	1.00	1.00
		Never hinged	2.00	
NJ17	D3	20 l lilac	1.00	1.00
		Never hinged	2.00	
NJ18	D3	30 l deep violet	5.00	5.00
		Never hinged	10.00	
a.		Inverted overprint (reading down)	35.00	60.00
		Never hinged	70.00	

NJ19	D3	40 l dark brown	1.50	1.50
		Never hinged	3.00	
NJ20	D3	50 l red brown	1.50	1.50
		Never hinged	3.00	
NJ21	D3	1d black	10.00	10.00
		Never hinged	20.00	
NJ22	D3	2d bronze	20.00	20.00
		Never hinged	40.00	
NJ23	D3	3d silver	25.00	25.00
		Never hinged	50.00	
NJ24	D3	5d gold	60.00	60.00
		Never hinged	120.00	

Carmine Overprint, Reading Up

NJ25	D3	2 l gray	10.00	12.00
		Never hinged	25.00	
NJ26	D3	3 l orange	200.00	225.00
		Never hinged	25.00	
NJ27	D3	1d black	110.00	120.00
		Never hinged	275.00	
a.		Double overprint, one inverted	300.00	
		Never hinged	750.00	
NJ28	D3	2d bronze	500.00	
		Never hinged	1,250.	
NJ29	D3	3d silver		2,000.

Carmine Overprint, Reading Down

NJ30	D3	2 l gray	7.00	7.00
		Never hinged	17.50	
NJ31	D3	3 l orange	18.00	18.00
		Never hinged	45.00	
NJ32	D3	5 l yellow green	15.00	15.00
		Never hinged	37.50	
NJ33	D3	10 l scarlet	15.00	15.00
		Never hinged	37.50	
NJ34	D3	1d black	75.00	75.00
		Never hinged	190.00	
a.		Double overprint	500.00	
		Never hinged	1,250.	
NJ35	D3	2d bronze	140.00	140.00
		Never hinged	350.00	
NJ36	D3	3d silver	500.00	500.00
		Never hinged	1,250.	
NJ37	D3	5d gold	1,000.	1,000.

Some of the varieties of lettering that occur on the postage stamps are also found on the postage due stamps.

FOR USE IN NORTH EPIRUS (ALBANIA)

Postage Due Stamps of Greece, 1930, Surcharged or Overprinted in Black:

a　　　　　b

Perf. 13, 13x12½
1940　Litho.　Unwmk.

NJ38	D3(a)	50 l on 25d lt red	.45	.90
		Never hinged	.60	
NJ39	D3(b)	2d light red	1.10	1.80
		Never hinged	1.50	
a.		Inverted overprint	67.50	
		Never hinged	90.00	
NJ40	D3(b)	5d blue gray	.65	1.50
		Never hinged	.90	
NJ41	D3(b)	10d green	1.10	1.80
		Never hinged	1.50	
NJ42	D3(b)	15d red brown	1.10	2.00
		Never hinged	1.50	
		Nos. NJ27-NJ31 (5)	4.40	8.00

POSTAL TAX STAMPS

FOR USE IN NORTH EPIRUS (ALBANIA)

Postal Tax Stamps of Greece, Nos. RA61-RA63, Overprinted Type "b" in Black

1940　Unwmk.　Litho.　*Perf. 13½x12*

NRA1	PT7	10 l	.25	.30
		Never hinged	.30	
NRA2	PT7	50 l	.40	.65
		Never hinged	.50	
a.		Inverted overprint	67.50	
		Never hinged	95.00	
b.		Double overprint	67.50	
		Never hinged	95.00	
NRA3	PT7	1d	.95	1.80
		Never hinged	1.20	
		Nos. NRA1-NRA3 (3)	1.60	2.75

GREENLAND

'gren-lənd

LOCATION — North Atlantic Ocean
GOVT. — Danish
AREA — 840,000 sq. mi.
POP. — 52,347 (1984)

CAPITAL — Nuuk (Godthaab)
100 Ore = 1 Krone

Christian　　　　Polar Bear — A2
X — A1

Perf. 13x12½
1938-46　Unwmk.　Engr.

1	A1	1o olive black	.30	.30
		Never hinged	.55	
2	A1	5o rose lake	2.25	1.25
		Never hinged	5.25	
		On cover		55.00
3	A1	7o yellow green	4.00	4.00
		Never hinged	6.00	
		On cover		70.00
4	A1	10o dk violet	1.00	1.00
		Never hinged	1.95	
		On cover		62.50
a.		10o light violet ('45)	2.10	1.60
		On cover	4.00	
				70.00
5	A1	15o red	1.00	1.00
		Never hinged	2.50	
		On cover		42.50
6	A1	20o red ('46)	1.10	1.25
		Never hinged	3.00	
		On cover		27.50
7	A2	30o blue	4.75	7.50
		Never hinged	13.50	
		On cover		125.00
8	A2	40o blue ('46)	22.50	11.50
		Never hinged	82.50	
		On cover		110.00
9	A2	1k light brown	5.50	10.00
		Never hinged	19.00	
		On cover		140.00
		Nos. 1-9 (9)	42.40	37.80
		Set, never hinged	110.00	

Issued: Nov. 1, 1938; Aug. 1, 1946.
Nos. 1 and 2 exist in two engraving types.
For surcharges see Nos. 39-40 in Scott Standard catalogue, Vol. 3.

PARCEL POST STAMPS

Arms of
Greenland
PP1

1905-10　Unwmk.　Typo.　*Perf. 12¼*

Q1a		1o ol grn ('05)	775.00	775.00
Q3a		5o brown ('05-'10)	750.00	775.00
Q4a		10o blue ('05-'10)	950.00	625.00
		Set of 3	1,750.	1,625.

Perf. 11½
1915-28

Q1	PP1	1o ol grn ('15-'26)	57.50	60.00
Q2	PP1	2o green ('15-'24)	350.00	125.00
Q3	PP1	5o brown ('18-'28)	125.00	125.00
Q4b	PP1	10o blue ('18)	60.00	65.00
Q5	PP1	15o violet ('15-'28)	275.00	275.00
Q6	PP1	20o red ('15-'33)	17.00	13.00
		Nos. Q1-Q6 (6)	884.50	663.00

1930

Q7a	PP1	70o violet	275.00	275.00
Q8a	PP1	1k yellow	52.50	65.00
Q9	PP1	3k brown	140.00	175.00
		Nos. Q7a-Q9 (3)	467.50	515.00

1937　Litho.　*Perf. 10¾*

Q10	PP1	70o pale violet	42.50	150.00
Q11	PP1	1k yellow	50.00	77.50
		Nos. Q10-Q11, never hinged		150.00

1937　　　　Typo.

Q4	PP1	10o blue ('37)	40.00	72.50
Q6a	PP1	20o red	40.00	60.00
Q7	PP1	70o violet ('37)	40.00	125.00
Q8	PP1	1k yellow ('37)	40.00	140.00
		Nos. Q4-Q8 (4)	160.00	397.50

On lithographed stamps, PAKKE-PORTO is slightly larger, hyphen has rounded ends and lines in shield are fine, straight and evenly spaced.

On typographed stamps, hyphen has squared ends and shield lines are coarse, uneven and inclined to be slightly wavy.

Used values are for stamps postally used from Denmark. Numeral cancels indicate use as postal savings stamps and are usually worth as much or more than postally used examples. Greenland village cancels on Nos. Q6, Q6a and Q8a often reflect postal savings use. These are often worth as much or more than postally used examples. Parcel post stamps not regularly used for postal savings that have village cancellations are often worth much more.

Sheets of 25. Certain printings of Nos. Q1-Q2, Q3a, Q4a and Q5-Q6 were issued without sheet margins. Stamps from the outer rows are straight edged. Some of these sheets had the outer straight edges officially perforated in 1918. Stamps with falsified reperforations exist.

GRENADA

grə-'nā-də

LOCATION — Windward Islands, West Indies
GOVT. — Independent nation in the British Commonwealth
AREA — 133 sq. mi.
POP. — 115,000 (est. 1981)
CAPITAL — St. George's

Grenada consists of Grenada Island and the southern Grenadines, including Carriacou. This colony was granted associated statehood with Great Britain in 1967 and became an independent state Feb. 7, 1974.

12 Pence = 1 Shilling
100 Cents = 1 Dollar (1949)

> **Catalogue values for unused stamps in this country are for Never Hinged items, beginning with Scott 143 in the regular postage section, Scott J15 in the postage due section.**

Watermarks

Wmk. 5 — Small　　Wmk. 6 — Large
Star　　　　　　　Star

Wmk. 7 — Large
Star with Broad
Points

PRE-STAMP POSTAL MARKINGS

Crowned Circle handstamp type I is pictured in the Crowned Circle Handstamps and Great Britain Used Abroad section.

St. George's

1850-58

A2	I	"Grenada" crowned circle handstamp in red, on cover	2,250.

In 1846 a Crowned Circle handstamp was issued inscribed "Carriacou." No examples are known.

STAMPS OF GREAT BRITAIN USED IN GRENADA

Numeral cancellation type A is pictured in the Crowned Circle Handstamps and Great Britain Used Abroad section

1850.00

A15 (St. George's)

A3	A	1p rose red (#20)	500.00
A4	A	2p blue (#29, P7)	1,200.
A5	A	4p rose (#26)	325.00
A6	A	6p lilac (#27)	150.00
A7	A	1sh green (#28)	1,500.

Values for unused stamps are for examples with original gum as defined in the catalogue introduction. Very fine examples of Nos. 1-19, 27-29, and 31-38 will have perforations touching the design on at least one side due to the narrow spacing of the stamps on the plates. Stamps with perfs clear of the design on all four sides are scarce and will command higher prices.

Queen Victoria — A1

Rough Perf. 14 to 16
1861   Engr.   Unwmk.

1	A1	1p green	57.50	50.00
a.		1p blue green	5,250.	350.00
b.		As No. 1, horiz. pair, imperf. btwn.		
2	A1	6p rose	1,050.	110.00
b.		6p lake red, perf. 11-12½	1,000.	

No. 2b was not issued. No. 2 imperf is a proof.

> An example of the six pence rose (#2) with the barred oval "CANCELLED" handstamp realized $10,450 in a New York auction in 2003.

1863-71   Wmk. 5

3	A1	1p green ('64)	100.00	15.00
a.		1p yellow green	125.00	30.00
4	A1	6p rose	775.00	20.00
5	A1	6p vermilion ('71)	875.00	20.00
a.		6p dull red	4,000.	275.00
g.		Double impression		2,350.
i.		6p orange red ('66)	750.00	14.00

No. 5a always has sideways watermark. Other colors sometimes have sideways watermark.

1873-78   Clean-Cut Perf. about 15

5B	A1	1p deep green	120.00	50.00
j.		Pair, imperf between	13,000.	
c.		1p blue green ('78)	275.00	45.00
h.		Half used as ½p on cover		11,000.
5D	A1	6p vermilion ('75)	925.00	40.00
e.		6p dull red	950.00	40.00
f.		Double impression		2,350.

1873   Wmk. 6

6	A1	1p blue green	105.00	22.50
a.		Diagonal half used as ½p on cover		11,000.
7	A1	6p vermilion	775.00	35.00

1875   Perf. 14

7A	A1	1p yellow green	90.00	9.00
b.		Half used as ½p on cover		16,000.
c.		Perf. 15	10,000.	2,600.

> A cover bearing one example of the bisected 1p stamp (#7Ab), together with two singles and a 6p stamp, addressed to France, realized $15,400 in a New York auction in 2003.

A2   A2a

Revenue Designs Surcharged in Black
Perf. 14, 14½
1875-81

8	A2	½p purple ('81)	17.50	7.00
b.		Imperf., pair	350.00	
c.		"ALF"	4,000.	
d.		"PEN"		
e.		No hyphen between "HALF" and "PENNY"	225.00	150.00
f.		Double surcharge	350.00	350.00
9	A2a	2½p lake ('81)	75.00	10.00
a.		Imperf., pair	650.00	
b.		Imperf. vertically, pair	6,000.	
c.		"PENCF"	525.00	225.00
d.		No period after "PENNY"	290.00	90.00
e.		"PENOE"	175.00	
10	A2	4p blue ('81)	150.00	10.00

Revenue Designs Surcharged in Dark Blue

11	A2	1sh purple	775.00	20.00
a.		"SHLLIING"	6,500.	800.00
b.		"NE SHILLING"		3,250.
c.		"OSTAGE"	7,250.	3,000.
d.		Invtd. "S" in "POSTAGE"	4,500.	750.00

See Nos. 27-35.

1881   Wmk. 7

12	A2	2½p lake	200.00	57.50
a.		2½p claret	550.00	200.00
b.		As No. 12, "PENCF"	875.00	325.00
c.		As No. 12, No period after "PENNY"	650.00	230.00
d.		As "a," "PENCF"	1,850.	825.00
e.		As "a," no period after "PENNY"	1,275.	575.00
13	A2	4p blue	350.00	210.00

Revenue Stamp Overprinted "POSTAGE" in Black

A3   A4

A5

Revenue Stamp Handstamped "POSTAGE" in Manuscript

A6

1883   Wmk. 5
Denomination & Crown in 2nd Color

14	A3	½p orange & grn	900.00	275.00
a.		Unsevered pair	5,000.	1,500.
b.		"POSTAGE" inverted		1,500.
15	A4	½p orange & grn	325.00	150.00
a.		Unsevered pair	2,000.	525.00
16	A5	1p orange & grn	400.00	65.00
a.		Inverted overprint	3,500.	2,600.
b.		Double overprint	1,625.	1,275.
c.		Inverted "S" in "Postage"	1,150.	700.00
d.		Diagonal half used as ½p on cover		3,500.

"Postage" in Manuscript, Red or Black

18	A6	1p orange & grn (R)		21,000.
19	A6	1p orange & green	—	15,000.

On Nos. 14-19 the words "ONE PENNY" measure from 10-11¼mm in length.
On No. 15, the lower "POSTAGE" is always inverted.
It has been claimed that although Nos. 18 and 19 were used, they were not officially authorized by Grenada's postmaster.

A8

1883   Wmk. 2   Perf. 14

20	A8	½p green	2.25	1.25
a.		Tete beche pair	5.00	21.00
21	A8	1p rose	90.00	4.00
a.		Tete beche pair	300.00	325.00
22	A8	2½p ultra	9.00	1.25
a.		Tete beche pair	30.00	60.00
23	A8	4p slate	11.00	2.25
a.		Tete beche pair	27.50	
24	A8	6p	0.00	6.50
a.		Tete beche pair	21.00	65.00
25	A8	8p bister	10.50	14.00
a.		Tete beche pair	40.00	90.00
26	A8	1sh violet	160.00	65.00
a.		Tete beche pair	2,000.	2,250.
		Nos. 20-26 (7)	288.75	94.25

Stamps of types A8, A10 and D2 were printed with alternate horizontal rows inverted. For surcharges see Nos. 36-38, J4-J7.

Revenue Stamps Surcharged

1886   Wmk. 6

27	A2	1p on 1½ org & grn	60.00	47.50
a.		Inverted surcharge	350.00	350.00
b.		Diagonal half used as ½ on cover		2,250.
c.		Double surcharge	600.00	350.00
d.		"HALH" instead of "HALF"	300.00	275.00
e.		"F" for first "E" in "THREE"	300.00	225.00
f.		"PFNCE" for "PENCE"	300.00	225.00
28	A2	1p on 1sh org & grn	50.00	42.50
a.		"SHILLING" instead of "SHILLING"	525.00	450.00
b.		No period after "POSTAGE"	500.00	
c.		Half used as ½p on cover		2,350.

Wmk. 5

29	A2	1p on 4p org & grn	190.00	110.00

A10

1887   Wmk. 2

30	A10	1p rose	4.25	1.75
a.		Tete beche pair	10.00	27.50

Revenue Stamps Surcharged

h   i

j   k

l

1888-91   Wmk. 5   Perf. 14½

31	A2 (h)	½p on 2sh org & grn ('89)	17.50	30.00
a.		Double surcharge	350.00	375.00
b.		First "S" in "SHILLINGS" inverted	325.00	350.00
32	A2 (i)	4p on 2sh org & grn	50.00	22.50
a.		"4d" and "POSTAGE" 5mm apart	80.00	37.50
b.		"S" inverted, as in #31b	550.00	400.00
c.		As "a," inverted "S," as in #31b	750.00	650.00

"d" Vertical instead of Slanting

33	A2 (j)	4p on 2sh org & grn	875.00	475.00
34	A2 (k)	1p on 2sh org & grn ('90)	92.50	87.50
a.		Inverted surcharge	875.00	
b.		"S" inverted	825.00	750.00
35	A2 (l)	1p on 2sh org & grn ('91)	70.00	70.00
a.		Inverted surcharge		
b.		No period after "d"	450.00	—
c.		"S" inverted	575.00	575.00

No. 25 Surcharged in Black

Wmk. 2

36	A8	1p on 8p bister	12.00	17.00
a.		Tete beche pair	50.00	70.00
b.		Inverted surcharge	375.00	325.00
c.		No period after "d"	300.00	300.00

"2" of "½" Upright

37	A8	2½p on 8p bister	11.00	14.00
a.		Tete beche pair	50.00	70.00
b.		Inverted surcharge		
c.		Double surcharge	1,000.	925.00
d.		Triple surcharge		1,100.
e.		Double surcharge, one inverted	650.00	575.00

"2" of "½" Italic

38	A8	2½p on 8p bister	14.00	13.00
		Ovptd. "SPECIMEN"	75.00	
a.		Tete beche pair	50.00	70.00
b.		Tete beche pair, #37, 38	125.00	
c.		Inverted surcharge		
d.		Double surcharge	875.00	925.00
e.		Triple surcharge		1,050.
f.		Triple surch., two inverted		1,000.
g.		Double surcharge, one inverted	625.00	575.00

Queen Victoria — A17

1895-99   Wmk. 2   Typo.   Perf. 14

39	A17	½p lilac & green	3.50	2.00
40	A17	1p lilac & car rose	5.25	.90
41	A17	2p lilac & brown	47.50	37.50
42	A17	2½p lilac & ultra	9.50	1.75
43	A17	3p lilac & orange	8.00	18.00
44	A17	6p lilac & green	20.00	60.00
45	A17	8p lilac & black	15.00	52.50
46	A17	1sh green & org	22.50	60.00
		Nos. 39-46 (8)	131.25	232.65
		Set, ovptd. "SPECIMEN"	175.00	

Numerals of ½p, 3p, 8p and 1sh of type A17 are in color on colorless tablet.
Issue dates: 1p, May, 1896; ½p, 2p, Sept. 1899; others, Sept. 5, 1895.

Columbus' Flagship, La Concepcion A18   King Edward VII A19

1898, Aug. 15   Engr.   Wmk. 1

47	A18	2½p ultra	21.00	8.00
		Ovptd. "SPECIMEN"	100.00	
a.		Bluish paper	37.50	47.50

Discovery of the island by Columbus, Aug. 15th, 1498.

1902   Wmk. 2   Typo.

48	A19	½p violet & grn	4.00	1.50
49	A19	1p vio & car rose	7.50	.35
50	A19	2p vio & brown	4.50	11.50
51	A19	2½p vio & ultra	5.50	3.25
52	A19	3p vio & org	5.50	10.50
53	A19	6p vio & green	9.00	20.00
54	A19	1sh green & org	9.00	37.50
55	A19	2sh grn & ultra	32.50	65.00

56	A19	5sh grn & car rose	47.50	80.00
57	A19	10sh green & vio	160.00	300.00
		Nos. 48-57 (10)	285.00	529.60
		Set, ovptd. "SPECIMEN"	225.00	

Numerals of ½p, 3p, 1sh, 2sh and 10sh of type A19 are in color on colorless tablet.

1904-06   Wmk. 3   *Perf. 14*
Ordinary Paper

58	A19	½p vio & green	20.00	42.50
59	A19	1p vio & car rose	16.00	3.00
60	A19	2p vio & brown	65.00	130.00
61	A19	2½p vio & ultra	65.00	75.00
62	A19	3p vio & org	3.75	11.00
a.		Chalky paper	4.75	9.00
63	A19	6p vio & green	12.00	26.00
a.		Chalky paper	13.00	35.00
64	A19	1sh green & org	7.00	37.50
65	A19	2sh grn & ultra	60.00	85.00
a.		Chalky paper	45.00	80.00
66	A19	5sh grn & car rose	75.00	110.00
67	A19	10sh green & vio	190.00	300.00
		Nos. 58-67 (10)	513.75	820.00

Issued: Nos. 58, 60-62, 64, 1905; Nos. 63, 65-67, 1906.

Seal of Colony — A20

1906-11   Engr.

68	A20	½p green	5.25	.35
69	A20	1p carmine	8.00	.25
70	A20	2p yellow	3.50	3.50
71	A20	2½p blue	7.00	2.00
a.		2½p ultramarine	11.00	3.75

Typo.
Chalky Paper
Numerals white on dark ground

72	A20	3p vio, *yel* ('08)	5.50	1.90
73	A20	6p violet ('08)	22.50	25.00
74	A20	1sh blk, *grn* ('11)	8.00	5.00
75	A20	2sh vio & blue, *blue* ('08)	26.00	14.00
76	A20	5sh red & green, *yel* ('08)	67.50	80.00
		Nos. 68-76 (9)	153.25	132.00

1908   Wmk. 2

| 77 | A20 | 1sh black, *green* | 50.00 | 75.00 |
| 78 | A20 | 10sh red & grn, *grn* | 150.00 | 300.00 |

King George V — A21

1913   Ordinary Paper   Wmk. 3

79	A21	½p green	1.25	1.60
80	A21	1p carmine	2.50	.35
a.		1p scarlet ('16)	12.00	2.00
81	A21	2p orange	1.90	.35
82	A21	2½p ultra	2.00	2.00

Chalky Paper

83	A21	3p violet, *yel*	.75	1.00
84	A21	6p dull vio & red vio	1.75	10.00
85	A21	1sh black, *green*	1.10	11.50
a.		1sh black, *emerald*	1.75	20.00
b.		1sh blk, *bl grn*, olive back	52.50	90.00
c.		As "a," olive back	1.75	15.00
86	A21	2sh vio & ultra, *bl*	7.25	14.00
87	A21	5sh grn & red, *yel*	20.00	67.50
88	A21	10sh grn & red, *grn*	70.00	110.00
a.		10sh grn & red, *emer*	70.00	180.00
		Nos. 79-88 (10)	108.50	218.30

1914   Surface-colored Paper

| 89 | A21 | 3p violet, *yel* | .70 | 1.60 |
| 90 | A21 | 1sh black, *green* | 1.40 | 8.50 |

1921-29   Ordinary Paper   Wmk. 4

91	A21	½p green	1.40	.35
92	A21	1p rose red	.90	.85
93	A21	1p brown ('23)	1.75	.35
94	A21	1½p rose red	1.75	1.75
95	A21	2p orange	1.40	.35
96	A21	2p gray ('26)	2.75	3.00
97	A21	2½p ultramarine	7.50	10.00
98	A21	2½p gray ('22)	1.10	10.00
99	A21	3p ultra ('22)	1.75	12.50

Chalky Paper

100	A21	3p vio, *yel* ('26)	3.50	5.75
101	A21	4p blk & red, *yel* ('26)	1.10	4.25
102	A21	5p gray vio & ol grn ('22)	1.75	4.75
103	A21	6p dl vio & red vio	1.50	28.00
104	A21	6p blk & red ('26)	2.50	2.75
105	A21	9p gray vio & blk ('22)	2.50	11.00
106	A21	1sh blk, *emer* ('23)	3.00	60.00
107	A21	1sh org brn ('26)	4.50	11.00
108	A21	2sh vio & ultra, *bl* ('22)	7.00	19.00
109	A21	2sh6p blk & red, *bl* ('29)	8.00	22.50
110	A21	3sh grn & vio ('22)	6.75	30.00
111	A21	5sh green & red, *yel* ('23)	14.00	40.00
112	A21	10sh green & red, *emer* ('23)	57.50	150.00
		Nos. 91-112 (22)	133.90	428.15

Grand Anse Beach — A22

Seal of the Colony — A23

View of Grand Etang — A24

View of St. George's — A25

1934, Oct. 23   Engr.   *Perf. 12½*

| 114 | A22 | ½p green | .25 | 1.25 |
| a. | | Perf. 12½x13 ('36) | 8.50 | 70.00 |

Perf. 13½x12½

| 115 | A23 | 1p blk brn & blk | .65 | .35 |
| a. | | Perf 12½ | 2.00 | 3.50 |

Perf. 12½x13½

| 116 | A24 | 1½p car & black | 1.25 | .45 |
| a. | | Perf 12½ ('36) | 7.00 | 5.00 |

Perf. 12½

117	A23	2p org & black	1.10	.80
118	A25	2½p deep blue	.55	.55
119	A23	3p ol grn & blk	1.10	3.25
120	A23	6p claret & blk	2.75	2.00
121	A23	1sh brown & blk	3.00	4.50
122	A23	2sh6p ultra & blk	9.00	30.00
123	A23	5sh vio & black	50.00	55.00
		Nos. 114-123 (10)	69.65	98.15
		Set, never hinged	130.00	

Common Design Types pictured following the introduction.

Silver Jubilee Issue
Common Design Type

1935, May 6   *Perf. 11x12*

124	CD301	½p green & blk	1.10	1.50
125	CD301	1p black & ultra	1.25	2.25
126	CD301	1½p car & blue	1.25	3.25
127	CD301	1sh brn vio & ind	13.00	32.50
		Nos. 124-127 (4)	16.60	39.50
		Set, never hinged	25.00	

Coronation Issue
Common Design Type

1937, May 12   Wmk. 4   *Perf. 11x11½*

128	CD302	1p dark purple	.25	.25
129	CD302	1p dark carmine	.25	.25
130	CD302	2½p deep ultra	.50	.35
		Nos. 128-130 (3)	1.00	.85
		Set, never hinged	1.60	

George VI — A26

1937, July 12   Photo.   *Perf. 14½x14*

| 131 | A26 | ¼p chestnut | .50 | .75 |

Grand Anse Beach — A27

Seal of the Colony — A28

View of Grand Etang — A29

View of St. George's — A30

Seal of the Colony — A31

1938, Mar. 16   Engr.   *Perf. 12½*

132	A27	½p green	.80	1.40
133	A28	1p blk brn & blk	.55	.55
134	A29	1½p scarlet & blk	.25	.95
135	A28	2p orange & blk	.25	.55
136	A30	2½p ultramarine	.25	.35
137	A28	3p olive grn & blk	.25	2.10
138	A28	6p red vio & blk	.25	.45
139	A28	1sh org brn & blk	2.50	.45
140	A28	2sh ultra & black	15.00	2.00
141	A28	5sh purple & blk	2.25	2.75

Perf. 14

142	A31	10sh rose car & gray blue	20.00	13.00
a.		10sh deep car & gray blue, perf. 12 ('43)	700.00	1,750.
b.		Perf. 12x13	42.50	12.00
		Nos. 131-142 (12)	43.85	25.30
		Set, never hinged	67.50	

1938-42   *Perf. 12½x13½, 13½x12½*

132a	A27	½p	3.50	.90
133a	A28	1p	.30	.25
134a	A29	1½p car & blk	1.25	.40
135a	A28	2p	1.40	.75
136a	A30	2½p	7,500.	240.00
137a	A28	3p	2.50	1.00
138a	A28	6p ('42)	1.25	.35
139a	A28	1sh ('42)	2.50	1.50
140a	A28	2sh ('41)	17.50	2.00
141a	A28	5sh ('47)	2.00	4.50

> Catalogue values for unused stamps in this section, from this point to the end of the section, are for Never Hinged items.

Peace Issue
Common Design Type

1946, Sept. 25   *Perf. 13½x14*

| 143 | CD303 | 1½p carmine | .25 | .25 |
| 144 | CD303 | 3½p deep blue | .25 | .70 |

Silver Wedding Issue
Common Design Types

1948, Oct. 27   Photo.   *Perf. 14x14½*

| 145 | CD304 | 1½p scarlet | .25 | .25 |

Engr.; Name Typo.
Perf. 11½x11

| 146 | CD305 | 10sh gray green | 26.00 | 26.00 |

UPU Issue
Common Design Types
Engr.; Name Typo. on 6c, 12c
Perf. 13½, 11x11½

1949, Oct. 10   Wmk. 4

147	CD306	5c ultra	.25	.25
148	CD307	6c deep olive	1.50	2.25
149	CD308	12c red lilac	.30	.50
150	CD309	24c red brown	.25	.55
		Nos. 147-150 (4)	2.30	3.55

A32

A33

A34

1951, Jan. 8   Engr.   *Perf. 11½*
Center in Black

151	A32	½c chestnut	.25	1.50
152	A32	1c blue green	.25	.60
153	A32	2c dark brown	.25	.25
154	A32	3c carmine	.25	.25
155	A32	4c deep orange	.40	.25
156	A32	5c purple	.50	.30
157	A32	6c olive	.50	.65
158	A32	7c blue	2.00	.30
159	A32	12c red violet	2.25	.75

Perf. 11½x12½

160	A33	25c dark brown	2.50	1.00
161	A33	50c ultra	6.50	.60
162	A33	$1.50 orange	8.25	8.00

Perf. 11½x13
Center in Gray Blue

| 163 | A34 | $2.50 deep carmine | 9.50 | 6.50 |
| | | Nos. 151-163 (13) | 33.40 | 20.95 |

See Nos. 180-183, 202 in Scott Standard catalogue, Vol. 3. For overprints see Nos. 166-169.

University Issue
Common Design Types

1951, Feb. 16   *Perf. 14x14½*

| 164 | CD310 | 3c dp car & gray blk | .55 | 1.00 |
| 165 | CD311 | 6c olive & black | .65 | .60 |

Nos. 154-156 and 159 Overprinted in Black or Carmine

1951, Sept. 21   *Perf. 11½*

166	A32	3c carmine & black	.25	.40
167	A32	4c dp orange & black	.25	.40
168	A32	5c purple & black (C)	.30	.65
169	A32	12c red violet & black	.30	.90
		Nos. 166-169 (4)	1.10	2.35

Adoption of a new constitution for the Windward Islands.

POSTAGE DUE STAMPS

D1   D2

GRENADA (continued)

1892		Typo.	Wmk. 2	Perf. 14	
J1	D1	1p black		30.00	2.75
J2	D1	2p black		225.00	3.25
J3	D1	3p black		200.00	4.00
		Nos. J1-J3 (3)		455.00	10.00

Black Surcharge

J4	D2	1p on 6p red lilac	110.00	2.25
a.	Tete beche pair		2,750.	1,800.
b.	Double surcharge			225.00
c.	Same as "b," tete beche pair			
J5	D2	1p on 8p bister	1,600.	6.00
a.	Tete beche pair		8,500.	2,500.
J6	D2	2p on 6p red lilac	190.00	4.50
a.	Tete beche pair		3,500.	1,800.
J7	D2	2p on 8p bister	3,200.	12.00
a.	Tete beche pair		7,500.	5,000.
		Nos. J4-J7 (4)	5,100.	24.75

Nos. J4-J7 were printed with alternate horizontal rows inverted.

1906-11			Wmk. 3	
J8	D1	1p black ('11)	3.75	7.50
J9	D1	2p black	12.50	3.75
J10	D1	3p black	15.00	6.50
		Nos. J8-J10 (3)	31.25	17.75

D3

1921-22			Wmk. 4	
J11	D3	1p black	2.00	1.40
J12	D3	1½p black	10.00	25.00
J13	D3	2p black	3.00	4.50
J14	D3	3p black	3.00	4.75
		Nos. J11-J14 (4)	18.00	35.65

Issued: 1½p, Dec. 15, 1922, others, Dec. 1921.

> **Catalogue values for unused stamps in this section, from this point to the end of the section, are for Never Hinged items.**

1952, Mar. 1				
J15	D3	2c black	.50	9.00
a.	Wmk. 4a (error)		55.00	
J16	D3	4c black	.50	17.00
a.	Wmk. 4a (error)		60.00	
J17	D3	6c black	.65	13.00
a.	Wmk. 4a (error)		100.00	
J18	D3	8c black	.75	14.00
a.	Wmk. 4a (error)		200.00	
		Nos. J15-J18 (4)	2.40	53.00

WAR TAX STAMPS

Nos. 80a, 80
Overprinted

1916		Wmk. 3	Perf. 14	
MR1	A21	1p carmine	2.50	2.00
a.	1p scarlet		3.00	3.00
b.	Double overprint		325.00	
c.	Inverted overprint		325.00	

No. 80 Overprinted

MR2	A21	1p scarlet	.30	.25

GRIQUALAND WEST

'gri-kwə-ˌland 'west

LOCATION — In South Africa west of the Orange Free State and north of the Orange River
GOVT. — Former British Crown Colony
AREA — 15,197 sq. mi.
POP. — 83,375 (1891)
CAPITAL — Kimberley

Originally a territorial division of the Cape of Good Hope Colony, Griqualand West was declared a British Crown Colony in 1873 and together with Griqualand East was annexed to the Cape Colony in 1880.

12 Pence = 1 Shilling

Beware of forgeries.

Stamps of Cape of Good Hope 1864-65 (Type I, 4p, 6p, 1sh) and 1871-76 (Type II, ½p, 1p, 4p, 5sh) Surcharged or Overprinted

"Hope" — A1

Type I — With frame line around stamp.
Type II — Without frame line.

Manuscript Surcharge in Dark Red

1874		Wmk. 1		Perf. 14	
1	A1	1p on 4p blue (type I)		1,800.	2,500.

Overprinted

G. W.

1877		Black Overprint		
2		1p rose	700.00	100.00
a.	Double overprint			3,000.

Red Overprint

3		4p blue (type II)	450.00	85.00

Overprinted In Black on the One Penny, in Red on the Other Values

a   b   c   d

e   f   g

4	(a)	½p gray black	35.00	37.50
5	(a)	1p rose	35.00	26.00
6	(a)	4p blue (type I)	325.00	45.00
7	(a)	4p blue (type II)	250.00	32.50
8	(a)	6p dull violet	160.00	29.00
9	(a)	1sh green	190.00	27.50
a.	Inverted overprint			575.00
10	(a)	5sh orange	750.00	32.50
11	(b)	½p gray black	35.00	40.00
12	(b)	1p rose	35.00	25.00
13	(b)	4p blue (type I)	425.00	50.00
14	(b)	4p blue (type II)	275.00	30.00
15	(b)	6p dull violet	300.00	35.00
16	(b)	1sh green	375.00	27.50
17	(b)	5sh orange	1,000.	35.00
18	(c)	½p gray black	80.00	95.00
19	(c)	1p rose	85.00	55.00
20	(c)	4p blue (type I)	750.00	125.00
21	(c)	4p blue (type II)	500.00	80.00
22	(c)	6p dull violet	350.00	85.00
23	(c)	1sh green	425.00	65.00
24	(c)	5sh orange	1,100.	75.00
25	(d)	½p gray black	47.50	55.00
26	(d)	1p rose	47.50	35.00
27	(d)	4p blue (type I)	500.00	65.00
28	(d)	4p blue (type II)	375.00	37.50
29	(d)	6p dull violet	250.00	45.00
30	(d)	1sh green	350.00	37.50
31	(d)	5sh orange	950.00	45.00
32	(e)	½p gray black	80.00	95.00
33	(e)	1p rose	85.00	55.00
34	(e)	4p blue (type I)	775.00	135.00
35	(e)	4p blue (type II)	500.00	85.00
36	(e)	6p dull violet	375.00	90.00
37	(e)	1sh green	450.00	67.50
a.	Inverted overprint			950.00
38	(e)	5sh orange	1,250.	80.00
39	(f)	½p gray black	90.00	110.00
40	(f)	1p rose	95.00	70.00
41	(f)	4p blue (type I)	850.00	160.00
42	(f)	4p blue (type II)	625.00	110.00
43	(f)	6p dull violet	450.00	110.00
44	(f)	1sh green	550.00	82.50
45	(f)	5sh orange	1,750.	95.00
46	(g)	½p gray black	42.50	50.00
47	(g)	1p rose	35.00	24.00
48	(g)	4p blue (type I)	400.00	62.50
49	(g)	4p blue (type II)	350.00	37.50
50	(g)	6p dull violet	225.00	42.50
51	(g)	1sh green	325.00	32.50
a.	Inverted overprint			475.00
52	(g)	5sh orange	900.00	40.00

There are minor varieties of types e and f.

Overprinted in Black

i   k   l   m   n

o   p   q   r

1878				
54	(g)	4p blue (type II)	400.00	70.00
55	(g)	6p dull violet	525.00	110.00
56	(i)	1p rose	37.50	24.00
57	(i)	4p blue (type II)	160.00	27.50
58	(i)	6p dull violet	300.00	60.00
a.	Double overprint			—
59	(k)	1p rose	85.00	42.50
60	(k)	4p blue (type II)	375.00	57.50
61	(k)	6p dull violet	500.00	95.00
62	(l)	1p rose	42.50	29.00
63	(l)	4p blue (type II)	175.00	29.00
64	(l)	6p dull violet	400.00	75.00
a.	Double overprint			1,100.
65	(m)	1p rose	80.00	70.00
66	(m)	4p blue (type II)	400.00	82.50
67	(m)	6p dull violet	550.00	150.00
68	(n)	1p rose	100.00	80.00
69	(n)	4p blue (type II)	425.00	85.00
70	(n)	6p dull violet	750.00	160.00
a.	Double overprint			1,400.
71	(o)	1p rose	90.00	55.00
72	(o)	4p blue (type II)	400.00	75.00
73	(o)	6p dull violet	550.00	110.00
74	(p)	1p rose	90.00	70.00
75	(p)	4p blue (type II)	425.00	77.50
76	(p)	6p dull violet	550.00	140.00
77	(q)	1p rose	150.00	110.00
78	(q)	4p blue (type II)	650.00	160.00
79	(q)	6p dull violet	850.00	225.00
80	(r)	1p rose	500.00	350.00
81	(r)	4p blue (type II)	2,000.	475.00
82	(r)	6p dull violet	2,500.	650.00

There are two minor varieties of type i and one of type p.

Overprinted in Red

s

t

1878				
83	(s)	½p gray black	22.50	22.50
a.	Double overprint		70.00	85.00
b.	Inverted overprint		25.00	25.00
c.	Double overprint, inverted		140.00	160.00
84	(s)	4p blue (type II)	500.00	140.00
a.	Inverted overprint		550.00	130.00
85	(t)	½p gray black	24.00	24.00
a.	Double overprint		110.00	110.00
b.	Inverted overprint		24.00	25.00
86	(t)	4p blue (type II)	—	120.00
a.	Inverted overprint		500.00	120.00

Black Overprint

87	(s)	½p gray black	275.00	150.00
a.	Inverted overprint		300.00	
b.	With 2nd ovpt. (s) in red, invtd.		475.00	
c.	With 2nd ovpt. (t) in red, invtd.		250.00	
88	(s)	1p rose	22.00	16.00
a.	Double overprint		275.00	70.00
b.	Inverted overprint		22.00	22.00
c.	Double overprint, both inverted		275.00	82.50
d.	With second overprint (s) in red, both inverted		50.00	55.00
89	(s)	4p blue (type I)		200.00
90	(s)	4p blue (type II)	180.00	45.00
a.	Double overprint		—	260.00
b.	Inverted overprint		275.00	97.50
c.	Double overprint, both inverted		—	350.00
91	(s)	6p dull violet	190.00	37.50
92	(t)	½p gray black	60.00	60.00
a.	Inverted overprint		130.00	87.50
b.	With 2nd ovpt. inverted		225.00	
93	(t)	1p rose	18.00	14.50
a.	Double overprint		—	105.00
b.	Inverted overprint		100.00	37.50
c.	Double overprint, both inverted		—	130.00
d.	With 2nd ovpt. (t) in red, both invtd.		100.00	100.00
94	(t)	4p blue (type I)		200.00
95	(t)	4p blue (type II)	200.00	20.00
a.	Double overprint		—	240.00
b.	Inverted overprint		350.00	37.50
c.	Double overprint, both inverted		—	325.00
96	(t)	6p dull violet		37.50

Overprinted in Black

G

97		½p gray black	25.00	9.00
a.	Double overprint		475.00	300.00
98		1p rose	26.00	7.00
a.	Double overprint		—	150.00
b.	Triple overprint		—	275.00
c.	Inverted overprint		—	95.00
99		4p blue (type II)	50.00	7.00
a.	Double overprint		—	130.00
100		6p brt violet	190.00	11.00
a.	Double overprint		850.00	200.00
b.	Inverted overprint		—	45.00
101		1sh green	180.00	7.50
a.	Double overprint		450.00	100.00
102		5sh orange	600.00	20.00
a.	Double overprint		800.00	100.00
b.	Triple overprint		—	350.00

These stamps were declared obsolete in 1880 and the remainders were used in Cape of Good Hope offices as ordinary stamps. Prices for used stamps are for examples with such cancels.

GUADELOUPE

'gwä-dᵊl-ˌüp

LOCATION — In the West Indies lying between Montserrat and Dominica
GOVT. — French colony
AREA — 688 sq. mi.
POP. — 271,262 (1946)
CAPITAL — Basse-Terre

Guadeloupe consists of two large islands, Guadeloupe proper and Grande-Terre, together with five smaller dependencies.

100 Centimes = 1 Franc

FORERUNNERS

> Crowned Circle handstamp types are pictured in the Crowned Circle Handstamps and Great Britain Used Abroad section.

BRITISH POST OFFICES IN GUADELOUPE

Guadeloupe

British P.O. opened Oct. 1, 1848; closed 1874

Pre-Stamp Postal Markings

1841
A1   Crowned Circle handstamp Type I, on cover, inscribed "GUADELOUPE", *from*   2,500.

Earliest known use Mar. 9, 1849.

Issues under French Administration

Stamps of French Colonies Surcharged

1884 — Unwmk. — Imperf.

1 A8 20c on 30c brn, *bis* — 72.50 — 60.00
  Never hinged — 140.00
  On cover — 375.00
  On cover, single franking — 1,000.
  a. Large "2" — 325.00 — 260.00
  b. Pair, #1 and #1a — 425.00 — 375.00
2 A8 25c on 35c blk, *org* — 60.00 — 60.00
  Never hinged — 120.00
  On cover — 375.00
  On cover, single franking — 625.00
  a. Large "2" — 325.00 — 260.00
  b. Large "5" — 160.00 — 125.00
  c. Pair, #2 and #2a — 425.00 — 375.00
  d. Pair, #2 and #2b — 240.00 — 225.00

The 5c on 4c (French Colonies No. 40) was not regularly issued. Three examples exist. Value $42,500.

The 5c on 4c also exists as an essay, surcharge similar to the issued values. Value $1,000.

c   d

1889 — Perf. 14x13½

Surcharged Type c

3 A9 3c on 20c red, *grn* — 5.25 — 5.25
  Never hinged — 10.50
  On cover — 200.00
  On cover, single franking — 400.00
4 A9 15c on 20c red, *grn* — 32.50 — 27.50
  Never hinged — 65.00
  On cover — 225.00
  On cover, single franking — 400.00
5 A9 25c on 20c red, *grn* — 32.50 — 27.50
  Never hinged — 65.00
  On cover — 225.00
  On cover, single franking — 400.00
  Nos. 3-5 (3) — 70.25 — 60.25

Surcharged Type d

6 A9 5c on 1c blk, *lil bl* — 14.50 — 13.50
  Never hinged — 25.00
  On cover — 175.00
  On cover, single franking — 450.00
  a. Inverted surcharge — 1,400.
  b. Double surcharge — 450.00 — 450.00
7 A9 10c on 40c red, *straw* — 40.00 — 35.00
  Never hinged — 80.00
  On cover — 300.00
  On cover, single franking — 450.00
  a. Double surcharge — 475.00 — 475.00
8 A9 15c on 20c red, *grn* — 32.50 — 30.00
  Never hinged — 72.50
  On cover — 325.00
  On cover, single franking — 450.00
  a. Double surcharge — 475.00 — 475.00
9 A9 25c on 30c brn, *bis* — 52.50 — 45.00
  Never hinged — 100.00
  On cover — 350.00
  On cover, single franking — 450.00
  a. Double surcharge — 475.00 — 475.00
  Nos. 6-9 (4) — 139.50 — 123.50

The word "centimes" in surcharges "b" and "c" varies from 10 to 12½mm.
Issue dates: No. 6, June 25; others, Mar. 22.

Stamps of French Colonies Surcharged

1891

10 A9 5c on 10c blk, *lav* — 16.00 — 12.00
  Never hinged — 32.50
  On cover — 175.00
  On cover, single franking — 450.00
11 A9 5c on 1fr brnz grn, *straw* — 17.00 — 12.50
  Never hinged — 30.00
  On cover — 175.00
  On cover, single franking — 450.00

Stamps of French Colonies Overprinted in Black

1891 — Imperf.

12 A7 30c brn, *yelsh* — 350.00 — 375.00
  a. Double overprint — 725.00 — 725.00
13 A7 80c car, *pnksh* — 1,100. — 1,300.

Perf. 14x13½

14 A9 1c blk, *lil bl* — 1.75 — 1.60
  Never hinged — 3.25
  On cover — 160.00
15 A9 2c brn, *buff* — 2.60 — 2.00
  Never hinged — 4.50
  On cover — 160.00
  a. Double overprint — 45.00 — 40.00
16 A9 4c claret, *lav* — 6.00 — 5.25
  Never hinged — 10.50
  On cover — 160.00
17 A9 5c grn, *grnsh* — 8.75 — 7.25
  Never hinged — 16.00
  On cover — 85.00
  a. Double overprint — 45.00 — 40.00
  b. Inverted overprint — 160.00 — 160.00
18 A9 10c blk, *lavender* — 17.00 — 13.50
  Never hinged — 30.00
  On cover — 100.00
19 A9 15c blue — 52.50 — 6.00
  Never hinged — 110.00
  On cover — 55.00
  a. Double overprint — 110.00
20 A9 20c red, *grn* — 45.00 — 30.00
  Never hinged — 95.00
  On cover — 250.00
  a. Double overprint — 240.00 — 240.00
21 A9 25c blk, *rose* — 47.50 — 5.25
  Never hinged — 105.00
  On cover — 72.50
  a. Double overprint — 240.00 — 240.00
  b. Inverted overprint — 225.00 — 225.00
22 A9 30c brn, *bister* — 45.00 — 30.00
  Never hinged — 95.00
  On cover — 210.00
  a. Double overprint — 240.00 — 240.00
23 A9 35c dp vio, *org* — 87.50 — 72.50
  Never hinged — 200.00
  On cover — 425.00
  a. Double overprint — 675.00 — 675.00
24 A9 40c red, *straw* — 65.00 — 52.50
  Never hinged — 130.00
  On cover — 275.00
  a. Double overprint — 675.00 — 675.00
25 A9 75c car, *rose* — 130.00 — 125.00
  On cover — 625.00
26 A9 1fr brnz grn, *straw* — 92.50 — 72.50
  Never hinged — 200.00
  On cover — 625.00
  Nos. 14-26 (13) — 601.10 — 423.35

Overprinted "GNADELOUPE"

12c A7 30c brn, *yelsh* — 1,050. — 1,050.
13c A7 80c car, *pnksh* — 5,750. — 5,750.
14c A9 1c blk, *lil bl* — 10.50 — 10.50
  Never hinged — 21.00
15c A9 2c brn, *buff* — 11.00 — 11.00
  Never hinged — 22.50
16c A9 4c claret, *lav* — 16.50 — 16.50
  Never hinged — 32.50
17c A9 5c grn, *grnsh* — 18.00 — 18.00
  Never hinged — 45.00
18c A9 10c blk, *lavender* — 47.50 — 47.50
  Never hinged — 100.00
19c A9 15c blue — 95.00 — 95.00
  Never hinged — 190.00
20c A9 20c red, *grn* — 110.00 — 110.00
  Never hinged — 225.00
21c A9 25c blk, *rose* — 95.00 — 95.00
  Never hinged — 190.00
22c A9 30c brn, *bister* — 175.00 — 175.00
23c A9 35c dp vio, *org* — 500.00 — 500.00
24c A9 40c red, *straw* — 275.00 — 275.00
25c A9 75c car, *rose* — 450.00 — 450.00
26c A9 1fr brnz grn, *straw* — 300.00 — 300.00

Overprinted "GUADBLOUPE"

12d A7 30c brn, *yelsh* — 2,500. — 2,500.
13d A7 80c car, *pnksh* — 10,750. — 10,750.
14d A9 1c blk, *lil bl* — 10.50 — 10.50
  Never hinged — 21.00
15d A9 2c brn, *buff* — 11.00 — 11.00
  Never hinged — 22.50
16d A9 4c claret, *lav* — 16.50 — 16.50
  Never hinged — 32.50
17d A9 5c grn, *grnsh* — 18.00 — 18.00
  Never hinged — 45.00
18d A9 10c blk, *lavender* — 47.50 — 47.50
  Never hinged — 100.00
19d A9 15c blue — 95.00 — 95.00
  Never hinged — 190.00
20d A9 20c red, *grn* — 110.00 — 110.00
  Never hinged — 225.00
21d A9 25c blk, *rose* — 130.00 — 130.00
22d A9 30c brn, *bister* — 160.00 — 160.00
23d A9 35c dp vio, *org* — 525.00 — 525.00
24d A9 40c red, *straw* — 525.00 — 525.00
25d A9 75c car, *rose* — 675.00 — 675.00
26d A9 1fr brnz grn, *straw* — 300.00 — 300.00

Overprinted "GUADELONPE"

12e A7 30c brn, *yelsh* — 2,500. — 2,500.
13e A7 80c car, *pnksh* — 10,750. — 10,750.
14e A9 1c blk, *lil bl* — 10.50 — 10.50
  Never hinged — 21.00
15e A9 2c brn, *buff* — 11.00 — 11.00
  Never hinged — 22.50
16e A9 4c claret, *lav* — 20.00 — 20.00
  Never hinged — 40.00
17e A9 5c grn, *grnsh* — 25.00 — 25.00
  Never hinged — 52.50
18e A9 10c blk, *lavender* — 52.50 — 52.50
  Never hinged — 105.00
19e A9 15c blue — 105.00 — 105.00
  Never hinged — 200.00
20e A9 20c red, *grn* — 120.00 — 120.00
  Never hinged — 240.00
21e A9 25c blk, *rose* — 130.00 — 130.00
22e A9 30c brn, *bister* — 160.00 — 160.00
23e A9 35c dp vio, *org* — 550.00 — 550.00
24e A9 40c red, *straw* — 540.00 — 540.00
25e A9 75c car, *rose* — 700.00 — 700.00
26e A9 1fr brnz grn, *straw* — 350.00 — 350.00

Overprinted "GUADELOUEP"

12f A7 30c brn, *yelsh* — 3,000. — 3,000.
13f A7 80c car, *pnksh* — 12,500. — 12,500.
14f A9 1c blk, *lil bl* — 24.00 — 24.00
  Never hinged — 47.50
15f A9 2c brn, *buff* — 14.50 — 14.50
  Never hinged — 29.00
16f A9 4c claret, *lav* — 25.00 — 25.00
  Never hinged — 50.00
17f A9 5c grn, *grnsh* — 27.50 — 27.50
  Never hinged — 55.00
18f A9 10c blk, *lavender* — 65.00 — 65.00
  Never hinged — 130.00
19f A9 15c blue — 110.00 — 110.00
  Never hinged — 225.00
20f A9 20c red, *grn* — 135.00 — 135.00
21f A9 25c blk, *rose* — 160.00 — 160.00
22f A9 30c brn, *bister* — 200.00 — 200.00
23f A9 35c dp vio, *org* — 725.00 — 725.00
24f A9 40c red, *straw* — 650.00 — 650.00
25f A9 75c car, *rose* — 775.00 — 775.00
26f A9 1fr brnz grn, *straw* — — — —

Navigation and Commerce — A7

Perf. 14x13½

1892-1901 — Typo. — Unwmk.
Colony Name in Blue or Carmine

27 A7 1c blk, *lil bl* — 1.40 — 1.40
  Never hinged — 1.60
  a. 1c blk, *gray* — 1.50 — 1.50
  b. 1c blk, *blue* — 2.00 — 2.00
  c. 1c blk, *yellowish* — 1.50 — 1.50
28 A7 2c brn, *buff* — 1.50 — 1.40
  Never hinged — 1.60
  On cover — 100.00
29 A7 4c claret, *lav* — 1.75 — 1.50
  Never hinged — 2.75
  On cover — 97.50
30 A7 5c grn, *grnsh* — 3.50 — 1.50
  Never hinged — 6.00
  On cover — 40.00
31 A7 5c yel grn ('01) — 6.00 — 1.60
  Never hinged — 9.50
  On cover — 13.00
32 A7 10c blk, *lavender* — 10.00 — 3.25
  Never hinged — 17.50
  On cover — 25.00
  a. 10c blk, *rose* — 10.00 — 3.00
33 A7 10c red ('00) — 8.75 — 2.40
  Never hinged — 14.50
  On cover — 15.00
  a. Imperf. — 120.00
  b. As "a," country name omitted — 150.00
34 A7 15c blue, quadrille paper — 18.00 — 1.75
  Never hinged — 32.50
  On cover — 30.00
35 A7 15c gray, *lt gray* ('00) — 13.00 — 1.60
  Never hinged — 24.00
  On cover — 14.50
36 A7 20c red, *grn* — 11.00 — 6.50
  Never hinged — 19.00
  On cover — 65.00
  On cover, single franking — 120.00
37 A7 25c blk, *rose* — 11.00 — 3.00
  Never hinged — 19.00
  On cover — 37.50
  On cover, single franking — 80.00
38 A7 25c blue ('00) — 100.00 — 100.00
  Never hinged — 200.00
  On cover — 300.00
  On cover, single franking — 450.00
39 A7 30c brn, *bister* — 24.00 — 15.00
  Never hinged — 42.50
  On cover — 110.00
  On cover, single franking — 240.00
40 A7 40c red, *straw* — 24.00 — 15.00
  Never hinged — 45.00
  On cover — 175.00
  On cover, single franking — 450.00
41 A7 50c car, *rose* — 30.00 — 16.00
  Never hinged — 65.00
  On cover — 225.00
  On cover, single franking — 600.00
42 A7 50c brn, *az* ('00) — 45.00 — 42.50
  Never hinged — 80.00
  On cover — 340.00
  On cover, single franking — 600.00
43 A7 75c dp vio, *org* — 32.50 — 22.50
  Never hinged — 65.00
  On cover — 300.00
  On cover, single franking — 675.00
44 A7 1fr brnz grn, *straw* — 32.50 — 30.00
  Never hinged — 65.00
  On cover — 300.00
  On cover, single franking — 675.00
  Nos. 27-44 (18) — 373.90 — 266.90

Perf. 13½x14 stamps are counterfeits.
For surcharges see Nos. 45-53, 83-85.

Nos. 39-41, 43-44 Surcharged in Black

f   g

h

1903

45 A7 (f) 5c on 30c — 4.00 — 4.00
  Never hinged — 7.25
  On cover — 85.00
  a. "C" instead of "G" — 32.50 — 32.50
  Never hinged — 60.00
  b. Inverted surcharge — 45.00 — 45.00
  Never hinged — 80.00
  c. Double surcharge — 140.00 — 140.00
  d. Double surch., inverted — 160.00
46 A7 (g) 10c on 40c — 9.50 — 9.50
  Never hinged — 14.50
  On cover — 100.00
  a. "C" instead of "G" — 40.00 — 40.00
  Never hinged — 60.00
  b. "1" inverted — 60.00 — 60.00
  Never hinged — 120.00
  c. Inverted surcharge — 55.00 — 55.00
  Never hinged — 95.00
  d. Double surcharge — 200.00 — 200.00
47 A7 (f) 15c on 50c — 13.00 — 13.00
  Never hinged — 25.00
  On cover — 100.00
  a. "C" instead of "G" — 40.00 — 40.00
  Never hinged — 75.00
  b. Inverted surcharge — 110.00 — 110.00
  c. "15" inverted — 375.00 — 375.00
  d. Pair, tête-bêche surcharge — 375.00
  e. Double surcharge — 200.00 — 200.00
48 A7 (g) 40c on 1fr — 13.00 — 13.00
  Never hinged — 25.00
  On cover — 115.00
  a. "C" instead of "G" — 52.50 — 52.50
  Never hinged — 100.00
  b. "4" inverted — 120.00 — 120.00
  Never hinged — 225.00
  c. Inverted surcharge — 110.00 — 110.00
  d. Double surcharge — 240.00 — 240.00
  e. Double triple — 450.00 — 500.00
49 A7 (h) 1fr on 75c — 42.50 — 42.50
  Never hinged — 80.00
  On cover — 350.00
  a. "C" instead of "G" — 160.00 — 160.00
  Never hinged — 275.00
  b. "1" inverted — 160.00 — 160.00
  Never hinged — 275.00
  c. Value above "G & D" — 300.00 — 300.00
  Never hinged — 450.00
  d. Inverted surcharge — 125.00 — 125.00
  Nos. 45-49 (5) — 82.00 — 82.00

Letters and figures from several fonts were used for these surcharges, resulting in numerous minor varieties.

Nos. 48-49 With Additional Overprint "1903" in a Frame
1904, Mar.
Red Overprint

50 A7 (g) 40c on 1fr — 75.00 — 85.00
  Never hinged — 120.00
  On cover — 340.00
  a. "C" instead of "G" — 175.00 — 200.00
  Never hinged — 275.00
  b. Inverted surcharge — 600.00 — 650.00
  Never hinged — 1,000.
  c. Double surcharge — 1,250. — 1,250.
  Never hinged — 2,000.
51 A7 (h) 1fr on 75c — 92.50 — 100.00
  Never hinged — 160.00
  On cover — 340.00
  a. Double surcharge — 950.00 — 950.00
  b. Inverted surcharge — 1,000. — 800.00

Blue Overprint

52 A7 (g) 40c on 1fr — 60.00 — 65.00
  Never hinged — 120.00
  On cover — 275.00
  a. Double surcharge — 1,150. — 1,200.
  b. Double surcharge, one inverted — 1,150. — 1,150.
53 A7 (h) 1fr on 75c — 87.50 — 95.00
  Never hinged — 160.00
  On cover — 375.00
  a. Double surcharge — 750.00 — 800.00
  Never hinged — 1,500.
  Nos. 50-53 (4) — 315.00 — 345.00

The date "1903" may be found in 19 different positions and type faces within the frame. These stamps may also be found with the minor varieties of Nos. 48-49.

The 40c exists with black overprint. Value, $500 unused or used.

Harbor at Basse-Terre — A8

View of La Soufrière A9

Pointe-à-Pitre, Grand-Terre — A10

1905-27   Typo.   Perf. 14x13½

54	A8	1c blk, *bluish*	.30	.30
		Never hinged	.55	
		On cover		40.00
55	A8	2c vio brn, *straw*	.30	.30
		Never hinged	.55	
		On cover		40.00
56	A8	4c bis brn, *az*	.30	.30
		Never hinged	.55	
		On cover		35.00
57	A8	5c green	2.40	.65
		Never hinged	3.50	
		On cover		12.00
58	A8	5c dp blue ('22)	.25	.25
		Never hinged	.40	
		On cover		16.00
		On cover, single franking		40.00
59	A8	10c rose	2.25	.65
		Never hinged	2.90	
		On cover		8.50
60	A8	10c green ('22)	1.40	1.25
		Never hinged	2.25	
		On cover		9.00
61	A8	10c red, *bluish* ('25)	.25	.25
		Never hinged	.40	
		On cover		5.50
62	A8	15c violet	.55	.50
		Never hinged	.85	
		On cover		6.50
63	A9	20c red, *grn*	.55	.40
		Never hinged	.85	
		On cover		9.50
64	A9	20c bl grn ('25)	.65	.65
		Never hinged	1.20	
		On cover		6.50
65	A9	25c blue	.95	.65
		Never hinged	1.40	
		On cover		20.00
		On cover, single franking		67.50
66	A9	25c ol grn ('22)	.65	.65
		Never hinged	1.00	
		On cover		4.00
67	A9	30c black	5.00	3.25
		Never hinged	8.00	
		On cover		16.00
		On cover, single franking		80.00
68	A9	30c rose ('22)	.70	.70
		Never hinged	1.10	
		On cover		12.00
		On cover, single franking		47.50
69	A9	30c brn ol, *lav* ('25)	.55	.55
		Never hinged	.85	
		On cover		4.00
70	A9	35c blk, *yel* ('06)	.80	.80
		Never hinged	1.25	
		On cover		20.00
		On cover, single franking		80.00
71	A9	40c red, *straw*	.80	.80
		Never hinged	1.20	
		On cover		20.00
		On cover, single franking		47.50
72	A9	45c ol gray, *lil* ('07)	1.40	.80
		Never hinged	2.10	
		On cover		24.00
		On cover, single franking		60.00
73	A9	45c rose ('25)	.80	.80
		Never hinged	1.25	
		On cover		16.00
		On cover, single franking		60.00
74	A9	50c gray grn, *straw*	5.50	4.00
		Never hinged	8.50	
		On cover		40.00
		On cover, single franking		80.00
75	A9	50c dp bl ('22)	1.25	1.10
		Never hinged	2.10	
		On cover		16.00
		On cover, single franking		55.00
76	A9	50c violet ('25)	.70	.70
		Never hinged	1.10	
		On cover		14.50
		On cover, single franking		47.50
77	A9	65c blue ('27)	.70	.70
		Never hinged	1.10	
		On cover		17.50
		On cover, single franking		65.00
78	A9	75c car, *bl*	.90	.80
		Never hinged	1.40	
		On cover		32.50
		On cover, single franking		67.50
79	A10	1fr blk, *green*	1.75	1.50
		Never hinged	2.40	
		On cover		35.00
		On cover, single franking		67.50
80	A10	1fr lt bl ('25)	1.00	.95
		Never hinged	1.90	
		On cover		40.00
		On cover, single franking		67.50
81	A10	2fr car, *org*	2.25	2.00
		Never hinged	3.25	
		On cover		32.50
		On cover, single franking		52.50
82	A10	5fr dp bl, *org*	7.50	7.50
		Never hinged	12.00	
		On cover		72.50
		On cover, single franking		120.00
		Nos. 54-82 (29)	42.40	33.65

Nos. 57, 59 and 82 exist imperf. Value, Nos. 57 and 59 each $60, No. 82 $140.

For surcharges see Nos. 86-95, 167 (in Scott Standard catalogue, Vol. 3), B1-B2.

Nos. 29, 39 and 40 Surcharged in Carmine or Black

1912, Nov.

Spacing between figures of surcharge 1.5mm (5c), 2mm (10c)

83	A7	5c on 4c claret, *lav* (C)	1.50	1.50
		Never hinged	2.60	
		On cover		40.00
84	A7	5c on 30c brn, *bis* (C)	2.00	2.00
		Never hinged	3.40	
		On cover		47.50
85	A7	10c on 40c red, *straw*	2.25	2.25
		Never hinged	3.75	
		On cover		55.00
		Nos. 83-85 (3)	5.75	5.75

Spacing between figures of surcharge 2.25mm (5c), 2.75mm (10c)

83a	A7	5c on 4c claret, *lav* (C)	170.00	170.00
		Never hinged	240.00	
84a	A7	5c on 30c brn, *bis* (C)	225.00	225.00
		Never hinged	325.00	
85a	A7	10c on 40c red, *straw*	165.00	165.00
		Never hinged	260.00	
		Nos. 83a-85a (3)	560.00	560.00

Se-tenant Pairs, Both Ovpt. Settings

83b	A7	5c on 4c claret, *lav* (C), #83 + #83a	190.00	
		Never hinged	275.00	
84b	A7	5c on 30c brn, *bis* (C), #84 + #84a	250.00	
		Never hinged	325.00	
85b	A7	10c on 40c red, *straw*, #85 + 85a	190.00	

Stamps and Types of 1905-27 Surcharged with New Value and Bars

1924-27

86	A10	25c on 5fr dp bl, *org*	.75	.70
		Never hinged	1.10	
		On cover		6.50
87	A10	65c on 1fr gray grn	1.40	1.25
		Never hinged	2.00	
		On cover		17.50
		On cover, single franking		32.50
88	A10	85c on 1fr gray grn	1.50	1.40
		Never hinged	2.25	
		On cover		20.00
		On cover, single franking		40.00
89	A9	90c on 75c dl red	1.40	1.25
		Never hinged	2.25	
		On cover		20.00
		On cover, single franking		67.50
90	A10	1.05fr on 2fr ver (Bl)	1.00	.85
		Never hinged	1.75	
		On cover		20.00
		On cover, single franking		72.50
91	A10	1.25fr on 1fr lt bl (R)	.65	.65
		Never hinged	1.00	
		On cover		20.00
		On cover, single franking		80.00
92	A10	1.50fr on 1fr dk bl	1.25	1.25
		Never hinged	2.00	
		On cover		24.00
		On cover, single franking		85.00
93	A10	3fr on 5fr org brn	1.50	1.50
		Never hinged	2.40	
		On cover		32.50
		On cover, single franking		90.00
94	A10	10fr on 5fr vio rose, *org*	11.00	11.00
		Never hinged	16.00	
		On cover		47.50
		On cover, single franking		110.00
95	A10	20fr on 5fr rose lil, *pnksh*	14.00	13.00
		Never hinged	22.50	
		On cover		60.00
		On cover, single franking		130.00
		Nos. 86-95 (10)	34.45	32.85

Years issued: Nos. 87-88, 1925. Nos. 90-91, 1926. Nos. 89, 92-95, 1927.

Sugar Mill — A11

Saints Roadstead A12

Harbor Scene A13

Perf. 14x13½

1928-40		**Unwmk.**		**Typo.**
96	A11	1c yel & vio	.25	.25
		Never hinged	.30	
		On cover		27.50
97	A11	2c blk & lt red	.25	.25
		Never hinged	.30	
		On cover		27.50
98	A11	3c yel & red vio ('40)	.30	.30
		Never hinged	.450	
		On cover		32.50
99	A11	4c yel grn & org brn	.25	.25
		Never hinged	.30	
		On cover		24.00
100	A11	5c ver & grn	.25	.25
		Never hinged	.30	
		On cover		20.00
101	A11	10c bis brn & dp bl	.25	.25
		Never hinged	.30	
		On cover		16.00
102	A11	15c brn red & blk	.30	.30
		Never hinged	.45	
		On cover		16.00
103	A11	20c lil & ol brn	.50	.50
		Never hinged	.65	
		On cover		12.00
104	A12	25c grnsh bl & olvn	.55	.55
		Never hinged	.80	
		On cover		6.50
105	A12	30c gray grn & yel grn	.40	.40
		Never hinged	.05	
		On cover		8.00
106	A12	35c bl grn ('38)	.40	.40
		Never hinged	.55	
		On cover		9.50
107	A12	40c yel & vio	.40	.40
		Never hinged	.65	
		On cover		4.00
108	A12	45c vio brn & slate	.95	.80
		Never hinged	1.30	
		On cover		6.50
109	A12	45c bl grn & dl grn ('40)	1.10	1.00
		Never hinged	1.50	
		On cover		27.50
110	A12	50c dl grn & org	.30	.30
		Never hinged	.45	
		On cover		4.00
111	A12	55c ultra & car ('38)	1.40	1.25
		Never hinged	2.00	
		On cover		8.00
112	A12	60c ultra & car ('40)	.65	.65
		Never hinged	.80	
		On cover		20.00
113	A12	65c gray blk & ver	.55	.55
		Never hinged	.80	
		On cover		5.50
114	A12	70c gray blk & ver ('40)	.70	.70
		Never hinged	.95	
		On cover		8.00
115	A12	75c dl red & bl grn	.70	.70
		Never hinged	.95	
		On cover		5.50
116	A12	80c car & brn ('38)	.85	.65
		Never hinged	1.20	
		On cover		10.50
117	A12	90c dl red & dl rose	2.00	1.75
		Never hinged	2.75	
		On cover		16.00
		On cover, single franking		50.00
118	A12	90c rose red & bl ('39)	1.25	1.10
		Never hinged	1.50	
		On cover		9.50
119	A13	1fr lt rose & lt bl	5.25	3.75
		Never hinged	7.50	
		On cover		40.00
		On cover, single franking		65.00
120	A13	1fr rose red & org ('38)	1.75	1.50
		Never hinged	2.75	
		On cover		12.00
		On cover, single franking		20.00
121	A13	1fr bl gray & blk brn ('40)	.70	.70
		Never hinged	.95	
		On cover		5.50
122	A13	1.05fr lt bl & rose	1.25	1.10
		Never hinged	1.75	
		On cover		12.00
		On cover, single franking		27.50
123	A13	1.10fr lt red & grn	4.00	2.75
		Never hinged	6.75	
		On cover		47.50
		On cover, single franking		100.00
124	A13	1.25fr bl gray & blk brn ('33)	.65	.65
		Never hinged	.80	
		On cover		9.50
		On cover, single franking		16.00
125	A13	1.25fr brt rose & red org ('39)	.95	.95
		Never hinged	1.25	
		On cover		47.50
		On cover, single franking		80.00

126	A13	1.40fr lt bl & lil rose ('40)	.70	.70
		Never hinged	.95	
		On cover		32.50
		On cover, single franking		60.00
127	A13	1.50fr dl bl & bl	.40	.40
		Never hinged	.65	
		On cover		10.50
		On cover, single franking		20.00
128	A13	1.60fr lil rose & yel brn ('40)	.70	.70
		Never hinged	.95	
		On cover		32.50
		On cover, single franking		65.00
129	A13	1.75fr lil rose & yel brn ('33)	5.75	3.25
		Never hinged	8.25	
		On cover		32.50
		On cover, single franking		95.00
130	A13	1.75fr vio bl ('38)	6.00	4.00
		Never hinged	8.50	
		On cover		35.00
		On cover, single franking		110.00
131	A13	2fr bl grn & dk brn	.40	.40
		Never hinged	.65	
		On cover		21.00
		On cover, single franking		32.50
132	A13	2.25fr vio bl ('39)	1.25	1.25
		Never hinged	1.50	
		On cover		45.00
		On cover, single franking		80.00
133	A13	2.50fr pale org & grn ('40)	1.25	1.25
		Never hinged	1.50	
		On cover		35.00
		On cover, single franking		60.00
134	A13	3fr org brn & sl	.65	.65
		Never hinged	.85	
		On cover		26.00
		On cover, single franking		45.00
135	A13	5fr dl bl & org	1.25	1.00
		Never hinged	1.60	
		On cover		35.00
		On cover, single franking		60.00
136	A13	10fr vio & ol brn	1.25	1.00
		Never hinged	1.60	
		On cover		45.00
		On cover, single franking		67.50
137	A13	20fr green & mag	1.50	1.40
		Never hinged	2.00	
		On cover		52.50
		On cover, single franking		80.00
		Nos. 96-137 (42)	50.20	40.95

Nos. 96-103, 110, 119, 123, 134, 137 exist imperf. Values each $30-$60.

For surcharges see Nos. 161-166 in Scott Standard catalogue, Vol. 3.

For 10c, type A11, without "RF," see No. 163A in Scott Standard catalogue, Vol. 3.

Common Design Types pictured following the introduction.

Colonial Exposition Issue
Common Design Types

1931, Apr. 13   Engr.   Perf. 12½
Name of Country in Black

138	CD70	40c deep green	4.75	4.75
		Never hinged	6.50	
		On cover		40.00
139	CD71	50c violet	4.75	4.75
		Never hinged	6.50	
		On cover		32.50
140	CD72	90c red orange	4.75	4.75
		Never hinged	7.25	
		On cover		60.00
		On cover, single franking		85.00
141	CD73	1.50fr dull blue	4.75	4.75
		Never hinged	7.25	
		On cover		52.50
		On cover, single franking		80.00
		Nos. 138-141 (4)	19.00	19.00

Cardinal Richelieu Establishing French Antilles Co., 1635 — A14

Victor Hugues and his Corsairs — A15

1935   Perf. 13

142	A14	40c gray brown	10.00	10.00
		Never hinged	14.50	
		On cover		45.00
143	A14	50c dull red	10.00	10.00
		Never hinged	14.50	
		On cover		35.00
144	A14	1.50fr dull blue	10.00	10.00
		Never hinged	14.50	
		On cover		60.00
		On cover, single franking		90.00

145 A15 1.75fr lilac rose 10.00 10.00
Never hinged 14.50
On cover 50.00
On cover, single franking 80.00
146 A15 5fr dark brown 10.00 10.00
Never hinged 14.50
On cover 50.00
On cover, single franking 80.00
147 A15 10fr blue green 10.00 10.00
Never hinged 14.50
On cover 67.50
On cover, single franking 120.00
Nos. 142-147 (6) 60.00 60.00

Tercentenary of the establishment of the French colonies in the West Indies.

Paris International Exposition Issue
Common Design Types
1937 *Perf. 13*
148 CD74 20c deep violet 1.90 1.90
Never hinged 2.60
On cover 52.50
149 CD75 30c dark green 1.75 1.75
Never hinged 2.10
On cover 45.00
150 CD76 40c car rose 1.50 1.50
Never hinged 2.10
On cover 40.00
151 CD77 50c dk brn & blk 1.50 1.50
Never hinged 1.80
On cover 32.50
152 CD78 90c red 1.50 1.50
Never hinged 2.10
On cover 55.00
On cover, single franking 100.00
153 CD79 1.50fr ultra 1.90 1.90
Never hinged 2.60
On cover 47.50
On cover, single franking 85.00
Nos. 148-153 (6) 10.05 10.05

Colonial Arts Exhibition Issue
Souvenir Sheet
Common Design Type
1937 *Imperf.*
154 CD75 3fr dark blue 9.50 *11.00*
Never hinged 12.50
On cover 100.00
On cover, single franking 125.00

New York World's Fair Issue
Common Design Type
1939 **Engr.** *Perf. 12½x12*
155 CD82 1.25fr car lake 1.25 1.25
Never hinged 1.60
On cover 40.00
On cover, single franking 85.00
156 CD82 2.25fr ultra 1.25 1.25
Never hinged 1.60
On cover 40.00
On cover, single franking 85.00

For surcharges see Nos. 159-160 in Scott Standard catalogue, Vol. 3.

SEMI-POSTAL STAMPS

Nos. 59 and 62 Surcharged in Red

1915-17 **Unwmk.** *Perf. 14 x 13½*
B1 A8 10c + 5c rose 5.25 3.50
Never hinged 8.75
On cover 35.00
B2 A8 15c + 5c violet 5.25 3.50
Never hinged 8.75
On cover 35.00
a. Double surcharge 225.00 225.00
b. Triple surcharge 240.00 240.00
c. Inverted surcharge 240.00 240.00
d. In pair with unovptd. stamp 275.00

Curie Issue
Common Design Type
1938, Oct. 24 *Perf. 13*
B3 CD80 1.75fr + 50c brt ultra 11.00 10.50
Never hinged 15.00
On cover 60.00
On cover, single franking 100.00

French Revolution Issue
Common Design Type
Name and Value Typo. in Black
1939, July 5 **Photo.** *Perf. 13*
B4 CD83 45c + 25c green 10.00 10.00
Never hinged 15.00
On cover 80.00
B5 CD83 70c + 30c brown 10.00 10.00
Never hinged 15.00
On cover 60.00
B6 CD83 90c + 35c red org 10.00 10.00
Never hinged 15.00
On cover 55.00

B7 CD83 1.25fr + 1fr rose pink 10.00 10.00
Never hinged 15.00
On cover 80.00
On cover, single franking 130.00
B8 CD83 2.25fr + 2fr blue 10.00 10.00
Never hinged 15.00
On cover 72.50
On cover, single franking 120.00
Nos. B4-B8 (5) 50.00 50.00

POSTAGE DUE STAMPS

D1   D2   D3

1876 **Unwmk.** **Typeset** *Imperf.*
J1 D1 25c black 1,350. 925.
On cover 4,500.
J2 D2 40c black, *blue* 37,500.
On cover 60,000.
J3 D3 40c black 1,500. 1,200.
On cover 4,500.

Twenty varieties of each.
Nos. J1 and J3 have been reprinted on thinner and whiter paper than the originals.

D4   D5

1879
J4 D4 15c black, *blue* 55.00 52.50
Never hinged 110.00
On cover 4,500.
a. Period after "c" omitted 175.00 175.00
b. "c" of denomination omitted 200.00 200.00
c. "i" of "percevoir" omitted 200.00 200.00
d. Accent over "a" of "á percevoir" omitted 175.00 175.00
e. 15c black, *deep blue* 75.00 65.00
J5 D4 30c black 110.00 87.50
On cover 2,500.
a. Period after "c" omitted 240.00 225.00
b. "c" of denomination omitted 300.00 260.00
c. "i" of "percevoir" omitted 300.00 260.00

Twenty varieties of each.

1884
J6 D5 5c black 35.00 35.00
Never hinged 67.50
On cover 3,000.
a. Double impression 100.00 100.00
J7 D5 10c black, *blue* 75.00 65.00
Never hinged 135.00
On cover 3,250.
a. Double impression 150.00 150.00
J8 D5 15c black, *violet* 110.00 87.50
On cover 3,500.
a. Double impression 225.00 225.00
J9 D5 20c black, *rose* 160.00 100.00
On cover 3,500.
a. Italic "2" in "20" 1,000. 950.00
J10 D5 30c black, *yellow* 160.00 160.00
On cover 3,750.
a. Double impression 450.00 450.00
J11 D5 35c black, *gray* 60.00 52.50
On cover 3,250.
a. Double impression 225.00 225.00
J12 D5 50c black, *green* 32.50 27.50
Never hinged 67.50
On cover 3,000.
a. Double impression 200.00 200.00
Nos. J6-J12 (7) 632.50 527.50

There are ten varieties of the 35c, and fifteen of each of the other values, also numerous wrong font and missing letters.

Postage Due Stamps of French Colonies Surcharged in Black

Two surcharge types: I, wide font, "3" with rounded top; II, narrow font, "3" with flat top.

1903
Type I
J13 D1 30c on 60c brn, *cr* 325.00 325.00
a. Inverted surcharge 1,100. 1,100.
b. Bee corner ornament turned 1,150. 1,150.
c. As "b," inverted surcharge 1,700.

d. "G" omitted 800.00 800.00
e. As "d," inverted surcharge 1,250.
f. Corrected surcharge, "30" over "33" 10,500. 10,500.
J14 D1 30c on 1fr rose, *cr* 400.00 400.00
a. Inverted surcharge 1,150. 1,150.
b. "30" sideways 10,000. 10,000.
c. As "b," inverted surcharge 10,000. 10,000.

Type II
J13A D1 30c on 60c brn, *cr* 1,000. 1,000.
a. Inverted surcharge 1,900. 1,900.
b. Bee corner ornament turned 1,600. 1,600.
c. As "b," inverted surcharge 2,200.
d. "G" omitted 1,000. 1,000.
e. As "d," inverted surcharge 1,500.
f. Corrected surcharge, "30" over "33" 10,500. 10,500.
J14A D1 30c on 1fr rose, *cr* 400.00 400.00
a. Inverted surcharge 1,200. 1,200.
b. "30" sideways 10,500. 10,500.
c. As "b," inverted surcharge 10,500. 10,500.

Gustavia Bay — D6

1905-06 **Typo.** *Perf. 14x13½*
J15 D6 5c blue .55 .55
Never hinged .70
On cover 150.00
J16 D6 10c brown .55 .55
Never hinged .70
On cover 150.00
J17 D6 15c green 1.00 1.00
Never hinged 1.40
On cover 150.00
J18 D6 20c black, *yel ('06)* 1.00 1.00
Never hinged 1.40
On cover 150.00
J19 D6 30c rose 1.25 1.25
Never hinged 1.60
On cover 150.00
J20 D6 50c black 3.25 3.25
Never hinged 4.50
On cover 175.00
J21 D6 60c brown orange 1.75 1.75
Never hinged 2.40
On cover 175.00
J22 D6 1fr violet 3.25 3.25
Never hinged 4.50
On cover 225.00
Nos. J15-J22 (8) 12.60 12.60

Type of 1905-06 Issue Surcharged

1926-27
J23 D6 2fr on 1fr gray 2.00 2.00
Never hinged 3.25
On cover 120.00
J24 D6 3fr on 1fr ultra ('27) 2.75 2.75
Never hinged 4.00
On cover 140.00

Avenue of Royal Palms — D7

1928, June 18
J25 D7 2c olive brn & lil .25 .25
Never hinged .30
On cover 60.00
J26 D7 4c bl & org brn .25 .25
Never hinged .30
On cover 60.00
J27 D7 5c gray grn & dk brn .25 .25
Never hinged .30
On cover 45.00
J28 D7 10c dl vio & yel .30 .30
Never hinged .45
On cover 45.00
J29 D7 15c rose & olive grn .30 .30
Never hinged .45
On cover 50.00
J30 D7 20c brn org & ol grn .50 .50
Never hinged .65
On cover 50.00
J31 D7 25c brn red & bl grn .50 .50
Never hinged .65
On cover 50.00
J32 D7 30c slate & olivine .80 .80
Never hinged .95
On cover 55.00
J33 D7 50c ol brn & lt red .80 .80
Never hinged .95
On cover 60.00

J34 D7 60c dp bl & blk .80 .80
Never hinged .95
On cover 60.00
J35 D7 1fr green & orange 3.00 2.60
Never hinged 3.75
On cover 80.00
J36 D7 2fr bis brn & lt red 2.25 1.90
Never hinged 2.75
On cover 80.00
J37 D7 3fr vio & bl blk 1.25 1.10
Never hinged 1.60
On cover 90.00
Nos. J25-J37 (13) 11.25 10.35

GUATEMALA

ˌgwä-lə-ˈmä-lə

LOCATION — Central America, bordering on Atlantic and Pacific Oceans
GOVT. — Republic
AREA — 42,042 sq. mi.
POP. — 6,577,000 (est. 1984)
CAPITAL — Guatemala City

100 Centavos = 8 Reales = 1 Peso
100 Centavos de Quetzal = 1 Quetzal (1927)

Coat of Arms
A1   A2

Two types of 10c:
Type I — Both zeros in "10" are wide.
Type II — Left zero narrow.

Perf. 14x13½
1871, Mar. 1 **Typo.** **Unwmk.**
1 A1 1c ocher .80 *10.50*
a. Imperf., pair 5.00
b. Printed on both sides, imperf. 75.00
2 A1 5c lt bister brn 4.00 *8.00*
a. Imperf. pair 35.00
b. Tête bêche pair 150.00
c. Tête bêche pair, imperf. 2,600.
3 A1 10c blue (I) 5.00 *8.00*
a. Imperf., pair (I) 45.00
b. Type II 8.00 *10.50*
c. Imperf. pair (II) 60.00
4 A1 20c rose 4.00 *8.00*
a. Imperf., pair 45.00
b. 20c blue (error) 125.00 125.00
c. As "b," imperf. 800.00
Nos. 1-4 (4) 13.80 34.50

Forgeries exist. Forged cancellations abound. See No. C458 in Scott Standard catalogue, Vol. 3.

1873 **Litho.** *Perf. 12*
5 A2 4r dull red vio 325.00 85.00
6 A2 1p dull yellow 175.00 115.00

Forgeries exist.

Liberty
A3   A4

A5   A6

1875, Apr. 15 **Engr.**
7 A3 ¼r black 1.00 *3.50*
8 A4 ½r blue green 1.00 3.00
9 A5 1r blue 1.00 3.00
a. Half used as ½r on cover 1,700.
10 A6 2r dull red 1.00 3.00
Nos. 7-10 (4) 4.00 12.50

Nos. 7-10 normally lack gum. Unused values are for examples without gum.
Forgeries and forged cancellations exist.

Indian Woman — A7   Quetzal — A8

Typographed on Tinted Paper
1878, Jan. 10   Perf. 13
11	A7	½r yellow grn	.80	3.25
12	A7	2r carmine rose	1.25	4.00
13	A7	4r violet	1.25	4.75
14	A7	1p yellow	2.00	9.00
c.		Half used as 4r on cover		2,200.
		Nos. 11-14 (4)	5.30	21.00

Some sheets of Nos. 11-14 have papermaker's watermark, "LACROIX FRERES," in double-lined capitals appearing on six stamps.
Part perforate pairs of Nos. 11, 12 and 14 exist. Value for each, about $100.
Forgeries of Nos. 11-14 are plentiful. Forged cancellations exist.
For surcharges see Nos. 18, 20.

Imperf., Pairs
11a	A7	½r yellow green	50.00
12a	A7	2r carmine rose	50.00
13a	A7	4r violet	50.00
14a	A7	1p yellow	50.00

1879   Engr.   Perf. 12
15	A8	¼r brown & green	7.25	9.50
16	A8	1r black & green	10.50	13.50

For similar types see A11, A72, A103, A121, A146. For surcharges see Nos. 17, 19.

Nos. 11, 12, 15, 16 Surcharged in Black

1881   Perf. 12 and 13
17	A8	1c on ¼r brn & grn	12.00	16.00
a.		"ecntavo,"	40.00	47.50
b.		Pair, one without surcharge	200.00	
18	A7	5c on ½r yel grn	5.50	8.00
a.		"ecntavos,"	35.00	40.00
b.		"5" omitted	100.00	
c.		Double surcharge	95.00	120.00
19	A8	10c on 1r blk & grn	17.50	24.00
a.		"s" of "centavos" missing	75.00	75.00
b.		"ecntavos"	57.50	87.50
20	A7	20c on 2r car rose	32.50	87.50
a.		Horiz. pair, imperf. between	425.00	
		Nos. 17-20 (4)	67.50	135.50

The 5c had three settings.
Surcharge varieties found on Nos. 17-20 include: Period omitted; comma instead of period; "ecntavo." or "ecntavos."; "s" omitted; spaced "centavos."; wider "0" in "20."
Counterfeits of Nos. 17-20 are plentiful.

Quetzal — A11

1881, Nov. 7   Engr.   Perf. 12
21	A11	1c black & grn	3.00	2.00
22	A11	2c brown & grn	3.00	2.00
a.		Center inverted	400.00	250.00
23	A11	5c red & grn	6.00	2.60
a.		Center inverted	3,250.	1,300.
24	A11	10c gray vio & grn	2.75	2.00
25	A11	20c yellow & grn	2.75	2.40
a.		Center inverted	500.00	
		Nos. 21-25 (5)	17.50	11.00

Surcharged in Black

Gen. Justo Rufino Barrios — A12   A12a

A12b

1886, Mar. 6
26	A12	25c on 1p ver	.70	.70
a.		"centovos"	1.50	
b.		"centanos"	1.50	
c.		"255" instead of "25"	150.00	
e.		Inverted "S" in "Nacionales"	20.00	
f.		"cen avos"	20.00	
h.		"Corre cionales"	20.00	
i.		Inverted surcharge	75.00	
27	A12	50c on 1p ver	.70	.70
a.		"centovos"	1.50	
b.		"centanos"	1.50	
c.		"Carreos"	1.50	
d.		Inverted surcharge	50.00	
e.		Double surcharge	75.00	
f.		Inverted "S" in "Nacionales"	10.00	
g.		"centavo"	20.00	
h.		"cen avos"	20.00	
28	A12	75c on 1p ver	.70	.70
a.		"centovos"	1.50	
b.		"centanos"	1.50	
c.		"Carreos"	1.50	
d.		"50" for "75" at upper right	2.00	
e.		Inverted "S" in "Nacionales"	10.00	
f.		Double surcharge	75.00	
g.		"ales" inverted	100.00	
29	A12a	100c on 1p ver	1.40	1.40
a.		"110" at upper left and "á" at lower left, instead of "100"	5.00	
b.		Inverted surcharge	75.00	
c.		"Guatemala" bolder; 23mm instead of 18½mm wide	2.25	
d.		Double surcharge, one diagonal	100.00	
30	A12b	150c on 1p ver	1.40	1.40
a.		Inverted "G"	5.00	
b.		"Guatemala" and italic "5" in upper 4 numerals	5.00	
d.		Inverted surcharge	90.00	
e.		Pair, one without surcharge	100.00	
f.		Double surcharge	100.00	
		Nos. 26-30 (5)	4.90	4.90

There are many other minor varieties, such as wrong font letters, etc.
Used values of Nos. 26-30 are for canceled to order stamps. Postally used sell for much more.

National Emblem — A13

1886, July 1   Litho.   Perf. 12
31	A13	1c dull blue	5.00	2.00
32	A13	2c brown	5.00	3.00
33	A13	5c purple	37.50	.75
34	A13	10c red	10.00	.75
35	A13	20c emerald	15.00	1.25
36	A13	25c orange	15.00	1.50
37	A13	50c olive green	10.00	2.00
38	A13	75c carmine rose	10.00	3.00
39	A13	100c red brown	10.00	3.00
40	A13	150c dark blue	15.00	3.75
41	A13	200c orange yellow	18.50	4.75
		Nos. 31-41 (11)	151.00	25.75

Used values of Nos. 38-41 are for canceled to order stamps. Postally used sell for more.
See Nos. 43-50, 99-107. For surcharges see Nos. 42, 51-59, 75-85, 97-98, 108-110, 124-130.

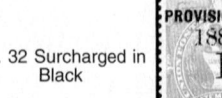

No. 32 Surcharged in Black

Two settings:
I — "1886" (no period).
II — "1886." (period).

1886, Nov. 12
42	A13	1c on 2c brown, I	2.00	2.50
a.		Date inverted, I	75.00	
b.		Date double, I	75.00	
c.		Date omitted, I	60.00	
d.		Date double, one invtd., I	100.00	
e.		Date triple, one inverted, I	100.00	
f.		Setting II	1.50	1.00
g.		Inverted surcharge, II	4.00	
h.		Double surcharge, II	100.00	

Forgeries exist.

 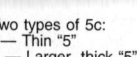

Type I   Type II

Two types of 5c:
I — Thin "5"
II — Larger, thick "5"

1886-95   Engr.   Perf. 12
43	A13	1c blue	.80	.25
44	A13	2c yellow brn	2.40	.25
a.		Half used as 1c on cover	100.00	
45	A13	5c purple (I)	52.50	1.00
46	A13	5c vio (II) ('88)	1.60	.25
47	A13	6c lilac ('95)	.65	.25
48	A13	10c red ('90)	1.60	.25
49	A13	20c green ('93)	3.25	.75
50	A13	25c red org ('93)	8.00	1.25
		Nos. 43-44,46-50 (7)	18.30	3.25

The impression of the engraved stamps is sharper than that of the lithographed. On the engraved stamps the top four lines at left are heavier than those below them. (This is also true of the 1c litho., which is distinguished from the engraved only by a slight color difference and the impression.)
The "2" and "5" (I) are more open than the litho. numerals. The "10" of the engraved is wider. The 20c and 25c of the engraved have a vertical line at right end of the "centavos" ribbon.

No. 38 Surcharged in Blue Black

"1894" 14½mm wide

1894, Apr. 25
51	A13	10c on 75c car rose	4.50	4.50
a.		Double surcharge	75.00	
b.		Inverted surcharge	100.00	

Same on Nos. 38-41 in Blue or Red "1894" 14mm wide
1894, June 13
52	A13	2c on 100c	7.50	4.25
53	A13	6c on 150c (R)	7.50	3.50
54	A13	10c on 75c	550.00	500.00
55	A13	10c on 200c	7.50	4.25
c.		Inverted surcharge	75.00	

Nos. 54-55 exist with thick or thin "1" in new value.

Same on Nos. 39-41 in Blue or Red "1894" 12mm wide
1894, July 14
52a	A13	2c on 100c red brn (Bk)	4.00	3.50
b.		Vert. pair, one without surcharge	150.00	
53a	A13	6c on 150c dk bl (R)	4.50	3.50
55a	A13	10c on 200c org yel (Bk)	5.00	3.50
d.		Inverted surcharge	100.00	
e.		Vert. pair, one without surcharge	150.00	

Nos. 44 and 46 Surcharged in Black, Blue Black, or Red

b   c

d   e

1894-96
56	A13 (b)	1c on 2c (Bk)	.75	.30
a.		"Centav"	5.00	5.00
b.		Double surcharge	75.00	
c.		As "a," dbl. surcharge	150.00	
d.		Blue black surcharge	20.00	20.00
e.		Dbl. surch., one inverted	150.00	

57	A13 (c)	1c on 5c (R) ('95)	.50	.25
a.		Inverted surcharge	3.00	3.00
b.		"1894" instead of "1895"	3.50	
c.		Double surcharge	50.00	
58	A13 (d)	1c on 5c (R) ('95)	.75	.25
a.		Inverted surcharge	50.00	
b.		Double surcharge	50.00	
59	A13 (e)	1c on 5c (R) ('96)	1.25	.40
a.		Inverted surcharge	50.00	
b.		Double surcharge	50.00	
		Nos. 56-59 (4)	3.25	1.20

Nos. 56-58 may be found with thick or thin "1" in the new value.

National Arms and President J. M. Reyna Barrios A21

1897, Jan. 1   Engr.   Unwmk.
60	A21	1c blk, gray	.55	.55
61	A21	2c blk, grnsh gray	.55	.55
62	A21	6c blk, brn org	.55	.55
63	A21	10c blk, dl bl	.55	.55
64	A21	12c blk, rose red	.55	.55
65	A21	18c blk, grysh white	9.50	9.50
66	A21	20c blk, scarlet	1.00	1.00
67	A21	25c blk, bis brn	1.60	1.00
68	A21	50c blk, redsh brn	1.00	1.00
69	A21	75c blk, gray	52.50	52.50
70	A21	100c blk, bl grn	1.00	1.00
71	A21	150c blk, dl rose	105.00	135.00
72	A21	200c blk, magenta	1.00	1.00
73	A21	500c blk, yel grn	1.00	1.00
		Nos. 60-73 (14)	176.35	205.75

Issued for Central American Exposition.
Stamps often sold as Nos. 65, 69 and 71 are examples with telegraph overprint removed.
Used values for Nos. 60-73 are for canceled-to-order stamps. Postally used examples are worth more.
The paper of Nos. 64 and 66 was originally colored on one side only, but has "bled through" on some examples.

No. 64 Surcharged in Violet

1897, Nov.
74	A21	1c on 12c rose red	1.00	1.00
a.		Inverted surcharge	30.00	30.00
b.		Pair, one without surcharge	75.00	
c.		Dbl. surch., one invtd.	100.00	

Stamps of 1886-93 Surcharged in Red

f   g

1898
75	(f)	1c on 5c violet	1.00	1.00
a.		Inverted surcharge	75.00	
76	(f)	1c on 50c ol grn	1.50	1.25
a.		Inverted surcharge	100.00	100.00
77	(f)	6c on 5c violet	4.50	4.50
78	(f)	6c on 150c dk bl	4.50	3.25
79	(g)	10c on 20c emerald	5.00	4.00
a.		Double surch., one inverted	125.00	125.00
		Nos. 75-79 (5)	16.50	11.00

Black Surcharge
80	(f)	1c on 25c red org	2.00	2.00
81	(f)	1c on 75c car rose	1.50	1.50
a.		Double surcharge	100.00	
82	(f)	6c on 10c red	10.00	9.00
83	(f)	6c on 20c emer	5.00	4.00
84	(f)	6c on 100c red brn	5.00	4.00
85	(f)	6c on 200c org yel	5.00	4.00
a.		Inverted surcharge	50.00	50.00
		Nos. 80-85 (6)	28.50	24.50

Information indicates that No. 77 inverted and double surcharges are counterfeits.

National Emblem — A24

Revenue Stamp Overprinted or Surcharged in Carmine

Perf. 12, 12x14, 14x12

1898, Oct. 8   **Litho.**

86	A24	1c dark blue	1.40	1.40
a.		Inverted overprint	12.50	12.50
87	A24	2c on 1c dk bl	2.25	2.25
a.		Inverted surcharge	12.50	12.50

Counterfeits exist.
See type A26.

National Emblem — A25

Revenue Stamps Surcharged in Carmine

1898   **Engr.**   **Perf. 12½ to 16**

88	A25	1c on 10c bl gray	.75	.75
a.		"ENTAVO"	5.00	5.00
89	A25	2c on 5c pur	1.25	1.00
90	A25	2c on 10c bl gray	6.50	7.00
a.		Double surch., car & blk	100.00	75.00
91	A25	2c on 50c dp bl	9.25	9.25
a.		Double surch., car & blk	100.00	100.00
		Nos. 88-91 (4)	17.75	18.00

Black Surcharge

92	A25	2c on 1c lil rose	3.50	2.00
93	A25	2c on 25c red	7.50	8.00
94	A25	6c on 1p purple	4.00	4.50
95	A25	6c on 5p gray vio	7.50	7.50
96	A25	6c on 10p emer	7.50	7.50
		Nos. 92-96 (5)	30.00	29.50

Nos. 88 and 90 are found in shades ranging from Prussian blue to slate blue.
Varieties other than those listed are bogus.
Counterfeits exist of No. 92.
Soaking in water causes marked fading.
See type A27.

No. 46 Surcharged in Red

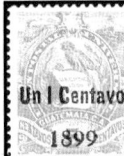

1899, Sept.   **Perf. 12**

97	A13	1c on 5c violet	.40	.25
a.		Inverted surcharge	7.50	7.50
b.		Double surcharge	15.00	15.00
c.		Double surcharge, one inverted	15.00	15.00

No. 48 Surcharged in Black

1900, Jan.

98	A13	1c on 10c red	.65	.50
a.		Inverted surcharge	10.00	10.00
b.		Double surcharge	75.00	75.00

Quetzal Type of 1886

1900-02   **Engr.**

99	A13	1c dark green	.60	.25
100	A13	2c carmine	.60	.25
101	A13	5c blue (II)	2.25	1.25
102	A13	6c lt green	.75	.25
103	A13	10c bister brown	7.50	1.00
104	A13	20c purple	7.50	7.50
105	A13	20c bister brn ('02)	7.50	7.50
106	A13	25c yellow	7.50	7.50
107	A13	25c blue green ('02)	7.50	7.50
		Nos. 99-107 (9)	41.70	33.00

No. 49 Surcharged in Black

1901, May

108	A13	1c on 20c green	.50	.50
a.		Inverted surcharge	22.50	22.50
b.		Double surch., one diagonal	50.00	
109	A13	2c on 20c green	1.50	1.50

No. 50 Surcharged in Black

1901, Apr.

110	A13	1c on 25c red org	.60	.60
a.		Inverted surcharge	25.00	25.00
b.		Double surcharge	50.00	50.00

A26   A27

Revenue Stamps Surcharged in Carmine or Black

1902, July   **Perf. 12, 14x12, 12x14**

111	A26	1c on 1c dk blue	1.10	1.10
a.		Double surcharge	20.00	
b.		Inverted surcharge	20.00	
112	A26	2c on 1c dk blue	1.10	1.10
a.		Double surcharge	90.00	
b.		Inverted surcharge	25.00	

Perf. 14, 15

113	A27	6c on 25c red (Bk)	2.50	2.50
a.		Double surch., one invtd.	75.00	75.00
		Nos. 111-113 (3)	4.70	4.70

National Emblem — A28

Statue of Justo Rufino Barrios — A29

"La Reforma" Palace — A30

Temple of Minerva — A31

Lake Amatitlán — A32

Cathedral in Guatemala — A33

Columbus Theater — A34

Artillery Barracks — A35

Monument to Columbus — A36

School for Indians — A37

1902   **Engr.**   **Perf. 12 to 16**

114	A28	1c grn & claret	.25	.25
a.		Horiz. pair, imperf. vert.	100.00	
115	A29	2c lake & blk	.25	.25
a.		Horiz. or vert. pair, imperf. btwn.	150.00	
116	A30	5c blue & blk	.30	.25
a.		5c ultra & blk	.75	.40
b.		Imperf., pair	100.00	100.00
c.		Horiz. pair, imperf. vert.	100.00	
117	A31	6c bister & grn	.30	.25
a.		Horiz. pair, imperf. btwn.	150.00	
118	A32	10c orange & bl	.40	.40
a.		Horiz. pair, imperf. vert.	100.00	
119	A33	20c rose lil & blk	.60	.40
a.		Horiz. pair, imperf. btwn.	100.00	
120	A34	50c red brn & bl	.45	.40
a.		Vert. pair, imperf. btwn.	350.00	
121	A35	75c gray lil & blk	.55	.40
a.		Horiz. pair, imperf. btwn.	150.00	
b.		Horiz. pair, imperf. vert.	100.00	
122	A36	1p brown & blk	.85	.40
a.		Horiz. pair, imperf. btwn.	150.00	
123	A37	2p ver & blk	1.00	.85
		Nos. 114-123 (10)	4.95	3.85

See Nos. 210, 212-214, 219, 223, 239-241, 243. For overprints and surcharges see Nos. 133, 135-139, 144-157, 168, 170-171, 178, 192-194, 298-299, 301 (in Scott Standard catalogue, Vol. 3), C19, C27, C123.

Issues of 1886-1900 Surcharged in Black or Carmine

1903, Apr. 18   **Perf. 12**

124	A13	25c on 1c dk grn	1.25	.55
a.		Inverted surcharge	50.00	50.00
125	A13	25c on 2c carmine	1.50	.55
126	A13	25c on 6c lt grn	2.50	1.75
a.		Inverted surcharge	40.00	40.00
127	A13	25c on 10c bis brn	7.50	7.00
128	A13	25c on 75c rose	10.00	10.00
129	A13	25c on 150c dk bl (C)	9.00	9.00
130	A13	25c on 200c yellow	10.00	10.00
		Nos. 124-130 (7)	41.75	38.85

Forgeries and bogus varieties exist.

Declaration of Independence A38

1907, Jan. 1   **Perf. 13½ to 15**

132	A38	12½c ultra & blk	.45	.45
a.		Horiz. pair, imperf. btwn.	150.00	

For surcharge see No. 134.

Nos. 118, 119 and 132 Surcharged in Black or Red

1908, May

133	A32	1c on 10c org & bl	.30	.30
a.		Double surcharge	25.00	
b.		Inverted surcharge	15.00	15.00
c.		Pair, one without surcharge	50.00	

134	A38	2c on 12½c ultra & blk (R)	.25	.25
a.		Horiz. or vert. pair, imperf. btwn.	100.00	
b.		Inverted surcharge	15.00	10.00
c.		Double surcharge	30.00	
135	A33	6c on 20c rose lil & blk	.45	.25
a.		Inverted surcharge	20.00	20.00
		Nos. 133-135 (3)	1.00	.80

Similar Surcharge, Dated 1909, in Red or Black on Nos. 121 and 120

1909, Apr.

136	A35	2c on 75c (R)	.55	.55
137	A34	6c on 50c (R)	62.50	62.50
a.		Double surcharge	125.00	125.00
138	A34	6c on 50c (Bk)	.30	.30
		Nos. 136-138 (3)	63.35	63.35

Counterfeits exist of Nos. 137, 137a.

No. 123 Surcharged in Black

139	A37	12½c on 2p ver & blk	.30	.30
a.		Inverted surcharge	25.00	25.00
b.		Period omitted after "1909"	12.50	12.50

Counterfeits exist.

Gen. Miguel García Granados, Birth Cent. (in 1909) — A39

1910, Feb. 11   **Perf. 14**

140	A39	6c bis & indigo	.55	.40
a.		Imperf., pair	55.00	

Some sheets used for this issue contained a two-line watermark, "SPECIAL POSTAGE PAPER / LONDON." For surcharge see No. 143.

General Post Office — A40

Pres. Manuel Estrada Cabrera — A41

1911, June   **Perf. 12**

141	A40	25c bl & blk	.55	.25
a.		Center inverted	1,750.	900.00
142	A41	5p red & blk	.65	.65
a.		Center inverted	30.00	27.50

Nos. 116, 118 and 140 Surcharged in Black or Red

h

i

j

1911   **Perf. 14**

143	A39	(h) 1c on 6c	25.00	9.75
a.		Double surcharge	75.00	75.00
144	A30	(i) 2c on 5c (R)	1.60	.85
145	A32	(j) 6c on 10c	1.25	1.25
a.		Double surcharge	50.00	
		Nos. 143-145 (3)	27.85	11.85

See watermark note after No. 140. Forgeries exist.

Nos. 119-121 Surcharged in Black

k

l

m

1912, Sept.

147 A33 (k) 1c on 20c		.40	.40
a.	Inverted surcharge	12.50	12.50
b.	Double surcharge	15.00	15.00
148 A34 (l) 2c on 50c		.40	.40
a.	Inverted surcharge	12.50	12.50
b.	Double surcharge	12.50	
c.	Double inverted surcharge	25.00	
149 A35 (m) 5c on 75c		.80	.80
a.	"191" for "1912"	7.50	7.50
b.	Double surcharge	15.00	15.00
c.	Inverted surcharge	10.00	
Nos. 147-149 (3)		1.60	1.60

Forgeries exist.

Nos. 120, 122 and 123 Surcharged in Blue, Green or Black

n

o

p

1913, July

151 A34 (n) 1c on 50c (Bl)		.25	.25
a.	Inverted surcharge	10.00	
b.	Double surcharge	17.50	
c.	Horiz. pair, imperf. btwn.	100.00	
152 A36 (o) 6c on 1p (G)		.30	.30
153 A37 (p) 12½c on 2p (Bk)		.30	.30
a.	Inverted surcharge	15.00	15.00
b.	Double surcharge	40.00	
c.	Horiz. pair, imperf. btwn.	100.00	
Nos. 151-153 (3)		.85	.85

Forgeries exist.

Nos. 114 and 115 Surcharged in Black

q

r

s

t

1916-17

154 A28 (q) 2c on 1c ('17)		.25	.25
155 A28 (r) 6c on 1c		.25	.25
156 A28 (s) 12½c on 1c		.25	.25
157 A29 (t) 25c on 2c		.25	.25
Nos. 154-157 (4)		1.00	1.00

Numerous errors of value and color, inverted and double surcharges and similar varieties are in the market. They were not regularly issued, but were surreptitiously made and sold.

Counterfeit surcharges abound.

"Liberty" and President Estrada Cabrera — A51

1917, Mar. 15 — Perf. 14, 15
158 A51 25c dp blue & brown .25 .25

Re-election of President Estrada Cabrera.

Estrada Cabrera and Quetzal — A52

1918 — Perf. 12
161 A52 1.50p dark blue .30 .25

Radio Station — A54

"Joaquina" Maternity Hospital — A55

"Estrada Cabrera" Vocational School — A56

National Emblem — A57

1919, May 3 — Perf. 14, 15

162 A54 30c red & blk		2.75	.75
163 A55 60c ol grn & blk		.80	.50
164 A56 90c red brn & blk		.80	.75
165 A57 3p dp grn & blk		1.75	.50
Nos. 162-165 (4)		6.10	2.50

See Nos. 215, 227. For surcharges see Nos. 166-167, 179-185, 188, 195-198, 245-246, C8-C11, C21-C22.

No. 162 Ovptd. in Blue & Srchd. in Black

1920, Jan. — Unwmk.

166 A54 2c on 30c red & blk		.30	.30
a.	Inverted surcharge	12.50	12.50
b.	"1920" double	10.00	10.00
c.	"1920" omitted	15.00	15.00
d.	"2 centavos" omitted	20.00	
e.	Imperf, pair	100.00	
f.	Pair, imperf. btwn.	100.00	

Nos. 123 and 163 Surcharged

u

v

1920

167 A55 2c on 60c (Bk & R)		.25	.25
a.	Inverted surcharge	10.00	10.00
b.	"1920" inverted	7.50	7.50
c.	"1920" omitted	10.00	10.00
d.	"1920" only	10.00	
e.	Double surcharge	25.00	
168 A37 25c on 2p (Bk)		.30	.25
a.	"35" for "25"	10.00	10.00
b.	Large "5" in "25"	10.00	10.00
c.	Inverted surcharge	15.00	15.00
d.	Double surcharge	25.00	

A61

1920

169 A61 25c green		.25	.25
a.	Double overprint	50.00	
b.	Double overprint, inverted	75.00	

See types A65-A66.

No. 119 Surcharged

1921, Apr.

170 A33 12½c on 20c		.25	.25
a.	Double surcharge	15.00	
b.	Inverted surcharge	15.00	

No. 121 Surcharged

1921, Apr.

171 A35 50c on 75c lil & blk		.50	.30
a.	Double surcharge	22.50	
b.	Inverted surcharge	25.00	25.00

Mayan Stele at Quiriguá — A62

Monument to President Granados — A63

"La Penitenciaria" Bridge — A64

1921, Sept. 1 — Perf. 13½, 14, 15

172 A62 1.50p blue & org		.85	.25
173 A63 5p brown & grn		2.75	1.25
174 A64 15p black & ver		22.50	12.50
Nos. 172-174 (3)		26.10	14.00

See Nos. 216, 228, 229. For surcharges see Nos. 186-187, 189-191, 199-201, 207, 231, 247-251, C1-C5, C12, C23-C24.

Telegraph Stamps Overprinted or Surcharged in Black or Red

A65

A66

1921 — Perf. 14

175 A65 25c green		.25	.25
176 A66 12½c on 25c grn (R)		.25	.25
177 A66 12½c on 25c grn		15.00	15.00
Nos. 175-177 (3)		15.50	15.50

Nos. 119, 163 and 164 Surcharged in Black or Red

w

x

1922, Mar.

178 A33(w) 12½c on 20c		.25	.25
a.	Inverted surcharge	10.00	
179 A55(w) 12½c on 60c		.50	.50
	(R)		
a.	Inverted surcharge	25.00	
180 A56(w) 12½c on 90c		.50	.50
a.	Inverted surcharge	25.00	
181 A55(x) 25c on 60c		1.00	1.00
a.	Inverted surcharge	20.00	
182 A55(x) 25c on 60c		125.00	125.00
	(R)		
183 A56(x) 25c on 90c		1.00	1.00
a.	Inverted surcharge	25.00	
184 A56(x) 25c on 90c		4.00	4.00
	(R)		
Nos. 178-181,183-184 (6)		7.25	7.25

Counterfeits exist.

Nos. 165, 173-174 Surcharged in Red or Dark Blue

1922, May

185 A57 12½c on 3p grn & blk		.25	.25
	(R)		
186 A63 12½c on 5p brn & grn		.50	.45
187 A64 12½c on 15p blk & ver		.50	.45
Nos. 185-187 (3)		1.25	1.15

Nos. 165, 173-174 Surcharged in Red or Black

Type I

Type II

Type III

Type IV

1922

188 A57	25c on 3p (I) (R)	.25	.25
a.	Type II	.60	.60
b.	Type III	.60	.60
c.	Type IV	.30	.30
d.	Inverted surcharge	40.00	
e.	Horiz. or vert. pair, imperf. btwn. (I)	125.00	
189 A63	25c on 5p (I)	1.00	2.00
a.	Type II	2.00	3.00
b.	Type III	2.00	3.00
c.	Type IV	1.00	2.00
190 A64	25c on 15p (I)	1.00	1.50
a.	Type II	2.00	3.00
b.	Type III	2.00	3.00
c.	Type IV	1.00	1.50
191 A64	25c on 15p (I) (R)	22.50	30.00
a.	Type II	40.00	45.00
b.	Type III	45.00	45.00
c.	Type IV	30.00	35.00
	Nos. 188-191 (4)	24.75	33.75

Stamps of 1902-21 Surcharged in Dark Blue or Red

Type V

Type VI

Type VII

Type VIII

Type IX

1922, Aug.   **On Nos. 121-123**

192 A35	25c on 75c (V)	.40	.40
a.	Type VII	.40	.40
b.	Type VII	1.75	1.75
c.	Type VIII	5.50	4.75
d.	Type IX	6.50	6.00
193 A36	25c on 1p (V)	.30	.30
a.	Type VI	.30	.30
b.	Type VII	1.25	1.25
c.	Type VIII	2.50	2.50
d.	Type IX	4.00	3.50
e.	Inverted surcharge	40.00	
194 A37	25c on 2p (V)	.45	.45
a.	Type VI	.45	.45
b.	Type VII	1.25	1.25
c.	Type VIII	4.00	4.00
d.	Type IX	6.50	6.50

On Nos. 162-165

195 A54	25c on 30c (V)	.45	.45
a.	Type VI	.45	.45
b.	Type VII	1.25	1.25
c.	Type VIII	5.50	5.50
d.	Type IX	6.50	6.50
196 A55	25c on 60c (V)	1.00	1.50
a.	Type VI	1.25	1.50
b.	Type VII	6.25	7.75
c.	Type VIII	8.50	9.50
d.	Type IX	10.00	11.00
197 A56	25c on 90c (V)	1.00	1.50
a.	Type VI	1.50	2.00
b.	Type VII	6.00	6.75
c.	Type VIII	8.50	9.50
d.	Type IX	10.00	11.00
198 A57	25c on 3p (R) (V)	.40	.40
a.	Type VI	.40	.40
b.	Type VII	1.25	1.00
c.	Type VIII	6.00	4.50
d.	Type IX	5.50	6.00
e.	Inverted surcharge	50.00	

On Nos. 172-174

199 A62	25c on 1.50p (V)	.30	.30
a.	Type VI	.30	.30
b.	Type VII	1.25	1.00
c.	Type VIII	3.00	3.00
d.	Type IX	4.50	4.50
e.	Inverted surcharge	40.00	
200 A63	25c on 5p (V)	.75	.90
a.	Type VI	.80	1.00
b.	Type VII	3.00	3.50
c.	Type VIII	5.50	6.00
d.	Type IX	8.00	8.50
201 A64	25c on 15p (V)	.85	.90
a.	Type VII	1.50	1.50
b.	Type VII	5.00	5.50
c.	Type VIII	6.50	6.50
d.	Type IX	12.00	12.00
	Nos. 192-201 (10)	5.90	7.10

Centenary Palace — A69

National Palace at Antigua — A70

Printed by Waterlow & Sons
1922   **Perf. 14, 14½**

202 A69	12½c green	.30	.25
a.	Horiz. or vert. pair, imperf. btwn.	100.00	
203 A70	25c brown	.30	.25

See Nos. 211, 221, 234.

Columbus Theater A71

Quetzal A72

Granados Monument — A73

Litho. by Castillo Bros.
1924, Feb.   **Perf. 12**

204 A71	50c rose	.50	.25
a.	Imperf., pair	7.50	
b.	Horiz. or vert. pair, imperf. btwn.	25.00	
205 A72	1p dark green	2.25	.25
a.	Imperf. vertically	15.00	
b.	Vert. pair, imperf. btwn.	20.00	
c.	Imperf., pair	7.50	
206 A73	5p orange	1.25	.50
a.	Imperf., pair	8.50	
b.	Horiz. pair, imperf. btwn.	20.00	
	Nos. 204-206 (3)	4.00	1.00

For surcharges see Nos. 208-209.

Nos. 172 and 206 Surcharged

1924, July

207 A62	1p on 1.50p bl & org	.30	.25
208 A73	1.25p on 5p orange	.50	.50
a.	"UN PESO 25 Cents." omitted	40.00	
b.	Horiz. pair, imperf. btwn.	25.00	

No. 208 Overprinted

1924

209 A73	1p on 5p orange	.50	.50

Types of 1902-22 Issues
Engr. by Perkins Bacon & Co.
1924, Aug.   **Re-engraved**   **Perf. 14**

210 A31	6c bister	.25	.25
211 A70	25c brown	.25	.25
212 A34	50c red	.25	.25
213 A36	1p orange brn	.25	.25
214 A37	2p orange	.35	.25
215 A57	3p deep green	2.00	.50
216 A64	15p black	5.00	2.75
	Nos. 210-216 (7)	8.35	4.50

The designs of the stamps of 1924 differ from those of the 1902-22 issues in many details which are too minute to illustrate. The re-engraved issue may be readily distinguished by the imprint "Perkins Bacon & Co. Ld. Londres."

Pres. Justo Rufino Barrios A74

Lorenzo Montúfar A75

1924, Aug.

217 A74	1.25p ultra	.25	.25
218 A75	2.50p dk violet	1.00	.25

See Nos. 224, 226. For surcharges see Nos. 232, C6, C20.

Aurora Park — A76

National Post Office — A77

National Observatory A78

Types of 1921-24 Re-engraved and New Designs Dated 1926
Engraved by Waterlow & Sons, Ltd.
1926, July-Aug.   **Perf. 12½**

219 A31	6c ocher	.25	.25
220 A76	12½c green	.25	.25
221 A70	25c brown	.25	.25
222 A77	50c red	.25	.25
223 A36	1p orange brn	.25	.25
224 A74	1.50p dk blue	.25	.25
225 A78	2p orange	1.25	1.00
226 A75	2.50p dk violet	1.50	1.25
227 A57	3p dark green	.45	.25
228 A63	5p brown vio	1.00	.40
229 A64	15p black	6.00	2.75
	Nos. 219-229 (11)	11.70	7.15

These stamps may be distinguished from those of the same designs in preceding issues by the imprint "Waterlow & Sons, Limited, Londres," the date, "1926," and the perforation.
See Nos. 233, 242. For surcharge see No. 230.

Nos. 225-226, 228 Surcharged in Various Colors

1928

230 A78	½c on 2p (Bl)	.65	.50
a.	Inverted surcharge	12.50	
231 A63	½c on 5p (Bk)	.35	.25
a.	Inverted surcharge	10.00	10.00
b.	Double surcharge	50.00	
c.	Blue surcharge	45.00	45.00
d.	Blue and black surcharge	50.00	50.00
232 A75	1c on 2.50p (R)	.35	.25
b.	Double surcharge	50.00	
	Nos. 230-232 (3)	1.35	1.00

Barrios — A79

Montúfar — A80

Granados A81

General Orellana A82

Coat of Arms of Guatemala City — A83

Engraved by T. De la Rue & Co.
1929, Jan.   **Perf. 14**

233 A78	½c yellow grn	.75	.25
234 A70	1c dark brown	.25	.25
235 A79	2c deep blue	.25	.25
236 A80	3c dark violet	.25	.25
237 A81	4c orange	.25	.25
238 A82	5c dk carmine	.50	.25
239 A31	10c brown	.40	.25
240 A36	15c ultra	.50	.25
241 A29	25c brown org	1.00	.25
242 A76	30c green	.90	.30
243 A32	50c pale rose	2.00	.60
244 A83	1q black	3.00	.40
	Nos. 233-244 (12)	10.05	3.55

Nos. 233, 234 and 239 to 243 differ from the illustrations in many minor details, particularly in the borders.
See No. 300 in Scott Standard catalogue (Vol. 3) for bisect of No. 235. For overprints and surcharges see Nos. 297, C13, C17-C18, C25-C26, C28, E1, RA17-RA18 (in Scott Standard catalogue, Vol. 3).

No. 227 Surcharged in Black or Red

1929, Dec. 28   **Perf. 12½, 13**

245 A57	3c on 3p dk grn (Bk)	1.25	1.90
a.	Inverted surcharge	15.00	15.00
246 A57	5c on 3p dk grn (R)	1.25	1.90
a.	Inverted surcharge	15.00	15.00

Inauguration of the Eastern Railroad connecting Guatemala and El Salvador.

No. 229 Surcharged in Red

1930, Mar. 30   **Unwmk.**

247 A64	1c on 15p black	1.25	1.40
248 A64	2c on 15p black	1.25	1.40
249 A64	3c on 15p black	1.25	1.40
250 A64	5c on 15p black	1.25	1.40
251 A64	15c on 15p black	1.25	1.40
	Nos. 247-251 (5)	6.25	7.00

Opening of Los Altos electric railway.

Hydroelectric Dam — A85

Los Altos
Railway
A86

Railroad
Station
A87

1930, Mar. 30   **Typo.**   **Perf. 12**
252	A85	2c brn vio & blk	1.40	1.90
a.		Horiz. pair, imperf. btwn.	125.00	
253	A86	3c dp red & blk	2.75	2.75
a.		Vert. pair, imperf. btwn.	125.00	
254	A87	5c buff & dk bl	2.75	2.75
		Nos. 252-254 (3)	6.90	7.40

Opening of Los Altos electric railway. Exist imperf.

Mayan Stele at
Quiriguá — A91

1932, Apr. 8   **Engr.**
258	A91	3c carmine rose	1.90	.40

See Nos. 302-303 in Scott Standard catalogue, Vol. 3.

Flag of
the Race,
Columbus
and
Tecum
Uman
A92

1933, Aug. 3   **Litho.**   **Perf. 12½**
259	A92	½c dark green	.75	.75
260	A92	1c dull brown	1.25	1.10
261	A92	2c deep blue	1.25	1.10
262	A92	3c dull violet	1.25	.75
263	A92	5c rose	1.25	1.10
		Nos. 259-263 (5)	5.75	4.80

Day of the Race and 441st anniv. of the sailing of Columbus from Palos, Spain, Aug. 3, 1492, on his 1st voyage to the New World. The 3c and 5c exist imperf.

Birthplace of
Barrios
A93

View of San
Lorenzo
A94

Justo Rufino
Barrios
A95

National
Emblem and
Locomotive
A96

General Post
Office — A97

Telegraph
Building and
Barrios
A98

Military
Academy
A99

National Police Headquarters — A100

Jorge Ubico
and J. R.
Barrios
A101

1935, July 19   **Photo.**
264	A93	½c yel grn & mag	.40	.45
265	A94	1c org red & pck bl	.40	.45
266	A95	2c orange & blk	.40	.55
267	A96	3c car rose & pck bl	4.50	2.25
268	A97	4c pck bl & org red	4.50	10.00
269	A98	5c bl grn & brn	3.25	4.25
270	A99	10c slate grn & rose lake	4.50	5.50
271	A100	15c ol grn & org brn	4.50	4.75
272	A101	25c scarlet & bl	4.50	4.75
		Nos. 264-272 (9)	26.95	32.95

General Barrios. See Nos. C29-C31.

Lake Atitlán   Quetzal
A102   A103

Legislative
Building — A104

1935, Oct. 10
273	A102	1c brown & crim	.25	.25
274	A103	3c rose car & pck grn	.70	.25
275	A103	3c red org & pck grn	.70	.25
276	A104	4c brt bl & dp rose	.35	.25
		Nos. 273-276 (4)	2.00	1.00

See No. 277. For surcharges see Nos. B1-B3.

No. 273 perforated diagonally through the center

1936, June   **Perf. 12½x12**
277	A102	(½c) brown & crimson	.25	.25
a.		Unsevered pair	.50	.60

Bureau of
Printing — A105

Map of
Guatemala
A106

1936, Sept. 24   **Perf. 12½**
278	A105	½c green & pur	.25	.25
279	A106	5c blue & dk brn	.90	.25

For surcharge see No. B4.

Quetzal   Union Park,
A107   Quezaltenango
          A108

Gen. Jorge
Ubico on
Horseback
A109

1c, Tower of the Reformer. 3c, National Post Office. 4c, Government Building, Retalhuleu. 5c, Legislative Palace entrance. 10c, Custom House. 15c, Aurora Airport Custom House. 25c, National Fair. 50c, Residence of Presidential Guard. 1.50q, General Ubico, portrait standing, no cap.

1937, May 20
280	A107	½c pck bl & car rose	.70	.45
281	A107	1c ol gray & red brn	.70	.35
282	A108	2c vio & car rose	.60	.35
283	A108	3c brn vio & brt bl	.50	.25
284	A108	4c yel & dl ol grn	3.00	3.00
285	A107	5c crim & brt vio	3.00	3.00
286	A107	10c mag & brn blk	4.00	4.00
287	A108	15c ultra & cop red	3.00	3.00
288	A108	25c red org & vio	4.00	4.00
289	A108	50c dk grn & org red	6.00	6.00
290	A109	1q magenta & blk	50.00	50.00
291	A109	1.50q red brn & blk	50.00	50.00
		Nos. 280-291 (12)	125.50	124.40

Second term of President Ubico.

Mayan Calendar   Natl. Flower
A119   (White Nun
             Orchid)
             A120

Quetzal — A121

Map of
Guatemala
A122

1939, Sept. 7   **Perf. 13x12, 12½**
292	A119	½c grn & red brn	.85	.25
293	A120	2c bl & gray blk	5.00	1.00
294	A121	3c red org & turq grn	6.50	1.75
295	A121	3c ol bis & turq grn	6.50	1.75
296	A122	5c blue & red	5.75	5.75
		Nos. 292-296 (5)	24.60	10.50

For overprints see Nos. 324, C157 in Scott Standard catalogue, Vol. 3.

No. 235 Surcharged
in Red

1939, Sept.   **Perf. 14**
297	A79	1c on 2c deep blue	.25	.25

Stamps of 1929 Surcharged in Blue

y

z

1940, June
298	A29	(y) 1c on 25c brn org	.25	.25
299	A32	(z) 5c on 50c pale rose (bar 10x¾mm)	.25	.25
a.		Bar 12½x2mm	.30	.25
b.		Bar 12½x1mm	50.00	5.00

SEMI-POSTAL STAMPS

Regular Issues of
1935-36
Surcharged in Blue
or Red similar to
illustration

1937, Mar. 15   **Unwmk.**   **Perf. 12½**
B1	A102	1c + 1c brn & crim	.75	1.00
B2	A103	3c + 1c rose car & pck grn	.75	1.00
B3	A103	3c + 1c red org & pck grn	.75	1.00
B4	A106	5c + 1c bl & dk brn (R)	.75	1.00
		Nos. B1-B4 (4)	3.00	4.00

1st Phil. Exhib. held in Guatemala, Mar. 15-20.

AIR POST STAMPS

Surcharged in
Red on No. 229

1929, May 20   Unwmk.   Perf. 12½
C1 A64 3c on 15p blk   1.10 *1.40*
C2 A64 5c on 15p blk   .55   .45
C3 A64 15c on 15p blk   1.50 .45
  a. Double surcharge (G & R) 100.00
C4 A64 20c on 15p blk   2.25 2.25
  a. Inverted surcharge   100.00
  b. Double surcharge   100.00

Surcharged in Red on No. 216

1929, May 20   Perf. 14
C5 A64 5c on 15p black   3.25 2.25
  Nos. C1-C5 (5)   8.65 6.80

Surcharged in Black
on No. 218

1929, Oct. 9
C6 A75 3c on 2.50p dk vio   1.00 1.00

Airplane
and Mt.
Agua
AP3

1930, June 4   Litho.   Perf. 12½
C7 AP3 6c rose red   4.50 *4.50*
  a. Double impression   25.00 25.00
  b. Imperf., pair   350.00

For overprint see No. C14.

Nos. 227, 229
Surcharged in
Black or Red

1930, Dec. 9   Perf. 12½
C8 A57 1c on 3p grn (Bk)   .40   .40
  a. Double surcharge   100.00
C9 A57 2c on 3p grn (Bk)   1.10 *1.50*
C10 A57 3c on 3p grn (R)   1.10 *1.50*
C11 A57 3c on 3p grn (R)   1.10 *1.50*
C12 A64 10c on 15p blk (R) 5.00 *5.00*
  a. Double surcharge   125.00
  Nos. C8-C12 (5)   8.70 *9.90*

No. 237 Overprinted

1931, May 19   Perf. 14
C13 A81 4c orange   .40   .30
  a. Double overprint   40.00 *50.00*

No. C7 Overprinted

Perf. 12½
C14 AP3 6c rose red   2.00 *2.00*
  a. On No. C7a   30.00 30.00
  b. Inverted overprint   7.00 *7.00*

Nos. 240, 242
Overprinted in
Red

1931, Oct. 21   Perf. 14
C15 A36 15c ultra   2.00 .25
  a. Double overprint   125.00 125.00
C16 A76 30c green   3.00 .95
  a. Double overprint   75.00 75.00

Nos. 235-236
Overprinted in Red
or Green

1931, Dec. 5
C17 A79 2c dp bl (R)   2.50 *3.00*
C18 A80 3c dk vio (G)   2.50 *3.00*

No. 240
Overprinted in
Red

C19 A36 15c ultra   2.75 *3.00*

Nos. C17-C19 were issued in connection
with the 1st postal flight from Barrios to Miami.

No. 224 Surcharged
in Red

1932-33   Perf. 12½
C20 A74 2c on 1.50p dk bl   .80   .55

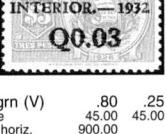

Nos. 227, 229
Surcharged in
Violet, Red or
Blue

C21 A57 3c on 3p grn (V)   .80   .25
  a. Inverted surcharge   45.00 45.00
  b. Vert. pair, imperf. horiz. 900.00
C22 A57 3c on 3p grn (R)   .80   .25
C23 A64 10c on 15p blk (R) 7.75 6.25
  b. First "I" of "Interior" missing 10.00 10.00
C24 A64 15c on 15p blk (Bl) 9.00 8.50
  a. First "I" of "Interior" missing 15.00 15.00
  Nos. C20-C24 (5)   19.15 15.80

Issued: No. C22, 1/1/33; others, 2/11/32.

No. 237 Overprinted
in Green

1933, Jan. 1   Perf. 14
C25 A81 4c orange   .40   .35
  a. Double overprint   40.00 40.00

Nos. 235, 238 and
240 Overprinted in
Red or Black

1934, Aug. 7
C26 A82 5c dk car (Bk)   1.50 .25
C27 A36 15c ultra (R)   1.50 .25

Overprinted in Red

C28 A79 2c deep blue   .55   .25

View of Port
Barrios — AP7

Designs: 15c, Tomb of Barrios. 30c,
Equestrian Statue of Barrios.

1935, July 19   Photo.   Perf. 12½
C29 AP7 10c yel brn & pck grn   6.00 4.50
C30 AP7 15c gray & brn   1.50 *1.75*
C31 AP7 30c car rose & bl vio   1.50 1.25
  Nos. C29-C31 (3)   9.00 7.50

Birth cent. of Gen. Justo Rufino Barrios.

Lake
Amatitlán
AP10

Designs: Nos. C36, C37, C45, C46. Different
views of Lake Amatitlan. 3c, Port Barrios.
No. C34, C35, Ruins of Fort San Felipe. 10c,
Port Livingston. No. C39, C40, Port San Jose.
No. C41, C42, View of Atitlan. No. C43, C44,
Aurora Airport.

Overprinted with Quetzal in Green

1935-37   Size: 37x17mm
C32 AP10 2c org brn   .25   .25
C33 AP10 3c blue   .25   .25
C34 AP10 4c black   .25   .25
C35 AP10 4c ultra ('37)   .25   .25
C36 AP10 6c yel grn   .25   .25
C37 AP10 6c blk vio ('37)   4.00 .25
C38 AP10 10c claret   .50   .25
C39 AP10 15c red org   .65   .40
C40 AP10 15c yel grn ('37) .65   .65
C41 AP10 30c olive grn   6.00 6.50
C42 AP10 30c ol bis ('37)   .75   .50
C43 AP10 50c rose vio   17.50 15.00
C44 AP10 50c Prus bl ('36) 4.00 3.00
C45 AP10 1q scarlet   17.50 20.00
C46 AP10 1q car ('36)   4.50 3.00
  Nos. C32-C46 (15)   57.30 50.80

Issue dates follow No. C69.
For overprints and surcharges see Nos.
C70-C79, CB1-CB2.

Central Park,
Antigua
AP11

Designs: 1c, Guatemala City. 2c, Central
Park, Guatemala City. 3c, Monastery. Nos.
C50-C51, Mouth of Dulce River. Nos. C52-
C53, Plaza Barrios. Nos. C54-C55, Los
Proceres Monument. No. C56, Central Park,
Antigua. No. C57, Dulce River. Nos. C58-
C59, Quezaltenango. Nos. C60-C61, Ruins at
Antigua. Nos. C62-C63, Dock at Port Barrios.
Nos. C64-C65, Port San Jose. Nos. C66-C67,
Aurora Airport. 2.50q, Island off Atlantic Coast.
5q, Atlantic Coast view.

Overprinted with Quetzal in Green

Size: 34x15mm
C47 AP11 1c yel brn   .25   .25
C48 AP11 2c vermilion   .25   .25
C49 AP11 3c magenta   .50   .25
C50 AP11 4c org yel ('36)   1.75 1.40
C51 AP11 4c car lake ('37) 1.00 .75
C52 AP11 5c dl bl   .25   .25
C53 AP11 5c org ('37)   .25   .25
C54 AP11 10c red brn   .50   .35
C55 AP11 10c ol grn ('37)   .50   .30
C56 AP11 15c rose red   .25   .25
C57 AP11 15c ver ('37)   .25   .25
C58 AP11 20c ultra   2.50 *3.00*
C59 AP11 20c dp cl ('37)   .50   .25
C60 AP11 25c gray blk   3.00 *3.50*
C61 AP11 25c bl grn ('37)   .45   .25
  a. Quetzal omitted   1,100.
C62 AP11 30c yel grn   1.50 *1.50*
C63 AP11 30c rose red ('37) 1.00 .25
C64 AP11 50c car rose   7.00 *8.00*
C65 AP11 50c pur ('36)   6.50 *7.50*
C66 AP11 1q dk bl   22.50 *25.00*

C67 AP11 1q dk grn ('36)   7.50 7.50
Size: 46x20mm
C68 AP11 2.50q rose red &
          ol grn
          ('36)   5.00 3.00
C69 AP11 5q org & ind
          ('36)   7.00 4.00
  a. Quetzal omitted   1,500. 1,250.
  Nos. C47-C69 (23)   70.20 *68.30*

Issued: Nos. C32-C34, C36, C38-C39, C41,
C43, C45, C47-C49, C52, C54, C56, C58,
C60, C62, 11/1/35; Nos. C44, C50, C67-C69,
10/1/36; Nos. C35, C37, C40, C42, C51, C53,
C55, C57, C59, C61, C63, 1/1/37.
Value for No. C61a is for a sound stamp.
For overprints and surcharges see Nos.
C80-C91, CB3-CB4.

Types of Air Post Stamps, 1935
Overprinted with Airplane in Blue

2c, Quezaltenango. 3c, Lake Atitlan. 4c,
Progressive Colony, Lake Amatitlan. 6c, Carmen Hill. 10c, Relief map. 15c, National University. 30c, Espana Plaza. 50c, Police Station, Aurora Airport. 75c, Amphitheater, Aurora
Airport. 1q, Aurora Airport.

1937, May 18
Center in Brown Black

C70 AP10 2c carmine   .25   .25
C71 AP10 3c blue   1.00 *1.25*
C72 AP10 4c citron   .25   .25
C73 AP10 6c yel grn   .35   .25
C74 AP10 10c red vio   2.00 *2.25*
C75 AP10 15c orange   1.50 1.00
C76 AP10 30c ol grn   3.75 3.00
C77 AP10 50c pck bl   5.00 4.25
C78 AP10 75c dk vio   10.00 *11.00*
C79 AP10 1q dp rose   11.00 *12.00*
  Nos. C70-C79 (10)   35.10 *35.50*

Overprinted with Airplane in Black

1c, 7th Ave., Guatemala City. 2c, Los
Proceres Monument. 3c, Natl. Printing Office.
5c, Natl. Museum. 10c, Central Park. 15c,
Escuintla. 20c, Motorcycle Police. 25c,
Slaughterhouse, Escuintla. 30c, Exhibition
Hall. 50c, Barrios Plaza. 1q, Polytechnic
School. 1.50q, Aurora Airport.

Size: 33x15mm
C80 AP11 1c yel brn & brt bl   .25   .25
C81 AP11 2c crim & dp vio   .25   .25
C82 AP11 3c red vio & red
          brn   .50   .50
C83 AP11 5c pck grn & cop
          red   4.00   3.00
C84 AP11 10c car & grn   1.25   1.00
C85 AP11 15c rose & dl ol grn .50   .25
C86 AP11 20c ultra & blk   3.00   1.75
C87 AP11 25c dk gray & scar   2.50   2.50
C88 AP11 30c grn & dp vio   1.25   1.25
C89 AP11 50c magenta & ultra 10.00 *12.00*
Size: 42x19mm
C90 AP11 1q ol grn & red
          vio   10.00 *12.00*
C91 AP11 1.50q scar & ol brn 10.00 *12.00*
  Nos. C80-C91 (12)   43.50 *46.75*

Second term of President Ubico.

Souvenir Sheet

AP12

1938, Jan. 10   Perf. 12½
C92 AP12 Sheet of 4   8.00 8.00
  a. 15c George Washington   1.50 1.50
  b. 4c Franklin D. Roosevelt 1.50 1.50
  c. 4c Map of the Americas 1.50 1.50
  d. 15c Pan American Union Build-
          ing, Washington, DC   .75   .75

150th anniv. of US Constitution.

President Arosemena, Panama AP13

Flags of Central American Countries — AP19

Designs: 2c, Pres. Cortés Castro, Costa Rica. 3c, Pres. Somoza, Nicaragua. 4c, Pres. Carias Andino, Honduras. 5c, Pres. Martinez, El Salvador. 10c, Pres. Ubico, Guatemala.

1938, Nov. 20   **Unwmk.**
C93	AP13	1c org & ol brn	.25 .25
C94	AP13	2c scar, pale pink & sl grn	.30 .25
C95	AP13	3c grn, buff & ol brn	.40 .30
C96	AP13	4c dk cl, pale lil & brn	.55 .35
C97	AP13	5c bis, pale grn & ol brn	.50 .60
C98	AP13	10c ultra, pale bl & brn	1.00 1.25
		Nos. C93-C98 (6)	3.00 3.00

Souvenir Sheet
C99	AP19	Sheet of 6	8.00 8.00
a.		1c Guatemala	.80 .80
b.		2c El Salvador	.80 .80
c.		3c Honduras	1.10 1.10
d.		4c Nicaragua	1.40 1.40
e.		5c Costa Rica	1.40 1.40
f.		10c Panama	2.40 2.40

1st Central American Phil. Exhib., Guatemala City, Nov. 20-27.
For overprints see Nos. CO1-CO7.

La Merced Church, Antigua AP20

Designs: 2c, Ruins of Christ School, Antigua. 3c, Aurora Airport. 4c, Drill ground, Guatemala City. 5c, Cavalry barracks. 6c, Palace of Justice. 10c, Customhouse, San José. 15c, Communications Building, Retalhuleu. 30c, Municipal Theater, Quezaltenango. 50c, Customhouse, Retalhuleu. 1q, Departmental Building.

Inscribed "Aéreo Interior"
Overprinted with Quetzal in Green

1939, Feb. 14
C100	AP20	1c ol bis & chnt	.25 .25
C101	AP20	2c rose red & sl grn	.25 .25
C102	AP20	3c dl bl & bis	.25 .25
C103	AP20	4c rose pink & yel grn	.25 .25
C104	AP20	5c brn lake & brt ultra	.30 .25
C105	AP20	6c org & gray brn	.35 .25
C106	AP20	10c bis brn & gray blk	.50 .25
C107	AP20	15c dl vio & blk	.75 .25
C108	AP20	30c dp bl & dk car	1.10 .25
C109	AP20	50c org & brt vio	1.50 .40
a.		Quetzal omitted	1,750.
C110	AP20	1q yel grn & brt ultra	2.50 1.25
		Nos. C100-C110 (11)	8.00 3.90

See Nos. C111-C122. For overprint and surcharge see No. C124, C132 in Scott Standard catalogue, Vol. 3.

Inscribed "Aéreo Internacional" or "Aérea Exterior"

1939, Feb. 14

Designs: 1c, Mayan Altar, Aurora Park. 2c, Sanitation Building. 3c, Lake Amatitlan. 4c, Lake Atitlan. 5c, Tamazulapa River bridge. 10c, Los proceres Monument. 15c, Palace of Captains General. 20c, Church on Carmen Hill. 25c, Barrios Park. 30c, Mayan Altar. 50c, Charles III fountain. 1q, View of Antigua.

Overprinted with Quetzal in Green
C111	AP20	1c ol grn & gldn brn	.25 .25
C112	AP20	2c lt grn & blk	.30 .25
C113	AP20	3c ultra & cob bl	.25 .25
C114	AP20	4c org brn & yel grn	.25 .25
C115	AP20	5c sage grn & red org	.35 .25
C116	AP20	10c lake & sl blk	1.75 .25
C117	AP20	15c ultra & brt rose	1.75 .25
C118	AP20	20c yel grn & ap grn	.60 .25
C119	AP20	25c dl vio & lt ol grn	.60 .25
C120	AP20	30c dl rose & blk	.80 .25
C121	AP20	50c scar & brt yel	1.50 .25
C122	AP20	1q org & yel grn	2.50 .35
		Nos. C111-C122 (12)	10.90 3.10

No. 240 Overprinted in Carmine

1940, Apr. 14   **Perf. 14**
C123	A36	15c ultra	.60 .25

Pan American Union, 50th anniversary.

AIR POST SEMI-POSTAL STAMPS

Air Post Stamps of 1937 Surcharged in Red or Blue

1937, Mar. 15   **Unwmk.**   **Perf. 12½**
CB1	AP10	4c + 1c ultra (R)	.90 1.25
CB2	AP10	6c + 1c blk vio (R)	.90 1.25
CB3	AP11	10c + 1c ol grn (Bl)	.90 1.25
CB4	AP11	15c + 1c ver (Bl)	.90 1.25
		Nos. CB1-CB4 (4)	3.60 5.00

1st Phil. Exhib. held in Guatemala, Mar. 15-20.

AIR POST OFFICIAL STAMPS

Nos. C93-C98 Overprinted in Black

1939, Apr. 29   **Unwmk.**   **Perf. 12½**
CO1	AP13	1c org & ol brn	1.10 1.10
CO2	AP13	2c multi	1.10 1.10
CO3	AP13	3c multi	1.10 1.10
CO4	AP13	4c multi	1.10 1.10
CO5	AP13	5c multi	1.10 1.10
CO6	AP13	10c multi	1.10 1.10
		Nos. CO1-CO6 (6)	6.60 6.60

No. C99 Overprinted in Black

1939
CO7	AP19	Sheet of 6	3.75 3.75
a.		1c yel org, blue & blk	.60 .60
b.		2c lake, org, blue & blk	.60 .60
c.		3c olive, blue & orange	.60 .60
d.		4c dk claret, bl, org & blk	.60 .60
e.		5c grnsh bl, bl, red, org & blk	.60 .60
f.		10c olive bister, red & org	.60 .60

SPECIAL DELIVERY STAMPS

No. 237 Overprinted in Red

1940, June   **Unwmk.**   **Perf. 14**
E1	A81	4c orange	1.50 .35

No. E1 paid for express service by motorcycle messenger between Guatemala City and Coban.

OFFICIAL STAMPS

Franqueo Oficial — O1

1902, Dec. 18   **Typeset**   **Perf. 12**
O1	O1	1c green	9.00 5.50
O2	O1	2c carmine	9.00 5.50
O3	O1	5c ultra	9.00 4.50
O4	O1	10c brown violet	12.00 4.50
O5	O1	25c orange	12.00 4.50
a.		Horiz. pair, imperf. between	125.00
		Nos. O1-O5 (5)	51.00 24.50

Nos. O1-O5 printed on thin paper with sheet watermark "AMERICAN LINEN BOND." Nos. O1-O3 also printed on thick paper with sheet watermark "ROYAL BANK BOND." Values are for copies that do not show the watermark. Counterfeits of Nos. O1-O5 exist.

During the years 1912 to 1926 the Post Office Department perforated the word "OFICIAL" on limited quantities of the following stamps: Nos. 114-123, 132, 141-149, 151-153, 158, 202, 210-229 and RA2. The perforating was done in blocks of four stamps at a time and was of two types.
A rubber handstamp "OFICIAL" was also used during the same period and was applied in violet, red, blue or black to stamps No. 117-118, 121-123, 163-165, 172 and 202-218.
Both perforating and handstamping were done in the post office at Guatemala City and use of the stamps was limited to that city.

National Emblem — O2

1929, Jan.   **Engr.**   **Perf. 14**
O6	O2	1c pale grnsh bl	.30 .30
O7	O2	2c dark brown	.30 .30
O8	O2	3c green	.30 .30
O9	O2	4c deep violet	.40 .35
O10	O2	5c brown car	.40 .35
O11	O2	10c brown orange	.70 .70
O12	O2	25c dark blue	1.40 1.10
		Nos. O6-O12 (7)	3.80 3.40

POSTAL TAX STAMPS

National Emblem — PT1

Perf. 13½, 14, 15

1919, May 3   **Engr.**   **Unwmk.**
RA1	PT1	12½c carmine	.30 .25

Tax for rebuilding post offices

G. P. O. and Telegraph Building — PT2

1927, Nov. 10   **Typo.**   **Perf. 14**
RA2	PT2	1c olive green	.55 .25

Tax to provide a fund for building a post office in Guatemala City.

No. RA2 Overprinted in Green

1936, June 30
RA3	PT2	1c olive green	5.75 4.00

Liberal revolution, 65th anniversary.

No. RA2 Overprinted in Blue

1936, Sept. 15
RA4	PT2	1c olive green	.55 .55

115th anniv. of the Independence of Guatemala.

No. RA2 Overprinted in Red Brown

1936, Nov. 15
RA5	PT2	1c olive green	.55 .45

National Fair.

No. RA2 Overprinted in Red

1937, Mar. 15
RA6	PT2	1c olive green	.55 .55

No. RA2 Overprinted in Blue

1938, Jan. 10   **Perf. 14x14½**
RA7	PT2	1c olive green	.30 .25
a.		"1937-1939" omitted	110.00

150th anniv. of the US Constitution.

No. RA2 Overprinted in Blue or Red

1938   **Perf. 14**
RA8	PT2	1c olive green (Bl)	.40 .30
RA9	PT2	1c olive green (R)	.40 .30

No. RA2
Overprinted in
Violet

1938, Nov. 20
RA10 PT2 1c olive green .40 .25
1st Central American Philatelic Exposition.

No. RA2
Overprinted in
Green or Black

1939
RA11 PT2 1c olive green (G) .40 .25
RA12 PT2 1c olive green (Bk) .40 .25

No. RA2
Overprinted in
Violet or Brown

1940
RA13 PT2 1c olive green (V) .40 .25
RA14 PT2 1c olive green (Br) .40 .25

No. RA2
Overprinted in
Red

1940, Apr. 14
RA15 PT2 1c olive green .40 .25
Pan American Union, 50th anniversary.

HAITI

'hā-tē

LOCATION — Western part of Hispaniola
GOVT. — Republic
AREA — 10,700 sq. mi.
POP. — 5,198,000 (est. 1984)
CAPITAL — Port-au-Prince

100 Centimes = 1 Piaster (1906)
100 Centimes = 1 Gourde

GREAT BRITAIN POST OFFICES IN HAITI

British postal agencies were opened in Jacmel in 1830 and in Port-au-Prince in 1842 and operated until June 30, 1881. During this period, British postal agencies also operated in Aux Cayes (1848-63), Cap Haitien (1842-63), Gonaives (1849-57), St. Marc (1854-61) and, possibly, Le Mole (ca. 1841). British stamps were used at the Jacmel agency from 1865 and at the Port-au-Prince agency from 1869.

Values are for clear cancellations on sound, fault-free stamps, with average to fine centering. In many cases, very fine copies are rare or non-existent.

JACMEL
Pre-Stamp Postmark

1843
Crowned Circle Handstamp Type II
A1 Inscribed "PAID AT JACMEL" in red, on cover 1,100.
Earliest known use 6/29/43.

Stamps of Great Britain
Canceled with barred oval "C59" obliterator

No. A31

1859-85
A2 ½p rose red, plates 4-6, 10-12, 14, 15 (#58), value from 65.00
A3 1p rose red, plates 74, 81, 84, 87, 95, 106, 107, 109, 122, 136, 137, 139, 146, 148, 150-152, 156, 157, 159, 160, 162, 164, 166, 167, 170, 171, 179, 181, 183, 186, 187, 189, 192, 194, 198, 200, 204, 206, 215, 219 (#33), value from 50.00
A4 1½p lake red, plate 3 (#32) 70.00
A5 2p blue, plate 9 (#29) 45.00
A6 2p blue, plates 13, 14, 15 (#30), value from 45.00
A7 2½p claret, plate 4 (#67) —
A8 3p rose, plates 5-10 (#49), value from 52.50
A9 3p rose, plates 11, 12, 14, 16-19 (#61), value from 55.00
A10 4p vermilion, hair lines (#34c) 130.00
A11 4p vermilion, plates 7-13 (#43), value from 52.50
A12 4p vermilion, plate 15 (#69) 325.00
A13 4p pale olive green, plate 15 (#70) 225.00
Plate 16 (#70) 210.00
A14 4p gray brown, plate 17 (#71) 350.00
A15 4p gray brown, plate 17 (#84) 60.00
A16 6p dull violet, plate 6 (#51) 85.00
A17 6p violet, plates 8, 9 (#51) 80.00
A18 6p brown plate 11 (#59)
a. 6p pale buff, plate 11 (#59b) 90.00
Plate 12 (#59b) 100.00
A19 6p gray, plate 12 (#60)
A20 6p gray, plates 13-17 (#62), value from 60.00
A21 8p orange (#73) 350.00
A22 9p straw (#40) 300.00
A23 9p straw (#46) 225.00
A24 10p red brown (#53) 325.00
A25 1sh green, plate 4 (#48) 150.00
A26 1sh green, plates 4-7 (#54), value from 50.00
A27 1sh green, plates 8-13 (#64), value from 75.00
A28 1sh salmon, plate 13 (#65) 425.00
A29 2sh blue (#55) 150.00
A30 2sh brown (#56) 2,500.
A31 5sh rose, plate 1 (#57) 500.00
Plate 2 (#57) 675.00

1880
A32 ½p deep green (#78) 80.00
A33 1p red brown (#79) 80.00
A34 1½p red brown (#80) 110.00
A35 2p lilac rose (#81) 150.00

PORT-AU-PRINCE
Pre-Stamp Postmark

1843
Crowned Circle Handstamp Type II
A40 Inscribed "PAID AT PORT-AU-PRINCE" in red, on cover 3,000.
Earliest known use 6/29/43.

Stamps of Great Britain
Canceled with barred oval "E53" obliterator

1865-81
A45 ½p rose red, plates 5,6, 10-14 (#58), value from 65.00
A46 1p rose red, plates 87, 134, 154, 159, 167, 171, 173, 174, 177, 181, 183, 187, 189, 192, 193, 199-202, 206, 210, 218, 219 (#33), value from 50.00
A47 1½p lake red, plate 3 (#32) 80.00
A48 2p blue, plate 9 (#29) 55.00
A49 2p blue, plates 14, 15 (#30), value from 55.00
A50 2½p claret, plates 3, 9 (#67), value from 165.00
A51 3p rose, plates 6, 7 (#49) —
A52 3p rose, plates 17, 18, 20 (#61), value from 55.00
A53 4p vermilion, plates 11-14 (#43), value from 55.00
A54 4p vermilion, plate 15 (#69) 325.00
A55 4p pale olive green, plate 15 (#70) 225.00
Plate 16 (#70) 210.00
A56 4p gray brown, plate 17 (#71) 350.00
A57 4p gray brown, plate 17 (#84) 60.00
A58 6p gray, plates 15, 16 (#62) —
A59 8p orange (#73) 350.00
A60 1sh green, plates 4-7 (#54), value from 50.00
A61 1sh green, plates 8-13 (#64), value from 75.00
A62 1sh salmon, plate 13 (#65) 425.00
A63 1sh salmon, plates 13, 14 (#87) 140.00
A64 2sh blue (#55) 175.00
A65 2sh brown (#56) 2,500.
A66 5sh rose, plate 1 (#57) 500.00
Plate 2 (#57) 675.00
A67 10sh slate (#74) 4,000.

1880
A68 ½p deep green (#78) 80.00
A69 1p red brown (#79) 80.00
A70 1½p red brown (#80) 110.00
A71 2p lilac rose (#81) 150.00

ISSUES OF THE REPUBLIC
Watermark

Wmk. 131 — RH

Liberty Head — A1

A3 A4

On A3 (Nos. 18, 19) there are crossed lines of dots on face. On A4 the "5" is 3mm wide, on A1 2½mm wide.

1881 Unwmk. Typo. Imperf.
Surface-colored Paper
1 A1 1c vermilion, yelsh 9.00 5.50
a. 1c carmine, yelsh 9.00 5.50
b. 1c rose red, cream 12.00 8.00
c. Vert. pair, tête-beche 3,000.
d. Paper colored on back only — 125.00

2 A1 2c violet, pale lil 11.00 5.50
a. 2c purple, pale lil 12.50 10.00
b. 2c purple, white 17.50
c. Vert. pair, tête-beche 1,250.
d. Paper colored on back only — 80.00
3 A1 3c olive bister, pale 20.00 8.00
bis
a. 3c olive bister, cream 20.00 10.00
4 A1 5c yel green, grnsh 32.50 16.00
a. 5c blue green, grnsh 32.50 16.00
5 A1 7c deep blue, grysh 22.00 4.00
a. 7c pale blue, grysh 22.00 4.00
6 A1 20c red brown, yelsh 82.50 30.00
a. 20c brown, cream 85.00 32.50
Nos. 1-6 (6) 177.00 69.00

Nos. 1-6 were printed from plate I, Nos. 7-13 from plates II and III.

1882 Perf. 13½
7 A1 1c dp ver, dp yelsh ('83) 5.75 2.10
a. Vert. pair imperf. btwn. 200.00 250.00
b. 1c pale ver, pale yelsh ('84) 5.75 2.25
c. As "b," vert. pair, imperf between 200.00 250.00
8 A1 2c dp purple, pale lil ('83) 11.00 3.25
a. 2c dark violet, white ('84) 12.00 6.50
b. As "a," vert. pair, imperf. between 175.00 250.00
c. As "a.," horiz. pair, imperf between 175.00 250.00
d. 2c red violet, pale lilac ('85) 7.25 2.60
e. As "d," vert. pair, imperf between 175.00 275.00
f. As "d," horiz. pair, imperf between 175.00 275.00
9 A1 3c gray bister, pale bis ('83) 11.50 3.25
a. 3c olive bister, bister ('85) 11.50 3.25
b. As "a," horiz. pair, imperf between 125.00 225.00
10 A1 5c blue grn, grnsh ('85) 8.25 1.60
a. 5c yellow green, greenish ('85) 7.75 1.40
b. 5c deep green, greenish ('85) 7.75 1.40
c. As "b," horiz. pair, imperf between 190.00 275.00
11 A1 7c deep blue, grysh ('85) 10.50 2.10
a. Horiz. pair, imperf. between 150.00 250.00
12 A1 7c ultra, grysh ('85) 16.00 3.25
a. Vert. pair, imperf. between 150.00 250.00
13 A1 20c pale brn, yelsh ('86) 15.00 4.50
a. Vert. pair, imperf. between 175.00 275.00
b. 20c red brown, yellowish ('84) 20.00 8.00
c. As "b," vert. pair, imperf between 150.00 300.00
d. As "b," horiz. pair, imperf between 150.00 300.00
Nos. 7-13 (7) 78.00 20.05

Stamps perf. 14, 16 are postal forgeries.

1886-87 Perf. 13½
18 A3 1c vermilion, yelsh 5.75 2.00
a. Horiz. pair, imperf. vert. — 175.00
b. Horiz. pair, imperf. between 200.00 190.00
19 A3 2c dk violet, lilac 42.50 7.00
20 A4 5c green ('87) 20.00 2.75
Nos. 18-20 (3) 68.25 11.75

General Louis Etienne
Félicité Salomon — A5

1887 Engr. Perf. 14
21 A5 1c lake .40 .30
22 A5 2c violet 1.00 .70
23 A5 3c blue .70 .45
24 A5 5c green 50.00 .55
a. Double impression 325.00
Nos. 21-24 (4) 52.10 2.00

Imperfs. of Nos. 21-24 are plate proofs. Value per pair, $50.
Nos. 21-22 are known overprinted "R:S" and postally used. Neither is known unused. Overprint is of a provisional or revolutionary government.

No. 23 Handstamp
Surcharged in Red

1890
25 A5 2c on 3c blue 3.50 3.00
a. Inverted surcharge 12.00 16.00
b. Double surcharge 12.00 14.00
c. Double surcharge, one inverted — 20.00

Missing letters are frequently found. This applies to succeeding surcharged issues.

Coat of Arms — A7

1891　　　　　　**Perf. 13**
26　A7　1c violet　　　　1.00　.30
27　A7　2c blue　　　　　1.50　.30
28　A7　3c gray lilac　　　2.00　.45
　a.　3c slate　　　　　　　1.75　.55
29　A7　5c orange　　　　5.50　.50
30　A7　7c red　　　　　20.00　2.75
　　Nos. 26-30 (5)　　　30.00　4.30

Nos. 26-30 exist imperf. Value of unused pairs, each $50.
The 2c, 3c and 7c exist imperf. vertically. Value, each $10 and up.

No. 28 Surcharged Like No. 25 in Red

1892
31　A7　2c on 3c gray lilac　3.00　2.00
　a.　2c on 3c slate　　　　　3.50　2.25
　b.　Inverted surcharge　　24.00
　c.　Double surcharge　　　32.50
　d.　Pair, one without surcharge　32.50

Coat of Arms (Leaves Drooping) — A9

1892-95　Engr., Litho. (20c)　Perf. 14
32　A9　1c lilac　　　　　.40　.25
　b.　Double impression　　375.00
33　A9　2c deep blue　　　.50　.25
34　A9　3c gray　　　　　.70　.45
35　A9　5c orange　　　　2.75　.50
36　A9　7c red　　　　　.50　.25
　a.　Imperf., pair　　　30.00
37　A9　20c brown　　　1.40　1.00
　　Nos. 32-37 (6)　　　6.25　2.70

Nos. 32, 33, 35 exist in horiz. pairs, imperf. vert., Nos. 33, 35, in vert. pairs, imperf. horiz. No. 32 exists imperf. It is a proof.

1896　Engr.　Perf. 13½
38　A9　1c light blue　　.55　.70
39　A9　2c red brown　　.65　1.20
40　A9　3c lilac brown　　.55　1.20
41　A9　5c slate green　　.65　1.20
42　A9　7c dark gray　　.90　1.75
43　A9　20c orange　　1.10　2.25
　　Nos. 38-43 (6)　　4.40　8.30

Nos. 32-37 are 23¾mm high, Nos. 38-43 23¼mm to 23½mm. The "C" is closed on Nos. 32-37, open on Nos. 38-43. Other differences exist. The stamps of the two issues may be readily distinguished by their colors and perfs.
Nos. 38-43 exist imperf. and in horiz. pairs, imperf. vert. The 1c, 3c, 5c, 7c exist in vert. pairs, imperf. horiz. or imperf. between. The 5c, 7c exist in horiz. pairs, imperf. between. Value of unused pairs, $9 and up.

Nos. 37, 43 Surcharged Like No. 25 in Red

1898
44　A9　2c on 20c brown　3.00　6.00
　a.　Inverted surcharge　　27.50
　b.　Double surcharge　　32.50
45　A9　2c on 20c orange　1.75　1.40
　a.　Inverted surcharge　　18.00
　b.　Double surcharge　　27.50
　c.　Double surcharge, one inverted　35.00

No. 45 exists in various part perf. varieties.

Coat of Arms — A11

1898　Wmk. 131　Perf. 11
46　A11　1c ultra　　　2.50　2.50
47　A11　2c brown carmine　.55　.40
48　A11　3c dull violet　2.50　2.50
49　A11　5c dark green　.55　.40
　a.　Double impression　　375.00
50　A11　7c gray　　　5.00　5.00
51　A11　20c orange　10.00　10.00
　　Nos. 46-51 (6)　21.10　20.80

Nos. 46-51 exist imperforate. They are plate proofs. Value, each $10 and up.

Pres. T. Augustin Simon Sam — A12 / Coat of Arms — A13

1898-99　Unwmk.　Perf. 12
52　A12　1c ultra　　　.25　.25
53　A13　1c yel green ('99)　.25　.25
54　A12　2c deep orange　.25　.25
55　A13　2c car lake ('99)　.25　.25
56　A12　3c green　　　.25　.25
57　A13　4c red　　　.25　.25
58　A12　5c red brown　.25　.25
59　A13　5c pale blue ('99)　.25　.25
60　A12　7c gray　　　.25　.25
61　A13　8c carmine　.25　.25
62　A13　10c orange red　.25　.25
63　A13　15c olive green　.60　.45
64　A12　20c black　　.60　.45
65　A12　50c rose brown　1.00　.50
66　A12　1g red violet　2.25　2.00
　　Nos. 52-66 (15)　7.20　6.15

For overprints see Nos. 67-81, 110-124, 169, 247-248.

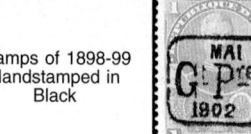

Stamps of 1898-99 Handstamped in Black

1902
67　A12　1c ultra　　　.60　1.50
　a.　Inverted overprint　3.50
　b.　Pair, one without overprint　40.00
68　A13　1c yellow green　.45　.30
　a.　Inverted overprint　3.50
　b.　Double overprint　30.00
　c.　Pair, one without overprint　50.00
69　A12　2c deep orange　.80　1.50
　a.　Inverted overprint　4.50
　b.　Double overprint　6.00
　c.　Pair, one without overprint　50.00
70　A13　2c carmine lake　.45　.30
　a.　Inverted overprint　4.00
　b.　Double overprint　6.00
71　A12　3c green　　　.45　.45
　a.　Inverted overprint　3.50
72　A13　4c red　　　.60　.90
　a.　Inverted overprint　3.50
　b.　Double overprint　6.00
　c.　Pair, one without overprint　50.00
73　A12　5c red brown　1.25　6.00
　a.　Inverted overprint　6.00
74　A13　5c pale blue　.45　.45
　a.　Inverted overprint　3.75
　b.　Double overprint　20.00
75　A12　7c gray　　　.95　.95
　a.　Inverted overprint　4.00
　b.　Double overprint　6.00
76　A13　8c carmine　.95　8.50
　a.　Inverted overprint　5.00
　b.　Double overprint　6.00
77　A13　10c orange red　.95　1.50
　a.　Inverted overprint　6.00
　b.　Double overprint　6.00
78　A13　15c olive green　5.00　7.00
　a.　Inverted overprint　18.00
　b.　Double overprint　10.00
79　A12　20c black　　5.00　6.00
　a.　Inverted overprint　14.00
　b.　Double overprint　16.00
80　A12　50c rose brown　17.50　37.50
　a.　Inverted overprint　45.00
81　A12　1g red violet　25.00　60.00
　a.　Inverted overprint　120.00
　b.　Pair, one without overprint　75.00
　　Nos. 67-81 (15)　60.40　132.85

Many forgeries exist of this overprint.
Specialists have called into question the existence of the double-overprint errors listed for this set except Nos. 68b and 74b. The editors would like to see documented evidence of the existence of Nos. 69b, 70b, 72b, 75b, 76b, 77b, 78b, 79b and 81b.

Centenary of Independence Issues

Coat of Arms — A14

Francois-Dominique Toussaint L'Ouverture — A15
Emperor Jean Jacques Dessalines A16
Pres. Alexandre Sabes Pétion A17

1903, Dec. 31　Engr.　Perf. 13¼, 14
82　A14　1c green　　.35　.35

Center Engr., Frame Litho.
83　A15　2c rose & blk　1.25　3.00
84　A15　5c dull blue & blk　1.25　3.00
85　A16　7c plum & blk　1.25　3.00
86　A16　10c yellow & blk　1.25　3.00
87　A17　20c slate & blk　1.25　3.00
88　A17　50c olive & blk　1.25　3.00
　　Nos. 82-88 (7)　7.85　18.35

Nos. 82 to 88 exist imperforate.
Nos. 83-88 exist with centers inverted. Some are known with head omitted.
Forgeries exist both perforated and imperf and constitute the great majority of Nos. 83-88 offered in the marketplace. Stamps perforated 13½ are forgeries. Many forgeries exist with heads lithographed instead of engraved.

Same Handstamped in Blue

1904
89　A14　1c green　　.50　1.50
90　A15　2c rose & blk　.50　1.50
91　A15　5c dull blue & blk　.50　1.50
92　A16　7c plum & blk　.50　1.50
93　A16　10c yellow & blk　.50　1.50
94　A17　20c slate & blk　.50　1.50
95　A17　50c olive & blk　.50　1.50
　　Nos. 89-95 (7)　3.50　10.50

Two dies were used for the handstamped overprint on Nos. 89-95. Letters and figures are larger on one than on the other. All values exist imperforate.

Pres. Pierre Nord-Alexis — A18

1904　Engr.　Perf. 13¼, 14
96　A18　1c green　　.35　.35
97　A18　2c carmine　.35　.35
98　A18　5c dark blue　.35　.35
99　A18　10c orange brown　.35　.35
100　A18　20c orange　.35　.35
101　A18　50c claret　.35　.35
　a.　Tête bêche pair　500.00
　　Nos. 96-101 (6)　2.10　2.10

Used values are for c-t-o's. Postally used examples are worth considerably more.
Nos. 96-101 exist imperforate. Value, set $10.
This issue, and the overprints and surcharges, exist in horiz. pairs, imperf. vert., and in vert. pairs, imperf. horiz.
For overprints and surcharges see Nos. 102-109, 150-161, 170-176, 217-218, 235-238, 240-242, 302-303.
Forgeries of Nos. 96, 101, 101a exist.
Reprints or very accurate imitations of this issue exist, including No. 101a. Some are printed in very bright colors on very white paper and are found both perforated and imperforate. The original stamps are perf. 13¼ or 14, the reprints (forgeries) perf. 13½, as well as numerous other perforations, including compound perfs.

Same Handstamped in Blue like Nos. 89-95

1904
102　A18　1c green　　.60　1.50
103　A18　2c carmine　.60　1.50
104　A18　5c dark blue　.60　1.50
105　A18　10c orange brown　.60　1.50
106　A18　20c orange　.60　1.50
107　A18　50c claret　.60　1.50
　　Nos. 102-107 (6)　3.60　9.00

The note after No. 95 applies also to Nos. 102-107. All values exist imperf.
Forgeries exist.

Regular Issue of 1904 Handstamp Surcharged in Black

1906, Feb. 20
108　A18　1c on 20c orange　.35　.25
　a.　1c on 50c claret　950.00
109　A18　2c on 50c claret　.35　.25

No. 108a is known only with inverted surcharge.
Forgeries exist.

Nos. 52-66 Handstamped in Red

1906
110　A12　1c ultra　　1.40　.95
　a.　Inverted overprint　3.00
111　A13　1c yellow green　.75　.75
　a.　Inverted overprint　25.00
112　A12　2c deep orange　2.50　2.25
　a.　Inverted overprint　3.00　25.00
113　A13　2c carmine lake　1.50　1.25
　a.　Inverted overprint　3.00
114　A12　3c green　　1.50　1.25
　a.　Inverted overprint　3.00　10.00
115　A13　4c red　　5.75　4.50
　a.　Pair, one without overprint　70.00
116　A12　5c red brown　7.00　5.50
　a.　Inverted overprint　10.00
117　A13　5c pale blue　1.10　.60
　a.　Inverted overprint　3.75
118　A12　7c gray　　5.00　4.50
　a.　Inverted overprint　20.00
119　A13　8c carmine　1.10　1.00
　a.　Inverted overprint　5.00
　b.　Double overprint　60.00
　c.　Pair, one without overprint　70.00
120　A13　10c orange red　2.00　1.25
　a.　Inverted overprint　6.00
　b.　Pair, one without overprint　70.00　100.00
121　A13　15c olive green　2.50　1.25
　a.　Inverted overprint　18.00
122　A12　20c black　5.75　4.50
123　A12　50c rose brown　5.50　3.50
　a.　Inverted overprint　45.00
124　A12　1g red violet　15.00　10.00
　a.　Inverted overprint　120.00
　　Nos. 110-124 (15)　58.35　43.05

Forgeries of this overprint are plentiful.

Coat of Arms — A19

President Nord-Alexis A20

Market at Port-au-Prince A21

Sans Souci Palace — A22

Independence Palace at Gonaives — A23

Entrance to Catholic College at Port-au-Prince A24

Monastery and Church at Port-au-Prince A25

Seat of Government at Port-au-Prince A26

Presidential Palace at Port-au-Prince A27

For Foreign Postage (centimes de piastre)

1906-13 — **Perf. 12**

125	A19	1c de p	green	.35	.25
126	A20	2c de p	ver	.45	.25
127	A21	3c de p	brown	.60	.25
128	A21	3c de p	org yel ('11)	6.00	6.00
129	A22	4c de p	car lake	.60	.35
130	A22	4c de p	lt ol grn ('13)	25.00	25.00
131	A20	5c de p	dk blue	2.50	.30
132	A23	7c de p	gray	1.75	.85
133	A23	7c de p	org red ('13)	65.00	65.00
134	A24	8c de p	car rose	1.75	.80
135	A24	8c de p	ol grn ('13)	55.00	35.00
136	A25	10c de p	org red	1.25	.30
137	A25	10c de p	red brn ('13)	27.50	22.50
138	A26	15c de p	sl grn	2.25	.90
139	A26	15c de p p	yel ('13)	20.00	12.00
140	A20	20c de p	blue grn	2.25	.90
141	A19	50c de p	red	3.25	2.25
142	A19	50c de p	org yel ('13)	20.00	12.00
143	A27	1p	claret	7.25	4.50
144	A27	1p	red ('13)	13.00	11.00
			Nos. 125-144 (20)	255.75	200.40

All 1906 values exist imperf. These are plate proofs.

For overprints and surcharges see Nos. 177-195, 213-216, 239, 245, 249-260, 263, 265-277, 279-284, 286-301, 304.

Nord-Alexis A28

Coat of Arms — A29

For Domestic Postage (centimes de gourde)

1906-10

145	A28	1c de g	blue	.35	.25
146	A29	2c de g	org yel	.45	.25
147	A29	2c de g	lemon ('10)	.65	.25
148	A28	3c de g	slate	.40	.25
149	A29	7c de g	green	1.25	.45
			Nos. 145-149 (5)	3.10	1.45

For overprints see Nos. 196-197.

Regular Issue of 1904 Handstamp Surcharged in Red like Nos. 108-109

1907

150	A18	1c on 5c	dk bl	.40	.35
151	A18	1c on 20c	org	.40	.25
152	A18	2c on 10c	org brn	.40	.40
153	A18	2c on 50c	claret	.50	.40

Black Surcharge

154	A18	1c on 5c	dk bl	.50	.40
155	A18	1c on 10c	org brn	.50	.25
156	A18	2c on 20c	org	.40	.40

Brown Surcharge

157	A18	1c on 5c	dk bl	1.50	1.25
158	A18	1c on 10c	org brn	1.50	1.25
159	A18	2c on 20c	org	5.00	4.00
160	A18	2c on 50c	claret	27.50	22.50

Violet Surcharge

161	A18	1c on 20c	org		150.00

The handstamps are found sideways, diagonal, inverted and double.
Forgeries exist.

A30

President Antoine T. Simon — A31

1910 — **For Foreign Postage**

162	A30	2c de p	rose red & blk	.65	.50
163	A30	5c de p	bl & blk	13.00	1.00
164	A30	20c de p	yel grn & blk	12.50	12.50

For Domestic Postage

165	A31	1c de g	lake & blk	.30	.25
			Nos. 162-165 (4)	26.45	14.25

For overprint and surcharges see Nos. 198, 262, 278, 285.

A32

A33

Pres. Cincinnatus Leconte — A34

1912

166	A32	1c de g	car lake	.40	.40
167	A33	2c de g	dp org	.50	.40

For Foreign Postage

168	A34	5c de p	dp blue	.90	.40
			Nos. 166-168 (3)	1.80	1.20

For overprints see Nos. 199-201.

Stamps of Preceding Issues Handstamped Vertically

1914 — **On No. 61**

169	A13	8c	carmine	13.00	10.00

On Nos. 96-101

170	A18	1c	green	35.00	30.00
171	A18	2c	carmine	35.00	30.00
172	A18	5c	dk blue	.65	.40
173	A18	10c	orange brn	.65	.40
174	A18	20c	orange	1.10	.50
175	A18	50c	claret	2.50	1.25
			Nos. 170-175 (6)	74.90	62.55

Perforation varieties of Nos. 172-175 exist. No. 175 overprinted "T. M." is a revenue stamp. The letters are the initials of "Timbre Mobile."

On No. 107

176	A18	50c	claret	10,000.	13,000.

Horizontally on Stamps of 1906-13

177	A19	1c de p	green	.55	.45
178	A20	2c de p	ver	.75	.45
179	A21	3c de p	brown	1.25	.65
180	A21	3c de p	org yel	.55	.45
181	A22	4c de p	car lake	1.25	.65
182	A22	4c de p	lt ol grn	3.00	1.60
183	A23	7c de p	gray	2.75	2.75
184	A23	7c de p	org red	7.25	6.75
185	A24	8c de p	car rose	5.00	4.50
186	A24	8c de p	ol grn	9.25	9.00
187	A25	10c de p	org red	1.50	.65
188	A25	10c de p	red brn	4.00	2.50
189	A26	15c de p	sl grn	4.25	3.75
190	A26	15c de p	yellow	3.00	1.60
191	A20	20c de p	bl grn	3.75	1.40
192	A19	50c de p	red	6.50	6.00
193	A19	50c de p	org yel	11.00	10.00
194	A27	1p	claret	6.50	6.00
195	A27	1p	red	12.00	11.00
196	A29	2c de g	lemon	.55	.45
197	A28	3c de g	slate	.55	.45
			Nos. 177-197 (21)	85.20	71.05

On No. 164

198	A30	20c de p	yel grn & blk	3.75	3.50

Vertically on Nos. 166-168

199	A32	1c de g	car lake	.50	.40
200	A33	2c de g	dp org	.65	.50
201	A34	5c de p	dp blue	1.10	.40
			Nos. 199-201 (3)	2.25	1.30

Two handstamps were used for the overprints on Nos. 169-201. They may be distinguished by the short and long foot of the "L" of "GL" and the position of the first "1" in "1914" with regard to the period above it. Both handstamps are found on all but Nos. 176, 294, 295, 306, 308.

Handstamp Surcharged

On Nos. 141 and 143

213	A19	1c de p on 50c de p	red	.50	.40
214	A27	1c de p on 1p	claret	.65	.50

On Nos. 142 and 144

215	A19	1c de p on 50c de p	org yel	.65	.50
216	A27	1c de p on 1p	red	.65	.50

Handstamp Surcharged

On Nos. 100 and 101

217	A18	7c on 20c	orange	.50	.25
218	A18	7c on 50c	claret	.45	.25

The initials on the preceding handstamps are those of Gen. Oreste Zamor; the date is that of his triumphal entry into Port-au-Prince.

Pres. Oreste Zamor

Coat of Arms

Pres. Tancrède Auguste

Owing to the theft of a large quantity of this 1914 issue, while in transit from the printers, the stamps were never placed on sale at post offices. A few stamps have been canceled through carelessness of favor. Value, set of 10, $8.50.

Preceding Issues Handstamp Surcharged in Carmine or Blue

1915-16 — **On Nos. 98-101**

235	A18	1c on 5c	dk bl (C)	2.00	2.25
236	A18	1c on 10c	org brn	.60	.75
237	A18	1c on 20c	orange	.60	.75
238	A18	1c on 50c	claret	.60	.75

On No. 132

239	A23	1c on 7c de p	gray (C)	.60	.75

On Nos. 106-107

240	A18	1c on 20c	orange	1.50	1.50
241	A18	1c on 50c	claret	3.50	1.50
242	A18	1c on 50c	cl (C)	125.00	125.00
			Nos. 235-242 (8)	134.40	133.25

Nos. 240-242 are known with two types of the "Post Paye" overprint. No. 237 with red surcharge and any stamps with violet surcharge are unofficial.

Values for Nos. 245-308 are for examples with the boxed "Gourde" surcharge partially on the stamp. Examples upon which this surcharge is fully present on the stamp command substantial premiums.

No. 143
Handstamp
Surcharged in
Red

1917-19
245 A27 2c on 1p claret .50 .50

Stamps of 1906-14 Handstamp Surcharged in Various Colors

1c, 5c

On Nos. 123-124
247 A12 1c on 50c (R) 90.00 40.00
248 A12 1c on 1g (R) 90.00 40.00

On #127, 129, 134, 136, 138, 140-141
249 A22 1c on 4c de p (Br) .65 .75
250 A25 1c on 10c de p (Bl) .65 .75
252 A20 1c on 20c de p (Bk) .65 .75
253 A20 1c on 20c de p (Bk) .65 .75
254 A19 1c on 50c de p (R) .65 .75
255 A19 1c on 50c de p (Bk) .65 .75
256 A21 2c on 3c de p (R) .65 .75
257 A24 2c on 8c de p (R) .65 .75
258 A24 2c on 8c de p (Bk) .65 .75
259 A26 2c on 15c de p (R) .65 .75
260 A20 2c on 20c de p (R) .65 .75
Nos. 249-260 (11) 7.15 8.25

The 1c on 10c de p stamp in black is actually a blue ink which bled into the stamps.

On Nos. 164, 128
262 A30 1c on 20c de p (Bk) 3.75 3.50
263 A21 2c on 3c de p (R) .60 .75

On #130, 133, 135, 137, 139, 142, 144
265 A22 1c on 4c de p (R) .70 .85
266 A23 1c on 7c de p (Br) .70 .85
267 A26 1c on 15c de p (R) .70 .85
268 A19 1c on 50c de p (Bk) 2.25 2.75
269 A27 1c on 1p (Bk) 2.25 2.75
270 A24 2c on 8c de p (R) .70 .85
271 A25 2c on 10c de p (Br) .70 .85
272 A26 2c on 15c de p (R) .70 .85
273 A25 5c on 10c de p (Bl) 2.25 2.75
274 A25 5c on 10c de p (VBk) .70 .85
275 A26 5c on 15c de p (R) 5.50 6.75
Nos. 265-275 (11) 17.15 20.95

"O. Z." Stamps of 1914 Handstamp Surcharged in Red or Brown

276 A26 1c on 15c de p sl grn .70 .85
277 A20 1c on 20c de p bl grn .70 .85
278 A30 1c on 20c de p yel grn & blk .70 .85
279 A27 1c on 1p claret (Br) .70 .85
280 A27 1c on 1p claret 2.25 2.75
281 A27 5c on 1p red (Br) .70 .85
Nos. 276-281 (6) 5.75 7.00

Srchd. in Violet, Green, Red, Magenta or Black 1 ct and 2 cts as in 1917-19 and

1919-20
282 A22 2c on 4c de p car lake (V) .70 .85
283 A24 2c on 8c de p car rose (G) .70 .85
284 A24 2c on 8c de p ol grn (R) .70 .85
285 A30 2c on 20c de p yel grn & blk (R) .85 1.10

286 A19 2c on 50c de p red (G)
288 A19 2c on 50c de p red (R) .70 .85
289 A19 2c on 50c de p org yel (R) .70 .85
290 A27 2c on 1pi red (R) 8.00 4.00
291 A27 2c on 1pi red (R) 2.25 2.75
292 A21 3c on 3c de p brn (R) .70 .85
293 A23 3c on 7c de p org red (R) .70 .85
294 A21 3c on 3c de p brn (R) .70 .85
295 A21 5c on 3c de p org yel (R) 2.25 2.75
296 A22 5c on 4c de p car lake (R) .70 .85
297 A22 5c on 4c de p ol grn (R) .70 .85
298 A23 5c on 7c de p gray (V) .70 .85
299 A23 5c on 7c de p org red (V) .70 .85
300 A25 5c on 10c de p org red (V) .70 .85
301 A26 5c on 15c de p yel (M) .70 .85
Nos. 282-301 (19) 19.35 23.35

Nos. 217 and 218 Handstamp Surcharged with New Value in Magenta
302 A18 5c on 7c on 20c orange .60 .75
303 A18 5c on 7c on 50c claret 3.50 4.00

No. 187
Handstamp
Surcharged in
Magenta

304 A25 5c de p on 10c de p .60 .75

Postage Due
Stamps of 1906-
14 Handstamp
Surcharged in
Black or
Magenta (#308)

On Stamp of 1906
305 D2 5c on 50c ol gray 15.00 15.00
On Stamp of 1914
306 D2 5c on 10c violet .60 .75
307 D2 5c on 50c olive gray .60 .75
308 D2 5c on 50c ol gray (M) 2.50 2.00
Nos. 305-308 (4) 18.70 18.50

Nos. 299 with red surcharge and 306-307 with violet are trial colors or essays.

Allegory of Agriculture A40

Allegory of Commerce A41

1920, Apr.   **Engr.**   **Perf. 12**
310 A40 3c deep orange .40 .40
311 A40 5c green .40 .40
312 A41 10c vermilion .50 .40
313 A41 15c violet .50 .40
314 A41 25c deep blue .65 .50
Nos. 310-314 (5) 2.45 2.10

Nos. 311-313 overprinted "T. M." are revenue stamps. The letters are the initials of "Timbre Mobile."

President Louis J. Borno — A42

Christophe's Citadel — A43

Old Map of West Indies — A44

Borno — A45

National Capitol — A46

1924, Sept. 3
315 A42 5c deep green .40 .25
316 A43 10c carmine .40 .25
317 A44 20c violet blue .90 .40
318 A45 50c orange & blk .90 .40
319 A46 1g olive green 1.60 .50
Nos. 315-319 (5) 4.20 1.80

For surcharges see Nos. 359 (in Scott Standard catalogue, Vol.3), C4A.

Coffee Beans and Flowers — A47

1928, Feb. 6
320 A47 35c deep green 3.75 .60
For surcharge see No. 337.

Pres. Louis Borno — A48

1929, Nov. 4
321 A48 10c carmine rose .50 .40
Signing of the "Frontier" treaty between Haiti and the Dominican Republic.

Presidents Salomon and Vincent — A49

Pres. Sténio Vincent — A50

1931, Oct. 16
322 A49 5c deep green 1.30 .50
323 A50 10c carmine rose 1.30 .50
50th anniv. of Haiti's joining the UPU.

President Vincent — A52

Aqueduct at Port-au-Prince A53

Fort National — A54

Palace of Sans Souci — A55

Christophe's Chapel at Milot — A56

King's Gallery Citadel — A57

Vallières Battery — A58

1933-40
325 A52 3c orange .30 .25
326 A52 3c dp ol grn ('39) .30 .25
327 A53 5c green .30 .25
  a. 5c emerald ('38) .30 .25
  b. 5c bright green ('39) .30 .25
  c. 5c brown olive ('40) .50 .25
329 A54 10c rose car .50 .25
  a. 10c vermilion .65 .25
330 A54 10c red brn ('40) .50 .25
331 A55 25c blue .90 .25
332 A56 50c brown 2.50 .55
333 A57 1g dark green 2.50 .55
334 A58 2.50g olive bister 4.50 .90
Nos. 325-334 (9) 12.30 3.50

For surcharges see Nos. 357-358, 360 in Scott Standard catalogue, Vol. 3.

Alexandre Dumas, His Father and Son — A59

1935, Dec. 29   **Litho.**   **Perf. 11½**
335 A59 10c rose pink & choc .90 .40
336 A59 25c blue & chocolate 1.60 .50
Nos. 335-336,C10 (3) 7.00 3.40

Visit of a delegation from France to Haiti. No. 335 exists imperf and in horiz. pair, imperf. between. No. 336 exists as pair, imperf horiz.

No. 320 Surcharged in Red

1939, Jan. 24   *Perf. 12*
337 A47 25c on 35c dp grn   .90 .40

SEMI-POSTAL STAMPS

Pierre de
Coubertin
SP1

Engraved & Litho (flag)
1939, Oct. 3   **Unwmk.**   *Perf. 12*
B1 SP1 10c + 10c multi   27.50 27.50
    Nos. B1,CB1-CB2 (3)   77.50 77.50

Pierre de Coubertin, organizer of the modern Olympic Games. The surtax was used to build a Sports Stadium at Port-au-Prince.

AIR POST STAMPS

Plane over Port-au-Prince — AP1

1929-30   **Unwmk.**   **Engr.**   *Perf. 12*
C1 AP1 25c dp grn ('30)   .50 .40
C2 AP1 50c dp vio   .65 .40
C3 AP1 75c red brn ('30)   1.75 1.25
C4 AP1 1g dp ultra   1.90 1.60
    Nos. C1-C4 (4)   4.80 3.65

AP1a

1933, July 6   **Red Surcharge**
C4A AP1a 60c on 20c blue   75.00 80.00

Non-stop flight of Capt. J. Errol Boyd and Robert G. Lyon from New York to Port-au-Prince.

Plane over Christophe's
Citadel — AP2

1933-40
C5 AP2 50c org brn   5.25 1.00
C6 AP2 50c ol grn ('35)   4.00 1.00
C7 AP2 50c car rose ('37)   3.50 2.00
C8 AP2 50c blk ('38)   2.00 1.00
C8A AP2 60c choc ('40)   1.10 .50
C9 AP2 1g ultra   1.75 .50
    Nos. C5-C9 (6)   17.60 6.00

For surcharge see No. C24 in Scott Standard catalogue, Vol. 3.

Dumas Type of Regular Issue

1935, Dec. 29   **Litho.**   *Perf. 11½*
C10 A59 60c brt vio & choc   4.50 2.50
   Visit of delegation from France to Haiti.

Arms of Haiti and Portrait of George
Washington — AP4

1938, Aug. 29   **Engr.**   *Perf. 12*
C11 AP4 60c deep blue   .70 .40
   150th anniv. of the US Constitution.

AIR POST SEMI-POSTAL STAMPS

Coubertin Semipostal Type of 1939
Unwmk.
1939, Oct. 3   **Engr.**   *Perf. 12*
CB1 SP1 60c + 40c multi   25.00 25.00
CB2 SP1 1.25g + 60c multi   25.00 25.00

POSTAGE DUE STAMPS

D1

1898, Aug. Unwmk. Engr.   *Perf. 12*
J1 D1 2c black   1.00 .75
J2 D1 5c red brown   1.50 1.00
J3 D1 10c brown orange   2.00 1.50
J4 D1 50c slate   3.00 2.50
    Nos. J1-J4 (4)   7.50 5.75

For overprints see Nos. J5-J9, J14-J16.

Stamps of 1898 Handstamped like Nos. 67-81

1902   **Black Overprint**
J5 D1 2c black   2.50 1.50
J6 D1 5c red brown   2.50 1.50
J7 D1 10c brown orange   2.50 1.50
J8 D1 50c slate   12.00 7.00

Red Overprint
J9 D1 2c black   3.50 3.50
    Nos. J5-J9 (5)   23.00 15.00

D2

1906
J10 D2 2c dull red   1.50 1.00
J11 D2 5c ultra   2.75 2.50
J12 D2 10c violet   2.75 2.50
J13 D2 50c olive gray   11.50 7.50
    Nos. J10-J13 (4)   18.50 13.50

For surcharges and overprints see Nos. 305-308, J17-J20.

Preceding Issues Handstamped like Nos. 169-201

1914   **On Stamps of 1898**
J14 D1 5c red brown   1.50 1.10
J15 D1 10c brown orange   1.50 1.10
J16 D1 50c slate   6.00 5.50
    Nos. J14-J16 (3)   9.00 7.70

On Stamps of 1906
J17 D2 2c dull red   1.25 1.00
J18 D2 5c ultra   2.25 2.25
J19 D2 10c violet   7.50 5.50
J20 D2 50c olive gray   45.00 45.00
    Nos. J17-J20 (4)   56.00 53.75

The note after No. 201 applies to Nos. J14-J20 also.

HATAY

hä-'tī

LOCATION — Northwest of Syria, bordering on Mediterranean Sea.
GOVT. — Former semi-independent republic
AREA — 10,000 sq. mi. (approx.)
POP. — 273,350 (1939)
CAPITAL — Antioch

Alexandretta, a semi-autonomous district of Syria under French mandate, was renamed Hatay in 1938 and transferred to Turkey in 1939.

100 Santims = 1 Kurush
40 Paras = 1 Kurush (1939)

Stamps of Turkey, 1931-38, Surcharged in Black

On A77   On A78

1939   **Unwmk.**   *Perf. 11½x12*
1 A77   10s on 20pa dp org   1.75 .35
   Never hinged   3.50
a.   "Sent" instead of "Sant"   135.00 22.50
   Never hinged   300.00
2 A78   25s on 1ku dk sl grn   2.00 .35
   Never hinged   4.00
a.   Small "25"   13.50 1.50
   Never hinged   28.00
3 A78   50s on 2ku dk vio   2.00 .35
   Never hinged   4.00
a.   Small "50"   6.00 2.00
   Never hinged   14.00
4 A77   75s on 2½ku green   1.75 .40
   Never hinged   3.50
5 A78   1ku on 4ku slate   10.00 4.25
   Never hinged   20.00
6 A78   1ku on 5ku rose red   5.50 1.40
   Never hinged   11.00
7 A78   1½ku on 3ku brn org   2.75 .80
   Never hinged   5.50
8 A78   2½ku on 4ku slate   3.75 1.00
   Never hinged   7.50
9 A78   5ku on 8ku brt blue   6.00 1.25
   Never hinged   12.00
10 A77   12½ku on 20ku ol grn   7.00 2.00
   Never hinged   14.00
11 A77   20ku on 25ku Prus bl   13.00 7.00
   Never hinged   30.00
    Nos. 1-11 (11)   55.50 19.15
   Set, never hinged   115.00

Map of
Hatay — A1

Flag of
Hatay
A3

Post Office
A4

1939   **Unwmk.**   **Typo.**   *Perf. 12*
12 A1   10p orange & aqua   2.50 .75
   Never hinged   5.00
13 A1   30p lt vio & aqua   2.50 .75
   Never hinged   5.00
14 A1   1½ku olive & aqua   2.50 .75
   Never hinged   5.00
15 A2   2½ku turq grn   3.00 1.00
   Never hinged   6.00
16 A2   3ku light blue   3.00 1.00
   Never hinged   6.00
17 A2   5ku chocolate   3.00 1.00
   Never hinged   6.00
18 A3   6ku brt blue & car   3.75 1.25
   Never hinged   7.50
19 A3   7½ku dp green & car   4.25 1.40
   Never hinged   8.50
20 A3   12ku violet & car   5.00 1.40
   Never hinged   10.00
21 A3   12½ku dk blue & car   4.00 1.50
   Never hinged   8.00
22 A4   17½ku brown car   8.00 3.00
   Never hinged   16.00
23 A4   25ku olive brn   9.00 3.50
   Never hinged   18.00
24 A4   50ku slate blue   18.00 8.50
   Never hinged   45.00
    Nos. 12-24 (13)   68.50 25.80
   Set, never hinged   146.00

Stamps of 1939
Overprinted in
Black

1939
25 A1   10p orange & aqua   1.75 .75
   Never hinged   3.50
a.   Overprint reading up   30.00
   Never hinged   45.00
26 A1   30p lt vio & aqua   1.75 .75
   Never hinged   3.50
27 A1   1½ku ol & aqua   2.50 .80
   Never hinged   5.00
28 A2   2½ku turq grn   2.50 .80
   Never hinged   5.00 5.00
29 A2   3ku light blue   2.75 .80
   Never hinged   5.50
30 A2   5ku chocolate   3.50 1.25
   Never hinged   7.00
a.   Overprint inverted   30.00
   Never hinged   45.00
31 A3   6ku brt bl & car   3.75 1.25
   Never hinged   7.50
32 A3   7½ku dp grn & car   4.00 1.25
   Never hinged   8.00
33 A3   12ku vio & car   4.00 1.25
   Never hinged   8.00
34 A3   12½ku dk bl & car   4.50 1.25
   Never hinged   9.00
35 A4   17½ku brn car   5.50 2.25
   Never hinged   11.00
a.   Overprint inverted   30.00
   Never hinged   45.00
36 A4   25ku olive brn   9.00 4.25
   Never hinged   22.00
37 A4   50ku slate blue   19.00 10.00
   Never hinged   50.00
    Nos. 25-37 (13)   64.50 26.65
   Set, never hinged   145.00

The overprint reads "Date of annexation to the Turkish Republic, June 30, 1939."
On Nos. 25-27, the overprint reads down. On Nos. 28-37, it is horizontal.

POSTAGE DUE STAMPS

Postage Due Stamps of
Turkey, 1936,
Surcharged or
Overprinted in Black

1939   **Unwmk.**   *Perf. 11½*
J1 D6   1ku on 2ku lt bl   3.75 .70
   Never hinged   7.50
J2 D6   3ku bright violet   4.25 1.25
   Never hinged   8.50
J3 D6   4ku on 5ku Prus bl   4.25 1.25
   Never hinged   8.50

Lions of
Antioch
A2

J4	D6	5ku on 12ku brt rose	4.75	1.25
		Never hinged	12.00	
J5	D6	12ku bright rose	52.50	35.00
		Never hinged	125.00	
		Nos. J1-J5 (5)	69.50	39.45
		Set, never hinged	100.00	

Castle at Antioch
D1

1939   **Typo.**   *Perf. 12*

J6	D1	1ku red orange	4.50	1.50
		Never hinged	9.00	
J7	D1	3ku dk olive brown	5.00	1.75
		Never hinged	10.00	
J8	D1	4ku turqoise green	5.50	2.00
		Never hinged	11.00	
J9	D1	5ku slate black	6.50	2.50
		Never hinged	13.00	
		Nos. J6-J9 (4)	21.50	7.75
		Set, never hinged	43.00	

Nos. J6-J9 Overprinted in Black like Nos. 25-37

1939

J10	D1	1ku red orange	4.25	1.50
		Never hinged	8.50	
J11	D1	3ku dk olive brown	5.00	1.75
		Never hinged	10.00	
J12	D1	4ku turqoise green	5.00	2.00
		Never hinged	10.00	
J13	D1	5ku slate black	7.25	2.50
		Never hinged	15.00	
a.		Overprint inverted	30.00	
		Never hinged	45.00	
		Nos. J10-J13 (4)	21.50	7.75
		Set, never hinged	44.00	

HELIGOLAND

'he-lə-gō-,land

LOCATION — An island in the North Sea near the northern coast of Germany
GOVT. — British Possession
AREA — ¼ sq. mi.
POP. — 2,307 (1900)

Great Britain ceded Heligoland to Germany in 1890. It became part of Schleswig-Holstein province. Stamps of Heligoland were superseded by those of the German Empire.

16 Schillings = 1 Mark
100 Pfennig = 1 Mark = 1 Schilling (1875)

REPRINTS
Most Heligoland issues were extensively reprinted between 1875 and 1895, and these comprise the great majority of Heligoland stamps in the marketplace. Such reprints sell for much less than the originals, usually for $1-$2 each. Expertization of Heligoland issues is strongly recommended by the editors.

Queen Victoria
A1   A2

A3   A4

HALF SCHILLING
A1: Curl below chignon is rounded.
A2: Curl resembles hook or comma.

Typo., Head Embossed

1867-68 **Unwmk.** *Rouletted*

1	A1	½sch bl grn & rose	325.00	*1,000.*
		On cover		*7,250.*
1A	A2	½sch bl grn & rose	800.00	*1,700.*
		On cover		*9,900.*
2	A1	1sch rose & dp grn	190.00	*200.00*
		On cover		*2,600.*
3	A3	2sch rose & pale grn	16.00	*60.00*
		On cover		*1,300.*
4	A3	6sch gray grn & rose	18.00	*475.00*
		On cover		*8,750.*

Reprints of No. 2 lack the large curl, those of No. 1A are not in blue green, and those of Nos. 3 and 4 are on slightly porous paper and the colors are either too deep or too bright. The 2sch and 6sch perforated exist only as reprints.

1869-71   *Perf. 13½x14½*
Thick Soft Paper

5	A2	½sch ol grn & car rose	125.00	*160.00*
		On cover		*1,300.*
a.		½sch blue green & rose	240.00	*250.00*
		On cover		*1,400.*
b.		½sch yellow green & rose	475.00	*450.00*
		On cover		*1,400.*
6	A2	1sch rose & yel grn	175.00	*300.00*
		On cover		*1,500.*

Reprints are on thinner paper and in too dark colors.

1873   **Thick Quadrille Paper**

7	A4	¼sch pale rose & pale grn	32.50	*2,250.*
		On cover		*6,000.*
a.		¼sch deep rose & pale grn	325.00	*2,250.*
		On cover		*6,000.*
8	A4	¼sch yel grn & rose	135.00	*3,600.*
		On cover		*10,500.*
9	A2	½sch brt grn & rose	125.00	*210.00*
		On cover		*1,100.*
10	A4	¾sch gray grn & pale rose	45.00	*2,250.*
		On cover		*5,250.*
11	A2	1sch rose & pale grn	210.00	*425.00*
		On cover		*1,400.*
12	A4	1½sch yel grn & rose	90.00	*325.00*
		On cover		*875.00*

Reprints are never on quadrille paper.

1874   **Thin Wove Paper**

13	A4	¼sch rose & yel grn		17.50

Originals have the large curl. The early reprints have the small curl. The later reprints are on thin hard paper with smooth white gum and the colors are too bright.

A5   A6

A7   Coat of Arms — A8

1875   **Wove Paper**

14	A5	1pf dk rose & dk grn	17.00	*600.00*
		On cover		*1,650.*
15	A5	2pf yel grn & dk rose	18.00	*875.00*
		On cover		*1,900.*
16	A6	5pf dk rose & dk grn	21.00	21.00
		On cover		*60.00*
17	A6	10pf blue grn & red	16.00	*37.50*
		On cover		*110.00*
a.		10pf yel green & dark rose	110.00	27.50
		On cover		*82.50*
b.		10pf lt green & pale red	140.00	25.00
		On cover		*82.50*
18	A7	25pf rose & dk green	24.00	*30.00*
		On cover		*87.50*
a.		25pf dk rose & dk green	24.00	30.00
		On cover		*87.50*

19	A7	50pf grn & brick red	25.00	*85.00*
		On cover		*190.00*
a.		50pf dl grn & dk rose	65.00	*37.50*
		On cover		*110.00*

The 1pf and 2pf have been reprinted on thin white paper with white gum. The colors are too bright and too light.

1876-88   **Typo.**

20	A8	3pf dp grn & dl red	275.00	*1,600.*
		On cover		*2,700.*
		On cover, single franking		*8,250.*
a.		3pf green & bright red ('77)	175.00	*1,000.*
		On cover		*2,000.*
		On cover, single franking		*8,250.*
21	A8	20pf ver & brt grn ('88)	20.00	*32.50*
		On cover		*92.50*
a.		20pf brn org & grn ('87)	425.00	*47.50*
		On cover		*140.00*
b.		20pf vio car & yel grn ('80)	240.00	*125.00*
		On cover		*360.00*
c.		20pf anil rose & dk grn ('85)	425.00	*65.00*
		On cover		*160.00*
d.		20pf lil rose & dk grn ('76)	240.00	*125.00*
		On cover		*410.00*
e.		20pf rose red & dk grn ('80)	240.00	*125.00*
		On cover		*360.00*

The coat-of-arms on Nos. 20, 21 and subvarieties is printed in three colors: varying shades of yellow, red and green.
The 3pf has been reprinted. The colors are usually too pale, especially the red, which is either orange or orange red.

A9   A10

1879   **Typo.**

22	A9	1m dp green & car	225.00	225.00
		On cover		*650.00*
a.		1m blue green & salmon	225.00	240.00
		On cover		*650.00*
b.		1m dark green & ver	80.00	
23	A10	5m blue grn & sal	200.00	*1,200.*
		On cover		*2,250.*

Perf. 11½

24	A9	1m dp grn & car	1,500.	*5,500.*
25	A10	5m bl grn & rose red	1,500.	*12,000.*
a.		Horiz. pair, imperf. vert.	5,000.	

Nos. 13, 22b, 24 and 25 were never placed in use. Forged cancellations of Nos. 1-23 are plentiful.
Covers: Values for Nos. 22, 22a, 23 are for overfranked complete covers, usually philatelic.
Heligoland stamps were replaced by those of the German Empire in 1890.

HONDURAS

hän-'dur-əs

LOCATION — Central America, between Guatemala on the north and Nicaragua on the south
GOVT. — Republic
AREA — 43,277 sq. mi.
POP. — 4,092,174 (est. 1983)
CAPITAL — Tegucigalpa

8 Reales = 1 Peso
100 Centavos = 1 Peso (1878)
100 Centavos = 1 Lempira (1933)

Values for unused stamps are for examples with original gum as defined in the catalogue introduction. Very fine examples of the locally printed Nos. 95-110, 127, 140, 151-210C, and 218-279 will have margins clear of the perforations but will be noticeably off center.

Watermark

Wmk. 209 — Multiple Ovals

Coat of Arms — A1

1865, Dec. **Unwmk.** **Litho.** *Imperf.*

1	A1	2r black, *green*	.65	—
2	A1	2r black, *pink*	.65	—

Nos. 1 and 2, although inscribed "DOS," were sold for one real.
Most used examples are pen cancelled with cross. Pre-philatelic handstamp cancellations command a premium.
One in 12 stamps has "LOS" for "DOS," and one stamp in each pane of 120 is inscribed "DGS" or "CORRFOS."
No covers are known bearing No. 1. Two covers bearing No. 2 are known.

Comayagua   Tegucigalpa

Medio real = ½ real
Un real = 1 real
Dos reales = 2 reales

Comayagua Issue
1877, May   **Red Surcharge**

3	A1	½r on 2r blk, *grn*	70.00	

Blue Surcharge

5	A1	2r on 2r blk, *grn*	150.00	—
6	A1	2r on 2r blk, *pink*	475.00	—

Black Surcharge

7	A1	1r on 2r blk, *grn*	150.00	
8	A1	2r on 2r blk, *grn*	800.00	
9	A1	2r on 2r blk, *pink*	500.00	

No. 5 may exist only as the base for No. 13a.

Tegucigalpa Issue
1877, July   **Black Surcharge**

13	A1	1r on 2r blk, *grn*	15.00	35.00
a.		Surcharged on #5	1000.	
14	A1	1r on 2r blk, *pink*	80.00	
16	A1	2r on 2r blk, *pink*		

Blue Surcharge

18	A1	½r on 2r blk, *grn*	*80.00*	
19	A1	1r on 2r blk, *pink*	*25.00*	
20	A1	1r on 2r blk, *grn*	*35.00*	
23	A1	2r on 2r blk, *pink*	15.00	*25.00*

Red Surcharge

24	A1	½r on 2r blk, *grn*	15.00	*35.00*
25	A1	½r on 2r blk, *pink*	60.00	

Only the stamps valued or dashed used are known to have been postally used. Nos. 3 and 7 may have been postally used, but to date no examples are recorded used. The other listed stamps were sold as remainders. No covers bearing Nos. 3 to 25 are known.
The blue surcharges range from light blue to violet black. The black surcharge has no tinge of blue. The red surcharges range from light to dark carmine. Some exist double or inverted, but genuine errors are rare. Normal cancel is a blue or black 7-bar killer. Target cancels on Nos. 1-24 are forgeries. Surcharges and cancels have been extensively forged.

Regular Issue

President Francisco Morazán — A4

Printed by National Bank Note Co. of N.Y.
Thin, hard paper, colorless gum
Various Frames

1878, July   Engr.   Perf. 12

30	A4	1c violet	.50	.50
		On cover		1,000.
31	A4	2c brown	.50	.50
		On cover		1,500.
32	A4	½r black	5.00	.50
		On cover		350.00
33	A4	1r green	25.00	.50
		On cover		450.00
34	A4	2r deep blue	3.00	5.00
		On cover		3,500.
35	A4	4r vermilion	5.00	10.00
36	A4	1p orange	6.00	25.00
		Nos. 30-36 (7)	45.00	42.00

Nos. 35 and 36 are not known on cover. Various counterfeit cancellations exist on Nos. 30-36. Most used examples of Nos. 35-36 offered are actually 35a-36a with fake or favor cancels.

Printed by American Bank Note Co. of N.Y.
Re-Issue Soft paper, yellowish gum
Various Frames

1889

30a	A4	1c deep violet	10.00
31a	A4	2c red brown	.25
32a	A4	½r black	.25
33a	A4	1r blue green	.25
34a	A4	2r ultramarine	5.00
35a	A4	4r scarlet vermilion	.25
36a	A4	1p orange yellow	.25
		Nos. 30a-36a (7)	16.25

Although Nos. 30a-36a were not intended for postal use, they were valid, and genuine cancels are known on Nos. 31a-34a.

Arms of Honduras — A5

1890, Jan. 6

40	A5	1c yellow green	.30	.30
41	A5	2c red	.30	.30
42	A5	5c blue	.30	.30
43	A5	10c orange	.35	.40
44	A5	20c ocher	.35	.40
45	A5	25c rose red	.35	.40
46	A5	50c purple	.50	.60
47	A5	40c dark blue	.50	.80
48	A5	50c brown	.55	.80
49	A5	75c blue green	.55	2.00
50	A5	1p carmine	.70	2.25
		Nos. 40-50 (11)	4.75	8.55

The tablets and numerals of Nos. 40 to 50 differ for each denomination.
For overprints see Nos. O1-O11.

Used values of Nos. 1-110 are for stamps with genuine cancellations applied while the stamps were valid. Various counterfeit cancellations exist.

A6

President Luis Bográn — A7

1891, July 31

51	A6	1c dark blue	.30	.30
52	A6	2c yellow brown	.30	.30
53	A6	5c blue green	.30	.30
54	A6	10c vermilion	.30	.30
55	A6	20c brown red	.30	.30
56	A6	25c magenta	.40	.55
57	A6	30c slate	.40	.55
58	A6	40c blue green	.40	.55
59	A6	50c black brown	.50	.80
60	A6	75c purple	.50	1.25
61	A6	1p brown	.75	1.60
62	A7	2p brn & black	2.25	5.00
a.		Head inverted	225.00	
63	A7	5p pur & black	2.00	5.75
a.		Head inverted	60.00	
64	A7	10p green & blk	2.00	5.75
a.		Head inverted	75.00	
		Nos. 51-64 (14)	10.70	23.30

Nos. 62, 64 exist with papermakers watermark.
For overprints see Nos. O12-O22.

Columbus Sighting Honduran Coast — A8

General Trinidad Cabanas — A9

1892, July 31

65	A8	1c slate	.40	.45
66	A8	2c deep blue	.40	.45
67	A8	5c yellow green	.40	.45
68	A8	10c blue green	.40	.45
69	A8	20c red	.40	.45
70	A8	25c orange brown	.50	.55
71	A8	30c ultramarine	.50	.60
72	A8	40c orange	.50	.90
73	A8	50c brown	.60	.85
74	A8	75c lake	.60	1.25
75	A8	1p purple	.60	1.40
		Nos. 65-75 (11)	5.30	7.80

Discovery of America by Christopher Columbus, 400th anniv.

1893, Aug.

76	A9	1c green	.25	1.50
77	A9	2c scarlet	.25	1.50
78	A9	5c dark blue	.25	1.50
79	A9	10c orange brn	.25	1.50
80	A9	20c brown red	.25	1.50
81	A9	25c dark blue	.30	1.50
82	A9	30c red orange	.50	1.50
83	A9	40c black	.50	1.50
84	A9	50c olive brn	.50	1.50
85	A9	75c purple	.75	1.50
86	A9	1p deep magenta	.75	1.75
		Nos. 76-86 (11)	4.55	16.75

"Justice" A10

President Celio Arias A11

1895, Feb. 15

87	A10	1c vermilion	.30	.30
88	A10	2c deep blue	.30	.30
89	A10	5c slate	.35	.50
90	A10	10c brown rose	.45	.50
91	A10	20c violet	.45	.50
92	A10	30c deep violet	.45	.85
93	A10	50c olive brown	.55	1.25
94	A10	1p dark green	.60	1.60
		Nos. 87-94 (8)	3.45	5.80

The tablets and numerals of Nos. 76-94 differ for each denomination.

1896, Jan. 1   Litho.   Perf. 11½

95	A11	1c dark blue	.30	.35
96	A11	2c yellow brn	.30	.35
97	A11	5c purple	1.10	.30
a.		5c red violet	.60	1.10
98	A11	10c vermilion	.40	.40
a.		10c red	4.50	4.50
99	A11	20c emerald	.75	.50
a.		20c deep green		
100	A11	30c ultramarine	.65	.70
101	A11	50c rose	.90	1.00
102	A11	1p black brown	1.25	1.50
		Nos. 95-102 (8)	5.65	5.10

Counterfeits are plentiful. Nos. 95-102 exist imperf. between horiz. or vertically.
Originals of Nos. 95 to 102 are on both thin, semi-transparent paper and opaque paper; reprints are on thicker, opaque paper and usually have a black cancellation "HONDURAS" between horizontal bars.

Railroad Train — A12

1898, Aug. 1

103	A12	1c brown	.50	.25
104	A12	2c rose	.50	.25
105	A12	5c dull ultra	1.00	.25
b.		5c red violet (error)	1.50	.70
106	A12	6c red violet	.90	.25
b.		6c dull rose (error)		
107	A12	10c dark blue	1.00	.30
108	A12	20c dull orange	1.25	.75
109	A12	50c orange red	2.00	1.25
110	A12	1p blue green	4.00	3.00
		Nos. 103-110 (8)	11.15	6.30

Excellent counterfeits of Nos. 103-110 exist.
For overprints see Nos. O23-O27.

Laid Paper

103a	A12	1c	1.00	.50
104a	A12	2c	1.25	.50
105a	A12	5c	1.60	.50
106a	A12	6c	1.60	.75
107a	A12	10c	1.60	1.00
		Nos. 103a-107a (5)	7.05	3.25

General Santos Guardiola A13

President José Medina A14

1903, Jan. 1   Engr.   Perf. 12

111	A13	1c yellow grn	.35	.25
112	A13	2c carmine rose	.35	.30
113	A13	5c blue	.35	.30
114	A13	6c dk violet	.35	.30
115	A13	10c brown	.40	.30
116	A13	20c dull ultra	.45	.40
117	A13	50c vermilion	1.25	1.10
118	A13	1p orange	1.25	1.10
		Nos. 111-118 (8)	4.75	4.05

"PERMITASE" handstamped on stamps of 1896-1903 was applied as a control mark by the isolated Pacific Coast post office of Amapala to prevent use of stolen stamps.

1907, Jan. 1   Perf. 14

119	A14	1c dark green	.25	.25
120	A14	2c scarlet	.25	.25
120A	A14	2c carmine	9.00	5.50
121	A14	5c blue	.30	.30
122	A14	6c purple	.35	.30
a.		6c dark violet	.80	.60
123	A14	10c gray brown	.40	.35
124	A14	20c ultra	.90	.85
a.		20c blue violet	110.00	110.00
125	A14	50c deep lake	1.10	1.10
126	A14	1p orange	1.50	1.50
a.		1p orange yellow	—	
		Nos. 119-126 (9)	14.05	10.40

All values of the above set exist imperforate, imperforate horizontally and in horizontal pairs, imperforate between. No. 124a imperf is worth only 10% of the listed perforated variety.
For surcharges see Nos. 128-130.

1909   Typo.   Perf. 11½

127	A14	1c green	1.25	1.00
a.		Imperf., pair	4.00	4.00
b.		Printed on both sides	7.50	10.00

The 1909 issue is roughly typographed in imitation of the 1907 design. It exists pin perf. 8, 13, etc.

No. 124 Handstamp Surcharged in Black, Green or Red

1910, Nov.   Perf. 14

128	A14	1c on 20c ultra	8.50	6.00
129	A14	5c on 20c ultra (G)	8.50	6.00
130	A14	10c on 20c ultra (R)	8.50	6.00
		Nos. 128-130 (3)	25.50	18.00

As is usual with handstamped surcharges inverts and double exist.

Honduran Scene — A15

1911, Jan.   Litho.   Perf. 14, 12 (1p)

131	A15	1c violet	.35	.25
132	A15	2c green	.35	.25
a.		Perf. 12	5.00	1.25
133	A15	5c carmine	.40	.25
a.		Perf. 12	8.00	3.50
134	A15	6c ultramarine	.50	.30
135	A15	10c blue	.60	.40
136	A15	20c yellow	.60	.50
137	A15	50c brown	2.00	1.75
138	A15	1p olive green	2.50	1.20
		Nos. 131-138 (8)	7.30	5.70

For overprints and surcharges see Nos. 139, 141-147, O28-O47.

No. 132a Overprinted in Red

1911, Sept. 19   Perf. 12

139	A15	2c green	20.00	18.00
a.		Inverted overprint	24.00	22.50

90th anniversary of Independence.
Counterfeit overprints on perf. 14 stamps exist.

President Manuel Bonilla — A16

1912, Feb. 1   Typo.   Perf. 11½

140	A16	1c orange red	12.00	12.00

Election of Pres. Manuel Bonilla.

Stamps of 1911 Surcharged in Black, Red or Blue

a   b

1913   Litho.   Perf. 14

141	A15(a)	2c on 1c violet	1.25	.75
a.		Double surcharge		3.25
b.		Inverted surcharge	4.50	
c.		Double surch., one invtd.	6.75	
d.		Red surcharge	40.00	40.00
142	A15(b)	2c on 1c violet	7.00	5.75
a.		Inverted surcharge	14.00	

143	A15(b)	2c on 10c blue	2.75 2.25
a.		Double surcharge	5.75 5.75
b.		Inverted surcharge	
144	A15(b)	2c on 20c yellow	7.00 6.75
145	A15(b)	5c on 1c violet	2.50 .75
146	A15(b)	5c on 10c bl (Bl)	2.75 1.50
147	A15(b)	6c on 1c violet	2.75 2.25

Counterfeit surcharges exist.

Terencio
Sierra — A17

Bonilla — A18

ONE CENTAVO:
Type I — Solid border at sides below numerals.
Type II — Border of light and dark stripes.

1913-14   **Typo.**   **Perf. 11½**

151	A17	1c dark brn, I	.25 .25
a.		1c brown, type II	.75 .45
152	A17	2c carmine	.25 .25
153	A18	5c blue	.40 .25
154	A18	5c ultra ('14)	.40 .25
155	A18	6c gray vio	.50 .25
156	A18	6c purple ('14)	.40 .25
a.		6c red lilac	.60 .35
157	A17	10c blue	.75 .75
158	A17	10c brown ('14)	1.25 .50
159	A17	20c brown	1.00 .75
160	A18	50c rose	2.00 2.00
161	A18	1p gray green	2.25 2.25
		Nos. 151-161 (11)	9.45 7.75

For overprints and surcharges see Nos. 162-173, O48-O57.

Surcharged in Black or Carmine

1914

162	A17	1c on 2c carmine	.75 .75
163	A17	5c on 2c carmine	1.25 .90
164	A18	5c on 6c gray vio	2.00 2.00
165	A17	10c on 2c carmine	2.00 2.00
166	A18	10c on 6c gray vio	2.00 2.00
a.		Double surcharge	10.00
167	A18	10c on 6c gray vio (C)	2.00 2.00
168	A18	10c on 50c rose	6.50 5.00
		Nos. 162-168 (7)	16.50 14.65

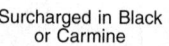
No. 158 Surcharged

1915

173	A17	5c on 10c brown	2.50 1.75

Ulua Bridge — A19

Bonilla Theater — A20

1915-16   **Typo.**

174	A19	1c chocolate	.25 .25
175	A19	2c carmine	.25 .25
a.		Tête bêche pair	1.00 1.00
176	A20	5c bright blue	.25 .25
177	A20	6c deep purple	.35 .25
178	A19	10c dull blue	.75 .25
179	A19	20c red brown	1.25 1.00
a.		Tête bêche pair	4.00 4.00
180	A20	50c red	1.50 1.50
181	A20	1p yellow grn	2.50 2.50
		Nos. 174-181 (8)	7.10 6.25

For overprints & surcharges see Nos. 183, 231-232, 237, 239-240, 285, 292, C1-C13, C25, C28, C31, C36, C57, CO21, CO30-CO32, CO42, O58-O65.

Imperf., Pairs

174a	A19	1c	2.00 2.00
175b	A19	2c	2.00 2.00
176a	A20	5c	3.50
178a	A19	10c	3.50
179b	A19	20c	5.25
180b	A20	50c	7.00
181a	A20	1p	8.75 8.75

Francisco Bertrand — A21

1916, Feb. 1

182	A21	1c orange	2.00 2.00

Election of Pres. Francisco Bertrand.
Unauthorized reprints exist.

Official Stamp No. O60 Overprinted

1918

183	A20	5c bright blue	2.00 1.50
a.		Inverted overprint	5.00 5.00

Statue to Francisco Morazán — A22

1919   **Typo.**

184	A22	1c brown	.25 .25
a.		Printed on both sides	2.00
b.		Imperf., pair	.70
185	A22	2c carmine	.25 .25
186	A22	5c lilac rose	.25 .25
187	A22	6c brt violet	.25 .25
188	A22	10c dull blue	.25 .25
189	A22	15c light blue	.75 .25
190	A22	15c dark violet	.60 .25
191	A22	20c orange brn	1.00 .30
a.		20c gray brown	10.00 .30
b.		Imperf., pair	2.75
192	A22	50c light brown	4.00 2.50
a.		Imperf. pair	15.00
193	A22	1p yellow green	7.50 20.00
a.		Imperf., pair	20.00
b.		Printed on both sides	9.00
c.		Tête bêche pair	15.00
		Nos. 184-193 (10)	15.10 24.55

See note on handstamp following No. 217.
Unauthorized reprints exist.
For overprints and surcharges see Nos. 201-210C, 230, 233, 235-236, 238, 241-243, 287, 289, C58, C61, CO23, CO25, CO33, CO36-CO38, CO39, CO40, O66-O74.

"Dawn of Peace" — A23

1920, Feb. 1   **Size: 27x21mm**

194	A23	2c rose	2.50 2.50
a.		Tête bêche pair	15.00 12.50
b.		Imperf., pair	15.00 12.50

Size: 51x40mm

195	A23	2c gold	10.00 10.00
196	A23	2c silver	10.00 10.00
197	A23	2c bronze	10.00 10.00
198	A23	2c red	12.00 12.00
		Nos. 194-198 (5)	44.50 44.50

Assumption of power by Gen. Rafael Lopez Gutierrez.
Nos. 195-198 exist imperf.
Unauthorized reprints of Nos. 195-198 exist.

Type of 1919, Dated "1920"

1921

201	A22	6c dark violet	10.00 5.00
a.		Tête bêche pair	15.00
b.		Imperf., pair	15.00

Unauthorized reprints exist.

No. 185 Surcharged in Antique Letters

1922

202	A22	6c on 2c carmine	.40 .40
a.		"ALE" for "VALE"	2.00 2.00
b.		Comma after "CTS"	2.00 2.00
c.		Without period after "CTS"	2.00 2.00
d.		"CT" for "CTS"	2.00 2.00
e.		Double surcharge	4.25
f.		Inverted surcharge	4.25

Stamps of 1919 Surcharged in Roman Figures and Antique Letters in Green

1923

203	A22	10c on 1c brown	1.50 1.50
204	A22	50c on 2c carmine	2.00 2.00
a.		Inverted surcharge	10.00 10.00
b.		"HABILTADO"	6.00 6.00

Surcharged in Black or Violet Blue

205	A22	1p on 5c lil rose (Bk)	3.50 3.50
a.		"PSEO"	20.00 20.00
b.		Inverted surcharge	20.00 20.00
206	A22	1p on 5c lil rose (VB)	20.00 20.00
a.		"PSEO"	70.00

On Nos. 205-206, "Habilitado Vale" is in Antique letters, "Un Peso" in Roman.

No. 185 Surcharged in Roman Letters in Green

207	A22	6c on 2c carmine	3.50 2.75

Nos. 184-185 Surcharged in Roman Letters in Green

208	A22	10c on 1c brown	1.75 1.25
a.		"DIES"	6.00
b.		"DEIZ"	6.00
c.		"DEIZ CAS"	6.00
d.		"TTS" for "CTS"	6.00
e.		"HABILTADO"	6.00
f.		"HABILTAD"	6.00
g.		"HABILITA"	6.00
h.		Inverted surcharge	30.00
209	A22	50c on 2c carmine	3.75 2.75
a.		"CAT" for "CTA"	10.00
b.		"TCA" for "CTA"	10.00
c.		"TTS" for "CTS"	10.00
d.		"CAS" for "CTS"	10.00
e.		"HABILTADO"	10.00

Surcharge on No. 209 is found in two spacings between value and HABILITADO: 5mm (illustrated) and 1½mm.

No. 186 Surcharged in Antique Letters in Black

210	A22	1p on 5c lil rose	25.00 25.00
a.		"PFSO"	75.00

In the surcharges on Nos. 202 to 210 there are various wrong font, inverted and omitted letters.

No. 184 Surcharged in Large Antique Letters in Green

210C	A22	10c on 1c brown	15.00 15.00
d.		"DIFZ"	55.00 55.00

Dionisio de Herrera A24

Pres. Miguel Paz Baraona A25

1924, June   **Litho.**   **Perf. 11, 11½**

211	A24	1c olive green	.30 .25
212	A24	2c deep rose	.35 .25
213	A24	6c red violet	.40 .25
214	A24	10c blue	.40 .25
215	A24	20c yellow brn	.80 .35
216	A24	50c vermilion	1.75 1.10
217	A24	1p emerald	4.00 2.75
		Nos. 211-217 (7)	8.00 5.20

In 1924 a facsimile of the signatures of Santiago Herrera and Francisco Caceres, covering four stamps, was handstamped in violet to prevent the use of stamps that had been stolen during a revolution.
Imperfs exist.
For overprints and surcharges see Nos. 280-281, 290-291, C14-C24, C26-C27, C29-C30, C32-C35, C56, C60, C73-C76, CO1-CO5, CO22, CO24, CO28-CO29, CO34-CO35, CO38A, CO39A, CO41, CO43, O75-O81.

1925, Feb. 1   **Typo.**   **Perf. 11½**

218	A25	1c dull blue	2.00 2.00
a.		1c dark blue	2.00 2.00
219	A25	1c car rose	5.00 5.00
a.		1c brown carmine	5.00 5.00
220	A25	1c olive brn	14.00 14.00
a.		1c orange brown	14.00 14.00
b.		1c dark brown	14.00 14.00
c.		1c black brown	14.00 14.00
221	A25	1c buff	12.00 12.00
222	A25	1c red	60.00 60.00
223	A25	1c green	40.00 40.00
		Nos. 218-223 (6)	133.00 133.00

Imperf

225	A25	1c dull blue	5.50 5.50
a.		1c dark blue	5.50 5.50
226	A25	1c car rose	8.75 8.75
a.		1c brown carmine	8.75 8.75
227	A25	1c olive brn	8.75 8.75
a.		1c orange brown	8.75 8.75
b.		1c deep brown	8.75 8.75
c.		1c black brown	8.75 8.75
228	A25	1c buff	8.75 8.75
229	A25	1c red	60.00 60.00
229A	A25	1c green	27.50 27.50
		Nos. 225-229A (6)	119.25 119.25

Inauguration of President Baraona.
Counterfeits and unauthorized reprints exist.

No. 187 Overprinted in Black and Red

1926, June   **Perf. 11½**

230	A22	6c bright violet	1.50 1.25

Many varieties of this two-part overprint exist: one or both inverted or double, and various combinations. Value, each $10.

Nos. 177 and 187 Overprinted in Black or Red

1926

231	A20	6c deep pur (Bk)	2.00 2.00
a.		Inverted overprint	5.50 5.50
b.		Double overprint	5.50 5.50
232	A20	6c deep pur (R)	2.50 2.50
a.		Double overprint	5.00 5.00
233	A22	6c lilac (Bk)	.60 .60
a.		6c violet	.75 .75
b.		Inverted overprint	5.00 5.00

c.	Double overprint	5.00	5.00
d.	Double ovpt., one inverted	5.00	5.00
e.	"192"	7.50	7.50
f.	Double ovpt., both inverted	7.50	7.50

Same Overprint on No. 230

235	A22 6c violet	20.00	20.00
a.	"1926" inverted	20.00	20.00
b.	"Habilitado" triple, one invtd.	20.00	20.00

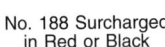

No. 188 Surcharged
in Red or Black

236	A22 6c on 10c blue (R)	.50	.25
c.	Double surcharge	5.00	4.00
d.	Without bar		
e.	Inverted surcharge	4.00	3.50
f.	"Vale" omitted		
g.	"6cts" omitted		
h.	"cts" omitted		
k.	Black surcharge	55.00	55.00

Nos. 175 and 185
Overprinted in
Green

237	A19 2c carmine	.25	.25
a.	Tête bêche pair	4.00	4.00
b.	Double overprint	2.00	1.40
c.	"HARILITADO"	2.00	1.40
d.	"1926" only	2.75	2.75
e.	Double overprint, one inverted	2.75	2.75
f.	"1926" omitted	3.50	3.50
g.	Triple overprint, two inverted	5.25	5.25
h.	Double on face, one on back	5.25	5.25
238	A22 2c carmine	.25	.25
a.	"HARILITADO"	.90	.90
b.	Double overprint	1.40	1.40
c.	Inverted overprint	2.00	2.00

No. 177
Overprinted in Red

1927	**Large Numerals, 12x5mm**		
239	A20 6c deep purple	25.00	25.00
a.	"1926" over "1927"	35.00	35.00
b.	Invtd. ovpt. on face of stamp, normal ovpt. on back	30.00	

No. 179 Surcharged

1927

240	A19 6c on 20c brown	.75	.75
a.	Tête bêche pair	2.75	2.75
c.	Interted surcharge	2.50	2.50
d.	Double surcharge	8.50	8.50

Nos. 8 and 10 in the setting have no period after "cts" and No. 50 has the "t" of "cts" inverted.

Same Surcharge on Nos. 189-191

241	A22 6c on 15c blue	27.50	27.50
a.	"c" of "cts" omitted		
242	A22 6c on 15c vio	.70	.70
a.	Double surcharge	1.75	1.75
b.	Double surch., one invtd.	2.00	2.00
c.	"L" of "Vale" omitted		
243	A22 6c on 20c yel brn	.60	.60
a.	6c on 20c deep brown		
b.	"6" omitted	1.75	1.75
c.	"Vale" and "cts" omitted	3.50	3.50
	Nos. 240-243 (4)	29.55	29.55

On Nos. 242 and 243 stamps Nos. 12, 16 and 43 in the setting have no period after "cts" and No. 34 often lacks the "s." On No. 243 the "c" of "cts" is missing on stamp No. 38. On No. 241 occur the varieties "ct" or "ts" for "cts." and no period.

Southern
Highway — A26

Ruins of
Copán — A27

Pine Tree — A28

Presidential
Palace — A29

Ponciano
Leiva — A30

Pres. M.A.
Soto — A31

Lempira — A32

Map of
Honduras — A33

President Juan
Lindo — A34

Statue of
Columbus — A35

1927-29	Typo.	Wmk. 209	
244	A26 1c ultramarine	.30	.25
a.	1c blue	.30	.25
245	A27 2c carmine	.30	.25
246	A28 5c dull violet	.30	.25
247	A28 5c bl gray ('29)	25.00	7.00
248	A29 6c blue black	.75	.50
a.	6c gray black	.75	.50
249	A29 6c dark bl ('29)	.40	.25
a.	6c light blue	.40	.25
250	A30 10c blue	.70	.25
251	A31 15c deep blue	1.00	.50
252	A32 20c dark blue	1.25	.60
253	A33 30c dark brown	1.50	1.00
254	A34 50c light blue	2.50	1.50
255	A35 1p red	5.00	2.50
	Nos. 244-255 (12)	39.00	14.85

In 1929 a quantity of imperforate sheets of No. 249 were stolen from the Litografia Nacional. Some of them were perforated by sewing machine and a few copies were passed through the post. To prevent the use of stolen stamps of the 1927-29 issues they were declared invalid and the stock on hand was overprinted "1929 a 1930."

For overprints and surcharges see Nos. 259-278, CO19-CO20B.

Pres. Vicente Mejia Colindres and
Vice-Pres. Rafael Diaz Chávez — A36

President Mejia
Colindres — A37

1929, Feb. 25

256	A36 1c dk carmine	3.00	3.00
257	A37 2c emerald	3.00	3.00

Installation of Pres. Vicente Mejia Colindres. Printed in sheets of ten.

Nos. 256 and 257 were surreptitiously printed in transposed colors. They were not regularly issued.

Stamps of 1927-29
Overprinted in
Various Colors

1929, Oct.

259	A26 1c blue (R)	.25	.25
a.	1c ultramarine (R)	.50	.25
b.	Double overprint	2.50	1.75
c.	As "a," double overprint	2.50	1.75
260	A26 1c blue (Bk)	6.50	6.50
a.	1c ultramarine (Bk)		
261	A27 2c car (R Br)	3.50	3.50
a.	Double overprint		
262	A27 2c car (Bl Gr)	1.00	1.00
a.	Double overprint		
263	A27 2c car (Bk)	1.00	.50
264	A27 2c car (V)	.50	.25
a.	Double overprint		
b.	Double ovpt., one inverted		
265	A27 2c org red (V)	1.50	
266	A28 5c dl vio (R)	.40	.30
a.	Double overprint (R+V)		
267	A28 5c bl gray (R)	1.00	.75
a.	Double overprint (R+Bk)		
269	A29 6c gray blk (R)	2.50	2.00
a.	Double overprint	6.00	6.00
272	A29 6c dk blue (R)	.40	.25
a.	6c light blue (R)	.40	.25
b.	Double overprint	2.00	2.00
c.	Double overprint (R+V)		
273	A30 10c blue (R)	.40	.25
a.	Double overprint	2.50	1.75
274	A31 15c dp blue (R)	.50	.25
a.	Double overprint	3.50	2.50
275	A32 20c dark bl (R)	.50	.35
276	A33 30c dark brn (R)	.75	.60
a.	Double overprint	3.50	2.50
277	A34 50c light bl (R)	2.00	1.00
278	A35 1p red (V)	5.00	2.50
	Nos. 259-278 (17)	27.70	20.25

Nos. 259-278 exist in numerous shades. There are also various shades of the red and violet overprints. The overprint may be found reading upwards, downwards, inverted, double, triple, tête bêche or combinations.

Status of both 6c stamps with overprint in black is questioned.

A38

1929, Dec. 10

279	A38 1c on 6c lilac rose	.70	.70
a.	"1992" for "1929"		
b.	"9192" for "1929"		
c.	Surcharge reading down	8.00	
d.	Dbl. surch., one reading down		

Varieties include "1992" reading down and pairs with one surcharge reading down, double or with "1992."

No. 214 Surcharged
in Red

Perf. 11, 11½

1930, Mar. 26		Unwmk.	
280	A24 1c on 10c blue	.35	.30
a.	"1093" for "1930"	1.40	
b.	"tsc" for "cts"	1.40	
281	A24 2c on 10c blue	.35	.30
a.	"tsc" for "cts"	2.00	
b.	"Vale 2" omitted		

Official Stamps of
1929 Overprinted
in Red or Violet

1930, Mar.	Wmk. 209	Perf. 11½	
282	O1 1c blue (R)	.50	.50
a.	Double overprint	2.00	2.00
284	O1 2c carmine (V)	.90	.90

Stamps of 1915-26
Overprinted in Blue

On No. 174

1930, July 19		Unwmk.	
285	A19 1c chocolate	.30	.25
a.	Double overprint	1.00	1.00
b.	Inverted overprint	1.40	1.40
c.	Dbl. ovpt., one inverted	1.40	1.40

On No. 184

287	A22 1c brown	15.00	15.00
a.	Double overprint		
c.	Inverted overprint		

On No. 204

289	A22 50c on 2c carmine	100.00	90.00
b.	Inverted surcharge		

On Nos. 211 and 212

290	A24 1c olive green	.25	.25
a.	Double overprint	1.75	1.75
b.	Inverted overprint	1.75	1.75
d.	On No. O75	12.00	
291	A24 2c carmine rose	.25	.25
a.	Double overprint	1.75	1.75
b.	Inverted overprint	1.75	1.75

On No. 237

292	A19 2c car (G & Bl)	100.00	100.00

From Title Page
of Government
Gazette, First
Issue — A39

1930, Aug. 11	Typo.	Wmk. 209	
295	A39 2c orange	2.00	2.00
296	A39 2c ultramarine	2.00	2.00
297	A39 2c red	2.00	2.00
	Nos. 295-297 (3)	6.00	6.00

Publication of the 1st newspaper in Honduras, cent. The stamps were on sale and available for postage on Aug. 11th, 1930, only. Not more than 5 examples of each color could be purchased by an applicant.

Nos. 295-297 exist imperf. and part-perforate. Unauthorized reprints exist.

For surcharges see Nos. CO15-CO18A.

Paz
Baraona — A40

Manuel
Bonilla — A41

Lake
Yojoa — A42

View of Palace at Tegucigalpa
A43

President Carías and Vice-President Williams — A49

1933, Apr. 29

318	A49	2c carmine rose	.50	.35
319	A49	6c deep green	.75	.40
320	A49	10c deep blue	1.00	.50
321	A49	15c red orange	1.25	.75
		Nos. 318-321 (4)	3.50	2.00

Inauguration of Pres. Tiburcio Carías Andino and Vice-Pres. Abraham Williams, Feb. 1, 1933.

Palace — A57

Designs: 3c, Map of Honduras. 5c, Bridge of Choluteca. 8c, Flag.

1939, Mar. 1　　　　**Perf. 12½**

336	A56	1c orange yellow	.25	.25
337	A57	2c red orange	.25	.25
338	A57	3c carmine	.30	.25
339	A57	5c orange	.30	.25
340	A56	8c dark blue	.50	.25
		Nos. 336-340 (5)	1.60	1.25
	Nos. 336-340,C89-C98 (15)		15.35	8.65

Nos. 336-340 exist imperf.
For overprints see Nos. 342-343.

1929　　　　　　　**Perf. 11, 11½**

C14	A24	25c on 50c ver	5.00	3.50

In the surcharges on Nos. C14 to C40 there are various wrong font and defective letters and numerals, also periods omitted.

Nos. 215-217 Surcharged in Green, Black or Red

1929, Oct.

C15	A24	5c on 20c yel brn (G)	1.40	1.40
a.	Double surcharge (R+G)		45.00	
C16	A24	10c on 50c ver (Bk)	2.25	1.90
C17	A24	15c on 1p emer (R)	3.50	3.50
		Nos. C15-C17 (3)	7.15	6.80

Nos. 214 and 216 Surcharged Vertically in Red or Black

　　　a　　　　　　　　b

1929, Dec. 10

C18	A24(a)	5c on 10c bl (R)	.60	.60
C19	A24(b)	20c on 50c ver	1.00	1.00
a.	"1299" for "1929"		190.00	
b.	"cts. cts." for "cts. oro."		190.00	
c.	"r" of "Aereo" omitted		2.00	
d.	Horiz. pair, imperf. btwn.		20.00	

Nos. 214, 215 and 180 Surcharged in Various Colors

1930, Feb.

C20	A24	5c on 10c (R)	.50	.50
a.	"1930" reading down		3.50	
b.	"1903" for "1930"		3.50	
c.	Surcharge reading down		10.00	
d.	Double surcharge		14.00	
e.	Dbl. surch., one downward		14.00	
C21	A24	5c on 10c (Y)	450.00	450.00
C22	A24	5c on 20c (Bl)	125.00	125.00
C23	A24	10c on 20c (Bk)	.70	.70
a.	"0" for "10"		3.50	
b.	Double surcharge		8.75	
c.	Dbl. surch., one downward		12.00	
d.	Horiz. pair, imperf. btwn.		70.00	
C24	A24	10c on 20c (V)	750.00	750.00
a.	"0" for "10"		1,600.	
C25	A24	20c on 50c (Bk)	.95	.95
a.	"Internaoical"		3.50	
b.	"o" for "oro"		3.50	
c.	Inverted surcharge		17.50	
d.	As "a," invtd. surch.		175.00	
e.	As "b," invtd. surch.		175.00	

Surcharge on Nos. C20-C24 are vertical.

Nos. 214, 215 and 180 Surcharged

1930, Apr. 1

C26	A24	5c on 10c blue	.50	.50
a.	Double surcharge		9.50	
b.	"Servicioa"		3.50	
C27	A24	15c on 20c yel brn	.55	.55
a.	Double surcharge		7.00	
C28	A20	20c on 50c red, surch. reading down	.95	.95
a.	Surcharge reading up		7.00	
		Nos. C26-C28 (3)	2.00	2.00

Nos. C22 and C23 Surcharged Vertically in Red

City of Amapala
A44

Mayan Stele at Copán
A45

Christopher Columbus
A46

Discovery of America
A47

Columbus' Fleet and Flag of the Race — A50

Wmk. 209

1933, Aug. 3　Typo.　　Perf. 11½

322	A50	2c ultramarine	1.00	.65
323	A50	6c yellow	1.00	.65
324	A50	10c lemon	1.40	.85

Perf. 12

325	A50	15c violet	2.00	1.50
326	A50	50c red	4.00	3.50
327	A50	1 l emerald	7.00	7.00
		Nos. 322-327 (6)	16.40	14.15

"Day of the Race," an annual holiday throughout Spanish-American countries. Also for the 441st anniv. of the sailing of Columbus to the New World, Aug. 3, 1492.

Loarque Bridge
A48

Unwmk.

1931, Jan. 2　Engr.　　Perf. 12

298	A40	1c black brown	.75	.25
299	A41	2c carmine rose	.75	.25
300	A42	5c dull violet	1.00	.25
301	A43	6c deep green	1.00	.25
302	A44	10c brown	1.50	.25
303	A45	15c dark blue	2.00	.30
304	A46	20c black	3.50	.40
305	A47	50c olive green	4.50	1.50
306	A48	1p slate black	9.00	2.50
		Nos. 298-306 (9)	24.00	5.95

Regular Issue of 1931 Overprinted in Black or Various Colors

1931

307	A40	1c black brown	.40	.30
308	A41	2c carmine rose	.60	.30
309	A45	15c dark blue	1.00	.30
310	A46	20c black	2.50	.40

Overprinted

311	A42	5c dull violet	.50	.30
312	A43	6c deep green	.50	.30
315	A44	10c brown	1.50	.35
316	A47	50c olive green	8.00	5.00
317	A48	1p slate black	10.00	7.50
		Nos. 307-317 (9)	25.00	14.75
	Nos. 307-317,C51-C55 (14)		50.00	35.75

The overprint is a control mark. It stands for "Tribunal Superior de Cuentas" (Superior Tribunal of Accounts).

Overprint varieties include: inverted; double; double, one or both inverted; on back; pair, one without overprint; differing colors (6c exists with overprint in orange, yellow and red).

Masonic Temple, Tegucigalpa — A51

Designs: 2c, President Carías. 5c, Flag. 6c, Tomás Estrada Palma.

Unwmk.

1935, Jan. 12　Engr.　　Perf. 12

328	A51	1c green	.40	.25
329	A51	2c carmine	.40	.25
330	A51	5c dark blue	.40	.25
331	A51	6c black brown	.40	.25
a.	Vert. pair, imperf. btwn.		20.00	20.00
		Nos. 328-331 (4)	1.60	1.00
	Nos. 328-331,C77-C83 (11)		15.20	6.50

Gen. Carías Bridge — A55

1937, June 4

332	A55	6c car & ol green	.90	.40
333	A55	21c grn & violet	1.50	.65
334	A55	46c orange & brn	2.10	1.50
335	A55	55c ultra & black	3.00	2.40
		Nos. 332-335 (4)	7.50	4.95

Prolongation of the Presidential term to Jan. 19, 1943.

Seal of Honduras
A56

AIR POST STAMPS

Regular Issue of 1915-16 Overprinted in Black, Blue or Red

1925　　Unwmk.　　Perf. 11½

C1	A20	5c lt blue (Bk)	87.50	87.50
C2	A20	5c lt blue (Bl)	300.00	300.00
a.	Inverted overprint		400.00	
b.	Vertical overprint		600.00	
c.	Double overprint		800.00	
C3	A20	5c lt blue (R)	7,250.	

Value for No. C3 is for an example without gum.

C4	A19	10c dk blue (R)	175.00	
a.	Inverted overprint		325.00	
b.	Overprint tête bêche, pair		800.00	
C5	A19	10c dk blue (Bl)	1,100.	
C6	A19	20c red brn (Bk)	175.00	175.00
a.	Inverted overprint		250.00	
b.	Tête bêche pair		400.00	
c.	Overprint tête bêche, pair		725.00	
d.	"AFRO"		1,400.	
e.	Double overprint		600.00	
C7	A19	20c red brn (Bl)	175.00	175.00
a.	Inverted overprint		700.00	
b.	Tête bêche pair		1,000	
c.	Vertical overprint		900.00	
C8	A20	50c red (Bk)	450.00	300.00
a.	Inverted overprint		550.00	
b.	Overprint tête bêche, pair		900.00	
C9	A20	1p yel grn (Bk)	600.00	600.00

Surcharged in Black or Blue

C10	A19	25c on 1c choc	125.00	125.00
a.	Inverted surcharge		700.00	
C11	A20	25c on 5c lt bl (Bl)	225.00	225.00
a.	Inverted surcharge		700.00	
b.	Double inverted surcharge		675.00	
C12	A19	25c on 10c dk bl	125,000.	
C13	A19	25c on 20c brn (Bl)	200.00	200.00
a.	Inverted surcharge		325.00	
b.	Tête bêche pair		450.00	

Counterfeits of Nos. C1-C13 are plentiful.

Monoplane and Lisandro Garay
AP1

1929, June 5　Engr.　　Perf. 12

C13C	AP1	50c carmine	2.00	1.75

No. 216 Surcharged in Blue

1930

C29	A24 10c on 5c on 20c (Bl+R)		.90	.90
a.	"1930" reading down		9.00	9.00
b.	"1903" for "1930"		9.00	9.00
c.	Red surcharge, reading down		14.00	
C30	A24 10c on 10c on 20c (Bk+R)		87.50	87.50
a.	"0" for "10"		190.00	

No. 181 Surcharged as No. C25 and Re-surcharged

C31	A20 50c on 25c on 1p grn	4.25	4.25
a.	"Internaoicnal"	7.00	
b.	"o" for "oro"	7.00	
c.	25c surcharge inverted	17.50	17.50
d.	50c surcharge inverted	17.50	17.50
e.	As "a" and "c"		
f.	As "a" and "d"		
g.	As "b" and "c"		
h.	As "b" and "d"		
	Nos. C29-C31 (3)	92.65	92.65

No. 215 Surcharged in Dark Blue

1930, May 22

C32	A24 5c on 20c yel brn	1.25	1.00
a.	Double surcharge	5.25	5.25
b.	Horiz. pair, imperf. btwn.	60.00	60.00
c.	Vertical pair, imperf. between	20.00	20.00

Nos. O78-O80 Surcharged like Nos. C20 to C25 in Various Colors

1930

C33	A24 5c on 10c (R)	450.00	350.00
a.	"1930" reading down	1,500.	
b.	"1903" for "1930"	1,500.	
C34	A24 5c on 20c (Bl)	400.00	400.00
C35	A24 25c on 50c (Bk)	225.00	225.00
a.	55c on 50c vermilion	325.00	325.00

No. C35 exists with inverted surcharge.

No. O64 Surcharged like No. C28

C36	A20 20c on 50c red, surcharge reading down	350.00	350.00
a.	Surcharge reading up	350.00	350.00
b.	Dbl. surch., reading down	350.00	350.00
c.	Dbl. surch., reading up	350.00	350.00

No. O87 Overprinted

1930, Feb. 21   Wmk. 209   Perf. 11½

C37	O1 50c yel, grn & blue	1.40	1.25
a.	"Internacinaj"	5.25	
b.	"luternacional"	5.25	
c.	Double overprint	5.25	

Nos. O86-O88 Overprinted in Various Colors

1930, May 23

C38	O1 20c on dark blue (R)	1.10	.85
a.	Double overprint	8.75	
b.	Triple overprint	12.00	
C39	O1 50c org, grn & bl (Bk)	1.10	.90
C40	O1 1p buff (Bl)	1.40	1.25
a.	Double overprint	10.50	
	Nos. C38-C40 (3)	3.60	3.00

National Palace AP3

Unwmk.

1930, Oct. 1   Engr.   Perf. 12

C41	AP3 5c yel orange	.50	.30
C42	AP3 10c carmine	.75	.60
C43	AP3 15c green	1.00	.75
C44	AP3 20c dull violet	1.25	.60
C45	AP3 1p light brown	4.00	4.00
	Nos. C41-C45 (5)	7.50	6.25

Overprinted in Various Colors

1931   Perf. 12

C51	AP3 5c yel orange (R)	2.00	1.50
C52	AP3 10c carmine (Bk)	3.00	2.50
C53	AP3 15c green (Br)	5.00	4.00
C54	AP3 20c dull vio (O)	5.00	4.25
C55	AP3 1p lt brown (G)	10.00	8.75
	Nos. C51-C55 (5)	25.00	21.00

See note after No. 317.

Stamps of Various Issues Surcharged in Blue or Black (#C59)

1931, Oct.   Perf. 11½

On No. 215

C56	A24 15c on 20c yel brn	3.50	2.75
a.	Horiz. pair, imperf. btwn.	42.50	
b.	Green surcharge	20.00	20.00

On No. O64

C57	A20 15c on 50c red	4.25	3.50
a.	Inverted surcharge	10.50	10.50

On No. O72

C58	A22 15c on 20c brn	4.25	4.25
a.	Vert. pair, imperf. between	12.00	

On Nos. C57 and C58 the word "OFICIAL" is canceled by two bars.

On No. O88

Wmk. 209

C59	O1 15c on 1p buff	4.25	4.25
a.	Vert. pair, imperf. horiz.	25.00	
b.	"Sevricio"	14.00	14.00

The varieties "Vaie" for "Vale," "aereo" with circumflex accent on the first "e" and "Interior" with initial capital "I" are found on Nos. C56, C58-C59. No. C57 is known with initial capital in "Interior."

A similar surcharge, in slightly larger letters and with many minor varieties, exists on Nos. 215, O63, O64 and O73. The authenticity of this surcharge is questioned.

Nos. 215, O73, O87-O88 Surcharged in Green, Red or Black

1931, Nov.   Unwmk.

C60	A24 15c on 20c (G)	3.50	2.75
a.	Inverted surcharge	6.25	
b.	"Xl" omitted	6.25	
c.	"X" for "Xl"	6.25	
d.	"Pl" for "Xl"	6.25	
C61	A22 15c on 50c (R)	3.50	2.75
a.	"Xl" omitted	6.75	
b.	"Pl" for "Xl"	6.75	
c.	Double surcharge	20.00	20.00

On No. C61 the word "OFICIAL" is not barred out.

Wmk. 209

C62	O1 15c on 50c (Bk)	2.75	2.50
a.	"1391" for "1931"	10.50	10.50
b.	Double surcharge	8.75	8.75
C63	O1 15c on 1p (Bk)	2.50	2.25
a.	"1391" for "1931"	12.50	
b.	Surcharged on both sides	7.00	

Nos. O76-O78 Surcharged in Black or Red

1932   Unwmk.   Perf. 11, 11½

C73	A24 15c on 2c	.80	.80
a.	Double surcharge	5.50	
b.	Inverted surcharge	4.25	
c.	"Ae" of "Aero" omitted	1.00	
d.	On No. 212 (no "Official")		
C74	A24 15c on 6c	.80	.80
a.	Double surcharge	3.50	
b.	Horiz. pair, imperf. btwn.	17.50	
c.	"Aer" omitted	1.00	
d.	"A" omitted		
e.	Inverted surcharge	3.50	
C75	A24 15c on 10c (R)	.80	.80
a.	Double surcharge	5.50	
b.	Inverted surcharge	3.50	
c.	"r" of "Aereo" omitted	1.00	

Same Surcharge on No. 214 in Red

C76	A24 15c on 10c dp bl	150.00	100.00

There are various broken and missing letters in the setting.
A similar surcharge with slightly larger letters exists.

Post Office and National Palace AP4

View of Tegucigalpa — AP5

Designs: 15c, Map of Honduras. 20c, Mayol Bridge. 40c, View of Tegucigalpa. 50c, Owl. 1 l, Coat of Arms.

1935, Jan. 10   Perf. 12

C77	AP4 8c blue	.25	.25
C78	AP5 10c gray	.25	.25
C79	AP5 15c olive gray	.40	.25
C80	AP5 20c dull green	.50	.25
C81	AP5 40c brown	.70	.25
C82	AP4 50c yellow	8.25	1.60
C83	AP4 1 l green	3.25	2.75
	Nos. C77-C83 (7)	13.55	5.35

Flags of US and Honduras — AP11

Engr. & Litho.

1937, Sept. 17   Unwmk.

C84	AP11 46c multicolored	2.75	1.40

US Constitution, 150th anniv.

Comayagua Cathedral AP12

Founding of Comayagua AP13

Alonzo Cáceres and Pres. Carías — AP14

Lintel of Royal Palace AP15

1937, Dec. 7   Engr.

C85	AP12 2c copper red	.25	.25
C86	AP13 8c dark blue	.35	.25
C87	AP14 15c slate black	.70	.70
C88	AP15 50c dark brown	4.25	2.75
	Nos. C85-C88 (4)	5.55	3.95

City of Comayagua founding, 400th anniv. For surcharges see Nos. C144-C146 in Scott Standard catalogue, Vol. 3.

Mayan Stele at Copán AP16

Mayan Temple, Copán AP17

Designs: 15c, President Carias. 30c, José C. de Valle. 40c, Presidential House. 46c, Lempira. 55c, Church of Our Lady of Suyapa. 66c, J. T. Reyes. 1 l, Hospital at Choluteca. 2 l, Ramón Rosa.

1939, Mar. 1   Perf. 12½

C89	AP16 10c orange brn	.25	.25
C90	AP16 15c grnsh blue	.30	.25
C91	AP17 21c gray	.50	.25
C92	AP16 30c dk blue grn	.55	.25
C93	AP17 40c dull violet	1.00	.25
C94	AP16 46c dk gray brn	1.00	.65
C95	AP16 55c orange	1.25	1.00
a.	Imperf., pair	22.50	
C96	AP16 66c black	1.75	1.25
C97	AP16 1 l olive grn	3.00	1.00
C98	AP16 2 l henna red	4.25	2.50
	Nos. C89-C98 (10)	13.80	7.45

For surcharges see Nos. C118-C119, C147-C152 in Scott Standard catalogue, Vol. 3.

Souvenir Sheets

AP26

14c, Francisco Morazan. 16c, George Washington. 30c, J. C. de Valle. 40c, Simon Bolivar.

1940, Apr. 13   Engr.   Perf. 12
Centers of Stamps Lithographed

C99	AP26 Sheet of 4	10.00	10.00
a.	14c black, yellow, ultra & rose	1.40	1.40
b.	16c black, yellow, ultra & rose	1.75	1.75
c.	30c black, yellow, ultra & rose	2.40	2.40

d.	40c black, yellow, ultra & rose	2.75	2.75

Imperf

C100	AP26 Sheet of 4	16.00	16.00
a.	14c black, yellow, ultra & rose	2.25	2.25
b.	16c black, yellow, ultra & rose	2.10	2.10
c.	30c black, yellow, ultra & rose	4.00	4.00
d.	40c black, yellow, ultra & rose	4.50	4.50

Pan American Union, 50th anniv.

For overprints see Nos. C153-C154, C187 in Scott Standard catalogue, Vol. 3.

Air Post Official Stamps of 1939 Overprinted in Red

1940, Oct. 12   **Perf. 12½**

C101	OA2	2c dp bl & green	.25	.25
C102	OA2	5c dp blue & org	.25	.25
C103	OA2	8c deep bl & brn	.30	.30
C104	OA2	15c dp blue & car	.50	.50
C105	OA2	46c dp bl & ol grn	.80	.80
C106	OA2	50c dp bl & vio	.90	.90
C107	OA2	1 l dp bl & red brn	3.75	3.75
C108	OA2	2 l dp bl & red org	7.50	7.50
	Nos. C101-C108 (8)		14.25	14.25

Erection and dedication of the Columbus Memorial Lighthouse.

AIR POST SEMI-POSTAL STAMPS

No. C13C Surcharged in Black

Unwmk.

1929, June 5   **Engr.**   **Perf. 12**

CB1	AP1	50c + 5c carmine	.65	.30
CB2	AP1	50c + 10c carmine	.70	.35
CB3	AP1	50c + 15c carmine	.95	.55
CB4	AP1	50c + 20c carmine	1.40	.75
	Nos. CB1-CB4 (4)		3.70	1.95

AIR POST OFFICIAL STAMPS

Official Stamps Nos. O78 to O81 Overprinted in Red, Green or Black

1930   **Perf. 11, 11½**

CO1	A24	10c deep blue (R)	1.25	1.25
CO2	A24	20c yellow brown	1.25	1.25
a.		Vert. pair, imperf. btwn.	14.00	
CO3	A24	50c vermilion (Bk)	1.40	1.40
CO4	A24	1p emerald (R)	1.25	1.25
	Nos. CO1-CO4 (4)		5.15	5.15

OA1

Green Surcharge

CO5	OA1	5c on 6c red vio	1.00	1.00
a.		"1910" for "1930"	2.75	2.75
b.		"1920" for "1930"	2.75	2.75

The overprint exists in other colors and on other denominations but the status of these is questioned.

Official Stamps of 1931 Overprinted

1931   **Unwmk.**   **Perf. 12**

CO6	O2	1c ultra	.35	.35
CO7	O2	2c black brown	.85	.85
CO8	O2	5c olive gray	1.00	1.00
CO9	O2	6c orange red	1.00	1.00
a.		Inverted overprint	24.00	24.00
CO10	O2	10c dark green	1.25	1.25
CO11	O2	15c olive brown	2.00	1.75
a.		Inverted overprint	20.00	20.00
CO12	O2	20c red brown	2.00	1.75
CO13	O2	50c gray violet	1.40	1.40
CO14	O2	1p deep orange	2.00	1.75
	Nos. CO6-CO14 (9)		11.85	11.10

In the setting of the overprint there are numerous errors in the spelling and punctuation, letters omitted and similar varieties.

This set is known with blue overprint. A similar overprint is known in larger type, but its status has not been fully determined.

Postage Stamps of 1918-30 Surcharged Type "a" or Type "b" (#CO22-CO23) in Green, Black, Red and Blue

     a   b

1933   **Wmk. 209, Unwmk.**

CO15	A39	20c on 2c #295 (G)	3.25	3.25
CO16	A39	20c on 2c #296 (G)	3.25	3.25
CO17	A39	20c on 2c #297 (G)	3.25	3.25
CO17A	A39	40c on 2c #295	2.00	2.00
CO18	A39	40c on 2c #297	7.00	7.00
CO18A	A39	40c on 2c #297 (G)	4.25	4.25
CO19	A28	40c on 5c #246	4.25	4.25
CO19A	A28	40c on 5c #247	7.00	7.00
CO20	A28	40c on 5c #266	15.00	15.00
CO20A	A28	40c on 5c #267	9.00	9.00
CO20B	A28	40c on 5c #267 (R)	14.00	14.00
CO21	A20	70c on 5c #183	3.00	3.00
CO22	A24	70c on 10c #214 (R)	3.25	3.25
CO23	A22	1 l on 20c #191 (Bl)	3.25	3.25
CO24	A24	1 l on 50c #216 (Bl)	14.00	14.00
CO25	A22	1.20 l on 1p #193 (Bl)	1.00	1.00
	Nos. CO15-CO25 (16)		96.75	96.75

Official Stamps of 1915-29 Surcharged Type "a" or Type "b" (#CO28-CO29, CO33-CO41, CO43) in Black, Red, Green, Orange, Carmine or Blue

CO26	O1	40c on 5c #O84 (Bk)	1.00	1.00
CO27	O1	40c on 5c #O84 (R)	25.00	25.00
CO28	A24	60c on 6c #O77 (Bk)	.70	.70
CO29	A24	60c on 6c #O77 (G)	25.00	25.00
CO30	A20	70c on 5c #O60 (Bk)	5.25	5.25
CO31	A19	70c on 10c #O62 (R)	9.00	9.00
CO32	A19	70c on 10c #O62 (Bk)	7.75	7.75
CO33	A22	70c on 10c #O70 (R)	4.50	4.00
CO34	A24	70c on 10c #O78 (O)	3.50	3.50
CO35	A24	70c on 10c #O78 (C)	4.50	4.50
CO36	A22	70c on 15c #O71 (R)	87.50	87.50
CO37	A22	90c on 10c #O70 (R)	5.25	5.25
CO38	A22	90c on 15c #O71 (R)	8.00	8.00
CO38A	A24	1 l on 2c #O76	1.40	1.40
CO39	A22	1 l on 10c #O72	2.50	2.50
CO39A	A24	1 l on 20c #O79	3.75	3.75
CO40	A22	1 l on 50c #O73	1.90	1.90

CO41	A24	1 l on 50c #O80	4.25	4.25
CO42	A20	1.20 l on 1p #O65	9.00	7.00
CO43	A24	1.20 l on 1p #O81	3.00	3.00
	Nos. CO26-CO43 (20)		212.75	210.25

Varieties of foregoing surcharges exist.

Merchant Flag and Seal of Honduras OA2

1939, Feb. 27   **Unwmk.**   **Perf. 12½**

CO44	OA2	2c dp blue & grn	.25	.25
CO45	OA2	5c dp blue & org	.25	.25
CO46	OA2	8c dp blue & brn	.25	.25
CO47	OA2	15c dp blue & car	.30	.25
CO48	OA2	46c dp blue & ol grn	.40	.30
CO49	OA2	50c dp blue & vio	.50	.30
CO50	OA2	1 l dp blue & red brn	1.75	1.25
CO51	OA2	2 l dp blue & red org	3.75	2.25
	Nos. CO44-CO51 (8)		7.45	5.10

For overprints and surcharges see Nos. C101-C117.

OFFICIAL STAMPS

Type of Regular Issue of 1890 Overprinted in Red

1890   **Unwmk.**   **Perf. 12**

O1	A5	1c pale yellow	.25
O2	A5	2c pale yellow	.25
O3	A5	5c pale yellow	.25
O4	A5	10c pale yellow	.25
O5	A5	20c pale yellow	.25
O6	A5	25c pale yellow	.25
O7	A5	30c pale yellow	.25
O8	A5	40c pale yellow	.25
O9	A5	50c pale yellow	.25
O10	A5	75c pale yellow	.25
O11	A5	1p pale yellow	.25
	Nos. O1-O11 (11)		2.75

Type of Regular Issue of 1891 Overprinted in Red

1891

O12	A6	1c yellow	.25
O13	A6	2c yellow	.25
O14	A6	5c yellow	.25
O15	A6	10c yellow	.25
O16	A6	20c yellow	.25
O17	A6	25c yellow	.25
O18	A6	30c yellow	.25
O19	A6	40c yellow	.25
O20	A6	50c yellow	.25
O21	A6	75c yellow	.25
O22	A6	1p yellow	.25
	Nos. O12-O22 (11)		2.75

Nos. O1 to O22 were never placed in use. Cancellations were applied to remainders. They exist with overprint inverted, double, triple and omitted; also, imperf. and part perf.

 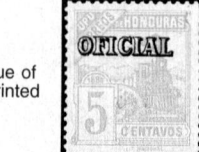

Regular Issue of 1898 Overprinted

1898-99   **Perf. 11½**

O23	A12	5c dl ultra	.40
O24	A12	10c dark bl	.80
O25	A12	20c dull org	1.25
O26	A12	50c org red	2.40
O27	A12	1p blue grn	3.00
	Nos. O23-O27 (5)		7.85

Counterfeits of basic stamps and of overprint exist.

Regular Issue of 1911 Overprinted

1911-15   **Perf. 12, 14**

Carmine Overprint

O28	A15	1c violet	1.50	.65
a.		Inverted overprint	2.40	2.40
b.		Double overprint	2.00	
O29	A15	6c ultra	2.50	2.00
a.		Inverted overprint	2.75	2.75
O30	A15	10c blue	1.50	1.25
a.		"OFICAIL"	2.50	
b.		Double overprint	3.50	
O31	A15	20c yellow	15.00	12.00
O32	A15	50c brown	8.00	7.00
O33	A15	1p ol grn	12.00	10.00
	Nos. O28-O33 (6)		40.50	32.90

Black Overprint

O34	A15	2c green	1.00	.70
a.		"OFICIAL"	5.00	
O35	A15	5c carmine	1.50	1.00
a.		Perf. 12	7.50	7.50
O36	A15	6c ultra	4.50	4.50
O37	A15	10c blue	4.00	4.00
O38	A15	20c yellow	5.00	5.00
O39	A15	50c brown	5.50	4.00
	Nos. O34-O39 (6)		21.50	19.20

Counterfeits of overprint of Nos. O28-O39 exist.

With Additional Surcharge

1913-14

O40	A15	1c on 5c car	1.75	1.50
O41	A15	2c on 5c car	2.00	1.50
O42	A15	10c on 1c vio	4.00	3.50
a.		"OFICIAL" inverted	7.50	
O43	A15	20c on 1c vio	3.00	2.00
	Nos. O40-O43 (4)		10.75	9.00

On No. O40 the surcharge reads "1 cent." Nos. O40-O43 exist with double surcharge.

No. O43 Surcharged Vertically in Black, Yellow or Maroon

1914

O44	A15	10c on 20c on 1c	20.00	20.00
a.		Maroon surcharge	20.00	20.00
O45	A15	10c on 20c on 1c (Y)	40.00	40.00

No. O35 Surcharged

1915

O46	A15	10c on 5c car	20.00	20.00

No. O39 Surcharged

O47	A15	20c on 50c brn	5.00	5.00

Regular Issues of 1913-14 Overprinted in Red or Black

1915			Perf. 11½	
O48	A17	1c brn (R)	.40	.40
a.		"OFICAIL"	5.00	
O49	A17	2c car (Bk)	.40	.40
a.		"OFICAIL"	5.00	
b.		Double overprint	4.00	
O50	A18	5c ultra (Bk)	.45	.45
a.		"OFIC"	4.00	
O51	A18	5c ultra (R)	1.00	1.00
a.		"OFIC"		
b.		"OFICAIL"	5.00	
O52	A18	6c pur (Bk)	1.50	1.50
a.		6c red lil (Bk)		
O53	A17	10c brn (Bk)	1.25	1.25
O54	A17	20c brn (Bk)	3.00	3.00
O55	A17	20c brn (R)	3.00	3.00
a.		Double overprint (R+Bk)	10.00	
b.		"OFICAIL"	5.00	
O56	A18	50c rose (Bk)	6.00	6.00
		Nos. O48-O56 (9)	17.00	17.00

The 10c blue has the overprint "OFICIAL" in different type from the other stamps of the series. It is stated that forty stamps were overprinted for the Postmaster General but the stamp was never put in use or on sale at the post office.

No. 152 Surcharged

O57	A17	1c on 2c car	2.00	2.00
a.		"0.10" for "0.01"	4.25	4.25
b.		"0.20" for "0.01"	4.25	4.25
c.		Double surcharge	8.50	8.50
d.		As "a," double surcharge	77.50	
e.		As "b," double surcharge	77.50	

Regular Issue of 1915-16 Overprinted in Black or Red

1915-16				
O58	A19	1c choc (Bk)	.25	.25
O59	A19	2c car (Bk)	.25	.25
a.		Tête bêche pair	1.25	1.25
b.		Double overprint	2.00	
c.		Double overprint, one inverted	2.00	
d.		"b" and "c" in tête bêche pair		
O60	A20	5c brt blue (R)	.30	.30
a.		Inverted overprint	3.00	
O61	A20	6c deep pur (R)	.40	.40
a.		Black overprint	3.00	
b.		Inverted overprint	2.00	2.00
O62	A19	10c dl bl (R)	.40	.40
O63	A19	20c red brn (Bk)	.60	.60
a.		Tête bêche pair	2.50	
O64	A20	50c red (Bk)	1.75	1.75
O65	A20	1p yel grn (C)	3.75	3.75
		Nos. O58-O65 (8)	7.70	7.70

The 6c, 10c and 1p exist imperf.

Regular Issue of 1919 Overprinted

1921				
O66	A22	1c brown	2.25	2.25
a.		Inverted overprint	3.00	3.00
O67	A22	2c carmine	6.50	6.50
a.		Inverted overprint	3.00	3.00
O68	A22	5c lilac rose	6.50	6.50
a.		Inverted overprint	3.00	
O69	A22	6c brt vio	.50	.50
a.		Inverted overprint		
O70	A22	10c dull blue	.60	.60
a.		Double overprint		
O71	A22	15c light blue	.70	.70
a.		Inverted overprint	2.00	
b.		Double ovpt., one inverted	4.00	
O72	A22	20c brown	1.00	1.00
O73	A22	50c light brown	1.50	1.50
O74	A22	1p yellow green	3.00	3.00
		Nos. O66-O74 (9)	22.55	22.55

Regular Issue of 1924 Overprinted

1924			Perf. 11, 11½	
O75	A24	1c olive brn	.25	.25
O76	A24	2c deep rose	.25	.25
O77	A24	6c red vio	.30	.30
O78	A24	10c deep bl	.45	.45
O79	A24	20c yel brn	.60	.60
O80	A24	50c vermilion	1.25	1.25
O81	A24	1p emerald	2.00	2.00
		Nos. O75-O81 (7)	5.10	5.10

J. C. del Valle — O1

Designs: 2c, J. R. Molina. 5c, Coffee tree. 10c, J. T. Reyes. 20c, Tegucigalpa Cathedral. 50c, San Lorenzo Creek. 1p, Radio station.

1929	Litho.	Wmk. 209	Perf. 11½	
O82	O1	1c blue	.25	.25
O83	O1	2c carmine	.25	.25
a.		2c rose	.25	
O84	O1	5c purple	.35	.35
O85	O1	10c emerald	.50	.35
O86	O1	20c dk bl	.60	.60
O87	O1	50c org, grn & bl	1.00	1.00
O88	O1	1p buff	1.75	1.75
		Nos. O82-O88 (7)	4.70	4.55

Nos. O82-O88 exist imperf.
For overprints and surcharges see Nos. 282, 284, C37-C40, C59, C62-C63, CO26-CO27.

View of Tegucigalpa O2

1931	Unwmk.	Engr.	Perf. 12	
O89	O2	1c ultra	.30	.25
O90	O2	2c black brn	.30	.25
O91	O2	5c olive gray	.35	.25
O92	O2	6c orange red	.40	.30
O93	O2	10c dark green	.50	.35
O94	O2	15c olive brn	.65	.40
O95	O2	20c red brown	.75	.50
O96	O2	50c gray vio	1.00	.65
O97	O2	1p dp orange	1.75	1.75
		Nos. O89-O97 (9)	6.00	4.70

For overprints see Nos. CO6-CO14, O98-O105.

Official Stamps of 1931 Overprinted in Black

1936-37				
O98	O2	1c ultra	.25	.25
O99	O2	2c black brn	.25	.25
a.		Inverted overprint	10.00	
O100	O2	5c olive gray	.30	.30
O101	O2	6c red orange	.40	.40
O102	O2	10c dark green	.40	.40
O103	O2	15c olive brown	.50	.50
a.		Inverted overprint	5.00	
O104	O2	20c red brown	1.00	1.00
		"1938-1935"		
O105	O2	50c gray violet	4.00	3.00
		Nos. O98-O105 (8)	7.10	6.10

Double overprints exist on 1c and 2c. No. O97 with this overprint is fraudulent.

HONG KONG

ˈhäŋˌkäŋ

LOCATION — A peninsula and island in southeast China at the mouth of the Canton River
GOVT. — British Crown Colony
AREA — 426 sq. mi.
POP. — 5,313,000 (est. 1983)
CAPITAL — Victoria

100 Cents = 1 Dollar

Catalogue values for unused stamps in this country are for Never Hinged items, beginning with Scott 174 in the regular postage section.

Pre-Stamp Postal Markings

1843-52		
A1	Crowned Circle handstamp Type II, on cover, inscribed "PAID AT HONG KONG" in red	1,500.
A2	Crowned Circle handstamp Type I, on cover, inscribed "PAID AT HONG KONG" in red	1,200.
A3	Crowned Circle handstamp Type IV, on cover, inscribed "PAID AT HONG KONG" in red	550.00

Earliest known uses: A1, 10/17/43; A2, 8/21/44; A3, 6/16/52.

Values for unused stamps are for examples with original gum as defined in the catalogue introduction. Very fine examples of Nos. 1-25, 29-48, 61-66 and 69-70a will have perforations touching the design on at least one side due to the narrow spacing of the stamps on the plates. Stamps with perfs clear of the design on all four sides are scarce and will command higher prices.

Queen Victoria — A1

		Unwmk.		
1862, Dec. 8		**Typo.**	**Perf. 14**	
1	A1	2c pale brown	575.00	125.00
		On cover		650.00
a.		2c deep brown	775.00	170.00
		On cover		800.00
2	A1	8c buff	775.00	90.00
		On cover		500.00
3	A1	12c blue	700.00	72.50
		On cover		425.00
4	A1	18c lilac	700.00	67.50
		On cover		475.00
5	A1	24c green	1,250.	140.00
		On cover		800.00
6	A1	48c rose	3,000.	450.00
		On cover		3,000.
7	A1	96c gray	4,000.	525.00
		On cover		
1863-80			**Wmk. 1**	
8	A1	2c brown ('65)	145.00	8.50
		On cover		50.00
a.		2c deep brown ('64)	370.00	35.00
		On cover		165.00
b.		2c pale yellowish brown	180.00	14.00
		On cover		75.00

9	A1	2c dull rose ('80)	260.00	40.00
		On cover		210.00
a.		2c rose	290.00	40.00
		Never hinged		210.00
10	A1	4c slate	135.00	9.50
		On cover		50.00
a.		4c greenish grey	370.00	325.00
		On cover		325.00
b.		4c bluish slate	525.00	27.50
		On cover		135.00
11	A1	5c ultra ('80)	775.00	57.50
		On cover		135.00
12	A1	6c lilac	475.00	20.00
		On cover		175.00
a.		6c violet	675.00	21.00
		On cover		175.00
13	A1	8c org buff ('65)	625.00	13.50
		On cover		170.00
a.		8c bright orange	500.00	16.50
		On cover		150.00
b.		8c brownish orange	525.00	16.50
		On cover		150.00
14	A1	10c violet ('80)	825.00	19.00
		On cover		130.00
15	A1	12c light blue	37.50	9.00
		On cover		55.00
a.		12c light greenish blue	1,500.	40.00
		On cover		350.00
b.		12c deep blue	300.00	14.50
		On cover		145.00
16	A1	16c yellow ('77)	2,200.	77.50
		On cover		525.00
17	A1	18c lilac ('66)	7,750.	350.00
		On cover		3,250.
18	A1	24c green ('65)	675.00	12.50
		On cover		110.00
a.		24c deep green	1,350.	37.50
		On cover		140.00
b.		24c pale green	800.00	17.50
		On cover		180.00
19	A1	30c vermilion	1,050.	14.50
		On cover		180.00
a.		30c orange vermilion	925.00	17.50
		On cover		180.00
20	A1	30c violet ('71)	300.00	7.00
		On cover		110.00
21	A1	48c rose carmine	1,100.	50.00
		On cover		275.00
a.		48c pale rose	1,400.	65.00
		On cover		300.00
22	A1	48c brown ('80)	1,600.	120.00
		On cover		
23	A1	96c bister ('65)	85,000.	800.00
		On cover		45,000.
24	A1	96c gray ('66)	1,750.	67.50
		On cover		8,250.
a.		96c brownish black	2,100.	62.50

Imperfs. are plate proofs.

1874			Perf. 12½	
25	A1	4c slate	13,500.	300.00
		On cover		

See Nos. 36-49. For surcharges or overprints on stamps of type A1 see Nos. 29-35B, 51-56, 61-66, 69-70.

A2   A3

A4

1874		Engr. Wmk. 1	Perf. 15½x15	
26	A2	$2 sage green	425.00	67.50
		On cover		
a.		$2 Thin translucent paper	425.00	67.50
27	A3	$3 violet	400.00	52.50
		On cover		
a.		$3 Thin translucent paper	400.00	42.50
28	A4	$10 rose	9,500.	725.00

Nos. 26-28 are revenues which were used postally. Used values are for postally canceled examples. Black "Paid All" cancels are fiscal usage.

See Nos. 57-59. For surcharges see Nos. 50, 67. For type surcharged see No. 60.

Nos. 17 and 20 Surcharged in Black

1876			Perf. 14	
29	A1	16c on 18c lilac	2,350.	160.00
		On cover		2,750.
a.		Wide space btwn. "n" & "t"	8,250.	1,000.
b.		Wide space btwn. "s" & period	8,250.	1,000.
c.		Broken "1" in "16"	4,000.	475.00
30	A1	28c on 30c violet	1,750.	62.50
		On cover		1,450.

Stamps of 1863-80 Surcharged in Black

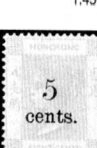

1879-80				
31	A1	5c on 8c org ('80)	1,150.	115.00
		On cover		1,450.
a.		Inverted surcharge		21,000.
b.		Double surcharge		22,000.
32	A1	5c on 18c lilac	1,050.	70.00
		On cover		2,500.
33	A1	10c on 12c pale blue	1,100.	65.00
		On cover		825.00
a.		10c on 12c blue	1,750.	115.00
b.		Double surcharge		52,500.
34	A1	10c on 16c yellow	4,750.	175.00
		On cover		2,500.
a.		Inverted surcharge		95,000.
b.		Double surcharge		85,000.
35	A1	10c on 24c green ('80)	1,550.	100.00
		On cover		1,650.

Most examples of No. 31a are damaged.

Nos. 16-17, 35B Surcharged in Black

A5   A6

1879				
35A	A5	3c on 16c on card	425.	2,200.
		Stamp off card		475.
d.		White card, red printing	475.	
e.		Yellow card, black printing	525.	
f.		As No. 35A, short "T" in "CENTS"	575.	
35B	A5	5c on 18c on card	425.	2,600.
		Stamp off card		550.
g.		White card, red printing	475.	
h.		Blue card, white printing	525.	
i.		As No. 35B, short "T" in "CENTS"	575.	
35C	A6	3c on 5c on 18c on card	8,500.	9,500.
		Stamp off card	8,000.	8,250.
j.		Short "T" in "CENTS"	9,000.	

Nos. 35A-35C were sold affixed to postal cards. Most used examples are found off card so values are given for these.

Type of 1862

1882-1902		Wmk. 2	Perf. 14	
36	A1	2c rose lake	290.00	35.00
		On cover		45.00
a.		2c rose pink	235.00	35.00
		On cover		50.00
b.		2c carmine ('84)	57.50	2.75
		On cover		25.00
c.		2c aniline carmine ('84)	57.50	2.75
		On cover		25.00
37	A1	2c green ('00)	32.50	1.10
		On cover		25.00
38	A1	4c slate ('96)	28.00	3.00
		On cover		42.50
39	A1	4c car rose ('00)	22.50	1.25
		On cover		25.00
40	A1	5c ultramarine	45.00	1.25
		On cover		32.50
41	A1	5c yellow ('00)	27.50	8.00
		On cover		82.50
42	A1	10c lilac	1,050.	22.00
		On cover		80.00
43	A1	10c green	190.00	2.25
		On cover		25.00
a.		10c blue green	2,000.	45.00
		On cover		1,225.
44	A1	10c vio, red ('91)	45.00	2.25
		On cover		25.00
45	A1	10c ultra ('00)	57.50	2.75
		On cover		30.00
46	A1	12c blue ('02)	55.00	72.50
		On cover		775.00
47	A1	30c gray grn ('91)	105.00	27.50
		On cover		165.00
a.		30c yellow green	150.00	47.50
		On cover		275.00
48	A1	30c brown ('01)	62.50	27.50
		On cover		275.00
a.		Pair, imperf.	2,000.	
		Nos. 36-48 (13)	2,010.	206.35

No. 47 has fugitive ink. Both colors will turn dull green upon soaking.
The 2c rose, perf 12, is a proof.

No. 28 Surcharged in Black

1880		Wmk. 1	Perf. 15½x15	
50	A4	12c on $10 rose	1,000.	375.00
		On cover		

Surcharged in Black

1885-91		Wmk. 2	Perf. 14	
51	A1	20c on 30c ver	200.00	7.00
		On cover		250.00
a.		Double surcharge		
52	A1	20c on 30c gray grn ('91)	125.00	175.00
		On cover		1,250.
a.		20c on 30c yellow green	200.00	180.00
		On cover		400.00
53	A1	50c on 48c brown	450.00	45.00
		On cover		400.00
54	A1	50c on 48c lil ('91)	300.00	325.00
		On cover		1,650.
55	A1	$1 on 96c ol gray	825.00	90.00
		On cover		1,000.

56	A1	$1 on 96c vio, red ('91)	550.00	24.00
		On cover		900.00

For overprints see Nos. 61-63.

Types of 1874 and

A7

1890-1902		Wmk. 2	Perf. 14	
56A	A7	2c dull purple	65.00	17.50
		On cover		125.00

		Wmk. 1		
57	A2	$2 gray green	475.00	300.00
58	A3	$3 lilac ('02)	625.00	525.00
a.		Bluish paper	2,100.	
59	A4	$10 gray grn ('92)	12,500.	12,000.

Due to a shortage of 2c postage stamps, No. 56A was authorized for postal use December 24-30, 1890.

Fake postmarks are known on No. 59. Beware also of fiscal cancels altered to resemble postal cancels.

For surcharge see No. 68.

Type of 1874 Surcharged in Black

1891, Jan. 1			Wmk. 2	
60	A4	$5 on $10 vio, red	400.00	125.00

Nos. 36b, 44 Overprinted

a   b

1891, Jan. 1				
60A	A1	2c carmine (a)	1,100.	425.00
60B	A1	2c carmine (b)	525.00	225.00
a.		Inverted overprint		9,000.
60C	A1	10c vio, red (a)	1,900.	475.00

Nos. 60A-60C were overprinted for use as fiscal stamps, "S.O." denoting "Stamp Office" and "S.D." denoting "Stamp Duty." They were authorized for postal use Jan. 1, 1891-1893. Examples of No. 60A with "O" changed to "D" in manuscript are known.

Forged overprints are often encountered. Expertization is required.

Nos. 52, 54 and 56 Handstamped with Chinese characters

g   h

i

61	A1 (g)	20c on 30c	55.00	10.50
		On cover		165.00
a.		20c on 30c dull green	62.50	12.50
		On cover		130.00
b.		"20 CENTS" double	26,000.	26,000.
62	A1 (h)	50c on 48c	95.00	6.25
		On cover		575.00

63	A1 (i)	$1 on 96c	525.00	27.50
		On cover		825.00
a.		Chinese inscriptions both sides	750.00	

No. 61 may be found with Chinese character 2mm, 2½mm or 3mm high.

The handstamped Chinese surcharges on Nos. 61-63 exist in several varieties including inverted, double, triple, misplaced, omitted and (on No. 63) on both front and back.

Nos. 43 and 20
Surcharged

1891

64	A1	7c on 10c green	100.00	10.50
		On cover		300.00
a.		Double surcharge	6,750.	1,500.
		On cover		
b.		Antique "t" in "cents"	725.00	165.00
c.		Small "t" in "cents"	675.00	155.00
		On cover		—

Wmk. 1

65	A1	14c on 30c violet	210.00	82.50
		On cover		725.00
a.		Antique "t" in "cents"	2,900.	3,500.
		On cover		—
b.		Small "t" in "cents"	1,400.	500.00
		On cover		2,250.

Beware of faked varieties.

No. 36 Overprinted in
Black

1891, Jan. 22   **Wmk. 2**

66	A1	2c rose	525.00	140.00
		On cover		3,250.
a.		Double overprint	17,500.	13,500.
b.		"U" of "JUBILEE" shorter	825.00	210.00
c.		"J" of "JUBILEE" shorter	825.00	210.00
d.		Tall "K" in "KONG"	1,350.	500.00
e.		Wide space btwn. "o" & "n"	1,800.	800.00
		Never hinged	1,250.	
f.		Broken "1" in "1891"	1,000.	325.00

50th anniversary of the colony.
Beware of faked varieties.

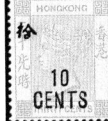

No. 26 Surcharged
(Chinese
Handstamped)

1897, Sept.   Wmk. 1   Perf. 15½x15

67	A2	$1 on 2c sage green	275.00	150.00
		On cover		—
a.		Without Chinese surcharges	4,500.	4,000.
		On cover		—
b.		Diagonal Chinese surcharge omitted	29,500.	

On No. 57
Perf. 14

68	A2	$1 on $2 gray green	275.00	160.00
		On cover		—
a.		Without Chinese surcharges	2,100.	1,800.
		On cover		—
b.		Diagonal Chinese surcharge omitted	22,000.	
c.		Vertical Chinese surcharge omitted Handstamped "SPECI-MEN"	160.00	

Handstamp Surcharged
in Black

1898   **Wmk. 2**

69	A1	10c on 30c gray grn	72.50	95.00
		On cover		500.00
a.		Large Chinese surcharge	1,400.	1,400.
b.		Without Chinese surcharge	600.00	1,200.
		On cover		—
c.		As #69, 1½mm between "1" & "0"	800.00	1,000.

d.		As #69b, 1½mm between "1" & "0"	8,000.	
70	A1	$1 on 96c black	240.00	32.50
		On cover		1,000.
a.		Without Chinese surcharge	3,000.	4,000.
		Overprinted "SPECIMEN"	625.00	

The Chinese surcharge is added separately. See notes below Nos. 61-63. The small Chinese surcharge is illustrated.

King Edward VII — A10

1903   **Wmk. 2**

71	A10	1c brown & lilac	2.25	.55
72	A10	2c gray green	20.00	2.10
73	A10	4c violet, red	23.00	.45
74	A10	5c org & gray grn	22.00	10.50
75	A10	8c violet & black	14.50	1.75
76	A10	10c ultra & lil, bl	62.50	2.00
77	A10	12c red vio & gray grn, yel	11.50	5.75
78	A10	20c org brn & blk	62.50	4.75
79	A10	30c blk & gray grn	62.50	24.00
80	A10	50c red vio & gray green	67.50	62.50
81	A10	$1 olive grn & lil	125.00	26.00
82	A10	$2 scar & black	375.00	375.00
83	A10	$3 dp blue & blk	450.00	450.00
84	A10	$5 blue grn & lil	625.00	575.00
85	A10	$10 org & blk, bl	1,450.	475.00
		Nos. 71-85 (15)	3,373.	2,015.

1904-11   **Wmk. 3**
Ordinary or Chalky Paper

86	A10	1c brown ('10)	9.00	1.10
a.		Booklet pane of 4		
87	A10	2c gray green	23.00	3.00
88	A10	2c deep green	42.00	2.00
a.		Booklet pane of 4		
b.		Booklet pane of 12		
89	A10	4c violet, red	34.00	.50
90	A10	4c carmine	18.00	.50
a.		Booklet pane of 4		
b.		Booklet pane of 12		
91	A10	5c org & gray grn	62.50	17.50
92	A10	6c red vio & org ('07)	34.00	8.25
93	A10	8c vio & blk ('07)	18.00	2.25
94	A10	10c ultra & lil, bl	32.00	1.50
95	A10	10c ultramarine	57.50	.50
96	A10	12c red vio & gray grn, yel ('07)	22.00	7.75
97	A10	20c org brn & blk	67.50	4.25
98	A10	20c ol grn & vio ('11)	57.50	50.00
99	A10	30c blk & gray grn	62.50	32.50
100	A10	30c blk & gray vio ('11)	67.50	42.50
101	A10	50c red vio & gray green	105.00	15.50
102	A10	50c blk, grn ('11)	52.50	19.00
103	A10	$1 ol grn & lil	200.00	42.00
104	A10	$2 scar & black	440.00	175.00
105	A10	$2 blk & car ('10)	420.00	440.00
106	A10	$3 dp bl & blk	340.00	320.00
107	A10	$5 bl grn & lil	525.00	500.00
108	A10	$10 org & blk, bl	2,000.	1,450.
		Nos. 86-108 (23)	4,689.	3,135.

Nos. 86, 88, 90, 94 and 95 are on ordinary paper only. Nos. 92, 93, 96, 98, 100, 102, 105, 106 and 107 are on chalky paper and the others of the issue are on both papers.

The 4c, 5c, 8c, 12c 20c, 50c, $2 and $5 denominations of type A10 are expressed in colored letters or numerals and letters on a colorless background.

King George V
A11   A12

A13   A14

A15

Type I — No. 117	Type II — No. 128

Two Types of 25c:
I: A short vertical stroke crosses the bottom of the top Chinese character in the left label.
II: The vertical stroke is absent from the character.

1912-14   **Ordinary Paper**

109	A11	1c brown	4.50	.60
a.		Booklet pane of 12		
110	A11	2c deep green	12.00	.40
a.		Booklet pane of 12		
111	A12	4c carmine	6.50	.40
a.		Booklet pane of 12		
b.		Booklet pane of 4		
112	A13	6c orange	6.00	2.25
113	A12	8c gray	27.50	8.00
114	A11	10c ultramarine	37.50	.35

Chalky Paper

115	A14	12c vio, yel	9.00	10.00
116	A14	20c ol grn & vio	12.00	1.50
117	A15	25c red vio & dl vio (I) ('14)	32.50	32.50
118	A13	30c org & violet	29.00	9.00
119	A14	50c black, bl grn, white back	25.00	2.00
a.		50c black, emerald	27.50	10.00
b.		50c black, bl grn, ol back	1,400.	32.50
c.		50c black, emer, ol back	32.50	10.00
120	A11	$1 blue & vio, bl	55.00	6.00
121	A14	$2 black & red	180.00	70.00
122	A13	$3 vio & green	275.00	100.00
123	A14	$5 red & grn, grn	725.00	400.00
a.		$5 red & grn, bl grn, ol back	1,300.	375.00
124	A13	$10 blk & vio, red	675.00	95.00
		Nos. 109-124 (16)	2,111.	738.00

For overprints see British Offices in China Nos. 1-27.

1914, May   Surface-colored Paper

125	A14	12c violet, yel	10.00	18.00
126	A14	50c black, green	25.00	5.00
127	A14	$5 red & grn, grn	675.00	350.00
		Nos. 125-127 (3)	710.00	373.00

Stamp of 1912-14 Redrawn (Type II)
1919, Aug.   Chalky Paper

128	A15	25c red vio & dl vio	250.00	80.00

Types of 1912-14 Issue
1921-37   **Wmk. 4**
Ordinary Paper

129	A11	1c brown	1.25	.50
130	A11	2c deep green	4.00	.75
131	A11	2c gray ('37)	22.50	8.00
132	A12	3c gray ('31)	10.00	1.50
133	A12	4c rose red	5.50	1.00
134	A11	5c violet ('31)	18.00	.40
135	A12	8c gray	21.00	40.00
136	A12	8c orange	5.75	2.00
137	A11	10c ultramarine	7.50	.45

Chalky Paper

138	A14	12c vio, yel ('33)	20.00	4.00
139	A14	20c ol grn & dl vio	8.50	.40
140	A15	25c red vio & dl vio, redrawn	7.50	1.50
141	A13	30c yel & violet	12.00	1.75
142	A14	50c blk, emerald	24.00	.45
143	A11	$1 ultra & vio, bl	45.00	.60
144	A14	$2 black & red	140.00	7.50
145	A13	$3 dl vio & grn ('26)	200.00	70.00
146	A14	$5 red & grn, emer ('25)	550.00	85.00
		Nos. 129-146 (18)	1,102.	225.80

Common Design Types
pictured following the introduction.

Silver Jubilee Issue
Common Design Type

1935, May 6   Engr.   Perf. 11x12

147	CD301	3c black & ultra	4.00	4.00
148	CD301	5c indigo & grn	10.00	3.00
149	CD301	10c ultra & brn	22.50	4.00
150	CD301	20c brn vio & ind	40.00	10.00
		Nos. 147-150 (4)	76.50	21.00
		Set, never hinged	200.00	

Coronation Issue
Common Design Type

1937, May 12   Perf. 11x11½

151	CD302	4c deep green	4.00	4.00
152	CD302	15c dark carmine	10.00	4.00
153	CD302	25c deep ultra	13.00	4.50
		Nos. 151-153 (3)	27.00	12.50
		Set, never hinged	40.00	

King George VI — A16

1938-48   **Typo.   Perf. 14**
Ordinary Paper

154	A16	1c brown	.75	1.00
155	A16	2c gray	1.25	.25
156	A16	4c orange	2.50	3.25
157	A16	5c green	1.10	.25
157B	A16	8c brown red ('41)	1.00	2.75
c.		Imperf., pair	30,000.	
158	A16	10c violet	3.50	.60
159	A16	15c carmine	1.00	.30
159A	A16	20c gray ('46)	.60	.30
159B	A16	25c rose red ('48)	3.75	.45
160	A16	25c ultramarine	17.00	3.50
160A	A16	25c gray ol ('46)	2.25	2.75
161	A16	30c olive bister	110.00	4.00
161B	A16	30c lt ultra ('46)	3.50	.25

Chalky Paper

162	A16	50c red violet	4.50	.40
b.		Ordinary paper	32.50	.75
162C	A16	80c lilac rose ('48)	2.50	1.00
163	A16	$1 lilac & ultra	4.50	3.75
a.		Ordinary paper	8.00	17.50
163B	A16	$1 dp org & grn ('46)	27.50	1.25
c.		Ordinary paper	12.50	.35
164	A16	$2 dp org & grn	52.50	27.50
164A	A16	$2 vio & red ('46)	25.00	1.10
b.		Ordinary paper	25.00	8.25
165	A16	$5 lilac & red	40.00	50.00
165A	A16	$5 grn & vio ('46)	60.00	4.75
b.		Ordinary paper	45.00	16.00
166	A16	$10 grn & vio	325.00	130.00
166A	A16	$10 vio & ultra ('46)	110.00	20.00
b.		Ordinary paper	80.00	50.00
		Nos. 154-166A (23)	799.70	259.40
		Set, never hinged	1,200.	

Coarse Impressions
Ordinary Rough-Surfaced Paper

1941-46   **Perf. 14½x14**

155a	A16	2c gray	1.10	6.00
156a	A16	4c orange ('46)	2.75	3.25
157a	A16	5c green	1.60	5.25
158a	A16	10c violet	6.00	.25
161a	A16	30c dull olive bister	17.50	9.50
162a	A16	50c red lilac	19.00	2.00
		Nos. 155a-162a (6)	47.95	26.25
		Set, never hinged	85.00	

A17

1938, Jan. 11   **Wmk. 4**

167	A17	5c green	65.00	14.50
		Never hinged	110.00	

No. 167 is a revenue stamp officially authorized to be sold and used for postal purposes. Used Jan. 11-20, 1938. The used price is for the stamp on cover. CTO covers exist.

Street Scene — A18

Hong Kong Bank — A22

Liner and Junk — A19

University of Hong Kong — A20

Harbor — A21

China Clipper and Seaplane A23

Perf. 13½x13, 13x13½

1941, Feb. 26   Engr.   Wmk. 4

168	A18	2c sepia & org	4.75	2.00
169	A19	4c rose car & vio	5.50	4.50
170	A20	5c yel grn & blk	2.25	.35
171	A21	15c red & black	5.75	2.50
172	A22	25c dp blue & dk brn	11.00	8.00
173	A23	$1 brn org & brt bl	32.00	12.00
		Nos. 168-173 (6)	61.25	29.35
		Set, never hinged	100.00	

Centenary of British rule.

Catalogue values for unused stamps in this section, from this point to the end of the section, are for Never Hinged items.

Peace Issue

Phoenix Rising from Flames A24

1946, Aug. 29   Perf. 13x12½

174	A24	30c car & dp blue	2.40	2.40
175	A24	$1 car & brown	2.75	.75
		Set, hinged	5.00	

Return to peace after WWII.

Silver Wedding Issue
Common Design Types
Perf. 14x14½

1948, Dec. 22   Photo.   Wmk. 4

178	CD304	10c purple	3.90	1.60

Engr.; Name Typo.
Perf. 11½x11

179	CD305	$10 rose car	360.00	135.00
		Set, hinged	275.00	

UPU Issue
Common Design Types
Engr.; Name Typo. on 20c & 30c

1949, Oct. 10   Perf. 13½, 11x11½

180	CD306	10c violet	4.75	1.10
181	CD307	20c deep car	18.00	6.25
182	CD308	30c indigo	15.50	6.25
183	CD309	80c red violet	36.00	10.00
		Nos. 180-183 (4)	74.25	23.60
		Set, hinged	25.00	

POSTAGE DUE STAMPS

Scales Showing Letter Overweight — D1

1923, Dec.   Typo.   Wmk. 4   Perf. 14

J1	D1	1c brown	2.75	.70
a.		Chalky paper, wmkd. sideways	1.60	3.50
J2	D1	2c green	40.00	9.50
J3	D1	4c red	52.50	7.25
J4	D1	6c orange	34.00	13.50
J5	D1	10c ultramarine	28.00	9.00
		Nos. J1-J5 (5)	157.25	39.95
		Set, never hinged	300.00	

No. J1a issued Mar. 21, 1956.

1938-47   Perf. 14

J6	D1	2c gray	6.75	9.50
J7	D1	4c orange yellow	10.00	5.25
J8	D1	6c carmine	3.50	5.75
J9	D1	8c fawn ('46)	3.00	34.00
J10	D1	10c violet	19.00	.55
J11	D1	20c black ('46)	3.75	2.50
J12	D1	50c blue ('47)	40.00	13.50
		Nos. J6-J12 (7)	86.00	71.05
		Set, never hinged	190.00	

Nos. J6-J7 and J10 exist on both ordinary and chalky paper.

OCCUPATION STAMPS

Issued under Japanese Occupation

War Factory Girl — A144

Gen. Maresuke Nogi — A84

Admiral Heihachiro Togo — A86

Stamps of Japan, 1942-43 Surcharged in Black

Wmk. 257

1945, Apr.   Typo.   Perf. 13

N1	A144	1½y on 1s org brn	37.50	32.00
N2	A84	3y on 2s ver	12.50	27.50
N3	A86	5y on 5s brn lake	1,000.	160.00
		Nos. N1-N3 (3)	1,050.	219.50

No. N1 has eleven characters.

TREATY PORTS

AMOY

Values for stamps of Hong Kong used at AMOY with "AMOY" c.d.s., "A1", "D27", or "AMOY" c.d.s.

1862   Unwmk.   Perf. 14
On Nos. 1-7

LAM1	A1	2c pale brown	285.00
a.		deep brown	300.00
LAM2	A1	8c buff	235.00
LAM3	A1	12c blue	210.00
LAM4	A1	18c lilac	160.00
LAM5	A1	24c green	260.00
LAM6	A1	48c rose	1,450.
LAM7	A1	96c gray	1,150.

1863-80   Wmk. 1   Perf. 14
On Nos. 8-25

LAM8	A1	2c brown	40.00
LAM9	A1	2c dull rose	57.50
LAM10	A1	4c slate	45.00
LAM11	A1	5c ultra	100.00
LAM12	A1	6c lilac	72.50
LAM13	A1	8c orange buff	52.50
LAM14	A1	10c violet	75.00
LAM15	A1	12c lt blue	25.00
LAM16	A1	16c yellow	150.00
LAM17	A1	18c lilac	110.00
LAM18	A1	24c green	67.50
LAM19	A1	30c vermilion	150.00
LAM20	A1	30c violet	22.50
LAM21	A1	48c rose carmine	85.00
LAM22	A1	48c brown	325.00
LAM23	A1	96c bister	3,750.
LAM24	A1	96c gray	400.00

Perf. 12½

LAM25	A1	4c slate	—

1874   Wmk. 1   Perf. 15½x15
On Nos. 26-27

LAM26	A2	$2 sage green	225.00
LAM27	A3	$3 dull violet	225.00

1876-77   On Nos. 29-30

LAM28	A1	16c on 18c lilac	375.00
LAM29	A1	28c on 30c violet	160.00

1879-80   On Nos. 31-35

LAM30	A1	5c on 8c orange	150.00
LAM31	A1	5c on 18c lilac	110.00
LAM32	A1	10c on 12c blue	110.00
LAM33	A1	10c on 16c yellow	250.00
LAM34	A1	10c on 24c green	150.00

1879   Wmk. 1   Perf. 14
On Nos. 35A-35B

LAM35	A5	3c on 16c yel on card	1,100.
LAM36	A5	5c on 18c lilac on card	1,100.

See note after No. 35C.

1882-1902   Wmk. 2   Perf. 14
On Nos. 36-48

LAM37	A1	2c rose lake	62.50
a.		carmine	5.50
LAM38	A1	2c green	5.50
LAM39	A1	4c slate	15.00
LAM40	A1	4c carmine rose	4.00
LAM41	A1	5c ultramarine	5.00
LAM42	A1	5c yellow	24.00
LAM43	A1	10c lilac	50.00
LAM44	A1	10c green	6.00
LAM45	A1	10c vio, red	6.00
LAM46	A1	10c ultra	6.50
LAM47	A1	12c blue	225.00
LAM48	A1	30c gray green	50.00
LAM49	A1	30c brown	90.00

1885-91   Wmk. 2   Perf. 14
On Nos. 51-56

LAM50	A1	20c on 30c vermilion	20.00
LAM51	A1	20c on 30c green	20.00
LAM52	A1	50c on 48c brown	90.00
LAM53	A1	50c on 48c lilac	20.00
LAM54	A1	$1 on 96c olive gray	150.00
LAM55	A1	$1 on 96c vio, red	57.50

1891   Wmk. 2   Perf. 14
On Nos. 60, 64-65

LAM56	A4	$5 on $10 red	350.00
LAM57	A1	7c on 10c green	27.50

Wmk. 1

LAM58	A1	14c on 30c violet	140.00

1891   Wmk. 2   Perf. 14
On No. 66

LAM59	A1	2c carmine	1,100.

50th anniv. of the colony.

1897   Wmk. 1   Perf. 15½x15
On Nos. 67-68

LAM60	A2	$1 on $2 sage grn	—

Perf. 14

LAM61	A2	$1 on $2 gray grn	450.00

1898   Wmk. 2   Perf. 14
On Nos. 69-70

LAM62	A1	10c on 30c gray green	275.00
LAM63	A1	$1 on 96c black	75.00

1903   Wmk. 2   Perf. 14
On Nos. 71-83

LAM64	A10	1c brown & lilac	5.50
LAM65	A10	2c gray green	5.50
LAM66	A10	4c violet, red	3.50
LAM67	A10	5c org & gray green	25.00
LAM68	A10	8c vio & blk	8.50
LAM69	A10	10c ultra & lilac, blue	5.00
LAM70	A10	12c red vio & gray grn, yel	18.00
LAM71	A10	20c org brn & blk	14.00
LAM72	A10	30c blk & gray grn	67.50
LAM73	A10	50c org & gray grn	115.00
LAM74	A10	$2 scarlet & blk	550.00
LAM75	A10	$3 dull blue & blk	900.00

1904-11   Wmk. 3   Perf. 14
On Nos. 86-107

LAM76	A10	1c brown	5.50
LAM77	A10	2c gray green	5.50
LAM78	A10	2c deep green	5.00
LAM79	A10	4c violet, red	3.50
LAM80	A10	4c carmine	3.50
LAM81	A10	5c org & gray grn	20.00
LAM82	A10	6c red vio & org	20.00
LAM83	A10	8c vio & blk	12.00
LAM84	A10	10c ultra & lil, blue	5.00
LAM85	A10	10c ultra	4.50
LAM86	A10	12c red vio & gray grn, yel	22.50
LAM87	A10	20c org brn & blk	14.00
LAM88	A10	20c olive grn & vio	80.00
LAM89	A10	30c blk & gray grn	45.00
LAM90	A10	30c org & vio	85.00
LAM91	A10	50c org & gray grn	45.00
LAM92	A10	50c blk, grn	85.00
LAM93	A10	$1 ol grn & lil	110.00
LAM94	A10	$2 scarlet & blk	450.00
LAM95	A10	$5 bl grn & lil	800.00

1912-15   Wmk. 3   Perf. 14
On Nos. 109-122

LAM96	A11	1c brown	7.00
LAM97	A11	2c deep green	6.50
LAM98	A12	4c carmine	3.50
LAM99	A13	6c orange	8.00
LAM100	A12	8c gray	25.00
LAM101	A11	10c ultramarine	5.00
LAM102	A14	12c vio, yel	35.00
LAM103	A14	20c ol grn & vio	8.50
LAM104	A15	25c red vio & dl vio	100.00
LAM105	A13	30c org & vio	30.00
LAM106	A14	50c blk, blue grn, white back	17.00
LAM107	A11	$1 blk & vio, blue	32.50
LAM108	A13	$3 vio & grn	250.00

ANPING

Values for stamps of Hong Kong used at ANPING

1882-91   Wmk. 2   Perf. 14
On Nos. 36b-44

LAP1	A1	2c carmine	1,100.
LAP2	A1	5c ultramarine	900.00
LAP3	A1	10c green	1,000.
LAP4	A1	10c vio, red	1,150.

1885-91   Wmk. 2   Perf. 14
On Nos. 51, 53

LAP5	A1	20c on 30c vermilion	1,100.
LAP6	A1	50c on 48c brown	1,900.

CANTON

Values for stamps of Hong Kong used at CANTON with "C1" or c.d.s.

1862   Unwmk.   Perf. 14
On No. 4

LCA1	A1	18c lilac	200.00

1863-80   Wmk. 1   Perf. 14
On Nos. 8-24

LCA2	A1	2c brown	42.50
LCA3	A1	2c dull rose	57.50
LCA4	A1	4c slate	45.00
LCA5	A1	5c ultra	90.00
LCA6	A1	6c lilac	72.50
LCA7	A1	8c orange buff	52.50
LCA8	A1	10c violet	65.00

LCA9	A1	12c lt blue	25.00
LCA10	A1	16c yellow	190.00
LCA11	A1	24c green	80.00
LCA12	A1	30c vermilion	—
LCA13	A1	30c violet	25.00
LCA14	A1	48c rose carmine	135.00
LCA15	A1	96c gray	325.00

1874   **Wmk. 1**   *Perf. 15½x15*
On No. 26

LCA16	A2	$2 sage green	225.00

1876-77   **On Nos. 29-30**

LCA17	A1	16c on 18c lilac	350.00
LCA18	A1	28c on 30c violet	150.00

1879-80   **On Nos. 31-35**

LCA19	A1	5c on 8c orange	190.00
LCA20	A1	5c on 18c lilac	145.00
LCA21	A1	10c on 12c blue	135.00
LCA22	A1	10c on 16c yellow	300.00
LCA23	A1	10c on 24c green	175.00

1879   **Wmk. 1**   *Perf. 14*
On Nos. 35A-35B

LCA24	A5	3c on 16c yel on card	850.00
LCA25	A5	5c on 18c lilac on card	1,000.

See note after No. 35C.

1882-1902   **Wmk. 2**   *Perf. 14*
On Nos. 36-48

LCA26	A1	2c rose lake	45.00
a.		carmine	4.00
LCA27	A1	2c green	5.00
LCA28	A1	4c slate	16.00
LCA29	A1	4c carmine rose	4.50
LCA30	A1	5c ultramarine	6.00
LCA31	A1	5c yellow	37.50
LCA32	A1	10c lilac	45.00
LCA33	A1	10c green	11.00
LCA34	A1	10c vio, *red*	5.50
LCA35	A1	10c ultra	5.00
LCA36	A1	12c blue	160.00
LCA37	A1	30c gray green	50.00
LCA38	A1	30c brown	80.00

1885-91   **Wmk. 2**   *Perf. 14*
On Nos. 51-56

LCA39	A1	20c on 30c vermilion	18.00
LCA40	A1	20c on 30c yel green	325.00
LCA41	A1	50c on 48c brown	90.00
LCA42	A1	50c on 48c lilac	25.00
LCA43	A1	$1 on 96c olive gray	160.00
LCA44	A1	$1 on 96c vio, *red*	75.00

1891   **Wmk. 2**   *Perf. 14*
On Nos. 60, 61a, 64-65

LCA45	A4	$5 on $10 vio, *red*	475.00
LCA46	A1(g)	20c on 30c dull grn	22.50
LCA47	A1	7c on 10c green	27.50
		Wmk. 1	
LCA48	A1	14c on 30c violet	150.00

1891   **Wmk. 2**   *Perf. 14*
On No. 66

LCA49	A1	2c carmine	*1,100.*

50th anniv. of the colony.

1897   **Wmk. 1**   *Perf. 15½x15*
On No. 67

LCA50	A2	$1 on $2 sage grn	—

1898   **Wmk. 2**   *Perf. 14*
On Nos. 69-70

LCA51	A1	10c on 30c gray green	200.00
LCA52	A1	$1 on 96c black	175.00

1903   **Wmk. 2**   *Perf. 14*
On Nos. 71-80

LCA53	A10	1c brown & lilac	5.00
LCA54	A10	2c gray green	5.50
LCA55	A10	4c violet, *red*	4.00
LCA56	A10	5c org & gray green	25.00
LCA57	A10	8c vio & blk	10.00
LCA58	A10	10c ultra & lilac, *blue*	5.00
LCA59	A10	12c red vio & gray grn, *yel*	20.00
LCA60	A10	20c org brn & blk	12.00
LCA61	A10	30c blk & gray grn	62.50
LCA62	A10	50c red vio & gray green	100.00

1904-11   **Wmk. 3**   *Perf. 14*
On Nos. 86-108

LCA63	A10	1c brown	5.00
LCA64	A10	2c gray green	5.00
LCA65	A10	2c deep green	5.00
LCA66	A10	4c violet, *red*	4.00
LCA67	A10	4c carmine	4.00
LCA68	A10	5c org & gray grn	24.00
LCA69	A10	6c red vio & org	24.00
LCA70	A10	8c vio & blk	16.00
LCA71	A10	10c ultra & lil, *blue*	5.00

LCA72	A10	10c ultra	5.00
LCA73	A10	12c red vio & gray grn, *yel*	26.00
LCA74	A10	20c org brn & blk	15.00
LCA75	A10	20c olive grn & vio	85.00
LCA76	A10	30c blk & gray grn	45.00
LCA77	A10	30c org & vio	72.50
LCA78	A10	50c red vio & gray grn	50.00
LCA79	A10	50c blk, *grn*	52.50
LCA80	A10	$1 ol grn & lil	90.00
LCA81	A10	$2 scarlet & blk	575.00
LCA82	A10	$2 carmine & blk	675.00
LCA83	A10	$3 dp blue & blk	750.00
LCA84	A10	$10 org & blk, *blue*	2,000.

1912-14   **Wmk. 3**   *Perf. 14*
On Nos. 109-124

LCA85	A11	1c brown	5.00
LCA86	A11	2c deep green	4.50
LCA87	A11	4c carmine	3.50
LCA88	A13	6c orange	7.50
LCA89	A12	8c gray	24.00
LCA90	A11	10c ultramarine	5.00
LCA91	A14	12c vio, *yel*	24.00
LCA92	A14	20c ol grn & vio	7.50
LCA93	A15	25c red vio & dl vio	100.00
LCA94	A10	30c org & vio	25.00
LCA95	A14	50c blk, *blue grn*	9.00
LCA96	A11	$1 blk & vio, *blue*	45.00
LCA97	A14	$2 blk & red	150.00
LCA98	A13	$3 vio & grn	275.00
LCA99	A13	$10 blk & vio, *red*	450.00

CHEFOO

**Values for stamps of Hong Kong
used at CHEFOO with c.d.s.**

1882-1902   **Wmk. 2**   *Perf. 14*
On Nos. 37-48

LCH1	A1	2c green	30.00
LCH2	A1	4c carmine rose	30.00
LCH3	A1	5c ultramarine	42.50
LCH4	A1	5c yellow	80.00
LCH5	A1	10c ultra	30.00
LCH6	A1	30c brown	180.00

1891   **Wmk. 2**   *Perf. 14*
On No. 52

LCH7	A1	20c on 30c gray green	62.50

1898   **Wmk. 2**   *Perf. 14*
On No. 70

LCH8	A1	$1 on 96c black	150.00

1903   **Wmk. 2**   *Perf. 14*
On Nos. 71-81

LCH9	A10	1c brown & lilac	12.50
LCH10	A10	2c gray green	11.00
LCH11	A10	4c violet, *red*	10.00
LCH12	A10	5c org & gray green	30.00
LCH13	A10	8c vio & blk	22.50
LCH14	A10	10c ultra & lilac, *blue*	14.00
LCH15	A10	12c red vio & gray grn, *yel*	40.00
LCH16	A10	20c org brn & blk	45.00
LCH17	A10	50c red vio & gray green	150.00
LCH18	A10	$1 ol grn & lilac	160.00

1904-11   **Wmk. 3**   *Perf. 14*
On Nos. 86-107

LCH19	A10	1c brown	12.50
LCH20	A10	2c gray green	11.00
LCH21	A10	2c deep green	11.50
LCH22	A10	4c violet, *red*	9.00
LCH23	A10	4c carmine	10.00
LCH24	A10	5c org & gray grn	22.50
LCH25	A10	6c red vio & org	40.00
LCH26	A10	8c vio & blk	20.00
LCH27	A10	10c ultra & lil, *blue*	11.00
LCH28	A10	10c ultra	11.00
LCH29	A10	12c red vio & gray grn, *yel*	35.00
LCH30	A10	20c org brn & blk	25.00
LCH31	A10	20c olive grn & vio	115.00
LCH32	A10	30c blk & gray grn	75.00
LCH33	A10	30c org & vio	90.00
LCH34	A10	50c red vio & gray grn	75.00
LCH35	A10	50c blk, *grn*	75.00
LCH36	A10	$1 ol grn & lil	125.00
LCH37	A10	$2 scarlet & blk	350.00
LCH38	A10	$2 carmine & blk	750.00
LCH39	A10	$3 dp blue & blk	675.00
LCH40	A10	$5 bl grn & lil	1,000.

1912-14   **Wmk. 3**   *Perf. 14*
On Nos. 109-124

LCH41	A11	1c brown	10.00
LCH42	A11	2c deep green	10.00
LCH43	A11	4c carmine	8.00
LCH44	A13	6c orange	20.00
LCH45	A12	8c gray	42.50
LCH46	A11	10c ultramarine	10.00
LCH47	A14	12c vio, *yel*	45.00
LCH48	A14	20c ol grn & vio	15.00
LCH49	A13	30c org & vio	27.50
LCH50	A14	50c blk, *blue grn,*	15.00

LCH51	A11	$1 blk & vio, *blue*	25.00
LCH52	A14	$2 blk & red	125.00
LCH53	A13	$3 vio & grn	190.00
LCH54	A14	$5 red & grn, *grn*	675.00
LCH55	A13	$10 blk & vio, *red*	450.00

FOOCHOW

**Values for stamps of Hong Kong
used at FOOCHOW with "F1" or
"FOOCHOWFOO" c.d.s.**

1862   **Unwmk.**   *Perf. 14*
On No. 4

LFO1	A1	18c lilac	225.00

1863-80   **Wmk. 1**   *Perf. 14*
On Nos. 8-24

LFO2	A1	2c brown	37.50
LFO3	A1	2c dull rose	50.00
LFO4	A1	4c slate	37.50
LFO5	A1	5c ultra	95.00
LFO6	A1	6c lilac	57.50
LFO7	A1	8c orange buff	52.50
LFO8	A1	10c violet	55.00
LFO9	A1	12c lt blue	22.50
LFO10	A1	16c yellow	175.00
LFO11	A1	18c lilac	1,050.
LFO12	A1	24c green	80.00
LFO13	A1	30c vermilion	250.00
LFO14	A1	30c violet	20.00
LFO15	A1	48c rose carmine	135.00
LFO16	A1	48c brpwn	300.00
LFO17	A1	96c gray	450.00

1874   **Wmk. 1**   *Perf. 15½x15*
On Nos. 26-27

LFO18	A2	$2 sage green	190.00
LFO19	A3	$3 violet	175.00

1876-77   **On Nos. 29-30**

LFO20	A1	16c on 18c lilac	375.00
LFO21	A1	28c on 30c violet	175.00

1879-80   **On Nos. 31-35**

LFO22	A1	5c on 8c orange	375.00
LFO23	A1	5c on 18c lilac	135.00
LFO24	A1	10c on 12c blue	135.00
LFO25	A1	10c on 16c yellow	—
LFO26	A1	10c on 24c green	180.00

1879   **Wmk. 1**   *Perf. 14*
On No. 35A

LFO27	A5	3c on 16c yel on card	1,100.

See note after No. 35C.

1882-1902   **Wmk. 2**   *Perf. 14*
On Nos. 36b-48

LFO28	A1	2c rose lake	42.50
a.		carmine	3.25
LFO29	A1	2c green	5.00
LFO30	A1	4c slate	9.50
LFO31	A1	4c carmine rose	5.50
LFO32	A1	5c ultramarine	4.00
LFO33	A1	5c yellow	25.00
LFO34	A1	10c lilac	47.50
LFO35	A1	10c green	11.50
LFO36	A1	10c vio, *red*	4.75
LFO37	A1	10c ultra	5.00
LFO38	A1	30c gray green	52.50
LFO39	A1	30c brown	100.00

1885-91   **Wmk. 2**   *Perf. 14*
On Nos. 51-56

LFO40	A1	20c on 30c vermilion	20.00
LFO41	A1	20c on 30c yel green	300.00
LFO42	A1	50c on 48c brown	90.00
LFO43	A1	50c on 48c lilac	30.00
LFO44	A1	$1 on 96c olive gray	150.00
LFO45	A1	$1 on 96c vio, *red*	75.00

1891   **Wmk. 2**   *Perf. 14*
On Nos. 61a, 64-65

LFO46	A1(g)	20c on 30c dull grn	25.00
LFO47	A1	7c on 10c green	70.00
		Wmk. 1	
LFO48	A1	14c on 30c violet	125.00

1898   **Wmk. 2**   *Perf. 14*
On Nos. 69-70

LFO49	A1	10c on 30c gray green	250.00
LFO50	A1	$1 on 96c black	110.00

1903   **Wmk. 2**   *Perf. 14*
On Nos. 71-81

LFO51	A10	1c brown & lilac	6.00
LFO52	A10	2c gray green	5.00
LFO53	A10	4c violet, *red*	3.50
LFO54	A10	5c org & gray green	24.00
LFO55	A10	8c vio & blk	14.00
LFO56	A10	10c ultra & lilac, *blue*	5.00
LFO57	A10	12c red vio & gray grn, *yel*	24.00

LFO58	A10	20c org brn & blk	15.00
LFO59	A10	30c blk & gray grn	57.50
LFO60	A10	50c red vio & gray green	95.00
LFO61	A10	$1 ol grn & lilac	85.00

1904-11   **Wmk. 3**   *Perf. 14*
On Nos. 86-103

LFO62	A10	1c brown	4.50
LFO63	A10	2c gray green	5.00
LFO64	A10	2c deep green	4.50
LFO65	A10	4c violet, *red*	3.50
LFO66	A10	4c carmine	3.50
LFO67	A10	5c org & gray grn	18.00
LFO68	A10	6c red vio & org	22.50
LFO69	A10	8c vio & blk	12.00
LFO70	A10	10c ultra & lil, *blue*	5.00
LFO71	A10	10c ultra	4.50
LFO72	A10	12c red vio & gray grn, *yel*	26.00
LFO73	A10	20c org brn & blk	12.50
LFO74	A10	20c olive grn & vio	85.00
LFO75	A10	30c blk & gray grn	52.50
LFO76	A10	30c org & vio	72.50
LFO77	A10	50c red vio & gray grn	45.00
LFO78	A10	50c blk, *grn*	52.50
LFO79	A10	$1 ol grn & lil	90.00

1912-14   **Wmk. 3**   *Perf. 14*
On Nos. 109-119

LFO80	A11	1c brown	6.00
LFO81	A11	2c deep green	4.75
LFO82	A12	4c carmine	3.50
LFO83	A13	6c orange	15.00
LFO84	A12	8c gray	27.50
LFO85	A11	10c ultramarine	5.00
LFO86	A14	12c vio, *yel*	37.50
LFO87	A14	20c ol grn & vio	8.00
LFO88	A15	25c red vio & dl vio	100.00
LFO89	A13	30c org & vio	27.50
LFO90	A14	50c blk, *blue grn,*	25.00

HANKOW

**Values for stamps of Hong Kong
used at HANKOW with "D29" or
c.d.s.**

1862   **Unwmk.**   *Perf. 14*
On No. 4

LHA1	A1	18c lilac	450.00

1863-80   **Wmk. 1**   *Perf. 14*
On Nos. 8-24

LHA2	A1	2c brown	135.00
LHA3	A1	2c dull rose	110.00
LHA4	A1	4c slate	135.00
LHA5	A1	5c ultra	125.00
LHA6	A1	6c lilac	180.00
LHA7	A1	8c orange buff	175.00
LHA8	A1	10c violet	135.00
LHA9	A1	12c lt blue	55.00
LHA10	A1	16c yellow	800.00
LHA11	A1	18c lilac	1,250.
LHA12	A1	24c green	275.00
LHA13	A1	30c violet	135.00
LHA14	A1	48c rose carmine	375.00
LHA15	A1	48c brown	500.00
LHA16	A1	96c gray	—

1874   **Wmk. 1**   *Perf. 15½x15*
On No. 26

LHA17	A2	$2 sage green	325.00

1876-77   **On Nos. 29-30**

LHA18	A1	16c on 18c lilac	550.00
LHA19	A1	28c on 30c violet	350.00

1879-80   **On Nos. 31-35**

LHA20	A1	5c on 8c orange	350.00
LHA21	A1	5c on 18c lilac	250.00
LHA22	A1	10c on 12c blue	275.00
LHA23	A1	10c on 16c yellow	525.00
LHA24	A1	10c on 24c green	325.00

1879   **Wmk. 1**   *Perf. 14*
On No. 35A

LHA25	A5	3c on 16c yel on card	1,750.

See note after No. 35C.

1882-1902   **Wmk. 2**   *Perf. 14*
On Nos. 36b-48

LHA26	A1	2c carmine	10.00
LHA27	A1	2c green	7.00
LHA28	A1	4c slate	22.50
LHA29	A1	4c carmine rose	7.50
LHA30	A1	5c ultramarine	11.00
LHA31	A1	5c yellow	37.50
LHA32	A1	10c lilac	110.00
LHA33	A1	10c green	14.00
LHA34	A1	10c vio, *red*	12.00
LHA35	A1	10c ultra	5.00
LHA36	A1	12c blue	200.00
LHA37	A1	30c gray green	80.00
LHA38	A1	30c brown	110.00

1885-91 — Wmk. 2 — Perf. 14 — On Nos. 51-56

LHA39	A1	20c on 30c vermilion	45.00
LHA40	A1	20c on 30c yel green	30.00
LHA41	A1	50c on 48c brown	110.00
LHA42	A1	50c on 48c lilac	32.50
LHA43	A1	$1 on 96c olive gray	225.00
LHA44	A1	$1 on 96c vio, red	100.00

1890 — Wmk. 1 — Perf. 14 — On No. 57

LHA45	A2	$2 gray green	550.00

1891 — Wmk. 1 — Perf. 14 — On Nos. 64-65

LHA46	A1	7c on 10c green	45.00

Wmk. 1

LHA47	A1	14c on 30c violet	175.00

1897 — Wmk. 1 — Perf. 15½x15 — On No. 67

LHA48	A2	$1 on $2 sage grn	800.00

1898 — Wmk. 2 — Perf. 14 — On Nos. 69-70

LHA49	A1	10c on 30c gray green	325.00
LHA50	A1	$1 on 96c black	125.00

1903 — Wmk. 2 — Perf. 14 — On Nos. 71-81

LHA51	A10	1c brown & lilac	7.50
LHA52	A10	2c gray green	7.00
LHA53	A10	4c violet, red	6.00
LHA54	A10	5c org & gray green	27.50
LHA55	A10	8c vio & blk	22.50
LHA56	A10	10c ultra & lilac, blue	6.50
LHA57	A10	12c red vio & gray grn, yel	27.50
LHA58	A10	20c org brn & blk	20.00
LHA59	A10	30c blk & gray grn	65.00
LHA60	A10	50c red vio & gray green	110.00
LHA61	A10	$1 ol grn & lilac	90.00

1904-11 — Wmk. 3 — Perf. 14 — On Nos. 86-108

LHA62	A10	1c brown	7.00
LHA63	A10	2c gray green	6.50
LHA64	A10	2c deep green	6.00
LHA65	A10	4c violet, red	5.50
LHA66	A10	4c carmine	4.50
LHA67	A10	5c org & gray grn	25.00
LHA68	A10	6c red vio & org	27.50
LHA69	A10	8c vio & blk	12.50
LHA70	A10	10c ultra & lil, blue	6.50
LHA71	A10	10c ultra	6.50
LHA72	A10	12c red vio & gray grn, yel	30.00
LHA73	A10	20c org brn & blk	20.00
LHA74	A10	20c olive grn & vio	110.00
LHA75	A10	30c blk & gray grn	55.00
LHA76	A10	30c org & vio	100.00
LHA77	A10	50c red vio & gray grn	45.00
LHA78	A10	$1 ol grn & lil	90.00
LHA79	A10	$2 scarlet & blk	525.00
LHA80	A10	$5 bl grn & lilac	1,000.
LHA81	A10	$10 org & blk, blue	2,400.

1912-14 — Wmk. 3 — Perf. 14 — On Nos. 109-123

LHA82	A11	1c brown	8.00
LHA83	A11	2c deep green	7.00
LHA84	A12	4c carmine	5.50
LHA85	A13	6c orange	16.00
LHA86	A11	10c ultramarine	6.50
LHA87	A14	20c ol grn & vio	16.00
LHA88	A13	30c org & vio	35.00
LHA89	A14	50c blk, blue grn	20.00
LHA90	A11	$1 blk & vio, blue	80.00
LHA91	A14	$5 red & grn, grn	900.00

KIUNGCHOW (HOIHAO)

Values for stamps of Hong Kong used at KIUNGCHOW (HOIHAO) with "D28", c.d.s. inscribed "KIUNG-CHOW" or c.d.s. inscribed "Hoi-Hao"

1863-80 — Wmk. 1 — Perf. 14 — On Nos. 8-24

LKC1	A1	2c brown	1,100.
LKC2	A1	4c slate	900.00
LKC3	A1	5c ultra	900.00
LKC4	A1	6c lilac	1,800.
LKC5	A1	8c orange buff	1,850.
LKC6	A1	10c violet	1,050.
LKC7	A1	12c lt blue	600.00
LKC8	A1	16c yellow	3,000.
LKC9	A1	24c green	1,800.
LKC10	A1	30c vermilion	
LKC11	A1	30c violet	325.00
LKC12	A1	48c rose carmine	2,750.
LKC13	A1	96c gray	2,750.

1874 — Wmk. 1 — Perf. 15½x15 — On No. 26

LKC14	A2	$2 sage green	525.00

1876-77 — On Nos. 29-30

LKC15	A1	16c on 18c lilac	1,900.
LKC16	A1	28c on 30c violet	1,600.

1879-80 — On Nos. 31-35

LKC17	A1	5c on 8c orange	1,250.
LKC18	A1	5c on 18c lilac	1,100.
LKC19	A1	10c on 12c blue	1,100.
LKC20	A1	10c on 16c yellow	2,250.
LKC21	A1	10c on 24c green	—

1882-1902 — Wmk. 2 — Perf. 14 — On Nos. 36b-48

LKC22	A1	2c carmine	65.00
LKC23	A1	2c green	85.00
LKC24	A1	4c slate	90.00
LKC25	A1	4c carmine rose	42.50
LKC26	A1	5c ultramarine	65.00
LKC27	A1	5c yellow	110.00
LKC28	A1	10c lilac	850.00
LKC29	A1	10c green	90.00
LKC30	A1	10c vio, red	75.00
LKC31	A1	10c ultra	47.50
LKC32	A1	30c gray green	150.00
LKC33	A1	30c brown	210.00

1885-91 — Wmk. 2 — Perf. 14 — On Nos. 51-56

LKC34	A1	20c on 30c vermilion	175.00
LKC35	A1	20c on 30c yel green	75.00
LKC36	A1	50c on 48c brown	190.00
LKC37	A1	50c on 48c lilac	100.00
LKC38	A1	$1 on 96c olive gray	350.00
LKC39	A1	$1 on 96c vio, red	210.00

1890 — Wmk. 1 — Perf. 14 — On No. 57

LKC40	A2	$2 gray green	775.00

1891 — Wmk. 2 — Perf. 14 — On No. 64

LKC41	A1	7c on 10c green	225.00

1891 — Wmk. 2 — Perf. 14 — On No. 66

LKC42	A1	2c carmine	3,250.

50th anniv. of the colony.

1897 — Wmk. 1 — Perf. 15½x15 — On No. 67

LKC43	A2	$1 on $2 sage grn	575.00

1898 — Wmk. 2 — Perf. 14 — On Nos. 69-70

LKC44	A1	10c on 30c gray green	575.00
LKC45	A1	$1 on 96c black	400.00

1903 — Wmk. 2 — Perf. 14 — On Nos. 71-82

LKC46	A10	1c brown & lilac	30.00
LKC47	A10	2c gray green	30.00
LKC48	A10	4c violet, red	21.00
LKC49	A10	5c org & gray green	62.50
LKC50	A10	8c vio & blk	52.50
LKC51	A10	10c ultra & lilac, blue	26.00
LKC52	A10	12c red vio & gray grn, yel	67.50
LKC53	A10	20c org brn & blk	80.00
LKC54	A10	30c blk & gray grn	145.00
LKC55	A10	50c red vio & gray green	225.00
LKC56	A10	$1 ol grn & lilac	350.00
LKC57	A10	$2 scar & blk	1,050.

1904-11 — Wmk. 3 — Perf. 14 — On Nos. 86-103

LKC58	A10	1c brown	27.50
LKC59	A10	2c gray green	27.50
LKC60	A10	2c deep green	26.00
LKC61	A10	4c violet, red	21.00
LKC62	A10	4c carmine	21.00
LKC63	A10	5c org & gray grn	62.50
LKC64	A10	6c red vio & org	67.50
LKC65	A10	8c vio & blk	37.50
LKC66	A10	10c ultra & lil, blue	24.00
LKC67	A10	10c ultra	24.00
LKC68	A10	12c red vio & gray grn, yel	67.50
LKC69	A10	20c org brn & blk	80.00
LKC70	A10	20c olive grn & vio	115.00
LKC71	A10	30c blk & gray grn	100.00
LKC72	A10	30c org & vio	100.00
LKC72	A10	$1 ol grn & lil	550.00

1912-14 — Wmk. 3 — Perf. 14 — On Nos. 109-120

LKC74	A11	1c brown	25.00
LKC75	A11	2c deep green	24.00
LKC76	A12	4c carmine	21.00
LKC77	A13	6c orange	40.00
LKC78	A12	8c gray	100.00
LKC79	A11	10c ultramarine	21.00
LKC80	A14	12c vio, yel	72.50
LKC81	A14	20c ol grn & vio	47.50
LKC82	A15	25c red vio & dl vio	135.00
LKC83	A13	30c org & vio	110.00
LKC84	A14	50c blk, blue grn	85.00
LKC85	A11	$1 blk & vio, blue	90.00

NINGPO

Values for stamps of Hong Kong used at LINGPO with "N1" or c.d.s.

1862 — Unwmk. — Perf. 14 — On No. 4

LNG1	A1	18c lilac	1,350.

1863-80 — Wmk. 1 — Perf. 14 — On Nos. 8-25

LNG2	A1	2c brown	500.00
LNG3	A1	4c slate	500.00
LNG4	A1	5c ultra	250.00
LNG5	A1	6c lilac	550.00
LNG6	A1	8c orange buff	550.00
LNG7	A1	10c violet	250.00
LNG8	A1	12c lt blue	180.00
LNG9	A1	16c yellow	675.00
LNG10	A1	18c lilac	
LNG11	A1	24c green	550.00
LNG12	A1	30c vermilion	650.00
LNG13	A1	30c violet	160.00
LNG14	A1	48c rose carmine	950.00
LNG15	A1	48c brown	1,100.
LNG16	A1	96c gray	1,100.

Perf. 12½

LNG17	A1	4c slate	

1874 — Wmk. 1 — Perf. 15½x15 — On No. 26

LNG19	A2	$2 sage green	500.00

1876-77 — On Nos. 29-30

LNG20	A1	16c on 18c lilac	800.00
LNG21	A1	28c on 30c violet	500.00

1879-80 — On Nos. 31-35

LNG22	A1	5c on 8c orange	550.00
LNG23	A1	5c on 18c lilac	475.00
LNG24	A1	10c on 12c blue	500.00
LNG25	A1	10c on 24c green	550.00

1879 — Wmk. 1 — Perf. 14 — On No. 35A

LNG26	A5	3c on 16c yellow on card	2,000.

See note after No. 35C.

1882-1902 — Wmk. 2 — Perf. 14 — On Nos. 36b-47

LNG27	A1	2c carmine	52.50
LNG28	A1	2c green	35.00
LNG29	A1	4c slate	90.00
LNG30	A1	4c carmine rose	35.00
LNG31	A1	5c ultramarine	52.50
LNG32	A1	10c lilac	250.00
LNG33	A1	10c green	67.50
LNG34	A1	10c vio, red	57.50
LNG35	A1	10c ultra	35.00
LNG36	A1	30c gray green	160.00

1890 — Wmk. 1 — Perf. 15½x15 — On No. 50

LNG37	A4	12c on $10 rose	—

1885-91 — Wmk. 2 — Perf. 14 — On Nos. 52-56

LNG38	A1	20c on 30c yel green	60.00
LNG39	A1	50c on 48c brown	200.00
LNG40	A1	50c on 48c lilac	100.00
LNG41	A1	$1 on 96c vio, red	190.00

1891 — Wmk. 2 — Perf. 14 — On Nos. 64-65

LNG42	A1	7c on 10c green	90.00

Wmk. 1

LNG43	A1	14c on 30c violet	325.00

1897 — Wmk. 1 — Perf. 15½x15 — On No. 67

LNG44	A2	$1 on $2 sage grn	—

1898 — Wmk. 2 — Perf. 14 — On Nos. 69-70

LNG45	A1	10c on 30c gray green	400.00
LNG46	A1	$1 on 96c black	225.00

1903 — Wmk. 2 — Perf. 14 — On Nos. 71-80

LNG47	A10	1c brown & lilac	35.00
LNG48	A10	2c gray green	35.00
LNG49	A10	4c violet, red	25.00
LNG50	A10	5c org & gray green	75.00
LNG51	A10	8c vio & blk	42.50
LNG52	A10	10c ultra & lilac, blue	27.50
LNG53	A10	12c red vio & gray grn, yel	85.00
LNG54	A10	50c red vio & gray green	160.00

1904-11 — Wmk. 3 — Perf. 14 — On Nos. 86-103

LNG55	A10	1c brown	25.00
LNG56	A10	2c gray green	30.00
LNG57	A10	2c deep green	25.00
LNG58	A10	4c violet, red	25.00
LNG59	A10	4c carmine	25.00
LNG60	A10	8c vio & blk	57.50
LNG61	A10	10c ultra	25.00
LNG62	A10	12c red vio & gray grn, yel	80.00
LNG63	A10	20c org brn & blk	75.00
LNG64	A10	20c olive grn & vio	135.00
LNG65	A10	30c blk & gray grn	110.00
LNG66	A10	30c org & vio	125.00
LNG67	A10	50c red vio & gray grn	100.00
LNG68	A10	$1 ol grn & lil	150.00

1912-14 — Wmk. 3 — Perf. 14 — On Nos. 109-120

LNG69	A11	1c brown	27.50
LNG70	A11	2c deep green	25.00
LNG71	A12	4c carmine	25.00
LNG72	A12	8c gray	85.00
LNG73	A11	10c ultramarine	25.00
LNG74	A14	20c ol grn & vio	65.00
LNG75	A13	30c org & vio	100.00
LNG76	A11	$1 blk & vio, blue	90.00

SHANGHAI

Values for stamps of Hong Kong used at SHANGHAI with "S1", "SHANGHAE" or "SHANGHAF" c.d.s.

The popular "Sunburst" cancellation was also applied at Shanghai in 1864-65. It is scarce and commands premiums starting at $350 for the least rare values. It can be found together with the "B62" canceller of Hong Kong, and in that combination has a premium of about $300 for the least rare values. These values assume clear and reasonably complete strikes.

1862 — Unwmk. — Perf. 14 — On Nos. 1-7

LSH1	A1	2c pale brown	175.00
a.		deep brown	190.00
LSH2	A1	8c buff	200.00
LSH3	A1	12c blue	150.00
LSH4	A1	18c lilac	125.00
LSH5	A1	24c green	240.00
LSH6	A1	48c rose	650.00
LSH7	A1	96c gray	850.00

1863-80 — Wmk. 1 — Perf. 14 — On Nos. 8-25

LSH8	A1	2c brown	12.50
LSH9	A1	2c dull rose	42.50
LSH10	A1	4c slate	12.00
LSH11	A1	5c ultra	72.50
LSH12	A1	6c lilac	25.00
LSH13	A1	8c orange buff	20.00
LSH14	A1	10c violet	24.00
LSH15	A1	12c lt blue	12.00
LSH16	A1	16c yellow	85.00
LSH17	A1	18c lilac	400.00
LSH18	A1	24c green	18.00
LSH19	A1	30c vermilion	27.50
LSH20	A1	30c violet	9.00
LSH21	A1	48c rose carmine	45.00
LSH22	A1	48c brown	160.00
LSH23	A1	96c bister	1,500.
LSH24	A1	96c gray	70.00

Perf. 12½

LSH25	A1	4c slate	300.00

1874 — Wmk. 1 — Perf. 15½x15 — On Nos. 26-28

LSH26	A2	$2 sage green	80.00
LSH27	A3	$3 dull violet	55.00
LSH28	A4	$10 rose	825.00

1876-77 — On Nos. 29-30

LSH29	A1	16c on 18c lilac	200.00
LSH30	A1	28c on 30c violet	60.00

1879-80   **On Nos. 31-35**

LSH31	A1	5c on 8c orange	115.00
LSH32	A1	5c on 18c lilac	75.00
LSH33	A1	10c on 12c blue	60.00
LSH34	A1	10c on 16c yellow	190.00
LSH35	A1	10c on 24c green	115.00

1879   **Wmk. 1**   *Perf. 14*
On Nos. 35A-35B

LSH36	A5	3c on 16c yel on card	575.00
LSH37	A5	5c on 18c lilac on card	700.00

See note after No. 35C.

1882-1902   **Wmk. 2**   *Perf. 14*
On Nos. 36-48

LSH38	A1	2c rose lake	40.00
a.		carmine	3.50
LSH39	A1	2c green	1.50
LSH40	A1	4c slate	3.75
LSH41	A1	4c carmine rose	1.50
LSH42	A1	5c ultramarine	2.00
LSH43	A1	5c yellow	10.00
LSH44	A1	10c lilac	27.50
LSH45	A1	10c green	2.50
LSH46	A1	10c vio, *red*	2.00
LSH47	A1	10c ultra	3.00
LSH48	A1	12c blue	110.00
LSH49	A1	30c gray green	42.50
LSH50	A1	30c brown	42.50

1890   **Wmk. 1**   *Perf. 15½x15*
On No. 50

LSH51	A4	12c on $10 rose	375.00

1885-91   **Wmk. 2**   *Perf. 14*
On Nos. 51-56

LSH52	A1	20c on 30c vermilion	10.00
LSH53	A1	20c on 30c green	
LSH54	A1	50c on 48c brown	75.00
LSH55	A1	50c on 48c lilac	350.00
LSH56	A1	$1 on 96c olive gray	125.00
LSH57	A1	$1 on 96c vio, *red*	450.00

1890   **Wmk. 1**   *Perf. 14*
On Nos. 57-58, 60

LSH58	A2	$2 gray green	300.00
LSH59	A3	$3 lilac	600.00

Wmk. 2

LSH60	A4	$5 on $10 vio, *red*	200.00

1891   **Wmk. 2**   *Perf. 14*
On Nos. 61-65

LSH61	A1(g)	20c on 30c gray grn	11.00
LSH62	A1(h)	50c on 48c lilac	8.50
LSH63	A1(i)	$1 on 96c vio, *red*	32.50
LSH64	A1	7c on 10c green	17.00

Wmk. 1

LSH65	A1	14c on 30c violet	100.00

1897   **Wmk. 1**   *Perf. 15½x15*
On Nos. 67-68

LSH66	A2	$1 on $2 sage grn	240.00

Perf. 14

LSH67	A2	$1 on $2 gray grn	325.00

1898   **Wmk. 2**   *Perf. 14*
On Nos. 69-70

LSH68	A1	10c on 30c gray green	125.00
LSH69	A1	$1 on 96c black	50.00

1903   **Wmk. 2**   *Perf. 14*
On Nos. 71-85

LSH70	A10	1c brown & lilac	1.10
LSH71	A10	2c gray green	2.75
LSH72	A10	4c violet, *red*	1.00
LSH73	A10	5c org & gray green	16.00
LSH74	A10	8c vio & blk	3.25
LSH75	A10	10c ultra & lilac, *blue*	2.25
LSH76	A10	12c red vio & gray grn, *yel*	9.00
LSH77	A10	20c org brn & blk	6.25
LSH78	A10	30c blk & gray grn	40.00
LSH79	A10	50c red vio & gray green	80.00
LSH80	A10	$1 ol grn & lil	42.50
LSH81	A10	$2 scarlet & blk	500.00
LSH82	A10	$3 dull blue & blk	700.00
LSH83	A10	$5 bl grn & lil	800.00
LSH84	A10	$10 org & blk, *blue*	900.00

1904-11   **Wmk. 3**   *Perf. 14*
On Nos. 86-108

LSH85	A10	1c brown	2.00
LSH86	A10	2c gray green	3.25
LSH87	A10	2c deep green	2.25
LSH88	A10	4c violet, *red*	1.00
LSH89	A10	4c carmine	1.00
LSH90	A10	5c org & gray grn	10.00
LSH91	A10	6c red vio & org	10.00
LSH92	A10	8c vio & blk	4.00
LSH93	A10	10c ultra & lil, *blue*	2.00
LSH94	A10	10c ultra	1.00

LSH95	A10	12c red vio & gray grn, *yel*	11.00
LSH96	A10	20c org brn & blk	5.00
LSH97	A10	20c olive grn & vio	62.50
LSH98	A10	30c blk & gray grn	32.50
LSH99	A10	30c org & vio	47.50
LSH100	A10	50c red vio & gray grn	21.00
LSH101	A10	50c blk, *grn*	30.00
LSH102	A10	$1 ol grn & lil	47.50
LSH103	A10	$2 scarlet & blk	225.00
LSH104	A10	$2 blk & carmine	575.00
LSH105	A10	$3 dp blue & blk	500.00
LSH106	A10	$5 bl grn & lil	725.00
LSH107	A10	$10 org & blk, *blue*	1,850.

1912-15   **Wmk. 3**   *Perf. 14*
On Nos. 109-120

LSH108	A11	1c brown	1.50
LSH109	A11	2c deep green	1.00
LSH110	A12	4c carmine	1.00
LSH111	A12	6c orange	3.75
LSH112	A12	8c gray	11.50
LSH113	A11	10c ultramarine	1.00
LSH114	A14	12c vio, *yel*	17.00
LSH115	A14	20c ol grn & vio	2.50
LSH116	A13	30c org & vio	16.00
LSH117	A14	50c blk, *emerald*	6.25
LSH118	A11	$1 blk & vio, *blue*	10.00

SWATOW

Values for stamps of Hong Kong used at SWATOW with "S2" or c.d.s.

1862   **Unwmk.**   *Perf. 14*
On No. 4

LSW1	A1	18c lilac	500.00

1863-80   **Wmk. 1**   *Perf. 14*
On Nos. 8-25

LSW2	A1	2c brown	170.00
LSW3	A1	2c dull rose	150.00
LSW4	A1	4c slate	160.00
LSW5	A1	5c ultra	175.00
LSW6	A1	6c lilac	625.00
LSW7	A1	8c orange buff	160.00
LSW8	A1	10c violet	180.00
LSW9	A1	12c lt blue	57.50
LSW10	A1	16c yellow	575.00
LSW11	A1	18c lilac	1,250.
LSW12	A1	24c green	200.00
LSW13	A1	30c vermilion	
LSW14	A1	30c violet	57.50
LSW15	A1	48c rose carmine	325.00
LSW16	A1	96c gray	1,150.

Perf. 12½

LSW17	A1	4c slate	

1874   **Wmk. 1**   *Perf. 15½x15*
On Nos. 26-27

LSW18	A2	$2 sage green	190.00
LSW19	A3	$3 violet	175.00

1876-77   **On Nos. 29-30**

LSW20	A1	16c on 18c lilac	575.00
LSW21	A1	28c on 30c violet	325.00

1879-80   **On Nos. 31-35**

LSW22	A1	5c on 8c orange	375.00
LSW23	A1	5c on 18c lilac	300.00
LSW24	A1	10c on 12c blue	325.00
LSW25	A1	10c on 16c yellow	325.00
LSW26	A1	10c on 24c green	425.00

1879   **Wmk. 1**   *Perf. 14*
On No. 35A

LSW27	A5	3c on 16c yel on card	1,500.

See note after No. 35C.

1882-1902   **Wmk. 2**   *Perf. 14*
On Nos. 36b-48

LSW28	A1	2c carmine	8.50
LSW29	A1	2c green	10.00
LSW20	A1	4c slate	26.00
LSW31	A1	4c carmine rose	8.00
LSW32	A1	5c ultramarine	10.00
LSW33	A1	5c yellow	30.00
LSW34	A1	10c lilac	135.00
LSW35	A1	10c green	12.50
LSW36	A1	10c vio, *red*	8.50
LSW37	A1	10c ultra	8.00
LSW38	A1	12c blue	225.00
LSW39	A1	30c gray green	72.50
LSW40	A1	30c brown	80.00

1885-91   **Wmk. 2**   *Perf. 14*
On Nos. 51-56

LSW41	A1	20c on 30c	24.00
LSW42	A1	20c on 30c yel green	35.00
LSW43	A1	50c on 48c lilac	475.00
LSW44	A1	$1 on 96c ol gray	225.00
LSW45	A1	$1 on 96c vio, *red*	700.00

1890   **Wmk. 1**   *Perf. 14*
On No. 57

LSW46	A2	$2 sage green	575.00

1891   **Wmk. 2**   *Perf. 14*
On Nos. 62-65

LSW47	A1(h)	50c on 48c lilac	35.00
LSW48	A1(i)	$1 on 96c vio, *red*	80.00
LSW49	A1	7c on 10c green	45.00

Wmk. 1

LSW50	A1	14c on 30c violet	175.00

1891   **Wmk. 2**   *Perf. 14*
On No. 66

LSW51	A1	2c carmine	1,500.

50th anniv. of the colony.

1898   **Wmk. 2**   *Perf. 14*
On Nos. 69-70

LSW52	A1	10c on 30c gray green	325.00
LSW53	A1	$1 on 96c black	110.00

1903   **Wmk. 2**   *Perf. 14*
On Nos. 71-81

LSW54	A10	1c brown & lilac	8.00
LSW55	A10	2c gray green	8.00
LSW56	A10	4c violet, *red*	7.00
LSW57	A10	5c org & gray green	24.00
LSW58	A10	8c vio & blk	16.00
LSW59	A10	10c ultra & lilac, *blue*	8.00
LSW60	A10	12c red vio & gray grn, *yel*	22.50
LSW61	A10	20c org brn & blk	11.50
LSW62	A10	30c blk & gray grn	65.00
LSW63	A10	50c red vio & gray green	115.00
LSW64	A10	$1 ol grn & lil	100.00

1904-11   **Wmk. 3**   *Perf. 14*
On Nos. 86-108

LSW65	A10	1c brown	10.00
LSW66	A10	2c gray green	8.00
LSW67	A10	2c deep green	10.00
LSW68	A10	4c violet, *red*	7.50
LSW69	A10	4c carmine	6.50
LSW70	A10	5c org & gray grn	24.00
LSW71	A10	6c red vio & org	20.00
LSW72	A10	8c vio & blk	15.00
LSW73	A10	10c ultra & lil, *bl*	8.00
LSW74	A10	10c ultra	7.50
LSW75	A10	12c red vio & gray grn, *yel*	25.00
LSW76	A10	20c org brn & blk	15.00
LSW77	A10	20c olive grn & vio	110.00
LSW78	A10	30c blk & gray grn	57.50
LSW79	A10	30c org & vio	90.00
LSW80	A10	50c red vio & gray grn	40.00
LSW81	A10	50c blk, *grn*	52.50
LSW82	A10	$1 ol grn & lil	100.00
LSW83	A10	$2 scar & blk	375.00
LSW84	A10	$10 org & blk, *bl*	2,250.

1912-14   **Wmk. 3**   *Perf. 14*
On Nos. 109-120

LSW85	A11	1c brown	7.50
LSW86	A11	2c deep green	6.00
LSW87	A12	4c carmine	5.00
LSW88	A12	6c orange	11.00
LSW89	A12	8c gray	30.00
LSW90	A11	10c ultramarine	5.00
LSW91	A14	12c vio, *yel*	24.00
LSW92	A14	20c ol grn & vio	8.00
LSW93	A14	25c red vio & dl vio	75.00
LSW94	A13	30c org & vio	35.00
LSW95	A14	50c blk, *emerald*	17.50
LSW96	A11	$1 blk & vio, *blue*	30.00

TIENTSIN

Values for stamps of Hong Kong used at TIENTSIN with c.d.s.

1903   **Wmk. 2**   *Perf. 14*
On Nos. 71-77

LTS1	A10	1c brown & lilac	17.50
LTS2	A10	4c violet, *red*	22.50
LTS3	A10	5c org & gray green	40.00
LTS4	A10	8c vio & blk	17.50
LTS5	A10	12c red vio & gray grn, *yel*	55.00

1904-11   **Wmk. 3**   *Perf. 14*
On Nos. 86-108

LTS6	A10	1c brown	8.00
LTS7	A10	2c gray green	7.50
LTS8	A10	2c deep green	6.00
LTS9	A10	4c violet, *red*	5.50
LTS10	A10	4c carmine	5.00
LTS11	A10	5c org & gray grn	22.50
LTS12	A10	6c red vio & org	25.00
LTS13	A10	8c vio & blk	17.50
LTS14	A10	10c ultra & lil, *bl*	7.50
LTS15	A10	10c ultra	6.00
LTS16	A10	12c red vio & gray grn, *yel*	27.50

LTS17	A10	20c org brn & blk	17.50
LTS18	A10	20c olive grn & vio	110.00
LTS19	A10	30c blk & gray grn	55.00
LTS20	A10	30c org & vio	100.00
LTS21	A10	50c red vio & gray grn	45.00
LTS22	A10	50c blk, *grn*	75.00
LTS23	A10	$1 ol grn & lil	80.00
LTS24	A10	$2 scar & blk	350.00
LTS25	A10	$2 blk & car	800.00
LTS26	A10	$3 dp bl & blk	875.00
LTS27	A10	$5 bl grn & lil	1,200.
LTS28	A10	$10 org & blk, *bl*	2,400.

1912-14   **Wmk. 3**   *Perf. 14*
On Nos. 109-123

LTS29	A11	1c brown	7.50
LTS30	A11	2c deep green	7.00
LTS31	A12	4c carmine	5.00
LTS32	A13	6c orange	10.00
LTS33	A12	8c gray	40.00
LTS34	A11	10c ultramarine	7.00
LTS35	A14	12c vio, *yel*	42.50
LTS36	A14	20c ol grn & vio	11.00
LTS37	A13	30c org & vio	24.00
LTS38	A14	50c blk, *emerald*	14.00
LTS39	A11	$1 blk & vio, *blue*	20.00
LTS40	A13	$3 vio & grn	250.00
LTS41	A14	$5 red & grn, *grn*	800.00

WEI HAI WEI (Liu Kung Tau)

Values for stamps of Hong Kong cancelled with "LIU KUNG TAU *POST OFFICE*" double oval.

1862   **Unwmk.**   *Perf. 14*
On No. 3

LWH1	A1	12c blue	—

1874   **Wmk. 1**   *Perf. 15½x15*
On No. 26

LWH2	A2	$2 sage green	1,150.

1882-1902   **Wmk. 2**   *Perf. 14*
On Nos. 36b-48

LWH3	A1	2c carmine	85.00
LWH4	A1	2c green	12.50
LWH5	A1	4c slate	100.00
LWH6	A1	4c carmine rose	12.50
LWH7	A1	5c ultramarine	85.00
LWH8	A1	5c yellow	37.50
LWH9	A1	10c vio, *red*	55.00
LWH10	A1	10c ultra	12.50
LWH11	A1	12c blue	180.00
LWH12	A1	30c gray green	100.00
LWH13	A1	30c brown	110.00

1885-91   **Wmk. 2**   *Perf. 14*
On Nos. 51, 54

LWH14	A1	20c on 30c yel green	67.50
LWH15	A1	50c on 48c lilac	72.50

1898   **Wmk. 2**   *Perf. 14*
On No. 70

LWH16	A1	$1 on 96c black	150.00

1903   **Wmk. 2**   *Perf. 14*
On Nos. 71-81

LWH17	A10	1c brown & lilac	10.00
LWH18	A10	2c gray green	10.00
LWH19	A10	4c violet, *red*	8.00
LWH20	A10	5c org & gray green	27.50
LWH21	A10	8c vio & blk	20.00
LWH22	A10	10c ultra & lilac, *blue*	12.50
LWH23	A10	12c red vio & gray grn, *yel*	42.50
LWH24	A10	20c org brn & blk	22.50
LWH25	A10	30c blk & gray grn	75.00
LWH26	A10	50c red vio & gray green	125.00
LWH27	A10	$1 ol grn & lil	110.00

1904-11   **Wmk. 3**   *Perf. 14*
On Nos. 86-102

LWH28	A10	1c brown	11.00
LWH29	A10	2c gray green	10.00
LWH30	A10	2c deep green	11.00
LWH31	A10	4c violet, *red*	10.00
LWH32	A10	4c carmine	8.00
LWH33	A10	8c vio & blk	18.00
LWH34	A10	10c ultra	9.00
LWH35	A10	20c org brn & blk	37.50
LWH36	A10	20c olive grn & vio	125.00
LWH37	A10	30c blk & gray grn	110.00
LWH38	A10	30c org & vio	110.00
LWH39	A10	50c red vio & gray grn	85.00
LWH40	A10	50c blk, *grn*	90.00

1912-14   **Wmk. 3**   *Perf. 14*
On Nos. 109-120

LWH41	A11	1c brown	12.50
LWH42	A11	2c deep green	10.00
LWH43	A12	4c carmine	8.00
LWH44	A13	6c orange	18.00

LWH45	A12 8c gray	42.50
LWH46	A11 10c ultramarine	10.00
LWH47	A11 $1 blk & vio, *blue*	42.50

**Values for stamps of Hong Kong
cancelled with "PORT EDWARD"
rectangular or c.d.s.**

**1882-1902　Wmk. 2　Perf. 14
On Nos. 37, 45**

LPE1	A1 2c green	100.00
LPE2	A1 10c ultra	125.00

**1903　Wmk. 2　Perf. 14
On Nos. 71-81**

LPE3	A10 1c brown & lilac	40.0
LPE4	A10 2c gray green	40.00
LPE5	A10 4c violet, *red*	35.00
LPE6	A10 5c org & gray green	55.00
LPE7	A10 8c vio & blk	55.00
LPE8	A10 10c ultra & lilac, *blue*	45.00
LPE9	A10 12c red vio & gray grn, *yel*	80.00
LPE10	A10 20c org brn & blk	110.00
LPE11	A10 30c blk & gray grn	110.00
LPE12	A10 50c red vio & gray green	145.00
LPE13	A10 $1 ol grn & lil	115.00

**1904-11　Wmk. 3　Perf. 14
On Nos. 86-102**

LPE14	A10 1c brown	22.50
LPE15	A10 2c gray green	22.50
LPE16	A10 2c deep green	22.50
LPE17	A10 4c violet, *red*	20.00
LPE18	A10 4c carmine	15.00
LPE19	A10 5c org & gray grn	35.00
LPE20	A10 6c red vio & org	45.00
LPE21	A10 8c vio & blk	27.50
LPE22	A10 10c ultra	17.50
LPE23	A10 20c org brn & blk	100.00
LPE24	A10 20c olive grn & vio	125.00
LPE25	A10 30c blk & gray grn	100.00
LPE26	A10 50c red vio & gray grn	100.00
LPE27	A10 50c blk, *grn*	75.00

**1912-14　Wmk. 3　Perf. 14
On Nos. 109-120**

LPE28	A11 1c brown	20.00
LPE29	A11 2c deep green	14.00
LPE30	A12 4c carmine	9.00
LPE31	A12 8c gray	40.00
LPE32	A11 10c ultramarine	10.00
LPE34	A10 50c blk, *grn*	35.00
LPE35	A11 $1 blk & vio, *blue*	35.00

BRITISH OFFICES IN JAPAN

HIOGO (KOBE)

**Values for stamps of Hong Kong
used at HIOGO (Kobe) with "D30"
or c.d.s.**

**1863-71　Wmk. 1　Perf. 14
On Nos. 8-24**

LHG1	A1 2c brown	6,750.
LHG2	A1 4c slate	5,000.
LHG3	A1 6c lilac	6,250.
LHG4	A1 8c orange buff	6,250.
LHG5	A1 12c lt blue	6,750.
LHG6	A1 16c yellow	8,000.
LHG7	A1 18c lilac	
LHG8	A1 24c green	5,250.
LHG9	A1 30c vermilion	
LHG10	A1 30c violet	6,750.
LHG11	A1 48c rose carmine	10,500.
LHG12	A1 96c bister	
LHG13	A1 96c gray	10,500.

1876　On No. 29

LHG14	A1 16c on 18c lilac	—

NAGASAKI

**Values for stamps of Hong Kong
used at NAGASAKI with "N2" or
c.d.s.**

**1862　Unwmk.　Perf. 14
On No. 4**

LNA1	A1 18c lilac	4,250.

**1863-77　Wmk. 1　Perf. 14
On Nos. 8-24**

LNA2	A1 2c brown	2,750.
LNA3	A1 4c slate	2,400.
LNA4	A1 6c lilac	2,400.
LNA5	A1 8c orange buff	2,400.
LNA6	A1 12c lt blue	2,400.
LNA7	A1 16c yellow	3,750.
LNA8	A1 18c lilac	5,000.
LNA9	A1 24c green	4,250.
LNA10	A1 30c vermilion	
LAN11	A1 30c violet	3,750.
LNA12	A1 48c rose carmine	4,750.
LNA13	A1 96c bister	—
LNA14	A1 96c gray	—

1876　On Nos. 29-30

LNA15	A1 16c on 18c lilac	*3,750.*
LNA16	A1 28c on 30c violet	*2,750.*

YOKOHAMA

**Values for stamps of Hong Kong
used at YOKOHAMA with "Y1" or
c.d.s.**

Two types of "Y1" canceller:
Type I: Tall, thin "Y".
Type II: Short, stubby "Y".

**1862　Unwmk.　Perf. 14
On Nos. 2, 4**

LYO1	A1 8c buff	475.00
LYO2	A1 18c lilac	150.00

**1863-77　Wmk. 1　Perf. 14
On Nos. 8-25
Type II "Y1" canceller**

LYO3	A1 2c brown	22.50
LYO4	A1 4c slate	24.00
LYO5	A1 6c lilac	30.00
LYO6	A1 8c orange buff	30.00
LYO7	A1 12c lt blue	22.50
LYO8	A1 16c yellow	135.00
LYO9	A1 18c lilac	725.00
LYO10	A1 24c green	27.50
LYO11	A1 30c vermilion	72.50
LYO12	A1 30c violet	22.50
LYO13	A1 48c rose carmine	62.50
LYO14	A1 96c bister	*6,000.*
LYO15	A1 96c gray	85.00

Perf. 12½

LYO16	A1 4c slate	575.00

Type I "Y1" canceller

LYO3a	brown	27.50
LYO4a	slate	27.50
LYO5a	lilac	35.00
LYO6a	orange buff	37.50
LYO7a	lt blue	25.00
LYO8a	yellow	150.00
LYO9a	lilac	800.00
LYO10a	green	32.50
LYO11a	vermilion	80.00
LYO12a	violet	27.50
LYO13a	rose carmine	75.00
LYO15a	gray	100.00

**1874　Wmk. 1　Perf. 15½x15
On Nos. 26-28**

LYO17	A2 $2 sage green	175.00
LYO18	A3 $3 dull violet	160.00
LYO19	A4 $10 rose	2,250.

**1876

On Nos. 29-30
Type II "Y1" cancel**

LYO20	A1 16c on 18c lilac	325.00
LYO21	A1 28c on 30c violet	100.00

Type I "Y1" cancel

LYO20a	on 18c lilac	400.00
LYO21a	on 30c violet	125.00

HORTA

ˈhor-tə

LOCATION — An administrative district
of the Azores, consisting of the
islands of Pico, Fayal, Flores and
Corvo
GOVT. — A district of the Republic of
Portugal
AREA — 305 sq. mi.
POP. — 49,000 (approx.)
CAPITAL — Horta

1000 Reis = 1 Milreis

**STAMPS OF PORTUGAL USED IN
HORTA**

Barred Numeral "49"

1853　Queen Maria II

A1	5r org brn (#1)	1,200.
A2	25r blue (#2)	60.
A3	50r dp yel grn (#3)	1,100.
a.	50r blue green (#3a)	1,500.
A4	100r lilac (#4)	2,250.

1855　King Pedro V (Straight Hair)

A5	5r red brn (#5)	1,200.
A6	25r blue, type II (#6)	57.50
a.	Type I (#6a)	60.00
A7	50r green (#7)	95.00
A8	100r lilac (#8)	110.00

**1856-58
King Pedro V (Curled Hair)**

A9	5r red brn (#9)	110.00
A10	25r blue, type II (#10)	70.00
a.	Type I (#10a)	67.50
A11	25r green, type II (#11 '58)	19.00

1862-64　King Luiz

A12	5r brown (#12)	60.00
A13	10r orange (#13)	67.50
A14	25r rose (#14)	13.50
A15	50r yel green (#15)	90.00
A16	100r lilac (#16; '64)	110.00

1866-67　King Luiz

Imperf.

A17	5r black (#17)	90.00
A18	10r yellow (#18)	140.00
A19	20r bister (#19)	140.00
A20	25r rose (#20; '67)	45.00
A21	50r green (#21)	125.00
A22	80r orange (#22)	125.00
A23	100r dk lilac (#23; '67)	150.00
A24	120r blue (#24)	125.00

Perf. 12½

A28	25r rose (#28)	125.00

**Issued under Portuguese
Administration**

King Carlos
A1　　　　A2
Chalk-surfaced Paper

Perf. 11½, 12½, 13½

		Typo.	Unwmk.	
1	A1	5r yellow	2.00	1.50
2	A1	10r reddish violet	2.00	1.75
3	A1	15r chocolate	2.00	2.00
4	A1	20r lavender	4.00	3.00
5	A1	25r dp grn, perf. 11½	4.25	1.00
a.		Perf. 13½	5.00	3.75
6	A1	50r blue	7.00	3.00
a.		Perf. 13½	9.00	5.25
7	A1	75r carmine	6.50	4.00
8	A1	80r yellow green	9.00	6.00
9	A1	100r brn, *yel* ('93)	35.00	10.00
a.		Perf. 12½	125.00	90.00
10	A1	150r car, *rose* ('93)	55.00	32.50
11	A1	200r dk bl, *bl* ('93)	60.00	32.50
12	A1	300r dark blue ('93)	60.00	35.00
		Nos. 1-12 (12)	246.75	132.25

Bisects of No. 1 were used in Aug. 1894.
Value, on newsprint, $16.
*The reprints have shiny white gum and
clean-cut perforation 13½. The white paper is
thinner than that of the originals. Value
unused, $12 each.*

**1897-1905　Perf. 11½
Name and Value in Black Except
500r**

13	A2	2½r gray	.50	.30
14	A2	5r orange	.50	.30
15	A2	10r lt green	.50	.30
16	A2	15r brown	4.00	2.50
17	A2	15r gray grn ('99)	1.25	.80
18	A2	20r gray violet	1.75	.85
19	A2	25r sea green	2.25	.45
20	A2	25r car rose ('99)	.90	.50
21	A2	50r blue	3.00	.70
22	A2	50r ultra ('05)	15.00	7.00
23	A2	65r slate blue ('98)	.70	.55
24	A2	75r rose	1.90	.95
25	A2	75r brn, *yel* ('05)	18.00	10.00
26	A2	80r violet	1.25	1.10
27	A2	100r dk blue, *bl*	1.75	.95
28	A2	115r org brn, *pink* ('98)	4.00	1.50
29	A2	130r gray brn, *buff* ('98)	4.00	1.50
30	A2	150r lt brn, *buff*	4.00	1.50
31	A2	180r sl, *pnksh* ('98)	4.00	1.75
32	A2	200r red vio, *pale lil*	10.00	4.00
33	A2	300r dk blue, *rose*	11.00	6.75
34	A2	500r blk & red, *bl*	20.00	8.50
		Nos. 13-34 (22)	110.25	52.75

Stamps of Portugal replaced those of Horta.

HUNGARY

ˈhəŋ-g̱ə-ˌrē

LOCATION — Central Europe
GOVT. — Republic
AREA — 35,911 sq. mi.
POP. — 10,679,000 (est. 1984)
CAPITAL — Budapest

Prior to World War I, Hungary
together with Austria comprised the
Austro-Hungarian Empire. The Hungarian post became independent on
May 1, 1867. During 1850-1871 stamps
listed under Austria were also used in
Hungary. Copies showing clear Hungarian cancels sell for substantially
more.

100 Krajczár (Kreuzer) = 1 Forint
100 Fillér = 1 Korona (1900)
100 Fillér = 1 Pengö (1926)

> Catalogue values for unused
> stamps in this country are for
> Never Hinged items, beginning
> with Scott 503 in the regular post-
> age section, Scott B92 in the semi-
> postal section, Scott C35 in the
> airpost section, and Scott J130 in
> the postage due section.

Watermarks

Wmk. 91 — "ZEITUNGS-MARKEN" in
Double-lined Capitals across the Sheet

Wmk. 106 —
Multiple Star

Wmk. 132 — kr in Oval

Wmk. 133
— Four
Double
Crosses

Wmk. 135 — Crown in Oval or Circle, Sideways

Wmk. 136

Wmk. 136a

Wmk. 137 — Double Cross

Wmk. 210 — Double Cross on Pyramid

Watermarks 132, 135, 136 and 136a can be found normal, reversed, inverted, or reversed and inverted.

Issues of the Monarchy

Franz Josef I — A1

1871   **Unwmk.**   **Litho.**   **Perf. 9½**

1	A1	2k orange	325.00	100.00
a.		2k yellow	1,200.	250.00
2	A1	3k lt green	1,000.	600.00
3	A1	5k rose	450.00	25.00
a.		5k brick red	900.00	75.00

4	A1	10k blue	1,250.	100.00
a.		10k pale blue	1,400.	150.00
5	A1	15k yellow brn	1,250.	125.00
6	A1	25k violet	1,000.	200.00
a.		25k bright violet	1,500.	300.00

The first printing of No. 1, in dark yellow, was not issued because of spots on the King's face. A few stamps were used at Pest in 1873. Value, $2,500.

1871-72   **Engr.**

7	A1	2k orange	40.00	7.50
a.		2k yellow	175.00	20.00
b.		Bisect on cover		—
8	A1	3k green	125.00	25.00
a.		3k blue green	150.00	30.00
9	A1	5k rose	110.00	1.75
a.		5k brick red	200.00	8.00
10	A1	10k deep blue	300.00	10.00
11	A1	15k brown	475.00	15.00
a.		15k copper brown	—	1,500.
b.		15k black brown	875.00	85.00
12	A1	25k lilac	200.00	40.00
		Nos. 7-12 (6)	1,250.	99.25

Reprints are perf. 11½ and watermarked "kr" in oval. Value, set $225.

Crown of St. Stephen — A2

1874-76   **Perf. 13**

13	A2	2k red violet	30.00	2.00
		Never hinged	60.00	
a.		2k violet	35.00	2.50
		Never hinged	70.00	
14	A2	3k yellow green	30.00	2.00
		Never hinged	60.00	
a.		3k blue green	37.50	2.50
		Never hinged	75.00	
15	A2	5k red	10.00	.50
		Never hinged	20.00	
a.		5k brick red	45.00	1.50
		Never hinged	90.00	
b.		5k lilac red	15.00	.75
		Never hinged	30.00	
c.		5k rose	10.00	.40
		Never hinged	20.00	
16	A2	10k blue	35.00	.75
		Never hinged	70.00	
17	A2	20k grnsh gray	700.00	9.00
		Never hinged	1,400.	
a.		20k gray	750.00	10.00
		Never hinged	1,500.	
		Nos. 13-17 (5)	805.00	14.25

Perf. 11½

13b	A2	2k red violet	45.00	5.00
		Never hinged	90.00	
c.		2k violet	—	6.00
d.		2k rose lilac	75.00	4.50
		Never hinged	150.00	
e.		2k gray blue	60.00	3.75
		Never hinged	120.00	
14b	A2	3k yellow green	50.00	4.00
		Never hinged	100.00	
c.		3k blue green	60.00	5.00
		Never hinged	120.00	
15d	A2	5k red	60.00	1.00
		Never hinged	120.00	
e.		5k rose	50.00	.75
		Never hinged	100.00	
16a	A2	10k blue	75.00	5.00
		Never hinged	150.00	
17b	A2	20k gray	700.00	45.00
		Never hinged	1,400.	

Perf. 13x11½

13f	A2	2k red violet	180.00	30.00
		Never hinged	360.00	
g.		2k rose lilac	200.00	30.00
		Never hinged	400.00	
14d	A2	3k yellow green	125.00	4.50
		Never hinged	250.00	
15f	A2	5k lilac red	250.00	12.00
		Never hinged	500.00	
g.		5k rose	300.00	15.00
		Never hinged	600.00	
16b	A2	10k blue	250.00	6.00
		Never hinged	500.00	
17c	A2	20k gray	800.00	50.00
		Never hinged	1,600.	

Perf. 11½x13

13h	A2	2k red violet	60.00	5.00
		Never hinged	120.00	
f.		2k rose lilac	100.00	4.00
		Never hinged	200.00	
g.		2k gray blue	75.00	3.75
		Never hinged	150.00	
15h	A2	5k red	75.00	1.00
		Never hinged	150.00	
17d	A2	20k gray	—	100.00

Perf. 9½

14e	A2	3k green	7,500.	2,500.

All examples of the 5k perf 9½ are counterfeit.

1881   **Wmk. 132**   **Perf. 11½**

18	A2	2k lilac	3.50	.40
		Never hinged	6.25	
a.		2k violet	3.50	.40
		Never hinged	6.25	
b.		2k gray blue	4.50	.50
		Never hinged	8.00	
19	A2	3k blue green	3.50	.40
		Never hinged	6.25	
a.		3k yellow green	4.50	.60
		Never hinged	8.00	

20	A2	5k rose	2.50	.25
		Never hinged	4.50	
21	A2	10k blue	6.00	.40
		Never hinged	11.00	
a.		10k pale blue	7.00	.60
		Never hinged	12.50	
22	A2	20k gray	4.50	.65
		Never hinged	8.00	
a.		20k greenish gray	5.00	.75
		Never hinged	9.00	
		Nos. 18-22 (5)	20.00	2.10

Perf. 13

18c	A2	2k violet	150.00	20.00
		Never hinged	275.00	
d.		2k gray blue	120.00	10.00
		Never hinged	225.00	
19b	A2	3k blue green	90.00	4.00
		Never hinged	175.00	
c.		3k yellow green	100.00	5.50
		Never hinged	175.00	
20a	A2	5k rose	120.00	4.00
		Never hinged	225.00	
21b	A2	10k blue	75.00	5.00
		Never hinged	130.00	
22b	A2	20k gray	350.00	15.00
		Never hinged	625.00	

Perf. 13x11½

18e	A2	2k violet	—	40.00
19d	A2	3k blue green	160.00	6.00
		Never hinged	275.00	
e.		3k yellow green	—	8.00
20b	A2	5k rose	—	15.00
21c	A2	10k blue	—	8.00
22c	A2	20k gray	—	12.50

Perf. 11½x13

18f	A2	2k violet	200.00	9.00
		Never hinged	350.00	
g.		2k gray blue	180.00	6.00
		Never hinged	325.00	
19f	A2	3k blue green	—	60.00
		Never hinged	—	75.00
20c	A2	5k rose	150.00	1.00
		Never hinged	250.00	
21d	A2	10k blue	—	1.75
22d	A2	20k gray	—	40.00

Perf. 12x11½

18h	A2	2k lilac	1.00	.25
		Never hinged	1.75	
i.		2k violet	15.00	1.20
		Never hinged	25.00	
19h	A2	3k blue green	1.00	.25
		Never hinged	1.75	
20d	A2	5k rose	2.50	.25
		Never hinged	4.00	
21e	A2	10k blue	3.00	.25
		Never hinged	5.00	
22e	A2	20k gray	300.00	7.50
		Never hinged	500.00	

Crown of St. Stephen — A3

Design A3 has an overall burelage of dots. Compare with design N3.

1888-98   **Typo.**   **Perf. 12x11½**

Numerals in Black

22A	A3	1k black, one plate	1.25	.30
		Never hinged	2.50	
c.		"1" printed separately	15.00	3.00
		Never hinged	30.00	
23	A3	2k red violet	1.50	.50
		Never hinged	3.00	
a.		Perf. 11½	725.00	50.00
		Never hinged	3.00	
24	A3	3k green	1.75	.40
		Never hinged	3.50	
a.		Perf. 11½	50.00	15.00
25	A3	5k rose	2.00	.25
		Never hinged	4.00	
a.		Perf. 11½	65.00	1.75
26	A3	8k orange	6.00	.60
		Never hinged	12.00	
a.		"8" double	150.00	
27	A3	10k blue	5.00	1.25
		Never hinged	10.00	
a.		Perf. 11½	450.00	325.00
28	A3	12k brown & green	12.50	1.00
		Never hinged	25.00	
29	A3	15k claret & blue	10.00	.40
		Never hinged	20.00	
30	A3	20k gray	7.50	2.00
		Never hinged	15.00	
a.		Perf. 11½	1,400.	600.00
31	A3	24k brn vio & red	22.50	1.25
		Never hinged	45.00	
32	A3	30k ol grn & brn	25.00	.35
		Never hinged	50.00	
33	A3	50k red & org	40.00	1.50
		Never hinged	80.00	

Numerals in Red

34	A3	1fo gray bl & sil	175.00	2.25
		Never hinged	350.00	
a.		Perf. 11½	190.00	3.50
		Nos. 22A-34 (13)	310.00	12.05

Perf. 11½

22i	A3	1k black, one plate	1.00	.40
		Never hinged	2.00	
j.		"1" printed separately	500.00	125.00
		Never hinged	1,000.	
23i	A3	2k red violet	600.00	50.00
		Never hinged	1,200.	
24i	A3	3k green	60.00	20.00
		Never hinged	120.00	
25i	A3	5k rose	60.00	20.00
		Never hinged	120.00	
26i	A3	8k orange	10.00	.75
		Never hinged	20.00	

27i	A3	10k blue	1,750.	750.00
28i	A3	12k brown & green	12.50	2.00
		Never hinged	25.00	
29i	A3	15k claret & green	14.00	.40
		Never hinged	27.50	
30i	A3	20k gray	2,000.	900.00
31i	A3	24k brn vio & red	25.00	2.00
		Never hinged	50.00	
32i	A3	30k ol grn & brn	275.00	.50
		Never hinged	550.00	
33i	A3	50k red & org	40.00	3.00
		Never hinged	80.00	

Numerals in Red

34i	A3	1fo gray blue & sil	190.00	3.00
		Never hinged	375.00	
35	A3	3fo lilac brn & gold	25.00	12.00
		Never hinged	50.00	

1898-99   **Perf. 12x11½**

Numerals in Black

Wmk. 135 (Oval)

35A	A3	1k black	1.50	.50
		Never hinged	3.00	
36	A3	2k violet	6.00	.50
		Never hinged	12.00	
37	A3	3k green	4.00	.60
		Never hinged	8.00	
38	A3	5k rose	5.00	.40
		Never hinged	10.00	
39	A3	8k orange	17.50	4.00
		Never hinged	35.00	
40	A3	10k blue	5.00	1.00
		Never hinged	10.00	
41	A3	12k red brn & grn	75.00	9.00
		Never hinged	150.00	
42	A3	15k rose & blue	5.00	.75
		Never hinged	10.00	
43	A3	20k gray	35.00	2.00
		Never hinged	70.00	
44	A3	24k vio brn & red	6.00	4.75
		Never hinged	12.00	
45	A3	30k ol grn & brn	40.00	1.50
		Never hinged	80.00	
46	A3	50k dull red & org	100.00	15.00
		Never hinged	200.00	
		Nos. 35A-46 (12)	300.00	40.00

Perf. 11½

35Ab	A3	1k black	40.00	7.50
			80.00	
36a	A3	2k violet	125.00	20.00
			250.00	
37a	A3	3k green	100.00	15.00
			200.00	
38a	A3	5k rose	140.00	15.00
			275.00	
39a	A3	8k orange	250.00	120.00
			500.00	
40a	A3	10k blue	150.00	60.00
			300.00	
41a	A3	12k red brn & grn	375.00	100.00
			750.00	
42a	A3	15k rose & blue	250.00	60.00
			500.00	
43a	A3	20k gray	375.00	75.00
			750.00	
44a	A3	24k vio brn & red	450.00	200.00
		Never hinged	900.00	
45a	A3	30k ol grn & brn	250.00	60.00
		Never hinged	500.00	
46a	A3	50k dull red & org	500.00	250.00
		Never hinged	1,000.	

Wmk. 135 (Circle)

Perf. 12x11½

35Ac	A3	1k black	14.00	2.50
		Never hinged	27.50	
36b	A3	2k violet	7.50	1.50
		Never hinged	15.00	
37b	A3	3k green	8.50	2.00
		Never hinged	17.00	
38b	A3	5k rose	10.00	1.00
		Never hinged	20.00	
39b	A3	8k orange	50.00	25.00
		Never hinged	100.00	
40b	A3	10k blue	75.00	4.00
		Never hinged	150.00	
41b	A3	12k red brn & grn	60.00	30.00
		Never hinged	120.00	
42b	A3	15k rose & blue	250.00	60.00
		Never hinged	500.00	
43b	A3	20k gray	5.00	6.00
		Never hinged	10.00	
44b	A3	24k vio brn & red	1,250.	45.00
		Never hinged	2,500.	
45b	A3	30k ol grn & brn	5.00	4.00
		Never hinged	10.00	
46b	A3	50k dull red & org	15.00	35.00
		Never hinged	30.00	

Perf. 11½

35Ad	A3	1k black	50.00	15.00
		Never hinged	100.00	
36c	A3	2k violet	200.00	25.00
		Never hinged	400.00	
37c	A3	3k green	200.00	40.00
		Never hinged	400.00	
38c	A3	5k rose	100.00	15.00
		Never hinged	200.00	
39c	A3	8k orange	80.00	12.50
		Never hinged	160.00	
40c	A3	10k blue	450.00	80.00
		Never hinged	900.00	
41c	A3	12k red brn & grn	750.00	300.00
		Never hinged	1,500.	
42c	A3	15k rose & blue	450.00	200.00
		Never hinged	950.00	
43c	A3	20k gray	1,500.	350.00
		Never hinged	3,000.	
44c	A3	24k vio brn & red	2,250.	600.00
		Never hinged	4,500.	
45c	A3	30k ol grn & brn	750.00	150.00
		Never hinged	1,500.	
46c	A3	50k dull red & org	500.00	400.00

In the watermark with circles, a four-pointed star and "VI" appear four times in the sheet in the large spaces between the intersecting circles. The paper with the circular watermark is often yellowish and thinner than that with the oval watermark.

Values for unused stamps are for examples with original gum as defined in the catalogue introduction. Very fine examples of Nos. 1-12 will have perforations touching the framelines on one or two sides due to imperfect perforating methods. Stamps with perfs clear on all four sides are very scarce and will command substantial premiums.

"Turul" and
Crown of St.
Stephen — A4

Franz Josef I
Wearing
Hungarian
Crown — A5

1900-04 Wmk. 135 Perf. 12x11½
Numerals in Black

47	A4	1f gray	.75	.30
		Never hinged	1.50	
a.		1f dull lilac	.75	.30
			1.50	
48	A4	2f olive yel	1.00	.75
		Never hinged	2.00	
49	A4	3f orange	.75	.25
		Never hinged	1.50	
50	A4	4f violet	1.00	.25
		Never hinged	2.00	
a.		Booklet pane of 6	60.00	
51	A4	5f emerald	2.50	.25
		Never hinged	5.00	
a.		Booklet pane of 6	35.00	
52	A4	6f claret	1.50	.60
		Never hinged	3.00	
a.		6f violet brown	2.50	.50
		Never hinged	5.00	
53	A4	6f bister ('01)	20.00	1.20
		Never hinged	40.00	
54	A4	6f olive grn ('02)	7.50	.50
		Never hinged	15.00	
55	A4	10f carmine	4.00	.25
		Never hinged	8.00	
a.		Booklet pane of 6	35.00	
56	A4	12f violet ('04)	2.00	1.25
		Never hinged	4.00	
57	A4	20f brown ('01)	4.00	.60
		Never hinged	8.00	
58	A4	25f blue	5.00	.60
		Never hinged	10.00	
a.		Booklet pane of 6	60.00	
59	A4	30f orange brn	24.00	.25
		Never hinged	47.50	
60	A4	35f red vio ('01)	14.00	1.00
		Never hinged	27.50	
a.		Booklet pane of 6	100.00	
61	A4	50f lake	12.00	1.00
		Never hinged	24.00	
62	A4	60f green	45.00	.30
		Never hinged	90.00	
63	A5	1k brown red	37.50	.75
		Never hinged	75.00	
64	A5	2k gray blue ('01)	600.00	22.50
		Never hinged	1,200.	
65	A5	3k sea green	90.00	3.75
		Never hinged	175.00	
66	A5	5k vio brown ('01)	125.00	40.00
		Never hinged	175.00	
		Nos. 47-66 (20)	997.50	76.35

The watermark on Nos. 47 to 66 is always the circular form of Wmk. 135 described in the note following No. 46.

Pairs imperf between of Nos. 47-49, 51 were favor prints made for an influential Budapest collector. Value, $90 each.

For overprints & surcharges see Nos. B35-B52, 2N1-2N3, 6N1-6N6, 6NB127N1-7N6, 7NB1, 10N1.

Perf. 11½

47b	A4	1f gray	350.00	80.00
		Never hinged	700.00	
48a	A4	2f olive yel	350.00	60.00
		Never hinged	700.00	
49a	A4	3f orange	100.00	20.00
		Never hinged	200.00	
50b	A4	4f violet	225.00	12.50
		Never hinged	450.00	
51b	A4	5f emerald	50.00	3.75
		Never hinged	100.00	
52b	A4	6f claret	—	60.00
53a	A4	6f bister ('01)	—	110.00
54a	A4	6f olive grn ('02)	—	300.00
55b	A4	10f carmine	400.00	25.00
		Never hinged	800.00	
56a	A4	12f violet ('04)	250.00	80.00
		Never hinged	500.00	
57a	A4	20f brown ('01)	—	150.00
58b	A4	25f blue	—	75.00
59a	A4	30f orange brn	—	125.00
60b	A4	35f red vio ('01)	—	275.00
61a	A4	50f lake	400.00	75.00
		Never hinged	800.00	
62a	A4	60f green	600.00	150.00
		Never hinged	1,200.	
63a	A5	1k brown red	175.00	15.00
		Never hinged	350.00	
64a	A5	2k gray blue ('01)	—	600.00
		Never hinged		
65a	A5	3k sea green	—	4,000.
		Never hinged		
66a	A5	5k vio brown ('01)	—	1,000.
		Never hinged		

1908-13 Wmk. 136 Perf. 15

67	A4	1f slate	.30	.25
		Never hinged	.60	
68	A4	2f olive yellow	.25	.25
		Never hinged	.50	
69	A4	3f orange	.30	.25
		Never hinged	.60	
70	A4	5f emerald	.30	.25
		Never hinged	.60	
c.		Booklet pane of 6	100.00	

71	A4	6f olive green	.30	.25
		Never hinged	.60	
72	A4	10f carmine	.40	.25
		Never hinged	.80	
c.		Booklet pane of 6	100.00	
73	A4	12f violet	.40	.25
		Never hinged	.80	
74	A4	16f gray green ('10)	.50	.60
		Never hinged	1.00	
75	A4	20f dark brown	7.50	.25
		Never hinged	15.00	
76	A4	25f blue	6.25	.25
		Never hinged	12.50	
77	A4	30f orange brown	7.50	.25
		Never hinged	15.00	
78	A8	35f red violet	10.00	.25
		Never hinged	20.00	
79	A4	50f lake	3.00	.30
		Never hinged	6.00	
80	A4	60f green	9.00	.25
		Never hinged	17.50	
81	A5	1k brown red	12.50	.25
		Never hinged	25.00	
82	A5	2k gray blue	90.00	.40
		Never hinged	175.00	
83	A5	5k violet brown	125.00	9.00
		Never hinged	250.00	
		Nos. 67-83 (17)	273.50	13.45

Nos. 67-73, 75-83 exist imperf. Value, set $1,000.

1904-05 Wmk. 136a Perf. 12x11½

67a	A4	1f slate	2.50	2.50
		Never hinged	5.00	
68a	A4	2f olive yellow	5.00	.30
		Never hinged	10.00	
69a	A4	3f orange	2.00	.40
		Never hinged	4.00	
70a	A4	5f emerald	4.00	.25
		Never hinged	8.00	
71a	A4	6f olive green	2.50	.40
		Never hinged	5.00	
72a	A4	10f carmine	7.50	.25
		Never hinged	15.00	
73a	A4	12f violet	4.00	3.00
		Never hinged	8.00	
75a	A4	20f dark brown	20.00	1.00
		Never hinged	40.00	
76a	A4	25f blue	40.00	1.00
		Never hinged	80.00	
77a	A4	30f orange brown	9.00	.40
		Never hinged	17.50	
78a	A4	35f red violet	22.50	.40
		Never hinged	45.00	
79a	A4	50f lake	15.00	4.00
		Never hinged	30.00	
c.		50f magenta	1.00	10.00
		Never hinged	2.00	
80a	A4	60f green	250.00	.40
		Never hinged	500.00	
81a	A5	1k brown red	250.00	.75
		Never hinged	500.00	
82a	A5	2k gray blue	900.00	50.00
		Never hinged	1,750.	
c.		Perf. 11½	2,000.	150.00
83a	A5	5k violet brown	240.00	10.00
		Nos. 67a-83a (16)	1,774.	140.05

1906 Perf. 15

67b	A4	1f slate	2.50	.50
		Never hinged	5.00	
68b	A4	2f olive yellow	1.75	.25
		Never hinged	3.50	
69b	A4	3f orange	2.25	.25
		Never hinged	4.50	
70b	A4	5f emerald	2.00	.25
		Never hinged	4.00	
71b	A4	6f olive green	2.00	.25
		Never hinged	4.00	
72b	A4	10f carmine	2.50	.25
		Never hinged	5.00	
73b	A4	12f violet	4.00	.25
		Never hinged	8.00	
75b	A4	20f dark brown	10.00	.30
		Never hinged	20.00	
76b	A4	25f blue	8.00	.30
		Never hinged	16.00	
77b	A4	30f orange brown	10.00	.25
		Never hinged	20.00	
78b	A4	35f red violet	50.00	.25
		Never hinged	100.00	
79b	A4	50f lake	5.00	1.00
		Never hinged	10.00	
80b	A4	60f green	62.50	.25
		Never hinged	125.00	
81b	A5	1k brown red	60.00	.60
		Never hinged	120.00	
82b	A5	2k gray blue	225.00	8.00
		Never hinged	450.00	
		Nos. 67b-82b (15)	447.50	12.95

1913-16 Wmk. 137 Vert. Perf. 15

84	A4	1f slate	.25	.25
		Never hinged	.50	
85	A4	2f olive yellow	.25	.25
		Never hinged	.50	
86	A4	3f orange	.25	.25
		Never hinged	.50	
87	A4	5f emerald	.50	.25
		Never hinged	1.00	
88	A4	6f olive green	.25	.25
		Never hinged	.50	
89	A4	10f carmine	.25	.25
		Never hinged	.50	
90	A4	12f violet, yel	.30	.25
		Never hinged	.60	
91	A4	16f gray green	.35	.90
		Never hinged	.70	
92	A4	20f dark brown	1.00	.25
		Never hinged	2.00	
93	A4	25f ultra	1.20	.25
		Never hinged	2.50	
94	A4	30f orange brown	.90	.25
		Never hinged	1.75	
95	A4	35f red violet	.90	.25
		Never hinged	1.75	
96	A4	50f lake, blue	.30	.25
		Never hinged	.60	
a.		Cliché of 35f in plate of 50f	325.00	—

97	A4	60f green	5.75	2.00
		Never hinged	11.50	
98	A4	60f green, salmon	.80	.30
		Never hinged	1.60	
99	A4	70f red brn, grn ('16)	.25	.25
		Never hinged	.50	
100	A4	80f dull violet ('16)	.25	.25
		Never hinged	.50	
101	A5	1k dull red	2.50	.25
		Never hinged	5.00	
102	A5	2k dull blue	4.25	.25
		Never hinged	8.50	
103	A5	5k violet brown	20.00	5.00
		Never hinged	40.00	
		Nos. 84-103 (20)	40.50	12.20

Nos. 89-97, 99-103 exist imperf. Value, set $1,200.

For overprints and surcharges see Nos. 2N1-2N3, 6N1-6N6, 6NB12, 7N1-7N6, 7NB1, 10N1.

Wmk. 137 Horiz.

84a	A4	1f slate	.75	.60
		Never hinged	1.50	
85a	A4	2f olive yellow	2.00	.40
		Never hinged	4.00	
87a	A4	5f emerald	.50	.25
		Never hinged	1.00	
88a	A4	6f olive green	1.00	.25
		Never hinged	2.00	
89b	A4	10f carmine	1.00	.25
		Never hinged	2.00	
90a	A4	12f violet, yellow	2.00	.25
		Never hinged	4.00	
92a	A4	20f dark brown	6.25	.25
		Never hinged	12.50	
94a	A4	30f orange brown	50.00	.25
		Never hinged	100.00	
95a	A4	35f red violet	200.00	.25
		Never hinged	400.00	
96b	A4	50f lake, blue	15.00	6.25
		Never hinged	30.00	
97a	A4	60f green	4.25	1.75
		Never hinged	8.50	
98a	A4	60f green, salmon	1.50	.25
		Never hinged	3.00	
101a	A5	1k dull red	16.00	.25
		Never hinged	32.50	
102a	A5	2k dull blue	100.00	1.00
		Never hinged	200.00	
		Nos. 84a-102a (14)	400.25	12.25

A5a

1916, July 1 Perf. 15
103A A5a 10f violet brown .25 .25

Although issued as a postal savings stamp, No. 103A was also valid for postage. Used value is for postal usage.

Exists imperf. Value $10.

For overprints and surcharges see Nos. 2N59, 5N23, 6N50, 8N13, 10N42.

Queen	Charles
Zita — A6	IV — A7

1916, Dec. 30
104	A6	10f violet	1.25	1.25
		Never hinged	2.00	
105	A7	15f red	1.25	1.25
		Never hinged	2.00	

Coronation of King Charles IV and Queen Zita on Dec. 30, 1916.

Exist imperf. Value, set $20.

During 1921-24 the two center rows of panes of various stamps then current were punched with three holes forming a triangle. These were sold at post offices. Collectors and dealers who wanted the stamps unpunched would have to purchase them through the philatelic agency at a 10% advance over face value.

Harvesting (White
Numerals) — A8

1916
106	A8	10f rose	.75	.25
		Never hinged	1.25	
107	A8	15f violet	.75	.25
		Never hinged	1.25	

Exist imperf. Value, set $20.
For overprints and surcharges see Nos. B56-B57, 2N4-2N5, 5N1.

Harvesting	Parliament Building
Wheat — A9	at Budapest — A10

1916-18 Perf. 15

108	A9	2f brown orange	.25	.25
		Never hinged	.30	
109	A9	3f red lilac	.25	.25
		Never hinged	.30	
110	A9	4f slate gray ('18)	.25	.25
		Never hinged	.30	
111	A9	5f green	.25	.25
		Never hinged	.30	
112	A9	6f grnsh blue	.25	.25
		Never hinged	.30	
113	A9	10f rose red	1.40	.25
		Never hinged	3.50	
114	A9	15f violet	.25	.25
		Never hinged	.30	
115	A9	20f gray brown	.25	.25
		Never hinged	.30	
116	A9	25f dull blue	.30	.25
		Never hinged	.75	
117	A9	35f brown	.25	.25
		Never hinged	.30	
118	A9	40f olive green	.25	.25
		Never hinged	.30	

Perf. 14

119	A10	50f red vio & lil	.25	.25
		Never hinged	.35	
120	A10	75f brt bl & pale bl	.25	.25
		Never hinged	.35	
121	A10	80f grn & pale grn	.25	.25
		Never hinged	.35	
122	A10	1k red brn & claret	.25	.25
		Never hinged	.35	
123	A10	2k ol brn & bister	.25	.25
		Never hinged	.50	
124	A10	3k dk vio & indigo	.60	.25
		Never hinged	1.75	
125	A10	5k dk brn & lt brn	.60	.25
		Never hinged	1.75	
126	A10	10k vio brn & vio	1.20	.25
		Never hinged	3.00	
		Nos. 108-126 (19)	7.60	4.75

Three-Hole Punch

115a	A9	20f gray brown	.25	.40
		Never hinged	.50	
118a	A9	40f olive green	.25	.40
		Never hinged	.50	
122a	A10	1k red brn & claret	.25	.25
		Never hinged	.65	
123a	A10	2k ol brn & bister	.50	.25
		Never hinged	1.25	
124a	A10	3k dk vio & indigo	2.10	.25
		Never hinged	5.25	
125a	A10	5k dk brn & lt brn	2.25	.25
		Never hinged	5.50	
126a	A10	10k vio brn & vio	4.25	.40
		Never hinged	10.50	
		Nos. 115a-126a (7)	9.85	2.20

Nos. 108-126 exist imperf. Value, set $100.

See Nos. 335-377, 388-396. For overprints and surcharges see Nos. 153, 167, C1-C5, J76-J99, 1N1-1N21, 1N26-1N30, 1N33, 1N36-1N39, 2N6-2N27, 2N33-2N38, 2N41, 2N43-2N48, 4N1-4N4, 5N2-5N17, 6N7-6N24, 6N29-6N39, 7N7-7N30, 7N38, 7N41-7N42, 8N1-8N4, 9N1-9N2, 9N4, 10N2-10N16, 10N25-10N29, 10N31, 10N33-10N41, 11N1-15, 11N20-24, 11N27, 11N30, 11N32-33.

Charles	Queen
IV — A11	Zita — A12

1918 Perf. 15
127	A11	10f scarlet	.30	.25
		Never hinged	.35	
128	A11	15f deep violet	.35	.75
		Never hinged	.75	
129	A11	20f dark brown	.30	.30
		Never hinged	.35	

130 A11 25f brt blue .30 .30
Never hinged .35
131 A12 40f olive green .30 *.30*
Never hinged .35
132 A12 50f lilac .30 *.30*
Never hinged .35
Nos. 127-132 (6) 1.85 2.20

Exist imperf. Value, set $35.

For overprints see Nos. 168-173, 1N32, 1N34-1N35, 2N28-2N32, 2N39-2N40, 2N42, 2N49-2N51, 5N18-5N22, 6N25-6N28, 6N40-6N43, 7N31-7N37, 7N39-7N40, 8N5, 9N3, 10N17-10N21, 10N30, 10N32, 11N16-19, 11N25-26, 11N28-29, 11N31.

Issues of the Republic

Hungarian Stamps of 1916-18 Overprinted in Black

1918-19   Wmk. 137   Perf. 15, 14
On Stamps of 1916-18
153 A9 2f brown orange .25 .25
Never hinged .30
154 A9 3f red lilac .25 .25
Never hinged .30
155 A9 4f slate gray .25 .25
Never hinged .30
156 A9 5f green .25 .25
Never hinged .30
157 A9 6f grnsh blue .25 .25
Never hinged .30
158 A9 10f rose red .25 .25
Never hinged .30
159 A9 20f gray brown .25 .25
Never hinged .30
162 A9 40f olive green .25 .25
Never hinged .30
163 A10 1k red brn & claret .25 .25
Never hinged .30
164 A10 2k ol brn & bis .25 .25
Never hinged .45
165 A10 3k dk violet & ind .40 1.00
Never hinged .60
166 A10 5k dk brn & lt brn 2.00 5.00
Never hinged 4.00
167 A10 10k vio brn & vio .65 1.50
Never hinged .90

On Stamps of 1918
168 A11 10f scarlet .25 .25
Never hinged .30
169 A11 15f deep violet .25 .25
Never hinged .30
170 A11 20f dark brown .25 .25
Never hinged .30
171 A11 25f brt blue .25 .25
Never hinged .30
172 A12 40f olive green .30 .60
Never hinged .40
173 A12 50f lilac .25 .30
Never hinged .30
Nos. 153-173 (19) 7.10 11.90

Nos. 153-164 exist imperf. Value, set $90.
Nos. 153-162, 168-173 exist with overprint inverted. Value, each $6.

A13   A14

1919-20   Perf. 15
174 A13 2f brown orange .25 .25
Never hinged .30
176 A13 4f slate gray .25 .25
Never hinged .30
177 A13 5f yellow grn .25 .25
Never hinged .30
178 A13 6f grnsh blue .25 .25
Never hinged .30
179 A13 10f red .25 .25
Never hinged .30
180 A13 15f violet .25 .25
Never hinged .30
181 A13 20f dark brown .25 .25
Never hinged .30
182 A13 20f green ('20) .25 .25
Never hinged .30
183 A13 25f dull blue .25 .25
Never hinged .30
184 A13 40f olive green .25 .25
Never hinged .30
185 A13 40f rose red ('20) .25 .25
Never hinged .30
186 A13 45f orange .25 .25
Never hinged .30

Perf. 14
187 A14 50f brn vio & pale vio .25 .25
Never hinged .30
188 A14 60f brown & bl ('20) .25 .25
Never hinged .30
189 A14 95f dk bl & bl .25 .25
Never hinged .30
190 A14 1k red brn .25 .25
Never hinged .30

191 A14 1k dk bl & dull bl
('20) .25 .25
Never hinged .30
192 A14 1.20k dk grn & grn .25 .25
Never hinged .30
193 A14 1.40k yellow green .25 .25
Never hinged .30
194 A14 2k ol brn & bis .25 .25
Never hinged .30
195 A14 3k dk vio & ind .25 .25
Never hinged .30
196 A14 5k dk brn & brn .25 .85
Never hinged .30
197 A14 10k vio brn & red vio .50 .75
Never hinged .95
Nos. 174-197 (23) 6.00 6.85

The 3f red lilac, type A13, was never regularly issued without overprint (Nos. 204 and 312). In 1923 a small quantity was sold by the Government at public auction. Value $3.
For overprints see Nos. 203-222, 306-330, 1N40, 2N52-2N58, 6N44-6N49, 8N6-8N12, 10N22-10N24, 11N34-35.
Nos. 174, 177-179, 181-197 exist imperf. Value set $60.

Issues of the Soviet Republic

Karl Marx — A15

Sándor Petöfi — A16

Ignác Martinovics — A17

György Dózsa — A18

Friedrich Engels — A19

Wmk. 137 Horiz.
1919, June 14   Litho.   Perf. 12½x12
198 A15 20f rose & brown .50 *1.00*
Never hinged 1.00
199 A16 45f brn org & dk grn .50 *1.00*
Never hinged 1.00
200 A17 60f blue gray & brn 1.50 *3.00*
Never hinged 3.00
201 A18 75f claret & vio brn 1.50 *3.00*
Never hinged 3.00
202 A19 80f olive db & blk
brn 1.50 *3.00*
Never hinged 3.00
Nos. 198-202 (5) 5.50 11.00

Used values are for favor cancels.
Exist imperf. Value, Set $150.

Wmk. Vertical
198a A15 20f 6.25 12.50
Never hinged 13.00
199a A16 45f 6.25 12.50
Never hinged 13.00
200a A17 60f 6.25 12.50
Never hinged 13.00

201a A18 75f 6.25 12.50
Never hinged 13.00
202a A19 80f 12.50 25.00
Never hinged 25.00
Nos. 198a-202a (5) 37.50

Nos. 198a-202a were not used postally. Used examples are favor canceled.

Stamps of 1919 Overprinted in Red

1919, July 21   Typo.   Perf. 15
203 A13 2f brown orange .25 .25
Never hinged .30
204 A13 3f red lilac .25 .25
Never hinged .30
205 A13 4f slate gray .25 .25
Never hinged .30
206 A13 5f yellow green .25 .25
Never hinged .30
207 A13 6f grnsh blue .25 .25
Never hinged .30
208 A13 10f red .25 .25
Never hinged .30
209 A13 15f violet .25 .25
Never hinged .30
210 A13 20f dark brown .25 .25
Never hinged .30
211 A13 25f dull blue .25 .25
Never hinged .30
212 A13 40f olive green .25 .25
Never hinged .35
213 A13 45f orange .25 .25
Never hinged .35

Overprinted in Red

Perf. 14
214 A14 50f brn vio & pale vio .25 .30
Never hinged .30
215 A14 95f dk blue & blue .25 .30
Never hinged .30
216 A14 1k red brown .25 .30
Never hinged .30
217 A14 1.20k dk grn & grn .25 .40
Never hinged .40
218 A14 1.40k yellow green .25 .40
Never hinged .40
219 A14 2k ol brn & bister .40 1.25
Never hinged .80
220 A14 3k dk vio & ind .65 1.00
Never hinged 1.00
221 A14 5k dk brn & brn .50 .80
Never hinged .80
222 A14 10k vio brn & red vio .75 1.75
Never hinged 1.50
Nos. 203-222 (20) 6.30 9.25

"Magyar Tanacsköztarsasag" on Nos. 198 to 222 means "Hungarian Soviet Republic."
Nos. 203-218, 221-222 exist imperf. Value, set $125.

Issues of the Kingdom

Stamps of 1919 Overprinted in Black

1919, Nov. 16
306 A13 5f green .65 1.00
Never hinged 1.00
307 A13 10f rose red .65 1.00
Never hinged 1.00
308 A13 15f violet .65 1.00
Never hinged 1.00
309 A13 20f gray brown .65 1.00
Never hinged 1.00
310 A13 25f dull blue .65 1.00
Never hinged 1.00
Nos. 306-310 (5) 3.25 11.50

Issued to commemorate the Romanian evacuation. The overprint reads: "Entry of the National Army-November 16, 1919."
Forged overprints exist.

Nos. 203 to 213 Overprinted in Black

1920, Jan. 26   Perf. 15
311 A13 2f brown orange 1.25 1.60
Never hinged 1.60

312 A13 3f red lilac .25 .30
Never hinged .30
313 A13 4f slate gray 1.25 1.60
Never hinged 1.60
314 A13 5f yellow green .25 .25
Never hinged .30
315 A13 6f blue green .25 .40
Never hinged .40
316 A13 10f red .25 .25
Never hinged .30
317 A13 15f violet .25 .25
Never hinged .30
318 A13 20f dark brown .25 .25
Never hinged .30
319 A13 25f dull blue .25 .30
Never hinged .30
320 A13 40f olive green 1.50 2.00
Never hinged 1.75
321 A13 45f orange 1.50 2.00
Never hinged 1.75

Nos. 214 to 222 Overprinted in Black

Perf. 14
322 A14 50f brn vio & pale
vio 1.50 *2.00*
Never hinged 1.75
323 A14 95f dk bl & bl 1.50 *2.00*
Never hinged 1.75
324 A14 1k red brown 1.50 *2.00*
Never hinged 1.75
325 A14 1.20k dk grn & grn 1.50 *2.50*
Never hinged 1.75
326 A14 1.40k yellow green 1.50 *2.50*
Never hinged 1.75
327 A14 2k ol brn & bis 8.50 *17.50*
Never hinged 14.00
328 A14 3k dk vio & ind 8.50 *17.50*
Never hinged 11.00
329 A14 5k dk brn & brn .25 *.50*
Never hinged .35
330 A14 10k vio brn & red
vio 8.50 *17.50*
Never hinged 11.00
Nos. 311-330 (20) 40.50 73.20

Counterfeit overprints exist.

Types of 1916-18 Issue
Denomination Tablets Without Inner Frame on Nos. 350 to 363
1920-24   Wmk. 137   Perf. 15
335 A9 5f brown orange .25 .25
Never hinged .30
336 A9 10f red violet .25 .25
Never hinged .35
337 A9 40f rose red .25 .25
Never hinged .30
338 A9 50f yellow green .25 .25
Never hinged .30
339 A9 50f blue vio ('22) .25 .25
Never hinged .30
340 A9 60f black .25 .25
Never hinged .30
341 A9 1k green ('22) .25 .25
Never hinged .35
342 A9 1½k brown vio ('22) .25 .25
Never hinged .30
343 A9 2k grnsh blue
('22) .25 .25
Never hinged .30
344 A9 2½k dp green ('22) .25 .25
Never hinged .30
345 A9 3k brown org ('22) .25 .25
Never hinged .40
346 A9 4k lt red ('22) .25 .25
Never hinged .40
347 A9 4½k dull violet ('22) .25 .25
Never hinged .40
348 A9 5k dp brn ('22) .25 .25
Never hinged .40
349 A9 6k dark blue ('22) .25 .25
Never hinged .40
350 A9 10k brown ('23) .25 .25
Never hinged .40
351 A9 15k slate ('23) .25 .25
Never hinged .50
352 A9 20k red vio ('23) .25 .25
Never hinged .50
353 A9 25k orange ('23) .25 .25
Never hinged .50
354 A9 40k gray grn ('23) .25 .25
Never hinged .50
355 A9 50k dark blue ('23) .25 .25
Never hinged .50
356 A9 100k claret ('23) .25 .25
Never hinged .60
357 A9 150k dark green
('23) .30 .25
Never hinged .55
358 A9 200k green ('23) .30 .25
Never hinged .55
359 A9 300k rose red ('24) .80 .30
Never hinged 1.00
360 A9 350k violet ('23) 1.50 .30
Never hinged 4.00
361 A9 500k dark gray ('24) 2.50 .30
Never hinged 5.75
362 A9 600k olive bis ('24) 2.50 .30
Never hinged 5.75
363 A9 800k org yel ('24) 2.50 .30
Never hinged 5.50

Perf. 14
364 A10 2.50k bl & gray bl .25 .25
Never hinged .30
365 A10 3.50k gray .25 .25
Never hinged .35

366	A10	10k brown ('22)		.50	.25
		Never hinged		1.00	
367	A10	15k dk gray ('22)		.25	.25
		Never hinged		.30	
368	A10	20k red vio ('22)		.25	.25
		Never hinged		.30	
369	A10	25k orange ('22)		.25	.25
		Never hinged		.75	
370	A10	30k claret ('22)		.75	.25
		Never hinged		.35	
371	A10	40k gray grn ('22)		.75	.25
		Never hinged		.40	
372	A10	50k dp blue ('22)		.75	.25
		Never hinged		.40	
373	A10	100k yel brn ('22)		.75	.25
		Never hinged		.50	
374	A10	400k turq bl ('23)		.75	.30
		Never hinged		1.50	
375	A10	500k brt vio ('23)		1.10	.25
		Never hinged		1.25	
376	A10	1000k lilac ('24)		1.50	.25
		Never hinged		3.00	
377	A10	2000k car ('24)		2.00	.60
		Nos. 335-377 (43)		26.00	11.40

Three-Hole Punch

335a	A9	5f brown orange		.50	1.25
		Never hinged		1.00	
336a	A9	10f red violet		.40	1.00
		Never hinged		.75	
338a	A9	50f yellow green		.25	.25
		Never hinged		.40	
339a	A9	50f blue vio ('22)		.25	.25
		Never hinged		.40	
340a	A9	60f black		.25	.25
		Never hinged		.40	
341a	A9	1k green ('22)		.25	.25
		Never hinged		.45	
342a	A9	1½k brown vio ('22)		.25	.45
		Never hinged		.45	
343a	A9	2k grnsh blue ('22)		.25	.40
		Never hinged		.40	
344a	A9	2½k dp green ('22)		.25	.40
		Never hinged		.40	
345a	A9	3k brown org ('22)		.25	.60
		Never hinged		.45	
346a	A9	4k lt red ('22)		.25	.60
		Never hinged		.45	
347a	A9	4½k dull violet ('22)		.25	.50
		Never hinged		.40	
348a	A9	5k deep brown ('22)		.25	.40
		Never hinged		.50	
349a	A9	6k dark blue ('22)		.25	.50
		Never hinged		.40	
350a	A9	10k brown ('23)		.25	.25
		Never hinged		.40	
351a	A9	15k slate ('23)		.25	.50
		Never hinged		.45	
352a	A9	20k red vio ('23)		.25	.35
		Never hinged		.45	
353a	A9	25k orange ('23)		.25	.35
		Never hinged		.45	
354a	A9	40k gray grn ('23)		.25	.35
		Never hinged		.50	
355a	A9	50k dark blue ('23)		.25	.40
		Never hinged		.40	
356a	A9	100k claret ('23)		.40	.50
		Never hinged		.75	
357a	A9	150k dark green ('23)		.50	.40
		Never hinged		1.00	
358a	A9	200k green ('23)		.50	.40
		Never hinged		1.00	
360a	A9	350k violet ('23)		2.00	1.75
		Never hinged		3.75	
364a	A10	2.50k bl & gray bl		.30	.30
		Never hinged		.50	
365a	A10	3.50k gray		.30	.30
		Never hinged		.50	
366a	A10	10k brown ('22)		.75	.35
		Never hinged		1.00	
367a	A10	15k dk gray ('22)		.30	.40
		Never hinged		.50	
368a	A10	20k red vio ('22)		.30	.40
		Never hinged		.50	
369a	A10	25k orange ('22)		.35	.30
		Never hinged		.60	
370a	A10	30k claret ('22)		.35	.40
		Never hinged		.60	
371a	A10	40k gray grn ('22)		.35	.30
		Never hinged		.60	
372a	A10	50k dp blue ('22)		.35	.30
		Never hinged		.60	
373a	A10	100k yel brn ('22)		.35	.30
		Never hinged		.60	
374a	A10	400k turq bl ('23)		1.25	.50
		Never hinged		2.50	
375a	A10	500k brt vio ('23)		1.25	.50
		Never hinged		2.50	
		Nos. 335a-375a (36)		15.00	16.75

Nos. 372 to 377 have colored numerals. Nos. 335-338, 340, 350-365, 368, 370, 372-377 exist imperf. Value, set $200.

Madonna and
Child — A23

1921-25   Typo.   Perf. 12

378	A23	50k dk brn & bl		.25	.25
		Never hinged		.50	
379	A23	100k ol bis & yel brn		.40	.35
		Never hinged		.75	

Wmk. 133

380	A23	200k dk bl & ultra		.40	.25
		Never hinged		.75	
381	A23	500k vio brn & vio		.75	.40
		Never hinged		1.50	

382	A23	1000k vio & red vio		1.00	.35
		Never hinged		2.00	
383	A23	2000k grnsh bl & vio		1.75	.50
		Never hinged		3.00	
384	A23	2500k ol brn & buff		2.00	.25
		Never hinged		4.00	
385	A23	3000k brn red & vio		2.00	.25
		Never hinged		4.00	
386	A23	5000k dk grn & yel grn		2.00	.25
		Never hinged		4.00	
a.		Center inverted		15,000.	8,000.
		Never hinged		17,500.	
387	A23	10000k gray vio & pale bl		2.00	.25
		Never hinged		4.00	
		Nos. 378-387 (10)		12.55	3.10

Three-Hole Punch

378a	A23	50k dk brn & bl		.55	.40
		Never hinged		1.00	
379a	A23	100k ol bis & yel brn		.85	.60
		Never hinged		1.50	
380a	A23	200k dk bl & ultra		.85	.50
		Never hinged		1.50	
381a	A23	500k vio brn & vio		1.40	.75
		Never hinged		2.50	
382a	A23	1000k vio & red vio		2.25	1.25
		Never hinged		4.00	
383a	A23	2000k grnsh bl & vio		2.50	2.50
		Never hinged		4.50	
		Nos. 378a-383a (6)		8.40	6.00

Nos. 380-387 exist imperf. Value, set of 8 $175.
Issue dates: 50k, 100k, Feb. 27, 1921; 2500k, 10,000k, 1925; others, 1923.

Types of 1916-18
Denomination Tablets Without Inner
Frame on Nos. 388-394

1924   Wmk. 133   Perf. 15

388	A9	100k claret		.40	.25
		Never hinged		.80	
389	A9	200k yellow grn		.25	.25
		Never hinged		.50	
390	A9	300k rose red		.30	.35
		Never hinged		.60	
391	A9	400k deep blue		.30	.35
		Never hinged		.60	
392	A9	500k dark gray		.40	.25
		Never hinged		.75	
393	A9	600k olive bister		.45	.25
		Never hinged		.90	
a.		"800" in upper right corner		110.00	260.00
		Never hinged		150.00	
394	A9	800k org yel		.50	.25
		Never hinged		1.00	

Perf. 14½x14

395	A10	1000k lilac		1.50	.25
		Never hinged		3.00	
396	A10	2000k carmine		2.00	.25
		Never hinged		4.00	
		Nos. 388-396 (9)		6.10	2.45

Nos. 395 and 396 have colored numerals.
Exist imperf. Value, set $37.50.

Maurus Jókai
(1825-1904),
Novelist
A24

1925, Feb. 1   Unwmk.   Perf. 12

400	A24	1000k dp grn & blk brn		1.75	3.25
		Never hinged		3.00	
401	A24	2000k lt brn & blk brn		.80	1.00
		Never hinged		1.00	
402	A24	2500k dk bl & blk brn		1.75	3.25
		Never hinged			
		Nos. 400-402 (3)		4.30	7.50

Exist imperf. Value, set $90.

Crown of St.
Stephen
A25

Matthias
Cathedral
A26

Palace at
Budapest — A27

1926-27   Wmk. 133   Litho.   Perf. 15

403	A25	1f dk gray		.45	.25
		Never hinged		.60	
404	A25	2f lt blue		.55	.25
		Never hinged		.80	
405	A25	3f orange		.55	.25
		Never hinged		.80	
406	A25	4f violet		.65	.25
		Never hinged		.90	
407	A25	6f lt green		.90	.25
		Never hinged		1.25	
408	A25	8f lilac rose		1.60	.25
		Never hinged		2.25	

Typo.

409	A26	10f deep blue		2.75	.25
		Never hinged		4.00	
410	A26	16f dark violet		2.25	.25
		Never hinged		3.25	
411	A26	20f carmine		2.75	.25
		Never hinged		4.00	
412	A26	25f lt brown		2.75	.25
		Never hinged		4.00	

Perf. 14¼x14

413	A27	32f dp vio & brt vio		4.25	.25
		Never hinged		6.00	
414	A27	40f dk blue & blue		5.00	.25
		Never hinged		8.00	
		Nos. 403-414 (12)		24.45	3.00

Perf. 14x14¼

403a	A25	1f dk gray		.85	.25
		Never hinged		1.50	
404a	A25	2f lt blue		14.00	2.50
		Never hinged		25.00	
405a	A25	3f orange		1.00	.25
		Never hinged		1.75	
406a	A25	4f violet		1.00	.25
		Never hinged		1.75	
407a	A25	6f lt green		1.40	.25
		Never hinged		2.50	
408a	A25	8f lilac rose		2.75	.25
		Never hinged		5.00	

Typo.

409a	A26	10f deep blue		1.00	.25
		Never hinged		1.75	
410a	A26	16f dark violet		.85	.25
		Never hinged		1.50	
411a	A26	20f carmine		1.10	.25
		Never hinged		2.00	
412a	A26	25f lt brown		1.10	.25
		Never hinged		2.00	

See Nos. 428-436. For surcharges see Nos. 450-456, 466-467.
Nos. 403-414, 418-421 exist imperf. Value, set $250.

Madonna and
Child — A28

1926-27   Engr.   Perf. 14

415	A28	1p violet		15.00	.65
		Never hinged		30.00	
416	A28	2p red		17.50	.85
		Never hinged		30.00	
417	A28	5p blue ('27)		17.50	4.00
		Never hinged		30.00	
		Nos. 415-417 (3)		50.00	5.50

Exist imperf. Value, set $400.

Palace at Budapest
A29

St. Stephen
A30

1926-27   Typo.   Perf. 14x14¼

418	A29	30f blue grn ('27)		4.00	.25
		Never hinged		6.00	
419	A29	46f ultra ('27)		5.25	.30
		Never hinged		6.50	
420	A29	50f brown blk ('27)		6.00	.25
		Never hinged		7.50	
421	A29	70f scarlet		9.75	.25
		Never hinged		12.50	
		Nos. 418-421 (4)		25.00	1.05

For surcharge see No. 480.

1928-29   Engr.   Perf. 15

422	A30	8f yellow grn		.65	.30
		Never hinged		1.10	
423	A30	8f rose lake ('29)		.65	.30
		Never hinged		1.10	
424	A30	16f orange red		.85	.30
		Never hinged		1.10	
425	A30	16f violet ('29)		.85	.30
		Never hinged		1.10	
426	A30	32f ultra		2.50	4.00
		Never hinged		4.50	

427	A30	32f bister ('29)		2.50	4.00
		Never hinged		4.50	
		Nos. 422-427 (6)		8.00	9.20

890th death anniversary of St. Stephen, the first king of Hungary.
Exist imperf. Value, set $300.

Types of 1926-27 Issue

1928-30   Typo.   Wmk. 210   Perf. 15

428	A25	1f black		.25	.25
		Never hinged		.50	
429	A25	2f blue		.35	.25
		Never hinged		.60	
430	A25	3f orange		.35	.25
		Never hinged		.60	
431	A25	4f violet		.45	.25
		Never hinged		.75	
432	A25	6f blue grn		.60	.25
		Never hinged		1.00	
433	A25	8f lilac rose		1.25	.25
		Never hinged		1.75	
434	A26	10f dp blue ('30)		4.50	.25
		Never hinged		6.00	
435	A26	16f violet		1.50	.25
		Never hinged		3.00	
436	A26	20f dull red		1.25	.25
		Never hinged		2.50	
		Nos. 428-436 (9)		10.50	2.25

Perf. 14x14¼

429a	A25	2f blue		5.00	1.50
		Never hinged		9.00	
433a	A25	8f lilac rose		3.00	.50
		Never hinged		5.50	

On Nos. 428-433 the numerals have thicker strokes than on the same values of the 1926-27 issue.
Exist imperf. Value, set $110.

Palace at
Budapest — A31

Type A31 resembles A27 but the steamer is nearer the right of the design. A31, A29 & A27 are similar but the frame borders are different.

1928-31   Perf. 14¼x14

437	A31	30f emerald ('31)		4.00	.25
		Never hinged		6.00	
438	A31	32f red violet		4.00	.25
		Never hinged		6.00	
439	A31	40f deep blue		5.00	.25
		Never hinged		8.00	
440	A31	46f apple green		4.50	.25
		Never hinged		6.75	
441	A31	50f ocher ('31)		4.50	.25
		Never hinged		6.75	
		Nos. 437-441 (5)		22.00	1.25

Exist imperf. Value, set $110.

Admiral Nicholas
Horthy — A32

1930, Mar. 1   Litho.   Perf. 15

445	A32	8f myrtle green		.75	.25
		Never hinged		1.50	
446	A32	16f purple		1.00	.25
		Never hinged		2.00	
447	A32	20f carmine		6.00	1.10
		Never hinged		12.00	
448	A32	32f olive brown		4.00	1.25
		Never hinged		8.00	
449	A32	40f dull blue		7.00	.50
		Never hinged		14.00	
		Nos. 445-449 (5)		18.75	3.35

10th anniv. of the election of Adm. Nicholas Horthy as Regent, Mar. 1, 1920.
Exist imperf. Value, set, $200.

Stamps of 1926-28
Surcharged

1931, Jan. 1   Perf. 14¼, 15

450	A25	2f on 3f orange		.50	.40
		Never hinged		1.00	
451	A25	6f on 8f magenta		.50	.25
		Never hinged		1.00	
a.		Perf. 14x14¼		30.00	30.00
		Never hinged		42.50	
452	A26	10f on 16f violet		.50	.25
		Never hinged		1.00	

Wmk. 133

453	A25	2f on 3f orange		2.50	5.00
		Never hinged		5.00	
a.		Perf. 14x14¼		3.00	6.00
		Never hinged		6.00	

454	A25	6f on 8f magenta	2.00 4.00
		Never hinged	4.00
a.		Perf. 14x14¼	50.00 100.00
		Never hinged	100.00
455	A26	10f on 16f dk vio	1.75 3.50
		Never hinged	3.50
a.		Perf. 14x14¼	2.00 4.00
		Never hinged	4.00
456	A26	20f on 25f lt brn	1.25 2.50
		Never hinged	3.00
a.		Perf. 14x14¼	1.25 2.25
		Never hinged	3.00
		Nos. 450-456 (7)	9.00 15.90

For surcharges see Nos. 466-467.

St. Elizabeth
A33

Ministering to Children
A34

Wmk. 210

1932, Apr. 21   Photo.   Perf. 15

458	A33	10f ultra	.75 .25
		Never hinged	1.50
459	A33	20f scarlet	.75 .25
		Never hinged	1.50

Perf. 14

460	A34	32f deep violet	1.50 2.50
		Never hinged	3.00
461	A34	40f deep blue	2.00 1.00
		Never hinged	4.00
		Nos. 458-461 (4)	5.00 4.00

700th anniv. of the death of St. Elizabeth of Hungary.
Exist imperf. Value, set $100.

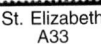

Madonna, Patroness of Hungary — A35

1932, June 1   Perf. 12

462	A35	1p yellow grn	30.00 .25
		Never hinged	60.00
463	A35	2p carmine	30.00 .40
		Never hinged	60.00
464	A35	5p deep blue	42.50 3.00
		Never hinged	90.00
465	A35	10p olive bister	42.50 22.50
		Never hinged	90.00
		Nos. 462-465 (4)	145.00 26.15

Exist imperf. Value, set $1,000.

Nos. 451 and 454 Surcharged

1932, June 14   Wmk. 210   Perf. 15

466	A25	2f on 6f on 8f mag	.25 .25
		Never hinged	.50

Wmk. 133

467	A25	2f on 6f on 8f mag	50.00 100.00
		Never hinged	100.00

Imre Madách — A36

Designs: 2f, Janos Arany. 4f, Dr. Ignaz Semmelweis. 6f, Baron Lorand Eotvos. 10f, Count Stephen Szechenyi. 16f, Ferenc Deak. 20f, Franz Liszt. 30f, Louis Kossuth. 32f, Stephen Tisza. 40f, Mihaly Munkacsy. 50f, Alexander Csoma. 70f, Farkas Bolyai.

1932   Wmk. 210   Perf. 15

468	A36	1f slate violet	.25 .25
		Never hinged	.30
469	A36	2f orange	.25 .25
		Never hinged	.30
470	A36	4f ultra	.25 .25
		Never hinged	.30
471	A36	6f yellow grn	.25 .25
		Never hinged	.30
472	A36	10f Prus green	.35 .25
		Never hinged	.75
473	A36	16f dull violet	.35 .25
		Never hinged	.75
474	A36	20f deep rose	.30 .25
		Never hinged	.60
475	A36	30f brown	.50 .25
		Never hinged	1.00
476	A36	32f brown vio	.70 .25
		Never hinged	1.20
477	A36	40f dull blue	.85 .25
		Never hinged	1.60
478	A36	50f deep green	1.10 .25
		Never hinged	2.25
479	A36	70f cerise	1.50 .25
		Never hinged	2.50
		Nos. 468-479 (12)	6.65 3.00
		Set, never hinged	11.50

Issued in honor of famous Hungarians.
Exist imperf. Value, set $125.
See Nos. 509-510.

No. 421 Surcharged

1933, Apr. 15   Wmk. 133   Perf. 14

480	A29	10f on 70f scarlet	3.00 .40
		Never hinged	6.00

Leaping Stag and Double Cross — A47

Wmk. 210

1933, July 10   Photo.   Perf. 15

481	A47	10f dk green	.75 .80
		Never hinged	1.50
482	A47	16f violet brn	2.00 2.50
		Never hinged	4.00
483	A47	20f car lake	1.50 1.25
		Never hinged	3.00
484	A47	32f yellow	5.00 6.00
		Never hinged	8.50
485	A47	40f deep blue	5.00 4.00
		Never hinged	10.50
		Nos. 481-485 (5)	14.25 14.55
		Set, never hinged	27.50

Boy Scout Jamboree at Gödöllö, Hungary, July 20 - Aug. 20, 1933.
Exists imperf. Value, set $150.

Souvenir Sheet

Franz Liszt — A48

1934, May 6   Perf. 15

486	A48	20f lake	70.00 90.00
		Never hinged	140.00

2nd Hungarian Phil. Exhib., Budapest, and Jubilee of the 1st Hungarian Phil. Soc. Sold for 90f, including entrance fee. Size: 64x76mm.
Exists imperf. Value $2,500.

Francis II Rákóczy (1676-1735), Prince of Transylvania A49

Cardinal Pázmány — A50

Signing the Charter — A51

1935, Apr. 8   Perf. 12

487	A49	10f yellow green	.75 .40
		Never hinged	1.25
488	A49	16f brt violet	4.50 3.50
		Never hinged	6.25
489	A49	20f dark carmine	2.00 1.25
		Never hinged	4.00
490	A49	32f brown lake	6.00 7.00
		Never hinged	10.00
491	A49	40f blue	7.50 8.00
		Never hinged	11.00
		Nos. 487-491 (5)	20.75 20.15
		Set, never hinged	32.50

Exists imperf. Value, set $400.

1935, Sept. 25

492	A50	6f dull green	1.10 1.00
		Never hinged	2.00
493	A51	10f dark green	.25 .25
		Never hinged	.50
494	A50	16f slate violet	1.50 1.60
		Never hinged	3.00
495	A50	20f magenta	.25 .40
		Never hinged	.50
496	A51	32f deep claret	2.50 3.25
		Never hinged	5.00
497	A51	40f dark blue	2.00 3.25
		Never hinged	4.00
		Nos. 492-497 (6)	7.60 9.75
		Set, never hinged	15.00

Tercentenary of the founding of the University of Budapest by Peter Cardinal Pázmány.
Exists imperf. Value, set $400.

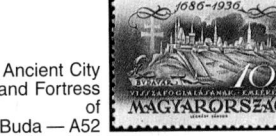

Ancient City and Fortress of Buda — A52

Guardian Angel over Buda — A53

Shield of Buda, Cannon and Massed Flags — A54

First Hungarian Soldier to Enter Buda — A55

1936, Sept. 2   Perf. 11½x12½

498	A52	10f dark green	.40 .25
		Never hinged	.75
499	A53	16f deep violet	2.50 3.50
		Never hinged	4.50
500	A54	20f car lake	.40 .25
		Never hinged	.75
501	A55	32f dark brown	2.50 3.25
		Never hinged	5.00
502	A52	40f deep blue	2.50 3.25
		Never hinged	5.00
		Nos. 498-502 (5)	8.30 10.50
		Set, never hinged	16.00

250th anniv. of the recapture of Budapest from the Turks.

Exists imperf. Value, set $400.

Catalogue values for unused stamps in this section, from this point to the end of the section, are for Never Hinged items.

Budapest International Fair — A56

1937, Feb. 22   Perf. 12

503	A56	2f deep orange	.25 .25
504	A56	6f yellow green	.40 .25
505	A56	10f myrtle green	.55 .25
506	A56	20f deep cerise	1.25 .40
507	A56	32f dark violet	2.00 .55
508	A56	40f ultra	1.60 .40
		Nos. 503-508 (6)	6.05 2.50

Exist imperf. Value, set $250.

Portrait Type of 1932

5f, Ferenc Kolcsey. 25f, Mihaly Vorosmarty.

1937, May 5   Perf. 15

509	A36	5f brown orange	.80 .25
510	A36	25f olive green	1.60 .25

Exist imperf. Value, set $400.

Pope Sylvester II, Archbishop Astrik — A59

Designs: 2f, 16f, Stephen the Church builder. 4f, 20f, St. Stephen enthroned. 5f, 25f, Sts. Gerhardt, Emerich, Stephen. 6f, 30f, St. Stephen offering holy crown to Virgin Mary. 10f, same as 1f. 32f, 50f, Portrait of St. Stephen. 40f, Madonna and Child. 70f, Crown of St. Stephen.

See designs A75-A77 for smaller stamps of designs similar Nos. 521-524, but with slanted "MAGYAR KIR POSTA."

1938, Jan. 1   Perf. 12

511	A59	1f deep violet	.40 .25
512	A59	2f olive brown	.40 .25
513	A59	4f brt blue	.80 .25
514	A59	5f magenta	1.25 .25
515	A59	6f dp yel grn	1.60 .25
516	A59	10f red orange	1.25 .25
517	A59	16f gray violet	2.00 .55
518	A59	20f car lake	1.25 .25
519	A59	25f dark green	1.60 .80
520	A59	30f olive bister	2.50 .25
521	A59	32f dp claret, buff	2.50 2.00
522	A59	40f Prus green	2.50 .25
523	A59	50f rose vio, grnsh	2.75 .25
524	A59	70f ol grn, bluish	4.50 .55
		Nos. 511-524 (14)	25.30 6.40

900th anniv. of the death of St. Stephen.
Exists imperf. Value, set $400.
For overprints see Nos. 535-536.

Admiral Horthy — A67

1938, Jan. 1   Perf. 12½x12

525	A67	1p peacock green	2.75 .25
526	A67	2p brown	3.25 .35
527	A67	5p sapphire blue	4.00 1.90
		Nos. 525-527 (3)	10.00 2.50

Exist imperf. Value, set $475.

Souvenir Sheet

St. Stephen — A68

1938, May 22 Wmk. 210 ***Perf. 12***

528	A68	20f carmine lake	32.50	25.00

3rd Hungarian Phil. Exhib., Budapest. Sheet sold only at exhibition with 1p ticket.
Exists imperf. Value $4,500.

College of Debrecen A69

Three Students — A71

George Marothy — A73

10f, 18th cent. view of College. 20f, 19th cent. view of College. 40f, Stephen Hatvani.

Perf. 12x12½, 12½x12

1938, Sept. 24 Wmk. 210

529	A69	6f deep green	.40	.25
530	A69	10f brown	.40	.25
531	A71	16f brown car	.40	.30
532	A69	20f crimson	.40	.25
533	A73	32f slate green	1.10	.75
534	A73	40f brt blue	1.10	.60
		Nos. 529-534 (6)	3.80	2.40

Founding of Debrecen College, 400th anniv.
Exists imperf. Value $300.

Types of 1938 Overprinted in Blue (#535) or Carmine (#536)

a

b

1938 ***Perf. 12***

535	A59(a)	20f salmon pink	2.00	1.60
536	A59(b)	70f brn, *grnsh*	2.00	1.60
a.		Overprint omitted	*12,500.*	*7,500.*

Restoration of the territory ceded by Czechoslovakia.
Exists imperf. Value $135.
Forgeries exist of No. 536a.

Crown of St. Stephen A75

St. Stephen A76

Madonna, Patroness of Hungary A77

Coronation Church, Budapest A78

Reformed Church, Debrecen A79

Cathedral, Esztergom A80

Deak Square Evangelical Church, Budapest — A81

Cathedral of Kassa — A82

Wmk. 210

1939, June 1 Photo. ***Perf. 15***

537	A75	1f brown car	.25	.25
538	A75	2f Prus green	.25	.25
539	A75	4f ocher	.25	.25
540	A75	5f brown violet	.25	.25
541	A75	6f yellow green	.25	.25
542	A75	10f bister brn	.25	.25
543	A75	16f rose violet	.25	.25
544	A76	20f rose red	.25	.25
545	A77	25f blue gray	.25	.25

Perf. 12

546	A78	30f red violet	.40	.25
547	A79	32f brown	.25	.25
548	A80	40f greenish blue	.40	.25
549	A81	50f olive	.50	.25
550	A82	70f henna brown	.50	.25
		Nos. 537-550 (14)	4.30	3.50

See Nos. 521-524, 578-596. For overprints see Nos. 559-560 in Scott. Post 1940 issues in Scott Standard catalogue, Vol. 3.
Exists imperf. Value, set $250.

Girl Scout Sign and Olive Branch — A83

6f, Scout lily, Hungary's shield, Crown of St. Stephen. 10f, Girls in Scout hat & national headdress. 20f, Dove & Scout emblems.

1939, July 20 Photo. ***Perf. 12***

551	A83	2f brown orange	.50	.35
552	A83	6f green	.50	.35
553	A83	10f brown	.80	.45
554	A83	20f lilac rose	1.25	.80
		Nos. 551-554 (4)	3.05	1.95

Girl Scout Jamboree at Gödöllő.
Exists imperf. Value, set $300.

Admiral Horthy at Szeged, 1919 — A87

Admiral Nicholas Horthy A88

Cathedral of Kassa and Angel Ringing "Bell of Liberty" A89

1940, Mar. 1

555	A87	6f green	.25	.25
556	A88	10f ol blk & ol bis	.25	.25
557	A89	20f brt rose brown	.80	.55
		Nos. 555-557 (3)	1.30	1.05

20th anniversary of the election of Admiral Horthy as Regent of Hungary.
Exists imperf. Value, set $100.

Crown of St. Stephen A90

1940, Sept. 5

558	A90	10f dk green & yellow	.40	.40

Issued in commemoration of the recovery of northeastern Transylvania from Romania.
Exists imperf. Value $25.

SEMI-POSTAL STAMPS

Issues of the Monarchy

"Turul" and St. Stephen's Crown — SP1

Franz Josef I Wearing Hungarian Crown — SP2

Wmk. Double Cross (137)

1913, Nov. 20 Typo. ***Perf. 14***

B1	SP1	1f slate	.40	.25
		Never hinged	.80	
B2	SP1	2f olive yellow	.40	.25
		Never hinged	.80	
B3	SP1	3f orange	.40	.25
		Never hinged	.80	
B4	SP1	5f emerald	.40	.25
		Never hinged	.80	
B5	SP1	6f olive green	.40	.25
		Never hinged	.80	
B6	SP1	10f carmine	.60	.25
		Never hinged	1.25	
B7	SP1	12f violet, *yellow*	.50	.25
		Never hinged	1.00	
B8	SP1	16f gray green	.75	.25
		Never hinged	1.50	
B9	SP1	20f dark brown	3.00	.40
		Never hinged	6.00	
B10	SP1	25f ultra	1.75	.25
		Never hinged	3.50	
B11	SP1	30f orange brown	2.00	.25
		Never hinged	4.00	
B12	SP1	35f red violet	2.00	.25
		Never hinged	4.00	
B13	SP1	50f lake, *blue*	3.75	.60
		Never hinged	7.50	
B14	SP1	60f green, *salmon*	3.75	.50
		Never hinged	7.50	
B15	SP2	1k dull red	25.00	2.00
		Never hinged	50.00	
B16	SP2	2k dull blue	75.00	40.00
		Never hinged	150.00	
B17	SP2	5k violet brown	30.00	30.00
		Never hinged	60.00	
		Nos. B1-B17 (17)	150.10	76.25

Nos. B1-B17 were sold at an advance of 2f over face value, as indicated by the label at bottom. The surtax was to aid flood victims.
For overprints see Nos. 5NB1-5NB10, 6NB1-6NB11.
Exist imperf. Value, set $1,000.

Semi-Postal Stamps of 1913 Surcharged in Red, Green or Brown

a

b

1914

B18	SP1(a)	1f slate	.25	.25
		Never hinged	.50	
B19	SP1(a)	2f olive yel	.25	.25
		Never hinged	.50	
B20	SP1(a)	3f orange	.25	.25
		Never hinged	.50	
B21	SP1(a)	5f emerald	.25	.25
		Never hinged	.50	
B22	SP1(a)	6f olive green	.25	.25
		Never hinged	.50	
B23	SP1(a)	10f carmine (G)	.35	.25
		Never hinged	.70	
B24	SP1(a)	12f violet, *yel*	.25	.25
		Never hinged	.50	
B25	SP1(a)	16f gray green	.30	.25
		Never hinged	.60	
B26	SP1(a)	20f dark brown	.90	.25
		Never hinged	2.00	
B27	SP1(a)	25f ultra	.90	.25
		Never hinged	2.00	
B28	SP1(a)	30f orange brn	1.10	.25
		Never hinged	2.75	
B29	SP1(a)	35f red violet	1.90	.25
		Never hinged	4.50	
B30	SP1(a)	50f lake, *bl*	1.50	.50
		Never hinged	3.00	
B31	SP1(a)	60f green, *salmon*	2.00	.55
		Never hinged	4.00	
B32	SP2(b)	1k dull red (Br)	60.00	25.00
		Never hinged	125.00	
B33	SP2(b)	2k dull blue	37.50	26.00
		Never hinged	75.00	
B34	SP2(b)	5k violet brn	30.00	21.00
		Never hinged	60.00	
		Nos. B18-B34 (17)	137.95	76.05

Exist imperf. Value, set $800.

Regular Issue of 1913 Surcharged in Red or Green

c

d

1915, Jan. 1

B35	A4(c)	1f slate	.25	.25
		Never hinged	.50	
B36	A4(c)	2f olive yel	.25	.25
		Never hinged	.50	
B37	A4(c)	3f orange	.25	.25
		Never hinged	.50	
B38	A4(c)	5f emerald	.25	.25
		Never hinged	.50	
B39	A4(c)	6f olive grn	.25	.25
		Never hinged	.50	
B40	A4(c)	10f carmine (G)	.25	.25
		Never hinged	.50	
B41	A4(c)	12f violet, *yel*	.25	.25
		Never hinged	.50	
B42	A4(c)	16f gray green	.25	.25
		Never hinged	.50	
B43	A4(c)	20f dark brown	.25	.25
		Never hinged	.50	
B44	A4(c)	25f ultra	.25	.25
		Never hinged	.50	
B45	A4(c)	30f orange brn	.40	.25
		Never hinged	.80	
B46	A4(c)	35f red violet	.45	.25
		Never hinged	.90	
B47	A4(c)	50f lake, *bl*	.65	.25
		Never hinged	1.25	
a.		On No. 96a	*5,000.*	
B48	A4(c)	60f green, *salmon*	.80	.30
		Never hinged	1.60	
B49	A5(d)	1k dull red	1.10	3.00
		Never hinged	2.25	
B50	A5(d)	2k dull blue	3.00	7.50
		Never hinged	6.00	
B51	A5(d)	5k violet brown	9.50	17.50
		Never hinged	18.50

Surcharged as Type "c" but in Smaller Letters

B52 A4   60f green, *salmon*   2.25   1.25
    Never hinged   9.50
    Nos. B35-B52 (18)   20.65   32.80

Nos. B18-B52 were sold at an advance of 2f over face value. The surtax to aid war widows and orphans.
Exist imperf. Value, set $200.

Soldiers Fighting
SP3   SP4

Eagle with Sword SP5   Harvesting SP6

1916-17   *Perf. 15*

B53 SP3 10f + 2f rose red   .25   .30
    Never hinged   .50
B54 SP4 15f + 2f dull violet   .25   .30
    Never hinged   .50
B55 SP5 40f + 2f brn car ('17)   .25   .40
    Never hinged   .50
    Nos. B53-B55 (3)   .75   1.00

Exist imperf. Value, set $15.
For overprints and surcharge see Nos. B58-B60. 1NB1-1NB3, 2NB1-2NB6, 4NJ1, 5NB11-5NB13, 6NB13-6NB15, 7NB2-7NB3, 9NB1, 10NB1-10NB4, 11NB1-B4.

1917, Sept. 15
Surcharge in Red

B56 SP6 10f + 1k rose   .60   *1.00*
    Never hinged   1.00
B57 SP6 15f + 1k violet   .60   *1.00*
    Never hinged   1.00

Nos. B56 and B57 were issued in connection with the War Exhibition of Archduke Josef.

Issues of the Republic

Semi-Postal Stamps of 1916-17 Overprinted in Black

1918

B58 SP3 10f + 2f rose red   .25   .25
    Never hinged   .50
B59 SP4 15f + 2f dull violet   .25   .25
    Never hinged   .50
B60 SP5 40f + 2f brown car   .25   .25
    Never hinged   .50
    Nos. B58-B60 (3)   .75   .75

Nos. B58-B60 exist with inverted overprint.
Exist imperf. Value, set $12.50.

> Postally used examples of Nos. B69-B130 sell for more.

Issues of the Kingdom

Released Prisoner Walking Home — SP7

Prisoners of War — SP8

Homecoming of Soldier — SP9

Wmk. 137 Vertical
1920, Mar. 10   *Perf. 12*

B69 SP7 40f + 1k dull red   5.00   10.00
    Never hinged   10.00
B70 SP8 60f + 2k gray brown   3.50   3.50
    Never hinged   7.00
B71 SP9 1k + 5k dk blue   1.75   3.50
    Never hinged   3.50
    Nos. B69-B71 (3)   10.25   17.00
    Nos. B69a-B71 (1)   1.75   3.50
    Set, never hinged   20.00

Wmk. 137 Horizontal

B69a SP7 40f + 1k dull red   1.75   3.50
    Never hinged   3.50
B70a SP8 60f + 2k gray brown   3.00   6.00
    Never hinged   6.00
B71a SP9 1k + 5k dk blue   3.50   3.50
    Never hinged   7.00
    Nos. B69a-B71a (1)   3.50   3.50
    Set, never hinged   18.50

The surtax was used to help prisoners of war return home from Siberia.
Exist imperf. Value, set $100.

Statue of Petöfi — SP10   Griffin — SP11

Sándor Petöfi — SP12

Petöfi Dying — SP13

Petöfi Addressing People — SP14

1923, Jan. 23 *Perf. 14 (10k, 40k), 12*

B72 SP10 10k slate green   .50   *1.00*
    Never hinged   1.00
B73 SP11 15k dull blue   1.00   *2.75*
    Never hinged   2.00
B74 SP12 25k gray brown   .50   *1.00*
    Never hinged   1.00
B75 SP13 40k brown violet   1.50   3.00
    Never hinged   3.00
B76 SP14 50k violet brown   1.50   3.00
    Never hinged   3.00
    Nos. B72-B76 (5)   5.00   10.75
    Set, never hinged   10.00

Birth centenary of the Hungarian poet Sándor Petöfi. The stamps were on sale at double face value, for a limited time and in restricted quantities, after which the remainders were given to a charitable organization.
Exist imperf. Value, set $100.

Child with Symbols of Peace — SP15

Mother and Infant — SP16

Instruction in Archery — SP17

Wmk. 133
1924, Apr. 8 Engr.   *Perf. 12*

B77 SP15 300k dark blue   1.50   *4.00*
    Never hinged   4.00
  a. Perf. 11½   35.00   30.00
B78 SP16 500k black brown   1.50   *4.00*
    Never hinged   4.00
B79 SP17 1000k black green   1.50   *4.00*
    Never hinged   4.00
    Nos. B77-B79 (3)   4.50   12.00
    Set, never hinged   12.00

Each stamp has on the back an inscription stating that it was sold at a premium of 100 per cent over the face value.
Exist imperf. Value, set $90.

Parade of Athletes SP18

Skiing — SP19

Skating — SP20

Diving — SP21

Fencing SP22

Scouts Camping — SP23

Soccer SP24

Hurdling — SP25

Perf. 12, 12½ and Compound
1925   Typo.   Unwmk.

B80 SP18 100k bl grn & brn   2.25   *2.00*
    Never hinged   4.50
B81 SP19 200k lt brn & myr grn   2.90   *2.50*
    Never hinged   5.50
B82 SP20 300k dark blue   3.50   *3.50*
    Never hinged   6.50
B83 SP21 400k dp bl & dp grn   3.80   *3.50*
    Never hinged   7.50
B84 SP22 500k purple brown   7.50   *10.00*
    Never hinged   10.50
B85 SP23 1000k red brown   6.25   *7.00*
    Never hinged   12.00
B86 SP24 2000k brown violet   7.50   *7.50*
    Never hinged   13.50
B87 SP25 2500k olive brown   7.50   *9.00*
    Never hinged   15.00
    Nos. B80-B87 (8)   41.20   *45.00*
    Set, never hinged   75.00

These stamps were sold at double face value, plus a premium of 10 per cent on orders sent by mail. They did not serve any postal need and were issued solely to raise funds to aid athletic associations. An inscription regarding the 100 per cent premium is printed on the back of each stamp.
Exist imperf. Value, set $450.

St. Emerich SP26   Sts. Stephen and Gisela SP27

St. Ladislaus SP28   Sts. Gerhardt and Emerich SP29

1930, May 15 Wmk. 210 *Perf. 14*

B88 SP26 8f + 2f deep green   .45   .40
    Never hinged   1.00
B89 SP27 16f + 4f brt violet   .65   *.60*
    Never hinged   1.10
B90 SP28 20f + 4f deep rose   1.90   *2.00*
    Never hinged   3.75
B91 SP29 32f + 8f ultra   2.50   *4.50*
    Never hinged   5.50
    Nos. B88-B91 (4)   5.50   *7.50*
    Set, never hinged   11.00

900th anniv. of the death of St. Emerich, son of Stephen I, king, saint and martyr.

Exist imperf. Value, set $150.

Catalogue values for unused stamps in this section, from this point to the end of the section, are for Never Hinged items.

St. Ladislaus — SP30

Holy Sacrament SP31

SP32

1938 May 16   Photo.   Perf. 12

B92	SP30	16f + 16f dull slate bl	3.00	3.00
B93	SP31	20f + 20f dk car	3.00	3.00

Souvenir Sheet

B94	SP32	Sheet of 7	50.00	32.50
a.		6f + 6f St. Stephen	4.00	3.00
b.		10f + 10f St. Emerich	4.00	3.00
c.		16f + 16f slate blue (B92)	4.00	3.00
d.		20f + 20f dark carmine (B93)	4.00	3.00
e.		32f + 32f St. Elizabeth	4.00	3.00
f.		40f + 40f St. Maurice	4.00	3.00
g.		50f + 50f St. Margaret	4.00	3.00

Printed in sheets measuring 136½x155mm. Nos. B94c and B94d are slightly smaller than B92 and B93.

Eucharistic Cong. in Budapest, May, 1938. Exist imperf. Value: set $125; souvenir sheet $3,750.

St. Stephen, Victorious Warrior SP33

St. Stephen, Offering Crown SP34

SP35

1938, Aug. 12   Perf. 12

B95	SP33	10f + 10f violet brn	3.00	3.00
B96	SP34	20f + 20f red org	3.00	3.00

Souvenir Sheet

B97	SP35	Sheet of 7	32.50	20.00
a.		6f + 6f St. Stephen the Missionary	3.25	2.00
b.		10f + 10f violet brown (B95)	3.25	2.00
c.		16f + 16f Seated Upon Throne	3.25	2.00
d.		20f + 20f red orange (B96)	3.25	2.00
e.		32f + 32f Receives Bishops and Monks	3.25	2.00
f.		40f + 40f St. Gisela, St. Stephen and St. Emerich	3.25	2.00
g.		50f + 50f St. Stephen on Bier	3.25	2.00

Death of St. Stephen, 900th anniversary. No. B97 is on brownish paper, Nos. B95-B96 on white.

Nos. B95-B97 exist imperf. Values: Nos. B95-B96 $150; No. B97 $4,500.

Statue Symbolizing Recovered Territories SP36

Castle of Munkács SP37

Admiral Horthy Entering Komárom SP38

Cathedral of Kassa SP39

Girl Offering Flowers to Soldier — SP40

1939, Jan. 16

B98	SP36	6f + 3f myrtle grn	1.00	.65
B99	SP37	10f + 5f olive grn	.65	.45
B100	SP38	20f + 10f dark red	.65	.45
B101	SP39	30f + 15f grnsh blue	1.25	.80
B102	SP40	40f + 20f dk bl gray	1.75	.80
		Nos. B98-B102 (5)	5.30	3.15

The surtax was for the aid of "Hungary for Hungarians" patriotic movement. Exist imperf. Value, set $175.

Memorial Tablets SP41

Gáspár Károlyi, Translator of the Bible into Hungarian SP42

Albert Molnár de Szenci, Translator of the Psalms SP43

Prince Gabriel Bethlen — SP44

Susanna Lórántffy SP45

Perf. 12x12½, 12½x12

1939   Photo.   Wmk. 210

B103	SP41	6f + 3f green	.70	.70
B104	SP42	10f + 5f claret	1.00	1.00
B105	SP43	20f + 10f copper red	1.00	1.00
B106	SP44	32f + 16f bister	1.00	1.00
B107	SP45	40f + 20f chalky blue	1.00	1.00
		Nos. B103-B107 (5)	4.70	4.70

Souvenir Sheets

Perf. 12

B108	SP44	32f olive & vio brn	30.00	15.00

Imperf

B109	SP44	32f bl grn, cop red & gold	30.00	15.00

National Protestant Day. The surtax was used to erect an Intl. Protestant Institute. The souvenir sheets sold for 1.32p each. Nos. B103-B108 exist imperf. Values: Nos. B103-B107 $350; No. B108 $4,000. Issue dates: Nos. B103-B107, Oct. 2. Nos. B108-B109, Oct. 27.

Boy Scout Flying Kite — SP47

Allegory of Flight — SP48

Archangel Gabriel from Millennium Monument, Budapest, and Planes — SP49

1940, Jan. 1   Perf. 12½x12

B110	SP47	6f + 6f yellow grn	.75	1.00
B111	SP48	10f + 10f chocolate	.95	1.25
B112	SP49	20f + 20f copper red	1.40	1.25
		Nos. B110-B112 (3)	3.10	3.50

The surtax was used for the Horthy National Aviation Fund. Exist imperf. Value, set $150.

Souvenir Sheet

SP50

Wmk. 210

1940, May 6   Photo.   Perf. 12

B113	SP50	20f + 1p dk blue grn	6.00	6.00

Exist imperf. Value $4,250.

Soldier Protecting Family from Floods SP51

1940, May

B114	SP51	10f + 2f gray brown	.40	.25
B115	SP51	20f + 4f orange red	.40	.25
B116	SP51	20f + 50f red brown	1.25	1.25
		Nos. B114-B116 (3)	2.05	1.75

The surtax on Nos. B113-B116 was used to aid flood victims. Exist imperf. Value, set $150.

Hunyadi Coat of Arms SP52

King Matthias SP54

Hunyadi Castle SP53

Equestrian Statue of King Matthias SP55

Corvin Codex — SP56

Equestrian Statue of King
Matthias — SP57

1940   **Perf. 12½x12, 12x12½**

B117	SP52	6f + 3f blue grn	.60	.60
B118	SP53	10f + 5f gldn brn	.60	.60
B119	SP54	16f + 8f dk ol bis	.80	.80
B120	SP55	20f + 10f brick red	.80	.80
B121	SP56	32f + 16f dk gray	1.25	1.10
	Nos. B117-B121 (5)		4.05	3.90

Souvenir Sheet

B122	SP57	20f + 1p dk bl grn &		
		pale grn	6.00	6.00

King Matthias (1440-1490) at Kolozsvar,
Transylvania. The surtax was used for war
relief.
Nos. B117-B122 exist imperf. Values: Nos.
B117-B121 $220; No. B122 $4,250.
Issued: Nos. B117-B121, July 1. No. B122.
Nov. 7.

Hungarian
Soldier — SP58

20f+50f, Virgin Mary and Szekley, symbol-
izing the return of transylvania. 32f+50f,
Szekley Mother Offering Infant Son to the
Fatherland.

1940, Dec. 2   **Photo.**   **Perf. 12½x12**

B123	SP58	10f + 50f dk blue grn	.95	.95
B124	SP58	20f + 50f brown car	1.00	1.00
B125	SP58	32f + 50f yellow brn	1.25	1.25
	Nos. B123-B125 (3)		3.20	3.20

Occupation of Transylvania. The surtax was
for the Pro-Transylvania movement.
Exist imperf. Value, set $200.

Symbol for
Drama
SP61

Symbol for
Sculpture — SP62

Symbols: 16f+16f, Art. 20f+20f, Literature.

1940, Dec. 15   **Perf. 12x12½, 12½x12**

B126	SP61	6f + 6f dark green	1.40	1.25
B127	SP62	10f + 10f olive bis	1.40	1.25
B128	SP62	16f + 16f dk violet	1.40	1.25
B129	SP61	20f + 20f fawn	1.40	1.25
	Nos. B126-B129 (4)		5.60	5.00

AIR POST STAMPS

Issues of the Monarchy

Nos. 120, 123
Surcharged in
Red or Blue

Wmk. 137

1918, July 4   **Typo.**   **Perf. 14**

C1	A10	1k 50f on 75f (R)	25.00	27.50
		Never hinged	37.50	
C2	A10	4k 50f on 2k (Bl)	25.00	27.50
		Never hinged	37.50	

Counterfeits exist.
Exist imperf. Value, set $350.

No. 126
Surcharged

1920, Nov. 7

C3	A10	3k on 10k (G)	1.40	2.25
		Never hinged	2.50	
		On cover		40.00
C4	A10	8k on 10k (R)	1.40	2.25
		Never hinged	2.50	
		On cover		7.50
C5	A10	12k on 10k (Bl)	1.40	2.25
		Never hinged	2.50	
		On cover		7.50
	Nos. C3-C5 (3)		4.20	6.75
	Set, never hinged		7.50	

Icarus — AP3

1924-25   **Perf. 14**

C6	AP3	100k red brn & red	1.25	2.50
		Never hinged	2.75	
C7	AP3	500k bl grn & yel		
		grn	1.25	2.50
		Never hinged	2.75	
C8	AP3	1000k bis brn & brn	1.25	2.50
		Never hinged	2.75	
C9	AP3	2000k dk bl & lt bl	1.25	2.50
		Never hinged	2.75	

Wmk. 133

C10	AP3	5000k dl vio & brt		
		vio	2.00	2.50
		Never hinged	3.50	
C11	AP3	10000k red & dl vio	2.00	4.00
		Never hinged	5.50	
	Nos. C6-C11 (6)		9.00	16.50
	Set, never hinged		20.00	

Issue dates: 100k-2000k, 4/11/24. Others,
4/20/25.
Exist imperf. Value, set $100.
Forgeries exist.
For surcharges see Nos. J112-J116.

Mythical
"Turul" — AP4

"Turul" Carrying Messenger
AP5   AP6

1927-30   **Engr.**   **Perf. 14**

C12	AP4	4f orange ('30)	.25	.40
		Never hinged	.50	
C13	AP4	12f deep green	.45	.40
		Never hinged	.50	
C14	AP4	16f red brown	.45	.40
		Never hinged	.50	
C15	AP4	20f carmine	.45	.40
		Never hinged	.50	
C16	AP4	32f brown vio	1.75	1.20
		Never hinged	3.50	
C17	AP4	40f dp ultra	1.40	.80
		Never hinged	3.50	
C18	AP5	50f claret	1.40	.80
		Never hinged	3.50	

C19	AP5	72f olive grn	1.90	1.20
		Never hinged	3.50	
C20	AP5	80f dp violet	1.90	1.20
		Never hinged	4.00	
C21	AP5	1p emerald ('30)	2.25	.50
		Never hinged	6.50	
C22	AP5	2p red ('30)	4.50	3.00
		Never hinged	8.50	
C23	AP5	5p dk blue ('30)	16.50	27.50
		Never hinged	20.00	
	Nos. C12-C23 (12)		33.20	37.80
	Set, never hinged		55.00	

Exist imperf. Value, set $250.

1931, Mar. 27   **Overprinted**

C24	AP6	1p orange (Bk)	40.00	65.00
		Never hinged	80.00	
C25	AP6	2p dull vio (G)	40.00	65.00
		Never hinged	80.00	
	Set, never hinged		160.00	

Exist imperf. Value, set $375.

Monoplane over
Danube
Valley — AP7

Worker
Welcoming
Plane, Double
Cross and Sun
Rays — AP8

Spirit of Flight
on Plane Wing
AP9

"Flight" Holding
Propeller
AP10

Wmk. 210

1933, June 20   **Photo.**   **Perf. 15**

C26	AP7	10f blue green	2.90	.25
		Never hinged	4.75	
C27	AP7	16f purple	2.00	.25
		Never hinged	3.25	

Perf. 12½x12

C28	AP8	20f carmine	4.50	.25
		Never hinged	8.00	
C29	AP8	40f blue	4.00	1.25
		Never hinged	7.50	
C30	AP9	48f gray black	9.50	1.50
		Never hinged	8.00	
C31	AP9	72f bister brn	20.00	2.75
		Never hinged	25.00	
C32	AP10	1p yellow grn	25.00	2.50
		Never hinged	45.00	
C33	AP10	2p violet brn	47.50	17.50
		Never hinged	135.00	
C34	AP10	5p dk gray	82.50	140.00
		Never hinged	135.00	
	Nos. C26-C34 (9)		197.90	166.25
	Set, never hinged		375.00	

Exist imperf. Value, set $2,600.

> **Catalogue values for unused
> stamps in this section, from this
> point to the end of the section, are
> for Never Hinged items.**

Fokker F VII
over Mail
Coach
AP11

Plane over
Parliament
AP12

Airplane
AP13

1936, May 8   **Perf. 12x12½**

C35	AP11	10f brt green	.80	.40
C36	AP11	20f crimson	.80	.40
C37	AP11	36f brown	.90	.40
C38	AP12	40f brt blue	.90	.40
C39	AP12	52f red org	3.25	.85
C40	AP12	60f brt violet	20.00	2.00
C41	AP12	80f dk sl grn	4.00	.60
C42	AP13	1p dk yel grn	4.75	.55
C43	AP13	2p brown car	7.50	2.00
C44	AP13	5p dark blue	24.00	19.50
	Nos. C35-C44 (10)		66.90	27.10
	Set, hinged		27.50	

Exist imperf. Value, set $675.

SPECIAL DELIVERY STAMPS

Issue of the Monarchy

SD1

1916   **Typo.**   **Wmk. 137**   **Perf. 15**

E1	SD1	2f gray green & red	.25	.25
		Never hinged	.30	

Exists imperf. Value $7.50.
For overprints and surcharges see Nos.
1NE1, 2NE1, 4N5, 5NE1, 6NE1, 7NE1, 8NE1,
10NE1, 11NE1, 11NJ7-J8.

Issues of the Republic

Special Delivery Stamp
of 1916 Overprinted

1919

E2	SD1	2f gray green & red	.25	.75
		Never hinged	.30	

Exists imperf. Value $12.50.

General Issue

SD2

1919

E3	SD2	2f gray green & red	.25	.75
		Never hinged	.30	

Exists imperf. Value $10.

POSTAGE DUE STAMPS

Issues of the Monarchy

D1

Perf. 11¾x12

1903   **Typo.**   **Wmk. 135**

J1	D1	1f green & blk	.50	.50
		Never hinged	1.00	
J2	D1	2f green & blk	3.00	1.50
		Never hinged	6.00	
J3	D1	5f green & blk	15.00	6.50
		Never hinged	30.00	
J4	D1	6f green & blk	12.00	6.00
		Never hinged	24.00	
J5	D1	10f green & blk	80.00	3.00
		Never hinged	160.00	

J6	D1	12f green & blk		2.50	2.50
		Never hinged		5.00	
J7	D1	20f green & blk		20.00	1.50
		Never hinged		40.00	
J8	D1	50f green & blk		16.00	12.50
		Never hinged		32.50	
J9	D1	100f green & blk		1.00	1.00
		Never hinged		2.00	
		Nos. J1-J9 (9)		150.00	35.00

Perf. 11½

J1a	D1	1f green & blk		1.00	1.00
		Never hinged		2.00	
J2a	D1	2f green & blk		15.00	7.50
		Never hinged		30.00	
J3a	D1	5f green & blk		14.00	6.00
		Never hinged		27.50	
J4a	D1	6f green & blk		15.00	9.00
		Never hinged		30.00	
J5a	D1	10f green & blk		90.00	10.00
		Never hinged		175.00	
J6a	D1	12f green & blk		225.00	150.00
		Never hinged		450.00	
J7a	D1	20f green & blk		300.00	60.00
		Never hinged		600.00	
J8a	D1	50f green & blk		400.00	450.00
		Never hinged		800.00	

See Nos. J10-J26, J28-J43. For overprints and surcharges see Nos. J27, J44-J50, 1NJ1-1NJ5, 2NJ1-2NJ16, 4NJ2-4NJ3, 5NJ1-5NJ8, 6NJ1-6NJ9, 7NJ1-7NJ4, 9NJ1-9NJ3, 10NJ1-10NJ6, 11NJ1-J6.

1908-09   Wmk. 136   Perf. 15

J10	D1	1f green & black		.75	.50
		Never hinged		1.50	
J11	D1	2f green & black		1.00	.50
		Never hinged		2.00	
J12	D1	5f green & black		2.50	.75
		Never hinged		5.00	
J13	D1	6f green & black		1.50	.50
		Never hinged		3.00	
J14	D1	10f green & black		1.50	.50
		Never hinged		3.00	
J15	D1	12f green & black		1.25	.50
		Never hinged		2.50	
J16	D1	20f green & black		10.00	.50
		Never hinged		20.00	
c.		Center inverted		9,000.	9,000.
J17	D1	50f green & black		1.75	.75
		Never hinged		3.50	
		Nos. J10-J17 (8)		20.25	4.50

1905   Wmk. 136a   Perf. 11½x12

J12a	D1	5f green & black		175.00	70.00
		Never hinged		350.00	
J13a	D1	6f green & black		14.00	7.50
		Never hinged		27.50	
J14a	D1	10f green & black		175.00	5.00
		Never hinged		350.00	
J15a	D1	12f green & black		25.00	16.00
		Never hinged		50.00	
J17a	D1	50f green & black		6.00	2.50
		Never hinged		12.00	
J18	D1	100f green & black		5.00	
		Never hinged		10.00	

1906   Perf. 15

J11b	D1	2f green & black		3.50	3.50
		Never hinged		7.00	
J12b	D1	5f green & black		2.50	2.00
		Never hinged		5.00	
J13b	D1	6f green & black		2.50	2.00
		Never hinged		5.00	
J14b	D1	10f green & black		15.00	.60
		Never hinged		30.00	
J15b	D1	12f green & black		.75	.60
		Never hinged		1.50	
J16b	D1	20f green & black		25.00	.60
		Never hinged		50.00	
d.		Center inverted		9,000.	9,000.
J17b	D1	50f green & black		1.00	1.00
		Never hinged		2.00	
		Nos. J11b-J17b (7)		50.25	10.30

1914   Wmk. 137 Horiz.   Perf. 15

J19	D1	1f green & black		.35	.25
		Never hinged		.50	
J20	D1	2f green & black		.25	.25
		Never hinged		.35	
J21	D1	5f green & black		.40	.40
		Never hinged		.60	
J22	D1	6f green & black		.80	.60
		Never hinged		1.20	
J23	D1	10f green & black		.90	.70
		Never hinged		1.40	
J24	D1	12f green & black		.40	.25
		Never hinged		.60	
J25	D1	20f green & black		.35	.25
		Never hinged		.50	
J26	D1	50f green & black		.70	.25
		Never hinged		2.00	
		Nos. J19-J26 (8)		4.15	2.95

1914   Wmk. 137 Vert.

J20a	D1	2f green & black		57.50	57.50
		Never hinged		85.00	
J21a	D1	5f green & black		4.50	4.50
		Never hinged		6.50	
J22a	D1	6f green & black		9.00	7.50
		Never hinged		13.50	
J25a	D1	20f green & black		2,250.	900.00
		Never hinged		3,250.	
J26a	D1	50f green & black		2.50	2.50
		Never hinged		3.75	

During 1921-24, a number of Postage Due stamps were punched with three holes prior to sale. See note following No. 105 in the Regular Postage section.

No. J9 Surcharged in Red

1915   Wmk. 135

J27	D1	20f on 100f grn & blk		.50	2.00
		Never hinged		1.00	
a.		On No. J18, Wmk. 136a		15.00	37.50
		Never hinged		30.00	

1915-22   Wmk. 137

J28	D1	1f green & red		.25	.25
		Never hinged		.30	
J29	D1	2f green & red		.25	.25
		Never hinged		.30	
J30	D1	5f green & red		.35	.25
		Never hinged		.75	
J31	D1	6f green & red		.25	.25
		Never hinged		.30	
J32	D1	10f green & red		.25	.25
		Never hinged		.30	
J33	D1	12f green & red		.25	.25
		Never hinged		.30	
J34	D1	15f green & red		.35	.50
		Never hinged		.60	
J35	D1	20f green & red		.25	.25
		Never hinged		.30	
J36	D1	30f green & red		.25	.25
		Never hinged		.30	
J37	D1	40f green & red ('20)		.25	.25
		Never hinged		.30	
J38	D1	50f green & red ('20)		.25	.25
		Never hinged		.30	
a.		Center inverted		60.00	
J39	D1	120f green & red ('20)		.25	.25
		Never hinged		.30	
J40	D1	200f green & red ('20)		.25	.25
		Never hinged		.30	
J41	D1	2k green & red ('22)		.25	.90
		Never hinged		.60	
J42	D1	5k green & red ('22)		.25	.25
		Never hinged		.30	
J43	D1	50k green & red ('22)		.50	.30
		Never hinged		.30	
		Nos. J28-J43 (16)		4.45	4.95

Three-Hole Punch

J32a	D1	10f green & red		.25	.40
		Never hinged		.40	
J35a	D1	20f green & red		.25	.35
		Never hinged		.40	
J37a	D1	40f green & red ('20)		.25	.40
		Never hinged		.40	
J38a	D1	50f green & red ('20)		.25	.40
		Never hinged		.40	
J39a	D1	120f green & red ('20)		.25	.25
		Never hinged		.40	
J40a	D1	200f green & red ('20)		.25	.25
		Never hinged		.40	
J41a	D1	2k green & red ('22)		.45	1.10
		Never hinged		.90	
J42a	D1	5k green & red ('22)		.25	.40
		Never hinged		.40	
J43a	D1	50k green & red ('22)		.25	.40
		Never hinged		.40	
		Nos. J32a-J43a (9)		2.45	3.95

Issues of the Republic

Postage Due Stamps of 1914-18 Overprinted in Black

1918-19   On Issue of 1914

J44	D1	50f green & black		3.00	5.50
		Never hinged		6.00	

On Stamps and Type of 1915-18

J45	D1	2f green & red		.25	.75
		Never hinged		.40	
J46	D1	3f green & red		.25	.75
		Never hinged		.40	
a.		"KOZTARSASAG" omitted		650.00	
J47	D1	10f green & red		.25	.75
		Never hinged		.40	
J48	D1	20f green & red		.25	.75
		Never hinged		.40	
J49	D1	40f green & red		.25	.75
		Never hinged		.40	
a.		Inverted overprint		60.00	60.00
J50	D1	50f green & red		.25	.75
		Never hinged		.40	
a.		Center and overprint inverted		75.00	75.00
		Nos. J44-J50 (7)		4.50	10.00

Issues of the Kingdom

D3

1919-20   Typo.

J65	D3	2f green & black		.25	.50
		Never hinged		.30	
a.		Inverted center		2,100.	
		Never hinged		3,000.	
J66	D3	3f green & black		.25	.50
		Never hinged		.30	
J67	D3	20f green & black		.25	.50
		Never hinged		.30	
J68	D3	40f green & black		.25	.50
		Never hinged		.30	

J69	D3	50f green & black		.25	.50
		Never hinged		.30	
		Nos. J65-J69 (5)		1.25	2.50

Postage Due Stamps of this type have been overprinted "Magyar Tancskztarsasag" but have not been reported as having been issued without the additional overprint "heads of wheat."
For overprints see Nos. J70-J75.

Additional Overprint in Black

1920

J70	D3	2f green & black		.85	1.50
		Never hinged		1.50	
J71	D3	3f green & black		.85	1.50
		Never hinged		1.50	
J72	D3	10f green & black		1.40	2.50
		Never hinged		2.50	
J73	D3	20f green & black		.85	1.50
		Never hinged		1.50	
J74	D3	40f green & black		.85	1.50
		Never hinged		1.50	
J75	D3	50f green & black		.85	1.50
		Never hinged		1.50	
		Nos. J70-J75 (6)		5.65	10.00

Postage Issues Surcharged

a   b

c

1921-25   Red Surcharge

J76	A9(a)	100f on 15f violet		.25	.25
		Never hinged		.30	
J77	A9(a)	500f on 15f violet		.25	.25
		Never hinged		.30	
J78	A9(b)	2½k on 10f red vio		.25	.25
		Never hinged		.30	
J79	A9(b)	3k on 15f violet		.25	.25
		Never hinged		.30	
J80	A9(c)	6k on 1½k violet		.25	1.50
		Never hinged		.30	
J81	A9(b)	9k on 40f ol grn		.25	.25
		Never hinged		.30	
J82	A9(c)	10k on 2½k green		.25	1.25
		Never hinged		.30	
J83	A9(b)	12k on 60f blk brn		.25	.25
		Never hinged		.30	
J84	A9(c)	15k on 1½k vio		.25	.25
		Never hinged		.30	
J85	A9(c)	20k on 2½k grn		.25	1.10
		Never hinged		.30	
J86	A9(c)	25k on 1½k vio		.25	.25
		Never hinged		.30	
J87	A9(c)	30k on 1½k vio		.25	.25
		Never hinged		.30	
J88	A9(c)	40k on 2½k grn		.25	1.25
		Never hinged		.30	
J89	A9(c)	50k on 1½k vio		.25	.25
		Never hinged		.30	
J90	A9(c)	100k on 4½k dl vio		.25	.25
		Never hinged		.30	
J91	A9(c)	200k on 4½k dl vio		.25	.25
		Never hinged		.35	
J92	A9(c)	300k on 4½k dl vio		.25	.25
		Never hinged		.35	
J93	A9(c)	500k on 2k grnsh bl		.60	.25
		Never hinged		1.00	
J94	A9(c)	500k on 3k org brn		2.10	.30
		Never hinged		3.50	
J95	A9(c)	1000k on 2k grnsh bl		1.20	.25
		Never hinged		2.00	
J96	A9(c)	1000k on 3k org brn		1.75	.25
		Never hinged		3.00	
J97	A9(c)	2000k on 2k grnsh bl		1.20	.40
		Never hinged		2.00	
J98	A9(c)	2000k on 3k org brn		2.10	.35
		Never hinged		3.50	
J99	A9(c)	5000k on 5k brown		.90	1.75
		Never hinged		1.50	
		Nos. J76-J99 (24)		14.10	11.90

Three-Hole Punch

J78a	A9	2½k on 10f red vio		.25	.30
		Never hinged		.40	
J80a	A9	6k on 1½k violet		.25	1.50
		Never hinged		.40	
J81a	A9	9k on 40f ol grn		.25	.30
		Never hinged		.40	
J82a	A9	10k on 2½k green		.25	2.00
		Never hinged		.40	
J83a	A9	12k on 60f blk brn		.25	.30
		Never hinged		.40	

J84a	A9	15k on 1½k vio		.25	.30
		Never hinged		.40	
J85a	A9	20k on 2½k grn		.25	2.00
		Never hinged		.40	
J86a	A9	25k on 1½k vio		.25	.30
		Never hinged		.40	
J87a	A9	30k on 1½k vio		.25	.30
		Never hinged		.40	
J88a	A9	40k on 2½k grn		.25	2.00
		Never hinged		.40	
J89a	A9	50k on 1½k vio		.25	.30
		Never hinged		.40	
J90a	A9	100k on 4½k dl vio		.25	.25
		Never hinged		.40	
J91a	A9	200k on 4½k dl vio		.30	.25
		Never hinged		.50	
J92a	A9	300k on 4½k dl vio		.30	.25
		Never hinged		.50	
J93a	A9	500k on 2k grnsh bl		1.25	.50
		Never hinged		2.10	
J94a	A9	500k on 3k org brn		4.25	.60
		Never hinged		7.00	
J95a	A9	1000k on 2k grnsh bl		2.50	.50
		Never hinged		4.00	
J96a	A9	1000k on 3k org brn		3.50	.25
		Never hinged		5.75	
J97a	A9	2000k on 2k grnsh bl		2.50	.80
		Never hinged		4.00	
J98a	A9	2000k on 3k org brn		4.25	.70
		Never hinged		7.00	
J99a	A9	5000k on 5k brown		1.75	3.50
		Nos. J78a-J99a (21)		23.60	17.20

Year of issue: 6k, 15k, 25k, 30k, 50k, 1922. 10k, 20k, 40k, 100k - No. J93, Nos. J95, J97, 1923. 5,000k, 1924. Nos. J94, J96, J98, 1925. Others, 1921.

D6

1926   Wmk. 133   Litho.   Perf. 15

J100	D6	1f rose red		.25	.25
		Never hinged		.30	
J101	D6	2f rose red		.25	.25
		Never hinged		.30	
J102	D6	3f rose red		.30	.60
		Never hinged		.60	
J103	D6	4f rose red		.25	.25
		Never hinged		.30	
J104	D6	5f rose red		1.75	2.50
		Never hinged		3.50	
J105	D6	8f rose red		.25	.25
		Never hinged		.40	
J106	D6	10f rose red		1.25	.25
		Never hinged		2.50	
J107	D6	16f rose red		.30	.25
		Never hinged		.60	
J108	D6	32f rose red		.50	.25
		Never hinged		1.00	
J109	D6	40f rose red		.75	.25
		Never hinged		1.25	
J110	D6	50f rose red		.90	.40
		Never hinged		1.40	
J111	D6	80f rose red		1.25	.65
		Never hinged		2.50	
		Nos. J100-J111 (12)		8.00	6.15

Perf. 14x14½

J103a	D6	4f rose red		.25	.25
		Never hinged		.30	
J104a	D6	5f rose red		1.25	2.50
		Never hinged		2.50	
J105a	D6	8f rose red		.25	.25
		Never hinged		.30	
J106a	D6	10f rose red		.25	.25
		Never hinged		.30	
J107a	D6	16f rose red		.25	.25
		Never hinged		.30	

Exist imperf. Value, set $100.
See Nos. J117-J123. For surcharges see Nos. J124-J129.

Nos. C7-C11 Surcharged in Red or Green

1926   Wmk. 137   Perf. 14

J112	AP3	1f on 500k (R)		.25	.30
		Never hinged		.30	
J113	AP3	2f on 1000k (G)		.25	.30
		Never hinged		.30	
J114	AP3	3f on 2000k (R)		.25	.30
		Never hinged		.30	

Wmk. 133

J115	AP3	5f on 5000k (G)		.65	1.50
		Never hinged		1.00	
J116	AP3	10f on 10000k (G)		.50	1.10
		Never hinged		.90	
		Nos. J112-J116 (5)		1.90	3.50

Type of 1926 Issue

1928-32   Wmk. 210   Perf. 15

J117	D6	2f rose red		.25	.25
		Never hinged		.30	
J118	D6	4f rose red ('32)		.25	.25
		Never hinged		.30	
J119	D6	8f rose red		.25	.25
		Never hinged		.40	
J120	D6	10f rose red		.25	.25
		Never hinged		.40	

J121	D6	16f rose red	.35 .25
		Never hinged	.60
J122	D6	20f rose red	.60 .25
		Never hinged	1.00
J123	D6	40f rose red	.50 .25
		Never hinged	.80
		Nos. J117-J123 (7)	2.45 1.75
		Exist imperf. Value, set $60.	

Postage Due Stamps
of 1926 Surcharged in
Black

1931-33   **Wmk. 133**

J124	D6	4f on 5f rose red	.25 .25
		Never hinged	.30
J125	D6	10f on 16f rose red	1.50 3.75
		Never hinged	2.50
J126	D6	10f on 80f rose red ('33)	.30 .25
		Never hinged	.50
J127	D6	12f on 50f rose red ('33)	.35 .25
		Never hinged	.60
J128	D6	20f on 32f rose red	.35 .30
		Nos. J124-J128 (5)	2.75 4.80

Perf. 14x14½

J124a	D6	4f on 5f rose red	.45 .45
		Never hinged	.75
J125a	D6	10f on 16f rose red	2.25 3.75
		Never hinged	3.75

Surcharged on No. J121

1931   **Wmk. 210**   *Perf. 15*

J129	D6	10f on 16f rose red	.85 *1.25*
		Never hinged	1.50

Catalogue values for unused stamps in this section, from this point to the end of the section, are for Never Hinged items.

Figure of Value — D7

1934   **Photo.**   **Wmk. 210**

J130	D7	2f ultra	.25 .25
J131	D7	4f ultra	.25 .25
J132	D7	6f ultra	.25 .25
J133	D7	8f ultra	.25 .25
J134	D7	10f ultra	.25 .25
J135	D7	12f ultra	.25 .25
J136	D7	16f ultra	.25 .25
J137	D7	20f ultra	.40 .25
J138	D7	40f ultra	.60 .25
J139	D7	80f ultra	2.00 .50
		Nos. J130-J139 (10)	4.75 2.75
		Exist imperf. Value, set $60.	

OFFICIAL STAMPS

During 1921-24, a number of Official stamps were punched with three holes prior to sale. See note following No. 105 in the Regular Postage section.

O1

1921-23   **Wmk. 137**   **Typo.**   *Perf. 15*

O1	O1	10f brn vio & blk	.25 .25
		Never hinged	.30
O2	O1	20f ol brn & blk	.25 .25
		Never hinged	.30
	a.	"HIVATALOS" inverted	10,000.
O3	O1	60f blk brn & blk	.25 .25
		Never hinged	.30
O4	O1	100f dl rose & blk	.25 .25
		Never hinged	.30
O5	O1	250f bl & blk	.25 .25
		Never hinged	.30
O6	O1	350f gray & blk	.25 .25
		Never hinged	.30
O7	O1	500f lt brn & blk	.25 .25
		Never hinged	.30
O8	O1	1000f lil brn & blk	.25 .25
		Never hinged	.30
O9	O1	5k brn ('23)	.25 .25
		Never hinged	.30

O10	O1	10k choc ('23)	.25 .25
		Never hinged	.30
O11	O1	15k gray blk ('23)	.25 .25
		Never hinged	.30
O12	O1	25k org ('23)	.25 .25
		Never hinged	.30
O13	O1	50k brn & red ('22)	.25 .25
		Never hinged	.30
O14	O1	100k bis & red ('22)	.25 .25
		Never hinged	.30
O15	O1	150k grn & red ('23)	.25 .25
		Never hinged	.30
O16	O1	300k dl red & red ('23)	.25 .25
		Never hinged	.30
O17	O1	350k vio & red ('23)	.30 .25
		Never hinged	.50
O18	O1	500k org & red ('22)	.30 .25
		Never hinged	.50
O19	O1	600k ol bis & red ('23)	.80 .60
		Never hinged	1.25
O20	O1	1000k bl & red ('22)	1.20 .25
		Never hinged	1.75
		Nos. O1-O20 (20)	6.60 5.35

Three-Hole Punch

O1a	O1	10f brn vio & blk	.25 .50
		Never hinged	.30
O2b	O1	20f ol brn & blk	.25 .25
		Never hinged	.30
O3a	O1	60f blk brn & blk	.25 .40
		Never hinged	.35
O4a	O1	100f dl rose & blk	.25 .25
		Never hinged	.35
O5a	O1	250f bl & blk	.25 .25
		Never hinged	.40
O6a	O1	350f gray & blk	.35 .25
		Never hinged	.45
O7a	O1	500f lt brn & blk	.35 .25
		Never hinged	.45
O8a	O1	1000f lil brn & blk	.35 .50
		Never hinged	.50
O9a	O1	5k brn ('23)	.30 .50
		Never hinged	.40
O10a	O1	10k choc ('23)	.30 .25
		Never hinged	.40
O11a	O1	15k gray blk ('23)	.35 .25
		Never hinged	.50
O12a	O1	25k org ('23)	.35 .25
		Never hinged	.50
O13a	O1	50k brn & red ('22)	.35 .25
		Never hinged	.50
O14a	O1	100k bis & red ('22)	.35 .25
		Never hinged	.50
		Nos. O1a-O14a (14)	4.30 4.15

Counterfeits of No. O2a exist.

Stamps of 1921
Surcharged in Red

1922

O21	O1	15k on 20f ol brn & blk	.25 .25
		Never hinged	.30
O22	O1	25k on 60f blk brn & blk	.25 .25
		Never hinged	.30

Stamps of 1921
Overprinted in Red

1923

O23	O1	350k gray & blk	.25 .25
		Never hinged	.50

**With Additional Surcharge
of New Value in Red**

O24	O1	150k on 100f dl rose & blk	.30 .25
		Never hinged	.50
O25	O1	2000k on 250f bl & blk	1.50 .40
		Never hinged	2.50
		Nos. O23-O25 (3)	2.05 .90

1923-24
Paper with Gray Moiré on Face

O26	O1	500k org & red ('23)	2.10 .25
		Never hinged	3.50
O27	O1	1000k bl & red ('23)	2.10 .25
		Never hinged	3.50
O28	O1	3000k vio & red ('24)	2.10 1.25
		Never hinged	3.50
O29	O1	5000k bl & red ('24)	2.40 1.50
		Never hinged	4.00
		Nos. O26-O29 (4)	8.70 3.25

Three-Hole Punch

O26a	O1	500k org & red ('23)	3.00 .50
		Never hinged	5.00
O27a	O1	1000k bl & red ('23)	3.00 .50
		Never hinged	5.00

1924   **Wmk. 133**

O30	O1	500k orange & red	1.40 1.00
		Never hinged	2.25
O31	O1	1000k blue & red	1.40 1.00
		Never hinged	2.25

NEWSPAPER STAMPS

Issues of the Monarchy

St. Stephen's Crown and
Post Horn

N1   N2

Litho. (#P1), Typo. (#P2)

1871-72   **Unwmk.**   *Imperf.*

P1	N1	(1k) ver red	50.00 20.00
P2	N2	(1k) rose red ('72)	20.00 6.00
	a.	(1k) vermilion	10.00 2.00
	b.	Printed on both sides	

Reprints of No. P2 are watermarked. Value, $450.

Letter with
Crown and
Post
Horn — N3

N5

1874

P3	N3	1k orange	3.75 .35

1881   **Wmk. "kr" in Oval (132)**

P4	N3	1k orange	1.25 .25
	a.	1k lemon yellow	16.00 3.50
	b.	Printed on both sides	

1898   **Wmk. 135**

P5	N3	1k orange	1.25 .25

See watermark note after No. 46.

1900   **Wmk. Crown in Circle (135)**

P6	N5	(2f) red orange	.75 .75
		Never hinged	1.50

1905   **Wmk. Crown (136a)**

P7	N5	(2f) red orange	1.00 .25
		Never hinged	2.00
	a.	Wmk. 136 ('08)	1.00 .25
		Never hinged	2.00

1914-22   **Wmk. Double Cross (137)**

P8	N5	(2f) orange	.25 .25
		Never hinged	.30
	a.	Wmk. horiz.	4.50 3.75
		Never hinged	9.00
P9	N5	(10f) deep blue ('20)	.25 .25
		Never hinged	.30
P10	N5	(20f) lilac ('22)	.25 .25
		Never hinged	.300
		Nos. P8-P10 (3)	.75 .75

For overprints and surcharges see Nos. 1NJ6-1NJ10, 1NP1, 2NP1, 5NP1, 6NP1, 8NP1, 10NP1, 11NP1.

NEWSPAPER TAX STAMPS

Issues of the Monarchy

NT1   NT2

Wmk. 91; Unwmk. from 1871

1868   **Typo.**   *Imperf.*

PR1	NT1	1k blue	4.00 1.00
	a.	Pair, one sideways	
PR2	NT2	2k brown	20.00 10.00
	a.	2k red brown	275.00 47.50

NT3

1868

PR2B	NT3	1k blue	*15,000. 11,000.*

No. PR2B was issued for the Military Border District only. All used stamps are precanceled (newspaper text printed on the stamp). A similar 2k was not issued.

1889-90   **Wmk. "kr" in Oval (132)**

PR3	NT1	1k blue	2.00 .80
PR4	NT2	2k brown	5.50 5.50

1898   **Wmk. Crown in Oval (135)**

PR5	NT1	1k blue	6.00 7.50

These stamps did not pay postage, but represented a fiscal tax collected by the postal authorities on newspapers.
Nos. PR3 and PR5 have a tall "k" in "kr."

OCCUPATION STAMPS

Issued under French Occupation

ARAD ISSUE

The overprints on this issue have been extensively forged. Even the inexpensive values are difficult to find with genuine overprints. Values are for genuine overprints. Collectors should be aware that stamps sold "as is" are likely to be forgeries, and unexpertized collections should be assumed to consist of mostly forged stamps. Education plus working with knowledgeable dealers is mandatory in this collecting area. More valuable stamps should be expertized.

Stamps of Hungary
Overprinted in Red or
Blue

On Issue of 1916-18

1919   **Wmk. 137**   *Perf. 15, 14*

1N1	A9	2f brn org (R)	1.60 1.60
1N2	A9	3f red lil (R)	.75 .75
1N3	A9	5f green (R)	20.00 20.00
1N4	A9	6f grnsh bl (R)	1.90 1.90
	a.	Inverted overprint	30.00 30.00
1N5	A9	10f rose red	4.00 4.00
1N6	A9	15f violet (R)	1.75 1.75
	a.	Double overprint	50.00 50.00
1N7	A9	20f gray brn (R)	50.00 50.00
1N8	A9	35f brown (R)	65.00 65.00
1N9	A9	40f ol grn (R)	37.50 37.50
1N10	A10	50f red vio & lil	6.00 6.00
1N11	A10	75f brt bl & pale bl	2.00 2.00
1N12	A10	80f grn & pale grn	2.75 2.75
1N13	A10	1k red brn & cl	15.00 15.00
1N14	A10	2k ol brn & bis	3.00 3.00
	a.	Inverted overprint	50.00 50.00
1N15	A10	3k dk vio & ind	17.50 17.50
1N16	A10	5k dk brn & lt brn	13.50 13.50
1N17	A10	10k vio brn & vio	70.00 70.00
		Nos. 1N1-1N17 (17)	312.25 312.25

With Additional Surcharges

a   b

c   d

1N18	A9 (a)	45f on 2f brn org	
1N19	A9 (b)	45f on 2f brn org	8.00 8.00
1N20	A9 (c)	50f on 3f red lil	8.00 8.00
1N21	A9 (d)	50f on 3f red lil	8.00 8.00
		Nos. 1N18-1N21 (4)	32.00 32.00

Overprinted On Issue of 1918

1N22	A11	10f scarlet (Bl)	60.00 60.00
1N23	A11	20f dk brn	.90 .90
1N24	A11	25f brt bl	2.40 2.40
a.		Inverted overprint	30.00 30.00
1N25	A12	40f ol grn	3.25 3.25
		Nos. 1N22-1N25 (4)	66.55 66.55

Ovptd. On Issue of 1918-19, Overprinted "Koztarsasag"

1N26	A9	2f brn org	2.00 2.00
a.		Inverted overprint	50.00 50.00
1N27	A9	4f slate gray	2.00 2.00
1N28	A9	5f green	.60 .60
1N29	A9	6f grnsh bl	12.00 12.00
a.		Inverted overprint	30.00 30.00
1N30	A9	10f rose red (Bl)	60.00 60.00
1N31	A9	20f gray brn	15.00 15.00
1N32	A11	25f brt bl	2.75 2.75
a.		Inverted overprint	30.00 30.00
1N33	A9	40f ol grn	2.00 2.00
1N34	A12	40f ol grn	60.00 60.00
a.		Inverted overprint	125.00 125.00
1N35	A12	50f lilac	8.00 8.00
1N36	A10	1k red brn & cl (Bl)	3.25 3.25
1N37	A10	3k dk vio & ind (Bl)	15.00 15.00
		Nos. 1N26-1N37 (12)	182.60 182.60

No. 1N36 With Additional Surcharge

    e

    f

1N38	A10 (e)	10k on 1k	13.50 13.50
1N39	A10 (f)	10k on 1k	13.50 13.50

On Issue of 1919
Inscribed "MAGYAR POSTA"

1N40	A13	5f red (R)	55.00 55.00
1N41	A13	10f red (Bl)	6.50 6.50

SEMI-POSTAL STAMPS

Hungarian Semi-Postal Stamps of 1916-17 Overprinted "Occupation francaise" in Blue or Red

1919		Wmk. 137	Perf. 15
1NB1	SP3	10f + 2f rose red	65.00 65.00
1NB2	SP4	15f + 2f dl vio (R)	9.50 9.50
1NB3	SP5	40f + 2f brn car	12.50 12.50
		Nos. 1NB1-1NB3 (3)	87.00 87.00

SPECIAL DELIVERY STAMP

Hungarian Special Delivery Stamp of 1916 Overprinted "Occupation francaise"

1919		Wmk. 137	Perf. 15
1NE1	SD1	2f gray green & red	.60 .60

POSTAGE DUE STAMPS

Hungarian Postage Due Stamps of 1915 Overprinted "Occupation francaise"

1919		Wmk. 137	Perf. 15
1NJ1	D1	2f green & red	7.50 7.50
1NJ2	D1	10f green & red	4.00 4.00
1NJ3	D1	12f green & red	32.50 32.50

1NJ4	D1	15f green & red	42.50 42.50
1NJ5	D1	20f green & red	3.00 3.00

Hungarian Newspaper Stamp of 1914 Surcharged

1NJ6	N5	12f on 2f orange	8.00 8.00
1NJ7	N5	15f on 2f orange	8.00 8.00
1NJ8	N5	30f on 2f orange	8.00 8.00
a.		Double surcharge	50.00 50.00
1NJ9	N5	50f on 2f orange	8.00 8.00
1NJ10	N5	100f on 2f orange	8.00 8.00
		Nos. 1NJ1-1NJ10 (10)	129.50 129.50

NEWSPAPER STAMP

Hungarian Newspaper Stamp of 1914 Overprinted "Occupation francaise"

1919		Wmk. 137	Imperf.
1NP1	N5	(2f) orange	1.25 1.25

ISSUED UNDER ROMANIAN OCCUPATION

FIRST DEBRECEN ISSUE

The overprints on this issue have been extensively forged. Even the inexpensive values are difficult to find with genuine overprints. The more extensive note before No. 1N1 also applies to Nos. 2N1-2NP16.

Hungarian Stamps of 1913-19 Overprinted in Blue, Red or Black

1919		Wmk. 137	Perf. 15, 14½x14

On Stamps of 1913

2N1	A4	2f olive yellow	90.00 90.00
2N2	A4	3f orange	125.00 125.00
2N3	A4	6f olive grn (R)	50.00 50.00

On Stamps of 1916

2N4	A8	10f rose	75.00 75.00
2N5	A8	15f violet (Bk)	65.00 65.00

On Stamps of 1916-18

2N6	A9	2f brown org	1.50 1.50
2N7	A9	3f red lilac	.70 .70
2N8	A9	5f green	4.75 4.75
2N9	A9	6f grnsh bl (R)	1.60 1.60
2N10	A9	15f violet (Bk)	.80 .80
a.		Red overprint	75.00 75.00
2N11	A9	20f gray brn	125.00 125.00
2N12	A9	25f dull bl (Bk)	4.50 4.50
2N13	A9	35f brown	60.00 60.00
2N14	A9	40f olive grn	3.75 3.75
2N15	A10	50f red vio & lil	8.25 8.25
2N16	A10	75f brt bl & pale bl (Bk)	2.00 2.00
2N17	A10	80f grn & pale grn (R)	3.50 3.50
2N18	A10	1k red brn & cl	4.75 4.75
2N19	A10	2k ol brn & bis (Bk)	1.75 1.75
2N20	A10	3k dk vio & ind (R)	30.00 30.00
a.		Blue overprint	65.00 65.00
b.		Black overprint	250.00 250.00
2N21	A10	5k dk brn & lt brn (Bk)	27.50 27.50
2N22	A10	10k vio brn & vio	160.00 160.00

With New Value Added

2N23	A9	35f on 3f red lil	2.00 2.00
2N24	A9	45f on 2f brn org	2.00 2.00
2N25	A10	3k on 75f brt bl & pale bl (Bk)	4.00 4.00

2N26	A10	5k on 75f brt bl & pale bl (Bk)	3.75 3.75
2N27	A10	10k on 80f grn & pale grn (H)	3.50 3.50

On Stamps of 1918

2N28	A11	10f scarlet	60.00 60.00
2N28A	A11	15f violet (R)	75.00 75.00
b.		Black overprint	125.00 125.00
2N29	A11	20f dk brown (R)	6.25 6.25
a.		Black overprint	30.00 30.00
b.		Blue overprint	75.00 75.00
2N30	A11	25f brt blue	7.00 7.00
a.		Black overprint	75.00 75.00
2N31	A12	40f olive green	3.00 3.00
2N32	A12	50f lilac	50.00 50.00

On Stamps of 1918-19, Overprinted "Koztarsasag"

2N33	A9	2f brn org	3.00 3.00
2N34	A9	3f red lilac	65.00 65.00
2N35	A9	4f sl gray (R)	1.75 1.75
2N36	A9	5f green	.65 .65
2N37	A9	6f grnsh bl (R)	30.00 30.00
2N38	A9	10f rose red	37.50 37.50
2N39	A11	10f scarlet	25.00 25.00
2N40	A11	15f dp vio (Bk)	45.00 45.00
a.		Red overprint	125.00 125.00
2N41	A9	20f gray brn	3.25 3.25
2N42	A11	20f dk brn (Bk)	37.50 37.50
b.		Red overprint	50.00 50.00
2N43	A9	40f olive grn	1.75 1.75
2N44	A10	1k red brn & cl	2.75 2.75
2N45	A10	2k ol brn & bis (Bk)	60.00 60.00
a.		Blue overprint	125.00 125.00
2N46	A10	3k dk vio & ind (R)	9.75 9.75
a.		Blue overprint	60.00 60.00
b.		Black overprint	200.00 200.00
2N47	A10	5k dk & lt brn (Bk)	225.00 225.00
2N48	A10	10k vio brn & vio	500.00 500.00
2N49	A11	25f brt bl (R)	3.25 3.25
a.		Black overprint	25.00 25.00
2N50	A12	40f olive grn	125.00 125.00
2N51	A12	50f lilac	2.25 2.25

On Stamps of 1919

2N52	A13	5f green	.50 .50
2N53	A13	6f grnsh bl (Bk)	22.50 22.50
2N54	A13	10f red	.25 .25
2N55	A13	20f dk brown	.25 .25
2N56	A13	25f dl bl (Bk)	1.25 1.25
2N56A	A13	40f olive green	125.00 125.00
2N57	A13	45f orange	15.00 15.00
2N57A	A14	95f dark blue & blue	125.00 125.00
2N57B	A14	1.20k dark green & green	125.00 125.00
2N57C	A14	1.40k yellow green	125.00 125.00

No. 2N58

2N58	A14	5k dk brn & brn	3,000. 3,000.

#2N58 is handstamped. Counterfeits exist. Expertization is required.

On No. 103A

2N59	A5a	10f violet brn (R)	50.00 50.00

On No. 208

2N60	A13	10f red	75.00 75.00
		Nos. 2N1-2N57,2N59-2N60 (61)	2,530. 2,530.

SEMI-POSTAL STAMPS

Hungary Nos. B36, B37 Overprinted like Regular Issues in Blue

1919		Wmk. 137	Perf. 14
2NB1	A4(c)	2f olive yellow	125.00 125.00
2NB1A	A4(c)	3f orange	125.00 125.00

Same Overprint in Blue or Black on Hungary Nos. B53--B55

1919		Wmk. 137	Perf. 15
2NB1B	SP3	10f + 2f rose red	4.00 4.00
2NB2	SP4	15f + 2f dl vio (Bk)	17.00 17.00

2NB3	SP5	40f + 2f brown car	11.00 11.00
		Nos. 2NB1B-2NB3 (3)	32.00 32.00

Same Overprint on Hungary Nos. B58-B60 (with "Köztarsasag")

1919			
2NB4	SP3	10f + 2f rose red	42.50 42.50
2NB5	SP4	15f + 2f dl vio (Bk)	75.00 75.00
2NB6	SP5	40f + 2f brown car	32.50 32.50
		Nos. 2NB4-2NB6 (3)	150.00 150.00

SPECIAL DELIVERY STAMP

Hungarian Special Delivery Stamp of 1916 Overprinted like Regular Issues

1919		Wmk. 137	Perf. 15
2NE1	SD1	2f gray grn & red (Bl)	3.00 3.00

POSTAGE DUE STAMPS

Hungarian Postage Due Stamps of 1914-19 Overprinted in Black like Regular Issues

1919		Wmk. 137	Perf. 15

On Stamp of 1914

2NJ1	D1	50f grn & blk	125.00 125.00

On Stamps of 1915

2NJ2	D1	1f green & red	62.50 62.50
2NJ3	D1	2f green & red	2.00 2.00
2NJ4	D1	5f green & red	225.00 225.00
2NJ5	D1	6f green & red	125.00 125.00
2NJ6	D1	10f green & red	.80 .80
2NJ7	D1	12f green & red	125.00 125.00
2NJ8	D1	15f green & red	20.00 20.00
2NJ9	D1	20f green & red	4.50 4.50
2NJ10	D1	30f green & red	13.50 13.50

On Stamps of 1918-19, Overprinted "Koztarsasag"

2NJ11	D1	2f green & red	25.00 25.00
2NJ12	D1	3f green & red	30.00 30.00
2NJ13	D1	10f green & red	30.00 30.00
2NJ14	D1	20f green & red	30.00 30.00
2NJ15	D1	40f green & red	30.00 30.00
2NJ16	D1	50f green & red	30.00 30.00
		Nos. 2NJ1-2NJ16 (16)	878.30 878.30

NEWSPAPER STAMP

Hungarian Newspaper Stamp of 1914 Overprinted like Regular Issues

1919		Wmk. 137	Imperf.
2NP1	N5	(2f) orange (Bl)	.55 .55
a.		Inverted overprint	50.00 50.00
b.		Double overprint	125.00 125.00

SECOND DEBRECEN ISSUE

Complete forgeries exist of this issue and are often found in large multiples or even complete sheets. Values are for genuine stamps.

Mythical "Turul" — OS5

Throwing
Lariat
OS6

Hungarian
Peasant
OS7

1920   Unwmk.   Typo.   Perf. 11½

3N1	OS5	2f lt brown	2.25	2.25
3N2	OS5	3f red brown	2.25	2.25
3N3	OS5	4f gray	2.25	2.25
3N4	OS5	5f lt green	.50	.50
3N5	OS5	6f slate	2.25	2.25
3N6	OS5	10f scarlet	.50	.50
3N7	OS5	15f dk violet	3.00	3.00
3N8	OS5	20f dk brown	.60	.60
3N9	OS6	25f ultra	1.25	1.25
3N10	OS6	30f buff	.65	.65
3N11	OS6	35f claret	1.25	1.25
3N12	OS6	40f olive grn	.75	.75
3N13	OS6	45f salmon	1.00	1.00
3N14	OS6	50f pale vio	.75	.75
3N15	OS6	60f yellow grn	.90	.90
3N16	OS6	75f Prus blue	.75	.75
3N17	OS7	80f gray grn	.85	.85
3N18	OS7	1k brown red	3.00	3.00
3N19	OS7	2k chocolate	3.00	3.00
3N20	OS7	3k brown vio	2.25	2.25
3N21	OS7	5k bister brn	2.25	2.25
3N22	OS7	10k dull vio	2.25	2.25
		Nos. 3N1-3N22 (22)	34.50	34.50

Thick, Glazed Paper

3N23	OS5	2f lt brown	3.00	3.00
3N24	OS5	3f red brown	3.00	3.00
3N25	OS5	4f gray	3.00	3.00
3N26	OS5	5f lt green	3.00	3.00
3N27	OS5	6f slate	3.00	3.00
3N28	OS5	10f scarlet	.75	.75
3N29	OS5	15f dk vio	3.00	3.00
3N30	OS5	20f dk brown	1.00	1.00
3N31	OS7	80f gray grn	1.50	1.50
3N32	OS7	1k brown red	4.00	4.00
3N33	OS7	1.20k orange	8.00	8.00
3N34	OS7	2k chocolate	4.50	4.50
		Nos. 3N23-3N34 (12)	37.75	37.75

SEMI-POSTAL STAMPS

Carrying Wounded — SP1

1920   Unwmk.   Typo.   Perf. 11½

3NB1	SP1	20f green	1.25	1.25
3NB2	SP1	50f gray brn	2.25	2.25
3NB3	SP1	1k blue green	2.25	2.25
3NB4	SP1	2k blue green	2.25	2.25

Colored Paper

3NB5	SP1	20f green, bl	3.00	3.00
3NB6	SP1	50f brn, rose	3.00	3.00
3NB7	SP1	1k dk grn, grn	3.00	3.00
		Nos. 3NB1-3NB7 (7)	17.00	17.00

POSTAGE DUE STAMPS

D1

1920   Typo.   Perf. 15

3NJ1	D1	5f blue green	1.50	1.50
3NJ2	D1	10f blue green	1.50	1.50
3NJ3	D1	20f blue green	.75	.75
3NJ4	D1	30f blue green	.75	.75
3NJ5	D1	60f blue green	1.25	1.25
		Nos. 3NJ1-3NJ5 (5)	5.75	5.75

TEMESVAR ISSUE

Issued under Romanian Occupation

Forgeries exist of the inverted and color error surcharges.

Hungary Nos. 108, 155, 109, 111, E1 Surcharged

1919   Wmk. 137   Perf. 15

4N1	A9	30f on 2f brn org (Bl)	.40	.40
a.		Red surcharge	2.00	2.00
b.		Inverted surcharge (R)	25.00	25.00
4N2	A9	1k on 4f sl gray (R)	.30	.30
4N3	A9	150f on 3f red lil (Bk)	.25	.25
4N4	A9	150f on 5f emer (Bk)	.40	.40
4N5	SD1	3k on 2f gray grn & red (Bk)	2.00	2.00
a.		Blue surcharge	.80	.80
		Nos. 4N1-4N5 (5)	3.35	3.35

POSTAGE DUE STAMPS

D1   D2

1919   Wmk. 137   Perf. 15

4NJ1	D1	40f on 15f + 2f vio (Bk)	.50	.50
a.		Red surcharge	2.00	2.00
4NJ2	D2	60f on 2f grn & red (Bk)	2.50	2.50
a.		Red surcharge	8.00	8.00
4NJ3	D2	60f on 10f grn & red (Bk)	1.25	1.25
a.		Red surcharge	4.00	4.00
		Nos. 4NJ1-4NJ3 (3)	4.25	4.25

FIRST TRANSYLVANIA ISSUE

Issued under Romanian Occupation

The scarcer values of this issue have been extensively forged. Genuine common values are more easily found.

Issued in Kolozsvar (Cluj)

Hungarian Stamps of
1916-18 Overprinted

1919   Wmk. 137   Perf. 15, 14
On Stamp of 1916, White Numerals

5N1	A8	15b violet	4.75	4.75
		On Stamps of 1916-18		
5N2	A9	2b brown org	.25	.25
5N3	A9	3b red lilac	.25	.25
5N4	A9	5b green	.25	.25
5N5	A9	6b grnsh blue	.40	.40
5N5A	A9	10b rose red	60.00	60.00
5N6	A9	15b violet	.25	.25
5N7	A9	25b dull blue	.25	.25
5N8	A9	35b brown	.25	.25
5N9	A9	40b olive grn	.50	.50
5N10	A10	50b red vio & lil	1.00	1.00
5N11	A10	75b brt bl & pale bl		
5N12	A10	80b grn & pale grn	.30	.30
5N13	A10	1 l red brn & cl	.25	.25
5N14	A10	2 l ol brn & bis	.60	.60
5N15	A10	3 l dk vio & ind	3.50	3.50
5N16	A10	5 l dk brn & lt brn	2.50	2.50
5N17	A10	10 l vio brn & vio	3.00	3.00
		On Stamps of 1918		
5N18	A11	10b scarlet	40.00	40.00
5N19	A11	15b dp violet	20.00	20.00
5N20	A11	20b dk brown	.25	.25
a.		Gold overprint	75.00	75.00
b.		Silver overprint	75.00	75.00
5N21	A11	25b brt blue	.65	.65
5N22	A12	40b olive grn	.30	.30
		On No. 103A		
5N23	A5a	10b violet brn	.35	.35
		Nos. 5N1-5N23 (24)	140.10	140.10

SEMI-POSTAL STAMPS

Hungarian Semi-Postal Stamps of 1913-17 Overprinted like Regular Issues
On Issue of 1913

1919   Wmk. 137   Perf. 14

5NB1	SP1	1 l on 1f slate	27.50	27.50
5NB2	SP1	1 l on 2f ol yel	70.00	70.00
5NB3	SP1	1 l on 3f org	37.50	37.50
5NB4	SP1	1 l on 5f emer	3.25	3.25
5NB5	SP1	1 l on 10f car	4.50	4.50
5NB6	SP1	1 l on 12f vio, yel	16.00	16.00
5NB7	SP1	1 l on 16f gray grn	6.25	6.25
5NB8	SP1	1 l on 25f ultra	60.00	60.00
5NB9	SP1	1 l on 35f red vio	10.00	10.00
5NB10	SP2	1 l on 1k dl red	60.00	60.00

On Issue of 1916-17
Perf. 15

5NB11	SP3	10b + 2b rose red	.25	.25
5NB12	SP4	15b + 2b dull vio	.25	.25
5NB13	SP5	40b + 2b brn car	.25	.25
		Nos. 5NB1-5NB13 (13)	295.75	295.75

SPECIAL DELIVERY STAMP

Hungarian Special Delivery Stamp of 1916 Overprinted like Regular Issues

1919   Wmk. 137   Perf. 15

5NE1	SD1	2b gray grn & red	.30	.30

POSTAGE DUE STAMPS

Hungarian Postage Due Stamps of 1914-18 Overprinted like Regular Issues
On Stamp of 1914

1919   Wmk. 137   Perf. 15

5NJ1	D1	50b green & blk	13.00	13.00
		On Stamps of 1915		
5NJ2	D1	1b green & red	350.00	350.00
5NJ3	D1	2b green & red	.70	.70
5NJ4	D1	5b green & red	60.00	60.00
5NJ5	D1	10b green & red	.45	.45
5NJ6	D1	15b green & red	20.00	20.00
5NJ7	D1	20b green & red	.40	.40
5NJ8	D1	30b green & red	30.00	30.00
		Nos. 5NJ1-5NJ8 (8)	474.55	474.55

NEWSPAPER STAMP

Hungarian Newspaper Stamp of 1914 Overprinted like Regular Issues

1919   Wmk. 137   Imperf.

5NP1	N5	2b orange	3.75	3.75

SECOND TRANSYLVANIA ISSUE

The scarcer values of this issue have been extensively forged. Genuine common values are more easily found.

Issued in Nagyvarad (Oradea)

Hungarian Stamps of
1916-19 Overprinted

1919   Wmk. 137   Perf. 15, 14
On Stamps of 1913-16

6N1	A4	2b olive yel	7.00	7.00
6N2	A4	3b orange	13.00	13.00
6N3	A4	6b olive grn	1.75	1.75
6N4	A4	16b gray grn	37.50	37.50
6N5	A4	50b lake, bl	1.75	1.75
6N6	A4	70b red brn & grn	26.00	26.00

On Stamp of 1916 (White Numerals)

6N6A	A8	15b violet	125.00	125.00

On Stamps of 1916-18

6N7	A9	2b brown org	.25	.25
6N8	A9	3b red lilac	.25	.25
6N9	A9	5b green	.30	.30
6N10	A9	6b grnsh blue	1.60	1.60
6N11	A9	10b rose red	2.10	2.10
6N12	A9	15b violet	.25	.25
6N13	A9	20b gray brn	20.00	20.00
6N14	A9	25b dull blue	.30	.30
6N15	A9	35b brown	.45	.45
6N16	A9	40b olive grn	.30	.30
6N17	A10	50b red vio & lil	.60	.60
6N18	A10	75b brt bl & pale bl	.25	.25
6N19	A10	80b grn & pale grn	.30	.30
6N20	A10	1 l red brn & cl	.75	.75
6N21	A10	2 l ol brn & bis	.25	.25
6N22	A10	3 l dk vio & ind	6.50	6.50
6N23	A10	5 l dk brn & lt brn	3.25	3.25
6N24	A10	10 l vio brn & vio	1.50	1.50

On Stamps of 1918

6N25	A11	10b scarlet	3.25	3.25
6N26	A11	20b dk brown	.25	.25
6N27	A11	25b brt blue	.75	.75
6N28	A12	40b olive grn	1.10	1.10

On Stamps of 1918-19, Overprinted "Koztarsasag"

6N29	A9	2b brown org	4.00	4.00
6N30	A9	3b red lilac	.25	.25
6N31	A9	4b slate gray	.25	.25
6N32	A9	5b green	.50	.50
6N33	A9	6b grnsh bl	3.00	3.00
6N34	A9	10b rose red	17.50	17.50
6N35	A9	20b gray brn	2.50	2.50
6N36	A9	40b olive grn	.50	.50
6N37	A10	1 l red brn & cl	.25	.25
6N38	A10	3 l dk vio & ind	.75	.75
6N39	A10	5 l dk brn & lt brn	4.50	4.50
6N40	A11	10b scarlet	75.00	75.00
6N41	A11	20b dk brown	4.50	4.50
6N42	A11	25b brt blue	1.25	1.25
6N43	A12	50b lilac	.25	.25

On Stamps of 1919
Inscribed "MAGYAR POSTA"

6N44	A13	5b yellow grn	.25	.25
6N45	A13	10b red	.25	.25
6N46	A13	20b dk brown	.40	.40
6N47	A13	25b dull blue	2.00	2.00
6N48	A13	40b olive grn	.65	.65
6N49	A14	5 l dk brn & brn	6.50	6.50

On No. 103A

6N50	A5a	10b violet brn	.85	.85
		Nos. 6N1-6N50 (51)	382.45	382.45

SEMI-POSTAL STAMPS

Hungarian Semi-Postal Stamps of 1913-17 Overprinted like Regular Issues
On Stamps of 1913

1919   Wmk. 137   Perf. 14

6NB1	SP1	1 l on 1f slate	2.25	2.25
6NB2	SP1	1 l on 2f olive yel	8.50	8.50
6NB3	SP1	1 l on 3f orange	2.75	2.75
6NB4	SP1	1 l on 5f emerald	.25	.25
6NB5	SP1	1 l on 6f olive grn	2.25	2.25
6NB6	SP1	1 l on 10f carmine	.30	.30
6NB7	SP1	1 l on 12f vio, yel	60.00	60.00
6NB8	SP1	1 l on 16f gray grn	2.50	2.50
6NB9	SP1	1 l on 20f dk brn	11.00	11.00
6NB10	SP1	1 l on 25f ultra	7.50	7.50
6NB11	SP1	1 l on 35f red vio	7.75	7.75

On Stamp of 1915

Wmk. 135   Perf. 11½

6NB12	A4	5b emerald	20.00	20.00

On Stamps of 1916-17

	Wmk. 137		Perf. 15	
6NB13	SP3	10b + 2b rose red	1.25	1.25
6NB14	SP4	15b + 2b dull vio	.45	.45
6NB15	SP5	40b + 2b brown car	.25	.25
Nos. 6NB1-6NB15 (15)			127.00	127.00

SPECIAL DELIVERY STAMP

Hungarian Special Delivery Stamp of 1916 Overprinted like Regular Issues

	Wmk. 137		Perf. 15	
1919				
6NE1	SD1	2b gray grn & red	.40	.40

POSTAGE DUE STAMPS

Hungarian Postage Due Stamps of 1915 Overprinted like Regular Issues

	Wmk. 137		Perf. 15	
1919				
6NJ1	D1	1b green & red	30.00	30.00
6NJ2	D1	2b green & red	.25	.25
6NJ3	D1	5b green & red	9.75	9.75
6NJ4	D1	6b green & red	6.75	6.75
6NJ5	D1	10b green & red	.25	.25
6NJ6	D1	12b green & red	1.50	1.50
6NJ7	D1	15b green & red	1.50	1.50
6NJ8	D1	20b green & red	.25	.25
6NJ9	D1	30b green & red	1.60	1.60
Nos. 6NJ1-6NJ9 (9)			51.85	51.85

On Hungary No. J27

Perf. 11½x12
Wmk. 135

6NJ10	D1	20b on 100b grn & blk	350.00	350.00

NEWSPAPER STAMP

Hungarian Newspaper Stamp of 1914 Overprinted like Regular Issues

	Wmk. 137		Imperf.	
1919				
6NP1	N5	2b orange	.45	.45

FIRST BARANYA ISSUE

Issued under Serbian Occupation

The scarcer values of this issue have been extensively forged. Genuine common values are more easily found.

Hungarian Stamps of 1913-18 Overprinted in Black or Red

On A4, A9,　　　On A10
A11, A12

	Wmk. 137		Perf. 15	
1919				
On Issue of 1913-16				
7N1	A4	6f olive grn (R)	.90	.90
7N2	A4	50f lake, bl	.25	.25
7N3	A4	60f grn, salmon	.75	.75
7N4	A4	70f red brn & grn (R)	2.00	2.00
7N5	A4	70f red brn & grn (Bk)	.25	.25
7N6	A4	80f dl vio (R)	3.25	3.25
On Issue of 1916-18				
7N7	A9	2f brown org (Bk)	4.25	4.25
7N8	A9	2f brown org (R)	.25	.25
7N9	A9	3f red lilac (Bk)	.25	.25
7N10	A9	3f red lilac (R)	.80	.80
7N11	A9	5f green (Bk)	.80	.80
7N12	A9	5f green (R)	.25	.25
7N13	A9	6f grnsh bl (Bk)	1.75	1.75
7N14	A9	6f grnsh bl (R)	2.00	2.00
7N15	A9	15f violet	.35	.35
7N16	A9	20f gray brn	20.00	20.00
7N17	A9	25f dull blue	3.50	3.50
7N18	A9	35f brown	5.75	5.75
7N19	A9	40f olive grn	20.00	20.00
7N20	A10	50f red vio & lil	2.00	2.00

7N21	A10	75f brt bl & pale bl	.40	.40
7N22	A10	80f grn & pale grn	.65	.65
7N23	A10	1k red brn & cl	.55	.55
7N24	A10	2k ol brn & bis	.65	.65
7N25	A10	3k dk vio & ind	.65	.65
7N26	A10	5k dk brn & lt brn	1.25	1.25
7N27	A10	10k vio brn & vio	4.00	4.00

7N28	A9	45f on 2f brn org	.35	.35
7N29	A9	45f on 5f green	.25	.25
7N30	A9	45f on 15f violet	.25	.25
On Issue of 1918				
7N31	A11	10f scarlet (Bk)	.25	.25
7N32	A11	20f dk brn (Bk)	.25	.25
7N34	A11	25f dp blue (Bk)	1.90	1.90
7N35	A11	25f dp blue (R)	1.10	1.10
7N36	A12	40f olive grn (Bk)	4.50	4.50
7N37	A12	40f olive grn (R)	30.00	30.00
On Issue of 1918-19 (Koztarsasag)				
7N38	A9	2f brown org (Bk)	3.50	3.50
7N39	A12	40f ol grn (Bk)	125.00	125.00
7N40	A12	40f ol grn (R)	20.00	20.00
With New Value Added				
7N41	A9	45f on 2f rose org (Bk)	2.00	2.00
7N42	A9	45f on 2f brn org (R)	.45	.45

The overprints were set in groups of 25. In each group two stamps have the figures "1" of "1919" with serifs.

SEMI-POSTAL STAMPS

Hungarian Semi-Postal Stamps Overprinted Regular Issue First Type On Stamp of 1915

	Wmk. 137		Perf. 15	
1919				
7NB1	A4	50f + 2f lake, bl	16.00	16.00
On Stamps of 1916				
7NB2	SP3	10f + 2f rose red	.30	.30
7NB3	SP4	15f + 2f dull vio	.40	.40
Nos. 7NB1-7NB3 (3)			16.70	16.70

SPECIAL DELIVERY STAMP

SD1

	Wmk. 137		Perf. 15	
1919				
7NE1	SD1	105f on 2f gray grn & red	1.25	1.25

POSTAGE DUE STAMPS

Overprinted or Surcharged on Hungary Nos. J29, J32, J35

	Wmk. 137		Perf. 15	
1919				
7NJ1	D1	2f green & red	3.75	3.75
7NJ2	D1	10f green & red	1.25	1.25
7NJ3	D1	20f green & red	1.60	1.60
With New Value Added				
7NJ4	D1	40f on 2f grn & red	1.50	1.50
Nos. 7NJ1-7NJ4 (4)			8.10	8.10

SECOND BARANYA ISSUE

The scarcer values of this issue have been extensively forged. Genuine common values are more easily found.

Hungarian Stamps of 1916-19 Surcharged in Black and Red

1919	On Stamps of 1916-18			
8N1	A9	20f on 2f brn org	4.25	4.25
8N2	A9	50f on 5f green	2.00	2.00
8N3	A9	150f on 15f violet	2.00	2.00
8N4	A10	200f on 75f brt bl & pale bl	.75	.75
On Stamp of 1918-19, Overprinted "Koztarsasag"				
8N5	A11	150f on 15f dp vio	.50	.50
On Stamps of 1919				
8N6	A13	20f on 2f brn org	.35	.35
8N7	A13	30f on 6f grnsh bl	.70	.70
8N8	A13	50f on 5f yel grn	.25	.25
8N9	A13	100f on 25f dull bl	.25	.25
8N10	A13	100f on 40f ol grn	.25	.25
8N11	A13	100f on 45f orange	1.10	1.10
8N12	A13	150f on 20f dk brn	1.40	1.40
On No. 103A				
8N13	A5a	10f on 10f vio brn	.75	.75
Nos. 8N1-8N13 (13)			14.55	14.55

SPECIAL DELIVERY STAMP

Hungarian Special Delivery Stamp of 1916 Surcharged like Regular Issues

1919	Wmk. 137		Perf. 15	
8NE1	SD1	10f on 2f gray grn & red	.65	.65

NEWSPAPER STAMP

Hungarian Newspaper Stamp of 1914 Surcharged like Regular Issues

1919	Wmk. 137		Imperf.	
8NP1	N5	10f on 2f orange	.80	.80

TEMESVAR ISSUES

Issued under Serbian Occupation

Forgeries exist of the inverted and color error surcharges.

Hungarian Stamps of 1916-18 Surcharged in Black, Blue or Brown

a　　　　　　b

1919				
9N1	A9(a)	10f on 2f brn org (Bl)	.25	.25
a.		Black surcharge	15.00	15.00
9N2	A9(b)	30f on 2f brn org	.25	.25
a.		Inverted surcharge	75.00	75.00
9N3	A11(b)	50f on 20f dk brn (Bl)	.25	.25
a.		Inverted surcharge		
9N4	A9(b)	1k 50f on 15f vio	.30	.30
a.		Brown surcharge	.75	.75
b.		Double surcharge (Bk)	50.00	50.00
Nos. 9N1-9N4 (4)			1.05	1.05

SEMI-POSTAL STAMP

Hungarian Semi-Postal Stamp of 1916 Surcharged in Blue

1919	Wmk. 137		Perf. 15	
9NB1	SP3	45f on 10f + 2f rose red	.25	.25

POSTAGE DUE STAMPS

Hungarian Postage Due Stamps of 1915 Surcharged

1919	Wmk. 137		Perf. 15	
9NJ1	D1	40f on 2f grn & red	.80	.80
9NJ2	D1	60f on 2f grn & red	.80	.80
9NJ3	D1	100f on 2f grn & red	.80	.80
Nos. 9NJ1-9NJ3 (3)			2.40	2.40

BANAT, BACSKA ISSUE

Issued under Serbian Occupation

Postal authorities at Temesvar applied these overprints. The stamps were available for postage, but were chiefly used to pay postal employees' salaries.

The overprints on this issue have been extensively forged. Even the inexpensive values are difficult to find with genuine overprints. The more extensive note before 1N1 also applies to Nos. 10N1-10NP1.

Hungarian Stamps of 1913-19 Overprinted in Black or Red

a　　　　　　　b

1919				
Type "a" on Stamp of 1913				
10N1	A4	50f lake, blue	4.00	4.00
Type "a" on Stamps of 1916-18				
10N2	A9	2f brown org	4.00	4.00
10N3	A9	3f red lilac	4.00	4.00
10N4	A9	5f green	4.00	4.00
10N5	A9	6f grnsh blue	4.00	4.00
10N6	A9	15f violet	4.00	4.00
10N7	A9	35f brown	35.00	35.00
Type "b"				
10N8	A10	50f red vio & lil (R)	30.00	30.00
10N9	A10	75f brt bl & pale bl	4.00	4.00
10N10	A10	80f grn & pale grn	4.00	4.00
a.		Red overprint	37.50	37.50
10N11	A10	1k red brn & cl	4.00	4.00
10N12	A10	2k ol brn & bis	4.00	4.00
a.		Red overprint	37.50	37.50
10N14	A10	3k dk vio & ind	65.00	65.00
10N15	A10	5k dk brn & lt brn	4.00	4.00
10N16	A10	10k vio brn & vio	4.00	4.00
Type "a" on Stamps of 1918				
10N17	A11	10f scarlet	4.00	4.00
10N18	A11	20f dk brown	4.00	4.00
10N19	A11	25f brt blue	4.00	4.00
10N20	A12	40f olive grn	4.00	4.00
10N21	A12	50f lilac	4.00	4.00
Type "a" on Stamps of 1919				
Inscribed "Magyar Posta"				
10N22	A13	10f red	30.00	30.00
10N23	A13	20f dk brown	30.00	30.00
10N24	A13	25f dull blue	37.50	37.50

Type "a" on Stamps of 1918-19
Overprinted "Koztarsasag"

10N25	A9	4f slate gray	3.50	3.50
10N26	A9	4f sl gray (R)	42.50	42.50
10N27	A9	5f green	4.00	4.00
10N28	A9	6f grnsh blue	4.00	4.00
10N29	A9	10f rose red	30.00	30.00
10N30	A11	15f dp violet	30.00	30.00
10N31	A9	20f gray brn	30.00	30.00
10N32	A11	25f brt blue	30.00	30.00
10N33	A9	40f olive grn	3.50	3.50
10N34	A9	40f ol grn (R)	32.50	32.50

Type "b"

10N35	A10	1k red brn & cl	4.00	4.00
10N36	A10	2k ol brn & bis	30.00	30.00
10N37	A10	3k dk vio & ind	30.00	30.00
10N38	A10	5k dk brn & lt brn	30.00	30.00
10N39	A10	10k vio brn & vio	30.00	30.00

Type "a" on Temesvár Issue

10N40	A9	10f on 2f brn org (Bl & Bk)	4.00	4.00
10N41	A9	1k50f on 15f vio	4.00	4.00

10N42	A5a	50f on 10f vio brn	4.00	4.00
a.		Red overprint	75.00	75.00
		Nos. 10N1-10N42 (41)	641.50	641.50

SEMI-POSTAL STAMPS

Semi-Postal Stamps of 1916-17 Overprinted Type "a" in Black

1919

10NB1	SP3	10f + 2f rose red	4.00	4.00
10NB2	SP4	15f + 2f dull vio	4.00	4.00
10NB3	SP5	40f + 2f brn car	4.00	4.00

Same Overprint on Temesvar Issue

10NB4	SP3	45f on 10f + 2f rose red (Bl & Bk)	4.00	4.00
		Nos. 10NB1-10NB4 (4)	16.00	16.00

SPECIAL DELIVERY STAMP

Hungary No. E1 Surcharged in Black

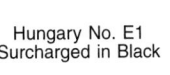

1919

10NE1	SD1	30f on 2f gray grn & red	4.00	4.00
a.		Red overprint	75.00	75.00

POSTAGE DUE STAMPS

Postage Due Stamps of 1914-15 Overprinted Type "a" in Black

1919

10NJ1	D1	2f green & red	4.00	4.00
10NJ2	D1	10f green & red	4.00	4.00
10NJ3	D1	15f green & red	32.50	32.50
10NJ4	D1	20f green & red	4.00	4.00
10NJ5	D1	30f green & red	30.00	30.00
10NJ6	D1	30f green & blk	30.00	30.00
		Nos. 10NJ1-10NJ6 (6)	104.50	104.50

NEWSPAPER STAMP

Stamp of 1914 Overprinted Type "a" in Black

1919

10NP1	N5	(2f) orange	4.00	4.00

SZEGED ISSUE

The "Hungarian National Government, Szeged, 1919," as the overprint reads, was an anti-Bolshevist government which opposed the Soviet Republic then in control at Budapest.

The overprints on this issue have been extensively forged. Even the inexpensive stamps are difficult to find with genuine overprints. The more extensive note before No. 1N1 also applies to Szeged Nos. 11N1-11NP1.

Hungary Stamps of 1916-19 Overprinted in Green, Red and Blue

On Stamps of 1916-18

1919   *Perf. 15, 14*

11N1	A9	2f brn org (G)	2.25	2.25
11N2	A9	3f red lilac (G)	.75	.75
11N3	A9	5f green	2.75	2.75
11N4	A9	6f grnsh blue	32.50	32.50
11N5	A9	15f violet	3.50	3.50
11N6	A10	50f red vio & lil	19.00	19.00
11N7	A10	75f brt bl & pale bl	4.25	4.25
11N8	A10	80f grn & pale grn	18.00	18.00
11N9	A10	1k red brn & cl (G)	2.25	2.25
11N10	A10	2k ol brn & bis	4.75	4.75
11N11	A10	3k dk vio & ind	7.25	7.25
11N12	A10	5k dk brn & lt brn	60.00	60.00
11N13	A10	10k vio brn & vio	60.00	60.00

With New Value Added

11N14	A9	45f on 3f red lil (R & G)	.80	.80
11N15	A10	10k on 1k red brn & cl (Bl & G)	8.00	8.00

On Stamps of 1918

11N16	A11	10f scarlet (G)	2.50	2.50
11N17	A11	20f dk brown	.60	.60
11N18	A11	25f brt blue	22.50	22.50
11N19	A12	40f olive grn	11.00	11.00

On Stamps of 1918-19 Overprinted "Koztarsasag"

11N20	A9	3f red lil (G)	42.50	42.50
11N21	A9	4f slate gray	11.00	11.00
11N22	A9	5f green	25.00	25.00
11N23	A9	6f grnsh blue	15.00	15.00
11N24	A9	10f rose red (G)	32.50	32.50
11N25	A11	10f scarlet)	30.00	30.00
11N26	A11	15f dp violet	10.00	10.00
11N27	A9	20f gray brown	50.00	50.00
11N28	A11	20f dk brown	65.00	65.00
11N29	A11	25f brt blue	20.00	20.00
11N30	A9	40f olive	2.25	2.25
11N31	A12	50f lilac	1.75	1.75
11N32	A10	3k dk vio & ind	37.50	37.50

With New Value Added

11N33	A9	20f on 2f brn org (R & G)	.80	.80

On Stamps of 1919 Inscribed "Magyar Posta"

11N34	A13	20f dk brown	60.00	60.00
11N35	A13	25f dull blue	1.75	1.75
		Nos. 11N1-11N35 (35)	667.70	667.70

SEMI-POSTAL STAMPS

Szeged Overprint on Semi-Postal Stamps of 1916-17 in Green or Red

1919

11NB1	SP3	10f + 2f rose red (G)	.85	.85
11NB2	SP4	15f + 2f dl vio (R)	3.75	3.75
11NB3	SP5	40f + 2f brn car (G)	10.00	10.00

With Additional Overprint "Koztarsasag"

11NB4	SP5	40f + 2f brn car (Bk & G)	15.00	15.00
		Nos. 11NB1-11NB4 (4)	29.60	29.60

SPECIAL DELIVERY STAMP

Szeged Overprint on Special Delivery Stamp of 1916 in Red

1919

11NE1	SD1	2f gray grn & red	11.00	11.00

POSTAGE DUE STAMPS

Szeged Overprint on Stamps of 1915-18 in Red

1919

11NJ1	D1	2f green & red	3.00	3.00
11NJ2	D1	6f green & red	9.75	9.75
11NJ3	D1	10f green & red	3.75	3.75
11NJ4	D1	12f green & red	4.75	4.75
11NJ5	D1	20f green & red	6.00	6.00
11NJ6	D1	30f green & red	9.00	9.00

Red Surcharge

11NJ7	SD1	50f on 2f gray grn & red	2.75	2.75
11NJ8	SD1	100f on 2f gray grn & red	2.75	2.75
		Nos. 11NJ1-11NJ8 (8)	41.75	41.75

NEWSPAPER STAMP

Szeged Overprint on Stamp of 1914 in Green

1919		**Wmk. 137**		*Imperf.*
11NP1	N5	(2f) orange	.85	.85

WESTERN HUNGARY

Following World War I, under the terms of the Trianon Treaty of 1920, four districts of western Hungary were transferred to Austrian administration. Three of these districts were German-speaking and joined Austria as the province of Burgenland. In the fourth district, which included the city of Sopron, Hungarian militia resisted incorporation into Austria, and in a plebiscite held Dec. 14-16, 1921, the area's citizens, although mostly German-speaking, overwhelmingly voted for the district to remain a part of Hungary.

During Sept.-Dec., the following stamps were issued by the local authorities and were sold at post offices within the area controlled by the Hungarian partisans.

Overprinted on Hungarian Stamps of 1916-20

1921, Sept. 4

1	A9	10f red violet	12.50	12.50
2	A9	20f gray brown	.65	.65
a.		Inverted overprint	50.00	50.00
3	A9	25f dull blue	75.00	75.00
a.		Inverted overprint	125.00	125.00
4	A9	40f olive green	1.40	1.40
a.		Inverted overprint	50.00	50.00
5	A9	50f yellow green	1.00	1.00
a.		Inverted overprint	50.00	50.00
6	A9	60f black	.90	.90
7	A10	1k red brn & cl	1.60	1.60
a.		Inverted overprint	50.00	50.00
8	A10	2k ol brn & bis	25.00	25.00
a.		Inverted overprint	75.00	75.00
9	A10	2.50k bl & gray bl	60.00	60.00
10	A10	3k dk vio & ind	25.00	25.00
a.		Inverted overprint	125.00	125.00
		Nos. 1-10 (10)	203.05	203.05

This overprint was also applied to 21 other contemporaneous Hungarian stamps, including 5 postage due stamps, but these were not issued. Value, each $10.

Nos. 1-10, and all of the Western Hungary overprints on Hungarian stamps, exist with the three-hole control punch described after Hungary No. 126. Values are for unpunched examples. Stamps with the control punch sell for 20-50 percent more.

1921, Sept. 19

11	A9	5f brown orange	23.00	23.00
12	A9	10f red violet	30.00	30.00
13	A9	15f violet	75.00	75.00
14	A9	20f gray brown	75.00	75.00
15	A9	40f olive green	75.00	75.00
16	A9	50f yellow green	19.00	19.00
a.		Inverted overprint	125.00	125.00
17	A9	60f black	20.00	20.00
18	A10	1k red brn & cl	20.00	20.00
19	A10	2k ol brn & bister	75.00	75.00
		Nos. 11-19 (9)	412.00	412.00

The text overprinted on Nos. 11-19 was machine-overprinted in black. The skull and crossed bones emblem was separately hand-stamped in red.

1921, Oct. 5

20	A9	10f red violet	.50	.50
21	A9	15f violet	1.00	1.00
22	A9	20f gray brown	.50	.50
23	A9	40f olive green	.50	.50
24	A9	50f yellow green	1.00	1.00
25	A9	60f black	1.00	1.00
26	A10	1k red brn & cl	1.50	1.50
27	A10	2k ol brn & bis	1.00	1.00
28	A9	2.50k on 2f brn org	50.00	50.00
29	A9	2.50k on 5f brn org	1.00	1.00
30	A10	3k dk vio & ind	2.00	2.00
31	A10	5k dk brn & lt brn	2.00	2.00
32	A10	10k vio brn & vio	2.00	2.00
		Nos. 20-32 (13)	64.00	64.00

1921, Oct. 16

33	A9	5f brown orange	2.00	2.00
34	A9	10f red violet	2.00	2.00
35	A9	15f violet	2.00	2.00
36	A9	20f gray brown	2.00	2.00
37	A9	40f olive green	2.00	2.00
38	A9	50f yellow green	2.00	2.00
39	A9	60f black	2.00	2.00
40	A10	1k red brn & cl	2.00	2.00
41	A10	2k ol brn & bis	3.50	3.50
42	A10	2.50k bl & gray bl	7.50	7.50
43	A10	3.50k gray	5.00	5.00
		Nos. 33-43 (11)	32.00	32.00

1921, Oct. 10

44	A9	5f brown orange	60.00	60.00
45	A9	10f red violet	65.00	65.00
46	A9	15f violet	65.00	65.00
47	A9	20f gray brown	65.00	65.00
48	A9	40f olive green	20.00	20.00
49	A9	50f yellow green	4.00	4.00
a.		Inverted overprint	50.00	50.00
50	A9	60f black	4.00	4.00
a.		Inverted overprint	50.00	50.00
51	A10	1k red brn & cl	4.00	4.00
a.		Inverted overprint	50.00	50.00
		Double overprint	50.00	50.00
52	A10	2k ol brn & bis	65.00	65.00
53	A10	2.50k bl & gray bl	20.00	20.00
54	A10	3k dk vio & ind	20.00	20.00
55	A10	3.50k gray	20.00	20.00
56	A10	5k dk brn & lt brn	125.00	125.00
57	A10	10k vio brn & vio	125.00	125.00
58	A23	50k dk brn & bl	125.00	125.00

59	A23	100k ol bis & yel brn	125.00	125.00

Nos. 44-59 (16)   912.00   912.00

See Nos. J1-J3.

A9a   A9b

1921, Oct. 12

60	A9a	20f on 20f gray brn	.40	.40
61	A9a	50f on 50f yel grn	.40	.40
62	A9b	1k on 10f red vio	.40	.40
63	A9b	2k on 40f ol grn	.40	.40
64	A9b	3k on 60f black	.80	.80
65	A9b	5k on 5f brn org	.80	.80
66	A9b	10k on 15f violet	.80	.80
a.		"01" for "10" in surcharge	40.00	40.00

Nos. 60-66 (7)   4.00   4.00

The large numerals on korona values are surcharged in red.

Arms — A1   M.M. Pronay — A2

Frakno — A3

Némétujvár A4

Városszal A5

Arms — A6

1921, Nov. 11

67	A1	10f violet brown	.45	.60
68	A2	20f green	.50	.75
69	A3	40f red brown	.50	.75
70	A4	50f green	.45	.60
71	A3	60f black	.50	.75
72	A5	Tête bêche pair	25.00	25.00
72	A5	1k vermilion	.40	.60
73	A1	2.50k blue	.50	.75
74	A4	5k dark brown	.50	.75
a.		Tête bêche pair	3.50	3.50
75	A2	10k red violet	.50	.75
a.		Tête bêche pair	18.00	18.00
76	A5	50k red violet	.50	.75
a.		Tête bêche pair	27.50	27.50
77	A6	100k lilac	.45	.60
a.		Tête bêche pair	12.00	12.00

Nos. 67-77 (11)   5.25   7.65

The 10f-40f, 60f, 1k, 2.50k, 50k and 100k exist imperf. Value, each $2. Tête bêche pairs of the 60f, 10k and 50k also exist imperf. Value, each $50.

Nos. 67-77 in different colors are proofs. Value: 10f-50k, each $5; 100k, $20.

See Nos. J4-J9.

Soproni népszavazás ❋ 1921. ❋ dec. 14

1921, Dec. 14

78	A9	10f red violet	1.00	1.00
a.		Inverted overprint	10.00	10.00
79	A9	20f gray brown	1.00	1.00
a.		Inverted overprint	10.00	10.00
80	A9	40f olive green	1.00	1.00
a.		Inverted overprint	10.00	10.00
81	A9	50f yellow green	.50	.50
a.		Inverted overprint	10.00	10.00
82	A9	60f black	.50	.50
a.		Inverted overprint	10.00	10.00
83	A10	1k red brn & claret	.50	.50
a.		Inverted overprint	10.00	10.00
84	A10	2k ol brn & bis	1.00	1.00
a.		Inverted overprint	10.00	10.00
85	A10	2.50k bl & gray bl	1.00	1.00
a.		Inverted overprint	10.00	10.00
86	A10	3.50k gray	1.00	1.00
a.		Inverted overprint	10.00	10.00
87	A10	5k dk brn & lt brn	1.00	1.00
a.		Inverted overprint	10.00	10.00
88	A10	10k vio brn & vio	1.50	1.50

Nos. 78-88 (11)   10.00   10.00

Six stamps in this design were prepared in 1921 but not issued. Value, each $40.

POSTAGE DUE STAMPS

1921, Oct. 10

J1	D1	2f green & red	75.00	75.00
J2	D1	120f green & red ('20)	30.00	30.00
a.		Inverted overprint	125.00	125.00
J3	D1	200f green & red ('20)	50.00	50.00

D2

1921, Nov. 11

J4	D2	50f green & black	.35	.50
a.		Inverted overprint	75.00	75.00
J5	D2	100f green & black	.35	.50
a.		Inverted overprint	75.00	75.00
J6	D2	200f green & black	.35	.50
a.		Inverted overprint	75.00	75.00
J7	D2	500f green & black	.35	.50
a.		Inverted overprint	75.00	75.00
J8	D2	1000f green & black	.35	.50
a.		Inverted overprint	75.00	75.00

Nos. J4-J8 (5)   1.75   2.50

Type D2 exists without denomination. Value $50.

Nos. J4-J8 printed in blue are color proofs. Value, each $35.

No. J6 Surcharged in Red

1921, Nov. 11

J9	D2	50f on 200f green & black	30.00	40.00

ICELAND

'is-lənd

LOCATION — Island in the North Atlantic Ocean, east of Greenland
AREA — 39,758 sq. mi.
POP. — 238,175 (1983)
CAPITAL — Reykjavik

Iceland became a republic on June 17, 1944. Formerly this country was united with Denmark under the government of King Christian X who, as a ruling sovereign of both countries, was assigned the dual title of king of each. Although the two countries were temporarily united in certain affairs beyond the king's person, both were acknowledged as sovereign states.

96 Skillings = 1 Rigsdaler

100 Aurar (singular "Eyrir") = 1 Krona (1876)

Watermarks

Wmk. 112 — Crown   Wmk. 113 — Crown

Wmk. 47 — Multiple Rosette   Wmk. 114 — Multiple Crosses

Values for unused stamps are for examples with original gum as defined in the catalogue introduction. Very fine examples of Nos. 1-33A and O1-O12 will have centering with perforations clear of the framelines but with design noticeably off center, and Nos. 1-7 and O1-O3 additionally will have some irregular or shorter perforations. Well centered stamps are quite scarce and will command higher prices.

A1

Perf. 14x13½

	1873	**Typo.**	**Wmk. 112**
1	A1	2s ultra	1,300.	3,000.
	On cover		50,000.
a.	Imperf.	850.	
2	A1	4s dark carmine	225.	1,250.
	On cover		44,000.
a.	Imperf.	850.	
3	A1	8s brown	425.	1,500.
	On cover		44,000.
a.	Imperf.	450.	
4	A1	16s yellow	2,000.	3,000.
	On cover		625.00
a.	Imperf.	550.	

Perf. 12½

5	A1	3s gray	650.	2,000.
	On cover		
a.	Imperf.	1,000.	

6	A1	4s carmine	1,900.	2,900.
	On cover		
7	A1	16s yellow	175.	850.
	On cover		

Filler and poor cancellations are often found on Nos. 1-7. Nos. 1-7 were valid until 7/31/76. Favor cancellations were applied starting in 1882. These cancels have sans-serif letters and dates with lines between the month and day. Values of stamps with favor cancellations range from $75 (Nos. 2, 7) to $575 (No. 4). The imperforate varieties lack gum.

A2

1876

8	A2	5a blue	475.00	1,000.

Perf. 14x13½

9	A2	5a blue	600.00	1,200.
	On cover		9,000.
a.	Imperf.	2,450.	
10	A2	6a gray	200.00	40.00
	On cover		1,500.
11	A2	10a carmine	300.00	10.00
	On cover		1,000.
a.	Imperf.	850.00	1,000.
12	A2	16a brown	175.00	67.50
	On cover		875.00
13	A2	20a dark violet	45.00	675.00
	On cover		3,100.
14	A2	40a green	140.00	300.00
	On cover		

Fake and favor cancellations are often found on No. 13, and value is considerably less than that shown.

Small "3" — A3   Large "3" — A3a

1882-98

15	A3	3a orange	82.50	35.00
	On cover		650.00
16	A2	5a green	75.00	18.00
	On cover		650.00
17	A2	20a blue	425.00	67.50
	On cover		1,000.
a.	20a ultramarine	1,000.	375.00
	On cover		1,600.
18	A2	40a red violet	75.00	57.50
	On cover		4,500.
a.	Perf. 13 ('98)	6,750.	
19	A2	50a bl & car ('92)	120.00	140.00
	On cover		1,900.
20	A2	100a brn & vio ('92)	110.00	175.00
	On cover		2,250.

Nos. 15-20 (6)   887.50   493.00

See note after No. 68.

1896-1901   **Perf. 13**

21	A3	3a orange ('97)	145.00	15.00
	On cover		600.00
22	A3a	3a yellow ('01)	11.00	30.00
	On cover		1,200.
23	A2	4a rose & gray ('99)	24.00	27.50
	On cover		1,000.
24	A2	5a green	5.25	3.75
	On cover		600.00
25	A2	6a gray ('97)	22.50	24.00
	On cover		1,250.
26	A2	10a carmine ('97)	18.00	3.75
	On cover		625.00
27	A2	16a brown	97.50	140.00
	On cover		1,100.
28	A2	20a dull blue ('98)	62.50	50.00
	On cover		775.00
a.	20a dull ultramarine	675.00	57.50
	On cover		1,250.
29	A2	25a yel brown & blue ('00)	30.00	42.50
	On cover		3,100.
30	A2	50a bl & car ('98)	600.00	900.00

Value for No. 30 used is for a canceled-to-order example after the stamp was invalidated in 1902. Stamps genuinely used before invalidation are rare and sell for much more.

See note after No. 68.

For surcharges see Nos. 31-33A, 45-68.

Black and Red Surcharge

Large "prir"

1897 Perf. 13

31	A2	3a on 5a green	900.	750.
	On cover			700.
a.	Perf. 14x13½		26,500.	4,750.
b.	Inverted surcharge		1,500.	1,250.
	On cover			1,500.
c.	As "a," inverted surcharge			7,500.

Large "prir" is 6.1mm to 6.3mm wide by 3.5mm tall.

Small "prir"

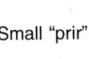

32	A2	3a on 5a green	900.	750.
	On cover			625.
a.	Inverted surcharge		1,650.	1,350.
	On cover			1,500.
b.	Perf. 14x13½		13,500.	3,000.
c.	In vert. pair with #31		2,250.	2,000.
d.	As "b," in vert. pair with #31a			—

All 5 known unused examples of No. 32b lack gum.
Small "prir" is 5.5mm to 5.6mm wide by 3.1mm tall.

Black Surcharge

Large "prir"

33	A2	3a on 5a green	1,450.	1,050.
	On cover			1,000.
b.	Inverted surcharge		1,950.	1,650.

Large "prir" is 6.1mm to 6.3mm wide by 3.5mm tall.

Small "prir"

33A	A2	3a on 5a green	1,100.	750.
	On cover			750.
c.	Inverted surcharge		1,800.	1,500.

Excellent counterfeits are known.
Small "prir" is 5.5mm to 5.6mm wide by 3.1mm tall.

King Christian IX — A4

1902-04 Wmk. 113 Perf. 13

34	A4	3a orange	7.00	4.50
	On cover			50.00
35	A4	4a gray & rose	4.50	1.60
	On cover			55.00
36	A4	5a yel green	40.00	1.40
	On cover			30.00
37	A4	6a gray brown	24.00	13.00
	On cover			110.00
38	A4	10a car rose	7.00	1.40
	On cover			50.00
39	A4	16a chocolate	10.00	13.00
	On cover			140.00
40	A4	20a deep blue	3.50	5.50
				42.50
a.	Inscribed "PJONUSTA"		75.00	110.00
	On cover			250.00
41	A4	25a brn & grn	5.00	8.25
				310.00
42	A4	40a violet	5.50	7.75
				440.00
43	A4	50a gray & bl blk	7.00	29.00
				500.00
44	A4	1k sl bl & yel brn	8.25	13.00
				550.00
44A	A4	2k olive brn & brt blue ('04)	32.50	87.50
	On cover			1,050.

44B	A4	5k org brn & slate blue ('04)	175.00	275.00
	On cover			1,500.
	Nos. 34-44B (13)		329.25	460.90

For surcharge see No. 142.

Stamps of 1882-1901 Overprinted

1902-03 Wmk. 112 Perf. 13
Red Overprint

45	A2	5a green	1.75	13.50
a.	Inverted overprint		100.00	140.00
b.	"I" before Gildi omitted		225.00	
c.	'03-'03		990.00	
d.	02'-'03		850.00	
e.	Pair, one without overprint		225.00	
46	A2	6a gray	1.50	13.50
a.	Double overprint		175.00	
b.	Inverted overprint		100.00	
c.	'03-'03		675.00	
d.	02'-'03		675.00	
e.	Pair, one with invtd. ovpt.		525.00	
f.	Pair, one without overprint		300.00	
g.	As "f," inverted		525.00	
47	A2	20a dull blue	1.50	16.50
a.	Inverted overprint		100.00	135.00
b.	"I" before Gildi omitted		225.00	
c.	02'-'03		900.00	
48	A2	25a yel brn & bl	1.50	24.00
a.	Inverted overprint		97.50	110.00
b.	'03-'03		600.00	
c.	02'-'03		600.00	
d.	Double overprint		525.00	

Black Overprint

49	A3	3a orange	300.00	675.00
b.	Inverted overprint		375.00	850.00
c.	"I" before Gildi omitted		850.00	
d.	'03-'03		850.00	
e.	02'-'03		850.00	
50	A3a	3a yellow	1.75	3.25
a.	Double overprint		525.00	
b.	Inverted overprint		110.00	135.00
c.	"I" before Gildi omitted		850.00	
d.	02'-'03		975.00	
51	A2	4a rose & gray	52.50	75.00
a.	Double overprint		525.00	
b.	Inverted overprint		150.00	
c.	Dbl. ovpt., one invtd.		525.00	
d.	"I" before Gildi omitted		375.00	
e.	'03-'03		675.00	
f.	02'-'03		675.00	
g.	Pair, one with invtd. ovpt.		525.00	
52	A2	5a green	450.00	1,200.
a.	Inverted overprint		525.00	
b.	Pair, one without overprint		675.00	
c.	As "b," inverted		825.00	
53	A2	6a gray	990.00	1,500.
a.	Inverted overprint		1,050.	
b.	Pair, one without overprint		1,050.	
c.	Double overprint		1,150.	
54	A2	10a carmine	1.75	16.50
a.	Inverted overprint		100.00	140.00
b.	Pair, one without overprint		275.00	
55	A2	16a brown	35.00	52.50
a.	Inverted overprint		225.00	
b.	"I" before Gildi omitted		375.00	
c.	'03-'03		900.00	
d.	02'-'03		850.00	
56	A2	20a dull blue	14,500.	
a.	Inverted overprint		13,000.	
57	A2	25 yel brn & bl	13,700.	
a.	Inverted overprint		14,500.	
58	A2	40a red vio	1.50	52.50
a.	Inverted overprint		120.00	
59	A2	50a bl & car	4.50	90.00
a.	Double overprint		335.00	
b.	02'-'03		1,100.	
c.	'03-'03		1,100.	

Perf. 14x13½
Red Overprint

60	A2	5a green	2,750.	—
a.	'03-'03		45,500.	
b.	02'-'03		45,500.	
61	A2	6a gray	2,750.	—
a.	02'-'03		45,000.	
62	A2	20a blue	7,500.	—
b.	02'-'03		15,000.	

Black Overprint

63	A3	3a orange	1,800.	2,750.
a.	Inverted overprint		2,300.	
b.	02'-'03		2,750.	
c.	'03-'03		3,000.	
64	A2	10a carmine	13,000.	—
65	A2	16a brown	2,000.	2,300.
a.	Inverted overprint		2,400.	
b.	02'-'03		3,000.	
c.	'03-'03		22,000.	
65C	A2	20a dull blue	12,000.	—
a.	Inverted overprint		15,500.	
66	A2	40a red vio	27.50	135.00
a.	Inverted overprint		450.00	
b.	'03-'03		675.00	
c.	02'-'03		675.00	

67	A2	50a bl & car	67.50	175.00
a.	Inverted overprint		450.00	
b.	'03-'03		600.00	
c.	02'-'03		600.00	
d.	As "c," inverted		—	
68	A2	100a brn & vio	75.00	110.00
a.	Inverted overprint		275.00	
b.	02'-'03		750.00	
c.	'03-'03		900.00	

"I GILDI" means "valid."
In 1904 Nos. 20, 22-30, 45-59 (except 49, 52, 53, 56 and 57) and No. 68 were reprinted for the Postal Union. The reprints are perforated 13 and have watermark type 113. Value $120 each. Without overprint, $250 each.

Kings Christian IX and Frederik VIII — A5

Typo., Center Engr.
1907-08 Wmk. 113 Perf. 13

71	A5	1e yel grn & red	2.00	1.40
72	A5	3a yel brn & ocher	4.75	1.75
73	A5	4a gray & red	2.60	2.10
74	A5	5a green	95.00	1.40
75	A5	6a gray & gray brn	60.00	4.00
76	A5	10a scarlet	165.00	1.60
77	A5	15a red & green	8.50	1.50
78	A5	16a brown	9.75	47.50
79	A5	20a blue	9.00	6.75
80	A5	25a bis brn & grn	7.25	14.00
81	A5	40a claret & vio	7.00	17.00
82	A5	50a gray & vio	8.00	17.00
83	A5	1k blue & brn	32.50	77.50
84	A5	2k dk brn & dk grn	42.50	90.00
85	A5	5k brn & slate	225.00	425.00
	Nos. 71-85 (15)		678.85	708.50

See Nos. 99-107.
For surcharges and overprints see Nos. 130-138, 143, C2, O69.

Jon Sigurdsson A6

Frederik VIII A7

1911 Typo. and Embossed

86	A6	1e olive green	3.00	2.75
87	A6	3a light brown	5.75	17.50
88	A6	4a ultramarine	2.25	2.25
89	A6	6a gray	14.50	30.00
90	A6	15a violet	17.50	2.25
91	A6	25a orange	32.50	57.50
	Nos. 86-91 (6)		75.50	112.25

Sigurdsson (1811-79), statesman and author. For surcharge see No. 149.

1912, Feb. 17

92	A7	5a green	37.50	14.00
93	A7	10a red	37.50	14.00
94	A7	20a pale blue	52.50	20.00
95	A7	50a claret	10.50	40.00
96	A7	1k yellow	32.50	80.00
97	A7	2k rose	30.00	80.00
98	A7	5k brown	175.00	250.00
	Nos. 92-98 (7)		375.50	498.00

For surcharges and overprints see Nos. 140-141, O50-O51.

Type of 1907-08
Typo., Center Engr.
1915-18 Wmk. 114 Perf. 14x14½

99	A5	1e yel grn & red	9.50	20.00
100	A5	3a bister brn	4.75	3.25
101	A5	4a gray & red	4.75	10.50
102	A5	5a green	110.00	1.50
103	A5	6a gray & gray brn	22.50	150.00
104	A5	10a scarlet	4.25	1.40
107	A5	20a blue	275.00	26.00
	Nos. 99-107 (7)		430.75	212.65

Revenue cancellations consisting of "TOLLUR" boxed in frame are found on stamps used to pay the tax on parcel post packages entering Iceland.

Christian X — A8

1920-22 Typo.

108	A8	1e yel grn & red	1.00	1.25
109	A8	3a bister brn	9.00	18.50
110	A8	4a gray & red	5.25	2.75
111	A8	5a green	2.50	2.25
112	A8	5a ol green ('22)	5.25	1.75
113	A8	6a dark gray	15.00	9.50
114	A8	8a dark brown	9.00	2.50
115	A8	10a red	2.75	12.50
116	A8	10a green ('21)	3.75	2.00
117	A8	15a violet	45.00	1.60
118	A8	20a deep blue	3.00	19.00
119	A8	20a choc ('22)	65.00	1.75
120	A8	25a brown & grn	19.00	2.00
121	A8	25a red ('21)	19.00	62.50
	Revenue cancellation			4.25
122	A8	30a red & green	57.50	3.75
	Revenue cancellation			8.75
123	A8	40a claret	50.00	3.25
	Revenue cancellation			9.50
124	A8	40a dk bl ('21)	87.50	15.00
	Revenue cancellation			11.00
125	A8	50a dk gray & cl	240.00	14.00
	Revenue cancellation			13.50
126	A8	1k dp bl & dk brn	110.00	2.00
	Revenue cancellation			1.75
127	A8	2k ol brn & myr green	300.00	37.50
	Revenue cancellation			3.50
128	A8	5k brn & ind	62.50	20.00
	Revenue cancellation			3.50
	Nos. 108-128 (21)		1,112.	235.35

See Nos. 176-187, 202.
For surcharges and overprints see Nos.139, 150, C1, C9-C14, O52, O70-O71.

A9

A10

A11

1921-25 Wmk. 113 Perf. 13

130	A9	5a on 16a brown	5.25	34.00
131	A11	5a on 16a brown	3.00	9.75
132	A10	20a on 25a brn & green	11.00	10.00
a.	Double surcharge		600.00	
133	A11	20a on 25a bis brn & green	6.50	9.25
134	A9	20a on 40a violet	11.00	25.00
135	A11	20a on 40a cl & vio	18.00	27.50
137	A9	30a on 50a gray & bl blk ('25)	45.00	40.00
	Revenue cancellation			22.50
138	A9	50a on 5k org brn & sl bl ('25)	82.50	62.50
	Revenue cancellation			35.00
	Nos. 130-138 (8)		182.25	218.00

No. 111 Surcharged

1922 Wmk. 114 Perf. 14x14½

139	A8	10a on 5a green	10.00	4.00

Nos. 95-96, 44A, 85 Surcharged

1924-30 Wmk. 113 Perf. 13

140	A7	10k on 50a ('25)	375.00	575.00
	Revenue cancellation			45.00
141	A7	10k on 1k	500.00	850.00
	Revenue cancellation			90.00
142	A4	10k on 2k ('29)	100.00	40.00
	Revenue cancellation			13.50
143	A5	10k on 5k ('30)	600.00	750.00
	Revenue cancellation			45.00

"Tollur" is a revenue cancellation.

Landing the Mail — A12

638

ICELAND

Designs: 7a, 50a, Landing the mail. 10a, 35a, View of Reykjavik. 20a, Museum building.

1925, Sept. 12   Typo.   Wmk. 114

144	A12	7a yel green	52.50	10.00
145	A12	10a dk bl & brn	90.00	10.00
146	A12	20a vermilion	52.50	1.00
147	A12	35a deep blue	90.00	12.00
148	A12	50a yel grn & brn	90.00	2.25
		Nos. 144-148 (5)	337.50	26.25

No. 91 Surcharged

1925   Wmk. 113   Perf. 13

149	A6	2k on 25a orange	180.00	190.00
		Revenue cancellation		22.50

No. 124 Surcharged in Red

1926

150	A8	1k on 40a dark blue	200.00	45.00
		Revenue cancellation		30.00

Parliament Building A15

Designs: 5a, Viking ship in storm. 7a, Parliament meeting place, 1690. 10a, Viking funeral. 15a, Vikings naming land. 20a, The dash for Thing. 25a, Gathering wood. 30a, Thingvalla Lake. 35a, Iceland woman in national costume. 40a, Iceland flag. 50a, First Althing, 930 A.D. 1k, Map of Iceland. 2k, Winter-bound home. 5k, Woman spinning. 10k, Viking Sacrifice to Thor.

Perf. 12½x12

1930, Jan. 1   Litho.   Unwmk.

152	A15	3a dull vio & gray vio	4.75	12.00
153	A15	5a dk bl & sl grn	4.75	12.00
154	A15	7a grn & gray grn	4.75	12.00
155	A15	10a dk vio & lilac	11.50	25.00
156	A15	15a dp ultra & bl gray	3.50	13.50
157	A15	20a rose red & sal	55.00	110.00
a.		Double impression	400.00	
158	A15	25a dk brn & lt brown	9.25	17.50
159	A15	30a dk grn & sl grn	7.75	17.00
160	A15	35a ultra & bl gray	8.50	16.50
161	A15	40a dk ultra, red & slate grn	7.50	17.00
162	A15	50a red brn & cinnamon	75.00	195.00
163	A15	1k ol grn & gray green	75.00	195.00
164	A15	2k turq bl & gray green	105.00	240.00
165	A15	5k org & yellow	60.00	190.00
166	A15	10k mag & dl rose	60.00	190.00
		Nos. 152-166 (15)	492.25	1,262.

Millenary of the "Althing," the Icelandic Parliament, oldest in the world.
Imperfs were privately printed.
For overprints see Nos. O53-O67.

Gullfoss (Golden Falls) — A30

1931-32   Unwmk.   Engr.   Perf. 14

170	A30	5a gray	17.50	1.10
171	A30	20a red	15.00	.25
172	A30	35a ultramarine	30.00	16.00
		Revenue cancellation		2.25
173	A30	60a red lil ('32)	18.00	1.25
174	A30	65a red brn ('32)	3.00	1.25
175	A30	75a grnsh bl ('32)	120.00	40.00
		Revenue cancellation		6.00
		Nos. 170-175 (6)	203.50	59.85

Issued: 5a-35a, Dec. 15; 60a-75a, May 30.

Type of 1920 Christian X Issue Redrawn

Perf. 14x14½

1931-33   Typo.   Wmk. 114

176	A8	1e yel grn & red	1.00	1.75
177	A8	2k water brown	10.00	78.50
		Revenue cancellation		8.00
178	A8	4a gray & red	2.50	2.50
179	A8	6a dark gray	2.00	4.25
180	A8	7a yel grn ('33)	.65	1.75
181	A8	10a chocolate	175.00	1.10
182	A8	25a brn & green	19.00	4.25
		Revenue cancellation		4.50
183	A8	30a red & green	30.00	6.50
		Revenue cancellation		11.00
184	A8	40a claret	300.00	24.00
		Revenue cancellation		15.00
185	A8	1k dk bl & lt brn	47.50	8.00
		Revenue cancellation		4.50
186	A8	2k choc & dk grn	300.00	90.00
		Revenue cancellation		11.00
187	A8	10k yel grn & blk	350.00	225.00
		Revenue cancellation		22.50
		Nos. 176-187 (12)	1,243.	385.60

On the redrawn stamps the horizontal lines of the portrait and the oval are closer together than on the 1920 stamps and are crossed by many fine vertical lines.
See No. 202.

Dynjandi Falls — A31   Mount Hekla — A32

Perf. 12½

1935, June 28   Engr.   Unwmk.

193	A31	10a blue	30.00	.25
		Never hinged	100.00	
194	A32	1k greenish gray	52.50	.25
		Never hinged	170.00	

Matthias Jochumsson — A33

1935, Nov. 11

195	A33	3a gray green	.75	4.50
196	A33	5a gray	15.00	1.50
197	A33	7a yel green	22.50	2.50
198	A33	35a blue	.65	1.50
		Nos. 195-198 (4)	38.90	10.00
		Set, never hinged	130.00	

Birth cent. of Matthias Jochumsson, poet.
For surcharges see Nos. 212, 236.

King Christian X — A34

1937, May 14   Perf. 13x12½

199	A34	10a green	2.50	27.50
200	A34	30a brown	2.50	12.00
201	A34	40a claret	2.50	12.00
		Nos. 199-201 (3)	7.50	51.50
		Set, never hinged	15.00	

Reign of Christian X, 25th anniv.

Christian X Type of 1931-33

1937   Unwmk.   Typo.   Perf. 11½

202	A8	1e yel grn & red	1.00	2.25
		Never hinged	3.75	

Geyser
A35   A36

1938-47   Engr.   Perf. 14

203	A35	15a dp rose vio	7.00	13.00
a.		Imperf., pair	900.00	
		Never hinged	1,050.	
204	A35	20a rose red	27.50	.30
205	A35	35a ultra	.85	1.10
206	A36	40a dk brn ('39)	17.00	32.50
207	A36	45a brt ultra ('40)	1.00	1.10
208	A36	50a dk slate grn	26.00	1.10
208A	A36	60a brt ultra ('19)	7.00	1.75
b.		Perf. 11½ ('47)	3.75	15.00
		Never hinged (#208Ac)	9.00	
208B	A36	1k indigo ('45)	2.50	.50
d.		Perf. 11½ ('47)	3.75	15.00
		Never hinged (#208Bd)	9.00	
		Nos. 203-208B (8)	88.85	50.85
		Set, never hinged	190.00	

University of Iceland A37

1938, Dec. 1   Perf. 13½

209	A37	25a dark grn	8.50	18.00
210	A37	30a brown	8.50	18.00
211	A37	40a brt red vio	8.50	18.00
		Nos. 209-211 (3)	25.50	54.00
		Set, never hinged	40.00	

20th anniversary of independence.

No. 198 Surcharged with New Value

1939, Mar. 17   Perf. 12½

212	A33	5a on 35a blue	1.00	1.75
		Never hinged	2.00	
a.		Double surcharge	325.00	
		Never hinged	675.00	

Trylon and Perisphere A38   Leif Ericsson's Ship and Route to America A39

Statue of Thorfinn Karlsefni — A40

1939   Engr.   Perf. 14

213	A38	20a crimson	4.00	7.75
214	A39	35a bright ultra	4.50	9.75
215	A40	45a bright green	4.75	13.00
216	A40	2k dark gray	62.50	160.00
		Nos. 213-216 (4)	75.75	190.50
		Set, never hinged	140.00	

New York World's Fair.
For overprints see Nos. 232-235.

Codfish — A41   Herring — A42

Flag of Iceland — A43

1939-45   Engr.   Perf. 14, 14x13½

217	A41	1e Prussian blue	.55	.70
a.		Perf. 14x13½	2.00	5.50
218	A41	3a dark violet	.55	1.25
a.		Perf. 14x13½	2.75	10.00
219	A41	5a dark brown	.55	.50
c.		Perf. 14x13½	2.75	1.40
220	A42	7a dark green	7.00	12.00
221	A42	10a green ('40)	45.00	1.75
b.		Perf. 14x13½	77.50	4.50
		Never hinged		
222	A42	10a slate gray ('45)	.40	.25
223	A42	12a dk grn ('43)	.50	1.00

224	A41	25a brt red ('40)	32.50	.70
b.		Perf. 14x13½	65.00	3.00
		Never hinged (#224b)	210.00	
225	A41	25a hn brn ('45)	.45	.45
226	A42	35a carmine ('43)	.60	.75
227	A41	50a dk bl grn ('45)	.90	1.10

Typo.

228	A43	10a car & ultra	2.50	1.60
		Nos. 217-228 (12)	91.40	25.65
		Set, never hinged	240.00	

Statue of Thorfinn Karlsefni — A44

1939-45   Engr.   Perf. 14

229	A44	2k dark gray	3.50	.50
230	A44	5k dk brn ('43)	27.50	.65
231	A44	10k brn yel ('45)	15.00	2.10
		Nos. 229-231 (3)	46.00	3.25
		Set, never hinged	200.00	

1947   Perf. 11½

229a	A44	2k	9.25	1.90
230a	A44	5k	35.00	2.50
231a	A44	10k	15.00	55.00
		Nos. 229a-231a (3)	59.25	59.40
		Set, never hinged	200.00	

New York World's Fair Issue of 1939 Overprinted "1940" in Black

1940, May 11   Perf. 14

232	A38	20a crimson	10.00	32.50
233	A39	35a bright ultra	10.00	32.50
234	A40	45a bright green	10.00	32.50
235	A40	2k dark gray	125.00	500.00
		Nos. 232-235 (4)	155.00	597.50
		Set, never hinged	300.00	

SEMI-POSTAL STAMPS

Shipwreck and Rescue by Breeches Buoy SP1

Children Gathering Rock Plants SP2

Old Fisherman at Shore SP3

Unwmk.

1933, Apr. 28   Engr.   Perf. 14

B1	SP1	10a + 10a red brown	2.25	7.50
B2	SP2	20a + 20a org red	2.25	7.50
B3	SP1	35a + 25a ultra	2.25	7.50
B4	SP3	50a + 25a blue grn	2.25	7.50
		Nos. B1-B4 (4)	9.00	30.00
		Set, never hinged	18.00	

Receipts from the surtax were devoted to a special fund for use in various charitable works especially those indicated on the stamps: "Slysavarnir" (Rescue work), "Barnaheli" (Asylum for scrofulous children), "Ellhaeli" (Asylum for the Aged).

Souvenir Sheets

King Christian X — SP4

1937, May 15 **Typo.**
B5 SP4 Sheet of 3   55.00   *375.00*
    Never hinged   105.00
  a.   15a violet   12.00   *67.50*
  b.   25a red   12.00   *67.50*
  c.   50a blue   12.00   *67.50*

Reign of Christian X, 25th anniv. Sheet sold for 2kr.

SP5

Designs: 30a, 40a, Ericsson statue, Reykjavik. 60a, Iceland's position on globe.

1938, Oct. 9 **Photo.** **Perf. 12**
B6 SP5 Sheet of 3   6.00   *32.50*
    Never hinged   10.00
  a.   30a scarlet   1.40   *13.00*
  b.   40a purple   1.40   *13.00*
  c.   60a deep green   1.40   *13.00*

Leif Ericsson Day, Oct. 9, 1938.

AIR POST STAMPS

No. 115 Overprinted

Perf. 14x14½
1928, May 31 **Wmk. 114**
C1 A8 10a red   1.10   *15.00*
    Never hinged   2.25

Same Overprint on No. 82
1929, June 29 **Wmk. 113** **Perf. 13**
C2 A5 50a gray & violet   75.00   *145.00*
    Never hinged   230.00

Gyrfalcon
AP1

Perf. 12½x12
1930, Jan. 1 **Litho.** **Unwmk.**
C3 AP1 10a dp ultra & gray
      blue   30.00   *90.00*
    Never hinged   60.00

Imperfs were privately printed.
For overprint see No. CO1.

Snaefellsjokull, Extinct Volcano — AP2

Parliament Millenary: 20a, Fishing boat. 35a, Iceland pony. 50a, Gullfoss (Golden Falls). 1k, Ingolfour Arnarson Statue.

Wmk. 47
1930, June 1 **Typo.** **Perf. 14**
C4 AP2 15a org brn & dl bl   37.50   *72.50*
C5 AP2 20a bis brn & sl bl   37.50   *72.50*
C6 AP2 35a olive grn & brn   72.50   *145.00*
C7 AP2 50a dp grn & dp bl   72.50   *145.00*
C8 AP2 1k olive grn & dk
      red   72.50   *145.00*
    Nos. C4-C8 (5)   292.50   *580.00*
    Set, never hinged   600.00

Regular Issue of 1920 Overprinted

Perf. 14x14½
1931, May 25 **Wmk. 114**
C9 A8 30a red & green   50.00   *175.00*
C10 A8 1k dp bl & dk brn   17.50   *175.00*
C11 A8 2k ol brn & myr
      grn   75.00   *175.00*
    Nos. C9-C11 (3)   142.50   *525.00*
    Set, never hinged   335.00

Nos. 185, 128 and 187 Overprinted in Red

1933, June 16
C12 A8 1k dk bl & lt brn   235.   *850.*
    Never hinged   525.
C13 A8 5k brn & indigo   775.   *2,000.*
    Never hinged   1,800.
C14 A8 10k yel grn & blk   1,650.   *3,750.*
    Never hinged   4,000.

Excellent counterfeit overprints exist.
Visit of the Italian Flying Armada en route from Rome to Chicago; also for the payment of the charges on postal matter sent from Iceland to the US via the Italian seaplanes.

Plane over
Thingvalla
Lake — AP7

10a-20a, Plane over Thingvalla Lake. 25a-50a, Plane and Aurora Borealis. 1k-2k, Map of Iceland.

Perf. 12½x14
1934, Sept. 1 **Engr.** **Unwmk.**
C15 AP7 10a blue   2.30   *4.00*
C16 AP7 20a emerald   5.00   *9.00*
  a.   Perf. 14   37.50   *27.00*
    Never hinged   135.00
C17 AP7 25a dark violet,
      perf. 14   13.00   *20.00*
    Revenue cancellation   50.00
  a.   Perf. 12½x14   37.50   *45.00*
    Never hinged   135.00
C18 AP7 50a red vio, perf. 14   4.00   *9.00*
C19 AP7 1k dark brown   22.50   *40.00*
    Revenue cancellation   30.00
C20 AP7 2k red orange   11.50   *25.00*
    Nos. C15-C20 (6)   58.30   *97.00*
    Set, never hinged   165.00

AIR POST OFFICIAL STAMPS

No. C3
Overprinted
In Red

1930, Jan. 1 **Unwmk.** **Perf. 12½x12**
CO1 AP1 10a dp ultra & gray
      blue   30.00   *170.00*
    Never hinged   55.00

Imperfs were privately printed.

OFFICIAL STAMPS

For Nos. O1-O12, see note on condition before No. 1.

   O1   O2

Perf. 14x13½
1873 **Typo.** **Wmk. 112**
O1 O1 4s green   *10,500.*   *12,000.*
  a.   Imperf.   150.
O2 O1 8s red lilac   750.   *900.*
    On cover   —
  a.   Imperf.   750.

Perf. 12½
O3 O1 4s green   120.   *525.*
    On cover   *37,500.*

False and favor cancellations are often found on Nos. O1-O37. Nos. O1-O3 were valid until 7/31/76. Favor cancellations were applied starting in 1882. These cancels have sans-serif letters and dates with lines between the month and day. Values of stamps with favor cancellations range from $60 (#O3) to $1,250 (#O1). The imperforate varieties lack gum.

1876-95 **Perf. 14x13½**
O4 O2 3a yellow   55.00   *82.50*
    On cover   *7,500.*
O5 O2 5a brown   13.00   *22.50*
    On cover   *6,250.*
  a.   Imperf.   450.00
O6 O2 10a blue   95.00   *21.00*
    On cover   *6,250.*
  a.   10a ultramarine   600.00   *85.00*
    On cover   *22,500.*
O7 O2 16a carmine   35.00   *70.00*
O8 O2 20a yellow green   35.00   *62.50*
    On cover   *6,250.*
O9 O2 50a rose lilac ('95)   110.00   *115.00*
    Nos. O4-O9 (6)   343.00   *373.50*

1898-1902 **Perf. 13**
O10 O2 3a yellow   18.00   *47.50*
O11 O2 4a gray ('01)   47.50   *60.00*
    On cover   —
O12 O2 10a ultra ('02)   87.50   *150.00*
    Nos. O10-O12 (3)   153.00   *257.50*

A 5a brown and 20a yellow green, both perf. 13 with Wmk. 112, exist. They were not regularly issued.
See note after No. O30.
For overprints see Nos. O20-O30.

O3

1902 **Wmk. 113** **Perf. 13**
O13 O3 3a buff & black   6.25   *3.75*
    On cover   500.00
O14 O3 4a dp grn & blk   6.25   *3.25*
    On cover   500.00
O15 O3 5a org brn & blk   5.00   *5.50*
    On cover   500.00
O16 O3 10a ultra & black   5.50   *5.50*
    On cover   500.00
O17 O3 16a carmine & blk   5.00   *20.00*
    On cover   500.00
O18 O3 20a green & blk   25.00   *10.00*
    On cover   625.00
O19 O3 50a violet & blk   10.00   *15.00*
    On cover   625.00
    Nos. O13-O19 (7)   63.00   *63.00*

Stamps of 1876-1901 Overprinted in Black

1902-03 **Wmk. 112** **Perf. 13**
O20 O2 3a yellow   1.50   *3.25*
  a.   "I" before Gildi omitted   210.00
  b.   Inverted overprint   52.50   *82.50*
  c.   As "a," invtd.   250.00
  d.   Pair, one with invtd.
      ovpt.   225.00
  e.   '03-'03   600.00
  f.   '02-'03   600.00
O21 O2 4a gray   1.50   *3.25*
  a.   "I" before Gildi omitted   210.00
  b.   Inverted overprint   75.00   *97.50*
  e.   '03-'03   675.00
  f.   '02-'03   675.00

---

  g.   Pair, one without ovpt.   275.00
  h.   Pair, one with invtd.
      ovpt.   125.00
  i.   "L" only of "I GILDI" in-
      verted   15,000.
O22 O2 5a brown   1.25   *3.25*
O23 O2 10a ultramarine   1.25   *3.25*
  a.   "I" before Gildi omitted   325.00
  b.   Inverted overprint   67.50   *97.50*
  c.   '03-'03   525.00
  d.   '02-'03   525.00
  e.   "L" only of "I GILDI"   60.00
  f.   As "e," inverted   525.00
  g.   "IL" only of "I GILDI"   275.00
O24 O2 20a yel green   1.20   *30.00*
    Nos. O20-O24 (5)   6.70   *43.00*

Perf. 14x13½
O25 O2 3a yellow   400.00   *1,800.*
  a.   "02'-'03"   700.00
  b.   '03-'03   700.00
O26 O2 5a brown   11.00   *210.00*
  a.   Inverted overprint   115.00
  b.   '03-'03   525.00
  c.   02'-'03   525.00
  d.   "L" only of "I GILDI" in-
      verted   15,000.
O27 O2 10a blue   550.00   *990.00*
  a.   "I" before Gildi omitted   30,000.
  b.   Inverted overprint   825.00   *1,150.*
  c.   '03-'03   1,200.
  d.   02'-'03   1,200.
O28 O2 16a carmine   22.50   *90.00*
  a.   "I" before Gildi omitted   825.00
  b.   Double overprint   150.00
  c.   Dbl. ovpt., one inverted   525.00
  d.   Inverted overprint   240.00   *325.00*
  e.   '03-'03   900.00
  f.   02'-'03   900.00
O29 O2 20a yel green   37.50   *120.00*
  a.   Inverted overprint   225.00   *240.00*
  b.   '03-'03   600.00
  c.   02'-'03   600.00
O30 O2 50a red lilac   7.50   *75.00*
  a.   "I" before Gildi omitted   60.00   *135.00*
  b.   Inverted overprint   225.00
    Nos. O25-O30 (6)   1,028.   *3,285.*

Nos. O10-O12, O20-O24, O28 and O30 were reprinted in 1904. They have the watermark of 1902 (type 113) and are perf. 13. Value $70 each. Without overprint $90 each.

Christian IX,   Christian
Frederik   X — O5
VIII — O4

Engraved Center
1907-08 **Wmk. 113** **Perf. 13**
O31 O4 3a yellow & gray   9.50   *11.00*
O32 O4 4a green & gray   5.00   *11.50*
O33 O4 5a brn org & gray   15.00   *5.50*
O34 O4 10a deep bl & gray   3.25   *4.25*
O35 O4 15a lt blue & gray   6.50   *11.50*
O36 O4 16a carmine & gray   6.50   *40.00*
O37 O4 20a yel grn & gray   19.00   *7.50*
O38 O4 50a violet & gray   10.00   *14.00*
    Nos. O31-O38 (8)   74.75   *105.25*

1918 **Wmk. 114** **Perf. 14x14½**
O39 O4 15a lt bl & gray   18.00   *45.00*

1920-30 **Typo.**
O40 O5 3a yellow & gray   7.00   *4.75*
O41 O5 4a dp grn & gray   1.75   *4.50*
O42 O5 5a orange & gray   1.75   *1.50*
O43 O5 10a dk bl & gray   22.50   *1.75*
O44 O5 15a lt blue & gray   1.10   *1.50*
O45 O5 20a yel grn & gray   70.00   *5.50*
O46 O5 50a violet & gray   65.00   *2.75*
O47 O5 1k car & gray   65.00   *2.75*
O48 O5 2k bl & blk ('30)   11.00   *25.00*
O49 O5 5k brn & blk ('30)   57.50   *70.00*
    Nos. O40-O49 (10)   302.60   *120.00*

See No. O68.

Nos. 97 and 98 Overprinted

1922, May **Wmk. 113** **Perf. 13**
O50 A7 2k rose, larger let-
      ters, no period   37.50   *75.00*
  a.   Smaller letters, with period   120.00   *75.00*
O51 A7 5k brown   300.00   *335.00*

No. 115 Surcharged

1923   Wmk. 114   *Perf. 14x14½*
O52 A8 20a on 10a red   37.50 3.00

Parliament Millenary Issue

#152-166
Overprinted
in Red or
Blue

1930, Jan. 1   Unwmk.   *Perf. 12½x12*
O53 A15   3a (R)   18.00   52.50
O54 A15   5a (R)   18.00   52.50
O55 A15   7a (R)   18.00   52.50
O56 A15 10a (Bl)   18.00   52.50
O57 A15 15a (R)   18.00   52.50
O58 A15 20a (Bl)   18.00   52.50
O59 A15 25a (Bl)   18.00   52.50
O60 A15 30a (R)   18.00   52.50
O61 A15 35a (R)   18.00   52.50
O62 A15 40a (Bl)   18.00   52.50
O63 A15 50a (Bl)   170.00   440.00
O64 A15   1k (R)   170.00   440.00
O65 A15   2k (R)   225.00   470.00
O66 A15   5k (Bl)   225.00   470.00
O67 A15 10k (Bl)   170.00   440.00
     Nos. O53-O67 (15)   1,140.   2,785.

Type of 1920 Issue Redrawn
1931   Wmk. 114   Typo.
O68 O5 20a yel grn & gray   52.50 3.75

For differences in redrawing see note after
No. 187.

No. 82 Overprinted in
Black

Overprint 15mm long
1936, Dec. 7   Wmk. 113   *Perf. 13*
O69 A5 50a gray & vio   30.00 37.50
**Same Overprint on Nos. 180 and
115**
Perf. 14x14½
Wmk. 114
O70 A8   7a yellow green   3.75 32.50
O71 A8 10a red   15.00   2.75
     Nos. O69-O71 (3)   48.75 72.75

INDIA

'in-dē-ə

LOCATION — Southern, central Asia
GOVT. — Republic
AREA — 1,266,732 sq. mi.
POP. — 683,810,051 (1981)
CAPITAL — New Delhi

On August 15, 1947, India was divided into two self-governing dominions: Pakistan and India. India became a republic in 1950.

The stamps of pre-partition India fall into three groups:

1) Issues inscribed simply "East India" (to 1881) and "India" (from 1882), for use mainly in British India proper, but available and valid throughout the country;

2) Issues as above and overprinted with one of the names of the six "Convention" states (Chamba, Faridkot, Gwalior, Jind, Nabha and Patiala) which had a postal convention with British India, for use in these states.

3) Issues of the feudatory states, over which the British India government exercised little internal control, valid for use only within the states issuing them.

12 Pies = 1 Anna
16 Annas = 1 Rupee

Catalogue values for unused stamps in this country are for Never Hinged items, beginning with Scott 168 in the regular postage section, Scott 51 in Hyderabad regular issues, Scott O54 in Hyderabad officials, Scott 49 in Jaipur regular issues, Scott O30 in Jaipur officials, Scott 39 in Soruth regular issues and Scott O19 in Soruth official

All of the values are for Never Hinged for all of the items in the sections for Jasdan, Rajasthan, and Travancore-Cochin.

Watermarks

Wmk. 36 —
Crown and INDIA

Wmk. 37 — Coat of Arms in Sheet.
(Reduced illustration. Watermark covers a large section of the sheet.)

Wmk. 38 —
Elephant's Head

Wmk. 39 — Star

Wmk. 40

Wmk. 41 — Small Umbrella

Wmk. 42 — Urdu Characters

Wmk. 43 — Shell

Wmk. 43A — Shell

Wmk. 196 — Multiple Stars

Wmk. 211 — Urdu Characters

Wmk. 294 — Letters and Ornaments in Sheet (size reduced)

SCINDE DISTRICT POST

A1

				Imperf.
1852, July 1		**Embossed**		
A1	A1	½a white	12,000.	2,000.
		On cover		12,000.
A2	A1	½a blue	40,000.	8,000.
		On cover		22,500.
A3	A1	½a red	105,000.	26,000.
		On cover		

Obsolete October, 1854.

Nos. A1-A3 were issued without gum. No. A3 is embossed on red wafer. It is usually found with cracks and these examples are worth somewhat less than the values given, depending on the degree of cracking.

Two examples of No. 3 are known unused, three on cover or part of cover.

Covers: On cover values are for very fine examples. Average to fine examples sell for approximately 40% of the values given.

GENERAL ISSUES

Unused stamps of India are valued with original gum as defined in the catalogue introduction except for Nos. 1-7 which are valued without gum.

East India Company

A1

A2

A3

A4

A5

Queen Victoria
Litho.; Typo. (#5)

					Imperf.
1854			**Wmk. 37**		
1	A1	½a red	1,200.		
2	A2	½a blue	85.00		30.00
		On cover			100.00
		On cover, pair			250.00
a.		½a deep blue	95.00		35.00
b.		Printed on both sides			11,000.
4	A3	1a red	125.00		60.00
		On cover			200.00
		On cover, pair			500.00
a.		1a scarlet	175.00		70.00
5	A4	2a green	120.00		32.50
		On cover			240.00
		On cover, pair			600.00
a.		Half used as 1a on cover			200,000.
6	A5	4a red & blue	4,500.		500.00
		On cover			625.00
		On cover, pair			1,500.
a.		4a deep red & blue	4,500.		575.00
		Cut to shape			42.50
c.		Head inverted			225,000.
		As "c," cut to shape			165,000.
e.		Double impression of head			25,000.

No. 1 was not placed in use.

Nos. 2, 4, 5 and 6 are known with unofficial perforation.

There are 3 dies of No. 2, and 2 dies of No. 4, showing slight differences.

There are 4 dies of the head and 2 dies of the frame of No. 6.

No. 5 is known with the watermark having the words "One Anna" in place of the lions and shield, with Urdu and Bengali characters. Values: $625 unused; $450 used.

Beware of forgeries.

A6

1855				
7	A6	1a red	1,300.	175.00
		On cover		525.00

No. 7 was printed from a lithographic transfer made from the original die retouched. The lines of the bust at the lower left are nearly straight and meet in a point.

Beware of forgeries.

Nos. 9-35 are normally found with very heavy cancellations, and values are for stamps so canceled. Lightly canceled stamps are seldom seen. The same holds true for Nos. O1-O26.

Diadem includes
Maltese Crosses — A7

1855-64 Unwmk. Typo. Perf. 14
Blue Glazed Paper

9	A7	4a black	725.00	22.50
		On cover		125.00
a.		Imperf., pair	5,500.	5,500.
		Half used as 2a on cover		12,000.
10	A7	8a rose	650.00	19.00
		On cover		175.00
a.		Imperf., pair	3,000.	
b.		Half used as 4a on cover		80,000.

See Nos. 11-18, 20, 22-25, 31. For overprints see Nos. O1-O5, O7-O9, O16-O19, O22-O24.

1855-64 **White Paper**

11	A7	½a blue	95.00	4.50
a.		Imperf., pair	475.00	1,750.
12	A7	1a brown	80.00	3.00
a.		Imperf., pair	800.00	2,200.
b.		Vert. pair, imperf between		
c.		Half used as ½a on cover		85,000.
13	A7	2a dull rose	750.00	37.50
a.		Imperf., pair	2,500.	2,000.
14	A7	2a yellow green	725.00	825.00
a.		Imperf., pair	2,000.	
15	A7	2a buff	450.00	37.50
a.		2a orange	700.00	45.00
b.		Imperf., pair	1,750.	3,250.
16	A7	4a black	450.00	10.00
a.		Imperf., pair	2,750.	2,750.
b.		Diagonal half used as 2a on cover		35,000.
17	A7	4a green ('64)	1,750.	45.00
18	A7	4a rose	600.00	27.50
		Half used as 4a on cover		80,000.

No. 14 was not regularly issued. See note after No. 25.

Many stamps of types A7-A90 are overprinted "Service" or "On H. M. S." For these, see listings of Official stamps.

Crown Colony

Queen Victoria — A8

1860-64 Unwmk. Perf. 14

19	A8	8p lilac	55.00	6.00
a.		Diagonal half used as 4p on cover		85,000.
b.		Imperf., pair	4,000.	5,000.
19C	A8	8p lilac, bluish	275.00	100.00

See No. 21. For overprint see No. O6 and footnote after No. O4.

1865-67 Wmk. 38

20	A7	½a blue	19.00	1.25
a.		Imperf., pair		1,600.
21	A8	8p lilac	10.00	12.00
22	A7	1a brown	9.00	1.50
23	A7	2a brownish orange	27.50	2.00
a.		2a yellow	175.00	7.00
b.		Imperf., pair		4,250.
24	A7	4a green	575.00	27.50
25	A7	8a rose	2,000.	85.00

No. 21 was variously surcharged locally, "NINE" or "NINE PIE," to indicate that it was being sold for 9 pies (the soldier's letter rate had been raised from 8 to 9 pies). These surcharges were made without government authorization.

Stamps of types A7 and A9 overprinted with crown and surcharged with new values were for use in Straits Settlements.

A9

A10

Diadem: Rows of pearls & diamonds — A11

FOUR ANNAS
Type I — Slanting line at corner of mouth extends downward only. Shading about mouth and chin. Pointed chin.
Type II — Line at corner of mouth extends both up and down. Upper lip and chin are defined by a colored line. Rounded chin.

1866-68

26	A9	4a green, type I	95.00	4.25
26B	A9	4a blue grn, type II	30.00	3.50
27	A10	6a8p slate	70.00	27.50
a.		Imperf., pair	3,000.	
28	A11	8a rose ('68)	45.00	7.00
		Nos. 26-28 (4)	240.00	42.25

Type A11 is a redrawing of type A7. Type A7 has Maltese crosses in the diadem, while type A11 has shaded lozenges.
For overprints see Nos. O10, O20-O21, O25-O26.

For designs A9-A85 overprinted CHAMBA, FARIDKOT, GWALIOR, JIND (JHIND, JEEND), NABHA, PATIALA (PUTTIALLA), see the various Convention States.

A12

SIX ANNAS
Type I — "POSTAGE" 3½mm high
Type II — "POSTAGE" 2½mm high

Blue Glazed Paper
Green Overprint
Perf. 14 Vert.

1866, June 28 Wmk. 36

29	A12	6a violet, type I	1,000.	140.00
		On cover		700.
a.		Inverted overprint		14,000.
30	A12	6a violet, type II	1,850.	175.00
		On cover		1,000.

Nos. 29 and 30 were made from revenue stamps with the labels at top and bottom cut off. Most and sometimes all of the watermark was removed with the labels. Twenty different varieties of this overprint exist.
These stamps are often found with cracked surface or scuffs. Such examples sell for somewhat less.

A13

A14

A15

A16

1873-76 Wmk. 38 Perf. 14

31	A7	½a blue, redrawn	7.50	1.00
32	A13	9p lilac ('74)	19.00	19.00
33	A14	6a bister ('76)	8.50	2.50
34	A15	12a red brown ('76)	12.00	27.50
35	A16	1r slate ('74)	65.00	30.00
		Nos. 31-35 (5)	112.00	80.00

In the redrawn ½ anna the lines of the mouth are more deeply cut, making the lips appear fuller and more open, and the nostril is defined by a curved line.

Victorian and Edwardian stamps overprinted "Postal Service" and new denominations were customs fee due stamps, not postage stamps.

Empire

A17 A18

A19 A20

A21 A22

A23 A24

A25 A26

A27

1882-87 Wmk. 39

36	A17	½a green	4.50	.25
a.		Double impression	750.00	1,000.
37	A18	9p rose	1.10	2.25
38	A19	1a maroon	5.25	.35
a.		1a violet brown	5.25	.35
39	A20	1a6p bister brown	1.10	1.40
40	A21	2a ultra	4.00	.35
a.		Double impression	1,050.	1,400.
41	A22	3a brown org	9.50	1.75
a.		3a orange	14.00	6.25
42	A23	4a olive green	15.00	1.60
43	A24	4a6p green	30.00	5.50
44	A25	8a red violet	27.50	2.25
a.		8a rose lilac	25.00	2.25
45	A26	12a violet, red	8.00	3.50
46	A27	1r gray	27.50	6.00
		Nos. 36-46 (11)	133.45	25.20

A 6a die essay was prepared, but no stamps were printed.
A postal counterfeit exists of No. 46. Examples are scarce.
No. 40a used value is for copy with postal cancellation.
See Nos. 56-58. For surcharges see Nos. 47, 53 and British East Africa No. 59. For overprints see Nos. M2-M4, M6-M9, Gwalior Nos. O1-O5.

Beginning with the 1882-87 issue, higher denomination stamps exist used for telegrams. The telegraph cancellation has concentric circles. These sell for 10-15% of the postally used values.

No. 43 Surcharged

2½ As.

1891, Jan. 1

47	A24	2½a on 4a6p green	4.00	.65

A28 A29

1892

48	A28	2a6p green	3.25	.45
49	A29	1r aniline car & grn	17.50	2.25
a.		1r carmine rose & green	20.00	5.00

See No. 59. For overprints see Nos. M5, M10 and Gwalior No. O6.

Queen Victoria
A30 A31

1895, Sept. 1

50	A30	2r yel brn & rose	42.50	10.00
a.		Brn & rose	50.00	10.00
51	A30	3r green & brown	37.50	11.00
52	A30	5r violet & ultra	47.50	30.00
		Nos. 50-52 (3)	127.50	51.00

Used high values such as Nos. 50-52, 71-76, 95-98, 124-125, as well as similar high value official issues are for postally used examples. Stamps bearing telegraph or revenue cancellations sell for much lower prices. Most telegraph cancellations on issues of Edward VII and George V can be recognized by the appearance of "T," "TEL" or "GTO" or if they contain the concentric circles of a target.

No. 36 Surcharged

1/4

1898

53	A17	¼a on ½a green	.25	.55
a.		Double surcharge	250.00	
b.		Double impression of stamp	260.00	

For Nos. 61, 81 with this overprint see Nos. 77, 105.

1899

54	A31	3p carmine rose	.45	.25

For overprint see No. M1, Gwalior No. O11.

1900

55	A31	3p gray	.80	1.40
56	A17	½a light green	1.75	.50
57	A19	1a carmine rose	2.50	.25
58	A21	2a violet	4.50	2.50
59	A28	2a6p ultramarine	3.75	4.25
		Nos. 55-59 (5)	13.30	8.90

For overprints see Nos. M11, Gwalior O7-O10.

Edward
VII — A32 A33

A34

A35

A36

A37

A38

A39

A40

A41

A42

A43

1902-09

60	A32	3p gray	1.10	.25
61	A33	½a green	1.75	.25
a.		Booklet pane of 6 ('04)	32.50	
62	A34	1a carmine rose	1.60	.25
a.		Booklet pane of 6 ('04)	92.50	
63	A35	2a violet	4.25	.45
64	A36	2a6p ultra	5.00	.65
65	A37	3a brown org	5.00	.65
66	A38	4a olive green	3.25	.65
67	A39	6a bister	12.50	4.75
68	A40	8a red violet	8.75	1.10
69	A41	12a violet, *red*	9.50	2.25
70	A42	1r car rose & grn	6.75	.75
a.		1r rose & green ('11)	40.00	4.50
71	A43	2r brown & rose	47.50	4.50
72	A43	3r green & brn ('04)	30.00	20.00
73	A43	5r violet & ultra ('04)	72.50	40.00
74	A43	10r carmine rose & green ('09)	125.00	30.00
75	A43	15r olive gray & ultra ('09)	175.00	45.00
76	A43	25r ultra & org brown	925.00	925.00
		Never hinged	1,800.	
		Telegraph cancel		300.00
		Nos. 60-75 (16)	509.45	151.50

For overprints see Nos. M12-M20, Gwalior Nos. O12-O18.

No. 61 Surcharged Like No. 53

1905

77	A33	¼a on ½a green	.60	.25
a.		Inverted surcharge	925.00	

A44

A45

1906

78	A44	½a green	3.25	.25
a.		Booklet pane of 4	17.50	
79	A45	1a carmine rose	1.90	.25
a.		Booklet pane of 4	25.00	

For overprints see Nos. O45-O46, Gwalior Nos. O19-O20.

A46

A47

A48

A49

A50

A51

A52

A53

A54

A55

George V — A56

1911-23   **Wmk. 39**

80	A46	3p gray	1.50	.25
a.		Booklet pane of 4	25.00	
81	A47	½a green	2.25	.25
a.		Double impression	175.00	
b.		Booklet pane of 4	21.00	
82	A48	1a carmine rose	2.75	.25
a.		Printed on both sides		
b.		Booklet pane of 4	35.00	
83	A48	1a dk brown ('22)	.85	.25
a.		Booklet pane of 4	42.50	

84	A49	2a dull violet	3.50	.40
a.		Booklet pane of 4	42.50	
85	A50	2a6p ultramarine	2.90	3.25
86	A51	3a brown org	4.25	.25
87	A51	3a ultra ('23)	13.00	.65
88	A52	4a olive green	8.00	.55
89	A53	6a yel bister	4.25	1.50
90	A53	6a bister ('15)	4.25	1.10
91	A54	8a red violet	6.25	1.25
92	A55	12a claret	6.50	2.40
93	A56	1r grn & red brn	19.00	1.75
94	A56	2r brn & car rose	22.50	1.90
95	A56	5r vio & ultra	55.00	7.00
96	A56	10r car rose & grn	82.50	13.00
97	A56	15r ol grn & ultra	115.00	26.00
98	A56	25r ultra & brn org	190.00	37.50
		Nos. 80-98 (19)	544.25	99.50

See Nos. 106-125. For type surcharged see No. 104. For overprints see Nos. M23-M25, M27, M29-M37, M39-M43, Gwalior No. O29. Nos. 93-98 also were used to pay for radio licenses, and stamps so used include "WIRE-LESS" in the cancel. Used values so canceled are worth 10-15% of the values shown, which are for postally used examples.

A57

1913-26

99	A57	2a6p ultramarine	2.90	.25
100	A57	2a6p brown org ('26)	6.00	6.00

See No. 112. For overprints see Nos. M28, M38.

"One and Half" — A58　　　"One and a Half" — A59

1919

101	A58	1½a chocolate	3.75	.45
a.		Booklet pane of 4	35.00	

For overprint and surcharge see Nos. M26, O75.

1921-26

102	A59	1½a chocolate	3.50	4.75
103	A59	1½a rose ('26)	3.25	.35

See No. 109. For surcharge see No. O76.

Type of 1911-26 Surcharged

1921

104	A48	9p on 1a rose	.90	.35
a.		Surcharged "NINE-NINE"	80.00	150.00
b.		Surcharged "PIES-PIES"	80.00	150.00
c.		Double surcharge	175.00	210.00
e.		Booklet pane of 4	27.50	

Forgeries exist of Nos. 104a-104c.

No. 81 Surcharged Like No. 53
1922

105	A47	¼a on ½a green	.60	.40
a.		Inverted surcharge	10.00	
b.		Pair, one without surcharge	240.00	

Types of 1911-26 Issues
1926-36　　　　　　　　Wmk. 196

106	A46	3p slate	.35	.25
107	A47	½a green	1.40	.25
108	A48	1a dark brown	.55	.25
a.		Tete beche pair	1.50	11.00
b.		Booklet pane of 4	16.00	
109	A59	1½a car rose ('29)	3.50	.25
110	A49	2a dull violet	2.00	.25
a.		Booklet pane of 4	32.50	
111	A49	2a ver ('34)	4.00	.55
a.		Small die ('36)	5.00	.35
112	A57	2a6p buff	2.50	
113	A51	3a ultramarine	11.50	1.25
114	A51	3a blue ('30)	10.00	.25
115	A51	3a car rose ('32)	9.75	.25

116	A52	4a olive green	1.60	.25
117	A53	6a bister ('35)	9.50	2.00
118	A54	8a red violet	4.25	.25
119	A55	12a claret	5.25	.35
120	A56	1r green & brown	5.50	.50
121	A56	2r brn org & car rose	15.00	.85
122	A56	5r dk vio & ultra	30.00	1.40
123	A56	10r carmine & grn	62.50	3.50
124	A56	15r ol grn & ultra	28.00	32.50
125	A56	25r blue & ocher	115.00	40.00
		Nos. 106-125 (20)	322.15	85.40

No. 111 measures 19x22½mm, while the small die, No. 111a, measures 18½x22mm. For overprints see Gwalior Nos. O30-O39, O44-O45.

A60　　　　　　　　　　A61

1926-32　　　　　　　　　　Typo.

126	A60	2a dull violet	.55	.25
a.		Tete beche pair	10.00	37.50
b.		2a rose violet	.45	.25
c.		Booklet pane of 4	19.00	
127	A60	2a vermilion ('32)	11.00	7.00
128	A61	4a olive green	6.25	.25
		Nos. 126-128 (3)	17.80	7.50

For overprints see Gwalior Nos. O33-O34.

Fortress of Purana Qila — A62

George V Flanked by Dominion Columns A67

½a, War Memorial Arch. 1a, Council Building. 2a, Viceroy's House. 3a, Parliament Building.

Wmk. 196 Sideways
1931, Feb. 9　Litho.　Perf. 13½x14

129	A62	¼a brown & ol grn	3.00	4.50
130	A62	½a green & violet	1.75	.60
131	A62	1a choc & red vio	1.75	.30
132	A62	2a blue & green	2.25	1.50
133	A62	3a car & choc	5.25	3.00
134	A67	1r violet & green	13.50	30.00
		Nos. 129-134 (6)	27.50	39.90
		Set, never hinged	66.00	

Change of the seat of Government from Calcutta to New Delhi.

A68　　　　　　　　　　A69

A70

Wmk. 196
1932, Apr. 22　Litho.　Perf. 14

135	A68	9p dark green	1.90	.25
136	A69	1a3p violet	.95	.25
137	A70	3a6p deep blue	4.75	.25
		Nos. 135-137 (3)	7.60	.75

No. 135 exists both litho. and typo. For overprints see Nos. O94, O96, O104 and Gwalior Nos. O41 and O43.

A71　　　　　　　　　　A72

1934　　　　　　　　　　Typo.

138	A71	½a green	5.75	.25
139	A72	1a dark brown	4.00	.25

For overprints see Nos. O93, O95 and Gwalior Nos. O40 and O42.

Silver Jubilee Issue

Gateway of India, Bombay A73

Designs: 9p, Victoria Memorial, Calcutta. 1a, Rameswaram Temple, Madras. 1¼a, Jain Temple, Calcutta. 2½a, Taj Mahal, Agra. 3½a, Golden Temple, Amritsar. 8a, Pagoda, Mandalay.

Wmk. 196 Sideways
1935　Litho.　Perf. 13½x14

142	A73	½a lt green & black	1.50	.55
143	A73	9p dull green & blk	1.50	.55
144	A73	1a brown & black	2.25	.55
145	A73	1¼a violet & black	1.00	.55
146	A73	2½a brown org & blk	3.25	1.10
147	A73	3½a blue & black	6.50	2.50
148	A73	8a rose lilac & blk	7.25	6.00
		Nos. 142-148 (7)	23.25	11.80
		Set, never hinged	50.00	

25th anniv. of the reign of George V.

King George VI
A80　　　　　　　　　　A82

Dak Runner A81

Mail transport: 2a6p, Dak bullock cart. 3a, Dak tonga. 3a6p, Dak camel. 4a, Mail train. 6a, Mail steamer. 8a, Mail truck. 12a, 14a, Mail plane.

Perf. 13½x14 or 14x13½
1937-40　Typo.　Wmk. 196

150	A80	3p slate	.40	.25
151	A80	½a brown	1.10	.25
152	A80	9p green	3.00	.30
153	A80	1a carmine	.35	.25
a.		Tete beche pair	3.50	2.10
b.		Booklet pane of 4	5.25	
154	A81	2a scarlet	2.10	.35
155	A81	2a6p purple	.65	.30
156	A81	3a yellow green	3.75	.35
157	A81	3a6p ultramarine	2.50	.60
158	A81	4a dark brown	10.00	.30
159	A81	6a peacock blue	10.00	.95
160	A81	8a blue violet	6.00	.60
161	A81	12a car lake	13.00	1.25
161A	A81	14a rose vio ('40)	15.00	1.50
162	A82	1r brown & slate	.90	.25
163	A82	2r dk brn & dk violet	3.25	.40
164	A82	5r dp ultra & dk green	14.00	.70
165	A82	10r rose car & dk violet	14.00	1.10
166	A82	15r dk green & dk brown	70.00	90.00
167	A82	25r dk vio & blue violet	100.00	24.00
		Nos. 150-167 (19)	270.00	123.70
		Set, never hinged	580.00	

The King's portrait is larger on No. 161A than on other stamps of type A81.

For overprints see Nos. O97-O103, Gwalior Nos. O48-O51.

A83　　　　　　　　　　A84

A85

Perf. 13½x14
1941-43　Typo.　Wmk. 196

168	A83	3p slate ('42)	1.00	.25
169	A83	½a rose vio ('42)	3.50	.25
170	A83	9p light green	3.50	.25
171	A83	1a car rose ('43)	3.50	.25
172	A84	1a3p bister	3.50	.25
172A	A84	1½a dark pur ('42)	4.00	.25
173	A84	2a scarlet	5.00	.25
174	A84	3a violet	10.00	.25
175	A84	3½a ultramarine	3.50	.65
176	A85	4a chocolate	2.50	.25
177	A85	6a peacock blue	11.50	.25
178	A85	8a blue violet	5.00	.65
179	A85	12a carmine lake	10.50	1.10
		Nos. 168-179 (13)	67.00	4.90

Early printings of the 1½a and 3a were lithographed. For surcharge see No. 199.

For stamps with this overprint, or a smaller type, see Oman (Muscat).

Symbols of Victory A86

1946, Jan. 2　Litho.　Perf. 13

195	A86	9p green	.80	1.10
196	A86	1½a dull purple	.45	.40
197	A86	3½a ultramarine	1.00	1.00
198	A86	12a brown lake	2.50	1.10
		Nos. 195-198 (4)	4.75	3.60

Victory of the Allied Nations in WWII.

No. 172 Surcharged With New Value and Bars
1946, Aug. 8　Perf. 13½x14

199	A84	3p on 1a3p bister	.35	.25

Dominion of India

Asoka Pillar — A87

National Flag A88

Four-Motor Plane A89

Perf. 14x13½, 13½x14

1947 **Litho.** **Wmk. 196**
200	A87	1½a greenish gray	1.50	.45
201	A88	3½a multicolored	4.50	4.75
202	A89	12a ultramarine	6.00	4.75
		Nos. 200-202 (3)	12.00	9.95

Elevation to dominion status, Aug. 15, 1947.

Mahatma Gandhi — A90

Design: 10r, Gandhi profile.

Perf. 11½

1948, Aug. 15 **Unwmk.** **Photo.**
Size: 22x32½mm
203	A90	1½a brown	8.25	1.25
204	A90	3½a violet	18.00	5.00
205	A90	12a dark gray green	21.00	3.00

Size: 22x37mm
206	A90	10r rose brn & brn	260.00	95.00
		Nos. 203-206 (4)	307.25	104.25

Mohandas K. Gandhi, 1869-1948.
For overprints see Nos. O112A-O112D.

Ajanta Panel — A91

Konarak Horse — A92

Bodhisattva A93

Tomb of Muhammad Adil Shah, Bijapur A95

Sanchi Stupa A94

Victory Tower, Chittorgarh A96

Red Fort, Delhi A97

Satrunjaya Temple, Palitana A98

9p, Trimurti. 2a, Nataraja. 3½a, Bodh Gaya Temple. 4a, Bhuvanesvara. 8a, Kandarya Mahadeva Temple. 12a, Golden Temple, Amritsar. 5r, Taj Mahal. 10r, Qutb Minar.

Perf. 13½x14, 14x13½

1949, Aug. 15 **Typo.** **Wmk. 196**
207	A91	3p gray violet	.30	.25
208	A92	6p red brown	.35	.25
209	A93	9p green	.60	.25
210	A93	1a turquoise	.85	.25
211	A93	2a carmine	1.25	.25
212	A94	3a red orange	3.00	.25
213	A94	3½a ultramarine	2.50	5.00
214	A94	4a brown lake	6.00	.35
215	A95	6a purple	2.75	.90
216	A95	8a blue green	2.25	.25
217	A95	12a blue	3.00	.35

Litho.
218	A96	1r dk green & pur	22.50	.25
219	A97	2r pur & rose red	20.00	.50
220	A97	5r brn car & dk grn	45.00	2.00
221	A96	10r dp bl & brn car	80.00	12.00

Perf. 13½x13
222	A98	15r dp car & dk brn	32.50	35.00
		Nos. 207-222 (16)	222.85	58.10

See Nos. 231, 235-236. For overprints see Nos. M44-M46, M48-M55 and Intl. Commission in Indo-china issues for Cambodia, Nos. 1, 3-5, Laos Nos. 1, 3-5 and Vietnam Nos. 1, 3-5.

Symbols of UPU and Asoka Pillar — A99

1949, Oct. **Litho.** **Perf. 13½x13**
223	A99	9p dull green	2.75	1.75
224	A99	2a carmine rose	2.75	1.75
225	A99	3½a ultramarine	6.00	3.00
226	A99	12a red brown	24.00	4.00
		Nos. 223-226 (4)	35.50	10.50

75th anniv. of the formation of the UPU.

AIR POST STAMPS

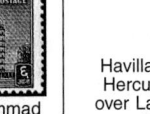

De Havilland Hercules over Lake AP1

Wmk. 196 Sideways

1929-30 **Typo.** **Perf. 14**
C1	AP1	2a dull green	1.00	.50
C2	AP1	3a deep blue	1.40	.90
C3	AP1	4a gray olive	4.00	1.90
a.		4a olive green ('30)	5.00	1.90
C4	AP1	6a bister	5.00	1.10
C5	AP1	8a red violet	5.75	5.75
C6	AP1	12a brown red	17.50	17.50
		Nos. C1-C6 (6)	34.65	27.65
		Set, never hinged	60.00	

Catalogue values for unused stamps in this section, from this point to the end of the section, are for Never Hinged items.

Dominion of India

Lockheed Constellation — AP2

Perf. 13½x14

1948, May 29 **Litho.** **Wmk. 196**
C7	AP2	12a ultra & slate blk	3.25	3.25

Bombay-London flight of June 8, 1948.

MILITARY STAMPS

China Expeditionary Force

Regular Issues of India, 1882-99, Overprinted

C. E. F.

1900 **Wmk. 39** **Perf. 14**
M1	A31	3p carmine rose	.70	2.10
M2	A17	½a dark green	1.25	.45
M3	A19	1a maroon	7.00	2.50
M4	A21	2a ultra	5.25	15.00
M5	A28	2a6p green	4.75	21.00
M6	A22	3a orange	4.75	27.50
M7	A23	4a olive green	4.75	13.00
M8	A25	8a red violet	4.75	30.00
M9	A26	12a violet, red	30.00	30.00
M10	A29	1r car rose & grn	37.50	37.50
a.		Double overprint		
		Nos. M1-M10 (10)	100.70	179.05

The 1a6p of this set was overprinted, but not issued. Value $250.

Overprinted on 1900 Issue of India

1904, Feb. 27
M11	A19	1a carmine rose	55.00	15.00

Overprinted on 1902-09 Issue of India

1904
M12	A32	3p gray	8.00	10.00
M13	A34	1a carmine rose	12.00	1.10
M14	A35	2a violet	22.50	3.75
M15	A36	2a6p ultra	5.25	8.00
M16	A37	3a brown org	5.75	6.50
M17	A38	4a olive green	13.50	19.00
M18	A40	8a red violet	13.00	12.00
M19	A41	12a violet, red	18.00	30.00
M20	A42	1r car rose & grn	20.00	45.00
		Nos. M12-M20 (9)	118.00	135.35

Overprinted on 1906 Issue of India

1909
M21	A44	½a green	1.50	1.00
M22	A45	1a carmine rose	1.50	.40

Overprinted on 1911-19 Issues of India

1913-21
M23	A46	3p gray	8.00	35.00
M24	A47	½a green	6.25	7.50
M25	A48	1a carmine rose	7.25	4.75
M26	A58	1½a chocolate	40.00	95.00
M27	A49	2a violet	27.50	80.00
M28	A57	2a6p ultra	20.00	30.00
M29	A51	3a brown org	40.00	240.00
M30	A52	4a olive green	37.50	210.00
M31	A54	8a red violet	40.00	400.00
M32	A55	12a claret	37.50	140.00
M33	A56	1r grn & red brn	110.00	375.00
		Nos. M23-M33 (11)	374.00	1,617.

Issue dates: No. M23, 1913; others, 1921.

Indian Expeditionary Force

Regular Issues of India, 1911-13, Overprinted

I. E. F.

1914 **Wmk. 39** **Perf. 14**
M34	A46	3p gray	.30	.55
a.		Double overprint	70.00	55.00
M35	A47	½a green	.80	.55
a.		Double overprint	175.00	300.00
M36	A48	1a carmine rose	2.10	.55
M37	A49	2a violet	2.10	.55
M38	A57	2a6p ultra	2.50	4.00
M39	A51	3a brown org	1.75	2.75
M40	A52	4a olive green	1.75	2.75
M41	A54	8a red violet	2.10	4.25
M42	A55	12a claret	3.75	10.50
a.		Double overprint, one albino	65.00	
M43	A56	1r grn & red brn	4.50	7.25
a.		Double overprint, one albino	115.00	
		Nos. M34-M43 (10)	21.65	33.70

OFFICIAL STAMPS

Nos. O1-O26 are normally found with very heavy cancellations, and values are for stamps so canceled. Lightly canceled stamps are seldom seen.

Regular Issues Overprinted in Black

Service.

1866, Aug. 1 **Unwmk.** **Perf. 14**
O1	A7	½a blue	1,100.	140.00
a.		Inverted overprint		
O3	A7	1a brown		140.00
O4	A7	8a rose	22.50	50.00

The 8p lilac unwatermarked (No. 19) with "Service" overprint was not officially issued.

Wmk. 38
O5	A7	½a blue	300.00	12.50
a.		Inverted overprint		
b.		Without period		210.00
O6	A8	8p lilac	20.00	52.50
O7	A7	1a brown	300.00	15.00
a.		Inverted overprint		
O8	A7	2a yellow	300.00	85.00
a.		Imperf.		
b.		Inverted overprint		
O9	A7	4a green	200.00	80.00
a.		Inverted overprint		
O10	A9	4a green (I)	1,000.	250.00

Reprints were made of Nos. O5, O7, O10 (type II).

Revenue Stamps Surcharged or Overprinted

Queen Victoria — O1

Blue Glazed Paper Black Surcharge

1866 **Wmk. 36** **Perf. 14 Vertically**
O11	O1	2a violet	350.00	250.00

The note after No. 30 will apply here also.

No. O11 is often found with cracked surface or scuffs. Such examples sell for somewhat less.

Reprints of No. O11 are surcharged in either black or green, and have the word "SERVICE" 16½x2½mm, instead of 16½x2¾mm and "TWO ANNAS" 18x3mm, instead of 20x3¼mm.

O2   O3

O4

1866   Green Overprint
O12	O2	2a violet	1,000. 325.
O13	O3	4a violet	4,500. 1,250.
O14	O4	8a violet	5,000. 5,000.

The note after No. 30 will apply here also.

These stamps are often found with cracked surface or scuffs. Such examples sell for somewhat less.

Reprints of No. O12 have the overprint in sans-serif letters 2¼mm high, instead of Roman letters 2½mm high. On the reprints of No. O13 "SERVICE" measures 16½x2¼mm, instead of 20¼x3mm and "POSTAGE" 18x2¼mm, instead of 22x3mm.

On No. O14 "SERVICE" is 20½mm long, instead of 20mm and "POSTAGE" is 23mm long, instead of 22mm. All three overprints are in a darker green than on the original stamps.

O5

Green Overprint
1866   Wmk. 40   Perf. 15½x15
Lilac Paper
O15	O5	½a violet	425.00 85.00
a.		Double overprint	3,000.

Regular Issues Overprinted in Black

Service.

1866-73   Wmk. 38   Perf. 14
O16	A7	½a blue	30.00 .35
O17	A7	½a bl, re-engraved	140.00 67.50
a.		Double overprint	
O18	A7	1a brown	32.50 .40
O19	A7	2a orange	4.50 2.00
a.		2a yellow	20.00 2.25
O20	A9	4a green (I)	2.75 1.50
O21	A11	8a rose	4.25 1.50
		Nos. O16-O21 (6)	212.75 73.25

The 6a8p with this overprint was not issued. Value $25.

On H.M.S.

Overprinted in Black

1874-82
O22	A7	½a blue, re-engraved	8.00 .25
a.		Blue overprint	350.00 45.00
O23	A7	1a brown	12.50 .25
a.		Blue overprint	550.00 120.00
O24	A7	2a orange	40.00 17.50
O25	A9	4a green (I)	12.50 2.75
O26	A11	8a rose	4.25 4.00
		Nos. O22-O26 (5)	77.25 24.75

Same Overprint on Nos. 36, 38, 40, 42, 44, 49
1883-97   Wmk. 39
O27	A17	½a green	.40 .25
a.		Pair, one without overprint	
b.		Double overprint	1,150.
O28	A19	1a maroon	.75 .25
a.		Inverted overprint	350.00 475.00
b.		Double overprint	1,150.
c.		1a violet brown	2.25 .35
O29	A21	2a ultramarine	4.50 .50
O30	A23	4a olive green	15.00 .40
O31	A25	8a red violet	7.00 .40
O32	A29	1r car rose & grn	11.00 .40
		Nos. O27-O32 (6)	38.65 2.20

Same Overprint on No. 54
1899
O33	A31	3p carmine rose	.25 .25

Same Overprint on Nos. 56-58
1900
O34	A17	½a light green	1.25 .30
O35	A19	1a carmine rose	2.50 .25
a.		Double overprint	1,350.
b.		Inverted overprint	1,400.
O36	A21	2a violet	27.50 .50
		Nos. O34-O36 (3)	31.25 1.05

Same Overprint on Nos. 60-63, 66-68, 70
1902-09
O37	A32	3p gray	.85 .25
O38	A33	½a green	1.00 .25
O39	A34	1a carmine rose	.85 .25
O40	A35	2a violet	2.50 .25
O41	A38	4a olive green	4.25 .25
O42	A39	6a bister	2.25 .25
O43	A40	8a red lilac	5.25 .50
O44	A42	1r car rose & green ('05)	4.50 .25
		Nos. O37-O44 (8)	21.45 2.25

Same Overprint on Nos. 78-79
1906-07
O45	A44	½a green	1.00 .25
O46	A45	1a carmine rose	1.75 .25
a.		Pair, one without overprint	—
b.		Overprint on back	

Same Overprint on Nos. 71, 73-76
1909
O47	A43	2r brown & rose	*6.50* .90
O48	A43	5r violet & ultra	*11.00* 1.00
O49	A43	10r car rose & grn	*21.00* 8.50
a.		10r red & green	*52.50* 6.00
O50	A43	15r ol gray & ultra	*52.50* 30.00
O51	A43	25r ultra & org brn	130.00 50.00
		Nos. O47-O51 (5)	221.00 90.40

For surcharges see Nos. O67-O69.

Regular Issues Overprinted in Black

SERVICE

1912-22
O52	A46	3p gray	.25 .25
O53	A47	½a green	.25 .25
a.		Double overprint	110.00
O54	A48	1a carmine rose	.75 .25
a.		Double overprint	950.00
O55	A48	1a dark brown ('22)	1.00 .25
a.		Imperf., pair	75.00
O56	A49	2a violet	.50 .25
O57	A52	4a olive green	.75 .25
O58	A53	6a bister	1.25 *1.75*
O59	A54	8a red violet	1.75 .75

Overprinted in Black

SERVICE

O60	A56	1r green & red brn	2.00 .80
O61	A56	2r yel brn & car rose	2.50 *3.50*
O62	A56	5r violet & ultra	10.50 *13.50*
O63	A56	10r car rose & grn	35.00 32.50
O64	A56	15r ol grn & ultra	80.00 *95.00*
O65	A56	25r ultra & brn org	180.00 150.00
		Nos. O52-O65 (14)	316.50 299.30

For surcharge see No. O69b.

O6

1921   Black Surcharge
O66	O6	9p on 1a rose	.75 .60

For overprint see Gwalior No. O28.

Official Stamps of 1909 Surcharged

1925
O67	A43	1r on 15r ol gray & ultra	4.00 3.00
O68	A43	1r on 25r ultra & org brn	20.00 *60.00*
O69	A43	2r on 10r red & grn	3.50 3.50
a.		2r on 10r car rose & green	210.00 55.00
b.		Surcharge on #O63 (error)	800.00

Official Stamps of 1912-13 Surcharged

O70	A56	1r on 15r ol grn & ultra	19.00 *65.00*
a.		Inverted surcharge	
O71	A56	1r on 25r ultra & brn org	5.00 *9.00*
a.		Inverted surcharge	600.00
		Nos. O67-O71 (5)	51.50 *140.50*

O7

1926   Black Surcharge
O73	O7	1a on 6a bister	.40 .40

Regular Issues of 1911-26 Surcharged

O74	A48	1a on 1a dk brn (error)	180.00 180.00
O75	A58	1a on 1½a choc	.25 .25
O76	A59	1a on 1½a choc	1.75 *4.00*
b.		Double surcharge	30.00
O77	A57	1a on 2a6p ultra	.50 .50
		Nos. O73-O77 (5)	182.90 185.15

Nos. O74, O75 and O76 have short bars over the numerals in the upper corners.

Regular Issues of 1926-35 Overprinted

SERVICE

1926-35   Wmk. 196
O78	A46	3p slate ('29)	.25 .25
O79	A47	½a green ('31)	5.00 .40
O80	A48	1a dark brown	.25 .25
a.		Overprint as on No. O55	100.00 4.75
O81	A49	2a vermilion ('35)	1.00 1.00
a.		Small die	.85 .25
O82	A60	2a dull violet	.25 .25
O83	A60	2a vermilion ('32)	.90 2.00
O84	A57	2a6p buff ('32)	.25 .25
O85	A52	4a olive green ('35)	1.00 .25
O86	A61	4a olive green	.35 .25
O87	A53	6a bister ('35)	18.00 9.00
O88	A54	8a red violet	.50 .25
O89	A55	12a claret	.50 *1.75*

Nos. 120-121, 123 Overprinted

SERVICE

O90	A56	1r green & brn ('30)	2.25 .90
O91	A56	2r brn org & car rose ('30)	6.00 6.00

O92	A56	10r car & green ('31)	70.00 50.00
		Nos. O78-O92 (15)	106.50 72.80

Regular Issues of 1932-34 Overprinted Type "a"
1932-35
O93	A71	½a green ('35)	.60 .25
O94	A68	9p dark green	.25 .25
O95	A72	1a dark brown ('35)	1.90 .25
O96	A69	1a3p violet	.25 .25
		Nos. O93-O96 (4)	3.00 1.00

Regular Issue of 1937 Overprinted Type "a"
1937-39   Perf. 13½x14
O97	A80	½a brown ('38)	22.50 .45
O98	A80	9p green	25.00 .60
O99	A80	1a carmine	4.75 .35

Type "b" Overprint
O100	A82	1r brown & slate ('38)	.70 .55
O101	A82	2r dk brown & dk ('38)	1.90 *3.25*
O102	A82	5r dp ultra & dk green ('38)	3.25 *7.50*
O103	A82	10r rose car & dark violet ('39)	19.00 6.75
		Nos. O97-O103 (7)	77.10 19.45

No. 136 Surcharged in Black

SERVICE 1A

1939, May   Wmk. 196   Perf. 14
O104	A69	1a on 1a3p violet	*17.00* 3.00

King George VI — O8

1939-43   Typo.   Perf. 13½x14
O105	O8	3p slate	.40 .40
O106	O8	½a brown	8.00 .40
O106A	O8	½a dk rose vio ('43)	.40 .40
O107	O8	9p green	.40 .40
O108	O8	1a car rose	.40 .40
O108A	O8	1a3p bister ('41)	7.00 1.25
O108B	O8	1½a dull pur ('43)	.40 .40
O109	O8	2a scarlet	.40 .40
O110	O8	2½a purple	.40 .40
O111	O8	4a dark brown	.40 .40
O112	O8	8a blue violet	.60 .40
		Nos. O105-O112 (11)	18.80 5.25

For overprints see Gwalior Nos. O52-O61. Stamps overprinted "Postal Service" or "I. P. N." were not used as postage stamps.

Nos. 203-206 (Gandhi Issue) Overprinted Type "a"
Perf. 11½
1948, Aug.   Unwmk.   Photo.
O112A	A90	1½a brown	65.00 45.00
O112B	A90	3½a violet	1,300. 750.00
O112C	A90	12a dk gray green	4,000. 2,500.
O112D	A90	10r rose brn & brown	25,000.

Overprint forgeries exist.

INDIA - CONVENTION STATES

CHAMBA

'chəm-bə

LOCATION — A State of India located in the north Punjab, south of Kashmir.
AREA — 3,127 sq. mi.
POP. — 168,908 (1941)
CAPITAL — Chamba

The varieties with small letters in the overprint are not listed as the letters are merely broken and not from another font of type.

Indian Stamps
Overprinted in Black

1887-95		Wmk. 39		Perf. 14
1	A17	½a green	1.50	1.75
a.		"CHMABA"	600.00	950.00
c.		Double overprint	950.00	
2	A19	1a violet brown	3.75	3.75
a.		"CHMABA"	700.00	950.00
b.		1a plum	4.25	3.75
3	A20	1a6p bis brown ('95)	4.50	21.00
4	A21	2a ultramarine	2.00	3.25
a.		"CHMABA"	2,750.	4,000.
5	A28	2a6p green ('95)	52.50	150.00
6	A22	3a brn org	4.50	9.00
a.		3a orange	16.00	35.00
b.		Inverted overprint		
c.		"CHMABA"	7,500.	11,000.
7	A23	4a olive green	8.25	14.00
a.		"CHMABA"	2,400.	4,000.
8	A25	8a red violet	13.50	18.00
a.		"CHMABA"	6,000.	6,250.
9	A26	12a vio, red ('90)	10.50	24.00
a.		"CHMABA"	12,500.	
b.		1st "T" of "STATE" invtd.	12,500.	
10	A27	1r gray	72.50	225.00
a.		"CHMABA"	21,000.	
11	A29	1r car rose & grn ('95)	14.00	25.00
12	A30	2r brown & rose ('95)	150.00	600.00
13	A30	3r grn & brown ('95)	175.00	525.00
14	A30	5r vio & bl ('95)	190.00	825.00
		Wmk. 38		
15	A14	6a bister ('90)	8.25	32.50
a.		6a bister brn	21.00	25.00
		Nos. 1-15 (15)	710.75	2,477.

1900			Wmk. 39
15B	A31	3p carmine rose	.90 1.40

1902-04			
16	A31	3p gray ('04)	.90 3.25
a.		Inverted overprint	120.00
17	A17	½a light green	1.00 2.50
18	A19	1a carmine rose	1.00 .60
19	A21	2a violet ('03)	16.00 52.50
		Nos. 16-19 (4)	18.90 58.85

1903-05			
20	A32	3p gray	.35 2.40
21	A33	½a green	1.20 .90
22	A34	1a carmine rose	2.40 1.40
23	A35	2a violet	2.75 5.25
24	A37	3a brown org ('05)	7.00 9.00
25	A38	4a olive green ('04)	10.50 32.50
26	A39	6a bister ('05)	6.50 35.00
27	A40	8a red violet ('04)	9.00 35.00
28	A41	12a violet, red	12.00 47.50
29	A42	1r car rose & grn ('05)	11.00 35.00
		Nos. 20-29 (10)	62.70 203.95

1907			
30	A44	½a green	3.75 6.00
31	A45	1a carmine rose	3.75 6.00

1913-24			
32	A46	3p gray	.60 1.90
33	A47	½a green	1.50 1.90
34	A48	1a carmine rose	15.00 17.50
35	A48	1a dark brown ('22)	5.25 8.25
36	A49	2a violet	6.00 17.50
37	A51	3a brown orange	7.00 13.00
38	A51	3a ultra ('24)	6.25 35.00
39	A52	4a olive green	6.00 8.25
40	A53	6a bister	6.50 11.00
41	A54	8a red violet	9.00 24.00
42	A55	12a claret	8.25 19.00
43	A56	1r green & red brown	27.50 47.50
		Nos. 32-43 (12)	98.85 204.80

India No. 104
Overprinted

1921			
44	A48	9p on 1a rose	1.50 27.50

India Stamps of 1913-
26 Overprinted

1922-27			
45	A58	1½a chocolate	40.00 190.00
46	A59	1½a chocolate	3.75 9.50
47	A59	1½a rose	1.40 35.00
48	A57	2a6p ultramarine	.90 6.50
49	A57	2a6p brown orange	4.00 35.00
		Nos. 45-49 (5)	50.05 276.00

India Stamps of 1926
Overprinted

1927-28			Wmk. 196
50	A46	3p slate	.30 2.50
51	A47	½a green	.45 3.75
52	A48	1a dark brown	2.50 2.25
53	A60	2a dull violet	3.25 6.00
54	A51	3a ultramarine	1.90 32.50
55	A61	4a olive green	1.90 10.00
57	A54	8a red violet	2.40 17.50
58	A55	12a claret	2.40 24.00

Overprinted

59	A56	1r green & brown	17.50 45.00
		Nos. 50-55,57-59 (9)	32.60 143.50

India Stamps of 1926-
35 Overprinted

1932-37			
60	A71	½a green	1.60 16.00
61	A68	9p dark green	7.50 32.50
62	A72	1a dark brown	2.50 2.25
63	A69	1a3p violet	2.10 9.50
64	A59	1½a carmine rose	9.50 11.00
65	A49	2a vermilion	1.90 37.50
a.		Small die	175.00 210.00
66	A57	2a6p buff	5.00 30.00
67	A51	3a carmine rose	3.25 17.50
68	A52	4a olive green ('36)	8.25 25.00
69	A53	6a bister ('37)	45.00 250.00
		Nos. 60-69 (10)	86.60 431.25

Same Overprint on India Stamps of 1937

1938			Wmk. 196	Perf. 13½x14
70	A80	3p slate	14.00	32.50
71	A80	½a brown	2.00	21.00
72	A80	9p green	12.50	57.50
73	A80	1a carmine	2.50	5.50

74	A81	2a scarlet	10.00	24.00
75	A81	2a6p purple	11.00	47.50
76	A81	3a yellow green	11.50	42.50
77	A81	3a6p ultra	11.50	45.00
78	A81	4a dark brown	30.00	45.00
79	A81	6a peacock blue	32.50	100.00
80	A81	8a blue violet	30.00	97.50
81	A81	12a carmine lake	22.50	97.50

Overprinted

82	A82	1r brown & slate	45.00	110.00
83	A82	2r dk brn & dk vio	75.00	525.00
84	A82	5r dp ultra & dk green	120.00	700.00
85	A82	10r rose car & dk vio	190.00	1,100.
86	A82	15r dk grn & dk brown	200.00	1,500.
87	A82	25r dk vio & bl vio	290.00	1,600.
		Nos. 70-87 (18)	1,110.	6,150.
		Set, never hinged	1,300.	

India Nos. 151 and 153
Overprinted

1942			
87B	A80	½a brown	62.50 67.50
		Never hinged	75.00
88	A80	1a carmine	95.00 90.00
		Never hinged	110.00

Same Ovpt. on India Stamps of 1941-42

1942-44			
89	A83	3p slate	1.50 8.25
90	A83	½a rose violet ('43)	1.00 9.50
91	A83	9p lt green ('43)	1.40 30.00
92	A83	1a car rose ('43)	2.50 8.25
93	A84	1½a dk purple ('44)	3.00 21.00
94	A84	2a scarlet ('43)	11.00 24.00
95	A84	3a violet ('43)	26.00 72.50
96	A84	3½a ultra ('43)	14.00 67.50
97	A85	4a chocolate ('43)	19.00 75.00
98	A85	6a pck blue ('43)	21.00 62.50
99	A85	8a blue violet ('43)	22.50 75.00
100	A85	12a car lake ('43)	30.00 97.50
		Nos. 89-100 (12)	152.90 551.00
		Set, never hinged	200.00

India Nos. 162-
167 Overprinted

1943		Wmk. 196	Perf. 13½x14
101	A82	1r brown & slate	26.00 97.50
102	A82	2r dk brown & dk vio	30.00 400.00
103	A82	5r dp ultra & dk grn	55.00 450.00
104	A82	10r rose car & dk vio	85.00 700.00
105	A82	15r dk grn & dk brn	190.00 1,250.
106	A82	25r dk vio & bl vio	175.00 1,250.
		Nos. 101-106 (6)	561.00 4,147.
		Set, never hinged	850.00

India No.
161A
Ovptd.

1947			
107	A81	14a rose violet	17.50 4.50

OFFICIAL STAMPS

Indian Stamps
Overprinted in Black

1887-98		Wmk. 39		Perf. 14
O1	A17	½a green	.90	.25
a.		"CHMABA"	375.00	375.00
c.		"SERV CE"		
O2	A19	1a violet brown	3.00	2.25
a.		"CHMABA"	600.00	600.00
c.		"SERV CE"	5,250.	
d.		"SERVICE" double	3,000.	1,600.
O3	A21	2a ultra	3.75	3.00
a.		"CHMABA"	1,500.	3,250.
O4	A22	3a brown orange	3.00	19.00
a.		3a orange	—	—
b.		"CHMABA"	4,500.	5,250.
O5	A23	4a olive green	4.50	12.00
a.		"CHMABA"	1,600.	3,250.
c.		"SERV CE"	6,000.	
O6	A25	8a red violet	4.50	4.50
a.		"CHMABA"	12,000.	12,000.
O7	A26	12a vio, red ('90)	12.50	72.50
a.		"CHMABA"	11,000.	
b.		1st "T" of "STATE" invtd.	10,000.	
O8	A27	1r gray ('90)	19.00	225.00
a.		"CHMABA"	7,500.	
O9	A29	1r car rose & grn ('98)	9.00	62.50
		Wmk. 38		
O10	A14	6a bister	6.25	22.50
		Nos. O1-O10 (10)	66.40	423.50

1902-04			Wmk. 39
O11	A31	3p gray ('04)	.75 1.20
O12	A17	½a light green	1.50 6.00
O13	A19	1a carmine rose	1.90 .90
O14	A21	2a violet ('03)	14.50 52.50
		Nos. O11-O14 (4)	18.65 60.60

1903-05			
O15	A32	3p gray	.40 .25
O16	A33	½a green	.30 .25
O17	A34	1a carmine rose	1.50 .45
O18	A35	2a violet	1.50 2.25
O19	A38	4a olive green ('05)	4.25 30.00
O20	A40	8a red violet ('05)	10.00 30.00
O21	A42	1r car rose & grn ('05)	2.00 21.00
		Nos. O15-O21 (7)	19.95 84.20

1907			
O22	A44	½a green	.85 1.10
a.		Inverted overprint	6,750. 8,250.
O23	A45	1a carmine rose	4.75 3.75

1913			
O24	A49	2a violet	22.50
O25	A52	4a olive green	20.00

India No. 63
Overprinted

O26	A35	2a violet	60.00

No. O26 was never placed in use.

India Stamps of 1911-29 Overprinted

a   b

1913-25

O27	A46	(a) 3p gray	.30	.60
O28	A47	(a) ½a green	.30	.90
O29	A48	(a) 1a carmine rose	.30	.25
O30	A48	(a) 1a dk brown	6.50	1.00
O31	A46	(a) 2a violet ('14)	1.60	22.50
O32	A52	(a) 4a olive green	1.60	30.00
O33	A54	(a) 8a red violet	2.50	30.00
O34	A56	(b) 1r grn & red brn	8.25	47.50
		Nos. O27-O34 (8)	21.35	132.75

India No. O66 Overprinted

1921

O35	O6	9p on 1a rose	.25	12.50

India Stamps of 1926-35 Overprinted

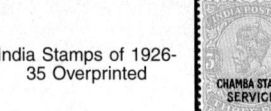

1927-39   **Wmk. 196**

O36	A46	3p slate	.65	.60
O37	A47	½a green	.40	.25
O38	A68	9p dark green ('32)	5.00	16.00
O39	A48	1a dark brown	.25	.25
O40	A69	1a3p violet ('32)	7.50	1.50
O41	A60	2a dull violet	3.25	.90
O42	A61	4a olive green	1.90	4.00
O43	A54	8a red violet	10.00	16.00
O44	A55	12a claret	6.50	37.50

Overprinted

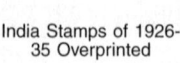

O45	A56	1r green & brown	19.00	72.50
O45A	A56	2r brn org & car rose ('39)	30.00	375.00
O45B	A56	5r dk vio & ultra ('39)	52.50	450.00
O45C	A56	10r car & grn ('39)	82.50	450.00
		Nos. O36-O45C (13)	219.45	1,424.

India Stamps of 1926-35 Overprinted

1935-36

O46	A71	½a green	7.00	.75
O47	A72	1a dark brown	6.75	.65
O48	A49	2a vermilion	7.00	1.90
O49	A52	4a olive grn ('36)	10.00	9.50
a.		Small die	9.50	30.00
		Nos. O46-O49 (4)	30.75	12.80

Same Overprint on India Stamps of 1937

1938   **Perf. 13½x14**

O50	A80	9p green	30.00	100.00
		Never hinged	37.50	
O51	A80	1a carmine	37.50	9.00
		Never hinged	45.00	

India Stamps of 1937 Overprinted

1940-41

O51A	A82	1r brn & sl ('41)	300.00	1,100.
O52	A82	2r dk brn & dk vio	52.50	600.00
O53	A82	5r dp ultra & dk grn	75.00	650.00
O54	A82	10r rose car & dk vio	105.00	1,200.
		Set, never hinged	625.00	

India Official Stamps of 1939-43 Overprinted

1941-46   **Wmk. 196**

O55	O8	3p slate ('44)	.85	1.90
O56	O8	½a brown	37.50	5.50
O57	O8	½a dk rose vio ('44)	.85	5.50
O58	O8	9p green	8.75	17.50
O59	O8	1a carmine rose	1.25	4.50
O60	O8	1a3p bister ('46)	105.00	32.50
O61	O8	1½a dull pur ('46)	9.50	12.50
O62	O8	2a scarlet ('44)	9.50	12.50
O63	O8	2½a purple ('44)	5.50	35.00
O64	O8	4a dark brown ('44)	9.50	27.50
O65	O8	8a blue vio ('41)	21.00	100.00
		Nos. O55-O65 (11)	209.20	254.90
		Set, never hinged	250.00	

India Nos. 162-165 Overprinted

1944

O66	A82	1r brown & slate	27.50	325.00
O67	A82	2r dk brn & dk vio	42.50	450.00
O68	A82	5r dp ultra & dk grn	80.00	650.00
O69	A82	10r rose car & dk grn	95.00	1,100.
		Nos. O66-O69 (4)	245.00	2,525.
		Set, never hinged	295.00	

FARIDKOT

fe-'rēd-ˌkōt

LOCATION — A State of India lying northeast of Nabha in the central Punjab.
AREA — 638 sq. mi.
POP. — 164,364
CAPITAL — Faridkot

Previous stamp issues are listed under Feudatory States. Stamps of Faridkot were superseded by those of India in 1901.

The varieties with small letters in the overprint are not listed as the letters are merely broken and not from another font.

India Stamps Overprinted in Black

1887-93   **Wmk. 39**   **Perf. 14**

4	A17	½a green	3.75	2.50
a.		"ARIDKOT"		
b.		"FAR DKOT"	—	2,500.
5	A19	1a violet brown	2.25	3.75
6	A21	2a ultramarine	4.75	10.50
7	A22	3a orange	5.50	9.00

8	A23	4a olive green	12.50	27.50
a.		"ARIDKOT"	2,100.	
9	A25	8a red violet	22.50	67.50
a.		"ARIDKOT"	4,500.	
10	A27	1r gray	67.50	550.00
a.		"ARIDKOT"	6,750.	
11	A29	1r car rose & grn ('93)	60.00	175.00

Wmk. 38

12	A14	6a bister	3.00	27.50
a.		"ARIDKOT"	2,750.	
		Nos. 4-12 (9)	181.75	873.25

1900   **Wmk. Star. (39)**

13	A31	3p car rose	2.25	67.50
14	A26	12a violet, red	67.50	625.00

OFFICIAL STAMPS

India Stamps Overprinted in Black

1886   **Wmk. 39**   **Perf. 14**

O1	A17	½a green	.90	1.10
a.		"SERV CE"	3,750.	
b.		"FAR DKOT"	3,500.	
c.		"ESRVICE"	3,500.	
O2	A19	1a violet brown	1.50	3.00
a.		"SERV CE"	5,500.	
O3	A21	2a ultramarine	3.00	16.00
a.		"SERV CE"	5,500.	
O4	A22	3a orange	6.00	57.50
O5	A23	4a olive green	7.00	45.00
a.		"SERV CE"	4,750.	
O6	A25	8a red lilac	15.00	45.00
a.		"SERV CE"	4,500.	
O7	A27	1r gray	82.50	400.00

Wmk. 38

O8	A14	6a bister	37.50	42.50
a.		"ARIDKOT"	2,100	
b.		"SERVIC"	4,500.	
		Nos. O1-O8 (8)	153.40	610.10

1896   **Wmk. 39**

O9	A29	1r car rose & green	140.00	1,000.
		Obsolete March 31, 1901.		

GWALIOR

'gwäl-ē-ˌoˌəˌr

LOCATION — One of the Central Provinces of India
AREA — 26,008 sq. mi.
POP. — 4,006,159 (1941)
CAPITAL — Lashkar

The varieties with small letters in the overprint are not listed as the letters are merely broken and not from another font.

India Stamps Overprinted in Black

Lines Spaced 16-17mm

1885   **Wmk. 39**   **Perf. 14**

1	A17	½a green	90.00
2	A19	1a violet brown	97.50
3	A20	1a6p bister brown	125.00
4	A21	2a ultramarine	100.00
5	A25	8a red lilac	110.00
6	A27	1r gray	110.00

Wmk. 38

7	A9	4a green	140.00
8	A14	6a bister	140.00
		Nos. 1-8 (8)	912.50

The Hindi overprint measures 13½-14x2mm and 15-15½x2½mm.
The two sizes are found in the same sheet in the proportion of one of the smaller to three of the larger.
The ½a, 1a, 2a, also exist with lines 13mm apart and the short Hindi overprint.
Reprints of the ½a and 1a have the 13mm spacing, the short Hindi overprint and usually carry the overprint "Specimen."

India Stamps Overprinted

Red Overprint

1885   **Wmk. 39**

9	A17	½a green	1.90	.25
10	A21	2a ultramarine	35.00	27.50
11	A27	1r gray	12.50	37.50

Wmk. 38

12	A9	4a green	42.50	24.00
		Nos. 9-12 (4)	91.90	89.25

Nos. 9-12 have been reprinted. They have the short Hindi overprint. Most stamps bear the word "Reprint." Those without it cannot be distinguished from the originals.

Black Overprint

1885-91   **Wmk. 39**

13	A17	½a green	.75	.25
a.		"GWALICR"	125.00	150.00
b.		Double overprint		1,400.
c.		Small raised "R"	100.00	
14	A18	9p rose	47.50	82.50
15	A19	1a violet brown	3.00	.25
c.		Small raised "R"	110.00	
16	A20	1a6p bister brown	3.25	2.00
17	A21	2a ultramarine	4.00	.25
c.		Small raised "R"	240.00	
18	A22	3a orange	7.00	.25
c.		Small raised "R"	1,300.	
19	A23	4a olive green	8.50	2.00
c.		Small raised "R"	600.00	
20	A25	8a red violet	9.00	2.00
21	A26	12a violet, red	5.00	1.00
22	A27	1r gray	6.50	5.25

Wmk. 38

23	A14	6a bister	7.50	18.00
		Nos. 13-23 (11)	102.00	113.75

The Hindi overprint measures 13½-14x2mm and 15-15½x2½mm as in the preceding issue.

1896   **Wmk. 39**

24	A28	2a6p green	14.00	30.00
a.		"GWALICR"	1,000.	
25	A29	1r car rose & grn	12.00	8.50
a.		"GWALICR"	1,350	2,400.
26	A30	2r bis brn & rose	8.25	4.50
c.		Small raised "R"	540.00	300.00
27	A30	3r grn & brown	11.00	5.25
c.		Small raised "R"	650.00	325.00
28	A30	5r violet & blue	21.00	9.50
c.		Small raised "R"	700.00	400.00
		Nos. 24-28 (5)	66.25	57.75

The Hindi inscription varies from 13 to 15½mm long.

1899

29	A31	3p carmine rose	.75	.25
a.		Inverted overprint	1,650.	825.00

1901-04

30	A31	3p gray ('04)	11.00	90.00
31	A17	½a light green	2.10	2.40
32	A19	1a carmine rose	1.90	.50
33	A21	2a violet	4.00	8.25
34	A28	2a6p ultra ('03)	2.25	9.50
		Nos. 30-34 (5)	21.25	110.65

1903-08

35	A32	3p gray	2.10	.25
36	A33	½a green	2.25	.45
37	A34	1a carmine rose	.30	.25
38	A35	2a violet	3.00	1.50
39	A36	2a6p ultra ('05)	37.50	120.00
40	A37	3a brown org ('04)	3.00	3.00
41	A38	4a olive green	3.75	.60
42	A39	6a bister ('06)	9.00	2.10
43	A40	8a red violet	7.50	2.40
44	A41	12a vio, red ('05)	4.50	30.00
45		1r car rose & grn ('05)	4.50	2.50
46	A43	2r brown & rose	13.50	16.50
47	A43	3r grn & brn ('08)	42.50	75.00
48	A43	5r vio & bl ('08)	27.50	40.00
		Nos. 35-48 (14)	160.90	292.05

There are two settings of the overprint on Nos. 35, 37-46. In the first (1903), "GWALIOR" is 14mm long and lines are spaced 1¾mm. In the second (1908), "GWALIOR" is 13mm long and lines are 2¾mm apart. No. 36 exists only with first overprint, Nos. 47-48 only with second.

1907
49 A44 ½a green .30 1.00
50 A45 1a carmine rose 2.25 .25

No. 49 exists with both settings of overprint. See note below No. 48.

1912-23
51 A46 3p gray .30 .25
52 A47 ½a green .30 .25
  a. Inverted overprint 600.00
53 A48 1a car rose .35 .25
  a. Double overprint 37.50
54 A48 1a dk brown ('23) 1.60 .25
55 A49 2a violet 1.20 .25
56 A51 3a brown orange 1.00 .25
57 A52 4a olive grn ('13) .90 .90
58 A53 6a bister 1.90 2.10
59 A54 8a red vio ('13) 3.25 1.20
60 A55 12a claret ('14) 2.10 6.00
61 A56 1r green & red brn 13.50 .65
62 A56 2r brn & car rose 7.50 6.50
63 A56 5r violet & ultra 35.00 9.50
  Nos. 51-63 (13) 68.90 28.35

India No. 104 Overprinted

1921
64 A48 9p on 1a rose 1.00 .75
  a. Inverted overprint

India Stamps of 1911-26 Overprinted

Hindi Overprint 15mm Long

1923-27
66 A59 1½a choc ('25) 3.25 .75
67 A59 1½a rose ('27) .30 .25
  a. Inverted overprint —
68 A57 2a6p ultra ('25) 3.25 2.50
69 A57 2a6p brown org ('27) .50 .75
70 A51 3a ultra ('24) 3.75 .90
  Nos. 66-70 (5) 11.05 5.15

Similar Ovpt. on India Stamps of 1926-35
Hindi Overprint 13½mm Long

1928-32   **Wmk. 196**
71 A46 3p slate ('32) 1.25 .25
72 A47 ½a green ('30) 1.90 .25
73 A48 1a dark brown 1.10 .25
74 A60 2a dull violet .70 .45
75 A51 3a ultramarine 1.25 .60
76 A61 4a olive green 1.60 1.50
77 A54 8a red violet 1.60 1.60
78 A55 12a claret 2.75 5.25

Overprinted

79 A56 1r green & brown 3.75 6.00
80 A56 2r brn org & car rose 6.75 6.50
81 A56 5r dk vio & ultra ('29) 24.00 37.50
82 A56 10r car & grn ('30) 82.50 62.50
83 A56 15r olive green & ultra ('30) 130.00 100.00
84 A56 25r bl & ocher ('30) 275.00 250.00
  Nos. 71-84 (14) 534.15 472.65

India Stamps of 1932-35 Overprinted in Black

Hindi Overprint 13½mm Long

1933-36
85 A71 ½a green ('36) .65 .25
86 A68 9p dk green ('33) 3.75 .45
87 A72 1a dk brown ('36) .30 .25
88 A69 1a3p violet ('36) .65 .25
89 A49 2a vermilion ('36) 3.75 5.25
  Nos. 85-89 (5) 9.10 6.45

Same Ovpt. on India Stamps of 1937

1938-40   **Perf. 13½x14**
90 A80 3p slate ('40) 10.00 .25
91 A80 ½a brown 11.00 .25
92 A80 9p green ('40) 60.00 6.00
93 A80 1a carmine 10.00 .25

94 A81 3a yel green ('39) 35.00 7.50
95 A81 4a dark brown 55.00 5.25
96 A81 6a pck blue ('39) 5.00 16.50
  Nos. 90-96 (7) 186.00 36.00
  Set, never hinged 225.00

Same Overprinted on India Stamps of 1941-43

1942-49
100 A83 3p slate ('44) .55 .25
101 A83 ½a rose vio ('46) 1.25 .25
102 A83 9p light green .55 .25
103 A83 1a car rose ('44) 1.25 .25
104 A84 1½a dk purple ('44) 8.75 .25
105 A84 2a scarlet ('44) 1.90 .25
106 A84 3a violet ('44) 20.00 2.50
108 A85 4a choc ('44) 4.00 .25
109 A85 6a pck blue ('48) 17.50 40.00
110 A85 8a blue violet 4.75 4.00
111 A85 12a carmine lake 7.00 35.00

India Nos. 162-167 Overprinted

Perf. 13½x14
112 A82 1r brn & sl ('45) 15.00 2.50
113 A82 2r dk brn & dk vio ('49) 62.50 14.00
114 A82 5r dp ultra & dk grn ('49) 40.00 60.00
115 A82 10r rose car & dk vio ('49) 40.00 62.50
116 A82 15r dk grn & dk brn ('48) 110.00 250.00
117 A82 25r dk vio & blue vio ('48) 110.00 190.00
  Nos. 100-106,108-117 (17) 445.00 662.25
  Set, never hinged 525.00

India Stamps of 1941-43 Overprinted

1949
118 A83 3p slate 2.50 .75
119 A83 ½a rose violet 2.50 .75
120 A83 1a carmine rose 2.25 .90
121 A84 2a scarlet 32.50 3.25
122 A84 3a violet 80.00 45.00
123 A85 4a chocolate 9.25 5.00
124 A85 6a pck blue 67.50 97.50
125 A85 8a blue violet 140.00 82.50
126 A85 12a carmine lake 525.00 225.00
  Nos. 118-126 (9) 861.50 460.65
  Set, never hinged 1,050.

OFFICIAL STAMPS

India Stamps Overprinted in Black

1895   **Wmk. 39**   **Perf. 14**
O1 A17 ½a green .75 .25
  a. Double overprint 1,400.
O2 A19 1a maroon 18.00 2.10
O3 A21 2a ultramarine 5.00 .60
O4 A23 4a olive green 5.25 2.25
O5 A25 8a red violet 6.50 5.00
O6 A29 1r car rose & grn 12.50 4.50
  Nos. O1-O6 (6) 48.00 14.70

Nos. O1 to O6 inclusive are known with the last two characters of the lower word transposed.

1901-04
O7 A31 3p gray ('04) 3.75 5.25
O8 A17 ½a light green 1.10 .25
O9 A19 1a carmine rose 9.00 .25
O10 A21 2a violet ('03) 2.50 2.25
  Nos. O7-O10 (4) 16.35 8.00

1902
O11 A31 3p carmine rose 1.90 .35

1903-05
O12 A32 3p gray .90 .25
O13 A33 ½a green 4.00 .25
O14 A34 1a carmine rose 1.40 .25
O15 A35 2a violet 2.25 .45

O16 A38 4a olive grn ('05) 22.50 2.50
O17 A40 8a red violet 9.50 1.00
O18 A42 1r car rose & grn ('05) 3.50 3.00
  Nos. O12-O18 (7) 44.05 7.70

1907
O19 A44 ½a green 2.50 .25
O20 A45 1a carmine rose 10.00 .25

Two spacings of the overprint lines, 10mm and 8mm, are found on Nos. O12-O20.

1913
O21 A46 3p gray .35 .25
O22 A47 ½a green .30 .25
O23 A48 1a carmine rose .45 .25
  a. Double overprint 97.50
O24 A49 2a violet 2.25 .25
O25 A52 4a olive green .90 2.25
O26 A54 8a red violet 1.90 1.50
O27 A56 1r grn & red brn 40.00 35.00
  Nos. O21-O27 (7) 46.15 39.75

India No. O66 Overprinted

1921
O28 O6 9p on 1a rose .25 .45

India No. 83 Overprinted

1923
O29 A481a dark brown 5.50 .25

Similar Ovpt. on India Stamps of 1926-35

1927-35   **Wmk. 196**
O30 A46 3p slate .30 .25
O31 A47 ½a green .30 .25
O32 A48 1a dark brown .30 .25
O33 A60 2a dull violet .30 .25
O34 A61 4a olive green 1.00 .45
O35 A54 8a red violet .90 1.60

Overprinted

O36 A56 1r green & brown 1.50 2.50
O37 A56 2r brn org & car rose ('35) 29.00 30.00
O38 A56 5r dk vio & ultra ('32) 35.00 250.00
O39 A56 10r car & grn ('32) 240.00 650.00
  Nos. O30-O39 (10) 308.60 935.55

India Stamps of 1926-35 Overprinted

1933-37   **Perf. 13½x14, 14**
O40 A71 ½a green ('36) .35 .25
O41 A68 9p dk green ('35) .30 .25
O42 A72 1a dk brown ('36) .30 .25
O43 A69 1a3p violet ('33) .75 .25
O44 A49 2a ver ('36) .30 .60
  a. Small die ('36) 3.75 1.90
O45 A52 4a olive green ('37) .90 1.10
  Nos. O40-O45 (6) 2.90 2.70

For surcharge see No. O62.

Same Overprint on India Stamps

1938   **Perf. 13½x14**
O46 A80 ½a brown 8.00 .45
  Never hinged 9.50
O47 A80 1a carmine 2.00 .25
  Never hinged 2.25

India Nos. 162-165 Overprinted

1945-48   **Wmk. 196**   **Perf. 13½x14**
O48 A82 1r brown & slate 12.50 32.50
O49 A82 2r dk brn & dk vio 22.50 140.00
O50 A82 5r dp ultra & dk grn ('46) 37.50 825.00
O51 A82 10r rose car & dk vio ('48) 100.00 1,650.
  Nos. O48-O51 (4) 172.50 2,647.
  Set, never hinged 200.00

India Official Stamps of 1939-43 Overprinted

1940-44   **Wmk. 196**   **Perf. 13½x14**
O52 O8 3p slate .65 .25
O53 O8 ½a brown 5.50 .35
O54 O8 ½a dk rose vio ('43) .75 .25
O55 O8 9p green ('43) .85 1.00
O56 O8 1a car rose ('41) 2.75 .25
O57 O8 1a3p bister ('42) 55.00 2.50
O58 O8 1½a dull purple ('43) 1.50 .45
O59 O8 2a scarlet ('41) 1.50 .45
O60 O8 4a dark brown ('44) 1.50 5.00
O61 O8 8a blue vio ('44) 6.00 14.00
  Nos. O52-O61 (10) 76.00 24.50
  Set, never hinged 95.00

Gwalior No. O43 with Additional Surcharge in Black

1942
O62 A69 1a on 1a3p violet 30.00 4.50
  Never hinged 37.50

JIND

'jind

(Jhind)

LOCATION — A State of India in the north Punjab.
AREA — 1,299 sq. mi.
POP. — 361,812 (1941)
CAPITAL — Sangrur

Previous stamp issues are listed under Feudatory States.

The varieties with small letters are not listed as the letters are merely broken and not from another font.

India Stamps Overprinted in Black

1885   **Wmk. 39**   **Perf. 14**
33 A17 ½a green 7.00 8.25
  a. Overprint reading down 140.00 160.00
34 A19 1a violet brown 62.50 90.00
  a. Overprint reading down 1,400. 1,500.
35 A21 2a ultra 29.00 32.50
  a. Overprint reading down 1,000. 1,200.
36 A25 8a red lilac 625.00
  a. Overprint reading down 18,000.
37 A27 1r gray 700.00
  a. Overprint reading down 21,000.

Wmk. 38
38 A9 4a green 97.50 140.00
  Nos. 33-38 (6) 1,521. 270.75

On the reprints of Nos. 33 to 38 "Jhind" measures 8mm instead of 9mm and "State" 9mm instead of 9½mm.

India Stamps Overprinted in Red or Black

1885   **Wmk. 39**

39	A17	½a green (R)	210.00
40	A19	1a violet brown	210.00
41	A21	2a ultra (R)	210.00
42	A25	8a red lilac	290.00
43	A27	1r gray (R)	290.00

Wmk. 00

44	A9	4a green (R)	290.00
		Nos. 39-44 (6)	1,500.

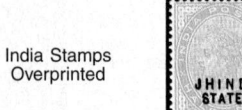

India Stamps
Overprinted

1886   **Wmk. 39**   **Red Overprint**

45	A17	½a green	52.50
a.		"JEIND"	1,800.
46	A21	2a ultramarine	57.50
a.		"JEIND"	1,800.
47	A27	1r gray	90.00
a.		"JEIND"	2,750.

Wmk. 38

48	A9	4a green	90.00
		Nos. 45-48 (4)	290.00

Nos. 46, 47 and 48 were not placed in use.

1886-98   **Wmk. 39**   **Black Overprint**

49	A17	½a green ('88)	1.20	.25
a.		Inverted overprint	300.00	
50	A19	1a violet brown	3.75	.25
a.		"JEIND"	750.00	
51	A20	1a6p bister brn ('97)	3.75	5.50
52	A21	2a ultra	3.75	.60
53	A22	3a orange	5.00	1.00
54	A23	4a olive green	6.00	3.25
55	A25	8a red violet	12.50	30.00
a.		"JEIND"	2,400.	
56	A26	12a vio, red ('97)	10.00	07.50
57	A27	1r gray ('91)	17.50	82.50
58	A29	1r car rose & green ('98)	16.50	90.00
59	A30	2r brn & rose ('97)	525.00	1,500.
60	A30	3r grn & brn ('97)	750.00	1,350.
61	A30	5r vio & bl ('97)	750.00	1,250.

Wmk. 38

62	A14	6a bister	6.50	21.00
		Nos. 49-62 (14)	2,111.	4,371.

1900   **Wmk. 39**

63	A31	3p carmine rose	1.60 2.50

1902-04

64	A31	3p gray ('04)	.60	6.00
65	A17	½a light green	7.00	10.00
66	A19	1a carmine rose	1.90	10.00
		Nos. 64-66 (3)	9.50	26.00

1903-09

67	A32	3p gray	.35	.25
68	A33	½a green	2.50	2.50
69	A34	1a car rose ('09)	2.75	2.40
70	A35	2a violet ('06)	4.25	3.25
70A	A36	2a6p ultra ('09)	.85	10.00
71	A37	3a brown orange	3.25	.60
a.		Double overprint	175.00	325.00
72	A38	4a olive green	11.50	14.00
73	A39	6a bister ('05)	9.25	32.50
74	A40	8a red violet	4.00	32.50
75	A41	12a vio, red ('05)	4.25	17.50
76	A42	1r car rose & grn ('05)	4.75	32.50
		Nos. 67-76 (11)	47.70	148.00

1907

77	A44	½a green	.60	.25
78	A45	1a carmine rose	2.25	1.00

1913

80	A46	3p gray	.30	3.50
81	A47	½a green	.30	1.10
82	A48	1a carmine rose	.30	.25
83	A49	2a violet	.30	6.25
84	A51	3a brown orange	2.25	21.00
85	A53	6a bister	12.50	42.50
		Nos. 80-85 (6)	15.95	75.00

India Stamps of 1911-26 Overprinted

1913-14

88	A46	3p gray	1.50	.25
89	A47	½a green	3.75	.25
90	A48	1a carmine rose	2.40	.25
91	A49	2a violet	6.50	1.90
92	A51	3a brown orange		
93	A52	4a olive green	3.00	14.00
94	A53	6a bister	6.00	24.00
95	A54	8a red violet	8.25	24.00
96	A55	12a claret	7.50	30.00
97	A56	1r grn & red brn	17.50	35.00
		Nos. 88-97 (10)	57.15	135.65

India No. 104 Overprinted

1921

98	A48	9p on 1a rose	1.90	22.50

India Stamps of 1913-19 Overprinted

1922

99	A58	1¼a chocolate	5.00	9.00
100	A57	2a6p ultramarine	.75	7.00

Same Overprint on India Stamps of 1911-26

1924

101	A48	1a dark brown	9.00	4.50
102	A59	1½a chocolate	.75	2.25

Same Overprint on India No. 87

1925

103	A51	3a ultramarine	3.00	7.50

Same Overprint on India Stamps of 1911-26

1927

104	A59	1½a rose	.30	2.25
105	A57	2a6p brown orange	1.90	12.00
106	A56	2r yel brn & car rose	9.50	225.00
107	A56	5r violet & ultra	67.50	450.00
		Nos. 104-107 (4)	79.20	689.25

India Stamps of 1926-35 Overprinted

1927-32   **Wmk. 196**

108	A46	3p slate	.30	.25
109	A47	½a green	.30	.50
110	A68	9p dark green ('32)	2.75	.60
111	A48	1a dark brown	.30	.25
112	A69	1a3p violet ('32)	.35	.45
113	A59	1½a carmine rose	.75	5.50
114	A60	2a dull violet	4.25	.60
115	A57	2a6p buff	2.00	16.00
116	A51	3a ultramarine	8.00	27.50
117	A61	4a olive green	2.00	5.25
118	A54	8a red violet	7.50	3.25
119	A55	12a claret	12.00	32.50

Indian Stamps of 1911-23 Overprinted

120	A56	1r green & brown	6.50	9.00
121	A56	2r buff & car rose	55.00	225.00
122	A56	5r dk vio & ultra	16.00	62.50
123	A56	10r car rose & ultra	19.00	27.50
124	A56	15r ol grn & blue	120.00	1,050.
125	A56	25r blue & ocher	190.00	1,250.
		Nos. 108-125 (18)	447.00	2,716.

India Stamps of 1926-35 Overprinted

1934-37

126	A71	½a green	.45	.35
127	A72	1a dark brown	2.50	.45
128	A49	2a vermilion	4.75	.90
129	A51	3a carmine rose	1.00	.25
130	A70	8a6p deep blue ('37)	3.25	30.00
131	A52	4a olive green	4.25	2.25
132	A53	6a bister ('37)	.85	32.50
		Nos. 126-132 (7)	20.30	67.05

Same Overprint on India Stamps of 1937

1937-38   **Wmk. 196**   **Perf. 13½x14**

133	A80	3p slate ('38)	11.00	3.75
134	A80	½a brown ('38)	.80	7.50
135	A80	9p green	.80	6.00
136	A80	1a carmine	.80	.90
137	A81	2a scarlet ('38)	1.75	27.50
138	A81	2a6p purple ('38)	1.40	35.00
139	A81	3a yel grn ('38)	6.75	30.00
140	A81	3a6p ultra ('38)	4.25	45.00
141	A81	4a dk brown ('38)	10.00	27.50
142	A81	6a pck blue ('38)	6.50	42.50
143	A81	8a blue vio ('38)	5.25	35.00
144	A81	12a car lake ('38)	3.00	45.00

India Stamps of 1937-40 Overprinted

1938

145	A82	1r brown & slate	13.00	62.50
146	A82	2r dk brn & violet	16.00	190.00
147	A82	5r dp ultra & dk green	25.00	125.00
148	A82	10r rose car & dk violet	50.00	120.00
149	A82	15r dk grn & dk brown	110.00	1,200.
150	A82	25r dk vio & bl vio	575.00	1,400.
		Nos. 133-150 (18)	841.30	3,393.
		Set, never hinged	1,200.	

India Stamps of 1937 Overprinted

1942-43   **Wmk. 196**   **Perf. 13½x14**

155	A80	3p slate	17.50	32.50
156	A80	½a brown	1.25	3.75
157	A80	9p green	16.00	30.00
158	A80	1a carmine	1.25	9.00
159	A82	1r brn & slate	11.00	40.00
160	A82	2r dk brn & dk violet	22.50	52.50
161	A82	5r dp ultra & dk green	50.00	140.00
162	A82	10r rose car & dk vio ('43)	75.00	140.00
163	A82	15r dk grn & dk brn ('43)	160.00	250.00
164	A82	25r dk vio & bl vio	75.00	525.00
		Nos. 155-164 (10)	429.50	1,222.
		Set, never hinged	510.00	

Same Overprint on India Stamps of 1941-43

165	A83	3p slate	.60	2.10
166	A83	½a rose vio ('43)	.60	3.25
167	A83	9p light green	.95	6.50
168	A83	1a car rose ('43)	1.25	2.25
169	A84	1a3p bister ('43)	1.25	7.50
170	A84	1½a dark purple	10.00	7.50
171	A84	2a scarlet	2.25	7.50
172	A84	3a violet ('43)	30.00	9.00
173	A84	3½a ultramarine	11.00	17.50
174	A85	4a chocolate	7.50	9.00
175	A85	6a peacock blue	8.00	25.00
176	A85	8a blue violet	5.25	22.50
177	A85	12a carmine lake	17.50	27.50
		Nos. 165-177 (13)	96.15	147.10
		Set, never hinged	115.00	

OFFICIAL STAMPS

India Stamps Overprinted in Black

1885   **Wmk. 39**   **Perf. 14**

O1	A17	½a green	3.00	.60
a.		"JHIND STATE" reading down	150.00	90.00
O2	A19	1a violet brown	1.00	.25
a.		"JHIND STATE" reading down	17.50	11.00
O3	A21	2a ultra	60.00	72.50
a.		"JHIND STATE" reading down	1,500.	1,750.
		Nos. O1-O3 (3)	64.00	73.35

The reprints may be distinguished by the same measurements as the reprints of the corresponding regular issue.

India Stamps Overprinted in Red or Black

1885

O4	A17	½a green (R)	150.00	
O5	A19	1a violet brown	125.00	
O6	A21	2a ultra (R)	140.00	
		Nos. O4-O6 (3)	415.00	

India Stamps Overprinted

1886   **Red Overprint**

O7	A17	½a green	42.50	
a.		"JEIND"	1,050.	
b.		"ERVICE"	6,000.	
O8	A21	2a ultramarine	47.50	
a.		"JEIND"	1,750.	
b.		"ERVICE"	3,750.	

No. O8 was not placed in use.

1886-96   **Black Overprint**

O9	A17	½a green ('88)	2.50	.25
O10	A19	1a violet brown	16.00	2.25
a.		"JEIND"	750.00	
b.		"ERVICE"		
O11	A21	2a ultramarine	4.25	1.50
O12	A23	4a olive green	4.50	3.00
O13	A25	8a red violet	7.00	12.50
O14	A29	1r car rose & grn ('96)	8.00	75.00
		Nos. O9-O14 (6)	42.25	94.50

1902

O15	A17	½a light green	3.75	.45

1903-06

O16	A32	3p gray	.85	.25
O17	A33	½a green	4.50	.25
a.		"HIND"	4,500.	450.00
O18	A34	1a carmine rose	3.75	.25
a.		"HIND"	5,250.	400.00
O19	A35	2a violet	2.50	.25
O20	A38	4a olive green	2.10	.65
O21	A40	8a red violet	7.50	2.25
O22	A42	1r car rose & grn ('06)	3.25	3.25
		Nos. O16-O22 (7)	24.45	7.15

1907

O23	A44	½a green	1.50	.25
O24	A45	1a carmine rose	2.50	.25

Indian Stamps of 1911-26 Overprinted

a   b

1914-27

O25	A46(a)	3p gray	.30	.25
O26	A47(a)	½a green	.40	.25
O27	A48(a)	1a car rose	1.00	.25
O28	A49(a)	2a violet	.35	.45
O29	A52(a)	4a olive green	1.90	.25
O30	A54(a)	8a red violet	1.00	1.50
O31	A56(b)	1r grn & red brn	3.75	2.50
O32	A56(b)	2r yel brn & car rose ('27)	27.50	100.00
O33	A56(b)	5r vio & ultra ('27)	35.00	375.00
		Nos. O25-O33 (9)	71.20	480.45

India Nos. 83 and 89 Overprinted Type "a"

1924-27

O34	A48	1a dark brown	.90	.25
O35	A53	6a bister ('27)	2.50	3.25

India Stamps of 1926-35 Overprinted — c

1927-32

O36	A46	3p slate	.25	.25
O37	A47	½a green	.25	1.50
O38	A68	9p dark green ('32)	.90	.25
O39	A48	1a dark brown	.25	.25
O40	A69	1a3p violet ('32)	.60	.25
O41	A60	2a dull violet	.35	.25
O42	A61	4a olive green	.50	.35
O43	A54	8a red violet	.90	2.50
O44	A55	12a claret	3.25	27.50

Indian Stamps of 1911-23 Overprinted — d

O45	A56	1r green & brown	7.50	8.25
O46	A56	2r buff & car rose	75.00	62.50
O47	A56	5r dk vio & ultra	19.00	400.00
O48	A56	10r car rose & grn	57.50	225.00
		Nos. O36-O48 (13)	166.25	728.85

India Stamps of 1926-35 Overprinted Type "c"

1934-37

O49	A71	½a green	.30	.25
O50	A72	1a dark brown	.30	.25
O51	A49	2a vermilion	.45	.25
O52	A57	2a6p buff ('37)	1.90	30.00
O53	A52	4a olive green	9.00	.45
O54	A53	6a bister ('37)	5.50	25.00
		Nos. O49-O54 (6)	17.45	56.20

India Nos. 151-153 Overprinted Type "c"

1937-42   Perf. 13½x14

O55	A80	½a brown ('42)	67.50	.45
O56	A80	9p green	2.50	24.00
O57	A80	1a carmine	1.90	.45

India Nos. 162-165 Overprinted Type "d"

O58	A82	1r brn & sl ('40)	45.00	67.50
O59	A82	2r dk brn & dk vio ('40)	47.50	375.00
O60	A82	5r dp ultra & dk grn ('40)	100.00	600.00
O61	A82	10r rose car & dk vio ('40)	450.00	1,500.
		Nos. O55-O61 (7)	714.40	2,567.
		Set, never hinged	875.00	

India Official Stamps of 1939-43 Overprinted

1940-43

O62	O8	3p slate	.65	3.00
O63	O8	½a brown	2.10	1.90
O64	O8	½a dk rose vio ('43)	.65	.45
O65	O8	9p green	3.25	19.00
O66	O8	1a car rose	3.75	.25
O67	O8	1½a dull pur ('43)	9.25	2.40
O68	O8	2a scarlet	8.50	.45
O69	O8	2½a purple	5.25	14.00
O70	O8	4a dark brown	9.50	7.00
O71	O8	8a blue violet	9.50	12.00

India Nos. 162-165 Overprinted

1942   Wmk. 196   Perf. 13½x14

O72	A82	1r brown & slate	19.00	82.50
O73	A82	2r dk brn & dk violet	45.00	250.00
O74	A82	5r dp ultra & dk green	75.00	625.00
O75	A82	10r rose car & dk violet	150.00	825.00
		Nos. O62-O75 (14)	341.40	1,842.
		Set, never hinged	500.00	

NABHA

'näb-hə

LOCATION — A State of India in the eastern and southeastern Punjab
AREA — 966 sq. mi.
POP. — 340,044 (1941)
CAPITAL — Nabha

The varieties with small letters in the overprint are not listed as the letters are merely broken and not from another font.

Indian Stamps Overprinted in Black

1885   Wmk. 39   Perf. 14

1	A17	½a green	6.25	9.00
2	A19	1a violet brown	82.50	290.00
3	A21	2a ultramarine	37.50	97.50
4	A25	8a red lilac	475.00	
5	A27	1r gray	550.00	

Wmk. 38

6	A9	4a green	125.00	375.00

On the reprints "Nabha" and "State" each measure 9½mm. On the originals they measure 11 and 10mm respectively.

Indian Stamps Overprinted

1885   Wmk. 39   Red Overprint

7	A17	½a green	1.90	1.50
8	A21	2a ultramarine	3.75	3.25
9	A27	1r gray	190.00	450.00

Wmk. 38

10	A9	4a green	67.50	325.00

1885-97   Wmk. 39   Black Overprint

11	A17	½a green	.90	.25
12	A18	9p rose ('92)	.30	5.25
13	A19	1a violet brown	4.50	1.90
14	A20	1a6p bister brn	2.50	6.00
a.		"ABHA"	450.00	
15	A21	2a ultramarine	4.50	3.00
16	A22	3a orange	16.00	32.50
17	A23	4a olive green	9.00	5.00
18	A25	8a red lilac	6.00	5.25
19	A26	12a vio, red ('89)	7.00	8.25
20	A27	1r gray	22.50	90.00
21	A29	1r car rose & grn ('93)	21.00	10.50
a.		"N BHA"		—
22	A30	2r brn & rose ('97)	210.00	450.00
23	A30	3r grn & brn ('97)	210.00	550.00
24	A30	5r vio & blk ('97)	225.00	825.00

Wmk. 38

25	A14	6a bister ('89)	5.50	6.50
		Nos. 11-25 (15)	744.70	1,999.

Nos. 7, 8, 9, 10, 13, and 18 have been reprinted. They usually bear the overprint "Specimen."

1900   Wmk. 39

26	A31	3p carmine rose	.45	.25

1903-09

27	A32	3p gray	.95	.25
28	A33	½a green	1.40	1.00
a.		"NABH"	1,650.	
29	A34	1a car rose	2.10	2.25
30	A35	2a violet	3.25	5.25
30A	A36	2a6p ultra	24.50	130.00
31	A37	3a brown orange	2.00	.60
32	A38	4a olive green	6.00	2.50
33	A39	6a bister	5.00	30.00
34	A40	8a red violet	13.00	40.00
35	A41	12a violet, red	5.50	40.00
36	A42	1r car rose & grn	12.00	27.50
		Nos. 27-36 (11)	75.70	279.35

1907

37	A44	½a green	2.25	1.90
38	A45	1a carmine rose	2.25	1.00

1913

40	A46	3p gray	.75	.75
41	A47	½a green	.75	.45
42	A48	1a carmine rose	1.60	.25
43	A49	2a violet	1.50	1.50
44	A51	3a brown orange	.75	.45
45	A52	4a olive green	1.00	3.00
46	A53	6a bister	1.90	9.50
47	A54	8a red violet	9.50	9.00
48	A55	12a claret	4.50	35.00
49	A56	1r green & red brn	15.00	11.00
		Nos. 40-49 (10)	37.25	70.90

1924

50	A48	1a dark brown	10.00	6.00

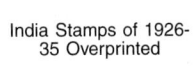

India Stamps of 1926-35 Overprinted

1927-32   Wmk. 196

51	A46	3p slate ('32)	2.50	.25
52	A47	½a green	1.50	.45
53	A48	1a dark brown	2.25	.25
54	A60	2a dull violet ('32)	3.75	.50
55	A57	2a6p buff ('32)	1.75	14.00
56	A51	3a blue ('30)	4.50	2.10
57	A61	4a olive green ('32)	6.75	3.75

Indian Stamps of 1937-40 Overprinted

58	A56	2r brown org & car rose ('32)	47.50	210.00
59	A56	5r dk violet & ultra ('32)	110.00	600.00
		Nos. 51-59 (9)	180.50	831.30

India Stamps of 1926-35 Overprinted

1936-37

63	A71	½a green	.75	.60
64	A68	9p dark green ('37)	3.00	1.60
65	A72	1a dark brown	.75	.45
66	A69	1a3p violet ('37)	3.50	11.00
67	A51	3a car rose ('37)	5.00	25.00
68	A52	4a olive green ('37)	7.50	7.50
		Nos. 63-68 (6)	20.50	46.15
		Set, never hinged	25.00	

Same Overprint in Black on 1937 Stamps of India

1938-39   Perf. 13½x14

69	A80	3p slate	9.50	2.25
70	A80	½a brown	7.50	2.50
71	A80	9p green	21.00	7.50
72	A80	1a carmine	3.25	1.50
73	A81	2a scarlet	1.25	12.00
74	A81	2a6p purple	1.25	17.50
75	A81	3a yel green	1.50	9.00
76	A81	3a6p ultramarine	1.75	37.50
77	A81	4a dark brown	8.00	10.50
78	A81	6a peacock blue	3.50	40.00
79	A81	8a blue violet	2.25	37.50
80	A81	12a car lake	3.00	37.50

Overprinted

81	A82	1r brown & slate	13.00	52.50
82	A82	2r brn & dk vio	32.50	175.00
83	A82	5r dp ultra & dk green	42.50	300.00
84	A82	10r rose car & dk vio ('39)	65.00	600.00
85	A82	15r dk grn & dk brn ('39)	200.00	1,250.
86	A82	25r dk vio & blue vio ('39)	150.00	1,250.
		Nos. 69-86 (18)	566.75	3,842.
		Set, never hinged	1,200.	

India Stamps of 1937 Overprinted in Black

1942   Perf. 13½x14

87	A80	3p slate	50.00	9.00
88	A80	½a brown	100.00	10.50
89	A80	9p green	14.00	24.00
90	A80	1a carmine	15.00	6.50
		Nos. 87-90 (4)	179.00	50.00
		Set, never hinged	210.00	

Same on India Nos. 168-179

1942-46   Wmk. 196

100	A83	3p slate	1.25	1.25
101	A83	½a rose vio ('43)	3.25	2.50
102	A83	9p lt green ('43)	2.50	2.50
103	A83	1a car rose ('46)	1.10	6.50
104	A84	1a3p bister ('44)	1.10	5.50
105	A84	1½a dark pur ('43)	2.50	4.50
106	A84	2a scarlet ('44)	1.20	6.50
107	A84	3a violet ('44)	7.00	7.00
108	A84	3½a ultramarine ('44)	18.00	100.00
109	A85	4a choc ('43)	1.90	1.50
110	A85	6a pck blue ('44)	15.00	82.50
111	A85	8a blue vio ('44)	13.50	62.50
112	A85	12a car lake ('44)	12.00	100.00
		Nos. 100-112 (13)	80.30	382.75
		Set, never hinged	110.00	

OFFICIAL STAMPS

Indian Stamps Overprinted in Black

1885   Wmk. 39   Perf. 14

O1	A17	½a green	7.50	2.25
O2	A19	1a violet brown	1.00	.30
O3	A21	2a ultra	125.00	250.00
		Nos. O1-O3 (3)	133.50	252.55

The reprints have the same measurements as the reprints of the regular issue of the same date.

Indian Stamps Overprinted

1885   Red Overprint

O4	A17	½a green	11.00	8.25
O5	A21	2a ultramarine	2.40	.80

1885-97		**Black Overprint**	
O6	A17	½a green	.60	.60
a.		Period after "SERVICE"	190.00	3.25
O7	A19	1a violet brown	3.00	.35
b.		Period after "SERVICE"	13.50	1.10
O8	A21	2a ultra	5.00	2.50
O9	A22	3a orange	81.00	140.00
O10	A23	4a olive green	5.25	2.25
O11	A25	8a red vio ('89)	4.00	2.25
O12	A26	12a vio, red ('89)	9.50	32.50
O13	A27	1r gray ('89)	62.50	525.00
O14	A29	1r car rose & grn ('97)	24.00	35.00

Wmk. 38

O15	A14	6a bister ('89)	32.50	52.50
		Nos. O6-O15 (10)	183.85	792.60

Nos. O4, O5, and O7 have been reprinted. They usually bear the overprint "Specimen."

1903-06		**Wmk. 39**	
O16	A32	3p gray ('06)	3.75	25.00
O17	A33	½a green	1.20	.50
O18	A34	1a carmine rose	1.20	.25
O19	A35	2a violet	5.00	2.10
O20	A38	4a olive green	2.40	.75
O21	A40	8a red violet	2.50	2.25
O22	A42	1r car rose & grn	2.50	3.75
		Nos. O16-O22 (7)	18.55	34.60

1907				
O23	A44	½a green	2.50	.75
O24	A45	1a carmine rose	1.00	.40

1913				
O25	A52	4a olive green	17.50	100.00
O26	A56	1r grn & red brn	92.50	750.00

Indian Stamps of 1911-26 Overprinted

a   b

1913				
O27	A46(a)	3p gray	1.40	15.00
O28	A47(a)	½a green	.85	.25
O29	A48(a)	1a carmine rose	.75	.25
O30	A49(a)	2a violet	1.60	.25
O31	A52(a)	4a olive green	1.25	.90
O32	A54(a)	8a red violet	2.10	3.00
O33	A56(b)	1r grn & red brn	8.50	6.50
		Nos. O27-O33 (7)	16.45	26.15

India Stamps of 1926-35 Overprinted

Perf. 13½x14, 14

1932-45		**Wmk. 196**	
O34	A46	3p slate	.30	.25
O35	A72	1a dark brown ('35)	.30	.25
O36	A52	4a olive green ('45)	35.00	3.75
O37	A54	8a red violet ('37)	1.50	4.00
		Nos. O34-O37 (4)	37.10	8.25

Same Overprint in Black on India Stamps of 1937

1938				
O38	A80	9p green	6.00	6.00
		Never hinged	7.00	
O39	A80	1a carmine	22.50	1.60
		Never hinged	27.50	

Official Stamps of India 1939-43 Overprinted in Black

1942-44		**Perf. 13½x14**	
O40	O8	3p slate	1.25	3.00
O41	O8	½a brown ('43)	1.20	.45
O42	O8	½a dk rose vio ('44)	4.75	2.25
O43	O8	9p green ('43)	1.25	.45
O44	O8	1a car rose ('43)	.65	.25
O45	O8	1 ½a dull purple ('43)	.70	.60
O46	O8	2a scarlet ('43)	2.25	2.25

O47	O8	4a dark brown ('43)	3.50	5.25
O48	O8	8a blue violet ('43)	6.75	30.00

India Nos. 162-164 Overprinted in Black

O49	A82	1r brown & slate	9.00	62.50
O50	A82	2r dk brn & dk vio	32.50	275.00
O51	A82	5r dp ultra & dk green	175.00	825.00
		Nos. O40-O51 (12)	238.80	1,207.
		Set, never hinged	300.00	

PATIALA

¸pət-ē-'äl-ə

LOCATION — A State of India in the central Punjab
AREA — 5,942 sq. mi.
POP. — 1,936,259 (1941)
CAPITAL — Patiala

The varieties with small letters in the overprint are not listed as the letters are merely broken and not from another font.

Indian Stamps Overprinted in Red

1884		**Wmk. 39**		**Perf. 14**
1	A17	½a green	6.00	7.00
a.		Double ovpt., one horiz.	4,750.	1,200.
2	A19	1a violet brown	75.00	110.00
a.		Double overprint		
b.		Double ovpt., one in black	1,050.	
c.		Pair, one as "b," one without overprint		
3	A21	2a ultra	19.00	24.00
4	A25	8a red lilac	650.00	1,600.
a.		Double ovpt., one in black	190.00	650.00
c.		Overprint reversed		
d.		Pair like "a," one with overprint reversed		
5	A27	1r gray	225.00	950.00

Wmk. 38

6	A9	4a green	140.00	150.00
		Nos. 1-6 (6)	1,115.	2,841.

Indian Stamps Overprinted in Red

1885		**Wmk. 39**		
7	A17	½a green	3.25	.45
a.		"AUTTIALLA"	24.00	52.50
c.		"STATE" only		
8	A21	2a ultra	9.00	2.50
a.		"AUTTIALLA"	62.50	
9	A27	1r gray	24.00	125.00
a.		"AUTTIALLA"	650.00	

Wmk. 38

10	A9	4a green	6.00	6.25
a.		Double overprint, one in black		
b.		Pair, one as "a," one with black overprint	375.00	

Same, Overprinted in Black
Wmk. 39

11	A19	1a violet brown	.90	.45
a.		"AUTTIALLA"	100.00	
c.		Double overprint, one in red	17.50	140.00
d.		Pair, one as "c," one without overprint		
12	A25	8a red lilac	35.00	82.50
a.		"AUTTIALLA"	550.00	
		Nos. 7-12 (6)	78.15	217.15

Nos. 7-12 have been reprinted. Most of them bear the word "Reprint." The few stamps that escaped the overprint cannot be distinguished from the originals.
The error "AUTTIALLA" has been reprinted in entire sheets, in red on the ½, 2, 4a and 1r and in black on the ½, 1, 2, 4, 8a and 1r. "STATE" is 7¾mm long, instead of 8½mm. Most stamps are overprinted "Reprint."

Same, Overprinted in Black

1891-96				
13	A17	½a green	.75	.25
14	A18	9p rose	1.50	3.25
15	A19	1a violet brown	2.10	.45
a.		"STATE" only	300.00	625.00
16	A20	1a6p bister brown	2.10	3.00
17	A21	2a ultra	3.25	1.50
18	A22	3a orange	3.75	1.10
19	A23	4a olive grn ('96)	3.75	1.10
a.		"STATE" only	750.00	375.00
20	A25	8a red violet ('96)	5.50	24.00
21	A26	12a violet, red ('96)	3.75	24.00
22	A29	1r car rose & grn ('96)	6.50	82.50
23	A30	2r brn & rose ('95)	210.00	1,250.
24	A30	3r grn & brn ('95)	290.00	1,350.
25	A30	5r vio & bl ('95)	325.00	1,400.

Wmk. 38

26	A14	6a bister	3.75	22.50
		Nos. 13-26 (14)	861.70	4,163.

1899		**Wmk. 39**		
27	A31	3p carmine rose	.45	.25
a.		Pair, one without overprint	6,000.	

1902				
28	A17	½a light green	1.50	.90
29	A19	1a carmine rose	3.75	2.50

1903-06				
31	A32	3p gray	.50	.25
32	A33	½a green	1.40	.25
33	A34	1a carmine rose	1.75	.25
a.		Pair, one without overprint	1,500.	
34	A35	2a ultra	2.00	1.00
35	A37	3a brown orange	2.00	.50
36	A38	4a olive green ('06)	3.50	2.25
37	A39	6a bister ('05)	4.25	15.00
38	A40	8a red violet ('06)	4.75	4.50
39	A41	12a vio, red ('06)	9.25	40.00
40	A42	1r car rose & grn ('05)	5.50	9.00
		Nos. 31-40 (10)	34.90	73.00

1908				
41	A44	½a green	.60	.35
42	A45	1a carmine rose	2.50	1.50

1912-14				
43	A46	3p gray	.35	.25
44	A47	½a green	.85	.25
45	A48	1a carmine rose	2.00	.25
46	A49	2a violet	1.90	2.25
47	A51	3a brown orange	3.25	2.50
48	A52	4a olive green	4.50	5.25
49	A53	6a bister	2.50	6.50
50	A54	8a red violet	3.75	3.75
51	A55	12a claret	4.75	15.00
52	A56	1r green & red brn	12.00	22.50
		Nos. 43-52 (10)	35.85	58.50

1922-26				
53	A48	1a dk brown ('23)	3.50	.75
54	A58	1 ½a chocolate	.35	.85
55	A51	3a ultra ('26)	4.25	14.00
56	A56	2r yel brn & car rose ('26)	18.00	225.00
57	A56	5r vio & ultra ('26)	45.00	300.00
		Nos. 53-57 (5)	71.10	540.60

India Stamps of 1926-35 Overprinted

1928-34		**Wmk. 196**		
60	A46	3p slate	2.50	.25
61	A47	½a green	.35	.25
62	A68	9p dark green	2.75	1.50
63	A48	1a dark brown	.95	.35
64	A60	1a3p violet	3.75	.25
65	A60	2a dull violet	2.10	.60
66	A57	2a6p buff	6.00	4.00
67	A51	3a blue	3.75	4.00
68	A61	4a olive green	6.50	3.00
69	A54	8a red violet	10.50	6.00

Indian Stamps of 1911-23 Overprinted

70	A56	1r green & brown	9.00	15.00
71	A56	2r buff & car rose	13.50	82.50
		Nos. 60-71 (12)	61.65	117.70

India Stamps of 1926-35 Overprinted Like Nos. 60-69

1935-37			**Perf. 14**	
75	A71	½a green ('37)	1.00	.45
76	A72	1a dk brown ('36)	1.40	.25
77	A49	2a ver ('36)	.50	2.25
78	A51	3a car rose ('37)	7.00	8.00
79	A52	4a olive green	2.25	3.50
		Nos. 75-79 (5)	12.15	14.45
		Set, never hinged	29.00	

Same Overprint in Black on Stamps of India, 1937

1937-38			**Perf. 13½x14**	
80	A80	3p slate ('38)	21.00	.50
81	A80	½a brown ('38)	8.50	.75
82	A80	9p green ('38)	5.25	1.50
83	A80	1a carmine ('38)	3.00	.25
84	A81	2a scarlet ('38)	1.60	14.00
85	A81	2a6p purple ('38)	6.00	30.00
86	A81	3a yel green ('38)	6.50	13.50
87	A81	3a6p ultra ('38)	6.75	37.50
88	A81	4a dark brown ('38)	24.00	25.00
89	A81	6a pck blue ('38)	25.00	90.00
90	A81	8a blue violet ('38)	27.50	62.50
91	A81	12a car lake ('38)	25.00	105.00

Overprinted Like Nos. 70-71

1938				
92	A82	1r brown & slate	30.00	62.50
93	A82	2r dk brn & dk vio	30.00	160.00
94	A82	5r dp ultra & dk green	40.00	375.00
95	A82	10r rose car & dk vio	52.50	600.00
96	A82	15r dk grn & dk brn	130.00	950.00
97	A82	25r dk vio & bl vio	150.00	950.00
		Nos. 80-97 (18)	592.60	3,478.
		Set, never hinged	850.00	

India Nos. 150-153 Overprinted in Black

1942-43			**Perf. 13½x14**	
98	A80	3p slate	11.50	4.00
99	A80	½a brown ('43)	6.75	3.25
100	A80	9p green ('43)	320.00	12.00
101	A80	1a carmine	25.00	3.75
		Nos. 98-101 (4)	363.25	23.00
		Set, never hinged	515.00	

India Stamps of 1941-43 with same Overprint in Black

1942-47			**Perf. 13½x14**	
102	A83	3p slate	4.25	.25
103	A83	½a rose violet ('43)	4.25	.25
104	A83	9p lt green ('43)	1.60	.25
a.		Pair, one without overprint	4,750.	
105	A83	1a car rose ('46)	1.10	.25
106	A84	1a3p bister ('43)	1.75	5.25
107	A84	1 ½a dk purple ('43)	13.50	5.50
108	A84	2a scarlet ('46)	9.50	.75
109	A84	3a violet ('46)	8.50	3.75
110	A84	3 ½a ultra ('46)	20.00	57.50
111	A85	4a choc ('46)	9.25	6.50
112	A85	6a pck blue ('46)	3.50	45.00
113	A85	8a blue vio ('46)	3.25	22.50
114	A85	12a car lake ('45)	30.00	125.00

No. 102 India No. 162 Overprinted in Black

115 A82 1r brown & slate
('47) 16.00 *120.00*
Nos. 102-115 (14) 126.45 *392.75*
Set, never hinged 170.00

OFFICIAL STAMPS

Indian Stamps Overprinted in Black and Red

1884   Wmk. 39   *Perf. 14*
O1 A17 ½a green 27.50 .60
O2 A19 1a vio brown 1.50 .25
  a. "SERVICE" double 3,000. 950.00
  b. "SERVICE" inverted 2,500.
  c. "PUTTIALLA STATE" dbl. 175.00
  d. "PUTTIALLA STATE" invtd. 3,000. 400.00
O3 A21 2a ultra *7,500.* 175.00

Overprinted in Red or Black

   a   b

1885-90
O4 A17(a) ½a green (R & Bk) 2.25 .35
  a. "AUTTIALLA" 80.00 25.00
  d. "SERVICE" double 1,050.
O5 A17(b) ½a green (Bk) 2.25 .25
O6 A19(a) 1a vio brn (Bk) 2.25 .25
  a. "AUTTILLA" 1,050. 72.50
  c. "SERVICE" dble., one invtd. 900.00
  d. "SERVICE" double 3,000.
O7 A21(b) 2a ultra (R) 1.10 .60
  c. "SERVICE" dbl., one invtd. 45.00 *290.00*
Nos. O4-O7 (4) 7.85 1.45

There are reprints of Nos. O4, O6 and O7. That of No. O4 has "SERVICE" overprinted in red in large letters and that of No. O6 has the same overprint in black. The originals have the word in small black letters. The reprints of No. O7, except those overprinted "Reprint," cannot be distinguished from the originals. These three reprints also exist with the error "AUTTIALLA."

Same, Overprinted in Black

1891-1900
O8 A17 ½a green ('95) .75 .25
  b. "SERVICE" inverted 90.00
O9 A19 1a vio brown ('00) 9.00 .25
  a. "SERVICE" inverted 90.00
O10 A21 2a ultramarine 5.00 3.25
  a. "SERVICE" inverted 90.00 *300.00*
O11 A22 3a orange 3.75 5.00
O12 A23 4a olive green 3.00 .45
O13 A25 8a red violet 5.25 2.50
O14 A26 12a violet, *red* 3.50 .80
O15 A27 1r gray 3.75 1.00
           Wmk. 38
O16 A14 6a bister 2.40 .50
Nos. O8-O16 (9) 36.40 14.00

1902   Wmk. 39
O17 A19 1a carmine rose 1.40 .25

1903
O18 A29 1r car rose & green 9.00 15.00

1903-09
O19 A32 3p gray .60 .25
O20 A33 ½a green 1.50 .25
O21 A34 1a carmine rose .90 .25
O22 A35 2a violet 1.20 .25
O23 A37 3a brown orange 6.00 5.25
O24 A38 4a olive green ('05) 4.00 .25
O25 A40 8a red violet 2.50 1.10
O26 A42 1r car rose & grn ('06) 3.00 1.20
Nos. O19-O26 (8) 19.70 8.80

1907
O27 A44 ½a green .75 .25
O28 A45 1a carmine rose .90 .25

India Stamps of 1911-26 Overprinted

   a   b

1913-26
O29 A46(a) 3p gray .30 .25
O30 A47(a) ½a green .25 .25
O31 A48(a) 1a car rose .25 .25
O32 A49(a) 2a violet 1.20 1.10
O33 A52(a) 4a olive green .75 .50
O34 A54(a) 8a red violet .80 *1.00*
O35 A56(b) 1r grn & red brn 1.75 2.10
O36 A56(b) 2r yel brn & car rose ('26) 24.00 *75.00*
O37 A56(b) 5r vio & ultra ('26) 15.00 *35.00*
Nos. O29-O37 (9) 44.30 *115.45*

Same Overprint on India Nos. 83 and 89

1925-26
O38 A48(a) 1a dark brown 9.50 1.50
O39 A53(a) 6a bister ('26) 2.10 *3.75*

India Stamps of 1926-35 Overprinted

1927-36   Wmk. 196
O40 A46 3p slate .25 .25
O41 A47 ½a green 1.25 .80
O42 A48 1a dark brown .25 .25
O43 A69 1a3p violet .60 .25
O44 A60 2a dull violet .25 *.45*
O45 A60 2a vermilion .45 .50
O46 A57 2a6p buff 3.75 .50
O47 A61 4a olive green .75 *.45*
O48 A54 8a red violet 1.60 1.00

Indian Stamps of 1911-23 Overprinted

O49 A56 1r green & brown 6.50 5.00
O50 A56 2r brn org & car rose ('36) 20.00 *62.50*
Nos. O40-O50 (11) 35.65 *71.95*

India Stamps of 1926-34 Overprinted

1935-36
O51 A71 ½a green ('36) .25 .25
O52 A72 1a dark brown ('36) .45 .45
O53 A49 2a vermilion .30 *.45*
  a. Small die 21.00 7.50
O54 A52 4a olive green ('36) 3.50 2.50
Nos. O51-O54 (4) 4.50 *3.65*
Set, never hinged 5.00

Same Overprint on India Nos. 151-153

1938-39   *Perf. 13½x14*
O55 A80 ½a brown ('39) .95 .30
O56 A80 9p green ('39) 16.00 *95.00*
O57 A80 1a carmine .95 .60
Nos. O55-O57 (3) 17.90 *95.90*
Set, never hinged 22.00

India No. 136 Surcharged in Black

1939   *Perf. 14*
O58 A69 1a on 1a3p violet 15.00 5.25
  Never hinged 18.00
"SERVICE" measures 9 ¼mm.

No. 64 Surcharged in Black

1940
O59 A69 1a on 1a3p violet 12.50 5.00
  Never hinged 15.00
"SERVICE" measures 8 ½mm.

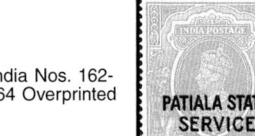

India Nos. 162-164 Overprinted

Perf. 13½x14
O60 A82 1r brown & slate 1.25 *10.50*
O61 A82 2r dk brn & dk vio 7.50 7.50
O62 A82 5r dp ultra & dk grn 21.00 *95.00*
Set, never hinged 36.00

India Official Stamps of 1939-43 Overprinted

1940-45
O63 O8 3p slate ('41) 1.90 .25
O64 O8 ½a brown 5.25 .25
O65 O8 ½a dk rose vio ('43) 1.10 .25
O66 O8 9p green 1.10 .75
O67 O8 1a carmine rose 3.50 .25
O68 O8 1a3p bister ('41) 1.25 .35
O69 O8 1½a dull purple ('45) 6.75 1.90
O70 O8 2a scarlet ('41) 11.00 .50
O71 O8 2½a purple ('41) 4.00 1.50
O72 O8 4a dk brown ('45) 1.90 *3.75*
O73 O8 8a blue violet ('45) 5.25 *9.00*

India Nos. 162-164 Overprinted in Black

O74 A82 1r brn & slate ('43) 5.25 16.00
O75 A82 2r dk brn & dk vio ('45) 13.50 95.00
O76 A82 5r dp ultra & dk grn ('45) 22.00 *125.00*
Nos. O63-O76 (14) 83.75 *254.75*
Set, never hinged 145.00

INDIA - FEUDATORY STATES
ALWAR
'əl-wər

LOCATION — A Feudatory State of India, lying southwest of Delhi in the Jaipur Residency.
AREA — 3,158 sq. mi.
POP. — 749,751.
CAPITAL — Alwar

Katar (Indian Dagger) — A1

1877   Unwmk.   Litho.   *Rouletted*
1 A1 ¼a ultramarine 7.00 1.60
  a. ¼a blue 7.00 1.60
2 A1 1a brown 5.25 1.90
  a. 1a yellow brown 16.00 8.25
  b. 1a red brown 5.00 2.25

Redrawn
1899-1901   *Pin-perf. 12*
3 A1 ¼a sl blue, wide margins 12.50 4.50
  a. Horiz. pair, imperf. between 600.00 *750.00*
  b. Vert. pair, imperf. between 1,200. *1,250.*
4 A1 ¼a yel grn, narrow margins ('01) 11.00 4.00
  a. Horiz. pair, imperf. between 950.00
  b. Imperf. pair 950.00
  c. ¼a emer, wide margins ('99) 600.00
  d. ¼a emer, narrow margins 5.25 4.75
  e. As "d," imperf. pair 550.00
  f. As "d," vert. pair, imperf horiz. 500.00
  g. As "d," horiz. pair, imperf vert. 450.00 *525.00*
  h. As "d," vert. pair, imperf horiz. 450.00 *525.00*

Nos. 3 and 4b are printed farther apart in the sheet.
On Nos. 3 and 4, the shading of the left border line is missing.
Nos. 1 to 4 occasionally show portions of the papermaker's watermark, W. T. & Co.
Alwar stamps became obsolete in 1902.

BAMRA

'bäm-rə

LOCATION — A Feudatory State in the Eastern States, Orissa States Agency, Bengal.
AREA — 1,988 sq. mi.
POP. — 151,259
CAPITAL — Deogarh

Stamps of Bamra were issued without gum.

A1   A2

1888   Unwmk.   Typeset   Imperf.

1	A1	¼a black, *yellow*	700.00	
a.		"g" inverted	7,000.	
2	A1	½a black, *rose*	125.00	
a.		"g" inverted	2,400.	
3	A1	1a black, *blue*	100.00	
a.		"g" inverted	2,100.	
4	A1	2a black, *green*	140.00	550.00
a.		"postge"	2,400.	
5	A1	4a black, *yellow*	120.00	550.00
a.		"postge"	2,250.	
6	A1	8a black, *rose*	72.50	
a.		"postge"	1,900.	
		Nos. 1-6 (6)	1,257.	

All values may be found with the scroll inverted, and with the long end of the scroll pointing to the right or left.
On No. 5 the last character on the 3rd line is a vertical line. On No. 1 it is not vertical.
On No. 2 the last character on the 3rd line looks like a backwards "R" with a bent leg. On No. 6 it looks like an apostrophe.
Nos. 1 and 2 have been reprinted in blocks of 8 and Nos. 1-6 in blocks of 20. In the reprints the 4th character of the native inscription often has the curved upper line broken at the left, but in many instances comparison with photographic reproductions of the original settings is the only certain test.

1890

7	A2	¼a black, *rose lilac*	7.00	9.00
a.		"Quatrer"	32.50	57.50
b.		"e" of "Postage" inverted	32.50	57.50
c.		"Eeudatory"	32.50	57.50
8	A2	2a black, *green*	5.25	5.25
a.		"Eeudatory"	90.00	110.00
b.		"postage" with small "p"	5.25	5.25
9	A2	1a black, *yellow*	6.50	5.00
a.		"Eeudatory"	195.00	225.00
b.		"postage" with small "p"	6.50	5.00
c.		"annas"	300.00	325.00
10	A2	2a black, *rose lilac*	30.00	57.50
a.		"Eeudatory"	275.00	550.00
11	A2	4a black, *bright rose*	9.50	12.50
a.		"Eeudatory"	6,750.	
12	A2	8a black, *rose lilac*	40.00	100.00
a.		"BAMBA"	375.00	550.00
b.		"Foudatory" & "Postage"	375.00	550.00
c.		"postage" with small "p"	40.00	100.00
13	A2	1r black, *rose lilac*	100.00	160.00
a.		"BAMBA"	650.00	825.00
b.		"Eeudatory"	825.00	1,050.
c.		"postage" with small "p"	100.00	160.00
		Nos. 7-13 (7)	198.25	349.25

1893

14	A2	¼a black, *rose*	3.00	4.50
a.		"postage" with small "p"	3.00	4.50
15	A2	¼a black, *magenta*	3.00	4.00
a.		"postage" with small "p"	3.00	4.00
b.		"AM" of "BAMRA" invtd.		
c.		"M" OF "BAMRA" invtd.		
d.		"AMRA" of "BAMRA" inverted	100.00	100.00
e.		"M" and 2nd "A" of "BAMRA" inverted	140.00	140.00
f.		First "a" of "anna" inverted	72.50	82.50
16	A2	2a black, *rose*	21.00	12.00
a.		"postage" with small "p"	21.00	12.00
17	A2	4a black, *rose*	16.00	12.00
a.		"postage" with small "p"	16.00	12.00
b.		"BAMBA"	1,600.	1,800.
18	A2	8a black, *rose*	42.50	29.00
a.		"postage" with small "p"	42.50	29.00
19	A2	1r black, *rose*	35.00	35.00
a.		"postage" with small "p"	35.00	35.00
		Nos. 14-19 (6)	120.50	96.50

The central ornament varies in size and may be found in various positions.
Bamra stamps became obsolete Dec. 31, 1894.

BARWANI

bər-'wän-ē

LOCATION — A Feudatory State of Central India, in the Malwa Agency.
AREA — 1,178 sq. mi.
POP. — 141,110
CAPITAL — Barwani

The stamps of Barwani were all typographed and normally issued in booklets containing panes of four. Exceptions are noted (Nos. 14-15, 20-25). The majority were completely perforated, but some of the earlier printings were perforated only between the stamps, leaving one or two sides imperf. Nos. 1-25 were issued without gum. Many shades exist.

Rana Ranjit Singh
A1   A2

1921, April (?)   Unwmk.   Pin-Perf 7
Toned Medium Wove Paper
Clear Impression

1	A1	¼a dull Prus green	225.00	625.00
2	A1	½a dull blue	500.00	950.00

1921   Coarse Perf. 7 x Imperf.
White Thin Wove Paper
Blurred Impression

3	A1	¼a dull green	37.50	190.00
4	A1	½a pale blue	25.00	275.00

1921   Toned Laid Paper   Imperf.

5	A1	¼a light green	30.00	125.00
6	A1	½a light green	8.25	
a.		Perf. 11, top or bottom only	7.00	

1921   Coarse Perf. 7, 7 x Imperf.
Thick Wove Paper
Very Blurred Impression

7	A1	¼a dull blue	25.00	
8	A1	½a dull green	22.50	

In 1927 Nos. 7-8 were printed on thin hard paper.

1922   Perf. 7 x Imperf.
Thick Glazed Paper

9	A1	¼a dull ultra	160.00	

Rough Perf. 11 x Imperf.

10	A2	1a vermilion	3.75	30.00
11	A2	2a violet	3.25	37.50
a.		Double impression	450.00	
		Nos. 9-11 (3)	167.00	67.50

Shades of No. 11 include purple. No. 11 was also printed on thick dark toned paper.

1923-26   Wove, Laid Paper   Perf.

12	A1	¼a grayish ultra, perf. 8½	2.40	72.50
13	A1	¼a black, perf. 7 x imperf.	110.00	550.00
14	A1	¼a dull rose, perf. 11½-12	3.75	21.00
15	A1	¼a dk bl, perf. 11 ('26)	2.25	16.00
16	A1	¼a grn, perf. 11 x imperf.	1.90	30.00
		Nos. 12-16 (5)	120.30	689.50

No. 12 was also printed on pale gray thin toned paper.
No. 14 was printed on horizontally laid paper in horizontal sheets of 12 containing three panes of 4.
No. 15 was printed on vertically laid paper in horizontal sheets of 8.

Rana Ranjit Singh — A3

1927-28   Thin Wove Paper   Perf. 7

17	A3	4a dull orange	200.00	675.00

No. 17 was also printed in light brown on thick paper, pin-perf. 6, and in orange brown on thick paper, rough perf. 7.

1928   Coarse Perf. 7
Thick Glazed Paper

18	A1	¼a bright blue	16.00	
19	A1	½a bright yel green	37.50	

1928, Nov.   Rough Perf. 10½

20	A1	¼a deep ultra	9.50	
a.		Tête bêche pair	19.00	
21	A1	½a yellow green	7.00	
a.		Tête bêche pair	14.00	

1929-31   Perf. 11

22	A1	¼a blue	3.25	21.00
a.		¼a ultramarine	3.00	21.00
23	A1	½a emerald green	4.00	24.00
24	A2	1a car pink ('31)	24.00	67.50
25	A3	4a salmon	120.00	325.00
		Nos. 22-25 (4)	151.25	437.50

Nos. 20-25 were printed in sheets of 8 (4x2).
No. 22 had five printings in various shades (bright to deep blue) in horizontal or vertical format.
No. 23 also printed in dark myrtle green.

Rana Devi Singh
A4   A5

1932-48   Glazed Paper   Perf. 11, 12

26	A4	¼a dark gray	3.75	35.00
27	A4	½a blue green	6.00	35.00
28	A4	1a brown	6.00	32.50
a.		1a chocolate, perf. 8½ ('48)	21.00	75.00
29	A4	2a deep red violet	5.50	62.50
a.		Perf. 12x11		
b.		2a red lilac	12.50	
30	A4	4a olive green	9.00	62.50
		Nos. 26-30 (5)	30.25	227.50

Types of 1921-27

1934-48   Perf. 11

31	A1	¼a slate gray	6.00	47.50
32	A1	½a blue green	6.50	60.00
33	A2	1a dark brown	16.00	29.00
a.		1a brown, perf. 8½ ('48)	15.00	75.00
34	A2	2a brt purple ('38)	125.00	490.00
35	A2	2a rose car ('46)	35.00	190.00
36	A3	4a olive green	20.00	67.50
		Nos. 31-36 (6)	208.50	884.00

In the nine printings of Nos. 26-36, several plate settings spaced the cliches from 2 to 9mm apart. Hence the stamps come in different overall sizes. Not all values were in each printing. Values are for the commonest varieties.
No. 36 was also printed in pale sage green.

1938

37	A5	1a dark brown	50.00	110.00
a.		Booklet pane of 4		

Stamps of type A5 in red are revenues.
Barwani stamps became obsolete July 1, 1948.

BHOPAL

bō-'päl

LOCATION — A Feudatory State of Central India, in the Bhopal Agency.
AREA — 6,924 sq. mi.
POP. — 995,175
CAPITAL — Bhopal

Inscription in Urdu in an octagon embossed on Nos. 1-83, in a circle embossed on Nos. 84-90. On designs A1-A3, A7, A11-A12, A14-A15, A19-A21 the embossing makes up the central part of the design.

The embossing may be found inverted or sideways.
Expect irregular perfs on the perforated stamps, Nos. 13-77, due to a combination of imperfect perforating methods and the fragility of the papers.
Nos. 1-90 issued without gum.

A1   A2

Double Lined Frame

1876   Unwmk.   Litho.   Imperf.

1	A1	¼a black	950.00	700.00
a.		"EGAM"	2,750.	2,400.
b.		"BFGAM"	2,750.	2,400.
c.		"BEGAN"	1,500.	1,250.
2	A1	½a red	30.00	72.50
a.		"EGAM"	110.00	250.00
b.		"BFGAM"	110.00	250.00
c.		"BEGAN"	72.50	160.00

1877   Single Lined Frame

3	A2	¼a black		9,000.
4	A2	½a red	52.50	110.00
a.		"NWAB"	250.00	490.00

A3   A4

1878

5	A3	¼a black	12.00	24.00
a.		"J" diagonal, plate II	13.50	27.50

All stamps of type A3 are lettered "EEGAM" for "BEGAM."

1878

6	A4	½a pale red	10.50	24.00
a.		"a brown red"	42.50	67.50
b.		"NWAB"	35.00	
c.		"JAHN"	57.50	
d.		"EECAM"	57.50	

A5   A6

1879-80

7	A5	¼a green	21.00	40.00
8	A5	½a red	27.50	35.00

Perf.

9	A5	¼a green	16.00	27.50
10	A5	½a red	160.00	
		Nos. 7-10 (4)	224.50	102.50

Nos. 7 and 9 have the value in parenthesis; Nos. 8 and 10 are without parenthesis.

1881   Imperf.

11	A6	¼a green	13.50	
a.		"NAWA"	42.50	
b.		"CHAH"	120.00	

Perf.

12	A6	¼a green	18.00	
a.		"NAWA"	67.50	
b.		"CHAH"	160.00	

A7

1881-89   Imperf.

13	A7	¼a black	9.00	35.00
a.		"NWAB"	22.50	
14	A7	½a red	7.50	25.00
a.		"NWAB"	18.00	

15	A7	1a brown	6.50 *29.00*
a.		"NWAB"	14.00
16	A7	2a blue	5.00 *29.00*
a.		"NWAB"	9.50
17	A7	4a yellow	30.00 *100.00*
a.		"NWAB"	82.50
		Nos. 13-17 (5)	58.00 *218.00*

A8   A9

1884 **Perf.**

19	A8	¼a green	225.00 *275.00*
a.		"JAN"	225.00 *275.00*
b.		"BEGM"	450.00 *625.00*
c.		"NWAB"	950.00
d.		"SHAHAN"	950.00
f.		"JAHA"	450.00
20	A9	¼a green	8.25 *27.50*

On type A9 there is a dash at the left of "JA" of "JAHAN" instead of a character like a comma as on types A5 and A6.

Imitations of No. 19 were printed about 1904 in black on wove paper and in red on laid paper, both imperf. and pin-perf.

A10

1884   Laid Paper   Imperf.

21	A10	¼a blue green	240.00 *275.00*
a.		"NWAB"	675.00
b.		"NAWAJANAN"	675.00
c.		"SAH"	675.00
22	A10	½a black	3.25 *3.75*
a.		"NWAB"	15.00 *18.00*
b.		"NAWAJANAN"	15.00 *18.00*
c.		"SAH"	15.00 *18.00*

Perf.

23	A10	¼a blue green	1.50 *6.00*
a.		"NWAB"	6.00
b.		"NAWAJANAN"	6.00
c.		"SAH"	6.00
24	A10	½a black	1.40 *5.00*
a.		"NWAB"	5.50 *12.50*
b.		"NAWAJANAN"	5.50 *12.50*
c.		"SAH"	5.50 *12.50*
		Nos. 21-24 (4)	246.15 *289.75*

Type Redrawn

1886   Wove Paper   Imperf.

25	A10	¼a grayish green	.80 *5.00*
a.		¼a green	.80 *5.00*
b.		"NWAB"	4.50 *13.50*
c.		"NAWAA"	3.00 *10.50*
d.		"NAWAA"	4.50 *13.50*
e.		"NAWABABEGAAM"	4.50 *13.50*
f.		"NWABA"	4.50 *13.50*
26	A10	½a red	1.00 *2.50*
a.		"SAH"	6.00 *9.50*
b.		"NAWABA"	4.50 *7.50*

Perf.

27	A10	¼a green	3.75 *6.00*
a.		"NWAB"	20.00
b.		"NAWA"	12.00
c.		"NAWAA"	20.00
d.		"NAWABABEGAAM"	20.00
e.		"NWABA"	20.00
28	A10	½a red	1.20 *3.00*
a.		"SAH"	9.00
b.		"NAWABA"	12.00
		Nos. 25-28 (4)	6.75 *16.50*

On Nos. 25-28 the inscriptions are closer to the value than on Nos. 21-24.

A11

A12

1886   Imperf.

29	A11	½a red	4.00 *15.00*
a.		"BEGAM"	18.00 *47.50*

---

b.		"NWAB"	18.00

Laid Paper

30	A12	4a yellow	18.00 *57.50*
a.		"EEGAM"	24.00
b.		Wove paper	1,500.
c.		As "a," wove paper	1,900.

Perf.

31	A12	4a yellow	6.50 *30.00*
a.		"EEGAM"	9.50 *42.50*
		Nos. 29-31 (3)	28.50

A13   A14

1889   Wove Paper   Imperf.

32	A13	¼a green	1.50 *3.00*
a.		"SAH"	6.50 *10.50*
b.		"NAWA"	6.50 *10.50*
33	A14	¼a black	3.25 *8.25*
a.		"EEGAN"	27.50 *47.50*

Perf.

34	A13	¼a green	3.00 *4.00*
a.		"SAH"	11.00 *13.50*
b.		"NAWA"	11.00 *13.50*
c.		Vert. pair, imperf between	325.00
35	A14	¼a black	2.50 *8.25*
a.		"EEGAN"	22.50 *47.50*
b.		Horiz. pair, imperf. between	400.00
		Nos. 32-35 (4)	10.25 *23.50*

Type A13 has smaller letters in the upper corners than Type A10.

A15   A16

1890   Imperf.

36	A15	¼a black	3.25 *3.00*
37	A15	1a brown	3.25 *7.00*
a.		"EEGAM"	21.00 *40.00*
b.		"BBGAM"	21.00 *40.00*
38	A7	2a greenish blue	3.00 *3.25*
a.		"BBEGAM"	12.50 *21.00*
b.		"NAWAH"	12.50 *21.00*
39	A7	4a yellow	3.75 *5.50*
40	A16	8a blue	100.00 *180.00*
a.		"HAH"	110.00 *190.00*
b.		"JABAN"	120.00
		Nos. 36-40 (5)	113.25 *198.75*

An imperf. imitation of Nos. 36 and 41 was printed about 1904 in black on wove paper.

Perf.

41	A15	¼a black	4.50 *6.25*
a.		Pair, imperf. between	500.00
42	A15	1a brown	6.50 *11.00*
a.		"EECAM"	37.50 *52.50*
b.		"BBGAM"	37.50 *52.50*
43	A7	2a greenish blue	3.75 *5.50*
a.		"BBEGAM"	14.00 *27.50*
b.		"NAWAH"	14.00 *27.50*
44	A7	4a yellow	4.50 *12.00*
45	A16	8a blue	100.00 *180.00*
a.		"HAH"	110.00
b.		"JABAN"	120.00
		Nos. 41-45 (5)	119.25 *214.75*

Nos. 40 and 45 have a frame line around each stamp.

Imperf

46	A12	½a red (BECAM)	3.00 *5.50*
47	A13	½a red (NWAB)	3.00 *2.25*
a.		Inverted "N"	
b.		"SAH"	9.00

Perf.

48	A12	½a red (BECAM)	2.50 *7.00*
a.		Without embossing	
49	A13	½a red (NWAB)	1.20 *3.00*
a.		Inverted "N"	
b.		"SAH"	7.50
		Nos. 46-49 (4)	9.70 *17.75*

1891-93   Laid Paper   Imperf.

50	A16	8a deep green	110.00 *225.00*
a.		"HAH"	125.00
b.		"JABAN"	150.00

Perf.

51	A16	8a deep green	110.00 *225.00*
a.		"HAH"	125.00
b.		"JABAN"	140.00

For overprint, see No. 83.

1894   Redrawn   Imperf.

53	A10	¼a green	2.25 *2.50*
a.		"NAWAH"	11.00 *12.00*
54	A11	½a brick red	3.25 *3.25*
55	A16	8a blue black	32.50 *32.50*
a.		Laid paper	300.00 *450.00*

56	A10	¼a green	4.50 *3.25*
a.		"NAWAH"	19.00 *16.00*
57	A11	½a brick red	1.20 *3.00*
58	A16	8a blue black	45.00 *60.00*
		Nos. 53-58 (6)	88.70 *104.50*

The ¼a redrawn has letters in corners larger; value in very small characters.
The 8a redrawn has no frame to each stamp but a frame to the sheet.

1898   Imperf.

60	A16	8a black	62.50 *82.50*
b.		"E" of "BEGAM" inverted	140.00 *150.00*

A17   A18

A19

A20   A21

1895   Laid Paper

61	A17	¼a green	2.25 *2.50*
62	A18	¼a red	10.50 *5.00*
63	A19	½a black	5.25 *4.50*
a.		"A" inserted in "NAW B"	12.50 *10.00*
64	A20	½a black	2.25 *2.50*
65	A21	½a red	3.25 *3.25*

Perf.

66	A17	¼a green	4.50 *3.25*
67	A18	¼a red	1,250.
		Nos. 61-67 (7)	28.00 *1,271.*

On No. 63a, the second "A" in "NAWAB" has been inserted by hand and varies somewhat in size.

Imperf. imitations of No. 65 were printed about 1904 in deep red on laid paper and in black on wove paper.

Stamps of types A16 and A19-A21 with a circular embossed seal and perforated, were prepared but not issued.

A22   A23

1898   Imperf.

72	A22	¼a black	.75 *.75*
a.		"SHAN"	5.00 *5.00*
73	A22	¼a green	1.10 *1.20*
a.		"SHAN"	5.25 *5.25*
74	A23	¼a black	2.10 *2.10*
		Nos. 72-74 (3)	3.95 *4.05*

1899

75	A13	½a black ("NWAB")	6.50 *9.50*
b.		"NWASBAHJAHNJ"	32.50 *42.50*
d.		"SBAH"	15.00 *22.50*
e.		"SBAN"	32.50 *42.50*
f.		"NWIB"	32.50 *42.50*
g.		"BEIAM"	32.50 *42.50*

A24   Coat of
                     Arms — A25

1902

76	A24	¼a red	5.50 *9.00*
77	A24	½a black	6.00 *10.00*
a.		Printed on both sides	1,100.
78	A24	1a brown	10.00 *25.00*
79	A24	2a blue	12.50 *22.50*
80	A24	4a orange	110.00 *160.00*
81	A24	8a violet	150.00 *290.00*
82	A24	1r rose	400.00 *600.00*
		Nos. 76-82 (7)	694.00 *1,116.*

No. 50 Overprinted
in Red

1903

83	A16	8a deep green	210.00 *225.00*
a.		Inverted overprint	550.00 *600.00*

There are two types of the overprint which is the Arabic S, initial of the Begum.

**Inscription in Circle
Embossed on Each Stamp**

1903   Wove Paper

84	A24	¼a red	2.25 *7.50*
85	A24	½a black	1.90 *7.50*
86	A24	1a brown	4.50 *11.00*
87	A24	2a blue	10.00 *37.50*
88	A24	4a orange	27.50 *75.00*
89	A24	8a violet	82.50 *190.00*
90	A24	1r rose	125.00 *290.00*
		Nos. 84-90 (7)	253.65 *618.50*

Laid Paper

84a	A24	¼a red	1.50 *12.00*
85a	A24	½a black	1.50 *12.50*
86a	A24	1a brown	10.00
87a	A24	2a blue	250.00 *325.00*
88a	A24	4a orange	500.00 *500.00*
89a	A24	8a violet	2,400.
90a	A24	1r rose	1,900.
		Nos. 84a-90a (7)	5,063. *849.50*

The embossing in a circle, which was first used in 1903, has been applied to many early stamps and impressions from redrawn plates of early issues. So far as is now known, these should be classed as reprints.

1908   Engr.   Perf. 13½

99	A25	1a yellow green	5.50 *6.75*
a.		Printed on both sides	180.00

OFFICIAL STAMPS

O1

Overprinted

Size: 20½x25mm

1908   Unwmk.   Engr.   Perf. 13½

O1	O1	½a yellow green	3.25 *.25*
a.		Pair, one without ovpt.	950.00
b.		Inverted overprint	275.00 *225.00*
c.		Double ovpt., one invtd.	160.00
O2	O1	1a carmine	6.25 *.60*
a.		Inverted overprint	180.00 *150.00*
O3	O1	2a blue	36.00 *.25*
O4	O1	4a red brown	21.00 *.80*
		Nos. O1-O4 (4)	66.50 *1.90*

Overprinted

O5	O1	½a yellow green	11.00	1.90
O6	O1	1a carmine	14.00	1.40
O7	O1	2a blue	6.00	.90
a.		Inverted overprint	37.50	
O8	O1	4a red brown	120.00	2.25
a.		Inverted overprint	30.00	100.00
		Nos. O5-O8 (4)	151.00	6.45

The difference in the two overprints is in the shape of the letters, most noticeable in the "R."

Type of 1908 Issue

Overprinted

Size: 25½x30½mm

1930-31		**Litho.**		**Perf. 14**
O9	O1	½a gray green ('31)	18.00	2.50
O10	O1	1a carmine	16.00	.25
O11	O1	2a blue	14.00	.65
O12	O1	4a brown	15.00	1.40
		Nos. O9-O12 (4)	63.00	4.80

½a, 2a, 4a are inscribed "POSTAGE" on the left side; 1a "POSTAGE AND REVENUE."

Similar to Type O1
Size: 21x25mm
"POSTAGE" at left
"BHOPAL STATE" at right

1932-33		**Perf. 11½, 13, 13½, 14**		
O13	O1	¼a orange yellow	3.75	.75
a.		Pair, one without overprint	180.00	
b.		Perf. 13½	16.00	.45
c.		Perf. 14	18.00	.45

"BHOPAL GOVT." at right
Perf. 13½

O14	O1	½a yellow green	11.00	.25
a.		Perf 14 ('34)	24.00	.60
O15	O1	1a brown red	16.00	.25
O16	O1	2a blue	16.00	.65
O17	O1	4a brown	16.00	1.50
a.		Perf 14 ('34)	24.00	16.00
		Nos. O13-O17 (5)	62.75	3.40

No. O14, O16-O17 Surcharged in Red, Violet, Black or Blue

a   b

c

1935-36			**Perf. 13½**	
O18	O1(a)	¼a on ½a (R)	47.50	21.00
a.		Inverted surcharge	300.00	125.00
O19	O1(b)	3p on ½a (R)	5.50	5.25
O20	O1(a)	¼a on 2a (R)	42.50	30.00
a.		Inverted surcharge	300.00	110.00
O21	O1(b)	3p on 2a (R)	6.75	6.75
a.		Inverted surcharge	120.00	60.00
O22	O1(a)	¼a on 4a (R)	1,500.	500.00
O23	O1(a)	¼a on 4a (Bk) ('36)	120.00	40.00
O24	O1(a)	¼a on 4a (R)	210.00	100.00
O25	O1(b)	3p on 4a (Bk) ('36)	3.75	5.00
O26	O1(c)	1a on ½a (V)	7.50	2.25
a.		Inverted surcharge	100.00	67.50
O27	O1(c)	1a on 4a (R)	3.25	3.00
a.		Inverted surcharge	140.00	140.00
O28	O1(c)	1a on 2a (Bk) ('36)	1.00	3.75
O29	O1(c)	1a on 4a (Bl)	10.50	7.50
		Nos. O18-O29 (12)	1,958.	724.50

Nos. O18-O25 are arranged in composite sheets of 100. The 2 top horizontal rows of

each value are surcharged "a" and the next 5 rows are "b." The next 3 rows as "b" but in a narrower setting.
Various errors of spelling or inverted letters are found on Nos. O18-O29.

Arms of Bhopal — O2

1935			**Litho.**	
O30	O2	1a3p claret & blue	5.25	2.25

Inscribed: "Bhopal State Postage"
Ovptd. "SERVICE" 11mm long

1937			**Perf. 12**	
O31	O2	1a6p dk claret & blue	3.75	1.50
a.		Overprint omitted	275.00	210.00
b.		Double overprint, one inverted	750.00	750.00
c.		Blue printing double		250.00
d.		Imperf, pair		275.00
e.		Pair, imperf between	300.00	325.00

See Nos. O42, O45.

Arms of Bhopal — O3

Brown or Black Overprint

1936-38			**Typo.**	
O32	O3	¼a orange (Br)	1.40	.90
a.		Inverted overprint	525.00	400.00
b.		Vert. pair, imperf between	250.00	
c.		Horiz. pair, imperf between		450.00
d.		Black overprint	12.50	1.10
e.		As "d," inverted ovpt.		600.00
f.		As "d," double ovpt.		450.00
O32B	O3	¼a yellow (Br) ('38)	5.25	2.25
O33	O3	1a carmine	1.90	.25
a.		Horiz. pair, imperf vert.		250.00
b.		Vert. pair, imperf between		490.00
c.		Horiz. pair, imperf between	200.00	225.00
d.		Block of 4, imperf between	625.00	625.00
		Nos. O32-O33 (3)	8.55	3.40

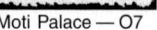

Moti Mahal O4

Overprinted in Black

1936			**Perf. 11½**	
O34	O4	½a green & chocolate	.85	1.20
a.		Double impression of stamp	150.00	22.50
b.		Double overprint	350.00	250.00
c.		Vert. pair, imperf between		325.00
d.		Horiz. pair, imperf between		325.00

Moti Masjid — O5

4a, Taj Mahal and Be-Nazir Palaces.

Overprinted in Black

1937			**Perf. 11½**	
O35	O5	2a dk blue & brown	2.50	1.40
a.		Inverted overprint	375.00	550.00
b.		Vert. pair, imperf between		525.00
c.		Horiz. pair, imperf between		375.00
O36	O5	4a bister brn & blue	4.50	.75
a.		Double overprint		240.00
b.		Center double		600.00
c.		Horiz. pair, imperf between		1,000.
d.		Overprint omitted		490.00

Types of 1937
Overprinted "SERVICE" in Black or Brown

Designs: 4a, Taj Mahal. 8a, Ahmadabad Palace. 1r, Rait-Ghat.

1938-44				
O37	O4	½a dp green & brown	.90	.60
O38	O5	2a violet & dp grn	15.00	.45
O39	O5	4a red brn & brt bl	4.25	.80
a.		Frame double		450.00
O40	O5	8a red vio & blue	7.00	3.25
a.		"SERAICE"	550.00	825.00
b.		Overprint omitted		250.00
c.		Double overprint		240.00
d.		Vert. pair, imperf between		625.00
e.		"1" for "I" in "SERVICE"	550.00	825.00
O41	O5	1r bl & red vio (Br)	27.50	12.50
a.		Black overprint ('44)	21.00	6.50
b.		"SREVICE"	160.00	375.00
c.		Overprint omitted	1,100.	
d.		Vert. pair, imperf horiz.		2,250.
		Nos. O37-O41 (5)	54.65	17.60

No. O39 measures 36½x22½mm, No. O40 39x24mm, No. O41 45½x27¾mm.

Type of 1935

1939			**Perf. 12**	
O42	O2	1a6p dark claret	7.50	2.50
a.		Overprint omitted		625.00
b.		Double overprint		625.00
c.		Double overprint, one inverted		625.00
d.		Pair, imperf between	250.00	325.00

Tiger — O6

Design: 1a, Deer.

1940		**Typo.**	**Perf. 11½**	
O43	O6	¼a ultramarine	6.00	2.50
O44	O6	1a red violet	35.00	4.50

Type of 1935
Inscribed: "Bhopal State Postage"

1941				
O45	O2	1a3p emerald	2.50	3.25
a.		Pair, imperf between	550.00	700.00

Moti Palace — O7   Coat of Arms — O8

2a, Moti Mosque. 4a, Be-Nazir Palaces.

		Perf. 11½, 12		
1944-46		**Unwmk.**	**Typo.**	
O46	O8	3p ultramarine	1.25	1.25
O47	O7	½a light green	1.10	1.50
O48	O8	9p orange brn ('46)	12.00	5.00
a.		Imperf., pair		290.00
O49	O8	1a brt red vio ('45)	6.25	2.60
O50	O8	1½a deep plum	1.90	1.90
O51	O7	2a red violet ('45)	13.50	6.00
O52	O8	3a yellow ('46)	16.00	21.00
a.		Imperf., pair		290.00
O53	O7	4a brown ('45)	8.75	3.25
O54	O8	6a brt rose ('46)	24.00	75.00
a.		Imperf., pair		400.00
		Nos. O46-O54 (9)	84.75	117.50

For surcharges see Nos. O58-O59.

1946-47		**Unwmk.**	**Perf. 11½**	
O55	O8	1a violet	11.00	4.75
O56	O8	2a violet ('47)	13.50	22.50
O57	O8	3a deep orange	125.00	160.00
a.		Imperf., pair	—	275.00
		Nos. O55-O57 (3)	149.50	187.25

No. O50 Surcharged "2 As." and Bars

1949			**Perf. 12**	
O58	O8	2a on 1½a dp plum	3.00	11.00
c.		Imperf., pair	300.00	450.00

Same Surcharged "2 As." and Rosettes

1949			**Imperf.**	
O59	O8	2a on 1½a dp plum	1,250.	1,500.
b.			1,000.	7,000.

Three or more types of "2" in surcharge. Bhopal stamps became obsolete in 1950.

BHOR
ˈbōˌər

LOCATION — A Feudatory State in the Kolhapur Residency and Deccan States Agency.
AREA — 910 sq. mi.
POP. — 141,546
CAPITAL — Bhor

A1

A2

1879		**Handstamped Unwmk.**		**Imperf.**
		Without Gum		
1	A1	½a carmine	5.50	7.50
2	A2	1a carmine	8.25	12.00

Pant Sachiv Shankarrao — A3

1901		**Without Gum**	**Typo.**
3	A3	½a red	24.00	60.00

BIJAWAR
bi-ˈjä-wər

LOCATION — A Feudatory State in the Bundelkhand Agency of Central India.
AREA — 973 sq. mi.
POP. — 115,852
CAPITAL — Bijawar

Maharaja Sir Sawant Singh — A1

1935-36	**Typo.**	**Unwmk.**	**Perf. 10½**	
1	A1	3p brown	11.00	8.25
a.		Imperf., pair	13.50	
b.		Rouletted 7 ('36)	9.00	9.00
2	A1	6p carmine	9.50	8.25
a.		Rouletted 7 ('36)	12.00	32.50
3	A1	9p purple	12.50	7.50
a.		Rouletted 7 ('36)	9.00	160.00
4	A1	1a dark blue	14.00	8.25
a.		Rouletted 7 ('36)	15.00	180.00
5	A1	2a slate green	13.50	7.50
a.		Rouletted 7 ('36)	19.00	190.00

Maharaja Sir
Sawant
Singh — A2

1937			Perf. 9	
6	A2	4a red orange	22.50	140.00
7	A2	6a yellow	22.50	140.00
8	A2	8a emerald	24.00	180.00
9	A2	12a turquoise blue	24.00	200.00
10	A2	1r purple	62.50	250.00
a.		"1Rs" instead of "1R"	75.00	500.00
		Nos. 1-10 (10)	216.00	949.75

Bijawar stamps became obsolete in 1939.

BUNDI

'bün-dē

LOCATION — A Feudatory State in the
Rajputana Agency of India.
AREA — 2,220 sq. mi.
POP. — 216,722
CAPITAL — Bundi

Katar (Indian
Dagger) — A1

Laid Paper
Without Gum
Gutters between Stamps

1894		Unwmk.	Litho.	Imperf.	
1	A1	½a slate		19,000.	3,250.

**Redrawn; Blade Does Not Touch
Oval**

No Gutters between Stamps
Wove Paper

1A	A1	½a slate	67.50	72.50
b.		Value above, name below	400.00	525.00
c.		Top right ornament omitted	3,750.	4,000.

On No. 1A, the dagger is thinner and its
point does not touch the oval inner frame.

A2

Without Gum

1896			**Laid Paper**	
2	A2	½a slate	9.00	14.00

A3

1897-98			**Without Gum**	
3	A3	1a red	18.00	27.50
4	A3	2a yellow green	21.00	40.00
5	A3	4a yellow green	100.00	140.00
6	A3	8a red	160.00	450.00
7	A3	1r yellow, blue	500.00	825.00
		Nos. 3-7 (5)	799.00	1,482.

A4 A5

**Redrawn; Blade Wider and
Diamond-shaped**

1898-1900			**Without Gum**	
8	A3	½a slate	7.00	7.00
9	A3	1a red	5.50	5.50
10	A3	2a emerald	19.00	25.00
a.		1st 2 characters of value omitted	3,000.	3,000.
11	A3	4a yel grn	42.50	100.00
12	A4	8a red	21.00	27.50
13	A5	1r yellow, blue	47.50	82.50
a.		Wove paper	24.00	40.00
		Nos. 8-13 (6)	142.50	247.50

On Nos. 9-10, the blade is wider and nearly
diamond-shaped.

Point of Dagger to Left

14	A3	4a green	5.00	5.00

Maharao Rajah
with Symbols of
Spiritual and
Temporal
Power — A6

Rouletted 11 to 13 in Color

1915		Typo.	**Without Gum**	

**"Bundi" in 3 Characters (word at
top right)**

15	A6	¼a blue	2.90	6.25
a.		Laid paper	6.75	35.00
16	A6	½a black	4.00	9.00
17	A6	1a vermilion	5.50	18.00
a.		Laid paper	15.00	45.00
18	A6	2a emerald	11.00	35.00
19	A6	2½a yellow	11.00	40.00
20	A6	3a brown	12.50	67.50
21	A6	4a yel green	5.25	62.50
23	A6	6a ultramarine	21.00	160.00
a.		6a deep blue	11.00	180.00
24	A6	8a orange	11.00	160.00
25	A6	10a olive	24.00	150.00
26	A6	12a dark green	19.00	140.00
27	A6	1r violet	40.00	250.00
28	A6	2r car brn & blk	125.00	325.00
29	A6	3r blue & brown	210.00	450.00
30	A6	4r pale grn & red brown	400.00	550.00
31	A6	5r ver & pale grn	400.00	550.00
		Nos. 15-31 (16)	1,302.	2,973.

Minor differences in lettering in top and bottom
panels may be divided into 8 types, but
not all values come in each type. In one subtype
the top appears as one word. Nos. 30-31
have an ornamental frame around the design.
For overprints see Nos. O1-O39.

1941			**Perf. 11**	

**"Bundi" in 4 Characters (word at
top right)**

32	A6	¼a light blue	2.25	62.50
33	A6	½a black	40.00	47.50
34	A6	1a carmine	15.00	75.00
35	A6	2a yellow green	20.00	110.00
		Nos. 32-35 (4)	77.25	295.00

The 4-character spelling of "Bundi" is found
also on stamps rouletted in color: on ½a and
4a in small characters, and on ¼a, ½a, 1a, 4a,
4r and 5r in large characters like those on Nos.
32-35.
For overprints see Nos. O41-O48.

Arms of Bundi — A7

1941-45		Typo.	**Perf. 11**	
36	A7	3p bright ultra	3.50	7.50
37	A7	6p indigo	5.25	12.50
38	A7	1a red orange	8.00	15.00
39	A7	2a fawn	10.50	27.50
a.		2a brown ('45)	19.00	30.00
40	A7	4a brt yel green	19.00	82.50
41	A7	8a dull green	25.00	300.00
42	A7	1r royal blue	52.50	450.00
		Nos. 36-42 (7)	123.75	895.00

The 1st printing of Nos. 36-42 was gummed.
All later printings were without gum. **Values
are for stamps without gum.**
For overprints see Nos. O49-O55.

Maj. Maharao Rajah Bahadur Singh — A9

View of Bundi — A10

1947   *Perf. 11*

43	A8	¼a deep green	2.75	57.50
44	A8	½a purple	2.50	47.50
45	A8	1a yellow green	2.50	47.50
46	A9	2a red	2.40	97.50
47	A9	4a deep orange	2.75	140.00
48	A10	8a violet blue	3.75	
49	A10	1r chocolate	19.00	
		Nos. 43-49 (7)	35.65	

For overprints see Rajasthan Nos. 1-14.

OFFICIAL STAMPS
Regular Issue of 1915 Handstamped in Black, Red or Green

a

Rouletted 11 to 13 in Color

1918   Unwmk.   Without Gum

O1	A6	¼a dark blue	1.90
O2	A6	½a black	1.10
O3	A6	1a vermilion	1.90
O4	A6	2a emerald	9.50
O5	A6	2½a yellow	6.00
O6	A6	3a brown	5.50
O7	A6	4a yel green	18.00
O8	A6	6a blue	22.50
O9	A6	8a orange	22.50
O10	A6	10a olive green	75.00
O11	A6	12a dark green	75.00
O12	A6	1r violet	90.00
O13	A6	2r car brn & blk	600.00
O14	A6	3r blue & brown	525.00
O15	A6	4r pale grn & red brn	450.00
O16	A6	5r ver & pale grn	490.00
		Nos. O1-O16 (16)	2,393.

All values come with black handstamp and most exist in red. The overprint is found in various positions, double, inverted, etc.

Several denominations exist in two or more types. See notes following Nos. 31 and 35.

Regular Issue of 1915 Handstamped in Black, Red or Green

b

1919   Without Gum

O17	A6	¼a dark blue	2.60
O18	A6	½a black	4.50
O19	A6	1a vermilion	16.00
O20	A6	2a emerald	29.00
O21	A6	2½a yellow	30.00
O22	A6	3a brown	35.00
O23	A6	4a yel green	100.00
O24	A6	6a blue	45.00
O25	A6	8a orange	52.50
O26	A6	10a olive green	140.00
O27	A6	12a dark green	120.00
O28	A6	1r violet	82.50
O29	A6	2r car brn & blk	275.00
O30	A6	3r blue & brown	325.00
O31	A6	4r pale grn & red brn	450.00
O32	A6	5r ver & pale grn	490.00
		Nos. O17-O32 (16)	2,217.

Note following No. O16 applies to this issue.

Regular Issue of 1915 Handstamped in Carmine or Black

c

1919   *Rouletted in Color*

Without Gum

O33	A6	¼a blue	11.00
O34	A6	½a black	18.00
O35	A6	1a vermilion	35.00
O36	A6	2a yel green	140.00
O37	A6	8a orange	450.00
O38	A6	10a olive	700.00
O39	A6	12a dark green	900.00
		Nos. O33-O39 (7)	2,254.

Nos. 33 and 35 Handstamped Type "a" In Black or Carmine

1941   *Perf. 11*

O41	A6	½a black	24.00
O42	A6	2a yellow green	825.00

Nos. 32 and 35 Handstamped Type "b" in Black or Carmine

1941

O43	A6	¼a light blue	90.00
O44	A6	2a yellow green	210.00

Nos. 32-35 Handstamped Type "c" in Black or Carmine

1941

O45	A6	¼a light blue	190.00
O46	A6	½a black	375.00
O47	A6	1a carmine	700.00
O48	A6	2a yellow green	625.00
		Nos. O45-O48 (4)	1,890.

Nos. 36 to 42 Overprinted in Black or Carmine

1941   *Perf. 11*

O49	A7	3p brt ultra (C)	7.50	24.00
O50	A7	6p indigo (C)	20.00	24.00
O51	A7	1a red orange	19.00	16.00
O52	A7	2a fawn	20.00	19.00
O53	A7	4a brt yel green	72.50	160.00
O54	A7	8a dull green	225.00	950.00
O55	A7	1r royal blue (C)	310.00	950.00
		Nos. O49-O55 (7)	674.00	2,143.

BUSSAHIR
'bus-ə-,hiə,r

(Bashahr)

LOCATION — A Feudatory State in the Punjab Hill States Agency
AREA — 3,439 sq. mi.
POP. — 100,192
CAPITAL — Bashahr

Tiger

A1   A2

A3   A4

A5   A6

A7   A8

Overprinted "R S" in Violet, Rose, or Blue Green (BG)

Laid Paper

1895	Unwmk.		Litho.	*Imperf.*
1	A1	¼a pink (V)	3,750.	
2	A2	½a slate (R)	750.00	1,000.
3	A3	1a red (V)	300.00	
4	A4	2a yellow (V,R)	110.00	300.00
5	A5	4a violet (V,R)	190.00	
6	A6	8a brown (V,BG)	210.00	375.00
a.		Without overprint	400.00	
7	A7	12a green (R)	450.00	
8	A8	1r ultra (R)	190.00	
		Nos. 1-8 (8)	5,950.	

Perf. 7 to 14				
9	A1	¼a pink (V,BG)	100.00	150.00
10	A2	½a slate (R)	35.00	210.00
11	A3	1a red (V)	35.00	140.00
a.		Pin-perf.	275.00	300.00
12	A4	2a yel (V,R,BG)	47.50	140.00
a.		Pin-perf. (V,R)	100.00	240.00
13	A5	4a vio (V,R,BG)	37.50	140.00
a.		Pin-perf. (R)	450.00	
14	A6	8a brown (V,BG)	35.00	160.00
15	A7	12a green (V,R)	120.00	200.00
a.		Pin-perf. (R)	650.00	825.00
b.		Without overprint	325.00	
16	A8	1r ultra (V,R)	65.00	180.00
a.		Pin-perf. (R)	700.00	
		Nos. 9-16 (8)	475.00	1,320.

"R. S." are the initials of Tika Raghunath Singh, son of the Raja.

Overprinted "R S" Like Nos. 1-16

A9   A10

A11   A12

A13   A14

Wove Paper

1896		Engr.	*Pin-perf.*
17	A9	¼a dk gray vio (R)	— 1,500.
18	A10	½a blue gray (R)	1,200. 450.00

1900		Litho.	*Imperf.*
19	A9	¼a red (V,BG)	7.50	16.00
20	A9	¼a violet (V,R)	12.50	
21	A10	½a blue (V,R)	15.00	40.00
22	A11	1a olive (R)	27.50	65.00
23	A11	1a red (V,BG)	7.00	24.00
24	A12	2a yellow (V)	75.00	
a.		2a ocher (V)	75.00	
25	A13	2a yellow (V)	90.00	
26	A14	4a brn vio (V,R,BG)	82.50	180.00
		Nos. 19-26 (8)	317.00	

Pin-perf.				
27	A9	¼a red (V,BG)	6.25	16.00
28	A9	¼a violet (R)	30.00	27.50
29	A10	½a blue (V,R)	90.00	140.00
30	A11	1a olive (V,R)	40.00	
31	A11	1a red (V)		300.00
32	A11	1a vermilion (BG)	11.00	22.50
33	A12	2a yellow (BG)	1,250.	1,300.
34	A13	2a yellow (V,R)	75.00	120.00
a.		2a ocher (V)	100.00	
35	A14	4a brn vio (V,R,BG)	120.00	
		Nos. 27-35 (9)	1,622.	

Obsolete March 31, 1901.

Stamps overprinted with the monogram above (RNS) or with the monogram "PS" were never issued for postal purposes. They are either reprints or remainders to which this overprint has been applied. Many other varieties have appeared since the stamps became obsolete. It is probable that all or nearly all of them are reprints.

CHARKHARI
chər-'kär-ē

LOCATION — A Feudatory State in the Bundelkhand Agency in Central India.
AREA — 880 sq. mi.
POP. — 120,351
CAPITAL — Maharajnagar

A1

Thin White or Blue Wove Paper

1894   Unwmk.   Typo.   *Imperf.*

Value in the Plural

Without Gum

1	A1	1a green	2,750.	3,750.
2	A1	2a green	3,250.	
3	A1	4a green	2,250.	

Value in the Singular

1897   Without Gum

3A	A1	¼a rose	1,800.	1,100.
4	A1	¼a purple	5.50	5.50
5	A1	½a purple	3.75	4.50
6	A1	1a green	6.50	9.50
7	A1	2a green	11.00	12.50
8	A1	4a green	17.50	27.50
		Nos. 4-8 (5)	44.25	59.50

In a later printing, the numerals of Nos. 4-8 are smaller or of different shape.

Proofs are known on paper of various colors.

A2

A3

Size: 19½x23mm

1909		Litho.		Perf. 11
9	A2	1p red brown	7.00	57.50
10	A2	1p pale blue	.90	.65
11	A2	½a scarlet	1.50	1.90
12	A2	1a light green	3.75	2.40
13	A2	2a ultra	4.50	5.25
14	A2	4a deep green	6.25	8.25
15	A2	8a brick red	11.00	30.00
16	A2	1r red brown	19.00	62.50
		Nos. 9-16 (8)	53.90	168.45

See Nos. 22-27, 39-43. For surcharges see Nos. 37-38A.

1912-17		Handstamped	Imperf.
		Without Gum	
21	A3	1p violet ('17)	10.50	7.50
c.		Double frameline	1,050.	125.00

The 1p black, type A3, is a proof.

A3a

Wove Paper
Handstamped

1922		Without Gum	Imperf.
21A	A3a	1a violet	120.00	125.00
b.		Perf. 11, laid paper	110.00	210.00

Type of 1909 Issue Redrawn
Size: 20x23½mm

1930-40				Typo.
		Without Gum		
22	A2	1p dark blue	.90	21.00
23	A2	½a olive green	3.75	21.00
23A	A2	½a cop brown ('40)	9.00	37.50
24	A2	1a light green	3.75	24.00
25	A2	1a chocolate	19.00	40.00
25A	A2	1a dull red ('40)	190.00	100.00
26	A2	2a light blue	1.90	25.00
a.		Tête bêche pair	14.00	
27	A2	4a carmine	4.50	30.00
a.		Tête bêche pair	21.00	
		Nos. 22-27 (8)	232.80	298.50

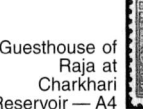
Guesthouse of Raja at Charkhari Reservoir — A4

Imlia Palace — A5

Industrial School — A6

View of City — A7

Maharajnagar Fort, Charkhari City — A8

Guesthouse A9

Palace Gate — A10

Temples at Rampur — A11

Govordhan Temple — A12

1931		Perf. 11, 11½, 12	
28	A4	½a dull green	3.25	.25
29	A5	1a black brown	2.40	.25
30	A6	2a purple	2.50	.25
31	A7	4a olive green	2.25	.25
32	A8	8a magenta	3.00	.25
33	A9	1r rose & green	4.00	.30
34	A10	2r brown & red	6.00	.35
35	A11	3r bl grn & choc	22.50	.60
36	A12	5r violet & blue	14.00	.75
		Nos. 28-36 (9)	59.90	3.25

Size range of A4-A12: 30-31x19½-24mm.
Many errors of perforation and printing exist.
Used values are for canceled to order stamps.

Nos. 15-16
Surcharged in Black

1940		Perf. 11	
37	A2	½a on 8a brick red	52.50	200.00
a.		Surcharge inverted	450.00	600.00
b.		"1" of "½" inverted	400.00	
38	A2	1a on 1r red brown	175.00	625.00
b.		Surcharge inverted	490.00	
38A	A2	"1 ANNA" on 1r red brown	400.00	450.00

Type of 1930

1943		Unwmk.	Typo.	Imperf.
		Size: 20x23½mm		
39	A2	1p violet	32.50	240.00
a.		Tête bêche pair	82.50	
40	A2	1p apple green	90.00	325.00
41	A2	½a orange red	30.00	62.50
42	A2	½a black	90.00	290.00
43	A2	2a grayish green	140.00	290.00
a.		Tête bêche pair	180.00	
		Nos. 39-43 (5)	382.50	1,207.

COCHIN

kō-'chin

LOCATION — A Feudatory State in the Madras States Agency in Southern India.
AREA — 1,480 sq. mi.
POP. — 1,422,875 (1941)
CAPITAL — Ernakulam

See the United State of Travancore and Cochin.

6 Puttans = 5 Annas
12 Pies = 1 Anna
16 Annas = 1 Rupee

A1　　　　　　　A1a

State Seal

1892		Unwmk.	Typo.	Perf. 12	
1	A1	½p yellow		3.75	4.50
a.		Imperf., pair		—	
b.		Laid paper		800.00	200.00
c.		½p orange buff		4.25	3.00
d.		½p orange buff, laid paper		700.00	200.00
e.		½p buff		3.00	3.50
f.		½p orange, laid paper		775.00	200.00
2	A1	1p red violet		4.50	4.00
a.		Vert. pair, imperf. between		—	4,000.
b.		1p purple (error)		175.00	125.00
3	A1	2p purple		3.00	3.25
a.		Imperf.		—	
		Nos. 1-3 (3)		11.25	11.75

Nos. 1 to 3 sometimes have watermark large umbrella in the sheet.

Wmk. Coat of Arms and Inscription in Sheet

1896				
4	A1a	1p violet	145.00	160.00

		Wmk. 43		
4A	A1a	1p violet	27.50	47.50

Originally intended for revenue use, Nos. 4-4A were later authorized for postal use. Beware of fraudulently removed fiscal markings.

1894		Wmk. 41		Thin Paper	
5	A1	½p orange		4.00	2.25
a.		Imperf., pair		—	
b.		½p buff		11.00	5.50
c.		½p yellow		7.75	2.25
6	A1	1p magenta		12.00	10.50
7	A1	2p purple		9.00	5.00
a.		Imperf., pair		—	
b.		Double impression		—	2,000.
c.		Printed on both sides		2,500.	
d.		Tete beche pair		6,250.	
		Nos. 5-7 (3)		25.00	17.75

A2

A3

A4

A5

1898			Thin Paper	
8	A2	3p ultra	2.10	1.60
a.		Double impression	950.00	
b.		Horiz. pair, imperf. between	800.00	
c.		Vert. pair, imperf. between	900.00	
9	A3	½p gray green	2.50	2.25
a.		Pair, one sideways	3,750.	
b.		Horiz. pair, imperf. between	1,750.	1,700.
10	A4	1p rose	5.50	2.50
a.		Laid paper	2,400.	
b.		Tete beche pair	5,250.	3,250.
c.		As "a," tete beche pair		12,000.

11	A5	2p purple		5.00	3.25
a.		Vert. pair, imperf. between		850.00	
b.		Vert. strip of 3, imperf. between		1,000.	
		Nos. 8-11 (4)		15.10	9.60

1903			Thin Paper	
12	A2	3p ultra	1.80	.25
d.		Horiz. pair, imperf. between		1,350.
i.		Double impression		450.00
12A	A3	½p gray green	1.90	.60
e.		Double impression		450.00
f.		Pair, one sideways	1,350.	1,350.
j.		Horiz. pair, imperf. between		1,750.
12B	A4	1p rose	2.50	.25
g.		Tete beche pair		5,250.
12C	A5	2p purple	3.75	.75
h.		Double impression	1,250.	450.00
		Nos. 12-12C (4)	9.95	1.85

Beware of fake overprint surcharge varieties, such as double, inverted, etc. This applies also to early Official varieties. Such varieties require expertization.

Type of 1898 Surcharged

1909				
13	A2	2p on 3p red violet	.25	.75
a.		Inverted surcharge	160.00	160.00
b.		Pair, stamps tete beche	250.00	300.00
c.		Pair, stamps & surch. tete beche	300.00	400.00

The surcharge is also known in a thin "2" measuring 5½x7mm, with curving foot. Values: unused $1,200; used $600.

Sri Rama Varma I — A6

1911-13		Engr.		Perf. 14	
14	A6	2p brown		.55	.25
a.		Imperf., pair		—	
15	A6	3p blue		3.00	.25
a.		Perf. 14x12½		40.00	3.00
16	A6	4p yel green		3.25	.25
16A	A6	4p apple green		4.00	.75
17	A6	9p car rose		2.75	.25
18	A6	1a orange buff		4.50	.25
19	A6	1½a lilac		11.00	.65
20	A6	2a gray		11.00	.60
21	A6	3a vermilion		57.50	57.50
		Nos. 14-21 (8)		93.55	60.00

For surcharge and overprints see Nos. 34, O2-O9, O23-O24, O27.

Sri Rama Varma II
A7　　　　　　　A8

1918-23		Engr.		Perf. 14	
23	A7	2p brown		12.00	.25
a.		Imperf., pair		750.00	
24	A7	4p green		1.50	.25
25	A7	6p red brown ('22)		3.75	.25
26	A7	8p black brown ('23)		2.50	.25
27	A7	9p carmine rose		32.50	.50
28	A7	10p deep blue		9.00	.25
29	A8	1a brown orange		27.50	5.00
30	A7	1½a red violet ('21)		5.50	.30
31	A7	2a gray		6.25	.25
32	A7	2¼a yel green ('22)		10.50	4.75
33	A7	3a vermilion		17.50	.50
		Nos. 23-33 (11)		128.50	12.55

The 2p and 1a are found in two types, the difference lying in the first of the three characters directly above the maharaja's head.

For surcharges and overprints see Nos. 36-40, 52-53, O10-O22, O25-O26, O28-O36, O71A.

No. 15 Surcharged

Type I — Numeral 8mm high. Curved foot. Top begins with a ball. (As illustrated.)
Type II — Numeral 9mm high. Curved foot. Top begins with a curved line.
Type III — Numeral 6mm high. Straight foot. "Two pies" 15mm wide.
Type IV — "2" as in type III. Capital "P" in "Pies." "Two Pies" 13mm wide.
Type V — Heavy gothic numeral. Capital "P" in "Pies."

1922-29

34	A6	2p on 3p blue		
		(Type I)	.60	.45
a.		Type II	5.00	1.25
b.		Type III	10.50	.50
c.		Type IV	17.50	20.00
d.		Type V	120.00	225.00
e.		Double surcharge, I	500.00	500.00
f.		Double surcharge II	1,100.	
g.		As "b," perf. 14x12½	17.50	20.00

Types II and III exist with a capital "P" in "Pies." It occurs once in each sheet of the second and third settings. There are four settings.

Type V is the first stamp, fourth row, of the fourth setting.

No. 32 Surcharged

1928

36	A7	1a on 2¼a yel green	9.00	18.00
a.		Double surcharge		
b.		"REVENUF" for "REVENUE"	85.00	125.00

Nos. 24, 26 and 28 Surcharged in Black

1932-33

38	A7	3p on 4p green	1.90	2.10
a.		"r" in "Three" inverted		575.00
39	A7	3p on 8p black brown	3.25	4.00
40	A7	9p on 10p deep blue	2.25	5.00
		Nos. 38-40 (3)	7.40	11.10

Sri Rama Varma III
A9　　　　　　　A10

1933-38		Engr.		Perf. 13x13½	
41	A9	2p brown ('36)		1.50	.75
42	A9	4p green		.90	.25
43	A9	6p red brown		1.00	.25
44	A10	1a brown org ('34)		2.00	.30
45	A9	1a8p rose red		4.50	9.50
46	A9	2a gray black ('38)		9.00	2.40
47	A9	2¼a yellow green		2.50	.45
48	A9	3a red org ('38)		8.25	2.40
49	A9	3a4p violet		2.50	2.10
50	A9	6a8p black brown		2.50	22.50
51	A9	10a deep blue		4.50	25.00
		Nos. 41-51 (11)		39.15	65.90

See Nos. 55-58. For overprints and surcharges see Nos. 54, 59-62, 73A-74, 76-77, 89, O37-O57, O70-O71, O72-O77A, O89.

Nos. 26 and 28 Surcharged in Red

1934			Perf. 13½	
52	A7	6p on 8p black brown	1.10	.90
53	A7	6p on 10p dark blue	2.50	3.00

No. 44 Overprinted in Black — a

1939			Engr.	
54	A10	1a brown orange	10.00	2.50

Types of 1933-38

1938-41		Litho.		Perf. 11	
55	A9	2p dull brown		1.25	.60
56	A9	4p dull green ('41)		1.25	.50
57	A9	6p red brown		4.50	.25
57A	A10	1a brown orange		95.00	140.00
58	A10	2¼a yellow green		7.50	.35
		Nos. 55-58 (5)		109.50	141.70

			Perf. 13x13½		
55B	A9	2p dull brown		11.00	1.00
56B	A9	4p dull green ('41)		10.00	20.00
57C	A10	6p red brown			5,250.
57D	A10	1a brown orange		160.00	200.00
58B	A10	2¼a yellow green		22.50	8.00

Type of 1934 Overprinted in Black Type "a" or — b

1941-42			Perf. 11 (#59), 13 (#60)	
59	A10(a)	1a brown orange	525.00	2.50
a.		Perf. 13		525.00
60	A10(b)	1a brown org ('42)	20.00	1.00
a.		Perf. 11	1.25	2.50

No. 45 Surcharged in Black — c

1943-44		Engr.		Perf. 13x13½	
61	A9	3p on 1a8p rose red ('44)		12.50	25.00
62	A9	1a3p on 1a8p rose red		1.25	.75

Maharaja Sri Kerala Varma
A11　　　　　　　A12

1943		Litho.	Wmk. 294	Perf. 11, 13	
63	A11	2p dull gray brn, wmk. 41		8.00	9.00
a.		Wmk. 294		42.50	6.25
b.		#63, Perf. 11			3,500.
c.		As "a," perf. 11			4,500.
64	A11	4p gray green, wmk. 294		8.00	25.00
a.		Wmk. 41		1,750.	625.00
b.		#64, perf. 11		4.75	6.25

65	A11	6p red brown	7.50	.25
a.		Perf. 11	10.00	2.00
66	A11	9p ultramarine	75.00	1.90
a.		Horiz. pair, imperf. between	3,500.	
67	A12	1a brown orange, wmk. 294	27.50	85.00
a.		Wmk. 41	150.00	175.00
b.		Perf. 13x13½	225.00	275.00
68	A11	2¼a lt ol green	35.00	10.00
a.		Perf. 13x13½	40.00	6.00
		Nos. 63-68 (6)	161.00	131.15

For surcharges and overprints see Nos. 69-73, 75, 78, 78B, O58-O69.

No. 64 Surcharged Type "c"

69	A11	3p on 4p gray green	9.50	.25
a.		Wmk. 41	140.00	35.00

Nos. 64, 64a and 65 Surcharged in Black — d

1944-48 **Wmk. 294**

70	A11	2p on 6p red brown	.95	6.00
a.		Perf. 11	1.20	3.50
71	A11	3p on 4p gray green	12.50	.25
72	A11	3p on 6p red brown	1.00	1.00
a.		Perf. 13x13½	2.50	.25
73	A11	4p on 6p red brown	8.50	18.00
		Nos. 70-73 (4)	22.95	25.25

Nos. 57A, 67a Surcharged in Black

1944 **Litho.** **Wmk. 41**

73A	A10	6p on 1a brown org	250.00	100.00
b.		Perf. 11	450.00	275.00
74	A10	9p on 1a brown org	550.00	60.00
75	A12	9p on 1a brown org	12.00	6.25
		Nos. 73A-75 (3)	812.00	166.25

No. 56 Surcharged Type "c" in Black

76	A9	3p on 4p dull green	8.75	6.00
a.		Perf. 13x13½	25.00	5.00

Nos. 57A, 67a Surcharged in Black

1944

77	A10	9p on 1a brown orange	45.00	12.50
78	A12	9p on 1a brown orange	14.00	5.00

No. 67a Surcharged Type "c"

1944 **Wmk. 41**

78B	A12	1a3p on 1a brn org	7,750.

Maharaja Ravi Varma
A13   A15

1944-46 **Wmk. 294** **Perf. 13**

79	A13	9p ultra ('46)	32.50	27.50
a.		Perf. 11	27.50	8.00
b.		Perf. 13x13½	62.50	7.00
80	A13	1a3p magenta	12.50	12.50
a.		Perf. 13x13½	500.00	110.00
81	A13	1a9p ultra ('46)	12.00	24.00
		Nos. 79-81 (3)	57.00	64.00

For overprints and surcharges see Nos. O78-O80, Travancore 12, 14, O10.

1946-50 **Litho.** **Perf. 13**

82	A15	2p dull brown	4.00	.25
a.		Perf. 11	10.00	.90
b.		Perf. 11x13	550.00	210.00
c.		Vert. pair, imperf. horiz.	4,250.	4,250.
83	A15	3p carmine rose	.60	.45
83A	A15	4p gray green ('50)	4,000.	120.00
84	A15	6p red brown ('47)	30.00	11.00
a.		Perf. 11	250.00	8.25
85	A15	9p ultramarine	3.50	.25
a.		Horiz. pair, imperf. between		4,000.
86	A15	1a dp orange ('47)	11.00	47.50
a.		Perf. 11	750.00	
87	A15	2a gray ('47)	175.00	12.50
a.		Perf. 11	225.00	10.00
88	A15	3a vermilion	110.00	4.00
		Nos. 82-83, 84-88 (7)	334.10	75.95

For surcharges and overprints see Nos. 98-99, O81-O88, Travancore 8, 13, 15-15A, O11.

No. 45 Surcharged Type "d"
Perf. 13x13½

1947-48 **Wmk. 41** **Engr.**

89	A9	6p on 1a8p rose red	6.00	30.00

Maharaja Sri Kerala Varma II — A16

Die I   Die II

Two dies on 2p: Die I, back of headdress almost touches value tablet; Die II, back of headdress farther away from value tablet.

Die I   Die II

Two dies on 3a4p: Die I, white frame line around head is continuous, and two white lines beneath value inscriptions at bottom; Die II, white frame line around head broken by value tablets at the sides, and single white line beneath value inscriptions at bottom. Die II comes from the first two stamps of the bottom row of the sheet.

1948-49 **Wmk. 294** **Perf. 11**

90	A16	2p olive brown	2.25	.25
a.		Die II	190.00	4.50
b.		#90, horiz. pair, imperf. vert.		4,000.
91	A16	3p car ('49)	4.00	.25
a.		#90, vert. pair, imperf. between		2,900.
92	A16	4p gray green	21.00	6.25
a.		Horiz. pair, imperf. vert.	375.00	500.00
93	A16	6p red brown	27.50	.35
94	A16	9p ultra ('49)	3.00	.90
95	A16	2a black	90.00	3.75
96	A16	3a ver ('49)	100.00	1.50
97	A16	3a4p violet ('49)	87.50	525.00
a.			350.00	
		Nos. 90-97 (8)	335.25	538.25

For overprints see Nos. O90-O97, Travancore 9-11, O8-O9.

No. 86 Surcharged Type "d" in Black

1949

98	A15	6p on 1a dp orange	90.00	225.00
99	A15	9p on 1a dp orange	150.00	225.00

Dutch Palace A17

Design: 2a, Chinese fishing net.

1949 **Unwmk.** **Perf. 11**

100	A17	2a gray	9.00	15.00
a.		Imperf. vert., horiz. pair	750.00	
101	A17	2¼a gray green	3.50	15.00
a.		Imperf. vert., horiz. pair	750.00	600.00

See Travancore-Cochin for succeeding issues.

OFFICIAL STAMPS

See note above No. 13.

Stamps and Type of 1911-14 Overprinted — h

1913-14 **Wmk. 41** **Engr.** **Perf. 14**

O2	A6	4p yel green	15.00	.25
a.		Inverted overprint	—	450.00
O3	A6	9p car rose	25.00	.25
O4	A6	1½a red violet	72.50	.25
a.		Double overprint	—	1,100.
O5	A6	2a gray	19.00	.25
O6	A6	3a vermilion	82.50	.65
O7	A6	6a violet	90.00	3.00
O8	A6	12a blue	60.00	10.00
O9	A6	1½r deep green	52.50	110.00
		Nos. O2-O9 (8)	416.50	124.65

Values for Nos. O2 and O3 are for the cheaper varieties with watermark sideways.

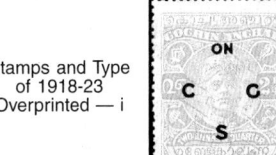

Stamps and Type of 1918-23 Overprinted — i

1918-34

O10	A7	4p green	6.25	.25
a.		Double overprint	—	825.00
O11	A7	6p red brn ('22)	22.50	.25
a.		Double overprint	—	750.00
O12	A7	8p blk brn ('26)	16.00	.25
O13	A7	9p carmine rose	97.50	.25
O14	A7	10p dp blue ('23)	22.50	.25
O16	A7	1½a red vio ('21)	8.25	.25
a.		Double overprint	—	1,100.
O17	A7	2a gray	62.50	.45
O18	A7	2¼a yel grn ('22)	20.00	.25
b.		Double overprint	—	750.00
O19	A7	3a ver ('22)	27.50	.35
a.		Double overprint	—	750.00
O20	A7	6a violet ('22)	57.50	.75
O21	A7	12a blue ('29)	25.00	7.50
O22	A7	1½r dk green ('34)	37.50	175.00
		Nos. O10-O22 (12)	403.00	185.80

On Nos. O2-O22, width of overprint varies from 14¾mm to 16½mm.

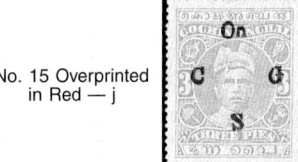

No. 15 Overprinted in Red — j

1921

O23	A6	3p blue	175.00	.25
a.		Overprint in black		1,900.
b.		Double overprint (R)		750.00
c.		Inverted "S" (R)		75.00

Nos. O3 and O13 Surcharged with New Values

1923-29

O24	A6	8p on 9p car rose	525.00	2.50
a.		Double surcharge		500.00
b.		Uppercase "P" in "pies"	1,600.	75.00
O25	A7	8p on 9p car rose	150.00	.25
a.		Double surcharge		400.00
b.		Uppercase "P" in "pies"	250.00	15.00
O26	A7	10p on 9p car rose ('25)	120.00	1.50
a.		Double surcharge		
b.		Surcharge measures 25mm		450.00
c.		As "b," double surcharge		500.00

O27	A6	10p on 9p car rose ('29)	2,200.	27.50
a.		Double surcharge		900.00
		Nos. O24-O27 (4)	2,995.	31.75

Surcharge measures 27½ mm.

Regular Issue of 1918-23 Overprinted — k

1929-31

O28	A7	4p green ('31)	32.50	3.00
O29	A7	6p red brown ('30)	21.00	.25
O30	A7	8p black brown ('30)	10.00	.25
O31	A7	10p deep blue ('30)	9.00	.25
O32	A7	2a gray ('30)	60.00	.35
O33	A7	3a vermilion ('30)	12.50	.30
O34	A7	6a dk violet ('30)	150.00	4.50
		Nos. O28-O34 (7)	295.00	8.90

Inverted "S" in Overprint

O28a	A7	4p green ('31)	325.00	25.00
O29a	A7	6p red brown ('30)	175.00	5.50
O30a	A7	8p black brown ('30)	85.00	6.00
O31a	A7	10p deep blue	85.00	6.00
O32a	A7	2a gray ('30)	400.00	15.00
O33a	A7	3a vermilion ('30)	150.00	10.00
O34a	A7	6a dk violet ('30)	950.00	125.00
		Nos. O28a-O34a (7)	2,170.	192.50

Same with Additional Surcharge on Type of Regular Issue of 1918-23 in Red

1933

O35	A7	6p on 8p black brown	3.75	.25
a.		Inverted "S"	32.50	6.00
O36	A7	6p on 10p dk blue	6.00	.25
a.		Inverted "S"	60.00	5.00

Regular Issue of 1933 Overprinted Type "k" in Black as in 1933-34

1933-35 **Perf. 13x13½**

O37	A9	4p green	8.50	.25
O38	A9	6p red brown	7.50	.25
O39	A10	1a brown orange	27.50	.25
O40	A9	1a8p rose red	2.25	.45
O41	A9	2a gray	35.00	.25
O42	A9	2¼a yellow green	12.50	.25
O43	A9	3a vermilion	67.50	.25
O44	A9	3a4p violet	2.25	.25
O45	A9	6a8p black brown	2.25	.30
O46	A9	10a deep blue	2.25	2.00
		Nos. O37-O46 (10)	167.50	4.50

Regular Stamps of 1934-38 Overprinted in Black — m

1937-38 **Perf. 11, 13x13½**

O47	A10	1a brown orange	50.00	.90
O48	A9	2a gray black	27.50	3.00
O49	A9	3a red orange	13.50	3.75
		Nos. O47-O49 (3)	91.00	7.65

Similar Overprint on Types of 1933-36

Perf. 11, 13x13½

1938-44 **Litho.** **Wmk. 294**

O50	A9	4p dull green, perf. 13x13½	3.00	1.00
a.		Perf. 11 ('42)	110.00	24.00
			Wmk. 41	
O51	A9	6p red brown ('41)	18.00	7.00
a.		Wmk. 294	25.00	1.50
b.		As "a," perf. 11	250.00	12.50
c.		Printed both sides		250.00
O52	A10	1a brown orange	1.25	.25
a.		Wmk. 294	3.00	6.50
b.		As "a," perf. 11	15.00	6.00
c.		Printed both sides		250.00
O53	A9	3a orange ('40)	3.75	3.25
b.		Wmk. 294	30.00	12.50
		Nos. O50-O53 (4)	26.00	11.50

Similar Overprint in
Narrow Serifed
Capitals on No. 57

Wmk. 41   **Perf. 11**
O53A A9 6p red brown   1,250. 600.00

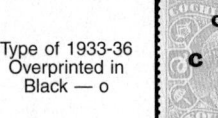

Type of 1933-36
Overprinted in
Black — o

Perf. 10½, 11, 13x13½

O54	A9	4p dull green, perf. 13x13½ ('41)	27.50	3.25
a.		Perf. 11	40.00	4.00
b.		Inverted "S"	55.00	4.00
O55	A9	6p red brown ('41)	40.00	.60
a.		Inverted "S"	50.00	3.00
O56	A9	2a gray black	25.00	1.50
a.		Inverted "S"	27.50	2.00
		Nos. O54-O56 (3)	92.50	5.35

Type of 1934
Overprinted in
Black — p

1941   **Perf. 11**
O57 A10 1a brown orange   425.00 3.75

Stamps and Types
of 1944
Overprinted in
Black — q

Perf. 11, 13x13½

1944-48				**Wmk. 294**
O58	A11	4p gray green	75.00	12.50
a.		Perf. 11	200.00	8.25
b.		Perf. 13	750.00	90.00
O59	A11	6p red brown, perf. 11	3.50	.25
a.		Perf. 13x13½	5.50	.25
b.		Perf. 13	10.00	3.50
c.		As "a," double overprint	175.00	8.25
d.		As "b," double overprint		120.00
O59E	A11	1a brown orange, perf. 13x13½	17,000.	85.00
O60	A11	2a gray black	8.75	1.50
O61	A11	2¼a dull yel green	5.25	1.60
a.		Additional ovpt. on reverse		200.00
O62	A11	3a red orange, perf. 13x13½	13.50	3.75
a.		Perf. 11	16.00	.50
		Nos. O58-O62 (5)	106.00	19.60

Same Overprint
with Additional
Surcharge

O63	A11	3p on 4p gray green, perf. 13x13½	5.50	.25
a.		Perf. 11	12.50	.75
b.		As "a," additional overprint on reverse		210.00
O64	A12	3p on 1a brown org	40.00	12.50
O65	A11	9p on 6p red brown	17.00	6.00
a.		Additional overprint on reverse		750.00

O66	A12	1a3p on 1a brown org	26.00	5.00
		Nos. O63-O66 (4)	88.50	23.75

Same Overprint in Black on Types of 1944 Surcharged Type "c"

O67	A11	3p on 4p gray green, perf. 13½x13	8.00	.80
a.		Perf. 11	600.00	225.00
O68	A11	9p on 6p red brown	7.50	1.00
O69	A12	1a3p on 1a brown org	5.50	.25
		Nos. O67-O69 (3)	21.00	2.05

Nos. O52 and O16 Surcharged Type "d"

1944		Wmk. 41 Perf. 11, 13x13½, 14		
O70	A10	3p on 1a brown org	5.00	5.00
O71	A10	9p on 1a brown org	475.00	87.50
		Engr.		
O71A	A7	9p on 1½a red vio	1,000.	40.00

No. O52 Surcharged Type "c"

1944				
O72	A10	1a3p on 1a brn org	500.00	150.00

No. 76 Overprinted
in Black

Perf. 13x13½

O72A	A9	3p on 4p dull green	250.00	90.00

No. 45 Overprinted Type "k" and Surcharged Type "d"

1944-48		Wmk. 41 Perf. 13x13½		
O73	A9	9p on 1a8p rose red	200.00	50.00
O74	A9	1a9p on 1a8p rose red	5.00	4.00

No. 45 Overprinted Type "k" and Surcharged Type "c"

O75	A9	3p on 1a8p rose red	8.00	4.50
O76	A9	1a9p on 1a8p rose red	3.50	.60

Type of 1939-41
Overprinted in
Black

1946		Wmk. 294 Perf. 11		
O77	A9	2a gray	110.00	1.20
b.		Overprint omitted		2,000.
O77A	A9	2¼a yellow green	2,900.	12.00

Same Overprint in Black on Nos. 79-81

1946		Litho. Perf. 13		
O78	A13	9p ultramarine	4.00	.25
a.		Perf. 13x13½	7.50	.25
b.		Additional overprint on reverse		900.00
O79	A13	1a3p magenta	2.00	.25
a.		Double overprint	25.00	18.00
b.		Additional overprint on reverse		200.00
c.		As "b," overprint doubled and inverted	110.00	100.00
O80	A13	1a9p ultramarine	.50	1.50
a.		Double overprint		
b.		Pair, one without overprint		2,750.
		Nos. O78-O80 (3)	6.50	2.00

Types and Stamps of 1946-48 Overprinted Type "h"

1946-48				
O81	A15	3p car rose	2.75	.25
a.		Additional overprint on reverse		950.00
O82	A15	4p gray green	40.00	10.00
O83	A15	6p red brown	25.00	4.00
O84	A15	9p ultra	1.00	.25
a.		Additional overprint on reverse, inverted		
O85	A15	1a3p magenta	7.50	2.10
O86	A15	1a9p ultra	8.50	.60
O87	A15	2a gray black	19.00	4.50
O88	A15	2¼a olive green	35.00	10.00
		Nos. O81-O88 (8)	138.75	31.70

No. 56 Overprinted Type "q" and Surcharged Type "d"

1947		Wmk. 41 Engr. Perf. 13x13½		
O89	A9	3p on 4p dull green	50.00	17.50
a.		Double surcharge	650.00	300.00

Stamps and Type of 1948-49 Overprinted Type "o"

1948-49		Wmk. 294 Litho. Perf. 11		
O90	A16	3p carmine ('49)	1.50	.25
O91	A16	4p gray green	3.00	.60
b.		Additional overprint on reverse	120.00	120.00
c.		Horizontal pair, imperf. between		2,500.
d.		Vertical pair, imperf. between		2,500.
O92	A16	6p red brown	5.00	.45
b.		Vertical pair, imperf. between		3,250.
O93	A16	9p ultramarine	6.00	.25
O94	A16	2a black ('49)	4.50	.25
O95	A16	2¼a lt ol green ('49)	6.00	9.50
O96	A16	3a vermilion ('49)	1.50	1.75
O97	A16	3a4p deep pur ('49)	75.00	70.00
		Nos. O90-O97 (8)	102.50	83.05

See Travancore-Cochin for succeeding issues.

"C" for "G" in Overprint

O90a	A16	3p carmine	25.00	5.00
O91a	A16	4p gray green	27.50	7.00
O92a	A16	6p red brown	45.00	5.00
O93a	A16	9p ultramarine	50.00	5.00
O94a	A16	2a black ('49)	42.50	5.25
O95a	A16	2¼a light olive green ('49)	50.00	85.00
O96a	A16	3a vermilion ('49)	30.00	17.50
O97a	A16	3a4p deep purple ('49)	425.00	450.00
		Nos. O90a-O97a (8)	695.00	579.75

DHAR

'där

LOCATION — A Feudatory State in the Malwa Agency in Central India.
AREA — 1,800 sq. mi.
POP. — 243,521
CAPITAL — Dhar

A1   Arms of
Dhar — A2

The stamps of type A1 have an oval control mark handstamped in black.

1897-1900		**Unwmk. Typeset Without Gum**		**Imperf.**
1	A1	½p black, red	4.50	5.00
a.		Characters for "pice" transposed	100.00	
b.		Four characters in first word	4.00	6.00
c.		Without control mark	500.00	
2	A1	¼a black, org red ('00)	5.50	7.50
a.		Without control mark	375.00	
3	A1	½a black, lil rose	6.75	8.25
4	A1	1a black, bl grn	12.50	25.00
5	A1	2a black, yel ('00)	42.50	75.00
		Nos. 1-5 (5)	71.75	120.75

1898-1900		**Typo.**		**Perf. 11½**
6	A2	½a red	7.00	9.50
7	A2	½a rose ('00)	6.25	9.00
a.		Imperf., pair		60.00
8	A2	1a maroon	6.25	12.00
9	A2	1a violet ('00)	6.25	22.50
10	A2	1a claret ('00)	6.25	12.00
11	A2	2a dark green ('00)	11.00	37.50
		Nos. 6-11 (6)	43.00	102.50

Obsolete Mar. 31, 1901.

DUNGARPUR

LOCATION — A princely state in Rajasthan, in northwestern India.
AREA — 1,447 sq. mi.
POP. — 100,103 (1901)
CAPITAL — Dungarpur

Arms of
Dungarpur — A1

1933-1947		**Unwmk. Litho. Perf. 11**		
1	A1	¼a bister yellow	2,000.	400.00
		On cover		1,000.
a.		¼a lemon yellow ('34)	2,500.	500.00
		On cover		1,250.
2	A1	¼a salmon ('35)	5,000.	1,000.
		On cover		2,500.
a.		¼a red brown ('36)	3,750.	750.00
		On cover		1,900.
b.		¼a orange red ('38)	6,250.	1,250.
		On cover		3,100.
3	A1	1a pale turquoise blue	1,500.	300.00
		On cover		750.00
		1a turquoise blue	2,000.	400.00
		On cover		1,000.
4	A1	1a3p deep red violet ('35)	3,000.	600.00
		On cover		2,400.
5	A1	2a deep dull green ('47)	3,750.	750.00
		On cover		3,000.
6	A1	4a dull rose red	6,250.	1,250.
		On cover		5,000.
a.		4a rose red ('34)	7,000.	1,400.
		On cover		5,500.

A2   A3

A4   A5

A6   A7

A8   A9

A10

Maharawal Lakshman Singh

1934-38		**Typo.**		**Perf. 12**
7	A2	¼a org buff ('36)	1,750.	200.00
		On cover		450.00
8	A3	½a vermilion, Die I	500.00	125.00
		On cover		350.00
9	A4	1a blue		
a.		Perf 11½ ('38)	750.00	125.00
		On cover		350.00
10	A5	4a gray brown	2,000.	650.00

There are three dies of the ½ anna: Die I measures 21x25½mm, and width of turban is 7½mm; Die II measures 20x20½mm; Die III measures 21x25½mm, and width of turban is 6½mm. There are 4 distinct cliches of Die III, printed in a block of 4, differing in the space between the top of the turban and the frame: Pos. 1 = 2mm; Pos. 2 = 2.5mm; Pos. 3 = 1mm; Pos. 4 = 1.5mm.

1940-41   *Perf. 11, 11½ (#15)*

11	A2	¼a dull org('41)	1,500.	150.00
		On cover		300.00
12	A3	½a carmine, Die I	500.00	150.00
		On cover		450.00
13	A4	1a blue	500.00	100.00
		On cover		250.00
14	A6	2a bright green	2,500.	900.00
		On cover		2,500.
15	A5	4a gray brown	1,800.	450.00
		On cover		1,350.

1943   *Pin-Perf 11½*

16	A6	2a bright green	2,500.	900.00
		On cover		2,500.

1943-44   *Perf. 10½*

17	A2	¼a dull org('44)	1,500.	150.00
		On cover		300.00
18	A3	½a vermilion, Die I ('44)	600.00	175.00
		On cover		550.00
19	A7	½a vermilion, Die II ('44)	600.00	175.00
		On cover		550.00
a.		Horiz. pair, #18 + #19	1,300.	450.
		On cover		1,000.
b.		Vert. pair, imperf between		5,000.
20	A4	1a blue ('44)	500.00	100.00
		On cover		250.00
21	A8	1a3p mauve	2,000.	450.00
		On cover		1,500.
22	A5	4a pale brown ('44)	2,400.	650.00
		On cover		2,000.

1945   *Perf. 10*

23	A2	¼a orange	2,000.	150.00
		On cover		300.00
24	A9	½a vermilion, Die III ('44)	800.00	100.00
		On cover		250.00
25	A4	1a blue	500.00	100.00
		On cover		250.00
26	A8	1a3p bright mauve	2,000.	450.00
		On cover		1,500.
27	A10	1½a deep violet	2,000.	450.00
		On cover		1,350.
28	A5	4a brown	1,600.	400.00
		On cover		1,000.

The stamps of Dungarpur became obsolete in Sept. 1949.

DUTTIA

'dət-ē-ə,

(Datia)

LOCATION — A Feudatory State in the Bundelkhand Agency in Central India.
AREA — 912 sq. mi.
POP. — 158,834
CAPITAL — Datia

Ganesh, Elephant-headed God
A1   A2

All Duttia stamps have a circular control mark, about 23mm in diameter, handstamped in blue or black. All were issued without gum.

1893   **Typeset   Unwmk.   Imperf.**

1	A1	¼a black, *org red*	6,250.	
2	A1	½a blk, *grysh grn*	24,000.	
3	A2	1a black, *red*	4,750.	7,500.
4	A1	2a black, *yellow*	5,250.	
5	A1	4a black, *rose*	1,900.	

Type A2 with Frameline around God, Rosettes in Lower Corners

1896 (?)

5A	A2	½ black, *green*	15,000.	
5C	A2	2a dk blue, *lemon*	3,750.	

A 1a in this revised type has been reported.

1897

6	A2	½a black, *green*	100.00	675.00
7	A2	1a black	150.00	525.00
a.		Laid paper	32.50	
8	A2	2a black, *yellow*	42.50	500.00
9	A2	4a black, *rose*	40.00	325.00
		Nos. 6-9 (4)	332.50	2,025.

A3   A4

10	A3	½a black, *green*	150.00	825.00
11	A3	1a black	290.00	
12	A3	2a black, *yellow*	175.00	825.00
13	A3	4a black, *rose*	175.00	825.00
		Nos. 10-13 (4)	790.00	2,475.

1899-1900
Rouletted in Colored Lines on 2 or 3 Sides

14	A4	¼a red (shades)	5.00	32.50
b.		Tete beche pair	4,900.	
15	A4	½a black, *green*	4.00	30.00
16	A4	1a black	4.50	30.00
17	A4	2a black, *yellow*	5.25	35.00
18	A4	4a black, *rose red*	5.00	32.50
a.		Tete beche pair		
		Nos. 14-18 (5)	23.75	160.00

1904   *Imperf.*

22	A4	¼a carmine	5.50	47.50
23	A4	½a black, *green*		27.50
24	A4	1a black	21.00	75.00
		Nos. 22-24 (3)	54.00	122.50

1911   *Perf. 13½*

25	A4	¼a carmine	9.50	75.00

1916   *Imperf.*

26	A4	¼a dull blue	8.25	40.00
27	A4	½a green	8.25	40.00
28	A4	1a violet	10.00	42.50
a.		Tete beche pair	35.00	
29	A4	2a brown	22.50	52.50
29A	A4	4a brick red	110.00	
		Nos. 26-29A (5)	159.00	175.00

1918

31	A4	½a ultramarine	5.25	27.50
32	A4	1a rose	5.25	27.50
33	A4	2a violet	11.00	40.00
		Perf. 12		
34	A4	¼a black	7.50	37.50
		Nos. 31-34 (4)	29.00	132.50

1920   *Rouletted*

35	A4	¼a blue	4.00	21.00
36	A4	½a rose	5.25	24.00
		Perf. 7		
37	A4	½a dull red	24.00	62.50
		Nos. 35-37 (3)	33.25	107.50

Duttia stamps became obsolete in 1921.

FARIDKOT

fe-'rēd-ˌkōt

LOCATION — A Feudatory State in the Punjab Agency of India.
AREA — 638 sq. mi.
POP. — 164,364
CAPITAL — Faridkot

4 Folus or Paisas = 1 Anna

A1   A2

A3

Handstamped

1879-86   **Unwmk.   Imperf.**
Without Gum

1	A1	1f ultramarine	4.00	6.00
a.		Laid paper	21.00	24.00
b.		Tete beche pair	400.00	
2	A2	1p ultramarine	7.50	16.00
a.		Laid paper	125.00	150.00
3	A3	1p ultramarine	2.25	
a.		Tete beche pair	340.00	
		Nos. 1-3 (3)	13.75	22.00

Several other varieties exist, but it is believed that only the stamps listed here were issued for postal use. They became obsolete Dec. 31, 1886. See Faridkot under Convention States for issues of 1887-1900.

HYDERABAD (DECCAN)

ˈhīd-ə-ˌrə-ˌbad

LOCATION — Central India
AREA — 82,313 sq. mi.
POP. — 16,338,534 (1941)
CAPITAL — Hyderabad

This independent princely state was occupied and annexed by India in 1948.

> **Catalogue values for unused stamps in this State are for Never Hinged items, beginning with Scott 51 in the regular postage section, and Scott O54 in the officials section.**

Expect irregular perfs on the Nos. 1-14 and O1-O20 due to the nature of the paper.

A1   A2

1869-71   **Engr.   Unwmk.   *Perf. 11½***

1	A1	½a brown ('71)	6.00	6.50
2	A2	1a olive green	27.50	11.00
a.		Imperf. horiz., pair	900.00	175.00
3	A1	2a green ('71)	90.00	72.50
		Nos. 1-3 (3)	123.50	90.00

For overprints see Nos. O1-O3, O11-O13.
The reprints are perforated 12½.

A3

Wove Paper

1871-1909   *Perf. 12½*

4	A3	½a orange brown	4.00	.25
a.		½a red brown	4.00	.25
b.		½a magenta (error)	75.00	12.00
c.		Perf. 11½	27.50	30.00
d.		½a rose	4.00	.30
e.		½a bright vermilion	4.00	.25
5	A3	1a dark brown	1.90	.25
a.		Imperf., pair	550.00	
b.		Horiz. pair, imperf. vert.	1,350.	
c.		Vert. pair, imperf. horiz.	1,350.	
d.		Perf. 11½	180.00	200.00
6	A3	1a black ('09)	3.50	.25
7	A3	2a green	5.50	.25
a.		2a olive green ('09)	5.50	.50
b.		Perf. 11½	1,900.	
8	A3	3a yellow brown	4.50	2.25
a.		Perf. 11½	60.00	82.50
9	A3	4a slate	11.00	5.25
a.		Imperf. horiz., pair	1,350.	1,350.
b.		Perf. 11½	225.00	225.00
10	A3	4a deep green	8.25	5.00
a.		4a olive green	9.00	3.75
11	A3	8a bister brown	5.25	6.50
a.		Perf. 11½		
12	A3	12a blue	7.00	12.00
a.		Perf. 11½	500.00	
b.		12a slate green	7.50	7.50
		Nos. 4-12 (9)	50.90	32.00

For overprints see Nos. 13, O4-O10, O14-O20, O25-O26.

Surcharged

1900

13	A3	¼a on ½a brt ver	.75	1.25
a.		Inverted surcharge	57.50	35.00

A4

1900, Sept. 20

14	A4	¼a blue	8.25	5.25

Seal of the Nizam
A5   A6
Engraved by A. G. Wyon

1905   **Wmk. 42**

17	A5	¼a blue	3.75	.90
18	A5	½a red	6.00	.35
19	A5	½a orange	9.00	.50
		Nos. 17-19 (3)	18.75	1.75

For overprints see Nos. O21-O23.

Perf. 11, 11½, 12½, 13½ and Compound

1908-11

20	A5	¼a gray	1.50	.25
21	A5	½a green	7.00	.25
22	A5	1a carmine	5.25	.25
23	A5	2a lilac	2.40	.25
24	A5	3a brn orange ('09)	4.00	1.50
25	A5	4a olive green ('09)	4.50	1.90
26	A5	8a violet ('11)	1.90	1.20
27	A5	12a blue green ('11)	10.50	6.00
		Nos. 20-27 (8)	37.05	11.60

For overprints see Nos. O24, O27-O38.

Engr. by Bradbury, Wilkinson & Co.

1912

28	A5	¼a brown violet	1.20	.25
29	A5	½a deep green	2.50	.25
a.		Imperf., pair	550.00	

The frame of type A5 differs slightly in each denomination.
Nos. 20-21 measure 19½x20½mm.
Nos. 28-29 measure 20x21½mm.
For overprints see Nos 37, O39-O40, O44.

1915-16

30	A6	½a green	1.50	.25
31	A6	1a carmine rose	3.75	.25
32	A6	1a red	2.50	.25
		Nos. 30-32 (3)	7.75	.75

Unless used, imperf. stamps of types A5 and A6 are from plate proof sheets.
See No. 58. For overprints see Nos. 38, O41-O43, O45.

A7

1927   **Wmk. 211**   *Perf. 13½*

36	A7	1r yellow	13.50	18.00

Stamps of 1912-16 Surcharged in Red

(4 pies)   (8 pies)

1930

37	A5	4p on ¼a brown violet	.45	.25
a.		Perf. 11		675.00
b.		Double surcharge		350.00
38	A6	8p on ½a green	.60	.25
a.		Perf. 11	400.00	210.00

For overprints see Nos. O44-O45.

Seal of Nizam — A8

Char Minar — A9

High Court of Justice A10

Reservoir for City of Hyderabad A11

Bidar College — A13

Entrance to Ajanta Caves A12

Victory Tower at Daulatabad A14

Wmk. 211
1931-48   Engr.   Perf. 13½

39	A8	4p black	.45	.25
a.		Laid paper ('47)	3.75	8.25
39B	A8	6p car lake ('48)	15.00	12.50
40	A8	8p green	.75	.25
a.		8p yel grn, laid paper ('47)	4.50	6.75
b.		Imperf., pair	90.00	180.00
41	A9	1a dark brown	.75	.25
42	A10	2a dark violet	4.50	.25
a.		Imperf., pair	195.00	400.00
43	A11	4a ultramarine	2.40	1.00
a.		Imperf., pair	210.00	500.00
44	A12	8a deep orange	10.50	6.00
45	A13	12a scarlet	11.00	18.00
46	A14	1r yellow	7.50	7.00
		Nos. 39-46 (9)	52.85	45.50

On No. 39B, "POSTAGE" has been moved to ribbon at bottom of design.
Nos. 39a and 40a are printed from worn plates. The background of the design is unshaded.
See Bi, 59. For overprints see Nos. O46-O53, O56.

Unani General Hospital A15

Osmania General Hospital A16

Osmania University A17

Osmania Jubilee Hall — A18

Perf. 13½x14
1937, Feb. 13   Litho.   Unwmk.

47	A15	4p violet & black	.75	3.25
48	A16	8p brown & black	1.25	3.25
49	A17	1a dull orange & gray	1.75	2.10
50	A18	2a dull green & gray	2.25	6.75
		Nos. 47-50 (4)	6.00	15.35

The Nizam's Silver Jubilee.

> Catalogue values for unused stamps in this section, from this point to the end of the section, are for Never Hinged items.

Returning Soldier — A19

1946   Typo.   Perf. 13½

51	A19	1a dark blue	.25	.25

Wmk. 211

52	A19	1a blue	.25	.25

Wmk. Nizam's Seal in Sheet Laid Paper

53	A19	1a dark blue	1.00	1.20
		Nos. 51-53 (3)	1.50	1.70

Victory of the Allied Nations in WW II.

Town Hall, Hyderabad A20

1947, Feb. 17   Litho.   Wove Paper

54	A20	1a black	2.00	2.90

Inauguration of the Reformed Legislature, Feb. 17th, 1947.

Power House, Hyderabad A21

Designs: 3a, Kaktyai Arch, Warangal Fort. 6a, Golkunda Fort.

Perf. 13½x14
1947-49   Typo.   Wmk. 211

55	A21	1a4p dark green	1.50	3.25
56	A21	3a blue	2.50	6.50
57	A21	6a olive brown	5.50	27.50
a.		6a red brown ('49)	25.00	47.50
b.		Imperf., pair	190.00	
		Nos. 55-57 (3)	9.50	37.25

Seal Type of 1915
1947   Engr.   Perf. 13½

58	A6	½a rose lake	3.75	1.10

For overprint see No. O54.

Seal Type of 1931
1949   Litho.

59	A8	2p brown	3.00	3.50

For overprint see No. O55.

OFFICIAL STAMPS

Regular Issues of 1869-71 Overprinted

1873   Unwmk.   Perf. 11½, 12½
Red Overprint

O1	A1	½a brown	195.00	125.00
O2	A2	1a olive green	35.00	35.00
O3	A1	2a green	72.50	57.50
O4	A3	½a red brown	27.50	9.00
O5	A3	1a dark brown	195.00	125.00
O6	A3	2a green	72.50	57.50
O7	A3	3a yel brown	250.00	250.00
O8	A3	4a slate	120.00	72.50
O9	A3	8a bister	125.00	225.00
O10	A3	12a blue	195.00	240.00

Black Overprint

O11	A1	½a brown		52.50
O12	A2	1a olive green	4.50	3.75
O13	A1	2a green	7.50	9.00
O14	A3	½a red brown	16.00	5.25
O15	A3	1a dark brown	—	52.50
O16	A3	2a green	7.50	9.00
O17	A3	3a yel brown	62.50	52.50
O18	A3	4a slate	32.50	30.00
O19	A3	8a bister	75.00	62.50
O20	A3	12a blue	90.00	120.00

The above official stamps became obsolete in August, 1878. Since that date the "Official" overprint has been applied to the reprints and probably to original stamps. Two new varieties of the overprint have also appeared, both on the reprints and on the current stamps. These are overprinted in various colors, positions and combinations.

Same Ovpt. On Regular Issues of 1905-11
1908   Wmk. 42

O21	A5	½a green	30.00	.25
O22	A5	1a carmine	97.50	.25
O23	A5	2a lilac	97.50	.25
		Nos. O21-O23 (3)	225.00	.75

Perf. 11, 11½, 12½, 13½ and Compound
1909-11

O24	A5	½a red	210.00	.25
O25	A3	1a black	140.00	.75
O26	A3	2a olive green	150.00	1.50
O27	A3	3a brown orange	11.00	5.00
O28	A3	4a olive green ('11)	45.00	1.90
O29	A3	8a violet ('11)	19.00	5.25
O30	A5	12a blue green ('11)	15.00	5.00
		Nos. O24-O30 (7)	590.00	19.65

Regular Issue of 1908-11 Overprinted

1911-12

O31	A5	¼a gray	6.75	1.10
O32	A5	½a green	5.25	.25
O33	A5	1a carmine	3.00	.25
O34	A5	2a lilac	2.50	1.90
O35	A5	3a brown orange	27.50	1.10
O36	A5	4a olive green	7.00	.25
O37	A5	8a violet	11.00	.30
O38	A5	12a blue green	36.00	3.75
		Nos. O31-O38 (8)	99.00	8.90

Same Overprint on Regular Issue of 1912
1912

O39	A5	¼a brown violet	5.50	.25
a.		¼a gray violet	5.50	.25
O40	A5	½a deep green	5.25	.25

Same Ovpt. On Regular Issue of 1915-16
1917

O41	A6	½a green	5.25	.25
O42	A6	1a carmine rose	7.00	.25
O43	A6	1a red	4.00	.25
		Nos. O41-O43 (3)	16.25	.75

Same Overprint on Nos. 37 and 38
1930

O44	A5	4p on ¼a brown violet	3.25	.25
O45	A6	8p on ½a green	2.25	.25

Same Overprint on Regular Issue of 1931
1934-47   Wmk. 211   Perf. 13½

O46	A8	4p black	4.00	.25
a.		Laid paper ('47)		.30
b.		Imperf., pair	120.00	
O47	A8	8p green	1.90	.25
a.		8p yel grn, laid paper ('47)	10.00	7.50
b.		Inverted overprint		240.00
O48	A9	1a dark brown	3.00	.25
O49	A10	2a dark violet	11.00	.25
O50	A11	4a ultramarine	6.00	.35
O51	A12	8a deep orange	21.00	.90
O52	A13	12a scarlet	19.00	2.50
O53	A14	1r yellow	30.00	3.75
		Nos. O46-O53 (8)	95.90	8.50

> Catalogue values for unused stamps in this section, from this point to the end of the section, are for Never Hinged items.

Same Overprint on Nos. 58-59, 39B
1947-50   Perf. 13½

O54	A6	½a rose lake	9.00	10.50
O55	A8	2p brown ('49)	9.00	15.00
O56	A8	6p car lake ('50)	11.00	35.00
		Nos. O54-O56 (3)	29.00	60.50

IDAR

ˈē-dər

LOCATION — A Feudatory State in the Western India States Agency.
AREA — 1,669 sq. mi.
POP. — 262,660
CAPITAL — Himmatnagar

Stamps of Idar are in booklet panes of four. All stamps have one or two straight edges.

Maharaja Shri Himatsinhji
A1   A2

1939   Unwmk.   Typo.   Perf. 11

1	A1	½a light green	21.00	37.50

1941   Same Redrawn

2	A1	½a green	17.50	40.00

The panels containing denomination and name of state are shaded.

1944   Unwmk.   Perf. 12

3	A2	½a green	4.00	110.00
4	A2	1a purple	4.00	100.00
a.		Imperf., pair	250.00	
5	A2	2a blue	4.50	150.00
6	A2	4a red	4.75	160.00
		Nos. 3-6 (4)	17.25	

INDORE

in-ˈdōər

(Holkar)

LOCATION — A Feudatory State in the Indore Agency in Central India.
AREA — 9,902 sq. mi.
POP. — 1,513,966
CAPITAL — Indore

Maharaja Tukoji Rao II — A1

INDORE (continued)

A2

1886 Unwmk. Litho. Perf. 15
1 A1 ½a lilac 5.50 3.25

1889 Handstamped Imperf.
3 A2 ¼a black, *rose* 5.25 5.50

No. 3 exists in two types.

The originals of this stamp are printed in water color. The reprints are in oil color and on paper of a deeper shade of rose.

Maharaja Shivaji Rao — A3

1889-92 Engr. Perf. 15
4 A3 ¼a orange 2.25 1.20
5 A3 ½a brown violet 3.75 .25
6 A3 1a green 4.50 1.90
7 A3 2a vermilion 10.50 3.00
Nos. 4-7 (4) 21.00 6.35

For overprint see No. 14.

Maharaja Tukoji Rao III
A4 · A5

1904-08 Perf. 13½, 14
8 A4 ¼a orange .90 .25
9 A5 ½a lake ('08) 13.50 .25
  a. Imperf., pair 35.00
10 A5 1a green ('07) 3.75 .25
  a. Imperf., pair 175.00
11 A5 2a brown ('05) 22.50 1.50
  a. Imperf., pair 120.00
12 A5 3a violet 35.00 10.50
13 A5 4a ultramarine 7.50 2.10
Nos. 8-13 (6) 83.15 14.85

For overprints see Nos. O1-O7.

No. 5 Surcharged

1905 Perf. 15
14 A3 ¼a on ½a brown violet 9.00 30.00

Maharaja Yeshwant Rao II
A6 · A7

1928-38 Engr. Perf. 13½
15 A6 ¼a orange .90 .30
16 A6 ½a claret 3.25 .25
17 A6 1a green 4.00 .25
18 A6 1¼a green ('33) 6.00 1.25
19 A6 2a dark brown 19.00 3.25
20 A6 2a Prus blue ('36) 19.00 3.25
  a. Imperf, pair 37.50 275.00
21 A6 3a dull violet 3.00 14.00
22 A6 3½a dull violet ('34) 10.50 15.00
  a. Imperf, pair 100.00 650.00
23 A6 4a ultramarine 10.50 7.50
24 A6 4a bister ('38) 52.50 2.50
  a. Imperf, pair 45.00 500.00
25 A6 8a gray 9.50 6.50
26 A6 8a red orange ('38) 40.00 35.00
27 A6 12a rose red ('34) 7.50 15.00

Perf. 14
28 A7 1r lt blue & black 12.50 22.50
29 A7 2r car lake & black 82.50 90.00
30 A7 5r org brn & black 140.00 140.00
Nos. 15-30 (16) 420.65 356.55

Imperforates of types A6 and A7 were used with official sanction at Indore City during a stamp shortage in 1938. They were from sheets placed by the printers (Perkins, Bacon) on top of packets of 100 perforated sheets as identification.

Stamps of 1929-33 Surcharged in Black

1940 Perf. 13, 14
31 A7 ¼a on 5r org brn & blk 19.00 2.50
  a. Dbl. surch., black over green 700.00
32 A7 ½a on 2r car lake & blk 32.50 5.00
33 A6 1a on 1 ¼a green 32.50 1.20
  a. Inverted surcharge 110.00
Nos. 31-33 (3) 84.00 8.70

Stamps with green surcharge only are proofs.

A8

1941-47 Typo. Perf. 11
34 A8 ¼a orange 2.50 .25
35 A8 ½a rose lilac 4.75 .25
36 A8 1a dk olive green 12.50 .25
37 A8 1¼a yellow green 20.00 20.00
  a. Imperf., pair 275.00
38 A8 2a turquoise blue 14.00 1.75
39 A8 4a bister ('47) 20.00 20.00

Size: 23x28¼mm
40 A8 2r car lake & blk ('47) 16.00 250.00
41 A8 5r brn org & blk 15.00 325.00
Nos. 34-41 (8) 104.75 617.50

OFFICIAL STAMPS

Stamps and Type of 1904-08 Overprinted

1904-06 Perf. 13½, 14
O1 A5 ½a lake 1.10 1.90
  a. Inverted overprint 35.00 62.50
  b. Double overprint 35.00
  c. Imperf., pair 110.00
O2 A5 1a green .25 .25
O3 A5 2a brown ('05) .45 .45
O4 A5 3a violet ('06) 2.50 5.50
  a. Imperf., pair 425.00
O5 A5 4a ultra ('05) 7.50 2.25
Nos. O1-O5 (5) 11.80 10.35

Same Overprint on No. 8

1907
O6 A4 ¼a orange 1.10 1.90

No. 9 Overprinted

O7 A5 ½a lake .25 1.75

Nos. O1, O7 differ mainly in the shape of the "R."

JAIPUR

ˈjī-ˌpu̇ə̯r

LOCATION — A Feudatory State in the Jaipur Residency of India.
AREA — 15,610 sq. mi.
POP. — 3,040,876
CAPITAL — Jaipur

> **Catalogue values for unused stamps in this State are for Never Hinged items, beginning with Scott 49 in the regular postage section, and Scott O30 in the officials section.**

A1 · A1a

Chariot of Surya, Sun God

Pin-perf. 14x14½

1904 Typo. Unwmk.
1 A1 ½a ultramarine 290.00 275.00
  a. ½a pale blue 210.00 275.00
  b. ½a gray blue 3,250. 300.00
  c. As "b," imperf. 525.00 900.00
1D A1a ½a blue 5.00 10.00
  e. ½a ultramarine 5.50 10.00
  f. Imperf. 5.50 10.00
2 A1 1a dull red 8.25 21.00
  a. 1a chestnut 8.25 21.00
3 A1 2a pale green 8.25 21.00
  a. 2a emerald 9.00
Nos. 1-3 (4) 311.50 327.00

No. 1 has 36 varieties (on 2 plates), differing in minor details. Nos. 1b and 1c are from plate II. No. 1D has 24 varieties (one plate).

Chariot of Surya — A2

Perf. 12½x12 and 13½

1904-06 Engr.
4 A2 ¼a olive green ('06) 1.25 1.60
5 A2 ½a deep blue 2.75 .75
6 A2 1a carmine 3.75 6.75
7 A2 2a dark green 5.25 2.25
8 A2 4a red brown 11.00 3.25
9 A2 8a violet 6.00 4.00
10 A2 1r yellow 35.00 24.00
Nos. 4-10 (7) 65.00 42.60

For overprints see Nos. 21-22.

A3

A4

1911 Typo. Imperf. Without Gum
11 A3 ¼a yellow green 3.75 5.00
  a. ¼a olive green 3.75 5.00
  b. "¼" inverted 9.00
12 A3 ¼a olive yellow .45 1.50
  b. ¼a blue (error) —
13 A3 ½a ultramarine .45 1.50
  a. ½a dull blue 4.00 4.00
  b. "½" for "½" 7.00
14 A3 1a carmine .75 1.50
15 A3 2a deep green 3.00 9.50
  a. 2a gray green 4.00 8.25
Nos. 11-15 (5) 8.40 19.00

There are six types for each value and several settings of the ¼a and ½a in the 1911 issue.

Wmk. "Dorling & Co., London" in Sheet

1913-18 Perf. 11
16 A4 ¼a olive bister 1.00 2.25
  a. Vert. pair, imperf. between 300.00 300.00
  b. Horiz. pair, imperf. between — 240.00
17 A4 ½a ultramarine 2.25 1.90
18 A4 1a carmine ('18) 8.25 8.25
  a. 1a scarlet 6.00 5.50
  b. Vert. pair, imperf. btwn. 1,250. 1,250.
  c. Vert. pair, imperf. horiz. 1,250.
19 A4 2a green ('18) 6.00 7.50
20 A4 4a red brown 10.50 15.00
Nos. 16-20 (5) 28.00 34.90

For overprints see Nos. O1-O6, O9-O10.

Stamps of 1904-06 Surcharged

1926 Unwmk. Engr. Perf. 13½
21 A2 3a on 8a violet 3.00 5.25
  a. Inverted surcharge 275.00 210.00
22 A2 3a on 1r yellow 4.00 9.50
  a. Inverted surcharge 825.00 275.00

Wmk. "Overland Bank" in Sheet

1928 Typo. Perf. 12
17a A4 ½a ultramarine 4.75 4.00
18d A4 1a rose red 40.00 25.00
18e A4 1a scarlet 62.50 17.50
19a A4 2a green 140.00 45.00
20a A4 4a pale brown
23 A4 1r red orange 600.00 825.00

Durbar Commemorative Issue

Chariot of Surya, Sun God — A5

Maharaja Man Singh II — A6

Elephant with Standard — A7

Sowar in Armor — A8

Blue Peafowl — A9

Royal Bullock Carriage — A10

Royal Elephant Carriage — A11

Albert Museum — A12

Sireh-Deorhi Gate — A13

Chandra Palace — A14

Amber Palace — A15

Rajas Jai Singh II and Man Singh II — A16

Perf. 13½x14, 14, 14x13½

1931, Mar. 14   Typo.   Unwmk.

24	A5	¼a red brown & blk	4.50	4.00
25	A6	½a dull vio & blk	.75	.30
26	A7	1a blue & black	13.50	14.00
27	A8	2a ocher & black	13.50	14.00
28	A9	2½a rose & black	47.50	90.00
29	A10	3a dk green & blk	27.50	67.50
30	A11	4a dull grn & blk	27.50	82.50
31	A12	6a dk blue & blk	9.00	82.50
32	A13	8a brown & black	30.00	140.00
33	A14	1r olive & black	60.00	500.00
34	A15	2r lt green & blk	62.50	550.00
35	A16	5r violet & black	82.50	600.00
		Nos. 24-35 (12)	378.75	2,144.

Investiture of the Maharaja Man Singh II with full ruling powers.

Eighteen sets of this issue were overprinted in red "INVESTITURE—MARCH 14, 1931" for presentation to distinguished personages.

For surcharges see Nos. 47, 48, 58. For overprints see Nos. O12-O16, Rajasthan 16.

Man Singh II Type of 1931 and

Raja Man Singh II — A18

1932-46   Perf. 14

36	A6	¼a red brn & blk	.75	.75
36A	A6	¾a brn orange & black ('43)	12.00	6.25
37	A18	1a blue & black	5.00	2.50
37A	A6	1a blue & black	14.00	6.75
38	A18	2a ocher & black	6.75	4.00
38A	A6	2a ocher & blk ('45)	19.00	7.50
39	A6	2½a dk car & blk	6.75	5.00
40	A6	3a green & black	6.00	1.00
41	A18	4a gray grn & blk	6.75	17.50
41A	A6	4a gray green & blk ('45)	72.50	2.40
42	A6	6a blue & black	9.00	45.00
43	A18	8a choc & black	9.00	22.50
43A	A6	8a choc & blk ('45)	42.50	190.00
44	A18	1r bis & gray blk	40.00	175.00
44A	A6	1r bis & gray blk ('46)	30.00	240.00
45	A18	2r yel grn & blk	140.00	700.00
		Nos. 36-45 (16)	420.00	1,426.

For overprints see Nos. O17-O30, Rajasthan Nos. 15, 17-25.

Stamps of 1931-32 Surcharged in Red or Black

1936   Perf. 14x13½, 13½x14

46	A18	1r on 2r yel grn & blk (R)	15.00	160.00
47	A16	1r on 5r violet & blk	15.00	125.00

No. 25 Surcharged in Red

1938   Perf. 14x13½

48	A6	¼a on ½a dull vio & blk	17.50	25.00

Catalogue values for unused stamps in this section, from this point to the end of the section, are for Never Hinged items.

Amber Palace A19

Designs: ¼a, Palace gate. ¾a, Map of Jaipur. 1a, Observatory. 2a, Palace of the Winds. 3a, Arms of the Raja. 4a, Gate of Amber Fort. 8a, Chariot of the Sun. 1r, Raja Man Singh II.

1947-48   Unwmk.   Engr.   Perf. 14

49	A19	¼a dk green & red brn ('48)	2.25	7.50
50	A19	½a blue vio & dp grn	.75	6.75
51	A19	¾a dk car & blk ('48)	2.25	9.00
52	A19	1a dp ultra & choc	1.50	7.00
53	A19	2a car & blue vio	1.50	7.50
54	A19	3a dk gray & grn ('48)	2.50	9.50
55	A19	4a choc & dp ultra	1.50	7.50
56	A19	8a dk brown & red	1.50	9.00
57	A19	1r dk red vio & bl grn ('48)	4.00	67.50
		Nos. 49-57 (9)	17.75	131.25

25th anniv. of the enthronement of Raja Man Singh II.

No. 25 Surcharged in Carmine with New Value and Bars

1947

58	A6	3p on ½a	25.00	40.00
a.		"3 PIE"	75.00	160.00
b.		Inverted surcharge	72.50	62.50
c.		Double surch., one inverted	110.00	82.50
d.		As "a," inverted surcharge	375.00	325.00

For overprint see No. O31.

OFFICIAL STAMPS

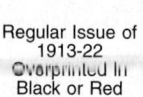

Regular Issue of 1913-22 Overprinted in Black or Red

1929   Unwmk.   Perf. 12½x12, 11

O1	A4	¼a olive green	3.75	4.00
O2	A4	½a ultramarine	1.90	.30
a.		Inverted overprint		675.00
O3	A4	½a ultra (R)	4.00	.45
O4	A4	1a red	2.25	.45
O5	A4	2a green	2.25	.60
O6	A4	4a red brown	3.00	2.50
O7	A4	8a purple	25.00	82.50
O8	A4	1r red orange	57.50	550.00
		Nos. O1-O8 (8)	99.65	640.80

The 8a and 1r not issued without overprint. For overprint see No. O11.

Regular Issue of 1913-22 Overprinted in Black or Red — b

1931   Perf. 11, 12½x12

O9	A4	½a ultra	575.00	.25
O10	A4	½a ultra (R)	300.00	.25
O10A	A4	8a purple	675.00	300.00
O10B	A4	1r red orange	700.00	400.00
		Nos. O9-O10B (4)	2,250.	700.50

No. O5 Surcharged

1932

O11	A4	½a on 2a green	225.00	3.00

Regular Issue of 1931 Overprinted in Red

1931-37   Perf. 13½x14, 14

O12	A6	¼a red brn & blk ('36)	.60	.25
O13	A6	½a dull vio & blk	.45	.25
O14	A7	1a blue & black	400.00	4.50
O15	A8	2a ocher & blk ('36)	6.75	8.25
O16	A11	4a dl grn & blk ('37)	72.50	60.00

For overprint see No. O32.

Same on Regular Issue of 1932 in Red

1932-37   Perf. 14

O17	A18	1a blue & black	6.75	.30
O18	A18	2a ocher & black	8.25	.30
O19	A18	4a gray grn & blk ('37)	550.00	16.00
O20	A18	8a choc & black	17.50	1.60
O21	A18	1r bister & gray blk	45.00	40.00
		Nos. O17-O21 (5)	627.50	58.20

No. 36 Overprinted Type "b" in Black

1939   Perf. 14

O22	A6	¼a red brown & blk	140.00	110.00

Nos. 36A, 38A, 39, 41A, 43A, 44A and Type of 1931 Overprinted in Carmine

1941-46   Unwmk.   Perf. 13½, 14

O23	A6	¾a brn org & blk ('43)	2.25	.75
O24	A6	1a blue & blk ('41)	6.75	.45
O25	A6	2a ocher & black	6.00	5.00
O26	A6	2½a dk car & blk ('46)	16.00	160.00
O27	A6	4a gray grn & blk ('46)	9.00	11.00
O28	A6	8a choc & black	6.00	12.50
O29	A6	1r bis & gray blk	60.00	
		Nos. O23-O28 (6)	46.00	189.70

Catalogue values for unused stamps in this section, from this point to the end of the section, are for Never Hinged items.

No. O24 Surcharged with New Value and Bars in Carmine

1947   Perf. 13½

O30	A6	9p on 1a blue & blk	5.50	5.50

No. 58 Overprinted in Red "SERVICE"   Perf. 14

O31	A6	3p on ½a	9.00	21.00
a.		Inverted surcharge		2,250.
b.		Double surch., one inverted	72.50	72.50
c.		"3 PIE"	400.00	450.00

No. O13 Surcharged "Three-quarter Anna" in Devanagari, similar to surcharge on No. 48, and Bars in Carmine

1949   Perf. 14x13½

O32	A6	¾a on ½a dl vio & blk	27.50	30.00

For later issues see Rajasthan.

JAMMU AND KASHMIR

ˈjəm-ˌü and ˈkash-ˌmi ə r

LOCATION — A Feudatory State in the Kashmir Residency in the extreme north of India.
AREA — 82,258 sq. mi.
POP. — 4,021,616 (1941)
CAPITAL — Srinagar

All stamps of Jammu and Kashmir were issued without gum.

½ Anna — A1

1 Anna — A2

4 Annas (¼ Rupee) — A3

Native Grayish Laid Paper
Handstamped
1866-67   Unwmk.   Imperf.
Printed in Water Colors

1	A1	½a gray black	375.00	150.00
		Cut to shape	75.00	30.00
2	A2	1a dull blue	900.00	180.00
a.		1a ultramarine	900.00	180.00
b.		1a royal blue	—	750.00
		Cut to shape	—	150.00
3	A2	1a gray black	2,400.	2,100.
		Cut to shape	475.00	425.00
4	A3	4a dull blue	4,500.	4,500.
a.		4a ultramarine	4,500.	4,500.
b.		4a indigo	4,500.	4,500.
		Cut to shape	900.00	900.00
5	A3	4a gray black	3,000.	
		Cut to shape	1,600.	
		Nos. 1-5 (5)	11,175.	6,930.

It has now been proved by the leading authorities on Indian stamps that all stamps of ½ anna and 1 anna printed from the so-called Die A are forgeries and that no such die was ever in use.

See Nos. 24-59.

JAMMU

A part of the Feudatory State of Jammu & Kashmir, both being ruled by the same sovereign.

½ Anna — A4   1 Anna — A5

Printed in blocks of four, three types of the ½a and one of the 1a.

Native Grayish Laid Paper
Printed in Water Colors

			Unwmk.	Imperf.
1867-77				
6	A4	½a black	1,800.	625.00
7	A4	½a indigo	625.00	490.00
a.		½a deep ultramarine	490.00	290.00
b.		½a deep violet blue	325.00	160.00
8	A4	½a red	12.50	6.75
a.		½a orange red	375.00	120.00
b.		½a orange	195.00	225.00
9	A5	1a black	3,750.	2,600.
10	A5	1a indigo	1,350	625.00
a.		1a deep ultramarine	1,200.	625.00
b.		1a deep violet blue	1,200.	625.00
11	A5	1a red	30.00	19.00
a.		1a orange red	1,250.	525.00
b.		1a orange	4,750.	2,750.

1876				
12	A4	½a emerald	3,750.	1,900.
13	A4	½a bright blue	2,400.	550.00
14	A5	1a emerald	5,250.	3,000.
15	A5	1a bright blue	700.00	750.00

Native Grayish Laid Paper

			Printed in Oil Colors	
1877				
16	A4	½a red	18.00	13.50
a.		½a brown red		67.50
17	A4	½a black		1,800.
18	A5	1a red	57.50	40.00
a.		1a brown red		225.00
19	A5	1a black	3,750.	2,750.

The formerly listed ½a dark blue, ½a dark green, 1a dark blue and 1a dark green are believed to be reprints.

European White Laid Paper

20	A4	½a red	—	1,600.
a.		Thin laid bâtonné paper		2,750.
21	A5	1a red	—	
a.		Thin laid bâtonné paper		6,750.

European White Wove Paper

22	A4	½a red		675.00
23	A5	1a red		

RE-ISSUES
For Jammu Only
Native Grayish Laid Paper
Printed in Water Colors

				Imperf.
1869-76				
24	A1	½a deep black	500.00	
25	A1	½a bright blue	550.00	675.00
26	A1	½a orange red	1,000.	1,100.
a.		½a orange to salmon	400.00	
b.		½a red	150.00	525.00
27	A1	½a emerald	175.00	450.00
28	A1	½a yellow	1,100.	1,400.
29	A2	1a deep black	500.00	
30	A2	1a bright blue	195.00	550.00
31	A2	1a orange red	1,000.	1,100.
b.		1a red	300.00	500.00
32	A2	1a emerald	195.00	450.00
33	A2	1a yellow	1,400.	
34	A3	4a deep black	450.00	—
35	A3	4a bright blue	325.00	—
a.		4a indigo		—
36	A3	4a orange red	325.00	425.00
a.		4a orange		425.00
b.		4a red	325.00	425.00
37	A3	4a emerald	450.00	1,000.
38	A3	4a yellow	900.00	

Native Grayish Laid Paper

			Printed in Oil Colors	
1877				
39	A1	½a red	52.50	90.00
40	A1	½a black	57.50	97.50
41	A1	½a slate blue	240.00	400.00
42	A1	½a sage green	210.00	
43	A2	1a red	72.50	290.00
45	A2	1a slate blue	57.50	450.00
46	A2	1a sage green	225.00	
47	A3	4a red	475.00	825.00
50	A3	4a sage green	225.00	

European White Laid Paper

51	A1	½a red		1,800.
52	A1	½a black	47.50	97.50
53	A1	½a slate blue	82.50	450.00
54	A1	½a yellow	240.00	
56	A2	1a slate blue	90.00	600.00
57	A3	4a red	650.00	750.00

58	A3	4a sage green		2,250.

European Brownish Wove Paper

59	A1	½a red		1,400.

It is probable that the issues of 1876, 1877 and the re-issues of the circular stamps were made to supply the demands of philatelists more than for postal needs. They were, however, available for postage.

There exist also reprints, printed in a variety of colors, on native and European thin wove paper. Collectors are warned against official imitations, which are very numerous. They are printed on several kinds of paper and in a great variety of colors.

A5a

Handstamped in Oil Color
1877, Nov.

60	A5a	(½a) red	1,900.

This provisional, made with a canceling device, was used only in Nov. 1877, at Jammu city.

KASHMIR

A part of the Feudatory State of Jammu & Kashmir, both being ruled by the same sovereign.

½ Anna — A6

Printed in Water Colors
Native Grayish Laid Paper
Printed from a Single Die

			Unwmk.	Imperf.
1866				
62	A6	½a black	5,250.	675.00

¼ Anna — A7   ½ Anna — A8

1 Anna A9   2 Annas A10

4 Annas — A11   8 Annas — A12

The ¼a, 1a and 2a are printed in strips of five varieties, the ½a in sheets of twenty varieties and the 4a and 8a from single dies.

1866-70				
63	A7	¼a black	6.75	7.00
64	A8	½a black	2,250.	300.00
65	A8	½a ultra	7.50	2.50
a.		½a blue	13.50	6.75
66	A9	1a black	4,000.	750.00
67	A9	1a red orange	22.50	17.50
68	A9	1a Venetian red	27.50	19.00
69	A9	1a orange brown	22.50	17.50
70	A9	1a ultra	6,500.	2,500.
71	A10	2a olive yellow	30.00	32.50
72	A11	4a emerald	75.00	72.50
73	A12	8a red	75.00	72.50

All the stamps printed in oil colors are reprints.

As in Jammu, official imitations are numerous and are found in many colors and on various papers.

JAMMU & KASHMIR

¼ Anna — A13   ½ Anna — A14

1 Anna — A15   2 Annas — A16

4 Annas — A17   8 Annas — A18

Laid Paper
Printed in Oil Colors

				Rough Perf. 10-14
1878				
74	A13	¼a red		
75	A14	½a red	21.00	25.00
a.		Wove paper		500.00
76	A14	½a slate blue	110.00	110.00
77	A15	1a red	1,900.	—
78	A15	1a bright violet		

				Imperf.
1878-80				
79	A13	¼a red	35.00	30.00
80	A14	½a red	15.00	16.00
81	A14	½a slate	27.50	24.00
82	A15	1a red	14.00	17.50
83	A15	1a violet	40.00	42.50
a.		1a dull purple	67.50	62.50
84	A16	2a red	140.00	140.00
85	A16	2a bright violet	60.00	57.50
86	A16	2a dull ultra	175.00	175.00
87	A17	4a red	340.00	290.00

Thick Wove Paper

88	A14	½a red	47.50	90.00
89	A15	1a red	75.00	37.50
90	A16	2a red	32.50	40.00

			Thin Toned Wove Paper	
1879-80				
91	A13	¼a red	5.50	6.75
92	A14	½a red	1.50	1.50
93	A15	1a red	3.75	5.25
94	A16	2a red	5.00	7.00
95	A17	4a red	16.00	16.00
96	A18	8a red	17.50	20.00
		Nos. 91-96 (6)	49.25	56.50

Thin Laid Bâtonné Paper
Printed in Water Color

1880				
97	A13	¼a ultramarine	1,350.	900.00

Thin Toned Wove Paper

			Printed in Oil Colors	
1881				
98	A13	¼a orange	17.50	24.00
99	A14	½a orange	35.00	25.00
100	A15	1a orange	37.50	21.00
101	A16	2a orange	27.50	21.00
102	A17	4a orange	67.50	82.50
103	A18	8a orange	110.00	120.00
		Nos. 98-103 (6)	295.00	293.50

⅛ Anna — A19

Thin White or Yellowish Wove Paper

1883-94				
104	A19	⅛a yellow brown	2.25	3.00
a.		⅛a yellow	2.25	3.00
105	A13	¼a brown	1.90	1.50
a.		Double impression	1,800.	

106	A14	½a red	1.90	1.25
a.		½a rose	2.40	1.50
106B	A19	⅛a bright blue	82.50	
c.		⅛a dull blue	12.00	
107	A15	1a bronze green	1.50	1.50
108	A15	1a yel green	1.50	1.50
109	A15	1a blue green	3.00	
110	A15	1a bister		
111	A17	4a green	6.50	6.00
112	A17	4a olive green	6.00	7.00
113	A18	8a deep blue	19.00	22.50
114	A18	8a dark ultra	18.00	21.00
115	A18	8a gray violet	15.00	32.50

Printed in Water Color

116	A18	8a gray blue	225.00	225.00

Printed in Oil Colors
Yellow Pelure Paper

117	A16	2a red	4.00	1.90

Yellow Green Pelure Paper

118	A16	2a red	5.50	6.00

Deep Green Pelure Paper

119	A16	2a red	27.50	27.50

Coarse Green Pelure Paper

120	A16	2a red	4.00	1.90
		Nos. 104-120 (18)	425.05	360.05

Thin Creamy Laid Paper

1886-94				
121	A19	⅛a yellow	90.00	100.00
122	A13	¼a brown	13.50	10.00
123	A14	½a vermilion	15.00	9.50
124	A14	½a rose red		110.00
125	A15	1a green	150.00	150.00
126	A17	4a green		

Printed in Water Color

127	A18	8a gray blue	160.00	150.00
		Nos. 121-127 (7)	428.50	529.50

Impressions of types A13 to A19 in colors other than the issued stamps are proofs. Forgeries to defraud the post exist, and some are common.

1/4 Anna

Stamps of the above type, printed in red or black, were never placed in use.

OFFICIAL STAMPS
Same Types as Regular Issues
White Laid Paper

			Unwmk.	Rough Perf. 10-14
1878				
O1	A14	½a black		3,000.

				Imperf
O3	A14	½a black	150.00	140.00
O4	A15	1a black	100.00	100.00
O5	A16	2a black	82.50	90.00
		Nos. O3-O5 (3)	332.50	330.00

Thin White or Yellowish Wove Paper

1880				
O6	A13	¼a black	2.50	3.00
O7	A14	½a black	.25	1.10
O8	A15	1a black	3.00	1.50
O9	A16	2a black	.45	.65
O10	A17	4a black	1.90	2.50
O11	A18	8a black	3.75	1.60
		Nos. O6-O11 (6)	11.85	10.35

Thin Creamy Laid Paper

1890-91				
O12	A13	¼a black	12.50	13.50
O13	A14	½a black	7.00	7.00
O14	A15	1a black	4.00	5.25
O15	A16	2a black	22.50	
O16	A17	4a black	82.50	97.50
O17	A18	8a black	42.50	75.00
		Nos. O12-O17 (6)	171.00	

Obsolete October 31, 1894.

JASDAN

LOCATION — A Feudatory State in the Kathiawar Agency in Western India.
AREA — 296 sq. mi.
POP. — 34,056 (1931)
CAPITAL — Jasdan

In 1948 Jasdan was incorporated in the United State of Saurashtra (see Soruth).

Catalogue values for all unused stamps in this state are for Never Hinged items.

Sun — A1

Perf. 8½ to 10½

1942		Unwmk.		Typo.	
1	A1	1a green		30.00	240.00

Issued in booklet panes of 4 and 8. The 1a carmine is a revenue stamp. Jasdan's stamp became obsolete Feb. 15, 1948.

JHALAWAR

'jäl-ə-,wär

LOCATION — A Feudatory State in the Rajputana Agency of India.
AREA — 813 sq. mi.
POP. — 107,890
CAPITAL — Jhalrapatan

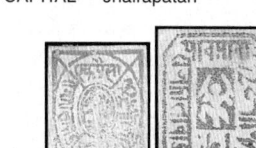

Apsaras, Hindu Nymph
A1   A2

Laid Paper

1887-90		Unwmk.		Imperf.	
		Without Gum			
1	A1	1p yellow green		7.00	22.50
2	A2	¼a green		1.90	3.75

Obsolete October 31, 1900.

JIND

'jind

(Jhind)

LOCATION — A State of India in the north Punjab.
AREA — 1,299 sq. mi.
POP. — 361,812 (1941)
CAPITAL — Sangrur

A1   A2

A3   A4

A5

1874		Unwmk. Litho.		Imperf.	
		Without Gum			
		Thin White Wove Paper			
1	A1	½a blue		10.00	6.25
2	A2	1a lilac		10.00	9.50
3	A3	2a yellow		1.50	8.75
4	A4	4a green		37.50	9.00
5	A5	8a dark violet		340.00	140.00
		Nos. 1-5 (5)		399.00	171.50

		Thick Blue Laid Paper			
1875				**Without Gum**	
6	A1	½a blue		1.50	7.00
7	A2	1a red violet		4.00	16.00
8	A3	2a brown orange		6.50	22.50
9	A4	4a green		5.50	22.50
10	A5	8a purple		13.50	32.50
		Nos. 6-10 (5)		31.00	100.50

Nos. 3 and 6 were perforated 12 in 1885 for use as fiscal stamps.

A6   A7

A8   A9

A10   A11

1882-84		Without Gum		Imperf.	
		Thin Yellowish Wove Paper			
12	A6	¼a buff		.45	2.25
a.		Double impression		75.00	
13	A7	½a yellow		3.75	2.50
14	A8	1a brown		2.50	5.00
15	A9	2a blue		3.00	13.50
16	A10	4a green		2.25	1.50
17	A11	8a red		9.50	6.75
		Nos. 12-17 (6)		21.45	31.50

		Perf. 12			
18	A6	¼a buff		1.50	4.00
19	A7	½a yellow		240.00	240.00
20	A8	1a brown		3.75	8.25
21	A9	2a blue		5.50	15.00
22	A10	4a green		7.50	16.00
23	A11	8a red		18.00	
a.		Thick white paper		15.00	
		Nos. 18-23 (6)		276.25	283.25

		Laid Paper			
		Imperf			
24	A6	¼a buff		1.90	
25	A7	½a yellow		1.90	
26	A8	1a brown		1.90	3.75
27	A9	2a blue		27.50	30.00
28	A11	8a red		3.75	16.00
		Nos. 24-28 (5)		36.95	49.75

		Perf. 12			
29	A6	¼a buff		12.50	
30	A7	½a yellow		190.00	40.00
31	A8	1a brown		2.25	
32	A11	8a red		3.75	15.00
		Nos. 29-32 (4)		208.50	55.00

As postage stamps these issues became obsolete in July, 1885, but some possibly remained in use as revenue stamps.
For later issues see Jind under Convention States.

KISHANGARH

'kish-ən-,gär

LOCATION — A Feudatory State in the Jaipur Residency of India.
AREA — 858 sq. mi.
POP. — 85,744
CAPITAL — Kishangarh

Kishangarh was incorporated in Rajasthan in 1947-49.
Stamps were issued without gum except Nos. 27-35.

Coat of Arms — A1

1899-1900		Unwmk. Typo.		Imperf.	
		Soft Porous Paper			
1	A1	1a green		32.50	90.00
2	A1	1a blue ('00)		600.00	
		Pin-perf			
3	A1	1a green		110.00	

A2   A3

Coat of   Maharaja
Arms — A4   Sardul
            Singh — A5

A6   A7

Coat of Arms—A9
A8

		Thin Wove Paper			
1899-1900		Handstamped		Imperf.	
4	A2	¼a rose pink		1.90	4.00
a.		¼a carmine		12.50	
5	A2	¼a green		825.00	1,200.
6	A3	½a light blue		1.90	2.50
7	A3	½a green		57.50	62.50
8	A3	½a carmine		3,750.	1,900.
9	A3	½a violet		240.00	490.00
10	A4	1a gray violet		1.60	1.50
a.		1a gray		7.50	7.50
11	A4	1a rose		110.00	300.00
11A	A5	2a orange		7.50	6.75
12	A6	4a chocolate		9.00	15.00
a.		Laid paper		125.00	125.00
13	A7	1r dull green		35.00	52.50
13A	A7	1r light brown		30.00	37.50
14	A8	2r brown red		125.00	190.00
a.		Laid paper		100.00	
15	A9	5r violet		120.00	150.00
a.		Laid paper		120.00	

		Pin-perf			
16	A2	¼a magenta		7.50	10.00
a.		¼a rose		.35	.60
17	A2	¼a green		400.00	700.00
a.		Imperf. vertically, pair		1,900.	
18	A3	½a blue		1.50	.75
a.		½a dark blue		3.75	5.00
19	A3	½a green		27.50	40.00
a.		Imperf. vert., pair		275.00	
20	A4	1a gray violet		1.10	1.50
a.		1a gray		8.25	5.25
b.		1a red lilac		2.25	3.00
d.		As "b," laid paper		62.50	19.00
20E	A4	1a rose		125.00	375.00
21	A5	2a orange		6.00	7.50
21B	A6	4a pale red brown		5.25	9.00
c.		4a chocolate		3.50	9.00
22	A7	1r dull green		16.00	22.50
b.		Laid paper		140.00	

23	A8	2r brown red		52.50	82.50
b.		Laid paper		67.50	
24	A9	5r red violet		52.50	82.50
d.		Laid paper		110.00	

Nos. 4-24 exist tête bêche and roll for a slight premium.
For overprints see Nos. O1-O11, Rajasthan Nos. 26-28, 30-32.

A9a   A9b

1901		Soft Porous Paper		Typo.	
24A	A9a	½a rose		12.00	9.00
24B	A9b	1a dull violet		72.50	40.00

For overprint see No. O12.

A10   A11

1903		Stout Hard Paper		Imperf.	
25	A10	½a pink		20.00	5.25
a.		Printed on both sides			2,100.

1904		Thin Wove Paper		Pin-perf.	
25B	A11	8a gray		7.50	11.00
c.		tête bêche pair		40.00	

For overprints see Nos. O13, O33, Rajasthan No. 29.

A11a   Maharaja Sardul
          Singh — A12

25D	A11a	1r green		27.50	27.50

For overprint see No. O13A.

1903		Stout Hard Paper		Imperf.	
26	A12	2a yellow		4.50	9.00

For overprints see Nos. O14, O34.

Maharaja Madan Singh
A13   A14

1904-05		Engr.		Perf. 12½, 13½	
27	A13	¼a carmine		.65	1.10
28	A13	½a chestnut		1.90	.45
29	A13	1a deep blue		3.75	4.00
30	A13	2a orange		22.50	10.00
31	A13	4a dark brown		22.50	25.00
32	A13	8a purple ('05)		19.00	37.50
33	A13	1r dark green		42.50	67.50
34	A13	2r lemon yellow		42.50	250.00
35	A13	5r purple brown		35.00	300.00
		Nos. 27-35 (9)		190.30	695.55

For overprints see Nos. O15-O22, O35-O38, Rajasthan Nos. 33-39.

		Thin Wove Paper			
1913		Typo.		Rouletted 9½	
37	A14	2 "ANNA" violet		8.25	13.50
a.		tête bêche pair		18.00	60.00

See Nos. 40-50. For overprint see Rajasthan No. 43.

Maharaja Madan Singh
A15   A16

Thick, Chalk-surfaced Paper

1913   *Rouletted 6½, 12*
38 A15 ¼a pale blue   .45   1.40
 a.   "Kishangahr"   7.50   10.00
 b.   Imperf., pair   11.00
39 A16 2a purple   12.50   27.50
 a.   "Kishangahr"   75.00 140.00

For overprint see No. O23.

1913-16   *Rouletted 12, 14½*
40 A14 ¼a pale blue   .30   .65
41 A14 ½a green ('15)   .30   1.50
 a.   Printed on both sides 350.00
42 A14 1a carmine   1.90   3.75
43 A14 2 "ANNAS" pur-
          ple   9.00   12.00
44 A14 4a ultramarine   9.00   12.00
45 A14 8a brown   10.00   60.00
46 A14 1r rose lilac   24.00 190.00
47 A14 2r dark green   150.00 525.00
48 A14 5r brown   60.00 675.00
     Nos. 40-48 (9)   264.50 1,479.

On Nos. 40-48 the halftone screen covers the entire design.
Nos. 41-48 have ornaments on both sides of value in top panel.
For overprints see Nos. O24-O30, O39-O43, Rajasthan Nos. 40-42, 44-48.

Type of 1913-16 Redrawn

1918   *Rouletted*
50 A14 1a rose red   2.25   8.25

The redrawn stamp is 24¾mm wide instead of 26mm. There is a white oval around the portrait with only traces of the red line. There is less shading outside the wreath.
For overprint see No. O44.

Maharaja Jagjanarajan Singh
A17   A18
Thick Glazed Paper

1928-29   *Pin-perf. 14½ to 16*
52 A17 ¼a light blue   1.90   3.00
53 A17 ½a lt yellow green 6.00   3.50
 a.   Imperf., pair   180.00 180.00
54 A18 1a carmine rose   1.10   2.25
55 A18 2a red violet   5.00   12.50
56 A17 4a yellow brown   2.50   2.50
57 A17 8a purple   8.25   42.50
58 A17 1r green   30.00   95.00
59 A17 2r lemon   42.50 340.00
60 A17 5r red brown   67.50 400.00
 a.   Imperf., pair   190.00
     Nos. 52-60 (9)   164.75 901.25

1945-47
Thick Soft Unglazed Paper
52a A17 ¼a gray blue   6.25   19.00
 b.   ¼a greenish blue ('47) 4.00   15.00
53b A17 ½a deep green   2.25   4.00
54a A18 1a dull carmine   12.50   6.50
55a A18 2a deep red violet 16.00   19.00
 b.   2a violet brown, imperf. 125.00 30.00
56a A17 4a brown   35.00   30.00
57a A17 8a violet   60.00 240.00
58a A17 1r deep green   75.00 250.00
59a A17 2r lemon
60b A17 5r red brown   875.00 1,100.

For overprints see Rajasthan Nos. 49-58.
For later issues see Rajasthan.

OFFICIAL STAMPS
Used values are for CTO stamps.

Regular Issues of 1899-1916 Handstamped in Black

On Issue of 1899-1900

1918   **Unwmk.**   *Imperf.*
O1 A2 ¼a carmine   12.00
O2 A4 1a gray violet   82.50   8.25
O3 A6 4a chocolate   —   190.00

               Pin-perf
O4 A2 ¼a carmine   3.25   .90
O4A A2 ¼a green   —   175.00
O4B A3 ½a blue   640.00 67.50
O6 A4 1a gray violet   67.50   2.25
O7 A5 2a orange   —   225.00
O8 A6 4a chocolate   100.00 24.00
O9 A7 1r dull green   250.00 180.00
O10 A8 2r brown red   —   1,400.
O11 A9 5r red violet   —   3,000.

See tete beche note after No. 24.

On Issue of 1901
O12 A9b 1a dull violet   75.00   2.25

On Issue of 1904
O13 A11 8a gray   140.00 35.00
O13A A11a 1r green   1,350.

                  Imperf.
O14 A12 2a yellow   125.00   7.50

On Issue of 1904-05
       Perf. 12½, 13
O15 A13 ¼a carmine   450.00
O16 A13 ½a chestnut   1.50   .50
O17 A13 1a deep blue   16.00   6.00
O18 A13 2a orange   1,500.
O19 A13 4a dark
           brown   90.00 27.50
O20 A13 8a purple   600.00 375.00
O21 A13 1r dark
           green   1,200. 1,100.
O22 A13 5r purple brn

On Issue of 1913
                  Rouletted
O23 A15 ¼a pale blue   11.00

On Issue of 1913-16
O24 A14 ¼a pale blue   .90   .75
O25 A14 ½a green   1.50   1.10
O26 A14 1a carmine   24.00 13.50
O27 A14 2a purple   12.50   6.00
O28 A14 4a ultra   42.50 22.50
O29 A14 8a brown   190.00 67.50
O30 A14 1r rose lilac 525.00 500.00
O31 A14 2r dark
           green
O32 A14 5r brown   2,750.

Red Handstamp
On Issue of 1904
                  Pin-perf
O33 A11 8a gray   —   450.00
                  Imperf
O34 A12 2a yellow   675.00 400.00

On Issue of 1904-05
       Perf. 12½, 13
O35 A13 1a deep blue   35.00 10.00
O36 A13 4a dark
           brown   140.00 62.50
O37 A13 8a purple   —   400.00
O38 A13 1r dark
           green   1,000.

On Issue of 1913-16
                  Rouletted
O39 A14 ¼a pale blue   3.00   2.50
O40 A14 ½a green   6.50   2.40
O41 A14 2a purple   210.00 100.00
O42 A14 4a ultra   —   52.50
O43 A14 8a brown   —   140.00

On Issue of 1918
Redrawn
O44 A14 1a rose red

The overprint on Nos. O1 to O44 is handstamped and, as usual with that style of overprint, is found inverted, double, etc. In this instance there is evidence that many of the varieties were deliberately made.

KOTAH

LOCATION — A Feudatory State in the Rajputana Agency of India.
AREA — 5714 sq. mi.
POP. — 526,827 (1880)
CAPITAL — Kotah City

All Kotah stamps are only known on cover, including the uncanceled

stamps. Values are for covers bearing a single stamp.

A1

A2   A3

              Handstamped
1883   **Unwmk.**   *Imperf.*
              Wove Paper
1 A1 2p green, *yellow*   20,000. 8,500.
 a.   Double impression   —
2 A2 2p black, *yellow*   20,000.
3 A3 2p indigo, *pink*   20,000.

A4

1886   **Wove Paper**
4 A4 1p green, *yellow*

The stamps of Kotah became obsolete in 1886.

LAS BELA
ləs 'bāl-ə

LOCATION — A Feudatory State in the Baluchistan District.
AREA — 7,132 sq. mi.
POP. — 63,008
CAPITAL — Bela

A1

A2

1897-98 **Unwmk. Typo.** *Perf. 12*
1 A1 ½a black, *white*   45.00 25.00
2 A1 ½a black, *gray*   25.00 16.00
3 A1 ½a black, *blue* ('98) 30.00 16.00
     Nos. 1-3 (3)   100.00 57.00

1901
4 A2 1a black, *red orange* 35.00 40.00

1904   *Pin-perf*
5 A1 ½a black, *lt blue*   24.00 13.50
Granite Paper
6 A1 ½a black, *greenish gray* 24.00 13.50
Las Bela stamps became obsolete in Mar. 1907.

MORVI
'mor-vē

LOCATION — A Feudatory State in the Kathiawar Agency, Western India.
AREA — 822 sq. mi.
POP. — 113,023
CAPITAL — Morvi

In 1948 Morvi was incorporated in the United State of Saurashtra (see Soruth).

Sir Lakhdhirji Waghji The Thakur Sahib of Morvi — A1

1931 **Unwmk. Typo.** *Perf. 12*
          Size: 21½x26½mm
1 A1 3p red   4.50 22.50
 a.   3p deep blue (error)   6.50 35.00
2 A1 ½a deep blue   40.00 67.50
3 A1 1a red brown   5.00 25.00
4 A1 2a yellow brown   6.00 60.00
     Nos. 1-4 (4)   55.50 175.00

Nos. 1-4 and 1a were printed in two blocks of four, with stamps 5½mm apart, and perforated on four sides. Nos. 1 and 2 were also printed in blocks of four, with stamps 10mm apart, and perforated on two or three sides.

A2   A3

1932 **Size: 21x25½mm** *Perf. 11*
5 A2 3p rose   7.50 21.00
6 A2 6p gray green   12.00 25.00
7 A2 6p emerald   9.50 21.00
8 A2 1a ultramarine   6.50 21.00
9 A2 2a violet   16.00 60.00
     Nos. 5-9 (5)   51.50 148.00

1934-48 *Perf. 14, Rough Perf. 11*
10 A3 3p carmine rose   3.75   5.25
 a.   3p red   2.50   6.50
11 A3 6p emerald   2.50 10.00
 a.   6p green   10.00 25.00
12 A3 1a red brown   2.75 21.00
 a.   1a brown   15.00 25.00
13 A3 2a violet   3.75 30.00
     Nos. 10-13 (4)   12.75 66.25

The 1934 London printing of Nos. 10-13 is perf. 14; the later Morvi Press printing is rough perf. 11.
Morvi stamps became obsolete Feb. 15, 1948.

NANDGAON
'nän͵d͵-gaun

LOCATION — A Feudatory State in the Chhattisgarh States Agency in Central India.
AREA — 871 sq. mi.
POP. — 182,380
CAPITAL — Rajnandgaon

A1

White Paper

1892, Feb. Unwmk. Typo. *Imperf.*
Without Gum

1	A1	½a blue	10.00	275.00
2	A1	2a rose	40.00	825.00

Some authorities claim that No. 2 was a revenue stamp.

For overprints see Nos. O1-O2.

A2

1893   **Without Gum**

4	A2	½a green	19.00	140.00
5	A2	2a rose	19.00	140.00

For overprint see No. O5.

Same Redrawn

1894   **Without Gum**

6	A2	½a yellow green	37.50	140.00
7	A2	1a rose	82.50	175.00
a.		Laid paper	375.00	

The redrawn stamps have smaller value characters and wavy lines between the stamps.
For overprints see Nos. O3-O4.

OFFICIAL STAMPS

Regular Issues Handstamped in Violet

1893-94   **Unwmk.**   *Imperf.*
Without Gum

O1	A1	½a blue	550.00	
O2	A1	2a red	1,350.	
O3	A2	½a yellow green	9.50	17.50
O4	A2	1a rose	16.00	37.50
a.		Laid paper	16.00	125.00
O5	A2	2a rose	3.00	3.00

Some authorities believe that this handstamp was used as a control mark, rather than to indicate a stamp for official mail.
The 1 anna has been reprinted in brown and in blue.
Nandgaon stamps became obsolete in July, 1895.

NOWANUGGUR

ˌnau-ə-ˈnəg-ər

(Navanagar)

LOCATION — A Feudatory State in the Kathiawar Agency, Western India.
AREA — 3,791 sq. mi.
POP. — 402,192
CAPITAL — Navanagar

Stamps of Nowanuggur were superseded by those of India.

6 Dokra = 1 Anna
16 Annas = 1 Rupee

Kandjar (Indian Dagger) — A1

1877   Unwmk.   Typo.   Imperf.
Without Gum
Laid Paper

1	A1	1d dull blue	1.00	37.50
a.		1d ultramarine	1.00	37.50
b.		Tete beche pair	1,900.	

Perf. 12½

2	A1	1d slate	120.00	175.00
a.		Tete beche pair	2,400.	

No. 2 on wove paper is of private origin.

A2

1877-88   Without Gum   Imperf.
Wove Paper

3	A2	1d black, *red violet*	5.25	16.00
a.		1d black, *rose*	5.25	
b.		Characters at beginning of 3rd line read "4102" instead of "418"		
4	A2	2d black, *green*	8.25	21.00
a.		2d black, *blue green*	12.50	
b.		"4102" instead of "418"		
5	A2	3d black, *yellow*	9.00	30.00
a.		3d black, *orange yellow*	19.00	
b.		"4102" instead of "418"		
c.		Laid paper	160.00	
d.		2d black, *yellow* (error in sheet of 3d)	600.00	
		Nos. 3-5 (3)	22.50	67.00

Nos. 3-5 range in width from 14 to 19mm.

Seal of the State — A3

1893   Thick Paper   Imperf.
Without Gum

6	A3	1d black	450.00

Perf. 12

7	A3	1d black	6.50
8	A3	3d orange	7.50

Imperf
Thin Paper

9	A3	1d black	350.00
10	A3	2d dark green	450.00
11	A3	3d orange	400.00
		Nos. 9-11 (3)	1,200.

Perf. 12

12	A3	1d black	2.50	9.00
13	A3	2d green	3.40	12.00
14	A3	3d orange	3.40	17.50
a.		Imperf. vert., pair		
		Nos. 12-14 (3)	9.30	38.50

Obsolete at end of 1895.

ORCHHA

ˈor-chə

(Orcha)

LOCATION — A Feudatory State in the Bundelkhand Agency in Central India.
AREA — 2,080 sq. mi.
POP. — 314,661
CAPITAL — Tikamgarh

Seal of Orchha — A1

1913-17   Unwmk.   Litho.   Imperf.
Without Gum

1	A1	¼a ultra ('15)	3.00	7.50
2	A1	½a emerald ('14)	.85	9.50
a.		Background of arms unshaded	52.50	150.00
3	A1	1a carmine ('14)	3.75	10.00
a.		Background of arms unshaded	30.00	275.00
4	A1	2a brown ('17)	6.75	35.00
5	A1	4a orange ('14)	12.00	57.50
		Nos. 1-5 (5)	26.35	119.50

Essays similar to Nos. 2-5 are in different colors.

A2

Maharaja Singh Dev — A3

1939-40   Perf. 13½, 13½x14

6	A2	¼a chocolate	5.00	12.00
7	A2	½a yellow green	4.50	100.00
8	A2	¾a ultramarine	7.00	150.00
9	A2	1a rose red	4.50	30.00
10	A2	1¼a deep blue	5.50	150.00
11	A2	1½a lilac	6.00	190.00
12	A2	2a vermilion	4.50	120.00
13	A2	2½a turq green	7.50	340.00
14	A2	3a dull violet	8.00	180.00
15	A2	4a blue gray	9.00	42.50
16	A2	8a rose lilac	15.00	340.00
17	A3	1r sage green	26.00	750.00
18	A3	2r lt violet ('40)	60.00	1,000.
19	A3	5r yel org ('40)	200.00	2,750.
20	A3	10r blue	700.00	4,500.
		Nos. 6-20 (15)	1,062.	10,654.

POONCH

ˈpünch

LOCATION — A Feudatory State in the Kashmir Residency in India.
AREA — 1,627 sq. mi.
POP. — 287,000 (estimated)
CAPITAL — Poonch

Poonch was feudatory to Jammu and Kashmir. Cancellations of Jammu and Kashmir are found on Poonch stamps, which became obsolete in 1894. The stamps are all printed in watercolor and handstamped from single dies. They may be found on various papers, including wove, laid, wove batonne, laid batonne and ribbed, in various colors and tones. Nearly all Poonch stamps exist tete beche and impressed sideways. Issued without gum.

A1

White Paper
Handstamped

1876   Unwmk.   Imperf.
Size: 22x21mm

1	A1	6p red	18,000.	240.

1877   Size: 19x17mm

1A	A1	½a red	22,500.	7,500.

1879   Size: 21x19mm

1B	A1	½a red	—	7,500.

A2   A3

A4   A5

A6

1880-88   **White Paper**

2	A2	1p red ('84)	40.00	40.00
3	A3	½a red	4.00	5.25
4	A4	1a red	6.75	
5	A5	2a red	16.00	19.00
6	A6	4a red	25.00	

Yellow Paper

7	A2	1p red	5.50	5.50
8	A3	½a red	9.50	9.50
9	A4	1a red	82.50	
10	A5	2a red	15.00	17.50
11	A6	4a red	7.50	7.50

Blue Paper

12	A2	1p red	4.00	3.75
13	A4	1a red	600.00	625.00

Orange Paper

14	A2	1p red	5.50	5.50
15	A3	½a red	42.50	
16	A5	2a red	150.00	
17	A6	4a red	37.50	

Green Paper

18	A3	½a red	67.50	
19	A4	1a red	5.00	7.50
20	A5	2a red	67.50	
21	A6	4a red	100.00	

Lavender Paper

22	A2	1p red	75.00	82.50
23	A4	1a red	125.00	160.00
24	A5	2a red	5.00	5.50

OFFICIAL STAMPS
White Paper
Handstamped

1888   Unwmk.   Imperf.

O1	A2	1p black	4.00	4.50
O2	A3	½a black	4.50	6.00
O3	A4	1a black	4.00	4.50
O4	A5	2a black	7.50	7.50
O5	A6	4a black	12.00	16.00
		Nos. O1-O5 (5)	32.00	38.50

1890   Yellowish Paper

O6	A2	1p black	3.75	
O7	A3	½a black	4.50	5.25
O8	A4	1a black	22.50	21.00
O9	A5	2a black	9.50	9.50
O10	A6	4a black	15.00	
		Nos. O6-O10 (5)	55.25	35.75

Obsolete since 1894.

RAJASTHAN

ˈrä-jə-ˌstän

(Greater Rajasthan Union)

AREA — 128,424 sq. miles
POP. — 13,085,000

The Rajasthan Union was formed in 1947-49 by 14 Indian States, including the stamp-issuing States of Bundi, Dungarpur, Jaipur and Kishangarh.

Catalogue values for all unused stamps in this state are for Never Hinged items.

Bundi Nos. 43 to 49 Overprinted — a

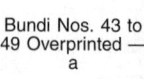

1948   Unwmk.   Perf. 11
Handstamped in Black

1	A8	¼a dp grn	8.25	50.00
a.		Pair, one without overprint	550.00	
2	A8	½a purple	8.25	50.00
a.		Pair, one without overprint	600.00	
3	A8	1a yel green	7.00	42.50
4	A9	2a red	21.00	125.00
5	A9	4a dp orange	72.50	450.00
6	A10	8a vio blue	13.50	80.00
		Nos. 1-6 (6)	130.50	797.50

Handstamped in Violet

1b	A8	¼a dp grn	9.00	55.00
2b	A8	½a purple	9.00	55.00
c.		Pair, one without overprint	550.00	
3a	A8	1a yel green	24.00	140.00
b.		Pair, one without overprint	550.00	

4a	A9	2a red	47.50	275.00
5a	A9	4a dp orange	47.50	275.00
6a	A10	8a vio blue	14.00	80.00
7	A10	1r chocolate	400.00	2,400.
		Nos. 1b-7 (7)	551.00	3,280.

Handstamped in Blue

1c	A8	¼a dp grn	52.50	300.00
2d	A8	½a purple	72.50	450.00
3c	A8	1a yel green	67.50	400.00
5b	A9	4a dp orange	190.00	1,100.
6b	A10	8a vio blue	120.00	725.00
7a	A10	1r chocolate	140.00	825.00
		Nos. 1c-7a (6)	642.50	3,800.

Typo. in Black

11	A9	2a red	15.00	100.00
a.		Inverted overprint	450.00	
12	A9	4a deep orange	6.00	100.00
a.		Double overprint	400.00	
13	A10	8a violet blue	27.50	
a.		Inverted overprint	950.00	
b.		Double overprint	600.00	
14	A10	1r chocolate	11.00	59.50
		Nos. 11-14 (4)		

Stamps of Jaipur, 1931-47, Overprinted in Blue or Carmine

1949   Center in Black   Perf. 14

15	A6	¼a red brown (Bl)	12.00	32.50
16	A6	½a dull violet	9.50	35.00
17	A6	¾a brown org (Bl)	15.00	40.00
18	A6	1a blue	11.00	72.50
19	A6	2a ocher	12.50	100.00
20	A6	2½a rose (Bl)	13.50	45.00
21	A6	3a green	16.00	110.00
22	A6	4a gray green	14.00	125.00
23	A6	6a blue	14.00	180.00
24	A6	8a chocolate	24.00	250.00
25	A6	1r bister	35.00	375.00
		Nos. 15-25 (11)	176.50	1,365.

Kishangarh Stamps and Types of 1899-1904 Handstamped Type "a" in Rose

1949   Pin-perf., Rouletted

26	A3	½a blue (#18)	900.00	
27	A4	1a dull lilac (#20)	21.00	62.50
28	A6	4a pale red brown (#21B)	125.00	160.00
29	A11	8a gray (#25B)	160.00	275.00
30	A7	1r dull green (#22)	450.00	500.00
31	A8	2r brown red (#23)	550.00	
32	A9	5r red violet (#24)	525.00	525.00
		Nos. 26-32 (7)	2,731.	

Kishangarh Nos. 28, 31-36 Handstamped Type "a" in Rose or Green

1949   Engr.   Perf. 13½, 12½

33	A13	½a chestnut (R)		300.00
34	A13	4a dark brown (G)	375.00	
35	A13	4a dark brown (R)	20.00	
36	A13	8a purple (R)	16.00	
37	A13	1r dark green (R)	21.00	
38	A13	2r lemon yellow (R)	27.50	
39	A13	5r purple brown (R)	47.50	

Kishangarh Nos. 40-42, 37, 43, 46-48 Handstamped Type "a" in Rose

1949   Typo.   Rouletted

40	A14	¼a pale blue	8.00	8.00
41	A14	½a orange	675.00	375.00
42	A14	1a carmine	—	450.00
43	A14	2 "anna" violet	825.00	
44	A14	2 "annas" purple	4.50	12.50
45	A14	8a brown	7.50	
46	A14	1r rose lilac	15.00	
47	A14	2r dark green	15.00	
48	A14	5r brown	675.00	
		Nos. 40-48 (9)	2,225.	

Kishangarh Stamps and Types of 1928-29 Handstamped Type "a" in Rose

1949   Pin-perf

49	A17	¼a greenish blue	75.00	75.00
50	A17	½a yel green	60.00	60.00
51	A18	1a car rose	110.00	110.00
52	A18	2a red violet	325.00	325.00
53	A17	4a yel brown	4.00	12.50
54	A17	8a purple	21.00	90.00
55	A17	1r deep green	10.00	
56	A17	2r lemon	140.00	
57	A17	5r red brown	75.00	
		Nos. 49-57 (9)	820.00	

Type of Kishangarh 1928-29, Handstamped Type "a" in Rose

1949   Pin-perf

58	A18	1a dark violet blue		140.00

No. 58 exists imperf.
Rajasthan stamps became obsolete Apr. 1, 1950.

RAJPEEPLA

räj-'pē-plə

(Rajpipla)

LOCATION — A Feudatory State near Bombay in the Gujarat States Agency in India.
AREA — 1,517 sq. mi.
POP. — 206,086
CAPITAL — Nandod

4 Paisas = 1 Anna

Kandjar (Indian Daggers) — A1

A2   A3

1880   Unwmk.   Litho.   Perf. 11, 12½
Without Gum

1	A1	1pa ultramarine	5.25	57.50
2	A2	2a green	45.00	160.00
a.		Horiz. pair, imperf. btwn.	900.00	900.00
3	A3	4a red	24.00	100.00
		Nos. 1-3 (3)	74.25	317.50

The stamps of Rajpeepla have been obsolete since 1886.

SIRMOOR

sir-'mu̇ə̇r

(Sirmur)

LOCATION — A Feudatory State in the Punjab District of India.
AREA — 1,046 sq. mi.
POP. — 148,568
CAPITAL — Nahan

A1   Raja Sir Shamsher Prakash — A2

1879   Unwmk.   Perf. 11½
Wove Paper

1	A1	1p green	24.00	500.00
a.		Imperf., pair		

Laid Paper

2	A1	1p blue	6.75	250.00
a.		Imperf., pair		

1885-88   Litho.   Perf. 14 and 14½.

3	A2	3p brown	1.00	.60
4	A2	3p orange	2.50	.45
5	A2	6p green	6.50	6.00
6	A2	1a blue	4.00	5.50
7	A2	2a carmine	6.25	21.00
		Nos. 3-7 (5)	20.25	33.55

There are several printings, dies and minor variations of this issue.
For overprints see Nos. O1-O16.

A3   Elephant — A4

1893   Perf. 11½

9	A3	1p yellow green	1.60	1.60
a.		1pa dark blue green	1.10	1.10
10	A3	1p ultramarine	1.90	1.20
b.		Imperf., pair	110.00	

Nos. 9 and 10 are re-issues, which were available for postage.
The printed perforation, which is a part of the design, is in addition to the regular perforation.

1895-99   Engr.   Perf. 14

11	A4	3p orange	5.45	.45
12	A4	6p green	1.10	.45
a.		Vert. pair, imperf between	15,000.	
13	A4	1a dull blue	6.50	5.25
14	A4	2a dull red	5.25	2.25
15	A4	3a yellow green	35.00	67.50
16	A4	4a dark green	24.00	35.00
17	A4	8a deep blue	27.50	42.50
18	A4	1r vermilion	57.50	110.00
		Nos. 11-18 (8)	162.30	263.40

No. 12a is unique.

Sir Surendar Bikram Prakash — A5

1899

19	A5	3a yellow green	6.25	32.50
20	A5	4a dark green	8.25	35.00
21	A5	8a blue	11.00	30.00
22	A5	1r vermilion	18.00	75.00
		Nos. 19-22 (4)	43.50	172.50

OFFICIAL STAMPS

Regular Stamps Overprinted in Black

1890-91   Unwmk.   Perf. 14, 14½

O1	A2	3p orange	4.50	52.50
O2	A2	6p green	2.25	2.25
a.		Double overprint	275.00	
b.		Double ovpt., one in red	1,250.	
O3	A2	1a blue	600.00	700.00
O4	A2	2a carmine	27.50	100.00
		Nos. O1-O4 (4)	634.25	

1890-92   Red Overprint

O5	A2	6p green	42.50	3.50
O6	A2	1a blue	37.50	47.50

O7	A2	6p green	8.25	.75
b.		Inverted overprint	210.00	150.00
O8	A2	1a blue	27.50	6.25
a.		Inverted overprint	500.00	300.00
b.		Double overprint	500.00	

1892   Black Overprint

O9	A2	3p orange	.90	.75
a.		Inverted overprint	375.00	
O10	A2	6p green	12.00	3.25
O11	A2	1a blue	18.00	1.50
a.		Double overprint	600.00	
O12	A2	2a carmine	10.00	10.00
a.		Inverted overprint	1,350.	1,350.
		Nos. O9-O12 (4)	40.90	15.50

Black Overprint

O13	A2	3p orange	19.00	1.90
a.		Inverted overprint		1,000.
b.		Double overprint		
O14	A2	6p green	8.25	.90
O15	A2	1a blue	11.00	1.90
O16	A2	2a carmine	25.00	21.00
		Nos. O13-O16 (4)	63.25	25.70

There are several settings of these overprints, differing in the sizes and shapes of the letters, the presence or absence of the periods, etc.
The overprints on Nos. O1-O16 are press printed. In addition, nine varieties of hand-stamped overprints were applied in 1894-96. Most of the handstamps are very similar to the press printed overprints.
Obsolete Mar. 31, 1901.

SORUTH

(Sorath)
(Junagarh)
(Saurashtra)

LOCATION — A Feudatory State near Bombay in the Western India States Agency in India.
AREA — 3,337 sq. mi.
POP. — 670,719
CAPITAL — Junagarh

The United State of Saurashtra (area 31,885 sq. mi.; population 2,900,000) was formed in 1948 by 217 States, including the stamp-issuing States of Jasdan, Morvi, Nowanuggur and Wadhwan.
Nos. 1-27 were issued without gum.

Catalogue values for unused stamps in this State are for Never Hinged items, beginning with Scott 39 in the regular postage section, and Scott O19 in the officials section.

Junagarh

A1   A2

Handstamped in Watercolor
1864   Unwmk.   Imperf.
Laid Paper

1	A1	(1a) black, bluish	950.00	125.00
a.		Wove paper		275.00
1B	A1	(1a) black, gray	950.00	125.00

Wove Paper

2	A1	(1a) black, cream		1,500.

1868   Typo.   Imperf.
Wove Paper
3	A2	1a black, *yellowish*		37,500.
4	A2	1a red, *green*		16,000.
5	A2	1a red, *blue*		12,500.
6	A2	1a black, *pink*	825.00	110.00
7	A2	2a black, *yellow*		16,000

Laid Paper
8	A2	1a black, *blue*	140.00	13.50
a.		Left character, 3rd line, omitted		
9	A2	1a red	32.50	37.50
a.		Left character, 3rd line, omitted		
10	A2	4a black	400.00	*675.00*
a.		Left character, 3rd line, omitted		

A 1a black on white laid paper exists in type A2. Value, used $9,500.

In 1890 official imitations of 1a and 4a stamps, type A2, were printed in sheets of 16 and 4. Original sheets have 20 stamps. Four of these imitations are perf. 12, six are imperf.

A3   A4

1877-86   Laid Paper   Imperf.
11	A3	1a green	1.50	.75
a.		Printed on both sides	750.00	825.00
12	A4	4a vermilion	4.00	2.50
a.		Printed on both sides	950.00	
13	A4	4a scarlet, *bluish*	5.50	5.00
		Nos. 11-13 (3)	11.00	8.25

Perf. 12
14	A3	1a green	.60	.25
a.		1a blue (error)	900.00	900.00
c.		Wove paper	5.25	2.25
d.		Imperf., pair	120.00	160.00
e.		As "a," wove paper	—	900.00
f.		As "a," vert. pair, imperf horiz.	240.00	
15	A3	1a green, *bluish*	5.25	*6.75*
a.		Vert. pair, imperf horiz.		525.00
b.		Horiz. pair, imperf vert.	210.00	
16	A4	4a red	4.00	1.90
a.		4a carmine	6.50	5.25
c.		Wove paper	7.50	18.00
d.		As "c," imperf., pair	340.00	450.00
17	A4	4a scarlet, *bluish*	16.00	*25.00*
		Nos. 14-17 (4)	25.85	33.90

Nos. 14d and 16c Surcharged

Three pies. / One anna.

1913-14   Perf. 12
18	A3	3p on 1a green	.25	.45
a.		Laid paper	110.00	45.00
b.		Inverted surcharge	52.50	30.00
c.		Imperf., pair	52.50	
19	A4	1a on 4a red	3.75	10.00
a.		Laid paper	11.00	*82.50*
b.		Imperf., pair	950.00	
c.		Double surcharge	1,000.	

A5   A6

1914   Perf. 12
20	A5	3p green	2.10	.50
a.		Imperf., pair	12.50	40.00
21	A6	1a rose carmine	2.25	*3.25*
a.		Imperf., pair	30.00	140.00
b.		Laid paper	375.00	160.00

Nawab Mahabat Khan III
A7   A8

1923-29   Wove Paper   Perf. 12
22	A7	3p violet	.50	.65
a.		Imperf, pair	450.00	
b.		Laid paper ('29)	7.50	6.50

c.		As "b," imperf, pair ('29)	5.25	*52.50*
d.		As "b," horiz. pair, imperf btwn.	4.50	*37.50*
23	A8	1a red	4.50	14.00
b.		Laid paper	4.50	14.00

Single examples of Nos. 23 and 23b cannot usually be distinguished.

Surcharged with New Value
27	A8	3p on 1a red	7.50	10.00

Two types of surcharge.

Junagarh City and The Girnar   A9

Gir Lion — A10

Nawab Mahabat Khan III — A11

Kathi Horse A12

1929   Perf. 14
30	A9	3p dk green & blk	1.50	.25
31	A10	½a dk blue & blk	9.00	.25
32	A11	1a claret & blk	7.50	1.50
33	A12	2a org buff & blk	19.00	3.00
34	A9	3a car rose & blk	9.00	19.00
35	A10	4a dull vio & blk	19.00	42.50
36	A12	8a apple grn & blk	25.00	35.00
37	A11	1r dull blue & blk	21.00	45.00
		Nos. 30-37 (8)	111.00	146.50

For surcharges see Nos. 40-42, O20-O25.
For overprints see Nos. O1-O14.

Type of 1929
Inscribed "Postage and Revenue"
1937
38	A11	1a claret & black	15.00	1.50

For overprint see No. O15.

> **Catalogue values for unused stamps in this section, from this point to the end of the section, are for Never Hinged items.**

United State of Saurashtra

A13

Bhavnagar Court Fee Stamp Overprinted in Black "U.S.S. Revenue & Postage Saurashtra"
1949   Unwmk.   Typo.   Perf. 11
39	A13	1a deep claret	16.00	15.00
a.		"POSTAGE" omitted	525.00	375.00
b.		Double overprint	525.00	*600.00*

Nos. 30, 31 Surcharged in Black or Carmine "POSTAGE & REVENUE ONE ANNA"
1949-50   Perf. 14
40	A9	1a on 3p dk grn & blk (bl) ('50)	60.00	82.50
a.		"OSTAGE"	750.00	900.00
41	A10	1a on ½a dk bl & blk (C)		7.50
a.		Double surcharge	14.00	825.00

For overprint see No. O19.

No. 33 Surcharged in Green "Postage & Revenue ONE ANNA"
1949
42	A12	1a on 2a org buff & blk	24.00	*40.00*
a.		"EVENUE" omitted	1,100.	

For overprint see No. O26.

OFFICIAL STAMPS
Regular Issue of 1929 Overprinted in Red

a

1929   Unwmk.   Perf. 14
O1	A9	3p dk green & black	2.50	.25
O2	A10	½a dk blue & black	6.00	.25
O3	A11	1a claret & black	6.00	.25
O4	A12	2a org buff & black	3.75	.90
O5	A9	3a car rose & black	1.10	.75
O6	A10	4a dull violet & blk	6.25	.65
O7	A12	8a apple green & blk	5.50	4.50
O8	A11	1r dull blue & blk	5.50	*35.00*
		Nos. O1-O8 (8)	36.60	42.55

For surcharges see Nos. O20-O24.

Regular Issue of 1929 Overprinted in Red

b

1933-49
O9	A9	3p dk grn & black ('49)	375.00	25.00
O10	A10	½a dk bl & black ('49)	900.00	22.50
O11	A9	3a car rose & blk	32.50	27.50
O12	A10	4a dull vio & blk	42.50	24.00
O13	A12	8a apple grn & blk	47.50	27.50
O14	A11	1r dull blue & blk	52.50	140.00

The 3p is also known with ms. "SARKARI" overprint in carmine.
For surcharge see No. O25.

No. 38 Overprinted Type "a" in Red
1938
O15	A11	1a claret & black	21.00	2.25

> **Catalogue values for unused stamps in this section, from this point to the end of the section, are for Never Hinged items.**

United State of Saurashtra
No. 41 with Manuscript "Service" in Carmine
1949
O19	A10	1a on ½a dk bl & blk (C)		225.00

Used value for No. O19 is for an example used on piece, cancelled at Gadhda or Una between June and December, 1949.
No. 42 is also known with carmine ms. "Service" overprint in English or Gujarati.

Nos. O4-O8 and O14 Surcharged "ONE ANNA" in Blue or Black
1949
Surcharge 2¼mm high
O20	A12	1a on 2a (Bl)	21,000.	40.00
O21	A9	1a on 3a	5,250.	100.00
O22	A10	1a on 4a	600.00	100.00
O23	A12	1a on 8a	525.00	72.50

Surcharge 4mm High, Handstamped
O24	A11	1a on 1r (#O8)	3,250.	72.50
O25	A11	1a on 1r (#O14)	1,350.	75.00
		Nos. O20-O25 (6)	31,975	460.00

No. 42 Overprinted Type "b" in Carmine
1949   Unwmk.   Perf. 14
O26	A12	1a on 2a	125.00	35.00

TONK
LOCATION — A Feudatory State in the Rajputana Agency of India.
AREA — 2509 sq. mi.
POP. — 307,528 (1900)
CAPITAL — Nimbahera

Three examples of Tonk No. 1 are known. All are on covers dated 1906.

A1

Handstamped with black octagonal control seal
1906   Unwmk.   Litho.   Imperf.
Wove Paper
1	A1	¼a yellow brown		—

The stamps of Tonk became obsolete in 1907.

TRAVANCORE
ˈtrav-ən-ˌkō̇r

LOCATION — A Feudatory State in the Madras States Agency, on the extreme southwest coast of India.
AREA — 7,662 sq. mi.
POP. — 6,070,018 (1941)
CAPITAL — Trivandrum

16 Cash = 1 Chuckram
2 Chuckrams = 1 Anna

Conch Shell (State Seal)
A1   A2

1888   Unwmk.   Typo.   Perf. 12
Laid Paper
1	A1	1ch ultramarine	7.00	6.50
2	A1	2ch orange red	9.00	*16.00*
3	A1	4ch scarlet	30.00	25.00
		Nos. 1-3 (3)	46.00	47.50

The frame and details of the central medallion differ slightly on each denomination of type A1.

Laid paper printings of Nos. 1-3, 5-7 in completely different colors are essays.

1889-99   Wmk. 43   Wove Paper
4	A1	½ch violet	.90	.35
a.		Vert. pair, imperf. between	450.00	450.00
b.		Double impression		450.00
c.		½ch slate lilac ('94)	3.25	.75
d.		As "c," double impression		450.00
e.		½ch purple ('99)	1.50	.35
f.		As "e," double impression		450.00
g.		½ch dull purple ('04)	1.75	.35
5	A1	1ch ultramarine	2.25	.25
a.		Vert. pair, imperf. between		675.00
b.		Horiz. pair, imperf. between		675.00
c.		Double impression		600.00
d.		Tete beche pair	3,750.	3,250.
e.		1ch pale ultra ('92)	3.25	.35
f.		1ch violet blue ('01)	5.00	.50
6	A1	2ch scarlet	5.00	1.25
a.		Horiz. pair, imperf. between	550.00	550.00
b.		Vert. pair, imperf. between	250.00	
c.		Double impression	300.00	
d.		2ch rose ('91)	4.00	.50
e.		As "d," imperf. pair		750.00
f.		2ch red ('04)	4.00	.50

7 A1 4ch dark green 5.00 1.00
  a. Double impression 650.00
  b. 4ch yellow green ('01) 3.00 1.00
  c. 4ch dull green ('04) 8.00 1.50
    Nos. 4-7 (4) 13.15 2.85

Shades exist for each denomination.
For surcharges see Nos. 20. For type surcharged see No. 20. For overprints see Nos. 10-11. For type surcharged see No. 20. For overprints see Nos. O1-O2, O4, O6, O18, O24-O25, O27B, O32-O33, O42.

1901-32   Handmade Wove Paper
8 A2 ¾ch black 3.00 2.10
9 A2 ¾ch brt violet ('32) .50 .25
  a. Horizontal pair, imperf. between 275.00
  b. ¾ch mauve, perf 12½ ('37) 17.50 1.00
  c. As "b," horiz. pair, imperf. between 225.00
  d. Perf. compound 12x12½ 25.00 10.00
  e. As "d," horiz. pair, imperf. between 325.00

Machine-made Paper
Wmk. 43A
8A A2 ¾ch black ('32) 11.50 .75

For overprints see Nos. O26-O27, O44, O52.

No. 4 Surcharged

1906   Wmk. 43
10 A1 ¼ch on ½ch violet 1.10 .25
  a. Inverted surcharge 100.00 55.00
  b. ¼ on ½ch reddish lilac 1.10 .45
  c. ¼ on ½ch reddish lilac 2.00 .45
11 A1 ¼ch on ½ch violet .60 .50
  a. Pair, one without surcharge —
  b. Inverted surcharge 90.00
  c. Double surcharge
  d. Figure "8" omitted in fraction 60.00
  e. ⅜ch on ½ch reddish lilac .60 .50
  f. ⅜ch on ½ch lilac 1.25 .50

A3   A4

1908-11
12 A3 4ca rose .45 .25
  a. Vertical pair, imperf. between 450.00 425.00
13 A1 6ca red brown ('10) .45 .25
  a. Printed on both sides 75.00
  b. Horizontal pair, imperf. between 425.00
14 A4 3ch purple ('11) 4.00 .30
  a. Vertical pair, imperf. between 450.00 425.00
  b. Vertical strip of 3, imperf. between 500.00
    Nos. 12-14 (3) 4.90 .80

For surcharge & overprints see Nos. 19, O3, O5, O8, O13, O15, O20, O22, O30-O31, O53.

A5   A6

1916
15 A5 7ch red violet 3.50 1.00
  a. 7ch carmine-red (error) 60.00
16 A6 14ch orange 4.00 3.75
  a. Horizontal strip of 3, imperf. vertically 625.00

For overprints see Nos. O11-O12, O34-O35.

A7

1920-33
17 A7 1¼ch claret .80 .80
  a. Horiz. pair, imperf. between 500.00 475.00

---

18 A7 1½ch light red ('33) 4.00 .25
  a. Horizontal strip of 3, imperf. between 325.00
  b. Perf. 12½ 25.00 3.25
  c. Perf. compound 12x12½ 60.00

For surcharges see Nos. 27-28. For overprints see Nos. O7, O17, O28-O29, O38, O56.

No. 12 and Type of
1888 Surcharged

1921
19 A3 1ca on 4ca rose .25 .25
  a. Inverted surcharge 37.50 25.00
20 A1 5ca on 1ch dull bl (R) 1.50 .25
  a. Inverted surcharge 19.00 12.50
  b. Double surcharge 100.00 75.00
  c. Vertical pair, imperf. between 425.00

A8

1921-32
21 A8 5ca bister 1.20 .25
  a. Horizontal pair, imperf. between 75.00
22 A8 5ca brown ('32) 4.00 .35
  a. Horizontal pair, imperf. between 55.00
  b. Vertical pair, imperf. between 300.00
23 A8 10ca rose .60 .25
    Nos. 21-23 (3) 5.80 .85

For surcharges & overprints see Nos. 29-30, O9-O10, O14, O16, O19, O21, O23, O36-O37.

Sri
Padmanabha
Shrine at
Trivandrum
A9

State
Chariot — A10

Maharaja Sir Bala
Rama Varma — A11

1931, Nov. 6
24 A9 6ca emerald & black 2.40 2.40
  a. Horizontal pair, imperf. between 225.00 225.00
25 A10 10ca ultra & black 1.90 1.00
  a. Vertical pair, imperf. between 750.00
26 A11 3ch violet & black 4.00 4.50
    Nos. 24-26 (3) 8.30 7.90

Investiture of Sir Bala Rama Varma with full ruling powers.

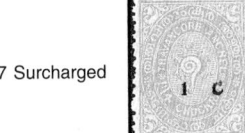

No. 17 Surcharged

1932, Jan. 14
27 A7 1ca on 1¼ch claret .25 .75
  a. Inverted surcharge 6.50 10.00
  b. Double surcharge 50.00 47.50
  c. Horizontal pair, imperf. between 190.00

---

  d. Pair, one without surcharge 175.00 190.00
  e. Letter "c" omitted 55.00 55.00
28 A7 2ca on 1¼ch claret .25 .25
  a. Inverted surcharge 6.50 10.00
  b. Double surcharge 42.50
  c. Pair, one without surcharge 180.00 190.00
  d. Double surcharge, one inverted 80.00
  e. Triple surcharge 100.00
  f. Triple surcharge, one inverted 85.00 85.00
  g. Numeral "2" omitted 55.00 55.00
  h. Letter "c" omitted 55.00 55.00
  i. Horizontal pair, imperf. between 180.00
  j. Vertical pair, imperf. between 190.00

Type of 1932 and No. 23 Surcharged like Nos. 19-20

1932, Mar. 5
29 A8 1ca on 5ca chocolate .25 .25
  a. Inverted surcharge 11.00 15.00
  b. Double surcharge
  c. Pair, one without surcharge 180.00
  d. Horizontal pair, imperf. between 190.00
  e. Surcharge inverted on reverse only 115.00
  f. Numeral "1" omitted 50.00
  g. Letter "c" omitted 45.00
30 A8 2ca on 10ca rose .25 .25
  a. Inverted surcharge 7.50 12.00
  b. Double surcharge 32.50 35.00
  c. Horizontal pair, imperf. between 200.00
  d. Double surcharge, one inverted 115.00 110.00
  e. Double surcharge, both inverted 65.00
31 A8 2ca on 5ca slate purple 2.25 .50
  a. Inverted surcharge 450.00
  b. Numeral "1" inverted 125.00 110.00

Untouchables Entering Temple and
Maharaja — A12

Designs: Different temples and frames.

1937, Mar. 29   Litho.   Perf. 11½
32 A12 6ca carmine 4.25 1.50
  b. Horizontal strip of 3, imperf. between 750.00
33 A12 12ca ultramarine 5.25 .90
34 A12 1½ch light green 2.25 3.50
  b. Vertical pair, imperf. between 525.00
35 A12 3ch purple 6.50 3.50
    Nos. 32-35 (4) 18.25 9.40

Temple Entry Bill.

Perf. 12½
32A A12 6ca carmine 3.75 3.00
  c. Compound perf. 75.00 82.50
33A A12 12ca ultramarine 7.00 1.25
  b. Vertical pair, imperf. between 700.00
  c. Compound perf. 110.00
34A A12 1½ch light green 40.00 11.50
  c. Compound perf. 175.00
35A A12 3ch purple 6.50 5.50
    Nos. 32A-35A (4) 57.25 21.25

Lake
Ashtamudi
A13

A14   A15

Sir Bala Rama
Varma — A16

Sri Padmanabha Shrine — A17

View of
Cape
Comerin
A18

Pachipara
Reservoir
A19

1939, May 9   Litho.   Perf. 12½
36 A13 1ch yellow green 12.00 .25
37 A14 1½ch carmine 7.00 7.00
  d. Perf. 13½ 27.50 100.00
38 A15 2ch orange 12.00 4.00
39 A16 3ch chocolate 11.00 .25
40 A17 4ch henna brown 14.00 .60
41 A18 7ch light blue 17.50 30.00
42 A19 14ch turq green 10.00 100.00
    Nos. 36-42 (7) 83.50 142.10

Perf. 11
36A A13 1ch yellow green 17.50 .25
37A A14 1½ch carmine 8.00 37.50
38A A15 2ch orange 27.50 2.75
39A A16 3ch chocolate 30.00 .50
40A A17 4ch henna brown 62.50 .75
41A A18 7ch light blue 150.00 62.50
42A A19 14ch turq green 18.00 180.00

Perf. 12
36B A13 1ch yellow green 37.50 3.75
37B A14 1½ch carmine 62.50 9.00
38B A15 2ch orange 175.00 10.00
39B A16 3ch chocolate 65.00 7.50
40B A17 4ch henna brown 55.00 14.00

Perf. Compound 11, 12, 12½
36C A13 1ch yellow green 45.00 5.00
37C A14 1½ch carmine 85.00 15.00
38C A15 2ch orange 175.00 10.00
39C A16 3ch chocolate 75.00 1.50
40C A17 4ch henna brown 275.00 200.00
41C A17 7ch light blue 175.00 75.00

27th birthday of Maharaja Sir Bala Rama Varma.
For surcharges and overprints see Nos. 45, O45-O51, Travancore-Cochin 3-7, O3-O7.

Maharaja
Sir Bala
Rama
Varma and
Aruvikara
Falls
A20

Maharaja
and
Marthanda
Varma
Bridge,
Alwaye
A21

1941, Oct. 20   Typo.   Perf. 12½
43 A20 6ca violet black 11.00 .25
  a. Perf. 11 9.00 .25
  b. As "a," vertical pair, imperf. between 35.00
  c. As "a," vertical pair, imperf. horiz. 80.00 100.00
  d. Perf. 12 80.00 100.00
  e. As "d," horiz. pair, imperf. between 37.50
  f. As "d," vert. pair, imperf. between 90.00
  g. As "d," vert. strip of 3, imperf. between 40.00
  h. Compound perf. 14.50 3.00
44 A21 ¾ch dull brown 12.50 .35
  a. Vertical pair, imperf. between 750.00
  b. Perf. 11 12.00 .25
  c. As "b," horizontal pair, imperf. between 350.00
  d. As "b," vert. pair, imperf. between 37.50 85.00
  e. As "b," vert. strip of 3, imperf. between 45.00
  f. As "b," block of 4, imperf. between horiz. & vert. 400.00
  g. Perf. 12 80.00 16.00
  h. Compound perf. 22.50 1.25

29th birthday of the Maharaja, Oct. 20, 1941.
For overprints & surcharges see Nos. 46-47, 49, O54-O55, Travancore-Cochin Nos. 1, O1.

Stamps and Types of
1939-41 Surcharged
in Black

Perf. 11, 12½

1943, Sept. 17   **Wmk. 43**

45	A14	2ca on 1½ch carmine	2.25	1.90
a.		Vertical pair, imperf. between	80.00	
b.		"2" omitted in surcharge	500.00	475.00
c.		"CA" omitted in surcharge	900.00	
d.		"ASH" omitted in surcharge	900.00	
e.		Perf. 11	.50	.50
f.		As "e," "CA" omitted in surcharge	900.00	
g.		As "e," horizontal pair, imperf. between		400.00
h.		Compound perf.	1.15	2.40
i.		As "h," vertical pair, imperf. between	240.00	
j.		As "h," numeral "2" omitted in surcharge	550.00	
46	A21	4ca on ¾ch dull brown	6.00	.45
a.		Perf. 11	8.00	1.00
b.		Perf. 12		225.00
c.		Compound perf.	10.00	2.00
47	A20	8ca on 6ca red	7.00	.25
a.		Perf. 11	7.00	.25
b.		As "a," horiz. pair, imperf. between	60.00	
c.		Perf. 12		125.00
d.		Compound perf.	25.00	13.50
		Nos. 45-47 (3)	15.25	2.60

For overprints see Nos. O57-O59.

Maharaja Sir Bala
Rama Varma — A22

1946, Oct. 24   **Typo.**   **Perf. 11**

48	A22	8ca rose red	3.50	3.00
a.		Perf. 12½	3.50	3.00
b.		Perf. 12	50.00	7.00
c.		As "b," horizontal pair, imperf. between	100.00	100.00
d.		As "b," horizontal strip of 3, imperf. between	100.00	
e.		Compound perf.		

For overprint see No. O60. For surcharges
see Travancore-Cochin Nos. 2, O2.

**No. O54 Overprinted "SPECIAL"
Vertically in Orange**

1946   **Perf. 12½**

49	A20	6ca violet black	9.50	5.00
a.		Perf. 11	55.00	9.00
b.		Compound perf.	10.00	9.00

OFFICIAL STAMPS

Nos. O1-O60 were issued without
gum.

Regular Issues of
1889-1911
Overprinted in Red or
Black

Perf. 12, 12½

1911, Aug. 16   **Wmk. 43**

O1	A1	1ch indigo (R)	1.65	.25
a.		Inverted overprint	10.00	6.50
b.		"nO" for "On"	120.00	120.00
c.		Double overprint	100.00	75.00
d.		Vertical pair, imperf. between		275.00
O2	A1	2ch scarlet	.50	.25
a.		Inverted overprint	12.00	12.00
b.		Blue overprint		180.00
O3	A4	3ch purple	.50	.25
a.		Inverted overprint	15.00	15.00
b.		Double overprint	120.00	100.00
c.		Vertical pair, imperf. between	325.00	300.00
d.		Horizontal pair, imperf. vertically	225.00	
e.		Blue overprint	225.00	110.00
O4	A1	4ch dark green	.80	.25
a.		Inverted overprint	82.50	19.00
b.		Double overprint	190.00	140.00
c.		Horizontal pair, imperf. between		400.00
		Nos. O1-O4 (4)	3.45	1.00

**Same Ovpt. on Regular Issues of
1889-1920**

1918-20

O5	A3	4ca rose	.25	.25
a.		Imperf., pair	450.00	450.00
b.		Inverted overprint		
c.		Double overprint	180.00	140.00
d.		Double impression		425.00
e.		"SS" inverted	60.00	30.00
O6	A1	½ch violet (R)	3.75	.50
a.		Inverted overprint	19.00	6.00
b.		"chucrram"	18.50	6.50
c.		Double overprint, both inverted	240.00	
d.		"On" omitted		210.00
e.		Double impression	75.00	
f.		Horizontal pair, imperf. between	240.00	210.00
g.		Vertical pair, imperf. between	100.00	100.00
O7	A7	1¼ch claret	.60	.25
a.		Inverted overprint	14.00	12.00
b.		Double overprint	67.50	
d.		Double impression		475.00
e.		A7 1¼ch carmine (error of color)	60.00	
		Nos. O5-O7 (3)	4.60	1.00

**Same Ovpt. on Regular Issues of
1909-21**

1921

O8	A1	6ca red brown	.45	.25
a.		Inverted overprint	200.00	18.00
b.		Double overprint	200.00	180.00
c.		Vertical pair, imperf. between		350.00
O9	A8	10ca rose	1.75	.25
a.		Inverted overprint	100.00	100.00
b.		Double overprint		
c.		Horizontal pair, imperf. between		225.00
d.		10ca scarlet ('25)		18.00

**Same Overprint on Regular Issue of
1921**

1922

O10	A8	5ca bister	2.00	.25
a.		Inverted overprint	21.00	13.50

For surcharge see No. O39B.

**Same Overprint on Regular Issue of
1916**

1925

O11	A5	7ch plum	2.50	.45
a.		7ch carmine red	75.00	
O12	A6	14ch orange	3.25	.60

**Same Overprint in Blue on Regular
Issues of 1889-1921**

O13	A3	4ca rose	80.00	1.00
O14	A8	5ca bister	.90	.25
O15	A1	6ca red brown	22.00	2.50
a.		Inverted overprint	180.00	160.00
O16	A8	10ca rose	120.00	32.50
a.		Inverted overprint		115.00
O17	A7	1¼ch claret	—	120.00
O18	A1	4ch dark green	—	100.00

Some authorities question the authenticity
of No. O14.

1930   **Black Overprint**

O19	A8	5ca brown	.35	.90
a.		Inverted overprint	27.50	
b.		Vertical pair, imperf. between		425.00

Regular Issues of
1889-1932
Overprinted in Black
or Red

1930-34

O20	A3	4ca rose	18.00	60.00
O21	A8	5ca brown	35.00	14.00
a.		Inverted overprint	100.00	100.00
O22	A1	6ca org brown	.25	.25
a.		Inverted overprint	30.00	
b.		Double overprint		100.00
c.		"nO" for "On"	200.00	200.00
d.		Vertical pair, imperf. between	100.00	100.00
O23	A8	10ca rose	6.50	4.50
a.		Horizontal pair, imperf. between	20.00	35.00
b.		Vertical pair, imperf. between	15.00	32.50
O24	A1	½ch violet ('34)	.85	.25
a.		"chucrram"	15.00	10.00
O25	A1	½ch purple (R)	.25	.25
a.		"chucrram"	15.00	10.00
b.		Vertical pair, imperf. between	180.00	175.00
O26	A2	¾ch black (R) ('32)	.60	.25
a.		Inverted overprint		375.00
b.		"N" omitted in overprint	160.00	155.00
O27	A2	¾ch brt vio ('33)	.45	.25
a.		Double overprint		200.00
c.		Vertical pair, imperf. between		240.00
d.		Compound perf. (12x12½)	50.00	32.50

O27B	A1	1ch gray blue (R) ('33)	1.50	.35
e.		Horizontal pair, imperf. between	200.00	200.00
f.		Vertical pair, imperf. between	32.50	47.50
g.		Perf. 11	15.00	8.50
h.		Compound perf. (12x12½)	37.50	17.50
i.		As "h," vertical pair, imperf. between		325.00
O28	A7	1¼ch claret	2.10	2.00
O29	A7	1½ch dull red ('32)	.60	.25
a.		Double overprint	80.00	80.00
b.		Perf. 12½	70.00	18.00
c.		Compound perf. (12x12½)		45.00
d.		As "c," double impression		350.00
O30	A4	3ch purple ('33)	1.90	.90
a.		Double overprint		150.00
O31	A4	3ch purple (R)	1.20	.25
a.		Inverted overprint		80.00
b.		Horizontal pair, imperf. between	150.00	75.00
c.		Vertical pair, imperf. between	110.00	65.00
d.		Perf. 12½		5.00
e.		As "d," vertical pair, imperf. between		325.00
O32	A1	4ch deep green (R)	3.00	.25
O33	A1	4ch deep green	2.75	7.50
O34	A5	7ch maroon	1.90	.45
a.		Vertical pair, imperf. between	65.00	65.00
b.		Perf. 12½		20.00
c.		Compound perf. (12x12½)	75.00	16.00
d.		As "c," vertical pair, imperf. between		190.00
O35	A6	14ch orange ('31)	2.50	.60
a.		Inverted overprint	500.00	425.00
b.		Horizontal pair, imperf. between	60.00	85.00
c.		Vertical pair, imperf. between	300.00	
		Nos. O20-O35 (17)	79.35	92.30

The overprint on Nos. O22, O26 and O28 is
smaller than the illustration. There are two
sizes of the overprint on No. O27.
For surcharges see Nos. O39, O40-O41.

Type of 1921-32 and
No. 17 Surcharged
and Overprinted

1932

O36	A8	6ca on 5ca dk brown	.25	.45
b.		Inverted surcharge	12.00	12.50
c.		Double surcharge	150.00	
d.		Double surcharge, one inverted	130.00	
e.		Pair, one without surcharge	500.00	
O36A	A8	6ca on 5ca bister	2.50	3.00
f.		Inverted surcharge	110.00	
O37	A8	12ca on 10a rose	.25	.25
a.		New value inverted	9.00	11.00
b.		Overprint and surcharge inverted	55.00	
c.		Double surcharge		160.00
O38	A7	1ch8ca on 1¼ch cl	.50	.30
a.		Inverted surcharge	17.50	17.50
b.		Double surcharge	75.00	
c.		Vertical pair, imperf. between		500.00
		Nos. O36-O38 (4)	3.50	4.00

Nos. O21, O10, O23
and O28 Surcharged
in Black

O39	A8	6ca on 5ca dk brown	.30	.45
a.		New value inverted	16.00	19.00
c.		Pair, one without surcharge	325.00	
O39B	A8	6ca on 5ca bis	50.00	20.00
O40	A8	12ca on 10a rose	3.00	2.25
a.		New value inverted	10.00	10.00
b.		"On S S" inverted	24.00	27.50
c.		Ovpt. & surch. inverted	60.00	70.00
d.		Ovpt. & surch. inverted	60.00	62.50
O41	A7	1ch8ca on 1¼ch cl	4.50	1.90
a.		New value inverted		160.00
		Nos. O39-O41 (4)	57.80	24.60

No. O39B can be distinguished from O36A
by the letters "S" in the overprint, which are
closer together on No. O39B.

Regular Issue of
1889-94 Overprinted

1933

O42	A1	½ch violet	5.50	.25
a.		Horizontal pair, imperf. between	130.00	100.00
b.		Horizontal strip of 3, imperf. between		250.00
c.		Vertical pair, imperf. between		200.00
d.		Double impression		325.00

Regular Issue of 1901
Overprinted in Red

1933

O44	A2	¾ch black	.50	.40
a.		Left "S" omitted	145.00	135.00
b.		Right "S" omitted	145.00	

No. O44 can be distinguished from No. O26
by its overprint, which is significantly smaller
than No. O26.

**Regular Issue of 1939 Overprinted
in Black**

a

SERVICE

1939   **Perf. 12½**

First Overprint
"SERVICE" 13mm wide, letter "R" with
curved tail

O45	A13	1ch yellow green	11.00	.50
O46	A14	1½ch carmine	16.00	2.40
a.		"SESVICE"	200.00	45.00
b.		Perf. 12	90.00	22.50
c.		As "b," "SESVICE"		300.00
d.		As "b," horizontal pair, imperf. between		450.00
O47	A15	2ch orange	32.50	5.00
a.		"SESVICE"	11.00	1.00
b.		Compound perf. (12x12½)	190.00	210.00
O48	A16	3ch chocolate	200.00	200.00
a.		"SESVICE"	9.50	.30
b.		Perf. 12	150.00	30.00
c.		As "b," "SESVICE"	50.00	.75
d.		Compound perf. (12x12½)	450.00	65.00
O49	A17	4ch henna brown	19.00	7.00
O50	A18	7ch light blue	24.00	8.50
O51	A19	14ch turq green	24.00	6.50
		Nos. O45-O51 (7)	35.00	12.00
			130.50	39.20

27th birthday of Maharaja Sir Bala Rama
Varma.

Second Overprint
Overprinted "SERVICE" 13½mm wide,
ketter "R" with straight tail

1941-42

Perf. 12½

O45F	A13	1ch yellow green	2.00	.25
a.		Inverted overprint		60.00
b.		Double overprint	30.00	
c.		Vertical pair, imperf. between	85.00	85.00
O46F	A14	1½ch scarlet	6.50	.25
a.		Horizontal pair, imperf. between	100.00	
O47F	A15	2ch orange	5.50	.35
O48F	A16	3ch chocolate	4.00	.25
a.		Vertical pair, imperf. between		1,000.
O49F	A17	4ch henna brown	5.50	1.25
O50F	A18	7ch light blue	11.00	.45
O51F	A19	14ch turq green	19.00	.85

Perf. 11

O45G	A13	1ch yellow green	1.25	.25
a.		Double overprint	225.00	210.00
b.		Vertical pair, imperf. between	65.00	
O46G	A14	1½ch scarlet	5.00	.25
a.		Vertical pair, imperf. between	240.00	225.00
b.		Vertical strip of 3, imperf. between	175.00	
c.		Horizontal pair, imperf. between		225.00
O47G	A15	2ch orange	20.00	4.00
a.		Vertical pair, imperf. between		1,000.

O48G	A16	3ch chocolate	4.25 .25
O49G	A17	4ch henna brown	6.50 .65
O50G	A18	7ch light blue	11.00 .45
a.		7ch blue	22.50 11.50
O51G	A19	14ch turq green	24.00 1.75

Perf. 12

- O45H A13 1ch yellow green 5.00 .60
  - a. Inverted overprint 210.00
  - b. Double overprint 27.50 42.50
  - c. Double impression 180.00
  - d. Vertical pair, imperf. between 140.00 135.00
- O46H A14 1½ch scarlet 11.00 1.25
  - a. Vertical strip of 3, imperf. between 350.00
- O47H A15 2ch orange 225.00 200.00
  - a. Vertical pair, imperf. between 1,100. 1,000.
- O48H A16 3ch chocolate 10.00 4.00
  - a. Vertical pair, imperf. between 1,000. 900.00
- O49H A17 4ch henna brown 32.50 9.00
- O50H A18 7ch light blue 37.50 15.00
  - a. 7ch blue 13.00 10.00
- O51H A19 14ch turq green 17.50 3.00

Perf. Compound (12x12½)

- O45I A13 1ch yellow green 10.00 3.00
- O46I A14 1½ch scarlet 5.00 .50
- O47I A15 2ch orange 200.00 200.00
- O48I A16 3ch chocolate 32.50 1.00
- O49I A17 4ch henna brown 80.00 32.50
- O50I A18 7ch light blue 25.00 6.00
- O51I A19 14ch turq green 125.00 20.00

"SERVICE" Overprint 13mm

No. 9 Overprinted — b

1939   Wmk. 43   Perf. 12.

- O52 A2 ¾ch violet 42.50 2.50
  - a. Perf. 12½ 260.00 125.00
  - b. Compound perf. (12x12½) 240.00 120.00

"SERVICE" 13½mm

1941   Perf. 12½

- O52F A2 ¾ch violet 25.00 .25
  - a. Horizontal pair, imperf. between 220.00 220.00
  - b. Perf. 11 100.00 1.25
  - c. Perf. 12 12.00 .25
  - d. Compound perf. (12x12½) 55.00 1.00

No. 13 Overprinted Type "b"

1941

- O53 A1 6ca red brown 1.25 .50
  - a. Perf. 11 2.00 .90
  - b. Perf. 12 1.00 .40
  - c. Compound perf. (12x12½) 1.00 1.25

Nos. 43-44 Overprinted Type "a"

1941   Perf. 12½

- O54 A20 6ca violet black .90 .75
  - a. Perf. 11 1.00 1.25
  - b. Perf. 12 110.00 17.50
  - c. Compound perf. (12x12½) 1.75 1.75
- O55 A21 ¾ch dull brown 9.50 .25
  - a. Vertical pair, imperf. between 750.00
  - b. Perf. 11 10.00 .25
  - c. Perf. 12 110.00 5.00
  - d. Compound perf. (12x12½) 12.50 1.00

29th birthday of the Maharaja, Oct. 20, 1941.
For overprint see No. 49.

No. 18 Overprinted Type "b"

1944   Perf. 12

- O56 A7 1½ch light red 6.50 1.25
  - a. Perf. 12½ ('44) 21.00 12.00
  - b. Compound perf. (12x12½) 28.50 17.50

Nos. 45-48 Overprinted Type "a"

1945-49   Perf. 11, 12

- O57 A14 2ca on 1½ch car .90 1.50
  - a. Pair, one without surcharge 500.00
  - b. Perf. 12½ .75 1.20
  - c. Compound perf. (12x12½) 1.00 1.50
  - d. As "c," "2" omitted in surcharge 750.00 750.00
  - e. Perf. 12
- O58 A21 4ca on ¾ch dull brn 6.00 .60
  - a. Perf. 12½ ('45) 8.00 .75
  - b. Compound perf. (12x12½) 4.50 1.75
- O59 A20 8ca on 6ca red 2.00 .25
  - a. Inverted surcharge 2,250.
  - b. Perf. 12½ 4.00 .75
  - c. Compound perf. (12x12½) 10.00 1.50
- O60 A22 8ca rose red ('49) 5.00 1.75
  - a. Double impression of stamp 47.50
  - b. Horizontal pair, imperf. between 65.00
  - c. Vertical pair, imperf. between 375.00
  - d. Perf. 12½ .75 1.20
  - e. As "d," double impression 50.00
  - f. Perf. 12 4.50 1.75
  - g. As "f," double impression 75.00
  - Nos. O57-O60 (4) 13.90 4.10

Travancore stamps became obsolete June 30, 1949.

TRAVANCORE-COCHIN

ˈtrav-ən-ˌkō͟ə̯r kō-ˈchin

LOCATION — Southern India
AREA — 9,155 sq. mi.
POP. — 7,492,000

The United State of Travancore-Cochin was established July 1, 1949.

> Catalogue values for all unused stamps in this state are for Never Hinged items.

Travancore Stamps of 1939-47 Surcharged in Red or Black

HALF ANNA
അര അണ

1949, July 1   Wmk. 43   Perf. 12

- 1 A20 2p on 6ca vio blk (R) .95 .30
  - a. Horiz. pair, imperf. between 110.00
  - b. Vert. pair, imperf. between 10.00 26.00
  - c. Inverted surcharge 200.00
  - d. Vert. strip of 3, imperf. between 47.50
  - e. Horiz. strip of 3, imperf. between 110.00
  - f. Block of 4, imperf. between (horiz. & vert.) 100.00
- 2 A22 4p on 8ca rose red 1.85 .40
  - a. Vert. pair, imperf. between 30.00
  - b. Inverted surcharge 250.00
  - c. Pair, one without surcharge 325.00
  - d. "FOUP" 225.00 125.00
  - e. "S" inverted 150.00
- 3 A13 ½a on 1ch yel grn 1.25 .50
  - a. Horiz. pair, imperf. between 110.00 110.00
  - b. Vert. pair, imperf. between 8.00 22.50
  - c. Inverted surcharge 7.50
  - d. "NANA" 400.00 200.00
  - e. Block of 4, imperf. between (horiz. & vert.) 80.00
- 4 A15 1a on 2ch orange 6.25 .65
  - a. Horiz. pair, imperf. between 17.50
  - b. Vert. pair, imperf. between 10.00 25.00
  - c. Block of 4, imperf. between (horiz. & vert.) 80.00
- 5 A17 2a on 4ch hn brn 6.25 .70
  - a. "O" inverted 85.00 27.50
- 6 A18 3a on 7ch lt blue 16.00 5.00
- 7 A19 6a on 14ch turq grn 35.00 55.00
  - a. Accent omitted from Malayalam surcharge 600.00 675.00
  - Nos. 1-7 (7) 67.55 62.55

For overprints see Nos. O1-O7, O12-O17.
For types overprinted see Nos. O18-O23.

Perf. 11

- 1g A20 2p on 6ca vio blk (R) 2.75 .50
  - h. Vert. pair, imperf. between 375.00 375.00
  - i. Pair, one without surcharge 190.00
- 2g A22 4p on 8ca rose red 3.50 .40
  - h. Vert. pair, imperf. between 325.00 325.00
  - i. Pair, one without surcharge 325.00
  - j. Inverted surcharge 200.00
  - k. "FOUP" 310.00 160.00
  - l. "S" inverted 150.00 62.50
- 3g A13 ½a on 1ch yel grn 4.25 .25
  - h. Vert. pair, imperf. between 55.00
  - i. Inverted surcharge 450.00
  - j. "NANA" 400.00 185.00
  - k. Inverted "H" in "HALF" 175.00
- 4g A15 1a on 2ch orange 1.85 .40
  - h. Double surcharge 67.50
- 5g A17 2a on 4ch hn brn 5.25 .75
  - h. "O" inverted 27.50
- 6g A18 3a on 2ch lt blue 8.00 5.50
  - h. Blue 100.00 6.25
  - i. "3" omitted 1,500.
- 7g A19 6a on 14ch turq grn 30.00 50.00
  - h. Accent omitted from Malayalam surcharge 550.00 650.00
  - Nos. 1g-7g (7) 55.60 57.80

Perf. 12½

- 1m A20 2p on 6ca vio blk (R) 4.25 2.25
  - n. Inverted surcharge 62.50
- 2m A22 4p on 8ca rose red 2.25 .50
  - n. Inverted surcharge 92.50
  - o. "S" inverted 150.00 62.50
- 3m A13 ½a on 1ch yel grn 5.25 .40
  - n. Vert. pair, imperf. between 325.00
  - o. "NANA" 350.00 135.00
  - p. Inverted "H" in "HALF" 175.00
- 4m A15 1a on 2ch orange 5.50 .40
- 5m A17 2a on 4ch hn brn 6.25 .75
  - n. "O" inverted 475.00
  - o. "O" inverted 75.00 25.00
- 6m A18 3a on 2ch lt blue 16.00 9.00
- 7m A19 6a on 14ch turq grn 35.00 67.50
  - n. Accent omitted from Malayalam surcharge 550.00 625.00
  - Nos. 1m-7m (7) 74.50 80.80

Perf. 14

- 1q A20 2p on 6ca vio blk (R) — 800.00
- 3q A13 ½a on 1ch yel grn — 775.00

Perf. 13½

- 2r A22 4p on 8ca rose red — 1,100.
- 4r A15 1a on 2ch orange 275.00 2.50

Compound Perforation

- 1s A20 2p on 6ca vio blk (R) — 62.50
- 2s A22 4p on 8ca rose red — 67.50
- 3s A13 ½a on 1ch yel grn — 67.50
- 4s A15 1a on 2ch orange 75.00 30.00
- 5s A17 2a on 4ch hn brn 85.00 52.50
- 6s A18 3a on 7ch lt blue — 125.00
  - t. Blue — 175.00
- 7s A19 6a on 14ch turq grn 92.50 110.00
  - t. Accent omitted from Malayalam surcharge 875.00
  - Nos. 1s-7s (7) 252.50 515.00

Imperforate Pairs

- 1u A20 2p on 6ca vio blk (R) 12.00 —
- 2u A22 4p on 8ca rose red 110.00 —
- 3u A13 ½a on 1ch yel grn 12.50 30.00
- 4u A15 1a on 2ch orange 15.00 —
- 7u A19 6a on 14ch turq grn 100.00 —
  - Nos. 1u-7u (5) 149.50 30.00

Cochin Nos. 80, 91 and Types of 1944-46 Surcharged in Black or Carmine — b

THREE PIES
COCHIN ANCHAL

1949-50   Wmk. 294   Perf. 11, 13

- 8 A15 3p on 9p ultra 18.00 35.00
- 9 A15 3p on 9p ultra 4.00 3.00
  - a. Vert. pair, imperf. between 4,000.
  - b. Double surcharge 975.00
  - c. Surcharged on both sides 725.00
- 10 A16 3p on 9p ultra (C) 8.25 4.00
- 11 A16 6p on 9p ultra (C) 2.50 .60
- 12 A15 6p on 1a3p mag ('50) 8.25 6.75
- 13 A15 6p on 1a3p magenta 24.00 22.50
  - a. Double surcharge 1,100.
- 14 A13 1a on 1a9p ultra (C) 3.50 2.10
- 15 A15 1a on 1a9p ultra (C) 5.25 3.50
  - b. Black surcharge 5,500.
  - c. Hindi characters 7.5mm long 7,500.
  - Nos. 8-15 (8) 73.75 77.45

The surcharge exists with line of Hindi characters varying from 16½ to 23mm wide.
For overprints see Nos. O10-O11, O24.

U.S.T.C.
Cochin No. 86 Overprinted

1949

- 15A A15 1a deep orange 11.00 125.00
  - d. No period after "S" 110.00
  - e. Raised period after "T" 110.00

Conch Shell — A23   View of River — A24

1950, Oct.   Litho.   Wmk. 196   Perf. 14

- 16 A23 2p rose red 4.50 5.50
- 17 A24 4p ultramarine 5.50 22.00

T-C.
Cochin No. 86 and Type of 1948-50 Overprinted in Black

1950, Apr. 1   Wmk. 294   Perf. 13, 11

- 18 A15 1a deep orange 11.00 110.00
  - a. No period after "T" 80.00 450.00
  - b. Inverted overprint 375.00
  - c. As No. 18b, raised period after "T" 2,450.

COCHIN T·C· SIX PIES
No. 18 Surcharged in Black

- 20 A15 6p on 1a deep orange 6.75 90.00
  - a. Surcharge on No. 15A 18.00
  - b. As No. 20a, no period after "S" 275.00
  - c. As No. 20a, raised period after "T" 275.00
- 21 A15 9p on 1a deep orange 6.50 72.50
  - a. Surcharge on No. 15A 275.00
  - b. As No. 21a, no period after "S" 1,150.
  - c. As No. 21a, raised period after "T" 1,150.

OFFICIAL STAMPS

Travancore Stamps of 1939-46 Surcharged Type "a" in Red or Black and Overprinted

BY TRAVANCORE SERVICE 6

1949   Wmk. 43   Perf. 12

- O1 A20 2p on 6ca vio blk (R) 1.80 .75
  - a. Horiz. pair, imperf. between 15.00 35.00
  - b. Vert. pair, imperf. between 8.00
  - c. Block of 4, imperf. between (horiz. & vert.) 35.00
- O2 A22 4p on 8ca rose red 7.25 1.25
  - a. "FOUB" 200.00 72.50
  - b. Pair, one without surcharge 1,350.
- O3 A13 ½a on 1ch yel grn 24.50 3.50
  - a. "NANA" 800.00 300.00
  - b. Pair, one without surcharge 220.00
  - c. Inverted surcharge on back only 600.00
- O4 A15 1a on 2ch orange — —
- O5 A17 2a on 4ch hn brn 12.00 6.75
  - a. Pair, one without surcharge 1,050.
- O6 A18 3a on 7ch lt blue 6.00 9.75
  - a. Horiz. pair, imperf. between 30.00
  - b. Vert. pair, imperf. between 11.00
  - c. Block of 4, imperf. between (horiz. & vert.) 60.00
  - d. blue 100.00 6.75
  - e. As "d," horiz. pair, imperf. between 1,000.
- O7 A19 6a on 14ch turq grn 80.00 13.50
  - a. Horiz. pair, imperf. between 40.00
  - b. Vert. pair, imperf. between 50.00
  - c. Block of 4, imperf. between (horiz. & vert.) 85.00
  - Nos. O1-O7 (7) 97.50 6.10

Perf. 11

- O1f A20 2p on 6ca vio blk (R) 1.50 .25
  - g. Vert. pair, imperf. between 375.00 375.00
- O2f A22 4p on 8ca rose red 6.00 .35
  - h. "FOUB" 160.00 40.00
- O3f A13 ½a on 1ch yel grn 3.75 .30
  - g. Inverted surcharge 110.00
  - h. "NANA" 500.00 160.00
  - i. Pair, one without surcharge 300.00
- O4f A15 1a on 2ch orange 19.50 9.00
  - g. Pair, one without surcharge 1,150.
- O5f A17 2a on 4ch hn brn 8.50 .75
  - g. Inverted surcharge 1,700.
- O6f A18 3a on 2ch lt blue 6.75 1.25
  - h. blue 100.00 22.00
- O7f A19 6a on 14ch turq grn 19.50 14.50
  - Nos. O1f-O7f (7) 65.50 26.40

Perf. 12½

- O1j A20 2p on 6ca vio blk (R) 2.50 1.00
  - k. Vert. pair, imperf. between 375.00 375.00
  - l. Pair, one without surcharge 325.00
- O2j A22 4p on 8ca rose red 8.50 1.50
  - k. "FOUB" 400.00 145.00
- O3J A13 ½a on 1ch yel grn 2.75 .30
  - k. "NANA" 500.00 135.00
  - l. Pair, one without surcharge 175.00
  - m. Inverted surcharge 50.00
- O4j A15 1a on 2ch orange 19.50 9.75
  - k. Pair, one without surcharge 1,050.
  - l. Inverted surcharge 125.00
- O5j A17 2a on 4ch hn brn 4.50 1.25
- O6j A18 3a on 2ch lt blue 8.50 4.00
  - k. Vert. pair, imperf. between 30.00
- O7j A19 6a on 14ch turq grn 24.50 16.00
  - k. Vert. pair, imperf. between 50.00
  - Nos. O1j-O7j (7) 73.25 33.80

Compound Perforation

O1n	A20	2p on 6ca vio blk (R)	100.00	—
O2n	A22	4p on 8ca rose red	35.00	30.00
O3n	A13	½a on 1ch yel grn		50.00
O5n	A17	2a on 4ch hn brn		67.50
		Nos. O1n-O5n (4)	135.00	147.50

Imperforate Pairs

O1o	A20	2p on 6ca vio blk (R)	10.00	35.00
O5o	A17	2a on 4ch hn brn	17.00	
O6o	A18	3a on 7ch lt blue	16.00	—
O7o	A19	6a on 14ch turq grn	20.00	—
		Nos. O1o-O7o (4)	63.00	35.00

Cochin Nos. O90-O91 Surcharged Type "b" in Black

1950		Wmk. 294	Perf. 11	
O8	A16	6p on 3p carmine	1.90	1.10
a.		Double surcharge		525.00
b.		Vert. pair, imperf. between		2,300.
c.		"C" in place of "G"	24.50	12.25
O9	A16	9p on 4p gray grn	1.60	4.00
a.		Horiz. pair, imperf. between	1,250.	1,350.
b.		Hindi characters 22mm long	1.35	1.55
c.		As "b," horiz. pair, imperf. between	1,175.	1,175.
d.		"C" in place of "G"	32.50	37.50

Hindi characters in surcharge on No. O9 are 18mm long.

Travancore-Cochin Nos. 14-15 Overprinted "ON C G S" Perf. 13

O10	A13	1a on 1a9p ultra	.90	1.00
O11	A15	1a on 1a9p ultra	37.50	25.00

Nos. 2-7 Overprinted in Black — d

1949-51		Wmk. 43	Perf. 12	
O12	A22	4p on 8ca rose red	.35	.25
O13	A13	½a on 1ch yel green	1.50	.25
a.		"AANA"	170.00	80.00
O14	A15	1a on 2ch orange	.60	.25
O15	A17	2a on 4ch hn brn	18.00	1.35
O16	A18	3a on 7ch lt blue	6.00	2.50
O17	A19	6a on 14ch turq grn	60.00	8.00
		Nos. O12-O17 (6)	86.45	12.60

Perf. 11

O12b	A22	4p on 8ca rose red	.60	.25
O13b	A13	½a on 1ch yel green	.60	.25
c.		"AANA"	110.00	50.00
O14b	A15	1a on 2ch orange	4.50	.60
O15b	A17	2a on 4ch hn brn	1.85	1.35
O16b	A18	3a on 7ch lt blue	1.85	1.35
O17b	A19	6a on 14ch turq grn	17.00	8.00
		Nos. O12b-O17b (6)	26.40	11.80

Perf. 12½

O12d	A22	4p on 8ca rose red	1.25	.25
O13d	A13	½a on 1ch yel green	2.75	.25
e.		"AANA"	400.00	90.00
O14d	A15	1a on 2ch orange	.50	.35
O15d	A17	2a on 4ch hn brn	5.25	1.00
O16d	A18	3a on 7ch lt blue	10.50	1.35
O17d	A19	6a on 14ch turq grn	1.85	5.50
		Nos. O12d-O17d (6)	22.10	8.70

Compound Perforation

O12f	A22	4p on 8ca rose red	14.50	14.50
O13f	A13	½a on 1ch yel green	57.50	32.00
g.		"AANA"		425.00
O14f	A15	1a on 2ch orange	36.50	32.00
O15f	A17	2a on 4ch hn brn	36.50	24.50
O16f	A18	3a on 7ch lt blue		100.00
O17f	A19	6a on 14ch turq grn	170.00	170.00
		Nos. O12f-O17f (6)	315.00	373.00

Imperforate Pairs

O12h	A22	4p on 8ca rose red	10.00	—
O13h	A13	½a on 1ch yel green	11.00	30.00
O14h	A15	1a on 2ch orange	29.00	—
O16h	A18	3a on 7ch lt blue	67.50	—
		Nos. O12h-O16h (4)	117.50	30.00

Types of 1949 Overprinted Type "d"

1951			Wmk. 294	
O18	A13	½a on 1ch yel green, perf. 12½	5.50	.80
a.		Perf. 11	.50	.50
b.		Perf. 12	28.00	19.50
c.		Compound perf.	21.00	3.75
O19	A15	1a on 2ch orange, perf. 12½	2.75	1.25
a.		Perf. 11	.60	1.50
b.		Perf. 12	16.00	5.00
c.		Perf. 13½	2.50	1.25
d.		Compound perf.	8.50	3.75

Type of 1949 Overprinted Type "c" Unwmk.

O20	A22	4p on 8ca rose red	1.40	1.10

No. O20 is not from an unwatermarked part of sheet with wmk. 294 but is printed on paper entirely without watermark.

Nos. 1, 3 and 5 Overprinted Type "c" Wmk. 294

O21	A13	½a on 1ch yel green	1.10	.50
O22	A20	2p on 6ca violet black, perf. 12½	.50	2.75
a.		"SERVICE" double	22.00	
b.		Perf. 11	.60	2.75
c.		Perf. 12	1.50	2.10
O23	A17	2a on 4ch henna brn, perf. 12½	4.00	3.25
a.		Perf. 11	1.85	1.35
b.		Vert. pair, imperf. between	525.00	150.00
c.		Perf. 12		115.00
d.		Compound perf.	90.00	55.00
		Nos. O21-O23 (3)	5.60	6.50

No. 9 Overprinted in Black

1951				
O24	A16	3p on 9p ultra	.90	1.20
a.		Horiz. pair, imperf. between		3,500.

WADHWAN

wə-'dwän

LOCATION — A Feudatory State in Kathiawar Agency, Western India.
AREA — 242 sq. mi.
POP. — 44,259
CAPITAL — Wadhwan

Coat of Arms — A1

1888		Litho. Unwmk. Pin-perf. Thin Paper		
1	A1	½p black	160.00	
		Perf. 12½		
2	A1	½p black	30.00	100.00
1889		**Perf. 12 and 12½ Thick Paper**		
3	A1	½p black	12.50	14.00
		Nos. 1-3 (3)	202.50	

INDO-CHINA

ˌin-ˌdō-'chī-nə

LOCATION — French possessions on the Cambodian Peninsula in southeastern Asia, bordering on the South China Sea and the Gulf of Siam
GOVT. — Former French Colony and Protectorate
AREA — 280,849 sq. mi.
POP. — 27,030,000 (estimated 1949)

CAPITAL — Hanoi

100 Centimes = 1 Franc
100 Cents = 1 Piaster (1918)

For French and French Colonies General Issue stamps used in Indo-China, values in the first column are for stamps with clear Indo-Chinese postmarks; values in the second column are for examples on cover. The numbers in parentheses are the catalogue numbers of the basic French or French Colonies stamp.

The Lozenge cancellations inscribed "CCH" were used in various post offices in Cochin China: Saigon, 1864-76; Bentre, 1872-73; Cholen, 1876; Go-Cong, 1872-73; Hatien, 1874-76; Mocai, 1870; Mytho, 1873-74; Sadec, 1875; Tan-an, 1868-75; Tayninh, 1874; Thaudumot, 1868; Vinh-Long, 1868; and Pnum-Penh (Cambodia) are rare. Uses other than Saigon are rare.

The "CCN" cancellations were used in the North Cochin China region: CCN2, Bien-Hoa (1863-74) and Tay-Ninh (1866-79); CCN3, Mytho (1864-70' 1872-75) and Sadec (1867-70s); CCN4, Baria (1864-75) and Cho-Len (1864-76); CCN5, Go-Cong (1864-73); CCN6, Tay-Ninh (1866-67) and Travinh (1868-72); CCN7, Tong-Keou (1864-76) and Chau-Doc (1867-76); and CCN8, Trang-Bang (1865-68(?)) and Tanan (1865-?).

STAMPS OF FRANCE USED IN INDO-CHINA

Canceled "CCH" or "CCN2" in Lozenge of Dots

1851				
1A1	A3	10c bistre (#14)		
		canceled "CCH"	325.00	3,500.
1A2	A3	20c blue (#15)		
		canceled "CCH"	175.00	3,250.
		canceled "CCN2"	450.00	
1A3	A3	40c orange (#18)		
		canceled "CCH"	325.00	
1A4	A3	80c rose (#19)		
		canceled "CCH"	400.00	

STAMPS OF FRENCH COLONIES GENERAL ISSUES USED IN INDO-CHINA

Eagle and Crown Issue Canceled "CCH" or "CCN" and number in Lozenge of Dots

1859-65				
2A1	A1	1c olive green, pale blue (#1)		
		canceled "CCH"	90.00	
		c.d.s. Saigon		
2A2	A1	5c yellow green, greenish (#2)		
		canceled "CCH"	35.00	525.00
		canceled "CCN3"	325.00	
		canceled "CCN7"	440.00	
2A3	A1	10c bister, yellow (#3)		
		canceled "CCH"	25.00	500.00
		canceled "CCN2"	130.00	
		canceled "CCN3"	210.00	
		canceled "CCN4"	325.00	
		canceled "CCN5"	525.00	
		canceled "CCN6"	350.00	
		canceled "CCN7"	360.00	
		canceled "CCN8"	440.00	
2A4	A1	20c blue, bluish (#4)		
		canceled "CCH"	25.00	350.00
		canceled "CCN2"	120.00	
		canceled "CCN3"	175.00	
		canceled "CCN4"	275.00	
		canceled "CCN6"	300.00	
		canceled "CCN7"	300.00	
		canceled "CCN8"	400.00	
2A5	A1	40c orange, yel (#5)		
		canceled "CCH"	35.00	600.00
		canceled "CCN2"	175.00	
		canceled "CCN3"	260.00	
		canceled "CCN4"	360.00	
2A6	A1	80c car rose, pinkish (#6)		
		canceled "CCH"	90.00	1,300.

Values for stamps on cover are for covers paying ordinary rates.

Ceres and Napoleon III Types

CCH in Lozenge of Dots

1871-72				
2A7	A2	1c olive green, pale blue (#7)		
		Lozenge "CCH"	90.00	
2A8	A3	5c yellow green, greenish (#8)		
		Lozenge "CCH"	400.00	
		Lozenge "CCN3"	475.00	
		Lozenge "CCN4"	525.00	
		Lozenge "CCN5"	640.00	
2A9	A4	10c bister, yelsh (#9)		
		Lozenge "CCH"	175.00	
		Lozenge "CCN4"	275.00	
2A10	A4	15c bister, yelsh (#10)		
		Lozenge "CCH"	47.50	
		c.d.s. Bien-Hoa	110.00	
		c.d.s. Ha-Noi	175.00	
		c.d.s. Hai-Phong	225.00	
		c.d.s. Hue	175.00	
		c.d.s. Quin-Hon	260.00	
		Military datestamp Saigon	90.00	
		Military datestamp Ha-Noi	175.00	
		Military datestamp Hai-Phong	225.00	
		Military datestamp Hue	160.00	
		Military datestamp dated January 1879	225.00	
		Military datestamp Quin-Hon	260.00	
		Military datestamp Tong-Keou	300.00	
		Military datestamp Vinh-Long	300.00	
2A11	A4	20c blue, bluish (#11)		
		Lozenge "CCH"	160.00	
		Lozenge "CCN2"	225.00	
		Lozenge "CCN6"	525.00	
		Lozenge "CCN7"	400.00	
2A12	A4	25c blue, bluish (#12)		
		Lozenge "CCH"	55.00	
		Lozenge "CCN6"	225.00	
		c.d.s. Bien-Hoa	100.00	
		c.d.s. Chaudoc	225.00	
		c.d.s. Ha-Noi	130.00	
		c.d.s. Hai-Phong	160.00	
		c.d.s. Hue	130.00	
		c.d.s. Pnum-Penh (Cambodia)	130.00	
		c.d.s. Quin-Hon	175.00	
		c.d.s. Vinh-Long	225.00	
		Military datestamp Cho-Len	260.00	
		Military datestamp Hue	120.00	
		Military datestamp Long-Xuyen	440.00	
		Military datestamp Quin-Hon	130.00	
		Military datestamp Tong-Keou	260.00	
		Military datestamp Traon	375.00	
		Military datestamp Vinh-Long	260.00	
2A13	A5	30c brown, yelsh (#13)		
		Lozenge "CCH"	100.00	
		c.d.s. Ha-Noi	300.00	
		c.d.s. Hai-Phong	360.00	
		c.d.s. Hue	340.00	
		c.d.s. Pnum-Penh (Cambodia)	440.00	
		c.d.s. Soctrang	300.00	
2A14	A4	40c orange, yel (#14)		
		Lozenge "CCH"	67.50	
		Lozenge "CCN4"	260.00	
		Lozenge "CCN6"	275.00	
		Military datestamp Vinh-Long	240.00	
2A15	A5	80c rose, pinkish (#15)		
		canceled "CCH"	130.00	

Ceres Types

Saigon c.d.s.

1872-77				
2A16	A6	1c olive green, pale blue (#16)		
		Lozenge "CCH"	120.00	
		With c.d.s. of Indo-China	—	
2A17	A6	2c red brown, yelsh (#17)		
		Lozenge "CCH"	875.00	18,500.
		c.d.s. Saigon	800.00	
		c.d.s. Pnum-Penh (Cambodia)	1,600.	
2A18	A6	4c gray (#18)		
		Lozenge "CCH"	525.00	12,000.
		c.d.s. Saigon	650.00	
		With other c.d.s. of Indo-China	—	
2A19	A6	5c green, pale blue (#19)		
		Lozenge "CCH"	35.00	
		c.d.s. Ha-Noi	160.00	

c.d.s. Hai-Phong	190.00		
c.d.s. Hue	175.00		
c.d.s. Pnum-Penh (Cambodia)	160.00		
c.d.s. Quin-Hon	260.00		
Military datestamp Saigon	120.00		
Military datestamp Cap St.-Jacques	150.00		
Military datestamp Ha-Noi	175.00		
Military datestamp Quin-Hon	260.00		
Military datestamp Tay-Ninh	240.00		

2A20 A7 10c bister, rose (#20)
Lozenge "CCH"	35.00
c.d.s. Ha-Noi	160.00
c.d.s. Hai-Phong	190.00
c.d.s. Hue	225.00
c.d.s. Quin-Hon	260.00
c.d.s. Soctrang	260.00
c.d.s. Traon	175.00
Military datestamp Saigon	110.00
Military datestamp Chaudoc	225.00
Military datestamp My-Tho	175.00
Military datestamp Quin-Hon	275.00
Military datestamp Tay-Ninh	225.00

2A22 A7 30c brown, yelsh (#22)
Lozenge "CCH"	60.00

2A23 A7 80c rose, pinkish (#23)
Lozenge "CCH"	175.00
Military datestamp Saigon	325.00

No. 2A17 was used only in Cochin-China and Pnum-Penh (Cambodia).

Beware of dangerous forgeries of Nos. 2A17 and 2A18.

Peace and Commerce Types Canceled with Circular Date Stamps

1877-78 — Type I

2A24 A8 1c green, grnsh (#24)
c.d.s. Saigon	90.00
c.d.s. Ha-Noi	110.00
c.d.s. Hai-Phong	125.00
Military datestamp Ha-Noi	225.00

2A25 A8 4c green, grnsh (#25)
c.d.s. Saigon	45.00
Military datestamp Ha-Noi	260.00

2A26 A8 30c brown, yelsh (#26)
c.d.s. Saigon	120.00
c.d.s. Ha-Noi	130.00
c.d.s. Hai-Phong	160.00

2A27 A8 40c ver, straw (#27)
c.d.s. Saigon	87.50
c.d.s. Ha-Noi	110.00
c.d.s. Hai-Phong	125.00
c.d.s. Soctrang	225.00

2A28 A8 75c rose, rose (#28)
c.d.s. Saigon	225.00
a. 75c carmine, rose (#28a)	225.00
c.d.s. Saigon	225.00

2A29 A8 1fr bronze grn, straw (#29)
c.d.s. Saigon	240.00
Military datestamp Hai-Phong	260.00

Type II

2A30 A8 2c green, grnsh (#30)
c.d.s. Saigon	67.50
c.d.s. Ha-Noi	130.00
c.d.s. Hai-Phong	160.00

2A31 A8 5c green, grnsh (#31)
c.d.s. Saigon	20.00
c.d.s. Ha-Noi	87.50
c.d.s. Hai-Phong	110.00
c.d.s. Hue	120.00
c.d.s. Pnum-Penh (Cambodia)	110.00
Military datestamp Saigon	67.50
Military datestamp Nien-Hoa	130.00
Military datestamp Chaudoc	175.00
Military datestamp My-Tho	130.00

2A32 A8 10c green, grnsh (#32)
c.d.s. Saigon	72.50
Military datestamp Saigon	90.00

2A33 A8 15c gray, grnsh (#33)
c.d.s. Saigon	140.00
c.d.s. Hue	225.00
Military datestamp Saigon	200.00
Military datestamp Hue	240.00

2A34 A8 20c red brn, straw (#34)
c.d.s. Saigon	45.00
c.d.s. Ha-Noi	90.00
c.d.s. Hai-Phong	110.00
c.d.s. Hue	160.00

2A35 A8 25c ultra, bluish (#35)
c.d.s. Saigon	35.00
c.d.s. Ha-Noi	87.50
c.d.s. Hai-Phong	110.00
c.d.s. Pnum-Penh (Cambodia)	87.50
Military datestamp Soctrang	350.00
Telegraph office, Poulocondor	140.00
a. 25c blue, bluish (#35a)	35.00
c.d.s. Saigon	87.50
c.d.s. Ha-Noi	110.00
c.d.s. Hai-Phong	87.50
c.d.s. Pnum-Penh (Cambodia)	87.50
Military datestamp Soctrang	350.00

2A36 A8 35c vio blk, org (#36)
c.d.s. Saigon	90.00

1878-80 — Type II

2A38 A8 1c black, lil blue (#38)
c.d.s. Saigon	67.50

2A41 A8 10c black, lav (#41)
c.d.s. Saigon	60.00

2A42 A8 15c blue (#42)
c.d.s. Saigon	45.00
c.d.s. Ha-Noi	87.50
c.d.s. Hai-Phong	110.00
c.d.s. Hue	175.00
c.d.s. Traon	160.00
Military datestamp Saigon	90.00
Military datestamp Baria	175.00
Military datestamp Hanoi	90.00
Military datestamp Hai-Phong	130.00
Military datestamp Hue	130.00
Military datestamp My-Tho	110.00
Military datestamp Pnum-Pehn (Cambodia)	360.00
Military datestamp Tai-Ninh	200.00
Military datestamp Tong-Keou	240.00

Commerce Type

1881-86

2A46 A9 1c black, lil blue (#46)
c.d.s. Saigon	24.00
c.d.s. Hanoi	27.50
c.d.s. Hai-Phong	35.00
c.d.s. Hue	110.00
c.d.s. Pnum-Penh (Cambodia)	52.50

2A47 A9 2c brn, buff (#47)
c.d.s. Saigon	24.00
c.d.s. Hanoi	27.50
c.d.s. Hai-Phong	35.00
c.d.s. Hue	110.00
c.d.s. Pnum-Penh (Cambodia)	52.50

2A48 A9 4c claret, lav (#48)
c.d.s. Saigon	24.00
c.d.s. Hanoi	27.50
c.d.s. Hai-Phong	35.00
c.d.s. Hue	110.00
c.d.s. Pnum-Penh (Cambodia)	52.50

2A49 A9 5c grn, grnsh (#49)
c.d.s. Saigon	20.00
c.d.s. Hanoi	24.00
c.d.s. Hai-Phong	27.50
c.d.s. Hue	87.50
c.d.s. Pnum-Penh (Cambodia)	45.00
c.d.s. Vinh-Long	160.00
Military datestamp Poulocondore	140.00
Steamship c.d.s.	130.00

2A50 A9 10c black, lav (#50)
c.d.s. Saigon	14.50
c.d.s. Hanoi	24.00
c.d.s. Hai-Phong	27.50
c.d.s. Hue	87.50
c.d.s. Pnum-Penh (Cambodia)	45.00
Military datestamp Poulocondore	140.00

2A51 A9 15c blue (#51)
c.d.s. Saigon	13.50
Chaudoc	120.00
Tonkin Expeditionary Force datestamp	65.00
c.d.s. Hanoi	24.00
c.d.s. Hai-Phong (2 types)	27.50
c.d.s. Hue	87.50
c.d.s. Pnum-Penh (Cambodia)	45.00
c.d.s. Rach-Gia	67.50
c.d.s. Soctrang	225.00
c.d.s. Traon	90.00
Military datestamp Saigon	52.50
Military datestamp Hai-Phong	87.50
Military datestamp Hatien	210.00
Military datestamp Poulocondore	140.00
Military datestamp Rach-Gia	130.00
Military datestamp Sadec	225.00
Military datestamp Tai-Ninh	120.00
Military datestamp Vinh Long	120.00
Steamship #2 datestamp (scalloped)	175.00
Telegraph office, Krochmar (Cambodia)	260.00
Telegraph office, Rocacon	240.00
Telegraph office, Takeo	275.00

2A52 A9 20c red, yel grn (#52)
c.d.s. Saigon	24.00
c.d.s. Hanoi	27.50
c.d.s. Hai-Phong	35.00
c.d.s. Hue	110.00
c.d.s. Pnum-Penh (Cambodia)	52.50

2A53 A9 25c yel, yel grn (#53)
c.d.s. Saigon	20.00
Tonkin Expeditionary Force datestamp	87.50
c.d.s. Dong-Dang	225.00
c.d.s. Hue	87.50
c.d.s. Lang-son	92.50
c.d.s. Pnum-Pehn (Cambodia)	45.00
Military datestamp Ha-Noi	67.50
Military datestamp Hai-Phong	110.00

2A54 A9 25c blk, rose (#54)
c.d.s. Saigon	12.00
c.d.s. Ha-Noi	16.00
c.d.s. Hai-Phong	20.00

c.d.s. Hue	60.00	
c.d.s. Pnum-Pehn (Cambodia)	27.50	
Telegraph office, Poulocondor	110.00	
Steamship #2 datestamp (scalloped)	175.00	

2A55 A9 30c brn, bister (#55)
c.d.s. Saigon	45.00
c.d.s. Hanoi	65.00
c.d.s. Hai-Phong	80.00
c.d.s. Hue	100.00
c.d.s. Pnum-Penh (Cambodia)	72.50

2A56 A9 35c vio blk, yel otg (#56)
c.d.s. Saigon	92.50
c.d.s. Hanoi	120.00
c.d.s. Hai-Phong	150.00

2A57 A9 40c ver, straw (#57)
c.d.s. Saigon	45.00
c.d.s. Hanoi	65.00
c.d.s. Hai-Duong	65.00
c.d.s. Hai-Phong	80.00
c.d.s. Hue	110.00
c.d.s. Pnum-Penh (Cambodia)	72.50

2A58 A9 75c car, rose (#58)
c.d.s. Saigon	110.00
c.d.s. Hanoi	160.00
c.d.s. Hai-Phong	190.00
c.d.s. Pnum-Penh (Cambodia)	150.00

2A59 A9 1fr brnz grn, straw (#59)
c.d.s. Saigon	90.00
c.d.s. Hanoi	120.00
c.d.s. Hai-Phong	150.00
c.d.s. Pnum-Penh (Cambodia)	110.00

Stamps of French Colonies Surcharged in Black or Red

a   b

1889   Unwmk.   **Perf. 14x13½**

1	A9(a)	5c on 35c dp vio, org	14.00	12.00
		On cover		1,000.
a.	"89" omitted		275.00	250.00
b.	Pair, #1 and #1a		425.00	425.00
c.	"86" instead of "89"		22,500.	
2	A9(b)	5c on 35c dp vio, org (R)	110.00	100.00
		On cover		1,200.
a.	Date in smaller type		250.00	250.00
b.	Inverted surcharge, #2		1,900.	1,900.
c.	Inverted surcharge, #2a		2,600.	2,600.
d.	Pair, #2 and #2a		575.00	575.00

Issue dates: No. 1, Jan. 8; No. 2, Jan. 10.
"R" is the Colonial Governor, P. Richaud, "D" is the Saigon P.M. General P. Demars.

For other overprints on designs A3-A27a see various issues of French Offices in China.

Navigation & Commerce — A3

Name of Colony in Blue or Carmine

1892-1900   Typo.   **Perf. 14x13½**

3	A3	1c blk, lil bl	1.25	1.25
		Never hinged	2.00	
		On cover		45.00
4	A3	2c brn, buff	1.75	1.75
		Never hinged	2.40	
		On cover		45.00
5	A3	4c claret, lav	1.75	1.75
		Never hinged	2.40	
		On cover		45.00
6	A3	5c grn, grnsh	2.50	2.50
		Never hinged	3.50	
		On cover		21.00
7	A3	5c yel grn ('00)	2.10	1.25
		Never hinged	3.25	
		On cover		17.00
8	A3	10c blk, lavender	8.00	2.00
		Never hinged	12.50	
		On cover		17.00
9	A3	10c red ('00)	3.75	2.25
		Never hinged	5.50	
		On cover		12.50
10	A3	15c blue, quadrille paper	40.00	2.25
		Never hinged	67.50	
		On cover		17.00
11	A3	15c gray ('00)	9.00	2.40
		Never hinged	15.00	
		On cover		12.50
12	A3	20c red, grn	12.00	7.25
		Never hinged	18.00	
		On cover		42.50
		On cover, single franking		75.00

13	A3	25c blk, rose	20.00	4.25
		Never hinged	35.00	
		On cover		35.00
		On cover, single franking		62.50
a.	"INDO-CHINE" omitted		7,250.	7,250.
14	A3	25c blue ('00)	24.00	5.00
		Never hinged	32.50	
		On cover		35.00
		On cover, single franking		62.50
15	A3	30c brn, bis	29.00	8.00
		Never hinged	47.50	
		On cover		35.00
		On cover, single franking		50.00
16	A3	40c red, straw	29.00	15.00
		Never hinged	47.50	
		On cover		37.50
		On cover, single franking		60.00
17	A3	50c car, rose	45.00	16.00
		Never hinged	75.00	
		On cover		72.50
		On cover, single franking		115.00
18	A3	50c brn, az ('00)	30.00	9.50
		Never hinged	55.00	
		On cover		55.00
		On cover, single franking		85.00
19	A3	75c dp vio, org	24.00	19.00
		Never hinged	42.50	
		On cover		115.00
		On cover, single franking		175.00
a.	"INDO-CHINE" inverted		7,500.	7,500.
20	A3	1fr brnz grn, straw	60.00	40.00
		Never hinged	110.00	
		On cover		150.00
		On cover, single franking		250.00
a.	"INDO-CHINE" double		1,200.	1,400.
21	A3	5fr red lil, lav ('96)	145.00	120.00
		Never hinged	250.00	
		On cover		300.00
		On cover, single franking		500.00
		Nos. 3-21 (19)	488.10	261.40

Perf. 13½x14 stamps are counterfeits.
For surcharges and overprints see Nos. 22-23, Q2-Q4.

Nos. 11 and 14 Surcharged in Black

1903

22	A3	5c on 15c gray	2.00	1.25
		Never hinged	3.25	
		On cover		12.50
23	A3	15c on 25c blue	2.50	1.60
		Never hinged	4.00	
		On cover		10.50

Issue dates: No. 22, Dec. 4; No. 23, Aug. 8.

France — A4

1904-06

24	A4	1c olive grn	.80	.80
		Never hinged	1.20	
		On cover		37.50
25	A4	2c vio brn, buff	1.25	.80
		Never hinged	1.60	
		On cover		37.50
26	A4	4c claret, bluish	.80	.80
		Never hinged	1.20	
		On cover		37.50
27	A4	5c deep green	1.25	.50
		Never hinged	1.60	
		On cover		12.50
28	A4	10c carmine	1.60	.75
		Never hinged	2.40	
		On cover		8.50
29	A4	15c org brn, bl	1.60	1.00
		Never hinged	2.40	
		On cover		8.50
30	A4	20c red, grn	3.50	1.60
		Never hinged	5.50	
		On cover		30.00
		On cover, single franking		50.00
31	A4	25c deep blue	15.00	1.60
		Never hinged	25.00	
		On cover		21.00
		On cover, single inverted		37.50
32	A4	30c pale brn	6.00	3.00
		Never hinged	10.00	
		On cover		21.00
		On cover, single franking		30.00
33	A4	35c blk, yel ('06)	22.00	3.25
		Never hinged	42.50	
		On cover		35.00
		On cover, single franking		47.50
34	A4	40c blk, bluish	5.75	1.60
		Never hinged	9.50	
		On cover		25.00
		On cover, single franking		37.50
35	A4	50c bister brn	11.00	3.00
		Never hinged	16.00	
		On cover		42.50
		On cover, single franking		72.50
36	A4	75c red, org	45.00	30.00
		Never hinged	80.00	
		On cover		85.00
		On cover, single franking		140.00
37	A4	1fr pale grn	22.50	8.50
		Never hinged	35.00	
		On cover		105.00
		On cover, single franking		175.00

38	A4	2fr brn, *org*	55.00	42.50
	Never hinged		90.00	
	On cover			175.00
	On cover, single franking			300.00
39	A4	5fr dp vio, *lil*	250.00	200.00
	On cover			400.00
	On cover, single franking			640.00
40	A4	10fr org brn, *grn*	225.00	190.00
	On cover			108.55
	On cover, single franking			750.00
	Nos. 24-40 (17)		668.05	489.70

For surcharges see Nos. 59-64.
Nos. 27, 29, 32, 34, 39-40 exist imperf.

Annamite
Girl — A5

Cambodian
Girl — A6

Cambodian
Woman — A7

Annamite
Women — A8

Hmong
Woman — A9

Laotian
Woman — A10

Cambodian
Woman — A11

1907   **Perf. 14x13½**

41	A5	1c ol brn & blk	.40	.40
	Never hinged		.55	
	On cover			17.00
42	A5	2c yel brn & blk	.40	.40
	Never hinged		.55	
	On cover			17.00
43	A5	4c blue & blk	1.25	1.25
	Never hinged		1.90	
	On cover			17.00
44	A5	5c grn & blk	1.60	.80
	Never hinged		2.40	
	On cover			10.00
45	A5	10c red & blk	1.60	.55
	Never hinged		2.40	
	On cover			6.75
46	A5	15c vio & blk	1.40	1.25
	Never hinged		2.10	
	On cover			6.75
47	A6	20c vio & blk	3.75	1.60
	Never hinged		5.25	
	On cover			10.00
48	A6	25c bl & blk	8.00	1.25
	Never hinged		12.00	
	On cover			17.00
	On cover, single franking			30.00
49	A6	30c brn & blk	12.50	7.50
	Never hinged		18.00	
	On cover			35.00
	On cover, single franking			55.00
50	A6	35c ol grn & blk	2.75	2.25
	Never hinged		4.75	
	On cover			21.00
	On cover, single franking			35.00
51	A6	40c yel brn & blk	4.50	2.00
	Never hinged		7.25	
	On cover			35.00
	On cover, single franking			72.50
52	A6	45c org & blk	11.00	7.00
	Never hinged		16.00	
	On cover			42.50
	On cover, single franking			62.50
53	A6	50c car & blk	16.00	6.00
	Never hinged		24.00	
	On cover			37.50

	On cover, single franking		60.00
	Perf. 13½x14		
54	A7	75c ver & blk	13.00	8.50
	Never hinged		20.00	
	On cover			42.50
	On cover, single franking			76.00
55	A8	1fr grn & blk	57.50	21.00
	Never hinged		95.00	
	On cover			85.00
	On cover, single franking			175.00
56	A9	2fr grn & blk	18.00	17.50
	Never hinged		27.50	
	On cover			97.50
	On cover, single franking			190.00
57	A10	5fr blue & blk	45.00	50.00
	Never hinged		72.50	
	On cover			125.00
	On cover, single franking			250.00
58	A11	10fr pur & blk	95.00	100.00
	Never hinged		160.00	
	On cover			225.00
	On cover, single franking			425.00
	Nos. 41-58 (18)		293.65	229.25

For surcharges see Nos. 65-93, B1-B7.
Nos. 41, 47-51, 54-55 exist imperf.

Stamps of 1904-06 Surcharged in Black or Carmine

There are two settings of surcharge. Type I:
2½mm between numerals. Type II: 3mm
between numerals.

1912, Nov.   **Perf. 14x13½**
**Spacing between figures of
surcharge 1.5mm (5c), 2mm (10c)**

59	A4	5c on 4c cl, *blu-ish*	6.00	6.00
	Never hinged		10.00	
	On cover			62.50
60	A4	5c on 15c org brn, *bl* (C)	1.25	1.25
	Never hinged		1.75	
	On cover			21.00
61	A4	5c on 30c pale brn	1.60	1.60
	Never hinged		2.50	
	On cover			42.50
62	A4	10c on 40c blk, *bluish* (C)	1.60	1.60
	Never hinged		2.50	
	On cover			42.50
63	A4	10c on 50c bis brn (C)	2.00	2.00
	Never hinged		3.50	
	On cover			45.00
64	A4	10c on 75c red, *org*	5.25	5.25
	Never hinged		8.50	
	On cover			55.00
	Nos. 59-64 (6)		17.70	17.70

**Spacing between figures of
surcharge 2.25mm (5c), 2.75mm (10c)**

59a	A4	5c on 4c cl, *bluish*	875.00	875.00
	Never hinged		1,450.	
60a	A4	5c on 15c org brn, *bl* (C)	35.00	35.00
	Never hinged		55.00	
61a	A4	5c on 30c pale brn	85.00	85.00
	Never hinged		140.00	
62a	A4	10c on 40c blk, *bluish* (C)	67.50	67.50
	Never hinged		120.00	
63a	A4	10c on 50c bis brn (C)	75.00	75.00
	Never hinged		55.00	
64a	A4	10c on 75c red, *org*	120.00	120.00
	Never hinged		190.00	
	Nos. 59a-64a (6)		1,257.	1,257.

Se-tenant Pairs, Both Ovpt. Settings

59b	A4	5c on 4c, #59 + #59a	1,050.	1,050.
	Never hinged		1,600.	
60b	A4	5c on 15c, #60 + #60a	42.50	42.50
	Never hinged		72.50	
61b	A4	5c on 30c, #61 + #61a	100.00	100.00
	Never hinged		160.00	
62b	A4	10c on 40c, #62 + #62a	77.50	77.50
	Never hinged		125.00	
63b	A4	10c on 50c, #63 + #63a	85.00	85.00
	Never hinged		140.00	
64b	A4	10c on 75c, #64 + #64a	140.00	140.00
	Never hinged		225.00	
	Nos. 59b-64b (6)		1,495.	1,495.

Nos. 41-58 Surcharged
in Cents or Piasters in
Black, Red or Blue

1919, Jan.

65	A5	⅖c on 1c	.85	.55
	Never hinged		1.20	
	On cover			21.00
66	A5	⅘c on 2c	1.40	.90
	Never hinged		2.00	
	On cover			21.00
67	A5	1⅗c on 4c (R)	2.00	.80
	Never hinged		3.25	
	On cover			20.00
68	A5	2c on 5c	1.75	.30
	Never hinged		2.40	
	On cover			12.50
a.	Inverted surcharge		135.00	
	Never hinged		200.00	
69	A5	4c on 10c (Bl)	1.60	.55
	Never hinged		2.40	
	On cover			8.50
a.	Closed "4"		9.00	3.25
	Never hinged		14.00	
	On cover			21.00
b.	Double surcharge		130.00	
	Never hinged		200.00	
c.	As "c," double surcharge		225.00	
	Never hinged		325.00	
70	A5	6c on 15c	6.75	1.25
	Never hinged		10.00	
	On cover			8.50
a.	Inverted surcharge		130.00	
	Never hinged		200.00	
71	A6	8c on 20c	5.50	1.90
	Never hinged		8.75	
	On cover			12.50
72	A6	10c on 25c	5.25	1.00
	Never hinged		8.00	
	On cover			14.50
73	A6	12c on 30c	7.00	1.10
	Never hinged		11.00	
	On cover			21.00
74	A6	14c on 35c	3.50	.75
	Never hinged		4.75	
	On cover			17.00
a.	Closed "4"		12.00	5.75
	Never hinged		19.00	
	On cover			37.50
75	A6	16c on 40c	6.75	2.00
	Never hinged		10.00	
	On cover			25.00
76	A6	18c on 45c	8.50	2.75
	Never hinged		12.50	
	On cover			30.00
77	A6	20c on 50c (Bl)	13.00	1.25
	Never hinged		18.00	
	On cover			25.00
78	A7	30c on 75c (Bl)	16.00	2.75
	Never hinged		24.00	
	On cover			30.00
79	A8	40c on 1fr (Bl)	25.00	2.75
	Never hinged		40.00	
	On cover			30.00
80	A9	80c on 2fr (R)	29.00	8.50
	Never hinged		47.50	
	On cover			47.50
a.	Double surcharge		350.00	275.00
81	A10	2pi on 5fr (R)	110.00	110.00
	Never hinged		210.00	
	On cover			250.00
82	A11	4pi on 10fr (R)	150.00	150.00
	Never hinged		250.00	
	On cover			340.00
	Nos. 65-82 (18)		393.85	289.10

Types of 1907 Issue Surcharged with New Values in Black or Red

Nos. 88-92   No. 93

1922

88	A5	1c on 5c ocher & blk	1.60	
	Never hinged		2.40	
89	A5	2c on 10c gray grn & blk	2.40	
	Never hinged		4.00	
90	A6	6c on 30c lt red & blk	2.75	
	Never hinged		4.75	
91	A6	10c on 50c lt bl & blk	2.75	
	Never hinged		4.75	
92	A6	11c on 55c vio & blk, *bluish*	3.00	
	Never hinged		4.75	
93	A6	12c on 60c lt bl & blk, *pnksh* (R)	3.00	
	Never hinged		4.75	
	Nos. 88-93 (6)		15.50	

Nos. 88-93 were sold officially in Paris but
were never placed in use in the colony.
   Nos. 88-93 exist without surcharge but were
not regularly issued in that condition. Value,
Nos. 88-89, each $190; Nos. 90-91, each
$140; Nos. 92-93, each $100.

A12

A13

Type 1   Type 2

Type 1   Type 2

Two types of "CENTS" for the 4c, 5c, 10c-
12c values: Type 1, thin font (April 1922); type
2, thicker font (Oct. 1922 and later printings).
All other denominations are type 2.

"CENTS" below Numerals

1922-23   **Perf. 14x13½**

94	A12	⅒c blk & sal ('23)	.25	.25
	Never hinged		.40	
	On cover			17.00
a.	Double impression of frame			
95	A12	⅕c blue & blk	.25	.25
	Never hinged		.40	
	On cover			17.00
96	A12	⅖c ol brn & blk	.25	.25
	Never hinged		.40	
	On cover			17.00
a.	Head and value doubled		260.00	260.00
	Never hinged		400.00	
97	A12	⅘c rose & blk, *lav*	.40	.35
	Never hinged		.50	
	On cover			10.00
98	A12	1c yel brn & blk	.25	.25
	Never hinged		.40	
	On cover			6.75
99	A12	2c gray grn & blk	.75	.55
	Never hinged		1.10	
	On cover			6.75
100	A12	3c vio & blk	.35	.35
	Never hinged		.50	
	On cover			4.25
101	A12	4c org & blk, type 2	.35	.35
	Never hinged		.45	
	On cover			4.00
a.	Type 1		.55	.55
	Never hinged		.85	
	On cover			6.50
b.	Head and value doubled		175.00	175.00
	Never hinged		250.00	
102	A12	5c car & blk, type 2	.35	.35
	Never hinged		.45	
	On cover			4.00
a.	Type 1		.65	.65
	Never hinged		.95	
	On cover			6.50
b.	Head and value doubled		290.00	290.00
	Never hinged		250.00	
	On cover			425.00
103	A13	6c dl red & blk	.50	.30
	Never hinged		.65	
	On cover			4.25
104	A13	7c grn & blk	.75	.65
	Never hinged		1.10	
	On cover			6.00
105	A13	8c blk, *lav*	2.00	1.25
	Never hinged		2.50	
	On cover			8.50
106	A13	9c ocher & blk, *grnsh*	1.50	.90
	Never hinged		1.90	
	On cover			8.50
107	A13	10c bl & blk, type 2	.80	.75
	Never hinged		1.20	
	On cover			8.50
a.	Type 1		.80	.75
	Never hinged		1.20	
	On cover			8.50
108	A13	11c vio & blk, type 2	.75	.75
	Never hinged		1.10	
	On cover			10.00
a.	Type 1		.75	.75
	Never hinged		1.10	
	On cover			10.00
109	A13	12c brn & blk, type 2	.55	.55
	Never hinged		.70	
	On cover			13.50
a.	Type 1		.55	.55
	Never hinged		.70	
	On cover			13.50
b.	Head and value double (11c+12c)		450.00	450.00
	Never hinged		625.00	
110	A13	15c org & blk	1.10	.80
	Never hinged		1.60	
	On cover			17.00
111	A13	20c bl & blk, *straw*	1.75	.80
	Never hinged		2.40	
	On cover			20.00

112 A13 40c ver & blk, *blu-ish* 2.75 1.40
Never hinged 4.00
On cover   21.00
113 A13 1pi bl grn & blk, *grnsh* 5.25 5.25
Never hinged 8.75
On cover   35.00
114 A13 2pi vio brn & blk, *pnksh* 13.00 13.00
Never hinged 21.00
On cover   45.00
Nos. 94-114 (21) 33.90 29.35

For overprints see Nos. O17-O32.

Plowing near Tower of Confucius
A14

Ha Long Bay
A15

Angkor Wat, Cambodia
A16

Carving Wood
A17

That Luang Temple, Laos
A18

Founding of Saigon
A19

1927, Sept. 26
115 A14 1/10c lt olive grn .25 .25
Never hinged .40
On cover   17.00
116 A14 1/5c yellow .25 .25
Never hinged .40
On cover   17.00
117 A14 2/5c light blue .25 .25
Never hinged .40
On cover   17.00
118 A14 4/5c dp brn .55 .55
Never hinged .80
On cover   10.00
119 A14 1c orange .65 .30
Never hinged .85
On cover   6.75
120 A14 2c blue grn 1.10 .50
Never hinged 1.60
On cover   6.75
121 A14 3c indigo .70 .30
Never hinged .95
On cover   4.25
122 A14 4c lil rose 1.60 1.25
Never hinged 2.00
On cover   5.00
123 A14 5c dp vio .80 .30
Never hinged 1.10
On cover   4.25
a. Booklet pane of 10 200.00
124 A15 6c deep red 2.25 .80
Never hinged 3.25
On cover   4.25
a. Booklet pane of 10 200.00
125 A15 7c lt brn 1.50 .80
Never hinged 2.00
On cover   6.00
126 A15 8c gray green 2.10 1.00
Never hinged 3.25
On cover   8.50
127 A15 9c red vio 1.50 1.00
Never hinged 2.00
On cover   8.50
128 A15 10c light blue 2.00 1.25
Never hinged 2.75
On cover   8.50
129 A15 11c orange 2.00 1.25
Never hinged 2.75
On cover   10.00
130 A15 12c myrtle grn 1.50 1.00
Never hinged 2.00
On cover   12.50
131 A16 15c dl rose & ol brn 8.00 7.50
Never hinged 12.00
On cover   30.00

132 A16 20c vio & slate 4.00 2.40
Never hinged 6.50
On cover   17.00
133 A17 25c org brn & lil rose 8.50 6.50
Never hinged 12.50
On cover   30.00
134 A17 30c dp bl & ol gray 5.00 4.00
Never hinged 8.00
On cover   21.00
135 A18 40c ver & lt bl 7.75 3.25
Never hinged 12.00
On cover   21.00
136 A18 50c lt grn & slate 10.00 3.25
Never hinged 14.50
On cover   21.00
137 A19 1pi dk bl, blk & yel 22.50 9.50
Never hinged 32.50
On cover   42.50
a. Yellow omitted 275.00
Never hinged 425.00
138 A19 2pi red, dp bl & org 30.00 16.50
Never hinged 47.50
On cover   55.00
Nos. 115-138 (24) 114.75 63.95

Common Design Types pictured following the introduction.

Colonial Exposition Issue
Common Design Types Surcharged

No. 140

No. 141

No. 142

1931, Apr. 13   Engr.   Perf. 12½
Name of Country in Black
140 CD71 4c on 50c violet 3.50 3.50
Never hinged 5.25
On cover   30.00
141 CD72 6c on 90c red org 3.50 3.50
Never hinged 5.25
On cover   42.50
142 CD73 10c on 1.50fr dl bl 4.50 4.50
Never hinged 7.00
On cover   42.50
Nos. 140-142 (3) 11.50 11.50
Set, never hinged 18.50

Junk — A20

Tower at Ruins of Angkor Thom — A21

Planting Rice — A22

Apsaras, Celestial Dancer
A23

1931-41   Photo.   Perf. 13½x13
143 A20 1/10c Prus blue .25 .25
Never hinged .40
On cover   12.50
144 A20 1/5c lake .25 .25
Never hinged .40
On cover   12.50
145 A20 2/5c org red .25 .25
Never hinged .40
On cover   12.50
146 A20 1/2c red brn .25 .25
Never hinged .40
On cover   12.50

147 A20 4/5c dk vio .25 .25
Never hinged .40
On cover   10.00
148 A20 1c blk brn .25 .25
Never hinged .40
On cover   6.75
149 A20 2c dk grn .25 .25
Never hinged .40
On cover   6.00
150 A21 3c dp brn .25 .25
Never hinged .40
On cover   4.25
151 A21 3c dk grn ('34) 6.00 1.60
Never hinged 8.00
On cover   8.50
152 A21 4c dk bl 1.25 .50
Never hinged 1.75
On cover   4.25
153 A21 4c dk grn ('38) .80 .55
Never hinged 1.10
On cover   5.00
153A A21 4c yel org ('40) .40 .40
Never hinged .50
On cover   8.50
154 A21 5c dp vio .30 .30
Never hinged .50
On cover   4.25
154A A21 5c dp grn ('41) .40 .40
Never hinged .60
On cover   6.75
155 A21 6c org red .25 .25
Never hinged .40
On cover   4.25
a. Bklt. pane 5 + 1 label 100.00
156 A21 7c blk ('38) .30 .30
Never hinged .50
On cover   4.25
157 A21 8c rose lake ('38) .40 .40
Never hinged .65
On cover   4.25
157A A21 9c blk, *yel* ('41) .75 .75
Never hinged 1.00
On cover   6.75
158 A22 10c dark blue .65 .50
Never hinged .85
On cover   4.25
158A A22 10c ultra, *pink* ('41) .55 .55
Never hinged .85
On cover   6.75
159 A22 15c dk brn 5.75 1.40
Never hinged 8.00
On cover   5.00
160 A22 15c dk bl ('33) .25 .25
Never hinged .40
On cover   4.25
161 A22 18c blue ('38) .75 .50
Never hinged .95
On cover   5.00
162 A22 20c rose .30 .25
Never hinged .50
On cover   8.50
163 A22 21c olive grn .30 .30
Never hinged .50
On cover   10.00
164 A22 22c dk grn ('38) .55 .55
Never hinged .65
On cover   5.00
165 A22 25c dp vio 3.50 1.60
Never hinged 4.75
On cover   12.50
165A A22 25c dk bl ('41) .55 .55
Never hinged .85
On cover   12.50
166 A22 30c org brn ('32) .50 .30
Never hinged .65
On cover   12.50

Perf. 13½
167 A23 50c dk brn .75 .25
Never hinged 1.00
On cover   12.50
168 A23 60c dl vio ('32) .90 .65
Never hinged 1.00
On cover   17.00
168A A23 70c lt bl ('41) .55 .55
Never hinged .95
On cover   17.00
169 A23 1pi yel grn .90 .65
Never hinged 1.25
On cover   17.00
170 A23 2pi red 1.10 .75
Never hinged 1.40
On cover   25.00
Nos. 143-170 (34) 30.70 17.05

Nos. 166, 167, 169 and 170 were issued without the letters "RF" in 1943, by the Vichy Government.

For surcharge & overprints see Nos. 214A (in Scott Standard catalogue, Vol. 3), O1-O16.

Emperor Bao-Dai
A24

King Sisowath Monivong
A25

For Use in Annam

1936, Nov. 20   Engr.   Perf. 13
171 A24 1c brown 1.00 1.00
Never hinged 1.25
On cover   10.00
172 A24 2c green 1.00 1.00
Never hinged 1.25
On cover   8.50

173 A24 4c violet 1.00 1.00
Never hinged 1.25
On cover   6.50
174 A24 5c red brn 1.50 1.50
Never hinged 1.90
On cover   6.00
175 A24 10c lil rose 2.00 2.00
Never hinged 2.60
On cover   6.00
176 A24 15c ultra 2.75 2.75
Never hinged 4.00
On cover   8.50
177 A24 20c scarlet 2.75 2.75
Never hinged 4.00
On cover   10.00
178 A24 30c plum 3.50 3.50
Never hinged 5.50
On cover   17.00
179 A24 50c slate grn 3.50 3.50
Never hinged 5.50
On cover   21.00
180 A24 1pi rose vio 4.75 4.75
Never hinged 6.50
On cover   30.00
181 A24 2pi black 5.75 5.75
Never hinged 7.25
On cover   35.00
Nos. 171-181 (11) 29.50 29.50

For Use in Cambodia
182 A25 1c brown 1.00 1.00
Never hinged 1.25
On cover   10.00
183 A25 2c green 1.00 1.00
Never hinged 1.25
On cover   8.50
184 A25 4c violet 1.10 1.10
Never hinged 1.40
On cover   6.75
185 A25 5c red brn 1.10 1.10
Never hinged 1.40
On cover   6.00
186 A25 10c lil rose 2.40 2.40
Never hinged 3.25
On cover   6.75
187 A25 15c ultra 3.25 3.25
Never hinged 4.75
On cover   8.50
188 A25 20c scarlet 2.75 2.75
Never hinged 4.00
On cover   10.00
189 A25 30c plum 3.25 3.25
Never hinged 4.75
On cover   16.00
190 A25 50c slate grn 3.25 3.25
Never hinged 4.75
On cover   19.00
191 A25 1pi rose vio 4.25 4.25
Never hinged 6.50
On cover   25.00
192 A25 2pi black 5.75 5.75
Never hinged 7.25
On cover   30.00
Nos. 182-192 (11) 29.10 29.10

Paris International Exposition Issue
Common Design Types

1937, Apr. 15
193 CD74 2c dp vio 1.60 1.60
Never hinged 2.50
On cover   30.00
194 CD75 3c dk grn 1.10 1.10
Never hinged 1.75
On cover   12.50
195 CD76 4c car rose 1.10 1.10
Never hinged 1.75
On cover   6.75
196 CD77 6c dk grn 1.10 1.10
Never hinged 1.75
On cover   12.50
197 CD78 9c red 1.40 1.40
Never hinged 1.75
On cover   12.50
198 CD79 15c ultra 1.40 1.40
Never hinged 2.00
On cover   12.50
Nos. 193-198 (6) 7.70 7.70
Set, never hinged 14.00

Colonial Arts Exhibition Issue
Souvenir Sheet
Common Design Type

1937, Apr. 15   Imperf.
199 CD79 30c dull violet 10.00 12.00
Never hinged 16.50
On cover   62.50
On cover, single franking 92.50

Governor-General Paul Doumer — A26

1938, June 8   Photo.   Perf. 13½x13
200 A26 5c rose car 1.00 .65
Never hinged 2.00
On cover   4.25
201 A26 6c brown 1.10 1.10
Never hinged 2.00
On cover   4.25
202 A26 18c brt bl 1.10 1.10
Never hinged 2.00
On cover   6.75
Nos. 200-202,C18 (4) 3.95 3.10
Set, never hinged 6.50

Trans-Indo-Chinese Railway, 35th anniv.

New York World's Fair Issue
Common Design Type

1939, May 10   Engr.   Perf. 12½x12

203	CD82	13c car lake	.80	.80
	Never hinged		1.40	
	On cover			35.00
204	CD82	23c ultra	1.25	1.25
	Never hinged		2.25	
	On cover			35.00

Mot Cot Pagoda, Hanoi — A27

1939, June 12   Perf. 13

205	A27	6c blk brn	1.10	1.10
	Never hinged		1.60	
	On cover			8.50
206	A27	9c vermilion	1.10	1.10
	Never hinged		1.60	
	On cover			4.25
207	A27	23c ultra	1.10	1.10
	Never hinged		1.60	
	On cover			6.75
208	A27	39c rose vio	1.50	1.50
	Never hinged		2.40	
	On cover			8.50
	Nos. 205-208 (4)		4.80	4.80

Golden Gate International Exposition.

SEMI-POSTAL STAMPS

No 45 Surcharged

Perf. 14x13½

1914, Oct. 28   Unwmk.

B1	A5	10c +5c red & blk	1.60	1.60
	Never hinged		2.40	
	On cover			12.50

Nos. 44-46 Surcharged

1915-17

B2	A5	5c + 5c grn & blk ('17)	1.60	1.60
	Never hinged		2.40	
	On cover			12.50
a.	Double surcharge		220.00	210.00
	Never hinged		325.00	
B3	A5	10c + 5c red & blk	2.50	2.00
	Never hinged		4.00	
	On cover			12.50
B4	A5	15c + 5c vio & blk ('17)	2.50	2.00
	Never hinged		4.00	
	On cover			14.50
a.	Triple surcharge		200.00	
	Never hinged		300.00	
b.	Quadruple surcharge		200.00	
	Never hinged		300.00	
	Nos. B2-B4 (3)		6.60	5.60

Nos. B2-B4 Surcharged with New Values in Blue or Black

1918-19

B5	A5	4c on 5c + 5c (Bl)	4.25	4.25
	Never hinged		6.50	
	On cover			30.00
a.	Closed "4"		220.00	
	Never hinged		325.00	
B6	A5	6c on 10c + 5c	3.75	4.00
	Never hinged		6.25	
	On cover			30.00
B7	A5	8c on 15c + 5c ('19)	15.00	15.00
	Never hinged		18.50	
	On cover			62.50
a.	Double surcharge		225.00	
	Never hinged		325.00	
	Nos. B5-B7 (3)		23.00	23.25

France Nos. B5-B10 Surcharged

1919 (?)

B8	SP5	10c on 15c + 10c	1.60	1.60
	Never hinged		3.00	
	On cover			17.00
a.	"10 CENTS" double		525.00	525.00
B9	SP5	16c on 25c + 10c	4.00	4.00
	Never hinged		7.50	
	On cover			21.00
B10	SP6	24c on 35c + 25c	7.25	7.25
	Never hinged		11.50	
	On cover			42.50
a.	Double surcharge		800.00	800.00
b.	CENTS" double		950.00	
B11	SP7	40c on 50c + 50c	12.50	12.50
	Never hinged			
	On cover			72.50
B12	SP8	80c on 1fr + 1fr	27.50	27.50
	Never hinged		50.00	
	On cover			85.00
B13	SP8	4pi on 5fr + 5fr	225.00	225.00
	Never hinged		450.00	
	On cover			425.00
a.	PIASTRES" double		6,250.	5,400.
	Nos. B8-B13 (6)		277.85	277.85

Curie Issue
Common Design Type
Inscription and Date in Upper Margin

1938, Oct. 24   Engr.   Perf. 13

B14	CD80	18c + 5c brt ultra	12.00	12.00
	Never hinged		20.00	
	On cover			42.50
	On cover, single franking			72.50

French Revolution Issue
Common Design Type
Name and Value Typo. in Black

1939, July 5   Photo.

B15	CD83	6c + 2c green	12.00	12.00
	Never hinged		22.50	
	On cover			75.00
B16	CD83	7c + 3c brown	12.00	12.00
	Never hinged		22.50	
	On cover			55.00
B17	CD83	9c + 4c red org	12.00	12.00
	Never hinged		22.50	
	On cover			45.00
B18	CD83	13c + 10c rose pink	12.00	12.00
	Never hinged		22.50	
	On cover			75.00
	On cover, single franking			115.00
B19	CD83	23c + 20c blue	12.00	12.00
	Never hinged		22.50	
	On cover			75.00
	On cover, single franking			115.00
	Nos. B15-B19 (5)		60.00	60.00
	Set, never hinged		112.50	

AIR POST STAMPS

Airplane AP1

1933-41   Unwmk.   Photo.   Perf. 13½

C1	AP1	1c ol brn	.25	.25
	Never hinged		.60	
	On cover			6.00
C2	AP1	2c dk grn	.30	.25
	Never hinged		.75	
	On cover			6.00
C3	AP1	5c yel grn	.30	.25
	Never hinged		.75	
	On cover			4.25
C4	AP1	10c red brn	.65	.30
	Never hinged		1.25	
	On cover			4.25
C5	AP1	11c rose car ('38)	.80	.30
	Never hinged		1.60	
	On cover			4.25
C6	AP1	15c dp bl	.70	.25
	Never hinged		1.50	
	On cover			4.25
C6A	AP1	16c brt pink ('41)	.35	.35
	Never hinged		.75	
	On cover			12.50
C7	AP1	20c grnsh gray	.50	.50
	Never hinged		.95	
	On cover			5.00
C8	AP1	30c org brn	.30	.25
	Never hinged		.75	
	On cover			5.00
C9	AP1	36c car rose	1.90	.35
	Never hinged		3.75	
	On cover			6.75
C10	AP1	37c ol grn ('38)	.80	.30
	Never hinged		1.60	
	On cover			6.00
C10A	AP1	39c dk ol grn ('41)	.35	.35
	Never hinged		.75	
	On cover			17.00
C11	AP1	60c dk vio	1.90	.35
	Never hinged		3.75	
	On cover			8.50
C12	AP1	66c olive grn	.55	.25
	Never hinged		1.25	
	On cover			8.50
C13	AP1	67c brt bl ('38)	1.20	1.00
	Never hinged		2.60	
	On cover			8.50

C13A	AP1	69c brt ultra ('41)	.65	.65
	Never hinged		1.25	
	On cover			21.00
C14	AP1	1pi black	.70	.25
	Never hinged		1.25	
	On cover			18.50
C15	AP1	2pi yel org	1.00	.35
	Never hinged		1.90	
	On cover			14.50
C16	AP1	5pi purple	1.90	.50
	Never hinged		3.75	
	On cover			17.00
C17	AP1	10pi deep red	3.75	.90
	Never hinged		7.50	
	On cover			21.00
	Nos. C1-C17 (20)		18.85	7.95

See Nos. C27-C28 in Scott Standard catalogue, Vol. 3.

Issue dates: 11c, 37c, June 8; 67c, Oct. 5; 16c, 39c, 69c, Feb. 5; others, June 1, 1933. Stamps of type AP1 without "RF" monogram were issued in 1942 and 1943 by the Vichy Government. On the Vichy stamps, the figure of value has been moved to the lower left corner of the vignette.

Trans-Indo-Chinese Railway Type

1938, June 8

C18	A26	37c red orange	.75	.25
	Never hinged		.95	
	On cover			7.50

AIR POST SEMI-POSTAL STAMP

French Revolution Issue
Common Design Type
Unwmk.

1939, July 5   Photo.   Perf. 13
Name and Value Typo. in Orange

CB1	CD83	39c + 40c brn blk	25.00	25.00
	Never hinged		45.00	
	On cover			100.00
	On cover, single franking			160.00

POSTAGE DUE STAMPS

Cover values are for examples bearing stamps used to pay correct postage due rates.

French Colonies No. J21 Surcharged

1904, June 26   Unwmk.   Imperf.

J1	D1	5c on 60c brn, *buff*	14.50	14.50
	On cover			800.00

French Colonies Nos. J10-J11 Surcharged in Carmine

1905, July 22

J2	D1	5c on 40c black	32.00	16.00
	On cover			500.00
J3	D1	10c on 60c black	32.00	20.00
	On cover			500.00
J4	D1	30c on 60c black	32.00	20.00
	On cover			500.00
	Nos. J2-J4 (3)		96.00	56.00

Dragon from Steps of Angkor Wat
D1   D2

1908   Typo.   Perf. 14x13½

J5	D1	2c black	1.40	1.00
	Never hinged		2.00	
	On cover			35.00
J6	D1	4c dp bl	1.40	1.00
	Never hinged		2.00	
	On cover			35.00
J7	D1	5c bl grn	1.75	1.10
	Never hinged		2.40	
	On cover			17.00
J8	D1	10c carmine	3.00	1.10
	Never hinged		4.25	
	On cover			12.50
J9	D1	15c violet	3.75	2.75
	Never hinged		5.50	
	On cover			21.00
J10	D1	20c chocolate	1.90	1.40
	Never hinged		2.75	
	On cover			17.00

J11	D1	30c ol grn	1.90	1.40
	Never hinged		2.75	
	On cover			25.00
J12	D1	40c claret	8.50	7.25
	Never hinged		18.00	
	On cover			62.50
J13	D1	50c grnsh bl	7.25	1.60
	Never hinged		11.00	
	On cover			50.00
J14	D1	60c orange	12.00	11.00
	Never hinged		17.50	
	On cover			72.50
J15	D1	1fr gray	24.00	18.50
	Never hinged		40.00	
	On cover			100.00
J16	D1	2fr yel brn	24.00	18.50
	Never hinged		40.00	
	On cover			100.00
J17	D1	5fr red	40.00	37.50
	Never hinged		65.00	
	On cover			175.00
	Nos. J5-J17 (13)		130.85	104.10

Surcharged in Cents or Piasters

1919

J18	D1	⅘c on 2c blk	1.75	1.25
	Never hinged		2.40	
	On cover			37.50
J19	D1	1⅗c on 4c dp bl	1.75	1.25
	Never hinged		2.40	
	On cover			37.50
J20	D1	2c on 5c bl grn	3.00	1.60
	Never hinged		4.25	
	On cover			21.00
J21	D1	4c on 10c car	4.25	1.25
	Never hinged		6.50	
	On cover			18.00
J22	D1	6c on 15c vio	9.50	3.00
	Never hinged		14.00	
	On cover			25.00
J23	D1	8c on 20c choc	6.75	2.40
	Never hinged		10.00	
	On cover			25.00
J24	D1	12c on 30c ol grn	9.50	2.40
	Never hinged		14.00	
	On cover			25.00
J25	D1	16c on 40c cl	9.50	2.00
	Never hinged		14.00	
	On cover			35.00
J26	D1	20c on 50c grnsh bl	12.50	6.50
	Never hinged		18.00	
	On cover			72.50
J27	D1	24c on 60c org	3.25	2.00
	Never hinged		4.75	
	On cover			55.00
a.	Closed "4"		20.00	16.00
	Never hinged		35.00	
	On cover			85.00
J28	D1	40c on 1fr gray	5.50	1.60
	Never hinged		8.00	
	On cover			55.00
a.	Closed "4"		20.00	16.00
	Never hinged		32.50	
	On cover			85.00
J29	D1	80c on 2fr yel brn	42.50	20.00
	Never hinged		67.50	
	On cover			110.00
J30	D1	2pi on 5fr red	62.50	42.50
	Never hinged		100.00	
	On cover			190.00
a.	Double surcharge		240.00	190.00
	Never hinged		350.00	
b.	Triple surcharge		225.00	180.00
	Never hinged		350.00	
	Nos. J18-J30 (13)		172.25	87.75

"CENTS" below Numerals

1922, Oct.

J31	D2	⅖c black	.25	.25
	Never hinged		.40	
	On cover			25.00
J32	D2	⅘c red	.30	.30
	Never hinged		.50	
	On cover			14.00
J33	D2	1c buff	.50	.40
	Never hinged		.65	
	On cover			12.50
J34	D2	2c gray grn	.65	.50
	Never hinged		.95	
	On cover			12.50
J35	D2	3c violet	.75	.75
	Never hinged		1.00	
	On cover			12.50
J36	D2	4c orange	.75	.40
	Never hinged			
	On cover			8.50
a.	"4 CENTS" omitted		700.00	
b.	"4 CENTS" double		105.00	105.00
	Never hinged		175.00	
J37	D2	6c ol grn	1.60	.65
	Never hinged		2.40	
	On cover			12.50
J38	D2	8c blk, *lav*	1.25	.65
	Never hinged		1.60	
	On cover			12.50
J39	D2	10c dp bl	2.00	.65
	Never hinged		2.75	
	On cover			12.50
J40	D2	12c ocher, *grnsh*	1.60	1.25
	Never hinged		2.40	
	On cover			12.50
J41	D2	20c dp bl, *straw*	2.00	.90
	Never hinged		2.60	
	On cover			21.00
J42	D2	40c red, *bluish*	2.00	1.10
	Never hinged		2.75	
	On cover			30.00

J43	D2	1pi brn vio, *pnksh*	6.75	3.75
		Never hinged	11.00	
		On cover		45.00
		Nos. J31-J43 (13)	20.40	11.55

Pagoda of
Mot Cot,
Hanoi — D3

Dragon of
Annam — D4

Perf. 14x13½, 13½x14

1927, Sept. 26

J44	D3	⅖c vio brn & org	.25	.25
		Never hinged	.40	
		On cover		25.00
J45	D3	⅘c vio & blk	.25	.25
		Never hinged	.40	
		On cover		14.50
J46	D3	1c brn red & sl	.90	.90
		Never hinged	1.25	
		On cover		12.50
J47	D3	2c grn & brn ol	1.00	1.00
		Never hinged	1.40	
		On cover		12.50
J48	D3	3c red brn & bl	1.60	1.60
		Never hinged	2.40	
		On cover		12.50
J49	D3	4c ind & brn	1.60	1.60
		Never hinged	2.40	
		On cover		12.50
J50	D3	6c dp red & ver	2.00	1.60
		Never hinged	2.75	
		On cover		14.50
J51	D3	8c ol brn & vio	1.60	1.25
		Never hinged	2.40	
		On cover		14.50
J52	D4	10c dp bl	2.50	1.25
		Never hinged	4.00	
		On cover		14.50
J53	D4	12c olive	5.75	4.75
		Never hinged	8.75	
		On cover		25.00
J54	D4	20c rose	4.00	2.00
		Never hinged	5.50	
		On cover		25.00
J55	D4	40c bl grn	4.00	3.50
		Never hinged	5.50	
		On cover		35.00
J56	D4	1pi red org	20.00	20.00
		Never hinged	26.00	
		On cover		85.00
		Nos. J44-J56 (13)	45.45	39.95

Surcharged in Black
or Blue — D5

1931-41   *Perf. 13*

J57	D5	⅒c red, *org* ('38)	.25	.25
		Never hinged	.40	
		On cover		17.00
J58	D5	⅖c red, *org*	.25	.25
		Never hinged	.40	
		On cover		17.00
J59	D5	⅘c red, *org*	.25	.25
		Never hinged	.40	
		On cover		8.50
J60	D5	1c red, *org*	.25	.25
		Never hinged	.40	
		On cover		8.50
J61	D5	2c red, *org*	.25	.25
		Never hinged	.40	
		On cover		8.50
J62	D5	2.5c red, *org* ('40)	.25	.25
		Never hinged	.40	
		On cover		10.00
J63	D5	3c red, *org* ('38)	.40	.25
		Never hinged	.55	
		On cover		8.50
J64	D5	4c red, *org*	.30	.30
		Never hinged	.50	
		On cover		8.50
J65	D5	5c red, *org* ('38)	.40	.30
		Never hinged	.65	
		On cover		8.50
J66	D5	6c red, *org*	.30	.30
		Never hinged	.50	
		On cover		8.50
J67	D5	10c red, *org*	.30	.30
		Never hinged	.50	
		On cover		8.50
J68	D5	12c red, *org*	.50	.30
		Never hinged	.65	
		On cover		10.00
J69	D5	14c red, *org* ('38)	.50	.30
		Never hinged	.80	
		On cover		8.50
J70	D5	18c red, *org* ('41)	.50	.50
		Never hinged	.65	
		On cover		12.50
J71	D5	20c red, *org*	.50	.50
		Never hinged	.65	
		On cover		12.50
J72	D5	50c red, *org*	.75	.50
		Never hinged	1.00	
		On cover		17.00
J72A	D5	1pi red, *org*	10.00	9.50
		Never hinged	13.50	
		On cover		42.50
J73	D5	1pi red, *org* (Bl)	2.25	1.25
		Never hinged	2.90	
		On cover		25.00
		Nos. J57-J73 (18)	18.20	15.80

OFFICIAL STAMPS

Regular Issues of
1931-32 Overprinted
in Blue or Red

Perf. 13, 13½

1933, Feb. 27   **Unwmk.**

O1	A20	1c black brown (Bl)	.80	.75
		Never hinged	1.10	
		On cover		10.00
O2	A20	2c dark green (Bl)	.90	.50
		Never hinged	1.20	
		On cover		8.50

Regular Issues of
1931-32 Overprinted
in Blue or Red

O3	A21	3c deep brown (Bl)	1.25	.65
		Never hinged	1.60	
		On cover		6.00
a.		Inverted overprint	160.00	
			210.00	
O4	A21	4c dark blue (R)	1.50	.90
		Never hinged	2.00	
		On cover		60.00
a.		Inverted overprint	160.00	
			210.00	
O5	A21	5c deep violet (Bl)	2.40	.90
		Never hinged	3.25	
		On cover		6.00
O6	A21	6c orange red (Bl)	2.40	1.25
		Never hinged	3.25	
		On cover		6.00

Regular Issues of
1931-32 Overprinted
in Blue or Red

O7	A22	10c dk blue (R)	1.25	1.00
		Never hinged	1.60	
		On cover		6.00
O8	A22	15c dk brown (Bl)	3.00	1.75
		Never hinged	3.50	
		On cover		7.50
O9	A22	20c rose (Bl)	3.25	.85
		Never hinged	4.00	
		On cover		12.50
O10	A22	21c olive grn (Bl)	3.00	1.75
		Never hinged	3.50	
		On cover		15.00
O11	A22	25c dp violet (Bl)	1.60	1.00
		Never hinged	2.40	
		On cover		18.50
O12	A22	30c orange brn (Bl)	3.25	.85
		Never hinged	4.50	
		On cover		18.50

Regular
Issues of
1931-32
Overprinted
in Blue or
Red

O13	A23	50c dark brown (Bl)	12.50	3.50
		Never hinged	18.00	
		On cover		21.00
O14	A23	60c dull violet (Bl)	2.75	2.40
		Never hinged	4.00	
		On cover		25.00
O15	A23	1pi yellow green (Bl)	30.00	11.00
		Never hinged	40.00	
		On cover		35.00
O16	A23	2pi red (Bl)	11.50	9.50
		Never hinged	16.00	
		On cover		37.50
		Nos. O1-O16 (16)	81.35	38.05

Type of 1922-23 Regular Issue
Overprinted diagonally in Black or
Red "SERVICE"

1934, Oct. 4   *Perf. 14x13*

O17	A13	1c olive green	1.25	.75
		Never hinged	1.25	
		On cover		10.00
O18	A13	2c brown orange	1.25	.75
		Never hinged	1.25	
		On cover		10.00
O19	A13	3c yellow green	1.40	.65
		Never hinged	1.75	
		On cover		6.00
O20	A13	4c cerise	2.50	1.30
		Never hinged	3.00	
		On cover		12.00
O21	A13	5c yellow	1.40	.75
		Never hinged	1.75	
		On cover		6.00
O22	A13	6c orange red	6.00	5.25
		Never hinged	8.50	
		On cover		30.00
O23	A13	10c gray grn (R)	3.50	2.25
		Never hinged	4.50	
		On cover		15.00
O24	A13	15c ultra	2.10	1.50
		Never hinged	2.90	
		On cover		12.50

O25	A13	20c gray black (R)	2.00	1.50
		Never hinged	2.50	
		On cover		14.50
O26	A13	21c light violet	11.00	9.25
		Never hinged	15.00	
		On cover		45.00
O27	A13	25c rose lake	13.00	11.00
		Never hinged	19.00	
		On cover		55.00
O28	A13	30c lilac gray	1.75	1.30
		Never hinged	2.10	
		On cover		17.00
O29	A13	50c brt violet	8.00	6.75
		Never hinged	12.00	
		On cover		35.00
O30	A13	60c gray	15.00	11.00
		Never hinged	22.00	
		On cover		55.00
O31	A13	1pi blue (R)	30.00	24.50
		Never hinged	42.50	
		On cover		67.50
O32	A13	2pi deep red	47.50	37.50
		Never hinged	67.50	
		On cover		100.00
		Nos. O17-O32 (16)	147.65	116.00

The value tablet has colorless numeral and
letters on solid background.

PARCEL POST STAMPS

French Colonies No. 50
Overprinted

1891   **Unwmk.**   *Perf. 14x13½*

Q1	A9	10c black, *lavender*	24.00	10.50
		Never hinged	55.00	
		On parcel post receipt card		400.00

The overprint on No. Q1 was also handstamped in shiny ink. Value unused, $750.

Indo-China No. 8
Overprinted

1898

Q2	A3	10c black, *lavender*	29.00	29.00
		Never hinged	65.00	
		On parcel post receipt card		400.00

Nos. 8 and 9
Overprinted

1902

Q3	A3	10c black, *lavender*	55.00	35.00
		Never hinged	120.00	
		On parcel post receipt card		400.00
a.		Inverted overprint	115.00	400.00
Q4	A3	10c red	55.00	24.00
		Never hinged	120.00	
		On parcel post receipt card		400.00
a.		Inverted overprint	85.00	50.00
b.		Double overprint	85.00	50.00

INHAMBANE

ˌin-yəm-ˈban-ə

LOCATION — East Africa
GOVT. — A district of Mozambique,
former Portuguese colony
AREA — 21,000 sq. mi. (approx.)
POP. — 248,000 (approx.)
CAPITAL — Inhambane

1000 Reis = 1 Milreis
100 Centavos = 1 Escudo (1913)

Stamps of
Mozambique
Overprinted

On 1886 Issue

1895, July 1   **Unwmk.**   *Perf. 12½*
Without Gum

1	A2	5r black	37.50	30.00
2	A2	10r green	50.00	25.00
a.		Perf. 13½	80.00	75.00
3	A2	20r rose	60.00	30.00
4	A2	25r lilac	700.00	250.00
5	A2	40r chocolate	60.00	40.00
6	A2	50r blue	60.00	32.50
a.		Perf. 13½	50.00	50.00
7	A2	100r yellow brown	700.00	400.00
8	A2	200r gray violet	75.00	40.00
9	A2	300r orange	75.00	40.00
		Nos. 1-9 (9)	1,817.	887.50

On 1894 Issue
Perf. 11½

10	A3	50r lt blue	42.50	35.00
a.		Perf. 12½	55.00	42.50
11	A3	75r rose	55.00	40.00
12	A3	80r yellow green	45.00	37.50
13	A3	100r brown, *buff*	175.00	60.00
14	A3	150r carmine, *rose*	50.00	45.00
		Nos. 10-14 (5)	367.50	217.50

700th anniv. of the birth of St. Anthony of
Padua.
The status of Nos. 4 and 7 is questionable.
No. 3 is always discolored.
Forged overprints exist. Genuine overprints
are 21mm high.

King Carlos — A1

1903, Jan. 1   **Typo.**   *Perf. 11½*
Name and Value in Black except
500r

15	A1	2½r gray	.30	.30
16	A1	5r orange	.30	.30
17	A1	10r lt green	.60	.40
18	A1	15r gray green	1.00	.75
19	A1	20r gray violet	.85	.55
20	A1	25r carmine	.70	.55
21	A1	50r brown	1.75	.55
22	A1	65r dull blue	20.00	15.00
23	A1	75r lilac	2.00	1.40
24	A1	100r dk blue, *blue*	2.75	1.25
25	A1	115r org brn, *pink*	5.00	5.00
26	A1	130r brown, *straw*	5.00	5.00
27	A1	200r red vio, *pink*	5.00	4.25
28	A1	400r dull bl, *straw*	8.25	7.50
29	A1	500r blk & red, *bl*	18.00	12.00
30	A1	700r gray blk, *straw*	20.00	13.00
		Nos. 15-30 (16)	91.50	68.50

For surcharge & overprints see Nos. 31-47,
88-101.

No. 22 Surcharged in
Black

1905

31	A1	50r on 65r dull blue	3.00	2.00

Nos. 15-21, 23-30
Overprinted in
Carmine or Green

1911

32	A1	2½r gray	.25	.25
33	A1	5r orange	.25	.25
34	A1	10r lt green	.25	.25
35	A1	15r gray green	.30	.30
36	A1	20r gray violet	.30	.30
37	A1	25r carmine (G)	.70	.50
38	A1	50r brown	.50	.50
39	A1	75r lilac	.50	.50
40	A1	100r dk blue, *bl*	.50	.50
41	A1	115r org brn, *pink*	1.00	.95
42	A1	130r brown, *straw*	1.00	.95
43	A1	200r red vio, *pink*	1.00	.95
44	A1	400r dull bl, *straw*	1.25	1.00
45	A1	500r blk & red, *bl*	1.50	1.00
46	A1	700r gray blk, *straw*	1.75	1.50
		Nos. 32-46 (15)	11.05	9.70

No. 31 Overprinted in Red

1914
47	A1 50r on 65r dull blue		1.75	1.25
a.	"Republica" inverted		25.00	25.00

Vasco da Gama Issue of Various Portuguese Colonies

Common
Design Types
CD20-CD27
Surcharged

REPUBLICA
INHAMBANE
¼ c.

1913   On Stamps of Macao
48	CD20	¼c on ½a bl grn	1.25	1.25
49	CD21	½c on 1a red	1.25	1.25
50	CD22	1c on 2a red vio	1.25	1.25
a.	Inverted surcharge		35.00	35.00
51	CD23	2½c on 4a yel grn	1.25	1.25
52	CD24	5c on 8a dk bl	1.25	1.25
53	CD25	7½c on 12a vio brn	2.25	2.25
54	CD26	10c on 16a bis brn	1.75	1.75
55	CD27	15c on 24a bis	1.75	1.75
	Nos. 48-55 (8)		12.00	12.00

On Stamps of Portuguese Africa
56	CD20	¼c on 2½r bl grn	1.00	1.00
57	CD21	½c on 5r red	1.00	1.00
58	CD22	1c on 10r red vio	1.00	1.00
59	CD23	2½c on 25r yel grn	1.00	1.00
60	CD24	5c on 50r dk bl	1.00	1.00
61	CD25	7½c on 75r vio brn	2.00	2.00
62	CD26	10c on 100r bis brn	1.50	1.50
63	CD27	15c on 150r bis	1.50	1.50
	Nos. 56-63 (8)		10.00	10.00

On Stamps of Timor
64	CD20	¼c on ½a bl grn	1.25	1.25
a.	Inverted surcharge		35.00	35.00
65	CD21	½c on 1a red	1.25	1.25
66	CD22	1c on 2a red vio	1.25	1.25
67	CD23	2½c on 4a yel grn	1.25	1.25
68	CD24	5c on 8a dk bl	1.25	1.25
69	CD25	7½c on 12a vio brn	2.50	2.50
70	CD26	10c on 16a bis brn	1.75	1.75
71	CD27	15c on 24a bis	1.75	1.75
	Nos. 64-71 (8)		12.25	12.25
	Nos. 48-71 (24)		34.25	34.25

Ceres — A2

1914   Typo.   Perf. 15x14
Name and Value in Black
Chalky Paper
72	A2	¼c olive brown	.50	.50
	Never hinged		.80	
73	A2	½c black	.50	.50
	Never hinged		.80	
a.	Imperf.			
74	A2	1c blue green	.50	.50
	Never hinged		.80	
75	A2	1½c lilac brown	.50	.50
	Never hinged		.80	
76	A2	2c carmine	.50	.50
	Never hinged		.80	
77	A2	2½c lt violet	.35	.35
	Never hinged		.55	
78	A2	5c deep blue	.80	.80
	Never hinged		1.25	
79	A2	7½c yellow brown	1.25	1.25
	Never hinged		2.00	
80	A2	8c slate	1.25	1.25
	Never hinged		2.00	
81	A2	10c orange brown	1.10	1.10
	Never hinged		1.75	
82	A2	15c plum	2.00	1.60
	Never hinged		3.25	
83	A2	20c yellow green	2.00	1.60
	Never hinged		3.25	
84	A2	30c brown, *grn*	3.00	2.50
	Never hinged		4.75	
85	A2	40c brown, *pink*	3.00	3.00
	Never hinged		4.75	
86	A2	50c orange, *sal*	5.00	5.00
	Never hinged		8.00	
87	A2	1e green, *blue*	6.00	6.00
	Never hinged		9.50	
	Nos. 72-87 (16)		28.25	26.95

No. 31 Overprinted in Carmine

1915   Perf. 11½
88	A1 50c on 65r dull blue		9.00	6.00

Nos. 15-21, 23-30
Overprinted Locally

1917
89	A1	2½r gray	25.00	25.00
90	A1	5r orange	25.00	25.00
91	A1	15r gray green	4.00	2.50
92	A1	20r gray violet	4.00	2.00
93	A1	50r brown	3.00	2.00
94	A1	75r lilac	3.00	2.00
95	A1	100r blue, *blue*	4.00	2.50
96	A1	115r org brn, *pink*	4.00	2.50
97	A1	130r brn, *straw*	4.00	2.50
98	A1	200r red vio, *pink*	4.00	2.50
99	A1	400r dull bl, *straw*	6.00	3.00
100	A1	500r blk & red, *bl*	7.00	3.00
101	A1	700r gray blk, *straw*	14.00	8.00
	Nos. 89-101 (13)	107.00	82.50

The stamps of Inhambane have been super-seded by those of Mozambique.

ININI

ĭ-ē-nĭ-'nē

LOCATION — In northeastern South America, adjoining French Guiana
GOVT. — Former territory of French Guiana
AREA — 30,301 sq. mi.
POP. — 5,024 (1946)
CAPITAL — St. Elie

Inini was separated from French Guiana in 1930 and reunited with it in when the colony became an integral part of the Republic, acquiring the same status as the departments of Metropolitan France, under a law effective Jan. 1, 1947.

100 Centimes = 1 Franc

Used values are for canceled-to-order stamps.

Stamps of French Guiana, 1929-40, Overprinted in Black, Red or Blue

Nos. 1-9

Nos. 10-26

GUYANE FRANÇAISE
Territoire de l'ININI

Nos. 27-40

1932-40   Unwmk.   Perf. 13½x14
1	A16	1c gray lil & grnsh bl	.40	.55
	Never hinged		.60	
	On cover, *from*		300.00	
2	A16	2c dk red & bl grn	.10	.05
	Never hinged		.60	
	On cover, *from*		300.00	
3	A16	3c gray lil & grnsh bl ('40)	.55	.70
	Never hinged		.75	
	On cover, *from*		340.00	
4	A16	4c ol brn & red vio ('38)	.55	.80
	Never hinged		.85	
	On cover, *from*		300.00	
5	A16	5c Prus bl & red org	.55	.80
	Never hinged		.85	
	On cover, *from*		290.00	
6	A16	10c magenta & brn	.40	.55
	Never hinged		.60	
	On cover, *from*		275.00	
7	A16	15c yel brn & red org	.40	.55
	Never hinged		.60	
	On cover, *from*		275.00	
8	A16	20c dk bl & ol grn	.40	.55
	Never hinged		.60	
	On cover, *from*		250.00	
9	A16	25c dk red & dk brn	.90	1.25
	Never hinged		1.20	
	On cover, *from*		250.00	

Perf. 14x13½
10	A17	30c dl grn & lt grn	2.40	2.40
	Never hinged		3.25	
	On cover, *from*		250.00	
11	A17	30c grn & brn ('40)	.60	.90
	Never hinged		.90	
	On cover, *from*		290.00	
12	A17	35c Prus grn & ol ('38)	1.20	1.40
	Never hinged		1.50	
	On cover, *from*		290.00	
13	A17	40c org brn & ol gray	.80	1.20
	Never hinged		1.20	
	On cover, *from*		250.00	
14	A17	45c ol grn & lt grn ('40)	1.40	1.50
	Never hinged		2.75	
	On cover, *from*		250.00	
15	A17	50c dk bl & ol gray	.70	1.05
	Never hinged		.95	
	On cover, *from*		290.00	
16	A17	55c vio bl & car ('38)	5.50	6.50
	Never hinged		7.00	
	On cover, *from*		250.00	
17	A17	60c sal & grn ('40)	.70	1.05
	Never hinged		.95	
	On cover, *from*		250.00	
18	A17	65c sal & grn ('38)	2.10	2.25
	Never hinged		3.00	
	On cover, *from*		250.00	
19	A17	70c ind & sl bl ('40)	1.00	1.10
	Never hinged		1.50	
	On cover, *from*		250.00	
20	A17	75c ind & sl bl (Bl)	4.25	3.50
	Never hinged		4.75	
	On cover, *from*		250.00	
21	A17	80c blk & vio bl (R) ('38)	1.25	1.25
	Never hinged		1.60	
	On cover, *from*		250.00	
22	A17	90c dk red & ver	3.50	2.25
	Never hinged		4.75	
	On cover, single franking, *from*		310.00	
			500.00	
23	A17	90c red vio & brn ('39)	1.75	1.40
	Never hinged		2.40	
	On cover, *from*		250.00	
24	A17	1fr lt vio & brn	22.50	24.00
	Never hinged		32.50	
	On cover, *from*		500.00	
	On cover, single franking, *from*		700.00	
25	A17	1fr car & lt red ('38)	2.75	1.75
	Never hinged		3.75	
	On cover, *from*		310.00	
	On cover, single franking, *from*		550.00	
26	A17	1fr blk & vio bl ('40)	1.00	1.40
	Never hinged		1.25	
	On cover, *from*		250.00	
27	A18	1.25fr blk brn & bl grn ('33)	2.25	1.60
	Never hinged		2.75	
	On cover, *from*		250.00	
	On cover, single franking, *from*		400.00	
28	A18	1.25fr rose & lt red ('39)	1.40	1.40
	Never hinged		2.00	
	On cover, *from*		250.00	
	On cover, single franking, *from*		475.00	
29	A18	1.40fr ol brn & red vio ('40)	1.25	1.40
	Never hinged		1.75	
	On cover, *from*		310.00	
	On cover, single franking, *from*		475.00	
30	A18	1.50fr dk bl & lt bl	1.05	1.50
	Never hinged		1.40	
	On cover, *from*		300.00	
	On cover, single franking, *from*		425.00	
31	A18	1.60fr ol brn & bl grn ('40)	1.00	1.40
	Never hinged		1.25	
	On cover, *from*		250.00	
	On cover, single franking, *from*		475.00	

32	A18	1.75fr brn, red & blk brn ('33)	30.00	27.50
	Never hinged		40.00	
	On cover, *from*		500.00	
	On cover, single frankinn		700.00	
33	A18	1.75fr vio bl ('38)	1.75	2.40
	Never hinged		2.50	
	On cover, single franking, *from*		250.00	
			425.00	
34	A18	2fr dk grn & rose red	1.25	1.75
	Never hinged		1.60	
	On cover, single franking, *from*		250.00	
			425.00	
35	A18	2.25fr vio bl ('39)	1.10	1.40
	Never hinged		1.50	
	On cover, single franking, *from*		250.00	
			400.00	
36	A18	2.50fr cop red & brn ('40)	1.00	1.40
	Never hinged		1.25	
	On cover, single franking, *from*		250.00	
			400.00	
37	A18	3fr brn red & red vio	1.50	1.75
	Never hinged		2.10	
	On cover, single franking, *from*		275.00	
			500.00	
38	A18	5fr dl vio & yel grn	1.25	1.75
	Never hinged		1.60	
	On cover, single franking, *from*		300.00	
			500.00	
39	A18	10fr ol gray & dp ultra (R)	1.75	2.10
	Never hinged		2.40	
	On cover, single franking, *from*		325.00	
			550.00	
40	A18	20fr indigo & ver	1.75	2.10
	Never hinged		2.40	
	On cover, *from*		450.00	
	On cover, single franking, *from*		750.00	
	Nos. 1-40 (40)		106.25	110.65

Cover values are for examples bearing stamps used to pay correct postage rates

Common Design Types pictured following the introduction.

Colonial Arts Exhibition Issue
Souvenir Sheet
Common Design Type
1937   Imperf.
41	CD75 3fr red brown		19.00	22.50
	Never hinged		28.00	
	On cover		275.00	
	On cover, single franking		375.00	

New York World's Fair Issue
Common Design Type
1939, May 10   Engr.   Perf. 12½x12
42	CD82 1.25fr car lake		3.75	4.50
	Never hinged		5.75	
	On cover		250.00	
	On cover, single franking		340.00	
43	CD82 2.25fr ultra		3.75	4.50
	Never hinged		5.75	
	On cover		250.00	
	On cover, single franking		325.00	

SEMI-POSTAL STAMPS

French Revolution Issue
Common Design Type
Photo.; Name & Value Typo. in Black
1939, July 5   Unwmk.   Perf. 13
B1	CD83	45c + 25c green	16.00	17.50
	Never hinged		23.00	
	On cover		190.00	
B2	CD83	70c + 30c brown	16.00	17.50
	Never hinged		23.00	
	On cover		160.00	
B3	CD83	90c + 35c red org	16.00	17.50
	Never hinged		23.00	
	On cover		140.00	
B4	CD83	1.25fr + 1fr rose pink	16.00	17.50
	Never hinged		23.00	
	On cover		225.00	
	On cover, single franking		310.00	
B5	CD83	2.25fr + 2fr blue	16.00	17.50
	Never hinged		23.00	
	On cover		210.00	
	On cover, single franking		275.00	
	Nos. B1-B5 (5)		80.00	87.50

POSTAGE DUE STAMPS

Cover values are for examples bear-ing stamps used to pay correct postage due rates.

Postage Due Stamps
of French Guiana,
1929, Overprinted in
Black

1932, Apr. 7   Unwmk.   Perf. 13½x14

J1	D3	5c indigo & Prus bl	.25	.40
		Never hinged	.40	
		On cover		1,250.
J2	D3	10c bis brn & Prus grn	.65	1.00
		Never hinged	.95	
		On cover		1,250.
J3	D3	20c grn & rose red	.65	1.00
		Never hinged	.95	
		On cover		1,250.
J4	D3	30c ol brn & rose red	.65	1.00
		Never hinged	.95	
		On cover		1,250.
J5	D3	50c vio & ol brn	1.00	1.50
		Never hinged	1.40	
		On cover		1,250.
J6	D3	60c brn red & ol brn	1.10	1.50
		Never hinged	1.40	
		On cover		1,250.

Overprinted in Black
or Red

J7	D4	1fr dp bl & org brn	1.75	1.75
		Never hinged	2.50	
		On cover		1,250.
J8	D4	2fr brn red & bluish grn	2.50	2.50
		Never hinged	3.50	
		On cover		1,250.
J9	D4	3fr vio & blk (R)	7.50	7.50
		Never hinged	14.00	
		On cover		1,250.
J10	D4	3fr vio & blk	4.25	5.00
		Never hinged	6.00	
		On cover		1,250.
		Nos. J1-J10 (10)	20.30	23.15

IONIAN ISLANDS

ī-'ō-nē-ən 'ī-lənds

LOCATION — A group of seven islands, of which six-Corfu, Paxos Lefkas (Santa Maura), Cephalonia, Ithaca and Zante-are in the Ionian Sea west of Greece, and a seventh-Kythera (Cerigo)-is in the Mediterranean south of Greece.
GOVT. — British Protectorate
AREA — 752 sq. mi.
POP. — 251,000 (approx.)

These islands were acquired by Great Britain in 1815 but in 1864 were ceded to Greece on request of the inhabitants.

10 Oboli = 1 Penny
12 Pence = 1 Shilling

Watermarks

Wmk. 138 — "2"   Wmk. 139 — "1"

PRE-STAMP POSTAL MARKINGS

No. A2

Cephalonia

1844

A1   Crowned Circle hand-
stamp Type I, on cover,
inscribed "PAID AT
CEPHALONIA" in black   2,000.

Corfu

A2   Crowned Circle hand-
stamp Type I, on cover,
inscribed "PAID AT COR-
FU" in black   675.00
A3   Crowned Circle hand-
stamp Type I, on cover,
inscribed "PAID AT COR-
FU" in green or blue   —

Zante

A4   Crowned Circle hand-
stamp Type I, on cover,
inscribed "PAID AT ZAN-
TE" in black   1,500.

Earliest known uses: A1, 4/19/44; A2, 4/19/44; A3, 1844; A4, 4/19/44.

ISSUES OF THE BRITISH PROTECTORATE

Queen Victoria — A1

1859   Unwmk.   Engr.   Imperf.

1	A1	(½p) orange	140.00	700.00

Wmk. 138

2	A1	(1p) blue	35.00	275.00

Wmk. 139

3	A1	(2p) lake	28.00	275.00
		Nos. 1-3 (3)	203.00	1,250.

Full margins = ¼mm at sides, ¾mm at top and bottom.

Forged cancellations are plentiful.

IRAN

i-'rän

(Persia)

LOCATION — Western Asia, bordering on the Persian Gulf and the Gulf of Oman
GOVT. — Islamic republic
AREA — 636,000 sq. mi.
POP. — 43,830,000 (est. 1984)
CAPITAL — Tehran

20 Shahis (or Chahis) = 1 Kran
10 Krans = 1 Toman
100 Centimes = 1 Franc = 1 Kran
(1881)
100 Dinars = 1 Rial (1933)
100 Rials = 1 Pahlavi

Beware of forgeries and/or reprints of most Iran stamps between the years 1870-1925. Scott values are for genuine stamps. Collectors should be aware that forgeries of many issues outnumber genuine examples by factors of 10 or 20 to one. Failing specialized knowledge on the part of the collector, these stamps should be examined or authenticated by acknowledged experts before purchase.

Watermark

Wmk. 161 — Lion

Many issues have handstamped surcharges. As usual with such surcharges there are numerous inverted, double and similar varieties.

Values of early stamps vary according to condition. Quotations for Nos. 1-20, 33-40 are for fine stamps. Very fine to superb examples sell at much higher prices, and inferior or poor examples sell at reduced prices, depending on the condition of the individual stamp.

Cracked gum on unused stamps does not detract from the value.

Coat of Arms
A1   A2

Design A2 has value numeral below lion.

1870   Unwmk.   Typo.   Imperf.

1	A1	1s dull violet	325.00	
2	A1	2s green	275.00	
3	A1	4s greenish blue	225.00	
		On cover, internal use		2,500.
4	A1	8s red	275.00	
		Nos. 1-4 (4)	1,100.	

Values for used examples of Nos. 1-4 are omitted, since this issue was only pen canceled. After 1875, postmarked remainders were sold to collectors. Values same as unused.
Printed in blocks of 4. Many shades exist. Forgeries exist.

Printed on Both Sides

1a	A1	1s	20,000.
2a	A1	2s	40,000.
3a	A1	4s	
4a	A1	8s	18,000.

Vertically Rouletted 10½ on 1 or 2 Sides

1875   Thick Wove Paper

11	A2	1s black	225.00	75.00
		On cover with #13, internal use		7,500.
a.		Imperf.	3,500.	5,000.
12	A2	2s blue	225.00	75.00
a.		Tête bêche pair	30,000.	
b.		Imperf.	—	

13	A2	4s vermilion	300.00	100.00
		On cover with #11, internal use		7,500.
a.		Imperf.	—	
b.		4s bright red, thin paper, imperf.	750.00	750.00
14	A2	8s yellow green	200.00	175.00
b.		Tête bêche pair	15,000.	10,000.
c.		Imperf.	2,000.	1,250.
		Nos. 11-14 (4)	950.00	425.00

Four varieties of each.

Nos. 11-14 were printed in horizontal strips of 4 with 3-10mm spacing between stamps. The strips were then cut very close all around (generally touching or cutting the outer frame-lines). Then they were hand-rouletted between the stamps. Values are for stamps with rouletting on both sides and margins clear at top and bottom. Stamps showing the rouletting on only one side sell for considerably less.

Nos. 11 to 14 also exist pin-perforated and percé en scie.

No. 13b has spacing of 2-3mm.

See Nos. 15-20, 33-40.

Medium to Thin White or Grayish Paper

1876   Imperf.

14A	A2	1s black	400.00	600.00
15	A2	1s gray black	50.00	175.00
		On cover, internal use		9,750.
a.		Printed on both sides	1,500.	
b.		Laid paper	1,000.	1,500.
16	A2	2s gray blue	550.00	750.00
a.		Printed on both sides	7,000.	
b.		Half used as 1s on cover		100,000.
17	A2	2s black	1,000.	
a.		Pair	7,500.	
		Tête bêche pair	6,000.	
18	A2	4s vermilion	500.00	150.00
a.		Printed on both sides	5,000.	5,000.
19	A2	1k rose	1,500.	100.00
a.		Printed on both sides		4,000.
b.		Laid paper	6,000.	1,200.
c.		1k yellow (error)	35,000.	15,000.
d.		Tête bêche pair		120,000.
20	A2	4k yellow	3,000.	300.00
a.		Printed on both sides		5,000.
b.		Laid paper	5,000.	300.00
c.		Tête bêche pair		18,000.

Nos. 15-16, 18-20 were printed in blocks of 4, and Nos. 14A and 17 in vertical strips of 4, with spacing of 2mm or less.

Nos. 14A and 17 are on medium to thick grayish wove paper. Forgeries exist.

Official reprints of the 1s and 4s are on thick coarse white paper without gum. Value, each $350.

Unofficial Reprints

1875 and 1876 issues.
The reprints of the 1s and 1k stamps are readily told; the pearls of the circle are heavier, the borders of the circles containing the Persian numeral of value are wider and the figure "1" below the lion is always Roman.

The reprints of the 2s have the outer line of the name at the left and at the bottom broken and on some specimens entirely missing.

A distinguishing mark by which to tell the 4s and 4k stamps is the frame, the outer line of which is of the same thickness as the inner line, while on the originals the inner line is very thin and the outer line thick; another feature of most of the reprints is a gash in the lower part of the circle below the figure "4."

In the reprints of the 8s stamps the small scroll nearest to the circles with Persian numerals at the bottom of the stamp touches the frame below it; the inner and outer lines of the frame are of equal thickness, while in the originals the outer line is much heavier than the inner one.

All reprints are found canceled to order.

Nasser-eddin Shah
Qajar — A3

Perf. 10½, 11, 12, 13, and Compounds
1876 — Litho.

27	A3	1s lilac & blk	30.00	6.00
28	A3	2s green & blk	35.00	7.50
29	A3	5s rose & blk	30.00	4.00
		On cover, internal use		175.00
		On cover, international use		2,200.
30	A3	10s blue & blk	45.00	8.00
		On cover		200.00
		Nos. 27-30 (4)	140.00	25.50

Bisects of the 5s and 1s, the latter used with 2s stamps, were used to make up the 2½ shahis postcard rate. Bisects of the 10s were used in the absence of 5s stamps to make up the letter rate.

The 10s was bisected and surcharged "5 Shahi" or "5 Shahy" for local use in Azerbaijan province and Khoy in 1877.

"Imperfs" of the 5s are envelope cutouts.

Forgeries and official reprints exist.

Very fine examples will have perforations cutting the background net on one side. Genuine stamps withs perfs clear of net on all four sides are very scarce.

1878 — Typo.

				Imperf.
33	A2	1k car rose	950.00	175.00
34	A2	1k red, *yellow*	5,000.	175.00
a.		Tête bêche pair		10,000.
35	A2	4k ultramarine	450.00	175.00
a.		Printed on both sides		4,000.
36	A2	5k violet	1,500.	350.00
37	A2	5k gold	8,500.	750.00
38	A2	5k red bronze	35,000.	2,500.
39	A2	5k vio bronze	65,000.	3,750.
a.		A2 5k slate-green bronze	—	—
40	A2	1t bronze, *bl*	75,000.	8,000.

Four varieties of each except for 4k which has 3.

Nos. 33 and 34 are printed from redrawn clichés. They have wide colorless circles around the corner numerals.

Nasser-eddin Shah
Qajar — A6

Perf. 10½, 12, 13, and Compounds
1879 — Litho.

41	A6	1k brown & blk	450.00	7.00
a.		Pair, imperf between		—
b.		Inverted center		5,000.
42	A6	5k blue & blk	400.00	5.00
a.		Imperf., pair	3,000.	600.00
b.		Inverted center		2,500.
c.		Inverted center, imperf		2,500.

1880

43	A6	1s red & black	50.00	15.00
a.		Pair, imperf between	4,500.	
44	A6	2s yellow & blk	85.00	10.00
a.		Imperf., pair		2,500.
45	A6	5s green & blk	350.00	2.00
46	A6	10s violet & blk	700.00	30.00
		Nos. 43-46 (4)	1,185.	57.00

Forgeries and official reprints exist.

The 2, 5 and 10sh of this issue and the 1 and 5kr of the 1879 issue have been reprinted

---

from a new die which resembles the 5 shahi envelope. The aigrette is shorter than on the original stamps and touches the circle above it.

Imperf., Pair

43a	A6	1s		1,500.
44a	A6	2s		2,000.
46a	A6	10s		3,000.

Sun — A7

1881 — Litho. Perf. 12, 13, 12x13

47	A7	5c dull violet	50.00	25.00
		On cover, single franking		125.00
48	A7	10c rose	50.00	25.00
49	A7	25c green	6,750.	100.00
		On cover, internal use		1,200.
		On cover, international use		2,750.
		Nos. 47-49 (3)	6,850.	150.00

1882 — Engr., Border Litho.

50	A7	5c blue vio & vio	50.00	60.00
51	A7	10c dp pink & rose	50.00	60.00
52	A7	25c deep grn & grn	1,400.	40.00
		On cover, internal use		125.00
		On cover, international use		325.00
		Nos. 50-52 (3)	1,500.	160.00

Very fine examples of Nos. 50-52 will have perforations cutting the outer colored border but clear of the inner framelines.

Counterfeits of Nos. 50-52, 53, 53a are plentiful and have been used to create forgeries of Nos. 66, 66a, 70 and 70a. They usually have a strong, complete inner frameline at right. On genuine stamps that line is weak or missing.

A8

Type I   Type II (error)

Shah Nasr-ed-Din
A9   A10

A11

Type I: Three dots at right end of scroll.
Type II: Two dots at right end of scroll.

1882-84 — Engr.

53	A8	5s green, type I	50.00	1.50
		On cover, internal use		75.00
a.		5s green, type II	100.00	10.00
54	A9	10s buff, org & blk	85.00	10.00
55	A10	50c buff, org & blk	700.00	80.00
56	A10	50c gray & blk ('84)	150.00	70.00
57	A10	1fr blue & black	150.00	10.00
58	A10	5fr rose red & blk	140.00	40.00
59	A11	10fr buff, red & blk	150.00	30.00
		Nos. 53-59 (7)	1,425.	231.50

Crude forgeries of Nos. 58-59 exist. Halves of the 10s, 50c and 1fr surcharged with Farsi characters in red or black are frauds. The 50c

---

and 1fr surcharged with a large "5" surrounded by rays are also frauds.

No. 59 used is valued for c-t-o.

For overprints and surcharges see Nos. 66-72.

Very fine examples of Nos. 53-59 will have perforations cutting the outer colored border but clear of the inner framelines.

A12   A13

Perf. 12-12½, 13
1885, March-May — Litho.

59A	A12	5c blue	1,200.	50.00
a.		5c violet blue	1,200.	75.00
b.		5c ultramarine	1,200.	75.00
c.		5c dp reddish lilac	2,000.	300.00
d.		As "a," imperf	6,000.	

No. 59A was issued because of an urgent need for 5c stamps, pending the arrival of No. 62 in July. No. 59A has 88 sunrays instead of the 124 sunrays on the typographed stamp, No. 62.

1885-86 — Typo.

60	A12	1c green	25.00	2.00
61	A12	2c rose	25.00	2.00
62	A12	5c dull blue	200.00	2.00
		On cover, internal use		45.00
63	A13	10c brown	40.00	2.00
64	A13	1k slate	100.00	3.00
65	A13	5k dull vio ('86)	800.00	40.00
		Nos. 60-65 (6)	1,190.	50.00

Nos. 53, 54, 56 and 58 Surcharged in Black

a   b

c   d

e   f

1885

66	(a)	6c on 5s grn, type I	150.00	30.00
		On cover, international use		4,500.
a.		6c on 5s green, type II	275.00	100.00
67	(b)	12c on 50c gray & blk	150.00	30.00
68	(c)	18c on 10s buff, org & black	150.00	30.00
69	(d)	1t on 5fr rose red & black	150.00	50.00
		Nos. 66-69 (4)	600.00	140.00

1887

70	(e)	3c on 5s grn, type I	150.00	30.00
		3c on 5s green, type II	275.00	100.00
71	(a)	6c on 10s buff, org & blk	150.00	30.00
		On cover, international use		4,500.
72	(f)	8c on 50c gray & blk	150.00	30.00
		Nos. 70-72 (3)	450.00	90.00

The word "OFFICIEL" indicated that the surcharged stamps were officially authorized. Surcharges on the same basic stamps of values other than those listed are believed to be bogus.

Counterfeits of Nos. 66-72 abound.

Very fine examples of Nos. 66-72 will have perforations cutting the outer colored border but clear of the inner framelines.

A14   A15

1889 — Typo. Perf. 11, 13½, 11x13½

73	A14	1c pale rose	2.50	.75
74	A14	2c pale blue	2.50	.75
75	A14	5c lilac	1.50	.50
		On cover, internal use		40.00
76	A14	7c brown	7.50	1.50
		On cover, international use		1,500.
77	A15	10c black	2.50	.75
78	A15	1k red orange	4.50	.75
79	A15	2k rose	40.00	6.00
80	A15	5k green	25.00	6.00
		Nos. 73-80 (8)	86.00	17.00

All values exist imperforate.
Canceled to order stamps of No. 76 abound.
For surcharges see Nos. 622-625.
Nos. 73-80 with average centering, faded colors and/or toned paper sell for much less.

A16   A17

1891 Perf. 10½, 11½

81	A16	1c black	2.50	1.00
82	A16	2c brown	2.50	1.00
83	A16	5c deep blue	2.50	.25
		On cover, internal use		45.00
84	A16	7c gray	350.00	12.00
		On cover, international use		550.00
85	A16	10c rose	2.50	.50
86	A16	14c orange	2.50	1.50
87	A17	1k green	30.00	2.00
88	A17	2k orange	700.00	25.00
89	A17	5k ocher yellow	8.00	*30.00*
		Nos. 81-89 (9)	1,100.	73.25

For surcharges see Nos. 626-629.

A18   Nasser-eddin
Shah
Qajar — A19

1894 Perf. 12½

90	A18	1c lilac	1.00	.25
91	A18	2c blue green	1.00	.25
92	A18	5c ultramarine	1.00	.25
		On cover, internal use		30.00
93	A18	8c brown	1.00	.25

Perf. 11½x11

94	A19	10c orange	1.25	.75
		On cover, international use		350.00
95	A19	16c rose	25.00	75.00
96	A19	1k red & yellow	3.00	.75
97	A19	2k brn org & pale bl	4.00	1.00
98	A19	5k violet & silver	10.00	1.00
99	A19	10k red & gold	20.00	10.00
100	A19	50k green & gold	50.00	15.00
		Nos. 90-100 (11)	117.25	105.00

Canceled to order stamps sell for one-third of listed values.

Reprints exist. They are hard to distinguish from the originals. Value, set $15.

See Nos. 104-112, 136-144. For overprints see Nos. 120-128, 152-167, 173-181. For surcharges see Nos. 101-103, 168, 206, 211.

Nos. 93, 98 With Violet or Magenta Surcharge

a

b

1897   **Perf. 12½, 11½x11**
101	A18(a)	5c on 8c brown (V)	30.00	5.00
a.		Inverted surcharge	150.00	25.00
102	A19(b)	1k on 5k vio & sil (V)	40.00	20.00
103	A19(b)	2k on 5k vio & sil (M)	60.00	35.00
		Nos. 101-103 (3)	130.00	60.00

Forgeries exist.

Lion Type of 1894 and

Mozaffar-eddin Shah Qajar — A22

1898   **Typo.**   **Perf. 12½**
104	A18	1c gray	5.00	.35
105	A18	2c pale brown	5.00	.35
106	A18	3c dull violet	10.00	3.00
107	A18	4c vermilion	10.00	3.00
108	A18	5c yellow	5.00	.25
		On cover, internal use		30.00
109	A18	8c orange	20.00	7.00
110	A18	10c light blue	5.00	.50
111	A18	12c rose	15.00	1.00
		On cover, international use		100.00
112	A18	16c green	20.00	7.00
113	A22	1k ultramarine	10.00	1.00
114	A22	2k pink	10.00	2.00
115	A22	3k yellow	10.00	3.00
116	A22	4k gray	10.00	5.00
117	A22	5k emerald	10.00	6.00
118	A22	10k orange	40.00	15.00
119	A22	50k bright vio	60.00	25.00
		Nos. 104-119 (16)	245.00	79.45

Unauthorized reprints of Nos. 104-119 were made from original clichés. Paper shows a vertical mesh. These abound unused and canceled to order. Value set, unused, hinged, $20.

See Nos. 145-151. For overprints see Nos. 129-135, 182-188. For surcharges see Nos. 169, 171, 207, 209, 215.

Reprints have been used to make counterfeits of Nos. 120-135, 152-167.

Stamps of 1898 Handstamped in Violet

a

b

c   d

---

e   f

g   h

1899
120	(a)	1c gray	5.00	5.00
121	(b)	2c pale brown	5.00	8.00
122	(b)	3c dull violet	12.00	15.00
123	(c)	4c vermilion	18.00	30.00
124	(c)	5c yellow	10.00	3.00
		On cover, internal use		65.00
125	(d)	8c orange	15.00	40.00
126	(d)	10c light blue	6.50	10.00
a.		Type "b" handstamp	500.00	500.00
127	(d)	12c rose	15.00	8.00
		On cover, international use		175.00
128	(d)	16c green	25.00	30.00
129	(e)	1k ultramarine	25.00	10.00
130	(f)	2k pink	30.00	25.00
131	(f)	3k yellow	80.00	250.00
132	(g)	4k gray	100.00	250.00
133	(g)	5k emerald	30.00	40.00
134	(h)	10k orange	60.00	60.00
135	(h)	50k brt violet	120.00	150.00
		Nos. 120-135 (16)	556.50	934.00

The handstamped control marks on Nos. 120-135 exist sideways, inverted and double. Counterfeits are plentiful.

Types of 1894-98

1899   **Typo.**   **Perf. 12½**
136	A18	1c gray, *green*	7.50	.75
137	A18	2c brown, *green*	7.50	.75
138	A18	3c violet, *green*	20.00	5.00
139	A18	4c red, *green*	12.00	5.00
140	A18	5c yellow, *green*	5.00	.30
		On cover, internal use		30.00
141	A18	8c orange, *green*	15.00	5.00
142	A18	10c pale blue, *grn*	5.00	.50
143	A18	12c lake, *green*	15.00	1.25
		On cover, international use		45.00
144	A18	16c green, *green*	25.00	5.00
145	A22	1k red	30.00	1.25
146	A22	2k deep green	35.00	8.50
147	A22	3k lilac brown	35.00	17.00
148	A22	4k orange red	35.00	17.00
149	A22	5k gray brown	40.00	17.00
150	A22	10k deep blue	400.00	100.00
151	A22	50k brown	75.00	30.00
		Nos. 136-151 (16)	762.00	214.30

Canceled to order stamps abound.

Unauthorized reprints of Nos. 136-151 were made from original clichés. Paper is chalky and has white gum. The design can be seen through the back of the reprints. Value unused, hinged, set, $30.

For surcharges and overprints see Nos. 171, 173-188, 206-207, 209, 211.

Nos. 104-111 Handstamped in Violet

(Struck once on every two stamps.)

1900
152	A18	1c gray	50.00	20.00
153	A18	2c pale brown	60.00	25.00
154	A18	3c dull violet	100.00	50.00
155	A18	4c vermilion	100.00	50.00
156	A18	5c yellow	25.00	10.00
		On cover, internal use		85.00
158	A18	10c light blue	2,000.	2,000.
159	A18	12c rose	100.00	50.00
		On cover, international use		375.00
		Nos. 152-159 (7)	2,435.	2,205.

Values are for single authenticated stamps. Pairs sell for much more.

This control mark, in genuine state, was not applied to the 8c orange (Nos. 109, 125).

Same Overprint Handstamped on Nos. 120-127 in Violet

(Struck once on each block of 4.)
160	A18	1c gray	100.00	50.00
163	A18	4c vermilion	300.00	140.00
164	A18	5c yellow	50.00	20.00
		On cover, internal use		225.00
166	A18	10c light blue	1,000.	500.00
a.		Type "b" handstamp	400.00	200.00
167	A18	12c rose	150.00	50.00
		On cover, international use		425.00
		Nos. 160-167 (5)		760.00

Values are for single authenticated stamps. Blocks are rare and worth much more.

Counterfeits exist of Nos. 152-167.

No. 93 Surcharged in Violet

1900
168	A18	5c on 8c brown	50.00	2.50
a.		Inverted surcharge	250.00	25.00

No. 145 Surcharged in Violet

1901
169	A22	12c on 1k red	100.00	100.00
a.		Blue surcharge	125.00	125.00

Counterfeits exist.

Some specialists state that No. 169 with black surcharge was made for collectors.

A23

1902   **Violet Surcharge**
171	A23	5k on 50k brown	200.00	80.00
a.		Blue surcharge	200.00	90.00

Counterfeits exist. See No. 207.

Nos. 136-151 Overprinted in Black

1902
173	A18	1c gray, *green*	50.00	20.00
174	A18	2c brown, *green*	50.00	20.00
175	A18	3c violet, *green*	150.00	100.00
176	A18	4c red, *green*	200.00	200.00
177	A18	5c yellow, *green*	20.00	5.00
178	A18	8c orange, *green*	200.00	200.00
179	A18	10c pale blue, *grn*	50.00	15.00
180	A18	12c lake, *green*	125.00	50.00
181	A18	16c green, *green*	300.00	100.00
182	A22	1k red	100.00	45.00
183	A22	2k deep green	250.00	100.00
188	A22	50k brown	400.00	125.00

Overprinted on No. 168
206	A18	5c on 8c brown	200.00	100.00

Overprinted on Nos. 171 and 171a
207	A23	5k on 50k brown	200.00	100.00
		On #171a	250.00	100.00

Overprinted on Nos. 169 and 169a
209	A22	12c on 1k red	100.00	50.00
a.		On #169a	100.00	50.00

Counterfeits of the overprint of Nos. 173-183, 188, 206-207, 209 are plentiful. Practically all examples with overprint sideways, inverted, double and double with one inverted are frauds.

Nos. 142 Surcharged in Violet

1902
211	A18	5c on 10c pale bl, *grn*	60.00	20.00

Surcharges in different colors were made for collectors.

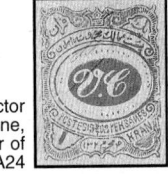

Initials of Victor Castaigne, Postmaster of Meshed — A24

1902   **Typo.**   **Imperf.**
222	A24	1c black	1,500.	450.00
a.		Inverted frame	—	3,000.
b.		Inverted center	—	3,000.
223	A24	2c black	1,250.	450.00
a.		Inverted frame	—	
b.		"2" in right upper corner	3,000.	1,750.
c.		Frame printed on both sides	—	
224	A24	3c black	3,250.	1,750.
225	A24	5c violet	750.00	200.00
a.		"5" in right upper corner	—	
b.		Frame printed on both sides	2,250.	1,000.
c.		Inverted center	—	
226	A24	5c black	900.00	350.00
a.		Persian "5" in lower left corner	—	
b.		Inverted center	—	
227	A24	12c dull blue	4,000.	1,500.
a.		Inverted frame	—	
b.		Inverted center	—	
228	A24	1k rose	30,000.	3,500.

Used values for Nos. 222-228 canceled to order are about ⅓ to ½ the values shown, which are for postally used stamps.

The design of No. 228 differs slightly from the illustration.

Nos. 222-228 were printed in three operations. Inverted centers have frames and numerals upright. Inverted frames have centers and numerals upright.

Pin-perforated
234	A24	12c dull blue	4,000.	1,500.

The post office at Meshed having exhausted its stock of stamps, the postmaster issued the above series provisionally. The center of the design is the seal of the postmaster who also wrote his initials upon the upper part, using violet ink for the 1k and red for the others.

Unauthorized reprints, including pinperforated examples of Nos. 222-226, and forgeries exist.

Expert knowledge or certificates of authenticity are required.

A25

TWO TYPES:

Type I — "CHAHI" or "KRANS" are in capital letters.

Type II — Only "C" of "Chahi" or "K" of "Krans" is a capital.

The 3c and 5c sometimes have a tall narrow figure in the upper left corner. The 5c is also found with the cross at the upper left broken or missing. These varieties are known with many of the overprints.

Stamps of Design A25 have a faint fancy background in the color of the stamp. All issued stamps have handstamped controls as listed.

Type I
Handstamp Overprinted in Black
1902   **Typeset**   **Imperf.**
235	A25	1c gray & buff	300.00	150.00
236	A25	2c brown & buff	400.00	150.00
237	A25	3c green & buff	400.00	150.00
238	A25	5c red & buff	300.00	100.00
239	A25	12c ultra & buff	500.00	150.00
		Nos. 235-239 (5)	1,900.	700.00

Counterfeits abound. Type II stamps with this overprint are forgeries.

The 3c with violet overprint is believed not to have been regularly issued.

Handstamp
Overprinted in Rose

			Type I
1902			
247	A25	1c gray & buff	25.00 2.00
a.		With Persian numerals "2"	100.00
248	A25	2c brown & buff	25.00 2.00
249	A25	3c dp grn & buff	25.00 2.00
250	A25	5c red & buff	25.00 .75
251	A25	10c ol yel & buff	50.00 3.00
252	A25	12c ultra & buff	75.00 5.00
253	A25	1k violet & bl	60.00 6.00
254	A25	2k ol grn & bl	100.00 12.50
256	A25	10k dk bl & bl	150.00 30.00
257	A25	50k red & blue	1,500. 800.00
		Nos. 247-257 (10)	2,035. 863.25

A 5k exists but its status is doubtful. Value $500.

Nos. 247-257 and the 12c on brown paper and on blue paper with blue quadrille lines are known without overprint but are not believed to have been regularly issued in this condition.

The 1c to 10k, A25 type I, with violet overprint are believed not to have been regularly issued. Five denominations also exist with overprint in blue, black or green.

			Type II
280	A25	1c gray & yellow	250.00 200.00
281	A25	2c brown & yel	200.00 200.00
282	A25	3c dk grn & yel	2,000. 750.00
a.		"Persans"	
283	A25	5c red & yellow	50.00 15.00
284	A25	10c ol yel & yel	100.00 15.00
285	A25	12c blue & yel	150.00 25.00
290	A25	50k org red & yel	1,250. 600.00

The 3c, inscribed "Persans," is not believed to have been regularly issued.

The same overprint in violet was applied to nine denominations of the Type II stamps, but these, too, are believed not to have been regularly issued. The overprint also exists in blue, black and green.

Reprints, counterfeits, counterfeit overprints, with or without cancellations, are plentiful for Nos. 247-257, 280-290.

Five stamps of type A25, type II, in high denominations (10, 20, 25, 50 and 100 tomans), with "Postes 1319" lion overprint in blue, were used only on money orders, not for postage. They are usually numbered on the back in red, blue or black.

> Beware of forgeries and/or reprints of most Iran stamps between the years 1870-1925. Scott values are for genuine stamps. Collectors should be aware that forgeries of many issues outnumber genuine examples by factors of 10 or 20 to one. Failing specialized knowledge on the part of the collector, these stamps should be examined or authenticated by acknowledged experts before purchase.

Handstamp
Surcharged in Black

			Type I
1902			
308	A25	5k on 5k ocher & bl	200.00 50.00

Counterfeits of No. 308 abound.
This surcharge in rose, violet, blue or green is considered bogus.
This surcharge on 50k orange red and blue, and on 5k ocher and blue, type II, is considered bogus.

Handstamp
Overprinted
Diagonally in Black

			Type I
1902			
315	A25	2c brown & buff	200.00 100.00
a.		Rose overprint	500.00 500.00

			Type II
316	A25	2c brown & yel	— —
a.		Rose overprint	— —

"P. L." stands for "Poste Locale."
Counterfeits of Nos. 315-316 exist.
Some specialists believe that Type II stamps were not used officially for this overprint.

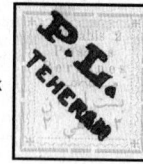

Handstamp
Overprinted in Black
or Rose

			Type II
1902			
317	A25	2c brn & yellow	200.00 100.00
318	A25	2c brown & yel (R)	500.00 500.00

Counterfeits of Nos. 317-318 exist.

Overprinted in Blue

			Type I
1903			
321	A25	1k violet & blue	125.00 125.00

			Type II
336	A25	1c gray & yellow	60.00 60.00
337	A25	2c brown & yellow	60.00 60.00
338	A25	5c red & yellow	40.00 40.00
339	A25	10c olive yel & yel	75.00 75.00
340	A25	12c blue & yellow	90.00 90.00
		Nos. 321-340 (6)	450.00 450.00

A 3c Type I exists but was not regularly issued. Value $250.
The overprint also exists in violet and black, but it is doubtful whether such items were regularly issued.
Forgeries of Nos. 321, 336-340 abound. Genuine unused examples are seldom found.

Arms of Persia — A26   Mozaffar-eddin Shah Qajar — A27

1902 (Dec.)-1904		**Typo.**	**Perf.**	**12½**
351	A26	1c violet	2.00	.25
352	A26	2c gray	2.00	.25
353	A26	3c green	2.00	.25
354	A26	5c rose	2.00	.25
355	A26	10c yellow brn	3.00	1.50
356	A26	12c blue	4.00	.50

			Engr.	
			Perf.	**11½x11**
357	A27	1k violet	15.00	.50
358	A27	2k ultramarine	25.00	1.25
359	A27	5k orange brn	40.00	2.00
360	A27	10k rose red	50.00	4.00
361	A27	20k orange ('04)	45.00	5.00
362	A27	30k green ('04)	70.00	12.50
363	A27	50k green	550.00	100.00
		Nos. 351-363 (13)	810.00	128.25

Nos. 351-363 used are valued canceled to order.
No. 355 exists with blue diagonal surcharge "1 CHAHI"; its status is questioned.
A government decree in November, 1903, required that all picture postcards be censored by the Central Post Office, which would apply a control mark on each card to show that the 2c tax for this service had been paid. No. 352 was overprinted "Controle" in several styles, for this purpose. Value: unused $100; used, from $25.
See Nos. 428-433. For surcharges and overprints see #364-420, 446-447, 464-469, O8-O28, P1.

No. 353 Surcharged in
Violet or Blue

1903			
364	A26	1c on 3c green (V)	50.00 20.00
365	A26	2c on 3c green (Bl)	50.00 20.00

A 2c surcharge on No. 354 exists, but its status is dubious.

No. 360 Surcharged
in Blue

366	A27	12c on 10k rose red	75.00 40.00
a.		Black surcharge	150.00 70.00
b.		Violet surcharge	150.00 70.00
		Nos. 364-366 (3)	175.00 80.00

Nos. 366, 366a and 366b used are valued canceled to order.

No. 363 Surcharged
in Blue or Black

1903			
368	A27	2t on 50k grn (Bl)	200.00 60.00
a.		Rose surcharge	225.00 100.00
b.		Black surcharge	225.00 100.00
370	A27	3t on 50k grn (Bk)	200.00 60.00
a.		Violet surcharge	225.00 60.00
b.		Rose surcharge	250.00 125.00

No. 363 Surcharged
in Blue or Black

1904			
372	A27	2t on 50k grn (Bl)	200.00 60.00
375	A27	3t on 50k grn (Bk)	200.00 60.00

The 2t on 50k also exists with surcharge in rose, violet, black and magenta; the 3t on 50k in rose, violet and blue. Values about the same unused; about 50 percent higher used.

No. 352 Overprinted in
Violet

		Perf. 12½
1904		
393 A26	2c gray	85.00 25.00
a.	Black overprint	100.00 30.00
b.	Rose overprint	90.00 25.00

This overprint also exists in blue, violet blue, maroon and gray, but these were not regularly issued.

Stamps of 1903 Surcharged in Black

a   b

c

1904			
400	A26(a)	3c on 5c rose	40.00 .75
401	A26(b)	6c on 10c brown	50.00 .75
402	A27(c)	9c on 1k violet	50.00 3.50
		Nos. 400-402 (3)	140.00 5.00

Stamps of 1903 Surcharged in Black, Magenta or Violet

1905-06			
404	A26	1c on 3c green ('06)	50.00 20.00
405	A27	1c on 1k violet	35.00 15.00
406	A27	2c on 5k orange brn	40.00 25.00
407	A26	1c on 3c grn (M) ('06)	15.00 5.00
408	A27	1c on 1k violet (M)	20.00 10.00
409	A27	2c on 5k org brn (V)	30.00 15.00
		Nos. 404-409 (6)	190.00 90.00

Nos. 355 and 358
Surcharged in Violet

1906			
419	A26	1c on 10c brown	150.00 —
420	A27	2c on 2k ultra	250.00 —

Forgeries of Nos. 419-420 are common. Forgeries of No. 420, especially, are hard to distinguish since the original handstamp was used. Genuine used stamps may, in some cases, be identified by the cancellation.

A28

Typeset; "Provisoire" Overprint Handstamped in Black

			Imperf.
1906			
422	A28	1c violet	17.50 1.00
a.		Irregular pin perf. or perf. 10½	50.00 17.50
423	A28	2c gray	60.00 10.00
424	A28	3c green	17.50 1.00
425	A28	6c red	17.50 .75
426	A28	10c brown	70.00 90.00
427	A28	13c blue	50.00 10.00
		Nos. 422-427 (6)	232.50 112.75

Stamps of type A28 have a faint background pattern of tiny squares within squares, an ornamental frame and open rectangles for the value corners.
The 3c and 6c also exist perforated.
Nos. 422-427 are known without overprint but were probably not issued in that condition. Nearly all values are known with overprint inverted and double.
Forgeries are plentiful.

Lion Type of 1903 and

Mohammed-Ali Shah Qajar
A29   A30

1907-09		Typo.	Perf. 12½	
428	A26	1c vio, *blue*	5.00	.25
429	A26	2c gray, *blue*	5.00	.25
430	A26	3c green, *blue*	5.00	.25
431	A26	6c rose, *blue*	5.00	.25
432	A26	9c org, *blue*	5.00	.30
433	A26	10c brown, *blue*	6.00	1.00

Engr.
Perf. 11, 11½

434	A29	13c dark blue	7.00	2.00
435	A29	1k red	8.00	1.50
436	A29	26c red brown	8.00	2.00
437	A29	2k deep grn	25.00	1.50
438	A29	3k pale blue	25.00	1.00
439	A29	4k brt yellow	450.00	20.00
440	A29	4k bister	25.00	3.00
441	A29	5k dark brown	25.00	3.00
442	A29	10k pink	30.00	3.00
443	A29	20k gray black	30.00	10.00
444	A29	30k dark violet	30.00	15.00
445	A30	50k gold, ver & black ('09)	150.00	30.00
		Nos. 428-445 (18)	844.00	94.30

Frame of No. 445 lithographed. Nos. 434-444 were issued in 1908.
Remainders canceled to order abound. Used values for Nos. 437-445 are for c-t-os.

Nos. 428-429 Overprinted in Black

1909			Perf. 12½	
446	A26	1c violet, *blue*	90.00	40.00
447	A26	2c gray, *blue*	80.00	30.00

Counterfeits of Nos. 446-447 exist.

Coat of Arms — A31

1909		Typo.	Perf. 12½x12	
448	A31	1c org & maroon	.50	.35
449	A31	2c vio & maroon	.50	.35
450	A31	3c yel grn & mar	.50	.35
451	A31	6c red & maroon	.50	.25
452	A31	9c gray & maroon	.50	.35
453	A31	10c red vio & mar	.50	.35
454	A31	13c dk blue & mar	.50	2.00
455	A31	1k sil, vio & bis brown	1.00	2.00
456	A31	26c dk grn & mar	1.00	3.00
457	A31	2k sil, dk grn & bis brown	1.00	2.00
458	A31	3k sil, gray & bis brown	1.00	3.50
459	A31	4k sil, by & bis brn	1.00	3.50
460	A31	5k gold, brn & bis brown	2.50	3.50
461	A31	10k gold, org & bis brown	5.00	10.00
462	A31	20k gold, ol grn & bister brn	7.00	20.00
463	A31	30k gold, car & bis brown	12.00	20.00
		Nos. 448-463 (16)	35.00	71.50

Unauthorized reprints of Nos. 448-463 abound. Originals have clean, bright colors, centers stand out clearly, and paper is much thinner. Nos. 460-463 have gleaming gold margins; reprint margins appear as blackish yellow. Centers of reprints of Nos. 448-454, 456 are brown.
Values above are for unused reprints or for authenticated used stamps. Original unused stamps sell for much higher prices.

For surcharges & overprints see Nos. 516-519, 541-549. 582-585, 588-594, 597, 601-606, 707-722, C1-C16, O31-O40.

In 1909 two sets of 16 stamps were prepared for the coronation of Ahmad Shad Qajar. The first set with lion and sun high values and gold borders was for postal use, while the second set with city gate high values and silver borders was inscribed "SERVICE". While neither set was placed in use, both were sold to collectors at a later date.

Nos. 428-444, Imperf., Surcharged in Red or Black

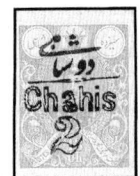

1910		Blue Paper	Imperf.	
464	A26	1c on 1c violet	200.00	140.00
465	A26	1c on 2c gray	200.00	140.00
466	A26	1c on 3c green	200.00	140.00
467	A26	1c on 6c rose (Bk)	200.00	140.00
468	A26	1c on 9c orange	200.00	140.00
469	A26	1c on 10c brown	200.00	140.00

White Paper

470	A29	2c on 13c dp bl	200.00	140.00
471	A29	2c on 26c red brown (Bk)	200.00	140.00
472	A29	2c on 1k red (Bk)	200.00	140.00
473	A29	2c on 2k dp grn	200.00	140.00
474	A29	2c on 3k pale bl	200.00	140.00
475	A29	2c on 4k brt yel	200.00	140.00
476	A29	2c on 4k bister	200.00	140.00
477	A29	2c on 5k dk brn	200.00	140.00
478	A29	2c on 10k pink (Bk)	200.00	140.00
479	A29	2c on 20k gray blk	200.00	140.00
480	A29	2c on 30k dk vio	200.00	140.00
		Nos. 464-480 (17)	3,400.	2,380.

Nos. 464-480 were prepared for use on newspapers, but nearly the entire printing was sold to stamp dealers. The issue is generally considered speculative. Counterfeit surcharges exist on trimmed stamps.
Used values are for c-t-o.

Ahmad Shah Qajar — A32

Perf. 11½, 11½x11, 11½x12
Engr. center, Typo. frame

1911-13				
481	A32	1c green & org	.50	.25
482	A32	2c red & sepia	.50	.25
483	A32	3c gray brn & grn	.50	.25
a.		3c bister brown & green	.50	1.00
484	A32	5c brn & car ('13)	.50	.75
485	A32	6c gray & car	.50	.25
486	A32	6c grn & red brown ('13)	.50	.25
487	A32	9c yel brn & vio	.75	.25
488	A32	10c red & org brn	.75	.25
489	A32	12c grn & ultra ('13)	.50	.50
490	A32	13c violet & ultra	1.00	2.00
491	A32	1k ultra & car	1.00	.50
492	A32	24c vio & grn ('13)	1.00	1.00
493	A32	26c ultra & green	1.00	5.00
494	A32	2k grn & red vio	2.00	1.00
495	A32	3k violet & blk	2.00	1.50
496	A32	4k ultramarine & gray ('13)	2.00	20.00
497	A32	5k red & ultra	3.00	1.00
498	A32	10k ol bis & cl	5.00	3.00
499	A32	20k vio brn & bis	6.00	4.00
500	A32	30k red & green	7.00	5.00
		Nos. 481-500 (20)	36.00	48.00

Values for Nos. 481-500 unused are for reprints, which cannot be distinguished from the late printings of the stamps. These are perf 11½ (11½x12 for the 4k) with the distance between the inner lines of the inscription tablets at top and bottom of the portrait being 19mm. Unused stamps with other perfs or a shorter vignette sell for much higher prices.

The reprints include inverted centers for some denominations. Values, each $30-$50.
For surcharges and overprints see Nos. 501-515, 520-540, 586-587, 595, 598, 600, 607-609, 630-634, 646-666.

Stamps of 1911 Overprinted in Black

1911				
501	A32	1c grn & orange	50.00	6.00
502	A32	2c red & sepia	50.00	6.00
503	A32	3c gray brn & grn	50.00	6.00
504	A32	6c gray & carmine	50.00	6.00
505	A32	9c yel brn & vio	50.00	6.00
506	A32	10c red & org brn	85.00	6.00
507	A32	13c vio & ultra	125.00	8.00
508	A32	1k ultra & car	175.00	10.00
509	A32	26c ultra & green	175.00	12.00
510	A32	2k grn & red vio	225.00	15.00
511	A32	3k vio & black	300.00	15.00
512	A32	5k red & ultra	350.00	20.00
513	A32	10k ol bis & claret	1,350.	40.00
514	A32	20k vio brn & bis	1,150.	50.00
515	A32	30k red & green	1,150.	50.00
		Nos. 501-515 (15)	5,335.	256.00

The "Officiel" overprint does not signify that the stamps were intended for use on official correspondence but that they were issued by authority. It was applied to the stocks in Tabriz and all post offices in the Tabriz region after a large quantity of stamps had been stolen during the Russian occupation of Tabriz.
The "Officiel" overprint has been counterfeited.

Stamps of 1909-11 Overprinted in Black

1911, Oct.		On #449-451, 454		
516	A31	2c vio & maroon	300.00	150.00
517	A31	3c yel grn & mar	300.00	150.00
518	A31	6c red & maroon	300.00	150.00
519	A31	13c dk blue & mar	300.00	150.00

		On #482-483, 485, 490		
520	A32	2c red & sepia	400.00	200.00
521	A32	3c gray brn & grn	400.00	200.00
522	A32	6c gray & car	400.00	200.00
523	A32	13c violet & ultra	400.00	200.00

Stamps were sold at a 10% discount to stagecoach station keepers on the Tehran-Recht route. To prevent speculation, these stamps were overprinted "Stagecoach Stations" in French and Farsi.
Forgeries exist, usually overprinted on reprints of the 1909 issue and used examples of the 1911 issue. Values are for authenticated stamps.

In 1912 this overprint, reading 'Sultan Mohammad Ali Shah Kajar,' was hand-stamped on outgoing mail in the Persian Kurdistan region occupied by the forces of the former Shah Mohammad Ali. It was applied after the stamps were on cover and is found on 8 of the Shah Ahmed stamps of 1911 (1c, 2c, 3c, 6c, 9c, 13c, 1k and 26c). Some specialists add the 10c. Forgeries are abundant.

Nos. 490 and 493 Surcharged

a   b

1914				
535	A32(a)	1c on 13c	30.00	2.00
536	A32(b)	3c on 26c	30.00	4.00

In 1914 a set of 19 stamps was prepared as a coronation issue. The 10 lower values each carry a different portrait; the 9 higher values show buildings and scenes. The same set printed with black centers was overprinted with red "SERVICE." The stamps were never placed in use, but were sold to stamp dealers in 1923.

Nos. 484 and 489 Surcharged in Black or Violet

c   d

1915				
537	A32(c)	1c on 5c	20.00	2.00
538	A32(c)	2c on 5c (V)	20.00	2.00
539	A32(c)	2c on 5c	200.00	40.00
540	A32(d)	6c on 12c	30.00	4.00
		Nos. 537-540 (4)	270.00	46.00

Nos. 455, 454 Surcharged

e   f

1915			Perf. 12½x12	
541	A31(e)	5c on 1k multi	60.00	5.00
542	A31(f)	12c on 13c multi	90.00	7.00

Counterfeit surcharges on reprints abound.

Nos. 448-453, 455 Overprinted

1915				
543	A31	1c org & maroon	70.00	5.00
544	A31	2c vio & maroon	50.00	5.00
545	A31	3c grn & maroon	60.00	5.00
546	A31	6c red & maroon	60.00	5.00
547	A31	9c gray & maroon	100.00	7.00
548	A31	10c red vio & mar	150.00	10.00
549	A31	1k sil, vio & bis brn	250.00	10.00
		Nos. 543-549 (7)	740.00	47.00

This overprint ("1333") also exists on the 2k, 10k, 20k and 30k, but they were not issued.

Counterfeit overprints, usually on reprints, abound.

Beware of forgeries and/or reprints of most Iran stamps between the years 1070-1077. ̣ ... prices are for genuine stamps. Collectors should be aware that forgeries of many issues outnumber genuine examples by factors of 10 or 20 to one. Failing specialized knowledge on the part of the collector, these stamps should be examined or authenticated by acknowledged experts before purchase.

Imperial Crown — A33

King Darius, Farohar overhead — A34

Ruins of Persepolis — A35

Perf. 11½ or Compound 11x11½
Engr., Typo.

1915, Mar.   **Wmk. 161**

560	A33	1c car & indigo	.25	2.00
561	A33	2c bl & carmine	.25	2.00
562	A33	3c dark green	.25	2.00
a.		Inverted center	—	
564	A33	5c red	.25	2.50
565	A33	6c olive grn & car	.25	2.00
a.		Inverted center	—	
566	A33	9c yel brn & vio	.25	2.00
567	A33	10c bl grn & yel brn	.25	2.00
568	A33	12c ultramarine	.25	2.00
569	A34	1k sil, yel brn & gray	.65	5.00
570	A33	24c yel brn & dk brn	.25	5.00
571	A34	2k silver, bl & rose	.65	5.00
572	A34	3k sil, vio & brn	.65	5.00
573	A34	5k sil, brn & green	.65	7.00
574	A35	1t gold, pur & blk	.65	10.00
575	A35	2t gold, grn & brn	1.00	10.00
576	A35	3t gold, cl & red brn	1.00	10.00
577	A35	5t gold, blue & ind	1.00	10.00
		Nos. 560-577 (17)	8.50	83.50

Coronation of Shah Ahmed.

Nos. 560-568, 570 are engraved. Nos. 569, 571-573 are engraved except for silver margins. Nos. 574-577 have centers engraved, frames typographed.

The 3c and 6c with inverted centers are considered genuine errors. Unauthorized reprints exist of these varieties and of other denominations with inverted centers. **Values unused for Nos. 560-577 are for reprints.**

For surcharges and overprints see Nos. 610-616, 635-646, O41-O57, Q19-Q35.

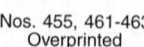

Nos. 455, 461-463 Overprinted

1915   **Unwmk.**   **Typo.**   **Perf. 12½x12**

582	A31	1k sil, vio & bis brn	2.00	20.00
583	A31	10k multicolored	5.00	30.00
584	A31	20k multicolored	10.00	100.00
585	A31	30k multicolored	12.00	60.00
		Nos. 582-585 (4)	29.00	210.00

Genuine unused examples are rare. Most unused stamps offered in the marketplace are reprints, and the unused values above are for authenticated stamps.

Forgeries abound of Nos. 582-585.

No. 491 Surcharged

1917   **Perf. 11½**

586	A32	12c on 1k multi	3,000.	3,500.
587	A32	24c on 1k multi	1,500.	1,750.

Issued during the Turkish occupation of Kermanshah. Forgeries exist.

Values for unused stamps are for reprints. Unused examples of the original stamps are rare, and most stamps offered in the marketplace are reprints.

No. 448 Overprinted "1335" in Persian Numerals

1917   **Perf. 12½x12**

588	A31	1c org & maroon	350.00	250.00

Overprint on No. 588 is similar to date in "k" and "l" surcharges. Forgeries exist.

Nos. 449, 452-453, 456 Surcharged

k   l

1917

589	A31(k)	1c on 2c	30.00	3.00
590	A31(k)	1c on 9c	40.00	4.00
591	A31(k)	1c on 10c	30.00	3.00
592	A31(l)	3c on 9c	50.00	4.00
593	A31(l)	3c on 10c	40.00	3.00
594	A31(l)	3c on 26c	40.00	5.00

Same Surcharge on No. 488

595	A32(k)	1c on 10c	75.00	1.50
596	A32(l)	3c on 10c	75.00	1.50

Nos. 454 & 491 Surcharged Type "e"

597	A31	5c on 13c	50.00	2.00
598	A32	5c on 1k	45.00	2.00

Counterfeit surcharges on "canceled" reprints of Nos. 449, 452-454, 456 abound.

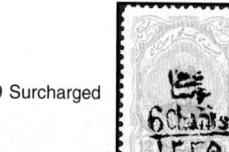

No. 489 Surcharged

600	A32	6c on 12c grn & ultra	125.00	15.00

No. 457 Overprinted

1918

601	A31	2k multi	125.00	20.00

Nos. 459-460 Surcharged

No. 491 Surcharged

1918

602	A31	24c on 4k multi	75.00	15.00
603	A31	10k on 5k multi	125.00	20.00

The surcharges of Nos. 602-603 have been counterfeited.

Nos. 457-463 Overprinted

1918

603A	A31	2k multicolored	3.00	65.00
604	A31	3k multicolored	3.00	15.00
604A	A31	4k multicolored	5.00	150.00
604B	A31	5k multicolored	5.00	75.00
605	A31	10k multicolored	8.00	50.00
605A	A31	20k multicolored	20.00	200.00
606	A31	30k multicolored	15.00	100.00
		Nos. 603A-606 (7)	59.00	655.00

Genuine unused examples are rare. Most unused stamps offered in the marketplace are reprints, and the unused values above are for reprints. Used values for for authenticated stamps.

Forgeries abound of Nos. 603A-606.

Nos. 489, 488 and 491 Surcharged

m   n

607	A32(m)	3c on 12c	75.00	1.50
608	A32(n)	6c on 10c	100.00	1.50
609	A32(n)	6c on 1k	75.00	1.50
		Nos. 607-609 (3)	250.00	4.50

Genuine unused examples are rare. Most unused stamps offered in the marketplace are reprints, and the unused values above are for reprints.

Nos. 571-577 Overprinted in Black or Red

1918   **Wmk. 161**

610	A34	2k sil, blue & rose	10.00	10.00
611	A34	3k sil, vio & brn (R)	10.00	10.00
612	A34	5k sil, brn & grn (R)	10.00	10.00
613	A35	1t gold, pur & black (R)	15.00	15.00
614	A35	2t gold, grn & brn	15.00	15.00
615	A35	3t gold, cl & red brn	15.00	15.00
616	A35	5t gold, bl & ind (R)	20.00	20.00
		Nos. 610-616 (7)	95.00	95.00

The overprint commemorates the end of World War I. Counterfeits of this overprint are plentiful.

A36

Color Litho., Black Typo.

1919   **Unwmk.**   **Perf. 11½**

617	A36	1c yel & black	20.00	1.00
618	A36	3c green & black	20.00	1.00
619	A36	5c rose & black	55.00	3.00
620	A36	6c vio & black	35.00	1.00
621	A36	12c blue & black	125.00	10.00
		Nos. 617-621 (5)	255.00	16.00

Nos. 617-621 exist imperf., in colors other than the originals, with centers inverted and double impressions. Some specialists call them fraudulent, others call them reprints.

This issue has been extensively counterfeited, and most examples in the marketplace are forgeries.

Counterfeits having double line over "POSTES" abound.

Nos. 75, 85-86 Surcharged in Various Colors

1919   **Perf. 10½, 11, 11½, 13½**

622	A14	2k on 5c lilac (Bk)	7.50	7.50
623	A14	3k on 5c lilac (Br)	7.50	7.50
624	A14	4k on 5c lilac (G)	7.50	7.50
625	A14	5k on 5c lilac (V)	7.50	7.50
626	A16	10k on 10c rose (Bl)	20.00	20.00
627	A16	20k on 10c rose (G)	20.00	20.00
628	A16	30k on 10c rose (Br)	20.00	20.00
629	A16	50k on 14c org (V)	20.00	20.00
		Nos. 622-629 (8)	110.00	110.00

Nos. 622-629 exist with inverted and double surcharge. Some specialists consider these fraudulent.

Nos. 486, 489 Handstamp Surcharged

1921   **Perf. 11½, 11½x11**

630	A32	10c on 6c	75.00	15.00
631	A32	1k on 12c	75.00	15.00

Counterfeits exist.

No. 489 Surcharged

632	A32	6c on 12c	400.00	20.00

Nos. 486, 489 Surcharged in Violet

1921

633	A32	10c on 6c	150.00	50.00
a.		Surcharge handstamped in black	350.00	350.00
634	A32	1k on 12c	150.00	50.00
a.		Surcharge handstamped in black	350.00	350.00

Counterfeits exist.

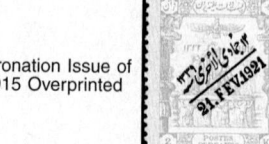

Coronation Issue of 1915 Overprinted

1921, May   **Wmk. 161**   **Perf. 11, 11½**

635	A33	3c dark grn	15.00	
a.		Center and overprint inverted		
636	A33	5c red	15.00	
637	A33	6c olive grn & car	15.00	
638	A33	10c bl grn & yel brn	15.00	
639	A33	12c ultramarine	15.00	
640	A34	1k sil, yel brn & gray	20.00	
641	A34	2k sil, blue & rose	20.00	
642	A34	5k sil, brn & green	20.00	

643	A35	2t gold, grn & brn	25.00	
644	A35	3t gold, cl & red		
		brn		30.00
645	A35	5t gold, blue & ind	30.00	
		Nos. 635-645 (11)	220.00	

Counterfeits of this Feb. 21, 1921, overprint are plentiful. Inverted overprints exist on all values; some specialists consider them fraudulent.

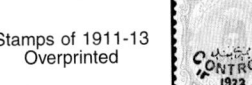

Stamps of 1911-13
Overprinted

1922 Unwmk. Perf. 11½, 11½x11

646	A32	1c grn & orange	10.00	.25
a.		Inverted overprint	250.00	
647	A32	2c red & sepia	10.00	.25
648	A32	3c brn & green	15.00	.25
a.		3c bister brown & green	10.00	.25
649	A32	5c brown & car	125.00	50.00
650	A32	6c grn & red brn	10.00	.25
651	A32	9c yel brn & vio	10.00	.25
652	A32	10c red & org brn	20.00	.25
a.		Double ovpt., one inverted	400.00	
653	A32	12c green & ultra	30.00	.50
a.		Double overprint	400.00	
654	A32	1k ultra & car	35.00	1.00
655	A32	24c vio & green	30.00	1.00
656	A32	2k grn & red vio	95.00	1.00
657	A32	3k vio & black	100.00	1.50
658	A32	4k ultra & gray	250.00	45.00
659	A32	5k red & ultra	200.00	2.00
660	A32	10k ol bis & cl	1,000.	5.00
661	A32	20k vio brn & bis	1,000.	7.00
662	A32	30k red & green	1,000.	10.00
		Nos. 646-662 (17)	3,940.	125.50

The status of inverted overprints on 5c and 12c is dubious. Unlisted inverts on other denominations are generally considered fraudulent. Counterfeits of this overprint exist.

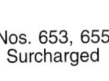

Nos. 653, 655
Surcharged

1922

663	A32	3c on 12c	95.00	1.00
664	A32	6c on 24c	125.00	2.00

Nos. 661-662 Surcharged

1923

665	A32	10c on 20k	150.00	10.00
666	A32	1k on 30k	175.00	15.00

Forgeries exist, generally made by handstamps applied to mint reprints or postally used original stamps.

Ahmed Shah
Qajar — A37

Perf. 11½, 11x11½, 11½x11

1924-25 Engr.

667	A37	1c orange	2.50	.25
668	A37	2c magenta	2.50	.25
a.		Imperf. btwn., pair		2,000.
669	A37	3c orange		
		brown	2.50	.25
670	A37	6c black		
		brown	2.50	.25
671	A37	9c dark green	2.00	5.00

672	A37	10c dark violet	2.00	.30
673	A37	12c red	2.00	.30
674	A37	1k dark blue	2.00	.35
675	A37	2k indigo &		
		red	5.00	5.00
a.		Center inverted	40,000.	6,000.
676	A37	3k dk vio &		
		red brown	17.00	2.00
677	A37	5k red &		
		brown	20.00	30.00
678	A37	10k choc & lilac	25.00	25.00
679	A37	20k dk grn &		
		brn	30.00	30.00
680	A37	30k org & blk		
		brn	40.00	40.00
		Nos. 667-680 (14)	155.00	138.95

For overprints see Nos. 703-706.

A38

SIX CHAHIS

Type I   Type II

Dated 1924
Color Litho., Black Typo.

1924 Perf. 11

681	A38	1c yel brn & blk	20.00	1.00
682	A38	2c gray & blk	20.00	1.00
683	A38	3c dp rose & blk	20.00	1.00
684	A38	6c orange & blk (I)	30.00	1.50
a.		6c orange & blk (II)	35.00	2.00
		Nos. 681-684 (4)	90.00	4.50

The 1c was surcharged "Chahis" by error. Later the "s" was blocked out in black.
Counterfeits having double line over "POSTES" are plentiful.

1925 Dated 1925

686	A38	2c yel grn & blk	10.00	1.00
687	A38	3c red & blk	10.00	1.00
689	A38	6c chalky bl & blk	10.00	1.00
690	A38	9c lt brn & blk	30.00	2.00
691	A38	10c gray & blk	75.00	5.00
694	A38	1k emer & blk	65.00	10.00
695	A38	2k lilac & blk	175.00	40.00
		Nos. 686-695 (7)	375.00	60.00

Counterfeits having double line over "POSTES" are plentiful.

A39

Gold Overprint on Treasury Department Stamps

1925

697	A39	1c red	15.00	6.00
698	A39	2c yellow	15.00	6.00
699	A39	3c yellow green	15.00	6.00
700	A39	5c dark gray	65.00	30.00
701	A39	10c deep orange	35.00	10.00
702	A39	1k ultramarine	35.00	15.00
		Nos. 697-702 (6)	180.00	73.00

Deposition of Ahmad Shah Qajar and establishment of provisional government of Reza Shah Pahlavi.
Nos. 697-702 have same center (Persian lion in sunburst) with 6 different frames. Overprint reads: "Post / Provisional Government / of Pahlavi / 9th Abanmah / 1304 / 1925."

Nos. 667-670
Overprinted

1926 Perf. 11½, 11x11½, 11½x11

703	A37	1c orange	5.00	3.00
704	A37	2c magenta	5.00	5.00
705	A37	3c orange brown	5.00	3.00
706	A37	6c black brown	125.00	85.00
		Nos. 703-706 (4)	140.00	96.00

Overprinted to commemorate the Pahlavi dynasty, dated 16 December 1925. Counterfeits exist.

Nos. 448-463
Overprinted

1926 Perf. 11½, 12½x12

707	A31	1c org & maroon	15.00	.25
a.		Inverted overprint	1,600.	
708	A31	2c vio & maroon	15.00	.25
709	A31	3c yel grn & mar	15.00	.25
a.		Inverted overprint	1,250.	
710	A31	6c red & maroon	15.00	.25
711	A31	9c gray & ma-roon	15.00	.25
712	A31	10c red vio & mar	20.00	.35
713	A31	13c dk bl & mar	25.00	.35
714	A31	1k multi	50.00	.35
715	A31	26c dk grn & mar	25.00	.35
716	A31	2k multi	65.00	1.00
717	A31	3k multi	150.00	2.00
718	A31	4k sil, bl & bis brn	500.00	35.00
719	A31	5k multi	200.00	10.00
720	A31	10k multi	700.00	15.00
721	A31	20k multi	750.00	15.00
722	A31	30k multi	800.00	20.00
		Nos. 707-722 (16)	3,360.	100.65

Overprinted to commemorate the Pahlavi government in 1926.
Values for Nos. 707-722 are for stamps perf. 11½, on thick paper. Stamps perf. 12½x12 on thin paper are worth substantially more.
Forgeries exist perf. 12½x12, with either machine overprints or handstamps. Most of these fakes can be identified by the absence of the top serif of the "1" in "1926."

A40   Reza Shah
Pahlavi — A41

1926-29 Typo. Perf. 11

723	A40	1c yellow green	6.00	.25
724	A40	2c gray violet	6.00	.25
725	A40	3c emerald	6.00	.25
727	A40	6c magenta	6.00	.25
728	A40	9c rose	12.00	.50
729	A40	10c bister brown	30.00	5.00
730	A40	12c deep orange	30.00	3.00
731	A40	15c pale ultra	35.00	2.00
733	A41	1k dull bl ('27)	60.00	15.00
734	A41	2k brt vio ('29)	180.00	75.00
		Nos. 723-734 (10)	371.00	101.50

1928 Redrawn

740	A40	1c yellow green	30.00	.25
741	A40	2c gray violet	30.00	.25
742	A40	3c emerald	30.00	.25
743	A40	6c rose	30.00	.50
		Nos. 740-743 (4)	120.00	1.25

On the redrawn stamps much of the shading of the face, throat, collar, etc., has been removed.
The letters of "Postes Persanes" and those in the circle at upper right are smaller. The redrawn stamps measure 20¼x25¾mm instead of 19¾x25¼mm.

A42

Reza Shah
Pahlavi — A43

Perf. 11½, 12, 12½, Compound

1929 Photo.

744	A42	1c yel grn & cer	3.50	.25
745	A42	2c scar & brt blue	3.50	.25
746	A42	3c mag & myr grn	3.50	.25
747	A42	6c yel brn & ol grn	3.50	.25
748	A42	9c Prus bl & ver	5.00	.25
749	A42	10c bl grn & choc	6.00	.25
750	A42	12c gray blk & pur	8.00	.30
751	A42	15c citron & ultra	10.00	.30
752	A42	1k dull bl & blk	15.00	.50
753	A42	24c ol grn & red brn	12.00	.50

Engr.
Perf. 11½

754	A42	2k brn org & dk vio	125.00	3.00
755	A42	3k dark grn & dp rose	150.00	5.00
756	A42	5k red brn & dp green	100.00	5.00
757	A42	1t ultra & dp rose	125.00	10.00
758	A42	2t carmine & blk	200.00	20.00

Engr. and Typo.

759	A43	3t gold & dp vio	175.00	35.00
		Nos. 744-759 (16)	945.00	81.10

For overprints see Nos. 810-817.

Reza Shah
Pahlavi — A44

1931-32 Litho. Perf. 11

760	A44	1c ol brn & ultra	6.00	.25
761	A44	2c red brn & blk	6.00	.25
762	A44	3c lilac rose & ol	6.00	.25
763	A44	6c red org & vio	6.00	.25
764	A44	9c ultra & red org	12.00	.40
765	A44	10c ver & gray	40.00	1.00
766	A44	11c bl & dull red	37.50	35.00
767	A44	12c turq blue & lil rose	45.00	.70
768	A44	16c black & red	50.00	1.75
769	A44	1k car & turq bl	85.00	1.75
770	A44	27c dk gray & dl bl	90.00	1.75
		Nos. 760-770 (11)	383.50	43.35

For overprints see Nos. 818-826.

A45   Reza Shah
Pahlavi — A46

1933-34

771	A45	5d olive brown	3.00	.25
772	A45	10d blue	3.00	.25
773	A45	15d gray	3.00	.25
774	A45	30d emerald	3.00	.25
775	A45	45d turq blue	3.00	.50
776	A45	50d magenta	4.00	.50
777	A45	60d green	5.00	.50
778	A45	75d brown	8.00	1.50
779	A45	90d red	10.00	2.50
780	A46	1r dk rose & blk	25.00	2.00

781	A46	1.20r gray blk & rose	30.00	2.00
782	A46	1.50 citron & bl	35.00	2.00
783	A46	2r lt bl & choc	45.00	2.00
784	A46	3r mag & green	60.00	4.00
785	A46	5r dk brn & red org	225.00	50.00

Nos. 771-785 (15)   462.00   68.50

For overprints see Nos. 795-809.

"Justice"
A47

"Education"
A49

Ruins of
Persepolis
A48

Tehran
Airport
A50

Sanatorium at Sakhtessar — A51

Cement Factory, Chah-Abdul-
Azim — A52

Gunboat
"Palang"
A53

Railway
Bridge
over
Karun
River
A54

Post
Office
and
Customs
Building,
Tehran
A55

1935, Feb. 21   **Photo.**   **Perf. 12½**

786	A47	5d red brn & grn	1.00	.75
787	A48	10d red org & gray black	1.00	.75
788	A49	15d mag & Prus bl	1.50	.75
789	A50	30d black & green	1.50	.75
790	A51	45d ol grn & red brn	2.00	.75
791	A52	75d grn & dark brn	6.00	1.25
792	A53	90d blue & car rose	20.00	5.00

793	A54	1r red brn & pur	60.00	30.00
794	A55	1½r violet & ultra	25.00	10.00

Nos. 786-794 (9)   118.00   50.00

Reign of Reza Shah Pahlavi, 10th anniv.

Stamps of 1933-34
Overprinted in Black

1935   **Perf. 11**

795	A45	5d olive brown	3.00	.50
796	A45	10d blue	3.00	.50
797	A45	15d gray	3.00	.50
798	A45	30d emerald	3.00	.50
799	A45	45d turq blue	10.00	3.00
800	A45	50d magenta	6.00	.50
801	A45	60d green	6.00	.50
802	A45	75d brown	10.00	10.00
803	A45	90d red	35.00	40.00
804	A46	1r dk rose & blk	125.00	200.00
805	A46	1.20r gray black & rose	15.00	2.00
806	A46	1.50r citron & bl	15.00	2.00
807	A46	2r lt bl & choc	40.00	2.00
808	A46	3r mag & green	75.00	10.00
809	A46	5r dk brn & red org	300.00	500.00

Nos. 795-809 (15)   649.00   772.00

Same Overprint on Stamps of 1929

1935   **Perf. 12, 12x12½**

810	A42	1c yel green & cer	500.00	600.00
811	A42	2c scar & brt blue	300.00	400.00
812	A42	3c mag & myr grn	200.00	200.00
813	A42	6c yel brn & ol grn	140.00	150.00
814	A42	9c Prus bl & ver	85.00	100.00

         Perf. 11½

815	A42	1t ultra & dp rose	50.00	75.00
816	A42	2t carmine & blk	50.00	40.00
817	A43	3t gold & dp vio	70.00	50.00

Nos. 810-817 (8)   1,395.   1,615.

No. 817 is overprinted vertically.
Forged overprints exist.

Same Ovpt. on Stamps of 1931-32

1935   **Perf. 11**

818	A44	1c ol brn & ultra	400.00	400.00
819	A44	2c red brn & blk	150.00	150.00
820	A44	3c lilac rose & ol	100.00	125.00
821	A44	6c red org & vio	200.00	200.00
822	A44	9c ultra & red org	200.00	225.00
823	A44	11c blue & dull red	12.50	3.50
824	A44	12c turq bl & lil rose	600.00	900.00
825	A44	16c black & red	15.00	5.00
826	A44	27c dk gray & dull bl	19.00	5.00

Nos. 818-826 (9)   1,696.   2,013.

Forged overprints exist.

Reza Shah
Pahlavi — A56

1935   **Photo.**   **Perf. 11**
        Size: 19x27mm

827	A56	5d violet	2.00	.25
828	A56	10d lilac rose	2.00	.25
829	A56	15d turquoise bl	2.00	.25
830	A56	30d emerald	2.00	.25
831	A56	45d orange	2.00	.25
832	A56	50d dull lt brn	2.75	.30
833	A56	60d ultramarine	10.00	.65
834	A56	75d red orange	10.00	.75
835	A56	90d rose	12.50	.75

        Size: 21½x31mm

836	A56	1r dull lilac	25.00	.50
837	A56	1.50r blue	40.00	.50
838	A56	2r dk olive grn	40.00	.75
839	A56	3r dark brown	45.00	2.00
840	A56	5r slate black	250.00	15.00

Nos. 827-840 (14)   445.25   23.95

Reza Shah Pahlavi
A57   A58

1936-37   **Litho.**   **Perf. 11**
       Size: 20x27mm

841	A57	5d bright vio	4.00	.25
842	A57	10d magenta	4.00	.25
843	A57	15d bright ultra	6.00	.25
844	A57	30d yellow green	25.00	.25
845	A57	45d vermilion	25.00	.25
846	A57	50d black brn ('37)	30.00	.25
847	A57	60d brown orange	25.00	.25
848	A57	75d rose lake	15.00	.25
849	A57	90d rose red	20.00	.35

       Size: 23x31mm

850	A57	1r turq green	20.00	.25
851	A57	1.50r deep blue	20.00	.35
852	A57	2r bright blue	35.00	.35
853	A57	3r violet brown	45.00	.80
854	A57	5r slate green	45.00	1.25
855	A57	10r dark brown & ultra ('37)	225.00	25.00

Nos. 841-855 (15)   544.00   30.35

1938-39   **Size: 20x27mm**   **Perf. 11**

856	A58	5d light violet	2.00	.25
857	A58	10d magenta	2.00	.25
858	A58	15d violet blue	2.00	.25
859	A58	30d bright green	3.00	.25
860	A58	45d vermilion	3.00	.25
861	A58	50d black brown	3.00	.25
862	A58	60d brown orange	3.00	.25
863	A58	75d rose lake	3.00	.25
864	A58	90d rose red ('39)	5.00	.25

       Size: 22½x30mm

865	A58	1r turq green	10.00	.25
866	A58	1.50r deep blue	15.00	.30
867	A58	2r lt blue ('39)	30.00	.30
868	A58	3r violet brown	30.00	.70
869	A58	5r gray grn ('39)	50.00	1.25
870	A58	10r dark brown & ultra ('39)	175.00	10.00

Nos. 856-870 (15)   335.00   15.05

Reza Shah
Pahlavi — A58a

1939, Mar. 15   **Perf. 13**

870A	A58a	5d gray blue	3.00	3.00
870B	A58a	10d brown	3.00	3.00
870C	A58a	30d green	3.00	3.00
870D	A58a	60d dark brown	3.00	3.00
870E	A58a	90d red	5.00	5.00
870F	A58a	1.50r blue	15.00	10.00
870G	A58a	5r lilac	35.00	30.00
870H	A58a	10r carmine	50.00	50.00

Nos. 870A-870H (8)   117.00   107.00

60th birthday of Reza Shah Pahlavi. Printed
in sheets of 4, perf. 13 and imperf. The 1r
violet and 2r orange were not available to the
public. Value, perf. 13 unused $35 each,
imperf. 35% more. Value of sheets (including
1r and 2r), perf. 13 $1,100, imperf. $1,500.

Crown
Prince and
Princess
Fawziya
A59

1939, Apr. 25   **Photo.**   **Perf. 11½**

871	A59	5d red brown	.50	.50
872	A59	10d bright violet	.50	.50
873	A59	30d emerald	1.50	.50
874	A59	90d red	12.00	2.00
875	A59	1.50r bright blue	20.00	4.00

Nos. 871-875 (5)   34.50   7.50

Wedding of Crown Prince Mohammad Reza
Pahlavi to Princess Fawziya of Egypt.

Type of 1909
Overprinted

1927   **Unwmk.**   **Typo.**   **Perf. 11½**

C1	A31	1c org & maroon	3.50	1.50
C2	A31	2c vio & maroon	3.50	1.50
C3	A31	3c grn & maroon	3.50	1.50
C4	A31	6c red & maroon	3.50	1.50
C5	A31	9c gray & maroon	5.00	2.00
C6	A31	10c red vio & mar	7.00	2.50
C7	A31	13c dk bl & mar	8.00	3.00
C8	A31	1k sil, vio & bis brown	8.00	3.00
C9	A31	26c dk grn & mar	8.00	4.00
C10	A31	2k sil, dk grn & bis brown	15.00	5.00
C11	A31	3k sil, gray & bis brown	25.00	7.50
C12	A31	4k sil, bl & bis brown	45.00	17.50
C13	A31	5k gold, brn & bis brown	45.00	15.00
C14	A31	10k gold, org & bis brown	275.00	300.00
C15	A31	20k gold, ol grn & bis brn	275.00	300.00
C16	A31	30k gold, car & bis brown	275.00	300.00

Nos. C1-C16 (16)   1,005.   965.50

Counterfeit overprints are plentiful. They
are found on Nos. 448-463, perf. 12½x12
instead of 11½.
Exist without overprint. Value, set $4,000.

AP1

AP2

AP3

AP4

AP5

Airplane, Value and "Poste aérièn"
Surcharged on Revenue Stamps

1928   **Perf. 11**

C17	AP1	3k yellow brn	125.00	40.00
C18	AP2	5k dark brown	30.00	20.00
C19	AP3	1t gray vio	30.00	20.00
C20	AP4	2t olive bister	30.00	20.00
C21	AP5	3t deep green	45.00	30.00

Nos. C17-C21 (5)   260.00   130.00

AP6   AP7

1928-29   **"Poste aerienne"**

C22	AP6	1c emerald	2.50	.50
	a.	1c yellow green	2.50	.50
	b.	Double overprint	35.00	

C23	AP6	2c light blue	2.50	.25
C24	AP6	3c bright rose	2.50	.25
C25	AP6	5c olive brn	1.25	.25
a.		"5" omitted	2,000.	1,500.
b.		Horiz. pair, imperf. btwn.	300.00	
C26	AP6	10c dark green	2.00	.25
a.		"10" omitted	40.00	
b.		"1" inverted	75.00	
C27	AP7	1k dull vio	3.00	1.00
a.		"1" inverted	100.00	
C28	AP7	2k orange	10.00	3.50
a.		"S" for "s" in "Krs"	200.00	175.00
		Nos. C22-C28 (7)	23.75	6.00

Counterfeits exist.

Revenue Stamps Similar to Nos. C17 to C21, Overprinted like Nos. C22 to C28: "Poste aerienne"

1929

C29	AP1	3k yellow brn	100.00	25.00
C30	AP2	5k dark brn	20.00	10.00
C31	AP3	10k violet	25.00	20.00
C32	AP4	20k olive grn	30.00	25.00
C33	AP5	30k deep grn	40.00	30.00
		Nos. C29-C33 (5)	215.00	110.00

Reza Shah Pahlavi and Eagle — AP8

1930, July 6   Photo.   Perf. 12½x11½

C34	AP8	1c ol bis & brt bl	1.00	1.00
C35	AP8	2c blue & gray blk	1.00	1.00
C36	AP8	3c ol grn & dk vio	1.00	1.00
C37	AP8	4c dk vio & pck bl	1.00	1.00
C38	AP8	5c lt grn & mag	1.00	1.00
C39	AP8	6c mag & bl grn	1.00	1.00
C40	AP8	8c dk gray & dp violet	1.00	1.00
C41	AP8	10c dp ultra & ver	1.00	1.00
C42	AP8	12c slate & org	1.00	1.00
C43	AP8	15c org brn & ol green	1.00	1.00
C44	AP8	1k Prus bl & scar	8.00	4.00

Engr.

C45	AP8	2k black & ultra	10.00	5.00
C46	AP8	3k dk brn & gray green	20.00	6.00
C47	AP8	5k dp red & gray black	15.00	5.00
C48	AP8	1t orange & vio	52.00	12.00
C49	AP8	2t dk grn & red brown	50.00	40.00
C50	AP8	3t brn vio & sl bl	250.00	85.00
		Nos. C34-C50 (17)	415.00	167.00

Nos. C34-C50 Overprinted in Black

1935   Photo.

C51	AP8	1c ol bis & brt bl	1.00	1.00
C52	AP8	2c blue & gray blk	1.00	1.00
C53	AP8	3c ol grn & dk vio	1.00	1.00
C54	AP8	4c dk vio & pck bl	1.00	1.00
C55	AP8	5c lt grn & mag	1.00	1.00
C56	AP8	6c mag & bl grn	1.00	1.00
C57	AP8	8c dk gray & dp violet	1.00	1.00
C58	AP8	10c dp ultra & ver	1.00	1.00
C59	AP8	12c slate & org	1.00	1.00
C60	AP8	15c org brn & ol green	1.00	1.00
C61	AP8	1k Prus bl & scar	75.00	100.00

Engr.

C62	AP8	2k blk & ultra	50.00	65.00
C63	AP8	3k dk brn & gray green	25.00	15.00
C64	AP8	5k dp red & gray black	10.00	10.00
C65	AP8	1t orange & vio	225.00	175.00
C66	AP8	2t dk grn & red brown	45.00	40.00
C67	AP8	3t brn vio & sl bl	75.00	50.00
		Nos. C51-C67 (17)	515.00	465.00

OFFICIAL STAMPS

Four bicolored stamps of this design (1s, 2s, 5s, 10s), with centers embossed, exist, but were never issued or used in Iran. Value $40. They are known imperforate and in many trial colors.

Shah Muzaffar-ed-Din
O1

No. 145 Surcharged in Black

1902   Perf. 12½

O5	O1	5c on 1k red	30.00	30.00
O6	O1	10c on 1k red	30.00	30.00
O7	O1	12c on 1k red	40.00	40.00
		Nos. O5-O7 (3)	100.00	100.00

Nos. 351-363 Overprinted in Black

1903-06

O8	A26	1c violet	5.00	.75
O9	A26	2c gray	5.00	.75
O10	A26	3c green	5.00	.75
O11	A26	5c rose	5.00	.75
O12	A26	10c yel brown	8.00	.75
O13	A26	12c blue	12.00	.75

Perf. 11½x11

O14	A27	1k violet	14.00	7.50
O15	A27	2k ultra	25.00	12.50
a.		Violet overprint	75.00	
O16	A27	5k org brown	40.00	20.00
O17	A27	10k rose red	50.00	19.00
a.		Violet overprint	75.00	
O18	A27	20k orange ('06)	200.00	40.00
O19	A27	30k green ('06)	250.00	90.00
O20	A27	50k green	250.00	125.00
		Nos. O8-O20 (13)	869.00	318.50

Two types of genuine handstamps exist. Type 2 was not regularly issued, and values are for stamps with type 2 handstamps. Values for stamps with type 1 handstamp are considerably higher.

Overprinted on Nos. 368, 370a

O21	A27	2t on 50k grn (Bl)	175.00	75.00
O22	A27	3t on 50k grn (V)	175.00	75.00

Overprinted on Nos. 372, 375, New Value Surcharged in Blue or Black

1905

O23	A27	2t on 50k grn (Bl)	200.00	75.00
O28	A27	3t on 50k grn (Bk)	200.00	75.00

The 2t on 50k also exists with surcharge in black and magenta; the 3t on 50k in violet and magenta. Values about the same.

Regular Issue of 1909 Overprinted

There is a space between the word "Service" and the Persian characters.

1911   Perf. 12½x12

O31	A31	1c org & maroon	15.00	7.50
O32	A31	2c vio & maroon	15.00	7.50
O33	A31	3c yel grn & mar	15.00	7.50
O34	A31	6c red & maroon	15.00	7.50
O35	A31	9c gray & maroon	25.00	13.00
O36	A31	10c multicolored	30.00	13.00

O38	A31	1k multicolored	60.00	45.00
O40	A31	2k multicolored	150.00	90.00
		Nos. O31-O40 (8)	325.00	191.00

The 13c, 26c and 3k to 30k denominations were not regularly issued with this overprint. Dangerous counterfeits exist, usually on reprints.

Regular Issue of 1915 Overprinted

1915   Wmk. 161   Perf. 11, 11½

O41	A33	1c car & indigo	2.50	4.00
O42	A33	2c bl & carmine	2.50	4.00
O43	A33	3c dark green	2.50	4.00
O44	A33	5c red	2.50	4.00
O45	A33	6c ol grn & car	2.50	4.00
O46	A33	9c yel brn & vio	2.50	4.00
O47	A33	10c multicolored	2.50	4.50
O48	A33	12c ultramarine	3.00	5.00
O49	A33	1k multicolored	7.00	10.00
O50	A33	24c multicolored	3.50	10.00
O51	A34	2k sil, bl & rose	7.00	15.00
O52	A34	3k sil, vio & brn	7.00	15.00
O53	A34	5k multicolored	7.50	15.00
O54	A35	1t gold, pur & blk	10.00	20.00
O55	A35	2t gold, grn & brn	10.00	27.50
O56	A35	3t multicolored	12.50	27.50
O57	A35	5t gold, bl & ind	15.00	30.00
		Nos. O41-O57 (17)	100.00	203.50

Coronation of Shah Ahmed.
Reprints have dull rather than shiny overprint. **Value, set, $17.50.**

NEWSPAPER STAMP

No. 429 Overprinted

1909   Typo.   Unwmk.   Perf. 12½

P1	A26	2c gray, *blue*	60.00	30.00

PARCEL POST STAMPS

Regular issues of 1907-08 (types A26, A29) with the handstamp above in blue, black or green are of questionable status as issued stamps. The handstamp probably is a cancellation.

No. 436 Overprinted in Black

1909   Engr.   Perf. 11½

Q18	A29	26c red brown	20.00	15.00

The overprint is printed.

Regular Issue of 1915 Overprinted in Black

1915   Wmk. 161   Perf. 11, 11½

Q19	A33	1c car & indigo	2.50	2.50
Q20	A33	2c bl & carmine	2.50	2.50
Q21	A33	3c dark green	2.50	2.50
Q22	A33	5c red	2.50	2.50
Q23	A33	6c ol green & car	2.50	2.50
Q24	A33	9c yel brn & vio	2.50	2.50
Q25	A33	10c bl grn & yel brn	2.50	2.50
Q26	A33	12c ultramarine	3.00	3.00
Q27	A33	24c multicolored	7.00	7.00
Q28	A33	24c multicolored	3.50	3.50
Q29	A34	2k multicolored	7.00	7.00
Q30	A34	3k multicolored	7.00	7.00
Q31	A34	5k multicolored	7.50	7.50
Q32	A35	1t multicolored	10.00	10.00
Q33	A35	2t gold, grn & brn	10.00	10.00
Q34	A35	3t multicolored	12.50	12.50
Q35	A35	5t multicolored	15.00	15.00
		Nos. Q19-Q35 (17)	100.00	100.00

Coronation of Shah Ahmed.
Reprints have dull rather than shiny overprint. **Value, set, $16.**

IRAQ
i-räk

LOCATION — In western Asia, bounded on the north by Syria and Turkey, on the east by Iran, on the south by Saudi Arabia, and on the west by Jordan
GOVT. — Republic
AREA — 167,925 sq. mi.
POP. — 12,029,700 (est. 1982)
CAPITAL — Baghdad

Iraq, formerly Mesopotamia, a province of Turkey, was mandated to Great Britain in 1920. The mandate was terminated in 1932. For earlier issues, see Mesopotamia.

16 Annas = 1 Rupee.
1000 Fils = 1 Dinar (1932)

Issues under British Mandate

Sunni Mosque — A1

Gufas on the Tigris — A2

Assyrian Winged Bull — A4

Ctesiphon Arch — A5

Motif of Assyrian Origin — A3 | Colors of the Dulaim Camel Corps — A6

Golden Shiah Mosque of Kadhimain — A7

Conventionalized Date Palm or "Tree of Life" — A8

1923-25   Engr.   Wmk. 4   Perf. 12

No.	Type	Description		
1	A1	½a olive grn	1.00	.25
		Never hinged	2.00	
2	A2	1a brown	1.75	.25
		Never hinged	3.50	
3	A3	1½a car lake	1.00	.25
		Never hinged	2.00	
4	A4	2a brown org	1.00	.25
		Never hinged	2.00	
5	A5	3a dp blue	2.00	.25
		Never hinged	4.00	
6	A6	4a dull vio		
		Never hinged	7.00	
7	A7	6a blue grn	2.75	.35
		Never hinged	5.50	
8	A6	8a olive bis	4.00	.75
		Never hinged	8.00	
9	A8	1r grn & brn	6.50	.90
		Never hinged	12.00	
10	A1	2r black	22.50	8.50
		Never hinged	42.50	
11	A1	2r bister ('25)	60.00	4.00
		Never hinged	115.00	
12	A6	5r orange	55.00	17.50
		Never hinged	105.00	
13	A7	10r carmine	67.50	25.00
		Never hinged	135.00	
		Nos. 1-13 (13)	229.50	58.60

For overprints see Nos. O1-O24, O42, O47, O51-O53.

King Faisal I — A9

1927

14	A9	1r red brown	15.00	2.00
		Never hinged	20.00	

See No. 27. For overprint and surcharges see Nos. 43, O25, O54.

King Faisal I
A10   A11

1931

15	A10	½a green	1.00	.30
		Never hinged	1.50	
16	A10	1a chestnut	1.00	.30
		Never hinged	1.50	
17	A10	1½a carmine	1.50	.45
		Never hinged	2.25	
18	A10	2a orange	1.25	.25
		Never hinged	1.90	
19	A10	3a light blue	1.50	.25
		Never hinged	2.25	
20	A10	4a pur brown	2.00	1.75
		Never hinged	3.00	
21	A10	6a Prus blue	2.50	.80
		Never hinged	3.75	
22	A10	8a dark green	3.00	2.00
		Never hinged	4.50	
23	A11	1r dark brown	5.50	1.75
		Never hinged	8.25	
24	A11	2r yel brown	7.75	5.00
		Never hinged	12.00	
25	A11	5r dp orange	27.50	35.00
		Never hinged	42.50	
26	A11	10r red	82.50	85.00
		Never hinged	125.00	
27	A9	25r violet	700.00	800.00
		Never hinged	1,050.	
		Nos. 15-27 (13)	837.00	932.85

See Nos. 44-60. For overprints see Nos. O26-O41, O43-O46, O48-O50, O54-O71.

Issues of the Kingdom
Nos. 6, 15-27 Surcharged in "Fils" or "Dinars" in Red, Black or Green

3 Fils | 25Fils
a | b

100Fils | 1 Dinar
c | d

1932, Apr. 1

28	A10(a)	2f on ½a (R)	.50	.25
29	A10(a)	3f on ½a	.50	.25
a.		Double surcharge	160.00	
b.		Inverted surcharge	160.00	
30	A10(a)	4f on 1a (R)	.75	.06
31	A10(a)	5f on 1a	.65	.25
a.		Double surcharge	275.00	
b.		Inverted Arabic "5"	35.00	40.00
32	A10(a)	8f on 1½a	.75	.50
a.		Inverted surcharge	160.00	
33	A10(a)	10f on 2a	.80	.25
34	A10(a)	15f on 3a	1.75	1.50
35	A10(a)	20f on 4a	2.75	1.50
36	A6(b)	25f on 4a	4.50	3.75
a.		"Flis" for "Fils"	350.00	425.00
b.		Inverted Arabic "5"	425.00	550.00
37	A10(a)	30f on 6a	5.00	.75
38	A10(a)	40f on 8a	4.25	2.75
39	A11(c)	75f on 1r	4.50	4.50
40	A11(c)	100f on 2r	10.00	4.75
41	A11(c)	200f on 5r	42.50	42.50
42	A11(d)	½d on 10r	125.00	95.00
a.		Bar in "½" omitted	1,200.	1,200.
43	A9(d)	1d on 25r	250.00	250.00
		Nos. 28-43 (16)	455.20	408.85

King Faisal I
A12   A13

A14

Values in "Fils" and "Dinars"

1932, May 9   Engr.

44	A12	2f ultra	.50	.25
45	A12	3f green	.50	.25
46	A12	4f vio brown	.50	.25
47	A12	5f gray green	.60	.25
48	A12	8f deep red	2.00	.25
49	A12	10f yellow	1.75	.25
50	A12	15f deep blue	1.90	.25
51	A12	20f orange	3.10	.55
52	A12	25f rose lilac	1.75	.55
53	A12	30f olive grn	5.00	.25
54	A12	40f dark violet	2.25	1.00
55	A13	50f deep brown	3.00	.30
56	A13	75f lt ultra	4.00	.25
57	A13	100f deep green	10.00	1.25
58	A13	200f dark red	25.00	7.00
59	A14	½d gray blue	90.00	40.00
60	A14	1d claret	175.00	150.00
		Nos. 44-60 (17)	326.85	154.65

For overprints see Nos. O55-O71.

A15   A16

King Ghazi — A17

1934-38   Unwmk.

61	A15	1f purple ('38)	.75	.25
62	A15	2f ultra	.45	.25
63	A15	3f green	.45	.25
64	A15	4f pur brown	.45	.25
65	A15	5f gray green	.45	.25
66	A15	8f deep red	.75	.25
67	A15	10f yellow	.95	.25
68	A15	15f deep blue	.95	.25
69	A15	20f orange	.95	.25
70	A15	25f brown vio	1.75	.35
71	A15	30f olive grn	1.50	.25
72	A15	40f dark vio	1.75	.25
73	A16	50f deep brown	3.50	.25
74	A16	75f ultra	4.00	.40
75	A16	100f deep green	5.00	.50
76	A16	200f dark red	7.50	3.00
77	A17	½d gray blue	27.50	20.00
78	A17	1d claret	85.00	30.00
		Nos. 61-78 (18)	143.65	57.25

For overprints see Nos. 226 (in Scott Standard Catalogue, Vol. 3), O72-O88.

OFFICIAL STAMPS

British Mandate
Regular Issue of 1923 Overprinted

ON STATE SERVICE | ON STATE SERVICE
k | l

1923   Wmk. 4   Perf. 12

O1	A1(k)	½a olive grn	1.25	.50
		Never hinged	1.60	
O2	A2(k)	1a brown	1.50	.25
		Never hinged	1.75	
O3	A3(l)	1½a car lake	3.25	.75
		Never hinged	4.50	
O4	A4(k)	2a brown org	2.25	.30
		Never hinged	3.00	
O5	A5(k)	3a deep blue	4.00	.75
		Never hinged	6.00	
O6	A6(l)	4a dull violet	4.25	.50
		Never hinged	7.00	
O7	A7(k)	6a blue green	6.00	1.40
		Never hinged	9.00	
O8	A6(l)	8a olive bister	6.50	1.30
		Never hinged	11.00	
O9	A8(l)	1r green & brn	7.50	1.40
		Never hinged	12.00	
O10	A1(k)	2r black (R)	22.50	9.00
		Never hinged	37.50	
O11	A6(l)	5r orange	65.00	27.50
		Never hinged	105.00	
O12	A7(k)	10r carmine	95.00	60.00
		Never hinged	160.00	
		Nos. O1-O12 (12)	219.00	103.65

Regular Issue of 1923-25 Overprinted

ON STATE SERVICE
m

ON STATE SERVICE
n

1924-25

O13	A1(m)	½a olive green	1.75	.30
		Never hinged	2.25	
O14	A2(m)	1a brown	1.50	.30
		Never hinged	7.00	
O15	A3(m)	1½a car lake	1.50	.30
		Never hinged	1.90	
O16	A4(m)	2a brown org	2.25	.30
		Never hinged	3.00	
O17	A5(m)	3a deep blue	2.75	.30
		Never hinged	3.75	
O18	A6(n)	4a dull violet	5.75	.30
		Never hinged	7.75	
O19	A7(m)	6a blue green	2.75	.30
		Never hinged	3.75	
O20	A6(n)	8a olive bister	5.75	.40
		Never hinged	7.75	
O21	A8(n)	1r green & brn	13.00	1.00
		Never hinged	18.00	
O22	A1(m)	2r bister ('25)	42.50	4.50
		Never hinged	70.00	
O23	A6(n)	5r orange	70.00	50.00
		Never hinged	110.00	
O24	A7(m)	10r brown red	100.00	52.50
		Never hinged	150.00	
		Nos. O13-O24 (12)	249.50	110.50

For overprint see Nos. O42, O47, O51-O53.

No. 14 Overprinted Type "n"
1927

O25	A9	1r red brown	10.00	2.00
		Never hinged	13.50	

Regular Issue of 1931 Overprinted Vertically

o

1931

O26	A10	½a green	.35	3.00
		Never hinged	.35	
O27	A10	1a chestnut	.35	.25
		Never hinged	.35	
O28	A10	1½a carmine	8.75	16.00
		Never hinged	12.00	
O29	A10	2a orange	.85	.25
		Never hinged	1.10	
O30	A10	3a light blue	1.50	.70
		Never hinged	2.10	
O31	A10	4a purple brown	1.75	.90
		Never hinged	2.25	
O32	A10	6a Pruss blue	5.75	12.50
		Never hinged	7.75	
O33	A10	8a dark green	5.75	12.50
		Never hinged	7.75	

Overprinted Horizontally

p

O34	A11	1r dark brown	11.00	12.50
		Never hinged	15.00	
O35	A11	2r yellow brown	22.50	45.00
		Never hinged	32.50	
O36	A11	5r deep orange	52.50	85.00
		Never hinged	75.00	
O37	A11	10r red	95.00	140.00
		Never hinged	140.00	
		Nos. O26-O37 (12)	206.05	328.60

Overprinted Vertically Reading Up

O38	A9(p)	25r violet	925.00	1,200.

For overprints see Nos. O39-O41, O43-O46, O48-O50, O54.

Kingdom

Nos. O15, O19, O22-O24, O26-O31, O33-O35, O38 Surcharged with New Values in Fils and Dinars, like Nos. 28-43

1932, Apr. 1

O39	A10	3f on ½a	4.25	4.00
O40	A10	4f on 1a (G)	3.00	.25
O41	A10	5f on 1a	3.00	.25
a.		Inverted Arabic "5"	52.50	35.00
O42	A3	8f on 1½a	6.75	.60
O43	A10	10f on 2a	4.00	.25
O44	A10	15f on 3a	5.25	2.75
O45	A10	20f on 4a	5.25	2.75
O46	A10	25f on 4a	5.50	2.25
O47	A7	30f on 6a	5.75	2.00
O48	A10	40f on 8a	5.00	4.00
a.		"Flis" for "Fils"	300.00	450.00
O49	A11	50f on 1r	6.75	4.00
O50	A11	75f on 1r	7.50	7.00
O51	A1	100f on 2r	22.00	4.00
O52	A6	200f on 5r	29.00	26.00
O53	A7	½d on 10r	8.00	100.00
a.		Bar in "½" omitted	850.00	975.00
O54	A9	1d on 25r	150.00	210.00
		Nos. O39-O54 (16)	271.00	370.10

Regular Issue of 1932 Overprinted Vertically like Nos. O26-O33

1932, May 9

O55	A12	2f ultramarine	1.10	.25
O56	A12	3f green	1.10	.25
O57	A12	4f violet brn	1.40	.25
O58	A12	5f gray	1.40	.25
O59	A12	8f deep red	1.40	.25
O60	A12	10f yellow	2.50	.25
O61	A12	15f deep blue	3.00	.25
O62	A12	20f orange	3.00	.25
O63	A12	25f rose lilac	3.00	.40
O64	A12	30f olive grn	4.25	.40
O65	A12	40f dark violet	6.50	.40

Overprinted Horizontally Like Nos. O34 to O37

O66	A13	50f deep brown	4.00	.50
O67	A13	75f lt ultra	3.00	1.00
O68	A13	100f deep green	13.50	1.90
O69	A13	200f dark red	25.00	8.75

Overprinted Vertically like No. O38

O70	A14	½d gray blue	17.50	22.50
O71	A14	1d claret	80.00	100.00
		Nos. O55-O71 (17)	171.65	137.45

Regular Issue of 1934-38 Overprinted Type "o" Vertically Reading up in Black

1934-38			**Unwmk.**	
O72	A15	1f purple ('38)	1.10	.50
O73	A15	2f ultramarine	1.10	.25
O74	A15	3f green	.65	.25
O75	A15	4f purple brn	1.10	.25
O76	A15	5f gray green	1.00	.25
O77	A15	8f deep red	4.50	.25
O78	A15	10f yellow	.45	.25
O79	A15	15f deep blue	10.00	1.50
O80	A15	20f orange	1.00	.25
O81	A15	25f brown violet	20.00	6.25
O82	A15	30f olive green	4.50	.25
O83	A15	40f dark violet	5.75	.40

Overprinted Type "p"

O84	A16	50f deep brown	1.00	.65
O85	A16	75f ultramarine	6.75	.90
O86	A16	100f deep green	1.75	1.00
O87	A16	200f dark red	4.50	2.75

Overprinted Type "p" Vertically Reading Up

O88	A17	½d gray blue	11.00	18.00
O89	A17	1d claret	45.00	55.00
		Nos. O72-O89 (18)	121.15	88.95

IRELAND

'īr-lənd

(Eire)

LOCATION — Comprises the entire island of Ireland, except 5,237 square miles at the extreme north
GOVT. — Republic
AREA — 27,136 sq. mi.
POP. — 3,443,405 (1981)
CAPITAL — Dublin

12 Pence = 1 Shilling

Catalogue values for unused stamps in this country are for Never Hinged items, beginning with Scott 99 in the regular postage section, and Scott J5 in the postage due section.

Watermarks

Wmk. 44 — SE in Monogram

Wmk. 262 — Multiple "e"

Overprinted by Dollard, Ltd.

Great Britain Nos. 159-167, 170-172, 179-181 Overprinted

Overprint means "Provisional Government of Ireland."

Overprint measures 15x17½mm Black or Gray Black Overprint

1922, Feb. 17		**Wmk. 33**	**Perf. 15x14**	
1	A82	½p green	1.50	1.50
		Never hinged	2.50	
a.		Inverted overprint	500.00	700.00
		Never hinged	750.00	
2	A83	1p scarlet	1.75	1.50
		Never hinged	2.50	
a.		Inverted overprint	300.00	550.00
b.		Double overprint		
3	A86	2½p ultra	3.75	16.00
		Never hinged	7.50	
4	A87	3p violet	10.00	13.00
		Never hinged	17.00	

5	A88	4p slate green	10.00	20.00
		Never hinged	17.00	
6	A89	5p yel brown	10.00	22.50
		Never hinged	17.50	
7	A90	9p black brown	29.00	40.00
		Never hinged	47.50	
8	A90	10p light blue	17.50	32.50
		Never hinged	30.00	
		Nos. 1-8 (8)	83.50	147.00

The ½p with red overprint is a proof. Value, $150.

Red or Carmine Overprint

1922, Apr.-July				
9	A86	2½p ultra	2.50	9.50
		Never hinged	5.00	
10	A88	4p slate green	17.00	30.00
		(R) Never hinged	30.00	
10A	A88	4p slate green	90.00	140.00
		(C) Never hinged	150.00	
11	A90	9p black brown	35.00	40.00
		(R) Never hinged	62.50	
11A	A90	9p black brown	150.00	175.00
		(C) Never hinged	225.00	
		Nos. 9-11A (5)	294.50	394.50

Overprinted in Black

There is a variation that is 21x14mm. The "h" and "é" are 1mm apart. See Nos. 36-38.

Overprint measures 21½x14mm

1922, Feb. 17		**Wmk. 34**	**Perf. 11x12**	
12	A91	2sh6p brown	57.50	110.00
		Never hinged	125.00	
13	A91	5sh car rose	100.00	200.00
		Never hinged	225.00	
14	A91	10sh gray blue	250.00	400.00
		Never hinged	450.00	
		Nos. 12-14 (3)	407.50	710.00

Overprinted by Alex. Thom & Co.

Overprinted in Black

TWO PENCE
Die I — Four horizontal lines above the head. Heavy colored lines above and below the bottom tablet. The inner frame line is closer to the central design than it is to the outer frame line.
Die II — Three lines above the head. Thinner lines above and below the bottom tablet. The inner frame line is midway between the central design and the outer frame line.

Overprint measures 14½x16mm

1922, Feb. 17		**Wmk. 33**	**Perf. 15x14**	
15	A84	1½p red brown	3.00	3.00
		Never hinged	5.00	
a.		"PENCF"	400.00	350.00
16	A85	2p orange (II)	4.00	2.00
		Never hinged	6.50	
a.		Inverted overprint (II)	400.00	500.00
b.		2p orange (I)	4.00	2.00
		As "b," never hinged	6.50	
c.		Inverted overprint (I)	210.00	300.00
17	A89	6p red violet	17.50	12.50
		Never hinged	30.00	
18	A90	1sh bister	25.00	22.50
		Never hinged	47.50	
		Nos. 15-18 (4)	49.50	40.00

Important: see Nos. 25-26, 31, 35.

Overprinted by Harrison & Sons

Overprinted in Black in Glossy Black Ink

Overprint measures 15¼x17mm

1922, June			**Coil Stamps**	
19	A82	½p green	6.00	25.00
		Never hinged	7.50	

20	A83	1p scarlet	5.00	20.00
		Never hinged	7.50	
21	A84	1½p red brown	8.00	57.50
		Never hinged	12.00	
22	A85	2p orange (I)	30.00	50.00
		Never hinged	47.50	
a.		2p orange (II)	30.00	47.50
		Never hinged	50.00	
		Nos. 19-22 (4)	49.00	152.50

In Harrison overprint, "i" of "Rialtas" extends below the base of the other letters.
The Harrison stamps were issued in coils, either horizontal or vertical. The paper is double where the ends of the strips were overlapped. Mint pairs with the overlap sell for about three times the price of a single. The perforations are often clipped.

Overprinted by Alex. Thom & Co.

Stamps of Great Britain, 1912-22 Overprinted as Nos. 15 to 18, in Shiny to Dull Blue Black, or Red

Note: The blue black overprints can best be distinguished from the black by use of 50-power magnification with a light source behind the stamp.

Overprint measures 14½x16mm

1922, July-Nov.			**Perf. 15x14**	
23	A82	½p green	1.50	2.00
		Never hinged	5.00	
24	A83	1p scarlet	2.25	2.25
		Never hinged	3.75	
25	A84	1½p red brown	6.50	10.00
		Never hinged	15.00	
26	A85	2p orange (II)	4.25	2.25
		Never hinged	7.25	
a.		Inverted overprint (II)	275.00	500.00
b.		2p orange (I)	35.00	4.25
		Never hinged	50.00	
27	A86	2½p ultra (R)	10.00	35.00
		Never hinged	20.00	
28	A87	3p violet	3.00	7.25
		Never hinged	6.50	
29	A88	4p slate green	4.50	4.75
		(R) Never hinged	10.00	
30	A89	5p yellow brown	10.00	17.00
		Never hinged	20.00	
31	A89	6p red violet	9.00	7.50
		Never hinged	20.00	
32	A90	9p blk brn (R)	22.50	26.00
		Never hinged	40.00	
33	A90	9p ol grn (R)	12.00	45.00
		Never hinged	22.50	
34	A90	10p light blue	30.00	60.00
		Never hinged	65.00	
35	A90	1sh bister	15.00	15.00
		Never hinged	35.00	
		Nos. 23-35 (13)	130.50	234.00

Nos. 23, 24, 28, 34 overprinted in dull black, rather than the normal blue-black, are believed to be proofs, pressed into use when supplies of the issued values ran low.

Overprinted as Nos. 12 to 14 in Blue Black (Shiny to Dull)

The "h" and "é" are ½mm apart.

Overprint measures 21x13½mm

1922		**Wmk. 34**	**Perf. 11x12**	
36	A91	2sh6p gray brown	325.	450.
		Never hinged	550.	
37	A91	5sh car rose	325.	500.
		Never hinged	575.	
38	A91	10sh gray blue	1,900.	2,250.
		Never hinged	3,000.	
		Nos. 36-38 (3)	2,550.	3,200.

Overprinted in Blue Black

Overprint measures 15¾x16mm

1922, Dec.		**Wmk. 33**	**Perf. 15x14**	
39	A82	½p green	1.50	2.75
		Never hinged	2.75	
40	A83	1p scarlet	1.50	5.00
		Never hinged	8.00	
41	A84	1½p red brown	3.50	17.50
		Never hinged	8.00	
42	A85	2p orange (II)	15.00	15.00
		Never hinged	25.00	
43	A90	1sh bister	50.00	62.50
		Never hinged	67.50	
		Nos. 39-43 (5)	71.50	102.75

Stamps of Great Britain, 1912-22, Overprinted in Shiny to Dull Blue Black or Red

This overprint means "Irish Free State"

The inner loop of the "9" is an upright oval. The measurement of "1922" is made across the bottom of the numerals and does not include the serif at the top of the "1."

There were 5 plates for printing the overprint on Nos. 44-55. In the impressions from plate I the 12th stamp in the 15th row has no accent on the 2nd "A" of "SAORSTAT." To correct this an accent was inserted by hand, sometimes this was in a reversed position.

On Nos. 56-58 the accent was omitted on the 2nd stamp in the 3rd and 8th rows. Damage to the plate makes the accent look reversed on the 4th stamp in the 7th row. The top of the "t" slants down in a line with the so-called accent.

Overprint measures 15x8½mm "1922" is 6¼mm long

1922-23	Wmk. 33	Perf. 15x14	
44	A82	½p green	1.50	1.50
	Never hinged		2.50	
a.	Accent omitted		1,300.	1,000.
b.	Accent added		125.00	150.00
45	A83	1p scarlet	1.50	1.50
	Never hinged		2.50	
a.	Accent omitted		14,000.	9,000.
b.	Accent added		150.00	175.00
c.	Accent and final "t" omitted		12,000.	7,500.
d.	Accent and final "t" added		250.00	300.00
46	A84	1½p red brown	3.50	17.50
	Never hinged		10.00	
47	A85	2p orange (II)	3.00	5.00
	Never hinged		7.50	
48	A86	2½p ultra (R)	5.00	10.00
	Never hinged		9.00	
a.	Accent omitted		160.00	200.00
49	A87	3p violet	10.00	12.50
	Never hinged		22.50	
a.	Accent omitted		325.00	425.00
50	A88	4p sl green (R)	5.00	9.00
	Never hinged		10.00	
a.	Accent omitted		225.00	300.00
51	A89	5p yel brown	5.75	10.00
	Never hinged		9.50	
52	A89	6p dull violet	3.50	3.00
	Never hinged		7.00	
a.	Accent added		900.00	900.00
53	A90	9p ol green (R)	5.50	12.50
	Never hinged		12.50	
a.	Accent omitted		275.00	350.00
54	A90	10p lt blue	20.00	57.50
	Never hinged		50.00	
55	A90	1sh bister	15.00	15.00
	Never hinged		40.00	
a.	Accent omitted		9,000.	10,000.
b.	Accent added		825.00	900.00

Perf. 11x12 Wmk. 34

56	A91	2sh6p lt brown	62.50	100.00
	Never hinged		140.00	
a.	Accent omitted		450.00	600.00
57	A91	5sh car rose	100.00	200.00
	Never hinged		250.00	
a.	Accent omitted		600.00	900.00
58	A91	10sh gray blue	225.00	500.00
	Never hinged		500.00	
a.	Accent omitted		3,000.	4,000.
	Nos. 44-58 (15)		466.75	955.00

Overprinted by Harrison & Sons Coil Stamps
Same Ovpt. in Black or Blue Black

1923	Wmk. 33	Perf. 15x14	
59	A82	½p green	3.25	15.00
	Never hinged		6.50	
a.	Tall "1"		10.00	55.00
	Never hinged		27.50	
60	A83	1p scarlet	8.50	21.00
	Never hinged		15.00	
a.	Tall "1"		45.00	160.00
	Never hinged		95.00	
61	A84	1½p red brown	8.50	50.00
	Never hinged		22.50	
a.	Tall "1"		95.00	250.00
	Never hinged		190.00	
62	A85	2p orange (II)	12.00	20.00
	Never hinged		17.00	
a.	Tall "1"		15.00	55.00
	Never hinged		30.00	
	Nos. 59-62 (4)		32.25	106.00

These stamps were issued in coils, made by joining horizontal or vertical strips of the stamps. See 2nd paragraph after No. 22. In some strips there were two stamps with the "1" of "1922" 2½mm high and with serif at foot.

In this setting the middle "e" of "eireann" is a trifle above the line of the other letters, making the word appear slightly curved. The lower end of the "1" of "1922" is rounded on Nos. 59-62 instead of flat as on Nos. 44-47.

The inner loop of the "9" is round.

See Nos. 77b, 78b and 79b.

Booklet Panes
For very fine, the perforation holes at top or bottom of the pane should be visible, though not necessarily perfect half circles.

"Sword of Light" — A1

Map of Ireland — A2

Coat of Arms — A3

Celtic Cross — A4

Perf. 15x14

1922-23	Typo.	Wmk. 44	
65	A1	½p emerald	1.50	1.50
	Never hinged		3.00	
a.	Booklet pane of 6		350.00	
66	A2	1p car rose	1.50	1.50
	Never hinged		3.00	
a.	Booklet pane of 6		350.00	
b.	Booklet pane of 3 + 3 labels		400.00	
67	A2	1½p claret	3.50	3.00
	Never hinged		8.00	
68	A2	2p deep green	1.50	.75
	Never hinged		2.50	
a.	Booklet pane of 6		350.00	
b.	Perf. 15 horiz. ('35)		12,500.	2,000.

No. 68b is valued in the grade of fine.

69	A3	2½p chocolate	4.00	8.50
	Never hinged		9.50	
70	A4	3p ultra	3.50	3.00
	Never hinged		7.25	
71	A3	4p slate	6.25	6.25
	Never hinged		12.50	
72	A1	5p deep violet	22.50	15.00
	Never hinged		57.50	
73	A1	6p red violet	7.25	5.75
	Never hinged		14.50	
74	A3	9p violet	35.00	25.00
	Never hinged		125.00	
75	A4	10p brown	17.00	35.00
	Never hinged		57.50	
76	A1	1sh light blue	35.00	17.00
	Never hinged		110.00	
	Nos. 65-76 (12)		138.50	122.25

The 2p was issued in 1922; other denominations in 1923.

No. 68b is a vertical coil stamp.

See Nos. 87, 91-92, 105-117, 137-138, 225-226, 326. For types overprinted see Nos. 118-119. Post 1940 issues in Scott Standard catalogue, Vol. 3.

Overprinted by the Government Printing Office, Dublin Castle and British Board of Inland Revenue at Somerset House, London

Great Britain Nos. 179-181 Ovptd. in Black or Gray Black

The measurement of "1922" is made across the bottom of the numerals and does not include the serif at the top of the "1."

"1922" is 5½mm long

1925	Wmk. 34	Perf. 11x12	
77	A91	2sh6p gray brown	70.00	175.00
	Never hinged		125.00	
78	A91	5sh rose red	95.00	275.00
	Never hinged		160.00	
79	A91	10sh gray blue	225.00	575.00
	Never hinged		425.00	
	Nos. 77-79 (3)		390.00	1,025.

In 1927 the 2sh6p, 5sh and 10sh stamps were overprinted from a plate in which the Thom and Castle clichés were combined, thus including wide and narrow "1922" in the same setting.

Overprinted by British Board of Inland Revenue at Somerset House, London
Pair with "1922" Wide and Narrow
1927

77a	A91	2sh6p	400.	
	Never hinged		775.	
78a	A91	5sh	700.	
	Never hinged		1,350.	
79a	A91	10sh	1,700.	
	Never hinged		3,750.	
	Nos. 77a-79a (3)		2,800.	

Wide "1922" "1922" is 6¼mm long
1927-28

77b	A91	2sh6p	60.00	60.00
	Never hinged		110.00	
78b	A91	5sh ('28)	90.00	140.00
	Never hinged		225.00	
79b	A91	10sh ('28)	250.00	425.00
	Never hinged		550.00	
	Nos. 77b-79b (3)		400.00	625.00

Daniel O'Connell — A5

Perf. 15x14

1929, June 22		Wmk. 44	
80	A5	2p dark green	.60	.55
	Never hinged		1.00	
81	A5	3p dark blue	4.25	14.00
	Never hinged		15.00	
82	A5	9p dark violet	4.75	13.50
	Never hinged		16.00	
	Nos. 80-82 (3)		9.60	28.05

Catholic Emancipation in Ireland, centenary.

Shannon River Hydroelectric Station — A6

1930, Oct. 15

83	A6	2p black brown	1.25	2.75
	Never hinged		4.25	

Opening of the hydroelectric development of the River Shannon.

Farmer with Scythe A7

Cross of Cong and Chalice A8

1931, June 12

84	A7	2p pale blue	1.00	1.50
	Never hinged		2.50	

Bicentenary of Royal Dublin Society.

1932, May 12

85	A8	2p dark green	2.00	.85
	Never hinged		3.00	
86	A8	3p bright blue	4.50	8.00
	Never hinged		7.00	

International Eucharistic Congress.

Type of 1922-23 Issue Coil Stamp

1933-34		Perf. 15 Horizontally	
87	A2	1p rose ('34)	27.50	60.00
	Never hinged		45.00	
a.	1p carmine rose		125.00	300.00
	Never hinged		200.00	

No. 87a has a single perforation at each side near the top, while No. 87 is perforated top and bottom only.
See No. 68b.

Adoration of the Cross A9

Hurling A10

1933, Sept. 18   Perf. 15x14

88	A9	2p slate green	.65	.55
	Never hinged		2.00	
89	A9	3p deep blue	3.00	6.00
	Never hinged		8.75	

Holy Year.

1934, July 27

90	A10	2p green	1.00	1.50
	Never hinged		2.50	

50th anniv. of the Gaelic Athletic Assoc.

Types of 1922-23 Coil Stamps Wmk. 44 Sideways

1934		Perf. 14 Vertically	
91	A1	½p green	30.00	75.00
	Never hinged		45.00	
92	A2	2p gray green	50.00	125.00
	Never hinged		85.00	

Overprinted by Harrison & Sons Great Britain Nos. 222-224 Overprinted in Black

1935   Wmk. 34   Perf. 11x12

93	A91	2sh6p brown	52.50	70.00
	Never hinged		100.00	
94	A91	5sh carmine	200.00	225.00
	Never hinged		350.00	
95	A91	10sh dark blue	400.00	650.00
	Never hinged		1,100.	
	Nos. 93-95 (3)		652.50	945.00

Waterlow printing can be distinguished by the crossed lines in the background of portrait. Previous issues have horizontal lines only.

St. Patrick and Paschal Fire — A11

1937, Sept. 8   Wmk. 44   Perf. 14x15

96	A11	2sh6p bright green	90.00	90.00
	Never hinged		225.00	
97	A11	5sh brown violet	110.00	110.00
	Never hinged		250.00	
98	A11	10sh dark blue	90.00	90.00
	Never hinged		225.00	
	Nos. 96-98 (3)		290.00	290.00

See Nos. 121-123 in Scott Standard catalogue, Vol. 3.

> **Catalogue values for unused stamps in this section, from this point to the end of the section, are for Never Hinged items.**

Allegory of Ireland and Constitution A12

1937, Dec. 29   Perf. 15x14

99	A12	2p plum	2.00	.30
100	A12	3p deep blue	7.00	7.00

Constitution Day.

See Nos. 169-170 in Scott Standard catalogue, Vol. 3.

Father
Theobald
Mathew
A13

1938, July 1
101	A13 2p black brown	2.00	.45
102	A13 3p ultramarine	9.00	9.00

Temperance Crusade by Father Mathew, centenary.

Washington, US Eagle and Harp — A14

1939, Mar. 1
103	A14 2p bright carmine	1.50	.50
104	A14 3p deep blue	13.00	12.00

US Constitution, 150th anniv.

Type of 1922-23
Coil Stamp
1940-46   Wmk. 262   Perf. 15 Horiz.
105	A2 1p car rose ('46)	40.00	32.50
a.	Perf. 14 horiz.	60.00	60.00

Types of 1922-23
1940-42   Perf. 15x14
Size: 18x22mm
106	A1 ½p emerald ('41)	2.75	1.40
a.	Booklet pane of 6	350.00	
107	A2 1p car rose ('41)	2.00	1.40
a.	Booklet pane of 6	6.00	
b.	Bkt. pane of 3 + 3 labels	3,500.	
108	A2 1½p claret ('41)	17.00	1.40
a.	Booklet pane of 6	140.00	
109	A2 2p deep green	2.50	1.40
a.	Booklet pane of 6	12.50	
110	A3 2½p choc ('41)	17.00	3.50
a.	Booklet pane of 6	95.00	
111	A4 3p dull blue ('41)	2.75	1.40
a.	Booklet pane of 6	40.00	
112	A3 4p slate	2.75	1.40
a.	Booklet pane of 6	65.00	
113	A1 5p deep violet	2.75	1.40
114	A1 6p red violet ('42)	2.75	1.40
115	A3 9p violet	2.75	1.40
116	A4 10p olive brown	2.75	1.40
117	A1 1sh blue	175.00	42.50
	Nos. 106-117 (12)	232.75	60.00

POSTAGE DUE STAMPS

D1

1925   Typo.   Wmk. 44   Perf. 14x15
J1	D1 ½p emerald	27.50	42.50
	Never hinged	140.00	
J2	D1 1p carmine	17.00	12.50
	Never hinged	60.00	
J3	D1 2p dark green	32.50	15.00
	Never hinged	125.00	
J4	D1 6p plum	10.50	14.00
	Never hinged	45.00	
	Nos. J1-J4 (4)	87.50	84.00

Catalogue values for unused stamps in this section, from this point to the end of the section, are for Never Hinged items.

1940-70   Wmk. 262
J5	D1 ½p emerald ('43)	27.50	22.50
J6	D1 1p brt carmine ('41)	1.10	.50
J7	D1 1½p vermilion ('52)	2.25	5.00
J8	D1 2p dark green	1.25	.55
J9	D1 3p blue ('52)	2.25	2.00
J10	D1 5p royal purple ('43)	3.50	7.50
J11	D1 6p plum ('60)	4.00	1.75
J12	D1 8p orange ('62)	7.50	7.50
J13	D1 10p red lilac ('65)	8.50	7.00
J14	D1 1sh lt yel grn ('69)	25.00	9.00
	Nos. J5-J14 (10)	82.85	63.30

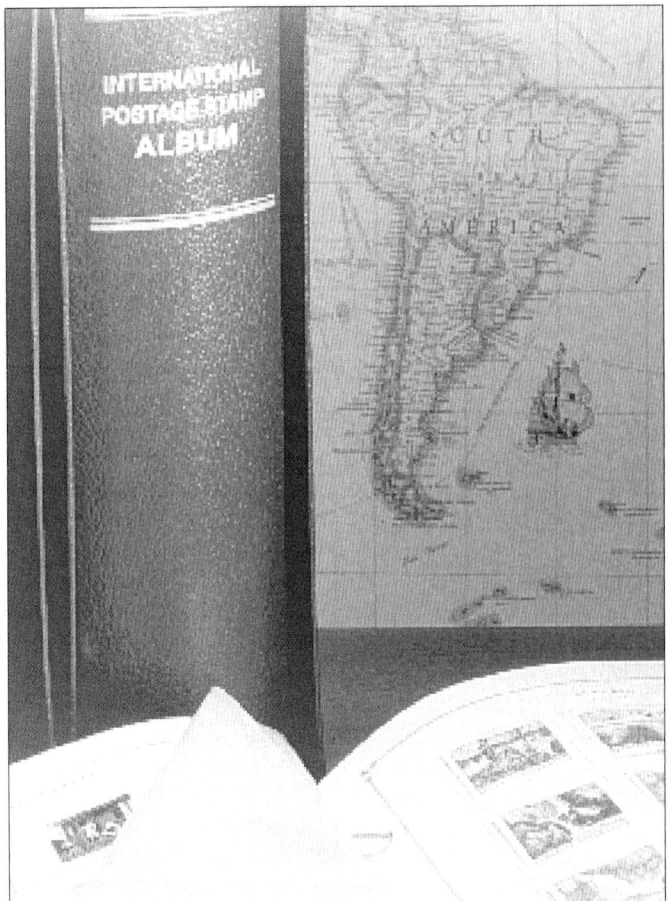

ITALIAN COLONIES

ə-'tal-yən 'kä-lə-nēz

General Issues for all Colonies

100 Centesimi = 1 Lira

Used values in italics are for postaly used stamps. CTO's or stamps with fake cancels sell for about the same as unused, hinged stamps.

Type of Italy, Dante Alighieri Society Issue, in New Colors

Overprinted in Red or Black

1932, July 11	Wmk. 140		Perf. 14
1	A126 10c gray blk	1.60	4.00
	Never hinged	4.00	
	On cover		100.00
2	A126 15c olive brn	1.60	4.00
	Never hinged	4.00	
	On cover		125.00
3	A126 20c slate grn	1.60	2.25
	Never hinged	4.00	
	On cover		100.00
4	A126 25c dk grn	1.60	2.25
	Never hinged	4.00	
	On cover		100.00
5	A126 30c red brn (Bk)	1.60	2.25
	Never hinged	4.00	
	On cover		175.00
6	A126 50c bl blk	1.60	1.50
	Never hinged	4.00	
	On cover		80.00
7	A126 75c car rose (Bk)	2.00	6.50
	Never hinged	5.00	
	On cover		125.00
8	A126 1.25 l dk bl	2.00	9.00
	Never hinged	5.00	
	On cover		240.00
9	A126 1.75 l violet	2.00	14.50
	Never hinged	5.00	
	On cover		525.00
10	A126 2.75 l org (Bk)	2.00	24.00
	Never hinged	5.00	
	On cover		600.00
11	A126 5 l + 2 l ol grn	2.00	27.50
	Never hinged	5.00	
	On cover		—
12	A126 10 l + 2.50 l dp bl	2.00	45.00
	Never hinged	5.00	
	On cover		—
Nos. 1-12,C1-C6 (18)		44.10	259.75

Nos. 1-12, set on overfranked philatelic cover   300.00

Types of Italy, Garibaldi Issue, in New Colors and Inscribed: "POSTE COLONIALI ITALIANE"

1932, July 1			Photo.
13	A138 10c green	4.75	17.50
	Never hinged	12.00	
	On cover		200.00
14	A138 20c car rose	4.75	11.00
	Never hinged	12.00	
	On cover		160.00
15	A138 25c green	4.75	11.00
	Never hinged	12.00	
	On cover		160.00
16	A138 30c green	4.75	17.50
	Never hinged	12.00	
	On cover		200.00
17	A138 50c car rose	4.75	11.00
	Never hinged	12.00	
	On cover		125.00
18	A141 75c car rose	4.75	19.00
	Never hinged	12.00	
	On cover		240.00
19	A141 1.25 l deep blue	4.75	19.00
	Never hinged	12.00	
	On cover		300.00
20	A141 1.75 l + 25c dp bl	9.50	25.00
	Never hinged	24.00	
	On cover		600.00
21	A144 2.55 l + 50c ol brn	9.50	45.00
	Never hinged	24.00	
	On cover		—
22	A145 5 l + 1 l dp bl	9.50	55.00
	Never hinged	24.00	
	On cover		—
Nos. 13-22,C8-C12 (15)		99.75	376.50

Nos. 13-22, set on overfranked philatelic cover   500.00

See Nos. CE1-CE2.

Plowing with Oxen — A1

Pack Camel — A2

Lioness — A3

1933, Mar. 27			Wmk. 140
23	A1 10c ol brn	16.00	22.50
	Never hinged	40.00	
	On cover		180.00
24	A2 20c dl vio	16.00	22.50
	Never hinged	40.00	
	On cover		125.00
25	A3 25c green	16.00	22.50
	Never hinged	40.00	
	On cover		180.00
26	A1 50c purple	16.00	22.50
	Never hinged	40.00	
	On cover		125.00
27	A2 75c carmine	16.00	26.00
	Never hinged	40.00	
	On cover		225.00
28	A3 1.25 l blue	16.00	26.00
	Never hinged	40.00	
	On cover		300.00
29	A1 2.75 l red orange	26.00	47.50
	Never hinged	60.00	
	On cover		650.00
30	A2 5 l + 2 l gray grn	35.00	95.00
	Never hinged	82.50	
	On cover		—
31	A3 10 l + 2.50 l org brn	35.00	145.00
	Never hinged	82.50	
	On cover		—
Nos. 23-31,C13-C19 (16)		381.00	864.50

Nos. 23-31, set on overfranked philatelic cover   800.00

Annexation of Eritrea by Italy, 50th anniv.

Agricultural Implements A4

Arab and Camel — A5

"Eager with New Life" — A7

Steam Roller — A6

1933		Photo.	Perf. 14
32	A4 5c orange	9.50	14.00
	Never hinged	22.50	
	On cover		90.00
33	A5 25c green	9.50	14.00
	Never hinged	22.50	
	On cover		180.00
34	A6 50c purple	9.50	12.50
	Never hinged	22.50	
	On cover		125.00
35	A4 75c carmine	9.50	24.00
	Never hinged	22.50	
	On cover		190.00
36	A5 1.25 l deep blue	9.50	24.00
	Never hinged	22.50	
	On cover		250.00
37	A6 1.75 l rose red	9.50	24.00
	Never hinged	22.50	
	On cover		325.00
38	A4 2.75 l dark blue	9.50	35.00
	Never hinged	22.50	
	On cover		450.00
39	A5 5 l brnsh blk	19.00	47.50
	Never hinged	40.00	
	On cover		—
40	A6 10 l bluish blk	19.00	60.00
	Never hinged	55.00	
	On cover		—
41	A7 25 l gray black	22.50	95.00
	Never hinged	55.00	
	On cover		—
Nos. 32-41,C20-C27 (18)		258.00	695.50

Nos. 32-41, set on overfranked philatelic cover   800.00

10th anniversary of Fascism. Each denomination bears a different inscription. Issue dates: 25 l, Dec. 26; others, Oct. 5.

Mercury and Fasces — A8

1934, Apr. 18			
42	A8 20c red orange	2.75	8.00
	Never hinged	6.00	
	On cover		125.00
43	A8 30c slate green	2.75	8.00
	Never hinged	6.00	
	On cover		180.00
44	A8 50c indigo	2.75	8.00
	Never hinged	6.00	
	On cover		180.00
45	A8 1.25 l blue	2.75	16.00
	Never hinged	6.00	
	On cover		350.00
Nos. 42-45 (4)		11.00	40.00

Nos. 42-45, set on overfranked philatelic cover   180.00

15th annual Trade Fair, Milan.

Scoring a Goal — A9

Soccer Kickoff — A10

1934, June 5			
46	A9 10c olive green	30.00	52.50
	Never hinged	65.00	
	On cover		450.00
47	A9 50c purple	65.00	35.00
	Never hinged	130.00	
	On cover		400.00
48	A9 1.25 l blue	65.00	125.00
	Never hinged	130.00	
	On cover		675.00
49	A10 5 l brown	90.00	400.00
	Never hinged	200.00	
	On cover		—
50	A10 10 l gray blue	90.00	400.00
	Never hinged	200.00	
	On cover		—
Nos. 46-50,C29-C35 (12)		700.00	2,027.

Nos. 46-50, set on overfranked philatelic cover   2,400.

2nd World Soccer Championship.

SEMI-POSTAL STAMPS

Many issues of Italy and Italian Colonies include one or more semi-postal denominations. To avoid splitting sets, these issues are generally listed as regular postage, airmail, etc., unless all values carry a surtax.

AIR POST STAMPS

Italian Air Post Stamps for Dante Alighieri Society Issue in New Colors and Overprinted in Red or Black Like #1-12

1932, July 11	Wmk. 140		Perf. 14
C1	AP10 50c gray blk (R)	3.25	8.00
	Never hinged	7.00	
	On cover		100.00
C2	AP11 1 l indigo (R)	3.25	8.00
	Never hinged	7.00	
	On cover		125.00
C3	AP11 3 l gray (R)	4.00	12.00
	Never hinged	8.50	
	On cover		525.00
C4	AP11 5 l ol brn (R)	4.00	17.50
	Never hinged	8.50	
	On cover		600.00
C5	AP10 7.70 l + 2 l car rose	4.00	24.00
	Never hinged	8.50	
C6	AP11 10 l + 2.50 l org	4.00	47.50
	Never hinged	8.50	
	On cover		—
Nos. C1-C6 (6)		22.50	117.00

Nos. C1-C6, set on flown cover   325.00

Leonardo da Vinci — AP1

1932, Sept. 7	Photo.		Perf. 14½
C7	AP1 100 l dp grn & brn	16.00	14.00
	Never hinged	40.00	
	On cover		725.00

Types of Italian Air Post Stamps, Garibaldi Issue, in New Colors and Inscribed: "POSTE AEREA COLONIALE ITALIANA"

1932, July 1			
C8	AP13 50c car rose	4.75	19.00
	Never hinged	12.00	
	On cover		160.00
C9	AP14 80c green	4.75	19.00
	Never hinged	12.00	
	On cover		240.00
C10	AP13 1 l + 25c ol brn	9.50	30.00
	Never hinged	24.00	
	On cover		450.00
C11	AP13 2 l + 50c ol brn	9.50	30.00
	Never hinged	24.00	
	On cover		—
C12	AP14 5 l + 1 l ol brn	9.50	47.50
	Never hinged	24.00	
Nos. C8-C12 (5)		28.25	122.00

Nos. C8-C12, set on flown cover   550.00

Eagle AP2

Savoia Marchetti 55 — AP3

Savoia Marchetti 55 Over Map of Eritrea AP4

1933			Perf. 14
C13	AP2 50c org brn	14.50	22.50
	On cover		175.00
C14	AP2 1 l blk vio	14.50	22.50
	Never hinged	35.00	
	On cover		200.00
C15	AP3 3 l carmine	27.50	45.00
	Never hinged	75.00	
	On cover		475.00
C16	AP3 5 l olive brn	27.50	45.00
	Never hinged	75.00	
	On cover		550.00
C17	AP2 7.70 l + 2 l slate	35.00	100.00
	Never hinged	85.00	
	On cover		

C18 AP3 10 l + 2.50 l dp
bl 35.00 *100.00*
Never hinged 85.00
On cover
C19 AP4 50 l dk vio 35.00 *100.00*
Never hinged 77.50
On cover —
Nos. C13-C19 (7) 154.50 *387.50*
Nos. C13-C19, set on
flown cover 800.00

50th anniv. of Italian Government of Eritrea.
Issue dates: 50 l, June 1; others, Mar. 27.

Macchi-Costoldi Seaplane — AP5

Savoia S73 — AP6

Winding Propeller AP7 — "More Efficient Machinery" AP8

1933-34
C20 AP5 50c org brn 13.00 21.00
Never hinged 30.00
On cover 180.00
C21 AP6 75c red vio 13.00 21.00
Never hinged 30.00
On cover 190.00
C22 AP5 1 l bis brn 13.00 21.00
Never hinged 30.00
On cover 250.00
C23 AP6 3 l olive gray 13.00 *40.00*
Never hinged 30.00
On cover 400.00
C24 AP5 10 l dp vio 13.00 *40.00*
Never hinged 30.00
On cover —
C25 AP6 12 l bl grn 13.00 *62.50*
Never hinged 30.00
On cover —
C26 AP7 20 l gray blk 19.00 *72.50*
Never hinged 42.50
On cover —
C27 AP8 50 l blue ('34) 34.00 *67.50*
Never hinged 77.50
On cover
Nos. C20-C27 (8) 109.50 *300.00*
Nos. C20-C27, set on flown
cover 800.00

Tenth anniversary of Fascism.
Issue dates: 50 l, Dec. 26; others, Oct. 5.

Natives Hailing Dornier Wal — AP9

1934, Apr. 24
C28 AP9 25 l brown olive 26.00 *240.00*
Never hinged 65.00
On flown cover 475.00
On flown cover, single franking 475.00

Issued in honor of Luigi Amadeo, Duke of the Abruzzi (1873-1933).

Airplane over Stadium AP10

Goalkeeper Leaping — AP11

Seaplane and Soccer Ball AP12

1934, June
C29 AP10 50c yel brn 17.50 *52.50*
Never hinged 37.50
On cover 400.00
C30 AP10 75c dp vio 17.50 *52.50*
Never hinged 37.50
On cover 525.00
C31 AP11 5 l brn blk 65.00 *120.00*
Never hinged 140.00
On cover 950.00
C32 AP11 10 l red org 65.00 *120.00*
Never hinged 140.00
On cover —
C33 AP10 15 l car rose 65.00 *120.00*
Never hinged 140.00
On cover —
C34 AP11 25 l green 65.00 *275.00*
Never hinged 140.00
On cover —
C35 AP12 50 l bl grn 65.00 *275.00*
Never hinged 140.00
On flown cover, single
franking 425.00
Nos. C29-C35 (7) 360.00 *1,015.*
Nos. C29-C35, set on
flown cover 2,400.

World Soccer Championship Games, Rome.
Issued: 50 l, June 21; others, June 5.

AIR POST SPECIAL DELIVERY STAMPS

Garibaldi Type of Italy
Wmk. 140
1932, Oct. 6 Photo. Perf. 14
CE1 APSD1 2.25 l + 1 l dk
vio & sl 11.00 *30.00*
Never hinged 27.50
On cover —
CE2 APSD1 4.50 l + 1.50 l dk
brn & grn 11.00 *47.50*
Never hinged 27.50
On cover —
Nos. CE1-CE2, set on
flown cover 375.00

ITALIAN EAST AFRICA

ə-'tal-yən 'ēst 'a-fri-kə

LOCATION — In eastern Africa, bordering on the Red Sea and Indian Ocean
GOVT. — Italian Colony
AREA — 665,977 sq. mi. (estimated)
POP. — 12,100,000 (estimated)
CAPITAL — Asmara

This colony was formed in 1936 and included Ethiopia and the former colonies of Eritrea and Italian Somaliland. For previous issues see listings under these headings.

100 Centesimi = 1 Lira

Used values in italics are for postaly used stamps. CTO's or stamps with fake cancels sell for about the same as unused, hinged stamps.

Grant's Gazelle — A1

Eagle and Lion — A2

Victor Emmanuel III — A3

Fascist Legionary — A5

Statue of the Nile — A4

Desert Road — A6

Wmk. 140
1938, Feb. 7 Photo. Perf. 14
1 A1 2c red orange 2.40 *1.10*
Never hinged 3.75
On cover 35.00
2 A2 5c brown 2.40 *.25*
Never hinged 3.75
On cover 24.00
3 A3 7½c dk violet 3.25 *4.75*
Never hinged 5.50
On cover 225.00
4 A4 10c olive brown 3.25 *.25*
Never hinged 6.00
On cover 9.50
5 A5 15c slate green 2.40 *.40*
Never hinged 3.75
On cover 35.00
6 A3 20c crimson 2.40 *.25*
Never hinged 3.75
On cover 24.00
7 A6 25c green 3.25 *.25*
Never hinged 6.00
On cover 9.50
8 A1 30c olive brown 2.40 *.80*
Never hinged 4.25
On cover 24.00
9 A2 35c sapphire 3.25 *12.00*
Never hinged 6.25
On cover 225.00
10 A3 50c purple 2.40 *.25*
Never hinged 3.75
On cover 5.50
Engr.
11 A5 75c carmine lake 3.25 *.40*
Never hinged 6.25
On cover 65.00
12 A6 1 l olive green 2.00 *.25*
Never hinged 4.40
On cover 5.50
13 A3 1.25 l deep blue 3.25 *.40*
Never hinged 6.25
On cover 24.00
14 A4 1.75 l orange 17.00 *.25*
Never hinged 42.50
On cover 5.50
15 A2 2 l cerise 3.25 *.40*
Never hinged 6.25
On cover 27.50
16 A6 2.55 l dark brown 20.00 *32.50*
Never hinged 50.00
On cover 450.00
17 A1 3.70 l purple 65.00 *95.00*
Never hinged 160.00
On cover 675.00
18 A5 5 l purple 20.00 *4.75*
Never hinged 42.50
On cover 400.00
19 A2 10 l henna brown 27.50 *20.00*
Never hinged 55.00
On cover 550.00
20 A4 20 l dull green 40.00 *47.50*
Never hinged 77.50
On cover
Nos. 1-20,C1-C11,CE1-CE2 (33) 466.90 *381.90*
Nos. 1-20, set on overfranked philatelic cover 1,100.

Augustus Caesar (Octavianus) A7

Goddess Abundantia A8

1938, Apr. 25 Photo. Perf. 14
21 A7 5c bister brn .85 *2.00*
Never hinged 2.10
On cover 180.00
22 A8 10c copper red .85 *1.25*
Never hinged 2.10
On cover 60.00
23 A7 25c deep green 1.60 *1.25*
Never hinged 3.75
On cover 95.00
24 A8 50c purple 1.60 *.85*
Never hinged 3.75
On cover 52.50
25 A7 75c crimson 1.60 *3.00*
Never hinged 3.75
On cover 210.00
26 A8 1.25 l deep blue 1.60 *8.50*
Never hinged 3.75
On cover 325.00
Nos. 21-26,C12-C13 (8) 9.70 *24.85*
Nos. 21-26, set on overfranked philatelic cover 200.00

Bimillenary of the birth of Augustus Caesar (Octavianus), first Roman emperor.

Rome-Berlin Axis.
Four stamps of type AP8, without "Posta Aerea," were prepared in 1941, but not issued. Value, each $2,400.

Native Boat — A9

Native Soldier — A10

Statue Suggesting Italy's Conquest of Ethiopia — A11

1940, May 11 Wmk. 140
27 A9 5c olive brown .85 *1.20*
Never hinged 2.10
On cover 125.00
28 A10 10c red orange .85 *1.20*
Never hinged 2.10
On cover 72.50
29 A11 25c green 2.40 *2.00*
Never hinged 4.75
On cover 95.00
30 A9 50c purple 2.40 *1.20*
Never hinged 4.75
On cover 72.50
31 A10 75c rose red 2.40 *8.00*
Never hinged 4.75
On cover 300.00
32 A11 1.25 l dark blue 2.40 *6.00*
Never hinged 4.75
On cover 340.00
33 A10 2 l + 75c carmine 2.40 *22.50*
Never hinged 4.75
Nos. 27-33,C14-C17 (11) 25.00 *58.10*
Nos. 27-33, set on overfranked philatelic cover 350.00

Issued in connection with the first Triennial Overseas Exposition held at Naples.

SEMI-POSTAL STAMPS
Many issues of Italy and Italian Colonies include one or more semi-postal denominations. To avoid splitting sets, these issues are generally listed as regular postage, airmail, etc., unless all values carry a surtax.

AIR POST STAMPS

Plane
Flying over
Mountains
AP1

Mussolini
Carved in
Stone
Cliff — AP2

Airplane
over Lake
Tsana
AP3

Bataleur
Eagle — AP4

Wmk. Crowns (140)

1938, Feb. 7　　Photo.　　Perf. 14

C1	AP1	25c slate green	3.25	4.75
		Never hinged	8.00	
		On cover		67.50
C2	AP2	50c olive brown	80.00	.25
		Never hinged	165.00	
		On cover		4.75
C3	AP3	60c red orange	3.25	14.50
		Never hinged	7.50	
		On cover		225.00
C4	AP1	75c orange brn	4.00	2.50
		Never hinged	9.50	
		On cover		27.50
C5	AP4	1 l slate blue	1.25	.25
		Never hinged	3.00	
		On cover		4.75

Engr.

C6	AP2	1.50 l violet	1.75	.40
		Never hinged	4.25	
		On cover		27.50
C7	AP3	2 l slate blue	1.75	1.75
		Never hinged	4.25	
		On cover		60.00
C8	AP1	3 l carmine lake	2.50	6.75
		Never hinged	6.25	
		On cover		140.00
C9	AP4	5 l red brown	80.00	47.50
		Never hinged	160.00	
		On cover		450.00
C10	AP2	10 l violet brn	12.00	14.50
		Never hinged	27.50	
		On cover		600.00
C11	AP1	25 l slate blue	32.50	35.00
		Never hinged	57.50	
		On cover		—
		Nos. C1-C11 (11)	173.75	95.55

Nos. C1-C11, set on over-
franked philatelic flown
cover 　　　　　　　　550.00

Eagle Attacking
Serpent — AP5

1938, Apr. 25　　　　　Photo.

C12	AP5	50c bister brown	.80	2.75
		Never hinged	3.00	
		On cover		60.00
C13	AP5	1 l purple	.80	5.25
		Never hinged	3.00	
		On cover		110.00

Nos. C12-C13, set on
overfranked philatelic
flown cover 　　　　　　87.50

Bimillenary of the birth of Augustus Caesar
(Octavianus), first Roman emperor.

Triennial Overseas Exposition Type

#C14, C16, Tractor. #C15, C17, Plane over
city.

1940, May 11

C14	A10	50c olive gray	2.40	8.00
		Never hinged	6.00	
		On cover		225.00
C15	A9	1 l purple	2.40	8.00
		Never hinged	6.00	
		On cover		300.00
C16	A10	3 l 75c gray		
		blue	3.25	—
		Never hinged	8.00	
		On cover		—
C17	A9	5 l + 2.50 l red		
		brn	3.25	—
		Never hinged	8.00	
		On cover		—
		Nos. C14-C17 (4)	10.50	16.00

Nos. C14-C17, set on
overfranked philatelic
flown cover 　　　　　　　—

AIR POST SPECIAL DELIVERY STAMPS

Plow and
Airplane — APSD1

Wmk. 140

1938, Feb. 7　Engr.　Perf. 14

CE1	APSD1	2 l slate blue	8.00	12.00
		Never hinged	19.00	
		On cover		1,000.
CE2	APSD1	2.50 l dark		
		brown	8.00	20.00
		Never hinged	19.00	
		On cover		—

SPECIAL DELIVERY STAMPS

Victor
Emmanuel
III — SD1

Wmk. 140

1938, Apr. 16　Engr.　Perf. 14

E1	SD1	1.25 l dark green	12.00	12.00
		Never hinged	28.00	
		On cover		325.00
E2	SD1	2.50 l dark carmine	12.00	35.00
		Never hinged	28.00	
		On cover		—

ITALIAN STATES

ə-'tal-yən 'stāts

Watermarks

Wmk. 157 —　　Wmk. 184 —
Large Letter "A"　Interlaced Wavy
　　　　　　　　Lines

Wmk. 184 has double lined letters diagonally across the sheet readiing: "II R R POSTE
TOSCANE."

Wmk. 185 — Crowns in the sheet

The watermark consists of twelve crowns,
arranged in four rows of three, with horizontal
and vertical lines between them. Only parts of
the watermark appear on each stamp.
(Reduced illustration.)

Wmk. 186 —
Fleurs-de-Lis in
Sheet

MODENA

LOCATION — In northern Italy
GOVT. — Duchy
AREA — 1,003 sq. mi.
POP. — 448,000 (approx.)
CAPITAL — Modena

In 1852, when the first postage
stamps were issued, Modena was
under the rule of Duke Francis V of the
House of Este-Lorraine. In June, 1859,
he was overthrown and the Duchy was
annexed to the Kingdom of Sardinia
which on March 17, 1861, became the
Kingdom of Italy.

100 Centesimi = 1 Lira

Values of Modena stamps vary tremendously according to condition. Values are for very fine examples, and values for unused stamps are for examples
with original gum as defined in the catalogue introduction. Extremely fine or
superb examples sell at much higher
prices, and fine or poor examples sell at
greatly reduced prices. In addition, very
fine unused examples without gum sell
for about 20% of the values shown.

Coat of Arms — A1

1852-57　Unwmk.　Typo.　Imperf.
Without Period After Figures of
Value

1	A1	5c blk, green	2,375.	125.00
		No gum	600.00	
		On cover		500.00
a.		Pair, Nos. 1, 6	2,950.	2,000.
		No gum	750.00	
		On cover		7,250.
2	A1	10c blk, rose	600.00	80.00
		No gum	150.00	
		On cover		325.00

---

a.	"EENT. 10"		9,000.	2,650.
	No gum		2,250.	
	On cover			13,500.
b.	"1" of "10" inverted		9,000.	2,650.
	No gum		2,250.	
	On cover			19,500.
c.	"CNET"		1,475.	1,650.
	No gum		375.00	
	On cover			7,500.
d.	No period after "CENT"		2,100.	725.00
	No gum		550.00	
	On cover			3,500.
e.	Pair, Nos. 2, 7		1,300.	2,500.
	No gum		325.00	
f.	Frame below figure of			
	value omitted			1,800.
3	A1	15c blk, yellow	70.00	32.50
		No gum	18.00	
		On cover		170.00
a.	"CETN 15."		9,000.	1,000.
	No gum		2,250.	
b.	No period after "CENT"		325.00	525.00
	No gum		82.50	
	On cover			2,650.
4	A1	25c blk, buff	120.00	45.00
		No gum	30.00	
		On cover		225.00
a.	No period after "CENT"		650.00	1,000.
	No gum		170.00	
	On cover			4,500.
b.	"ENT.25" omitted		1,000.	
	No gum		275.00	
c.	25c black, green (error)		3,600.	2,250.
d.	"N" of "CENT" omitted		725.00	1,650.
	No gum		225.00	
	On cover			7,500.
e.	Raised period after			
	"CENT"			1,500.
5	A1	40c blk, blue	450.00	110.00
		No gum	110.00	
		On cover		525.00
a.	40c black, pale blue		16,500.	1,650.
	No gum			8,250.
b.	No period after "CENT"		1,900.	1,500.
	No gum		575.00	
	On cover			7,500.
c.	As "a," no period after			
	"CENT"		—	—
d.	Pair, Nos. 5, 8		675.00	2,250.
	No gum		240.00	
	On cover			9,000.

Full margins = 1mm.
There are dividing lines between stamps.

Unused examples of No. 5a lack gum.
Used examples of No. 4c have a green
administrative cancellation.
See Nos. PR3-PR4.

Values for pairs

1	A1	5c black, green	4,750.	325.00
		On cover		1,300.
2	A1	10c black, rose	1,250.	300.00
		On cover		1,450.
3	A1	15c black, yellow	145.00	210.00
		On cover		1,350.
4	A1	25c black, buff	240.00	440.00
		On cover		2,200.
5	A1	40c black, blue	925.00	500.00
		On cover		2,500.
5a	A1	40c black, pale blue		16,500.

With Period After Figures of Value

6	A1	5c blk, green	42.50	47.50
		No gum	11.00	
		On cover		190.00
		Single franking, on		
		newspaper		2,250.
a.	5c black, olive green			
	('55)		475.00	145.00
	No gum		30.00	
	On cover			550.00
b.	"ENT"		—	2,750.
	On cover			13,500.
c.	"CNET"		4,350.	3,600.
	No gum		1,250.	
	On cover			16,500.
d.	As "a," "CNET"		2,250.	2,175.
	No gum		750.00	
	On cover			9,000.
e.	"E" of "CENT" sideways		—	5,750.
	No gum			
	On cover			25,000.
f.	As "a," "CEN1"		2,750.	2,500.
	No gum		800.00	
	On cover			10,500.
g.	As "a," no period after			
	"5"		725.00	575.00
	No gum		210.00	
	On cover			2,350.
h.	Double impression, no			
	gum		1,200.	—
i.	As "a," double impres-			
	sion		1,200.	—
	No gum		240.00	
j.	Pair, #6a, 6g		1,300.	2,350.
	No gum		550.00	
	On cover			9,750.
k.	No space between "T"			
	and "5"		12,000.	5,750.
	On cover			25,000.
7	A1	10c blk, rose		
		('57)	475.00	350.00
		No gum	120.00	
		On cover		1,100.
		On cover, single frank-		
		ing		4,400.
a.	"CENE"		1,500.	1,700.
	No gum		500.00	
	On cover			7,500.
b.	"CNET"		650.00	900.00
	No gum		200.00	
	On cover			3,600.
c.	"CE6T"		1,500.	1,700.
	No gum		500.00	
	On cover			7,500.
d.	"N" of "CENT" sideways		11,500.	4,350.
	No gum		3,100.	
	On cover			19,500.
e.	Double impression		1,200.	4,400.
	No gum		400.00	
f.	Raised period after "10"		1,500.	1,825.
	No gum		500.00	
	On cover			7,500.
g.	Pair, one with no period			
	after value		1,200.	2,500.
	No gum		550.00	
	On cover			10,500.

8 A1 40c blk, *blue* ('54) 50.00 125.00
  No gum 12.50
  On cover 550.00
  a. "CNET" 290.00 800.00
    No gum 95.00
    On cover 3,600.
  b. "CENE" 650.00 1,700.
    No gum 200.00
    On cover 7,500.
  c. "CE6T" 650.00 1,700.
    No gum 200.00
    On cover 7,500.
  d. "49" 290.00 900.00
    No gum 90.00
    On cover 3,600.
  e. "4C" 650.00 1,700.
    No gum 135.00
    On cover 7,500.
  f. "CEN.T" 37,500. —
    No gum 22,500.
  g. Space between "T" and period 290.00 825.00
    No gum 90.00
    On cover 9,000.
  h. Pair, one with no period after value 725.00 2,500.
    No gum 290.00
    On cover 10,500.

Values for pairs
6 A1 5c black, *green* 85.00 130.00
  On cover 650.00
6a A1 5c black, *olive green* 950.00 325.00
  On cover 1,300.
7 A1 10c black, *rose* 950.00 800.00
  On cover 2,500.
8 A1 40c black, *blue* 110.00 500.00
  On cover 2,500.
9 A1 1L black 125.00 11,000.
  On cover 37,500.

Wmk. 157
9 A1 1 l black ('53) 57.50 2,250.
  No gum 18.00
  On cover 9,000.
  On cover, single franking 55,000.
  a. With period after "LIRA" 165.00 4,250.
    No gum 47.50
    On cover 21,000.
  b. No period after "1" 145.00 3,600.
    No gum 47.50
    On cover 18,000.

Full margins = 1mm.
There are dividing lines between stamps.

Provisional Government

Coat of Arms — A2

1859 Unwmk.
10 A2 5c green 1,450. 700.00
  No gum 360.00
  On cover 3,250.
  On cover, single franking 37,500.
  a. 5c emerald 1,525. 800.00
    No gum 375.00
    On cover 3,600.
  b. 5c dark green 1,525. 800.00
    No gum 375.00
    On cover 3,600.
11 A2 15c brown 2,325. 4,000.
  No gum 575.00
  On cover 26,000.
  a. 15c gray brown 325.00
    No gum 82.50
  b. 15c black brown 2,625. 5,000.
    No gum 800.00
    On cover 36,500.
  c. No period after "15" 3,000. 4,750.
    No gum 900.00
  d. Period before "CENT" 4,000. 6,500.
    No gum 1,000.
  e. Double impression (#11a) 1,650.
    No gum 600.00
  f. As #11a, no period after "15" 400.00
    No gum 110.00
  g As #11a, period before "CENT" 650.00
    No gum 210.00
12 A2 20c lilac 75.00 1,350.
  No gum 18.00
  On cover 5,500.
  a. 20c violet 4,000. 180.00
    No gum 1,000.
    On cover 1,100.
  b. 20c blue violet 2,400. 180.00
    No gum 600.00
    On cover 1,100.
  c. As #12, no period after "20" 100.00 1,500.
    No gum 32.50
    On cover 7,500.
  d. As #12, "ECNT" 250.00 3,250.
    No gum 72.50
    On cover 16,500.
  e. As #12, "N" inverted 200.00 2,250.
    No gum 65.00
    On cover 11,500.
  f. Double impression (#12b) 6,500.
    No gum —
  g. As #12b, no period after "20" 3,100. 725.00
13 A2 40c carmine 190.00 1,350.
  No gum 47.50
  On cover 9,500.
  On cover, single franking 27,500.
  a. 40c brown rose 190.00 1,350.
    No gum 47.50
    On cover 9,500.
  b. No period after "40" 365.00 2,275.
    No gum 110.00
  c. Period before "CENT" 365.00 —
    No gum 110.00 2,275.
    On cover —
  d. Inverted "5" before the "C", no gum 36,000. 45,000.
14 A2 80c buff 190.00 21,000.
  No gum 47.50
  On cover 165,000.
  On cover, single franking 190,000.
  a. 80c brown orange 190.00 21,000.
    No gum 45.00
    On cover 165,000.
  b. "CENT 8" 365.00 —
    No gum 115.00
  c. "CENT 0" 1,200.
    No gum 375.00
  d. No period after "80" 365.00 —
    No gum 115.00
  e. "N" inverted 365.00 —
    No gum 115.00

Full margins = 1mm.
There are dividing lines between stamps.

Values for pairs
10 A2 5c green 3,100. 1,500.
  On cover 7,250.
11 A2 15c brown 5,250. 12,000.
  On cover —
11a A2 15c gray brown 750.00 —
12 A2 20c lilac 160.00 6,000.
  On cover 32,500.
12b A2 20c blue violet 5,250. 1,800.
  On cover 11,000.
13 A2 40c carmine 400.00 16,500.
  On cover 100,000.
14 A2 80c buff 400.00 —

The reprints of the 1859 issue have the word "CENT" and the figures of value in different type from the originals. There is no frame line at the bottom of the small square in the lower right corner.

NEWSPAPER TAX STAMPS

NT1

Type I

Type II

1853 Unwmk. Typo. *Imperf.*
PR1 NT1 9c blk, *violet* (I) — 3,000.
  On newspaper 16,500. 11,000.
PR2 NT1 9c blk, *violet* (II) 725.00 80.00
  No gum 180.00
  On newspaper 215.00
  a. No period after "9" 1,100. 275.00
    No gum 290.00
    On newspaper 1,100.

Full margins = 1mm.
There are dividing lines between stamps.

All known unused examples of #PR1 lack gum.

1855-57
PR3 A1 9c blk, *violet* 3.65
  No gum .90
  On cover 1.80
  a. No period after "9" 7.25
    No gum 2.75
  b. No period after "CENT" 11.00
    No gum 2.75
  c. Large period after "9" 8.75
    No gum 3.00
PR4 A1 10c blk, *gray vio* ('57) 72.50 250.00
  No gum 18.00
  On newspaper 1,600.
  On newspaper, un-canceled 40.00
  a. "CEN1" 365.00 1,450.
    No gum 100.00
    On newspaper 5,750.
  b. Frameline under value tablet missing 425.00 1,500.
    No gum 110.00
    On newspaper 5,750.

Full margins = 1mm.
There are dividing lines between stamps.

No. PR3 was never placed in use.

NT2

1859
PR5 NT2 10c black 1,100. 2,100.
  No gum 290.00
  On newspaper 8,250.
  On newspaper, un-cancelled 725.00
  a. Double impression 16,250. 20,000.
  b. Vert. guidelines between stamps 1,150.
    No gum 290.00
  c. Blurred and shifted impression 1,700. 3,100.
    On newspaper 11,750.

Full margins = 1 ½mm.
No. PR5 has horizontal guide lines between stamps. No. PR5b is a second printing, which was not issued.

Values for unused pairs
PR5 NT2 10c black 2,750.
PR5b NT2 10c black 2,750.

Values for unused blocks
PR5 NT2 10c black 8,000.
PR5b NT2 10c black 8,000.

These stamps did not pay postage, but were a fiscal tax collected by the postal authorities on newspapers arriving from foreign countries.
The stamps of Modena were superseded by those of Sardinia in February, 1860.

PARMA

LOCATION — Comprising the present provinces of Parma and Piacenza in northern Italy.
GOVT. — Independent Duchy
AREA — 2,750 sq. mi. (1860)
POP. — 500,000 (1860)
CAPITAL — Parma

Parma was annexed to Sardinia in 1860.

100 Centesimi = 1 Lira

Values of Parma stamps vary tremendously according to condition. Values are for very fine examples, and values for unused stamps are for examples with original gum as defined in the catalogue introduction except for No. 8 which is known only without gum. Extremely fine or superb copies sell at much higher prices, and fine or poor stamps sell at greatly reduced prices. In addition, very fine unused stamps without gum sell for about 20% of the values shown.

Crown and Fleur-de-lis
A1 A2

1852 Unwmk. Typo. *Imperf.*
1 A1 5c blk, *yellow* 130.00 150.00
  No gum 32.50
  On cover, single franking 450.00 4,500.
2 A1 10c blk, *white* 130.00 150.00
  No gum 32.50
  On cover 450.00
  On cover, single franking 9,000.
3 A1 15c blk, *pink* 4,200. 95.00
  No gum 1,050.
  On cover 240.00
  a. Tête bêche pair, horiz. 100,000.
    Tête bêche pair, vert., on cover 200,000. 265,000.
  b. Double impression 4,750.
4 A1 25c blk, *violet* 16,500. 235.00
  No gum 4,200.
  On cover 725.00
5 A1 40c blk, *blue* 3,500. 540.00
  No gum 900.00
  On cover 2,100.
  a. 40c black, *pale blue* 6,000. 800.00
    No gum 3,250.

Full margins = ½mm.

Values for pairs
1 A1 5c black, *yellow* 260.00 325.00
  On cover 1,100.
2 A1 10c black 275.00 325.00
  On cover 1,300.
3 A1 15c black, *pink* 8,000. 215.00
  On cover 850.00
4 A1 25c black, *violet* 32,500. 9,750.
  On cover 28,500.
5 A1 40c black, *blue* 6,250. 1,200.
  On cover 4,100.
5a A1 40c black, *pale blue* 14,250. 1,600.
  On cover 5,500.

1854-55
6 A1 5c org yel 9,500. 800.00
  No gum 2,350.
  On cover or newspaper, single franking 2,000.
  a. 5c lemon yellow 12,000. 1,000.
    No gum 3,000.
    On cover 21,000.
  b. Double impression 1,350. 19,000.
7 A1 15c red 12,000. 300.00
  No gum 3,000.
  On cover 450.00
8 A1 25c red brn ('55) — 450.00
  No gum 11,250.
  On cover 1,350.
  a. Double impression 38,000.

Full margins = ½mm.

No. 8 unused is without gum.

Values for pairs
6 A1 5c orange yellow — 1,600.
  On cover 4,500.
6a A1 5c lemon yellow — —
7 A1 15c red 23,500. 475.00
  On cover 1,100.
8 A1 25c red brown — 20,000.
  On cover 55,000.

1857-59
9 A2 15c red ('59) 385.00 360.00
  No gum 95.00
  On cover 1,100.
10 A2 25c red brown 650.00 210.00
  No gum 165.00
  On cover 525.00
11 A2 40c bl, wide "0" ('58) 90.00 550.00
  No gum 22.50
  On cover 2,100.
  a. Narrow "0" in "40" 95.00 650.00
    No gum 22.50
    On cover 2,350.
  b. Pair, #11, 11a 225.00 1,800.
    No gum 72.50
    On cover 7,250.

Full margins = 1mm.

Values for pairs
9 A2 15c red 790.00 850.00
  On cover 2,150.
10 A2 25c red brown 2,500. 4,500.
  On cover 18,000.
11 A2 40c blue 360.00 1,100.
  On cover 4,250.

Provisional Government

A3

1859
12 A3 5c yel grn 600.00 30,000.
  No gum 150.00
  On cover —
  a. 5c blue green 3,000. 5,400.
    No gum 750.00
    On cover 32,500.
13 A3 10c brown 1,200. 650.00
  No gum 300.00
  On cover 3,250.
  a. 10c deep brown 1,200. 650.00
    No gum 300.00
    On cover 3,250.
  b. "1" of "10" inverted 2,400. 5,000.
    No gum 600.00
    On cover 35,000.
  c. Thick "0" in "10" 1,500. 775.00
    No gum 375.00
    On cover 40,000.
14 A3 20c pale blue 1,200. 240.00
  No gum 375.00
  On cover 1,200.
  a. 20c deep blue 1,200. 265.00
    No gum 300.00
    On cover 1,350.
  b. Thick "0" in "20" 1,450. 265.00
    No gum 375.00
    On cover 1,350.
15 A3 40c red 650.00 10,000.
  No gum 180.00
  On cover 50,000.
  a. 40c brown red 24,000. 15,000.
    No gum 6,250.
    On cover 45,000.
  b. Thick "0" in "40" (#15) 775.00 11,250.
    No gum 210.00
    On cover 55,000.
  c. Thick "0" in "40", (#15a) 28,000. 17,000.
    No gum 8,000.
    On cover 50,000.
16 A3 80c olive yellow 8,000. 250,000.
  No gum 2,650.
  a. 80c orange yellow 11,000.
    No gum 3,000.
  b. 80c bister 9,000.
    No gum 2,600.
  c. 80c orange bister 9,750.

d.	No gum	3,000.	
	Thick "0" in "80" (#16)	9,000.	
	No gum	2,500.	
e.	Thick "0" in "80," (#16a)	12,000.	
	No gum	4,000.	

Full margins = 1 ¼mm.

Nos. 12-16 exist in two other varieties: with spelling "CFNTESIMI" and with small "A" in "STATI." These are valued about 50 per cent more than normal stamps.
See Nos. PR1-PR2.

Values for pairs

12	A3	5c yellow green	1,450.	48,500.
		On cover		100,000.
12a	A3	5c blue green	6,800.	10,000.
		On cover		55,000.
13	A3	10c brown	2,900.	1,450.
		On cover		6,750.
14	A3	20c pale blue	2,900.	5,000.
		On cover		30,000.
15	A3	40c red	1,600.	
15a	A3	40c brown red	55,000.	
16	A3	80c orange yel-low	18,000.	
16a	A3	80c olive yellow	27,500.	

NEWSPAPER TAX STAMPS

Type of 1859
Normal Paper ('53)

1853-57   Unwmk.   Typo.   Imperf.

PR1	A3	6c black, deep rose	2,100.	325.00
		No gum	525.00	
		On newspaper		13,500.
		On newspaper, un-canceled		775.00
PR2	A3	9c black, blue	1,100.	12,750.
		No gum	275.00	
		On newspaper		35,000.
		On newspaper, un-canceled		400.00

Full margins = 1 ¼mm.

Thin, Semitransparent Paper ('57)

PR1a	A3	6c black, rose ('57)	140.00	
		No gum	35.00	
PR2a	A3	9c black, blue	72.50	
		No gum	18.00	

These stamps belong to the same class as the Newspaper Tax Stamps of Modena, Austria, etc.
Note following #16 also applies to #PR1-PR2.
Nos. PR1a-PR2a were not issued.
The stamps of Parma were superseded by those of Sardinia in 1860.

ROMAGNA

LOCATION — Comprised the present Italian provinces of Forli, Ravenna, Ferrara and Bologna.
GOVT. — One of the Roman States
AREA — 5,626 sq. mi.
POP. — 1,341,091 (1853)
CAPITAL — Ravenna

Postage stamps were issued when a provisional government was formed pending the unification of Italy. In 1860 Romagna was annexed to Sardinia and since 1862 the postage stamps of Italy have been used.

100 Bajocchi = 1 Scudo

Values of Romagna stamps vary tremendously according to condition. Values are for very fine examples. Values for unused stamps are for examples with original gum as defined in the catalogue introduction. Extremely fine or superb stamps sell at much higher prices, and fine or poor stamps sell at greatly reduced prices. In addition, very fine unused stamps without gum sell for about 20% of the values shown.

A1

1859   Unwmk.   Typo.   Imperf.

1	A1	½b blk, straw	30.00	350.00
		No gum	9.00	
		On cover		1,800.
		On newspaper, single franking		18,000.
a.	Half used as ¼b on cov-er			130,000.
2	A1	1b blk, drab	30.00	180.00
		No gum	9.00	
		On cover		900.00
3	A1	2b blk, buff	42.50	210.00
		No gum	11.00	
		On cover		1,000.
a.	Half used as 1b on cover			6,250.
4	A1	3b blk, dk grn	50.00	360.00
		No gum	12.50	
		On cover		2,500.
5	A1	4b blk, fawn	550.00	165.00
		No gum	150.00	
		On cover		900.00
a.	Half used as 2b on cover			30,000.
6	A1	5b blk, gray vio	60.00	400.00
		No gum	18.00	
		On cover		4,000.
7	A1	6b blk, yel grn	400.00	8,500.
		No gum	120.00	
		On cover		87,500.
a.	Half used as 3b on cover			150,000.
8	A1	8b blk, rose	200.00	1,800.
		No gum	65.00	
		On cover		19,000.
a.	Half used as 4b on cover			150,000.
9	A1	20b blk, gray grn	200.00	2,400.
		No gum	65.00	
		On cover		24,000.

Full margins = 1mm.
There are dividing lines between stamps.

Forged cancellations are plentiful.
Bisects used Oct. 12, 1859 to Mar. 1, 1860.

Values for pairs

1	A1	½b black, straw	80.00	725.00
		On cover		3,650.
2	A1	1b black, drab	80.00	625.00
		On cover		3,000.
3	A1	2b black, buff	110.00	550.00
		On cover		2,200.
4	A1	3b black, dark green	125.00	2,000.
		On cover		10,000.
5	A1	4b black, fawn	1,500.	2,500.
		On cover		12,750.
6	A1	5b black, gray vio-let	165.00	
7	A1	6b black, yellow green		1,000.
8	A1	8b black, rose	475.00	
9	A1	20b black, gray green	475.00	

Values for blocks of 4

1	A1	½b black, straw	165.00	—
2	A1	1b black, drab	165.00	
3	A1	2b black, buff	225.00	
4	A1	3b black, dark green	250.00	
5	A1	4b black, fawn	2,900.	
6	A1	5b black, gray vio-let	325.00	
7	A1	6b black, yellow green	2,200.	
8	A1	8b black, rose	975.00	
9	A1	20b black, gray green	975.00	

These stamps have been reprinted several times. The reprints usually resemble the originals in the color of the paper but there are impressions on incorrect colors and also in colors on white paper. They often show broken letters and other injuries. The Y shaped ornaments between the small circles in the corners are broken and blurred and the dots outside the circles are often missing or joined to the circles.
The stamps of Romagna were superseded by those of Sardinia in February, 1860.

ROMAN STATES

LOCATION — Comprised most of the central Italian Peninsula, bounded by the former Kingdom of Lombardy-Venetia and Modena on the north, Tuscany on the west, and the Kingdom of Naples on the southeast.
GOVT. — Under the direct government of the See of Rome.
AREA — 16,000 sq. mi.
POP. — 3,124,758 (1853)
CAPITAL — Rome

Upon the formation of the Kingdom of Italy, the area of the Roman States was greatly reduced and in 1870 they disappeared from the political map of

Europe. Postage stamps of Italy have been used since that time.

100 Bajocchi = 1 Scudo
100 Centesimi = 1 Lira (1867)

Values of Roman States stamps vary tremendously according to condition. Values are for very fine examples, and values for unused stamps are for examples with original gum as defined in the catalogue introduction. Extremely fine or superb stamps sell at much higher prices, and fine or poor stamps sell at greatly reduced prices. In addition, very fine unused stamps without gum sell for about 20% of the values shown.

Papal Arms
A1   A2

A3   A4

A5   A6

A7   A8

A9   A10

A11

1852   Unwmk.   Typo.   Imperf.

1	A1	½b black, dull violet	65.00	150.00
		No gum	16.50	
		On cover, single franking		600.00
				1,200.
a.	½b black, gray blue	800.00	100.00
		No gum	200.00	
		On cover		300.00
		On cover, single franking		600.00
b.	½b black, gray lilac	800.00	400.00
		No gum	200.00	
		On cover		1,450.
		On cover, single franking		2,500.
c.	½b black, gray	800.00	100.00
		No gum	200.00	
		On cover		300.00
		On cover, single franking		625.00
d.	½b black, reddish vi-olet	4,250.	3,000.
		No gum	1,050.	
		On cover		9,000.
e.	½b black, dark violet	325.00	350.00
		No gum	82.50	
		On cover		1,425.
f.	Tête bêche pair		32,500.
				97,500.
h.	As "a," half used as ¼b on wrapper		60,000.
		As "h," pen canceled		10,000.
i.	As #1, double im-pression		6,750.
j.	Impression on both sides	—	14,500.
k.	As #1a, double im-pression		6,500.
l.	½b black, grayish vi-olet ('64)	67.50	150.00

		No gum	17.50	
		On cover		600.00
2	A2	1b black, gray green	360.00	10.00
		No gum	90.00	
		On cover		30.00
a.	1b black, blue green	180.00	110.00
		On cover		180.00
b.	As "a," half used as ½b on cover		475.00
c.	Grayish oily ink	1,300.	32.50
		No gum	650.00	
		On cover		100.00
d.	Double impression		6,500.
		On cover		32,500.
e.	Impression on both sides	—	14,250.
3	A3	2b black, greenish white	18.00	72.50
		No gum	4.50	
		On cover		210.00
a.	2b black, yellow green	265.00	18.00
		No gum	57.50	
		On cover		55.00
b.	As #3, half used as 1b on cover		6,000.
c.	As "a," half used as 1b on cover		400.00
d.	Grayish oily ink	1,425.	37.50
		No gum	725.00	
		On cover		110.00
e.	No period after "BAJ"	165.00	37.50
		No gum	42.50	
		On cover		130.00
f.	As "a" and "e"	540.00	35.00
		No gum	135.00	
		On cover		110.00
g.	Double impression		6,500.
4	A4	3b black, brown	300.00	60.00
		No gum	75.00	
		On cover		200.00
a.	3b black, light brown	6,000.	180.00
		No gum	1,500.	
		On cover		540.00
b.	3b black, yellow brown	2,675.	45.00
		No gum	675.00	
		On cover		135.00
c.	3b black, yellow buff	2,675.	45.00
		No gum	675.00	
		On cover		135.00
d.	3b black, chrome yellow	47.50	180.00
		No gum	12.00	
		On cover		575.00
e.	One-third used as 1b on circular		3,750.
f.	Two-thirds used as 2b on circular		11,500.
g.	Grayish oily ink	7,750.	235.00
		No gum	3,900.	
		On cover		725.00
h.	Impression on both sides	—	12,000.
i.	Double impression	—	6,600.
j.	Half used as 1½b on cover		12,500.
5	A5	4b black, lem-on	265.00	80.00
		No gum	67.50	
		On cover		210.00
a.	4b black, yellow	265.00	80.00
		No gum	67.50	
		On cover		210.00
b.	4b black, rose brown	12,500.	130.00
		No gum	3,000.	
		On cover		400.00
c.	4b black, gray brown	10,000.	80.00
		No gum	2,500.	
		On cover		210.00
d.	Half used as 2b on cover		2,500.
e.	One-quarter used as 1b on cover		24,000.
f.	Impression on both sides		12,000.
g.	Ribbed paper	325.00	90.00
		No gum	80.00	
		On cover		225.00
h.	Grayish oily ink	24,000.	360.00
		No gum	12,000.	
		On cover		1,100.
i.	As "a," half used as 2b on cover		4,250.
j.	As "a," one-quarter used as 1b on cover		23,500.
6	A6	5b black, rose	250.00	16.00
		No gum	62.50	
		On cover		50.00
a.	5b black, pale rose	265.00	17.50
		No gum	67.50	
		On cover		57.50
c.	Impression on both sides		12,500.
d.	Double impression		6,500.
		On cover		32,500.
e.	Grayish oily ink	1,550.	40.00
		No gum	850.00	
		On cover		140.00
f.	Half used as 2 ½b on cover		60,000.
7	A7	6b black, greenish gray	1,075.	75.00
		No gum	265.00	
		On cover		210.00
a.	6b black, gray	1,650.	80.00
		No gum	400.00	
		On cover		240.00
b.	6b black, grayish li-lac	1,575.	240.00
		No gum	400.00	
		On cover		950.00
c.	Grayish oily ink	4,250.	300.00
		No gum	2,100.	
		On cover		900.00
d.	Double impression		6,500.
		On cover		32,500.
e.	Half used as 3b on cover		4,750.
f.	One-third used as 2b on cover		18,000.

8 A8 7b black, *blue* 1,700. 80.00
No gum 425.00
On cover 300.00
On cover, single
 franking 4,250.
a. Half used as 3¼b on
 cover 30,000.
b. Double impression 6,500.
 On cover 13,000.
c. Grayish oily ink 5,500. 150.00
 No gum 2,750.
 On cover 600.00
9 A9 8b black 625.00 45.00
No gum 160.00
On cover 125.00
a. Half used as 4b on
 cover 9,000.
b. Quarter used as 2b
 on cover 90,000.
c. Double impression —
d. Grayish oily ink 2,500. 225.00
 No gum 1,300.
 On cover 650.00
10 A10 50b dull blue 16,000. 1,800.
No gum 4,000.
On cover 6,750.
On cover, single
 franking 32,500.
a. 50b deep blue
 (worn impression) 30,000. 3,250.
 No gum 5,750.
 On cover (from an
 1864 printing) 50,000.
11 A11 1sc rose 4,000. 3,600.
No gum 1,000.
On cover, with grill
 cancellation 55,000.
On cover, single
 franking, with
 c.d.s. 95,000.

Full margins: Nos. 1-2, 4-5, 10-11 = ½mm; Nos. 3, 6-8 = ¾mm; No. 9 = 1¼mm. There are double dividing lines between stamps on Nos. 1-2, 4-5, 9.

Counterfeits exist of Nos. 10-11. Fraudulent cancellations are found on No. 11.
Covers: Values for Nos. 1-2, 4-5, 9 are for covers bearing stamps with at least one frameline complete on each side; for Nos. 3, 6-8, 10-11, stamps are cut square clear of the design. Covers bearing stamps with framelines missing are worth much less; covers with stamps showing all 8 framelines intact are worth much more.

Nos. 1, 8, 10-11 single frankings are worth much more. Nos. 10-11 with circular datestamps are worth 10-20% more.

Grayish oily ink stamps are from specific 1854 printings. Covers usually are dated 1854.

A12   A13

A14   A15

A16   A17

A18

1867   **Glazed Paper**   *Imperf.*
12 A12 2c black,
 green 95.00 *350.00*
No gum 24.00
On cover 1,100.
On cover, single
 franking 2,150.
a. No period after "Cent" 120.00 *390.00*
 No gum 35.00
 On cover 1,200.
13 A13 3c black,
 gray 1,500. *9,000.*
No gum 275.00
On cover 105,000.
a. 3c black, lilac gray 3,600. *2,400.*
 No gum 900.00
 On cover 19,500.
14 A14 5c black, *light
 blue* 210.00 *240.00*
No gum 52.50
On cover 500.00
On cover, single
 franking 1,500.
a. No period after "5" 415.00 *500.00*
 No gum 105.00
 On cover 1,000.

15 A15 10c black, *ver-
 milion* 2,100. *105.00*
No gum 525.00
On cover 210.00
a. Double impression 6,500.
 On cover 32,500.
16 A16 20c black,
 *copper
 red* (un-
 glazed) 210.00 *135.00*
No gum 52.50
On cover 260.00
a. No period after "20" 600.00 *400.00*
 No gum 160.00
 On cover 800.00
b. No period after
 "CENT" 600.00 *400.00*
 No gum 160.00
 On cover 800.00
17 A17 40c black, *yel-
 low* 225.00 *180.00*
No gum 57.50
On cover 550.00
a. No period after "40" 285.00 *225.00*
 No gum 60.00
 On cover 700.00
18 A18 80c black, *lilac
 rose* 200.00 *500.00*
No gum 50.00
On cover 2,100.
On cover, single
 franking 4,200.
a. No period after "80" 300.00 *750.00*
 No gum 75.00
 On cover 3,150.

Values for stamps in pairs
12 A12 2c black, *green* 575.00
13 A13 3c black, *gray* 1,700.
 21,500.
13a A13 3c black, *lilac
 gray* 9,000.
 On cover —
14 A14 5c black, *light
 blue* 540.00
 On cover 1,100.
15 A15 10c black, *vermilion* 290.00
 On cover 1,150.
16 A16 20c black, *copper red*
 (unglazed) 725.00
 On cover 1,800.
17 A17 40c black, *yellow* 900.00
 On cover 3,600.
18 A18 80c black, *lilac
 rose* 1,250.
 On cover 5,000.

Full margins: No. 12 = 2mm; Nos. 13, 17 = 1¼mm; Nos. 14, 18 = 1½mm at sides, 1mm at top and bottom;
No. 15 = 2½mm at sides, 1mm at top and bottom; No. 16 = 1½mm at sides, ¼mm at top and bottom.
There are double dividing lines between stamps.

Imperforate stamps on unglazed paper, or in colors other than listed, are unfinished remainders of the 1868 issue.
Fraudulent cancellations are found on Nos. 13, 14, 17, 18.
Covers: Values for Nos. 12-18 are for covers bearing stamps with at least one frameline complete on each side.
Covers bearing stamps with framelines missing are worth much less; covers with stamps showing all 8 framelines intact are worth much more.

1868   **Glazed Paper**   **Perf. 13**
19 A12 2c black,
 green 9.00 *90.00*
No gum 2.25
On cover 225.00
On newspaper, sin-
 gle franking 450.00
a. No period after
 "CENT" 11.00 *110.00*
 No gum 2.75
 On cover 270.00
b. Figure "2" omitted 37,500. *16,500.*
c. Vert. pair, imperf
 horiz. 425.00
d. Horiz. pair, imperf
 vert. 425.00
e. Horiz. pair, imperf
 between 800.00
20 A13 3c black,
 gray 55.00 *3,250.*
No gum 13.50
On cover 27,000.
a. 3c black, lilac gray 10,000. *18,000.*
 No gum 2,500.
 On cover 215,000.
21 A14 5c black,
 *light
 blue* 60.00 *60.00*
No gum 15.00
On cover 150.00
On cover, single
 franking 1,350.
a. No period after "5" 75.00 *72.50*
 No gum 15.00
 On cover 180.00
b. No period after
 "Cent" 150.00 *350.00*
 No gum 37.50
 On cover 900.00
c. 5c black, lt bl (un-
 glazed, imperf.,
 without gum) 120.00 —
d. Horiz. pair, imperf
 vert. 425.00
e. Horiz. pair, imperf
 between 800.00 *4,250.*
22 A15 10c black, *orange
 ver* 3.00 *15.00*
No gum .90
On cover 30.00

a. 10c black, *vermilion* 60.00 15.00
 No gum 18.00
 On cover 45.00
b. 10c black, *ver* (un-
 glazed) 1.25 —
 No gum —
c. 10c black, *ver* (un-
 glazed, imperf.,
 without gum) 1.25 —
d. As #22, vert. pair,
 imperf horiz. 240.00
e. As "a," vert. pair,
 imperf vert. 500.00
f. As #22, horiz. pair,
 imperf vert. 275.00
g. As "a," horiz. pair,
 imperf vert. 400.00
h. As #22, horiz. pair,
 imperf between 425.00
i. As "a," horiz. pair,
 imperf between 900.00 *4,750.*
j. As "a," vert. pair,
 imperf between 1,100. *5,000.*
23 A16 20c black,
 *deep
 crimson* 4.75 *30.00*
No gum 1.50
On cover 105.00
a. 20c black, *magenta* 6.00 *42.50*
 No gum 1.50
 On cover 105.00
b. 20c black, *magenta*
 (unglazed) 300.00 *35.00*
 No gum 75.00
 On cover 100.00
c. 20c black, *magenta*
 (imperf., without
 gum) 2.50 —
d. 20c black, *copper
 red* (unglazed) 1,950. *42.50*
 No gum 500.00
 On cover 125.00
e. 20c black, *deep
 crimson* (imperf.,
 without gum) 2.50 —
f. No period after "20"
 (*copper red*) 2,800. *350.00*
 No gum 600.00
 On cover 900.00
g. No period after "20"
 (*mag*) 24.00 *180.00*
 No gum 6.00
 On cover 450.00
h. No period after "20"
 (*deep crimson*) 25.00 *180.00*
 No gum 6.25
 On cover 450.00
i. No period after
 "CENT" (*copper
 red*) 2,800. *375.00*
 No gum 550.00
 On cover 900.00
j. No period after
 "CENT" (*magen-
 ta*) 24.00 *180.00*
 No gum 6.00
 On cover 450.00
k. No period after
 "CENT" (*deep
 crimson*) 24.00 *180.00*
 No gum 6.00
 On cover 450.00
l. Horiz. pair, imperf
 vert. 275.00
m. As #23, horiz. pair,
 imperf between 425.00
n. As "d," horiz. pair,
 imperf between 5,000. *9,500.*
o. As #23, vert. pair,
 imperf between 550.00
p. As "d," vert. pair,
 imperf between —
24 A17 40c black,
 *green-
 ish yel-
 low* 11.00 *125.00*
No gum 2.75
On cover 375.00
a. 40c black, *yellow* 210.00 *75.00*
 No gum 55.00
 On cover 225.00
b. 40c black, *orange
 yellow* 90.00 *750.00*
 No gum 22.50
 On cover 2,250.
c. No period after "40" 15.00 *95.00*
 No gum 3.75
 On cover 290.00
d. Vert. pair, imperf
 horiz. 400.00
e. Horiz. pair, imperf
 vert. 400.00
25 A18 80c black,
 *rose li-
 lac* 210.00 *415.00*
No gum 52.50
On cover 1,650.
a. 80c black, *bright
 rose* 6,500. *60,000.*
 No gum 850.00
 On cover 240,000.
b. 80c black, *rose* (un-
 glazed) 65.00 —
 No gum 16.50
c. No period after "80"
 (*rose lilac*) 110.00 —
 No gum 27.50
 On cover —
d. 80c black, *pale rose
 lilac* (unglazed) 77.50 —
e. 80c black, *pale rose* 55.00 *425.00*
 No gum 13.50
 On cover 1,750.
f. As "e," no period af-
 ter "80" 65.00 *650.00*
 No gum 16.50
 On cover 3,000.
g. As "a," no period af-
 ter "80" 7,000. —
 No gum 1,800.
h. As "e," double im-
 pression —
i. As "e," vert. pair,
 imperf horiz. 400.00
j. As #25, vert. pair,
 imperf between 1,100.
k. As "b," vert. pair,
 imperf horiz. 500.00
l. As "b," horiz. pair,
 imperf vert. 575.00

m. As "e,"horiz. pair,
 imperf vert. 425.00
n. As "b," horiz. pair,
 imperf between —
o. As #25, vert. pair,
 imperf between 1,450.
p. As "e," vert. pair,
 imperf between 1,000.
Nos. 19-25 (7) 352.75 3,985.

Values for stamps in pairs
19 A12 2c black,
 green 24.00 *150.00*
 On cover 425.00
20 A13 3c black, *gray* 100.00 *8,250.*
 65,000.
20a A13 3c black, *lilac
 gray* 20,000.
21 A14 5c black, *light
 blue* 65.00 *125.00*
 On cover 260.00
22 A15 10c black, *orange ver-
 milion* 8.25 *32.50*
 On cover 100.00
23 A16 20c black,
 *deep
 crimson* 12.50 *290.00*
 On cover 1,150.
23d A16 20c black, *copper red*
 (un-
 glazed) 3,750. *290.00*
 On cover 1,150.
24 A17 40c black,
 *greenish
 yellow* 22.00 *325.00*
 On cover 1,350.
25a A18 80c black,
 *bright
 rose* 12,500.
25b A18 80c black, *rose
 lilac* (un-
 glazed) 145.00
25c A18 80c black, *pale
 rose* 100.00 *900.00*
 On cover 3,600.

All values except the 3c are known imperforate vertically or horizontally.
Double impressions are known of the 5c, 10c, 20c (all three colors), 40c and 80c.
Covers: Nos. 21, 25 single frankings are worth much more.
Fraudulent cancellations are found on Nos. 20, 24 and 25.
The stamps of the 1867 and 1868 issues have been privately reprinted; many of these reprints are well executed and it is difficult to distinguish them from the originals. Most reprints show more or less pronounced defects of the design. On the originals the horizontal lines between stamps are unbroken, while on most of the reprints these lines are broken. Most of the perforated reprints gauge 11½.

Roman States stamps were replaced by those of Italy in 1870.

SARDINIA

LOCATION — An island in the Mediterranean Sea off the west coast of Italy and a large area in northwestern Italy, including the cities of Genoa, Turin and Nice.
GOVT. — Kingdom

As a result of war and revolution, most of the former independent Italian States were joined to the Kingdom of Sardinia in 1859 and 1860. On March 17, 1861, the name was changed to the Kingdom of Italy.

100 Centesimi = 1 Lira

Values of Sardinia stamps vary tremendously according to condition. Values are for very fine examples, and values for unused stamps are for examples with original gum as defined in the catalogue introduction. Extremely fine or superb stamps sell at much higher prices, and fine or poor stamps sell at greatly reduced prices. In addition, very fine unused stamps without gum sell for about 20-30% of the values shown.

King Victor Emmanuel II — A1

1851   **Unwmk.**   **Litho.**   *Imperf.*
1 A1 5c gray black 13,000. *2,200.*
No gum 3,250.
On cover 6,500.
On cover, single franking 20,000.
a. 5c black 13,000. *2,200.*
 No gum 3,250.

	On cover		6,500.	
	On cover, single franking		20,000.	
2	A1	20c blue	9,000.	235.00
	No gum		2,250.	
	On cover			700.00
a.	20c deep blue		9,000.	235.00
	No gum		2,250.	
	On cover			700.00
b.	20c pale blue		9,000.	325.00
	No gum		4,000.	
	On cover			975.00
c.	20c deep sky blue		15,750.	1,600.
	No gum		4,000.	
	On cover			4,800.
3	A1	40c rose	19,000.	4,100.
	No gum		4,750.	
	On cover			16,500.
a.	40c violet rose		19,000.	5,850.
	No gum		4,750.	
	On cover			23,500.

Full margins = ½mm.

Values for pairs

1a	A1	5c black	21,500.	4,650.
	On cover			14,500.
2	A1	20c blue	17,750.	1,100.
	On cover			4,250.
3	A1	40c rose	42,500.	10,750.
	On cover			42,500.

Values for blocks of 4

1a	A1	5c black	57,500.
2	A1	20c blue	77,500.
3	A1	40c rose	120,000.

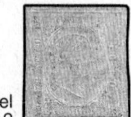

King Victor Emmanuel
II — A2

Vignette & Inscriptions Embossed
1853

4	A2	5c *blue green*	18,000.	1,200.
	No gum		4,500.	
	On cover			3,500.
	On cover, single franking			8,750.
a.	Double embossing			3,250.
	On cover			9,750.
5	A2	20c *dull blue*	19,000.	180.00
	No gum		4,750.	
	On cover			525.00
a.	Double embossing			1,350.
	On cover			4,000.
6	A2	40c *pale rose*	10,750.	900.00
	No gum		2,700.	
	On cover			3,750.
a.	40c *rose*		15,000.	1,450.
	No gum		3,750.	
	On cover			6,000.
b.	Double embossing			2,400.
	On cover			9,500.

Full margins = ¾mm.

Values for pairs

4	A2	5c *blue green*	36,000.	2,750.
	On cover			7,800.
5	A2	20c *dull blue*	40,000.	900.00
	On cover			2,700.
6	A2	40c *pale rose*	25,000.	2,700.
	On cover			10,750.

Values for blocks of 4

4	A2	5c *blue green*	72,500.
5	A2	20c *dull blue*	
6	A2	40c *pale rose*	57,500. 60,000.

King Victor Emmanuel
II — A3

Lithographed Frame in Color,
Colorless Embossed Vignette
1854

7	A3	5c yellow green	32,500.	650.00
	No gum		12,000.	
	On cover			2,750.
	On cover, single franking			6,500.
a.	Double embossing			1,350.
	On cover			5,250.
b.	5c grayish green		3,600.	
	On cover			900.00
c.	5c deep green		3,600.	
8	A3	20c blue	17,500.	175.00
	No gum		6,500.	
	On cover			525.00
a.	Double embossing			540.00
	On cover			1,800.
b.	20c indigo		800.00	
	No gum		190.00	
9	A3	40c rose	90,000.	3,250.
	No gum		40,000.	
	On cover			9,750.
a.	Double embossing			6,000.
	On cover			18,000.
b.	40c brown rose		200.00	
	No gum		45.00	

Full margins = ¾mm.

Values for pairs

7	A3	5c yellow green		1,450.
	On cover		5,750.
b.	5c grayish green	7,250.	
8	A3	20c blue		725.00
b.	20c indigo	2,150.	
9	A3	40c rose		8,250.
	On cover		28,500.

b.	40c brown rose	500.00	

Values for blocks of 4

7	A3	5c yellow green		110,000.
8	A3	5c grayish green	14,250.	
8	A3	20c blue		—
9	A3	20c indigo	4,000.	
9	A3	40c brown rose	9,000.	—

Nos. 7b, 8b and 9b, differing in shade from the original stamps, were prepared but not issued.

King Victor Emmanuel
II — A4

Stamps of this issue vary greatly in color, paper and sharpness of embossing as between the early (1855-59) printings and the later (1860-63) ones. Year dates after each color name indicate whether the stamp falls into the Early or Late printing group.

As a rule, early printings are on smooth thick paper with sharp embossing, while later printings are usually on paper varying from thick to thin and of inferior quality with embossing less distinct and printing blurred. The outer frame shows a distinct design on the early printings, while this design is more or less blurred or even a solid line on the later printings.

Typographed Frame in Color,
Colorless Embossed Vignette

1855-63		**Unwmk.**		*Imperf.*
10	A4	5c green ('62-63)	5.00	12.00
	No gum		1.50	
	On cover			47.50
	On cover, single franking			75.00
a.	5c yellow green ('62-63)		36.00	18.00
	No gum		9.00	
	On cover			75.00
	On cover, single franking			110.00
b.	5c olive green ('60-61)		450.00	75.00
	No gum		90.00	
	On cover			300.00
	On cover, single franking			400.00
c.	5c yellow green ('55-59)		1,000.	175.00
	No gum		250.00	
	On cover			700.00
	On cover, single franking			900.00
d.	5c myrtle green ('57)		6,500.	525.00
	No gum		1,650.	
	On cover			2,000.
	On cover, single franking			2,400.
e.	5c emerald ('55-57)		3,900.	425.00
	No gum		975.00	
	On cover			1,500.
	On cover, single franking			2,100.
f.	Head inverted		—	3,400.
	On cover			34,000.
g.	Double head, one inverted		—	3,400.
	On cover			34,000.
11	A4	10c bister ('63)	5.00	24.00
	No gum		1.50	
	On cover			70.00
a.	10c ocher ('62)		100.00	24.00
	No gum		27.00	
	On cover			70.00
b.	10c olive bister ('62)		210.00	24.00
	No gum		52.50	
	On cover			85.00
c.	10c olive green ('61)		210.00	32.50
	No gum		55.00	
	On cover			110.00
d.	10c reddish brown ('61)		1,650.	175.00
	No gum		425.00	
	On cover			525.00
e.	10c gray brown ('61)		150.00	45.00
	No gum		37.50	
	On cover			135.00
f.	10c olive gray ('60-61)		400.00	60.00
	No gum		100.00	
	On cover			190.00
g.	10c gray ('60)		1,500.	200.00
	No gum		375.00	
	On cover			600.00
h.	10c grayish brown ('59)		145.00	235.00
	No gum		37.50	
	On cover			700.00
i.	10c violet brown ('59)		650.00	325.00
	No gum		160.00	
	On cover			1,000.
j.	10c dark brown ('58)		825.00	400.00
	No gum		210.00	
	On cover			1,150.
k.	Head inverted		—	4,000.
	On cover			40,000.
l.	Double head, one inverted		—	4,000.
	On cover			40,000.
m.	Pair, one without embossing		2,250.	
n.	Half used as 5c on cover (15c rate)			115,000.
o.	Half used as 5c on cover (5c rate)			175,000.
12	A4	20c indigo ('62)	95.00	42.50
	No gum		24.00	
	On cover			125.00
a.	20c blue ('61)		180.00	18.00
	No gum		45.00	
	On cover			52.50
b.	20c light blue ('60-61)		180.00	18.00
	No gum		45.00	

	On cover			52.50
c.	20c Prussian bl ('59-60)		840.00	30.00
	No gum		210.00	
	On cover			90.00
d.	20c indigo ('57-58)		510.00	42.50
	No gum		130.00	
	On cover			190.00
e.	20c sky blue ('55-56)		6,500.	190.00
	No gum		1,650.	
	On cover			575.00
f.	20c cobalt ('55)		3,400.	110.00
	No gum		850.00	
	On cover			325.00
g.	Head inverted		3,250.	1,600.
	No gum		1,650.	
	On cover			16,000.
h.	Double head, one inverted		—	—
i.	Pair, one without embossing		1,200.	—
	No gum		600.00	
j.	Half used as 10c on cover			150,000.
13	A4	40c red ('63)	19.00	42.50
	No gum		4.75	
	On cover			140.00
a.	40c rose ('61-62)		150.00	65.00
	No gum		37.50	
	On cover			190.00
b.	40c carmine ('60)		775.00	385.00
	No gum		170.00	
	On cover			1,250.
c.	40c light red ('57)		3,600.	120.00
	No gum		900.00	
	On cover			375.00
d.	40c vermilion ('55-57)		6,500.	380.00
	No gum		1,650.	
	On cover			1,550.
e.	Head inverted		—	5,500.
	On cover			40,000.
f.	Double head, one inverted		—	5,900.
g.	Pair, one without embossing		1,800.	—
	No gum		900.00	
h.	Half used as 20c on cover			76,000.
14	A4	80c orange yellow ('62)	24.00	410.00
	No gum		6.00	
	On cover			2,800.
a.	80c yellow ('60-61)		27.50	400.00
	No gum		7.50	
	On cover			2,350.
b.	80c yellow ocher ('59)		950.00	760.00
	No gum		240.00	
	On cover			5,250.
c.	80c ocher ('58)		225.00	600.00
	No gum		50.00	
	On cover			4,250.
d.	80c brown orange ('58)		240.00	650.00
	No gum		60.00	
	On cover			4,500.
e.	Head inverted		—	22,000.
	On cover			11,000.
f.	Half used as 40c on cover			4,500.
15	A4	3 l bronze, thin paper ('61)	425.00	3,650.
	No gum		110.00	
	On cover			145,000.
	On cover, single franking			220,000.
a.	Thick, opaque paper		525.00	3,650.
	No gum		175.00	
	On cover			145,000.
	On cover, single franking			220,000.

Nos. 10-15 (6)   573.00   4,181.

Full margins = 1mm.

Values for pairs

10	A4	5c green	11.50	30.00
	On cover			130.00
a.	5c yellow green		72.50	45.00
	On cover			175.00
b.	5c olive green		850.00	190.00
	On cover			725.00
c.	5c yellow green		2,000.	430.00
	On cover			1,575.
d.	5c myrtle green		10,000.	1,100.
	On cover			4,000.
e.	5c emerald		7,250.	900.00
	On cover			4,300.
11	A4	10c bister	11.50	55.00
	On cover			160.00
a.	10c ocher		210.00	55.00
	On cover			160.00
b.	10c olive bister		360.00	80.00
	On cover			215.00
c.	10c olive green		500.00	200.00
	On cover			600.00
f.	10c olive gray		700.00	200.00
	On cover			600.00
h.	10c grayish brown		250.00	475.00
	On cover			1,425.
j.	10c dark brown		1,550.	875.00
	On cover			3,100.
12	A4	20c indigo	230.00	145.00
	On cover			500.00
b.	20c light blue		430.00	62.50
	On cover			260.00
c.	20c prussian blue		1,450.	110.00
	On cover			400.00
d.	20c indigo		1,100.	200.00
	On cover			800.00
f.	20c cobalt		5,750.	375.00
	On cover			1,300.
13	A4	40c red	45.00	160.00
	On cover			575.00
a.	40c rose		360.00	240.00
	On cover			800.00
b.	40c carmine		1,450.	650.00
	On cover			2,000.
c.	40c light red		6,500.	325.00
	On cover			975.00
d.	40c vermilion		10,000.	975.00
	On cover			3,750.
14	A4	80c orange yellow	57.50	1,150.
	On cover			7,900.
a.	80c yellow		65.00	975.00
	On cover			5,250.
b.	80c yellow ocher		1,800.	1,600.
	On cover			11,000.
c.	80c ocher		475.00	1,275.
	On cover			9,000.
d.	80c brown orange		475.00	1,300.
	On cover			9,000.

15	A4	3 l bronze, thin paper	1,000.	10,750.
a.	Thick opaque paper		1,200.	10,750.

Forgeries of the inverted and double head varieties have been made by applying a faked head embossing to printings made without head. These forgeries are plentiful.

Fraudulent cancellations are found on #13-15.

The 5c, 20c and 40c have been reprinted; the embossing of the reprints is not as sharp as that of the originals, the colors are dull and blurred.

NEWSPAPER STAMPS

N1

Typographed and Embossed

1861		**Unwmk.**		*Imperf.*
P1	N1	1c black	6.75	15.00
	No gum		2.00	
	On newspaper or cover			45.00
a.	Numeral "2"		600.00	2,500.
	No gum		550.00	
	On newspaper or cover			16,500.
b.	Figure of value inverted		2,400.	34,000.
c.	Double impression		2,750.	—
	No gum		1,800.	
P2	N1	2c black	180.00	105.00
	No gum		45.00	
	On newspaper or cover			215.00
a.	Numeral "1"		13,000.	32,500.
	No gum		6,500.	
b.	Figure of value inverted		2,400.	34,000.
	No gum		1,200.	

Full margins = 1mm.

Values for pairs

P1	N1	1c black	16.00	30.00
	On newspaper or cover			80.00
P2	N1	2c black	400.00	260.00
	On newspaper or cover			525.00

Forgeries of the varieties of the embossed numerals have been made from printer's waste without numerals.

See Italy No. P1 for 2c buff.

The stamps of Sardinia were superseded in 1862 by those of Italy, which were identical with the 1855 issue of Sardinia, but perforated. Until 1863, imperforate and perforated stamps were issued simultaneously.

TUSCANY

LOCATION — In the north central part of the Apennine Peninsula.

GOVT. — Grand Duchy

AREA — 8,890 sq. mi.

POP. — 2,892,000 (approx.)

CAPITAL — Florence

Tuscany was annexed to Sardinia in 1860.

60 Quattrini = 20 Soldi = 12 Crazie = 1 Lira

100 Centesimi = 1 Lira (1860)

Values of Tuscany stamps vary tremendously according to condition. Values are for very fine examples, and values for unused stamps are for examples with original gum as defined in the catalogue introduction. Extremely fine or superb stamps sell at much higher prices, and fine or poor stamps sell at greatly reduced prices. In addition, very fine unused stamps without gum sell for about 20% of the values shown.

Covers: Values are for covers bearing stamps with four margins. Covers with stamps lacking four margins are worth much less.

Dangerous counterfeits exist of #1-PR1c.

Lion of Tuscany — A1

1851-52   Typo.   Wmk. 185   Imperf.
Blue, Grayish Blue or Gray Paper

1 A1 1q black ('52) 17,500. 2,250.
  No gum 4,500.
  On cover 6,500.
  On newspaper, single franking 13,250.
  On circular, single franking 20,000.
a. 1q black, bluish ('51) 21,000. 2,500.
  No gum 5,500.
  On cover 8,000.
  On newspaper, single franking 14,000.
  On circular, single franking 20,000.
2 A1 1s ocher, grayish 22,000. 2,600.
  No gum 5,500.
  On cover 11,000.
a. 1s orange, grayish 24,000. 2,600.
  No gum 6,000.
  On cover 11,000.
b. 1s yellow, bluish 26,000. 2,900.
  No gum 6,900.
  On cover 12,000.
c. 1s yellow bister, bluish 26,000. 3,000.
  No gum 6,900.
  On cover 12,000.
d. 1s golden yellow, bluish 37,500. 3,100.
  No gum 9,800.
  On cover 12,000.
e. 1s bister orange, grayish 21,000. 2,750.
  No gum 5,500.
  On cover 11,000.
3 A1 2s scarlet 65,000. 10,500.
  No gum 17,000.
  On cover 26,000.
4 A1 1cr carmine 11,000. 180.00
  No gum 3,000.
  On cover 550.00
a. 1cr brown carmine 14,500. 180.00
  No gum 3,900.
  On cover 550.00
5 A1 2cr blue 6,500. 200.00
  No gum 1,700.
  On cover 775.00
a. 2cr greenish blue 14,000. 200.00
  No gum 3,600.
  On cover 900.00
6 A1 4cr green 11,000. 225.00
  No gum 3,000.
  On cover 900.00
a. 4cr bluish green 11,000. 225.00
  No gum 3,000.
  On cover 1,000.
7 A1 6cr slate blue 12,000. 350.00
  No gum 3,000.
  On cover 1,550.
a. 6cr blue 11,000. 350.00
  No gum 3,000.
  On cover 1,550.
b. 6cr indigo 12,000. 375.00
  No gum 3,250.
  On cover 1,550.
8 A1 9cr gray lilac 26,000. 375.00
  No gum 6,900.
  On cover 1,550.
a. 9cr deep violet 26,000. 375.00
  No gum 6,900.
  On cover 1,550.
9 A1 60cr red ('52) 120,000. 32,500.
  No gum 32,500.
  On cover 200,000.

Values for Pairs
1 A1 1q black ('52) 38,500. 5,500.
  On cover 16,500.
2 A1 1s ocher, grayish 50,000. 7,750.
  On cover 32,500.
3 A1 2s scarlet 22,500.
  On cover 55,000.
4 A1 1cr carmine 450.00
  On cover 1,350.
5 A1 2cr blue 700.00
  On cover 2,750.
6 A1 4cr green 27,500. 1,100.
  On cover 4,400.
7a A1 6cr blue 27,500. 1,550.
  On cover 6,000.
8a A1 9cr deep violet 900.00
  On cover 3,600.
9 A1 60cr red ('52) 120,000.

Full margins = ¼mm.

The first paper was blue, later paper more and more grayish. Stamps on distinctly blue paper sell about 20 percent higher, except Nos. 3 and 9 which were issued on blue paper only. Examples without watermark are proofs.
Reprints of Nos. 3 and 9 have re-engraved value labels, color is too brown and impressions blurred and heavy. Paper same as originals.

No. 14a

1857-59   Wmk. 184
White Paper
10 A1 1q black 2,200. 1,150.
  No gum 600.00
  On cover 4,000.
  On newspaper, single franking 7,750.
  On circular, single franking 15,500.
11 A1 1s yellow 65,000. 7,500.
  No gum 17,500.
  On cover 40,000.
12 A1 1cr carmine 14,500. 950.00
  No gum 3,850.
  On cover 2,800.
13 A1 2cr blue 4,800. 200.00
  No gum 1,300.
  On cover 775.00
a. 2cr greenish blue 5,000. 195.00
  No gum 1,300.
  On cover 775.00
b. 2cr yellowish gray green 5,000. 200.00
  No gum 1,300.
  On cover 775.00
14 A1 4cr green 11,000. 225.00
  No gum 3,000.
  On cover 1,000.
a. Inverted value tablet 1,100,000.
b. A1 4cr yellow green 12,000. 250.00
15 A1 6cr deep blue 15,500. 375.00
  No gum 4,000.
  On cover 1,550.
16 A1 9cr gray lilac ('59) 65,000. 7,500.
  No gum 17,000.
  On cover 39,000.

Full margins = ¼mm.

Values for pairs
10 A1 1q black 5,000. 2,750.
  On cover 8,250.
11 A1 1s yellow 19,500.
  On cover 100,000.
12 A1 1cr carmine 38,500. 1,750.
  On cover 5,000.
13 A1 2cr blue 11,000. 700.
  On cover 2,750.
14 A1 4cr green 27,500. 1,100.
  On cover 4,400.
15 A1 6cr deep blue 60,000. 1,550.
  On cover 6,000.
16 A1 9cr gray lilac 20,000.
  On cover 100,000.

Provisional Government

Coat of Arms — A2

1860
17 A2 1c brn lilac 4,150. 1,200.
  No gum 1,100.
  On cover 4,250.
  On newspaper or wrapper, single franking 6,250.
  On circular, single franking 8,250.
a. 1c red lilac 5,250. 1,350.
  No gum 1,400.
  On cover 4,750.
  On newspaper or wrapper, single franking 8,500.
  On circular, single franking 8,750.
b. 1c gray lilac 4,250. 1,200.
  No gum 1,100.
  On cover 4,250.
  On newspaper or wrapper, single franking 6,250.
  On circular, single franking 8,500.
18 A2 5c green 16,000. 325.00
  No gum 4,400.
  On cover 1,000.
  On cover, single franking 30,000.
a. 5c olive green 18,000. 350.00
  No gum 5,000.
  On cover 1,100.
b. 5c yellow green 22,000. 450.00
  No gum 6,000.
  On cover 1,500.
19 A2 10c deep brown 5,750. 75.00
  No gum 1,450.
  On cover 250.00
a. 10c gray brown 5,000. 75.00
  No gum 1,250.
  On cover 250.00
b. 10c purple brown 5,000. 75.00
  No gum 1,250.
  On cover 250.00
20 A2 20c blue 14,500. 225.00
  No gum 3,750.
  On cover 1,000.
a. 20c deep blue 14,500. 275.00
  No gum 3,750.
  On cover 1,200.
b. 20c gray blue 15,000. 275.00
  No gum 4,250.
  On cover 1,200.
21 A2 40c rose 22,000. 440.00
  No gum 5,500.
  On cover 2,200.
a. 40c carmine 22,000. 440.00
  No gum 5,500.
  On cover 2,200.
b. Half used as 20c on cover 300,000.
22 A2 80c pale red brn 40,000. 1,900.
  No gum 10,500.
  On cover 10,000.
  On cover, single franking 15,000.
a. 80c brown orange 40,000. 1,900.
  No gum 10,500.
  On cover 10,000.
  On cover, single franking 15,000.
23 A2 3 l ocher 300,000. 130,000.
  No gum 115,000.

Full margins = ¼mm.

Values for pairs
17b A2 1c gray lilac 8,500. 3,000.
  On cover 9,000.
18 A2 5c green 700.00
  On cover 2,000.
19a A2 10c deep brown 10,000. 250.00
  On cover 750.00
20 A2 20c blue 30,000. 825.00
  On cover 3,300.
21a A2 40c carmine 44,000. 2,750.
  On cover 14,000.
22 A2 80c pale red brown 5,500.
  On cover 27,500.

NEWSPAPER TAX STAMPS

NT1

1854   Unwmk.   Typo.   Imperf.
Yellowish Pelure Paper
PR1 NT1 2s black 100.00
  No gum 30.00
  On newsprint, uncanceled 400.00
a. Tête bêche pair 950.00
b. As "a," one stamp on back 950.00
c. Double impression 700.00

Full margins = 10mm.

This stamp represented a fiscal tax on newspapers coming from foreign countries. It was not canceled when used.

The stamps of Tuscany were superseded by those of Sardinia in 1861.

TWO SICILIES

LOCATION — Formerly comprised the island of Sicily and the lower half of the Apennine Peninsula.
GOVT. — Independent Kingdom
CAPITAL — Naples

The Kingdom was annexed to Sardinia in 1860.

200 Tornesi = 100 Grana = 1 Ducat

Values of Two Sicilies stamps vary tremendously according to condition. Values are for very fine examples, and values for unused stamps are for examples with original gum as defined in the catalogue introduction. Extremely fine or superb copies sell at much higher prices, and fine or poor copies sell at greatly reduced prices. In addition, very fine unused stamps without gum sell for about 20%-30% of the values shown.

Naples

Coat of Arms
A1   A2

A3   A4

A5   A6

A7

1858   Engr.   Wmk. 186   Imperf.
1 A1 ½g pale lake 2,100. 360.00
  No gum 525.00
  On cover 1,100.
  Single franking on newspaper or wrapper 1,600.
  Single franking on circular 2,150.
a. ½g rose lake 2,100. 360.00
  No gum 525.00
  On cover 1,100.
  Single franking on newspaper or wrapper 1,600.
  Single franking on circular 2,150.
b. ½g lake 2,700. 600.00
  No gum 675.00
  On cover 1,800.
  Single franking on newspaper or wrapper 2,650.
  Single franking on circular 3,500.
c. ½g carmine lake 3,275. 800.00
  No gum 825.00
  On cover 2,400.
  Single franking on newspaper or wrapper 3,500.
  Single franking on circular 4,750.
d. Half used as ¼g on newspaper 240,000.
2 A2 1g pale lake 1,050. 42.50
  No gum 260.00
  On cover 120.00
a. 1g rose lake 725.00 45.00
  No gum 180.00
  On cover 120.00
b. 1g brown lake 1,800. 90.00
  No gum 450.00
  On cover 275.00
c. 1g carmine lake 1,050. 72.50
  No gum 275.00
  On cover 215.00
d. Printed on both sides 2,000.
e. Printed on both sides, one inverted 1,000.
  On cover 4,000.
3 A3 2g pale lake 450.00 16.00
  No gum 110.00
  On cover 37.50
a. 2g rose lake 450.00 16.00
  No gum 110.00
  On cover 37.50
b. 2g lake 750.00 25.00
  No gum 160.00
  On cover 72.50
c. 2g carmine lake 900.00 25.00
  No gum 225.00
  On cover 65.00
d. Impression of 1g on reverse 1,800.
e. Double impression 10,000.
  On cover 32,750.
f. Printed on both sides 2,000.
4 A4 5g brown lake 3,600. 75.00
  No gum 900.00
  On cover 225.00
a. 5g rose lake 3,000. 75.00
  No gum 750.00
  On cover 225.00
b. 5g carmine lake 4,500. 75.00
  No gum 1,100.
  On cover 225.00
d. Printed on both sides 5,000.
e. 5g rose carmine 6,000. 180.00
  No gum 1,500.
  On cover 550.00
f. 5g bright carmine 6,500. 210.00
  No gum 1,650.
  On cover 650.00
g. 5g dark carmine 7,750. 300.00
  No gum 1,950.
  On cover 1,000.
5 A5 10g rose lake 6,500. 210.00
  No gum 1,650.
  On cover 600.00
a. 10g lake 7,250. 350.00
  No gum 1,800.
  On cover 1,100.
b. 10g carmine lake 7,250. 350.00
  No gum 1,800.
  On cover 1,100.
c. Printed on both sides 16,250.
d. Double impression 17,000.
  On cover 55,000.
6 A6 20g rose lake 6,000. 750.00
  No gum 1,500.
  On cover 3,000.
a. 20g lake 6,000. 900.00
  No gum 1,500.
  On cover 3,250.
b. Double impression 60,000.
c. 20g pale rose 9,000. 1,500.
  No gum 1,800.
  On cover 6,000.
d. 20g pale car rose 10,000. 1,800.
  No gum 2,500.
  On cover 7,000.
7 A7 50g rose lake 12,000. 2,700.
  No gum 3,000.
  On cover 32,500.

a.	50g lake	12,000.	2,700.
	No gum	2,900.	
	On cover		29,000.

Nos. 1-2, 4-7 have been reprinted in bright rose and Nos. 1, 7 in dull brown. The reprints are on thick unwatermarked paper. Value $8 each.

Values for pairs

1	A1	½g pale lake	4,200.	750.00
		On cover		2,200.
1b	A1	½g pale lake	5,500.	1,150.
		On cover		3,100.
2	A2	1g pale lake	2,200.	110.00
		On cover		275.00
2a	A2	1g rose lake	1,300.	110.00
		On cover		275.00
3	A3	2g pale lake	875.00	40.00
		On cover		100.00
3a	A3	2g rose lake	875.00	40.00
		On cover		100.00
4a	A4	5g rose lake	5,400.	440.00
		On cover		1,300.
4e	A4	5g rose carmine	11,500.	1,100.
		On cover		3,250.
5	A5	10g rose lake	12,750.	1,750.
		On cover		5,250.
5b	A5	10g carmine lake	13,250.	2,550.
		On cover		7,600.
6	A6	20g rose lake	11,000.	4,000.
		On cover		16,000.
6c	A6	20g pale car rose	16,250.	5,800.
		On cover		20,000.
7	A7	50g rose lake	25,000.	14,500.
		On cover		72,500.

Values for strips of 3

1	A1	½g pale lake	1,300.
		On cover	3,250.
1b	A1	½g pale lake	1,800.
		On cover	4,500.
2	A2	1g pale lake	360.00
		On cover	900.00
2a	A2	1g rose lake	360.00
		On cover	900.00
3	A3	2g pale lake	160.00
		On cover	500.00
3a	A3	2g rose lake	160.00
		On cover	500.00
4a	A4	5g rose lake	1,800.
		On cover	7,250.
4e	A4	5g rose carmine	3,250.
		On cover	13,000.
5	A5	10g rose lake	7,250.
		On cover	22,000.
5b	A5	10g carmine lake	12,750.
		On cover	—
6	A6	20g rose lake	23,500.
		On cover	—
6c	A6	20g pale car rose	35,000.
		On cover	—
7	A7	50g rose lake	50,000.
		On cover	—

Full margins = 1mm at sides, 1½mm at top and bottom.

Covers: Single frankings of Nos. 1, 2, 7 on newspapers, wrappers or circulars are worth much more.

Only one example of No. 6b is known.

As a secret mark, the engraver, G. Masini, placed a minute letter of his name just above the lower outer line of each stamp. There were three plates of the 2g, one plate of the 50g, and two plates of each of the other values.

Nos. 1-2, 4-7 have been reprinted in bright rose and Nos. 1, 7 in dull brown. The reprints are on thick unwatermarked paper. Value $8 each.

Provisional Government

A8   A9

1860

8	A8	½t deep blue	235,000.	11,000.
		No gum	80,000.	
		On newspaper		22,500.
		On circular		25,000.
		On official document		30,000.
9	A9	½t blue	47,500.	3,250.
		No gum	15,750.	
		On newspaper		12,750.
		On circular		26,000.
		On official document		17,000.
a.		½t deep blue	47,500.	3,250.
		No gum	15,750.	
		On newspaper		12,750.
		On circular		26,000.
		On official document		17,000.

Full margins = 1¼mm at sides, 2mm at top and bottom.

100 varieties of each.

No. 8 was made from the plate of No. 1, which was altered by changing the "G" to "T."

No. 9 was made from the same plate after a second alteration erasing the coat of arms and inserting the Cross of Savoy. Dangerous counterfeits exist of Nos. 8-9.

Covers: Nos. 8-10 on official documents are worth more than on newspapers.

Sicily

Ferdinand II — A10

1859   Unwmk.   Engr.   Imperf.
Soft Porous Paper, Brownish Gum
(Naples consignment)

10	A10	½g orange	800.00	800.00
		No gum	200.00	
		On cover		3,600.
		On circular, single franking		8,000.
		On newspaper, single franking		5,500.
a.		½g yellow	8,750.	2,500.
		No gum	2,100.	
		On cover		12,750.
		On circular, single franking		25,500.
		On newspaper, single franking		24,000.
b.		½g olive yellow	—	40,000.
		On cover		90,000.
		On circular, single franking		—
		On newspaper, single franking		145,000.
c.		Printed on both sides	—	40,000.
d.		½g brownish yellow	11,500.	6,000.
		No gum	5,000.	
		On cover		44,000.
e.		½g deep orange	1,300.	3,250.
		No gum	325.00	
		On cover		15,000.
f.		½g reddish orange		16,500.

> *A newspaper with single franking ½ grana orange, No. 10e, sold for the equivalent of U.S. $14,750 at a Turin auction in 2004.*

11	A10	1g dark brown	17,500.	700.00
		No gum	5,250.	
		On cover		3,500.
		On cover, single franking		18,250.
a.		1g olive brown (I)	40,000.	875.00
		No gum	10,500.	
		On cover		4,500.
		On cover, single franking		18,250.
12	A10	1g olive green (III)	1,800.	240.00
		No gum	500.00	
		On cover		725.00
		On cover, single franking		6,500.
a.		1g grysh olive grn (II)	3,650.	175.00
		No gum	925.00	
		On cover		550.00
		On cover, single franking		5,500.
b.		1g olive brown (II)	1,100.	125.00
		No gum	300.00	
		On cover		400.00
		On cover, single franking		5,500.
c.		Double impression	4,400.	4,400.
		On cover		32,500.
13	A10	2g blue	3,250.	115.00
		No gum	925.00	
		On cover		275.00
		On cover, single franking		4,000.
a.		2g deep blue	5,500.	440.00
		No gum	1,300.	
		On cover		1,100.
		On cover, single franking		1,100.
b.		Printed on both sides	—	26,000.
c.		2g greenish blue	1,100.	140.00
		No gum	275.00	
		On cover		375.00
d.		2g ultramarine	11,000.	875.00
		No gum	2,750.	
		On cover		2,200.
e.		2g cobalt	4,400.	190.00
		No gum	1,100.	
		On cover		450.00
f.		2g dark cobalt	11,000.	500.00
		No gum	2,750.	
		On cover		1,300.
14	A10	5g deep rose	725.00	600.00
		No gum	200.00	
		On cover		3,600.
		On cover, single franking		8,500.
a.		5g carmine	725.00	600.00
		No gum	190.00	
		On cover		3,500.
		On cover, single franking		8,500.
b.		5g brick red	13,000.	6,500.
		No gum	3,250.	
		On cover		25,000.
c.		5g dark carmine	3,650.	1,000.
		No gum	925.00	
		On cover		6,250.
d.		5g blood red	2,500.	1,100.
		No gum	640.00	
		On cover		6,250.
15	A10	5g vermilion	600.00	1,600.
		No gum	175.00	
		On cover		12,000.
		On cover, single franking		26,000.
a.		5g orange vermilion	400.00	1,825.
		No gum	80.00	
		On cover		13,500.
		On cover, single franking		18,000.
b.		5g bright vermilion	440.00	2,200.
		No gum	110.00	
		On cover		17,500.

16	A10	10g dark blue	800.00	375.00
		No gum	240.00	
		On cover		2,800.
		On cover, single franking		2,800.
a.		10g indigo	875.00	400.00
		No gum	240.00	
		On cover		2,800.
		On cover, single franking		2,800.
b.		10g indigo black	3,600.	1,800.
		No gum	800.00	
		On cover		11,000.
17	A10	20g dk gray vio	800.00	625.00
		No gum	225.00	
		On cover		4,250.
		On cover, single franking		13,500.
a.		20g slate black	3,000.	1,800.
		No gum	925.00	
		On cover		11,000.
b.		20g slate violet	3,250.	3,750.
		No gum	1,100.	
		On cover		22,000.
18	A10	50g dk brn red	800.00	4,750.
		No gum	240.00	
		On cover		90,000.
		On cover, single franking		
a.		50g dark purple lake	2,200.	—

Hard White Paper, White Gum
(Palermo consignment)

10g	A10	½g orange	575.00	4,000.
		No gum	175.00	
		On cover		—
10h	A10	½g bright orange	575.00	5,000.
		No gum	175.00	
		On cover		—
12g	A10	1g grayish olive (!!)	650.00	140.00
		No gum	200.00	
		On cover		400.00
12h	A10	1g pale olive green (III)	200.00	180.00
		No gum	60.00	
		On cover		600.00
12i	A10	1g olive green (III)	200.00	180.00
		No gum	60.00	
		On cover		600.00
13g	A10	2g blue	180.00	120.00
		No gum	55.00	
		On cover		275.00
13h	A10	2g pale blue	180.00	120.00
		No gum	55.00	
		On cover		275.00

Full margins = 1mm.

Covers: Single frankings of Nos. 11, 12, 15, 17 on newspapers or covers are worth more. Fraudulent cancellations are known on Nos. 10, 15, 15a and 18.

There were three plates each for the 1g and 2g, two each for the ½g and 5g and one plate each for the other values.

Nos. 10a, 10b, 11, 11a, 14, 14a, 14b and 15 are printed from Plate I on which the stamps are 2 to 2½mm apart. On almost all stamps from Plate I, the S and T of POSTA touch.

Nos. 12a, and 15a are from Plate II and No. 12 is from Plate III. On both Plates II and III stamps are spaced 1½mm apart. Most stamps from Plate II have a white line about 1mm long below the beard.

The ½g blue is stated to be a proof of which two examples are known. Both originated on the same cover. One stamp is sound and still on its original partial cover. This item was sold at auction in 2011, where it realized $2.6 million. The second stamp is a faulty, loose single.

Neapolitan Provinces

King Victor Emmanuel II — A11

Lithographed, Center Embossed
1861   Unwmk.   Imperf.

19	A11	½t green	18.50	325.00
		No gum	4.50	
		On cover		500.00
		On newspaper, single franking		500.00
		On circular, single franking		800.00
a.		½t yellow green	500.00	440.00
		No gum	125.00	
		On cover		650.00
		On circular, single franking		950.00
b.		½t emerald	8,750.	1,450.
		No gum	2,200.	
		On cover		2,200.
		On circular, single franking		3,100.
c.		½t black (error)	160,000.	180,000.
		No gum	40,000.	
d.		Head inverted (green)	255.00	
		No gum	80.00	
e.		Head inverted (yel grn)		14,500.
		On cover		44,000.
f.		Printed on both sides		40,000.
g.		½t olive green	3,650.	725.00
		No gum	900.00	
		On cover		1,250.

20	A11	½g bister	215.00	290.00
		No gum	45.00	
		On cover		575.00
		On cover, single franking		5,500.
a.		½g brown	215.00	400.00
		No gum	45.00	
		On cover		800.00
		On cover, single franking		5,500.
b.		½g gray brown	255.00	290.00
		No gum	55.00	
		On cover		575.00
		On cover, single franking		5,500.
c.		Head inverted	2,350.	
		No gum	1,000.	
21	A11	1g black	400.00	37.50
		No gum	100.00	
		On cover		110.00
		On cover, single franking		1,200.
a.		Head inverted		2,175.
		On cover		13,000.
b.		1g silver gray	21,750.	2,900.
		On cover		8,750.
22	A11	2g blue	145.00	14.50
		No gum	37.50	
		On cover		35.00
a.		2g deep blue	145.00	14.50
		No gum	35.00	
		On cover		37.50
b.		Head inverted	500.00	1,275.
		No gum	135.00	
		On cover		8,000.
c.		2g black (error)		180,000.
		On cover		—
d.		2g sky blue	3,250.	29.00
		No gum	825.00	
		On cover		72.50
e.		2g slate blue	5,000.	220.00
		No gum	1,275.	
		On cover		550.00
f.		2g indigo	8,000.	575.00
		No gum	2,100.	
		On cover		1,450.
23	A11	5g car rose	290.00	165.00
		No gum	72.50	
		On cover		500.00
a.		5g vermilion	290.00	200.00
		No gum	72.50	
		On cover		600.00
b.		5g lilac rose	325.00	325.00
		No gum	82.50	
		On cover		1,350.
c.		Head inverted	1,450.	11,000.
		No gum	550.00	
e.		Printed on both sides		25,000.
f.		5g lilac	365.00	475.00
		No gum	90.00	
		On cover		1,450.
g.		5g dark lilac	875.00	650.00
		No gum	215.00	
		On cover		2,000.
25	A11	10g orange	115.00	365.00
		No gum	30.00	
		On cover		1,100.
a.		10g ocher	1,450.	800.00
		No gum	365.00	
		On cover		2,350.
b.		10g bister	135.00	365.00
		No gum	37.50	
		On cover		1,100.
c.		10g olive bister	650.00	1,000.
		No gum	160.00	
		On cover		3,000.
26	A11	20g yellow	550.00	3,650.
		No gum	125.00	
		On cover		14,500.
a.		Head inverted		50,000.
b.		20g orange yellow	575.00	3,750.
		No gum	145.00	
		On cover		15,000.
27	A11	50g gray	45.00	11,000.
		No gum	11.00	
		On cover		175,000.
		On cover, single franking		215,000.
a.		50g slate	50.00	11,000.
		No gum	13.00	
		On cover		175,000.
b.		50g slate blue	57.50	14,500.
		No gum	14.50	
		On cover		215,000.
c.		50g blackish gray	160.00	
		No gum	40.00	
	Nos. 19-27 (8)		1,778.	15,847.

Full margins = 1mm.

Counterfeits of the inverted head varieties of this issue are plentiful. See note on forgeries after Sardinia No. 15.

Values for pairs

19	A11	½t green	40.00	525.00
		On cover		1,500.
20	A11	½t bister	400.00	500.00
		On cover		1,000.
21	A11	1g black	825.00	72.50
		On cover		240.00
22	A11	2g blue	250.00	55.00
		On cover		275.00
23	A11	5g carmine rose	500.00	550.00
		On cover		2,200.
25	A11	10g orange	240.00	2,200.
		On cover		8,750.
26	A11	20g yellow	1,100.	6,250.
		On cover		32,000.
27	A11	50g gray	85.00	27,500.

Values for blocks of 4

19	A11	½t green	80.00	22,000.
20	A11	½t bister	800.00	25,000.
21	A11	1g black	1,600.	15,000.
22	A11	2g blue	500.00	15,750.
23	A11	5g carmine rose	1,000.	—
25	A11	10g orange	500.00	—
26	A11	20g yellow	2,250.	—
27	A11	50g gray	160.00	

Fraudulent cancellations are found on Nos. 19-20, 23-27.

Stamps similar to those of Sardinia 1855-61, type A4 but with inscriptions in larger, clearer lettering, were prepared in 1861 for the Neapolitan Provinces. They were not officially issued although a few are known postally used. Denominations: 5c, 10c, 20c, 40c and 80c.

Stamps of Two Sicilies were replaced by those of Italy in 1862.

ITALY

'i-t^əl-ē

LOCATION — Southern Europe
GOVT. — Republic
AREA — 119,764 sq. mi.
POP. — 56,929,101 (est. 1983)
CAPITAL — Rome

Kingdom

100 Centesimi = 1 Lira

Watermarks

Wmk. 87 — Honeycomb

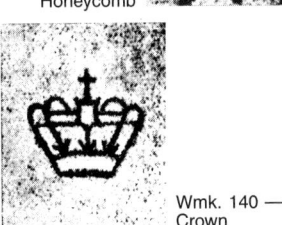

Wmk. 140 — Crown

Values of Italy stamps vary tremendously according to condition. Quotations are for very fine examples, and values for unused stamps are for examples with original gum as defined in the catalogue introduction. Extremely fine or superb examples sell at much higher prices, and fine or poor examples sell at greatly reduced prices.

Very fine examples of Nos. 17-21, 24-75, J2-J27, O1-O8 and Q1-Q6 will have perforations barely clear of the frameline or design due to the narrow spacing of the stamps on the plates.

Values for never hinged stamps are for examples centered clear of perfs. Premiums do not apply to stamps with perforations cutting the design.

King Victor Emmanuel II — A4

Typographed; Head Embossed
1862   Unwmk.   Perf. 11½x12

17	A4	10c bister	9,500.	360.00
		No gum	3,250.	
		Never hinged	14,500.	
		On cover		900.00
a.		10c yellow brown	16,000.	460.00
		No gum	6,400.	
		On cover		1,150.

b.		10c brown	23,000.	550.00
		No gum	9,500.	
		On cover		1,400.
c.		10c dk olive brn	31,500.	1,400.
		No gum	11,500.	
		On cover		3,500.
d.		10c dark brown	40,500.	1,400.
		No gum	14,000.	
		On cover		3,500.
e.		10c olive bister	29,000.	640.00
		No gum	11,000.	
		On cover		1,600.
f.		10c reddish org	29,000.	1,400.
		No gum	11,000.	
		On cover		3,500.
g.		Vert. half used as 5c		
		on cover		160,000.
19	A4	20c dark blue	24.00	40.00
		No gum	14.00	
		Never hinged	60.00	
		On cover		160.00
a.		20c blue	1,600.	1,000.
		No gum	950.00	
		On cover		4,000.
b.		20c pale blue	17,500.	4,400.
		No gum	7,750.	
		On cover		17,500.
c.		20c pale milky blue	25,000.	8,750.
		No gum	11,500.	
		On cover		35,000.
d.		20c gray blue	800.00	875.00
		No gum	400.00	
		On cover		2,350.
e.		20c dp dk blue	17,500.	4,400.
		No gum	8,250.	
		On cover		17,500.
f.		Vert. half used as		
		10c on cover		210,000.
20	A4	40c red	325.00	200.00
		No gum	72.50	
		Never hinged	650.00	
		On cover		400.00
a.		40c pale rose	725.00	550.00
		No gum	190.00	
		On cover		1,100.
b.		40c brt car red	360.00	240.00
		On cover		475.00
c.		40c deep car red	360.00	240.00
		On cover		475.00
21	A4	80c orange	65.00	2,400.
		No gum	42.50	
		Never hinged	175.00	
		On cover		9,600.
a.		80c bright yellow	87.50	2,400.
		No gum	42.50	
		On cover		9,600.
b.		80c dark yellow	95.00	2,400.
		No gum	47.50	
		On cover		9,300.
c.		80c olive yellow	10,200.	
		No gum	5,000.	

The outer frame shows a distinct design on the early printings, while this design is more or less blurred, or even a solid line, on the later printings.

The 20c and 40c exist perf. 11½. These are remainders of Sardinia with forged perforations.

Counterfeit cancellations are often found on No. 21.

Values for pairs

17	A4	10c bister	16,500.	750.00
		On cover		1,900.
19	A4	20c dark blue	50.00	100.00
		On cover		475.00
20	A4	40c red	700.00	900.00
		On cover		3,400.
21	A4	80c orange	160.00	7,200.
		On cover		44,000.

Values for strips of 3

17	A4	10c bister	—	2,200.
		On cover		11,000.
19	A4	20c dark blue	75.00	440.00
		On cover		2,350.
20	A4	40c red	1,100.	4,500.
		On cover		36,000.
21	A4	80c orange	250.00	—
		On cover		—

Values for strips of 4

17	A4	10c bister	—	8,750.
		On cover		44,000.
19	A4	20c dark blue	105.00	4,400.
		On cover		22,000.
20	A4	40c red	—	—
		On cover		—
21	A4	80c orange	—	—
		On cover		—

Values for blocks of 4

17	A4	10c bister	50,000.	—
		On cover		—
19	A4	20c dark blue	175.00	22,000.
		On cover		—
20	A4	40c red	2,100.	—
		On cover		—
21	A4	80c orange	475.00	—
		On cover		—

Values for strips of 5

17	A4	10c bister	—	—
		On cover		—

19	A4	20c dark blue	—	10,750.
		On cover		54,000.
20	A4	40c red	—	—
		On cover		—
21	A4	80c orange	—	—
		On cover		—

Lithographed; Head Embossed
1863   Imperf.

22	A4	15c blue	80.00	55.00
		No gum	35.00	
		Never hinged	200.00	
		On cover		140.00
a.		Head inverted		92,000.
		On cover		200,000.
b.		Double head	160.00	87.50
		No gum	50.00	
		On cover		225.00
c.		Head omitted	800.00	55,000.
		On cover		120,000.
d.		15c deep blue	80.00	55.00
		No gum	35.00	
		Never hinged	200.00	
		On cover		140.00
e.		15c pale blue	80.00	55.00
		No gum	35.00	
		Never hinged	200.00	
		On cover		140.00
f.		15c milky blue	240.00	1,100.
		No gum	87.50	
		On cover		3,400.
g.		15c sky blue	525.00	1,100.
		No gum	225.00	
		On cover		3,400.
h.		15c violet indigo	200.00	325.00
		No gum	75.00	
		On cover		950.00
i.		15c gray blue	2,550.	800.00
		No gum	750.00	
		On cover		2,400.
j.		Triple head	360.00	560.00
		No gum	140.00	
		On cover		1,400.

See note after Sardinia No. 15. No. 22c is valued with original gum only.

Values for a pair of stamps

22	A4	15c blue	200.00	175.00
		On cover		550.00

Values for used strip of 3

22	A4	15c blue		800.00
		On cover		3,250.

Values for used strip of 4

22	A4	15c blue		4,750.
		On cover		24,000.

Values for block of 4

22	A4	15c blue	625.00	28,000.
		On cover		112,000.

King Victor Emmanuel II — A5

Type I — First "C" in bottom line nearly closed.
Type II — "C" open. Line broken below "Q."

1863   Litho.

23	A5	15c blue, Type II	10.00	16.00
		No gum	3.25	
		Never hinged	20.00	
		On cover		35.00
a.		Type I	400.00	27.50
		No gum	47.50	
		Never hinged	800.00	
		On cover		70.00
b.		15c slate blue (II)	12.00	24.00
		No gum	4.75	
		On cover		60.00
c.		As "a," double impression		5,250.
		On cover		20,000.
d.		15c pale blue (I)	400.00	27.50
		No gum	47.50	
		On cover		70.00
e.		15c pale blue (II)	8.00	14.50
		No gum	3.25	
		On cover		35.00
f.		As "a," printed on both sides		24,000.

One example of No. 23f is known used, cancelled "Milano, 25-VII-1863." Unused examples always lack gum and are from printer's waste. They are of little value.

Values for pairs

23	A5	15c blue (II)	16.00	32.50
		On cover		80.00
a.		Type I	875.00	62.50

On cover 160.00

Values for used strips of 3

23	A5	15c blue (II)	125.00	
		On cover	525.00	
a.		Type I	175.00	
		On cover	725.00	

Values for used strips of 4

23	A5	15c blue (II)	525.00	
		On cover	2,200.	
a.		Type I	900.00	
		On cover	3,600.	

Values for blocks of 4

23	A5	15c blue (II)	60.00	26,000.
		On cover		46,000.
a.		Type I	2,800.	15,000.
		On cover		72,000.

Values for used strips of 5

23	A5	15c blue (II)	2,200.	
		On cover	13,200.	
a.		Type I	4,500.	
		On cover	26,000.	

Values for Nos. 24-33 are for well-centered stamps with perforations clear of frameline. Values for used stamps are for stamps canceled with legible circular date stamps. Examples with numeral and other cancellations sell for somewhat less.

Values for never hinged mint stamps are for examples with very fine centering. Never hinged premiums over hinged original gum values do not apply to stamps with perforations cutting into the design. This applies to all 19th century issues.

A6

A7

A8

A13

1863-77   Typo.   Wmk. 140   Perf. 14
Turin Printing

24	A6	1c gray green	8.00	4.00
		No gum	2.00	
		Never hinged	20.00	
		On cover		8.00
a.		Imperf., pair		12,000.
		On cover		37,500.
25	A7	2c org brn ('65)	32.50	2.75
		No gum	5.50	
		Never hinged	80.00	
		On cover		5.50
a.		Imperf., pair	150.00	200.00
		Imperf single, on cover		500.00
26	A8	5c slate grn	2,400.	4.50
		No gum	290.00	
		Never hinged	4,000.	
		On cover		8.75
27	A8	10c buff	4,000.	5.50
		No gum	475.00	
		Never hinged	6,750.	
a.		10c orange brown	4,000.	5.50
		No gum	475.00	
		Never hinged	6,750.	
		On cover, #27 or 27a		10.00
28	A8	10c blue ('77)	7,500.	6.50
		No gum	950.00	
		Never hinged	12,500.	
		On cover		16.00
29	A8	15c blue	3,000.	4.00
		No gum	350.00	
		Never hinged	4,600.	
		On cover		16.50
a.		Imperf, single		5,500.
		On cover		43,500.

30	A8	30c brown	12.00	12.00
		No gum	2.50	
		Never hinged	30.00	
		On cover		35.00
a.		Imperf, single		—
		Imperf single, on cover		—
31	A8	40c carmine	8,750.	8.00
		No gum	1,050.	
		[Never hinged]	14,500.	
a.		40c rose	8,750.	8.00
		No gum	1,050.	
		Never hinged	14,500.	
		On cover, #31 or 31a		24.00
32	A8	60c lilac	12.00	*19.00*
		No gum	2.40	
		Never hinged	30.00	
		On cover		75.00
33	A13	2 l vermilion	32.50	*125.00*
		No gum	18.00	
		Never hinged	80.00	
		On cover		3,000.
		On cover, single franking		4,750.

Nos. 26 to 32 have the head of type A8 but with different corner designs for each value.

Early printings of Nos. 24-27, 29-33 were made in London by De La Rue, later printings in Turin. Used examples can be determined by cancellation date. Unused singles cannot be distinguished.

For overprints see Italian Offices Abroad Nos. 1-5, 8-11.

De La Rue Printing

Stamps from De La Rue printing are distinguished by legible datestamps with dates between Dec. 1863 and Dec. 1865.

24	A6	1c		24.00
		On cover		47.50
		On cover, single franking		275.00
25	A7	2c		120.00
		On cover		240.00
26	A8	5c		24.00
		On cover		47.50
27	A8	10c		24.00
a.		10c		24.00
		On cover, #27 or 27a		47.50
		On cover, single franking, #27 or 27a		400.00
29	A8	15c		4.00
		On cover		16.00
30	A8	30c		100.00
		On cover		300.00
31	A8	40c		20.00
a.		40c		20.00
		On cover, #31 or 31a		60.00
32	A8	60c		47.50
		On cover		190.00
33	A13	2 l		475.00
		On cover		12,000.
		On cover, single franking		15,000.

Values for blocks of 4
Turin Printing

24	A6	1c	60.00	25.00
		On cover		95.00
25	A7	2c	260.00	35.00
		On cover		140.00
26	A8	5c	12,500.	62.50
		On cover		375.00
27	A8	10c	23,000.	140.00
a.		10c	23,000.	140.00
		On cover, #27 or 27a		900.00
28	A8	10c	45,000.	475.00
		On cover		2,400.
30	A8	30c	87.50	*600.00*
		On cover		4,800.
31	A8	40c	47,500.	775.00
a.		40c	47,500.	775.00
		On cover, #31 or 31a		4,800.
32	A8	60c	87.50	*2,100.*
		On cover		14,000.
33	A13	2 l	260.00	*5,000.*

Values for blocks of 4
De La Rue Printing

24	A6	1c	200.00
		On cover	1,200.
26	A8	5c	200.00
		On cover	1,200.
27	A8	10c	525.00
		On cover	2,750.
29	A8	15c	2,100.
		On cover	13,000.
30	A8	30c	*6,250.*
		On cover	25,000.
31	A8	40c	2,800.
		On cover	15,000.

Watermark Inverted
De La Rue Printing

24b	A6	1c	160.00
		On cover	650.00
25b	A7	2c	725.00
		On cover	—
29b	A8	15c	160.00
		On cover	650.00

Turin Printing

24c	A6	1c	55.00	32.50
		On cover		160.00
25c	A7	2c	160.00	95.00
		On cover		575.00
26a	A8	5c	—	120.00
		On cover		600.00
27b	A8	10c	—	95.00
		On cover		575.00
28a	A8	10c	—	95.00
		On cover		225.00
30b	A8	30c	110.00	350.00
		On cover		1,400.
31b	A8	40c	—	225.00
		On cover		1,100.
32a	A8	60c	—	325.00
		On cover		1,600.
33a	A13	2 l	—	725.00
		On cover		1,600.

No. 29 Surcharged in Brown

1865

Type I — Dots flanking stars in oval, and dot in eight check-mark ornaments in corners.
Type II — Dots in oval, none in corners.
Type III — No dots.

34	A8	20c on 15c bl (I)	750.00	4.75
		No gum	105.00	
		Never hinged	2,000.	
		On cover		12.00
a.		Type II	10,500.	20.00
		No gum	1,600.	
		Never hinged	19,000.	
		On cover		50.00
b.		Type III	2,100.	8.00
		No gum	400.00	
		Never hinged	4,000.	
		On cover		20.00
c.		Inverted surcharge (I)		80,000.

A15

1867-77   Typo.

35	A15	20c blue	800.00	1.60
		No gum	130.00	
		Never hinged	1,600.	
		On cover		3.25
36	A15	20c orange ('77)	5,500.	4.00
		No gum	675.00	
		Never hinged	9,500.	
		On cover		10.00

For overprints see Italian Offices Abroad Nos. 9-10.

Official Stamps Surcharged in Blue

1878

37	O1	2c on 2c lake	200.00	32.50
		No gum	25.00	
		On cover	390.00	
		On cover		65.00
38	O1	2c on 5c lake	240.00	40.00
		No gum	40.00	
		On cover	475.00	
		On cover		80.00
39	O1	2c on 20c lake	875.00	4.75
		No gum	140.00	
		Never hinged	1,800.	
		On cover		9.50
40	O1	2c on 30c lake	800.00	16.00
		No gum	85.00	
		Never hinged	1,600.	
		On cover		32.50
41	O1	2c on 1 l lake	650.00	4.75
		No gum	80.00	
		Never hinged	1,200.	
		On cover		9.50
42	O1	2c on 2 l lake	650.00	12.00
		No gum	80.00	
		Never hinged	1,200.	
		On cover		24.00
43	O1	2c on 5 l lake	875.00	16.00
		No gum	95.00	
		Never hinged	1,800.	
		On cover		32.50
44	O1	2c on 10 l lake	650.00	20.00
		No gum	80.00	
		Never hinged	1,200.	
		On cover		40.00
		Nos. 37-44 (8)	4,940.	146.00

Inverted Surcharge

37a	O1	2c on 2c		2,000.
		On cover		18,000.
38a	O1	2c on 5c		1,600.
		On cover		14,500.
39a	O1	2c on 20c	47,500.	1,000.
		On cover		9,500.
40a	O1	2c on 30c		1,600.
		On cover		14,500.
41a	O1	2c on 1 l	55,000.	1,400.
		On cover		13,000.
42a	O1	2c on 2 l	55,000.	1,600.
		On cover		14,500.
43a	O1	2c on 5 l		1,600.
		On cover		14,500.
44a	O1	2c on 10 l		1,600.
		On cover		14,500.

Values for blocks of 4

37	O1	2c on 2c lake	1,250.	375.00
		On cover		1,100.
38	O1	2c on 5c lake	1,600.	490.00
		On cover		1,400.
39	O1	2c on 20c lake	6,000.	125.00
		On cover		350.00
40	O1	2c on 30c lake	5,200.	210.00
		On cover		600.00
41	O1	2c on 1 l lake	3,900.	125.00
		On cover		350.00
42	O1	2c on 2 l lake	3,900.	290.00
		On cover		800.00

43	O1	2c on 5 l lake	6,000.	350.00
		On cover		1,000.
44	O1	2c on 10 l lake	3,900.	425.00
		On cover		1,200.

King Humbert I — A17

1879   Typo.   Perf. 14

45	A17	5c blue green	9.50	1.60
		No gum	2.40	
		Never hinged	24.00	
		On cover		4.75
46	A17	10c claret	475.00	1.75
		No gum	77.50	
		Never hinged	975.00	
		On cover		5.25
47	A17	20c orange	450.00	1.60
		No gum	72.50	
		Never hinged	950.00	
		On cover		4.75
48	A17	25c blue	800.00	9.50
		No gum	115.00	
		Never hinged	1,700.	
		On cover		24.00
49	A17	30c brown	175.00	*2,800.*
		No gum	110.00	
		Never hinged	260.00	
		On cover		16,750.
50	A17	50c violet	24.00	27.50
		No gum	6.00	
		Never hinged	52.50	
		On cover		72.50
51	A17	2 l vermilion	65.00	*400.00*
		No gum	35.00	
		Never hinged	125.00	
		On cover		120,000.

Values for blocks of 4

45	A17	5c blue green	65.00	52.50
		On cover		240.00
46	A17	10c claret	3,400.	77.50
		On cover		440.00
47	A17	20c orange	3,000.	175.00
		On cover		2,000.
48	A17	25c blue	5,700.	650.00
49	A17	30c brown	1,400.	
50	A17	50c violet	150.00	*1,400.*
51	A17	2 l vermilion	425.00	*26,000.*

Nos. 45-51 have the head of type A17 with different corner designs for each value.

Beware of forged cancellations on No. 49, on or off cover.

No. 51 on complete commercial covers is very rare. On large pieces or cover fronts, it is worth $1,500-$15,000, depending on the usage and on the individual piece.

For surcharges and overprints see Nos. 64-66, Italian Offices Abroad 12-17.

Arms of Savoy — A24

Humbert I — A25

A26   A27

A28   A29

1889

52	A24	5c dark green	875.00	3.25
		No gum	97.50	
		Never hinged	2,000.	
		On cover		8.00
53	A25	40c brown	14.50	20.00
		No gum	6.50	
		Never hinged	35.00	
		On cover		120.00
54	A26	45c gray green	2,600.	9.50
		No gum	500.00	
		Never hinged	6,600.	
		On cover		29.00
55	A27	60c violet	19.00	*47.50*
		No gum	8.00	
		Never hinged	47.50	
		On cover		575.00
		On cover, single franking		2,600.
56	A28	1 l brown & yel	19.00	24.00
		No gum	8.00	
		Never hinged	47.50	
		On cover		190.00
		On cover, single franking		1,350.

a.		1 l brown & orange	21.00	30.00
		No gum	8.00	
		Never hinged	47.50	
		On cover		240.00
		On cover, single franking		*1,350.*
57	A29	5 l grn & claret	30.00	*1,200.*
		No gum	16.00	
		Never hinged	87.50	
		On cover		175,000.

Values for blocks of 4

52	A24	5c dark green	6,750.	80.00
		On cover		350.00
53	A25	40c brown	110.00	*1,300.*
		On cover		12,000.
54	A26	45c gray green	26,000.	1,800.
		On cover		16,000.
55	A27	60c violet	150.00	*3,600.*
		On cover		32,000.
56	A28	1 l brown & yel	150.00	*1,600.*
		On cover		8,000.
57	A29	5 l grn & claret	260.00	

Forged cancellations exist on Nos. 51, 57.

No. 57 on complete commercial covers is very rare. On large pieces or cover fronts, it is worth $2,850-$20,000, depending on the usage and on the individual piece.

Parcel Post Stamps of 1884-86 Surcharged in Black

1890

58	PP1	2c on 10c ol gray	6.00	*8.00*
		No gum	3.60	
		Never hinged	24.00	
		On cover		32.50
a.		Inverted surcharge	550.00	3,600.
59	PP1	2c on 20c blue	6.00	*8.00*
		No gum	3.60	
		Never hinged	24.00	
		On cover		32.50
60	PP1	2c on 50c claret	65.00	47.50
		No gum	26.00	
		Never hinged	250.00	
		On cover		140.00
a.		Inverted surcharge		52,500.
61	PP1	2c on 75c blue grn	6.00	*8.00*
		No gum	3.60	
		Never hinged	24.00	
		On cover		32.50
62	PP1	2c on 1.25 l org	55.00	40.00
		No gum	22.00	
		Never hinged	225.00	
		On cover		120.00
a.		Inverted surcharge	95,000.	47,500.
63	PP1	2c on 1.75 l brn	24.00	*60.00*
		No gum	14.00	
		Never hinged	95.00	
		On cover		180.00
		Nos. 58-63 (6)	162.00	171.50

Values for blocks of 4

58	PP1	2c on 10c ol gray	65.00	72.50
		On cover		350.00
59	PP1	2c on 20c blue	65.00	72.50
		On cover		350.00
60	PP1	2c on 50c claret	725.00	325.00
		On cover		1,250.
61	PP1	2c on 75c blue grn	65.00	72.50
		On cover		350.00
62	PP1	2c on 1.25 l org	600.00	275.00
		On cover		1,100.
63	PP1	2c on 1.75 l brn	260.00	*350.00*
				1,400.

Covers: Single frankings of Nos. 58-63 on newspapers or circulars are worth more.

Stamps of 1879 Surcharged

1890-91

64	A17	2c on 5c bl grn ('91)	22.50	55.00
		No gum	16.00	
		Never hinged	55.00	
		On cover		110.00
a.		"2" with thin tail	140.00	325.00
		On cover		1,250.
65	A17	20c on 30c brown	475.00	12.00
		No gum	80.00	
		Never hinged	950.00	
		On cover		30.00
66	A17	20c on 50c violet	550.00	47.50
		No gum	87.50	
		Never hinged	1,100.	
		On cover		140.00
		Nos. 64-66 (3)	1,047.	114.50

Values for blocks of 4

64	A17	2c on 5c bl grn ('91)	160.00	*275.00*
		On cover		550.00
65	A17	20c on 30c brown	3,200.	*5,200.*
		On cover		21,000.
66	A17	20c on 50c violet	3,750.	*4,400.*
		On cover		17,500.

On Nos. 65-66 the period is omitted in the surcharge.

Arms of
Savoy — A33

Humbert
I — A34

A35

A36

A37

A38

1891-96 — Typo.

67	A33	5c green	550.00	2.40
	No gum		75.00	
	Never hinged		1,050.	
	On cover			7.25
68	A34	10c claret ('96)	9.50	2.40
	No gum		2.40	
	Never hinged		24.00	
	On cover			4.75
69	A35	20c orange ('95)	9.50	2.40
	No gum		2.40	
	Never hinged		24.00	
	On cover			4.75
70	A36	25c blue	9.50	10.00
	No gum		2.40	
	Never hinged		24.00	
	On cover			40.00
71	A37	45c ol grn ('95)	9.50	10.00
	No gum		2.40	
	Never hinged		24.00	
	On cover			40.00
72	A38	5 l blue & rose	95.00	240.00
	No gum		40.00	
	Never hinged		190.00	
	On cover			24,000.

Values for blocks of 4

67	A33	5c green	3,600.	35.00
	On cover			240.00
68	A34	10c claret ('96)	72.50	40.00
	On cover			250.00
69	A35	20c orange ('95)	72.50	175.00
	On cover			1,750.
70	A36	25c blue	72.50	325.00
	On cover			3,250.
71	A37	45c ol grn ('95)	72.50	600.00
	On cover			6,000.
72	A38	5 l blue & rose	650.00	2,800.

Value of No. 72 on cover is for a complete cover. Stamps on piece or cover fronts are more common and worth much less.

Arms of
Savoy — A39

A40

A41

1896-97

73	A39	1c brown	11.00	8.00
	No gum		3.25	
	Never hinged		27.50	
	On cover			16.00
a.	Half used as ½c on cover			1,600.
74	A40	2c orange brown	11.00	2.00
	No gum		2.40	
	Never hinged		27.50	
	On cover			4.00
75	A41	5c green ('97)	40.00	2.00
	No gum		8.00	
	Never hinged		100.00	
	On cover			4.00
	Nos. 73-75 (3)		62.00	12.00

Values for blocks of 4

73	A39	1c brown	85.00	40.00
	On cover			120.00
74	A40	2c orange brown	85.00	20.00
	On cover			120.00
75	A41	5c green ('97)	300.00	32.50
	On cover			190.00

A42

Coat of Arms
A43   A44

Victor Emmanuel III
A45   A46

1901-26

76	A42	1c brown	1.60	.40
	Never hinged		4.00	
	On cover			1.20
a.	Imperf., single		450.00	725.00
77	A43	2c org brn	1.60	.40
	Never hinged		4.00	
	On cover			1.20
a.	Double impression		125.00	225.00
b.	Imperf., single		125.00	175.00
78	A44	5c blue grn	87.50	.60
	Never hinged		200.00	
	On cover			1.60
a.	Imperf., single		2,000.	
79	A45	10c claret	120.00	1.25
	Never hinged		300.00	
	On cover			4.75
a.	Imperf., single		—	10,500.
80	A45	20c orange	24.00	1.25
	Never hinged		60.00	
	On cover			4.75
81	A45	25c ultra	275.00	4.00
	Never hinged		600.00	
	On cover			40.00
a.	25c dp blue		275.00	4.00
	Never hinged		600.00	
	On cover			40.00
82	A46	25c grn & pale grn ('26)	1.60	.35
	Never hinged		4.00	
	On cover			1.40
83	A45	40c brown	800.00	9.50
	Never hinged		2,000.	
	On cover			55.00
84	A45	45c olive grn	12.50	.40
	Never hinged		30.00	
	On cover			11.00
a.	Imperf., single		160.00	225.00
85	A45	50c violet	950.00	17.50
	Never hinged		2,000.	
	On cover			200.00
86	A46	75c dk red & rose ('26)	4.75	.35
	Never hinged		12.00	
	On cover			2.75
87	A46	1 l brown & grn	4.75	.40
	Never hinged		12.00	
	On cover			4.00
a.	Imperf., single		80.00	120.00
b.	Floral design (green) omitted		160.00	
c.	Double impression of vignette (brown)		80.00	110.00
88	A46	1.25 l bl & ultra ('26)	12.50	.35
	Never hinged		35.00	
	On cover			2.00
89	A46	2 l dk grn & org ('23)	24.00	8.00
	Never hinged		60.00	
	On cover			65.00
90	A46	2.50 l dk grn & org ('26)	65.00	8.00
	Never hinged		150.00	
	On cover			67.50
91	A46	5 l blue & rose	32.50	7.25
	Never hinged		80.00	
	On cover			240.00
	Nos. 76-91 (16)		2,417.	60.00

Values for Blocks of 4

76	A42	1c brown	12.00	2.60
77	A43	2c org brn	12.00	2.40
78	A44	5c blue grn	625.00	9.75
79	A45	10c claret	850.00	13.00
80	A45	20c orange	190.00	16.00
81	A45	25c ultra	1,725.	80.00
81a	A45	25c deep blue	1,725.	80.00
82	A46	25c grn & pale grn ('26)	8.75	5.00
83	A45	40c brown	5,500.	375.00
84	A45	45c olive grn	95.00	20.00
85	A45	50c violet	6,750.	550.00
86	A46	75c dk red & rose ('26)	50.00	2.50
87	A46	1 l brown & grn	40.00	2.75
88	A46	1.25 l bl & ultra ('26)	50.00	2.00
89	A46	2 l dk grn & org ('23)	140.00	110.00

90	A46	2.50 l dk grn & org l ('26)	260.00	35.00
91	A46	5 l blue & rose	240.00	80.00

Nos. 83, 85, unused, are valued in fine condition.

The borders of Nos. 79-81, 83-85, 87, 89 and 91 differ slightly for each denomination.

On Nos. 82, 86, 88 and 90, the value is expressed as "Cent. 25," etc.

See No. 87d in set following No. 174G.

For surcharges and overprints see Nos. 148-149, 152, 158, 174F-174G, B16; Austria N20-N21, N27, N30, N52-N53, N58, N60, N64-N65, N71, N74; Dalmatia 1, 6-7.

Overprints & Surcharges

See Castellorizo, Italian Offices in China, Crete, Africa, Turkish Empire (Albania to Valona) and Aegean Islands for types A36-A58 overprinted or surcharged.

No. 80 Surcharged in
Black

1905

92	A45	15c on 20c org	80.00	2.00
	Never hinged		200.00	
	Block of 4		350.00	110.00
	Never hinged		875.00	
	On cover			9.50
a.	Double surcharge			5,500.

A47

No.
93

No.
111

No.
123

1906   Unwmk.   Engr.   Perf. 12

93	A47	15c slate	80.00	1.00
	Never hinged		200.00	
	Block of 4		325.00	
	Never hinged		875.00	
	On cover			6.00
a.	Vert. pair, imperf horiz.		200.00	200.00
b.	Horiz. pair, imperf vert.		200.00	200.00
c.	Booklet pane of 6		3,750.	
	Complete bkt., 4 #93c		15,000.	

A48

A49

1906-19   Wmk. 140   Typo.   Perf. 14

94	A48	5c green	1.60	.35
	Never hinged		4.75	
	Block of 4		7.00	
	Never hinged		17.50	
				.80
a.	Imperf., single		40.00	40.00
b.	Printed on both sides		250.00	
	Never hinged		325.00	
95	A48	10c claret	3.25	.35
	Never hinged		11.00	
	Block of 4		14.00	
	Never hinged		35.00	
				.80
a.	Imperf., single		40.00	40.00
b.	Printed on both sides		250.00	
	Never hinged		325.00	
96	A48	15c slate ('19)	3.25	.40
	Never hinged		8.00	
	Block of 4		14.50	
	Never hinged		45.00	
				1.60
a.	Imperf., single		140.00	225.00
	Nos. 94-96 (3)		8.10	1.10

The frame of No. 95 differs in several details.
See Nos. 96b-96d following No. 174G.
For overprints and surcharge see Nos. 142A-142B, 150, 174A, B5, B9-B10; Austria N22-N23, N31, N54-N55, N61-N62, N66-N67; Dalmatia 2-5.

1908-27

97	A49	20c brn org ('25)	1.60	1.00
	Never hinged		4.00	
				4.75
98	A49	20c green ('25)	.40	.25
	Never hinged		1.00	
				1.00
99	A49	20c lil brn ('26)	3.20	.35
	Never hinged		8.00	
				1.20
100	A49	25c blue	2.40	.35
	Never hinged		6.00	
				1.00
a.	Imperf., pair		72.50	72.50
b.	Printed on both sides		225.00	360.00
101	A49	25c lt grn ('27)	8.00	20.00
	Never hinged		20.00	
				60.00
102	A49	30c org brn ('22)	3.20	.80
	Never hinged		8.00	
				4.75
a.	Imperf., single		250.00	—
103	A49	30c gray ('25)	4.75	.25
	Never hinged		12.00	
				3.25
104	A49	40c brown	4.00	.35
	Never hinged		10.00	
				1.00
a.	Imperf., pair		95.00	95.00
105	A49	50c violet	1.60	.35
	Never hinged		4.00	
				1.00
a.	Imperf., pair		87.50	87.50
106	A49	55c dl vio ('20)	19.00	40.00
	Never hinged		47.50	
				200.00
107	A49	60c car ('17)	2.40	.40
	Never hinged		6.00	
				2.40
108	A49	60c blue ('23)	9.50	87.50
	Never hinged		24.00	
	On cover			325.00
	On foreign postcard			225.00
109	A49	60c brn org ('26)	12.50	.60
	Never hinged		32.50	
				8.00
110	A49	85c red brn ('20)	24.00	32.50
	Never hinged		60.00	
	On cover			125.00
	Nos. 97-110 (14)		96.55	184.70

Values for Mint Never Hinged and Used Blocks of 4

97	A49	20c brn org ('25)	22.00	
98	A49	20c green ('25)	4.25	
99	A49	20c lil brn ('26)	42.50	
100	A49	25c blue	26.00	
101	A49	25c lt grn ('27)	87.50	200.00
102	A49	30c org brn ('22)	35.00	12.50
103	A49	30c gray ('25)	52.50	
104	A49	40c brown	45.00	
105	A49	50c violet	17.50	
106	A49	55c dl vio ('20)	210.00	
107	A49	60c car ('17)	32.50	
108	A49	60c blue ('23)	100.00	550.00
109	A49	60c brn org ('26)	140.00	
110	A49	85c red brn ('20)	260.00	

Hinged blocks of Nos. 97-110 do not command a premium above the value of the single stamps that comprise them. Similarly, used blocks not valued above are worth the combined value of 4 singles.

The upper panels of Nos. 104 and 105 are in solid color with white letters. A body of water has been added to the background.
See Nos. 100c-105j following No. 174G.
For overprints & surcharges see Nos. 142C-142D,147, 151, 153-157, 174B-174E, B7-B8, B12-B15A; Austria N24-N26, N28-N29, N32, N56-N57, N59, N63, N68-N70, N72-N73.

A50

A51

Redrawn
Perf. 13x13½, 13½x14

1909-17   Unwmk.

111	A50	15c slate black	300.00	2.40
	Never hinged		750.00	
	Block of 4		1,300.	80.00
	Never hinged		3,400.	
	On cover			8.75
112	A50	20c brown org ('16)	65.00	4.75
	Never hinged		160.00	
	Block of 4		290.00	175.00
	Never hinged		700.00	
	On cover			16.00

No. 111 is similar to No. 93, but the design has been redrawn and the stamp is 23mm high instead of 25mm. There is a star at each side of the coat collar, but one is not distinct. See illustrations next to A47.
For overprints see Nos. B6, B11.

Wmk. 140   Perf. 14

1917

113	A50	20c brn org ('17)	8.00	.40
	Never hinged		20.00	
	Block of 4		35.00	

Never hinged		87.50	
On cover			1.60
a. Imperf., pair		32.50	*40.00*

Stamps overprinted "Prestito Nazionale, 1917," or later dates, are Thrift or Postal Savings Stamps.

1910, Nov. 1
114	A51	10 l gray grn & red	80.00	35.00
	Never hinged		200.00	
	Block of 4		350.00	240.00
	Never hinged		875.00	
	On cover			1,800.
	On cover, single franking			5,400.
a.	Red inverted			7,250.

For surcharge see Dalmatia No. 8.

Giuseppe Garibaldi
A52   A53

Perf. 14x13½

1910, Apr. 15   Unwmk.
115	A52	5c green	32.50	27.50
	Never hinged		130.00	
	Block of 4		140.00	
	Never hinged		560.00	
	On cover			140.00
116	A52	15c claret	55.00	55.00
	Never hinged		225.00	
	Block of 4		240.00	
	Never hinged		975.00	
	On cover			275.00

50th anniversary of freedom of Sicily.

1910, Dec. 1
117	A53	5c claret	140.00	140.00
	Never hinged		560.00	
	Block of 4		600.00	
	Never hinged		2,400.	
	On cover			675.00
118	A53	15c green	250.00	200.00
	Never hinged		1,000.	
	Block of 4		1,100.	
	Never hinged		4,400.	
	On cover			1,100.
	#115-118, set of 2 commem covers			1,250.

50th anniversary of the plebiscite of the southern Italian provinces in 1860.
Nos. 115-118 sold for 5c above face value to benefit the anniversary committee. The stamps were valid only on mail to addresses within the Kingdom of Italy. Nos. 115-116 were valid to June 30, 1910; Nos. 117-118 were valid to Jan. 31, 1911.

Used values in italics are for postally used stamps. CTO's sell for about the same as unused, hinged stamps.

Symbols of Rome and Turin — A54

Symbol of Valor — A55

Genius of Italy — A56

Glory of Rome — A57

1911, May 1   Engr.   *Perf. 14x13½*
119	A54	2c brown	3.25	*6.50*
	Never hinged		8.00	
	Block of 4		14.00	28.00
	Never hinged		35.00	
	On cover			30.00

a.	Vert. pair, imperf horiz.		95.00	95.00
b.	Horiz. pair, imperf vert.		95.00	95.00
c.	Perf 13½		47.50	47.50
120	A55	5c deep green	45.00	40.00
	Never hinged		110.00	
	Block of 4		200.00	175.00
	Never hinged		500.00	
	On cover			130.00
c.	Perf 13½		35.00	35.00
121	A56	10c carmine	32.50	60.00
	Never hinged		80.00	
	Block of 4		140.00	360.00
	Never hinged		350.00	
	On cover			175.00
a.	Vert. pair, imperf horiz.		—	—
b.	Horiz. pair, imperf vert.		200.00	200.00
c.	Perf 13½			
122	A57	15c slate	42.50	*80.00*
	Never hinged		95.00	
	Block of 4		190.00	490.00
	Never hinged		475.00	
	On cover			175.00
	Nos. 119-122 (4)		123.25	*186.50*
	Set on commem cover			375.00

50th anniv. of the union of Italian States to form the Kingdom of Italy.
Nos. 119 to 122 were sold at a premium over their face value to benefit the anniversary committee. They were valid to Dec. 31, 1911. The stamps were valid only for mail to addresses within the Kingdom of Italy. They were used by military post offices in Libya. After 1913, No. 119 was sold without the premium.
For surcharges see Nos. 126-128.

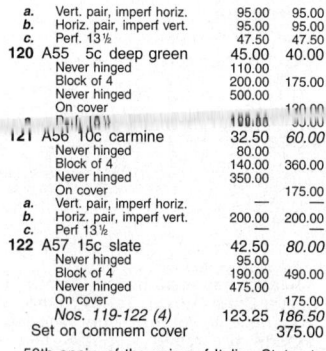

Victor Emmanuel III
A58

Campanile, Venice
A59

1911, Oct.   Re-engraved   *Perf. 13½*
123	A58	15c slate	32.50	1.25
	Never hinged		80.00	
	Block of 4		140.00	20.00
	Never hinged		350.00	
				3.25
a.	Imperf., single		95.00	125.00
b.	Printed on both sides		400.00	525.00
c.	Bklt. pane of 6		1,500.	
	Cplt. bklt., 4 #123c		6,000.	

The re-engraved stamp is 24mm high. The stars at each side of the coat collar show plainly and the "C" of "Cent" is nearer the frame than in No. 93. See illustrations next to A47.
For surcharge see No. 129.

1912, Apr. 25   *Perf. 14x13½*
124	A59	5c indigo	9.50	*14.50*
	Never hinged		24.00	
	Block of 4		40.00	72.50
	Never hinged		100.00	
	On cover			45.00
125	A59	15c dk brn	52.50	*67.50*
	Never hinged		140.00	
	Block of 4		225.00	400.00
	Never hinged		525.00	
	On cover			175.00
	Set on commem cover			160.00

Re-erection of the Campanile at Venice.
Nos. 124-125 were sold only in Venice and were valid to Dec. 31, 1912. The stamps were valid only for mail within Italy.

Nos. 120-121
Surcharged in Black

1913, Mar. 1
126	A55	2c on 5c dp grn	2.40	*6.75*
	Never hinged		6.00	
	Block of 4		10.50	27.50
	Never hinged		26.00	
	On cover			45.00
a.	On #120a		40.00	60.00
127	A56	2c on 10c car	2.40	*6.75*
	Never hinged		6.00	
	Block of 4		10.50	27.50
	Never hinged		26.00	
	On cover			45.00

No. 122 Surcharged in Violet

128	A57	2c on 15c slate	2.40	*6.75*
	Never hinged		6.00	
	Block of 4		10.50	27.50
	Never hinged		26.00	
	On cover			45.00
	Nos. 126-128 (3)		7.20	*20.25*
	Set, never hinged		18.00	
	Set on commem cover			87.50

No. 123 Surcharged

1916, Jan. 8
129	A58	20c on 15c slate	17.50	1.25
	Never hinged		45.00	
	Block of 4		75.00	18.00
	Never hinged		190.00	
	On cover			3.25
a.	Bklt. pane of 6		750.00	
	Cplt. bklt., 4 #129a		3,000.	
b.	Inverted surcharge		350.00	350.00
c.	Double surcharge		225.00	225.00
d.	Surcharge on reverse		225.00	
e.	Vert. pair, one without surcharge		1,750.	
	Never hinged		2,250.	
f.	Horiz. strip of 3, 2 without surcharge		1,900.	
	Never hinged		2,750.	
g.	Imperf, single		160.00	200.00
h.	Pair, one stamp with albino surcharge		550.00	

Old Seal of Republic of Trieste
A60

Allegory of Dante's Divine Comedy
A61

Italy Holding Laurels for Dante — A62

Dante Alighieri — A63

Wmk. 140
1921, June 5   Litho.   *Perf. 14*
130	A60	15c blk & rose	7.25	*55.00*
	Never hinged		18.00	
	Block of 4		30.00	
	Never hinged		77.50	
	On cover			675.00
a.	Horiz. pair, imperf btwn.		950.00	
131	A60	25c bl & rose	7.25	*55.00*
	Never hinged		18.00	
	Block of 4		30.00	
	Never hinged		77.50	
	On cover			675.00
132	A60	40c brn & rose	7.25	*55.00*
	Never hinged		18.00	
	Block of 4		30.00	
	Never hinged		77.50	
	On cover			675.00
	Nos. 130-132 (3)		21.75	*165.00*
	Set, never hinged		54.00	
	Set on commem cover			475.00

Reunion of Venezia Giulia with Italy.

1921, Sept. 28   Typo.
133	A61	15c vio brn	7.25	*35.00*
	Never hinged		18.00	
	Block of 4		30.00	
	Never hinged		77.50	

	On cover			175.00
a.	Imperf, single		40.00	40.00
	Imperf, pair		90.00	
134	A62	25c gray grn	7.25	*35.00*
	Never hinged		18.00	
	Block of 4		30.00	
	Never hinged		77.50	
	On cover			175.00
a.	Imperf, single		40.00	40.00
	Imperf, pair		90.00	
135	A63	40c brown	7.25	*35.00*
	Never hinged		18.00	
	Block of 4		30.00	
	Never hinged		77.50	
	On cover			175.00
a.	Imperf, single		40.00	40.00
	Imperf, pair		90.00	
	Nos. 133-135 (3)		21.75	*105.00*
	Set, never hinged		54.00	
	Set on commem cover			190.00

600th anniversary of the death of Dante. A 15c gray was not issued. Value: hinged $160, never hinged $400, used $550.
Nos. 133-135 exist in part perforate pairs.

"Victory" — A64

1921, Nov. 1   Engr.   *Perf. 14*
136	A64	5c olive green	1.60	*2.00*
	Never hinged		4.00	
	Block of 4		7.00	
	Never hinged		17.50	
	On cover			14.00
137	A64	10c red	2.40	2.40
	Never hinged		6.00	
	Block of 4		10.00	
	Never hinged		25.00	
	On cover			27.50
138	A64	15c slate green	4.00	*9.50*
	Never hinged		10.00	
	Block of 4		17.50	
	Never hinged		42.50	
	On cover			47.50
139	A64	25c ultra	2.40	*6.50*
	Never hinged		6.00	
	Block of 4		10.00	
	Never hinged		25.00	
	On cover			32.50
	Nos. 136-139 (4)		10.40	*20.40*
	Set, never hinged		26.00	
	Set on commem cover			60.00

Perf. 14x13¼
136a	A64	5c	2.40	*3.25*
	Never hinged		6.00	
137a	A64	10c	3.25	*4.00*
	Never hinged		8.00	
138a	A64	15c	8.00	*14.50*
	Never hinged		20.00	
139a	A64	25c	3.25	*8.00*
	Never hinged		8.00	

Perf. 13½
137b	A64	10c	125.00	*180.00*
139b	A64	25c	175.00	*225.00*

Imperf Singles
136b	A64	5c	250.00	275.00
	Never hinged		350.00	
137c	A64	10c	250.00	*525.00*
	Never hinged		350.00	
139c	A64	25c	190.00	190.00
	Never hinged		250.00	
d.	Double impression		650.00	—
	Never hinged		900.00	

Unwmk.
136c	A64	5c	5.25	*9.50*
	Never hinged		13.00	
137d	A64	10c	12.00	*20.00*
	Never hinged		30.00	
138b	A64	15c	27.50	*45.00*
	Never hinged		67.50	
139e	A64	25c	12.00	*20.00*
	Never hinged		30.00	

Wmk. Small Cross
136d	A64	5c	20.00	*32.50*
	Never hinged		50.00	
137e	A64	10c	40.00	*72.50*
	Never hinged		100.00	
138c	A64	15c	100.00	*160.00*
	Never hinged		250.00	
139f	A64	25c	40.00	*72.50*
	Never hinged		100.00	

3rd anniv. of the victory on the Piave.
For surcharges see Nos. 171-174.

Flame of Patriotism Tempering Sword of Justice — A65

Giuseppe Mazzini — A66

Mazzini's Tomb A67

1922, Sept. 20   Typo.   Perf. 14

140	A65 25c maroon	13.00	35.00
	Never hinged	32.50	
	Block of 4	55.00	
	Never hinged	140.00	
	On cover		300.00
141	A66 40c vio brn	25.00	45.00
	Never hinged	65.00	
	Block of 4	110.00	
	Never hinged	275.00	
	On cover		325.00
142	A67 80c dk bl	13.00	55.00
	Never hinged	32.50	
	Block of 4	55.00	
	Never hinged	140.00	
	On cover		475.00
	Nos. 140-142 (3)	*51.00*	*135.00*
	Set, never hinged	130.00	
	Set on commem cover		275.00

Mazzini (1805-1872), patriot and writer.

Nos. 95, 96, 100 and 104 Overprinted in Black

1922, June 4   Wmk. 140   Perf. 14

142A	A48 10c claret	475.00	475.00
	Never hinged	1,200.	
	On cover		1,300.
142B	A48 15c slate	250.00	250.00
	Never hinged	640.00	
	On cover		1,200.
142C	A49 25c blue	250.00	250.00
	Never hinged	625.00	
	On cover		1,200.
142D	A49 40c brown	400.00	400.00
	Never hinged	1,000.	
	On cover		1,300.
	Nos. 142A-142D (4)	*1,375.*	*1,375.*
	Set, never hinged	3,465.	
	Set on commem postal card		1,800.
	Set on commem cover		1,500.

Values for mint never hinged and used blocks of 4

142A	A48	10c claret	5,500.	3,100.
142B	A48	15c slate	2,900.	1,600.
142C	A49	25c blue	2,900.	1,600.
142D	A49	40c brown	4,600.	2,600.

9th Italian Philatelic Congress, Trieste. Nos. 142A-142D were on sale to Sept. 30, 1922. Counterfeits exist.

Christ Preaching The Gospel — A68

Portrait at upper right and badge at lower right differ on each value. Portrait at upper left is of Pope Gregory XV. Others: 20c, St. Theresa. 30c, St. Dominic. 50c, St. Francis of Assisi. 1 l, St. Francis Xavier.

1923, June 11

143	A68 20c ol grn & brn org	6.50	175.00
	Never hinged	16.00	
	Block of 4	28.00	
	Never hinged	70.00	
	On cover		1,100.

144	A68 30c claret & brn org	6.50	175.00
	Never hinged	16.00	
	Block of 4	28.00	
	Never hinged	70.00	
	On cover		1,100.
145	A68 50c vio & brn org	6.50	175.00
	Never hinged	16.00	
	Block of 4	28.00	
	Never hinged	70.00	
	On cover		1,100.
146	A68 1 l bl & brn org	6.50	175.00
	Never hinged	16.00	
	Block of 4	28.00	
	Never hinged	70.00	
	On cover		1,100.
	Nos. 143-146 (4)	*26.00*	*700.00*
	Set, never hinged	64.00	
	Set on commem cover		1,100.

Forged cancellations exist on Nos. 143-146.

Imperf Singles

143a	A68 20c	550.00	725.00
144a	A68 30c	550.00	725.00
145a	A68 50c	550.00	725.00
146a	A68 1 l	550.00	725.00

Perf. 14 Horiz., Singles

144b	A68 30c	125.00	350.00
145b	A68 50c	125.00	350.00
146b	A68 1 l	125.00	350.00

Horiz. Pairs, Imperf Between

144c	A68 30c	1,200.	1,650.
	Never hinged	1,600.	
145c	A68 50c	1,800.	2,400.
	Never hinged	2,400.	
146c	A68 1 l	1,200.	1,640.
	Never hinged	1,600.	

Vert. Pairs, Imperf Between

143b	A68 20c	1,200.	1,650.
	Never hinged	1,600.	
144d	A68 30c	1,200.	1,650.
	Never hinged	1,600.	
145d	A68 50c	1,200.	1,650.
	Never hinged	1,600.	
146d	A68 1 l	1,200.	1,650.
	Never hinged	1,600.	

300th anniv. of the Propagation of the Faith. Practically the entire issue was delivered to speculators.

Stamps of Previous Issues, Surcharged

Cent. 7½

a

b

10 CENTESIMI

DIECI

c

Cent. 25

d

Lire 1,75

e

Type I   Type II

Type I

Type II

Two types of 7½c surcharge:
Type I: Base of "1" level with top of "2."
Type II: Base of "1" higher than top of "2," fraction bar longer and thinner.

Two types of 25c on 60c surcharge:
Type I: Bars of obliterator long and widely spaced. Bars measure 3.5mm to 3.75mm wide, and the space between the bars measure 10.5mm to 11mm
Type II: Bars shorter and narrowly spaced. Bars measure 3mm wide, and the space between the bars measures 11.5mm.

1923-25

147	A49(a) 7½c on 85c (I)	.40	1.25
	Never hinged	1.00	
	On cover		24.00
	On cover, single franking		36.00
a.	Double surcharge	—	1,600.
b.	Type II	10.50	72.50
	Never hinged	26.00	
	On cover		275.00
	On cover, single franking		575.00
c.	As "b," double surcharge	450.00	—
148	A42(b) 10c on 1c	.40	.35
	Never hinged	1.00	
	On cover		3.25
a.	Inverted surcharge	24.00	40.00
149	A43(b) 10c on 2c	.40	.35
	Never hinged	1.00	
	On cover		3.25
a.	Inverted surcharge	60.00	95.00
b.	Vert. pair, one without surcharge	1,200.	—
150	A48(c) 10c on 15c	.40	.35
	Never hinged	1.00	
	On cover		4.00
a.	Vert. pair, one without surcharge	1,100.	—
151	A49(a) 20c on 25c	.40	.35
	Never hinged	1.00	
	On cover		4.00
152	A45(d) 25c on 45c	1.60	16.00
	Never hinged	4.00	
	On cover		125.00
a.	Vert. pair, one without surcharge	1,100.	
153	A49(a) 25c on 60c (I)	3.25	1.00
	Never hinged	8.00	
	On cover		24.00
a.	Vert. pair, one without surcharge	1,100.	—
b.	Type II	32.50	160.00
	Never hinged	80.00	
	On cover		525.00
	On cover, single franking		800.00
c.	As "a," Type II	1,100.	

Single franked covers bearing No. 153b were canceled between 2/15/25 and 3/16/25.

154	A49(a) 30c on 50c	.40	.35
	Never hinged	1.00	
	On cover		20.00
	On cover, single franking		67.50
155	A49(a) 30c on 55c	1.60	.35
	Never hinged	4.00	
	On cover		47.50
	On cover, single franking		110.00
156	A49(a) 50c on 40c	6.50	.40
	Never hinged	16.00	
	On cover		4.75
a.	Inverted surcharge	240.00	360.00
b.	Double surcharge	130.00	150.00
157	A49(a) 50c on 55c	22.50	16.00
	Never hinged	55.00	
	On cover		40.00
a.	Inverted surcharge	1,200.	2,250.
	Never hinged	1,400.	
158	A51(e) 1.75 l on 10 l	16.00	35.00
	Never hinged	40.00	
	On cover		475.00
	On cover, single franking		1,600.
a.	Vert. pair, one without surcharge	1,750.	
	Never hinged	2,000.	
	Nos. 147-158 (12)	*53.85*	*71.75*
	Set, never hinged	133.00	

Values for mint never hinged blocks of 4

147	A49(a)	7½c on 85c (I)	4.25
147b	A49(a)	7½c on 85c (II)	110.00
148	A42(b)	10c on 1c	4.25
149	A43(b)	10c on 2c	4.25
150	A48(c)	10c on 15c	4.25
151	A49(a)	20c on 25c	4.25
152	A45(d)	25c on 45c	17.00
153	A49(a)	25c on 60c (I)	35.00
153b	A49(a)	25c on 60c (II)	340.00
154	A49(a)	30c on 50c	4.25
155	A49(a)	30c on 55c	17.00

156	A49(a)	50c on 40c	70.00
157	A49(a)	50c on 55c	240.00
158	A51(e)	1.75 l on 10 l	170.00

Years of issue: Nos. 148-149, 156-157, 1923; Nos. 147, 152-153, 1924; others, 1925.

Emblem of the New Government A69

Wreath of Victory, Eagle and Fasces A70

Symbolical of Fascism and Italy — A71

Unwmk.

1923, Oct. 24   Engr.   Perf. 14

159	A69 10c dark green	4.75	11.00
	Never hinged	12.00	
	On cover		55.00
a.	Imperf, single	800.00	950.00
	Never hinged	1,200.	
160	A69 30c dark violet	4.75	11.00
	Never hinged	12.00	
	On cover		55.00
161	A69 50c brown carmine	9.50	20.00
	Never hinged	24.00	
	On cover		120.00

Wmk. 140   Typo.

162	A70 1 l blue	16.00	20.00
	Never hinged	40.00	
	On cover		175.00
163	A70 2 l brown	19.00	24.00
	Never hinged	47.50	
	On cover		275.00
164	A71 5 l blk & bl	32.50	65.00
	Never hinged	80.00	
	On cover		550.00
a.	Imperf, single	325.00	
	Nos. 159-164 (6)	*86.50*	*151.00*
	Set, never hinged	215.50	
	Set on commem cover		600.00

Values for mint never hinged blocks of 4

159	A69	10c dark green	52.50
160	A69	30c dark violet	52.50
161	A69	50c brown carmine	105.00
162	A70	1 l blue	175.00
163	A70	2 l brown	210.00
164	A71	5 l blk & bl	350.00

Anniv. of the March of the Fascisti on Rome.

Fishing Scene A72

Designs: 15c, Mt. Resegone. 30c, Fugitives bidding farewell to native mountains. 50c, Part of Lake Como. 1 l, Manzoni's home, Milan. 5 l, Alessandro Manzoni. The first four designs show scenes from Manzoni's work "I Promessi Sposi."

1923, Dec. 29   Perf. 14

165	A72 10c brn red & blk	24.00	200.00
	Never hinged	60.00	
	On cover		800.00
166	A72 15c bl grn & blk	24.00	200.00
	Never hinged	60.00	
	On cover		800.00
167	A72 30c blk & slate	24.00	200.00
	Never hinged	60.00	
	On cover		800.00
a.	Imperf, single	3,000.	
	Never hinged	4,500.	
	Imperf, pair	—	
168	A72 50c org brn & blk	24.00	200.00
	Never hinged	60.00	
	On cover		800.00
a.	Imperf, single	4,000.	
169	A72 1 l blue & blk	160.00	800.00
	Never hinged	400.00	
	On cover		2,750.
a.	Imperf, single, no gum	160.00	875.00
	As "a," with gum	300.00	
170	A72 5 l vio & blk	800.00	4,400.
	Never hinged	2,000.	
	On cover		—
a.	Imperf, single	950.00	

Never hinged	2,400.		
Imperf, pair			
Nos. 165-170 (6)	1,056.	6,000.	
Set, never hinged	2,640.		
Set on commem cover		16,000.	

Values for mint never hinged blocks of 4

165	A72	10c brn red & blk	300.00
166	A72	15c bl grn & blk	300.00
167	A72	30c blk & slate	300.00
168	A72	50c org brn & blk	300.00
169	A72	1 l blue & blk	2,100.
170	A72	5 l vio & blk	10,500.

50th anniv. of the death of Alessandro Manzoni.

Values are for stamps with perforations clear of the design. Very fine centered examples command a 50% premium.

Nos. 136-139 Surcharged

1924, Feb. — Perf. 14

171	A64	1 l on 5c ol grn	25.00	250.00
	Never hinged		62.50	
	On cover			1,600.
172	A64	1 l on 10c red	16.00	250.00
	Never hinged		40.00	
	On cover			1,600.
173	A64	1 l on 15c slate grn	25.00	250.00
	Never hinged		62.50	
	On cover			1,600.
174	A64	1 l on 25c ultra	16.00	250.00
	Never hinged		40.00	
	On cover			1,600.
	Nos. 171-174 (4)		82.00	1,000.
	Set, never hinged		205.00	
	Set on commem cover			4,750.

Surcharge forgeries exist.

Perf. 14x13½

171a	A64	1 l on 5c	35.00	350.00
	Never hinged		70.00	
172a	A64	1 l on 10c	20.00	350.00
	Never hinged		40.00	
173a	A64	1 l on 15c	35.00	350.00
	Never hinged		70.00	
174h	A64	1 l on 25c	20.00	350.00
	Never hinged		40.00	
	Nos. 171a-174h (4)		110.00	1,400.
	Set, never hinged		220.00	

Perf. 13½

171b	A64	1 l on 5c	175.00	1,000.
	Never hinged		350.00	
172c	A64	1 l on 10c	350.00	
174i	A64	1 l on 25c	175.00	—
	Never hinged		350.00	

Unwmk.

171c	A64	1 l on 5c	80.00	—
	Never hinged		275.00	
172b	A64	1 l on 10c	52.50	—
	Never hinged		165.00	
173b	A64	1 l on 15c	80.00	—
	Never hinged		275.00	
174j	A64	1 l on 25c	52.50	—
	Never hinged		165.00	

Nos. 95, 102, 105, 108, 110, 87 and 89 Overprinted in Black or Red

1924, Feb. 16

174A	A48	10c claret	2.40	47.50
	Never hinged		6.00	
	On cover			240.00
174B	A49	30c org brn	2.40	47.50
	Never hinged		6.00	
	On cover			240.00
174C	A49	50c violet	2.40	47.50
	Never hinged		6.00	
	On cover			240.00
174D	A49	60c bl (R)	16.00	140.00
	Never hinged		40.00	
	On cover			475.00
174E	A49	85c choc (R)	8.00	140.00
	Never hinged			
	On cover			475.00
174F	A46	1 l brn & grn	47.50	475.00
	Never hinged		120.00	
	On cover			2,400.
174G	A46	2 l dk grn & org	35.00	475.00
	Never hinged		87.50	
	On cover			3,250.
	Nos. 174A-174G (7)		113.70	1,372.
	Set, never hinged		285.00	
	Set on commem cover			4,200.

Values for mint never hinged blocks of 4

174A	A48	10c claret	26.00
174B	A49	30c org brn	26.00
174C	A49	50c violet	26.00
174D	A49	60c bl (R)	175.00
174E	A49	85c choc (R)	97.50
174F	A46	1 l brn & grn	325.00
174G	A46	2 l dk grn & org	400.00

These stamps were sold on an Italian merchant ship which made a cruise to South American ports in 1924.

Overprint forgeries exist of Nos. 174D-174G.

Stamps of 1901-22 with Advertising Labels Attached

Perf. 14 all around, Imperf. between

1924-25

96b	A48	15c + Bitter Campari	4.00	27.50
	Never hinged		10.00	
	On cover			120.00
96c	A48	15c + Cordial Campari	4.00	24.00
	Never hinged		10.00	
	On cover			100.00
96d	A48	15c + Columbia	65.00	55.00
	Never hinged		160.00	
	On cover			260.00
100c	A49	25c + Abrador	110.00	140.00
	Never hinged		225.00	
	On cover			925.00
100d	A49	25c + Coen	240.00	72.50
	Never hinged		600.00	
	On cover			450.00
100e	A49	25c + Piperno	1,600.	1,200.
	Never hinged		3,250.	
	On cover			4,000.
100f	A49	25c + Reinach	110.00	95.00
	Never hinged		225.00	
	On cover			625.00
100g	A49	25c + Tagliacozzo	950.00	1,200.
	Never hinged		1,900.	
	On cover			4,000.
102b	A49	30c + Columbia	32.50	45.00
	Never hinged		80.00	
	On cover			200.00
105b	A49	50c + Coen	1,600.	95.00
	Never hinged		3,250.	
	On cover			450.00
105c	A49	50c + Columbia	24.00	17.50
	Never hinged		60.00	
	On cover			80.00
105d	A49	50c + De Montel	4.00	17.50
	Never hinged		10.00	
	On cover			240.00
105e	A49	50c + Piperno	2,200.	350.00
	Never hinged		4,500.	
	On cover			1,200.
105f	A49	50c + Reinach	240.00	72.50
	Never hinged		600.00	
	On cover			325.00
105g	A49	50c + Siero Casali	24.00	52.50
	Never hinged		60.00	
	On cover			240.00
105h	A49	50c + Singer	4.00	12.00
	Never hinged		10.00	
	On cover			47.50
105i	A49	50c + Tagliacozzo	2,400.	675.00
	Never hinged		4,750.	
	On cover			2,500.
105j	A49	50c + Tantal	400.00	225.00
	Never hinged		1,000.	
	On cover			800.00
87d	A46	1 l + Columbia	950.00	1,050.
	Never hinged		1,900.	
	On cover			4,750.
	Nos. 96b-87d (19)		10,961.	5,426.
	Set, never hinged		22,700.	

No. 113 with Columbia label and No. E3 with Cioccolato Perugina label were prepared but not issued. Values: Columbia, unused $55, never hinged $140; Cioccolato, unused $20, never hinged $47.50.

King Victor Emmanuel III — A78

1925-26 — Engr. — Unwmk. — Perf. 11

175	A78	60c brn car	1.60	.80
	Never hinged		4.00	
	On cover			2.00
a.	Perf. 13½		8.00	2.40
	Never hinged		20.00	
	On cover			6.50
b.	Imperf., pair		260.00	260.00
	Never hinged		400.00	
c.	Perf. 11x13½		650.00	400.00
	Never hinged		975.00	
d.	Perf. 13½x11		650.00	400.00
	Never hinged		975.00	
176	A78	1 l dk bl	1.60	.80
	Never hinged		4.00	
	On cover			2.75
a.	Perf. 13½		16.00	16.00
	Never hinged		40.00	
	On cover			47.50
b.	Imperf., pair		260.00	260.00
	Never hinged		400.00	
c.	Perf. 11x13½		550.00	275.00
	Never hinged		825.00	
d.	Perf. 13½x11		550.00	275.00

	Never hinged	825.00	

Perf. 13½

177	A78	1.25 l dk bl ('26)	4.75	2.40
	Never hinged		12.00	
a.	Perf 11		11.00	18.00
	Never hinged		275.00	
	On cover			425.00
b.	Imperf., pair		600.00	600.00
	Never hinged		900.00	
c.	Perf. 11x13½		950.00	450.00
	Never hinged		1,150.	
d.	Perf. 13½x11		950.00	450.00
	Never hinged		1,150.	
	Nos. 175-177 (3)		7.95	4.00
	Set, never hinged		20.00	

25th year of the reign of Victor Emmanuel III.

Nos. 175 to 177 exist with sideways watermark of fragments of letters or a crown, which are normally on the sheet margin.

St. Francis and His Vision A79

Monastery of St. Damien A80

Assisi Monastery A81

St. Francis' Death A82

St. Francis — A83

1926, Jan. 30 — Wmk. 140 — Perf. 14

178	A79	20c gray grn	.80	1.00
	Never hinged		2.00	
	On cover			4.50
a.	Imperf single		1,200.	1,200.
	Never hinged		1,500.	
179	A80	40c dk vio	.80	1.00
	Never hinged		2.00	
	On cover			4.50
a.	Imperf single		550.00	550.00
	Never hinged		700.00	
180	A81	60c red brn	.80	1.00
	Never hinged		2.00	
	On cover			4.50

Unwmk. — Perf. 11

181	A83	30c slate blk	.80	1.00
	Never hinged		2.00	
	On cover			4.50
a.	Perf. 13½		12.00	22.50
	Never hinged		30.00	
	On cover			45.00
b.	Perf. 13½x11		550.00	
c.	Perf. 11x13½		550.00	450.00
182	A82	1.25 l dark blue	4.00	1.00
	Never hinged		10.00	
	On cover			9.50
a.	Perf. 13½		475.00	45.00
	Never hinged		1,200.	
	On cover			125.00

Perf. 13½

183	A83	5 l + 2.50 l dk brn	11.00	140.00
	Never hinged		27.50	
	On cover			—
	Nos. 178-183 (6)		18.20	145.00
	Set, never hinged		45.00	

700th anniv. of the death of St. Francis of Assisi.

Alessandro Volta — A84

1927 — Wmk. 140 — Typo. — Perf. 14

188	A84	20c dk car	3.25	1.25
	Never hinged		8.00	
	On cover			12.00
189	A84	50c grnsh blk	3.25	.80
	Never hinged		8.00	
	On cover			11.00
190	A84	60c chocolate	4.75	4.75
	Never hinged		12.00	
	On cover			52.50
191	A84	1.25 l ultra	16.00	8.00
	Never hinged		40.00	
	On cover			80.00
	Nos. 188-191 (4)		27.25	14.80
	Set, never hinged		68.00	

Cent. of the death of Alessandro Volta. The 20c in purple is Cyrenaica No. 25a.

A85

1927-29 — Size: 17½x22mm — Perf. 14

192	A85	50c brn & slate	3.25	.40
	Never hinged		8.00	
	On cover			1.40
a.	Imperf, pair		—	
	As "a," single		240.00	325.00
	Never hinged		350.00	

Unwmk. — Engr. — Perf. 11 — Size: 19x23mm

193	A85	1.75 l dp brn	4.00	.35
	Never hinged		10.00	
	On cover			1.25
a.	Perf. 13½ ('29)		42,500.	3,500.
	Never hinged		65,000.	
	On cover			10,500.
b.	Perf. 11x13½ ('29)		—	3,500.
c.	Perf. 13½x11 ('29)		—	3,500.
d.	Imperf, single		5,250.	
	Never hinged		7,750.	
194	A85	1.85 l black	3.25	.70
	Never hinged		9.00	
	On cover			45.00
195	A85	2.55 l brn car	4.00	9.50
	Never hinged		10.00	
	On cover			200.00
196	A85	2.65 l dp vio	6.50	80.00
	Never hinged		16.00	
	On cover			1,250.
	On cover, single franking			2,400.
a.	Imperf, single		3,500.	
	Never hinged		4,750.	
	Nos. 192-196 (5)		21.00	90.95
	Set, never hinged		45.00	

A86

1928-29 — Wmk. 140 — Typo. — Perf. 14

197	A86	7½c lt brown	3.25	12.00
	Never hinged		8.00	
	On cover			32.50
	On cover, single franking			200.00
198	A86	15c brown org ('29)	3.25	.35
	Never hinged		8.00	
	On cover			6.50
199	A86	35c gray blk ('29)	8.75	16.00
	Never hinged		22.00	
	On cover			67.50
	On cover, single franking			675.00
200	A86	50c dull violet	19.00	.35
	Never hinged		47.50	
	On cover			1.00
a.	Imperf single		250.00	
	Never hinged		360.00	
	Nos. 197-200 (4)		34.25	28.70
	Set, never hinged		85.50	

Emmanuel Philibert, Duke of Savoy — A87

Statue of Philibert, Turin — A88

Philibert and Italian Soldier of 1918 — A89

1928   *Perf. 11*
```
201 A87  20c red brn & ultra       9.50   16.00
         Never hinged    25.00
         On cover                         45.00
  a.     Perf. 13½       240.00  240.00
         Never hinged   500.00
         On cover                        600.00
202 A87  25c dp red & bl grn       9.50   16.00
         Never hinged    20.00
         On cover                         45.00
  a.     Perf. 13½        47.50   52.50
         Never hinged   160.00
         On cover                        160.00
203 A87  30c bl grn & red brn     16.00   32.00
         Never hinged    40.00
         On cover                         87.50
  a.     Center inverted 67,500. 9,200.
         No gum         75,000.
  b.     Perf. 13½        35.00   35.00
         Never hinged    80.00
         On cover                        110.00
```
Perf. 14
```
204 A89  50c org brn & bl          4.00    1.25
         Never hinged    10.00
         On cover                          5.50
205 A89  75c dp red               4.75    4.00
         Never hinged    12.00
         On cover                         20.00
206 A88  1.25 l bl & blk          4.75    4.00
         Never hinged    12.00
         On cover                         22.50
207 A89  1.75 l bl grn           32.50   40.00
         Never hinged    80.00
         On cover                        110.00
208 A87  5 l vio & bl grn (Perf. 11)  29.00  110.00
         Never hinged    72.50
         On cover                        550.00
209 A89  10 l blk & pink         35.00  225.00
         Never hinged    87.50
         On cover                       9,200.
210 A88  20 l vio & blk          70.00  725.00
         Never hinged   175.00
         On cover                      15,000.
Nos. 201-210 (10)               215.00  1,173.
Set, never hinged               535.00
```

400th anniv. of the birth of Emmanuel Philibert, Duke of Savoy; 10th anniv. of the victory of 1918; Turin Exhibition.

She-wolf Suckling Romulus and Remus

A90   A95a

Julius Caesar A91   Augustus Caesar A92

"Italia" — A93

A94   A95

1929-42 Wmk. 140 Photo. *Perf. 14*
```
213 A90  5c olive brn       .25    .25
         Never hinged      .50
         On cover                  .40
214 A91  7½c deep vio     1.60    .25
         Never hinged     4.00
         On cover                20.00
215 A92  10c dark brown     .25    .25
         Never hinged      .50
         On cover                  .40
216 A93  15c slate grn      .25    .25
         Never hinged      .50
         On cover                  .40
217 A91  20c rose red       .25    .25
         Never hinged      .50
         On cover                  .40
218 A94  25c dp green       .25    .25
         Never hinged      .50
         On cover                  .40
219 A95  30c olive brn      .25    .25
         Never hinged      .50
         On cover                  .40
  a.     Imperf., pair   1,100.
         Never hinged    2,250.
220 A93  35c dp blue        .25    .25
         Never hinged      .50
         On cover                32.50
221 A95  50c purple         .25    .25
         Never hinged      .50
         On cover                  .40
  a.     Imperf., pair    725.00  875.00
                         1,450.
222 A94  75c rose red       .25    .25
         Never hinged      .50
         On cover                  .40
222A A91 1 l dk pur ('42)   .25    .25
         Never hinged      .50
         On cover                20.00
223 A94  1.25 l dp blue     .25    .25
         Never hinged      .50
         On cover                  .40
224 A92  1.75 l red org     .25    .25
         Never hinged      .50
         On cover                  .40
225 A93  2 l car lake       .25    .25
         Never hinged      .50
         On cover                  .40
226 A95a 2.55 l slate grn   .25    .80
         Never hinged      .50
         On cover                32.50
226A A95a 3.70 l pur ('30)  .25    .80
         Never hinged      .50
         On cover                60.00
227 A95a 5 l rose red       .25    .25
         Never hinged      .50
         On cover                20.00
228 A93  10 l purple       4.00   4.00
         Never hinged    10.00
         On cover                72.50
229 A91  20 l lt green     4.75  12.00
         Never hinged    12.00
         On cover               325.00
230 A92  25 l bluish sl   11.00  35.00
         Never hinged    27.50
         On cover                2,400.
231 A94  50 l dp violet   13.00  40.00
         Never hinged    32.50
         On cover                2,400.
Nos. 213-231 (21)        38.35  96.35
Set, never hinged        94.00
```

Stamps of the 1929-42 issue overprinted "G.N.R." are 1943 local issues of the Guardia Nazionale Republicana.

See Nos. 427-438, 441-459 in Scott Standard catalogue, Vol. 3.

For surcharge and overprints see Nos. 460, M1-M13, 1N10-1N13, 1LN1-1LN1A, 1LN10, Italian Social Republic 1-5A, and Ionian Islands Nos. N18-N25 in Scott Standard catalogue, Vol. 3; Yugoslavia-Ljubljana N36-N54 in Scott Standard catalogue, Vol. 6.

Courtyard of Monte Cassino A96

Monks Laying Cornerstone — A98

St. Benedict of Nursia — A100

Designs: 25c, Fresco, "Death of St. Benedict." 75c+15c, 5 l+1 l, Monte Cassino Abbey.

1929, Aug. 1 Photo. Wmk. 140
```
232 A96  20c red orange      1.60   1.60
         Never hinged       4.00
         On cover                   8.00
233 A96  25c dk green        1.60   1.60
         Never hinged       4.00
         On cover                   8.00
234 A98  50c + 10c ol brn    4.00  30.00
         Never hinged      10.00
         On cover                  87.50
235 A98  75c + 15c crim      4.75  40.00
         Never hinged      12.00
         On cover                 110.00
236 A96  1.25 l + 25c saph   6.50  45.00
         Never hinged      16.00
         On cover                 125.00
237 A98  5 l + 1 l dk vio    9.50 175.00
         Never hinged      23.00
         On cover                 475.00
```
Unwmk.   Engr.
```
238 A100 10 l + 2 l slate grn  14.50  325.00
         Never hinged     35.00
         On cover                 2,750.
Nos. 232-238 (7)        42.45  618.20
Set, never hinged      105.00
Set on overfranked philatelic cover   1,200.
```

14th cent. of the founding of the Abbey of Monte Cassino by St. Benedict in 529 A.D. The premium on some of the stamps was given to the committee for the celebration of the centenary.

Prince Humbert and Princess Marie José A101

1930, Jan. 8 Photo. Wmk. 140
```
239 A101 20c orange red      .80    .60
         Never hinged      2.00
         On cover                   4.00
240 A101 50c + 10c ol brn   2.40   4.00
         Never hinged      6.00
         On cover                   9.50
241 A101 1.25 l + 25c dp bl 5.50  13.00
         Never hinged     14.00
         On cover                  32.50
Nos. 239-241 (3)         8.70  17.60
Set, never hinged       22.00
Set on overfranked philatelic cover    35.00
```

Marriage of Prince Humbert of Savoy with Princess Marie José of Belgium.

The surtax on Nos. 240 and 241 was for the benefit of the Italian Red Cross Society.

The 20c in green is Cyrenaica No. 35a.

Ferrucci Leading His Army A102

Fabrizio Maramaldo Killing Ferrucci A103

Francesco Ferrucci — A104

1930, July 10
```
242 A102 20c rose red        .80    .80
         Never hinged      2.00
         On cover                   9.50
243 A103 25c deep green     1.40    .80
         Never hinged      3.50
         On cover                   9.50
244 A103 50c purple          .80    .40
         Never hinged      2.00
         On cover                   4.75
245 A103 1.25 l deep blue  11.00   4.75
         Never hinged     27.50
         On cover                  60.00
246 A104 5 l + 2 l org red 22.50 140.00
         Never hinged     55.00
         On cover                 600.00
Nos. 242-246 (5)        36.50 146.75
Set, never hinged       90.00
Set on overfranked philatelic cover   550.00
Nos. 242-246,C20-C22 (8)  60.50 314.75
Set, never hinged      150.00
```

4th cent. of the death of Francesco Ferrucci, Tuscan warrior.

Overprints
See Castellorizo and Aegean Islands for types A103-A145 Overprinted.

Helenus and Aeneas A106

Designs: 20c, Anchises and Aeneas watch passing of Roman Legions. 25c, Aeneas feasting in shade of Albunea. 30c, Ceres and her children with fruits of Earth. 50c, Harvesters at work. 75c, Woman at loom, children and calf. 1.25 l, Anchises and his sailors in sight of Italy. 5 l+1.50 l, Shepherd piping by fireside. 10 l+2.50 l, Aeneas leading his army.

1930, Oct. 21 Photo. *Perf. 14*
```
248 A106 15c olive brn      2.40   2.40
         Never hinged      6.00
         On cover                  16.00
249 A106 20c orange         2.40   1.60
         Never hinged      6.00
         On cover                   8.00
250 A106 25c green          3.20   1.60
         Never hinged      8.00
         On cover                   8.00
251 A106 30c dull vio       9.50   4.00
         Never hinged     24.00
         On cover                  20.00
252 A106 50c violet        16.00    .80
         Never hinged     40.00
         On cover                   4.00
253 A106 75c rose red       4.00  12.00
         Never hinged     10.00
         On cover                  52.50
254 A106 1.25 l blue        4.00  12.00
         Never hinged     10.00
         On cover                  65.00
```
Unwmk.   Engr.
```
255 A106 5 l +1.50 l red brn  60.00  525.00
         Never hinged    150.00
         On cover                 1,200.
256 A106 10 l +2.50 l gray grn 60.00  725.00
         Never hinged    150.00
         On cover                 4,000.
Nos. 248-256 (9)       161.50  1,284.
Set, never hinged      405.00
Set on overfranked philatelic cover   3,250.
Nos. 248-256,C23-C26 (13) 332.00  2,019.
Set, never hinged      835.00
```

Bimillenary of the birth of Virgil. Surtax on Nos. 255-256 was for the National Institute Figli del Littorio.

Arms of Italy (Fascist Emblems Support House of Savoy Arms) — A115

1930, Dec. 16 Photo. Wmk. 140
```
257 A115 2c deep orange     1.60    .25
         Never hinged      4.00
         On cover                  12.00
```

St. Anthony being Installed as a Franciscan A116

Olivares Hermitage, Portugal A118

St. Anthony Freeing Prisoners A120

St. Anthony's Death A121

St. Anthony Succoring the Poor — A122

Designs: 25c, St. Anthony preaching to the fishes. 50c, Basilica of St. Anthony, Padua.

Wmk. 140

1931, Mar. 9   **Photo.**   **Perf. 14**

No.	Type	Description		
258	A116	20c dull violet	4.00	1.25
		Never hinged	10.00	
		On cover		4.75
259	A116	25c gray green	2.40	1.25
		Never hinged	6.00	
		On cover		4.75
260	A118	30c brown	6.50	2.40
		Never hinged	16.00	
		On cover		12.00
261	A118	50c violet	2.00	.80
		Never hinged	5.00	
		On cover		3.50
262	A120	1.25 l blue	20.00	9.50
		Never hinged	50.00	
		On cover		45.00

Unwmk.   **Engr.**

No.	Type	Description		
263	A121	75c brown red	9.50	16.00
		Never hinged	24.00	
		On cover		67.50
a.		Perf. 12	100.00	375.00
		Never hinged	240.00	
		On cover		750.00
264	A122	5 l + 2.50 l ol grn	40.00	325.00
		Never hinged	100.00	
		On cover		725.00
		Nos. 258-264 (7)	84.40	356.20

Set, never hinged   210.00
Set on overfranked philatelic cover   525.00

7th centenary of the death of Saint Anthony of Padua.

Tower of Meloria — A123

Training Ship "Amerigo Vespucci" A124

Cruiser "Trento" A125

1931, Nov. 29   **Photo.**   **Wmk. 140**

No.	Type	Description		
265	A123	20c rose red	8.75	2.00
		Never hinged	35.00	
		On cover		9.50
266	A124	50c purple	8.75	1.60
		Never hinged	35.00	
		On cover		8.00
267	A125	1.25 l dk bl	24.00	4.75
		Never hinged	95.00	
		On cover		40.00
		Nos. 265-267 (3)	41.50	8.35

Set, never hinged   165.00
Set on overfranked philatelic cover   45.00

Royal Naval Academy at Leghorn (Livorno), 50th anniv.

Giovanni Boccaccio A126

Designs: 15c, Niccolo Machiavelli. 20c, Paolo Sarpi. 25c, Count Vittorio Alfieri. 30c, Ugo Foscolo. 50c, Count Giacomo Leopardi. 75c, Giosue Carducci. 1.25 l, Carlo Giuseppe Botta. 1.75 l, Torquato Tasso. 2.75 l, Francesco Petrarca. 5 l+2 l, Ludovico Ariosto. 10 l+2.50 l, Dante Alighieri.

1932, Mar. 14   **Perf. 14**

No.	Type	Description		
268	A126	10c olive brn	3.25	1.60
		Never hinged	8.00	
		On cover		14.00
269	A126	15c slate green	3.25	2.00
		Never hinged	8.00	
		On cover		32.50
270	A126	20c rose red	3.25	1.60
		Never hinged	8.00	
		On cover		8.00
271	A126	25c dp green	3.25	1.25
		Never hinged	8.00	
		On cover		6.50
272	A126	30c olive brn	4.00	1.60
		Never hinged	10.00	
		On cover		20.00
273	A126	50c violet	2.40	.80
		Never hinged	6.00	
		On cover		3.50
274	A126	75c car rose	16.00	8.00
		Never hinged	40.00	
		On cover		40.00
275	A126	1.25 l dp blue	4.75	4.00
		Never hinged	12.00	
		On cover		32.50
276	A126	1.75 l orange	12.00	8.00
		Never hinged	30.00	
		On cover		47.50
277	A126	2.75 l gray	24.00	40.00
		Never hinged	60.00	
		On cover		175.00
278	A126	5 l + 2 l car rose	29.00	300.00
		Never hinged	72.50	
		On cover		1,100.
279	A126	10 l + 2.50 l ol grn	35.00	450.00
		Never hinged	87.50	
		On cover		2,750.
		Nos. 268-279 (12)	140.15	818.85

Set, never hinged   350.00
Set on overfranked philatelic cover   2,000.
Nos. 268-279,C28-C33,C34 (19)   237.90   2,426.
Set, never hinged   600.00

Dante Alighieri Society, a natl. literary association founded to promote development of the Italian language and culture. The surtax was added to the Society funds to help in its work.

View of Caprera A138

Garibaldi Carrying His Dying Wife A141

Garibaldi Memorial A144

Giuseppe Garibaldi A145

Designs: 20c, 30c, Garibaldi meeting Victor Emmanuel II. 25c, 50c, Garibaldi at Battle of Calatafimi. 1.25 l, Garibaldi's tomb. 1.75 l+25c, Rock of Quarto.

1932, Apr. 6

No.	Type	Description		
280	A138	10c gray blk	2.40	1.60
		Never hinged	6.00	
		On cover		14.50
281	A138	20c olive brn	2.40	1.25
		Never hinged	6.00	
		On cover		11.00
282	A138	25c dull grn	3.25	1.60
		Never hinged	8.00	
		On cover		8.00
283	A138	30c orange	3.25	2.40
		Never hinged	8.00	
		On cover		35.00
284	A138	50c violet	1.60	.40
		Never hinged	4.00	
		On cover		3.25
285	A141	75c rose red	16.00	9.50
		Never hinged	40.00	
		On cover		45.00
286	A141	1.25 l dp blue	32.50	4.00
		Never hinged	80.00	
		On cover		40.00
287	A141	1.75 l + 25c bl gray	40.00	87.50
		Never hinged	100.00	
		On cover		450.00
288	A144	2.55 l + 50c red brn	32.50	125.00
		Never hinged	80.00	
		On cover		500.00
289	A145	5 l + 1 l cop red	32.50	130.00
		Never hinged	80.00	
		On cover		675.00
		Nos. 280-289 (10)	166.40	363.25

Set, never hinged   410.00
Set on overfranked philatelic cover   950.00
Nos. 280-289,C35-C39,CE1-CE2 (17)   242.40   619.25
Set, never hinged   600.00

50th anniv. of the death of Giuseppe Garibaldi, patriot.

Plowing with Oxen and Tractor A146

10c, Soldier guarding mountain pass. 15c, Marine, battleship & seaplane. 20c, Head of Fascist youth. 25c, Hands of workers & tools. 30c, Flags, Bible & altar. 35c, "New roads for the new Legions." 50c, Mussolini statue, Bologna. 60c, Hands with spades. 75c, Excavating ruins. 1 l, Steamers & galleons. 1.25 l, Italian flag, map & points of compass. 1.75 l, Flag, athlete & stadium. 2.55 l, Mother & child. 2.75 l, Emblems of drama, music, art & sport. 5 l+2.50 l, Roman emperor.

1932, Oct. 27   **Photo.**

No.	Type	Description		
290	A146	5c dk brown	2.40	1.25
		Never hinged	6.00	
		On cover		27.50
291	A146	10c dk brown	2.40	.80
		Never hinged	6.00	
		On cover		9.50
292	A146	15c dk gray grn	2.40	1.25
		Never hinged	6.00	
		On cover		16.00
293	A146	20c car rose	2.40	.60
		Never hinged	6.00	
		On cover		3.25
294	A146	25c dp green	2.40	.40
		Never hinged	6.00	
		On cover		3.25
295	A146	30c dk brown	3.25	2.40
		Never hinged	8.00	
		On cover		20.00
296	A146	35c dk blue	8.00	9.50
		Never hinged	20.00	
		On cover		87.50
297	A146	50c purple	1.60	.40
		Never hinged	4.00	
		On cover		2.00
298	A146	60c orange brn	12.00	8.00
		Never hinged	30.00	
		On cover		55.00
299	A146	75c car rose	4.00	4.00
		Never hinged	10.00	
		On cover		20.00
300	A146	1 l black vio	16.00	6.50
		Never hinged	40.00	
		On cover		52.50
301	A146	1.25 l dp blue	4.00	1.60
		Never hinged	10.00	
		On cover		20.00
302	A146	1.75 l orange	24.00	2.00
		Never hinged	60.00	
		On cover		20.00
303	A146	2.55 l dk gray	29.00	40.00
		Never hinged	72.50	
		On cover		160.00
304	A146	2.75 l slate grn	29.00	40.00
		Never hinged	72.50	
		On cover		200.00
305	A146	5 l + 2.50 l car rose	40.00	450.00
		Never hinged	100.00	
		On cover		1,900.
		Nos. 290-305 (16)	182.85	568.70

Set, never hinged   455.00
Set on overfranked philatelic cover   1,650.
Nos. 290-305,C40-C41,E16-E17 (20)   700.00
Set, never hinged   520.00

10th anniv. of the Fascist government and the March on Rome.

Statue of Athlete — A162

Cross in Halo, St. Peter's Dome — A163

1933, Aug. 16   **Perf. 14**

No.	Type	Description		
306	A162	10c dk brown	.80	.80
		Never hinged	2.00	
		On cover		8.00
307	A162	20c rose red	.80	.80
		Never hinged	2.00	
		On cover		9.50
308	A162	50c purple	.80	.40
		Never hinged	2.00	
		On cover		4.75
309	A162	1.25 l blue	4.75	6.50
		Never hinged	12.00	
		On cover		4.75
		Nos. 306-309 (4)	7.15	8.50

Set, never hinged   18.00
Set on overfranked philatelic cover   52.50

Intl. University Games at Turin, Sept., 1933.

1933, Oct. 23

Designs: 25c, 50c, Angel with cross. 1.25 l, as 20c. 2.55 l, + 2.50 l, Cross with doves.

No.	Type	Description		
310	A163	20c rose red	4.75	1.25
		Never hinged	12.00	
		On cover		8.00
311	A163	25c green	12.00	1.60
		Never hinged	30.00	
		On cover		8.00
312	A163	50c purple	4.75	.40
		Never hinged	12.00	
		On cover		3.25
313	A163	1.25 l dp blue	12.00	4.75
		Never hinged	30.00	
		On cover		40.00
314	A163	2.55 l + 2.50 l blk	8.00	240.00
		Never hinged	20.00	
		On cover		725.00
		Nos. 310-314 (5)	41.50	248.00

Set, never hinged   105.00
Set on overfranked philatelic cover   725.00
Nos. 310-314,CB1-CB2 (7)   47.90   435.50
Set, never hinged   121.00

Issued at the solicitation of the Order of the Holy Sepulchre of Jerusalem to mark the Holy Year.

Anchor of the "Emanuele Filiberto" A166

Antonio Pacinotti A172

Designs: 20c, Anchor. 50c, Gabriele d'Annunzio. 1.25 l, St. Vito's Tower. 1.75 l, Symbolizing Fiume's annexation. 2.55 l+2 l, Victor Emmanuel III arriving aboard "Brindisi." 2.75 l+2.50 l, Galley, gondola and battleship.

1934, Mar. 12

No.	Type	Description		
315	A166	10c dk brown	8.00	4.00
		Never hinged	20.00	
		On cover		32.50
316	A166	20c rose red	1.60	1.60
		Never hinged	4.00	
		On cover		17.50
317	A166	50c purple	1.60	1.60
		Never hinged	4.00	
		On cover		16.00
318	A166	1.25 l blue	1.60	6.50
		Never hinged	4.00	
		On cover		60.00
319	A166	1.75 l + 1 l indigo	1.60	35.00
		Never hinged	4.00	
		On cover		475.00

320	A166 2.55 l + 2 l dull vio		1.60	*55.00*
	Never hinged		4.00	
	On cover			*600.00*
321	A166 2.75 l + 2.50 l ol grn		1.60	*55.00*
	Never hinged		4.00	
	On cover			*650.00*
	Nos. 315-321 (7)		17.60	*158.70*
	Set, never hinged		44.00	
	Set on overfranked philatelic cover			950.00
	Nos. 315-321,C56-C61,CE5-CE7 (16)		29.95	*308.60*
	Set, never hinged		66.50	

10th anniversary of annexation of Fiume.

1934, May 23

322	A172 50c purple		.80	.40
	Never hinged		2.00	
	On cover			4.00
323	A172 1.25 l sapphire		1.25	2.75
	Never hinged		3.00	
	On cover			35.00
	Set, never hinged		5.00	
	Set on overfranked philatelic cover			35.00

75th anniv. of invention of the dynamo by Antonio Pacinotti (1841-1912), scientist.

Guarding the Goal — A173   Players — A175

Soccer Players A174

1934, May 23

324	A173 20c red orange		6.50	*8.00*
	Never hinged		16.00	
	On cover			80.00
325	A174 25c green		6.50	2.40
	Never hinged		16.00	
	On cover			52.50
326	A174 50c purple		6.50	1.25
	Never hinged		16.00	
	On cover			40.00
327	A174 1.25 l blue		16.00	16.00
	Never hinged		40.00	
	On cover			240.00
328	A175 5 l + 2.50 l brn		95.00	*700.00*
	Never hinged		240.00	
	On cover			*4,000.*
	Nos. 324-328 (5)		130.50	*727.65*
	Set, never hinged		330.00	
	Set on overfranked philatelic cover			*3,750.*
	Nos. 324-328,C62-C65 (9)		264.00	*1,465.*
	Set, never hinged		625.00	

2nd World Soccer Championship.
For overprints see Aegean Islands Nos. 31-35.

Luigi Galvani — A176

1934, Aug. 16

329	A176 30c brown, *buff*		1.00	.80
	Never hinged		2.50	
	On cover			8.00
330	A176 75c carmine, *rose*		1.40	3.25
	Never hinged		3.50	
	On cover			35.00
	Set, never hinged		6.00	
	Set on overfranked philatelic cover			40.00

Intl. Congress of Electro-Radio-Biology.

Carabinieri Emblem — A177

Cutting Barbed Wire A178

Designs: 20c, Sardinian Grenadier and soldier throwing grenade. 25c, Alpine Infantry. 30c, Military courage. 75c, Artillery. 1.25 l, Acclaiming the Service. 1.75 l+1 l, Cavalry. 2.55 l+2 l, Sapping Detail. 2.75 l+2 l, First aid.

1934, Sept. 6   Photo.   Wmk. 140

331	A177 10c dk brown		2.40	2.40
	Never hinged		6.00	
	On cover			17.50
332	A177 15c olive grn		2.40	*4.00*
	Never hinged		6.00	
	On cover			24.00
333	A178 20c rose red		2.40	1.60
	Never hinged		6.00	
	On cover			12.00
334	A177 25c green		4.00	1.60
	Never hinged		10.00	
	On cover			12.00
335	A178 30c dk brown		4.00	*8.00*
	Never hinged		10.00	
	On cover			35.00
336	A178 50c purple		2.40	.80
	Never hinged		6.00	
	On cover			4.00
337	A178 75c car rose		40.00	12.00
	Never hinged		100.00	
	On cover			52.50
338	A178 1.25 l dk blue		40.00	8.00
	Never hinged		100.00	
	On cover			40.00
339	A177 1.75 l + 1 l red org		17.50	*60.00*
	Never hinged		42.50	
	On cover			550.00
340	A178 2.55 l + 2 l dp cl		17.50	*80.00*
	Never hinged		42.50	
	On cover			675.00
341	A178 2.75 l + 2 l vio		21.00	*80.00*
	Never hinged		52.50	
	On cover			950.00
	Nos. 331-341 (11)		153.60	*258.40*
	Set, never hinged		385.00	
	Set on overfranked philatelic cover			1,300.
	Nos. 331-341,C66-C72 (18)		202.10	*421.40*
	Set, never hinged		505.00	

Centenary of Military Medal of Valor.
For overprints see Aegean Islands Nos. 36-46.

Man Holding Fasces A187

Standard Bearer, Bayonet Attack A188

Design: 30c, Eagle and soldier.

1935, Apr. 23   Perf. 14

342	A187 20c rose red		.80	.80
	Never hinged		2.00	
	On cover			8.00
343	A187 30c dk brown		6.50	16.00
	Never hinged		16.00	
	On cover			65.00
344	A188 50c purple		.80	.40
	Never hinged		2.00	
	On cover			6.50
	Nos. 342-344 (3)		8.10	17.20
	Set, never hinged		20.00	
	Set on overfranked philatelic cover			65.00

Issued in honor of the University Contests.

Fascist Flight Symbolism A190

Leonardo da Vinci — A191

1935, Oct. 1

345	A190 20c rose red		20.00	2.00
	Never hinged		80.00	
	On cover			25.00
346	A190 30c brown		35.00	6.50
	Never hinged		140.00	
	On cover			87.50
347	A191 50c purple		72.50	1.25
	Never hinged		290.00	
	On cover			17.50
348	A191 1.25 l dk blue		80.00	7.25
	Never hinged		320.00	
	On cover			110.00
	Nos. 345-348 (4)		207.50	17.00
	Set, never hinged		830.00	
	Set on overfranked philatelic cover			200.00

International Aeronautical Salon, Milan.

Vincenzo Bellini — A192   Bellini's Villa — A194

Bellini's Piano A193

1935, Oct. 15

349	A192 20c rose red		16.00	4.00
	Never hinged		40.00	
	On cover			24.00
350	A192 30c brown		24.00	14.50
	Never hinged		60.00	
	On cover			40.00
351	A192 50c violet		24.00	1.60
	Never hinged		60.00	
	On cover			16.00
352	A192 1.25 l dk blue		40.00	20.00
	Never hinged		100.00	
	On cover			110.00
353	A193 1.75 l + 1 l red org		35.00	*325.00*
	Never hinged		90.00	
	On cover			725.00
354	A194 2.75 l + 2 l ol blk		65.00	*340.00*
	Never hinged		160.00	
	On cover			1,000.
	Nos. 349-354 (6)		204.00	*705.10*
	Set, never hinged		510.00	
	Set on overfranked philatelic cover			1,350.
	Nos. 349-354,C79-C83 (11)		287.00	*1,021.*
	Set, never hinged		710.00	

Bellini (1801-35), operatic composer.

Map of Italian Industries A195

Designs: 20c, 1.25 l, Map of Italian Industries. 30c, 50c, Cogwheel and plow.

1936, Mar. 23

355	A195 20c red		.80	.40
	Never hinged		2.00	
	On cover			4.75
356	A195 30c brown		.80	1.25
	Never hinged		2.00	
	On cover			12.00

357	A195 50c purple		.80	.35
	Never hinged		2.00	
	On cover			3.25
358	A195 1.25 l blue		4.75	3.25
	Never hinged		12.00	
	On cover			20.00
	Nos. 355-358 (4)		7.15	5.25
	Set, never hinged		18.00	
	Set on overfranked philatelic cover			24.00

The 17th Milan Trade Fair.

Flock of Sheep A197

Ajax Defying the Lightning A199   Bust of Horace A200

Designs: 20c, 1.25 l+1 l, Countryside in Spring. 75c, Capitol. 1.75 l+1 l, Pan piping. 2.55 l+1 l, Dying warrior.

Wmk. Crowns (140)

1936, July 1   Photo.   Perf. 14

359	A197 10c dp green		6.50	1.25
	Never hinged		16.00	
	On cover			9.50
360	A197 20c rose red		4.75	.80
	Never hinged		12.00	
	On cover			8.00
361	A199 30c olive brn		6.50	2.40
	Never hinged		16.00	
	On cover			20.00
362	A200 50c purple		6.50	.40
	Never hinged		16.00	
	On cover			4.75
363	A197 75c rose red		16.00	12.00
	Never hinged		40.00	
	On cover			45.00
364	A197 1.25 l + 1 l dk bl		27.50	*160.00*
	Never hinged		67.50	
	On cover			525.00
365	A199 1.75 l + 1 l car rose		32.50	*300.00*
	Never hinged		80.00	
	On cover			600.00
366	A197 2.55 l + 1 l sl blk		40.00	*350.00*
	Never hinged		100.00	
	On cover			800.00
	Nos. 359-366 (8)		140.25	*826.85*
	Set, never hinged		350.00	
	Set on overfranked philatelic cover			1,600.
	Nos. 359-366,C84-C88 (13)		202.00	*1,153.*
	Set, never hinged		500.00	

2000th anniv. of the birth of Quintus Horatius Flaccus (Horace), Roman poet.

Child Holding Wheat — A204   Child Giving Salute — A205

Child and Fasces — A206   "Il Bambino" by della Robbia — A207

1937, June 28
367	A204	10c yellow brn	3.25	1.60
		Never hinged	8.00	
		On cover		20.00
368	A205	20c car rose	3.25	1.25
		Never hinged	8.00	
		On cover		6.50
369	A204	25c green	3.25	2.00
		Never hinged	8.00	
		On cover		24.00
370	A206	30c dk brown	4.75	4.00
		Never hinged	12.00	
		On cover		30.00
371	A205	50c purple	3.25	.40
		Never hinged	8.00	
		On cover		4.00
372	A207	75c rose red	16.00	17.50
		Never hinged	40.00	
		On cover		80.00
373	A205	1.25 l dk blue	20.00	17.50
		Never hinged	50.00	
		On cover		72.50
374	A206	1.75 l + 75c org	40.00	250.00
		Never hinged	100.00	
		On cover		800.00
375	A207	2.75 l + 1.25 l dk bl grn	32.50	275.00
		Never hinged	80.00	
		On cover		1,000.
376	A205	5 l + 3 l bl gray	40.00	375.00
		Never hinged	100.00	
		On cover		2,200.
		Nos. 367-376 (10)	166.25	*944.25*
		Set, never hinged	415.00	
		Set on overfranked philatelic cover		2,750.
		Nos. 367-376,C89-C94 (16)	262.25	*1,377.*
		Set, never hinged	655.00	

Summer Exhibition for Child Welfare. The surtax on Nos. 374-376 was used to support summer camps for children.

Rostral Column — A208

15c, Army Trophies. 20c, Augustus Caesar (Octavianus) offering sacrifice. .25c, Cross Roman Standards. 30c, Julius Caesar and Julian Star. 50c, Augustus receiving acclaim. 75c, Augustus Caesar. 1.25 l, Symbolizing maritime glory of Rome. 1.75 l+1 l, Sacrificial Altar. 2.55 l+2 l, Capitol.

1937, Sept. 23
377	A208	10c myrtle grn	3.25	.80
		Never hinged	8.00	
		On cover		6.50
378	A208	15c olive grn	3.25	1.25
		Never hinged	8.00	
		On cover		16.00
379	A208	20c red	3.25	.60
		Never hinged	8.00	
		On cover		4.75
380	A208	25c green	3.25	.60
		Never hinged	8.00	
		On cover		4.75
381	A208	30c olive bis	4.00	.80
		Never hinged	10.00	
		On cover		12.00
382	A208	50c purple	3.25	.35
		Never hinged	8.00	
		On cover		3.50
383	A208	75c scarlet	3.25	4.75
		Never hinged	8.00	
		On cover		24.00
384	A208	1.25 l dk blue	8.00	5.50
		Never hinged	20.00	
		On cover		27.50
385	A208	1.75 l + 1 l plum	40.00	225.00
		Never hinged	100.00	
		On cover		550.00
386	A208	2.55 l + 2 l sl blk	52.50	300.00
		Never hinged	130.00	
		On cover		725.00
		Nos. 377-386 (10)	124.00	*539.65*
		Set, never hinged	300.00	
		Set on overfranked philatelic cover		1,000.
		Nos. 377-386,C95-C99 (15)	259.00	*812.65*
		Set, never hinged	625.00	

Bimillenary of the birth of Emperor Augustus Caesar (Octavianus) on the occasion of the exhibition opened in Rome by Mussolini, Sept. 22, 1937.

For overprints see Aegean Islands Nos. 47-56.

Gasparo Luigi Pacifico Spontini
A218

Antonius Stradivarius
A219

Count Giacomo Leopardi
A220

Giovanni Battista Pergolesi
A221

Giotto di Bondone — A222

1937, Oct. 25
387	A218	10c dk brown	1.60	.80
		Never hinged	4.00	
		On cover		6.50
388	A219	20c rose red	1.60	.80
		Never hinged	4.00	
		On cover		4.75
389	A220	25c dk green	1.60	.80
		Never hinged	4.00	
		On cover		4.75
390	A221	30c dk brown	1.60	1.60
		Never hinged	4.00	
		On cover		16.00
391	A220	50c purple	1.60	.80
		Never hinged	4.00	
		On cover		3.25
392	A221	75c crimson	2.25	4.75
		Never hinged	5.50	
		On cover		35.00
393	A222	1.25 l dp blue	3.25	4.75
		Never hinged	8.00	
		On cover		35.00
394	A218	1.75 l dp orange	3.25	4.75
		Never hinged	8.00	
		On cover		35.00
395	A219	2.55 l + 2 l gray grn	16.00	260.00
		Never hinged	40.00	
		On cover		675.00
396	A222	2.75 l + 2 l red brn	16.00	300.00
		Never hinged	40.00	
		On cover		725.00
		Nos. 387-396 (10)	48.75	*579.05*
		Set, never hinged	125.00	
		Set on overfranked philatelic cover		1,100.

Centennials of Spontini, Stradivarius, Leopardi, Pergolesi and Giotto.

For overprints see Aegean Islands Nos. 57-58.

Guglielmo Marconi
A223

Augustus Caesar (Octavianus)
A224

1938, Jan. 24
397	A223	20c rose pink	3.25	.80
		Never hinged	8.00	
		On cover		6.50
398	A223	50c purple	.80	.40
		Never hinged	2.00	
		On cover		4.75

399	A223	1.25 l blue	3.25	6.75
		Never hinged	8.00	
		On cover		45.00
		Nos. 397-399 (3)	7.30	*7.95*
		Set, never hinged	18.00	
		Set on overfranked philatelic cover		40.00

Guglielmo Marconi (1874-1937), electrical engineer, inventor of wireless telegraphy.

1938, Oct. 28

10c, Romulus Plowing. 25c, Dante. 30c, Columbus. 50c, Leonardo da Vinci. 75c, Victor Emmanuel II and Garibaldi. 1.25 l, Tomb of Unknown Soldier, Rome. 1.75 l, Blackshirts' March on Rome, 1922. 2.75 l, Map of Italian East Africa and Iron Crown of Monza. 5 l, Victor Emmanuel III.

400	A224	10c brown	2.40	.80
		Never hinged	6.00	
		On cover		8.00
401	A224	20c car rose	2.40	.80
		Never hinged	6.00	
		On cover		8.00
402	A224	25c dk green	2.40	.80
		Never hinged	6.00	
		On cover		8.00
403	A224	30c olive brn	2.40	2.00
		Never hinged	6.00	
		On cover		14.50
404	A224	50c lt violet	2.40	.80
		Never hinged	6.00	
		On cover		3.50
405	A224	75c rose red	3.25	3.25
		Never hinged	8.00	
		On cover		35.00
406	A224	1.25 l dp blue	6.50	3.25
		Never hinged	16.00	
		On cover		35.00
407	A224	1.75 l vio blk	8.00	4.00
		Never hinged	20.00	
		On cover		47.50
408	A224	2.75 l slate grn	27.50	47.50
		Never hinged	67.50	
		On cover		240.00
409	A224	5 l lt red brn	32.50	52.50
		Never hinged	82.50	
		On cover		400.00
		Nos. 400-409 (10)	89.75	*115.70*
		Set, never hinged	220.00	
		Set on overfranked philatelic cover		600.00
		Nos. 400-409,C100-C105 (16)	143.25	*284.20*
		Set, never hinged	350.00	

Proclamation of the Empire.

Wood-burning Engine and Streamlined Electric Engine — A234

1939, Dec. 15　Photo.　Perf. 14
410	A234	20c rose red	.80	.60
		Never hinged	2.00	
		On cover		9.50
411	A234	50c brt violet	1.60	.80
		Never hinged	4.00	
		On cover		8.00
412	A234	1.25 l dp blue	4.00	4.00
		Never hinged	10.00	
		On cover		40.00
		Nos. 410-412 (3)	6.40	*5.40*
		Set, never hinged	16.00	
		Set on overfranked philatelic cover		40.00

Centenary of Italian railroads.

SEMI-POSTAL STAMPS

Many issues of Italy and Italian Colonies include one or more semi-postal denominations. To avoid splitting sets, these issues are generally listed as regular postage, airmail, etc., unless all values carry a surtax.

Italian Flag — SP1

Italian Eagle Bearing Arms of Savoy — SP2

1915-16　Typo.　Perf. 14
B1	SP1	10c + 5c rose	8.50	12.00
		Never hinged	21.00	
		On cover		47.50

B2	SP2	15c + 5c slate	6.75	9.50
		Never hinged	17.00	
		On cover		47.50
		On cover, single franking		175.00
B3	SP2	20c + 5c orange	32.00	65.00
		Never hinged	85.00	
		On cover		175.00
		Nos. B1-B3 (3)	47.75	*86.50*
		Set, never hinged	125.00	

No. B2 Surcharged

1916
B4	SP2	20c on 15c + 5c	20.00	55.00
		Never hinged	50.00	
		On cover		240.00
a.		Double overprint	800.00	—
		Never hinged	—	
b.		Inverted overprint	800.00	1,400.
		Never hinged	—	
c.		Pair, one without surcharge	1,800.	
		Never hinged	2,600.	

Regular Issues of 1906-16 Overprinted in Blue or Red

1921
B5	A48	10c claret (Bl)	1,000.	1,600.
		No gum	475.00	
		Never hinged	2,000.	
		On BLP envelope	525.00	5,500.
a.		Double overprint	1,450.	
		Never hinged	—	
B6	A50	20c brn org (Bl)	1,400.	475.00
		No gum	575.00	
		Never hinged	2,800.	
		On BLP envelope	650.00	1,200.
B7	A49	25c blue (R)	240.00	200.00
		No gum	100.00	
		Never hinged	600.00	
		On BLP envelope	110.00	550.00
a.		Double overprint	400.00	
B8	A49	40c brn (Bl)	95.00	20.00
		No gum	35.00	
		Never hinged	240.00	
		On BLP envelope	40.00	65.00
a.		Inverted overprint	475.00	
b.		Violet ovpt.	160.00	27.50
		No gum	47.50	
		Never hinged	400.00	
		On BLP envelope	40.00	65.00
c.		Maroon ovpt.	110.00	24.00
		No gum	45.00	
		Never hinged	275.00	
		On BLP envelope	47.50	95.00
d.		Blue black ovpt.	240.00	72.50
		No gum	80.00	
		Never hinged	600.00	
		On BLP envelope	87.50	275.00
		Nos. B5-B8 (4)	2,735.	2,295.
		Set, never hinged	5,640.	

Regular Issues of 1901-22 Overprinted in Black, Blue, Brown or Red

1922-23

Typographed Ovpt.
B9	A48	10c cl ('23) (Bk)	125.00	110.00
		No gum	47.50	
		Never hinged	325.00	
		On BLP envelope	52.50	325.00
a.		Blue ovpt.	95.00	87.50
		No gum	40.00	
		Never hinged	240.00	
		On BLP envelope	45.00	1,050.
b.		Brown ovpt.	95.00	87.50
		No gum	40.00	
		Never hinged	240.00	
		On BLP envelope	45.00	1,600.
d.		Blk ovpt. double	175.00	
e.		As "b," ovpt. double	175.00	
B10	A48	15c slate (Org)	325.00	540.00
		No gum	140.00	
		Never hinged	800.00	
		On BLP envelope	160.00	7,250.
b.		Red overprint	400.00	650.00
		Never hinged	210.00	
		On BLP envelope	1,000.	
		On BLP envelope	240.00	8,750.
B11	A50	20c brn org (Bk)	400.00	540.00
		No gum	160.00	
		Never hinged	1,000.	
		On BLP envelope	175.00	2,450.
b.		Red overprint	325.00	540.00
		No gum	140.00	
		Never hinged	800.00	
		On BLP envelope	160.00	—
c.		Orange ovpt.	325.00	540.00
		No gum	140.00	

Never hinged		800.00	
On BLP envelope		160.00	—
B12A A49 30c org brn			
(Bk)		240.00	225.00
No gum		100.00	
Never hinged		600.00	
On BLP envelope		110.00	3,750.
B15A A49 85c choc (Bk)		325.00	540.00
No gum		140.00	
Never hinged		800.00	
On BLP envelope		160.00	14,000.

Litho. Ovpt.

B9c A48 10c Blk ovpt.		125.00	110.00
No gum		47.50	
Never hinged		325.00	
On BLP envelope		52.50	*325.00*
B10a A48 15c Blue ovpt.		1,000.	1,050.
No gum		450.00	
Never hinged		2,000.	
On BLP envelope		475.00	*8,000.*
c. Blk ovpt.		4,000.	
Never hinged		8,000.	
B11a A50 20c Blue ovpt.		875.00	525.00
No gum		325.00	
Never hinged		1,750.	
On BLP envelope		350.00	*1,300.*
b. Blk ovpt.		875.00	875.00
No gum		325.00	
Never hinged		1,750.	
On BLP envelope		350.00	*1,600.*
b. As "a," invtd. ovpt.		—	—
B12 A49 25c blue (Bk)		110.00	120.00
No gum		47.50	
Never hinged		275.00	
On BLP envelope		55.00	*950.00*
B13 A49 40c brn (Bl)		190.00	120.00
No gum		72.50	
Never hinged		475.00	
On BLP envelope		80.00	*950.00*
a. Black ovpt.		210.00	120.00
No gum		72.50	
Never hinged		475.00	
On BLP envelope		80.00	*950.00*
B14 A49 50c vio ('23)			
(Bk)		800.00	800.00
No gum		275.00	
Never hinged		1,600.	
On BLP envelope		325.00	*2,400.*
a. Blue overprint			
B15 A49 60c car (Bk)		2,200.	2,600.
No gum		1,050.	
Never hinged		4,500.	
On BLP envelope		1,200.	8,750.
B16 A46 1 l brn & grn			
('23) (Bk)		3,600.	3,000.
No gum		1,800.	
Never hinged		7,250.	
On BLP envelope		2,000.	5,500.
a. Inverted overprint		5,500.	
Never hinged		6,250.	
Nos. B9-B16 (10)		8,315.	8,595.
Set, never hinged		21,060.	
Set, #B9-B16, B12A,			
B15A, never hinged		17,625.	

The stamps overprinted "B. L. P." were sold by the Government below face value to the National Federation for Assisting War Invalids. Most of them were affixed to special envelopes (Buste Lettere Postali) which bore advertisements. The Federation was permitted to sell these envelopes at a reduction of 5c from the face value of each stamp. The profits for the war invalids were derived from the advertisements.

Values of Nos. B5-B16 unused are for stamps with original gum. Most copies without gum or with part gum sell for about a quarter of values quoted. Uncanceled stamps affixed to the special envelopes usually sell for about half value.

The overprint on Nos. B9-B16 is wider (13½mm) than that on Nos. B5-B8 (11mm). The 1922-23 overprint exists both typo. and litho. on 10c, 15c, 20c and 25c; only litho. on 40c, 50c, 60c and 1 l; and only typo. on 30c and 85c.

Counterfeits of the B.L.P. overprints exist.

Administering
Fascist
Oath — SP3

1923, Oct. 29   **Perf. 14x14½**

B17 SP3 30c + 30c brown		32.50	*160.00*
Never hinged		85.00	
On cover			550.00
B18 SP3 50c + 50c violet		32.50	*160.00*
Never hinged		85.00	
On cover			550.00
a. Horiz. pair, imperf between		1,900.	

B19 SP3 1 l + 1 l gray		32.50	*160.00*
Never hinged		85.00	
On cover			550.00
Nos. B17-B19 (3)		97.50	*480.00*
Set, never hinged		250.00	
Set on commem cover			925.00

The surtax was given to the Benevolent Fund of the Black Shirts (the Italian National Militia).

Anniv. of the March of the Fascisti on Rome.

St. Maria
Maggiore
SP4

Pope
Opening
Holy Door
SP8

Designs: 30c+15c, St. John Lateran. 50c+25c, St. Paul's Church. 60c+30c, St. Peter's Basilica. 5 l+2.50 l, Pope closing Holy Door.

1924, Dec. 24   **Perf. 12**

B20 SP4 20c + 10c dk grn & brn		4.50	*12.50*
Never hinged		10.50	
On cover			47.50
B21 SP4 30c + 15c dk brn & brn		4.50	*12.50*
Never hinged		10.50	
On cover			47.50
B22 SP4 50c + 25c vio & brn		4.50	*12.50*
Never hinged		10.50	
On cover			55.00
B23 SP4 60c + 30c dp rose & brn		4.50	*40.00*
Never hinged		10.50	
On cover			95.00
B24 SP8 1 l + 50c dp bl & vio		7.50	*40.00*
Never hinged		17.00	
On cover			175.00
B25 SP8 5 l + 2.50 l org brn & vio		9.50	*80.00*
Never hinged		23.00	
On cover			400.00
Nos. B20-B25 (6)		35.00	*197.50*
Set, never hinged		82.00	
Set on commem cover			350.00

The surtax was contributed toward the Holy Year expenses.

Castle of
St. Angelo
SP10

Designs: 50c+20c, 60c+30c, Aqueduct of Claudius. 1.25 l+50c, 1.25 l+60c, Capitol, Roman Forum. 5 l+2 l, 5 l+2.50 l, People's Gate.

Unwmk.

1926, Oct. 26   **Engr.**   **Perf. 11**

B26 SP10 40c + 20c dk brn & blk		3.25	*24.00*
Never hinged		8.00	
On cover			100.00
B27 SP10 60c + 30c brn red & ol brn		3.25	*24.00*
Never hinged		8.00	
On cover			100.00
B28 SP10 1.25 l + 60c bl grn & blk		3.25	*72.50*
Never hinged		8.00	
On cover			225.00
B29 SP10 5 l + 2.50 l dk bl & blk		6.50	*225.00*
Never hinged		16.00	
On cover			675.00
Nos. B26-B29 (4)		16.25	*345.50*
Set, never hinged		40.00	
Set on commem cover			650.00

Stamps inscribed "Poste Italiane" and "Fiere Campionaria di Tripoli" are listed in Libya.

1928, Mar. 1

B30 SP10 30c + 10c dl vio & blk		12.50	*65.00*
Never hinged		30.00	
On cover			125.00
B31 SP10 50c + 20c ol grn & sl		21.00	*65.00*
Never hinged		52.50	
On cover			125.00

B32 SP10 1.25 l + 50c dp bl & blk		25.00	*140.00*
Never hinged		62.50	
On cover			275.00
B33 SP10 5 l + 2 l brn red & blk		55.00	*450.00*
Never hinged		140.00	
On cover			875.00
Nos. B30-B33 (4)		113.50	*720.00*
Set, never hinged		275.00	
Set on commem cover			1,350.

The tax on Nos. B26 to B33 was devoted to the charitable work of the Voluntary Militia for National Defense.

See Nos. B35-B38.

Victor Emmanuel
II — SP14

1929, Jan. 4   **Photo.**   **Perf. 14**

B34 SP14 50c + 10c ol grn		4.75	*12.00*
Never hinged		12.00	
On cover			60.00

50th anniv. of the death of King Victor Emmanuel II. The surtax was for veterans.

Type of 1926 Issue

Designs in same order.

1930, July 1   **Engr.**

B35 SP10 30c + 10c dk grn & vio		2.40	*40.00*
Never hinged		6.00	
On cover			120.00
B36 SP10 50c + 10c dk grn & bl grn		3.25	*30.00*
Never hinged		8.00	
On cover			67.50
B37 SP10 1.25 l + 30c ind & grn		8.00	*95.00*
Never hinged		20.00	
On cover			240.00
B38 SP10 5 l + 1.50 l blk brn & ol brn		16.00	*450.00*
Never hinged		40.00	
On cover			1,250.
Nos. B35-B38 (4)		29.65	*615.00*
Set, never hinged		74.00	
Set on commem cover			1,200.

The surtax was for the charitable work of the Voluntary Militia for National Defense.

Militiamen at
Ceremonial
Fire with
Quotation from
Leonardo da
Vinci — SP15

Symbolical of
Pride for
Militia — SP16

Symbolical of
Militia Guarding
Immortality of
Italy
SP17

Militia Passing
Through Arch
of Constantine
SP18

1935, July 1   **Photo.**   **Wmk. 140**

B39 SP15 20c + 10c rose red		9.50	*12.50*
Never hinged		24.00	
On cover			95.00
B40 SP16 25c + 15c green		9.50	*20.00*
Never hinged		24.00	
On cover			95.00
B41 SP17 50c + 30c pur- ple		9.50	*28.00*
Never hinged		24.00	
On cover			325.00

B42 SP18 1.25 l + 75c blue		9.50	*42.50*
Never hinged		24.00	
On cover			500.00
Nos. B39-B42 (4)		38.00	*103.00*
Set, never hinged		96.00	
Set on commemorative cover			400.00
Nos. B39-B42,CB3 (5)		47.50	*143.00*
Set, never hinged		117.50	

The surtax was for the Militia.

AIR POST STAMPS

Used values for Nos. C1-C105 are for postally used stamps with legible cancellations. Forged cancels on these issues abound, and expertization is srongly recommended.

Special Delivery Stamp No. E1 Overprinted

1917, May   **Wmk. 140**   **Perf. 14**

C1 SD1 25c rose red		24.00	*40.00*
Never hinged		60.00	
On flown colored postcard			100.00
On flown white postcard			*1,300.*

Type of
SD3
Surcharged
in Black

1917, June 27

C2 SD3 25c on 40c violet		24.00	*47.50*
Never hinged		60.00	
On flown cover or postcard			105.00

Type SD3 was not issued without surcharge.

AP2

1926-28   **Typo.**

C3 AP2 50c rose red ('28)		19.00	12.00
Never hinged		47.50	
On commercial cover			40.00
C4 AP2 60c gray		4.75	*12.00*
Never hinged		12.00	
On commercial cover			40.00
C5 AP2 80c brn vio & brn ('28)		35.00	*120.00*
Never hinged		87.50	
On commercial cover			400.00
C6 AP2 1 l blue		12.00	*12.00*
Never hinged		30.00	
On commercial cover			40.00
C7 AP2 1.20 l brn ('27)		24.00	*120.00*
Never hinged		60.00	
On commercial cover			260.00
C8 AP2 1.50 l buff		19.00	32.50
Never hinged		47.50	
On commercial cover			100.00
C9 AP2 5 l gray grn		40.00	*105.00*
Never hinged		100.00	
On commercial cover			325.00
Nos. C3-C9 (7)		153.75	*413.50*
Set, never hinged		385.00	
Nos. C4, C6, C8, C9 on overfranked philatelic cover (Mar. 1926)			550.00

Nos. C4
and C6
Surcharged

1927, Sept. 16

C10 AP2 50c on 60c gray		24.00	*95.00*
Never hinged		50.00	
On commercial cover			190.00
a. Pair, one without surcharge		2,250.	
Never hinged		3,250.	

C11 AP2 80c on 1 l blue   60.00 *450.00*
   Never hinged   150.00
   On overfranked cover   875.00
   Set, never hinged   200.00
   On overfranked com-
   mem. cover   950.00

Pegasus
AP3

Wings
AP4

Spirit of Flight — AP5

Arrows
AP6

1930-32   Photo.   Wmk. 140

C12 AP4 25c dk grn ('32)   .25   .25
   Never hinged   .50
   On commercial cover   14.50
C13 AP3 50c olive brn   .25   .25
   Never hinged   .50
   On commercial cover   1.60
C14 AP5 75c org brn ('32)   .40   .25
   Never hinged   1.00
   On commercial cover   24.00
C15 AP4 80c org red   .25   .70
   Never hinged   .50
   On commercial cover   60.00
C16 AP5 1 l purple   .25   .25
   Never hinged   .50
   On commercial cover   1.60
C17 AP6 2 l deep blue   .40   .25
   Never hinged   1.00
   On commercial cover   27.50
C18 AP3 5 l dk green   .80   *1.60*
   Never hinged   2.00
   On commercial cover   52.50
C19 AP3 10 l dp car   1.60   *6.50*
   Never hinged   4.00
   On commercial cover   95.00
   Nos. C12-C19 (8)   4.20 10.05
   Set, never hinged   10.00

The 50c, 1 l and 2 l were reprinted in 1942 with labels similar to those of Nos. 427-438, but were not issued. Value, set of 3: unused $550; never hinged $1,400.

For overprints see Nos. MC1-MC5 in Scott Standard catalogue, Vol. 3. For overprints and surcharges on design AP6 see Nos. C52-C55; Yugoslavia-Ljubljana NB9-NB20, NC11-NC17 (in Scott Standard catalogue, Vol. 6).

Ferrucci Type of Postage

Statue of Ferrucci.

1930, July 10
C20 A104 50c purple   4.00 *17.50*
   Never hinged   10.00
   On commercial cover   95.00
C21 A104 1 l orange brn   4.00 *20.00*
   Never hinged   10.00
   On commercial cover   130.00
C22 A104 5 l + 2 l brn vio 16.00 *130.00*
   Never hinged   40.00
   On commercial cover   650.00
   Nos. C20-C22 (3)   24.00 *167.50*
   Set, never hinged   60.00
   Set, on flown overfranked
   commem. cover   450.00

For overprinted types see Aegean Islands Nos. C1-C3.

Virgil Type of Postage

Jupiter sending forth his eagle.

1930, Oct. 21   Photo.   Wmk. 140
C23 A106 50c lt brown   24.00 *40.00*
   Never hinged   60.00
   On commercial cover   87.50
C24 A106 1 l orange   24.00 *45.00*
   Never hinged   60.00
   On commercial cover   160.00

**Engr.
Unwmk.**

C25 A106 7.70 l + 1.30 l
       vio brn   55.00 *520.00*
   Never hinged   140.00
   On commercial cover   2,200.
C26 A106 9 l + 2 l indi-
       go   65.00 *600.00*
   Never hinged   160.00
   On commercial cover   3,000.
   Nos. C23-C26 (4)   168.00 *1,205.*

   Set, never hinged   430.00
   Set, on flown overfranked
   commem. cover   2,300.

The surtax on Nos. C25-C26 was for the National Institute Figli del Littorio.

For overprinted types see Aegean Islands Nos. C4-C7.

Trans-Atlantic Squadron — AP9

1930, Dec. 15   Photo.   Wmk. 140
C27 AP9 7.70 l Prus bl &
       gray   450.00 *1,600.*
   Never hinged   900.00
   On flown cover   2,000.
  a. Seven stars instead of
     six   2,000.   —
   Never hinged   4,000.
   On flown cover   36,000.

Flight by Italian aviators from Rome to Rio de Janeiro, Dec. 1930-Jan. 12, 1931.

Leonardo
da Vinci's
Flying
Machine
AP10

Leonardo
da Vinci
AP11

Leonardo da
Vinci — AP12

1932
C28 AP10 50c olive brn   4.75 *14.50*
   Never hinged   12.00
   On commercial cover   55.00
C29 AP11 1 l violet   6.50 *16.00*
   Never hinged   16.00
   On commercial cover   95.00
C30 AP11 3 l brown red   8.00 *40.00*
   Never hinged   20.00
   On commercial cover   160.00
C31 AP11 5 l dp green   13.00 *47.50*
   Never hinged   32.50
   On commercial cover   240.00
C32 AP10 7.70 l + 2 l dk bl 9.50 *200.00*
   Never hinged   24.00
   On commercial cover   2,000.
C33 AP11 10 l + 2.50 l blk
       brn   11.00 *340.00*
   Never hinged   27.50
   On commercial cover   2,600.
   Nos. C28-C33 (6)   52.75 *658.00*
   Set, never hinged   132.00
   Set, on flown overfranked
   commem. cover   1,600.

**Engr.
Unwmk.**

C34 AP12 100 l brt bl &
       grnsh blk 45.00 *950.00*
   Never hinged   110.00
   On flown cover   2,750.
  a. Thin paper   260.00 *1,800.*
   Never hinged   400.00
   On flown cover   525.00

Dante Alighieri Soc. and especially Leonardo da Vinci, to whom the invention of a flying machine has been attributed. Surtax was for the benefit of the Society.

Inscription on No. C34: "Man with his large wings by beating against the air will be able to dominate it and lift himself above it".

Issued: Nos. C28-C33, 3/14; No. C34, 8/6.
For overprinted types see Aegean Islands Nos. C8-C13.

Garibaldi's
Home at
Caprera
AP13

Farmhouse
where Anita
Garibaldi Died
AP14

50c, 1 l+25c, Garibaldi's home, Caprera. 2 l+50c, Anita Garibaldi. 5 l+1 l, Giuseppe Garibaldi.

1932, Apr. 6   Photo.   Wmk. 140
C35 AP13 50c copper red   4.75   *8.00*
   Never hinged   12.00
   On commercial cover   55.00
C36 AP14 80c deep green   5.00 *13.00*
   Never hinged   12.50
   On commercial cover   125.00
C37 AP13 1 l + 25c red brn   8.00 *32.50*
   Never hinged   20.00
   On commercial cover   175.00
C38 AP13 2 l + 50c dp bl   13.00 *45.00*
   Never hinged   32.50
   On commercial cover   240.00
C39 AP14 5 l + 1 l dp grn   13.00 *52.50*
   Never hinged   32.50
   On commercial cover   650.00
   Nos. C35-C39 (5)   43.75 *151.00*
   Set, never hinged   110.00
   Set, on flown overfranked
   commem. cover   475.00

50th anniv. of the death of Giuseppe Garibaldi, patriot. The surtax was for the benefit of the Garibaldi Volunteers.

For overprinted types see Aegean Islands Nos. C15-C19.

March on Rome Type of Postage

50c, Eagle sculpture and airplane. 75c, Italian buildings from the air.

1932, Oct. 27   Perf. 14
C40 A146 50c dark brown   3.25   *9.50*
   Never hinged   8.00
   On cover   40.00
C41 A146 75c orange brn   9.50 *32.50*
   Never hinged   24.00
   On cover   100.00
   Set, never hinged   32.00
   Set, on flown overfranked
   commem. cover   130.00

Graf Zeppelin Issue

Zeppelin
over
Pyramid
of Caius
Cestius
AP19

5 l, Tomb of Cecilia Metlella. 10 l, Stadium of Mussolini. 12 l, St. Angelo Castle and Bridge. 15 l, Roman Forum. 20 l, Imperial Avenue.

1933, Apr. 24
C42 AP19 3 l black &
       grn   22.50 *125.00*
   Never hinged   55.00
   On flown cover   300.00
C43 AP19 5 l green &
       brn   22.50 *140.00*
   Never hinged   55.00
   On flown cover   425.00
C44 AP19 10 l car & dl bl   22.50 *325.00*
   Never hinged   55.00
   On flown cover   950.00
C45 AP19 12 l dk bl & red
       org   22.50 *575.00*
   Never hinged   55.00
   On flown cover   1,250.
C46 AP19 15 l dk brn &
       gray   22.50 *725.00*
   Never hinged   55.00
   On flown cover   1,800.
C47 AP19 20 l org brn &
       bl   22.50 *800.00*
   Never hinged   55.00
   On flown cover   2,000.
  a. Vertical pair, imperf.
    between   10,000.
   Never hinged   15,000.
   Nos. C42-C47 (6)   135.00 *2,690.*
   Set, never hinged   330.00
   Set, on flown over-
   franked commem. cov-
   er   6,750.

Balbo's Trans-Atlantic Flight Issue

Italian Flag

King Victor Emmanuel III

Allegory "Flight" — AP25

No. C49, Colosseum at Rome, Chicago skyline. Nos. C48-C49 consist of 3 parts; Italian flag, Victor Emmanuel III, & scene arranged horizontally.

1933, May 20
C48 AP25 5.25 l + 19.75 l
       red, grn &
       ultra   125.00 *2,000.*
   Never hinged   250.00
   On flown cover   3,000.
  a. Left stamp without ovpt. 37,500.
   Never hinged   57,500.
C49 AP25 5.25 l + 44.75 l
       grn, red &
       ultra   160.00 *2,000.*
   Never hinged   325.00
   On flown cover   3,000.

Transatlantic Flight, Rome-Chicago, of 24-seaplane squadron led by Gen. Italo Balbo. Center and right sections paid postage. At left is registered air express label overprinted "APPARECCHIO" and abbreviated pilot's name. Twenty triptychs of each value differ in name overprint.

No. C49 overprinted "VOLO DI RITORNO/ NEW YORK-ROMA" was not issued; flight canceled. Value: unused $36,000; never hinged $54,000.

Nos. C48-C49 exist imperf. at bottom. Value, set $112,000.

For overprints see Nos. CO1, Aegean Islands C26-C27.

**Type of Air Post Stamp of 1930
Surcharged in Black**

1934, Jan. 18
C52 AP6 2 l on 2 l yel   10.50 *95.00*
   Never hinged   26.00
   On flight cover   160.00
C53 AP6 3 l on 2 l yel grn 10.50 *140.00*
   Never hinged   26.00
   On flight cover   190.00
C54 AP6 5 l on 2 l rose   10.50 *275.00*
   Never hinged   26.00
   On flight cover   600.00
C55 AP6 10 l on 2 l vio   10.50 *400.00*
   Never hinged   26.00
   On flight cover   875.00
   Nos. C52-C55 (4)   42.00 *910.00*
   Set, never hinged   104.00
   Set, on overfranked flown
   cover   1,600.

For use on mail carried on a special flight from Rome to Buenos Aires.

Annexation of Fiume Type

25c, 75c, View of Fiume Harbor. 50c, 1 l+50c, Monument to the Dead. 2 l+1.50 l, Venetian Lions. 3 l+2 l, Julian wall.

1934, Mar. 12
C56 A166 25c green   .95   *4.00*
   Never hinged   2.40
   On cover   67.50
C57 A166 50c brown   .95   *2.40*
   Never hinged   2.40
   On cover   52.50
C58 A166 75c org brn   .95   *9.50*
   Never hinged   2.40
   On cover   180.00

C59 A166 1 l + 50c dl vio .95 *16.00*
Never hinged 2.40
On cover 240.00
C60 A166 2 l + 1.50 l dl bl .95 *21.00*
Never hinged 2.40
On cover 400.00
C61 A166 3 l + 2 l blk brn .95 *23.00*
Never hinged 2.40
On cover 550.00
Nos. C56-C61 (6) 4.80 *76.40*
Set, never hinged 14.40
Nos. C56-C61, CE6-CE7
on overfranked commem.
cover 875.00
No. CE5 on commem. cover-
er (July 1934) 875.00

Airplane
and View of
Stadium
AP32

Soccer Player
and Plane
AP33

Airplane and
Stadium
Entrance
AP35

Airplane
over
Stadium
AP34

1934, May 24
C62 AP32 50c car rose 11.00 *52.50*
Never hinged 27.50
On cover 225.00
C63 AP33 75c gray blue 17.50 *65.00*
Never hinged 45.00
On cover 300.00
C64 AP34 5 l + 2.50 l ol
grn 52.50 *425.00*
Never hinged 130.00
On cover 1,900.
C65 AP35 10 l + 5 l brn blk 52.50 *650.00*
Never hinged 130.00
On cover 3,500.
Nos. C62-C65 (4) 133.50 *1,192.*
Set, never hinged 332.50
Set, on overfranked com-
mem. cover 3,750.
2nd World Soccer Championships.
For overprinted types see Aegean Islands
Nos. C28-C31.

Zeppelin
under Fire
AP36

Air Force
Memorial — AP40

Designs: 25c, 80c, Zeppelin under fire. 50c,
75c, Motorboat patrol. 1 l+50c, Desert infantry.
2 l+1 l, Plane attacking troops.

1934, Apr. 24
C66 AP36 25c dk green 3.25 *8.00*
Never hinged 8.00
On cover 60.00
C67 AP36 50c gray 3.25 *9.50*
Never hinged 8.00
On cover 52.50
C68 AP36 75c dk brown 3.25 *11.00*
Never hinged 8.00
On cover 160.00
C69 AP36 80c slate blue 3.25 *14.50*
Never hinged 8.00
On cover 225.00

C70 AP36 1 l + 50c red brn 8.00 *32.50*
Never hinged 20.00
On cover 325.00
C71 AP36 2 l + 1 l brt bl 11.50 *40.00*
Never hinged 29.00
On cover 550.00
C72 AP40 3 l + 2 l brn blk 16.00 *47.50*
Never hinged 40.00
On cover 600.00
Nos. C66-C72 (7) 48.50 *149.00*
Set, never hinged 120.00
Nos. C66-C72, CE8-CE9
on overfranked commem.
cover 1,200.
Cent. of the institution of the Military Medal
of Valor.
For overprinted types see Aegean Islands
Nos. C32-C38.

King Victor
Emmanuel
III — AP41

1934, Nov. 5
C73 AP41 1 l purple 3.25 *95.00*
Never hinged 8.00
On cover 210.00
C74 AP41 2 l brt blue 3.25 *105.00*
Never hinged 8.00
On cover 240.00
C75 AP41 4 l red brown 7.50 *325.00*
Never hinged 19.00
On cover 550.00
C76 AP41 5 l dull green 7.50 *425.00*
Never hinged 19.00
On cover 725.00
C77 AP41 8 l rose red 23.00 *525.00*
Never hinged 57.50
On cover 1,200.
C78 AP41 10 l brown 25.00 *800.00*
Never hinged 62.50
On cover 1,450.
Nos. C73-C78 (6) 69.50 *2,275.*
Set, never hinged 160.00
Set, on overfranked com-
mem. cover 3,250.
65th birthday of King Victor Emmanuel III
and the nonstop flight from Rome to
Mogadiscio.
For overprint see No. CO2.

Muse
Playing
Harp
AP42

Angelic
Dirge for
Bellini
AP43

Scene from Bellini Opera, La
Sonnambula — AP44

1935, Sept. 24
C79 AP42 25c dull yellow 4.75 *13.00*
Never hinged 12.00
On cover 52.50
C80 AP42 50c brown 4.75 *11.00*
Never hinged 12.00
On cover 110.00
C81 AP42 60c rose carmine 16.00 *32.50*
Never hinged 40.00
On cover 550.00
C82 AP43 1 l + 1 l purple 24.00 *240.00*
Never hinged 60.00
On cover 800.00
C83 AP44 5 l + 2 l green 32.50 *325.00*
Never hinged 80.00
On cover 800.00
Nos. C79-C83 (5) 82.00 *621.50*
Set, never hinged 204.00
Set, on overfranked com-
mem. cover 1,200.
Vincenzo Bellini, (1801-35), operatic
composer.

Quintus Horatius Flaccus Type

25c, Seaplane in Flight. 50c, 1 l+1 l, Monoplane over valley. 60c, Oak and eagle. 5 l+2 l,
Ruins of ancient Rome.

1936, July 1
C84 A197 25c dp green 3.25 *12.00*
Never hinged 8.00
On cover 52.50
C85 A197 50c dk brown 5.00 *12.00*
Never hinged 12.50
On cover 52.50
C86 A197 60c scarlet 8.50 *20.00*
Never hinged 21.00
On cover 120.00
C87 A197 1 l + 1 l vio 19.00 *240.00*
Never hinged 47.50
On cover 600.00
C88 A197 5 l + 2 l slate bl 24.00 *350.00*
Never hinged 60.00
On cover 1,200.
Nos. C84-C88 (5) 59.75 *634.00*
Set, never hinged 150.00
Set, on overfranked com-
mem. cover 1,250.

Child of the
Balilla
AP49

Heads of
Children
AP50

1937, June 28
C89 AP49 25c dk bl grn 8.00 *27.50*
Never hinged 20.00
On cover 110.00
C90 AP50 50c brown 16.00 *17.50*
Never hinged 40.00
On cover 87.50
C91 AP49 1 l purple 12.00 *35.00*
Never hinged 30.00
On cover 110.00
C92 AP50 2 l + 1 l dk bl 16.00 *200.00*
Never hinged 40.00
On cover 600.00
C93 AP49 3 l + 2 l org 20.00 *275.00*
Never hinged 50.00
On cover 1,050.
C94 AP50 5 l + 3 l rose
lake 24.00 *340.00*
Never hinged 60.00
On cover 2,000.
Nos. C89-C94 (6) 96.00 *895.00*
Set, never hinged 240.00
Set, on overfranked com-
mem. cover 2,600.
Summer Exhibition for Child Welfare. The
surtax on Nos. C92-C94 was used to support
summer camps for poor children.

Prosperous
Italy
AP51

50c, Prolific Italy. 80c, Apollo's steeds. 1 l+1
l, Map & Roman Standard. 5 l+1 l, Augustus
Caesar.

1937, Sept. 23
C95 AP51 25c red vio 8.00 *16.00*
Never hinged 20.00
On cover 47.50
C96 AP51 50c olive brn 8.00 *12.00*
Never hinged 20.00
On cover 47.50
C97 AP51 80c orange brn 24.00 *22.50*
Never hinged 60.00
On cover 87.50
C98 AP51 1 l + 1 l dk bl 30.00 *175.00*
Never hinged 75.00
On cover 450.00
C99 AP51 5 l + 1 l dl vio 65.00 *340.00*
Never hinged 160.00
On cover 725.00
Nos. C95-C99 (5) 135.00 *565.50*
Set, never hinged 335.00
Set, on overfranked com-
mem. cover 1,100.
Bimillenary of the birth of Augustus Caesar
(Octavianus) on the occasion of the exhibition
opened in Rome by Mussolini on Sept. 22nd,
1937.
For overprinted types see Aegean Islands
Nos. C39-C43.

King Victor
Emmanuel
III — AP56

25c, 3 l, King Victor Emmanuel III. 50c, 1 l,
Dante Alighieri. 2 l, 5 l, Leonardo da Vinci.

1938, Oct. 28
C100 AP56 25c dull green 4.75 *6.50*
Never hinged 12.00
On cover 40.00
C101 AP56 50c dk yel brn 4.75 *6.50*
Never hinged 12.00
On cover 32.50
C102 AP56 1 l violet 8.00 *9.50*
Never hinged 20.00
On cover 40.00
C103 AP56 2 l royal blue 8.00 *36.00*
Never hinged 20.00
On cover 95.00
C104 AP56 3 l brown car 13.00 *45.00*
Never hinged 32.50
On cover 200.00
C105 AP56 5 l dp green 15.00 *65.00*
Never hinged 37.50
On cover 275.00
Nos. C100-C105 (6) 54.00 *170.50*
Set, never hinged 134.00
Set, on overfranked com-
mem. cover 525.00
Proclamation of the Empire.

AIR POST SEMI-POSTAL STAMPS

Holy Year Type of Postage

Dome of St. Peter's, dove with olive branch,
Church of the Holy Sepulcher.

Wmk. 140
1933, Oct. 23 **Photo.** *Perf. 14*
CB1 A163 50c + 25c org
brn 2.40 *27.50*
Never hinged 6.00
On cover 72.50
CB2 A163 75c + 50c brn vio 4.00 *160.00*
Never hinged 10.00
On cover 275.00
Set, never hinged 16.00

Symbolical of Military
Air Force — SPAP2

1935, July 1
CB3 SPAP2 50c + 50c brown 9.50 *40.00*
Never hinged 24.00
On cover 240.00
The surtax was for the Militia.

AIR POST SPECIAL DELIVERY
STAMPS

Garibaldi,
Anita
Garibaldi,
Plane
APSD1

Wmk. 140
1932, June 2 **Photo.** *Perf. 14*
CE1 APSD1 2.25 l + 1 l 16.00 *52.50*
Never hinged 40.00
On cover 475.00
CE2 APSD1 4.50 l + 1.50 l 16.00 *52.50*
Never hinged 40.00
On cover 600.00
Set, never hinged 80.00
Death of Giuseppe Garibaldi, 50th anniv.
For overprinted types see Aegean Islands
Nos. CE1-CE2.

Airplane
and
Sunburst
APSD2

1933-34
CE3 APSD2 2 l gray blk
('34) .25 *3.25*
Never hinged .50
On cover 40.00

CE4 APSD2 2.25 l gray blk 4.75 *200.00*
  Never hinged 12.00
  On cover 875.00
  Set, never hinged 12.50

For overprint and surcharge see Nos. MCE1 in Scott Standard catalogue, Vol. 3; Yugoslavia-Ljubljana NCE1 in Scott Standard catalogue, Vol. 6.

Annexation of Fiume Type

Flag raising before Fascist headquarters.

1934, Mar. 12
CE5 A166 2 l + 1.25 l 4.75 *27.50*
  Never hinged 12.00
  On cover 875.00
CE6 A166 2.25 l + 1.25 l .95 *22.50*
  Never hinged 2.50
  On cover 650.00
CE7 A166 4.50 l + 2 l .95 *24.00*
  Never hinged 2.50
  On cover 725.00
  Nos. CE5-CE7 (3) 5.60 *77.00*
  Set, never hinged 17.00

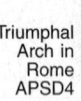
Triumphal Arch in Rome APSD4

1934, Aug. 31
CE8 APSD4 2 l + 1.25 l brown 16.00 *45.00*
  Never hinged 40.00
  On cover 725.00
CE9 APSD4 4.50 l + 2 l cop red 20.00 *45.00*
  Never hinged 50.00
  On cover 725.00
  Set, never hinged 90.00

Centenary of the institution of the Military Medal of Valor.
For overprinted types see Aegean Islands Nos. CE3-CE4.

AIR POST OFFICIAL STAMPS

Balbo Flight Type of Air Post Stamp of 1933 Overprinted

1933 Wmk. 140 Perf. 14
CO1 AP25 5.25 l + 44.75 l red, grn & red vio 3,300. *14,000.*
  Never hinged 5,000.
  On cover 21,000.

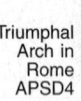
Air Post Stamp of 1934 Overprinted in Gold

1934
CO2 AP41 10 l blue blk 875.00 *14,000.*
  Never hinged 1,750.
  On cover 27,500.

65th birthday of King Victor Emmanuel III and the non-stop flight from Rome to Mogadiscio.

PNEUMATIC POST STAMPS

PN1

1913-28 Wmk. 140 Typo. Perf. 14
D1 PN1 10c brown 2.40 *32.50*
  Never hinged 6.00
  On cover 140.00
D2 PN1 15c brn vio ('28) 3.25 *16.00*
  Never hinged 8.00
  On cover 65.00
a. 15c dull violet ('21) 3.25 45.00

  Never hinged 8.00
  On cover 200.00
D3 PN1 15c rose red ('28) 16.00 *40.00*
  Never hinged 40.00
  On cover 160.00
D4 PN1 15c claret ('28) 4.75 *16.00*
  Never hinged 12.00
  On cover 65.00
D5 PN1 20c on 10c ('20) 24.00 *65.00*
  Never hinged 60.00
  On cover 260.00
D6 PN1 30c blue ('23) 8.00 *225.00*
  Never hinged 20.00
  On cover 875.00
D7 PN1 35c rose red ('27) 25.00 *475.00*
  Never hinged 62.50
  On cover 1,900.
D8 PN1 40c dp red ('26) 27.50 *450.00*
  Never hinged 67.50
  On cover 1,900.
  Nos. D1-D8 (8) 110.90 *1,319.*

Nos. D1, D2a, D5-D6, D8 Surcharged Like Nos. C10-C11

1924-27
D9 PN1 15c on 10c 4.75 *40.00*
  Never hinged 12.00
  On cover 160.00
D10 PN1 15c on 20c ('27) 9.50 *72.50*
  Never hinged 23.00
  On cover 275.00
D11 PN1 20c on 10c ('25) 9.50 *80.00*
  Never hinged 23.00
  On cover 325.00
D12 PN1 20c on 15c ('25) 12.50 *47.50*
  Never hinged 30.00
  On cover 200.00
D13 PN1 35c on 40c ('27) 21.00 *400.00*
  Never hinged 52.50
  On cover 1,600.
D14 PN1 40c on 30c ('25) 12.50 *425.00*
  Never hinged 30.00
  On cover 1,050.
  Nos. D9-D14 (6) 69.75 *1,065.*

Dante Alighieri PN2

Galileo Galilei PN3

1933, Mar. 29 Photo.
D15 PN2 15c dark violet .45 *1.60*
  Never hinged .75
  On cover 40.00
D16 PN3 35c rose red .45 *7.25*
  Never hinged .75
  On cover 375.00

SPECIAL DELIVERY STAMPS

Victor Emmanuel III — SD1

1903-26 Typo. Wmk. 140 Perf. 14
E1 SD1 25c rose red 47.50 1.20
  Never hinged 120.00
  On cover 9.50
a. Imperf., pair 475.00 600.00
E2 SD1 50c dl red ('20) 4.75 1.20
  Never hinged 12.00
  On cover 14.00
E3 SD1 60c dl red ('22) 9.50 1.20
  Never hinged 24.00
  On cover 12.00
E4 SD1 70c dl red ('25) 1.60 .35
  Never hinged 4.00
  On cover 6.50
E5 SD1 1.25 l dp bl ('26) .80 .25
  Never hinged 2.00
  On cover 1.60
  Nos. E1-E5 (5) 64.15 4.60

No. E1 is almost always found poorly centered, and it is valued thus.
For overprints and surcharges see Nos. C1, E11, E13, Austria NE1-NE2, Dalmatia E1, Offices in Crete, Offices in Africa, Offices in Turkish Empire.

Victor Emmanuel III — SD2

1908-26
E6 SD2 30c blue & rose 2.25 *4.00*
  Never hinged 5.50
  On cover 27.50
E7 SD2 2 l bl & red ('25) 8.00 *160.00*
  Never hinged 20.00
  On cover 600.00
E8 SD2 2.50 l bl & red ('26) 3.25 *10.50*
  Never hinged 8.00
  On cover
  Nos. E6-E8 (3) 13.50 *174.50*

The 1.20 lire blue and red (see No. E12) was prepared in 1922, but not issued. Value: unused $200; never hinged $400.
For surcharges and overprints see Nos. E10, E12, Austria NE3, Dalmatia E2, Offices in China, Offices in Africa, Offices in Turkish Empire.

SD3

1917, Nov.
E9 SD3 25c on 40c violet 40.00 125.00
  Never hinged 100.00
  On cover 450.00

Type SD3 not issued without surcharge. For surcharge see No. C2.

No. E6 Surcharged

1921, Oct.
E10 SD2 1.20 l on 30c 2.40 27.50
  Never hinged 6.00
  On cover 160.00
a. Comma in value omitted 12.50 55.00
b. Double surcharge 350.00

No. E2 Surcharged

1922, Jan. 9
E11 SD1 60c on 50c dull red 47.50 1.60
  Never hinged 120.00
  On cover 16.00
a. Inverted surcharge 275.00 275.00
b. Double surcharge 2,000.
c. Imperf., pair 475.00 600.00

Type of 1908 Surcharged

1924, May
E12 SD2 1.60 l on 1.20 l bl & red 3.25 *1.60*
  Never hinged 8.00
  On cover 800.00
a. Double surch., one inverted 350.00

No. E3 Surcharged like No. E11
1925, Apr. 11
E13 SD1 70c on 60c dull red 1.60 1.20
  Never hinged 4.00
  On cover 12.00
a. Inverted surcharge 340.00 400.00

Victor Emmanuel III — SD4

1932-33 Photo.
E14 SD4 1.25 l green .30 .25
  Never hinged .30
  On cover .60
E15 SD4 2.50 l dp org ('33) .30 6.60
  Never hinged
  On cover 47.50

For overprints and surcharges see Italian Social Republic Nos. E1-E2; Yugoslavia-Ljubljana NB5-NB8, NE1 (in Scott Standard catalogue, Vol. 6).

March on Rome Type of Postage

1.25 l Ancient Pillars and Entrenchments. 2.50 l, Head of Mussolini, trophies of flags, etc.

1932, Oct. 27
E16 A146 1.25 l deep green 2.40 1.60
  Never hinged 6.00
  On cover 20.00
E17 A146 2.50 l deep orange 8.00 *160.00*
  Never hinged 20.00
  On cover 675.00
  Set, never hinged 26.00

AUTHORIZED DELIVERY STAMPS

For the payment of a special tax for the authorized delivery of correspondence privately instead of through the post office.

AD1   Coat of Arms — AD2

1928 Wmk. 140 Typo. Perf. 14
EY1 AD1 10c dull blue 9.50 .60
  Never hinged 24.00
  On cover 6.00
a. Perf. 11 37.50 4.75
  Never hinged 95.00
  On cover 45.00

1930 Photo. Perf. 14
EY2 AD2 10c dark brown .25 .25
  Never hinged .25
  On cover 1.60

For surcharge and overprint see Nos. EY3, Italian Social Republic EY1 in Scott Standard catalogue, Vol. 3.

POSTAGE DUE STAMPS

Unused values for Postage Due stamps are for examples with full original gum. Stamps with part gum or privately gummed sell for much less.

D1   D2

1863 Unwmk. Litho. Imperf.
J1 D1 10c yellow 2,000. 240.00
  No gum 80.00
  Never hinged 3,000.
  On cover 725.00
  On cover, uncanceled 100.00
a. 10c yellow orange 2,250. 260.00
  No gum 90.00
  Never hinged 3,000.
  On cover 775.00
  On cover, uncanceled 100.00

1869 Wmk. 140 Typo. Perf. 14
J2 D2 10c buff 9,000. 80.00
  No gum 950.00
  Never hinged 18,000.
  On cover 240.00

D3

1870-1925
J3 D3 1c buff & mag 4.00 12.00
  No gum 1.60
  Never hinged 10.00
  On cover 120.00

J4	D3	2c buff & mag	8.00	24.00
	No gum		4.00	
	Never hinged		20.00	
	On cover			190.00
J5	D3	5c buff & mag	.80	.80
	No gum		.40	
	Never hinged		2.00	
	On cover			6.50
J6	D3	10c buff & mag	.80	.80
		('71)		
	No gum		.40	
	Never hinged		2.00	
	On cover			6.50
b.	Imperf, single			2,200.
J7	D3	20c buff & mag	8.00	.80
		('94)		
	No gum		40.00	
	Never hinged		20.00	
	On cover			6.50
a.	Imperf, pair		240.00	240.00
J8	D3	30c buff & mag	2.40	1.20
	No gum		1.20	
	Never hinged		6.00	
	On cover			12.00
b.	Imperf, pair		6,000.	3,600.
J9	D3	40c buff & mag	2.40	2.40
	No gum		1.20	
	Never hinged		6.00	
	On cover			47.50
J10	D3	50c buff & mag	2.40	1.20
	No gum		1.20	
	Never hinged		6.00	
	On cover			12.00
b.	Imperf, single			2,000.
J11	D3	60c buff & mag	120.00	4.75
	No gum		32.50	
	Never hinged		300.00	
	On cover			95.00
J12	D3	60c buff & brn	40.00	16.00
		('25)		
	Never hinged		100.00	
	On cover			65.00
J13	D3	1 l lt bl & brn	8,000.	20.00
	No gum		1,100.	
	Never hinged		16,000.	
	On cover			140.00
J14	D3	1 l bl & mag	45.00	1.25
		('94)		
	No gum		4.75	
	Never hinged		110.00	
	On cover			12.00
a.	Imperf., pair		400.00	350.00
J15	D3	2 l lt bl & brn	7,250.	32.50
	No gum		1,050.	
	Never hinged		14,500.	
	On cover			950.00
J16	D3	2 l bl & mag	65.00	9.50
		('03)		
	Never hinged		160.00	
	On cover			340.00
J17	D3	5 l bl & brn	500.00	35.00
		('74)		
	No gum		105.00	
	Never hinged		1,250.	
	On cover			40,000.
J18	D3	5 l bl & brn	250.00	55.00
		('03)		
	Never hinged		625.00	
	On cover			1,400.
J19	D3	10 l bl & brn	9,500.	35.00
		('74)		
	No gum		1,900.	
	Never hinged		19,000.	
	On cover			—
J20	D3	10 l bl & mag	225.00	8.00
		('94)		
	No gum		27.50	
	Never hinged		550.00	
	On cover			9,500.

Early printings of 5c, 10c, 30c, 40c, 50c and 60c were in buff and magenta, later ones (1890-94) in stronger shades. The earlier, paler shades and their inverted-numeral varieties sell for considerably more than those of the later shades. Values are for the later shades.

Covers: Covers bearing Nos. J5-J6, J8-J11 dated between Jan. 1870 and Dec. 1889 have stamps from early printings and are worth more.

For surcharges and overprints see Nos. J25-J27, Offices in China, Offices in Turkish Empire.

Numeral Inverted

J3a	D3	1c	4,750.	3,000.
J4a	D3	2c	12,000.	4,500.
	On cover			45,000.
J5a	D3	5c	6.50	12.00
	On cover			350.00
J6a	D3	10c	8.00	16.00
	On cover			475.00
J7b	D3	20c	65.00	60.00
	On cover			1,800.
J8a	D3	30c	12.00	24.00
	On cover			725.00
J9a	D3	40c	550.00	650.00
	On cover			19,000.
J10a	D3	50c	60.00	80.00
	On cover			2,400.
J11a	D3	60c	550.00	400.00
	On cover			12,000.
J13a	D3	1 l		
J14b	D3	1 l	5,200.	4,500.
	On cover			18,000.
J15a	D3	2 l		3,000.
J16a	D3	2 l	4,500.	4,500.
	On cover			13,000.
J17a	D3	5 l		1,400.
J19a	D3	10 l		450.00

D4

1884-1903

J21	D4	50 l green	87.50	95.00
	No gum		45.00	
	Never hinged		225.00	
J22	D4	50 l yellow ('03)	95.00	47.50
	No gum		240.00	
J23	D4	100 l claret	87.50	47.50
	No gum		22.50	
	Never hinged		225.00	
J24	D4	100 l blue ('03)	72.50	20.00
	Never hinged		175.00	
	Nos. J21-J24 (4)		342.50	210.00

Nos. J21-J24 were used for Post Office internal accounting purposes and are not known used on cover.

Nos. J3 & J4
Surcharged in Black

1890-91

J25	D3	10c on 2c	130.00	35.00
	No gum		27.50	
	Never hinged		250.00	
	On cover			225.00
J26	D3	20c on 1c	525.00	27.50
	No gum		80.00	
	Never hinged		1,000.	
	On cover			160.00
a.	Inverted surcharge			10,000.
J27	D3	30c on 2c	2,000.	12.00
	No gum		275.00	
	Never hinged		4,000.	
	On cover			120.00
a.	Inverted surcharge			2,750.
	Nos. J25-J27 (3)		2,655.	74.50

Coat of Arms
D6   D7

1934   Photo.

J28	D6	5c brown	.80	.40
	Never hinged		2.00	
	On cover			5.50
J29	D6	10c blue	.80	.40
	Never hinged		2.00	
	On cover			4.75
J30	D6	20c rose red	.80	.40
	Never hinged		2.00	
	On cover			3.25
J31	D6	25c green	.80	.40
	Never hinged		2.00	
	On cover			3.25
J32	D6	30c red org	.80	.40
	Never hinged		2.00	
	On cover			5.50
J33	D6	40c blk brn	.80	4.75
	Never hinged		2.00	
	On cover			12.00
J34	D6	50c violet	.80	.40
	Never hinged		2.00	
	On cover			2.40
J35	D6	60c slate blk	.80	14.00
	Never hinged		2.00	
	On cover			27.50
J36	D7	1 l red org	.80	.40
	Never hinged		2.00	
	On cover			2.40
J37	D7	2 l green	.80	.40
	Never hinged		2.00	
	On cover			9.50
J38	D7	5 l violet	1.60	.80
	Never hinged		4.00	
	On cover			24.00
J39	D7	10 l blue	6.50	12.00
	Never hinged		16.00	
	On cover			65.00
J40	D7	20 l car rose	12.50	40.00
	Never hinged		30.00	
	Nos. J28-J40 (13)		28.60	74.75

For overprints and surcharges see Italian Social Republic #J1-J13 in Scott Standard catalogue, Vol. 3; Yugoslavia-Ljubljana NJ14-NJ22 in Scott Standard catalogue, Vol. 6.

OFFICIAL STAMPS

O1

1875   Wmk. 140   Typo.   Perf. 14

O1	O1	2c lake	3.25	4.75
	No gum		.80	
	Never hinged		8.00	
	On cover			9.50
O2	O1	5c lake	3.25	4.75
	No gum		.80	
	Never hinged		8.00	
	On cover			14.50
O3	O1	20c lake	1.60	1.60
	No gum		.40	
	Never hinged		4.00	
	On cover			3.25
O4	O1	30c lake	1.60	3.25
	No gum		.40	
	Never hinged		4.00	
	On cover			6.50
O5	O1	1 l lake	4.75	20.00
	No gum		1.20	
	Never hinged		12.00	
	On cover			200.00
O6	O1	2 l lake	12.50	60.00
	No gum		3.25	
	Never hinged		32.50	
	On cover			600.00
O7	O1	5 l lake	55.00	225.00
	No gum		14.00	
	Never hinged		140.00	
	On cover			4,750.
O8	O1	10 l lake	95.00	160.00
	No gum		24.00	
	Never hinged		240.00	
	On cover			12,000.
	Nos. O1-O8 (8)		176.95	479.35

Covers: Values for Nos. O7-O8 are for over-franked covers.

For surcharges see Nos. 37-44.

Stamps inscribed "Servizio Commissioni" were used in connection with the postal service but not for the payment of postage.

NEWSPAPER STAMP

N1

Typographed, Numeral Embossed
1862   Unwmk.   Imperf.

P1	N1	2c buff	52.50	110.00
	No gum		27.50	
	Never hinged		110.00	
	On newspaper or cover			275.00
a.	Numeral double		475.00	1,650.
	On newspaper or cover			6,750.
b.	Printed on gummed side		500.00	

Black 1c and 2c stamps of similar type are listed under Sardinia.

PARCEL POST STAMPS

King Humbert
I — PP1

1884-86   Wmk. 140   Typo.   Perf. 14
Various Frames

Q1	PP1	10c olive gray	125.00	120.00
	No gum		32.50	
	Never hinged		525.00	
	On parcel post receipt card			1,500.
Q2	PP1	20c blue	260.00	175.00
	No gum		65.00	
	Never hinged		1,000.	
	On parcel post receipt card			4,250.
Q3	PP1	50c claret	9.50	14.50
	No gum		3.25	
	Never hinged		40.00	
	On parcel post receipt card			2,200.
Q4	PP1	75c blue grn	9.50	14.50
	No gum		3.25	
	Never hinged		40.00	
	On parcel post receipt card			2,200.
Q5	PP1	1.25 l orange	20.00	32.50
	No gum		8.00	
	Never hinged		80.00	
	On parcel post receipt card			3,000.
Q6	PP1	1.75 l brown	24.00	120.00
	No gum		14.50	
	Never hinged		95.00	
	On parcel post receipt card			—
	Nos. Q1-Q6 (6)		448.00	476.50

For surcharges see Nos. 58-63.

Parcel Post stamps from No. Q7 onward were used by affixing them to the waybill so that one half remained on it following the parcel, the other half staying on the receipt given the sender. Most used halves are right halves. Complete stamps were and are obtainable canceled, probably to order.

Both unused and used values are for complete stamps.

PP2

1914-22   Wmk. 140   Perf. 13

Q7	PP2	5c brown	4.75	20.00
Q8	PP2	10c deep blue	4.75	20.00
Q9	PP2	20c black ('17)	17.50	20.00
Q10	PP2	25c red	24.00	20.00
Q11	PP2	50c orange	35.00	40.00
Q12	PP2	1 l violet	40.00	16.00
Q13	PP2	2 l green	40.00	20.00
Q14	PP2	3 l bister	47.50	55.00
Q15	PP2	4 l slate	60.00	72.50
Q16	PP2	10 l lilac ('22)	95.00	72.50
a.	10 l brn lilac		95.00	72.50
b.	10 l rose brn			
Q17	PP2	12 l red brn ('22)	160.00	450.00
Q18	PP2	15 l ol grn ('22)	140.00	450.00
Q19	PP2	20 l brn vio ('22)	120.00	450.00
	Nos. Q7-Q19 (13)		788.50	1,706.

Halves Used

Q7-Q14, each	.40
Q15	.80
Q16	1.60
Q17	4.00
Q18	4.00
Q19	6.50

Imperfs exist. Value per pair: 20c, 25c, 50c, 2 l, 3l, 4 l: $50 each; 10l $225.

No. Q7 Surcharged

Q20	PP2	30c on 5c brown	1.60	24.00
	Half stamp			3.25
Q21	PP2	60c on 5c brown	1.60	24.00
	Half stamp			3.25
Q22	PP2	1.50 l on 5c brown	6.50	190.00
	Half stamp			6.50
a.	Double surcharge		250.00	

No. Q16 Surcharged

Q23	PP2	3 l on 10 l rose lilac	6.50	80.00
	Half stamp			3.25
	Nos. Q20-Q23 (4)		16.20	318.00

PP3

1927-39   Wmk. 140

Q24	PP3	5c brn ('38)	.80	3.25
Q25	PP3	10c dp bl ('39)	.80	3.25
Q26	PP3	25c red ('32)	.80	3.25
Q27	PP3	30c ultra	.80	4.00
Q28	PP3	50c org ('32)	.80	3.25
Q29	PP3	60c red	.80	4.00
Q30	PP3	1 l lilac ('31)	.80	3.25
Q31	PP3	1 l brn vio ('36)	24.00	87.50
Q32	PP3	2 l grn ('32)	.80	4.00
Q33	PP3	3 l yel bister	.80	9.50
a.	Printed on both sides		65.00	
Q34	PP3	4 l gray	.80	9.50
Q35	PP3	10 l rose lil ('34)	2.40	55.00
Q36	PP3	20 l lil brn ('33)	3.25	80.00
	Nos. Q24-Q36 (13)		37.65	269.75

Value of used halves: Nos. Q24-Q34, each 40c; Q35 80c; Q36 $4.

For overprints see Italian Social Republic Nos. Q1-Q12 in Scott Standard catalogue, Vol. 3.

OCCUPATION STAMPS

Issued under Austrian Occupation

Emperor Karl of Austria
OS1　　　　OS2

Austria Nos. M49-M67 Surcharged in Black

				Unwmk.	Perf. 12½
1918					
N1	OS1	2c on 1h grnsh bl		.25	.45
		Never hinged		.80	
		On cover			32.50
N2	OS1	3c on 2h red org		.25	.40
		Never hinged		.80	
		On cover			32.50
N3	OS1	4c on 3h ol gray		.25	.45
		Never hinged		.80	
		On cover			32.50
N4	OS1	6c on 5h ol grn		.25	.40
		Never hinged		.80	
		On cover			27.50
N5	OS1	7c on 6h vio		.25	.40
		Never hinged		.80	
		On cover			32.50
a.		Perf. 12½x11½		16.00	95.00
		Never hinged		47.50	
		On cover			—
N6	OS1	11c on 10h org brn		.25	.45
		Never hinged		.80	
		On cover			27.50
N7	OS1	13c on 12h blue		.25	.45
		Never hinged		.80	
		On cover			32.50
N8	OS1	16c on 15h brt rose		.25	.40
		Never hinged		.80	
		On cover			32.50
N9	OS1	22c on 20h red brn		.25	.45
		Never hinged		.80	
		On cover			32.50
a.		Perf. 11½		24.00	80.00
		Never hinged		55.00	
N10	OS1	27c on 25h ultra		.65	1.60
		Never hinged		2.40	
		On cover			75.00
N11	OS1	32c on 30h slate		.65	1.60
		Never hinged		2.40	
		On cover			60.00
N12	OS1	43c on 40h ol bis		.65	1.60
		Never hinged		2.40	
		On cover			45.00
a.		Perf. 11½		16.00	72.50
		Never hinged		47.50	
N13	OS1	53c on 50h dp grn		.65	1.60
		Never hinged		2.40	
		On cover			60.00
N14	OS1	64c on 60h rose		.65	1.60
		Never hinged		2.40	
		On cover			95.00
N15	OS1	85c on 80h dl bl		.65	1.20
		Never hinged		.80	
		On cover			80.00
N16	OS1	95c on 90h dk vio		.65	1.20
		Never hinged		2.40	
		On cover			95.00
N17	OS2	2 l 11c on 2k rose, straw		.65	2.40
		Never hinged		3.25	
		On cover			200.00
N18	OS2	3 l 16c on 3k grn, bl		1.20	3.25
		Never hinged		4.00	
N19	OS2	4 l 22c on 4k rose, grn		2.40	5.50
		Never hinged		5.50	
		Nos. N1-N19 (19)		11.05	25.45

Exist imperf. Values: unused, $160; never hinged, $325.

Emperor Karl — OS3

Austria Nos. M69-M81 Surcharged in Black

1918				
N20	OS3	2c on 1h grnsh bl		6.00
		Never hinged		20.00
N21	OS3	3c on 2h orange		6.00
		Never hinged		20.00
N22	OS3	4c on 3h ol gray		6.00
		Never hinged		20.00
N23	OS3	6c on 5h yel grn		6.00
		Never hinged		20.00
N24	OS3	11c on 10h dk brn		6.00
		Never hinged		20.00
N25	OS3	22c on 20h red		6.00
		Never hinged		20.00
N26	OS3	27c on 25h blue		6.00
		Never hinged		20.00
N27	OS3	32c on 30h bister		6.00
		Never hinged		20.00
N28	OS3	48c on 45h dk sl		6.00
		Never hinged		20.00
N29	OS3	53c on 50h dp grn		6.00
		Never hinged		20.00
N30	OS3	64c on 60h violet		6.00
		Never hinged		20.00
N31	OS3	85c on 80h rose		6.00
		Never hinged		20.00
N32	OS3	95c on 90h brn vio		6.00
		Never hinged		20.00
N33	OS3	1 l 60c on 1k al grn, grnish		6.00
		Never hinged		20.00
		Nos. N20-N33 (14)		84.00

Nos. N20 to N33 inclusive were never placed in use in the occupied territory. They were, however, on sale at the Post Office in Vienna for a few days before the Armistice.

Exist imperf. Values unused, $325; never hinged, $800.

OCCUPATION SPECIAL DELIVERY STAMPS

Bosnia Nos. QE1-QE2 Surcharged

			Unwmk.	Perf. 12½
1918				
NE1	SH1	3c on 2h ver	12.00	24.00
		Never hinged	47.50	
NE2	SH1	6c on 5h dp grn	12.00	24.00
		Never hinged	47.50	

Nos. NE1-NE2 are on yellowish paper. Reprints on white paper sell for about $1.25 a set.

OCCUPATION POSTAGE DUE STAMPS

Bosnia Nos. J16, J18-J19, J21-J24 Surcharged Like Nos. NE1-NE2

			Unwmk.	Perf. 12½
1918				
NJ1	D2	6c on 5h red	3.25	6.50
		Never hinged	6.50	
a.		Perf. 11½	8.00	12.00
		Never hinged	20.00	
NJ2	D2	11c on 10h red	2.40	8.00
		Never hinged	9.50	
a.		Perf. 11½	8.00	12.00
		Never hinged	20.00	
NJ3	D2	16c on 15h red	.80	3.25
		Never hinged	3.25	
NJ4	D2	27c on 25h red	.80	3.25
		Never hinged	3.25	
NJ5	D2	32c on 30h red	.80	4.00
		Never hinged	3.25	
NJ6	D2	43c on 40h red	.80	4.00
		Never hinged	3.25	
NJ7	D2	53c on 50h red	.80	4.00
		Never hinged	3.25	
		Nos. NJ1-NJ7 (7)	9.65	33.00

OCCUPATION NEWSPAPER STAMPS

Austrian Nos. MP1-MP4 Surcharged

			Unwmk.	Perf. 12½
1918				
NP1	MN1	3c on 2h blue	.80	1.20
		Never hinged	2.40	
a.		Perf. 11½	12.00	40.00
		Never hinged	40.00	
NP2	MN1	7c on 6h org	1.10	2.40
		Never hinged	3.25	
NP3	MN1	11c on 10h car	1.10	2.40
		Never hinged	3.25	
NP4	MN1	22c on 20h brn	1.10	2.75
		Never hinged	3.25	
a.		Perf. 11½	125.00	250.00
		Never hinged	250.00	
		Nos. NP1-NP4 (4)	4.10	8.75

ITALY OFFICES ABROAD

Stamps listed under this heading were issued for use in the Italian Post Offices which, for various reasons, were maintained from time to time in foreign countries.

100 Centesimi = 1 Lira

GENERAL ISSUE

Values of Italian Offices Abroad stamps vary tremendously according to condition. Quotations are for very fine examples, and values for unused stamps are for examples with original gum as defined in the catalogue introduction. Extremely fine or superb examples sell at much higher prices, and fine or poor examples sell at greatly reduced prices. In addition, unused examples without gum are discounted severely.

Very fine examples of Nos. 1-17 will have perforations barely clear of the frameline or design due to the narrow spacing of the stamps on the plates.

Italian Stamps with Corner Designs Slightly Altered and Overprinted

1874-78		**Wmk. 140**		**Perf. 14**
1	A6	1c ol grn	47.50	47.50
		No gum	9.50	
		Never hinged	120.00	
		On cover		725.00
		On newspaper, single franking		2,600.
a.		Inverted overprint	40,000.	
c.		2 dots in lower right corner	87.50	275.00
d.		Three dots in upper right corner	400.00	1,750.
e.		Without overprint	75,000.	
f.		1c gray green	95.00	
		On cover		725.00
2	A7	2c org brn	52.50	55.00
		No gum	12.50	
		Never hinged	130.00	
		On cover		800.00
a.		Without overprint	75,000.	
3	A8	5c slate grn	1,200.	55.00
		No gum	240.00	
		Never hinged	2,400.	
		On cover		550.00
		On newspaper, single franking		1,600.
a.		Lower right corner not altered	24,000.	2,600.
4	A8	10c buff	3,600.	120.00
		No gum	550.00	
		Never hinged	7,250.	
		On cover		600.00
		On newspaper, single franking		8,750.
a.		Upper left corner not altered	30,000.	1,800.
b.		None of the corners altered	—	75,000.
c.		Lower corners not altered		12,000.
5	A8	10c blue ('78)	725.00	35.00
		No gum	140.00	
		Never hinged	1,400.	
		On cover		540.00
6	A15	20c blue	2,800.	55.00
		No gum	525.00	
		Never hinged	5,500.	
		On newspaper, single franking		275.00
				2,000.
7	A15	20c org ('78)	13,000.	3,250.
		No gum	2,600.	
		Never hinged	19,500.	
		On cover		475.00
8	A8	30c brown	8.00	32.50
		No gum	2.40	
		Never hinged	20.00	
		On cover		260.00
a.		None of the corners altered		55,000.
b.		Right lower corner not altered		—
c.		Double overprint		—
9	A8	40c rose	8.00	32.50
		No gum	2.40	
		Never hinged	20.00	
		On cover		200.00
10	A8	60c lilac	27.50	350.00
		No gum	9.50	
		Never hinged	70.00	
		On cover		3,750.
a.		60c pale lilac	240.00	350.00
		On cover		3,800.
11	A13	2 l vermilion	350.00	1,100.
		No gum	95.00	
		Never hinged	725.00	
		On cover		27,500.

Values for pairs

1	A6	1c olive green	95.00	110.00
		On cover		1,600.
2	A7	2c org brn	105.00	120.00
		On cover		1,800.
3	A8	5c slate grn	2,400.	120.00
		On cover		1,200.
4	A8	10c buff	7,200.	260.00
		On cover		1,600.
5	A8	10c blue	1,450.	80.00
		On cover		1,200.
6	A15	20c blue	5,600.	120.00
		On cover		600.00

7	A15	20c orange	26,000.	160.00
		On cover		3,250.
8	A8	30c brown	16.00	240.00
		On cover		1,900.
9	A8	40c rose	16.00	72.50
		On cover		2,200.
10	A8	60c lilac	55.00	800.00
		On cover		9,000.
11	A13	2 l vermilion	700.00	2,800.

1881				
12	A17	5c green	47.50	20.00
		No gum	8.00	
		Never hinged	120.00	
		On cover		300.00
		On cover, single franking		1,400.
13	A17	10c claret	9.50	16.00
		No gum	2.40	
		Never hinged	24.00	
		On cover		400.00
14	A17	20c orange	9.50	9.50
		No gum	2.40	
		Never hinged	24.00	
a.		Double overprint, on piece		190.00
15	A17	25c blue	9.50	24.00
		No gum	2.40	
		Never hinged	24.00	
		On cover		1,200.
16	A17	50c violet	24.00	80.00
		No gum	4.75	
		Never hinged	60.00	
		On cover		2,750.
17	A17	2 l vermilion	47.50	—
		No gum	8.00	
		Never hinged	120.00	
		Nos. 12-17 (6)	147.50	
		Nos. 12-16 (5)		149.50

Values for Pairs

12	A17	5c green	95.00	45.00
				650.00
13	A17	10c claret	19.00	35.00
				900.00
14	A17	20c orange	19.00	47.50
				950.00
15	A17	25c blue	19.00	72.50
				3,500.
16	A17	50c violet	48.00	200.00
				6,500.
17	A17	2 l vermilion	95.00	

The "Estero" stamps were used in various parts of the world, South America, Africa, Turkey, etc.

Forged cancellations exist on Nos. 1-2, 9-11, 16.

OFFICES IN CHINA

100 Cents = 1 Dollar

PEKING

Italian Stamps of 1901-16 Handstamped

		Wmk. 140, Unwmk.		
1917			**Perf. 12, 13½, 14**	
1	A48	2c on 5c green	450.00	300.00
		Never hinged	875.00	
		On cover		600.00
a.		Inverted surcharge	400.00	275.00
		Never hinged	800.00	
b.		Double surcharge, one inverted	1,100.	875.00
c.		4c on 5c green	9,500.	
		Never hinged	14,000.	
d.		8c on 5c green	—	
e.		Pair, one with "PECHINO," one "TIENTSIN"	8,750.	
		Never hinged	12,500.	
3	A48	4c on 10c claret (No. 95)	800.00	475.00
		Never hinged	1,600.	
		On cover		950.00
a.		Inverted surcharge	725.00	450.00
		Never hinged	1,400.	
b.		Double surcharge, one inverted	1,750.	1,200.
c.		4c on 10c claret (No. 79)	—	
5	A58	6c on 15c slate	1,600.	1,100.
		Never hinged	3,250.	
		On cover		2,250.
b.		8c on 15c slate	5,500.	5,200.
		Never hinged	11,000.	
c.		Pair, one without surcharge	—	
d.		Pair, one with "PECHINO," one "TIENTSIN"	17,500.	
7	A58	8c on 20c on 15c slate	6,000.	4,500.
		Never hinged	12,000.	
a.		Inverted surcharge	5,500.	4,000.
		Never hinged	11,000.	
8	A50	8c on 20c brn org (No. 112)	12,000.	4,500.
		On cover	17,500.	
a.		Inverted surcharge	10,500.	4,200.
		Never hinged	16,000.	
9	A49	20c on 50c vio	60,000.	37,500.
		On cover	90,000.	
a.		Inverted surcharge	52,000.	34,000.
		Never hinged	77,500.	

b.	40c on 50c violet	24,000.	24,000.
	Never hinged	36,000.	
c.	As "b," inverted surcharge	22,000.	22,000.
	Never hinged	32,000.	
11	A46 40c on 1 l brn & grn	350,000.	60,000.
	Never hinged	440,000.	
	On cover		—
a.	Inverted surcharge	300,000.	52,000.

Excellent forgeries exist of the higher valued stamps of Offices in China.

Italian Stamps of 1901-16 Overprinted

1917-18

12	A42 1c brown	40.00	80.00
	Never hinged	90.00	
	On cover		650.00
13	A43 2c orange brown	40.00	80.00
	Never hinged	90.00	
	On cover		650.00
14	A48 5c green	12.00	27.50
	Never hinged	26.00	
	On cover		350.00
a.	Double overprint	275.00	
	Never hinged	400.00	
15	A48 10c claret	12.00	27.50
	Never hinged	26.00	
	On cover		350.00
16	A50 20c brn org (No. 112)	300.00	350.00
	Never hinged	650.00	
	On cover		—
17	A49 25c blue	12.00	35.00
	Never hinged	26.00	
	On cover		350.00
18	A49 50c violet	12.00	35.00
	Never hinged	26.00	
	On cover		600.00
19	A46 1 l brown & grn	27.50	72.50
	Never hinged	60.00	
	On cover		875.00
20	A46 5 l blue & rose	55.00	120.00
	Never hinged	120.00	
21	A51 10 l gray grn & red	400.00	675.00
	Never hinged	875.00	
	Nos. 12-21 (10)	*910.50*	*1,502.*

Italy No. 113, the watermarked 20c brown orange, was also overprinted "Pechino," but not issued. Value: hinged $32.50; never hinged $80.

Italian Stamps of 1901-16 Surcharged

Type I   Type II

TWO DOLLARS:
Type I — Surcharged "2 dollari Pechino"
Type II — Surcharged "2 DOLLARI."
Type III — Surcharged "2 dollari." "Pechino" measures 11 ½mm wide, instead of 13mm.

1918-19			**Perf. 14**
22	A42 ½c on 1c brown	350.00	350.00
	Never hinged	875.00	
	On cover		—
a.	Surcharged "1 cents"	1,100.	1,200.
	Never hinged	2,200.	
23	A43 1c on 2c org brn	12.00	24.00
	Never hinged	30.00	
	On cover		400.00
a.	Surcharged "1 cents"	550.00	650.00
	Never hinged	1,100.	
24	A48 2c on 5c green	12.00	24.00
	Never hinged	30.00	
	On cover		325.00
25	A48 4c on 10c claret	12.00	24.00
	Never hinged	30.00	
	On cover		325.00
26	A50 8c on 20c brn org (No. 112)	65.00	47.50
	Never hinged	160.00	
	On cover		525.00
a.	"8 CENTS" doubled	525.00	525.00
	Never hinged	800.00	
27	A49 10c on 25c blue	24.00	47.50
	Never hinged	60.00	
	On cover		525.00
a.	"10 CENTS" doubled	525.00	525.00
	Never hinged	800.00	

28	A49 20c on 50c violet	32.50	47.50
	Never hinged	80.00	
	On cover		675.00
29	A46 40c on 1 l brown & green	350.00	450.00
	Never hinged	875.00	
	On cover		—
30	A46 $2 on 5 l bl & rose (type I)	650.00	1,050.
	Never hinged	1,600.	
	On cover		—
a.	Type II	125,000.	100,000.
	Never hinged	185,000.	
b.	Type III	20,000.	16,000.
	Never hinged	30,000.	
	On cover		—
	Nos. 22-30 (9)	*1,507.*	*2,064.*

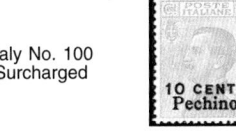

Italy No. 100 Surcharged

1919			
32	A49 10c on 25c blue	11.00	27.50
	Never hinged	27.50	
	On cover		275.00

Imperf. examples of No. 32 are proofs.

PEKING SPECIAL DELIVERY STAMPS

Italian Special Delivery Stamp 1908 Ovptd.

1917	**Wmk. 140**		**Perf. 14**
E1	SD2 30c blue & rose	16.00	60.00
	Never hinged	40.00	
	On cover		1,200.

No. E1 Surcharged

1918			
E2	SD2 12c on 30c bl & rose	125.00	450.00
	Never hinged	325.00	
	On cover		2,200.

PEKING POSTAGE DUE STAMPS

Italian Postage Due Stamps Overprinted Like Nos. 12-21

1917	**Wmk. 140**		**Perf. 14**
J1	D3 10c buff & magenta	5.50	14.00
	Never hinged	13.50	
a.	Double overprint	400.00	
J2	D3 20c buff & magenta	5.50	14.00
	Never hinged	13.50	
J3	D3 30c buff & magenta	5.50	14.00
	Never hinged	13.50	
J4	D3 40c buff & magenta	11.00	14.00
	Never hinged	27.50	
	Nos. J1-J4 (4)	*27.50*	*56.00*

Nos. J1-J4 Surcharged Like No. E2

1918			
J5	D3 4c on 10c	125,000.	100,000.
	Never hinged	160,000.	
J6	D3 8c on 20c	55.00	110.00
	Never hinged	140.00	
a.	Pair, one without surcharge	2,000.	
	Never hinged	3,000.	

J7	D3 12c on 30c	125.00	275.00
	Never hinged	300.00	
J8	D3 16c on 40c	550.00	950.00
	Never hinged	1,350.	

In 1919, the same new values were surcharged on Italy Nos. J6-J9 in a different style: four lines to cancel the denomination, and "-PECHINO- 4 CENTS." These were not issued. Value $17.50 each, never hinged $42.50 each.

TIENTSIN

Italian Stamps of 1906 Handstamped

	Wmk. 140, Unwmk.		
1917			**Perf. 12, 13½, 14**
1	A48 2c on 5c green	650.00	650.00
	Never hinged	1,300.	
	On cover		1,250.
a.	Surcharge inverted	600.00	600.00
	Never hinged	1,200.	
b.	Double surcharge	1,200.	875.00
	Never hinged	1,750.	
c.	4c on 5c green	16,000.	
	Never hinged		
d.	Double surcharge, one inverted	1,250.	950.00
	Never hinged	1,900.	
2	A48 4c on 10c claret	1,200.	1,000.
	Never hinged	2,400.	
	On cover		2,000.
a.	Surcharge inverted	1,100.	950.00
	Never hinged	2,200.	
b.	Double surcharge	1,900.	1,100.
	Never hinged	2,800.	
c.	Double surcharge, one inverted	2,000.	1,200.
	Never hinged	3,000.	
4	A58 6c on 15c slate	2,600.	2,000.
	Never hinged	5,200.	
	On cover		3,000.
a.	Surcharge inverted	2,400.	1,900.
	Never hinged	4,000.	
b.	4c on 15c slate	8,750.	8,000.
	Never hinged	13,000.	
	Nos. 1-4 (3)	*4,450.*	*3,650.*

Italian Stamps of 1901-16 Overprinted

1917-18

5	A42 1c brown	40.00	80.00
	Never hinged	100.00	
	On cover		650.00
a.	Inverted overprint	525.00	525.00
	Never hinged	1,050.	
6	A43 2c orange brn	40.00	80.00
	Never hinged	100.00	
	On cover		650.00
7	A48 5c green	12.00	27.50
	Never hinged	30.00	
	On cover		350.00
8	A48 10c claret	12.00	27.50
	Never hinged	30.00	
	On cover		350.00
a.	Double overprint	550.00	
	Never hinged	1,100.	
9	A50 20c brn org (#112)	300.00	350.00
	Never hinged	750.00	
	On cover		—
10	A49 25c blue	12.00	35.00
	Never hinged	30.00	
	On cover		350.00
11	A49 50c violet	12.00	35.00
	Never hinged	30.00	
	On cover		600.00
12	A46 1 l brown & grn	27.50	72.50
	Never hinged	67.50	
	On cover		875.00
13	A46 5 l blue & rose	55.00	120.00
	Never hinged	140.00	
	On cover		—
14	A51 10 l gray grn & red	400.00	675.00
	Never hinged	1,000.	
	Nos. 5-14 (10)	*910.50*	*1,502.*

Italy No. 113, the watermarked 20c brown orange was also overprinted "Tientsin," but not issued. Value: hinged $32.50; never hinged $80.

Type I

TWO DOLLARS:
Type I — Surcharged "2 Dollari Tientsin"
Type II — Surcharged "2 dollari."
Type III — Surcharged "2 Dollari." "Tientsin" measures 10mm wide instead of 13mm.

1918-21			**Perf. 14**
15	A42 ½c on 1c brown	350.00	350.00
	Never hinged	875.00	
	On cover		—
a.	Inverted surcharge	650.00	650.00
	Never hinged	1,300.	
b.	Surcharged "1 cents"	1,100.	1,200.
	Never hinged	2,100.	
c.	Vertical fraction bar	800.00	
	Never hinged	1,600.	
16	A43 1c on 2c org brn	12.00	24.00
	Never hinged	30.00	
	On cover		400.00
a.	Surcharged "1 cents"	550.00	650.00
	Never hinged	1,100.	
b.	Inverted surcharge	650.00	650.00
	Never hinged	1,300.	
17	A48 2c on 5c green	12.00	24.00
	Never hinged	30.00	
	On cover		325.00
18	A48 4c on 10c claret	12.00	24.00
	Never hinged	30.00	
	On cover		325.00
19	A50 8c on 20c brn org (#112)	65.00	55.00
	Never hinged	160.00	
	On cover		525.00
20	A49 10c on 25c blue	24.00	47.50
	Never hinged	60.00	
	On cover		525.00
21	A49 20c on 50c violet	32.50	47.50
	Never hinged	80.00	
	On cover		675.00
22	A46 40c on 1 l brn & grn	350.00	450.00
	Never hinged	875.00	
	On cover		—
23	A46 $2 on 5 l bl & rose (type I)	650.00	1,050.
	Never hinged	1,600.	
	On cover		—
a.	Type II	20,000.	20,000.
	Never hinged	30,000.	
	On cover		—
b.	Type III ('21)	17,500.	16,000.
	Never hinged	26,000.	
	Nos. 15-23 (9)	*1,507.*	*2,072.*

SPECIAL DELIVERY STAMPS

Italian Special Delivery Stamp of 1908 Overprinted

1917	**Wmk. 140**		**Perf. 14**
E1	SD2 30c blue & rose	16.00	60.00
	Never hinged	40.00	
	On cover		1,200.

No. E1 Surcharged

1918			
E2	SD2 12c on 30c bl & rose	125.00	450.00
	Never hinged	325.00	
	On cover		2,200.

POSTAGE DUE STAMPS

Italian Postage Due Stamps Overprinted

1917   **Wmk. 140**   *Perf. 14*

J1	D3	10c buff & magenta	5.50	*14.00*
		Never hinged	13.50	
a.		Double overprint	400.00	
		Never hinged	800.00	
J2	D3	20c buff & magenta	5.50	*14.00*
		Never hinged	13.50	
J3	D3	30c buff & magenta	5.50	*14.00*
		Never hinged		
		Double overprint	400.00	
		Never hinged	800.00	
J4	D3	40c buff & magenta	11.00	*14.00*
		Never hinged	27.50	
		Nos. J1-J4 (4)	*27.50*	*56.00*

Nos. J1-J4
Surcharged

1918

J5	D3	4c on 10c	*9,500.*	*9,500.*
		Never hinged	14,000.	
a.		"4 CENTS" handstamped	16,000.	17,500.
		Never hinged	20,000.	
J6	D3	8c on 20c	55.00	*110.00*
		Never hinged	140.00	
a.		"8 CENTS" double	2,750.	
		Never hinged	5,500.	
J7	D3	12c on 30c	120.00	*275.00*
		Never hinged	300.00	
J8	D3	16c on 40c	550.00	*950.00*
		Never hinged	1,350.	

In 1919, the same new values were surcharged on Italy Nos. J6-J9 in a different style: four lines to cancel the denomination, and "-TIENTSIN- 4 CENTS." These were not issued. Value $17 each, never hinged $42.50 each.

OFFICES IN CRETE

40 Paras = 1 Piaster
100 Centesimi = 1 Lira (1906)

Italy Nos. 70 and 81 Surcharged in Red or Black

    a   b

1900-01   **Wmk. 140**   *Perf. 14*

1	A36(a)	1pi on 25c blue	19.00	*87.50*
		Never hinged	47.50	
		No gum	6.50	
		On cover		2,200.
2	A45(b)	1pi on 25c dp bl (Bk) ('01)	4.75	*12.00*
		Never hinged	12.00	
		On cover		475.00

Values for pairs

1	A36(a)	1pi on 25c blue	38.00	225.00
2	A45(b)	1pi on 25c dp bl (Bk) ('01)	9.50	

Italian Stamps
Overprinted

1906

On Nos. 76-79, 92, 81, 83-85, 87, 91

3	A42	1c brown	3.25	*6.50*
		Never hinged	8.00	
		On cover		325.00
a.		Pair, one without ovpt.	1,600.	
b.		Double overprint	400.00	
4	A43	2c org brn	3.25	*6.50*
		Never hinged	8.00	
		On cover		300.00
a.		Imperf., pair	3,250.	
b.		Double overprint	400.00	
5	A44	5c bl grn	6.50	*8.00*
		Never hinged	16.00	
		On cover		175.00
6	A45	10c claret	450.00	*350.00*
		Never hinged	1,100.	
		On cover		—
7	A45	15c on 20c org	6.50	*8.00*
		Never hinged	16.00	
		On cover		325.00
8	A45	25c blue	24.00	*32.50*
		Never hinged	60.00	
		On cover		525.00
9	A45	40c brown	24.00	*32.50*
		Never hinged	60.00	
		On cover		875.00
10	A45	45c ol grn	16.00	*32.50*
		Never hinged	40.00	
		On cover		1,100.

11	A45	50c violet	24.00	*40.00*
		Never hinged	60.00	
		On cover		1,400.
12	A46	1 l brn & grn	95.00	*140.00*
		Never hinged	225.00	
13	A46	5 l bl & rose	550.00	*650.00*
		Never hinged	1,050.	
		Nos. 3-13 (11)	*1,202.*	*1,306.*
		Set on overfranked philatelic cover		2,500.

Values for blocks of four

6	A45	10c claret	4,250.	
13	A46	5 l bl & rose	4,300.	*3,250.*

On Nos. 94-95, 100, 104-105

1907-10

14	A48	5c green	3.25	*3.25*
		Never hinged	8.00	
		On cover		125.00
a.		Inverted overprint	400.00	
		Never hinged	750.00	
15	A48	10c claret	3.25	*3.25*
		Never hinged	8.00	
		On cover		200.00
a.		Double overprint	400.00	
16	A49	25c blue	4.75	*20.00*
		Never hinged	11.50	
		On cover		240.00
17	A49	40c brown	40.00	*52.50*
		Never hinged	100.00	
		On cover		475.00
18	A49	50c violet	4.75	*17.50*
		Never hinged	11.50	
		On cover		550.00
		Nos. 14-18 (5)	*56.00*	*96.50*

On No. 111 in Violet

1912   **Unwmk.**   *Perf. 13x13½*

19	A50	15c slate black	4.75	*6.50*
		Never hinged	11.00	
		On cover		240.00
		Nos. 14-19 on overfranked philatelic cover		275.00

SPECIAL DELIVERY STAMPS

Special
Delivery
Stamp of
Italy
Overprinted

1906   **Wmk. 140**   *Perf. 14*

E1	SD1	25c rose red	12.50	*32.50*
		Never hinged	32.50	
		On cover		725.00

Some sheets from the first printing have a second, albino overprint.

OFFICES IN AFRICA

40 Paras = 1 Piaster
100 Centesimi = 1 Lira (1910)

BENGASI

Italy No. 81 Surcharged
in Black

1901   **Wmk. 140**   *Perf. 14*

1	A45	1pi on 25c dp bl	65.00	*160.00*
		Never hinged	160.00	
		On cover		475.00

Same Surcharge on
Italy No. 100

1911

1A	A49	1pi on 25c blue	65.00	*160.00*
		Never hinged	160.00	
		On cover		475.00

TRIPOLI

Italian Stamps of 1901-
00 Overprinted in Black
or Violet

1909   **Wmk. 140**

2	A42	1c brown	4.75	*3.25*
		Never hinged	12.00	
		On cover		250.00
a.		Inverted overprint	275.00	
		Never hinged	550.00	
3	A43	2c orange brn	2.40	*3.25*
		Never hinged	6.00	
		On cover		200.00
4	A48	5c green	175.00	*9.50*
		Never hinged	425.00	
		On cover		80.00
a.		Double overprint	325.00	
		Never hinged	600.00	
5	A48	10c claret	3.25	*3.25*
		Never hinged	8.00	
		On cover		87.50
a.		Double overprint	225.00	*225.00*
		Never hinged	450.00	
6	A49	25c blue	2.40	*3.25*
		Never hinged	6.00	
		On cover		175.00
7	A49	40c brown	8.00	*8.00*
		Never hinged	20.00	
		On cover		450.00
8	A49	50c violet	9.50	*9.50*
		Never hinged	24.00	
		On cover		525.00

Perf. 13½x14
Unwmk.

9	A50	15c slate blk (V)	4.75	*4.75*
		Never hinged	12.00	
		On cover		240.00
		Nos. 2-9 (8)	*210.05*	*44.75*

Italian Stamps of 1901
Overprinted

1909   **Wmk. 140**   *Perf. 14*

10	A46	1 l brown & grn	140.00	*100.00*
		Never hinged	350.00	
		On cover		1,000.
11	A46	5 l blue & rose	47.50	*300.00*
		Never hinged	120.00	
		On cover		—
		Set of 10 on overfranked, philatelic cover		650.00

Same Overprint on Italy Nos. 76-77

1915

12	A42	1c brown		3.50
		Never hinged		8.75
13	A43	2c orange brown		3.50
		Never hinged		8.75

Nos. 12-13 were prepared but not issued. No. 12 exists as a pair, one without overprint, value $2,400 hinged, $3,600 never hinged. No. 12 also exists with inverted overprint. Value, $1,600.

SPECIAL DELIVERY STAMPS

Italy Nos.
E1, E6
Ovptd. Like
Nos. 10-11

1909   **Wmk. 140**   *Perf. 14*

E1	SD1	25c rose red	19.00	*12.00*
		Never hinged	47.50	
		On cover		325.00
E2	SD2	30c blue & rose	6.50	*16.00*
		Never hinged	16.00	
		On cover		475.00

Tripoli was ceded by Turkey to Italy in Oct., 1912, and became known as the Colony of Libia. Later issues will be found under Libya.

OFFICES IN TURKISH EMPIRE

40 Paras = 1 Piaster

Various powers maintained post offices in the Turkish Empire before World War I by authority of treaties which ended with the signing of the

---

Treaty of Lausanne in 1923. The foreign post offices were closed Oct. 27, 1923.

GENERAL ISSUE

Italian Stamps of 1906-
08 Surcharged

Printed at Turin

1908   **Wmk. 140**

1	A48	10pa on 5c green	8.00	*4.75*
		Never hinged	20.00	
		On cover		110.00
2	A48	20pa on 10c claret	8.00	*4.75*
		Never hinged	20.00	
		On cover		140.00
3	A49	40pa on 25c blue	3.25	*3.25*
		Never hinged	8.00	
		On cover		80.00
4	A49	80pa on 50c violet	6.50	*4.75*
		Never hinged	16.00	
		On cover		140.00

See Janina Nos. 1-4.

Surcharged in Violet

Unwmk.

5	A47	30pa on 15c slate	2.40	*2.40*
		Never hinged	6.00	
		On cover		65.00
		Nos. 1-5 (5)	*28.15*	*19.90*

Nos. 1, 2, 3 and 5 were first issued in Janina, Albania, and subsequently for general use. They can only be distinguished by the cancellations.

Italian Stamps of 1901-08 Surcharged

Nos. 6-8   No. 9

Nos. 10-12

Printed at Constantinople

1908   **First Printing**

6	A48	10pa on 5c green	400.00	*475.00*
		Never hinged	800.00	
		On cover		725.00
a.		Vert. pair, one without surcharge	4,000.	
		Never hinged	7,500.	
7	A48	20pa on 10c claret	400.00	*475.00*
		Never hinged	800.00	
		On cover		725.00
8	A47	30pa on 15c slate	1,200.	*1,400.*
		Never hinged	2,400.	
		On cover		2,100.
9	A49	1pi on 25c blue	1,200.	*1,400.*
		Never hinged	2,400.	
		On cover		2,900.
a.		"PIASTRE"	2,000.	2,000.
10	A49	2pi on 50c violet	3,250.	*4,000.*
		Never hinged	6,500.	
		On cover		8,000.
11	A46	4pi on 1 l brn & grn	17,500.	*12,000.*
		Never hinged	26,000.	
		On cover		17,500.
12	A46	20pi on 5 l bl & rose	40,000.	*35,000.*
		Never hinged	60,000.	
		On cover		54,000.

On Nos. 8, 9 and 10 the surcharge is at the top of the stamp. No. 11 has the "4" closed at the top. No. 12 has the "20" wide.

Second Printing
Italian Stamps of 1901-08 Surcharged

Nos. 13-15   No. 16

Nos. 17-19

13	A48	10pa on 5c green	40.00	52.50
		Never hinged	100.00	
		On cover		450.00
14	A48	20pa on 10c claret	40.00	52.50
		Never hinged	100.00	
		On cover		450.00
15	A47	30pa on 15c slate	160.00	120.00
		Never hinged	400.00	
		On cover		650.00
a.		Double surcharge	350.00	350.00
b.		Triple surcharge	800.00	800.00
16	A49	1pi on 25c blue	40.00	52.50
		Never hinged	100.00	
		On cover		675.00
a.		"PIPSTRA"	250.00	250.00
b.		"1" omitted	250.00	250.00
17	A49	2pi on 50c violet	240.00	240.00
		Never hinged	600.00	
		On cover		2,200.
a.		Surcharged "20 PIASTRE"	2,400.	2,400.
		Never hinged	3,600.	
b.		"20" with "0" scratched out	800.00	800.00
c.		"2" 5mm from "PIASTRE"	650.00	650.00
18	A46	4pi on 1 l brn & grn	1,600.	1,600.
		Never hinged	3,200.	
		On cover		4,000.
19	A46	20pi on 5 l bl & rose	9,500.	5,200.
		Never hinged	14,500.	
		On cover		16,000.
		Nos. 13-19 (7)	11,620.	7,317.

On No. 18 the "4" is open at the top.

Third Printing

Surcharged in Red

20	A47	30pa on 15c slate	9.50	9.50
		Never hinged	24.00	
		On cover		140.00
a.		Double surcharge	240.00	240.00

Fourth Printing

20B	A46	4pi on 1 l brn & grn	65.00	95.00
		Never hinged	160.00	
		On cover		—
c.		Inverted "S"	200.00	200.00
20D	A46	20pi on 5 l bl & rose	210.00	240.00
		Never hinged	525.00	
		On cover		—
i.		Inverted "S"	550.00	550.00

Fifth Printing

20E	A46	4pi on 1 l brn & grn	55.00	72.50
		Never hinged	140.00	
		On cover		—
f.		Surch. "20 PIASTRE"	2,750.	
		Never hinged	3,250.	
20G	A46	20pi on 5 l bl & rose	55.00	72.50
		Never hinged	140.00	
		On cover		—
h.		Double surcharge	1,600.	1,600.
		Never hinged	2,400.	

Italian Stamps of 1906-19 Surcharged

1921

21	A48	1pi on 5c green	350.00	475.00
		Never hinged	875.00	
		On cover		—
22	A48	2pi on 15c slate	8.00	12.00
		Never hinged	20.00	
		On cover		275.00
23	A50	4pi on 20c brn org (No. 113)	80.00	95.00
		Never hinged	200.00	
		On cover		—
24	A49	5pi on 25c blue	80.00	95.00
		Never hinged	200.00	
		On cover		—
a.		Double surcharge	350.00	
25	A49	10pi on 60c carmine	4.75	8.00
		Never hinged	12.00	
		Nos. 21-25 (5)	522.75	685.00
		Set of 5 on overfranked philatelic cover		1,000.

No. 21 is almost always found poorly centered, and it is valued thus.

On No. 25 the "10" is placed above "PIASTRE."

Italian Stamps of 1901-19 Surcharged

n   o

1922

26	A42(n)	10pa on 1c brown	2.40	2.75
		Never hinged	6.00	
		On cover		—
27	A43(n)	20pa on 2c org brn	2.40	2.75
		Never hinged	6.00	
28	A48(n)	30pa on 5c green	6.50	6.50
		Never hinged	16.00	
		On cover		300.00
29	A48(o)	1pi20pa on 15c slate	7.25	2.75
		Never hinged	18.00	
		On cover		175.00
30	A50(n)	3pi on 20c brn org (#113)	9.50	17.50
		Never hinged	24.00	
		On cover		200.00
31	A49(o)	3pi30pa on 25c blue	4.75	2.75
		Never hinged	12.00	
		On cover		160.00
32	A49(o)	7pi20pa on 60c carmine	9.50	6.50
		Never hinged	24.00	
		On cover		240.00
33	A46(n)	15pi on 1 l brn & grn	27.50	47.50
		Never hinged	67.50	
		On cover		—
		Nos. 26-33 (8)	69.80	89.00
		Set of 5 on overfranked philatelic cover		175.00

On No. 32, the distance between the two lines is 2mm. See note after No. 58A.

Italy No. 100 Surcharged

34	A49	3.75pi on 25c blue	2.40	2.75
		Never hinged	6.00	
		On cover		95.00

Italian Stamps of 1901-20 Surcharged

q   r

1922

35	A48	30pi on 5c green	4.00	17.50
		Never hinged	10.00	
		On cover		275.00
36	A49	1.50pi on 25c blue	2.40	9.50
		Never hinged	6.00	
		On cover		80.00
37	A49	3.75pi on 40c brown	3.25	11.00
		Never hinged	8.00	
		On cover		72.50
38	A49	4.50pi on 50c violet	8.00	24.00
		Never hinged	20.00	
		On cover		80.00
a.		Double surcharge	325.00	
39	A49	7.50pi on 60c carmine	6.50	17.50
		Never hinged	16.00	
		On cover		95.00
a.		Double surcharge	400.00	
b.		Pair, one without surcharge	1,750.	
40	A49	15pi on 85c red brn	12.00	40.00
		Never hinged	30.00	
		On cover		120.00
41	A46	18.75pi on 1 l brn & grn	5.50	32.50
		Never hinged	14.00	
		On cover		240.00

On No. 40 the numerals of the surcharge are above "PIASTRE."

Italian Stamps of 1901-20 Surcharged

42	A46	45pa on 5 l bl & rose	450.00	725.00
		Never hinged	1,100.	
		On cover		—
43	A51	90pi on 10 l gray grn & red	475.00	875.00
		Never hinged	1,200.	
		On cover		—

On No. 42 the figure "4" is open at top. See note after No. 61.

On No. 43 the figure "9" has a curved or arched bottom. See note after No. 62.

Italian Stamps of 1901-17 Surcharged Type "q" or:

44	A43	30pa on 2c org brn	2.40	6.50
		Never hinged	6.00	
		On cover		200.00
45	A50	1.50pi on 20c brn org (#113)	2.40	6.50
		Never hinged	6.00	
		On cover		95.00
		Nos. 35-45 (11)	971.45	1,765.
		Nos. 36-45, set of 10 on overfranked philatelic cover		2,600.

Italian Stamps of 1901-20 Surcharged in Black or Red

46	A48	30pa on 5c green	2.40	4.00
		Never hinged	6.00	
		On cover		275.00
a.		"RARA" instead of "PARA"	20.00	20.00
47	A48	1 ½pi on 10c claret	2.40	4.00
		Never hinged	6.00	
		On cover		175.00
48	A49	3pi on 25c blue	20.00	8.00
		Never hinged	50.00	
		On cover		225.00
49	A49	3¾pi on 40c brown	4.00	4.00
		Never hinged	10.00	
		On cover		250.00
50	A49	4 ½pi on 50c violet	47.50	45.00
		Never hinged	120.00	
		On cover		325.00
51	A49	7 ½pi on 85c red brn	9.50	12.00
		Never hinged	24.00	
		On cover		160.00
a.		"PIASIRE"	47.50	47.50
52	A46	7 ½pi on 1 l brn & grn (R)	12.00	14.00
		Never hinged	27.50	
		On cover		225.00
a.		Double surcharge	175.00	
b.		"PIASIRE"	55.00	55.00
53	A46	15pi on 1 l brn & grn	72.50	175.00
		Never hinged	175.00	
54	A46	45pi on 5 l blue & rose	110.00	110.00
		Never hinged	275.00	

55	A51	90pi on 10 l gray grn & red	87.50	200.00
		Never hinged	210.00	
		Nos. 46-55 (10)	367.80	576.00
		Set of 10 on overfranked philatelic cover		825.00

Italian Stamps of 1901-20 Surcharged Type "o" or

No. 58   No. 59

Nos. 61-62

1923

56	A49	1pi20pa on 25c blue	14.00	
			35.00	
57	A49	3pi30pa on 40c brown	14.00	
			35.00	
58	A49	4pi20pa on 50c violet	14.00	
		Never hinged	35.00	
58A	A49	7pi20pa on 60c car	40.00	
		Never hinged	100.00	
59	A49	15pi on 85c red brn	14.00	
		Never hinged	35.00	
60	A46	18pi30pa on 1 l brn & grn	14.00	
			35.00	
a.		Double surcharge	325.00	
61	A46	45pi on 5 l bl & rose	40.00	
		Never hinged	100.00	
62	A51	90pi on 10 l gray grn & red	35.00	
		Never hinged	87.50	
		Nos. 56-62 (8)	185.00	

On No. 58A the distance between the lines is 1.5mm. On No. 61 the figure "4" is closed at top. On No. 62 the figure "9" is nearly rectilinear at bottom.

Nos. 56-62 were not issued.

SPECIAL DELIVERY STAMPS

Italian Special Delivery Stamps Surcharged

1908   Wmk. 140   Perf. 14

E1	SD1	1pi on 25c rose red	3.25	4.75
		Never hinged	8.00	
		On cover		550.00

Surcharged

1910

E2	SD2	60pa on 30c blue & rose	6.50	8.00
		Never hinged	16.00	
		On cover		2,000.
		Nos. E1 and E2, set of two on overfranked philatelic cover		650.00

Surcharged

1922
E3   SD2 15pi on 1.20 l on
                30c bl & rose   35.00   87.50
        Never hinged   87.50
        On cover   875.00
    a.   Missing comma between "1"
          and "20" (position 13)   175.00 240.00

On No. E3 lines obliterate the first two denominations.

Surcharged

1922
E4   SD2 15pi on 30c bl &
                rose   525.00 1,050.
        Never hinged   1,300.

Surcharged

1923
E5   SD2 15pi on 1.20 l blue &
                red   16.00
        Never hinged   40.00

No. E5 was not regularly issued.

ALBANIA

Stamps of Italy
Surcharged in Black

ALBANIA
10 Para 10

1902   **Wmk. 140**   **Perf. 14**
1   A44 10pa on 5c green   4.75   2.40
        Never hinged   12.00
        On cover   175.00
2   A45 35pa on 20c orange 7.25   8.00
        Never hinged   18.00
        On cover   350.00
3   A45 40pa on 25c blue   14.00   8.00
        Never hinged   35.00
        On cover   325.00
        Nos. 1-3 (3)   26.00   18.40
    Set of 3 on overfranked
      philatelic cover   95.00

Nos. 1-3 with red surcharges are proofs.

1907
4   A48 10pa on 5c green   55.00   65.00
        Never hinged   140.00
        On cover   325.00
5   A48 20pa on 10c claret 35.00   27.50
        Never hinged   87.50
        On cover   275.00
6   A45 80pa on 50c violet 35.00   27.50
        Never hinged   87.50
        On cover   675.00
        Nos. 4-6 (3)   125.00 120.00
    Set of 3 on overfranked
      philatelic cover   275.00

No. 5 is almost always found poorly centered, and it is valued thus.

CONSTANTINOPLE

Stamps of Italy
Surcharged in Black or
Violet

Constantinopli
10 Para 10

Wmk. 140, Unwmk. (#3)
1909-11   **Perf. 14, 12**
1   A48 10pa on 5c green   2.40   2.40
        Never hinged   6.00
        On cover   87.50
2   A48 20pa on 10c claret 2.40   2.40
        Never hinged   6.00
        On cover   87.50

3   A47 30pa on 15c slate
                (V)   2.40   2.40
        Never hinged   6.00
        On cover   125.00
4   A49 1pi on 25c blue   2.40   2.40
        Never hinged   6.00
        On cover   125.00
5   A45 2pi on 50c violet 4.75   3.25
        Never hinged   12.00
        On cover   200.00

Surcharged

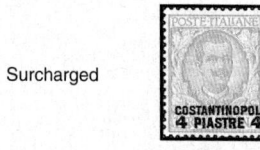

COSTANTINOPOLI
4 PIASTRE 4

6   A46 4pi on 1 l brn & grn 4.75   4.00
        Never hinged   12.00   —
7   A46 20pi on 5 l bl & rose 72.50 72.50
        Never hinged   175.00
8   A51 40pi on 10 l gray grn
                & red   8.00   32.50
        Never hinged   20.00
        On cover   —
        Nos. 1-8 (8)   99.60 121.85
    Set of 8 on overfranked
      philatelic cover   240.00

Italian Stamps of 1901-19
Surcharged

COSTANTINOPOLI   COSTANTINOPOLI
PIASTRE 1   PIASTRE 3
PARÀ 20

Nos. 10, 12-13   Nos. 9, 11

1922
9   A48 20pa on 5c green   20.00   32.50
        Never hinged   50.00
        On cover   875.00
10 A48 1pi20pa on 15c slate 2.40 2.40
        Never hinged   6.00
        On cover   240.00
11 A49 3pi on 30c org
                brn   2.40   2.40
        Never hinged   6.00
        On cover   87.50
12 A49 3pi30pa on 40c brown 2.40 2.40
        Never hinged   6.00
        On cover   200.00
13 A46 7pi20pa on 1 l brn &
                grn   2.40   2.40
        Never hinged   6.00
        On cover   225.00
        Nos. 9-13 (5)   29.60 42.10
    Set of 8 on overfranked
      philatelic cover   160.00

Italian Stamps of 1901-20 Surcharged

COSTANTINOPOLI
PIASTRE 1
PARÀ 20

1923
14 A48 30pa on 5c
                green   3.25   2.40
        Never hinged   8.00
        On cover   450.00
15 A49 1pi20pa on 25c
                blue   3.25   2.40
        Never hinged   8.00
        On cover   125.00
16 A49 3pi30pa on 40c
                brown   3.25   2.00
        Never hinged   8.00
        On cover   125.00
17 A49 4pi20pa on 50c vio-
                let   3.25   2.00
        Never hinged   8.00
        On cover   100.00
18 A49 7pi20pa on 60c car 3.25   2.00
        Never hinged   8.00
        On cover   160.00
19 A49 15pi on 85c red
                brn   3.25   3.25
        Never hinged   8.00
        On cover   275.00
20 A46 18pi30pa on 1 l brn
                & grn   3.25   3.25
        Never hinged   8.00
        On cover   450.00
21 A46 45pi on 5 l bl &
                rose   3.25   7.25
        Never hinged   8.00
        On cover   —
22 A51 90pi on 10 l
                gray grn
                & red   3.25   8.00
        Never hinged   7.00
        On cover   —
        Nos. 14-22 (9)   29.25 32.55
    Set of 9 on overfranked
      philatelic cover   125.00

CONSTANTINOPLE SPECIAL DELIVERY STAMP

Unissued
Special
Delivery
Stamp of
1922
Surcharged
in Black

COSTANTINOPOLI
EXPRES
15
PIASTRE

1923   **Wmk. 140**   **Perf. 14**
E1   SD2 15pi on 1.20 l bl &
                red   8.00   45.00
        Never hinged   20.00
        On cover   875.00

CONSTANTINOPLE POSTAGE DUE STAMPS

Italian Postage Due
Stamps of 1870-1903
Overprinted

Costantinopli

1922   **Wmk. 140**   **Perf. 14**
J1   D3 10c buff & mag   80.00 110.00
        Never hinged   160.00
J2   D3 30c buff & mag   80.00 110.00
        Never hinged   160.00
J3   D3 60c buff & mag   80.00 110.00
        Never hinged   160.00
J4   D3 1 l blue & mag   80.00 110.00
        Never hinged   160.00
J5   D3 2 l blue & mag   1,900.   3,400.
        Never hinged   3,800.
J6   D3 5 l blue & mag   875.00 1,200.
        Never hinged   1,750.
        Nos. J1-J6 (6)   3,095.   5,040.

A circular control mark with the inscription "Poste Italiane Constantinopoli" and with the arms of the Kingdom of Italy (Savoy Cross) in the center was applied to each block of four of these stamps in black. Value, set of 6 blocks of four with control marks: unused $20,000; used $28,000.

Without Control Mark
J1a D3 10c buff & mag   1,900.
        Never hinged   2,900.
J2a D3 30c buff & mag   1,900.
        Never hinged   2,900.
J3a D3 60c buff & mag   1,900.
        Never hinged   2,900.
J4a D3 1 l blue & mag   1,900.
        Never hinged   2,900.
J5a D3 2 l blue & mag   —
        Never hinged   —
J6a D3 5 l blue & mag   —
        Never hinged   —
        Nos. J1a-J4a (4)   7,200.

DURAZZO

Stamps of Italy
Surcharged in Black or
Violet

Durazzo
10 Parà 10

Wmk. 140, Unwmk. (#3)
1909-11   **Perf. 14, 12**
1   A48 10pa on 5c green   1.60   3.25
        Never hinged   4.00
        On cover   87.50
2   A48 20pa on 10c claret 1.60   3.25
        Never hinged   4.00
        On cover   87.50
3   A47 30pa on 15c slate
                (V)   80.00   4.00
        Never hinged   200.00
        On cover   175.00
4   A49 1pi on 25c blue   2.40   4.00
        Never hinged   6.00
        On cover   175.00
5   A49 2pi on 50c violet 2.40   4.00
        Never hinged   6.00
        On cover   350.00

Surcharged

DURAZZO
4 PIASTRE 4

6   A46 4pi on 1 l brn & grn 4.00   4.75
        Never hinged   10.00
        On cover   475.00

7   A46 20pi on 5 l bl & rose 325.00 275.00
        Never hinged   800.00
8   A51 40pi on 10 l gray grn
                & red   20.00 140.00
        Never hinged   50.00
        Nos. 1-8 (8)   437.00 438.25
    Set of 8 stamps on over-
      franked philatelic cover   650.00

CENT. 20

No. 3 Surcharged

1916   **Unwmk.**   **Perf. 12**
9   A47 20c on 30pa on 15c
                slate   4.75   20.00
        Never hinged   12.00
        On cover   120.00

JANINA

Stamps of Italy
Surcharged

10 Para 10

1902-07   **Wmk. 140**   **Perf. 14**
1   A44 10pa on 5c green   11.00   4.00
        Never hinged   27.50
        On cover   110.00
2   A45 35pa on 20c orange 8.00   4.75
        Never hinged   20.00
        On cover   225.00
3   A45 40pa on 25c blue   40.00   12.50
        Never hinged   100.00
        On cover   325.00
4   A45 80pa on 50c vio
                ('07)   67.50   47.50
        Never hinged   160.00
        On cover   475.00
        Nos. 1-4 (4)   126.50   68.75
    Nos. 1-3 on overfranked
      philatelic cover   140.00

Surcharged in Black or
Violet

Janina
10 Para 10

Wmk. 140, Unwmk. (#7)
1909-11   **Perf. 14, 12**
5   A48 10pa on 5c green   1.60   3.25
        Never hinged   4.00
        On cover   95.00
6   A48 20pa on 10c claret 1.60   3.25
        Never hinged   4.00
        On cover   95.00
7   A47 30pa on 15c slate
                (V)   1.60   3.25
        Never hinged   4.00
        On cover   175.00
8   A49 1pi on 25c blue   1.60   3.25
        Never hinged   4.00
        On cover   175.00
9   A49 2pi on 50c violet 1.60   4.00
        Never hinged   4.00
        On cover   350.00

Surcharged

JANINA
4 PIASTRE 4

10 A46 4pi on 1 l brn &
                grn   4.00   4.75
        Never hinged   10.00
        On cover   525.00
11 A46 20pi on 5 l bl &
                rose   375.00 425.00
        Never hinged   940.00
12 A51 40pi on 10 l gray
                grn & red   20.00 120.00
        Never hinged   50.00
        Nos. 5-12 (8)   407.00 566.75
    Set of 8 on overfranked
      philatelic cover   825.00

JERUSALEM

Stamps of Italy
Surcharged in Black or
Violet

Wmk. 140, Unwmk. (#3)
1909-11   *Perf. 14, 12*

1	A48	10pa on 5c green	8.00	20.00
		Never hinged	20.00	
		On cover		525.00
2	A48	20pa on 10c claret	8.00	20.00
		Never hinged	20.00	
		On cover		525.00
3	A47	30pa on 15c slate	8.00	27.50
		(V)		
		Never hinged	20.00	
		On cover		875.00
4	A49	1pi on 25c blue	8.00	20.00
		Never hinged	20.00	
		On cover		1,200.
5	A49	2pi on 50c violet	27.50	65.00
		Never hinged	67.50	
		On cover		1,800.

Surcharged

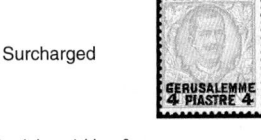

6	A46	4pi on 1 l brn &		
		grn	35.00	87.50
		Never hinged	87.50	
		On cover		4,750.
7	A46	20pi on 5 l bl &		
		rose	1,250.	1,400.
		Never hinged	3,100.	
8	A51	40pi on 10 l gray		
		grn & red	47.50	600.00
		Never hinged	120.00	
		Nos. 1-8 (8)	1,392.	2,240.
		Set of 8 on overfranked		
		philatelic cover		8,750.

Forged cancellations exist on Nos. 1-8.

SALONIKA

Stamps of Italy
Surcharged in Black or
Violet

Wmk. 140, Unwmk. (#3)
1909-11   *Perf. 14, 12*

1	A48	10pa on 5c green	1.60	3.25
		Never hinged	4.00	
		On cover		87.50
2	A48	20pa on 10c claret	1.60	3.25
		Never hinged	4.00	
		On cover		87.50
3	A47	30pa on 15c slate	2.40	3.25
		(V)		
		Never hinged	6.00	
		On cover		160.00
4	A49	1pi on 25c blue	2.40	3.25
		Never hinged	6.00	
		On cover		120.00
5	A49	2pi on 50c violet	2.40	4.00
		Never hinged	6.00	
		On cover		250.00

Surcharged

6	A46	4pi on 1 l brn &		
		grn	4.00	4.75
		Never hinged	10.00	
		On cover		475.00
7	A46	20pi on 5 l bl &		
		rose	550.00	740.00
		Never hinged	1,350.	
8	A51	40pi on 10 l gray		
		grn & red	20.00	125.00
		Never hinged	50.00	
		Nos. 1-8 (8)	584.40	886.75
		Set of 8 on overfranked		
		philatelic cover		1,100.

SCUTARI

Stamps of Italy
Surcharged in Black or
Violet

Wmk. 140, Unwmk. (#3)
1909-11   *Perf. 14, 12*

1	A48	10pa on 5c green	1.60	3.25
		Never hinged	4.00	
		On cover		87.50
2	A48	20pa on 10c claret	1.60	3.25
		Never hinged	4.00	
		On cover		87.50
3	A47	30pa on 15c slate	27.50	6.50
		(V)		
		Never hinged	67.50	
		On cover		200.00
4	A49	1pi on 25c blue	1.60	3.25
		Never hinged	4.00	
		On cover		125.00
5	A49	2pi on 50c violet	1.60	4.75
		Never hinged	4.00	
		On cover		525.00

Surcharged

6	A46	4pi on 1 l brn &		
		grn	3.25	4.75
		Never hinged	8.00	
		On cover		725.00
7	A46	20pi on 5 l bl &		
		rose	35.00	55.00
		Never hinged	87.50	
8	A51	40pi on 10 l gray		
		grn & red	75.00	175.00
		Never hinged	190.00	
		Nos. 1-8 (8)	147.15	255.75
		Set of 8 on overfranked		
		philatelic cover		350.00

Surcharged like Nos. 1-5
1915

9	A43	4pa on 2c orange		
		brn	2.40	5.50
		Never hinged	6.00	
		On cover		110.00

No. 3 Surcharged

1916   **Unwmk.**   *Perf. 12*

10	A47	20c on 30pa on 15c		
		slate	6.50	27.50
		Never hinged	16.00	
		On cover		275.00

SMYRNA

Stamps of Italy
Surcharged in Black or
Violet

Wmk. 140, Unwmk. (#3)
1909-11   *Perf. 14, 12*

1	A48	10pa on 5c green	1.60	1.60
		Never hinged	4.00	
		On cover		87.50
2	A48	20pa on 10c claret	1.60	1.60
		Never hinged	4.00	
		On cover		87.50
3	A47	30pa on 15c slate	3.25	4.75
		(V)		
		Never hinged	8.00	
		On cover		200.00
4	A49	1pi on 25c blue	3.25	4.75
		Never hinged	8.00	
		On cover		125.00
5	A49	2pi on 50c violet	4.00	6.50
		Never hinged	10.00	
		On cover		450.00

Surcharged

6	A46	4pi on 1 l brn &		
		grn	4.75	8.00
		Never hinged	12.00	
		On cover		525.00
7	A46	20pi on 5 l bl &		
		rose	190.00	240.00
		Never hinged	475.00	
8	A51	40pi on 10 l gray		
		grn & red	20.00	120.00
		Never hinged	50.00	
		Nos. 1-8 (8)	228.45	387.20
		Set of 8 on overfranked		
		philatelic cover		570.00

Italian Stamps of 1901-22 Surcharged

Nos. 10, 12-13

Nos. 9, 11

1922

9	A48	20pa on 5c green	32.50	
		Never hinged	80.00	
10	A48	1pi20pa on 15c slate	1.60	
		Never hinged	4.00	
11	A49	3pi on 30c org		
		brn	1.60	
		Never hinged	4.00	
12	A49	3pi30pa on 40c		
		brown	4.00	
		Never hinged	10.00	
13	A46	7pi20pa on 1 l brn &		
		grn	4.00	
		Never hinged	10.00	
		Nos. 9-13 (5)	43.70	

Nos. 9-13 were not issued.

VALONA

Stamps of Italy
Surcharged in Black or
Violet

Wmk. 140, Unwmk. (#3)
1909-11   *Perf. 14, 12*

1	A48	10pa on 5c green	1.60	3.25
		Never hinged	4.00	
		On cover		87.50
2	A48	20pa on 10c claret	1.60	3.25
		Never hinged	4.00	
		On cover		87.50
3	A47	30pa on 15c slate	20.00	6.50
		(V)		
		Never hinged	50.00	
		On cover		175.00
4	A49	1pi on 25c blue	2.40	3.25
		Never hinged	6.00	
		On cover		140.00
5	A49	2pi on 50c violet	2.40	4.00
		Never hinged	6.00	
		On cover		400.00

Surcharged

6	A46	4pi on 1 l brn &		
		grn	2.40	4.00
		Never hinged	6.00	
		On cover		600.00
7	A46	20pi on 5 l bl &		
		rose	55.00	65.00
		Never hinged	140.00	
8	A51	40pi on 10 l gray		
		grn & red	65.00	175.00
		Never hinged	160.00	
		Nos. 1-8 (8)	150.40	264.25
		Set of 8 on overfranked		
		philatelic cover		390.00

Italy No. 123
Surcharged in Violet
or Red Violet

1916

9	A58	30pa on 15c slate		
		(V)	4.75	14.00
		Never hinged	12.00	
		On cover		200.00
a.		Red violet surcharge	11.00	32.50
		Never hinged	27.50	

No. 9 Surcharged

10	A58	20c on 30pa on 15c		
		slate	2.40	20.00
		Never hinged	6.00	
		On cover		175.00

AEGEAN ISLANDS
(Dodecanese)

A group of islands in the Aegean Sea off the coast of Turkey. They were occupied by Italy during the Tripoli War and were ceded to Italy by Turkey in 1924 by the Treaty of Lausanne. Stamps of Italy overprinted with the name of the island were in use at the post offices maintained in the various islands.

Rhodes, on the island of the same name, was capital of the entire group.

100 Centesimi = 1 Lira

GENERAL ISSUE

Italian Stamps of 1907-08 Overprinted

1912   **Wmk. 140**   *Perf. 14*

1	A49	25c blue	55.00	35.00
		Never hinged	140.00	
		On cover		110.00
a.		Inverted overprint	300.00	300.00
2	A49	50c violet	55.00	35.00
		Never hinged	140.00	
		On cover		125.00
a.		Inverted overprint	300.00	300.00
		Set on overfranked phila-		
		telic cover		140.00

Virgil Issue

Italian
Stamps of
1930
Ovptd. in
Red or
Blue

1930   **Photo.**   **Wmk. 140**   *Perf. 14*

3	A106	15c vio blk	1.60	21.00
		Never hinged	4.00	
		On cover		125.00
4	A106	20c org brn	1.60	21.00
		Never hinged	4.00	
		On cover		120.00
5	A106	25c dk green	1.60	9.50
		Never hinged	4.00	
		On cover		100.00
6	A106	30c lt brown	1.60	9.50
		Never hinged	4.00	
		On cover		120.00
7	A106	50c dull vio	1.60	9.50
		Never hinged	4.00	
		On cover		100.00
8	A106	75c rose red	1.60	21.00
		Never hinged	4.00	
		On cover		225.00
9	A106	1.25 l gray bl	1.60	27.50
		Never hinged	4.00	
		On cover		300.00

Engr.
Unwmk.

10	A106	5 l + 1.50 l dk vio	4.75	52.50
		Never hinged	12.00	—
11	A106	10 l + 2.50 l ol	1.75	52.50
		Never hinged	12.00	—

Nos. 3-11,C4-C7 (13)   35.00 436.50
Set on overfranked phila-
telic cover   500.00

St. Anthony of Padua Issue

Italian
Stamps of
1931
Ovptd. in
Blue or
Red

1932   Photo.   Wmk. 140   Perf. 14

12	A116	20c black brn	32.50	27.50
		Never hinged	80.00	
		On cover		200.00
13	A116	25c dull grn	32.50	27.50
		Never hinged	80.00	
		On cover		180.00
14	A118	30c brown org	32.50	32.50
		Never hinged	80.00	
		On cover		200.00
15	A118	50c dull vio	32.50	24.00
		Never hinged	80.00	
		On cover		160.00
16	A120	1.25 l gray bl	32.50	47.50
		Never hinged	80.00	
		On cover		450.00

Engr.
Unwmk.

17	A121	75c lt red	32.50	35.00
		Never hinged	80.00	
		On cover		300.00
18	A122	5 l + 2.50 l dp org	32.50	175.00
		Never hinged	80.00	
		On cover		—

Nos. 12-18 (7)   227.50 369.00
Set on overfranked phila-
telic cover   675.00

Dante Alighieri Society Issue

Italian
Stamps of
1932
Overprinted

1932   Photo.   Wmk. 140

19	A126	10c grnsh gray	1.60	8.00
		Never hinged	4.00	
		On cover		95.00
20	A126	15c black vio	1.60	8.00
		Never hinged	4.00	
		On cover		120.00
21	A126	20c brown org	1.60	8.00
		Never hinged	4.00	
		On cover		120.00
22	A126	25c dp green	1.60	8.00
		Never hinged	4.00	
		On cover		80.00
23	A126	30c dp org	1.60	8.00
		Never hinged	4.00	
		On cover		120.00
24	A126	50c dull vio	1.60	4.00
		Never hinged	4.00	
		On cover		80.00
25	A126	75c rose red	1.60	11.00
		Never hinged	4.00	
		On cover		160.00
26	A126	1.25 l blue	1.60	9.50
		Never hinged	4.00	
		On cover		175.00
27	A126	1.75 l ol brn	3.25	11.00
		Never hinged	8.00	
		On cover		325.00
28	A126	2.75 l car rose	3.25	11.00
		Never hinged	8.00	
		On cover		375.00
29	A126	5 l + 2 l dp vio	3.25	25.00
		Never hinged	8.00	
		On cover		—
30	A126	10 l + 2.50 l dk brn	3.25	45.00
		Never hinged	8.00	
		On cover		—

Nos. 19-30 (12)   25.80 156.50
Set of on overfranked philatelic cover   450.00

See Nos. C8-C14.

Soccer Issue

Types of Italy,
"Soccer" Issue,
Overprinted in Black
or Red

1934

31	A173	20c brn rose (Bk)	87.50	100.00
		Never hinged	220.00	
		On cover		675.00
32	A174	25c green (R)	87.50	100.00
		Never hinged	220.00	
		On cover		550.00
33	A174	50c violet (R)	340.00	80.00
		Never hinged	850.00	
		On cover		450.00
34	A174	1.25 l gray bl (R)	87.50	190.00
		Never hinged	220.00	
		On cover		875.00
35	A175	5 l +2.50 l bl (R)	87.50	450.00
		Never hinged	220.00	

Nos. 31-35 (5)   690.00 920.00
Set on overfranked phila-
telic cover   2,200.

See Nos. C28-C31.

Same Overprint on Types of Medal of Valor Issue of Italy, in Red or Black

1935

36	A177	10c sl gray (R)	47.50	95.00
		Never hinged	120.00	
		On cover		275.00
37	A178	15c brn (Bk)	47.50	95.00
		Never hinged	120.00	
		On cover		275.00
38	A178	20c red org (Bk)	47.50	95.00
		Never hinged	120.00	
		On cover		275.00
39	A177	25c dp grn (R)	47.50	95.00
		Never hinged	120.00	
		On cover		275.00
40	A178	30c lake (Bk)	47.50	95.00
		Never hinged	120.00	
		On cover		275.00
41	A178	50c ol grn (Bk)	47.50	95.00
		Never hinged	120.00	
		On cover		275.00
42	A178	75c rose red (Bk)	47.50	95.00
		Never hinged	120.00	
		On cover		450.00
43	A178	1.25 l dp bl (R)	47.50	95.00
		Never hinged	120.00	
		On cover		550.00
44	A177	1.75 l + 1 l pur (R)	47.50	95.00
		Never hinged	120.00	
		On cover		—
45	A178	2.55 l + 2 l dk car (Bk)	47.50	95.00
		Never hinged	120.00	
		On cover		—
46	A178	2.75 l + 2 l org brn (Bk)	47.50	95.00
		Never hinged	120.00	

Nos. 36-46 (11)   522.50 1,045.
Set on overfranked phila-
telic cover   2,400.

See Nos. C32-C38, CE3-CE4.

Types of Italy, 1937,
Overprinted in Blue
or Red

1938   Wmk. 140   Perf. 14

47	A208	10c dk brn (Bl)	4.00	9.50
		Never hinged	10.00	
		On cover		200.00
48	A208	15c pur (R)	4.00	9.50
		Never hinged	10.00	
		On cover		190.00
49	A208	20c yel bis (Bl)	4.00	9.50
		Never hinged	10.00	
		On cover		140.00
50	A208	25c myr grn (R)	4.00	9.50
		Never hinged	10.00	
		On cover		175.00
51	A208	30c dp cl (Bl)	4.00	9.50
		Never hinged	10.00	
		On cover		200.00
52	A208	50c sl grn (R)	4.00	16.00
		Never hinged	10.00	
		On cover		140.00
53	A208	75c rose red (Bl)	4.00	16.00
		Never hinged	10.00	
		On cover		250.00
54	A208	1.25 l dk bl (R)	4.00	16.00
		Never hinged	10.00	
		On cover		425.00

55	A208	1.75 l + 1 l dp org (Bl)	6.50	30.00
		Never hinged	16.00	
56	A208	2.55 l + 2 l ol brn (R)	6.50	—
		Never hinged	16.00	

Nos. 47-56 (10)   45.00 155.50
Set on overfranked philatelic cover   550.00

Bimillenary of birth of Augustus Caesar
(Octavianus), first Roman emperor.
See Nos. C39-C43.

Same Overprint of Type of Italy, 1937, in Red

1938

57	A222	1.25 l deep blue	1.60	2.40
		Never hinged	4.00	
		On cover		110.00
58	A222	2.75 l + 2 l brown	1.75	9.50
		Never hinged	4.25	
		On cover		450.00

Set on overfranked philatelic cover   65.00

600th anniversary of the death of Giotto di
Bondone, Italian painter.

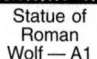

Statue of Roman Wolf — A1	Arms of Rhodes — A2

Dante's
House,
Rhodes
A3

1940   Photo.

59	A1	5c lt brown	.80	1.20
		Never hinged	2.00	
		On cover		160.00
60	A2	10c pale org	.80	1.20
		Never hinged	2.00	
		On cover		120.00
61	A3	25c blue grn	1.60	2.00
		Never hinged	4.00	
		On cover		100.00
62	A1	50c rose vio	1.60	2.00
		Never hinged	4.00	
		On cover		100.00
63	A2	75c dull ver	1.60	4.00
		Never hinged	4.00	
		On cover		240.00
64	A3	1.25 l dull blue	1.60	4.00
		Never hinged	4.00	
		On cover		325.00
65	A2	2 l + 75c rose	1.60	27.50
		Never hinged	4.00	

Nos. 59-65,C44-C47 (11)   18.60 81.40
Nos. 59-65 on overfranked
philatelic cover   120.00

Triennial Overseas Exposition, Naples.

AIR POST STAMPS

Ferrucci Issue

Types of Italian Air Post Stamps
of 1930 Overprinted in Blue or Red
Like Nos. 12-18

1930   Wmk. 140   Perf. 14

C1	A104	50c brn vio (Bl)	11.00	24.00
		Never hinged	27.50	
		On cover		175.00
C2	A104	1 l dk bl (R)	11.00	24.00
		Never hinged	27.50	
		On cover		300.00
C3	A104	5 l + 2 l dp car (Bl)	21.00	67.50
		Never hinged	52.50	
		On cover		—

Nos. C1-C3 (3)   43.00 115.50
Set on overfranked philatelic flown cover   340.00

Nos. C1-C3 were sold at Rhodes only.

Virgil Issue

Types of Italian Air Post Stamps of
1930 Overprinted in Red or Blue Like
Nos. C10, C11

1930   Photo.

C4	A106	50c dp grn (R)	2.40	40.00
		Never hinged	6.00	
		On cover		190.00
C5	A106	1 l rose red (Bl)	2.40	40.00
		Never hinged	6.00	
		On cover		325.00

Engr.
Unwmk.

C6	A106	7.70 l + 1.30 l dk brn (R)	4.75	52.50
		Never hinged	12.00	
		On cover		—
C7	A106	9 l + 2 l gray (R)	4.75	80.00
		Never hinged	12.00	
		On cover		—

Nos. C4-C7 (4)   14.30 212.50
Set on overfranked philatelic flown cover   500.00

Dante Alighieri Society Issue

Types of Italian Air Post Stamps of
1932 Overprinted Like Nos. 19-30

1932   Wmk. 140

C8	AP10	50c car rose	1.60	6.50
		Never hinged	4.00	
		On cover		160.00
C9	AP11	1 l dp grn	1.60	6.50
		Never hinged	4.00	
		On cover		175.00
C10	AP11	3 l dl vio	1.60	9.50
		Never hinged	4.00	
		On cover		325.00
C11	AP11	5 l dp org	1.60	9.50
		Never hinged	4.00	
		On cover		400.00
C12	AP10	7.70 l + 2 l ol brn	4.75	22.50
		Never hinged	12.00	
		On cover		—
C13	AP11	10 l + 2.50 l dk bl	4.75	30.00
		Never hinged	12.00	

Nos. C8-C13 (6)   15.90 84.50
Set on overfranked philatelic flown cover   325.00

Leonardo da
Vinci — AP12

1932   Photo.   Perf. 14½

C14	AP12	100 l dp bl & grnsh gray	21.00	140.00
		Never hinged	52.50	
		On flown cover		575.00

Garibaldi Types of
Italian Air Post
Stamps of 1932
Overprinted in Red or
Blue

1932

C15	AP13	50c deep green	60.00	140.00
		Never hinged	150.00	
		On cover		300.00
C16	AP14	80c copper red	60.00	140.00
		Never hinged	150.00	
		On cover		400.00
C17	AP13	1 l + 25c dl bl	60.00	140.00
		Never hinged	150.00	
		On cover		525.00
C18	AP13	2 l + 50c red brn	60.00	140.00
		Never hinged	150.00	
		On cover		650.00
C19	AP14	5 l + 1 l bluish sl	60.00	140.00
		Never hinged	150.00	

Nos. C15-C19 (5)   300.00 700.00
Set on overfranked phila-
telic flown cover   1,400.

See Nos. CE1-CE2.

Graf
Zeppelin
over
Rhodes
AP17

1933 **Perf. 14**

C20 AP17 3 l olive brn   95.00 *240.00*
  Never hinged   240.00
  On cover   475.00
C21 AP17 5 l dp vio   95.00 *275.00*
  Never hinged   240.00
  On cover   675.00
C22 AP17 10 l dk green   95.00 *450.00*
  Never hinged   240.00
  On cover   950.00
C23 AP17 12 l dk blue   95.00 *500.00*
  Never hinged   240.00
  On cover   1,200.
C24 AP17 15 l car rose   95.00 *500.00*
  Never hinged   240.00
  On cover   1,200.
C25 AP17 20 l gray blk   95.00 *500.00*
  Never hinged   240.00
  On cover   1,200.
  Nos. C20-C25 (6)   570.00 *2,465.*
  Set on overfranked phila-
   telic flown cover   4,750.
  Set of 6 flown covers   5,700.

Balbo Flight Issue

Italian Air
Post
Stamps of
1933
Ovptd.

1933 **Wmk. 140** **Perf. 14**

C26 AP25 5.25 l + 19.75 l
   grn, red &
   bl gray   60.00 *165.00*
  Never hinged   150.00
  On cover   4,200.
C27 AP25 5.25 l + 44.75 l
   red, grn &
   bl gray   60.00 *165.00*
  Never hinged   190.00
  On cover   4,200.
  Set on overfranked phila-
   telic flown cover   8,250.

Soccer Issue

Types of Italian Air Post Stamps of
1934 Overprinted in Black or Red Like
#31-35

1934

C28 AP32 50c brown (R)   20.00 *80.00*
  Never hinged   50.00
  On cover   600.00
C29 AP33 75c rose red)   20.00 *80.00*
  Never hinged   50.00
  On cover   550.00
C30 AP34 5 l + 2.50 l red
   org   32.50 *160.00*
  Never hinged   80.00
  On cover   —
C31 AP35 10 l + 5 l grn (R)   32.50 *190.00*
  Never hinged   80.00
  On cover   —
  Nos. C28-C31 (4)   105.00 *510.00*
  Set on overfranked phila-
   telic flown cover   2,050.

Types of Medal of Valor Issue of Italy Overprinted in Red or Black Like Nos. 31-35

1935

C32 AP36 25c dp grn   67.50 *110.00*
  Never hinged   170.00
  On cover   400.00
C33 AP36 50c blk brn (R)   67.50 *110.00*
  Never hinged   170.00
  On cover   350.00
C34 AP36 75c rose   67.50 *110.00*
  Never hinged   170.00
  On cover   400.00
C35 AP36 80c dk brn   67.50 *110.00*
  Never hinged   170.00
  On cover   525.00
C36 AP36 1 l + 50c ol grn   47.50 *110.00*
  Never hinged   120.00
  On cover   —
C37 AP36 2 l + 1 l dp bl
   (R)   47.50 *110.00*
  Never hinged   120.00
  On cover   —
C38 AP40 3 l + 2 l vio (R)   47.50 *110.00*
  Never hinged   120.00
  Nos. C32-C38 (7)   412.50 *770.00*
  Nos. C32-C38, CE3-CE4
   on overfranked philatelic
   flown cover   2,400.

Types of Italy Air Post Stamps, 1937, Overprinted in Blue or Red Like Nos. 47-56

1938 **Perf. 14**

C39 AP51 25c dl gray vio (R)   4.75 *9.50*
  Never hinged   12.00
  On cover   250.00
C40 AP51 50c grn (R)   4.75 *9.50*
  Never hinged   12.00
  On cover   175.00
C41 AP51 80c brt bl (R)   4.75 *30.00*
  Never hinged   12.00
  On cover   275.00
C42 AP51 1 l + 1 l rose lake   9.50 *30.00*
  Never hinged   24.00
  On cover   —

C43 AP51 5 l + 1 l rose red   12.50 *60.00*
  Never hinged   30.00
  On cover   —
  Nos. C39-C43 (5)   36.25 *139.00*
  Set on overfranked phila-
   telic flown cover   600.00

Bimillenary of the birth of Augustus Caesar
(Octavianus).

Statues of
Stag and
Roman
Wolf
AP18

Plane over Government Palace,
Rhodes — AP19

1940 **Photo.**

C44 AP18 50c olive blk   2.40 *4.00*
  Never hinged   6.00
  On cover   240.00
C45 AP19 1 l dk vio   2.40 *4.00*
  Never hinged   6.00
  On cover   250.00
C46 AP18 2 l + 75c dk bl   2.40 *12.00*
  Never hinged   6.00
  On cover   —
C47 AP19 5 l + 2.50 l cop
   brn   2.40 *22.50*
  Never hinged   6.00
  On cover   —
  Nos. C44-C47 (4)   9.60 *42.50*
  Set on overfranked philatel-
   ic flown cover   200.00

Triennial Overseas Exposition, Naples.

AIR POST SPECIAL DELIVERY STAMPS

Type of Italian Garibaldi Air Post Special Delivery Stamps Overprinted in Blue or Ocher Like Nos. 12-18

1932 **Wmk. 140** **Perf. 14**

CE1 APSD1 2.25 l + 1 l bl &
   rose &
   (Bl)   95.00 *260.00*
  Never hinged   240.00
  On cover   —
CE2 APSD1 4.50 l + 1.50 l
   ocher &
   gray (O)   95.00 *260.00*
  Never hinged   240.00
  On cover   —
  Set on overfranked philatel-
   ic flown cover   1,050.

Type of
Medal of
Valor Issue
of Italy,
Ovptd. in
Black

1935

CE3 APSD4   2 l + 1.25 l
   dp bl   47.50 *110.00*
  Never hinged   120.00
CE4 APSD4 4.50 l + 2 l grn   47.50 *110.00*
  Never hinged   120.00

ISSUES FOR THE INDIVIDUAL ISLANDS

Italian Stamps of 1901-20 Overprinted with Names of Various Islands as

a

b

c

The 1912-22 issues of each island have
type "a" overprint in black on all values except
15c (type A58) and 20c on 15c, which have
type "b" overprint in violet.

The 1930-32 Ferruci and Garibaldi issues
are types of the Italian issues overprinted type
"c." Stamps with type "c" overprints are also
listed in Castellorizo.

CALCHI

Overprinted "Karki" in Black or Violet

1912-22 **Wmk. 140** **Perf. 13½, 14**

1 A43 2c orange brn   8.00 *9.50*
  Never hinged   20.00
  On cover   110.00
 a. Double overprint   400.00 *600.00*
2 A48 5c green   4.75 *9.50*
  Never hinged   12.00
  On cover   65.00
3 A48 10c claret   1.60 *9.50*
  Never hinged   4.00
  On cover   65.00
4 A48 15c slate ('22)   4.75 *47.50*
  Never hinged   12.00
  On cover   475.00
 a. Double overprint   400.00
5 A50 20c brn org ('21)   4.75 *45.00*
  Never hinged   12.00
  On cover   450.00
6 A49 25c blue   1.60 *9.50*
  Never hinged   4.00
  On cover   110.00
7 A49 40c brown   1.60 *9.50*
  Never hinged   4.00
  On cover   240.00
8 A49 50c violet   1.60 *19.00*
  Never hinged   4.00
  On cover   275.00

Unwmk.

9 A58 15c slate (V)   47.50 *19.00*
  Never hinged   120.00
  On cover   180.00
10 A50 20c brn org ('17)   140.00 *175.00*
  Never hinged   350.00
  On cover   875.00
  Nos. 1-10 (10)   216.15 *353.00*
  Nos. 1-3, 6-9 on over-
   franked philatelic cover   160.00

No. 9 Surcharged

1916 **Perf. 13½**

11 A58 20c on 15c slate   2.40 *27.50*
  Never hinged   6.00
  On cover   140.00

Ferrucci Issue
Types of Italy
Overprinted in Red or Blue

1930 **Wmk. 140** **Perf. 14**

12 A102 20c vio (R)   4.00 *9.50*
  Never hinged   10.00
  On cover   140.00
13 A103 25c dk grn (R)   4.00 *9.50*
  Never hinged   10.00
  On cover   190.00
14 A103 50c blk (R)   4.75 *16.00*
  Never hinged   12.00
  On cover   125.00
15 A103 1.25 l dp bl (R)   4.75 *16.00*
  Never hinged   12.00
  On cover   300.00
16 A104 5 l + 2 l dp car
   (Bl)   11.00 *27.50*
  Never hinged   27.50
  On cover   —
  Nos. 12-16 (5)   28.50 *78.50*
  Set on overfranked philatel-
   ic cover   140.00

Garibaldi Issue
Types of Italy
Overprinted "CARCHI" in Red or Blue

1932

17 A138 10c brown   19.00 *36.00*
  Never hinged   47.50
  On cover   250.00
18 A138 20c red brn (Bl)   19.00 *36.00*
  Never hinged   47.50
  On cover   160.00
19 A138 25c dp grn   19.00 *36.00*
  Never hinged   47.50
  On cover   160.00

20 A138 30c bluish sl   19.00 *36.00*
  Never hinged   47.50
  On cover   240.00
21 A138 50c red vio (Bl)   19.00 *36.00*
  Never hinged   47.50
  On cover   125.00
22 A141 75c cop red (Bl)   19.00 *36.00*
  Never hinged   47.50
  On cover   350.00
23 A141 1.25 l dl bl   19.00 *36.00*
  Never hinged   47.50
  On cover   550.00
24 A141 1.75 l + 25c brn   19.00 *36.00*
  Never hinged   47.50
  On cover   —
25 A144 2.55 l + 50c org
   (Bl)   19.00 *36.00*
  Never hinged   47.50
  On cover   —
26 A145 5 l + 1 l dl vio   19.00 *36.00*
  Never hinged   47.50
  On cover   —
  Nos. 17-26 (10)   190.00 *360.00*
  Set on overfranked phila-
   telic cover   650.00

CALINO

Overprinted "Calimno" in Black or Violet

1912-21 **Wmk. 140** **Perf. 13½, 14**

1 A43 2c orange brn   9.50 *9.50*
  Never hinged   24.00
  On cover   110.00
2 A48 5c green   3.25 *9.50*
  Never hinged   8.00
  On cover   65.00
3 A48 10c claret   1.60 *9.50*
  Never hinged   4.00
  On cover   65.00
4 A48 15c slate ('21)   4.75 *55.00*
  Never hinged   12.00
  On cover   550.00
5 A50 20c brn org ('21)   4.75 *55.00*
  Never hinged   12.00
  On cover   400.00
6 A49 25c blue   9.50 *9.50*
  Never hinged   24.00
  On cover   110.00
7 A49 40c brown   1.60 *9.50*
  Never hinged   4.00
  On cover   240.00
8 A49 50c violet   1.60 *19.00*
  Never hinged   4.00
  On cover   275.00

Unwmk.

9 A58 15c slate (V)   40.00 *19.00*
  Never hinged   100.00
  On cover   180.00
10 A50 20c brn org ('17)   95.00 *225.00*
  Never hinged   240.00
  On cover   400.00
  Nos. 1-10 (10)   171.55 *420.50*
  Nos. 1-3, 6-9 on over-
   franked philatelic cover   160.00

No. 9 Surcharged Like Calchi No. 11

1916 **Perf. 13½**

11 A58 20c on 15c slate   17.50 *40.00*
  Never hinged   42.50
  On cover   200.00

Ferrucci Issue
Types of Italy
Overprinted in Red or Blue

1930 **Wmk. 140** **Perf. 14**

12 A102 20c violet (R)   4.00 *9.50*
  Never hinged   10.00
  On cover   140.00
13 A103 25c dk green (R)   4.00 *9.50*
  Never hinged   10.00
  On cover   190.00
14 A103 50c black (R)   4.75 *16.00*
  Never hinged   12.00
  On cover   125.00
15 A103 1.25 l dp bl (R)   4.75 *16.00*
  Never hinged   12.00
  On cover   300.00
16 A104 5 l + 2 l dp car
   (Bl)   11.00 *27.50*
  Never hinged   27.50
  Nos. 12-16 (5)   28.50 *78.50*
  Set on overfranked philatel-
   ic cover   140.00

Garibaldi Issue
Types of Italy
Overprinted in Red or Blue

1932

17 A138 10c brown   19.00 *35.00*
  Never hinged   47.50
  On cover   250.00
18 A138 20c red brn (Bl)   19.00 *35.00*
  Never hinged   47.50
  On cover   160.00
19 A138 25c dp grn   19.00 *35.00*
  Never hinged   47.50
  On cover   160.00
20 A138 30c bluish sl   19.00 *35.00*
  Never hinged   47.50
  On cover   240.00
21 A138 50c red vio (Bl)   19.00 *35.00*
  Never hinged   47.50
  On cover   120.00
22 A141 75c cop red (Bl)   19.00 *35.00*
  Never hinged   47.50
  On cover   350.00

23	A141	1.25 l dull blue	19.00	35.00
	Never hinged		47.50	
	On cover			550.00
24	A141	1.75 l + 25c brn	19.00	35.00
	Never hinged		47.50	
	On cover			—
25	A144	2.55 l + 50c org		
		(Bl)	19.00	35.00
	Never hinged		47.50	
	On cover			—
26	A145	5 l + 1 l dl vio	19.00	35.00
	Never hinged		47.50	
	On cover			—
	Nos. 17-26 (10)		190.00	350.00
	Set on overfranked philatelic cover			650.00

CASO

Overprinted "Caso" in Black or Violet

	1912-21	Wmk. 140	*Perf. 13½, 14*	
1	A43	2c orange brn	8.00	9.50
	Never hinged		20.00	
	On cover			110.00
2	A48	5c green	4.75	9.50
	Never hinged		12.00	
	On cover			65.00
3	A48	10c claret	1.60	9.50
	Never hinged		4.00	
	On cover			65.00
4	A48	15c slate ('21)	4.75	47.50
	Never hinged		12.00	
	On cover			475.00
5	A50	20c brn org ('20)	4.00	35.00
	Never hinged		10.00	
	On cover			9.50
6	A49	25c blue	1.60	9.50
	Never hinged		4.00	
	On cover			110.00
7	A49	40c brown	1.60	9.50
	Never hinged		4.00	
	On cover			240.00
8	A49	50c violet	1.60	19.00
	Never hinged		4.00	
	On cover			275.00

Unwmk.

9	A58	15c slate (V)	47.50	19.00
	Never hinged		120.00	
	On cover			180.00
10	A50	20c brn org ('17)	140.00	225.00
	Never hinged		350.00	
	On cover			650.00
	Nos. 1-10 (10)		215.40	393.00
	Nos. 1-3, 6-9 on overfranked philatelic cover			160.00

No. 9 Surcharged Like Calchi No. 11

	1916		*Perf. 13½*	
11	A58	20c on 15c slate	1.60	40.00
	Never hinged		4.00	
	On cover			200.00

Ferrucci Issue
Types of Italy
Overprinted in Red or Blue

	1930	Wmk. 140	*Perf. 14*	
12	A102	20c violet (R)	4.00	9.50
	Never hinged		10.00	
	On cover			140.00
13	A103	25c dk green (R)	4.00	9.50
	Never hinged		10.00	
	On cover			190.00
14	A103	50c black (R)	4.00	16.00
	Never hinged		10.00	
	On cover			125.00
15	A103	1.25 l dp bl (R)	4.00	16.00
	Never hinged		10.00	
	On cover			300.00
16	A104	5 l + 2 l dp car		
		(Bl)	11.00	27.50
	Never hinged		27.50	
	Nos. 12-16 (5)		27.00	78.50
	Set on overfranked philatelic cover			140.00

Garibaldi Issue
Types of Italy
Overprinted in Red or Blue

	1932			
17	A138	10c brown	19.00	35.00
	Never hinged		47.50	
	On cover			250.00
18	A138	20c red brn (Bl)	19.00	35.00
	Never hinged		47.50	
	On cover			160.00
19	A138	25c dp grn	19.00	35.00
	Never hinged		47.50	
	On cover			160.00
20	A138	30c bluish sl	19.00	35.00
	Never hinged		47.50	
	On cover			240.00
21	A138	50c red vio (Bl)	19.00	35.00
	Never hinged		47.50	
	On cover			125.00
22	A141	75c cop red (Bl)	19.00	35.00
	Never hinged		47.50	
	On cover			350.00
23	A141	1.25 l dull blue	19.00	35.00
	Never hinged		47.50	
	On cover			550.00
24	A141	1.75 l + 25c brn	19.00	35.00
	Never hinged		47.50	
	On cover			—
25	A144	2.55 l + 50c org		
		(Bl)	19.00	35.00
	Never hinged		47.50	

26	A145	5 l + 1 l dl vio	19.00	35.00
	Never hinged		47.50	
	On cover			—
	Nos. 17-26 (10)		190.00	350.00
	Set on overfranked philatelic cover			650.00

COO

(Cos, Kos)
Overprinted "Cos" in Black or Violet

	1912-22	Wmk. 140	*Perf. 13½, 14*	
1	A43	2c orange brn	8.00	9.50
	Never hinged		20.00	
	On cover			110.00
2	A48	5c green	100.00	9.50
	Never hinged		250.00	
	On cover			65.00
3	A48	10c claret	4.75	9.50
	Never hinged		12.00	
	On cover			65.00
4	A48	15c slate ('22)	4.75	55.00
	Never hinged		12.00	
	On cover			550.00
5	A50	20c brn org ('21)	4.00	35.00
	Never hinged		10.00	
	On cover			350.00
6	A49	25c blue	40.00	9.50
	Never hinged		100.00	
	On cover			110.00
7	A49	40c brown	1.60	9.50
	Never hinged		4.00	
	On cover			240.00
8	A49	50c violet	1.60	19.00
	Never hinged		4.00	
	On cover			275.00

Unwmk.

9	A58	15c slate (V)	60.00	19.00
	Never hinged		150.00	
	On cover			180.00
10	A50	20c brn org ('17)	65.00	225.00
	Never hinged		160.00	
	On cover			650.00
	Nos. 1-10 (10)		289.70	400.50
	Nos. 1-3, 6-9 on overfranked philatelic cover			160.00

No. 9 Surcharged Like Calchi No. 11

	1916		*Perf. 13½*	
11	A58	20c on 15c slate	19.00	40.00
	Never hinged		47.50	
	On cover			200.00

Ferrucci Issue
Types of Italy
Overprinted in Red or Blue

	1930	Wmk. 140	*Perf. 14*	
12	A102	20c violet (R)	4.00	9.50
	Never hinged		10.00	
	On cover			140.00
13	A103	25c dk green (R)	4.00	9.50
	Never hinged		10.00	
	On cover			190.00
14	A103	50c black (R)	4.00	16.00
	Never hinged		10.00	
	On cover			125.00
15	A103	1.25 l dp bl (R)	4.00	16.00
	Never hinged		10.00	
	On cover			300.00
16	A104	5 l + 2 l dp car		
		(Bl)	11.00	27.50
	Never hinged		27.50	
	Nos. 12-16 (5)		27.00	78.50
	Set on overfranked philatelic cover			140.00

Garibaldi Issue
Types of Italy
Overprinted in Red or Blue

	1932			
17	A138	10c brown	19.00	35.00
	Never hinged		47.50	
	On cover			250.00
18	A138	20c red brn (Bl)	19.00	35.00
	Never hinged		47.50	
	On cover			160.00
19	A138	25c dp grn	19.00	35.00
	Never hinged		47.50	
	On cover			160.00
20	A138	30c bluish sl	19.00	35.00
	Never hinged		47.50	
	On cover			240.00
21	A138	50c red vio (Bl)	19.00	35.00
	Never hinged		47.50	
	On cover			125.00
22	A141	75c cop red (Bl)	19.00	35.00
	Never hinged		47.50	
	On cover			350.00
23	A141	1.25 l dull blue	19.00	35.00
	Never hinged		47.50	
	On cover			550.00
24	A141	1.75 l + 25c brn	19.00	35.00
	Never hinged		47.50	
	On cover			—
25	A144	2.55 l + 50c org		
		(Bl)	19.00	35.00
	Never hinged		47.50	
	On cover			—
26	A145	5 l + 1 l dl vio	19.00	35.00
	Never hinged		47.50	
	On cover			—
	Nos. 17-26 (10)		190.00	350.00
	Set on overfranked philatelic cover			650.00

LERO

Overprinted "Leros" in Black or Violet

	1912-22	Wmk. 140	*Perf. 13½, 14*	
1	A43	2c orange brn	9.50	9.50
	Never hinged		24.00	
	On cover			110.00
2	A48	5c green	8.00	9.50
	Never hinged		24.00	
	On cover			65.00
3	A48	10c claret	3.25	9.50
	Never hinged		8.00	
	On cover			65.00
4	A48	15c slate ('22)	4.75	40.00
	Never hinged		12.00	
	On cover			400.00
5	A50	20c brn org ('21)	175.00	125.00
	Never hinged		425.00	
	On cover			525.00
6	A49	25c blue	72.50	9.50
	Never hinged		180.00	
	On cover			110.00
7	A49	40c brown	4.75	9.50
	Never hinged		12.00	
	On cover			240.00
8	A49	50c violet	1.60	19.00
	Never hinged		4.00	
	On cover			275.00

Unwmk.

9	A58	15c slate (V)	87.50	19.00
	Never hinged		220.00	
	On cover			180.00
10	A50	20c brn org ('17)	65.00	225.00
	Never hinged		160.00	
	On cover			650.00
	Nos. 1-10 (10)		431.85	475.50
	Nos. 1-3, 6-9 on overfranked philatelic cover			160.00

No. 9 Surcharged Like Calchi No. 11

	1916		*Perf. 13½*	
11	A58	20c on 15c slate	19.00	40.00
	Never hinged		47.50	
	On cover			200.00

Ferrucci Issue
Types of Italy
Overprinted in Red or Blue

	1930		*Perf. 14*	
12	A102	20c violet (R)	4.00	9.50
	Never hinged		10.00	
	On cover			140.00
13	A103	25c dk green (R)	4.00	9.50
	Never hinged		10.00	
	On cover			190.00
14	A103	50c black (R)	4.00	16.00
	Never hinged		10.00	
	On cover			125.00
15	A103	1.25 l dp bl (R)	4.00	16.00
	Never hinged		10.00	
	On cover			300.00
16	A104	5 l + 2 l dp car		
		(Bl)	11.00	27.50
	Never hinged		27.50	
	On cover			—
	Nos. 12-16 (5)		27.00	78.50
	Set on overfranked philatelic cover			140.00

Garibaldi Issue
Types of Italy
Overprinted in Red or Blue

	1932			
17	A138	10c brown	19.00	35.00
	Never hinged		47.50	
	On cover			250.00
18	A138	20c red brn (Bl)	19.00	35.00
	Never hinged		47.50	
	On cover			160.00
19	A138	25c dp grn	19.00	35.00
	Never hinged		47.50	
	On cover			160.00
20	A138	30c bluish sl	19.00	35.00
	Never hinged		47.50	
	On cover			240.00
21	A138	50c red vio (Bl)	19.00	35.00
	Never hinged		47.50	
	On cover			125.00
22	A141	75c cop red (Bl)	19.00	35.00
	Never hinged		47.50	
	On cover			350.00
23	A141	1.25 l dull blue	19.00	35.00
	Never hinged		47.50	
	On cover			550.00
24	A141	1.75 l + 25c brn	19.00	35.00
	Never hinged		47.50	
	On cover			—
25	A144	2.55 l + 50c org		
		(Bl)	19.00	35.00
	Never hinged		47.50	
	On cover			—
26	A145	5 l + 1 l dl vio	19.00	35.00
	Never hinged		47.50	
	Nos. 17-26 (10)		190.00	350.00
	Set on overfranked philatelic cover			650.00

LISSO

Overprinted "Lipso" in Black or Violet

	1912-22	Wmk. 140	*Perf. 13½, 14*	
1	A43	2c orange brn	8.00	9.50
	Never hinged		20.00	
	On cover			110.00
2	A48	5c green	4.75	9.50
	Never hinged		12.00	
	On cover			65.00
3	A48	10c claret	3.25	9.50
	Never hinged		8.00	
	On cover			65.00
4	A48	15c slate ('22)	4.75	40.00
	Never hinged		12.00	
	On cover			400.00
5	A50	20c brn org ('21)	4.75	47.50
	Never hinged		12.00	
	On cover			475.00
6	A49	25c blue	1.60	9.50
	Never hinged		4.00	
	On cover			110.00
7	A49	40c brown	3.25	9.50
	Never hinged		8.00	
	On cover			240.00
8	A49	50c violet	1.60	19.00
	Never hinged		4.00	
	On cover			275.00

Unwmk.

9	A58	15c slate (V)	47.50	19.00
	Never hinged		120.00	
	On cover			180.00
10	A50	20c brn org ('17)	95.00	225.00
	Never hinged		240.00	
	On cover			650.00
	Nos. 1-10 (10)		174.45	398.00
	Nos. 1-3, 6-9 on overfranked philatelic cover			160.00

No. 9 Surcharged Like Calchi No. 11

	1916		*Perf. 13½*	
11	A58	20c on 15c slate	1.60	40.00
	Never hinged		4.00	
	On cover			200.00

Ferrucci Issue
Types of Italy
Overprinted in Red or Blue

	1930	Wmk. 140	*Perf. 14*	
12	A102	20c violet (R)	4.00	9.50
	Never hinged		10.00	
	On cover			140.00
13	A103	25c dk green (R)	4.00	9.50
	Never hinged		10.00	
	On cover			190.00
14	A103	50c black (R)	4.00	16.00
	Never hinged		10.00	
	On cover			125.00
15	A103	1.25 l dp bl (R)	4.00	16.00
	Never hinged		10.00	
	On cover			300.00
16	A104	5 l + 2 l dp car		
		(Bl)	11.00	29.00
	Never hinged		27.50	
	On cover			—
	Nos. 12-16 (5)		27.00	80.00
	Set on overfranked philatelic cover			140.00

Garibaldi Issue
Types of Italy
Overprinted "LIPSO" in Red or Blue

	1932			
17	A138	10c brown	19.00	35.00
	Never hinged		47.50	
	On cover			250.00
18	A138	20c red brn (Bl)	19.00	35.00
	Never hinged		47.50	
	On cover			160.00
19	A138	25c dp grn	19.00	35.00
	Never hinged		47.50	
	On cover			160.00
20	A138	30c bluish sl	19.00	35.00
	Never hinged		47.50	
	On cover			240.00
21	A138	50c red vio (Bl)	19.00	35.00
	Never hinged		47.50	
	On cover			125.00
22	A141	75c cop red (Bl)	19.00	35.00
	Never hinged		47.50	
	On cover			350.00
23	A141	1.25 l dull blue	19.00	35.00
	Never hinged		47.50	
	On cover			550.00
24	A141	1.75 l + 25c brn	19.00	35.00
	Never hinged		47.50	
	On cover			—
25	A144	2.55 l + 50c org		
		(Bl)	19.00	35.00
	Never hinged		47.50	
	On cover			—
26	A145	5 l + 1 l dl vio	19.00	35.00
	Never hinged		47.50	
	On cover			—
	Nos. 17-26 (10)		190.00	350.00
	Set on overfranked philatelic cover			650.00

NISIRO

Overprinted "Nisiros" in Black or Violet

1912-22	Wmk. 140		Perf. 13½, 14
1	A43 2c orange brn	8.00	9.50
	Never hinged	20.00	
	On cover		110.00
2	A48 5c green	4.75	9.50
	Never hinged	12.00	
	On cover		65.00
3	A48 10c claret	1.60	9.50
	Never hinged	4.00	
	On cover		65.00
4	A48 15c slate ('22)	32.50	55.00
	Never hinged	80.00	
	On cover		400.00
5	A50 20c brn org ('21)	110.00	125.00
	Never hinged	275.00	
	On cover		650.00
6	A49 25c blue	3.25	9.50
	Never hinged	8.00	
	On cover		110.00
7	A49 40c brown	1.60	9.50
	Never hinged	4.00	
	On cover		240.00
8	A49 50c violet	4.00	19.00
	Never hinged	10.00	
	On cover		275.00

Unwmk.

9	A58 15c slate (V)	47.50	19.00
	Never hinged	120.00	
	On cover		180.00
10	A50 20c brn org ('17)	140.00	225.00
	Never hinged	350.00	
	On cover		650.00
	Nos. 1-10 (10)	353.20	490.50
	Nos. 1-3, 6-9 on over-franked philatelic cover		160.00

No. 9 Surcharged Like Calchi No. 11

1916			Perf. 13½
11	A58 20c on 15c slate	1.60	40.00
	Never hinged	4.00	
	On cover		200.00

Ferrucci Issue
Types of Italy
Overprinted in Red or Blue

1930	Wmk. 140		Perf. 14
12	A102 20c violet (R)	4.00	9.50
	Never hinged	10.00	
	On cover		140.00
13	A103 25c dk green (R)	4.00	9.50
	Never hinged	10.00	
	On cover		190.00
14	A103 50c black (R)	4.00	16.00
	Never hinged	10.00	
	On cover		125.00
15	A103 1.25 l dp bl (R)	4.00	16.00
	Never hinged	10.00	
	On cover		300.00
16	A104 5 l + 2 l dp car (Bl)	11.00	27.50
	Never hinged	27.50	
	On cover		—
	Nos. 12-16 (5)	27.00	78.50
	Set on overfranked philatelic cover		140.00

Garibaldi Issue
Types of Italy
Overprinted in Red or Blue

1932			
17	A138 10c brown	19.00	35.00
	Never hinged	47.50	
	On cover		250.00
18	A138 20c red brn (Bl)	19.00	35.00
	Never hinged	47.50	
	On cover		160.00
19	A138 25c dp grn	19.00	35.00
	Never hinged	47.50	
	On cover		160.00
20	A138 30c bluish sl	19.00	35.00
	Never hinged	47.50	
	On cover		240.00
21	A138 50c red vio (Bl)	19.00	35.00
	Never hinged	47.50	
	On cover		125.00
22	A141 75c cop red (Bl)	19.00	35.00
	Never hinged	47.50	
	On cover		350.00
23	A141 1.25 l dull blue	19.00	35.00
	Never hinged	47.50	
	On cover		550.00
24	A141 1.75 l + 25c brn	19.00	35.00
	Never hinged	47.50	
	On cover		—
25	A144 2.55 l + 50c org (Bl)	19.00	35.00
	Never hinged	47.50	
	On cover		—
26	A145 5 l + 1 l dl vio	19.00	35.00
	Never hinged	47.50	
	On cover		—
	Nos. 17-26 (10)	190.00	350.00
	Set on overfranked philatelic cover		650.00

PATMO

Overprinted "Patmos" in Black or Violet

1912-22	Wmk. 140		Perf. 13½, 14
1	A43 2c orange brn	8.00	9.50
	Never hinged	20.00	
	On cover		110.00
2	A48 5c green	4.75	9.50
	Never hinged	12.00	
	On cover		65.00
3	A48 10c claret	3.25	9.50
	Never hinged	8.00	
	On cover		65.00
4	A48 15c slate ('22)	4.75	52.50
	Never hinged	12.00	
	On cover		350.00
5	A50 20c brn org ('21)	175.00	225.00
	Never hinged	450.00	
	On cover		650.00
6	A49 25c blue	1.60	9.50
	Never hinged	4.00	
	On cover		110.00
7	A49 40c brown	4.00	9.50
	Never hinged	10.00	
	On cover		240.00
8	A49 50c violet	1.60	19.00
	Never hinged	4.00	
	On cover		275.00

Unwmk.

9	A58 15c slate (V)	47.50	19.00
	Never hinged	120.00	
	On cover		180.00
10	A50 20c brn org ('17)	95.00	225.00
	Never hinged	240.00	
	On cover		650.00
	Nos. 1-10 (10)	345.45	588.00
	Nos. 1-3, 6-9 on over-franked philatelic cover		140.00

No. 9 Surcharged Like Calchi No. 11

1916			Perf. 13½
11	A58 20c on 15c slate	19.00	40.00
	Never hinged	47.50	
	On cover		200.00

Ferrucci Issue
Types of Italy
Overprinted in Red or Blue

1930	Wmk. 140		Perf. 14
12	A102 20c violet (R)	4.00	9.50
	Never hinged	10.00	
	On cover		140.00
13	A103 25c dk green (R)	4.00	9.50
	Never hinged	10.00	
	On cover		190.00
14	A103 50c black (R)	4.00	16.00
	Never hinged	10.00	
	On cover		125.00
15	A103 1.25 l dp bl (R)	4.00	16.00
	Never hinged	10.00	
	On cover		300.00
16	A104 5 l + 2 l dp car (Bl)	11.00	29.00
	Never hinged	27.50	
	On cover		—
	Nos. 12-16 (5)	27.00	80.00
	Set on overfranked philatelic cover		140.00

Garibaldi Issue
Types of Italy
Overprinted in Red or Blue

1932			
17	A138 10c brown	19.00	35.00
	Never hinged	47.50	
	On cover		250.00
18	A138 20c red brn (Bl)	19.00	35.00
	Never hinged	47.50	
	On cover		160.00
19	A138 25c dp grn	19.00	35.00
	Never hinged	47.50	
	On cover		160.00
20	A138 30c bluish sl	19.00	35.00
	Never hinged	47.50	
	On cover		240.00
21	A138 50c red vio (Bl)	19.00	35.00
	Never hinged	47.50	
	On cover		125.00
22	A141 75c cop red (Bl)	19.00	35.00
	Never hinged	47.50	
	On cover		350.00
23	A141 1.25 l dull blue	19.00	35.00
	Never hinged	47.50	
	On cover		550.00
24	A141 1.75 l + 25c brn	19.00	35.00
	Never hinged	47.50	
	On cover		—
25	A144 2.55 l + 50c org (Bl)	19.00	35.00
	Never hinged	47.50	
	On cover		—
26	A145 5 l + 1 l dl vio	19.00	35.00
	Never hinged	47.50	
	On cover		—
	Nos. 17-26 (10)	190.00	350.00
	Set on overfranked philatelic cover		650.00

PISCOPI

Overprinted "Piscopi" in Black or Violet

1912-21	Wmk. 140		Perf. 13½, 14
1	A43 2c orange brn	8.00	9.50
	Never hinged	20.00	
	On cover		110.00
2	A48 5c green	4.75	9.50
	Never hinged	12.00	
	On cover		65.00
3	A48 10c claret	1.60	9.50
	Never hinged	4.00	
	On cover		180.00
4	A48 15c slate ('21)	19.00	52.50
	Never hinged	47.50	
	On cover		350.00
5	A50 20c brn org ('21)	65.00	72.50
	Never hinged	160.00	
	On cover		575.00
6	A49 25c blue	1.60	9.50
	Never hinged	4.00	
	On cover		110.00
7	A49 40c brown	1.60	9.50
	Never hinged	4.00	
	On cover		240.00
8	A49 50c violet	1.60	19.00
	Never hinged	4.00	
	On cover		275.00

Unwmk.

9	A58 15c slate (V)	47.50	19.00
	Never hinged	120.00	
	On cover		180.00
10	A50 20c brn org ('17)	95.00	225.00
	Never hinged	240.00	
	On cover		650.00
	Nos. 1-10 (10)	245.65	435.50
	Nos. 1-3, 6-9 on over-franked philatelic cover		160.00

No. 9 Surcharged Like Calchi No. 11

1916			Perf. 13½
11	A58 20c on 15c slate	1.60	40.00
	Never hinged	4.00	
	On cover		200.00

Ferrucci Issue
Types of Italy
Overprinted in Red or Blue

1930	Wmk. 140		Perf. 14
12	A102 20c violet (R)	4.00	9.50
	Never hinged	10.00	
	On cover		140.00
13	A103 25c dk green (R)	4.00	9.50
	Never hinged	10.00	
	On cover		190.00
14	A103 50c black (R)	4.00	16.00
	Never hinged	10.00	
	On cover		125.00
15	A103 1.25 l dp bl (R)	4.00	16.00
	Never hinged	10.00	
	On cover		300.00
16	A104 5 l + 2 l dp car (Bl)	11.00	29.00
	Never hinged	27.50	
	On cover		—
	Nos. 12-16 (5)	27.00	80.00
	Set on overfranked philatelic cover		140.00

Garibaldi Issue
Types of Italy
Overprinted in Red or Blue

1932			
17	A138 10c brown	19.00	35.00
	Never hinged	47.50	
	On cover		250.00
18	A138 20c red brn (Bl)	19.00	35.00
	Never hinged	47.50	
	On cover		160.00
19	A138 25c dp grn	19.00	35.00
	Never hinged	47.50	
	On cover		160.00
20	A138 30c bluish sl	19.00	35.00
	Never hinged	47.50	
	On cover		240.00
21	A138 50c red vio (Bl)	19.00	35.00
	Never hinged	47.50	
	On cover		125.00
22	A141 75c cop red (Bl)	19.00	35.00
	Never hinged	47.50	
	On cover		350.00
23	A141 1.25 l dull blue	19.00	35.00
	Never hinged	47.50	
	On cover		550.00
24	A141 1.75 l + 25c brn	19.00	35.00
	Never hinged	47.50	
	On cover		—
25	A144 2.55 l + 50c org (Bl)	19.00	35.00
	Never hinged	47.50	
	On cover		—
26	A145 5 l + 1 l dl vio	19.00	35.00
	Never hinged	47.50	
	On cover		—
	Nos. 17-26 (10)	190.00	350.00
	Set on overfranked philatelic cover		650.00

RHODES

(Rodi)
Overprinted "Rodi" in Black or Violet

1912-24	Wmk. 140		Perf. 13½, 14
1	A43 2c org brn	1.60	9.50
	Never hinged	4.00	
	On cover		87.50
2	A48 5c green	4.75	9.50
	Never hinged	12.00	
	On cover		52.50
a.	Double overprint	400.00	600.00
3	A48 10c claret	1.60	9.50
	Never hinged	4.00	
	On cover		52.50
4	A48 15c slate ('21)	175.00	72.50
	Never hinged	450.00	
	On cover		500.00
5	A45 20c org ('16)	3.25	8.00
	Never hinged	8.00	
	On cover		160.00
6	A50 20c brn org ('19)	6.50	20.00
	Never hinged	16.00	
	On cover		240.00
a.	Double overprint	87.50	
7	A49 25c blue	4.75	9.50
	Never hinged	12.00	
	On cover		110.00
8	A49 40c brown	6.50	9.50
	Never hinged	16.00	
	On cover		240.00
9	A49 50c violet	1.60	19.00
	Never hinged	4.00	
	On cover		275.00
10	A49 85c red brn ('22)	87.50	125.00
	Never hinged	225.00	
	On cover		375.00
11	A46 1 l brn & grn ('24)	3.25	
	Never hinged	8.00	

No. 11 was not regularly issued.

Unwmk.

12	A58 15c slate (V)	47.50	19.00
	Never hinged	120.00	
	On cover		180.00
13	A50 20c brn org ('17)	240.00	225.00
	Never hinged	600.00	
	On cover		650.00
	Nos. 1-13 (13)	583.80	536.00
	Nos. 1-3, 7-9, 12 on over-franked philatelic cover		160.00

No. 12 Surcharged Like Calchi No. 11

1916			Perf. 13½
14	A58 20c on 15c slate	140.00	175.00
	Never hinged	350.00	
	On cover		350.00

Windmill, Rhodes — A1

Medieval Galley — A2

Christian Knight — A3

Crusader Kneeling in Prayer — A4

Crusader's Tomb — A5

No Imprint

1929	Unwmk.	Litho.	Perf. 11
15	A1 5c magenta	11.00	2.40
	Never hinged	27.50	
	On cover		52.50
16	A2 10c olive brn	11.00	1.60
	Never hinged	27.50	
	On cover		20.00
17	A3 20c rose red	11.00	.80
	Never hinged	27.50	
	On cover		14.00
18	A3 25c green	11.00	.80
	Never hinged	27.50	
	On cover		14.00
19	A4 30c dk blue	72.50	2.40
	Never hinged	180.00	
	On cover		40.00
20	A5 50c dk brown	11.00	.80
	Never hinged	27.50	
	On cover		9.50

21	A5 1.25 l dk blue	11.00	2.40
	Never hinged	27.50	
	On cover		60.00
22	A4 5 l magenta	80.00	140.00
	Never hinged	200.00	
	On cover		1,400.
23	A4 10 l olive brn	240.00	340.00
	Never hinged	600.00	
	On cover		4,200.
	Nos. 15-23 (9)	458.50	491.20
	Set on overfranked phila-		
	telic cover		1,900.

Visit of the King and Queen of Italy to the Aegean Islands. The stamps are inscribed "Rodi" but were available for use in all the Aegean Islands.

Nos. 15-23 and C1-C4 were used in eastern Crete in 1941-42 with Greek postmarks. See Nos. 55-63.

Ferrucci Issue
Overprinted in Red or Blue

1930		**Wmk. 140**	**Perf. 14**
24	A102 20c violet (R)	4.00	9.50
	Never hinged	10.00	
	On cover		140.00
25	A103 25c dk green (R)	4.00	9.50
	Never hinged	10.00	
	On cover		190.00
26	A103 50c black (R)	4.00	16.00
	Never hinged	10.00	
	On cover		125.00
27	A103 1.25 l dp blue (R)	4.00	16.00
	Never hinged	10.00	
	On cover		300.00
28	A104 5 l + 2 l dp car (Bl)	11.00	29.00
	Never hinged	27.50	
	On cover		—
	Nos. 24-28 (5)	27.00	80.00
	Set on overfranked phila-		
	telic cover		140.00

Hydrological Congress Issue

Rhodes Issue of 1929 Overprinted

1930		**Unwmk.**	**Perf. 11**
29	A1 5c magenta	65.00	55.00
	Never hinged	160.00	
	On cover		525.00
30	A2 10c olive brn	65.00	55.00
	Never hinged	160.00	
	On cover		450.00
31	A3 20c rose red	72.50	55.00
	Never hinged	180.00	
	On cover		450.00
32	A3 25c green	80.00	55.00
	Never hinged	200.00	
	On cover		525.00
33	A4 30c dk blue	65.00	55.00
	Never hinged	160.00	
	On cover		525.00
34	A5 50c dk brown	600.00	95.00
	Never hinged	1,500.	
	On cover		400.00
35	A5 1.25 l dk blue	450.00	140.00
	Never hinged	1,100.	
	On cover		725.00
36	A4 5 l magenta	400.00	600.00
	Never hinged	1,000.	
	On cover		—
37	A4 10 l olive grn	400.00	650.00
	Never hinged	1,000.	
	On cover		—
	Nos. 29-37 (9)	2,197.	1,760.
	Set on overfranked phil-		
	atelic cover		3,250.

Rhodes Issue of 1929 Overprinted in Blue or Red

1931			
38	A1 5c mag (Bl)	9.50	22.50
	Never hinged	24.00	
	On cover		260.00
39	A2 10c ol brn (R)	9.50	22.50
	Never hinged	24.00	
	On cover		225.00
40	A3 20c rose red (Bl)	9.50	37.50
	Never hinged	24.00	
	On cover		225.00
41	A3 25c green (R)	9.50	37.50
	Never hinged	24.00	
	On cover		260.00
42	A4 30c dk blue (R)	9.50	37.50
	Never hinged	24.00	
	On cover		325.00
43	A5 50c dk brown (R)	65.00	87.50
	Never hinged	160.00	
	On cover		340.00

44	A5 1.25 l dk bl (R)	55.00	125.00
	Never hinged	140.00	
	On cover		600.00
	Nos. 38-44 (7)	167.50	370.00
	Set on overfranked phila-		
	telic cover		725.00

Italian Eucharistic Congress, 1931.

Garibaldi Issue
Types of Italy
Overprinted in Red or Blue

1932		**Wmk. 140**	**Perf. 14**
45	A138 10c brown	19.00	35.00
	Never hinged	47.50	
	On cover		250.00
46	A138 20c red brn (Bl)	19.00	35.00
	Never hinged	47.50	
	On cover		240.00
47	A138 25c dp grn	19.00	35.00
	Never hinged	47.50	
	On cover		160.00
48	A138 30c bluish sl	19.00	35.00
	Never hinged	47.50	
	On cover		240.00
49	A138 50c red vio (Bl)	19.00	35.00
	Never hinged	47.50	
	On cover		125.00
50	A141 75c cop red (Bl)	19.00	35.00
	Never hinged	47.50	
	On cover		350.00
51	A141 1.25 l dl bl	19.00	35.00
	Never hinged	47.50	
	On cover		550.00
52	A141 1.75 l + 25c brn	19.00	35.00
	Never hinged	47.50	
	On cover		—
53	A144 2.55 l + 50c org (Bl)	19.00	35.00
	Never hinged	47.50	
	On cover		—
54	A145 5 l + 1 l dl vio	19.00	35.00
	Never hinged	47.50	
	Nos. 45-54 (10)	190.00	350.00
	Set on overfranked phila-		
	telic cover		650.00

Types of Rhodes Issue of 1929
Imprint: "Officina Carte-Valori Roma"

1932			
55	A1 5c rose lake	1.60	.25
	Never hinged	4.00	
	On cover		16.00
56	A2 10c dk brn	1.60	.25
	Never hinged	4.00	
	On cover		6.00
57	A3 20c red	1.60	.25
	Never hinged	4.00	
	On cover		4.00
58	A3 25c dl grn	1.60	.25
	Never hinged	4.00	
	On cover		4.00
59	A4 30c dl bl	1.60	.25
	Never hinged	4.00	
	On cover		4.00
60	A5 50c blk brn	1.60	.25
	Never hinged	4.00	
	On cover		2.00
61	A5 1.25 l dp bl	1.60	.25
	Never hinged	4.00	
	On cover		6.00
62	A4 5 l rose lake	1.60	2.25
	Never hinged	2.40	
	On cover		600.00
63	A4 10 l ol brn	4.00	4.75
	Never hinged	10.00	
	On cover		1,800.
	Nos. 55-63 (9)	16.80	8.75

 Aerial View of Rhodes A6

 Map of Rhodes — A7

Deer and Palm — A8

1932		**Wmk. 140 Litho.**	**Perf. 11**
Shield in Red			
64	A6 5c blk & grn	9.50	24.00
	Never hinged	24.00	
	On cover		350.00
65	A6 10c blk & vio bl	9.50	20.00
	Never hinged	24.00	
	On cover		225.00
66	A6 20c blk & dl yel	9.50	20.00
	Never hinged	24.00	
	On cover		225.00
67	A6 25c lil & blk	9.50	20.00
	Never hinged	24.00	
	On cover		260.00

68	A6 30c blk & pink	9.50	20.00
	Never hinged	24.00	
	On cover		300.00
Shield and Map Dots in Red			
69	A7 50c blk & gray	9.50	20.00
	Never hinged	24.00	
	On cover		225.00
70	A7 1.25 l red brn & gray	9.50	40.00
	Never hinged	24.00	
	On cover		450.00
71	A7 5 l dk bl & gray	24.00	100.00
	Never hinged	60.00	
	On cover		—
72	A7 10 l dk grn & gray	65.00	180.00
	Never hinged	160.00	
	On cover		—
73	A7 25 l choc & gray	250.00	1,200.
	Never hinged	625.00	
	On cover		—
	Nos. 64-73 (10)	405.50	1,644.
	Set on overfranked phila-		
	telic cover		3,250.

20th anniv. of the Italian occupation and 10th anniv. of Fascist rule.

1935, Apr.		**Photo.**	**Wmk. 140**
74	A8 5c orange	27.50	35.00
	Never hinged	67.50	
	On cover		450.00
75	A8 10c brown	27.50	35.00
	Never hinged	67.50	
	On cover		250.00
76	A8 20c car rose	27.50	45.00
	Never hinged	67.50	
	On cover		275.00
77	A8 25c green	27.50	45.00
	Never hinged	67.50	
	On cover		300.00
78	A8 30c purple	27.50	52.50
	Never hinged	67.50	
	On cover		325.00
79	A8 50c red brn	27.50	52.50
	Never hinged	67.50	
	On cover		250.00
80	A8 1.25l blue	27.50	120.00
	Never hinged	67.50	
	On cover		475.00
81	A8 5 l yellow	240.00	450.00
	Never hinged	600.00	
	On cover		—
	Nos. 74-81 (8)	432.50	835.00
	Set on overfranked phila-		
	telic cover		1,200.

Holy Year.

RHODES AIR POST STAMPS

Symbolical of Flight — AP18

1935		**Typo.**	**Wmk. 140 Upright**	**Perf. 14¼**
C1	AP18 50c black & yel	.80	.40	
	Never hinged	2.00		
	On cover		2.40	
C2	AP18 80c black & mag	3.25	4.00	
	Never hinged	8.00		
	On cover		87.50	
C3	AP18 1 l black & grn	1.60	.40	
	Never hinged	4.00		
	On cover		4.00	
C4	AP18 5 l black & red vio	19.00	9.50	
	Never hinged	47.50		
	On cover		350.00	
	Nos. C1-C4 (4)	24.65	14.30	

1935-38		**Typo.**	**Wmk. 140 Sideways**	**Perf. 14**
C1a	AP18 50c black & yellow	—	.40	
	Never hinged	—		
	On cover		2.40	
C2a	AP18 80c black & mag	.80	2.40	
	Never hinged	2.00		
	On cover		80.00	
C3a	AP18 1 l black & green	.80	.40	
	Never hinged	2.00		
	On cover		4.00	
C4a	AP18 5 l black & red vio	1.60	4.75	
	Never hinged	4.00		
	On cover		350.00	
	Nos. C1a-C4a (4)	3.20	7.95	

RHODES SPECIAL DELIVERY STAMPS

 Stag — SD1

1936		**Photo.**	**Wmk. 140**	**Perf. 14**
E1	SD1 1.25 l green	4.75	4.75	
	Never hinged	12.00		
	On cover		200.00	
E2	SD1 2.50 l vermilion	8.00	8.00	
	Never hinged	20.00		
	On cover		650.00	

RHODES POSTAGE DUE STAMPS

 Maltese Cross PD1

 Immortelle PD2

1934		**Photo.**	**Wmk. 140**	**Perf. 13**
J1	PD1 5c vermilion	4.75	8.00	
	Never hinged	12.00		
	On cover		475.00	
J2	PD1 10c carmine	4.75	8.00	
	Never hinged	12.00		
	On cover		300.00	
J3	PD1 20c dk grn	4.75	6.50	
	Never hinged	12.00		
	On cover		300.00	
J4	PD1 30c purple	4.75	6.50	
	Never hinged	12.00		
	On cover		300.00	
J5	PD1 40c dk bl	4.75	12.50	
	Never hinged	12.00		
	On cover		475.00	
J6	PD2 50c vermilion	4.75	6.50	
	Never hinged	12.00		
	On cover		210.00	
J7	PD2 60c carmine	4.75	24.00	
	Never hinged	12.00		
	On cover		475.00	
J8	PD2 1 l dk grn	4.75	24.00	
	Never hinged	12.00		
	On cover		400.00	
J9	PD2 2 l purple	4.75	12.50	
	Never hinged	12.00		
	On cover		525.00	
	Nos. J1-J9 (9)	42.75	108.50	

RHODES PARCEL POST STAMPS

Both unused and used values are for complete stamps.

 PP1

 PP2

1934		**Photo.**	**Wmk. 140**	**Perf. 13**
Q1	PP1 5c vermilion	6.50	12.00	
	Never hinged	16.00		
Q2	PP1 10c carmine	6.50	12.00	
	Never hinged	16.00		
Q3	PP1 20c dk green	6.50	12.00	
	Never hinged	16.00		
Q4	PP1 25c purple	6.50	12.00	
	Never hinged	16.00		
Q5	PP1 50c dk blue	6.50	12.00	
	Never hinged	16.00		
Q6	PP1 60c black	6.50	12.00	
	Never hinged	16.00		
Q7	PP2 1 l vermilion	6.50	12.00	
	Never hinged	16.00		
Q8	PP2 2 l carmine	6.50	12.00	
	Never hinged	16.00		
Q9	PP2 3 l dk green	6.50	12.00	
	Never hinged	16.00		
Q10	PP2 4 l purple	6.50	12.00	
	Never hinged	16.00		
Q11	PP2 10 l dk blue	6.50	12.00	
	Never hinged	16.00		
	Nos. Q1-Q11 (11)	71.50	132.00	

Value of used halves, Nos. Q1-Q11, each 80 cents.

See note preceding No. Q7 of Italy.

SCARPANTO

Overprinted "Scarpanto" in Black or Violet

1912-22   Wmk. 140   Perf. 13½, 14

1	A43	2c org brn	9.50	9.50
		Never hinged	24.00	
		On cover		110.00
2	A48	5c green	3.25	9.50
		Never hinged	8.00	
		On cover		65.00
3	A48	10c claret	1.60	9.50
		Never hinged	4.00	
		On cover		65.00
4	A48	15c slate ('22)	19.00	40.00
		Never hinged	47.50	
		On cover		400.00
5	A50	20c brn org ('21)	65.00	65.00
		Never hinged	160.00	
		On cover		450.00
6	A49	25c blue	9.50	9.50
		Never hinged	24.00	
		On cover		110.00
7	A49	40c brown	1.60	9.50
		Never hinged	4.00	
		On cover		240.00
8	A49	50c violet	3.25	19.00
		Never hinged	8.00	
		On cover		275.00

Unwmk.

9	A58	15c slate (V)	40.00	19.00
		Never hinged	100.00	
		On cover		180.00
10	A50	20c brn org ('17)	140.00	225.00
		Never hinged	350.00	
		On cover		650.00
		Nos. 1-10 (10)	292.70	415.50
		Nos. 1-3, 6-9 on over-franked philatelic cover		160.00

No 9 Surcharged Like Calchi No. 11

1916   Perf. 13½

11	A58	20c on 15c slate	1.60	40.00
		Never hinged	4.00	
		On cover		200.00

Ferrucci Issue
Types of Italy
Overprinted in Red or Blue

1930   Wmk. 140   Perf. 14

12	A102	20c violet (R)	4.00	9.50
		Never hinged	10.00	
		On cover		140.00
13	A103	25c dk green (R)	4.00	9.50
		Never hinged	10.00	
		On cover		190.00
14	A103	50c black (R)	4.00	16.00
		Never hinged	10.00	
		On cover		120.00
15	A103	1.25 l dp bl (R)	4.00	16.00
		Never hinged	10.00	
		On cover		300.00
16	A104	5 l + 2 l dp car (Bl)	11.00	27.50
		Never hinged	27.50	
		On cover		—
		Nos. 12-16 (5)	27.00	78.50
		Set on overfranked philatelic cover		140.00

Garibaldi Issue
Types of Italy
Overprinted in Red or Blue

1932

17	A138	10c brown	19.00	35.00
		Never hinged	47.50	
		On cover		250.00
18	A138	20c red brn (Bl)	19.00	35.00
		Never hinged	47.50	
		On cover		160.00
19	A138	25c dp grn	19.00	35.00
		Never hinged	47.50	
		On cover		160.00
20	A138	30c bluish sl	19.00	35.00
		Never hinged	47.50	
		On cover		240.00
21	A138	50c red vio (Bl)	19.00	35.00
		Never hinged	47.50	
		On cover		125.00
22	A141	75c cop red (Bl)	19.00	35.00
		Never hinged	47.50	
		On cover		350.00
23	A141	1.25 l dull blue	19.00	35.00
		Never hinged	47.50	
		On cover		550.00
24	A141	1.75 l + 25c brn	19.00	35.00
		Never hinged	47.50	
		On cover		—
25	A144	2.55 l + 50c org (Bl)	19.00	35.00
		Never hinged	47.50	
		On cover		—
26	A145	5 l + 1 l dl vio	19.00	35.00
		Never hinged	47.50	
		On cover		—
		Nos. 17-26 (10)	190.00	350.00
		Set on overfranked philatelic cover		650.00

SIMI

Overprinted "Simi" in Black or Violet

1912-21   Wmk. 140   Perf. 13½, 14

1	A43	2c org brn	16.00	9.50
		Never hinged	40.00	
		On cover		110.00
2	A48	5c green	40.00	9.50
		Never hinged	100.00	
		On cover		65.00
3	A48	10c claret	1.60	9.50
		Never hinged	4.00	
		On cover		65.00
4	A48	15c slate ('21)	140.00	72.50
		Never hinged	350.00	
		On cover		450.00
5	A50	20c brn org ('21)	72.50	40.00
		Never hinged	180.00	
		On cover		400.00
6	A49	25c blue	9.50	9.50
		Never hinged	24.00	
		On cover		110.00
7	A49	40c brown	1.60	9.50
		Never hinged	4.00	
		On cover		240.00
8	A49	50c violet	1.60	19.00
		Never hinged	4.00	
		On cover		275.00

Unwmk.

9	A58	15c slate (V)	72.00	19.00
		Never hinged	180.00	
		On cover		180.00
10	A50	20c brn org ('17)	72.50	125.00
		Never hinged	180.00	
		On cover		525.00
		Nos. 1-10 (10)	427.30	323.00
		Nos. 1-3, 6-9 on over-franked philatelic cover		160.00

No 9 Surcharged Like Calchi No. 11

1916   Perf. 13½

11	A58	20c on 15c slate	9.50	40.00
		Never hinged	24.00	
		On cover		200.00

Ferrucci Issue
Types of Italy
Overprinted in Red or Blue

1930   Wmk. 140   Perf. 14

12	A102	20c violet (R)	4.75	9.50
		Never hinged	12.00	
		On cover		140.00
13	A103	25c dk green (R)	4.75	9.50
		Never hinged	12.00	
		On cover		190.00
14	A103	50c black (R)	4.75	16.00
		Never hinged	12.00	
		On cover		125.00
15	A103	1.25 l dp bl (R)	4.75	16.00
		Never hinged	12.00	
		On cover		300.00
16	A104	5 l + 2 l dp car (Bl)	11.00	27.50
		Never hinged	27.50	
		On cover		—
		Nos. 12-16 (5)	30.00	78.50
		Set on overfranked philatelic cover		140.00

Garibaldi Issue
Types of Italy
Overprinted in Red or Blue

1932

17	A138	10c brown	19.00	35.00
		Never hinged	47.50	
		On cover		250.00
18	A138	20c red brn (Bl)	19.00	35.00
		Never hinged	47.50	
		On cover		160.00
19	A138	25c dp grn	19.00	35.00
		Never hinged	47.50	
		On cover		160.00
20	A138	30c bluish sl	19.00	35.00
		Never hinged	47.50	
		On cover		240.00
21	A138	50c red vio (Bl)	19.00	35.00
		Never hinged	47.50	
		On cover		125.00
22	A141	75c cop red (Bl)	19.00	35.00
		Never hinged	47.50	
		On cover		350.00
23	A141	1.25 l dull blue	19.00	35.00
		Never hinged	47.50	
		On cover		550.00
24	A141	1.75 l + 25c brn	19.00	35.00
		Never hinged	47.50	
		On cover		—
25	A144	2.55 l + 50c org (Bl)	19.00	35.00
		Never hinged	47.50	
		On cover		—
26	A145	5 l + 1 l dl vio	19.00	35.00
		Never hinged	47.50	
		On cover		—
		Nos. 17-26 (10)	190.00	350.00
		Set on overfranked philatelic cover		650.00

STAMPALIA

Overprinted "Stampalia" in Black or Violet

1912-21   Wmk. 140   Perf. 13½, 14

1	A43	2c org brn	9.50	9.50
		Never hinged	24.00	
		On cover		110.00
2	A48	5c green	1.60	9.50
		Never hinged	4.00	
		On cover		65.00
3	A48	10c claret	1.60	9.50
		Never hinged	4.00	
		On cover		65.00
4	A48	15c slate ('21)	11.00	40.00
		Never hinged	27.50	
		On cover		400.00
5	A50	20c brn org ('21)	55.00	72.50
		Never hinged	140.00	
		On cover		500.00
6	A49	25c blue	1.60	9.50
		Never hinged	4.00	
		On cover		110.00
7	A49	40c brown	4.75	9.50
		Never hinged	12.00	
		On cover		240.00
8	A49	50c violet	1.60	19.00
		Never hinged	4.00	
		On cover		275.00

Unwmk.

9	A58	15c slate (V)	47.50	19.00
		Never hinged	120.00	
		On cover		180.00
10	A50	20c brn org ('17)	95.00	125.00
		Never hinged	240.00	
		On cover		525.00
		Nos. 1-10 (10)	229.15	323.00
		Nos. 1-3, 6-9 on over-franked philatelic cover		140.00

No 9 Surcharged Like Calchi No. 11

1916   Perf. 13½

11	A58	20c on 15c slate	1.60	40.00
		Never hinged	4.00	
		On cover		200.00

Ferrucci Issue
Types of Italy
Overprinted in Red or Blue

1930   Wmk. 140   Perf. 14

12	A102	20c violet (R)	4.00	9.50
		Never hinged	10.00	
		On cover		140.00
13	A103	25c dk green (R)	4.00	9.50
		Never hinged	10.00	
		On cover		190.00
14	A103	50c black (R)	4.00	16.00
		Never hinged	10.00	
		On cover		125.00
15	A103	1.25 l dp bl (R)	4.00	16.00
		Never hinged	10.00	
		On cover		300.00
16	A104	5 l + 2 l dp car (Bl)	11.00	27.50
		Never hinged	27.50	
		On cover		—
		Nos. 12-16 (5)	27.00	78.50
		Set on overfranked philatelic cover		140.00

Garibaldi Issue
Types of Italy
Overprinted in Red or Blue

1932

17	A138	10c brown	19.00	35.00
		Never hinged	47.50	
		On cover		250.00
18	A138	20c red brn (Bl)	19.00	35.00
		Never hinged	47.50	
		On cover		160.00
19	A138	25c dp grn	19.00	35.00
		Never hinged	47.50	
		On cover		160.00
20	A138	30c bluish sl	19.00	35.00
		Never hinged	47.50	
		On cover		240.00
21	A138	50c red vio (Bl)	19.00	35.00
		Never hinged	47.50	
		On cover		125.00
22	A141	75c cop red (Bl)	19.00	35.00
		Never hinged	47.50	
		On cover		350.00
23	A141	1.25 l dull blue	19.00	35.00
		Never hinged	47.50	
		On cover		550.00
24	A141	1.75 l + 25c brn	19.00	35.00
		Never hinged	47.50	
		On cover		—
25	A144	2.55 l + 50c org (Bl)	19.00	35.00
		Never hinged	47.50	
		On cover		—
26	A145	5 l + 1 l dl vio	19.00	35.00
		Never hinged	47.50	
		On cover		—
		Nos. 17-26 (10)	190.00	350.00
		Set on overfranked philatelic cover		650.00

IVORY COAST

ˈiv-rē ˈkōst

LOCATION — West coast of Africa, bordering on Gulf of Guinea

GOVT. — French Colony
AREA — 127,520 sq. mi.
POP. — 13,107,000 (est. 1991)
CAPITAL — Yamoussoukro

100 Centimes = 1 Franc

Navigation and Commerce — A1

Perf. 14x13½

1892-1900   Typo.   Unwmk.
Colony Name in Blue or Carmine

1	A1	1c black, lil bl	2.00	2.40
		Never hinged	3.25	
		On cover		105.00
2	A1	2c brown, buff	2.75	3.25
		Never hinged	4.50	
		On cover		105.00
3	A1	4c claret, lav	4.75	4.75
		Never hinged	8.25	
		On cover		105.00
4	A1	5c green, grnsh	13.50	9.00
		Never hinged	22.50	
		On cover		55.00
5	A1	10c black, lavender	20.00	12.50
		Never hinged	35.00	
		On cover		50.00
6	A1	10c red ('00)	130.00	110.00
		Never hinged	225.00	
		On cover		425.00
7	A1	15c blue, quadrille paper	32.50	13.50
		Never hinged	60.00	
		On cover		55.00
8	A1	15c gray ('00)	20.00	5.75
		Never hinged	35.00	
		On cover		42.50
9	A1	20c red, green	21.00	16.00
		Never hinged	40.00	
		On cover		92.50
		On cover, single franking		160.00
10	A1	25c black, rose	24.00	6.50
		Never hinged	45.00	
		On cover		42.50
11	A1	25c blue ('00)	40.00	37.50
		Never hinged	75.00	
		On cover		190.00
12	A1	30c brown, bister	35.00	27.50
		Never hinged	72.50	
		On cover		92.50
		On cover, single franking		140.00
13	A1	40c red, straw	27.50	16.00
		Never hinged	50.00	
		On cover		87.50
		On cover, single franking		125.00
14	A1	50c car, rose	80.00	65.00
		Never hinged	165.00	
		On cover		210.00
		On cover, single franking		275.00
15	A1	50c brn, azure ('00)	37.50	32.50
		Never hinged	67.50	
		On cover		300.00
		On cover, single franking		400.00
16	A1	75c deep vio, org	32.50	32.50
		Never hinged	65.00	
		On cover		340.00
		On cover, single franking		500.00
17	A1	1fr brnz grn, straw	52.50	45.00
		Never hinged	105.00	
		On cover		350.00
		On cover, single franking		550.00
		Nos. 1-17 (17)	575.50	439.65

Perf. 13½x14 stamps are counterfeits.
For surcharges see Nos. 18-20, 37-41.

Nos. 12, 16-17 Surcharged in Black

1904

18	A1	0,05c on 30c brn, bis	87.50	87.50
		Never hinged	175.00	
		On cover		500.00
19	A1	0,10c on 75c vio, org	18.00	18.00
		Never hinged	32.50	
		On cover		210.00
20	A1	0,15c on 1fr brnz grn, straw	26.00	26.00
		Never hinged	45.00	
		On cover		225.00
		Nos. 18-20 (3)	131.50	131.50

Gen. Louis Faidherbe A2

Oil Palm — A3

Dr. N.
Eugène
Ballay
A4

1906-07
Name of Colony in Red or Blue

No.	Type	Description		
21	A2	1c slate	2.00	2.00
		Never hinged	3.25	
		On cover		67.50
a.		"CÔTE D'IVOIRE" omitted	160.00	160.00
22	A2	2c chocolate	2.00	2.00
		Never hinged	3.25	
		On cover		67.50
23	A2	4c choc, gray bl	2.40	2.40
		Never hinged	3.75	
		On cover		67.50
a.		"CÔTE D'IVOIRE" double	225.00	
b.		"CÔTE D'IVOIRE" omitted	190.00	
24	A2	5c green	4.00	2.75
		Never hinged	7.25	
		On cover		42.50
a.		"CÔTE D'IVOIRE" omitted	110.00	92.50
25	A2	10c carmine (B)	9.50	6.50
		Never hinged	19.00	
		On cover		27.50
a.		"CÔTE D'IVOIRE" double	210.00	400.00
b.		"CÔTE D'IVOIRE" omitted		400.00
26	A3	20c black, azure	10.00	9.50
		Never hinged	20.00	
		On cover		42.50
27	A3	25c bl, pinkish	9.50	6.00
		Never hinged	20.00	
		On cover		42.50
28	A3	30c choc, pnksh	12.50	8.75
		Never hinged	25.00	
		On cover		42.50
		On cover, single franking		75.00
30	A3	35c black, yel	12.50	5.75
		Never hinged	25.00	
		On cover		42.50
		On cover, single franking		62.50
a.		"CÔTE D'IVOIRE" omitted	225.00	
31	A3	45c choc, grnsh	18.00	12.50
		Never hinged	25.00	
		On cover		92.50
		On cover, single franking		125.00
32	A3	50c deep violet	16.00	12.50
		Never hinged	35.00	
		On cover		67.50
		On cover, single franking		110.00
33	A3	75c blue, org	16.00	12.50
		Never hinged	35.00	
		On cover		100.00
		On cover, single franking		225.00
34	A4	1fr black, azure	40.00	35.00
		Never hinged	80.00	
		On cover		150.00
		On cover, single franking		300.00
35	A4	2fr blue, pink	52.50	50.00
		Never hinged	110.00	
		On cover		200.00
		On cover, single franking		350.00
36	A4	5fr car, straw (B)	100.00	95.00
		Never hinged	190.00	
		On cover		275.00
		On cover, single franking		425.00
		Nos. 21-36 (15)	306.90	263.15

Stamps of 1892-1900 Surcharged in Carmine or Black

1912
Spacing between figures of surcharge 1.5mm (5c), 2mm (10c)

No.	Type	Description		
37	A1	5c on 15c gray (C)	1.60	1.60
		Never hinged	2.50	
		On cover		55.00
38	A1	5c on 30c brn, bis (C)	2.40	2.75
		Never hinged	3.75	
		On cover		75.00
39	A1	10c on 40c red, straw	2.40	2.75
		Never hinged	3.75	
		On cover		75.00
a.		Pair, one without surcharge	75.00	75.00
40	A1	10c on 50c brn, az (C)	4.00	4.75
		Never hinged	6.75	
		On cover		95.00
41	A1	10c on 75c dp vio, org	9.00	10.00
		Never hinged	15.00	
		On cover		145.00
		Nos. 37-41 (5)	19.40	21.85

Spacing between figures of surcharge 2.25mm (5c), 2.75mm (10c)

No.	Type	Description		
37a	A1	5c on 15c gray (C)	8.50	8.50
		Never hinged	17.50	
38a	A1	5c on 30c brn, bis (b)	8.50	8.50
		Never hinged	24.00	
39b	A1	10c on 40c red, straw	50.00	50.00
		Never hinged	125.00	
40a	A1	10c on 50c brn, az (C)	92.50	92.50
		Never hinged	210.00	
41a	A1	10c on 75c dp vio, org	200.00	200.00
		Never hinged	200.00	—
		Nos. 37a-41a (5)	359.50	359.50

River Scene A5

1913-35

No.	Type	Description		
42	A5	1c vio brn & vio	.25	.25
			.40	
		On cover		55.00
43	A5	2c brown & blk	.25	.25
			.40	
		On cover		55.00
44	A5	4c vio & vio brn	.30	.30
			.55	
		On cover		55.00
45	A5	5c yel grn & bl grn	1.10	.50
		Never hinged	1.60	
		On cover		22.50
a.		Chalky paper	1.90	1.25
		Never hinged	3.50	
46	A5	5c choc & ol brn ('22)	.30	.30
		Never hinged	.45	
		On cover		25.00
47	A5	10c red org & rose	2.00	.95
		Never hinged	3.00	
		On cover		14.00
a.		Chalky paper	2.25	1.60
		Never hinged	3.75	
48	A5	10c yel grn & bl grn ('22)	.70	.70
		Never hinged	1.00	
		On cover		42.50
49	A5	10c car rose, bluish ('26)	.30	.30
		Never hinged	.50	
		On cover		42.50
50	A5	15c org & rose ('17)	1.75	.80
		Never hinged	1.60	
		On cover		14.00
a.		Chalky paper	1.10	.60
		Never hinged	1.90	
		On cover		15.00
51	A5	20c black & gray	.80	.55
		Never hinged	1.25	
		On cover		25.00
52	A5	25c ultra & bl	11.00	6.50
		Never hinged	16.00	
		On cover		37.50
		On cover, single franking		67.50
a.		Chalky paper	11.00	6.50
		Never hinged	16.00	
		On cover		37.50
53	A5	25c blk & vio ('22)	.55	.55
			.90	
		On cover		7.50
54	A5	30c choc & brn	2.40	2.00
		Never hinged	3.50	
		On cover		30.00
		On cover, single franking		75.00
55	A5	30c red org & rose ('22)	2.75	2.75
		Never hinged	4.25	
		On cover		30.00
		On cover, single franking		55.00
56	A5	30c lt bl & rose red ('26)	.50	.50
			.75	
		On cover		10.00
a.		Chalky paper	1.50	1.50
		Never hinged	2.00	
		On cover		14.00
57	A5	30c dl grn & grn ('27)	.80	.80
			1.25	
		On cover		25.00
58	A5	35c vio & org	.95	.80
		Never hinged	1.40	
		On cover		37.50
		On cover, single franking		75.00
a.		Chalky paper	1.10	.75
		Never hinged	1.65	
		On cover		37.50
59	A5	40c gray & bl grn	1.60	.80
		Never hinged	2.40	
		On cover		42.50
		On cover, single franking		92.50
60	A5	45c red org & choc	1.00	.80
		Never hinged	1.50	
		On cover		50.00
		On cover, single franking		110.00
61	A5	45c dp rose & mar ('34)	6.25	5.00
		Never hinged	9.00	
		On cover		55.00
		On cover, single franking		125.00
62	A5	50c black & vio	5.00	3.50
		Never hinged	7.25	
		On cover		62.50
		On cover, single franking		125.00

No.	Type	Description		
63	A5	50c ultra & bl ('22)	2.00	2.00
		Never hinged	3.00	
		On cover		25.00
		On cover, single franking		55.00
64	A5	50c ol grn & bl ('36)	.00	.60
		Never hinged	1.00	
		On cover		7.50
65	A5	60c vio, pnksh ('25)	.80	.80
		Never hinged	1.10	
		On cover		25.00
		On cover, single franking		62.50
66	A5	65c car rose & ol grn ('26)	1.60	1.60
		Never hinged	2.40	
		On cover		14.00
		On cover, single franking		22.50
67	A5	75c brn & rose	1.00	.80
		Never hinged	1.50	
		On cover		42.50
		On cover, single franking		105.00
68	A5	75c ind & ultra ('34)	4.50	4.00
		Never hinged	5.50	
		On cover		32.50
69	A5	85c red vio & blk ('26)	1.60	1.60
		Never hinged	2.40	
		On cover		35.00
		On cover, single franking		92.50
70	A5	90c brn red & rose ('30)	17.50	13.50
		Never hinged	21.00	
		On cover		67.50
		On cover, single franking		165.00
71	A5	1fr org & black	1.10	1.00
		Never hinged	1.60	
		On cover		55.00
		On cover, single franking		140.00
72	A5	1.10fr dl grn & dk brn ('28)	7.75	7.00
		Never hinged	11.00	
		On cover		110.00
		On cover, single franking		275.00
73	A5	1.50fr lt bl & dp bl ('30)	10.00	7.50
		Never hinged	13.50	
		On cover		50.00
		On cover, single franking		140.00
74	A5	1.75fr lt ultra & mag ('35)	17.50	9.50
		Never hinged	21.00	
		On cover		62.50
		On cover, single franking		87.50
75	A5	2fr brn & blue	6.00	2.90
		Never hinged	8.00	
		On cover		67.50
		On cover, single franking		140.00
76	A5	3fr red vio ('30)	11.00	7.50
		Never hinged	13.50	
		On cover		87.50
		On cover, single franking		190.00
77	A5	5fr dk bl & choc	10.00	5.75
		Never hinged	12.00	
		On cover		87.50
		On cover, single franking		165.00
		Nos. 42-77 (36)	133.70	95.15

Nos. 45, 47, 50, 52, 56 and 58 exist on both ordinary and chalky paper.
For surcharges see Nos. 78-91, B1.
Nos. 45, 47 and 52, pasted on cardboard and overprinted "Valeur d'echange" and value of basic stamp, were used as emergency currency in 1920.

Stamps and Type of 1913-34 Srchd.

1922-34

No.	Type	Description		
78	A5	50c on 45c dp rose & maroon ('34)	4.00	2.75
		Never hinged	5.75	
		On cover		16.00
79	A5	50c on 75c indigo & ultra ('34)	2.40	2.00
		Never hinged	3.25	
		On cover		14.00
80	A5	50c on 90c brn red & rose ('34)	2.40	2.40
		Never hinged	3.50	
		On cover		14.00
81	A5	60c on 75c vio, pnksh	.65	.65
		Never hinged	1.00	
		On cover		16.00
		On cover, single franking		275.00
a.		Surcharge omitted	160.00	175.00
		Never hinged	225.00	
82	A5	65c on 15c orange & rose ('25)	1.25	1.25
		Never hinged	1.75	
		On cover		55.00
		On cover, single franking		125.00
a.		Chalky paper (on #50a)	2.25	2.10
		Never hinged	3.75	
83	A5	85c on 75c brown & rose ('25)	1.60	1.25
		Never hinged	2.75	
		On cover		42.50
		On cover, single franking		80.00
		Nos. 78-83 (6)	12.30	10.30

Stamps and Type of 1913 Surcharged with New Value and Bars

No.	Type	Description		
84	A5	25c on 2fr (R)	1.10	1.10
		Never hinged	1.60	
		On cover		7.50
85	A5	25c on 5fr	1.10	1.10
		Never hinged	1.60	
		On cover		7.50
86	A5	90c on 75c brn red & cer ('27)	2.00	1.60
		Never hinged	2.75	
		On cover		42.50
		On cover, single franking		80.00
a.		Surcharge omitted	240.00	
		Never hinged	325.00	
87	A5	1.25fr on 1fr dk bl & ultra (R) ('26)	1.25	1.25
		Never hinged	1.75	
		On cover		50.00
		On cover, single franking		92.50
88	A5	1.50fr on 1fr lt bl & dk blue ('27)	2.00	2.00
		Never hinged	2.75	
		On cover		37.50
		On cover, single franking		62.50
89	A5	3fr on 5fr brn red & bl grn ('27)	6.00	6.00
		Never hinged	8.75	
		On cover		67.50
		On cover, single franking		140.00
a.		Double surcharge	160.00	
90	A5	10fr on 5fr dl red & rose lil ('27)	17.50	16.00
		Never hinged	26.00	
		On cover		92.50
		On cover, single franking		190.00
91	A5	20fr on 5fr bl grn & ver ('27)	21.00	19.00
		Never hinged	35.00	
		On cover		105.00
		On cover, single franking		225.00
		Nos. 84-91 (8)	51.95	48.05

Common Design Types pictured following the introduction.

Colonial Exposition Issue
Common Design Types
Name of Country in Black

1931		Engr.	Perf. 12½	
92	CD70	40c deep green	4.00	4.00
		Never hinged	6.75	
		On cover		87.50
93	CD71	50c violet	6.50	6.50
		Never hinged	10.00	
		On cover		75.00
94	CD72	90c red orange	5.50	5.50
		Never hinged	8.50	
		On cover		125.00
		On cover, single franking		190.00
95	CD73	1.50fr dull blue	6.50	6.50
		Never hinged	10.00	
		On cover		110.00
		On cover, single franking		165.00
		Nos. 92-95 (4)	22.50	22.50

Stamps of Upper Volta 1928, Overprinted

1933   Perf. 13½x14

No.	Type	Description		
96	A5	2c brown & lilac	.25	.25
		Never hinged	.40	
		On cover		42.50
a.		Inverted overprint	27.50	
		Never hinged	40.00	
b.		Double overprint	40.00	47.50
		Never hinged	50.00	
		On cover		67.50
97	A5	4c blk & yellow	.35	.35
		Never hinged	.50	
		On cover		42.50
a.		Inverted overprint	100.00	
		Never hinged	150.00	
b.		Double overprint	65.00	72.50
		Never hinged	100.00	
		On cover		100.00
98	A5	5c ind & gray bl	.65	.50
		Never hinged	.90	
		On cover		37.50
a.		Inverted overprint	47.50	
		Never hinged	100.00	
b.		Double overprint	65.00	
		Never hinged	100.00	
99	A5	10c indigo & pink	.50	.50
		Never hinged	.65	
		On cover		30.00
100	A5	15c brown & blue	1.25	1.00
		Never hinged	1.75	
		On cover		37.50
a.		Double overprint	65.00	
		Never hinged	90.00	
101	A5	20c brown & green	1.25	1.00
		Never hinged	1.75	
		On cover		17.50
102	A6	25c brn & yellow	2.25	1.90
		Never hinged	3.00	
		On cover		42.50
103	A6	30c dp grn & brn	2.75	2.00
		Never hinged	3.00	
		On cover		50.00

a.	Double overprint	75.00		
	Never hinged	110.00		
104	A6 45c brown & blue	10.00	6.50	
	Never hinged	11.00		
	On cover		62.50	
a.	Inverted overprint	80.00		
	Never hinged	110.00		
b.	Double overprint	120.00		
	Never hinged	175.00		
105	A6 65c indigo & bl	4.00	2.90	
	Never hinged	4.50		
	On cover		75.00	
a.	Double overprint	95.00		
	Never hinged	150.00		
106	A6 75c black & lilac	4.75	2.50	
	Never hinged	5.50		
	On cover		40.00	
a.	Double overprint	95.00		
	Never hinged	150.00		
107	A6 90c brn red & lil	4.00	2.90	
	Never hinged	4.50		
	On cover		75.00	
	On cover, single franking		140.00	

Burkina Faso Nos. 58 & 60 Ovptd.

108	A7 1fr brown & green	4.75	3.25	
	Never hinged	5.50		
	On cover		50.00	
	On cover, single franking		67.50	
a.	Inverted overprint	150.00	160.00	
	Never hinged	200.00		
	On cover		260.00	
109	A7 1.50fr ultra & grysh	4.50	2.90	
	Never hinged	5.25		
	On cover		50.00	
	On cover, single franking		110.00	
a.	Inverted overprint	150.00		
	Never hinged	225.00		
b.	Double overprint	95.00		
	Never hinged	140.00		

Burkina Faso Nos. 52 & 54 Surcharged

110	A6 1.25fr on 40c blk & pink	3.00	2.25	
	Never hinged	4.00		
	On cover		27.50	
	On cover, single franking		67.50	
a.	Double overprint	100.00		
	Never hinged	150.00		
111	A6 1.75fr on 50c blk & green	5.25	3.25	
	Never hinged	5.50		
	On cover		27.50	
	On cover, single franking		42.50	
a.	Double overprint	100.00		
	Never hinged	150.00		
	Nos. 96-111 (16)	49.50	33.95	

Baoulé Woman — A6   Rapids on Comoe River — A9

Mosque at Bobo-Dioulasso — A7

Coastal Scene A8

1936-44 Perf. 13

112	A6 1c carmine rose	.25	.25	
	Never hinged	.40		
	On cover		25.00	

113	A6 2c ultramarine	.25	.25	
	Never hinged	.40		
	On cover		25.00	
114	A6 3c dp grn ('40)	.25	.25	
	Never hinged	.40		
	On cover		25.00	
115	A6 4c chocolate	.25	.25	
	Never hinged	.40		
	On cover		25.00	
116	A6 5c violet	.25	.25	
	Never hinged	.40		
	On cover		21.00	
117	A6 10c Prussian bl	.25	.25	
	Never hinged	.40		
	On cover		19.00	
118	A6 15c copper red	.25	.25	
	Never hinged	.40		
	On cover		12.50	
119	A7 20c ultramarine	.35	.25	
	Never hinged	.50		
	On cover		12.50	
120	A7 25c copper red	.50	.25	
	Never hinged	.60		
	On cover		8.75	
121	A7 30c blue green	.35	.35	
	Never hinged	.50		
	On cover		19.00	
122	A7 30c brown ('40)	.25	.25	
	Never hinged	.40		
	On cover		7.50	
123	A6 35c dp grn ('38)	.85	.65	
	Never hinged	1.00		
	On cover		27.50	
124	A7 40c carmine rose	.50	.35	
	Never hinged	.60		
	On cover		7.50	
125	A7 45c brown	.65	.65	
	Never hinged	.90		
	On cover		25.00	
126	A7 45c blue grn ('40)	.35	.35	
	Never hinged	.50		
	On cover		19.00	
127	A7 50c plum	.50	.50	
	Never hinged	.65		
	On cover		6.25	
128	A7 55c dark vio ('38)	.60	.60	
	Never hinged	.75		
	On cover		8.75	
129	A8 60c car rose ('40)	.40	.40	
	Never hinged	.55		
	On cover		19.00	
130	A8 65c red brown	.65	.50	
	Never hinged	.90		
	On cover		45.00	
131	A8 70c red brn ('40)	.65	.65	
	Never hinged	.85		
	On cover		21.00	
132	A8 75c dark violet	1.25	.75	
	Never hinged	1.50		
	On cover		10.00	
133	A8 80c blk brn ('38)	1.50	.95	
	Never hinged	1.50		
	On cover		50.00	
	On cover, single franking		87.50	
134	A8 90c carmine rose	10.00	5.50	
	Never hinged	11.00		
	On cover		30.00	
	On cover, single franking		55.00	
135	A8 90c dk grn ('39)	.85	.80	
	Never hinged	1.00		
	On cover		35.00	
	On cover, single franking		67.50	
136	A8 1fr dark green	5.00	2.75	
	Never hinged	4.75		
	On cover		15.00	
	On cover, single franking		25.00	
137	A8 1fr car rose ('38)	1.75	.95	
	Never hinged	1.60		
	On cover		37.50	
	On cover, single franking		67.50	
138	A8 1fr dk vio ('40)	.65	.65	
	Never hinged	.85		
	On cover		6.25	
139	A8 1.25fr copper red	.50	.40	
	Never hinged	.65		
	On cover		21.00	
	On cover, single franking		37.50	
140	A8 1.40fr ultra ('40)	.65	.65	
	Never hinged	.85		
	On cover		30.00	
	On cover, single franking		67.50	
141	A8 1.50fr ultramarine	.60	.40	
	Never hinged	.65		
	On cover		19.00	
	On cover, single franking		32.50	
141A	A8 1.50fr grnsh blk ('42)	2.25	2.00	
	Never hinged	2.40		
	On cover		9.25	
142	A8 1.60fr blk brn ('40)	1.25	1.00	
	Never hinged	1.40		
	On cover		30.00	
	On cover, single franking		80.00	
143	A9 1.75fr carmine rose	.65	.40	
	Never hinged	.65		
	On cover		10.00	
	On cover, single franking		19.00	
144	A9 1.75fr dull bl ('38)	1.25	.85	
	Never hinged	1.20		
	On cover		37.50	
	On cover, single franking		100.00	
145	A9 2fr ultramarine	.85	.60	
	Never hinged	1.10		
	On cover		14.00	
	On cover, single franking		22.50	
146	A9 2.25fr dark bl ('39)	1.25	1.25	
	Never hinged	1.40		
	On cover		50.00	
	On cover, single franking		92.50	
147	A9 2.50fr rose red ('40)	1.75	1.40	
	Never hinged	1.90		
	On cover		27.50	
	On cover, single franking		50.00	
148	A9 3fr green	.95	.60	
	Never hinged	1.00		
	On cover		30.00	
	On cover, single franking		55.00	
149	A9 5fr chocolate	1.00	.65	
	Never hinged	1.05		
	On cover		37.50	
	On cover, single franking		67.50	
150	A9 10fr violet	1.50	1.00	
	Never hinged	1.60		
	On cover		42.50	
	On cover, single franking		80.00	

151	A9 20fr copper red	2.75	1.80	
	Never hinged	2.75		
	On cover		55.00	
	On cover, single franking		92.50	
	Nos. 112-151 (41)	46.55	32.85	

Stamps of types A7-A9 without "RF" were issued in 1944 and are listed Nos.166A-166D in Vol. 3 of the *Scott Standard Postage Stamp Catalogue.*
For surcharges see Nos. B8-B11 in the same volume.

Paris International Exposition Issue
Common Design Types

1937 Perf. 13

152	CD74 20c deep violet	2.00	2.00	
	Never hinged	3.00		
	On cover		95.00	
153	CD75 30c dark green	2.00	2.00	
	Never hinged	3.00		
	On cover		80.00	
154	CD76 40c carmine rose	2.00	2.00	
	Never hinged	3.00		
	On cover		62.50	
155	CD77 50c dk brn & bl	1.60	1.60	
	Never hinged	2.75		
	On cover		55.00	
156	CD78 90c red	1.60	1.60	
	Never hinged	2.75		
	On cover		100.00	
	On cover, single franking		190.00	
157	CD79 1.50fr ultra	2.00	2.00	
	Never hinged	3.00		
	On cover		87.50	
	On cover, single franking		165.00	
	Nos. 152-157 (6)	11.20	11.20	

Colonial Arts Exhibition Issue
Souvenir Sheet
Common Design Type

1937 Imperf.

158	CD76 3fr sepia	8.75	10.00	
	Never hinged	13.50		
	On cover		125.00	
	On cover, single franking		190.00	

Louis Gustave Binger A10

1937 Perf. 13

159	A10 65c red brown	.65	.65	
	Never hinged	.85		
	On cover		6.75	

Death of Governor General Binger; 50th anniv. of his exploration of the Niger.

Caillie Issue
Common Design Type

1939 Engr. Perf. 12½x12

160	CD81 90c org brn & org	.80	.80	
	Never hinged	1.10		
	On cover		6.25	
161	CD81 2fr bright violet	1.20	1.20	
	Never hinged	1.50		
	On cover		22.50	
	On cover, single franking		45.00	
162	CD81 2.25fr ultra & dk bl	1.20	1.20	
	Never hinged	1.50		
	On cover		22.50	
	On cover, single franking		45.00	
	Nos. 160-162 (3)	3.20	3.20	

New York World's Fair Issue
Common Design Type

1939

163	CD82 1.25fr carmine lake	1.50	1.50	
	Never hinged	2.00		
	On cover		67.50	
	On cover, single franking		140.00	
164	CD82 2.25fr ultramarine	1.50	1.50	
	Never hinged	2.00		
	On cover		67.50	
	On cover, single franking		125.00	

SEMI-POSTAL STAMPS

No. 47 Surcharged in Red

1915 Unwmk. Perf. 14x13½

B1	A5 10c + 5c	1.60	1.60	
	Never hinged	2.40		
	On cover		37.50	
a.	Double surcharge	80.00	80.00	

	Never hinged	125.00		
b.	Chalky paper (on #47a)	1.75	1.75	
	Never hinged	2.75		

Issued on ordinary and chalky paper.

Curie Issue
Common Design Type

1938 Perf. 13

B2	CD80 1.75fr + 50c brt ultra	11.00	9.50	
	Never hinged	19.00		
	On cover		95.00	
	On cover, single franking		165.00	

French Revolution Issue
Common Design Type

1939 Photo.
Name and Value Typo. in Black

B3	CD83 45c + 25c grn	8.75	8.75	
	Never hinged	14.00		
	On cover		140.00	
B4	CD83 70c + 30c brn	8.75	8.75	
	Never hinged	14.00		
	On cover		100.00	
B5	CD83 90c + 35c red org	8.75	8.75	
	Never hinged	14.00		
	On cover		87.50	
B6	CD83 1.25fr + 1fr rose pink	8.75	8.75	
	Never hinged	14.00		
	On cover, single franking		225.00	
B7	CD83 2.25fr + 2fr blue	8.75	8.75	
	Never hinged	17.50		
	On cover		140.00	
	On cover, single franking		200.00	
	Nos. B3-B7 (5)	43.75	43.75	

AIR POST STAMPS

Common Design Type

1940 Unwmk. Engr. Perf. 12½x12

C1	CD85 1.90fr ultramarine	.40	.40	
	Never hinged	.55		
	On cover		35.00	
C2	CD85 2.90fr dark red	.40	.40	
	Never hinged	.55		
	On cover		35.00	
C3	CD85 4.50fr dk gray grn	.75	.75	
	Never hinged	1.00		
	On cover		40.00	
C4	CD85 4.90fr yel bister	1.00	1.00	
	Never hinged	1.20		
	On cover		45.00	
C5	CD85 6.90fr deep orange	1.50	1.50	
	Never hinged	1.90		
	On cover		62.50	
	Nos. C1-C5 (5)	4.05	4.05	

POSTAGE DUE STAMPS

Natives — D1   D2

Perf. 14x13½

1906-07 Unwmk. Typo.

J1	D1 5c grn, *greenish*	4.00	4.00	
	Never hinged	7.25		
	On cover		95.00	
J2	D1 10c red brown	4.00	4.00	
	Never hinged	7.25		
	On cover		87.50	
J3	D1 15c dark blue	6.50	6.50	
	Never hinged	13.50		
	On cover		100.00	
J4	D1 20c blk, *yellow*	9.50	9.50	
	Never hinged	20.00		
	On cover		105.00	
J5	D1 30c red, *straw*	9.50	9.50	
	Never hinged	20.00		
	On cover		110.00	
J6	D1 50c violet	7.25	7.25	
	Never hinged	14.50		
	On cover		80.00	
J7	D1 60c black, *buff*	32.50	32.50	
	Never hinged	67.50		
	On cover		160.00	
J8	D1 1fr blk, *pinkish*	35.00	35.00	
	Never hinged	75.00		
	On cover		190.00	
	Nos. J1-J8 (8)	108.25	108.25	

1914

J9	D2 5c green	.25	.25	
	Never hinged	.40		
	On cover		50.00	
J10	D2 10c rose	.30	.30	
	Never hinged	.55		
	On cover		50.00	
J11	D2 15c gray	.30	.30	
	Never hinged	.55		
	On cover		50.00	
J12	D2 20c brown	.55	.55	
	Never hinged	.80		
	On cover		55.00	

J13	D2	30c blue	.55	.55
		Never hinged	.80	
		On cover		55.00
J14	D2	50c black	.90	.90
		Never hinged	1.20	
		On cover		62.50
J15	D2	60c orange	1.25	1.25
		Never hinged	1.60	
		On cover		|||||
J16	D2	1fr violet	1.50	1.50
		Never hinged	2.10	
		On cover		80.00
		Nos. J9-J16 (8)	5.60	5.60

Type of 1914 Issue
Surcharged

1927

J17	D2	2fr on 1fr lilac rose	2.75	2.75
		Never hinged	3.75	
		On cover		95.00
J18	D2	3fr on 1fr org brown	2.75	2.75
		Never hinged	3.75	
		On cover		100.00

PARCEL POST STAMPS

Postage Due Stamps of French Colonies Overprinted

Overprinted In Black

1903   Unwmk.   *Imperf.*

Q1	D1	50c lilac	42.50	40.00
		Never hinged	60.00	
Q2	D1	1fr rose, *buff*	42.50	40.00
		Never hinged	60.00	

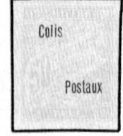

Overprinted In Black

Q3	D1	50c lilac	3,300.	3,400.
Q4	D1	1fr rose, *buff*	3,300.	3,400.

Accents on "O" of "COTE"

Nos. Q7-Q8, Q11-Q12, Q15, Q17-Q18, Q21-Q22, Q24-Q25 exist with or without accent.

Overprinted In Red and Black

Red Overprint

Q5	D1	50c lilac	120.00	120.00
		Never hinged	160.00	
a.		Inverted overprint	425.00	425.00

Blue Black Overprint

Q6	D1	1fr rose, *buff*	87.50	87.50
		Never hinged	100.00	
a.		Inverted overprint	350.00	350.00

Surcharged in Black

a   b

c   d

e   f

g   h

1903

Q7	D1	50c on 15c pale grn	16.00	16.00
		Never hinged	24.00	
a.		Inverted surcharge	225.00	225.00
Q8	D1	50c on 60c brn, *buff*	35.00	35.00
		Never hinged	52.50	
a.		Inverted surcharge	225.00	225.00
Q9	(a)	1fr on 5c blue	4,400.	3,600.
Q10	(b)	1fr on 5c blue	4,400.	2,800.
Q11	(c)	1fr on 5c blue	18.00	16.00
		Never hinged	25.00	
a.		Inverted surcharge	950.00	950.00
Q12	(c)	1fr on 5c blue	27.50	24.00
		Never hinged	45.00	
Q13	(e)	1fr on 5c blue	4,800.	4,000.
Q14	(f)	1fr on 5c blue	12,000.	9,500.
Q15	(g)	1fr on 5c blue	110.00	110.00
		Never hinged	150.00	
Q16	(h)	1fr on 5c blue	3,750.	3,850.
Q17	(c)	1fr on 10c gray brn	27.50	24.00
		Never hinged	32.50	
a.		Inverted surcharge	325.00	325.00
Q18	(d)	1fr on 10c gray brn	47.50	45.00
		Never hinged	72.50	
a.		Inverted surcharge	475.00	475.00
Q19	(g)	1fr on 10c gray brn	4,000.	3,850.
Q20	(h)	1fr on 10c gray brn	46,000.	

Some authorities regard Nos. Q9 and Q10 as essays. A sub-type of type "a" has smaller, bold "XX" without serifs.

Surcharged in Black

j   k

l

Q21	(j)	4fr on 60c brn, *buff*	140.00	140.00
		Never hinged	175.00	
a.		Double surcharge		5,600.
Q22	(k)	4fr on 60c brn, *buff*	375.00	375.00
		Never hinged	525.00	
Q23	(l)	4fr on 60c brn, *buff*	1,200.	1,000.

Surcharged in Black

Q24	D1	4fr on 15c green	130.00	130.00
		Never hinged	175.00	
a.		One large star	525.00	525.00
b.		Two large stars	300.00	300.00
Q25	D1	4fr on 30c rose	130.00	130.00
		Never hinged	175.00	
a.		One large star	525.00	525.00
b.		Two large stars	300.00	300.00

Overprinted in Black

1904

Q26	D1	50c lilac	45.00	45.00
		Never hinged	50.00	
a.		Inverted overprint		
Q27	D1	1fr rose, *buff*	45.00	45.00
		Never hinged	50.00	
a.		Inverted overprint		

Overprinted in Black

Q28	D1	50c lilac	42.50	42.50
		Never hinged	50.00	
a.		Inverted overprint	225.00	225.00
Q29	D1	1fr rose, *buff*	42.50	42.50
		Never hinged	50.00	
a.		Inverted overprint	225.00	225.00

Surcharged in Black

Q30	D1	4fr on 5c blue	240.00	240.00
		Never hinged	310.00	
Q31	D1	8fr on 15c green	240.00	240.00
		Never hinged	310.00	

Overprinted in Black

1905

Q32	D1	50c lilac	92.50	92.50
		Never hinged	125.00	
Q33	D1	1fr rose, *buff*	92.50	92.50
		Never hinged	125.00	

Surcharged in Black

Q34	D1	2fr on 1fr rose, *buff*	240.00	240.00
		Never hinged	350.00	
Q35	D1	4fr on 1fr rose, *buff*	240.00	240.00
		Never hinged	350.00	
a.		Italic "4"	2,200.	2,200.
Q36	D1	8fr on 1fr rose, *buff*	700.00	700.00

JAMAICA

jə-'mā-kə

LOCATION — Caribbean Sea, about 90 miles south of Cuba
GOVT. — Independent state in the British Commonwealth
AREA — 4,411 sq. mi.
POP. — 2,230,000 (est. 1982)
CAPITAL — Kingston

Jamaica administered two dependencies: Cayman Islands and Turks and Caicos Islands.

12 Pence = 1 Shilling
20 Shillings = 1 Pound

Catalogue values for unused stamps in this country are for Never Hinged items, beginning with Scott 129 in the regular postage section.

Watermark

Wmk. 45 — Pineapple

STAMPS OF GREAT BRITAIN USED IN JAMAICA

For information on these cancels, see the Crowned Circle Handstamps and Great Britain Used Abroad section.

A01 (Kingston)

Type A Cancel

Short letter and numbers.

1858-60

A1	A	1p rose red, perf. 16 (#18)	700.00
A2	A	1p rose red, perf. 14 (#20)	95.00
A3	A	4p rose (#26)	75.00
A4	A	6p lilac (#27)	75.00
A5	A	1sh green (#28)	375.00

See note after No. A13.

Duplex cancel

Tall letter and numbers.

1859-60

A6		1p rose red (#20)	350.00
A7		4p rose (#26)	77.50
A8		6p lilac (#27)	77.50
A9		1sh green (#28)	750.00

Double Numeral cancel

As type A but bolder letter and numbers.

A10		1p rose red (#20)	450.00
A11		4p rose (#26)	325.00
a.		Thick glazed paper (#26b)	600.00
A12		6p lilac (#27)	325.00
A13		1sh green (#28)	

Single examples of Nos. A10-A12 can be difficult to distinguish from Nos. A2-A4.

A27 (Alexandria)

A14	A	1p rose red (#20)	950.00
A15	A	2p blue (#21)	1,600.
A16	A	4p rose (#26)	375.00
A17	A	6p lilac (#27)	700.00

A28 (Anotto Bay)

A18	A	1p rose red (#20)	500.00
A19	A	4p rose (#26)	200.00
A20	A	6p lilac (#27)	425.00

A29 (Bath)

A21	A	1p rose red (#20)	300.00
A22	A	4p rose (#26)	200.00
A23	A	6p lilac (#27)	600.00

A30 (Black River)

A24	A	1p rose red (#20)	300.00
A25	A	4p rose (#26)	150.00
A26	A	6p lilac (#27)	275.00

A31 (Brown's Town)

A27	A	1p rose red (#20)	425.00
A28	A	4p rose (#26)	375.00
A29	A	6p lilac (#27)	375.00

A32 (Buff Bay)
A30	A	1p rose red (#20)	350.00
A31	A	4p rose (#26)	275.00
A32	A	6p lilac (#27)	275.00

A33 (Chapelton)
A33	A	1p rose red (#20)	375.00
A34	A	4p rose (#26)	250.00
A35	A	6p lilac (#27)	350.00

A34 (Claremont)
A36	A	1p rose red (#20)	600.00
A37	A	4p rose (#26)	300.00
A38	A	6p lilac (#27)	350.00

A35 (Clarendon)
A39	A	1p rose red (#20)	475.00
A40	A	4p rose (#26)	300.00
A41	A	6p lilac (#27)	375.00

A36 (Dry Harbour)
A42	A	1p rose red (#20)	700.00
A43	A	4p rose (#26)	475.00
A44	A	6p lilac (#27)	425.00

A37 (Duncans)
A45	A	1p rose red (#20)	800.00
A46	A	4p rose (#26)	650.00
A47	A	6p lilac (#27)	450.00

A39 (Falmouth)
A48	A	1p rose red (#20)	200.00
A49	A	4p rose (#26)	120.00
A50	A	6p lilac (#27)	140.00
A51	A	1sh green (#28)	1,300.

A40 (Flint River)
A52	A	1p rose red (#20)	400.00
A53	A	4p rose (#26)	275.00
A54	A	6p lilac (#27)	325.00
A55	A	1sh green (#28)	1,300.

A41 (Gayle)
A56	A	1p rose red (#20)	750.00
A57	A	4p rose (#26)	225.00
A58	A	6p lilac (#27)	275.00
A59	A	1sh green (#28)	850.00

A42 (Golden Spring)
A60	A	1p rose red (#20)	500.00
A61	A	4p rose (#26)	375.00
A62	A	6p lilac (#27)	650.00
A63	A	1sh green (#28)	1,200.

A43 (Gordon Town)
A64	A	1p rose red (#20)	—
A65	A	4p rose (#26)	—
A66	A	6p lilac (#27)	750.00

A44 (Goshen)
A67	A	1p rose red (#20)	275.00
A68	A	4p rose (#26)	250.00
A69	A	6p lilac (#27)	130.00

A45 (Grange Hill)
A70	A	1p rose red (#20)	375.00
A71	A	4p rose (#26)	120.00
A72	A	6p lilac (#27)	150.00
A73	A	1sh green (#28)	1,200.

A46 (Green Island)
A74	A	1p rose red (#20)	500.00
A77	A	4p rose (#26)	300.00
A76	A	6p lilac (#27)	425.00
A77	A	1sh green (#28)	1,200.

A47 (Highgate)
A78	A	1p rose red (#20)	325.00
A79	A	4p rose (#26)	225.00
A80	A	6p lilac (#27)	400.00

A48 (Hope Bay)
A81	A	1p rose red (#20)	700.00
A82	A	4p rose (#26)	325.00
A83	A	6p lilac (#27)	700.00

A49 (Lilliput)
A84	A	1p rose red (#20)	300.00
A85	A	4p rose (#26)	325.00
A86	A	6p lilac (#27)	175.00

A51 (Lucea)
A87	A	1p rose red (#20)	475.00
A88	A	4p rose (#26)	140.00
A89	A	6p lilac (#27)	325.00

A52 (Manchioneal)
A90	A	1p rose red (#20)	550.00
A91	A	4p rose (#26)	325.00
A92	A	6p lilac (#27)	550.00

A53 (Mandeville)
A93	A	1p rose red (#20)	325.00
A94	A	4p rose (#26)	130.00
A95	A	6p lilac (#27)	275.00

A54 (May Hill)
A96	A	1p rose red (#20)	200.00
A97	A	4p rose (#26)	180.00
A98	A	6p lilac (#27)	130.00
A98A	A	1sh green (#28)	1,600.

A55 (Mile Gulley)
A99	A	1p rose red (#20)	450.00
A100	A	4p rose (#26)	375.00
A101	A	6p lilac (#27)	375.00

A56 (Moneague)
A102	A	1p rose red (#20)	400.00
A103	A	4p rose (#26)	375.00
A104	A	6p lilac (#27)	700.00

A57 (Montego Bay)
A105	A	1p rose red (#20)	325.00
A106	A	4p rose (#26)	100.00
A107	A	6p lilac (#27)	120.00
A108	A	1sh green (#28)	1,100.

A58 (Montpelier)
A109	A	1p rose red (#20)	—
A110	A	4p rose (#26)	—
A111	A	6p lilac (#27)	1,100.

A59 (Morant Bay)
A112	A	1p rose red (#20)	550.00
A113	A	4p rose (#26)	130.00
A114	A	6p lilac (#27)	150.00

A60 (Ocho Rios)
A115	A	1p rose red (#20)	1,100.
A116	A	4p rose (#26)	180.00
A117	A	6p lilac (#27)	375.00

A61 (Old Harbour)
A118	A	1p rose red (#20)	325.00
A119	A	4p rose (#26)	225.00
A120	A	6p lilac (#27)	275.00

A62 (Plantain Garden River)
A121	A	1p rose red (#20)	275.00
A122	A	4p rose (#26)	180.00
A123	A	6p lilac (#27)	275.00

A64 (Port Antonio)
A124	A	1p rose red (#20)	600.00
A125	A	4p rose (#26)	400.00
A126	A	6p lilac (#27)	425.00

A65 (Port Morant)
A127	A	1p rose red (#20)	425.00
A128	A	4p rose (#26)	190.00
A129	A	6p lilac (#27)	375.00

A66 (Port Maria)
A130	A	1p rose red (#20)	350.00
A131	A	4p rose (#26)	140.00
A132	A	6p lilac (#27)	400.00

A67 (Port Royal)
A133	A	1p rose red (#20)	550.00
A134	A	2p blue (#27, P9)	2,750.
A135	A	4p rose (#26)	600.00
A136	A	6p lilac (#27)	550.00

A68 (Porus)
A137	A	1p rose red (#20)	350.00
A138	A	4p rose (#26)	160.00
A139	A	6p lilac (#27)	500.00

A69 (Ramble)
A140	A	1p rose red (#20)	350.00
A141	A	4p rose (#26)	300.00
a.		Thick glazed paper (#26b)	600.00
A142	A	6p lilac (#27)	425.00

A70 (Rio Bueno)
A143	A	1p rose red (#20)	400.00
A144	A	4p rose (#26)	300.00
A145	A	6p lilac (#27)	200.00

A71 (Rodney Hall)
A146	A	1p rose red (#20)	300.00
A147	A	4p rose (#26)	190.00
A148	A	6p lilac (#27)	225.00

A72 (St. David's)
A149	A	1p rose red (#20)	375.00
A150	A	4p rose (#26)	500.00
A151	A	6p lilac (#27)	—

A73 (St. Ann's Bay)
A152	A	1p rose red (#20)	325.00
A153	A	4p rose (#26)	170.00
A154	A	6p lilac (#27)	275.00
A154A	A	1sh green (#28)	1,500.

A74 (Salt Gut)
A155	A	1p rose red (#20)	400.00
A156	A	4p rose (#26)	250.00
A157	A	6p lilac (#27)	350.00

A75 (Savannah-la-Mar)
A158	A	1p rose red (#20)	180.00
A159	A	4p rose (#26)	120.00
A160	A	6p lilac (#27)	275.00
A161	A	1sh green (#28)	1,100.

A76 (Spanish Town)
A162	A	1p rose red (#20)	190.00
A163	A	4p rose (#26)	110.00
A164	A	6p lilac (#27)	180.00
A165	A	1sh green (#28)	900.00

A77 (Stewart Town)
A166	A	1p rose red (#20)	600.00
A167	A	4p rose (#26)	450.00
A168	A	6p lilac (#27)	325.00

A78 (Vere)
A169	A	1p rose red (#20)	450.00
A170	A	4p rose (#26)	175.00
A171	A	6p lilac (#27)	120.00
A172	A	1sh green (#28)	1,300.

Cancels A38 (Ewarton) and A50 (Little River) were received after the post offices were closed. The numbers were reallocated in 1862 to Falmouth and Malvern, respectively. Cancel A63 (Pear Tree Grove) has not been found canceling stamps of Great Britain, even though its allocation is well documented.

Issued under British Administration

Values for unused stamps are for examples with original gum as defined in the catalogue introduction. Very fine examples of Nos. 1-12 will have perforations touching the design on at least one side due to the narrow spacing of the stamps on the plates. Stamps with perfs clear on all four sides are scarce and will command higher prices.

Queen Victoria

A1   A2

A3   A4

A5   A6

1860-63   Typo.   Wmk. 45   Perf. 14
1	A1	1p blue	72.50	16.00
a.		Diagonal half used as ½p on cover		825.00
b.		1p deep blue	145.00	37.50
c.		1p pale blue	77.50	22.50
d.		1p pale greenish blue	100.00	24.00
2	A2	2p rose	250.00	65.00
a.		2p deep rose	175.00	65.00
3	A3	3p green ('63)	170.00	32.50
4	A4	4p brown org	275.00	62.50
a.		4p orange	250.00	28.00
5	A5	6p lilac	240.00	28.00
a.		6p deep lilac	1,050.	65.00
b.		6p gray lilac	350.00	40.00
6	A6	1sh brown	230.00	35.00
a.		1sh lilac brown	700.00	30.00
b.		1sh yellow brown	575.00	32.50

All except No. 3 exist imperforate.

1870-71   Wmk. 1
7	A1	1p blue	105.00	.90
a.		1p deep blue	85.00	1.75
8	A2	2p rose	110.00	.85
a.		2p brownish rose	120.00	1.10
9	A3	3p green	155.00	9.25
10	A4	4p brown org ('72)	325.00	13.50
a.		4p red orange	450.00	6.50
11	A5	6p lilac ('71)	100.00	6.75
12	A6	1sh brown ('73)	27.50	9.50
		Nos. 7-12 (6)	822.50	40.75

The 1p and 4p exist imperf.
See Nos. 17-23, 40, 43, 47-53.

A7

1872, Oct. 29
13	A7	½p claret	21.00	4.00
a.		½p deep claret	26.50	6.00

Exists imperf. See No. 16.

A8   A9

1875, Aug. 27   Perf. 12½
14	A8	2sh red brown	50.00	30.00
15	A9	5sh violet	135.00	175.00

Exist imperf.
See Nos. 29-30, 44, 54.

1883-90   Wmk. 2   Perf. 14
16	A7	½p blue green ('85)	9.00	1.75
a.		½p gray green	2.75	.25
17	A1	1p blue ('84)	350.00	7.75
18	A1	1p carmine ('85)	72.50	.75
a.		1p rose	87.50	2.25
19	A2	2p rose ('84)	240.00	5.25
20	A2	2p slate ('85)	110.00	.70
a.		2p green	160.00	9.00
21	A3	3p ol green ('86)	2.75	2.25
a.		3p sage green ('86)	4.00	1.00
22	A4	4p red brown	2.25	.40
a.		4p orange brown	450.00	25.00
23	A5	6p orange yel ('90)	6.00	5.00
a.		6p yellow	40.00	8.75
		Nos. 16-23 (8)	792.50	23.85

Nos. 18 and 20 exist imperf. Perf. 12 stamps are considered to be proofs.
For surcharge, see No. 27.

Nos. 16-26, O1-O4 used in Cayman Islands.
See Cayman Islands for stamps with Grand Cayman and Cayman Brac cancellations.

A10

1889-91
24	A10	1p lilac & red vio	10.00	.25
25	A10	2p deep green	22.50	8.00
a.		2p green	37.50	9.50
26	A10	2½p lilac & ultra ('91)	8.75	.75
		Nos. 24-26 (3)	41.25	9.00

Unused examples of No. 25 may be distinguished from No. 25a by their brown gum.

No. 22 Surcharged in Black

TWO PENCE
HALF-PENNY

1890, June
27	A4	2½p on 4p red brn	40.00	17.50
a.		1.5mm btw lines of surcharge	45.00	20.00
b.		Double surcharge	350.00	250.00
d.		"PFNNY"	100.00	70.00
f.		As "d," double surcharge	—	

Three settings of surcharge.

1897
28	A6	1sh brown	9.50	6.50
29	A8	2sh red brown	32.50	30.00
30	A9	5sh violet	70.00	100.00
		Nos. 28-30 (3)	112.00	136.50

The 2sh exists imperf.

Llandovery
Falls — A12

1900, May 1   Engr.   Wmk. 1
31	A12	1p red	11.50	.25

1901, Sept. 25
32	A12	1p red & black	9.50	.25
a.		Pair, imperf. horiz.	22,000.	
b.		Bluish paper	120.00	110.00

Arms of Jamaica — A13

1903-04   Typo.   Wmk. 2
33	A13	½p green & black	1.75	.40
b.		"SERv ET" for "SERVIET"	45.00	50.00
34	A13	1p car & black ('04)	4.50	.25
b.		"SERv ET" for "SERVIET"	35.00	40.00
35	A13	2½p ultra & black	8.25	.45
a.		"SERv ET" for "SERVIET"	72.50	85.00

36	A13	5p yel & black ('04)	17.50	26.00
a.		"SERv ET" for "SERVIET"	875.00	1,100.
		Nos. 33-36 (4)	32.00	27.10
		Set, overprinted "SPECI-MEN"	90.00	

1905-11 Chalky Paper Wmk. 3

37	A13	½p green & black	5.00	.25
b.		"SERv ET" for "SERVIET"	32.50	45.00
38	A13	1p car & black	20.00	2.00
39	A13	2½p ultra & blk ('07)	3.75	6.25
39A	A3	3p vio, *yel* ('10)	2.25	1.60
40	A4	4p black, *yel* ('10)	14.00	60.00
		Overprinted "SPECI-MEN"	50.00	
41	A13	5p yel & black ('07)	70.00	80.00
a.		"SERv ET" for "SERVIET"	1,400.	1,600.
42	A13	6p red vio & vio ('11)	15.50	19.00
		Overprinted "SPECI-MEN"	50.00	
42A	A5	6p purple ('10)	11.50	30.00
43	A6	1sh black, *green* ('10)	10.00	10.00
		Overprinted "SPECI-MEN"	50.00	
44	A8	2sh vio, *blue* ('10)	12.00	6.50
		Overprinted "SPECI-MEN"	50.00	
45	A13	5sh vio & black ('10)	55.00	55.00
		Overprinted "SPECI-MEN"	40.00	
		Nos. 37-45 (11)	219.00	270.60

1905-11 Ordinary Paper

46	A13	2½p ultra ('10)	5.00	1.40
a.		2½p deep ultramarine	2.75	1.90
		Overprinted "SPECIMEN"	50.00	
47	A3	3p sage green ('07)	7.00	3.25
a.		3p olive green ('05)	9.50	4.50
48	A3	3p pale purple, *yel* ('10)	8.00	3.75
		Overprinted "SPECIMEN"	50.00	
49	A4	4p red brn ('08)	77.50	80.00
50	A4	4p red, *yel* ('11)	1.75	8.50
		Overprinted "SPECIMEN"	45.00	
51	A5	6p dull vio ('09)	30.00	45.00
		Overprinted "SPECIMEN"	45.00	
52	A5	6p org yel ('09)	35.00	57.50
a.		6p orange ('06)	17.00	27.50
53	A6	1sh brown ('06)	25.00	45.00
a.		1sh deep brown	32.50	55.00
54	A8	2sh red brn ('08)	125.00	170.00
		Nos. 46-54 (9)	314.25	436.90

 A14

 A15

1906

58	A14	½p green	4.00	.25
a.		Booklet pane of 6	—	
b.		½p yellow green	10.00	.55
		Overprinted "SPECIMEN"	37.50	
c.		½p deep green	5.00	.25
59	A15	1p carmine	1.60	.25
		Overprinted "SPECIMEN"	47.50	

For overprints see Nos. MR1, MR4, MR7, MR10.

 Edward VII — A16

1911, Feb. 3

60	A16	2p gray	7.00	15.00
		Overprinted "SPECIMEN"	52.50	

 George V — A17

1912-20

61	A17	1p scarlet ('16)	7.50	.80
a.		1p carmine ('12)	1.75	.25
b.		Booklet pane of 6	—	
62	A17	1½p brown org ('16)	1.25	.70
a.		1½p yellow orange	17.00	1.25
63	A17	2p gray	2.25	2.00
a.		2p slate gray	2.50	3.00

64	A17	2½p dp br blue	.75	1.25
a.		2½p ultra ('13)	1.75	.25

Chalky Paper

65	A17	3p violet, *yel*	.60	.50
a.		3p violet, *lemon* ('16)	4.25	1.75
66	A17	4p scar & blk, *yel* ('10)	.60	4.00
a.		4p scar & blk, *lemon* ('16)	26.00	21.00
b.		4p scar & blk, *pale yel* ('19)	24.00	17.00
67	A17	6p red vio & dl vio	2.00	2.00
a.		6p dull purple & bright purple ('12)	4.50	10.50
b.		6p dull purple & bright magenta ('20)	5.25	2.50
68	A17	1sh black, *green*	2.60	2.25
a.		1sh blk, *bl grn*, olive back ('20)	2.60	7.75
69	A17	2sh ultra & vio, *blue* ('19)	22.50	32.50
70	A17	5sh scarlet & green, *yel* ('19)	82.50	105.00
a.		5sh scarlet & green, pale yellow ('20)	95.00	115.00
b.		5sh scarlet & green, orange buff ('20)	160.00	200.00

Surface-colored Paper

71	A17	3p violet, *yel* ('13)	.65	.45
72	A17	4p scar & black, *yel* ('14)	1.50	4.50
73	A17	1sh black, *green* ('15)	2.75	5.50
		Nos. 61-73 (13)	127.45	161.45

See Nos. 101-102. For overprints see Nos. MR2-MR3, MR5-MR6, MR8-MR9, MR11.

Exhibition Buildings of 1891 — A18

Arawak Woman Preparing Cassava — A19

World War I Contingent Embarking for Overseas Duty — A20

King's House, Spanish Town — A21

Return of Overseas Contingent, 1919 — A22

Columbus Landing in Jamaica — A23

Cathedral in Spanish Town — A24

Statue of Queen Victoria — A26

Memorial to Admiral Rodney — A27

Monument to Sir Charles Metcalfe — A28

Woodland Scene — A29

King George V — A30

1919-21 Typo. Wmk. 3 Perf. 14

Chalky Paper

75	A18	½p ol grn & dk grn ('20)	1.10	1.10
76	A19	1p org & car ('21)	2.00	1.90

Engr.

Ordinary Paper

77	A20	1½p green	.45	1.10
78	A21	2p grn & bl ('21)	1.25	4.50
79	A22	2½p blue-black & blue	1.50	1.75
a.		2½p blue & dark blue ('21)	15.00	3.50
80	A23	3p blue & grn ('21)	4.50	2.75
81	A24	4p green & dk brown ('21)	2.75	10.00
83	A26	1sh brt org & org ('20)	4.25	5.75
a.		Frame inverted	37,500.	25,000.
		As "a," revenue cancel		2,500.
84	A27	2sh brn & bl ('20)	12.50	30.00
85	A28	3sh org & violet ('20)	24.00	120.00
86	A29	5sh ocher & blue ('21)	55.00	82.50
87	A30	10sh dk myrtle grn ('20)	85.00	160.00
		Nos. 75-87 (12)	194.30	421.35

See note after No. 100. Watermark varieties exist and sell for much higher values.

A 6p stamp depicting the abolition of slavery was sent to the Colony but was not issued. "Specimen" examples exist with wmk. 3 or 4. Value $750 each.

Without "Specimen," values: wmk. 3, $52,500; wmk. 4, $32,500.

Port Royal in 1853 A31

1921-23 Typo. Wmk. 4 Perf. 14

Chalky Paper

88	A18	½p ol grn & dk grn ('22)	.60	.60
a.		Booklet pane of 4		
89	A19	1p orange & car ('22)	1.75	.25
a.		Booklet pane of 6		

Engr.

Ordinary Paper

90	A20	1½p green	2.50	.55
91	A21	2p grn & blue	7.50	.90
92	A22	2½p bl & dk bl	6.50	2.00
93	A23	3p bl & grn ('22)	2.75	.80
94	A24	4p grn & dk brn	1.25	.35
95	A31	6p bl & blk ('22)	15.00	2.25
96	A26	1sh brn org & dl org		.90
97	A27	2sh brn & bl ('22)	3.75	.75
98	A28	3sh org & violet	17.50	11.00
99	A29	5sh ocher & bl ('23)	35.00	29.00
a.		5sh orange & blue	75.00	80.00

100	A30	10sh dk myrtle green ('22)	60.00	80.00
		Nos. 88-100 (13)	156.10	129.35
		Set, never hinged	375.00	

... all differ from No. 76 in having the words "Postage and Revenue" at the bottom. On No. 79 the horizontal bar of the flag at the left has a broad white line below the colored line. On No. 92 this has been corrected and the broad white line placed above the colored line.

Watermark is sideways on Nos. 76-77, 87, 89-90.

Type of 1912-19 Issue

1921-27 Typo. Wmk. 4

101	A17	½p green ('27)	3.00	.25
a.		Booklet pane of 6		
102	A17	6p red vio & dl vio	16.00	4.50

No. 102 is on chalky paper.

A32

Type I

Type II

Type II — Cross shading beneath "Jamaica."

1929-32 Engr. Perf. 13½x14, 14

103	A32	1p red, type I	13.00	.25
a.		1p red, type II ('32)	13.00	.25
b.		Booklet pane of 6, type II		
104	A32	1½p brown	7.50	.25
105	A32	9p violet brown	7.50	1.25
		Nos. 103-105 (3)	28.00	1.75
		Set, never hinged	35.00	

The frames on Nos. 103 to 105 differ.

Coco Palms at Columbus Cove — A33

Scene near Castleton, St. Andrew — A34

Priestman's River, Portland Parish — A35

1932 Perf. 12½

106	A33	2p grn & gray blk	32.50	3.50
a.		Vertical pair, imperf. between	14,500.	
107	A34	2½p ultra & sl blue	6.50	1.75
a.		Vertical pair, imperf. between	21,000.	21,000.
108	A35	6p red vio & gray black	32.50	4.50
		Nos. 106-108 (3)	71.50	9.75
		Set, never hinged	115.00	

Common Design Types pictured following the introduction.

Silver Jubilee Issue

Common Design Type

1935, May 6 Perf. 11x12

109	CD301	1p car & blue	.55	.25
a.		Booklet pane of 6	175.00	
110	CD301	1½p black & ultra	.75	1.75
111	CD301	6p indigo & grn	12.00	20.00
112	CD301	1sh brn vio & ind	8.50	13.00
		Nos. 109-112 (4)	21.80	35.00
		Set, never hinged	32.50	

Coronation Issue
Common Design Type

1937, May 12   **Perf. 13½x14**

113	CD302	1p carmine	.25	.25
114	CD302	1½p gray black	.40	.30
115	CD302	2½p bright ultra	.70	.70
		Nos. 113-115 (3)	1.35	1.25
		Set, never hinged	2.25	

King George
VI — A36

Coco Palms at
Columbus
Cove — A37

Scene near
Castleton, St.
Andrew — A38

Bananas
A39

Citrus
Grove
A40

Priestman's
River, Portland
Parish — A41

Kingston
Harbor
A42

Sugar
Industry
A43

Bamboo
Walk — A44

Woodland
Scene — A45

King George
VI — A46

1938-51   **Perf. 13½x14**

116	A36	½p dk blue grn	1.40	.25
a.		Booklet pane of 6	9.00	
b.		Wmkd. sideways	—	9,000.
117	A36	1p carmine	1.00	.25
a.		Booklet pane of 6	13.00	
118	A36	1½p brown	1.00	.25

Perf. 12½, 13x13½, 13½x13, 12½x13

119	A37	2p grn & gray blk, perf. 12½	1.00	1.00
a.		Perf. 13x13½ ('39)	2.25	.60
b.		Perf. 12½x13 ('51)	1.00	.25
120	A38	2½p ultra & sl bl	5.00	2.25
121	A39	3p grn & lt ultra	.90	1.75
122	A40	4p grn & yel brn	.65	.25
123	A41	6p red vio & gray blk, perf. 13½x13 ('50)	2.00	.25
a.		Perf. 12½	5.50	.35
b.		As "a," double impression of gray blk	—	
124	A42	9p rose lake	.65	.55
125	A43	1sh dk brn & brt grn	8.00	.25
126	A44	2sh brn & brt bl	22.50	1.25

Perf. 13, 14

127	A45	5sh ocher & bl, perf. 13 ('50)	6.00	4.25
a.		Bluish paper, perf. 13 ('49)	6.00	3.50
b.		Perf. 14	11.50	4.00
128	A46	10sh dk myrtle grn, perf. 14	9.00	10.50
a.		Perf. 13 ('50)	11.50	8.00
		Nos. 116-128 (13)	59.10	23.05
		Set, never hinged	110.00	

See Nos. 140, 148, 149, 152.

> **Catalogue values for unused stamps in this section, from this point to the end of the section, are for Never Hinged items.**

Courthouse,
Falmouth
A47

Kings Charles
II and
George VI
A48

House of
Assembly,
1762-1869
A50

Institute of
Jamaica — A49   Allegory of Labor
and
Learning — A51

Constitution
and Flag of
Jamaica
A52

Perf. 12½

1945, Aug. 20   **Engr.**   **Wmk. 4**

129	A47	1½p brown	.30	.35
a.		Booklet pane of 4	37.50	
b.		Perf. 12½x13½ ('46)	10.00	1.75
130	A48	2p dp grn, perf. 12½x13½	.35	.55
a.		Perf. 12½	14.00	1.10
131	A49	3p bright ultra	.25	.55
a.		Perf. 13 ('46)	3.25	3.25
132	A50	4½p slate black	.60	.35
a.		Perf. 13 ('46)	4.50	4.75

133	A51	2sh chocolate	1.25	.50
134	A52	5sh deep blue	3.50	1.10
135	A49	10sh green	3.00	2.60
		Nos. 129-135 (7)	9.25	6.00

Granting of a new Constitution in 1944.

Peace Issue
Common Design Type

1946, Oct. 14   **Wmk. 4**   **Perf. 13½**

136	CD303	1½p black brown	.30	4.50
a.		Perf. 13½x14	2.75	.25

Perf. 13½x14

137	CD303	3p deep blue	7.00	3.00
a.		Perf. 13½x14	.60	8.00

Silver Wedding Issue
Common Design Types

1948, Dec. 1   **Photo.**   **Perf. 14x14½**

138	CD304	1½p red brown	.35	.25

Engr.; Name Typo.
Perf. 11½x11

139	CD305	£1 red	32.50	75.00

Type of 1938 and

Tobacco
Industry
A53

1949, Aug. 15   **Engr.**   **Perf. 12½**

140	A39	3p ultra & slate blue	4.25	1.25
141	A53	£1 purple & brown	60.00	40.00

UPU Issue
Common Design Types
Perf. 13½, 11x11½

1949, Oct. 10   **Wmk. 4**

142	CD306	1½p red brown	.25	.25
143	CD307	2p dark green	1.40	2.75
144	CD308	3p indigo	.50	1.25
145	CD309	6p rose violet	.55	1.75
		Nos. 142-145 (4)	2.70	6.00

University Issue
Common Design Types

1951, Feb. 16   **Perf. 14x14½**

146	CD310	2p brown & gray blk	.35	.35
147	CD311	6p rose lilac & gray blk	.60	.50

George VI Type of 1938

1951, Oct. 25   **Perf. 13½x14**

148	A36	½p orange	2.75	.35
a.		Booklet pane of 6	16.50	
149	A36	1p blue green	3.50	.25
a.		Booklet pane of 6	22.50	

Boy Scout Emblem
with Map — A54

Map and
Emblem
A55

Perf. 13½x13, 13x13½

1952, Mar. 5   **Typo.**   **Wmk. 4**

150	A54	2p blk, yel grn & blue	.30	.25
151	A55	6p blk, yel grn & dk red	.70	.60

1st Caribbean Boy Scout Jamboree, 1952.

Banana Type of 1938

1952, July 1   **Engr.**   **Perf. 12½**

152	A39	3p rose red & green	4.50	.40

SEMI-POSTAL STAMPS

Native Girl — SP1   Native Boy — SP2

Native Boy and
Girl — SP3

1923, Nov. 1   **Engr.**   **Perf. 12**

B1	SP1	½p green & black	1.00	6.25
B2	SP2	1p car & black	2.50	11.50
B3	SP3	2½p blue & black	17.50	20.00
		Nos. B1-B3 (3)	21.00	37.75
		Set, overprinted "SPECIMEN"	125.00	

Each stamp was sold for ½p over face value. The surtax benefited the Child Saving League of Jamaica.

WAR TAX STAMPS

Regular Issues of 1906-19 Overprinted

1916   **Wmk. 3**   **Perf. 14**

MR1	A14	½p green	.25	.40
a.		Without period	16.00	27.50
b.		Double overprint	140.00	160.00
c.		Inverted overprint	130.00	150.00
d.		As "c," without period	350.00	
MR2	A17	3p violet, yel	2.25	22.00
a.		Without period	32.50	100.00

Surface-colored Paper

MR3	A17	3p violet, yel	27.50	45.00
		Nos. MR1-MR3 (3)	30.00	67.40

Regular Issues of 1906-18 Overprinted

MR4	A14	½p green	.25	.30
a.		Without period	18.00	50.00
b.		Pair, one without ovpt.	5,500.	4,750.
c.		"R" inserted by hand	1,800.	1,500.
d.		"WAR" only	125.00	
MR5	A17	1½p orange	.25	.25
a.		Without period	5.75	8.50
b.		"TAMP"	180.00	190.00
c.		"S" inserted by hand	425.00	
d.		"R" omitted	3,250.	3,000.
e.		"R" inserted by hand	1,500.	1,200.
MR6	A17	3p violet, yel	6.50	1.10
a.		Without period	65.00	70.00
b.		"TAMP"	1,000.	1,000.
c.		"S" inserted by hand	225.00	225.00
d.		Inverted overprint	325.00	175.00
e.		As "a," inverted		
		Nos. MR4-MR6 (3)	7.00	1.65

Regular Issues of 1906-19 Overprinted

1917, Mar.

MR7	A14	½p green	1.75	.35
a.		Without period	16.00	27.00
b.		Overprinted on back instead of face	250.00	
c.		Inverted overprint	24.00	57.50
MR8	A17	1½p orange	.25	.25
a.		Without period	4.00	20.00
b.		Double overprint	92.50	100.00
c.		Inverted overprint	92.50	85.00
d.		As "a," inverted	400.00	

MR9	A17	3p violet, *yel*	2.00	1.60
a.		Without period	25.00	50.00
b.		Vertical overprint	425.00	425.00
c.		Inverted overprint	160.00	
d.		As "a," inverted	450.00	
		Nos. MR7-MR9 (3)	4.00	2.20

There are many minor varieties of Nos. MR1-MR9.

Regular Issues of 1906-19 Overprinted in Red

1919, Oct. 4

MR10	A14	½p green	.25	.25
MR11	A17	3p violet, *yel*	5.25	3.00

OFFICIAL STAMPS

No. 16 Overprinted in Black

Type I — Word 15 to 16mm long.
Type II — Word 17 to 17½mm long.

1890   Wmk. 2   Perf. 14

O1	A7	½p green (II)	18.00	2.25
a.		Type I	42.50	29.00
b.		Inverted overprint (II)	100.00	110.00
c.		Double overprint (II)	100.00	110.00
d.		Dbl. ovpt., one invtd. (II)	550.00	550.00
e.		Dbl. ovpt., one vert. (II)	1,100.	
f.		Double overprint (I)	800.00	
g.		Missing "O"	700.00	
h.		Missing "L"	800.00	800.00
i.		Missing both "I"s	850.00	850.00

Missing "O," "L" or one or both "I's known.

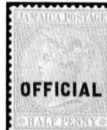

No. 16 and Type of 1889 Overprinted

1890-91

O2	A7	½p green	11.00	1.75
O3	A10	1p carmine rose	8.00	1.50
O4	A10	2p slate	24.00	1.50
		Nos. O2-O4 (3)	43.00	4.75

JAPAN
jə-'pan

LOCATION — North Pacific Ocean, east of China
GOVT. — Constitutional monarchy
AREA — 142,726 sq. mi.
POP. — 120,020,000 (est. 1984)
CAPITAL — Tokyo

1000 Mon = 10 Sen
100 Sen = 1 Yen (or En)
10 Rin = 1 Sen

Watermarks

Wmk. 141 — Zigzag Lines   Wmk. 142 — Parallel Lines

Wmk. 257 — Curved Wavy Lines

Counterfeits of Nos. 1-71 are plentiful. Some are excellent and deceive many collectors.
Nos. 1-54A were printed from plates of 40 with individually engraved subjects. Each stamp in the sheet is slightly different.

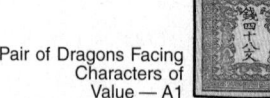
Pair of Dragons Facing Characters of Value — A1

Plate I   Plate II

48 mon:
Plate I — Solid dots in inner border.
Plate II — Tiny circles replace dots.

Plate I

Plate II

100 mon:
Plate I — Lowest dragon claw at upper right and at lower left point upward.
Plate II — Same two claws point downward.

Plate I   Plate II

200 mon:
Plate I — Dot in upper left corner.
Plate II — No dot. (Some Plate I copies show dot faintly; these can be mistaken for Plate II.)

Plate I   Plate II

Plate I   Plate II

Plate I   Plate II

500 mon:
Plate I — Lower right corner of Greek-type border incomplete

Plate II — Short horizontal line completes corner border pattern.

Unwmk.
1871, Apr. 20   Engr.   *Imperf.*
Native Laid Paper Without Gum
Denomination in Black

1	A1	48m brown (I)	260.	260.
a.		48m red brown (I)	375.	375.
b.		Wove paper (I)	300.	300.
c.		48m brown (II)	350.	350.
d.		Wove paper (II)	400.	400.
2	A1	100m blue (I)	260.	260.
a.		Wove paper (I)	350.	350.
b.		Plate II	550.	550.
c.		Wove paper (II)	800.	800.
3	A1	200m vermilion	450.	425.
a.		Wove paper (I)	525.	450.
b.		Plate II	2,500.	2,000.
c.		Wove paper (II)		4,000.
4	A1	500m blue green	650.	650.
a.		500m greenish blue (I)	700.	675.
b.		500m green (I)	2,000.	1,400.
c.		500m yellow green (I)	2,250.	1,500.
d.		Wove paper (I)	750.	650.
e.		500m blue green (II)	775.	4,000.
f.		500m greenish blue (II)	775.	4,000.
g.		Wove paper (II)	2,750.	5,000.
h.		Denomination inverted (I)		175,000.

Perforations, Nos. 5-8
Perforations on Nos. 5-8 generally are rough and irregular due to the perforating equipment used and the quality of the paper. Values are for stamps with rough perfs that touch the frameline on one or more sides.

Dragons and Denomination — A1a

½ sen:
Plate I — Same as 48m Plate II. Measures not less than 19.8x19.8mm. Some subjects on this plate measure 20.3x20.2mm.
Plate II — Same as 48m Plate II. Measures not more than 19.7x19.3mm. Some subjects measure 19.3x18.7mm.

 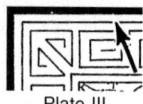
Plate I & II   Plate III

1 sen:
Plate I — Same as 100m Plate I. Narrow space between frameline and Greek-type border.
Plate II — Same as 100m Plate II. Same narrow space between frameline and border.
Plate III — Space between frameline and border is much wider. Frameline thinner. Shading on dragon heads heavier than on Plates I and II.

Native Laid Paper With or Without Gum
1872   Perf. 9-12 & compound
Denomination in Black

5	A1a	½s brown (II)	130.00	130.00
a.		½s red brown (II)	130.00	130.00
b.		½s gray brown (II)	130.00	130.00
c.		Wove paper (II)	725.00	675.00
d.		½s brown (I)	200.00	200.00
e.		½s red brown (I)	200.00	200.00
f.		½s gray brown (I)	200.00	200.00
g.		Wove paper (I)	275.00	275.00
6	A1a	1s blue (II)	425.00	425.00
a.		Wove paper (II)	675.00	675.00
b.		Plate I	1,400.	3,000.
c.		Wove paper (I)	7,000.	
d.		Plate III	10,000.	2,500.
e.		Wove paper (III)		7,500.
7	A1a	2s vermilion	575.00	575.00
a.		Wove paper	625.00	625.00
8	A1a	5s blue green	850.00	850.00
a.		5s yellow green	875.00	875.00
b.		Wove paper	900.00	900.00

In 1896 the government made imperforate imitations of Nos. 6-7 to include in a presentation book.

Beginning with No. 9, Japanese stamps intended for distribution outside the Postal Ministry were overprinted with three characters, as shown above reading "Million (specimen). These specimens were included in ministry announcements detailing forthcoming issues and were in presentation booklets given to government officials, foreign governments, etc.

Expect perforations on Nos. 9-71 to be rough and irregular.

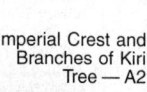
Imperial Crest and Branches of Kiri Tree — A2

Dragons and Chrysanthemum Crest — A3

Imperial Chrysanthemum Crest — A4

Imperial Crest and Branches of Kiri Tree — A5

Perf. 9 to 13 and Compound
1872-73
Native Wove or Laid Paper of Varying Thickness

9	A2	½s brown, *hard*		
		wove	25.00	20.00
a.		Upper character in left label has 2 diagonal top strokes missing	2,100.	1,250.
b.		Laid paper	80.00	
c.		As "a," laid paper	2,200.	
d.		½s gray brown, *soft porous native wove*	80.00	—

Nos. 9, 9a are on stiff, brittle wove paper. Nos. 9b, 9c and 9d on a soft, fibrous paper. Nos. 9b, 9c and 9d probably were never put in use, though genuine used examples do exist.

10	A2	1s blue, *wove*	50.00	26.00
a.		Laid paper	52.50	29.00
11	A2	2s ver, *wove*	100.00	50.00
12	A2	2s dull rose, *laid*	75.00	35.00
a.		Wove paper	100.00	50.00
13	A2	2s yel, *laid* ('73)	75.00	21.00
a.		Wove paper ('73)	175.00	26.00
14	A2	4s rose, *laid* ('73)	67.50	26.00
a.		Wove paper ('73)	210.00	32.00
15	A3	10s blue grn, *wove*	260.00	160.00
16	A3	10s yel grn, *laid*	475.00	325.00
a.		Wove paper ('73)	1,150.	500.00
17	A4	20s lilac, *wove*	700.00	425.00
a.		20s violet, *wove*	750.00	425.00
b.		20s red violet, *laid*		
18	A5	30s gray, *wove*	625.00	375.00

See Nos. 24-25, 30-31, 37-39, 51-52.

1874   Foreign Wove Paper

24	A2	4s rose	650.	300.
25	A5	30s gray	*30,000.*	*7,500.*

A6

A7

A8

Design A6 differs from A2 by the addition of a syllabic character in a box covering crossed kiri branches above SEN. Stamps of design A6 differ for each value in border and spandrel designs.

In design A7, the syllabic character appears just below the buckle. In design A8, it appears in an oval frame at bottom center below SE of SEN.

With Syllabic Characters

イ	ロ	ハ	ニ	ホ	ヘ	ト	チ
i	ro	ha	ni	ho	he	to	chi
1	2	3	4	5	6	7	8

リ	ヌ	ル	ヂ	ワ	カ	ヨ	タ
ri	nu	ru	wo	wa	ka	yo	ta
9	10	11	12	13	14	15	16

レ	ソ	ツ	子	ナ	ラ	ム
re	so	tsu	ne	na	ra	mu
17	18	19	20	21	22	23

Perf. 9½ to 12½ and Compound
1874   Native Laid or Wove Paper

28	A6	2s yellow (syll. 1)	27,000.	400.00
		Syllabic 16	425.00	
29	A7	6s vio brn (Syll. 1)	1,700.	475.00
		Wove paper	1,500.	400.00
		Syllabic 2	1,900.	500.00
		Wove paper	1,750.	500.00
		Syllabic 3	20,000.	1,100.
		Wove paper	20,000.	1,150.
		Syllabic 4	20,000.	600.00
		Wove paper	20,000.	575.00
		Syllabic 5	20,000.	600.00
		Wove paper	20,000.	625.00
		Syllabic 6	20,000.	700.00
		Wove paper	20,000.	775.00
		Syllabic 7	25,000.	550.00
		Wove paper	25,000.	550.00
		Syllabic 8	25,000.	550.00
		Wove paper	25,000.	500.00
		Syllabic 9	20,000.	700.00
		Wove paper	20,000.	675.00
		Syllabic 10		3,500.
		Wove paper		3,000.
		Syllabic 11		3,000.
		Wove paper		3,000.
		Syllabic 12	20,000.	1,900.
		Wove paper	20,000.	1,800.
30	A4	20s red vio (Syll. 3)	10,000.	
		Specimen overprint	10,000.	
		Syllabic 1	150,000.	
		Syllabic 2	10,000.	
		Specimen overprint	10,000.	
31	A5	30s gray (Syll. 1)	3,000.	3,000.
a.		Very thin laid paper	3,000.	3,000.

No. 30, syll. 1, comes only with small, elliptical specimen dot (*Sumiten*, "secret mark").
Specimen overprints on No. 30, Syllabics 2 and 3, consist of the three-character *Mihon* overprint.

Perf. 11 to 12½ and Compound
1874   Foreign Wove Paper

32	A6	½s brown (Syll. 1)	25.00	20.00
		Syllabic 2	40.00	40.00
33	A6	1s blue (Syll. 4)	160.00	40.00
		Syllabic 1	150.00	35.00
		Syllabic 2	225.00	40.00
		Syllabic 3	200.00	40.00
		Syllabic 5	650.00	150.00
		Syllabic 6, 9	150.00	45.00
		Syllabic 7	350.00	50.00
		Syllabic 8	150.00	40.00
		Syllabic 10	225.00	70.00
		Syllabic 11	215.00	60.00
		Syllabic 12	250.00	65.00
34	A6	2s yel (Syll. 2-4, 15, 17, 20)	200.00	30.00
		Syllabic 5	400.00	35.00
		Syllabic 6	450.00	30.00
		Syllabic 7	2,000.	50.00
		Syllabic 8	2,000.	30.00
		Syllabic 9	200.00	55.00
		Syllabic 10	200.00	35.00
		Syllabic 11	2,750.	50.00
		Syllabic 12,22	200.00	30.00
		Syllabic 13	2,650.	30.00
		Syllabic 14	2,500.	30.00
		Syllabic 16	2,650.	45.00
		Syllabic 18,19	2,500.	35.00
		Syllabic 21	200.00	30.00
		Syllabic 23	250.00	30.00
		Syllabic 23	265.00	30.00
35	A6	4s rose (Syll. 1)	3,500.	475.00
36	A7	6s vio brn (Syll. 16)	200.00	70.00
		Syllabic 10	650.00	650.00
		Syllabic 11	500.00	
		Syllabic 13	14,000.	5,000.
		Syllabic 14	300.00	275.00

		Syllabic 15	25,000.	3,000.
		Syllabic 17	240.00	85.00
		Syllabic 18	325.00	115.00
37	A3	10s yel grn (Syll. 2)	425.00	100.00
		Syllabic 1	525.00	85.00
		Syllabic 3	1,000.	300.00
38	A4	20s violet (Syll. 5)	500.00	95.00
		Syllabic 4	525.00	100.00
39	A5	30s gray (Syll. 1)	575.00	100.00

1875   Perf. 9 to 13 and Compound

40	A6	½s gray (Syll. 2, 3)	25.00	20.00
		Syllabic 4	30.00	1,000.
41	A6	1s brn (Syll. 15)	35.00	22.50
		Syllabic 5	375.00	50.00
		Syllabic 7	2,250.	275.00
		Syllabic 8	32,500.	275.00
		Syllabic 12	1,300.	225.00
		Syllabic 13	50.00	22.50
		Syllabic 14	50.00	22.50
		Syllabic 16-17	45.00	25.00
42	A6	4s green (Syll. 1)	130.00	29.00
		Syllabic 2	200.00	29.00
		Syllabic 3	130.00	29.00
43	A7	6s orange (Syll. 16,17)	90.00	25.00
		Syllabic 10	175.00	55.00
		Syllabic 11	150.00	50.00
		Syllabic 13	325.00	45.00
		Syllabic 14	160.00	32.50
		Syllabic 15		162,500.
44	A8	6s orange (Syll. 20)	90.00	25.00
		Syllabic 19	125.00	25.00
		Syllabic 21	100.00	25.00
		Syllabic 22	4,250.	1,750.

Dragons
A9

Wild Goose
A10

Wagtail — A11

Imperial Crest — A11a

Kiri Branches — A11b

Goshawk — A12

45	A9	10s ultra (Syll. 4)	175.00	27.50
		Syllabic 5	4,150.	350.00
46	A10	12s rose (Syll. 1)	450.00	150.00
		Syllabic 2	500.00	175.00
		Syllabic 3	3,500.	500.00
47	A11	15s lilac (Syll. 1)	350.00	160.00
		Syllabic 2	400.00	165.00
		Syllabic 3	350.00	175.00
48	A11a	20s rose (Syll. 8)	140.00	25.00
		Syllabic 9		—
49	A11b	30s vio (Syll. 2-4)	180.00	70.00
50	A12	45s lake (Syll. 1)	600.00	275.00
		Syllabic 2	1,250.	550.00
		Syllabic 3	1,200.	425.00

Issued: No. 46, syll. 2, 1882; No. 46, syll. 3, 1883; others, 1875.
The 1s brown on laid paper, type A6, formerly listed as No. 50A, is one of several stamps of the preceding issue which exist on a laid type paper. They are difficult to identify and mainly of interest to specialists.

1875   Without Syllabic Characters

51	A2	1s brown	6,500.	700.00
52	A2	4s green	525.00	100.00

Branches of Kiri Tree Tied with Ribbon
A13

Imperial Crest and Kiri Branches
A14

1875-76

53	A13	1s brown	80.00	12.00
54	A13	2s yellow	95.00	20.00
54A	A14	5s green ('76)	200.00	100.00
		Nos. 53-54A (3)	375.00	132.00

Postal Cancellations

Beta Cancel

Postal Cancel

Telegraph Cancellation

Nos. 58, 61-62, 64-65, 71-84 are found with telegraph or telephone office cancellations. These sell at considerably lower prices than postally used examples.

A15

A16

Imperial Crest, Star and Kiri Branches
A17

Sun, Kikumon and Kiri Branches
A18

Imperial Crest and Kiri Branches
A19

Kikumon
A20

Perf. 8 to 14 and Compound
1876-77   Typo.

55	A15	5r slate	25.00	10.00
56	A16	1s black	37.50	4.75
a.		Horiz. pair, imperf. btwn.		
57	A16	2s brown ol	52.50	3.00
58	A16	4s blue grn	42.50	5.00
a.		4s green	42.50	5.00
59	A17	5s brown	65.00	25.00

60	A17	6s orange ('77)	160.00	65.00
61	A17	8s vio brn ('77)	67.50	6.00
62	A17	10s blue ('77)	55.00	2.50
63	A17	12s rose ('77)	250.00	150.00
64	A18	15s yel grn ('77)	160.00	2.50
65	A18	20s dk blue ('77)	175.00	12.00
66	A18	30s violet ('77)	250.00	110.00
67	A18	45s carmine ('77)	775.00	525.00

1879

68	A16	1s maroon	15.00	1.25
69	A16	2s dk violet	40.00	2.00
70	A16	3s orange	60.00	30.00
71	A18	50s carmine	225.00	15.00
		Nos. 68-71 (4)	340.00	48.25

1883

72	A16	1s green	11.50	.80
73	A16	2s car rose	15.00	.25
74	A17	5s ultra	25.00	.60
		Nos. 72-74 (3)	51.50	1.65

1888-92

75	A15	5r gray blk ('89)	5.00	.45
76	A16	3s lilac rose ('92)	15.00	.45
77	A16	4s olive bis	13.00	.45
78	A17	8s blue lilac	19.00	1.60
79	A17	10s brown org	17.00	.45
80	A18	15s purple	57.50	.50
81	A18	20s orange	75.00	1.50
a.		20s yellow	75.00	1.50
82	A19	25s blue green	150.00	1.50
83	A19	50s brown	100.00	3.25
84	A20	1y carmine	160.00	4.25
		Nos. 75-84 (10)	611.50	14.40

Stamps of types A16-A18 differ for each value, in backgrounds and ornaments.

Cranes and Imperial Crest — A21

Perf. 11½ to 13 and Compound

1894, Mar. 9

85	A21	2s carmine	24.00	3.00
86	A21	5s ultra	37.50	11.00

25th wedding anniv. of Emperor Meiji (Mutsuhito) and Empress Haru.

Gen. Yoshihisa Kitashirakawa
A22   A23

Field Marshal Akihito Arisugawa
A24   A25

1896, Aug. 1   **Engr.**

87	A22	2s rose	26.00	3.00
88	A23	5s deep ultra	52.50	3.00
89	A24	2s rose	26.00	3.00
90	A25	5s deep ultra	52.50	3.00
		Nos. 87-90 (4)	157.00	12.00

Victory in Chinese-Japanese War (1894-95).

A26   A27

A28   A29

Perf. 11½ to 14 and Compound

1899-1907   **Typo.**

91	A26	5r gray	5.50	1.00
92	A26	½s gray ('01)	3.00	.25
93	A26	1s lt red brn	3.50	.25
94	A26	1½s ultra ('00)	12.00	.85
95	A26	1½s violet ('06)	9.00	.25
96	A26	2s lt green	9.00	.25
97	A26	3s violet brn	8.50	.25
a.		Double impression		
98	A26	3s rose ('06)	5.00	.25
99	A26	4s rose	6.00	1.25
a.		4s pink ('06)	7.00	1.75
100	A26	5s orange yel	18.00	.25
101	A27	6s maroon ('07)	32.50	3.50
102	A27	8s olive grn	34.00	5.00
103	A27	10s deep blue	11.00	.25
104	A27	15s purple	42.50	2.00
105	A27	20s red orange	21.00	.25
106	A28	25s blue green	67.50	1.00
107	A28	50s red brown	70.00	2.25
108	A29	1y carmine	80.00	3.25
		Nos. 91-108 (18)	438.00	22.35

For overprints see Nos. M1, Offices in China, 1-18, Offices in Korea, 1-14.

Boxes for Rice Cakes and Marriage Certificates — A30

Perf. 11½ to 12½ and Compound

1900, May 10

109	A30	3s carmine	28.00 2.50

Wedding of the Crown Prince Yoshihito and Princess Sadako.

For overprints see Offices in China No. 19, Offices in Korea No. 15.

Symbols of Korea and Japan — A31

1905, July 1

110	A31	3s rose red	80.00 20.00

Issued to commemorate the amalgamation of the postal services of Japan and Korea. Korean stamps were withdrawn from sale June 30, 1905, but remained valid until Aug. 31. No. 110 was used in the Korea and China Offices of Japan, as well as in Japan proper.

Field-piece and Japanese Flag — A32

1906, Apr. 29

111	A32	1½s blue	26.00 4.00
112	A32	3s carmine rose	55.00 16.00

Triumphal military review following the Russo-Japanese War.

Empress Jingo — A33

1908   **Engr.**

113	A33	5y green	875.00 6.00
114	A33	10y dark violet	1,200. 10.00

The frame of No. 114 differs slightly from the illustration.
See Nos. 146-147.

For overprints see Offices in China Nos. 20-21, 48-49.

A34   A35

A36

Perf. 12, 12x13, 13x13½

1913   **Typo.**   **Unwmk.**

115	A34	½s brown	7.00	.85
116	A34	1s orange	14.00	.85
117	A34	1½s lt blue	18.00	1.25
a.		Booklet pane of 6	175.00	
118	A34	2s green	19.00	.85
119	A34	3s rose	26.00	.45
a.		Booklet pane of 6	175.00	
120	A35	4s red	27.50	14.00
121	A35	5s violet	35.00	1.25
122	A35	10s deep blue	110.00	.60
123	A35	20s claret	110.00	1.25
124	A35	25s olive green	110.00	2.75
125	A36	1y yel grn & mar	775.00	45.00
		Nos. 115-125 (11)	1,251.	69.10

1914-25   **Wmk. 141**   **Granite Paper**
Size: 19x22½mm ("Old Die")

127	A34	½s brown	2.10	.25
128	A34	1s orange	2.10	.25
129	A34	1½s blue	2.10	.25
a.		Booklet pane of 6	72.50	
d.		As "a," imperf.		
130	A34	2s green	4.25	.25
a.		Booklet pane of 6	72.50	
131	A34	3s rose	1.60	.25
a.		Booklet pane of 6	60.00	
132	A35	4s red	14.00	1.00
a.		Booklet pane of 6	72.50	
133	A35	5s violet	13.00	.45
134	A35	6s brown ('19)	18.00	2.40
136	A35	8s gray ('19)	15.00	9.00
137	A35	10s deep blue	17.50	.25
a.		Booklet pane of 6	110.00	
138	A35	13s olive brn ('25)	35.00	1.90
139	A35	20s claret	80.00	.60
140	A35	25s olive grn	12.00	.85
141	A36	30s orange brn ('19)	18.00	.50
143	A36	50s dk brown ('19)	26.00	1.00
145	A36	1y yel grn & mar	140.00	1.50
b.		Imperf., pair		
146	A33	5y green	475.00	6.00
147	A33	10y violet	650.00	9.50
		Nos. 127-147 (18)	1,525.	36.20

"New Die" Size: 18½x22mm (Flat Plate) or 18½x22½mm (Rotary)

1924-33

127a	A34	½s brown	1.75	.95
128a	A34	1s orange	1.75	.95
129b	A34	1½s blue	2.75	.30
c.		Bklt. pane of 6 ('30)	19.00	
131b	A34	3s rose	1.10	.25
c.		Bklt. pane of 6 ('28)	45.00	
133a	A35	5s violet	15.00	.25
135	A35	7s red org ('30)	7.75	.25
138a	A35	13s bister brn ('25)	6.00	.25
140a	A35	25s olive green	45.00	.25
142	A36	30s org & grn ('29)	17.00	.30
144	A36	50s yel brn & dk bl ('29)	12.00	.60
145a	A36	1y yel grn & mar	67.50	1.00
		Nos. 127a-145a (11)	177.60	5.25

See Nos. 212-213, 239-241, 243, 245, 249-252, 255. For overprints see Nos. C1-C2, M2-M5, Offices in China, 22-47.

Ceremonial Cap — A37   Imperial Throne — A38

Enthronement Hall, Kyoto — A39

Perf. 12½

1915, Nov. 10   **Typo.**   **Unwmk.**

148	A37	1½s red & blk	2.00	.55
149	A38	3s orange & vio	2.50	.80

Engr.
Perf. 12x12½

150	A39	4s carmine rose	12.00	10.00
151	A39	10s ultra	25.00	16.00
		Nos. 148-151 (4)	41.50	27.35

Enthronement of Emperor Yoshihito.

Mandarin Duck — A40   Ceremonial Cap — A41

1916, Nov. 3   **Typo.**   **Perf. 12½**

152	A40	1½s green, red & yel	4.00	1.75
153	A40	3s red & yellow	7.00	2.00
154	A41	10s ultra & dk blue	825.00	275.00

Nomination of the Prince Heir Apparent, later Emperor Hirohito.

A42

Dove and Olive Branch — A43

Perf. 12, 12½, 13½x13

1919, July 1   **Engr.**

155	A42	1½s dark brown	2.00	.60
156	A43	3s gray green	2.50	1.00
157	A42	4s rose	5.50	3.75
158	A43	10s dark blue	23.00	12.00
		Nos. 155-158 (4)	33.00	17.35

Restoration of peace after World War I.

Census Officer, A.D. 652 — A44

Perf. 12½

1920, Sept. 25   **Typo.**   **Unwmk.**

159	A44	1½s red violet	6.50	2.75
160	A44	3s vermilion	7.00	3.60

Taking of the 1st modern census in Japan. Not available for foreign postage except to China.

Meiji Shrine,
Tokyo — A45

1920, Nov. 1   **Engr.**
161 A45 1½s dull violet   2.50 1.10
162 A45 3s rose   2.50 1.10

Dedication of the Meiji Shrine. Not available for foreign postage except to China.

National and
Postal
Flags — A46

Ministry of Communications Building,
Tokyo — A47

Typographed (A46), Engraved (A47)
1921, Apr. 20   *Perf. 12½, 13x13½*
163 A46 1½s gray grn & red   1.60   .90
164 A47 3s violet brn   2.10 1.00
165 A46 4s rose & red   42.50 18.00
166 A47 10s dark blue   200.00 125.00
   Nos. 163-166 (4)   246.20 144.90

50th anniv. of the establishment of postal service and Japanese postage stamps.

Battleships
"Katori" and
"Kashima" — A48

1921, Sept. 3   **Litho.**   *Perf. 12½*
167 A48 1½s violet   2.00 1.00
168 A48 3s olive green   2.25 1.00
169 A48 4s rose red   32.50 15.00
170 A48 10s deep blue   45.00 18.00
   Nos. 167-170 (4)   81.75 35.00

Return of Crown Prince Hirohito from his European visit.

Mount Fuji — A49

Perf. 13x13½
1930-37   **Typo.**   **Wmk. 141**
Granite Paper
Size: 18½x22mm ("New Die")
171 A49 4s green ('37)   2.40   .35
172 A49 4s orange   5.50   .25
174 A49 8s olive green   8.50   .25
175a A49 20s blue ('37)   19.00 26.00
176 A49 20s brown violet   26.00   .25
   Nos. 171-176 (5)   61.40 27.10

1922-29
Size: 19x22½mm ("Old Die")
171a A49 4s green   7.50 2.60
172a A49 4s orange ('29)   75.00 7.50
173 A49 8s rose   15.00 5.25
174a A49 8s olive green ('29)   225.00 70.00
175 A49 20s deep blue   17.00   .50
176a A49 20s brown vio ('29)   75.00 1.25
   Nos. 171a-176a (6)   414.50 87.10

See Nos. 242, 246, 248.

Mt. Niitaka,
Taiwan — A50

Perf. 12½
1923, Apr. 16   **Unwmk.**   **Engr.**
177 A50 1½s orange   9.50 6.75
178 A50 3s dark violet   14.00 5.75

1st visit of Crown Prince Hirohito to Taiwan. The stamps were sold only in Taiwan, but were valid throughout the empire.

Cherry   Sun and
Blossoms   Dragonflies
A51   A52

Without Gum; Granite Paper
1923   **Wmk. 142**   **Litho.**   *Imperf.*
179 A51 ½s gray   4.50 2.25
180 A51 1½s lt blue   5.00 1.00
181 A51 2s red brown   4.50 1.00
182 A51 3s brt rose   3.25   .80
183 A51 4s gray green   40.00 12.00
184 A51 5s dull violet   15.00 1.00
185 A51 8s red orange   65.00 21.00
186 A52 10s deep brown   27.50 1.00
187 A52 20s deep blue   30.00 1.50
   Nos. 179-187 (9)   194.75 41.55

Nos. 179-187 exist rouletted and with various perforations. These were made privately.

Empress Jingo — A53

Granite Paper
Perf. 12, 13x13½
1924   **Engr.**   **Wmk. 141**
188 A53 5y gray green   250.00 3.50
189 A53 10y dull violet   375.00 3.00

See Nos. 253-254.

Cranes — A54

Phoenix — A55

Perf. 10½ to 13½ and Compound
1925, May 10   **Litho.**   **Unwmk.**
190 A54 1½s gray violet   2.00 1.00
191 A55 3s silver & brn org   2.60 1.50
  a. Vert. pair, imperf. btwn.   425.00
192 A54 8s light red   20.00 11.00
193 A55 20s silver & gray
        grn   45.00 35.00
   Nos. 190-193 (4)   69.60 48.50

25th wedding anniv. of the Emperor Yoshihito (Taisho) and Empress Sadako.

Mt. Fuji — A56   Yomei Gate,
          Nikko — A57

Nagoya
Castle — A58

Perf. 13½x13
1926-37   **Typo.**   **Wmk. 141**
Granite Paper
194 A56 2s green   1.60   .25
195 A57 6s carmine   6.00   .25
196 A58 10s dark blue   7.00   .25
197 A58 10s carmine ('37)   8.00 7.00
   Nos. 194-197 (4)   22.60 7.75

See Nos. 244, 247. For surcharges see People's Republic of China No. 2L5-2L6 in Scott Standard catalogue, Vol. 2.

Baron Hisoka
Maeshima — A59

Map of World on Mollweide's
Projection — A60

Perf. 12½, 13x13½
1927, June 20   **Unwmk.**
198 A59 1½s lilac   2.50 1.00
199 A59 3s olive green   2.50 1.00
200 A60 6s carmine rose   55.00 45.00
201 A60 10s blue   67.50 45.00
   Nos. 198-201 (4)   127.50 92.00

50th anniv. of Japan's joining the UPU. Baron Maeshima (1835-1919) organized Japan's modern postal system and was postmaster general.

Phoenix — A61   Enthronement Hall,
            Kyoto — A62

1928, Nov. 10   **Engr.**   *Perf. 12½*
Yellow Paper
202 A61 1½s deep green   1.25   .50
203 A62 3s red violet   1.25   .50
204 A61 6s carmine rose   2.25 1.60
205 A62 10s deep blue   3.00 2.10
   Nos. 202-205 (4)   7.75 4.70

Enthronement of Emperor Hirohito.

Great Shrines of
Ise — A63

1929, Oct. 2   *Perf. 12½*
206 A63 1½s gray violet   1.00 1.00
207 A63 3s carmine   1.50 1.10

58th rebuilding of the Ise Shrines.

Map of Japanese
Empire — A64

1930, Sept. 25   **Unwmk.**
208 A64 1½s deep violet   2.00 1.25
209 A64 3s deep red   2.25 1.50

2nd census in the Japanese Empire.

Meiji Shrine — A65

1930, Nov. 1   **Litho.**
210	A65	1½s green	1.50	.85
211	A65	3s brown org	2.00	1.00

10th anniv. of dedication of Meiji Shrine.

Coil Stamps
Wmk. Zigzag Lines (141)
1933		**Typo.**	**Perf. 13 Horiz.**
212	A34	1½s light blue	13.00	17.00
213	A34	3s rose	14.00	21.00

Japanese Red Cross Badge — A66   Red Cross Building, Tokyo — A67

Perf. 12½
1934, Oct. 1		**Engr.**	**Unwmk.**
214	A66	1½s green & red	1.50	1.00
215	A67	3s dull vio & red	1.75	1.25
216	A66	6s dk car & red	8.00	5.00
217	A67	10s blue & red	12.00	8.00
		Nos. 214-217 (4)	23.25	15.25

15th International Red Cross Congress. Sheets of 20 with commemorative marginal inscription. One side of sheet is perf. 13.

White Tower of Liaoyang and Warship "Hiei" — A68   Akasaka Detached Palace, Tokyo — A69

1935, Apr. 2
218	A68	1½s olive green	1.00	.60
219	A69	3s red brown	1.50	1.00
220	A68	6s carmine	6.25	3.00
221	A69	10s blue	9.00	6.00
		Nos. 218-221 (4)	17.75	10.60

Visit of Emperor Kang Teh of Manchukuo (Henry Pu-yi) to Tokyo, April 6, 1935. Sheets of 20 with commemorative marginal inscription. One side of sheet is perf. 13.

Mt. Fuji — A70

1935   **Typo.**   **Perf. 13x13½**
Granite Paper
222	A70	1½s rose carmine	10.00	.75
a.		Miniature sheet of 20	700.00	500.00

Issued to pay postage on New Year's cards from Dec. 1-31, 1935. After Jan. 1, 1936, used for ordinary letter postage. No. 222 was issued in sheets of 100.

Mt. Fuji A71

Lake Ashi A72

Fuji from Lake Kawaguchi — A73

Fuji from Mishima A74

1936, July 10   **Photo.**   **Wmk. 141**
Granite Paper
223	A71	1½s red brown	3.00	2.00
224	A72	3s dark green	4.50	3.00
225	A73	6s carmine rose	10.00	8.00
226	A74	10s dark blue	12.00	10.00
		Nos. 223-226 (4)	29.50	23.00

Fuji-Hakone National Park.

Dove, Map of Manchuria and Kwantung — A75   Shinto Shrine, Port Arthur — A76

Headquarters of Kwantung Government A77

1936, Sept. 1   **Litho.**   **Perf. 12½**
Granite Paper
227	A75	1½s gray violet	18.00	10.00
228	A76	3s red brown	14.00	12.00
229	A77	10s dull green	210.00	135.00
		Nos. 227-229 (3)	242.00	157.00

30th anniv. of Japanese administration of Kwantung Leased Territory and the South Manchuria Railway Zone.

Imperial Diet Building A78

Grand Staircase A79

1936, Nov. 7   **Engr.**   **Perf. 13**
230	A78	1½s green	2.00	1.00
231	A79	3s brown vio	3.00	1.50
232	A79	6s carmine	6.00	4.00
233	A78	10s blue	10.00	5.75
		Nos. 230-233 (4)	21.00	12.25

Opening of the new Diet Building, Tokyo.

"Wedded Rocks," Futamigaura — A80

1936, Dec. 10   **Photo.**
234	A80	1½s rose carmine	3.50	.25

Issued to pay postage on New Year's greeting cards.

Types of 1913-26
Perf. 13½x13, 13x13½
1937		**Typo.**	**Wmk. 257**
239	A34	½s brown	1.90	1.00
240	A34	1s orange yel	2.75	1.25
241	A34	3s rose	1.00	.25
242	A49	4s green	3.75	.25
243	A35	5s violet	5.00	.25
244	A57	6s crimson	8.00	.95
245	A35	7s red org	8.00	.25
246	A49	8s olive bister	8.50	.50
247	A58	10s carmine	7.00	.25
248	A49	20s blue	13.50	.50
249	A35	25s olive grn	40.00	2.00
250	A36	30s org & grn	30.00	.50
251	A36	50s brn org & dk bl	125.00	2.00
252	A36	1y yel grn & mar	60.00	1.50
		Nos. 239-252 (14)	314.40	11.45

Engr.
253	A53	5y gray green	300.00	3.25
254	A53	10y dull violet	425.00	30.00

For overprint see People's Republic of China No. 2L6 in Scott Standard catalogue, Vol. 2.

Coil Stamps
1938		**Typo.**	**Perf. 13 Horiz.**
255	A34	3s rose	4.00	4.00

New Year's Decoration — A81

1937, Dec. 15   **Photo.**   **Perf. 13**
256	A81	2s scarlet	6.25	.25

Issued to pay postage on New Year's cards, later for ordinary use.

Trading Ship A82

Harvesting A83

Gen. Maresuke Nogi — A84

Power Plant — A85

Admiral Heihachiro Togo A86

Mount Hodaka A87

Garambi Lighthouse, Taiwan — A88

Diamond Mountains, Korea — A89

Meiji Shrine, Tokyo — A90   Yomei Gate, Nikko — A91

Plane and Map of Japan — A92   Kasuga Shrine, Nara — A93

Mount Fuji and Cherry Blossoms A94   Horyu Temple, Nara A95

Miyajima Torii, Itsukushima Shrine — A96   Golden Pavilion, Kyoto — A97

Great Buddha, Kamakura A98

Kamatari Fujiwara A99

Plum Blossoms — A100

Typographed or Engraved
1937-45		**Wmk. 257**	**Perf. 13**
257	A82	½s purple	.50	.30
258	A83	1s fawn	1.50	.25
259	A84	2s crimson	.35	.25
a.		Booklet pane of 20	50.00	
b.		2s pink, perf. 12 ('45)	1.25	.85
c.		2s vermilion ('44)	2.10	1.60
260	A85	3s green ('39)	.35	.25
261	A86	4s dark green	.75	.25
a.		Booklet pane of 20	13.00	
262	A87	5s dark ultra ('39)	.75	.25
263	A88	6s orange ('39)	1.50	.60
264	A89	7s deep green ('39)	.50	.25
265	A90	8s dk pur & pale vio ('39)	.45	.25
266	A91	10s lake ('38)	2.50	.25
267	A92	12s indigo ('39)	.50	.30
268	A93	14s rose lake & pale rose ('38)	.50	.25
269	A94	20s ultra ('40)	.50	.25
270	A95	25s dk brn & pale brn ('38)	.50	.25
271	A96	30s pck blue ('39)	1.25	.25
a.		Imperf., pair	400.00	
272	A97	50s ol & pale ol ('39)	.60	.25
a.		Pale olive (forest) omitted		

273	A98	1y brn & pale brn ('39)	3.50 1.00
274	A99	5y dp gray grn ('39)	25.00 2.50
275	A100	10y dk brn vio ('39)	16.50 2.00
		Nos. 257-275 (19)	58.00 9.95

Nos. 257-261, 265, 268, 270, 272- 273 are typographed; the others are engraved.

Coil Stamps

1938-39   Typo.   Perf. 13 Horiz.

276	A82	½s purple ('39)	2.75 4.50
277	A84	2s crimson	3.25 4.25
278	A86	4s dark green	3.75 4.25
279	A93	14s rose lake & pale rose	125.00 80.00
		Nos. 276-279 (4)	134.75 93.00

See Nos. 329, 331, 333, 341, 351, 360 and 361 in Scott Standard catalogue, Vol. 4. For surcharges see Nos. B4-B5, Burma 2N4-2N27, China-Taiwan 8-9 and People's Republic of China 2L3, 2L7, 2L9-2L10, 2L39 in Scott Vol. 2, Korea 55-56 in Scott Vol. 4. For overprints see Ryukyu Islands (Scott US Specialized catalogue) Nos. 2X1-2X2, 2X4-2X7, 2X10, 2X13-2X14, 2X17, 2X20, 2X23, 2X27, 2X29, 2X33-2X34, 3X2-3X7, 3X10-3X11, 3X14, 3X17, 3X19, 3X21, 3X23, 3X26-3X30, 5X1-5X3, 5X5-5X8, 5X10.

Mount Nantai — A101   Kegon Falls — A102

Sacred Bridge, Nikko A103

Mount Hiuchi A104

Unwmk.

1938, Dec. 25   Photo.   Perf. 13

280	A101	2s brown orange	1.00 .50
281	A102	4s olive green	1.00 .50
282	A103	10s deep rose	5.75 3.75
283	A104	20s dark blue	5.75 3.75
a.		Souvenir sheet of 4, #280-283	45.00 75.00
		Never hinged	80.00
		Nos. 280-283 (4)	13.50 8.50
		Set, never hinged	32.50

Nikko National Park.
No. 283a sold for 50s.

Many souvenir sheets were sold in folders. Values are for sheets without folders.

Mount Daisen A106

Yashima Plateau, Inland Sea A107

Abuto Kwannon Temple A108

Tomo Bay, Inland Sea A109

1939, Apr. 20

285	A106	2s lt brown	1.00 .50
286	A107	4s yellow grn	1.60 1.00
287	A108	10s dull rose	6.50 4.00
288	A109	20s blue	6.50 4.00
a.		Souvenir sheet of 4, #285-288	25.00 40.00
		Never hinged	50.00
		Nos. 285-288 (4)	15.60 9.50
		Set, never hinged	32.50

Daisen and Inland Sea National Parks.
No. 288a sold for 50s.

View from Kuju Village, Kyushu A111

Mount Naka A112

Crater of Mount Naka A113

Volcanic Cones of Mt. Aso A114

1939, Aug. 15

290	A111	2s olive brown	1.00 .50
291	A112	4s yellow green	3.00 2.00
292	A113	10s carmine	15.00 9.00
293	A114	20s sapphire	22.50 10.00
a.		Souvenir sheet of 4, #290-293	85.00 100.00
		Never hinged	140.00
		Nos. 290-293 (4)	41.50 21.50
		Set, never hinged	85.00

Aso National Park. No. 293a sold for 50s.

Globe — A116   Tsunetami Sano — A117

1939, Nov. 15   Perf. 12½

Cross in Carmine

295	A116	2s brown	1.50 .90
296	A117	4s yellow green	1.60 1.00
297	A116	10s crimson	7.00 6.50
298	A117	20s sapphire	7.00 6.50
		Nos. 295-298 (4)	17.10 14.90
		Set, never hinged	32.50

Intl. Red Cross Society founding, 75th anniv.

Sacred Golden Kite — A118   Mount Takachiho — A119

Five Ayu Fish and Sake Jar — A120   Kashiwara Shrine — A121

1940   Engr.   Perf. 12

299	A118	2s brown orange	.80 .80
300	A119	4s dark green	.60 .60
301	A120	10s dark carmine	3.25 3.00
302	A121	20s dark ultra	.80 .80
		Nos. 299-302 (4)	5.45 5.20
		Set, never hinged	7.50

2,600th anniv. of the legendary date of the founding of Japan.

Mt. Hokuchin, Hokkaido A122

Mt. Asahi, Hokkaido A123

Sounkyo Gorge — A124

Tokachi Mountain Range A125

1940, Apr. 20   Photo.   Perf. 13

303	A122	2s brown	1.00 1.00
304	A123	4s yellow green	2.75 2.00
305	A124	10s carmine	6.00 5.25
306	A125	20s sapphire	6.00 5.50
a.		Souvenir sheet of 4, #303-306	190.00 200.00
		Never hinged	350.00
		Nos. 303-306 (4)	15.75 13.75
		Set, never hinged	32.50

Daisetsuzan National Park. No. 306a sold for 50s.

Mt. Karakuni, Kyushu A127

Mt. Takachiho A128

Torii of Kirishima Shrine A129

Lake of the Six Kwannon A130

1940, Aug. 21

308	A127	2s brown	1.00 .75
309	A128	4s green	1.75 1.50
310	A129	10s carmine	6.00 4.75
311	A130	20s deep ultra	7.00 5.75
a.		Souvenir sheet of 4, #308-311	175.00 175.00
		Never hinged	325.00
		Nos. 308-311 (4)	15.75 12.75
		Set, never hinged	37.50

Kirishima National Park.
No. 311a sold for 50s.

Education Minister with Rescript on Education A132   Characters Signifying Loyalty and Filial Piety A133

1940, Oct. 25   Engr.   Perf. 12½

313	A132	2s purple	.75 .75
314	A133	4s green	1.00 1.00
		Set, never hinged	2.25

50th anniv. of the imperial rescript on education, given by Emperor Meiji to clarify Japan's educational policy.

SEMI-POSTAL STAMPS

Douglas Plane over Japan Alps — SP1

Wmk. Zigzag Lines (141)

1937, June 1   Photo.   Perf. 13

B1	SP1	2s + 2s rose carmine	1.75 .75
B2	SP1	3s + 2s purple	1.75 1.25
B3	SP1	4s + 2s green	2.50 1.00
		Nos. B1-B3 (3)	6.00 3.00
		Set, never hinged	8.00

The surtax was for the Patriotic Aviation Fund to build civil airports.

AIR POST STAMPS

Regular Issue of 1914 Overprinted in Red or Blue

Wmk. Zigzag Lines (141)
1919, Oct. 3   *Perf. 13x13½*
Granite Paper

C1	A34	1½s blue (R)	260.00 72.50
C2	A34	3s rose (Bl)	450.00 210.00

Excellent counterfeits exist.

Passenger Plane
over Lake
Ashi — AP1

1929-34   **Engr.**   *Perf. 13½x13*
Granite Paper

C3	AP1	8½s orange brn	27.50 14.00
C4	AP1	9½s rose	9.00 3.75
C5	AP1	16½s yellow grn	9.00 4.00
C6	AP1	18s ultra	10.00 3.75
C7	AP1	33s gray	20.00 3.25
		Nos. C3-C7 (5)	75.50 28.75
		Set, never hinged	190.00

Souvenir Sheet

C8	AP1	Sheet of 4, #C4-C7	1,250. 1,250.
		Never hinged	2,000.

Issued: 9½s, 3/1/34; No. C8, 4/20/34; others, 10/6/29. No. C8 for Communications Commemoration Day (1st observance of establishment of the postal service and issuance of #1-4). Sold only at Phil. Exhib. p.o., Tokyo, 4/20-27. Size: 110x100mm.

MILITARY STAMPS

Nos. 98, 119, 131
Overprinted

1910-14   **Unwmk.**   *Perf. 11½ to 13½*

M1	A26	3s rose	225.00 35.00
M2	A34	3s rose ('13)	350.00 140.00

Wmk. 141

M3	A34	3s rose ('14)	35.00 16.00
		Nos. M1-M3 (3)	610.00 191.00

Nos. M1-M3 overprint type I has 3.85mm between characters; type II, 4-4.5mm (movable type).

1921   **On Offices in China No. 37**

M4	A34	3s rose	5,750. 4,750.

No. M4 is a provisional military stamp issued at the Japanese Post Office, Tsingtao, China. The overprint differs from the illustration, being 12mm high with thicker characters. Counterfeits are plentiful.

Overprint 16mm High

1924   **On No. 131**

M5	A34	3s rose	100.00 72.50
a.		3s rose (#131b)	100.00 72.50

Excellent forgeries exist of Nos. M1-M5.

JAPANESE OFFICES ABROAD

Offices in China

1899-1907 Regular
Issues of Japan
Overprinted in Red or
Black

Perf. 11½, 12, 12½, 13½, 13x13½

1900-06   **Unwmk.**

1	A26	5r gray (R)	3.50 2.75
2	A26	½s gray (R) ('01)	2.10 .70
3	A26	1s lt red brn (R)	2.10 .70
4	A26	1½s ultra	9.50 2.10
5	A26	1½s vio ('06)	5.25 .95
6	A26	2s lt grn (R)	5.25 .70
7	A26	3s violet brn	5.75 .70
8	A26	3s rose ('06)	4.25 .50
9	A26	4s rose	4.75 1.25
10	A26	5s org yel (R)	9.50 1.25

11	A27	6s maroon ('06)	18.00 12.00
12	A27	8s ol grn (R)	9.50 6.00
13	A27	10s deep blue	9.50 1.00
14	A27	15s purple	20.00 1.75
15	A27	20s red org	18.00 1.00
16	A28	25s blue grn (R)	37.50 4.00
17	A28	50s red brown	40.00 4.00
18	A29	1y carmine	60.00 3.00
		Nos. 1-18 (18)	264.45 43.35

No. 6 with black overprint is bogus.
Nos. 5, 6, 8, 9 and 13 exist as booklet panes of 6, made from sheet stamps. They are rare.

1900

19	A30	3s carmine	27.50 15.00

Wedding of Crown Prince Yoshihito and Princess Sadako.

Japan Nos. 113 & 114
Overprinted

1908

20	A33	5y green	400.00 47.50
21	A33	10y dark violet	700.00 110.00

On #20-21 the space between characters of the overprint is 6½mm instead of 1½mm.

Stamps of 1913-33
Issues Overprinted

1913   *Perf. 12, 12x13, 13x13½*

22	A34	½s brown	15.00 15.00
23	A34	1s orange	16.00 16.00
24	A34	1½s lt blue	42.50 19.00
25	A34	2s green	50.00 21.00
26	A34	3s rose	24.00 8.00
27	A35	4s red	70.00 70.00
28	A35	5s violet	70.00 55.00
29	A35	10s deep blue	70.00 22.50
30	A35	20s claret	275.00 150.00
31	A35	25s olive green	100.00 22.50
32	A36	1y yel grn & mar	825.00 550.00
		Nos. 22-32 (11)	1,557. 949.00

Nos. 24, 25, 26, 27 and 29 exist in booklet panes of 6, made from sheet stamps. The No. 26 pane is very rare.

Japan Nos. 127-137, 139-147
Overprinted

1914-21   **Wmk. 141**
Granite Paper

33	A34	½s brown	3.25 .80
34	A34	1s orange	3.75 .80
35	A34	1½s blue	4.25 .80
36	A34	2s green	2.75 .95
37	A34	3s rose	2.40 .80
38	A35	4s red	10.50 4.75
39	A35	5s violet	1.90 1.75
40	A35	6s brown ('20)	32.50 19.00
41	A35	8s gray ('20)	40.00 21.00
42	A35	10s dp blue	13.50 1.25
43	A35	20s claret	45.00 3.25
44	A35	25s olive grn	55.00 3.50
45	A36	30s org brn ('20)	80.00 29.00
46	A36	50s dk brn ('20)	95.00 32.50
47	A36	1y yel grn & mar ('18)	140.00 6.75
48	A33	5y green	1,900. 550.00
49	A33	10y violet ('21)	2,700. 1,700.
		Nos. 33-49 (17)	5,146. 2,376.

On Nos. 48-49 the space between characters of overprint is 4½mm, instead of 6½mm on Nos. 20-21 and 1½mm on all lower values. See No. M4.
No. 42 exists as a booklet pane of 6, made from sheet stamps. It is very rare.
Counterfeit overprints exist of Nos. 1-49.

Offices in Korea

Regular Issue of Japan
Overprinted in Red or
Black

1900   **Unwmk.**   *Perf. 11½, 12, 12½*

1	A26	5r gray (R)	19.00 8.75
2	A26	½s lt red brn (R)	20.00 5.00
3	A26	1½s ultra	250.00 130.00
4	A26	2s lt green (R)	19.00 10.00
5	A26	3s violet brn	1.90 1.15
6	A26	4s rose	65.00 27.50
7	A26	5s org yel (R)	67.50 27.50
8	A27	8s ol grn (R)	250.00 120.00
9	A27	10s deep blue	35.00 9.00
10	A27	15s purple	62.50 6.00
11	A27	20s red orange	62.50 5.00
12	A28	25s blue grn (R)	220.00 55.00
13	A28	50s red brown	175.00 18.00
14	A29	1y carmine	475.00 14.00
		Nos. 1-14 (14)	1,737. 440.50

1900

15	A30	3s carmine	125.00 55.00

Wedding of Crown Prince Yoshihito and Princess Sadako.
Counterfeit overprints exist of Nos. 1-15.

JORDAN

'jor-d^ən

Trans-Jordan

LOCATION — In the Near East, separated from the Mediterranean Sea by Israel
GOVT. — Kingdom
AREA — 38,400 sq. mi.
POP. — 3,750,000 (est. 1982)
CAPITAL — Amman

The former Turkish territory was mandated to Great Britain following World War I. It became an independent state in 1946.

10 Milliemes = 1 Piaster
1000 Mils = 1 Palestine Pound (1930)

British Mandate

Stamps and Type of Palestine 1918 Overprinted in Black or Silver

Perf. 14, 15x14

1920, Nov.   **Wmk. 33**

1	A1	1m dark brown	2.00 3.00
a.		Inverted overprint	140.00 275.00
b.		Perf. 14	2.50 2.50
c.		As "b," inverted overprint	170.00
2	A1	2m blue green	2.00 2.00
a.		Perf. 15x14	20.00 21.00
b.		2m blue green (S)	
3	A1	3m light brown	2.50 2.50
a.		Perf. 14	20.00 25.00
4	A1	4m scarlet	2.75 2.75
a.		Perf. 14	19.00 40.00
5	A1	5m orange	5.00 1.00
a.		Perf. 15x14	5.75 2.00
6	A1	1pi dark blue (S)	3.75 2.50
a.		Perf. 15x14	2,250.
7	A1	2pi olive green	6.00 5.00
a.		Perf. 15x14	7.00 11.00
8	A1	5pi plum	5.50 7.50
a.		Perf. 15x14	40.00 50.00
9	A1	9pi bister	7.25 30.00
a.		Perf. 15x14	1,000. 1,500.
10	A1	10pi ultramarine	9.25 30.00
11	A1	20pi gray	17.50 50.00
		Nos. 1-11 (11)	63.50 136.25

The overprint reads "Sharqi al-ardan" (East of Jordan).
For overprints see Nos. 12-63, 83A.

Stamps of 1920 Issue Handstamp Surcharged "Ashir el qirsh" (tenth of piaster) and numeral in Black, Red or Violet

1922

12	A1	¹⁄₁₀pi on 1m dk brn	35.00 32.50
13	A1	¹⁄₁₀pi on 1m dk brn (R)	90.00 67.50
13A	A1	¹⁄₁₀pi on 1m dk brn	77.50 70.00
14	A1	²⁄₁₀pi on 2m bl grn	40.00 29.00
a.		³⁄₁₀pi on 2m bl grn (error)	125.00 110.00
15	A1	³⁄₁₀pi on 2m bl grn (R)	100.00 80.00

16	A1	³⁄₁₀pi on 2m bl grn (V)	135.00 100.00
17	A1	³⁄₁₀pi on 3m lt brn	17.50 15.00
17A	A1	³⁄₁₀pi on 3m lt brn	175.00 160.00
18	A1	³⁄₁₀pi on 4m scar	70.00 50.00
19	A1	³⁄₁₀pi on 5m org	225.00 100.00
c.		Perf. 15x14	200.00 100.00
19A	A1	³⁄₁₀pi on 5m dp org	250.00
19B	A1	³⁄₁₀pi on 5m org (V)	325.00

For overprint see No. 83B.

Handstamp Surcharged "El qirsh" (piaster) and numeral in Black, Red or Violet

20	A1	1pi dk bl (R)	210.00 60.00
20A	A1	1pi dk bl (V)	425.00
21	A1	2pi ol grn (Bk)	300.00 75.00
22	A1	2pi ol grn (R)	350.00 80.00
22A	A1	2pi ol grn (V)	325.00 90.00
23	A1	5pi plum (Bk)	65.00 70.00
23A	A1	5pi plum (V)	325.00
24	A1	9pi bister (Bk)	350.00 350.00
25	A1	9pi bister (R)	175.00 140.00
a.		Perf. 14	600.00 600.00
26	A1	10pi ultra (Bk)	975.00 1,000.
27	A1	20pi gray (Bk)	800.00 850.00
27A	A1	20pi gray (V)	1,000. 950.00

Same Surcharge in Black on Palestine Nos. 13-14

28	A1	10pi on 10pi ultra	2,000. 2,500.
29	A1	20pi on 20pi gray	2,600. 3,000.

For overprints see Nos. 86, 88, 94, 97, 98.

Stamps of 1920 Handstamped in Violet, Black or Red

1922, Dec.   *Perf. 15x14, 14*

30	A1	1m dk brn (V)	32.50 20.00
31	A1	1m dk brn (Bk)	27.50 18.00
32	A1	1m dk brn (R)	17.50 15.00
33	A1	2m bl grn (V)	12.50 10.00
34	A1	2m bl grn (Bk)	15.00 15.00
35	A1	2m bl grn (R)	32.50 25.00
36	A1	3m lt brn (V)	12.50 9.00
37	A1	3m lt brn (Bk)	14.00 10.00
38	A1	3m lt brn (R)	55.00 40.00
39	A1	4m scar (V)	65.00 65.00
39A	A1	4m scar (Bk)	60.00 60.00
40	A1	4m scar (R)	60.00 60.00
41	A1	5m orange (V)	22.50 12.00
42	A1	5m orange (R)	45.00 12.00
a.		Perf. 14	325.00 75.00
43	A1	1pi dk blue (V)	22.50 9.00
44	A1	1pi dk blue (R)	37.50 15.00
45	A1	2pi ol grn (V)	30.00 15.00
a.		Perf. 14	82.50 80.00
46	A1	2pi ol grn (Bk)	17.50 10.00
47	A1	2pi ol grn (R)	75.00 40.00
48	A1	5pi plum (V)	80.00 85.00
a.		Perf. 14	110.00 120.00
49	A1	5pi plum (R)	100.00 120.00
50	A1	9pi bister (V)	250.00 250.00
50A	A1	9pi bister (Bk)	72.50 85.00
50B	A1	9pi bister (R)	450.00 450.00
51	A1	10pi ultra (V)	1,250. 1,600.
51A	A1	10pi ultra (R)	2,000. 1,900.
52	A1	20pi gray (V)	1,250. 1,800.
52A	A1	20pi gray (R)	1,750. 2,000.

The overprint reads "Hukumat al Sharqi al Arabia" (Arab Government of the East) and date, 1923. The surcharges or overprints on Nos. 12 to 52A inclusive are handstamped and, as usual, are found inverted and double.
Ink pads of several colors were in use at the same time and the surcharges and overprints frequently show a mixture of two colors.
For overprints see Nos. 84, 87, 89, 92-93, 95-96.

Stamps of 1920 Overprinted in Gold or Black

1923, Mar. 1   *Perf. 14, 15x14*

53	A1	1m dark brn (G)	22.50 32.50
a.		Inverted overprint	750.00
b.		Perf. 15x14	1,600. 1,800.
54	A1	2m blue grn (G)	20.00 20.00
a.		Double overprint	300.00
b.		Inverted overprint	375.00 350.00
c.		Black overprint	300.00
d.		As "c," inverted overprint	300.00

55	A1	3m lt brn (G)	17.50	*15.00*
a.		Double overprint	550.00	
b.		Inverted overprint	550.00	
c.		Black overprint	82.50	*85.00*
56	A1	4m scarlet (Bk)	20.00	17.50
57	A1	5m orange (Bk)	17.50	12.00
a.		Perf. 15x14	60.00	50.00
58	A1	1pi dk blue (G)	17.50	17.50
a.		Double overprint	500.00	475.00
b.		Black overprint	875.00	850.00
59	A1	2pi ol grn (G)	23.00	*21.00*
a.		Black overprint	275.00	250.00
b.		Overprint on back	275.00	
60	A1	5pi plum (G)	75.00	*100.00*
a.		Inverted overprint	250.00	
b.		"922" for "921"		
c.		Black overprint (inverted)	1,500.	
61	A1	9pi bister (Bk)	95.00	*130.00*
a.		Perf. 15x14		
62	A1	10pi ultra (G)	85.00	*130.00*
63	A1	20pi gray (G)	85.00	*130.00*
a.		Inverted overprint	400.00	
b.		Double overprint	475.00	
c.		Double ovpt., one inverted	475.00	
d.		Black overprint	850.00	
e.		As "d," inverted	1,100.	
f.		As "d," double, one inverted	1,300.	

The overprint reads "Hukumat al Sharqi al Arabia, Nissan Sanat 921" (Arab Government of the East, April, 1921).
For overprints see Nos. 85, 99, 100, 102.

Stamps of Hejaz, 1922, Overprinted in Black

Coat of Arms (Hejaz A7)

1923, Apr.   Unwmk.   Perf. 11½

64	A7	⅛pi orange brn	4.50	*3.75*
a.		Double overprint	225.00	
b.		Inverted overprint	100.00	
65	A7	½pi red	4.50	*3.75*
a.		Inverted overprint	125.00	
66	A7	1pi dark blue	3.75	*1.50*
a.		Inverted overprint	140.00	140.00
67	A7	1½pi violet	3.75	*2.50*
a.		Double overprint	160.00	
b.		Pair, one without overprint	250.00	
c.		Pair, imperf. between	175.00	
68	A7	2pi orange	4.50	*8.00*
69	A7	3pi olive brn	5.00	*13.00*
a.		Inverted overprint	250.00	
b.		Double overprint	250.00	
c.		Pair, one without overprint	400.00	
70	A7	5pi olive green	22.50	*32.50*
		Nos. 64-70 (7)	48.50	*65.00*

The overprint is similar to that on the preceding group but is differently arranged. There are numerous varieties in the Arabic letters.
For overprints see Nos. 71-72, 91, J1-J5.

With Additional Surcharge of New Value in Arabic

a   b

71	A7(a)	¼pi on ⅛pi	11.00	*11.00*
		Never hinged	15.00	
a.		Inverted surcharge	175.00	
b.		Surcharge doubled	—	200.00
72	A7(b)	10pi on 5pi	32.50	*37.50*
		Never hinged	45.00	

Independence Issue

Palestine Stamps and Type of 1918 Overprinted Vertically in Black or Gold

1923, May   Wmk. 33   Perf. 15x14

73	A1	1m dark brn (Bk)	22.50	*17.00*
a.		Double ovpt., one reversed	725.00	650.00
73B	A1	1m dark brn (G)	175.00	175.00
c.		Double ovpt., one reversed	1,000.	
74	A1	2m blue grn	42.50	*50.00*
75	A1	3m lt brown	14.00	*17.50*
76	A1	4m scarlet	14.00	*17.50*
77	A1	5m orange	70.00	*80.00*
78	A1	1pi dk blue (G)	95.00	*110.00*
a.		Double overprint	750.00	850.00

79	A1	2pi olive grn	70.00	*90.00*
80	A1	5pi plum (G)	80.00	*90.00*
a.		Double overprint (G)	725.00	
b.		Double overprint (Bk)	1,500.	
81	A1	9pi bis, perf. 14	70.00	*85.00*
82	A1	10pi ultra, perf. 14	80.00	*100.00*
83	A1	20pi gray	85.00	*110.00*
		Nos. 73-83 (12)	818.00	*942.00*

The overprint reads, "Arab Government of the East (abbreviated), Souvenir of Independence, 25th, May, 1923 ('923')."
There were printed 480 complete sets and a larger number of the 1, 2, 3 and 4m. A large number of these sets were distributed to high officials. The overprint was in a setting of twenty-four and the error "933" instead of "923" occurs once in the setting. Value about five times the "923" stamps.
The overprint exists reading downward on all values, as illustrated, and reading upward on all except the 5m and 2pi.
Forged overprints exist.
For overprint see No. 101.

Stamps of Preceding Issues, Handstamp Surcharged

83A	A1	2½/10ths pi on 5m dp org	175.00	*175.00*
83B	A1	5/10pi on 3m (#17)		
84	A1	5/10pi on 3m (#36)	50.00	*60.00*
85	A1	5/10pi on 3m (#55)	27.50	*40.00*
86	A1	5/10pi on 5pi (#23)	75.00	*85.00*
87	A1	5/10pi on 5pi (#48)	10.00	*17.50*
88	A1	5/10pi on 5pi (#23)	75.00	*85.00*
89	A1	1pi on 5pi (#48)	2,500.	

Same Surcharge on Palestine Stamp of 1918

90	A1	5/10pi on 3m lt brn	17,000.	

No. 90 is valued in the grade of fine-very fine. Very fine examples are not known.
As is usual with handstamped surcharges these are found double, inverted, etc.

No. 67 Surcharged by Handstamp

Unwmk.   Perf. 11½

91	A7	½pi on 1½pi vio	12.00	*14.00*
		Never hinged	5.00	
a.		Surcharge typographed	55.00	*55.00*
b.		As "a," inverted surcharge	150.00	
c.		As "a," double surcharge	180.00	
d.		As "a," pair, one with surcharge	500.00	

The surcharge reads: "Nusf el qirsh" (half piastre). See note after No. 90.
Handstamped surcharge exists double; inverted; double, one inverted, etc.

Stamps of Preceding Issues Surcharged by Handstamp

No. 92

Perf. 14, 15x14
1923, Nov.   Wmk. 33

92	A1	½pi on 2pi (#45)	60.00	*80.00*
93	A1	½pi on 2pi (#47)	100.00	*120.00*
94	A1	½pi on 2pi (#23)	75.00	*85.00*
95	A1	½pi on 5pi (#48)	3,000.	2,000.
96	A1	½pi on 5pi (#49)	2,000.	2,750.
97	A1	½pi on 9pi (#24)	6,500.	
98	A1	½pi on 9pi (#25)	95.00	*160.00*
99	A1	½pi on 9pi (#61)	200.00	160.00

Surcharged by Handstamp

No. 102

100	A1	1pi on 10pi (#62)	2,250.	2,500.
101	A1	1pi on 10pi (#82)	3,000.	3,000.
102	A1	2pi on 20pi (#63)	65.00	80.00

Of the 25 examples of No. 100, a few were handstamped in violet. Value, unused $2,750.

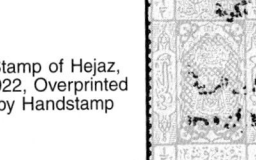
Stamp of Hejaz, 1922, Overprinted by Handstamp

1923, Dec.   Unwmk.   Perf. 11½

103	A7	½pi red	7.50	*4.25*
		Never hinged	5.50	

Two settings of No. 103 exist. They differ in the spacing of the characters and the position of the bottom line of the overprint, either to the left or centered.
Nos. 92-103 handstamps exist inverted, doubled, etc.

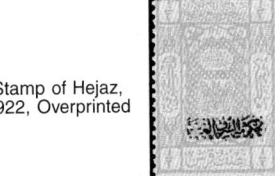
Stamp of Hejaz, 1922, Overprinted

1924   Typo.

104	A7	½pi red	13.50	*14.00*

King Hussein Issue

Stamps of Hejaz, 1922, Overprinted

1924   Gold Overprint

105	A7	½pi red	3.25	3.25
		Never hinged	2.50	
a.				
106	A7	1pi dark blue	3.50	3.25
		Never hinged	3.25	
107	A7	1½pi violet	4.25	*4.50*
		Never hinged	3.00	
108	A7	2pi orange	10.00	10.00
		Never hinged	4.00	

Black Overprint

109	A7	½pi red	2.50	2.50
		Never hinged	1.50	
110	A7	1pi dark blue	3.00	3.00
		Never hinged	1.75	
111	A7	1½pi violet	3.25	3.25
		Never hinged	2.00	
112	A7	2pi orange	10.00	10.00
		Never hinged	2.50	
		Nos. 105-112 (8)	39.75	39.75

The overprint reads: "Arab Government of the East. In commemoration of the visit of H. M. the King of the Arabs, 11 Jemad el Than i 1342 (17th Jan. 1924)." The overprint was in a setting of thirty-six and the error "432" instead of "342" occurs once in the setting and is found on all values. Value, $75 each.

Stamps of Hejaz, 1922-24, Overprinted in Black or Red

Coat of Arms (Hejaz A8)

1924

113	A7	⅛pi red brown	1.00	.50
		Never hinged	1.25	
a.		Inverted overprint	130.00	—
114	A7	¼pi yellow green	1.00	.65
		Never hinged	.50	
a.		Tête bêche pair	9.00	12.00
b.		As "a," one overprint inverted	300.00	—
c.		Inverted overprint	85.00	—
115	A7	½pi red	1.00	.65
		Never hinged	.50	
116	A7	1pi dark blue	7.50	2.50
		Never hinged	6.50	
a.		Inverted overprint	100.00	—
b.		Pair, imperf. between	130.00	—
117	A7	1½pi violet	5.75	5.75
		Never hinged	5.50	
118	A7	2pi orange	4.25	3.50
		Never hinged	5.00	
a.		Double overprint		
119	A7	3pi red brown	3.75	3.75
		Never hinged	4.00	
a.		Double overprint	100.00	—
b.		Inverted overprint	100.00	—
120	A7	5pi olive green	5.00	*5.75*
		Never hinged	4.50	
121	A8	10pi vio & dk brn (R)	11.50	*13.00*
		Never hinged	9.00	
a.		Pair, one without overprint	250.00	—
b.		Black overprint		
		Nos. 113-121 (9)	40.75	36.05

The overprint reads: "Hukumat al Sharqi al Arabia, 1342." (Arab Government of the East, 1924.)

Stamps of Hejaz, 1925, Overprinted in Black or Red

(Hejaz A9)

(Hejaz A10)

(Hejaz A11)

1925, Aug.

122	A9	⅛pi chocolate	.80	1.25
		Never hinged	1.25	
a.		Inverted overprint	70.00	
b.		Pair, imperf. vert.	130.00	*150.00*
123	A9	¼pi ultramarine	1.00	*1.50*
		Never hinged	1.25	
a.		Inverted overprint	70.00	—
124	A9	½pi carmine rose	1.10	.65
		Never hinged	1.25	
a.		Inverted overprint	70.00	—
125	A10	1pi yellow green	1.00	.65
		Never hinged	1.25	
126	A10	1½pi orange	2.50	*.85*
		Never hinged	3.00	
a.		Inverted overprint	70.00	—
127	A10	2pi deep blue	4.00	*4.50*
		Never hinged	4.00	
a.		Triple overprint	160.00	225.00
128	A11	3pi dark green (R)	4.25	*7.00*
		Never hinged	4.50	
a.		Inverted overprint	90.00	—
b.		Pair, imperf. vert.	130.00	170.00
c.		3 pi dark green (Bk)	130.00	160.00
129	A11	5pi orange brn	7.75	*12.00*
		Never hinged	6.50	
a.		Inverted overprint	85.00	—
		Nos. 122-129 (8)	22.40	28.40

The overprint reads: "Hukumat al Sharqi al Arabi. 1343 Sanat." (Arab Government of the East, 1925). Nos. 122-129 exist imperforate, and with overprint double.

Type of Palestine, 1918

1925, Nov. 1   Wmk. 4   Perf. 14

130	A1	1m dark brown	.40	2.75
131	A1	2m yellow	.65	.50
132	A1	3m Prussian bl	1.50	1.25
133	A1	4m rose	1.50	2.75
134	A1	5m orange	2.00	.55
135	A1	6m blue green	1.50	2.00
136	A1	7m yel brown	1.50	2.00
137	A1	8m red	1.50	1.10
138	A1	1pi gray	1.50	.70
139	A1	13m ultramarine	1.75	1.75
140	A1	2pi olive green	3.25	3.50
141	A1	5pi plum	6.00	8.00
142	A1	9pi bister	8.75	19.00
143	A1	10pi light blue	22.50	320.00
a.		"E.F.F." in bottom panel (error)	800.00	3,000.
144	A1	20pi violet	35.00	50.00
		Nos. 130-144 (15)	89.30	415.85

This overprint reads: "Sharqi al-ardan" (East of Jordan).

For overprints see Nos. J12-J23.

Perf. 15x14

142a	A1	9pi	900.	1,425.
143a	A1	10pi	100.	110.
144a	A1	20pi	1,100.	1,100.
		Nos. 142a-144a (3)	2,100.	2,635.

Amir Abdullah ibn Hussein
A1   A2

1927-29   Engr.   Perf. 14

145	A1	2(m) Prus blue	1.00	1.00
146	A1	3(m) rose	1.75	1.75
147	A1	4(m) green	2.25	3.00
148	A1	5(m) orange	1.50	.35
149	A1	10(m) red	1.75	2.00
150	A1	15(m) ultra	1.75	.35
151	A1	20(m) olive grn	2.00	2.00
152	A2	50(m) claret	3.75	7.50
153	A2	90(m) bister	9.75	17.50
154	A2	100(m) lt blue	11.00	16.00
155	A2	200(m) violet	22.50	37.50
156	A2	500(m) dp brn ('29)	87.50	110.00
157	A2	1000(m) gray ('29)	175.00	210.00
		Nos. 145-157 (13)	321.50	408.95

For overprints see Nos. 158-168, B1-B12, J24-J29.

Stamps of 1927 Overprinted in Black

1928, Sept. 1

158	A1	2(m) Prus blue	1.75	2.00
159	A1	3(m) rose	2.00	3.00
160	A1	4(m) green	2.25	4.00
161	A1	5(m) orange	2.25	2.25
162	A1	10(m) red	2.50	5.00
163	A1	15(m) ultra	2.50	2.00
164	A1	20(m) olive grn	7.50	12.50
165	A2	50(m) claret	14.00	15.00
166	A2	90(m) bister	22.50	45.00
167	A2	100(m) lt blue	32.50	65.00
168	A2	200(m) violet	90.00	160.00
		Nos. 158-168 (11)	179.75	315.75

The overprint is the Arabic word "Dastour," meaning "Constitution." The stamps were in commemoration of the enactment of the law setting forth the Constitution.

A3

"MILS" or "L. P." at lower right and Arabic equivalents at upper left.

1930-36   Engr.   Perf. 14
Size: 17¼x21mm

169	A3	1m red brn ('34)	1.00	1.10
170	A3	2m Prus blue	.50	.60
171	A3	3m rose	1.50	.85
172	A3	3m green ('34)	2.00	1.25
173	A3	4m green	1.75	3.75
174	A3	4m rose ('34)	3.75	1.50
175	A3	5m orange	1.25	.35
a.		Perf. 13½x14 (coil) ('36)	32.50	18.00
176	A3	10m red	2.00	.25
177	A3	15m ultra	2.00	.25
a.		Perf. 13½x14 (coil) ('36)	30.00	17.50
178	A3	20m olive grn	3.00	.55

Size: 19¼x23½mm

179	A3	50m red violet	3.50	2.00
180	A3	90m bister	4.25	6.00
181	A3	100m light blue	5.00	6.00
182	A3	200m violet	16.00	18.00
183	A3	500m deep brown	30.00	57.50
184	A3	£1 gray	82.50	125.00
		Nos. 169-184 (16)	160.00	224.95

See Nos. 199-220, 230-235 in Scott Standard catalogue, Vol. 4. For overprint see No. N15a in Scott Vol. 4.

1939   Perf. 13½x13
Size: 17¼x21mm

169a	A3	1m red brown	6.00	4.00
170a	A3	2m Prussian blue	15.00	3.75
172a	A3	3m green	25.00	6.50
174a	A3	4m rose	90.00	27.50
175b	A3	5m orange	75.00	4.00
176a	A3	10m red	150.00	5.75
177b	A3	15m ultramarine	47.50	5.50
178a	A3	20m olive green	72.50	17.50
		Nos. 169a-178a (8)	481.00	75.00

For overprint see No. N3a in Scott Standard catalogue, Vol. 4.

Mushetta — A4

Nymphaeum, Jerash — A5

Kasr Kharana — A6

Kerak Castle — A7

Temple of Artemis, Jerash — A8

Aijalon Castle — A9

Khazneh, Rock-hewn Temple, Petra — A10

Allenby Bridge, River Jordan — A11

Ancient Threshing Floor — A12

Amir Abdullah ibn Hussein — A13

1933, Feb. 1   Perf. 12

185	A4	1m dk brn & blk	1.50	1.25
		Never hinged	1.50	
186	A5	2m claret & blk	2.00	1.00
		Never hinged	1.60	
187	A6	3m blue green	2.50	1.50
		Never hinged	1.90	
188	A7	4m bister & blk	3.00	3.00
		Never hinged	3.00	
189	A8	5m orange & blk	3.50	1.25
		Never hinged	3.50	
190	A9	10m brown red	4.00	3.50
		Never hinged	4.25	
191	A10	15m dull blue	4.50	1.75
		Never hinged	5.75	
192	A11	20m ol grn & blk	6.50	5.50
		Never hinged	8.25	
193	A12	50m brn vio & blk	20.00	15.00
		Never hinged	18.00	
194	A6	90m yel & black	22.50	27.50
		Never hinged	26.00	
195	A8	100m blue & blk	25.00	30.00
		Never hinged	30.00	
196	A9	200m dk vio & blk	60.00	80.00
		Never hinged	85.00	
197	A10	500m brn & ver	180.00	250.00
		Never hinged	260.00	
198	A13	£1 green & blk	600.00	900.00
		Never hinged	900.00	
		Nos. 185-198 (14)	935.00	1,321.

Nos. 194-197 are larger than the lower values in the same designs.

SEMI-POSTAL STAMPS

Locust Campaign Issue

Nos. 145-156 Overprinted

1930, Apr. 1   Wmk. 4   Perf. 14

B1	A1	2(m) Prus blue	1.75	3.50
		Never hinged	2.40	
a.		Inverted overprint	200.00	
B2	A1	3(m) rose	1.75	3.50
		Never hinged	2.40	
B3	A1	4(m) green	2.00	4.75
		Never hinged	2.60	
B4	A1	5(m) orange	20.00	16.75
		Never hinged	27.50	
a.		Double overprint	300.00	
B5	A1	10(m) red	2.25	3.50
		Never hinged	2.90	
B6	A1	15(m) ultra	2.25	3.50
		Never hinged	2.90	
a.		Inverted overprint	200.00	
B7	A1	20(m) olive grn	2.25	5.00
		Never hinged	2.90	
B8	A2	50(m) claret	7.50	11.50
		Never hinged	10.00	
B9	A2	90(m) bister	16.00	45.00
		Never hinged	22.50	
B10	A2	100(m) lt blue	20.00	47.50
		Never hinged	27.50	
B11	A2	200(m) violet	47.50	110.00
		Never hinged	65.00	
B12	A2	500(m) brown	150.00	160.00
		Never hinged	190.00	
a.		"C" of "Locust" omitted	750.00	
		Nos. B1-B12 (12)	273.25	414.50

These stamps were issued to raise funds to help combat a plague of locusts.

POSTAGE DUE STAMPS

Stamps of Regular Issue (Nos. 69, 66-68 Surcharged with New Value like No. 91) Overprinted

This overprint reads: "Mustahaq" (Tax or Due)

1923   Unwmk.   Perf. 11½
Typo. Ovpt. "Mustahaq" 10mm long

J1	A7	½pi on 3pi ol brn	47.50	55.00
		Never hinged	72.50	
a.		Inverted overprint	175.00	175.00
b.		Double overprint	175.00	175.00

Handstamped Overprint 12mm long

J2	A7	½pi on 3pi ol brn	13.50	15.00
		Never hinged	20.00	
a.		Inverted overprint	50.00	—
b.		Double overprint	50.00	—
J3	A7	1pi dark blue	9.00	9.50
		Never hinged	13.50	
a.		Inverted overprint	45.00	—
b.		Double overprint	50.00	—
J4	A7	1½pi violet	9.00	9.50
		Never hinged	13.50	
a.		Inverted overprint	45.00	—
b.		Double overprint	50.00	—
J5	A7	2pi orange	10.00	11.00
		Never hinged	15.00	
a.		Inverted overprint	60.00	—
b.		Double overprint	65.00	—
		Nos. J1-J5 (5)	89.00	100.00

Stamps of Hejaz Handstamped

J6	A7	½pi red	1.50	1.75
		Never hinged	2.25	
J7	A7	1pi dark blue	1.60	2.00
		Never hinged	2.50	
J8	A7	1½pi violet	2.00	2.25
		Never hinged	3.00	
J9	A7	2pi orange	2.50	3.00
		Never hinged	3.75	
J10	A7	3pi olive brown	3.50	5.50
		Never hinged	5.25	
J11	A7	5pi olive green	6.00	8.00
		Never hinged	9.00	
		Nos. J6-J11 (6)	17.10	22.50

Type of Palestine, 1918, Overprinted

1925   Wmk. 4   Perf. 14

J12	A1	1m dark brown	2.25	5.00
		Never hinged	3.50	
J13	A1	2m yellow	3.00	3.25
		Never hinged	4.50	
J14	A1	4m rose	4.75	5.00
		Never hinged	7.25	
J15	A1	8m red	5.50	8.50
		Never hinged	8.25	
J16	A1	13m ultramarine	7.50	8.50
		Never hinged	11.00	
J17	A1	5pi plum	8.25	11.50
		Never hinged	12.50	
a.		Perf. 15x14	67.50	77.50
		Nos. J12-J17 (6)	31.25	41.75

The overprint reads: "Mustahaq. Sharqi al'Ardan." (Tax. Eastern Jordan).

Stamps of Palestine, 1918, Surcharged

1926

J18	A1	1m on 1m dk brn	4.00	5.00
		Never hinged	6.00	
J19	A1	2m on 1m dk brn	4.00	5.00
		Never hinged	6.00	
J20	A1	4m on 3m Prus bl	4.00	6.75
		Never hinged	6.00	

J21	A1	8m on 3m Prus bl	4.25	7.50
		Never hinged	6.25	
J22	A1	13m on 13m ultra	4.25	8.50
		Never hinged	6.25	
J23	A1	5pi on 13m ultra	5.75	10.50
		Never hinged	8.75	
		Nos. J18-J23 (6)	26.25	43.25

The surcharge reads "Tax—Eastern Jordan" and New Value.

Stamps of Regular Issue, 1927, Overprinted

1929

J24	A1	2m Prussian bl	2.50	6.00
		Never hinged	2.25	
J25	A1	10m red	2.50	6.00
		Never hinged	3.50	
J26	A2	50m claret	6.50	19.00
		Never hinged	13.00	
		Nos. J24-J26 (3)	11.50	31.00

With Additional Surcharge

J27	A1	1(m) on 3(m) rose	1.75	7.00
		Never hinged		
J28	A1	4(m) on 15(m) ultra	3.00	7.50
		Never hinged		
a.		Inverted surch. and ovpt.	95.00	
J29	A2	20(m) on 100(m) lt bl	6.50	19.00
		Never hinged	9.50	
		Nos. J27-J29 (3)	11.25	33.50

D1

1929 Engr. Perf. 14
Size: 17¼x21mm

J30	D1	1m brown	1.00	3.25
		Never hinged	1.25	
a.		Perf. 13½x13	90.00	45.00
J31	D1	2m orange	1.00	3.75
		Never hinged	1.25	
J32	D1	4m green	1.00	4.25
		Never hinged	1.25	
J33	D1	10m carmine	2.25	4.75
		Never hinged	2.75	
J34	D1	20m olive green	8.50	15.00
		Never hinged	11.00	
J35	D1	50m blue	10.50	19.00
		Never hinged	13.00	
		Nos. J30-J35 (6)	24.25	50.00

See Nos. J39-J43 design with larger type in Scott Standard catalogue, Vol. 4. For surcharge see No. J52 in same volume. For overprints see Nos. NJ1a, NJ3, NJ5a, NJ6-NJ7 in same volume.

OFFICIAL STAMP

Saudi Arabia No. L34 Overprinted

1924, Jan. Typo. Perf. 11½

O1	A7	½pi red	100.00	—
		Never hinged	200.00	
a.		Arabic date "1242"	200.00	
		Never hinged	400.00	

Overprint reads: "(Government) the Arabian East 1342."

KARELIA

kə-'rē-lə-ə

LOCATION — In northwestern Soviet Russia.
GOVT. — An autonomous republic of the Soviet Union.
AREA — 55,198 sq. mi. (approx.).
POP. — 270,000 (approx.).
CAPITAL — Petrozavodsk (Kalininsk).

In 1921 the Karelians rebelled and for a short period a form of sovereignty independent of Russia was maintained.

100 Pennia = 1 Markka

Bear — A1

1922 Unwmk. Litho. Perf. 11½, 12

1	A1	5p dark gray	15.00	50.00
2	A1	10p light blue	15.00	50.00
3	A1	20p rose red	15.00	50.00
4	A1	25p yellow brown	16.00	50.00
5	A1	40p magenta	16.00	50.00
6	A1	50p gray green	16.00	50.00
7	A1	75p orange yellow	25.00	50.00
8	A1	1m pink & gray	25.00	50.00
9	A1	2m yel grn & gray	30.00	110.00
10	A1	3m lt blue & gray	30.00	140.00
11	A1	5m red lil & gray	30.00	175.00
12	A1	10m lt brn & gray	35.00	275.00
13	A1	15m green & car	35.00	275.00
14	A1	20m rose & green	37.50	275.00
15	A1	25m yellow & blue	60.00	275.00
		Nos. 1-15 (15)	400.50	1,925.
		Set, never hinged	475.00	

Nos. 1-15 were valid Jan. 31-Feb. 16, 1922. Use probably ended Feb. 3, although cancellations of the 4th and 5th exist. Counterfeits abound.

KENYA, UGANDA, & TANZANIA

'ke-nyə, ü-'gan-də, ˌtan-zə-'nē-ə

LOCATION — East Africa, bordering on the Indian Ocean
GOVT. — States in British Commonwealth
AREA — 679,802 sq. mi.
POP. — 42,760,000 (est. 1977)
CAPITAL — Nairobi (Kenya), Kampala (Uganda), Dar es Salaam (Tanzania)

Kenya became a crown colony in 1906, including the former East Africa Protectorate leased from the Sultan of Zanzibar and known as the Kenya Protectorate.
The inland Uganda Protectorate, lying west of Kenya Colony, was declared a British Protectorate in 1894.
Tanganyika, a trust territory larger than Kenya or Uganda, was grouped with them postally from 1935 under the East African Posts & Telecommunications Admin.

100 Cents = 1 Rupee
100 Cents = 1 Shilling (1922)
20 Shillings = 1 Pound

> Catalogue values for unused stamps in this country are for Never Hinged items, beginning with Scott 90.

East Africa and Uganda Protectorates

King George V
A1   A2

1921 Typo. Wmk. 4 Perf. 14
Ordinary Paper

1	A1	1c black	.90	1.90
2	A1	3c green	6.75	12.00
3	A1	6c rose red	8.50	17.50
4	A1	10c orange	9.75	1.40
5	A1	12c gray	8.50	140.00
6	A1	15c ultramarine	12.50	19.00

Chalky Paper

7	A1	50c gray lilac & blk	16.50	120.00
8	A2	2r blk & red, *blue*	82.50	190.00
9	A2	3r green & violet	150.00	350.00
10	A2	5r gray lil & ultra	175.00	275.00
11	A2	50r gray grn & red	5,250.	7,500.
		Nos. 1-10 (10)	470.90	1,126.

The name of the colony was changed to Kenya in August, 1920, but stamps of the East Africa and Uganda types were continued in use. Stamps of types A1 and A2 watermarked Multiple Crown and C A (3) are listed under East Africa and Uganda Protectorates.
For stamps of Kenya and Uganda overprinted "G. E. A." used in parts of former German East Africa occupied by British forces, see Tanganyika Nos. 1-9.

Kenya and Uganda

King George V
A3   A4

1922-27 Wmk. 4

18	A3	1c brown	1.10	3.50
19	A3	5c violet	4.50	1.00
20	A3	5c green ('27)	2.40	.55
21	A3	10c green	1.75	.35
22	A3	10c black ('27)	4.50	.25
23	A3	12c black	11.00	29.00
24	A3	15c car rose	1.40	.25
25	A3	20c orange	3.75	.25
26	A3	30c ultra	4.25	.60
27	A3	50c gray	2.75	.25
28	A3	75c ol bister	8.50	15.00
29	A4	1sh green	4.75	3.00
30	A4	2sh gray lilac	10.00	17.50
31	A4	2sh50c black ('25)	24.00	110.00
32	A4	3sh gray black	20.00	7.50
33	A4	4sh gray ('25)	32.50	110.00
34	A4	5sh carmine	27.50	27.50
35	A4	7sh50c org ('25)	110.00	250.00
36	A4	10sh ultra	70.00	70.00
37	A4	£1 org & blk	225.00	300.00
		Revenue cancel		20.00
38	A4	£2 brn vio & grn ('25)	1,100.	1,800.
		Revenue cancel		120.00
39	A4	£3 yel & dl vio ('25)	1,650.	—
		Revenue cancel		180.00
40	A4	£4 rose lil & blk ('25)	5,000.	—
		Revenue cancel		225.00
41	A4	£5 blue & blk	6,000.	—
		Revenue cancel		375.00
41A	A4	£10 grn & blk	14,000.	—
		Revenue cancel		475.00
41B	A4	£20 grn & red ('25)	34,500.	—
		Revenue cancel		850.00
41C	A4	£25 red & blk	30,000.	—
		Revenue cancel		800.00
41D	A4	£50 brn & blk	37,500.	—
		Revenue cancel		900.00
41E	A4	£75 gray & purple	110,000.	—
		Revenue cancel		1,500.
41F	A4	£100 blk & red	120,000.	—
		Revenue cancel		1,600.
		Nos. 18-37 (20)	569.65	946.50

Nos. 37 and 38 are commonly found with court or fiscal cancellations. Values are much lower than those shown, which are for postally used stamps.
Nos. 39-41F are likely to bear court or fiscal cancels only.
High face value stamps are known with revenue cancellations removed and forged postal cancellations added.

Common Design Types pictured following the introduction.

Kenya, Uganda, Tanganyika
Silver Jubilee Issue
Common Design Type

1935, May Engr. Perf. 13½x14

42	CD301	20c ol grn & lt bl	1.75	.25
43	CD301	30c blue & brown	2.75	3.50
44	CD301	65c indigo & green	2.00	3.25
45	CD301	1sh brt vio & indigo	2.50	4.00
		Nos. 42-45 (4)	9.00	11.00
		Set, never hinged	16.00	

Kavirondo Cranes — A5

Dhow on Lake Victoria — A6

Lion — A7

Mount Kilimanjaro — A8   Jinja Bridge by Ripon Falls — A9

Mount Kenya — A10

Lake Naivasha A11

Type I

FIVE CENTS
Type I — Left rope does not touch sail.
Type II — Left rope touches sail.

Perf. 13, 14, 11½x13, 13x11½
Engr.; Typo. (10c, £1)
1935, May 1

46	A5	1c red brn & blk	1.00	1.50
47	A6	5c grn & blk (I)	3.00	.50
a.		Type II	32.50	3.50
b.		Perf. 13x11½ (I)	8,500.	900.00
c.		Perf. 13x11½ (II)	800.00	225.00
48	A7	10c black & yel	6.00	.65
49	A8	15c red & black	3.25	.25
50	A5	20c red org & blk	3.50	.25
51	A9	30c dk ultra & blk	4.25	1.00
52	A6	50c blk & red vio	4.75	.25
53	A10	65c yel brn & blk	6.50	2.00
54	A11	1sh grn & black	5.00	1.00
a.		Perf. 13x11½ ('36)	1,400.	130.00
55	A8	2sh red vio & rose brn	11.00	4.50
56	A11	3sh blk & ultra	16.00	17.50
a.		Perf. 13x11½	2,250.	

57	A9	5sh car & black	24.00	35.00
58	A5	10sh ultra & red vio	95.00	120.00
59	A7	£1 blk & scar	250.00	350.00
		Nos. 46-59 (14)	433.25	534.40
		Set, never hinged		900.00

Coronation Issue
Common Design Type

1937, May 12   Engr.   Perf. 13½x14

60	CD302	5c deep green	.25	.25
61	CD302	20c deep orange	.30	.35
62	CD302	30c brt ultra	.50	1.00
		Nos. 60-62 (3)	1.05	1.60
		Set, never hinged		2.00

Kavirondo Cranes — A12

Dhow on Lake Victoria — A13

Lake Naivasha — A14

Jinja Bridge, Ripon Falls — A16

Mt. Kilimanjaro A15

Lion — A17

Type II

FIFTY CENTS:
Type I — Left rope does not touch sail.
Type II — Left rope touches sail.

1938-54   Engr.   Perf. 13½x13½

66	A12	1c vio brn & blk ('42)	.25	.50
a.		1c red brown & gray black, perf. 13	2.75	.85

Perf. 13x11½

67	A13	5c grn & blk	3.00	.50
68	A13	5c red org & brn ('49)	.90	5.50
a.		Perf. 13x12½ ('50)	1.75	4.00
69	A14	10c org & brn	2.00	.25
a.		Perf. 14 ('41)	95.00	10.00
70	A14	10c grn & blk ('49)	.25	1.75
a.		Perf. 13x12½ ('50)	2.40	.25

Perf. 13x12½

71	A14	10c gray & red brn ('52)	.80	.55

Perf. 13½x13, 13x13½

72	A15	15c car & gray blk ('43)	3.50	3.75
a.		Booklet pane of 4	15.00	
b.		Perf. 13	25.00	.55
73	A15	15c grn & blk ('52)	1.75	6.00
74	A12	20c org & gray blk ('42)	5.75	.25
a.		Booklet pane of 4	24.00	
b.		Imperf., pair		
c.		Perf. 13	35.00	.30
d.		Perf. 14 ('41)	50.00	3.00

Perf. 13x12½

75	A13	25c car & blk ('52)	1.25	2.25

Perf. 13x13½

76	A16	30c dp bl & gray blk ('42)	2.00	.35
a.		Perf. 14 ('41)	130.00	12.50
b.		Perf. 13	40.00	.40
77	A16	30c brn & pur ('52)	1.25	.40
78	A12	40c brt bl & gray blk ('52)	1.50	5.00

Perf. 13x12½

79	A13	50c gray blk & red vio (II) ('49)	5.75	.60
a.		Perf. 13x11½ (II)	14.00	1.10
b.		Perf. 13x11½ (I)	175.00	250.00

Perf. 13x11½

80	A14	1sh yel brn & gray blk	18.00	.30
a.		Perf. 13x12½ ('49)	10.00	.60

Perf. 13½x13

81	A15	2sh red vio & org brn ('44)	27.50	.30
a.		Perf. 13	110.00	2.50
b.		Perf. 14 ('41)	62.50	16.00

Perf. 13x12½

82	A14	3sh gray blk & ultra ('50)	30.00	7.50
a.		Perf. 13x11½	35.00	7.50

Perf. 13x13½

83	A16	5sh car rose & gray blk ('44)	30.00	1.75
a.		Perf. 13	125.00	18.00
b.		Perf. 14 ('41)	35.00	2.75
84	A12	10sh ultra & red vio ('44)	40.00	7.00
a.		Perf. 13	110.00	29.00
b.		Perf. 14 ('41)	32.50	22.00

**Typo.
Perf. 14**

85	A17	£1 blk & scar ('41)	22.50	23.00
a.		Perf. 11½x13	300.00	150.00
b.		Perf. 12½ ('54)	12.00	37.50
		Nos. 66-85 (20)	197.95	67.50
		Set, never hinged		300.00

Nos. 85-85b were printed on chalky paper. No. 85 also exists on ordinary paper, from a 1944 printing. Values are the same.
See Nos. 98-99.

South Africa Nos. 48, 57, 60 and 62 Surcharged

Basic stamps of Nos. 86-89 are inscribed alternately in English and Afrikaans.

1941-42   Wmk. 201   Perf. 15x14, 14

86	A6	5c on 1p car & gray, pair	1.00	2.00
a.		Single, English	.25	.25
b.		Single, Afrikaans	.25	.25
87	A17	10c on 3p ultra, pair	3.00	10.00
a.		Single, English	.30	.35
b.		Single, Afrikaans	.30	.35
88	A7	20c on 6p org & grn, pair	2.50	3.75
a.		Single, English	.25	.25
b.		Single, Afrikaans	.25	.25
89	A11	70c on 1sh lt bl & ol brn, pair	15.00	7.00
a.		Single, English	.50	.45
b.		Single, Afrikaans	.50	.45
		Nos. 86-89 (4)	21.50	22.75
		Set, never hinged		30.00

Issued: Nos. 86-88, 7/1/41; No. 89, 4/20/42. Values are for horizontal pairs. Vertical pairs are worth substantially less.

Catalogue values for unused stamps in this section, from this point to the end of the section, are for Never Hinged items.

Peace Issue
Common Design Type

1946, Nov. 11   Engr.   Wmk. 4

90	CD303	20c red orange	.25	.25
91	CD303	30c deep blue	.40	.40

Silver Wedding Issue
Common Design Types

1948, Dec. 1   Photo.   Perf. 14x14½

92	CD304	20c orange	.25	.25

**Engr.; Name Typo.
Perf. 11½x11**

93	CD305	£1 red	52.50	72.50

UPU Issue
Common Design Types
Engr.; Typo. on Nos. 95 and 96

1949, Oct. 10   Perf. 13, 11x11½

94	CD306	10c red orange	.25	.25
95	CD307	30c indigo	1.75	2.25
96	CD308	50c gray	.40	.40
97	CD309	1sh red brown	.50	.50
		Nos. 94-97 (4)	2.90	3.40

Type of 1949 with Added Inscription: "Royal Visit 1952"

1952, Feb. 1   Engr.   Perf. 13x12½

98	A14	10c green & black	.30	1.60
99	A14	1sh yel brn & gray blk	1.25	2.25

Visit of Princess Elizabeth, Duchess of Edinburgh, and the Duke of Edinburgh, 1952.

POSTAGE DUE STAMPS

Kenya and Uganda

D1

Perf. 14½x14

1928-33   Typo.   Wmk. 4

J1	D1	5c deep violet	2.75	1.00
J2	D1	10c orange red	2.75	.60
J3	D1	20c yel green	3.25	4.00
J4	D1	30c ol brn ('31)	22.50	16.00
J5	D1	40c dull blue	7.50	15.00
J6	D1	1sh grnsh gray ('33)	72.50	140.00
		Nos. J1-J6 (6)	111.25	176.60
		Set, never hinged		200.00

Kenya, Uganda, Tanganyika

D2

1935, May 1   Perf. 13½x14

J7	D2	5c violet	3.25	2.00
J8	D2	10c red	.35	.65
J9	D2	20c green	.55	.65
J10	D2	30c brown	1.25	.80
J11	D2	40c ultramarine	1.75	3.50
J12	D2	1sh gray	22.50	25.00
		Nos. J7-J12 (6)	29.65	32.60
		Set, never hinged		50.00

KIAUCHAU
(Kiautschou)

LOCATION — A district of China on the south side of the Shantung peninsula.

GOVT. — A former German colony.

AREA — 200 sq. mi.

POP. — 192,000 (approx. 1914).

The area was seized by Germany in 1897 and through negotiations that followed was leased to Germany by China.

100 Pfennig = 1 Mark
100 Cents = 1 Dollar (1905)

STAMPS OF GERMAN OFFICES IN CHINA USED IN KIAUCHAU

Type A

Type B

Type C

Stamps of Germany canceled Type A, Type B or Type C

1898

A1	A8	2m brownish purple	400.00
		On cover	5,000.
a.		2m carmine lilac	575.00
		On cover	165.00
		On cover	
A2	A9	3pf brown	57.50
		On cover	165.00
		3pf yellow brown	57.50
		On cover	165.00
b.		3pf ocher brown	165.00
		On cover	325.00
c.		3pf olive brown	82.50
		On cover	250.00
A3	A9	5pf blue green	50.00
		On cover	175.00
A4	A10	10pf carmine	20.00
		On cover	62.50
a.		dark carmine	22.50
		On cover	65.00
A5	A10	20pf ultramarine	100.00
		On cover	250.00
A6	A10	25pf orange	250.00
		On cover	575.00
A7	A9	50 red brown	290.00
		On cover	650.00

Stamps of 1898 German Offices in China Canceled Type B or Type C

1898

56 degree Angle

A8	A9	3pf dark brown (#1)	20.00
		On cover	40.00
a.		3pf yellow brown (#1a)	16.00
		On cover	32.50
b.		3pf reddish brown (#1b)	165.00
		On cover	275.00
A9	A9	5pf green (#2)	13.00
		On cover	20.00
A10	A10	10pf carmine (#3)	16.00
		On cover	25.00
A11	A10	20pf ultramarine (#4)	260.00
		On cover	375.00
A12	A10	25pf 25pf orange (#5)	125.00
		On cover	250.00
A13	A10	50pf red brown (#6)	90.00
		On cover	260.00

**Canceled Type A
45 degree Angle**

A14	A9	3pf yellow brown (#1c)	12,500.
A15	A9	5pf green (#2a)	20.00
		On cover	30.00
A16	A10	10pf carmine (#3a)	16.00
		On cover	25.00
A17	A10	20pf ultramarine (#4a)	16.00
		On cover	32.50
A18	A10	25pf orange (#5a)	82.50
		On cover	165.00
A19	A10	50pf red brown (#6a)	75.00
		On cover	260.00

Cancellations other than Types A-C are scarce and command premiums.

TSINGTAU ISSUES

Stamps of Germany, Offices in China 1898, with Additional Surcharge

a

b

c

On Nos. 1-9, a blue or violet line is drawn through "PF. 10 PF." All exist without this line. All examples of Nos. 1b, 2b and 3b lack the colored line.

The three surcharge types can most easily be distinguished by the differences in the lower loop of the "5."

1900
"China" Overprint at 56 degree Angle

No.		Description	Unused	Used
1	A10(a)	5pfg on 10pf car	45.00	52.50
		Never hinged	140.00	
		On cover		200.00
c.		Dbl. surch., one inverted	750.00	
		Never hinged	1,650.00	
2	A10(b)	5pfg on 10pf car	45.00	52.50
		Never hinged	140.00	
		On cover		200.00
c.		Dbl. surch., one inverted	750.00	
		Never hinged	1,650.00	
3	A10(c)	5pfg on 10pf car	45.00	52.50
		Never hinged	140.00	
		On cover		200.00
c.		Dbl. surch., one inverted	750.00	
		Never hinged	1,650.00	
		Nos. 1-3 (3)	135.00	157.50

"China" Overprint at 45 degree Angle

No.		Description	Unused	Used
1a	A10(a)	5pfg on 10pf car	145.00	130.00
		Never hinged	350.00	
		On cover		325.00
b.		Double surcharge	450.00	575.00
		Never hinged	975.00	
2a	A10(b)	5pfg on 10pf car	145.00	130.00
		Never hinged	350.00	
		On cover		325.00
b.		Double surcharge	450.00	575.00
		Never hinged	975.00	
3a	A10(c)	5pfg on 10pf car	145.00	130.00
		Never hinged	350.00	
		On cover		325.00
b.		Double surcharge	450.00	575.00
		Never hinged	975.00	
		Nos. 1a-3a (3)	435.00	390.00

Surcharged

d   e

5 Pf.

f

"China" Overprint at 48 degree Angle on Nos. 4-9

No.		Description	Unused	Used
4	A10(d)	5pf on 10pf car	3,250.	4,000.
		Never hinged	5,000.	
		On cover		7,500.
a.		Double surcharge	8,250.	18,000.
		On cover		24,000.
5	A10(e)	5pf on 10pf car	3,250.	4,000.
		Never hinged	5,000.	
		On cover		7,500.
a.		Double surcharge	8,250.	18,000.
		On cover		32,500.
6	A10(f)	5pf on 10pf car	3,250.	4,000.
		Never hinged	5,000.	
		On cover		7,500.
a.		Double surcharge	8,250.	18,000.
		On cover		32,500.
b.		5fP		18,000.
		On cover		
c.		As "b," double surcharge	—	—

5

With Additional Handstamp

No.		Description	Unused	Used
7	A10(d)	5pf on 10pf car	40,000.	50,000.
		Never hinged	57,500.	
		On cover		90,000.
8	A10(f)	5pf on 10pf car	40,000.	50,000.
		Never hinged	57,500.	
		On cover		90,000.
a.		On No. 6b		

With Additional Handstamp

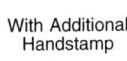

No.		Description	Unused	Used
9	A10(f)	5pf on 10pf car	8,250.	12,500.
		Never hinged	13,000.	
		On cover		20,000.
a.		Double surcharge	37,500.	

b. On No. 6a
c. On No. 6b
d. On No. 6c

On Nos. 1-9, a blue or violet line is drawn through "PF. 10 PF." All exist without this line. All examples of Nos. 1b, 2b and 3b lack the colored line.

A1   A2

Kaiser's Yacht "Hohenzollern"

1901, Jan. Unwmk. Typo. Perf. 14

No.		Description	Unused	Used
10	A1	3pf brown	2.00	2.00
		Never hinged	5.00	
		On cover		40.00
11	A1	5pf green	2.00	1.75
		Never hinged	5.00	
		On cover		16.50
12	A1	10pf carmine	2.50	2.10
		Never hinged	6.50	
		On cover		16.50
13	A1	20pf ultra	7.50	8.50
		Never hinged	20.00	
		On cover		24.00
14	A1	25pf org & blk, yel	13.50	17.00
		Never hinged	32.50	
		On cover		50.00
15	A1	30pf org & blk, sal	13.50	16.50
		Never hinged	40.00	
		On cover		52.50
16	A1	40pf lake & blk	16.00	21.00
		Never hinged	40.00	
		On cover		52.50
17	A1	50pf pur & blk, sal	16.00	22.50
		Never hinged	40.00	
		On cover		52.50
18	A1	80pf lake & blk, rose	30.00	52.50
		Never hinged	70.00	
		On cover		115.00

Engr. Perf. 14½x14

No.		Description	Unused	Used
19	A2	1m carmine	50.00	92.50
		Never hinged	135.00	
		On cover		165.00
20	A2	2m blue	75.00	110.00
		Never hinged	190.00	
		On cover		180.00
21	A2	3m blk vio	75.00	200.00
		Never hinged	190.00	
		On cover		375.00
22	A2	5m slate & car	210.00	650.00
		Never hinged	575.00	
		On cover		1,250.
		Nos. 10-22 (13)	513.00	1,196.
		Set, never hinged	1,350.	
		Set, ovptd. "SPECIMEN"	1,100.	
		Set, ovptd. "SPECIMEN," never hinged	2,100.	

Covers: Values for Nos. 17-22 are for overfranked complete covers, usually philatelic.

A3

A4

1905 Typo.

No.		Description	Unused	Used
23	A3	1c brown	1.25	1.75
		Never hinged	4.25	
		On cover		19.00
24	A3	2c green	2.00	1.75
		Never hinged	5.25	
		On cover		16.50
25	A3	4c carmine	4.50	1.75
		Never hinged	11.50	
		On cover		16.00
26	A3	10c ultra	8.50	5.50
		Never hinged	20.00	
		On cover		24.00
27	A3	20c lake & blk	34.00	20.00
		Never hinged	105.00	
		On cover		52.50
28	A3	40c lake & blk, rose	100.00	100.00
		Never hinged	250.00	
		On cover		175.00

Engr.

No.		Description	Unused	Used
29	A4	$½ carmine	72.50	85.00
		Never hinged	170.00	
		On cover		175.00
30	A4	$1 blue, 26x17 holes	190.00	125.00
		Never hinged	525.00	
		On cover		200.00
a.		$1 blue, 25x16 holes	150.00	130.00
		Never hinged	375.00	
		On cover		200.00
31	A4	$1½ blk vio	1,200.	1,700.
		Never hinged	2,600.	
		On cover		2,450.
32	A4	$2½ slate & car, 26x17 holes	1,500.	5,000.
		Never hinged	4,300.	
		On cover		7,500.
a.		$2½ slate & car, 25x16 holes	2,100.	3,500.
		Never hinged	4,900.	
		On cover		5,600.
		Nos. 23-32 (10)	3,112.	7,040.
		Set, never hinged	8,000.	

Values for Nos. 27-32 on cover are for overfranked, usually philatelic, covers.

1905-16 Wmk. 125 Typo.

No.		Description	Unused	Used
33	A3	1c brown ('06)	1.25	1.50
		Never hinged	3.25	
		On cover		32.50
a.		1c yellow brown ('16)	.50	—
		Never hinged	2.00	
34	A3	2c green ('09)	1.10	1.10
		Never hinged	2.75	
		On cover		14.50
a.		2c dark green ('14)	.50	1.75
		Never hinged	2.00	
		On cover		20.00
35	A3	4c carmine ('09)	1.00	1.10
		Never hinged	2.50	
		On cover		16.00
36	A3	10c ultra ('09)	1.10	3.25
		Never hinged	2.50	
		On cover		22.50
a.		10c blue	12.00	5.00
		Never hinged	25.00	
		On cover		15.00
37	A3	20c lake & blk ('08)	3.00	16.00
		Never hinged	6.00	
		On cover		52.50
a.		20c red & black ('18)	1.60	
		Never hinged	4.00	
38	A3	40c lake & blk, rose	3.25	52.50
		Never hinged	8.00	
		On cover		120.00

Engr.

No.		Description	Unused	Used
39	A4	$½ carmine, 26x17 holes ('07)	10.00	65.00
		Never hinged	32.50	
		On cover		140.00
a.		$½ pale rose, 25x17 holes ('18)	6.50	
		Never hinged	22.50	
40	A4	$1 blue, 26x17 holes ('06)	12.50	67.50
		Never hinged	65.00	
		On cover		150.00
a.		$1 bright blue, 25x17 holes ('18)	8.00	
		Never hinged	27.50	
41	A4	$1½ blk violet	11.00	225.00
		Never hinged	125.00	
		On cover		—
a.		$1½ gray violet, 25x17 holes ('18)	20.00	
		Never hinged	82.50	
42	A4	$2½ slate & car	60.00	475.00
		Never hinged	300.00	
		On cover		825.00
		Nos. 33-42 (10)	104.20	907.95
		Set, never hinged	550.00	

Nos. 37a, 39a, 40a and 41a were not placed in use.

Unused examples with original gum are worth approximately 50% more than the values shown.

KIONGA

'kyoŋ-gə

LOCATION — Southeast Africa and northeast Mozambique, on Indian Ocean south of Rovuma River
GOVT. — Part of German East Africa
AREA — 400 sq. mi.

This territory, occupied by Portuguese troops during World War I, was allotted to Portugal by the Treaty of Versailles. Later it became part of Mozambique.

100 Centavos = 1 Escudo

Lourenco Marques No. 149 Surcharged in Red

1916, May 29 Unwmk. Perf. 11½

No.		Description	Unused	Used
1	A2	½c on 100r bl, bl	30.00	20.00
2	A2	1c on 100r bl, bl	24.00	17.00
3	A2	2½c on 100r bl, bl	24.00	17.00
4	A2	5c on 100r bl, bl	24.00	17.00
		Nos. 1-4 (4)	102.00	71.00

Most of the stock of Lourenço Marques No. 149 used for these surcharges lacked gum.

KOREA

kə-'rē-ə

(Corea)

(Chōsen, Tyosen, Tae Han)

LOCATION — Peninsula extending from Manchuria between the Yellow Sea and the Sea of Japan
GOVT. — Republic
AREA — 38,221 sq. mi.
POP. — 39,950,743 (1983)
CAPITAL — Seoul

Korea (or Corea) an independent monarchy for centuries under Chinese influence, came under Japanese influence in 1895. Japanese stamps were used there as early as 1875. Administrative control was assumed by Japan in 1904 and annexation followed in 1910. Postage stamps of Japan were used in Korea from 1905 to early 1946.

100 Mon = 1 Tempo
5 Poon = 1 Cheun
100 Sen = 1 Yen
1000 Re = 100 Cheun = Weun

Stylized Yin Yang
A1   A2

Perf. 8½ to 11½

1884		Typo.		Unwmk.
1	A1	5m rose	65.00	6,750.
2	A2	10m blue	55.00	6,750.

Reprints and counterfeits of Nos. 1-2 exist.

These stamps were never placed in use. Values: 25 and 50 mon, each $19; 100 mon $20.
Counterfeits exist.

Yin Yang — A6

Two types of 50p:
I — No period after "50."
II — Period after "50."

Perf. 11½, 12, 12½, 13 and Compound

1895				Litho.
6	A6	5p green	27.50	16.00
a.		5p pale yellow green	75.00	27.50
b.		Vert. pair, imperf horiz.	425.00	
c.		Horiz. pair, imperf. vert.	425.00	

---

	d.	Vertical pair, imperf. between	425.00	—
	e.	Horiz. pair, imperf. btwn.	425.00	—
7	A6	10p deep blue	150.00	40.00
a.		Horiz. pair, imperf. between	425.00	
b.		Vert. pair, imperf. horiz.	425.00	
8	A6	25p maroon	30.00	30.00
a.		Horiz. pair, imperf. between	375.00	375.00
b.		Vert. pair, imperf. horiz.	375.00	375.00
9	A6	50p purple (II)	24.00	14.00
a.		Horiz. pair, imperf. between	400.00	400.00
b.		Vert. pair, imperf. horiz.	400.00	400.00
c.		Horiz. pair, imperf. vert.	400.00	400.00
d.		Type I	75.00	40.00
		Nos. 6-9 (4)	269.00	100.00

For overprints and surcharges see Nos. 10-17C, 35-38.
Counterfeits exist of Nos. 6-9 and all surcharges and overprints.

Overprinted "Tae Han" in Korean and Chinese Characters

1897			**Red Overprint**	
10	A6	5p green	100.00	10.00
a.		5p pale yellow green	200.00	150.00
b.		Inverted overprint	150.00	150.00
c.		Without ovpt. at bottom	150.00	130.00
d.		Without overprint at top	150.00	130.00
f.		Double overprint at top	140.00	140.00
g.		Overprint at bottom in blk	160.00	160.00
h.		Pair, one without overprint	450.00	450.00
i.		Double overprint at top, inverted at bottom	550.00	
11	A6	10p deep blue	110.00	15.00
a.		Without overprint at top	150.00	150.00
b.		Without overprint at top	150.00	150.00
c.		Double overprint at top	150.00	150.00
d.		Bottom overprint inverted	140.00	140.00
e.		Top ovpt. dbl., one in blk	210.00	210.00
f.		Top overprint omitted, bottom overprint inverted	450.00	
12	A6	25p maroon	120.00	17.00
a.		Overprint at bottom invtd.	150.00	150.00
b.		Overprint at bottom in blk	210.00	210.00
c.		Bottom overprint omitted	150.00	150.00
e.		Top ovpt. dbl., one in blk	225.00	225.00
f.		Top and bottom overprints double, one of each in blk	250.00	250.00
g.		Pair, one without overprint	425.00	425.00
13	A6	50p purple	100.00	12.00
a.		Without ovpt. at bottom	120.00	110.00
b.		Without overprint at top	120.00	110.00
c.		Bottom overprint double	120.00	110.00
e.		Pair, one without overprint	275.00	275.00
		Nos. 10-13 (4)	430.00	54.00

1897			**Black Overprint**	
13F	A6	5p green	400.00	85.00
13G	A6	10p deep blue	400.00	100.00
h.		Without ovpt. at bottom	450.00	
14	A6	25p maroon	400.00	100.00
a.		Without ovpt. at bottom	450.00	
b.		Without overprint at top	450.00	
c.		Double overprint at bottom	450.00	
15	A6	50p purple	400.00	80.00
a.		Without ovpt. at bottom	450.00	
		Nos. 13F-15 (4)	1,600.	

These stamps with black overprint, also No. 16A, are said not to have been officially authorized.

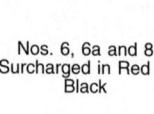

Nos. 6, 6a and 8 Surcharged in Red or Black

1900				
15B	A6	1p on 5p grn (R)	3,500.	750.00
c.		Yellow green		
16	A6	1p on 25p mar	100.00	60.00

Same Surcharge in Red or Black on Nos. 10, 10a, 12, 12c and 14

16A	A6	1p on 5p grn (R)	1,000.	
b.		1p on 5p pale yellow green	1,000.	
17	A6	1p on 25p (#12)	60.00	22.50
a.		Figure "1" omitted	100.00	
b.		On #12c	90.00	70.00
17C	A6	1p on 25p (#14)	775.00	175.00

Counterfeit overprints and surcharges of Nos. 10-17C exist. See note after No. 15.

A8   A9

A10

A11

A12

A13

A14

A15

A16   A17

A18   A19

A20   A21

1900-01		**Typo.**		**Perf. 11**
18	A8	2re gray	8.00	3.50
19	A9	1ch yellow grn	12.00	4.50
20B	A11	2ch pale blue	27.50	12.00
21	A12	3ch orange red	12.00	10.00
a.		Vert. pair, imperf. horiz.	200.00	200.00
b.		Horiz. pair, imperf. btwn.		500.00
c.		3c brnsh org	12.00	10.00
d.		As "c," vert. pair, imperf. btwn.		500.00
22	A13	4ch carmine	40.00	16.00
23	A14	5ch pink	32.50	8.00
24	A15	6ch dp blue	40.00	7.25
25	A16	10ch purple ('01)	47.50	27.50
26	A17	15ch gray vio	72.50	45.00
27	A18	20ch red brown	140.00	47.50
31	A19	50ch ol grn & pink	600.00	240.00
32	A20	1wn rose, blk & bl	1,200.	300.00
33	A21	2wn pur & yel grn	1,500.	650.00
		Nos. 18-33 (13)	3,732.	1,371.

Nos. 22, 23, 25, 26, 33 exist imperf.
Some examples of Nos. 18-27 exist with forged Tae Han overprints in red. It is believed that Nos. 18 and 21 exist with genuine Tae Han overprints.
Reprints of No. 24 were made in light blue, perf. 12x13, in 1905 for a souvenir booklet. See note after No. 54.
See Nos. 52-54.

Perf. 10

18a	A8	2re	17.50	5.25
19a	A9	1ch	17.50	5.50
20	A10	2ch blue	75.00	45.00
a.		Horiz. pair, imperf. btwn.	725.00	
20Ba	A11	2ch pale blue	50.00	45.00
21e	A12	3ch	16.00	9.00
22a	A13	4ch	45.00	20.00
23a	A14	5ch	40.00	10.00
24a	A15	6ch	47.50	12.00
26a	A17	15ch	160.00	140.00
27a	A18	20ch	225.00	225.00
		Nos. 18a-27a (10)	693.50	516.75

Emperor's Crown — A22

1902, Oct. 18   **Perf. 11½**
34	A22	3ch orange	67.50	35.00

40th year of the reign of Emperor Kojong. An imperf. single was part of the 1905 souvenir booklet. See note following No. 54.
Counterfeits exist.

Nos. 8 and 9 Handstamp Surcharged in Black

1ch   2ch

3ch

Perf. 11½, 12, 12½, 13 and Compound

1902				
35	A6	1ch on 25p maroon	25.00	6.00
b.		Horiz. pair, imperf. btwn.	275.00	
c.		Imperf.	90.00	
d.		Vert. pair, imperf. horiz.	275.00	
e.		On No. 12	—	—
36	A6	2ch on 25p maroon	29.00	7.00
b.		Imperf.	75.00	
d.		On No. 12	90.00	90.00
36E	A6	2ch on 50p purple	175.00	175.00
f.		Character "cheun" unabbreviated (in two rows instead of one)	250.00	175.00
37	A6	3ch on 50p purple	27.50	8.00
b.		With character "cheun" unabbreviated (in two rows instead of one)	2,400.	950.00
d.		Horiz. pair, imperf. btwn.		200.00
e.		Vert. pair, imperf. btwn.		200.00
g.		On No. 13		240.00
38	A6	3ch on 25p maroon	65.00	65.00
		Nos. 35-38 (5)	321.50	261.00

There are several sizes of these surcharges. Being handstamped, inverted and double surcharges exist.
Counterfeit surcharges exist.

Falcon — A23

1903			**Perf. 13½x14**	
39	A23	2re slate	10.00	6.25
40	A23	1ch violet brn	11.00	7.50
41	A23	2ch green	15.00	7.50
42	A23	3ch orange	13.00	7.50
43	A23	4ch rose	22.50	9.50
44	A23	5ch yellow brn	22.50	11.00
45	A23	6ch lilac	26.00	12.50
46	A23	10ch blue	32.50	16.00
47	A23	15ch red, straw	45.00	22.50
48	A23	20ch vio brn, straw	67.50	32.50
49	A23	50ch red, grn	210.00	120.00
50	A23	1wn vio, lav	550.00	300.00
51	A23	2wn vio, org	550.00	300.00
		Nos. 39-51 (13)	1,575.	852.75

Values are for stamps with perfs touching the design.

Types of 1901

1903   *Perf. 12½*
Thin, Semi-Transparent Paper

52	A19	50ch pale ol grn & pale pink	400.00	160.00
53	A20	1wn rose, blk & bl	600.00	200.00
54	A21	2wn lt vio & lt grn	875.00	250.00
		Nos. 52-54 (3)	1,875.	610.00

No. 24, perf. 12x13, No. 34 imperf. and most examples of Nos. 52-54 unused are from souvenir booklets made up in 1905 when the Japanese withdrew all Korean stamps from circulation.

KUWAIT

ku-'wāt

LOCATION — Northwestern coast of the Persian Gulf
GOVT. — Sheikdom under British Protection
AREA — 7,000 sq. mi.
POP. — 1,910,856 (est. 1985)
CAPITAL — Kuwait

16 Annas = 1 Rupee

> Catalogue values for unused stamps in this country are for Never Hinged items, beginning with Scott 72 in the regular postage section.

There was a first or trial setting of the overprint with the word "Koweit." Twenty-four sets of regular and official stamps were printed with this spelling. Value for set, $10,000.

> Catalogue values for Nos. 1-71 used, are for postally used examples. Stamps with telegraph cancellations are worth less.

Iraqi Postal Administration
Stamps of India, 1911-23, Overprinted

a   b

1923-24   **Wmk. 39**   *Perf. 14*

1	A47(a)	½a green	4.75	12.00
		Never hinged	7.25	
2	A48(a)	1a dk brown	7.00	4.75
		Never hinged	9.00	
3	A58(a)	1½a chocolate	5.00	9.00
		Never hinged	7.25	
4	A49(a)	2a violet	5.00	7.50
		Never hinged	7.50	
5	A57(a)	2a6p ultra	3.75	10.00
		Never hinged	5.75	
6	A51(a)	3a brown org	5.00	24.00
		Never hinged	7.50	
7	A51(a)	3a ultra ('24)	12.50	3.75
		Never hinged	19.00	
8	A52(a)	4a ol green	11.50	27.50
		Never hinged	17.00	
9	A53(a)	6a bister	13.00	16.00
		Never hinged	19.50	
10	A54(a)	8a red violet	12.00	50.00
		Never hinged	18.00	
11	A55(a)	12a claret	16.00	55.00
		Never hinged	24.00	
12	A56(b)	1r grn & red brown	40.00	50.00
		Never hinged	55.00	
13	A56(b)	2r brn & car rose	60.00	110.00
		Never hinged	90.00	
14	A56(b)	5r vio & ultra	140.00	250.00
		Never hinged	195.00	

15	A56(b)	10r car & green	225.00	500.00
		Never hinged	315.00	
		Nos. 1-15 (15)	560.50	1,129.

Overprint "a" on India No. 102 is generally considered unofficial.
Nos. 1-4, 6-7 exist with inverted overprint. None of these are believed to have been sold at the Kuwait post office.
For overprints see Nos. O1-O13.

Stamps of India, 1926-35, Overprinted Type "a"

1929-37   **Wmk. 196**

17	A47	½a green	4.00	1.75
		Never hinged	6.00	
18	A71	½a green ('34)	7.00	2.00
		Never hinged	10.50	
19	A48	1a dark brown	7.00	3.25
		Never hinged	16.50	
20	A72	1a dk brown ('34)	7.00	1.25
		Never hinged	10.50	
21	A60	2a dk violet	7.00	1.50
		Never hinged	9.00	
22	A60	2a vermilion	27.50	95.00
		Never hinged	37.50	
23	A49	2a ver ('34)	17.50	6.75
		Never hinged	26.00	
a.		Small die	5.50	2.50
24	A51	3a ultramarine	6.00	2.00
		Never hinged	9.00	
25	A51	3a car rose ('34)	9.00	4.50
		Never hinged	13.50	
26	A61	4a olive green	40.00	100.00
		Never hinged	60.00	
27	A52	4a ol green ('34)	13.00	14.50
		Never hinged	16.00	
28	A53	6a bister ('37)	27.50	65.00
		Never hinged	42.50	
29	A54	8a red violet	12.00	15.00
		Never hinged	18.00	
30	A55	12a claret	35.00	47.50
		Never hinged	52.50	

Overprinted — c

31	A56	1r green & brown	24.00	45.00
		Never hinged	35.00	
32	A56	2r buff & car rose	25.00	72.50
		Never hinged	37.50	
33	A56	5r dk vio & ultra ('37)	130.00	300.00
		Never hinged	180.00	
34	A56	10r car & grn ('34)	275.00	500.00
		Never hinged	375.00	
35	A56	15r ol grn & ultra ('37)	900.00	1,100.
		Never hinged	1,275.	
		Nos. 17-35 (19)	1,573.	2,377.

For overprints see Nos. O15-O25.

Stamps of India, 1937, Overprinted Type "a" (A80, A81) or "c" (A82)

1939   **Wmk. 196**   *Perf. 13½x14*

45	A80	½a brown	4.25	2.75
46	A80	1a carmine	4.25	3.00
47	A81	2a scarlet	4.50	4.00
48	A81	3a yel green	6.00	2.75
49	A81	4a dark brown	25.00	27.50
50	A81	6a peacock blue	16.00	18.00
51	A81	8a blue violet	17.50	37.50
52	A81	12a car lake	12.00	85.00
53	A82	1r brown & slate	16.00	7.50
a.		Elongated "T"	725.00	525.00
54	A82	2r dk brown & dk violet	5.00	25.00
a.		Elongated "T"	725.00	800.00
55	A82	5r dp ultra & dk green	12.00	29.00
a.		Elongated "T"	1,000.	
56	A82	10r rose car & dk violet	50.00	100.00
a.		Double overprint	450.00	450.00
b.		Elongated "T"	1,450.	
57	A82	15r dk green & dk brown	70.00	225.00
a.		Elongated "T"	1,900.	
		Nos. 45-57 (13)	242.50	567.00
		Set, never hinged	400.00	

The elongated "T" variety was corrected in later printings.

Indian Postal Administration

From May 24, 1941, until August 1947, the Kuwaiti postal service was administered by India, and during 1941-45 unoverprinted Indian stamps were used in Kuwait.

Kuwaiti postal services were administered by Pakistan from August 1947 through March 1948. Control was transferred to Great Britain on April 1, 1948.

Stamps of India 1940-43, Overprinted in Black

1945   **Wmk. 196**   *Perf. 13½x14*

59	A83	3p slate	2.75	9.00
60	A83	½a rose violet	1.75	5.00
61	A83	9p lt green	2.75	17.50
62	A83	1a car rose	2.00	2.50
63	A84	1½a dark purple	2.75	11.00
64	A84	2a scarlet	3.00	8.00
65	A84	3a violet	4.00	15.00
66	A84	3½a ultramarine	3.75	16.00
67	A85	4a chocolate	4.00	4.75
68	A85	6a peacock blue	11.00	20.00
69	A85	8a blue violet	5.75	14.00
70	A85	12a car lake	6.00	8.50
71	A81	14a rose violet	11.00	22.50
		Nos. 59-71 (13)	60.50	153.75
		Set, never hinged	110.00	

> Catalogue values for unused stamps in this section, from this point to the end of the section, are for Never Hinged items.

British Postal Administration

See Oman (Muscat) for similar stamps with surcharge of new value only.

Great Britain Nos. 258 to 263, 243 and 248 Surcharged in Black

1948-49   **Wmk. 251**   *Perf. 14½x14*

72	A101	½a on ½p grn	3.50	4.00
73	A101	1a on 1p ver	3.50	2.50
74	A101	1½a on 1½p lt red brown	4.50	2.50
75	A101	2a on 2p lt org	3.50	2.50
76	A101	2½a on 2½p ultra	4.00	1.25
77	A101	3a on 3p violet	3.50	1.10
a.		Pair, one without surcharge		
78	A102	6a on 6p rose lil	3.50	1.00
79	A103	1r on 1sh brown	7.50	2.50

Great Britain Nos. 249A, 250 and 251A Surcharged in Black

		Wmk. 259		*Perf. 14*
80	A104	2r on 2sh6p yel grn	8.50	9.00
81	A104	5r on 5sh dull red	11.00	9.00
81A	A105	10r on 10sh ultra	60.00	11.50
		Nos. 72-81A (11)	113.00	46.85

Issued: Nos. 72-81, 4/48; 10r, 7/4/49.
Bars of surcharge at bottom on No. 81A.

Silver Wedding Issue

Great Britain Nos. 267 and 268 Surcharged in Black

1948   *Perf. 14½x14, 14x14½*
Wmk. 251

82	A109	2½a on 2½p brt ultra	3.00	3.00
83	A110	15r on £1 deep chalky blue	42.50	42.50

Three bars obliterate the original denomination on No. 83.

Olympic Games Issue

Great Britain Nos. 271 to 274 Surcharged "KUWAIT" and New Value in Black

1948   *Perf. 14½x14*

84	A113	2½a on 2½p brt ultra	1.75	3.25
85	A114	3a on 3p dp violet	2.00	3.50
86	A115	6a on 6p red violet	2.10	4.00
87	A116	1r on 1sh dk brown	2.50	4.50
		Nos. 84-87 (4)	8.35	15.25

A square of dots obliterates the original denomination on No. 87.

UPU Issue

Great Britain Nos. 276 to 279 Surcharged "KUWAIT", New Value and Square of Dots in Black

1949, Oct. 10   **Photo.**

89	A117	2½a on 2½p brt ultra	1.25	2.50
90	A118	3a on 3p brt vio	1.50	3.00
91	A119	6a on 6p red vio	1.60	3.00
92	A120	1r on 1sh brown	1.75	1.75
		Nos. 89-92 (4)	6.10	10.25

Great Britain Nos. 280-285 Surcharged Like Nos. 72-79 in Black

Great Britain Nos. 280-285 Surcharged Like Nos. 72-79 in Black

1950-51   **Wmk. 251**   *Perf. 14½x14*

93	A101	½a on ½p lt org	2.75	1.60
94	A101	1a on 1p ultra	2.75	1.60
95	A101	1½a on 1½p green	2.75	2.25
96	A101	2a on 2p lt red brown	2.75	1.50
97	A101	2½a on 2½p ver	2.75	2.75
98	A102	4a on 4p ultra ('50)	2.75	1.50

Great Britain Nos. 286-288 Surcharged in Black

Perf. 11x12
Wmk. 259

99	A121	2r on 2sh6p green	24.00	8.75
100	A121	5r on 5sh dl red	30.00	10.00
101	A122	10r on 10sh ultra	50.00	11.00
		Nos. 93-101 (9)	120.50	40.85

Longer bars, at lower right, on No. 101.
Issued: 4a, 10/2/50; others, 5/3/51.

AIR POST STAMPS

Air Post Stamps of India, 1929-30, Overprinted type "c"

1933-34   **Wmk. 196**   *Perf. 14*

C1	AP1	2a dull green	22.50	27.50
C2	AP1	3a deep blue	4.75	3.50
C3	AP1	4a gray olive	150.00	225.00
C4	AP1	6a bister ('34)	7.00	4.50
		Nos. C1-C4 (4)	184.25	260.50

Counterfeits of Nos. C1-C4 exist.

OFFICIAL STAMPS

Stamps of India, 1911-23, Overprinted

Nos. O1-O9   Nos. O10-O14

1923-24		Wmk. 39	Perf. 14	
O1	A47	½a green	6.00	45.00
		Never hinged	7.50	
O2	A48	1a brown	5.50	24.00
		Never hinged	6.75	
O3	A58	1½a chocolate	5.00	60.00
		Never hinged		
O4	A49	2a violet	10.00	45.00
		Never hinged	13.00	
O5	A57	2a6p ultra	7.00	75.00
		Never hinged	9.00	
O6	A51	3a brown org	7.50	70.00
		Never hinged	9.75	
O7	A51	3a ultra ('24)	7.75	70.00
		Never hinged	10.00	
O8	A52	4a olive grn	6.25	70.00
		Never hinged	8.00	
O9	A54	8a red violet	9.50	110.00
		Never hinged	13.00	
O10	A56	1r grn & brn	32.50	190.00
		Never hinged	42.50	
O11	A56	2r brn & car rose	37.50	275.00
		Never hinged	42.50	
O12	A56	5r vio & ultra	125.00	450.00
		Never hinged	150.00	
O13	A56	10r car & grn	235.00	400.00
		Never hinged	300.00	
O14	A56	15r ol grn & ultra	375.00	600.00
		Never hinged	450.00	
		Nos. O1-O14 (14)	869.50	2,484.

Stamps of India, 1926-30, Overprinted

Nos. O15-O20

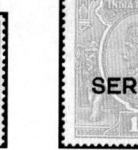
Nos. O21-O25

1929-33		Wmk. 196		
O15	A48	1a dk brown	6.00	40.00
O16	A60	2a violet	70.00	250.00
O17	A51	3a blue	6.00	50.00
O18	A61	4a ol green	6.75	85.00
O19	A54	8a red violet	9.00	120.00
O20	A55	12a claret	42.50	200.00
O21	A56	1r green & brn	13.00	250.00
O22	A56	2r buff & car rose	17.50	375.00
O23	A56	5r dk vio & ultra	45.00	450.00
O24	A56	10r car & green	80.00	750.00
O25	A56	15r olive grn & ultra	275.00	1,300.
		Nos. O15-O25 (11)	570.75	3,870.

LABUAN

lə-ˈbü-ən

LOCATION — An island in the East Indies, about six miles off the northwest coast of Borneo

GOVT. — A British possession, administered as a part of the North Borneo Colony

AREA — 35 sq. mi.

POP. — 8,963 (estimated)

CAPITAL — Victoria

The stamps of Labuan were replaced by those of Straits Settlements in 1906.

100 Cents = 1 Dollar

Covers: There are no known covers bearing Nos. 1-4. Except for Nos. 19, 19a, 29, 29a, covers bearing Nos. 5-32 are very rare. Values for listed covers are for properly franked commercial covers or postal cards. Philatelic covers also exist and sell for much less.

Watermark

Wmk. 46 — C A over Crown

Queen Victoria — A1

On Nos. 1, 2, 3, 4 and 11 the watermark is 32mm high. It is always placed sideways and extends over two stamps.

1879, May		Engr.	Wmk. 46	Perf. 14	
1	A1	2c green		1,600.	975.00
2	A1	6c orange		240.00	215.00
a.		Missing dot in upper left panel (position 2/4).		550.00	500.00
3	A1	12c carmine		1,925.	850.00
a.		Missing right foot in second Chinese character (position 2/3).		4,250.	1,750.
4	A1	16c blue		77.50	190.00
		Nos. 1-4 (4)		3,842.	2,230.

Covers: Covers bearing Nos. 1-4 are not known.

See Nos. 5-10, 16-24, 33-39, 42-48. For surcharges see Nos. 12-15, 25, 31, 40-41.

1880-82			Wmk. 1		
5	A1	2c green		29.00	47.50
6	A1	6c orange		135.00	145.00
a.		Missing dot in upper left panel (position 2/4).		275.00	275.00
7	A1	8c carmine ('82)		135.00	135.00
a.		Missing dot at lower left		250.00	250.00
8	A1	10c yel brown		195.00	100.00
9	A1	12c carmine		330.00	400.00
a.		Missing right foot in second Chinese character (position 2/3).		600.00	700.00
10	A1	16c blue ('81)		100.00	100.00
		Nos. 5-10 (6)		924.00	927.50

Covers: Covers bearing Nos. 5-10 are very rare.

A2

A3

A3a

A4

1880-83				Wmk. 46		
11	A2	6c on 16c blue (with additional "6" across original value) R)			3,750.	1,200.
a.		One "6"				
			Wmk. 1			
12	A2	8c on 12c carmine			1,800.	1,000.
a.		Original value not obliterated			3,500.	2,000.
b.		Additional surcharge "8" across original value			2,175.	1,450.
c.		"8" inverted			2,100.	1,200.
d.		As "a," "8" inverted			3,750.	
e.		Missing right foot in second Chinese character (position 2/3).			3,500.	2,000.
13	A3	8c on 12c car ('81)			450.00	500.00
14	A3a	8c on 12c car ('81)			145.00	155.00
a.		"Eighr"			22,500.	
b.		Inverted surcharge			15,000.	
c.		Double surcharge			2,500.	2,250.
e.		Missing right foot in second Chinese character (position 2/3).			330.00	400.00
15	A4	$1 on 16c blue (R) ('83)			4,800.	

Covers: Covers bearing Nos. 11-15 are very rare.

On No. 12 the original value is obliterated by a pen mark in either black or red.

1883-86				Wmk. 2		
16	A1	2c green			27.50	45.00
a.		Horiz. pair, imperf. btwn.			17,000.	
17	A1	2c rose red ('85)			4.25	16.00
a.		2c pale rose red ('86)			4.25	14.00
18	A1	8c carmine			325.00	160.00
a.		Missing dot at lower left			600.00	225.00
19	A1	8c dk violet ('85)			45.00	45.00
		On cover				1,500.
a.		8c mauve ('86)			35.00	10.00
		On cover				1,500.
b.		Missing dot at lower left			75.00	25.00
c.		As "a," Missing dot at lower left			77.50	27.50

20	A1	10c yellow brn		55.00	55.00
21	A1	10c black brn ('86)		30.00	70.00
22	A1	16c blue		115.00	215.00
23	A1	16c gray blue ('86)		120.00	180.00
24	A1	40c ocher		27.50	140.00
		Nos. 16-24 (9)		719.25	960.00

Covers: Covers bearing Nos. 16-18, 20-24 are very rare.

Nos. 1-10, 16-24 are in sheets of 10. For surcharges see Nos. 26-30, 32.

A5

A6

A7

A8

1885			Wmk. 1		
25	A5	2c on 16c blue		1,150.	1,100.
			Wmk. 2		
26	A5	2c on 8c car		275.00	500.00
a.		Double surcharge			
27	A6	2c on 16c blue		135.00	200.00
a.		Double surcharge			7,500.
28	A7	2c on 8c car		80.00	145.00
a.		Missing dot at lower left		170.00	350.00

Covers: Covers bearing Nos. 25-28 are very rare.

1891

Black or Red Surcharge

29	A8	6c on 8c violet	16.00	14.00
		On cover		1,500.
a.		6c on 8c dark violet	180.00	160.00
		On cover		1,750.
b.		Double surcharge	390.00	
c.		As "a," "Cents" omitted	550.00	550.00
d.		Inverted surcharge	90.00	85.00
e.		Dbl. surch., one inverted	1,100.	
f.		Dbl. surch., both inverted	1,100.	
g.		"6" omitted	600.00	
h.		Pair, one without surcharge	1,800.	1,800.
i.		Invt. surcharge, "Cents" omitted	600.00	
j.		As "d," one without surcharge	2,000.	2,000.
k.		As "a," inverted surcharge	300.00	275.00
m.		As "a," double surcharge	600.00	
n.		As "a," double surcharge, one inverted	1,200.	
p.		As "a," pair, one inverted, one omitted	2,000.	
q.		As "a," horiz. pair, imperf,. btwn.	15,000.	
30	A8	6c on 8c dk vio (R)	1,325.	675.00
a.		Inverted surcharge	1,800.	850.00
			Wmk. 46	
31	A8	6c on 16c blue	2,750.	2,200.
a.		Inverted surcharge	14,000.	8,000.
			Wmk. 2	
32	A8	6c on 40c ocher	13,000.	5,750.
a.		Inverted surcharge	12,000.	9,000.

Covers: Covers bearing Nos. 30-32 are very rare. Values for Nos. 29 and 29a on cover are for properly franked commercial covers or postal cards. Philatelic covers exist and sell for much less.

1892		Engr.	Unwmk.	
33	A1	2c rose	7.25	4.25
		On cover		500.00
34	A1	6c yellow green	12.00	5.75
		On cover		550.00
35	A1	8c violet	9.50	16.00
		On cover		1,500.
a.		8c pale violet ('93)	9.50	15.00
		On cover		1,500.
36	A1	10c brown	24.00	9.50
		On cover		1,000.
a.		10c dk sepia brown ('93)	20.00	17.00
		On cover		
37	A1	12c deep ultra	13.00	8.00
		On cover		800.00
38	A1	16c gray	22.00	45.00
		On cover		1,500.
39	A1	40c ocher	27.50	42.50
a.		40c brown buff ('93)	55.00	30.00
		On cover		
		Nos. 33-39 (7)	115.25	131.00

The 2c, 8c and 10c are in sheets of 30; others in sheets of 10.

Values for covers are for properly franked commercial usages. Philatelic covers exist and sell for lower prices.

Remainders of the 1892 issue were canceled to order, but in most cases cannot be distinguished from postally used examples.

Nos. 39 and 38 Surcharged

1893					
40	A1	2c on 40c ocher		200.00	110.00
		On cover			1,600.
a.		Inverted surcharge		500.00	675.00
41	A1	6c on 16c gray		450.00	180.00
		On cover			2,500.
a.		Inverted surcharge		675.00	350.00
b.		Surcharge sideways		675.00	375.00
c.		"Six" omitted		—	
d.		"Cents" omitted		—	
e.		Handstamped "Six Cents"		2,275.	

Surcharges on Nos. 40-41 each exist in 10 types. Counterfeits exist.

No. 41e was handstamped on examples of No. 41 on which the surcharge failed to print or was printed partially or completely albino.

Values for covers are for properly franked commercial usages.

From Jan. 1, 1890, to Jan. 1, 1906, Labuan was administered by the British North Borneo Co. Late in that period, unused remainders of Nos. 42-83, 53a, 63a, 64a, 65a, 66a, 68a, 85-86, 96-118, 103a, 107a, J1-J9, J3a and J6a were canceled to order by bars forming an oval. Values for these stamps used are for those with this form of cancellation, unless described as postally used, which are for stamps with dated town cancellations. Nos. 63b, 64b, 65b, 104a, J6a, and possibly others, only exist c.t.o.

1894, Apr.			Litho.	
42	A1	2c bright rose	2.00	.65
		Postally used		16.00
		On cover		1,000.
43	A1	6c yellow green	25.00	.65
		Postally used		50.00
		On cover		3,000.
a.		Horiz. pair, imperf. btwn.	10,000.	
44	A1	8c bright violet	25.00	.65
		Postally used		50.00
		On cover		2,750.
45	A1	10c brown	60.00	.65
		Postally used		65.00
		On cover		3,750.
46	A1	12c light ultra	32.50	.80
		Postally used		85.00
		On cover		4,750.
47	A1	16c gray	37.50	.65
		Postally used		150.00
		On cover		
48	A1	40c orange	60.00	.65
		Postally used		160.00
		On cover		
		Nos. 42-48 (7)	242.00	4.70
		Set, ovptd. "SPECIMEN"	145.00	

Counterfeits exist.

Values for covers are for properly franked commercial usages. Philatelic covers exist and sell for lower prices.

Dyak Chieftain — A9   Malayan Sambar — A10

Sago Palm A11   Argus Pheasant A12

Arms of North Borneo — A13   Dhow — A14

Saltwater
Crocodile — A15

Mt.
Kinabalu — A16

Arms of North
Borneo — A17

Perf. 14 ½-15

1894, May-1896   **Engr.**

49	A9	1c lilac & black	2.00	.65
		Postally used		11.50
		On cover		180.00
a.		Vert. pair, imperf. between	1,300.	575.00
50	A10	2c blue & black	3.00	.65
		Postally used		12.00
		On cover		180.00
a.		Imperf., pair	725.00	
51	A11	3c bister & black	4.50	.65
		Postally used		21.00
		On cover		325.00
52	A12	5c green & black	38.50	1.10
		Postally used		32.50
		On cover		425.00
a.		Horiz. pair, imperf. between	1,800.	
53	A13	6c brn red & blk	3.00	.65
		Postally used		20.00
		On cover		275.00
a.		Imperf., pair	725.00	350.00
54	A14	8c rose & black	9.00	.65
		Postally used		30.00
		On cover		450.00
a.		8c red & black	29.00	1.40
		Postally used		35.00
		On cover		525.00
55	A15	12c orange & black	27.50	.65
		Postally used		57.50
56	A16	18c ol brn & blk	26.50	.65
		Postally used		65.00
		On cover		
a.		18c olive bister & black	67.50	.55
		Postally used		85.00
b.		Vert. pair, imperf. between		2,500.
57	A17	24c lilac & blue	18.00	.65
		Postally used		55.00
		On cover		900.00
a.		24c mauve & blue	30.00	.55
		Postally used		65.00
	Nos. 49-57 (9)		132.00	6.30
	Set, ovptd. "SPECIMEN"		150.00	

Perf. 13½-14

49b	A9	1c lilac & black	13.00	
		Postally used		12.00
		On cover		200.00
50b	A10	2c blue & black	5.50	
		Postally used		12.00
		On cover		200.00
51a	A11	3c bister & black	14.00	
		Postally used		11.00
		On cover		250.00
52b	A12	5c green & black	45.00	
		Postally used		20.00
		On cover		300.00
53b	A13	6c brn red & blk		2.25
54b	A14	8c rose & black	37.50	1.10
		Postally used		37.50
		On cover		625.00
54c	A14	8c red & black	35.00	
		Postally used		55.00
		On cover		800.00
55a	A15	12c orange & black	77.50	2.40
		Postally used		85.00
56c	A16	18c ol brn & blk	85.00	
56d	A16	18c ol bister & blk	32.50	
		Postally used		77.50
		On cover		
57b	A17	24c lilac & blue	16.00	.60
		Postally used		55.00
57c	A17	24c mauve & blue	30.00	
		Postally used		60.00

Perf. 13½-14 compound 14½-15

49c	A9	1c lilac & black	32.50	
50c	A10	2c blue & black	32.50	
51b	A11	3c bister & black	—	
53c	A13	6c brn red & blk	—	—

Perf. 13½-14 compound 12-13

49d	A9	1c lilac & black	30.00	1.10
		Postally used		14.50
		On cover		275.00
50d	A10	2c blue & black	—	
51c	A11	3c bister & black	47.50	
52c	A12	5c green & black	60.00	
53d	A13	6c brown red & blk	—	

55b	A15	12c orange & black	250.00	—
		Postally used		
		On cover		—
56e	A16	18c bister & blk	—	

Perf. 12-13

49e	A9	1c lilac & black	—	
50e	A10	2c blue & black	150.00	
51d	A11	3c bister & black	—	
52d	A12	5c green & black	175.00	
53e	A13	6c brown red & blk	250.00	
55c	A15	12c orange & black	—	

Values for covers are for properly franked commercial usages.
For overprints see Nos. 66-71.

A18

A19

A20

A21

1895, June   **Litho.**   **Perf. 14**

58	A18	4c on $1 red	2.75	.50
		Postally used		3.50
59	A18	10c on $1 red	9.50	.50
		Postally used		1.75
60	A18	20c on $1 red	45.00	.50
		Postally used		14.00
61	A18	30c on $1 red	47.50	1.50
		Postally used		55.00
62	A18	40c on $1 red	47.50	1.50
		Postally used		45.00
	Nos. 58-62 (5)		152.25	4.50
	Set, ovptd. "SPECIMEN"		95.00	

1896

63	A19	25c blue green	37.50	.80
		Postally used		40.00
a.		Imperf, pair	32.50	72.50
b.		Without overprint	60.00	2.00
c.		As "b," imperf, pair		
64	A20	50c claret	37.50	.80
		Postally used		40.00
a.		Imperf, pair	30.00	72.50
b.		Without overprint	52.50	2.00
c.		As "b," imperf, pair		
65	A21	$1 dark blue	80.00	1.00
		Postally used		75.00
a.		Imperf, pair	45.00	72.50
b.		Without overprint	60.00	2.00
c.		As "b," imperf, pair		
	Nos. 63-65 (3)		155.00	2.60
	Set, ovptd. "SPECIMEN"		65.00	

For surcharges and overprint see Nos. 93-95, 116-118, 120.

Nos. 49-54
Overprinted

1896   **Perf. 14½-15**

66	A9	1c lilac & black	24.00	1.25
		Postally used		27.50
a.		"JEBILEE"	1,450.	360.00
		Postally used		675.00
b.		"JUBILE"	3,000.	
c.		Orange overprint	325.00	24.00
		Postally used		240.00
67	A10	2c blue & black	52.50	1.75
		Postally used		30.00
a.		Vert. pair, imperf. btwn.	1,200.	1,150.
b.		"JEBILEE"	1,800.	1,325.
c.		"JUBILE"	3,500.	
d.		Vert. strip of 3, imperf between	8,000.	
68	A11	3c bister & black	50.00	1.25
		Postally used		27.50
a.		"JEBILEE"	2,250.	850.00
		Postally used		1,800.
b.		"JUBILE"	—	
69	A12	5c green & black	72.50	1.35
		Postally used		19.50
a.		Double overprint	925.00	600.00

70	A13	6c brown red & blk	42.50	1.00
		Postally used		27.50
a.		Double overprint	975.00	600.00
		Postally used		
b.		"JUBILE"	3,500.	
71	A14	8c rose & black	57.50	1.00
		Postally used		18.50
a.		Double overprint	—	3,000.
		Postally used		3,500.
	Nos. 66-71 (6)		299.00	7.60
	Set, ovptd. "SPECIMEN"		150.00	

Perf. 13½-14

66d	A9	1c lilac & black	30.00	
		Postally used		26.00
e.		Double overprint	450.00	400.00
		Postally used		
f.		Orange overprint	325.00	240.00
		Postally used		
67e	A10	2c blue & black	47.50	
		Postally used		21.00
68c	A11	3c bister & black	50.00	1.10
		Postally used		35.00
d.		Triple overprint	1,150.	
69b	A12	5c green & black	72.50	1.35
		Postally used		27.50
70c	A13	6c brown red & blk	—	
		Postally used		100.00
71b	A14	8c rose & black	50.00	1.00
		Postally used		16.00

Perf. 13½-14 compound 14½-15

67f	A10	2c blue & black	—	50.00
		Postally used		
68e	A11	3c bister & black	—	
70d	A13	6c brown red & blk	—	
71c	A14	8c rose & black	60.00	21.00
		Postally used		

Perf. 13½-14 compound 12-13

66g	A9	1c lilac & black	37.50	
		Postally used		25.00
h.		Orange overprint	—	240.00
		Postally used		
67g	A10	2c blue & black	55.00	
68f	A11	3c bister & black	450.00	200.00
		Postally used		450.00
g.		Double overprint	925.00	
h.		Triple overprint	775.00	
69c	A12	5c green & black	—	

Perf. 12-13

66i	A9	1c lilac & black	—	

Cession of Labuan to Great Britain, 50th anniv.

Dyak Chieftain
A22

Malayan
Sambar
A23

Sago Palm
A24

Argus Pheasant
A25

Dhow — A27

Saltwater
Crocodile — A28

Mt. Kinabalu
"Postal
Revenue" — A29

Coat of
Arms — A30

1897-1900   **Engr.**   **Perf. 14½-15**

72	A22	1c lilac & black	6.00	.60
		Postally used		5.75
72A	A22	1c red brn & blk	3.75	.80
73	A23	2c blue & black	30.00	.90
a.		Vert. pair, imperf between		950.00
b.		Horiz. pair, imperf between		1,300.
75	A24	3c bister & blk	10.00	.60
		Postally used		8.00
a.		Vert. pair, imperf between	1,300.	675.00
76	A25	5c green & blk	60.00	.85
		Postally used		67.50
78	A26	6c brn red & blk	11.00	.60
		Postally used		
a.		Vert. pair, imperf between		850.00
79	A27	8c red & black	22.00	
		Postally used		14.50
80	A28	12c red & black	40.00	2.00
		Postally used		60.00
82	A30	24c gr lilac & bl	14.50	.60
		Postally used		60.00
	Nos. 72-82 (9)		197.25	6.95
	Set (Nos. 72, 73-82), ovptd. "SPECIMEN"		220.00	

Perf. 13½-14

72Ab	A22	1c red brn & blk	22.50	.80
				24.00
73c	A23	2c blue & black	21.00	.80
				5.50
74	A23	2c grn & blk ('00)	4.50	.35
				3.00
a.		Horiz. pair, imperf between		3,000.
75b	A24	3c bister & blk	10.00	.60
				27.50
76b	A25	5c green & blk	67.50	.90
				67.50
77	A25	5c lt bl & blk ('00)	27.50	.80
				21.00
78b	A26	6c brn red & blk	8.00	.60
		Postally used		45.00
79a	A27	8c red & black	60.00	.60
79b	A27	8c vermilion & black	14.50	.60
80a	A28	12c red & black	110.00	2.25
				130.00
81	A29	18c ol bis & blk	15.00	.60
				55.00
82a	A30	24c gr lilac & bl	57.50	1.35
		Postally used		100.00

Perf. 13½-14 compound 14½-15

72c	A22	1c lilac & black	—	

Perf. 13½-14 compound 12-13

73d	A23	2c blue & black	55.00	
		Postally used		25.00
74b	A23	2c grn & blk ('00)	—	
75c	A24	3c bister & blk	25.00	2.00
				35.00
76c	A25	5c green & blk	100.00	
77a	A25	5c lt bl & blk ('00)	—	
78c	A26	6c brn red & blk	7.00	
79c	A27	8c red & black	45.00	3.25

Perf. 16

72Ad	A22	1c red brn & blk	18.50	
				16.00
73e	A23	2c blue & black		8.50
79d	A27	8c red & black		6.50
81a	A29	18c ol bis & blk	10.00	
		Postally used		—
b.		Vert. pair, imperf between		3,750.

For surcharges see Nos. 87-89, 110-112.

"Postage &
Revenue" — A31

"Postage &
Revenue" — A32

1897, Nov.   **Perf. 14½-15**

83	A31	18c bister & black	95.00	2.40
		Postally used		72.50
84	A32	24c brn lilac & blue	42.50	3.00
		Postally used		67.50
		Overprinted "SPECIMEN"	27.50	
a.		24c ocher & blue	42.50	4.00

Perf. 13½-14

83a	A31	18c bister & black	—	
84b	A32	24c brn lilac & blue	42.50	2.40
		Postally used		67.50

Perf. 13½-14 compound 12-13

91a	A06 24c brn lilac & blue			
		Postally used		77.50

Perf. 16

83b	A31	18c bister & black		10.00
84d	A32	24c brn lilac & blue	45.00	

No. 84a only exists cto.
For surcharges see Nos. 92, 115.

"Postage &
Revenue" — A33

"Postage &
Revenue" — A34

1898, Mar.   Perf. 14½-15

85	A33	12c red & black	57.50	4.00
86	A34	18c bister & black	72.50	—
		Postally used		72.50

Perf. 13½-14

85a	A33	12c red & black	50.00	
		Postally used		60.00
86a	A34	18c bister & black	38.50	3.25
		Postally used		75.00

Perf. 13½-14 compound 14½-15

85b	A33 12c red & black			

Perf. 13½-14 compound 12-13

86b	A34	18c bister & black	52.50	
		Postally used		67.50

Perf. 12-13

86c	A34 18c bister & black		—	

Perf. 16

85c	A33	12c red & black	67.50	
		Postally used		72.50
86d	A34	18c bister & black	45.00	

For surcharges see Nos. 90-91, 113-114.

Regular Issue
Surcharged in Black

1899   Perf. 14½-15

87	A25	4c on 5c grn & blk	55.00	30.00
88	A26	4c on 6c brn red & blk	27.50	22.50
89	A27	4c on 8c red & blk	72.50	48.00
90	A33	4c on 12c red & blk	60.00	42.50
91	A34	4c on 18c bis & blk	35.00	21.50
a.		Double surcharge	500.00	600.00
92	A32	4c on 24c lil & bl	32.50	36.00

Perf. 14

93	A19	4c on 25c blue grn	7.25	8.00
94	A20	4c on 50c claret	8.50	8.00
95	A21	4c on $1 dk blue	8.50	8.00
		Nos. 87-95 (9)	306.75	224.50
		Set, ovptd. "SPECIMEN"	175.00	

Perf. 13½-14

88a	A26	4c on 6c brn red & blk	37.50	45.00
89a	A27	4c on 8c red & blk	42.00	37.50
90a	A33	4c on 12c red & blk	55.00	50.00
92a	A32	4c on 24c lil & bl	32.50	36.00

Perf. 13½-14 compound 12-13

88b	A26	4c on 6c brn red & blk	60.00	72.50
89b	A27	4c on 8c red & blk	35.00	42.50
90b	A33	4c on 12c red & blk	67.50	77.50
92b	A32	4c on 24c lil & bl	40.00	35.00

Perf. 12-13

89c	A27	4c on 8c red & blk		—

Perf. 16

90c	A33	4c on 12c red & blk	55.00	47.50
92c	A32	4c on 24c lil & bl	55.00	57.50

Orangutan
A35

Sun Bear
A36

Railroad
Train — A37

Crown — A38

1899-1901   Perf. 13½-14

96	A35	4c yel brown & blk	10.00	.75
		Postally used		60.00
a.	Vert. pair, imperf. btwn.		1,350.	
b.	Perf 13½-14 compound 12-13		42.50	
97	A35	4c car & blk ('00)	14.50	.90
				3.50
a.	Perf 14½-15		6.00	.60
				13.00
b.	Perf 13½-14 compound 12-13		40.00	.90
				10.00
c.	Perf 16		—	
98	A36	10c gray vio & dk brn ('01)	60.00	.75
				100.00
99	A37	16c org brn & grn (G) ('01)	60.00	3.00
				140.00
a.	Perf 14½-15		160.00	
b.	Perf 13½-14 compound 12-13		95.00	
				140.00
c.	Perf 12-13		350.00	
		Nos. 96-99 (4)	144.50	5.40
		Set, ovptd. "SPECIMEN"	180.00	

1902-03   Engr.   Perf. 13½-14

99A	A38	1c vio & black	6.00	.60
				8.50
100	A38	2c green & blk	5.00	.35
		Postally used		6.00
100A	A38	3c sepia & blk	4.00	.35
		Postally used		18.50
101	A38	4c car & black	4.00	.35
		Postally used		4.25
102	A38	8c org & black	15.00	.60
		Postally used		11.00
103	A38	10c sl blue & brn	4.00	.35
		Postally used		18.50
a.	Vert. pair, imperf. between		850.00	
104	A38	12c yel & black	12.00	.35
		Postally used		21.00
a.	Vert. strip of 3, imperf. horiz.		4,000.	
105	A38	16c org brn & grn	5.75	.35
		Postally used		27.50
a.	Vert. pair, imperf. between		—	2,300.
106	A38	18c bis brn & blk	4.00	.35
		Postally used		30.00
107	A38	25c grnsh bl & grn	9.00	.60
		Postally used		24.00
a.	25c greenish blue & black		600.00	
108	A38	50c gray lil & vio	12.00	2.25
		Postally used		55.00
109	A38	$1 org & red brn	10.00	2.00
		Postally used		60.00
		Nos. 99A-109 (12)	90.75	8.50
		Set, ovptd. "SPECIMEN"	230.00	

Perf. 14½-15

99Ab	A38	1c vio & black	95.00	
		Postally used		9.00
100b	A38	2c green & blk	120.00	
				6.00
101a	A38	4c car & black	8.50	
				12.00
102a	A38	8c org & black	9.50	
103b	A38	10c sl blue & brn	7.25	.60
		Postally used		20.00

107b	A38	25c grnsh bl & grn	18.00	.75
				42.50
109a	A38	$1 org & red brn	12.00	2.00

Perf. 13½-14 compound 12-13

99Ac	A38	1c vio & black	92.50	
		Postally used		60.00
101b	A38	4c car & black	82.50	
		Postally used		60.00
108a	A38	50c gray lil & vio	19.50	
		Postally used		65.00

Perf. 16

104b	A38	12c yel & black	11.00	
		Postally used		25.00

Line Through "B" of "LABUAN"

Perf. 13½-14

99Ad	A38	1c vio & black	80.00	9.50
		Postally used		110.00
100c	A38	2c green & blk	75.00	9.50
		Postally used		90.00
100Ac	A38	3c sepia & blk	75.00	9.75
		Postally used		150.00
101c	A38	4c car & black	75.00	9.75
		Postally used		77.50
102b	A38	8c org & black	110.00	9.75
		Postally used		120.00
103c	A38	10c sl blue & brn	75.00	9.50
		Postally used		170.00
104c	A38	12c yel & black	120.00	9.75
		Postally used		200.00
105b	A38	16c org brn & grn	100.00	9.75
		Postally used		240.00
106a	A38	18c bis brn & blk	85.00	9.75
		Postally used		250.00
107c	A38	25c grnsh bl & grn	120.00	11.00
		Postally used		230.00
108b	A38	50c gray lil & vio	200.00	20.00
		Postally used		500.00
109b	A38	$1 org & red brn	190.00	20.00
		Postally used		525.00
		Nos. 99Ad-109b (12)	1,305.	138.00

There are 3 known examples of No. 104a, all cto.
The "line through B" variety is a constant plate flaw in position R5/10.
For overprints and surcharges see Brunei Nos. 1-12.

Regular Issue of
1896-97 Surcharged
in Black

1904   Perf. 14½x15

110	A25	4c on 5c green & blk	55.00	17.00
		Postally used		47.50
111	A26	4c on 6c brown red & black	14.50	17.00
		Postally used		47.50
112	A27	4c on 8c red & blk	30.00	17.00
		Postally used		55.00
113	A33	4c on 12c red & blk	27.50	17.00
		Postally used		50.00
a.	Perf 16		35.00	55.00
		Postally used		50.00
114	A34	4c on 18c bis & blk	30.00	17.00
		Postally used		55.00
a.	Perf 13½-14, comp. 12-13		32.50	55.00
b.	Perf 12-13		—	
115	A32	4c on 24c brn lil & bl	19.25	17.00
		Postally used		60.00
a.	Perf 13½-14		32.50	45.00
b.	Perf 13½-14, comp. 12-13		35.00	
				57.50
c.	Perf 16		32.50	17.00
		Postally used		50.00

Perf. 14

116	A19	4c on 25c blue green	10.00	17.00
				29.00
117	A20	4c on 50c claret	10.00	17.00
		Postally used		30.00
a.	Double surcharge		400.00	
118	A21	4c on $1 dark blue	10.00	17.00
		Postally used		30.00
		Nos. 110-118 (9)	206.25	153.00

Stamps of North Borneo, 1893, and Labuan No. 65a Overprinted in Black

      a   b

c

1905

119	A30(a)	25c slate blue	1,325.	1,100.
120	A21(c)	$1 blue		1,050.
121	A33(b)	$2 gray green	4,000.	
		Postally used		4,000.
122	A34(c)	$5 red violet	7,250.	1,700.
		Postally used		8,000.
a.	$5 dull purple		7,000.	1,800.
		Postally used		7,250.
123	A35(c)	$10 brown	50,000.	13,000.

Nos. 119, 120 and 123 do not exist used. No. 120 exists only cto.

POSTAGE DUE STAMPS

Regular Issues
Overprinted

1901   Unwmk.   Perf. 14

J1	A23	2c green & black	24.00	1.10
		Postally used		37.50
a.	Double overprint		425.00	
J2	A24	3c bister & black	30.00	1.00
		Postally used		130.00
J3	A35	4c car & black	52.50	2.50
a.	Double overprint		875.00	
J4	A25	5c lt blue & black	60.00	1.50
		Postally used		150.00
J5	A26	6c brown red & blk	50.00	1.10
		Postally used		135.00
J6	A27	8c red & black	100.00	2.75
a.	Center inverted, ovpt. reading down			12,000.
d.	8c rose red & blk		100.00	155.00
J7	A33	12c red & black	140.00	6.00
a.	Overprint reading down			1,100.
J9	A32	24c brown lil & bl	70.00	7.00
		Postally used		155.00
c.	24c ocher & blue		100.00	1.75
		Nos. J1-J9 (8)	526.50	22.95

Perf. 14½-15

J3b	A35	4c car & black	60.00	.60
		Postally used		120.00
J4a	A25	5c lt blue & black		1.35
J5a	A26	6c brown red & blk	65.00	
		Postally used		120.00
J6b	A27	8c red & black	100.00	1.00
		Postally used		170.00
J6e	A27	8c rose red & blk	150.00	9.00
J7b	A33	12c red & black	120.00	14.50
		Postally used		175.00
J8	A34	18c ol bister & blk	35.00	1.75
		Postally used		145.00
J9a	A32	24c brown lil & bl	45.00	

Perf. 14½-15, Compound 12-13

J1b	A23	2c green & black	95.00	12.00
		Postally used		100.00

J2a	A24	3c bister & black	95.00	2.75
J4b	A25	5c lt blue & black	100.00	
		Postally used		190.00

Perf. 16

J5b	A26	6c brown red & blk	72.50	.80
J6c	A27	8c red & black	97.50	
		Postally used		130.00
J9d	A32	24c ocher & blue	70.00	
		Postally used		130.00

Perf. 13½-14, Compound 12-13

J9b	A32	24c brown lil & bl	100.00	

See note after No. 41.

The stamps of Labuan were superseded by those of Straits Settlements in 1906.

LAGOS

'lā-ˌgäs

LOCATION — West Africa, bordering on the former Southern Nigeria Colony
GOVT. — British Crown Colony and Protectorate
AREA — 3,460 sq. mi. (approx.)
POP. — 1,500,000 (1901)
CAPITAL — Lagos

This territory was purchased by the British in 1861 and placed under the Governor of Sierra Leone. In 1874 it was detached and formed part of the Gold Coast Colony until 1886 when the Protectorate of Lagos was established. It was chartered to the Royal Niger Company until 1899 when all territories of this Company were surrendered to the Crown of Great Britain and formed into the Northern and Southern Nigeria Protectorates. In 1906 Lagos and Southern Nigeria were united to form the Colony and Protectorate of Southern Nigeria.

12 Pence = 1 Shilling

GREAT BRITAIN POST OFFICES IN LAGOS

British postal agencies were opened in Lagos in April 1852, and a distinctive postal marking was intoduced in 1859.

Pre-Stamp Postmark

1859
Crowned Circle Handstamp Type V
A1 Inscribed "PAID AT LAGOS" in black, on cover 4,250.
Earliest known use 12/12/71.

Queen Victoria — A1

1874-75	**Typo.**	**Wmk. 1**	**Perf.**	**12½**
1	A1	1p lilac	80.00	47.50
2	A1	2p blue	80.00	42.50
3	A1	3p red brown ('75)	130.00	47.50
4	A1	4p rose	140.00	47.50
5	A1	6p blue green	140.00	17.50
6	A1	1sh orange ('75)	425.00	70.00
a.		Value 15½mm instead of 16½mm long	700.00	160.00
		Nos. 1-6 (6)	995.00	272.50

1876			**Perf.**	**14**
7	A1	1p lilac	50.00	21.00
8	A1	2p blue	75.00	15.00
9	A1	3p red brown	120.00	30.00
a.		3p chestnut	125.00	40.00

10	A1	4p rose	225.00	12.50
11	A1	6p green	130.00	7.00
12	A1	1sh orange	950.00	95.00
		Nos. 7-12 (6)	1,550.	180.50

The 4p exists with watermark sideways.

#19, 53a

#19b, 53

1882-1902				**Wmk. 2**
13	A1	½p green ('86)	2.25	.95
14	A1	1p lilac	30.00	22.50
15	A1	1p car rose	2.25	.95
16	A1	2p blue	200.00	8.00
17	A1	2p gray	95.00	9.00
18	A1	2p lil & bl ('87)	7.50	3.25
19	A1	2½p ultra ('91)	7.50	2.00
a.		2½p blue	90.00	57.50
b.		As No. 19, larger letters of value	25.00	19.00
20	A1	3p orange brn	27.50	7.50
21	A1	3p lilac & brn orange ('91)	3.00	3.75
22	A1	4p rose	200.00	14.00
23	A1	4p violet	160.00	9.50
24	A1	4p lil & blk ('87)	2.50	2.00
25	A1	5p lil & grn ('94)	3.00	12.50
26	A1	6p olive green	9.00	55.00
27	A1	6p lilac & red violet ('87)	5.50	3.50
28	A1	6p lilac & car rose ('02)	5.75	13.50
29	A1	7½p lilac & car rose ('94)	3.75	35.00
30	A1	10p lil & yel ('94)	4.00	15.00
31	A1	1sh orange ('85)	15.00	22.50
32	A1	1sh yellow green & blk ('87)	6.50	32.50
a.		1sh blue green & black	5.75	29.00
33	A1	2sh6p ol brn ('86)	375.00	325.00
34	A1	2sh6p green & car rose ('87)	27.50	92.50
35	A1	5sh blue ('86)	700.00	500.00
36	A1	5sh green & ultra ('87)	47.50	175.00
37	A1	10sh brn vio ('86)	1,700.	1,150.
38	A1	10sh grn & brn ('87)	120.00	250.00

Excellent forgeries exist of Nos. 33, 35 and 37 on paper with genuine watermark.

No. 24 Surcharged in Black

1893				
39	A1	½p on 4p lilac & blk	9.00	3.00
a.		Double surcharge	70.00	62.50
b.		Triple surcharge	170.00	
c.		½p on 2p lilac & blue (#18)	—	25,000.

Four settings of surcharge.
Only one used example is known of No. 39c. The two unused examples are in museums.

King Edward VII — A3

#43a

#43

1904, Jan. 22				
40	A3	½p grn & bl grn	2.25	*6.25*
41	A3	1p vio & blk, red	1.25	.25
42	A3	2p violet & ultra	6.75	7.00
43	A3	2½p vio & ultra,	1.50	*1.75*
a.		Smaller letters of value	5.00	*9.75*
44	A3	3p vio & org brn	3.25	2.00
45	A3	6p vio & red vio	40.00	11.50
46	A3	1sh green & blk	40.00	47.50
47	A3	2sh6p grn & car rose	160.00	*325.00*
48	A3	5sh grn & ultra	150.00	*325.00*
49	A3	10sh green & brn	350.00	*950.00*
		Nos. 40-49 (10)	755.00	*1,676.*
		Set, ovptd. "SPECIMEN"	200.00	

1904-05				**Wmk. 3**

Ordinary Paper

50	A3	½p grn & bl grn	12.00	3.00
51	A3	1p vio & blk, *red*	8.00	.25
52	A3	2p violet & ultra	3.75	3.00
53	A3	2½p vio & ultra, *bl,* smaller letters of value	62.50	*140.00*
54	A3	3p vio & org brn	4.00	1.50
55	A3	6p vio & red vio	7.50	4.00
56	A3	1sh green & blk	17.50	26.00
57	A3	2sh6p grn & car rose	25.00	*75.00*
58	A3	5sh grn & ultra	26.00	*110.00*
59	A3	10sh green & brn	90.00	*250.00*
		Nos. 50-59 (10)	246.25	*608.00*

Chalky Paper

50a	A3	½p grn & bl grn	11.50	2.00
51a	A3	1p vio & blk, *red*	1.75	.25
52a	A3	2p violet & ultra	15.00	11.50
53a	A3	2½p vio & ultra, *bl*	2.00	*18.50*
54a	A3	3p vio & org brn	17.50	2.00
55a	A3	6p vio & red vio	5.00	1.75
56a	A3	1sh green & blk	26.00	2.50
57a	A3	2sh6p grn & car rose	40.00	67.50
58a	A3	5sh grn & ultra	77.50	190.00
59a	A3	10sh green & brn	90.00	*225.00*
		Nos. 50a-59a (10)	286.25	*521.00*

The stamps of Lagos were superseded by those of Southern Nigeria.

LATAKIA

ˌla-tə-ˈkē-ə

LOCATION — A division of Syria in Western Asia
GOVT. — French Mandate
AREA — 2,500 sq. mi.
POP. — 278,000 (approx. 1930)
CAPITAL — Latakia

This territory, included in the Syrian Mandate to France under the Versailles Treaty, was formerly known as Alaouites. The name Latakia was adopted in 1930. See Alaouites and Syria.

100 Centimes = 1 Piaster

Stamps of Syria Overprinted in Black or Red

		Perf. 12x12½, 13½		
1931-33				**Unwmk.**
1	A6	10c red violet	1.25	1.25
		Never hinged	1.60	
		On cover		37.50
2	A6	10c vio brn ('33)	1.60	1.60
		Never hinged	2.40	
		On cover		37.50
3	A7	20c dk blue (R)	1.25	1.25
		Never hinged	1.60	
		On cover		30.00
4	A7	20c brown org ('33)	1.60	1.60
		Never hinged	2.40	
		On cover		30.00
5	A8	25c gray grn (R)	1.25	1.25
		Never hinged	1.60	
		On cover		30.00
6	A8	25c dk bl gray (R) ('33)	1.60	1.60
		Never hinged	2.40	
		On cover		30.00
7	A9	50c violet	2.00	2.00
		Never hinged	2.75	
		On cover		25.00
8	A15	75c org red ('32)	3.25	3.25
		Never hinged	4.75	
		On cover		25.00
9	A10	1p green (R)	2.40	2.40
		Never hinged	3.50	
		On cover		25.00
10	A11	1.50p bis brn (R)	3.25	3.25
		Never hinged	5.25	
		On cover		30.00
11	A11	1.50p dp grn (R) ('33)	4.00	4.00
		Never hinged	6.50	
		On cover		25.00
12	A12	2p dk vio (R)	4.00	4.00
		Never hinged	6.50	
		On cover		30.00
13	A13	3p yel grn (R)	6.00	6.00
		Never hinged	10.00	
		On cover		42.50
14	A14	4p orange	5.50	5.50
		Never hinged	9.00	
		On cover		55.00
15	A15	4.50p rose car	5.75	5.75
		Never hinged	10.00	
		On cover		62.50
16	A16	6p grnsh blk (R)	5.75	5.75
		Never hinged	10.00	
		On cover		75.00
17	A17	7.50p dl blue (R)	5.50	5.50
		Never hinged	8.00	
		On cover		80.00
18	A18	10p dp brown (R)	9.50	9.50
		Never hinged	15.00	
		On cover		105.00
a.		Inverted overprint	650.00	
19	A19	15p dp green (R)	11.00	11.00
		Never hinged	17.50	
		On cover		125.00
20	A20	25p violet brn	24.00	24.00
		Never hinged	40.00	
		On cover		165.00
21	A21	50p dk brown (R)	22.50	22.50
		Never hinged	37.50	
		On cover		190.00
a.		Inverted overprint	650.00	
22	A22	100p red orange	55.00	55.00
		Never hinged	92.50	
		On cover		300.00
		Nos. 1-22 (22)	177.95	177.95

AIR POST STAMPS

Air Post Stamps of Syria, 1931, Overprinted in Black or Red

1931-33		**Unwmk.**		**Perf. 13½**
C1	AP2	50c ocher	1.25	1.25
		Never hinged	1.60	
		On cover		30.00
a.		Inverted overprint	1,200.	1,200.
C2	AP2	50c blk brn (R) ('33)	2.50	2.50
		Never hinged	4.25	
		On cover		25.00
C3	AP2	1p chestnut brn	2.50	2.50
		Never hinged	4.25	
		On cover		25.00
C4	AP2	2p Prus blue (R)	4.00	4.00
		Never hinged	6.25	
		On cover		37.50
C5	AP2	3p blue grn (R)	5.50	5.50
		Never hinged	9.00	
		On cover		42.50
C6	AP2	5p red violet	7.00	7.00
		Never hinged	12.00	
		On cover		62.50
C7	AP2	10p slate grn (R)	8.75	8.75
		Never hinged	13.50	
		On cover		92.50
C8	AP2	15p orange red	12.50	12.50
		Never hinged	20.00	
		On cover		140.00
C9	AP2	25p orange brn	24.00	24.00
		Never hinged	37.50	
		On cover		200.00
C10	AP2	50p black (R)	40.00	40.00
		Never hinged	67.50	
		On cover		275.00
C11	AP2	100p magenta	42.50	42.50
		Never hinged	70.00	
		On cover		290.00
		Nos. C1-C11 (11)	150.50	150.50

POSTAGE DUE STAMPS

Postage Due Stamps of Syria, 1931, Overprinted like Regular Issue

1931			Unwmk.	Perf. 13½	
J1	□□	▯□ ▯□, gray b/ (R)		24.00	24.00
		Never hinged		40.00	
		On cover			300.00
J2	D8	15p blk, dl rose (R)		24.00	24.00
		Never hinged		40.00	
		On cover			300.00

Stamps of Latakia were superseded in 1937 by those of Syria.

LATVIA

ˈlat-vē-ə

(Lettonia, Lettland)

LOCATION — Northern Europe, bordering on the Baltic Sea and the Gulf of Riga
GOVT. — Independent Republic
AREA — 25,395 sq. mi.
POP. — 1,994,506 (estimated 1939)
CAPITAL — Riga

Latvia was created a sovereign state following World War I and was admitted to the League of Nations in 1922. In 1940 it became a republic in the Union of Soviet Socialist Republics.

100 Kapeikas = 1 Rublis
100 Santims = 1 Lat (1923)

Watermarks

Wmk. 108
Honeycomb

Wmk. 145 —
Wavy Lines

Wmk.
181
Wavy
Lines

Wmk. 197 — Star and Triangles

Wmk. 212
Multiple
Swastikas

Wmk. 265 — Multiple Waves

Arms — A1

Printed on the Backs of German Military Maps

Unwmk.

1918, Dec. 18   Litho.   Imperf.

1	A1	5k carmine	1.00	2.00

Perf. 11½

2	A1	5k carmine	1.00	2.00

Values given are for stamps where the map on the back is printed in brown and black. Maps printed only in black are valued at: No. 1 unused $2.00; No. 2 unused $1.20, used $2.50. Stamps with no map at all valued: No. 1 unused $1.50, used $3.28; No. 2 unused $1.20, used $2.50. Stamps with no printing on the back are from the outer rows of some sheets.

Redrawn
Paper with Ruled Lines

1919			Imperf.	
3	A1	5k carmine	.25	.25
4	A1	10k dark blue	.25	.25
5	A1	15k green	.50	.50

Perf. 11½

6	A1	5k carmine	2.40	4.00
7	A1	10k dark blue	2.40	4.00
8	A1	15k deep green	7.25	9.50
		Nos. 3-8 (6)	13.05	18.50

In the redrawn design the wheat heads are thicker, the ornament at lower left has five points instead of four, and there are minor changes in other parts of the design.

The sheets of this and subsequent issues were usually divided in half by a single line of perforation gauging 10. Thus stamps are found with this perforation on one side.

1919		Pelure Paper	Imperf.	
9	A1	3k lilac	4.75	4.50
10	A1	5k carmine	.25	.25
11	A1	10k deep blue	.25	.25
12	A1	15k dark green	.25	.25
13	A1	20k orange	.25	.25
13A	A1	25k gray	40.00	40.00
14	A1	35k dark brown	.25	.25
15	A1	50k purple	.25	.25
16	A1	75k emerald	2.50	2.50
		Nos. 9-16 (9)	48.75	48.50

Perf. 11½, 9½

17	A1	3k lilac	35.00	35.00
18	A1	5k carmine	.80	.80
19	A1	10k deep blue	4.00	4.00
20	A1	15k dark green	3.00	3.00
21	A1	20k orange	3.75	3.75
22	A1	35k dark brown	4.50	4.50
23	A1	50k purple	5.50	5.50
24	A1	75k emerald	8.00	8.00
		Nos. 17-24 (8)	64.55	64.55

Values are for perf 11½. Examples Perf 9½ sell for more.

Nos. 17-24 are said to be unofficially perforated varieties of Nos. 9-16.

1919		Wmk. 108	Imperf.	
25	A1	3k lilac	.30	.25
26	A1	5k carmine	.30	.25
27	A1	10k deep blue	.30	.25
28	A1	15k deep green	.30	.25
29	A1	20k orange	.35	.25
30	A1	25k gray	.40	.35
31	A1	35k dark brown	.35	.25
32	A1	50k purple	.35	.25
33	A1	75k emerald	.35	.25
		Nos. 25-33 (9)	3.00	2.35

The variety "printed on both sides" exists for 3k, 10k, 15k, 20k and 35k. Value, $20 each.

See Nos. 57-58, 76-82. For surcharges and overprints see Nos. 86, 132-133, 2N1-2N8, 2N12-2N19.

Liberation of
Riga — A2

Rising
Sun — A4

1919			Wmk. 108	
43	A2	5k carmine	.25	.25
44	A2	15k deep green	.25	.25
45	A2	35k brown	.35	.80
		Nos. 43-45 (3)	.85	1.30

Unwmk.
Pelure Paper

49	A2	5k carmine	9.50	16.00
50	A2	15k deep green	9.50	16.00
51	A2	35k brown	21.00	16.00
		Nos. 49-51 (3)	40.00	48.00

For surcharge and overprints see Nos. 87, 2N9-2N11, 2N20-2N22.

1919			Imperf.	
55	A4	10k gray blue	.85	.60

Perf. 11½

56	A4	10k gray blue	1.00	1.50

Type of 1918

1919 Laid Paper			Perf. 11½	
57	A1	3r slate & org	1.00	1.00
58	A1	5r gray brn & org	1.00	1.00

Independence Issue

Allegory of One
Year of
Independence
A5

1919, Nov. 18   Unwmk.
Wove Paper
Size: 33x45mm

59	A5	10k brown & rose	1.75	1.75

Laid Paper

60	A5	10k brown & rose	1.75	1.75

Size: 28x38mm

61	A5	10k brown & rose	.40	.40
a.		Imperf.	50.00	
62	A5	35k indigo & grn	.40	.40
a.		Vert. pair, imperf. btwn.	50.00	45.00

Wmk. 197
Thick Wove Paper
Blue Design on Back

63	A5	1r green & red	.55	.55
		Nos. 59-63 (5)	4.85	4.85

There are two types of Nos. 59 and 60. In type I the trunk of the tree is not outlined. In type II it has a distinct white outline.

No. 63 was printed on the backs of unfinished 5r bank notes of the Workers and Soldiers Council, Riga.

For surcharges see Nos. 83-85, 88, 94.

Warrior Slaying
Dragon — A6

1919-20   Unwmk.   Perf. 11½
Wove Paper

64	A6	10k brown & car	.50	.50
a.		Horiz. pair, imperf. btwn.	55.00	45.00
65	A6	25k ind & yel grn	.50	.50
a.		Pair, imperf. btwn.	55.00	45.00
66	A6	35k black & bl ('20)	.50	.50
a.		Horiz. pair, imperf. btwn.	55.00	45.00
67	A6	1r dk grn & brn ('20)	.50	.50
a.		Horiz. pair, imperf. vert.	50.00	40.00
b.		Horiz. pair, imperf. btwn.	50.00	40.00
		Nos. 64-67 (4)	2.00	2.00
		Set, never hinged	5.75	

Issued in honor of the liberation of Kurzeme (Kurland). The paper sometimes shows impressed quadrille lines.

For surcharges see Nos. 91-93.

Latgale Relief Issue

Latvia Welcoming
Home Latgale
Province — A7

1920, Mar.
Brown and Green Design on Back

68	A7	50k dk green & rose	1.00	.50
a.		Horiz. pair, imperf. vert.	50.00	
69	A7	1r slate grn & brn	.50	.50
a.		Horiz. pair, imperf. vert.	50.00	
		Set, never hinged	10.00	

No. 68-69 were printed on the backs of unfinished bank notes of the government of Colonel Bermondt-Avalov and on the so-called German "Ober-Ost" money.

For surcharges see Nos. 95-99.

First National Assembly Issue

Latvia Hears Call
to Assemble — A8

1920

70	A8	50k rose	.50	.30
a.		Imperf., pair	5.00	5.00
71	A8	1r blue	.50	.30
a.		Vert. pair, imperf. btwn.	45.00	45.00
b.		Imperf., pair	20.00	15.00
72	A8	3r dk brn & grn	.50	.75
73	A8	5r slate & vio brn	.80	.80
		Nos. 70-73 (4)	2.30	2.15
		Set, never hinged	10.00	

For surcharges see Nos. 90, 134.

Type of 1918 Issue
Wove Paper

1920-21		Unwmk.	Perf. 11½	
76	A1	5k carmine	.25	.25
78	A1	20k orange	.25	.25
79	A1	40k lilac ('21)	.30	.25
80	A1	50k violet	.35	.25
81	A1	75k emerald	.35	.25
82	A1	5r gray brn & org ('21)	1.50	1.00
		Nos. 76-82 (6)	3.00	2.25
		Set, never hinged	6.00	

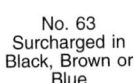

No. 63 Surcharged in Black, Brown or Blue

1920, Sept. 1
83	A5	10r on 1r grn & red (Bk)	1.60	1.60
84	A5	20r on 1r grn & red (Br)	4.00	4.00
85	A5	30r on 1r grn & red (Bl)	5.50	4.00
		Nos. 83-85 (3)	11.10	9.60
		Set, never hinged	20.00	

Types of 1919 Surcharged

1920-21 Wmk. 108 Perf. 11½
86	A1	2r on 10k dp blue	2.00	7.25
87	A2	2r on 35k brown	.75	5.50
		Set, never hinged	5.00	

No. 62 Surcharged in Red

Unwmk.
88	A5	2r on 35k ind & grn	.40	.50
		Never hinged		.75

No. 70 Surcharged in Blue

1921
90	A8	2r on 50k rose	.50	.60
		Never hinged		1.00

Nos. 64-66 Surcharged in Red or Blue

1920-21
91	A6	1r on 35k blk & bl (R)	.35	.35
92	A6	2r on 10k brn & rose (Bl)	.70	.75
93	A6	2r on 25k ind & grn (R)	.40	.40
a.		Imperf.		—
		Nos. 91-93 (3)	1.45	1.50
		Set, never hinged	3.50	

On Nos. 92 and 93 the surcharge reads "DIVI 2 RUBLI."

No. 83 with Added Surcharge

1921 Wmk. 197
94	A5	10r on 10r on 1r	1.50	1.00
		Never hinged	5.00	

Latgale Relief Issue of 1920 Surcharged in Black or Blue

1921, May 31 Unwmk.
95	A7	10r on 50k	1.25	1.00
a.		Imperf.		
96	A7	20r on 50k	3.50	4.00
97	A7	30r on 50k	5.00	4.00
98	A7	50r on 50k	7.50	5.00
99	A7	100r on 50k (Bl)	17.50	16.00
		Nos. 95-99 (5)	34.75	30.00
		Set, never hinged	60.00	

Excellent counterfeits exist.

Arms and Stars for Vidzeme, Kurzeme & Latgale — A10

Coat of Arms — A11

Type I, slanting cipher in value.
Type II, upright cipher in value.

Perf. 10, 11½ and Compound
Wmk. Similar to 181

1921-22 Typo.
101	A10	50k violet (II)	.50	.30
102	A10	1r orange yel	.50	.50
103	A10	2r deep green	.25	.25
104	A10	3r brt green	.65	.45
105	A10	5r rose	1.40	.40
106	A10	6r dp claret	2.00	.80
107	A10	9r orange	1.25	.55
108	A10	10r blue (I)	1.25	.25
109	A10	15r ultra	3.25	.50
a.		Printed on both sides	50.00	
110	A10	20r dull lilac (II)	20.00	2.00

1922, Aug. 21 Perf. 11½
111	A11	50r dk brn & pale brn (I)	30.00	4.50
112	A11	100r dk bl & pale bl (I)	35.00	4.50
		Nos. 101-112 (12)	96.05	15.00
		Set, never hinged	200.00	

Nos. 101-131 sometimes show letters and numerals of the paper maker's watermark "PACTIEN LIGAT MILLS 1858." Stamps showing part of the inscription command a 100 percent premium. Pairs with the complete year "1858" command a 300 percent premium.
See Nos. 126-131, 152-154.

A12

2 SANTIMS
Type A, tail of "2" ends in an upstroke.
Type B, tail of "2" is nearly horizontal.

1923-25 Perf. 10, 11, 11½
113	A12	1s violet	.40	.25
114	A12	2s org yel (A)	.60	.35
115	A12	4s dark green	.60	.25
a.		Horiz. pair, imperf. btwn.	55.00	50.00
116	A12	5s lt green ('25)	2.50	.65
117	A12	6s grn, red ('25)	3.50	.25
118	A12	10s rose red (I)	1.50	.25
a.		Horiz. pair, imperf. btwn.	55.00	50.00
119	A12	12s claret	.25	.40
120	A12	15s brn, sal	3.50	.25
a.		Horiz. pair, imperf. btwn.	55.00	50.00
121	A12	20s dp blue (II)	1.50	.25
122	A12	25s ultra ('25)	.50	.25
123	A12	30s pink (I) ('25)	5.00	.25
124	A12	40s lilac (I)	2.00	.25
125	A12	50s lil gray (II)	3.75	.35
126	A11	1 l dk brn & pale brn	12.50	1.00
127	A11	2 l dk blue & blue	20.00	1.60
130	A11	5 l dp grn & pale grn	60.00	5.00
131	A11	10 l car rose & pale rose (I)	3.00	6.00
		Nos. 113-131 (17)	121.10	17.60
		Set, never hinged	250.00	

Value in "Santims" (1s); "Santimi" (2s-6s) or "Santimu" (others).
See note after No. 110.
See Nos. 135-151, 155-157. For overprints and surcharges see Nos. 164-167, B21-B23.

Nos. 79-80 Surcharged

No. 72 Surcharged

1927 Unwmk. Perf. 11½
132	A1	15s on 40k lilac	.45	.45
133	A1	15s on 50k violet	1.40	1.60
134	A8	1 l on 3r brn & grn	11.00	8.00
		Nos. 132-134 (3)	12.85	10.05
		Set, never hinged	25.00	

Types of 1923-25 Issue

1927-33 Wmk. 212 Perf. 10, 11½
135	A12	1s dull violet	.25	.25
136	A12	2s org yel (A)	.35	.25
137	A12	2s org yel (B) ('33)	.30	.25
138	A12	3s org red ('31)	.25	.25
139	A12	4s dk green ('29)	3.50	2.25
140	A12	5s lt green ('31)	.50	.25
141	A12	6s grn, yel	.25	.25
142	A12	7s dk green ('33)	.50	.25
143	A12	10s red (I)	2.50	.70
144	A12	10s grn, yel (I) ('32)	10.00	.25
145	A12	15s brn, sal	3.50	.45
146	A12	20s pink (I)	5.00	.25
147	A12	20s pink (II)	6.00	.25
148	A12	30s lt blue (I)	1.25	.40
149	A12	35s dk blue ('31)	1.50	.25
150	A12	40s dl lil (I) ('29)	2.25	.25
151	A12	50s gray (II)	2.50	.45
152	A11	1 l dk brn & pale brn	8.00	.30
153	A11	2 l dk bl & bl ('31)	30.00	2.25
154	A11	5 l grn & pale grn ('33)	140.00	30.00
		Nos. 135-154 (20)	218.40	39.80
		Set, never hinged	400.00	

The paper of Nos. 141, 144 and 145 is colored on the surface only.
See note above No. 113 for types A and B, and note above No. 101 for types I and II.

Type of 1927-33 Issue
Paper Colored Through

1931-33 Perf. 10
155	A12	6s grn, yel	.25	.25
156	A12	10s grn, yel (I) ('33)	15.00	.25
157	A12	15s brn, salmon	18.25	.25
		Nos. 155-157 (3)	18.25	.75
		Set, never hinged	37.50	

View of Rezekne — A13

Designs (Views of Cities): 15s, Jelgava. 20s, Cesis (Wenden). 30s, Liepaja (Libau). 50s, Riga. 1 l, Riga Theater.

1928, Nov. 18 Litho.
158	A13	6s dp grn & vio	1.00	.40
159	A13	15s dk brn & ol grn	1.00	.40
160	A13	20s cerise & bl grn	1.25	.45
161	A13	30s ultra & vio brn	1.50	.40
162	A13	50s dk gray & plum	1.50	1.00
163	A13	1 l blk brn & brn	3.75	1.75
		Nos. 158-163 (6)	10.00	4.40
		Set, never hinged	20.00	

10th anniv. of Latvian Independence.

Riga Exhibition Issue

Stamps of 1927-33 Overprinted

1932, Aug. 30 Perf. 10, 11
164	A12	3s orange	.95	.50
165	A12	10s green, yel	.95	.50
166	A12	20s pink (I)	1.90	1.00
167	A12	35s dark blue	4.25	2.00
		Nos. 164-167 (4)	8.05	4.00
		Set, never hinged	30.00	

Riga Castle — A19

Arms and Shield — A20

Allegory of Latvia — A21

Ministry of Foreign Affairs — A22

1934, Dec. 15 Litho. Perf. 10½, 10
174	A19	3s red orange	.25	.25
175	A20	5s yellow grn	.25	.25
176	A20	10s gray grn	1.00	.25
177	A21	20s deep rose	1.00	.25
178	A22	35s dark blue	.35	.25
179	A19	40s brown	.35	.25
		Nos. 174-179 (6)	3.20	1.50
		Set, never hinged	6.00	

Atis Kronvalds A23

A. Pumpurs A24

Juris Maters A25

Mikus Krogzemis (Auseklis) A26

1936, Jan. 4 Wmk. 212 Perf. 11½
180	A23	3s vermilion	3.00	4.75
181	A24	10s green	3.00	4.75
182	A25	20s rose pink	3.00	6.00
183	A26	35s dark blue	3.00	6.00
		Nos. 180-183 (4)	12.00	21.50
		Set, never hinged	40.00	

President Karlis
Ulmanis — A27

1937, Sept. 4   Litho.   Perf. 10, 11½

184	A27	3s org red & brn org	.25	.25
185	A27	5s yellow grn	.25	.25
186	A27	10s dk sl grn	.75	.60
187	A27	20s rose lake & brn lake	1.50	.60
188	A27	25s black vio	2.25	1.25
189	A27	30s dark blue	2.25	1.25
190	A27	35s indigo	1.00	1.00
191	A27	40s lt brown	2.00	1.25
192	A27	50s olive blk	2.25	1.50
		Nos. 184-192 (9)	12.50	7.95
		Set, never hinged	25.00	

60th birthday of President Ulmanis.

Independence
Monument,
Rauna
(Ronneburg)
A28

Monument
Entrance
to
Cemetery
at Riga
A29

Independence
Monument,
Jelgava — A30

War Memorial,
Valka — A31

Independence
Monument,
Iecava — A32

Independence
Monument,
Riga — A33

Tomb of Col.
Kalpaks — A34

Unwmk.
1937, July 12   Litho.   Perf. 10
Thick Paper

193	A28	3s vermilion	.60	.90
194	A29	5s yellow grn	.60	.90
195	A30	10s deep grn	.60	.90
196	A31	20s carmine	1.50	1.00
197	A32	30s lt blue	2.00	2.00

Wmk. 212
Engr.   Perf. 11½
Thin Paper

198	A33	35s dark blue	2.00	2.00
199	A34	40s brown	3.25	3.00
		Nos. 193-199 (7)	10.55	10.30
		Set, never hinged	22.50	

View of
Vidzeme — A35

General J.
Balodis
A37

President
Karlis
Ulmanis
A38

Views: 5s, Latgale. 30s, Riga waterfront.
35s, Kurzeme. 40s, Zemgale.

1938, Nov. 17   Perf. 10, 10½x10

200	A35	3s brown org	.25	.25
a.		Booklet pane of 4	40.00	
201	A35	5s yellow grn	.25	.25
a.		Booklet pane of 4	40.00	
202	A37	10s dk green	.25	.25
a.		Booklet pane of 2	40.00	
203	A38	20s red lilac	.25	.25
a.		Booklet pane of 2	40.00	
204	A35	30s deep blue	.90	.25
205	A35	35s indigo	.90	.25
a.		Booklet pane of 2	40.00	
206	A35	40s rose violet	1.25	.25
		Nos. 200-206 (7)	4.05	1.75
		Set, never hinged	9.00	

The 20th anniversary of the Republic.

School,
Riga — A42

Independence
Monument,
Riga — A45

President
Karlis Ulmanis
A49

Designs: 5s, Castle of Jelgava. 10s, Riga
Castle. 30s, Symbol of Freedom. 35s, Community House Daugavpils. 40s, Powder Tower
and War Museum, Riga.

1939, May 13   Photo.   Perf. 10

207	A42	3s brown orange	.25	.80
208	A42	5s deep green	.50	.80
209	A42	10s dk slate grn	.75	.80
210	A45	20s dk car rose	1.50	1.60
211	A42	30s brt ultra	1.00	.80
212	A42	35s dark blue	1.50	1.60
213	A45	40s brown violet	2.00	1.00
214	A49	50s grnsh black	3.00	1.00
		Nos. 207-214 (8)	10.50	8.40
		Set, never hinged	20.00	

5th anniv. of National Unity Day.

Harvesting
Wheat — A50

Apple — A51

1939, Oct. 8

215	A50	10s slate green	.90	.60
216	A51	20s rose lake	.90	.65
		Set, never hinged	3.00	

8th Agricultural Exposition held near Riga.

Arms and Stars for
Vidzeme, Kurzeme and
Latgale — A52

1940

217	A52	1s dk vio brn	.30	.30
218	A52	2s ocher	.40	.30
219	A52	3s red orange	.25	.25
220	A52	5s dk olive brn	.25	.25
221	A52	7s dk green	.30	.30
222	A52	10s dk blue grn	.75	.25
224	A52	20s rose brown	.75	.25
225	A52	30s dp red brn	1.25	.30
226	A52	35s brt ultra	.25	.80
228	A52	40s brown violet	1.75	.80
229	A52	1 l olive green	3.50	2.40
		Nos. 217-229 (11)	9.75	6.20
		Set, never hinged	20.00	

SEMI-POSTAL STAMPS

"Mercy"
Assisting
Wounded
Soldier — SP1

1920   Unwmk.   Typo.   Perf. 11½
Brown and Green Design on Back

B1	SP1	20(30)k dk brn & red	.50	1.00
B2	SP1	40(55)k dk bl & red	.50	1.00
B3	SP1	50(70)k dk grn & red	.50	1.00
B4	SP1	1(1.30)r dl sl & red	.50	1.50

Wmk. 197
Blue Design on Back

B5	SP1	20(30)k dk brn & red	.70	1.00
B6	SP1	40(55)k dk bl & red	.70	1.00
a.		Vert. pair, imperf. btwn.	40.00	
B7	SP1	50(70)k dk grn & red	.70	1.25
B8	SP1	1(1.30)r dk sl & red	.70	2.00

Wmk. Similar to 145
Pink Paper   Imperf.
Brown, Green and Red Design on Back

B9	SP1	20(30)k dk brn & red	1.00	2.50
B10	SP1	40(55)k dk bl & red	1.00	2.50
B11	SP1	50(70)k dk grn & red	1.00	2.50
B12	SP1	1(1.30)r dk sl & red	2.00	4.25
		Nos. B1-B12 (12)	9.80	21.50
		Set, never hinged	17.50	

These semi-postal stamps were printed on
the backs of unfinished bank notes of the
Workers and Soldiers Council, Riga, and the
Bermondt-Avalov Army. Blocks of stamps
showing complete banknotes on reverse are
worth approximately three times the catalogue
value of the stamps.

Nos. B1-B8
Surcharged

1921   Unwmk.   Perf. 11½
Brown and Green Design on Back

B13	SP1	20k + 2r dk brn & red	2.50	4.00
B14	SP1	40k + 2r dk bl & red	2.50	4.00
B15	SP1	50k + 2r dk grn & red	2.50	4.00
B16	SP1	1r + 2r dk sl & red	2.50	4.00

Wmk. 197
Blue Design on Back

B17	SP1	20k + 2r dk brn & red	10.00	40.00
B18	SP1	40k + 2r dk bl & red	10.00	40.00
B19	SP1	50k + 2r dk grn & red	10.00	40.00
B20	SP1	1r + 2r dk sl & red	10.00	40.00
		Nos. B13-B20 (8)	50.00	176.00
		Set, never hinged	140.00	

Regular Issue of
1923-25 Surcharged
in Blue

1923   Wmk. Similar to 181   Perf. 10

B21	A12	1s + 10s violet	.75	1.75
B22	A12	2s + 10s yellow	.75	1.75
B23	A12	4s + 10s dk green	.75	1.75
		Nos. B21-B23 (3)	2.25	5.25
		Set, never hinged	5.00	

The surtax benefited the Latvian War
Invalids Society.

Lighthouse
and Harbor,
Liepaja
(Libau)
SP2

Church at
Liepaja — SP5

Coat of Arms of
Liepaja — SP6

Designs: 15s (25s), City Hall, Liepaja. 25s
(35s), Public Bathing Pavilion, Liepaja.

1925, July 23   **Perf. 11½**

B24	SP2	6s (12s) red brown & deep blue	2.50	5.50
B25	SP2	15s (25s) dk bl & brn	1.50	4.00
B26	SP2	25s (35s) violet & dark green	2.50	4.00
B27	SP5	30s (40s) dark blue & lake	4.50	12.00
B28	SP6	50s (60s) dark grn & violet	6.50	16.00
		Nos. B24-B28 (5)	17.50	41.50
		Set, never hinged	40.00	

Tercentenary of Liepaja (Libau). The surtax
benefited that city. Exist imperf. Value, unused
set $500.

President Janis
Cakste — SP7

1928, Apr. 18   **Engr.**

B29	SP7	2s (12s) red orange	2.50	3.25
B30	SP7	6s (16s) deep green	2.50	3.25
B31	SP7	15s (25s) red brown	2.50	3.25
B32	SP7	25s (35s) deep blue	2.50	3.25
B33	SP7	30s (40s) claret	2.50	3.25
		Nos. B29-B33 (5)	12.50	16.25
		Set, never hinged	27.50	

The surtax helped erect a monument to
Janis Cakste, 1st pres. of the Latvian
Republic.

Venta
River — SP8

Allegory,
"Latvia" — SP9

View of Jelgava
SP10

National
Theater,
Riga — SP11

View of Cesis
(Wenden)
SP12

Riga Bridge
and Trenches
SP13

Perf. 11½, Imperf.

1928, Nov. 18   Wmk. 212   Litho.

B34	SP8	6s (16s) green	2.50	2.75
B35	SP9	10s (20s) scarlet	2.50	2.75
B36	SP10	15s (25s) maroon	2.50	2.75
B37	SP11	30s (40s) ultra	2.50	2.75
B38	SP12	50s (60s) dk gray	2.50	2.75
B39	SP13	1 l (1.10 l) choc	3.75	2.75
		Nos. B34-B39 (6)	16.25	16.50
		Set, never hinged	35.00	

The surtax was given to a committee for the
erection of a Liberty Memorial.

Z. A. Meierovics
SP14

1929, Aug. 22   **Perf. 11½, Imperf.**

B46	SP14	2s (4s) orange	3.50	2.75
B47	SP14	6s (12s) dp grn	3.50	2.75
B48	SP14	15s (25s) red brown	3.50	2.75
B49	SP14	25s (35s) deep blue	3.50	2.75
B50	SP14	30s (40s) ultra	3.50	2.75
		Nos. B46-B50 (5)	17.50	13.75
		Set, never hinged	35.00	

The surtax was used to erect a monument
to Z. A. Meierovics, Latvian statesman.

Tuberculosis
Cross — SP15

Allegory of Hope
for the
Sick — SP16

Gustavs
Zemgals — SP17

Riga
Castle — SP18

Daisies and
Double-barred
Cross — SP20

Tuberculosis Sanatorium, near
Riga — SP22

Cakste,
Kviesis
and
Zemgals
SP23

Designs: No. B61, Janis Cakste, 1st pres. of
Latvia. No. B63, Pres. Alberts Kviesis.

1930, Dec. 4   Typo.   Perf. 10, 11½

B56	SP15	1s (2s) dk vio & red orange	.75	.85
B57	SP15	2s (4s) org & red orange	.75	.85
a.		Cliché of 1s (2s) in plate of 2s (4s)	700.00	700.00
B58	SP16	4s (8s) dk grn & red	.75	.85
B59	SP17	5s (10s) brt grn & dk brown	1.50	1.75
B60	SP18	6s (12s) ol grn & bister	1.50	1.75
B61	SP17	10s (20s) dp red & black	2.20	2.25
B62	SP20	15s (30s) mar & dl green	2.25	2.25
B63	SP17	20s (40s) rose lake & ind	2.25	2.25
B64	SP22	25s (50s) multi	3.00	3.50
B65	SP23	30s (60s) multi	3.50	5.00
		Nos. B56-B65 (10)	18.45	21.30
		Set, never hinged	45.00	

Surtax for the Latvian Anti-Tuberculosis Soc.
For surcharges see Nos. B72-B81.

J. Rainis
and New
Buildings,
Riga
SP24

Character
from Play
and
Rainis
SP25

Characters from Plays — SP26

Rainis
and Lyre
SP27

Flames,
Flag and
Rainis
SP28

1930, May 23   Wmk. 212   Perf. 11½

B66	SP24	1s (2s) dull violet	.75	3.25
B67	SP25	2s (4s) yellow org	.75	3.25
B68	SP26	4s (8s) dp green	.75	3.25
B69	SP27	6s (12s) yel grn & red brown	.75	3.25
B70	SP28	10s (20s) dark red	22.50	47.50
B71	SP27	15s (30s) red brn & yellow green	22.50	47.50
		Nos. B66-B71 (6)	48.00	108.00
		Set, never hinged	95.00	

Sold at double face value, surtax going to
memorial fund for J. Rainis (Jan Plieksans,
1865-1929), writer and politician.
Exist imperf. Value twice that of perf.
stamps.

Nos. B56 to B65
Surcharged in Black
With Bars

Nos. B56 to B65
Surcharged in
Black Without Bars

1931, Aug. 19   **Perf. 10, 11½**

B72	SP18	9s on 6s (12s)	1.00	2.00
B73	SP15	16s on 1s (2s)	12.50	24.00
B74	SP15	17s on 2s (4s)	1.25	2.00
B75	SP16	19s on 4s (8s)	3.75	8.50
B76	SP17	20s on 5s (10s)	2.50	8.50
B77	SP20	23s on 15s (30s)	1.00	1.50
B78	SP17	25s on 10s (20s)	2.50	4.50
B79	SP17	35s on 20s (40s)	3.75	7.00
B80	SP22	45s on 25s (50s)	10.00	20.00
B81	SP23	55s on 30s (60s)	12.50	32.50
		Nos. B72-B81 (10)	50.75	110.50
		Set, never hinged	110.00	

The surcharge replaces the original total
price, including surtax.
Nos. B73-B81 have no bars in the
surcharge. The surtax aided the Latvian Anti-
Tuberculosis Society.

Lacplesis,
the Deliverer
SP29

Designs: 1s, Kriva telling stories under Holy
Oak. 2s, Enslaved Latvians building Riga
under knight's supervision. 4s, Death of Black
Knight. 5s, Spirit of Lacplesis over freed Riga.

**Inscribed: "AIZSARGI" (Army
Reserve)**

1932, Feb. 10   **Perf. 10½, Imperf.**

B82	SP29	1s (11s) vio brn & bluish	2.50	2.50
B83	SP29	2s (17s) ocher & ol green	2.50	2.50
B84	SP29	3s (23s) red brn & org brown	2.50	2.50
B85	SP29	4s (34s) dk green & green	2.50	2.50
B86	SP29	5s (45s) green & emerald	2.50	2.50
		Nos. B82-B86 (5)	12.50	12.50
		Set, never hinged	22.00	

Surtax aided the Militia Maintenance Fund.

Marching
Troops
SP30

Infantry in
Action
SP31

Nurse Binding
Soldier's
Wound — SP32

Army Soup
Kitchen — SP33

Gen. J.
Balodis — SP34

1932, May   **Perf. 10½, Imperf.**

B87	SP30	6s (25s) ol brn & red violet	4.50	6.50
B88	SP31	7s (35s) dk bl grn & dark blue	4.50	6.50
B89	SP32	10s (45s) ol green & black brown	4.50	6.50
B90	SP33	12s (55s) lake & ol green	4.50	6.50
B91	SP34	15s (75s) red org & brown violet	4.50	6.50
		Nos. B87-B91 (5)	22.50	32.50
		Set, never hinged	45.00	

The surtax aided the Latvian Home Guards.

Symbolical of
Unified
Latvia — SP35

Symbolical of
the Strength of
the Latvian
Union — SP36

Aid to the Sick
SP37

"Charity"
SP38

Wmk. 212

1936, Dec. 28   **Litho.**   **Perf. 11½**

B92	SP35	3s orange red	1.50	3.50
B93	SP36	10s green	1.50	3.50
B94	SP37	20s rose pink	1.50	4.50
B95	SP38	35s blue	1.50	4.50
		Nos. B92-B95 (4)	6.00	16.00
		Set, never hinged	12.00	

Souvenir Sheets

SP39

1938, May 12   **Wmk. 212**   **Perf. 11**

B96	SP39	Sheet of 2	12.00	20.00
		Never hinged	22.50	
a.		35s Justice Palace, Riga	2.00	5.00
b.		40s Power Station, Kegums	2.00	5.00

Sold for 2 l. The surtax of 1.25 l was for the National Reconstruction Fund.
No. B96 exists imperf.

Overprinted in Blue with Dates 1934
1939 and "15" over "V"

1939

B97	SP39	Sheet of 2	15.00	55.00
		Never hinged	45.00	

5th anniv. of Natl. Unity Day. Sold for 2 lats.
Surtax for the Natl. Reconstruction Fund.

AIR POST STAMPS

Blériot
XI — AP1

Wmk. Wavy Lines Similar to 181

1921, July 30   **Litho.**   **Perf. 11½**

C1	AP1	10r emerald	3.00	4.50
a.		Imperf.	6.00	35.00
C2	AP1	20r dark blue	3.00	4.50
a.		Imperf.	6.00	35.00
		Set, perf, never hinged	12.00	
		Set, imperf, never hinged	25.00	

1928, May 1

C3	AP1	10s deep green	4.50	1.60
C4	AP1	15s red	2.00	1.60
C5	AP1	25s ultra	3.75	2.50
a.		Pair, imperf. btwn.	35.00	
		Nos. C3-C5 (3)	10.25	5.70
		Set, never hinged	16.00	

Nos. C1-C5 sometimes show letters of a paper maker's watermark "PACTIEN LIGAT MILLS."

1931-32   **Wmk. 212**   **Perf. 11½**

C6	AP1	10s deep green	1.00	.90
a.		Perf. 11	12.00	14.50
C7	AP1	15s red	1.50	1.00
a.		Perf. 11	120.00	32.50
C8	AP1	25s deep blue ('32)	8.50	1.25
a.		Perf. 11	28.00	14.50
		Nos. C6-C8 (3)	11.00	3.15
		Set, never hinged	22.50	

Type of 1921 Overprinted or Surcharged in Black

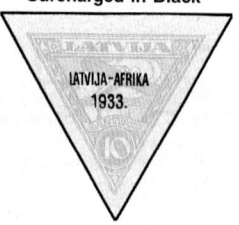

1933, May 26   **Wmk. 212**   **Imperf.**

C9	AP1	10s deep green	40.00	80.00
C10	AP1	15s red	40.00	80.00
C11	AP1	25s deep blue	40.00	80.00
C12	AP1	50s on 15s red	200.00	525.00
C13	AP1	100s on 25s dp blue	200.00	525.00
		Nos. C9-C13 (5)	520.00	1,290.
		Set, never hinged	800.00	

Honoring and financing a flight from Riga to Bathurst, Gambia. The plane crashed at Neustettin, Germany.
Counterfeits exist of Nos. C1-C13.

AIR POST SEMI-POSTAL STAMPS

Durbes Castle, Rainis
Birthplace — SPAP1

Wmk. 212

1930, May 26   **Litho.**   **Perf. 11½**

CB1	SPAP1	10s (20s) red & olive green	6.50	14.50
CB2	SPAP1	15s (30s) dk yel green & copper red	6.50	14.50
		Set, never hinged	25.00	

Surtax for the Rainis Memorial Fund.

Imperf.

CB1a	SPAP1	10s (20s)	10.00	27.50
CB2a	SPAP1	15s (30s)	10.00	27.50
		Set, never hinged	40.00	

Nos. C6-C8 Surcharged in Magenta, Blue or Red

1931, Dec. 5

CB3	AP1	10s + 50s deep green (M)	6.50	7.50
CB4	AP1	15s + 1 l red (Bl)	6.50	7.50
CB5	AP1	25s + 1.50 l deep blue	6.50	7.50
		Nos. CB3-CB5 (3)	19.50	22.50
		Set, never hinged	40.00	

Surtax for the Latvian Home Guards.

Imperf.

CB3a	AP1	10s + 50s	10.00	11.00
CB4a	AP1	15s + 1 l	10.00	11.00
CB5a	AP1	25s + 1.50 l	10.00	11.00
		Nos. CB3a-CB5a (3)	30.00	33.00
		Set, never hinged	55.00	

SPAP2

1932, June 17   **Perf. 10½**

CB6	SPAP2	10s (20s) dk sl grn & green	12.50	25.00
CB7	SPAP2	15s (30s) brt red & buff	12.50	25.00
CB8	SPAP2	25s (50s) dp bl & gray	12.50	25.00
		Nos. CB6-CB8 (3)	37.50	75.00
		Set, never hinged	75.00	

Surtax for the Latvian Home Guards.

Imperf.

CB6a	SPAP2	10s (20s)	12.50	25.00
CB7a	SPAP2	15s (30s)	12.50	25.00
CB8a	SPAP2	25s (50s)	12.50	25.00
		Nos. CB6a-CB8a (3)	37.50	75.00
		Set, never hinged	75.00	

Icarus — SPAP3

Leonardo da
Vinci — SPAP4

Charles
Balloon — SPAP5

Wright
Brothers
Biplane
SPAP6

Blériot
Monoplane
SPAP7

1932, Dec.   **Perf. 10, 11½**

CB9	SPAP3	5s (25s) ol bister & green	17.50	20.00
CB10	SPAP4	10s (50s) ol brn & gray grn	17.50	20.00
CB11	SPAP5	15s (75s) red brown & gray grn	17.50	20.00
CB12	SPAP6	20s (1 l) gray grn & lil rose	17.50	20.00
CB13	SPAP7	25s (1.25 l) brn & bl	17.50	20.00
		Nos. CB9-CB13 (5)	87.50	100.00
		Set, never hinged	150.00	

Issued to honor pioneers of aviation. The surtax of four times the face value was for wounded Latvian aviators.

Imperf.

CB9a	SPAP3	5s (25s)	17.50	20.00
CB10a	SPAP4	10s (50s)	17.50	20.00
CB11a	SPAP5	15s (75s)	17.50	20.00
CB12a	SPAP6	20s (1 l)	17.50	20.00
CB13a	SPAP7	25s (1.25 l)	17.50	20.00
		Nos. CB9a-CB13a (5)	87.50	100.00
		Set, never hinged	150.00	

Icarus Falling
SPAP8

Monument to
Aviators
SPAP9

Proposed Tombs for Aviators
SPAP10   SPAP11

1933, Mar. 15   **Perf. 11½**

CB14	SPAP8	2s (52s) blk & ocher	14.00	20.00
CB15	SPAP9	3s (53s) blk & red org	14.00	20.00
CB16	SPAP10	10s (60s) blk & dk yel green	14.00	20.00
CB17	SPAP11	20s (70s) blk & cerise	14.00	20.00
		Nos. CB14-CB17 (4)	56.00	80.00
		Set, never hinged	125.00	

50s surtax for wounded Latvian aviators.

Imperf.

CB14a	SPAP8	2s (52s)	15.00	21.00
CB15a	SPAP9	3s (53s)	15.00	21.00
CB16a	SPAP10	10s (60s)	15.00	21.00
CB17a	SPAP11	20s (70s)	15.00	21.00
		Nos. CB14a-CB17a (4)	60.00	84.00
		Set, never hinged	135.00	

Monoplane
Taking Off
SPAP12

Designs: 7s (57s), Biplane under fire at Riga. 35s (1.35 l), Map and planes.

1933, June 15   **Wmk. 212**   **Perf. 11½**

CB18	SPAP12	3s (53s) org & sl blue	19.00	40.00

CB19	SPAP12	7s (57s) sl bl & dk brn	19.00	40.00
CB20	SPAP12	35s (1.35 l) dp ul- tra & ol black	19.00	40.00
	Nos. CB18-CB20 (3)		57.00	*120.00*
	Set, never hinged		125.00	

Surtax for wounded Latvian aviators. Counterfeits exist.

Imperf.

CB18a	SPAP12	3s (53s)	22.50	42.50
CB19a	SPAP12	7s (57s)	22.50	42.50
CB20a	SPAP12	35s (1.35 l)	22.50	42.50
	Nos. CB18a-CB20a (3)		67.50	*127.50*
	Set, never hinged		130.00	

American Gee-Bee SPAP13

English Seaplane S6B SPAP14

Graf Zeppelin over Riga SPAP15

DO-X SPAP16

1933, Sept. 5   **Perf. 11½**

CB21	SPAP13	8s (68s) brn & gray black	40.00	85.00
CB22	SPAP14	12s (1.12 l) brn car & ol green	40.00	85.00
CB23	SPAP15	30s (1.30 l) blue & gray black	50.00	90.00
CB24	SPAP16	40s (1.90 l) brn vio & indi- go	40.00	85.00
	Nos. CB21-CB24 (4)		170.00	*345.00*
	Set, never hinged		275.00	

Surtax for wounded Latvian aviators.

Imperf.

CB21a	SPAP13	8s (68s)	40.00	85.00
CB22a	SPAP14	12s (1.12 l)	40.00	85.00
CB23a	SPAP15	30s (1.30 l)	50.00	95.00
CB24a	SPAP16	40s (1.90 l)	40.00	90.00
	Nos. CB21a-CB24a (4)		170.00	*355.00*
	Set, never hinged		275.00	

OCCUPATION STAMPS

Issued under German Occupation

German Stamps of 1905-18 Handstamped

1919   **Wmk. 125**   **Perf. 14, 14½**
Red Overprint

1N1	A22	2½pf gray	275.00	325.00
1N2	A16	5pf green	225.00	100.00
1N3	A22	15pf dk vio	375.00	100.00
1N4	A16	20pf blue vio	135.00	65.00
1N5	A16	25pf org & blk, yel	475.00	325.00
1N6	A16	50pf pur & blk, buff	475.00	325.00

Blue Overprint

1N7	A22	2½pf gray	275.00	325.00
1N8	A16	5pf green	225.00	120.00
1N9	A16	10pf carmine	190.00	47.50
1N10	A22	15pf dk vio	325.00	325.00
1N11	A16	20pf bl vio	135.00	65.00
1N12	A16	25pf org & blk, yel	675.00	525.00
1N13	A16	50pf pur & blk, buff	675.00	525.00
	Nos. 1N1-1N13 (13)		4,460.	*3,172.*

Inverted and double overprints exist, as well as counterfeit overprints.

Some experts believe that Nos. 1N1-1N7 were not officially issued. All used examples are canceled to order.

ISSUED UNDER RUSSIAN OCCUPATION

Fake overprints/surcharges exist on Nos. 2N1-2N36.

The following stamps were issued at Mitau during the occupation of Kurland by the West Russian Army under Colonel Bermondt-Avalov.

Stamps of Latvia Handstamped

1919   **Wmk. 108**   **Imperf.**
On Stamps of 1919

2N1	A1	3k lilac	40.00	52.50
2N2	A1	5k carmine	40.00	52.50
2N3	A1	10k dp blue	140.00	240.00
2N4	A1	20k orange	40.00	52.50
2N5	A1	25k gray	40.00	52.50
2N6	A1	35k dk brown	40.00	52.50
2N7	A1	50k purple	40.00	52.50
2N8	A1	75k emerald	40.00	80.00

On Riga Liberation Stamps

2N9	A2	5k carmine	40.00	52.50
2N10	A2	15k dp green	20.00	40.00
2N11	A2	35k brown	20.00	40.00

Stamps of Latvia Overprinted

On Stamps of 1919

2N12	A1	3k lilac	6.00	9.50
2N13	A1	5k carmine	6.00	9.50
2N14	A1	10k dp blue	120.00	200.00
2N15	A1	20k orange	12.00	20.00
2N16	A1	25k gray	27.50	60.00
2N17	A1	35k dk brown	20.00	27.50
2N18	A1	50k purple	20.00	27.50
2N19	A1	75k emerald	20.00	27.50

On Riga Liberation Stamps

2N20	A2	5k carmine	4.00	8.00
2N21	A2	15k dp green	4.00	8.00
2N22	A2	35k brown	4.00	8.00
a.	Inverted overprint		200.00	
	Nos. 2N1-2N22 (22)		743.50	*1,173.*

The letters "Z. A." are the initials of "Zapadnaya Armiya"-i.e. Western Army.

Russian Stamps of 1909-17 Surcharged

Perf. 14, 14½x15
Unwmk.
On Stamps of 1909-12

2N23	A14	10k on 2k grn	6.00	8.00
a.	Inverted surcharge		30.00	
2N24	A15	30k on 4k car	8.00	8.00
2N25	A14	40k on 5k cl	8.00	9.50
2N26	A15	50k on 10k dk bl	6.00	8.00
2N27	A11	70k on 15k red brn & bl	6.00	8.00
a.	Inverted surcharge		200.00	
2N28	A8	90k on 20k bl & car	12.00	16.00

2N29	A11	1r on 25k grn & vio	6.00	8.00
2N30	A11	1½r on 35k red brn & grn	47.50	65.00
2N31	A8	2r on 50k vio & grn	12.00	16.00
a.	Inverted surcharge		120.00	
2N32	A11	4r on 70k brn & org	20.00	27.50

Perf. 13½

2N33	A9	6r on 1r pale brn, brn & org	27.50	40.00

On Stamps of 1917
Imperf

2N34	A14	20k on 3k red	6.00	8.00
2N35	A14	40k on 5k claret	95.00	100.00
2N36	A12	10r on 3.50r mar & lt grn	80.00	80.00
a.	Inverted surcharge		300.00	
	Nos. 2N23-2N36 (14)		340.00	*402.00*

Eight typographed stamps of this design were prepared in 1919, but never placed in use. They exist both perforated and imperforate. Value, set, imperf. $1, perf. $2.

Reprints and counterfeits exist.

> **Catalogue values for unused stamps in this section, from this point to the end of the section, are for Never Hinged items.**

Arms of Soviet Latvia — OS1

1940   **Typo.**   **Wmk. 265**   **Perf. 10**

2N45	OS1	1s dk violet	.25	.25
2N46	OS1	2s orange yel	.25	.25
2N47	OS1	3s orange ver	.25	.25
2N48	OS1	5s dk olive grn	.25	.25
2N49	OS1	7s turq green	.25	.80
2N50	OS1	10s slate green	2.00	.40
2N51	OS1	20s brown lake	1.20	.25
2N52	OS1	30s light blue	2.40	.40
2N53	OS1	35s brt ultra	.25	.40
2N54	OS1	40s chocolate	2.00	1.20
2N55	OS1	50s lt gray	2.50	1.20
2N56	OS1	1 l lt brown	3.25	1.50
2N57	OS1	5 l brt green	24.00	13.50
	Nos. 2N45-2N57 (13)		38.85	*20.65*

Used values of Nos. 2N45-2N57 are for CTOs. Commercially used examples are worth three times as much.

LEBANON

'le-bə-nən

(Grand Liban)

LOCATION — Asia Minor, bordering on the Mediterranean Sea
GOVT. — Republic
AREA — 4,036 sq. mi.
POP. — 3,500,000 (est. 1984)
CAPITAL — Beirut

Formerly a part of the Syrian province of Turkey, Lebanon was occupied by French forces after World War I. It was mandated to France after it had been declared a separate state. Limited autonomy was granted in 1927 and full independence achieved in 1941. The French issued two sets of occupation stamps (with T.E.O. overprint) for Lebanon in late 1919. The use of these and later occupation issues (of 1920-24, with overprints "O.M.F." and "Syrie-Grand Liban") was extended to Syria,

Cilicia, Alaouites and Alexandretta. By custom, these are all listed under Syria.

100 Centimes = 1 Piaster
100 Piasters = 1 Pound

Issued under French Mandate

Stamps of France 1900-21 Surcharged

Type 1   Type 2

Two types each exist for surcharges on the centime surcharges and on the piastre surcharges on type A18. Centimes: type 1, serif on upper curve of "C"; type 2, serifs on both lower and upper curves of "C." Piastres: type 1, 1.5-2mm space between value and "P," except for 3p (3mm); type 2, 4mm between value and "P."

1924   **Unwmk.**   **Perf. 14x13½**

1	A16	10c on 2c vio brn (1)	1.60	1.60
	Never hinged		3.25	
	On cover			16.00
a.	Inverted surcharge		45.00	45.00
	Never hinged		90.00	
b.	Type 2		2.40	2.40
	Never hinged		4.75	
	On cover			20.00
c.	As "b," double surcharge		45.00	45.00
	Never hinged		90.00	
d.	As "b," in pair with un-surcharged stamp		260.00	
2	A22	25c on 5c orange (1)	1.60	1.60
	Never hinged		3.25	
	On cover			13.50
a.	Type 2		3.50	3.50
	Never hinged		7.00	
	On cover			24.00
3	A22	50c on 10c green (1)	1.60	1.60
	Never hinged		3.25	
	On cover			12.00
a.	"S" of "CENTIEMES" inverted		17.50	17.50
	Never hinged		35.00	
b.	Double surcharge		45.00	45.00
	Never hinged		80.00	
c.	Type 2		3.50	3.50
	Never hinged		7.00	
	On cover			24.00
d.	As "c," "R" omitted from "GRAND"		60.00	45.00
	Never hinged		120.00	
4	A20	75c on 15c sl grn (1)	2.75	2.40
	Never hinged		5.50	
	On cover			12.00
a.	Inverted surcharge		45.00	45.00
	Never hinged		90.00	
b.	Type 2		3.50	3.25
	Never hinged		7.00	
	On cover			24.00
5	A22	1p on 20c red brn	1.60	1.60
	Never hinged		3.25	
	On cover			16.00
a.	Double surcharge		45.00	45.00
	Never hinged		90.00	
b.	Inverted surcharge		45.00	45.00
	Never hinged		90.00	
6	A22	1.25p on 25c blue	4.50	2.40
	Never hinged		9.00	
	On cover			16.00
a.	Double surcharge		40.00	40.00
	Never hinged		80.00	
7	A22	1.50p on 30c org	2.75	2.00
	Never hinged		5.50	
	On cover			9.50
8	A22	1.50p on 30c red	2.75	2.40
	Never hinged		5.50	
	On cover			12.00
9	A20	2.50p on 50c dl bl	2.40	2.00
	Never hinged		4.75	
	On cover			16.00
	On cover, single franking			24.00
a.	Inverted surcharge		35.00	35.00
	Never hinged		70.00	
b.	"0" of "2,50" omitted		35.00	35.00
	Never hinged		70.00	
c.	"2" of "2,50" omitted		65.00	65.00
	Never hinged		130.00	
d.	Comma of "2,50" omitted		13.50	13.50
	Never hinged		27.50	

Surcharged

GRAND LIBAN 2 PIASTRES

10	A18	2p on 40c red & pale bl	5.50	3.75
	Never hinged		11.00	
a.	Inverted surcharge		27.50	27.50
11	A18	3p on 60c violet & ultra	8.00	6.75
	Never hinged		16.00	

12	A18	5p on 1fr cl & ol green	10.00	7.50
		Never hinged	20.00	
13	A18	10p on 2fr org & pale bl	15.00	12.00
		Never hinged	30.00	
	a.	*Inverted surcharge*		
14	A18	25p on 5fr dk bl & buff	22.50	19.00
		Never hinged	45.00	
	a.	*Inverted surcharge*	85.00	85.00
		Nos. 1-14 (14)	82.55	66.60

Broken and missing letters and varieties of spacing are numerous in these surcharges.
For overprints see Nos. C1-C4.

Stamps of France, 1923, (Pasteur) Surcharged "GRAND LIBAN" and New Values

15	A23	50c on 10c green	3.50	1.10
		Never hinged	7.00	
	a.	*Inverted surcharge*	35.00	25.00
16	A23	1.50p on 30c red	4.50	2.25
		Never hinged	9.00	
17	A23	2.50p on 50c blue	3.75	1.10
		Never hinged	7.50	
	a.	*Inverted surcharge*	30.00	27.50
		Nos. 15-17 (3)	11.75	4.45

Commemorative Stamps of France, 1924, (Olympic Games) Surcharged "GRAND LIBAN" and New Values

18	A24	50c on 10c gray grn & yel grn	32.50	32.50
		Never hinged	65.00	
	a.	*Inverted surcharge*	350.00	
19	A25	1.25p on 25c rose & dk rose	32.50	32.50
		Never hinged	65.00	
	a.	*Inverted surcharge*	350.00	
20	A26	1.50p on 30c brn red & blk	32.50	32.50
		Never hinged	65.00	
	a.	*Inverted surcharge*	350.00	
21	A27	2.50p on 50c ultra & dk bl	32.50	32.50
		Never hinged	65.00	
	a.	*Inverted surcharge*	350.00	
		Nos. 18-21 (4)	130.00	130.00

Stamps of France, 1900-24, Surcharged

1924-25

22	A16	10c on 2c vio brn	1.00	.50
		Never hinged	1.50	
23	A22	25c on 5c orange	1.25	.75
		Never hinged	1.75	
24	A22	50c on 10c green	2.00	1.40
		Never hinged	2.60	
25	A20	75c on 15c gray grn	1.75	1.10
		Never hinged	2.60	
26	A22	1p on 20c red brn	1.50	.95
		Never hinged	2.25	
27	A22	1.25p on 25c blue	2.25	1.60
		Never hinged	3.50	
28	A22	1.50p on 30c red	2.00	1.25
		Never hinged	3.00	
29	A22	1.50p on 30c orange	62.50	57.50
		Never hinged	100.00	
30	A22	2p on 35c vio ('25)	2.25	1.60
		Never hinged	3.50	
31	A20	3p on 60c lt vio ('25)	3.00	2.10
		Never hinged	4.50	
32	A20	4p on 85c ver	3.50	2.50
		Never hinged	5.50	

Surcharged

33	A18	2p on 40c red & pale bl	2.25	1.60
		Never hinged	4.25	
	a.	*2nd line of Arabic reads "2 Piastre" (singular)*	2.50	.50
34	A18	2p on 45c green & blue ('25)	27.50	22.50
		Never hinged	42.50	
35	A18	3p on 60c violet & ultra	3.50	2.50
		Never hinged	6.00	
36	A18	5p on 1fr cl & ol green	4.25	3.25
		Never hinged	8.00	
37	A18	10p on 2fr org & pale bl	9.75	8.50
		Never hinged	17.00	
38	A18	25p on 5fr dk bl & buff	15.00	13.50
		Never hinged	27.50	
		Nos. 22-38 (17)	145.25	123.10

Last line of surcharge on No. 33 has four characters, with a 9-like character between the third and fourth in illustration. Last line on No. 33a is as illustrated.

The surcharge may be found inverted on most of Nos. 22-38, and double on some values.
For overprints see Nos. C5-C8.

Stamps of France 1923-24 (Pasteur) Surcharged as Nos. 22-32

39	A23	50c on 10c green	2.00	.85
		Never hinged	3.00	
	a.	*Inverted surcharge*	35.00	25.00
	b.	*Double surcharge*	40.00	21.00
40	A23	75c on 15c green	2.25	1.40
		Never hinged	3.25	
41	A23	1.50p on 30c red	2.75	1.40
		Never hinged	4.25	
	a.	*Inverted surcharge*	35.00	25.00
42	A23	2p on 45c red	5.00	3.50
		Never hinged	8.00	
	a.	*Inverted surcharge*	35.00	21.00
43	A23	2.50p on 50c blue	2.00	.95
		Never hinged	4.25	
	a.	*Inverted surcharge*	35.00	21.00
	b.	*Double surcharge*	40.00	21.00
44	A23	4p on 75c blue	5.00	3.50
		Never hinged	8.00	
		Nos. 39-44 (6)	19.00	11.60

France Nos. 198 to 201 (Olympics) Surcharged as Nos. 22-32

45	A24	50c on 10c	32.50	32.50
		Never hinged	50.00	
46	A25	1.25p on 25c	32.50	32.50
		Never hinged	50.00	
47	A26	1.50p on 30c	32.50	32.50
		Never hinged	50.00	
48	A27	2.50p on 50c	32.50	32.50
		Never hinged	50.00	
		Nos. 45-48 (4)	130.00	130.00

France No. 219 (Ronsard) Surcharged

49	A28	4p on 75c bl, *bluish*	3.50	3.50
		Never hinged	5.00	
	a.	*Inverted surcharge*	65.00	50.00

Cedar of Lebanon — A1

Crusader Castle, Tripoli — A3

View of Beirut — A2

Designs: 50c, Crusader Castle, Tripoli. 75c, Beit-ed-Din Palace. 1p, Temple of Jupiter, Baalbek. 1.25p, Mouktara Palace. 1.50p, Harbor of Tyre. 2p, View of Zahle. 2.50p, Ruins at Baalbek. 3p, Square at Deir-el-Kamar. 5p, Castle at Sidon. 25p, Square at Beirut.

1925		**Litho.**	*Perf.*	*12½, 13½*
50	A1	10c dark violet	.50	.25
		Never hinged	.75	
		Photo.		
51	A2	25c olive black	.95	.25
		Never hinged	1.30	
52	A2	50c yellow grn	.75	.25
		Never hinged	1.25	
53	A2	75c brn orange	.75	.25
		Never hinged	1.25	
54	A2	1p magenta	2.00	.80
		Never hinged	3.00	
55	A2	1.25p deep green	2.25	1.40
		Never hinged	3.50	
56	A2	1.50p rose red	1.00	.25
		Never hinged	1.50	
57	A2	2p dark brown	1.25	.25
		Never hinged	2.00	
58	A2	2.50p peacock bl	2.00	.80
		Never hinged	3.00	
59	A2	3p orange brn	2.75	1.10
		Never hinged	3.75	
60	A2	5p violet	3.00	1.40
		Never hinged	4.50	
61	A3	10p violet brn	7.50	2.10
		Never hinged	9.50	
62	A2	25p ultramarine	20.00	12.00
		Never hinged	30.00	
		Nos. 50-62 (13)	44.70	21.10

For surcharges and overprints see Nos. 63-107, B1-B12, C9-C38, CB1-CB4.

Stamps of 1925 with Bars and Surcharged

1926

63	A2	3.50p on 75c brn org	1.50	1.50
		Never hinged	2.50	
64	A2	4p on 25c ol blk	2.50	2.50
		Never hinged	4.00	
65	A2	6p on 2.50p pck bl	2.00	2.00
		Never hinged	3.50	
66	A2	12p on 1.25p dp grn	1.40	1.40
		Never hinged	2.75	
67	A2	20p on 1.25p dp grn	6.75	6.75
		Never hinged	9.25	

Stamps of 1925 with Bars and Surcharged

68	A2	4.50p on 75c brn org	2.75	2.75
		Never hinged	4.50	
69	A2	7.50p on 2.50p pck bl	2.75	2.75
		Never hinged	4.50	
70	A2	15p on 25p ultra	2.75	2.75
		Never hinged	4.50	
		Nos. 63-70 (8)	22.40	22.40

No. 51 with Bars and Surcharged

1927

71	A2	4p on 25c ol blk	2.50	2.50
		Never hinged	4.00	

Issues of Republic under French Mandate

Stamps of 1925 Issue Overprinted in Black or Red

1927

72	A1	10c dark vio (R)	.55	.25
		Never hinged	1.00	
	a.	*Black overprint*	35.00	
	b.	*Inverted overprint*	35.00	
73	A2	50c yellow grn	.55	.25
		Never hinged	1.00	
74	A2	1p magenta	.55	.25
		Never hinged	1.00	
75	A2	1.50p rose red	.80	.60
		Never hinged	1.50	
76	A2	2p dark brown	1.10	.90
		Never hinged	1.50	
77	A2	3p orange brn	.90	.25
		Never hinged	1.60	
78	A2	5p violet	1.75	1.00
		Never hinged	3.00	
79	A3	10p violet brn	2.25	1.10
		Never hinged	4.00	
80	A2	25p ultramarine	19.00	8.00
		Never hinged	30.00	
		Nos. 72-80 (9)	27.45	12.60

On Nos. 72 and 79 the overprint is set in two lines. On all stamps the double bar obliterates GRAND LIBAN.

Same Overprint on Provisional Issues of 1926-27

15 PIASTERS ON 25 PIASTERS
TYPE I — "République Libanaise" at foot of stamp.
TYPE II — "République Libanaise" near top of stamp.

81	A2	4p on 25c ol blk	.75	.25
		Never hinged	1.25	
82	A2	4.50p on 75c brn org	.85	.25
		Never hinged	1.50	

83	A2	7.50p on 2.50p pck bl	1.10	.25
		Never hinged	2.00	
84	A2	15p on 25p ultra (I)	7.50	5.25
		Never hinged	11.00	
	a.		11.50	
		Nos. 81-84 (4)	10.20	6.00

Most of Nos. 72-84 are known with overprint double, inverted or on back as well as face.

Stamps of 1927 Overprinted in Black or Red

1928

86	A1	10c dark vio (R)	.80	.60
		Never hinged	1.25	
	a.	*French overprint omitted, on #50*		
	b.	*Overprinted on No. 72b*		
87	A2	50c yel grn (Bk)	2.00	1.50
		Never hinged	3.00	
	a.	*Arabic overprint inverted*	35.00	25.00
88	A2	1p magenta (Bk)	1.00	.70
		Never hinged	1.50	
	a.	*Inverted overprint*	35.00	25.00
89	A2	1.50p rose red (Bk)	2.00	1.50
		Never hinged	3.00	
90	A2	2p dark brown (R)	2.75	2.10
90A	A2	2p dk brn (Bk+R)	110.00	110.00
91	A2	3p org brown (Bk)	1.90	1.40
		Never hinged	3.50	
92	A2	5p violet (Bk+R)	3.50	2.75
		Never hinged	5.50	
93	A2	5p violet (R)	3.00	2.40
		Never hinged	4.50	
	a.	*French ovpt. below Arabic*	30.00	14.00
94	A3	10p vio brn (Bk)	5.00	4.25
		Never hinged	8.00	
	a.	*Double overprint*	100.00	90.00
	b.	*Double overprint inverted*		
	c.	*Inverted overprint*	100.00	70.00
95	A2	25p ultra (Bk+R)	11.50	10.50
		Never hinged	17.50	
95A	A2	25p ultra (R)	13.00	13.00
		Never hinged	20.00	
		Nos. 86-95A (12)	156.45	150.70

On all stamps the double bar with Arabic overprint obliterates Arabic inscription.

Same Overprint on Nos. 81-84

96	A2	4p on 25c (Bk+R)	2.00	1.50
		Never hinged	3.00	
97	A2	4.50p on 75c (Bk)	2.00	1.50
		Never hinged	8.00	
98	A2	7.50p on 2.50p (Bk+R)	4.50	3.50
		Never hinged	8.00	
99	A2	7.50p on 2.50p (R)	7.00	6.00
		Never hinged	11.00	
100	A2	15p on 25p (II) (Bk+R)	11.00	9.50
		Never hinged	17.50	
	a.	*Arabic overprint inverted*		
101	A2	15p on 25p (I) (R)	14.00	12.00
		Never hinged	22.50	
		Nos. 96-101 (6)	40.50	34.00

The new values are surcharged in black. The initials in ( ) refer to the colors of the overprints.

Stamps of 1925 Srchd. in Red or Black

1928-29			*Perf.*	*13½*
102	A2	50c on 75c brn org (Bk) ('29)	1.50	1.90
		Never hinged	2.25	
103	A2	2p on 1.25p dp grn	1.50	1.90
		Never hinged	2.25	
104	A2	4p on 25c ol blk	1.50	1.90
		Never hinged	2.25	
	a.	*Double surcharge*	35.00	25.00
105	A2	7.50p on 2.50p pck bl	2.50	2.75
		Never hinged	3.75	
	a.	*Double surcharge*	40.00	25.00
	b.	*Inverted surcharge*	55.00	25.00
106	A2	15p on 25p ultra	22.50	10.00
		Never hinged	35.00	
		Nos. 102-106 (5)	29.50	18.45

On Nos. 103, 104 and 105 the surcharged numerals are 3¼mm high, and have thick strokes.

No. 86 Surcharged in Red

1928
107 A1 5c on 10c dk vio ... 1.75 .30
Never hinged ... 3.00

Silkworm, Cocoon and Moth — A4

1930, Feb. 11   Typo.   Perf. 11
108 A4 4p black brown ... 15.00 15.00
Never hinged ... 35.00
109 A4 4½p vermilion ... 15.00 15.00
Never hinged ... 35.00
110 A4 7½p dark blue ... 15.00 15.00
Never hinged ... 35.00
111 A4 10p dk violet ... 15.00 15.00
Never hinged ... 35.00
112 A4 15p dark green ... 15.00 15.00
Never hinged ... 35.00
113 A4 25p claret ... 15.00 15.00
Never hinged ... 35.00
Nos. 108-113 (6) ... 90.00 90.00

Sericultural Congress, Beirut. Presentation imperfs exist.

Pigeon Rocks, Ras Beirut — A5

View of Bickfaya A8

Beit-ed-Din Palace A10

Crusader Castle, Tripoli A11

Ruins of Venus Temple, Baalbek A12

Ancient Bridge, Dog River A13

Belfort Castle A14

Afka Falls — A19

20c, Cedars of Lebanon. 25c, Ruins of Bacchus Temple, Baalbek. 1p, Crusader Castle, Sidon Harbor. 5p, Arcade of Beit-ed-Din Palace. 6p, Tyre Harbor. 7.50p, Ruins of Sun Temple, Baalbek. 10p, View of Hasbeya. 25p, View of Deir-el-Kamar. 75c, 100p, Ruins at Baalbek.

1930-35   Litho.   Perf. 12½, 13½
114 A5 10c brown orange ... .60 .25
Never hinged ... 1.00
115 A5 20c yellow brn ... .60 .25
Never hinged ... 1.00
116 A5 25c deep blue ... .75 .45
Never hinged ... 1.25

Photo.
117 A8 50c orange brn ... 3.00 1.50
Never hinged ... 4.25
118 A11 75c ol brn ('32) ... 1.50 1.00
Never hinged ... 2.50
119 A8 1p deep green ... 1.75 1.25
Never hinged ... 3.00
120 A8 1p brn vio ('35) ... 3.00 1.00
Never hinged ... 4.25
121 A10 1.50p violet brn ... 3.25 1.90
Never hinged ... 4.75
122 A10 1.50p dp grn ('32) ... 3.50 1.50
Never hinged ... 5.00
123 A11 2p Prussian bl ... 4.50 1.60
Never hinged ... 6.50
124 A12 3p black brown ... 4.50 1.60
Never hinged ... 6.50
125 A13 4p orange brn ... 4.75 1.60
Never hinged ... 7.00
126 A14 4.50p carmine ... 5.00 1.60
Never hinged ... 7.50
127 A13 5p greenish blk ... 3.00 1.50
Never hinged ... 5.00
128 A13 6p brn violet ... 5.25 2.75
Never hinged ... 7.50
129 A10 7.50p deep blue ... 5.00 1.60
Never hinged ... 8.00
130 A10 10p dk ol grn ... 9.00 1.60
Never hinged ... 13.00
131 A19 15p blk violet ... 11.50 3.50
Never hinged ... 15.00
132 A19 25p blue green ... 20.00 6.00
Never hinged ... 27.50
133 A8 50p apple grn ... 60.00 15.00
Never hinged ... 95.00
134 A11 100p black ... 65.00 19.00
Never hinged ... 100.00
Nos. 114-134 (21) ... 215.45 66.45

See Nos. 135, 144, 152-155. For surcharges see Nos. 147-149; 161, 173-174 in Scott Standard catalogue, Vol 4.

Pigeon Rocks Type of 1930-35 Redrawn
1934   Litho.   Perf. 12½x12
135 A5 10c dull orange ... 6.75 4.00

Lines in rocks and water more distinct. Printer's name "Hélio Vaugirard, Paris," in larger letters.

Cedar of Lebanon A23

President Emile Eddé A24

Dog River Panorama A25

1937-40   Typo.   Perf. 14x13½
137 A23 10c rose car ... .50 .25
Never hinged ... .75
137A A23 20c aqua ('40) ... .50 .25
Never hinged ... .75
137B A23 25c pale rose lilac ('40) ... .50 .25
Never hinged ... .75
138 A23 50c magenta ... .50 .25
Never hinged ... .75
138A A23 75c brown ('40) ... .50 .25
Never hinged ... .75

Engr.
Perf. 13
139 A24 3p dk violet ... 4.00 .75
Never hinged ... 5.00
140 A24 4p black brown ... .75 .25
Never hinged ... 1.25
141 A24 4.50p carmine ... 1.00 .25
Never hinged ... 1.50
142 A25 10p brn carmine ... 2.25 .25
Never hinged ... 3.00
142A A25 12½p dp ultra ('40) ... 1.00 .25
Never hinged ... 1.50
143 A25 15p dk grn ('38) ... 4.00 .75
Never hinged ... 5.50
143A A25 20p chestnut ('40) ... 1.00 .25
Never hinged ... 1.50
143B A25 25p crimson ('40) ... 1.50 .60
Never hinged ... 2.25

143C A25 50p dk vio ('40) ... 5.00 1.60
Never hinged ... 6.50
143D A25 100p sepia ('40) ... 3.50 2.25
Never hinged ... 5.00
Nos. 137-143D (15) ... 26.50 8.45

Nos. 137A, 137B, 138A, 142A, 143A, 143B, 143C, and 143D exist imperforate.
For surcharges see Nos. 145-146A, 150-151; 160, 162, 175-176 in Scott Standard catalogue, Vol. 4.

View of Bickfaya A26

Type A8 Redrawn
1935 (?)   Photo.   Perf. 13½
144 A26 50c orange brown ... 17.50 9.75
Never hinged ... 20.00

Arabic inscriptions more condensed.

Stamps of 1930-37 Surcharged in Black or Red

1937-42   Perf. 13, 13½
145 A24 2p on 3p dk vio ... 1.50 1.50
Never hinged ... 2.25
146 A24 2½p on 4p blk brn ... 1.50 1.50
Never hinged ... 2.25
146A A24 2½p on 4p black brown (R) ('42) ... 1.50 1.50
Never hinged ... 2.25
147 A10 6p on 7.50p dp bl (R) ... 4.00 4.00
Never hinged ... 6.00

Stamps of 1930-35 and Type of 1937-40 Surcharged in Black or Red

Perf. 13½, 13
148 A8 7.50p on 50p ap grn ... 2.50 2.50
Never hinged ... 3.50
149 A11 7.50p on 100p blk (R) ... 2.50 2.50
Never hinged ... 3.50
150 A25 12.50p on 7.50p dk bl (R) ... 5.00 5.00
Never hinged ... 7.00

Type of 1937-40 Srchd. in Red

1939   Engr.   Perf. 13
151 A25 12½p on 7.50p dk bl ... 2.00 2.00
Never hinged ... 3.00
Nos. 145-151 (8) ... 20.50 20.50

Type of 1930-35 Redrawn Imprint: "Beiteddine-Imp.-Catholique-Beyrouth-Liban."
1939   Litho.   Perf. 11½
152 A10 1p dk slate grn ... 2.25 .25
Never hinged ... 3.25
153 A10 1.50p brn violet ... 2.25 .75
Never hinged ... 3.25
154 A10 7.50p carmine lake ... 2.25 1.10
Never hinged ... 3.25
Nos. 152-154 (3) ... 6.75 2.10

Bridge Type of 1930-35 Imprint: "Degorce" instead of "Hélio Vaugirard"
1940   Engr.   Perf. 13
155 A13 5p grnsh blue ... 1.50 .25
Never hinged ... 2.50

Exists imperforate.

SEMI-POSTAL STAMPS

Stamps of 1925 Srchd. in Red or Black

1926   Unwmk.   Perf. 14x13½
B1 A2 25c + 25c ol blk ... 4.25 4.25
Never hinged ... 6.25
B2 A2 50c + 25c yellow green (B) ... 4.25 4.25
Never hinged ... 6.25
B3 A2 75c + 25c brown orange (B) ... 4.25 4.25
Never hinged ... 6.25
B4 A2 1p + 50c mag ... 4.25 4.25
Never hinged ... 6.25
B5 A2 1.25p + 50c dp grn ... 4.75 4.75
Never hinged ... 6.75
B6 A2 1.50p + 50c rose red (B) ... 4.75 4.75
Never hinged ... 6.75
a. Double surcharge ... 40.00 30.00
B7 A2 2p + 75c dk brn ... 4.25 4.25
Never hinged ... 6.75
B8 A2 2.50p + 75c pck bl ... 4.75 4.75
Never hinged ... 6.75
B9 A2 3p + 1p org brn ... 4.75 4.75
Never hinged ... 6.75
B10 A2 5p + 1p vio (B) ... 4.75 4.75
Never hinged ... 6.75
B11 A3 10p + 2p violet brown (B) ... 4.75 4.75
Never hinged ... 6.75
B12 A2 25p + 5p ultra ... 4.75 4.75
Never hinged ... 6.75
Nos. B1-B12 (12) ... 54.50 54.50

On No. B11 the surcharge is set in six lines to fit the shape of the stamp. All values of this series exist with inverted surcharge. Value each, $14.
See Nos. CB1-CB4.

AIR POST STAMPS

Nos. 10-13 with Additional Overprint

1924   Unwmk.   Perf. 14x13½
C1 A18 2p on 40c ... 13.00 13.00
Never hinged ... 20.00
a. Double surcharge ... 52.50 52.50
C2 A18 3p on 60c ... 13.00 13.00
Never hinged ... 20.00
a. Invtd. surch. and ovpt. ... 87.50 87.50
C3 A18 5p on 1fr ... 13.00 13.00
Never hinged ... 20.00
a. Dbl. surch. and ovpt. ... 72.50 72.50
b. "5" omitted ... 300.00
C4 A18 10p on 2fr ... 13.00 13.00
Never hinged ... 20.00
a. Invtd. surch. and ovpt. ... 110.00 110.00
b. Dbl. surch. and ovpt. ... 60.00 60.00
Nos. C1-C4 (4) ... 52.00 52.00

Nos. 33, 35-37 Overprinted

C5 A18 2p on 40c ... 13.00 13.00
Never hinged ... 20.00
a. Overprint reversed ... 45.00
C6 A18 3p on 60c ... 13.00 13.00
Never hinged ... 20.00
a. Overprint reversed ... 45.00
C7 A18 5p on 1fr ... 13.00 13.00
Never hinged ... 20.00
a. Overprint reversed ... 45.00
C8 A18 10p on 2fr ... 13.50 13.50
Never hinged ... 21.00
a. Overprint reversed ... 45.00
b. Double surcharge ... 45.00
Nos. C5-C8 (4) ... 52.50 52.50

Nos. 57, 59-61 Overprinted in Green

1925
C9 A2 2p dark brown ... 4.50 4.50
Never hinged ... 6.75

C10	A2	3p orange brown	4.50	4.50
	Never hinged		6.75	
C11	A2	5p violet	4.50	4.50
	Never hinged		6.75	
a.	Inverted overprint			
C12	A3	10p violet brown	4.50	4.50
	Never hinged		6.75	
	[illegible] (4)		18.00	18.00

Nos. 57,
59-61
Ovptd. in
Red — c

1926

C13	A2	2p dark brown	4.75	4.75
	Never hinged		7.00	
C14	A2	3p orange brown	4.75	4.75
	Never hinged		7.00	
C15	A2	5p violet	4.75	4.75
	Never hinged		7.00	
C16	A3	10p violet brown	4.75	4.75
	Never hinged		7.00	
	Nos. C13-C16 (4)		19.00	19.00

Airplane pointed down on No. C16.
Exist with inverted overprint. Value, each
$45.

Issues of Republic under French Mandate

Nos. C13-
C16
Overprinted
— d

1927

C17	A2	2p dark brown	5.50	5.50
	Never hinged		8.50	
C18	A2	3p orange brown	5.50	5.50
	Never hinged		8.50	
C19	A2	5p violet	5.50	5.50
	Never hinged		8.50	
C20	A3	10p violet brown	5.50	5.50
	Never hinged		8.50	
	Nos. C17-C20 (4)		22.00	22.00

On No. C19 "Republique Libanaise" is
above the bars. Overprint set in two lines on
No. C20.

Nos. C17-
C20 with
Additional
Ovpt. — e

1928   **Black Overprint**

C21	A2	2p brown	12.50	10.00
	Never hinged		19.00	
a.	Double overprint		65.00	65.00
b.	Inverted overprint		65.00	65.00
C22	A2	3p orange brown	12.50	10.00
	Never hinged		19.00	
a.	Double overprint		65.00	65.00
C23	A2	5p violet	12.50	10.00
	Never hinged		19.00	
a.	Double overprint		65.00	65.00
C24	A3	10p violet brown	12.50	10.00
	Never hinged		19.00	
a.	Double overprint		65.00	65.00
	Nos. C21-C24 (4)		50.00	40.00

On Nos. C21-C24 the airplane is always in
red.

Nos. 52,
54, 57, 59-
62 Ovptd.
in Red or
Black — f

1928

C25	A2	2p dark brown	4.50	4.50
	Never hinged		6.75	
C26	A2	3p orange brown	3.00	3.00
	Never hinged		4.50	
C27	A2	5p violet	4.50	4.50
	Never hinged		6.75	
C28	A3	10p violet brown	4.50	4.50
	Never hinged		6.75	

1929

C33	A2	50c yellow green	1.25	1.25
	Never hinged			
a.	Inverted overprint		45.00	45.00
C34	A2	1p magenta (Bk)	1.00	1.00
	Never hinged		1.50	
a.	Inverted overprint		45.00	45.00

C35	A2	25p ultra	190.00	160.00
	Never hinged		390.00	
a.	Inverted overprint		525.00	525.00
	Nos. C25-C34 (6)		18.75	18.75
	Nos. C25-C35 (7)		208.75	178.75

On Nos. C25-C28 the airplane is always in
red.

On No. C28 the overprinted orientation is
horizontal. The bars covering the old country
names are at the left.

The red overprint of a silhouetted plane and
"Republique Libanaise," as on Nos. C25-C27,
was also applied to Nos. C9-C12. These are
believed to have been essays, and were not
regularly issued.

No. 62 with
Surcharge
Added in
Red

Two types of surcharge:
I — The "5" of "15 P." is italic. The "15" is
4mm high. Arabic characters for "Lebanese
Republic" and for "15 P." are on same line in
that order.
II — The "5" is in Roman type (upright) and
smaller; "15" is 3½mm high. Arabic for "Lebanese Republic" is centered on line by itself,
with Arabic for "15 P." below right end of line.

C36	A2	15p on 25p ultra (I)	225.00	175.00
a.	Type II (#106)		800.00	800.00

Nos. 102 Overprinted Type "c" in Blue

C37	A2	50c on 75c	1.00	1.00
	Never hinged		1.50	
a.	Airplane inverted		45.00	
b.	French and Arabic surch. intvd.			
c.	"P" omitted			
d.	Airplane double		50.00	

No. 55 Surcharged in Red

1930

C38	A2	2p on 1.25p dp green	1.75	1.25
	Never hinged		3.00	
a.	Inverted surcharge		72.50	45.00

Airplane
over
Racheya
AP2

Designs: 1p, Plane over Broumana. 2p,
Baalbek. 3p, Hasroun. 5p, Byblos. 10p,
Kadicha River. 15p, Beirut. 25p, Tripoli. 50p,
Kabeljas. 100p, Zahle.

1930-31   **Photo.**   *Perf. 13½*

C39	AP2	50c dk violet ('31)	.50	.50
	Never hinged		1.00	
C40	AP2	1p yellow grn ('31)	.80	.80
	Never hinged		1.60	
C41	AP2	2p dp orange ('31)	2.50	2.50
	Never hinged		5.00	
C42	AP2	3p magenta ('31)	2.50	2.50
	Never hinged		5.00	
C43	AP2	5p indigo	2.50	2.50
	Never hinged		5.00	
C44	AP2	10p orange red	3.25	3.25
	Never hinged		6.50	
C45	AP2	15p orange brn	3.25	3.25
	Never hinged		6.50	
C46	AP2	25p gray vio ('31)	4.75	4.75
	Never hinged		9.50	
C47	AP2	50p dp claret	9.00	9.00
	Never hinged		18.00	
C48	AP2	100p olive brown	12.00	12.00
	Never hinged		24.00	
	Nos. C39-C48 (10)		41.05	41.05

Nos. C39-C48 exist imperforate. Value, set
$200.

Tourist Publicity Issue

Skiing in
Lebanon
AP12

Bay of
Jounie
AP13

1936, Oct. 12

C49	AP12	50c slate grn	3.00	3.00
	Never hinged		6.00	
C50	AP13	1p red orange	3.75	3.75
	Never hinged		7.50	
C51	AP12	2p black violet	3.75	3.75
	Never hinged		7.50	
C52	AP13	3p yellow grn	4.00	4.00
	Never hinged		8.00	
C53	AP12	5p brown car	4.00	4.00
	Never hinged		8.00	
C54	AP13	10p orange brn	4.00	4.00
	Never hinged		8.00	
C55	AP13	15p dk carmine	37.50	37.50
	Never hinged		75.00	
C56	AP12	25p green	125.00	125.00
	Never hinged		250.00	
	Nos. C49-C56 (8)		185.00	185.00

Nos. C49-C56 exist imperforate. Value, set
$650.

Lebanese
Pavilion at
Exposition
AP14

1937, July 1   *Perf. 13½*

C57	AP14	50c olive black	1.50	1.50
	Never hinged		3.00	
C58	AP14	1p yellow green	1.50	1.50
	Never hinged		3.00	
C59	AP14	2p dk red orange	1.50	1.50
	Never hinged		3.00	
C60	AP14	3p dk olive grn	1.50	1.50
	Never hinged		4.00	
C61	AP14	5p deep green	2.00	2.00
	Never hinged		4.00	
C62	AP14	10p carmine lake	9.00	9.00
	Never hinged		18.00	
C63	AP14	15p rose lake	10.00	10.00
	Never hinged		20.00	
C64	AP14	25p orange brn	17.50	17.50
	Never hinged		35.00	
	Nos. C57-C64 (8)		44.50	44.50

Paris International Exposition.

Arcade of
Beit-ed-Din
Palace
AP15

Ruins of
Baalbek
AP16

1937-40   **Engr.**   *Perf. 13*

C65	AP15	50c ultra ('38)	.35	.25
	Never hinged		.70	
C66	AP15	1p henna brn ('40)	.35	.25
	Never hinged		.70	
C67	AP15	2p sepia ('40)	.35	.25
	Never hinged		.70	
C68	AP15	3p rose ('40)	3.25	1.25
	Never hinged		6.50	
C69	AP15	5p lt green ('40)	.35	.25
	Never hinged		.70	
C70	AP16	10p dull violet	.35	.25
	Never hinged		.70	
C71	AP16	15p turq bl ('40)	2.75	1.75
	Never hinged		5.50	
C72	AP16	25p violet ('40)	6.00	5.00
	Never hinged		12.00	
C73	AP16	50p yellow grn ('40)	11.00	7.00
	Never hinged		22.00	
C74	AP16	100p brown ('40)	6.00	3.50
	Never hinged		12.00	
	Nos. C65-C74 (10)		30.75	19.75

Nos. C65-C74 exist imperforate.

Medical
College of
Beirut
AP17

1938, May 9   **Photo.**   *Perf. 13*

C75	AP17	2p green	3.00	*3.50*
	Never hinged		6.00	
C76	AP17	3p orange	6.00	*7.00*
	Never hinged			
C77	AP17	5p lilac gray	5.50	*6.50*
	Never hinged		11.00	
C78	AP17	10p lake	10.50	*12.00*
	Never hinged		21.00	
	Nos. C75-C78 (4)		22.00	25.50

Medical Congress.

Maurice Noguès and View of
Beirut — AP18

1938, July 15   *Perf. 11*

C79	AP18	10p brown carmine	4.00	1.50
	Never hinged		8.00	
a.	Souv. sheet of 4, perf. 13½		35.00	20.00
b.	Perf. 13½		7.50	4.00

10th anniversary of first Marseille-Beirut
flight, by Maurice Noguès.
No. C79a has marginal inscriptions in
French and Arabic. Exists imperf.; value $250.

AIR POST SEMI-POSTAL STAMPS

Nos. C13-C16 Surcharged Like Nos. B1-B12

1926   *Perf. 13½*

CB1	A2	2pi +1pi dark brown	12.00	8.00
CB2	A2	3pi + 2pi orabge brown	12.00	8.00
CB3	A2	5pi +3pi violet	12.00	8.00
CB4	A3	10pi +5pi violet brown	12.00	8.00
	Nos. CB1-CB4 (4)		48.00	32.00

These stamps were sold for their combined
values, original and surcharged. The latter
represented their postal franking value and the
former was a contribution to the relief of refugees from the Djebel Druze War.

POSTAGE DUE STAMPS

Postage Due Stamps of France, 1893-1920, Surcharged like Regular Issue

1924   **Unwmk.**   *Perf. 14x13½*

J1	D2	50c on 10c choc	6.75	4.25
J2	D2	1p on 20c ol grn	6.75	4.25
J3	D2	2p on 30c red	6.75	4.25
J4	D2	3p on 50c vio brn	6.75	4.25
J5	D2	5p on 1fr red brn, straw	6.75	4.25
	Nos. J1-J5 (5)		33.75	21.25

Postage Due Stamps of
France, 1893-1920,
Surcharged

1924

J6	D2	50c on 10c choc	7.25	4.00
	Never hinged		12.00	
J7	D2	1p on 20c ol grn	7.25	4.00
	Never hinged		12.00	
J8	D2	2p on 30c red	7.25	4.00
	Never hinged		12.00	
J9	D2	3p on 50c vio brn	7.25	4.00
	Never hinged		12.00	
J10	D2	5p on 1fr red brn, straw	7.25	4.00
	Never hinged		12.00	
	Nos. J6-J10 (5)		36.25	20.00

Ancient
Bridge
across Dog
River — D3

Designs: 1p, Village scene. 2p, Pigeon
Rocks, near Beirut. 3p, Belfort Castle. 5p,
Venus Temple at Baalbek.

1925 Photo. Perf. 13½

J11	D3	50c brown, *yellow*	.95	.45
J12	D3	1p violet, *rose*	1.35	.65
J13	D3	2p black, *blue*	2.25	.90
J14	D3	3p black, *red org*	3.50	2.00
J15	D3	5p black, *bl grn*	5.75	3.75
		Nos. J11-J15 (5)	13.80	7.75
		Set, never hinged	42.50	

Nos. J11 to J15 Overprinted

1927

J16	D3	50c brown, *yellow*	1.50	.40
J17	D3	1p violet, *rose*	2.50	.85
J18	D3	2p black, *blue*	3.50	1.25
J19	D3	3p black, *red org*	7.25	3.00
J20	D3	5p black, *bl grn*	9.50	4.50
		Nos. J16-J20 (5)	24.25	10.00
		Set, never hinged	35.00	

Nos. J16-J20 with Additional Ovpt.

1928

J21	D3	50c brn, *yel* (Bk+R)	1.75	1.25
J22	D3	1p vio, *rose* (Bk)	1.75	1.25
J23	D3	2p blk, *bl* (Bk+R)	3.00	2.00
J24	D3	3p blk, *red org* (Bk)	6.00	3.50
J25	D3	5p blk, *bl grn* (Bk+R)	6.75	4.25
		Nos. J21-J25 (5)	19.25	12.25
		Set, never hinged	65.00	

No. J23 has not the short bars in the upper corners.

Postage Due Stamps of 1925 Overprinted in Red like Nos. J21-J25

1928

J26	D3	50c brn, *yel* (R)	1.00	.50
J27	D3	2p blk, *bl* (R)	4.25	3.50
J28	D3	5p blk, *bl grn* (R)	11.50	7.50
		Nos. J26-J28 (3)	16.75	11.50
		Set, never hinged	32.50	

No. J28 has not the short bars in the upper corners.

D4

Bas-relief of a Ship — D5

D6

D7

D8

Bas-relief from Sarcophagus of King Ahiram — D9

D10

1930-40 Photo.; Engr. (No. J35)

J29	D4	50c black, *rose*	.75	.50
J30	D5	1p blk, *gray bl*	1.25	1.00
J31	D6	2p blk, *yellow*	1.75	1.25
J32	D7	3p blk, *bl grn*	1.75	1.25
J33	D8	5p blk, *orange*	7.25	5.50
J34	D9	8p blk, *lt rose*	5.00	3.50
J35	D8	10p dk green ('40)	7.75	4.50
J36	D10	15p black	6.25	2.75
		Nos. J29-J36 (8)	31.75	20.25
		Set, never hinged	65.00	

Nos. J29-J36 exist imperf.

LEEWARD ISLANDS

'lē-wərd 'ī-lənds

LOCATION — A group of islands in the West Indies, southeast of Puerto Rico
GOVT. — British Colony
AREA — 423 sq. mi.
POP. — 108,847 (1946)
CAPITAL — St. John

While stamps inscribed "Leeward Islands" were in use, 1890-1956, the colony consisted of the presidencies (now colonies) of Antigua, Montserrat, St. Christopher (St. Kitts) with Nevis and Anguilla, the British Virgin Islands and Dominica (which became a separate colony in 1940).
Each presidency issued its own stamps, using them along with the Leeward Islands general issues.

12 Pence = 1 Shilling
20 Shillings = 1 Pound

Catalogue values for unused stamps in this country are for Never Hinged items, beginning with Scott 116.

Queen Victoria — A1

1890 Typo. Wmk. 2 Perf. 14

1	A1	½p lilac & green	3.75	1.40
2	A1	1p lilac & car	8.00	.25
3	A1	2½p lilac & ultra	8.50	.30
4	A1	4p lilac & org	10.00	9.50
5	A1	6p lilac & brown	12.50	14.00
6	A1	7p lilac & slate	11.00	18.00
7	A1	1sh green & car	24.00	55.00
8	A1	5sh green & ultra	140.00	300.00
		Nos. 1-8 (8)	217.75	398.45
		Set, ovptd. "SPECIMEN"	275.00	

Denomination of Nos. 7-8 are in color on plain tablet: "ONE SHILLING" or "FIVE SHILLINGS."
For overprints and surcharges see Nos. 9-19.

Jubilee Issue

Regular Issue of 1890 Handstamp Overprinted

1897, July 22

9	A1	½p lilac & green	7.50	22.50
10	A1	1p lilac & car	8.50	22.50
11	A1	2½p lilac & ultra	9.00	22.50
12	A1	4p lilac & org	55.00	80.00
13	A1	6p lilac & brown	60.00	130.00
14	A1	7p lilac & slate	60.00	130.00
15	A1	1sh green & car	130.00	275.00
16	A1	5sh green & ultra	525.00	850.00
		Nos. 9-16 (8)	855.00	1,532.

Double Overprints

9a	A1	½p	1,400.	
b.		Triple overprint	10,000.	
10a	A1	1p	1,150.	
b.		Triple overprint	5,500.	
11a	A1	2½p	1,350.	
12a	A1	4p	1,350.	
13a	A1	6p	1,700.	4,500.
14a	A1	7p	1,700.	
15a	A1	1sh	2,250.	
16a	A1	5sh	6,000.	

60th year of Queen Victoria's reign.
Excellent counterfeits of Nos. 9-16 exist.

Stamps of 1890 Surcharged in Black or Red

One Penny / One Penny
b c

1902, Aug.

17	A1(b)	1p on 4p lilac & org	6.00	9.00
a.		Tall narrow "O" in "One"	45.00	85.00
18	A1(b)	1p on 6p lilac & brn	7.50	14.00
a.		Tall narrow "O" in "One"	60.00	140.00
19	A1(c)	1p on 7p lilac & sl	6.00	11.00
		Nos. 17-19 (3)	19.50	34.00

King Edward VII — A4

Numerals of ¼p, 2p, 3p and 2sh6p of type A4 are in color on plain tablet. The 1sh and 5sh denominations are expressed as "ONE SHILLING" and "FIVE SHILLINGS" on plain tablet.

1902

20	A4	½p violet & green	6.00	1.10
21	A4	1p vio & car rose	8.50	.25
22	A4	2p violet & bister	3.00	4.50
23	A4	2½p violet & ultra	6.00	2.50
24	A4	3p violet & black	9.00	8.00
25	A4	6p violet & brown	2.75	8.50
26	A4	1sh grn & car rose	8.50	25.00
27	A4	2sh6p green & blk	29.00	80.00
28	A4	5sh green & ultra	65.00	90.00
		Nos. 20-28 (9)	137.75	219.85
		Set, ovptd. "SPECIMEN"	170.00	

1905-11 Wmk. 3
Chalky Paper (Ordinary Paper #29, 33)

29	A4	½p vio & grn ('06)	4.00	2.25
a.		Chalky paper ('08)	32.50	19.00
30	A4	1p vio & car rose	9.50	.90
31	A4	2p vio & bis ('08)	11.00	24.00
32	A4	2½p vio & ultra	80.00	50.00
33	A4	3p violet & black	22.50	55.00
a.		Chalky paper ('08)	60.00	95.00
34	A4	3p violet, *yel* ('10)	3.75	8.00
35	A4	6p vio & brn ('08)	55.00	85.00
36	A4	6p violet & red violet ('11)	9.00	7.50
37	A4	1sh grn & car rose ('08)	47.50	130.00
38	A4	1sh blk, *grn* ('11)	7.00	22.50
39	A4	2sh6p blk & red, *blue* ('11)	42.50	55.00
40	A4	5sh grn & red, *yel* ('11)	47.50	70.00
		Nos. 29-40 (12)	339.25	510.15

1907-11 Ordinary Paper

41	A4	¼p brown ('09)	3.00	1.90
42	A4	½p green	4.50	1.40
43	A4	1p red	12.00	.85
a.		1p rose carmine	45.00	3.75
44	A4	2p gray ('11)	4.75	10.00
45	A4	2½p ultramarine	8.00	4.50
		Nos. 41-45 (5)	32.25	18.65

A5

King George V — A6

For description of dies I and II, see "Dies of British Colonial Stamps" in Table of Contents.
The ½p, 1p, 2½p and 6p denominations of type A5 show the numeral on horizontally-lined tablet. The 1sh and 5sh denominations are expressed as "ONE SHILLING" and "FIVE SHILLINGS" on plain tablet.

Die I
1912 Ordinary Paper

46	A5	¼p brown	1.90	1.10
47	A5	½p green	5.50	1.75
48	A5	1p carmine	5.25	1.10
a.		1p scarlet	12.00	1.10
49	A5	2p gray	4.25	5.75
50	A5	2½p ultramarine	3.50	7.25

1912-22 Chalky Paper

51	A5	3p violet, *yel*	2.25	20.00
52	A5	4p blk & red, *yel* (Die II) ('22)	7.00	22.50
53	A5	6p vio & red vio	3.75	8.50
54	A5	1sh blk, *bl grn*, ol back	14.00	8.50
a.		1sh black, *green*	3.25	8.50
55	A5	2sh vio & ultra, *bl* (Die II) ('22)	18.00	65.00
56	A5	2sh6p black & red, *blue* ('14)	20.00	55.00
57	A5	5sh green & red, *yellow* ('14)	65.00	120.00
a.		5sh green & red, *lemon* ('15)	45.00	85.00
		Nos. 46-57 (12)	150.40	316.45
		Set, ovptd. "SPECIMEN"	300.00	

1913, Nov. Surface-colored Paper

58	A5	3p violet, *yel*	90.00	180.00
59	A5	1sh black, *green*	85.00	40.00
60	A5	5sh green & red, *yel*	55.00	90.00
		Nos. 58-60 (3)	230.00	310.00

Die II
1921-32 Wmk. 4 Ordinary Paper

61	A5	¼p dk brown ('22)	2.50	1.10
a.		¼p dark brown (I) ('32)	14.00	21.00
62	A5	½p green	1.25	.80
a.		½p green (I) ('32)	27.50	60.00
63	A5	1p carmine	2.50	.60
a.		1p rose red (I) ('32)	45.00	1.00
b.		1p bright scarlet (II) ('29)	14.00	2.50
64	A5	1p dp violet ('22)	2.50	1.10
65	A5	1½p rose red ('26)	6.00	2.10
66	A5	1½p red brn ('29)	1.50	.25
a.		1½p red brown (I) ('32)	4.50	3.00
68	A5	2p gray ('22)	2.50	.85
69	A5	2½p orange ('23)	11.00	60.00
70	A5	2½p ultra ('27)	3.75	1.40
a.		Die I ('32)	7.50	3.75
71	A5	3p ultra ('23)	14.00	30.00
a.		3p deep ultramarine ('25)	65.00	65.00

Chalky Paper

72	A5	3p violet, *yel*	6.00	6.75
73	A5	4p black & red, *yel* ('23)	3.25	22.50
74	A5	5p vio & olive grn ('22)	2.75	4.50
75	A5	6p vio & red vio ('23)	17.50	42.50
a.		Die I ('32)	30.00	95.00
76	A5	1sh blk, *emerald* ('23)	11.00	8.50
a.		1sh black, *green* (I) ('32)	60.00	85.00
77	A5	2sh vio & ultra, *bl* ('22)	22.50	45.00
a.		2sh red purple & blue, *blue* ('26)	9.50	52.50
78	A5	2sh6p blk & red, *bl* ('23)	9.50	24.00
79	A5	3sh green & vio	12.50	37.50
80	A5	4sh black & scar	18.00	42.50
81	A5	5sh grn & red, *yel*	50.00	85.00
82	A6	10sh red & grn, *emer* ('28)	80.00	140.00

Wmk. 3

83	A6	£1 black & vio, *red* ('28)	240.00	325.00
		Nos. 61-66,68-83 (22)	520.50	881.95

Common Design Types
pictured following the introduction.

Silver Jubilee Issue
Common Design Type
Perf. 11x12

1935, May 6		**Engr.**	**Wmk. 4**	
96	CD301	1p car & dk blue	1.75	3.25
97	CD301	1½p blk & ultra	2.75	1.60
98	CD301	2½p ultra & brn	4.00	4.75
99	CD301	1sh brn vio & ind	22.50	25.00
	Nos. 96-99 (4)		31.00	34.60
	Set, never hinged		42.50	
	Set, perf "SPECIMEN"		130.00	

Coronation Issue
Common Design Type

1937, May 12			**Perf. 13½x14**	
100	CD302	1p carmine	.50	.90
101	CD302	1½p brown	.50	1.50
102	CD302	2½p bright ultra	.55	1.50
	Nos. 100-102 (3)		1.55	3.90
	Set, never hinged		2.75	
	Set, perf "SPECIMEN"		110.00	

King George VI
A7   A8

1938-51		**Typo.**	**Perf. 14**	
103	A7	¼p brown	.40	1.50
	Never hinged		.55	
a.	¼p deep brown, chalky paper ('49)		.25	1.75
	Never hinged		.30	
104	A7	½p green	.75	.75
	Never hinged		.65	
105	A7	1p carmine	1.25	1.75
	Never hinged		1.40	
a.	1p scarlet ('42)		1.40	12.00
	Never hinged		2.00	
b.	1p red ('48)		3.75	6.50
	Never hinged		5.50	
106	A7	1½p red brown	.80	.50
	Never hinged		.90	
107	A7	2p gray	2.00	2.25
	Never hinged		2.75	
a.	2p slate gray ('42)		4.00	3.25
	Never hinged		5.00	
108	A7	2½p ultramarine	.60	2.25
	Never hinged		.75	
a.	2½p bright blue		18.00	4.00
	Never hinged		18.00	
109	A7	3p dl org ('42)	.40	.90
	Never hinged		4.50	
a.	3p brown orange		22.50	2.75
	Never hinged		22.50	
110	A7	6p vio & red vio	6.00	3.50
	Never hinged		7.25	
a.	6p deep dull purple & bright purple		16.00	7.00
	Never hinged		21.00	
b.	6p purple & deep magenta ('47)		9.00	5.00
	Never hinged		8.75	
111	A7	1sh blk, *emerald* ('42)	3.50	1.50
	Never hinged		4.00	
a.	1sh black, *emerald*, chalky paper		10.00	5.50
	Never hinged		17.50	
112	A7	2sh vio & ultra, *bl*	7.75	2.25
	Never hinged		9.00	
a.	2sh reddish purple & blue, *blue*, chalky paper		17.00	3.00
	Never hinged		22.50	
113	A7	5sh grn & red, *yel*	21.00	18.00
	Never hinged		30.00	
a.	5sh green & red, *yel*, chalky paper		30.00	22.50
	Never hinged		50.00	
114	A8	10sh dp ver & dp grn, *emer*, ordinary paper ('47)	82.50	100.00
	Never hinged		130.00	
a.	10sh dp red & bluish grn, *green*, chalky paper		125.00	140.00
	Never hinged		225.00	
b.	10sh dull red & pale grn, *green*, ordinary paper ('44)		475.00	375.00
	Never hinged		600.00	
c.	10sh red & green, *green*, ordinary paper ('45)		100.00	90.00
	Never hinged		160.00	

Two dies were used for the 1p, differing in thickness of shading line at base of "1."

	Wmk. 3		**Perf. 13**	
115	A8	£1 blk & vio, *scar* ('51)	22.50	37.50
	Never hinged		50.00	
a.	£1 black & brown purple, *red*, perf. 14 ('41)		225.00	375.00
	Never hinged		375.00	
b.	£1 black & purple, *carmine*, perf. 14 ('41)		55.00	55.00
	Never hinged		90.00	
c.	£1 black & brown purple, *salmon*, perf. 14 ('43)		27.50	29.00

d.	Never hinged		45.00
	Wmkd. sideways (as #115, perf. 13)		3,600.
	Never hinged		6,000.
	Nos. 103-115 (13)	149.45	172.65
	Set, never hinged		240.00

The 3p&1 were issued on chalky paper in 1938 and on ordinary paper in 1942. Values are for the most common varieties.
Issued: #115, 12/13/51; others, 11/25/38. See Nos. 120-125.

> **Catalogue values for unused stamps in this section, from this point to the end of the section, are for Never Hinged items.**

Peace Issue
Common Design Type
Perf. 13½x14

1946, Nov. 1		**Wmk. 4**	**Engr.**	
116	CD303	1½p brown	.25	.25
117	CD303	3p deep orange	.25	.25
	Set, perf "SPECIMEN"		100.00	

Silver Wedding Issue
Common Design Types

1949, Jan. 2		**Photo.**	**Perf. 14x14½**	
118	CD304	2½p bright ultra	.25	.25

Perf. 11½x11
Engr.; Name Typographed

119	CD305	5sh green	6.50	6.50

George VI Type of 1938

1949, July 1		**Typo.**	**Perf. 13½x14**	
120	A7	½p gray	2.00	1.50
121	A7	1p green	.55	.25
122	A7	1½p orange & black	1.75	.40
123	A7	2p crimson rose	1.40	1.25
124	A7	2½p black & plum	1.00	1.00
125	A7	3p ultramarine	1.00	.25
	Nos. 120-125 (6)		7.70	3.90

UPU Issue
Common Design Types
Engr.; Name Typo. on 3p and 6p

1949, Oct. 10			**Perf. 13½, 11x11½**	
126	CD306	2½p slate	.25	.75
127	CD307	3p indigo	2.00	1.00
128	CD308	6p red lilac	.40	1.00
129	CD309	1sh blue green	.40	1.00
	Nos. 126-129 (4)		3.05	3.75

University Issue
Common Design Types
Perf. 14x14½

1951, Feb. 16		**Engr.**	**Wmk. 4**	
130	CD310	3c gray black & org	.35	.75
131	CD311	12c lilac & rose car	1.00	1.25

LIBERIA

lī-'bir-ē-ə

LOCATION — West coast of Africa, between Ivory Coast and Sierra Leone
GOVT. — Republic
AREA — 43,000 sq. mi.
POP. — 1,900,000 (est. 1984)
CAPITAL — Monrovia

100 Cents = 1 Dollar

Values for unused stamps are for examples with original gum as defined in the catalogue introduction. Any exceptions will be noted. Very fine examples of Nos. 1-3, 13-21 and 157-159 will have perforations just clear of the design due to the narrow spacing of the stamps on the plates and/or imperfect perforating methods.

Watermarks

Wmk. 116 —
Crosses and
Circles

Wmk. 143

"Liberia" — A1

Thick Paper

1860	**Unwmk.**	**Litho.**	**Perf. 12**	
1	A1	6c red	400.00	300.00
a.	Imperf, pair		500.00	
2	A1	12c deep blue	25.00	50.00
a.	Imperf, pair		250.00	
3	A1	24c green	50.00	50.00
a.	Imperf, pair		300.00	
	Nos. 1-3 (3)		475.00	400.00

Stamps set very close together. Examples of the 12c occasionally show traces of a frame line around the design.

Medium to Thin Paper
With a single-line frame around each stamp, about 1mm from the border

1864			**Perf. 11, 12**	
7	A1	6c red	62.50	85.00
a.	Imperf, pair		225.00	
8	A1	12c blue	80.00	95.00
a.	Imperf, pair		225.00	
9	A1	24c lt green	87.50	100.00
a.	Imperf, pair		225.00	
	Nos. 7-9 (3)		230.00	280.00

Stamps set about 5mm apart. Margins large and perforation usually outside the frame line.

1866-69		**Without Frame Line**		
13	A1	6c lt red	25.00	40.00
14	A1	12c lt blue	25.00	40.00
15	A1	24c lt yellow grn	25.00	40.00
	Nos. 13-15 (3)		75.00	120.00

Stamps set 2-2½mm apart with small margins. Stamps are usually without frame line but those from one transfer show broken and irregular parts of a frame.

1880	**With Frame Line**		**Perf. 10½**	
16	A1	1c ultra	5.00	8.00
17	A1	2c rose	5.00	5.25
a.	Imperf, pair		175.00	
18	A1	6c violet	5.00	5.25
19	A1	12c yellow	5.00	5.25
20	A1	24c rose red	6.00	5.50
	Nos. 16-20 (5)		26.00	29.25

Unused values for Nos. 16-20 are for stamps without gum.
For surcharges see Nos. 157-159.

Counterfeits
Counterfeits exist of Nos. 1-28, 32 and 64.

From Arms of
Liberia — A2

1881				
21	A2	3c black	15.00	10.00

Unused value is for a stamp without gum.

A3

A4

1882			**Perf. 11½, 12, 14**	
22	A3	8c blue	50.00	10.00
23	A4	16c red	8.00	5.00

The "1" in "22" and the openings in the figure "8" enclose a pattern of slanting lines. Compare with No. 32.

Canceled to Order
Beginning with the issue of 1885, values in the used column are for "canceled to order" stamps. Postally used examples sell for much more.

A5   A6

From Arms of
Liberia — A7

Perf. 10½, 11, 12, 11½x10½, 14, 14½

1885				
24	A5	1c carmine	2.00	2.00
a.	1c rose		2.00	2.00
25	A5	2c green	2.00	2.00
26	A5	3c violet	2.00	2.00
27	A5	4c brown	2.00	2.00
28	A5	6c olive gray	2.00	2.00
29	A6	8c bluish gray	4.00	4.00
a.	8c lilac		7.00	7.00
30	A6	16c yellow	15.00	12.00
31	A7	32c deep blue	35.00	29.00
	Nos. 24-31 (8)		64.00	55.00

In the 1885 printing, the stamps are spaced 2mm apart and the paper is medium. In the 1892 printing, the stamps are 4½mm apart. For surcharges see Nos. J1-J2.

Imperf., Pair

24b	A5	1c	3.00	
25a	A5	2c	4.75	
26a	A5	3c	5.00	
27a	A5	4c	5.00	
28a	A5	6c	4.25	4.25
29b	A6	8c	12.50	
30a	A6	16c	30.00	
31a	A7	32c	50.00	

Imperf. pairs with 2mm spacing sell for higher prices.

A8

1889			**Perf. 12, 14**	
32	A8	8c blue	4.25	4.25
a.	Imperf., pair		20.00	

The openings in the figure "8" are filled with network. See No. 22.

A9   Elephant — A10

Oil Palm — A11

Pres. Hilary R. W. Johnson — A12

Vai Woman in Full Dress — A13

Coat of Arms — A14

Liberian Star — A15

Coat of Arms — A16

Hippopotamus A17

Liberian Star — A18

President Johnson — A19

1892-96 Wmk. 143 Engr. Perf. 15

33	A9	1c vermilion	.50	.40
a.		1c blue (error)	40.00	
34	A9	2c blue	.50	.40
a.		2c vermilion (error)	40.00	
35	A10	4c green & blk	1.75	1.00
a.		Center inverted	200.00	
36	A11	6c blue green	.70	.50
37	A12	8c brown & blk	.95	.95
a.		Center inverted	500.00	500.00
b.		Center sideways	750.00	
38	A12	10c chrome yel & indigo ('96)	.95	.65
39	A13	12c rose red	.95	.65
40	A13	15c slate ('96)	.95	.65
41	A14	16c lilac	3.50	1.75
a.		16c deep greenish blue (error)	110.00	
42	A14	20c vermilion ('96)	3.50	1.75
43	A15	24c ol grn, yel	2.00	1.10
44	A15	25c yel grn ('96)	2.00	1.40
45	A16	30c steel bl ('96)	6.25	4.50
46	A16	32c grnsh blue	3.50	2.75
a.		32c lilac (error)	110.00	
47	A17	$1 ultra & blk	12.00	9.00
a.		$1 blue & black	13.50	11.00
48	A18	$2 brown, yel	9.00	8.00
49	A19	$5 carmine & blk	10.00	10.00
a.		Center inverted	400.00	400.00
		Nos. 33-49 (17)	59.00	45.45

Many imperforates, part-perforated and mis-perforated varieties exist.

The 1c, 2c and 4c were issued in sheets of 60; 6c, sheet of 40; 8c, 10c, sheets of 30; 12c, 15c, 24c, 25c, sheets of 20; 16c, 20c, 30c, sheets of 15; $1, $2, $5, sheets of 10.

For overprints & surcharges see Nos. 50, 64B-64F, 66, 71-77, 79-81, 85-93, 95-100, 160, O1-O13, O15-O25, O37-O41, O44-O45.

No. 36 Surcharged

a   b

1893
50	A11 (a)	5c on 6c blue grn	1.75	1.10
a.		"5" with short flag	6.00	6.00
b.		Both 5's with short flags	5.00	5.00
c.		"i" dot omitted	19.00	19.00
d.		Surcharge "b"	30.00	30.00

"Commerce," Globe and Krumen — A22

1894 Unwmk. Engr. Imperf.
52	A22	5c carmine & blk	5.00	5.00

Rouletted
53	A22	5c carmine & blk	10.00	7.50

For overprints see Nos. 69, O26-O27.

Oil Palm A23

Hippopotamus A24

Elephant — A25   Liberty — A26

1897-1905 Wmk. 143 Perf. 14 to 16
54	A23	1c lilac rose	1.00	.65
a.		1c violet	1.00	.65
55	A23	1c deep green		
		('00)	1.25	.95
56	A23	1c lt green ('05)	3.00	1.60
57	A24	2c bister & blk	3.00	1.60
58	A24	2c org red & blk ('00)	6.00	2.10
59	A24	2c rose & blk ('05)	3.00	1.60
60	A25	5c lake & black	3.00	1.60
a.		5c lilac rose & black	3.00	1.60
61	A25	5c gray bl & blk ('00)	6.00	5.00
62	A25	5c ultra & blk ('05)	4.25	2.75
a.		Center inverted	1,500.	
63	A26	50c red brn & blk	4.00	3.50
		Nos. 54-63 (10)	34.50	21.35

For overprints & surcharges see Nos. 65, 66A-68. 70, 78, 82-84, M1, O28-O36, O42, O92.

A27

Two types:
I — 13 pearls above "Republic Liberia."
II — 10 pearls.

1897 Unwmk. Litho. Perf. 14
64	A27	3c red & green (I)	.25	.60
a.		Type II	20.00	.25

No. 64a is considered a reprint, unissued. "Used" examples are CTO.

For surcharge see No. 128.

Official Stamps Handstamped in Black

1901-02 Wmk. 143
On Nos. O7-O8, O10-O12
64B	A14	16c lilac	525.00	525.00
64C	A15	24c ol grn, yel	575.00	400.00
64D	A17	$1 blue & blk	3,000.	2,000.
64E	A18	$2 brown, yel	—	—
64F	A19	$5 carmine & blk	—	—

On Stamps with "O S" Printed
65	A23	1c green	37.50	40.00
66	A9	2c blue	100.00	100.00
66A	A24	2c bister & blk	—	150.00
67	A24	2c org red & blk	45.00	40.00
68	A25	5c gray bl & blk	37.50	35.00
69	A22	5c vio & grn (No. O26)	300.00	300.00
70	A25	5c lake & blk	275.00	225.00
71	A12	10c yel & blue blk	37.50	60.00
a.		"O S" omitted		
72	A13	15c slate	40.00	60.00
73	A14	16c lilac	550.00	350.00
74	A14	20c vermilion	42.50	50.00
75	A15	24c ol grn, yel	52.50	50.00
76	A15	25c yellow grn	42.50	50.00
a.		"O S" omitted	750.00	
77	A16	30c steel blue	42.50	40.00
78	A26	50c red brn & blk	100.00	52.50
79	A17	$1 ultra & blk	325.00	275.00
a.		"O S" omitted		
80	A18	$2 brn, yel	2,000.	1,800.
81	A19	$5 car & blk	2,500.	2,000.
a.		"O S" omitted	3,000.	2,750.

On Stamps with "O S" Handstamped
82	A23	1c deep green	62.50	—
83	A24	2c org red & blk	75.00	—
84	A25	5c lake & blk	200.00	—
85	A12	10c yel & bl blk	125.00	—
86	A14	20c vermilion	140.00	—
87	A15	24c ol grn, yel	140.00	—
88	A15	25c yel grn	160.00	—
89	A16	30c steel blue	525.00	—
90	A16	32c grnsh blue	210.00	—

Varieties of Nos. 65-90 include double and inverted overprints.

Nos. 47, O10, O23a Surcharged in Carmine

1902
91	A17	75c on $1 #47	15.00	13.00
a.		Thin "C" and comma	20.00	20.00
b.		Inverted surcharge	62.50	62.50
c.		As "a," inverted		
92	A17	75c on $1 #O10	2,750.	
a.		Thin "C" and comma	3,750.	
93	A17	75c on $1 #O23a	4,000.	
a.		Thin "C" and comma	4,750.	

Liberty — A29

1903 Unwmk. Engr. Perf. 14
94	A29	3c black	.30	.25
a.		Printed on both sides	45.00	
b.		Perf. 12	20.00	6.00

For overprint see No. O43.

Stamps of 1892 Surcharged in Blue

a   b

1903 Wmk. 143
95	A14 (a)	10c on 16c lilac	3.00	5.00
96	A15 (b)	15c on 24c ol grn, yel	4.50	6.00
97	A16 (b)	20c on 32c grnsh bl	6.25	8.50
		Nos. 95-97 (3)	13.75	19.50

Nos. 50, O3 and 45 Surcharged in Black or Red

1904
98	A11	1c on 5c on 6c bl grn	.70	.55
a.		"5" with short flag	4.25	4.25
b.		Both 5's with short flags	8.75	8.75
c.		"i" dot omitted	10.00	10.00
d.		Surcharge on #50d	12.50	12.50
e.		Inverted surcharge	6.75	6.75
99	A10	2c on 4c grn & blk	2.75	4.00
a.		Pair, one without surcharge	35.00	
b.		Double surcharge		
c.		Double surcharge, red and blk	62.50	
d.		Surcharged on back also	19.00	
e.		"Official" overprint missing	30.00	
100	A16	2c on 30c stl bl (R)	9.50	15.00
		Nos. 98-100 (3)	12.95	19.55

African Elephant — A33

Mercury — A34

Chimpanzee A35

Great Blue Touraco — A36

Agama — A37

Egret — A38

Head of Liberty
From Coin — A39

A40

Liberian
Flag — A41

Pygmy
Hippopotamus
A42

Liberty with Star
of Liberia on
Cap — A43

Mandingos — A44

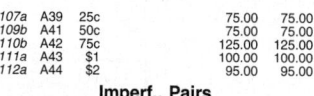

Executive
Mansion and
Pres. Arthur
Barclay — A45

1906   Unwmk.   Engr.   Perf. 14

101	A33	1c green & blk	1.50	.50
102	A34	2c carmine & blk	.30	.25
103	A35	5c ultra & blk	2.75	.85
104	A36	10c red brn & blk	4.00	.85
105	A37	15c pur & dp grn	14.50	3.00
106	A38	20c orange & blk	8.50	2.50
107	A39	25c dull blue & gray	.85	.25
108	A40	30c deep violet	1.00	.25
109	A41	50c dp green & blk	1.00	.25
110	A42	75c brown & blk	12.00	2.50
111	A43	$1 rose & gray	3.00	.25
112	A44	$2 dp green & blk	4.50	.35
113	A45	$5 red brown & blk	9.25	.50
		Nos. 101-113 (13)	63.15	12.30

For surcharges see Nos. 114, 129, 130,
141, 145-149, 161, M2, M5, O72-O73, O82-
O85, O96. For overprints see Nos. O46-O58.

Center Inverted

101a	A33	1c	110.00	55.00
102a	A34	2c	120.00	35.00
103a	A35	5c	175.00	175.00
104a	A36	10c	80.00	80.00
105a	A37	15c	175.00	175.00
106b	A38	20c	175.00	175.00

107a	A39	25c	75.00	75.00
109b	A41	50c	75.00	75.00
110b	A42	75c	125.00	125.00
111a	A43	$1	100.00	100.00
112a	A44	$2	95.00	95.00

Imperf., Pairs

101b	A33	1c	13.50	
102b	A34	2c	14.00	
106a	A38	20c	20.00	
107b	A39	25c	55.00	45.00
109a	A41	50c	20.00	
110a	A42	75c	20.00	
113a	A45	$5	27.00	

No. 104 Surcharged
in Black

1909

114 A36 3c on 10c red brn & blk   6.00 6.00

Coffee
Plantation — A46

Pres.
Barclay — A47

S. S. Pres. Daniel
E. Howard, former
Gunboat
Lark — A48

Commerce with Caduceus — A49

Vai Woman
Spinning
Cotton — A50

Blossom and
Fruit of Pepper
Plants — A51

Circular
House — A52

President
Barclay — A53

Men in
Canoe — A54

Liberian
Village — A55

1909-12   Perf. 14

115	A46	1c yel grn & blk	.70	.55
116	A47	2c lake & blk	.70	.55
117	A48	5c ultra & blk	.70	.55
118	A49	10c plum & blk, perf. 12½	.70	.55
a.		Imperf., pair	19.00	
b.		Perf 14 ('12)	2.25	2.25
c.		As "b," pair, imperf between	27.50	
d.		Perf 12½x14	2.75	2.25
119	A50	15c indigo & blk	3.50	.60
120	A51	20c rose & grn	4.50	.60
b.		Imperf.		
121	A52	25c dk brn & blk	1.40	.60
b.		Imperf.		
122	A53	30c dark brown	4.50	.60
123	A54	50c green & blk	4.50	.60
124	A55	75c red brn & blk	4.50	.60
		Nos. 115-124 (10)	25.70	5.80

Rouletted

125	A49	10c plum & blk	.75	.45

For surcharges see Nos. 126-127E, 131-
133, 136-140, 142-144, 151-156, 162, B1-B2,
M3-M4, M6-M7, O70-O1, O74-O81, O86-O91,
O97.

For overprints see Nos. O59-O69.

Center Inverted

116a	A47	2c	70.00	60.00
117a	A48	5c	62.50	55.00
119a	A50	15c	100.00	60.00
120a	A51	20c	70.00	55.00
121b	A52	25c	47.50	42.50
123a	A54	50c	95.00	80.00

**Stamps and Types of 1909-12
Surcharged in Blue or Red**

1910-12   Rouletted

126	A49	3c on 10c plum & blk (Bl)	.40	.25
a.		"3" inverted		
126B	A49	3c on 10c blk & ultra (R)	30.00	5.00

No. 126B is roulette 7. It also exists in roulette 13.

Perf. 12½, 14, 12½x14

127	A49	3c on 10c plum & blk (Bl) ('12)	.40	.25
a.		Imperf., pair	22.50	
b.		Double surcharge, one invtd.	22.50	
c.		Double vertical surcharge		
127E	A49	3c on 10c blk & ultra (R) ('12)	17.00	.55
		Nos. 126-127E (4)	47.80	6.05

Nos. 64, 64a
Surcharged in
Dark Green

1913

128	A27	8c on 3c red & grn (I)	.30	.25
a.		Surcharge on No. 64a	3.00	.25
b.		Double surcharge	6.25	
c.		Imperf., pair	20.00	
d.		Inverted surcharge	25.00	

**Stamps of Preceding Issues
Surcharged**

a

b

1914   On Issue of 1906

129	A39 (a)	2c on 25c dl bl & gray	11.50	3.25
130	A40 (b)	5c on 30c dp violet	11.50	3.25

On Issue of 1909

131	A52 (a)	2c on 25c brn & blk	11.50	3.25
132	A53 (b)	5c on 30c dk brown	11.50	3.25
133	A54 (c)	10c on 50c grn & blk	11.50	3.25
		Nos. 129-133 (5)	57.50	16.25

Liberian
House
A57

Providence
Island,
Monrovia
Harbor
A58

1915   Engr.   Wmk. 116   Perf. 14

134	A57	2c red	.25	.25
135	A58	3c dull violet	.25	.25

For overprints see Nos. 196-197, O113-
O114, O128-O129.

**Nos. 109, 111-113, 119-124
Surcharged in Dark Blue, Black or
Red**

c

d

e

f

g

1915-16   Unwmk.

136	A50 (c)	2c on 15c (R)	.90	.90
137	A52 (d)	2c on 25c (R)	8.50	8.50
138	A51 (e)	5c on 20c (Bk)	1.10	6.25
139	A53 (f)	5c on 30c (R)	4.50	4.50
a.		Double surcharge	15.00	15.00
140	A53 (g)	5c on 30c (R)	40.00	40.00

h

i

141	A41 (h)	10c on 50c (R)	8.00	8.00
a.		Double surch., one invtd.		
142	A54 (i)	10c on 50c (R)	15.00	15.00
a.		Double surcharge red & blk	35.00	35.00
b.		Blue surcharge	35.00	35.00
143	A54 (i)	10c on 50c (Bk)	20.00	15.00

j

k

144 A55 (j) 20c on 75c (Bk) 4.00 7.50
145 A43 (k) 25c on $1 (Bk) 42.50 42.50

l　　m

146 A44 (l) 50c on $2 (R) 12.00 12.00
　a. "Ceuts" 22.50 22.50
147 A44 (m) 50c on $2 (R) 800.00 800.00

n

148 A45 $1 on $5 (Bk) 65.00 65.00
　a. Double surcharge 90.00 90.00

o

149 A45 $1 on $5 (R) 52.50 52.50

The color of the red surcharge varies from light dull red to almost brown.

Handstamped Surcharge, Type "i"
150 A54 10c on 50c (Dk Bl) 14.00 14.00

No. 119 Surcharged in Black

151 A50 2c on 15c 650.00 650.00

No. 119 Surcharged in Red

152 A50 2c on 15c 45.00 40.00
　a. Double surcharge 92.50

Nos. 116-117 Surcharged in Black or Red

a　b

c　d

e　f

g　h

i　j

k

l

m

n

o

p

q

r

s

t

Types A-J are for No. 153. Types K-T are for No. 154.

153 A47 1c on 2c lake & blk 2.50 2.50
　a. Strip of 10 types 35.00
154 A48 2c on 5c ultra & blk 3.50 2.50
　(R)
　a. Black surcharge 14.00 14.00
　b. Strip of 10 types (R) 35.00
　c. Strip of 10 types (Bk) 175.00

The 10 types of surcharge are repeated in illustrated sequence on 1c on 2c in each horiz. row and on 2c on 5c in each vert. row of sheets of 100 (10x10).

No. 116 and Type of 1909 Surcharged

155 A47 1c on 2c lake & blk 190.00 190.00

No. 117 Surcharged

156 A48 2c on 5c turq & blk 140.00 140.00

Nos. 18-20 Surcharged

1916
157 A1 3c on 6c violet 45.00 45.00
　a. Inverted surcharge 100.00 75.00
158 A1 5c on 12c yellow 3.00 3.00
　a. Inverted surcharge 12.50 12.50
　b. Surcharge sideways 12.50
159 A1 10c on 24c rose red 2.75 3.00
　a. Inverted surcharge 15.00 15.00
　b. Surcharge sideways
　Nos. 157-159 (3) 50.75 51.00

Unused values for Nos. 157-159 are for examples without gum.

Nos. 44 and 108 Surcharged

p　r

1917 **Wmk. 143**
160 A15 (p) 4c on 25c yel grn 12.00 12.00
　a. "OUR" 27.50 27.50
　b. "FCUR" 27.50 27.50

Unwmk.
161 A40 (r) 5c on 30c dp vio 90.00 90.00

No. 118 Surcharged in Red

1918
162 A49 3c on 10c plum & blk 2.75 4.25
　a. "3" inverted 9.25 9.25

Bongo Antelope — A59

Symbols of Liberia — A61

Two-spot Palm Civet A60

A62

Palm-nut Vulture — A66

Oil Palm — A63

Mercury — A64

Traveler's Tree — A65

"Mudskipper" or Bommi Fish — A67

Mandingos A68　　"Liberia" A71

Coast Scene A69

Liberia College A70

1918　　Engr.　　Perf. 12½, 14

163	A59	1c dp grn & blk	.65	.25
164	A60	2c rose & blk	.80	.25
165	A61	5c gray bl & blk	.25	.25
166	A62	10c dark green	.25	.25
167	A63	15c blk & dk grn	3.00	.25
168	A64	20c claret & blk	.35	.25
169	A65	25c dk grn & grn	3.25	.25
170	A66	30c red vio & blk	15.00	.80
171	A67	50c ultra & blk	26.50	3.50
172	A68	75c ol bis & blk	.90	.25
173	A69	$1 yel brn & bl	7.25	.25
174	A70	$2 lt vio & blk	6.50	.25
175	A71	$5 dark brown	7.00	.40
		Nos. 163-175 (13)	71.70	7.20

For surcharges see Nos. 176-177, 228-229, 248-270, B3-B15, O111-O112, O155-O157.
For overprints see Nos. O98-O110.

Nos. 163-164, F10-F14 Surcharged

1920

176	A59	3c on 1c grn & blk	1.10	1.10
a.		"CEETS"	17.00	17.00
b.		Double surcharge	10.00	10.00
c.		Triple surcharge	15.00	15.00
177	A60	4c on 2c rose & blk	1.10	1.10
a.		Inverted surcharge	20.00	20.00
b.		Double surcharge	10.00	10.00
c.		Double surcharge, one invtd.	18.00	
d.		Triple surcharge, one inverted	25.00	25.00
e.		Quadruple surcharge	30.00	30.00
f.		Typewritten surcharge		
g.		Same as "f" but inverted		
h.		Printed and typewritten surcharges, both inverted		

178	R6	5c on 10c bl & blk	2.50	2.75
a.		Inverted surcharge	10.00	10.00
b.		Double surcharge	10.00	10.00
c.		Double surcharge, one invtd.	15.00	15.00
d.		Typewritten surcharge ("five")		100.00
e.		Printed and typewritten surcharge	100.00	
179	R6	5c on 10c org red & blk	2.50	2.75
a.		5c on 10c orange & black	4.00	2.75
b.		Inverted surcharge	15.00	
c.		Double surcharge	15.00	
d.		Double surcharge, one invtd.	18.00	15.00
e.		Typewritten surch. in violet	100.00	100.00
f.		Typewritten surch. in black		
g.		Printed and typewritten surcharges	100.00	
180	R6	5c on 10c grn & blk	2.50	2.75
a.		Double surcharge	10.00	10.00
b.		Double surcharge, one invtd.	18.00	18.00
c.		Inverted surcharge		18.00
d.		Quadruple surcharge	25.00	25.00
e.		Typewritten surcharge		100.00
f.		Printed and typewritten surcharges		
181	R6	5c on 10c vio & blk (Monrovia)	4.00	5.00
a.		Double surcharge, one invtd.	25.00	25.00
182	R6	5c on 10c mag & blk (Robertsport)	2.25	2.40
a.		Double surcharge	15.00	15.00
b.		Double surcharge, one invtd.	15.00	15.00
c.		Double surcharge, both invtd.	25.00	
		Nos. 176-182 (7)	15.95	17.85

Cape Mesurado A75

Pres. Daniel E. Howard — A76　　Arms of Liberia — A77

Crocodile A78

Pepper Plant — A79

Leopard A80

Village Scene — A81

Krumen in Dugout A82

Rapids in St. Paul's River — A83

Bongo Antelope A84

Hornbill A85

Elephant A86

1921　　Wmk. 116　　Perf. 14

183	A75	1c green	.25	.25
184	A76	5c dp bl & blk	.25	.25
185	A77	10c red & dl bl	.25	.25
186	A78	15c dl vio & grn	6.50	.55
187	A79	20c rose red & grn	2.75	.25
188	A80	25c org & blk	7.50	.55
189	A81	30c grn & dl vio	.40	.25
190	A82	50c org & ultra	.45	.25
191	A83	75c red & blk brn	.80	.25
a.		Center inverted	70.00	
192	A84	$1 red & blk	20.00	1.75
193	A85	$2 yel & ultra	16.00	1.25
194	A86	$5 car rose & vio	32.50	1.50
		Nos. 183-194 (12)	87.65	7.35

For overprints see Nos. 195, 198-208, O115-O127, O130-O140.

Nos. 134-135, 183-194 Ovptd.

195	A75	1c green	22.50	.40
196	A57	2c red	22.50	.40
197	A58	3c dull violet	32.50	.40
198	A76	5c dp bl & blk	3.50	.30
199	A77	10c red & dull bl	50.00	.40
200	A78	15c dull vio & grn	22.50	1.40
201	A79	20c rose red & grn, ovpt. invtd.	7.25	.75
202	A80	25c orange & blk	22.50	1.40
203	A81	30c grn & dull vio	2.50	.30
204	A82	50c orange & ultra	3.50	.30
205	A83	75c red & blk brn	4.75	.30
206	A84	$1 red & blk	62.50	2.10
207	A85	$2 yellow & ultra	22.50	2.10
208	A86	$5 car rose & vio	60.00	2.75
		Nos. 195-208 (14)	339.00	13.30

Overprint exists inverted in Nos. 195-208 and normal on No. 201.

First Settlers Landing at Cape Mesurado from U. S. S. Alligator A87

1923　　Litho.

209	A87	1c lt blue & blk	18.00	.45
210	A87	2c claret & ol gray	26.00	.45
211	A87	5c ol grn & ind	26.00	.45
212	A87	10c bl grn & vio	1.00	.45
213	A87	$1 rose & brn	3.25	.45
		Nos. 209-213 (5)	74.25	2.25

Centenary of founding of Liberia.

Memorial to J. J. Roberts, 1st Pres. — A88

Hall of Representatives, Monrovia — A89

Liberian Star — A90

A91

Pres. Charles Dunbar Burgess King — A92

Hippopotamus — A93

Antelope A94

West African Buffalo A95

Grebos
Making
Dumboy
A96

Pineapple
A97

Carrying
Ivory Tusk
A98

Rubber Planter's House — A99

Stockton Lagoon — A100

Grebo Houses — A101

1923 Perf. 13½x14½, 14½x13½
White Paper

214	A88	1c yel grn & dp grn	7.50	1.25
215	A89	2c claret & brn	7.50	.25
216	A90	3c lilac & blk	.35	.25
217	A91	5c bl vio & blk	115.00	.25
218	A92	10c slate & brn	.35	.25
219	A93	15c bister & bl	35.00	.50
220	A94	20c bl grn & vio	2.50	.35
221	A95	25c org red & brn	160.00	.60
222	A96	30c dk brn & vio	.60	.25
223	A97	50c dull vio & org	1.25	.25
224	A98	75c gray & bl	1.90	.40
225	A99	$1 dp red & dk vio	30.00	.60
226	A100	$2 orange & blue	7.50	.80
227	A101	$5 dp grn & brn	30.00	.55
		Nos. 214-227 (14)	399.45	6.55

Brownish Paper

222a	A96	30c dk brn & vio	.60	.25
223a	A97	50c dull vio & org	1.00	.25
224a	A98	75c gray & bl	1.90	.45
225a	A99	$1 dp red & dk vio	4.50	.60
226a	A100	$2 orange & blue	5.75	.60
227a	A101	$5 dp grn & brn	8.00	.90

Nos. 222-227 also exist on a light buff paper. Values are the same as for examples on brownish paper.
For overprints see Nos. O141-O154.

No. 163 Surcharged
in Black

1926 Unwmk. Perf. 14
228 A59 2c on 1c dp grn & blk 3.50 3.50
a. Surcharge with ornamental design as on #O155 17.00

No. 163 Surcharged
in Red

1927
229 A59 2c on 1c dp grn & blk 9.50 9.50
a. "Ceuts" 14.00
b. "Vwo" 14.00
c. "Twc" 14.00
d. Double surcharge 27.50
e. Wavy lines omitted 17.50

Palms
A102

Map of
Africa — A103

President
King — A104

1928 Engr. Perf. 12
230 A102 1c green .75 .50
231 A102 2c dark violet .50 .35
232 A102 3c bister brn .50 .35
a. Horiz. pair, imperf vert. —
233 A103 5c ultra 1.00 .55
234 A104 10c olive gray 1.40 .55
235 A103 15c dull violet 6.25 2.25
236 A103 $1 red brown 77.50 26.50
Nos. 230-236 (7) 87.90 31.05

For surcharges & overprints see Nos. 288A, 289A, 290A-291, 292A, C1-C3, O158-O165. Post 1940 issues are in Scott Standard catalogue, Vol. 4.

Nos. 164-168, 170-175 Surcharged in Various Colors and Styles

No. 248

No. 250

1936 Perf. 12½, 14
248 A60 1c on 2c (Bl) .55 3.50
249 A61 3c on 5c (Bl) .25 2.00
250 A62 4c on 10c (Br) .25 2.00
251 A63 6c on 15c (Bl) .55 3.50
252 A64 8c on 20c (V) .25 2.00

253 A66 12c on 30c (V) 1.00 9.75
254 A67 14c on 50c (Bl) 1.10 11.00
255 A68 16c on 75c (Br) .55 5.50
256 A69 18c on $1 (Bk) .55 5.50
a. 22c on $1 yellow brown & blue 7.25
257 A70 22c on $2 (V) .75 7.75
258 A71 24c on $5 (Bk) 1.00 9.75
Nos. 248-258 (11) 6.80 62.25

Official Stamps, Nos. O99-O110, Srchd. or Ovptd. in Various Colors & Styles

1936
259 A60 1c on 2c (Bl) .40 4.00
260 A61 3c on 5c (Bl) .40 4.00
261 A62 4c on 10c (Bl) .40 4.00
262 A63 6c on 15c (Bl) .40 4.00
263 A64 8c on 20c (V) .40 4.00
264 A66 12c on 30c (V) 1.50 20.00
a. "193" instead of "1936" 19.00
265 A67 14c on 50c (Bl) 2.00 21.00
266 A68 16c on 75c (Bk) 1.00 12.00
267 A69 18c on $1 (Bk) 1.00 12.00
268 A70 22c on $2 (Bl) 1.25 15.00
269 A71 24c on $5 (Bk) 1.50 17.00
270 A65 25c (Bk) 2.00 21.00
Nos. 259-270 (12) 12.25 138.00

Hornbill — A106

Designs: 2c, Bushbuck. 3c, West African dwarf buffalo. 4c, Pygmy hippopotamus. 5c, Lesser egret. 6c, Pres. E. J. Barclay.

Perf. Compound of 11½, 12, 12½, 14
1937, Apr. 10 Engr. Unwmk.
271 A106 1c green & blk 1.50 .80
272 A106 2c carmine & blk 1.50 .25
273 A106 3c violet & blk 1.50 .80
274 A106 4c orange & blk 2.25 1.25
275 A106 5c blue & blk 2.25 .95
276 A106 6c green & blk .80 .25
Nos. 271-276 (6) 9.80 4.30

Coast
Line of
Liberia,
1839
A107

Seal of
Liberia,
Map
and
Farming
Scenes
A108

Thomas Buchanan and Residence at Bassa Cove — A109

1940, July 29 Engr. Perf. 12
277 A107 3c dark blue .35 .35
278 A108 5c dull red brn .35 .35
279 A109 10c dark green .35 .35
Nos. 277-279 (3) 1.05 1.05

100th anniv. of the founding of the Commonwealth of Liberia.
For overprints & surcharges see Nos. 280-282, B16-B18, C14-C16, CB1-CB3, CE1, CF1, E1, F35 in the Scott Standard Catalogue, Vol. 4.

SEMI-POSTAL STAMPS

No. 127 Surcharged in Red

1915 Unwmk. Perf. 14
B1 A49 2c + 3c on 10c 1.00 3.50
a. Double red surcharge
b. Double blue surcharge
c. Both surcharges double
d. Pair, one without "2c"

Same Surcharge On Official Stamp of 1912
B2 A49 2c + 3c on 10c blk & ultra 1.00 3.50
a. Double surcharge

Regular Issue of 1918 Surcharged in Black and Red

1918 Perf. 12½, 14
B3 A59 1c + 2c dp grn & blk 1.40 10.50
B4 A60 2c + 2c rose & blk 1.40 10.50
a. Double surch., one inverted
b. Invtd. surch., cross double
c. Invtd. surch., cross omitted 17.00
B5 A61 5c + 2c gray bl & blk .65 3.00
a. Imperf., pair 19.00
B6 A62 10c + 2c dk green 1.25 3.00
a. Inverted surcharge 5.75 27.50
B7 A63 15c + 2c blk & dk grn 5.25 10.50
B8 A64 20c + 2c claret & blk 2.10 8.50
B9 A65 25c + 2c dk grn & grn 4.25 15.00
B10 A66 30c + 2c red vio & blk 10.00 10.50
B11 A67 50c + 2c ultra & blk 8.50 16.00
B12 A68 75c + 2c ol bis & blk 3.75 30.00
B13 A69 $1 + 2c yel brn & bl 6.25 57.50
B14 A70 $2 + 2c lt vio & blk 8.50 80.00
B15 A71 $5 + 2c dk brown 20.00 200.00
Nos. B3-B15 (13) 73.30 455.00

Used values are for postally canceled stamps.

AIR POST STAMPS

Regular
Issue of
1928 Srchd.
in Black

1936, Feb. 28 Unwmk. Perf. 12
C1 A102 6c on 2c violet 250.00 275.00
C2 A102 6c on 3c bis brn 250.00 275.00

Same Srch.
on Official
Stamp of
1928

C3 A102 6c on 1c green 250.00 275.00
m. On No. 230 (error) 750.00
Nos. C1-C3 (3) 750.00 825.00

Values are for stamps with disturbed gum. Many counterfeits exist.

Waco Plane — AP1

1936, Sept. 30   Engr.   Perf. 14

C3A	AP1	1c yellow grn & blk	.25	.25
C3B	AP1	2c carmine & blk	.25	.25
C3C	AP1	3c purple & blk	.25	.25
C3D	AP1	4c orange & blk	.25	.25
C3E	AP1	5c blue & blk	.25	.25
C3F	AP1	6c green & blk	.25	.25
		Nos. C3A-C3F (6)	1.50	1.50

Liberia's 1st air mail service of Feb. 28, 1936.

Nos. C3A-C3F exist in pairs imperf. between (value, $50 each) and in pairs imperf. (value $15 each).

Eagle in Flight — AP2

Trimotor Plane AP3

Egrets — AP4

Sikorsky Amphibian — AP5

Designs: 3c, 30c, Albatross.

1938, Sept. 12   Photo.   Perf. 12½

C4	AP2	1c green	.25	.25
C5	AP3	2c red orange	.40	.25
C6	AP3	3c olive green	.50	.25
C7	AP4	4c orange	.60	.25
C8	AP4	5c brt blue grn	1.00	.25
C9	AP3	10c violet	1.00	.25
C10	AP3	20c magenta	1.25	.25
C11	AP3	30c gray black	2.25	.25
C12	AP2	50c brown	3.00	.25
C13	AP5	$1 blue	5.25	.25
		Nos. C4-C13 (10)	15.50	2.50

For surcharges see Nos. C17-C36, C45-C46, C47-C48, C49-C50 in Scott Standard catalogue, Vol. 4.

REGISTRATION STAMPS

R1

1893   Unwmk.   Litho.   Perf. 14, 15
Without Value Surcharged

F1	R1	(10c) blk (Buchanan)	250.	250.
F2	R1	(10c) blk (Greenville)	*2,500.*	—
F3	R1	(10c) blk (Harper)	*2,500.*	—
F4	R1	(10c) blk (Monrovia)	30.	30.
F5	R1	(10c) blk (Roberts-port)	1,000.	1,000.

Types of 1893 Surcharged in Black

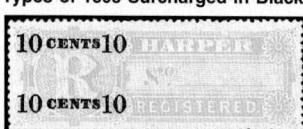

1894   Perf. 14

F6	R1	10c bl, *pink* (Buchanan)	5.50	5.50
F7	R1	10c grn, *buff* (Harper)	5.50	5.50
F8	R1	10c red, *yel* (Monrovia)	5.50	5.50
F9	R1	10c rose, *blue* (Roberts - port)	5.50	5.50
		Nos. F6-F9 (4)	22.00	22.00

Exist imperf or missing one 10. Value, each $10.

President Garretson W. Gibson — R6

1903   Engr.   Perf. 14

F10	R6	10c bl & blk (Buchanan)	1.75	.25
a.		Center inverted	100.00	
F11	R6	10c org red & blk ("Grenville")	1.75	
a.		Center inverted	100.00	
b.		10c orange & black	1.90	.25
F12	R6	10c grn & blk (Harper)	1.75	.25
a.		Center inverted	100.00	
F13	R6	10c vio & blk (Monrovia)	1.75	.25
a.		Center inverted	100.00	
b.		10c lilac & black	1.90	
F14	R6	10c magenta & blk (Robertsport)	1.75	.25
a.		Center inverted	100.00	
		Nos. F10-F14 (5)	8.75	
		Nos. F10, F11b, F12-F14		.75

For surcharges see Nos. 178-182.

S.S. Quail on Patrol — R7

1919   Litho.   Serrate Roulette 12

F15	R7	10c blk & bl (Buchanan)	1.40	2.75

Serrate Roulette 12, Perf. 14

F16	R7	10c ocher & blk ("Grenville")	1.40	2.75
F17	R7	10c grn & blk (Harper)	1.40	2.75
F18	R7	10c vio & bl (Monrovia)	1.40	2.75
F19	R7	10c rose & blk (Robertsport)	1.40	2.75
		Nos. F15-F19 (5)	7.00	13.75

Gabon Viper — R8

Wmk. Crosses and Circles (116)
1921   Engr.   Perf. 13x14

F20	R8	10c cl & blk (Buchanan)	90.00	3.50
F21	R8	10c red & blk (Greenville)	22.50	3.50
F22	R8	10c ultra & blk (Harper)	22.50	3.50

F23	R8	10c org & blk (Monrovia)	22.50	3.50
a.		Imperf., pair	225.00	
F24	R8	10c grn & blk (Robertsport)	22.50	3.50
a.		Imperf., pair	225.00	
		Nos. F20-F24 (5)	180.00	17.50

Nos. F20-F24 Overprinted in Black

F25	R8	10c (Buchanan)	25.00	6.25
F26	R8	10c (Greenville)	25.00	6.25
F27	R8	10c (Harper)	70.00	6.25
F28	R8	10c (Monrovia)	25.00	6.25
F29	R8	10c (Robertsport)	25.00	6.25
		Nos. F25-F29 (5)	170.00	31.25

Nos. F25-F29 exist with "1921" inverted. Value same as normal.

Passengers Going Ashore from Ship — R9

Designs: No. F31, Transporting merchandise, shore to ship (Greenville). No. F32, Sailing ship (Harper). No. F33, Ocean liner (Monrovia). No. F34, Canoe in surf (Robertsport).

1924   Litho.   Perf. 14

F30	R9	10c gray & carmine	7.00	.60
F31	R9	10c gray & blue grn	7.00	.60
F32	R9	10c gray & orange	7.00	.60
F33	R9	10c gray & blue	7.00	.60
F34	R9	10c gray & violet	7.00	.60
		Nos. F30-F34 (5)	35.00	3.00

POSTAGE DUE STAMPS

Nos. 26, 28 Surcharged

1892   Unwmk.   Perf. 11

J1	A5	3c on 3c violet	6.50	4.25
a.		Imperf., pair	30.00	
b.		Inverted surcharge	45.00	45.00
c.		As "a," inverted surcharge	110.00	

Perf. 12

J2	A5	6c on 6c olive gray	15.00	13.50
a.		Imperf., pair	40.00	
b.		Inverted surcharge	52.50	35.00

D2

Engr.; Figures of Value Typographed in Black

1893   Wmk. 143   Perf. 14, 15

J3	D2	2c org, *yel*	2.00	1.00
J4	D2	4c rose, *rose*	2.00	1.00
J5	D2	6c brown, *buff*	2.00	1.25
J6	D2	8c blue, *blue*	2.00	1.25
J7	D2	10c grn, *lil rose*	2.25	1.50

J8	D2	20c vio, *gray*	2.25	1.50
a.		Center inverted	110.00	110.00
J9	D2	40c ol brn, *grnsh*	4.50	3.00
		Nos. J3-J9 (7)	17.00	10.50

All values of the above set exist imperforate. Each value also exists with center inverted

MILITARY STAMPS

Issues of 1905, 1906 and 1909 Surcharged

1916   Wmk. 143

M1	A23	1c on 1c lt grn	190.00	190.00
a.		2nd "F" inverted	250.00	250.00
b.		"FLF"	250.00	250.00
c.		Inverted surcharge	250.00	250.00

Unwmk.

M2	A33	1c on 1c grn & blk	550.00	550.00
a.		2nd "F" inverted	600.00	600.00
b.		"FLF"	600.00	600.00
M3	A46	1c on 1c yel grn & blk	4.00	4.75
a.		2nd "F" inverted	7.50	7.50
b.		"FLF"	7.50	7.50
M4	A47	1c on 2c lake & blk	4.00	4.75
a.		2nd "F" inverted	7.50	7.50
b.		"FLF"	7.50	7.50

Surcharge exists sideways on Nos. M2, M5; double on Nos. M1-M4; inverted on Nos. M2-M4.

Nos. O46, O59-O60 Surcharged

M5	A33	1c on 1c	475.00	475.00
a.		2nd "F" inverted	650.00	650.00
b.		"FLF"	650.00	650.00
M6	A46	1c on 1c	4.75	5.50
a.		2nd "F" inverted	9.00	9.00
b.		"FLF"	9.00	9.00
c.		"LFF 1c" inverted	12.50	12.50
d.		As "a" and "1c" inverted		15.00
e.		"FLF 1c" inverted		15.00
M7	A47	1c on 2c	3.25	4.00
a.		2nd "F" inverted	6.50	6.50
b.		"FLF"	6.50	6.50
c.		Pair, one without "LFF 1c"		

OFFICIAL STAMPS

Types of Regular Issues Overprinted in Various Colors

Perf. 12½ to 15 and Compound
1892   Wmk. 143

O1	A9	1c vermilion	.80	.80
O2	A9	2c blue	.80	.80
O3	A10	4c grn & blk	.80	.80
O4	A11	6c bl grn	.80	.80
O5	A12	8c brn & blk	.80	.80
O6	A13	12c rose red	2.00	2.00
O7	A14	16c red lilac	2.00	2.00
O8	A15	24c ol grn, *yel*	2.00	2.00
O9	A16	32c grnsh bl	2.00	2.00
O10	A17	$1 bl & blk	40.00	16.00
O11	A18	$2 brn, *yel*	16.00	11.50
O12	A19	$5 car & blk	24.00	9.00
		Nos. O1-O12 (12)	92.00	48.50

a   "5" With Short Flag

1893

O13	A11	5c on 6c bl grn		
		(a) (No. 50)	1.20	1.20
a.		"5" with short flag	6.00	6.00
b.		Both 5's with short flags	6.00	6.00
c.		"i" dot omitted	20.00	20.00
d.		Overprinted on #50d	45.00	45.00

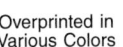

Overprinted in Various Colors

1894

O15	A9	1c vermilion	.70	.35
O16	A9	2c blue	.85	.40
a.		Imperf.		
O17	A10	4c grn & blk	1.00	.55
O18	A12	8c brn & blk	1.00	.55
O19	A13	12c rose red	1.40	.60
O20	A14	16c red lilac	1.40	.60
O21	A15	24c ol grn, *yel*	1.40	.70
O22	A16	32c grnsh bl	2.75	.80
O23	A17	$1 bl & blk	27.50	21.00
a.		$1 ultra & black	27.50	21.00
O24	A18	$2 brn, *yel*	27.50	21.00
O25	A19	$5 car & blk	125.00	87.50
		Nos. O15-O25 (11)	190.50	134.05

Unwmk.

Imperf

O26	A22	5c vio & grn	3.50	2.25

Rouletted

O27	A22	5c vio & grn	3.50	2.25

Regular Issue of 1896-1905 Overprinted in Black or Red

1898-1905   Wmk. 143   *Perf. 14, 15*

O28	A23	1c lil rose	.90	.90
O29	A23	1c dp grn ('00)	.90	.90
O30	A23	1c lt grn (R) ('05)	.90	.90
O31	A24	2c bis & blk	1.75	.60
a.		Pair, one without overprint	900.00	
O32	A24	2c org red & blk ('00)	2.75	1.50
O33	A24	2c rose & blk ('05)	4.50	2.75
O34	A25	5c lake & blk	3.00	1.50
O35	A25	5c gray bl & blk ('00)	3.50	1.50
O36	A25	5c ultra & blk (R) ('05)	6.00	3.75
O37	A12	10c chr yel & ind	1.75	1.75
O38	A13	15c slate	1.75	1.75
O39	A14	20c vermilion	3.00	2.10
O40	A15	25c yel grn	1.75	1.75
O41	A16	30c steel blue	4.50	2.75
O42	A26	50c red brn & blk	4.50	2.75
		Nos. O28-O42 (15)	41.45	27.15

For surcharge see No. O92.

Official stamps overprinted "ORDINARY" or with a bar with an additional surcharge are listed as Nos. 64B-90, 92-93, 99.

Red Overprint

1903   Unwmk.   *Perf. 14*

O43	A29	3c green	.25	.25
a.		Overprint omitted	5.00	
b.		Inverted overprint		

Two overprint types: I — Thin, sharp, dark red. II — Thick, heavier, orange red. Same value.

On No. 50   O3

1904   Black Surcharge   Wmk. 143

O44	A11	1c on 5c on 6c bl grn	1.60	2.00
a.		"5" with short flag	4.25	
b.		Both "5s" with straight flag	8.00	8.00

Red Surcharge

O45	O3	2c on 30c steel blue	9.50	9.50
a.		Double surcharge, red and black		
b.		Surcharge also on back		

Types of Regular Issue Overprinted in Various Colors

a

1906   Unwmk.

O46	A33	1c grn & blk (R)	.65	.40
O47	A34	2c car & blk (Bl)	.25	.25
a.		Center and overprint inverted	30.00	3.00
b.		Inverted overprint	6.00	
O48	A35	5c ultra & blk (Bk)	.65	.40
a.		Inverted overprint	15.00	15.00
b.		Center and overprint invtd.	50.00	
O49	A36	10c dl vio & blk (R)	.75	.55
a.		Inverted overprint	10.00	10.00
b.		Center and overprint invtd.	50.00	
O50	A37	15c brn & blk (Bk)	3.00	.55
a.		Inverted overprint	4.50	
b.		Overprint omitted	12.00	6.00
c.		Center and overprint invtd.	60.00	
O51	A38	20c dp grn & blk (R)	.55	.55
a.		Overprint omitted	15.00	
O52	A39	25c plum & gray (Bl)	.50	.25
a.		With 2nd ovpt. in blue, invtd.	15.00	
O53	A40	30c dk brn (Bk)	.55	.25
O54	A41	50c org brn & dp grn (G)	.75	.25
a.		Inverted overprint	5.00	4.00
O55	A42	75c ultra & blk (Bk)	1.40	.95
a.		Inverted overprint	9.50	5.75
b.		Overprint omitted	22.50	
O56	A43	$1 dp grn & gray (R)	.90	.25
O57	A44	$2 plum & blk (Bl)	2.75	.25
a.		Inverted overprint	22.50	15.00
O58	A45	$5 org & blk (Bk)	5.50	.25
a.		Overprint omitted	11.00	
b.		Inverted overprint	12.00	8.00
		Nos. O46-O58 (13)	18.40	5.15

Nos. O52, O54, O55, O56 and O58 are known with center inverted.

For surcharges see Nos. O72, O82-O85, O96.

b

1909-12

O59	A46	1c emer & blk (R)	.40	.25
O60	A47	2c car rose & brn (Bl)	.40	.25
O61	A48	5c turq & blk (Bk)	.45	.25
a.		Double overprint, one inverted	7.50	
O62	A49	10c blk & ultra (R) ('12)	.60	.25
O63	A50	15c cl & blk (Bl)	.60	.45
O64	A51	20c bis & grn (Bk)	1.10	.55
O65	A52	25c ultra & grn (Bk)	1.10	.55
a.		Double overprint	4.75	4.75
O66	A53	30c dk bl (R)	.85	.25
O67	A54	50c brn & grn (Bk)	1.40	.40
a.		Center inverted	27.50	
b.		Inverted overprint	4.00	2.75
O68	A55	75c pur & blk (R)	1.50	.25
		Nos. O59-O68 (10)	8.40	3.45

Nos. O63, O64, O67 and O68 are known without overprint and with center inverted.

For surcharges see Nos. O74-O81, O86-O90, O97.

Rouletted

O69	A49	10c blk & ultra (R)	1.00	.95

Nos. 126B and 127E Overprinted type "a" ("OS") in Red

1910-12   Rouletted

O70	A49	3c on 10c blk & ultra	.70	1.25

Perf. 12½, 14, 12½x14

O71	A49	3c on 10c blk & ultra ('12)	.70	.40
a.		Pair, one without surch., the other with dbl. surch., one invtd.		
b.		Double surcharge, one inverted	4.00	

Stamps of Preceding Issues Srchd. with New Values like Regular Issue and — c

1914

On Nos. O52 and 110

O72	A39	(a) 2c on 25c plum & gray	25.00	10.50
O73	A42	(c) 20c on 75c brn & blk	8.75	5.25

On Nos. O66 and O68

O74	A53	(b) 5c on 30c dk bl	8.75	5.25
O75	A55	(c) 20c on 75c pur & blk (R)	13.00	5.25
		Nos. O72-O75 (4)	55.50	26.25

Official Stamps of 1906-09 Surcharged Like Regular Issues of Same Date

1915-16

O76	A50	(c) 2c on 15c (Bk)	.95	.50
O77	A52	(d) 2c on 25c (Bk)	5.25	5.25
O78	A51	(e) 2c on 20c (Bk)	.95	.65
O79	A53	(g) 5c on 30c (R)	8.50	8.50
O80	A54	(i) 10c on 50c (Bk)	5.50	3.25
O81	A55	(j) 20c on 75c (R)	2.75	2.75
O82	A43	(k) 25c on $1 (R)	20.00	20.00
a.		"25" double	25.00	
b.		"OS" inverted	25.00	
O83	A44	(l) 50c on $2 (Bk)	50.00	50.00
a.		"Ceuts"	70.00	70.00
O84	A44	(m) 50c on $2 (Br)	22.50	22.50
O85	A45	(n) $1 on $5 (Bk)	21.00	21.00

Handstamped Surcharge

O86	A54	(i) 10c on 50c (Bk)	11.00	11.00

Nos. O60-O61 Surcharged like Nos. 153-154 in Black or Red

a1, b1

c1, d1

e1, f1

g1, h1

---

i1, j1

O87	A47	1c on 2c	2.75	2.75
		Strip of 10 types	30.00	
O88	A48	2c on 5c (R)	2.75	2.75
		Strip of 10 types (R)	30.00	
a.		Black surcharge	10.00	10.00
		Strip of 10 types (Bk)	140.00	

See note following Nos. 153-154.

Nos. O60-O61 Surcharged

O90	A47	1c on 2c	125.00	125.00
O91	A48	2c on 5c	100.00	100.00

No. O42 Surcharged

O92	A26	10c on 50c (Bk)	11.00	11.00

No. O53 Surcharged

1917

O96	A40	5c on 30c dk brn	21.00	21.00
a.		"FIV"	35.00	35.00

The editors consider the 1915-17 issues unnecessary and speculative.

No. O62 Surcharged in Red like No. 162

1918

O97	A49	3c on 10c blk & ultra	2.40	2.40

Types of Regular Issue of 1918 Ovptd. Type "a" in Black, Blue or Red

1918   Unwmk.   *Perf. 12½, 14*

O98	A59	1c dp grn & red brn (Bk)	.60	.25
O99	A60	2c red & blk (Bl)	.60	.25
O100	A61	5c ultra & blk (R)	1.10	.25
O101	A62	10c ultra (R)	.60	.25
O102	A63	15c choc & dk grn (Bl)	2.75	.60
O103	A64	20c gray lil & blk (R)	.85	.25
O104	A65	25c choc & grn (Bk)	5.25	.65
O105	A66	30c brt vio & blk (R)	6.50	.65
O106	A67	50c mar & blk (Bl)	7.75	.65
a.		Overprint omitted	11.00	
O107	A68	75c car brn & blk (Bl)	3.00	.25
O108	A69	$1 ol bis & turq bl	6.00	.25
O109	A70	$2 ol bis & blk (R)	9.25	.25
O110	A71	$5 yel grn (Bk)	12.00	.40
		Nos. O98-O110 (13)	56.25	4.95

For surcharges see Nos. 259-269, O111-O112, O155-O157. For overprint see No. 270.

Official Stamps of 1918 Surcharged like Regular Issue

1920
FOUR CENTS

1920

O111	A59	3c on 1c grn & red brn	1.10	.70
a.		"CEETS"	15.00	15.00
b.		Double surcharge	8.00	8.00
c.		Double surch., one invtd.	15.00	15.00
d.		Triple surcharge	20.00	20.00
O112	A60	4c on 2c red & blk	.70	.70
a.		Inverted surcharge	12.00	12.00
b.		Double surcharge	12.00	12.00
c.		Double surch., one invtd.	10.00	10.00
d.		Triple surcharge	15.00	15.00

Types of Regular Issues of 1915-21 Overprinted

OFFICIAL

1921   **Wmk. 116**   **Perf. 14**

O113	A57	2c rose red	8.25	.25
O114	A58	3c brown	1.75	.25
O115	A79	20c brn & ultra	2.25	.40

O   S

Same, Overprinted "O S"

O116	A75	1c dp grn	1.75	.25
O117	A76	5c dp bl & brn	1.75	.25
O118	A77	10c red vio & blk	.85	.25
O119	A78	15c blk & grn	4.75	.60
a.		Double overprint		
O120	A80	25c org & grn	6.50	.60
O121	A81	30c brn & red	1.75	.25
O122	A82	50c grn & blk	1.75	.25
a.		Overprinted "S" only		
O123	A83	75c bl & vio	3.25	.25
O124	A84	$1 bl & blk	22.50	.65
O125	A85	$2 grn & org	12.00	.95
O126	A86	$5 grn & bl	13.50	2.10
		Nos. O113-O126 (14)	82.60	7.30

O   S
1921

Preceding Issues Overprinted "1921"

1921

O127	A75	1c dp grn	7.50	.25
O128	A57	2c rose red	7.50	.25
O129	A58	3c brown	7.50	.25
O130	A76	5c dp bl & brn	4.50	.25
O131	A77	10c red vio & blk	7.50	.25
O132	A78	15c blk & grn	8.50	.25
O133	A79	20c brn & ultra	8.50	.40
O134	A80	25c org & grn	8.25	.80
O135	A81	30c brn & red	7.50	.25
O136	A82	50c grn & blk	8.75	.25
O137	A83	75c bl & vio	5.50	.25
O138	A84	$1 bl & blk	15.00	2.00
O139	A85	$2 org & grn	19.00	2.25
O140	A86	$5 grn & bl	15.00	3.25
		Nos. O127-O140 (14)	130.50	10.95

O   S

Types of Regular Issue of 1923 Ovptd.

1923   **Perf. 13½x14½, 14½x13½**

White Paper

O141	A88	1c bl grn & blk	8.75	.25
O142	A89	2c dl red & yel brn	8.75	.25
O143	A90	3c gray bl & blk	8.75	.25
O144	A91	5c dl grn	8.75	.25
O145	A92	10c ol bis & dk vio	8.75	.25
O146	A93	15c yel grn & bl	1.10	.40
O147	A94	20c vio & ind	1.10	.40
O148	A95	25c brn & red brn	32.50	.40

White, Buff or Brownish Paper

O149	A96	30c dp ultra & brn	1.50	.25
O150	A97	50c dl bis & red brn	1.50	.40
O151	A98	75c gray & grn	2.25	.25
O152	A99	$1 red org & grn	3.00	.45
b.		Overprint omitted	11.00	
O153	A100	$2 red lil & ver	6.00	.25
O154	A101	$5 bl & brn vio	5.00	1.50
		Nos. O141-O154 (14)	97.70	5.55
		Nos. O141-O154a (10)	86.70	2.60

Brownish Paper

O149a	A96	30c dp ultra & brn	1.10	.30
b.		Overprint omitted	2.00	
O150a	A97	50c dl bis & red brn	2.25	.45
O151a	A98	75c gray & grn	1.50	.30
O152a	A99	$1 red org & grn	2.25	.65
c.		Overprint omitted	11.00	
O153a	A100	$2 red lil & ver	2.50	1.00
O154a	A101	$5 bl & brn vio	4.50	2.25

Nos. O149-O154 also exist on a light buff paper. Values are the same as for stamps on brownish paper.

No. O98 Surcharged in Red Brown

Two Cents

1926   **Unwmk.**   **Perf. 14**

O155	A59	2c on 1c	2.25	2.25
a.		"Gents"	15.00	
b.		Surcharged in black	5.75	
c.		As "b," "Gents"	15.00	

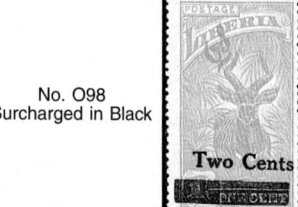

No. O98 Surcharged in Black

Two Cents

1926

O156	A59	2c on 1c	1.00	1.00
a.		Inverted surcharge	20.00	
b.		"Gents"	10.00	

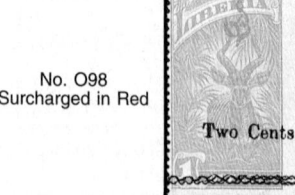

No. O98 Surcharged in Red

Two Cents

1927

O157	A59	2c on 1c	35.00	35.00
a.		"Ceuts"	55.00	
b.		"Vwo"	55.00	
c.		"Twc"	55.00	

Regular Issue of 1928 Overprinted in Red or Black

OFFICIAL SERVICE
ONE CENT

1928   **Perf. 12**

O158	A102	1c grn (R)	1.10	.55
O159	A102	2c gray vio (R)	3.50	2.10
O160	A102	3c bis brn (Bk)	3.75	4.25
O161	A103	5c ultra (R)	1.10	.55
O162	A104	10c ol gray (R)	3.50	1.75
O163	A103	15c ol grn (R)	3.50	1.50
O164	A103	$1 red brn (Bk)	77.50	22.50
		Nos. O158-O164 (7)	93.95	32.70

For surcharges see Nos. C3, O165 (in Scott Standard catalogue, Vol. 4).

LIBYA

'li-bē-ə,

(Libia)

LOCATION — North Africa, bordering on the Mediterranean Sea
GOVT. — Republic
AREA — 679,358 sq. mi.
POP. — 3,500,000 (est. 1982)
CAPITAL — Tripoli

In 1939, the four northern provinces of Libya, a former Italian colony, were incorporated in the Italian national territory. Included in the territory is the former Turkish Vilayet of Tripoli, annexed in 1912. See Cyrenaica and Tripolitania.

100 Centesimi = 1 Lira

Watermarks

Wmk. 140 — Crown

Used values in italics are for postally used stamps. CTO's sell for about the same as unused, hinged stamps.

POSTE
Libia

Stamps of Italy Overprinted in Black

Libia   *Libia*

Type I   Type II

Two types of overprint. Type I: bold letters, dots close within letter "i." Type II: thinner letters, dots further away within letter "i."

1912-22   **Wmk. 140**   **Perf. 14**

Type I

1	A42	1c brown ('15)	1.60	1.00
		Never hinged	4.00	
		On cover		24.00
a.		Double overprint	260.00	260.00
		Never hinged	360.00	
2	A43	2c orange brn	1.60	.60
		Never hinged	4.00	
		On cover		24.00
3	A48	5c green	1.60	.40
		Never hinged	4.00	
		On cover		8.00
a.		Double overprint	95.00	95.00
		Never hinged	150.00	
b.		Imperf., pair	400.00	
		Never hinged	500.00	
c.		Inverted overprint		—
d.		Pair, one without overprint	425.00	425.00
		Never hinged	650.00	
4	A48	10c claret	16.00	.40
		Never hinged	40.00	
		On cover		8.00
a.		Pair, one without overprint	425.00	425.00
		Never hinged	650.00	
b.		Double overprint	175.00	175.00
		Never hinged	225.00	
5	A48	15c slate ('22)	6.50	9.50
		Never hinged	16.00	
		On cover		72.50
6	A45	20c orange ('15)	6.50	.40
		Never hinged	16.00	
		On cover		22.50

a.		Double overprint	200.00	200.00
		Never hinged	325.00	
b.		Pair, one without overprint	750.00	750.00
		Never hinged	1,100.	
7	A50	20c brn org ('18)	4.75	6.50
		On cover		55.00
8	A49	25c blue	6.50	.40
		Never hinged	16.00	
		On cover		55.00
9	A49	40c brown	16.00	1.25
		Never hinged	40.00	
		On cover		200.00
10	A45	45c ol grn ('17)	45.00	35.00
		Never hinged	110.00	
		On cover		125.00
a.		Inverted overprint	675.00	
		Never hinged	925.00	
11	A49	50c violet	40.00	1.60
		Never hinged	100.00	
		On cover		275.00
12	A49	60c brn car ('18)	22.50	27.50
		Never hinged	55.00	
		On cover		175.00
13	A46	1 l brown & green ('15)	72.50	2.00
		Never hinged	180.00	
		On cover		110.00
14	A46	5 l bl & rose ('15)	475.00	575.00
		Never hinged	1,400.	
		On cover		4,750.
15	A51	10 l gray green & red ('15)	40.00	225.00
		Never hinged	100.00	
		Nos. 1-15 (15)	756.05	886.55

Type II

1b	A42	1c brown ('15)	1.60	2.00
		Never hinged	4.00	
		On cover		95.00
3e	A48	5c green	1.60	.80
		Never hinged	4.00	
		On cover		22.50
f.		Double overprint	87.50	87.50
		Never hinged	125.00	
g.		Imperf., pair	325.00	
		Never hinged	425.00	
h.		Pair, one without overprint	325.00	325.00
		Never hinged	425.00	
4c	A48	10c claret	16.00	.80
		Never hinged	40.00	
		On cover		22.50
d.		Pair, one without overprint	325.00	325.00
		Never hinged	425.00	
e.		Double overprint	160.00	160.00
		Never hinged	240.00	
6c	A45	20c orange ('15)	6.50	.80
		Never hinged	16.00	
		On cover		40.00
8a	A49	25c blue	6.50	1.60
		Never hinged	16.00	
		On cover		100.00
b.		Double overprint, both type II	160.00	160.00
		Never hinged	250.00	
11a	A49	50c violet	175.00	2.00
		Never hinged	625.00	
		On cover		475.00
13a	A46	1 l brown & green ('15)	72.50	4.00
		Never hinged	180.00	
		On cover		160.00
14a	A46	5 l bl & rose ('15)	475.00	725.00
		Never hinged	1,200.	
		On cover		5,500.
15a	A51	10 l gray green & red ('15)	4,750.	
		Never hinged	9,500.	

For surcharges see Nos. 37-38.

POSTE ITALIANE 15
LIBIA

Overprinted in Violet

1912   **Unwmk.**

16	A58	15c slate	300.00	2.00
		Never hinged	750.00	
		On cover		72.50
a.		Blue black overprint	24,000.	47.50
		Never hinged	36,000.	
		On cover		140.00

POSTE ITALIANE
CENT. 20

No. 16 Surcharged

1916, Mar.   **Unwmk.**

19	A58	20c on 15c slate	65.00	12.00
		Never hinged	160.00	
		On cover		35.00
a.		Blue-black surcharge	100.00	27.50
		Never hinged	275.00	
		On cover		85.00

Roman
Legionary — A1

Diana of
Ephesus — A2

Ancient Galley
Leaving
Tripoli — A3

"Victory" — A4

1921   Engr.   Wmk. 140   Perf. 14

20	A1	1c blk & gray brn	3.25	8.00
		Never hinged	8.00	
		On cover		95.00
21	A1	2c blk & red brn	3.25	8.00
		Never hinged	8.00	
		On cover		95.00
22	A1	5c black & green	4.00	.80
		Never hinged	10.00	
		On cover		2.40
a.		5c black & red brown (error)	2,100.	
		Never hinged	2,600.	
b.		Center inverted	60.00	87.50
		Never hinged	120.00	
c.		Imperf., pair	600.00	600.00
		Never hinged	1,200.	
23	A2	10c blk & rose	4.00	.80
		Never hinged	10.00	
		On cover		2.40
a.		Center inverted	60.00	87.50
		Never hinged	120.00	
24	A2	15c blk brn & brn org	87.50	3.25
		Never hinged	225.00	
		On cover		20.00
a.		Center inverted	125.00	260.00
		Never hinged	260.00	
25	A2	25c dk bl & bl	4.00	.25
		Never hinged	10.00	
		On cover		2.40
a.		Center inverted	20.00	27.50
		Never hinged	40.00	
b.		Imperf., pair	875.00	875.00
		Never hinged	1,750.	
26	A3	30c blk & blk brn	35.00	.80
		Never hinged	87.50	
		On cover		4.00
a.		Center inverted	3,000.	3,000.
		Never hinged	3,900.	
27	A3	50c blk & ol grn	16.00	.25
		Never hinged	40.00	
		On cover		2.40
a.		50c black & brown (error)	650.00	
		Never hinged	1,300.	
b.		Center inverted		4,750.
28	A3	55c black & vio	16.00	27.50
		Never hinged	40.00	
		On cover		525.00
29	A4	1 l dk brn & brn	47.50	.25
		Never hinged	120.00	
		On cover		2.40
30	A4	5 l blk & dk blue	32.50	24.00
		Never hinged	80.00	
		On cover		1,100.
31	A4	10 l dk bl & ol grn	350.00	180.00
		Never hinged	875.00	
		On cover		2,500.
		Nos. 20-31 (12)	603.00	253.90

See No. 47-61. For surcharges see No. 102-121 in Scott Standard catalogue, Vol. 4.

20d	A1	1c blk & gray brn	6.50	14.50
		Never hinged	16.00	
21d	A1	2c blk & red brn	6.50	14.50
		Never hinged	16.00	
22d	A1	5c blk & red green	8.00	1.60
		Never hinged	20.00	
23d	A2	10c blk & rose	8.00	1.60
		Never hinged	20.00	
24d	A2	15c blk & brn org	175.00	6.50
		Never hinged	425.00	
25d	A2	25c dk bl & bl	8.00	.40
		Never hinged	20.00	
26d	A3	30c blk & blk brn	72.50	1.60
		Never hinged	180.00	
27d	A3	50c blk & ol grn	32.50	.40
		Never hinged	80.00	
28d	A3	55c blk & vio	32.50	55.00
		Never hinged	80.00	
29d	A4	1 l dk brn & brn	95.00	.40
		Never hinged	240.00	
30d	A4	5 l blk & dk blue	65.00	35.00
		Never hinged	160.00	
31d	A4	10 l blk & ol grn	725.00	225.00
		Never hinged	1,800.	

Italy Nos. 136-139
Overprinted

1922, Apr.

33	A64	5c olive green	2.00	7.25
		Never hinged	5.00	
		On cover		125.00
a.		Double overprint	450.00	450.00
		Never hinged	750.00	
34	A64	10c red	2.00	7.25
		Never hinged	5.00	
		On cover		240.00
a.		Double overprint	450.00	450.00
		Never hinged	750.00	
b.		Inverted overprint	950.00	950.00
		Never hinged	1,250.	
35	A64	15c slate green	2.00	11.00
		Never hinged	5.00	
		On cover		250.00
36	A64	25c ultramarine	2.00	11.00
		Never hinged	5.00	
		On cover		300.00
		Nos. 33-36 (4)	8.00	36.50

3rd anniv. of the victory of the Piave.

Nos. 11, 8 Surcharged

1922, June 1

37	A49	40c on 50c violet	4.00	2.40
		Never hinged	10.00	
		On cover		95.00
38	A49	80c on 25c blue	4.00	9.50
		Never hinged	10.00	
		On cover		350.00

Libyan Sibyl — A6

1924-31   Unwmk.   Perf. 14½x14

39	A6	20c deep green	.80	.25
		Never hinged	2.00	
		On cover		2.00
c.		Vert. pair, imperf between and top	1,440.	
		Never hinged	1,850.	
d.		Horiz. pair, imperf between and at right	1,440.	
		Never hinged	1,850.	
e.		Horiz. pair, imperf between and at left	1,440.	
		Never hinged	1,850.	
40	A6	40c brown	2.40	.80
		Never hinged	6.00	
		On cover		17.50
b.		Imperf single	350.00	475.00
		Never hinged	525.00	
41	A6	60c deep blue	.80	.25
		Never hinged	2.00	
		On cover		22.50
b.		Imperf single	325.00	
		Never hinged	475.00	
42	A6	1.75 l orange ('31)	1.60	.25
		Never hinged	4.00	
		On cover		4.75
43	A6	2 l carmine	4.75	1.20
		Never hinged	12.00	
		On cover		27.50
b.		Imperf single	325.00	400.00
		Never hinged	550.00	
44	A6	2.55 l violet ('31)	9.50	20.00
		Never hinged	24.00	
		On cover		240.00
		Nos. 39-44 (6)	19.85	22.75

1926-29   Perf. 11

39a	A6	20c	47.50	.35
		Never hinged	120.00	
		On cover		9.50
40a	A6	40c	35.00	2.75
		Never hinged	85.00	
		On cover		22.50
41a	A6	60c	35.00	.55
		Never hinged	85.00	
		On cover		45.00
43a	A6	2 l ('29)	16.00	6.00
		Never hinged	42.50	
		On cover		52.50
		Nos. 39a-43a (4)	133.50	9.65

Type of 1921

1924-40   Unwmk.   Perf. 13½ to 14

47	A1	1c blk & gray brown	3.25	6.50
		Never hinged	8.00	
		On cover		160.00
48	A1	2c blk & red brn	3.25	6.50
		Never hinged	8.00	
		On cover		160.00

49	A1	5c blk & green	4.00	.80
		Never hinged	10.00	
		On cover		2.40
50	A1	7½c blk & brown ('31)	1.60	16.00
		Never hinged	4.00	
		On cover		110.00
51	A2	10c blk & dl red	3.25	.35
		Never hinged	8.00	
		On cover		2.40
b.		10c blk & carmine	3.25	.35
		Never hinged	8.00	
		On cover		2.40
c.		As "b," center inverted	200.00	
		Never hinged	375.00	
52	A2	15c blk brn & org	9.50	1.25
		Never hinged	22.50	
		On cover		20.00
b.		Center inverted, perf. 11	4,750.	7,250.
		Never hinged	7,000.	
53	A2	25c dk bl & bl	47.50	.60
		Never hinged	120.00	
		On cover		2.40
a.		Center inverted	275.00	400.00
		Never hinged	425.00	
54	A3	30c blk & blk brn	3.25	.60
		Never hinged	8.00	
		On cover		4.00
55	A3	50c blk & ol grn	3.25	.35
		Never hinged	8.00	
		On cover		2.40
b.		Center inverted	4,750.	
		Never hinged	7,000.	
56	A3	55c black & vio	725.00	950.00
		Never hinged	1,800.	
57	A4	75c violet & red ('31)	6.50	.25
		Never hinged	16.00	
		On cover		16.00
58	A4	1 l dk brn & brn	12.00	.40
		Never hinged	30.00	
		On cover		3.25
59	A3	1.25 l indigo & ultra ('31)	1.60	.25
		Never hinged	4.00	
		On cover		12.00
60	A4	5 l blk & dark blue ('40)	175.00	200.00
		Never hinged	450.00	
		On cover		1,000.
		Nos. 47-60 (14)	998.95	1,183.

Perf. 11

47a	A1	1c	450.00	
		Never hinged	1,100.	
48a	A1	2c	450.00	
		Never hinged	1,100.	
49a	A1	5c	80.00	20.00
		Never hinged	250.00	
				60.00
51a	A2	10c	40.00	8.00
		Never hinged	100.00	
				24.00
52a	A2	15c	550.00	52.50
		Never hinged	1,350.	
				160.00
54a	A3	30c	160.00	2.50
		Never hinged	400.00	
				8.00
55a	A3	50c	875.00	.25
		Never hinged	2,200.	
				2.40
58a	A4	1 l	400.00	.40
		Never hinged	1,000.	
				14.50
60a	A4	5 l ('37)	2,750.	525.00
		Never hinged	3,750.	
		On cover		1,600.
61	A4	10 l dk bl & olive grn ('37)	725.00	600.00
		Never hinged	1,800.	
		On cover		2,600.

Nos. 47a and 48a were not sent to the colony. A few philatelically inspired covers exist.

Italy Nos. 197 and 88 Overprinted Like Nos. 1-15

1929   Wmk. 140   Perf. 14

62	A86	7½c light brown	12.00	65.00
		Never hinged	30.00	
		On cover		350.00
a.		Double overprint	—	—
63	A46	1.25 l blue & ultra	67.50	24.00
		Never hinged	160.00	
		On cover		175.00
a.		Inverted overprint	4,000.	
		Never hinged	4,500.	

Italy No. 193 Overprinted Like Nos. 33-36

1929   Unwmk.   Perf. 11

64	A85	1.75 l deep brown	87.50	2.40
		Never hinged	210.00	
		On cover		67.50
h.		Perf 13¾	12,000.	
		On cover		36,000.

No. 64h is not known unused.

Water
Carriers
A7

Man of Tripoli — A8

Designs: 25c, Minaret. 30c, 1.25 l, Tomb of Holy Man near Tagiura. 50c, Statue of Emperor Claudius at Leptis. 75c, Ruins of gardens.

1934, Feb. 17   Photo.   Perf. 14

64A	A7	10c brown	4.75	20.00
		Never hinged	12.00	
		On cover		190.00
64B	A8	20c car rose	4.75	17.50
		Never hinged	12.00	
		On cover		210.00
64C	A8	25c green	4.75	17.50
		Never hinged	12.00	
		On cover		225.00
64D	A7	30c dark brown	4.75	17.50
		Never hinged	12.00	
		On cover		260.00
64E	A8	50c purple	4.75	16.00
		Never hinged	12.00	
		On cover		210.00
64F	A7	75c rose	4.75	32.50
		Never hinged	12.00	
		On cover		325.00
64G	A7	1.25 l blue	65.00	110.00
		Never hinged	160.00	
		On cover		650.00
		Nos. 64A-64G (7)	93.50	231.00
		Nos. 64A-64G,C14-C18 (12)	580.50	1,131.
		Nos. 64A-64G on overfranked philatelic cover		2,200.

8th Sample Fair, Tripoli.

Bedouin
Woman — A15

Highway
Memorial
Arch — A16

1936, May 11   Wmk. 140   Perf. 14

65	A15	50c purple	2.00	3.25
		Never hinged	5.00	
		On cover		52.50
66	A15	1.25 l deep blue	2.00	8.75
		Never hinged	5.00	
		On cover		175.00
		Nos. 65-66 on overfranked philatelic cover		55.00

10th Sample Fair, Tripoli.

1937, Mar. 15

67	A16	50c copper red	3.25	6.50
		Never hinged	8.00	
		On cover		190.00
68	A16	1.25 l sapphire	3.25	14.50
		Never hinged	8.00	
		On cover		275.00
		Nos. 67-68,C28-C29 (4)	13.00	41.50

Coastal road to the Egyptian frontier, opening.

Nos. 67-68
Overprinted in Black

1937, Apr. 24

69	A16	50c copper red	16.00	40.00
		Never hinged	40.00	
		On cover		210.00
70	A16	1.25 l sapphire	16.00	40.00
		Never hinged	40.00	
		On cover		325.00
		Nos. 69-70,C30-C31 (4)	64.00	160.00

11th Sample Fair, Tripoli.

Roman Wolf and Lion of St. Mark A17

View of Fair Buildings A18

1938, Feb. 20

71	A17	5c brown	.30	1.25
	Never hinged		.75	
	On cover			87.50
72	A18	10c olive brown	.80	.80
	Never hinged		.75	
	On cover			47.50
73	A17	25c green	.65	1.40
	Never hinged		1.60	
	On cover			87.50
74	A18	50c purple	.65	.65
	Never hinged		1.60	
	On cover			40.00
75	A17	75c rose red	1.60	3.25
	Never hinged		4.00	
	On cover			190.00
76	A18	1.25 l dark blue	1.60	8.00
	Never hinged		4.00	
	On cover			225.00
	Nos. 71-76,C32-C33 (8)		8.80	25.10
	Nos. 71-76 on overfranked philatelic cover			120.00

12th Sample Fair, Tripoli.

Augustus Caesar (Octavianus) A19
Goddess Abundantia A20

1938, Apr. 25

77	A19	5c olive brown	.25	1.60
	Never hinged		.65	
	On cover			210.00
78	A20	10c brown red	.25	1.60
	Never hinged		.65	
	On cover			72.50
79	A19	25c dk yel green	.55	.75
	Never hinged		1.40	
	On cover			100.00
80	A20	50c dk violet	.55	.55
	Never hinged		1.40	
	On cover			60.00
81	A19	75c orange red	1.60	2.00
	Never hinged		4.00	
	On cover			225.00
82	A20	1.25 l dull blue	1.60	3.25
	Never hinged		4.00	
	On cover			275.00
	Nos. 77-82,C34-C35 (8)		6.45	16.25
	Nos. 77-82 on overfranked philatelic cover			140.00

Birth bimillenary of Augustus Caesar (Octavianus), first Roman emperor.

Desert City — A21

View of Ghadames A22

1939, Apr. 12 **Photo.**

83	A21	5c olive brown	.80	1.25
	Never hinged		2.00	
	On cover			67.50
84	A22	20c red brown	.80	1.25
	Never hinged		2.00	
	On cover			47.50
85	A21	50c rose violet	.80	1.25
	Never hinged		2.00	
	On cover			20.00
86	A22	75c scarlet	.80	4.00
	Never hinged		2.00	
	On cover			120.00
87	A21	1.25 l gray blue	1.60	4.75
	Never hinged		4.00	
	On cover			210.00
	Nos. 83-87,C36-C38 (8)		7.60	20.55
	Nos. 83-87 on overfranked philatelic cover			60.00

13th Sample Fair, Tripoli.

Modern City — A23

Oxen and Plow A24

Mosque — A25

1940, June 3 **Wmk. 140** *Perf. 14*

88	A23	5c brown	.80	1.25
	Never hinged		2.00	
	On cover			95.00
89	A24	10c red orange	.80	.80
	Never hinged		2.00	
	On cover			67.50
90	A25	25c dull green	.80	1.25
	Never hinged		2.00	
	On cover			87.50
91	A23	50c dark violet	.80	.80
	Never hinged		2.00	
	On cover			45.00
92	A24	75c crimson	.80	4.00
	Never hinged		2.00	
	On cover			225.00
93	A25	1.25 l ultramarine	1.60	6.50
	Never hinged		4.00	
	On cover			325.00
94	A24	2 l + 75c rose lake	1.60	19.00
	Never hinged		4.00	
	On cover			600.00
	Nos. 88-94,C39-C42 (11)		11.30	59.10
	Nos. 88-94 on overfranked philatelic cover			200.00

Triennial Overseas Exposition, Naples.

SEMI-POSTAL STAMPS

Many issues of Italy and Italian Colonies include one or more semipostal denominations. To avoid splitting sets, these issues are generally listed as regular postage, semipostals or airmails, etc.

Semi-Postal Stamps of Italy Overprinted

1915-16 **Wmk. 140** *Perf. 14*

B1	SP1	10c + 5c rose	4.00	16.00
	Never hinged		10.00	
	On cover			120.00
a.	Double overprint		875.00	
	Never hinged		1,250.	
B2	SP2	15c + 5c slate	32.50	27.50
	Never hinged		80.00	
	On cover			225.00
B3	SP2	20c + 5c org ('16)	4.75	35.00
	Never hinged		12.00	
	On cover			325.00
a.	Double overprint, one albino		550.00	
	Never hinged		850.00	
	Nos. B1-B3 (3)		41.25	78.50

No. B2 with Additional Surcharge

1916, Mar.

B4	SP2	20c on 15c + 5c slate	32.50	35.00
	Never hinged		80.00	
	On cover			240.00
a.	Double surcharge		875.00	
	Never hinged		1,250.	
	Nos. B1-B4 on overfranked philatelic cover			275.00

View of Port, Tripoli SP1

Designs: B5, B6, View of port, Tripoli. B7, B8, Arch of Marcus Aurelius. B9, B10, View of Tripoli.

1927, Feb. 15 **Litho.**

B5	SP1	20c + 5c brn vio & black	4.00	17.50
	Never hinged		10.00	
	On cover			175.00
B6	SP1	25c + 5c bl grn & black	4.00	17.50
	Never hinged		10.00	
	On cover			225.00
B7	SP1	40c + 10c blk brn & black	4.00	17.50
	Never hinged		10.00	
	On cover			225.00
B8	SP1	60c + 10c org brn & black	4.00	17.50
	Never hinged		10.00	
	On cover			250.00
B9	SP1	75c + 20c red & black	4.00	17.50
	Never hinged		10.00	
	On cover			325.00
B10	SP1	1.25 l + 20c bl & blk	27.50	47.50
	Never hinged		67.50	
	On cover			800.00
	Nos. B5-B10 (6)		47.50	135.00
	Set on overfranked philatelic cover			450.00

First Sample Fair, Tripoli. Surtax aided fair. See Nos. EB1-EB2.

View of Tripoli — SP2

Knights of Malta Castle SP3

Designs: 50c+20c, Date palm. 1.25 l+20c, Camel riders. 2.55 l+50c, View of Tripoli. 5 l+1 l, Traction well.

1928, Feb. 20 **Wmk. 140** *Perf. 14*

B11	SP2	30c + 20c mar & blk	4.00	17.50
	Never hinged		10.00	
	On cover			210.00
B12	SP2	50c + 20c bl grn & blk	4.00	17.50
	Never hinged		10.00	
	On cover			250.00
B13	SP2	1.25 l + 20c red & blk	4.00	17.50
	Never hinged		10.00	
	On cover			325.00
B14	SP3	1.75 l + 20c bl & blk	4.00	17.50
	Never hinged		10.00	
	On cover			475.00
B15	SP3	2.55 l + 50c brn & blk	8.00	25.00
	Never hinged		20.00	
	On cover			600.00
B16	SP3	5 l + 1 l pur & blk	11.00	40.00
	Never hinged		27.50	
	On cover			
	Nos. B11-B16 (6)		35.00	135.00
	... on overfranked philatelic cover			375.00

2nd Sample Fair, Tripoli, 1928. The surtax was for the aid of the Fair.

Olive Tree — SP4

Herding SP5

Designs: 50c+20c, Dorcas gazelle. 1.25 l+20c, Peach blossoms. 2.55 l+50c, Camel caravan. 5 l+1 l, Oasis with date palms.

1929, Apr. 7

B17	SP4	30c + 20c mar & blk	16.00	32.50
	Never hinged		40.00	
	On cover			325.00
B18	SP4	50c + 20c bl grn & blk	16.00	32.50
	Never hinged		40.00	
	On cover			300.00
B19	SP4	1.25 l + 20c scar & blk	16.00	32.50
	Never hinged		40.00	
	On cover			550.00
B20	SP5	1.75 l + 20c bl & blk	16.00	32.50
	Never hinged		40.00	
	On cover			800.00
B21	SP5	2.55 l + 50c yel brn & blk	16.00	32.50
	Never hinged		40.00	
	On cover			1,100.
B22	SP5	5 l + 1 l pur & blk	150.00	340.00
	Never hinged		375.00	
	On cover			—
	Nos. B17-B22 (6)		230.00	502.50
	Set on overfranked philatelic cover			1,400.

3rd Sample Fair, Tripoli, 1929. The surtax was for the aid of the Fair.

Harvesting Bananas — SP6

Water Carriers SP7

Designs: 50c, Tobacco plant. 1.25 l, Venus of Cyrene. 2.55 l+45c, Black bucks. 5 l+1 l, Motor and camel transportation. 10 l+2 l, Rome pavilion.

1930, Feb. 20 **Photo.**

B23	SP6	30c dark brown	4.75	20.00
	Never hinged		12.00	
	On cover			300.00
B24	SP6	50c violet	4.75	20.00
	Never hinged		12.00	
	On cover			260.00
B25	SP6	1.25 l deep blue	4.75	20.00
	Never hinged		12.00	
	On cover			400.00
B26	SP7	1.75 l + 20c scar	8.00	30.00
	Never hinged		20.00	
	On cover			550.00
B27	SP7	2.55 l + 45c dp grn	19.00	45.00
	Never hinged		47.50	
	On cover			800.00
B28	SP7	5 l + 1 l dp org	19.00	55.00
	Never hinged		47.50	
B29	SP7	10 l + 2 l dk vio	19.00	72.50
	Never hinged		47.50	
	Nos. B23-B29 (7)		79.25	262.50
	Set on overfranked philatelic cover			725.00

4th Sample Fair at Tripoli, 1930. The surtax was for the aid of the Fair.

Statue of
Ephebus — SP8

Exhibition
Pavilion
SP9

Designs: 25c, Arab musician. 50c, View of
Zeughet. 1.25 l, Snake charmer. 1.75 l+25c,
Windmill. 2.75 l+45c, "Zaptie." 5 l+1 l,
Mounted Arab.

1931, Mar. 8
B30	SP8	10c black brown	6.50	11.00
	Never hinged		16.00	
	On cover			240.00
B31	SP8	25c green	6.50	11.00
	Never hinged		16.00	
	On cover			275.00
B32	SP8	50c purple	6.50	11.00
	Never hinged		16.00	
	On cover			240.00
B33	SP8	1.25 l blue	6.50	16.00
	Never hinged		16.00	
	On cover			400.00
B34	SP8	1.75 l + 25c car rose	6.50	19.00
	Never hinged		16.00	
	On cover			—
B35	SP8	2.75 l + 45c org	6.50	27.50
	Never hinged		16.00	
	On cover			—
B36	SP8	5 l + 1 l dl vio	17.50	40.00
	Never hinged		42.50	
	On cover			—
B37	SP9	10 l + 2 l brn	55.00	80.00
	Never hinged		140.00	
	Nos. B30-B37 (8)		111.50	215.50
	Nos. B30-B37,C3,EB3 (10)		119.60	264.00
	Nos. B30-B37 on overfranked philatelic cover			875.00

Fifth Sample Fair, Tripoli. Surtax aided fair.

Papaya Tree
SP10

Dorcas Gazelle
SP12

Ar Tower,
Mogadiscio
SP11

Designs: 10c, 50c, Papaya tree. 20c, 30c,
Euphorbia abyssinica. 25c, Fig cactus. 75c,
Mausoleum, Ghirza. 1.75 l+25c, Lioness.
5 l+1 l, Bedouin with camel.

1932, Mar. 8
B38	SP10	10c olive brn	8.00	19.00
	Never hinged		20.00	
	On cover			190.00
B39	SP10	20c brown red	8.00	19.00
	Never hinged		20.00	
	On cover			125.00
B40	SP10	25c green	8.00	19.00
	Never hinged		20.00	
	On cover			190.00
B41	SP10	30c olive blk	8.00	19.00
	Never hinged		20.00	
	On cover			240.00
B42	SP10	50c dk violet	8.00	19.00
	Never hinged		20.00	
	On cover			125.00
B43	SP10	75c carmine	9.50	19.00
	Never hinged		24.00	
	On cover			375.00
B44	SP11	1.25 l dk blue	9.50	27.50
	Never hinged		24.00	
	On cover			525.00
B45	SP11	1.75 l + 25c ol brn	32.50	87.50
	Never hinged		80.00	
	On cover			675.00
B46	SP11	5 l + 1 l dp bl	32.50	225.00
	Never hinged		80.00	

B47	SP12	10 l + 2 l brn violet	140.00	400.00
	Never hinged		350.00	
	Nos. B38-B47 (10)		264.00	854.00
	Nos. B38-B47,C4-C7 (14)		471.50	1,349.
	Nos. B38-B47 on overfranked philatelic cover			2,500.

Sixth Sample Fair, Tripoli. Surtax aided fair.

Ostrich — SP13

Arab
Musician
SP14

Designs: 25c, Incense plant. 30c, Arab
musician. 50c, Arch of Marcus Aurelius. 1.25 l,
African eagle. 5 l+1 l, Leopard. 10 l+2.50 l,
Tripoli skyline and fasces.

1933, Mar. 2   Photo.   Wmk. 140
B48	SP13	10c dp violet	45.00	47.50
	Never hinged		110.00	
	On cover			275.00
B49	SP13	25c dp green	24.00	47.50
	Never hinged		60.00	
	On cover			225.00
B50	SP14	30c orange brn	24.00	47.50
	Never hinged		60.00	
	On cover			275.00
B51	SP13	50c purple	24.00	47.50
	Never hinged		60.00	
	On cover			225.00
B52	SP13	1.25 l dk blue	55.00	87.50
	Never hinged		140.00	
	On cover			650.00
B53	SP14	5 l + 1 l ol brn	125.00	200.00
	Never hinged		300.00	
	On cover			—
B54	SP13	10 l + 2.50 l car	125.00	350.00
	Never hinged		300.00	
	On cover			—
	Nos. B48-B54 (7)		422.00	827.50
	Nos. B48-B54,C8-C13 (13)		547.00	1,217.
	Nos. B48-B54 on overfranked philatelic cover			2,400.

Seventh Sample Fair, Tripoli. Surtax aided
fair.

Pomegranate
Tree — SP15

Designs: 50c+10c, 2 l+50c, Musician.
75c+15c, 1.25 l+25c, Tribesman.

1935, Feb. 16
B55	SP15	10c + 10c brown	2.00	5.50
	Never hinged		5.00	
	On cover			210.00
B56	SP15	20c + 10c rose red	2.00	5.50
	Never hinged		5.00	
	On cover			225.00
B57	SP15	50c + 10c purple	2.00	5.50
	Never hinged		5.00	
	On cover			210.00
B58	SP15	75c + 15c car	2.00	5.50
	Never hinged		5.00	
	On cover			275.00
B59	SP15	1.25 l + 25c dl blue	2.00	5.50
	Never hinged		5.00	
	On cover			475.00

B60	SP15	2 l + 50c ol grn	2.00	14.50
	Never hinged		5.00	
	On cover			—
	Nos. B55-B60 (6)		12.00	42.00
	Nos. B55-B60,C19-C24 (12)		31.00	123.50
	Nos. B55-B60 on overfranked philatelic cover			800.00

Ninth Sample Fair, Tripoli. Surtax aided fair.

AIR POST STAMPS

Italy Nos.
C3 and C5
Overprinted

1928-29   Wmk. 140   Perf. 14
C1	AP2	50c rose red	16.00	27.50
	Never hinged		40.00	
	On cover			125.00
C2	AP2	80c brn vio & brn ('29)	55.00	80.00
	Never hinged		140.00	
	On cover			475.00

Airplane
AP1

1931, Mar. 8   Photo.   Wmk. 140
C3	AP1	50c blue	1.60	16.00
	Never hinged		4.00	
	On flown cover			180.00

See note after No. B37.

Seaplane
over
Bedouin
Camp
AP2

Designs: 50c, 1 l, Seaplane over Bedouin
camp. 2 l+1 l, 5 l+2 l, Seaplane over Tripoli.

1932, Mar. 1   Perf. 14
C4	AP2	50c dark blue	17.50	47.50
	Never hinged		45.00	
	On cover			240.00
C5	AP2	1 l org brown	17.50	47.50
	Never hinged		45.00	
	On cover			275.00
C6	AP2	2 l + 1 l dk gray	32.50	140.00
	Never hinged		80.00	
C7	AP2	5 l + 2 l car	140.00	260.00
	Never hinged		350.00	
	Nos. C4-C7 (4)		149.00	332.00
	Set on overfranked philatelic cover			950.00

See note after No. B47.

Seaplane
Arriving at
Tripoli
AP3

Designs: 50c, 2 l+50c, Seaplane arriving at
Tripoli. 75c, 10 l+2.50 l, Plane over Tagiura. 1 l,
5 l+1 l, Seaplane leaving Tripoli.

1933, Mar. 1
C8	AP3	50c dp green	12.50	25.00
	Never hinged		30.00	
	On cover			240.00
C9	AP3	75c carmine	12.50	25.00
	Never hinged		30.00	
	On cover			300.00
C10	AP3	1 l dk blue	12.50	25.00
	Never hinged		30.00	
	On cover			350.00
C11	AP3	2 l + 50c pur	20.00	60.00
	Never hinged		50.00	
C12	AP3	5 l + 1 l org brn	35.00	95.00
	Never hinged		87.50	
	On cover			—

C13	AP3	10 l + 2.50 l gray blk	32.50	160.00
	Never hinged		75.00	
	Nos. C8-C13 (6)		99.50	315.00
	Set on overfranked philatelic cover			1,000.

See note after No. B54.

Seaplane
over Tripoli
Harbor
AP4

Airplane and
Camel — AP5

Designs: 50c, 5 l+1 l, Seaplane over Tripoli
harbor. 75c, 10 l+2 l, Plane and minaret.

1934, Feb. 17   Photo.   Wmk. 140
C14	AP4	50c slate bl	16.00	35.00
	Never hinged		40.00	
	On cover			275.00
C15	AP4	75c red org	16.00	35.00
	Never hinged		40.00	
	On cover			325.00
C16	AP4	5 l + 1 l dp grn	140.00	240.00
	Never hinged		350.00	
	On cover			—
C17	AP4	10 l + 2 l dl vio	140.00	240.00
	Never hinged		350.00	
	On cover			—
C18	AP5	25 l + 3 l org brn	175.00	350.00
	Never hinged		425.00	
	Nos. C14-C18 (5)		352.00	627.00
	Set on overfranked philatelic cover			2,100.

Eighth Sample Fair, Tripoli. Surtax aided
fair. See Nos. CE1-CE2.

Plane and Ancient
Tower — AP6

Camel
Train
AP7

Designs: 25c+10c, 3 l+1.50 l, Plane and
ancient tower. 50c+10c, 2 l+30c, Camel train.
1 l+25c, 10 l+5 l, Arab watching plane.

1935, Apr. 12
C19	AP6	25c + 10c green	1.60	6.50
	Never hinged		4.00	
	On cover			250.00
C20	AP7	50c + 10c slate bl	1.60	6.50
	Never hinged		4.00	
	On cover			250.00
C21	AP7	1 l + 25c blue	1.60	6.50
	Never hinged		4.00	
	On cover			325.00
C22	AP7	2 l + 30c rose red	1.60	11.00
	Never hinged		4.00	
	On cover			—
C23	AP6	3 l + 1.50 l brn	1.60	11.00
	Never hinged		4.00	
	On cover			—
C24	AP7	10 l + 5 l dl vio	11.00	40.00
	Never hinged		27.50	
	Nos. C19-C24 (6)		15.50	64.50
	Set on overfranked philatelic cover			400.00

See note after No. B60.

Cyrenaica No. C6
Overprinted in Black

1936, Oct.

C25	AP2 50c purple	24.00	.40
	Never hinged	60.00	
	On cover		2.40

Same on Tripolitania Nos. C8 and C12

1937

C26	AP1 50c rose carmine	.80	.25
	Never hinged	2.00	
	On cover		2.00
C27	AP2 1 l deep blue	2.40	1.00
	Never hinged	6.00	
	On cover		5.50
	Set, never hinged	8.00	

See Nos. C45-C50 in Scott Standard catalogue, Vol. 4.

Ruins of Odeon Theater, Sabrata AP8

1937, Mar. 15   **Photo.**

C28	AP8 50c dark violet	3.25	8.00
	Never hinged	8.00	
	On cover		175.00
C29	AP8 1 l vio black	3.25	12.50
	Never hinged	8.00	
	On cover		275.00
	Set, never hinged	16.00	
	Set on overfranked philatelic cover		120.00

Opening of a coastal road to the Egyptian frontier.

Nos. C28-C29 Overprinted "XI FIERA DI TRIPOLI"

1937, Mar. 15

C30	AP8 50c dark violet	16.00	40.00
	Never hinged	40.00	
	On cover		120.00
C31	AP8 1 l violet blk	16.00	40.00
	Never hinged	40.00	
	On cover		250.00
	Set, never hinged	80.00	
	Set on overfranked philatelic cover		325.00

11th Sample Fair, Tripoli.

View of Tripoli   Eagle Attacking
AP9   Serpent AP10

1938, Mar. 12   **Perf. 14**

C32	AP9 50c dk olive grn	1.60	3.25
	Never hinged	4.00	
	On cover		65.00
C33	AP9 1 l slate blue	1.60	6.50
	Never hinged	4.00	
	On cover		125.00
	Set, never hinged	8.00	

12th Sample Fair, Tripoli.

1938, Apr. 25   **Wmk. 140**

C34	AP10 50c olive brown	.40	2.00
	Never hinged	1.00	
	On cover		60.00
C35	AP10 1 l brn violet	1.25	4.50
	Never hinged	3.25	
	On cover		120.00
	Set, never hinged	4.25	

Birth bimillenary Augustus Caesar (Octavianus), first Roman emperor.

Arab and Camel AP11

Design: 50c, Fair entrance.

1939, Apr. 12   **Photo.**

C36	AP11 25c green	.80	2.40
	Never hinged	2.00	
	On cover		87.50
C37	AP11 50c olive brown	.80	2.40
	Never hinged	2.00	
	On cover		60.00
C38	AP11 1 l rose violet	1.20	3.25
	Never hinged	3.00	
	On cover		175.00
	Nos. C36-C38 (3)	1.90	6.70
	Set, never hinged	7.00	

13th Sample Fair, Tripoli.

Plane Over Modern City AP12

Design: 1 l, 5 l+2.50 l, Plane over oasis.

1940, June 3

C39	AP12 50c brn blk	.80	1.00
	Never hinged	2.00	
	On cover		87.50
C40	AP12 1 l brn vio	.80	2.00
	Never hinged	2.00	
	On cover		125.00
C41	AP12 2 l + 75c indigo	1.25	8.00
	Never hinged	3.25	
	On cover		—
C42	AP12 5 l + 2.50 l copper brn	1.25	14.50
	Never hinged	3.25	
	On cover		—
	Nos. C39-C42 (4)	3.70	21.35
	Set, never hinged	10.50	
	Set on overfranked philatelic cover		160.00

Triennial Overseas Exposition, Naples.

AIR POST SPECIAL DELIVERY STAMPS

APSD1

Wmk. 140

1934, Feb. 17   **Photo.**   **Perf. 14**

CE1	APSD1 2.25 l olive blk	65.00	80.00
	Never hinged	160.00	
	On cover		2,000.
CE2	APSD1 4.50 l + 1 l gray blk	65.00	80.00
	Never hinged	160.00	
	On cover		—
	Set, never hinged	320.00	
	Set, on overfranked flown cover		2,100.

8th Sample Fair at Tripoli. The surtax was for the aid of the Fair.

SPECIAL DELIVERY STAMPS

Special Delivery Stamps of Italy Overprinted

Two types of overprint. See note preceding No. 1 for descriptions.

1915-16.   **Wmk. 140**   **Perf. 14**

E1	SD1 25c rose red, ovpt. type I	95.00	35.00
	Never hinged	220.00	
	On cover		240.00
a.	Overprinted type II	27.50	20.00
	Never hinged	67.50	
	On cover		125.00

E2	SD2 30c blue & rose, ovpt. type I	8.00	35.00
	Never hinged	20.00	
	On cover		450.00
a.	Overprinted type II	22.50	35.00
	Never hinged	55.00	
	On cover		450.00
	Never hinged		240.00

Issued: Nos. E1, E2, Nov. 1915; Nos. E1a, E2a, Dec. 1916.
For surcharges see Nos. E7-E8.

"Italia" SD3

1921-23   **Engr.**   **Perf. 13½**

E3	SD3 30c blue & rose	2.40	8.00
	Never hinged	6.00	
	On cover		175.00
E4	SD3 50c rose red & brn	4.75	12.00
	Never hinged	12.00	
	On cover		200.00
E5	SD3 60c dk red & brn ('23)	8.00	18.00
	Never hinged	20.00	
	On cover		260.00
E6	SD3 2 l dk bl & red ('23)	16.00	32.50
	Never hinged	40.00	
	On cover		525.00
	Nos. E3-E6 (4)	31.15	70.50
	Set, never hinged	78.00	

30c, 2 l inscribed "EXPRES."
For surcharges see Nos. E9-E12.

Nos. E1-E2 Surcharged

1922, June 1

E7	SD1 60c on 25c rose red	14.50	20.00
	Never hinged	35.00	
	On cover		300.00
E8	SD2 1.60 l on 30c bl & rose	17.50	40.00
	Never hinged	40.00	
	On cover		675.00
	Set, never hinged	75.00	

Nos. E5-E6 Surcharged in Blue or Red

No. E9

Nos. E10, E12

No. E11

1926-36

E9	SD3 70c on 60c	8.00	18.00
	Never hinged	20.00	
	On cover		225.00
E10	SD3 2.50 l on 2 l (R)	16.00	32.50
	Never hinged	40.00	

	On cover		725.00

Perf. 11

E11	SD3 1.25 l on 60c	6.50	2.00
	Never hinged	16.00	
	On cover		20.00
a.	Perf. 14 ('36)	24.00	4.00
	Never hinged	60.00	
	On cover		130.00
b.	Black surcharge	150,000.	19,000.
	Never hinged	190,000.	
	On cover		47,500.
E12	SD3 2.50 l on 2 l (R)	275.00	950.00
	Never hinged	690.00	
	On cover		3,750.
	Nos. E9-E12 (4)	305.50	1,002.
	Set, never hinged	775.00	

Issued: Nos. E9-E10, July 1926; Nos. E11-E12, 1927.

SEMI-POSTAL SPECIAL DELIVERY STAMPS

Camel Caravan SPSD1

Wmk. 140

1927, Feb. 15   **Litho.**   **Perf. 14**

EB1	SPSD1 1.25 l + 30c pur & blk	9.50	47.50
	Never hinged	24.00	
	On cover		325.00
EB2	SPSD1 2.50 l + 1 l yel & blk	9.50	47.50
	Never hinged	24.00	
	On cover		325.00
	Set, never hinged	48.00	

See note after No. B10.
No. EB2 is inscribed "EXPRES."

War Memorial SPSD2

1931, Mar. 8   **Photo.**

EB3	SPSD2 1.25 l + 20c car rose	6.50	32.50
	Never hinged	16.00	

See note after No. B37.

AUTHORIZED DELIVERY STAMPS

Italy No. EY1 Overprinted in Black

1929, May 11   **Wmk. 140**   **Perf. 14**

EY1	AD1 10c dull blue	35.00	80.00
	Never hinged	90.00	
	On cover		800.00
a.	Perf. 11	140.00	325.00
	Never hinged	350.00	
	On cover		1,600.

POSTAGE DUE STAMPS

Italian Postage Due Stamps, 1870-1903 Overprinted in Black

1915, Nov.   **Wmk. 140**   **Perf. 14**

J1	D3 5c buff & magenta	2.40	12.00
	Never hinged	4.75	
	On cover		325.00
J2	D3 10c buff & magenta	2.40	6.50
	Never hinged	4.75	
	On cover		190.00

J3	D3 20c buff & ma-		
	genta	3.25	*9.50*
	Never hinged	6.50	
	On cover		*190.00*
a.	Double overprint	550.00	
	Never hinged	800.00	
b.	Inverted overprint	550.00	
	Never hinged	850.00	
J4	D3 30c buff & ma-		
	genta	8.00	*12.00*
	Never hinged	16.00	
	On cover		*240.00*
J5	D3 40c buff & ma-		
	genta	12.00	*14.50*
	Never hinged	24.00	
	On cover		*325.00*
a.	"40" in black	5,250.	
	Never hinged	10,500.	
J6	D3 50c buff & ma-		
	genta	8.00	*9.50*
	Never hinged	16.00	
	On cover		*190.00*
J7	D3 60c buff & ma-		
	genta	12.00	*22.50*
	Never hinged	24.00	
	On cover		*325.00*
J8	D3 1 l blue & ma-		
	genta	8.00	*22.50*
	Never hinged	16.00	
	On cover		*350.00*
a.	Double overprint	11,000.	*17,500.*
J9	D3 2 l blue & ma-		
	genta	65.00	*125.00*
	Never hinged	130.00	
	On cover		—
J10	D3 5 l blue & ma-		
	genta	87.50	*225.00*
	Never hinged	175.00	
	On cover		—
	Nos. J1-J10 (10)	208.55	*459.00*

1926

J11	D3 60c buff & brown	175.00	*325.00*
	Never hinged	350.00	
	On cover		*650.00*

Postage Due Stamps
of Italy, 1934,
Overprinted in Black

1934

J12	D6 5c brown	.40	*3.25*
	Never hinged	1.00	
	On cover		*260.00*
J13	D6 10c blue	.40	*3.25*
	Never hinged	1.00	
	On cover		*160.00*
J14	D6 20c rose red	1.60	*1.60*
	Never hinged	4.00	
	On cover		*160.00*
J15	D6 25c green	1.60	*1.60*
	Never hinged	4.00	
	On cover		*125.00*
J16	D6 30c red orange	1.60	*6.50*
	Never hinged	4.00	
	On cover		*240.00*
J17	D6 40c black brn	1.60	*4.00*
	Never hinged	4.00	
	On cover		*260.00*
J18	D6 50c violet	2.00	*.40*
	Never hinged	5.00	
	On cover		*110.00*
J19	D6 60c black	2.00	*20.00*
	Never hinged	5.00	
	On cover		*350.00*
J20	D7 1 l red orange	1.60	*.40*
	Never hinged	4.00	
	On cover		*160.00*
J21	D7 2 l green	47.50	*20.00*
	Never hinged	115.00	
	On cover		*350.00*
J22	D7 5 l violet	110.00	*45.00*
	Never hinged	275.00	
	On cover		—
J23	D7 10 l blue	14.50	*60.00*
	Never hinged	35.00	
	On cover		—
J24	D7 20 l carmine	14.50	*80.00*
	Never hinged	35.00	
	On cover		—
	Nos. J12-J24 (13)	199.30	*246.00*

PARCEL POST STAMPS

These stamps were used by affixing them to the way bill so that one half remained on it following the parcel, the other half staying on the receipt given the sender. Most used halves are right halves. Complete stamps were obtainable canceled, probably to order. Both unused and used values are for complete stamps.

Italian Parcel Post
Stamps, 1914-22,
Overprinted

1915-24   Wmk. 140   Perf. 13½

Q1	PP2 5c brown	8.00	*16.00*
	Never hinged	16.00	
a.	Double overprint	450.00	
	Never hinged	675.00	

Q2	PP2 10c deep blue	8.00	*16.00*
	Never hinged	16.00	
Q3	PP2 20c blk ('18)	9.50	*16.00*
	Never hinged	19.00	
Q4	PP2 25c red	9.50	*16.00*
	Never hinged	19.00	
Q5	PP2 50c orange	12.00	*16.00*
	Never hinged	24.00	
Q6	PP2 1 l violet	12.00	*24.00*
	Never hinged	24.00	
Q7	PP2 2 l green	16.00	*24.00*
	Never hinged	32.00	
Q8	PP2 3 l bister	24.00	*24.00*
	Never hinged	47.50	
Q9	PP2 4 l slate	24.00	*24.00*
	Never hinged	47.50	
Q10	PP2 10 l rose lil		
	('24)	80.00	*140.00*
	Never hinged	160.00	
Q11	PP2 12 l red brn		
	('24)	160.00	*300.00*
	Never hinged	325.00	
Q12	PP2 15 l ol grn		
	('24)	160.00	*475.00*
	Never hinged	325.00	
Q13	PP2 20 l brn vio		
	('24)	240.00	*550.00*
	Never hinged	475.00	
	Nos. Q1-Q13 (13)	763.00	*1,641.*

Halves Used

Q1	1.00
Q2	1.50
Q3	1.50
Q4	1.50
Q5	1.50
Q6	1.50
Q7	1.50
Q8	1.50
Q9	1.50
Q10	10.00
Q11	11.00
Q12	25.00
Q13	65.00

Same Overprint on Parcel Post Stamps of Italy, 1927-36

1927-38

Q14	PP3 10c dp bl ('36)	8.00	*12.00*
	Never hinged	16.00	
Q15	PP3 25c red ('36)	8.00	*12.00*
	Never hinged	16.00	
Q16	PP3 30c ultra ('29)	4.00	*8.00*
	Never hinged	8.00	
Q17	PP3 50c orange	55.00	*400.00*
	Never hinged	110.00	
a.	Overprint 8¾x2mm		
	('31)	100.00	*525.00*
	Never hinged	200.00	
Q18	PP3 60c red ('29)	4.00	*8.00*
	Never hinged	8.00	
Q19	PP3 1 l lilac ('36)	45.00	*160.00*
	Never hinged	90.00	
Q20	PP3 2 l grn ('38)	62.50	*160.00*
	Never hinged	125.00	
Q21	PP3 3 l bister	4.75	*16.00*
	Never hinged	9.50	
Q22	PP3 4 l gray	4.75	*24.00*
	Never hinged	9.50	
Q23	PP3 10 l rose lil		
	('36)	325.00	*725.00*
	Never hinged	650.00	
Q24	PP3 20 l brn vio		
	('36)	360.00	*950.00*
	Never hinged	725.00	
	Nos. Q14-Q24 (11)	881.00	*2,475.*

Halves Used

Q14	.50
Q15	.50
Q16	.50
Q17	12.50
Q17a	22.50
Q18	.50
Q19	7.50
Q20	7.50
Q21	1.50
Q22	2.50
Q23	30.00
Q24	35.00

The overprint measures 10x1½mm on No. Q17.

Same Overprint on Italy No. Q24

1939

Q25	PP3 5c brown	17,500.	
	Never hinged	26,500.	

The overprint was applied to the 5c in error. Few examples exist.

LIECHTENSTEIN

ˈlik-tən-ˌshtin

LOCATION — Central Europe southeast of Lake Constance, between Austria and Switzerland
GOVT. — Principality
AREA — 61.8 sq. mi.
POP. — 4,896 (est. 1984)
CAPITAL — Vaduz

The Principality of Liechtenstein is a sovereign state consisting of the two counties of Schellenberg and Vaduz. Since 1921 the post office has been administered by Switzerland.

100 Heller = 1 Krone
100 Rappen = 1 Franc (1921)

Watermark

Greek Cross —
Wmk. 183

Austrian Administration of the Post Office

Prince Johann
II — A1

Perf. 12½x13

1912, Feb. 1   Unwmk.   Typo.
Thick Chalky Paper

1	A1	5h yellow green	42.50	17.50
		Never hinged	175.00	
		On cover		32.50
2	A1	10h rose	85.00	17.50
		Never hinged	400.00	
		On cover		32.50
3	A1	25h dark blue	85.00	55.00
		Never hinged	325.00	
		On cover		210.00
		Nos. 1-3 (3)	212.50	90.00
		Set, never hinged	900.00	
		First day cover, #1-3		325.00

Nos. 1-3 exist imperf. Value set, $525 unused with original gum, $2,100 never hinged.

Values for blocks of 4 (NH, used)

1	A1	5h yellow green	750.00	105.00
2	A1	10h rose	1,750.	105.00
3	A1	25h dark blue	1,350.	390.00

1915   Thin Unsurfaced Paper

1a	A1	5h yellow green	14.00	21.00
		Never hinged	42.50	
		On cover		32.50
2a	A1	10h rose	85.00	32.50
		Never hinged	325.00	
		On cover		62.50
3a	A1	25h dark blue	600.00	200.00
		Never hinged	2,450.	
		On commercial cover, single franking		600.00
b.		25h ultramarine	350.00	425.00
		Never hinged	1,550.	
		On commercial cover, single franking		10,500.
		#1a-3a, never hinged	2,500.	

Nos. 1a-3a exist imperf. Value set, $1,150 unused with original gum, $2,000 never hinged.

Values for blocks of 4 (NH, used)

1b	A1	5h yellow green	140.00	105.00
2b	A1	10h rose	1,050.	175.00
3b	A1	25h dark blue	8,800.	1,050.
c.		25h ultramarine	5,200.	2,500.

Coat of
Arms — A2

Prince Johann
II — A3

1917-18

4	A2	3h violet	2.00	2.00
		Never hinged	8.50	
		On cover		32.50
5	A2	5h yellow green	2.00	2.00
		Never hinged	8.50	
		On cover		25.00
6	A3	10h claret	2.00	2.00
		Never hinged	8.50	
		On cover		37.50
7	A3	15h dull red	2.00	2.00
		Never hinged	8.50	
		On cover		37.50
8	A3	20h dark green	2.00	2.00
		Never hinged	8.50	
		On cover		42.50
9	A3	25h deep blue	2.00	2.00
		Never hinged	8.50	
		On cover		42.50
		Nos. 4-9 (6)	12.00	12.00
		Set, never hinged	51.00	
		Nos. 4-7, 9, set of 5 on fdc (6/14/17)		750.00

Exist imperf. Value set unused original gum, $525; never hinged, $1,150.
For surcharges see Nos. 11-16.

Prince Johann
II — A4

1918, Nov. 12
Dates in Upper Corners

10	A4	20h dark green	.70	2.75
		Never hinged	5.50	
		On cover		37.50
		First day cover		175.00

Accession of Prince Johann II, 60th anniv.
Exists imperf. Value, unused original gum, $225; never hinged, $560.

National Administration of the Post Office
Stamps of 1917-18 Overprinted or Surcharged

a

b

c

1920

11	A2(a)	5h yellow green	2.75	8.75
		Never hinged	11.00	
		On cover		625.00
		On cover, overfranked		175.00
a.		Inverted overprint	70.00	175.00
		Never hinged	140.00	
b.		Double overprint	14.00	85.00
		Never hinged	35.00	
		On cover		700.00
12	A3(a)	10h claret	2.75	9.50
		Never hinged	12.00	
		On cover		625.00
		On cover, overfranked		175.00
a.		Inverted overprint	70.00	175.00
		Never hinged	140.00	
b.		Double overprint	14.00	105.00
		Never hinged	35.00	
		On cover		850.00
c.		Overprint type "c"	14.00	105.00
		Never hinged	27.50	
		On cover		625.00

13	A3(a)	25h deep blue	2.75	9.50
		Never hinged	14.00	
		On cover		625.00
		On cover, overfranked		175.00
a.		Inverted overprint	70.00	175.00
		Never hinged	140.00	
b.		Double overprint	14.00	105.00
		Never hinged	27.50	
		On cover		850.00
14	A2(b)	40h on 3h violet	2.75	9.50
		Never hinged	11.00	
		On cover		625.00
		On cover, overfranked		175.00
a.		Inverted surcharge	70.00	175.00
		Never hinged	140.00	
15	A3(c)	1k on 15h dull red	2.75	9.50
		Never hinged	11.00	
		On cover		625.00
		On cover, overfranked		175.00
a.		Inverted surcharge	70.00	175.00
		Never hinged	140.00	
b.		Overprint type "a"	87.50	350.00
		Never hinged	315.00	
				1,050.
16	A3(c)	2½k on 20h dk grn	2.75	9.50
		Never hinged	12.00	
		On cover		625.00
		On cover, overfranked		175.00
a.		Inverted surcharge	70.00	175.00
		Never hinged	140.00	
		Nos. 11-16 (6)	16.50	56.25
		Set, never hinged	71.00	

Coat of Arms
A5

Chapel of St.
Mamertus
A6

Coat of Arms with Supporters
A15

Designs: 40h, Gutenberg Castle. 50h, Courtyard, Vaduz Castle. 60h, Red Tower, Vaduz. 80h, Old Roman Tower, Schaan. 1k, Castle at Vaduz. 2k, View of Bendern. 5k, Prince Johann I. 7½k, Prince Johann II.

1920   Engr.   Imperf.

18	A5	5h olive bister	.35	5.75
		Never hinged	.80	
		On cover		160.00
19	A5	10h deep orange	.35	5.75
		Never hinged	.85	
		On cover		140.00
20	A5	15h dark blue	.35	5.75
		Never hinged	.85	
		On cover		160.00
21	A5	20h deep brown	.35	5.75
		Never hinged	1.00	
		On cover		105.00
22	A5	25h dark green	.35	5.75
		Never hinged	1.00	
		On cover		125.00
23	A5	30h gray black	.35	5.75
		Never hinged	1.10	
		On cover		160.00
24	A5	40h dark red	.35	5.75
		Never hinged	1.50	
		On cover		105.00
25	A6	1k blue	.35	5.75
		Never hinged	2.75	
		On cover		160.00
		#18-25, set of 8 on fdc (5/5/20)		1,400.

Perf. 12½

32	A5	5h olive bister	.35	.70
		Never hinged	.70	
		On cover		125.00
33	A5	10h deep orange	.35	.70
		Never hinged	.70	
		On cover		105.00
34	A5	15h deep blue	.35	.70
		Never hinged	.70	
		On cover		125.00
35	A5	20h red brown	.35	.70
		Never hinged	.70	
		On cover		90.00
36	A6	25h olive green	.35	.70
		Never hinged	.70	
		On cover		105.00
37	A5	30h dark gray	.35	.70
		Never hinged	.70	
		On cover		140.00
38	A6	40h claret	.35	.70
		Never hinged	.70	
		On cover		125.00
39	A6	50h yellow green	.35	.70
		Never hinged	.70	
		On cover		125.00
40	A6	60h red brown	.35	.70
		Never hinged	.70	
		On cover		160.00

41	A6	80h rose	.35	.70
		Never hinged	.70	
		On cover		77.50
42	A6	1k dull violet	.70	1.00
		Never hinged	1.10	
		On cover		125.00
43	A6	2k light blue	.70	1.25
		Never hinged	2.00	
		On cover		160.00
44	A6	5k black	.70	1.50
		Never hinged	3.50	
		On cover		425.00
45	A6	7½k slate	.70	1.75
		Never hinged	4.25	
		On cover		525.00
46	A15	10k ocher	.70	3.00
		Never hinged	14.00	
		On cover		625.00
		Nos. 18-46 (23)	9.80	61.50
		Set, never hinged	41.00	

No. 25 perf. 12½ was not officially issued. It is known mint, used and on cover.
Used values for Nos. 18-46 are for canceled to order stamps. Value with postal cancels approximately $95.
Many denominations of Nos. 32-46 are found imperforate, imperforate vertically and imperforate horizontally.
For surcharges see Nos. 51-52.

Madonna and
Child — A16

1920, Oct. 5

47	A16	50h olive green	1.00	2.10
		Never hinged	3.50	
		On cover		210.00
48	A16	80h brown red	1.00	2.10
		Never hinged	3.50	
		On cover		210.00
49	A16	2k dark blue	1.00	2.75
		Never hinged	3.50	
		On cover		210.00
		Nos. 47-49 (3)	3.00	6.95
		Set, never hinged	10.50	
		Set of 3 on fdc		160.00
		Set of 3 on overfranked cover		25.00

80th birthday of Prince Johann II.

Imperf., Singles

47a	A16	50h	7.00	1,400.
		Never hinged	21.00	
48a	A16	80h	7.00	1,400.
		Never hinged	21.00	
49a	A16	2k	7.00	1,400.
		Never hinged	21.00	
		Set, never hinged	63.00	
		Set of 3 singles on fdc		2,500.

On 1/31/21 the Swiss took over the Post Office administration. Previous issues were demonetized and remainders of Nos. 4-49 were sold.

Swiss Administration of the Post Office
No. 19 Surcharged

No. 51

No. 52

1921   Unwmk.   Engr.   Imperf.

51	A5	2rp on 10h dp org	1.40	50.00
		Never hinged	7.00	
		On cover		700.00
		First day cover (2/1/21)		1,500.
a.		Double surcharge	105.00	140.00
		Never hinged	140.00	
		On cover		850.00
b.		Inverted surcharge	105.00	160.00
		Never hinged	140.00	
		On cover		850.00
c.		Double surch., one inverted	105.00	175.00
		Never hinged	140.00	
		On cover		850.00
d.		Comma after "Rp"	70.00	160.00
		Never hinged	100.00	
		On cover		850.00
e.		Inverted comma after "Rp"	70.00	160.00
		Never hinged	100.00	
		On cover		850.00
52	A5	2rp on 10h dp org	.70	50.00
		Never hinged	5.50	
		On cover		450.00
		First day cover (2/27/21)		875.00
a.		Double surcharge	72.50	160.00
		Never hinged	105.00	

	On cover		850.00
b.	Inverted surcharge	72.50	160.00
	Never hinged	105.00	
	On cover		850.00
c.	Double surch., one inverted	87.50	190.00
	Never hinged	140.00	
	On cover		850.00

Arms with Supporters A19

Chapel of St. Mamertus A20

View of Vaduz A21

Designs: 25rp, Castle at Vaduz. 30rp, View of Bendern. 35rp, Prince Johann II. 40rp, Old Roman Tower at Schaan. 50rp, Gutenberg Castle. 80rp, Red Tower at Vaduz.

1921 Perf. 12½, 9½ (2rp, 10rp, 15rp) Surface Tinted Paper (#54-61)

54	A19	2rp lemon	1.40	14.00
		Never hinged	3.75	
		On cover		32.50
55	A19	2½rp black	2.10	17.50
		Never hinged	7.00	
		On cover		32.50
a.		Perf. 9½	1.40	70.00
		Never hinged	3.50	
		On cover		75.00
56	A19	3rp orange	2.10	17.50
		Never hinged	7.00	
		On cover		35.00
a.		Perf. 9½	140.00	5,000.
		Never hinged	425.00	
		On cover		6,750.
57	A19	5rp olive green	14.00	2.10
		Never hinged	42.50	
		On cover		11.00
a.		Perf. 9½	70.00	27.50
		Never hinged	225.00	
		On cover		42.50
58	A19	7½rp dark blue	7.00	42.50
		Never hinged	25.00	
		On cover		95.00
a.		Perf. 9½	275.00	1,050.
		Never hinged	675.00	
		On cover		3,500.
59	A19	10rp yellow green	27.50	17.50
		Never hinged	70.00	
		On cover		27.50
a.		Perf. 12½	27.50	14.00
		Never hinged	140.00	
		On cover		21.00
60	A19	13rp brown	10.50	90.00
		Never hinged	27.50	
		On cover		140.00
a.		Perf. 9½	100.00	2,450.
		Never hinged	250.00	
		On cover		5,250.
b.		Perf. 12½x9½	210.00	—
		Never hinged	425.00	
61	A19	15rp dark violet	25.00	70.00
		Never hinged	40.00	
		On cover		110.00
a.		Perf. 12½	27.50	27.50
		Never hinged	50.00	
		On cover		62.50
62	A20	20rp dull vio & blk	70.00	2.10
		Never hinged	210.00	
		On cover		11.00
63	A20	25rp rose red & blk	3.50	5.00
		Never hinged	11.00	
		On cover		17.50
64	A20	30rp dp grn & blk	85.00	21.00
		Never hinged	275.00	
		On cover		52.50
65	A20	35rp brn & blk, straw	7.00	17.50
		Never hinged	17.50	
		On cover		42.50
66	A20	40rp dk blue & blk	10.50	7.00
		Never hinged	30.00	
		On cover		21.00
67	A20	50rp dk grn & blk	17.50	10.50
		Never hinged	42.50	
		On cover		27.50
68	A20	80rp gray & blk	32.00	85.00
		Never hinged	70.00	
		On cover		160.00
69	A21	1fr dp claret & blk	55.00	55.00
		Never hinged	160.00	
		On cover		140.00
		Nos. 54-69 (16)	370.10	474.20
		Set, never hinged	1,039.	

Nos. 54-69 exist imperforate; Nos. 54-61, partly perforated. See Nos. 73, 81. For surcharges see Nos. 70-71.

Nos. 58, 60a Surcharged in Red

1924 Perf. 12½, 9½

70	A19	5rp on 7½rp	1.40	3.50
		Never hinged	4.25	
		On cover		42.50
a.		Perf. 9½	19.00	17.50
		Never hinged	50.00	
		On cover		85.00
71	A19	10rp on 13rp	1.75	3.50
		Never hinged	5.25	
		On cover		42.50
a.		Perf. 12½	20.00	52.50
		Never hinged	60.00	
		On cover		260.00

Type of 1921 Granite Paper

1924 Wmk. 183 Perf. 11½

73	A19	10rp green	21.00	3.50
		Never hinged	85.00	
		On cover		35.00

Peasant A28

Government Palace and Church at Vaduz A30

10rp, 20rp, Courtyard, Vaduz Castle.

1924-28 Typo. Perf. 11½

74	A28	2½rp ol grn & red vio ('28)	1.40	5.50
		Never hinged	4.25	
		On cover		21.00
75	A28	5rp brown & blue	2.75	.75
		Never hinged	8.50	
		On cover		5.00
76	A28	7½rp bl grn & brn ('28)	2.10	5.50
		Never hinged	5.00	
		On cover		17.50
77	A28	15rp red brn & bl grn ('28)	10.50	35.00
		Never hinged	35.00	
		On cover		70.00

Engr.

78	A28	10rp yellow grn	11.25	.70
		Never hinged	35.00	
		On cover		5.00
79	A28	20rp deep red	42.50	.70
		Never hinged	140.00	
		On cover		70.00
80	A30	1½fr blue	85.00	110.00
		Never hinged	275.00	
		On cover		325.00
		Nos. 74-80 (7)	155.50	158.15
		Set, never hinged	503.00	

Bendern Type of 1921

1925

81	A20	30rp blue & blk	17.50	3.50
		Never hinged	55.00	
		On cover		35.00

Prince Johann II — A31

Prince Johann II as Boy and Man A32

1928, Nov. 12 Typo. Wmk. 183

82	A31	10rp lt brn & ol grn	7.00	7.00
		Never hinged	12.50	
		On cover		17.50
83	A31	20rp org red & ol grn	10.50	14.00
		Never hinged	22.50	
		On cover		28.00
84	A31	30rp sl bl & ol grn	35.00	25.00
		Never hinged	90.00	
		On cover		70.00

85	A31	60rp red vio & ol grn	70.00	70.00
		Never hinged	175.00	
		On cover		210.00

Engr. Unwmk.

86	A32	1.20fr ultra	50.00	87.50
		Never hinged	110.00	
		On cover		425.00
87	A32	1.50fr black brown	87.50	210.00
		Never hinged	210.00	
		On cover		700.00
88	A32	2fr deep car	87.50	210.00
		Never hinged	210.00	
		On cover		700.00
89	A32	5fr dark green	87.50	245.00
		Never hinged	210.00	
		On cover		1,550.
		Nos. 82-89 (8)	435.00	868.50
		Set, never hinged	1,040.	
		Set of 8 on fdc	2,800.	

70th year of the reign of Prince Johann II.

Prince Francis I, as a Child — A33

Prince Francis I as a Man — A34

Princess Elsa — A35

Prince Francis and Princess Elsa — A36

1929, Dec. 2 Photo.

90	A33	10rp olive green	.55	4.25
		Never hinged	1.40	
		On cover		11.00
91	A34	20rp carmine	.85	7.00
		Never hinged	2.10	
		On cover		17.50
92	A35	30rp ultra	1.40	17.50
		Never hinged	3.50	
		On cover		52.50
93	A36	70rp brown	25.00	110.00
		Never hinged	70.00	
		On cover		210.00
		Nos. 90-93 (4)	27.80	138.75
		Set, never hinged	77.00	
		Set of 4 on fdc	700.00	

Values for used blocks of 4

90	A33	10rp olive green		21.00
91	A34	20rp carmine		35.00
92	A35	30rp ultra		105.00
93	A36	70rp brown		560.00

Accession of Prince Francis I, Feb. 11, 1929.

Grape Girl — A37

Chamois Hunter — A38

Mountain Cattle — A39

Courtyard, Vaduz Castle — A40

Mt. Naafkopf — A41

Chapel at Steg — A42

Rofenberg Chapel — A43

Chapel of St. Mamertus — A44

Alpine Hotel, Malbun — A45

Gutenberg Castle — A46

Schellenberg Monastery — A47

Castle at Vaduz — A48

Mountain Cottage — A49

Prince Francis and Princess Elsa — A50

1930 — Perf. 10½

No.	Type	Description	Unused	Used
94	A37	3rp brown lake	1.10	2.80
		Never hinged	3.50	
		On cover		11.00
95	A38	5rp deep green	2.80	7.00
		Never hinged	15.00	
		On cover		11.00
96	A39	10rp dark violet	14.50	7.00
		Never hinged		
		On cover		14.00
97	A40	20rp dp rose red	42.50	7.00
		Never hinged	105.00	
		On cover		14.00
98	A41	25rp black	8.50	45.00
		Never hinged	27.50	
		On cover		70.00
99	A42	30rp dp ultra	8.50	10.50
		Never hinged	27.50	
		On cover		21.00
103	A46	60rp olive blk	105.00	42.50
		Never hinged	280.00	
		On cover		70.00
104	A47	90rp violet brn	105.00	350.00
		Never hinged	350.00	
		On cover		525.00
105	A48	1.20fr olive brn	125.00	375.00
		Never hinged	390.00	
		On cover		525.00
106	A49	1.50fr black violet	70.00	77.50
		Never hinged	175.00	
		On cover		210.00
107	A50	2fr gray grn & red brn	85.00	140.00
		Never hinged	210.00	
		On cover		210.00

Perf. 11½

No.	Type	Description	Unused	Used
95a	A38	5rp dp grn	3.50	2.75
		Never hinged	14.00	
		On cover		7.00
96b	A39	10rp dp vio	3.50	2.75
		Never hinged	14.00	
		On cover		7.00
97a	A40	20rp dp rose red	27.50	3.50
		Never hinged	77.50	
		On cover		8.50
98a	A41	25rp blk	105.00	350.00
		Never hinged	350.00	
		On cover		525.00
99b	A42	30rp dp ultra	8.50	5.00
		Never hinged	27.50	
		On cover		17.50
100a	A43	35rp dk grn	8,750.	14,000.
		Never hinged	13,500.	
102a	A45	50rp blk brn	165.00	245.00
		Never hinged	600.00	
		On cover		350.00
103a	A46	60rp olive blk	105.00	35.00
		Never hinged	275.00	
		On cover		70.00
104a	A47	90rp vio brn	110.00	140.00
		Never hinged	350.00	
		On cover		275.00
105b	A48	1.20fr ol brn	160.00	275.00
		Never hinged	390.00	
		On cover		425.00
106a	A49	1.50fr blk vio	55.00	70.00
		Never hinged	140.00	
		On cover		210.00
107b	A50	2fr gray grn & red brn	85.00	140.00
		Never hinged	245.00	
		On cover		225.00

Perf. 11½x10½

No.	Type	Description	Unused	Used
96a	A39	10rp dk violet	11.00	120.00
		Never hinged	28.00	
		On cover		160.00
99a	A42	30rp dp ultra	1,050.	2,500.
		Never hinged	2,175.	
		On cover		5,750.
100	A43	35rp dark green	11.00	21.00
		Never hinged	35.00	
		On cover		52.50
101	A44	40rp lt brown	11.00	11.00
		Never hinged	35.00	
		On cover		32.50
102	A45	50rp black brown	105.00	21.00
		Never hinged	300.00	
		On cover		42.50
105a	A48	1.20fr ol brn	8,750.	14,000.
		Never hinged	13,500.	
107a	A50	2fr ol grn & red brn	3,850.	7,750.
		Never hinged	6,750.	
		On cover		10,500.
		Nos. 94-107 (11)	555.90	1,064.
		Set, never hinged	1,600.	

For overprints see Nos. O1-O8.

Values for used blocks of 4

Perf. 10½

No.	Type	Description	Value
94	A37	3rp brn lake	14.00
95	A38	5rp dp grn	35.00
96	A39	10rp dk vio	35.00
97	A40	20rp dp rose red	35.00
98	A41	25rp blk	210.00
99	A42	30rp dp ultra	50.00
103	A46	60rp ol blk	175.00
104	A47	90rp vio brn	1,550.
105	A48	1.20fr ol brn	1,750.
106	A49	1.50fr blk vio	390.00
107	A50	2fr ol grn & red brn	700.00

Perf. 11½

No.	Type	Description	Value
95a	A38	5rp dp grn	14.00
96b	A39	10rp dk vio	14.00
97a	A40	20rp dp rose red	21.00
98a	A41	25rp blk	1,750.
99b	A42	30rp dp ultra	35.00
100a	A43	35rp dk grn	—
102a	A45	50rp blk brn	1,150.
103a	A46	60rp ol blk	160.00
104a	A47	90rp vio brn	700.00
105b	A48	1.20fr ol brn	1,400.
106a	A49	1.50fr blk vio	350.00
107b	A50	2fr ol grn & red brn	700.00

Perf. 11½x10½

No.	Type	Description	Value
96a	A39	10rp dk vio	500.00
99a	A42	30rp dp ultra	11,250.
100	A43	35rp dk grn	105.00
101	A44	40rp lt brn	55.00
102	A45	50rp blk brn	125.00
105a	A48	1.20fr ol brn	125.00
107a	A50	2fr ol grn & red brn	—

Mt. Naafkopf A51

Gutenberg Castle A52

Vaduz Castle — A53

1933, Jan. 23 — Perf. 14½

No.	Type	Description	Unused	Used
108	A51	25rp red orange	200.00	87.50
		Never hinged	560.00	
		On cover		125.00
109	A52	90rp dark green	10.50	105.00
		Never hinged	20.00	
		On cover		210.00
110	A53	1.20fr red brown	85.00	300.00
		Never hinged	260.00	
		On cover		525.00
		Nos. 108-110 (3)	295.50	492.50
		Set, never hinged	840.00	
		Set of 3 on fdc	3,150.	

For overprints see Nos. O9-O10.

Values for used blocks of 4

No.	Type	Description	Value
108	A51	25rp red org	450.00
109	A52	90rp dk grn	525.00
110	A53	1.20fr red brn	1,400.

Prince Francis I A54

A55

1933, Aug. 28 — Perf. 11

No.	Type	Description	Unused	Used
111	A54	10rp purple	21.00	42.50
		Never hinged	60.00	
		On cover		70.00
112	A54	20rp brown carmine	21.00	42.50
		Never hinged	60.00	
		On cover		70.00
113	A54	30rp dark blue	21.00	42.50
		Never hinged	60.00	
		On cover		70.00
		Nos. 111-113 (3)	63.00	127.50
		Set, never hinged	180.00	
		Set of 3 on fdc		200.00

Values for used blocks of 4

No.	Type	Description	Value
111	A54	10rp pur	175.00
112	A54	20rp brn car	175.00
113	A54	30rp dk bl	175.00

80th birthday of Prince Francis I.

1933, Dec. 15 — Engr. — Perf. 12½

No.	Type	Description	Unused	Used
114	A55	3fr violet blue	125.00	250.00
		Never hinged	250.00	
		On cover		700.00
		First day cover		3,250.

See No. 152.

Agricultural Exhibition Issue
Souvenir Sheet

Arms of Liechtenstein — A56

1934, Sept. 29 — Perf. 12
Granite Paper

No.	Type	Description	Unused	Used
115	A56	5fr brown	1,400.	2,500.
		Never hinged	2,250.	
		On cover		3,500.
		First day cover		3,250.
		Single stamp	1,000.	1,750.
		Never hinged	1,400.	
		On cover		3,500.
		First day cover		4,250.

See No. 131.

Coat of Arms A57

"Three Sisters" (Landmark) A58

Church of Schaan A59

Bendern A60

Rathaus, Vaduz — A61

Samina Valley — A62

Samina Valley in Winter A63

Ruin at Schellenberg — A64

Government Palace — A65

Vaduz Castle A66

Gutenberg Castle A68

Alpine Hut — A69

Princess Elsa — A70

Coat of Arms — A71

60rp, Vaduz castle, diff. 1.50fr, Valuna.

1934-35 — Photo. — Perf. 11½

No.	Type	Description	Unused	Used
116	A57	3rp copper red	.35	.70
		Never hinged	.70	
		On cover		1.90
117	A58	5rp emerald	5.50	2.10
		Never hinged	17.50	
		On cover		2.75
a.		Grilled gum	5.00	11.00
		Never hinged	14.00	
		On cover		14.00
118	A59	10rp deep violet	2.75	1.40
		Never hinged	14.00	
		On cover		2.75
a.		Grilled gum	.70	8.50
		Never hinged	1.75	
		On cover		14.00
119	A60	15rp red org	.35	1.40
		Never hinged	1.40	
		On cover		7.00
120	A61	20rp red	.70	1.40
		Never hinged	2.10	
		On cover		3.50
121	A62	25rp brown	28.00	65.00
		Never hinged	70.00	
		On cover		90.00
122	A63	30rp dk blue	5.50	2.10
		Never hinged	17.50	
		On cover		6.25
123	A64	35rp gray grn	2.75	8.50
		Never hinged	3.50	
		On cover		17.50
124	A65	40rp brown	1.75	7.00
		Never hinged	4.25	
		On cover		14.00
125	A66	50rp lt brown	25.00	21.00
		Never hinged	85.00	
		On cover		42.50
126	A66	60rp claret	2.10	9.00
		Never hinged	7.00	
		On cover		21.00
127	A68	90rp deep green	8.50	32.00
		Never hinged	21.00	
		On cover		52.50
128	A69	1.20fr deep blue	3.50	32.00
		Never hinged	14.00	
		On cover		52.50
129	A69	1.50fr brn car	4.25	35.00
		Never hinged	17.50	
		On cover		70.00
		Nos. 116-129 (14)	91.00	218.60
		Set, never hinged	275.00	
		#125-128 on fdc (6/18/34)		400.00
		#116-118 on fdc (12/17/34)		525.00
		#120-121 on fdc (1/3/35)		525.00
		#119, 122-124, 129 on fdc (12/9/35)		600.00

Engr.
Perf. 12½

No.	Type	Description	Unused	Used
130	A70	2fr henna brn ('35)	85.00	250.00
		Never hinged	140.00	
		On cover		525.00

131	A71	5fr dk vio ('35)	425.00	*1,050.*
		Never hinged	700.00	
		On cover		*2,800.*

No. 131 has the same design as the 5fr in the souvenir sheet, No. 115. See No. 226 (in Scott Standard catalogue, Vol. 4), B14. For overprints see Nos. O11-O20.

Bridge at Malbun
A72

Labor: 20rp, Constructing Road to Triesenberg. 30rp, Binnen Canal. 50rp, Bridge near Planken.

1937, June 30   **Photo.**

132	A72	10rp brt violet	1.75	2.10
		Never hinged	5.25	
		On cover		6.00
133	A72	20rp red	1.75	*2.75*
		Never hinged	5.25	
		On cover		6.00
134	A72	30rp brt blue	1.75	3.50
		Never hinged	5.25	
		On cover		8.00
135	A72	50rp yellow brown	1.75	4.25
		Never hinged	5.25	
		On cover		11.00
		Nos. 132-135 (4)	7.00	12.60
		Set, never hinged	21.00	
		Set of 4 on fdc		165.00

Ruin at Schalun — A76

Peasant in Rhine Valley
A77

Ruin at Schellenberg — A78

Knight and Gutenberg Castle
A79

Baron von Brandis and Vaduz Castle
A80

Designs: 5rp, Chapel at Masescha. 10rp, Knight and Vaduz Castle. 15rp, Upper Valüna Valley. 20rp, Wooden Bridge over Rhine, Bendern. 25rp, Chapel at Steg. 90rp, "The Three Sisters". 1fr, Frontier stone. 1.20fr, Gutenberg Castle and Harpist. 1.50fr, Alpine View of Lawena and Schwartzhorn.

1937-38

136	A76	3rp yellow brown	.35	*.70*
		Never hinged	.70	
		On cover		2.00

Pale Buff Shading

137	A76	5rp emerald	.35	.35
		Never hinged	.70	
		On cover		2.00
138	A76	10rp violet	.35	.35
		Never hinged	.70	
		On cover		2.00
139	A76	15rp dk slate grn	.35	*.70*
		Never hinged	.70	
		On cover		2.75
140	A76	20rp brn org	.35	*.70*
		Never hinged	.70	
		On cover		2.75

141	A76	25rp chestnut	.70	3.50
		Never hinged	2.00	
		On cover		5.50
142	A77	30rp blue & gray	3.50	1.40
		Never hinged	14.50	
		On cover		4.25
144	A78	40rp dark green	2.10	2.75
		Never hinged	7.00	
		On cover		8.50
145	A79	50rp dark brown	1.40	*7.00*
		Never hinged	3.50	
		On cover		*7.00*
146	A80	60rp dp claret ('38)	2.75	*3.50*
		Never hinged	7.00	
		On cover		11.00
147	A80	90rp gray vio ('38)	7.00	42.50
		Never hinged	14.00	
		On cover		42.50
148	A80	1fr red brown	2.10	17.50
		Never hinged	7.00	
		On cover		32.50
149	A80	1.20fr dp brn ('38)	7.00	32.00
		Never hinged	27.50	
		On cover		65.00
a.		Imperf, single	800.00	3,250.
		Never hinged	1,400.	
		On cover		8,750.
150	A80	1.50fr slate bl ('38)	4.25	32.50
		Never hinged	11.00	
		On cover		62.50
		Nos. 136-150 (14)	32.55	145.45
		Set, never hinged	97.00	

For overprints see Nos. O21-O29.

Souvenir Sheet

Josef Rheinberger — A91

1938, July 30   **Engr.**   **Perf. 12**

151		Sheet of 4	27.50	27.50
		Never hinged	70.00	
		On cover		70.00
		On first day cover		90.00
a.	A91	50rp slate gray	3.50	5.25
		Never hinged	7.00	
		On cover		11.00
		On first day cover		160.00

Third Philatelic Exhibition of Liechtenstein. Sheet size: 99¾x135mm. See No. 153.

Francis Type of 1933
Thick Wove Paper

1938, Aug. 15   **Perf. 12½**

152	A55	3fr black, *buff*	10.50	100.00
		Never hinged	21.00	
		On cover		250.00
		On first day cover		700.00

Issued in memory of Prince Francis I, who died July 25, 1938. Sheets of 20.

Josef Gabriel Rheinberger (1839-1901), German Composer and Organist — A92

1939, Mar. 31

153	A92	50rp slate green	1.10	*6.25*
		Never hinged	2.40	
		On cover		11.00
		On first day cover		140.00

Issued in sheets of 20. See No. 151.

Scene of Homage, 1718 — A93

1939, May 29

154	A93	20rp brown lake	1.40	2.75
		Never hinged	5.50	
		On cover		5.00
155	A93	30rp slate blue	1.40	2.75
		Never hinged	4.25	
		On cover		5.50
156	A93	50rp gray green	1.40	2.75
		Never hinged	4.25	
		On cover		5.00
		Nos. 154-156 (3)	4.20	8.25
		Set, never hinged	14.00	
		Set of 3 on fdc		17.50

Honoring Prince Franz Joseph II. Sheets of 20.

Cantonal Coats of Arms — A94

Prince Franz Joseph II — A96

Design: 3fr, Arms of Principality.

1939

157	A94	2fr dk green, *buff*	7.00	*42.50*
		Never hinged	17.50	
		On cover		90.00
158	A94	3fr indigo, *buff*	4.50	*42.50*
		Never hinged	10.50	
		On cover		90.00
159	A96	5fr brown, *buff*	14.00	*27.50*
		Never hinged	35.00	
		On cover		105.00
a.		Sheet of 4	90.00	140.00
		Never hinged	175.00	
		On first day cover		70.00
		Nos. 157-159 (3)	25.50	112.50
		Set, never hinged	63.00	
		Set of 3 on fdc		700.00

2fr, 3fr issued in sheets of 12; 5fr in sheets of 4.

Prince Johann as a Child
A100

Memorial Tablet
A101

Prince Johann II — A102

30rp, Prince Johann and Tower at Vaduz. 50rp, Prince Johann and Gutenberg Castle. 1fr, Prince Johann in 1920 and Vaduz Castle.

1940   **Photo.**   **Perf. 11½.**

160	A100	20rp henna brown	.70	2.75
		Never hinged	1.50	
161	A100	30rp indigo	.70	4.25
		Never hinged	1.75	
		On cover		8.50
162	A100	50rp dk slate grn	1.40	10.50
		Never hinged	3.25	
		On cover		21.00
163	A100	1fr brown vio	10.50	70.00
		Never hinged	21.00	
		On cover		135.00
164	A101	1.50fr violet blk	14.00	62.50
		Never hinged	27.50	
		On cover		125.00
165	A102	3fr brown	5.00	21.00
		Never hinged	11.00	
		On cover		55.00
		On first day cover		52.50
		Nos. 160-165 (6)	32.30	171.00
		Set, never hinged	66.00	
		Nos. 160-164 on fdc		475.00

Birth centenary of Prince Johann II. Nos. 160-164 issued in sheets of 25; No. 165 in sheets of 12.
Issue dates: 3fr, Oct. 5; others Aug. 10.

SEMI-POSTAL STAMPS

Prince Johann II — SP1   Coat of Arms — SP2

Wmk. 183

1925, Oct. 5   **Engr.**   **Perf. 11½**

B1	SP1	10rp yellow green	42.50	22.50
		Never hinged	120.00	
		On cover		52.50
B2	SP1	20rp deep red	21.00	22.50
		Never hinged	70.00	
		On cover		52.50
B3	SP1	30rp deep blue	7.00	7.00
		Never hinged	20.00	
		On cover		21.00
		Nos. B1-B3 (3)	70.50	52.00
		Set, never hinged	210.00	
		Set of 3 on fdc		625.00

85th birthday of the Prince Regent. Sold at a premium of 5rp each, the excess being devoted to charities.

1927, Oct. 5   **Typo.**

B4	SP2	10rp multicolored	10.50	*25.00*
		Never hinged	24.50	
		On cover		52.50
B5	SP2	20rp multicolored	10.50	*25.00*
		Never hinged	24.50	
		On cover		52.50
B6	SP2	30rp multicolored	5.00	*21.00*
		Never hinged	13.00	
		On cover		52.50
		Nos. B4-B6 (3)	26.00	71.00
		Set, never hinged	62.00	
		Set of 3 on fdc		525.00

87th birthday of Prince Johann II. These stamps were sold at premiums of 5, 10 and 20rp respectively. The money thus obtained was devoted to charity.

Railroad Bridge Demolished by Flood
SP3

Designs: 10rp+10rp, Inundated Village of Ruggel. 20rp+10rp, Austrian soldiers rescuing refugees. 30rp+10rp, Swiss soldiers salvaging personal effects.

1928, Feb. 6   **Litho.**   **Unwmk.**

B7	SP3	5rp + 5rp brn vio & brn	17.50	26.00
		Never hinged	55.00	
		On cover		52.50
B8	SP3	10rp + 10rp bl grn & brn	25.00	26.00
		Never hinged	55.00	
		On cover		52.50
B9	SP3	20rp + 10rp dl red & brn	25.00	26.00
		Never hinged	55.00	
		On cover		52.50

B10 SP3 30rp + 10rp dp bl
　　　& brn　　　　　　　21.00　26.00
　　Never hinged　　　　55.00
　　On cover　　　　　　　　　　52.50
　　Nos. B7-B10 (4)　　88.50　104.00
　　Set, never hinged　220.00
　　Set of 4 on fdc　　　　　　650.00

The surtax on these stamps was used to aid the sufferers from the Rhine floods.

Coat of Arms — SP7　　　Princess Elsa — SP8

Design: 30rp, Prince Francis I.

1932, Dec. 21　　　　　　**Photo.**
B11 SP7 10rp (+ 5rp) olive
　　　grn　　　　　　　　21.00　35.00
　　Never hinged　　　　55.00
　　On cover　　　　　　　　　　70.00
B12 SP8 20rp (+ 5rp) rose
　　　red　　　　　　　　21.00　37.50
　　Never hinged　　　　55.00
　　On cover　　　　　　　　　　70.00
B13 SP8 30rp (+ 10rp) ultra　28.00　37.50
　　Never hinged　　　　62.50
　　On cover　　　　　　　　　　70.00
　　Nos. B11-B13 (3)　70.00　110.00
　　Set, never hinged　172.50
　　Set of 3 on fdc　　　　　　850.00

The surtax was for the Child Welfare Fund.

Postal Museum Issue
Souvenir Sheet

SP10

1936, Oct. 24　**Litho.**　**Imperf.**
B14 SP10 Sheet of 4　17.50　50.00
　　Never hinged　　　　70.00
　　On cover　　　　　　　　　　85.00
　　On first day cover　　　　425.00

Sheet contains 2 each, Nos. 120, 122. Sold for 2fr.

AIR POST STAMPS

Airplane over Snow-capped Mountain Peaks — AP1

Airplane above Vaduz Castle — AP2

Airplane over Rhine Valley — AP3

Perf. 10½, 10½x11½
1930, Aug. 12　**Photo.**　**Unwmk.**
Gray Wavy Lines in Background
C1 AP1 15rp dark brown　10.50　17.50
　　Never hinged　　　　28.00
　　On cover　　　　　　　　　　28.00
C2 AP1 20rp slate　　　£5.00　25.00
　　Never hinged　　　　70.00
　　On cover　　　　　　　　　　35.00
C3 AP2 25rp olive brown　14.00　45.00
　　Never hinged　　　　42.50
　　On cover　　　　　　　　　　52.50
C4 AP2 35rp slate blue　21.00　42.50
　　Never hinged　　　　62.50
　　On cover　　　　　　　　　　52.50
C5 AP3 45rp olive green　50.00　87.50
　　Never hinged　　　　140.00
　　On cover　　　　　　　　　　105.00
C6 AP3 1fr lake　　　　55.00　62.50
　　Never hinged　　　　175.00
　　On cover　　　　　　　　　　92.50
　　Nos. C1-C6 (6)　175.50　280.00
　　Set, never hinged　518.00
　　Set of 6 on fdc　　　　　1,000.

For surcharge see No. C14.

Zeppelin over Naafkopf, Falknis Range AP4

Design: 2fr, Zeppelin over Valüna Valley.

1931, June 1　　　　**Perf. 11½**
C7 AP4 1fr olive black　70.00　125.00
　　Never hinged　　　　175.00
　　On cover　　　　　　　　　　140.00
C8 AP4 2fr blue black　140.00　400.00
　　Never hinged　　　　390.00
　　On cover　　　　　　　　　　425.00
　　Set, never hinged　565.00

Golden Eagle — AP6

15rp, Golden Eagle in flight, diff. 20rp, Golden Eagle in flight, diff. 30rp, Osprey. 50rp, Eagle.

1934-35
C9 AP6 10rp brt vio ('35)　10.50　55.00
　　Never hinged　　　　70.00
　　On cover　　　　　　　　　　62.50
C10 AP6 15rp red org ('35)　28.00　55.00
　　Never hinged　　　　77.50
　　On cover　　　　　　　　　　62.50
C11 AP6 20rp red ('35)　28.00　55.00
　　Never hinged　　　　90.00
　　On cover　　　　　　　　　　62.50
C12 AP6 30rp brt bl ('35)　28.00　55.00
　　Never hinged　　　　77.50
　　On cover　　　　　　　　　　62.50
C13 AP6 50rp emerald　17.50　62.50
　　Never hinged　　　　70.00
　　On cover　　　　　　　　　　65.00
　　Nos. C9-C13 (5)　112.00　282.50
　　Set, never hinged　385.00

With Grilled Gum

1936
C9a AP6　10rp brt vio　7.00　24.50
　　Never hinged　　　　21.00
　　On cover　　　　　　　　　　28.00
C10a AP6　15rp red org　21.00　55.00
　　Never hinged　　　　55.00
　　On cover　　　　　　　　　　62.50
C11a AP6　20rp red　25.00　55.00
　　Never hinged　　　　70.00
　　On cover　　　　　　　　　　62.50
C12a AP6　30rp brt bl　25.00　55.00
　　Never hinged　　　　70.00
　　On cover　　　　　　　　　　62.50
C13a AP6　50rp emerald　21.00　42.50
　　Never hinged　　　　32.50
　　On cover　　　　　　　　　　42.50
　　Nos. C9a-C13a (5)　99.00　232.00
　　Set, never hinged　250.00

No. C6 Surcharged with New Value

1935, June 24　**Perf. 10½x11½**
C14 AP3 60rp on 1fr lake　42.50　50.00
　　Never hinged　　　　160.00
　　On cover　　　　　　　　　　55.00
　　On first day cover　　　　1,750.

Airship "Hindenburg" — AP11

Design: 2fr, Airship "Graf Zeppelin."

1936, May 1　　　　**Perf. 11½**
C15 AP11 1fr rose carmine　50.00　105.00
　　Never hinged　　　　125.00
　　On cover　　　　　　　　　　105.00
C16 AP11 2fr violet　35.00　105.00
　　Never hinged　　　　35.00
　　On cover　　　　　　　　　　105.00
　　Set, never hinged　160.00

AP13

10rp, Barn swallows. 15rp, Black-headed Gulls. 20rp, Gulls. 30rp, Eagle. 50rp, Northern Goshawk. 1fr, Lammergeier. 2fr, Lammergeier.

1939, Apr. 3　　　　　　**Photo.**
C17 AP13 10rp violet　　.70　　.70
　　Never hinged　　　　1.40
　　On cover　　　　　　　　　　2.75
　　a. Grilled gum　　　　1.40　1.40
　　Never hinged　　　　2.10
C18 AP13 15rp red orange　.70　2.50
　　Never hinged　　　　1.40
　　On cover　　　　　　　　　　6.50
C19 AP13 20rp dark red　2.75　1.40
　　Never hinged　　　　8.50
　　On cover　　　　　　　　　　3.50
C20 AP13 30rp dull blue　1.75　2.75
　　Never hinged　　　　3.50
　　On cover　　　　　　　　　　5.50
C21 AP13 50rp brt green　4.25　5.00
　　Never hinged　　　　16.00
　　On cover　　　　　　　　　　10.00
C22 AP13　1fr rose car　2.75　17.50
　　Never hinged　　　　8.75
　　On cover　　　　　　　　　　32.50
C23 AP13　2fr violet　2.75　17.50
　　Never hinged　　　　8.75
　　On cover　　　　　　　　　　32.50
　　Nos. C17-C23 (7)　15.65　47.35
　　Set, never hinged　48.00

POSTAGE DUE STAMPS

National Administration of the Post Office

D1

1920　**Unwmk.**　**Engr.**　**Perf. 12½**
J1 D1 5h rose red　　.35　　.40
　　Never hinged　　　.50
　　On cover　　　　　　　　2,100.
J2 D1 10h rose red　.35　　.40
　　Never hinged　　　.50
　　On cover　　　　　　　　2,100.
J3 D1 15h rose red　.35　　.40
　　Never hinged　　　.50
　　On cover　　　　　　　　2,300.
J4 D1 20h rose red　.35　　.55
　　Never hinged　　　.50
　　On cover　　　　　　　　2,300.
J5 D1 25h rose red　.35　　.55
　　Never hinged　　　.70
　　On cover　　　　　　　　2,300.
J6 D1 30h rose red　.35　　.55
　　Never hinged　　　.70
　　On cover　　　　　　　　2,300.
J7 D1 40h rose red　.35　　.55
　　Never hinged　　　.70
　　On cover　　　　　　　　2,300.
J8 D1 50h rose red　.35　　.55
　　Never hinged　　　.70
　　On cover　　　　　　　　2,300.
J9 D1 80h rose red　.35　　.55
　　Never hinged　　　.70
　　On cover　　　　　　　　2,300.
J10 D1 1k dull blue　.40　1.40
　　Never hinged　　　1.75
　　On cover　　　　　　　　2,450.
J11 D1 2k dull blue　.40　1.40
　　Never hinged　　　1.75
　　On cover　　　　　　　　2,650.

J12 D1 5k dull blue　　.40　1.75
　　Never hinged　　　3.50
　　On cover　　　　　　　　　—
　　Nos. J1-J12 (12)　4.35　9.05
　　Set, never hinged　12.50

Nos. J1-J12 exist imperf. (value, unused, set $260) and part perf. (value, unused or used, set $7.50).

Swiss Administration of the Post Office

D2　　　　　Post Horn — D3

1928　**Litho.**　**Wmk. 183**　**Perf. 11½**
Granite Paper
J13 D2 5rp purple & or-
　　　ange　　　　　　1.40　3.50
　　Never hinged　　　3.50
　　On cover　　　　　　　　21.00
J14 D2 10rp purple & or-
　　　ange　　　　　　1.40　3.50
　　Never hinged　　　3.50
　　On cover　　　　　　　　21.00
J15 D2 15rp purple & or-
　　　ange　　　　　　2.10　14.00
　　Never hinged　　　7.00
　　On cover　　　　　　　　50.00
J16 D2 20rp purple & or-
　　　ange　　　　　　2.10　3.50
　　Never hinged　　　7.00
　　On cover　　　　　　　　21.00
J17 D2 25rp purple & or-
　　　ange　　　　　　7.00　8.50
　　Never hinged　　　21.00
　　On cover　　　　　　　　32.50
J18 D2 30rp purple & or-
　　　ange　　　　　　7.00　14.00
　　Never hinged　　　21.00
　　On cover　　　　　　　　52.50
J19 D2 40rp purple & or-
　　　ange　　　　　　7.00　14.00
　　Never hinged　　　21.00
　　On cover　　　　　　　　85.00
J20 D2 50rp purple & or-
　　　ange　　　　　　7.00　17.50
　　Never hinged　　　27.50
　　On cover　　　　　　　　140.00
　　Nos. J13-J20 (8)　35.00　78.50
　　Set, never hinged　105.00

Engraved; Value Typographed in Dark Red
1940　**Unwmk.**　**Perf. 11½**
J21 D3 5rp gray blue　1.75　2.75
　　Never hinged　　　3.50
J22 D3 10rp gray blue　.70　1.40
　　Never hinged　　　1.50
　　On cover　　　　　　　　17.50
J23 D3 15rp gray blue　1.00　5.00
　　Never hinged　　　2.00
　　On cover　　　　　　　　21.00
J24 D3 20rp gray blue　1.00　2.00
　　Never hinged　　　2.50
　　On cover　　　　　　　　17.50
J25 D3 25rp gray blue　2.00　3.50
　　Never hinged　　　4.50
　　On cover　　　　　　　　21.00
J26 D3 30rp gray blue　4.50　5.50
　　Never hinged　　　9.00
　　On cover　　　　　　　　32.50
J27 D3 40rp gray blue　4.50　5.50
　　Never hinged　　　9.00
　　On cover　　　　　　　　52.50
J28 D3 50rp gray blue　5.25　5.50
　　Never hinged　　　10.00
　　On cover　　　　　　　　70.00
　　Nos. J21-J28 (8)　20.70　31.15
　　Set, never hinged　42.00

OFFICIAL STAMPS

Regular Issue of 1930 Overprinted in Various Colors

Perf. 11½, 11½x10½ (#O5, O6)
1932　　　　　　　　　**Unwmk.**
O1 A38　5rp dk grn (Bk)　10.50　15.50
　　Never hinged　　　35.00
　　On cover　　　　　　　　32.50
　　a. Perf 10½　　　　14.00　55.00
　　Never hinged　　　55.00
　　On cover　　　　　　　　65.00
O2 A39　10rp dark vio (R)　75.00　15.50
　　Never hinged　　　275.00
　　On cover　　　　　　　　28.00
　　b. Perf 11½x10½　875.00　2,000.

Column 1 (Liechtenstein)

	Never hinged		1,400.	
	On cover			2,500.
c.	Perf 10½		100.00	42.50
	Never hinged		275.00	
	On cover			42.50
O3	A40	20rp dp rose red (Bl)	90.00	15.50
	Never hinged		275.00	
	On cover			28.00
a.	Perf. 10½		250.00	92.50
	Never hinged		675.00	
	On cover			140.00
O4	A42	30rp ultra (R)	17.50	21.00
	Never hinged		50.00	
	On cover			28.00
a.	Perf. 10½		21.00	70.00
	Never hinged		70.00	
	On cover			85.00
O5	A43	35rp dp grn (Bk) (Perf. 11½x10½)	14.00	*35.00*
	Never hinged		35.00	
	On cover			65.00
a.	Perf 11½		8,500.	*12,750.*
	Never hinged		13,500.	
	On cover			21,000.
O6	A45	50rp blk brn (Bl) (Perf. 11½x10½)	77.50	*21.00*
	Never hinged		210.00	
	On cover			42.50
a.	Perf. 11½		135.00	*325.00*
	Never hinged		550.00	
	On cover			350.00
O7	A46	60rp olive blk (R)	14.00	*50.00*
	Never hinged		42.50	
	On cover			105.00
a.	Perf 10½		14.00	*50.00*
	Never hinged		42.50	
	On cover			85.00
O8	A48	1.20fr olive brn (G)	150.00	425.00
	Never hinged		500.00	
	On cover			500.00
a.	Perf 10½		150.00	425.00
	Never hinged		460.00	
	On cover			500.00
	Nos. O1-O8 (8)		448.50	598.50
	Set, never hinged		1,763.	

Nos. 108, 110
Overprinted in Black

1933			**Perf. 14½**	
O9	A51	25rp red orange	42.50	52.50
	Never hinged		125.00	
	On cover			75.00
a.	Imperf		260.00	*525.00*
	Never hinged		525.00	
O10	A53	1.20fr red brown	85.00	*350.00*
	Never hinged		235.00	
	On cover			310.00
a.	Double overprint			475.00
	Set, never hinged		360.00	

Regular Issue of 1934-35 Ovptd. in Various Colors

1934-36			**Perf. 11½**	
O11	A58	5rp emerald (R)	2.10	*3.50*
	Never hinged		7.00	
	On cover			5.25
a.	Grilled gum		6.00	*12.00*
	Never hinged		21.00	
	On cover			15.00
O12	A59	10rp dp vio (Bk)	4.25	*3.50*
	Never hinged		14.00	
	On cover			5.25
a.	Grilled gum		1.40	*62.50*
	Never hinged		7.00	
	On cover			52.50
O13	A60	15rp red org (V)	.70	*3.50*
	Never hinged		2.10	
	On cover			5.25
O14	A61	20rp red (Bk)	.70	*3.50*
	Never hinged		2.75	
	On cover			5.25
O15	A62	25rp brown (R)	42.50	*115.00*
	Never hinged		115.00	
	On cover			97.50
O16	A62	25rp brown (Bk)	3.50	*21.00*
	Never hinged		21.00	
	On cover			22.50
O17	A63	30rp dark bl (R)	5.00	*10.50*
	Never hinged		17.50	
	On cover			15.00
O18	A66	50rp lt brown (V)	1.40	*17.50*
	Never hinged		3.50	
	On cover			9.75
O19	A68	90rp dp grn (Bk)	10.50	*10.50*
	Never hinged		35.00	
	On cover			60.00
a.	Double overprint		150.00	
	Never hinged		300.00	
O20	A69	1.50fr brown car (Bl)	42.50	*280.00*
	Never hinged		140.00	
	On cover			210.00
	Nos. O11-O20 (10)		113.15	*468.50*
	Set, never hinged		358.00	

Column 2 (Liechtenstein / Lithuania)

Regular Issue of 1937-38 Overprinted in Black, Red or Blue

1937-41				
O21	A76	5rp emerald (Bk)	.35	.75
	Never hinged		1.00	
	On cover			1.50
O22	A76	10rp vio & buff (R)	.70	2.00
	Never hinged		2.75	
	On cover			3.00
O23	A76	20rp brn org (Bl)	.70	2.00
	Never hinged		3.25	
	On cover			3.75
O24	A76	20rp brn org (Bk) ('41)	1.40	2.75
	Never hinged		4.25	
	On cover			3.75
O25	A76	25rp chestnut (Bk)	.75	2.75
	Never hinged		3.25	
	On cover			3.75
O26	A77	30rp blue & gray (Bk)	1.75	2.75
	Never hinged		8.50	
	On cover			3.00
O27	A79	50rp dk brn & buff (R)	1.00	2.10
	Never hinged		3.50	
	On cover			3.00
O28	A80	1fr red brown (Bk)	1.00	*12.00*
	Never hinged		5.50	
	On cover			15.00
O29	A80	1.50fr slate bl (Bk) ('38)	2.75	*17.50*
	Never hinged		17.50	
	On cover			19.00
	Nos. O21-O29 (9)		10.40	*44.60*
	Set, never hinged		49.50	

LITHUANIA

|li-thə-ˈwā-nē-ə

(Lietuva)

LOCATION — Northern Europe bordering on the Baltic Sea
GOVT. — Independent republic
AREA — 22,959 sq. mi.
POP. — 2,879,070 (1940)
CAPITAL — Vilnius

Lithuania was under Russian rule when it declared its independence in 1918. The League of Nations recognized it in 1922. In 1940 it became a republic in the Union of Soviet Socialist Republics.

100 Skatiku = 1 Auksinas
100 Centai = 1 Litas (1922)

Nos. 1-26 were printed in sheets of 20 (5x4) which were imperf. at the outer sides, so that only 6 stamps in each sheet were fully perforated. Values are for the stamps partly imperf. The stamps fully perforated sell for at least double these values. There was also a printing of Nos. 19-26 in a sheet of 160, composed of blocks of 20 of each stamp. Pairs or blocks with different values se-tenant sell for considerably more than the values for the stamps singly.
Nos. 1-26 are without gum.

Watermarks

Wmk. 109 — Webbing

Wmk. 144 — Network

Column 3 (Lithuania)

Wmk. 145 — Wavy Lines

Wmk. 146 — Zigzag Lines Forming Rectangles

Wmk. 147 — Parquetry

Wmk. 198 — Intersecting Diamonds

Wmk. 209 — Multiple Ovals

Wmk. 238 — Multiple Letters

First Vilnius Printing

A1

Thin Figures

Perf. 11½

1918, Dec. 27		**Unwmk.**	**Typeset**	
1	A1	10sk black	125.00	100.00
2	A1	15sk black	125.00	100.00

Second Vilnius Printing

1918, Dec. 31			**Thick Figures**	
3	A1	10sk black	70.00	55.00
4	A1	15sk black	70.00	55.00
5	A1	20sk black	30.00	16.00
6	A1	30sk black	35.00	17.50
7	A1	40sk black	50.00	25.00
8	A1	50sk black	40.00	17.50
	Nos. 3-8 (6)		295.00	186.00

Column 4 (Lithuania)

First Kaunas Issue

A2

1919, Jan. 29				
9	A2	10sk black	8.00	4.50
10	A2	15sk black	8.00	4.50
a.	"5" for "15"		95.00	72.50
11	A2	20sk black	8.00	4.50
12	A2	30sk black	8.00	4.50
	Nos. 9-12 (4)		32.00	18.00

Second Kaunas Issue

A3

1919, Feb. 18				
13	A3	10sk black	4.25	2.50
14	A3	15sk black	4.25	2.50
15	A3	20sk black	4.25	2.50
a.	"astas" for "pastas"		80.00	75.00
16	A3	30sk black	4.25	2.50
17	A3	40sk black	4.25	2.50
18	A3	50sk black	4.25	2.50
19	A3	60sk black	4.25	2.50
	Nos. 13-19 (7)		29.75	17.50

Third Kaunas Issue

A4

1919, Mar. 1				
20	A4	10sk black	4.25	2.50
21	A4	15sk black	4.25	2.50
22	A4	20sk black	4.25	2.50
23	A4	30sk black	4.25	2.50
24	A4	40sk black	4.25	2.50
25	A4	50sk black	4.25	2.50
26	A4	60sk black	4.25	2.50
	Nos. 20-26 (7)		29.75	17.50

The White Knight "Vytis"
A5   A6

A7   A8

	Perf. 10½ to 14 & Compound			
1919		**Litho.**	**Wmk. 144**	
		Gray Granite Paper		
30	A5	10sk deep rose	1.25	.40
a.	Wmk. vert.		17.50	15.00
31	A5	15sk violet	1.25	.40
a.	Wmk. vert.		17.50	15.00
32	A5	20sk dark blue	1.60	.40
33	A5	30sk deep orange	1.60	.40
a.	Wmk. vert.		17.50	15.00
34	A5	40sk dark brown	1.60	.40
35	A6	50sk blue green	1.60	.50
36	A6	75sk org & dp rose	1.60	.50
37	A7	1auk gray & rose	3.25	.50
38	A7	3auk bis brn & rose	3.25	.50
39	A7	5auk blue grn & rose	3.25	.80
	Nos. 30-39 (10)		20.25	4.80

Nos. 30a, 31a and 33a are from the first printing with watermark vertical showing points to left; various perforations.
Nos. 30-39 exist imperf. Value in pairs, $100.
Issued: Nos. 30a, 31a, 33a, 2/17/19; Nos. 30-36, 3/20/19.

Thick White Paper

1919			Wmk. 145	
40	A5	10sk dull rose	.35	.25
41	A5	15sk violet	.35	.25
42	A5	20sk dark blue	.35	.25
43	A5	30sk orange	.35	.25
44	A5	40sk red brown	.35	.25
45	A6	50sk green	.35	.25
46	A6	75sk yel & dp rose	.35	.25
47	A7	1auk gray & rose	.95	.35
48	A7	3auk yellow brn & rose, perf. 12½	.60	.40
49	A7	5auk bl grn & rose	1.00	.40
		Nos. 40-49 (10)	5.00	2.90

Nos. 40-49 exist imperf. Value in pairs, $90.

Perf. 10½ to 14 & Compound

1919, May 8			Thin White Paper	
50	A5	10sk red	.40	.25
51	A5	15sk lilac	.40	.25
52	A5	20sk dull blue	.40	.25
53	A5	30sk buff	.40	.25
54	A5	40sk gray brn	.40	.25
55	A6	50sk lt green	.40	.25
56	A6	60sk violet & red	.40	.25
57	A6	75sk bister & red	.40	.25
58	A8	1auk gray & red	.40	.25
59	A8	3auk lt brown & red	.40	.30
60	A8	5auk blue grn & red	.40	.45
		Nos. 50-60 (11)	4.40	3.00

Nos. 50-60 exist imperf. Value, pairs $150.
See Nos. 93-96. For surcharges see Nos. 114-115, 120-139, 149-150.

"Lithuania" Receiving Benediction — A9

The Spirit of Lithuania Rises — A10

"Lithuania" with Chains Broken — A11

White Knight — A12

1920, Feb. 16		Wmk. 146	Perf. 11½	
70	A9	10sk dp rose	3.75	2.25
71	A9	15sk lt violet	3.75	2.25
72	A9	20sk gray blue	3.75	2.25
73	A10	30sk yellow brn	3.75	2.25
74	A11	40sk brown & grn	3.75	2.25
75	A10	50sk deep rose	3.75	2.25
76	A10	60sk lt violet	3.75	2.25
77	A11	80sk purple & red	3.75	2.25
78	A11	1auk green & red	3.75	2.25
79	A12	3auk brown & red	3.75	2.25
80	A12	5auk green & red	3.75	2.25
a.		Right "5" dbl., grn and red	90.00	90.00
		Nos. 70-80 (11)	41.25	24.75

Anniv. of natl. independence. The stamps were on sale only 3 days in Kaunas. The stamps were available in other cities after that. Only a limited number of stamps was sold at post offices but 40,000 sets were delivered to the bank of Kaunas.
All values exist imperforate.

White Knight — A13

Grand Duke Vytautas — A14

Grand Duke Gediminas A15

Sacred Oak and Altar A16

1920, Aug. 25				
81	A13	10sk rose	.95	.50
a.		Imperf., pair	40.00	
82	A13	15sk dark violet	.95	.50
83	A14	20sk grn & lt grn	.95	.50
84	A13	30sk brown	.95	.50
a.		Pair, #82, 84	40.00	
85	A14	40sk gray grn & vio	.95	.50
86	A14	50sk brn & brn org	2.75	1.25
87	A14	60sk red & org	1.50	1.00
88	A15	80sk blk, db & red	1.50	1.00
89	A16	1auk orange & blk	1.75	1.00
90	A16	3auk green & blk	1.75	1.00
91	A16	5auk gray vio & blk	4.50	2.00
		Nos. 81-91 (11)	18.50	9.75

Opening of Lithuanian National Assembly. On sale for three days.

1920				
92	A14	20sk green & lilac	150.00	
92A	A15	40sk gray grn, buff & vio	150.00	
92B	A14	50sk brown & gray lil	150.00	
92C	A14	60sk red & green	150.00	
92D	A15	80sk black, grn & red	150.00	
		Nos. 92-92D (5)	750.00	

Nos. 92 to 92D were trial printings. By order of the Ministry of Posts, 2,000 examples of each were placed on sale at post offices.

Type of 1919 Issue

1920		Unwmk.	Perf. 11½	
93	A5	15sk lilac	5.25	4.00
94	A5	20sk deep blue	5.25	4.00

		Wmk. 109		
95	A5	20sk deep blue	4.50	4.50
96	A5	40sk gray brown	9.75	7.50
		Nos. 93-96 (4)	24.75	20.00
		Set, never hinged	35.00	

Watermark horizontal on Nos. 95-96. No. 96 exists perf. 10½x11½.

Imperf., Pairs

93a	A5	15sk	32.00	32.00
94a	A5	20sk	32.00	32.00
95a	A5	20sk	17.00	17.00
96a	A5	40sk	48.00	48.00

Sower A17

Peasant Sharpening Scythe A18

Prince Kestutis A19

Black Horseman A20

Perf. 11, 11½ and Compound

1921-22				
97	A17	10sk brt rose	.85	.55
98	A17	15sk violet	.35	.70
99	A17	20sk ultra	.25	.25
100	A18	30sk brown	2.50	1.10
101	A19	40sk red	.25	.25
102	A18	50sk olive	.35	.25
103	A18	60sk grn & vio	2.50	1.65
104	A19	80sk brn org & car	.35	.25
105	A19	1auk brown & grn	.35	.25
106	A19	2auk gray bl & red	.35	.25
107	A20	3auk yel brn & dk bl	1.00	.40
108	A17	4auk yel & dk bl ('22)	.45	.25
109	A20	5auk gray blk & rose	1.00	1.50

110	A17	8auk grn & blk ('22)	.45	.25
111	A20	10auk rose & vio	1.00	.55
112	A20	25auk bis brn & grn	1.25	.85
113	A20	100auk dl red & gray blk	12.50	8.00
		Nos. 97-113 (17)	25.75	17.30
		Set, never hinged	60.00	

Imperf., Pairs

97a	A17	10sk	—	
98a	A17	15sk	—	
99a	A17	20sk	—	
100a	A18	30sk	—	
101a	A19	40sk	25.00	
102a	A18	50sk	25.00	
103a	A18	60sk	—	
104a	A19	80sk	—	
105a	A19	1auk	—	
106a	A19	2auk	120.00	
107a	A20	3auk	120.00	
108a	A20	4auk	120.00	
110a	A17	8auk	10.00	10.00
111a	A20	10auk	50.00	
112a	A20	25auk	50.00	
113a	A20	100auk	50.00	

For surcharges see Nos. 140-148, 151-160.

No. 57 Surcharged

Perf. 12½x11½

1922, May			Wmk. 145	
114	A6	4auk on 75sk bis & red	.90	.25
		Never hinged	1.50	
a.		Inverted surcharge	35.00	35.00

Same with Bars over Original Value

115	A6	4auk on 75sk bis & red	4.00	8.00
		Never hinged	6.50	
a.		Double surcharge	30.00	30.00

Povilas Luksis — A20a

Justinas Staugaitis, Antanas Smetona, Stasys Silingas — A20b

Portraits: 40s, Lt. Juozapavicius. 50s, Dr. Basanavicius. 60s, Mrs. Petkeviciute. 1auk, Prof. Voldemaras. 2auk, Pranas Dovidaitis. 3auk, Dr. Slezevicius. 4auk, Dr. Galvanauskas. 5auk, Kazys Grinius. 6auk, Dr. Stulginskis. 8auk, Pres. Smetona.

1922		Litho.	Unwmk.	
116	A20a	20s blk & car rose	1.25	.90
		Never hinged	2.00	
116A	A20a	40s bl grn & vio	1.25	.90
		Never hinged	2.00	
116B	A20a	50s plum & grnsh bl	1.25	.90
		Never hinged	2.00	
117	A20a	60s pur & org	1.25	.90
		Never hinged	2.00	
117A	A20a	1auk car & lt bl	1.25	.90
		Never hinged	2.00	
117B	A20a	2auk dp bl & yel brn	1.25	.90
		Never hinged	2.00	
c.		Center inverted	100.00	100.00
118	A20a	3auk mar & ultra	1.25	.90
		Never hinged	2.00	
118A	A20a	4auk dk grn & red vio	1.25	.90
		Never hinged	2.00	
118B	A20a	5auk blk brn & dp rose	1.25	.90
		Never hinged	2.00	
119	A20a	6auk dk bl & grnsh bl	1.25	.90
		Never hinged	2.00	
a.		Cliché of 8auk in sheet of 6auk	175.00	175.00
119B	A20a	8auk ultra & bis	1.25	.90
		Never hinged	2.00	

119C	A20b	10auk dk vio & bl grn	1.25	.90
		Never hinged	2.00	
		Nos. 116-119C (12)	15.00	10.80

League of Nations' recognition of Lithuania. Nos. 116-119C, $1,000.

Forty sheets of the 6auk each included eight examples of the 8auk.

Stamps of 1919-22 Surcharged in Black, Carmine or Green

On Nos. 37-39

1922		Wmk. 144	Perf. 11½x12	
		Gray Granite Paper		
120	A7	3c on 1auk	125.00	225.00
		Never hinged	175.00	
121	A7	3c on 3auk	125.00	225.00
		Never hinged	175.00	
122	A7	3c on 5auk	100.00	140.00
		Never hinged	200.00	
		Nos. 120-122 (3)	350.00	590.00

White Paper
Perf. 14, 11½, 12½x11½
Wmk. 145

123	A5	1c on 10sk red	.55	1.50
124	A5	1c on 15sk lilac	.80	1.50
125	A5	1c on 20sk dull bl	.50	1.50
126	A5	1c on 30sk org	250.00	110.00
		Never hinged	350.00	
127	A5	1c on 30sk buff	.25	.40
128	A5	1c on 40sk gray brn	1.60	1.50
129	A6	2c on 50sk green	.70	1.50
130	A6	2c on 60sk vio & red	.25	.25
131	A6	2c on 75sk bis & red	.40	1.50
132	A8	3c on 1auk gray & red	.25	.25
133	A8	3c on 3auk brn & red	.25	.25
134	A8	3c on 5auk bl grn & red	.25	.25
		Nos. 123-125,127-134 (11)	5.80	10.40
		Set, never hinged, Nos. 123-125, 127-134)	24.00	

On Stamps of 1920

1922		Unwmk.	Perf. 11	
136	A5	1c on 20sk dp bl (C)	3.75	2.00

Wmk. Webbing (109)
Perf. 11, 11½

138	A5	1c on 20sk dp bl (C)	3.50	2.00
139	A5	1c on 40sk gray brn (C)	7.50	1.25

On Stamps of 1921-22

140	A18	1c on 50sk ol (C)	.25	.25
a.		Imperf., pair	45.00	
b.		Inverted surcharge	40.00	
141	A17	3c on 10sk	11.00	8.00
142	A17	3c on 15sk	.25	.25
143	A17	3c on 20sk	.40	1.50
144	A18	3c on 30sk	18.50	12.00
145	A19	3c on 40sk	.40	.40
a.		Imperf., pair		
146	A18	5c on 50sk	.25	.25
147	A18	5c on 60sk	18.50	18.50
148	A19	5c on 80sk	.55	.55
a.		Imperf., pair	35.00	15.00

Wmk. Wavy Lines (145)
Perf. 12½x11½

149	A6	5c on 4auk on 75sk (No. 114) (G)	1.60	10.00
150	A6	5c on 4auk on 75sk (No. 115) (G)	16.00	17.50

Wmk. Webbing (109)
Perf. 11, 11½

151	A19	10c on 1auk	.80	.25
a.		Inverted surcharge	55.00	
152	A19	10c on 2auk	.25	.25
a.		Inverted surcharge	50.00	
b.		Imperf., pair	45.00	
153	A17	15c on 4auk	.25	.25
a.		Inverted surcharge	45.00	
154	A20	25c on 3auk	18.50	18.50
155	A20	25c on 5auk	11.00	5.00
156	A20	25c on 10auk	2.25	1.50
a.		Imperf., pair	45.00	
157	A20	30c on 8auk (C)	1.15	.35
a.		Inverted surcharge	45.00	25.00
158	A20	50c on 25auk	3.75	2.50
160	A20	1 l on 100auk	4.00	2.50
		Nos. 136-160 (23)	124.40	105.55
		Set, never hinged	140.00	

A21

Ruin — A22

Seminary Church,
Kaunas — A23

1923	Litho.	Wmk. 109	Perf. 11	
165	A21	10c violet	6.00	.25
		Never hinged	8.50	
166	A21	15c scarlet	2.25	.25
		Never hinged	3.00	
167	A21	20c olive brown	2.25	.25
		Never hinged	3.00	
168	A21	25c deep blue	2.25	.25
		Never hinged	3.00	
169	A22	50c yellow green	2.25	.25
		Never hinged	3.00	
170	A22	60c red	2.25	.25
		Never hinged	3.00	
171	A23	1 l orange & grn	10.00	.25
		Never hinged	14.50	
172	A23	3 l red & gray	13.50	.45
		Never hinged	19.00	
173	A23	5 l brown & blue	21.00	1.00
		Never hinged	28.00	
		Nos. 165-173 (9)	61.75	3.20
		Set, never hinged	85.00	

See Nos. 189-209, 281-282. For surcharges
see Nos. B1-B42.

Memel Coat of
Arms — A24

Lithuanian Coat of Arms — A25

Biruta
Chapel — A26

Kaunas, War
Memorial
A27

Trakai
Ruins
A28

Memel Lighthouse — A29

Memel
Harbor
A30

Perf. 11, 11½, 12

1923,	Aug.		Unwmk.	
176	A24	1c rose, grn & blk	1.25	1.60
		Never hinged	2.50	
177	A25	2c dull vio & blk	1.25	1.60
		Never hinged	2.50	
178	A26	3c yellow & blk	1.25	1.60
		Never hinged	2.50	
179	A24	5c bl, buff & blk	2.50	1.90
		Never hinged	4.50	
180	A27	10c orange & blk	1.90	1.90
		Never hinged	3.50	
181	A27	15c green & blk	1.90	2.50
		Never hinged	3.50	
182	A28	25c brt vio & blk	1.90	2.50
		Never hinged	3.50	
183	A25	30c red vio & blk	4.00	5.00
		Never hinged	7.50	
184	A29	60c ol grn & blk	2.25	2.75
		Never hinged	4.00	
185	A30	1 l bl grn & blk	2.25	2.75
		Never hinged	4.00	
186	A26	2 l red & black	8.25	7.50
		Never hinged	15.00	
187	A28	3 l blue & black	8.25	7.50
		Never hinged	16.00	
188	A29	5 l ultra & black	8.25	7.50
		Never hinged	16.00	
		Nos. 176-188 (13)	45.20	46.60
		Set, never hinged	85.00	

This series was issued ostensibly to commemorate the incorporation of Memel with
Lithuania.

Type of 1923

1923		Unwmk.	Perf. 11	
189	A21	5c pale green	3.75	.50
		Never hinged	9.00	
190	A21	10c violet	5.00	.50
		Never hinged	12.00	
a.		Imperf., pair	50.00	
191	A21	15c scarlet	6.00	.50
		Never hinged	14.00	
a.		Imperf., pair	50.00	
193	A21	25c blue	10.00	.50
		Never hinged	25.00	
		Nos. 189-193 (4)	24.75	2.00
		Set, never hinged	60.00	

1923			Wmk. 147	
196	A21	2c pale brown	.50	.25
		Never hinged	1.40	
197	A21	3c olive bister	.75	.25
		Never hinged	1.60	
198	A21	5c pale green	.75	.25
		Never hinged	1.60	
199	A21	10c violet	1.50	.25
		Never hinged	3.50	
202	A21	25c deep blue	3.50	.25
		Never hinged	7.00	
a.		Imperf., pair	40.00	
204	A21	36c orange brown	5.50	.75
		Never hinged	11.00	
		Nos. 196-204 (6)	12.50	2.00
		Set, never hinged	26.00	

Perf. 11½, 14½, 11½x14½

1923-25			Wmk. 198	
207	A21	25c deep blue	750.00	450.00
		Never hinged	1,000.	
208	A22	50c deep green ('25)	25.00	.50
		Never hinged	75.00	
209	A22	60c carmine ('25)	25.00	.50
		Never hinged	75.00	

Double-barred
Cross — A31

Dr. Jonas
Basanavicius — A32

1927,	Jan.		Perf. 11½, 14½	
210	A31	2c orange	1.00	.30
		Never hinged	2.00	
211	A31	3c deep brown	1.00	.30
		Never hinged	2.00	
212	A31	5c green	1.50	.30
		Never hinged	3.50	
a.		Imperf., pair	25.00	
213	A31	10c violet	2.25	.30
		Never hinged	4.50	
214	A31	15c red	2.25	.30
		Never hinged	4.50	
a.		Imperf., pair	25.00	
215	A31	25c blue	2.25	.30
		Never hinged	4.50	
		Nos. 210-215 (6)	10.25	1.80
		Set, never hinged	21.00	

1927-29		Wmk. 147	Perf. 14½	
216	A31	5c green	30.00	150.00
		Never hinged	100.00	
217	A31	30c blue ('30)	25.00	10.00
		Never hinged	100.00	

See Nos. 233-240, 278-280.

1927	Unwmk.	Perf. 11½, 14½x11½		
219	A32	15c claret & blk	2.00	1.25
		Never hinged	4.00	
220	A32	25c dull blue & blk	2.00	1.25
		Never hinged	4.00	
221	A32	50c dk green & blk	2.00	1.25
		Never hinged	4.00	
222	A32	60c dk violet & blk	3.75	2.00
		Never hinged	8.00	
		Nos. 219-222 (4)	9.75	5.75
		Set, never hinged	20.00	

Dr. Jonas Basanavicius (1851-1927), patriot
and folklorist.

National
Arms — A33

1927,	Dec. 23	Wmk. 109	Perf. 14½	
223	A33	1 l blue grn & gray	1.25	.75
		Never hinged	3.00	
224	A33	3 l vio & pale grn	3.25	.75
		Never hinged	8.00	
225	A33	5 l brown & gray	4.50	1.25
		Never hinged	10.00	
		Nos. 223-225 (3)	9.00	2.75
		Set, never hinged	21.00	

Pres. Antanas
Smetona — A34

Decade of
Independence
A35

Dawn of
Peace — A36

1928,	Feb.		Wmk. 109	
226	A34	5c org brn & grn	1.00	.30
		Never hinged	1.50	
227	A34	10c violet & blk	1.25	.30
		Never hinged	1.90	
228	A34	15c orange & brn	1.25	.35
		Never hinged	1.90	
229	A34	25c blue & indigo	1.25	.35
		Never hinged	1.90	
230	A35	50c ultra & dl vio	1.50	.45
		Never hinged	2.25	
231	A35	60c carmine & blk	1.75	.55
		Never hinged	2.50	
232	A36	1 l blk brn & drab	2.00	.70
		Never hinged	3.00	
		Nos. 226-232 (7)	10.00	3.00
		Set, never hinged	15.00	

10th anniv. of Lithuanian independence.

Type of 1926

1929-31				
233	A31	2c orange ('31)	10.00	1.00
		Never hinged	18.50	
234	A31	5c green	2.40	.25
		Never hinged	4.75	
235	A31	10c violet ('31)	7.50	1.00
		Never hinged	14.00	
237	A31	15c red	2.75	.25
		Never hinged	5.50	
a.		Tête bêche pair	45.00	35.00
239	A31	30c dark blue	4.25	.25
		Never hinged	8.50	

			Unwmk.	
240	A31	15c red ('30)	7.50	.60
		Never hinged	14.00	
		Nos. 233-240 (6)	34.40	3.35
		Set, never hinged	65.00	

Grand Duke
Vytautas
A37

Grand Duke, Mounted
A38

1930,	Feb. 16		Perf. 14	
242	A37	2c yel brn & dk brn	.30	.25
		Never hinged	.70	
243	A37	3c dk brn & vio	.30	.25
		Never hinged	.70	
244	A37	5c yel grn & dp org	.30	.25
		Never hinged	.70	
245	A37	10c vio & emer	.30	.25
		Never hinged	.70	
246	A37	15c dp rose & vio	.30	.25
		Never hinged	.70	
247	A37	30c dk bl & brn vio	.50	.25
		Never hinged	1.25	
248	A37	36c brn vio & ol blk	.75	.30
		Never hinged	1.90	
249	A37	50c dull grn & ultra	.50	.35
		Never hinged	1.25	
250	A37	60c dk blue & rose	.50	.40
		Never hinged	1.25	
251	A38	1 l bl grn, db & red brn	2.10	1.00
		Never hinged	5.50	
252	A38	3 l dk brn, sal & dk vio	3.25	1.75
		Never hinged	8.25	
253	A38	5 l ol brn, gray & red	7.50	2.75
		Never hinged	19.00	
254	A38	10 l multicolored	20.00	16.00
		Never hinged	50.00	
255	A38	25 l multicolored	42.50	55.00
		Never hinged	110.00	
		Nos. 242-255 (14)	79.10	79.05
		Set, never hinged	200.00	

5th cent. of the death of the Grand Duke
Vytautas.

Kaunas,
Railroad
Station
A39

Cathedral at
Vilnius — A39a

Designs: 15c, 25c, Landscape on the
Neman River. 50c, Main Post Office, Kaunas.

Perf. 14, Imperf.

1932,	July 21		Wmk. 238	
256	A39	10c dk red brn & ocher	.40	.45
		Never hinged	.55	
257	A39	15c dk brown & ol	.75	.80
		Never hinged	1.10	

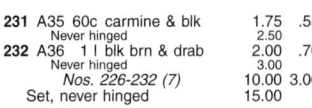

258	A39	25c dk blue & ol	1.15	1.25
		Never hinged	1.60	
259	A39	50c gray blk & ol	2.50	2.50
		Never hinged	3.50	
260	A39a	1 l dk blue & ol	6.50	5.00
		Never hinged	9.25	
261	A39a	3 l red brn & gray grn	6.50	6.50
		Never hinged	9.25	

Wmk. 198

262	A39	5c vio bl & ocher	.40	.45
		Never hinged	.55	
263	A39a	60c grnsh blk & lil	6.50	5.00
		Never hinged	9.25	
		Nos. 256-263 (8)	24.70	21.95
		Set, never hinged	35.00	

Issued for the benefit of Lithuanian orphans.

In September, 1935, a red overprint was applied to No. 259: "ORO PASTAS / LITUANICA II / 1935 / NEW YORK-KAUNAS." Value, $400.

Vytautas Fleeing from Prison, 1382 A40

Designs: 15c, 25c, Conversion of Ladislas II Jagello and Vytautas (1386). 50c, 60c, Battle at Tannenberg (1410). 1 l, 3 l, Meeting of the Nobles (1429).

1932   Wmk. 209   Perf. 14, Imperf.

264	A40	5c red & rose lake	.30	.35
		Never hinged	.75	
265	A40	10c ol bis & org brn	.35	.35
		Never hinged	.85	
266	A40	15c rose lil & ol grn	.50	.50
		Never hinged	1.00	
267	A40	25c dk vio brn & ocher	1.10	1.25
		Never hinged	2.25	
268	A40	50c dp grn & bis brn	1.10	1.75
		Never hinged	2.25	
269	A40	60c ol grn & brn car	2.25	2.50
		Never hinged	5.50	
270	A40	1 l ultra & ol grn	2.40	3.00
		Never hinged	6.00	
271	A40	3 l dk brn & dk grn	2.50	4.00
		Never hinged	6.50	
		Nos. 264-271 (8)	10.50	13.70
		Set, never hinged	25.00	

15th anniversary of independence.

A. Visteliauskas A41

Designs: 15c, 25c, Petras Vileisis. 50c, 60c, Dr. John Sliupas. 1 l, 3 l, Jonas Basanavicius.

1933   Perf. 14, Imperf.

272	A41	5c yel grn & car	.35	.30
		Never hinged	.60	
273	A41	10c ultra & car	.45	.40
		Never hinged	.80	
274	A41	15c orange & red	.55	.50
		Never hinged	1.00	
275	A41	25c dk bl & blk brn	.85	.90
		Never hinged	1.50	
276	A41	50c ol gray & dk bl	1.40	1.50
		Never hinged	2.50	
277	A41	60c org brn & chnt	4.50	4.00
		Never hinged	8.00	
277A	A41	1 l red & vio brn	5.50	4.75
		Never hinged	10.00	
277B	A41	3 l turq grn & vio brn	6.25	6.00
		Never hinged	11.00	
		Nos. 272-277B (8)	19.85	18.35
		Set, never hinged	35.00	

50th anniv. of the 1st newspaper, "Ausra," in lithuanian language.

Mother and Child — A42

Designs: 15c, 25c, Boy reading. 50c, 60c, Boy playing with blocks. 1 l, 3 l, Woman and boy at the Spinning Wheel.

1933, Sept.   Perf. 14, Imperf.

277C	A42	5c dp yel grn &	.30	.25
		Never hinged	.50	
277D	A42	10c rose brn & ultra	.30	.30
		Never hinged	.55	
277E	A42	15c ol grn & plum	.30	.45
		Never hinged	.55	
277F	A42	25c org & gray blk	1.10	1.25
		Never hinged	1.90	
277G	A42	50c ol grn & car	1.45	2.00
		Never hinged	2.50	
277H	A42	60c blk & yel org	4.75	3.25
		Never hinged	8.50	
277I	A42	1 l dk brn & ultra	5.50	3.75
		Never hinged	9.50	
277K	A42	3 l rose lil & ol grn	6.50	10.00
		Never hinged	11.00	
		Nos. 277C-277K (8)	20.20	21.25
		Set, never hinged	35.00	

Issued for the benefit of Lithuanian orphans.

Types of 1923-26

1933-34   Wmk. 238   Perf. 14

278	A31	2c orange	42.50	6.50
		Never hinged	75.00	
279	A31	10c dark violet	60.00	9.50
		Never hinged	100.00	
280	A31	15c red	42.50	4.50
		Never hinged	75.00	
281	A22	50c green	42.50	9.50
		Never hinged	75.00	
282	A22	60c red	42.50	9.50
		Never hinged	75.00	
		Nos. 278-282 (5)	230.00	39.50
		Set, never hinged	400.00	

Pres. Antanas Smetona, 60th Birthday — A43

1934   Unwmk.   Engr.   Perf. 11½

283	A43	15c red	6.50	.25
		Never hinged	11.00	

Unwmk.

284	A43	30c green	8.25	.35
		Never hinged	8.25	

Unwmk.

285	A43	60c blue	10.00	.50
		Never hinged	10.00	

Unwmk.

		Nos. 283-285 (3)	24.75	1.10
		Set, never hinged	42.50	

A44   Arms — A45

Girl with Wheat — A46

A47

Knight A48

Wmk. 198; Wmk. 209 (35c, 10 l)

1934-35   Litho.   Perf. 14

286	A44	2c rose & dull org	1.50	.25
		Never hinged	3.00	
287	A44	5c bl grn & grn	1.50	.25
		Never hinged	3.00	
288	A45	10c chocolate	3.50	.25
		Never hinged	7.50	
289	A46	25c dk brn & emer	5.50	.25
		Never hinged	10.00	
290	A46	60c Carmine	5.50	.25
		Never hinged	12.00	
291	A46	50c dk blue & blue	10.00	.25
		Never hinged	20.00	
292	A47	1 l salmon & mar	92.50	.25
		Never hinged	190.00	
293	A47	3 l grn & gray grn	.45	.25
		Never hinged	1.00	
294	A48	5 l maroon & gray bl	.65	.45
		Never hinged	1.25	
295	A48	10 l choc & yel	4.50	3.75
		Never hinged	10.00	
		Nos. 286-295 (10)	125.60	6.20
		Set, never hinged	260.00	

No. 290 exists imperf. Value, pair $65.
For overprint see No. 2N9.

1936-37   Wmk. 238   Perf. 14
Size: 17½x23mm

296	A44	2c orange ('37)	.25	.25
		Never hinged	.25	
297	A44	5c green	.30	.25
		Never hinged	.25	

Pres. Smetona A49   Arms A50

1936-37   Unwmk.

298	A49	15c carmine	5.50	.25
		Never hinged	9.00	
299	A49	30c green ('37)	7.50	.25
		Never hinged	12.00	
300	A49	60c ultra ('37)	6.75	.25
		Never hinged	11.00	
		Nos. 298-300 (3)	19.75	.75
		Set, never hinged	32.00	

Paper with Gray Network

No. 304 exists in two types:
I — "50" is fat and broad, with "0" leaning to right.
II — "50" is thinner and narrower, with "0" straight.

1937-39   Wmk. 238   Perf. 14

301	A50	10c green	.85	.25
		Never hinged	1.90	
302	A50	25c magenta	.25	.25
		Never hinged	.25	
303	A50	35c red	.50	.25
		Never hinged	1.00	
304	A50	50c brown	.30	.25
		Never hinged	.60	
305	A50	1 l dp vio bl ('39)	.35	.45
		Never hinged	.75	
		Nos. 301-305 (5)	2.25	1.45
		Set, never hinged	4.50	

For overprint see No. 2N10.

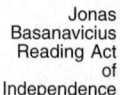

Jonas Basanavicius Reading Act of Independence A51

President Antanas Smetona A52

Perf. 13x13½
1939, Jan. 15   Engr.   Unwmk.

306	A51	15c dark red	.25	.30
		Never hinged	.50	
307	A52	30c deep green	.50	.30
		Never hinged	1.00	
308	A51	35c red lilac	.60	.45
		Never hinged	1.25	
309	A52	60c dark blue	.75	.60
		Never hinged	1.50	
a.		Souvenir sheet of 2, #308-309	5.00	15.00
		Never hinged	10.00	
b.		As "a," imperf.	35.00	72.50
		Never hinged	72.50	
		Nos. 306-309 (4)	2.10	1.65
		Set, never hinged	4.25	

20th anniv. of Independence.
Nos. 309a, 309b sold for 2 l.

Same Overprinted in Blue

1939

310	A51	15c dark red	.40	.90
		Never hinged	.85	
311	A52	30c deep green	.45	.90
		Never hinged	.90	
312	A51	35c red lilac	1.00	1.00
		Never hinged	2.00	
313	A52	60c dark blue	1.10	1.00
		Never hinged	2.25	
		Nos. 310-313 (4)	2.95	3.80
		Set, never hinged	6.00	

Recovery of Vilnius.

View of Vilnius A53

Gediminas — A54

Trakai Ruins A55

Unwmk.
1940, May 6   Photo.   Perf. 14

314	A53	15c brn & pale brn	.30	.25
		Never hinged	.75	
315	A54	30c dk grn & lt grn	.60	.85
		Never hinged	1.25	
316	A55	60c dk bl & lt bl	1.10	1.00
		Never hinged	2.25	
a.		Souv. sheet of 3, #314-316, imperf.	8.00	16.00
		Never hinged	16.00	
		Nos. 314-316 (3)	2.00	2.10
		Set, never hinged	4.25	

Return of Vilnius to Lithuania, Oct. 10, 1939.
Exist imperf.
No. 316a has simulated perforations in gold.
Sold for 2 l.

White Knight — A56   Angel — A57

Woman Releasing Dove A58   Mother and Children A59

Liberty Bell — A60   Mythical Animal — A61

1940

317	A56	5c brown carmine	.25	.30
		Never hinged	.40	
318	A57	10c green	.40	.45
		Never hinged	1.25	
319	A58	15c dull orange	.25	.30
		Never hinged	.40	
320	A59	25c light brown	.25	.40
		Never hinged	.40	
321	A60	30c Prussian green	.25	.30
		Never hinged	.45	
322	A61	35c red orange	.25	.35
		Never hinged	.60	
		Nos. 317-322 (6)	1.65	2.10
		Set, never hinged	3.00	

Nos. 317-322 exist imperf.
For overprints see Nos. 2N11-2N16.

SEMI-POSTAL STAMPS

Regular Issue of 1923-24
Surcharged in Blue, Violet or Black

On A21 On A22

On A23

1924, Feb. Wmk. 147 Perf. 11

B1	A21	2c + 2c pale brn (Bl)	.90	2.25
B2	A21	3c + 3c ol bis (Bl)	.90	2.25
B3	A21	5c + 5c pale grn (V)	.90	2.25
B4	A21	10c + 10c vio (Bk)	2.25	3.25
B5	A21	36c + 34c org brn (V)	4.75	12.00

Wmk. Webbing (109)

B6	A21	10c + 10c vio (Bk)	7.50	20.00
B7	A21	15c + 15c scar (V)	1.10	2.50
B8	A21	20c + 20c ol brn (Bl)	2.25	4.00
B9	A21	25c + 25c bl (Bk)	21.00	55.00
B10	A21	50c + 50c yel grn (V)	5.25	12.00
B11	A22	60c + 60c red (V)	5.25	12.00
B12	A23	1 l + 1 l org & grn (V)	6.00	16.00
B13	A23	3 l + 2 l red & gray (V)	9.00	32.50
B14	A23	5 l + 3 l brn & bl (V)	15.00	40.00

Unwmk.

B15	A21	25c + 25c dp bl (Bk)	4.75	12.00
		Nos. B1-B15 (15)	86.80	228.00
		Set, never hinged	225.00	

For War Invalids

Semi-Postal Stamps of 1924 Surcharged in Gold or Copper

1926, Dec. 3 Wmk. 147

B16	A21	1 + 1c on #B1	1.00	1.25
a.		Inverted surcharge	40.00	
B17	A21	2 + 2c on #B2 (C)	1.00	1.25
B19	A21	2 + 2c on #B3	1.00	1.25
a.		Double surch., one inverted	40.00	
B20	A21	5 + 5c on #B4	2.00	2.00
B21	A21	14 + 14c on #B5	6.00	7.00

Wmk. Webbing (109)

B22	A21	5 + 5c on #B6	10.00	10.00
B23	A21	5 + 5c on #B7	2.00	2.00
B24	A21	10 + 10c on #B8	2.00	2.00
B25	A21	10 + 10c on #B9	65.00	65.00

Unwmk.

B26	A21	10 + 10c on #B15	4.00	5.00

Surcharged in Copper or Silver

On A22 On A23

Wmk. Webbing (109)

B27	A22	20 + 20c on #B10	4.00	5.00
B28	A22	25 + 25c on #B11 (S)	6.00	7.00
B29	A23	30 + 30c on #B12 (S)	9.00	11.00
		Nos. B16-B29 (13)	113.00	119.75
		Set, never hinged	225.00	

For War Orphans

Surcharged in Gold

1926, Dec. 3 Wmk. 147

B30	A21	1 + 1c on #B1	.90	.90
B31	A21	2 + 2c on #B2	.90	.90
B32	A21	2 + 2c on #B3	.90	.90
a.		Inverted surcharge	30.00	
B33	A21	5 + 5c on #B4	2.00	2.25
B34	A21	19 + 19c on #B5	4.00	5.00

Wmk. Webbing (109)

B35	A21	5 + 5c on #B6	10.00	10.00
B36	A21	10 + 10c on #B7	1.75	2.00
B37	A21	15 + 15c on #B8	2.00	2.25
B38	A21	15 + 15c on #B9	65.00	65.00

Unwmk.

B39	A21	15 + 15c on #B15	3.00	3.00

Surcharged in Gold

On A22 On A23

Wmk. 109

B40	A22	25c on #B10	5.00	6.00
B41	A22	30c on #B11	8.00	7.00
B42	A23	50c on #B12	10.00	11.00
		Nos. B30-B42 (13)	113.45	116.20
		Set, never hinged	225.00	

Javelin throwing — SP1

Natl. Olympiad, July 15-20: 5c+5c, Archery. 30c+10c, Diving. 60c+15c, Running.

Unwmk.

1938, July 13 Photo. Perf. 14

B43	SP1	5c + 5c grn & dk grn	2.50	6.50
		Never hinged	6.50	
B44	SP1	15c + 5c org & red org	2.50	6.50
		Never hinged	6.50	
B45	SP1	30c + 10c bl & dk bl	4.50	12.00
		Never hinged	12.00	
B46	SP1	60c + 15c tan & brn	5.75	16.00
		Never hinged	17.50	
		Nos. B43-B46 (4)	15.25	41.00
		Set, never hinged	42.50	

Same Overprinted in Red, Blue or Black

Nos. B47, B50 Nos. B48-B49

1938, July 13

B47	SP1	5c + 5c (R)	6.00	7.50
		Never hinged	12.00	
B48	SP1	15c + 5c (Bl)	6.00	7.50
		Never hinged	12.00	
B49	SP1	30c + 10c (R)	7.50	7.50
		Never hinged	16.00	
B50	SP1	60c + 15c (Bk)	10.00	12.50
		Never hinged	20.00	
		Nos. B47-B50 (4)	29.50	35.00
		Set, never hinged	60.00	

National Scout Jamboree, July 12-14. Forged cancellations exist.

Basketball Players
SP6 SP7

Flags of Competing Nations and Basketball — SP8

1939 Photo. Perf. 14

B52	SP6	15c + 10c copper brn & brn	3.25	6.50
		Never hinged	6.50	
B53	SP7	30c + 15c myrtle grn & grn	3.25	6.50
		Never hinged	6.50	
B54	SP8	60c + 40c blue vio & gray vio	6.00	12.00
		Never hinged	12.00	
		Nos. B52-B54 (3)	12.50	25.00
		Set, never hinged	25.00	

3rd European Basketball Championships held at Kaunas. The surtax was used for athletic equipment. Nos. B52-B54 exist imperf. Value, set pairs, $500.

AIR POST STAMPS

Winged Posthorn AP1

Airplane over Neman River — AP2

Air Squadron AP3

Plane over Gediminas Castle — AP4

1921 Litho. Wmk. 109 Perf. 11½

C1	AP1	20sk ultra	1.25	.75
		Never hinged	3.25	
C2	AP1	40sk red orange	1.00	.75
		Never hinged	2.50	
C3	AP1	60sk green	1.10	.75
		Never hinged	2.75	
a.		Imperf., pair	45.00	
C4	AP1	80sk lt rose	1.50	.75
		Never hinged	3.75	
a.		Horiz. pair, imperf. vert.	50.00	40.00
C5	AP2	1auk green & red	1.50	.75
		Never hinged	3.75	
a.		Imperf., pair	90.00	175.00
C6	AP3	2auk brown & blue	1.60	.75
		Never hinged	4.00	
C7	AP4	5auk slate & yel	2.00	1.75
		Never hinged	5.00	
		Nos. C1-C7 (7)	9.95	6.25
		Set, never hinged	25.00	

For surcharges see Nos. C21-C26, C29.

Allegory of Flight — AP5

1921, Nov. 6

C8	AP5	20sk org & gray bl	1.40	1.50
		Never hinged	2.50	
C9	AP5	40sk dl bl & lake	1.40	1.50
		Never hinged	2.50	
C10	AP5	60sk vio bl & ol grn	1.40	1.50
		Never hinged	2.50	
C11	AP5	80sk ocher & dp grn	1.40	1.50
		Never hinged	2.50	
a.		Vert. pair, imperf. btwn.	35.00	35.00
C12	AP5	1auk bl grn & bl	1.40	1.50
		Never hinged	2.50	
C13	AP5	2auk gray & brn org	1.40	1.50
		Never hinged	2.50	
C14	AP5	5auk dl lil & Prus bl	1.40	1.50
		Never hinged	2.50	
		Nos. C8-C14 (7)	9.80	10.50
		Set, never hinged	17.50	

Opening of airmail service.

Plane over Kaunas — AP6

Black Overprint

1922, July 16 Perf. 11, 11½

C15	AP6	1auk ol brn & red	1.00	2.75
		Never hinged	3.25	
a.		Imperf., pair	60.00	
C16	AP6	3auk violet & grn	1.00	2.75
		Never hinged	3.25	
C17	AP6	5auk dp blue & yel	1.00	4.00
		Never hinged	3.25	
		Nos. C15-C17 (3)	3.00	9.50
		Set, never hinged	9.75	

Nos. C15-C17, without overprint, were to be for the founding of the Air Post service but they were not put in use at that time. Subsequently the word "ZENKLAS" (stamp) was overprinted over "ISTEIGIMAS" (founding) and the date "1921, VI, 25" was obliterated by short vertical lines.
For surcharge see No. C31.

Plane over Gediminas Castle — AP7

1922, July 22

C18	AP7	2auk blue & rose	1.10	.85
		Never hinged	1.60	
C19	AP7	4auk brown & rose	1.10	.85
		Never hinged	1.60	
C20	AP7	10auk black & gray bl	1.25	1.40
		Never hinged	1.80	
		Nos. C18-C20 (3)	3.45	3.10
		Set, never hinged	10.00	

For surcharges see Nos. C27-C28, C30.

Nos. C1-C7, C17-C20 Surcharged like Regular Issues in Black or Carmine

1922

C21	AP1	10c on 20sk	3.25	2.50
		Never hinged	5.75	
C22	AP1	10c on 40sk	1.75	1.50
		Never hinged	3.00	
C23	AP1	10c on 60sk	1.75	1.50
		Never hinged	3.00	
a.		Inverted surcharge	45.00	
C24	AP1	10c on 80sk	1.75	1.50
		Never hinged	3.00	
C25	AP2	20c on 1auk	11.00	6.00
		Never hinged	20.00	
C26	AP3	20c on 2auk	11.00	7.50
		Never hinged	20.00	
a.		Without "CENT"	200.00	140.00
C27	AP7	25c on 2auk	1.00	*1.00*
		Never hinged	1.75	
a.		Inverted surcharge	45.00	40.00
C28	AP7	30c on 4auk (C)	1.00	*1.00*
		Never hinged	1.75	
a.		Double surcharge	50.00	45.00
C29	AP4	50c on 5auk	2.00	1.50
		Never hinged	3.50	
C30	AP7	50c on 10auk	1.00	*1.00*
		Never hinged	1.75	
a.		Inverted surcharge	50.00	45.00
C31	AP6	1 l on 5auk	16.00	15.00
		Never hinged	29.00	
a.		Double surcharge	50.00	
		Nos. C21-C31 (11)	51.50	40.00
		Set, never hinged	92.50	

Airplane and Carrier Pigeons AP8

"Flight" AP9

1924, Jan. 28　　Wmk. 147　　*Perf. 11*

C32	AP8	20c yellow	1.15	.75
		Never hinged	5.00	
C33	AP8	40c emerald	1.15	.75
		Never hinged	5.00	
a.		Horiz. or vert. pair, imperf. between	60.00	
C34	AP8	60c rose	1.15	.75
		Never hinged	5.00	
a.		Imperf., pair	75.00	
C35	AP9	1 l dk brown	2.50	.75
		Never hinged	10.00	
		Nos. C32-C35 (4)	5.95	3.00
		Set, never hinged	25.00	

Most stamps, if not all, of the "unwatermarked" varieties show faint traces of watermark, according to experts.

For surcharges see Nos. CB1-CB4.

Swallow — AP10

1926, June 17　　Wmk. 198　　*Perf. 14½*

C37	AP10	20c carmine rose	1.10	.75
		Never hinged	1.50	
a.		Horiz. or vert. pair, imperf. between	55.00	
C38	AP10	40c violet & red org	1.10	.75
		Never hinged	1.50	
a.		Horiz. or vert. pair, imperf. between	55.00	
C39	AP10	60c blue & black	2.25	.75
		Never hinged	3.00	
a.		Horiz. or vert. pair, imperf. between	55.00	
c.		Center inverted	250.00	160.00
		Nos. C37-C39 (3)	4.45	2.25
		Set, never hinged	6.00	

Juozas Tubelis — AP11

Vytautas and Airplane over Kaunas AP12

Vytautas and Antanas Smetona AP13

1930, Feb. 16　　Wmk. 109　　*Perf. 14*

C40	AP11	5c blk, bis & brn	.70	.35
		Never hinged	1.75	
C41	AP11	10c dk bl, db & blk	.70	.35
		Never hinged	1.75	
C42	AP11	15c mar, gray & bl	.70	.35
		Never hinged	1.75	
C43	AP12	20c dk brn, org & dl red	.70	.80
		Never hinged	1.75	
C44	AP12	40c dk bl, lt bl & vio	1.25	.80
		Never hinged	3.25	
C45	AP13	60c bl grn, lil & blk	2.00	.85
		Never hinged	5.50	
C46	AP13	1 l dl red, lil & blk	3.75	1.60
		Never hinged	9.50	
		Nos. C40-C46 (7)	9.80	5.10
		Set, never hinged	25.00	

5th cent. of the death of the Grand Duke Vytautas.

Map of Lithuania, Klaipeda and Vilnius — AP14

15c, 20c, Airplane over Neman. 40c, 60c, City Hall, Kaunas. 1 l, 2 l, Church of Vytautas, Kaunas.

Wmk. Multiple Letters (238)

1932, July 21　　*Perf. 14, Imperf.*

C47	AP14	5c ver & ol grn	.25	*.65*
		Never hinged	1.00	
C48	AP14	10c dk red brn & ocher	.25	*.65*
		Never hinged	1.00	
C49	AP14	15c dk bl & org yel	.25	*.65*
		Never hinged	1.00	
C50	AP14	20c sl blk & org	1.40	.90
		Never hinged	1.00	
C51	AP14	60c ultra & ocher	1.90	*3.50*
		Never hinged	7.50	
C52	AP14	2 l dk bl & yel	2.00	*4.50*
		Never hinged	8.50	

Wmk. 198

C53	AP14	40c vio brn & yel	1.60	*5.00*
		Never hinged	6.50	
C54	AP14	1 l vio brn & grn	2.25	*5.75*
		Never hinged	8.50	
		Nos. C47-C54 (8)	9.90	21.60
		Set, never hinged	40.00	

Issued for the benefit of Lithuanian orphans.

Mindaugas in the Battle of Shauyai, 1236 — AP15

15c, 20c, Coronation of Mindaugas (1253). 40c, Grand Duke Gediminas and his followers. 60c, Founding of Vilnius by Gediminas (1332).

1 l, Gediminas capturing the Russian Fortifications. 2 l, Grand Duke Algirdas before Moscow (1368).

Perf. 14, Imperf.

1932, Nov. 28　　　　Wmk. 209

C55	AP15	5c grn & red lil	.25	.75
		Never hinged	.90	
C56	AP15	10c emer & rose	.25	.75
		Never hinged	.90	
C57	AP15	15c rose vio & bis brn	.25	.75
		Never hinged	.90	
C58	AP15	20c rose red & blk brn	1.00	*1.00*
		Never hinged	3.75	
C59	AP15	40c choc & dk gray	1.50	*3.50*
		Never hinged	5.50	
C60	AP15	60c org & gray blk	1.90	*6.50*
		Never hinged	7.00	
C61	AP15	1 l rose vio & grn	2.25	*5.50*
		Never hinged	8.00	
C62	AP15	2 l dp bl & brn	2.50	*7.50*
		Never hinged	9.00	
		Nos. C55-C62 (8)	9.90	26.25
		Set, never hinged	36.00	

Anniv. of independence.

Nos. C58-C62 exist with overprint "DARIUS-GIRENAS / NEW YORK-1933- KAUNAS" below small plane. The overprint was applied in New York with the approval of the Lithuanian consul general. Lithuanian postal authorities seem not to have been involved in the creation or release of these overprints.

Trakai Castle, Home of the Grand Duke Kestutis — AP16

Designs: 15c, 20c, Meeting of Kestutís and the Hermit Birute. 40c, 60c, Hermit Birute. 1 l, 2 l, Kestutis and his Brother Algirdas.

1933, May 6　　　　*Perf. 14, Imperf.*

C63	AP16	5c ol gray & dp bl	.50	.45
		Never hinged	.70	
C64	AP16	10c gray vio & org brn	.50	.45
		Never hinged	.70	
C65	AP16	15c dp blue & lilac	.80	.60
		Never hinged	1.10	
C66	AP16	20c org brn & lilac	1.75	1.00
		Never hinged	2.50	
C67	AP16	40c lt ultra & lilac	3.50	1.75
		Never hinged	5.00	
C68	AP16	60c brown & lt ultra	5.00	3.50
		Never hinged	7.00	
C69	AP16	1 l ol gray & dp bl	6.00	4.00
		Never hinged	8.50	
C70	AP16	2 l vio gray & yel grn	7.00	8.00
		Never hinged	9.50	
		Nos. C63-C70 (8)	25.05	19.75
		Set, never hinged	35.00	

Reopening of air service to Berlin-Kaunas-Moscow, and 550th anniv. of the death of Kestutis.

Joseph Maironis — AP17

Joseph Tumas-Vaizgantas — AP17a

Designs: 40c, 60c, Vincas Kudirka. 1 l, 2 l, Julia A. Zemaite.

1933, Sept. 15　　　　*Perf. 14, Imperf.*

C71	AP17	5c crim & dp bl	.35	*.65*
		Never hinged	1.10	
C72	AP17	10c bl vio & grn	.35	*.65*
		Never hinged	1.10	

C73	AP17a	15c dk grn & choc	.35	*.65*
		Never hinged	1.10	
C74	AP17a	20c brn car & ultra	.55	*.90*
		Never hinged	1.75	
C75	AP17	40c red brn & ol grn	1.25	*1.50*
		Never hinged	3.75	
C76	AP17	60c dk bl & choc	1.50	*2.50*
		Never hinged	4.50	
C77	AP17	1 l citron & indigo	2.25	*3.50*
		Never hinged	6.75	
C78	AP17	2 l dp grn & red brn	3.50	*5.75*
		Never hinged	10.00	
		Nos. C71-C78 (8)	10.10	16.10
		Set, never hinged	30.00	

Issued for the benefit of Lithuanian orphans.

Capts. Steponas Darius and Stasys Girenas AP18

Ill-Fated Plane "Lituanica" AP19

The Dark Angel of Death — AP20

"Lituanica" over Globe — AP21

"Lituanica" and White Knight — AP22

Perf. 11½

1934, May 18　　Unwmk.　　Engr.

C79	AP18	20c scarlet & blk	.25	.25
		Never hinged	.25	
C80	AP19	40c dp rose & bl	.25	.25
		Never hinged	.25	
C81	AP18	60c dk vio & blk	.25	.25
		Never hinged	.25	
C82	AP20	1 l black & rose	.35	.25
		Never hinged	.35	
C83	AP21	3 l gray grn & org	.45	.50
		Never hinged	.90	
C84	AP22	5 l dk brn & bl	1.75	3.25
		Never hinged	3.50	
		Nos. C79-C84 (6)	3.30	4.75
		Set, never hinged	5.50	

Death of Capts. Steponas Darius and Stasys Girenas on their New York-Kaunas flight of 1933.

No. C80 exists with diagonal overprint: "F. VAITKUS / nugalejo Atlanta / 21-22-IX-1935." Value $300.

Felix Waitkus and Map of Transatlantic Flight — AP23

Wmk. 238

1936, Mar. 24　　Litho.　　*Perf. 14*

C85	AP23	15c brown lake	2.25	.85
		Never hinged	3.25	
C86	AP23	30c dark green	3.25	.85
		Never hinged	4.50	
C87	AP23	60c blue	4.50	2.50
		Never hinged	6.00	
		Nos. C85-C87 (3)	10.00	4.20
		Set, never hinged	13.75	

Transatlantic Flight of the Lituania II, Sept. 21-22, 1935.

AIR POST SEMI-POSTAL STAMPS

Nos. C32-C35 Surcharged like Nos. B1-B9 (No. CB1), Nos. B10-B11 (Nos. CB2-CB3), and Nos. B12-B14 (No. CB4) in Red, Violet or Black

1924		**Wmk. 147**		**Perf. 11**
CB1	AP8	20c + 20c yellow (R)	12.00	12.00
		Never hinged	20.00	
CB2	AP8	40c + 40c emerald (V)	12.00	12.00
		Never hinged	20.00	
CB3	AP8	60c + 60c rose (V)	12.00	12.00
		Never hinged	20.00	
CB4	AP9	1 l + 1 l dk brown	12.00	12.00
		Never hinged	20.00	
		Nos. CB1-CB4 (4)	48.00	48.00
		Set, never hinged	80.00	

Surtax for the Red Cross. See note following No. C35.

SOUTH LITHUANIA

GRODNO DISTRICT

Russian Stamps of 1909-12 Surcharged in Black or Red

1919		**Unwmk.**	**Perf. 14, 14½x15**	
L1	A14	50sk on 3k red	60.00	57.50
a.		Double surcharge	250.00	250.00
L2	A14	50sk on 5k claret	60.00	57.50
a.		Imperf., pair	550.00	475.00
L3	A15	50sk on 10k dk bl (R)	60.00	57.50
L4	A11	50sk on 15k red brn & bl	60.00	57.50
a.		Imperf., pair	650.00	550.00
L5	A11	50sk on 25k grn & gray vio (R)	60.00	57.50
L6	A11	50sk on 35k red brn & grn	60.00	57.50
L7	A8	50sk on 50k vio & grn	60.00	57.50
L8	A11	50sk on 70k brn & org	60.00	57.50
		Nos. L1-L8 (8)	480.00	460.00

Excellent counterfeits are plentiful.
This surcharge exists on Russia No. 119, the imperf. 1k orange of 1917. Value, unused $90, used $60.

OCCUPATION STAMPS

The issue formerly listed as Lithuania 1N1-1N12 is now listed as Russia 1N1-1N12.

Issued under Russian Occupation

Lithuanian Stamps of 1937-40 Overprinted in Red or Blue

1940		**Wmk. 238**		**Perf. 14**
2N9	A44	2c orange (Bl)	.25	.25
		Never hinged	.30	
2N10	A50	50c brown (Bl)	.25	.25
		Unwmk.		
		Never hinged	.75	
2N11	A56	5c brown car (Bl)	.25	.40
		Never hinged	.30	
2N12	A57	10c green (R)	3.75	3.75
		Never hinged	10.00	
2N13	A58	15c dull orange (Bl)	.25	.25
		Never hinged	.30	
2N14	A59	25c lt brown (R)	.25	.25
		Never hinged	.65	
2N15	A60	30c Prus green (R)	.25	.25
		Never hinged	.65	
2N16	A61	35c red orange (Bl)	.35	.35
		Never hinged	.90	
		Nos. 2N9-2N16 (8)	5.60	5.75
		Set, never hinged	13.50	

Values for used stamps are for CTOs. Postally used examples are considerably more.
The Lithuanian Soviet Socialist Republic was proclaimed July 21, 1940.

LOURENCO MARQUES

lə-'ren͜t͜s-͜ə͜sō-͜mär-'kes

LOCATION — In the southern part of Mozambique in Southeast Africa
GOVT. — Part of Portuguese East Africa Colony
AREA — 28,800 sq. mi. (approx.)
POP. — 474,000 (approx.)
CAPITAL — Lourenço Marques

Stamps of Mozambique replaced those of Lourenço Marques in 1920. See Mozambique.

1000 Reis = 1 Milreis
100 Centavos = 1 Escudo (1913)

King Carlos — A1

Perf. 11½, 12½, 13½

			Typo.	**Unwmk.**	
1895					
1	A1	5r yellow		1.00	.25
2	A1	10r redsh violet		1.00	.35
3	A1	15r chocolate		1.50	.50
4	A1	20r lavender		1.50	.50
5	A1	25r blue green		1.50	.30
a.		Perf. 11½		3.50	1.00
6	A1	50r light blue		2.00	1.00
a.		Perf. 13½		15.00	5.00
b.		Perf. 11½		—	—
7	A1	75r rose		3.00	1.25
8	A1	80r yellow grn		4.75	3.00
9	A1	100r brn, yel		3.50	1.00
a.		Perf. 12½		5.00	3.25
10	A1	150r car, rose		5.00	3.00
11	A1	200r dk bl, bl		6.00	3.00
12	A1	300r dk bl, sal		7.50	4.00
		Nos. 1-12 (12)		38.25	18.15

For surcharges and overprints see Nos. 29, 58-69, 132-137, 140-143, 156-157, 160.

Saint Anthony of Padua Issue

Regular Issues of Mozambique, 1886 and 1894, Overprinted in Black

1895		**Without Gum**	**Perf. 12½**	
		On 1886 Issue		
13	A2	5r black	20.00	12.00
14	A2	10r green	25.00	12.00
15	A2	20r rose	35.00	14.00
16	A2	25r lilac	40.00	14.00
17	A2	40r chocolate	35.00	15.00
18	A2	50r bl, perf. 13½	30.00	14.00
a.		Perf. 12½	50.00	27.50
19	A2	100r yellow brn	110.00	90.00
20	A2	200r gray vio	42.50	32.50
21	A2	300r orange	70.00	40.00
		On 1894 Issue		
		Perf. 11½		
22	A3	5r yellow	35.00	25.00
23	A3	10r redsh vio	40.00	15.00
24	A3	50r light blue	50.00	32.50
a.		Perf. 12½	275.00	275.00
25	A3	75r rose, perf. 12½	65.00	50.00
26	A3	80r yellow grn	80.00	65.00
27	A3	100r brown, buff	350.00	160.00
28	A3	150r car, rose, perf. 12½	50.00	40.00
		Nos. 13-28 (16)	1,077.	631.00

No. 12 Surcharged in Black

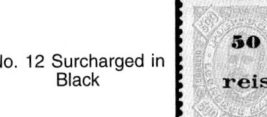

1897, Jan. 2

29	A1	50r on 300r	200.00	150.00

Most examples of No. 29 were issued without gum.

King Carlos — A2

1898-1903			**Perf. 11½**	
		Name, Value in Black except 500r		
30	A2	2½r gray	.35	.30
31	A2	5r orange	.35	.30
32	A2	10r lt green	.35	.30
33	A2	15r brown	1.25	.85
34	A2	15r gray green ('03)	.75	.50
a.		Imperf.		
35	A2	20r gray violet	.65	.40
a.		Imperf.		
36	A2	25r sea green	.70	.40
a.		Perf. 13½	25.00	8.50
b.		25r light green (error)	30.00	30.00
c.		Perf. 12½	40.00	35.00
37	A2	25r car ('03)	.35	.30
a.		Imperf.		
38	A2	50r blue	2.00	.50
39	A2	50r brown ('03)	.90	.75
40	A2	65r dull bl ('03)	25.00	8.50
41	A2	75r rose	2.00	1.50
42	A2	75r lilac ('03)	1.25	.95
a.		Imperf.		
43	A2	80r violet	2.50	1.25
44	A2	100r dk blue, blue	1.75	.65
a.		Perf. 13½	14.50	5.00
45	A2	115r org brn, pink ('03)	6.00	5.00
46	A2	130r brn, straw ('03)	6.00	5.00
47	A2	150r brn, straw	2.25	1.40
48	A2	200r red lil, pnksh	2.75	1.25
49	A2	300r dk bl, rose	3.25	1.50
50	A2	400r dl bl, straw ('03)	7.00	5.00
51	A2	500r blk & red, bl ('01)	6.00	3.00
52	A2	700r vio, yelsh ('01)	12.00	7.00
		Nos. 30-52 (23)	85.40	46.60

For surcharges and overprints see Nos. 57, 71-74, 76-91, 138, 144-155.

Coat of Arms — A3

Surcharged On Upper and Lower Halves of Stamp

1899			**Imperf.**	
53	A3	5r on 10r grn & brn	20.00	7.00
54	A3	25r on 10r grn & brn	20.00	7.00
55	A3	50r on 30r grn & brn	30.00	11.00
a.		Inverted surcharge		
56	A3	50r on 800r grn & brn	40.00	20.00
		Nos. 53-56 (4)	110.00	45.00

The lower half of No. 55 can be distinguished from that of No. 56 by the background of the label containing the word "REIS." The former is plain, while the latter is formed of white intersecting curved horizontal lines over vertical shading of violet brown.

Values are for undivided stamps. Halves sell for ¼ as much.

Most examples of Nos. 53-56 were issued without gum. Values are for stamps without gum. Values for stamps with gum are two times the values shown.

No. 41 Surcharged in Black

1899			**Perf. 11½**	
57	A2	50r on 75r rose	6.00	2.50

Most examples of No. 57 were issued without gum. Values are for stamp without gum.

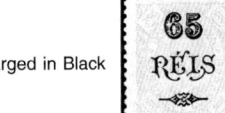

Surcharged in Black

On Issue of 1895

1902			**Perf. 11½, 12½**	
58	A1	65r on 5r yellow	6.00	2.50
59	A1	65r on 15r choc	6.00	2.50
60	A1	65r on 20r lav	7.00	2.50
a.		Perf. 12½	25.00	15.00
61	A1	115r on 10r red vio	7.00	3.00
62	A1	115r on 200r bl, bl	7.00	3.00
63	A1	115r on 300r bl, sal	7.00	3.00
64	A1	130r on 25r grn, perf. 12½	4.00	2.00
a.		Perf. 11½	30.00	22.50
65	A1	130r on 80r yel grn	4.00	3.00
66	A1	130r on 150r car, rose	5.00	3.00
67	A1	400r on 50r lt bl	8.00	6.00
68	A1	400r on 75r rose	8.00	6.00
69	A1	400r on 100r brn, buff	9.00	6.00

On Newspaper Stamp of 1893

70	N1	65r on 2½ brn	5.00	2.00
		Nos. 58-70 (13)	81.00	44.50

Surcharge exists inverted on Nos. 61, 70.
Nos. 64, 67 and 68 have been reprinted on thin white paper with shiny white gum and clean-cut perforation 13½. Value $6 each.
For overprints see Nos. 132-137, 140-143, 156-157, 160.

Issue of 1898-1903 Overprinted in Black

1903			**Perf. 11½**	
71	A2	15r brown	2.00	.85
72	A2	25r sea green	1.50	.85
73	A2	50r blue	2.50	.85
74	A2	75r rose	3.00	1.40
a.		Inverted overprint	50.00	50.00
		Nos. 71-74 (4)	9.00	3.95

Surcharged in Black

1905				
76	A2	50r on 65r dull blue	4.00	2.00

Regular Issues Overprinted in Carmine or Green

1911				
77	A2	2½r gray	.30	.25
78	A2	5r orange	.30	.25
a.		Double overprint	10.00	10.00
b.		Inverted overprint	10.00	10.00
79	A2	10r lt grn	.40	.35
80	A2	15r gray grn	.40	.35
a.		Inverted overprint	10.00	10.00
81	A2	20r dl vio	.40	.40
82	A2	25r car (G)	.90	.50
83	A2	50r brown	.80	.50
84	A2	75r lilac	1.00	.50
85	A2	100r dk bl, bl	.80	.55
86	A2	115r org brn, pink	9.00	3.50
87	A2	130r brn, straw	.80	.60
88	A2	200r red lil, pnksh	.85	.60
89	A2	400r dl bl, straw	1.25	1.10
90	A2	500r blk & red, bl	1.50	1.10
91	A2	700r vio, yelsh	1.75	1.25
		Nos. 77-91 (15)	20.45	11.80

Vasco da Gama Issue of Various Portuguese Colonies Common Design Types Surcharged

1913			**Perf. 12½-16**	
		On Stamps of Macao		
92	CD20	¼c on ½a bl grn	2.25	2.25
93	CD21	½c on 1a red	2.25	2.25
94	CD22	1c on 2a red vio	2.25	2.25
95	CD23	2½c on 4a yel grn	2.25	2.25
96	CD24	5c on 8a dk bl	2.25	2.25
97	CD25	7½c on 12a vio brn	4.25	4.25

98	CD26	10c on 16a bis brn	3.50	3.50
a.		Inverted surcharge	40.00	40.00
99	CD27	15c on 24a bister	3.75	3.75
		Nos. 92-99 (8)	22.75	22.75

On Stamps of Portuguese Africa

100	CD20	¼c on 2½r bl grn	1.75	1.75
101	CD21	½c on 5r red	1.75	1.75
102	CD22	1c on 10r red vio	1.75	1.75
103	CD23	2½c on 25r yel grn	1.75	1.75
104	CD24	5c on 50r dk bl	1.75	1.75
105	CD25	7½c on 75r vio brn	4.00	4.00
106	CD26	10c on 100r bis brn	2.75	2.75
107	CD27	15c on 150r bis	2.75	2.75
		Nos. 100-107 (8)	18.25	18.25

On Stamps of Timor

108	CD20	¼c on ½a bl grn	1.75	1.75
109	CD21	½c on 1a red	1.75	1.75
110	CD22	1c on 2a red vio	1.75	1.75
111	CD23	2½c on 4a yel grn	1.75	1.75
112	CD24	5c on 8a dk bl	2.00	1.75
113	CD25	7½c on 12a vio brn	4.00	4.00
114	CD26	10c on 16a bis brn	2.75	2.75
115	CD27	15c on 24a bister	2.75	2.75
		Nos. 108-115 (8)	18.50	18.25
		Nos. 92-115 (24)	59.50	59.25

Ceres — A4

1914   Typo.   Perf. 15x14
Name and Value in Black
Chalky Paper

116	A4	¼c olive brn	.35	.35
		Never hinged	.60	
117	A4	½c black	.35	.35
		Never hinged	.60	
118	A4	1c blue grn	.35	.35
		Never hinged	.60	
119	A4	1½c lilac brn	.75	.75
		Never hinged	1.25	
120	A4	2c carmine	.75	.75
		Never hinged	1.25	
121	A4	2½c lt vio	.75	.75
		Never hinged	1.25	
122	A4	5c dp blue	.75	.75
		Never hinged	1.25	
123	A4	7½c yellow brn	.95	.75
		Never hinged	1.60	
124	A4	8c slate	.95	.75
		Never hinged	1.60	
125	A4	10c orange brn	1.50	.85
		Never hinged	2.50	
126	A4	15c plum	2.00	.70
		Never hinged	3.50	
127	A4	20c yellow grn	2.50	.90
		Never hinged	4.25	
128	A4	30c brown, green	3.50	1.00
		Never hinged	6.00	
129	A4	40c brown, pink	9.00	4.00
		Never hinged	15.00	
130	A4	50c orange, sal	8.00	3.00
		Never hinged	13.50	
131	A4	1e green, blue	10.00	3.00
		Never hinged	17.00	
		Nos. 116-131 (16)	39.25	16.00

Glazed Paper

131A	A4	1c blue grn	1.75	1.45
		Never hinged	3.25	
131B	A4	2½c lt vio	1.75	1.45
		Never hinged	3.25	

1918   Ordinary Paper

131C	A4	¼c olive brn	.25	.25
		Never hinged	.40	
131D	A4	½c black	.25	.25
		Never hinged	.40	
a.		Value omitted	20.00	
		Never hinged	22.50	
131E	A4	1c blue grn	.25	.25
		Never hinged	.40	
131F	A4	1½c lilac brn	.25	.25
		Never hinged	.40	
a.		Imperf.		
131G	A4	2c carmine	.25	.25
		Never hinged	.40	
131H	A4	2½c lt vio	.25	.25
		Never hinged	.40	
131I	A4	5c dp blue	.25	.25
		Never hinged	.40	
131J	A4	7½c yellow brn	.50	.40
		Never hinged	.80	
131K	A4	8c slate	.50	.40
		Never hinged	.80	
131L	A4	10c orange brn	25.00	18.50
		Never hinged	40.00	
131M	A4	15c plum	2.00	.70
		Never hinged	3.25	
		Nos. 131C-131M (11)	29.75	21.75

For surcharges see Nos. 139, 159, 161-162, B1-B12.

In 1921 Nos. 131D and 131F were surcharged 10c and 30c respectively, for use in Mozambique as Nos. 230 and 231. These same values, surcharged 5c and 10c respectively, with the addition of the word "PORTEADO," were used in Mozambique as postage dues, Nos. J44 and J45.

Provisional Issue of
1902 Overprinted
Locally in Carmine

1914   Perf. 11½, 12½

132	A1	115r on 10r red vio	1.00	.45
a.		"Republica" inverted	20.00	
133	A1	115r on 200r bl, bl	1.00	.45
134	A1	115r on 300r bl, sal	1.10	.45
a.		Double overprint	40.00	40.00
135	A1	130r on 25r grn	1.50	.70
a.		Perf. 12½	3.25	1.60
136	A1	130r on 80r yel grn	1.10	.35
137	A1	130r on 150r car, rose	1.10	.35
		Nos. 132-137 (6)	6.80	2.75

No. 135a was issued without gum.

Nos. 78 and 117
Perforated Diagonally
and Surcharged in
Carmine

1915   Perf. 11½

138	A2	¼c on half of 5r org, pair	5.00	5.00
a.		Pair without dividing perfs.	20.00	20.00

Perf. 15x14

139	A4	¼c on half of ½c blk, pair	9.00	9.00
		Never hinged	3.25	

The added perforation on Nos. 138-139 runs from lower left to upper right corners, dividing the stamp in two. Values are for pairs, both halves of the stamp.

Provisional Issue of
1902 Overprinted in
Carmine

1915   Perf. 11½, 12½

140	A1	115r on 10r red vio	.55	.40
141	A1	115r on 200r bl, bl	.70	.40
142	A1	115r on 300r bl, sal	.70	.40
143	A1	130r on 150r car, rose	.75	.40
		Nos. 140-143 (4)	2.70	1.60

Nos. 34 and 80
Surcharged

1915   On Issue of 1903

144	A2	2c on 15r gray grn	.90	.80

On Issue of 1911

145	A2	2c on 15r gray grn	.90	.80
a.		New value inverted	22.50	

Regular Issues of
1898-1903
Overprinted Locally
in Carmine

1916

146	A2	15r gray grn	1.50	1.00
147	A2	50r brown	3.50	2.00
a.		Inverted overprint		
148	A2	75r lilac	3.50	2.00
149	A2	100r blue, bl	3.00	1.00
150	A2	115r org brn, pink	2.50	1.00
151	A2	130r brown, straw	10.00	5.00
152	A2	200r red lil, pnksh	7.00	2.00
153	A2	400r dull bl, straw	12.00	4.00
154	A2	500r blk & red, bl	7.00	3.00
155	A2	700r vio, yelsh	12.00	5.00
		Nos. 146-155 (10)	62.00	26.00

Same Overprint on Nos. 67-68
1917

156	A1	400r on 50r lt blue	1.25	.65
a.		Perf. 13½	11.50	9.00
157	A1	400r on 76r bl	9.00	1.00

No. 69 exists with this overprint. It was not officially issued.

Type of 1914
Surcharged in Red

1920   Perf. 15x14

159	A4	4c on 2½c violet	1.00	.30

Stamps of 1914 Surcharged in
Green or Black

a   b

1921

160	A1(a)	¼c on 115r on 10r red vio (G)	.80	.80
		Never hinged	1.25	
161	A4(a)	1c on 2½c vio (Bk)	.60	.40
		Never hinged	.95	
a.		Inverted surcharge	40.00	
		Never hinged	65.00	
162	A4(b)	1½c on 2½c vio (Bk)	.80	.60
		Never hinged	1.25	
		Nos. 160-162 (3)	2.20	1.80

Nos. 159-162 were postally valid throughout Mozambique. No. 162 exists on glazed paper. Value the same as No. 162.

SEMI-POSTAL STAMPS

Regular Issue of 1914 Overprinted
or Surcharged

a   b

c

1918   Perf. 15x14½

B1	A4(a)	¼c olive brn	3.00	3.00
		Never hinged	5.00	
B2	A4(a)	½c black	3.00	4.00
		Never hinged	5.00	
B3	A4(a)	1c bl grn	3.00	4.00
		Never hinged	5.00	
B4	A4(a)	2½c violet	4.00	4.00
		Never hinged	6.75	
B5	A4(a)	5c blue	4.00	6.00
		Never hinged	6.75	

Chalky Paper

B5A	A4(a)	5c blue	4.00	6.00
		Never hinged	6.75	
B6	A4(a)	10c org brn	5.00	7.00
		Never hinged	8.50	
B7	A4(b)	20c on 1½c lil brn	5.00	8.00
		Never hinged	8.50	
B8	A4(a)	30c brn, grn	6.00	9.00
		Never hinged	10.00	
B9	A4(b)	40c on 2c car	6.00	10.00
		Never hinged	10.00	
B10	A4(b)	50c on 7½c bis	10.00	12.00
		Never hinged	13.50	
B11	A4(b)	70c on 8c slate	12.00	15.00
		Never hinged	17.00	
B12	A4(c)	$1 on 15c mag	18.00	15.00
		Never hinged	25.00	
		Nos. B1-B12 (13)	83.00	103.00

Nos. B1-B12 were used in place of ordinary postage stamps on Mar. 9, 1918. Nos. B3 and B4 also exist on glazed paper. The unsurfaced

paper on which Nos. B1-B5 were printed show a diamond pattern when held to the light. This pattern is used to determine genuine stamps.

NEWSPAPER STAMPS

Numeral of
Value — N1

**   Perf. 11½**
1893, July 28   Typo.   Unwmk.

P1	N1	2½r brown	.25	.65
a.		Perf. 12½	17.00	17.50

For surcharge see No. 70.

Saint Anthony of Padua Issue

Mozambique No. P6
Overprinted

1895, July 1   Perf. 11½, 13½

P2	N3	2½r brown	20.00	17.50
a.		Inverted overprint	30.00	30.00

LUXEMBOURG

ˈlək-səm-ˌbərg

LOCATION — Western Europe between southern Belgium, Germany and France
GOVT. — Grand Duchy
AREA — 998 sq. mi.
POP. — 365,800 (est. 1984)
CAPITAL — Luxembourg

12½ Centimes = 1 Silbergroschen
100 Centimes = 1 Franc

Watermarks

Wmk. 110 — Octagons

Wmk. 149 — W

Wmk. 213 — Double Wavy Lines

Wmk. 216 — Multiple Airplanes

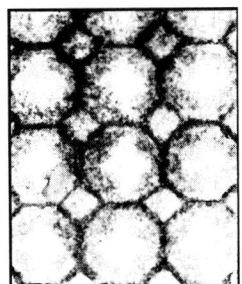

Wmk. 246 — Multiple Cross Enclosed in Octagons

Wmk. 247 — Multiple Letters

Unused values of Nos. 1-47 are for stamps without gum. Though these stamps were issued with gum, most examples offered are without gum. Stamps with original gum sell for more.

Grand Duke William III — A1

Luxembourg Print

Wmk. 149

1852, Sept. 15	Engr.		Imperf.
1	A1 10c gray black	2,100.	55.00
	With gum	3,500.	
	On cover		465.00
a.	10c greenish black ('53)	2,250.	55.00
	With gum	3,900.	
	On cover		525.00
b.	10c intense black ('54)	2,400.	120.00
	With gum		
	On cover		1,400.
2	A1 1sg brown red ('53)	1,500.	75.00
	With gum	2,500.	
	On cover		900.00
a.	1sg brick red	1,500.	80.00
	With gum	2,500.	
	On cover		900.00
b.	1sg orange red ('54)	1,300.	87.50
	With gum	2,500.	
	On cover		1,000.
c.	1sg blood red	2,750.	475.00
	With gum		
	On cover		1,850.
3	A1 1sg rose ('55)	1,350.	87.50
	With gum	2,500.	
	On cover		750.00
a.	1sg carmine rose ('56)	1,250.	80.00
	With gum	2,500.	
	On cover		850.00
b.	1sg dark carmine rose, thin paper ('59)	1,400.	240.00
	With gum	3,500.	
	On cover		2,000.
	Nos. 1-3 (3)		217.50

Full margins = 1mm.

Reprints of both values exist on watermarked paper. Some of the reprints show traces of lines cancelling the plates, but others can be distinguished only by an expert. See Nos. 278-279, 603 in Scott Standard catalogue, Vol. 4.

Values for pairs

1	A1 10c gray black	—	125.00
	On cover		1,100.
2b	A1 1sg orange red	—	275.00
	On cover		1,750.
3	A1 1sg rose	—	300.00
	On cover		1,750.

Values for strips of 3

1	A1 10c gray black	—	575.00
	On cover		1,600.
2b	A1 1sg orange red	—	—
	On cover		—
3	A1 1sg rose	—	450.00
	On cover		2,000.

Values for strips of 4

1	A1 10c gray black	—	1,250.
	On cover		2,200.
2b	A1 1sg orange red	—	—
	On cover		—
3	A1 1sg rose	—	1,800.
	On cover		3,500.

Values for blocks of 4

1	A1 10c gray black	—	6,000.
	On cover		10,000.
2b	A1 1sg orange red	—	—
	On cover		—
3	A1 1sg rose	—	7,250.
	On cover		12,000.

Coat of Arms
A2   A3

A4   A5

Frankfurt Print

1859-64	Typo.		Unwmk.
4	A2 1c buff ('63)	130.00	450.00
	With gum	195.00	
	On cover		2,400.
5	A2 2c black ('60)	95.00	550.00
	With gum	140.00	
	On cover		2,900.
6	A2 4c yellow ('64)	175.00	175.00
	With gum	260.00	
	On cover		2,400.
a.	4c orange ('64)	190.00	190.00
	With gum	270.00	
	On cover		2,200.
7	A3 10c blue	175.00	20.00
	With gum	260.00	
	On cover		250.00
a.	10c dark blue	1,700.	40.00

	With gum	1,775.	
	On cover		225.00
8	A3 12½c rose	275.00	160.00
	With gum	400.00	
	On cover		1,100.
9	A3 25c brown	350.00	275.00
	With gum	500.00	
	On cover		2,400.
10	A3 30c rose lilac	290.00	225.00
	With gum	405.00	
	On cover		2,100.
11	A3 37½c green	325.00	200.00
	With gum	440.00	
	On cover		1,400.
12	A3 40c red orange	875.00	240.00
	With gum	1,275.	
	On cover		1,100.

Full margins = ½mm.

Counterfeits of Nos. 1-12 exist.

See Nos. 13-25, 27-38, 40-47. For surcharges and overprints see Nos. 26, 39, O1-O51.

Values for pairs

4	A2 1c buff	360.00	1,500.
	On cover		9,000.
5	A2 2c black	575.00	1,700.
	On cover		8,500.
6	A2 4c yellow	650.00	640.00
	On cover		7,000.
a.	4c orange	675.00	650.00
	On cover		7,000.
7	A3 10c blue	850.00	225.00
	On cover		1,050.
a.	10c dark blue	3,000.	90.00
			—
8	A3 12½c rose	800.00	475.00
	On cover		3,350.
9	A3 25c brown	1,400.	1,200.
	On cover		4,250.
10	A3 30c rose lilac	1,150.	725.00
	On cover		8,250.
11	A3 37½c green	1,400.	925.00
	On cover		6,750.
12	A3 40c red orange	3,200.	750.00
	On cover		3,600.

1865-71			Rouletted
13	A2 1c red brown	200.00	240.00
	With gum	310.00	
	On cover		1,600.
14	A2 2c black ('67)	20.00	13.50
	With gum	35.00	
	On cover		540.00
15	A2 4c yellow ('67)	600.00	175.00
	With gum	1,025.	
	On cover		2,350.
16	A2 4c green ('71)	40.00	24.00
	With gum	62.50	
	On cover		290.00
	Nos. 13-16 (4)	860.00	452.50

Values for pairs

13	A2 1c red brown	500.00	750.00
	On cover		2,500.
14	A2 2c black ('67)	60.00	55.00
	On cover		700.00
15	A2 4c yellow ('67)	2,500.	750.00
	On cover		2,750.
16	A2 4c green ('71)	115.00	100.00
	On cover		625.00

Values for strips of 3

13	A2 1c red brown	750.00	1,450.
	On cover		3,600.
14	A2 2c black ('67)	140.00	190.00
	On cover		1,200.
15	A2 4c yellow ('67)	—	1,750.
	On cover		1,750.
16	A2 4c green ('71)	250.00	300.00
	On cover		1,000.

1865-74			Rouletted in Color
17	A2 1c red brn ('72)	35.00	8.00
	With gum	42.50	
	On cover		140.00
18	A2 1c orange ('69)	40.00	8.00
	With gum	50.00	
	On cover		140.00
a.	1c brown orange ('67)	120.00	35.00
	With gum	145.00	
	On cover		—
b.	1c red orange ('69)	1,350.	325.00
	With gum	1,725.	
	On cover		—
19	A3 10c rose lilac	120.00	4.00
	With gum	180.00	
	On cover		40.00
a.	10c lilac	100.00	4.00
	With gum	115.00	
	On cover		40.00
b.	10c gray lilac	100.00	4.00
	With gum	115.00	
	On cover		42.50
20	A3 12½c carmine ('71)	175.00	8.00
	With gum	190.00	
	On cover		140.00
a.	12½c rose	175.00	8.00
	With gum	225.00	
	On cover		140.00
21	A3 20c gray brown ('72)	120.00	8.00
	With gum	150.00	
	On cover		225.00
a.	20c yellow brown ('69)	125.00	8.00
	With gum	160.00	
	On cover		240.00
22	A3 25c blue ('72)	1,100.	11.00
	With gum	1,300.	
	On cover		275.00
22A	A3 25c ultra ('65)	1,100.	11.00
	With gum	1,300.	
	On cover		290.00
23	A3 30c lilac rose	1,200.	80.00
	With gum	1,400.	
	On cover		1,800.
24	A3 37½c bister ('66)	750.00	240.00
	With gum	930.00	
	On cover		3,600.

25	A3 40c pale orange ('74)	40.00	80.00
	With gum	52.50	
	On cover		1,400.
a.	40c orange red ('66)	1,050.	60.00
	With gum	1,250.	
	On cover		1,300.
26	A4 1fr on 37½c bis ('73)	875.00	80.00
	With gum	1,075.	
	On cover		1,400.
a.	Surcharge inverted		3,600.

Luxembourg Print

1874	Typo.		Imperf.
27	A2 4c green	110.00	110.00
	With gum	145.00	
	On cover		925.00

1875-79			Perf. 13
		Narrow Margins	
29	A2 1c red brown ('78)	35.00	8.00
	With gum	45.00	
	On cover		225.00
30	A2 2c black	125.00	27.50
	With gum	160.00	
	On cover		300.00
31	A2 4c green	2.40	9.50
	With gum	3.25	
	On cover		425.00
32	A2 5c yellow ('76)	175.00	24.00
	With gum	215.00	
	On cover		145.00
a.	5c orange yellow	600.00	125.00
	With gum	725.00	
	On cover		1,100.
b.	Imperf.	925.00	1,100.
	On cover		1,100.
33	A3 10c gray lilac	475.00	2.40
	With gum	600.00	
	On cover		30.00
b.	10c lilac	1,350.	29.00
	With gum	1,575.	
	On cover		275.00
c.	Imperf.	2,700.	3,250.
	On cover		3,000.
34	A3 12½c lilac rose ('77)	600.00	20.00
	With gum	750.00	
	On cover		240.00
35	A3 12½c car rose ('76)	400.00	27.50
	With gum	535.00	
	On cover		250.00
36	A3 25c blue ('77)	800.00	14.00
	With gum	1,025.	
	On cover		550.00
37	A3 30c dull rose ('78)	750.00	450.00
	With gum	990.00	
	On cover		1,900.
38	A3 40c orange ('79)	1.60	9.50
	With gum	3.25	
	On cover		1,300.
39	A5 1fr on 37½c bis ('79)	8.00	27.50
	With gum	11.00	
	On cover		1,350.
a.	"Pranc"	5,250.	6,400.
	With gum	6,000.	
b.	Without surcharge	475.00	
	With gum	630.00	
c.	As "b," imperf.	700.00	
	With gum	775.00	
	As "c," pair	1,400.	
	With gum	1,600.	

In the Luxembourg print the perforation is close to the border of the stamp. Excellent forgeries of No. 39a are plentiful, as well as faked cancellations on Nos. 31, 38 and 39.

Nos. 32b and 33c are said to be essays; Nos. 39b and 39c printer's waste.

Haarlem Print

Perf. 12½x12, 13½ (5c, 12½c)

1880-81			
		Wide Margins	
40	A2 1c yel brn ('81)	8.75	6.00
	With gum	10.00	
	On cover		175.00
a.	Perf. 11½x12	14.00	11.00
	With gum	19.50	
b.	Perf. 13½	10.50	6.00
	With gum	14.00	
	On cover		190.00
41	A2 2c black	7.25	1.60
	With gum	8.50	
	On cover		190.00
a.	Perf. 11½x12	13.50	8.50
	With gum	16.00	
b.	Perf. 13½	9.50	1.75
	With gum	11.00	
	On cover		190.00
42	A2 5c yellow ('81)	200.00	95.00
	With gum	235.00	
	On cover		350.00
b.	Perf. 12½x12	760.00	390.00
	With gum	960.00	
c.	Perf. 11½x12	960.00	575.00
	With gum	1,150.	
43	A3 10c gray lilac	160.00	1.60
	With gum	190.00	
	On cover		19.00
b.	Perf. 11½x12	190.00	5.00
	With gum	230.00	
c.	Perf. 13½	175.00	2.10
	With gum	230.00	
	On cover		30.00
44	A3 12½c rose ('81)	190.00	190.00
	With gum	245.00	
	On cover		825.00
b.	Perf. 12½x12	210.00	190.00
	With gum	245.00	
	On cover		825.00
c.	Perf. 11½x12	245.00	210.00
	With gum	295.00	

45	A3	20c gray brown ('81)	45.00	20.00
		With gum	52.50	
		On cover		250.00
a.		Perf. 11½x12	52.50	27.00
		With gum	57.50	17.00
b.		Perf. 13½	50.00	17.00
		With gum	57.50	
		On cover		300.00
46	A3	25c blue	240.00	4.75
		With gum	290.00	
		On cover		160.00
b.		Perf. 11½x12	290.00	20.00
		With gum	375.00	
c.		Perf. 13½	270.00	5.00
		With gum	325.00	
		On cover		210.00
47	A3	30c dull rose ('81)	8.00	24.00
		With gum	4.25	
		On cover		750.00
a.		Perf. 11½x12	8.25	32.50
		With gum	10.00	

Gray Yellowish Paper
Perf. 12½

42a	A2	5c	7.25	
		With gum	8.75	
43a	A3	10c	4.00	
		With gum	5.00	
44a	A3	12½c	9.50	
		With gum	11.50	
46a	A3	25c	5.50	
		With gum	6.25	
		Nos. 42a-46a (4)	26.25	

Nos. 42a-46a were not regularly issued.

"Industry" and "Commerce" A6

Grand Duke Adolphe — A7

1882, Dec. 1   Typo.   Perf. 12½

48	A6	1c gray lilac	.25	.40
		Never hinged	.50	
		On cover		6.00
49	A6	2c olive gray	.25	.40
		Never hinged	.40	
		On cover		5.00
d.		2c olive brown	.90	.50
		Never hinged	2.50	
		On cover		11.00
50a	A6	4c olive bister	.60	2.75
		Never hinged	1.50	
		On cover		8.50
51	A6	5c lt green	.80	.40
		Never hinged	2.75	
		On cover		6.00
52	A6	10c rose	8.00	.40
		Never hinged	67.50	
		On cover		25.00
53	A6	12½c slate	1.25	24.00
		Never hinged	6.75	
		On cover		60.00
54	A6	20c orange	3.25	1.60
		Never hinged	13.00	
		On cover		25.00
55	A6	25c ultra	175.00	1.60
		Never hinged	925.00	
		On cover		27.50
57	A6	50c bister brown	1.20	12.00
		Never hinged	4.75	
		On cover		60.00
d.		50c gray brown	25.00	9.50
		Never hinged	50.00	
		On cover		60.00

For overprints see Nos. O52-O64.

Perf. 12½x12

48a	A6	1c gray lilac	.30	.60
		Never hinged	.80	
49a	A6	2c olive gray	.45	.80
		Never hinged	1.00	
50	A6	4c olive bister	.25	2.00
		Never hinged	1.40	
51a	A6	5c lt green	.85	1.50
		Never hinged	2.50	
52a	A6	10c rose	8.00	1.00
		Never hinged	50.00	
53a	A6	12½c slate	1.75	30.00
		Never hinged	5.50	
54a	A6	20c orange	4.00	5.00
		Never hinged	13.00	
55a	A6	25c ultra	175.00	1.90
		Never hinged	1,000.	
56a	A6	30c gray green	25.00	14.00
		Never hinged	90.00	
57a	A6	50c bister brown	2.40	12.00
		Never hinged	9.50	
58	A6	1fr pale violet	1.60	24.00
		Never hinged	7.50	
59a	A6	5fr brown orange	37.50	190.00
		Never hinged	65.00	

Perf. 11½x12

48b	A6	1c gray lilac	1.20	6.00
		Never hinged	3.00	
49b	A6	2c olive gray	1.20	6.00
		Never hinged	3.00	
50b	A6	4c olive bister	.90	4.00
		Never hinged	2.25	
51b	A6	5c lt green	3.50	7.00
		Never hinged	8.50	
52b	A6	10c rose	10.00	7.00
		Never hinged	50.00	
53b	A6	12½c slate	4.50	40.00
		Never hinged	11.50	
54b	A6	20c orange	6.00	10.00
		Never hinged	19.00	
55b	A6	25c ultra	200.00	6.00
		Never hinged	1,150.	
56b	A6	30c gray green	25.00	35.00
		Never hinged	95.00	

57b	A6	50c bister brown	4.00	12.00
		Never hinged	11.50	
58b	A6	1fr pale violet	2.00	29.00
		Never hinged	5.50	
59b	A6	5fr brown orange	60.00	225.00
		Never hinged	100.00	

Perf. 13½

48c	A6	1c gray lilac	8.00	1.20
		Never hinged	16.00	
49c	A6	2c olive gray	1.20	2.50
		Never hinged	2.40	
50c	A6	4c olive bister	.80	2.50
		Never hinged	2.00	
51c	A6	5c lt green	1.50	1.50
		Never hinged	4.25	
52c	A6	10c rose	8.00	4.00
		Never hinged	47.50	
53c	A6	12½c slate	3.50	30.00
		Never hinged	9.50	
54c	A6	20c orange	4.00	6.00
		Never hinged	11.50	
55c	A6	25c ultra	175.00	3.00
		Never hinged	1,000.	
56	A6	30c gray green	24.00	12.00
		Never hinged	105.00	
57c	A6	50c bister brown	1.90	12.00
		Never hinged	7.00	
58c	A6	1fr pale violet	3.00	30.00
		Never hinged	10.00	
59	A6	5fr brown orange	37.50	160.00
		Never hinged	60.00	

Perf. 11, 11½x11, 12½
1891-93   Engr.

60	A7	10c carmine	.80	.40
		Never hinged	2.25	
		On cover		5.50
a.		Sheet of 25, perf. 11½	125.00	
b.		10c dark carmine	9.50	1.75
		Never hinged	19.00	
		On cover		30.00
61	A7	12½c slate grn ('93)	1.20	.80
		Never hinged	6.00	
		On cover		11.00
62	A7	20c orange ('93)	8.00	.80
		Never hinged	35.00	
		On cover		22.50
a.		20c brown, perf. 11½	160.00	240.00
		Never hinged	275.00	
63	A7	25c blue	.80	.80
		Never hinged	3.50	
		On cover		8.75
a.		Sheet of 25, perf. 11½	1,000.	
		Never hinged	1,750.	
64	A7	30c olive grn ('93)	1.60	1.25
		Never hinged	3.25	
		On cover		27.50
65	A7	37½c green ('93)	3.25	3.25
		Never hinged	7.00	
		On cover		37.50
66	A7	50c brown ('93)	7.25	4.00
		Never hinged	25.00	
		On cover		37.50
67	A7	1fr dp violet ('93)	14.50	6.50
		Never hinged	65.00	
		On cover		85.00
c.		1fr reddish violet	55.00	11.00
		Never hinged	110.00	
		On cover		150.00
d.		1fr bluish violet	65.00	11.00
		Never hinged	130.00	
		On cover		175.00
68	A7	2½fr black ('93)	1.60	20.00
		Never hinged	3.25	
		On cover		290.00
69	A7	5fr lake ('93)	29.00	72.50
		Never hinged	65.00	
		On cover		850.00
		Nos. 60-69 (10)	68.00	110.30

No. 62a was never on sale at any post office, but exists postally used.

Covers: Cover values are for postally used and correctly franked covers. Low denomination stamps on ordinary postcards sell for somewhat less. Overfranked philatelic covers sell for much less.

For overprints see Nos. O65-O74.

Grand Duke Adolphe — A8

1895, May 4   Typo.   Perf. 12½

70	A8	1c pearl gray	3.25	.40
		Never hinged	19.00	
		On cover		8.50
71	A8	2c gray brown	.40	.25
		Never hinged	1.20	
		On cover		4.00
72	A8	4c olive bister	.40	.90
		Never hinged	1.75	
		On cover		8.50
73	A8	5c green	5.50	.25
		Never hinged	30.00	
		On cover		6.00
74	A8	10c carmine	14.50	.25
		Never hinged	50.00	
		On cover		5.00
		Nos. 70-74 (5)	24.05	2.05

For overprints see Nos. O75-O79.

Coat of Arms — A9

Grand Duke William IV — A10

1906-26   Typo.   Perf. 12½

75	A9	1c gray ('07)	.25	.25
		Never hinged	.30	
		On cover		2.50
76	A9	2c olive brn ('07)	.25	.25
		Never hinged	.30	
		On cover		2.50
77	A9	4c bister ('07)	.25	.25
		Never hinged	.40	
		On cover		3.00
78	A9	5c green ('07)	.25	.25
		Never hinged	1.20	
		On cover		2.50
79	A9	5c lilac ('26)	.25	.25
		Never hinged	.30	
		On cover		2.25
80	A9	6c violet ('07)	.25	.25
		Never hinged	1.00	
		On cover		5.00
81	A9	7½c orange ('19)	.25	3.25
		Never hinged	.30	
		On cover		25.00

Engr.
Perf. 11, 11½x11

82	A10	10c scarlet	1.60	.25
		Never hinged	2.75	
		On cover		11.00
a.		Souvenir sheet of 10	450.00	1,200.
		Never hinged	700.00	
				1,650.
b.		Perf. 11	2.40	25.00
		Never hinged	13.00	—
83	A10	12½c slate grn ('07)	1.60	.40
		Never hinged	9.25	
		On cover		6.00
84	A10	15c orange brn ('07)	1.60	.65
		Never hinged	6.50	
		On cover		9.50
85	A10	20c orange ('07)	2.75	.55
		Never hinged	16.00	
		On cover		9.50
86	A10	25c ultra ('07)	72.50	.40
		Never hinged	390.00	
		On cover		9.50
87	A10	30c olive grn ('08)	1.20	.55
		Never hinged	3.00	
		On cover		9.50
88	A10	37½c green ('07)	1.20	.80
		Never hinged	3.50	
		On cover		16.50
a.		Perf. 12½	16.00	12.00
		Never hinged	110.00	
		On cover		90.00
89	A10	50c brown ('07)	4.00	.80
		Never hinged	14.00	
		On cover		16.50
90	A10	87½c dk blue ('08)	1.60	12.00
		Never hinged	5.50	
		On cover		65.00
91	A10	1fr violet ('08)	4.75	1.60
		Never hinged	20.00	
		On cover		40.00
a.		1fr deep violet	14.00	3.25
		Never hinged	60.00	
		On cover		65.00
92	A10	2½fr vermilion ('08)	72.50	80.00
		Never hinged	210.00	
		On cover		45.00
93	A10	5fr claret ('08)	12.00	65.00
		Never hinged	32.50	
		On cover		250.00
		Nos. 75-93 (19)	179.05	167.75

No. 82a for accession of Grand Duke William IV to the throne.
Set of 12 stamps, imperf on thick paper $1,200.
For surcharges and overprints see Nos. 94-96, 112-117, O80-O98.

Nos. 90, 92-93 Surcharged in Red or Black

62½ cts.

1912-15

94	A10	62½c on 87½c (R)	3.25	2.00
		Never hinged	6.50	
		On cover		60.00
95	A10	62½c on 2½fr (Bk) ('15)	3.25	4.00
		Never hinged	6.00	
		On cover		17.50
96	A10	62½c on 5fr (Bk) ('15)	1.60	2.75
		Never hinged	2.50	
		On cover		7.00
		Nos. 94-96 (3)	8.10	8.75

Grand Duchess Marie Adelaide — A11

1914-17   Engr.   Perf. 11½, 11½x11

97	A11	10c lake	.25	.25
		Never hinged	.30	
		On cover		1.20
98	A11	12½c dull green	.25	.25
		Never hinged	.30	
		On cover		1.75
99	A11	15c sepia	.25	.25
		Never hinged	.30	
		On cover		3.00
100	A11	17½c dp brown ('17)	.25	.40
		Never hinged	.30	
		On cover		8.50
101	A11	25c ultra	.25	.25
		Never hinged	.30	
		On cover		1.75
102	A11	30c bister	.25	.40
		Never hinged	.30	
		On cover		4.00
103	A11	35c dark blue	.25	.40
		Never hinged	.30	
		On cover		3.00
104	A11	37½c black brn	.25	.40
		Never hinged	.30	
		On cover		4.00
105	A11	40c orange	.25	.40
		Never hinged	.30	
		On cover		4.00
106	A11	50c dark gray	.25	.40
		Never hinged	.30	
		On cover		7.00
107	A11	62½c blue green	.40	2.40
		Never hinged	.50	
		On cover		25.00
108	A11	87½c orange ('17)	.40	2.40
		Never hinged	.50	
		On cover		25.00
109	A11	1fr orange brown	2.00	.55
		Never hinged	2.40	
		On cover		25.00
110	A11	2½fr red	.40	2.00
		Never hinged	.50	
		On cover		90.00
111	A11	5fr dark violet	9.50	47.50
		Never hinged	37.50	
		On cover		190.00
		Nos. 97-111 (15)	15.20	58.25
		Set, never hinged	42.50	

For surcharges and overprints see Nos. 118-124, B7-B10, O99-O113. Nos. 97, 98, 101, 107, 109 and 111 overprinted "Droits de statistique" are revenue stamps.

Stamps of 1906-19 Surcharged with New Value and Bars in Black or Red
1916-24

112	A9	2½c on 5c ('18)	.25	.25
		Never hinged	.40	
		On cover		1.75
a.		Double surcharge	75.00	
		On cover		90.00
113	A9	3c on 2c ('21)	.25	.25
		Never hinged	.40	
		On cover		1.75
114	A9	5c on 1c ('23)	.25	.25
		Never hinged	.40	
		On cover		1.75
115	A9	5c on 4c ('23)	.25	.40
		Never hinged	.40	
		On cover		2.50
116	A9	5c on 7½c ('24)	.25	.25
		Never hinged	.40	
		On cover		2.50
117	A9	6c on 2c (R) ('22)	.25	.25
		Never hinged	.50	
		On cover		2.50
118	A11	7½c on 10c ('18)	.25	.25
		Never hinged	.40	
		On cover		1.75
119	A11	17½c on 30c	.25	.40
		Never hinged	.40	
		On cover		6.00
120	A11	20c on 17½c ('21)	.25	.25
		Never hinged	.40	
		On cover		2.50
121	A11	25c on 37½c ('23)	.25	.25
		Never hinged	.40	
		On cover		2.50
a.		Double surcharge	90.00	
		Never hinged	120.00	
122	A11	75c on 62½c (R) ('22)	.25	.25
		Never hinged	.40	
		On cover		3.50
123	A11	80c on 87½c ('22)	.25	.25
		Never hinged	.40	
		On cover		5.00
124	A11	87½c on 1fr	.55	5.50
		Never hinged	1.60	
		On cover		30.00
		Nos. 112-124 (13)	3.55	8.80

Grand Duchess Charlotte — A12

1921, Jan. 6   Engr.   Perf. 11½

125 A12 15c rose	.25	.25
Never hinged	.40	
On cover		3.00
a. Sheet of 5, perf 11	150.00	250.00
Never hinged	350.00	
Perf. 11, single	6.00	12.00
Never hinged	9.50	
b. Sheet of 25, perf. 11½,		
11x11½, 12x11½	5.50	17.00
Never hinged	7.00	

Birth of Prince Jean, first son of Grand Duchess Charlotte, Jan. 5 (No. 125a). No. 125 was printed in sheets of 100.

See Nos. 131-150. For surcharges and overprints see Nos. 154-158, O114-O131, O136.

Vianden Castle — A13

Foundries at Esch — A14

Adolphe Bridge — A15

1921-34   Perf. 11½

126 A13 1fr carmine	.25	.40
Never hinged	.50	
On cover		15.00
a. Perf. 11x11½	.25	1.20
Never hinged	.30	
On cover		35.00
127 A13 1fr dk blue ('26)	.25	.45
Never hinged	.60	
On cover		17.50

Perf. 11½x11; 11½ (#129, 130)

128 A14 2fr indigo	.30	.80
Never hinged	.85	
On cover		30.00
129 A14 2fr dk brown ('26)	7.00	2.00
Never hinged	12.00	
On cover		60.00
130 A15 5fr dk violet	20.00	9.50
Never hinged	50.00	
On cover		150.00
a. Perf. 12½ ('34)	14.00	11.00
Never hinged	70.00	
On cover		175.00
b. Perf. 11½x11	12.00	12.00
Never hinged	60.00	
On cover		175.00
Nos. 126-130 (5)	27.80	13.15

For overprints see Nos. O132-O135, O137-138, O140.
See No. B85.

Charlotte Type of 1921

1921-26   Perf. 11½

131 A12 2c brown	.25	.25
Never hinged	.30	
On cover		3.00
132 A12 3c olive green	.25	.25
Never hinged	.30	
On cover		3.00
a. Sheet of 25	10.00	25.00
Never hinged	25.00	
133 A12 6c violet	.25	.25
Never hinged	.30	
On cover		3.00
a. Sheet of 25	10.00	25.00
Never hinged	25.00	
134 A12 10c yellow grn	.25	.25
Never hinged	.30	
On cover		3.00
135 A12 10c olive brn ('24)	.25	.25
Never hinged	.30	
On cover		3.00
136 A12 15c brown olive	.25	.25
Never hinged	.40	
On cover		3.00
137 A12 15c pale green ('24)	.25	.25
Never hinged	.50	
On cover		3.00
138 A12 15c dp orange ('26)	.25	.25
Never hinged	.40	
On cover		3.00
139 A12 20c dp orange	.25	.25
Never hinged	.40	
On cover		3.00
a. Sheet of 25	60.00	110.00
Never hinged	95.00	
140 A12 20c yellow grn ('26)	.25	.25
Never hinged	.40	
On cover		3.00
141 A12 25c dk green	.25	.25
Never hinged	.40	
On cover		1.75
142 A12 30c carmine rose	.25	.25
Never hinged	.40	
On cover		3.00

143 A12 40c brown orange	.25	.25
Never hinged	.40	
On cover		3.00
144 A12 50c deep blue	.40	.45
Never hinged	1.00	
On cover		5.50
145 A12 50c red ('24)	.25	.25
Never hinged	.40	
On cover		3.00
146 A12 75c red	.25	1.20
Never hinged	.60	
On cover		12.00
a. Sheet of 25	325.00	
Never hinged	450.00	
147 A12 75c deep blue ('24)	.25	.25
Never hinged	.40	
On cover		6.00
148 A12 80c black	.65	1.25
Never hinged	4.00	
On cover		15.00
a. Sheet of 25	325.00	
Never hinged	450.00	
Nos. 131-148 (18)	5.05	6.65

For surcharges and overprints see Nos. 154-158, O114-O131, O136.

Philatelic Exhibition Issue

1922, Aug. 27   Imperf.

Laid Paper

149 A12 25c dark green	2.25	6.00
Never hinged	6.75	
150 A12 30c carmine rose	2.25	6.00
Never hinged	6.75	

Nos. 149 and 150 were sold exclusively at the Luxembourg Phil. Exhib., Aug. 1922.

Souvenir Sheet

View of Luxembourg — A16

1923, Jan. 3   Perf. 11

151 A16 10fr dp grn, sheet	1,000.	2,400.
Never hinged	1,600.	

Birth of Princess Elisabeth.

1923, Mar.   Perf. 11½

152 A16 10fr black	9.50	13.50
Never hinged	29.00	
a. Perf. 12½ ('34)	8.00	12.00
Never hinged	17.00	

For overprint see No. O141.

The Wolfsschlucht near Echternach — A17

1923-34   Perf. 11½

153 A17 3fr dk blue & blue	2.75	.80
Never hinged	13.50	
a. Perf. 12½ ('34)	2.75	.80
Never hinged	13.50	

For overprint see No. O139.

Stamps of 1921-26 Surcharged with New Values and Bars

1925-28

154 A12 5c on 10c yel grn	.25	.30
Never hinged	.30	
155 A12 15c on 20c yel grn ('28)	.25	.25
Never hinged	.30	
a. Bars omitted		
156 A12 35c on 40c brn org ('27)	.25	.25
Never hinged	.30	
157 A12 60c on 75c dp bl ('27)	.25	.25
Never hinged	.60	
158 A12 60c on 80c blk ('28)	.40	.35
Never hinged	.60	
Nos. 154-158 (5)	1.40	1.40

Grand Duchess Charlotte — A18

1926-35   Engr.   Perf. 12

159 A18 5c dk violet	.25	.25
Never hinged	.30	
160 A18 10c olive grn	.25	.25
Never hinged	.30	
161 A18 15c black ('30)	.25	.25
Never hinged	.50	
162 A18 20c orange	.40	.50
Never hinged	.50	
163 A18 25c yellow grn	.40	.40
Never hinged	.75	
164 A18 25c vio brn ('27)	.35	.25
Never hinged	.75	
165 A18 30c yel grn ('27)	.35	.50
Never hinged	.75	
166 A18 30c gray vio ('30)	.30	.25
Never hinged	.75	
167 A18 35c gray vio ('28)	3.00	.25
Never hinged	3.50	
168 A18 35c yel grn ('30)	.25	.25
Never hinged	.40	
169 A18 40c olive gray	.25	.30
Never hinged	.30	
170 A18 50c red brown	.25	.30
Never hinged	.30	
171 A18 60c blue grn ('28)	3.00	.25
Never hinged	.50	
172 A18 65c black brn	.25	1.10
Never hinged	.60	
173 A18 70c blue vio ('35)	.25	.25
Never hinged	.30	
174 A18 75c rose	.25	.65
Never hinged	.60	
175 A18 75c bis brn ('27)	.25	.25
Never hinged	.30	
176 A18 80c bister brn	.35	1.60
Never hinged	.60	
177 A18 90c rose ('27)	1.50	1.40
Never hinged	4.00	
178 A18 1fr black	1.25	.60
Never hinged	3.50	
179 A18 1fr rose ('30)	.60	.25
Never hinged	1.50	
180 A18 1¼fr dk blue	.25	.45
Never hinged	.40	
181 A18 1¼fr yellow ('30)	15.00	1.60
Never hinged	17.50	
182 A18 1¼fr blue grn ('31)	.45	.25
Never hinged	2.50	
183 A18 1¼fr rose car ('34)	22.50	2.00
Never hinged	40.00	
184 A18 1½fr dp blue ('27)	3.00	1.40
Never hinged	7.00	
185 A18 1¾fr dk blue ('30)	.75	.25
Never hinged	1.50	
Nos. 159-185 (27)	55.95	15.95
Set, never hinged	90.00	

For surcharges and overprints see Nos. 186-193, N17-N29, O142-O178.

Stamps of 1926-35, Surcharged with New Values and Bars

1928-39

186 A18 10(c) on 30c yel grn ('29)	.50	.40
Never hinged	1.30	
187 A18 15c on 25c yel grn	.40	.55
Never hinged	1.50	
187A A18 30c on 60c bl grn ('39)	.30	1.60
Never hinged	.80	
188 A18 60c on 65c blk brn	.25	.40
Never hinged	.65	
189 A18 60c on 75c rose	.25	.40
Never hinged	.65	
190 A18 60c on 80c bis brn	.35	.65
Never hinged	.80	
191 A18 70(c) on 75c bis brn ('35)	12.00	.40
Never hinged	23.00	
192 A18 75(c) on 90c rose ('29)	2.00	.40
Never hinged	5.25	
193 A18 1¾(fr) on 1½fr dp bl ('29)	5.50	1.60
Never hinged	11.50	
Nos. 186-193 (9)	21.55	6.40
Set, never hinged	45.00	

The surcharge on No. 187A has no bars.

View of Clervaux A19

1928-34   Perf. 12½

194 A19 2fr black ('34)	1.75	.80
Never hinged	4.00	
a. Perf. 11½ ('28)	2.75	.80
Never hinged	6.00	

See No. B66. For overprint see No. O179.

Coat of Arms — A20

1930, Dec. 20   Typo.   Perf. 12½

195 A20 5c claret	.85	.40
196 A20 10c olive green	1.10	.25
Set, never hinged	5.50	

View of the Lower City of Luxembourg A21

Gate of "Three Towers" A22

1931, June 20   Engr.

197 A21 20fr deep green	3.50	17.50
Never hinged	8.50	

For overprint see No. O180.

1934, Aug. 30   Perf. 14x13½

198 A22 5fr blue green	3.00	9.50
Never hinged	8.50	

For surcharge and overprint see Nos. N31, O181.

Castle From Our Valley A23

1935, Nov. 15   Perf. 12½x12

199 A23 10fr green	3.00	14.00
Never hinged	6.50	

For surcharge and overprint see Nos. N32, O182.

Municipal Palace — A24

1936, Aug. 26   Photo.   Perf. 11½

Granite Paper

200 A24 10c brown	.25	.45
201 A24 35c green	.35	.90
202 A24 70c red orange	.40	1.40
203 A24 1fr carmine rose	2.00	8.50
204 A24 1.25fr violet	2.50	12.00
205 A24 1.75fr brt ultra	1.60	9.00
Nos. 200-205 (6)	7.10	32.25
Set, never hinged	16.00	

11th Cong. of Intl. Federation of Philately.

Arms of Luxembourg A25

William I A26

Designs: 70c, William II. 75c, William III. 1fr, Prince Henry. 1.25fr, Grand Duke Adolphe. 1.75fr, William IV. 3fr, Regent Marie Anne. 5fr,

Grand Duchess Marie Adelaide. 10fr, Grand Duchess Charlotte.

1939, May 27 Engr. Perf. 12½x12
206	A26	35c brt green	.25	.25
207	A26	50c orange	.25	.25
208	A26	70c slate green	.25	.25
209	A26	75c sepia	.65	.95
210	A26	1fr red	1.60	2.00
211	A26	1.25fr brown violet	.25	.25
212	A26	1.75fr dark blue	.25	.25
213	A26	3fr lt brown	.25	.50
214	A26	5fr gray black	.50	8.00
215	A26	10fr copper red	.75	10.00
		Nos. 206-215 (10)	5.00	22.70
		Set, never hinged	8.50	

Centenary of Independence.

Allegory of Medicinal Baths — A35

1939, Sept. 18 Photo. Perf. 11½
216	A35	2fr brown rose	.50	4.00
		Never hinged	1.25	

Elevation of Mondorf-les-Bains to town status.
See No. B104. For surcharge see No. N30.

Souvenir Sheet

A36

1939, Dec. 20 Engr. Perf. 14x13
217	A36	Sheet of 3	45.00	110.00
		Sheet, never hinged	110.00	
a.		2fr vermilion, buff	7.00	22.50
b.		3fr dark green, buff	7.00	22.50
c.		5fr blue, buff	7.00	22.50

20th anniv. of the reign of Grand Duchess Charlotte (Jan. 15, 1919) and her marriage to Prince Felix (Nov. 6, 1919).
See Nos. B98-B103.

SEMI-POSTAL STAMPS

Clervaux Monastery SP1

Designs: 15c+10c, View of Pfaffenthal. 25c+10c, View of Luxembourg.

Engr.; Surcharge Typo. in Red
1921, Aug. 2 Unwmk. Perf. 11½
B1	SP1	10c + 5c green	.30	4.50
B2	SP1	15c + 10c org red	.30	6.00
B3	SP1	25c + 10c dp grn	.30	4.50
		Nos. B1-B3 (3)	.90	15.00
		Set, never hinged	2.50	

The amount received from the surtax on these stamps was added to a fund for the erection of a monument to the soldiers from Luxembourg who died in World War I.

Nos. B1-B3 with Additional Surcharge in Red or Black

1923, May 27
B4	SP1	25c on #B1 (R)	1.10	14.50
B5	SP1	25c on #B2	1.25	20.00
B6	SP1	25c on #B3	1.10	14.50
		Nos. B4-B6 (3)	3.45	49.00
		Set, never hinged	10.00	

Unveiling of the monument to the soldiers who died in World War I.

Regular Issue of 1914-15 Surcharged in Black or Red

1924, Apr. 17 Perf. 11½x11
B7	A11	12½c + 7½c grn	.25	2.75
B8	A11	35c + 10c dk bl (R)	.25	2.75
B9	A11	2½fr + 1fr red	1.75	27.50
B10	A11	5fr + 2fr dk vio	.55	17.50
		Nos. B7-B10 (4)	2.80	50.50
		Set, never hinged	6.25	

Nurse and Patient SP4   Prince Jean SP5

1925, Dec. 21 Litho. Perf. 13
B11	SP4	5c (+ 5c) dl vio	.25	.70
B12	SP4	30c (+ 5c) org	.25	3.00
B13	SP4	50c (+ 5c) red brn	.25	5.50
B14	SP4	1fr (+ 10c) dp bl	.40	14.00
		Nos. B11-B14 (4)	1.15	23.20
		Set, never hinged	1.75	

1926, Dec. 15 Photo. Perf. 12½x12
B15	SP5	5c (+ 5c) vio & blk	.25	.55
B16	SP5	40c (+ 10) grn & blk	.25	.90
B17	SP5	50c (+ 15c) lem & blk	.25	.95
B18	SP5	75c (+ 20c) lt red & blk	.25	11.00
B19	SP5	1.50fr (+ 30c) gray bl & blk	.35	12.00
		Nos. B15-B19 (5)	1.35	25.40
		Set, never hinged	2.50	

Grand Duchess Charlotte and Prince Felix — SP6

1927, Sept. 4 Engr. Perf. 11½
B20	SP6	25c dp vio	1.10	10.00
B21	SP6	50c green	1.50	16.00
B22	SP6	75c rose lake	1.10	10.00
B23	SP6	1fr gray blk	1.10	10.00
B24	SP6	1½fr dp bl	1.10	10.00
		Nos. B20-B24 (5)	5.90	56.00
		Set, never hinged	17.00	

Introduction of postage stamps in Luxembourg, 75th anniv. These stamps were sold exclusively at the Luxembourg Philatelic Exhibition, September 4-8, 1927, at a premium of 3 francs per set, which was donated to the exhibition funds.

Princess Elisabeth SP7   Princess Marie Adelaide SP8

1927, Dec. 1 Photo. Perf. 12½
B25	SP7	10c (+ 5c) turq bl & blk	.25	.55
B26	SP7	50c (+ 10c) dk brn & blk	.25	.95
B27	SP7	75c (+ 20c) org & blk	.25	1.50
B28	SP7	1fr (+ 30c) brn lake & blk	.25	11.00
B29	SP7	1½fr (+ 50c) ultra & blk	.25	11.00
		Nos. B25-B29 (5)	1.25	25.00
		Set, never hinged	4.00	

The surtax was for Child Welfare societies.

1928, Dec. 12 Perf. 12½x12
B30	SP8	10c (+ 5c) ol grn & brn vio	.25	1.10
B31	SP8	60c (+ 10c) brn & ol grn	.40	2.75
B32	SP8	75c (+ 15c) vio rose & bl grn	.70	7.25
B33	SP8	1fr (+ 25c) dk grn & brn	1.75	22.50
B34	SP8	1½fr (+ 50c) cit & bl	1.75	22.50
		Nos. B30-B34 (5)	4.85	56.10
		Set, never hinged	12.00	

Princess Marie Gabrielle SP9   Prince Charles SP10

1929, Dec. 14 Perf. 13
B35	SP9	10c (+ 10c) mar & dp brn	.25	1.10
B36	SP9	35c (+ 15c) dk grn & red brn	1.50	7.25
B37	SP9	75c (+ 30c) ver & blk	1.75	9.00
B38	SP9	1¼fr (+ 50c) mag & bl grn	2.25	22.50
B39	SP9	1¾fr (+ 75c) Prus bl & sl	2.75	27.50
		Nos. B35-B39 (5)	8.50	67.35
		Set, never hinged	24.00	

The surtax was for Child Welfare societies.

1930, Dec. 10 Perf. 12½
B40	SP10	10c (+ 5c) bl grn & ol brn	.25	1.10
B41	SP10	75c (+ 10c) vio brn & bl grn	1.10	4.75
B42	SP10	1fr (+ 25c) car rose & vio	2.50	17.50
B43	SP10	1¼fr (+ 75c) ol bis & dk brn	4.00	22.50
B44	SP10	1¾fr (+ 1.50fr) ultra & red brn	4.50	22.50
		Nos. B40-B44 (5)	12.35	68.35
		Set, never hinged	40.00	

The surtax was for Child Welfare societies.

Princess Alix SP11   Countess Ermesinde SP12

1931, Dec. 10
B45	SP11	10c (+ 5c) brn org & gray	.30	1.10
B46	SP11	75c (+ 10c) claret & bl grn	4.50	14.50
B47	SP11	1fr (+ 25c) dp grn & gray	9.00	29.00
B48	SP11	1¼fr (+ 75c) dk vio & bl grn	6.00	29.00
B49	SP11	1¾fr (+ 1.50fr) bl & gray	16.00	55.00
		Nos. B45-B49 (5)	35.80	128.60
		Set, never hinged	110.00	

The surtax was for Child Welfare societies.

1932, Dec. 8
B50	SP12	10c (+ 5c) ol bis	.40	1.10
B51	SP12	75c (+ 10c) dp vio	2.75	14.50
B52	SP12	1fr (+ 25c) scar	11.00	32.50
B53	SP12	1¼fr (+ 75c) red brn	11.00	32.50
B54	SP12	1¾fr (+ 1.50fr) dp bl	11.00	32.50
		Nos. B50-B54 (5)	36.15	113.10
		Set, never hinged	92.50	

The surtax was for Child Welfare societies.

Count Henry VII — SP13   John the Blind — SP14

1933, Dec. 12
B55	SP13	10c (+ 5c) yel brn	.40	1.10
B56	SP13	75c (+ 10c) dp vio	4.75	14.50
B57	SP13	1fr (+ 25c) car rose	11.00	35.00
B58	SP13	1¼fr (+ 75c) org	14.50	47.50
B59	SP13	1¾fr (+ 1.50fr) brt bl	14.50	50.00
		Nos. B55-B59 (5)	45.15	148.10
		Set, never hinged	125.00	

1934, Dec. 5
B60	SP14	10c (+ 5c) dk vio	.25	1.10
B61	SP14	35c (+ 10c) dp grn	2.50	9.00
B62	SP14	75c (+ 15c) rose lake	2.50	9.00
B63	SP14	1fr (+ 25c) dp rose	14.50	47.50
B64	SP14	1¼fr (+ 75c) org	14.50	47.50
B65	SP14	1¾fr (+ 1.50fr) brt bl	14.50	47.50
		Nos. B60-B65 (6)	48.75	161.60
		Set, never hinged	125.00	

Teacher SP15

Sculptor and Painter — SP16

Journalist SP17

Engineer SP18

Scientist
SP19

Lawyer — SP20

Savings Bank
and Adolphe
Bridge — SP21

Surgeon
SP22

1935, May 1   Unwmk.   Perf. 12½

B65A	SP15	5c violet	.25	1.10
B65B	SP16	10c brn red	.25	1.10
B65C	SP17	15c olive	.40	1.75
B65D	SP18	20c orange	.55	3.50
B65E	SP19	35c yel grn	.70	3.25
B65F	SP20	50c gray blk	.95	4.75
B65G	SP21	70c dk green	1.40	5.50
B65H	SP22	1fr car red	1.75	7.25
B65J	SP19	1.25fr turq	7.25	50.00
B65K	SP18	1.75fr blue	9.00	52.50
B65L	SP16	2fr lt brown	27.50	110.00
B65M	SP17	3fr dk brown	37.50	150.00
B65N	SP20	5fr lt blue	65.00	275.00
B65P	SP15	10fr red vio	160.00	450.00
B65Q	SP22	20fr dk green	175.00	550.00
		Nos. B65A-B65Q (15)	487.50	1,665.
		Set, never hinged		1,250.

Sold at double face, surtax going to intl. fund to aid professional people.

Philatelic Exhibition Issue
Type of Regular Issue of 1928
Wmk. 246

1935, Aug. 15   Engr.   Imperf.

B66	A19	2fr (+ 50c) blk	4.75	16.00
		Never hinged	13.00	

Philatelic exhibition held at Esch-sur-Alzette.

Charles I — SP23

Perf. 11½
1935, Dec. 2   Photo.   Unwmk.

B67	SP23	10c (+ 5c) vio	.25	.40
B68	SP23	35c (+ 10c) grn	.40	.55
B69	SP23	70c (+ 20c) dk brn	.95	1.50
B70	SP23	1fr (+ 25c) rose lake	14.50	37.50
B71	SP23	1.25fr (+ 75c) org brn	14.50	37.50
B72	SP23	1.75fr (+ 1.50fr) bl	14.50	47.50
		Nos. B67-B72 (6)	45.10	124.95
		Set, never hinged	110.00	

Wenceslas I, Duke of
Luxembourg — SP24

1936, Dec. 1   Perf. 11½x13

B73	SP24	10c + 5(c) blk brn	.25	.25
B74	SP24	35c + 10(c) bl grn	.25	.55
B75	SP24	70c + 20(c) blk	.40	.90
B76	SP24	1fr + 25(c) rose car	2.50	14.50

B77	SP24	1.25fr + 75(c) vio	2.25	29.00
B78	SP24	1.75fr + 1.50(fr) saph	1.60	17.50
		Nos. B73-B78 (6)	7.25	62.70
		Set, never hinged	37.50	

Wenceslas II — SP25

1937, Dec. 1   Perf. 11½x12½

B79	SP25	10c + 5c car & blk	.25	.40
B80	SP25	35c + 10c red vio & grn	.25	.55
B81	SP25	70c + 20c ultra & red brn	.25	.55
B82	SP25	1fr + 25c dk grn & scar	1.60	17.00
B83	SP25	1.25fr + 75c dk brn & vio	2.25	17.00
B84	SP25	1.75fr + 1.50fr blk & ultra	2.75	17.50
		Nos. B79-B84 (6)	7.35	53.00
		Set, never hinged	23.00	

Souvenir Sheet

SP26

Wmk. 110

1937, July 25   Engr.   Perf. 13

B85	SP26	Sheet of 2	4.00	11.50
		Never hinged	11.00	
a.		2fr red brown, single stamp	1.50	5.50

National Philatelic Exposition at Dudelange on July 25-26.
Sold for 5fr per sheet, of which 1fr was for the aid of the exposition.

Portrait of St.
Willibrord — SP28

St. Willibrord,
after a
Miniature
SP29

Abbey at Echternach — SP30

Designs: No, B87, The Rathaus at Echternach. No. B88, Pavilion in Abbey Park, Echternach. No. B91, Dancing Procession in Honor of St. Willibrord.

Perf. 14x13, 13x14

1938, June 5   Engr.   Unwmk.

B86	SP28	35c + 10c dk bl grn	.40	.55
B87	SP28	70c + 10c ol gray	.70	.55
B88	SP28	1.25fr + 25c brn car	1.50	2.50
B89	SP29	1.75fr + 50c sl bl	2.50	2.75
B90	SP30	3fr + 2fr vio brn	5.50	9.00
B91	SP30	5fr + 5fr dk vio	6.50	7.25
		Nos. B86-B91 (6)	17.10	22.60
		Set, never hinged	60.00	

12th centenary of the death of St. Willibrord. The surtax was used for the restoration of the ancient Abbey at Echternach.

Duke
Sigismond
SP32

Prince Jean
SP33

1938, Dec. 1   Photo.   Perf. 11½

B92	SP32	10c + 5c lil & blk	.25	.40
B93	SP32	35c + 10c grn & blk	.25	.55
B94	SP32	70c + 20c buff & blk	.25	.55
B95	SP32	1fr + 25c red org & blk	2.40	14.50
B96	SP32	1.25fr + 75c gray bl & blk	2.40	14.50
B97	SP32	1.75fr + 1.50fr bl & blk	3.50	22.50
		Nos. B92-B97 (6)	9.05	53.00
		Set, never hinged	25.00	

1939, Dec. 1   Litho.   Perf. 14x13

Designs: Nos. B99, B102, Prince Felix. Nos. B100, B103, Grand Duchess Charlotte.

B98	SP33	10c + 5c red brn, *buff*	.25	.40
B99	SP33	35c + 10c sl grn, *buff*	.25	1.10
B100	SP33	70c + 20c blk, *buff*	.95	1.50
B101	SP33	1fr + 25c red org, *buff*	4.00	32.50
B102	SP33	1.25fr + 75c vio brn, *buff*	4.75	50.00
B103	SP33	1.75fr + 1.50fr lt bl, *buff*	5.50	65.00
		Nos. B98-B103 (6)	15.70	150.50
		Set, never hinged	45.00	

See No. 217 (souvenir sheet).

Allegory of
Medicinal
Baths — SP36

1940, Mar. 1   Photo.   Perf. 11½

B104	SP36	2fr + 50c gray, blk & slate grn	1.25	20.00
		Never hinged	4.50	

AIR POST STAMPS

Airplane over Luxembourg — AP1

1931-33   Unwmk.   Engr.   Perf. 12½

C1	AP1	50c green ('33)	.55	1.10
C2	AP1	75c dark brown	.55	1.50
C3	AP1	1fr red	.55	1.50
C4	AP1	1¼fr dark violet	.55	1.50
C5	AP1	1¾fr dark blue	.55	1.50
C6	AP1	3fr gray black ('33)	1.10	6.00
		Nos. C1-C6 (6)	3.85	13.10
		Set, never hinged	8.25	

POSTAGE DUE STAMPS

Coat of Arms — D1

1907   Unwmk.   Typo.   Perf. 12½

J1	D1	5c green & black	.25	.25
J2	D1	10c green & black	.95	.25
J3	D1	12½c green & black	.25	.80
J4	D1	20c green & black	.55	.80
J5	D1	25c green & black	16.00	1.20
J6	D1	50c green & black	.45	3.50
J7	D1	1fr green & black	.25	3.50
		Nos. J1-J7 (7)	18.70	10.30
		See Nos. J10-J22.		

Nos. J3, J5
Surcharged

1920

J8	D1	15c on 12½c	.50	7.25
J9	D1	30c on 25c	.60	9.00
		Set, never hinged	3.50	

Arms Type of 1907
1921-35

J10	D1	5c green & red	.25	.40
J11	D1	10c green & red	.25	.35
J12	D1	20c green & red	.25	.35
J13	D1	25c green & red	.25	.35
J14	D1	30c green & red	.55	.60
J15	D1	35c green & red ('35)	.55	.35
J16	D1	50c green & red	.55	.60
J17	D1	60c green & red ('28)	.45	.50
J18	D1	70c green & red ('35)	.55	.35
J19	D1	75c green & red ('30)	.55	.25
J20	D1	1fr green & red	.55	1.10
J21	D1	2fr green & red ('30)	.55	6.50
J22	D1	3fr green & red ('30)	1.60	18.00
		Nos. J10-J22 (13)	6.90	29.70
		Set, never hinged	27.50	

OFFICIAL STAMPS

Forged overprints on Nos. O1-O64 abound.

Unused values of Nos. O1-O51 are for stamps without gum. Though these stamps were issued with gum, most examples offered are without gum. Stamps with original gum sell for somewhat more.

Regular Issues
Overprinted Reading
Diagonally Up or Down

Frankfurt Print

Rouletted in Color except 2c

1875   Unwmk.

O1	A2	1c red brown	27.50	37.50
O2	A2	2c black	27.50	37.50
O3	A3	10c lilac	2,400.	2,400.
O4	A3	12½c rose	475.00	600.00
O5	A3	20c gray brn	37.50	57.50
O6	A3	25c blue	250.00	140.00
O7	A3	25c ultra	2,100.	1,400.
O8	A3	30c lilac rose	32.50	75.00

O9	A3	40c pale org	160.00	240.00
a.		40c org red, thick paper	250.00	325.00
c.		As "a," thin paper	1,650.	1,400.
O10	A3	1fr on 37½c		
		blk	100.00	22.50

Double overprints exist on Nos. O1-O6, O8-O10.

Overprints reading diagonally down sell for more.

Inverted Overprint

O1a	A2	1c	190.00	225.00
O2a	A2	2c	190.00	225.00
O3a	A3	10c	2,500.	2,500.
O4a	A3	12½c	650.00	925.00
O5a	A3	20c	55.00	75.00
O6a	A3	25c	1,100.	1,300.
O7a	A3	25c	2,100.	1,500.
O8a	A3	30c	650.00	925.00
O9b	A3	40c pale orange	325.00	450.00
O10a	A3	1fr on 37½c	175.00	75.00

Luxembourg Print

1875-76   *Perf. 13*

O11	A2	1c red brown	9.50	27.50
O12	A2	2c black	12.00	32.50
O13	A2	4c green	90.00	160.00
O14	A2	5c yellow	65.00	80.00
a.		5c orange yellow	75.00	110.00
O15	A3	10c gray lilac	92.50	120.00
O16	A3	12½c lilac	85.00	120.00
O17	A3	12½c lilac rose	225.00	275.00
O18	A3	25c blue	11.00	32.50
O19	A3	1fr on 37½c bis	35.00	60.00
	Nos. O11-O19 (9)		625.00	907.50

Double overprints exist on Nos. O11-O15.

Inverted Overprint

O11a	A2	1c	92.50	110.00
O12a	A2	2c	150.00	190.00
O13a	A2	4c	160.00	190.00
O14b	A2	5c	500.00	650.00
O15a	A3	10c	500.00	190.00
O16a	A3	12½c	400.00	550.00
O17a	A3	12½c	450.00	525.00
O18a	A3	25c	125.00	175.00
O19a	A3	1fr on 37½c	190.00	250.00
	Nos. O11a-O19a (9)		2,567.	2,830.

Haarlem Print

1880   *Perf. 11½x12, 12½x12, 13½*

O22	A3	25c blue	2.25	2.75

Overprinted

Frankfurt Print

1878   *Rouletted in Color*

O23	A2	1c red brown	140.00	160.00
O25	A2	20c gray brn	190.00	400.00
O26	A3	30c lilac rose	750.00	575.00
O27	A3	40c orange	325.00	400.00
O28	A3	1fr on 37½c bis	550.00	110.00
	Nos. O23-O28 (5)		1,955.	1,520.

Inverted Overprint

O23a	A2	1c	225.00	300.00
O25a	A3	20c	325.00	400.00
O26a	A3	30c	925.00	700.00
O27a	A3	40c	875.00	925.00
O28a	A3	1fr on 37½c	650.00	200.00

Luxembourg Print

1878-80   *Perf. 13*

O29	A2	1c red brown	750.00	925.00
O30	A2	2c black	190.00	225.00
O31	A2	4c green	190.00	225.00
O32	A2	5c yellow	375.00	450.00
O33	A3	10c gray lilac	375.00	400.00
O34	A3	12½c rose	65.00	110.00
O35	A3	25c blue	525.00	550.00
	Nos. O29-O35 (7)		2,470.	2,885.

Inverted Overprint

O29a	A2	1c	140.00	160.00
O30a	A2	2c	14.50	27.50
O31a	A2	4c	150.00	190.00
O32a	A2	5c	1,500.	1,500.
O33a	A3	10c	92.50	110.00
O34a	A3	12½c	525.00	600.00
O35a	A3	25c	850.00	1,000.

Overprinted

Frankfurt Print

1881   *Rouletted in Color*

O39	A3	40c orange	37.50	75.00
a.		Inverted overprint	210.00	275.00

"S.P." are initials of "Service Public."

Luxembourg Print
Perf. 13

O40	A2	1c red brown	125.00	160.00
O41	A2	4c green	175.00	200.00
a.		Inverted overprint	250.00	
O42	A2	5c yellow	600.00	750.00
O43	A3	1fr on 37½c bis	32.50	47.50
	Nos. O40-O43 (4)		932.50	1,157.

Haarlem Print
Perf. 11½x12, 12½x12, 13½

O44	A2	1c yellow brn	8.50	9.25
O45	A2	2c black	9.25	9.25
O46	A2	5c yellow	160.00	200.00
a.		Inverted overprint	225.00	
O47	A3	10c gray lilac	160.00	200.00
O48	A3	12½c rose	175.00	240.00
O49	A3	20c gray brown	72.50	92.50
O50	A3	25c blue	72.50	92.50
O51	A3	30c dull rose	75.00	120.00
	Nos. O44-O51 (8)		732.75	963.50

Stamps of the 1881 issue with the overprint of the 1882 issue shown below were never issued.

Overprinted

Perf. 11½x12, 12½x12, 12½, 13½

1882

O52	A6	1c gray lilac	.25	.40
O53	A6	2c ol gray	.25	.40
a.		"S" omitted	110.00	
O54	A6	4c ol bister	.25	.45
O55	A6	5c lt green	.25	.55
O56	A6	10c rose	12.00	16.00
O57	A6	12½c slate	1.60	4.75
O58	A6	20c orange	1.60	4.00
O59	A6	25c ultra	19.00	24.00
O60	A6	30c gray grn	4.00	8.75
O61	A6	50c bis brown	.95	2.75
O62	A6	1fr pale vio	.95	4.00
O63	A6	5fr brown org	16.00	40.00
	Nos. O52-O63 (12)		57.10	106.05

Nos. O52-O63 exist without one or both periods, also with varying space between "S" and "P." Nine denominations exist with double overprint, six with inverted overprint.

Overprinted

1883   *Perf. 13½*

O64	A6	5fr brown org	2,200.	2,200.

Overprinted

1891-93   *Perf. 11, 11½, 11½x11, 12½*

O65	A7	10c carmine	.25	.50
a.		Sheet of 25	55.00	
O66	A7	12½c slate grn	8.00	7.25
O67	A7	20c orange	13.00	8.50
O68	A7	25c blue	.25	.45
a.		Sheet of 25	65.00	
O69	A7	30c olive grn	8.00	8.00
O70	A7	37½c green	8.00	8.00
O71	A7	50c brown	6.00	8.75
O72	A7	1fr dp vio	8.00	9.50
O73	A7	2½fr black	45.00	72.50
O74	A7	5fr lake	40.00	55.00
	Nos. O65-O74 (10)		136.50	178.45

1895   *Perf. 12½*

O75	A8	1c pearl gray	1.90	1.90
O76	A8	2c gray brn	1.00	1.60
O77	A8	4c olive bis	1.00	1.60
O78	A8	5c green	4.00	5.00
O79	A8	10c carmine	24.00	35.00
	Nos. O75-O79 (5)		31.90	45.10

Nos. O66-O79 exist without overprint and perforated "OFFICIEL" through the stamp. Values for set: unused, $12; used, $45.

Nos. O65a and O68a were issued to commemorate the coronation of Grand Duke Adolphe.

Regular Issue of 1906-26 Overprinted

1908-26   *Perf. 11x11½, 12½*

O80	A9	1c gray	.25	.40
a.		Inverted overprint	125.00	
O81	A9	2c olive brn	.25	.40
O82	A9	4c bister	.25	.40
a.		Double overprint	140.00	
O83	A9	5c green	.25	.40
O84	A9	5c lilac ('26)	.25	.40
O85	A9	6c violet	.25	.40
O86	A9	7½c org ('19)	.25	.40
O87	A10	10c scarlet	.25	.40
O88	A10	12½c slate grn	.25	.55
O89	A10	15c orange brn	.25	.55
O90	A10	20c orange	.25	.75
O91	A10	25c ultra	.25	.75
O92	A10	30c olive grn	2.75	6.50
O93	A10	37½c green	.45	.75
O94	A10	50c brown	.75	1.50
O95	A10	87½c dk blue	2.00	3.50
O96	A10	1fr violet	2.75	4.00
O97	A10	2½fr vermilion	65.00	65.00
O98	A10	5fr claret	55.00	45.00
	Nos. O80-O98 (19)		131.70	132.05

On Regular Issue of 1914-17
1915-17

O99	A11	10c lake	.25	.75
O100	A11	12½c dull grn	.25	.75
O101	A11	15c olive blk	.25	.75
O102	A11	17½c dp brn ('17)	.25	.75
O103	A11	25c ultra	.25	.75
O104	A11	30c bister	1.40	5.00
O105	A11	35c dk blue	.25	1.20
O106	A11	37½c blk brn	.25	1.60
O107	A11	40c orange	.30	1.20
O108	A11	50c dk gray	.30	.95
O109	A11	62½c blue grn	.30	1.60
O110	A11	87½c org ('17)	.30	1.60
O111	A11	1fr orange brn	.30	1.60
O112	A11	2½fr red	.30	2.50
O113	A11	5fr dk violet	.30	2.75
	Nos. O99-O113 (15)		5.25	23.75

On Regular Issues of 1921-26 in Black
1922-26   *Perf. 11½, 11½x11, 12½*

O114	A12	2c brown	.25	.25
O115	A12	3c olive grn	.25	.25
O116	A12	6c violet	.25	.40
O117	A12	10c yellow grn	.25	.40
O118	A12	10c ol grn ('24)	.25	.40
O119	A12	15c brown ol	.25	.40
O120	A12	15c pale grn ('24)	.25	.40
O121	A12	15c dp org ('26)	.25	.40
O122	A12	20c orange	.25	.40
O123	A12	20c yel grn ('26)	.25	.40
O124	A12	25c dk green	.25	.40
O125	A12	30c car rose	.25	.40
O126	A12	40c brown org	.25	.40
O127	A12	50c dp brown	.25	.45
O128	A12	50c red ('24)	.25	.55
O129	A12	75c red	.25	.55
O130	A12	75c dp bl ('24)	.25	.45
O131	A12	80c black	4.75	8.00
O132	A13	1fr carmine	.40	2.00
O133	A14	2fr indigo	3.00	6.00
O134	A14	2fr dk brn ('26)	1.75	5.00
O135	A15	5fr dk vio	17.50	40.00
	Nos. O114-O135 (22)		31.65	67.90

On Regular Issues of 1921-26 in Red
1922-34   *Perf. 11, 11½, 11½x11, 12½*

O136	A12	80c blk, perf. 11½	.25	.45
O137	A13	1fr dk bl, perf. 11½ ('26)	.25	1.20
O138	A14	2fr ind, perf. 11½x11	.55	2.00
O139	A17	3fr dk bl & bl, perf. 11	2.75	2.75
a.		Perf. 11½	.60	1.40
b.		Perf. 12½	1.40	1.40
O140	A15	5fr dk vio, perf. 11½x11	4.00	9.00
a.		Perf. 12½ ('34)	12.00	20.00
O141	A16	10fr blk, perf. 11½	12.00	24.00
a.		Perf. 12½	12.00	27.50
	Nos. O136-O141 (6)		19.80	39.40

On Regular Issue of 1926-35
1926-27   *Perf. 12*

O142	A18	5c dk violet	.25	.25
O143	A18	10c olive grn	.25	.25
O144	A18	20c orange	.25	.25
O145	A18	25c yellow grn	.25	.25
O146	A18	25c blk brn ('27)	.35	.55
O147	A18	30c yel grn ('27)	.65	1.20
O148	A18	40c olive gray	.25	.25
O149	A18	50c red brown	.25	.25
O150	A18	65c black brn	.25	.25
O151	A18	75c rose	.25	.25
O152	A18	75c bis brn ('27)	.35	.55
O153	A18	80c bister brn	.25	.40
O154	A18	90c rose ('27)	.35	.55
O155	A18	1fr black	.25	.45

O156	A18	1¼fr dk blue	.25	.45
O157	A18	1½fr dp blue ('27)	.55	1.20
	Nos. O142-O157 (16)		5.00	7.35

Type of Regular Issue, 1926-35, Overprinted

1928-35   *Wmk. 213*

O158	A18	5c dk violet	.25	.40
O159	A18	10c olive grn	.25	.40
O160	A18	15c black ('30)	.25	1.20
O161	A18	20c orange	.45	.75
O162	A18	25c violet brn	.45	.75
O163	A18	30c yellow grn	.50	1.40
O164	A18	30c gray vio ('30)	.25	1.20
O165	A18	35c yel grn ('30)	.25	1.20
O166	A18	35c gray vio	.35	.90
O167	A18	40c olive gray	.35	.75
O168	A18	50c red brown	.35	.75
O169	A18	60c blue grn	.35	.75
O170	A18	70c blue vio ('35)	3.50	7.25
O171	A18	75c bister brn	.35	.75
O172	A18	90c rose	.35	1.20
O173	A18	1fr black	.35	1.20
O174	A18	1fr rose ('30)	.45	2.40
O175	A18	1¼fr yel ('30)	4.00	6.50
O176	A18	1¼fr bl grn ('31)	1.50	4.00
O177	A18	1½fr dep blue	.35	1.40
O178	A18	1¾fr dk blue ('30)	.45	1.60
	Nos. O158-O178 (21)		15.35	36.75

Type of Regular Issues of 1928-31 Overprinted Like Nos. O80-O98
1928-31   *Wmk. 216*   *Perf. 11½*

O179	A19	2fr black	.50	1.60

    Wmk. 110   *Perf. 12½*

O180	A21	20fr dp green ('31)	2.25	8.00

No. 198 Overprinted Like Nos. O80-O98
1934   *Unwmk.*   *Perf. 14x13½*

O181	A22	5fr blue green	1.50	6.00

Type of Regular Issue of 1935 Overprinted Like Nos. O158-O178 in Red
1935   *Wmk. 247*   *Perf. 12½x12*

O182	A23	10fr green	1.60	7.00

OCCUPATION STAMPS

Issued under German Occupation

Stamps of Germany, 1933-36, Overprinted in Black

1940, Oct. 1   *Wmk. 237*   *Perf. 14*

N1	A64	3pf olive bis	.25	.50
N2	A64	4pf dull blue	.25	.55
N3	A64	5pf bright green	.25	.50
N4	A64	6pf dark green	.25	.50
N5	A64	8pf vermilion	.25	.50
N6	A64	10pf chocolate	.25	.50
N7	A64	12pf deep carmine	.25	.50
N8	A64	15pf maroon	.35	.70
a.		Inverted overprint	450.00	1,300.
N9	A64	20pf bright blue	.40	1.10
N10	A64	25pf ultra	.40	1.60
N11	A64	30pf olive green	.40	1.60
N12	A64	40pf red violet	.55	1.60
N13	A64	50pf dk green & blk	.95	3.00
N14	A64	60pf claret & blk	1.10	3.00
N15	A64	80pf dk blue & blk	2.00	6.50
N16	A64	100pf orange & blk	3.50	6.50
	Nos. N1-N16 (16)		11.40	29.15
	Set, never hinged		32.50	

Nos. 159-162, 164, 168-171, 173, 175, 179, 182, 216, 198-199 Surcharged in Black

a   b

c

d

Perf. 12, 14x13½, 12½x12, 11½

1940, Dec. 5   **Unwmk.**

N17	A18(a)	3rpf on 15c	.25	.35
N18	A18(a)	4rpf on 20c	.25	.35
N19	A18(a)	5rpf on 35c	.25	.35
N20	A18(a)	6rpf on 10c	.25	.35
N21	A18(a)	8rpf on 25c	.25	.35
N22	A18(a)	10rpf on 40c	.25	.35
N23	A18(a)	12rpf on 60c	.25	.35
N24	A18(a)	15rpf on 1fr rose	.25	.35
N25	A18(a)	20rpf on 50c	.25	.60
N26	A18(a)	25rpf on 5c	.25	1.20
N27	A18(a)	30rpf on 70c	.25	.60
N28	A18(a)	40rpf on 75c	.30	1.20
N29	A18(a)	50rpf on 1¼fr	.25	.60
N30	A35(b)	60rpf on 2fr	1.40	9.50
N31	A22(c)	80rpf on 5fr	.40	2.00
N32	A23(d)	100rpf on 10fr	.65	2.75
		Nos. N17-N32 (16)	5.75	21.25
		Set, never hinged	9.00	

OCCUPATION SEMI-POSTAL STAMPS

Semi-Postal Stamps of Germany, 1940 Overprinted in Black

1941, Jan. 12   **Unwmk.**   ***Perf. 14***

NB1	SP153	3pf + 2pf dk brn	.25	.60
NB2	SP153	4pf + 3pf bluish blk	.25	.60
NB3	SP153	5pf + 3pf yel grn	.25	.60
NB4	SP153	6pf + 4pf dk grn	.25	.60
NB5	SP153	8pf + 4pf dp org	.25	.60
NB6	SP153	12pf + 6pf carmine	.25	.60
NB7	SP153	15pf + 10pf dk vio brn	.30	1.60
NB8	SP153	25pf + 15pf dp ultra	.55	3.50
NB9	SP153	40pf + 35pf red lil	.85	6.00
		Nos. NB1-NB9 (9)	3.20	14.70
		Set, never hinged	8.00	

MACAO

mə-'kau

LOCATION — Off the Chinese coast at the mouth of the Canton River
GOVT. — Portuguese Overseas Territory
AREA — 6 sq. mi.

POP. — 261,680 (1981)
CAPITAL — Macao

The territory includes the two small adjacent islands of Coloane and Taipa.

1000 Reis = 1 Milreis
78 Avos = 1 Rupee (1894)
100 Avos = 1 Pataca (1913)

PRE-STAMP POSTAL MARKINGS
British Post Office Crowned Paid Postmarks

1844
A1   Crowned double circle handstamp, on cover, inscribed "PAID AT MACAO" in red   35,000.

1881
A2   Crown and "MACAO" in double circle, with date on two lines, on cover   —

Watermark

Wmk. 232 — Maltese Cross

Portuguese Crown — A1

1884-85   **Typo.**   **Unwmk.**   ***Perf. 13½***

1	A1	5r black	13.00	9.00
2a	A1	10r orange	25.00	9.00
3a	A1	10r green ('85)	82.50	60.00
4	A1	20r bister	32.50	22.50
5	A1	20r rose ('85)	45.00	18.00
6	A1	25r rose	22.50	5.25
7a	A1	25r violet ('85)	140.00	60.00
8	A1	40r blue	115.00	40.00
9a	A1	40r yellow ('85)	140.00	60.00
10	A1	50r green	250.00	75.00
11a	A1	50r blue ('85)	225.00	70.00
12	A1	80r gray ('85)	57.50	30.00
13	A1	100r red lilac	75.00	24.00
a.		100r lilac	75.00	24.00
14	A1	200r orange	70.00	20.00
15a	A1	300r chocolate	250.00	100.00

Perf. 12½

1a	A1	5r black	20.00	10.00
2	A1	10r orange	25.00	12.00
3	A1	10r green ('85)	30.00	9.00
4a	A1	20r bister	40.00	25.00
6a	A1	25r rose	30.00	7.50
7	A1	25r violet ('85)	30.00	13.50
8a	A1	40r blue	140.00	45.00
9	A1	40r yellow ('85)	42.50	20.00
10a	A1	50r green	450.00	150.00
11	A1	50r blue ('85)	57.50	25.00
12a	A1	80r gray ('85)	75.00	40.00
13b	A1	100r red lilac	40.00	15.00
c.		100r lilac	40.00	15.00
14a	A1	200r orange	125.00	40.00
15	A1	300r chocolate	100.00	25.00

The reprints of the 1885 issue are printed on smooth, white chalky paper, ungummed and on thin white paper with shiny white gum and clean-cut perforation 13½.

For surcharges see Nos. 16-28, 108-109.

Nos. 12, 13a and 14 Surcharged in Black

1884   **Without Gum**   ***Perf. 12½***

16	A1	80r on 100r lilac	90.00	45.00
a.		Inverted surcharge	200.00	75.00
b.		Without accent on "e" of "reis"	80.00	47.50
c.		Perf. 13½	125.00	55.00
d.		As "b," perf. 13½	140.00	62.50

Nos. 6, 6a, 10, 10a Surcharged in Black, Blue or Red

b   c

1885   **Without Gum**

17	A1(b)	5r on 25r rose, perf. 12½ (Bk)	21.00	6.50
a.		With accent on "e" of "Reis"	35.00	12.00
b.		Double surcharge	200.00	150.00
c.		Inverted surcharge	175.00	110.00
d.		Perf. 13½	125.00	100.00
e.		As "d," inverted surcharge	175.00	125.00
f.		Thin bar	21.00	6.50
g.		As "a," thin bar	22.50	15.00
h.		As "c," thin bar	225.00	175.00
18	A1(b)	10r on 25r rose (Bl)	47.50	18.00
a.		Accent on "e" of "Reis"		
b.		Pair, one without surcharge	—	
19	A1(b)	10r on 50r grn, perf. 13½ (Bl)	625.00	225.00
a.		Perf. 12½	625.00	260.00
20	A1(b)	20r on 50r green, perf. 12½ (Bk)	47.50	10.00
a.		Double surcharge		150.00
b.		Accent on "e" of "Reis"	—	—
c.		Perf. 13½	50.00	12.50
21	A1(b)	40r on 50r grn, perf. 12½ (R)	175.00	50.00
a.		Perf. 13½	240.00	50.00
		Nos. 17-21 (5)	916.00	309.50

1885   **Without Gum**

22	A1(c)	5r on 25r rose (Bk)	32.50	18.00
a.		Original value not obliterated		
23	A1(c)	10r on 50r green (Bk)	32.50	18.00
a.		Inverted surcharge		
b.		Perf. 12½	32.50	18.00
c.		Thin bar	100.00	100.00
d.		As "b," thin bar	125.00	125.00

Nos. 12, 12a, 13, 13a, 14, 14a Surcharged in Black

1887   **Without Gum**   **Perf. 13½, 12½**

24	A1	5r on 80r gray	32.50	9.00
a.		"R" of "Reis" 4mm high	125.00	50.00
b.		Perf. 12½	150.00	45.00
25	A1	5r on 100r lilac	150.00	90.00
a.		Perf. 12½	95.00	50.00
26	A1	10r on 80r gray	65.00	20.00
a.		"R" 4mm high	140.00	47.50
27	A1	10r on 200r orange	160.00	62.50
a.		"R" 4mm high, "e" without accent	200.00	80.00
b.		Perf. 13½	140.00	62.50
28	A1	20r on 80r gray	125.00	35.00
a.		"R" 4mm high	175.00	47.50
b.		Perf. 12½	100.00	50.00
c.		"R" 4mm high, "e" without accent	160.00	47.50
		Nos. 24-28 (5)	532.50	216.50

The surcharges with larger "R" (4mm) have accent on "e." Smaller "R" is 3mm high.
Occasionally Nos. 24, 26 and 28 may be found with original gum. Values the same.

Coat of Arms — A6

Red Surcharge
Without Gum

1887, Oct. 20   ***Perf. 12½***

32	A6	5r green & buff	15.00	7.00
a.		With labels, 5r on 10r	77.50	65.00
b.		With labels, 5r on 20r	90.00	65.00
c.		With labels, 5r on 60r	77.50	65.00

33	A6	10r green & buff	22.50	9.00
a.		With labels, 10r on 10r	95.00	75.00
b.		With labels, 10r on 60r	110.00	75.00
34	A6	40r green & buff	37.50	14.00
a.		With labels, 40r on 20r	150.00	110.00
		Nos. 32-34 (3)	75.00	30.00

Nos. 32-34 were local provisionals, created by perforating contemporary revenue stamps to remove the old value inscriptions and then surcharging the central design portion. The unused portion of the design was normally removed prior to use. For simplicity's sake, we refer to these extraneous portions of the original revenue stamps as "labels."
The 10r also exists with 20r labels, and 40r with 10r labels. Value, $250 each.

King Luiz — A7

Typographed and Embossed
1888, Jan.   ***Perf. 12½, 13½***
Chalk-surfaced Paper

35	A7	5r black	21.00	4.00
36	A7	10r green	21.00	6.00
a.		Perf. 13½	75.00	37.50
37	A7	20r carmine	35.00	13.00
38	A7	25r violet	35.00	13.00
39	A7	40r chocolate	35.00	18.00
a.		Perf. 13½	60.00	26.00
40	A7	50r blue	60.00	13.50
41	A7	80r gray	95.00	22.50
a.		Imperf., pair		
42	A7	100r brown	45.00	22.50
43	A7	200r gray lilac	90.00	45.00
44	A7	300r orange	72.50	45.00
		Nos. 35-44 (10)	509.50	202.50

Nos. 37-44 were issued without gum.
For surcharges and overprints see Nos. 45, 58-66B, 110-118, 164-170, 239.

No. 43 Surcharged in Red

1892   **Without Gum**   ***Perf. 13½***

45	A7	30r on 200r gray lilac	75.00	24.00
a.		Inverted surcharge	275.00	165.00
b.		Perf. 12½	60.00	20.00

King Carlos — A9

1894, Nov. 15   **Typo.**   ***Perf. 11½***

46	A9	5r yellow	8.25	3.75
47	A9	10r redsh violet	8.25	3.75
48	A9	15r chocolate	12.50	5.25
49	A9	20r lavender	14.00	6.00
50	A9	25r green	35.00	11.25
51	A9	50r lt blue	37.50	22.50
a.		Perf. 13½	500.00	300.00
52	A9	75r carmine	70.00	30.00
53	A9	80r yellow green	37.50	22.50
54	A9	100r brown, *buff*	40.00	22.50
55	A9	150r carmine, *rose*	45.00	22.50
56	A9	200r dk blue, *blue*	62.50	34.00
57	A9	300r dk blue, *sal*	82.50	45.00
		Nos. 46-57 (12)	453.00	229.00

Nos. 49-57 were issued without gum, No. 49 with or without gum.
For surcharges and overprints see Nos. 119-130, 171-181, 183-186, 240-251, 257-258.

Stamps of 1888 Surcharged in Red, Green or Black

1894   **Without Gum**   ***Perf. 12½***

58	A7	1a on 5r black (R)	11.00	4.50
a.		Short "1"	11.00	4.50
b.		Inverted surcharge	100.00	100.00
c.		Double surcharge	400.00	

d.	Surch. on back instead of face	200.00	200.00
59	A7 3a on 20r carmine (G)	19.00	4.50
a.	Inverted surcharge		
60	A7 4a on 50r violet (Bk)	21.00	9.00
a.	Inverted surcharge	60.00	50.00
61	A7 6a on 40r choc (Bk)	25.00	6.75
a.	Perf. 13½	19.00	12.00
62	A7 8a on 50r blue (R)	55.00	18.00
a.	Double surch., one inverted		
b.	Inverted surcharge	125.00	60.00
c.	Perf. 13½	62.50	40.00
63	A7 13a on 80r gray (Bk)	24.00	7.00
a.	Double surcharge	—	—
64	A7 16a on 100r brown (Bk)	50.00	18.00
a.	Inverted surcharge	—	—
b.	Perf. 13½	115.00	110.00
65	A7 31a on 200r gray lil (Bk)	72.50	25.00
a.	Inverted surcharge	150.00	125.00
b.	Perf. 13½	75.00	25.00
66	A7 47a on 300r orange (G)	72.50	11.00
a.	Double surcharge	—	—
	Nos. 58-66 (9)	350.00	103.75

The style of type used for the word "PROVISORIO" on Nos. 58 to 66 differs for each value.

A 2a on 10r green was unofficially surcharged and denounced by the authorities. Value, $500.

On No. 45

66B	A7 5a on 30r on 200r	150.00	50.00
c.	Perf. 13½	150.00	50.00

Vasco da Gama Issue
Common Design Types

1898, Apr. 1	**Engr.**	**Perf. 12½ to 16**	
67	CD20 ½a blue green	7.00	2.25
68	CD21 1a red	7.00	3.75
69	CD22 2a red violet	7.00	5.25
70	CD23 4a yellow green	10.00	7.50
71	CD24 8a dark blue	19.00	12.00
72	CD25 12a violet brown	30.00	22.00
73	CD26 16a bister brown	26.00	22.00
74	CD27 24a bister	30.00	22.00
	Nos. 67-74 (8)	136.00	96.75

For overprints and surcharges see Nos. 187-194.

King Carlos — A11

1898-1903	**Typo.**	**Perf. 11½**	
	Name and Value in Black except #103		
75	A11 ½a gray	4.50	1.00
a.	Perf. 12½	15.00	7.50
76	A11 1a orange	4.50	1.00
a.	Perf. 12½	15.00	7.50
77	A11 2a yellow green	5.75	1.50
78	A11 2a gray green ('03)	6.25	1.50
79	A11 2½a red brown	7.50	2.25
80	A11 3a gray violet	7.50	2.25
81	A11 3a slate ('03)	6.25	1.65
82	A11 4a sea green	9.00	5.00
83	A11 4a carmine ('03)	6.25	1.50
84	A11 5a gray brn ('00)	15.00	3.75
85	A11 5a pale yel brn ('03)	9.00	2.25
86	A11 6a brown ('03)	10.00	2.00
87	A11 8a blue	12.50	3.75
88	A11 8a gray brn ('03)	16.00	4.00
89	A11 10a slate blue ('00)	15.00	3.75
90	A11 12a rose	15.00	6.50
91	A11 12a red lilac ('03)	62.50	15.00
92	A11 13a violet	18.00	6.50
93	A11 13a gray lilac ('03)	22.50	6.00
94	A11 15a pale ol grn ('00)	90.00	23.00
95	A11 16a dk blue, *bl*	17.00	7.50
96	A11 18a org brn, *pink* ('03)	32.50	11.50
97	A11 20a brn, *yelsh* ('00)	45.00	11.50
98	A11 24a brown, *buff*	27.50	7.50
99	A11 31a red lilac	27.50	9.00
100	A11 31a red lil, *pink* ('03)	32.50	11.50
101	A11 47a dk blue, *rose*	50.00	11.50
102	A11 47a dull bl, *straw*	60.00	13.00
103	A11 78a blk & red, *bl* ('00)	77.50	17.50
	Nos. 75-103 (29)	712.50	194.65

Issued without gum: Nos. 76a, 77, 79-80, 82, 84, 89, 94, 97 and 103.
For surcharges and overprints see Nos. 104-107, 132-136, 141, 147-157D, 159-161, 182, 195-209, 253-255, 258A.

Nos. 92, 95, 98-99
Surcharged in Black.

1900		**Without Gum**	
104	A11 5a on 13a violet	20.00	3.50
105	A11 10a on 16a dk bl, *bl*	22.50	5.00
106	A11 15a on 24a brn, *buff*	22.50	8.25
107	A11 20a on 31a red lilac	25.00	13.50
	Nos. 104-107 (4)	90.00	30.25

Nos. 106-107 were issued with and without gum.

Regular Issues
Surcharged

On Stamps of 1884-85

1902	**Black Surcharge**	**Perf. 11½**	
108	A1 6a on 10r orange	30.00	9.75
a.	Double surcharge	300.00	175.00
109	A1 6a on 10r green	21.00	6.00

On Stamps of 1888
Red Surcharge
Perf. 12½, 13½

110	A7 6a on 5r black	10.00	3.50
a.	Inverted surcharge	110.00	60.00

Black Surcharge

111	A7 6a on 10r green	8.25	3.50
112	A7 6a on 40r choc	8.25	3.50
a.	Double surcharge	125.00	50.00
b.	Perf. 13½	30.00	10.00
113	A7 18a on 20r rose	17.00	4.50
a.	Double surcharge	160.00	70.00
b.	Inverted surcharge	175.00	
114	A7 18a on 25r violet	200.00	60.00
115	A7 18a on 80r gray	225.00	67.50
a.	Double surcharge	240.00	175.00
116	A7 18a on 100r brown	42.50	26.00
a.	Perf. 13½	90.00	35.00
117	A7 18a on 200r gray lil	200.00	67.50
a.	Perf. 12½	190.00	60.00
118	A7 18a on 300r orange	30.00	10.00
a.	Perf. 13½	57.50	25.00

Issued without gum: Nos. 110-118.
Nos. 109 to 118 inclusive, except No. 111, have been reprinted. The reprints have white gum and clean-cut perforation 13½ and the colors are usually paler than those of the originals.

On Stamps of 1894

1902-10		**Perf. 11½, 13½**	
119	A9 6a on 5r yellow	7.75	2.75
a.	Inverted surcharge	82.50	65.00
120	A9 6a on 10r red vio	26.00	5.25
121	A9 6a on 15r choc	26.00	5.25
122	A9 6a on 25r green	7.75	2.75
123	A9 6a on 80r yel grn	7.75	2.75
124	A9 6a on 100r brn, *buff*	15.00	6.00
a.	Perf. 11½	26.00	10.00
125	A9 6a on 200r bl, *bl*	10.00	2.75
a.	Vert. half used as 3a on cover ('10)		40.00
126	A9 18a on 20r lavender	21.00	6.75
127	A9 18a on 50r lt blue	26.00	6.75
a.	Perf. 13½	77.50	17.00
128	A9 18a on 75r carmine	21.00	6.00
129	A9 18a on 150r car, *rose*	21.00	7.50
130	A9 18a on 300r bl, *salmon*	26.00	6.75

On Newspaper Stamp of 1893
Perf. 12½

131	N3 18a on 2½r brown	10.00	3.25
a.	Perf. 13½	27.50	9.00
b.	Perf. 11½	45.00	14.00
	Nos. 108-131 (24)	1,017.	327.00

Issued without gum: Nos. 122-130, 131b.

Stamps of 1898-1900
Overprinted in Black

1902		**Perf. 11½**	
132	A11 2a yellow green	21.00	4.00
133	A11 4a sea green	32.50	10.00
134	A11 8a blue	21.00	7.00

135	A11 10a slate blue	26.00	8.00
136	A11 12a rose	70.00	26.00
	Nos. 132-136 (5)	170.50	55.00

Issued without gum: Nos. 133, 135.
Reprints of Nos. 132-136 have white gum and clean-cut perforation 13½. Value $1.

No. 91 Surcharged

1905		**Without Gum**	
141	A11 10a on 12a red lilac	30.00	12.50

Nos. J1-J3
Overprinted

1910, Oct.		**Perf. 11½x12**	
144	D1 ½a gray green	10.00	6.75
a.	Inverted overprint	30.00	25.00
b.	Double overprint	40.00	40.00
145	D1 1a yellow green	12.00	6.75
a.	Inverted overprint	30.00	25.00
146	D1 2a slate	20.00	7.50
a.	Inverted overprint	60.00	25.00
	Nos. 144-146 (3)	42.00	21.00

No. 144 issued without gum, Nos. 145-146 with and without gum.

Stamps of 1898-1903
Overprinted in
Carmine or Green

Overprint 24½mm long. "A" has flattened top.

Lisbon Overprint

1911, Apr. 2		**Perf. 11½**	
147	A11 ½a gray	2.10	.75
a.	Inverted overprint	20.00	20.00
147B	A11 1a orange	2.00	.75
a.	Inverted overprint	20.00	20.00
148	A11 2a gray green	2.00	.75
a.	Inverted overprint	5.00	5.00
149	A11 3a slate	6.25	.75
a.	Inverted overprint	12.50	5.00
150	A11 4a carmine (G)	6.25	2.00
a.	4a pale yel brn (error)	75.00	50.00
b.	As No. 150, inverted overprint	25.00	25.00
151	A11 5a pale yel brn	6.25	4.00
152	A11 6a red brown	6.25	4.00
153	A11 8a gray brown	6.25	4.00
154	A11 10a slate blue	6.25	4.00
155	A11 13a gray lilac	10.00	5.00
a.	Inverted overprint	60.00	60.00
156	A11 16a dk blue, *bl*	10.00	5.00
a.	Inverted overprint	60.00	60.00
157	A11 18a org brn, *pink*	16.00	6.00
157A	A11 20a brown, *straw*	16.00	6.00
157B	A11 31a red lil, *pink*	30.00	8.00
157C	A11 47a dull bl, *straw*	50.00	10.00
157D	A11 78a blk & red, *bl*	82.50	12.00
	Nos. 147-157D (16)	258.10	73.00

Issued without gum: Nos. 151, 153-157D.

Coat of Arms — A14

Red Surcharge

1911		**Perf. 11½x12**	
158	A14 1a on 5r brn & buff	32.50	12.50
a.	"1" omitted	67.50	50.00
b.	Inverted surcharge	45.00	25.00
c.	Larger "1"	52.50	26.50

Stamps of 1900-03
Surcharged

Diagonal Halves
Black Surcharge

1911	**Without Gum**	**Perf. 11½**	
159	A11 2a on half of 4a car	32.50	32.50
a.	"2" omitted	80.00	80.00
b.	Inverted surcharge	150.00	82.50
d.	Entire stamp	67.50	65.00
159C	A11 5a on half of 10a sl bl (#89)	4,000.	
e.	Entire stamp	8,500.	—

Red Surcharge

160	A11 5a on half of 10a sl bl (#89)	4,500.	1,500.
a.	Inverted surcharge	5,000.	1,750.
b.	Entire stamp	11,000.	5,000.
161	A11 5a on half of 10a sl bl (#135)	125.00	80.00
a.	Inverted surcharge	350.00	200.00
b.	Entire stamp	275.00	165.00

A15

Laid or Wove Paper

1911		**Perf. 12x11½**	
162	A15 1a black	525.00	—
a.	"Correio"	1,900.	—
163	A15 2a black	600.00	—
a.	"Correio"	1,900.	—

The vast majority of used stamps were not canceled.

Surcharged Stamps
of 1902 Overprinted
in Red or Green

Overprint 23mm long. "A" has pointed top.

Local Overprint

1913	**Without Gum**	**Perf. 11½**	
164	A1 6a on 10r green (R)	37.50	12.00
a.	"REPUBLICA" double	65.00	65.00
		Perf. 12½, 13½	
165	A7 6a on 5r black (G)	15.00	3.50
166	A7 6a on 10r green (R)	31.00	8.00
a.	Perf. 13½	50.00	20.00
167	A7 6a on 40r choc (R)	10.50	3.00
a.	Perf. 13½	50.00	20.00
168	A7 18a on 20r car (G)	21.00	6.00
169	A7 18a on 100r brown (R)	82.50	40.00
a.	Perf. 13½	100.00	50.00
170	A7 18a on 300r org (R)	32.50	9.00
a.	Perf. 13½	50.00	10.00
	Nos. 164-170 (7)	230.00	81.50

"Republica" overprint exists inverted on Nos. 164-170.
"Republica" overprint exists double on No. 164.

"REPUBLICA" Inverted

164b	A1 6a on 10r green (R)	65.00	65.00
165a	A7 6a on 5r black (G)	65.00	60.00
166a	A7 6a on 10r green (R)	65.00	60.00
167b	A7 6a on 40r choc (R)	65.00	60.00
168a	A7 18a on 20r car (G)	66.00	60.00
169a	A7 18a on 100r brown (R)	95.00	60.00
170b	A7 18a on 300r org (R)	65.00	60.00

1913	**Without Gum**	**Perf. 11½, 13½**	
171	A9 6a on 10r red vio (G)	14.50	4.50
172	A9 6a on 10r red vio (R)	175.00	26.00
173	A9 6a on 15r choc (R)	14.50	5.00
174	A9 6a on 25r green (R)	16.00	5.00
175	A9 6a on 80r yel grn (R)	14.50	5.00
176	A9 6a on 100r brn, *buff* (R)	30.00	7.00
a.	Perf. 11½	32.50	8.00

177	A9	18a on 20r lav (R)	19.00	5.00
178	A9	18a on 50r lt bl (R)	19.00	5.00
a.		Perf. 13½	21.00	6.00
179	A9	18a on 75r car (G)	19.00	5.50
180	A9	18a on 150r car, rose (G)	21.00	6.00
181	A9	18a on 300r dk bl, sal (R)	32.50	10.00

On No. 141

182	A11	10a on 12a red lil (R)	13.00	4.50
		Nos. 171-182 (12)	388.00	88.50

"Republica" overprint exists inverted on Nos. 171-181.

"REPUBLICA" Inverted

171a	A9	6a on 10r red vio (G)	65.00	60.00
172a	A9	6a on 10r red vio (R)	65.00	60.00
174a	A9	6a on 25r green (R)	65.00	60.00
175a	A9	6a on 80r yel grn (R)	65.00	60.00
176b	A9	6a on 100r brn, buff (R)	65.00	60.00
177a	A9	18a on 20r lav (R)	65.00	60.00
178b	A9	18a on 50r lt bl (R)	65.00	60.00
179a	A9	18a on 75r car (R)	65.00	60.00
180a	A9	18a on 150r car, rose (R)	65.00	60.00
181a	A9	18a on 300r dk bl, buff (R)	65.00	60.00

Stamps of Preceding Issue Surcharged

1913 Without Gum Perf. 11½

183	A9	2a on 18a on 20r (R)	10.00	4.00
184	A9	2a on 18a on 50r (R)	10.00	4.00
a.		Perf. 13½	11.00	4.25
185	A9	2a on 18a on 75r (G)	10.00	4.00
186	A9	2a on 18a on 150r (G)	10.00	4.00
		Nos. 183-186 (4)	40.00	16.00

"REPUBLICA" Inverted

183b	A9	2a on 18a on 20r (R)	20.00	—
184b	A9	2a on 18a on 50r (R)	20.00	—
185b	A9	2a on 18a on 75r (G)	20.00	—
186b	A9	2a on 18a on 150r (G)	20.00	—

"2" Surcharge Inverted

183c	A9	2a on 18a on 20r (R)	30.00	32.50
184c	A9	2a on 18a on 50r (R)	30.00	32.50
185c	A9	2a on 18a on 75r (G)	30.00	32.50
186c	A9	2a on 18a on 150r (G)	30.00	32.50

"2" Surcharge Double

183d	A9	2a on 18a on 20r (R)	30.00	27.50
184d	A9	2a on 18a on 50r (R)	30.00	30.00
185d	A9	2a on 18a on 75r (G)	32.50	35.00
186d	A9	2a on 18a on 150r (G)	35.00	35.00

Vasco da Gama Issue Overprinted or Surcharged

j

k

187	CD20 (j)	½a blue green	7.75	2.00
188	CD21 (j)	1a red	8.50	2.00
189	CD22 (j)	2a red violet	8.50	2.00
a.		Double ovpt., one inverted	100.00	
190	CD23 (j)	4a yellow grn	7.75	2.00
191	CD24 (j)	8a dk blue	13.00	2.00
192	CD25 (k)	10a on 12a vio brn	24.00	5.00
193	CD26 (j)	16a bister brn	17.00	4.00
194	CD27 (j)	24a bister	27.50	5.00
		Nos. 187-194 (8)	114.00	24.00

Stamps of 1898-1903 Overprinted in Red or Green

1913 Without Gum Perf. 11½

195	A11	4a carmine (G)	250.00	100.00
196	A11	5a yellow brn	30.00	20.00
a.		Inverted overprint	50.00	40.00
197	A11	6a red brown	77.50	40.00
198	A11	8a gray brown	625.00	300.00
198A	A11	10a dull blue	—	
199	A11	13a violet	77.50	32.50
a.		Inverted overprint	95.00	
200	A11	13a gray lilac	40.00	20.00
201	A11	16a blue, bl	50.00	20.00
202	A11	18a org brn, pink	50.00	20.00
203	A11	20a brown, yelsh	50.00	20.00
204	A11	31a red lil, pink	67.50	30.00
205	A11	47a dull bl, straw	100.00	40.00

Only 20 examples of No. 198A were sold by the Post Office.

Stamps of 1911-13 Surcharged

On Stamps of 1911 With Lisbon "Republica"

1913

206	A11	½a on 5a yel brn (R)	15.00	3.00
a.		"½ Avo" inverted	125.00	70.00
207	A11	4a on 8a gray brn (R)	30.00	4.00
a.		"4 Avos" inverted	110.00	70.00

On Stamps of 1913 With Local "Republica"

208	A11	1a on 13a violet (R)	150.00	30.00
209	A11	1a on 13a gray lil (R)	15.00	3.00
		Nos. 206-209 (4)	210.00	40.00

Issued without gum: Nos. 207-209.

"Ceres" — A16

Name and Value in Black
Chalky Paper

1913 Perf. 15x14

210	A16	½a olive brown	1.75	.25
		Never hinged	2.75	
211	A16	1a black	1.75	.25
		Never hinged	2.75	
212	A16	2a blue green	1.75	.25
		Never hinged	2.75	
213	A16	4a carmine	6.75	1.00
		Never hinged	11.00	
214	A16	5a lilac brown	7.75	3.00
		Never hinged	12.50	
215	A16	6a lt violet	7.75	3.00
		Never hinged	12.50	
216	A16	8a lilac brown	7.75	3.00
		Never hinged	12.50	
217	A16	10a deep blue	7.75	3.00
		Never hinged	12.50	
218	A16	12a yellow brn	11.00	3.00
		Never hinged	17.50	
219	A16	16a slate	20.00	5.00
		Never hinged	32.50	
220	A16	20a orange brn	20.00	5.00
		Never hinged	32.50	
221	A16	40a plum	21.00	5.00
		Never hinged	35.00	
222	A16	58a brown, grn	35.00	12.00
		Never hinged	55.00	
223	A16	76a brown, pink	50.00	14.00
		Never hinged	80.00	
224	A16	1p orange, sal	67.50	20.00
		Never hinged	110.00	
225	A16	3p green, bl	200.00	55.00
		Never hinged	325.00	
		Nos. 210-225 (16)	467.50	132.75

Nos. 210, 211 and 212 exist on glazed paper.

Ordinary Paper

1919 Perf. 15x14

226	A16	½a olive brown	5.50	2.25
		Never hinged	8.25	
a.		Inscriptions inverted	50.00	
227	A16	1a black	5.50	2.25
		Never hinged	8.25	
a.		Inscriptions inverted	50.00	
b.		Inscriptions double	50.00	
228	A16	2a blue green	14.50	7.00
		Never hinged	22.50	
		Inscriptions inverted	40.00	
229	A16	4a carmine	42.50	21.00
		Never hinged	22.50	
		Nos. 226-229 (4)	68.00	32.50

1922-24 Perf. 12x11½

230	A16	½a olive brown	2.75	1.10
		Never hinged	4.25	

231	A16	1a black	2.75	1.10
		Never hinged	4.25	
232	A16	1½a yellow green ('24)	1.75	.25
		Never hinged	2.75	
233	A16	2a blue green	6.00	3.00
		Never hinged	9.00	
234	A16	3a orange brown	10.00	3.00
		Never hinged	15.00	
235	A16	4a carmine	20.00	5.00
		Never hinged	32.50	
236	A16	4a lemon ('24)	14.00	5.00
		Never hinged	21.00	
237	A16	6a gray ('23)	47.50	7.50
		Never hinged	72.50	
238	A16	8a lilac brown	17.50	5.50
		Never hinged	26.00	
238A	A16	10a pale blue ('23)	27.50	6.00
		Never hinged	42.50	
238B	A16	12a yellow brown	30.00	6.50
		Never hinged	45.00	
238C	A16	14a lilac ('24)	42.50	12.00
		Never hinged	65.00	
238D	A16	16a slate	67.50	20.00
		Never hinged	100.00	
238E	A16	24a slate green ('23)	25.00	7.00
		Never hinged	37.50	
238F	A16	32a orange brown ('24)	25.00	8.00
		Never hinged	37.50	
238G	A16	56a dull rose ('24)	50.00	15.00
		Never hinged	75.00	
238H	A16	72a brown ('23)	67.50	20.00
		Never hinged	100.00	
238I	A16	1p orange ('24)	200.00	30.00
		Never hinged	300.00	

Glazed Paper

238J	A16	3p pale turq ('24)	425.00	95.00
		Never hinged	725.00	
238K	A16	5p carmine rose ('24)	350.00	82.50
		Never hinged	600.00	
		Nos. 230-238K (20)	1,432.	333.45

For surcharges see Nos. 256, 259-267.

Preceding Issues and No. P4 Overprinted in Carmine

On Stamps of 1902

Perf. 11½, 12, 12½, 13½, 11½x12

1915

239	A7	6a on 10r green	14.50	4.00
240	A9	6a on 5r yellow	14.50	4.00
241	A9	6a on 10r red vio	14.50	4.00
242	A9	6a on 15r choc	12.50	3.25
243	A9	6a on 25r green	12.00	4.00
244	A9	6a on 80r yel grn	12.00	4.00
245	A9	6a on 100r brn, buff	21.00	4.00
246	A9	6a on 200r bl, bl	11.00	6.00
247	A9	18a on 20r lav	21.00	6.00
248	A9	18a on 50r lt bl	45.00	6.75
249	A9	18a on 75r car	40.00	6.75
250	A9	18a on 150r car, rose	45.00	8.00
251	A9	18a on 300r bl, sal	40.00	10.00
252	N3	18a on 2½r brn	32.50	6.00

With Additional Overprint

253	A11	8a blue	14.50	8.25
254	A11	10a slate blue	14.50	6.00
a.		"Provisorio" double	110.00	

On Stamp of 1905

255	A11	10a on 12a red lilac	19.00	9.75
		Nos. 239-255 (17)	383.50	100.75

Issued without gum: Nos. 243-251 and 255.

No. 217 Surcharged

Without Gum

1919-20 Perf. 15x14

256	A16	½a on 5a lilac brn	100.00	32.50
		Never hinged	125.00	

Nos. 243 and 244 Surcharged

257	A9	2a on 6a on 25r green	500.00	125.00
258	A9	2a on 6a on 80r yel grn	100.00	70.00

No. 152 Surcharged

258A	A11	2a on 6a red brown	175.00	70.00
		Nos. 256-258A (4)	875.00	297.50

Issued without gum: Nos. 256-258A.

Stamps of 1913-24 Surcharged

1931-33 Perf. 12x11½

259	A16	1a on 24a slate green ('33)	14.50	4.00
		Never hinged	26.00	
260	A16	2a on 32a orange brown ('33)	14.50	4.00
		Never hinged	26.00	
261	A16	4a on 12a bister brown ('33)	14.50	4.00
		Never hinged	26.00	
262	A16	5a on 6a light gray ('33)	57.50	20.00
		Never hinged	100.00	
264	A16	7a on 8a lilac brown	24.00	5.00
		Never hinged	45.00	
265	A16	12a on 14a lilac	24.00	5.00
		Never hinged	45.00	
266	A16	15a on 16a dark gray ('33)	24.00	5.00
		Never hinged	45.00	
267	A16	20a on 56a dull rose ('33)	50.00	11.00
		Never hinged	90.00	

Chalky Paper
Perf. 15x14

263	A16	5a on 6a light violet ('33)	30.00	11.00
		Never hinged	47.50	
		Nos. 259-267 (9)	253.00	69.00

"Portugal" and Vasco da Gama's Flagship "San Gabriel" — A17

Wmk. 232

1934, Feb. 1 Typo. Perf. 11½

268	A17	½a bister	.45	.40
269	A17	1a olive brown	.45	.25
270	A17	2a blue green	1.10	.50
271	A17	3a violet	1.40	.50
272	A17	4a black	1.75	.50
273	A17	5a gray	1.75	.80
274	A17	6a brown	1.75	.80
275	A17	7a brt rose	3.25	1.00
276	A17	8a brt blue	3.25	1.00
277	A17	10a red orange	7.25	2.00
278	A17	12a dark blue	7.25	2.00
279	A17	14a olive green	7.25	2.00
280	A17	15a maroon	7.25	2.00
281	A17	20a orange	7.25	2.00
282	A17	30a apple green	14.00	3.50
283	A17	40a violet	14.00	3.50
284	A17	50a olive bister	21.00	5.00
285	A17	1p lt blue	110.00	27.50
286	A17	2p brown org	140.00	35.00
287	A17	3p emerald	225.00	40.00
288	A17	5p dark violet	350.00	87.50
		Nos. 268-288 (21)	925.40	217.75

See Nos. 316-323. For overprints and surcharges see Nos. 306-315, C1-C6, J43-J49. Post 1940 listings are in Scott Standard catalogue, Vol. 4.

Common Design Types
Perf. 13½x13
1938, Aug. 1   Engr.   Unwmk.
Name and Value in Black

289	CD34	1a gray green	1.00	.35
290	CD34	2a orange brown	1.25	.55
291	CD34	3a dk vio brn	1.25	.55
292	CD34	4a brt green	1.25	.55
293	CD35	5a dk carmine	1.25	.55
294	CD35	6a slate	1.25	.55
295	CD35	8a rose violet	2.10	2.25
296	CD36	10a brt red vio	2.50	2.25
297	CD36	12a red	3.25	2.60
298	CD36	15a orange	3.25	2.60
299	CD37	20a blue	16.50	2.90
300	CD37	40a gray black	16.50	3.50
301	CD37	50a brown	16.50	3.75
302	CD38	1p brown car	50.00	7.25
303	CD38	2p olive green	100.00	11.00
304	CD38	3p blue violet	125.00	22.50
305	CD38	5p red brown	250.00	37.50
		Nos. 289-305 (17)	592.85	101.20

For surcharge see No. 315A in Scott Standard catalogue, Vol. 4.

AIR POST STAMPS

Stamps of 1934 Overprinted or Surcharged in Black

a   b

1936   Wmk. 232   *Perf. 11½*

C1	A17 (a)	2a blue green	2.50	.75
C2	A17 (a)	3a violet	4.25	.75
C3	A17 (b)	5a on 6a brown	4.25	.75
C4	A17 (a)	7a brt rose	4.25	.75
C5	A17 (a)	8a brt blue	11.00	1.00
C6	A17 (a)	15a maroon	27.50	4.00
		Nos. C1-C6 (6)	53.75	8.00

Common Design Type
Name and Value in Black
Perf. 13½x13
1938, Aug. 1   Engr.   Unwmk.

C7	CD39	1a scarlet	.90	.50
C8	CD39	2a purple	1.10	.50
C9	CD39	3a orange	1.60	.90
C10	CD39	5a ultra	3.25	1.25
C11	CD39	10a lilac brn	5.50	1.25
C12	CD39	20a dk green	11.00	3.00
C13	CD39	50a red brown	18.00	4.00
C14	CD39	70a rose car	22.50	5.00
C15	CD39	1p magenta	45.00	18.00
		Nos. C7-C15 (9)	108.85	34.40

No. C13 exists with overprint "Exposicao Internacional de Nova York, 1939-1940" and Trylon and Perisphere. Value $325.

POSTAGE DUE STAMPS

Numeral of Value — D1

Name and Value in Black
Perf. 11½x12
1904, July   Typo.   Unwmk.

J1	D1	½a gray green	1.50	1.25
a.		Name & value inverted	125.00	60.00
J2	D1	1a yellow grn	2.00	1.25
J3	D1	2a slate	2.00	1.25
J4	D1	4a pale brown	2.75	1.25
J5	D1	5a red orange	3.50	2.00
J6	D1	8a gray brown	4.00	2.00
J7	D1	12a red brown	6.00	2.00
J8	D1	20a dull blue	10.00	4.50
J9	D1	40a carmine	20.00	6.00
J10	D1	50a orange	26.50	12.00
J11	D1	1p gray violet	52.50	25.00
		Nos. J1-J11 (11)	130.75	58.50

Issued without gum: Nos. J7-J11. Issued with or without gum: No. J4. Others issued with gum.

For overprints see Nos. 144-146, J12-J32.

Issue of 1904 Overprinted in Carmine or Green

Overprint 24½mm long. "A" has flattened top.

1911   Lisbon Overprint

J12	D1	½a gray green	.50	.30
J13	D1	1a yellow green	1.00	.50
J14	D1	2a slate	1.25	.65
J15	D1	4a pale brown	1.50	.75
J16	D1	5a orange	2.00	1.00
J17	D1	8a gray brown	4.00	1.75
J18	D1	12a red brown	7.00	2.00
J19	D1	20a dull blue	9.50	3.00
J20	D1	40a carmine (G)	12.50	4.00
J21	D1	50a orange	16.00	5.00
J22	D1	1p gray violet	30.00	7.50
		Nos. J12-J22 (11)	85.25	26.45

Issued without gum: Nos. J19-J22.

Issue of 1904 Overprinted in Red or Green

Overprint 23mm long. "A" has pointed top.

1911   Local Overprint

J22A	D1	½a gray green	1,600.	600.00
J23	D1	1a yellow green	3.00	.50
J24	D1	2a slate	3.00	.50
J25	D1	4a pale brown	3.00	.75
J26	D1	5a orange	3.50	.75
J27	D1	8a gray brown	3.50	.90
J28	D1	12a red brown	3.50	.80
J29	D1	20a dull blue	12.50	3.00
J30	D1	40a car (G)	35.00	5.00
a.		Double ovpt., red and green	100.00	27.50
J31	D1	50a orange	35.00	8.00
J32	D1	1p gray violet	70.00	10.00
		Nos. J23-J32 (10)	172.00	30.20

Issued without gum: Nos. J28, J30-J32.

WAR TAX STAMPS

Victory
WT1

1919, Aug. 11   Unwmk.   *Perf. 15x14*
Overprinted in Black or Carmine

MR1	WT1	2a green	2.25	1.00
MR2	WT1	11a green (C)	3.50	1.40

Nos. MR1-MR2 were also for use in Timor. A 9a value was issued for revenue use. Value $15.

NEWSPAPER STAMPS

Nos. P1-P2   No. P3

Typographed and Embossed
1892-93   Unwmk.   *Perf. 12½*
Black Surcharge
Without Gum

P1	A7	2½r on 40r choc	6.00	2.50
a.		Inverted surcharge	45.00	30.00
b.		Perf. 13½	7.00	4.50
P2	A7	2½r on 80r gray	9.00	4.00
a.		Inverted surcharge	60.00	50.00
b.		Double surcharge		
c.		Perf. 13½	45.00	35.00

P3	A7	2½r on 10r grn ('93)	6.00	4.00
a.		Double surcharge		
b.		Perf. 13½	7.00	5.75
		Nos. P1-P3 (3)	21.00	10.50

N3   N4

1893-94   Typo.   *Perf. 11½*

P4	N3	2½r brown	3.25	2.00
a.		Perf. 12½	3.25	2.25
b.		Perf. 13½	3.50	2.00
P5	N4	½a on 2½r brn (Bk) ('94)	4.50	2.75
a.		Double surcharge		

For surcharges see Nos. 131, 252.

POSTAL TAX STAMPS

Pombal Commemorative Issue
Common Design Types
Perf. 12½
1925, Nov. 3   Engr.   Unwmk.

RA1	CD28	2a red org & blk	3.25	.70
RA2	CD29	2a red org & blk	3.25	.70
RA3	CD30	2a red org & blk	3.25	.70
		Nos. RA1-RA3 (3)	9.75	2.10

PT1

Symbolical of Charity
1930, Dec. 25   Litho.   *Perf. 11*

RA4	PT1	5a dk brown, *yel*	7.00	5.00

POSTAL TAX DUE STAMPS

Pombal Commemorative Issue
Common Design Types
1925   Unwmk.   *Perf. 12½*

RAJ1	CD28	4a red orange & blk	3.25	.70
RAJ2	CD29	4a red orange & blk	3.25	.70
RAJ3	CD30	4a red orange & blk	3.25	.70
		Nos. RAJ1-RAJ3 (3)	9.75	2.10

MADAGASCAR

ˌma-də-ˈgas-kər

LOCATION — Large island off the coast of southeastern Africa
GOVT. — French colony.
AREA — 226,658 sq. mi.
POP. — 3,797,936 (est. 1940)
CAPITAL — Antananarivo

Madagascar became a French protectorate in 1885 and a French colony in 1896 following several years of dispute among France, Great Britain, and the native government. The colony administered the former protectorates of Anjouan, Grand Comoro, Mayotte, Diego-Suarez, Nossi-Be and Sainte-Marie de Madagascar. Previous issues

---

of postage stamps are found under these individual headings.

12 Pence = 1 Shilling
100 Centimes = 1 Franc

British Consular Mail stamps of Madagascar were gummed only in one corner. Unused values are for stamps without gum. Examples having the original corner gum will command higher prices. Most used examples of these stamps have small faults and values are for stamps in this condition. Used stamps without faults are scarce and are worth more. Used stamps are valued with the commonly used crayon or pen cancellations.

"B C M" and Arms — A1

Handstamped "British Vice-Consulate"
Black Seal Handstamped

1884		Unwmk. Typo. *Rouletted*		
1	A1	1p violet	525.	450.
b.		Seal omitted	9,000.	9,000.
2	A1	2p violet	210.	325.
3	A1	3p violet	425.	350.
4	A1	4p violet 1 oz.	5,750.	5,250.
a.		"1 oz." corrected to "4 oz." in mss.	1,000.	725.
b.		Seal omitted	7,250.	7,250.
5	A1	6p violet	475.	500.
6	A1	1sh violet	525.	475.
7	A1	1sh6p violet	525.	525.
8	A1	2sh violet	850.	900.
9	A1	1p on 1sh vio		
10	A1	4½ on 1sh vio		
11	A1	6p red	1,150.	825.

1886		Violet Seal Handstamped		
12	A1	4p violet	1,650.	—
13	A1	6p violet	2,600.	—

Handstamped "British Consular Mail" as on A3
Black Seal Handstamped

14	A1	4p violet	1,850.	

Violet Seal Handstamped

15	A1	4p violet	7,250.	—

The 1, 2, 3 and 4 pence are inscribed "POSTAL PACKET," the other values of the series are inscribed "LETTER."

"British Vice-Consulate" — A2

Three types of A2 and A3:
I — "POSTAGE" 29½mm. Periods after "POSTAGE" and value.
II — "POSTAGE" 29½mm. No periods.
III — "POSTAGE" 24½mm. Period after value.

1886   Violet Seal Handstamped

16	A2	1p rose, I	400.	—
a.		Type II	1,250.	
17	A2	1½p rose, I	1,350.	875.
a.		Type II	2,850.	
18	A2	2p rose, I	400.	—
19	A2	3p rose, I	575.	400.
a.		Type I	1,350.	—
20	A2	4p rose, III	500.	—
21	A2	4½p rose, I	725.	350.
a.		Type III	2,100.	—
22	A2	6p rose, II	1,550.	—
23	A2	8p rose, II	2,350.	1,900.
a.		Type III	625.	
24	A2	9p rose	1,350.	—
24A	A2	1sh rose, III	19,000.	—
24B	A2	1sh6p rose, III	10,500.	—
25	A2	2sh rose, III	5,750.	—

Black Seal Handstamped
Type I

26	A2	1p rose	135.	210.
27	A2	1½p rose	2,600.	1,250.
28	A2	2p rose	200.	—
29	A2	3p rose	3,400.	1,150.
30	A2	4½p rose	3,400.	575.
31	A2	8p rose	4,500.	3,150.
32	A2	9p rose	4,250.	2,900.
32A	A2	2sh rose, III	—	—

"British Consular Mail" — A3

1886   Violet Seal Handstamped

33	A3	1p rose, II	150.	—
34	A3	1½p rose, II	240.	—
35	A3	2p rose, II	260.	—
36	A3	3p rose, II	210.	—
37	A3	4p rose, III	475.	—
38	A3	4½p rose, II	210.	—
39	A3	6p rose, II	450.	—
40	A3	8p rose, III	1,350.	—
a.		Type I	1,650.	—
41	A3	9p rose, II	475.	—
42	A3	1sh rose, III	1,650.	—
43	A3	1sh6p rose, III	1,550.	—
44	A3	2sh rose, III	1,600.	—

Black Seal Handstamped

45	A3	1p rose, I	115.	—
a.		Type II	115.	175.
46	A3	1½p rose, I	150.	250.
a.		Type II	125.	165.
47	A3	2p rose, I	155.	—
a.		Type II	135.	165.
48	A3	3p rose, I	155.	240.
a.		Type I	145.	175.
49	A3	4p rose, III	340.	—
50	A3	4½p rose, I	165.	210.
a.		Type I	145.	165.
51	A3	6p rose, II	145.	190.
52	A3	8p rose, I	190.	—
a.		Type III	1,675.	—
53	A3	9p rose, I	200.	325.
54	A3	1sh rose, III	575.	—
55	A3	1sh6p rose, III	675.	—
56	A3	2sh rose, III	700.	—

Seal Omitted

45b	A3	1p rose, II	4,200.	
46b	A3	1½p rose, II	4,400.	
48b	A3	3p rose, II	6,250.	
49a	A3	4p rose, III	5,000.	
50b	A3	4½p rose, II	7,250.	
51a	A3	6p rose, II	7,800.	
52b	A3	8p rose, II	5,000.	
53a	A3	9p rose, I	6,750.	
54a	A3	1sh rose, III	6,750.	
55a	A3	1sh6p rose, III	5,750.	
56a	A3	2sh rose, III	6,750.	

Some students of these issues doubt that the 1886 "seal omitted" varieties were regularly issued.

Red Seal Handstamped

57	A3	3p rose, I	—	15,500.
58	A3	4½p rose, I	—	10,500.

FRENCH OFFICES IN MADAGASCAR

The general issues of French Colonies were used in these offices in addition to the stamps listed here.

Stamps of French Colonies Surcharged in Black

a   b

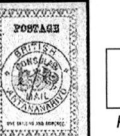

c

Overprint Type "a"

1889   Unwmk.   Perf. 14x13½

1	A9	05c on 10c blk, lav	725.	220.
a.		Inverted surcharge	1,950.	1,300.
b.		Vertical surcharge	1,200.	1,200.
c.		05c and 25c on 10c blk, lav	2,750.	1,450.
d.		Pair, one without surcharge		2,750.

2	A9	05c on 25c blk, rose	725.	220.
a.		Inverted surcharge	1,950.	1,300.
b.		25c on 10c lav (error)	11,500.	10,000.
c.		Double surcharge	1,400.	1,250.
3	A9	25c on 40c red, straw	650.	200.
		On cover		900.
a.		Inverted surcharge	1,700.	1,300.
b.		Double surcharge	1,750.	1,450.
c.		Vertical surcharge		1,400.

Covers: Values are for commercial covers paying correct rates. Philatelic covers sell for less.

1891   Overprint Type "b"

4	A9	05c on 40c red, straw	235.00	100.00
a.		Double "5" in surcharge	725.00	700.00
5	A9	15c on 25c blk, rose	235.00	110.00
a.		Surcharge vertical	275.00	145.00
b.		Double surcharge	725.00	650.00

Overprint Type "c"

6	A9	5c on 10c blk, lav	275.00	125.00
a.		Double surcharge	1,000.	900.00
7	A9	5c on 25c blk, rose	275.00	125.00

See Senegal Nos. 4, 8 for similar surcharge on 20c, 30c.
Forgeries of Nos. 1-7 exist.

A4

1891   Type-set   Imperf.
Without Gum

8	A4	5c blk, green	165.00	32.50
9	A4	10c blk, lt bl	125.00	40.00
		On cover		575.00
10	A4	15c ultra, pale bl	125.00	47.50
		On cover		575.00
11	A4	25c brn, buff	30.00	22.50
		On cover		400.00
12	A4	1fr blk, yellow	1,300.	300.00
13	A4	5fr vio & blk, lil	2,400.	1,275.

Ten varieties of each. Nos. 12-13 have been extensively forged.
Nos. 12 and 13 have a printed network of circles on the colored paper.
Most examples of Nos. 12-13 are defective due to the frail paper. Thinned examples sell for about 25% of the values quoted which are for stamps without damage.

POSTE FRANÇAISE Madagascar

Stamps of France 1876-90, Overprinted in Red or Black

1895   Perf. 14x13½

14	A15	5c grn, grnsh (R)	22.50	11.00
		On cover		175.00
15	A15	10c blk, lav (R)	50.00	32.50
		On cover		175.00
16	A15	15c bl (R)	72.50	22.00
		On cover		175.00
17	A15	25c blk, rose (R)	100.00	25.00
		On cover		140.00
18	A15	40c red, straw (Bk)	95.00	45.00
		On cover		225.00
19	A15	50c rose, rose (Bk)	110.00	55.00
		On cover		240.00
20	A15	75c dp vio, org (R)	125.00	62.50
		On cover		400.00
21	A15	1fr brnz grn, straw (Bk)	135.00	72.50
		On cover		450.00
22	A15	5fr vio, lav (Bk)	220.00	100.00
		On cover		500.00
		Nos. 14-22 (9)	930.00	425.50

Majunga Issue
Stamps of France, 1876-86, Surcharged with New Value

1895
Manuscript Surcharge in Red

22A	A15	0,15c on 25c blk, rose	8,000.
22B	A15	0,15c on 1fr brnz grn, straw	6,000.

Handstamped in Black

22C	A15	15c on 25c blk, rose	12,750.
22D	A15	15c on 1fr brnz grn, straw	11,750.

On most of No. 22C and all of No. 22D the manuscript surcharge of Nos. 22A-22B was washed off. Three types of "15" were used for No. 22C.

Stamps of France,
1876-84, Surcharged

1896

23	A15	5c on 1c blk, *bl*	6,400.	2,500.
		On cover		6,000.
24	A15	5c on 2c brn, *buff*	2,600.	1,000.
		On cover		3,250.
25	A15	25c on 3c gray, *grysh*	3,400.	1,100.
		On cover		3,250.
26	A15	25c on 4c cl, *lav*	6,400.	1,950.
		On cover		5,500.
27	A15	25c on 40c red, *straw*	1,650.	875.
		On cover		2,750.

The oval of the 5c and 15c surcharges is smaller than that of the 25c, and it does not extend beyond the edges of the stamp as the 25c surcharge does.

Excellent counterfeits of the surcharges on Nos. 22A to 27 exist.

Issues of the Colony

Navigation and
Commerce — A7

1896-1906   Typo.   Perf. 14x13½
Colony Name in Blue or Carmine

28	A7	1c blk, *lil bl*	1.50	1.10
		On cover		80.00
a.		Name double	525.00	
29	A7	2c brn, *buff*	2.25	1.50
		On cover		80.00
a.		Name in blue black	4.25	4.50
30	A7	4c claret, *lav*	2.50	1.80
		On cover		65.00
31	A7	5c grn, *grnsh*	8.00	1.50
		On cover		40.00
32	A7	5c yel grn ('01)	1.80	1.10
		On cover		11.00
33	A7	10c blk, *lav*	8.00	2.25
		On cover		30.00
34	A7	10c red ('00)	3.00	1.10
		On cover		11.00
35	A7	15c blue, quadrille paper	14.00	1.50
		On cover		32.50
36	A7	15c gray ('00)	2.50	1.50
		On cover		11.00
37	A7	20c red, *grn*	7.25	2.25
		On cover		55.00
38	A7	25c blk, *rose*	11.00	4.50
		On cover		30.00
39	A7	25c blue ('00)	25.00	32.50
		On cover		100.00
40	A7	30c brn, *bis*	8.75	3.75
		On cover		55.00
41	A7	35c blk, *yel* ('06)	45.00	7.25
		On cover		65.00
a.		Name inverted		15,000.
42	A7	40c red, *straw*	11.00	6.00
		On cover		55.00
43	A7	50c car, *rose*	14.50	3.00
		On cover		60.00
44	A7	50c brn, *az* ('00)	32.50	45.00
		On cover		95.00
45	A7	75c dp vio, *org*	6.25	4.50
		On cover		92.50
a.		Thin, translucent paper	7.50	5.00
46	A7	1fr brnz grn, *straw*	14.50	3.75
		On cover		110.00
a.		Name in blue ('99)	30.00	22.00
47	A7	5fr red lil, *lav* ('99)	37.50	32.50
		On cover		250.00
		Nos. 28-47 (20)	256.80	158.35

Perf. 13½x14 stamps are counterfeits.
For surcharges see Nos. 48-55, 58-60, 115-118, 127-128.

Nos. 32, 43, 44 and 46, affixed to pressboard with animals printed on the back, were used as emergency currency in the Comoro Islands in 1920.

Surcharged in Black

1902

48	A7	05c on 50c car, *rose*	7.25	6.00
		On cover		45.00
a.		Inverted surcharge	120.00	120.00
49	A7	10c on 5fr red lil, *lav*	25.00	22.00
		On cover		110.00
a.		Inverted surcharge	125.00	125.00

50	A7	15c on 1fr ol grn, *straw*	9.50	8.75
		On cover		45.00
a.		Inverted surcharge	120.00	120.00
b.		Double surcharge	400.00	400.00
c.		Pair, one w/o srch (?)	11.75	66.75

Surcharged in Black

51	A7	0,01 on 2c brn, *buff*	11.50	11.50
		On cover		72.50
a.		Inverted surcharge	72.50	72.50
b.		"00,1" instead of "0,01"	150.00	155.00
c.		As "b" inverted	—	—
d.		Comma omitted	210.00	210.00
e.		Name in blue black	11.50	11.50
52	A7	0,05 on 30c brn, *bis*	11.50	11.50
		On cover		65.00
a.		Inverted surcharge	72.50	72.50
b.		"00,5" instead of "0,05"	100.00	100.00
c.		As "b" inverted	2,550.	
d.		Comma omitted	210.00	210.00
53	A7	0,10 on 50c car, *rose*	9.50	9.50
		On cover		65.00
a.		Inverted surcharge	72.50	72.50
b.		Comma omitted	210.00	210.00
54	A7	0,15 on 75c vio, *org*	7.25	7.25
		On cover		62.50
a.		Inverted surcharge	72.50	72.50
b.		Comma omitted	210.00	210.00
c.		As "b," inverted	725.00	725.00
55	A7	0,15 on 1fr ol grn, *straw*	14.50	14.50
		On cover		72.50
a.		Inverted surcharge	110.00	110.00
b.		Comma omitted	275.00	275.00
		Nos. 51-55 (5)	54.25	54.25

Surcharged On Stamps of Diego-Suarez

56	A11	0,05 on 30c brn, *bis*	165.00	145.00
		On cover		400.00
a.		"00,5" instead of "0,05"	1,350.	1,350.
b.		Inverted surcharge	1,450.	1,450.
57	A11	0,10 on 50c car, *rose*	5,000.	5,000.

Counterfeits of Nos. 56-57 exist with surcharge both normal and inverted.

Surcharged in Black

58	A7	0,01 on 2c brn, *buff*	11.50	11.50
		On cover		72.50
a.		Inverted surcharge	72.50	72.50
b.		Comma omitted	210.00	210.00
59	A7	0,05 on 30c brn, *bis*	11.50	11.50
		On cover		65.00
a.		Inverted surcharge	72.50	72.50
b.		Comma omitted	210.00	210.00
60	A7	0,10 on 50c car, *rose*	9.50	9.50
		On cover		65.00
a.		Inverted surcharge	72.50	72.50
b.		Comma omitted	210.00	210.00
		Nos. 58-60 (3)	32.50	32.50

Surcharged On Stamps of Diego-Suarez

61	A11	0,05 on 30c brn, *bis*	165.00	145.00
		On cover		400.00
a.		Inverted surcharge	1,450.	1,450.
62	A11	0,10 on 50c car, *rose*	5,000.	5,000.

Se-tenant Pairs

51g	0,01	#51 + #58	25.00
52g	0,05	#52 + #59	30.00
53g	0,10	#53 + #60	30.00
56g	0,05	#56 + #62	550.00
57g	0,10	#57 + #63	—

BISECTS

During alleged stamp shortages at several Madagascar towns in 1904, it is claimed that bisects were used. After being affixed to letters, these bisects were handstamped "Affranchissement - exceptionnel - (faute de timbres)" and other inscriptions of similar import. The stamps bisected were 10c, 20c, 30c and 50c denominations of Madagascar type A7 and Diego-Suarez type A11. The editors believe these provisionals were unnecessary and speculative.

Zebu, Traveler's Tree
and Lemur — A8

1903   Engr.   Perf. 11½

63	A8	1c dk violet	1.10	1.10
a.		On bluish paper	8.00	6.50
64	A8	2c olive brn	1.10	1.10
65	A8	4c brown	1.45	1.50
66	A8	5c yellow grn	7.25	2.25
67	A8	10c red	13.25	1.50
68	A8	15c carmine	17.00	1.50
a.		On bluish paper	185.00	185.00
69	A8	20c orange	6.50	3.00
70	A8	25c dull blue	30.00	6.00
71	A8	30c pale red	45.00	16.00
72	A8	40c gray vio	30.00	6.50
73	A8	50c brown org	50.00	30.00
74	A8	75c orange yel	65.00	30.00
75	A8	1fr dp green	65.00	30.00
76	A8	2fr slate	87.50	32.50
77	A8	5fr gray black	100.00	105.00
		Nos. 63-77 (15)	520.15	267.95

Nos. 63-77 exist imperf. Value of set, $600.
For surcharges see Nos. 119-124, 129.

Transportation by
Sedan Chair — A9

1908-28   Typo.   Perf. 13½x14

79	A9	1c violet & ol	.25	.25
80	A9	2c red & ol	.25	.25
81	A9	4c ol brn & brn	.25	.25
82	A9	5c bl grn & ol	1.10	.30
83	A9	5c blk & rose ('22)	.30	.30
84	A9	10c rose & brown	1.10	.35
85	A9	10c bl grn & ol grn ('22)	.65	.45
86	A9	10c org brn & vio ('25)	.35	.35
87	A9	15c dl vio & rose ('16)	.35	.35
88	A9	15c dl grn & lt grn ('27)	.75	.75
89	A9	15c dk bl & rose red ('28)	1.90	1.10
90	A9	20c org & brn	.75	.50
91	A9	25c blue & blk	3.25	1.10
92	A9	25c vio & blk ('22)	.45	.35
93	A9	30c brown & blk	3.25	1.50
94	A9	30c rose red & brn ('22)	.60	.45
95	A9	30c grn & red vio ('25)	.60	.50
96	A9	30c dp grn & yel grn ('27)	1.50	1.10
97	A9	35c red & black	2.25	1.10
98	A9	40c vio brn & blk	1.50	.75
99	A9	45c bl grn & blk	1.10	.75
100	A9	45c red & ver ('25)	.50	.50
101	A9	45c gray lil & mag ('27)	1.45	1.10
102	A9	50c violet & blk	1.10	.75
103	A9	50c blue & blk ('22)	.95	.65
104	A9	50c blk & org ('25)	1.10	.45
105	A9	60c vio, *pnksh* ('25)	.75	.75
106	A9	65c black & bl ('25)	1.10	.85
107	A9	75c rose red & blk	1.10	.75
108	A9	85c grn & ver ('25)	1.50	.95
109	A9	1fr brown & ol	1.10	.75
110	A9	1fr dull blue ('25)	1.10	1.10
111	A9	1fr rose & grn ('28)	6.25	5.00
112	A9	1.10fr bis & bl grn ('28)	2.25	3.25
113	A9	2fr blue & olive	4.50	1.80
114	A9	5fr vio & vio brn	14.00	6.00
		Nos. 79-114 (36)	61.25	37.45

75c violet on pinkish stamps of type A9 are No. 138 without surcharge.
For surcharges and overprints see Nos. 125-126, 130-146, 178-179, B1, 212-214.

Preceding Issues Surcharged in Black or Carmine

1912, Nov.   Perf. 14x13½

115	A7	5c on 15c gray (C)	1.10	1.10
a.		Wide spacing in surcharge	8.75	1.45
116	A7	5c on 20c red, *grn*	1.50	1.50
a.		Inverted surcharge	175.00	
b.		As #116, wide spacing in surcharge	10.00	10.00
c.		As #116a, wide spacing in surcharge	2,200.	
117	A7	5c on 30c brn, *bis* (C)	1.90	1.90
a.		Wide spacing in surcharge	12.50	12.50
118	A7	10c on 75c vio, *org*	10.00	11.50
a.		Double surcharge	310.00	
b.		As #118, wide spacing in surcharge	210.00	210.00
c.		As #118a, wide spacing in surcharge	3,000.	
119	A8	5c on cl brn (C)	1.10	1.10
120	A8	5c on 20c org	1.10	1.10
121	A8	5c on 30c pale red	1.90	1.90
122	A8	10c on 40c gray vio (C)	1.90	1.90
123	A8	10c on 50c brn org	3.75	4.50
124	A8	10c on 75c org yel	6.50	8.00
a.		Inverted surcharge	230.00	
		Nos. 115-124 (10)	30.75	34.50

Two spacings between the surcharged numerals are found on Nos. 115 to 118: Narrow spacing between figures of surcharge 1.5mm (5c), 2mm (10c); Wide spacing between figures of surcharge 2.25mm (5c), 2.75mm (10c). Values for Nos. 115-118 are for stamps with narrow spacing.

Stamps of Anjouan, Grand Comoro Island, Mayotte and Mohéli with similar surcharges were also available for use in Madagascar and the entire Comoro archipelago.

Preceding Issues Surcharged in Red or Black

g

h

1921   On Nos. 98 & 107

125	A9 (g)	30c on 40c (R)	2.50	2.50
126	A9 (g)	60c on 75c	3.25	3.25

On Nos. 45 & 47

127	A7 (g)	60c on 75c (R)	12.50	12.50
a.		Inverted surcharge	220.00	220.00
128	A7 (h)	1fr on 5fr	1.10	1.10

On No. 77

129	A8 (h)	1fr on 5fr (R)	100.00	100.00
		Nos. 125-129 (5)	119.35	119.35

Stamps and Type of 1908-16 Surcharged in Black or Red

130	A9	1c on 15c dl vio & rose	1.10	1.10
131	A9	25c on 35c red & blk	6.50	6.50
132	A9	25c on 35c red & blk (R)	32.50	32.50
133	A9	25c on 40c brn & blk	5.00	5.00
134	A9	25c on 45c grn & blk	4.50	4.50
		Nos. 130-134 (5)	49.60	49.60
		Nos. 125-134 (10)	109.45	109.45

Stamps and Type of 1908-28 Surcharged with New Value and Bars

1922-27

135	A9	25c on 15c dl vio & rose	.35	.35
a.		Double surcharge	95.00	
136	A9	25c on 2fr bl & ol	.50	.50
137	A9	25c on 5fr vio & vio brn	.35	.35
138	A9	60c on 75c vio, *pnksh*	.60	.60
139	A9	65c on 75c rose red & blk	1.10	1.10
140	A9	85c on 45c bl grn & blk	1.90	1.45
141	A9	90c on 75c dl red & rose red	1.10	1.10

142	A9	1.25fr on 1fr lt bl (R)	.75	.50
143	A9	1.50fr on 1fr dp bl & dl bl	.75	.60
144	A9	3fr on 5fr grn & vio	2.25	1.45
145	A9	10fr on 5fr org & rose lil	9.50	6.00
146	A9	20fr on 5fr rose & sl bl	10.00	8.00
		Nos. 135-146 (12)	29.15	22.00

Years of issue: No. 138, 1922; Nos. 136, 137, 1924; Nos. 135, 139-140, 1925; No. 142, 1926; Nos. 141, 142-146, 1927.
See Nos. 178-179.

Sakalava Chief — A10   Hova Woman — A12

Hova with Oxen A11

Bétsiléo Woman A13

Perf. 13½x14, 14x13½

1930-44			**Typo.**	
147	A11	1c dk bl & bl grn ('33)	.25	.25
148	A10	2c brn red & dk brn	.25	.25
149	A10	4c dk brn & vio	.25	.25
150	A11	5c lt grn & red	.40	.25
151	A12	10c ver & dp grn	.40	.25
152	A13	15c dp red	.25	.25
153	A11	20c yel brn & dk bl	.25	.25
154	A12	25c vio & dk brn	.25	.25
155	A13	30c Prus blue	.65	.45
156	A10	40c grn & red	.75	.50
157	A13	45c dull violet	.90	.55
158	A11	65c brn & vio	1.10	.80
159	A13	75c dk brown	.85	.50
160	A11	90c brn red & dk red	1.40	.90
161	A12	1fr yel brn & dk bl	1.75	1.10
162	A12	1fr dk red & car rose ('38)	.95	.90
163	A12	1.25fr dp bl & dk brn ('33)	1.60	.90
164	A10	1.50fr dk & dp bl	5.50	1.10
165	A10	1.50fr brn & dk red ('38)	.75	.50
165A	A10	1.50fr dk red & brn ('44)	.50	.50
166	A10	1.75fr dk brn & dk red ('33)	4.25	1.60
167	A10	5fr vio & dk brn	1.25	.70
168	A10	20fr yel brn & dk bl	2.00	1.75
		Nos. 147-168 (23)	26.35	14.75

For surcharges and overprints see Nos. 211, 215, 217-218, 222-223, 228-229, 233, 235, 239, 257 and note after No. B10 in Scott Standard catalogue, Vol. 4.

Common Design Types pictured following the introduction.

Colonial Exposition Issue
Common Design Types

1931	**Engr.**		**Perf. 12½**
Name of Country in Black			
169	CD70	40c deep green	1.40 1.00
170	CD71	50c violet	2.00 1.25
171	CD72	90c red orange	2.00 1.25
172	CD73	1.50fr dull blue	2.50 1.50
		Nos. 169-172 (4)	7.90 5.00

General Joseph Simon Galliéni — A14

1931	**Engr.**		**Perf. 14**
Size: 21½x34½mm			
173	A14	1c ultra	.50 .45
174	A14	50c orange brn	1.40 .35
175	A14	2fr deep red	5.75 4.25
176	A14	3fr emerald	5.50 3.00
177	A14	10fr dp orange	4.00 3.00
		Nos. 173-177 (5)	17.15 11.05

See Nos. 180-190. For overprints and surcharges see Nos. 216, 219, 221, 224, 232, 258 in Scott Standard catalogue, Vol. 4.

Nos. 113 and 109 Surcharged

1932			**Perf. 13½x14**
178	A9	25c on 2fr bl & ol	.75 .50
179	A9	50c on 1fr brn & ol	.75 .50

No. 178 has numerals in thick block letters.
No. 136 has thin shaded numerals.

Galliéni Type of 1931

1936-40	**Photo.**	**Perf. 13½, 13x13½**	
Size: 21x34mm			
180	A14	3c sapphire ('40)	.25 .25
181	A14	45c brt green ('40)	.50 .40
182	A14	50c yellow brown	.25 .25
183	A14	60c brt red lil ('40)	.40 .25
184	A14	70c brt rose ('40)	.60 .40
185	A14	90c copper brn ('39)	.50 .40
186	A14	1.40fr org yel ('40)	.90 .50
187	A14	1.60fr purple ('40)	.90 .60
188	A14	2fr dk carmine	.50 .25
189	A14	3fr green	4.50 2.25
190	A14	3fr olive blk ('39)	.90 .70
		Nos. 180-190 (11)	10.20 6.25

For overprint see note after No. B10 in Scott Standard catalogue, Vol. 4.

Paris International Exposition Issue
Common Design Types

1937, Apr. 15	**Engr.**		**Perf. 13**
191	CD74	20c dp violet	1.90 1.90
192	CD75	30c dk green	1.90 1.90
193	CD76	40c car rose	1.60 1.60
194	CD77	50c dk brn & blk	1.40 1.40
195	CD78	90c red	1.75 1.75
196	CD79	1.50fr ultra	1.75 1.75
		Nos. 191-196 (6)	10.30 10.30

Colonial Arts Exhibition Issue
Common Design Type
Souvenir Sheet

1937			**Imperf.**
197	CD74	3fr orange red	7.25 *8.00*

Jean Laborde A15

1938-40			**Perf. 13**
198	A15	35c green	.65 .40
199	A15	55c dp purple	.65 .40
200	A15	65c orange red	.90 .40
201	A15	80c violet brn	.65 .40
202	A15	1fr rose car	.90 .40
203	A15	1.25fr rose car ('39)	.40 .25
204	A15	1.75fr dk ultra	1.75 1.75
205	A15	2.15fr yel brn	2.50 1.75
206	A15	2.25fr dk ultra ('39)	.60 .50
207	A15	2.50fr blk brn ('40)	.65 .50
208	A15	10fr dk green ('40)	1.25 .90
		Nos. 198-208 (11)	10.90 6.60

Nos. 198-202, 204, 205 commemorate the 60th anniv. of the death of Jean Laborde, explorer.

For overprints and surcharges see Nos. 220, 225-227, 230-231, 234, 236-237 in Scott Standard catalogue, Vol. 4.

New York World's Fair Issue
Common Design Type

1939, May 10	**Engr.**	**Perf. 12½x12**	
209	CD82	1.25fr car lake	1.25 1.25
210	CD82	2.25fr ultra	2.50 2.50

For surcharge see No. 240 in Scott Standard catalogue, Vol. 4.

SEMI-POSTAL STAMPS

No. 84 Surcharged in Red

1915, Feb.	**Unwmk.**	**Perf. 13½x14**	
B1	A9	10c + 5c rose & brn	1.50 1.50

Curie Issue
Common Design Type

1938, Oct. 24			**Perf. 13**
B2	CD80	1.75fr + 50c brt ultra	11.00 11.00

French Revolution Issue
Common Design Type
Name and Value Typographed in Black

1939, July 5			**Photo.**
B3	CD83	45c + 25c grn	9.50 9.50
B4	CD83	70c + 30c brn	9.50 9.50
B5	CD83	90c + 35c red org	9.50 9.50
B6	CD83	1.25fr + 1fr rose pink	9.50 9.50
B7	CD83	2.25fr + 2fr blue	9.50 9.50
		Nos. B3-B7 (5)	47.50 47.50

Nos. 162, 190 Surcharged "SECOURS +50c NATIONAL"

AIR POST STAMPS

Airplane and Map of Madagascar — AP1

		Perf. 13x13½	
1935-41	**Photo.**	**Unwmk.**	
		Map in Red	
C1	AP1	50c yellow green	.65 .45
C2	AP1	90c yel grn ('41)	.50
C3	AP1	1.25fr claret	.50 .50
C4	AP1	1.50fr bright blue	.50 .50
C5	AP1	1.60fr brt blue ('41)	.25 .25
C6	AP1	1.75fr orange	8.75 3.75
C7	AP1	2fr Prus blue	.85 .45
C8	AP1	3fr dp org ('41)	.25 .25
C9	AP1	3.65fr ol blk ('38)	.85 .50
C10	AP1	3.90fr turq grn ('41)	.25 .25
C11	AP1	4fr rose	45.00 3.25
C12	AP1	4.50fr black	27.50 2.50
C13	AP1	5.50fr ol blk ('41)	.25 .25
C14	AP1	6fr rose lil ('41)	.35 .25
C15	AP1	6.90fr dl vio ('41)	.25 .25
C16	AP1	8fr rose lilac	1.50 .90
C17	AP1	8.50fr green	1.50 1.10
C18	AP1	9fr ol grn ('41)	.35 .35
C19	AP1	12fr violet brown	.80 .55
C20	AP1	12.50fr dull violet	1.90 .90
C21	AP1	15fr org yel ('41)	.80 .55
C22	AP1	16fr olive green	1.75 1.10
C23	AP1	20fr dark brown	2.50 1.75

C24	AP1	50fr brt ultra ('38)	4.75	4.50
		Nos. C1,C3-C24 (23)	102.05	25.10

According to some authorities the 90c was not placed on sale in Madagascar.

AIR POST SEMI-POSTAL STAMPS

French Revolution Issue
Common Design Type
Unwmk.

1939, July 13	**Photo.**		**Perf. 13**
Name and Value in Orange			
CB1	CD83	4.50fr + 4fr brn blk	18.00 18.00

POSTAGE DUE STAMPS

Postage Due Stamps of French Colonies Overprinted in Red or Blue — D1

1896		**Unwmk.**		**Imperf.**
J1	D1	5c blue (R)	12.00	9.50
		On cover		300.00
J2	D1	10c brown (R)	11.00	8.00
		On cover		300.00
J3	D1	20c yellow (Bl)	10.00	8.00
		On cover		300.00
J4	D1	30c rose red (Bl)	11.00	8.00
		On cover		300.00
J5	D1	40c lilac (R)	80.00	50.00
		On cover		750.00
J6	D1	50c gray vio (Bl)	14.50	10.00
		On cover		400.00
J7	D1	1fr dk grn (R)	80.00	65.00
		On cover		65.00
		Nos. J1-J7 (7)	218.50	158.50

Governor's Palace — D2

1908-24		**Typo.**		**Perf. 13½x14**
J8	D2	2c vio brn	.25	.25
J9	D2	4c violet	.25	.25
J10	D2	5c green	.25	.25
J11	D2	10c deep rose	.25	.25
J12	D2	20c olive green	.40	.40
J13	D2	40c brn, *straw*	.45	.45
J14	D2	50c brn, *bl*	.60	.60
J15	D2	60c orange ('24)	.60	.60
J16	D2	1fr dark blue	1.10	1.10
		Nos. J8-J16 (9)	4.15	4.15

Type of 1908 Issue Surcharged

1924-27				
J17	D2	60c on 1fr org	1.90	1.90

Surcharged

J18	D2	2fr on 1fr lil rose ('27)	.90	.90
J19	D2	3fr on 1fr ultra ('27)	.90	.90

MADEIRA

mə-'dir-ə

LOCATION — A group of islands in the Atlantic Ocean northwest of Africa
GOVT. — Part of the Republic of Portugal
AREA — 314 sq. mi.
POP. — 150,574 (1900)
CAPITAL — Funchal

These islands are considered an integral part of Portugal and since 1898 postage stamps of Portugal have been in use.

1000 Reis = 1 Milreis
100 Centavos = 1 Escudo (1925)

STAMPS OF PORTUGAL USED IN MADEIRA

PRE-STAMP POSTAL MARKINGS
British Post Office Crowned Paid Postmarks

1842
A1   Crowned double circle handstamp, on cover, inscribed "PAID AT MADEIRA" in red   20,000.

Earliest known use: 2/28/42.

Stamps of Portugal Used in Madeira
Barred Numeral "51"

1853   **Queen Maria II**
A1	5r org brn (#1)	2,300.
A2	25r blue (#2)	150.
A3	50r dp yel grn (#3)	2,250.
A4	100r lilac (#4)	5,000.

1855   King Pedro V (Straight Hair)
A5	5r red brn (#5)	2,300.
A6	25r blue, type II (#6)	110.00
	On cover	500.00
a.	Type I (#6a)	120.00
	On cover	450.00
A7	50r green (#7)	175.00
	On cover	900.00
A8	100r lilac (#8)	190.00

1856-58
King Pedro V (Curled Hair)
A9	5r red brn (#9)	290.00
A10	25r blue, type II (#10)	165.00
	On cover	500.00
a.	Type I (#10a)	165.00
	On cover	475.00
A11	25r rose, type II (#11; '58)	60.00
	On cover	300.00

1862-64   King Luiz
A12	5r brown (#12)	175.00
A13	10r orange (#13)	190.00
A14	25r rose (#14)	65.00
	On cover	175.00
A15	50r yel green (#15)	180.00
	On cover	500.00
A16	100r lilac (#16; '64)	165.00

1866-67   King Luiz
Imperf.
A17	5r black (#17)	190.00
A18	10r yellow (#18)	290.00
A19	20r bister (#19)	290.00
A20	25r rose (#20)	210.00
	On cover	375.00
A21	50r green (#21)	290.00
	On cover	475.00
A22	80r orange (#22)	290.00
	On cover	625.00
A23	100r dk lilac (#23; '67)	375.00
A24	120r blue (#24)	190.00
	On cover	625.00

Perf. 12½
A28	25r rose (#28)	160.00

Issued under Portuguese Administration

It is recommended that the rare overprinted 1868-81 stamps be purchased accompanied by certificates of authenticity from competent experts.

King Luiz — A1

Stamps of Portugal Overprinted

1868, Jan. 1   Unwmk.   Imperf.
Black Overprint
2	A1	20r bister	210.00	120.00
a.	Inverted overprint			
b.	Rouletted			—
3	A1	50r green	210.00	120.00
4	A1	80r orange	225.00	125.00
a.	Double overprint			—
5	A1	100r lilac	225.00	125.00
	Nos. 2-5 (4)		870.00	490.00

The 5r black does not exist as a genuinely imperforate original.
Reprints of 1885 are on stout white paper, ungummed. (Also, 5r, 10r and 25r values were overprinted.) Reprints of 1905 are on ordinary white paper with shiny gum and have a wide "D" and "R." Value, $12 each.

Lozenge Perf.
2c	A1	20r	—
3a	A1	50r	—
4b	A1	50r	—
5a	A1	100r	—

Overprinted in Red or Black

1868-70   Perf. 12½
6	A1	5r black (R)	50.00	37.50
8	A1	10r yellow	90.00	80.00
9	A1	20r bister	140.00	110.00
10	A1	25r rose	50.00	12.00
a.	Inverted overprint			—
11	A1	50r green	200.00	140.00
a.	Inverted overprint			—
12	A1	80r orange	180.00	140.00
13	A1	100r lilac	190.00	140.00
a.	Inverted overprint			—
14	A1	120r blue	110.00	80.00
15	A1	240r violet ('70)	500.00	425.00
	Nos. 6-15 (9)		1,510.	1,164.

Two types of 5r differ in the position of the "5" at upper right.
The reprints are on stout white paper, ungummed, with rough perforation 13½, and on thin white paper with shiny white gum and clean-cut perforation 13½. The overprint has the wide "D" and "R" and the first reprints included the 5r with both black and red overprint. Value $10 each.

King Luiz — A2

Overprinted in Red or Black

1871-80   Perf. 12½, 13½
16	A2	5r black (R)	11.00	8.00
a.	Inverted overprint			
b.	Double overprint	55.00	55.00
c.	Perf. 14	90.00	55.00
18	A2	10r yellow	35.00	22.50
19	A2	10r bl grn ('79)	140.00	110.00
a.	Perf. 13½	160.00	140.00
20	A2	10r yel grn ('80)	65.00	52.50
21	A2	15r brn ('75)	19.00	11.50
22	A2	20r bister	30.00	22.50
23	A2	25r rose	13.50	4.50
a.	Inverted overprint	50.00	40.00
b.	Double overprint	50.00	40.00
24	A2	50r green ('72)	67.50	30.00
a.	Double overprint		—
b.	Inverted overprint	200.00	200.00
25	A2	50r blue ('80)	125.00	55.00
26	A2	80r orange ('72)	77.50	67.50
27	A2	100r pale lil ('73)	90.00	60.00
a.	Perf. 14	200.00	85.00
b.	Perf. 13½	60.00	75.00
28	A2	120r blue	110.00	80.00
29	A2	150r blue ('76)	160.00	140.00
a.	Perf. 13½	175.00	150.00
30	A2	150r yel ('79)	300.00	240.00
31	A2	240r violet ('74)	700.00	500.00
32	A2	300r vio ('76)	75.00	67.50
	Nos. 16-32 (16)	2,018.	1,471.

There are two types of the overprint, the second one having a broad "D."
The reprints have the same characteristics as those of the 1868-70 issues.

A3

A4

King Luiz — A5

1880-81
33	A3	5r black	40.00	21.00
34	A4	25r pearl gray	50.00	21.00
a.	Inverted overprint	75.00	75.00
35	A5	25r lilac	50.00	11.00
a.	25r purple brown	32.50	11.00
b.	25r gray	35.00	10.00
	Nos. 33-35 (3)	140.00	53.00

Nos. 33, 34 and 35 have been reprinted on stout white paper, ungummed, and the last three on thin white paper with shiny white gum. The perforations are as previously described.

Common Design Types pictured following the introduction.

Vasco da Gama Issue
Common Design Types

1898, Apr. 1   Engr.   Perf. 14-15
37	CD20	2½r blue grn	2.40	1.25
38	CD21	5r red	2.40	1.25
39	CD22	10r red violet	3.00	1.50
40	CD23	25r yel green	2.75	1.25
41	CD24	50r dk blue	6.00	3.25
42	CD25	75r vio brown	8.00	7.00
43	CD26	100r bister brn	8.00	7.00
44	CD27	150r bister	12.00	11.50
	Nos. 37-44 (8)	44.55	34.00

Nos. 37-44 with "REPUBLICA" overprint and surcharges are listed as Portugal Nos. 199-206.

Ceres — A6

1928, May 1   Engr.   Perf. 13½
Value Typographed in Black
45	A6	3c deep violet	.40	.60
	Never hinged	.50	
46	A6	4c orange	.40	.60
	Never hinged	.50	
47	A6	5c light blue	.40	.60
	Never hinged	.50	
48	A6	6c brown	.40	.60
	Never hinged	.50	
49	A6	10c red	.40	.60
	Never hinged	.50	
50	A6	15c yel green	.40	.60
	Never hinged	.50	
51	A6	16c red brown	.40	.60
	Never hinged	.55	
52	A6	25c violet rose	1.00	.60
	Never hinged	1.20	
53	A6	32c blue grn	1.00	.60
	Never hinged	1.20	
54	A6	40c yel brown	1.50	1.75
	Never hinged	2.40	
55	A6	50c slate	1.50	1.75
	Never hinged	2.40	
56	A6	64c Prus blue	1.50	3.00
	Never hinged	2.40	
57	A6	80c dk brown	1.50	5.00
	Never hinged	2.40	
58	A6	96c carmine rose	5.00	3.00
	Never hinged	8.00	
59	A6	1e black	1.25	3.00
a.	Value omitted	42.50	45.00
	Never hinged	75.00	
60	A6	1.20e light rose	1.25	3.00
	Never hinged	2.00	
61	A6	1.60e ultra	1.25	3.00
	Never hinged	2.00	
62	A6	2.40e yellow	2.00	3.50
	Never hinged	3.25	
63	A6	3.36e dull green	3.00	5.75
	Never hinged	4.75	
64	A6	4.50e brown red	5.00	9.00
	Never hinged	8.00	
65	A6	7e dark blue	6.00	17.50
	Never hinged	9.00	
	Nos. 45-65 (21)	35.55	64.65

It was obligatory to use these stamps in place of those in regular use on May 1, June 5, July 1 and Dec. 31, 1928, Jan. 1 and 31, May

1 and June 5, 1929. The amount obtained from this sale was donated to a fund for building a museum.
Less than very fine examples sell for much less.

NEWSPAPER STAMP

Numeral of Value — N1

Newspaper Stamp of Portugal Overprinted in Black
Perf. 12½, 13½
1876, July 1   Unwmk.
P1	N1	2½r olive	9.00	4.25
a.	Inverted overprint	30.00	

The reprints have the same papers, gum, perforations and overprint as the reprints of the regular issues.

POSTAL TAX STAMPS

Pombal Commemorative Issue
Common Design Types

1925   Unwmk.   Engr.   Perf. 12½
RA1	CD28	15c gray & black	.60	.65
RA2	CD29	15c gray & black	.60	.65
RA3	CD30	15c gray & black	.60	.65
	Nos. RA1-RA3 (3)	1.80	1.95

POSTAL TAX DUE STAMPS

Pombal Commemorative Issue
Common Design Types

1925   Unwmk.   Perf. 12½
RAJ1	CD28	30c gray & black	.85	3.50
RAJ2	CD29	30c gray & black	.85	3.50
RAJ3	CD30	30c gray & black	.85	3.50
	Nos. RAJ1-RAJ3 (3)	2.55	10.50

MALAYA

mə-ˈlā-ə

Federated Malay States

LOCATION — Malay peninsula
GOVT. — British Protectorate
AREA — 27,585 sq. mi.
CAPITAL — Kuala Lumpur

The Federated Malay States consisted of the sultanates of Negri Sembilan, Pahang, Perak and Selangor. Stamps of the Federated Malay States replaced those of the individual states and were used until 1935, when individual issues were resumed.

100 Cents = 1 Dollar

> **Catalogue values for unused stamps in this country are for Never Hinged items, beginning with Scott J20 in the postage due section, Scott 55 in Kedah, Scott 44 in Kelantan, Scott 1 in Malacca, Scott 36 in Negri Sembilan, Scott 44 in Pahang, Scott 1 in Penang, Scott 99 in Perak, Scott 1 in Perlis, Scott 74 in Selangor, and Scott 47 in Trengganu.**

Watermarks

Wmk. 47 —
Multiple Rosettes

Wmk. 71 —
Rosette

Stamps of Straits Settlements overprinted "BMA MALAYA" are listed in Straits Settlements.

Stamps and Type of Negri Sembilan Overprinted in Black

1900   Wmk. 2   Perf. 14

1	A2	1c lilac & green	3.50	10.00
2	A2	2c lilac & brown	35.00	77.50
3	A2	3c lilac & black	3.25	6.00
4	A2	5c lilac & olive	85.00	200.00
5	A2	10c lilac & org	15.00	45.00
6	A2	20c green & olive	100.00	125.00
7	A2	25c grn & car rose	300.00	425.00
8	A2	50c green & black	110.00	160.00
		Nos. 1-8 (8)	651.75	1,048.
		Set, ovptd. "SPECIMEN"	225.00	

Overprinted on Perak Nos. 51, 53, 57-58, 60-61

1900

9	A9	5c lilac & olive	27.50	70.00
10	A9	10c lilac & org	90.00	80.00

Wmk. 1

11	A10	$1 green & lt grn	210.00	275.00
12	A10	$2 green & car rose	175.00	300.00
13	A10	$5 green & ultra	500.00	800.00
		Revenue cancel		75.00
13A	A10	$25 green & org		13,000.
		Revenue cancel		450.00
		Overprinted "SPECIMEN"	500.00	
		Nos. 9-13 (5)	1,002.	1,525.

No. 10 with bar omitted is an essay.

Elephants and Howdah — A3

Tiger — A4

1900   Typo.

14	A3	$1 green & lt green	170.	170.
15	A3	$2 grn & car rose	170.	190.
16	A3	$5 green & ultra	400.	425.
a.		$5 green & pale ultramarine	350.	375.
		Revenue cancel		20.
17	A3	$25 grn & orange	3,750.	1,950.
		Revenue cancel		100.
		Overprinted "SPECIMEN"	375.	
		Nos. 14-17 (4)	4,490.	2,735.
		Nos. 14-16, ovptd. "SPECIMEN"	190.00	

High values with revenue cancellations are plentiful and inexpensive.

1901   Wmk. 2

Stamps of type A4 are watermarked sideways.

18	A4	1c blue grn & blk	11.00	9.00
a.		1c green & gray	4.75	1.25
b.		1c green & gray brown	12.00	.40
19	A4	3c brown & gray	7.25	.45
a.		3c brown & black	14.50	5.00
b.		3c brown & gray brown	7.75	.25
20	A4	4c rose & black	19.00	8.50
a.		4c carmine & gray	10.00	5.75
b.		4c carmine & gray brown	30.00	5.75
21	A4	5c scar & grn, yel	3.00	3.75
22	A4	8c ultra & blk	55.00	22.50
a.		8c ultramarine & gray	24.00	6.50
b.		8c ultramarine & gray brown	32.50	4.50
23	A4	10c violet & blk	135.00	55.00
a.		10c violet & gray	90.00	10.00
b.		10c purple & black	170.00	50.00
c.		10c purple & gray	97.50	15.00
d.		10c purple & gray brown	105.00	8.50
24	A4	20c black & gray vio	26.00	12.00
25	A4	50c brn org & black	195.00	155.00
a.		50c brown orange & gray	120.00	60.00
b.		50c brown orange & gray brown	110.00	50.00
		Nos. 18-25 (8)	451.25	266.20
		Set, ovpted. "SPECIMEN"	240.00	

1904-10   Wmk. 3 Sideways

26	A4	1c green & black	85.00	10.00
a.		1c green & gray brown	45.00	.85
27	A4	3c brown & gray	77.50	1.25
a.		3c brn & gray brn ('05)	55.00	2.10
b.		As "a," chalky paper ('05)	50.00	3.25
28	A4	4c rose & black	7.75	1.00
a.		Chalky paper	26.00	3.25
b.		4c scarlet & black	26.00	3.00
c.		4c scarlet & gray brown	47.50	4.00
d.		4c scarlet & gray	60.00	5.75
29	A4	5c scar & grn, yel	13.00	3.25
a.		Chalky paper	35.00	6.50
b.		5c carmine & deep green, yel	17.00	4.00
c.		5c car & dp grn, org buff ('21)	20.00	10.00
d.		5c car & dp grn, pale yel ('22)	15.00	7.75
30	A4	8c ultra & black ('05)	85.00	25.00
a.		8c ultra & gr brn ('05)	22.50	5.00
b.		As "a," chalky paper ('05)	85.00	16.00
c.		As "b," wmk upright ('07)	11.00	5.75
31	A4	10c violet & black	110.00	6.00
a.		10c claret & gray brown	90.00	9.00
b.		As "a," chalky paper ('05)	120.00	13.00
c.		10c claret & black	32.50	.75
d.		10c purple & gray brown ('05)	85.00	4.00
e.		10c purple & black	35.00	3.25
32	A4	20c blk & gray vio ('05)	11.50	1.50
a.		Chalky paper	18.00	3.50
33	A4	50c brn org & blk ('05)	105.00	20.00
a.		Chalky paper	85.00	12.00
b.		50c orange & gray ('05)	18.00	11.50
c.		50c org brn & gray brn ('06)	60.00	9.00
d.		As "b," chalky paper	135.00	25.00
e.		50c org brn & jet blk ('14)	72.50	11.50

The 1c and 4c are on ordinary paper, the other values on both ordinary and chalky papers.

Chalky Paper

34	A3	$1 green & lt green ('07)	110.00	57.50
35	A3	$2 green & car rose ('06)	120.00	140.00
36	A3	$5 grn & ultra ('06)	300.00	160.00
		Revenue cancellation		25.00
37	A3	$25 grn & org ('10)	1,700.	900.00
		Revenue cancellation		60.00
		Nos. 26-36 (11)	1,024.	425.50

High values with revenue cancellations are plentiful and inexpensive.

1906-22   Ordinary Paper

Two dies for Nos. 38 and 44:
I — Thick line under "Malay."
II — Thin line under "Malay."

38	A4	1c dull grn, die II	9.50	.25
b.		Die I	17.00	.55
39	A4	1c brown ('19)	3.00	1.25
40	A4	2c green ('19)	2.50	.55
41	A4	3c brown	10.50	.25

42	A4	3c carmine ('09)	4.50	.25
43	A4	3c dp gray ('19)	2.50	.25
44	A4	4c scar, die II	2.25	.25
b.		Die I ('19)	3.75	5.50
45	A4	6c orange ('19)	3.25	3.25
46	A4	8c ultra ('09)	16.00	1.40
47	A4	10c ultra ('19)	9.00	2.25
48	A4	35c red, yellow	7.50	15.00
		Nos. 38-48 (11)	70.50	24.95
		Set, ovptd. "SPECIMEN"	600.00	

1922-32   Wmk. 4   Ordinary Paper

49	A4	1c brown ('22)	2.25	3.50
50	A4	1c black ('23)	.85	.25
51	A4	2c dk brown ('25)	6.50	9.00
52	A4	2c green ('26)	3.00	.25
53	A4	3c dp gray ('23)	2.50	7.50
54	A4	3c green ('24)	2.75	2.00
55	A4	3c brown ('27)	3.00	.50
56	A4	4c scar (II) ('23)	3.50	.60
57	A4	4c orange ('26)	1.50	.25
c.		Unwatermarked	475.00	300.00
58	A4	5c vio, yel ('22)	1.25	.25
59	A4	5c dk brown ('32)	3.50	.25
60	A4	6c orange ('22)	1.00	.55
61	A4	6c scarlet ('26)	1.50	.25
62	A4	10c ultra ('23)	1.75	8.00
63	A4	10c ultra & blk ('23)	2.50	.80
64	A4	10c vio, yel, chalky paper ('31)	6.00	.55
65	A4	12c ultra ('22)	1.75	.25

Chalky Paper

66	A4	20c blk & vio ('23)	5.00	1.75
a.		Ordinary paper	50.00	3.50
67	A4	25c red vio & ol vio ('29)	3.50	2.75
68	A4	30c yel & dl vio ('29)	4.00	4.75
69	A4	35c red, yel, ordinary paper ('28)	6.00	26.00
70	A4	35c dk vio & car ('31)	17.00	15.00
71	A4	50c org & blk ('24)	17.00	17.00
72	A4	50c blk, bl grn ('31)	5.50	2.50
73	A3	$1 gray grn & yel grn ('26)	23.00	55.00
a.		$1 green & blue green	24.00	100.00
74	A3	$2 grn & car ('26)	37.50	95.00
75	A3	$5 grn & ultra ('25)	150.00	250.00
76	A3	$25 grn & org ('28)	1,500.	1,800.
		Revenue cancel		120.00
		Nos. 49-75 (27)	313.60	504.50

1931-34

77	A4	$1 red & blk, blue	15.00	4.75
78	A4	$2 car & green, yel ('34)	60.00	50.00
79	A4	$5 car & green, emer ('34)	300.00	250.00
		Nos. 77-79 (3)	375.00	304.75
		Set (#49-79), ovptd. "SPECIMEN"	600.00	

POSTAGE DUE STAMPS

D1

D2

Perf. 14½x14

1924-26		**Typo.**		**Wmk. 4**
J1	D1	1c violet	4.75	40.00
J2	D1	2c black	2.25	7.00
J3	D1	4c green ('26)	3.25	8.00
J4	D1	8c red	6.00	37.50
J5	D1	10c orange	10.00	17.50
J6	D1	12c ultramarine	10.00	27.50
		Nos. J1-J6 (6)	36.25	137.50
		Set, ovptd. "SPECIMEN"	250.00	

The Malayan Postal Union (MPU), established in 1934, linked the postal services of the federated states and Straits Settlements. MPU postage due stamps for common use were issued using the D1 design. Stamps with this design continued to be issued well after the war and were only gradually replaced by postage due stamps issued by Singapore and Malaysia.

1936-38   Perf. 14½x14

J7	D2	1c dk violet ('38)	7.00	1.10
J8	D2	4c yellow green	19.00	1.40
J9	D2	8c scarlet	9.00	5.00
J10	D2	10c yel orange	13.00	.50
J11	D2	12c blue violet	16.00	17.50
J12	D2	50c black ('38)	20.00	8.00
		Nos. J7-J12 (6)	84.00	33.50

Nos. J7-J12 were also used in Straits Settlements.

For overprints see Nos. NJ1-NJ20, Malacca Nos. NJ1-NJ6.

1945-49

J13	D2	1c reddish violet	2.50	2.25
J14	D2	3c yel green	5.00	6.00
J15	D2	5c org scarlet	4.50	3.50
J16	D2	8c yel org ('49)	9.00	16.00
J17	D2	9c yel orange	27.50	50.00
J18	D2	15c blue vio	77.50	35.00
J19	D2	20c dk blue ('48)	6.00	10.00
		Nos. J13-J19 (7)	132.00	122.75

For surcharge see No. J34.

> **Catalogue values for unused stamps in this section, from this point to the end of the section, are for Never Hinged items.**

1951-54   Wmk. 4   Perf. 14

J20	D2	1c dull violet ('52)	.70	1.75
J21	D2	2c dk gray ('53)	1.25	2.25
J22	D2	3c green ('52)	28.00	15.00
J23	D2	4c dk brown ('53)	.70	7.00
J24	D2	5c vermilion	50.00	13.00
J25	D2	8c yel orange	2.50	6.00
J26	D2	12c magenta ('54)	1.25	6.50
J27	D2	20c deep blue	7.00	6.75
		Nos. J20-J27 (8)	91.40	58.25

Nos. J13-J27 were used throughout the Federation and in Singapore, later in Malaysia.

1957-63 Ordinary Paper   Perf. 12½

J21a	D2	2c ('60)	2.50	20.00
b.		2c, chalky paper ('62)	1.75	13.00
J23a	D2	4c ('60)	2.00	21.00
b.		4c, chalky paper ('62)	1.00	18.00
J26a	D2	12c, chalky paper ('62)	3.25	27.50
J27a	D2	20c	8.00	29.00
		~~, ~~ ('00)	8.88	78.00
		Nos. J21a-J27a (4)	15.75	97.50

OCCUPATION STAMPS

Issued Under Japanese Occupation

Malayan Fruit
and Fronds
OS1

Tin Dredging
OS2

Monument to
Japanese
War Dead
OS3

Malayan
Plowman
OS4

1943   Unwmk.   Litho.   Perf. 12½

N30	OS1	2c emerald	1.00	.25
a.		Rouletted	2.25	2.25
b.		Imperf., pair	6.50	6.50
N31	OS2	4c rose red	3.00	.25
a.		Rouletted	2.25	2.25
b.		Imperf., pair	6.50	6.50
N32	OS3	8c dull blue	.50	.25
		Nos. N30-N32 (3)	4.50	.75

1943, Sept. 1

N33	OS4	8c violet	11.00	3.50
N34	OS4	15c carmine red	8.00	3.50

Publicity for Postal Savings which had reached a $10,000,000 total in Malaya.

Rubber
Tapping
OS5

Seaside
Houses
OS6

Japanese
Shrine,
Singapore
OS7

Sago Palms
OS8

Johore Bahru
and Strait of
Johore
OS9

Malay Mosque,
Kuala Lumpur
OS10

1943, Oct. 1

N35	OS5	1c gray green	1.75	.70
N36	OS5	3c olive gray	1.00	.25
N37	OS6	10c red brown	1.25	.25
N38	OS7	15c violet	1.75	5.00
N39	OS8	30c olive green	1.50	.50
N40	OS9	50c blue	5.00	5.00
N41	OS10	70c dull blue	22.50	16.00
		Nos. N35-N41 (7)	34.75	27.70

Rice Planting and Map
of Malaysia — OS11

1944, Feb. 15

N42	OS11	8c carmine	16.00	4.00
N43	OS11	15c violet	5.00	4.00

Issued on the anniversary of the fall of Singapore to commemorate the "Birth of New Malaya".

OCCUPATION POSTAGE DUE STAMPS

Stamps and Type of Postage Due Stamps of 1936-38 Handstamped in Black, Red or Brown

No. NJ7

1942   Wmk. 4   Perf. 14½x14

NJ1	D2	1c violet	14.00	30.00
a.		Brown overprint	160.00	170.00
b.		Red overprint	190.00	190.00
NJ2	D2	3c yellow green	85.00	90.00
a.		Red overprint	375.00	400.00
NJ3	D2	4c yellow green	80.00	47.50
a.		Brown overprint	200.00	200.00
b.		Red overprint	65.00	60.00
NJ4	D2	8c red	140.00	110.00
a.		Brown overprint	275.00	275.00
b.		Red overprint	200.00	150.00
NJ5	D2	10c yellow orange	32.50	55.00
a.		Brown overprint	100.00	110.00
b.		Red overprint	375.00	375.00
NJ6	D2	12c blue violet	27.50	52.50
a.		Red overprint	400.00	400.00
NJ7	D2	50c black	75.00	100.00
a.		Red overprint	600.00	650.00
		Nos. NJ1-NJ7 (7)	454.00	485.00

Overprinted in Black

1942

NJ8	D2	1c violet	3.50	10.50
NJ9	D2	3c yel green	20.00	26.00
NJ10	D2	4c yel green	18.00	12.50
NJ11	D2	8c red	30.00	22.50
NJ12	D2	10c yel orange	2.00	17.00
NJ13	D2	12c blue violet	2.00	40.00
		Nos. NJ8-NJ13 (6)	75.50	128.50

The 9c and 15c with this overprint were not regularly issued.

Postage Due Stamps of 1936-45 Overprinted

1943

NJ14	D2	1c reddish vio	2.25	5.00
NJ15	D2	3c yel green	2.25	4.50
NJ15A	D2	4c yel green	60.00	52.50
NJ16	D2	5c scarlet	1.50	5.00
NJ17	D2	9c yel orange	.90	8.50
NJ18	D2	10c yel orange	2.25	9.00
NJ19	D2	12c blue violet	2.25	18.00
NJ20	D2	15c blue violet	2.25	9.00
		Nos. NJ14-NJ20 (8)	73.65	111.50

No. NJ15A is said to have been extensively forged.

ISSUED UNDER THAI OCCUPATION

For use in Kedah, Kelantan, Perlis and Trengganu

War Memorial — OS1

Perf. 12½

		Unwmk.		Litho.
1943, Dec.				
2N1	OS1	1c pale yellow	35.00	37.50
2N2	OS1	2c buff	14.00	24.00
2N3	OS1	3c pale green	22.50	45.00
a.		Imperf., pair	975.00	
2N4	OS1	4c dull lilac	16.00	32.50
2N5	OS1	8c rose	16.00	24.00
2N6	OS1	15c lt blue	45.00	72.50
		Nos. 2N1-2N6 (6)	148.50	235.50

These stamps, in cent denominations, were for use only in the four Malayan states ceded to Thailand by the Japanese. The states reverted to British rule in September 1945.

JOHORE

jə-'hōr

LOCATION — At the extreme south of the Malay Peninsula. Linked to Singapore by a causeway.
AREA — 7,330 sq. mi.
POP. — 1,009,649 (1960)
CAPITAL — Johore Bahru

Stamps of the Straits Settlements Overprinted in Black

Overprinted

1876   Wmk. 1   Perf. 14

1	A2	2c brown	20,000.	5,750.
b.		Double overprint		

Overprinted

Overprint 13 to 14mm Wide

1884-86   Wmk. 2

1A	A2	2c rose	210.00	225.00
c.		Double overprint	1,200.	

No. 2d

Without Period
Overprint 16¾x2mm ("H" & "E" wide)

2	A2	2c rose	2,500.	750.00
a.		Double overprint		2,200.
b.		"J" raised	2,200.	825.00
c.		As "b," double overprint	4,000.	2,200.
d.		"H" wide & "E" narrow, ovpt. 16mm	2,750.	850.00
e.		As "d," double overprint		
f.		All ovpt. letters narrow	7,250.	

Overprinted

Overprint 11x2½mm

3	A2	2c rose ('86)	115.00	125.00

Overprinted

Overprint 17½x2¾mm

4	A2	2c rose ('85)	9,000.	2,000.

Overprinted

Overprint 12½ to 15x2¾mm

5	A2	2c rose	18.00	22.50
a.		"H" wide ('85)	100.00	100.00

Overprinted

Overprint 9x2½mm

7	A2	2c rose ('86)	67.50	60.00
a.		Double overprint	850.00	

Overprinted

Overprint 9x3mm

8	A2	2c rose ('86)	57.50	57.50

Overprinted

Overprint 14 to 15x3mm

9	A2	2c rose	16.00	13.00
a.		2c bright rose ('90)	12.50	12.50
		Tall "J" 3½mm high		
10	A2	2c rose	225.00	200.00

Overprinted

1888
Overprint 15 to 15½x3mm
With Period

11	A2	2c rose	175.00	70.00
a.		Tall "J" in "Johor"	900.00	450.00
b.		Double overprint	950.00	

Overprinted

1890-91
Overprint 12½ to 13x2½mm

12	A2	2c rose	20.00	20.00
		Overprint 12x2¾mm		
13	A2	2c rose ('91)	10,500.	

Surcharged in Black

a

b

c

d

a

b

c

d

1891

14	A3(a)	2c on 24c green	47.50	62.50
15	A3(b)	2c on 24c green	150.00	160.00
a.		Thin, narrow "J"	550.00	550.00
16	A3(c)	2c on 24c green	30.00	45.00
a.		"CENST"	1,000.	525.00
17	A3(d)	2c on 24c green	140.00	150.00
		Nos. 14-17 (4)	367.50	417.50

Sultan Abubakar — A5

1891-94   Typo.   Unwmk.

18	A5	1c lilac & vio ('94)	.85	.60
19	A5	2c lilac & yellow	.75	1.75
20	A5	3c lilac & car rose ('94)	.75	.60
21	A5	4c lilac & black	3.25	22.50
22	A5	5c lilac & green	8.50	22.50
23	A5	6c lilac & blue	9.50	22.50
24	A5	$1 green & car rose	90.00	190.00
		Nos. 18-24 (7)	113.60	260.45

For surcharges and overprints see Nos. 26-36.

Stamps of 1892-94 Surcharged in Black

3 cents.

1894

26	A5	3c on 4c lilac & blk	3.00	.65
a.		No period after "Cents"	115.00	85.00
27	A5	3c on 5c lilac & grn	2.40	4.25
a.		No period after "Cents"	275.00	175.00
28	A5	3c on 6c lilac & bl	4.00	5.00
a.		No period after "Cents"	210.00	240.00
29	A5	3c on $1 green & car	14.50	85.00
a.		No period after "Cents"	500.00	900.00
		Nos. 26-29 (4)	23.90	94.90

Coronation of Sultan Ibrahim
Stamps of 1892-94 Overprinted

Overprinted "KEMAHKOTAAN"
1896

30	A5	1c lilac & violet	.60	1.25
31	A5	2c lilac & yellow	.60	1.25
32	A5	3c lilac & car rose	.65	1.25
33	A5	4c lilac & black	1.00	3.00
34	A5	5c lilac & green	6.00	8.00
35	A5	6c lilac & blue	4.00	7.00
36	A5	$1 green & car rose	60.00	125.00
		Nos. 30-36 (7)	72.85	146.75

Overprinted "KETAHKOTAAN"

30a	A5	1c	4.50	6.00
31a	A5	2c	5.75	8.50
32a	A5	3c	11.00	14.00
33a	A5	4c	3.50	15.00
34a	A5	5c	4.25	8.50
35a	A5	6c	9.00	14.00
36a	A5	$1	42.50	190.00
		Nos. 30a-36a (7)	80.50	256.00

Sultan Ibrahim — A7

1896-99   Typo.   Wmk. 71

37	A7	1c green	1.00	1.75
38	A7	2c green & blue	.60	1.00
39	A7	3c green & vio	4.75	3.00
40	A7	4c green & car rose	1.25	2.40
41	A7	4c yel & red ('99)	1.75	1.75
42	A7	5c green & brn	2.40	3.75
43	A7	6c green & yel	2.40	5.00
44	A7	10c green & black	8.50	55.00
45	A7	25c green & vio	10.00	50.00
46	A7	50c grn & car rose	19.00	52.50
47	A7	$1 lilac & green	37.50	85.00
48	A7	$2 lilac & car rose	47.50	100.00
49	A7	$3 lilac & blue	42.50	140.00
50	A7	$4 lilac & brn	42.50	100.00
51	A7	$5 lilac & orange	92.50	150.00
		Nos. 37-51 (15)	314.15	751.15

On Nos. 44-46 the numerals are on white tablets. Numerals of Nos. 48-51 are on tablets of solid color.

Stamps of 1896-1926 with revenue cancellations sell for a fraction of those used postally.
For surcharges see Nos. 52-58.

Nos. 40-41 Surcharged in Black

3 cents.

1903

52	A7	3c on 4c yel & red	.80	1.25
a.		Without bars	4.00	24.00
53	A7	10c on 4c grn & car rose	3.00	10.00
a.		Without bars	27.50	75.00

Bars on Nos. 52-53 were handruled with pen and ink.

Surcharged

50 Cents.

54	A7	50c on $3 lilac & blue	35.00	87.50

Surcharged

One Dollar

55	A7	$1 on $2 lilac & car rose	75.00	140.00
a.		Inverted "e" in "one"	1,800.	

Surcharged

10 CENTS.

1904

56	A7	10c on 4c yel & red	25.00	42.50
a.		Double surcharge	8,750.	
57	A7	10c on 4c grn & car rose	10.50	65.00
58	A7	50c on $5 lil & org	80.00	170.00
		Nos. 56-58 (3)	115.50	277.50

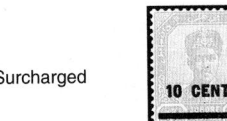

Sultan Ibrahim — A8

The 10c, 21c, 25c, 50c, and $10 to $500 denominations of type A8 show the numerals on white tablets. The numerals of the 8c, 30c, 40c, and $2 to $5 denominations are shown on tablets of solid colors.

1904-10   Typo.   Wmk. 71
Ordinary Paper

59	A8	1c violet & green	2.00	.40
a.		Chalky paper ('09)	12.00	11.00
60	A8	2c violet & brn org	3.00	4.25
a.		Chalky paper ('10)	14.00	17.00
61	A8	3c violet & black	4.75	.60
62	A8	4c violet & red	9.25	3.25
63	A8	5c violet & ol grn	2.50	3.00
64	A8	8c violet & blue	4.25	13.00
65	A8	10c violet & black	50.00	11.00
a.		Chalky paper ('10)	120.00	80.00
66	A8	25c violet & green	8.50	40.00
67	A8	50c violet & red	45.00	17.50
68	A8	$1 green & vio	19.00	72.50
69	A8	$2 green & car	27.50	62.50
70	A8	$3 green & blue	32.50	87.50
71	A8	$4 green & brn	35.00	125.00
72	A8	$5 green & org	50.00	100.00
73	A8	$10 green & blk	85.00	175.00
74	A8	$50 green & blue	300.00	400.00
75	A8	$100 green & scar	450.00	700.00
		Revenue cancel		50.00
		Nos. 59-73 (15)	378.25	715.50

Nos. 74 and 75 were theoretically available for postage but were mostly used for revenue purposes.
For surcharge see No. 86.

1912-19   Wmk. 47   Chalky Paper

76	A8	1c violet & green	1.25	.25
77	A8	2c violet & orange	6.00	1.00
78	A8	3c violet & black	10.00	.70
79	A8	4c violet & red	18.00	1.00
80	A8	5c violet & ol grn	8.50	2.75
81	A8	8c violet & blue	4.50	10.00
82	A8	10c violet & black	60.00	3.00
83	A8	25c violet & green	18.00	50.00
84	A8	50c violet & red ('19)	72.50	140.00
85	A8	$1 green & vio ('18)	100.00	120.00
		Nos. 76-85 (10)	298.75	328.70

No. 64 Surcharged

3 CENTS.

1912   Wmk. 71

86	A8	3c on 8c vio & blue	7.50	9.00
a.		"T" of "CENTS" omitted	1,600.	

1918-20   Typo.
Chalky Paper   Wmk. 3

87	A8	2c violet & orange	.75	1.75
88	A8	2c violet & grn ('19)	1.00	5.50
89	A8	4c violet & red	1.75	.70
90	A8	5c vio & olive grn ('20)	2.00	10.00
91	A8	10c violet & blue	2.00	1.75
92	A8	21c violet & orange ('19)	3.00	3.25
93	A8	25c vio & grn ('20)	9.00	30.00
94	A8	50c vio & red ('19)	24.00	65.00
95	A8	$1 grn & red vio	14.00	75.00
96	A8	$2 green & scar	27.50	60.00
97	A8	$3 green & blue	65.00	125.00
98	A8	$4 green & brn	80.00	175.00
99	A8	$5 green & org	120.00	200.00
100	A8	$10 green & blk	350.00	500.00
		Nos. 87-100 (14)	700.00	1,252.
		Set, ovptd. "SPECIMEN"	750.00	

1921-40   Wmk. 4

101	A8	1c violet & black	.30	.25
102	A8	2c violet & brn ('24)	1.25	4.25
103	A8	2c green & dk grn ('28)	.50	.40
104	A8	3c green ('25)	2.25	4.75
105	A8	3c dull vio & brn ('28)	1.40	1.50
106	A8	4c vio & red	2.50	.25
107	A8	5c vio & ol grn	.50	.25
108	A8	6c vio & red brown	.50	.50
109	A8	10c vio & blue	20.00	37.50
110	A8	10c vio & yel ('22)	.50	.25
111	A8	12c vio & black	1.25	1.60
111A	A8	12c ultra ('40)	47.50	4.00
112	A8	21c dull vio & org ('28)	2.75	3.50
113	A8	25c vio & green	4.25	1.25
114	A8	30c dull vio & org ('36)	9.50	10.00
115	A8	40c dull vio & brn ('36)	9.50	11.00
116	A8	50c violet & red	3.75	1.60
117	A8	$1 grn & red violet	3.75	1.25
118	A8	$2 grn & red	10.00	5.00
119	A8	$3 grn & blue	75.00	95.00
120	A8	$4 grn & brn ('26)	110.00	190.00
121	A8	$5 grn & org	62.50	52.50
122	A8	$10 grn & blk	275.00	400.00
123	A8	$50 grn & ultra	1,200.	
		Revenue cancel		100.00

124	A8	$100 grn & red	1,800.	150.00
		Revenue cancel		
125	A8	$500 ultra & org brn ('26)	23,000.	300.00
		Revenue cancel		
		Nos. 101-122 (23)	644.45	826.60

Nos. 123, 124 and 125 were available for postage but were probably used only fiscally.

A9

A10

1935, May 15   Engr.   Perf. 12½

126	A9	8c Sultan Ibrahim, Sultana	5.00	3.00
		Never hinged	8.00	

1940, Feb.   Perf. 13½

127	A10	8c Sultan Ibrahim	17.00	1.00
		Never hinged	26.00	

Catalogue values for unused stamps in this section, from this point to the end of the section, are for Never Hinged items.

Silver Wedding Issue
Common Design Types
Inscribed: "Malaya Johore"
Perf. 14x14½

1948, Dec. 1   Wmk. 4   Photo.

128	CD304	10c purple	.25	.75

Perf. 11½x11
Engr.; Name Typo.

129	CD305	$5 green	29.00	52.50

Common Design Types
Pictured following the introduction.

Sultan Ibrahim — A11

1949-55   Wmk. 4   Typo.   Perf. 18

130	A11	1c black	.50	.25
131	A11	2c orange	.30	.30
132	A11	3c green	1.10	1.10
133	A11	4c chocolate	1.25	.25
134	A11	5c rose vio ('52)	1.25	.30
135	A11	6c gray	1.25	.25
a.		Wmk. 4a (error)	2,500.	1,800.
136	A11	8c rose red	4.00	1.40
137	A11	8c green ('52)	7.50	2.25
138	A11	10c plum	1.00	.25
a.		Imperf., pair	3,500.	
139	A11	12c rose red ('52)	8.00	6.50
140	A11	15c ultra	3.50	.45
141	A11	20c dk grn & blk	2.25	1.25
142	A11	20c ultra ('52)	1.50	.30
143	A11	25c org & rose lil	3.50	.25
144	A11	30c plum & rose red ('55)	2.50	2.75
145	A11	35c dk vio & rose red ('52)	8.50	2.25
146	A11	40c dk vio & rose red	6.50	15.00
147	A11	50c ultra & blk	4.00	.30
148	A11	$1 vio brn & blk	9.00	2.50
149	A11	$2 rose red & emer	22.50	11.00
150	A11	$5 choc & emer	47.50	16.00
		Nos. 130-150 (21)	137.40	64.90

UPU Issue
Common Design Types
Inscribed: "Malaya-Johore"
Engr.; Name Typo. on 15c, 25c

1949, Oct. 10   Perf. 13½, 11x11½

151	CD306	10c rose violet	.30	.40
152	CD307	15c indigo	2.00	1.25
153	CD308	25c orange	.80	3.50
154	CD309	50c slate	1.60	3.75
		Nos. 151-154 (4)	4.70	8.90

POSTAGE DUE STAMPS

D1

Perf. 12½

1938, Jan. 1   Typo.   Wmk. 4

J1	D1	1c rose red	18.00	47.50
J2	D1	4c green	42.50	45.00
J3	D1	8c dull yellow	50.00	160.00
J4	D1	10c bister brown	50.00	57.50
J5	D1	12c rose violet	60.00	140.00
		Nos. J1-J5 (5)	220.50	450.00

OCCUPATION POSTAGE DUE STAMPS

Issued under Japanese Occupation

Johore Nos. J1-J5
Overprinted in Black,
Brown or Red

1942   Wmk. 4   Perf. 12½

NJ1	D1	1c rose red	25.00	75.00
NJ2	D1	4c green	70.00	85.00
NJ3	D1	8c dull yellow	85.00	100.00
NJ4	D1	10c bister brown	18.00	55.00
NJ5	D1	12c rose violet	47.50	60.00
		Nos. NJ1-NJ5 (5)	245.50	375.00

Johore Nos. J1-J5
Overprinted in Black

1943

NJ6	D1	1c rose red	10.00	32.50
a.		Second character sideways	350.00	700.00
NJ7	D1	4c green	8.00	37.50
a.		Second character sideways	375.00	700.00
NJ8	D1	8c dull yellow	10.00	37.50
a.		Second character sideways	425.00	750.00
NJ9	D1	10c bister brown	9.50	47.50
a.		Second character sideways	400.00	850.00
NJ10	D1	12c rose violet	11.00	65.00
a.		Second character sideways	500.00	950.00
		Nos. NJ6-NJ10 (5)	48.50	220.00

KEDAH

'ke-də

LOCATION — On the west coast of the Malay Peninsula.
AREA — 3,660 sq. mi.
POP. — 752,706 (1960)
CAPITAL — Alor Star

Sheaf of
Rice — A1

Native
Plowing — A2

Council
Chamber — A3

1912-21   Engr.   Wmk. 3   Perf. 14

1	A1	1c green & black	.70	.30
2	A1	1c brown ('19)	.65	.60
3	A1	2c green ('19)	.60	.35
4	A1	3c car & black	5.00	.35
5	A1	3c dk violet ('19)	.75	2.25
6	A1	4c slate & car	12.00	.30
7	A1	4c scarlet ('19)	5.50	.40
8	A1	5c org brown & grn	2.75	3.50
9	A1	8c ultra & blk	4.25	4.00
10	A2	10c black brn & bl	2.75	1.25
11	A2	20c yel grn & blk	6.50	4.50
12	A2	21c red vio & vio ('19)	6.25	70.00
13	A2	25c red vio & bl ('21)	2.10	32.50
14	A2	30c car & black	3.50	12.00
15	A2	40c lilac & blk	4.00	18.00
16	A2	50c dull bl & brn	10.00	14.00
17	A3	$1 scar & blk, yel	17.50	24.00
18	A3	$2 dk brn & dk grn	24.00	95.00
19	A3	$3 dk bl & blk, bl	100.00	190.00
20	A3	$5 car & black	110.00	200.00
		Nos. 1-20 (20)	318.80	673.30
		Set, ovptd. "SPECIMEN"	550.00	

There ave two types of No. 7, one printed from separate plates for frame and center, the other printed from a single plate.

Overprints are listed after No. 45.

Stamps of 1912
Surcharged

1919

21	A3	50c on $2 dk brn & dk grn	80.00	90.00
a.		"C" of ovpt. inserted by hand	1,450.	1,650.
22	A3	$1 on $3 dk bl & blk, blue	22.50	110.00

1921-36   Wmk. 4

Two types of 1c:
I — The 1's have rounded corners, small top serif. Small letters "c."
II — The 1's have square-cut corners, large top serif. Large letters "c."

Two types of 2c:
I — The 2's have oval drops. Letters "c" are fairly thick and rounded.
II — The 2's have round drops. Letters "c" thin and slightly larger.

23	A1	1c brown	.90	.25
24	A1	1c blk (I) ('22)	1.00	.25
a.		1c black (II) ('39)	77.50	5.00
25	A1	2c green (I)	1.50	.25
a.		2c green (II) ('40)	160.00	8.00
26	A1	3c dk violet	1.00	.80
27	A1	3c green ('22)	2.75	1.00
28	A1	4c carmine	7.50	.25
29	A1	4c dull vio ('26)	1.50	.25
30	A1	5c yellow ('22)	2.25	.25
31	A1	6c scarlet ('26)	2.50	.80
32	A1	8c gray ('36)	18.00	.25
33	A2	10c blk brn & bl	3.25	1.00
34	A2	12c dk ultra & blk ('26)	6.50	5.00
35	A2	20c green & blk	5.25	3.00
36	A2	21c red vio & vio	3.25	17.50
37	A2	25c red vio & bl	3.25	9.00
38	A2	30c red & blk ('22)	4.00	11.00
39	A2	35c claret ('26)	12.00	45.00
40	A2	40c red vio & blk	6.00	60.00
41	A2	50c dp blue & brn	4.50	21.00
42	A3	$1 scar & blk, yel ('24)	75.00	80.00
43	A3	$2 brn & green	17.50	125.00
44	A3	$3 dk bl & blk, bl	75.00	110.00
45	A3	$5 car & black	97.50	200.00
		Nos. 23-45 (23)	351.90	691.85

For overprints see Nos. N1-N6.

Stamps of 1912-21 Overprinted in Black: "MALAYA-BORNEO EXHIBITION." in Three Lines

1922   Wmk. 3

3a	A1	2c green	5.00	27.50
12a	A2	21c red vio & vio	35.00	95.00
13a	A2	25c red vio & blue	35.00	110.00
b.		Inverted overprint	1,500.	
16a	A2	50c dull blue & brn	35.00	125.00

Wmk. 4

23a	A1	1c brown	5.50	25.00
26a	A1	3c dark violet	4.75	47.50
28a	A1	4c carmine	4.75	30.00
33a	A2	10c blk brn & blue	9.25	55.00
		Nos. 3a-33a (8)	134.25	515.00

Industrial fair at Singapore, Mar. 31-Apr. 15, 1922.

On Nos. 12a, 13a and 16a, "BORNEO" exists both 14mm and 15mm wide.

Sultan of Kedah,
Sir Abdul Hamid
Halim Shah — A4

1937, July   Wmk. 4   Perf. 12½

46	A4	10c sepia & ultra	3.25	2.25
47	A4	12c gray vio & blk	27.50	5.50
48	A4	25c brn vio & ultra	6.00	5.50
49	A4	30c dp car & yel grn	5.50	11.50
50	A4	40c brn vio & blk	3.00	16.00
51	A4	50c dp blue & sepia	5.50	5.00
52	A4	$1 dk green & blk	3.00	11.00
53	A4	$2 dk brn & yel grn	75.00	85.00
54	A4	$5 dp car & black	22.50	170.00
		Nos. 46-54 (9)	151.25	311.75
		Set, never hinged	265.00	

For overprints see Nos. N7-N15.

> Catalogue values for unused stamps in this section, from this point to the end of the section, are for Never Hinged items.

Silver Wedding Issue
Common Design Types
Inscribed: "Malaya Kedah"

1948, Dec. 1   Photo.   Perf. 14x14½

55	CD304	10c purple	.25	.25

Perf. 11½x11
Engraved; Name Typographed

56	CD305	$5 rose car	35.00	50.00

UPU Issue
Common Design Types
Inscribed: "Malaya-Kedah"

Engr.; Name Typo. on 15c, 25c
1949, Oct. 10   Perf. 13½, 11x11½

57	CD306	10c rose violet	.25	1.25
58	CD307	15c indigo	2.25	1.75
59	CD308	25c orange	.80	2.50
60	CD309	50c slate	1.50	4.75
		Nos. 57-60 (4)	4.80	10.25

Sheaf of
Rice
A5

Sultan
Tungku
Badlishah
A6

1950-55   Wmk. 4   Typo.   Perf. 18

61	A5	1c black	.70	.30
62	A5	2c orange	.50	.25
63	A5	3c green	2.00	1.00
64	A5	4c chocolate	.75	.25
65	A5	5c rose vio ('52)	3.50	2.50
66	A5	6c gray	.70	.25
67	A5	8c rose red	2.25	4.50
68	A5	8c green ('52)	3.25	2.00
69	A5	10c plum	.70	.25
70	A5	12c rose red ('52)	3.25	3.00
71	A5	15c ultramarine	3.00	.70
72	A5	20c dk green & blk	3.00	3.00
73	A5	20c ultra ('52)	1.50	.35
74	A6	25c org & rose lilac	1.50	.50
75	A6	30c plum & rose red ('55)	4.50	1.50
76	A6	35c dk vio & rose red ('52)	4.00	2.00
77	A6	40c dk vio & rose red	4.75	8.50
78	A6	50c ultra & black	4.00	.35
79	A6	$1 vio brown & ultra	5.00	6.50
80	A6	$2 rose red & emer	30.00	35.00
81	A6	$5 choc & emerald	50.00	65.00
		Nos. 61-81 (21)	128.85	137.70

OCCUPATION STAMPS

Issued Under Japanese Occupation

Stamps of Kedah 1922-36, Overprinted in Red or Black

1942, May 13   Wmk. 4   Perf. 14

N1	A1	1c black (R)	7.00	10.00
N2	A1	2c green (R)	35.00	45.00
N3	A1	4c dull violet (R)	7.00	4.00
N4	A1	5c yellow (R)	5.50	5.50
a.		Black overprint	300.00	325.00
N5	A1	6c scarlet (Bk)	4.25	18.00
N6	A1	8c gray (R)	4.75	4.00

Nos. 46 to 54
Overprinted in Red

Perf. 12½

N7	A4	10c sepia & ultra	16.00	18.00
N8	A4	12c gray vio & blk	37.50	55.00
N9	A4	25c brn vio & ultra	12.00	19.00
a.		Black overprint	375.00	325.00
N10	A4	30c dp car & yel grn	75.00	85.00
N11	A4	40c brn vio & blk	37.50	55.00
N12	A4	50c dp blue & sep	35.00	50.00
N13	A4	$1 dk grn & blk	160.00	160.00
a.		Inverted overprint	750.00	850.00
N14	A4	$2 dk brn & yel green	210.00	190.00
N15	A4	$5 dp car & blk	90.00	125.00
a.		Black overprint	1,300.	1,100.
		Nos. N1-N15 (15)	736.50	838.50

KELANTAN

kə-'lan-ˌtan

LOCATION — On the eastern coast of the Malay Peninsula.
AREA — 5,750 sq. mi.
POP. — 545,620 (1960)
CAPITAL — Kota Bharu

Symbols of
Government — A1

1911-15   Typo.   Wmk. 3   Perf. 14
Ordinary Paper

1	A1	1c gray green	8.00	1.25
a.		1c green	7.25	.35
2	A1	3c rose red	5.00	.25
3	A1	4c black & red	1.90	.25
4	A1	5c grn & red, yel	12.00	1.25
5	A1	8c ultramarine	6.25	1.25
6	A1	10c black & violet	35.00	.90

Chalky Paper

7	A1	30c violet & red	12.50	3.00
8	A1	50c black & org	10.00	3.00
9	A1	$1 green & emer	55.00	45.00
10	A1	$1 grn & brn ('15)	75.00	2.40
11	A1	$2 grn & car rose	1.90	3.75
12	A1	$5 green & ultra	4.75	4.00
13	A1	$25 green & org	55.00	105.00
		Nos. 1-13 (13)	282.30	171.30
		Set, ovptd. "SPECIMEN"	325.00	

For overprints see listings after No. 26. For surcharges see Nos. N20-N22.

1921-28   Wmk. 4
Ordinary Paper

14	A1	1c green	5.00	.75
15	A1	1c black ('23)	1.00	.60
16	A1	2c brown	7.50	4.75
17	A1	2c green ('26)	5.50	.25
18	A1	3c brown ('27)	5.00	1.50
19	A1	4c black & red	3.50	.25
20	A1	5c grn & red, yel	1.75	.25
21	A1	6c claret	3.50	2.00
22	A1	6c rose red ('28)	5.00	5.00
23	A1	10c black & violet	3.00	.25

Chalky Paper

24	A1	30c dull vio & red ('26)	5.00	6.00
25	A1	50c black & orange	7.25	52.50
26	A1	$1 green & brown	35.00	90.00
		Nos. 14-26 (13)	88.00	164.45

Stamps of 1911-21 Overprinted in Black in Three Lines

1922   **Wmk. 3**

3a	A1	4c black & red	6.50	50.00
4a	A1	5c green & red, yel	7.00	80.00
7a	A1	30c violet & red	8.00	80.00
8a	A1	50c black & orange	11.00	90.00
10a	A1	$1 green & brown	35.00	125.00
11a	A1	$2 green & car rose	90.00	225.00
12a	A1	$5 green & ultra	225.00	525.00

Wmk. 4

14a	A1	1c black & red	3.50	55.00
23a	A1	10c black & violet	7.25	75.00
		Nos. 3a-23a (9)	393.25	1,275.

Industrial fair at Singapore. Mar. 31-Apr. 15, 1922.

Sultan Ismail
A2   A2a

1928-33   **Engr.**   **Perf. 12**
Size: 21½x30mm

27	A2	$1 ultramarine	17.50	85.00

Perf. 14

28	A2	$1 blue ('33)	60.00	47.50

1937-40   **Perf. 12**
Size: 22½x34½mm

29	A2a	1c yel & ol green	1.40	.65
30	A2a	2c deep green	3.50	.25
31	A2a	4c brick red	3.50	1.00
32	A2a	5c red brown	3.00	.25
33	A2a	6c car lake	8.75	10.00
34	A2a	8c gray green	3.00	.25
35	A2a	10c dark violet	14.50	3.50
36	A2a	12c deep blue	3.50	6.50
37	A2a	25c vio & red org	4.50	4.75
38	A2a	30c scar & dk vio	27.50	24.00
39	A2a	40c blue grn & org	5.75	35.00
40	A2a	50c org & ol grn	42.50	9.50
41	A2a	$1 dp grn & dk violet	30.00	16.00
42	A2a	$2 red & red brn ('40)	175.00	275.00
43	A2a	$5 rose lake & org ('40)	350.00	650.00
		Nos. 29-43 (15)	676.40	1,036.
		Set, never hinged		1,200.

For overprints see Nos. N1-N19.

> Catalogue values for unused stamps in this section, from this point to the end of the section, are for Never Hinged items.

Common Design Types pictured following the introduction.

Silver Wedding Issue
Common Design Types
Inscribed: "Malaya Kelantan"
Perf. 14x14½
1948, Dec. 1   **Wmk. 4**   **Photo.**

44	CD304	10c purple	.75	2.75

Perf. 11½x11
Engraved; Name Typographed

45	CD305	$5 rose car	35.00	60.00

UPU Issue
Common Design Types
Inscribed: "Malaya-Kelantan"
Engr.; Name Typo. on 15c, 25c
1949, Oct. 10   **Perf. 13½, 11x11½**

46	CD306	10c rose violet	.40	.40
47	CD307	15c indigo	2.25	2.25
48	CD308	25c orange	.60	5.50
49	CD309	50c slate	1.00	3.00
		Nos. 46-49 (4)	4.25	11.15

Sultan Ibrahim — A3

Perf. 18
1951, July 11   **Wmk. 4**   **Typo.**

50	A3	1c black	.50	.40
51	A3	2c orange	1.25	.40
52	A3	3c green	5.25	1.75
53	A3	4c chocolate	1.75	.30
54	A3	6c gray	.75	.30
55	A3	8c rose red	4.25	4.25
56	A3	10c plum	.50	.30
57	A3	15c ultramarine	6.00	.80
58	A3	20c dk green & blk	4.50	11.00
59	A3	25c orange & plum	1.50	.80
60	A3	40c vio brn & rose red	14.00	20.00
61	A3	50c dp ultra & blk	6.00	.60
62	A3	$1 vio brown & ultra	10.00	11.00
63	A3	$2 rose red & emer	37.50	50.00
64	A3	$5 choc & emer	72.50	72.50

1952-55

65	A3	5c rose violet	1.50	.50
66	A3	8c green	4.50	2.25
67	A3	12c rose red	4.50	3.00
68	A3	20c ultramarine	1.50	.25
69	A3	30c plum & rose red ('55)	1.60	5.00
70	A3	35c dk vio & rose red	2.00	1.75
		Nos. 50-70 (21)	181.85	187.15

Compare with Pahang A8, Perak A16, Selangor A15, Trengganu A5.

OCCUPATION STAMPS

Issued Under Japanese Occupation

Kelantan No. 35 Handstamped in Black

1942   **Wmk. 4**   **Perf. 12**

N1	A2a	10c dark violet	400.00	500.00

Some authorities believe No. N1 was not regularly issued.

Kelantan Nos. 29-40 Surcharged in Black or Red and Handstamped with Oval Seal "a" in Red

Sunakawa-a   Handa-b

1942

N2		1c on 50c org & ol green	225.00	150.00
a.		With "b" seal	160.00	200.00
N3		2c on 40c bl grn & orange	300.00	200.00
a.		With "b" seal	160.00	200.00

N4		5c on 12c dp bl (R)	200.00	200.00
N5		8c on 5c red brn (R)	175.00	100.00
a.		With "b" seal (R)	110.00	175.00
N6		10c on 6c car lake	475.00	500.00
a.		With "b" seal	120.00	200.00
N7		12c on 8c gray green (R)	60.00	140.00
N8		30c on 4c brick red	2,500.	2,250.
N9		40c on 2c dk grn (R)	70.00	100.00
N10		50c on 1c yel & ol green	1,800.	1,500.

Kelantan Nos. 29-40, 19-20, 22 Surcharged in Black or Red and Handstamped with Oval Seal "b" in Red

N10A		1c on 50c org & ol green	350.00	200.00
N11		2c on 40c bl grn & orange	900.00	350.00
N11A		4c on 30c scar & dark vio	2,500.	1,400.
N12		5c on 12c dp bl (R)	350.00	200.00
N13		6c on 25c vio & red org	375.00	200.00
N14		8c on 5c red brown (R)	500.00	150.00
N15		10c on 6c car lake	100.00	125.00
N16		12c on 8c gray grn (R)	225.00	375.00
a.		Seal omitted	70.00	120.00
N17		25c on 10c dk vio	1,600.	1,500.
N17A		30c on 4c brick red	2,500.	2,250.
N18		40c on 2c dp grn (R)	70.00	100.00
N19		50c on 1c yel & ol green	1,800.	1,500.

Perf. 14

N20		$1 on 4c blk & red (R)	60.00	85.00
N21		$2 on 5c grn & red, yel	60.00	85.00
N22		$5 on 6c rose red	60.00	85.00

Examples of Nos. N2-N22 without handstamped seal are from the remainder stocks sent to Singapore after Kelantan was ceded to Thailand. Some authorities believe stamps without seals were used before June 1942.

ISSUED UNDER THAI OCCUPATION

OS1

1943, Nov. 15   **Perf. 11**

2N1	OS1	1c violet & black	240.00	375.00
2N2	OS1	2c violet & black	300.00	300.00
a.		Violet (arms) omitted	900.00	
2N3	OS1	4c violet & black	300.00	375.00
a.		Violet (arms) omitted	1,000.	
2N4	OS1	8c violet & black	300.00	300.00
a.		Violet (arms) omitted	700.00	
2N5	OS1	10c violet & black	300.00	550.00
		Nos. 2N1-2N5 (5)	1,590.	1,900.

Stamps with centers in red are revenues.

MALACCA

mə-'la-kə

Melaka

LOCATION — On the west coast of the Malay peninsula.
AREA — 640 sq. mi.
POP. — 318,110 (1960)

CAPITAL — Malacca

> Catalogue values for unused stamps in this section are for Never Hinged items.

Common Design Types pictured following the introduction.

Silver Wedding Issue
Common Design Types
Inscribed: "Malaya Malacca"
Perf. 14x14½
1948, Dec. 1   **Wmk. 4**   **Photo.**

1	CD304	10c purple	.40	2.25

Engraved; Name Typographed
Perf. 11½x11

2	CD305	$5 lt brown	35.00	47.50

Type of Straits Settlements, 1937-41, Inscribed "Malacca"
Perf. 18
1949, Mar. 1   **Wmk. 4**   **Typo.**

3	A29	1c black	.40	.85
4	A29	2c orange	1.00	.60
5	A29	3c green	.40	2.25
6	A29	4c chocolate	.40	.25
7	A29	6c gray	.90	1.10
8	A29	8c rose red	.90	7.50
9	A29	10c plum	.40	.25
10	A29	15c ultramarine	3.50	.85
11	A29	20c dk green & blk	.60	7.00
12	A29	25c org & rose lil	.60	.85
13	A29	40c dk vio & rose red	1.50	13.00
14	A29	50c ultra & black	1.50	1.50
15	A29	$1 vio brn & ultra	15.00	26.00
16	A29	$2 rose red & emer	27.50	27.50
17	A29	$5 choc & emer	60.00	50.00
		Nos. 3-17 (15)	114.60	139.50

See Nos. 22-26.

UPU Issue
Common Design Types
Inscribed: "Malaya-Malacca"
Engr.; Name Typo. on 15c, 25c
Perf. 13½, 11x11½
1949, Oct. 10   **Wmk. 4**

18	CD306	10c rose violet	.35	.55
19	CD307	15c indigo	2.40	2.75
20	CD308	25c orange	.50	8.50
21	CD309	50c slate	1.00	5.50
		Nos. 18-21 (4)	4.25	17.30

Type of Straits Settlements, 1937-41, Inscribed "Malacca"
1952, Sept. 1   **Wmk. 4**   **Perf. 18**

22	A29	5c rose violet	1.25	1.75
23	A29	8c green	6.00	5.25
24	A29	12c rose red	6.00	9.50
25	A29	20c ultramarine	7.50	3.00
26	A29	35c dk vio & rose red	6.00	3.75
		Nos. 22-26 (5)	26.75	23.25

OCCUPATION STAMPS

Issued Under Japanese Occupation
Stamps of Straits Settlements, 1937-41 Handstamped in Carmine

The handstamp covers four stamps. Values are for single stamps. Blocks of four showing complete handstamp sell for six times the price of singles.

1942   **Wmk. 4**   **Perf. 14**

N1	A29	1c black	125.00	90.00
N2	A29	2c brown orange	75.00	75.00
N3	A29	3c green	80.00	90.00
N4	A29	5c brown	175.00	175.00

N5	A29	8c gray	300.00	150.00
N6	A29	10c dull violet	125.00	125.00
N7	A29	12c ultramarine	140.00	140.00
N8	A29	15c ultramarine	100.00	125.00
N9	A29	30c org & vio	3,500.	—
N10	A29	40c dk vio & rose	100.00	100.00
N11	A29	50c blk, emerald	1,100.	1,100.
N12	A29	$1 red & blk, bl	1,350.	1,250.
N13	A29	$2 rose red & gray grn	3,500.	—
N14	A29	$5 grn & red, grn	3,500.	—

Some authorities believe Nos. N9, N13, and N14 were not regularly issued.

OCCUPATION POSTAGE DUE STAMPS

Malaya Postage Due Stamps and Type of 1936-38, Handstamped Like Nos. N1-N14 in Carmine

1942 Wmk. 4 Perf. 14½x14

NJ1	D2	1c violet	250.00	225.00
NJ2	D2	4c yel green	275.00	275.00
NJ3	D2	8c red	3,500.	2,250.
NJ4	D2	10c yel orange	550.00	525.00
NJ5	D2	12c blue violet	800.00	725.00
NJ6	D2	50c black	3,000.	2,000.
		Nos. NJ1-NJ6 (6)	8,375.	6,000.

Pricing note above No. N1 also applies to Nos. NJ1-NJ6.

NEGRI SEMBILAN

'ne-grē səm-'bē-lən

LOCATION — South of Selangor on the west coast of the Malay Peninsula, bordering on Pahang on the east and Johore on the south.
AREA — 2,580 sq. mi.
POP. — 401,742 (1960)
CAPITAL — Seremban

Stamps of the Straits Settlements Overprinted in Black

1891 Wmk. 2 Perf. 14
Overprint 14½ to 15mm Wide

1	A2	2c rose	3.50	8.00

Tiger — A1

Tiger Head — A2

1891-94 Typo.

2	A1	1c green ('93)	4.00	1.25
3	A1	2c rose	4.00	11.00
4	A1	5c blue ('94)	35.00	47.50
		Nos. 2-4 (3)	43.00	59.75
		Set, ovptd. "SPECIMEN"	100.00	

1895-99

5	A2	1c lilac & green	18.00	8.50
6	A2	2c lilac & brown	42.50	140.00
7	A2	3c lilac & car rose	18.00	1.50
8	A2	5c lilac & olive	10.00	11.50
9	A2	8c lilac & blue	35.00	20.00
10	A2	10c lilac & orange	32.50	17.00
11	A2	15c green & vio	50.00	90.00
12	A2	20c grn & ol ('99)	80.00	45.00
13	A2	25c grn & car rose	85.00	110.00
14	A2	50c green & black	90.00	80.00
		Nos. 5-14 (10)	461.00	523.50
		Set, ovptd. "SPECIMEN"	275.00	

For surcharges see Nos. 15-16, 19-20; Federated Malay States Nos. 1-8.

Stamps of 1891-99 Surcharged

1899 Blue-green Surcharge

15	A2	4c on 8c lil & blue	8.50	5.00
a.		Double surcharge	2,750.	2,500.
b.		Pair, one without surcharge	7,250.	4,500.
c.		Double surcharge, 1 green, 1 red	1,000.	1,100.

Black Surcharge

16	A2	4c on 8c lil & blue	1,400.	1,500.

Surcharge on No. 16 is thinner and sharper than on No. 15.

Same Surcharge and Bar in Black

17	A1	4c on 1c green	3.00	20.00
18	A1	4c on 5c blue	1.50	17.00
19	A2	4c on 3c lil & car rose	4.00	24.00
a.		Double surcharge	2,750.	1,200.
b.		Pair, one without surcharge	12,000.	6,000.
c.		Bar omitted	1,000.	800.00
d.		Bar double		975.00
e.		"Four" double (at right)	2,750.	2,400.
f.		"cents" double (at left)	2,750.	2,500.
g.		Inverted surcharge	2,100.	1,600.
h.		As "g," one surcharge albino		1,200.

Bar at bottom on Nos. 17-18, at top on No. 19.

No. 11 Surcharged in Black

One cent.

1900

20	A2	1c on 15c grn & vio	125.00	350.00
a.		Inverted period	500.00	1,300.

Arms of Negri Sembilan — A4

1935-41 Typo. Wmk. 4

21	A4	1c black ('36)	1.40	.25
22	A4	2c dp green ('36)	1.40	.25
22A	A4	2c brown org ('41)	2.25	75.00
22B	A4	3c green ('41)	4.25	11.00
23	A4	4c brown orange	1.25	.25
24	A4	5c chocolate	1.25	.25
25	A4	6c rose red	9.25	2.75
25A	A4	6c gray ('41)	3.00	140.00
26	A4	8c gray	1.10	.40
27	A4	10c dull vio ('36)	1.10	.25
28	A4	12c ultra ('36)	1.75	.75
28A	A4	15c ultra ('41)	5.50	75.00
29	A4	25c rose red & dull vio ('36)	2.00	1.00
30	A4	30c org & dull vio ('36)	3.00	2.00
31	A4	40c dull vio & car	2.00	3.00
32	A4	50c blk, emer ('36)	5.00	2.25
33	A4	$1 red & blk, bl ('36)	3.00	5.00
34	A4	$2 rose red & grn ('36)	30.00	20.00
35	A4	$5 brn red & grn, emer ('36)	20.00	100.00
		Nos. 21-35 (19)	98.50	439.40
		Set, never hinged	175.00	

For overprints see Nos. N1-N31.

Catalogue values for unused stamps in this section, from this point to the end of the section, are for Never Hinged items.

Common Design Types pictured following the introduction.

Silver Wedding Issue
Common Design Types
Inscribed: "Malaya Negri Sembilan"

1948, Dec. 1 Photo. Perf. 14x14½

36	CD304	10c purple	.60	.70

Perf. 11½x11
Engraved; Name Typographed

37	CD305	$5 green	27.50	37.50

Arms of Negri Sembilan — A5

1949-55 Wmk. 4 Typo. Perf. 18

38	A5	1c black	1.25	.25
39	A5	2c orange	1.00	.25
40	A5	3c green	.60	.45
41	A5	4c chocolate	.30	.25
42	A5	5c	1.00	.45
43	A5	6c gray	2.25	.25
44	A5	8c rose red	.80	.95
45	A5	8c green	5.50	2.25
46	A5	10c plum	.40	.25
47	A5	12c rose red	5.50	3.25
48	A5	15c ultramarine	4.25	.45
49	A5	20c dk green & blk	2.25	2.00
50	A5	20c ultramarine	2.00	.35
51	A5	25c org & rose lilac	1.00	.35
52	A5	30c plum & rose red ('55)	2.00	2.75
53	A5	35c dk vio & rose red	1.50	3.75
54	A5	40c dk vio & rose red	4.75	6.00
55	A5	50c ultra & black	5.00	.45
56	A5	$1 vio brn & ultra	6.00	2.25
57	A5	$2 rose red & emer	18.00	27.50
58	A5	$5 choc & emerald	60.00	75.00
		Nos. 38-58 (21)	125.35	129.45

UPU Issue
Common Design Types
Inscribed: "Malaya-Negri Sembilan"
Engr.; Name Typo. on 15c, 25c

1949, Oct. 10 Perf. 13½, 11x11½

59	CD306	10c rose violet	.25	.25
60	CD307	15c indigo	1.40	3.50
61	CD308	25c orange	.75	3.00
62	CD309	50c slate	1.10	4.00
		Nos. 59-62 (4)	3.50	10.75

OCCUPATION STAMPS

Issued under Japanese Occupation

Stamps and Type of Negri Sembilan, 1935-41, Handstamped in Red, Black, Brown or Violet

1942 Wmk. 4 Perf. 14

N1	A4	1c black	25.00	16.00
N2	A4	2c brown org	16.00	17.50
N3	A4	3c green	21.00	21.00
N4	A4	5c chocolate	29.00	27.50
N5	A4	6c rose red	600.00	600.00
N6	A4	6c gray	150.00	150.00
N7	A4	8c gray	87.50	87.50
N8	A4	8c rose red	55.00	47.50
N9	A4	10c dark violet	110.00	110.00
N10	A4	12c ultramarine	900.00	900.00
N11	A4	15c ultramarine	20.00	11.00
N12	A4	25c rose red & dk vio	35.00	40.00
N13	A4	30c org & dk vio	175.00	190.00
N14	A4	40c dk vio & car	750.00	750.00
N15	A4	$1 red & blk, bl	140.00	140.00
N16	A4	$5 brn red & grn, emerald	325.00	350.00

The 8c rose red is not known to have been issued without overprint.
Some authorities believe Nos. N5 and N7 were not regularly issued.

Stamps of Negri Sembilan, 1935-41, Overprinted in Black

DAI NIPPON 2602 MALAYA

N17	A4	1c black	1.40	1.40
a.		Inverted overprint	17.00	27.50
b.		Dbl. ovpt., one invtd.	47.50	67.50
N18	A4	2c brown orange	1.60	1.40
N19	A4	3c green	1.40	1.00
N20	A4	5c chocolate	.90	.90
N21	A4	6c gray	2.00	2.00
a.		Inverted overprint		1,000.
N22	A4	8c rose red	2.75	2.75
N23	A4	10c dk violet	5.50	5.50
N24	A4	15c ultramarine	8.00	4.75
N25	A4	25c rose red & dk vio	2.00	6.75
N26	A4	30c org & dk vio	4.00	5.00
N27	A4	$1 red & blk, bl	140.00	175.00
		Nos. N17-N27 (11)	169.55	206.45

The 8c rose red is not known to have been issued without overprint.

Negri Sembilan, Nos. 21, 24 and 29, Overprinted or Surcharged in Black

a   b

c

1943

N28	A4	1c black	.65	.65
a.		Inverted overprint	17.00	24.00
N29	A4	2c on 5c choc	.55	.65
N30	A4	6c on 5c choc	.65	.90
a.		"6 cts." inverted	350.00	400.00
N31	A4	25c rose red & dk violet	2.00	2.75
		Nos. N28-N31 (4)	3.85	4.95

The Japanese characters read: "Japanese Postal Service."

PAHANG

pə-'haŋ

LOCATION — On the east coast of the Malay Peninsula, bordering Johore on the south, Parak and Selangor on the west, and Trengganu on the north.
AREA — 13,820 sq. mi.
POP. — 338,210 (1960)
CAPITAL — Kuala Lipis

Stamps of the Straits Settlements Overprinted in Black

Overprinted

Overprint 16x2¾mm
1889 Wmk. 2 Perf. 14

1	A2	2c rose	140.00	60.00
2	A3	8c orange	2,200.	2,000.
3	A7	10c slate	250.00	300.00

Overprinted

Overprint 12½x2mm

4	A2	2c rose	9.00	10.00
a.		Antique letters	1,000.	
b.		2c pale rose	18.00	23.00

Overprinted

1890 Overprint 15x2½mm

5	A2	2c rose	9,000.	2,500.

Pahang

Overprinted

Overprint 16x2¾mm

6 A2 2c rose   125.00 16.00

Surcharged in Black

a   b

c   d

1891

7	A3 (a)	2c on 24c green	1,100.	1,250.
8	A3 (b)	2c on 24c green	425.00	475.00
9	A3 (c)	2c on 24c green	225.00	275.00
10	A3 (d)	2c on 24c green	1,100.	1,250.
		Nos. 7-10 (4)	2,850.	3,250.

A5   A6

1892-95   Typo.

11	A5	1c green	5.00	4.00
12	A5	2c rose	5.50	4.00
13	A5	5c blue	12.50	47.50
		Nos. 11-13 (3)	23.00	55.50
		Set, ovptd. "SPECIMEN"	97.50	

For surcharges see Nos. 21-22.

1895-99

14	A6	3c lilac & car rose	9.75	3.25
14A	A6	4c lil & car rose ('99)	20.00	14.50
15	A6	5c lilac & olive	35.00	25.00
		Nos. 14-15 (3)	64.75	42.75
		Set of 3, ovptd. "SPECIMEN"	80.00	

For surcharge see No. 28.

Stamps of Perak,
1895-99, Overprinted

1898-99

16	A9	10c lilac & orange	25.00	30.00
17	A9	25c green & car rose	95.00	190.00
18	A9	50c green & black	500.00	575.00
18A	A9	50c lilac & black	350.00	425.00

Overprinted

Pahang.

Wmk. 1

19	A10	$1 green & lt grn	425.	600.
20	A10	$5 green & ultra	1,700.	2,700.
		Nos. 16-20 (6)	3,095.	4,520.

No. 13 Cut in Half
Diagonally & Srchd. in
Red & Initials "JFO" in
ms.

1897, Aug. 2   Wmk. 2
Red Surcharge

21	A5	2c on half of 5c blue	1,750.	450.
a.		Black surcharge	9,500.	3,500.
b.		Bisected horizontally		2,500.
22	A5	3c on half of 5c blue	1,750.	450.
a.		Black surcharge	9,500.	3,500.
b.		Bisected horizontally	5,000.	2,400.
c.		Unsevered pair, #21, 22	12,000.	4,800.
d.		Se-tenant pair, #21, 22	5,500.	1,200.

Used at Kuala Lipis. No. 22c consists a
complete, unsevered, stamp. No. 22d consists
of halves of two separate stamps perfed
between.

Perak No. 52
Surcharged

Pahang
Four cents

1898

25	A9	4c on 8c lilac & blue	7.50	7.50
a.		Double surcharge	1,100.	
b.		Inverted surcharge	4,250.	1,700.

Surcharged on pieces
of White Paper

Pahang
Five cents

1898   Without Gum   Imperf.

26	4c black		4,500.
27	5c black	3,000.	

Pahang No. 15
Surcharged

Four cents.

1899   Perf. 14

28	A6	4c on 5c lilac & olive	21.00	70.00

Sultan Abu Bakar — A7

1935-41   Typo. Wmk. 4   Perf. 14

29	A7	1c black ('36)	.25	.25
30	A7	2c dp green ('36)	1.40	.25
30A	A7	3c green ('41)	10.00	19.00
31	A7	4c brown orange	.70	.25
32	A7	5c chocolate	.70	.25
33	A7	6c rose red ('36)	12.00	3.50
34	A7	6c gray	2.00	.25
34A	A7	6c rose red ('41)	3.00	60.00
35	A7	10c dk violet ('36)	1.75	.25
36	A7	12c ultra ('36)	2.10	2.00
36A	A7	15c ultra ('41)	14.00	65.00
37	A7	25c rose red & pale vio ('36)	3.00	1.25
38	A7	30c org & dk vio ('36)	1.50	1.25
39	A7	40c dk vio & car	1.25	2.40
40	A7	50c black, emer ('36)	2.50	2.00
41	A7	$1 red & blk, blue ('36)	2.50	8.00
42	A7	$2 rose red & green ('36)	15.00	50.00
43	A7	$5 brn red & grn, emer ('36)	6.00	87.50
		Nos. 29-43 (18)	79.65	303.65

The 3c was printed on both ordinary and
chalky paper; the 15c only on ordinary paper;
other values only on chalky paper.

Values for Nos. 34A used and 36A used are
for stamps with legible postmarks dated in
1941.

A 2c brown orange and 6c gray, type A7,
exist, but are not known to have been regularly
issued.

For overprints see Nos. N1-N21.

> **Catalogue values for unused
> stamps in this section, from this
> point to the end of the section, are
> for Never Hinged items.**

Common Design Types
pictured following the introduction.

Silver Wedding Issue
Common Design Types
Inscribed: "Malaya Pahang"
Perf. 14x14½

1948, Dec. 1	Photo.	Wmk. 4		
44	CD304	10c purple	.50	.55

Perf. 11½x11

Engraved; Name Typopgraphed

45	CD305	$5 green	27.50	37.50

UPU Issue
Common Design Types
Inscribed: "Malaya-Pahang"
Engr.; Name Typo. on 15c, 25c

1949, Oct. 10	Perf. 13½, 11x11½			
46	CD306	10c rose violet	.30	.25
47	CD307	15c indigo	1.10	1.50
48	CD308	25c orange	.60	2.50
49	CD309	50c slate	1.00	3.00
		Nos. 46-49 (4)	3.00	7.25

Sultan Abu Bakar — A8

Perf. 18

1950, June 1	Wmk. 4		Typo.	
50	A8	1c black	.30	.30
51	A8	2c orange	.30	.30
52	A8	3c green	.30	.80
53	A8	4c chocolate	2.25	.35
54	A8	6c gray	.50	.35
55	A8	8c rose red	.50	2.00
56	A8	10c plum	.30	.30
57	A8	15c ultramarine	.75	.35
58	A8	20c dk green & blk	1.00	3.00
59	A8	25c org & rose lilac	.50	.30
60	A8	40c dk vio & rose red	2.25	8.50
61	A8	50c dp ultra & black	1.50	.35
62	A8	$1 vio brn & ultra	3.50	3.50
63	A8	$2 rose red & emer	16.00	30.00
64	A8	$5 choc & emer	65.00	90.00

1952-55

65	A8	5c rose violet	.50	.70
66	A8	8c green	1.25	1.10
67	A8	12c rose red	1.50	1.25
68	A8	20c ultramarine	2.50	.30
69	A8	30c plum & rose red ('55)	2.75	.50
70	A8	35c dk vio & rose red	1.00	.35
		Nos. 50-70 (21)	104.45	144.60

OCCUPATION STAMPS

Issued under Japanese Occupation

Stamps of Pahang,
1935-41,
Handstamped in Black,
Red, Brown or Violet

1942		Wmk. 4	Perf. 14	
N1	A7	1c black	35.00	40.00
N1A	A7	3c green	125.00	140.00
N2	A7	5c chocolate	15.00	9.50
N3	A7	8c rose red	26.00	11.00
N3A	A7	8c gray	240.00	240.00
N4	A7	10c dk violet	60.00	60.00
N5	A7	12c ultramarine	1,200.	1,200.
N6	A7	15c ultramarine	87.50	87.50
N7	A7	25c rose red & pale vio	21.00	37.50
N8	A7	30c org & dk vio	17.00	32.50
N9	A7	40c dk vio & car	17.50	35.00
N10	A7	50c blk, emerald	300.00	350.00
N11	A7	$1 red & blk, bl	100.00	125.00
N12	A7	$5 brown red & grn, emer	575.00	625.00

Some authorities claim the 2c green, 4c
brown orange, 6c rose red and $2 rose red

and green were not regularly issued with this
overprint.

Stamps of Pahang,
1935-41, Overprinted
in Black

N13	A7	1c black	2.00	1.10
N14	A7	5c chocolate	2.00	2.00
N15	A7	8c rose red	35.00	3.75
N16	A7	10c violet brown	20.00	9.00
N17	A7	12c ultramarine	2.00	3.00
N18	A7	25c rose red & pale vio	7.50	10.50
N19	A7	30c org & dk vio	2.75	5.50
		Nos. N13-N19 (7)	71.25	34.85

**Pahang No. 32 Overprinted and
Surcharged in Black**

e   f

1943

N20	A7(e)	6c on 5c chocolate	1.40	1.40
N21	A7(f)	6c on 5c chocolate	2.00	1.50

The Japanese characters read: "Japanese
Postal Service."

PENANG

pə-naŋ

LOCATION — An island off the west
coast of the Malay Peninsula, plus a
coastal strip called Province
Wellesley.
AREA — 400 sq. mi.
POP. — 616,254 (1960)
CAPITAL — Georgetown

> **Catalogue values for unused
> stamps in this section are for
> Never Hinged items.**

Common Design Types
pictured following the introduction.

Silver Wedding Issue
Common Design Types
Inscribed: "Malaya Penang"
Perf. 14x14½

1948, Dec. 1	Wmk. 4		Photo.	
1	CD304	10c purple	.50	.30

Perf. 11½x11

Engraved; Name Typographed

2	CD305	$5 lt brown	40.00	37.50

**Type of Straits Settlements, 1937-
41, Inscribed "Penang"**

1949-52			Perf. 18	
3	A29	1c black	1.50	.30
4	A29	2c orange	1.50	.30
5	A29	3c green	.60	1.25
6	A29	4c chocolate	.50	.25
7	A29	5c rose vio ('52)	4.25	4.00
8	A29	6c gray	1.50	.30
9	A29	8c rose red	1.25	5.00
10	A29	8c green ('52)	4.00	3.00
11	A29	10c plum	.50	.25
12	A29	12c rose red ('52)	4.50	9.00
13	A29	15c ultramarine	2.00	.40
14	A29	20c dk grn & blk	2.75	1.50
15	A29	20c ultra ('52)	3.25	1.50
16	A29	25c org & rose lilac	3.00	1.25
17	A29	35c dk vio & rose red ('52)	3.25	1.50
18	A29	40c dk vio & rose red	4.25	15.00
19	A29	50c ultra & black	5.50	.30
20	A29	$1 vio brn & ultra	20.00	3.00
21	A29	$2 rose red & emer	26.00	2.50
22	A29	$5 choc & emerald	52.50	3.75
		Nos. 3-22 (20)	142.60	54.35

UPU Issue
Common Design Types
Inscribed: "Malaya-Penang"
Engr.; Name Typo. on 15c, 25c

1949, Oct. 10   Perf 13½, 11x11½

23	CD306	10c rose violet	.25	.25
24	CD307	15c indigo	2.50	3.75
25	CD308	25c orange	.60	3.75
26	CD309	50c slate	1.75	4.00
		Nos. 23-26 (4)	5.10	11.75

OCCUPATION STAMPS

Issued under Japanese Occupation

Stamps of Straits Settlements, 1937-41, Overprinted in Red or Black

1942   Wmk. 4   Perf. 14

N1	A29	1c black (R)	7.00	3.75
a.		Inverted overprint	600.00	600.00
b.		Double overprint	350.00	350.00
N2	A29	2c brown orange	6.00	4.75
a.		Inverted overprint	175.00	
b.		Double overprint	575.00	
c.		"PE" for "PENANG"	120.00	100.00
N3	A29	3c green (R)	6.00	7.00
a.		Double overprint, one inverted	450.00	
N4	A29	5c brown (R)	3.50	9.00
a.		Double overprint	575.00	475.00
b.		"N PPON" for "NIPPON"	200.00	
N5	A29	8c gray (R)	2.50	1.60
a.		Double overprint, one inverted	525.00	
b.		"N PPON" for "NIPPON"	60.00	65.00
N6	A29	10c dull vio (R)	1.75	2.50
a.		Double overprint	500.00	500.00
b.		Double overprint, one inverted	450.00	450.00
N7	A29	12c ultra (R)	4.75	18.00
a.		Double overprint	450.00	
b.		Double overprint, one inverted	675.00	675.00
c.		"N PPON" for "NIPPON"	550.00	
N8	A29	15c ultra (R)	2.00	4.50
a.		Inverted overprint	450.00	475.00
b.		Double overprint	600.00	600.00
c.		"N PPON" for "NIPPON"	120.00	130.00
N9	A29	40c dk vio & rose red	6.00	18.00
N10	A29	50c black, emer (R)	4.25	35.00
N11	A29	$1 red & blk, bl	7.00	47.50
a.		Inverted overprint	1,200.	
N12	A29	$2 rose red & gray grn	65.00	100.00
N13	A29	$5 grn & red, grn	675.00	750.00
		Nos. N1-N13 (13)	790.75	1,001.

Stamps of Straits Settlements Handstamped Okugawa Seal in Red

1942   Wmk. 4   Perf. 14

N14	A29	1c black	12.00	13.50
N15	A29	2c brown orange	27.50	25.00
N16	A29	3c green	22.50	25.00
N17	A29	5c brown	27.50	32.50
N18	A29	8c gray	30.00	42.50
N19	A29	10c dull violet	55.00	55.00
N20	A29	12c ultramarine	47.50	55.00
N21	A29	15c ultramarine	55.00	55.00
N22	A29	40c dk vio & rose red	110.00	125.00
N23	A29	50c blk, emerald	250.00	250.00
N24	A29	$1 red & blk, bl	275.00	300.00
N25	A29	$2 rose red & gray grn	900.00	800.00
N26	A29	$5 grn & red, grn	2,750.	1,700.
		Nos. N14-N26 (13)	4,562.	3,478.

Uchibori Seal Handstamped in Red

N14a	A29	1c	190.00	150.00
N15a	A29	2c	190.00	130.00
N16a	A29	3c	125.00	125.00
N17a	A29	5c	2,750.	2,750.
N18a	A29	8c	100.00	110.00
N19a	A29	10c	190.00	190.00
N20a	A29	12c	125.00	140.00
N21a	A29	15c	140.00	150.00
		Nos. N14a-N21a (8)	3,810.	3,745.

PERAK
ˈper-ə-ˌak

LOCATION — On the west coast of the Malay Peninsula.
AREA — 7,980 sq. mi.
POP. — 1,327,120 (1960)
CAPITAL — Taiping

Straits Settlements No. 10 Handstamped in Black

1878   Wmk. 1   Perf. 14

1	A2	2c brown	2,200.	1,800.

Overprinted

Overprint 17x3½mm Wide
1880-81

2	A2	2c brown	40.00	80.00

Overprinted

Overprint 10 to 14½mm Wide

3	A2	2c brown, ovpt. 12-13.5mm ('81)	190.00	200.00
a.		"R" narrow, "A" wide	195.00	215.00
b.		"R" narrow, "A" narrow	300.00	325.00
c.		"P" wide, "K" wide	675.00	500.00
d.		2c brown, ovpt. 10.25mm ('80)	600.00	675.00
e.		2c brown, ovpt. 11mm ('80)	2,300.	850.00
f.		2c brown, ovpt. 14.5mm ('80)	2,750.	1,200.

Same Overprint on Straits Settlements Nos. 40, 41a
1883   Wmk. 2

4	A2	2c brown	22.50	72.50
a.		Double overprint	750.00	
5	A2	2c rose	35.00	60.00
a.		"A" wide	32.50	95.00
b.		"E" wide	32.50	80.00
c.		Double overprint	750.00	
d.		As "b," double overprint	850.00	

Overprinted

Overprint 14 to 15½mm Wide

6	A2	2c rose	5.50	4.00
a.		Inverted overprint	475.00	600.00
b.		Double overprint	700.00	700.00
c.		"E" in overprint narrow	80.00	80.00
d.		As "c," inverted overprint	1,800.	1,950.

For surcharge, see No. 19E

Overprinted

Overprint 12¾ to 14mm Wide
1886-90

7	A2	2c rose	2.75	8.00
a.		"FERAK" corrected by pen	425.00	550.00
b.		2c pale rose	175.00	35.00

Overprinted

Overprint 10x1¾mm

8	A2	2c rose	22.50	60.00

Overprinted

Overprint 12-12½x2¾mm

10	A2	2c rose	9.50	40.00
a.		Double overprint	1,800.	

Overprinted

Overprint 10½-10¾x2½mm

11	A2	2c rose	160.00	175.00

Overprinted

Overprint 13x2¾mm

11A	A2	2c rose	3,000.	

Straits Settlements Nos. 11, 41a, 42 Surcharged in Black or Blue

q   r
s   t

12	A2(q)	2c on 4c rose, as #3 ('83)	725.00	300.00
a.		2c on 4c rose, as #5b ('83)	1,200.	525.00
b.		2c on 4c rose, Sts. Setts. #42 (q)	4,000.	
c.		2c on 4c rose, Sts. Setts. #11 (q)	10,000.	
13	A2(t)	1c on 2c rose	350.00	150.00
a.		Without period after "CENT" ('90)	—	300.00
14	A2(r)	1c on 2c rose	75.00	95.00
a.		Without period after "PERAK"	800.00	850.00
b.		Double surcharge	1,250.	
c.		Both "N"s wide ('86)	135.00	155.00
15	A2(s)	1c on 2c rose (Bl)	65.00	85.00
15A	A2(s)	1c on 2c rose (Bk)	2,100.	1,600.

In type "r" PERAK is 11½ to 14mm wide.
No. 12 was first overprinted with the type of No. 3 and then surcharged "TWO CENTS."
No. 12a was first overprinted with the type of No. 5c and subsequently surcharged "TWO CENTS." Nos. 12b and 12c were surcharged and overprinted in one operation.
Nos. 13 and 13a were created in two operations, surcharging No. 6.
Nos. 14, 14a, 15 and 15A were overprinted in one operation.

Surcharged in Black

16	A2	1c on 2c rose	175.00	175.00
a.		Double surcharge	2,000.	2,000.

Surcharged

18	A2	1c on 2c rose	2,750.	2,750.
b.		Double surcharge, one inverted		

Surcharged

18A	A2	1c on 2c rose	1,100.	800.00

Surcharged

19	A2	1c on 2c rose	4.50	14.00
a.		Double surcharge, one inverted		
b.		Inverted surcharge		
c.		"One" inverted	3,500.	
d.		Double surcharge	1,400.	

No. 6 surcharged "1 CENT" in Italic Serifed Capital Letters
1886

19E	A2	1c on 2c rose	3,300.	2,750.

Straits Settlements No. 41a Surcharged

u   v
w   x
y   z

h

1889-90

20	A2(u)	1c on 2c rose	4.00	7.75
a.		Italic Roman "K" in "PERAK"	425.00	550.00
b.		Double surcharge	1,400.	
c.		2c bright rose	3.25	3.50
21	A2(v)	1c on 2c rose	800.00	975.00
23	A2(w)	1c on 2c rose	20.00	50.00
a.		"PREAK"	775.00	975.00
b.		2c bright rose	22.50	50.00
c.		As "b," "PREAK"	800.00	975.00

24	A2(x)	1c on 2c rose	150.00	*175.00*
25	A2(y)	1c on 2c rose	11.00	*19.00*
a.		2c bright rose	5.50	*19.00*
26	A2(z)	1c on 2c rose	13.00	*22.50*
a.		2c bright rose	5.50	*22.50*
27	A2(h)	1c on 2c rose	24.00	*45.00*
a.		2c bright rose	20.00	*37.50*

**Straits Settlements Nos. 41a, 48, 54
Surcharged in Black**

a   b

c   d

e   f

g

1891   **Wmk. 2**

28	A2(a)	1c on 2c rose	2.75	10.00
a.		Bar omitted	215.00	
b.		As #28, narrow "O" in "One"	30.00	*85.00*
c.		As #28a, narrow "O" in "One"	2,750.	
29	A2(a)	1c on 6c violet	60.00	42.50
30	A3(b)	2c on 24c green	22.50	14.50
31	A2(c)	1c on 2c rose	9.75	37.50
a.		Bar omitted	1,000.	
32	A2(d)	1c on 2c rose	2.75	14.50
a.		Bar omitted	425.00	
33	A2(d)	1c on 6c violet	100.00	95.00
34	A3(d)	2c on 24c green	85.00	42.50
35	A2(e)	1c on 2c rose	9.75	37.50
a.		Bar omitted	1,000.	
36	A2(e)	1c on 6c violet	210.00	210.00
37	A3(e)	2c on 24c green	140.00	80.00
38	A2(f)	1c on 6c violet	210.00	200.00
39	A3(f)	2c on 24c green	140.00	95.00
40	A2(f)	1c on 6c violet	210.00	200.00
41	A3(g)	2c on 24c green	140.00	95.00
		Nos. 28-41 (14)	*1,342.*	*1,174.*

A7

1892-95   **Typo.**   **Perf. 14**

42	A7	1c green	2.75	.40
43	A7	2c rose	2.25	.40
44	A7	2c orange ('95)	.70	*5.25*
45	A7	5c blue	4.00	8.50
		Nos. 42-45 (4)	*9.70*	*14.55*
		Set, ovptd. "SPECIMEN"	135.00	

For overprint see No. O10.

**Type of 1892
Surcharged in Black**

3 CENTS

1895

46	A7	3c on 5c rose	4.25	3.75
		Overprinted "SPECIMEN"	37.50	

A9   A10

1895-99   **Wmk. 2**   *Perf. 14*

47	A9	1c lilac & green	3.25	.60
48	A9	2c lilac & brown	3.50	.60
49	A9	3c lilac & car rose	3.75	.25
50	A9	4c lil & car rose ('99)	14.50	6.00
51	A9	5c lilac & olive	6.00	.70
52	A9	8c lilac & blue	50.00	.70
53	A9	10c lilac & orange	17.00	.65
54	A9	25c grn & car rose ('96)	200.00	14.00
55	A9	50c lilac & black	52.50	45.00
56	A9	50c grn & blk ('99)	240.00	190.00

Wmk. 1

57	A10	$1 green & lt grn	250.00	225.00
58	A10	$2 grn & car rose ('96)	400.00	375.00
59	A10	$3 green & ol ('96)	475.00	475.00
60	A10	$5 green & ultra ('96)	575.00	575.00
61	A10	$25 grn & org ('96)	10,000.	3,750.
		Overprinted "SPECIMEN"	350.00	
		Nos. 47-57 (11)	*840.50*	*483.50*
		Nos. 47-60 ovptd. "SPECIMEN"	500.00	

For surcharges and overprint see Nos. 62-68, O11, Malaya Nos. 9-13A.

**Stamps of 1895-99 Surcharged in
Black**

One Cent.   ONE CENT.

i   k

Three Cent.

m

Three Cent.

n

1900   **Wmk. 2**

62	A9(i)	1c on 2c lilac & brown	.75	2.75
63	A9(k)	1c on 4c lilac & car rose	1.25	14.50
a.		Double surcharge	1,250.	
64	A9(i)	1c on 5c lilac & ol	3.00	17.00
65	A9(i)	3c on 8c lilac & blue	7.00	13.00
a.		No period after "Cent"	190.00	*300.00*
b.		Double surcharge	575.00	650.00
66	A9(i)	3c on 50c green & black	4.00	8.50
a.		No period after "Cent"	150.00	*225.00*

Wmk. 1

67	A10(m)	3c on $1 grn & lt green	62.50	*175.00*
a.		Double surcharge	1,700.	
b.		A10(n) Thin "t" in "Cent."	325.00	*600.00*
68	A10(m)	3c on $2 grn & car rose	42.50	*95.00*
		Nos. 62-68 (7)	*121.00*	*325.75*

Sultan Iskandar
A14   A15

1935-37   **Typo.**   **Wmk. 4**
Chalky Paper

69	A14	1c black ('36)	1.00	.25
70	A14	2c dp green ('36)	1.00	.25
71	A14	4c brown orange	1.10	.25
72	A14	5c chocolate	.30	.25
73	A14	6c rose red ('37)	6.00	4.25
74	A14	8c gray	.50	.30
75	A14	10c dk vio ('36)	.40	.25
76	A14	12c ultra ('36)	2.00	1.25
77	A14	25c rose red & pale vio ('36)	1.50	1.25
78	A14	30c org & dark vio ('36)	2.00	2.00
79	A14	40c dk vio & car ('36)	2.75	5.00
80	A14	50c blk, *emerald* ('36)	3.75	2.00
81	A14	$1 red & blk, *bl*	1.50	1.25
82	A14	$2 rose red & green ('36)	17.50	9.00
83	A14	$5 brn red & grn, *emer* ('36)	70.00	37.50
		Nos. 69-83 (15)	*111.30*	*65.05*
		Set, never hinged	200.00	

1938-41

84	A15	1c black ('39)	7.00	.25
85	A15	2c dp green ('39)	4.50	.25
85A	A15	2c brn org ('41)	1.75	*18.00*
85B	A15	3c green ('41)	1.50	8.00
86	A15	4c brn org ('39)	20.00	.25
87	A15	5c choc ('39)	3.50	.25
88	A15	6c rose red ('39)	14.00	.25
89	A15	8c gray	16.00	.25
89A	A15	8c rose red ('41)	.55	*50.00*
90	A15	10c dk violet	18.00	.25
91	A15	12c ultramarine	13.00	2.00
91A	A15	15c ultra ('41)	2.25	*20.00*
92	A15	25c rose red & pale vio ('39)	27.50	4.00
93	A15	30c org & dk vio	5.00	3.00
94	A15	40c dk vio & rose red	27.50	3.00
95	A15	50c blk, *emerald*	17.50	.75
96	A15	$1 red & blk, *bl* ('40)	75.00	25.00
97	A15	$2 rose red & grn ('40)	100.00	75.00
98	A15	$5 red, *emer* ('40)	160.00	*425.00*
		Nos. 84-98 (19)	*514.55*	*635.50*
		Set, never hinged	950.00	

For overprints see Nos. N1-N40.

> **Catalogue values for unused stamps in this section, from this point to the end of the section, are for Never Hinged items.**

Common Design Types
pictured following the introduction.

Silver Wedding Issue
Common Design Types
Inscribed: "Malaya Perak"

1948, Dec. 1   **Photo.**   *Perf. 14x14½*
99	CD304	10c purple	.30	.25

Perf. 11½x11
Engraved; Name Typographed
100	CD305	$5 green	27.50	37.50

UPU Issue
Common Design Types
Inscribed: "Malaya-Perak"
Engr.; Name Typo. on 15c, 25c
Perf. 13½, 11x11½

1949, Oct. 10   **Wmk. 4**
101	CD306	10c rose violet	.25	.25
102	CD307	15c indigo	1.50	2.00
103	CD308	25c orange	.40	5.00
104	CD309	50c slate	1.50	3.50
		Nos. 101-104 (4)	*3.65*	*10.75*

**Sultan Yussuf Izuddin
Shah — A16**

1950, Aug. 17   **Typo.**   *Perf. 18*
105	A16	1c black	.25	.40
106	A16	2c orange	.25	.40
107	A16	3c green	3.00	1.40
108	A16	4c chocolate	.75	.40
109	A16	6c gray	.40	.40
110	A16	8c rose red	1.60	2.25
111	A16	10c plum	.25	.40
112	A16	15c ultramarine	1.10	.50
113	A16	20c dk grn & blk	1.60	.75
114	A16	25c org & plum	.90	.30

115	A16	40c vio brn & rose red	5.00	7.00
116	A16	50c dp ultra & blk	5.00	.30
117	A16	$1 vio brn & ultra	7.00	1.10
118	A16	$2 rose red & emer	17.00	7.50
119	A16	$5 choc & emerald	42.50	22.50

1952-55

120	A16	5c rose violet	.50	2.00
121	A16	8c green	1.40	1.25
122	A16	12c rose red	1.40	5.00
123	A16	20c ultramarine	1.10	.30
124	A16	30c plum & rose red ('55)	2.25	.30
125	A16	35c dk vio & rose red	1.40	.40
		Nos. 105-125 (21)	*94.65*	*54.85*

OFFICIAL STAMPS

P.G.S.

Stamps and Types of
Straits Settlements
Overprinted in Black

1890   **Wmk. 1**   *Perf. 14*
O1	A3	12c blue	240.00	300.00
O2	A3	24c green	800.00	*900.00*

Wmk. 2

O3	A2	2c rose	5.50	7.50
a.		No period after "S"	85.00	105.00
b.		Double overprint	950.00	950.00
O4	A2	4c brown	22.50	27.50
a.		No period after "S"	200.00	*225.00*
O5	A2	6c violet	32.50	60.00
O6	A3	8c orange	42.50	75.00
O7	A7	10c slate	85.00	85.00
O8	A3	12c vio brown	250.00	325.00
O9	A3	24c green	210.00	*250.00*

Wide Spacing Between "G" and "S"

O1a	A3	12c blue	900.00	
O2a	A3	24c green	2,750.	
O3c	A2	2c rose	85.00	*105.00*
O4b	A2	4c brown	115.00	*155.00*
O5a	A2	6c violet	180.00	*225.00*
O6a	A3	8c orange	215.00	*350.00*
O7a	A7	10c slate	400.00	400.00
O8a	A3	12c vio brown	1,050.	
O9a	A3	24c green	850.00	

P.G.S. stands for Perak Government Service.

Perak No. 45
Overprinted

Service.

1894
O10	A7	5c blue	90.00	1.25
a.		Inverted overprint	1,200.	550.00

Same Overprint on No. 51
1897
O11	A9	5c lilac & olive	3.50	.60
a.		Double overprint	700.00	450.00

OCCUPATION STAMPS

Issued under Japanese Occupation

Stamps of Perak,
1938-41,
Handstamped in Black,
Red, Brown or Violet

1942   **Wmk. 4**   *Perf. 14*
N1	A15	1c black	50.00	35.00
N2	A15	2c brn orange	35.00	21.00
N3	A15	3c green	35.00	37.50
N4	A15	5c chocolate	11.50	11.00
N5	A15	8c gray	55.00	37.50
N6	A15	8c rose red	25.00	35.00
N7	A15	10c dk violet	22.50	27.50
N8	A15	12c ultramarine	150.00	150.00
N9	A15	15c ultramarine	30.00	35.00
N10	A15	25c rose red & pale vio	27.50	30.00
N11	A15	30c org & dk vio	35.00	40.00
N12	A15	40c dk vio & rose red	175.00	190.00
N13	A15	50c blk, *emerald*	57.50	*60.00*

N14	A15	$1 red & blk, bl	275.00	300.00
N15	A15	$2 rose red &		
		blk	1,500.	1,500.
N16	A15	$5 red, emerald	750.00	750.00

Some authorities claim No. N8 was not regularly issued. This overprint also exists on No. 85

Stamps of Perak, 1938-41, Overprinted in Black

N16A	A15	1c black	40.00	40.00
N17	A15	2c brn org	1.60	1.60
a.		Inverted overprint	27.50	29.00
N18	A15	3c green	1.25	1.40
a.		Inverted overprint	27.50	30.00
N18B	A15	5c chocolate	40.00	
N19	A15	8c rose red	1.25	.65
a.		Inverted overprint	10.00	10.00
b.		Dbl. ovpt., one invtd.	250.00	275.00
c.		Pair, one without ovpt.	500.00	475.00
N20	A15	10c dk violet	8.50	9.50
N21	A15	15c ultramarine	6.00	6.75
N21A	A15	30c org & dk vio	35.00	35.00
N22	A15	50c blk, emerald	4.00	6.00
N23	A15	$1 red & blk, bl	350.00	375.00
N24	A15	$5 red, emerald	60.00	67.50
a.		Inverted overprint	350.00	400.00

Some authorities claim Nos. N16A, N18B and N21A were not regularly issued.

Overprinted on Perak No. 87 and Surcharged in Black "2 Cents"

N25	A15	2c on 5c chocolate	2.00	1.40

Perak Nos. 84 and 89A Overprinted in Black

N26	A15	1c black	3.25	4.00
a.		Inverted overprint	35.00	40.00
N27	A15	8c rose red	3.25	2.00
a.		Inverted overprint	20.00	24.00

Overprinted on Perak No. 87 and Surcharged in Black "2 Cents"

N28	A15	2c on 5c chocolate	5.00	5.00
a.		Inverted overprint	35.00	47.50
b.		As "a," "2 Cents" omitted	50.00	57.50

Stamps of Perak, 1938-41, Overprinted or Surcharged in Black

n   No. N31

No. N32

1943

N29	A15	1c black	.65	.65
N30	A15	2c brn orange	35.00	35.00
N31	A15	2c on 5c choc	1.00	1.00
a.		"2 Cents" inverted	35.00	40.00
b.		Entire surcharge inverted	35.00	40.00
N32	A15	2c on 5c choc	1.40	1.40
a.		Vertical characters invtd.	35.00	40.00
b.		Entire surcharge inverted	35.00	40.00
N33	A15	3c green	37.50	37.50
N34	A15	5c chocolate	1.00	1.00
a.		Inverted overprint	50.00	60.00
N35	A15	8c gray	35.00	35.00
N36	A15	8c rose red	1.00	1.00
a.		Inverted overprint	35.00	40.00
N37	A15	10c dk violet	1.25	1.25
N38	A15	30c org & dk vio	2.75	4.00
N39	A15	50c blk, emerald	5.50	9.50
N40	A15	$5 red, emerald	75.00	85.00
		Nos. N29-N40 (12)	197.05	212.30

No. N34 was also used in the Shan States of Burma. The Japanese characters read: "Japanese Postal Service."

Some authorities claim Nos. N30, N33 and N35 were not regularly issued.

PERLIS

'per-ləs

LOCATION — On the west coast of the Malay peninsula, adjoining Siam and Kedah.
AREA — 310 sq. mi.
POP. — 97,645 (1960)
CAPITAL — Kangar

> Catalogue values for unused stamps in this section are for Never Hinged items.

Common Design Types pictured following the introduction.

Silver Wedding Issue
Common Design Types
Inscribed: "Malaya Perlis"
Perf. 14x14½

1948, Dec. 1		**Photo.**		**Wmk. 4**
1	CD304	10c purple	1.00	3.00

Engraved; Name Typographed
Perf. 11½x11

2	CD305	$5 lt brown	32.50	55.00

UPU Issue
Common Design Types
Inscribed: "Malaya-Perlis"
Engr.; Name Typo. on 15c, 25c

1949, Oct. 10		**Perf. 13½, 11x11½**		
3	CD306	10c rose violet	.40	2.00
4	CD307	15c indigo	1.40	4.50
5	CD308	25c orange	.65	3.50
6	CD309	50c slate	1.50	4.25
		Nos. 3-6 (4)	3.95	14.25

Raja Syed Putra — A1

Perf. 18

			Typo.	
1951, Mar. 26		**Wmk. 4**		
7	A1	1c black	.25	1.00
8	A1	2c orange	.75	.70
9	A1	3c green	1.75	5.25
10	A1	4c chocolate	1.75	1.50
11	A1	6c gray	1.50	2.50
12	A1	8c rose red	3.75	7.50
13	A1	10c plum	1.25	.50
14	A1	15c ultramarine	5.00	8.50
15	A1	20c dk green & blk	4.50	11.50
16	A1	25c org & rose lilac	2.25	3.75
17	A1	40c dk vio & rose red	5.00	29.00
18	A1	50c ultra & black	4.75	7.00
19	A1	$1 vio brn & ultra	10.00	27.50
20	A1	$2 rose red & emer	20.00	60.00
21	A1	$5 choc & emerald	70.00	125.00
1952-55				
22	A1	5c rose violet	.75	3.75
23	A1	8c green	2.75	4.50
24	A1	12c rose red	2.00	6.25
25	A1	20c ultramarine	1.25	1.75
26	A1	30c plum & rose red ('55)	2.75	15.00
27	A1	35c dk vio & rose red	3.00	8.50
		Nos. 7-27 (21)	145.00	330.95

SELANGOR

sə-'laŋ-ər

LOCATION — South of Perak on the west coast of the Malay Peninsula.
AREA — 3,160 sq. mi.
POP. — 1,012,891 (1960)
CAPITAL — Kuala Lumpur

Stamps of the Straits Settlements Overprinted

Handstamped in Black or Red

1878		**Wmk. 1**	**Perf. 14**	
1	A2	2c brown (Bk)	—	
		Wmk. 2	**Perf.**	
2	A2	2c brown (R)	600.00	

The authenticity of Nos. 1-2 is questioned.

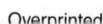

Overprinted in Black

1882				
3	A2	2c brown	—	3,300.

Overprinted

Overprint 16 to 16¾mm Wide				
1881			**Wmk. 1**	
5	A2	2c brown	140.00	140.00
a.		Double overprint		
b.		"S" inverted	675.00	725.00
c.		"S" wide	225.00	250.00
d.		"N" wide	9,000.	2,750.
e.		"SE" and "AN" wide ('82)	275.00	300.00
f.		"SEL" and "N" wide ('82)	275.00	300.00
g.		"SELAN" wide ('82)	275.00	300.00

Overprint 16 to 17mm Wide				
1882-83			**Wmk. 2**	
"S" wide, all other letters narrow				
6	A2	2c brown	200.00	160.00
a.		All letters narrow	375.00	160.00
b.		"SEL" and "NG" wide	325.00	375.00
c.		"E" and "ANG" wide	325.00	375.00
d.		"ELANG" wide	325.00	375.00
e.		"S" and "L" wide		4,250.
f.		"S" and "A" wide	725.00	600.00
g.		"E" wide	500.00	375.00
h.		"EL" wide	500.00	375.00
i.		"SE" and "N" wide	215.00	210.00
j.		"S" and "N" wide	215.00	210.00
7	A2	2c rose	160.00	125.00
a.		"N" wide	240.00	210.00
b.		"S" and "L" wide	275.00	210.00
c.		"E" wide	160.00	135.00
d.		"EL" wide	140.00	115.00
e.		As "d," double overprint	1,200.	
f.		As "d," triple overprint		
g.		"E" and "A" wide	160.00	125.00
h.		"A" wide	500.00	215.00
i.		"L" wide	600.00	275.00
j.		All wide letters, "L" narrow	120.00	110.00
k.		All wide letters, "A" narrow	230.00	195.00
l.		All wide letters	575.00	275.00

Overprinted

Overprint 14¼x3mm				
8	A2	2c rose	11.50	24.00
a.		Double overprint	975.00	850.00

Overprinted

Overprint 14½ to 15½mm Wide				
1886-89				
9	A2	2c rose	42.50	55.00

Overprinted

Overprint 16½x1¾mm				
9A	A2	2c rose	67.50	72.50
b.		Double overprint	1,000.	

Overprinted

Overprint 15½ to 17mm Wide				
With Period				
10	A2	2c rose	140.00	90.00
Without Period				
11	A2	2c rose	14.50	3.25
Same Overprint, but Vertically				
12	A2	2c rose	22.50	37.50

12A	A2	2c rose	150.00	3.75

Overprinted

Overprint 17mm Wide				
13	A2	2c rose	1,700.	1,850.

Overprinted

14	A2	2c rose	400.00	175.00

Overprinted Vertically

1889				
15	A2	2c rose	725.00	40.00

Overprinted Vertically

Overprint 19 to 20¾mm Wide				
16	A2	2c rose	325.00	95.00
Similar Overprint, but Diagonally				
17	A2	2c rose	3,000.	

Overprinted Vertically

18	A2	2c rose	90.00	6.75
Same Overprint Horizontally				
18A	A2	2c rose	4,500.	

Surcharged in Black

a   b

c

d

e

1891

19	A3 (a)	2c on 24c green	40.00	75.00
20	A3 (b)	2c on 24c green	225.00	275.00
21	A3 (c)	2c on 24c green	225.00	250.00
22	A3 (d)	2c on 24c green	125.00	150.00
a.		Overprinted "SE-LANGCR"		
23	A3 (e)	2c on 24c green	225.00	275.00
		Nos. 19-23 (5)	840.00	1,025.

No. 22a occurred ijn the first printing in one position (R. 8/3) in the sheet.

A6

1891-95   Typo.   Wmk. 2

24	A6	1c green	1.75	.30
25	A6	2c rose	4.00	1.25
26	A6	2c orange ('95)	3.00	1.00
27	A6	5c blue	27.50	5.25
		Nos. 24-27 (4)	36.25	7.80
		Set, ovptd. "SPECIMEN"	115.00	

Type of 1891
Surcharged

3 CENTS

1894

28	A6	3c on 5c rose	5.00	.70
		Overprinted "SPECIMEN" in black	42.50	

A8

A9

1895-99   Wmk. 2   Perf. 14

29	A8	3c lilac & car rose	7.00	.35
30	A8	5c lilac & olive	8.50	.35
31	A8	8c lilac & blue	55.00	8.50
32	A8	10c lilac & orange	13.50	2.50
33	A8	25c grn & car rose	90.00	60.00
34	A8	50c lilac & black	80.00	29.00
35	A8	50c green & black	475.00	140.00

Wmk. 1

36	A9	$1 green & lt grn	65.00	150.00
37	A9	$2 grn & car rose	250.00	300.00
38	A9	$3 green & olive	600.00	500.00
39	A9	$5 green & ultra	300.00	400.00
40	A9	$10 grn & brn vio	800.00	1,000.
		Overprinted "SPECIMEN"	175.00	
41	A9	$25 green & org	4,000.	4,000.
		Overprinted "SPECIMEN"	325.00	
		Nos. 29-39, Ovpt. "SPECIMEN"	450.00	

High values with revenue cancellations are plentiful and inexpensive.

Surcharged in Black

One cent.

Three cents.

1900   Wmk. 2

42	A8	1c on 5c lilac & olive	75.00	125.00
43	A8	1c on 50c grn & blk	3.50	29.00
a.		Surcharge reading "cent One cent."	3,500.	
44	A8	3c on 50c grn & blk	6.00	26.00
a.		Antique "t" in "Cents"	160.00	250.00
		Nos. 42-44 (3)	84.50	180.00

Mosque at Klang
A12

Sultan Sulaiman
A13

1935-41   Typo.   Wmk. 4   Perf. 14

45	A12	1c black ('36)	.30	.25
46	A12	2c dp green ('36)	.55	.25
46A	A12	2c org brn ('41)	2.25	1.25
46B	A12	3c green ('41)	1.25	8.00
47	A12	4c orange brown	.30	.25
48	A12	5c chocolate	.70	.25
49	A12	6c rose red ('37)	4.00	.25
50	A12	8c gray	.35	.25
51	A12	10c dk violet ('36)	.35	.25
52	A12	12c ultra ('36)	.90	.25
52A	A12	15c ultra ('41)	7.00	35.00
53	A12	25c rose red & pale vio ('36)	.60	.80
54	A12	30c org & dk vio ('36)	.60	1.10
55	A12	40c dk vio & car	1.50	1.25
56	A12	50c blk, emer ('36)	1.00	.50
57	A13	$1 red & black, blue ('36)	6.00	1.10
58	A13	$2 rose red & green ('36)	17.50	9.50
59	A13	$5 brn red & grn, emer ('36)	55.00	30.00
		Nos. 45-59 (18)	100.15	90.50

Nos. 46A-46B were printed on both ordinary and chalky paper; 15c only on ordinary paper; other values only on chalky paper.

An 8c rose red was prepared but not issued.

For overprints see Nos. N1-N15, N18A-N24, N26-N39.

Sultan Hisam-ud-Din Alam Shah — A14

1941

72	A14	$1 red & blk, blue	11.50	7.00
73	A14	$2 car & green	30.00	40.00
		Set, never hinged	70.00	

A $5 stamp of type A14, issued during the Japanese occupation with different overprints (Nos. N18, N25A, N42), also exists without overprint. The unoverprinted stamp was not issued. Value $125.

For overprints see Nos. N16-N17, N24A, N25, N40-N41.

> **Catalogue values for unused stamps in this section, from this point to the end of the section, are for Never Hinged items.**

Common Design Types pictured following the introduction.

Silver Wedding Issue
Common Design Types
Inscribed: "Malaya Selangor"
Perf. 14x14½

1948, Dec. 1   Photo.   Wmk. 4

74	CD304	10c purple	.25	.30

Perf. 11½x11

Engraved; Name Typographed

75	CD305	$5 green	30.00	25.00

UPU Issue
Common Design Types
Inscribed: "Malaya-Selangor"
Engr.; Name Typo. on Nos. 77 & 78

1949, Oct. 10   Perf. 13½, 11x11½

76	CD306	10c rose violet	.40	.30
77	CD307	15c indigo	2.50	2.50
78	CD308	25c orange	.50	4.50
79	CD309	50c slate	1.50	5.00
		Nos. 76-79 (4)	4.90	12.30

Sultan Hisam-ud-Din Alam Shah — A15

1949, Sept. 12   Typo.   Perf. 18

80	A15	1c black	.25	.60
81	A15	2c orange	.30	1.50
82	A15	3c green	4.00	.30
83	A15	4c chocolate	.50	.35
84	A15	6c gray	.35	.35
85	A15	8c rose red	2.00	1.25
86	A15	10c plum	.25	.25
87	A15	15c ultramarine	8.00	.35
88	A15	20c dk grn & black	5.00	.50
89	A15	25c orange & rose lil	2.00	.35
90	A15	40c dk vio & rose red	11.00	8.00
91	A15	50c ultra & black	3.50	.35
92	A15	$1 vio brn & ultra	4.00	.60
93	A15	$2 rose red & emer	15.00	1.10
94	A15	$5 choc & emerald	55.00	3.00

1952-55

95	A15	5c rose violet	1.00	2.75
96	A15	8c green	1.00	1.75
97	A15	12c rose red	1.25	3.50
98	A15	20c ultramarine	1.25	.35
99	A15	30c plum & rose red ('55)	2.25	2.25
100	A15	35c dk vio & rose red	1.50	1.50
		Nos. 80-100 (21)	119.40	32.65

OCCUPATION STAMPS

Issued under Japanese Occupation

Stamps of Selangor 1935-41 Handstamped Vertically or Horizontally in Black, Red, Brown or Violet

1942, Apr. 3   Wmk. 4   Perf. 14

N1	A12	1c black	15.00	21.00
N2	A12	2c deep green	600.00	600.00
N3	A12	2c orange brown	55.00	55.00
N4	A12	3c green	35.00	17.00
N5	A12	5c chocolate	10.00	10.00
N6	A12	6c rose red	200.00	200.00
N7	A12	8c gray	27.50	27.50
N8	A12	10c dark violet	22.50	27.50
N9	A12	12c ultramarine	47.50	47.50
N10	A12	15c ultramarine	17.00	20.00
N11	A12	25c rose red & pale vio	80.00	95.00
N12	A12	30c org & dk vio	15.00	30.00
N13	A12	40c dk vio & car	100.00	140.00
N14	A12	50c blk, emerald	40.00	47.50
N15	A13	$5 brn red & grn, emer	275.00	275.00

Some authorities believe No. N15 was not issued regularly.

Handstamped Vertically on Stamps and Type of Selangor 1941 in Black or Red

N16	A14	$1 red & blk, bl	67.50	80.00
N17	A14	$2 car & green	80.00	110.00
N18	A14	$5 brn red & grn, emer	110.00	110.00

Stamps and Type of Selangor, 1935-41, Overprinted in Black

1942, May

N18A	A12	1c black	110.00	110.00
N19	A12	3c green	1.00	1.00
N19A	A12	5c chocolate	110.00	110.00
N20	A12	10c dark violet	35.00	35.00
N21	A12	12c ultramarine	2.75	5.00
N22	A12	15c ultramarine	5.50	4.00
N23	A12	30c org & dk vio	35.00	35.00
N24	A12	40c dk vio & car	4.00	4.00
N24A	A14	$1 red & blk, bl	35.00	35.00
N25	A14	$2 car & green	24.00	30.00
N25A	A14	$5 brn red & grn, emer	55.00	55.00
		Nos. N18A-N25A (11)	417.25	424.00

Overprint is horizontal on $1, $2, $5.

On Nos. N18A and N19 the overprint is known reading up, instead of down.

Some authorities claim Nos. N18A, N19A, N20, N23, N24A and N25A are not regularly issued.

Selangor No. 46B Overprinted in Black

1942, Dec.

N26	A12	3c green	400.00	400.00

Stamps and Type of Selangor, 1935-41, Ovptd. or Srchd. in Black or Red

i

k

l

m

1943

N27	A12(i)	1c black	1.40	1.40
N28	A12(k)	1c black (R)	.90	.90
N29	A12(l)	2c on 5c choc (R)	.90	.90
N30	A12(i)	3c green	1.00	1.00
N31	A12(l)	3c on 5c choc	.65	1.00
N32	A12(k)	5c choc (R)	.65	1.00
N33	A12(l)	6c on 5c choc	.25	.90
N34	A12(m)	6c on 5c choc	.25	1.00
N35	A12(i)	12c ultra	1.40	1.60
N36	A12(i)	15c ultra	6.75	10.00
N37	A12(l)	15c ultra	13.50	13.50
N38	A12(m)	$1 on 10c dk vio	.50	1.40
N39	A12(m)	$1.50 on 30c org & dk vio	.50	1.40
N40	A14(i)	$1 red & blk, blue	6.75	8.50
N41	A14(i)	$2 car & grn	24.00	24.00
N42	A14(i)	$5 brn red & grn, emer	50.00	55.00
		Nos. N27-N42 (16)	109.40	123.50

The "i" overprint is vertical on Nos. N40-N42 and is also found reading in the opposite direction on Nos. N30, N35 and N36.

The overprint reads: "Japanese Postal Service."

Singapore is listed following Sierra Leone.

SUNGEI UJONG

ˈsu̇n-ji ü-jun

Formerly a nonfederated native state on the Malay Peninsula, which in 1895 was consolidated with the Federated State of Negri Sembilan.

Stamps of the Straits Settlements Overprinted in Black

Overprinted

1878   Wmk. 1   Perf. 14

2	A2	2c brown	3,600.	3,900.

Overprinted

4	A2	2c brown	400.00	
a.		"UJONG" printed twice	2,200.	
b.		All letters narrow, evenly spaced	500.00	

c. "S" wide, "UJ" close together   1,200.
d. Both "N"s wide   3,600.   3,000.
e. "N" of "SUNGEI" narrow, "N" of "UJONG" wide   5,500.   4,250.
5   A2 4c rose   1,950.   2,000.

No. 5 is no longer recognized by some experts.

All Letters Narrow, "UJ" Close Together "SUNGEI" 14mm, "UJONG" approx. 14mm

4F   A2 2c brown   275.00
g. "N" and "E" of "SUNGEI" and "U" and "NG" of "UJONG" wide   425.00
h. "SUN" and "E" of "SUNGEI" and "U" and "NG" of "UJONG" wide   450.00
i. "SUN" of "SUNGEI" and "U" and "NG" of "UJONG" wide   425.00
j. "S" of "SUNGEI" wide   400.00
k. As "S" inverted   4,500.

Overprinted

1882-83   **Wmk. 2**
6   A2 2c brown   375.00
7   A2 4c rose   4,250.   4,800.

This overprint on the 2c brown, wmk. 1, is probably a trial printing.

Overprinted

11   A2 2c brown   325.00   400.00

Overprinted

1881-84
14   A2 2c brown   1,200.   550.00
15   A2 2c rose   140.00   140.00
a. "Ujong" printed sideways
b. "Sungei" printed twice
16   A2 4c brown   325.00   425.00
17   A3 8c orange   2,250.   1,700.
18   A7 10c slate   725.00   625.00

Overprinted

19   A2 2c brown   57.50   160.00

Overprinted

1885-90   **Without Period**
20   A2 2c rose   45.00   77.50

With Period
21   A2 2c rose   125.00   90.00
a. "UNJOG"   5,750.   4,000.

Overprinted

22   A2 2c rose   95.00   110.00
a. Double overprint   775.00   775.00

Overprinted

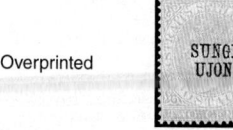

23   A2 2c rose   125.00   150.00

Overprinted

24   A2 2c rose   30.00   47.50
a. Double overprint

25   A2 2c rose   110.00   125.00

Overprinted

26   A2 2c rose   175.00   175.00
c. Double overprint

Overprint 14-16x3mm
26A A2 2c rose   12.00   16.00

Overprinted

26B A2 2c rose   50.00   21.00

Stamp of 1883-91 Surcharged

SUNGEI UJONG Two CENTS	SUNGEI UJONG Two CENTS
a	b
SUNGEI UJONG Two CENTS	SUNGEI UJONG Two CENTS
c	d

1891
27   A3 (a) 2c on 24c green   240.   275.
a. Antique "G" in "SUNGEI"   1,300.
b. Antique "G" in "UJONG"   1,300.
28   A3 (b) 2c on 24c green   1,100.   1,200.
29   A3 (c) 2c on 24c green   425.   500.
30   A3 (d) 2c on 24c green   1,100.   1,200.
Nos. 27-30 (4)   2,865.   3,175.

On Nos. 27-28, SUNGEI is 14½mm, UJONG 12¾x2½mm.

A3

1891-94   **Typo.**   **Perf. 14**
31   A3 2c rose   40.00   35.00
32   A3 2c orange ('94)   2.25   5.50
33   A3 5c blue ('93)   6.50   7.75
Nos. 31-33 (3)   48.75   48.25
Set, ovptd. "SPECIMEN"   77.50

Type of 1891 Surcharged in Black

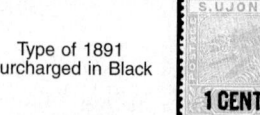

1894
34   A3 1c on 5c green   1.40   .90
35   A3 3c on 5c rose   3.25   6.00

 A4

1895
36   A4 3c lilac & car rose   15.00   4.75

Stamps of Sungei Ujong were superseded by those of Negri Sembilan in 1895.

TRENGGANU

treṇ·'gä-ˌnü

LOCATION — On the eastern coast of the Malay Peninsula.
AREA — 5,050 sq. mi.
POP. — 302,171 (1960)
CAPITAL — Kuala Trengganu

Sultan Zenalabidin
A1   A2

1910-19   **Typo.**   **Wmk. 3**   **Perf. 14**
Ordinary Paper
1   A1 1c gray green   3.25   1.50
a. 1c blue green   2.10   1.25
2   A1 2c red vio & brn ('15)   1.25   1.10
3   A1 3c rose red   2.75   2.75
4   A1 4c brn orange   4.25   6.75
5   A1 4c grn & org brn ('15)   2.50   5.75
6   A1 4c scarlet ('19)   1.50   2.10
7   A1 5c gray   1.75   4.50
8   A1 5c choc & gray ('15)   3.00   2.40
9   A1 8c ultramarine   1.75   11.00
10   A1 10c red & grn, yel ('15)   1.75   2.75

Chalky Paper
11   A1 10c violet, yel   5.75   15.00
a. 10c violet, pale yel   4.00   9.00
12   A1 20c red vio & vio   4.25   5.75
13   A1 25c dl vio & grn ('15)   9.75   42.50
14   A1 30c blk & dl vio ('15)   8.50   65.00
15   A1 50c blk & sep, grn   5.75   11.50
16   A1 $1 red & blk, blue   22.50   29.00
17   A1 $3 red & grn, grn ('15)   225.00   500.00
18   A2 $5 lil & blue grn   225.00   675.00

19   A2 $25 green & car   1,200.   2,750.
  Revenue Cancel   300.00
  Overprinted "SPECIMEN"   290.00
Nos. 1-18 (18)   530.25   1,384.
Nos. 1a-18 (10)   1,727.   4,128.
Nos. 1-18 ovptd. "SPECIMEN"   725.00

On No. 19 the numerals and Arabic inscriptions at top, left and right are in color on a colorless background.
Overprints are listed after No. 41. For surcharges see Nos. B1-B4.

Sultan Badaru'l-alam
A3   A4

1921-38   **Wmk. 4**   **Perf. 14**
Chalky Paper
20   A3 1c black ('25)   2.75   1.75
21   A3 2c deep green   1.75   2.40
22   A3 3c dp grn ('25)   3.00   1.10
23   A3 3c lt brn ('38)   32.50   22.50
24   A3 4c rose red   2.40   2.00
25   A3 5c choc & gray   3.25   8.00
26   A3 5c vio, yel ('25)   2.75   2.00
27   A3 6c orange ('24)   6.00   .85
28   A3 8c gray ('38)   42.50   9.50
29   A3 10c ultramarine   3.25   1.50
30   A3 12c ultra ('25)   7.00   7.25
31   A3 20c org & dl vio   3.50   2.40
32   A3 25c dk vio & grn   3.75   5.00
33   A3 30c blk & dl vio   5.50   6.00
34   A3 35c red ('25)   7.75   12.50
35   A3 50c car & green   11.50   5.25
36   A3 $1 ultra & vio, bl ('29)   15.00   6.00
37   A3 $3 red & green, emer ('25)   87.50   240.00
38   A4 $5 red & grn, yel ('38)   500.00   2,800.
39   A4 $25 blue & lil   750.00   1,250.
  Overprinted "SPECIMEN"   160.00
40   A4 $50 org & green   1,850.   3,200.
  Overprinted "SPECIMEN"   350.00
41   A4 $100 red & green   5,750.   7,500.
  Overprinted "SPECIMEN"   625.00
Nos. 20-37 (18)   241.65   336.00
Nos. 20-38 ovptd. or perf "SPECIMEN"   800.00

On Nos. 39 to 41 the numerals and Arabic inscriptions at top, left and right are in color on a colorless background.
A 2c orange, 6c gray, 8c rose red and 15c ultramarine, type A3, exist, but are not known to have been regularly issued.
For surcharges and overprints see Nos. 45-46, N1-N60.

Stamps of 1910-21 Overprinted in Black

1922, Mar.   **Wmk. 3**
8a   A1 5c chocolate & gray   4.75   37.50
10a A1 10c red & green, red   4.75   37.50
12a A1 20c red vio & violet   4.25   50.00
13a A1 25c dull vio & green   4.25   50.00
14a A1 30c black & dull vio   4.25   50.00
15a A1 50c blk & sepia, grn   4.25   50.00
16a A1 $1 red & blk, blue   20.00   95.00
17a A1 $3 red & grn, green   210.00   575.00
18a A2 $5 lil & blue green   300.00   575.00

Wmk. 4
21a A3 2c deep green   2.75   47.50
24a A3 4c rose red   7.75   47.50
Nos. 8a-24a (11)   567.00   1,615.

Industrial fair at Singapore, Mar. 31-Apr. 15.

1921   **Wmk. 3**   **Chalky Paper**
42   A3 $1 ultra & vio, bl   20.00   40.00
43   A3 $3 red & grn, emer   140.00   160.00
44   A4 $5 red & green, yel   140.00   150.00
Nos. 42-44 (3)   300.00   350.00

Types of 1921-25 Surcharged in Black

1941, May 1 Wmk. 4 Perf. 13½x14

45	A3	2c on 5c magenta, yel	5.50	6.50
46	A3	8c on 10c lt ultra	9.50	6.50

For overprints see Nos. N30-N33, N46-N47, N59-N60.

> Catalogue values for unused stamps in this section, from this point to the end of the section, are for Never Hinged items.

Common Design Types pictured following the introduction.

Silver Wedding Issue
Common Design Types
Inscribed: "Malaya Trengganu"

1948, Dec. 1 Photo. Perf. 14x14½

47	CD304	10c purple	.25	.25

Engraved; Name Typographed
Perf. 11½x11

48	CD305	$5 rose car	35.00	62.50

UPU Issue
Common Design Types
Inscribed: "Malaya-Trengganu"
Engr.; Name Typo. on 15c, 25c
Perf. 13½, 11x11½

1949, Oct. 10 Wmk. 4

49	CD306	10c rose violet	.65	.65
50	CD307	15c indigo	.80	2.10
51	CD308	25c orange	1.40	3.50
52	CD309	50c slate	2.10	3.50
		Nos. 49-52 (4)	4.95	9.75

Sultan Ismail
Nasiruddin Shah — A5

1949, Dec. 27 Typo. Perf. 18

53	A5	1c black	.40	.45
54	A5	2c orange	.40	.50
55	A5	3c green	1.25	1.50
56	A5	4c chocolate	.60	.50
57	A5	6c gray	1.25	1.25
58	A5	8c rose red	1.60	1.90
59	A5	10c plum	.60	.50
60	A5	15c ultramarine	1.75	1.60
61	A5	20c dk grn & black	2.40	5.00
62	A5	25c org & rose lilac	2.25	3.25
63	A5	40c dk vio & black	4.50	27.50
64	A5	50c dp ultra & black	2.75	2.75
65	A5	$1 vio brn & ultra	5.50	10.00
66	A5	$2 rose red & emer	30.00	24.50
67	A5	$5 choc & emerald	80.00	67.50

1952-55

68	A5	5c rose violet	.40	.50
69	A5	8c green	1.60	3.25
70	A5	12c rose red	1.60	6.75
71	A5	20c ultramarine	1.60	1.50
72	A5	30c plum & rose red ('55)	3.00	6.75
73	A5	35c dk vio & rose red	3.50	6.75
		Nos. 53-73 (21)	146.95	174.20

SEMI-POSTAL STAMPS

Nos. 3, 4 and 9
Surcharged

1917, Oct. Wmk. 3 Perf. 14

B1	A1	3c + 2c rose red	1.50	8.00
a.		"CSOSS"	65.00	100.00
b.		Comma after "2c"	10.00	10.50
c.		Pair, one without surcharge	2,900.	2,900.
B2	A1	4c + 2c brn org	2.25	12.50
a.		"CSOSS"	275.00	275.00
b.		Comma after "2c"	16.00	42.50
B3	A1	8c + 2c ultra	3.50	24.00
a.		"CSOSS"	175.00	210.00
b.		Comma after "2c"	13.00	45.00
		Nos. B1-B3 (3)	7.25	44.50

Same Surcharge on No. 5
1918

B4	A1	4c + 2c grn & org brn	4.25	11.50
a.		Pair, one without surcharge	2,300.	

POSTAGE DUE STAMPS

D1

Perf. 14
1937, Aug. 10 Typo. Wmk. 4

J1	D1	1c rose red	8.25	65.00
		Never hinged	11.50	
J2	D1	4c green	9.00	72.50
		Never hinged	11.50	
J3	D1	8c lemon	47.50	400.00
		Never hinged	67.50	
J4	D1	10c light brown	92.50	115.00
		Never hinged	125.00	
		Nos. J1-J4 (4)	157.25	652.50
		Set, never hinged	215.00	
		Set, perf "SPECIMEN"	180.00	

For overprints see Nos. NJ1-NJ4.

OCCUPATION STAMPS

Issued under Japanese Occupation

No. N6   No. N17A

**Stamps of Trengganu, 1921-38,
Handstamped in Black or Brown**

1942 Wmk. 4 Perf. 14

N1	A3	1c black	110.00	110.00
N2	A3	2c deep green	190.00	275.00
N3	A3	3c lt brown	140.00	110.00
N4	A3	4c rose red	275.00	190.00
N5	A3	5c violet, yel	17.50	19.00
N6	A3	6c orange	13.50	20.00
N7	A3	8c gray	17.50	25.00
N8	A3	10c ultramarine	13.50	27.50
N9	A3	12c ultramarine	15.00	25.00
N10	A3	20c org & dl vio	15.00	22.50
N11	A3	25c dk vio & grn	13.50	27.50
N12	A3	30c blk & dl vio	13.50	25.00
N13	A3	35c red, yel	22.50	27.50
N14	A3	50c car & grn	125.00	95.00
N15	A3	$1 ultra & vio, blue	1,650.	1,750.
N16	A3	$3 red & grn, emerald	125.00	140.00
N17	A4	$5 red & grn, yellow	240.00	240.00
N17A	A4	$25 blue & lil	1,500.	
N17B	A4	$50 org & grn	8,800.	
N17C	A4	$100 red & grn	950.00	

Handstamped in Red

N18	A3	1c black	275.00	225.00
N19	A3	2c dp green	140.00	160.00
N20	A3	5c violet, yel	35.00	20.00
N21	A3	6c orange	20.00	20.00
N22	A3	8c gray	275.00	240.00
N23	A3	10c ultramarine	275.00	275.00
N24	A3	12c ultramarine	55.00	55.00
N25	A3	20c org & dl vio	35.00	35.00
N26	A3	25c dk vio & grn	40.00	40.00
N27	A3	30c blk & dl vio	35.00	35.00
N28	A3	35c red, yellow	35.00	20.00
N29	A3	$3 red & grn, emerald	100.00	40.00
N29A	A3	$25 blue & lil	500.00	500.00

**Handstamped on Nos. 45 and 46 in
Black or Red**

N30	A3	2c on 5c (Bk)	140.00	140.00
N31	A3	2c on 5c (R)	100.00	100.00
N32	A3	8c on 10c (Bk)	25.00	35.00
N33	A3	8c on 10c (R)	35.00	40.00

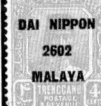

Stamps of Trengganu,
1921-38, Overprinted in
Black

1942

N34	A3	1c black	15.00	17.00
N35	A3	2c deep green	100.00	140.00
N36	A3	3c light brown	16.00	29.00
N37	A3	4c rose red	15.00	20.00
N38	A3	5c violet, yel	10.00	20.00
N39	A3	6c orange	10.00	17.00
N40	A3	8c gray	67.50	60.00
N41	A3	12c ultramarine	10.00	13.50
N42	A3	20c org & dl vio	13.50	25.00
N43	A3	25c dk vio & grn	13.50	17.00
N44	A3	30c blk & dl vio	13.50	20.00
N45	A3	$3 red & grn, emer	100.00	140.00

**Overprinted on Nos. 45 and 46 in
Black**

N46	A3	2c on 5c mag, yel	13.50	17.00
N47	A3	8c on 10c lt ultra	11.50	20.00
		Nos. N34-N47 (14)	409.00	515.50

Stamps of Trengganu,
1921-38, Overprinted in
Black

1943

N48	A3	1c black	13.50	19.00
N49	A3	2c deep green	13.50	27.50
N50	A3	5c violet, yel	11.50	27.50
N51	A3	6c orange	15.00	27.50
N52	A3	8c gray	95.00	67.50
N53	A3	10c ultramarine	100.00	175.00
N54	A3	12c ultramarine	19.00	35.00
N55	A3	20c org & dl vio	20.00	35.00
N56	A3	25c dl vio & grn	19.00	35.00
N57	A3	30c blk & dl vio	20.00	35.00
N58	A3	35c red, yellow	20.00	40.00

**Overprinted on Nos. 45 and 46 in
Black**

N59	A3	2c on 5c mag, yel	11.00	35.00
N60	A3	8c on 10c lt ultra	27.50	25.00
		Nos. N48-N60 (13)	385.00	584.00

The Japanese characters read: "Japanese Postal Service."

**OCCUPATION POSTAGE DUE
STAMPS**

Trengganu Nos. J1-J4
Handstamped in
Black or Brown

1942 Wmk. 4 Perf. 14

NJ1	D1	1c rose red	67.50	95.00
NJ2	D1	4c green	125.00	125.00
NJ3	D1	8c lemon	25.00	67.50
NJ4	D1	10c light brown	25.00	50.00
		Nos. NJ1-NJ4 (4)	242.50	337.50

The handstamp reads: "Seal of Post Office of Malayan Military Department."

MALDIVE ISLANDS

ˈmol-ˌdīv ˈī-lənds

LOCATION — A group of 2,000 islands in the Indian Ocean about 400 miles southwest of Ceylon.
GOVT. — Republic
AREA — 115 sq. mi.
POP. — 168,000 (est. 1983)
CAPITAL — Male

Maldive Islands was a British Protectorate as a dependency of Ceylon.

100 Cents = 1 Rupee

> Catalogue values for unused stamps in this country are for Never Hinged items, beginning with Scott 20.

Watermarks

Wmk. 47 —
Multiple Rosette

Wmk. 233 — "Harrison & Sons,
London" in Script

Stamps of Ceylon,
1904-05, Overprinted

1906, Sept. 9 Wmk. 3 Perf. 14

1	A36	2c orange brown	22.00	50.00
2	A37	3c green	30.00	50.00
3	A37	4c yellow & blue	50.00	90.00
4	A38	5c dull lilac	5.00	6.50
5	A40	15c ultramarine	100.00	180.00
6	A40	25c bister	110.00	190.00
		Nos. 1-6 (6)	317.00	566.50

Minaret of Juma
Mosque, near
Male — A1

1909 Engr. Wmk. 47

7	A1	2c orange brown	2.25	4.00
8	A1	3c green	.50	.70
9	A1	5c red violet	.50	.35
10	A1	10c carmine	7.50	.80
		Nos. 7-10 (4)	10.75	5.85

Type of 1909 Issue Redrawn
Perf. 14½x14
1933 Photo. Wmk. 233

11	A1	2c gray	2.75	2.50
12	A1	3c yellow brown	.75	1.75
13	A1	5c brown lake	40.00	10.00
14	A1	6c brown red	1.75	5.50
15	A1	10c green	1.00	1.75
16	A1	15c gray black	6.50	22.00
17	A1	25c brown	6.50	22.00
18	A1	50c red violet	6.50	22.00
19	A1	1r blue black	12.50	5.00
		Nos. 11-19 (9)	78.25	91.30

On the 6c, 15c, 25c and 50c, the right hand panel carries only the word "CENTS."
Nos. 11-19 exist with watermark vert. or horiz. The 5c with vert. watermark sells for twice the price of the horiz. watermark.

> Catalogue values for unused stamps in this section, from this point to the end of the section, are for Never Hinged items.

Palm Tree and
Seascape — A2

Unwmk.
1950, Dec. 24 Engr. Perf. 13

20	A2	2 l olive green	2.25	4.00
21	A2	3 l deep blue	12.50	.85
22	A2	5 l dp blue green	12.50	.85
23	A2	6 l red brown	1.25	1.25
24	A2	10 l red	1.25	1.00
25	A2	15 l orange	1.25	1.00
26	A2	25 l rose violet	1.25	2.75

27	A2	50 l violet blue	1.50	4.00
28	A2	1r dark brown	14.00	37.50
		Nos. 20-28 (9)	47.75	53.20

Maldive Fish — A3

1952

29	A3	3 l shown	2.00	.75
30	A3	5 l Urns	1.10	2.00

MALTA

'mol-tə

LOCATION — A group of islands in the Mediterranean Sea off the coast of Sicily

GOVT. — Republic within the British Commonwealth

AREA — 122 sq. mi.

POP. — 329,189 (1983)

CAPITAL — Valletta

The former colony includes the islands of Malta, Gozo, and Comino.

4 Farthings = 1 Penny
12 Pence = 1 Shilling
20 Shillings = 1 Pound

Catalogue values for unused stamps in this country are for Never Hinged items, beginning with Scott 206 in the regular postage section.

FORERUNNERS

Values are for clear cancellations on sound, fault-free stamps, with average to fine centering. In many cases, very fine copies are rare or non-existent.

STAMPS OF GREAT BRITAIN USED IN MALTA
Canceled with seven-line wavy obliterator

1855-56

A1	1p red brown, Die I (#8)	950.00
A2	1p red brown, Die II (#12)	925.00
A3	1p red brown, Die II (#14)	950.00
A4	1p red brown, Die II (#16)	925.00
A5	2p blue (#17)	—
A6	6p red violet (#7)	4,750.
A7	1sh green (#5)	5,250.

Canceled with oval barred "M" obliterator

1857-59

A8	1p red brown (#3)	2,500.
A9	1p red brown, Die I (#8)	175.00
A10	1p red brown, Die II (#9)	1,050.
A11	1p red brown, Die II (#12)	265.00
A12	1p red brown, Die II (#16)	87.50
A13	1p rose red (#20)	24.00
A14	2p blue (#4)	4,000.
A15	2p blue (#10)	875.00
A16	2p blue (#17)	70.00
A17	2p blue (#19)	350.00
A18	2p blue, Plate 7 (#29)	67.50
	Plate 8	57.50
	Plate 9	47.50
A19	4p rose (#26)	50.00
a.	Thick glazed paper (#26b)	240.00
A20	6p red violet (#7)	4,250.
A21	6p lilac (#27)	60.00
a.	Thick paper (#27d)	250.00
b.	Bluish paper (#27c)	1,000.
A22	1sh green (#28)	140.00
a.	Thick paper (#28d)	210.00

Canceled "A25" in barred oval

No. A77

1860-84

A23	½p rose red, plates 4-6, 8-15, 19 (#58), *value from*	32.50
A24	1p red brown (#3)	3,250.
A25	1p red brown, Die I (#8)	375.00
A26	1p red brown, Die I (#16)	87.50
A27	1p rose red (#20)	9.00
A28	1p rose red, (#33), plates 71-74, 76, 78-125, 127, 129-224 *value from*	19.00
A29	1 ½p lake red, plates 1, 3 (#32), *value from*	600.00
A30	2p blue (#4)	4,750.
A31	2p blue (#17)	82.50
A32	2p blue, plates 7, 8, 9, 12 (#29), *value from*	19.00
A33	2p blue, plates 13, 14, 15 (#30), *value from*	19.00
A34	2 ½p claret, plates 1, 2, 3 (#00), *value from*	37.50
a.	Bluish paper, plates 1, 2 (#66a), *value from*	82.50
b.	Lettered "LH-FL" (#66b)	3,500.
A35	2 ½p claret, plates 3-17 (#67), *value from*	19.00
A36	2 ½p blue plates 17-20 (#68), *value from*	22.50
A37	2 ½p blue plates 21-23 (#82), *value from*	12.50
A38	3p rose (#37)	140.00
A39	3p rose (#44)	87.50
A40	3p rose, plates 4-10 (#49), *value from*	30.00
A41	3p rose, plates 11-20 (#61), *value from*	37.50
A42	3p rose, plates 20, 21 (#83), *value from*	1,050.
A43	3p on 3d violet (#94)	550.00
A44	4p rose (#26)	45.00
a.	Thick glazed paper (#26b)	175.00
A45	4p vermilion, plate 3 (#34)	45.00
a.	Hair lines (#34c)	55.00
A46	4p vermilion, plates 7-14 (#43), *value from*	27.50
A47	4p vermilion, plate 15 (#69)	225.00
A48	4p pale olive green, plate 15 (#70)	175.00
	Plate 16 (#70)	175.00
A49	4p gray brown, plate 17 (#71)	240.00
A50	4p gray brown, plates 17, 18 (#84), *value from*	57.50
A51	6p red violet (#7)	3,750.
A52	6p lilac (#27)	55.00
a.	Thick paper (#27d)	—
A53	6p lilac, plate 3 (#39)	45.00
a.	Hairlines, plate 4 (#39d)	100.00
A54	6p lilac (#45)	45.00
	Plate 6 (#45)	100.00
a.	Wmk. 3 (#45c)	1,400.
	Plate 6 (#45c)	
A55	6p dull violet, plate 6 (#50)	50.00
A56	6p violet, plates 6, 8, 9 (#51)	40.00
A57	6p brown plate 11 (#59), *value from*	37.50
a.	6p pale buff, plate 11 (#59b)	120.00
	Plate 12 (#59b)	140.00
A58	6p gray, plate 12 (#60)	140.00
A59	6p gray, plates 13-17 (#62), *value from*	37.50
A60	6p gray, plates 17, 18 (#86), *value from*	80.00
A61	6p on 6p violet (#95)	150.00
A62	8p orange (#73)	475.00
A63	9p straw (#40)	700.00
a.	9p bister (#40a)	650.00
A64	9p straw (#46)	650.00
A65	9p bister (#52)	825.00

A66	10p red brown (#53)	190.00
A67	1sh green (#5)	4,000.
A68	1sh green (#28)	160.00
a.	Thick paper (#28d)	325.00
A69	1sh green (#42)	95.00
A70	1sh green (#10)	85.00
A71	1sh green, plates 4-7 (#54), *value from*	32.50
A72	1sh green, plates 8-13 (#64), *value from*	47.50
A73	1sh salmon, plate 13 (#65)	300.00
A74	1sh salmon, plates 13, 14 (#87), *value from*	90.00
A75	2sh blue (#55)	165.00
A76	2sh brown (#56)	3,250.
A77	5sh rose, plate 1 (#57)	475.00
	Plate 2 (#57)	575.00
A78	5sh rose, *bluish* (#90)	2,500.
a.	White paper (#90a)	1,900.
A79	10sh gray green (#74)	3,500.

1880

A80	½p deep green (#78)	16.00
a.	½p green (#78c)	16.00
A81	1p red brown (#79)	15.00
A82	1 ½p red brown (#80)	500.00
A83	2p lilac rose (#81)	45.00
a.	2p deep lilac rose (#81a)	45.00
A84	5p indigo (#85)	77.50

1881

A85	1p lilac, 14 dots (#88)	35.00
A86	1p lilac, 16 dots (#89)	10.00

1883-84

A87	½p slate blue (#98)	19.00
A88	1 ½p lilac (#99)	
A89	2p lilac (#100)	110.00
A90	2 ½p lilac (#101)	14.00
A91	3p lilac (#102)	
A92	4p dull green (#103)	190.00
A93	5p dull green (#104)	165.00
A94	6p dull green (#105)	—
A95	9p dull green (#106)	—
A96	1sh dull green (#107)	400.00
A97	5sh rose, white paper (#108)	1,150.
a.	Bluish paper (#108a)	2,000.

Postal Fiscal stamps of Great Britain are found used in Malta. They are rare.

STAMPS OF FRANCE USED IN MALTA

1853-60

A98	5c green (#13)	—
	On cover	—
A99	10c bister (#14)	125.00
	On cover	1,400.
A100	20c blue (#15)	115.00
	On cover	1,300.
A101	40c orange (#18)	92.50
	On cover	1,050.
A102	80c lake, *yellowish* (#19)	145.00
	On cover	1,650.
A103	80c rose, *pinkish* (#20)	145.00
	On cover	1,650.

1862-67

A104	5c green (#23)	57.50
	On cover	1,250.
A105	10c bister (#25)	37.50
	On cover	975.00
A106	20c blue (#26)	92.50
	On cover	1,175.
A107	40c orange (#27)	100.00
	On cover	1,300.
A108	80c rose, *pinkish* (#28)	150.00
	On cover	1,550.
a.	80c carmine rose (#28b)	175.00
	On cover	1,600.

1863-70

A109	10c bister (#32)	80.00
	On cover	1,500.
A110	20c blue (#33)	57.50
	On cover	1,350.
A111	30c brown, *yellowish* (#34)	80.00
	On cover	1,650.
A112	40c orange, *yellowish* (#35)	100.00
	On cover	1,500.
A113	80c rose, *pinkish* (#36)	150.00

Stamps of Italy, and occasionally those of other Mediterranean countries, are found obliterated by the A25 cancellations, usually originating in ship mail.

Issued under British Administration

Values for unused stamps are for examples with original gum as defined in the catalogue introduction. Very fine examples of Nos. 1-7 will have perforations touching the frameline on one or more sides due to the narrow spacing of the stamps on the plate. Stamps with perfs clear of the frameline are scarce and will command higher prices.

Queen Victoria
A1   A2

A3   A4

1860-61   **Unwmk.**   **Typo.**   *Perf. 14*

1	A1 ½p buff ('63)	850.00	400.00
	On cover		1,650.
a.	½p pale buff ('63)	850.00	400.00
	On cover		1,650.
b.	½p brown orange ('61)	1,300.	475.00
	On cover		1,750.
2	A1 ½p buff, *bluish*	1,300.	650.00
	On cover		2,400.
a.	Imperf. (single)	12,000.	

1863-80   **Wmk. 1**

3	A1 ½p yellow buff ('75)	85.00	65.00
a.	½p buff	120.00	75.00
b.	½p brown orange ('67)	425.00	110.00
c.	½p orange yellow ('80)	250.00	110.00
d.	½p bright orange ('64)	800.00	200.00
e.	½p dull orange ('70)	300.00	90.00
f.	½p orange buff ('72)	180.00	80.00
g.	½p pale buff ('77)	190.00	75.00
h.	½p yellow ('81)	130.00	75.00
4	A1 ½p golden yel (aniline) ('74)	350.00	400.00

1865   *Perf. 12½*

5	A1 ½p buff	160.00	110.00
a.	½p yellow buff	375.00	190.00

1878   *Perf. 14x12½*

6	A1 ½p buff	200.00	100.00
a.	Perf. 12 ½x14	—	
b.	½p yellow ('79)	225.00	110.00

No. 6a unused is believed to be unique. It has a small fault.

1882   **Wmk. 2**   *Perf. 14*

7	A1 ½p reddish orange ('84)	21.00	57.50
a.	½p orange	42.50	40.00

1885, Jan. 1

8	A1 ½p green	4.50	.60
9	A2 1p car rose	11.00	.40
a.	1p rose	100.00	30.00
10	A3 2p gray	8.50	2.25
11	A4 2 ½p ultramarine	50.00	1.25
a.	2 ½p bright ultramarine	50.00	1.25
b.	2 ½p dull blue	65.00	3.00
12	A3 4p brown	13.00	5.50
a.	Imperf., pair	6,000.	6,000.
13	A3 1sh violet	60.00	22.50
a.	1sh pale dull violet ('90)	70.00	22.50
	Nos. 8-13 (6)	147.00	30.50
	Set of 6, overprinted "SPECIMEN"	4,250.	

Do not confuse faded examples of No. 13 for No. 13a.

For surcharge see No. 20.

Queen Victoria within Maltese Cross — A5

1886   **Wmk. 1**

14	A5 5sh rose	125.00	95.00
	Overprinted "SPECIMEN"	700.00	

Gozo Fishing Boat — A6

Ancient Galley — A7

1899, Feb. 4   Engr.   Wmk. 2

15	A6	4½p	black brown	24.00 16.00
16	A7	5p	brown red	47.50 19.00

See Nos. 42-45.

"Malta" — A8
St. Paul after Shipwreck — A9

1899   Wmk. 1

17	A8	2sh6p	olive gray	47.50 15.00
18	A9	10sh	blue black	105.00 75.00

See No. 64. For overprint see No. 85.

Valletta Harbor — A10

1901, Jan. 1   Wmk. 2

19	A10	1f	red brown	1.75 .55
a.			1f brown	8.00 3.00

See Nos. 28-29.

No. 11 Surcharged in Black

1902, July 4

20	A4	1p on 2½p dull blue		1.50 2.00
a.		"Pnney"		32.50 65.00
b.		Double surcharge		17,500. 4,500.
d.		1p on 2½p bright ultra		1.10 2.00
e.		As "d," "Pnney"		35.00 65.00
		Overprinted "SPECIMEN"		82.50

King Edward VII — A12

1903-04   Typo.

21	A12	½p	dark green	10.00 1.00
22	A12	1p	car & black	17.50 .50
23	A12	2p	gray & red vio	32.50 7.00
24	A12	2½p	ultra & brn vio	32.50 5.25
25	A12	3p	red vio & gray	2.00 .60
26	A12	4p	brown & blk ('04)	30.00 19.00
27	A12	1sh	violet & gray	27.50 8.25
		Nos. 21-27 (7)		152.00 41.60
		Set of 7 ovptd "SPECIMEN"		175.00

1904-11   Wmk. 3

28	A10	1f	red brown ('05)	9.00 2.25
29	A10	1f	dk brown ('10)	7.00 .25
30	A12	½p	green	6.00 .35
31	A12	1p	car & blk ('05)	22.50 .25
32	A12	1p	carmine ('07)	3.50 .25
33	A12	2p	gray & red vio ('05)	13.00 3.00
34	A12	2p	gray ('11)	4.75 6.50
35	A12	2½p	ultra & brn vio ('11)	32.50 .70
36	A12	2½p	ultra ('11)	6.50 4.25
37	A12	4p	brn & blk ('06)	13.00 7.50
38	A12	4p	scar & blk, yel ('11)	4.75 4.50
39	A12	1sh	violet & gray	57.50 2.40
40	A12	1sh	blk, grn ('11)	8.75 4.25

41	A12	5sh	scar & grn, yel ('11)	75.00 87.50

Engr.

42	A6	4½p	black brn ('05)	40.00 7.00
43	A6	4½p	orange ('11)	5.25 4.00
44	A7	5p	red ('04)	37.50 7.00
45	A7	5p	ol green ('10)	5.00 4.00
a.		5p deep sage green ('14)		13.00 16.00
		Nos. 28-45 (18)		351.50 145.95

A13   A15

King George V — A16

1914-21   Ordinary Paper   Typo.

49	A13	¼p	brown	1.25 .25
50	A13	½p	green	2.50 .35
51	A13	1p	scarlet ('15)	1.75 .45
a.		1p carmine ('14)		1.75 .25
52	A13	2p	gray ('15)	12.00 6.00
53	A13	2½p	ultramarine	2.50 .60

Chalky Paper

54	A15	3p	vio, yel	3.00 17.50
a.		3p violet, orange yellow		70.00 50.00
58	A13	6p	dull vio & red vio	13.00 21.00
59	A15	1sh	black, green	14.00 22.00
a.		1sh black, bl grn, ol back		22.50 27.50
b.		1sh black, emerald ('21)		37.50 85.00
c.		As "b," olive back		10.00 32.50
60	A16	2sh	ultra & dl vio, bl	57.50 37.50
61	A16	5sh	scar & grn, yel	105.00 115.00

Surface-colored Paper

62	A15	1sh	blk, grn ('15)	16.00 37.50
		Nos. 49-54,58-62 (11)		228.50 258.15

See Nos. 66-68, 70-72. For overprints see Nos. 77-82, 84.

Valletta Harbor — A17

1915   Ordinary Paper   Engr.

63	A17	4p	black	17.50 7.00

St. Paul A18
George V A19

1919

64	A8	2sh6p	olive green	75.00 95.00
65	A18	10sh	black	3,500. 4,400.
		Revenue cancel		85.00
		Overprinted "SPECIMEN"		950.00

For overprint see No. 83.

1921-22   Typo.   Wmk. 4

Ordinary Paper

66	A13	¼p	brown	6.00 35.00
67	A13	½p	green	6.00 32.50
68	A13	1p	rose red	6.00 2.50
69	A19	2p	gray	8.00 2.00
70	A13	2½p	ultramarine	7.00 40.00

Chalky Paper

71	A13	6p	dull vio & red vio	35.00 85.00
72	A16	2sh	ultra & dull vio, bl	70.00 225.00

Engr.
Ordinary Paper

73	A18	10sh	black	400.00 800.00
		Nos. 66-73 (8)		538.00 1,222.

For overprints and surcharge see Nos. 86-93, 97.

Stamps of 1914-19 Overprinted in Red or Black

1922   Ordinary Paper   Wmk. 3

Overprint 21mm

77	A13	½p	green	1.25 3.00
78	A13	2½p	ultra	15.00 45.00

Chalky Paper

79	A15	3p	violet, yel	4.50 27.50
80	A13	6p	dull lil & red vio	4.50 24.00
81	A15	1sh	black, emer	4.75 24.00

Overprint 28mm

82	A16	2sh	ultra & dull vio, bl (R)	250.00 525.00

Ordinary Paper

83	A8	2sh6p	olive grn	32.50 55.00

Chalky Paper

84	A16	5sh	scar & grn, yel	57.50 100.00
		Nos. 77-84 (8)		370.00 803.50

Wmk. 1

85	A9	10sh	blue black (R)	225.00 400.00

Same Overprint on Stamps of 1921

1922   Ordinary Paper   Wmk. 4

Overprint 21mm

86	A13	¼p	brown	.35 .75
87	A13	½p	green	4.00 9.50
88	A13	1p	rose red	1.10 .25
89	A19	2p	gray	4.25 .50
90	A13	2½p	ultramarine	1.25 1.75

Chalky Paper

91	A13	6p	dull vio & red vio	21.00 50.00

Overprint 28mm

92	A16	2sh	ultra & dull vio, bl (R)	50.00 100.00

Ordinary Paper

93	A18	10sh	black (R)	160.00 250.00
		Nos. 86-93 (8)		241.95 412.75

No. 69 Surcharged

1922, Apr. 15

97	A19	1f on 2p gray		.85 .50

"Malta" — A20
Britannia and Malta — A21

1922-26   Chalky Paper   Typo.

98	A20	¼p	brown	3.00 .70
99	A20	½p	green	3.00 .25
100	A20	1p	buff & plum	4.50 .25
101	A20	1p	violet ('24)	4.25 .90
102	A20	1½p	org brn ('23)	5.50 .25
103	A20	2p	ol brn & turq	3.25 1.40
104	A20	2½p	ultra ('26)	4.50 13.00
105	A20	3p	ultramarine	5.00 2.00
a.		3p blue		6.00 2.50
106	A20	3p	blk, yel ('26)	4.25 20.00
107	A20	4p	yel & ultra	3.00 4.25
108	A20	6p	ol grn & vio	4.50 3.75
109	A20	1sh	ol brn & blue	10.00 3.50
110	A21	2sh	ultra & ol brn	14.00 18.00
111	A21	2sh6p	blk & red vio	12.50 16.00
112	A21	5sh	ultra & org	24.00 47.50
113	A21	10sh	ol brn & gray	65.00 175.00

Engr.
Ordinary Paper

114	A20	£1	car red & blk ('25)	125.00 500.00
a.		£1 rose car & blk ('22)		150.00 350.00
		Nos. 98-114 (17)		295.25 806.75

No. 114a has watermark sideways.
For overprints and surcharges see Nos. 115-129.

No. 105 Surcharged

1925, Dec.

115	A20	2½p on 3p ultramarine		2.00 4.50

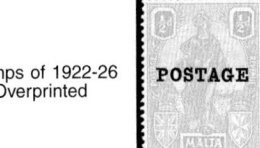
Stamps of 1922-26 Overprinted

1926

116	A20	¼p	brown	.80 5.50
117	A20	½p	green	.80 .25
118	A20	1p	violet	1.10 .25
119	A20	1½p	orange brown	1.25 .70
120	A20	2p	ol brn & turq	.85 2.00
121	A20	2½p	ultramarine	1.40 1.00
122	A20	3p	black, yel	.85 .90
a.		Inverted overprint		200.00 550.00
123	A20	4p	yel & ultra	17.00 28.00
124	A20	6p	ol grn & vio	3.25 5.50
125	A21	1sh	ol brn & blk	6.25 18.00
126	A21	2sh	ultra & ol brown	60.00 160.00
127	A21	2sh6p	blk & red vio	18.50 47.50
128	A21	5sh	ultra & org	11.00 47.50
129	A21	10sh	ol brn & gray	8.50 21.00
		Nos. 116-129 (14)		131.55 338.10

George V — A22
Valletta Harbor — A23

St. Publius — A24
Notabile (Mdina) — A25

Gozo Fishing Boat — A26
Statue of Neptune — A27

Ruins at Mnaidra — A28
St. Paul — A29

1926-27   Typo.   Perf. 14½x14

131	A22	¼p brown	.90	.25
132	A22	½p green	.70	.25
133	A22	1p red	3.50	1.10
134	A22	1½p orange brn	2.25	.25
135	A22	2p gray	5.25	15.00
136	A22	2½p blue	4.50	1.50
137	A22	3p dark violet	5.00	4.00
138	A22	4p org red & blk	3.75	16.00
139	A22	4½p yel buff & vio	4.00	4.50
140	A22	6p red & violet	5.00	6.00

Engr.   Perf. 12½
Inscribed: "Postage"

141	A23	1sh black	7.50	8.50
142	A24	1sh6p green & blk	7.50	18.00
143	A25	2sh dp vio & blk	7.50	23.00
144	A26	2sh6p ver & black	19.00	55.00
145	A27	3sh blue & blk	20.00	35.00
146	A28	5sh green & blk	25.00	70.00
147	A29	10sh car & blk	65.00	110.00
		Nos. 131-147 (17)	186.35	368.35

See Nos. 167-183. For overprints see Nos. 148-166.

Stamps and Type of 1926-27 Overprinted in Black

1928   Perf. 14½x14

148	A22	¼p brown	1.75	.25
149	A22	½p green	1.75	.25
150	A22	1p red	2.00	3.75
151	A22	1p orange brown	5.25	.25
152	A22	1½p yel brown	2.25	1.00
153	A22	1½p red	5.00	.25
154	A22	2p gray	5.00	10.50
155	A22	2½p blue	2.25	.25
156	A22	3p dark violet	2.25	1.00
157	A22	4p org red & blk	2.25	2.00
158	A22	4½p yel & violet	2.50	1.10
159	A22	6p red & violet	2.50	1.75

Overprinted in Red

Perf. 12½

160	A23	1sh black	6.25	3.00
161	A24	1sh6p green & blk	11.00	11.00
162	A25	2sh dp vio & blk	27.50	70.00
163	A26	2sh6p ver & black	20.00	26.00
164	A27	3sh ultra & blk	22.50	35.00
165	A28	5sh yel grn & blk	37.50	75.00
166	A29	10sh car rose & black	70.00	100.00
		Nos. 148-166 (19)	229.50	342.35

Issued: Nos. 151, 153, Dec. 5; others, Oct. 1.

Types of 1926-27 Issue
Inscribed: "Postage & Revenue"
1930, Oct. 20   Typo.   Perf. 14½x14

167	A22	¼p brown	.70	.25
168	A22	½p green	.70	.25
169	A22	1p yel brown	.70	.25
170	A22	1½p red	.80	.25
171	A22	2p gray	1.40	.60
172	A22	2½p blue	2.25	.25
173	A22	3p dark violet	1.75	.25
174	A22	4p org red & blk	1.40	5.00
175	A22	4½p yel & violet	3.75	1.40
176	A22	6p red & violet	3.25	1.40

Engr.   Perf. 12½

177	A23	1sh black	11.00	19.00
178	A24	1sh6p green & blk	9.75	25.00
179	A25	2sh dp vio & blk	12.00	27.00
180	A26	2sh6p ver & black	20.00	60.00
181	A27	3sh ultra & blk	40.00	62.50
182	A28	5sh yel grn & blk	47.50	75.00
183	A29	10sh car rose & blk	100.00	180.00
		Nos. 167-183 (17)	256.95	458.40

Common Design Types pictured following the introduction.

Silver Jubilee Issue
Common Design Type
1935, May 6   Perf. 11x12

184	CD301	½p green & blk	.50	.70
185	CD301	2½p ultra & brn	2.50	4.50
186	CD301	6p ol grn & lt bl	7.00	7.00
187	CD301	1sh brn vio & ind	15.00	22.50
		Nos. 184-187 (4)	25.00	34.70
		Set, never hinged	45.00	

Coronation Issue
Common Design Type
1937, May 12   Wmk. 4   Perf. 13½x14

188	CD302	½p deep green	.25	.25
189	CD302	1½p carmine	.55	.60
190	CD302	2½p bright ultra	.55	.80
		Nos. 188-190 (3)	1.35	1.65
		Set, never hinged	2.25	

Valletta Harbor — A30

Fort St. Angelo — A31

Verdala Palace — A32

Neolithic Ruins — A33

Victoria and Citadel, Gozo — A34

De l'Isle Adam Entering Mdina — A35

St. John's Co-Cathedral A36

Mnaidra Temple — A37

Statue of Antonio Manoel de Vilhena — A38

Woman in Faldetta — A39

St. Publius — A40

Mdina Cathedral A41

Statue of Neptune — A42

Palace Square — A43

St. Paul — A44

1938-43   Wmk. 4   Perf. 12½

191	A30	1f brown	.25	.25
192	A31	½p green	1.75	.30
192A	A31	½p chnt ('43)	.55	.30
193	A32	1p chestnut	3.50	.40
193A	A32	1p grn ('43)	.30	.25
194	A33	1½p rose red	1.00	2.00
194A	A33	1½p dk gray ('43)	.25	.25
195	A34	2p dark gray	1.10	.30
195A	A34	2p rose red ('43)	.40	.25
196	A35	2½p blue	2.00	.60
196A	A35	2½p violet ('43)	.35	.35
197	A36	3p violet	1.25	.80
197A	A36	3p blue ('43)	.40	.25
198	A37	4½p ocher & ol green	.30	.30
199	A38	6p rose red & ol green	1.10	.30
200	A39	1sh black	.90	.55
201	A40	1sh6p sage grn & black	5.00	4.00
202	A41	2sh dk bl & lt grn	2.50	6.00
203	A42	2sh6p rose red & black	5.00	5.50
204	A43	5sh bl grn & blk	4.75	8.00
205	A44	10sh dp rose & blk	15.00	16.00
		Nos. 191-205 (21)	47.65	46.95
		Set, never hinged	75.00	

See No. 236a. For overprints see Nos. 208-222.

> **Catalogue values for unused stamps in this section, from this point to the end of the section, are for Never Hinged items.**

Peace Issue
Common Design Type
Inscribed: "Malta" and Crosses
Perf. 10½x14
1946, Dec. 3   Engr.   Wmk. 4

206	CD303	1p bright green	.25	.25
207	CD303	3p dark ultra	.40	1.75

Stamps of 1938-43 Overprinted in Black or Carmine

a

1948, Nov. 25   Perf. 12½

208	A30	1f brown	.35	.25
209	A31	½p chestnut	.35	.25
210	A32	1p green	.35	.25
211	A33	1½p dk gray (C)	1.40	.25
212	A34	2p rose red	1.40	.30
213	A35	2½p violet (C)	.90	.30
214	A36	3p blue (C)	3.00	.25
215	A37	4½p ocher & ol grn	2.75	1.75
216	A38	6p rose red & ol green	3.50	.45
217	A39	1sh black	3.75	.70
218	A40	1sh6p sage grn & blk	2.75	1.25
219	A41	2sh dk bl & lt grn (C)	5.75	2.75
220	A42	2sh6p rose red & blk	14.00	2.75
221	A43	5sh bl grn & blk (C)	26.00	5.00
222	A44	10sh dp rose & blk	26.00	25.00
		Nos. 208-222 (15)	92.25	41.50

The overprint is smaller on No. 208. It reads from lower left to upper right on Nos. 209 and 221.

See Nos. 235-240.

Silver Wedding Issue
Common Design Types
Inscribed: "Malta" and Crosses
1949, Jan. 4   Photo.   Perf. 14x14½

223	CD304	1p dark green	.55	.25

Perf. 11½x11
Engr.

224	CD305	£1 dark blue	40.00	45.00

UPU Issue
Common Design Types
Inscribed: "Malta" and Crosses
Perf. 13½, 11x11½
1949, Oct. 10   Engr.   Wmk. 4

225	CD306	2½p violet	.30	.25
226	CD307	3p indigo	3.00	1.25
227	CD308	6p dp carmine	.60	1.10
228	CD309	1sh slate	.60	2.75
		Nos. 225-228 (4)	4.50	5.35

Princess Elizabeth — A45

Madonna and Child — A46

1950, Dec. 1   Engr.   Perf. 12x11½

229	A45	1p emerald	.25	.25
230	A45	3p bright blue	.25	.25
231	A45	1sh gray black	1.10	2.00
		Nos. 229-231 (3)	1.60	2.50

Visit of Princess Elizabeth.

1951, July 12

232	A46	1p green	.25	.25
233	A46	3p purple	.55	.25
234	A46	1sh slate black	1.60	1.40
		Nos. 232-234 (3)	2.40	1.90

700th anniv. of the presentation of the scapular to St. Simon Stock.

AIR POST STAMPS

No. 140 Overprinted

Perf. 14½x14

1928, Apr. 1		**Typo.**		**Wmk. 4**
C1	A22	6p red & violet	2.00	1.00

POSTAGE DUE STAMPS

D1

1925		**Typeset**	**Unwmk.**	**Imperf.**
J1	D1	½p black, *white*	1.40	8.00
J2	D1	1p black, *white*	3.75	11.00
J3	D1	1½p black, *white*	3.50	4.25
J4	D1	2p black, *white*	12.00	21.00
J5	D1	2½p black, *white*	3.25	3.25
a.		"2" of "½" omitted	1,000.	1,400.
J6	D1	3p black, *gray*	10.50	17.00
J7	D1	4p black, *orange*	5.75	11.00
J8	D1	6p black, *orange*	5.75	22.50
J9	D1	1sh black, *orange*	8.50	25.00
J10	D1	1sh6p black, *orange*	16.00	62.50
		Nos. J1-J10 (10)	70.40	178.00
		Set, never hinged	130.00	

These stamps were typeset in groups of 42. In each sheet there were four impressions of a group, two of them being inverted and making tete beche pairs.

Forged examples of No. J5a are known.

Maltese Cross — D2

Wmk. 4 Sideways

1925		**Typo.**		**Perf. 12**
J11	D2	½p blue green	1.40	.70
J12	D2	1p violet	1.40	.50
J13	D2	1½p yellow brown	1.75	1.00
J14	D2	2p gray	12.50	1.25
J15	D2	2½p orange	2.25	1.40
J16	D2	3p dark blue	4.25	1.40
J17	D2	4p olive green	14.00	18.00
J18	D2	6p claret	3.50	4.75
J19	D2	1sh gray black	7.50	14.00
J20	D2	1sh6p deep rose	9.75	42.50
		Nos. J11-J20 (10)	58.30	85.50
		Set, never hinged	85.00	

In 1953-57 six values (½p-2p, 3p, 4p) were reissued on chalky paper in slightly different colors.

WAR TAX STAMPS

Nos. 50, 25 Overprinted

1918		**Wmk. 3**		**Perf. 14**
MR1	A13	½p green	2.00	.30
		Wmk. 2		
MR2	A12	3p red violet & gray	3.00	12.00

MANCHUKUO

ˈman-ˈchü-ˈkwō

LOCATION — Covering Manchuria, or China's three northeastern provinces

— Fengtien, Kirin and Heilungkiang — plus Jehol province.
GOVT. — Independent state under Japanese influence
AREA — 503,013 sq. mi. (estimated)
POP. — 43,233,954 (est. 1940)
CAPITAL — Hsinking (Changchun)

Manchukuo was formed in 1932 with the assistance of Japan. In 1934 Henry Pu-yi, Chief Executive, was enthroned as Emperor Kang Teh.

100 Fen = 1 Yuan

Watermarks

Wmk. 141 —
Horizontal Zigzag
Lines

Wmk. 239 —
Curved Wavy
Lines

Wmk. 242 —
Characters

Pagoda at
Liaoyang
A1

Chief
Executive
Henry Pu-yi
A2

Five characters in top label.
Inscription reads "Manchu State Postal Administration."

Lithographed
Perf. 13x13½

1932, July 26			**Unwmk.**
		White Paper	
1	A1	½f gray brown	1.75	.75
2	A1	1f dull red	2.00	.75
3	A1	1½f lilac	6.50	4.00
4	A1	2f slate	6.50	1.00
5	A1	3f dull brown	8.25	5.00
6	A1	4f olive green	3.00	.50
7	A1	5f green	4.00	.90
8	A1	6f rose	11.00	3.50
9	A1	7f gray	4.75	2.50
10	A1	8f ocher	18.00	11.00
11	A1	10f orange	6.75	1.10
12	A2	13f dull brown	15.00	7.00
13	A2	15f rose	18.00	4.00
14	A2	16f turquoise grn	27.50	9.00
15	A2	20f gray brown	11.00	1.90
16	A2	30f orange	12.00	2.50
17	A2	50f olive green	27.50	3.25
18	A2	1y violet	42.50	12.00
		Nos. 1-18 (18)	226.00	69.65
		Set, never hinged	300.00	

A local provisional overprint of a horizontal line of four characters in red or black, reading "Chinese Postal Administration," was applied to Nos. 1-18 by followers of Gen. Su Ping-wen, who rebelled against the Manchukuo government in September, 1932. Many counterfeits exist.

See Nos. 23-31. For surcharges see Nos. 36, 59-61.
See note on local handstamps at end of the Manchukuo listings.

Flags, Map and
Wreath — A3

Old State Council
Building — A4

1933, Mar. 1			**Perf. 12½**	
19	A3	1f orange	6.50	4.00
20	A4	2f dull green	17.50	12.00
21	A3	4f light red	6.50	4.50
22	A4	10f deep blue	37.50	30.00
		Nos. 19-22 (4)	68.00	50.50
		Set, never hinged	100.00	

1st anniv. of the establishing of the State. Nos. 19-22 were printed in sheets of 100 with a special printing in sheets of 20.

Type of 1932
Perf. 13x13½

1934, Feb.		**Engr.**	**Wmk. 239**	
		Granite Paper		
23	A1	½f dark brown	4.00	1.65
24	A1	1f red brown	4.00	2.00
25	A1	1½f dark violet	6.00	3.00
26	A1	2f slate	7.50	2.00
27	A1	3f brown	4.00	.60
28	A1	4f olive brown	32.50	5.00
29	A1	10f deep orange	14.50	2.50
30	A2	15f rose	525.00	225.00
31	A2	1y violet	55.00	14.00
		Nos. 23-31 (9)	652.50	255.75

For surcharge see No. 60.

Emperor's
Palace — A5

Phoenix — A6

1934, Mar. 1			**Perf. 12½**	
32	A5	1½f orange brown	6.00	5.00
33	A6	3f carmine	5.00	4.00
34	A6	6f green	14.50	10.00
35	A6	10f dark blue	26.00	17.50
		Nos. 32-35 (4)	51.50	36.50
		Set, never hinged	75.00	

Enthronement of Emperor Kang Teh. Nos. 32-35 were printed in sheets of 100, with a special printing in sheets of 20.

No. 6 Surcharged in
Black

1934		**Unwmk.**	**White Paper**	
36	A1	1f on 4f olive grn	6.00	4.00
		Never hinged	11.00	
a.		Brown surcharge	45.00	45.00
b.		Upper left character of surcharge omitted		
c.		Inverted surcharge	175.00	175.00

Pagoda at
Liaoyang
A7

Emperor Kang
Teh
A8

Six characters in top label instead of five as in 1932-34 issues.
Inscription reads "Manchu Empire Postal Administration."

Perf. 13x13½

1934-36		**Wmk. 239**	**Engr.**	
		Granite Paper		
37	A7	½f brown	.50	.35
38	A7	1f red brown	1.00	.30
39	A7	1½t dk violet	1.00	.50
41	A7	3f brown ('35)	.75	.35
a.		Booklet pane of 6	80.00	
42	A7	5f dk blue ('35)	10.00	2.00
43	A7	5f gray ('36)	5.00	2.00
44	A7	6f rose ('35)	3.00	2.00
45	A7	7f dk gray ('36)	2.50	2.00
47	A7	9f red orange ('35)	2.50	.75
50	A8	15f ver ('35)	2.50	.85
51	A8	18f Prus grn ('35)	25.00	5.00
52	A8	20f dk brown ('35)	4.00	.90
53	A8	30f orange brn ('35)	4.50	.90
54	A8	50f ol grn ('35)	6.00	2.00
55	A8	1y dk violet ('35)	24.00	6.00
a.		1y violet	26.00	8.00
		Nos. 37-55 (15)	92.25	24.50
		Set, never hinged	125.00	

Booklet pane of 6 — 90.00 (for No. 39a)

4f and 8f, type A7, were prepared but not issued. Values $45 and $15, respectively.

1935		**Wmk. 242**	**Perf. 13x13½**	
57	A7	10f deep blue	13.00	2.00
58	A8	13f light brown	16.00	8.00
		Set, never hinged	42.00	

Nos. 6 and 28
Surcharged in Black

1935		**White Paper**	**Unwmk.**	
59	A1	3f on 4f ol grn	70.00	60.00
		Never hinged	100.00	

1935		**Granite Paper**	**Wmk. 239**	
60	A1	3f on 4f olive brn	9.00	5.50
		Never hinged	16.00	

Similar Surcharge on No. 14

1935		**White Paper**	**Unwmk.**	
61	A2	3f on 16f turq grn	15.00	10.00
		Never hinged	22.50	
		Nos. 59-61 (3)	94.00	75.50

Orchid Crest
of Manchukuo
A9

Sacred White
Mountains
and Black
Waters
A10

1935, Jan. 1		**Litho.**	**Wmk. 141**	
		Granite Paper		
62	A9	2f green	5.50	2.00
63	A10	4f dull ol grn	2.75	1.75
64	A9	8f ocher	4.50	3.25
65	A10	12f brown red	14.00	17.50
		Nos. 62-65 (4)	26.75	24.50
		Set, never hinged	44.00	

Nos. 62-65 exist imperforate.

1935			**Wmk. 242**	
66	A9	2f yellow green	3.50	1.00
68	A9	8f ocher	6.00	4.00
70	A10	12f brown red	12.50	10.00
		Nos. 66-70 (3)	22.00	15.00
		Set, never hinged	30.00	

Nos. 62-70 issued primarily to pay postage to China, but valid for any postal use.
See Nos. 75-78, 113, 115, 158 (in Scott Standard catalogue, Vol. 4). For surcharges see Nos. 101, 103-104, 106-109, People's Republic of China No. 2L19 (in Scott Standard catalogue, Vol. 2).

Mt. Fuji — A11

Phoenix — A12

Perf. 11, 12½ and Compound

1935, Apr. 1	Engr.	Wmk. 242	
71	A11	1½f dull green	2.50	2.00
72	A12	3f orange	3.50	3.25
a.		3f red orange	6.00	5.00
73	A11	6f dk carmine	5.50	4.75
a.		Horiz. pair, imperf. btwn.	250.00	
b.		Perf. 11x12½	45.00	37.50
74	A12	10f dark blue	7.50	6.00
a.		Perf. 12½x11	50.00	37.50
b.		Perf. 12½	22.50	25.00
	Nos. 71-74 (4)	19.00	16.00
	Set, never hinged	27.50	

Visit of the Emperor of Manchukuo to Tokyo.

Orchid Crest — A13

Types of A9 & A10 Redrawn and Engraved

1936	Wmk. 242	Perf. 13x13½	
75	A13	1½f lt green	1.00	.30
76	A10	4f olive green	3.25	.75
77	A13	8f ocher	3.00	1.25
78	A10	12f orange brn	42.50	32.50
	Nos. 75-78 (4)	49.75	34.80
	Set, never hinged	67.50	

Unbroken lines of shading in the background of Nos. 76 and 78. Shading has been removed from right and left of the mountains. Nearly all lines have been removed from the lake. There are numerous other alterations in the design.

Issued primarily to pay postage to China, but valid for any postal use.

See No. 112. For surcharges see Nos. 102-106.

Wild Goose over Sea of Japan — A14

Communications Building at Hsinking — A15

Perf. 12x12½, 12½x12

1936, Jan. 26		Wmk. 242	
79	A14	1½f black brown	4.00	2.50
80	A15	3f rose lilac	4.00	2.00
81	A14	6f carmine rose	8.00	7.00
82	A15	10f blue	10.00	8.50
	Nos. 79-82 (4)	26.00	20.00
	Set, never hinged	42.50	

Postal convention with Japan.

New State Council Building A16

Carting Soybeans A17

North Mausoleum at Mukden A18

Summer Palace at Chengteh A19

1936-37	Wmk. 242	Perf. 13x13½	
83	A16	½f brown	.40	.25
84	A16	1f red brown	.40	.25
85	A16	1½f violet	4.25	2.75
a.		Booklet pane of 6	85.00	
86	A17	2f lt green ('37)	.40	.25
a.		Booklet pane of 6	20.00	
87	A16	3f chocolate	.40	.25
a.		Booklet pane of 6	200.00	
88	A18	4f lt ol grn ('37)	.45	.25
a.		Booklet pane of 6	25.00	
89	A16	5f gray black	25.00	7.50
90	A17	6f carmine	.45	.25
91	A18	7f brown blk	.75	.30
92	A18	9f red orange	.80	.25
93	A19	10f blue	.70	.25
94	A18	12f dp orange ('37)	.55	.25
95	A18	13f brown	40.00	37.50
96	A18	15f carmine	3.00	.55
97	A17	20f dk brown	1.10	.35
98	A19	30f chestnut brn	1.10	.35
99	A17	50f olive green	1.60	.50
100	A19	1y violet	4.25	.60
	Nos. 83-100 (18)	85.60	52.75
	Set, never hinged	120.00	

Nos. 83, 84, 86, 88 and 93 are known imperforate but were not regularly issued.

See Nos. 159-163 in Scott Standard catalogue, Vol. 4. For overprints see Nos. 140-141, 148-151 in Scott Vol. 4. For surcharges see People's Republic of China Nos. 2L1-2L2, 2L11-2L18, 2L20-2L37, 2L40-2L52 in Scott Standard catalogue, Vol. 2.

a

b

c

d

1937		Surcharged on No. 66	
101	A9 (a)	2½f on 2f	3.50	3.00

Surcharged on Nos. 75, 76 and 78

102	A13 (a)	2½f on 2f	4.00	2.75
103	A10 (b)	5f on 4f	4.75	4.00
104	A10 (c)	13f on 12f	12.50	12.50

Surcharged in Black on Nos. 75, 76 and 70

Space between bottom characters of surcharge 4½mm

105	A13 (d)	2½f on 2f	2.00	1.90
a.		Inverted surcharge	400.00	425.00
b.		Vert. pair, one without surch.	95.00	
106	A10 (b)	5f on 4f	3.50	2.75
107	A10 (c)	13f on 12f	12.00	10.00

Surcharged on No. 70

Space between characters 6½mm

| 108 | A10 (c) | 13f on 12f | 225.00 | 200.00 |

Same Surcharge on No. 63

Space between characters 4½mm

Wmk. 141

109	A10 (b)	5f on 4f	7.25	6.00
	Nos. 101-109 (9)	274.50	241.40
	Set, never hinged	310.00	

Nos. 101-109 were issued primarily to pay postage to China, but were valid for any postal use.

Rising Sun over Manchurian Plain — A20

Composite Picture of Manchurian City — A21

Perf. 12½

1937, Mar. 1	Litho.	Unwmk.	
110	A20	1½f carmine rose	3.50	3.00
111	A21	3f blue green	3.00	2.75
	Set, never hinged	10.00	

5th anniv. of the founding of the State of Manchukuo.

Types of 1936

Perf. 13x13½

1937	Wmk. 242	Engr.	
112	A13	2½f dk violet	1.00	.40
113	A10	5f black	.25	.25
115	A10	13f dk red brown	1.00	.60
	Nos. 112-115 (3)	2.25	1.25
	Set, never hinged	2.50	

Issued primarily to pay postage to China, but were valid for any postal use.

Pouter Pigeon — A22

National Flag and Buildings — A23

Perf. 12x12½

1937, Sept. 16		Unwmk.	
116	A22	2f dark violet	2.50	1.60
117	A23	4f rose carmine	2.50	1.25
118	A22	10f dark green	5.75	3.25
119	A23	20f dark blue	7.50	5.25
	Nos. 116-119 (4)	18.25	11.35
	Set, never hinged	24.00	

Completion of the national capital, Hsinking, under the first Five-Year Construction Plan.

Map — A24

Dept. of Justice Building — A27

Japanese Residents' Association Building — A25

Postal Administration Building — A26

Perf. 12x12½, 13

1937, Dec. 1	Litho.	Unwmk.	
121	A24	2f dark carmine	1.75	.90
122	A25	4f green	2.50	1.10
123	A25	8f orange	5.00	3.50
124	A26	10f blue	6.00	4.00
125	A27	12f lt violet	7.00	5.50
126	A26	20f lilac brown	10.00	6.25
	Nos. 121-126 (6)	32.25	21.25
	Set, never hinged	45.00	

Issued in commemoration of the abolition of extraterritorial rights within Manchukuo.

New Year Greetings — A28

Map and Cross — A29

1937, Dec. 15	Engr.	Perf. 12x12½	
127	A28	2f dk blue & red	2.50	1.00
		Never hinged	3.75	
a.		Double impression of border	12.50	

Issued to pay postage on New Year's greeting cards.

Wmk. 242

1938, Oct. 15	Litho.	Perf. 13	
128	A29	2f lake & scarlet	1.75	1.25
129	A29	4f slate grn & scar	1.75	1.25
	Set, never hinged	5.00	

Founding of the Red Cross Soc. in Manchukuo.

Network of State Railroads in Manchukuo A30

Express Train "Asia" A31

1939, Oct. 21			
130	A30	2f dk org, blk & dp bl	2.00	1.50
131	A31	4f dp blue & indigo	2.00	1.50
	Set, never hinged	6.00	

Attainment of 10,000 kilometers in the railway mileage in Manchuria.

Stork Flying above Mast of Imperial Flagship — A32

1940	Photo.	Unwmk.	
132	A32	2f brt red violet	.80	.80
133	A32	4f brt green	.80	.80
	Set, never hinged	2.00	

Second visit of Emperor Kang Teh to Emperor Hirohito of Japan.

Census Taker and Map of Manchukuo A33

Census Form A34

1940, Sept. 10	Litho.	Wmk. 242	
134	A33	2f vio brn & org	.70	.70
135	A34	4f black & green	.75	.75
a.		Double impression of green	50.00	
	Set, never hinged	2.00	

National census starting Oct. 1.

Message of Congratulation from Premier Chang Chinghui — A35

Dragon Dance A36

1940, Sept. 18   Engr.   Perf. 13x13½

136	A35 2f carmine	.55	.55

Perf. 13½x13

137	A36 4f indigo	.70	.70
a.	Imperf., pair	100.00	
	Set, never hinged	1.75	

2600th anniversary of the birth of the Japanese Empire.

Soldier — A37

Perf. 13x13½

1941, May 25   Photo.   Unwmk.

138	A37 2f deep carmine	.60	.60
139	A37 4f bright ultra	.60	.60
	Set, never hinged	2.00	

Conscription Law, effective June 1, 1941.

AIR POST STAMPS

Sheep Grazing AP1

Railroad Bridge AP2

Wmk. Characters (242)

1936-37   Engr.   Perf. 13x13½
Granite Paper

C1	AP1 18f green	15.00	12.50
C2	AP1 19f blue green ('37)	5.00	3.50
C3	AP2 38f blue	16.00	15.00
C4	AP2 39f deep blue ('37)	1.60	1.75
	Nos. C1-C4 (4)	37.60	32.75
	Set, never hinged	50.00	

With the end of World War II and the collapse of Manchukuo, the Northeastern Provinces reverted to China. In many Manchurian towns and cities, the Manchukuo stamps were locally handstamped in ideograms: "Republic of China," "China Postal Service" or "Temporary Use for China." A typical example is shown above. Many of these local issues also were surcharged.

MARIANA ISLANDS

ˌmar-ē-ˈa-nə ˈī-lənds

LOCATION — A group of 14 islands in the West Pacific Ocean, about 1500 miles east of the Philippines.

GOVT. — Possession of Spain, then of Germany
AREA — 246 sq. mi.
POP. — 44,025 (1935)
CAPITAL — Saipan

Until 1899 this group belonged to Spain but in that year all except Guam were ceded to Germany.

100 Centavos = 1 Peso
100 Pfennig = 1 Mark (1899)

Values for unused stamps are for examples with original gum as defined in the catalogue introduction. Very fine examples of Nos. 1-6 will have perforations touching or just cutting into the design. Stamps with perfs clear on all sides and well centered are rare and sell for substantially more.

Issued under Spanish Dominion

Philippines Stamps Hstmpd. Vert. in Blackish Violet Reading Up or Down

1899, Sept.   Unwmk.   Perf. 14

1	A39	2c dark blue green	800.	300.
		On cover		2,500.
2	A39	3c dark brown	500.	250.
		On cover		2,500.
3	A39	5c car rose	700.	300.
		On cover		3,000.
4	A39	6c dark blue	5,500.	3,000.
		On cover		6,500.
5	A39	8c gray brown	500.	175.
		On cover		2,500.
6	A39	15c dull ol grn	1,900.	1,100.
		On cover		5,000.

Overprint forgeries of Nos. 1-6 exist.
No. 4 was issued in a quantity of 50 stamps.

Issued under German Dominion

Stamps of Germany, 1889-90, Overprinted in Black at 56 degree Angle

1900, May   Unwmk.   Perf. 13½x14½

11	A9	3pf dark brown	12.00	30.00
		Never hinged	25.00	
		On cover		160.00
12	A9	5pf green	16.00	32.50
		Never hinged	32.50	
		On cover		160.00
13	A10	10pf carmine	19.00	45.00
		Never hinged	40.00	
		On cover		95.00
14	A10	20pf ultra	25.00	125.00
		Never hinged	60.00	
		On cover		275.00
15	A10	25pf orange	62.50	160.00
		Never hinged	160.00	
		On cover		475.00
b.		Inverted overprint	2,400.	
		Never hinged	3,600.	
16	A10	50pf red brn	65.00	210.00
		Never hinged	160.00	
		On cover		475.00
		Nos. 11-16 (6)	199.50	602.50

Forged cancellations exist on Nos. 11-16, 17-29.
Covers: Value for No. 16 on cover is for overfranked complete cover, usually philatelic.

Stamps of Germany, 1889-90, Overprinted in Black at 48 degree Angle

1899, Nov. 18

11a	A9	3pf light brown	2,000.	2,000.
		Never hinged	3,600.	
		On cover		5,600.
12a	A9	5pf green	2,500.	1,700.
		Never hinged	4,750.	
		On cover		2,800.
13a	A10	10pf carmine	190.	200.00
		Never hinged	550.00	
		On cover		800.00
14a	A10	20pf ultra	190.	200.00
		Never hinged	550.00	
		On cover		800.00
15a	A10	25pf orange	2,750.	2,750.
		Never hinged	6,000.	
		On cover		6,500.

16a	A10	50pf red brown	2,750.	2,750.
		Never hinged	6,000.	
		On cover		5,250.

Covers: Value for No. 16a on cover is for overfranked complete cover, usually philatelic.

Kaiser's Yacht "Hohenzollern"
A4   A5

1901, Jan.   Typo.   Perf. 14

17	A4	3pf brown	1.10	1.75
		Never hinged	2.00	
		On cover		105.00
18	A4	5pf green	1.10	1.90
		Never hinged	2.00	
		On cover		45.00
19	A4	10pf carmine	1.10	4.25
		Never hinged	2.00	
		On cover		52.50
20	A4	20pf ultra	1.25	7.25
		Never hinged	2.50	
		On cover		175.00
21	A4	25pf org & blk, yel	1.75	12.50
		Never hinged	3.50	
		On cover		175.00
22	A4	30pf org & blk, sal	1.75	13.50
		Never hinged	3.50	
		On cover		175.00
23	A4	40pf lake & blk	1.75	13.50
		Never hinged	4.00	
		On cover		175.00
24	A4	50pf pur & blk, sal	2.00	15.00
		Never hinged	4.50	
		On cover		55.00
25	A4	80pf lake & blk, rose	2.50	25.00
		Never hinged	6.00	
		On cover		82.50

Engr.
Perf. 14½x14

26	A5	1m carmine	4.00	72.50
		Never hinged	20.00	
		On cover		100.00
27	A5	2m blue	5.50	92.50
		Never hinged	24.00	
		On cover		200.00
28	A5	3m blk vio	8.00	140.00
		Never hinged	32.50	
		On cover		290.00
29	A5	5m slate & car	140.00	500.00
		Never hinged	400.00	
		On cover		725.00
		Nos. 17-29 (13)	171.80	899.65

Covers: Values for Nos. 24-29 on cover are for overfranked complete covers, usually philatelic.

Wmk. Lozenges (125)

1916-19   Typo.   Perf. 14

30	A4	3pf brown ('19)	1.00	
		On cover		2.00

Engr.
Perf. 14½x14

31	A5	5m slate & carmine, 25x17 holes	30.00	
		Never hinged	175.00	
a.		5m slate & carmine, 26x17 holes	35.00	
		Never hinged	225.00	

Nos. 30 and 31 were never placed in use.

MARIENWERDER

mä-ˈrē-ən-ˌveˌəˌrd-ər

LOCATION — Northeastern Germany, bordering on Poland
GOVT. — District of West Prussia

By the Versailles Treaty the greater portion of West Prussia was ceded to Poland but the district of Marienwerder was allowed a plebiscite which was held in 1920 and resulted in favor of Germany.

100 Pfennig = 1 Mark

Plebiscite Issues

Symbolical of Allied Supervision of the Plebiscite — A1

1920   Unwmk.   Litho.   Perf. 11½

1	A1	5pf green	.75	1.75
		Never hinged	2.10	
		On cover		4.00
2	A1	10pf rose red	.75	1.50
		Never hinged	2.10	
		On cover		4.00
3	A1	15pf gray	.75	1.75
		Never hinged	2.10	
		On cover		4.00
4	A1	20pf brn org	.75	1.50
		Never hinged	2.10	
		On cover		4.00
5	A1	25pf deep blue	.75	1.50
		Never hinged	2.10	
		On cover		8.00
6	A1	30pf orange	.95	1.75
		Never hinged	2.60	
		On cover		9.50
7	A1	40pf brown	.75	1.75
		Never hinged	2.10	
		On cover		6.50
8	A1	50pf violet	.75	1.50
		Never hinged	2.10	
		On cover		6.50
9	A1	60pf red brown	4.25	3.00
		Never hinged	11.50	
		On cover		20.00
10	A1	75pf chocolate	.95	1.50
		Never hinged	2.60	
		On cover		12.00
11	A1	1m brn & grn	.75	1.50
		Never hinged	2.10	
		On cover		12.00
12	A1	2m dk vio	2.10	3.75
		Never hinged	5.25	
		On cover		35.00
13	A1	3m red	5.00	5.50
		Never hinged	14.00	
		On cover		40.00
14	A1	5m blue & rose	27.50	22.00
		Never hinged	77.50	
		On cover		80.00
a.		5m ultramarine & pale red	22.50	21.00
		Never hinged	65.00	
		Nos. 1-14 (14)	46.75	50.25
		Set, never hinged	130.00	

These stamps occasionally show parts of two papermakers" watermarks, consisting of the letters "O. B. M." with two stars before and after, or "P. & C. M."
Nos. 1-14 exist imperf.; value for set, $700. Nearly all exist part perf.

Stamps of Germany, 1905-19, Overprinted

1920   Wmk. 125   Perf. 14, 14½

24	A16	5pf green	15.00	30.00
		Never hinged	30.00	
		On cover		65.00
a.		Inverted overprint	125.00	
		Never hinged	210.00	
26	A16	20pf bl vio	7.25	27.50
		Never hinged	20.00	
		On cover		40.00
a.		Inverted overprint	62.50	
		Never hinged	125.00	
b.		Double overprint	85.00	
		Never hinged	150.00	
28	A16	50pf vio & blk, buff	375.00	850.00
		Never hinged	800.00	
		On cover		1,600.
a.		50pf vio & blk, pale yel org	800.00	2,750.
		Never hinged	2,750.	
		On cover		3,500.
29	A16	75pf grn & blk	4.75	8.75
		Never hinged	9.00	
		On cover		20.00
a.		Inverted overprint	62.50	
		Never hinged	125.00	
30	A16	80pf lake & blk, rose	75.00	120.00
		Never hinged	150.00	
		On cover		300.00
31	A17	1m car rose	85.00	160.00
		Never hinged	160.00	
		On cover		400.00
a.		Inverted overprint	425.00	
		Never hinged	850.00	
		Nos. 24-31 (6)	562.00	1,196.
		Set, never hinged	1,200.	

Trial impressions were made in red, green and lilac, and with 2½mm instead of 3mm space between the lines of the overprint. These were printed on the 75pf and 80pf. The 1 mark was overprinted with the same words in 3 lines of large sans-serif capitals. All these are essays. Some were passed through the post, apparently with speculative intent.

Stamps of Germany, 1905-18, Surcharged

32	A22	1m on 2pf gray	22.50	47.50
		Never hinged	80.00	
		On cover		80.00

33	A22	2m on 2½pf gray	12.00	20.00
		Never hinged	50.00	
		On cover		80.00
a.		Inverted surcharge	55.00	100.00
		Never hinged	100.00	
34	A16	3m on 3pf brown	12.00	20.00
		Never hinged	40.00	
		On cover		95.00
a.		Double surcharge	55.00	100.00
		Never hinged	100.00	
b.		Inverted surcharge	55.00	100.00
		Never hinged	100.00	
35	A22	5m on 7½pf org	12.00	21.00
		Never hinged	50.00	
		On cover		120.00
a.		Inverted surcharge	55.00	100.00
		Never hinged	100.00	
b.		Double surcharge	55.00	100.00
		Never hinged	100.00	
		Nos. 32-35 (4)	58.50	108.50
		Set, never hinged	220.00	

There are two types of the letters "M," "C," "i" and "e" and of the numerals "2" and "5" in these surcharges.

Counterfeits exist of Nos. 24-35.

Stamps of Germany, 1920, Overprinted

1920, July			**Perf. 15x14½**	
36	A17	1m red	2.50	7.25
		Never hinged	6.50	
		On cover		60.00
37	A17	1.25m green	3.25	8.00
		Never hinged	8.00	
		On cover		60.00
38	A17	1.50m yellow brown	4.25	9.75
		Never hinged	10.50	
		On cover		60.00
39	A21	2.50m lilac rose	2.50	8.00
		Never hinged	7.50	
		On cover		80.00
		Nos. 36-39 (4)	12.50	33.00
		Set, never hinged	32.50	

A2

1920		**Unwmk.**	**Perf. 11½**	
40	A2	5pf green	3.25	2.00
		Never hinged	6.00	
		On cover		12.00
41	A2	10pf rose red	3.25	2.00
		Never hinged	6.00	
		On cover		16.00
42	A2	15pf gray	11.00	13.50
		Never hinged	27.00	
		On cover		40.00
43	A2	20pf brn org	2.00	2.00
		Never hinged	4.50	
		On cover		12.00
44	A2	25pf dp bl	12.50	17.50
		Never hinged	32.50	
		On cover		40.00
45	A2	30pf orange	1.60	1.60
		Never hinged	2.75	
		On cover		6.50
46	A2	40pf brown	.80	1.60
		Never hinged	2.00	
		On cover		6.50
47	A2	50pf violet	1.60	2.00
		Never hinged	4.00	
		On cover		8.00
48	A2	60pf red brn	6.00	5.50
		Never hinged	13.50	
		On cover		20.00
49	A2	75pf chocolate	6.00	5.50
		Never hinged	14.50	
		On cover		27.50
50	A2	1m brn & grn	1.60	1.60
		Never hinged	2.75	
		On cover		12.00
51	A2	2m dk vio	1.60	1.60
		Never hinged	3.25	
		On cover		27.50
52	A2	3m light red	2.00	2.00
		Never hinged	4.75	
		On cover		47.50
53	A2	5m blue & rose	3.25	2.75
		Never hinged	6.50	
		On cover		80.00
		Nos. 40-53 (14)	56.45	61.15
		Set, never hinged	130.00	

MARSHALL ISLANDS

ˈmär-shəl ˈī-ləndz

LOCATION — Two chains of islands in the West Pacific Ocean, northwest of the Gilbert and Ellice group
GOVT. — German possession
AREA — 176 sq. mi.

POP. — 15,179 (1913)
CAPITAL — Jaluit

100 Pfennig = 1 Mark

Watermark

Wmk. 125 — Lozenges

Issued under German Dominion

A1   A2

Stamps of Germany Overprinted "Marschall-Inseln" in Black

Two printings of Nos. 1-4: Berlin printing, white, smooth shiny gum; Jaluit printing, yellowish, dull gum.

1897		**Unwmk.**	**Perf. 13½x14½**	
1	A1	3pf dark brown (Berlin)	140.00	725.00
		Never hinged	525.00	
		On cover		950.00
a.		3pf light yellowish brown (Jaluit)	4,250.	2,200.
		Never hinged	7,250.	
		On cover		12,000.
b.		3pf reddish ochre (Jaluit)	3,600.	5,250.
		Never hinged	7,250.	
		On cover		12,000.
2	A1	5pf green (Berlin)	120.00	550.00
		Never hinged	325.00	
		On cover		875.00
a.		5pf green (Jaluit)	525.00	440.00
		Never hinged	1,350.	
		On cover		950.00
3	A1	10pf carmine (Berlin)	55.00	150.00
		Never hinged	150.00	
		On cover		250.00
a.		Vertical half used as 5pf on postcard		27,500.
b.		As "a," on newspaper wrapper		34,000.
c.		10pf carmine (Jaluit)	60.00	85.00
		Never hinged	175.00	
		On cover		240.00
4	A2	20pf ultra (Berlin)	50.00	150.00
		Never hinged	140.00	
		On cover		250.00
a.		20pf ultra (Jaluit)	60.00	95.00
		Never hinged	175.00	
		On cover		275.00
5	A2	25pf orange (Berlin)	160.00	925.00
		Never hinged	550.00	
		On cover		2,400.
6	A2	50pf red brown (Berlin)	140.00	925.00
		Never hinged	475.00	
		On cover		2,000.
		Nos. 1-6 (6)	665.00	3,425.

Nos. 5 and 6 were not placed in use, but canceled stamps and covers exist.

Value for No. 6 on cover is for complete, overfranked covers, usually philatelic.

Forged cancellations are found on almost all Marshall Islands stamps.

Overprinted "Marschall-Inseln"

1899-1900				
7	A1	3pf dk brn ('00)	4.50	5.50
		Never hinged	12.00	
		On cover		20.00
a.		3pf light brown	275.00	775.00
		Never hinged	650.00	
		On cover		—
8	A1	5pf green	9.25	12.50
		Never hinged	24.00	
		On cover		20.00
9	A2	10pf car ('00)	12.00	16.00
		Never hinged	40.00	
		On cover		30.00
a.		Half used as 5pf on post-card		8,000.
10	A2	20pf ultra ('00)	17.00	25.00
		Never hinged	45.00	
		On cover		42.50
11	A2	25pf orange	19.00	42.50
		Never hinged	65.00	
		On cover		72.50
12	A2	50pf red brown	30.00	47.50
		Never hinged	110.00	
		On cover		95.00
a.		Half used as 25pf on cover		35,000.
		Nos. 7-12 (6)	91.75	149.00

Values for Nos. 9a and 12a are for properly used items, addressed and sent to Germany.

Kaiser's Yacht "Hohenzollern"
A3   A4

1901		**Unwmk.** **Typo.**	**Perf. 14**	
13	A3	3pf brown	.65	1.75
		Never hinged	1.40	
		On cover		47.50
14	A3	5pf green	.65	1.75
		Never hinged	1.40	
		On cover		20.00
15	A3	10pf carmine	.65	5.00
		Never hinged	1.40	
		On cover		27.50
16	A3	20pf ultra	.95	9.25
		Never hinged	1.40	
		On cover		85.00
17	A3	25pf org & blk, *yel*	1.00	16.00
		Never hinged	2.00	
		On cover		85.00
18	A3	30pf org & blk, *sal*	1.00	16.00
		Never hinged	2.00	
		On cover		80.00
19	A3	40pf lake & blk	1.00	16.00
		Never hinged	2.00	
		On cover		80.00
20	A3	50pf pur & blk, *sal*	1.40	25.00
		Never hinged	4.00	
		On cover		60.00
21	A3	80pf lake & blk, *rose*	2.50	35.00
		Never hinged	12.00	
		On cover		80.00

Engr.
Perf. 14½x14

22	A4	1m carmine	4.00	85.00
		Never hinged	17.00	
		On cover		125.00
23	A4	2m blue	5.50	120.00
		Never hinged	20.00	
		On cover		150.00
24	A4	3m blk vio	8.50	200.00
		Never hinged	27.50	
		On cover		240.00
25	A4	5m slate & car	140.00	500.00
		Never hinged	490.00	
		On cover		725.00
		Nos. 13-25 (13)	167.80	1,030.

Covers: Values for Nos. 20-25 on cover are for overfranked complete covers, usually philatelic.

Wmk. Lozenges (125)

1916		**Typo.**	**Perf. 14**	
26	A3	3pf brown	.85	
		Never hinged	1.90	

Engr.
Perf. 14½x14

27	A4	5m slate & carmine, 25x17 holes	35.00	
		Never hinged	120.00	
a.		5m slate & carmine, 26x17 holes	32.00	
		Never hinged	140.00	

Nos. 26 and 27 were never placed in use. The stamps of Marshall Islands overprinted "G. R. I." and new values in British currency were all used in New Britain and are listed among the issues for that country.

MARTINIQUE

ˌmär-tᵊn-ˈēk

LOCATION — Island in the West Indies, southeast of Puerto Rico
GOVT. — French Colony
AREA — 385 sq. mi.
POP. — 261,595 (1946)
CAPITAL — Fort-de-France

100 Centimes = 1 Franc

Stamps of French Colonies 1881-86 Surcharged in Black

Nos. 1, 7   No. 2

No. 3

No. 4

Nos. 5-6, 8

Nos. 9-20

1886-91		**Unwmk.**	**Perf. 14x13½**	
1	A9	5 on 20c	65.00	55.00
		Never hinged	135.00	
		On cover		375.00
		On cover, single franking		625.00
a.		Double surcharge	750.00	750.00
2	A9	5c on 20c	15,000.	15,000.
3	A9	15c on 20c ('87)	275.00	240.00
		On cover		1,100.
		On cover, single franking		1,900.
a.		Inverted surcharge	2,350.	2,500.
4	A9	15c on 20c ('87)	100.00	100.00
		Never hinged	215.00	
		On cover		675.00
		On cover, single franking		1,100.
a.		Inverted surcharge	1,500.	1,500.
b.		Se-tenant pair, #3-4	475.00	425.00
c.		Se-tenant pair, #3a-4a	4,750.	4,750.
5	A9	01 on 20c ('88)	20.00	19.00
		Never hinged	42.50	
		On cover		275.00
		On cover, single franking		500.00
a.		Inverted surcharge	350.00	350.00
6	A9	05 on 20c	16.00	13.00
		Never hinged	32.50	
		On cover		150.00
		On cover, single franking		500.00
7	A9	15 on 20c ('88)	200.00	180.00
		On cover		550.00
		On cover, single franking		925.00
c.		Inverted surcharge	700.00	750.00
8	A9	015 on 20c ('87)	60.00	65.00
		Never hinged	135.00	
		On cover		375.00
		On cover, single franking		625.00
a.		Inverted surcharge	875.00	825.00
9	A9	01c on 2c ('88)	4.75	3.25
		Never hinged	9.75	
		On cover		55.00
		On cover, single franking		500.00
a.		Double surcharge	475.00	475.00
b.		"MARTINIQUE" below "01"	30.00	30.00
10	A9	01c on 4c ('88)	15.00	4.75
		Never hinged	29.00	
		On cover		75.00
		On cover, single franking		375.00
11	A9	05c on 4c ('88)	1,500.	1,375.
12	A9	05c on 10c ('90)	120.00	72.50
		On cover		250.00
		On cover, single franking		450.00
a.		Slanting "5"	300.00	240.00
13	A9	05c on 20c ('88)	28.00	20.00
		Never hinged	60.00	
		On cover		150.00
		On cover, single franking		375.00
a.		Slanting "5"	150.00	120.00
		On cover		450.00
b.		Inverted surcharge	425.00	375.00
14	A9	05c on 30c ('91)	35.00	28.00
		Never hinged	72.50	
		On cover		150.00
		On cover, single franking		375.00
a.		Slanting "5"	160.00	150.00
15	A9	05c on 35c ('91)	20.00	16.00
		Never hinged	72.50	
		On cover		125.00
		On cover, single franking		375.00
a.		Slanting "5"	160.00	150.00
b.		Inverted surcharge	325.00	300.00
c.		"MARTINIQUE" below "05"	60.00	60.00
d.		"MARTINIQUE" omitted	60.00	60.00
e.		05c on 35c violet, *yel* ('91)	22.50	18.50
16	A9	05c on 40c ('91)	65.00	47.00
		Never hinged	135.00	
		On cover		190.00
		On cover, single franking		425.00
a.		Slanting "5"	260.00	165.00
17	A9	15c on 4c ('88)	12,000.	11,000.
18	A9	15c on 20c ('87)	150.00	120.00
		On cover		550.00
		On cover, single franking		950.00
a.		Slanting "5"	500.00	425.00
b.		Double surcharge	700.00	700.00
c.		"MARTINIQUE" below "15"	350.00	350.00
d.		"MARTINIQUE" omitted	2,100.	
19	A9	15c on 25c ('90)	32.50	20.00
		Never hinged	65.00	
		On cover		75.00
		On cover, single franking		425.00
a.		Slanting "5"	150.00	130.00
b.		Inverted surcharge	325.00	275.00
c.		Double surcharge	450.00	450.00
20	A9	15c on 75c ('91)	210.00	175.00
		On cover		675.00
		On cover, single franking		1,100.
a.		Slanting "5"	550.00	450.00

French Colonies No. 47 Surcharged

1891
21　A9　01c on 2c brn, *buff*　11.00　11.00
　　Never hinged　22.50
　　On cover　　150.00
　　On cover, single franking　　375.00
　a.　No dot after "c"　40.00　40.00

French Colonies Nos.
J5-J9 Surcharged

1891-92　Black Surcharge　*Imperf.*
22　D1　05c on 5c blk ('92)　17.50　17.00
　　Never hinged　52.50
　　On cover　　150.00
　　On cover, single franking　　375.00
　a.　Slanting "5"　72.50　65.00
　b.　#22, "Martinique" omitted　75.00　75.00
23　D1　05c on 15c blk　16.00　16.00
　　Never hinged　47.50
　　On cover　　120.00
　　On cover, single franking　　375.00
　b.　Slanting "5"　72.50　65.00
　c.　#23, "Martinique" omitted　130.00　130.00
24　D1　15c on 20c blk　20.00　16.00
　　Never hinged　60.00
　　On cover　　125.00
　　On cover, single franking　　375.00
　a.　Inverted surcharge　300.00　300.00
　b.　Double surcharge　300.00　300.00
　c.　#24, "Martinique" omitted　175.00　175.00
25　D1　15c on 30c blk　20.00　16.00
　　Never hinged　60.00
　　On cover　　125.00
　　On cover, single franking　　375.00
　a.　Inverted surcharge　300.00　300.00
　b.　Slanting "5"　80.00　72.50
　c.　#25, "Martinique" omitted　175.00　175.00
　　Nos. 22-25 (4)　73.50　65.00

Red Surcharge
26　D1　05c on 10c blk　14.50　11.00
　　Never hinged　40.00
　　On cover　　190.00
　　On cover, single franking　　375.00
　a.　Inverted surcharge　300.00　300.00
　b.　#26, "Martinique" omitted　100.00　100.00
27　D1　05c on 15c blk　16.00　16.00
　　Never hinged　47.50
　　On cover　　200.00
　　On cover, single franking　　375.00
28　D1　15c on 20c blk　52.50　45.00
　　Never hinged　135.00
　　On cover　　225.00
　　On cover, single franking　　375.00
　a.　Inverted surcharge　450.00　450.00
　　Nos. 26-28 (3)　83.00　72.00

**French Colonies No. 54 Surcharged
in Black**

j　　k

1892　　Perf. 14x13½
29　A9 (j)　05c on 25c　65.00　65.00
　　Never hinged　125.00
　　On cover　　375.00
　　On cover, single franking　　625.00
　a.　Slanting "5"　300.00　300.00
30　A9 (j)　15c on 25c　36.00　36.00
　　Never hinged　82.50
　　On cover　　210.00
　　On cover, single franking　　325.00
　a.　Slanting "5"　275.00　275.00
31　A9 (k)　05c on 25c　65.00　65.00
　　Never hinged　135.00
　　On cover　　375.00
　　On cover, single franking　　625.00
　a.　"1882" instead of "1892"　675.00　600.00
　b.　"95" instead of "05"　850.00　800.00
　c.　Slanting "5"　300.00　300.00
32　A9 (k)　15c on 25c　32.50　32.50
　　Never hinged　70.00
　　On cover　　210.00
　　On cover, single franking　　325.00
　a.　"1882" instead of "1892"　600.00　600.00
　　On cover, single franking　　750.00
　　　　　　1,250.
　b.　Slanting "5"　160.00　160.00
　　Nos. 29-32 (4)　198.50　198.50

Navigation and
Commerce — A15

**1892-1906　Typo.　Perf. 14x13½
"MARTINIQUE" Colony in Carmine
or Blue**
33　A15　1c blk, *lil bl*　1.50　1.40
　　Never hinged　2.25
　　On cover　　75.00
　　On cover, single franking　　125.00
　a.　"MARTINIQUE" in blue　1,000.　1,000.
　b.　"MARTINIQUE" omitted　　5,500.
34　A15　2c brn, *buff*　1.75　1.40
　　Never hinged　2.50
　　On cover　　75.00

　　On cover, business card,
　　printed notice　　125.00
35　A15　4c claret, *lav*　2.00　1.50
　　Never hinged　3.25
　　On cover　　67.50
36　A15　5c grn, *grnsh*　2.40　1.50
　　Never hinged　4.00
　　On cover　　30.00
　　On cover, single franking　　50.00
37　A15　5c yel grn ('99)　3.50　1.10
　　Never hinged　5.75
　　On cover　　12.00
　　On cover, single franking　　20.00
38　A15　10c blk, *lav*　11.00　2.00
　　Never hinged　20.00
　　On cover　　22.50
　　On cover, single franking　　37.50
　　On cover, single frank-
　　　ing, military letter,
　　　from　　375.00
39　A15　10c red ('99)　5.25　1.50
　　Never hinged　9.00
　　On cover　　16.00
　　On cover, single franking　　22.50
40　A15　15c blue, qua-
　　　drille paper　42.50　8.00
　　Never hinged　72.50
　　On cover　　27.50
　　On cover, single franking　　45.00
　　On cover, single frank-
　　　ing, military letter,
　　　from　　300.00
41　A15　15c gray ('99)　13.50　2.10
　　Never hinged　22.50
　　On cover　　16.00
　　On cover, single franking　　37.50
42　A15　20c red, *grn*　20.00　10.00
　　Never hinged　40.00
　　On cover　　55.00
　　On cover, single franking　　95.00
43　A15　25c blk, *rose*　24.00　3.25
　　Never hinged　42.50
　　On cover　　60.00
　　On cover, single franking　　115.00
44　A15　25c blue ('99)　16.00　14.50
　　Never hinged　27.50
　　On cover　　275.00
　　On cover, single franking　　500.00
45　A15　30c brn, *bis*　36.00　19.00
　　Never hinged　65.00
　　On cover　　175.00
　　On cover, single franking　　310.00
46　A15　35c blk, *yel* ('06)　16.00　9.50
　　Never hinged　27.50
　　On cover　　125.00
　　On cover, single franking　　700.00
47　A15　40c red, *straw*　36.00　19.00
　　Never hinged　65.00
　　On cover　　240.00
　　On cover, single franking　　450.00
48　A15　50c car, *rose*　40.00　24.00
　　Never hinged　70.00
　　On cover　　275.00
　　On cover, single franking　　500.00
49　A15　50c brn, *az* ('99)　42.50　32.50
　　Never hinged　82.50
　　On cover　　500.00
　　On cover, single franking　　625.00
50　A15　75c dp vio, *org*　32.50　20.00
　　Never hinged　62.50
　　On cover　　300.00
　　On cover, single franking　　700.00
51　A15　1fr brnz grn,
　　　straw　32.50　21.00
　　Never hinged　62.50
　　On cover　　300.00
　　On cover, single franking　　700.00
52　A15　2fr vio, *rose*
　　　　('04)　92.50　75.00
　　Never hinged　190.00
　　On cover　　925.00
　　On cover, single franking　　1,500.
53　A15　5fr lil, *lav* ('03)　110.00　95.00
　　Never hinged　205.00
　　On cover　　1,050.
　　On cover, single franking　　1,900.
　　Nos. 33-53 (21)　581.40　363.25

Perf. 13½x14 stamps are counterfeits.
For surcharges see Nos. 54-61, 101-104.

Stamps of 1892-1903
Surcharged in Black

Two types of surcharge: type 1, end of top of
"C" round; type 2, end of top of "C" barred
serif.

1904
54　A15　10c on 30c brn, *bis*
　　　　(1)　14.50　14.50
　　Never hinged　24.00
　　On cover　　75.00
　　On cover, single franking　　125.00
　a.　Double surcharge　525.00　525.00
　b.　Inverted surcharge　1,600.　1,600.
　c.　Type 2　70.00　70.00
　　Never hinged　135.00
　d.　Pair, types 1 and 2　110.00　110.00
　　Never hinged　210.00
55　A15　10c on 5fr lil, *lav*
　　　　(1)　16.00　16.00
　　Never hinged　27.50
　　On cover　　125.00
　　On cover, single franking　　130.00
　b.　Type 2　140.00　140.00
　　Never hinged　220.00
　c.　Pair, types 1 and 2　220.00　220.00
　　Never hinged　325.00

Surcharged

56　A15　10c on 30c brn, *bis*　24.00　24.00
　　Never hinged　42.50
　　On cover　　115.00
　　On cover, single franking　　190.00
57　A15　10c on 40c red,
　　　straw　24.00　24.00
　　Never hinged　42.50
　　On cover　　125.00
　　On cover, single franking　　195.00
　a.　Double surcharge　600.00　600.00
58　A15　10c on 50c car,
　　　rose　28.00　28.00
　　Never hinged　55.00
　　On cover　　195.00
59　A15　10c on 75c dp vio,
　　　org　20.00　20.00
　　Never hinged　35.00
　　On cover　　110.00
　　On cover, single franking　　175.00
60　A15　10c on 1fr brnz
　　　grn, *straw*　24.00　24.00
　　Never hinged　42.50
　　On cover　　125.00
　　On cover, single franking　　195.00
　a.　Double surcharge　350.00　350.00
61　A15　10c on 5fr lil, *lav*　200.00　200.00
　　On cover　　1,000.
　　On cover, single franking　　1,500.
　　Nos. 54-61 (8)　350.50　350.50

Martinique
Woman — A16

Girl Bearing
Pineapple in
Cane
Field — A18

View of Fort-de-France — A17

1908-30　　Typo.
62　A16　1c red brn &
　　　brn　.25　.25
　　Never hinged　.30
　　On cover　　40.00
　　On cover, single franking　　62.50
63　A16　2c ol grn & brn　.30　.25
　　Never hinged　.45
　　On cover　　40.00
　　On cover, single franking　　62.50
64　A16　4c vio brn & brn　.30　.30
　　Never hinged　.45
　　On cover　　40.00
　　On cover, single franking　　55.00
65　A16　5c grn & brn　1.10　.40
　　Never hinged　1.60
　　On cover　　15.00
　　On cover, single franking　　21.00
　a.　Perf 11　140.00
　　Never hinged　190.00
66　A16　5c org & brn
　　　　('22)　.50　.40
　　Never hinged　.65
　　On cover　　5.00
　　On cover, single franking　　6.25
67　A16　10c car & brn　1.10　.50
　　Never hinged　1.60
　　On cover　　8.00
　　On cover, single franking　　12.50
68　A16　10c bl grn & grn
　　　　('22)　.55　.40
　　Never hinged　.80
　　On cover　　30.00
　　On cover, single franking　　45.00
69　A16　10c brn vio &
　　　rose ('25)　.55　.40
　　Never hinged　.80
　　On cover　　15.00
　　On cover, single franking　　20.00
70　A16　15c brn vio &
　　　rose ('17)　.65　.40
　　Never hinged　1.10
　　On cover　　10.00
　　On cover, single franking　　12.50
71　A16　15c bl grn & gray
　　　grn ('25)　.50　.40
　　Never hinged　.75
　　On cover　　10.00
　　On cover, single franking　　12.50
72　A16　15c dp bl & red
　　　org ('28)　1.60　1.60
　　Never hinged　2.40
　　On cover　　10.00
　　On cover, single franking　　12.50

73　A16　20c vio & brn　1.40　1.10
　　Never hinged　2.00
　　On cover　　12.50
　　On cover, single franking　　16.00
74　A17　25c bl & brn　2.25　1.10
　　Never hinged　3.25
　　On cover　　30.00
　　On cover, single franking　　105.00
75　A17　25c org & brn
　　　　('22)　.90　.55
　　Never hinged　1.20
　　On cover　　10.00
　　On cover, single franking　　12.50
76　A17　30c brn org &
　　　brn　2.25　1.10
　　Never hinged　3.25
　　On cover　　50.00
　　On cover, single franking　　110.00
77　A17　30c dl red & brn
　　　　('22)　.75　.65
　　Never hinged　.95
　　On cover　　25.00
　　On cover, single franking　　95.00
78　A17　30c rose & ver
　　　　('24)　.55　.55
　　Never hinged　.80
　　On cover　　7.50
　　On cover, single franking　　10.00
79　A17　30c ol brn & brn
　　　　('25)　.55　.55
　　Never hinged　.95
　　On cover　　6.00
　　On cover, single franking　　8.75
80　A17　30c sl bl & bl grn
　　　　('27)　1.60　1.60
　　Never hinged　2.40
　　On cover　　10.00
　　On cover, single franking　　12.50
81　A17　35c vio & brn　.90　.65
　　Never hinged　1.20
　　On cover　　30.00
　　On cover, single franking　　125.00
　a.　White chalky paper　4.50　2.75
　　　7.00
82　A17　40c gray grn &
　　　brn　.90　.65
　　Never hinged　1.20
　　On cover　　30.00
　　On cover, single franking　　62.50
83　A17　45c dk brn & brn　.90　.65
　　Never hinged　1.20
　　On cover　　30.00
　　On cover, single franking　　75.00
　a.　White chalky paper　2.00　1.60
　　　3.25
84　A17　50c rose & brn　2.25　1.10
　　Never hinged　3.25
　　On cover　　45.00
　　On cover, single franking　　95.00
　a.　50c red and brown　2.40　1.20
　　Never hinged　4.00
　　On cover　　45.00
　　On cover, single franking　　95.00
85　A17　50c bl & brn ('22)　1.40　1.30
　　Never hinged　2.00
　　On cover　　25.00
　　On cover, single franking　　87.50
86　A17　50c org & grn
　　　　('25)　.90　.40
　　Never hinged　1.20
　　On cover　　12.50
87　A17　60c dk bl & lil
　　　rose ('25)　.75　.75
　　Never hinged　2.00
　　On cover　　30.00
　　On cover, single franking　　105.00
88　A17　65c vio & ol brn
　　　　('27)　2.00　2.00
　　Never hinged　2.75
　　On cover　　10.00
　　On cover, single franking　　15.00
89　A17　75c slate & brn　1.40　1.10
　　Never hinged　2.15
　　On cover　　50.00
　　On cover, single franking　　105.00
90　A17　75c ind & dk bl
　　　　('25)　.90　.90
　　Never hinged　1.20
　　On cover　　25.00
　　On cover, single franking　　95.00
91　A17　75c org brn & lt
　　　bl ('27)　2.75　2.75
　　Never hinged　4.25
　　On cover　　16.00
92　A17　90c brn red & brt
　　　red ('30)　5.50　5.50
　　Never hinged　9.00
　　On cover　　62.50
　　On cover, single franking　　110.00
93　A18　1fr dl bl & brn　1.20　1.00
　　Never hinged　1.90
　　On cover　　55.00
　　On cover, single franking　　105.00
94　A18　1fr dk bl ('25)　1.00　.90
　　Never hinged　1.35
　　On cover　　25.00
　　On cover, single franking　　75.00
95　A18　1fr ver & ol grn
　　　　('27)　2.75　2.75
　　Never hinged　4.25
　　On cover　　45.00
　　On cover, single franking　　62.50
96　A18　1.10fr vio & dk brn
　　　　('28)　3.75　*4.50*
　　Never hinged　5.50
　　On cover　　80.00
　　On cover, single franking　　225.00
97　A18　1.50fr ind & ultra
　　　　('30)　5.50　5.50
　　Never hinged　9.00
　　On cover　　55.00
　　On cover, single franking　　95.00
98　A18　2fr gray & brn　4.50　2.00
　　Never hinged　7.00
　　On cover　　55.00
　　On cover, single franking　　95.00
99　A18　3fr red vio ('30)　9.50　9.50
　　Never hinged　14.50
　　On cover　　95.00
　　On cover, single franking　　160.00

100 A18   5fr org red &
              brn   10.50   8.00
     Never hinged   18.00
     On cover   125.00
     On cover, single franking   200.00
     Nos. 62-100 (39)   76.90   64.40

For surcharges see Nos. 105-128, B1.

Nos. 41, 43, 47 and 53 Surcharged in Carmine or Black

1912, Aug.
Spacing between figures of surcharge 1.5mm (5c), 2mm (10c)

101 A15   5c on 15c gray
          (C)   1.00   1.00
     Never hinged   1.60
     On cover   40.00
     On cover, single franking   62.50
102 A15   5c on 25c blk,
          rose (C)   1.50   1.50
     Never hinged   2.40
     On cover   50.00
     On cover, single franking   80.00
103 A15   10c on 40c red,
          straw   2.40   2.40
     Never hinged   4.00
     On cover   110.00
     On cover, single franking   175.00
104 A15   10c on 5fr lil, *lav* 3.00   3.00
     Never hinged   4.75
     On cover   120.00
     On cover, single franking   190.00
     Nos. 101-104 (4)   7.90   7.90

Spacing between figures of surcharge 2.25mm (5c), 2.75mm (10c)

101a A15   5c on 15c gray
          (C)   37.50 37.50
     Never hinged   92.50
102a A15   5c on 25c blk,
          rose (C)   77.50 77.50
     Never hinged   190.00
103a A15   10c on 40c red,
          straw   125.00 125.00
     Never hinged   280.00
104a A15   10c on 5fr lil, *lav* 77.50 77.50
     Never hinged   280.00
     Nos. 101a-104a (4) 317.50 317.50

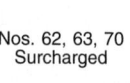

Nos. 62, 63, 70
Surcharged

1920, June 15
105 A16   5c on 1c   2.10   2.10
     Never hinged   3.15
     On cover   35.00
     On cover, single franking   50.00
  a. Double surcharge   45.00 45.00
     Never hinged   70.00
  b. Inverted surcharge   32.50 32.50
     Never hinged   57.50
     On cover   75.00
106 A16   10c on 2c   2.10   2.10
     Never hinged   3.15
     On cover   40.00
     On cover, single franking   62.50
  a. Double surcharge   130.00
     Never hinged   200.00
  b. Inverted surcharge   45.00 45.00
     Never hinged   70.00
  c. Double surcharge, one in-
     verted   95.00
     Never hinged   150.00
107 A16   25c on 15c   2.25   2.25
     Never hinged   3.25
     On cover   62.50
  a. Double surcharge   55.00 55.00
     Never hinged   100.00
  b. Inverted surcharge   55.00 55.00
     Never hinged   100.00
  c. Double surcharge, one in-
     verted   100.00
     Never hinged   150.00
  d. Pair, one stamp without
     surcharge   160.00 160.00
     Never hinged   275.00
     Nos. 105-107 (3)   6.45   6.45

No. 70 Surcharged in Various Colors

1922, Dec.
108 A16   1c on 15c (Bk)   .50   .50
     Never hinged   .65
     On cover   75.00
     On cover, single franking   110.00
  a. Double surcharge   190.00 190.00
109 A16   2c on 15c (Bl)   .50   .50
     Never hinged   .65
     On cover   75.00
     On cover, single franking   110.00
110 A16   5c on 15c (R)   .65   .65
     Never hinged   .95
     On cover   25.00
     On cover, single franking   37.50
  a. Imperf., pair   260.00
     Never hinged   400.00
     Nos. 108-110 (3)   1.65   1.65

Types of
1908-30
Surcharged

1923-25
111 A17   60c on 75c bl & rose .65   .65
     Never hinged   .95
     On cover   30.00
     On cover, single franking   60.00
112 A17   65c on 45c ol brn &
          brn ('25)   1.45   1.45
     Never hinged   2.40
     On cover   30.00
     On cover, single franking   60.00
113 A17   85c on 75c blk & brn
          (R) ('25)   1.75   1.75
     Never hinged   2.75
     On cover   37.50
     On cover, single franking   90.00
     Nos. 111-113 (3)   3.85   3.85

Nos. 63,
73, 76-77,
84-85
Surcharged
in Brown

Surcharge is horiz. on #114-115, vert. reading up on #116, 119 and down on #117-118.

1924, Feb. 14
114 A16   1c on 2c   3.25   3.25
     Never hinged   5.75
     On cover   75.00
     On cover, single franking   125.00
  a. Double surcharge   550.00 550.00
  b. Inverted surcharge 100.00 100.00
     Never hinged   160.00
     On cover   275.00
     On cover, single franking   295.00
115 A16   5c on 20c   4.00   4.00
     Never hinged   6.50
     On cover   150.00
     On cover, single franking   450.00
  a. Inverted surcharge 100.00 100.00
     Never hinged   160.00
116 A17   15c on 30c (#76) 16.00 16.00
     Never hinged   27.50
     On cover   100.00
     On cover, single franking   160.00
  a. Surcharge reading down 57.50 57.50
     Never hinged   90.00
117 A17   15c on 30c (#77) 22.50 22.50
     Never hinged   37.50
     On cover   125.00
     On cover, single franking   210.00
  a. Surcharge reading up   67.50 67.50
     Never hinged   120.00
118 A17   25c on 50c (#84) 325.00 350.00
     Never hinged   650.00
119 A17   25c on 50c (#85) 10.50 10.50
     Never hinged   18.00
     On cover   65.00
     On cover, single franking   110.00
  a. Double surcharge   400.00 400.00
  b. Surcharge reading down 47.50
     Never hinged   80.00
     Nos. 114-119 (6) 381.25 406.25

Stamps and Types of
1908-30 Surcharged

1924-27
120 A16   25c on 15c brn vio
          & rose ('25) .55   .55
     Never hinged   .80
     On cover   6.00
     On cover, single franking   9.00
121 A18   25c on 2fr gray &
          brn   .50   .50
     Never hinged   .65
     On cover   6.00
     On cover, single franking   9.00
122 A18   25c on 5fr org red &
          brn (Bl)   2.10   1.75
     Never hinged   3.00
     On cover   9.00
     On cover, single franking   14.00
123 A17   90c on 75c brn red
          & red ('27) 3.75   2.75
     Never hinged   5.75
     On cover   27.50
     On cover, single franking   45.00
124 A18   1.25fr on 1fr dk bl
          ('26)   1.10   1.00
     Never hinged   1.75
     On cover   24.00
     On cover, single franking   37.50
125 A18   1.50fr on 1fr dk bl &
          ultra ('27) 2.00   1.10
     Never hinged   2.75
     On cover   50.00
     On cover, single franking   125.00
126 A18   3fr on 5fr dl red &
          grn ('27)   3.00   3.00
     Never hinged   4.25
     On cover   55.00
     On cover, single franking   140.00
  a. Period after "F" omitted 13.50 13.50
     Never hinged   24.00
127 A18   10fr on 5fr dl grn &
          dp red ('27) 12.00 12.00
     Never hinged   19.00
     On cover   75.00
     On cover, single franking   175.00
  a. Period after "F" omitted 35.00 35.00
     Never hinged   57.50
128 A18   20fr on 5fr org brn &
          red vio ('27) 18.50 17.50
     Never hinged   27.50
     On cover   95.00
     On cover, single franking   200.00
  a. Period after "F" omitted 47.50 47.50
     Never hinged   75.00
     Nos. 120-128 (9) 43.50 40.15

Common Design Types
pictured following the introduction.

Colonial Exposition Issue
Common Design Types
1931, Apr. 13   Engr.   Perf. 12½
Name of Country in Black
129 CD70   40c deep green 5.25 5.25
     Never hinged   7.25
     On cover   37.50
     On cover, single franking   62.50
130 CD71   50c violet   5.25 5.25
     Never hinged   7.25
     On cover   30.00
     On cover, single franking   50.00
131 CD72   90c red orange 5.25 5.25
     Never hinged   7.25
     On cover   95.00
     On cover, single franking   140.00
132 CD73   1.50fr dull blue 5.25 5.25
     Never hinged   7.25
     On cover   80.00
     On cover, single franking   125.00
     Nos. 129-132 (4) 21.00 21.00

Village of Basse-Pointe — A19

Government Palace, Fort-de-
France — A20

Martinique
Women
A21

1933-40   Photo.   Perf. 13½
133 A19   1c red, *pink*   .25   .25
     Never hinged   .30
     On cover   27.50
     On cover, single franking   42.50
134 A20   2c dull blue   .25   .25
     Never hinged   .30
     On cover   27.50
     On cover, single franking   42.50
135 A20   3c sepia ('40)   .35   .35
     Never hinged   .40
     On cover   30.00
     On cover, single franking   50.00
136 A19   4c olive grn   .25   .25
     Never hinged   .30
     On cover   25.00
     On cover, single franking   37.50
137 A20   5c dp rose   .35   .35
     Never hinged   .45
     On cover   20.00
     On cover, single franking   30.00
138 A19   10c blk, *pink*   .35   .35
     Never hinged   .45
     On cover   15.00
     On cover, single franking   25.00
139 A20   15c blk, *org*   .35   .35
     Never hinged   .45
     On cover   15.00
     On cover, single franking   22.50
140 A21   20c org brn   .35   .35
     Never hinged   .45
     On cover   10.00
     On cover, single franking   15.00
141 A19   25c brn vio   .35   .35
     Never hinged   .45
     On cover   8.00
     On cover, single franking   10.00
142 A20   30c green   .50   .50
     Never hinged   .65
     On cover   8.00
     On cover, single franking   12.50
143 A20   30c lt ultra ('40) .40   .40
     Never hinged   .60
     On cover   20.00
     On cover, single franking   30.00
144 A21   35c dl grn ('38) 1.00   .90
     Never hinged   1.25
     On cover   10.00
     On cover, single franking   15.00
145 A21   40c olive brn   .65   .50
     Never hinged   .80
     On cover   5.00
     On cover, single franking   6.25
146 A20   45c dk brn   2.00   1.90
     Never hinged   2.40
     On cover   12.50
     On cover, single franking   19.00
147 A20   45c grn ('40)   .65   .65
     Never hinged   .80
     On cover   25.00
     On cover, single franking   37.50
148 A20   50c red   .50   .30
     Never hinged   .65
     On cover   5.00
     On cover, single franking   6.25
149 A19   55c brn red ('38) 1.30 1.00
     Never hinged   1.75
     On cover   10.00
     On cover, single franking   12.50
150 A19   60c lt bl ('40) .95   .95
     Never hinged   1.20
     On cover   20.00
     On cover, single franking   30.00
151 A21   65c red, *grn*   .50   .50
     Never hinged   .65
     On cover   7.50
     On cover, single franking   10.00
152 A21   70c brt red vio
          ('40)   .75   .75
     Never hinged   .95
     On cover   7.50
     On cover, single franking   12.50
153 A19   75c dk brn   1.10   .90
     Never hinged   2.10
     On cover   7.50
     On cover, single franking   25.00
154 A20   80c vio ('38)   .75   .65
     Never hinged   .90
     On cover   7.50
     On cover, single franking   12.50
155 A19   90c carmine   1.90   1.75
     Never hinged   2.25
     On cover   15.00
     On cover, single franking   25.00
156 A19   90c brt red vio
          ('39)   .95   .95
     Never hinged   1.25
     On cover   7.50
     On cover, single franking   12.50
157 A20   1fr blk, *grn*   1.90   1.40
     Never hinged   2.25
     On cover   12.50
     On cover, single franking   19.00
158 A20   1fr rose red ('38) .75   .65
     Never hinged   .90
     On cover   12.50
     On cover, single franking   21.00
159 A21   1.25fr dk vio   .80   .80
     Never hinged   1.20
     On cover   12.50
     On cover, single franking   30.00
160 A21   1.25fr dp rose ('39) .75   .75
     Never hinged   .95
     On cover   62.50
     On cover, single franking   100.00
161 A19   1.40fr lt ultra ('40) .80   .80
     Never hinged   1.20
     On cover   45.00
     On cover, single franking   87.50
162 A20   1.50fr dp bl   .65   .55
     Never hinged   .80
     On cover   15.00
     On cover, single franking   30.00

163 A20 1.60fr chnt ('40) .80 .80
  Never hinged 1.10
  On cover 45.00
  On cover, single franking 87.50
164 A21 1.75fr ol grn 9.50 5.25
  Never hinged 13.50
  On cover 50.00
  On cover, single franking 80.00
165 A21 1.75fr dp bl ('38) .75 .75
  Never hinged .90
  On cover 16.00
  On cover, single franking 37.50
166 A19 2fr dk bl,grn .50 .40
  Never hinged .65
  On cover 30.00
  On cover, single franking 50.00
167 A21 2.25fr blue ('39) .75 .75
  Never hinged .95
  On cover 55.00
  On cover, single franking 100.00
168 A19 2.50fr sepia ('40) .95 .95
  Never hinged 1.20
  On cover 55.00
  On cover, single franking 95.00
169 A21 3fr brn vio .65 .60
  Never hinged .80
  On cover 37.50
  On cover, single franking 67.50
170 A21 5fr red, pink 1.30 1.10
  Never hinged 1.60
  On cover 45.00
  On cover, single franking 75.00
171 A19 10fr dk bl, bl 1.10 .80
  Never hinged 1.40
  On cover 62.50
  On cover, single franking 100.00
172 A20 20fr red, yel 1.35 .95
  Never hinged 1.90
  On cover 80.00
  On cover, single franking 125.00
  Nos. 133-172 (40) 40.05 32.75

For surcharges see Nos. 190-195 in Scott Standard catalogue, Vol. 4.

Landing of Bélain d'Esnambuc — A22

Freed Slaves Paying Homage to Victor Schoelcher A23

1935, Oct. 22 Engr. Perf. 13
173 A22 40c blk brn 3.25 3.25
  Never hinged 4.50
  On cover 42.50
  On cover, single franking 67.50
174 A22 50c dl red 3.25 3.25
  Never hinged 4.50
  On cover 35.00
  On cover, single franking 57.50
175 A22 1.50fr ultra 12.00 12.00
  Never hinged 16.50
  On cover 95.00
  On cover, single franking 140.00
176 A23 1.75fr lil rose 12.00 12.00
  Never hinged 16.50
  On cover 80.00
  On cover, single franking 125.00
177 A23 5fr brown 12.00 12.00
  Never hinged 16.50
  On cover 80.00
  On cover, single franking 125.00
  a. 5fr ultramarine (error) 950.00
178 A23 10fr blue grn 9.50 9.50
  Never hinged 12.50
  On cover 105.00
  On cover, single franking 150.00
  Nos. 173-178 (6) 52.00 52.00

Tercentenary of French possessions in the West Indies.

Colonial Arts Exhibition Issue
Common Design Type
Souvenir Sheet
1937 Imperf.
179 CD74 3fr brt grn 8.75 10.50
  Never hinged 11.00
  On cover 140.00
  On cover, single franking 200.00
  a. "MARTINIQUE" omitted 3,100.
  b. Inscriptions inverted 2,200.
     Never hinged 3,250.

Paris International Exposition Issue
Common Design Types
1937, Apr. 15 Perf. 13
180 CD74 20c dp vio 2.10 2.10
  Never hinged 3.15
  On cover 50.00
  On cover, single franking 85.00
181 CD75 30c dk grn 1.75 1.75
  Never hinged 2.75
  On cover 42.50
  On cover, single franking 70.00

182 CD76 40c car rose 1.75 1.75
  Never hinged 2.75
  On cover 37.50
  On cover, single franking 62.50
183 CD77 50c dk brn & blk 1.60 1.60
  Never hinged 2.50
  On cover 40.00
  On cover, single franking 50.00
184 CD78 90c red 2.00 2.00
  Never hinged 3.00
  On cover 87.50
  On cover, single franking 160.00
185 CD79 1.50fr ultra 2.00 2.00
  Never hinged 3.00
  On cover 75.00
  On cover, single franking 140.00
  Nos. 180-185 (6) 11.20 11.20

New York World's Fair Issue
Common Design Type
1939, May 10 Perf. 12½x12
186 CD82 1.25fr car lake 1.10 1.10
  Never hinged 1.40
  On cover 62.50
  On cover, single franking 140.00
187 CD82 2.25fr ultra 1.25 1.25
  Never hinged 1.60
  On cover 62.50
  On cover, single franking 125.00

SEMI-POSTAL STAMPS

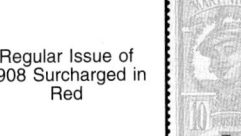

Regular Issue of 1908 Surcharged in Red

Perf. 13½x14
1915, May 15 Unwmk.
B1 A16 10c + 5c car & brn 2.75 2.00
  Never hinged 4.00
  On cover 110.00

Curie Issue
Common Design Type
1938, Oct. 24 Perf. 13
B2 CD80 1.75fr + 50c brt ultra 13.00 13.00
  Never hinged 17.50
  On cover 95.00
  On cover, single franking 160.00

French Revolution Issue
Common Design Type
Photo.; Name & Value Typo. in Black
1939, July 5
B3 CD83 45c + 25c grn 10.50 10.50
  Never hinged 15.00
  On cover 125.00
B4 CD83 70c + 30c brn 10.50 10.50
  Never hinged 15.00
  On cover 95.00
B5 CD83 90c + 35c red org 10.50 10.50
  Never hinged 15.00
  On cover 87.50
B6 CD83 1.25fr + 1fr rose pink 10.50 10.50
  Never hinged 15.00
  On cover 125.00
  On cover, single franking 200.00
B7 CD83 2.25fr + 2fr blue 10.50 10.50
  Never hinged 15.00
  On cover 110.00
  On cover, single franking 190.00
  Nos. B3-B7 (5) 52.50 52.50

POSTAGE DUE STAMPS

The set of 14 French Colonies postage due stamps (Nos. J1-J14) overprinted "MARTINIQUE" diagonally in red in 1887 was not an official issue.

Postage Due Stamps of France, 1893-1926 Overprinted

1927, Oct. 10 Perf. 14x13½
J15 D2 5c light blue 1.75 1.75
  Never hinged 2.75
  On cover 125.00
J16 D2 10c brown 2.10 2.00
  Never hinged 3.75
  On cover 125.00
J17 D2 20c olive green 2.10 2.00
  Never hinged 3.75
  On cover 125.00
J18 D2 25c rose 2.75 2.60
  Never hinged 4.75
  On cover 140.00
J19 D2 30c red 3.75 3.50
  Never hinged 6.00
  On cover 145.00
J20 D2 45c green 5.25 5.00
  Never hinged 8.00
  On cover 160.00
J21 D2 50c brn violet 6.50 6.00
  Never hinged 11.00
  On cover 165.00
J22 D2 60c blue green 6.50 6.00
  Never hinged 11.00
  On cover 175.00
J23 D2 1fr red brown 8.75 8.25
  Never hinged 14.50
  On cover 190.00
J24 D2 2fr bright vio 12.00 11.00
  Never hinged 19.00
  On cover 225.00
J25 D2 3fr magenta 13.00 12.00
  Never hinged 21.00
  On cover 250.00
  Nos. J15-J25 (11) 64.45 60.10

 Tropical Fruit — D3

1933, Feb. 15 Photo. Perf. 13½
J26 D3 5c dk bl, green .50 .50
  Never hinged .65
  On cover 95.00
J27 D3 10c orange brown .50 .50
  Never hinged .65
  On cover 80.00
J28 D3 20c dk blue .95 .95
  Never hinged 1.25
  On cover 80.00
J29 D3 25c red, pink 1.40 1.40
  Never hinged 1.75
  On cover 75.00
J30 D3 30c dk vio 1.40 1.40
  Never hinged 1.75
  On cover 75.00
J31 D3 45c red, yel 1.10 1.10
  Never hinged 1.40
  On cover 75.00
J32 D3 50c dk brn 1.75 1.75
  Never hinged 2.25
  On cover 75.00
J33 D3 60c dl grn 1.75 1.75
  Never hinged 2.25
  On cover 80.00
J34 D3 1fr blk, org 1.75 1.75
  Never hinged 2.25
  On cover 95.00
J35 D3 2fr dp rose 1.75 1.75
  Never hinged 2.25
  On cover 110.00
J36 D3 3fr dk blue, bl 1.75 1.75
  Never hinged 2.25
  On cover 125.00
  Nos. J26-J36 (11) 14.60 14.60

PARCEL POST STAMP

Postage Due Stamp of French Colonies Surcharged in Black

1903, Oct. Unwmk. Imperf.
Q1 D1 5fr on 60c brn, buff 550.00 675.00
  a. Inverted surcharge 875.00 950.00

MAURITANIA

mor-ə-ta-nē-ə

LOCATION — Northwestern Africa, bordering on the Atlantic Ocean
GOVT. — French Colony
AREA — 398,000 sq. mi.
POP. — 1,834,500 (est. 1984)
CAPITAL — Nouakchott
  100 Centimes = 1 Franc

 General Louis Faidherbe A1

 Oil Palms — A2

 Dr. Noel Eugène Ballay A3

Perf. 14x13½
1906-07 Typo. Unwmk.
"Mauritanie" in Red or Blue
1 A1 1c slate .80 .80
  Never hinged 1.50
  On cover 87.50
2 A1 2c chocolate 1.60 1.60
  Never hinged 2.50
  On cover 87.50
3 A1 4c choc, gray bl 2.40 2.00
  Never hinged 3.75
  On cover 87.50
4 A1 5c green 1.20 1.20
  Never hinged 2.25
  On cover 40.00
5 A1 10c carmine (B) 13.50 4.75
  Never hinged 26.00
  On cover 60.00
7 A2 20c black, azure 28.00 20.00
  Never hinged 50.00
  On cover 87.50
8 A2 25c blue, pnksh 8.75 7.25
  Never hinged 17.00
  On cover 50.00
9 A2 30c choc, pnksh 120.00 67.50
  Never hinged 215.00
  On cover 225.00
  On cover, single franking 350.00
10 A2 35c black, yellow 9.25 5.50
  Never hinged 17.00
  On cover 130.00
11 A2 40c car, az (B) 9.50 8.75
  Never hinged 18.00
  On cover 130.00
12 A2 45c choc, grnsh ('07) 10.50 8.75
  Never hinged 20.00
  On cover 130.00
13 A2 50c deep violet 9.50 8.00
  Never hinged 20.00
  On cover 130.00
14 A2 75c blue, org 8.75 9.50
  Never hinged 17.00
  On cover 95.00
  On cover, single franking 225.00
15 A3 1fr black, azure 28.00 30.00
  Never hinged 50.00
  On cover 150.00
  On cover, single franking 300.00
16 A3 2fr blue, pink 65.00 65.00
  Never hinged 135.00
  On cover 225.00
  On cover, single franking 400.00
17 A3 5fr car, straw (B) 160.00 160.00
  Never hinged 310.00
  On cover 475.00
  On cover, single franking 625.00
  Nos. 1-17 (16) 476.75 400.60

 Crossing Desert A4

1913-38
18 A4 1c brn vio & brn .30 .55
  Never hinged .55
  On cover 70.00
19 A4 2c black & blue .40 .65
  Never hinged .70
  On cover 70.00
20 A4 4c violet & blk .40 .65
  Never hinged .70
  On cover 70.00
21 A4 5c yel grn & bl grn 1.20 .80
  Never hinged 1.75
  On cover 27.50
  a. Chalky paper 3.00 2.25
     Never hinged 3.00
     On cover 37.50
22 A4 5c brn vio & rose ('22) .30 .40
  Never hinged .45
  On cover 25.00
23 A4 10c rose & red org 2.75 2.00
  Never hinged 4.75
  On cover 25.00

a.   Chalky paper   4.00   2.75
Never hinged   4.50
On cover   25.00
24   A4   10c yel grn & bl grn ('22)   .65   .80
Never hinged   .85
On cover   45.00
25   A4   10c lil rose, *bluish* ('25)   .50   .65
Never hinged   .80
On cover   47.50
26   A4   15c dk brn & blk ('17)   .80   .80
Never hinged   1.15
On cover   15.00
a.   Chalky paper   1.20   1.20
Never hinged   1.75
On cover   17.50
27   A4   20c bis brn & org   .80   .80
Never hinged   1.15
On cover   27.50
28   A4   25c blue & vio   1.60   1.20
Never hinged   2.50
On cover   27.50
On cover, single franking   75.00
29   A4   25c grn & rose ('22)   .40   .40
Never hinged   .50
On cover   10.00
30   A4   30c bl grn & rose   1.60   1.60
Never hinged   2.25
On cover   35.00
On cover, single franking   87.50
31   A4   30c rose & red org ('22)   2.00   2.40
Never hinged   2.50
On cover   37.50
On cover, single franking   75.00
32   A4   30c black & yel ('26)   .30   .40
Never hinged   .45
On cover   16.00
33   A4   30c bl grn & yel grn ('28)   1.60   1.60
Never hinged   2.15
On cover   37.50
34   A4   35c brown & vio   .90   .90
Never hinged   1.40
On cover   40.00
On cover, single franking   95.00
35   A4   35c dp grn & lt grn ('38)   1.60   1.60
Never hinged   2.15
On cover   45.00
36   A4   40c gray & bl grn   3.25   2.75
Never hinged   4.50
On cover   45.00
On cover, single franking   100.00
37   A4   45c org & bis brn   1.60   2.00
Never hinged   2.50
On cover   55.00
On cover, single franking   125.00
38   A4   50c brn vio & rose   1.20   1.60
Never hinged   1.75
On cover   62.50
On cover, single franking   140.00
39   A4   50c dk brn & ultra ('22)   .65   .80
Never hinged   .85
On cover   30.00
On cover, single franking   45.00
40   A4   50c gray grn & dp bl ('26)   .90   .90
Never hinged   1.40
On cover   10.00
41   A4   60c vio, *pnksh* ('25)   .80   1.20
Never hinged   1.15
On cover   27.50
On cover, single franking   80.00
42   A4   65c yel brn & lt bl ('26)   1.20   1.90
Never hinged   1.60
On cover   17.50
On cover, single franking   30.00
43   A4   75c ultra & brown   1.20   1.60
Never hinged   1.60
On cover   50.00
On cover, single franking   125.00
44   A4   85c myr grn & lt brn ('26)   1.10   1.75
Never hinged   1.75
On cover   35.00
On cover, single franking   100.00
45   A4   90c brn red & rose ('30)   2.40   2.40
Never hinged   4.00
On cover   50.00
On cover, single franking   95.00
46   A4   1fr rose & black   1.20   1.60
Never hinged   1.75
On cover   70.00
On cover, single franking   160.00
47   A4   1.10fr vio & ver ('28)   12.00   14.50
Never hinged   19.00
On cover   160.00
On cover, single franking   340.00
48   A4   1.25fr dk bl & blk brn ('33)   2.60   2.60
Never hinged   3.50
On cover   27.50
On cover, single franking   87.50
49   A4   1.50fr lt bl & dp bl ('30)   1.60   1.60
Never hinged   2.50
On cover   45.00
On cover, single franking   80.00
50   A4   1.75fr bl grn & brn red ('33)   2.10   2.10
Never hinged   3.00
On cover   22.50
On cover, single franking   35.00
51   A4   1.75fr dk bl & ultra ('38)   2.40   2.40
Never hinged   3.00
On cover   45.00
On cover, single franking   75.00
52   A4   2fr red org & vio   2.00   2.40
Never hinged   3.25
On cover   80.00
On cover, single franking   175.00
53   A4   3fr red violet ('30)   2.40   2.40
Never hinged   3.50
On cover   62.50
On cover, single franking   140.00

54   A4   5fr violet & blue   3.50   *4.50*
Never hinged   5.75
On cover   105.00
On cover, single franking   225.00
Nos. 18-54 (37)   62.20   69.20

Stamp and Type of 1913-38 Srchd.

1922-25
55   A4   60c on 75c violet, *pnksh*   1.20   *1.60*
Never hinged   1.75
On cover   21.00
On cover, single franking   35.00
56   A4   65c on 15c dk brn & blk ('25)   2.00   *2.40*
Never hinged   3.00
On cover   62.50
On cover, single franking   140.00
57   A4   85c on 75c ultra & brn ('25)   2.00   *2.40*
Never hinged   3.00
On cover   45.00
On cover, single franking   87.50
Nos. 55-57 (3)   5.20   6.40

Type of 1913-38 Srchd.

1924-27
58   A4   25c on 2fr red org & vio   1.20   1.60
Never hinged   1.75
On cover   10.00
a.   Left bars and "2" omitted   400.00
Never hinged   600.00
59   A4   90c on 75c brn red & cer ('27)   2.75   *3.25*
Never hinged   4.50
On cover   50.00
On cover, single franking   87.50
60   A4   1.25fr on 1fr dk bl & ultra ('26)   .80   *.80*
Never hinged   .90
On cover   55.00
On cover, single franking   105.00
61   A4   1.50fr on 1fr bl & dp bl ('27)   1.60   *2.00*
Never hinged   2.75
On cover   45.00
On cover, single franking   75.00
62   A4   3fr on 5fr ol brn & red vio ('27)   7.25   8.00
Never hinged   12.50
On cover   95.00
On cover, single franking   190.00
63   A4   10fr on 5fr mag & bl grn ('27)   7.25   9.00
Never hinged   12.50
On cover   105.00
On cover, single franking   225.00
64   A4   20fr on 5fr bl vio & dp org ('27)   8.50   *9.25*
Never hinged   13.00
On cover   120.00
On cover, single franking   250.00
a.   Period after "F" omitted   26.00   26.00
Never hinged   45.00
Nos. 58-64 (7)   29.35   33.90

Common Design Types pictured following the introduction.

Colonial Exposition Issue
Common Design Types
Engr.; Name of Country Typo. in Black

1931, Apr. 13   **Perf. 12½**
65   CD70   40c deep green   8.00   8.00
Never hinged   13.00
On cover   110.00
66   CD71   50c violet   5.50   5.50
Never hinged   7.75
On cover   95.00
67   CD72   90c red orange   5.50   5.50
Never hinged   7.75
On cover   165.00
On cover, single franking   240.00
68   CD73   1.50fr dull blue   5.50   5.50
Never hinged   9.00
On cover   150.00
On cover, single franking   225.00
Nos. 65-68 (4)   24.50   24.50

Paris International Exposition Issue
Common Design Types

1937, Apr. 15   **Perf. 13**
69   CD74   20c deep violet   2.00   2.00
Never hinged   3.25
70   CD75   30c dark green   2.00   2.00
Never hinged   3.25
On cover   95.00

71   CD76   40c carmine rose   2.00   2.00
Never hinged   3.25
On cover   75.00
72   CD77   50c dk brn & blk   1.60   1.60
Never hinged   2.75
On cover   70.00
73   CD78   90c red   1.60   1.60
Never hinged   2.75
On cover   105.00
On cover, single franking   175.00
74   CD79   1.50fr ultra   2.00   2.00
Never hinged   3.25
On cover   95.00
On cover, single franking   160.00
Nos. 69-74 (6)   11.20   11.20

Colonial Arts Exhibition Issue
Common Design Type
Souvenir Sheet

1937   *Imperf.*
75   CD76   3fr dark blue   8.75   *10.50*
Never hinged   14.00
On cover   125.00
On cover, single franking   190.00
a.   Marginal inscription inverted   1,100.
Never hinged   1,500.

Camel Rider — A5

Mauri Couple — A8

Mauris on Camels A6

Family Before Tent — A7

1938-40   **Perf. 13**
76   A5   2c violet blk   .30   .30
Never hinged   .45
On cover   35.00
77   A5   3c dp ultra   .30   .30
Never hinged   .45
On cover   35.00
78   A5   4c rose violet   .30   .30
Never hinged   .45
On cover   35.00
79   A5   5c orange red   .30   .30
Never hinged   .45
On cover   27.50
80   A5   10c brown car   .40   .40
Never hinged   .55
On cover   27.50
81   A5   15c dk violet   .40   .40
Never hinged   .55
On cover   22.50
82   A6   20c red   .40   .40
Never hinged   .55
On cover   9.75
83   A6   25c deep ultra   .50   .50
Never hinged   .70
On cover   12.50
84   A6   30c deep brown   .30   .30
Never hinged   .45
On cover   8.25
85   A6   35c Prus green   .80   .80
Never hinged   1.25
On cover   27.50
86   A6   40c rose car ('40)   .30   .30
Never hinged   .45
On cover   14.50
87   A6   45c Prus grn ('40)   .40   .40
Never hinged   .55
On cover   30.00
88   A6   50c purple   .55   .55
Never hinged   .70
On cover   16.00
89   A7   55c rose violet   1.00   1.20
Never hinged   1.40
On cover   40.00
90   A7   60c violet ('40)   .55   .55
Never hinged   .75
On cover   25.00
91   A7   65c deep green   1.00   1.20
Never hinged   1.40
On cover   40.00
92   A7   70c red ('40)   .90   .90
Never hinged   1.10
On cover   27.50
93   A7   80c deep blue   1.40   1.50
Never hinged   1.75
On cover   45.00

94   A7   90c rose violet ('39)   .90   .90
Never hinged   1.25
On cover   45.00
On cover, single franking   100.00
95   A7   1fr red   2.40   2.40
Never hinged   3.25
On cover   40.00
On cover, single franking   75.00
96   A7   1fr dp green ('40)   .95   .95
Never hinged   1.40
On cover   7.50
97   A7   1.25fr rose car ('39)   1.50   1.50
Never hinged   2.25
On cover   62.50
On cover, single franking   125.00
98   A7   1.40fr dp blue ('40)   .95   .95
Never hinged   1.40
On cover   45.00
On cover, single franking   100.00
99   A7   1.50fr violet   .95   .95
Never hinged   1.40
On cover   40.00
On cover, single franking   105.00
99A   A7   1.50fr red brn ('40)   110.00   110.00
Never hinged   160.00
On cover   350.00
100   A7   1.60fr black brn ('40)   2.00   2.00
Never hinged   2.40
On cover   45.00
On cover, single franking   105.00
101   A8   1.75fr deep ultra   1.50   *1.60*
Never hinged   2.00
On cover   40.00
On cover, single franking   105.00
102   A8   2fr rose violet   .95   *1.00*
Never hinged   1.10
On cover   27.50
On cover, single franking   50.00
103   A8   2.25fr dull ultra ('39)   .80   .80
Never hinged   1.10
On cover   55.00
On cover, single franking   110.00
104   A8   2.50fr black brn ('40)   1.10   1.10
Never hinged   1.40
On cover   35.00
On cover, single franking   70.00
105   A8   3fr deep green   .90   *1.00*
Never hinged   1.10
On cover   45.00
On cover, single franking   80.00
106   A8   5fr scarlet   1.00   *1.20*
Never hinged   1.40
On cover   45.00
On cover, single franking   87.50
107   A8   10fr deep brown   1.90   *2.10*
Never hinged   2.75
On cover   55.00
On cover, single franking   105.00
108   A8   20fr brown car   2.25   *2.60*
Never hinged   2.75
On cover   70.00
On cover, single franking   120.00
Nos. 76-108 (34)   140.15   141.65

Nos. 91 and 109 surcharged with new values are listed under French West Africa.
For surcharges see Nos. B9-B12 in Scott Standard catalogue, Vol. 4.

Caillie Issue
Common Design Type

1939, Apr. 5   **Engr.**   **Perf. 12½x12**
109   CD81   90c org brn & org   1.10   1.10
Never hinged   1.50
On cover   11.00
110   CD81   2fr brt violet   1.40   1.40
Never hinged   1.90
On cover   27.50
On cover, single franking   50.00
111   CD81   2.25fr ultra & dk bl   1.40   1.40
Never hinged   1.90
On cover   35.00
On cover, single franking   55.00
Nos. 109-111 (3)   3.90   3.90

New York World's Fair Issue
Common Design Type

1939, May 10
112   CD82   1.25fr carmine lake   .80   .80
Never hinged   1.20
On cover   75.00
On cover, single franking   160.00
113   CD82   2.25fr ultra   .80   .80
Never hinged   1.20
On cover   75.00
On cover, single franking   145.00

SEMI-POSTAL STAMPS

Nos. 23 and 26 Surcharged in Red

1915-18   **Unwmk.**   **Perf. 14x13½**
B1   A4   10c + 5c rose & red org   2.00   *2.40*
Never hinged   3.25
On cover   60.00
a.   Double surcharge   225.00
Never hinged   350.00
B2   A4   15c + 5c dk brn & blk ('18)   2.00   *2.40*
Never hinged   3.25
On cover   60.00
a.   Double surcharge   210.00

	Never hinged	350.00	
b.	Inverted surcharge	170.00	
	Never hinged	275.00	

Curie Issue
Common Design Type

1938, Oct. 24   *Perf. 13*

B3	CD80	1.75fr + 50c brt ul-tra	8.75	8.75
	Never hinged		14.50	
	On cover			100.00
	On cover, single franking			170.00

French Revolution Issue
Common Design Type

**Photo.; Name and Value
Typographed in Black**

1939, July 5   Unwmk.

B4	CD83	45c + 25c grn	9.50	9.50
	Never hinged		15.00	
	On cover			160.00
B5	CD83	70c + 30c brn	9.50	9.50
	Never hinged		15.00	
	On cover			120.00
B6	CD83	90c + 35c red org	9.50	9.50
	Never hinged		15.00	
	On cover			100.00
B7	CD83	1.25fr + 1fr rose pink	9.50	9.50
	Never hinged		15.00	
	On cover			170.00
	On cover, single franking			250.00
B8	CD83	2.25fr + 2fr bl	9.50	9.50
	Never hinged		15.00	
	On cover			160.00
	On cover, single franking			225.00
	Nos. B4-B8 (5)		47.50	47.50

AIR POST STAMPS

Common Design Type
Perf. 12½x12

1940, Feb. 8   Engr.   Unwmk.

C1	CD85	1.90fr ultra	.55	.55
	Never hinged		.70	
	On cover			37.50
C2	CD85	2.90fr dk red	.55	.55
	Never hinged		.70	
	On cover			37.50
a.	"MAURITANIE" double		150.00	
	Never hinged		225.00	
C3	CD85	4.50fr dk gray grn	.70	.70
	Never hinged		.90	
	On cover			45.00
C4	CD85	4.90fr yel bister	1.00	1.00
	Never hinged		1.25	
	On cover			50.00
a.	"MAURITANIE" inverted		225.00	
	Never hinged		300.00	
C5	CD85	6.90fr deep org	1.10	1.10
	Never hinged		1.50	
	On cover			62.50
	Nos. C1-C5 (5)		3.90	3.90

POSTAGE DUE STAMPS

D1

D2

Perf. 14x13½

1906-07   Unwmk.   Typo.

J1	D1	5c grn, *grnsh*	2.75	2.75
	Never hinged		4.25	
	On cover			200.00
J2	D1	10c red brn	4.50	4.50
	Never hinged		7.75	
	On cover			200.00
J3	D1	15c dk bl	8.75	8.00
	Never hinged		18.50	
	On cover			200.00
J4	D1	20c blk, *yellow*	11.00	9.50
	Never hinged		24.00	
	On cover			200.00
J5	D1	30c red, *straw*	13.00	12.00
	Never hinged		28.00	
	On cover			200.00

J6	D1	50c violet	20.00	19.00
	Never hinged		42.50	
	On cover			200.00
J7	D1	60c blk, *buff*	14.50	13.50
	Never hinged		28.00	
	On cover			200.00
J8	D1	1fr blk, *pinkish*	22.00	18.50
	Never hinged		50.00	
	On cover			200.00
	Nos. J1-J8 (8)		96.50	87.75

Issue dates: 20c, 1906; others 1907.
Regular postage stamps canceled "T" in a triangle were used for postage due.

1914

J9	D2	5c green	.25	.40
	Never hinged		.40	
	On cover			150.00
J10	D2	10c rose	.30	.55
	Never hinged		.55	
	On cover			150.00
J11	D2	15c gray	.50	.70
	Never hinged		.85	
	On cover			150.00
J12	D2	20c brown	.50	.70
	Never hinged		.85	
	On cover			150.00
J13	D2	30c blue	.80	1.20
	Never hinged		1.40	
	On cover			150.00
J14	D2	50c black	1.50	2.00
	Never hinged		2.25	
	On cover			150.00
J15	D2	60c orange	1.30	1.60
	Never hinged		1.75	
	On cover			150.00
J16	D2	1fr violet	1.30	1.60
	Never hinged		1.75	
	On cover			150.00
	Nos. J9-J16 (8)		6.45	8.75

Type of 1914 Issue
Surcharged

1927, Oct. 10

J17	D2	2fr on 1fr lil rose	3.50	3.50
	Never hinged		5.75	
a.	Period after "F" omitted		16.00	17.50
	Never hinged		27.50	
J18	D2	3fr on 1fr org brn	3.75	4.50
	Never hinged		5.75	

MAURITIUS

mo-'ri-sh ē-əs

LOCATION — Island in the Indian Ocean about 550 miles east of Madagascar
GOVT. — British Colony
AREA — 720 sq. mi.
POP. — 969,191 (est. 1983)

CAPITAL — Port Louis

12 Pence = 1 Shilling
100 Cents = 1 Rupee (1878)

Nos. 1-6, 14-17 unused are valued without gum.

Nos. 3a-8, 14-15 are printed on fragile paper with natural irregularities which might be mistaken for faults.

Very fine examples of Nos. 22-58 will have perforations touching the design on one or more sides. Examples with perfs clear on four sides are scarce and will sell for more. Inferior examples will sell for much reduced prices.

> **Catalogue values for unused stamps in this country are for Never Hinged stamps, beginning with Scott 223 in the regular postage section, Scott J1 in the postage due section.**

Queen Victoria
A1   A2

1847   Unwmk.   Engr.   *Imperf.*

1	A1	1p orange	1,250,000.	1,150,000.
2	A1	2p dark blue		1,700,000.

Nos. 1 and 2 were engraved and printed in Port Louis. There is but one type of each value. The initials "J. B." on the bust are those of the engraver, J. Barnard.

All unused examples of the 2p are in museums. There is one unused example of the 1p in private hands. There are two used examples of the 1p in private hands, both of which have small faults and are valued thus.

Earliest Impressions

1848   **Thick Yellowish Paper**

3	A2	1p orange	62,500.	18,000.
4	A2	2p dark blue	57,500.	23,000.
d.	"PENOE"	115,000.	40,000.

Early Impressions
Yellowish White Paper

3a	A2	1p orange	29,000.	7,250.
4a	A2	2p blue	31,000.	8,000.
e.	"PENOE"	57,500.	14,500.

Bluish Paper

5	A2	1p orange	29,000.	7,250.
6	A2	2p blue	31,000.	8,000.
c.	"PENOE"	57,500.	14,500.

Intermediate Impressions
Yellowish White Paper

3b	A2	1p red orange	19,000.	2,850.
4b	A2	2p blue	19,000.	3,750.
f.	"PENOE"	31,500.	7,250.

Bluish Paper

5a	A2	1p red orange	18,500.	2,900.
6a	A2	2p blue	19,000.	3,750.
d.	"PENOE"	32,500.	7,250.
f.	Double impression		

Worn Impressions
Yellowish White Paper

3c	A2	1p orange red	6,750.	900.
d.	1p brownish red	6,750.	900.
4c	A2	2p blue	8,500.	1,550.
g.	"PENOE"	11,000.	3,150.

Bluish Paper

5b	A2	1p orange red	6,250.	850.
c.	1p brownish red	6,250.	850.
d.	Double impression		
6b	A2	2p blue	8,250.	1,450.
e.	"PENOE"	12,500.	3,000.

**Latest Impressions
Yellowish or Grayish Paper**

3e	A2	1p orange red	5,250.	725.
f.	1p brownish red	5,250.	725.
4h	A2	2p blue	6,250.	1,050.
i.	"PENOE"	11,500.	2,000.

Bluish Paper

5e	A2	1p orange red	5,250.	725.
f.	1p brownish red	5,250.	725.
6g	A2	2p blue	6,250.	1,050.
h.	"PENOE"	11,500.	2,000.

These stamps were printed in sheets of twelve, four rows of three, and each position differs in details. The "PENOE" error is the most pronounced variety on the plates and is from position 7.

The stamps were in use until 1859. Earliest impressions, Nos. 3-4, show the full background of diagonal and vertical lines with the diagonal lines predominant. Early impressions, Nos. 3a-4a, 5-6, show the full background with the vertical lines predominating. As the plate became worn the vertical lines disappeared, giving the intermediate impressions, Nos. 3b-4b, 5a-6a.

Worn impressions, Nos. 3c-4c, 5b-6b, have little background remaining, and latest impressions, Nos. 3e-4h, 5e-6g, have also lost details of the frame and head. The paper of the early impressions is usually rather thick, that of the worn impressions rather thin. Expect natural fibrous inclusions in the paper of all impressions.

"Britannia"
A3   A4

1849-58

7	A3	red brown, *blue*	26.00	
8	A3	blue ('58)	9.00	

Nos. 7-8 were never placed in use.

1858-59

9	A3	(4p) green, *bluish*	550.00	240.00
10	A3	(6p) red	57.50	*125.00*
11	A3	(9p) magenta ('59)	850.00	240.00
a.	Used as 1p ('62)		200.00

No. 11 was re-issued in Nov. 1862, as a 1p stamp (No. 11a). When used as such it is always canceled "B53." Price so used, $200.

1858   **Black Surcharge**

12	A4	4p green, *bluish*	1,650.	525.00

Queen Victoria — A5

1859, Mar.   **Early Impressions**

14	A5	2p blue, *grayish*	12,500.	2,900.
a.	2p deep blue, *grayish*	14,500.	3,400.
14B	A5	2p blue, *bluish*	12,500.	2,900.
c.	Intermediate impression	8,000.	1,250.
d.	Worn impression	4,250.	850.00

Type A5 was engraved by Lapirot, in Port Louis, and was printed locally. There were twelve varieties in the sheet.

Early impressions have clear and distinct background lines. In the intermediate impressions, the lines are somewhat blurred, and white patches appear. In the worn impressions, the background lines are discontinuous, with many white patches. Analogous wear is also obvious in the background of the inscriptions on all four sides. Values depend on the state of wear. One should expect natural fibrous inclusions in the paper on all printings.

A6

A7

1859, Oct.
15   A6   2p blue, *bluish*   190,000.   11,000.

No. 15 was printed from the plate of the 1848 issue after it had been entirely re-engraved by Sherwin. It is commonly known as the "fillet head." The plate of the 1p, 1848, was also re-engraved but was never put in use.

1859, Dec.   Litho.   Laid Paper
16   A7   1p vermilion   8,000.   1,350.
   a.   1p deep red   13,500.   2,350.
   b.   1p red   10,000.   1,675.
17   A7   2p pale blue   4,500.   850.
   a.   2p slate blue   8,500.   1,250.
   b.   2p blue   5,000.   950.

Lithographed locally by Dardenne.

"Britannia" — A8

1859   Wove Paper   Engr.   Imperf.
18   A8   6p blue   800.00   57.50
19   A8   1sh vermilion   3,150.   62.50

1861
20   A8   6p gray violet   37.50   67.50
21   A8   1sh green   675.00   160.00

1862   Perf. 14 to 16
22   A8   6p slate   34.00   110.00
   a.   Horiz. pair, imperf between   8,500.
23   A8   1sh deep green   2,900.   400.00

Following the change in currency in 1878, a number of issues denominated in sterling were overprinted "CANCELLED" in serifed type and sold as remainders.

A9

A10

1860-63   Typo.   Perf. 14
24   A9   1p brown lilac   375.00   37.50
25   A9   2p blue   400.00   60.00
26   A9   4p rose   400.00   42.50
27   A9   6p green ('62)   1,050.   175.00
28   A9   6p lilac ('63)   425.00   125.00
29   A9   9p dull lilac   190.00   50.00
   Overprinted "CANCELLED"   120.00
30   A9   1sh buff ('62)   400.00   100.00
31   A9   1sh green ('63)   900.00   200.00

For surcharges see Nos. 43-45.

1863-72   Wmk. 1
32   A9   1p lilac brown   85.00   17.50
   Overprinted "CANCELLED"   60.00
   a.   1p bister brown   160.00   17.00
   b.   1p brown   110.00   13.00
33   A9   2p blue   100.00   13.00
   Overprinted "CANCELLED"   70.00
   a.   Imperf., pair   1,950.   2,350.
34   A9   3p vermilion   90.00   20.00
   Overprinted "CANCELLED"   42.50
   a.   3p deep red   190.00   32.50
35   A9   4p rose   100.00   4.00
   Overprinted "CANCELLED"   80.00
36   A9   6p lilac ('64)   425.00   45.00
37   A9   6p blue grn ('65)   235.00   7.25
   Overprinted "CANCELLED"   110.00
   a.   6p yellow green ('65)   285.00   16.75
38   A9   9p green ('72)   200.00   375.00
39   A9   1sh org yel ('64)   365.00   29.00
   Overprinted "CANCELLED"   165.00
   a.   1sh yellow   285.00   14.50
40   A9   1sh blue ('70)   155.00   28.50
41   A9   5sh red violet   260.00   65.00
   Overprinted "CANCELLED"   145.00

---

   a.   5sh bright violet   325.00   65.00
   Overprinted "CANCELLED"   180.00
   Nos. 32-41 (10)   2,015.   604.25

For surcharges see Nos. 48-49, 51-58, 87.

1872
42   A10   10p claret   375.00   57.50
   Overprinted "CANCELLED"   110.00

For surcharges see Nos. 46-47.

No. 29 Surcharged in Black or Red

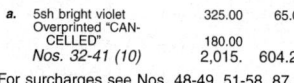

HALF PENNY   ½ d   HALF PENNY
     a   b

1876   Unwmk.
43   A9(a)   ½p on 9p   24.00   22.00
   Overprinted "CANCELLED"   11.00
   a.   Inverted surcharge   800.00
   b.   Double surcharge   2,350.
44   A9(b)   ½p on 9p   5,000.
   Overprinted "CANCELLED"   325.00
45   A9(b)   ½p on 9p (R)   3,400.
   Overprinted "CANCELLED"   140.00
   a.   "PRNNY" instead of "PENNY"   140.00

Nos. 44 and 45 were never placed in use. No. 45 is valued with perfs cutting into the design.

Stamps of 1863-72 Surcharged in Black

HALF PENNY   One Penny
   c   d

1876-77   Wmk. 1
46   A10(a)   ½p on 10p claret   4.25   27.50
47   A10(c)   ½p on 10p cl ('77)   10.00   47.50
   Overprinted "CANCELLED"   4.75
48   A9(d)   1p on 4p rose ('77)   23.00   25.00
49   A9(d)   1sh on 5sh red vio ('77)   340.00   125.00
   Overprinted "CANCELLED"   60.00
   a.   1sh on 5sh violet ('77)   340.00   160.00
   Overprinted "CANCELLED"   50.00
   Nos. 46-49 (4)   377.25   225.00

A16

1878   Black Surcharge
50   A16   2c claret   15.50   10.00

Stamps and Type of 1863-72 Surcharged in Black — e

51   A9   4c on 1p bister brn   25.00   9.00
52   A9   8c on 2p blue   90.00   4.00
53   A9   13c on 3p org red   24.00   45.00
54   A9   17c on 4p rose   200.00   4.25
55   A9   25c on 6p sl blue   290.00   7.75
56   A9   38c on 9p violet   45.00   100.00
57   A9   50c on 1sh green   100.00   4.75
58   A9   2r50c on 5sh violet   20.00   24.00
   Nos. 50-58 (9)   809.50   208.75

For surcharge see No. 87.

A18

A19

A20   A21

A22   A23

A24   A25

A26

1879-80   Wmk. 1
59   A18   2c red brn ('80)   55.00   25.00
60   A19   4c orange   72.50   4.25
61   A20   8c blue ('80)   37.50   4.50
62   A21   13c slate ('80)   175.00   325.00
63   A22   17c rose ('80)   90.00   9.50
64   A23   25c bister   475.00   17.00
65   A24   38c violet ('80)   200.00   375.00
66   A25   50c green ('80)   5.25   4.50
67   A26   2r50c brn vio ('80)   57.50   85.00
   Nos. 59-67 (9)   1,167.   849.75

Nos. 59-67 are known imperforate.
For surcharges & overprints see #76-78, 83-86, 122-123.

1882-93   Wmk. 2
68   A18   1c violet ('93)   2.10   .55
   Overprinted "SPECIMEN"   95.00
69   A18   2c red brown   38.50   6.00
70   A18   2c green ('85)   4.25   .75
   Overprinted "SPECIMEN"   95.00
71   A19   4c orange   95.00   5.25
72   A19   4c rose ('85)   4.50   1.25
   Overprinted "SPECIMEN"   95.00
73   A20   8c blue ('91)   4.25   1.80
74   A23   25c bister ('83)   11.50   3.75
75   A25   50c dp orange ('87)   42.50   18.00
   Overprinted "SPECIMEN"   100.00
   Nos. 68-75 (8)   202.60   37.35

For surcharges and overprint see #88-89, 121.

Nos. 63 and Type of 1882 Surcharged in Black

16 CENTS   SIXTEEN CENTS
   f   g

1883   Wmk. 1
Surcharge Measures 14x3½mm
76   A22(f)   16c on 17c rose   180.00   60.00
   a.   Double surcharge   2,900.
Surcharge Measures 15½x3½mm
77   A22(f)   16c on 17c rose   190.00   60.00
   a.   Double surcharge   3,150.
   b.   Horiz. pair (#76, #77)   850.00   750.00
Surcharge Measures 15½x2¾mm
78   A22(f)   16c on 17c rose   375.00   135.00
Wmk. 2
79   A22(g)   16c on 17c rose   115.00   2.40
   Nos. 76-79 (4)   860.00   257.40

Queen Victoria — A29

1885-94
80   A29   15c orange brown ('92)   9.00   1.50
81   A29   15c blue ('94)   10.00   1.50
82   A29   16c orange brown   9.50   2.75
   Nos. 80-82 (3)   28.50   5.75
   Set of 3, ovptd "SPECIMEN"   345.00

For surcharges see Nos. 90, 116.

Various Stamps Surcharged in Black or Red

2 CENTS   2 CENTS
   h   j

1885-87   Wmk. 1
83   A24(h)   2c on 38c violet   170.00   47.50
   a.   Inverted surcharge   1,250.   1,000.
   b.   Double surcharge   1,350.
   c.   Without bar   275.00
84   A21(j)   2c on 13c sl (R) ('87)   80.00   130.00
   a.   Inverted surcharge   260.00   300.00
   b.   Double surcharge   975.00   850.00
   c.   As "b," one on back   1,000.
   d.   Double surcharge, both inverted   1,750.

TWO CENTS   TWO CENTS
                 38 CENTS
   k   l

1891
85   A22(k)   2c on 17c rose   145.00   155.00
   a.   Inverted surcharge   575.00   —
   b.   Double surcharge   950.00   950.00
86   A24(k)   2c on 38c vio   10.50   14.50
   a.   Double surcharge   240.00   260.00
   b.   Dbl. surch., one invtd   260.00   300.00
   c.   Inverted surcharge   1,250.   —
87   A9(e+l)   2c on 38c on 9p vio   12.50   6.75
   a.   Double surcharge   850.00   850.00
   b.   Inverted surcharge   625.00   —
   c.   Dbl. surch., one invtd   200.00   225.00

Wmk. 2
88   A19(k)   2c on 4c rose   1.80   .85
   a.   Double surcharge   95.00   90.00
   b.   Inverted surcharge   90.00   —
   c.   Dbl. surch., one invtd   95.00   90.00
   Nos. 85-88 (4)   169.80   177.10

ONE CENT   ONE CENT
   m   n

1893, Jan.
89   A18(m)   1c on 2c violet   2.75   1.35
   Overprinted "SPECIMEN"   37.50
90   A29(n)   1c on 16c org brown   2.75   4.00

Coat of Arms — A38

1895-1904   Wmk. 2
91   A38   1c lilac & ultra   .90   1.80
92   A38   1c gray blk & black   .60   .25
93   A38   2c lilac & orange   6.75   .60
94   A38   2c dull lil & vio   1.00   .25
95   A38   3c lilac   .85   .60
96   A38   3c grn & scar, *yel*   4.50   1.50
97   A38   4c lilac & green   4.50   .60
98   A38   4c dull lil & car, *yel*   1.80   .50
99   A38   4c gray green & pur   1.90   2.40

100	A38	4c black & car, blue	16.00	.75
101	A38	5c lilac & vio, *buff*	10.00	85.00
102	A38	5c lilac & blk, *buff*	3.00	3.00
103	A38	6c grn & rose	5.75	5.00
104	A38	6c violet & scar, red	3.50	1.00
105	A38	8c gray grn & blk, *buff*	4.00	12.50
106	A38	12c black & car rose	2.75	2.75
107	A38	15c grn & org	26.00	10.00
108	A38	15c blk & ultra, blue	65.00	1.50
109	A38	18c gray grn & ultra	19.00	4.25
110	A38	25c grn & car, *grn*, chalky paper	5.00	25.00
a.		Ordinary paper ('02)	22.50	37.50
111	A38	50c green, *yel*	20.00	80.00
		Nos. 91-111 (21)	202.80	239.25
		Set of 21, ovptd "SPECIMEN"	600.00	

The 25c is on both ordinary and chalky paper. Ornaments in lower panel omitted on #106-111.

Year of issue: #103, 107, 1899; #92, 94, 98, 1900; #96, 99, 101-102, 104-106, 110-111, 1902; #100, 108, 1904; others, 1895.

See #128-135. For surcharges and overprints see #113, 114, 117-120.

Diamond Jubilee Issue

Arms
A39

1898, May 23   Wmk. 46

112	A39	36c brown org & ultra	13.00	25.00
		Overprinted "SPECIMEN"	55.00	

60th year of Queen Victoria's reign.
For surcharges see Nos. 114 and 127.

No. 109 Surcharged in Red

1899   Wmk. 2

113	A38	6c on 18c	1.50	1.20
a.		Inverted surcharge	725.00	340.00

No. 112 Surcharged in Blue

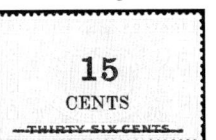

Wmk. 46

114	A39	15c on 36c	3.00	2.10
a.		Without bar	525.00	

Admiral Mahe de
La Bourdonnais
A40

1899, Dec.   Engr.   Wmk. 1

115	A40	15c ultra	30.00	5.00
		Overprinted "SPECIMEN"	85.00	

Birth bicent. of Admiral Mahe de La Bourdonnais, governor of Mauritius, 1734-46.

No. 82 Surcharged in Black

1900   Wmk. 2

116	A29	4c on 16c orange brown	13.50	24.00

No. 109 Surcharged in Black — r

1902

117	A38	12c on 18c grn & ultra	3.00	9.00

Preceding Issues Overprinted in Black

1902

118	A38	4c lilac & car, yel	1.50	.35
119	A38	6c green & rose	1.50	3.25
120	A38	15c green & org	6.25	1.35
121	A23	25c bister	8.00	3.25

Wmk. 1

122	A25	50c green	20.00	6.25
123	A26	2r50c brown violet	135.00	225.00
		Nos. 118-123 (6)	172.25	239.45

Coat of
Arms — A41

1902   Wmk. 1

124	A41	1r blk & car rose	62.50	60.00

Wmk. 2 Sideways

125	A41	2r50c grn & blk, *bl*	35.00	160.00
126	A41	5r blk & car, *red*	100.00	170.00
		Nos. 124-126 (3)	197.50	390.00
		Set of 3, ovptd "SPECIMEN"	145.00	

No. 112 Surcharged type "r" but with longer bar

1902   Wmk. 46

127	A39	12c on 36c	2.00	1.50
a.		Inverted surcharge	775.00	525.00

Arms Type of 1895-1904

1904-07   Wmk. 3   Chalky Paper

128	A38	1c gray blk & black ('07)	8.75	5.00
129	A38	2c dl lil & vio ('05)	34.00	10.50
130	A38	3c grn & scar, yel	22.50	10.50
131	A38	4c blk & car, blue	15.00	.25
132	A38	6c vio & scar, red ('06)	12.50	.35
133	A38	15c blk & ultra, *bl*	4.50	.40
135	A38	50c green, *yel*	3.00	5.25
136	A41	1r black & car rose ('07)	47.50	65.00
		Nos. 128-136 (8)	147.75	88.75

The 2c, 4c, 6c also exist on ordinary paper. Ornaments in lower panel omitted on 15c and 50c.

Arms — A42   Edward VII — A43

1910   Wmk. 3   Ordinary Paper

137	A42	1c black	3.25	.30
138	A42	2c brown	3.00	.25
139	A42	3c green	3.25	.25
140	A42	4c ol grn & rose	4.00	.25
141	A42	5c gray & rose	3.00	3.25
142	A42	6c carmine	5.25	.25
a.		A42 6c pale red	9.00	2.40
143	A42	8c brown orange	3.25	1.60
144	A43	12c gray	3.75	3.00
145	A42	15c ultramarine	21.00	.25

Chalky Paper

146	A43	25c blk & scar, yel	2.25	13.00
147	A43	50c dull vio & blk	2.60	20.00
148	A43	1r blk, green	17.75	13.00
149	A43	2r50c blk & car, *bl*	27.50	75.00

150	A43	5r grn & car, *yel*	42.50	100.00
151	A43	10r grn & car, *grn*	165.00	250.00
		Nos. 137-151 (15)	307.35	480.40

Numerals of 12c, 25c and 10r of type A43 are in color on plain tablet.
See Nos. 161-178.

King George V — A44

Die I

For description of dies I and II see "Dies of British Colonial Stamps" in table of contents.
Numeral tablet of 5c, 50c, 1r, 2.50r or 5r of type A44 has lined background with colorless denomination.

1912-22   Wmk. 3   Ordinary Paper

152	A44	5c gray & rose	3.00	4.50
a.		A44 5c slate gray & carmine	11.00	11.50
153	A44	12c gray	8.00	1.10

Chalky Paper

154	A44	25c blk & red, yel	.45	1.50
a.		25c gray black & red, yellow, Die II	1.10	25.00
		Overprinted "SPECIMEN"	47.50	
155	A44	50c dull vio & blk	52.50	125.00
156	A44	1r black, emerald, die II	2.50	8.00
		Overprinted "SPECIMEN"	50.00	
a.		1r black, emer, olive back, die I ('21)	11.50	60.00
b.		1r blk, bl grn, olive back, die I	6.75	21.00
157	A44	2r50c blk & red, *bl*	42.50	75.00
158	A44	5r grn & red, *yel*	115.00	175.00
a.		Die II ('22)	115.00	200.00
159	A44	10r grn & red, emer, die II ('21)	47.50	180.00
		Overprinted "SPECIMEN"	67.50	
a.		10r grn & red, bl grn, olive back, die I	1,150.	
b.		10r green & red, emer, die I	85.00	200.00
c.		10r grn & red, emer, olive back, die I	145.00	210.00
d.		10r grn & red, grn, die I	105.00	210.00

Surface-colored Paper

160	A44	25c blk & red, yel ('16)	2.75	21.00
		Nos. 152-160 (9)	274.20	591.10

1921-26   Wmk. 4   Ordinary Paper

161	A42	1c black	1.10	1.10
162	A42	2c brown	1.10	.25
163	A42	2c violet, *yel* ('25)	3.50	2.00
164	A42	3c green ('25)	3.50	3.50
165	A42	4c ol grn & rose	1.60	2.00
166	A42	4c green	1.10	.25
167	A42	4c brown ('25)	4.50	2.50
168	A42	6c rose red	13.50	7.25
169	A42	6c violet	1.35	.25
170	A42	8c brown org ('25)	2.50	24.00
171	A42	10c gray ('22)	2.25	3.75
172	A42	10c rose red ('25)	12.00	6.75
173	A42	12c rose red	1.70	1.60
174	A42	12c gray ('25)	1.90	5.00
175	A42	15c ultramarine	6.00	5.50
176	A42	15c dull blue ('25)	1.60	.25
177	A42	20c ultra ('22)	2.25	.90
178	A42	20c dull vio ('25)	9.50	16.00
		Nos. 161-178 (18)	70.95	82.85

Ornaments in lower panel omitted on #171-178.
For surcharges see Nos. 201-203.

Die II

1922-34   Ordinary Paper

179	A44	1c black	2.40	3.00
180	A44	2c brown	1.10	.25
181	A44	3c green	2.10	.45
182	A44	4c olive grn & red ('27)	3.25	.30
a.		Die I ('32)	18.00	62.50
183	A44	4c green, die I ('33)	13.50	.50
184	A44	5c gray & car	1.10	.25
a.		Die I ('32)	10.00	6.50
185	A44	6c olive brn ('28)	5.50	.65
186	A44	8c orange	2.10	15.50
187	A44	10c rose red ('26)	4.25	.25
a.		Die I ('32)	15.50	16.75
188	A44	12c gray, small "c" ('22)	5.00	23.00
		Overprinted "SPECIMEN"	47.50	
189	A44	12c gray, "c" larger & thinner ('34)	17.50	.25
190	A44	12c rose red	.70	3.75
191	A44	15c dk blue ('28)	4.75	.25
192	A44	20c dull vio	4.75	.45

193	A44	20c dk blue ('34)	28.00	.45
a.		Die I ('27)	11.00	2.60
194	A44	25c black & red, yel	1.10	.25
a.		Die I ('32)	7.25	67.50

Chalky Paper

195	A44	50c dull vio & blk	8.00	3.75
196	A44	1r blk, emerald	6.75	.55
a.		Die I ('32)	25.00	62.50
197	A44	2r50c blk & red, *bl*	22.00	19.00
198	A44	5r green & red, *yel*	47.50	95.00
199	A44	10r green & red, *emer* ('28)	145.00	340.00
		Nos. 179-199 (21)	326.35	507.85

A45

1924

200	A45	50r lilac & green	1,000.	2,750.
		Overprinted "SPECIMEN"	400.00	

Nos. 166, 173, 177 Surcharged

1925

201	A42	3c on 4c green	8.00	6.25
202	A42	10c on 12c rose red	.50	1.60
203	A42	15c on 20c ultra	.65	1.75
		Nos. 201-203 (3)	9.15	9.60
		Set, ovpted. "SPECIMEN"	92.50	

Common Design Types pictured following the introduction.

Silver Jubilee Issue
Common Design Type

1935, May 6   Engr.   Perf. 13½x14

204	CD301	5c gray black & ultra	.60	.25
205	CD301	12c indigo & green	5.50	.25
206	CD301	20c blue & brown	6.50	.25
207	CD301	1r brt vio & indigo	35.00	57.50
		Nos. 204-207 (4)	47.60	58.25
		Set, never hinged	60.00	
		Set, ovpted "SPECIMEN"	145.00	

Coronation Issue
Common Design Type

1937, May 12   Wmk. 4   Perf. 13½x14

208	CD302	5c dark purple	.30	.25
		Never hinged	.45	
209	CD302	12c carmine	.50	2.40
		Never hinged	.90	
210	CD302	20c bright ultra	1.25	1.10
		Never hinged	1.90	
		Nos. 208-210 (3)	2.05	3.75
		Set, never hinged	3.25	
		Set, perforated "SPECIMEN"	85.00	
		Set, never hinged, perforated "SPECIMEN"	110.00	

King George VI — A46

1938-43   Typo.   Perf. 14

211	A46	2c gray ('43)	.25	.25
		Never hinged	.30	
a.		Perf. 15x14 ('43)	.70	.25
		Never hinged	1.10	
212	A46	3c rose vio & car ('43)	1.50	2.15
		Never hinged	2.10	
213	A46	4c green ('43)	3.25	2.15
		Never hinged	5.75	
214	A46	5c violet ('43)	2.10	.25
		Never hinged	3.50	
a.		Perf. 15x14 ('43)	40.00	.25
		Never hinged	62.50	
215	A46	10c carmine ('43)	1.90	.25
		Never hinged	2.75	
a.		Perf. 15x14 ('43)	25.00	2.50
		Never hinged	42.50	
216	A46	12c salmon pink ('43)	.70	.25
		Never hinged	1.10	
a.		Perf. 15x14 ('43)	40.00	1.35
		Never hinged	60.00	

217	A46	20c blue ('43)	.70	.25
		Never hinged	1.10	
218	A46	25c maroon ('43)	6.00	.25
		Never hinged	9.00	
a.		A46 25c brown purple, chalky paper ('38)	14.00	.25
		Never hinged	20.00	
219	A46	1r brown black ('43)	14.00	2.00
		Never hinged	20.00	
a.		A46 1r gray brown, chalky paper ('38)	30.00	3.25
		Never hinged	45.00	
220	A46	2.50r pale violet ('43)	25.00	26.00
		Never hinged	37.50	
a.		A46 2.50r pale violet, chalky paper ('38)	40.00	28.00
		Never hinged	62.50	
221	A46	5r olive green ('43)	21.00	42.50
		Never hinged	30.00	
a.		A46 5r olive green, chalky paper ('38)	35.00	42.50
		Never hinged	57.50	
222	A46	10r rose violet ('43)	9.75	42.50
		Never hinged	14.00	
a.		A46 10r reddish purple, chalky paper ('38)	52.50	57.50
		Never hinged	80.00	
		Nos. 211-222 (12)	86.15	118.80
		Set, never hinged	127.00	
		Set, perforated "SPECIMEN"	300.00	
		Set, never hinged, perforated "SPECIMEN"	400.00	

> Catalogue values for unused stamps in this section, from this point to the end of the section, are for Never Hinged items.

Peace Issue
Common Design Type
Perf. 13½x14

			Wmk. 4
1946, Nov. 20		**Engr.**	
223	CD303	5c lilac	.25 .80
224	CD303	20c deep blue	.25 .25

"Post Office" Stamp of 1847 — A47

1948, Mar. 22   *Perf. 11½*

225	A47	5c red vio & orange	.25	.55
226	A47	12c green & orange	.25	.25
227	A47	20c blue & dp blue	.25	.25
228	A47	1r lt red brn & dp blue	.35	.35
		Nos. 225-228 (4)	1.10	1.40

Cent. of the 1st Mauritius postage stamps.

Silver Wedding Issue
Common Design Types

1948, Oct. 25   **Photo.**   *Perf. 14x14½*
229   CD304   5c violet   .25   .25

Perf. 11½x11
Engraved; Name Typographed
230   CD305   10r lilac rose   17.50   45.00

UPU Issue
Common Design Types
Engr.; Name Typo. on 20c, 35c
Perf. 13½, 11x11½

			Wmk. 4
1949, Oct. 10			
231	CD306	12c rose carmine	.65 2.10
232	CD307	20c indigo	2.40 2.75
233	CD308	35c rose violet	.65 1.60
234	CD309	1r sepia	.65 .25
		Nos. 231-234 (4)	4.35 6.70

Sugar Factory — A48

Aloe Plant — A49

Designs: 2c, Grand Port. 4c, Tamarind Falls. 5c, Rempart Mountain. 10c, Transporting cane. 12c, Map and dodo. 20c, "Paul et Virginie." 25c, Statue of Mahe La Bourdonnais. 35c, Government House. 50c, Pieter Both Mountain. 1r, Sambar. 2.50r, Port Louis. 5r, Beach scene. 10r, Arms.

Perf. 13½x14½, 14½x13½

1950, July 1				**Photo.**
235	A48	1c red violet	.25	.55
236	A48	2c cerise	.25	.25
237	A49	3c yel green	.70	4.50
238	A49	4c green	.25	3.25
239	A48	5c greenish blue	.25	.25
240	A48	10c red	.30	.80
241	A48	12c olive green	1.60	3.25
242	A49	20c brt ultra	1.10	.25
243	A49	25c vio brown	2.15	.25
244	A48	35c rose violet	.45	.25
245	A48	50c emerald	3.00	.55
246	A48	1r sepia	10.00	.25
247	A48	2.50r orange	22.00	17.50
248	A48	5r red brown	23.00	17.50
249	A48	10r gray blue	18.00	37.50
		Nos. 235-249 (15)	83.30	87.10

SPECIAL DELIVERY STAMPS

SD1

1903		**Wmk. 1**		**Perf. 14**
		Red Surcharge		
E1	SD1	15c on 15c ultra	14.50	37.50

SD2   SD3

EXPRESS DELIVERY (INLAND)

New Setting with Smaller "15c" without period — SD3a   **15 c**

1904				
E2	SD2	15c on 15c ultra	62.50	95.00
a.		"INLAND" inverted		3,400.
b.		Inverted "A" in "INLAND"	1,700.	1,250.
E3	SD3	15c on 15c ultra	9.00	3.75
a.		Double surcharge, both inverted	1,875.	1,900.
b.		Inverted surcharge	1,250.	800.00
c.		Vert. pair, imperf between	6,250.	
E3F	SD3a	15c on 15c ultra	840.00	800.00
g.		Inverted surcharge		1,775.
h.		Double surcharge		3,750.
i.		Double surcharge, both inverted	—	5,500.
j.		"c" omitted		2,750.

To make No. E2 the word "INLAND" was printed on No. E1. For Nos. E3 and E3F, new settings of the surcharge were made with different spacing between the words.

SD4   SD5

E4	SD4	15c green & red	18.00	6.25
a.		Double surcharge	800.00	800.00
b.		Inverted surcharge	1,000.	900.00
c.		"LNIAND."		

d.		As "c," double surcharge	900.00	800.00
E5	SD5	18c green & black	3.00	32.50
a.		Exclamation point (!) instead of "I" in "FOREIGN"	800.00	

POSTAGE DUE STAMPS

> Catalogue values for unused stamps in this section are for Never Hinged items.

Numeral — D1

Perf. 14½x14

			Wmk. 4
1933-54		**Typo.**	
J1	D1	2c black	1.50 .60
		On cover	625.00
J2	D1	4c violet	.60 .80
		On cover	625.00
J3	D1	6c red	.70 .95
		On cover	625.00
J4	D1	10c green	.85 2.40
		On cover	625.00
J5	D1	20c ultramarine	.75 2.60
		On cover	750.00
J6	D1	50c dp red lilac ('54)	.65 19.00
		On cover	900.00
J7	D1	1r orange ('54)	.85 19.00
		On cover	1,000.
		Nos. J1-J7 (7)	5.90 45.35

Covers: Values are for properly franked commercial covers. Philatelic covers sell for less.

MAYOTTE

mä-'yät

LOCATION — One of the Comoro Islands situated in the Mozambique Channel midway between Madagascar and Mozambique (Africa)
GOVT. — French Colony
AREA — 140 sq. mi.
POP. — 13,783 (1914)
CAPITAL — Dzaoudzi
See Comoro Islands

100 Centimes = 1 Franc

Stamps of Mayotte were replaced successively by those of Madagascar, Comoro Islands and France.

Navigation and Commerce — A1

Perf. 14x13½

			Unwmk.
1892-1907		**Typo.**	
	Name of Colony in Blue or Carmine		
1	A1	1c blk, *lil bl*	1.40 .90
		Never hinged	2.40
		On cover	190.00
2	A1	2c brn, *buff*	1.90 1.40
		Never hinged	3.00
		On cover	190.00
a.		Name double	575.00 500.00
3	A1	4c claret, *lav*	2.40 1.75
		Never hinged	4.00
		On cover	190.00
4	A1	5c grn, *grnsh*	4.75 3.25
		Never hinged	9.00
		On cover	125.00
5	A1	10c blk, *lavender*	9.00 4.75
		Never hinged	16.00
		On cover	160.00
6	A1	10c red ('00)	67.50 52.50
		Never hinged	140.00
		On cover	190.00
7	A1	15c blue, quadrille paper	17.50 10.50
		Never hinged	35.00
		On cover	250.00
8	A1	15c gray ('00)	125.00 110.00
		Never hinged	275.00
		On cover	340.00
9	A1	20c red, *grn*	13.50 10.50
		Never hinged	27.50
		On cover	225.00

10	A1	25c blk, *rose*	14.50	9.75
		Never hinged	30.00	
		On cover		225.00
		On cover, single franking		310.00
11	A1	25c blue ('00)	16.00	13.50
		Never hinged	95.00	
		On cover		95.00
		On cover, single franking		160.00
12	A1	30c brn, *bis*	22.00	16.00
		Never hinged	42.50	
		On cover		190.00
		On cover, single franking		225.00
13	A1	35c blk, *yel*	11.00	8.00
		Never hinged	24.00	
		On cover		62.50
		On cover, single franking		110.00
14	A1	40c red, *straw*	22.50	16.00
		Never hinged	42.50	
		On cover		225.00
		On cover, single franking		310.00
15	A1	45c blk, *gray grn* ('07)	21.00	20.00
		Never hinged	42.50	
		On cover		110.00
		On cover, single franking		190.00
16	A1	50c carmine, *rose*	32.00	22.50
		Never hinged	62.50	
		On cover		250.00
		On cover, single franking		375.00
17	A1	50c brn, *az* ('00)	30.00	30.00
		Never hinged	57.50	
		On cover		160.00
		On cover, single franking		275.00
18	A1	75c dp vio, *org*	30.00	21.00
		Never hinged	67.50	
		On cover		300.00
		On cover, single franking		450.00
19	A1	1fr brnz grn, *straw*	32.00	22.50
		Never hinged	67.50	
		On cover		310.00
		On cover, single franking		440.00
20	A1	5fr red lil, *lav* ('99)	150.00	130.00
		Never hinged	325.00	
		On cover		440.00
		On cover, single franking		625.00
		Nos. 1-20 (20)	623.95	504.80

Perf. 13½x14 stamps are counterfeits.

Issues of 1892-1907 Surcharged in Black or Carmine

1912				
	Spacing between figures of surcharge 1.5mm (5c), 2mm (10c)			
22	A1	5c on 2c brn, *buff*	3.25	4.00
		Never hinged	5.75	
		On cover		125.00
23	A1	5c on 4c cl, *lav* (C)	2.00	2.00
		Never hinged	3.50	
		On cover		95.00
24	A1	5c on 15c bl (C)	2.00	2.00
		Never hinged	3.50	
		On cover		95.00
25	A1	5c on 20c red, *grn*	2.00	2.40
		Never hinged	3.50	
		On cover		105.00
26	A1	5c on 25c blk, *rose* (C)	1.60	1.60
		Never hinged	2.50	
		On cover		95.00
a.		Double surcharge	300.00	
b.		Pair, one stamp without surcharge	1,000.	
27	A1	5c on 30c brn, *bis* (C)	2.00	2.00
		Never hinged	3.50	
		On cover		100.00
28	A1	10c on 40c red, *straw*	2.00	2.40
		Never hinged	3.50	
		On cover		110.00
a.		Double surcharge	300.00	
29	A1	10c on 45c blk, *gray grn* (C)	2.00	2.00
		Never hinged	3.50	
		On cover		105.00
a.		Double surcharge	300.00	325.00
30	A1	10c on 50c car, *rose*	4.50	5.00
		Never hinged	7.50	
		On cover		170.00
31	A1	10c on 75c dp vio, *org*	3.50	4.25
		Never hinged	6.50	
		On cover		160.00
32	A1	10c on 1fr brnz grn, *straw*	3.50	4.25
		Never hinged	6.50	
		On cover		160.00
		Nos. 22-32 (11)	28.35	31.90

	Spacing between figures of surcharge 2.25mm (5c), 2.75mm (10c)			
22a	A1	5c on 2c brn, *buff*	19.00	19.00
		Never hinged	30.00	
23a	A1	5c on 4c cl, *lav* (C)	13.50	13.50
		Never hinged	24.00	
24a	A1	5c on 15c bl (C)	13.50	13.50
		Never hinged	24.00	
25a	A1	5c on 20c red, *grn*	13.50	13.50
		Never hinged	24.00	
26c	A1	5c on 25c blk, *rose* (C)	13.00	13.00
		Never hinged	22.50	
d.		Double surcharge	2,800.	2,750.

27a A1   5c on 30c brn, *bis*
  (C)   13.50   13.50
  Never hinged   24.00
28b A1 10c on 40c red,
  straw   65.00   65.00
  Never hinged   125.00
  c. Double surcharge   3,500. 3,000.
29b A1 10c on 45c blk, *gray*
  grn (C)   60.00   60.00
  Never hinged   115.00
  c. Double surcharge   3,500. 3,000.
30a A1 10c on 50c car, *rose*   87.50   87.50
  Never hinged   160.00
31a A1 10c on 75c dp vio,
  org   87.50   87.50
  Never hinged   160.00
32a A1 10c on 1fr brnz grn,
  straw   150.00 150.00
  Nos. 22a-32a (11)   536.00 536.00

Se-tenant Pairs, Both Ovpt. Settings

22b A1   5c on 2c, #22 +
  #22a   22.50   22.50
  Never hinged   37.50
23b A1   5c on 4c, #23 +
  #23a   17.50   17.50
  Never hinged   27.50
24b A1   5c on 15c, #24 +
  #24a   17.50   17.50
  Never hinged   27.50
25b A1   5c on 20c, #25 +
  #25a   17.50   17.50
  Never hinged   27.50
26b A1   5c on 25c, #26 +
  #26a   16.50   16.50
  Never hinged   26.00
27b A1   5c on 30c, #27 +
  #27a   17.50   17.50
  Never hinged   27.50
28b A1 10c on 40c, #28 +
  #28a   75.00   75.00
  Never hinged   140.00
29b A1 10c on 45c, #29 +
  #29a   65.00   65.00
  Never hinged   125.00
30b A1 10c on 50c, #30 +
  #30a   95.00   95.00
  Never hinged   175.00
31b A1 10c on 75c, #31 +
  #31a   95.00   95.00
  Never hinged   175.00
32b A1 10c on 1fr, #32 +
  #32a   175.00 175.00
  Never hinged   280.00
  Nos. 22b-32b (11)   614.00 614.00

Nos. 22-32 were available for use in Madagascar and the entire Comoro archipelago.

MEMEL

'mā-məl

LOCATION — In northern Europe, bordering on the Baltic Sea
GOVT. — Special commission (see below)
AREA — 1099 sq. mi.
POP. — 151,960

Following World War I this territory was detached from Germany and by Treaty of Versailles assigned to the government of a commission of the Allied and Associated Powers (not the League of Nations), which administered it until January, 1923, when it was forcibly occupied by Lithuania. In 1924 Memel became incorporated as a semi-autonomous district of Lithuania with the approval of the Allied Powers and the League of Nations.

100 Pfennig = 1 Mark
100 Centu = 1 Litas (1923)

Excellent counterfeits of all Memel stamps exist.

Stamps of Germany, 1905-20, Overprinted

Wmk. Lozenges (125)

1920, Aug. 1   **Perf. 14, 14½**

1	A16	5pf green	1.25	9.00
		Never hinged	6.00	
		On cover		22.50
2	A16	10pf car rose	2.75	10.00
		Never hinged	9.00	
		On cover		18.00
3	A16	10pf orange	.30	2.75
		Never hinged	1.10	
		On cover		6.00
4	A22	15pf violet brown	2.75	13.00
		Never hinged	12.50	
		On cover		22.50
5	A16	20pf blue violet	1.20	5.50
		Never hinged	4.50	
		On cover		6.00
6	A16	30pf org & blk, *buff*	1.40	8.75
		Never hinged	6.75	
		On cover		8.00
7	A16	30pf dull blue	.40	3.50
		Never hinged	1.50	
		On cover		10.50
8	A16	40pf lake & blk	.25	3.50
		Never hinged	.75	
		On cover		6.00
9	A16	50pf pur & blk, *buff*	.30	3.50
		Never hinged	1.10	
		On cover		8.00
10	A16	60pf olive green	1.60	6.50
		Never hinged	4.75	
		On cover		10.50
11	A16	75pf grn & blk	2.75	21.00
		Never hinged	13.50	
		On cover		30.00
12	A16	80pf blue violet	1.60	10.00
		Never hinged	6.50	
		On cover		19.00

Overprinted

13	A17	1m car rose	.40	3.50
		Never hinged	1.10	
		On cover		20.00
14	A17	1.25m green	13.50	52.50
		Never hinged	37.50	
		On cover		100.00
15	A17	1.50m yel brn	4.75	32.50
		Never hinged	21.00	
		On cover		40.00
16	A21	2m blue	2.00	14.50
		Never hinged	7.50	
		On cover		32.50
17	A21	2.50m red lilac	12.00	65.00
		Never hinged	45.00	
		On cover		150.00
		Nos. 1-17 (17)	49.20	265.00

Stamps of France, Surcharged in Black

On A22

On A18

1920   **Unwmk.**   **Perf. 14x13½**

18	A22	5pf on 5c green	.80	3.25
		Never hinged	4.75	
		On cover		4.50
19	A22	10pf on 10c red	.30	2.75
		Never hinged	1.50	
		On cover		4.50
20	A22	20pf on 25c blue	1.25	3.75
		Never hinged	5.25	
		On cover		7.50
21	A22	30pf on 30c org	.40	3.00
		Never hinged	1.90	
		On cover		4.50
22	A22	40pf on 20c red brn	1.25	3.00
		Never hinged	7.00	
		On cover		7.50
23	A22	50pf on 35c vio	.30	2.75
		Never hinged	1.50	
		On cover		4.50
24	A18	60pf on 40c red & pale bl	.35	3.00
		Never hinged	1.50	
		On cover		6.00
25	A18	80pf on 45c grn & bl	1.25	4.00
		Never hinged	6.25	
		On cover		9.00
26	A18	1m on 50c brn & lav	.55	4.00
		Never hinged	2.50	
		On cover		9.00
27	A18	1m 25pf on 60c vio & ultra	1.30	9.00
		Never hinged	5.50	
		On cover		19.00
28	A18	2m on 1fr cl & ol grn	.35	2.75
		Never hinged	1.50	
		On cover		4.50
29	A18	3m on 5fr bl & buff	18.50	67.50
		Never hinged	67.50	
		On cover		140.00
		Nos. 18-29 (12)	26.60	108.75

For stamps with additional surcharges and overprints see Nos. 43-49, C1-C4.

French Stamps of 1900-20 Surcharged like Nos. 24 to 29 in Red or Black

On A18

Type I

Type II

1920-21   **Unwmk.**   **Perf. 14x13½**

30	A18	3m on 2fr org & pale bl	24.00	67.50
		Never hinged	95.00	
		On cover		125.00
31	A18	4m on 2fr org & pale bl (I) (Bk)	.50	2.75
		Never hinged	1.60	
		On cover		8.00
a.		Type II	52.50	160.00
		Never hinged	160.00	
32	A18	10m on 5fr bl & buff	3.00	16.00
		Never hinged	12.00	
		On cover		72.50
33	A18	20m on 5fr bl & buff	40.00	160.00
		Never hinged	170.00	225.00
		On cover		210.00
		Nos. 30-33 (4)	67.50	246.25

For stamps with additional overprints see Nos. C5, C19.

New Value with Initial Capital

1921

39	A18	60Pf on 40c red & pale bl	4.75	20.00
		Never hinged	15.00	
		On cover		32.50

40	A18	3M on 60c vio & ultra	2.40	8.00
		Never hinged	9.50	
		On cover		11.00
41	A18	10M on 5fr bl & buff	2.40	8.00
		Never hinged	9.50	
		On cover		20.00
42	A18	20M on 45c grn & bl	4.75	26.00
		Never hinged	20.00	
		On cover		72.50
		Nos. 39-42 (4)	14.30	62.00

The surcharged value on No. 40 is in italics. For stamps with additional overprints see Nos. C6-C7, C18.

Stamps of 1920 Surcharged with Large Numerals in Dark Blue or Red

No. 43

No. 49

1921-22

43	A22	15pf on 10pf on 10c	.50	2.00
		Never hinged	2.25	
		On cover		4.75
a.		Inverted surcharge	67.50	100.00
		Never hinged	150.00	
44	A22	15pf on 20pf on 25c	.50	3.00
		Never hinged	2.25	
		On cover		5.25
a.		Inverted surcharge	72.50	175.00
		Never hinged	175.00	
45	A22	15pf on 50pf on 35c (R)	.50	3.00
		Never hinged	2.25	
		On cover		5.25
a.		Inverted surcharge	72.50	175.00
		Never hinged	175.00	
46	A22	60pf on 40pf on 20c	.50	2.00
		Never hinged	2.25	
		On cover		4.00
a.		Inverted surcharge	67.50	160.00
		Never hinged	150.00	
47	A18	75pf on 60pf on 40c	.60	2.40
		Never hinged	2.25	
		On cover		16.00
48	A18	1.25m on 1m on 50c	.50	2.25
		Never hinged	1.90	
		On cover		7.50
49	A18	5.00m on 2m on 1fr	1.25	3.75
		Never hinged	3.75	
		On cover		19.00
a.		Inverted surcharge	200.00	625.00
		Never hinged	375.00	
		Nos. 43-49 (7)	4.35	18.40

Stamps of France Surcharged in Black or Red

On A20, A22

1922

50	A22	5pf on 5c org	.25	1.40
		Never hinged	1.10	
		On cover		8.00
51	A22	10pf on 10c red	.80	5.50
		Never hinged	4.50	
		On cover		16.00
52	A22	10pf on 10c grn	.50	1.40
		Never hinged	1.10	
		On cover		8.00
53	A22	15pf on 10c grn	.25	1.40
		Never hinged	1.10	
		On cover		8.00
54	A22	20pf on 20c red brn	8.00	40.00
		Never hinged	32.50	
		On cover		67.50
55	A22	20pf on 25c bl	8.00	40.00
		Never hinged	32.50	
		On cover		67.50
56	A22	25pf on 5c org	.25	1.40
		Never hinged	1.10	
		On cover		8.00
57	A22	30pf on 30c red	1.20	5.50
		Never hinged	4.75	
		On cover		16.00
58	A22	35pf on 35c vio	.25	.80
		Never hinged	.75	
		On cover		9.50
59	A22	50pf on 50c dl bl	.30	1.40
		Never hinged	1.10	
		On cover		6.00
60	A20	75pf on 15c grn	.25	.80
		Never hinged	.75	
		On cover		8.00
61	A22	75pf on 35c vio	.30	1.40
		Never hinged	1.10	
		On cover		8.00

62	A22	1m on 25c blue	.25	.80
		Never hinged	.75	
		On cover		6.00
63	A22	1¼m on 30c red	.30	1.40
		Never hinged	.75	
		On cover		8.00
64	A22	3m on 5c org	.30	4.50
		Never hinged	1.40	
		On cover		8.00
65	A20	6m on 15c grn (R)	.55	5.50
		Never hinged	2.60	
		On cover		8.00
66	A22	8m on 30c red	.70	13.50
		Never hinged	3.25	
		On cover		26.00

On A18

67	A18	40pf on 40c red & pale bl	.25	1.40
		Never hinged	1.10	
		On cover		8.00
68	A18	80pf on 45c grn & bl	.30	1.40
		Never hinged	1.10	
		On cover		4.50
69	A18	1m on 40c red & pale bl	.30	1.40
		Never hinged	1.10	
		On cover		4.50
70	A18	1.25m on 60c vio & ultra (R)	.30	1.40
		Never hinged	1.10	
		On cover		6.00
71	A18	1.50m on 45c grn & bl (R)	.30	1.40
		Never hinged	1.10	
		On cover		6.00
72	A18	2m on 45c grn & bl	.50	2.25
		Never hinged	2.25	
		On cover		6.00
73	A18	2m on 1fr cl & ol grn	.30	1.40
		Never hinged	1.10	
		On cover		4.50
74	A18	2¼m on 40c red & pale bl	.25	.80
		Never hinged	.75	
		On cover		8.00
75	A18	2½m on 60c vio & ultra	.45	2.40
		Never hinged	2.25	
		On cover		16.00
76	A18	3m on 60c vio & ultra (R)	1.20	5.50
		Never hinged	4.50	
		On cover		9.00
77	A18	4m on 45c grn & bl	.25	.80
		Never hinged	.75	
		On cover		8.00
78	A18	5m on 1fr cl & ol grn	.30	1.60
		Never hinged	1.20	
		On cover		6.00
79	A18	6m on 60c vio & ultra	.25	.80
		Never hinged	.75	
		On cover		8.00
80	A18	6m on 2fr org & pale bl	.35	1.60
		Never hinged	1.20	
		On cover		8.00
81	A18	9m on 1fr cl & ol grn	.40	.80
		Never hinged	.75	
		On cover		8.00
82	A18	9m on 5fr bl & buff (R)	.40	2.75
		Never hinged	2.25	
		On cover		9.50
83	A18	10m on 45c grn & bl (R)	.70	5.25
		Never hinged	3.25	
		On cover		8.00
84	A18	12m on 40c red & pale bl	.25	2.00
		Never hinged	1.20	
		On cover		8.00
85	A18	20m on 40c red & pale bl	.70	5.25
		Never hinged	3.25	
		On cover		8.00
86	A18	20m on 2fr org & pale bl	.25	2.00
		Never hinged	1.20	
		On cover		8.00
87	A18	30m on 60c vio & ultra	.70	5.25
		Never hinged	3.25	
		On cover		8.00
88	A18	30m on 5fr dk bl & buff	2.75	20.00
		Never hinged	12.00	
		On cover		60.00
89	A18	40m on 1fr cl & ol grn	.70	6.75
		Never hinged	3.25	
		On cover		11.00
90	A18	50m on 2fr org & pale bl	11.00	47.50
		Never hinged	35.00	
		On cover		90.00
91	A18	80m on 2fr org & pale bl (R)	.70	6.75
		Never hinged	3.25	
		On cover		11.00

92 A18 100m on 5fr bl & buff   .95   *13.50*
  Never hinged   4.00
  On cover   47.50
  Nos. 50-92 (43)   47.25   *268.65*

A 500m on 5fr dark blue and buff was prepared, but not officially issued. Value: unused $950; never hinged $2,400.
For stamps with additional surcharges and overprints see Nos. 93-99, C8-C17, C20-C29.

Nos. 52, 54, 67, 59 Surcharged "Mark"

1922-23
93 A22 10m on 10pf on 10c   .90   *8.00*
  Never hinged   3.75
  On cover   24.00
 a. Double surcharge   110.00   *275.00*
  Never hinged   260.00
94 A22 20m on 20pf on 20c   .40   *4.75*
  Never hinged   2.25
  On cover   11.00
95 A18 40m on 40pf on 40c   .80   *5.25*
  ('23)
  Never hinged   3.75
  On cover   20.00
96 A20 50m on 50pf on 50c   2.40   *13.50*
  Never hinged   10.00
  On cover   26.00
  Nos. 93-96 (4)   4.50   *31.50*

Nos. 72, 61, 70 Srchd. in Red or Black

1922-23
97 A18 10m on 2m on 45c   2.00   *13.50*
  Never hinged   9.00
  On cover   22.50
98 A22 25m on 1m on 25c   2.00   *13.50*
  Never hinged   9.00
  On cover   22.50
99 A18 80m on 1.25m on 60c   1.20   *7.50*
  (Bk) ('23)
  Never hinged   4.50
  On cover   72.50
  Nos. 97-99 (3)   5.20   *34.50*

For No. 99 with additional surcharges see Nos. N28-N30.

AIR POST STAMPS

Nos. 24-26, 28, 31, 39-40 Ovptd. in Dark Blue

1921, July 6   Unwmk.   Perf. 14x13½
C1 A18 60pf on 40c   40.00   *160.00*
  Never hinged   120.00
  On cover   225.00
C2 A18 80pf on 45c   4.00   *20.00*
  Never hinged   16.00
  On cover   75.00
C3 A18 1m on 50c   4.75   *12.00*
  Never hinged   20.00
  On cover   52.50
C4 A18 2m on 1fr   4.50   *16.00*
  Never hinged   15.00
  On cover   60.00
 a. "Flugpost" inverted   170.00
  Never hinged   375.00
C5 A18 4m on 2fr (I)   4.25   *20.00*
  Never hinged   15.00
  On cover   75.00
 a. Type II   120.00   *275.00*
  Never hinged   240.00
  On cover   1,200.
 b. Pair, type I and type II   150.00
  New Value with Initial Capital
C6 A18 60Pf on 40c   4.00   *20.00*
  Never hinged   15.00
  On cover   75.00
 a. "Flugpost" inverted   190.00
  Never hinged   450.00
C7 A18 3M on 60c   3.50   *15.00*
  Never hinged   11.00
  On cover   60.00
 a. "Flugpost" inverted   175.00
  Never hinged   375.00
  Nos. C1-C7 (7)   65.00   *263.00*

The surcharged value on No. C7 is in italics.

Nos. 67-71, 73, 76, 78, 80, 82 Ovptd. in Dark Blue

1922, May 12
C8 A18 40pf on 40c   .40   *2.75*
  Never hinged   1.90
  On cover   40.00

C9 A18 80pf on 45c   .40   *2.75*
  Never hinged   1.90
  On cover   40.00
C10 A18 1m on 40c   .40   *2.75*
  Never hinged   1.90
  On cover   40.00
C11 A18 1.25m on 60c   .80   *4.75*
  Never hinged   3.50
  On cover   40.00
C12 A18 1.50m on 45c   .80   *4.75*
  Never hinged   3.50
  On cover   40.00
C13 A18 2m on 1fr   .80   *4.75*
  Never hinged   3.50
  On cover   40.00
C14 A18 3m on 60c   .80   *4.75*
  Never hinged   3.50
  On cover   40.00
C15 A18 5m on 1fr   1.20   *4.75*
  Never hinged   4.25
  On cover   60.00
C16 A18 6m on 2fr   1.20   *4.75*
  Never hinged   4.25
  On cover   60.00
C17 A18 9m on 5fr   1.20   *4.75*
  Never hinged   4.25
  On cover   60.00
  Same Overprint On Nos. 40, 31
C18 A18 3m on 60c   130.00   *1,100.*
  Never hinged   325.00
  On cover   2,400.
C19 A18 4m on 2fr   .80   *4.50*
  Never hinged   3.50
  On cover   47.50
  Nos. C8-C17,C19 (11)   8.80   *46.00*

Nos. 67, 69-71, 73, 76, 78, 80, 82 Ovptd. in Black or Red

1922, Oct. 17
C20 A18 40pf on 40c   1.20   *16.00*
  Never hinged   4.50
  On cover   100.00
C21 A18 1m on 40c   1.20   *16.00*
  Never hinged   4.50
  On cover   100.00
C22 A18 1.25m on 60c (R)   1.20   *16.00*
  Never hinged   4.50
  On cover   100.00
C23 A18 1.50m on 45c (R)   1.20   *16.00*
  Never hinged   4.50
  On cover   100.00
C24 A18 2m on 1fr   1.20   *16.00*
  Never hinged   4.50
  On cover   100.00
C25 A18 3m on 60c (R)   1.20   *16.00*
  Never hinged   4.50
  On cover   100.00
C26 A18 4m on 2fr   1.20   *16.00*
  Never hinged   4.50
  On cover   100.00
C27 A18 5m on 1fr   1.20   *16.00*
  Never hinged   4.50
  On cover   100.00
C28 A18 6m on 2fr   1.20   *16.00*
  Never hinged   4.50
  On cover   100.00
C29 A18 9m on 5fr (R)   1.20   *16.00*
  Never hinged   4.50
  On cover   100.00
  Nos. C20-C29 (10)   12.00   *160.00*

No. C26 is not known without the "FLUGPOST" overprint.

OCCUPATION STAMPS

Issued under Lithuanian Occupation
Surcharged in Various Colors on Unissued Official Stamps of Lithuania Similar to Type O4

On Nos. N1-N6   On Nos. N7-N11

Memel Printing
1923   Unwmk.   Litho.   Perf. 11
N1 O4 10m on 5c bl (Bk)   1.20   *12.00*
  Never hinged   11.50
  On cover   37.50
 a. Double overprint   40.00   *275.00*
  Never hinged   150.00
 b. "Memel" and bars omitted   5.75   *60.00*
  Never hinged   22.50
  On cover   160.00
N2 O4 25m on 5c bl (R)   1.20   *12.00*
  Never hinged   11.50
  On cover   30.00
 a. Double overprint   40.00   *160.00*
  Never hinged   150.00
N3 O4 50m on 25c red   1.20   *12.00*
  (Bk)
  Never hinged   11.50
  On cover   32.50
 a. Double overprint   40.00   *275.00*
  Never hinged   150.00

N4 O4 100m on 25c red   1.20   *12.00*
  (G)
  Never hinged   11.50
  On cover   32.50
 a. Double overprint   40.00   *275.00*
  Never hinged   150.00
N5 O4 400m on 1 l brn (R)   1.60   *16.00*
  Never hinged   19.00
  On cover   60.00
 a. Double overprint   40.00   *275.00*
  Never hinged   150.00
N6 O4 500m on 1 l brn (Bl)   1.60   *16.00*
  Never hinged   19.00
  On cover   80.00
 a. Double overprint   40.00   *275.00*
  Never hinged   150.00
  Nos. N1-N6 (6)   8.00   *80.00*

Kaunas Printing
Black Surcharge
N7 O4 10m on 5c blue   .80   *7.25*
  Never hinged   11.00
  On cover   15.00
N8 O4 25m on 5c blue   .80   *7.25*
  Never hinged   11.00
  On cover   15.00
N9 O4 50m on 25c red   .80   *7.25*
  Never hinged   11.00
  On cover   15.00
N10 O4 100m on 25c red   .95   *7.25*
  Never hinged   13.50
  On cover   16.00
N11 O4 400m on 1 l brn   1.60   *11.00*
  Never hinged   21.00
  On cover   80.00
  Nos. N7-N11 (5)   4.95   *40.00*

No. N8 has the value in "Markes," others of the group have it in "Markiu."
For additional surcharge see No. N87.

Surcharged in Various Colors on Unissued Official Stamps of Lithuania Similar to Type O4

1923
N12 O4 10m on 5c bl (R)   1.60   *9.50*
  Never hinged   15.00
  On cover   60.00
 a. "Markes" instead of "Markiu"   20.00   *110.00*
  Never hinged   90.00
N13 O4 20m on 5c bl (R)   1.60   *9.50*
  Never hinged   15.00
  On cover   60.00
N14 O4 25m on 25c red (Bl)   1.60   *13.00*
  Never hinged   15.00
  On cover   60.00
N15 O4 50m on 25c red (Bl)   3.25   *13.00*
  Never hinged   26.00
  On cover   60.00
 a. Inverted surcharge   40.00   *160.00*
  Never hinged   150.00
N16 O4 100m on 1 l brn (Bk)   3.25   *17.50*
  Never hinged   30.00
  On cover   80.00
 a. Inverted surcharge   40.00   *160.00*
  Never hinged   150.00
N17 O4 200m on 1 l brn (Bk)   4.00   *17.50*
  Never hinged   37.50
  On cover   80.00
  Nos. N12-N17 (6)   15.30   *80.00*

No. N14 has the value in "Markes," others of the group have it in "Markiu."

"Vytis"
O4   O5

1923, Mar.
N18 O4 10m lt brown   .40   *6.75*
  Never hinged   2.60
  On cover   19.00
N19 O4 20m yellow   .40   *6.75*
  Never hinged   2.60
  On cover   19.00
N20 O4 25m orange   .40   *8.00*
  Never hinged   2.60
  On cover   19.00
N21 O4 40m violet   .40   *6.75*
  Never hinged   2.60
  On cover   19.00
N22 O4 50m yellow grn   1.20   *14.50*
  Never hinged   9.00
  On cover   30.00
N23 O5 100m carmine   .55   *7.25*
  Never hinged   3.75
  On cover   30.00
N24 O5 300m olive grn   6.00   *145.00*
  Never hinged   65.00
  On cover   275.00
N25 O5 400m olive brn   .55   *7.25*
  Never hinged   4.50
  On cover   30.00
N26 O5 500m lilac   6.00   *145.00*
  Never hinged   65.00
  On cover   275.00

N27 O5 1000m blue   1.10   *12.00*
  Never hinged   7.50
  On cover   95.00
  Nos. N18-N27 (10)   17.00   *359.25*

No. N20 has the value in "Markes."
For surcharges see Nos. N44-N69, N88-N114.

No. 99 Surcharged in Green

1923, Apr. 13
N28 A18 100m on No. 99   5.00   *72.50*
  Never hinged   13.50
  On cover   725.00
 a. Inverted overprint   110.00
  Never hinged   260.00
N29 A18 400m on No. 99   3.75   *72.50*
  Never hinged   15.00
  On cover   725.00
 a. Inverted overprint   110.00
  Never hinged   260.00
N30 A18 500m on No. 99   5.00   *72.50*
  Never hinged   13.50
  On cover   725.00
 a. Inverted overprint   110.00
  Never hinged   260.00
  Nos. N28-N30 (3)   13.75   *217.50*

The normal position of the green surcharge is sideways, up-reading, with the top at the left. Inverted varieties are reversed, with the overprint down-reading.

Ship — O7   Seal — O8

Lighthouse — O9

1923, Apr. 12   Litho.
N31 O7 40m olive grn   4.50   *40.00*
  Never hinged   33.00
  On cover   275.00
N32 O7 50m brown   4.50   *40.00*
  Never hinged   33.00
  On cover   275.00
N33 O7 80m green   4.50   *40.00*
  Never hinged   33.00
  On cover   275.00
N34 O7 100m red   4.50   *40.00*
  Never hinged   33.00
  On cover   275.00
N35 O8 200m deep blue   4.50   *40.00*
  Never hinged   33.00
  On cover   275.00
N36 O8 300m brown   4.50   *40.00*
  Never hinged   33.00
  On cover   275.00
N37 O8 400m lilac   4.50   *40.00*
  Never hinged   33.00
  On cover   275.00
N38 O8 500m orange   4.50   *40.00*
  Never hinged   33.00
  On cover   275.00
N39 O8 600m olive grn   4.50   *40.00*
  Never hinged   33.00
  On cover   275.00
N40 O9 800m deep blue   4.50   *40.00*
  Never hinged   33.00
  On cover   275.00
N41 O9 1000m lilac   4.50   *40.00*
  Never hinged   33.00
  On cover   275.00
N42 O9 2000m red   4.50   *40.00*
  Never hinged   33.00
  On cover   275.00
N43 O9 3000m green   4.50   *40.00*
  Never hinged   33.00
  On cover   275.00
  Nos. N31-N43 (13)   58.50   *520.00*

Union of Memel with Lithuania. Forgeries exist.
For surcharges see Nos. N70-N86.

Nos. N20, N24, N26 Surcharged in Various Colors

1923   Thin Figures

N44	O5 2c on 300m (R)	6.50	16.00
	Never hinged	35.00	
	On cover		52.50
a.	Double surcharge	80.00	400.00
	Never hinged	225.00	
N45	O5 3c on 300m (R)	7.25	30.00
	Never hinged	37.50	
	On cover		52.50
a.	Double surcharge	175.00	475.00
	Never hinged	250.00	
N46	O4 10c on 25m (Bk)	7.25	16.00
	Never hinged	37.50	
	On cover		52.50
a.	Double surcharge	80.00	400.00
	Never hinged	225.00	
b.	Inverted surcharge	110.00	325.00
	Never hinged	240.00	
N47	O4 15c on 25m (Bk)	7.25	16.00
	Never hinged	37.50	
	On cover		52.50
N48	O5 20c on 500m (Bl)	11.00	32.50
	Never hinged	50.00	
	On cover		75.00
N49	O5 30c on 500m (Bk)	8.75	16.00
	Never hinged	37.50	
	On cover		52.50
a.	Double surcharge		—
	On cover		
N50	O5 50c on 500m (G)	20.00	32.50
	Never hinged	75.00	
	On cover		120.00
a.	Inverted surcharge	65.00	240.00
	Never hinged	190.00	
b.	Double surcharge	160.00	725.00
	Never hinged	450.00	
	Nos. N44-N50 (7)	68.00	149.00

Nos. N19, N21-N27 Surcharged

N51	O4 2c on 20m yellow	3.25	16.00
	Never hinged	15.00	
	On cover		32.50
N52	O4 2c on 50c yel grn	3.25	16.00
	Never hinged	15.00	
	On cover		32.50
a.	Double surcharge	65.00	325.00
	Never hinged	165.00	
b.	Vert. pair, imperf between	80.00	350.00
	Never hinged	225.00	
N53	O4 3c on 40m violet	4.75	14.50
	Never hinged	22.50	
	On cover		45.00
a.	Double surcharge	65.00	325.00
	Never hinged	175.00	
N54	O5 3c on 300m ol grn	3.25	12.00
	Never hinged	15.00	
	On cover		32.50
a.	Double surcharge	160.00	550.00
	Never hinged	450.00	
N55	O5 5c on 100m carmine	8.00	12.00
	Never hinged	37.50	
	On cover		32.50
N56	O5 5c on 300m ol grn (R)	4.00	20.00
	Never hinged	26.00	
	On cover		50.00
a.	Double surcharge	110.00	400.00
	Never hinged	300.00	
N57	O5 10c on 400m ol brn	12.00	24.00
	Never hinged	60.00	
	On cover		52.50
N58	O5 30c on 500m lilac	6.50	28.00
	Never hinged	42.50	
	On cover		67.50
a.	Double surcharge	110.00	400.00
	Never hinged	300.00	
b.	Inverted surcharge	120.00	450.00
	Never hinged	350.00	
N59	O5 1 l on 1000m blue	20.00	75.00
	Never hinged	105.00	
	On cover		110.00
a.	Double surcharge	160.00	550.00
	Never hinged	450.00	
	Nos. N51-N59 (9)	65.00	217.50

There are several types of the numerals in these surcharges. Nos. N56 and N58 have "CENT" in short, thick letters, as on Nos. N44 to N50.

Nos. N18-N23, N25, N27 Surcharged

Thick Figures

N60	O4 2c on 10m lt brn	6.50	80.00
	Never hinged	24.00	
	On cover		150.00
N61	O4 2c on 20m yellow	20.00	140.00
	Never hinged	80.00	
	On cover		275.00
N62	O4 2c on 50m yel grn	8.00	95.00
	Never hinged	37.50	
	On cover		150.00
N63	O4 3c on 10m lt brn	20.00	130.00
	Never hinged	80.00	
	On cover		190.00
a.	Double surcharge	160.00	650.00
	Never hinged	450.00	

N64	O4 3c on 40m violet	24.00	225.00
	Never hinged	100.00	
	On cover		375.00
N65	O5 5c on 100m car	12.00	40.00
	Never hinged	50.00	
	On cover		75.00
a.	Double surcharge	110.00	950.00
N66	O5 10c on 400m ol brn	145.00	675.00
	On cover	600.00	
			1,600.
N67	O4 15c on 25m orange	145.00	675.00
	On cover	600.00	
			1,600.
N68	O5 50c on 1000m blue	6.50	12.00
	Never hinged	22.50	
	On cover		32.50
a.	Double surcharge	110.00	350.00
	Never hinged	325.00	
N69	O5 1 l on 1000m blue	8.00	24.00
	Never hinged	40.00	
	On cover		60.00
a.	Double surcharge	110.00	350.00
	Never hinged	325.00	
	Nos. N60-N69 (10)	395.00	2,096.

No. N69 is surcharged like type "b" in the following group.

Nos. N31-N43 Surcharged

a	b

N70	O7(a) 15c on 40m ol grn	5.50	32.50
	Never hinged	22.50	
	On cover		55.00
N71	O7(a) 30c on 50m brown	5.25	24.00
	Never hinged	24.50	
	On cover		45.00
a.	Double surcharge	65.00	275.00
	Never hinged	200.00	
N72	O7(a) 30c on 80m green	5.25	40.00
	Never hinged	24.50	
	On cover		67.50
N73	O7(a) 30c on 100m red	5.50	16.00
	Never hinged	24.50	
	On cover		37.50
N74	O8(a) 50c on 200m dp blue	6.00	32.50
	Never hinged	24.50	
	On cover		55.00
N75	O8(a) 50c on 300m brn	5.25	20.00
	Never hinged	24.50	
	On cover		37.50
a.	Double surcharge	65.00	275.00
	Never hinged	200.00	
b.	Inverted surcharge	67.50	325.00
	Never hinged	200.00	
N76	O8(a) 50c on 400m lilac	5.50	28.00
	Never hinged	24.50	
	On cover		52.50
a.	Inverted surcharge	72.50	325.00
	Never hinged	200.00	
N77	O8(a) 50c on 500m org	5.50	16.00
	Never hinged	24.50	
	On cover		37.50
a.	Double surcharge	65.00	275.00
	Never hinged	160.00	
N78	O8(b) 1 l on 600m ol grn	5.50	36.00
	Never hinged	26.00	
	On cover		67.50
N79	O9(b) 1 l on 800m dp blue	6.50	36.00
	Never hinged	26.00	
	On cover		67.50
N80	O9(b) 1 l on 1000m lil	6.00	36.00
	Never hinged	26.00	
	On cover		67.50
N81	O9(b) 1 l on 2000m red	6.00	36.00
	Never hinged	26.00	
	On cover		75.00
N82	O9(b) 1 l on 3000m grn	6.50	36.00
	Never hinged	26.00	
	On cover		67.50
	Nos. N70-N82 (13)	74.25	389.00

These stamps are said to have been issued to commemorate the institution of autonomous government.

Nos. N32, N34, N36, N38 Surcharged in Green

1923

N83	O7 15c on 50m brn	275.	2,000.
	Never hinged	1,050.	
	On cover		3,350.
a.	Thick numerals in surcharge	950.	4,750.
	Never hinged	3,250.	
N84	O7 25c on 100m red	150.	1,200.
	Never hinged	350.	
	On cover		2,500.

a.	Thick numerals in surcharge	550.	3,250.
	Never hinged	2,400.	
N85	O8 30c on 300m brn	250.	1,300.
	Never hinged	650.	
	On cover		2,800.
a.	Thick numerals in surcharge	725.	3,500.
	Never hinged	2,400.	
N86	O8 60c on 500m org	150.	1,200.
	Never hinged	350.	
	On cover		2,800.
a.	Thick numerals in surcharge	550.	2,400.
	Never hinged	1,600.	

Surcharges on Nos. N83-N86 are of two types, differing in width of numerals. Values are for stamps with narrow numerals, as illustrated.

Nos. N8, N10-N11, N3 Surcharged in Red or Green

N87	O4 10c on 25m on 5c bl (R)	35.00	120.00
	Never hinged	375.00	
	On cover		225.00
N88	O4 15c on 100m on 25c red (G)	40.00	350.00
	Never hinged	450.00	
	On cover		600.00
a.	Inverted surcharge	400.00	2,250.
	Never hinged	1,900.	
N89	O4 30c on 400m on 1 l brn (R)	17.50	47.50
	Never hinged	60.00	
	On cover		90.00
N90	O4 00c on 50m on 25c red (G)	40.00	325.00
	Never hinged	400.00	
	On cover		600.00
	Nos. N87-N90 (4)	132.50	842.50

Nos. N18-N22 Surcharged in Green or Red

N91	O4 15c on 10m	32.50	210.00
	Never hinged	150.00	
	On cover		260.00
N92	O4 15c on 20m	3.50	32.50
	Never hinged	15.00	
	On cover		110.00
N93	O4 15c on 25m	5.25	65.00
	Never hinged	22.50	
	On cover		110.00
N94	O4 15c on 40m	3.50	32.50
	Never hinged	15.00	
	On cover		110.00
N95	O4 15c on 50m (R)	2.75	24.50
	Never hinged	11.00	
	On cover		90.00
a.	Inverted surcharge	65.00	250.00
	Never hinged	200.00	
N96	O4 25c on 10m	11.00	120.00
	Never hinged	52.50	
	On cover		260.00
N97	O4 25c on 20m	3.50	32.50
	Never hinged	11.00	
	On cover		90.00
a.	Double surcharge	160.00	600.00
N98	O4 25c on 25m	5.25	47.50
	Never hinged	26.00	
	On cover		110.00
N99	O4 25c on 40m	4.50	47.50
	Never hinged	22.50	
	On cover		90.00
a.	Inverted surcharge	60.00	
	Never hinged	190.00	
N100	O4 25c on 50m (R)	2.60	24.50
	Never hinged	13.50	
	On cover		90.00
a.	Inverted surcharge	65.00	
	Never hinged	200.00	
N101	O4 30c on 10m	32.50	200.00
	Never hinged	150.00	
	On cover		300.00
N102	O4 30c on 20m	3.75	40.00
	Never hinged	16.50	
	On cover		140.00
N103	O4 30c on 25m	5.25	65.00
	Never hinged	22.50	
	On cover		140.00
N104	O4 30c on 40m	3.75	24.00
	Never hinged	15.00	
	On cover		140.00
N105	O4 30c on 50m (R)	2.60	24.50
	Never hinged	11.00	
	On cover		140.00
a.	Inverted surcharge	65.00	
	Never hinged	200.00	
	Nos. N91-N105 (15)	122.20	989.50

Nos. N23, N25, N27 Surcharged in Green or Red

N106	O5 15c on 100m	2.75	22.50
	Never hinged	11.00	
	On cover		90.00
a.	Inverted surcharge	60.00	
	Never hinged	190.00	
N107	O5 15c on 400m	2.50	18.50
	Never hinged	9.00	
	On cover		90.00
N108	O5 15c on 1000m (R)	65.00	400.00
	Never hinged	325.00	
	On cover		875.00
a.	Inverted surcharge	200.00	800.00
	Never hinged	600.00	
N109	O5 25c on 100m	2.50	22.50
	Never hinged	9.00	
	On cover		90.00
N110	O5 25c on 400m	2.50	22.50
	Never hinged	9.00	
	On cover		90.00
a.	Double surcharge	160.00	
	Never hinged	350.00	
N111	O5 25c on 1000m (R)	65.00	400.00
	Never hinged	300.00	
	On cover		875.00
a.	Inverted surcharge	200.00	800.00
	Never hinged	375.00	
N112	O5 30c on 100m	2.60	24.50
	Never hinged	11.00	
	On cover		140.00
a.	Inverted surcharge	60.00	
	Never hinged	190.00	
N113	O5 30c on 400m	2.60	24.50
	Never hinged	11.00	
	On cover		140.00
N114	O5 00c on 1000m (R)	65.00	175.00
	Never hinged	300.00	
	On cover		875.00
a.	Inverted surcharge	200.00	800.00
	Never hinged	600.00	
	Nos. N106-N114 (9)	210.45	1,410.

Nos. N96 to N100 and N109 to N111 are surcharged "Centai," the others "Centu."

MESOPOTAMIA

ˌme-sˌə-pə-'tä-mē-ə

LOCATION — In Western Asia, bounded on the north by Syria and Turkey, on the east by Persia, on the south by Saudi Arabia and on the west by Trans-Jordan.
GOVT. — A former Turkish Province
AREA — 143,250 (1918) sq. mi.
POP. — 2,849,282 (1920)
CAPITAL — Baghdad

During World War I this territory was occupied by Great Britain. It was recognized as an independent state and placed under British Mandate but in 1932 the Mandate was terminated and the country admitted to membership in the League of Nations as the Kingdom of Iraq. Postage stamps of Iraq are now in use.

16 Annas = 1 Rupee

Watermark

Wmk. 48 — Diagonal Zigzag Lines

Issued under British Occupation

Baghdad Issue
Stamps of Turkey 1901-16 Surcharged

N1

N2

N3

N4

N5

The surcharges were printed from slugs which were arranged to fit the various shapes of the stamps.

1917   Unwmk.   Perf. 12, 13½
On Turkey Nos. 254, 256, 258-260

N1	¼a on 2pa red lil	325.00	375.00
a.	"IN BRITISH" omitted	14,000.	
N2	¼a on 5pa vio brown	225.00	250.00
a.	"¼ An" omitted	11,000.	

N3	½a on 10pa green	1,200.	1,400.
N4	1a on 20pa red	800.00	900.00
a.	"BAGHDAD" double	2,150.	
N5	2a on 1pi blue	375.00	400.00
	Nos. N1-N5 (5)	2,925.	3,325.

On Turkey No. 249

N6	A22 2a on 1pi ultra	700.00	875.00
a.	"IN BRITISH" omitted	13,000.	

On Turkey No. 251

N7	A23 ½a on 10pa green	1,850.	2,100.

On Turkey Nos. 272-273

N8	A29 1a on 20pa red	425.	500.
a.	"OCCUPATION" omitted	10,000.	
b.	"BAGHDAD" double	2,150.	
N9	A30 2a on 1pi blue	5,250.	6,000.

On Turkey Nos. 346-348

N10	A41 ½a on 10pa car, perf 12½	700.00	800.00
a.	Perf 13½	1,500.	1,600.
N11	A41 1a on 20pa ultra, perf 12½	1,500.	2,000.
a.	"1 An" omitted	13,000.	
b.	Perf 13½	7,500.	
N12	A41 2a on 1pi vio & black, perf 13½	190.00	200.00
a.	"BAGHDAD" omitted	9,750.	
b.	Perf 12½	400.00	425.00

On Turkey Nos. 297, 300

N13	A17 ¼a on 5pa purple	10,000.	
N14	A17 2a on 1pi blue	300.	350.
a.	"OCCUPATION" omitted	13,000.	

On Turkey No. 306

N15	A18 1a on 20pa car	700.	825.
a.	Value omitted	13,000.	

On Turkey Nos. 329-331

N16	A22 ½a on 10pa bl grn	175.00	190.00
N17	A22 1a on 20pa car rose	650.00	700.00
a.	"1 An" omitted	7,000.	5,750.
b.	With additional "Behie"	8,000.	8,250.
N18	A22 2a on 1pi ultra	190.00	200.00
a.	"BAGHDAD" omitted	—	

On Turkey No. 337

N19	A22 1a on 20pa car rose	6,000.	7,500.

On Turkey No. P125

N20	A17 1a on 20pa car	—	

On Turkey Nos. B1, B8

Inscription in crescent is obliterated by another crescent handstamped in violet black on Nos. N21-N27.

N21	A18 ½a on 10pa dull grn	200.00	250.00
a.	"OCCUPATION" omitted	12,500.	
N22	A21 1a on 20pa car rose	700.00	750.00

On Turkey No. B29

N23	A21 2a on 1pi ultra	2,500.	2,750.

On Turkey Nos. B33-B34

N24	A22 1a on 20pa car rose	200.00	250.00
N25	A22 2a on 1pi ultra	300.00	350.00
a.	"OCCUPATION" omitted	12,000.	
b.	"BAGHDAD" omitted	11,000.	

On Turkey No. B42

N26	A41 ½a on 10pa car, perf 12½	300.00	325.00
a.	"BAGHDAD" double		
b.	Perf 13½	550.00	650.00

On Turkey No. B38

N27	A11 1a on 10pa on 20pa vio brn	325.00	350.00
a.	"OCCUPATION" omitted	12,000.	11,000.

Iraq Issue

N28

N29

N30

N31

N32

N33

N34

N35

N36

N37

N38

N39

N40

N41

Turkey Nos. 256, 258-269 Surcharged

1918-20			**Perf. 12**
N28	¼a on 5pa vio brn	.55	1.10
N29	½a on 10pa grn	.75	.25
N30	1a on 20pa red	.55	.25
N31	1½a on 5pa vio brn	8.75	5.50
N32	2½a on 1pi blue	1.35	1.50
a.	Inverted surcharge	8,500.	
N33	3a on 1½pi car & black	1.60	.25
a.	Double surcharge, red & blk	3,500.	4,500.
N34	4a on 1¾pi slate & red brn	1.60	.30
a.	Center inverted		30,000.
N35	6a on 2pi grn & black	1.75	2.00
N36	8a on 2½pi org & ol grn	2.25	2.25
N37	12a on 5pi dl vio	2.00	5.00
N38	1r on 10pi red brown	2.50	1.50
N39	2r on 25pi ol grn	8.00	2.75

N40 5r on 50pi car 26.00 30.00
N41 10r on 100pi dp blue 92.50 18.50
Nos. N28-N41 (14) 150.15 71.15

See #N50-N53. For overprints see #NO1-NO21.

Mosul Issue

A13

A14

A15

A16

A17

A18

A19

1919 Unwmk. Perf. 11½, 12
N42 A13 ½a on 1pi grn & brn red 2.40 2.10
N43 A14 1a on 20pa *rose* 1.50 1.90
  a. "POSTAGE" omitted
N44 A15 1a on 20pa *rose* 4.50 4.50
  a. Double surcharge 725.00

Turkish word at right of tughra ("reshad") is large on No. N43, small on No. N44.

Wmk. Turkish Characters
Perf. 12½
N45 A16 2½a on 1pi vio & yel 1.60 1.60
N46 A17 3a on 20pa grn & yel 75.00 100.00

Wmk. 48
N47 A17 3a on 20pa green 1.75 4.25
N48 A18 4a on 1pi dull vio 3.50 3.75
  a. Double surcharge 1,100.
  b. "4" omitted 2,000.
  c. As "b," double surcharge
N49 A19 8a on 10pa claret 4.25 5.50
  a. Double surcharge 700.00 875.00
  b. Inverted surcharge 800.00 1,000.
  c. 8a on 1pi dull violet 3,250.
  Nos. N42-N49 (8) 94.50 123.60

Value for No. 49c is for a stamp with the perfs cutting into the design.

Iraq Issue
Types of 1918-20 Issue
1921 Wmk. 4 Perf. 12
N50 A28 ½a on 10pa green 3.25 2.25
N51 A26 1½a on 5pa dp brn 2.50 1.10
N52 A37 2r on 25pi ol grn 24.00 13.00
  Nos. N50-N52 (3) 29.75 16.35
  Set of 3, ovptd "SPECI-MEN" 120.00

Type of 1918-20 without "Reshad"
1922 Unwmk.
N53 A36 1r on 10pi red brn 220.00 26.00
"Reshad" is the small Turkish word at right of the tughra in circle at top center.

For overprint see No. NO22.

OFFICIAL STAMPS

Nos. N29-N41 Overprinted

1920 Unwmk. Perf. 12
NO1 A28 ½a on 10pa grn 13.00 2.00
NO2 A29 1a on 20pa red 5.50 .65
NO3 A26 1½a on 5pa vio brown 37.50 2.75
NO4 A30 2½a on 1pi blue 5.50 6.00
NO5 A31 3a on 1½pi car & black 26.00 .85
NO6 A32 4a on 1¾pi sl & red brn 37.50 4.00
NO7 A33 6a on 2pi grn & black 32.50 8.00
NO8 A34 8a on 2½pi org & ol grn 35.00 5.00
NO9 A35 12a on 5pi dull vio 25.00 16.00
NO10 A36 1r on 10pi red brown 32.50 12.00
NO11 A37 2r on 25pi ol green 32.50 17.50
NO12 A38 5r on 50pi car 65.00 48.00
NO13 A39 10r on 100pi dp blue 92.50 *120.00*
  Nos. NO1-NO13 (13) 440.00 242.75

Same Overprint on Types of Regular Issue of 1918-20

1921-22 Wmk. 4
NO14 A28 ½a on 10pa grn 1.10 1.10
NO15 A29 1a on 20pa red 7.50 1.10
NO16 A26 1½a on 5pa dp brn 3.00 .75
NO17 A32 4a on 1¾pi gray & red brn 2.25 *2.75*
NO18 A33 6a on 2pi grn & black 30.00 *140.00*
NO19 A34 8a on 2½pi org & yel grn 3.50 2.25
NO20 A35 12a on 5pi dl vio 30.00 *85.00*
NO21 A37 2r on 25pi ol grn 85.00 *130.00*
  Nos. NO14-NO21 (8) 162.35 *362.95*
  Set of 8, ovptd "SPECI-MEN" 325.00

Same Overprint on No. N53

1922 Unwmk.
NO22 A36 1r on 10pi red brn 37.50 7.50

MEXICO

ˈmek-si-ˌkō

LOCATION — Extreme southern part of the North American continent, south of the United States
GOVT. — Republic
AREA — 756,198 sq. mi.
POP. — 76,791,819 (est. 1984)
CAPITAL — Mexico, D.F

8 Reales = 1 Peso
100 Centavos = 1 Peso

GREAT BRITAIN POST OFFICES IN MEXICO

British postal agencies were opened in Veracruz in 1825 and in Tampico in 1842. British stamps were used at Tampico from 1867 but were not provided for the agency at Veracruz. The British Veracruz office was closed in 1874 and the Tampico office in 1876.

Values are for clear cancellations on sound, fault-free stamps, with average to fine centering. In many cases, very fine copies are rare or non-existent.

TAMPICO
Pre-Stamp Postmark
1841
Crowned Circle Handstamp Type II
A1 Inscribed "PAID AT TAM-PICO" in red, on cover 2,250.
  Earliest known use 11/13/41.

Stamps of Great Britain Cancelled with barred oval "C63" obliterator
1859-85
A4 1p rose red, plates 81, 89, 103, 117, 139, 147 (#33), *value from* 150.00
A5 2p blue, plate 9 (#29) 200.00
A6 2p blue, plate 14 (#30), *value from* 200.00
A7 4p vermilion, plates 7-14 (#43), *value from* 150.00
A8 1sh green, plates 4, 5, 7, 8 (#54), *value from* 200.00
A9 2sh blue (#55) 600.00

VERACRUZ
Pre-Stamp Postal Markings
1841-45
Crowned Circle Handstamp Type II
A10 Inscribed "PAID AT VERA-CRUZ" in red, on cover 2,000.
A11 Inscribed "PAID AT VERA-CRUZ" in black, on cover 1,100.
  Earliest known use: A10, 11/13/41; A11, 1845.

District Overprints
Nos. 1-149 are overprinted with names of various districts, and sometimes also with district numbers and year dates. Some of the district overprints are rare and command high prices. Values given for Nos. 1-149 are for the more common district overprints.

Watermarks

Wmk. 150 — PAPEL SELLADO in Sheet

Wmk. 151 — R. P. S. in the Sheet (R.P.S. stands for "Renta Papel Sellado")

Wmk. 152 — "CORREOS E U M" on Every Horizontal Line of Ten Stamps

Wmk. 153 — "R M" Interlaced

Wmk. 154 — Eagle and R M

Wmk. 155 — SERVICIO POSTAL DE LOS ESTADOS UNIDOS MEXICANOS

Wmk. 156 — CORREOS MEXICO

Wmk. 248 — SECRETARIA DE HACIENDA MEXICO

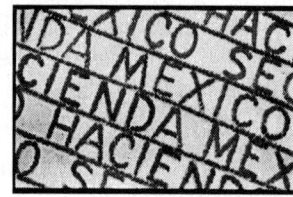
Wmk. 260 — Lines and SECRETARIA DE HACIENDA MEXICO

Miguel Hidalgo y Costilla — A1

Handstamped with District Name
1856 Unwmk. Engr. Imperf.
1 A1 ½r blue 50.00 40.00
  b. Without overprint 45.00 45.00
  c. Double impression 150.00
2 A1 1r yellow 30.00 5.00
  b. Half used as ½r on cover 10,000.
  c. Without overprint 25.00 30.00
  d. 1r green (error)
3 A1 2r yellow grn 27.50 3.50
  a. 2r blue green 275.00 40.00
  b. 2r emerald 250.00 50.00
  c. Half used as 1r on cover 600.00
  d. Without overprint 40.00 22.50
  e. As "a," without overprint 250.00 45.00
  f. As "b," without overprint 75.00
  g. Printed on both sides (yel green) 300.00
4 A1 4r red 175.00 110.00
  a. Half used as 2r on cover 250.00
  b. Quarter used as 1r on cover 700.00
  c. Without overprint 140.00 160.00
  d. Three quarters used as 3r on cover 12,000.
5 A1 8r red lilac 350.00 200.00
  a. 8r violet 300.00 200.00
  b. Without overprint 225.00 225.00
  c. Eighth used as 1r on cover 17,500.

d. Quarter used as 2r on
   cover   225.00
e. Half used as 4r on cover   900.00
   Nos. 1-5 (5)   632.50   358.50

The 1r and 2r were printed in sheets of 60 with wide spacing between stamps, and in sheets of 190 or 200 with narrow spacing.

No. 3a can be distinguished from the other 2r stamps by the horizontal grain of the paper. The plate for No. 3b has framelines.

All values, except the 1r, have been reprinted, some of them several times. The reprints usually show signs of wear and the impressions are often smudgy. The paper is usually thicker than that of the originals. Reprints are usually on very white paper. Reprints are found with and without overprints and with cancellations made both from the original handstamps and from forged ones.

Counterfeits exist.

See Nos. 6-12. For overprints see Nos. 35-45.

1861

6	A1 ½r black, *buff*	50.00	45.00
a.	Without overprint	34.00	62.50
7	A1 1r black, *green*	20.00	5.50
a.	Impression of 2r on back		450.00
b.	Without overprint	5.00	22.50
d.	As "b," blk, *pink* (error)	8,000	*9,000.*
f.	Double impression		150.00
8	A1 2r black, *pink*	15.00	4.50
a.	Impression of 1r on back	2,000.	
b.	Half used as 1r on cover		750.00
c.	Without overprint	3.50	22.50
d.	Printed on both sides		2,250.
e.	Double impression		100.00
f.	As "e," without overprint		—
9	A1 4r black, *yellow*	200.00	100.00
a.	Half used as 2r on cover		190.00
b.	Without overprint	50.00	100.00
c.	Quarter used as 1r on cover		700.00
d.	Three-quarters used as 3r on cover		*35,000.*
10	A1 4r dull rose, *yel*	200.00	70.00
a.	Half used as 2r on cover		*950.00*
b.	Without overprint	110.00	140.00
c.	Printed on both sides		*9,000.*
d.	Quarter used as 1r on cover		10,000.
11	A1 8r black, *red brn*	375.00	250.00
a.	⅛ used as 1R on cover front		11,000.
b.	Quarter used as 2r on cover		250.00
c.	Half used as 4r on cover		750.00
d.	Without overprint	110.00	225.00
e.	Three quarters used as 6r on cover		*45,000.*
12	A1 8r grn, *red brn*	500.00	240.00
a.	Half used as 4r on cover		30,000.
b.	Without overprint	150.00	200.00
c.	Quarter used as 2r on cover		40,000.
d.	Printed on both sides	*12,500.*	*12,500.*
	Nos. 6-12 (7)	1,360.	715.00

Nos. 6, 9, 10, 11 and 12 have been reprinted. Most reprints of the ½r, 4r and 8r are on vertically grained paper. Originals are on horizontally grained paper. The original ½r stamps are much worn but the reprints are unworn. The paper of the 4r is too deep and rich in color and No. 10 is printed in too bright red.

Reprints of the 8r can only be told by experts. All these reprints are found in fancy colors and with overprints and cancellations as in the 1856 issue.

Counterfeits exist.

Hidalgo — A3

With District Name

1864   *Perf. 12*

14	A3 1r red	750.	3,000.
a.	Without District Name	.75	
15	A3 2r blue	1,100.	1,750.
a.	Without District Name	.75	
16	A3 4r brown	1,250.	2,400.
a.	Without District Name	1.25	
b.	Vert. pair, imperf. between		
17	A3 1p black	3,250.	22,500.
a.	Without District Name	2.00	

Nos. 14 to 17 were issued with district overprints of Saltillo or Monterrey on the toned paper of 1864. Overprints on the 1867 white paper are fraudulent. Counterfeits and counterfeit cancellations are plentiful. The 1r red with "½" surcharge is bogus.

Coat of Arms — A4

Overprint of District Name, etc.

Five types of overprints:

I — District name only.

II — District name, consignment number and "1864" in large figures.

III — District name, number and "1864" in small figures.

IV — District name, number and "1865."

V — District name, number and "1866."

1864-66   *Imperf.*

18	A4 3c brn (IV, V)	1,300.	*2,500.*
a.	Without overprint	700.00	
b.	Laid paper	*4,500.*	6,000.
19	A4 ½r brown (I)	400.00	250.00
a.	Type II	2,200.	2,250.
b.	Without overprint	200.00	650.00
20	A4 ½r lilac (IV)	60.00	55.00
a.	Type III	140.00	75.00
b.	Type II	200.00	200.00
c.	Type V		3,000.
d.	½r gray (V)	70.00	80.00
e.	Without overprint	5.75	
f.	½r gray lilac	250.00	100.00
21	A4 1r blue (IV, V)	15.00	9.00
a.	Type III		80.00
b.	Without overprint	2.50	
c.	Half used as ½r on cover		3,000.
22	A4 1r ultra (I, II)	120.00	30.00
a.	Type III	90.00	40.00
b.	Without overprint	160.00	150.00
c.	Half used as ½r on cover		*7,250.*
23	A4 2r org (III, IV, V)	10.00	4.00
a.	Type II	20.00	6.00
b.	Type I	50.00	7.00
c.	2r dp org, without ovpt., early plate	175.00	65.00
d.	Without ovpt., late plate	2.00	
e.	Half used as 1r on cover		6,000.
24	A4 4r grn (III, IV, V)	100.00	50.00
a.	Types I, II	160.00	77.50
b.	4r dk grn, without ovpt.	4.75	*1,700.*
d.	Half used as 2r on cover		700.00
25	A4 8r red (IV, V)	150.00	90.00
a.	Types II, III	175.00	125.00
b.	Type I	400.00	175.00
c.	8r dk red, without ovpt.	7.00	*575.00*
f.	Quarter used as 2r on cover		15,000.
g.	Three-quarters used as 6r on cover		

The 2r printings from the early plates are 25½mm high; those from the late plate, 24½mm.

Varieties listed as "Without overprint" in unused condition are remainders.

Besides the overprints of district name, number and date, Nos. 18-34 often received, in the district offices, additional overprints of numbers and sometimes year dates. Stamps with these "sub-consignment numbers" sell for more than stamps without them.

Genuine examples of No. 20c should bear Mexico district name overprint, together with consignment numbers 1-1866 or 17-1866. Gray lilac stamps of other consignments are examples of No. 20f.

Value unused for No. 18 is for an example without gum. Examples with original gum sell for more. Examples of No. 18a on laid paper are forgeries.

No. 25g does not exist on full cover.

Faked quarterlings and bisects of 1856-64 are plentiful.

The 3c has been reprinted from a die on which the words "TRES CENTAVOS," the outlines of the serpent and some of the background lines have been retouched.

Emperor
Maximilian — A5

Overprinted with District Name, Number and Date 1866 or 866; also with Number and Date only, or with Name only

1866   *Litho.*

26	A5 7c lilac gray	65.00	125.00
a.	7c deep gray	85.00	140.00
27	A5 13c blue	35.00	35.00
a.	Half used as 7c on cover	25.00	25.00
b.	13c cobalt blue	25.00	
c.	Without overprint	2,500.	
28	A5 25c buff	12.50	9.00
a.	Half used as 13c on cover	2,500.	
b.	Without overprint		

29	A5 25c orange	12.00	12.00
a.	25c red orange	20.00	27.50
b.	25c red brown	85.00	47.50
c.	25c brown	*110.00*	85.00
30	A5 50c green	25.00	30.00
	Nos. 26-30 (5)	149.50	211.00

Litho. printings have round period after value numerals.

Overprinted with District Name, Number and Date 866 or 867; also with Number and Date only Engr.

31	A5 7c lilac	450.00	*5,500.*
a.	Without overprint	3.50	
32	A5 13c blue	12.00	12.00
a.	Without overprint	1.25	
33	A5 25c orange brown	12.00	11.00
a.	Without overprint	1.25	
34	A5 50c green	700.00	70.00
a.	Without overprint	2.50	

See "sub-consignment" note after No. 25.

Engraved printings have square period after value numerals.

Varieties listed as "Without overprint" in unused condition are remainders.

1867

35	A1 ½r blk, *buff*	2,500.	*4,000.*
36	A1 1r blk, *green*	60.00	10.00
37	A1 2r blk, *pink*	22.50	5.00
a.	Printed on both sides		140.00
38	A1 4r red, *yel*	625.00	50.00
a.	Printed on both sides		175.00
39	A1 4r red	*6,000.*	*3,250.*
40	A1 8r blk, *red brn*	3,500.	275.00
41	A1 8r grn, *red brn*		*4,000.*

Dangerous counterfeits exist of the "Mexico" overprint.

Examples of No. 38 with yellow removed are offered as No. 39.

Same Overprint Thin Gray Blue Paper Wmk. 151

42	A1 ½r gray	275.00	190.00
a.	Without overprint	175.00	175.00
43	A1 1r blue	400.00	65.00
a.	Without overprint	300.00	125.00
44	A1 2r green	200.00	30.00
a.	Printed on both sides	6,000.	3,500.
b.	Without overprint	300.00	50.00
45	A1 4r rose	3,000.	75.00
a.	Without overprint	*5,000.*	225.00

Most examples of Nos. 42-45 do not show the watermark. Values are for such stamps. Examples showing the watermark sell for more.

Reprints of the ½r and 4r exist on watermarked paper. Reprints of ½r and 8r also exist in gray on thick grayish wove paper, unwatermarked.

Hidalgo — A6

Thin Figures of Value, without Period after Numerals

Overprinted with District Name, Number and Abbreviated Date

1868 Unwmk.   Litho.   *Imperf.*

46	A6 6c blk, *buff*	40.00	20.00
47	A6 12c blk, *green*	45.00	20.00
a.	Period after "12"	65.00	55.00
48	A6 25c bl, *pink*	75.00	20.00
a.	Without overprint	125.00	
49	A6 50c blk, *yellow*	600.00	60.00
50	A6 100c blk, *brown*	775.00	140.00
a.	Half used as 50c on cover		3,000.
51	A6 100c brn, *brn*		1,750. 500.00

			Perf.
52	A6 6c blk, *buff*	35.00	35.00
a.	Without overprint	150.00	
b.	Period after "6"	100.00	75.00
53	A6 12c blk, *green*	35.00	12.00
a.	Period after "12"	85.00	30.00
b.	Very thick paper	50.00	25.00
c.	Without overprint	110.00	
54	A6 25c blue, *pink*	55.00	10.00
b.	Without overprint	150.00	
55	A6 50c blk, *yellow*	325.00	45.00
a.	Half used as 50c on cover		3,000.
56	A6 100c blk, *brown*	375.00	110.00
c.	Without overprint	350.00	
57	A6 100c brn, *brn*	1,000.	375.00
a.	Printed on both sides	1,250.	1,000.

Four kinds of perforation are found in the 1868 issue: serrate, square, pin and regular. The narrow spacing between stamps was inadequate for some of these perforation types.

Thick Figures of Value, with Period after Numerals

Overprinted with District Name, Number and Abbreviated Date
Imperf

58	A6	6c blk, *buff*	9.50	4.50
59	A6	12c blk, *green*	4.25	1.25
b.		12c black, *buff* (error)	575.00	575.00
d.		Printed on both sides		3,000.
e.		No period after "12"		
61	A6	25c blue, *pink*	8.00	1.25
a.		No period after "25"		90.00
c.		Very thick paper	25.00	6.00
d.		"85" for "25"	75.00	50.00
e.		"35" for "25"		75.00
f.		Printed on both sides		
62	A6	50c blk, *yellow*	125.00	15.00
a.		No period after "50"	225.00	30.00
b.		50c blue, *lt pink* (error)	3,000.	2,000.
c.		Half used as 25c on cover		1,000.
d.		Very thick paper		50.00
e.		"30" for "50"	750.00	750.00
64	A6	100c blk, *brown*	150.00	90.00
a.		No period after "100"	175.00	
b.		Very thick paper		75.00
c.		Quarter used as 25c on cover		2,000.
		Nos. 58-64 (5)	296.75	112.00

Perf.

65	A6	6c blk, *buff*	40.00	20.00
a.		Very thick paper	60.00	35.00
66	A6	12c blk, *green*	5.50	5.50
a.		Very thick paper	20.00	15.00
b.		12c black, *buff* (error)	575.00	575.00
c.		No period after "12"	—	
68	A6	25c blue, *pink*	20.00	2.50
a.		No period after "25"	80.00	80.00
b.		Thick paper	30.00	15.00
d.		"85" for "25"	80.00	40.00
69	A6	50c blk, *yellow*	200.00	25.00
a.		No period after "50"	200.00	30.00
b.		50c blue, *lt pink* (error)	2,500.	1,500.
c.		Thick paper		60.00
70	A6	100c blk, *brown*	200.00	60.00
a.		No period after "100"	200.00	65.00
b.		Very thick paper		80.00
		Nos. 65-70 (5)	465.50	113.00

Postal forgeries of Nos. 58-70 were printed from original plates with district name overprints forged. These include the pelure paper varieties and some thick paper varieties. The "Anotado" handstamp was applied to some of the confiscated forgeries and they were issued, including Nos. 73a and 78a.

Stamps of 1868 Handstamped

Overprinted with District Name, Number and Abbreviated Date
Thick Figures with Period
1872 — *Imperf.*

71	A6	6c blk, *buff*	650.00	675.00
72	A6	12c blk, *green*	85.00	75.00
73	A6	25c bl, *pink*	40.00	45.00
a.		Pelure paper	55.00	65.00
b.		"85" for "25"		125.00
74	A6	50c blk, *yellow*	850.00	475.00
a.		No period after "50"	900.00	475.00
75	A6	100c blk, *brown*	1,250.	1,000.
a.		No period after "100"		1,100.

Perf.

76	A6	6c blk, *buff*		750.00
77	A6	12c blk, *green*	90.00	80.00
78	A6	25c blk, *pink*	35.00	42.50
a.		Pelure paper	65.00	90.00
79	A6	50c blk, *yellow*	850.00	600.00
a.		No period after "50"		550.00
80	A6	100c blk, *brown*		1,200.

Counterfeit "Anotado" overprints abound. Genuine cancellations other than Mexico City or of the Diligencias de Puebla are unknown. It is recommended that these be purchased accompanied by certificates of authenticity from competent experts.

The stamps of the 1872 issue are found perforated with square holes, pin-perf. 13, 14 or 15, and with serrate perforation.

The counterfeits of the 1868 6c, 12c buff, 50c and 100c (both colors) from new plates have clear, sharp impressions and more facial shading lines than the originals. These counterfeits are found perf. and imperf., with thick and thin numerals, and with the "Anotado" overprint.

Hidalgo — A8

Moiré on White Back
Overprinted with District Name, Number and Abbreviated Date
White Wove Paper
1872 — **Wmk. 150** — **Imperf.**

81	A8	6c green	325.00	275.00
82	A8	12c blue	250.00	125.00
a.		Laid paper	2,000.	350.00
83	A8	25c red	400.00	125.00
a.		Laid paper	2,000.	350.00
84	A8	50c yellow	2,000.	850.00
a.		50c blue (error)		3,000.
b.		Laid paper		4,000.
c.		As "a," without ovpt.	130.00	
86	A8	100c gray lilac	1,000.	650.00
		Nos. 81-86 (5)	3,975.	2,025.

Wmk. "LA + F"

81a	A8	6c green	2,000.	1,000.
82b	A8	12c blue	450.00	325.00
83b	A8	25c red	575.00	575.00
c.		Without overprint	500.00	
84d	A8	50c yellow	3,500.	2,000.
86a	A8	100c gray lilac	4,000.	1,500.

1872 — **Wmk. 150** — **Pin-perf.**

87	A8	6c green	2,500.	2,000.
88	A8	12c blue	475.00	175.00
89	A8	25c red	550.00	275.00
b.		Laid paper		1,000.
90	A8	50c yellow	1,500.	950.00
a.		50c blue (error)	1,000.	1,250.
b.		As "a," without overprint	200.00	
92	A8	100c gray lilac	1,200.	1,200.
		Nos. 87-92 (5)	6,225.	4,600.

Wmk. "LA + F"

87a	A8	6c green	2,500.	2,000.
88a	A8	12c blue	450.00	400.00
89a	A8	25c red	950.00	350.00
90c	A8	50c yellow	4,000.	2,500.
92a	A8	100c gray lilac	3,600.	2,750.

The watermark "LA+F" stands for La Croix Frères, the paper manufacturers, and is in double-lined block capitals 13mm high. A single stamp will show only part of this watermark.

Values for Nos. 87-92a are for examples with visible perfs on all sides.

1872 — **Unwmk.** — **Imperf.**

93	A8	6c green	12.50	12.50
a.		Without moiré on back, without overprint	60.00	
b.		Vertically laid paper	3,000.	1,300.
c.		Bottom label retouched	100.00	90.00
d.		Very thick paper	37.50	37.50
94	A8	12c blue	2.00	1.75
a.		Without moiré on back, without overprint	30.00	35.00
b.		Vertically laid paper	350.00	210.00
c.		Thin gray bl paper of 1867 (Wmk 151)		2,000.
95	A8	25c red	8.50	2.00
a.		Without moiré on back, without overprint	30.00	35.00
b.		Vertically laid paper	450.00	500.00
c.		Thin gray bl paper of 1867 (Wmk 151)		1,500.
96	A8	50c yellow	140.00	35.00
a.		50c orange	140.00	
b.		Without moiré on back, without overprint	50.00	70.00
c.		Vertically laid paper		2,000.
d.		50c blue (error)		650.00
e.		As "d," without overprint	45.00	
f.		As "e," without moiré on back	65.00	
g.		Half used as 25c on cover		5,000.
98	A8	100c gray lilac	90.00	50.00
a.		100c lilac	100.00	42.50
b.		Without moiré on back, without overprint	50.00	110.00
c.		Vertically laid paper		1,250.
		Nos. 93-98 (5)	253.00	101.25

Counterfeits of these stamps are 24½mm high instead of 24mm. The printing is sharper and more uniform than the genuine. Forged district names and consignment numbers exist.

Pin-perf. and Serrate Perf.

99	A8	6c green	90.00	75.00
100	A8	12c blue	3.50	3.00
a.		Vertically laid paper		350.00
b.		Horiz. pair, imperf. vert.	100.00	100.00
c.		Vert. pair, imperf. between		150.00
101	A8	25c red	3.25	1.50
a.		Vertically laid paper		500.00
b.		Horiz. pair, imperf. vert.	100.00	100.00
102	A8	50c yellow	175.00	50.00
a.		50c orange	160.00	50.00
b.		50c blue (error)	475.00	500.00
c.		As "b," without overprint	45.00	
104	A8	100c lilac	150.00	80.00
a.		100c gray lilac	125.00	80.00
		Nos. 99-104 (5)	421.75	209.50

Values for Nos. 99-104a are for examples with visible perfs on all sides.

A11

A12

A13

A14

Overprinted with District Name and Number and Date; also with Number and Date only
Thick Wove Paper, Some Showing Vertical Ribbing
1874-80 — **Unwmk.** — **Engr.** — **Perf. 12**

105	A9	4c org ('80)	12.50	12.00
a.		Vert. pair, imperf. btwn.	60.00	
b.		Without overprint	6.50	12.50
c.		Half used as 2c on cover		1,000.
106	A10	5c brown	4.50	3.00
a.		Horizontally laid paper	100.00	55.00
b.		Imperf., pair	60.00	
c.		Horiz. pair, imperf. btwn.	50.00	300.00
d.		Vert. pair, imperf. btwn.	110.00	110.00
e.		Without overprint	37.50	37.50
f.		As "a," wmkd. "LACROIX"	1,750.	1,000.
107	A11	10c black	2.00	1.25
a.		Horizontally laid paper	2.50	2.50
b.		Horiz. pair, imperf. btwn.	75.00	75.00
c.		Without overprint	35.00	27.50
d.		Half used as 5c on cover		2,000.
f.		As "a," wmkd. "LACROIX"	350.00	250.00
108	A11	10c org ('78)	2.00	1.25
a.		10c yellow bister	7.50	4.25
b.		Imperf., pair		
c.		Without overprint	55.00	50.00
d.		Half used as 5c on cover		100.00
109	A12	25c blue	.85	.70
a.		Horizontally laid paper	2.25	1.75
c.		Imperf., pair	50.00	25.00
d.		Without overprint	35.00	20.00
f.		Horiz. pair, imperf. btwn.	125.00	
g.		As "b," horiz. pair, imperf. vert.		200.00
h.		As "b," wmkd. "LACROIX"	300.00	250.00
i.		Printed on both sides		1,500.
j.		Half used as 10c on cover		2,000.
110	A13	50c green	13.00	13.00
a.		Without overprint	50.00	
b.		Half used as 25c on cover		2,500.
111	A14	100c carmine	18.00	15.00
a.		Imperf., pair	200.00	200.00
b.		Without overprint	50.00	
c.		Quartef used as 25c on cover		3,000.
		Nos. 105-111 (7)	52.85	46.20

The "LACROIX" watermark is spelled out "LACROIX FRERES" in 2 lines of block capitals without serifs once to a sheet of horiz. laid paper. 6-12 stamps may have a portion of the wmk.

1875-77 — **Wmk. 150**

112	A10	5c brown	110.00	70.00
113	A11	10c black	110.00	70.00
114	A12	25c blue	110.00	70.00
115	A13	50c green	650.00	450.00
116	A14	100c carmine	600.00	400.00
		Nos. 112-116 (5)	1,580.	1,060.

1881 — **Unwmk.** — **Thin Wove Paper**

117	A9	4c orange	70.00	70.00
a.		Without overprint	20.00	20.00
118	A10	5c brown	10.00	6.50
a.		Without overprint	.50	20.00
b.		As "a," vert. pair, imperf. horiz.	1,000.	
119	A11	10c orange	6.00	3.50
a.		Imperf., pair		
b.		Vert. pair, imperf. horiz.		
c.		Without overprint	.75	4.50
d.		Vert. pair, imperf. btwn.		
e.		Half used as 5c on cover		1,500.
120	A12	25c blue	4.00	2.25
a.		Imperf., pair	100.00	
b.		Without overprint	.50	8.00
c.		Double impression		65.00
d.		Printed on both sides		1,500.
121	A13	50c green	45.00	40.00
a.		Without overprint	4.00	30.00
122	A14	100c carmine	50.00	50.00
a.		Without overprint	6.00	300.00

The stamps of 1874-81 are found with number and date wide apart, close together or omitted, and in various colors.

The thin paper is fragile and easily damaged. Values for Nos. 117-122 are for undamaged, fine examples.

Benito Juárez — A15

Overprinted with District Name and Number and Date; also with Number and Date only
Thick Wove Paper, Some Showing Vertical Ribbing
1879 — *Perf. 12*

123	A15	1c brown	4.00	4.00
a.		Without overprint	75.00	140.00
b.		1c gray	20.00	15.00
124	A15	2c dk violet	4.00	4.50
a.		Without overprint	75.00	150.00
b.		Printed on both sides		
c.		2c dark gray	20.00	14.00
125	A15	5c orange	2.25	1.50
a.		Without overprint	75.00	90.00
b.		Double impression		500.00
126	A15	10c blue	3.00	2.50
a.		Without overprint	75.00	150.00
b.		10c ultra	160.00	160.00
127	A15	25c rose	8.00	30.00
a.		Without overprint	1.75	150.00
128	A15	50c green	15.00	50.00
a.		Without overprint	1.25	150.00
b.		Printed on both sides		165.00
129	A15	85c violet	20.00	250.00
a.		Without overprint	2.50	
130	A15	100c black	25.00	75.00
a.		Without overprint	3.00	150.00
		Nos. 123-130 (8)	81.25	417.50

Used values for Nos. 127-130 are for stamps with postal cancellations. Pen cancelled examples are worth the same as unused stamps.

Forged cancellations on Nos. 127-130 are plentiful.

1882 — **Thin Wove Paper**

131	A15	1c brown	40.00	37.50
a.		Without overprint	125.00	
132	A15	2c dk violet	27.50	24.00
a.		2c slate	47.50	50.00
b.		Without overprint	110.00	
133	A15	5c orange	9.00	6.00
a.		Without overprint	1.25	
b.		Half used as 2c on cover		
c.		As "a," vert. pair, imperf. btwn.		
134	A15	10c blue	9.00	6.00
a.		Without overprint	1.25	
b.		Half used as 5c on cover		
135	A15	10c brown	9.00	
a.		Imperf., pair	3.00	
136	A15	12c brown	7.50	8.00
a.		Without overprint	2.50	22.50
b.		Imperf., pair	75.00	
c.		Half used as 6c on cover		
137	A15	18c orange brn	9.00	15.00
a.		Horiz. pair, imperf. btwn.	100.00	
b.		Without overprint	2.25	18.00
138	A15	24c violet	9.00	11.00
a.		Without overprint	2.25	17.50
139	A15	25c rose	45.00	250.00
a.		Without overprint	4.50	
140	A15	25c orange brn	5.50	
141	A15	50c green	45.00	75.00
a.		Without overprint	6.25	
142	A15	50c yellow	80.00	350.00
a.		Without overprint	150.00	
143	A15	85c red violet	55.00	
a.		Without overprint	5.00	
144	A15	100c black	75.00	250.00
a.		Without overprint	5.00	
b.		Vert. pair, imperf. btwn.	165.00	165.00
145	A15	100c orange	95.00	400.00
a.		Without overprint	175.00	
		Nos. 131-145 (15)	520.50	1,432.

No. 135, 140 and 143 exist only without overprint. They were never placed in use.

Used values for Nos. 139, 141, 142, 144 and 145 are for postally used stamps. Forged cancellations are plentiful. Pen cancelled examples are worth the same as unused stamps.

See note on thin paper after No. 122.

A16

Overprinted with District Name, Number and Abbreviated Date
1882-83

146	A16	2c green	11.00	8.00
a.		Without overprint	27.50	20.00
147	A16	3c car lake	11.00	8.00
a.		Without overprint	5.25	8.50
148	A16	6c blue ('83)	30.00	40.00
a.		Without overprint	30.00	50.00

Hidalgo
A9   A10

149	A16 6c ultra	6.00	8.50
a.	Without overprint	3.50	6.00
b.	As "a," imperf. pair	50.00	
	Nos. 146-149 (4)	58.00	64.50

See note on thin paper after No. 122.

Hidalgo — A17

1884 Wove or Laid Paper *Perf. 12*

150	A17 1c green	4.00	.75
a.	Imperf., pair	125.00	
b.	1c blue (error)	600.00	475.00
c.	1c black green	75.00	40.00
151	A17 2c green	6.75	2.00
a.	Imperf., pair	200.00	225.00
b.	Half used as 1c on cover	75.00	40.00
c.	2c black green	12.50	2.00
152	A17 3c green	200.00	250.00
a.	Imperf., pair	225.00	250.00
b.	Horiz. pair, imperf. vert.	75.00	40.00
c.	3c black green	16.00	2.00
153	A17 4c green	200.00	250.00
a.	Imperf., pair	200.00	250.00
b.	Half used as 2c on cover	400.00	
c.	Horiz. pair, imperf. btwn.	200.00	250.00
154	A17 5c green	17.50	1.50
a.	Imperf., pair	200.00	250.00
b.	5c black green	75.00	40.00
c.	Horiz. pair, imperf. btwn.		250.00
d.	Vert. pair, imperf. btwn.		275.00
155	A17 6c green	15.00	1.50
a.	Imperf., pair	200.00	250.00
b.	6c black green	80.00	50.00
156	A17 10c green	16.00	.75
a.	Imperf., pair	125.00	150.00
b.	10c black green	50.00	25.00
157	A17 12c green	30.00	3.50
a.	Vert. pair, imperf. between	250.00	350.00
b.	Half used as 6c on cover		300.00
c.	12c black green	90.00	60.00
158	A17 20c green	90.00	2.50
a.	Diagonal half used as 10c on cover		300.00
b.	Imperf., pair	350.00	350.00
159	A17 25c green	150.00	5.00
a.	Imperf., pair	300.00	300.00
160	A17 50c green	.60	5.00
a.	Imperf., pair	150.00	150.00
b.	Horiz. pair, imperf. btwn.	300.00	
c.	Double impression	200.00	200.00
161	A17 1p blue	.60	11.00
a.	Imperf., pair	250.00	250.00
b.	Vert. pair, imperf. between	100.00	
c.	1p with 1c printed on back	300.00	
d.	Horiz. pair, imperf. btwn.	250.00	
162	A17 2p blue	.60	22.50
a.	Imperf., pair	175.00	200.00
163	A17 5p blue	350.00	300.00
164	A17 10p blue	500.00	225.00
	Nos. 150-162 (13)	359.55	60.00

Imperforate varieties should be purchased in pairs or larger. Single imperforates are usually trimmed perforated stamps.

Beware of examples of No. 150 that have been chemically changed to resemble No. 150b.

Bisects were not officially authorized. Nos. 155 and 160 exist as bisects on piece.

Forged cancels on Nos. 161-162 are plentiful.

Some values exist perf. 11.

See Nos. 165-173, 230-231.

1885

165	A17 1c pale green	35.00	7.00
166	A17 2c carmine	25.00	3.50
a.	Diagonal half used as 1c on cover		350.00
167	A17 3c orange brn	25.00	6.00
a.	Imperf., pair	250.00	250.00
b.	Horiz. pair, imperf. btwn.		300.00
168	A17 4c red orange	42.50	19.00
a.	Half used as 2c on cover		350.00
169	A17 5c ultra	27.50	3.50
170	A17 6c dk brown	32.50	6.00
a.	Half used as 3c on cover		350.00
171	A17 10c orange	27.50	1.50
a.	10c yellow	30.00	1.50
b.	Horiz. pair, imperf. btwn.	250.00	250.00
c.	Imperf., pair	300.00	
172	A17 12c olive brn	57.50	9.00
a.	Printed on both sides	300.00	
173	A17 25c grnsh blue	225.00	22.50
	Nos. 165-173 (9)	497.50	78.00

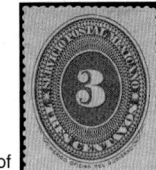

Numeral of
Value — A18

1886 *Perf. 12*

174	A18 1c yellow green	2.25	.75
a.	1c blue grn	5.50	4.50
b.	Horiz. pair, imperf. btwn.	200.00	200.00
c.	Perf. 11	45.00	45.00
175	A18 2c carmine	2.60	.90
a.	Horiz. pair, imperf. btwn.	80.00	75.00
b.	Vert. pair, imperf. between	200.00	200.00
c.	Perf. 11	45.00	45.00
d.	Half used as 1c on cover		100.00
176	A18 3c lilac	12.00	7.50
177	A18 4c lilac	18.00	5.25
a.	Perf. 11	50.00	55.00
b.	Horiz. pair, imperf. btwn.	450.00	
178	A18 5c ultra	2.25	1.00
a.	5c blue	2.25	.75
179	A18 6c lilac	30.00	7.50
180	A18 10c lilac	22.50	1.10
a.	Perf. 11		125.00
181	A18 12c lilac	25.00	14.00
182	A18 20c lilac	190.00	110.00
183	A18 25c lilac	75.00	19.00
	Nos. 174-183 (10)	379.60	167.00

Nos. 175, 191, 194B, 196, 202 exist with blue or black surcharge "Vale 1 Cvo." These were made by the Colima postmaster.

1887

184	A18 3c scarlet	1.90	.60
a.	Imperf., pair	75.00	
185	A18 4c scarlet	7.50	2.25
a.	Imperf., pair	500.00	
b.	Horiz. pair, imperf. btwn.	400.00	
186	A18 6c scarlet	12.50	2.25
a.	Horiz. pair, imperf. btwn.	200.00	
187	A18 10c scarlet	2.75	.60
a.	Imperf., pair	75.00	
b.	Horiz. pair, imperf. btwn.	200.00	
188	A18 20c scarlet	18.00	1.50
a.	Horiz. pair, imperf. btwn.	275.00	
b.	Vert. pair, imperf. btwn.	350.00	
189	A18 25c scarlet	15.00	4.00
	Nos. 184-189 (6)	57.65	11.20

Perf. 6

190	A18 1c blue grn	45.00	45.00
191	A18 2c brown car	22.50	42.00
192	A18 5c ultra	15.00	4.50
a.	5c blue	15.00	4.50
193	A18 10c lilac	15.00	4.25
193A	A18 10c brown lilac	15.00	3.00
194	A18 10c scarlet	35.00	15.00

Perf. 6x12

194A	A18 1c blue grn	62.50	42.50
194B	A18 2c brown car	85.00	75.00
194C	A18 3c scarlet	300.00	350.00
194D	A18 5c ultra	60.00	45.00
194E	A18 5c lilac	90.00	75.00
194F	A18 10c scarlet	80.00	60.00
194G	A18 10c brown lilac	90.00	75.00

Many shades exist.

Paper with colored ruled lines on face or reverse of stamp

1887 *Perf. 12*

195	A18 1c green	75.00	45.00
196	A18 2c brown car	190.00	47.50
198	A18 5c ultra	110.00	30.00
199	A18 10c scarlet	110.00	25.00

Perf. 6

201	A18 1c green	60.00	20.00
202	A18 2c brown car	60.00	24.00
204	A18 5c ultra	50.00	12.00
205	A18 10c brown lil	42.50	10.00
206	A18 10c scarlet	250.00	40.00
	Nos. 201-206 (5)	462.50	106.00

Perf. 6x12

207	A18 1c green	225.00	140.00
208	A18 2c brown car	325.00	140.00
209	A18 5c ultra	225.00	140.00
210	A18 10c brown lil	290.00	135.00
211	A18 10c scarlet	350.00	225.00
	Nos. 207-211 (5)	1,415.	780.00

1890-95 Wmk. 152 *Perf. 11 & 12*
Wove or Laid Paper

212	A18 1c yellow grn	.75	.35
a.	1c blue grn	.75	.35
b.	Horiz. pair, imperf. btwn.	125.00	125.00
c.	Laid paper	2.50	2.50
d.	Horiz. pair, imperf. vert.	125.00	125.00
213	A18 2c carmine	1.50	.75
a.	2c brown car	1.25	1.00
b.	Horiz. pair, imperf. btwn.	150.00	
c.	Imperf., pair	200.00	
214	A18 3c vermilion	1.00	.60
a.	Horiz. pair, imperf. btwn.	200.00	
215	A18 4c vermilion	3.25	2.10
a.	Horiz. pair, imperf. btwn.	200.00	
216	A18 5c ultra	.60	.50
a.	5c dull blue	1.00	.50
217	A18 6c vermilion	3.75	2.75
a.	Horiz. pair, imperf. btwn.	300.00	
218	A18 10c vermilion	.50	.35
b.	Horiz. or vert. pair, imperf. btwn.	175.00	175.00
c.	Vert. pair, imperf. horiz.	175.00	
d.	Imperf., pair	200.00	
219	A18 12c ver ('95)	14.00	18.00
a.	Imperf., pair	450.00	
220	A18 20c vermilion	3.50	1.50
220A	A18 20c dk violet	160.00	190.00
221	A18 25c vermilion	5.00	2.50
	Nos. 212-220,221 (10)	33.85	29.40

No. 219 has been reprinted in slightly darker shade than the original.

1892

222	A18 3c orange	4.00	2.00
223	A18 4c orange	4.25	3.00
224	A18 6c orange	5.75	2.00
225	A18 10c orange	27.50	2.00
226	A18 20c orange	50.00	6.00
227	A18 25c orange	16.00	4.50
	Nos. 222-227 (6)	107.50	19.50

1892

228	A18 5p carmine	1,250.	900.
229	A18 10p carmine	1,900.	1,250.
230	A17 5p blue green	3,500.	1,200.
231	A17 10p blue green	7,000.	2,700.

1894 *Perf. 5½, 6*

232	A18 1c yellow grn	3.00	3.00
233	A18 3c vermilion	9.00	9.00
234	A18 4c vermilion	40.00	37.50
235	A18 5c ultra	12.50	5.00
236	A18 10c vermilion	7.50	3.00
236A	A18 20c vermilion	110.00	110.00
237	A18 25c vermilion	62.50	62.50
	Nos. 232-237 (7)	244.50	230.00

Perf. 5½x11, 11x5½, Compound and Irregular

238	A18 1c yellow grn	7.00	7.00
238A	A18 2c brown car	16.00	16.00
238B	A18 3c vermilion	47.50	32.50
238C	A18 4c vermilion	55.00	55.00
239	A18 5c ultra	17.50	12.50
a.	5c blue	12.50	12.50
239C	A18 6c vermilion	75.00	75.00
240	A18 10c vermilion	20.00	7.00
240A	A18 20c vermilion	200.00	200.00
241	A18 25c vermilion	62.50	62.50
	Nos. 238-241 (9)	500.50	467.50

The stamps of the 1890 to 1895 issues are also to be found unwatermarked, as part of the sheet frequently escaped the watermark.

Letter Carrier — A20

Mounted Courier with Pack Mule — A21

Statue of Cuauhtémoc A22

Mail Coach A23

Mail Train — A24

Regular or Pin Perf. 12

1895 Wmk. 152
Wove or Laid Paper

242	A20 1c green	3.00	.75
a.	Vert. pair, imperf. horiz.	175.00	
d.	Watermarked sideway ('97)	125.00	15.00
243	A20 2c carmine	3.75	1.00
a.	Half used as 1c on cover		250.00
c.	Watermarked sideways ('97)	80.00	10.00
244	A20 3c orange brown	3.75	1.00
a.	Vert. pair, imperf. horiz.		250.00
d.	Watermarked sideways ('97)	125.00	10.00
e.	Horiz. or vert. pair, imperf. between		300.00
246	A21 4c orange	12.50	1.50
a.	4c orange red	7.50	1.25
247	A22 5c ultra	7.00	.35
a.	Imperf., pair	175.00	200.00
b.	Horiz. or vert. pair, imperf. between	175.00	200.00
e.	Half used as 2c on cover		400.00
f.	Watermarked sideways ('97)	15.00	5.00
248	A23 10c lilac rose	4.50	1.00
a.	Horiz. or vert. pair, imperf. btwn.		250.00
b.	Watermarked sideways ('97)		250.00
c.	Half used as 5c on cover		250.00
249	A21 12c olive brown	50.00	12.50
251	A23 15c brt blue	27.50	3.00
b.	Watermarked sideways ('97)		100.00
c.	Imperf., pair		300.00

252	A23 20c brown rose	32.50	3.00
b.	Half used as 10c on cover		200.00
c.	Watermarked sideways ('97)	1,000.	750.00
253	A23 50c purple	70.00	16.00
254	A24 1p brown	90.00	35.00
a.	Watermarked sideways ('97)	750.00	900.00
255	A24 5p scarlet	300.00	190.00
256	A24 10p deep blue	650.00	350.00
	Nos. 242-256 (13)	1,254.	615.10

No. 248 exists in perf. 11.

Nos. 242d, 243c, 244d, 247f, 251b, 252c and 254a was a special printing, made in Jan. 1897. The watermark is sideways, the grain of the paper is horizontal (rather than vertical, as appears on Nos. 242-256), and the design is somewhat shorter than the other stamps in this series. The sideways orientation of the watermark is the most easily identifable feature of this printing.

Important: For unwatermarked examples of Nos. 242-256, see the footnote after No. 291.

Perf. 6

242b	A20 1c green	60.00	35.00
243b	A20 2c carmine	125.00	60.00
244b	A20 3c orange brown	90.00	60.00
247c	A22 5c ultra	90.00	50.00
248c	A23 10c lilac rose	125.00	55.00
249a	A21 12c olive brown	60.00	50.00

Perf. 6x12, 12x6 & Compound or Irregular

242c	A20 1c green	30.00	20.00
244c	A20 3c orange brown	35.00	20.00
246b	A21 4c orange	75.00	50.00
247d	A22 5c ultra	75.00	50.00
248d	A23 10c lilac rose	35.00	20.00
249b	A21 12c olive brown	50.00	25.00
251a	A23 15c brt blue	60.00	40.00
252a	A23 20c brown rose	100.00	50.00
253b	A23 50c purple	150.00	100.00

See Nos. 257-291. For overprints see Nos. O10-O48A.

"Irregular" Perfs.

Some stamps perf. 6x12, 12x6, 5½x11 and 11x5½ have both perf. 6 and 12 or perf. 5½ and 11 on one or more sides of the stamp. These are known as irregular perfs.

1896-97 Wmk. 153 *Perf. 12*

257	A20 1c green	14.00	1.25
c.	Imperf., pair		250.00
258	A20 2c carmine	17.50	1.50
a.	Horiz. pair, imperf. vert.		
259	A20 3c orange brn	20.00	1.50
c.	Horiz. pair, imperf. between		300.00
260	A21 4c orange	32.50	1.75
a.	4c deep orange	30.00	6.00
261	A22 5c ultra	9.00	1.25
a.	Imperf., pair	200.00	200.00
b.	Vert. pair, imperf. btwn.	200.00	
262	A21 12c olive brn	160.00	80.00
263	A23 15c brt blue	200.00	13.00
264	A23 20c brown rose	750.00	275.00
265	A23 50c purple	175.00	110.00
266	A24 1p brown	300.00	250.00
267	A24 5p scarlet	800.00	600.00
268	A24 10p dp blue	900.00	525.00
	Nos. 257-268 (12)	3,378.	1,860.

Perf. 6

257a	A20 1c green	35.00	25.00
259a	A20 3c orange brown	35.00	20.00
260a	A21 4c orange	40.00	25.00
261c	A22 5c ultra	110.00	70.00
263a	A23 15c bright blue	75.00	35.00

Perf. 6x12, 12x6 and Compound or Irregular

257b	A20 1c green	25.00	20.00
258b	A20 2c carmine	50.00	25.00
259b	A20 3c orange brown	40.00	20.00
260b	A21 4c orange	45.00	20.00
261d	A22 5c ultra	40.00	20.00
262a	A21 12c olive brown	125.00	80.00
263b	A23 15c bright blue	250.00	125.00
264a	A23 20c brown rose		
265a	A23 50c purple		

1897-98 Wmk. 154 *Perf. 12*

269	A20 1c green	20.00	3.00
270	A20 2c scarlet	35.00	4.50
a.	Horiz. pair, imperf. btwn.		250.00
271	A21 4c orange	52.50	3.75
a.	Horizontal pair, imperf. vertical	—	
272	A22 5c ultra	50.00	3.75
a.	Imperf., pair	85.00	
273	A21 12c olive brown	200.00	45.00
275	A23 15c brt blue	275.00	85.00
276	A23 20c brown rose	175.00	15.00
c.	Horiz. pair, imperf. btwn.		300.00

277	A23	50c purple	375.00	75.00
278	A24	1p brown	425.00	200.00
278A	A24	5p scarlet	—	4,000.
		Nos. 269-278 (9)	1,607.	435.00

Perf. 6

269a	A20	1c green	48.00	25.00
270a	A20	2c scarlet	45.00	25.00
272b	A22	5c ultra	60.00	25.00
273a	A21	12c olive brown	110.00	60.00
276a	A23	20c brown rose	—	650.00

Perf. 6x12, 12x6 and Compound or Irregular

269b	A20	1c green	25.00	15.00
270b	A20	2c scarlet	30.00	22.50
271b	A21	4c orange	65.00	12.50
272c	A22	5c ultra	50.00	15.00
273b	A21	12c olive brown	125.00	65.00
275a	A23	15c bright blue	125.00	65.00
276b	A23	20c brown rose	240.00	30.00
277a	A23	50c purple	125.00	50.00

1898   Unwmk.   Perf. 12

279	A20	1c green	3.00	.50
a.		Horiz. pair, imperf. vert	300.00	
b.		Imperf., pair	250.00	
280	A20	2c scarlet	6.25	.75
a.		2c green (error)	475.00	
281	A20	3c orange brn	6.00	.75
a.		Imperf., pair	250.00	250.00
b.		Pair, imperf. between	80.00	80.00
282	A21	4c orange	30.00	3.00
b.		4c deep orange	37.50	7.00
c.		Imperf., pair		300.00
283	A22	5c ultra	2.00	.50
a.		Imperf., pair	200.00	200.00
b.		Pair, imperf. between	200.00	
284	A23	10c lilac rose	550.00	175.00
285	A21	12c olive brn	80.00	27.50
a.		Imperf., pair	200.00	
286	A23	15c brt blue	175.00	8.00
287	A23	20c brown rose	35.00	3.00
a.		Imperf., pair	250.00	
288	A23	50c purple	150.00	42.50
289	A24	1p brown	175.00	80.00
290	A24	5p carmine rose	550.00	425.00
291	A24	10p deep blue	800.00	575.00
		Nos. 279-291 (13)	2,562.	1,341.

Warning: Sheets of Nos. 242-256 (watermarked "CORREOS E U M") have a column of stamps without watermarks, because the watermark did not fit the sheet size. As a result, be careful not to confuse unwatermarked examples of Nos. 242-256 with Nos. 279-291. This is especialy important for No. 284. Nos. 242-256 and the watermarked 1895-97 overprinted Officials, Nos. O10-O39, have a vertical grain or mesh to the paper. Nos. 279-291 and the unwatermarked 1898 overprinted Officials, Nos. O40-O48B, have a horizontal grain or mesh to the paper. Be careful not to confuse unwatermarked examples of Nos. O10-O39 with Nos. O40-O48B.

Perf. 6

279c	A20	1c green	85.00	35.00
280b	A20	2c scarlet	75.00	30.00
281c	A20	3c orange brown	50.00	35.00
283c	A22	5c ultra	65.00	30.00
287b	A23	20c brown rose	125.00	75.00
291a	A24	10p deep blue		

Perf. 6x12, 12x6 and Compound or Irregular

279d	A20	1c green	25.00	20.00
280c	A20	2c scarlet	25.00	20.00
281d	A20	3c orange brown	30.00	20.00
282a	A21	4c orange	40.00	25.00
283d	A22	5c ultra	20.00	10.00
284a	A23	10c lilac rose	125.00	85.00
285b	A21	12c olive brown	90.00	60.00
286a	A23	15c bright blue	75.00	50.00
287c	A23	20c brown rose	100.00	50.00
288a	A23	50c purple	575.00	575.00

Forgeries of the 6 and 6x12 perforations of 1895-98 are plentiful.

Coat of Arms
A25   A26

A27   A28

A29   A30

A31

View of Mt. Popocatépetl — A33

Juanacatlán Falls — A32

Cathedral, Mexico, D. F. — A34

1899, Nov. 1   Wmk. 155   Perf. 14, 15

294	A25	1c green	1.90	.35
295	A26	2c vermilion	4.50	.35
296	A27	3c orange brn	3.00	.35
297	A28	5c dark blue	4.75	.35
298	A29	10c violet & org	6.00	.35
299	A30	15c lav & claret	8.00	.35
300	A31	20c rose & dk bl	9.00	.40
301	A32	50c red lil & blk	35.00	2.25
a.		50c lilac & black	42.50	2.25
302	A33	1p blue & blk	80.00	3.50
303	A34	5p carmine & blk	275.00	12.00
		Nos. 294-303 (10)	427.15	20.25
		Set, never hinged	1,500.	

See Nos. 304-305, 307-309. For overprints see Nos. 420-422, 439-450, 452-454, 482-483, 515-516, 539, 550, O49-O60, O62-O66, O68-O74, O101.

A35

1903

304	A25	1c violet	1.50	.35
a.		Booklet pane of 6	55.00	
305	A26	2c green	2.00	.35
a.		Booklet pane of 6	82.50	
306	A35	4c carmine	5.00	.45
307	A28	5c orange	1.25	.35
a.		Booklet pane of 6	82.50	
308	A29	10c blue & org	5.00	.35
309	A32	50c carmine & blk	75.00	6.50
		Nos. 304-309 (6)	89.75	8.35
		Set, never hinged	350.00	

For overprints see Nos. 451, O61, O67.

Independence Issue

Josefa Ortiz — A36   Leona Vicario — A37

López Rayón — A38   Juan Aldama — A39

Miguel Hidalgo — A40   Ignacio Allende — A41

Epigmenio González A42   Mariano Abasolo A43

Declaration of Independence A44

Mass on the Mount of Crosses A45

Capture of Granaditas A46

1910   Perf. 14

310	A36	1c dull violet	.35	.35
a.		Booklet pane of 4	40.00	
311	A37	2c green	.35	.35
a.		Booklet pane of 8	40.00	
312	A38	3c orange brn	.60	.35
313	A39	4c carmine	2.50	.45
314	A40	5c orange	.35	.35
a.		Booklet pane of 8	27.50	
315	A41	10c blue & org	1.50	.35
316	A42	15c gray bl & cl	8.00	.50
317	A43	20c red & bl	5.00	.40
318	A44	50c red brn & blk	12.00	1.60
319	A45	1p blue & blk	15.00	2.00
320	A46	5p car & blk	57.50	16.50
		Nos. 310-320 (11)	103.15	23.20
		Set, never hinged	325.00	

Independence of Mexico from Spain, cent.

For overprints and surcharges see Nos. 370-380, 423-433, 455-465, 484-494, 517-538, 540-549, 551-558, 577-590, O75-O85, O102-O112, O191-O192, O195, RA13, Merida 1.

CIVIL WAR ISSUES

During the 1913-16 Civil War, provisional issues with various handstamped overprints were circulated in limited areas.

Sonora

A47

Seal

Typeset in a row of five varieties. Two impressions placed tête bêche (foot to foot) constitute a sheet. The settings show various wrong font and defective letters, "!" for "1" in "1913," etc. The paper occasionally has a manufacturer's watermark.

a   b   c   d

Four Types of the Numerals.
a — Wide, heavy-faced numerals.
b — Narrow Roman numerals.
c — Wide Roman numerals.
d — Gothic or sans-serif numerals.

Nos. 321-346 Issued Without Gum
Embossed "CONSTITUCIONAL"

1913   Typeset   Unwmk.   Perf. 12

321	A47(a)	5c black & red	4,250.	800.00
a		"CENTAVOB"	4,750.	850.00

Colorless Roulette

322	A47(b)	1c black & red	22.00	25.00
a.		With green seal	1,500.	1,250.
b.		Peerless Mills watermark	75.00	75.00
323	A47(a)	2c black & red	18.00	15.00
a.		With green seal	2,000.	2,000.
b.		Peerless Mills watermark	75.00	75.00
324	A47(c)	2c black & red	87.50	72.50
a.		With green seal	5,000.	5,000.
b.		Peerless Mills watermark	150.00	150.00
325	A47(a)	3c black & red	97.50	77.50
a.		With green seal	750.00	750.00
b.		Peerless Mills watermark	250.00	250.00
326	A47(a)	5c black & red	190.00	77.50
a.		"CENTAVOB"	200.00	50.00
b.		Peerless Mills watermark	800.00	800.00
327	A47(a)	5c black & red	1,200.	350.00
a.		With green seal		1,000.
b.		Peerless Mills watermark	4,500.	1,500.
328	A47(b)	10c black & red	35.00	37.50
a.		Peerless Mills watermark	75.00	75.00

Black Roulette

329	A47(d)	5c black & red	300.00	140.00
a.		"MARO"	87.50	52.50
b.		Yukon Aurora watermark	2,500.	2,500.

Stamps are known with the embossing double or omitted.

The varieties with green seal are from a few sheets embossed "Constitucional" which were in stock at the time the green seal control was adopted.

Nos. 322-329 are known with papermakers' watermark ("Peerless Mills" or "Yukon Aurora").

No. 339

Without Embossing
With Green Seal
Colorless Roulette

336	A47(b)	1c black & red	15.00	10.00
a.		Peerless Mills watermark	60.00	40.00
337	A47(a)	3c black & red	14.50	9.00
a.		Imperf.	350.00	
b.		Peerless Mills watermark	60.00	40.00

338	A47(a)	5c black & red	750.00	250.00
a.		"CENTAVOB"	800.00	275.00
b.		Peerless Mills watermark	3,000.	1,000.
339	A47(b)	10c black & red	8.00	7.50
a.		Peerless Mills watermark	35.00	35.00

Colored Roulette

340	A47(d)	5c brnsh blk & red	25.00	6.00
a.		5c lilac brown & red	75.00	22.50
b.		Double seal		1,250.
c.		Red printing omitted		1,000.
d.		Yukon Aurora watermark	3,500.	2,500.

Nos. 336-340 are known with papermaker's watermark ("Peerless Mills" or "Yukon Aurora").

1913-14 Black Roulette
With Green Seal

341	A47(a)	1c black & red	4.00	4.00
b.		"erano" ('14)	100.00	60.00
342	A47(d)	2c black & red	4.50	4.00
a.		"erano" ('14)	30.00	35.00
343	A47(a)	3c black & red	4.75	4.00
a.		"CENTAVO"	25.00	25.00
b.		"erano" ('14)	35.00	35.00
344	A47(a)	5c black & red	4.75	4.00
b.		Heavy black penetrating roulette	2.75	1.75
c.		As "b," "MARO"	10.50	5.00
d.		Without green seal	2,250.	
		Nos. 341-344 (4)	18.00	16.00

Stamps without seal are unfinished remainders.

On Nos. 341-344 the rouletting cuts the paper slightly or not at all. On Nos. 344b-344c the rouletting is heavy, cutting deeply into the paper.

1914

345	A47(a)	5c black & red	5.00	5.00
346	A47(b)	10c black & red	4.25	5.00

Coat of Arms — A49

Revenue Stamps Used for Postage

1913	**Litho.**	**Rouletted 14, 14x7**		
347	A49	1c yellow grn	2.00	2.50
		Never hinged	7.00	
a.		With coupon	7.00	6.00
		Never hinged	40.00	
348	A49	2c violet	3.50	4.00
		Never hinged	14.00	
a.		With coupon	17.50	14.50
		Never hinged	95.00	
349	A49	5c brown	.60	.75
		Never hinged	2.50	
a.		With coupon	2.00	1.50
		Never hinged	15.00	
350	A49	10c claret	2.50	3.50
		Never hinged	12.00	
a.		With coupon	15.00	12.00
		Never hinged	100.00	
351	A49	20c gray grn	3.00	3.50
		Never hinged	12.00	
a.		With coupon	20.00	18.00
		Never hinged	125.00	
352	A49	50c ultra	11.00	16.00
		Never hinged	47.50	
a.		With coupon	60.00	47.50
		Never hinged	325.00	
353	A49	1p orange	45.00	55.00
		Never hinged	180.00	
a.		With coupon	175.00	120.00
		Never hinged	750.00	
		Nos. 347-353 (7)	67.60	85.25

For a short time these stamps (called "Ejercitos") were used for postage with coupon attached. Later this was required to be removed unless they were to be used for revenue. Stamps overprinted with district names are revenues. Values above 1p were used for revenue. Imperfs exist of all values, but were not issued.

Many examples do not have gum because of a flood.

Use of typeset Sonora revenue stamps for postage was not authorized or allowed.

Coat of Arms
A50   A51
5c (A50): "CINCO CENTAVOS"
14x2mm

1914		**Rouletted 9½x14**		
354	A50	1c deep blue	.45	.45
355	A50	2c yellow grn	.60	.35
a.		2c green	3.00	1.75
356	A50	4c blue vio	11.00	2.50
a.		Horiz. pair, imperf. btwn.	250.00	
357	A50	5c gray grn	11.00	3.00
a.		Horiz. pair imperf. btwn.	250.00	
358	A50	10c red	.45	.45
359	A50	20c yellow brn	.60	.60
a.		20c deep brown	2.25	2.25
b.		Horiz. pair, imperf. btwn.	250.00	
360	A50	50c claret	2.50	3.50
a.		Horiz. pair, imperf. btwn.	250.00	
361	A50	1p brt violet	14.00	16.00
a.		Horiz. pair, imperf. btwn.	250.00	
		Nos. 354-361 (8)	40.60	26.85
		Set, never hinged	175.00	

Nos. 354-361 (called "Transitorios") exist imperf. but were not regularly issued.

Many examples do not have gum because of a flood.

See Note after No. 465.

See No. 369. For overprints see Nos. 362-368, 559-565.

Overprinted in Black

1914				
362	A50	1c deep blue	200.00	175.00
		Never hinged	750.00	
363	A50	2c yellow green	225.00	200.00
		Never hinged	825.00	
364	A50	4c blue violet	250.00	300.00
		Never hinged	900.00	
365	A50	5c gray green	35.00	50.00
		Never hinged	115.00	
a.		Horiz. pair, imperf. btwn.	550.00	
366	A50	10c red	150.00	150.00
		Never hinged	560.00	
367	A50	20c yellow brn	2,500.	2,500.
368	A50	50c claret	3,500.	3,500.

Values are for stamps with design close to, or just touching, the perfs.

Excellent counterfeits of this overprint exist.

Redrawn
"CINCO CENTAVOS" 16x2½mm

1914		**Perf. 12**		
369	A51	5c gray green	1.00	.35
		Never hinged	1.50	

Imperfs are printers' waste.

Regular Issue of
1910 Overprinted in
Violet, Magenta,
Black or Green

1914	**Wmk. 155**	**Perf. 14**		
370	A36	1c dull violet	1.50	.60
a.		Booklet pane of 4	75.00	
371	A37	2c green	3.00	1.25
a.		Booklet pane of 8	75.00	
372	A38	3c orange brn	3.00	1.25
373	A39	4c carmine	5.00	2.00
374	A40	5c orange	1.00	.35
a.		Booklet pane of 8	60.00	
375	A41	10c blue & org	6.00	2.00
376	A42	15c gray bl & cl	10.00	3.00
377	A43	20c red & blue	20.00	6.00
378	A44	50c red brn & blk	25.00	8.00
379	A45	1p blue & blk	55.00	11.00
380	A46	5p carmine & blk	190.00	160.00
		Nos. 370-380 (11)	319.50	195.45
		Set, never hinged	1,000.	

Overprinted On Postage Due
Stamps of 1908

381	D1	1c blue	27.50	30.00
382	D1	2c blue	27.50	30.00
383	D1	4c blue	27.50	30.00

384	D1	5c blue	27.50	30.00
385	D1	10c blue	27.50	30.00
		Nos. 381-385 (5)	137.50	150.00
		Set, never hinged	375.00	

This overprint is found double, inverted, sideways and in pairs with and without the overprint.

There are two or more types of this overprint.

The Postage Due Stamps and similar groups of them which follow were issued and used as regular postage stamps.

Values are for stamps where the overprint is clear enough to be expertised.

Counterfeits abound.

A52   A53

1914	**Unwmk.**	**Litho.**	**Perf. 12**	
386	A52	1c pale blue	.35	.50
387	A52	2c light green	.35	.45
388	A52	3c orange	.50	.50
389	A52	5c deep rose	.50	.35
390	A52	10c rose	.70	.85
391	A52	15c rose lilac	1.20	1.75
392	A52	50c yellow	2.00	2.50
a.		50c ocher	1.75	
393	A52	1p violet	8.50	12.00
		Nos. 386-393 (8)	14.10	18.90
		Set, never hinged	50.00	

Nos. 386-393, are known imperforate.

This set is usually called the Denver Issue because it was printed there.

See Note after No. 465.

For overprints and surcharges see Nos. 566-573, 591-592.

Revenue Stamps Used for Postage

1914, July		**Perf. 12**		
393A	A53	1c rose	40.00	
393B	A53	2c lt green	35.00	
393C	A53	3c lt orange	75.00	
393D	A53	5c red	15.00	
393E	A53	10c gray green	70.00	
393F	A53	25c blue	150.00	
		Nos. 393A-393F (6)	385.00	

Nos. 393A-393F were used in the northeast. Values are for examples with postal cancellations.

Unused examples are to be considered as revenues.

Pres. Madero

Stamps in this design, featuring Pres. Madero, within a frame very similar to that of the Denver Issue (Nos. 386-393), were ordered in 1915 by Francisco Villa, to be used by the Constitutionalist government. Five values (1c green, 2c brown, 3c carmine, 5c blue, and 10c yellow) were printed by Ellis Brothers & Co., El Paso, Texas. By the time of the stamps' arrival in Mexico City, the Constitutionalist regime had fallen, and the new Conventionist government returned them to the printer, who later sold the unissued stamps within the philatelic market. Value, set $10.

Background as
A55 — A54   A55

Nos. 394-413 Issued Without Gum

1914		**Imperf.**

Values and Inscriptions in Black
Inscribed "SONORA"

394	A54	1c blue & red	.35	.35
a.		Double seal	20.00	
395	A54	2c green & org	.35	.35
a.		Without seal	100.00	
396	A54	5c yellow & grn	.35	.35
a.		5c orange & green	1.50	1.25
b.		Without seal		300.00
397	A54	10c lt bl & red	3.50	1.75
a.		10c blue & red	40.00	15.00
398	A54	20c yellow & grn	1.75	2.00
399	A54	20c orange & bl	15.00	17.50
400	A54	20c yellow & org	1.25	1.25
		Nos. 394-400 (7)	22.55	23.55

Shades. Stamps of type A54 are usually termed the "Coach Seal Issue."

Inscribed "DISTRITO SUR DE LA BAJA CAL"

401	A54	1c yellow & blue	2.00	30.00
a.		Without seal	50.00	
402	A54	2c gray & ol grn	2.50	25.00
403	A54	5c olive & rose	2.00	25.00
404	A54	10c pale red & dl vio	2.00	20.00
a.		Without seal	50.00	
		Nos. 401-404 (4)	8.50	95.00

Counterfeit cancellations exist.

Inscribed "SONORA"

405	A55	1c blue & red	6.00	
a.		Without seal	50.00	
406	A55	2c green & org	.50	
407	A55	5c yellow & grn	.50	2.50
a.		Without seal	75.00	
408	A55	10c blue & red	.50	2.50
409	A55	20c yellow & grn	75.00	15.00
a.		Without seal	95.00	
b.		Double seal	80.00	
		Nos. 405-409 (5)	82.50	20.00

With "PLATA" added to the inscription

410	A55	1c blue & red	1.00	
a.		"PLATA" inverted	60.00	
b.		Pair, one without "PLATA"	15.00	
411	A55	10c blue & red	1.00	
412	A55	20c yellow & grn	2.50	
a.		"PLATA" double	50.00	
413	A55	50c gray grn & org	1.75	
a.		Without seal	50.00	
b.		As "a," "P" of "PLATA" missing	150.00	
		Nos. 410-413 (4)	6.25	

Stamps of type A55 are termed the "Anvil Seal Issue".

Nos. 410-413 were not placed in use.

Oaxaca

Coat of Arms — A56

5c:
Type I — Thick numerals, 2mm wide.
Type II — Thin numerals, 1½mm wide.

1915	**Typo.**		**Perf. 8½ to 14**	
				Unwmk.
414	A56	1c dull violet	2.00	1.25
415	A56	2c emerald	3.00	2.25
a.		Inverted numeral	30.00	
e.		Numeral omitted	35.00	
416	A56	3c red brown	4.00	3.50
b.		Inverted numeral	30.00	
417	A56	5c org (type I)	77.50	77.50
a.		Tête bêche pair	175.00	175.00
418	A56	5c org (type II)	.50	.75
a.		Types I and II in pair	70.00	
419	A56	10c blue & car	4.00	4.00
		Nos. 414-419 (6)	91.00	89.25
		Set, never hinged	275.00	

Many printing errors, imperfs and part perfs exist. Mostly these are printers' waste, private reprints or counterfeits.

Nos. 414-419 printed on backs of post office receipt forms.

Regular Issues of
1899-1910
Overprinted in Black

1914 Wmk. 155 Perf. 14
On Issues of 1899-1903

420	A28	5c orange		
421	A30	15c lav & claret	250.00	250.00
		Never hinged	700.00	
422	A31	20c rose & dk bl	7,000.	500.00

Counterfeits exist.
The listing of No. 420 is being re-evaluated. The Catalogue Editors would appreciate any information on the stamp.

On Issue of 1910

423	A36	1c dull violet	.35	.35
424	A37	2c green	.35	.35
425	A38	3c orange brown	.40	.40
426	A39	4c carmine	.50	.50
427	A40	5c orange	.35	.35
428	A41	10c blue & orange	.35	.35
429	A42	15c gray bl & claret	.70	.60
430	A43	20c red & blue	.75	.70

Overprinted

431	A44	50c red brn & blk	1.75	1.50
432	A45	1p blue & blk	8.00	5.50
433	A46	5p carmine & blk	42.50	32.50
		Nos. 423-433 (11)	56.00	43.10
		Set, never hinged	170.00	

In the first setting of the overprint on 1c to 20c, the variety "GONSTITUCIONALISTA" occurs 4 times in each sheet of 100. In the second setting it occurs on the last stamp in each row of 10.
The overprint exists reading downward on Nos. 423-430; inverted on Nos. 431-433; double on Nos. 423-425, 427.
See Note after No. 465.
For overprints see Nos. 528-538.

Postage Due Stamps of 1908 Overprinted

434	D1	1c blue	4.75	5.00
435	D1	2c blue	6.00	5.00
436	D1	4c blue	25.00	25.00
437	D1	5c blue	25.00	25.00
438	D1	10c blue	5.50	5.00
a.		Double overprint		
		Nos. 434-438 (5)	66.25	65.00
		Set, never hinged	200.00	

Preceding Issues Overprinted

This is usually called the "Villa" monogram. Counterfeits abound.

1915 On Issue of 1899

439	A25	1c green	210.00	
440	A26	2c vermilion	210.00	
441	A27	3c orange brn	175.00	
442	A28	5c dark blue	210.00	
443	A29	10c violet & org	210.00	
444	A30	15c lav & claret	750.00	750.00
445	A31	20c rose & bl	1,000.	—
446	A32	50c red lil & blk	500.00	—
447	A33	1p blue & blk	500.00	—
448	A34	5p car & blk	750.00	—
		Nos. 439-448 (10)	4,515.	

On Issue of 1903

449	A25	1c violet	200.00	
450	A26	2c green	200.00	
451	A35	4c carmine	200.00	
452	A28	5c orange	45.00	
a.		Inverted overprint	75.00	
453	A29	10c blue & org	750.00	—
454	A32	50c car & blk	—	—
		Nos. 449-453 (5)	1,395.	

In Sept. 1915 Postmaster Hinojosa ordered a special printing of Nos. 439-454 (as valued) for sale to collectors. Earlier a small quantity of Nos. 444-445, 448 and 452-454 was regularly issued. They are hard to distinguish and sell for much more. Counterfeits abound.

On Issue of 1910

455	A36	1c dull violet	.85	1.00
456	A37	2c green	.40	.60
457	A38	3c orange brown	.60	.75
458	A39	4c carmine	4.00	4.50
459	A40	5c orange	.35	.35
460	A41	10c blue & orange	7.00	7.50
461	A42	15c gray bl & cl	3.00	4.00
462	A43	20c red & blue	5.50	7.00
463	A44	50c red brn & blk	13.00	14.00
464	A45	1p blue & blk	17.00	20.00
465	A46	5p carmine & blk	150.00	
		Never hinged	300.00	
		Nos. 455-464 (10)	51.70	59.70

Nos. 455-464, never hinged 175.00

Nos. 455-465 exist with overprint inverted, double and other variations. Most were ordered by Postmaster General Hinojosa for philatelic purposes. They were sold at a premium. This applies to Nos. 354-361, 386-393, 431-433 with this monogram as well.

Overprinted On Postage Due Stamps of 1908

466	D1	1c blue	15.00	20.00
467	D1	2c blue	15.00	20.00
468	D1	4c blue	15.00	20.00
469	D1	5c blue	15.00	20.00
470	D1	10c blue	15.00	20.00
		Nos. 466-470 (5)	75.00	100.00
		Set, never hinged	225.00	

Nos. 466 to 470 are known with inverted overprint. All other values of the 1899 and 1903 issues exist with this overprint. See note after No. 465.

Issues of 1899-1910 Overprinted

This is called the "Carranza" or small monogram. Counterfeits abound.

On Issues of 1899-1903

482	A28	5c orange	40.00	20.00
		Never hinged	125.00	
483	A30	15c lav & claret	200.00	80.00
		Never hinged	650.00	

On Issue of 1910

484	A36	1c dull violet	.70	.70
485	A37	2c green	.70	.60
486	A38	3c orange brn	.75	.75
487	A39	4c carmine	2.00	2.00
488	A40	5c orange	.35	.35
489	A41	10c blue & org	1.50	1.50
a.		Double ovpt., one invtd.	25.00	
490	A42	15c gray bl & cl	1.50	1.50
491	A43	20c red & blue	1.50	1.50
492	A44	50c red brn & blk	10.00	10.00
493	A45	1p blue & blk	15.00	15.00
494	A46	5p car & blk	150.00	150.00
		Nos. 484-494 (11)	184.00	183.90
		Set, never hinged	550.00	

All values exist with inverted overprint; all but 5p with double overprint.

Overprinted On Postage Due Stamps of 1908

495	D1	1c blue	22.00	25.00
496	D1	2c blue	22.00	25.00
497	D1	4c blue	22.00	25.00
498	D1	5c blue	22.00	25.00
499	D1	10c blue	22.00	25.00
		Nos. 495-499 (5)	110.00	125.00
		Set, never hinged	325.00	

Nos. 495-499 exist with inverted overprint.
It is stated that, in parts of Mexico occupied by the revolutionary forces, instructions were given to apply a distinguishing overprint to all stamps found in the post offices. This overprint was usually some arrangement or abbreviation of "Gobierno Constitucionalista". Such overprints as were specially authorized or were in general use in large sections of the country are listed. Numerous other handstamped overprints were used in one town or locality. They were essentially military faction control marks necessitated in most instances by the chaotic situation following the split between Villa and Carranza. The fact that some were often struck in a variety of colors and positions suggests the influence of philatelists.

Coat of Arms
A57

Statue of Cuauhtémoc
A58

Ignacio Zaragoza
A59

José María Morelos
A60

Francisco Madero — A61

Benito Juárez — A62

1915 Unwmk. Litho. Rouletted 14

500	A57	1c violet	.25	.25
501	A58	2c green	.25	.25
502	A59	3c brown	.50	.25
503	A60	4c carmine	.50	.25
504	A61	5c orange	.75	.25
505	A62	10c ultra	.35	.30
		Nos. 500-505 (6)	2.60	1.55
		Set, never hinged	4.00	

Nos. 500-505 exists imperf.; some exist imperf. vertically or horizontally; some with rouletting and perforation combined. These probably were not regularly issued in these forms.
See Nos. 506-511. For overprints see Nos. O86-O97.

Map of Mexico — A63

Veracruz Lighthouse A64

Post Office, Mexico, D.F. — A65

TEN CENTAVOS:
Type I — Size 19½x24mm. Crossed lines on coat.
Type II — Size 19x23½mm. Diagonal lines only on coat.

1915-16 Perf. 12

506	A57	1c violet	.40	.25
507	A58	2c green	.40	.30
508	A59	3c brown	.50	.30
509	A60	4c carmine	.50	.35
a.		"CEATRO"	7.50	7.50
510	A61	5c orange	.75	.35
511	A62	10c ultra, type I	1.00	.35
a.		10c ultra, type II	.50	.25

Engr.

512	A63	40c slate	.75	.35
513	A64	1p brown & blk	1.00	.75
a.		Inverted center	200.00	275.00
514	A65	5p cl & ultra ('16)	12.00	4.00
a.		Inverted center	450.00	
		Nos. 506-514 (9)	17.30	7.00
		Set, never hinged	60.00	

Nos. 507-508, 510-514, exist imperf; Nos. 513-514 imperf with inverted center. These varieties were not regularly issued.

See Nos. 626-628, 647. For overprints see Nos. O92-O100, O121-O123, O132-O133, O142-O144, O153-O154, O162-O164, O174, O188, O193, O207, O222.

Issues of 1899-1910 Overprinted in Blue, Red or Black

1916 Wmk. 155 Perf. 14
On Issues of 1899-1903

515	A28	5c orange (Bl)	125.00	175.00
		Never hinged	400.00	
516	A30	15c lav & cl (Bl)	775.00	775.00
		Never hinged	2,250.	

On Issue of 1910

517	A36	1c dull vio (R)	10.00	10.00
518	A37	2c green (R)	.50	.35
519	A38	3c orange brn (Bl)	.55	.40
a.		Double overprint		500.00
520	A39	4c carmine (Bl)	6.00	8.00
521	A40	5c orange (Bl)	.25	.25
a.		Double overprint	75.00	
522	A41	10c blue & org (R)	1.25	1.50
523	A42	15c gray bl & cl (Bk)	1.75	3.00
524	A43	20c red & bl (Bk)	1.75	3.00
525	A44	50c red brn & blk (R)	8.50	5.00
526	A45	1p blue & blk (R)	15.00	6.50
527	A46	5p car & blk (R)	175.00	175.00
		Nos. 517-527 (11)	220.55	213.00
		Nos. 517-527, never hinged	650.00	

Nos. 519-524 exist with this overprint (called the "Corbata") reading downward and Nos. 525-527 with it inverted. Of these varieties only Nos. 519-521 were regularly issued.

On Nos. 423-430

528	A36	1c dull vio (R)	2.50	4.00
529	A37	2c green (R)	.75	.60
530	A38	3c orange brn (Bl)	.60	.60
531	A39	4c carmine (R)	.60	.60
532	A40	5c orange (Bl)	1.00	.30
533	A41	10c blue & org (R)	.75	.60
534	A42	15c gray bl & cl (Bk)	.80	.80
535	A43	20c red & bl (Bk)	.80	.80

On Nos. 431-433 in Red

536	A44	50c red brn & blk	7.50	6.00
537	A45	1p blue & blk	16.00	16.00
538	A46	5p carmine & blk	150.00	140.00
a.		Tablet inverted	300.00	
		Nos. 528-538 (11)	181.30	170.30
		Set, never hinged	550.00	

Nos. 529 to 535 are known with the overprint reading downward and Nos. 536 to 538 with it inverted.

On No. 482

539	A28	5c orange (Bl)	400.00	400.00

On Nos. 484-494

540	A36	1c dull vio (R)	6.00	6.00
541	A37	2c green (R)	.75	.75
a.		Monogram inverted	100.00	
542	A38	3c orange brn (Bl)	.75	.75
543	A39	4c carmine (Bl)	8.50	10.00
544	A40	5c orange (R)	1.25	.25
545	A41	10c blue & org (R)	2.00	2.50
546	A42	15c gray bl & cl (Bk)	1.75	.75
a.		Tablet double	750.00	750.00
b.		Monogram double		750.00
547	A43	20c red & bl (Bk)	1.75	1.50
548	A44	50c red brn & blk (R)	9.00	10.00
a.		Monogram inverted	75.00	
b.		Tablet inverted	85.00	
549	A45	1p blue & blk (R)	13.00	14.00
a.		Tablet double	200.00	
b.		Monogram inverted	70.00	
		Nos. 539-549 (11)	444.75	446.60
		Set, never hinged	1,300.	

Nos. 541-547 exist with overprint reading downward. A few 5p were overprinted for the Post Office collection.

On No. 452

550	A28	5c orange (Bl)	125.00	125.00
		Never hinged	275.00	

On Nos. 455-462

551	A36	1c dull vio (R)	11.00	15.00
552	A37	2c green (R)	1.50	.90
553	A38	3c org brn (Bl)	3.25	4.50
554	A39	4c carmine (Bl)	13.00	15.00
555	A40	5c orange (Bl)	4.50	6.00
556	A41	10c bl & org (R)	12.00	14.00
a.		Monogram inverted	250.00	
557	A42	15c gray bl & cl (Bk)	12.00	14.00
a.		Monogram inverted	250.00	

558 A43 20c red & bl (Bk) 12.00 14.00
   a. Monogram inverted 250.00
   Nos. 550-558 (9) 194.25 208.40
   Set, never hinged 650.00

Stamps of 50c, 1p and 5p were overprinted for the Post Office collection but were not regularly issued.

Issues of 1914
Overprinted

On "Transitorio" Issue
Rouletted 9½x14
Unwmk.

559 A50 1c dp blue (R) 24.00 24.00
   Never hinged 75.00
560 A50 2c yellow grn (R) 12.00 18.00
   Never hinged 27.50
561 A50 4c blue vio (R) 425.00 375.00
   Never hinged 1,200.
562 A50 10c red (Bl) 2.00 6.00
   Never hinged 4.00
   a. Vertical overprint 125.00
563 A50 20c yellow brn (Bl) 3.00 6.00
   Never hinged 7.50
564 A50 50c claret (Bl) 15.00 20.00
   Never hinged 45.00
565 A50 1p violet (Bl) 24.00 24.00
   Never hinged 100.00
   a. Horiz. pair, imperf. btwn.
   Nos. 559-565 (7) 505.00 473.00

Overprinted in Blue
On "Denver" Issue
Perf. 12

566 A52 1c pale blue 3.75
567 A52 2c lt green 3.75
568 A52 3c orange .45 5.00
569 A52 5c deep rose .45 5.00
570 A52 10c rose .45 5.00
571 A52 15c rose lilac .45 5.00
572 A52 50c yellow 1.10 15.00
573 A52 1p violet 9.50 25.00
   Nos. 566-573 (8) 19.90
   Set, never hinged 65.00

Many of the foregoing stamps exist with the "G. P. DE M." overprint printed in other colors than those listed. These "trial color" stamps were not regularly on sale at post offices but were available for postage and used copies are known.

There appears to have been speculation in Nos. 516, 517, 520, 528, 539, 540, 543, 566, and 567. A small quantity of each of these stamps was sold at post offices but subsequently they could be obtained only from officials or their agents at advanced prices.

Venustiano
Carranza — A66

Coat of
Arms — A67

1916, June 1   **Engr.**   ***Perf. 12***
574 A66 10c blue 1.75 1.00
   a. Imperf., pair 25.00
575 A66 10c lilac brown 15.00 15.00
   a. Imperf., pair 50.00
   Nos. 574-575, never hinged 32.50

Entry of Carranza into Mexico, D.F.
Stamps of type A66 with only horizontal lines in the background of the oval are essays.

1916
576 A67 1c lilac .35 .25
   Never hinged .80

Issue of 1910
Surcharged in
Various Colors

This overprint is called the "Barril."

1916   **Wmk. 155**   ***Perf. 14***
577 A36 5c on 1c dl vio (Br) .50 .50
   a. Vertical surcharge 1.25 1.25
   b. Double surcharge 150.00

---

578 A36 10c on 1c dl vio (Bl) .50 .50
   a. Double surcharge 100.00
579 A40 20c on 5c org (Br) .50 .50
   a. Double surcharge 90.00
580 A40 25c on 5c org (G) .40 .50
581 A37 60c on 2c grn (R) 27.50 20.00
   Nos. 577-581 (5) 29.40 22.00
   Set, never hinged 100.00

On Nos. 423-424, 427
582 A36 5c on 1c (Br) .50 .50
   a. Double tablet, one vertical 100.00
   b. Inverted tablet 250.00 250.00
583 A36 10c on 1c (Bl) 1.00 1.00
584 A40 25c on 5c (G) .50 .50
   a. Inverted tablet 225.00 225.00
585 A37 60c on 2c (R) 650.00 425.00
   Never hinged 1,750.
   Nos. 582-584, never hinged 4.50

No. 585 was not regularly issued.
The variety "GONSTITUCIONALISTA" is found on Nos. 582 to 585.

On No. 459
586 A40 25c on 5c org (G) .25 .25
   Never hinged .70

On Nos. 484-485, 488
587 A36 5c on 1c (Br) 15.00 20.00
   a. Vertical tablet 100.00 125.00
588 A36 10c on 1c (Bl) 5.00 7.50
589 A40 20c on 5c (G) 1.00 1.50
   a. Inverted tablet 225.00
590 A37 60c on 2c (R) 650.00
   Never hinged 1,750.
   Nos. 587-589, never hinged 60.00

No. 590 was not regularly issued.

Surcharged on "Denver" Issue of 1914

1916   **Unwmk.**   ***Perf. 12***
591 A52 60c on 1c pale bl (Br) 3.00 6.00
592 A52 60c on 2c lt grn (Br) 3.00 6.00
   a. Inverted surcharge 1,250.
   Set, never hinged 18.00

Postage Due Stamps Surcharged Like Nos. 577-581

1916   **Wmk. 155**   ***Perf. 14***
593 D1 5c on 1c blue (Br) 2.50
594 D1 10c on 2c blue (V) 2.50
595 D1 20c on 4c blue (Br) 2.50
596 D1 25c on 5c blue (G) 2.50
597 D1 60c on 10c blue (R) 1.50
598 D1 1p on 1c blue (C) 1.50
599 D1 1p on 2c blue (C) 1.50
600 D1 1p on 4c blue (C) .80 .80
601 D1 1p on 5c blue (C) 2.50
602 D1 1p on 10c blue (C) 2.50
   Nos. 593-602 (10) 20.30
   Set, never hinged

There are numerous "trial colors" and "essays" of the overprints and surcharges on Nos. 577 to 602. They were available for postage though not regularly issued.

Postage Due Stamps
Surcharged

1916
603 D1 2.50p on 1c blue 1.25 1.25
604 D1 2.50p on 2c blue 10.00
605 D1 2.50p on 4c blue 10.00 250.00
606 D1 2.50p on 5c blue 10.00
607 D1 2.50p on 10c blue 10.00
   a. Inverted surcharge 1,500.
   Nos. 603-607 (5) 41.25
   Set, never hinged 125.00

Regular Issue

Ignacio
Zaragoza
A68

Ildefonso
Vázquez
A69

J. M. Pino
Suárez
A70

Jesús
Carranza
A71

Maclovio
Herrera — A72

F. I.
Madero — A73

Belisario
Domínguez
A74

Aquiles Serdán
A75

Rouletted 14½
1917-20   **Engr.**   **Unwmk.**
Thick Paper
608 A68 1c dull violet 2.00 1.00
   Never hinged 4.00
609 A68 1c lilac gray ('20) 5.00 .75
   Never hinged 9.50
   a. 1c gray ('20) 5.00 5.00
610 A69 2c gray green 1.50 .50
   Never hinged 3.00
611 A70 3c bister brn 1.50 1.00
   Never hinged 3.00
612 A71 4c carmine 2.50 1.00
   Never hinged 7.50
613 A72 5c ultra 2.50 .50
   Never hinged 5.00
   a. Horiz. pair, imperf. btwn. 75.00
   b. Imperf., pair 35.00 75.00
614 A73 10c blue 4.00 .50
   Never hinged 10.00
   a. Without imprint 7.50 1.00
   Never hinged 16.00
615 A74 20c brown rose 40.00 2.00
   Never hinged 90.00
   a. 20c rose 40.00 2.00
   Never hinged 80.00
616 A75 30c gray brown 90.00 3.00
   Never hinged 250.00
617 A75 30c gray blk ('20) 100.00 4.00
   Never hinged 250.00
   Nos. 608-617 (10) 249.00 14.25

Perf. 12
Thick or Medium Paper
618 A68 1c dull violet 35.00 25.00
   Never hinged 100.00
619 A69 2c gray green 10.00 6.00
   Never hinged 20.00
620 A70 3c bis brn ('17) 200.00 200.00
   Never hinged 400.00
622 A72 5c ultra 5.00 .25
   Never hinged 10.00
623 A73 10c blue ('17) 5.00 .25
   Never hinged 10.00
   a. Without imprint ('17) 20.00 15.00
   Never hinged 40.00
624 A74 20c rose ('20) 140.00 3.00
   Never hinged 350.00
625 A75 30c gray blk ('20) 140.00 2.00
   Never hinged 350.00

Thin or Medium Paper
626 A63 40c violet 65.00 1.00
   Never hinged 200.00
627 A64 1p blue & blk 50.00 1.50
   Never hinged 150.00
   a. With center of 5p 800.00
   b. 1p bl & dark blue (error) 500.00 20.00
   Never hinged 800.00
   c. Vert. pair, imperf. btwn. 250.00
628 A65 5p green & blk 1.50 10.00
   Never hinged 3.00
   a. With violet or red control number 25.00 10.00
   b. With center of 1p 800.00

The 1, 2, 3, 5 and 10c are known on thin paper perforated. It is stated they were printed for Postal Union and "specimen" purposes.

All values exist imperf; these are not known to have been regularly issued. Nos. 627a and 628b were not regularly issued.

All values except 3c have an imprint.
For overprints and surcharges see Nos. B1-B2, O113-O165.

Meeting of
Iturbide and
Guerrero
A77

Entering City
of Mexico
A78

1921
632 A77 10c blue & brn 25.00 3.00
   Never hinged 82.50
   a. Center inverted 40,000.
633 A78 10p black brn & blk 22.50 37.50
   Never hinged 75.00

Commemorating the meeting of Agustín de Iturbide and Vicente Guerrero and the entry into City of Mexico in 1821.
For overprint see No. O194.

"El Salto de
Agua," Public
Fountain
A79

Pyramid of the
Sun at
Teotihuacán
A80

Chapultepec
Castle
A81

Columbus
Monument
A82

Juárez Colonnade,
Mexico, D. F.
A83

Monument to
Josefa Ortiz
de Dominguez
A84

Cuauhtémoc
Monument — A85

1923   **Unwmk.**   ***Rouletted 14½***
634 A79 2c scarlet 2.00 .25
635 A80 3c bister brn 2.00 .25
636 A81 4c green 2.50 .75
637 A82 5c orange 5.00 .25
638 A83 10c brown 3.75 .25
639 A85 10c claret 3.50 .25
640 A84 20c dk blue 52.50 1.75
641 A85 30c dk green 52.50 2.00
   Nos. 634-641 (8) 123.75 5.75
   Set, never hinged 300.00

See Nos. 642-646, 650-657, 688-692, 727A, 735A-736. For overprints see Nos. O166-O173, O178-O181, O183-O187, O196-O197, O199-O206, O210, O212-O214, O217-O222.

Communications Building — A87

Palace of Fine Arts (National Theater) A88

Two types of 1p:
I — Eagle on palace dome.
II — Without eagle.

1923   Wmk. 156   Perf. 12

642	A79	2c scarlet	10.00	10.00
643	A81	4c green	1.40	.30
644	A82	5c orange	10.00	7.00
645	A85	10c brown lake	12.50	6.00
646	A83	30c dark green	.95	.25
647	A63	40c violet	1.25	.25
648	A87	50c olive brn	1.00	.25
649	A88	1p red brn & bl (I)	1.00	1.00
a.		Type II	3.00	10.00
		Nos. 642-649 (8)	38.10	25.05
		Set, never hinged	90.00	

Most of Nos. 642-649 are known imperforate or part perforate but probably were not regularly issued.
For overprints see Nos. O175-O176, O189-O190, O208-O209, O223.

1923-34   Rouletted 14½

650	A79	2c scarlet	.25	.25
651	A80	3c bis brn ('27)	.25	.25
652	A81	4c green	47.50	35.00
653	A82	4c green ('27)	.25	.25
654	A82	5c orange	.25	.25
655	A85	10c lake	.25	.25
656	A84	20c deep blue	.75	.30
657	A83	30c dk green ('34)	.75	.30
		Nos. 650-657 (8)	50.25	36.85
		Set, never hinged	125.00	

Nos. 650 to 657 inclusive exist imperforate.

Medallion A90

Map of Americas A91

Francisco García y Santos — A92

Post Office, Mexico, D. F. — A93

1926   Perf. 12

658	A90	2c red	2.50	1.00
659	A91	4c green	2.50	1.00
660	A90	5c orange	2.50	.75
661	A91	10c brown red	4.00	1.00
662	A92	20c dk blue	4.00	1.25
663	A92	30c dk green	7.50	4.00
664	A92	40c violet	13.50	3.00
665	A93	1p brown & blue	27.50	10.00
a.		1p red & blue	37.50	15.00
		Nos. 658-665 (8)	64.00	22.00
		Set, never hinged	150.00	

Pan-American Postal Congress.
Nos. 658-665 were also printed in black, on unwatermarked paper, for presentation to delegates to the Universal Postal Congress at London in 1929. Remainders were overprinted in 1929 for use as airmail official stamps, and are listed as Nos. CO3-CO10.
For overprints see Nos. 667-674, 675A-682, CO3-CO10.

Benito Juárez — A94

1926   Rouletted 14½

666	A94	8c orange	.30	.25
		Never hinged		.70

For overprint see No. O182.

Nos. 658-665 Overprinted **HABILITADO 1930**

1930   Perf. 12

667	A90	2c red	4.00	2.25
a.		Reading down	15.00	15.00
668	A91	4c green	4.00	2.50
a.		Reading down	15.00	15.00
669	A90	5c orange	4.00	2.00
a.		Reading down	15.00	35.00
b.		Double overprint	75.00	75.00
670	A91	10c brown red	7.50	2.50
671	A92	20c dk blue	9.50	3.50
672	A92	30c dk green	8.50	4.00
a.		Reading down	10.00	12.00
673	A92	40c violet	12.50	8.50
a.		Reading down	47.50	50.00
674	A93	1p red brn & bl	11.00	7.00
a.		Double overprint	250.00	
b.		Triple overprint	200.00	
		Nos. 667-674 (8)	61.00	32.25
		Set, never hinged	150.00	

Overprint horizontal on 1p.

Arms of Puebla — A95

1931, May 1   Engr.

675	A95	10c dk bl & dk brn	3.00	.50
		Never hinged		7.50

400th anniversary of Puebla.

Nos. 658-665a Overprinted **HABILITADO 1931**

1931

676	A91	4c green	70.00	75.00
a.		Inverted overprint	750.00	
677	A90	5c orange	13.00	17.00
678	A91	10c brown red	13.00	14.00
679	A92	20c dk blue	13.00	18.00
680	A92	30c dk green	22.50	25.00
681	A92	40c violet	32.50	35.00
682	A93	1p brown & bl	30.00	35.00
a.		1p red & blue	42.50	45.00
		Nos. 676-682 (7)	194.00	219.00
		Set, never hinged	475.00	

Overprint horizontal on 1p.
Nos. 676 and 682 are not known to have been sold to the public through post offices. Forgeries of overprint exist.

Bartolomé de las Casas A96

Emblem of Mexican Society of Geography and Statistics A97

1933, Mar. 3   Engr.   Rouletted 14½

683	A96	15c dark blue	.30	.25
		Never hinged		.70

For overprint see No. O215.

1933, Oct.   Rouletted 14½

684	A97	2c deep green	1.50	.60
685	A97	5c dark brown	1.75	.50
686	A97	10c dark blue	.75	.25
687	A97	1p dark violet	100.00	65.00
		Nos. 684-687 (4)	104.00	66.35
		Set, never hinged	250.00	

XXI Intl. Congress of Statistics and the 1st centenary of the Mexican Society of Geography and Statistics.

Types of 1923 and PT1

1934   Perf. 10½, 11 (4c)

687A	PT1	1c brown	1.00	.30
688	A79	2c scarlet	.35	.25
689	A82	4c green	.35	.25
690	A85	10c brown lake	.35	.25
691	A84	20c dark blue	.75	.75
692	A83	30c dk blue grn	1.00	1.25
		Nos. 687A-692 (6)	3.80	3.05
		Set, never hinged	9.00	

See 2nd note after Postal Tax stamp No. RA3.

Indian Archer — A99

Indian — A100

Woman Decorating Pottery A101

Peon A102

Potter A103

Sculptor A104

Offering to the Gods A106

Craftsman A105

Worshiper — A107

1934, Sept. 1   Wmk. 156   Perf. 10½

698	A99	5c dk green	10.00	3.00
699	A100	10c brown lake	17.00	4.00
700	A101	20c ultra	30.00	20.00
701	A102	30c black	60.00	42.50
702	A103	40c black brn	37.50	25.00
703	A104	50c dull blue	175.00	160.00
704	A105	1p brn lake & blk	350.00	175.00
705	A106	5p brn blk & red brn	750.00	725.00
706	A107	10p brown & vio	2,000.	2,500.
a.		Unwatermarked	3,250.	
		Never hinged	5,000.	
		Nos. 698-706 (9)	3,429.	3,654.
		Set, never hinged	7,500.	

National University.
The design of the 1p is wider than the rest of the set. Values are for copies with perfs just touching the design.
See Nos. C54-C61, RA13B.

Yalalteca Indian — A108

Tehuana Indian — A109

Arch of the Revolution A110

Tower of Los Remedios A111

Cross of Palenque A112

Independence Monument A113

Independence Monument, Puebla A114

Monument to the Heroic Cadets A115

Stone of Tizoc — A116

Ruins of Mitla — A117

Coat of Arms A118

Charro A119

Imprint: "Oficina Impresora de Hacienda-Mexico"

1934-40   Wmk. 156   Perf. 10½
Size: 20x26mm

707	A108	1c orange	.65	.25
a.		Unwmkd.		—
708	A109	2c green	.65	.25
a.		Unwmkd.	3.75	3.75
709	A110	4c carmine	.90	.25
710	A111	5c olive brn	.65	.25
a.		Unwmkd.	400.00	350.00
711	A112	10c dk blue	.80	.25
712	A112	10c violet ('35)	1.25	.25
a.		Unwmkd.	200.00	40.00
713	A113	15c lt blue	4.00	.30
714	A114	20c gray green	1.90	.25
a.		20c olive green	2.00	.25
715	A114	20c ultra ('35)	1.40	.25
a.		Unwmkd.		150.00
716	A115	30c lake	.90	.25
a.		Unwmkd.	350.00	
716B	A115	30c lt ultra ('40)	1.00	.25
717	A116	40c red brown	1.00	.25
718	A117	50c grnsh black	.90	.25
a.		Imperf., pair		375.00
b.		Unwmkd.		
719	A118	1p dk brn & org	2.50	.25
a.		Imperf., pair	350.00	
720	A119	5p org & vio	7.75	.75
		Nos. 707-720 (15)	26.25	4.30
		Set, never hinged	70.00	

No. 718a was not regularly issued.
The existence of No. 707a has been questioned.

See Nos. 729-733, 733B, 735, 784-788, 795A-800A, 837-838, 840-841, 844, 846-851 (post 1940 listings are in Scott Standard catalogue, Vol. 4). For overprints see Nos. 728, O224-O232.

Tractor — A120

1935, Apr. 1   Wmk. 156   Perf. 10½
721   A120   10c violet   4.00   .50
   Never hinged   9.00

Industrial census of Apr. 10, 1935.

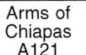

Arms of Chiapas
A121

Emiliano Zapata
A122

1935, Sept. 14
722   A121   10c dark blue   .50   .25
   Never hinged   1.40
  a.   Unwmkd.   125.00   100.00

The 111th anniversary of the joining of the state of Chiapas with the federal republic of Mexico. See No. 734.

1935, Nov. 20   Wmk. 156
723   A122   10c violet   .75   .25
   Never hinged   2.00

25th anniversary of the Plan of Ayala.

US and Mexico Joined by Highways
A123

Matalote Bridge
A124

View of Nuevo Laredo Highway — A125

1936   Wmk. 248   Perf. 14
725   A123   5c blue grn & rose   .35   .25
726   A124   10c slate bl & blk   .50   .25
727   A125   20c brn & dk grn   1.50   1.00
   Nos. 725-727,C77-C79 (6)   3.60   2.50
   Set, never hinged   8.50

Opening of the Mexico City - Nuevo Laredo Highway.

Monument Type of 1923
1936   Wmk. 248   Engr.   Perf. 10½
727A   A85   10c brown lake   2,500.   650.00

No. 712 Overprinted in Green

1936, Dec. 15   Wmk. 156
728   A112   10c violet   .60   .50
   Never hinged   1.50

1st National Congress of Industrial Hygiene and Medicine.

Type of 1934
Redrawn size: 17½x21mm
Imprint: "Talleres de Imp. de Est. y Valores-Mexico"

1937   Photo.   Wmk. 156   Perf. 14
729   A108   1c orange   .60   .25
  a.   Imperf., pair   12.50   12.50
   Never hinged   25.00
730   A109   2c dull green   .60   .25
  a.   Imperf., pair   12.50   12.50
   Never hinged   30.00
731   A110   4c carmine   .90   .25
  a.   Imperf., pair   12.50   12.50
   Never hinged   30.00
732   A111   5c olive brn   .80   .25
  a.   Unwmkd.   300.00
733   A112   10c violet   .70   .25
  a.   Imperf., pair   10.00   12.50
   Never hinged   12.00
   Nos. 729-733 (5)   3.60   1.25
   Set, never hinged   9.00

The imperfs were not regularly issued.

Types of 1934-35
1937   Wmk. 260   Size: 17½x21mm
733B   A111   5c olive brown   4,000.   250.00
   Never hinged   9,000.

1937   Engr.   Perf. 10½
734   A121   10c dark blue   35.00   35.00
   Never hinged   75.00

1937   Size: 20x26mm
735   A112   10c violet   350.00   55.00

Types of 1923
1934-37   Wmk. 260   Perf. 10½
735A   A79   2c scarlet   6,000.
735B   A85   10c brown lake   —

Forged perforations exist.
The listing of No. 735B is being re-evaluated. The Catalogue Editors would appreciate any information on the stamp.

Rouletted 14½
736   A85   10c claret   5,500.   175.00

Blacksmith
A126

Revolutionary Soldier
A127

Revolutionary Envoy — A128

Wmk. 156
1938, Mar. 26   Photo.   Perf. 14
737   A126   5c black & brn   .80   .25
738   A127   10c red brown   .35   .25
739   A128   20c maroon & org   6.00   1.00
   Nos. 737-739,C82-C84 (6)   13.15   5.00
   Set, never hinged   32.00

Plan of Guadalupe, 25th anniv.

Arch of the Revolution
A129

Independence Monument
A131

Design: 10c, National Theater.

1938, July 1
740   A129   5c bister brn   4.25   .60
741   A129   5c red brown   25.00   2.25
742   A129   10c orange   15.00   11.00
743   A129   10c chocolate   1.00   .25
744   A131   20c brown lake   6.00   4.00
745   A131   20c black   18.00   15.00
   Nos. 740-745 (6)   69.25   33.10
   Nos. 740-745,C85-C90 (12)   129.60   63.30
   Set, never hinged   275.00

16th Intl. Congress of Planning & Housing.

Arch of the Revolution
A132

1939, May 1
746   A132   10c Prus blue   .65   .25
   Nos. 746,C91-C93 (4)   4.75   3.00
   Set, never hinged   11.00

New York World's Fair.

Indian — A133

1939, May 17
747   A133   10c red orange   .45   .25
   Nos. 747,C94-C96 (4)   5.55   2.80
   Set, never hinged   13.00

Tulsa World Philatelic Convention.

Juan Zumárraga
A134

First Printing Shop in Mexico, 1539
A135

Design: 10c, Antonio de Mendoza.

1939, Sept. 1   Engr.   Perf. 10½
748   A134   2c brown blk   .75   .25
749   A135   5c green   .75   .25
750   A134   10c red brown   .25   .25
   Nos. 748-750,C97-C99 (6)   3.75   1.95
   Set, never hinged   11.50

400th anniversary of printing in Mexico.

View of Taxco
A137

Allegory of Agriculture
A138

10c, Two hands holding symbols of commerce.

1939, Oct. 1   Photo.   Perf. 12x13
751   A137   2c dark carmine   1.25   .25
752   A138   5c sl grn & gray grn   .25   .25
753   A138   10c org brn & buff   .25   .25
   Nos. 751-753,C100-C102 (6)   6.25   2.00
   Set, never hinged   14.00

Census Taking.

"Penny Black" of 1840
A140

Roadside Monument
A141

1940, May   Perf. 14
754   A140   5c black & lemon   .90   .50
755   A140   10c dark violet   .25   .25
756   A140   20c lt blue & car   .25   .25
757   A140   1p gray & red org   7.00   4.00
758   A140   5p black & Prus bl   50.00   50.00
   Nos. 754-758,C103-C107 (10)   141.00   116.05
   Set, never hinged   340.00

Postage stamp centenary.

1940   Wmk. 156
759   A141   6c deep green   .50   .25
   Never hinged   1.25

Opening of the highway between Mexico, D. F., and Guadalajara. See Nos. 789, 842 in Scott Standard catalogue, Vol. 4.

Vasco de Quiroga — A142

Melchor Ocampo — A143

College Seal — A144

1940, July 15   Engr.   Perf. 10½
760   A142   2c violet   1.30   .50
761   A143   5c copper red   .80   .25
762   A144   10c olive bister   .80   .30
  a.   Imperf., pair   150.00
   Nos. 760-762,C108-C110 (6)   5.10   2.60
   Set, never hinged   11.00

Founding of the National College of San Nicolas de Hidalgo, 400th anniv.

Coat of Arms of Campeche
A145

1940, Aug. 7   Photo.   Perf. 12x13
763   A145   10c bis brn & dk car   5.00   1.25
   Never hinged   8.50
   Nos. 763,C111-C113 (4)   12.60   6.70
   Set, never hinged   30.00

400th anniversary of the founding of Campeche.

MEXICO

Man at Helm
A146

1940, Dec. 1

764	A146	2c red org & blk	1.60	.60
765	A146	5c peacock bl & red brn	8.00	3.50
766	A146	10c slate grn & dk brn	4.00	.85

Nos. 764-766,C114-C116 (6) 21.00 9.45
Set, never hinged 45.00

Inauguration of Pres. Manuel Avila Camacho.

SEMI-POSTAL STAMPS

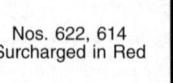

Nos. 622, 614
Surcharged in Red

1918, Dec. 25 Unwmk. Perf. 12

B1	A72	5c + 3c ultra	20.00	25.00

Rouletted 14½

B2	A73	10c + 5c blue	25.00	25.00

Set, never hinged 57.50

AIR POST STAMPS

Eagle
AP1

Unwmk.
1922, Apr. 2 Engr. Perf. 12

C1	AP1	50c blue & red brn	67.50	50.00
		Never hinged	160.00	
a.		50c dark blue & claret ('29)	90.00	90.00
		Never hinged	200.00	

See #C2-C3. For overprints and surcharges see #C47-C48, CO1-CO2B, CO18-CO19, CO29.

1927, Oct. 13 Wmk. 156

C2	AP1	50c dk bl & red brn	.75	.25
		Never hinged	2.50	
a.		50c dark blue & claret ('29)	.75	.25
		Never hinged	3.00	
b.		Vert. strip of 3, imperf. btwn.	7,500.	

The vignettes of Nos. C1a and C2a fluoresce a bright rose red under UV light.

1928

C3	AP1	25c brn car & gray brn	.45	.25
C4	AP1	25c dk grn & gray brn	.45	.25

Set, never hinged 2.50

On May 3, 1929, certain proofs or essays were sold at the post office in Mexico, D. F. They were printed in different colors from those of the regularly issued stamps. There were 7 varieties perf. and 2 imperf. and a total of 225 copies. They were sold with the understanding that they were for collections but the majority of them were used on air mail sent out that day.

Capt. Emilio Carranza and his
Airplane "México Excelsior"
AP2

1929, June 19

C5	AP2	5c ol grn & sepia	1.10	.65
C6	AP2	10c sep & brn red	1.25	.70
C7	AP2	15c vio & dk grn	3.00	1.25
C8	AP2	20c brown & blk	1.25	.75
C9	AP2	50c brn red & blk	7.50	5.00
C10	AP2	1p black & brn	15.00	10.00

Nos. C5-C10 (6) 29.10 18.35
Set, never hinged 75.00

1st anniv. of death of Carranza (1905-28).
For overprints see Nos. C29-C36, C40-C44.

Coat of
Arms and
Airplane
AP3

1929-34 Perf. 11½, 12

C11	AP3	10c violet	.35	.25
C12	AP3	15c carmine	1.35	.25
C13	AP3	20c brown olive	37.50	1.25
C14	AP3	30c gray black	.25	.25
C15	AP3	35c blue green	.35	.25
a.		Imperf., pair	1,200.	
C16	AP3	50c red brn ('34)	1.25	.65
C17	AP3	1p blk & dk bl	1.25	.65
C18	AP3	5p claret & dp bl	4.00	3.50
C19	AP3	10p vio & ol brn	6.00	7.00

Nos. C11-C19 (9) 52.30 14.05
Set, never hinged 130.00

1930-32 Rouletted 13, 13½

C20	AP3	5c lt blue ('32)	.35	.25
C21	AP3	10c violet	.35	.25
C22	AP3	15c carmine	.35	.25
a.		15c rose carmine	.40	
C23	AP3	20c brown olive	1.50	.25
a.		20c brown	.50	.25
b.		20c yellow brown	.50	.25
c.		Horiz. pair, imperf. btwn.		
C24	AP3	25c violet	.95	.80
C25	AP3	50c red brown	.90	.75

Nos. C20-C25 (6) 4.40 2.55
Set, never hinged 13.00

Trial impressions of No. C20 were printed in orange but were never sold at post offices.
See Nos. C62-C64, C75. For overprints and surcharges see Nos. C28, C38-C39, C46, C49-C50, CO17, CO20-CO28, CO30.

Plane over
Plaza,
Mexico
City — AP4

1929, Dec. 10 Wmk. 156 Perf. 12

C26	AP4	20c black violet	1.25	1.00
C27	AP4	40c slate green	85.00	75.00

Set, never hinged 210.00

Aviation Week, Dec. 10-16.
For overprint see No. CO11.

No. C21 Overprinted in Red

1930, Apr. 20 Rouletted 13, 13½

C28	AP3	10c violet	2.00	1.25
		Never hinged	5.50	

National Tourism Congress at Mexico, D. F., Apr. 20-27, 1930.

Nos. C5 and C7 Overprinted

1930, Sept. 1 Perf. 12

C29	AP2	5c ol grn & sepia	5.50	4.50
a.		Double overprint	225.00	250.00
C30	AP2	15c violet & dk grn	9.00	7.75

Set, never hinged 45.00

Nos. C5-C10 Overprinted

1930, Dec. 18

C31	AP2	5c ol grn & sepia	7.00	6.50
C32	AP2	10c sep & brn red	3.50	4.00
a.		Double overprint	60.00	60.00
C33	AP2	15c vio & dk grn	7.50	7.00
C34	AP2	20c brown & blk	7.00	5.50
C35	AP2	50c brn red & blk	14.00	10.00
C36	AP2	1p black & brn	4.00	2.75

Nos. C31-C36 (6) 43.00 35.75
Set, never hinged 130.00

Plane
over
Flying
Field
AP5

1931, May 15 Engr. Perf. 12

C37	AP5	25c lake	4.00	4.50
		Never hinged	11.00	
a.		Imperf., pair	80.00	72.50
		Never hinged	175.00	

Aeronautic Exhibition of the Aero Club of Mexico. Of the 25c, 15c paid air mail postage and 10c went to a fund to improve the Mexico City airport.
For surcharge see No. C45.

Nos. C13 and C23 Srchd. in Red

1931

C38	AP3	15c on 20c brn ol	32.50	35.00
		Never hinged	80.00	

Rouletted 13, 13½

C39	AP3	15c on 20c brn ol	.30	.25
		Never hinged	1.00	
a.		Inverted surcharge	150.00	200.00
b.		Double surcharge	150.00	200.00
c.		Pair, one without surcharge	350.00	

Nos. C5 to C9 Overprinted

1932, July 13 Perf. 12

C40	AP2	5c ol grn & sep	6.00	5.00
a.		Imperf., pair	60.00	60.00
C41	AP2	10c sep & brn red	5.00	3.00
a.		Imperf., pair	60.00	60.00
C42	AP2	15c vio & bk grn	6.00	4.00
a.		Imperf., pair	60.00	60.00
C43	AP2	20c brn & blk	5.00	2.75
a.		Imperf., pair	60.00	60.00
C44	AP2	50c brn red & blk	35.00	35.00
a.		Imperf., pair	60.00	60.00

Nos. C40-C44 (5) 57.00 49.75
Set, never hinged 170.00
Set, C40a-C44a never hinged 650.00

Death of Capt. Emilio Carranza, 4th anniv.

No. C37 Surcharged

1932

C45	AP5	20c on 25c lake	.70	.30
		Never hinged	2.50	
a.		Imperf., pair	72.50	72.50
		Never hinged	150.00	

No. C13 Surcharged

C46	AP3	30c on 20c brn ol	30.00	30.00
		Never hinged	75.00	

Similar Surcharge on Nos. C3 and C4

C47	AP1	40c on 25c (#C3)	.90	.90
		Never hinged	3.00	
a.		Inverted surcharge	11,000.	
C48	AP1	40c on 25c (#C4)	50.00	50.00
		Never hinged	125.00	

Surcharged on Nos. C23 and C24
Rouletted 13, 13½

C49	AP3	30c on 20c brn ol	.35	.25
		Never hinged	1.00	
a.		Inverted surcharge		2,750.
C50	AP3	80c on 25c dl vio	1.75	1.25
		Never hinged	5.00	

Nos. C45-C50 (6) 83.70 82.70

Palace of
Fine Arts
AP6

1933, Oct. 1 Engr. Perf. 12

C51	AP6	20c dk red & dl vio	3.50	1.40
C52	AP6	30c dk brn & dl vio	7.00	6.00
C53	AP6	1p grnsh blk & dl vio	72.50	70.00

Nos. C51-C53 (3) 83.00 77.40
Set, never hinged 190.00

21st Intl. Cong. of Statistics and the cent. of the Mexican Soc. of Geography and Statistics.

National University Issue

Nevado de
Toluca
AP7

Pyramids
of the Sun
and Moon
AP8

View of
Ajusco
AP9

Volcanoes Popocatepetl and
Iztaccíhuatl — AP10

Bridge over
Tepecayo
AP11

Chapultepec Fortress — AP12

Orizaba Volcano (Citlaltépetl) AP13

Mexican Girl and Aztec Calendar Stone AP14

1934, Sept. 1   Wmk. 156   Perf. 10½

C54	AP7	20c orange	15.00	10.00
C55	AP8	30c red lilac & vio	20.00	20.00
C56	AP9	50c ol grn & bis brn	20.00	25.00
C57	AP10	75c blk & yel grn	25.00	25.00
C58	AP11	1p blk & pck bl	30.00	30.00
C59	AP12	5p bis brn & dk bl	225.00	250.00
C60	AP13	10p indigo & mar	550.00	525.00
C61	AP14	20p brn & brn lake	1,800.	1,800.
		Nos. C54-C61 (8)	2,685.	2,685.
		Set, never hinged	4,750.	

Type of 1929-34

1934-35   Perf. 10½, 10½x10

C62	AP3	20c olive green	.35	.25
a.		20c slate	500.00	500.00
		Never hinged	600.00	
C63	AP3	30c slate	.40	.40
C64	AP3	50c red brn ('35)	2.00	2.00
		Nos. C62-C64 (3)	2.75	2.65
		Set, never hinged	7.00	

Symbols of Air Service AP15

Tláloc, God of Water (Quetzalcóatl Temple) — AP16

Orizaba Volcano (Citlaltépetl) AP17

"Eagle Man" AP18

Symbolical of Flight AP19

Aztec Bird-Man — AP20

Allegory of Flight and Pyramid of the Sun AP21

"Eagle Man" and Airplanes AP22

Natives Looking at Airplane and Orizaba Volcano — AP23

Imprint: "Oficina Impresora de Hacienda-Mexico"

Perf. 10½x10, 10x10½

1934-35   Wmk. 156

C65	AP15	5c black	.45	.25
a.		Imperf., pair		
C66	AP16	10c red brown	.90	.25
C67	AP17	15c gray green	1.25	.25
a.		Imperf., pair	400.00	
C68	AP18	20c brown car	3.00	.25
a.		20c lake	4.00	.25
b.		Imperf., pair		
C69	AP19	30c brown olive	.70	.25
C70	AP20	40c blue ('35)	1.25	.25
C71	AP21	50c green	2.50	.25
a.		Imperf., pair	275.00	
C72	AP22	1p gray grn & red brn	3.50	.25
C73	AP23	5p dk car & blk	7.25	.70
		Nos. C65-C73 (9)	20.80	2.70
		Set, never hinged	45.00	

See Nos. C76A, C80, C81; C132-C140, C170-C177A in Scott Standard catalogue, Vol. 4. For overprint see No. C74.

No. C68 Overprinted in Violet

1935, Apr. 16

C74	AP18	20c lake	3,250.	4,000.
		Never hinged	6,000.	

Amelia Earhart's goodwill flight to Mexico. No. C74 with "Muestra" to left of "Mexico" was not issued for postage.

Arms-Plane Type of 1929-34

1935   Wmk. 248   Perf. 10½x10

C75	AP3	30c slate	3.00	5.00
		Never hinged	5.00	

Francisco I. Madero AP24

1935, Nov. 20   Wmk. 156

C76	AP24	20c scarlet	.30	.25
		Never hinged	.75	

Plan of San Luis, 25th anniv. See No. C76B.

Eagle Man Type of 1934-35

1936   Wmk. 260

C76A	AP18	20c lake	4,500.	60.00
		Never hinged	7,500.	

Madero Type of 1935

C76B	AP24	20c scarlet	12,500.

Tasquillo Bridge AP25

Corona River Bridge AP26

Bridge on Nuevo Laredo Highway AP27

Wmk. 248

1936, July 1   Photo.   Perf. 14

C77	AP25	10c slate bl & lt bl	.35	.25
C78	AP26	20c dl vio & org	.35	.25
C79	AP27	40c dk bl & dk grn	.55	.50
		Nos. C77-C79 (3)	1.25	.90
		Set, never hinged	2.75	

Opening of Nuevo Laredo Highway.

Eagle Man Type of 1934-35

Perf. 10½x10

1936, June 18   Engr.   Unwmk.

C80	AP18	20c brown carmine	10.00	7.00
		Never hinged	25.00	

Imprint: "Talleres de Imp. de Est. y Valores-Mexico"

1937   Wmk. 156   Photo.   Perf. 14

C81	AP18	20c rose red	1.25	.25
		Never hinged	2.50	
a.		20c brown carmine	1.50	.25
		Never hinged	3.00	
b.		20c dark carmine	2.00	.25
		Never hinged	4.50	
c.		Imperf., pair	37.50	50.00
		Never hinged	75.00	

There are two sizes of watermark 156. No. C81c was not regularly issued.

Cavalryman AP28

Early Biplane over Mountains AP29

Venustiano Carranza on Horseback AP30

1938, Mar. 26

C82	AP28	20c org red & bl	.50	.25
C83	AP29	40c bl & org red	.75	1.00
C84	AP30	1p bl & bis brn	4.75	2.25
		Nos. C82-C84 (3)	6.00	3.45
		Set, never hinged	18.00	

Plan of Guadalupe, 25th anniversary.

Reconstructed edifices of Chichén Itzá — AP31

Designs: Nos. C85, C86, The Zócalo and Cathedral, Mexico City. Nos. C89, C90, View of Acapulco.

1938, July 1

C85	AP31	20c carmine rose	.35	.25
C86	AP31	20c purple	20.00	10.00
C87	AP31	40c brt green	10.00	5.00
C88	AP31	40c dark green	10.00	5.00
C89	AP31	1p light blue	10.00	5.00
C90	AP31	1p slate blue	10.00	5.00
		Nos. C85-C90 (6)	60.35	30.25
		Set, never hinged	130.00	

16th Intl. Cong. of Planning & Housing.

Statue of José María Morelos — AP34

1939   Engr.   Perf. 10½

C91	AP34	20c green	.70	.50
		Never hinged	1.00	
C92	AP34	40c red violet	2.00	1.25
		Never hinged	5.00	
C93	AP34	1p vio brn & car	1.40	1.00
		Never hinged	1.75	
		Nos. C91-C93 (3)	4.10	2.75
		Set, never hinged	9.50	

New York World's Fair. Released in New York May 2, in Mexico May 24.

Type of 1939 Overprinted in Cerise

1939, May 23

C93A	AP34	20c blue & red	425.00	425.00
		Never hinged	800.00	

Issued for the flight of Francisco Sarabia from Mexico City to New York on May 25.

Statue of Pioneer Woman, Ponca City, OK — AP35

1939, May 17

C94	AP35	20c gray brown	1.00	.40
		Never hinged	2.00	
C95	AP35	40c slate green	2.50	1.25
		Never hinged	7.00	
C96	AP35	1p violet	1.60	.90
		Never hinged	3.00	
		Nos. C94-C96 (3)	5.10	2.55
		Set, never hinged	12.00	

Tulsa World Philatelic Convention.

First Engraving Made in Mexico, 1544 — AP36

First Work of Legislation Printed in America, 1563 — AP37

Designs: 1p, Reproduction of oldest preserved Mexican printing.

1939, Sept. 7   **Wmk. 156**
C97 AP36 20c slate blue   .25   .25
  a.   Unwmkd.   50.00 25.00
C98 AP37 40c slate green   .65   .25
  a.   Imperf., pair   700.00
C99 AP37 1p dk brn & car   1.10   .70
     Nos. C97-C99 (3)   2.00   1.10
     Set, never hinged   6.00

400th anniversary of printing in Mexico.

Alternated Perforations
Nos. 763-766, 774-779, 792-795, 801-804, 806-811, 813-818, C100-C102, C111-C116, C123-C128, C143-C162, C430-C431 have alternating small and large perforations. See Scott Standard catalogue, Vol. 4, for post 1940 listings.

Transportation — AP39

Designs: 40c, Finger counting and factory. 1p, "Seven Censuses."

Perf. 12x13, 13x12
1939, Oct. 2   **Photo.**
C100 AP39 20c dk bl & bl   1.00   .25
C101 AP39 40c red org & org   .75   .25
C102 AP39 1p ind & vio bl   2.75   .75
     Nos. C100-C102 (3)   4.50   1.20
     Set, never hinged   10.00

National Census of 1939-40.

Penny Black Type of Regular Issue, 1940

1940, May   **Perf. 14**
C103 A140 5c blk & dk grn   .65   .55
C104 A140 10c bis brn & dp bl   .55   .25
C105 A140 20c car & bl vio   .40   .25
C106 A140 1p car & choc   6.00   5.00
C107 A140 5p gray grn & red brn   75.00 55.00
     Nos. C103-C107 (5)   82.60 61.00
     Set, never hinged   200.00

Issue dates: 5c-1p, May 2; 5p, May 15.

Part of Original College at Pátzcuaro AP43

College at Morelia (18th Century) — AP44

College at Morelia (1940) AP45

1940, July 15   **Engr.**   **Perf. 10½**
C108 AP43 20c brt green   .45   .25
C109 AP44 40c orange   .50   .30
C110 AP45 1p dp pur, red brn & org 1.25   1.00
     Nos. C108-C110 (3)   2.20   1.50
     Set, never hinged   5.00

400th anniv. of the founding of the National College of San Nicolas de Hidalgo.

Pirate Ship AP46

Designs: 40c, Castle of San Miguel. 1p, Temple of San Francisco.

Perf. 12x13, 13x12
1940, Aug. 7   **Photo.**
C111 AP46 20c red brn & bis brn   1.10   .70
C112 AP46 40c blk & sl grn   1.50   .75
C113 AP46 1p vio bl & blk   5.00   4.00
     Nos. C111-C113 (3)   7.60   5.45
     Set, never hinged   20.00

400th anniversary of Campeche.

Inauguration Type of Regular Issue, 1940

1940, Dec. 1   **Perf. 12x13**
C114 A146 20c gray blk & red org   1.90   1.00
C115 A146 40c chnt brn & dk sl   2.00   1.50
C116 A146 1p brt vio bl & rose   3.50   2.00
     Nos. C114-C116 (3)   7.40   4.50
     Set, never hinged   20.00

AIR POST OFFICIAL STAMPS

Nos. C4 and C3 Overprinted in Black or Red

1929   **Wmk. 156**   **Perf. 12**
CO1 AP1 25c dk grn & gray brn   4.50   3.25
  a.   Without period   20.00 20.00
CO2 AP1 25c dk grn & gray brn (R)   4.00   5.00
  a.   Without period   21.00 21.00
CO2B AP1 25c brn car & gray brn   10.00 12.50
  c.   Without period   25.00 25.00
     Nos. CO1-CO2B (3)   18.50 20.75
     Set, never hinged   35.00

Types of Regular Issue of 1926 Overprinted in Red

1929, Oct. 15   **Unwmk.**
CO3 A90 2c black   75.00 90.00
CO4 A91 4c black   75.00 90.00
CO5 A90 5c black   75.00 90.00
CO6 A91 10c black   75.00 90.00
CO7 A92 20c black   75.00 90.00
CO8 A92 30c black   75.00 90.00
CO9 A92 40c black   75.00 90.00
     Nos. CO3-CO9 (7)   525.00 630.00
     Set, never hinged   1,100.

Horizontal Overprint
CO10 A93 1p black   2,250. 2,250.
     Never hinged   4,000.

Nos. CO3-CO9 also exist with overprint reading up.

No. C26 Overprinted in Black

1930   **Wmk. 156**
CO11 AP4 20c black violet   1.10   1.75
     Never hinged   2.25
  a.   Without period   20.00 20.00
  b.   Inverted overprint   18.00 18.00
  c.   As "a," inverted overprint 210.00 210.00

No. CO11 with red overprint is believed not to have been issued for postal purposes.

Plane over Mexico City OA1

1930   **Engr.**
CO12 OA1 20c gray black   6.00   6.00
CO13 OA1 35c lt violet   1.10   1.90
CO14 OA1 40c ol brn & dp bl   1.25   1.75
CO15 OA1 70c vio & ol gray   1.25   1.75
     Nos. CO12-CO15 (4)   9.60 11.40
     Set, never hinged   22.50

No. CO12 Surcharged in Red

HABILITADO Quince centavos

1931
CO16 OA1 15c on 20c   .85   1.40
     Never hinged   1.60
  a.   Inverted surcharge   140.00
  b.   Double surcharge   140.00

No. C20 Overprinted

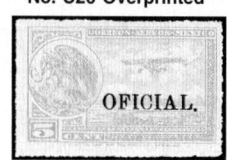

OFICIAL.

1932   **Rouletted 13, 13½**
CO17 AP3 5c light blue   .80   .90
     Never hinged   1.75

Air Post Stamps of 1927-32 Overprinted

SERVICIO OFICIAL

On No. C1a
1932   **Unwmk.**   **Perf. 12**
CO18 AP1 50c dk bl & cl   1,000. 1,000.
     Never hinged   2,000.

On Nos. C2, C2a
                                        Wmk. 156
CO19 AP1 50c dk bl & red brn   1.25   1.50
     Never hinged   2.25
  a.   50c dark blue & claret   1.40   1.60
     See note after No. C2.

On Nos. C11 and C12
                                        Perf. 12
CO20 AP3 10c violet   22.50 25.00
     Never hinged   45.00
CO21 AP3 15c carmine   350.00 375.00
     Never hinged   700.00

On Nos. C21 to C23
                                     Rouletted 13, 13½
CO22 AP3 10c violet   .35   .55
CO23 AP3 15c carmine   1.40   2.00
CO24 AP3 20c brn olive   1.40   2.00

Nos. C20, C21 C23 and C25 Overprinted

SERVICIO OFICIAL

1933-34   **Rouletted 13½**
CO25 AP3 5c light blue   .30   .55
CO26 AP3 10c violet ('34)   .30   .90
CO27 AP3 20c brown olive   .75   1.25
CO28 AP3 50c red brn ('34)   1.25   1.90

On No. C2
Perf. 12
CO29 AP1 50c dk bl & red brn   1.10   2.00
  a.   50c dark blue & claret   1.60   2.50

On No. C11
Perf. 12
CO30 AP3 10c violet ('34)   140.00 175.00
  a.   Double overprint   325.00

Forgeries exist.

SPECIAL DELIVERY STAMPS

Motorcycle Postman SD1

1919   **Unwmk.   Engr.   Perf. 12**
E1 SD1 20c red & black   70.00   2.75

1923   **Wmk. 156**
E2 SD1 20c blk car & blk   .30   .25

For overprint see No. E7.

Messenger with Quipu — SD2

1934
E3 SD2 10c brn red & blue   .30   .50

Indian Archer — SD3

Imprint: "Oficina Impresora de Hacienda Mexico."

1934   **Perf. 10x10½**
E4 SD3 10c black violet   1.50   .50

See Nos. E5-E6, E8-E9 (in Scott Standard catalogue, Vol. 4).

Redrawn
Imprint: "Talleres de Imp. de Est. y Valores-Mexico."

1938-41   **Photo.**   **Perf. 14**
E5 SD3 10c slate violet   .75   .25
  a.   Unwatermarked   50.00
E6 SD3 20c orange red ('41)   .50   .25

Imperforate examples of No. E6 were not regularly issued.

No. E2 Overprinted "1940" in Violet
1940   **Engr.**   **Perf. 12**
E7 SD1 20c red & black   .40   .25

INSURED LETTER STAMPS

Insured Letters — IL1   Registered Mailbag — IL2

Safe — IL3

1935	**Engr.**	**Wmk. 156**	***Perf. 10½***	
G1	IL1	10c vermilion	1.75	.75
a.		Perf. 10x10½		
G2	IL2	50c dk bl	10.00	.60
G3	IL3	1p turq grn	1.25	.85
	Nos. G1-G3 (3)		13.00	2.20

Nos. G1 and G4 were issued both with and without imprint.

POSTAGE DUE STAMPS

D1

1908	**Engr.**	**Wmk. 155**	***Perf. 14***	
J1	D1	1c blue	1.00	3.00
J2	D1	2c blue	1.00	3.00
J3	D1	4c blue	1.00	3.00
J4	D1	5c blue	1.00	3.00
J5	D1	10c blue	1.00	3.00
	Nos. J1-J5 (5)		5.00	15.00

For overprints and surcharges see Nos. 381-385, 434-438, 466-470, 495-499, 593-607.

PORTE DE MAR STAMPS

These stamps were used to indicate the amount of cash to be paid to the captains of the mail steamers taking outgoing foreign mail.

PM2   PM3

1875	**Unwmk.**	**Litho.**	***Imperf.***	
JX9	PM2	2c black	.60	50.00
a.		"5" added to make 25c	12.00	100.00
JX10	PM2	10c black	.80	30.00
JX11	PM2	12c black	.80	50.00
JX12	PM2	20c black	1.00	50.00
JX13	PM2	25c black	3.25	50.00
JX14	PM2	35c black	3.25	60.00
JX15	PM2	50c black	3.00	60.00
JX16	PM2	60c black	3.00	75.00
JX17	PM2	75c black	3.50	75.00
JX18	PM2	85c black	3.25	100.00
JX19	PM2	100c black	4.00	100.00
	Nos. JX9-JX19 (11)		26.45	700.00

Same, Numerals Larger

JX20	PM2	5c black	1.00	50.00
JX21	PM2	25c black	1.65	50.00
JX22	PM2	35c black	250.00	
JX23	PM2	50c black	1.00	50.00
JX24	PM2	60c black	125.00	
JX25	PM2	100c black	.60	100.00
	Nos. JX20-JX25 (6)		379.25	

In Nos. JX9-JX19 the figures of value are 7mm high and "CENTAVOS" is 7½mm long. On Nos. JX20-JX25 the figures of value are 8mm high and "CENTAVOS" is 9½mm long.

Nos. JX9-JX25 exist with overprints of district names.

Counterfeits exist of Nos. JX9-JX31.

1879

JX26	PM3	2c brown	.50	
JX27	PM3	5c yellow	.50	
JX28	PM3	10c red	.50	
JX29	PM3	25c blue	.50	
JX30	PM3	50c green	.50	
JX31	PM3	100c violet	.50	
	Nos. JX26-JX31 (6)		3.00	

Nos. JX26-JX31 were never put in use.

Nos. JX26-JX31 were printed on paper watermarked "ADMINISTRACION GENERAL DE CORREOS MEXICO." Approximately ¾ of the stamps do not show any of the watermark.

Stamps of this design were never issued. Examples appeared on the market in 1884. Value, set, $22.

All were printed in same sheet of 49 (7x7). Sheet consists of 14 of 10c; 7 each of 25c, 35c, 50c; 4 each of 60c, 85c; 3 each of 75c, 100c. There are four varieties of 10c, two of 25c, 35c and 50c.

OFFICIAL STAMPS

Hidalgo — O1

Wove or Laid Paper

1884-93	**Unwmk.**	**Engr.**	***Perf. 12***	
O1	O1	red	1.40	1.00
a.		Vert. pair, imperf. betwn.	120.00	
O1B	O1	scarlet ('85)	1.40	1.00
O2	O1	olive brn ('87)	.90	.70
a.		Horiz. pair, imperf. betwn.		
b.		Blue ruled lines on paper		
O3	O1	orange ('88)	2.50	.90
a.		Vert. pair, imperf. betwn.	110.00	
b.		Perf. 11	15.00	12.00
O4	O1	blue grn ('93)	1.40	.80
a.		Imperf., pair	15.00	12.00
b.		Perf. 11	15.00	12.00
	Nos. O1-O4 (5)		7.60	4.40

Pin-perf. 6

O5	O1	olive brown ('87)	100.00	50.00

Wmk. "Correos E U M" on every Vertical Line of Ten Stamps (152)

1894			***Perf. 5½***	
O6	O1	ultra	3.00	2.75
a.		Vert. pair, imperf. horiz.	35.00	
b.		Imperf., pair	45.00	

Perf. 11, 12

O7	O1	ultra	1.75	1.60

Perf. 5½x11, 11x5½

O9	O1	ultra	12.00	8.00
	Nos. O6-O9 (3)		16.75	12.35

Regular Issues with Handstamped Overprint in Black

1895		**Wmk. 152**	***Perf. 12***	
O10	A20	1c green	17.50	6.00
O11	A20	2c carmine	20.00	6.00
O12	A20	3c orange brn	17.50	6.00
O13	A21	4c red orange	26.00	12.00
a.		4c orange	42.50	14.00
O14	A22	5c ultra	35.00	12.00
O15	A23	10c lilac rose	32.50	3.00
O16	A21	12c olive brn	70.00	30.00
O17	A23	15c brt blue	42.50	18.00
O18	A23	20c brown rose	42.50	18.00
O19	A23	50c purple	90.00	42.50
O20	A24	1p brown	200.00	90.00
O21	A24	5p scarlet	475.00	250.00
O22	A24	10p deep blue	750.00	500.00
	Nos. O10-O22 (13)		1,818.	993.50

Similar stamps with red overprint were not officially placed in use. Nos. O10-O22 have a vertical grain or mesh to the paper.

1896-97			**Wmk. 153**	
		Black Overprint		
O23	A20	1c green	60.00	10.00
O24	A20	2c carmine	60.00	12.00
O25	A20	3c orange brn	60.00	12.00
O26	A21	4c red orange	60.00	12.00
a.		4c orange	75.00	22.50
O27	A22	5c ultra	60.00	12.00
O28	A21	12c olive brn	80.00	30.00
O29	A23	15c brt blue	100.00	30.00
O29A	A23	50c purple	650.00	650.00
	Nos. O23-O29A (8)		1,130.	768.00

Nos. O23-O29A have a vertical grain or mesh to the paper.

1897	**Wmk. 154**	**Black Overprint**		
O30	A20	1c green	100.00	30.00
O31	A20	2c scarlet	90.00	35.00
O33	A21	4c orange	125.00	60.00
O34	A22	5c ultra	100.00	35.00
O35	A21	12c olive brn	125.00	42.50
O36	A23	15c brt blue	160.00	42.50
O37	A23	20c brown rose	110.00	18.00
O38	A23	50c purple	150.00	30.00
O39	A24	1p brown	375.00	125.00
	Nos. O30-O39 (9)		1,335.	418.00

Nos. O30-O39 have a vertical grain or mesh to the paper.

1898	**Unwmk.**	**Black Overprint**		
O40	A20	1c green	35.00	9.50
O41	A20	2c scarlet	35.00	9.50
O42	A20	3c orange brn	35.00	9.50
O43	A21	4c orange	60.00	12.00
O44	A22	5c ultra	60.00	20.00
O45	A23	10c lilac rose	650.00	500.00
O46	A21	12c olive brn	125.00	30.00
O47	A23	15c brt blue	125.00	30.00
O48	A23	20c brown rose	225.00	75.00
O48A	A23	50c purple	375.00	150.00
O48B	A24	10p deep blue	—	
	Nos. O40-O48A (10)		1,725.	845.50

The existence of No. O45 has been questioned by specialists. The editors would like to see authenticated evidence of this stamp. See note following No. 291.

		Black Overprint		
1900	**Wmk. 155**	***Perf. 14, 15***		
O49	A25	1c green	37.50	2.50
O50	A26	2c vermilion	50.00	4.00
O51	A27	3c yellow brn	50.00	2.50
O52	A28	5c dark blue	50.00	4.50
O53	A29	10c violet & org	65.00	5.50
O54	A30	15c lavender & cl	65.00	5.50
O55	A31	20c rose & dk bl	75.00	2.50
O56	A32	50c red lil & blk	150.00	25.00
O57	A33	1p blue & blk	300.00	25.00
O58	A34	5p carmine & blk	575.00	75.00
	Nos. O49-O58 (10)		1,417.	152.00

		Black Overprint		
1903		**Black Overprint**		
O59	A25	1c violet	35.00	4.00
O60	A26	2c green	35.00	4.00
O61	A35	4c carmine	65.00	2.50
O62	A28	5c orange	65.00	13.00
O63	A29	10c blue & org	70.00	4.00
O64	A32	50c carmine & blk	200.00	25.00
	Nos. O59-O64 (6)		470.00	52.50

Regular Issues Overprinted

1910		**On Issues of 1899-1903**		
O65	A26	2c green	175.00	6.50
O66	A27	3c orange brn	175.00	4.00
O67	A35	4c carmine	200.00	10.00
O68	A28	5c orange	225.00	50.00
O69	A29	10c blue & org	200.00	4.00
O70	A30	15c lav & claret	225.00	6.50
O71	A31	20c rose & dk bl	275.00	3.00
O72	A32	50c carmine & blk	375.00	35.00
O73	A33	1p blue & blk	575.00	125.00
O74	A34	5p carmine & blk	200.00	125.00
	Nos. O65-O74 (10)		2,625.	369.00

1911		**On Issue of 1910**		
O75	A36	1c violet	5.00	5.00
O76	A37	2c green	3.75	2.25
O77	A38	3c orange brn	5.00	2.50
O78	A39	4c carmine	5.50	2.25
O79	A40	5c orange	12.50	7.00
O80	A41	10c blue & org	5.50	2.50
O81	A42	15c gray bl & cl	13.00	8.50
O82	A43	20c red & blue	10.00	2.50
O83	A44	50c red brn & blk	35.00	15.00
O84	A45	1p blue & blk	60.00	25.00
O85	A46	5p carmine & blk	300.00	125.00
	Nos. O75-O85 (11)		455.25	197.50

Nos. 500 to 505 Overprinted

1915	**Unwmk.**	***Rouletted 14½***		
O86	A57	1c violet	1.00	2.00
O87	A58	2c green	1.00	2.00
O88	A59	3c brown	1.25	2.00
O89	A60	4c carmine	1.00	2.00
O90	A61	5c orange	1.00	2.00
O91	A62	10c ultra	1.25	2.00
	Nos. O86-O91 (6)		6.50	12.00

All values are known with inverted overprint. All values exist imperforate and part perforate but were not regularly issued in these forms.

On Nos. 506 to 514

1915-16			***Perf. 12***	
O92	A57	1c violet	1.50	2.00
O93	A58	2c green	1.50	2.00
O94	A59	3c brown	1.50	2.00
O95	A60	4c carmine	1.50	2.00
a.		"CEATRO"	21.00	30.00
O96	A61	5c orange	1.50	2.00
O97	A62	10c ultra, type II	1.50	2.00
a.		Double overprint	475.00	
O98	A63	40c slate	8.00	14.50
a.		Inverted overprint	24.00	25.00
b.		Double overprint	40.00	
O99	A64	1p brown & blk	10.00	14.50
a.		Inverted overprint	27.50	27.50
O100	A65	5p claret & ultra	60.00	60.00
a.		Inverted overprint	80.00	
	Nos. O92-O100 (9)		87.00	101.00

Nos. O98 and O99 exist imperforate but probably were not issued in that form.

Preceding Issues Overprinted in Red, Blue or Black

On No. O74

1916			**Wmk. 155**	
O101	A34	5p carmine & blk	900.00	

On Nos. O75 to O85

O102	A36	1c violet	6.50	
O103	A37	2c green	1.25	
O104	A38	3c orange brn (Bl)	1.75	
O105	A39	4c carmine (Bl)	7.00	
O106	A40	5c orange (Bl)	1.75	
O107	A41	10c blue & org	1.75	
O108	A42	15c gray bl & cl (Bk)	1.75	
O109	A43	20c red & bl (Bk)	1.90	
O110	A44	50c red brn & blk	200.00	
O111	A45	1p blue & blk	11.00	
O112	A46	5p carmine & blk	3,250.	
	Nos. O102-O111 (10)		234.65	

No. O102 with blue overprint is a trial color. Counterfeits exist of Nos. O110, O112.

Nos. 608, 610 to 612,
615 and 616
Overprinted Vertically
in Red or Black

Thick Paper

1918		Unwmk.	**Rouletted 14½**	
O113	A68	1c violet (R)	60.00	35.00
O114	A69	2c gray grn (R)	65.00	35.00
O115	A70	3c bis brn (R)	60.00	35.00
O116	A71	4c carmine (Bk)	60.00	35.00
O117	A74	20c rose (Bk)	125.00	90.00
O118	A75	30c gray brn (R)	190.00	175.00

On Nos. 622-623
Medium Paper
Perf. 12

O119	A72	5c ultra (R)	40.00	40.00
O120	A73	10c blue (R)	35.00	25.00
a.		Double overprint	400.00	400.00
		Nos. O113-O120 (8)	635.00	470.00

Overprinted
Horizontally in
Red

On Nos. 626-628
Thin Paper

O121	A63	40c violet (R)	35.00	27.50
O122	A64	1p bl & blk (R)	85.00	70.00
O123	A65	5p grn & blk (R)	575.00	600.00
		Nos. O121-O123 (3)	695.00	697.50

Nos. 608 and 610 to
615 Ovptd. Vertically
Up in Red or Black

Thick Paper

1919			**Rouletted 14½**	
O124	A68	1c dull vio (R)	6.00	6.00
a.		"OFICIAN"	70.00	80.00
O125	A69	2c gray grn (R)	9.50	3.50
a.		"OFICIAN"	70.00	80.00
O126	A70	3c bis brn (R)	14.00	6.00
a.		"OFICIAN"	95.00	100.00
O127	A71	4c car (Bk)	29.00	13.00
c.		"OFICIAN"		—
O127A	A72	5c ultra	200.00	125.00
b.		"OFICIAN"	500.00	
O128	A73	10c blue (R)	9.50	2.50
a.		"OFICIAN"	85.00	60.00
O129	A74	20c rose (Bk)	60.00	47.50
a.		"OFICIAN"		140.00

On Nos. 618, 622
Perf. 12

O130	A68	1c dull violet (R)	47.50	47.50
a.		"OFICIAN"	140.00	100.00
O131	A72	5c ultra (R)	47.50	22.50
a.		"OFICIAN"	140.00	100.00

Overprinted Horizontally
On Nos. 626-627
Thin Paper

O132	A63	40c violet (R)	47.50	35.00
O133	A64	1p bl & blk (R)	60.00	50.00
		Nos. O124-O133 (11)	530.50	358.50

Nos. 608 to 615 and
617 Ovptd. Vertically
down in Black, Red or
Blue

Size: 17½x3mm

1921			**Rouletted 14½**	
O134	A68	1c gray (Bk)	30.00	12.00
a.		1c dull violet (Bk)	17.00	7.00
O135	A69	2c gray grn (R)	5.00	3.00
O136	A70	3c bis brn (R)	8.50	4.50
O137	A71	4c carmine (Bk)	27.50	21.00
O138	A72	5c ultra (R)	25.00	12.00
O139	A73	10c bl, reading down (R)	32.50	12.00
a.		Overprint reading up	60.00	60.00
O140	A74	20c rose (Bl)	47.50	27.50
O141	A75	30c gray blk (R)	25.00	25.00

Overprinted Horizontally
On Nos. 626-628
Perf. 12

O142	A63	40c violet (R)	32.50	32.50
O143	A64	1p bl & blk (R)	25.00	25.00
O144	A65	5p grn & blk (Bk)	600.00	600.00
		Nos. O134-O144 (11)	858.50	774.50

Nos. 609 to 615
Overprinted Vertically
Down in Black

1921-30			**Rouletted 14½**	
O145	A68	1c gray	5.00	2.50
a.		1c lilac gray	1.00	.70
O146	A69	2c gray green	1.75	.70
O147	A70	3c bister brn	.80	.70
a.		"OFICAL"	47.50	25.00
b.		"OIFICAL"	47.50	25.00
c.		Double overprint	140.00	
O148	A71	4c carmine	22.50	2.50
O149	A72	5c ultra	1.00	.70
O150	A73	10c blue	1.00	.70
a.		"OFICIAN"	50.00	
O151	A74	20c brown rose	9.00	9.50
a.		20c rose	5.00	2.50

On No. 625
Perf. 12

O152	A75	30c gray black	7.25	2.50

Overprinted Horizontally
On Nos. 626, 628

O153	A63	40c violet	7.00	5.00
a.		"OFICAL"	60.00	60.00
b.		"OICIFAL"	60.00	60.00
c.		Inverted overprint	90.00	125.00
O154	A65	5p grn & blk ('30)	375.00	375.00
		Nos. O145-O154 (10)	430.30	399.80

Ovptd. Vertically Down
in Red On Nos. 609,
610, 611, 613 and
614

1921-24			**Rouletted 14½**	
O155	A68	1c lilac	1.60	1.00
O156	A69	2c gray green	1.50	.90
O157	A70	3c bister brown	4.00	1.00
O158	A72	5c ultra	1.60	.80
O159	A73	10c blue	35.00	3.50
a.		Double overprint		

On Nos. 624-625
Perf. 12

O160	A74	20c rose	7.25	1.60
O161	A75	30c gray black	19.00	5.00

Overprinted Horizontally
On Nos. 626-628

O162	A63	40c violet	14.00	7.50
a.		Vert. pair, imperf. btwn.		
O163	A64	1p blue & blk	35.00	25.00
O164	A65	5p green & blk	300.00	300.00

Overprinted Vertically Down in Blue
on No. 612
Rouletted 14½

O165	A71	4c carmine	7.00	3.50
		Nos. O155-O165 (11)	425.95	349.80

Same Overprint Vertically Down in
Red on Nos. 635 and 637

1926-27			**Rouletted 14½**	
O166	A80	3c bis brn, ovpt. horiz.	12.00	12.00
a.		Period omitted	30.00	30.00
O167	A82	5c orange	27.50	30.00

Same Overprint Vertically Down in
Blue or Red 0n Nos. 650, 651, 655
and 656
Wmk. 156

O168	A79	2c scarlet (Bl)	20.00	20.00
a.		Overprint reading up	30.00	30.00
O169	A80	3c bis brn, ovpt. horiz. (R)	5.00	5.00
a.		Inverted overprint	60.00	
O170	A85	10c claret (Bl)	35.00	16.00
O171	A84	20c deep blue (R)	14.00	12.00
a.		Overprint reading up	14.00	12.00

Overprinted Horizontally in Red
On Nos. 643, 646-649
Perf. 12

O172	A81	4c green	6.00	6.00
O173	A83	30c dk grn	6.00	6.00
O174	A63	40c violet	16.00	16.00
a.		Inverted overprint	80.00	

O175	A87	50c olive brn	1.50	1.50
		50c yellow brown	18.00	18.00
O176	A88	1p red brn & bl	15.00	15.00
		Nos. O168-O176 (9)	118.50	97.50

Same Overprint Horizontally on No.
651, Vertically Up on Nos. 650, 653-
656, 666, RA1

1927-31			**Rouletted 14½**	
O177	PT1	1c brown ('31)	.70	1.00
O178	A79	2c scarlet	.70	1.00
a.		"OFICAIL"	30.00	30.00
b.		Overprint reading down	1.50	2.00
O179	A80	3c bis brn	2.00	1.50
a.		"OFICIAL"	40.00	30.00
O180	A82	4c green	1.50	1.00
a.		"OFICIAL"	40.00	40.00
b.		Overprint reading down	10.00	2.00
O181	A82	5c orange	4.00	3.00
a.		Overprint reading up	4.00	2.50
O182	A94	8c orange	12.00	8.00
a.		Overprint reading up	7.00	6.00
O183	A85	10c lake	2.00	2.00
a.		Overprint reading up	2.00	2.00
O184	A84	20c dark blue	10.00	4.00
a.		"OFICIAL"	40.00	40.00
b.		Overprint reading down	20.00	20.00
		Nos. O177-O184 (8)	32.90	21.50

Overprinted Vertically Up on #O186,
Horizontally
On Nos. 643 and 645 to 649

1927-33			**Perf. 12**	
O185	A81	4c green	6.00	5.00
a.		Inverted overprint	30.00	30.00
O186	A85	10c brown lake	55.00	45.00
O187	A83	30c dark green	1.40	1.00
a.		Inverted overprint	30.00	30.00
b.		Pair, tête bêche overprints	35.00	35.00
c.		"OFICIAL"	35.00	35.00
O188	A63	40c violet	12.00	8.00
O189	A87	50c olive brn ('33)	3.25	4.00
O190	A88	1p red brn & bl	24.00	20.00
		Nos. O185-O190 (6)	101.65	83.00

The overprint on No. O186 is vertical.

Nos. 320,
628, 633
Overprinted
Horizontally

On Stamp No. 320

1927-28		**Wmk. 155**	**Perf. 14, 15**	
O191	A46	5p car & blk (R)	175.00	250.00
O192	A46	5p car & blk (Bl)	175.00	250.00

		Unwmk.	**Perf. 12**	
O193	A65	5p grn & blk (Bk)	375.00	500.00
a.		Inverted overprint	—	—
O194	A78	10p blk brn & blk (Bl)	200.00	300.00

No. 320
Overprinted
Horizontally

		Wmk. 155	**Perf. 14**	
O195	A46	5p carmine & blk	300.00	

Nos. 650 and 655
Overprinted
Horizontally

1928-29		**Wmk. 156**	**Rouletted 14½**	
		Size: 16x2½mm		
O196	A79	2c dull red	18.00	12.00
O197	A85	10c rose lake	27.50	12.00

Nos. RA1, 650-651,
653-656 Overprinted

1932-33				
O198	PT1	1c brown	.70	1.00
O199	A79	2c dull red	.80	1.00
O200	A80	3c bister brn	3.00	3.00

O201	A82	4c green	10.00	8.00
O202	A82	5c orange	12.00	8.00
O203	A85	10c rose lake	3.25	4.00
O204	A84	20c dark blue	15.00	10.00
a.		Double overprint	200.00	90.00
		Nos. O198-O204 (7)	44.75	34.00

Nos. 651,
646 649
Overprinted
Horizontally

1933			**Rouletted 14½**	
O205	A80	3c bister brn	3.00	3.00
		Perf. 12		
O206	A83	30c dk green	8.00	3.00
O207	A63	40c violet	15.00	6.00
O208	A87	50c olive brn	2.50	3.00
a.		"OFICIAL OFICIAL"	50.00	50.00
O209	A88	1p red brn & bl, type I	3.00	3.00
a.		Type II	2.75	3.50

Overprinted Vertically On No. 656
Rouletted 14½

O210	A84	20c dark blue	18.00	10.00
		Nos. O205-O210 (6)	49.50	28.00

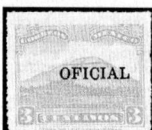

Nos. RA1, 651,
653, 654, 683
Overprinted
Horizontally

1934-37			**Rouletted 14½**	
		Size: 13x2mm		
O211	PT1	1c brown	5.00	6.00
O212	A80	3c bister brn	.70	.70
O213	A82	4c green	12.00	10.00
O214	A82	5c orange	.70	.70
O215	A96	15c dk blue ('37)	1.00	1.00
		Nos. O211-O215 (5)	19.40	18.40

See No. O217a.

Same Overprint on Nos. 687A-692

1934-37			**Perf. 10½**	
O216	PT1	1c brown ('37)	1.00	1.25
O217	A79	2c scarlet	1.00	1.50
a.		On No. 650 (error)	350.00	
b.		Double overprint	275.00	
O218	A82	4c green ('35)	1.40	1.60
O219	A85	10c brown lake	1.00	1.00
O220	A84	20c dk blue ('37)	1.25	1.25
O221	A83	30c dk bl grn ('37)	2.00	2.00

On Nos. 647 and 649
Perf. 12, 11½x12

O222	A63	40c violet	3.00	3.50
O223	A88	1p red brn & bl (I)	5.00	6.00
a.		Type II	4.00	4.00
		Nos. O216-O223 (8)	15.65	18.10

On Nos. 707 to 709, 712, 715, 716,
717, 718 and 719

O224	A108	1c orange	2.00	4.00
O225	A109	2c green	1.25	2.00
O226	A110	4c carmine	1.25	1.40
O227	A112	10c violet	1.25	2.50
O228	A114	20c ultra	1.60	2.50
O229	A115	30c lake	2.00	4.00
O230	A116	40c red brown	2.50	4.00
O231	A117	50c black	2.75	2.75
O232	A118	1p dk brn & org	8.00	12.00
		Nos. O224-O232 (9)	22.60	35.15

POSTAL TAX STAMPS

Morelos
Monument — PT1

1925		**Engr.**	**Wmk. 156**	
		Rouletted 14½		
RA1	PT1	1c brown	.35	.25
a.		Imperf.	30.00	

1926 — Perf. 12
RA2 PT1 1c brown .75 5.00
   a. Booklet pane of 2 12.00

1925 — Unwmk. — Rouletted 14½
RA3 PT1 1c brown 75.00 19.00

It was obligatory to add a stamp of type PT1 to the regular postage on every article of domestic mail matter. The money obtained from this source formed a fund to combat a plague of locusts.

In 1931, 1c stamps of type PT1 were discontinued as Postal Tax stamps. It was subsequently used for the payment of postage on drop letters (announcement cards and unsealed circulars) to be delivered in the city of cancellation. See No. 687A.

For overprints see Nos. O177, O198, O211, O216, RA4.

No. RA1 Overprinted in Red

1929 — Wmk. 156
RA4 PT1 1c brown .35 .25
   a. Overprint reading down 75.00 75.00

There were two settings of this overprint. They may be distinguished by the two lines being spaced 4mm or 6mm apart.

The money from sales of this stamp was devoted to child welfare work.

Mother and Child — PT3

1929 — Litho. — Rouletted 13, 13½
RA5 PT3 1c violet .35 .25

PT4

1929 — Size: 18x24½mm — Unwmk.
RA6 PT4 2c deep green .40 .25
RA7 PT4 5c brown .40 .25
   a. Imperf., pair 60.00 60.00

For surcharges see Nos. RA10-RA11.

PT5

Two types of 1c:

Type I — Background lines continue through lettering of top inscription. Denomination circle hangs below second background line. Paper and gum white.

Type II — Background lines cut away behind some letters. Circle rests on second background line. Paper and gum yellowish.

1929 — Size: 19x25¼mm
RA8 PT5 1c violet, type I .35 .25
   a. Booklet pane of 4 10.00
   b. Booklet pane of 2 18.00
   c. Type II .40 .25
   d. Imperf., pair 50.00 50.00
RA9 PT5 2c deep green .65 .25
   a. Imperf., pair 12.00

The use of these stamps, in addition to the regular postage, was compulsory. The money obtained from their sale was used for child welfare work.

For surcharge see No. RA12.

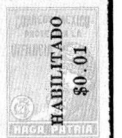

Nos. RA6, RA7, RA9 Surcharged

1930
RA10 PT4 1c on 2c dp grn .75 .40
RA11 PT4 1c on 5c brown 1.00 .60
RA12 PT5 1c on 2c dp grn 2.00 1.00
   Nos. RA10-RA12 (3) 3.75 2.00

Used stamps exist with surcharge double or reading down.

No. 423 Overprinted

1931, Jan. 30 — Wmk. 155 — Perf. 14
RA13 A36 1c dull violet .40 .40
   a. "PRO INFANCIA" double 50.00

Indian Mother and Child — PT6

Mosquito Attacking Man — PT7

Wmk. 156
1934, Sept. 1 — Engr. — Perf. 10½
RA13B PT6 1c dull orange .30 .25

1939 — Photo. — Wmk. 156 — Perf. 14
RA14 PT7 1c Prus blue 1.50 .25
   a. Imperf. 3.00 3.00

This stamp was obligatory on all mail, the money being used to aid in a drive against malaria.

See Nos. RA16, RA19 in Scott Standard catalogue, Vol. 4.

PROVISIONAL ISSUES

During the struggle led by Juarez to expel the Emperor Maximilian, installed June, 1864 by Napoleon III and French troops, a number of towns when free of Imperial forces issued provisional postage stamps. Maximilian was captured and executed June 19, 1867, but provisional issues continued current for a time pending re-establishment of Republican Government.

Campeche

A southern state in Mexico, comprising the western part of the Yucatan peninsula.

White Paper
Numerals in Black

1876 — Handstamped — Imperf.
1 A1 5c gray blue & blue 2,000.
2 A1 25c gray blue & blue 1,100.
3 A1 50c gray blue & blue 4,500.

The stamps printed in blue-black and blue on yellowish paper, formerly listed as issued in 1867, are now known to be an unofficial production of later years. They are reprints, but produced without official sanction.

Chiapas

A southern state in Mexico, bordering on Guatemala and the Pacific Ocean.

A1

1866 — Typeset
1 A1 ½r blk, gray bl 2,000. 1,300.
2 A1 1r blk, lt grn 850.
3 A1 2r blk, rose 900.
4 A1 4r blk, lt buff 2,000.
   a. Vertical half used as 2r on cover 3,000.
5 A1 8r blk, rose 15,000.
   a. Quarter used as 2r on cover 4,000.
   b. Half used as 4r on cover 5,000.

Chihuahua

A city of northern Mexico and capital of the State of Chihuahua.

A1

A2

1872 — Handstamped
1 A1 12(c) black 3,000.
   On cover
2 A2 25(c) black 3,000.

Cuautla

A town in the state of Morelos.

A1

1867 — Handstamped
1 A1 (2r) black 7,000.

All known examples on cover are uncancelled. Examples are known without the "73" inside the oval.

Cuernavaca

A city of Mexico, just south of the capital, and the capital of the State of Morelos.

A1

1867 — Handstamped
1 A1 (1r) black 1,750.
2 A1 (2r) black 40,000.

No. 1 was canceled at Cuernavaca with the district name overprint. Supplies of overprinted stamps were sent to the Tetecala and Yquala sub-offices, where they were canceled with the usual local postmarks.

No. 2 was created by doubling the impression of the basic stamp and applying the district name overprint twice.

Unused examples of Nos. 1 and 2 do not exist.

Counterfeits exist.

Guadalajara

A city of Mexico and capital of the State of Jalisco.

A1

Dated "1867"
1st Printing
Medium Wove Paper

1867 — Handstamped — Imperf.
1 A1 Medio r blk, white 350.00 250.00
2 A1 un r blk, gray bl 750.00 350.00
   a. Overprinted "Cd. Guzman" 1,000.
3 A1 un r blk, dk bl 450.00
4 A1 un r blk, white 250.00
   a. Overprinted "Cd. Guzman" 750.00
5 A1 2r blk, dk grn 250.00 21.00
   a. Overprinted "Cd. Guzman" 500.00
6 A1 2r blk, white 125.00
   a. Overprinted "Cd. Guzman" 400.00
   b. Double print 250.00
7 A1 4r blk, rose 250.00 300.00
   a. Half used as 2r on cover 500.00
   b. Overprinted "Cd. Guzman" 900.00
8 A1 4r blk, white 500.00
   a. Half used as 2r on cover 2,500.
9 A1 un p blk, lilac 250.00 300.00

Serrate Perf.
10 A1 un r blk, gray bl 400.00
11 A1 2r blk, dk grn 700.00
12 A1 4r blk, rose 350.00
12A A1 un p blk, lilac 1,750.

2nd Printing
No Period after "2" or "4"
Thin Quadrille Paper
Imperf
13 A1 2r blk, green 30.00 20.00
   a. Half used as 1r on cover 400.00

Serrate Perf.
14 A1 2r blk, green 225.00

Thin Laid Batonné Paper
Imperf
15 A1 2r blk, green 45.00 24.00

Serrate Perf.
16 A1 2r blk, green 225.00

3rd Printing
Capital "U" in "Un" on 1r, 1p
Period after "2" and "4"
Thin Wove Paper
Imperf
16A A1 Un r blk, white 125.00
17 A1 Un r blk, blue 90.00
17A A1 Un r blk, lilac 100.00
18 A1 2r blk, rose 50.00
18A A1 4r blk, blue 500.00 1,000.
18B A1 Un p blue 1,750.

Serrate Perf.
19 A1 Un r blk, blue 300.00
19A A1 2r blk, rose 750.00
19B A1 4r blue 500.00

Thin Quadrille Paper
Imperf
20 A1 2r blk, rose 42.50 42.50
21 A1 4r blk, blue 15.00 30.00
22 A1 4r blk, white 200.00
23 A1 Un p blk, lilac 15.00 60.00
24 A1 Un p blk, rose 65.00
24A A1 Un p blk, white 1,500.

Serrate Perf
24B A1 2r blk, rose 500.00
25 A1 Un p blk, lilac 750.00 750.00
25A A1 Un p blk, rose 700.00 300.00

Thin Laid Batonné Paper
Imperf
26	A1	Un r blk, *green*		22.50	17.50
27	A1	2r blk, *rose*		27.50	22.50
27A	A1	2r blk, *green*			47.50
28	A1	4r blk, *blue*		17.50	42.50
29	A1	4r blk, *lilac*		100.00	
30	A1	Un p blk, *lilac*		30.00	52.50
31	A1	Un p blk, *rose*		65.00	

Serrate Perf.
32	A1	Un r blk, *green*		65.00	
33	A1	2r blk, *rose*		400.00	200.00
34	A1	4r blk, *blue*			425.00
34A	A1	4r blk, *white*			1,750.
34B	A1	Un p blk, *lilac*			700.00

Thin Oblong Quadrille Paper
Imperf
35	A1	Un r blk, *blue*		250.00	22.50
35A	A1	Un r blk, *white*			1,500.
36	A1	4r blk, *blue*		600.00	

Serrate Perf.
37	A1	Un r blk, *blue*		300.00	

4th Printing
Dated "1868"
Wove Paper

1868   *Imperf.*
38	A1	2r blk, *lilac*		30.00	14.00
a.	Half used as 1r on cover				500.00
39	A1	2r blk, *rose*		52.50	65.00

Serrate Perf.
40	A1	2r blk, *lilac*			52.50
41	A1	2r blk, *rose*		750.00	95.00

Laid Batonné Paper
Imperf
42	A1	un r blk, *green*		12.50	12.50
43	A1	2r blk, *lilac*		12.50	12.50
a.	Half used as 1r on cover				1,500.
43A	A1	2r blk, *rose*		750.00	

Serrate Perf.
44	A1	un r blk, *green*		250.00	200.00
44A	A1	2r blk, *rose*		500.00	

Quadrille Paper.
Imperf
45	A1	2r blk, *lilac*		25.00	14.00

Serrate Perf.
46	A1	2r blk, *lilac*		300.00	300.00

Laid Paper
Imperf
47	A1	un r blk, *green*		13.00	17.00
a.	Watermarked "LA + F"		750.00		1,000.
b.	"nu" instead of "un"				750.00
c.	Dated "1863"				300.00
48	A1	2r blk, *lilac*		32.50	32.50
49	A1	2r blk, *rose*		37.50	37.50

Serrate Perf.
50	A1	un r blk, *green*		750.00	55.00
51	A1	2r blk, *rose*		475.00	

Counterfeits of Nos. 1-51 abound.

Merida

A city of southeastern Mexico, capital of the State of Yucatan.

Mexico No. 521 Surcharged **25**

1916   Wmk. 155   *Perf. 14*
1	A40	25(c) on 5c org, on cover	500.00

The G.P.DE.M. overprint reads down.

Authorities consider the Monterrey, Morelia and Patzcuaro stamps to be bogus.

Tlacotalpan

A village in the state of Veracruz.

A1

Handstamped Monogram, Value in Manuscript

1856, Oct.
1	A1	½(r) black	30,000.

REVOLUTIONARY ISSUES

SINALOA

A northern state in Mexico, bordering on the Pacific Ocean. Stamps were issued by a provisional government.

Coat of Arms — A1

1929   Unwmk.   Litho.   *Perf. 12*
1	A1	10c blk, red & bl	5.00	
a.	Tête bêche pair		35.00	
2	A1	20c blk, red & gray	5.00	

Just as Nos. 1 and 2 were ready to be placed on sale the state was occupied by the Federal forces and the stamps could not be used. At a later date a few stamps were canceled by favor.

A recent find included a number of errors or printer's waste.

YUCATAN

A southeastern state of Mexico.

Chalchihuitlicue, Nahuatl Water Goddess — A1   "Casa de Monjas" — A2

Temple of the Tigers — A3

Without Gum
1924   Unwmk.   Litho.   *Imperf.*
1	A1	5c violet	10.00	15.00
2	A2	10c carmine	40.00	50.00
3	A3	50c olive green	175.00	

Perf. 12
4	A1	5c violet	50.00	60.00
5	A2	10c carmine	50.00	75.00
6	A3	50c olive green	200.00	

Nos. 3 and 6 were not regularly issued.

MIDDLE CONGO

ˈmi-dᵊl ˈkäŋ‿ɡō

LOCATION — Western Africa at the Equator, bordering on the Atlantic Ocean

GOVT. — French Colony

AREA — 166,069

POP. — 746,805 (1936)

CAPITAL — Brazzaville

In 1910 Middle Congo, formerly a part of French Congo, was declared a separate colony. It was grouped with Gabon and the Ubangi-Shari and Chad Territories and officially designated French Equatorial Africa. This group

became a single administrative unit in 1934. See Gabon.

100 Centimes = 1 Franc

Leopard — A1

Bakalois Woman — A2   Coconut Grove — A3

Perf. 14x13½
1907-22   Typo.   Unwmk.
1	A1	1c ol gray & brn	.45	.45
	Never hinged		.60	
	On cover			87.50
a.	Perf 11		45.00	
	Never hinged		65.00	
b.	Chalky paper		.60	.45
	Never hinged		.55	
	On cover			87.50
2	A1	2c vio & brn	.45	.45
	Never hinged		.60	
	On cover			87.50
a.	Chalky paper		.40	.45
	Never hinged		.55	
	On cover			87.50
3	A1	4c blue & brn	.90	1.00
	Never hinged		1.40	
	On cover			87.50
a.	Perf 11		45.00	
	Never hinged		65.00	
b.	Chalky paper		.80	.85
	Never hinged		1.40	
	On cover			87.50
4	A1	5c dk grn & bl	1.00	.80
	Never hinged		1.40	
	On cover			35.00
a.	Perf 11		45.00	
	Never hinged		65.00	
b.	Chalky paper		.90	.70
	Never hinged		1.40	
	On cover			35.00
5	A1	5c yel & bl ('22)	1.00	.90
	Never hinged		1.60	
	On cover			25.00
6	A1	10c car & bl	1.25	.80
	Never hinged		1.75	
	On cover			20.00
a.	Perf 11		45.00	
	Never hinged		65.00	
b.	Chalky paper		.90	.70
	Never hinged		1.40	
	On cover			20.00
7	A1	10c dp grn & bl grn ('22)	4.50	4.00
	Never hinged		5.50	
	On cover			50.00
8	A1	15c brn vio & rose ('17)	2.75	1.25
	Never hinged		4.00	
	On cover			20.00
9	A1	20c brown & bl	3.50	3.25
	Never hinged		5.25	
	On cover			35.00
a.	Chalky paper		3.25	3.25
	Never hinged		5.25	
	On cover			35.00
10	A2	25c blue & grn	1.75	1.25
	Never hinged		2.75	
	On cover			40.00
	On cover, single franking			105.00
a.	Chalky paper		1.60	1.00
	Never hinged		2.75	
	On cover			40.00
11	A2	25c bl grn & gray ('22)	1.25	1.10
	Never hinged		1.90	
	On cover			14.00
12	A2	30c scar & grn	2.60	2.00
	Never hinged		4.00	
	On cover			45.00
	On cover, single franking			87.50
a.	Chalky paper		2.40	1.75
	Never hinged		4.00	
	On cover			45.00
13	A2	30c dp rose & rose ('22)	2.25	2.40
	Never hinged		3.25	
	On cover			45.00
	On cover, single franking			80.00
14	A2	35c vio brn & bl	2.25	1.60
	Never hinged		3.25	
	On cover			50.00
	On cover, single franking			75.00
15	A2	40c dl grn & brn	2.25	2.00
	Never hinged		3.25	
	On cover			45.00
	On cover, single franking			105.00
a.	Chalky paper		2.25	2.00
	Never hinged		3.25	
16	A2	45c violet & red	6.50	4.25
	Never hinged		9.50	
	On cover			62.50
	On cover, single franking			87.50
a.	Chalky paper		6.50	4.25
	Never hinged		9.50	
	On cover			62.50
17	A2	50c bl grn & red	2.75	2.40
	Never hinged		4.00	
	On cover, single franking			70.00
	On cover			140.00
a.	Perf 11		45.00	
	Never hinged		65.00	
b.	Chalky paper		3.25	2.40
	Never hinged		5.50	
	On cover			75.00
18	A2	50c bl & grn ('22)	2.75	2.40
	Never hinged		5.50	
	On cover			37.50
	On cover, single franking			75.00
19	A2	75c brown & bl	11.00	5.75
	Never hinged		16.50	
	On cover			62.50
	On cover, single franking			140.00
a.	Chalky paper		10.00	13.00
	Never hinged		16.50	
	On cover			62.50
20	A3	1fr dp grn & vio	16.50	10.50
	Never hinged		27.50	
	On cover			75.00
	On cover, single franking			175.00
a.	Chalky paper		15.00	13.00
	Never hinged		27.50	
	On cover			75.00
21	A3	2fr vio & gray grn	17.50	12.50
	Never hinged		30.00	
	On cover			87.50
	On cover, single franking			190.00
a.	Chalky paper		16.00	15.00
	Never hinged		30.00	
	On cover			87.50
22	A3	5fr blue & rose	55.00	35.00
	Never hinged		90.00	
	On cover			140.00
	On cover, single franking			250.00
a.	Perf 11		72.50	
	Never hinged		120.00	
b.	Chalky paper		50.00	40.00
	Never hinged		90.00	
	On cover			140.00
	Nos. 1-22 (22)		140.15	96.05

For stamps of types A1-A3 in changed colors, see Chad and Ubangi-Shari. French Congo A4-A6 are similar but inscribed "Congo Francais."

For overprints and surcharges see Nos. 23-60, B1-B2.

Stamps and Types of 1907-22 Overprinted in Black, Blue or Red

1924-30
23	A1	1c ol gray & brn	.35	.50
	Never hinged		.50	
	On cover			62.50
a.	Double surcharge		150.00	
	Never hinged		200.00	
24	A1	2c violet & brn	.35	.50
	Never hinged		.50	
	On cover			62.50
a.	Chalky paper		.30	.40
	Never hinged		.45	
	On cover			62.50
25	A1	4c blue & brn	.35	.50
	Never hinged		.50	
	On cover			62.50
a.	Chalky paper		.30	.40
	Never hinged		.50	
	On cover			62.50
26	A1	5c yellow & bl	.55	.50
	Never hinged		.80	
	On cover			27.50
27	A1	10c grn & bl grn (R)	1.10	.40
	Never hinged		2.00	
	On cover			20.00
28	A1	10c car & gray ('25)	.45	.55
	Never hinged		.80	
	On cover			25.00
29	A1	15c brn vio & rose (Bl)	.90	.50
	Never hinged		1.20	
	On cover			16.00
a.	Double surcharge		130.00	
	Never hinged		200.00	
30	A1	20c brown & blue	.80	.70
	Never hinged		1.00	
	On cover			27.50
a.	Chalky paper		.80	
	Never hinged		1.00	
	On cover			27.50
31	A1	20c bl grn & yel grn ('26)	.45	.45
	Never hinged		.75	
	On cover			19.00
32	A1	20c dp brn & rose lil ('27)	1.75	1.20
	Never hinged		3.00	
	On cover			37.50

Nos. 10-22
Overprinted in Black,
Red (R), and Blue
(Bl)

33	A2	25c bl grn & gray	1.10	.50
		Never hinged	1.75	
		On cover		14.00
34	A2	30c rose & pale rose (Bl)	1.75	.80
		Never hinged	2.75	
		On cover		45.00
		On cover, single franking		75.00
35	A2	30c gray & bl vio (R) ('25)	.90	.70
		Never hinged	1.20	
		On cover		12.50
36	A2	30c dk grn & grn ('27)	2.25	1.60
		Never hinged	3.25	
		On cover		37.50
37	A2	35c choc & bl	.80	.80
		Never hinged	1.10	
		On cover		45.00
		On cover, single franking		75.00
38	A2	40c ol grn & brn	1.75	1.60
		Never hinged	3.25	
		On cover		50.00
		On cover, single franking		80.00
a.		Double overprint	275.00	
		Never hinged	450.00	
39	A2	45c vio & pale red (Bl)	1.75	1.20
		Never hinged	3.00	
		On cover		16.00
		On cover, single franking		27.50
a.		Inverted overprint	160.00	
		Never hinged	250.00	
40	A2	50c blue & grn (R)	1.75	1.20
		Never hinged	3.25	
		On cover		15.00
		On cover, single franking		22.50
41	A2	50c org & blk ('25)	.90	.70
		Never hinged	1.20	
		On cover		12.50
a.		Without overprint	250.00	275.00
		Never hinged	325.00	
42	A2	65c org brn & bl ('27)	3.00	2.40
		Never hinged	4.75	
		On cover		30.00
		On cover, single franking		62.50
43	A2	75c brown & blue	1.40	1.25
		Never hinged	2.00	
		On cover		35.00
		On cover, single franking		75.00
44	A2	90c brn red & pink ('30)	5.50	4.00
		Never hinged	8.00	
		On cover		55.00
		On cover, single franking		100.00
45	A3	1fr green & vio	2.25	1.60
		Never hinged	3.50	
		On cover		35.00
		On cover, single franking		70.00
a.		Double overprint	250.00	
		Never hinged	400.00	
46	A3	1.10fr vio & brn ('28)	5.50	4.75
		Never hinged	8.00	
		On cover		160.00
		On cover, single franking		340.00
47	A3	1.50fr ultra & bl ('30)	8.75	5.50
		Never hinged	12.50	
		On cover		50.00
		On cover, single franking		87.50
48	A3	2fr vio & gray grn	2.25	1.60
		Never hinged	3.00	
		On cover		62.50
		On cover, single franking		125.00
a.		Chalky paper	2.00	1.60
		Never hinged	3.00	
		On cover		62.50
49	A3	3fr red violet ('30)	10.00	7.25
		Never hinged	15.00	
		On cover		87.50
		On cover, single franking		170.00
50	A3	5fr blue & rose	7.25	5.25
		Never hinged	13.00	
		On cover		75.00
		On cover, single franking		140.00
a.		Chalky paper	6.50	6.50
		Never hinged	12.00	
		On cover		75.00
		Nos. 23-50 (28)	65.90	48.50

Nos. 48 and 50 Surcharged with New
Values

1924

51	A3	25c on 2fr vio & gray grn	1.20	1.20
		Never hinged	2.00	
		On cover		16.00
52	A3	25c on 5fr bl & rose (Bl)	1.20	1.20
		Never hinged	2.00	
		On cover		16.00
a.		Chalky paper	1.20	1.20
		Never hinged	2.00	
		On cover		16.00

**Types of 1924-27 Surcharged with
New Values in Black or Red**

1925-27

53	A3	65c on 1fr red org & ol brn	1.20	1.20
		Never hinged	2.00	
		On cover		75.00
		On cover, single franking		170.00
a.		Without surcharge	250.00	
		Never hinged	375.00	

54	A3	85c on 1fr red org & ol brn	1.20	1.20
		Never hinged	2.00	
		On cover		62.50
		On cover, single franking		125.00
a.		Double surcharge	175.00	
		Never hinged	240.00	
55	A2	90c on 75c brn red & rose red ('27)	2.00	2.40
		Never hinged	4.00	
		On cover		62.50
		On cover, single franking		110.00
56	A3	1.25fr on 1fr dl bl & ultra (R)	1.20	1.20
		Never hinged	2.00	
		On cover		70.00
		On cover, single franking		140.00
a.		Without surcharge	180.00	200.00
		Never hinged	300.00	
57	A3	1.50fr on 1fr ultra & bl ('27)	2.00	2.00
		Never hinged	3.75	
		On cover		55.00
		On cover, single franking		100.00
a.		Without surcharge	200.00	225.00
		Never hinged	300.00	
58	A3	3fr on 5fr org brn & dl red ('27)	4.50	4.00
		Never hinged	7.25	
		On cover		105.00
		On cover, single franking		225.00
a.		Without surcharge	325.00	
		Never hinged	450.00	
b.		Period after "F" omitted	24.00	24.00
		Never hinged	40.00	
59	A3	10fr on 5fr ver & bl grn ('27)	13.00	13.00
		Never hinged	22.50	
		On cover		125.00
		On cover, single franking		225.00
60	A3	20fr on 5fr org brn & vio ('27)	13.50	13.50
		Never hinged	24.00	
		On cover		140.00
		On cover, single franking		275.00
a.		Period after "F" omitted	40.00	40.00
		Never hinged	65.00	
		Nos. 53-60 (8)	38.60	38.50

Bars cover old values on Nos. 56-60.

Common Design Types
pictured following the introduction.

Colonial Exposition Issue
Common Design Types

1931		Engr.	Perf. 12½
Name of Country in Black			
61	CD70	40c deep green	5.00	5.00
		Never hinged	8.00	
		On cover		105.00
62	CD71	50c violet	4.00	4.00
		Never hinged	7.25	
		On cover		87.50
63	CD72	90c red orange	4.00	4.00
		Never hinged	7.25	
		On cover		150.00
		On cover, single franking		225.00
64	CD73	1.50fr dull blue	5.50	5.50
		Never hinged	9.00	
		On cover		140.00
		On cover, single franking		210.00
		Nos. 61-64 (4)	18.50	18.50

Viaduct at
Mindouli
A4

Pasteur
Institute at
Brazzaville
A5

Government Building, Brazzaville — A6

1933		Photo.	Perf. 13½
65	A4	1c lt brown	.30	.25
		Never hinged	.45	
		On cover		27.50
66	A4	2c dull blue	.30	.25
		Never hinged	.45	
		On cover		27.50
67	A4	4c olive grn	.35	.30
		Never hinged		
		On cover		25.00
68	A4	5c red violet	.60	.40
		Never hinged	.85	
		On cover		14.00
69	A4	10c slate	.90	.50
		Never hinged	1.30	
		On cover		16.00

70	A4	15c dk violet	1.75	1.20
		Never hinged	2.50	
		On cover		22.50
71	A4	20c red, pink	9.25	7.25
		Never hinged	13.00	
		On cover		45.00
72	A4	25c orange	1.40	1.10
		Never hinged	1.75	
		On cover		27.50
73	A4	30c yellow grn	3.00	2.00
		Never hinged	4.50	
		On cover		37.50
74	A5	40c orange brn	3.00	2.00
		Never hinged	4.50	
		On cover		11.00
75	A5	45c blk, green	3.00	2.00
		Never hinged	4.50	
		On cover		55.00
76	A5	50c black violet	1.10	.80
		Never hinged	1.75	
		On cover		7.50
77	A5	65c brn red, grn	3.00	2.00
		Never hinged	4.50	
		On cover		87.50
78	A5	75c black, pink	16.50	11.00
		Never hinged	27.50	
		On cover		50.00
79	A5	90c carmine	3.00	2.00
		Never hinged	3.75	
		On cover		45.00
		On cover, single franking		125.00
80	A5	1fr dark red	1.30	.80
		Never hinged	1.90	
		On cover		35.00
		On cover, single franking		50.00
81	A5	1.25fr Prus blue	2.75	1.60
		Never hinged	4.50	
		On cover		35.00
		On cover, single franking		95.00
82	A5	1.50fr dk blue	14.50	6.50
		Never hinged	26.00	
		On cover		75.00
		On cover, single franking		190.00
83	A6	1.75fr dk violet	3.50	1.60
		Never hinged	6.00	
		On cover		35.00
		On cover, single franking		50.00
84	A6	2fr grnsh blk	2.75	1.60
		Never hinged	3.75	
		On cover		35.00
		On cover, single franking		62.50
85	A6	3fr orange	6.50	4.75
		Never hinged	9.75	
		On cover		55.00
		On cover, single franking		110.00
86	A6	5fr slate blue	35.00	25.00
		Never hinged	65.00	
		On cover		140.00
		On cover, single franking		240.00
87	A6	10fr black	60.00	36.00
		Never hinged	120.00	
		On cover		170.00
		On cover, single franking		275.00
88	A6	20fr dark brown	40.00	32.50
		Never hinged	70.00	
		On cover		170.00
		On cover, single franking		300.00
		Nos. 65-88 (24)	213.75	143.40

SEMI-POSTAL STAMPS

No. 6
Surcharged
in Black

1916		Unwmk.	Perf. 14x13½
B1	A1	10c + 5c car & blue	1.60	1.60
		Never hinged	2.75	
		On cover		70.00
a.		Double surcharge	160.00	160.00
		Never hinged	240.00	
b.		Inverted surcharge	140.00	140.00
		Never hinged	210.00	
c.		"c" omitted	52.50	52.50
		Never hinged	90.00	
d.		Period below "c" omitted	47.50	47.50
		Never hinged	80.00	
e.		As "a," One inverted	200.00	200.00
		Never hinged	325.00	
f.		In pair with unsurcharged stamp	425.00	
		Never hinged	640.00	

A printing with the surcharge placed lower
and more to the left was made and used in
Ubangi.

No. 6
Surcharged
in Red

B2	A1	10c + 5c car & blue	1.60	1.60
		Never hinged	2.50	
		On cover		70.00

POSTAGE DUE STAMPS

Postage Due Stamps of
France Overprinted

1928		Unwmk.	Perf. 14x13½
J1	D2	5c light blue	.50	.80
		Never hinged	1.00	
		On cover		95.00
J2	D2	10c gray brn	.70	.80
		Never hinged	1.50	
		On cover		95.00
J3	D2	20c olive grn	1.20	1.60
		Never hinged	2.00	
		On cover		95.00
J4	D2	25c brt rose	1.60	2.00
		Never hinged	2.75	
		On cover		100.00
J5	D2	30c lt red	1.60	2.00
		Never hinged	2.75	
		On cover		100.00
J6	D2	45c blue grn	1.60	2.00
		Never hinged	2.75	
		On cover		105.00
J7	D2	50c brown vio	1.60	2.00
		Never hinged	2.75	
		On cover		110.00
a.		Period after "F" omitted	16.00	20.00
		Never hinged	27.50	
J8	D2	60c yellow brn	2.00	2.00
		Never hinged	4.75	
		On cover		120.00
J9	D2	1fr red brn	2.75	3.25
		Never hinged	4.75	
		On cover		125.00
J10	D2	2fr orange red	4.00	4.75
		Never hinged	6.50	
		On cover		140.00
J11	D2	3fr brt violet	5.50	8.00
		Never hinged	10.00	
		On cover		160.00
		Nos. J1-J11 (11)	23.05	29.20

Village on
Ubangi,
Dance
Mask — D3

Steamer
on Ubangi
River — D4

1930			Typo.
J12	D3	5c dp bl & ol	.80	1.20
		Never hinged	1.20	
		On cover		37.50
J13	D3	10c dp red & brn	1.20	1.60
		Never hinged	2.00	
		On cover		37.50
J14	D3	20c green & brn	2.25	3.25
		Never hinged	4.50	
		On cover		37.50
J15	D3	25c lt bl & brn	3.50	4.00
		Never hinged	6.00	
		On cover		45.00
J16	D3	30c bis brn & Prus bl	5.25	5.50
		Never hinged	8.00	
		On cover		45.00
J17	D3	45c Prus bl & ol	6.00	6.50
		Never hinged	9.50	
		On cover		50.00
J18	D3	50c red vio & brn	6.00	6.75
		Never hinged	9.50	
		On cover		50.00
J19	D3	60c gray lil & bl blk	8.00	8.75
		Never hinged	13.50	
		On cover		55.00
J20	D4	1fr bis brn & bl blk	12.00	13.50
		Never hinged	19.00	
		On cover		70.00
J21	D4	2fr violet & brn	13.00	15.00
		Never hinged	20.00	
		On cover		80.00
J22	D4	3fr dk red & brn	13.50	17.50
		Never hinged	21.00	
		On cover		95.00
		Nos. J12-J22 (11)	71.50	83.55

Rubber
Trees and
Djoué
River — D5

1933		Photo.	Perf. 13½
J23	D5	5c apple green	.80	.80
		Never hinged	1.20	
		On cover		37.50
J24	D5	10c dk bl, bl	.80	.80
		Never hinged	1.20	
		On cover		37.50

J25	D5 20c red, *yel*	1.60	1.60
	Never hinged	2.40	
	On cover		37.50
J26	D5 25c chocolate	1.60	1.60
	Never hinged	2.40	
	On cover		37.50
J27	D5 30c orange red	2.00	2.40
	Never hinged	2.75	
	On cover		40.00
J28	D5 45c dk violet	2.00	2.40
	Never hinged	2.75	
	On cover		45.00
J29	D5 50c gray black	2.75	3.25
	Never hinged	4.00	
	On cover		50.00
J30	D5 60c blk, *orange*	4.50	4.75
	Never hinged	7.25	
	On cover		50.00
J31	D5 1fr brown rose	6.50	7.25
	Never hinged	9.50	
	On cover		62.50
J32	D5 2fr orange yel	8.00	9.50
	Never hinged	11.00	
	On cover		70.00
J33	D5 3fr Prus blue	13.50	17.50
	Never hinged	19.00	
	On cover		87.50
	Nos. J23-J33 (11)	44.05	51.85

MOHELI

mo-'ā-lē

LOCATION — One of the Comoro Islands, situated in the Mozambique Channel midway between Madagascar and Mozambique (Africa)
GOVT. — French Colony
AREA — 89 sq. mi.
POP. — 4,000
CAPITAL — Fomboni
See Comoro Islands

100 Centimes = 1 Franc

Navigation and
Commerce — A1

Perf. 14x13½

	1906-07	**Typo.**	**Unwmk.**
	Name of Colony in Blue or Carmine		
1	A1 1c blk, *lil bl*	3.75	2.40
	Never hinged	5.50	
	On cover		250.00
2	A1 2c brn, *buff*	2.00	1.75
	Never hinged	2.40	
	On cover		250.00
3	A1 4c claret, *lav*	3.25	2.40
	Never hinged	5.25	
	On cover		250.00
4	A1 5c yellow grn	4.25	2.40
	Never hinged	7.50	
	On cover		225.00
5	A1 10c carmine	5.50	2.40
	Never hinged	9.50	
	On cover		250.00
6	A1 20c red, *green*	13.00	7.25
	Never hinged	24.00	
	On cover		250.00
	On cover, single franking		440.00
7	A1 25c blue	13.00	5.50
	Never hinged	24.00	
	On cover		125.00
	On cover, single franking		225.00
8	A1 30c brn, *bister*	17.50	14.50
	Never hinged	32.50	
	On cover		160.00
	On cover, single franking		225.00
9	A1 35c blk, *yellow*	10.50	4.00
	Never hinged	21.00	
	On cover		225.00
	On cover, single franking		300.00
10	A1 40c red, *straw*	17.50	13.50
	Never hinged	32.50	
	On cover		250.00
	On cover, single franking		400.00
11	A1 45c blk, *gray grn* ('07)	75.00	60.00
	Never hinged	150.00	
	On cover		500.00
	On cover, single franking		690.00
12	A1 50c brn, *az*	24.00	14.50
	Never hinged	47.50	
	On cover		300.00
	On cover, single franking		440.00
13	A1 75c dp vio, *org*	26.00	24.00
	Never hinged	52.50	
	On cover		375.00
	On cover, single franking		525.00
14	A1 1fr brnz grn, *straw*	24.00	17.50
	Never hinged	47.50	
	On cover		340.00
	On cover, single franking		525.00
15	A1 2fr vio, *rose*	35.00	35.00
	Never hinged	67.50	
	On cover		440.00
	On cover, single franking		625.00
16	A1 5fr lil, *lavender*	130.00	130.00
	Never hinged	275.00	
	On cover		800.00
	On cover, single franking		1,100.
	Nos. 1-16 (16)	404.25	337.10

Perf. 13½x14 stamps are counterfeits.

No. 12, affixed to pressboard with animals printed on the back, was used as emergency currency in the Comoro Islands in 1920.

Issue of 1906-07 Surcharged in Carmine or Black

1912

Spacing between figures of surcharge 1.5mm (5c), 2mm (10c)

17	A1 5c on 4c cl, *lav* (C)	2.40	3.25
	Never hinged	4.00	
	On cover		190.00
18	A1 5c on 20c red, *grn*	4.00	4.75
	Never hinged	7.25	
	On cover		200.00
19	A1 5c on 30c brn, *bis* (C)	2.75	3.50
	Never hinged	4.00	
	On cover		200.00
20	A1 10c on 40c red, *straw*	2.75	3.50
	Never hinged	4.00	
	On cover		200.00
21	A1 10c on 45c blk, *gray grn* (C)	2.00	2.00
	Never hinged	3.25	
	On cover		80.00
a.	"Moheli" double	475.00	
b.	"Moheli" triple	475.00	
d.	As "a," in pair with normal stamp	850.00	
e.	As "b," in pair with normal stamp	850.00	
22	A1 10c on 50c brn, *az* (C)	3.50	4.50
	Never hinged	5.50	
	On cover		200.00
	Nos. 17-22 (6)	17.40	21.50

Spacing between figures of surcharge 2.25mm (5c), 2.75mm (10c)

17a	A1 5c on 4c cl, *lav* (C)	20.00	20.00
	Never hinged	32.50	
18a	A1 5c on 20c red, *grn*	55.00	55.00
	Never hinged	100.00	
19a	A1 5c on 30c brn, *bis* (C)	55.00	55.00
	Never hinged	100.00	
20a	A1 10c on 40c red, *straw*	175.00	175.00
	Never hinged	260.00	
21c	A1 10c on 45c blk, *gray grn* (C)	75.00	75.00
	Never hinged	140.00	
22a	A1 10c on 50c brn, *az*	150.00	150.00
	Never hinged	240.00	
	Nos. 17a-22a (6)	530.00	530.00

Se-tenant Pairs, Both Ovpt. Settings

17b	A1 5c on 4c, #17 + #17a	24.00	24.00
	Never hinged	40.00	
18b	A1 5c on 20c, #18 + #18a	65.00	65.00
	Never hinged	120.00	
19b	A1 5c on 30c, #19 + #19a	65.00	65.00
	Never hinged	120.00	
20b	A1 10c on 40c, #20 + #20a	190.00	190.00
	Never hinged	300.00	
21f	A1 10c on 45c, #21 + #21a	87.50	57.50
	Never hinged	120.00	
22b	A1 10c on 50c, #22 + #22a	180.00	180.00
	Never hinged	275.00	

The stamps of Moheli were supposed to have been superseded by those of Madagascar, January, 1908. However, Nos. 17-22 were surcharged in 1912 to use up remainders. These were available for use in Madagascar and the entire Comoro archipelago. In 1950 stamps of Comoro Islands came into use.

MONACO

'mä-nə-ˌkō

LOCATION — Southern coast of France, bordering on the Mediterranean Sea
GOVT. — Principality
AREA — 481 acres
POP. — 27,063 (1982)
CAPITAL — Monaco

100 Centimes = 1 Franc

STAMPS OF SARDINIA

CANCELED WITH SARDINIAN "MENTONE" C.D.S.

1851

A1	20c blue (#2) on cover, stamp pen cancelled		7,500.

No. A1 is unique.

1853

A2	20c blue (#5)		—

1854

A3	20c blue (#8)		—

1855-60

A4	5c yellow green (#10a)	925.00	
	On cover		—
A5	10c bister (#11)	450.00	
A6	20c light blue (#12b)	450.00	
	On cover		8,100.
A7	40c red (#13)	600.00	
A8	80c orange yellow (#14)	2,750.	

With French Small Figures "4220" for Menton

A9	10c bister (#11)	1,500.	
A10	80c orange yellow (#14)	5,100.	

STAMPS OF SARDINIA CANCELED WITH SARDINIAN "MONACO" C.D.S.

1853

A12	20c blue (#5) on cover		9,000.

One cover and four singles of No. A12 are known.

1854

A13	20c blue (#8) on cover		—

One example of No. A13 is known.

1855-60

A14	5c yellow green (#10a)	1,900.	
	On cover		21,500.
A15	10c bister (#11)	900.00	
	On cover		16,250.
A16	20c light blue (#12b)	750.00	
	On cover, from		10,800.
A17	40c red (#13)	1,200.	
	On cover, from		16,250.
A18	80c orange yellow (#14)	5,400.	
	On cover		21,500.

With French Small Figures "4222" for Monaco

A19	10c bister (#11)	2,200.	
A20	10c blue (#12a)	1,800.	
A21	40c red (#13)	2,900.	
A22	80c orange yellow (#14)	4,000.	

STAMPS OF FRANCE CANCELED WITH SARDINIAN "MENTONE" C.D.S.

A23	10c bister (#14)	875.00	
	On cover, from		4,800.
A24	20c blue(#15)	425.00	
	On cover, from		3,000.
A25	40c orange (#18)	1,450.	
	On cover, from		10,000.
A26	80c carmine(#19)	1,450.	
	On cover, from		10,000.

STAMPS OF FRANCE CANCELED WITH SARDINIAN "MONACO" C.D.S.

A27	10c bister (#14)	1,325.	
	On cover, from		11,000.
A28	20c blue(#15)	725.00	
	On cover, from		11,000.
A29	40c orange (#18)	1,600.	
A30	80c carmine(#19)	2,900.	

STAMPS OF FRANCE CANCELED WITH VARIOUS FRENCH POSTMARKS OF MONACO
"4222" SMALL FIGURES

1853-60		***Empire, Imperf***	
A31	1c olive green (#12)	1,600.	
A32	5c green (#13)	1,325.	
A33	10c bister (#14)	550.	
	On cover, from		5,750.
A34	20c blue (#15)	375.	
	On cover, from		3,300.
A35	40c orange (#18)	1,100.	
	On cover, from		13,800.
A36	80c carmine(#19)	1,750.	
A37	20c blue (#26)	16,500.	

"2387" LARGE FIGURES

1853-60		***Empire, Imperf***	
A38	1c olive green (#12)		—
A39	5c green (#13)	1,000.	
A40	10c bister (#14)	550.00	
A41	20c blue (#15)	450.00	
A42	40c orange (#18)	1,000.	
A43	80c carmine(#19)		—

1862-71		***Empire, Perforated***	
A44	1c olive green (#22)	725.00	
A45	5c yellow green (#23)	300.00	
	On cover, from		2,600.
A46	10c bister (#25)	60.00	
	On cover, from		725.00
A47	20c blue (#26)	110.00	
	On cover, from		300.00
A48	40c orange (#27)	210.00	
	On cover, from		3,600.
A49	80c rose (#28)	850.00	
	On cover, from		10,800.

1863-70		***Empire, "Laureated"***	
A50	1c bronze green, *pale blue* (#29)	210.00	
	On cover, from		3,000.
A51	2c red brown, *yellowish* (#30)	290.00	
A52	4c gray (#31)	325.00	
	On cover, from		3,300.
A53	10c bister, *yellowish* (#32)	110.00	
	On cover, from		725.00
A54	20c blue, *bluish* (#33)	70.00	
	On cover, from		290.00
A55	30c brown, *yelsh* (#34)	160.00	
	On cover, from		1,450.
A56	40c orange, *yelsh* (#35)	140.00	
	On cover, from		1,200.
A57	80c rose, *pinkish* (#36)	210.00	
	On cover, from		1,900.
A58	5fr gray lilac, *lav* (#37)	1,900.	

1870-71		***Bordeaux Issue***	
A59	1c olive green, *pale blue* (#38)	450.00	
A60	2c red brown, *yellowish* (B) (#39)	1,000.	
A61	4c gray (#40)	1,000.	
A62	5c green, *greenish* (#41)	400.00	
	On cover, from		400.00
A63	10c bister, *yellowish* (A) (#42)	290.00	
	On cover, from		2,150.
A64	20c blue, *bluish* (#43)	8,400.	
A65	20c blue, *bluish* (#44)	290.00	
	On cover, from		2,200.
A66	20c blue, *bluish* (#45)	290.00	
	On cover, from		2,150.
A67	30c brown, *yelsh* (#46)	550.00	
A68	40c orange, *yellow* (#47)	450.00	
A69	80c rose, *pinkish* (#48)	600.00	

1870-73		***Ceres***	
A70	1c olive green, *pale blue* (#50)	210.00	
A71	2c red brown, *yellowish* (#51)	300.00	
A72	4c gray (#52)	240.00	
A73	5c yellow green, *pale blue* (#53)	140.00	
	On cover, from		1,600.
A74	10c bister, *yellowish* (#54)	700.00	
A75	10c bister, *rose* ('73) (#55)	150.00	
	On cover, from		1,400.
A76	15c bister, *yellowish* ('71) (#56)	110.00	
	On cover, from		1,100.
A77	20c dull blue, *bluish* (#57)	200.00	
	On cover, from		1,950.
A78	40c orange, *yelsh* (I) (#59)	110.00	
	On cover, from		1,100.

1872-75		***Ceres, Larger Figures of Value***	
A79	10c bister, *rose* ('75) (#60)	150.00	
	On cover, from		1,500.
A80	15c bister ('73) (#61)	140.00	
	On cover, from		1,600.
A81	30c brown, *yellowish* (#62)	150.00	
	On cover, from		1,900.
A82	80c rose, *pinkish* (#63)	210.00	
	On cover, from		1,900.

"2387" SMALL FIGURES

1862-71		***Empire, Imperf***	
A83	10c bister (#25)	725.00	
	On cover, from		16,500.
A84	20c blue (#26)	450.00	
	On cover, from		7,200.
A85	40c orange (#27)	450.00	
	On cover, from		7,200.

1863-70		***Empire, "Laureated"***	
A86	20c blue, *bluish* (#33)	600.00	
	On cover, from		8,400.
A87	30c brown, *yelsh* (#34)	450.00	
	On cover, from		6,600.
A88	40c orange, *yelsh* (#35)	240.00	
	On cover, from		4,900.
A89	80c rose, *pinkish* (#36)	290.00	
A90	5fr gray lilac, *lav* (#37)	2,100.	

1870-71		***Bordeaux Issue***	
A91	5c green, *greenish* (#41)	925.00	
A92	10c bister, *yellowish* (A) (#42)	325.00	
	On cover, from		7,200.
A93	20c blue, *bluish* (#43)	1,100.	
A94	20c blue, *bluish* ('71) (#45)	1,100.	
A95	30c brown, *yelsh* (#46)	1,100.	
	On cover, from		7,200.
A96	40c orange, *yelsh* (#47)	500.00	
	On cover, from		6,300.
A97	80c rose, *pinkish* (#48)	600.00	
	On cover		1,600.

Ceres, Larger Figures of Value

1872-75

A98	30c brown, *yellowish* (#62)	
A99	80c rose, *pinkish* (#63)	400.00

"MONACO / (87)" DOUBLE CIRCLE DATESTAMP, DATE IN 3 LINES, WITHOUT TIME INDICIA

1853-60   *Empire, Imperf*

A100	1c olive green (#12)	210.00
A101	5c yellow green (#13)	325.00
A102	10c bister (#14)	275.00
A103	20c blue (#15)	275.00
A104	40c orange (#18)	

1862-71   *Empire, Perforated*

A105	1c olive green (#22)	200.00
A106	5c yellow green (#23)	200.00
	On cover	425.00
A107	5c green, *pale blue* ('71) (I) (#24)	—
A108	10c bister (#25)	160.00
A109	20c blue (#26)	290.00
	On cover, from	2,900.
A110	40c orange (#27)	200.00
	On cover, from	2,900.
A111	80c rose (#28)	650.00

1863-70   *Empire, "Laureated"*

A112	1c bronze green, *pale blue* (#29)	—
A113	2c red brown, *yellowish* (#30)	87.50
	On cover, from	1,600.
A114	4c gray (#31)	87.50
	On cover, from	1,400.
A115	10c bister, *yellowish* (#32)	140.00
A116	20c blue, *bluish* (#33)	290.00
	On cover, from	2,200.
A117	30c brown, *yelsh* (#34)	—
A118	40c orange, *yelsh* (#35)	—
A119	80c rose, *pinkish* (#36)	—
A120	5fr gray lilac, *lav* (#37)	1,900.

"MONACO / (87)" SINGLE CIRCLE DATESTAMP, DATE IN 3 LINES, WITH TIME INDICIA

1862-71   *Empire, Perforated*

A121	10c bister (#25)	400.00

1863-70   *Empire, "Laureated"*

A122	1c brnz grn, *pale blue* (#29)	160.00
A123	2c red brn, *yelsh* (#30)	130.00
A124	4c gray (#31)	130.00
A125	10c bister, *yellowish* (#32)	400.00
A126	20c blue, *bluish* (#33)	325.00

1870-71   *Bordeaux Issue*

A127	5c green, *greenish* (#41)	500.00

1870-73   *Ceres*

A128	1c ol grn, *pale blue* (#50)	290.00
A129	2c red brn, *yelsh* (#51)	290.00
A130	4c gray (#52)	290.00
A131	5c yel grn, *pale blue* (#53)	290.00

"MONACO / (87)" DOUBLE CIRCLE DATESTAMP, DATE IN 3 LINES, WITH TIME INDICIA

1862-71   *Empire, Perforated*

A132	1c olive green (#22)	200.00
A133	5c yellow green (#23)	200.00
	On cover, from	450.00
A134	5c green, *pale blue* ('71) (I) (#24)	210.00
A135	10c bister (#25)	200.00
A136	20c blue (#26)	300.00
A137	40c orange (#27)	—
A138	80c rose (#28)	—

1863-70   *Empire, "Laureated"*

A139	1c brnz grn, *pale blue* (#29)	125.00
A140	2c red brn, *yelsh* (#30)	85.00
	On cover, from	1,000.
A141	4c gray (#31)	110.00
	On cover, from	1,100.
A142	10c bister, *yellowish* (#32)	125.00
	On cover, from	3,000.
A143	20c blue, *bluish* (#33)	240.00
A144	30c brown, *yelsh* (#34)	325.00
A145	40c orange, *yelsh* (#35)	240.00
A146	80c rose, *pinkish* (#36)	325.00
A147	5fr gray lilac, *lav* (#37)	1,900.

1870-71   *Bordeaux Issue*

A148	1c ol grn, *pale blue* (#38)	325.00
	On cover	3,250.
A149	2c red brn, *yelsh* (B) (#39)	450.00
A150	4c gray (#40)	725.00
	On cover, from	4,900.
A151	5c green, *greenish* (#41)	400.00
A152	10c bister, *yelsh* (A) (#42)	210.00
	On cover	—
A153	20c blue, *bluish* (#44)	210.00
	On cover, from	4,400.

A154	20c blue, *bluish* (#45)	210.00
	On cover, from	3,800.
A155	30c brown, *yelsh* (#46)	725.00
A156	40c orange, *yelsh* (#47)	325.00
A157	80c rose, *pinkish* (#48)	500.00

1870-73   *Ceres*

A158	1c ol grn, *pale blue* (#50)	110.00
A159	2c red brn, *yelsh* (#51)	110.00
	On cover, from	1,600.
A160	4c gray (#52)	110.00
A161	5c yel grn, *pale blue* (#53)	72.50
	On cover	1,200.
A162	10c bister, *rose* ('73) (#55)	140.00
	On cover	1,200.
A163	15c bister, *yelsh* ('71) (#56)	92.50
	On cover	1,400.
A164	20c dull blue, *bluish* (#57)	160.00
A165	25c blue, *bluish* ('71) (#58)	92.50
	On cover, from	725.00
A166	40c orange, *yelsh* (I) (#59)	190.00
	On cover	2,100.

Ceres, Larger Figures of Value

1872-75

A167	10c bister, *rose* ('75) (#60)	140.00
	On cover, from	1,200.
A168	15c bister ('73) (#61)	92.50
	On cover, from	1,400.
A169	30c brown, *yellowish* (#62)	140.00
	On cover	1,800.
A170	80c rose, *pinkish* (#63)	290.00
	On cover	—

"MONACO / PRINCIPAUTE" DOUBLE CIRCLE DATESTAMP, DATE IN 3 LINES, WITH TIME INDICIA

1863-70   *Empire, "Laureated"*

A171	5fr gray lilac, *lav* (#37)	1,600.

1870-73   *Ceres*

A172	1c ol grn, *pale blue* (#50)	110.00
A173	2c red brn, *yelsh* (#51)	110.00
	On cover, from	1,600.
A174	4c gray (#52)	110.00
A175	5c yel grn, *pale blue* (#53)	85.00
	On cover, from	1,200.
A176	15c bister, *yelsh* ('71) (#56)	140.00
A177	20c dull blue, *bluish* (#57)	—
A178	25c blue, *bluish* ('71) (#58)	85.00
	On cover, from	725.00
A179	40c orange, *yelsh* (I) (#59)	290.00
	On cover	—

Ceres, Larger Figures of Value

1872-75

A180	10c bister, *rose* ('75) (#60)	140.00
	On cover, from	1,200.
A181	15c bister ('73) (#61)	85.00
	On cover, from	1,400.
A182	30c brown, *yellowish* (#62)	140.00
	On cover, from	1,800.
A183	80c rose, *pinkish* (#63)	290.00
	On cover	—

"MONACO / PRINCIPAUTE" DOUBLE CIRCLE DATESTAMP, DATE IN 3 LINES, WITH TIME INDICIA IN SANS SERIF CHARACTERS

Peace & Commerce Issue, Type I ("N" under "B")

1876-78

A184	1c green, *greenish* (#64)	290.00
	On cover	—
A185	2c green, *greenish* (#65)	1,200.
A186	4c green, *greenish* (#66)	210.00
	On cover	—
A187	5c green, *greenish* (#67)	210.00
	On cover	6,600.
A188	10c green, *greenish* (#68)	2,100.
A189	15c gray lilac, *grayish* (#69)	160.00
	On cover	875.00
A190	20c red brown, *straw* (#70)	210.00
	On cover	—
A191	25c ultramarine, *bluish* (#72)	210.00
	On cover	1,200.
A192	30c brown, *yellowish* (#73)	140.00
	On cover	875.00
A193	40c red, *straw* (#74)	150.00
	On cover	1,200.

A194	75c carmine, *rose* (#75)	210.00
	On cover	550.00
A195	1fr bronze green, *straw* (#76)	110.00
	On cover	2,100.

Peace & Commerce Issue, Type II ("N" under "U")

1876-90

A196	2c green, *greenish* (#77)	210.00
A197	5c green, *greenish* (#78)	40.00
	On cover	500.00
A198	10c green, *greenish* (#79)	725.00
A199	15c gray lilac, *grayish* (#80)	42.50
	On cover	325.00
A200	25c ultramarine, *bluish* (#81)	42.50
	On cover	210.00
A201	25c blue, *bluish* (#81a)	55.00
	On cover	290.00
A202	30c yel brn, *yelsh* (#82)	110.00
A203	75c car, *rose* ('77) (#83)	—
A204	1fr brnz grn, *straw* ('77) (#84)	110.00
	On cover	1,400.
A205	1c black, *lilac blue* (#86)	210.00
	On cover	2,800.
A206	2c brown, *straw* (#88)	160.00
	On cover	—
A207	3c yellow, *straw* ('78) (#89)	210.00
A208	4c claret, *lavender* (#90)	72.50
	On cover	1,600.
A209	10c black, *lavender* (#91)	72.50
	On cover	1,100.
A210	15c blue ('78) (#92)	40.00
	On cover	210.00
A211	25c black, *red* ('78) (#93)	85.00
	On cover	1,300.
A212	35c black, *yellow* ('78) (#94)	725.00
	On cover	—
A213	40c red, *straw* ('80) (#95)	65.00
	On cover	850.00
A214	5fr violet, *lavender* (#96)	290.00
	On cover	7,200.
A215	3c gray, *grayish* ('80) (#97)	160.00
A216	20c red, *yellow green* (#98)	110.00
	On cover	—
A217	25c yellow, *straw* (#99)	42.50
	On cover	425.00

"MONACO / ALPES-MARITIMES" DOUBLE CIRCLE DATESTAMP, DATE IN 3 LINES, WITH TIME INDICIA

1870-73   *Ceres*

A218	4c gray (#52)	1,900.
A219	5c yel grn, *pale blue* (#53)	1,900.
A220	25c blue, *bluish* ('71) (#58)	1,100.
	On cover	10,000.

"MONTE-CARLO / PTE. DE MONACO" DOUBLE CIRCLE DATESTAMP, DATE IN 3 LINES, WITH TIME INDICIA

Peace & Commerce Issue, Type II ("N" under "U")

1876-90

A221	2c green, *greenish* (#77)	—
A222	5c green, *greenish* (#78)	—
A223	10c green, *greenish* (#79)	72.50
A224	15c gray lilac, *grayish* (#80)	—
A225	25c ultramarine, *bluish* (#81)	—
A226	25c blue, *bluish* (#81a)	—
A227	30c yel brn, *yelsh* (#82)	190.00
A228	75c carm, *rose* ('77) (#83)	—
A229	1fr brnz grn, *straw* ('77) (#84)	110.00
A230	1c black, *lilac blue* (#86)	110.00
A231	2c brown, *straw* (#88)	72.50
A232	3c yellow, *straw* ('78) (#89)	—
A233	4c claret, *lavender* (#90)	72.50
A234	10c black, *lavender* (#91)	72.50
A235	15c blue ('78) (#92)	65.00
	On cover	875.00
A236	25c black, *red* ('78) (#93)	85.00
	On cover	1,100.
A237	35c black, *yellow* ('78) (#94)	—

A238	40c red, *straw* ('80) (#95)	110.00
A239	5fr violet, *lavender* (#96)	475.00
A240	3c gray, *grayish* ('80) (#97)	110.00
A241	20c red, *yellow green* (#98)	110.00
A242	25c yellow, *straw* (#99)	72.50

Other "Monte-Carlo" cancelations exist, used at mail transit offices.

POSTAGE DUE STAMPS OF FRANCE

"MONACO / PRINCIPAUTE" DOUBLE CIRCLE DATESTAMP, DATE IN 3 LINES, WITH TIME INDICIA

1859-95   *Empire, "Laureated"*

AJ1	10c black (#J3)	—
AJ2	15c black ('63) (#J4)	900.00
AJ3	25c black ('71) (#J6)	1,300.
AJ4	30c black ('78) (#J7)	1,300.
AJ5	1c black (#J11)	42.50
	On cover	300.00
AJ6	2c black (#J12)	72.50
	On cover	875.00
AJ7	3c black (#J13)	72.50
	On cover	950.00
AJ8	4c black (#J14)	110.00
AJ9	5c black (#J15)	35.00
	On cover	290.00
AJ10	10c black (#J16)	35.00
	On cover	290.00
AJ11	15c black (#J17)	55.00
	On cover	325.00
AJ12	20c black (#J18)	160.00
AJ13	30c black (#J19)	55.00
	On cover	290.00
AJ14	40c black (#J20)	140.00
	On cover	—
AJ15	50c black ('92) (#J21)	160.00
	On cover	1,100.
AJ16	60c black ('84) (#J22)	130.00
	On cover	725.00
AJ17	2fr black ('84) (#J24)	850.00
AJ18	5fr black ('84) (#J25)	1,400.
AJ19	1fr brown (#J26)	475.00
AJ20	2fr brown (#J27)	475.00
AJ21	5fr brown (#J28)	725.00
AJ22	5c blue ('94) (#J29)	29.00
	On cover	72.50
AJ23	10c brown (#J30)	29.00
	On cover	90.00
AJ24	15c light green ('94) (#J31)	29.00
	On cover	110.00
AJ25	30c red ('94) (#J34)	29.00
	On cover	90.00
AJ26	50c brn violet ('95) (#J38)	35.00
	On cover	140.00

"MONTE-CARLO / PTE. DE MONACO" DOUBLE CIRCLE DATESTAMP, DATE IN 3 LINES, WITH TIME INDICIA

1882-95

AJ27	1c black (#J11)	42.50
	On cover	290.00
AJ28	2c black (#J12)	72.50
	On cover	950.00
AJ29	3c black (#J13)	85.00
AJ30	4c black (#J14)	—
AJ31	5c black (#J15)	55.00
	On cover	325.00
AJ32	10c black (#J16)	55.00
	On cover	290.00
AJ33	15c black (#J17)	32.50
	On cover	290.00
AJ34	20c black (#J18)	240.00
AJ35	30c black (#J19)	55.00
	On cover	325.00
AJ36	40c black (#J20)	160.00
AJ37	50c black ('92) (#J21)	160.00
	On cover	875.00
AJ38	60c black ('84) (#J22)	—
AJ39	1fr brown (#J26)	360.00
AJ40	2fr brown (#J27)	—
AJ41	5fr brown (#J28)	475.00
AJ42	5c blue ('94) (#J29)	21.00
	On cover	55.00
AJ43	10c brown (#J30)	29.00
	On cover	85.00
AJ44	15c light green ('94) (#J31)	29.00
	On cover	85.00
AJ45	30c red ('94) (#J34)	21.00
	On cover	55.00
AJ46	50c brn violet ('95) (#J38)	35.00
	On cover	110.00

Other "Monte-Carlo" cancelations exist, used at mail transit offices.

Issues of the Principality

Values for unused stamps are for examples with original gum as defined in the catalogue introduction. Very fine examples of Nos. 1-181, B1-B50, C1 and J1-J27 will have perforations clear of the design and/or frameline. Very well centered are worth more than the values quoted.

Prince Charles III — A1

1885 Unwmk. Typo. Perf. 14x13½

1	A1	1c olive green	25.00	17.50
		Never hinged	37.50	
		On cover with other values		290.00
		On postal stationery to up-grade rate		525.00
a.		1c bronze green	30.00	21.00
		Never hinged	45.00	
2	A1	2c dull lilac	57.50	27.50
		Never hinged	72.50	
		On cover with other values		290.00
		On postal stationery to up-grade rate		525.00
a.		2c slate violet	62.50	32.50
		Never hinged	92.50	
3	A1	5c blue	70.00	35.00
		Never hinged	95.00	
		On cover with other values		175.00
		On postal stationery to up-grade rate		290.00
4	A1	10c brown, straw	85.00	40.00
		Never hinged	125.00	
		On cover with other values		225.00
		On postal stationery to up-grade rate		225.00
5	A1	15c rose	350.00	18.00
		Never hinged	490.00	
		On cover		175.00
6	A1	25c green	700.00	75.00
		Never hinged	925.00	
		On cover		350.00
7	A1	40c slate, rose	85.00	45.00
		Never hinged	110.00	
		On cover		225.00
		On cover, single franking		400.00
8	A1	75c black, rose	275.00	125.00
		Never hinged	400.00	
		On cover		800.00
		On cover, single franking		1,150.
9	A1	1fr black, yellow	1,750.	500.00
		Never hinged	2,300.	
		On cover		4,000.
		Philatelic cover, single franking		2,900.
10	A1	5fr rose, green	3,000.	2,000.
		Never hinged	4,400.	
		On registered cover		11,500.
		On money letter		10,500.
		Philatelic cover, single franking		7,750.

Values for blocks of 4

1	A1	1c olive green	125.00	110.00
		Never hinged	190.00	
		On cover		190.00
2	A1	2c dull lilac	275.00	300.00
		Never hinged	375.00	
		On cover		450.00
3	A1	5c blue	400.00	240.00
		Never hinged	600.00	
		On cover		600.00
4	A1	10c brown, straw	400.00	250.00
		Never hinged	600.00	
		On cover		625.00
5	A1	15c rose	2,200.	165.00
		Never hinged	2,750.	
6	A1	25c green	5,500.	800.00
		Never hinged	7,000.	
7	A1	40c slate, rose	425.00	375.00
		Never hinged	550.00	
		On cover		1,450.
8	A1	75c black, rose	1,700.	750.00
		Never hinged	2,400.	
9	A1	1fr black, yellow	12,000.	10,000.

No blocks of No. 10 are known. A few pairs do exist. Values: unused $17,500; used $6,750.

Prince Albert I — A2

1891-1921

11	A2	1c olive green	.70	.70
		Never hinged	1.20	
		On cover		8.50
		On printed matter		175.00
12	A2	2c dull violet	.80	.80
		Never hinged	1.25	
		On cover		8.50
		On printed matter		115.00
13	A2	5c blue	50.00	6.00
		Never hinged	85.00	
		On cover		24.00
		On cover, single franking		90.00

14	A2	5c yellow grn ('01)	.40	.35
		Never hinged	.80	
		On cover		7.00
		On cover, single franking		57.50
15	A2	10c brown, straw	100.00	16.00
		Never hinged	160.00	
		On cover		85.00
		On cover, with #13 (15c rate)		175.00
		On cover, single franking		—
a.		10c dark brown, yellow	110.00	17.50
		Never hinged	175.00	
16	A2	10c carmine ('01)	3.25	.70
		Never hinged	6.75	
		On cover		29.00
		On postcard		29.00
a.		10c rose	3.50	.60
		Never hinged	7.00	
		On cover		29.00
17	A2	15c rose	175.00	10.00
		Never hinged	275.00	
		On cover		30.00
		On cover, single franking		85.00
a.		Double impression	1,400.	
18	A2	15c vio brn, straw ('01)	3.00	1.00
		Never hinged	6.50	
		On cover		30.00
19	A2	15c gray green ('21)	2.00	2.50
		Never hinged	4.00	
		On cover		18.00
		On cover, single franking		30.00
20	A2	25c green	275.00	32.50
		Never hinged	425.00	
		On cover		90.00
		On cover, single franking		175.00
21	A2	25c deep blue ('01)	15.00	5.00
		Never hinged	27.50	
		On cover		57.50
22	A2	40c slate, rose ('94)	3.50	2.40
		Never hinged	5.50	
		On cover		57.50
		On cover, single franking		85.00
23	A2	50c violet brown (shades), orange	7.00	4.75
		Never hinged	12.00	
		On cover		29.00
		On cover, single franking		57.50
a.		50c brown, orange	12.50	12.50
		Never hinged	21.00	
		On cover		35.00
24	A2	75c vio brn, buff ('94)	27.50	18.00
		Never hinged	50.00	
		On cover		140.00
		On cover, single franking		290.00
a.		75c lilac brown, buff	36.00	27.50
		Never hinged	65.00	
		On cover		50.00
25	A2	75c ol brn, buff ('21)	20.00	24.00
		Never hinged	40.00	
		On cover		115.00
		On cover, single franking		—
26	A2	1fr black, yellow	19.00	11.00
		Never hinged	32.50	
		On cover		115.00
		On cover, single franking		125.00
a.		1fr black, pale yel straw	17.00	11.50
		Never hinged	32.50	
		On cover		125.00
27	A2	5fr rose, grn	100.00	87.50
		Never hinged	175.00	
		On cover		975.00
		Philatelic cover, over-franked		350.00
a.		5fr carmine rose, green	160.00	120.00
		Never hinged	350.00	
		Philatelic cover, over-franked		350.00
28	A2	5fr dull violet ('21)	200.00	250.00
		Never hinged	350.00	
		On cover		1,600.
		Philatelic cover, over-franked		850.00
29	A2	5fr dark green ('21)	22.50	27.50
		Never hinged	47.50	
		On cover		290.00
		Philatelic cover, over-franked		115.00
a.		5fr pale green ('21)	400.00	275.00
		Never hinged	575.00	
		Nos. 11-29 (19)	1,024.	500.70

The handstamp "OL" in a circle of dots is a cancellation, not an overprint.

On cover values for Nos. 27-29 are for over-franked philatelic covers.

See No. 1782 in Scott Standard catalogue, Vol. 4. For overprints and surcharges see Nos. 30-35, 57-59, B1.

Stamps of 1901-21 Overprinted or Surcharged

1921, Mar. 5

30	A2	5c lt green	.70	.70
		Never hinged	1.20	
		On cover		40.00

31	A2	75c brown, buff	5.25	6.25
		Never hinged	8.00	
		On cover		70.00
32	A2	2fr on 5fr dull vio	32.50	52.50
		Never hinged	60.00	
		On cover		85.00
		On cover, single franking©		225.00
		Nos. 30-32 (3)	38.45	59.45

Issued to commemorate the birth of Princess Antoinette, daughter of Princess Charlotte and Prince Pierre, Comte de Polignac.

Stamps and Type of 1891-1921 Surcharged

25c.

1922

33	A2	20c on 15c gray green	1.10	1.40
		Never hinged	2.00	
		On cover		17.50
34	A2	25c on 10c rose	.70	.90
		Never hinged	1.20	
		On cover		17.50
35	A2	50c on 1fr black, yel	6.00	6.50
		Never hinged	9.50	
		On cover		35.00
		Nos. 33-35 (3)	7.80	8.80

Prince Albert I — A5

Oceanographic Museum — A6

"The Rock" of Monaco — A7

Royal Palace — A8

1922-24 Engr. Perf. 11

40	A5	25c deep brown	4.00	4.75
		Never hinged	6.75	
		On cover		7.25
a.		25c olive brown	12.00	12.00
		Never hinged	21.00	
		On cover		24.00
41	A6	30c dark green	.90	.90
		Never hinged	1.75	
		On cover		2.00
a.		30c gray green	2.75	2.75
		Never hinged	4.00	
		On cover		16.00
42	A6	30c scarlet ('23)	.50	.45
		Never hinged	.75	
		On cover		2.00
a.		30c salmon	.75	1.75
		Never hinged	1.25	
		On cover		2.40
43	A6	50c ultra	4.25	4.25
		Never hinged	8.00	
		On cover		8.00
a.		50c pale ultra	7.25	7.50
		Never hinged	12.00	
		On cover		13.50
b.		50c greenish blue	5.50	6.00
		Never hinged	9.50	
		On cover		—
44	A7	60c black brown	.35	.35
		Never hinged	.55	
		On cover		1.60
a.		60c pale gray	.70	.70
		Never hinged	1.20	
		On cover		2.40
45	A7	1fr black, yellow	.25	.25
		Never hinged	.40	
		On cover		1.20
a.		1fr gray black, yellow	.40	.25
		Never hinged	.70	
		On cover		1.60
46	A7	2fr scarlet ver	.50	.45
		Never hinged	.85	
		On cover		4.00
a.		2fr carmine	2.50	3.00
		Never hinged	4.50	
		On cover		6.50
47	A8	5fr red brown	32.50	37.50
		Never hinged	55.00	
		On cover		92.50
a.		5fr deep brown	55.00	65.00
		Never hinged	95.00	
		On cover		175.00
48	A8	5fr green, bluish	10.50	10.50
		Never hinged	21.00	
		On cover		40.00
a.		5fr dk green, lil ('24)	12.00	12.00
		Never hinged	24.00	
		On cover		35.00

Prince Louis II
A9   A10

St. Dévote Viaduct ("Bridge of Suicides") A11

49	A8	10fr carmine	14.00	18.00
		Never hinged	30.00	
		On cover		40.00
a.		10fr rose	65.00	72.50
		Never hinged	105.00	
		On cover		125.00
		Nos. 40-49 (10)	67.75	77.40

Nos. 40-49 exist imperf.

1923-24 Engr.

50	A9	10c deep green	.35	.55
		Never hinged	.55	
		On cover		1.15
51	A9	15c car rose ('24)	.45	.70
		Never hinged	.70	
		On cover		1.15
52	A9	20c red brown	.35	.55
		Never hinged	.65	
		On cover		1.15
53	A9	25c violet	.25	.45
		Never hinged	.45	
		On cover		1.15
a.		Without engraver's name	27.50	27.50
		Never hinged	40.00	
		On cover		—
54	A11	40c orange brn ('24)	.65	.55
		Never hinged	.85	
		On cover		1.15
55	A10	50c ultra	.35	.45
		Never hinged	.55	
		On cover		1.60
		Nos. 50-55 (6)	2.40	3.25

The 25c comes in 2 types, one with larger "5" and "c" touching frame of numeral tablet.

Stamps of the 1922-24 issues sometimes show parts of the letters of a papermaker's watermark.

The engraved stamps of type A11 measure 31x21½mm. The typographed stamps of that design measure 36x21½mm.

See #86-88. For surcharges see #95-96.

Stamps and Type of 1891-1921 Surcharged

45

1924, Aug. 5 Perf. 14x13½

57	A2	45c on 50c brn ol, buff	.50	.70
		Never hinged	.80	
		On cover		1.60
		On cover, single franking		3.25
a.		Double surcharge	775.00	775.00
		Never hinged	1,050.	
58	A2	75c on 1fr blk, yel	.50	.70
		Never hinged	.80	
		On cover		2.00
		On cover, single franking		3.50
a.		Double surcharge	550.00	550.00
		Never hinged	1,050.	
59	A2	85c on 5fr dk green	.50	.70
		Never hinged	.80	
		On cover		2.00
		On cover, single franking		3.25
a.		Double surcharge	650.00	650.00
		Never hinged	700.00	
		Nos. 57-59 (3)	1.50	2.10
		Set, never hinged	2.25	

Grimaldi Family Coat of Arms — A12

Prince Louis II — A13

Louis II — A14

View of Monaco A15

1924-33   Typo.

60	A12	1c gray black	.25	.25
61	A12	2c red brown	.25	.25
62	A12	3c brt violet ('33)	2.75	1.90
63	A12	5c orange ('26)	.35	.30
64	A12	10c blue	.25	.25
65	A13	15c apple green	.25	.25
66	A13	15c dull vio ('29)	2.75	1.90
67	A13	20c violet	.25	.25
68	A13	20c rose	.35	.25
69	A13	25c rose	.25	.25
70	A13	25c red, *yel*	.25	*.25*
71	A13	30c orange	.25	.25
72	A13	40c black brown	.25	.25
73	A13	40c lt bl, *bluish*	.35	.35
74	A13	45c gray black ('26)	.90	.70
75	A14	50c myrtle grn ('25)	.25	*.25*
76	A14	50c brown, *org* ('25)	.25	.25
77	A14	60c yellow brn ('25)	.25	*.25*
78	A13	60c ol grn, *grnsh* ('26)	.25	*.25*
79	A13	75c ol grn, *grnsh* ('26)	.70	.35
80	A13	75c car, *straw* ('26)	.35	.25
81	A13	75c slate	.90	.55
82	A13	80c red, *yel* ('26)	.40	.30
83	A13	90c rose, *straw* ('27)	2.00	1.60
84	A13	1.25fr bl, *bluish* ('26)	.25	.25
85	A13	1.50fr bl, *bluish* ('27)	3.75	1.90

Size: 36x21½mm

86	A11	1fr blk, *orange*	.25	*.25*
87	A11	1.05fr red violet ('26)	.25	*.25*
88	A11	1.10fr blue grn ('27)	8.00	6.00
89	A15	2fr vio & ol brn ('25)	2.75	1.00
90	A15	3fr rose & ultra, *yel* ('27)	25.00	12.00
91	A15	5fr green & rose ('25)	8.50	6.00
92	A15	10fr yel brn & bl ('25)	25.00	17.50
		Nos. 60-92 (33)	88.80	56.85
		Set, never hinged	175.00	

Nos. 60 to 74 and 76 exist imperforate.
For surcharges see Nos. 93-94, 97-99, C1.

Type of 1924-33
Surcharged in Black

1926-31

93	A13	30c on 25c rose	.30	.25
94	A13	50c on 60c ol grn, *grnsh* ('28)	1.50	.35
95	A11	50c on 1.05fr red vio ('28)	1.10	.70
a.		Double surcharge	65.00	
96	A11	50c on 1.10fr bl grn ('31)	14.00	8.75
97	A13	50c on 1.25fr bl, *bluish* (R) ('28)	1.60	.65
98	A13	1.25fr on 1fr bl, *bluish*	.80	.50
99	A15	1.50fr on 2fr vio & ol brn ('28)	7.00	5.25
		Nos. 93-99 (7)	26.30	16.45
		Set, never hinged	40.00	

Princes Charles III, Louis II and Albert I A17

1928, Feb. 18   Engr.   Perf. 11

100	A17	50c dull carmine	2.50	4.75
101	A17	1.50fr dark blue	2.50	4.75
102	A17	3fr dark violet	2.50	4.75
		Nos. 100-102 (3)	7.50	14.25
		Set, never hinged	18.00	

Nos. 100-102 were sold exclusively at the Intl. Phil. Exhib. at Monte Carlo, Feb., 1928. One set was sold to each purchaser of a ticket of admission to the exhibition which cost 5fr. Exist imperf. Value, set $27.50.

Old Watchtower A20

Royal Palace A21

Church of St. Dévote — A22

Prince Louis II — A23

"The Rock" of Monaco A24

Gardens of Monaco A25

Fortifications and Harbor — A26

1932-37   Perf. 13, 14x13½

110	A20	15c lilac rose	.80	.25
111	A20	20c orange brn	.80	.25
112	A21	25c olive blk	1.10	.35
113	A22	30c yellow grn	1.40	.35
114	A23	40c dark brown	3.25	1.40
115	A24	45c brown red	3.50	1.10
a.		45c red	425.00	425.00
116	A23	50c purple	3.25	.85
117	A25	65c blue green	3.50	1.10
118	A26	75c deep blue	4.00	1.75
119	A23	90c red	9.50	3.25
120	A22	1fr red brown ('33)	27.50	7.75
121	A26	1.25fr rose lilac	6.75	4.50
122	A23	1.50fr ultra	40.00	10.50
123	A21	1.75fr rose lilac	35.00	9.50
124	A21	1.75fr car rose ('37)	24.00	13.00
125	A24	2fr dark blue	13.50	4.75
126	A20	3fr purple	20.00	9.00
127	A21	3.50fr orange ('35)	47.50	32.50
128	A22	5fr violet	27.50	20.00
129	A21	10fr deep blue	125.00	70.00
130	A25	20fr black	175.00	140.00
		Nos. 110-130 (21)	572.85	332.15
		Set, never hinged	1,150.	

Postage Due Stamps of 1925-32 Surcharged or Overprinted in Black

1937-38   Perf. 14x13

131	D3	5c on 10c violet	1.00	1.00
132	D3	10c violet	1.00	1.00
133	D3	15c on 30c bister	1.00	1.00
134	D3	20c on 30c bister	1.00	1.00
135	D3	25c on 60c red	1.50	1.50
136	D3	30c bister	2.40	2.40
137	D3	40c on 60c red	2.40	2.40
138	D3	50c on 60c red	2.40	2.40
139	D3	65c on 1fr lt bl	2.25	2.00
140	D3	85c on 1fr lt bl	5.00	4.50
141	D3	1fr light blue	7.75	7.75
142	D3	2.15fr on 2fr dl red	7.75	7.75
143	D3	2.25fr on 2fr dl red ('38)	19.00	19.00
144	D3	2.50fr on 2fr dl red ('38)	29.00	29.00
		Nos. 131-144 (14)	83.45	82.70
		Set, never hinged	175.00	

Grimaldi Arms — A27

Prince Louis II — A28

1937-43   Engr.

145	A27	1c dk vio brn ('38)	.25	.25
146	A27	2c emerald	.25	.25
147	A27	3c brt red violet	.25	.25
148	A27	5c red	.25	.25
149	A27	10c ultra	.25	.25
149A	A27	10c black ('43)	.25	.25
150	A27	15c violet ('39)	1.75	1.50
150A	A27	30c dull green ('43)	.25	.25
150B	A27	40c rose car ('43)	.25	.25
150C	A27	50c brt violet ('43)	.25	.25
151	A28	55c red brown ('38)	5.75	2.25
151A	A27	60c Prus blue ('43)	.25	.25
152	A28	65c violet ('38)	30.00	13.00
153	A28	70c red brown ('39)	.35	.35
153A	A27	70c red brown ('43)	.25	.25
154	A28	90c violet ('39)	.35	.30
155	A28	1fr rose red ('38)	18.50	10.50
156	A28	1.25fr rose red ('39)	.35	.35
157	A28	1.75fr ultra ('38)	18.50	10.50
158	A28	2.25fr ultra ('39)	.35	.25
		Nos. 145-158 (20)	78.65	41.75
		Set, never hinged	150.00	

Nos. 151, 152, 155, 157 exist imperf.

Souvenir Sheet

Prince Louis II — A29

1938, Jan. 17   Unwmk.   Imperf.

159	A29	10fr magenta	65.00	65.00
		Never hinged	175.00	

"Fête Nationale" 1/17/38. Size: 99x120mm.

Cathedral of Monaco — A30

St. Nicholas Square — A31

Palace Gate — A32

Palace of Monaco — A34

Panorama of Monaco A33

Harbor of Monte Carlo A35

1939-46   Perf. 13

160	A30	20c rose lilac	.25	.25
161	A31	25c gldn brown	.45	.30
162	A32	30c dk blue grn	.35	.30
162A	A32	30c brown red ('40)	.35	.25
163	A31	40c henna brn	.70	.50
164	A33	45c brt red vio	.50	.50
165	A34	50c dk blue grn	.35	.25
166	A32	60c rose carmine	.40	.35
166A	A32	60c dk green ('40)	.90	.70
166B	A35	70c brt red vio ('41)	.40	.25
167	A35	75c dark green	.40	.25
167A	A30	80c dull green ('43)	.25	*.25*
168	A34	1fr brown black	.40	.25
168A	A33	1fr claret ('43)	.25	.25
168B	A35	1.20fr ultra ('46)	.25	*.35*
168C	A34	1.30fr brown blk ('41)	.40	.35
168D	A31	1.50fr ultra ('46)	.40	.40
169	A31	2fr rose violet	.40	.30
169A	A35	2fr lt ultra ('43)	.25	.25
169B	A34	2fr green ('46)	.35	.25
170	A33	2.50fr red	27.50	17.50
171	A33	2.50fr dp blue ('40)	1.75	1.75
172	A35	3fr brown red	.45	.35
172A	A31	3fr black ('43)	.25	.25
172B	A30	4fr rose lilac ('46)	1.25	.55
172C	A34	4.50fr brt violet ('43)	.25	.25
173	A30	5fr Prus blue	5.25	4.00
173A	A32	5fr deep green ('43)	.25	.25
173B	A34	6fr lt violet ('46)	.70	.55
174	A33	10fr green	1.40	*1.60*
174A	A30	10fr deep blue ('43)	.25	*.25*
174B	A35	15fr rose pink ('43)	.40	*.25*
175	A32	20fr brt ultra	1.60	1.25
175A	A33	20fr sepia ('43)	.40	.25
175B	A35	25fr blue green ('46)	1.40	1.25
		Nos. 160-175B (35)	51.10	36.85
		Set, never hinged	100.00	

See Nos. 214-221, 228-232, 274-275, 319-320, 407-408, 423, 426, 428-429 in Scott Standard catalogue, Vol. 4; B36-B50.

Louis II Stadium A36

1939, Apr. 23   **Engr.**
176 A36 10fr dark green   100.00   110.00
   Never hinged   175.00

Inauguration of Louis II Stadium.

Louis II
Stadium
A37

1939, Aug. 15
177 A37 40c dull green   1.25   1.25
178 A37 70c brown black   1.60   1.60
179 A37 90c dark violet   2.25   2.25
180 A37 1.25fr copper red   3.00   3.00
181 A37 2.25fr dark blue   4.25   4.25
   Nos. 177-181 (5)   12.35   12.35
   Set, never hinged   22.50

8th International University Games.

Imperforates
Many Monaco stamps from 1940 to 1999 exist imperforate. Officially 20 sheets, ranging from 25 to 100 subjects, were left imperforate.

SEMI-POSTAL STAMPS

No. 16 Surcharged in
Red

1914, Oct.   **Unwmk.**   *Perf. 14x13½*
B1 A2 10c + 5c carmine   8.00   8.00
   Never hinged   17.50
   On cover, 10c rate   57.50

View of Monaco — SP2

1919, Sept. 20   **Typo.**
B2 SP2 2c + 3c lilac   32.50   35.00
   Never hinged   60.00
   On Cover   55.00
B3 SP2 5c + 5c green   21.00   20.00
   Never hinged   45.00
   On Cover   40.00
B4 SP2 15c + 10c rose   21.00   20.00
   Never hinged   45.00
   On Cover   40.00
B5 SP2 25c + 15c blue   39.00   40.00
   Never hinged   65.00
   On Cover   65.00
B6 SP2 50c + 50c brn,
    buff   190.00   175.00
   Never hinged   350.00
   On Cover   240.00
B7 SP2 1fr + 1fr blk, *yel*   300.00   375.00
   Never hinged   550.00
   On Cover   550.00
B8 SP2 5fr + 5fr dull
    red   1,000.   1,200.
   Never hinged   2,000.
   On Cover   2,000.
   Nos. B2-B8 (7)   1,603.   1,865.

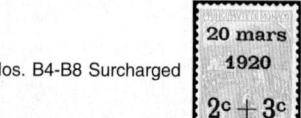

Nos. B4-B8 Surcharged
20 mars 1920 2c + 3c

1920, Mar. 20
B9 SP2 2c + 3c on #B4   40.00   45.00
   Never hinged   75.00
   On Cover   80.00
   a. "c" of "3c" inverted   1,500.   1,850.
    Never hinged   2,400.
   b. Pair, Nos. 9, 9a   2,250.   2,600.
    Never hinged   3,000.
B10 SP2 2c + 3c on #B5   40.00   45.00
   Never hinged   75.00
   On Cover   80.00
   a. "c" of "3c" inverted   1,500.   1,850.
    Never hinged   2,400.
   b. Pair, Nos. 10, 10a   2,250.   2,600.
    Never hinged   3,000.
B11 SP2 2c + 3c on #B6   40.00   45.00
   Never hinged   75.00
   On Cover   80.00
   a. "c" of "3c" inverted   1,500.

---

   b. Never hinged   2,400.
    Pair, Nos. 11, 11a   2,250.   2,600.
    Never hinged   3,000.
B12 SP2 5c + 5c on #B7   40.00   45.00
   Never hinged   75.00
   On Cover   80.00
B13 SP2 5c + 5c on #B8   40.00   45.00
   Never hinged   70.00
   On Cover   80.00

Overprinted
20 mars 1920

B14 SP2 15c + 10c rose   25.00   25.00
   Never hinged   50.00
   On Cover   40.00
B15 SP2 25c + 15c blue   16.00   16.00
   Never hinged   27.50
   On Cover   24.00
B16 SP2 50c + 50c
    brown,
    buff   55.00   55.00
   Never hinged   95.00
   On Cover   120.00
B17 SP2 1fr + 1fr black,
    yel   75.00   75.00
   Never hinged   150.00
   On Cover   325.00
B18 SP2 5fr + 5fr red   6,500.   6,500.
   Never hinged   10,000.
   Nos. B9-B17 (9)   371.00   396.00

Marriage of Princess Charlotte to Prince Pierre, Comte de Polignac.

Palace Gardens SP3

"The Rock" of Monaco SP4

Bay of Monaco SP5

Prince Louis II — SP6

1937, Apr.   **Engr.**   *Perf. 13*
B19 SP3 50c + 50c green   3.00   3.00
B20 SP4 90c + 90c car   3.00   3.00
B21 SP5 1.50fr + 1.50fr blue   6.00   6.00
B22 SP6 2fr + 2fr violet   11.50   11.50
B23 SP6 5fr + 5fr brn red   100.00   100.00
   Nos. B19-B23 (5)   123.50   123.50
   Set, never hinged   250.00

The surtax was used for welfare work.

Pierre and Marie Curie — SP7

1939, June 26
B26 SP9   5c + 5c brown
    blk   1.90   1.10
B27 SP10 10c + 10c rose
    vio   1.90   1.10

Monaco
Hospital,
Date Palms
SP8

1938, Nov. 15   *Perf. 13*
B24 SP7 65c + 25c dp bl grn   11.00   11.00
B25 SP8 1.75fr + 50c dp ultra   11.00   11.00
   Set, never hinged   40.00

B24 and B25 exist imperforate.
The surtax was for the International Union for the Control of Cancer.

Lucien — SP9

Honoré II — SP10

Louis I — SP11

Charlotte de Gramont — SP12

Antoine I — SP13

Marie de Lorraine — SP14

Jacques I SP15

Louise-Hippolyte SP16

Honoré III — SP17

"The Rock," 18th Century SP18

B28 SP11 45c + 15c brt
    green   6.75   5.00
B29 SP12 70c + 30c brt
    red vio   10.00   9.00
B30 SP13 90c + 35c vio   10.00   9.00
B31 SP14 1fr + 1fr ultra   20.00   24.00
B32 SP15 2fr + 2fr brn
    org   25.00   24.00
B33 SP16 2.25fr + 1.25fr
    Prus bl   30.00   30.00
B34 SP17 3fr + 3fr dp
    rose   40.00   42.50
B35 SP18 5fr + 5fr red   75.00   77.50
   Nos. B26-B35 (10)   225.55   223.20
   Set, never hinged   450.00

Types of Regular
Issue, 1939
Surcharged in Red

1940, Feb. 10   **Engr.**   *Perf. 13*
B36 A30 20c + 1fr violet   2.75   2.75
B37 A31 25c + 1fr dk grn   2.75   2.75
B38 A32 30c + 1fr brn red   2.75   2.75
B39 A31 40c + 1fr dk blue   2.75   2.75
B40 A33 45c + 1fr rose
    car   2.75   2.75
B41 A34 50c + 1fr brown   2.75   2.75
B42 A32 60c + 1fr dk grn   3.50   3.50
B43 A35 75c + 1fr brn blk   3.50   3.50
B44 A34 1fr + 1fr scarlet   4.50   4.50
B45 A31 2fr + 1fr indigo   4.50   4.50
B46 A33 2.50fr + 1fr dk grn   11.00   11.00
B47 A35 3fr + 1fr dk blue   11.00   11.00
B48 A30 3fr + 1fr brn blk   15.00   15.00
B49 A33 10fr + 5fr lt blue   28.00   28.00
B50 A32 20fr + 5fr brn vio   29.00   29.00
   Nos. B36-B50 (15)   126.50   126.50
   Set, never hinged   300.00

The surtax was used to purchase ambulances for the French government.

AIR POST STAMPS

No. 91
Srchd. in
Black

    Perf. 14x13½
1933, Aug. 22   **Unwmk.**
C1 A15 1.50fr on 5fr   25.00   25.00
   a. Imperf., pair   375.00

POSTAGE DUE STAMPS

D1   Prince Albert I — D2

    Perf. 14x13½
1905-43   **Unwmk.**   **Typo.**
J1 D1 1c olive green   .45   .55
J2 D1 5c green   .45   .55
   On cover   57.50
J3 D1 10c rose   .45   .55
   On cover   57.50
J4 D1 10c brn ('09)   350.00   125.00
   On cover   175.00
J5 D1 15c vio brn, *straw*   3.50   1.75
J6 D1 20c bis brn, *buff*
    ('26)   .35   .35
J7 D1 30c blue   .45   .55
   On cover   57.50
J8 D1 40c red vio ('26)   .35   .35
J9 D1 50c brn, *org*   4.50   4.00
   On cover   57.50
J10 D1 50c blue grn ('27)   .35   .35
J11 D1 60c gray blk ('26)   .35   .65
J12 D1 60c brt vio ('34)   21.00   27.50
J13 D1 1fr red brn, *straw*
    ('26)   .35   .25
J14 D1 2fr red org ('27)   1.00   1.50

J15	D1	3fr mag ('27)	1.00	1.50
J15A	D1	5fr ultra ('43)	.80	1.00
		Nos. J1-J15A (16)	385.35	166.40

For surcharge see No. J27.

1910

J16	D2	1c olive green	.25	.45
J17	D2	10c light violet	.45	.60
J18	D2	30c bister	190.00	160.00

In January, 1917, regular postage stamps overprinted "T" in a triangle were used as postage due stamps.

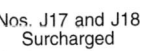

Nos. J17 and J18 Surcharged

1918

J19	D2	20c on 10c lt vio	4.00	7.50
a.		Double surcharge	1,000.	
J20	D2	40c on 30c bister	4.50	8.50

D3

1925-32

J21	D3	1c gray green	.40	.50
J22	D3	10c violet	.40	.55
J23	D3	30c bister	.50	.75
J24	D3	60c red	.70	.75
J25	D3	1fr lt bl ('32)	80.00	80.00
J26	D3	2fr dull red ('32)	80.00	80.00
		Nos. J21-J26 (6)	162.00	162.55

Nos. J25 and J26 have the numerals of value double-lined.

"Recouvrements" stamps were used to recover charges due on undelivered or refused mail which was returned to the sender.

No. J9 Surcharged

1925

J27	D1	1fr on 50c brn, org	.80	.55
a.		Double surcharge	750.00	

MONGOLIA

män-'gōl-yə

(Outer Mongolia)

LOCATION — Central Asia, bounded on the north by Siberia, on the west by Sinkiang, on the south and east by China proper and Manchuria
GOVT. — Republic
AREA — 604,250 sq. mi.
POP. — 1,820,000 (est. 1984)
CAPITAL — Ulan Bator

Outer Mongolia, which had long been under Russian influence although nominally a dependency of China, voted at a plebescite on October 20, 1945, to sever all ties with China and become an independent nation. See Tannu Tuva.

100 Cents = 1 Dollar
100 Mung = 1 Tugrik (1926)

Watermark

Wmk. 170 — Greek Border and Rosettes

Scepter of Indra — A1

1924　Litho.　Unwmk.　Perf. 10, 13½
Surface Tinted Paper

1	A1	1c multi, bister	12.00	12.00
2	A1	2c multi, brnsh	10.50	5.50
a.		Perf. 13½	47.50	40.00
3	A1	5c multi	40.00	24.00
a.		Perf. 10	47.50	35.00
4	A1	10c multi, gray bl	20.00	16.00
a.		Perf. 10	20.00	16.00
5	A1	20c multi, gray	27.50	17.50
6	A1	50c multi, salmon	40.00	24.00
7	A1	$1 multi, yellow	55.00	40.00
b.		Perf. 10	650.00	190.00
		Nos. 1-7 (7)	205.00	139.00

These stamps vary in size from 19x25mm (1c) to 30x39mm ($1). They also differ in details of the design.

Errors of perforating and printing exist.

Some quantities of Nos. 1-2, 4-7 were defaced with horizontal perforation across the center.

The 5c exists perf 11½. Value, $325 unused, hinged; $190 used.

Revenue Stamps Handstamp

A2

Sizes: 1c to 20c: 22x36mm
50c, $1: 26x43½mm
$5: 30x45½mm

Overprinted in Violet

		1926	**Perf. 11**	
16	A2	1c blue	12.00	12.00
17	A2	2c orange	16.00	11.00
18	A2	5c plum	16.00	13.00
19	A2	10c green	20.00	17.00
20	A2	20c yel brn	24.00	20.00
21	A2	50c brn & ol grn	190.00	175.00
22	A2	$1 brn & salmon	550.00	475.00
23	A2	$5 red, yel & gray	650.00	
		Nos. 16-23 (8)	1,478.	723.00

Black Overprint

16a	A2	1c blue	20.00	13.50
17a	A2	2c orange	32.50	20.00
18a	A2	5c plum	36.00	20.00
19a	A2	10c green	47.50	24.00
20a	A2	20c yellow brown	65.00	45.00
21a	A2	50c brown & olive grn	1,200.	325.00
22a	A2	$1 brown & salmon	600.00	400.00
23a	A2	$5 red, yellow & gray		
		Nos. 16a-22a (7)	2,001.	847.50

Red Overprint

16b	A2	1c blue	
17b	A2	2c orange	
18b	A2	5c plum	
19b	A2	10c green	
20b	A2	20c yellow brown	

The preceding handstamped overprints may be found inverted, double, etc. Counterfeits abound.

For overprints and surcharges see #48-61.

A3

A4

Soyombo

TYPE I — The pearl above the crescent is solid. The devices in the middle of the stamp are not outlined.
TYPE II — The pearl is open. The devices and panels are all outlined in black.

1926-29　　　　　　Perf. 11

Type I
Size: 22x28mm

32	A3	5m lilac & blk	12.00	12.00
33	A3	20m blue & blk	20.00	24.00

Type II
Size: 22x29mm

34	A3	1m yellow & blk	3.25	3.25
35	A3	2m brn org & blk	4.00	3.25
36	A3	5m lilac & blk	4.75	4.00
37	A3	10m lt blue & blk	4.00	2.00
a.		Imperf, pair		
38	A3	25m yel grn & blk	8.00	4.00
a.		Imperf, pair	125.00	110.00

Size: 26x34mm

40	A3	40m lemon & blk	11.00	4.75
41	A3	50m buff & blk	16.00	6.50

Size: 28x37mm

42	A4	1t brown, grn & blk	32.50	12.00
43	A4	3t red, yel & blk	72.50	47.50
44	A4	5t brn vio, rose & blk	95.00	60.00
		Nos. 32-44 (12)	283.00	183.25

In 1929 a change was made in the perforating machine. Every fourth pin was removed, which left the perforation holes in groups of three with blank spaces between the groups. Nos. 44A-44D have only this interrupted perforation. Nos. 37 and 39 are found with both perforations.

For overprints and surcharges see #45-47.

Soyombo — A5

1929, July　　Interrupted Perf 11

44A	A5	5m lilac & black	25.00	20.00
44B	A5	10m lt grnish blue & black	100.00	65.00
a.		imperf, pair		
44C	A5	20m blue & black	35.00	27.50
a.		imperf, pair		
b.		Horiz. pair, imperf btwn.		
44D	A5	25m yel grn & black	32.50	27.50
a.		imperf, pair		

See note after No. 44.

Nos. 34, 35, 40 Handstamped With New Values in Black

1930

45	A3	10m on 1m	32.50	30.00
46	A3	20m on 2m	45.00	40.00
47	A3	25m on 40m	52.50	47.50
		Nos. 45-47 (3)	130.00	117.50

Soyombo — A6

Violet Overprint, Handstamped

1931

48	A6	1c blue	24.00	12.00
a.		Blue overprint	87.50	47.50
49	A6	2c orange	27.50	9.50
50	A6	5c brown vio	35.00	9.50
a.		Blue overprint	65.00	22.50
51	A6	10c green	32.50	9.50
a.		Blue overprint	65.00	37.50
52	A6	20c bister brn	47.50	12.00
53	A6	50c brown & ol yel	130.00	120.00
54	A6	$1 brown & salmon	200.00	160.00
		Nos. 48-54 (7)	496.50	332.50

Soyombo — A7

Revenue Stamps Surcharged in Black, Red or Blue

1931

59	A7	5m on 5c brn vio (Bk)	40.00	16.00
a.		Inverted surcharge		35.00
b.		Imperf., pair	225.00	225.00
60	A7	10m on 10c green (R)	55.00	27.50
a.		Inverted surcharge	90.00	50.00
b.		Imperf., pair	225.00	225.00
61	A7	20m on 20c bis brn (Bl)	65.00	35.00
a.		Inverted surcharge		55.00
b.		Imperf., pair	225.00	225.00
		Nos. 59-61 (3)	160.00	78.50

On Nos. 59-61, "Postage" is always diagonal, and may read up or down.

Weaver at Loom — A8

Telegrapher A9

Sukhe Bator A10

Lake and Mountains — A11

Designs: 5m, Mongol at lathe. 10m, Government building, Ulan Bator. 15m, Young Mongolian revolutionary. 20m, Studying Latin alphabet. 25m, Mongolian soldier. 50m, Monument to Sukhe Bator. 3t, Sheep shearing. 5t, Camel caravan. 10t, Chasing wild horses.

Perf. 12½x12

		1932　Photo.	**Wmk. 170**	
62	A8	1m brown	3.25	1.50
63	A9	2m red violet	3.25	1.50
64	A8	5m indigo	2.00	.80
65	A8	10m dull green	2.00	.80
66	A9	15m dp brown	2.00	.80

67	A9	20m rose red	2.40	.80
68	A9	25m dull violet	2.40	.80
69	A10	40m gray black	2.00	1.20
70	A10	50m dull blue	2.40	.80

Perf. 11x12

71	A11	1t dull green	2.75	1.20
72	A11	3t dull violet	5.50	2.00
73	A11	5t brown	19.50	12.00
74	A11	10t ultra	40.00	20.00
		Nos. 62-74 (13)	89.45	44.20

Used values are for canceled-to-order stamps.

MONTENEGRO

ˌmän-tə-ˈnē-ˌgrō

LOCATION — Southern Europe, bordering on the Adriatic Sea
GOVT. — Kingdom
AREA — 5,603 sq. mi.
POP. — 516,000 (estimated)
CAPITAL — Cetinje

This kingdom, formerly a Turkish Protectorate, later became independent. On December 1, 1918, Montenegro united with Serbia, Bosnia and Herzegovina, Croatia, Dalmatia and Slovenia to form the Kingdom of the Serbs, Croats and Slovenes which became Yugoslavia in 1929.

100 Novcic = 1 Florin
100 Helera = 1 Kruna (1902)
100 Para = 1 Kruna (1907)
100 Para = 1 Perper (1910)

Canceled to Order

Used values for Nos. 1-110, H1-H5, J1-J26, and stamps issued under German occupation (Nos. 3N1-3NCB6) are for canceled-to-order stamps. Postally used examples sell for considerably more.

Watermark

Wmk. 91 — "BRIEF-MARKEN" (#1-14) or "ZEITUNGS-MARKEN" (#15-21) in Double-lined Capitals once across sheet

Prince Nicholas I — A1

Early Printings
Narrow Spacing (2-2½mm)
Perf. 10½ Large Holes, pointed teeth

			Typo.	Wmk. 91
1874				
1	A1	2n yellow	40.00	40.00
2	A1	3n green	55.00	40.00
3	A1	5n rose red	50.00	40.00
4	A1	7n lt lilac	50.00	32.50
5	A1	10n blue	120.00	80.00
6	A1	15n yel bister	135.00	120.00
7	A1	25n lilac gray	280.00	210.00
		Nos. 1-7 (7)	730.00	562.50

Middle Printings (1879)
Narrow spacing
Perf. 12, 12½, 13 and Compound

8	A1	2n yellow	10.00	7.00
a.		Perf. 12-13x10½	65.00	65.00
9	A1	3n green	7.50	5.50
10	A1	5n red	7.50	5.50
11	A1	7n rose lilac	7.50	5.50
a.		7n lilac	19.00	14.00
12	A1	10n blue	16.00	11.00
a.		Perf. 12-13x10½	65.00	52.50

13	A1	15n bister brn	19.00	11.00
14	A1	25n gray lilac	25.00	16.00
		Nos. 8-14 (7)	92.50	61.50

Late Printings (1893?)
Narrow and wide spacing (2¾-3½mm)
Perf. 10½, 11½ Small holes, broad teeth
(Perf. 11½ also with pointed teeth)

15	A1	2n yellow	4.00	2.75
a.		Perf. 11 ('94)	27.50	20.00
16	A1	3n green	4.00	2.75
17	A1	5n red	4.75	3.25
18	A1	7n rose	2.75	2.00
a.		Perf. 11 ('94)	12.00	9.00
19	A1	10n blue	4.00	2.75
20	A1	15n brown	4.00	3.25
21	A1	25n brown violet	4.75	3.00
		Nos. 15-21 (7)	28.25	19.75

Dates of issue of the late printings are still being researched.

Types of 1874-93 Overprinted in Black or Red

1893			Perf. 10½, 11½	
22	A1	2n yellow	35.00	6.50
a.		Perf. 11	35.00	35.00
23	A1	3n green	6.50	3.25
24	A1	5n red	2.40	1.60
25	A1	7n rose	4.00	2.50
a.		Perf. 12	60.00	50.00
b.		7n rose lilac	5.00	3.00
c.		7n lilac; perf. 12	125.00	
d.		Perf. 11	40.00	30.00
26	A1	10n blue	4.00	3.25
27	A1	10n blue (R)	6.00	4.00
28	A1	15n brown	4.50	3.25
a.		Perf. 12	50.00	42.50
29	A1	15n brown (R)	2,400.	1,600.
30	A1	25n brown violet	4.00	2.40
31	A1	25n brn vio (R)	6.00	4.00
a.		Perf. 12½		225.00
		Nos. 22-28,30-31 (9)	72.40	30.75

Introduction of printing to Montenegro, 400th anniversary.

This overprint had many settings. Several values exist with "1494" or "1495" instead of "1493", or with missing letters or numerals due to wearing of the clichés. Double and inverted overprints exist. Some printings were made after 1893 to supply a philatelic demand, but were available for postage.

The 7n with red overprint was not issued.

1894-98		Wmk. 91	Perf. 10½, 11½	
32	A1	1n gray blue	.40	.40
33	A1	2n emerald ('98)	.40	.40
34	A1	3n carmine rose ('98)	.40	.40
35	A1	5n orange ('98)	2.40	.55
36	A1	7n gray lilac ('98)	.50	.50
37	A1	10n magenta ('98)	.50	.50
38	A1	15n red brown ('98)	.40	.40
39	A1	20n brown orange	.40	.40
40	A1	25n dull blue ('98)	.40	.40
41	A1	30n maroon	.40	.25
42	A1	50n ultra	.55	.55
43	A1	1fl deep green	.80	.80
44	A1	2fl red brown	1.25	1.25
		Nos. 32-44 (13)	8.80	6.80

Monastery at Cetinje (Royal Mausoleum) A3

Perf. 10½, 11½

1896, Sept. 1			Litho.	Unwmk.
45	A3	1n dk blue & bis	.40	.40
46	A3	2n magenta & yel	.40	.40
47	A3	3n org brn & yel grn	.40	.40
48	A3	5n bl grn & bis	.40	.40
49	A3	10n yellow & ultra	.40	.40
50	A3	15n dk blue & grn	.40	.40
a.		Perf. 11½	60.00	60.00
51	A3	20n bl grn & ultra	.40	.40
a.		Perf. 11½	40.00	40.00
52	A3	25n dk blue & yel	.50	.50
53	A3	30n magenta & bis	.55	.55
54	A3	50n red brn & gray bl	.55	.55
55	A3	1fl rose & gray bl	1.00	1.00
56	A3	2fl brown & black	1.40	1.40
		Nos. 45-56 (12)	6.80	6.80

Bicentenary of the ruling dynasty, founded by the Vladika, Danilo Petrovich of Nyegosh. Inverted centers and other errors exist, but experts believe these to be printer's waste.

Perf. 11½ counterfeits are common.

Prince Nicholas I — A4

Perf. 13x13½, 13x12½ (2h, 5h, 50h, 2k, 5k), 12½ (1h, 25h)

1902, July 12				
57	A4	1h ultra	.40	.40
58	A4	2h rose lilac	.40	.40
59	A4	5h green	.40	.40
60	A4	10h rose	.40	.40
61	A4	25h dull blue	.55	.55
62	A4	50h gray green	.80	.80
63	A4	1k chocolate	.80	.80
64	A4	2k pale brown	.80	.80
65	A4	5k buff	.95	.95
		Nos. 57-65 (9)	5.50	5.50

The 2h black brown and 25h indigo were not issued. The 25h, perf. 12½, probably was never issued.

Constitution Issue

Same Overprinted in Red or Black "Constitution" 15mm

1905, Dec. 5				
66	A4	1h ultra (R)	.40	.40
67	A4	2h rose lilac	.40	.40
68	A4	5h green (R)	.80	.80
69	A4	10h rose	.95	.95
70	A4	25h dull blue (R)	.55	.55
71	A4	50h gray green (R)	.55	.55
72	A4	1k chocolate (R)	.55	.55
73	A4	2k pale brown (R)	.80	.80
74	A4	5k buff	1.25	1.25
		Nos. 66-74 (9)	6.25	6.25

Overprints in other colors are proofs.

1906			"Constitution" 16½mm	
66a	A4	1h ultra (R)	.55	.55
67a	A4	2h rose lilac	.55	.55
68a	A4	5h green (R)	.80	.80
69a	A4	10h rose	1.25	1.25
70a	A4	25h dull blue (R)	.80	.80
71a	A4	50h gray green (R)	.80	.80
72a	A4	1k chocolate (R)	1.25	1.25
73a	A4	2k pale brown (R)	1.25	1.25
74a	A4	5k buff	1.25	1.25
		Nos. 66a-74a (9)	8.50	8.50

Three settings of Nos. 66a-74a containing four types of "ЧСТАВ": I, 9¾mm, II, 11¼mm, III, 10¼mm, IV, 8½mm. Type IV occurs only in one setting, at two positions. Nos. 67a, 69a-74a, H3a exist in type IV.

Two errors occur: "Constitutton" and "Coustitution." Many other varieties including reversed color overprints exist.

Values are for types I and II.

Prince Nicholas I — A5

1907, June 1			Engr.	Perf. 12½
75	A5	1pa ocher	.45	.45
76	A5	2pa black	.45	.45
77	A5	5pa yellow green	1.40	.45
78	A5	10pa rose red	2.25	.45
79	A5	15pa ultra	.45	.45
80	A5	20pa red orange	.45	.45
81	A5	25pa indigo	.45	.45
82	A5	35pa bister brown	.55	.45
83	A5	50pa dull violet	.80	.50
84	A5	1kr carmine rose	.80	.50
85	A5	2kr green	.80	.50
86	A5	5kr red brown	1.75	1.20
		Nos. 75-86 (12)	10.60	6.60

Many Montenegro stamps exist imperforate or part perforate. Experts believe these to be printer's waste.

King Nicholas I as a Youth — A6　　　King Nicholas I and Queen Milena — A7

King Nicholas I — A11　　　Prince Nicholas — A12

5pa, 10pa, 25pa, 35pa, Nicholas in 1910. 15pa, Nicholas in 1878. 20pa, King and Queen, diff.

1910, Aug. 28			Engr.	
87	A6	1pa black	.65	.65
88	A7	2pa purple brown	.65	.65
89	A6	5pa dark green	.65	.65
90	A6	10pa carmine	.65	.65
91	A6	15pa slate blue	.65	.65
92	A7	20pa olive green	.65	.65
93	A6	25pa deep blue	.65	.65
94	A6	35pa chestnut	1.20	.80
95	A11	50pa violet	1.20	.80
96	A11	1per lake	.65	.80
97	A11	2per yellow green	1.30	.80
98	A12	5per pale blue	1.60	1.25
		Nos. 87-98 (12)	10.50	9.00

Proclamation of Montenegro as a kingdom, the 50th anniv. of the reign of King Nicholas and the golden wedding celebration of the King and Queen.

King Nicholas I — A13

1913, Apr. 1			Typo.	
99	A13	1pa orange	.65	.65
100	A13	2pa plum	.65	.65
101	A13	5pa deep green	.65	.65
102	A13	10pa deep rose	.65	.65
103	A13	15pa blue gray	.65	.65
104	A13	20pa dark brown	.65	.65
105	A13	25pa deep blue	.65	.65
106	A13	35pa vermilion	.65	.65
107	A13	50pa pale blue	.80	.80
108	A13	1per yellow brown	.80	.80
109	A13	2per gray violet	.80	.80
110	A13	5per yellow green	.80	.80
		Nos. 99-110 (12)	8.40	8.40

ACKNOWLEDGMENT OF RECEIPT STAMPS

Prince Nicholas I
AR1　　　　AR2
Perf. 10½, 11½

1895			Litho.	Wmk. 91
H1	AR1	10n ultra & rose	.95	.95

1902			Unwmk.	Perf. 12½
H2	AR2	25h orange & carmine	.95	.95

Constitution Issue

No. H2 Overprinted in Black

1905
H3	AR2	25h orange & carmine	1.20	1.20
a.		"Constitution" 16½mm ('06)	1.60	1.60

See note after 74a.

AR3

Nicholas I — AR4

1907 Engr.
H4	AR3	25pa olive	.80	.80

1913 Typo.
H5	AR4	25pa olive green	.80	.80

POSTAGE DUE STAMPS

D1

D2

Perf. 10½, 11, 11½
1894 Litho. Wmk. 91
J1	D1	1n red	3.25	3.25
J2	D1	2n yellow green	1.10	1.10
J3	D1	3n orange	.85	.80
J4	D1	5n olive green	.55	.55
J5	D1	10n violet	.55	.55
J6	D1	20n ultra	.55	.55
J7	D1	30n emerald	.55	.55
J8	D1	50n pale gray grn	.55	.55
		Nos. J1-J8 (8)	7.95	7.90

1902 Unwmk. Perf. 12½
J9	D2	5h orange	.40	.40
J10	D2	10h olive green	.40	.40
J11	D2	25h dull lilac	.40	.40
J12	D2	50h emerald	.40	.40
J13	D2	1k pale gray green	.80	.40
		Nos. J9-J13 (5)	2.40	2.00

Constitution Issue
Postage Due Stamps of 1902 Overprinted in Black or Red Like Nos. 66-74

1905
J14	D2	5h orange	.80	.80
J15	D2	10h olive green (R)	.80	.80
J16	D2	25h dull lilac	.80	.80
J17	D2	50h emerald	.80	.80
J18	D2	1k pale gray green	.80	.80
		Nos. J14-J18 (5)	4.00	4.00

The 10h with "Constitution" 16½mm is not known used. It is an unissued stamp.

D3

D4

1907 Typo. Perf. 13x13½
J19	D3	5pa red brown	.40	.40
J20	D3	10pa violet	.40	.40
J21	D3	25pa rose	.40	.40
J22	D3	50pa green	.40	.40
		Nos. J19-J22 (4)	1.60	1.60

1913 Perf. 12½
J23	D4	5pa gray	1.20	1.20
J24	D4	10pa violet	.80	.80
J25	D4	25pa blue gray	.80	.80
J26	D4	50pa lilac rose	1.20	1.20
		Nos. J23-J26 (4)	4.00	4.00

ISSUED UNDER AUSTRIAN OCCUPATION

Austrian Military Stamps of 1917 Overprinted

1917 Unwmk. Perf. 12½
1N1	M1	10h blue	14.50	12.00
1N2	M1	15h car rose	14.50	12.00

Austrian Military Stamps of 1917 Overprinted in Black

1918
1N3	M1	10h blue	40.00	
1N4	M1	15h car rose	1.90	

Nos. 1N3-1N4 were never placed in use. This overprint exists on other stamps of Austria and Bosnia and Herzegovina, and in blue or red.

MONTSERRAT

ˌmän(t)-sə-ˈrat

LOCATION — West Indies southeast of Puerto Rico
GOVT. — British Crown Colony
AREA — 39 sq. mi.
POP. — 12,074 (1980)
CAPITAL — Plymouth

Montserrat was one of the four presidencies of the former Leeward Islands colony until it became a colony itself in 1956.

Montserrat stamps were discontinued in 1890 and resumed in 1903. In the interim, stamps of Leeward Islands were used. In 1903-56, stamps of

---

Montserrat and Leeward Islands were used concurrently.

> 12 Pence = 1 Shilling
> 20 Shillings = 1 Pound
> 100 Cents = 1 Dollar (1951)

Catalogue values for unused stamps in this country are for Never Hinged items, beginning with Scott 104 in the regular postage section.

PRE-STAMP POSTAL MARKINGS

Crowned Circle handstamp type VI is pictured in the Crowned Circle Handstamps and Great Britain Used Abroad section.

Plymouth

1852-58
A1	VI	"Montserrat" crowned circle handstamp in red, on cover		4,500.

The handstamp was used, in black, as a provisional in 1886.

STAMPS OF GREAT BRITAIN USED IN MONTSERRAT

Numeral cancellation type A is pictured in the Crowned Circle Handstamps and Great Britain Used Abroad section.

1858-60 A08 (Plymouth)
A2	A	1p rose red (#20)	1,300.
A3	A	4p rose (#26)	
A4	A	6p lilac (#27)	550.00
A5	A	1sh green (#28)	2,750.

Issued under British Administration

Values for unused stamps are for examples with original gum as defined in the catalogue introduction. Very fine examples of Nos. 1-2, 6 and 11 will have perforations touching the design on at least one side due to the narrow spacing of the stamps on the plates. Stamps with perfs clear of the framelines on all four sides are scarce and will command higher prices.

Stamps of Antigua Overprinted in Black — a

1876 Engr. Wmk. 1 Perf. 14
1	A1	1p red	27.50	19.00
a.		Vert. or diag. half used as ½p on cover		1,650.
c.		"S" inverted	1,250.	875.00
2	A1	6p green	75.00	50.00
a.		Vertical half used as 3p on cover		—
b.		Vertical third used as 2p on cover		6,000.
c.		"S" inverted	1,900.	1,350.
d.		6p blue green	1,350.	
e.		As "d," "S" inverted	13,000.	

Some experts consider Nos. 2d, 2e to be from a trial printing.

Queen Victoria — A2

1880 Typo.
3	A2	2½p red brown	300.00	225.00
4	A2	4p blue	160.00	47.50

See Nos. 5, 7-10.

1884 Wmk. 2
5	A2	½p green	1.25	11.00

Antigua No. 18 Overprinted type "a"
1884 Engr.
6	A1	1p rose red	27.00	20.00
a.		Vert. half used as ½p on cover		1,550.
b.		"S" inverted	1,100.	1,100.

Type of 1880
1884-85 Typo.
7	A2	2½p red brown	275.00	77.50
8	A2	2½p ultra ('85)	27.50	22.50
9	A2	4p blue	2,100.	300.00
10	A2	4p red lilac ('85)	6.00	3.50

Antigua No. 20 Overprinted type "a"
1884 Engr. Perf. 12
11	A1	1p red	82.50	65.00
a.		"S" inverted	2,350.	1,550.
b.		Vert. half used as ½p on cover		1,900.

Symbol of the Colony — A3

King Edward VII — A4

1903 Wmk. 2 Typo. Perf. 14
12	A3	½p gray green	.90	19.00
13	A3	1p car & black	.90	.90
14	A3	2p brown & black	6.50	50.00
15	A3	2½p ultra & black	1.75	2.10
16	A3	3p dk vio & brn orange	6.50	50.00
17	A3	6p ol grn & vio	11.00	65.00
18	A3	1sh vio & gray grn	12.00	22.00
19	A3	2sh brn org & gray green	37.50	23.00
20	A3	2sh6p blk & gray grn	26.00	55.00
		Wmk. 1		
21	A4	5sh car & black	160.00	225.00
		Nos. 12-21 (10)	263.05	511.60
		Set of 10, ovptd "SPECIMEN"	190.00	

1904-08 Wmk. 3 Chalky Paper
22	A3	½p grn & gray grn ('06)	1.00	1.25
a.		Ordinary paper	11.00	3.00
23	A3	1p car & blk ('07)	17.00	30.00
24	A3	2p brown & black ('06)	2.50	1.40
a.		Ordinary paper	2.00	11.00
25	A3	2½p ultra & blk ('05)	3.00	7.75
26	A3	3p dk vio & brn orange ('08)	11.00	2.75
a.		Ordinary paper	9.00	8.00
27	A3	6p ol grn & vio ('08)	13.00	6.50
a.		Ordinary paper	8.50	37.50
28	A3	1sh violet & gray grn ('08)	11.50	8.50
29	A3	2sh brn org & gray grn ('08)	55.00	52.50

(continued)

30	A3	2sh6p blk & gray grn ('08)	60.00	57.50
31	A4	5sh car & blk ('07)	160.00	170.00
		Nos. 22-31 (10)	334.00	338.15
		Set of 10, ovptd "SPECIMEN"	300.00	

1903-10   **Ordinary Paper**

31A	A3	½p deep green	9.50	1.10
32	A3	1p carmine	1.75	.35
33	A3	2p gray	2.00	20.00
34	A3	2½p ultramarine	2.50	4.25

Chalky Paper

35	A3	3p vio, *yellow*	1.10	22.50
36	A3	6p red vio & gray vio	11.00	60.00
37	A3	1sh blk, *green*	10.00	55.00
38	A3	2sh bl & vio, *bl*	45.00	67.50
39	A3	2sh6p car & blk, *blue*	37.50	87.50
40	A4	5sh grn & scar, *yel*	65.00	92.50

Surface-colored Paper

41	A3	3p vio, *yel* ('13)	4.50	37.50
		Overprinted "SPECIMEN"	26.00	
		Nos. 31A-41 (11)	189.85	448.20
		#31A-40, ovptd "SPECIMEN"	250.00	

King George V
A5   A6

1913   **Chalky Paper**

42	A5	5sh green & scar, *yel*	90.00	150.00
		Overprinted "SPECIMEN"	85.00	

1916-22   **Wmk. 3**   **Perf. 14**
Ordinary Paper

43	A6	½p green	.45	2.75
44	A6	1p scarlet	1.75	.90
a.		1p carmine red	28.00	9.00
45	A6	2p gray	2.25	5.00
46	A6	2½p ultramarine	2.50	26.00

Chalky Paper

47	A6	3p violet, *yel*	1.40	21.00
48	A6	4p blk & red, *yel* ('22)	7.00	42.50
49	A6	6p dl vio & red violet	3.50	28.00
50	A6	1sh blk, *bl grn, ol back*	3.50	32.00
51	A6	2sh vio & ultra, *bl*	18.00	55.00
52	A6	2sh6p blk & red, *bl*	35.00	85.00
53	A6	5sh grn & red, *yel*	55.00	90.00
		Nos. 43-53 (11)	130.35	388.15
		Set of 11, ovptd "SPECIMEN"	200.00	

For overprints see Nos. MR1-MR3.

1922-29   **Wmk. 4**   **Ordinary Paper**

54	A6	¼p brown	.35	6.25
55	A6	½p green ('23)	.30	.30
56	A6	1p dp violet ('23)	.80	.70
57	A6	1p carmine ('29)	1.10	1.75
58	A6	1½p orange	2.50	11.00
59	A6	1½p rose red ('23)	.60	5.00
60	A6	1½p fawn ('29)	2.25	.55
61	A6	2p gray	.80	2.25
62	A6	2½p ultramarine	9.25	18.00
63	A6	2½p orange ('23)	2.75	21.00
64	A6	3p ultra ('23)	.80	18.00

Chalky Paper

65	A6	3p vio, *yel* ('26)	2.00	5.50
66	A6	4p black & red, *yel* ('23)	1.75	14.00
67	A6	5p dull vio & ol grn	4.50	11.00
68	A6	6p dull vio & red vio ('23)	3.50	8.50
69	A6	1sh blk, *emer* ('23)	3.50	8.00
70	A6	2sh vio & ultra, *bl*	8.00	18.00
71	A6	2sh6p blk & red, *bl* ('23)	14.00	60.00
72	A6	3sh green & vio	14.00	60.00
73	A6	4sh black & scar	17.50	42.50
74	A6	5sh grn & red, *yel* ('23)	35.00	60.00
		Nos. 54-74 (21)	125.25	333.30
		Set of 21, ovptd or perforated "SPECIMEN"	350.00	

Tercentenary Issue

Plymouth and Harbor
A7

1932, Apr. 18   **Engr.**

75	A7	½p green	.85	12.00
76	A7	1p red	.85	6.50
77	A7	1½p orange brown	1.40	2.75
78	A7	2p gray	1.90	22.50
79	A7	2½p ultra	1.40	18.00
80	A7	3p orange	1.90	21.00
81	A7	6p violet	2.50	37.50
82	A7	1sh olive green	14.50	50.00
83	A7	2sh6p lilac rose	52.50	87.50
84	A7	5sh dark brown	115.00	200.00
		Nos. 75-84 (10)	192.80	457.75
		Set, never hinged	400.00	
		Set of 10, perforated "SPECIMEN"	250.00	

300th anniv. of the colonization of Montserrat.

Common Design Types
pictured following the introduction.

Silver Jubilee Issue
Common Design Type

1935, May 6   **Perf. 11x12**

85	CD301	1p car & dk blue	1.25	4.25
86	CD301	1½p gray blk & ultra	2.00	3.75
87	CD301	2½p ultra & brn	2.75	4.25
88	CD301	1sh brn vio & ind	4.25	18.00
		Nos. 85-88 (4)	10.25	30.25
		Set, never hinged	19.00	
		Set, perforated "SPECIMEN"	100.00	

Coronation Issue
Common Design Type

1937, May 12   **Perf. 13½x14**

89	CD302	1p carmine	.25	1.50
90	CD302	1½p brown	.40	.35
91	CD302	2½p bright ultra	.35	1.50
		Nos. 89-91 (3)	1.00	3.35
		Set, never hinged	1.75	

Carr's Bay — A8

Sea Island Cotton — A9

Botanic Station A10

1941-48   **Perf. 14**

92	A8	½p dk grn ('42)	.25	.25
93	A9	1p car ('42)	.40	.35
94	A9	1½p rose vio ('42)	.40	.55
95	A10	2p red orange	1.20	.80
96	A9	2½p brt ultra ('43)	.40	.35
97	A8	3p brown ('42)	1.50	.45
98	A10	6p dull vio ('42)	2.00	.70
99	A8	1sh brn lake ('42)	1.75	.35
100	A10	2sh6p slate bl ('43)	13.50	3.00
101	A8	5sh car rose ('42)	16.00	3.50

Perf. 12

102	A10	10sh blue ('48)	10.00	30.00
103	A8	£1 black ('48)	10.00	35.00
		Nos. 92-103 (12)	57.40	75.30
		Set, never hinged	85.00	

1938, Aug. 2   **Perf. 13**

92a	A8	½p	2.50	2.00
93a	A8	1p	2.50	.40
94a	A9	1½p	11.00	1.00
95a	A10	2p	11.00	1.00
96a	A9	2½p	1.25	1.50
97a	A8	3p	3.00	3.25
98a	A10	6p	11.50	1.00
99a	A8	1sh	11.50	1.25
100a	A10	2sh6p	20.00	1.00
101a	A8	5sh	24.00	10.00
		Nos. 92a-101a (10)	98.25	22.65
		Set, never hinged	200.00	

> **Catalogue values for unused stamps in this section, from this point to the end of the section, are for Never Hinged items.**

Peace Issue
Common Design Type

1946, Nov. 1   **Engr.**   **Perf. 13½x14**

104	CD303	1½p deep magenta	.25	.25
105	CD303	3p brown	.25	.25

Silver Wedding Issue
Common Design Types

1949, Jan. 3   **Photo.**   **Perf. 14x14½**

106	CD304	2½p ultra	.25	.25

Engraved; Name Typographed
Perf. 11½x11

107	CD305	5sh rose carmine	9.00	18.00

UPU Issue
Common Design Types
Engr.; Name Typo. on 3p and 6p
Perf. 13½, 11x11½

1949, Oct. 10   **Wmk. 4**

108	CD306	2½p ultramarine	.45	1.00
109	CD307	3p chocolate	1.10	.75
110	CD308	6p lilac	.75	.85
111	CD309	1sh rose violet	1.10	1.25
		Nos. 108-111 (4)	3.40	3.85

University Issue
Common Design Types

1951, Feb. 16   **Engr.**   **Perf. 14x14½**

112	CD310	3c rose lil & gray blk	.25	.60
113	CD311	12c violet & black	.60	.90

Government House
A11

Designs (portrait at right on 12c, 24c and $2.40): 2c, $1.20, Cotton field. 3c, Map of Presidency. 4c, 24c, Picking tomatoes. 5c, 12c, St. Anthony's Church. 6c, $4.80, Badge of Presidency. 8c, 60c, Cotton ginning.

Perf. 11½x11

1951, Sept. 17   **Engr.**   **Wmk. 4**

114	A11	1c gray	.30	.30
115	A11	2c green	.30	.30
116	A11	3c orange brown	.30	.30
117	A11	4c rose carmine	.30	.30
118	A11	5c red violet	.30	.30
119	A11	6c dark brown	.40	.40
120	A11	8c dark blue	.60	.60
121	A11	12c red brn & blue	1.25	1.25
122	A11	24c emer & rose carmine	1.75	1.75
123	A11	60c rose car & gray black	3.50	3.50
124	A11	$1.20 dp bl & emer	11.00	11.00
125	A11	$2.40 dp grn & gray black	14.00	14.00
126	A11	$4.80 pur & gray blk	28.00	28.00
		Nos. 114-126 (13)	62.00	62.00

WAR TAX STAMPS

No. 43 Overprinted in Red or Black

1917-18   **Wmk. 3**   **Perf. 14**

MR1	A6	½p green (R)	.25	1.75
MR2	A6	½p green ('18)	.25	2.00

Type of Regular Issue of 1919 Overprinted

1918

MR3	A6	1½p orange & black	.30	.35
		Set of 3, ovptd "SPECIMEN"	100.00	

Denomination on No. MR3 in black on ... ground. Two dots under "d."

MOROCCO

mə-'rä-ˌkō

LOCATION — Northwest coast of Africa
GOVT. — Kingdom
AREA — Approx. 170,000 sq. mi.
POP. — 4,442,000 (1912 est.)
CAPITAL — Rabat

In 1892 the Sultan of Morocco established a postal service for most of the country's chief towns and cities. This service, utilizing handstruck franks, carried official correspondence, as well as some private correspondence. With French guidance, it was reorganized as the *Administration Cherifienne des Postes, Telegraphes et Telephones* in Sept. 1911. In 1912 Morocco became a French protectorate, and on Oct. 1, 1913, the Cherifian PTT was merged with the French *Administration des Postes et Telegraphes*.

Stamps were issued by the Moroccan post office in 1912, and these remained in use throughout the country until 1915 and in Tangier until 1919.

400 Moussonats = 1 Rial

Aissaouas Mosque, Tangier — A1a

On White Paper
Narrow Margins

1912, May 25   **Litho.**   **Perf. 11**

A1	A1a	1m light gray	9.25	8.50
		Never hinged	17.00	
		On cover		325.00
A2	A1a	2m lilac	10.00	9.25
		Never hinged	19.00	
		On cover		325.00
A3	A1a	5m blue green	12.50	8.50
		Never hinged	24.00	
		On cover		275.00
A4	A1a	10m vermilion	19.00	8.50
		Never hinged	35.00	
		On cover		275.00
A5	A1a	25m blue	29.00	24.00
		Never hinged	55.00	
		On cover		400.00
A6	A1a	50m violet	42.50	37.50
		Never hinged	75.00	
		On cover		475.00
		Nos. A1-A6 (6)	122.25	96.25

On Nos. A1-A12, the 5m and 10m values always have the name of the engraver beneath the design, while the 1m, 25m and 50m always lack name, and the 2m value exists both with and without name.

Aissaouas Mosque, Tangier — A1b

On Lightly Tinted Paper

1913, Feb.   **Wide Margins**

A7	A1b	1m gray	1.25	1.25
		Never hinged	2.00	
		On cover		275.00
A8	A1b	2m brown lilac	1.25	1.25
		Never hinged	2.00	
		On cover		275.00
A9	A1b	5m blue green	1.75	1.75
		Never hinged	2.75	
		On cover		240.00
A10	A1b	10m vermilion	1.75	1.75
		Never hinged	2.75	
		On cover		240.00
A11	A1b	25m blue	3.75	3.75
		Never hinged	6.50	
		On cover		260.00
A12	A1b	50m gray violet	4.50	4.50
		Never hinged	8.00	
		On cover		325.00
		Nos. A7-A12 (6)	14.25	14.25

No. A6 Surcharged

1913, Nov.

A13	A1a	.05 on 50c violet	1,750.	2,000.
		On cover		2,600.
A14	A1a	.10 on 50c violet	1,750.	2,000.
		On cover		2,600.

MOZAMBIQUE

mō-zəm-'bēk

LOCATION — Southeastern Africa, bordering on the Mozambique Channel
GOVT. — Portuguese Colony
AREA — 308,642 sq. mi.
POP. — 14,140,000 (est. 1983)
CAPITAL — Maputo

Mozambique, or Portuguese East Africa, was divided into eight districts: Lourenco Marques, Inhambane, Quelimane, Tete, Mozambique, Zambezia, Nyassa and the Manica and Sofala region formerly administered by the Mozambique Company. At various times the districts issued their own stamps which were eventually replaced by those inscribed "Mocambique."

1000 Reis = 1 Milreis
100 Centavos = 1 Escudo (1913)

Portuguese Crown — A1

Perf. 12½, 13½

		1877-85	**Typo.**	**Unwmk.**
1	A1	5r black	2.00	1.00
a.		Perf. 13½	3.00	1.60
2	A1	10r yellow	15.00	4.50
3	A1	10r green ('81)	1.50	.60
4	A1	20r bister	1.50	.75
a.		Perf. 13½	3.00	2.00
5	A1	20r rose ('85)	300.00	125.00
6	A1	25r rose	1.00	.35
a.		Perf. 13½	6.75	1.60
7	A1	25r violet ('85)	3.00	2.00
8	A1	40r blue	25.00	15.00
9	A1	40r yel buff ('81)	2.00	1.60
10	A1	50r green	60.00	20.00
a.		Perf. 12½	125.00	60.00
11	A1	50r blue ('81)	.75	.40
12	A1	100r lilac	1.00	.50
13	A1	200r orange	2.00	1.40
a.		Perf. 12½	5.25	4.50
14	A1	300r chocolate	2.25	2.00
		Nos. 1-4,6-14 (13)	117.00	50.10

The reprints of the 1877-85 issues are printed on a smooth white chalky paper, ungummed, with rough perforation 13½, also on thin white paper, with shiny white gum and clean-cut perforation 13½.

King Luiz — A2

Typographed and Embossed

		1886		**Perf. 12½**
15	A2	5r black (R)	1.50	.60
16	A2	10r green	1.50	.70
17	A2	20r rose	2.00	1.50
18	A2	25r dull lilac	9.00	1.40
19	A2	40r chocolate	1.75	.85
20	A2	50r blue	2.25	.50
21	A2	100r yellow brn	2.50	.50
22	A2	200r gray violet	4.25	1.75
23	A2	300r orange	4.50	2.00
		Nos. 15-23 (9)	29.25	9.80

Perf. 13½

15a	A2	5r	4.00	2.75
16a	A2	10r	4.25	2.75
17a	A2	20r	13.00	6.00
18a	A2	25r	13.00	6.00
19a	A2	40r	15.00	9.50
20a	A2	50r	16.00	4.50
22a	A2	200r	15.00	12.50
		Nos. 15a-22a (7)	80.25	44.00

Nos. 15, 18, 19, 20, 21 and 23 have been reprinted. The reprints have shiny white gum and clean-cut perforation 13½. Many of the colors are paler than those of the originals.
For surcharges and overprints see Nos. 23A, 36-44, 46-48, 72-80, 192, P1-P5.

No. 19 Surcharged in Black

Type I   Type II

Type III

There are three varieties of No. 23A:
I — "PROVISORIO" 19mm long, numerals 4½mm high.
II — "PROVISORIO" 19½mm long, numerals 5mm high.
III — "PROVISORIO" 19½mm long, numerals of both sizes.

1893, Jan.   **Perf. 12½**
Without Gum

23A	A2	5r on 40r choc	125.00	50.00

King Carlos I — A3

		1894	**Typo.**	**Perf. 11½, 12½**
24	A3	5r yellow	.50	.45
25	A3	10r red lilac	.50	.35
26	A3	15r red brown	1.25	.75
27	A3	20r gray lilac	1.25	.50
28	A3	25r blue green	1.25	.25
29	A3	50r lt blue	5.00	1.50
a.		Perf. 12½	7.50	2.00
30	A3	75r rose	1.75	1.25
31	A3	80r yellow grn	2.00	1.00
32	A3	100r brown, buff	1.75	1.25
33	A3	150r car, rose	8.00	4.00
a.		Perf. 11½		
34	A3	200r dk blue, blue	5.00	3.00
35	A3	300r dk blue, salmon	7.00	3.00
		Nos. 24-35 (12)	35.25	17.30

Nos. 28 and 31-33 have been reprinted with shiny white gum and clean-cut perf. 13½.
For surcharges and overprints see Nos. 45, 81-92, 193-198, 201-205, 226-228, 238-239.

Stamps of 1886 Overprinted in Red or Black

1895, July 1   **Perf. 12½**
Without Gum

36	A2	5r black (R)	11.00	5.50
37	A2	10r green	12.50	6.50
38	A2	20r rose	14.00	6.00
39	A2	25r violet	16.00	6.50
a.		Double overprint	200.00	
40	A2	40r chocolate	17.50	7.50
41	A2	50r blue	17.50	7.50
a.		Double overprint	80.00	55.00
42	A2	100r yellow brown	17.50	8.25
43	A2	200r gray violet	27.50	13.00
a.		Perf. 13½	100.00	65.00
44	A2	300r orange	37.50	17.50
		Nos. 36-44 (9)	171.00	78.25

Birth of Saint Anthony of Padua, 7th cent.

No. 35 Surcharged in Black

1897, Jan. 2   **Perf. 12½**
Without Gum

45	A3	50r on 300r dk bl, sal	150.00	40.00

Nos. 17, 19 Surcharged

a   b

c

		1898	**Without Gum**
46	A2 (a)	2½r on 20r rose	42.50	11.00
47	A2 (b)	2½r on 20r rose	27.50	10.00
a.		Inverted surcharge	55.00	45.00
48	A2 (c)	5r on 40r choc	35.00	10.00
a.		Inverted surcharge	90.00	45.00
		Nos. 46-48 (3)	105.00	31.00

King Carlos I — A4

Name and Value in Black except 500r

		1898-1903	**Typo.**	**Perf. 11½**
49	A4	2½r gray	.25	.25
50	A4	5r orange	.25	.25
51	A4	10r lt green	.25	.25
52	A4	15r brown	2.00	1.50
53	A4	15r gray grn ('03)	.70	.55
54	A4	20r gray violet	.85	.40
55	A4	25r sea green	.85	.40
56	A4	25r carmine ('03)	.70	.30
57	A4	50r dark blue	1.50	.50
58	A4	50r brown ('03)	2.00	1.50
59	A4	65r dull blue ('03)	15.00	12.00
60	A4	75r rose	7.00	2.75
61	A4	75r red lilac ('03)	3.00	1.75
62	A4	80r violet	6.00	3.25
63	A4	100r dk blue, bl	2.00	1.00
64	A4	115r dk blue, pink ('03)	10.00	5.00
65	A4	130r brown, straw ('03)	10.00	5.00
66	A4	150r brown, straw	10.00	2.75
67	A4	200r red lilac, pnksh	2.00	1.40
68	A4	300r dk blue, rose	8.00	3.25
69	A4	400r dl bl, straw ('03)	13.00	7.50
70	A4	500r blk & red, bl ('01)	20.00	8.00
71	A4	700r vio, yelsh ('01)	25.00	9.00
		Nos. 49-71 (23)	140.35	68.55

For overprints and surcharges see Nos. 94-113, 200, 207-220.

Stamps of 1886-94 Surcharged

On Stamps of 1886
Red Surcharge

		1902		**Perf. 12½, 13½**
72	A2	115r on 5r blk	5.00	2.00

Black Surcharge

73	A2	65r on 20r rose	5.00	2.50
a.		Double surcharge	50.00	50.00
74	A2	65r on 40r choc	6.00	4.00
75	A2	65r on 200r violet	5.00	1.75
76	A2	115r on 50r blue	2.00	1.00
77	A2	130r on 25r red vio	3.00	.90
78	A2	130r on 300r orange	3.00	.90
79	A2	400r on 10r green	7.50	3.25
80	A2	400r on 100r yel brn	40.00	25.00
		Nos. 72-80 (9)	76.50	41.30

The reprints of Nos. 74, 75, 76, 77, 79 and 80 have shiny white gum and clean-cut perforation 13½.

On Stamps of 1894
Perf. 11½

81	A3	65r on 10r red lil	3.50	2.00
82	A3	65r on 15r red brn	3.50	2.00
a.		Pair, one without surcharge		
83	A3	65r on 20r gray lil	3.75	2.00
84	A3	115r on 5r yel	4.00	2.00
a.		Inverted surcharge		
85	A3	115r on 25r bl grn	3.50	2.00
86	A3	130r on 75r rose	4.00	2.25
87	A3	130r on 100r brn, buff	6.00	5.00
88	A3	130r on 150r car, rose	4.00	2.00
89	A3	130r on 200r bl, bl	5.00	3.50
90	A3	400r on 50r lt bl	1.00	1.40
91	A3	400r on 80r yel grn	1.00	1.40
92	A3	400r on 300r bl, sal	1.00	1.40

On Newspaper Stamp of 1893
Perf. 13½

93	N3	115r on 2½r brn	2.00	2.25
		Nos. 81-93 (13)	42.25	29.20

Reprints of No. 87 have shiny white gum and clean-cut perforation 13½.

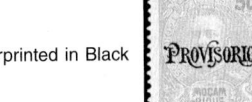

Overprinted in Black

On Stamps of 1898
Perf. 11½

94	A4	15r brown	2.00	.85
95	A4	25r sea green	2.50	.85
96	A4	50r blue	3.00	1.75
97	A4	75r rose	5.00	2.00
		Nos. 94-97 (4)	12.50	5.45

No. 59 Surcharged in Black

1905

98	A4	50r on 65r dull blue	3.00	2.00

Stamps of 1898-1903 Overprinted in Carmine or Green

1911

99	A4	2½r gray	.30	.25
a.		Inverted overprint	15.00	15.00
100	A4	5r orange	.30	.25
101	A4	10r lt green	2.00	.50
102	A4	15r gray grn	.30	.25
103	A4	20r gray vio	2.00	.40
104	A4	25r carmine (G)	.30	.25
a.		25r gray violet (error)		
105	A4	50r brown	.50	.25
106	A4	75r red lilac	1.00	.50
107	A4	100r dk blue, bl	1.00	.50
108	A4	115r org brn, pink	1.50	.50
109	A4	130r brown, straw	1.50	.85
a.		Double overprint		
110	A4	200r red lil, pnksh	3.00	.70
111	A4	400r dull bl, straw	3.50	.85
112	A4	500r blk & red, bl	4.00	.85
113	A4	700r vio, straw	4.50	.85
		Nos. 99-113 (15)	25.70	8.10

King Manoel — A5

Overprinted in Carmine or Green

		1912		**Perf. 11½x12**
114	A5	2½r violet	.25	.25
115	A5	5r black	.25	.25
116	A5	10r gray grn	.25	.25

117	A5	20r carmine (G)	.55	.40
118	A5	25r vio brn	.25	.25
119	A5	50r dp blue	.50	.35
120	A5	75r bis brn	.50	.35
121	A5	100r brn, *lt grn*	.50	.35
122	A5	200r dk grn, *salmon*	1.00	.70
123	A5	300r black, *azure*	1.00	.70

Perf. 14x15

124	A5	500r ol grn & vio brn	2.00	1.25
		Nos. 114-124 (11)	7.05	5.10

Vasco da Gama Issue of Various Portuguese Colonies Common Design Types Surcharged

1913   **On Stamps of Macao**

125	CD20	¼c on ½a bl grn	1.50	1.50
126	CD21	½c on 1a red	1.50	1.50
127	CD22	1c on 2a red vio	1.50	1.50
128	CD23	2½c on 4a yel grn	1.50	1.50
a.		Double surcharge	50.00	50.00
129	CD24	5c on 8a dk bl	2.50	2.50
130	CD25	7½c on 12a vio brn	2.00	2.00
131	CD26	10c on 16a bis brn	1.75	1.50
132	CD27	15c on 24a bis	1.50	1.50
		Nos. 125-132 (8)	13.75	13.50

On Stamps of Portuguese Africa

133	CD20	¼c on 2½a bl grn	1.25	1.25
134	CD21	½c on 5r red	1.25	1.25
135	CD22	1c on 10r red vio	1.25	1.25
a.		Inverted surcharge	45.00	45.00
136	CD23	2½c on 25r yel grn	1.25	1.25
137	CD24	5c on 50r dk bl	1.25	1.25
138	CD25	7½c on 75r vio brn	1.75	1.75
139	CD26	10c on 100r bis brn	1.50	1.50
140	CD27	15c on 150r bis	1.50	1.50
		Nos. 133-140 (8)	11.00	11.00

On Stamps of Timor

141	CD20	¼c on ½a bl grn	1.50	1.50
142	CD21	½c on 1a red	1.50	1.50
143	CD22	1c on 2a red vio	1.50	1.50
144	CD23	2½c on 4a yel grn	1.50	1.50
145	CD24	5c on 8a dk bl	1.50	1.50
146	CD25	7½c on 12a vio brn	3.00	3.00
147	CD26	10c on 16a bis brn	1.50	1.50
148	CD27	15c on 24a bis	2.00	2.00
		Nos. 141-148 (8)	14.00	14.00
		Nos. 125-148 (24)	38.75	38.50

Ceres — A6

1914   **Typo.**   **Perf. 15x14**
Name and Value in Black
Chalky Paper

149	A6	¼c olive brown	.35	.25
		Never hinged	.55	
150	A6	½c black	.35	.25
		Never hinged	.55	
151	A6	1c blue green	.35	.25
		Never hinged	.55	
152	A6	1½c lilac brown	.35	.25
		Never hinged	.55	
153	A6	2c carmine	.40	.25
		Never hinged	.65	
154	A6	2½c lt vio	.40	.25
		Never hinged	.65	
155	A6	5c deep blue	.40	.25
		Never hinged	.65	
156	A6	7½c yel brn	1.45	.75
		Never hinged	2.25	
157	A6	8c slate	1.45	.75
		Never hinged	2.25	
158	A6	10c org brn	1.45	.75
		Never hinged	2.25	
159	A6	15c plum	3.00	1.40
		Never hinged	4.75	
160	A6	20c yellow green	1.45	.95
		Never hinged	2.25	
161	A6	30c brown, *grn*	1.50	1.10
		Never hinged	2.40	
163	A6	40c brn, *pink*	1.25	.85
		Never hinged	2.00	
164	A6	50c org, *salmon*	2.75	3.00
		Never hinged	4.50	
165	A6	1e black, *bl,*	18.00	7.00
		Never hinged	29.00	
		Nos. 149-165 (16)	34.90	18.30

1919-26   **Ordinary Paper**

166	A6	¼c olive brown	.25	.25
		Never hinged	.40	
a.		Name and value printed twice	12.00	
		Never hinged	19.00	
b.		Name and value printed triple		
c.		Thick carton paper	8.00	
		Never hinged	13.00	

167	A6	½c black	.25	.25
		Never hinged	.40	
168	A6	1c blue green	.25	.25
		Never hinged	.40	
169	A6	1½c lilac brown	.25	.25
		Never hinged	.40	
170	A6	2c carmine	.25	.25
		Never hinged	.40	
171	A6	2½c lt vio	.25	.25
		Never hinged	.40	
172	A6	3c org ('21)	.25	.25
		Never hinged	.40	
a.		Name and value printed twice	—	
173	A6	4c pale rose ('21)	.25	.25
		Never hinged	.40	
174	A6	4½c gray ('21)	.25	.25
		Never hinged	.40	
175	A6	5c deep blue	.25	.25
		Never hinged	.40	
176	A6	7c ultra ('21)	.25	.25
		Never hinged	.40	
177	A6	7½c yel brn	.25	.25
		Never hinged	.40	
178	A6	8c slate	.25	.25
		Never hinged	.40	
179	A6	10c org brn	.25	.25
		Never hinged	.40	
180	A6	30c deep green ('21)	.75	.50
		Never hinged	1.20	
181	A6	1e rose	1.40	.85
		Never hinged	2.25	
		Nos. 166-181 (16)	5.65	4.85

Perf. 12x11½

182	A6	¼c olive brown	.30	.25
		Never hinged	.50	
183	A6	½c black	.25	.25
		Never hinged	.40	
184	A6	1c blue green	.50	.25
		Never hinged	.80	
a.		Name and value printed twice	16.00	
		Never hinged	26.00	
185	A6	1½c lilac brown	.25	.25
		Never hinged	.40	
186	A6	2c carmine	.25	.25
		Never hinged	.40	
187	A6	2c gray ('26)	.25	.25
		Never hinged	.40	
188	A6	2½c lt vio	.25	.25
		Never hinged	.40	
189	A6	3c org ('21)	.25	.25
		Never hinged	.40	
190	A6	4c pale rose ('21)	.25	.25
		Never hinged	.40	
a.		Name and value printed twice	16.00	
		Never hinged	26.00	
b.		Value omitted	15.00	
		Never hinged	24.00	
c.		4c carmine rose	.25	.25
		Never hinged	.40	
191	A6	4½c gray ('21)	.25	.25
		Never hinged	.40	
191A	A6	6c lilac ('21)	.25	.25
		Never hinged	.40	
191B	A6	7c ultra ('21)	.25	.25
		Never hinged	.40	
a.		Name and value printed twice		
191C	A6	7½c yel brn	.25	.25
		Never hinged	.40	
191D	A6	8c slate	.25	.25
		Never hinged	.40	
191E	A6	10c org brn	.25	.25
		Never hinged	.40	
191F	A6	12c gray brn ('21)	.25	.25
		Never hinged	.40	
191G	A6	12c blue grn ('22)	.25	.25
		Never hinged	.40	
191H	A6	15c plum	.65	.35
		Never hinged	1.05	
191I	A6	15c brn rose ('22)	.25	.25
		Never hinged	.40	
191J	A6	20c yel grn	.25	.25
		Never hinged	.40	
191K	A6	24c ultra ('26)	4.50	2.00
		Never hinged	7.25	
191L	A6	25c choc ('26)	1.50	1.25
		Never hinged	2.40	
191M	A6	30c deep green ('21)	1.00	.25
		Never hinged	1.60	
191N	A6	40c turq blue ('22)	1.00	.30
		Never hinged	1.60	
191O	A6	50c lt violet ('26)	.50	.25
		Never hinged	.80	
191P	A6	60c dk blue ('22)	1.00	.30
		Never hinged	1.60	
191Q	A6	60c rose ('26)	1.10	.25
		Never hinged	1.75	
191R	A6	80c brt rose ('22)	1.60	1.25
		Never hinged	2.50	
191S	A6	80c rose ('22)	1.00	.25
		Never hinged	1.60	
191T	A6	1e rose ('22)	1.60	.50
		Never hinged	2.50	
		Nos. 182-191T (30)	20.50	11.70

For surcharges see Nos. 232-234, 236-237, 249-250, J46-50.

1921   **Chalky Paper**

191U	A6	40c brown, *pink* ('21)	1.25	.85
		Never hinged	2.00	
191V	A6	60c red brn, *pink*	1.00	.60
		Never hinged	1.60	
191W	A6	80c dk brn, *bl* ('21)	1.40	.60
		Never hinged	2.25	
191X	A6	1e grn, *bl,*	1.40	.60
		Never hinged	2.25	
191Y	A6	2e brt vio, *pink*	1.40	.60
		Never hinged	2.25	

Perf. 15x14

191Z	A6	30c gray bl, *pink* ('21)	1.50	1.25
		Never hinged	2.40	
		Nos. 191U-191Z (6)	7.95	4.50

Stamps of 1902 Overprinted Locally in Carmine

1915
On Provisional Stamps of 1902

192	A2	115r on 5r black	175.00	100.00
193	A3	115r on 5r yellow	1.25	.75
194	A3	115r on 25r bl grn	1.25	.75
195	A3	130r on 75r rose	1.25	.75
196	A3	130r on 100r brn, *buff*	1.25	.75
197	A3	130r on 150r car, *rose*	1.25	.75
198	A3	130r on 200r bl, *bl*	1.25	.75
199	N3	115r on 2½r brn	.80	.40

On No. 97

200	A4	75r rose	1.50	1.10
		Nos. 192-200 (9)	184.80	106.00

Stamps of 1902-05 Overprinted in Carmine

1915
On Provisional Stamps of 1902

201	A3	115r on 5r yellow	.80	.50
202	A3	115r on 25r bl grn	.80	.55
203	A3	130r on 75r rose	.80	.55
204	A3	130r on 150r car, *rose*	1.00	.50
205	A3	130r on 200r bl, *bl*	1.00	.50
206	N3	115r on 2½r brn	1.00	.50

On No. 96

207	A4	50r blue	1.00	.50

On No. 98

208	A4	50r on 65r dull blue	1.00	.50
		Nos. 201-208 (8)	7.40	4.10

Stamps of 1898-1903 Overprinted Locally in Carmine Like Nos. 192-200

1917

209	A4	2½r gray	20.00	17.50
210	A4	15r gray grn	15.00	12.50
211	A4	20r gray vio	15.00	12.50
212	A4	50r brown	14.00	11.00
213	A4	75r red lilac	32.50	25.00
214	A4	100r blue, *bl*	6.00	2.50
215	A4	115r org brn, *pink*	8.00	2.50
216	A4	130r brown, *straw*	7.50	3.00
217	A4	200r red lil, *pnksh*	7.50	2.50
218	A4	400r dull bl, *straw*	7.50	3.00
219	A4	500r blk & red, *bl*	7.00	2.50
220	A4	700r vio, *yelsh*	15.00	6.00
		Nos. 209-220 (12)	155.00	101.00

War Tax Stamps of 1916-18 Surcharged

1918   **Rouletted 7**

221	WT2	2½c on 5c rose	2.50	1.50

Perf. 11, 12

222	WT2	2½c on 5c red	1.10	.70
a.		"PETRIA"	3.00	2.00
b.		"PEPUBLICA"	3.00	2.00
c.		"1910" for "1916"	9.00	4.00

War Tax Stamps of 1916-18 Surcharged

1919   **Perf. 11**

224	WT1	1c on 1c gray grn	.75	.40
a.		"PEPUBLICA"	4.75	4.00

b.		Rouletted 7	300.00	100.00

Perf. 12

225	WT2	1½c on 5c red	.40	.35
a.		"PETRIA"	3.00	2.00
b.		"PEPUBLICA"	3.00	2.50

Stamps of 1902 Overprinted Locally in Carmine Like Nos. 192-200

1920

226	A3	400r on 50r lt blue	1.25	1.25
227	A3	400r on 80r yel grn	1.25	1.25
228	A3	400r on 300r bl, *sal*	1.25	1.25
		Nos. 226-228 (3)	3.75	3.75

War Tax Stamp of 1918 Surcharged in Green

1920   **Perf. 12**

229	WT2	6c on 5c red	.60	.50
a.		"1910" for "1916"	9.00	5.00
b.		"PETRIA"	2.50	2.00
c.		"PEPUBLICA"	2.50	2.00

Lourenco Marques Nos. 117, 119 Surcharged in Red or Bue

1921   **Perf. 15x14**

230	A4	10c on ½c blk (R)	.75	.40
		Never hinged	1.20	
231	A4	30c on 1½c brn (Bl)	1.25	.70
		Never hinged	2.00	

Same Surcharge on Mozambique Nos. 150, 152, 155 in Red, Blue or Green

232	A6	10c on ½c blk (R)	1.00	.85
		Never hinged	1.60	
233	A6	30c on 1½c brn (Bl)	1.10	.70
		Never hinged	1.75	
a.		Double surcharge	30.00	30.00
		Never hinged	47.50	
234	A6	60c on 2½c vio (G)	1.50	.80
		Never hinged	2.40	
		Nos. 230-234 (5)	5.60	3.45

War Tax Stamp of 1918 Surcharged in Green

1921   **Perf. 12**

235	WT2	2e on 5c red	1.00	.50
a.		"PETRIA"	2.50	2.25
b.		"PEPUBLICA"	4.25	2.50
c.		"1910" for "1916"	9.00	6.50

No. 157 Surcharged

1923   **Perf. 12x11½**

236	A6	50c on 4c pale rose	1.00	.55
		Never hinged	1.60	

No. 183 Overprinted in Green

1924

237	A6	80c bright rose	1.00	.60
		Never hinged	1.60	

4th centenary of the death of Vasco da Gama.

Nos. 90 and 91
Surcharged

1925 *Perf. 11½*
238 A3 40c on 400r on 50r .70 .70
239 A3 40c on 400r on 80r .60 .50
  a. "a" omitted 42.50 42.50

Glazed Paper
1922-26 *Perf. 12x11½*
240 A6 1e blue ('26) 1.60 .65
  Never hinged 2.50
241 A6 2e dk violet ('22) 1.00 .35
  Never hinged 1.60
242 A6 5e buff ('26) 8.00 2.50
  Never hinged 16.00
243 A6 10e pink ('26) 15.00 5.00
  Never hinged 24.00
244 A6 20e pale turq ('26) 40.00 17.50
  Never hinged 65.00

Postage Due Stamp
of 1917 Overprinted
in Black and Bars in
Red

1929, Jan. *Perf. 12*
247 D1 50c gray .85 .55

No. 188 Surcharged

1931 *Perf. 11½*
249 A6 70c on 2e dk vio 1.00 .50
  Never hinged 1.60
250 A6 1.40e on 2e dk vio 1.50 .50
  Never hinged 2.40

"Portugal" Holding
Volume of the
"Lusiads" — A7

Wmk. Maltese Cross (232)
1933, July 13 Typo. *Perf. 14*
Value in Red or Black
251 A7 1c bister brn (R) .25 .25
252 A7 5c black brn .25 .25
253 A7 10c dp violet .25 .25
254 A7 15c black (R) .25 .25
255 A7 20c light gray .25 .25
256 A7 30c blue green .25 .25
257 A7 40c orange red .25 .25
258 A7 45c brt blue .40 .25
259 A7 50c dk brown .30 .25
260 A7 60c olive grn .25 .25
261 A7 70c orange brn .25 .25
262 A7 80c emerald .25 .25
263 A7 85c deep rose 1.00 .50
264 A7 1e red brown .75 .25
265 A7 1.40e dk blue (R) 7.00 1.10
266 A7 2e dk violet 2.00 .35
267 A7 5e apple green 3.00 .50
268 A7 10e olive bister 7.00 1.00
269 A7 20e orange 22.50 2.00
  Nos. 251-269 (19) 46.45 8.70

See Nos. 298-299 in Scott Standard catalogue, Vol. 4.

Common Design Types
pictured following the introduction.

Common Design Types
Perf. 13½x13
1938, Aug. Engr. Unwmk.
Name and Value in Black
270 CD34 1c gray green .25 .25
271 CD34 5c orange brn .25 .25
272 CD34 10c dk carmine .25 .25
273 CD34 15c dk vio brn .25 .25
274 CD34 20c slate .25 .25
275 CD34 30c rose vio .25 .25
276 CD35 35c brt green .30 .25
277 CD35 40c brown .40 .25

---

278 CD35 50c brt red vio .40 .25
279 CD36 60c gray black .50 .25
280 CD36 70c brown vio .50 .25
281 CD36 80c orange .75 .25
282 CD36 1e red .70 .25
283 CD37 1.75e blue 1.75 .30
284 CD37 2e brown car 1.50 .30
285 CD37 5e olive green 3.50 .50
286 CD38 10e blue vio 9.00 1.00
287 CD38 20e red brown 22.50 1.40
  Nos. 270-287 (18) 43.30 6.75

For surcharges see Nos. 297, 301 in Scott Standard catalogue, Vol. 4.

No. 258 Surcharged in
Black

1938, Jan. 16 Wmk. 232 Perf. 14
288 A7 40c on 45c brt blue 2.50 1.40

Map of Africa —
A7a

Perf. 11½x12
1939, July 17 Litho. Unwmk.
289 A7a 80c vio, *pale rose* 1.50 1.25
290 A7a 1.75e bl, *pale bl* 4.00 2.75
291 A7a 3e grn, *yel grn* 6.00 4.00
292 A7a 20e brn, *buff* 30.00 50.00
  Nos. 289-292 (4) 41.50 58.00

Presidential visit.

SEMI-POSTAL STAMPS

"History"
Pointing
out to "the
Republic"
Need for
Charity
SP1

Nurse
Leading
Wounded
Soldiers
SP2

Veteran Relating Experiences — SP3

Perf. 11½
1920, Dec. 1 Litho. Unwmk.
B1 SP1 ¼c olive 3.50 3.50
B2 SP1 ½c olive blk 3.50 3.50
B3 SP1 1c dp bister 3.50 3.50
B4 SP1 2c lilac brn 3.50 3.50
B5 SP1 3c lilac 3.50 3.50
B6 SP1 4c green 3.50 3.50
B7 SP2 5c grnsh blue 3.50 3.50
B8 SP2 6c light blue 3.50 3.50
B9 SP2 7½c red brown 3.50 3.50
B10 SP2 8c lemon 3.50 3.50
B11 SP2 10c gray lilac 3.50 3.50
B12 SP2 12c pink 3.50 3.50
B13 SP3 18c rose 3.50 3.50
B14 SP3 24c vio brn 3.50 3.50
B15 SP3 30c pale ol grn 3.50 3.50
B16 SP3 40c dull red 3.50 3.50

B17 SP3 50c yellow 3.50 3.50
B18 SP3 1e ultra 3.50 3.50
  Nos. B1-B18 (18) 63.00 63.00

Nos. B1-B18 were used Dec. 1, 1920, in place of ordinary stamps. The proceeds were for war victims.

AIR POST STAMPS

Common Design Type
Perf. 13½x13
1938, Aug. Engr. Unwmk.
Name and Value in Black
C1 CD39 10c scarlet .30 .25
C2 CD39 20c purple .30 .25
C3 CD39 50c orange .30 .25
C4 CD39 1e ultra .40 .30
C5 CD39 2e lilac brn 1.00 .30
C6 CD39 3e dk green 1.75 .40
C7 CD39 5e red brown 2.10 .70
C8 CD39 9e rose car 4.25 .75
C9 CD39 10e magenta 7.25 1.25
  Nos. C1-C9 (9) 17.65 4.45

No. C7 exists with overprint "Exposicao Internacional de Nova York, 1939-1940" and Trylon and Perisphere.

POSTAGE DUE STAMPS

D1

1904 Unwmk. Typo. Perf. 11½x12
Name and Value in Black
J1 D1 5r yellow grn .40 .25
J2 D1 10r slate .40 .25
J3 D1 20r yellow brn .40 .25
J4 D1 30r orange .80 .70
J5 D1 50r gray brn .70 .55
J6 D1 60r red brown 3.50 1.75
J7 D1 100r red lilac 3.00 1.75
J8 D1 130r dull blue 1.50 1.20
J9 D1 200r carmine 2.00 1.20
J10 D1 500r violet 2.50 1.20
  Nos. J1-J10 (10) 15.20 9.10

See J34-J43. For overprints see Nos. 247, J11-J30.

Same Overprinted in
Carmine or Green

1911
J11 D1 5r yellow green .25 .25
J12 D1 10r slate .40 .25
J13 D1 20r yellow brn .30 .25
J14 D1 30r orange .30 .25
J15 D1 50r gray brown .40 .30
J16 D1 60r red brown .60 .35
J17 D1 100r red lilac .80 .55
J18 D1 130r dull blue 1.10 .80
J19 D1 200r carmine (G) 1.20 .95
J20 D1 500r violet 1.60 .95
  Nos. J11-J20 (10) 6.95 4.90

Nos. J1-J10
Overprinted Locally in
Carmine

1916
J21 D1 5r yellow grn 4.00 3.25
J22 D1 10r slate 5.50 3.25
J23 D1 20r yellow brn 80.00 60.00
J24 D1 30r orange 22.50 17.50
J25 D1 50r gray brown 80.00 55.00
J26 D1 60r red brown 65.00 45.00
J27 D1 100r red lilac 80.00 60.00
J28 D1 130r dull blue 2.40 2.25
J29 D1 200r carmine 2.75 3.00
J30 D1 500r violet 5.50 4.75
  Nos. J21-J30 (10) 347.65 249.00

War Tax
Stamps of
1916 Ovptd.
Diagonally

1918 *Rouletted 7*
J31 WT1 1c gray green .95 .80
J32 WT2 5c rose .95 .80
  a. Inverted overprint 8.25 7.50
Perf. 11
J33 WT1 1c gray green .95 .80
  a. "PEPUBLICA" 50.00 40.00
  Nos. J31-J33 (3) 2.85 2.40

**Type of 1904 Issue With Value in
Centavos**
1917 *Perf. 12*
J34 D1 ½c yellow green .30 .30
J35 D1 1c slate .30 .30
J36 D1 2c orange brown .30 .30
J37 D1 3c orange .30 .30
J38 D1 5c gray brown .30 .30
J39 D1 6c pale brn .30 .30
J40 D1 10c red violet .30 .30
J41 D1 13c deep blue .55 .55
J42 D1 20c rose .55 .55
J43 D1 50c gray .55 .55
  Nos. J34-J43 (10) 3.75 3.75

Lourenco Marques Nos.
117, 119 Surcharged in
Red

1921
J44 A4 5c on ½c blk 1.60 .95
J45 A4 10c on 1½c brn 1.60 .95

**Same Surcharge on Mozambique
Nos. 151, 155, 157 in Red or Green**
J46 A6 6c on 1c bl grn (R) 1.60 .95
  Never hinged 2.50
J47 A6 20c on 2½c vio (R) 1.00 .85
  Never hinged 1.60
  a. Inverted surcharge 7.50 7.50
  Never hinged 12.00
J48 A6 50c on 4c rose (G) 1.00 .85
  Never hinged 1.60
  a. Inverted surcharge 8.50 8.50
  Never hinged 13.50
  Nos. J44-J48 (5) 6.80 4.55

Regular Issues of 1921-
22 Surcharged in Black
or Red

1924 *Perf. 12x11½*
J49 A6 20c on 30c ol grn (Bk) 1.10 .45
  Never hinged 1.75
  a. Perf. 15x14 19.00 4.50
  Never hinged 30.00
J50 A6 50c on 60c dk bl (R) 1.00 1.00
  Never hinged 1.60

WAR TAX STAMPS

Coats of Arms of Portugal and
Mozambique on Columns, Allegorical
Figures of History of Portugal and the
Republic Holding Scroll with Date of
Declaration of War — WT1

No. 258 Surcharged in Black (40 centavos)

Prow of Galley of Discoveries. Left, "Republic" Teaching History of Portugal; Right "History" with Laurels (Victory) and Sword (Symbolical of Declaration of War) — WT2

1916   Unwmk.   Litho.   Rouletted 7

MR1	WT1	1c gray green	2.25	.55
a.		Imperf., pair	15.00	
MR2	WT2	5c rose	2.25	.55
a.		Imperf., pair	15.00	

1918   Perf. 11, 12

MR3	WT1	1c gray green	.85	.55
a.		"PEPUBLICA"	8.50	4.75
MR4	WT2	5c red	1.00	.70
a.		"PETRIA"	3.50	3.50
b.		"PEPUBLICA"	3.50	3.50
c.		"1910" for "1916"	11.00	5.50
d.		Imperf., pair	6.35	2.35
		Nos. MR1-MR4 (4)	6.35	2.35

For surcharges and overprints see Nos. 221-225, 229, 235, J31-J33.

NEWSPAPER STAMPS

No. 19 Surcharged in Black, Red or Blue

      a   b

1893   Unwmk.   Perf. 11½, 12½, 13½

P1	A2 (a)	2½r on 40r	200.00	90.00
P2	A2 (a)	5r on 40r	175.00	90.00
P3	A2 (a)	5r on 40r (R)	150.00	75.00
P4	A2 (a)	5r on 40r (Bl)	180.00	75.00
P5	A2 (b)	2½r on 40r	22.50	16.00
		Nos. P1-P5 (5)	727.50	346.00

Nos. P1-P5 exist with double surcharge, Nos. P2-P4 with inverted surcharge.

N3

1893   Typo.   Perf. 11½, 13½

P6	N3	2½r brown	.35	.30

For surcharge and overprint see Nos. 93, 199, 206.

No. P6 has been reprinted on chalk-surfaced paper with clean-cut perforation 13½. Value, 50 cents.

POSTAL TAX STAMPS

Pombal Commemorative Issue
Common Design Types

1925   Engr.   Perf. 12½

RA1	CD28	15c brown & black	.30	.25
RA2	CD29	15c brown & black	.30	.25
RA3	CD30	15c brown & black	.30	.25
		Nos. RA1-RA3 (3)	.90	.75

Seal of Local Red Cross Society
PT7   PT8

Surcharged in Various Colors

1925   Typo.   Perf. 11½

RA4	PT7	50c slate & yel (Bk)	1.60	1.60

1926

RA5	PT8	100 slate & yel (Dk)	3.25	3.25
RA6	PT8	50c slate & yel (R)	3.25	3.25
RA7	PT8	60c slate & yel (V)	3.25	3.25
RA8	PT8	80c slate & yel (Br)	3.25	3.25
RA9	PT8	1e slate & yel (Bl)	3.25	3.25
RA10	PT8	2e slate & yel (G)	3.25	3.25
		Nos. RA5-RA10 (6)	19.50	19.50

Obligatory on mail certain days of the year. The tax benefited the Cross of the Orient Society.

Type of 1926 Issue

1927   Black Surcharge

RA11	PT8	5c red & yel	3.25	3.25
RA12	PT8	10c green & yel	3.25	3.25
RA13	PT8	20c gray & yel	3.25	3.25
RA14	PT8	30c lt bl & yel	3.25	3.25
RA15	PT8	40c vio & yel	3.25	3.25
RA16	PT8	50c car & yel	3.25	3.25
RA17	PT8	60c brown & yel	3.25	3.25
RA18	PT8	80c blue & yel	3.25	3.25
RA19	PT8	1e olive & yel	3.25	3.25
RA20	PT8	2e yel brn & yel	3.25	3.25
		Nos. RA11-RA20 (10)	32.50	32.50

See note after No. RA10.

PT9

1928   Litho.

RA21	PT9	5c grn, yel & blk	4.50	4.50
RA22	PT9	10c sl bl, yel & blk	4.50	4.50
RA23	PT9	20c gray blk, yel & blk	4.50	4.50
RA24	PT9	30c brn rose, yel & blk	4.50	4.50
RA25	PT9	40c cl brn, yel & blk	4.50	4.50
RA26	PT9	50c red org, yel & blk	4.50	4.50
RA27	PT9	60c brn, yel & blk	4.50	4.50
RA28	PT9	80c dk brn, yel & blk	4.50	4.50
RA29	PT9	1e gray, yel & blk	4.50	4.50
RA30	PT9	2e red, yel & blk	4.50	4.50
		Nos. RA21-RA30 (10)	45.00	45.00

See note after RA10.

Mother and Children — PT10

1929   Photo.   Perf. 14

RA31	PT10	40c ultra, cl & blk	2.75	2.75

The use of this stamp was compulsory on all correspondence to Portugal and Portuguese Colonies for eight days beginning July 24, 1929.
See Nos. RA39-RA47.

Mousinho de Albuquerque
PT11

1930-31   Perf. 14½x14

Inscribed: "MACONTENE"

RA32	PT11	50c lake, red & gray	3.50	4.00

Inscribed: "COOLELA"

RA33	PT11	50c red vio, red brn & gray	3.50	4.00

Inscribed: "MUJENGA"

RA34	PT11	50c org red, red & gray	3.50	4.00

Inscribed: "CHAIMITE"

RA35	PT11	50c dp grn, bl grn		

Inscribed: "IBRAHIMO"

RA36	PT11	50c dk bl, blk & gray	3.50	4.00

Inscribed: "MUCUTO-MUNO"

RA37	PT11	50c ultra, blk & gray	3.50	4.00

Inscribed: "NAGUEMA"

RA38	PT11	50c dk vio, lt vio & gray	3.50	4.00
		Nos. RA32-RA38 (7)	24.50	28.00

The portrait is that of Mousinho de Albuquerque, the celebrated Portuguese warrior, and the names of seven battles in which he took part appear at the foot of the stamps. The stamps were issued for the memorial fund bearing his name and their use was obligatory on all correspondence posted on eight specific days in the year.

Type of 1929 Issue
Denominations in Black
No. RA42 Without Denomination

1931   Perf. 14

RA39	PT10	40c rose & vio	4.00	3.25
RA40	PT10	40c ol grn & vio ('32)	5.50	4.50
RA41	PT10	40c bis brn & rose ('33)	5.50	4.50
RA42	PT10	bl grn & rose ('34)	3.75	3.50
RA43	PT10	40c org & ultra ('36)	5.50	4.50
RA44	PT10	40c choc & ultra ('37)	5.50	4.50
RA45	PT10	40c grn & brn car ('38)	7.50	5.50
RA46	PT10	40c yel & blk ('39)	7.50	5.50
RA47	PT10	40c gray brn ('40)	7.50	5.50
		Nos. RA39-RA47 (9)	52.25	41.25

POSTAL TAX DUE STAMPS

Pombal Commemorative Issue
Common Design Types

1925   Unwmk.   Perf. 12½

RAJ1	CD28	30c brown & black	.55	.65
RAJ2	CD29	30c brown & black	.55	.65
RAJ3	CD30	30c brown & black	.55	.65
		Nos. RAJ1-RAJ3 (3)	1.65	1.95

MOZAMBIQUE COMPANY

mō-zəm-'bēk 'kəmp-nē

LOCATION — Comprises the territory of Manica and Sofala of the Mozambique Colony in southeastern Africa
GOVT. — A part of the Portuguese Colony of Mozambique
AREA — 51,881 sq. mi.
POP. — 368,447 (1939)
CAPITAL — Beira

The Mozambique Company was chartered by Portugal in 1891 for 50 years. The territory was under direct administration of the Company until July 18, 1941

1000 Reis = 1 Milreis
100 Centavos = 1 Escudo (1916)

Mozambique Nos. 15-23 Overprinted in Carmine or Black

1892   Unwmk.   Perf. 12½, 13½

1	A2	5r black (C)	2.00	2.00
a.		Pair, one without overprint	50.00	22.50
2	A2	10r green	2.00	.50
3	A2	20r rose	2.00	.50
a.		Perf. 13½	45.00	30.00
4	A2	25r violet	2.00	.45
a.		Double overprint	27.50	

5	A2	40r chocolate	2.00	.45
a.		Double overprint	20.00	
6	A2	50r blue	2.00	.50
7	A2	100r yellow brown	2.00	.75
8	A2	200r gray violet	2.50	.90
9	A2	300r orange	3.50	.90
		Nos. 1-9 (8)	20.00	5.45

Nos. 1 to 6, 8-9 were reprinted in 1905. These reprints have white gum and clean-cut perf. 13½ and the colors are usually paler than those of the originals.

Company Coat of Arms — A2

Perf. 11½, 12½, 13½

1895-1907   Typo.

Black or Red Numerals

10	A2	2½r olive yellow	.25	.25
11	A2	2½r gray ('07)	1.50	1.50
12	A2	5r orange	.25	.25
a.		Value omitted	15.00	
b.		Perf. 13½	2.00	1.10
13	A2	10r red lilac	.40	.30
14	A2	10r yel grn ('07)	2.50	.40
a.		Value inverted at top of stamp	20.00	20.00
15	A2	15r red brown	1.00	.30
16	A2	15r dk green ('07)	2.50	.40
17	A2	20r gray lilac	1.50	.30
18	A2	25r green	.75	.30
a.		Perf. 13½	1.90	1.25
19	A2	25r carmine ('07)	2.50	.60
a.		Value omitted	15.00	10.00
20	A2	50r blue	.90	.30
21	A2	50r brown ('07)	2.50	.60
a.		Value omitted	15.00	
22	A2	65r slate blue ('02)	.75	.30
23	A2	75r rose	.70	.30
24	A2	75r red lilac ('07)	5.00	1.00
25	A2	80r yellow green	.50	.30
26	A2	100r brown, buff	1.00	.30
27	A2	100r dk bl, bl ('07)	4.00	1.00
28	A2	115r car, pink ('04)	1.25	.70
29	A2	115r org brn, pink ('07)	6.00	1.40
30	A2	130r grn, pink ('04)	1.50	.70
31	A2	130r brn, yel ('07)	6.00	1.40
32	A2	150r org brn, pink	1.00	.60
33	A2	200r dk blue, bl	1.00	.90
a.		Perf. 13½	2.00	1.60
34	A2	200r red lil, pink ('07)	7.00	1.40
35	A2	300r dk brn, salmon	1.10	.90
a.		Perf. 13½	2.50	1.40
36	A2	400r brn, bl ('04)	2.50	1.10
37	A2	400r dl bl, yel ('07)	8.00	3.25
38	A2	500r blk & red	1.10	.75
39	A2	500r blk & red, bl ('07)	8.00	1.90
a.		500r pur & red, yel (error)		
40	A2	700r slate, buff ('04)	8.50	2.00
41	A2	700r pur, yel ('07)	5.00	2.00
42	A2	1000r violet & red	1.50	1.00
		Nos. 10-42 (33)	87.95	28.75

#12b, 18a, 33a, 35a were issued without gum.
For overprints & surcharges see #43-107, B1-B7.

Nos. 25 and 6 Surcharged or Overprinted in Red

      b   c

1895   Perf. 12½, 13½

43	A2(b)	25r on 80r yel grn	22.50	16.00
44	A2(c)	50r blue	9.00	4.00

Overprint "c" on No. 44 also exists reading from upper left to lower right.

Stamps of 1895 Overprinted in Bister, Orange, Violet, Green, Black or Brown

1898   Perf. 12½, 13½
Without Gum

45	A2	2½r olive yel (Bi)	5.00	1.50
a.		Double overprint	40.00	25.00
b.		Red overprint	60.00	50.00

46	A2	5r orange (O)	7.00	1.50
47	A2	10r red lilac (V)	7.00	1.50
48	A2	15r red brown (V)	10.00	3.00
a.		Red overprint		
49	A2	20r gray lilac (V)	10.00	3.00
50	A2	25r green (G)	12.00	3.00
a.		Inverted overprint	65.00	40.00
51	A2	50r blue (Bk)	12.00	4.00
a.		Inverted overprint	60.00	40.00
52	A2	75r rose (V)	12.50	5.00
a.		Inverted overprint	75.00	40.00
b.		Red overprint		
53	A2	80r yellow grn (G)	17.50	5.00
a.		Inverted overprint		
54	A2	100r brn, buff (Br)	17.50	5.00
55	A2	150r org brn, pink (O)	17.50	5.00
a.		Inverted overprint	75.00	30.00
b.		Double overprint		
56	A2	200r dk blue, bl (Bk)	16.00	7.50
57	A2	300r dk blue, sal (Bk)	20.00	10.00
a.		Inverted overprint	60.00	50.00
b.		Green overprint		
		Nos. 45-57 (13)	164.00	55.00

Vasco da Gama's discovery of route to India, 400th anniversary.
No. 57b was prepared but not issued.
Nos. 45 and 49 were also issued with gum.
The "Centenario" overprint on stamps perf. 11½ is forged.

Nos. 23, 12, 17 Surcharged in Black, Carmine or Violet

e

f   g

1899 *Perf. 12½*
| 59 | A2(e) | 25r on 75r rose (Bk) | 4.00 | 2.50 |

1900 *Perf. 12½, 12½x11½*
60	A2(f)	25r on 5r org (C)	2.10	1.40
61	A2(g)	50r on half of 20r gray lil (V)	2.00	1.00
b.		Entire stamp	15.00	9.00

No. 61b is perf. 11½ vertically through center.

Stamps of 1895-1907 Overprinted Locally in Carmine or Green

1911 *Perf. 11½, 13½*
61A	A2	2½r gray (C)	7.00	3.00
62	A2	5r orange (G)	6.00	3.00
63	A2	10r yellow grn (C)	.70	.50
64	A2	15r dk green (C)	.90	.50
a.		Double overprint	40.00	20.00
65	A2	20r gray lilac (G)	1.25	.60
a.		Perf. 13½	1.40	.80
66	A2	25r carmine (G)	1.25	.60
67	A2	50r brown (G)	.70	.45
68	A2	75r red lilac (G)	1.10	.45
69	A2	100r dk bl, bl (C)	1.25	.50
70	A2	115r org brn, pink (G)	2.00	1.25
71	A2	130r brn, yel (G)	3.00	1.25
72	A2	200r red lil, pink (G)	3.00	1.25
73	A2	400r dull bl, yel (C)	3.00	1.00
74	A2	500r blk & red, bl (C)	4.00	1.40
75	A2	700r pur, yel (C)	4.00	1.40
		Nos. 61A-75 (15)	39.15	16.75

Nos. 63, 67 and 71 exist with inverted overprint; Nos. 63, 72 and 75 with double overprint.

Overprinted in Lisbon in Carmine or Green

1911 *Perf. 11½, 12½*
75B	A2	2½r gray	.30	.25
76	A2	5r orange	.30	.25
77	A2	10r yellow grn	.25	.25
78	A2	15r dark green	.35	.25
79	A2	20r gray lilac	.40	.25
80	A2	25r carmine (G)	.35	.25
a.		Value inverted at top of stamp	18.00	
81	A2	50r brown	.70	.25
82	A2	75r red lilac	.70	.25
a.		Value omitted	15.00	
83	A2	100r dk blue, bl	1.00	.25
84	A2	115r org brn, pink	2.50	.40
85	A2	130r brown, yel	3.00	.40
a.		Double overprint	30.00	
86	A2	200r red lil, pink	3.00	.40
87	A2	400r dull bl, yel	5.00	.40
88	A2	500r blk & red, bl	7.50	.40
89	A2	700r pur, yel	5.00	.55
		Nos. 75B-89 (15)	30.35	4.80

Nos. 75B-89 Surcharged

1916 *Perf. 11½*
90	A2	¼c on 2½r gray	.25	.25
91	A2	½c on 5r org	.25	.25
a.		"½c" double	20.00	
92	A2	1c on 10r yel grn	.40	.25
93	A2	1½c on 15r dk grn	.40	.25
a.		Imperf., pair	35.00	
94	A2	2c on 20r gray lil	.50	.25
95	A2	2½c on 25r car	1.00	.25
96	A2	5c on 50r brn	.40	.25
a.		Imperf., pair	40.00	
97	A2	7½c on 75r red lil	.65	.25
98	A2	10c on 100r dk bl, bl	1.25	.95
a.		Inverted surcharge	40.00	40.00
99	A2	11½c on 115r org brn, pink	3.50	.95
a.		Inverted surcharge	50.00	50.00
100	A2	13c on 130r brn, yel	6.50	.95
101	A2	20c on 200r red lil, pink	5.50	1.10
102	A2	40c on 400r dl bl, yel	6.50	.50
103	A2	50c on 500r blk & red, bl (R)	8.00	.70
104	A2	70c on 700r pur, yel	8.00	1.25
		Nos. 90-104 (15)	43.10	8.40

Nos. 87 to 89 Surcharged

1918 *Perf. 11½*
105	A2	½c on 700r pur, yel	2.50	1.30
106	A2	2½c on 500r blk & red, bl (Bl)	3.50	1.30
107	A2	5c on 400r dl bl, yel	4.50	1.30
		Nos. 105-107 (3)	10.50	3.90

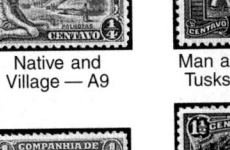

Native and Village — A9

Man and Ivory Tusks — A10

Corn — A11

Tapping Rubber Tree — A12

Tobacco Field — A15

View of Beira — A16

Coffee Plantation A17

Orange Tree A18

Cotton Field A19

Sisal Plantation A20

Scene on Beira R. R. — A21

Court House at Beira — A22

Coconut Palm A23

Mangroves A24

Cattle — A25

Company Arms — A26

1918-31 *Engr.* *Perf. 14, 15, 12½*
108	A9	¼c brn & yel grn	.55	.50
109	A9	¼c ol grn & blk ('25)	.30	.25
110	A10	½c black	.55	.50
111	A11	1c green & blk	.55	.50
112	A12	1½c black & grn	.55	.50
113	A13	2c carmine & blk	.55	.50
114	A13	2c ol blk & blk ('25)	.30	.25
115	A14	2½c lilac & blk	.55	.50
116	A11	3c ocher & blk ('23)	.30	.25
a.		3p orange & black ('25)	.30	.25
117	A15	4c grn & brn ('21)	.30	.25
118	A15	4c red & blk ('25)	.30	.25
119	A9	4½c gray & blk ('23)	.30	.25
120	A16	5c blue & blk	.55	.50
121	A17	6c claret & bl ('21)	.80	.30
122	A17	6c lilac & blk ('25)	.30	.25
123	A21	7c ultra & blk ('23)	1.00	.50
124	A18	7½c orange & grn	.75	.70
125	A19	8c violet & blk	1.50	1.10
126	A20	10c red org & blk	1.50	1.10
127				
128	A19	12c brn & blk ('23)	1.00	.50
129	A19	12c bl grn & blk ('25)	2.00	.35
130	A21	15c carmine & blk	1.00	.95
131	A22	20c dp green & blk	1.60	.65
132	A23	30c red brn & blk	3.50	.95
133	A23	30c gray grn & blk ('25)	2.00	.55
134	A23	30c bl grn & blk ('31)	3.50	.55
135	A24	40c yel grn & blk	1.90	1.10
136	A24	40c grnsh bl & blk ('25)	.70	.85
137	A25	50c orange & blk	2.25	1.10
138	A25	50c lt vio & blk ('25)	2.25	.80
139	A25	60c rose & brn ('23)	1.50	.80
140	A20	80c ultra & brn ('23)	4.00	.80
141	A20	80c car & blk ('25)	1.10	.80
142	A26	1e dk green & blk	2.25	2.00
143	A26	1e blue & blk ('25)	2.25	.80

144	A16	2e rose & vio ('23)	5.00	1.30
145	A16	2e lilac & blk ('25)	4.00	.80
		Nos. 108-145 (37)	53.30	24.80

Shades exist of several denominations.
For surcharges see Nos. 146-154, RA1.

Nos. 132, 142, 115, 120, 131, 135, 125, 137 Surcharged with New Values in Red, Blue, Violet or Black

h   i

j

1920 *Perf. 14, 15*
146	A23(h)	½c on 30c (Bk)	6.00	5.00
147	A26(h)	½c on 1e (R)	6.00	5.00
148	A14(h)	1½c on 2½c (Bl)	5.00	2.25
149	A16(h)	1½c on 5c (V)	5.00	2.25
150	A14(h)	2c on 2½c (R)	5.00	2.25
151	A22(i)	4c on 20c (V)	5.75	4.50
152	A24(i)	4c on 40c (V)	5.75	4.50
153	A19(j)	6c on 8c (R)	7.00	4.50
154	A25(j)	6c on 50c (Bk)	8.00	4.50
		Nos. 146-154 (9)	53.50	34.75

The surcharge on No. 148 is placed vertically between two bars. On No. 154 the two words of the surcharge are 13mm apart.

Native — A27

View of Beira — A28

Tapping Rubber Tree — A29

Picking Tea — A30

Zambezi River — A31

1925-31 *Engr.* *Perf. 12*
155	A27	24c ultra & blk	1.25	1.00
156	A28	25c choc & ultra	1.25	1.00
157	A27	85c brn red & blk ('31)	.95	.80
158	A28	1.40e dl bl & blk ('31)	.90	.80
159	A29	5e yel brn & ultra	1.75	.65
160	A30	10e rose & blk	2.75	.95
161	A31	20e green & blk	3.25	1.20
		Nos. 155-161 (7)	12.10	6.40

Sugar Refinery — A13

Buzi River Scene — A14

Ivory Tusks — A32

Panning Gold — A33

1931 *Litho.* *Perf. 14*
| 162 | A32 | 45c lt blue | 2.50 | 1.30 |
| 163 | A33 | 70c yellow brn | 1.40 | .70 |

Zambezi
Railroad
Bridge
A34

1935   Engr.   Perf. 12½
164 A34 1e dk blue & blk   8.75 1.60

Opening of a new bridge over the Zambezi
River.

Airplane over Beira — A35

1935
165 A35 5c blue & blk   .55 .55
166 A35 10c red org & blk   .55 .40
167 A35 15c red & blk   .55 .40
  a. Square pair, imperf. between   50.00
168 A35 20c yel grn & blk   .55 .40
169 A35 30c green & blk   .55 .40
170 A35 40c gray bl & blk   .70 .55
171 A35 45c blue & blk   .70 .55
172 A35 50c violet & blk   .70 .70
  a. Square pair, imperf. btwn.   60.00
173 A35 60c carmine & brn   1.10 .65
174 A35 80c carmine & blk   1.10 .65
        Nos. 165-174 (10)   7.05 5.25

Issued to commemorate the opening of the
Blantyre-Beira Salisbury air service.

Giraffe — A36

Thatched
Huts — A37

Rock Python — A41

Coconut
Palms
A50

Zambezi
Railroad
Bridge
A52

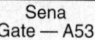
Sena
Gate — A53

Company
Arms — A54

Designs: 10c, Dhow. 15c, St. Caetano Fortress, Sofala. 20c, Zebra. 40c, Black rhinoceros. 45c, Lion. 50c, Crocodile. 60c, Leopard. 70c, Mozambique woman. 80c,
Hippopotami. 85c, Vasco da Gama's flagship.
1e, Man in canoe. 2e, Greater kudu.

1937, May 16   Perf. 12½
175 A36 1c yel grn & vio   .30 .25
176 A37 5c blue & yel grn   .30 .25
177 A36 10c ver & ultra   .30 .25
178 A37 15c carmine & blk   .30 .25
179 A36 20c green & ultra   .30 .25
180 A41 30c dk grn & ind   .30 .30
181 A41 40c grn & vio   .30 .30
182 A41 45c blue & brn   .30 .30
183 A41 50c dk vio & emer   .30 .30
184 A37 60c carmine & bl   .30 .30
185 A36 70c yel brn & pale
          grn   .30 .30
186 A37 80c car & pale grn   .40 .35
187 A41 85c org red & blk   .50 .40
188 A41 1e dp bl & blk   .50 .40
189 A50 1.40e dk bl & pale
          grn   .90 .40
190 A41 2e pale lilac & brn   1.50 .50
191 A52 5e yel brn & bl   1.25 .75
192 A53 10e carmine & blk   2.25 1.50
193 A54 20e grn & brn vio   3.00 2.75
        Nos. 175-193 (19)   13.60 10.10

Stamps of 1937 Overprinted in Red or Black

1939, Aug. 28
194 A41 30c dk grn & ind (R)   2.00 .85
195 A41 40c gray bl & blk (R)   2.00 .85
196 A41 45c blue & brn (Bk)   2.00 .85
197 A41 50c dk vio & emer (R)   3.00 1.00
198 A41 85c org red & blk (Bk) 3.00 1.00
199 A41 1e dp bl & blk (R)   3.00 1.25
200 A41 2e pale lil & brn (Bk) 3.50 1.75
        Nos. 194-200 (7)   18.50 7.55

Visit of the President of Portugal to Beira in
1939.

King Alfonso   King John IV
Henriques   A56
A55

1940, Feb. 16 Typo. Perf. 11½x12
201 A55 1.75e blue & lt blue   1.50 .75

800th anniv. of Portuguese independence.

1941   Engr.   Perf. 12½
202 A56 40c gray grn & blk   .65 .50
203 A56 50c dk vio & brt grn   .65 .50
204 A56 60c brt car & dp bl   .65 .50
205 A56 70c brn org & dk grn   .65 .50
206 A56 80c car & dp grn   .65 .50
207 A56 1e dk bl & blk   .65 .50
        Nos. 202-207 (6)   3.90 3.00

300th anniv. of the restoration of the Portu-
guese Monarchy.
  Mozambique Company's charter terminated
July 18th, 1941 after which date its stamps
were superseded by those of the territory of
Mozambique.

SEMI-POSTAL STAMPS

Lisbon Issue of 1911
Overprinted in Red

1917   Unwmk.   Perf. 11½
B1 A2 2½r gray   7.50 10.50
  a. Double overprint   75.00 75.00
B2 A2 10r yellow grn   8.75 15.00
B3 A2 20r gray lilac   12.00 20.00
B4 A2 50r brown   20.00 25.00
B5 A2 75r red lilac   65.00 70.00

B6 A2 100r dk blue, bl   75.00 80.00
B7 A2 700r purple, yel   175.00 225.00
    Nos. B1-B7 (7)   363.25 445.50

Nos. B1-B7 were used on July 31, 1917, in
place of ordinary stamps. The proceeds were
given to the Red Cross.

AIR POST STAMPS

Airplane over
Beira — AP1

1935 Unwmk. Engr.   Perf. 12½
C1   AP1 5c blue & blk   .25 .25
C2   AP1 10c org red & blk   .25 .25
C3   AP1 15c red & blk   .25 .25
C4   AP1 20c yel grn & blk   .25 .25
C5   AP1 30c green & blk   .25 .25
C6   AP1 40c gray bl & blk   .25 .25
C7   AP1 45c blue & blk   .25 .25
C8   AP1 50c dk vio & blk   .40 .25
C9   AP1 60c car & brn   .40 .25
C10 AP1 80c car & blk   .50 .25
C11 AP1 1e blue & blk   .50 .25
C12 AP1 2e mauve & blk   1.25 .40
C13 AP1 5e bis brn & bl   1.25 .50
C14 AP1 10e car & blk   1.40 .75
C15 AP1 20e bl grn & blk   2.75 1.00
        Nos. C1-C15 (15)   10.20 5.40

POSTAGE DUE STAMPS

D1

1906 Unwmk. Typo. Perf. 11½x12
Denominations in Black
J1   D1 5r yellow grn   .70 .40
J2   D1 10r slate   .70 .55
J3   D1 20r yellow brn   1.25 .55
J4   D1 30r orange   1.50 1.00
J5   D1 50r gray brown   1.50 1.00
J6   D1 60r red brown   22.50 9.00
J7   D1 100r red lilac   4.00 2.50
J8   D1 130r dull blue   32.50 12.00
J9   D1 200r carmine   13.00 4.00
J10 D1 500r violet   18.00 5.00
        Nos. J1-J10 (10)   95.65 36.00

Nos. J1-J10
Overprinted in
Carmine or Green

1911
J11 D1 5r yellow grn   .30 .30
J12 D1 10r slate   .30 .30
J13 D1 20r yellow brn   .30 .30
J14 D1 30r orange   .30 .30
J15 D1 50r gray brown   .30 .30
J16 D1 60r red brown   .50 .50
J17 D1 100r red lilac   .50 .50
J18 D1 130r dull blue   2.00 1.40
J19 D1 200r carmine (G)   1.30 1.35
J20 D1 500r violet   2.50 1.40
        Nos. J11-J20 (10)   8.30 6.65

D2

Company
Arms — D3

1916   Typo.
With Value in Centavos in Black
J21 D2 ½c yellow grn   .30 .30
J22 D2 1c slate   .30 .30
J23 D2 2c orange brn   .30 .30
J24 D2 3c orange   .70 .30
J25 D2 5c gray brown   .70 .35
J26 D2 ...
J27 D2 10c red lilac   .70 .55
J28 D2 13c gray blue   1.40 1.30
J29 D2 20c rose   1.40 1.30
J30 D2 50c gray   3.25 1.50
        Nos. J21-J30 (10)   9.75 6.50

1919 Engr. Perf. 12½, 13½, 14, 15
J31 D3 ½c green   .25 .25
J32 D3 1c slate   .25 .25
J33 D3 2c red brown   .25 .25
J34 D3 3c orange   .25 .25
J35 D3 5c gray brown   .25 .25
J36 D3 6c lt brown   .50 .50
J37 D3 10c lilac rose   .50 .50
J38 D3 13c dull blue   .50 .50
J39 D3 20c rose   .50 .50
J40 D3 50c gray   .50 .50
        Nos. J31-J40 (10)   3.75 3.75

NEWSPAPER STAMP

Newspaper Stamp of
Mozambique
Overprinted

COMP.ª DE
MOÇAMBIQUE

1894   Unwmk.   Perf. 11½
P1 N3 2½r brown   .65 .55
  a. Inverted overprint   30.00 30.00
  b. Perf. 12½   1.50 1.10

Reprints are on stout white paper with
clean-cut perf. 13½. Value $1.

POSTAL TAX STAMPS

No. 116
Surcharged in
Black

1932   Perf. 12½
RA1 A11 2c on 3c org & blk   1.40 2.00

Charity — PT2

1933   Litho.   Perf. 11
RA2 PT2 2c magenta & blk   1.40 2.00

PT3

1940   Unwmk.   Perf. 10½
RA3 PT3 2c black & ultra   15.00 16.00

NATAL

nə-ˈtal

LOCATION — Southern coast of Africa, bordering on the Indian Ocean
GOVT. — British Crown Colony
AREA — 35,284 sq. mi.
POP. — 1,206,386 (1908)
CAPITAL — Pietermaritzburg

Natal united with Cape of Good Hope, Orange Free State and the Transvaal in 1910 to form the Union of South Africa.

12 Pence = 1 Shilling
20 Shillings = 1 Pound

Values for Nos. 1-7 are for examples with complete margins and free from damage. Unused values for No. 8 on are for stamps with original gum as defined in the catalogue introduction. Very fine examples of Nos. 8-49, 61-63 and 79 will have perforations touching the design on one or more sides due to the narrow spacing of the stamps on the plates. Stamps with perfs clear of the design on all four sides are scarce and will command higher prices.

Watermark

Wmk. 5 — Small Star

Crown and V R (Victoria Regina) — A1   Crown and V R (Victoria Regina) — A2

Crown and Laurel — A3

A4

A5

Colorless Embossing

1857	Unwmk.		Imperf.	
1	A1	3p *rose*	725.	
a.	Tete beche pair		55,000.	
2	A2	6p *green*	2,000.	
a.	Diagonal half used as 3p on cover		16,500.	
3	A3	9p *blue*	65,000.	13,000.
4	A4	1sh *buff*	10,500.	
1858				
5	A5	1p *blue*	1,400.	
6	A5	1p *rose*	2,200.	
a.	No. 1 embossed over No. 6			
7	A5	1p *buff*	1,450.	

Reprints: The paper is slightly glazed, the embossing sharper and the colors as follows: 1p pale blue, deep blue, carmine rose or yellow; 3p pale rose or carmine rose; 6p bright green or yellow green; 1sh pale buff or pale yellow. Bogus cancellations are found on the reprints.
The stamps printed on surface-colored paper are revenue stamps with trimmed perforations.

Queen Victoria — A6

1860	Engr.		Perf. 14	
8	A6	1p rose	190.00	95.00
9	A6	3p blue	225.00	60.00
a.	Vert. pair, imperf betwn.		13,000.	
1863			**Perf. 13**	
10	A6	1p red	130.00	35.00
a.	1p carmine lake		130.00	35.00
1861	**Clean-cut Perf. 14 to 16**			
11	A6	3p blue	350.00	82.50
1862	**Rough Perf. 14 to 16**			
12	A6	3p blue	175.00	45.00
a.	Imperf., pair		4,500.	
b.	Imperf. horiz. or vert., pair		6,500.	
13	A6	6p gray	275.00	75.00
1862			**Wmk. 5**	
14	A6	1p rose	180.00	82.50

Imperforate copies of the 1p and 3p on paper watermarked small star are proofs.

1864	Wmk. 1		Perf. 12½	
15	A6	1p carmine red	140.00	50.00
a.	1p brown red		200.00	50.00
b.	1p rose		135.00	45.00
16	A6	6p violet	87.50	37.50
a.	6p dull reddish violet		110.00	22.50

No. 15 imperf is a proof.

Queen Victoria — A7

1867	Typo.		Perf. 14	
17	A7	1sh green	275.00	52.50

For types A6 and A7 overprinted or surcharged see Nos. 18-50, 61-63, 76, 79.

Stamps of 1860-67 Overprinted

1869		Overprint 12¾mm		
18	A6	1p carmine red (#15)	525.00	100.00
a.	1p rose (#15b)		550.00	105.00
b.	Double overprint		—	
19	A6	3p blue (#12)	700.00	110.00
19A	A6	3p blue (#9)	—	550.00
19B	A6	3p blue (#11)	1,050.	325.00
20	A6	6p violet (#16)	650.00	110.00
a.	6p dull reddish violet (#16a)		775.00	100.00
21	A7	1sh green (#17)	30,000.	2,100.
		Same Overprint 13¾mm		
22	A6	1p rose (#15b)	1,200.	325.00
a.	1p carmine red (#15)		1,200.	300.00
23	A6	3p blue (#12)	2,800.	550.00
a.	Inverted overprint			

23B	A6	3p blue (#9)	—	—
23C	A6	3p blue (#11)	—	1,100.
24	A6	6p violet (#16)	2,750.	225.00
a.	6p dull reddish violet (#16a)		3,000.	225.00
25	A7	1sh green (#17)	35,000.	3,250.
	Same Overprint 14½ to 15½mm			
26	A6	1p rose (#15b)	1,050.	250.00
a.	1p carmine red (#15)		1,050.	210.00
27	A6	3p blue (#12)	—	450.00
27A	A6	3p blue (#11)	—	775.00
27B	A6	3p blue (#9)	—	—
28	A6	6p violet (#16)	2,100.	140.00
a.	6p dull reddish violet (#16a)		—	150.00
29	A7	1sh green (#17)	32,000.	2,750.

Overprinted

30	A6	1p rose (#15b)	150.00	55.00
a.	1p carmine red (#15)		210.00	55.00
31	A6	3p blue (#12)	250.00	55.00
a.	Double overprint			1,800.
31B	A6	3p blue (#11)	225.00	62.50
31C	A6	3p blue (#9)	400.00	95.00
32	A6	6p violet (#16)	210.00	77.50
a.	6p dull reddish violet (#16a)		275.00	87.50
33	A7	1sh green (#17)	350.00	87.50

Overprinted

34	A6	1p rose (#15b)	650.00	120.00
a.	1p carmine red (#15)		550.00	110.00
35	A6	3p blue (#12)	825.00	120.00
35A	A6	3p blue (#11)	1,200.	375.00
35B	A6	3p blue (#9)	4,250.	925.00
36	A6	6p violet (#16)	825.00	120.00
a.	6p dull reddish violet (#16a)		875.00	100.00
b.	Inverted overprint			
37	A7	1sh green (#17)	37,500.	2,000.

Overprinted in Black or Red

1870-73	Wmk. 1		Perf. 12½	
38	A6	1p red	120.00	16.50
39	A6	3p ultra (R) ('72)	130.00	16.50
40	A6	6p lilac ('73)	250.00	45.00
		Nos. 38-40 (3)	500.00	78.00

Overprinted in Red, Black or Green — g

1870			Perf. 14	
41	A7	1sh green (R)	—	9,500.
42	A7	1sh green (Bk)	—	1,750.
a.	Double overprint			3,900.
43	A7	1sh green (G)	150.00	13.00

See No. 76.

Type of 1867 Overprinted

1873				
44	A7	1sh brown lilac	400.00	30.00

No. 44 without overprint is a revenue.

Type of 1864 Overprinted

1874			Perf. 12½	
45	A6	1p rose red	400.00	95.00
a.	Double overprint			

Overprinted

1875				
46	A6	1p rose red	185.00	70.00
a.	1p carmine		175.00	82.50
b.	Double overprint		1,900.	650.00

Overprinted

1875	Overprint 14½mm		Perf. 12½	
47	A6	1p yellow	100.00	100.00
a.	Double overprint, one albino			275.00
48	A6	1p rose red	140.00	87.50
a.	Inverted overprint		2,250.	575.00
49	A6	6p violet	95.00	10.00
a.	Inverted overprint		900.00	190.00
b.	Double overprint			1,050.
			Perf. 14	
50	A7	1sh green	140.00	—
a.	Double overprint			425.00
		Nos. 47-50 (4)	475.00	206.50

The 1p yellow without overprint is a revenue.

A8   A9

A10   A11

Queen Victoria — A12

1874-78	Typo.	Wmk. 1	Perf. 14	
51	A8	1p dull rose	50.00	7.50
a.	1p bright rose		50.00	7.50
52	A9	3p ultramarine	190.00	37.50
a.	Perf. 14x12½		2,250.	1,100.
53	A10	4p brown ('78)	210.00	17.50
54	A11	6p violet	105.00	9.00
			Perf. 15½x15	
55	A12	5sh claret	525.00	120.00
			Perf. 14	
56	A12	5sh claret ('78)	450.00	120.00
57	A12	5sh carmine	120.00	42.50
		Handstamped "SPECIMEN"	250.00	
a.	5sh rose ('78)		150.00	45.00
			Perf. 12½	
58	A10	4p brown ('78)	400.00	82.50

See Nos. 65-71. For types A8-A10 surcharged see Nos. 59-60, 72-73, 77, 80.

Surcharged in Black

n

No. 60

o

1877   **Perf. 14**
59 A8(n) ½p on 1p rose   45.00 82.50
  a. Double surcharge "1/2"
60 A8(n) ½p on 1p rose   110.00

Surcharge "n" exists in 3 or more types each of the large "1/2" (No. 59) and the small "1/2" (No. 60).
"HALF" and "½" were overprinted separately; "½" may be above, below or overlapping.

           Perf. 12½
61 A6(o) ½p on 1p yel   12.50   25.00
  a. Double surcharge   400.00 230.00
  b. Inverted surcharge   400.00 240.00
  c. Pair, one without
     surcharge   4,750. 3,000.
  d. "POTAGE"   350.00 250.00
  e. "POSAGE"   350.00 325.00
  f. "POSTAGE" omitted   2,500.   —
62 A6(o) 1p on 6p vio   82.50   13.00
  a. "POSTAGE" omitted
  b. "POTAGE"   650.00 190.00
63 A6(o) 1p on 6p rose   150.00   60.00
  a. Inverted surcharge   1,750. 600.00
  b. Double surcharge   —   350.00
  c. Dbl. surch., one invert-
     ed   400.00 250.00
  d. Triple surch., one invtd.
  e. Quadruple surcharge   550.00 300.00
  f. "POTAGE"   1,000. 390.00
     Nos. 61-63 (3)   245.00   98.00

No. 63 without overprint is a revenue.

A14

1880   **Typo.**   **Perf. 14**
64 A14 ½p blue green   22.50   27.50
  a. Vertical pair, imperf. between

1882-89   **Wmk. Crown and CA (2)**
65 A14 ½p blue green ('84)   120.00   20.00
66 A14 ½p gray green ('84)   5.50   1.40
67 A8 1p rose ('84)   7.25   .30
  a. 1p carmine   7.00   .40
68 A9 3p ultra ('84)   170.00   22.00
69 A9 3p gray ('89)   10.00   5.25
70 A10 4p brown   14.00   1.90
71 A11 6p violet   11.00   2.75
     Nos. 65-71 (7)   337.75   53.60

Surcharged in Black

p

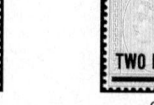

q

1885-86
72 A8(p) ½p on 1p rose   24.00   14.00
  a. Hyphen after "HALF" omit-
     ted   120.00   55.00
73 A9(q) 2p on 3p gray
     ('86)   32.50   7.00

A17

1887
74 A17 2p olive green, die
     B ('89)   6.00   1.75
     Handstamped "SPECIMEN"   87.50
  a. Die A   60.00   2.90
     Overprinted "SPECIMEN" 110.00

For explanation of dies A and B see "Dies of B ̶l̶i̶t̶ ̶O̶ ̶a̶l̶ ̶S̶t̶a̶m̶p̶s̶" in the catalogue introduction.

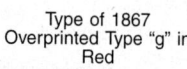

Type of 1867
Overprinted Type "g" in Red

1888
76 A7 1sh orange   10.00   1.90
     Handstamped "SPECI-
     MEN"   130.00
  a. Double overprint   3,250.

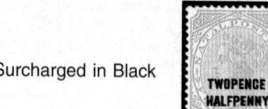

Surcharged in Black

1891
77 A10 2½p on 4p brown   17.50   17.50
     Handstamped "SPECIMEN" 130.00
  a. "PENGE"   77.50
  b. "PENN"   325.00 275.00
  c. Double surcharge   400.00 350.00
  d. As "c," in vert. pair with
     normal stamp   650.00 750.00
  e. Inverted surcharge   550.00 475.00
  f. Vert. pair, surcharge tete-
     beche   2,250. 3,000.

A20

1891, June
78 A20 2½p ultramarine   11.00   1.60
     Handstamped "SPECIMEN"   82.50

Surcharged in Red or Black

No. 79   No. 80

1895, Mar.   **Wmk. 1**   **Perf. 12½**
79 A6 ½p on 6p vio (R)   3.00   10.00
     Handstamped "SPECIMEN"   65.00
  a. "Ealf"   27.50   75.00
  b. "Penn"   27.50   75.00
  c. Double surcharge, one verti-
     cal   350.00
  d. Double surcharge   350.00

Stamps with fancy "P," "T" or "A" in surcharge sell for twice as much.

      Wmk. 2   **Perf. 14**
80 A8 ½p on 1p rose (Bk)   3.50   2.50
     Handstamped "SPECIMEN"   70.00
  a. Double surcharge   525.00 550.00
  b. Pair, one without surcharge
     and the other with double
     surcharge   —

A23   King Edward
                       VII — A24

1902-03 **Typo.** **Wmk. 2** **Perf. 14**
81 A23 ½p blue green   6.50   .55
82 A23 1p rose   12.00   .20
83 A23 1½p blk & blue grn   4.50   5.50
84 A23 2p ol grn & scar   5.25   .45
85 A23 2½p ultramarine   1.90   6.00
86 A23 3p gray & red vio   1.60   2.75

87 A23 4p brown & scar   10.50   27.50
88 A23 5p org & black   4.00   4.00
89 A23 6p mar & bl grn   4.00   5.00
90 A23 1sh pale bl & dp
     rose   5.25   5.25
91 A23 2sh vio & bl grn   62.50   11.50
92 A23 2sh6p red violet   50.00   15.00
93 A23 4sh val & dp rose   85.00   85.00
     *Nos. 81-93, ovptd. "SPECI-
     MEN"*   225.00

         Wmk. 1
94 A24 5sh car lake
     & dk
     blue   60.00   14.00
     Overprinted "SPECI-
     MEN"   65.00
95 A24 10sh brn & dp
     rose   120.00   42.50
     Overprinted "SPECI-
     MEN"   65.00
96 A24 £1 ultra &
     blk   350.00   85.50
     Overprinted "SPECI-
     MEN"   65.00
97 A24 £1 10sh vio
     & bl
     green   600.00 140.00
     Overprinted "SPECI-
     MEN"   120.00
     Revenue cancel   15.00
98 A24 £5 black &
     vio   5,500. 1,400.
     Overprinted "SPECI-
     MEN"   250.00
     Revenue cancel   110.00
99 A24 £10 org &
     green   12,500. 6,000.
     Overprinted "SPECI-
     MEN"   450.00
     Revenue cancel   180.00
100 A24 £20 green &
     car   27,500. 17,500.
     Overprinted "SPECI-
     MEN"   550.00
     Revenue cancel   325.00
     Nos. 81-96 (16)   793.00 320.75

1904-08   **Wmk. 3**
101 A23 ½p blue green   11.00   .25
102 A23 1p rose   11.00   .25
  a. Booklet pane of 6   550.00
     Complete booklet of 5
     #102a   3,500.
  b. Booklet pane of 5 + 1
     label   500.00
     Complete booklet of 5
     #102b   3,500.
103 A23 2p ol green &
     scar   18.50   4.00
104 A23 4p brn & scar   3.50   1.60
105 A23 5p org & blk
     ('08)   5.50   5.00
106 A23 1sh pale bl & dp
     rose   100.00   9.00
107 A23 2sh vio & bl grn   75.00   55.00
108 A23 2sh6p red violet   70.00   55.00
109 A24 £1 10sh vio &
     org brn,
     chalky paper   1,900. 5,000.
     Overprinted "SPECI-
     MEN"   350.00
     Revenue cancel   55.00
     Nos. 101-108 (8)   294.50 130.10

A25   A26

1908-09
110 A25 6p red violet   5.75   3.50
111 A25 1sh blk, *grn*   7.75   3.25
112 A25 2sh bl & vio, *bl*   19.00   3.75
113 A25 2sh6p red & blk, *bl* 32.00   3.75
114 A26 5sh red & grn, *yell* 30.00   45.00
115 A26 10sh red & grn, *grn* 135.00 135.00
116 A26 £1 blk & vio, *red* 440.00 400.00
     Nos. 110-116 (7)   669.50 594.25

OFFICIAL STAMPS

Nos. 101-103, 106 and
Type A23 Overprinted

1904   **Wmk. 3**   **Perf. 14**
O1 A23 ½p blue green   3.75   .45
O2 A23 1p rose   10.00   1.10
O3 A23 2p ol grn & scar   45.00   22.50
O4 A23 3p gray & red vio   25.00   5.50
O5 A23 6p mar & bl grn   87.50   82.50

O6 A23 1sh pale bl & dp
     rose   250.00 275.00
     Nos. O1-O6 (6)   421.25 387.05

Stamps of Natal were replaced by those of the Union of South Africa.

NAURU

nä-'ü-₍e₎rü

LOCATION — An island on the Equator in the west central Pacific Ocean, midway between the Marshall and Solomon Islands.
GOVT. —
AREA — 8 ½ sq. mi.
POP. — 8,421 (est. 1983)
CAPITAL — None. Parliament House is in Yaren District.

The island, a German possession, was captured by Australian forces in 1914 and, following World War I, was mandated to the British Empire. It was administered jointly by Great Britain, Australia and New Zealand.
See North West Pacific Islands.

12 Pence = 1 Shilling

Great Britain Stamps of 1912-13 Overprinted at Bottom of Stamp

1916-23		**Wmk. 33**	**Perf. 14½x14**	
1	A82	½p green	3.50	10.00
a.	Double ovpt, one albino		70.00	
2	A83	1p scarlet	2.25	12.00
a.	1p carmine red		16.00	
b.	Double ovpt, one albino		260.00	
3	A84	1½p red brn ('23)	57.50	85.00
4	A85	2p org (die I)	3.00	15.00
a.	Double ovpt, one albino		135.00	
b.	Triple ovpt, two albino		350.00	
c.	2p deep orange (die II) ('23)	75.00	110.00
6	A86	2½p ultra	5.00	12.00
a.	Double ovpt, one albino		300.00	
7	A87	3p violet	3.00	11.00
a.	Double ovpt, one albino		375.00	
8	A88	4p slate green	3.00	14.50
a.	Double ovpt, one albino		260.00	
9	A89	5p yel brown	4.50	15.00
a.	Double ovpt, one albino		175.00	
10	A89	6p dull violet	10.00	17.00
a.	Double ovpt, one albino		400.00	
11	A90	9p black brown	14.00	24.00
a.	Double ovpt, one albino		375.00	
12	A90	1sh bister	13.00	22.50
a.	Double ovpt, one albino		425.00	
		Nos. 1-12 (11)	118.75	238.00

Great Britain Stamps of 1915 Overprinted

Nos. of basic British stamps are in parentheses.

		Wmk. 34	**Perf. 11x12**	
13	A91	2sh6p light brown (#173d)	90.00	125.00
a.	2sh6p black brown (#173e)	625.00	1,600.
b.	As "a," double ovpt, one albino	1,950.	
c.	As "a," triple ovpt, two albino	1,950.	
d.	2sh6p pale brown (worn plate) (#173a)	80.00	115.00
14	A91	5sh carmine (#174b)	150.00	200.00
a.	As "a," triple ovpt, one albino	1,500.	
b.	5sh rose carmine (#174)	3,000.	2,750.
15	A91	10sh light blue (R) (#175a)	375.00	400.00
a.	Double ovpt, one albino	1,500.	
b.	Triple ovpt, one black, one red, one albino	3,750.	
c.	10sh indigo blue (#175)	12,500.	6,000.
d.	Double ovpt, one albino	14,000.	8,000.

e.	10sh deep bright blue (#175c)	575.00	625.00

Same Ovpt. on Great Britain No. 179a and 179b

1920				
16	A91	2sh6p gray brown (#179a)	92.50	160.00
a.	Double ovpt, one albino	550.00	
b.	2sh6p chocolate brown (#179b)	105.00	175.00
c.	As "b", double ovpt, one albino	550.00	
		Nos. 13-16 (4)	707.50	885.00
		Nos. 1-16 (15)	826.25	1,109.

1923			**Overprint Centered**	
1b	A82	½p	8.00	55.00
2c	A83	1p	22.50	40.00
3a	A84	1½p	35.00	57.50
b.	Double ovpt, one albino	200.00	
4d	A85	2p As No. 4a	40.00	80.00
		Nos. 1b-4d (4)	105.50	232.50

On Nos. 1-12 "NAURU" is usually 12¾mm wide and at the foot of the stamp. In 1923 four values were overprinted with the word 13½mm wide and across the middle of the stamp.
Forged overprints exist.

Freighter — A1

1924-48		**Unwmk. Engr.**	**Perf. 11**	
Unsurfaced grayish paper '24-'34				
17	A1	½p orange brown	2.25	3.00
18	A1	1p green	4.00	3.00
19	A1	1½p red	4.50	4.50
20	A1	2p orange	4.50	12.00
21	A1	2½p blue	6.50	27.50
b.	2½ greenish blue ('34)	13.00	25.00
22	A1	3p pale blue	4.50	14.50
23	A1	4p olive green	8.50	22.50
24	A1	5p dk brown	4.50	7.50
25	A1	6p dark violet	5.25	13.00
26	A1	9p brown olive	10.50	21.00
27	A1	1sh brown red	7.00	14.00
28	A1	2sh6p slate green	32.50	55.00
29	A1	5sh claret	55.00	110.00
30	A1	10sh yellow	140.00	200.00
		Nos. 17-30 (14)	289.50	507.50
Glazed surfaced white paper '37-'48				
17a	A1	½p orange brown	4.75	15.00
b.	Perf. 14 ('47)	1.40	10.00
18a	A1	1p green	2.50	4.00
19a	A1	1½p red	1.10	2.00
20a	A1	2p orange	4.00	4.00
21a	A1	2½p blue ('48)	3.50	4.00
c.	Horiz. pair, imperf between	14,000.	20,000.
d.	Vert. pair, imperf between	14,000.	20,000.
22a	A1	3p grnsh gray ('47)	5.00	16.00
23a	A1	4p olive green	4.25	15.00
24a	A1	5p dk brown	5.25	5.00
25a	A1	6p dark violet	5.75	6.00
26a	A1	9p brown olive	9.50	21.00
27a	A1	1sh brown red	7.50	4.50
28a	A1	2sh6p slate green	32.00	40.00
29a	A1	5sh claret	37.50	60.00
30a	A1	10sh yellow	85.00	125.00
		Nos. 17a-30a (14)	207.60	325.50
		Set #17a-30a, never hinged	205.00	

Stamps of Type A1 Overprinted in Black

1935, July 12			**Perf. 11**	
Glazed Paper				
31	A1	1½p red	1.10	1.10
32	A1	2p orange	2.50	6.00
33	A1	2½p blue	2.50	1.75
34	A1	1sh brown red	6.50	5.00
		Nos. 31-34 (4)	12.60	13.85
		Set, never hinged	20.00	

25th anniv. of the reign of George V.

George VI — A2

1937, May 10			**Engr.**	
35	A2	1½p salmon rose	.25	1.00
36	A2	2p dull orange	.25	2.00
37	A2	2½p blue	.25	1.25
38	A2	1sh brown violet	.40	1.25
		Nos. 35-38 (4)	1.15	5.50
		Set, never hinged	2.25	

Coronation of George VI & Elizabeth.

NEPAL

nə-'pol

LOCATION — In the Himalaya Mountains between India and Tibet
GOVT. — Kingdom
AREA — 56,136 sq. mi.
POP. — 16,100,000 (est. 1982)
CAPITAL — Kathmandu

Nepal stamps were valid only in Nepal and India until April 1959, when they became valid to all parts of the world.

4 Pice = 1 Anna
64 Pice = 16 Annas = 1 Rupee

Nos. 1-24, 29A were issued without gum.

Sripech and Crossed Khukris — A1

1881		**Typo. Unwmk.**	**Pin-perf.**	
European Wove Paper				
1	A1	1a ultramarine	250.00	450.00
2	A1	2a purple	350.00	350.00
a.	Tete beche pair	500.00	
3	A1	4a green	500.00	600.00
Imperf				
4	A1	1a blue	175.00	140.00
5	A1	2a purple	175.00	200.00
a.	Tete beche pair	500.00	
6	A1	4a green	275.00	500.00

1886		**Native Wove Paper**	**Imperf.**	
7	A1	1a ultramarine	22.50	30.00
a.	Tete beche pair	150.00	175.00
8	A1	2a violet	35.00	35.00
a.	Tete beche pair	200.00	200.00
9	A1	4a green	55.00	50.00
a.	Tete beche pair	300.00	250.00
		Nos. 7-9 (3)	112.50	115.00

Used values for Nos. 9-49 are for telegraph cancels.

Siva's Bow and Two Khukris — A2

1899-1917			**Imperf.**	
Native Wove Paper				
10	A2	½a black	10.00	3.00
a.	Tete beche pair	100.00	10.00
11	A2	½a red orange ('17)	1,750.	350.00
a.	Tete beche pair		
Pin-perf.				
12	A2	½a black	10.00	
a.	Tete beche pair	50.00	

No. 11 is known postally used on six covers.

Type of 1881				
1898-1917			**Imperf.**	
13	A1	1a pale blue	12.50	6.00
a.	1a bluish green	50.00	50.00
b.	Tete beche pair	150.00	150.00
14	A1	2a gray violet	25.00	10.00
a.	Tete beche pair	100.00	100.00
15	A1	2a claret ('17)	30.00	12.00
a.	Tete beche pair	100.00	100.00
16	A1	2a brown ('17)	10.00	
a.	Tete beche pair	25.00	

17	A1	4a dull green	10.00	15.00
a.	Tete beche pair	70.00	350.00
b.	Cliche of 1a in plate of 4a ('04)	350.00	350.00
		Nos. 13-17 (5)	87.50	43.00

#17b has the recut frame of the 1904 issue. #17b probably was used only on telegraph/telephone forms.

Pin-perf.

18	A1	1a pale blue	17.50	10.00
a.	Tete beche pair	75.00	50.00
19	A1	2a gray violet	25.00	12.00
a.	Tete beche pair	75.00	75.00
20	A1	2a claret ('17)	8.75	6.00
a.	Tete beche pair	30.00	30.00
21	A1	2a brown ('17)	7.50	
a.	Tete beche pair	30.00	30.00
22	A1	4a dull green	50.00	18.00
a.	Tete beche pair	100.00	100.00

Frame Recut on All Cliches, Fewer Lines

1903-04		**Native Wove Paper**	**Imperf.**	
23	A1	1a bright blue		10.00
a.	Tete beche pair		50.00
Pin-perf.				
24	A1	1a bright blue		15.00
a.	Tete beche pair		100.00
European Wove Paper				
23b	A1	1a blue	800.00	300.00
23c		Tete beche pair	1,750.	
Pin-perf.				
24b	A1	1a blue	950.00	
24c		Tete beche pair	2,750.	

Siva Mahadeva — A3

1907		**Engr.**	**Perf. 13½**	
European Wove Paper				
26	A3	2p brown	6.00	.50
27	A3	4p green	6.50	.50
28	A3	8p carmine	14.00	.50
29	A3	16p violet	27.50	1.50
		Nos. 26-29 (4)	54.00	3.50

Type A3 has five characters in bottom panel, reading "Gurkha Sirkar." Date divided in lower corners is "1964." Outer side panels carry denomination (also on A5).

A4

1917-18			**Imperf.**	
29A	A4	1a bright blue	9.00	3.00
b.	1a indigo	10.00	4.00
c.	Pin-perf.	13.00	11.00

No. 29A may not have been used postally.

In 1917 a telephone and telegraph system was started and remainder stocks and further printings of designs A1 and A2 were used to pay telegrams fees. Design A4 was designed for telegraph use but was valid for postal use. After 1929 design A3 was used for telegrams. The usual telegraph cancellation is crescent-shaped.

Type of 1907 Redrawn

A5

Nine characters in bottom panel reading "Nepal Sirkar"

1929			**Perf. 14, 14½**	
Size: 24¾x18¾mm				
30	A5	2p dark brown	6.00	.30
31	A5	4p green	6.00	.50
32	A5	8p deep red	20.00	1.25
33	A5	16p dark red vio	13.50	2.00
34	A5	24p orange yellow	11.00	2.00
35	A5	32p dark ultra	13.50	2.00
Size: 26x19½mm				
36	A5	1r orange red	16.50	4.00

Size: 28x21mm

37	A5	5r brown & black	32.50	25.00
		Nos. 30-37 (8)	119.00	36.05

On Nos. 30-37 the date divided in lower corners is "1986."

Type of 1929 Redrawn

Date characters in Lower Corners read "1992"

1935		Unwmk. Engr.	Perf. 14	
38	A5	2p dark brown	2.75	.45
39	A5	4p green	3.00	.75
40	A5	8p bright red	150.00	8.00
41	A5	16p dk red violet	4.75	1.25
42	A5	24p orange yellow	4.75	2.00
43	A5	32p dark ultra	10.00	3.25
		Nos. 38-43 (6)	175.25	15.70

NETHERLANDS

'ne-thər-lən d z

(Holland)

LOCATION — Northwestern Europe, bordering on the North Sea
GOVT. — Kingdom
AREA — 13,203 sq. mi.
POP. — 14,394,589 (1984)
CAPITAL — Amsterdam

100 Cents = 1 Gulden
(Guilder or Florin)

Catalogue values for unused stamps in this country are for Never Hinged items, beginning with Scott 216 in the regular postage section, and Scott B123 in the semi-postal section.

Values for unused stamps are for examples with original gum as defined in the catalogue introduction. Very fine examples of Nos. 4-12 will have perforations touching the frameline on one or more sides due to the narrow spacing of the stamps on the plates. Stamps with perfs clear on all four sides are very scarce and command higher prices.

Watermarks

Wmk. 158   Wmk. 202 — Circles

Syncopated Perforations

Type A   Type B

Type C

These special "syncopated" or "interrupted" perforations, devised for coil stamps, are found on Nos. 142-156, 158-160, 164-166, 168-185, 187-193 and certain semipostals of 1925-33, between Nos. B9 and B69. There are four types:

A (1st stamp is #142a). On two shorter sides, groups of four holes separated by blank spaces equal in width to two or three holes.

B (1st stamp is #164a). As "A," but on all four sides.

C (1st stamp is #181f). On two shorter sides, end holes are omitted.

D (1st stamp is #174c). Four-hole sequence on horiz. sides, three-hole on vert. sides.

King William III
A1   A2

Wmk. 158

1852, Jan. 1		Engr.	Imperf.	
1	A1	5c blue	400.00	35.00
		No gum	200.00	
		On cover, single franking		95.00
		Handstamped "SPECIMEN"	1,900.	
a.		5c light blue	450.00	40.00
b.		5c steel blue (Plates 1-2, '53)	750.00	100.00
c.		5c dark blue	450.00	35.00
d.		5c greenish blue (Plate 5, '62)	—	125.00
e.		Thin paper (Plate 6, '63)	425.00	32.50
f.		Ribbed paper (Plate 2, '54)		200.00
2	A1	10c lake	450.00	27.50
		No gum	220.00	
		On cover, single franking		82.50
		Handstamped "SPECIMEN"	1,900.	
a.		10c deep rose red	575.00	47.50
b.		10c brownish red	700.00	77.50
c.		10c car lake (see "f.")	1,550.	40.00
d.		10c dp rose red, thin paper	525.00	35.00
e.		Ribbed paper (Plate 3, '54)	—	
f.		As "c," horn on forehead	450.00	27.50
3	A1	15c orange yellow	775.00	130.00
		No gum	380.00	
		On cover, single franking		400.00
		Handstamped "SPECIMEN"	1,900.	
a.		15c dark orange	950.00	175.00
b.		15c dark yel org, thin paper	950.00	300.00

Full margins = 1¼mm.

In 1895 the 10c was privately reprinted in several colors on unwatermarked paper by Joh. A. Moesman, whose name appears on the back.

Values for pairs

1	A1	5c blue	975.00	155.00
		On cover		235.00
2	A1	10c lake	1,000.	140.00
		On cover		225.00
3	A1	15c orange yellow	1,650.	350.00
		On cover, single franking		550.00

Values for strips of 3

1	A1	5c blue	2,100.	425.00
		On cover		750.00
2	A1	10c lake	2,100.	350.00
		On cover		750.00
3	A1	15c orange yellow	2,750.	775.00
		On cover		1,250.

Values for strips of 4

1	A1	5c blue	4,000.	1,325.
2	A1	10c lake	3,000.	775.00
3	A1	15c orange yellow	5,500.	1,425.

Values for strips of 5

1	A1	5c blue	5,250.	3,600.
2	A1	10c lake	4,500.	2,750.
3	A1	15c orange yellow	7,000.	2,500.

Values for blocks of 4

1	A1	5c blue	5,250.	3,100.
2	A1	10c lake	5,250.	3,000.
3	A1	15c orange yellow	6,500.	5,750.

Values for Vert. or Horiz. Gutter Pairs

1	A1	5c blue	12,500.
2	A1	10c lake	24,000.
3	A1	15c orange yellow	19,500.

Gutter = 10mm.

1864		Unwmk.	Perf. 12½x12	
4	A2	5c blue	300.00	16.00
		No gum	100.00	
		On cover, single franking		40.00
		Handstamped "SPECIMEN"	1,050.	
5	A2	10c lake	425.00	8.00
		No gum	150.00	
		On cover, single franking		30.00
		Handstamped "SPECIMEN"	1,050.	
6	A2	15c orange	1,050.	100.00
		No gum	350.00	
		On cover, single franking		135.00
		Handstamped "SPECIMEN"	1,050.	
a.		15c yellow ('66)	450.00	115.00
		On cover, single franking		200.00

The paper varies considerably in thickness. It is sometimes slightly bluish, also vertically ribbed.

Values for used pairs

4	A2	5c blue	52.50
5	A2	10c lake	25.00
6	A2	15c orange	225.00

Values for used strips of 3

4	A2	5c blue	100.00
5	A2	10c lake	50.00
6	A2	15c orange	375.00

Values for used strips of 4

4	A2	5c blue	200.00
5	A2	10c lake	175.00
6	A2	15c orange	700.00

Values for blocks of 4

4	A2	5c blue	2,400.	900.00
5	A2	10c lake	2,900.	1,150.
6	A2	15c orange	5,500.	2,750.

William III — A3

1867			Perf. 12¾x11¾	
7a	A3	5c ultra	115.00	2.75
		No gum	29.00	
		On cover, single franking		8.00
8a	A3	10c lake	225.00	4.75
		No gum	55.00	
		On cover, single franking		8.00
9	A3	15c orange brn	640.00	35.00
		No gum	200.00	
		On cover, single franking		47.50
10	A3	20c dk green	625.00	24.00
		No gum	175.00	
		Overprinted "SPECIMEN"	3,850.	
		On cover, single franking		37.50
11	A3	25c dk violet	2,100.	110.00
		No gum	525.00	
		On cover, single franking		325.00
12	A3	50c gold	2,500.	160.00
		No gum	625.00	
		On cover, single franking		1,125.

The paper of Nos. 7-22 sometimes has an accidental bluish tinge of varying strength. During its manufacture a chemical whitener (bluing agent) was added in varying quantities. No particular printing was made on bluish paper.

Two varieties of numerals in each value, differing chiefly in the thickness.

Oxidized examples of the 50c are worth much less.

Imperforate varieties of Nos. 7-12 are proofs.

Values for blocks of 4

7a	A3	5c ultra	600.00	110.00
8a	A3	10c lake	1,000.	175.00
9	A3	15c orange brn		23,000.
10	A3	20c dk green	7,000.	7,000.
11	A3	25c dk violet	11,500.	1,100.
12	A3	50c gold	12,500.	1,100.

1867-68

			Perf. 14	
7	A3	5c ultra	115.00	2.75
8	A3	10c lake	225.00	4.75
9a	A3	15c org brn	650.00	37.50
10a	A3	20c dk grn	1,150.	24.00
11a	A3	25c dk vio	4,000.	
12a	A3	50c gold	11,500.	

			Perf. 13½	
7b	A3	5c ultra	1,050.	700.00
d.		5c blue	115.00	2.40
8b	A3	10c car lake	175.00	3.25
9b	A3	15c org brn	675.00	32.50
10b	A3	20c dk grn	1,150.	24.00
11b	A3	25c dk vio	9,000.	
7c	A3	5c ultra	225.00	11.50
8c	A3	10c lake	230.00	7.75
9c	A3	15c orange brown	2,700.	1,150.
10c	A3	20c dark green	1,550.	155.00

			Perf. 13¼x14	
7e	A3	5c ultra	97.50	2.40
8d	A3	10c lake	160.00	3.25
9d	A3	15c orange brown	650.00	32.50
10d	A3	20c dark green	625.00	24.00

Coat of Arms — A4

1869-71		Typo.	Perf. 13¼, 14	
17	A4	½c red brown ('71)	24.00	3.75
		Never hinged	210.00	
		No gum	7.75	
		On cover, single franking		275.00
		On cover, two singles		160.00
		Overprinted "SPECIMEN"	250.00	
c.		Perf. 14	2,300.	875.00
18	A4	1c black	210.00	70.00
		Never hinged	1,150.	
		No gum	85.00	
		On cover, single franking		220.00
		On cover, two singles		500.00
		Overprinted "SPECIMEN"	250.00	
19	A4	1c green	15.50	2.25
		Never hinged	190.00	
		No gum	5.00	
		On cover, single franking		85.00
		On cover, two singles		37.50
		Overprinted "SPECIMEN"	250.00	
c.		Perf. 14	27.50	5.50
20	A4	1½c rose	150.00	...
		Never hinged	850.00	
		No gum	72.50	
		On cover, single franking		1,150.
		On cover, two singles		750.00
		Overprinted "SPECIMEN"	250.00	
b.		Perf. 14	175.00	97.50
21	A4	2c buff	60.00	15.00
		Never hinged	275.00	
		No gum	19.00	
		On cover, single franking		140.00
		On cover, two singles		275.00
		Overprinted "SPECIMEN"	250.00	
c.		Perf. 14	55.00	14.00
22	A4	2½c violet ('70)	475.00	70.00
		Never hinged	1,950.	
		No gum	115.00	
		On cover, single franking		175.00
		On cover, two singles		200.00
		Overprinted "SPECIMEN"	250.00	
c.		Perf. 14	775.00	425.00

Imperforate varieties are proofs.

Values for blocks of 4

17	A4	½c red brown ('71)	110.00	77.50
18	A4	1c black	1,125.	775.00
19	A4	1c green	57.50	57.50
20	A4	1½c rose	875.00	575.00
21	A4	2c buff	250.00	155.00
22	A4	2½c violet ('70)	2,400.	775.00

A5   A6

Perf. 12½, 13, 13½, 13x14, 14, 12½x12 and 11½x12

1872-88				
23	A5	5c blue	11.50	.30
		Never hinged	130.00	
		No gum	3.00	
		On cover, single franking		4.00
		On cover, two singles		7.00
		Overprinted "SPECIMEN"	62.50	
a.		5c ultra	14.00	1.25
		Never hinged	77.50	
		No gum	3.50	
		On cover, single franking		20.00
		On cover, two singles		27.50
24	A5	7½c red brn ('88)	35.00	18.00
		Never hinged	200.00	
		No gum	15.00	
		On cover, single franking		—
		On cover, two singles		105.00
		Overprinted "SPECIMEN"	40.00	
25	A5	10c rose	57.50	1.60
		Never hinged	275.00	
		No gum	14.50	
		On cover, single franking		7.75
		On cover, two singles		32.00
		Overprinted "SPECIMEN"	100.00	
26	A5	12½c gray ('75)	62.50	2.40
		Never hinged	275.00	
		No gum	16.00	
		On cover, single franking		22.50
		On cover, two singles		37.50
		Overprinted "SPECIMEN"	92.50	
27	A5	15c brn org	350.00	5.25
		Never hinged	2,750.	
		No gum	87.50	
		On cover, single franking		70.00
		On cover, two singles		105.00
		Overprinted "SPECIMEN"	92.50	
28	A5	20c green	425.00	5.00
		Never hinged	2,750.	
		No gum	105.00	
		On cover, single franking		70.00
		On cover, two singles		105.00
		Overprinted "SPECIMEN"	125.00	
29	A5	22½c dk grn ('88)	77.50	42.50
		Never hinged	750.00	
		No gum	40.00	
		On cover, single franking		575.00
		Overprinted "SPECIMEN"	80.00	
30	A5	25c dull vio	525.00	4.00
		Never hinged	2,950.	
		No gum	130.00	
		On cover, single franking		110.00
		On cover, two singles		195.00
		On parcel post receipt card		105.00
		Overprinted "SPECIMEN"	125.00	
31	A5	50c bister	650.00	11.00
		Never hinged	3,750.	
		No gum	165.00	
		On cover, two singles		275.00
		On parcel post receipt card		125.00
		Overprinted "SPECIMEN"	150.00	
32	A5	1g gray vio ('88)	480.00	40.00
		Never hinged	1,750.	
		No gum	120.00	
		On cover, single franking		—
		On parcel post receipt card		175.00
		Overprinted "SPECIMEN"	110.00	
33	A6	2g50c rose & ultra	900.00	105.00
		Never hinged	4,000.	
		No gum	425.00	
		On cover, single franking		—
		On cover, two singles		—
		On parcel post receipt card		550.00
		Overprinted "SPECIMEN"		

Imperforate varieties are proofs.

Values for blocks of 4

23	A5	5c blue	57.50	20.00
a.		5c ultra	75.00	20.00
24	A5	7½c red brown	175.00	350.00
25	A5	10c rose	275.00	65.00
26	A5	12½c gray	325.00	70.00
27	A5	15c brown orange	2,300.	115.00
28	A5	20c green	2,450.	125.00
29	A5	22½c dark green	350.00	325.00
30	A5	25c dull violet	3,000.	75.00
31	A5	50c bister	3,250.	75.00
32	A5	1g gray violet	2,800.	750.00
33	A6	2g50c rose & ultra	4,400.	550.00

Numeral of Value — A7

HALF CENT:
Type I — Fraction bar 8 to 8½mm long.
Type II — Fraction bar 9mm long and thinner.

Perf. 12½, 13½, 14, 12½x12, 11½x12
1876-94

34	A7	½c rose (II)	11.50	.30
		Never hinged	40.00	
		On cover		47.50
		On cover, single franking		70.00
a.		½c rose (I)	15.00	.50
		Never hinged	45.00	
		On cover		57.50
		On cover, single franking		77.50
c.		Laid paper		60.00
d.		Perf. 14 (I)	1,950.	575.00
35	A7	1c emer grn ('94)	2.75	.25
		Never hinged	15.00	
		On cover, single franking		5.00
b.		As "c," laid paper	70.00	7.25
c.		1c green	8.00	.25
		Never hinged	75.00	
		On cover, single franking		5.50
36	A7	2c olive yel ('94)	32.50	2.75
		Never hinged	145.00	
		On cover, single franking		55.00
a.		2c yellow	65.00	3.50
		Never hinged	300.00	
		On cover, single franking		55.00
37	A7	2½c violet ('94)	14.00	.30
		Never hinged	110.00	
		On cover, single franking		2.75
b.		2½c dark violet ('94)	17.50	.45
		Never hinged	150.00	
		On cover, single franking		3.50
c.		2½c lilac	100.00	.80
		Never hinged	700.00	
		On cover, single franking		4.00
		Nos. 34-37 (4)	60.75	3.60

Imperforate varieties are proofs.

Values for blocks of 4

34	A7	½c rose (II)	57.50	62.50
b.		½c red brn	525.00	175.00
35	A7	1c emerald grn	11.00	25.00
		1c grn	47.50	27.50
36	A7	2c ol yel	160.00	60.00
a.		2c yel	325.00	62.50
37	A7	2½c vio	70.00	85.00
b.		2½c dk vio	90.00	100.00
c.		2½c lilac	475.00	50.00

Princess Wilhelmina — A8

1891-94 Perf. 12½

40	A8	3c orange ('94)	8.00	2.30
		Never hinged	35.00	
		On cover, single franking		52.50
		Overprinted "SPECIMEN"	52.50	
a.		3c orange yellow ('92)	11.50	2.75
		Never hinged	52.50	
		On cover, single franking		57.50
41	A8	5c lt ultra ('94)	4.00	.25
		Never hinged	26.00	
		On cover, single franking		2.75
		Overprinted "SPECIMEN"	52.50	
a.		5c dull blue	5.00	.25
		Never hinged	29.00	
		On cover, single franking		3.00
42	A8	7½c brown ('94)	15.00	6.25
		Never hinged	75.00	
		On postcard		42.50
		On cover		50.00
		On cover, single franking		190.00
		Overprinted "SPECIMEN"	52.50	
a.		7½c red brown	27.50	6.25
		Never hinged	135.00	
		On postcard		42.50
		On cover		50.00
		On cover, single franking		190.00
43	A8	10c brt rose ('94)	23.50	1.60
		Never hinged	125.00	
		On cover, single franking		9.25
		Overprinted "SPECIMEN"	52.50	
a.		10c brick red	45.00	2.40
		Never hinged	175.00	
		On cover, single franking		14.00
44	A8	12½c bluish gray ('94)	23.50	1.60
		Never hinged	130.00	
		On cover, single franking		12.50
		Overprinted "SPECIMEN"	52.50	
a.		12½c gray	40.00	1.75

		Never hinged	175.00	
		On cover, single franking		30.00
45	A8	15c yel brn ('94)	60.00	5.00
		Never hinged	300.00	
		On cover, single franking		100.00
		Overprinted "SPECIMEN"	52.50	
a.		15c orange brown	80.00	5.50
		Never hinged	400.00	
		On cover, single franking		150.00
46	A8	20c green ('94)	70.00	3.00
		Never hinged	325.00	
		On cover, single franking		125.00
		Overprinted "SPECIMEN"	52.50	
a.		20c yellow green	80.00	3.00
		Never hinged	400.00	
		On cover, single franking		160.00
47	A8	22½c dk grn ('94)	32.50	13.50
		Never hinged	165.00	
		On cover, single franking		175.00
		Overprinted "SPECIMEN"	55.00	
a.		22½c deep blue green	55.00	13.50
		Never hinged	275.00	
		On cover, single franking		290.00
48	A8	25c dl vio ('94)	110.00	6.00
		Never hinged	575.00	
		On cover, single franking		77.50
		Overprinted "SPECIMEN"	77.50	
a.		25c dark violet	110.00	6.00
		Never hinged	575.00	
		On cover, single franking		77.50
49	A8	50c yel brn ('94)	550.00	20.00
		Never hinged	2,600.	
		On parcel post receipt card		275.00
		On cover, single franking		450.00
		Overprinted "SPECIMEN"	150.00	
a.		50c bister	575.00	27.50
		Never hinged	2,750.	
		On parcel post receipt card		325.00
		On cover, single franking		500.00
50	A8	1g gray vio	625.00	77.50
		Never hinged	2,750.	
		On cover		875.00
		On cover, single franking		2,750.
		Overprinted "SPECIMEN"	1,250.	

The paper used in 1891-93 was white, rough and somewhat opaque. In 1894, a thinner, smooth and sometimes transparent paper was introduced.
The 5c orange was privately produced.

Values for blocks of 4

40	A8	3c org	50.00	14.00
a.		3c org yel	70.00	50.00
41	A8	5c lt ultra	21.00	11.50
a.		5c dull bl	32.50	11.50
42	A8	7½c brn	100.00	72.50
a.		7½c red brn	160.00	77.50
43	A8	10c br rose	145.00	40.00
a.		10c brick red	240.00	50.00
44	A8	12½c bluish gray	145.00	57.50
a.		12½c gray	200.00	70.00
45	A8	15c yel brn	325.00	85.00
a.		15c org brn	500.00	100.00
46	A8	20c green	400.00	57.50
a.		20c yel grn	475.00	77.50
47	A8	22½c dk grn	200.00	160.00
a.		22½c dp bl grn	225.00	155.00
48	A8	25c dull vio	625.00	57.50
a.		25c dk vio	625.00	57.50
49	A8	50c yel brn	2,750.	160.00
a.		50c bister	3,500.	275.00
50	A8	1g gray vio	3,250.	500.00

Princess Wilhelmina — A9

1893-96 Perf. 11½x11

51	A9	50c emer & yel brn ('96)	80.00	15.00
		On cover		550.00
a.		Perf. 11	2,500.	200.00
52	A9	1g brn & ol grn ('96)	200.00	22.50
		On cover		2,200.
a.		Perf. 11	225.00	60.00
53	A9	2g 50c brt rose & ultra	400.00	130.00
		On cover		6,000.
a.		2g 50c lil rose & ultra, perf. 11	475.00	130.00
b.		Perf. 11½	500.00	140.00

Perf. 11

54	A9	5g brnz grn & red brn ('96)	700.00	425.00

Values for blocks of 4

51	A9	50c emer & yel brn	375.00	72.50
52	A9	1g brn & ol grn	850.00	200.00
a.		Perf. 11	1,100.	250.00
53	A9	2g 50c brt rose & ultra	1,900.	650.00
a.		2g 50c lil rose & ultra	2,200.	675.00
b.		Perf. 11½	2,250.	750.00
54	A9	5g brnz grn & red brn	3,500.	2,600.

A10

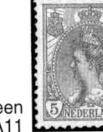

Queen Wilhelmina — A11

Perf. 12½ (#70, 73, 75-77, 81-82), 11½, 11½x11, 11x11½
1898-1924

55	A10	½c violet	.45	.25
		Never hinged	.80	
		On cover		2.50
		On cover, single franking		50.00
56	A10	1c red	.90	.25
		Never hinged	3.00	
		On cover, pair		1.00
		On cover, single franking		.50
b.		Imperf., pair	2,000.	
57	A10	1½c ultra ('08)	6.00	.85
		Never hinged	15.00	
		On cover		3.25
		On cover, single franking		2.50
58	A10	1½c dp blue ('13)	3.00	.35
		Never hinged	8.00	
		On cover		2.00
		On cover, single franking		1.00
59	A10	2c yellow brn	3.75	.25
		Never hinged	16.00	
		On cover		3.25
		On cover, single franking		1.75
60	A10	2½c deep green	3.25	.25
		Never hinged	9.50	
		On cover, pair		.75
		On cover, single franking		.50
b.		Imperf., pair	6,250.	
61	A11	3c orange	16.50	3.25
		Never hinged	70.00	
		On cover		30.00
		On cover, single franking		25.00
62	A11	3c pale ol grn ('01)	1.10	.25
		Never hinged	2.50	
		On cover		1.75
		On cover, single franking		.50
63	A11	4c claret ('21)	1.60	1.10
		Never hinged	2.50	
		On cover		8.00
		On cover, single franking		32.50
a.		4c lilac	2.50	1.50
		Never hinged	5.25	
		On cover		65.00
64	A11	4½c violet ('19)	3.75	3.75
		Never hinged	5.25	
		On cover		10.00
		On cover, single franking		65.00
65	A11	5c car rose	1.60	.25
		Never hinged	3.75	
		On cover		1.00
		On cover, single franking		.50
a.		5c pale rose	2.50	.25
66	A11	7½c brown	.75	.25
		Never hinged	1.60	
		On cover		1.00
		On cover, single franking		.50
a.		Tête bêche pair ('24)	80.00	72.50
		Never hinged	115.00	
		On cover, overfranked		325.00
b.		7½c dark brown	1.50	.30
67	A11	10c gray lilac	6.25	.25
		Never hinged	15.00	
		On cover		6.50
		On cover, single franking		1.00
a.		10c dark gray	7.25	.30
68	A11	12½c blue	3.25	.30
		Never hinged	11.00	
		On cover		5.00
		On cover, single franking		3.25
69	A11	15c yellow brn	100.00	3.25
		Never hinged	500.00	
		On cover		32.50
		On cover, single franking		65.00
70	A11	15c bl & car ('08)	6.25	.25
		Never hinged	22.00	
		On cover		15.00
		On cover, single franking		25.00
a.		Perf. 11½	7.25	.80
b.		Perf. 11½x11	75.00	16.50
c.		Perf 11x11½	1,100.	525.00
71	A11	17½c vio ('06)	50.00	12.00
		Never hinged	100.00	
		On cover		40.00
		On cover, single franking		150.00
73	A11	17½c ultra & brn ('10)	15.00	.90
		Never hinged	60.00	
		On cover		20.00
		On cover, single franking		30.00
a.		17½c ultra & blk brn	18.00	.90
b.		Perf 11½	18.00	3.00
c.		Perf 11½x11	18.00	3.00
74	A11	20c yellow green	150.00	.75
		Never hinged	1,200.	
		On cover		35.00
		On cover, single franking		65.00
75	A11	20c ol grn & gray ('08)	10.00	.50
		Never hinged	45.00	
		On cover		30.00
		On cover, single franking		25.00
a.		Perf 11½	12.00	1.40
76	A11	22½c brn & ol grn	9.25	.60
		Never hinged	45.00	
		On cover		25.00
		On cover, single franking		30.00
a.		Perf 11½	9.25	1.90
b.		Perf 11½x11	9.25	.50
77	A11	25c car & blue	9.25	.45
		Never hinged	45.00	
		On cover		16.50
		On cover, single franking		22.50
a.		25c rose & blue	18.00	.50
b.		Perf 11½	10.00	.75
c.		Perf 11½x11	10.00	.75
78	A11	30c lil & vio brn ('17)	24.00	.50
		Never hinged	65.00	
		On cover		16.50
		On cover, single franking		26.00

79	A11	40c grn & org ('20)	34.00	1.10
		Never hinged	92.50	
		On cover		30.00
		On cover, single franking		65.00
80	A11	50c brnz grn & red brn	110.00	1.10
		Never hinged	400.00	
		On cover		32.50
		On cover, single franking		100.00
81	A11	50c gray & vio ('14)	70.00	1.10
		Never hinged	175.00	
		On cover		32.50
		On cover, single franking		80.00
		On parcel post receipt card, multiple		165.00
a.		Perf 11½x11	70.00	16.50
		On cover, single franking		125.00
b.		50c gray blk & vio	72.50	1.90
82	A11	60c ol grn & grn ('20)	34.00	1.10
		Never hinged	92.50	
		On cover		50.00
		On cover, single franking		115.00
a.		Perf 11½	200.00	20.00
b.		Perf 11½x11	40.00	1.40
		Nos. 55-82 (27)	673.90	35.20
		Set, never hinged	3,000.	

See Nos. 107-112. For overprints and surcharges see Nos. 102-103, 106, 117-123, 135-136, O1-O8.

Values for blocks of 4

55	A10	½c vio	2.25	5.25
56	A10	1c red	4.75	5.25
57	A10	1½c ultra	30.00	10.00
58	A10	1½c dp bl	14.00	5.25
59	A10	2c yel brn	19.00	5.25
60	A10	2½c dp grn	17.00	5.25
61	A11	3c org	85.00	60.00
62	A11	3c pale ol grn	5.50	3.00
63	A11	4c claret	7.50	5.00
64	A11	4½c vio	18.00	18.00
65	A11	5c car rose	7.00	1.50
66	A11	7½c brn	3.00	1.75
67	A11	10c gray lil	32.50	2.00
68	A11	12½c bl	17.00	5.25
69	A11	15c yel brn	450.00	45.00
70	A11	15c bl & car	30.00	4.50
71	A11	17½c vio	250.00	62.50
73	A11	17½c ultra & brn	75.00	11.00
74	A11	20c yel grn	725.00	32.50
75	A11	20c ol grn & gray	52.50	6.00
76	A11	22½c brn & ol grn	47.50	7.25
77	A11	25c car & bl	47.50	6.00
78	A11	30c lil & vio brn	120.00	9.00
79	A11	40c grn & org	175.00	15.00
80	A11	50c brnz grn & red brn	500.00	18.50
81	A11	50c gray & vio	350.00	11.00
82	A11	60c ol grn & grn	175.00	11.00

A12

          I   II

Type I — The figure "1" is 3¾mm high and 2¾mm wide.

Type II — The figure "1" is 3½mm high and 2½mm wide, it is also thinner than in type I.

Perf. 11, 11x11½, 11½, 11½x11
1898-1905   Engr.

83	A12	1g dk grn, II ('99)	52.50	.75
	Never hinged		375.00	
	On parcel post receipt card			65.00
	On parcel post receipt card, single franking			225.00
a.	Type I ('98)		190.00	110.00
	Never hinged		1,000.	
	On cover, overfranked			225.00
84	A12	2½g brn lil ('99)	100.00	3.25
	Never hinged		275.00	
	On parcel post receipt card			100.00
	On flight cover			55.00
85	A12	5g claret ('99)	225.00	6.00
	Never hinged		675.00	
	On parcel post receipt card			150.00
	On flight cover			100.00
86	A12	10g orange ('05)	775.00	675.00
	Never hinged		1,650.	
	On parcel post receipt card			—
	On flight cover			675.00
	Set, never hinged		2,975.	

For surcharge see No. 104.

Values for blocks of 4

83	A12	1g dk grn (II)	240.00	5.00
a.	Type I		925.00	750.00
84	A12	2½g brnn lil	475.00	14.50
85	A12	5g claret	1,000.	30.00
86	A12	10g org	4,250.	3,400.

Admiral M. A. de Ruyter and Fleet — A13   King William I — A14

1907, Mar. 23   Typo.   Perf. 12x12½

87	A13	½c blue	2.00	1.25
	Never hinged		5.25	
	On cover			22.50
	On cover, single franking			65.00
88	A13	1c claret	3.50	2.25
	Never hinged		15.00	
	On cover			19.00
	On cover, single franking			27.50
89	A13	2½c vermilion	6.00	2.25
	Never hinged		17.00	
	On cover			24.00
	On cover, single franking			37.50
	Nos. 87-89 (3)		11.50	5.75
	Set, never hinged		37.00	

De Ruyter (1607-1676), naval hero.
For surcharges see Nos. J29-J41.

Perf. 11½x11, 11½ (#97, 100-101)
1913, Nov. 29   Engr.

Designs: 2½c, 12½c, 1g, King William I. 3c, 20c, 2½g, King William II. 5c, 25c, 5g, King William III. 10c, 50c, 10g, Queen Wilhelmina.

90	A14	2½c green, grn	.80	.80
	Never hinged		2.25	
	On cover			10.00
	On cover, single franking			8.00
91	A14	3c buff, straw	1.80	1.50
	Never hinged		1.60	
	On cover			20.00
	On cover, single franking			20.00
92	A14	5c rose red, sal	1.25	.90
	Never hinged		1.90	
	On cover			11.00
	On cover, single franking			6.50
93	A14	10c gray blk	4.25	2.40
	Never hinged		6.50	
	On cover			22.50
	On cover, single franking			32.50
94	A14	12½c dp blue, bl	3.00	1.90
	Never hinged		5.50	
	On cover			22.50
	On cover, single franking			26.00
95	A14	20c orange brn	13.00	11.00
	Never hinged		32.50	
	On cover			25.00
	On cover, single franking			72.50
96	A14	25c pale blue	15.00	8.75
	Never hinged		32.50	
	On cover			60.00
	On cover, single franking			90.00

97	A14	50c yel grn	32.50	27.50
			82.50	
	On cover			120.00
	On cover, single franking			145.00
	On parcel post receipt card			190.00
98	A14	1g claret	47.50	20.00
	Never hinged		175.00	
	On cover			120.00
	On parcel post receipt card			190.00
	Never hinged		190.00	
99	A14	2½g dull violet	120.00	50.00
	Never hinged		325.00	
	On parcel post receipt card			180.00
100	A14	5g yel, straw	225.00	40.00
	Never hinged		525.00	
	On parcel post receipt card			160.00
101	A14	10g red, straw	800.00	725.00
	Never hinged			
	Nos. 90-101 (12)		1,264.	889.75
	Set, never hinged		2,285.	

90a	A14	2½c grn, grn	1.10	.90
91a	A14	5c buff, straw	1.40	1.35
92a	A14	5c rose red, salmon	1.50	.90
93a	A14	10c gray blk	4.25	2.50
94a	A14	12½c dp bl, bl	3.25	2.25
95a	A14	20c org brn	13.00	11.00
98a	A14	1g claret	60.00	20.00
	Never hinged		140.00	

Centenary of Dutch independence.
For surcharge see No. 105.

No. 78 Surcharged in Red or Black

       a   b

1919, Dec. 1   Perf. 12½

102	A11 (a) 40c on 30c (R)		22.50	3.25
	Never hinged		80.00	
	On cover			75.00
	On cover, single franking			110.00
103	A11 (b) 60c on 30c (Bk)		25.00	3.75
	Never hinged		80.00	
	On cover			80.00
	On cover, single franking			130.00
	Set, never hinged		140.00	
	Set on overfranked philatelic cover			55.00

Nos. 86 and 101 Surcharged in Black

1920, Aug. 17   Perf. 11, 11½

104	A12 2.50g on 10g		145.00	110.00
	Never hinged		300.00	
	On parcel post receipt card, single franking			300.00
	On parcel post receipt card, multiple franking			500.00
	On overfranked philatelic cover			375.00
105	A14 2.50g on 10g		160.00	100.00
	Never hinged		325.00	
	On parcel post receipt card, single franking			300.00
	On parcel post receipt card, multiple franking			350.00
	On overfranked philatelic cover			375.00
	Set, never hinged		625.00	
	Set on overfranked philatelic cover			375.00

No. 64 Surcharged in Red

1921, Mar. 1   Typo.   Perf. 12½

106	A11 4c on 4½c vio		4.00	1.60
	Never hinged		8.00	
	On cover			19.00
	On cover, single franking			16.00

A17

1921-22   Typo.   Perf. 12½

107	A17	5c green ('22)	11.00	.25
	Never hinged		35.00	
	On cover			1.75
	On cover, single franking			1.75
108	A17	12½c vermilion ('22)	18.00	1.75
	Never hinged		55.00	
	On cover, single franking			18.00
109	A17	20c blue	27.50	.25
	Never hinged		125.00	
	On cover			15.00
	On cover, single franking			5.00
	Nos. 107-109 (3)		56.50	2.25
	Set, never hinged		215.00	

Queen Type of 1898-99, 10c Redrawn

1922   Perf. 12½

110	A11	10c gray	29.00	.25
	Never hinged		75.00	

Imperf

111	A11	5c car rose	7.25	7.25
	Never hinged		13.50	
	On cover			30.00
	On cover, single franking			65.00
112	A11	10c gray	7.25	7.25
	Never hinged		14.00	
	On cover			30.00
	On cover, single franking			55.00
	Nos. 110-112 (3)		43.50	14.75
	Set (Nos. 111-112) on overfranked philatelic cover			35.00

In redrawn 10c the horizontal lines behind the Queen's head are wider apart.

Orange Tree and Lion of Brabant   Post Horn and Lion
A18   A19

Numeral of Value — A20

1923, Mar. 9   Perf. 12½

113	A18	1c dark violet	.55	.60
	Never hinged		1.75	
	On cover			7.25
	On cover, single franking			
114	A18	2c orange	6.00	.25
	Never hinged		9.00	
	On cover			2.75
	On cover, single franking			.55
115	A19	2½c bluish green	1.75	.65
	Never hinged		3.50	
	On cover			9.00
116	A20	4c deep blue	1.25	.60
	Never hinged		2.75	
	On cover			—
	On cover, single franking			13.00
	Nos. 113-116 (4)		9.55	2.10
	Set, never hinged		17.00	
	Set on overfranked philatelic cover			6.00

Nos. 56, 58, 62, 65, 68, 73, 76 Surcharged in Various Colors

      c   d

1923, July   Perf. 12½

117	A10(c) 2c on 1c (Bl)		.45	.25
	Never hinged		.90	
	On cover			2.75
	On cover, single franking			3.75
118	A10(c) 2c on 1½c (Bk)		.45	.25
	Never hinged		.90	
	On cover			2.75
	On cover, single franking			3.75
119	A11(d) 10c on 3c (Br)		4.25	.25
	Never hinged		10.00	
	On cover			16.00
	On cover, single franking			6.40
120	A11(d) 10c on 5c (Bk)		8.00	.50
	Never hinged		17.50	
	On cover			22.50
	On cover, single franking			9.00
121	A11(d) 10c on 12½c (R)		7.25	.90
	Never hinged		19.00	
	On cover			22.50

	On cover, single franking			15.00
	Perf. 11½x11			
122	A11(d) 10c on 17½c (R)		4.00	4.00
	Never hinged		8.00	
	On cover			30.00
	On cover, single franking			45.00
a.	Perf. 11½		1,600.	800.00
	Never hinged		8.00	
	On cover, single franking			35.00
	On cover, single franking			60.00
123	A11(d) 10c on 22½c (R)		4.00	4.00
	Never hinged		6.50	
	On cover			30.00
	On cover, single franking			45.00
a.	Perf. 11½		3.00	3.50
	Never hinged		6.50	
	On cover			30.00
	On cover, single franking			45.00
b.	Perf. 11½		4.00	4.00
	Never hinged		8.00	
	On cover			35.00
	On cover, single franking			55.00
	Nos. 117-123 (7)		28.40	10.15
	Set, never hinged		62.50	
	Set on overfranked philatelic cover			13.00

Queen Wilhelmina
A21   A22

Perf. 11½x12½, 11½x12 (5c)
1923, Oct.   Engr.

124	A22	2c myrtle green	.25	.25
	Never hinged		1.10	
	On cover			5.50
	On cover, single franking			1.15
a.	Vert. pair, imperf. between		2,400.	
125	A21	5c green	.35	.25
	Never hinged		1.10	
	On cover			11.00
	On cover, single franking			1.10
a.	Vert. pair, imperf. between		1,800.	
126	A22	7½c carmine	.50	.25
	Never hinged		2.00	
	On cover			5.50
	On cover, single franking			1.10
127	A22	10c vermilion	.40	.25
	Never hinged		1.50	
	On cover			3.75
	On cover, single franking			.90
a.	Vert. pair, imperf. between		550.00	575.00
128	A22	20c ultra	3.50	1.00
	Never hinged		1.50	
	On cover			3.75
	On cover, single franking			.90
129	A22	25c yellow	5.50	1.10
	Never hinged		15.00	
	On cover			32.50
	On cover, single franking			65.00
	Perf. 11½			
130	A22	35c orange	5.00	3.00
	Never hinged		15.00	
	On cover			35.00
	On cover, single franking			30.00
131	A22	50c black	17.00	.50
	Never hinged		45.00	
	On cover			100.00
	On cover, single franking			150.00
132	A21	1g red	30.00	7.25
	Never hinged		60.00	
	On cover			350.00
	On cover, single franking			200.00
133	A21	2½g black	210.00	200.00
	Never hinged		450.00	
	on parcel post receipt card, single franking			310.00
	on parcel post receipt card, single franking			550.00
134	A21	5g dark blue	200.00	175.00
	Never hinged		375.00	
	on parcel post receipt card, single franking			300.00
	Nos. 124-134 (11)		472.50	388.85
	Set, never hinged		975.00	

25th anniv. of the assumption as monarch of the Netherlands by Queen Wilhelmina at the age of 18.

No. 119 Overprinted in Red

No. 73 With Additional Surcharge in Blue

1923 Typo. Perf. 12½
135	A11 10c on 3c	1.10	1.00
	Never hinged	8.00	
	On cover		27.50
	On cover, single franking		27.50
136	A11 1g on 17½c	62.50	15.00
	Never hinged	160.00	
	On cover		240.00
	On cover, single franking		320.00
a.	Perf. 11½	95.00	40.00
b.	Perf. 11½x11	80.00	30.00

Stamps with red surcharge were prepared for use as Officials but were not issued.

Queen Wilhelmina — A23

1924, Sept. 6 Photo. Perf. 12½
137	A23 10c slate green	32.50	35.00
	Never hinged	55.00	
	On cover		170.00
	On cover, single franking		180.00
138	A23 15c gray black	42.50	45.00
	Never hinged	80.00	
	On cover		200.00
139	A23 35c brown orange	32.50	35.00
	Never hinged	60.00	
	On cover		250.00
	Nos. 137-139 (3)	107.50	115.00

These stamps were available solely to visitors to the International Philatelic Exhibition at The Hague and were not obtainable at regular post offices. Set of three on international philatelic exhibition cover dataed Sept. 6-12, 15-17, 1924, value, $110. Set of three on Netherland Philatelic Exhibition cover dated Sept. 13-14, value, $150.

See Nos. 147-160, 172-193. For overprints and surcharge see Nos. 194, O11, O13-O15.

Ship in Distress — A23a

Lifeboat — A23b

1924, Sept. 15 Litho. Perf. 11½
140	A23a 2c black brn	3.75	2.50
	Never hinged	7.25	
	On cover		7.25
	On cover, single franking		13.00
141	A23b 10c orange brn	6.50	2.00
	Never hinged	13.00	
	On cover		7.25
	On cover, single franking		13.00

Centenary of Royal Dutch Lifeboat Society.

Type A23 and

Gull — A24

1924-26 Perf. 12½
142	A24 1c deep red	.75	.90
	Never hinged	.90	
	On cover		1.90
143	A24 2c red orange	2.50	.25
	Never hinged	3.75	
	On cover		.75
	On cover, single franking		.80
144	A24 2½c deep green	3.00	.80
	Never hinged	5.00	
	On cover		1.75
	On cover, single franking		4.50
145	A24 3c yel grn ('25)	15.00	1.00
	Never hinged	50.00	
	On cover		2.75
	On cover, single franking		5.50
146	A24 4c dp ultra	3.00	.70
	Never hinged	15.00	
	On cover		2.00
	On cover, single franking		7.25

Photo.
147	A23 5c dull green	3.50	.75
	Never hinged	8.00	
	On cover		2.00
148	A23 6c org brn ('25)	.75	.50
	Never hinged	1.40	
	On cover		7.00
	On cover, single franking		12.50
149	A23 7½c orange ('25)	.35	.25
	Never hinged	1.10	
	On cover		.50
	On cover, single franking		1.25

150	A23 9c org red & blk ('26)	1.50	1.25
	Never hinged	3.00	
	On cover		27.50
	On cover, single franking		110.00
151	A23 10c red, shades	1.50	.25
	Never hinged	5.50	
	On cover		.40
152	A23 12½c deep rose	1.60	.35
	Never hinged	4.50	
	On cover		11.00
	On cover, single franking		12.50
153	A23 15c ultra	6.00	.45
	Never hinged	15.00	
	On cover, single franking		.75
154	A23 20c dp blue ('25)	10.00	.60
	Never hinged	22.00	
	On cover		7.00
	On cover, single franking		12.50
155	A23 25c olive bis ('25)	22.50	.85
	Never hinged	40.00	
	On cover		8.00
	On cover, single franking		25.00
156	A23 30c violet	13.00	.65
	Never hinged	40.00	
	On cover		20.00
	On cover, single franking		25.00
157	A23 35c olive brn ('25)	30.00	6.00
	Never hinged	80.00	
	On cover		20.00
	On cover, single franking		85.00
158	A23 40c dp brown	35.00	.75
	Never hinged	200.00	
	On cover		25.00
	On cover, single franking		60.00
159	A23 50c blue grn ('25)	60.00	.60
	Never hinged	275.00	
	On cover		25.00
	On parcel post receipt card, single franking		70.00
160	A23 60c dk violet ('25)	27.50	.80
	Never hinged	100.00	
	On cover		65.00
	On cover, single franking		250.00
	Nos. 142-160 (19)	237.45	17.70
	Set, never hinged	725.00	

See Nos. 164-171, 243A-243Q. For overprints and surcharges see Nos. 226-243, O9-O10.

Syncopated, Type A (2 Sides)
1925-26
142a	A24 1c deep red	.75	.80
	Never hinged	1.45	
143a	A24 2c red orange	2.75	2.50
	Never hinged	4.50	
144a	A24 2½c deep green	2.75	1.25
	Never hinged	4.50	
145a	A24 3c yellow green	18.00	20.00
	Never hinged	40.00	
146a	A24 4c deep ultra	2.75	1.90
	Never hinged	7.00	
147a	A23 5c dull green	5.50	2.50
	Never hinged	10.00	
148a	A23 6c orange brown	110.00	100.00
	Never hinged	190.00	
149a	A23 7½c orange	1.10	1.00
	Never hinged	1.50	
150a	A23 9c org red & blk	1.75	1.25
	Never hinged	2.50	
151a	A23 10c red	11.00	2.75
	Never hinged	17.00	
152a	A23 12½c deep rose	1.75	1.50
	Never hinged	3.50	
153a	A23 15c ultra	67.50	6.00
	Never hinged	145.00	
154a	A23 20c deep blue	10.00	4.00
	Never hinged	20.00	
155a	A23 25c olive bister	42.50	45.00
	Never hinged	90.00	
156a	A23 30c violet	14.50	10.50
	Never hinged	27.50	
158a	A23 40c deep brown	45.00	36.00
	Never hinged	160.00	
159a	A23 50c blue green	55.00	20.00
	Never hinged	240.00	
160a	A23 60c dark violet	27.50	11.00
	Never hinged	70.00	
	Nos. 142a-160a (18)	420.10	267.95
	Set, never hinged	1,035.	

A25

1925-30 Engr. Perf. 11½
161	A25 1g ultra	8.00	.65
	Never hinged	25.00	
	On cover		18.00
	On parcel post receipt card, single franking		55.00
a.	Perf 12½ ('30)	8.75	.75
	Never hinged	27.50	
	As "a," on cover		20.00
	As "a," pn parcel post receipt card, single franking		55.00
162	A25 2½g car ('27)	90.00	3.00
	Never hinged	175.00	
	On cover		72.50
	On parcel post receipt card, single franking		110.00
a.	Perf 12½ ('30)	100.00	3.00
	Never hinged	175.00	
	As "a," on cover		72.50
	On parcel post receipt card, single franking		110.00
163	A25 5g gray blk	160.00	2.50
	On cover	300.00	
	On parcel post receipt card, single franking		55.00
			90.00
a.	Perf 12½ ('30)	175.00	1.90

	Never hinged	300.00	
	As "a," on cover		55.00
	As "a," on parcel post receipt card, single franking		90.00
	Nos. 161-163 (3)	258.00	6.15

Types of 1924-26 Issue
Perf. 12½, 13½x12½, 12½x13½
1926-39 Wmk. 202 Litho.
164	A24 ½c gray ('28)	.90	1.00
	Never hinged	1.60	
	On cover		4.00
165	A24 1c dp red ('27)	.25	.25
	Never hinged	.35	
	On cover		.80
166	A24 1½c red vio ('28)	1.10	.25
	Never hinged	2.50	
	On cover		.50
c.	"CEN" for "CENT"	165.00	275.00
	Never hinged	375.00	
	On cover		500.00
d.	"GENT" for "CENT"	120.00	115.00
	Never hinged	250.00	
167	A24 1½c gray ('35)	.25	.25
	Never hinged	.35	
	On cover		.50
a.	1½c dark gray	.25	.25
	Never hinged	.35	
	On cover		.50
168	A24 2c dp org	.25	.25
	Never hinged	.35	
	On cover		.50
a.	2c red orange	.25	.25
	Never hinged	.35	
	On cover		.50
169	A24 2½c green ('27)	2.75	.25
	Never hinged	6.50	
	On cover		.50
170	A24 3c yel grn ('27)	.25	.25
	Never hinged	.35	
	On cover		.65
171	A24 4c dp ultra ('27)	.25	.25
	Never hinged	.35	
	On cover		.65
			1.00

Photo.
172	A23 5c dp green	.25	.25
	Never hinged	.35	
	On cover		.50
173	A23 6c org brn ('27)	.25	.25
	Never hinged	.35	
	On cover		.50
174	A23 7½c dk vio ('27)	3.25	.25
	Never hinged	5.75	
	On cover		.65
175	A23 7½c red ('28)	.35	.25
	Never hinged	.65	
	On cover		.65
176	A23 9c org red & blk ('28)	11.00	12.00
	Never hinged	15.00	
	On cover		13.50
	On cover, single franking		82.50
b.	Value omitted	14,500.	
177	A23 10c red	1.30	.25
	Never hinged	2.60	
	On cover		.50
178	A23 10c dl vio ('29)	2.50	.25
	Never hinged	5.00	
	On cover		.50
179	A23 12½c dp rose ('27)	42.50	4.50
	Never hinged	82.50	
	On cover		15.00
180	A23 12½c ultra ('28)	.25	.25
	Never hinged	.50	
	On cover		3.25
181	A23 15c ultra	7.25	.25
	Never hinged	11.50	
	On cover		3.25
182	A23 15c orange ('29)	1.30	.25
	Never hinged	2.50	
	On cover		3.25
183	A23 20c dp blue ('28)	7.25	.25
	Never hinged	12.00	
	On cover		3.25
184	A23 21c ol brn ('31)	25.00	.90
	Never hinged	52.50	
	On cover		25.00
	On cover, single franking		30.00
185	A23 22½c ol brn ('27)	7.25	3.00
	Never hinged	17.00	
	On cover		25.00
	On cover, single franking		62.50
186	A23 22½c dp org ('39)	15.50	16.00
	Never hinged	20.00	
	On cover		40.00
	On cover, single franking		75.00
187	A23 25c ol bis ('27)	4.50	.25
	Never hinged	13.00	
	On cover		13.00
	On cover, single franking		21.00
188	A23 27½c gray ('28)	4.50	.90
	Never hinged	13.00	
	On cover		10.00
189	A23 30c violet	5.00	.25
	Never hinged	13.00	
	On cover		16.50
190	A23 35c olive brn	62.50	12.50
	Never hinged	145.00	
	On cover		22.50
191	A23 40c dp brown	9.00	.25
	Never hinged	24.00	
	On cover		26.00
	On cover, single franking		50.00
192	A23 50c blue grn	5.00	.25
	Never hinged	13.00	
	On parcel post receipt card		32.50
			50.00
193	A23 60c black ('29)	57.50	.90
	Never hinged	180.00	
	On parcel post receipt card		50.00
	On parcel post receipt card		75.00
	On parcel post receipt card, single franking		120.00
	Nos. 164-193 (30)	279.20	56.95
	Set, never hinged	640.00	

		300.00	
	As "a," on cover		55.00
	As "a," on parcel post receipt card, single franking		90.00
	Nos. 161-163 (3)	258.00	6.15

Syncopated, Type A (2 Sides), 12½
1926-27
168b	A24 2c deep orange	.40	.40
170a	A24 3c yellow green	.60	.60
171a	A24 4c deep ultra	.60	.60
172a	A23 5c deep green	.70	.60
173a	A23 6c orange brown	.40	.45
174a	A23 7½c dark violet	4.50	2.00
177a	A23 10c red	1.00	.85
181a	A23 15c ultra	7.00	3.00
185a	A23 22½c olive brown	7.00	2.50
187a	A23 25c olive bister	20.00	18.00
189a	A23 30c violet	19.00	12.00
190a	A23 35c olive brown	77.50	22.50
191a	A23 40c deep brown	50.00	40.00
	Nos. 168b-191a (13)	188.70	103.50
	Set, never hinged	360.00	

1928 Syncopated, Type B (4 Sides)
164a	A24 ½c gray	.80	.65
165a	A24 1c deep red	.30	.30
166a	A24 1½c red violet	.80	.25
168c	A24 2c deep orange	1.00	.60
169a	A24 2½c green	2.75	.25
170b	A24 3c yellow green	.75	.75
171b	A24 4c deep ultra	.75	.65
172b	A23 5c deep green	1.00	.75
173b	A23 6c orange brown	.75	.50
174b	A23 7½c dark violet	4.25	2.00
175a	A23 7½c red		
176a	A23 9c org red & blk	10.00	12.50
178a	A23 10c dull violet	5.25	5.00
179a	A23 12½c deep rose	80.00	80.00
180a	A23 12½c ultra	1.40	.40
181b	A23 15c ultra	9.00	2.00
182a	A23 15c orange	.75	.30
183a	A23 20c deep blue	7.00	3.75
187b	A23 25c olive bister	17.00	10.00
188a	A23 27½c gray	4.50	2.00
189b	A23 30c violet	15.00	8.00
191b	A23 40c deep brown	35.00	22.50
192a	A23 50c blue green	55.00	45.00
193a	A23 60c black	45.00	22.50
	Nos. 164a-193a (24)	298.30	220.15
	Set, never hinged	600.00	

Syncopated, Type C (2 Sides, Corners Only)
1930
164b	A24 ½c gray	1.00	.70
165b	A24 1c deep red	1.00	.40
166b	A24 1½c red violet	.90	.25
168d	A24 2c deep orange	.80	.70
169b	A24 2½c green	2.75	.25
170c	A24 3c yellow green	1.10	.50
171c	A24 4c deep ultra	.50	.25
172c	A23 5c deep green	.70	.70
173c	A23 6c orange brown	.70	.70
178b	A23 10c dull violet	8.00	7.00
183b	A23 20c deep blue	7.75	3.75
184a	A23 21c olive brown	25.00	9.00
189c	A23 30c violet	12.00	7.00
192b	A23 50c blue green	45.00	45.00
	Nos. 164b-192b (14)	107.20	76.20
	Set, never hinged	225.00	

Syncopated, Type D (3 Holes Vert., 4 Holes Horiz.)
1927
174c	A23 7½c dark violet	2,750.	2,100.
	Never hinged	3,750.	

No. 185 Surcharged in Red

1929, Nov. 11 Perf. 12½
194	A23 21c on 22½c ol brn	21.00	1.50
	Never hinged	47.50	

Queen Wilhelmina — A26

1931, Oct. Photo. Perf. 12½
195	A26 70c dk bl & red	30.00	.80
	Never hinged	120.00	
a.	Perf. 14½x13½ ('39)	36.00	8.00
	Never hinged	140.00	

See No. 201.

Arms of the House of Orange — A27

William I — A28

Designs: 5c, William I, Portrait by Goltzius. 6c, Portrait of William I by Van Key. 12½c, Portrait attributed to Moro.

1933, Apr. 1		Unwmk.	Engr.	
196	A27	1½c black	.55	.40
197	A28	5c dark green	1.75	.40
198	A28	6c dull violet	2.75	.30
199	A28	12½c deep blue	17.00	3.50
		Nos. 196-199 (4)	22.05	4.60
		Set, never hinged	55.00	

400th anniv. of the birth of William I, Count of Nassau and Prince of Orange, frequently referred to as William the Silent.

Star, Dove and Sword — A31

1933, May 18		Photo.	Wmk. 202	
200	A31	12½c dp ultra	9.00	.75
		Never hinged	27.50	

For overprint see No. O12.

Queen Wilhelmina Design of 1931

Queen Wilhelmina and ships.

Perf. 14½x13½

1933, July 26			Wmk. 202	
201	A26	80c Prus bl & red	110.00	3.25
		Never hinged	350.00	

Willemstad Harbor — A33

Van Walbeeck's Ship — A34

Perf. 14x12½

1934, July 2		Engr.	Unwmk.	
202	A33	6c violet blk	3.50	.25
203	A34	12½c dull blue	22.00	3.00
		Set, never hinged	77.50	

Tercentenary of Curacao.

Minerva — A35

Design: 12½c, Gisbertus Voetius.

		Wmk. 202		
1936, May 15		**Photo.**	**Perf. 12½**	
204	A35	6c brown lake	2.50	.25
205	A35	12½c indigo	4.50	4.50
		Set, never hinged	16.00	

300th anniversary of the founding of the University at Utrecht.

A37

A38

A39

1937, Apr. 1		Perf. 14½x13½		
206	A37	1½c Boy Scout Emblem	.40	.25
207	A38	6c "Assembly"	1.25	.25
208	A39	12½c Mercury	4.00	1.40
		Nos. 206-208 (3)	5.65	1.90
		Set, never hinged	12.00	

Fifth Boy Scout World Jamboree, Vogelenzang, Netherlands, 7/31-8/13/37.

Wilhelmina — A40

1938, Aug. 27		Perf. 12½x12		
209	A40	1½c black	.25	.25
210	A40	5c red orange	.30	.25
211	A40	12½c royal blue	4.00	1.60
		Nos. 209-211 (3)	4.55	2.10
		Set, never hinged	13.50	

Reign of Queen Wilhelmina, 40th anniv.

St. Willibrord — A41

Design: 12½c, St. Willibrord as older man.

Perf. 12½x14

1939, June 15		Engr.	Unwmk.	
212	A41	5c dk slate grn	.75	.25
213	A41	12½c slate blue	5.00	2.75
		Set, never hinged	14.00	

12th centenary of the death of St. Willibrord.

Woodburning Engine — A43

Design: 12½c, Streamlined electric car.

Perf. 14½x13½

1939, Sept. 1		Photo.	Wmk. 202	
214	A43	5c dk slate grn	.80	.25
215	A43	12½c dark blue	8.00	4.00
		Set, never hinged	22.50	

Centenary of Dutch Railroads.

Catalogue values for unused stamps in this section, from this point to the end of the section, are for Never Hinged items.

Queen Wilhelmina — A45

1940-47		Perf. 13½x12½		
216	A45	5c dk green	.25	.25
216B	A45	6c hn brn ('47)	.55	.25
217	A45	7½c brt red	.25	.25
218	A45	10c brt red vio	.25	.25
219	A45	12½c sapphire	.25	.25
220	A45	15c light blue	.25	.25
220B	A45	17½c slate bl ('46)	1.25	.70
221	A45	20c purple	.35	.25
222	A45	22½c olive grn	1.25	.85
223	A45	25c rose brn	.35	.25
224	A45	30c bister	.80	.35
225	A45	40c brt green	1.25	.60
225A	A45	50c orange ('46)	9.50	.60
225B	A45	60c pur brn ('46)	8.50	2.00
		Nos. 216-225B (14)	25.05	7.10

Imperf. examples of Nos. 216, 218-220 were released through philatelic channels during the German occupation, but were never issued at any post office. Value, set, $1.
For overprints see Nos. O16-O24 (O20-O24 in Scott Standard catalogue, Vol. 5).

Type of 1924-26 Surcharged in Black or Blue

Perf. 12½x13½

1940, Oct.		Photo.	Wmk. 202	
226	A24	2½c on 3c ver	2.00	.25
227	A24	5c on 3c lt grn	.25	.25
228	A24	7½c on 3c ver	.25	.25
a.		Pair, #226, 228	4.00	1.50
229	A24	10c on 3c lt grn	.25	.25
230	A24	12½c on 3c lt bl		
		(Bl)	.30	.25
231	A24	17½c on 3c lt grn	.60	.65
232	A24	20c on 3c lt grn	.40	.25
233	A24	22½c on 3c lt grn	.80	.85
234	A24	25c on 3c lt grn	.50	.25
235	A24	30c on 3c lt grn	.65	.30
236	A24	40c on 3c lt grn	.80	.60
237	A24	50c on 3c lt grn	.70	.40
238	A24	60c on 3c lt grn	1.60	.85
239	A24	70c on 3c lt grn	3.75	1.75
240	A24	80c on 3c lt grn	5.50	4.00
241	A24	1g on 3c lt grn	35.00	32.50
242	A24	2.50g on 3c lt grn	40.00	37.50
243	A24	5g on 3c lt grn	37.50	35.00
		Nos. 226-243 (18)	130.85	116.15
		Set, hinged	70.00	

No. 228a is from coils.

Gull Type of 1924-26

1941				
243A	A24	2½c dk green	1.25	.35
b.		Booklet pane of 6	10.00	
243C	A24	5c brt green	.25	.25
243E	A24	7½c henna	.25	.25
r.		Pair, #243A, 243E	1.00	1.00
243G	A24	10c brt violet	.25	.25
243H	A24	12½c ultra	.25	.25
243J	A24	15c lt blue	.25	.25
243K	A24	17½c red org	.25	.25
243L	A24	20c lt violet	.25	.25
243M	A24	22½c dk ol grn	.25	.25
243N	A24	25c lake	.25	.25
243O	A24	30c olive	3.50	.25
243P	A24	40c emerald	.25	.25
243Q	A24	50c orange brn	.25	.25
		Nos. 243A-243Q (13)	7.50	3.35

No. 243Er is from coils.

SEMI-POSTAL STAMPS

Design Symbolical of the Four Chief Means for Combating Tuberculosis: Light, Water, Air and Food — SP1

Perf. 12½

1906, Dec. 21		Typo.	Unwmk.	
B1	SP1	1c (+1c) rose red	20.00	11.00
B2	SP1	3c (+3c) pale ol grn	30.00	26.00
B3	SP1	5c (+5c) gray	30.00	15.00
		Nos. B1-B3 (3)	80.00	52.00
		Set, never hinged		

Surtax aided the Society for the Prevention of Tuberculosis.
Nos. B1-B3 canceled-to-order "AMSTERDAM 31.07 10-12 N," sell at $3 a set.

Symbolical of Charity SP2

SP3

1923, Dec. 15		Perf. 11½		
B4	SP2	2c (+5c) vio bl	17.00	17.00
B5	SP3	10c (+5c) org red	17.00	17.00
		Set, never hinged	75.00	

The surtax was for the benefit of charity.

Allegory, Charity Protecting Child — SP6

1924, Dec. 15		Photo.	Perf. 12½	
B6	SP6	2c (+2c) emer	1.80	1.80
B7	SP6	7½c (+3½c) dk brn	6.75	8.00
B8	SP6	10c (+2½c) vermilion	4.00	1.80
		Nos. B6-B8 (3)	12.55	11.60
		Set, never hinged	26.00	

These stamps were sold at a premium over face value for the benefit of Child Welfare Societies.

Arms of North Brabant SP7

Arms of Gelderland SP8

Arms of South Holland — SP9

1925, Dec. 17		Perf. 12½		
B9	SP7	2c (+2c) grn & org	.85	.75
B10	SP8	7½c (+3½c) vio & bl	4.25	4.50
B11	SP9	10c (+2½c) red & org	3.50	.45
		Nos. B9-B11 (3)	8.60	5.70
		Set, never hinged	18.50	

Surtax went to Child Welfare Societies.

Syncopated Perfs., Type A

B9a	SP7	2c (+2c)	18.50	22.00
B10a	SP8	7½c (+3½c)	37.50	37.50
B11a	SP9	10c (+2½c)	65.00	52.00
		Nos. B9a-B11a (3)	121.00	111.50
		Set, never hinged	250.00	

Arms of Utrecht SP10

Arms of Zeeland SP11

Arms of
North Holland
SP12

Arms of
Friesland
SP13

1926, Dec. 1   Wmk. 202   Perf. 12½

B12	SP10	2c (+2c) sil & red	.50	.40
B13	SP11	5c (+3c) grn & gray bl	1.40	1.10
B14	SP12	10c (+3c) red & gold	2.10	.25
B15	SP13	15c (+3c) ultra & yel	5.50	4.25
		Nos. B12-B15 (4)	9.50	6.00
		Set, never hinged	25.00	

The surtax on these stamps was devoted to
Child Welfare Societies.

Syncopated Perfs., Type A

B12a	SP10	2c (+2c)	4.75	4.75
B13a	SP11	5c (+3c)	7.25	7.25
B14a	SP12	10c (+3c)	13.50	13.50
B15a	SP13	15c (+3c)	14.50	14.50
		Nos. B12a-B15a (4)	40.00	40.00
		Set, never hinged	95.00	

King William
III — SP14

Red Cross and
Doves — SP18

Designs: 3c, Queen Emma. 5c, Prince Con-
sort Henry. 7½c, Queen Wilhelmina.

Perf. 11½, 11½x12 B

1927, June   Photo.   Unwmk.

B16	SP14	2c (+2c) scar	2.50	2.25
		Engr.		
B17	SP14	3c (+2c) dp grn	5.75	8.00
B18	SP14	5c (+3c) slate bl	1.00	1.00
		Photo.		
B19	SP14	7½c (+3½c) ultra	4.50	1.50
B20	SP18	15c (+5c) ultra & red	8.75	8.00
		Nos. B16-B20 (5)	22.50	20.75
		Set, never hinged	52.50	

60th anniversary of the Netherlands Red
Cross Society. The surtaxes in parentheses
were for the benefit of the Society.

Arms of
Drenthe
SP19

Arms of
Groningen
SP20

Arms of
Limburg
SP21

Arms of
Overijssel
SP22

1927, Dec. 15   Wmk. 202   Perf. 12½

B21	SP19	2c (+2c) dp rose & vio	.35	.30
B22	SP20	5c (+3c) ol grn & yel	1.50	1.25
B23	SP21	7½c (+3½c) red & blk	3.25	.35
B24	SP22	15c (+3c) ultra & org brn	4.75	4.25
		Nos. B21-B24 (4)	9.85	6.15
		Set, never hinged	26.00	

The surtax on these stamps was for the
benefit of Child Welfare Societies.

Syncopated Perfs., Type A

B21a	SP19	2c (+2c)	1.90	1.40
B22a	SP20	5c (+3c)	3.50	1.75
B23a	SP21	7½c (+3c)	4.25	1.75
B24a	SP22	15c (+3c)	12.50	9.00
		Nos. B21a-B24a (4)	22.15	13.90
		Set, never hinged	57.50	

Rowing — SP23

Fencing — SP24

Soccer
SP25

Yachting
SP26

Putting the
Shot
SP27

Running
SP28

Riding
SP29

Boxing
SP30

Perf. 11½, 12, 11½x12, 12x11½

1928, Mar. 27   Litho.

B25	SP23	1½c (+1c) dk grn	1.90	1.40
B26	SP24	2c (+1c) red vio	2.40	1.75
B27	SP25	3c (+1c) green	2.40	2.00
B28	SP26	5c (+1c) lt bl	3.00	1.40
B29	SP27	7½c (+2½c) org	3.00	1.75
B30	SP28	10c (+2c) scarlet	6.75	5.25
B31	SP29	15c (+2c) dk bl	6.75	3.75
B32	SP30	30c (+3c) dk brn	20.00	17.50
		Nos. B25-B32 (8)	46.20	34.80
		Set, never hinged	150.00	

The surtax on these stamps was used to
help defray the expenses of the Olympic
Games of 1928.

Jean Pierre
Minckelers — SP31

5c, Hermann Boerhaave. 7½c, Hendrik
Antoon Lorentz. 12½c, Christian Huygens.

1928, Dec. 10   Photo.   Perf. 12x12½

B33	SP31	1½c (+1½c) vio	.55	.40
B34	SP31	5c (+3c) grn	1.75	.60
		Perf. 12		
B35	SP31	7½c (+2½c) ver	3.50	.25
a.		Perf. 12x12½	4.75	.70
		Never hinged	11.00	
B36	SP31	12½c (+3½c) ultra	9.75	7.50
a.		Perf. 12x12½	77.50	7.75
		Never hinged	175.00	
		Nos. B33-B36 (4)	15.55	8.75
		Set, never hinged	37.50	

The surtax on these stamps was for the
benefit of Child Welfare Societies.

Child on
Dolphin — SP35

1929, Dec. 10   Litho.   Perf. 12½

B37	SP35	1½c (+1½c) gray	2.10	.45
B38	SP35	5c (+3c) blue grn	3.50	.75
B39	SP35	6c (+4c) scarlet	2.10	.35
B40	SP35	12½c (+3½c) dk bl	13.50	11.00
		Nos. B37-B40 (4)	21.20	12.55
		Set, never hinged	62.50	

Surtax for child welfare.

Syncopated Perfs., Type B

B37a	SP35	1½c (+1½c)	3.00	1.25
B38a	SP35	5c (+3c)	4.50	1.25
B39a	SP35	6c (+4c)	3.25	1.25
B40a	SP35	12½c (+3½c)	25.00	14.00
		Nos. B37a-B40a (4)	35.75	17.75
		Set, never hinged	72.50	

Rembrandt and
His "Cloth
Merchants of
Amsterdam"
SP36

Perf. 11½

1930, Feb. 15   Engr.   Unwmk.

B41	SP36	5c (+5c) bl grn	6.75	6.00
B42	SP36	6c (+5c) gray blk	5.25	3.50
B43	SP36	12½c (+5c) dp bl	9.00	8.00
		Nos. B41-B43 (3)	21.00	17.50
		Set, never hinged	52.50	

Surtax for the benefit of the Rembrandt Soc.

"Spring" — SP37

5c, Summer. 6c, Autumn. 12½c, Winter.

1930, Dec. 10   Perf. 12½

B44	SP37	1½c (+1½c) lt red	1.50	.45
B45	SP37	5c (+3c) gray grn	2.25	.60
B46	SP37	6c (+4c) claret	2.00	.45
B47	SP37	12½c (+3½c) lt ultra	16.00	8.50
		Nos. B44-B47 (4)	21.75	10.00
		Set, never hinged	52.50	

Surtax was for Child Welfare work.

Syncopated Perfs.,
Type C

B44a	SP37	1½c (+1½c)	2.40	1.25
B45a	SP37	5c (+3c)	3.50	1.25
B46a	SP37	6c (+4c)	2.40	1.25
B47a	SP37	12½c (+3½c)	19.00	12.50
		Nos. B44a-B47a (4)	27.30	16.25
		Set, never hinged	55.00	

Stained Glass Window
and Detail of Repair
Method — SP41

6c, Gouda Church and repair of window
frame.

Wmk. 202

1931, Oct. 1   Photo.   Perf. 12½

B48	SP41	1½c (+1½c) bl grn	17.00	15.00
B49	SP41	6c (+4c) car rose	20.00	17.00
		Set, never hinged	75.00	

Deaf Mute Learning Lip
Reading — SP43

Designs: 5c, Mentally retarded child. 6c,
Blind girl learning to read Braille. 12½c, Child
victim of malnutrition.

1931, Dec. 10   Perf. 12½

B50	SP43	1½c (+1½c) ver & ultra	1.90	1.25
B51	SP43	5c (+3c) Prus bl & vio	5.25	1.25
B52	SP43	6c (+4c) vio & grn	5.25	1.25
B53	SP43	12½c (+3½c) ultra & dp org	29.00	21.00
		Nos. B50-B53 (4)	41.40	24.75
		Set, never hinged	95.00	

The surtax was for Child Welfare work.

Syncopated Perfs., Type C

B50a	SP43	1½c (+1½c)	1.90	1.25
B51a	SP43	5c (+3c)	5.25	1.25
B52a	SP43	6c (+4c)	5.50	1.25
B53a	SP43	12½c (+3½c)	30.00	22.50
		Nos. B50a-B53a (4)	42.65	26.25
		Set, never hinged	105.00	

Drawbridge — SP47

Designs: 2½c, Windmill and Dikes. 6c,
Council House, Zierikzee. 12½c, Flower fields.

1932, May 23   Perf. 12½

B54	SP47	2½c (+1½c) turq grn & blk	7.00	5.00
B55	SP47	6c (+4c) gray blk & blk	10.50	5.00
B56	SP47	7½c (+3c) brt red & blk	30.00	12.50
B57	SP47	12½c (+2½c) ultra & blk	32.50	19.00
		Nos. B54-B57 (4)	80.00	41.50
		Set, never hinged	190.00	

The surtax was for the benefit of the
National Tourist Association.

Furze and Boy — SP51

Designs (Heads of children and flowers typi-
fying the seasons): 5c, Cornflower. 6c, Sunflower. 12½c, Christmas rose.

1932, Dec. 10   Perf. 12½

B58	SP51	1½c (+1½c) brn & yel	2.10	.45
B59	SP51	5c (+3c) red org & ultra	2.75	.75
B60	SP51	6c (+4c) dk grn & ocher	2.10	.35
B61	SP51	12½c (+3½c) ocher & ultra	27.50	18.00
		Nos. B58-B61 (4)	34.45	19.55
		Set, never hinged	90.00	

The surtax aided Child Welfare Societies.

Syncopated Perfs., Type C

B58a	SP51	1½c (+1½c)	2.75	1.60
B59a	SP51	5c (+3c)	3.50	1.60
B60a	SP51	6c (+4c)	3.50	1.60
B61a	SP51	12½c (+3½c)	35.00	22.50
		Nos. B58a-B61a (4)	44.75	27.30
		Set, never hinged	100.00	

Monument at
Den Helder
SP55

The "Hope," A
Church and
Hospital Ship
SP56

Lifeboat in a Storm SP57

Dutch Sailor and Sailors' Home SP58

1933, June 10   Perf. 14½x13½
B62 SP55 1½c (+1½c) dp red 3.50 1.60
B63 SP56 5c (+3c) bl grn & red org 10.50 3.00
B64 SP57 6c (+4c) dp grn 16.00 2.50
B65 SP58 12½c (+3½c) ultra 24.00 17.50
Nos. B62-B65 (4) 54.00 24.60
Set, never hinged 125.00
The surtax was for the aid of Sailors' Homes.

Child Carrying the Star of Hope, Symbolical of Christmas Cheer — SP59

1933, Dec. 11   Perf. 12½
B66 SP59 1½c (+1½c) sl & red orn 1.50 .55
B67 SP59 5c (+3c) dk brn & ocher 2.00 .65
B68 SP59 6c (+4c) bl grn & gold 2.50 .55
B69 SP59 12½c (+3½c) dk bl & sil 25.00 18.00
Nos. B66-B69 (4) 31.00 19.75
Set, never hinged 75.00
The surtax aided Child Welfare Societies.

Syncopated Perfs., Type C
B66a SP59 1½c (+1½c) 1.90 .70
B67a SP59 5c (+3c) 2.60 .90
B68a SP59 6c (+4c) 3.25 .90
B69a SP59 12½c (+3½c) 26.00 20.00
Nos. B66a-B69a (4) 33.75 22.50
Set, never hinged 87.50

Queen Wilhelmina SP60

Princess Juliana SP61

1934, Apr. 28   Engr.   Unwmk.
B70 SP60 5c (+4c) dk vio 11.50 3.25
B71 SP61 6c (+5c) blue 10.50 4.25
Set, never hinged 52.50
The surtax was for the benefit of the Anti-Depression Committee.

Dowager Queen Emma — SP62

1934, Oct. 1   Perf. 13x14
B72 SP62 6c (+2c) blue 11.50 1.40
Never hinged 27.50
Surtax for the Fight Tuberculosis Society.

Poor Child — SP63

Perf. 13½x13
1934, Dec. 10   Photo.   Wmk. 202
B73 SP63 1½c (+1½c) olive 1.40 .45
B74 SP63 5c (+3c) rose red 2.40 1.00
B75 SP63 6c (+4c) bl grn 2.40 .25
B76 SP63 12½c (+3½c) ultra 22.50 16.00
Nos. B73-B76 (4) 28.70 17.70
Set, never hinged 75.00
The surtax aided child welfare.

Henri D. Guyot SP64

A. J. M. Diepenbrock SP65

F. C. Donders SP66

J. P. Sweelinck SP67

Perf. 12½ x 12, 12
1935, June 17   Engr.   Unwmk.
B77 SP64 1½c (+1½c) dk car 1.50 1.25
B78 SP65 5c (+3c) blk brn 4.00 3.50
B79 SP66 6c (+4c) myr grn 4.50 .70
B80 SP67 12½c (+3½c) dp bl 24.00 4.00
Nos. B77-B80 (4) 34.00 9.45
Set, never hinged 87.50
Surtax for social and cultural projects.

Netherlands Map, DC-3 Planes' Shadows SP68

Perf. 14x13
1935, Oct. 16   Photo.   Wmk. 202
B81 SP68 6c (+4c) brn 24.00 7.50
Never hinged 60.00
Surtax for Natl. Aviation.

Girl Picking Apple — SP69

1935, Dec. 4   Perf. 14½x13½
B82 SP69 1½c (+1½c) crim .50 .30
B83 SP69 5c (+3c) dk yel 1.40 1.10
B84 SP69 6c (+4c) blk brn 1.25 .30
B85 SP69 12½c (+3½c) ultra 20.00 7.00
Nos. B82-B85 (4) 23.15 8.70
Set, never hinged 80.00
The surtax aided child welfare.

H. Kamerlingh Onnes — SP70

Dr. A. S. Talma — SP71

Msgr. H. J. A. M. Schaepman SP72

Desiderius Erasmus SP73

Perf. 12½x12
1936, May 1   Engr.   Unwmk.
B86 SP70 1½c (+1½c) brn blk .80 .75
B87 SP71 5c (+3c) dl grn .80 3.25
B88 SP72 6c (+4c) dk red 3.50 .50
B89 SP73 12½c (+3½c) dl bl 13.00 2.50
Nos. B86-B89 (4) 18.10 7.00
Set, never hinged 60.00
Surtax for social and cultural projects.

Cherub — SP74

Perf. 14½x13½
1936, Dec. 1   Photo.   Wmk. 202
B90 SP74 1½c (+1½c) lil gray .50 .30
B91 SP74 5c (+3c) turq grn 2.00 .75
B92 SP74 6c (+4c) dp red brn 1.90 .25
B93 SP74 12½c (+3½c) ind 14.00 4.75
Nos. B90-B93 (4) 18.40 6.05
Set, never hinged 45.00
The surtax aided child welfare.

Jacob Maris — SP75

Franciscus de la Boe Sylvius — SP76

Joost van den Vondel SP77

Anthony van Leeuwenhoek SP78

Perf. 12½x12
1937, June 1   Engr.   Unwmk.
B94 SP75 1½c (+1½c) blk brn .50 .40
B95 SP76 5c (+3c) dl grn 4.00 2.75
B96 SP77 6c (+4c) brn vio 1.00 .25
B97 SP78 12½c (+3½c) dl bl 7.00 .85
Nos. B94-B97 (4) 12.50 4.25
Set, never hinged 35.00
Surtax for social and cultural projects.

"The Laughing Child" after Frans Hals — SP79

Perf. 14½x13½
1937, Dec. 1   Photo.   Wmk. 202
B98 SP79 1½c (+1½c) blk .25 .25
B99 SP79 3c (+2c) grn 1.50 1.00
B100 SP79 4c (+2c) hn brn .60 .45

B101 SP79 5c (+3c) bl grn .50 .25
B102 SP79 12½c (+3½c) dk bl 7.25 1.40
Nos. B98-B102 (5) 10.10 3.35
Set, never hinged 32.50
The surtax aided child welfare.

Marnix van Sint Aldegonde SP80

Otto Gerhard Heldring SP81

Maria Tesselschade SP82

Hermann Boerhaave SP84

Harmenszoon Rembrandt van Rijn — SP83

Perf. 12½x12
1938, May 16   Engr.   Unwmk.
B103 SP80 1½c (+1½c) sep .30 .50
B104 SP81 3c (+2c) dk grn .55 .30
B105 SP82 4c (+2c) rose lake 1.75 1.50
B106 SP83 5c (+3c) dk sl grn 2.25 .30
B107 SP84 12½c (+3½c) dl bl 7.75 1.10
Nos. B103-B107 (5) 12.60 3.70
Set, never hinged 32.50
The surtax was for the benefit of cultural and social relief.

Child with Flowers, Bird and Fish — SP85

Perf. 14½x13½
1938, Dec. 1   Photo.   Wmk. 202
B108 SP85 1½c (+1½c) blk .25 .25
B109 SP85 3c (+2c) mar .30 .25
B110 SP85 4c (+2c) dk bl grn .60 .80
B111 SP85 5c (+3c) hn brn .25 .25
B112 SP85 12½c (+3½c) dp bl 9.00 1.75
Nos. B108-B112 (5) 10.40 3.30
Set, never hinged 35.00
The surtax aided child welfare.

Matthijs Maris — SP86

Anton Mauve SP87

Gerard van
Swieten
SP88

Nikolaas Beets
SP89

Peter
Stuyvesant — SP90

Perf. 12½x12

1939, May 1   Engr.   Unwmk.

B113	SP86	1½c (+1½c) sepia	.60 .60
B114	SP87	2½c (+2½c) gray grn	3.00 2.75
B115	SP88	3c (+3c) ver	.80 1.00
B116	SP89	5c (+3c) dk sl grn	2.00 .30
B117	SP90	12½c (+3½c) indigo	5.00 .85
		Nos. B113-B117 (5)	11.40 5.50
		Set, never hinged	40.00

The surtax was for the benefit of cultural and social relief.

Child Carrying
Cornucopia — SP91

Perf. 14½x13½

1939, Dec. 1   Photo.   Wmk. 202

B118	SP91	1½c (+1½c) blk	.25 .25
B119	SP91	2½c (+2½c) dk ol grn	3.75 2.00
B120	SP91	3c (+3c) hn brn	.40 .25
B121	SP91	5c (+3c) dk grn	.85 .25
B122	SP91	12½c (+3½c)c dk bl	4.00 1.00
		Nos. B118-B122 (5)	9.25 3.75
		Set, never hinged	40.00

The surtax was used for destitute children.

> Catalogue values for unused stamps in this section, from this point to the end of the section, are for Never Hinged items.

Vincent van
Gogh
SP92

E. J. Potgieter
SP93

Petrus Camper
SP94

Jan Steen
SP95

Joseph
Scaliger — SP96

Perf. 12½x12

1940, May 11   Engr.   Unwmk.

B123	SP92	1½c +1½c brn blk	1.90 .25
B124	SP93	2½c +2½c dk grn	6.00 1.40
B125	SP94	3c +3c car	3.75 1.10
B126	SP95	5c +3c dp grn	7.75 .25
a.		Booklet pane of 4	250.00
B127	SP96	12½c +3½c dp bl	6.75 .80

Surtax for social and cultural projects.

Type of 1940
Surcharged in Black

1940, Sept. 7

B128	SP95	7½c +2½c on 5c +3c dk red	.50 .25
		Nos. B123-B128 (6)	26.65 4.05

Child with Flowers and
Doll — SP97

Perf. 14½x13½

1940, Dec. 2   Photo.   Wmk. 202

B129	SP97	1½c +1½c dl bl gray	.65 .25
B130	SP97	2½c +2½c dp ol	2.50 .50
B131	SP97	4c +3c royal bl	2.50 .65
B132	SP97	5c +3c dk bl grn	2.50 .25
B133	SP97	7½c +3½c hn	.65 .25
		Nos. B129-B133 (5)	8.80 1.90

The surtax was used for destitute children.

AIR POST STAMPS

Stylized
Seagull — AP1

Perf. 12½

1921, May 1   Unwmk.   Typo.

C1	AP1	10c red	1.50 1.25
C2	AP1	15c yellow grn	6.25 2.50
C3	AP1	60c dp blue	19.00 .50
		Nos. C1-C3 (3)	26.75 4.25
		Set, never hinged	190.00

Nos. C1-C3 were used to pay airmail fee charged by the carrier, KLM.

Lt. G. A.
Koppen — AP2

Capt. Jan van
der Hoop — AP3

Wmk. Circles (202)

1928, Aug. 20   Litho.   Perf. 12

C4	AP2	40c orange red	.25 .25
C5	AP3	75c blue green	.25 .25
		Set, never hinged	1.25

Mercury
AP4

Queen
Wilhelmina
AP5

Perf. 11½

1929, July 16   Unwmk.   Engr.

C6	AP4	1½g gray	2.50 1.65
C7	AP4	4½g carmine	1.75 3.00
C8	AP4	7½g blue green	24.00 4.50
		Nos. C6-C8 (3)	28.25 9.15
		Set, never hinged	70.00

Perf. 12½, 14x13

1931, Sept. 24   Photo.   Wmk. 202

C9	AP5	36c org red & dk bl	10.00 .60
		Never hinged	70.00

Fokker
Pander
AP6

1933, Oct. 9   Perf. 12½

C10	AP6	30c dark green	.40 .60
		Never hinged	.80

Nos. C10-C12 were issued for use on special flights.

Crow in
Flight
AP7

1938-53   Perf. 13x14

C11	AP7	12½c dk blue & gray	.35 .25
C12	AP7	25c dk bl & gray ('53)	1.50 1.50
		Set, never hinged	4.25

MARINE INSURANCE STAMPS

Floating Safe
Attracting
Gulls — MI1

Floating Safe
with Night
Flare — MI2

Fantasy of Floating
Safe — MI3

Perf. 11½

1921, Feb. 2   Unwmk.   Engr.

GY1	MI1	15c slate grn	11.00 75.00
GY2	MI1	60c car rose	15.00 75.00
GY3	MI1	75c gray brn	18.50 75.00
GY4	MI2	1.50g dk blue	65.00 425.00
GY5	MI2	2.25g org brn	110.00 550.00
GY6	MI3	4½g black	165.00 675.00
GY7	MI3	7½g red	250.00 925.00
		Nos. GY1-GY7 (7)	634.50 2,800.
		Set, never hinged	1,500.

POSTAGE DUE STAMPS

Postage due types of Netherlands were also used for Netherlands Antilles, Netherlands Indies and Surinam in different colors.

D1

Unwmk.

1870, May 15   Typo.   Perf. 13

J1	D1	5c brown, org	72.50 15.00
		No gum	22.00
		On cover	140.00
		On postcard	80.00
J2	D1	10c violet, bl	150.00 20.00
		No gum	47.50
		On cover	225.00
a.		Perf 12½x12	300.00 32.50

D2

Type I — 34 loops. "T" of "BETALEN" over center of loop; top branch of "E" of "TE" shorter than lower branch.
Type II — 33 loops. "T" of "BETALEN" between two loops.
Type III — 32 loops. "T" of "BETALEN" slightly to the left of loop; top branch of first "E" of "BETALEN" shorter than lower branch.
Type IV — 37 loops. Letters of "PORT" larger than in the other three types.
Imperforate varieties are proofs.

Perf. 11½x12, 12½x12, 12½, 13½

1881-87   Value in Black

J3	D2	1c lt blue (III)	11.00 11.00
		No gum	4.00
a.		Type I	15.00 18.00
b.		Type II	20.00 20.00
c.		Type IV	47.50 52.50
J4	D2	1c lt blue (III)	15.00 15.00
		No gum	4.00
a.		Type I	18.00 18.00
b.		Type II	24.00 24.00
c.		Type IV	75.00 75.00
J5	D2	2½c lt blue (III)	37.50 5.00
		No gum	8.00
a.		Type I	45.00 5.50
b.		Type II	50.00 6.00
c.		Type IV	210.00 125.00
J6	D2	5c lt blue (III) ('87)	140.00 3.50
		No gum	20.00
a.		Type I	50.00 5.00
b.		Type II	130.00 5.25
c.		Type IV	1,250. 350.00
J7	D2	10c lt blue (III) ('87)	92.50 4.00
		No gum	22.50
a.		Type I	115.00 4.50
b.		Type II	125.00 5.00
c.		Type IV	2,500. 375.00
J8	D2	12½c lt blue (III)	95.00 25.00
		No gum	22.50
a.		Type I	165.00 40.00
b.		Type II	130.00 45.00
c.		Type IV	350.00 100.00
J9	D2	15c lt blue (III)	90.00 4.00
		No gum	17.00
a.		Type I	105.00 4.50
b.		Type II	120.00 5.00
c.		Type IV	130.00 25.00
J10	D2	20c lt blue (III)	35.00 4.00
		No gum	7.75
a.		Type I	47.50 4.25
b.		Type II	50.00 5.50
c.		Type IV	137.50 27.50
J11	D2	25c lt blue (III)	210.00 3.50
		No gum	47.50
a.		Type I	230.00 3.00
b.		Type II	275.00 4.50
c.		Type IV	425.00 170.00

Value in Red

J12	D2	1g lt blue (III)	85.00 30.00
		No gum	20.00
a.		Type I	85.00 37.50
b.		Type II	100.00 40.00
c.		Type IV	175.00 75.00
		Nos. J3-J12 (10)	811.00 105.00

See Nos. J13-J26, J44-J60. For surcharges see Nos. J27-J28, J42-J43, J72-J75.

1896-1910   Perf. 12½

Value in Black

J13	D2	½c dk bl (I) ('01)	.40 .35
J14	D2	1c dk blue (I)	1.65 .35
a.		Type III	2.50 3.25
J15	D2	1½c dk blue (I)	.75 .35
a.		Type III	2.50 2.50
J16	D2	2½c dk blue (I)	1.50 .75
a.		Type III	3.25 1.50
J17	D2	3c dk bl (I) ('10)	1.65 1.10
J18	D2	4c dk bl (I) ('09)	1.65 2.25
J19	D2	5c dk blue (I)	13.00 .35
a.		Type III	16.00 .55
J20	D2	6½c dk bl (I) ('07)	45.00 45.00
J21	D2	7½c dk bl (I) ('04)	1.75 .55
J22	D2	10c dk blue (I)	35.00 .55
a.		Type III	52.50 1.50
J23	D2	12½c dk blue (I)	30.00 1.10
a.		Type III	45.00 3.50

J24	D2	15c dk blue (I)	35.00	.90
a.		Type III	55.00	1.00
J25	D2	20c dk blue (I)	20.00	8.00
a.		Type III	20.00	8.75
J26	D2	25c dk blue (I)	45.00	.75
a.		Type III	50.00	1.00
		Nos. J13-J26 (14)	232.35	62.35

Surcharged in Black

1906, Jan. 10   *Perf. 12½*

J27	D2	50c on 1g lt bl (III)	125.00	110.00
a.		50c on 1g light blue (I)	165.00	140.00
b.		50c on 1g light blue (II)	175.00	150.00

Surcharged in Red

1906, Oct. 6

J28	D2	6½c on 20c dk bl (I)	5.50	5.00

Nos. 87-89
Surcharged

1907, Nov. 1

J29	A13	½c on 1c claret	1.25	1.25
J30	A13	1c on 1c claret	.50	.50
J31	A13	1½c on 1c claret	.50	.50
J32	A13	2½c on 1c claret	1.25	1.25
J33	A13	5c on 2½c ver	1.40	.40
J34	A13	6½c on 2½c ver	3.50	3.50
J35	A13	7½c on ½c blue	2.00	1.25
J36	A13	10c on ½c blue	1.75	.75
J37	A13	12½c on ½c blue	5.00	4.75
J38	A13	15c on 2½c ver	6.00	4.00
J39	A13	25c on ½c blue	9.00	8.50
J40	A13	50c on ½c blue	42.50	40.00
J41	A13	1g on ½c blue	60.00	55.00
		Nos. J29-J41 (13)	134.65	121.65

Two printings of the above surcharges were made. Some values show differences in the setting of the fractions; others are practically impossible to distinguish.

No. J20 Surcharged in
Red

1909, June

J42	D2	4c on 6½c dark blue	5.50	5.00
		Never hinged	20.00	

No. J12 Surcharged in
Black

1910, July 11

J43	D2	3c on 1g lt bl, type III	30.00	27.50
		Never hinged	100.00	
a.		Type I	37.50	40.00
		Never hinged	110.00	
b.		Type II	40.00	40.00
		Never hinged	125.00	

Type I

1912-21   *Perf. 12½, 13½x13*
Value in Color of Stamp

J44	D2	½c pale ultra	.25	.25
J45	D2	1c pale ultra ('13)	.25	.25
J46	D2	1½c pale ultra ('15)	1.90	1.50
J47	D2	2½c pale ultra	.25	.25
J48	D2	3c pale ultra	.40	.40
J49	D2	4c pale ultra ('13)	.25	.25
J50	D2	4½c pale ultra ('16)	5.25	5.00
J51	D2	5c pale ultra	.25	.25
J52	D2	5½c pale ultra ('16)	5.00	5.00
J53	D2	7c pale ultra ('21)	2.25	2.25
J54	D2	7½c pale ultra ('13)	2.50	1.00
J55	D2	10c pale ultra ('13)	.40	.40

J56	D2	12½c pale ultra ('13)	.40	.40
J57	D2	15c pale ultra ('13)	.40	.40
J58	D2	20c pale ultra ('20)	.40	.25
J59	D2	25c pale ultra ('17)	80.00	.60
J60	D2	50c pale ultra ('20)	.40	.25
		Nos. J44-J60 (17)	100.55	18.70
		Set, never hinged	450.00	

D3

1921-38 Typo.   *Perf. 12½, 13½x12½*

J61	D3	3c pale ultra ('28)	.25	.25
J62	D3	6c pale ultra ('27)	.25	.25
J63	D3	7c pale ultra ('28)	.40	.40
J64	D3	7½c pale ultra ('26)	.40	.40
J65	D3	8c pale ultra ('38)	.40	.40
J66	D3	9c pale ultra ('30)	.40	.40
J67	D3	11c ultra ('21)	13.00	3.50
J68	D3	12c pale ultra ('28)	.40	.25
J69	D3	25c pale ultra ('25)	.40	.25
J70	D3	30c pale ultra ('35)	.40	.25
J71	D3	1g ver ('21)	.50	.25
		Nos. J61-J71 (11)	16.80	6.60
		Set, never hinged	50.00	

Stamps of 1912-21
Surcharged

1923, Dec.   *Perf. 12½*

J72	D2	1c on 3c ultra	.75	.50
J73	D2	2½c on 7c ultra	1.20	.50
J74	D2	25c on 1½c ultra	8.00	.50
J75	D2	25c on 7½c ultra	10.00	.50
		Nos. J72-J75 (4)	19.95	2.00
		Set, never hinged	45.00	

Nos. 56, 58, 62, 65
Surcharged

1924, Aug.

J76	A11	4c on 3c olive grn	1.50	1.10
J77	A10	5c on 1c red	.75	.40
a.		Surcharge reading down	500.00	450.00
J78	A10	10c on 1½c blue	.95	.40
J79	A11	12½c on 5c carmine	.95	.50
a.		Tête bêche pair	10.00	10.00
		Nos. J76-J79 (4)	4.15	2.40

The 11c on 22½c and 15c on 17½c exist. These were used by the postal service for accounting of parcel post fees.

OFFICIAL STAMPS

Regular Issues of
1898-1908
Overprinted

1913 Typo. Unwmk.   *Perf. 12½*

O1	A10	1c red	4.00	2.75
O2	A10	1½c ultra	1.00	2.25
O3	A10	2c yellow brn	7.00	7.00
O4	A10	2½c dp green	16.00	12.00
O5	A11	3c olive grn	4.00	1.00
O6	A11	5c carmine rose	4.00	4.50
O7	A11	10c gray lilac	35.00	37.50
		Nos. O1-O7 (7)	71.00	67.00

Same Overprint in Red on No. 58
1919

O8	A10	1½c deep blue (R)	100.00	110.00

Nos. O1 to O8 were used to defray the postage on matter relating to the Poor Laws. Counterfeit overprints exist.

For the International Court of Justice
Regular Issue of 1926-33 Overprinted in Gold

1934   Wmk. 202   *Perf. 12½*

O9	A24	1½c red violet	1.00	1.00
O10	A24	2½c deep green		1.50
O11	A23	7½c red		2.25
O12	A31	12½c deep ultra		22.50
O13	A23	15c orange		2.00
O14	A23	30c violet		2.25
a.		Perf. 13½x12½		2.25
		Nos. O9-O14 (6)		32.00

Same Overprint on No. 180 in Gold

1937   *Perf. 13½x12½*

O15	A23	12½c ultra		16.00

"Mint" Officials
Nos. O9-O15, were sold to the public only canceled. Uncanceled, they were obtainable only by favor of an official or from UPU specimen stamps.

Same on Regular Issue of 1940 Overprinted in Gold

1940   *Perf. 13½x12½*

O16	A45	7½c bright red	22.50	8.75
O17	A45	12½c sapphire	22.50	8.75
O18	A45	15c lt blue	22.50	8.75
O19	A45	30c bister	22.50	8.75
		Nos. O16-O19 (4)	90.00	35.00

NETHERLANDS ANTILLES

'ne-thər-lənd͜z an-'ti-lēz

(Curaçao)

LOCATION — Two groups of islands about 500 miles apart in the West Indies, north of Venezuela
GOVT. — Dutch Colony
AREA — 383 sq. mi.
POP. — 260,000 (est. 1983)
CAPITAL — Willemstad

100 Cents = 1 Gulden

Values for unused examples of Nos. 1-44 are for stamps without gum.

Watermark

Wmk. 202 — Circles

King William III — A1

Regular Perf. 11½, 12½, 11½x12, 12½x12, 13½x13, 14

1873-79 Typo.			Unwmk.	
1	A1	2½c green	5.00	8.00
2	A1	3c bister	55.00	110.00
3	A1	5c rose	10.00	12.00
4	A1	10c ultra	60.00	10.00
5	A1	25c brown orange	45.00	10.00
6	A1	50c violet	1.75	2.50
7	A1	2.50g bis & pur ('79)	37.50	37.50
		Nos. 1-7 (7)	214.25	197.00

See bluish paper note with Netherlands #7-22.

The gulden denominations, Nos. 7 and 12, are of larger size.
See 8-12. For surcharges see #18, 25-26.

Perf. 14, Small Holes

1b	A1	2½c	12.00	15.00
2b	A1	3c	60.00	140.00
4b	A1	10c	1.00	1.00
5b	A1	25c	72.50	80.00
5b	A1	25c	65.00	45.00
6b	A1	50c	26.00	30.00
		Nos. 1b-6b (6)	250.00	331.00

"Small hole" varieties have the spaces between the holes wider than the diameter of the holes.

1886-89   *Perf. 11½, 12½, 12½x12*

8	A1	12½c yellow	95.00	52.50
9	A1	15c olive ('89)	27.50	19.00
10	A1	30c pearl gray ('89)	35.00	50.00
11	A1	60c olive bis ('89)	42.50	17.00
12	A1	1.50g lt & dk bl ('89)	100.00	18.50
		Nos. 8-12 (5)	300.00	218.50

Nos. 1-12 were issued without gum until 1890. Imperfs. are proofs.

Numeral — A2

1889   *Perf. 12½*

13	A2	1c gray	.85	1.00
14	A2	2c violet	.65	1.25
15	A2	2½c green	4.50	3.00
16	A2	3c bister	5.00	4.50
17	A2	5c rose	21.00	1.75
		Nos. 13-17 (5)	32.00	11.50

King William III — A3

Black Surcharge, Handstamped
1891   *Perf. 12½x12*
Without Gum

18	A3	25c on 30c pearl gray	15.00	14.00

No. 18 exists with dbl. surch., value $225, and with invtd. surch., value $275.

Queen Wilhelmina — A4

1892-96   *Perf. 12½*

19	A4	10c ultra ('95)	1.25	1.25
20	A4	12½c green	26.00	6.25
21	A4	15c rose ('93)	2.50	2.50
22	A4	25c brown orange	100.00	5.50
23	A4	30c gray ('96)	2.50	5.50
		Nos. 19-23 (5)	132.25	21.00

A5   A6

Magenta Surcharge, Handstamped
1895   *Perf. 12½, 13½x13*

25	A5	2½c on 10c ultra	13.00	8.00

Black Surcharge, Handstamped
Perf. 12½x12

26	A6	2½c on 30c gray	125.00	6.00

Nos. 25-26 exist with surcharge double or inverted.
No. 26 and No. 25, perf. 13½x13, were issued without gum.

Netherlands Nos. 77,
68 Surcharged in Black

1902, Jan. 1 *Perf. 12½*
27 A11 25c on 25c car & bl 2.00 2.00

Netherlands No. 84
Surcharged in Black

1901, May 1 **Engr.** *Perf. 11½x11*
28 A12 1.50g on 2.50g brn lil 20.00 21.00

1902, Mar. 1 **Typo.** *Perf. 12½*
29 A11 12½c on 12½c blue 25.00 7.00

A9

A10

1904-08
30 A9 1c olive green 1.40 .90
31 A9 2c yellow brown 12.00 3.00
32 A9 2½c blue green 4.00 .35
33 A9 3c orange 7.50 4.00
34 A9 5c rose red 7.00 .35
35 A9 7½c gray ('08) 27.50 6.00
36 A10 10c slate 11.00 3.00
37 A10 12½c deep blue 1.25 .50
38 A10 15c brown 14.00 10.00
39 A10 22½c brn & ol ('08) 14.00 8.50
40 A10 25c violet 14.00 1.90
41 A10 30c brown orange 32.50 13.00
42 A10 50c red brown 27.50 8.25
     Nos. 30-42 (13) 173.65 59.75

Queen
Wilhelmina — A11

1906, Nov. 1 **Engr.** *Perf. 11½*
Without Gum
43 A11 1½g red brown 35.00 25.00
44 A11 2½g slate blue 35.00 24.00

A12

A13

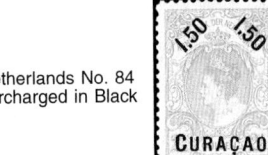

Queen
Wilhelmina — A14

Perf. 12½, 11, 11½, 11x11½
1915-33 **Typo.**
45 A12 ½c lilac ('20) 1.60 1.10
46 A12 1c olive green .25 .25
47 A12 1½c blue ('20) .25 .25
48 A12 2c yellow brn 1.25 1.40
49 A12 2½c green .90 .25
50 A12 3c yellow 2.25 1.50
51 A12 3c green ('26) 2.60 2.50
52 A12 5c rose 2.00 .25
53 A12 5c green ('22) 3.75 2.75
54 A12 5c lilac ('26) 2.00 .25
55 A12 7½c drab 1.10 .30
56 A12 7½c bister ('20) 1.10 .25
57 A12 10c lilac ('22) 5.00 4.50
58 A12 10c rose ('26) 4.25 1.25
59 A13 10c car rose 13.00 3.00
60 A13 12½c blue 2.25 .50
61 A13 12½c red ('22) 2.00 1.60
62 A13 15c olive grn .65 .65
63 A13 15c lt blue ('26) 4.00 2.50
64 A13 20c blue ('22) 6.50 3.00
65 A13 20c olive grn
          ('26) 2.50 2.25
66 A13 22½c orange 2.50 2.25
67 A13 25c red violet 3.25 .90
68 A13 30c slate 3.25 .65
69 A13 35c sl & red ('22) 3.25 4.25
    Perf. 11½x11, 11½, 12½, 11
          Engr.
70 A14 50c green 4.00 .25
71 A14 1½g violet 13.00 11.00
72 A14 2½g carmine 21.00 20.00
  a. Perf. 12½ ('33) 140.00 *300.00*
     Nos. 45-72 (28) 109.45 69.60

Some stamps of 1915 were also issued
without gum.
For surcharges see #74, 107-108, C1-C3.

A15

No. 60 Surcharged in
Black

Laid Paper, without Gum
1918, July 16 **Typo.** *Perf. 12*
73 A15 1c black, *buff* 6.75 3.75

"HAW" are the initials of Postmaster H. A.
Willemsen.

No. 60 Surcharged in
Black

1918, Sept. 1 *Perf. 12½*
74 A13 5c on 12½c blue 3.75 2.00
  a. "5" 2½mm wide 60.00 32.50
  b. Double surcharge 700.00

The "5" of No. 74 is 3mm wide. Illustration
shows No. 74a surcharge.

Queen
Wilhelmina — A16

1923 **Engr.** *Perf. 11½, 11x11½*
75 A16 5c green 1.00 2.00
76 A16 7½c olive grn 1.25 1.60
77 A16 10c car rose 1.75 2.00
78 A16 20c indigo 2.50 3.50
  a. Perf. 11x11½ 3.25 4.25
79 A16 1g brown vio 30.00 19.00
80 A16 2½g gray black 70.00 *170.00*
81 A16 5g brown 90.00 *200.00*
  a. Perf. 11x11½ 625.00
     Nos. 75-81 (7) 196.50 398.10

25th anniv. of the assumption of the government of the Netherlands by Queen Wilhelmina, at the age of 18.
Nos. 80-81 with clear cancel between Aug.
1, 1923 and Apr. 30, 1924, sell for considerably more.

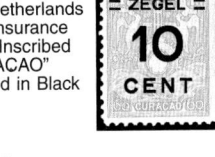

Types of Netherlands
Marine Insurance
Stamps, Inscribed
"CURACAO"
Surcharged in Black

1927, Oct. 3
87 MI1 3c on 15c dk
          green .25 .30
88 MI1 10c on 60c car
          rose .25 .45
89 MI1 12½c on 75c gray
          brn .25 .45
90 MI2 15c on 1.50g dk bl 3.00 2.50
  a. Double surcharge 500.00
91 MI2 25c on 2.25g org
          brn 6.50 6.25
92 MI3 30c on 4½g black 13.00 11.00
93 MI3 50c on 7½g red 7.50 7.25
     Nos. 87-93 (7) 30.75 28.20

Nos. 90, 91 and 92 have "FRANKEER-
ZEGEL" in one line of small capitals. Nos. 90
and 91 have a heavy bar across the top of the
stamp.

Queen
Wilhelmina — A17

1928-30 **Engr.** *Perf. 11½, 12½*
95 A17 6c orange red ('30) 1.50 .40
  a. Booklet pane of 6
96 A17 7½c orange red .60 .45
97 A17 10c carmine 1.50 .35
98 A17 12½c red brown 1.50 1.00
  a. Booklet pane of 6
99 A17 15c dark blue 1.50 .35
  a. Booklet pane of 6
100 A17 20c blue black 5.75 .55
101 A17 21c yellow grn ('30) 9.25 14.00
102 A17 25c brown vio 3.50 1.40
103 A17 27½c black ('30) 12.00 14.00
104 A17 30c deep green 5.75 .55
105 A17 35c brnsh black 2.00 1.75
     Nos. 95-105 (11) 44.85 34.80

No. 96 Surcharged
in Black with Bars
over Original Value

1929, Nov. 1
106 A17 6c on 7½c org red 1.40 1.00
  a. Inverted surcharge 275.00 260.00

No. 51 Surcharged
in Red

1931, Mar. 1 **Typo.** *Perf. 12½*
107 A12 2½c on 3c green 1.10 1.10

No. 49 Surcharged
in Red

1932, Oct. 29
108 A12 1½c on 2½c grn 3.50 3.50

Prince William I,
Portrait by Van
Key — A18

1933 **Photo.** *Perf. 12½*
109 A18 6c deep orange 1.75 1.40

400th birth anniv. of Prince William I, Count
of Nassau and Prince of Orange, frequently
referred to as William the Silent.

Willem
Usselinx
A19

Van Walbeeck's
Ship
A22

Designs: 2½c, 5c, 6c, Frederik Hendrik. 10c, 12½c, 15c, Jacob Binckes. 27½c, 30c, 50c, Cornelis Evertsen the Younger. 1.50g, 2.50g, Louis Brion.

1934, Jan. 1		Engr.	Perf. 12½	
110	A19	1c black	1.00	1.25
111	A19	1½c dull violet	.75	.90
112	A19	2c orange	1.00	1.25
113	A19	2½c dull green	.85	1.25
114	A19	5c black brn	.85	.85
115	A19	6c violet bl	.75	.25
116	A19	10c lake	2.00	1.00
117	A19	12½c bister brn	6.50	7.00
118	A19	15c blue	1.60	1.00
119	A22	20c black	3.00	2.00
120	A22	21c brown	11.00	13.00
121	A22	25c dull green	11.00	11.00
122	A19	27½c brown vio	14.00	16.00
123	A19	30c scarlet	11.00	5.25
124	A19	50c orange	11.00	8.25
125	A19	1.50g indigo	47.50	50.00
126	A19	2.50g yellow grn	52.50	47.50
		Nos. 110-126 (17)	176.30	167.15

3rd centenary of the founding of the colony.

Numeral
A25

Queen
Wilhelmina
A26

1936, Aug. 1		Litho.	Perf. 13½x13	
		Size: 18x22mm		
127	A25	1c brown black	.25	.25
128	A25	1½c deep ultra	.25	.25
129	A25	2c orange	.25	.25
130	A25	2½c green	.25	.25
131	A25	5c scarlet	.35	.25

		Engr.		
		Perf. 12½		
		Size: 20¼x30½mm		
132	A26	6c brown vio	.45	.25
133	A26	10c orange red	.85	.25
134	A26	12½c dk bl grn	1.50	.95
135	A26	15c dark blue	1.25	.60
136	A26	20c orange yel	1.25	.60
137	A26	21c dk gray	2.25	2.25
138	A26	25c brown lake	1.50	.75
139	A26	27½c violet brn	2.50	2.75
140	A26	30c olive brn	.60	.25

		Perf. 13x14		
		Size: 22x33mm		
141	A26	50c dull yel grn	3.00	.25
a.		Perf. 14	50.00	
142	A26	1.50g black brn	18.00	13.00
a.		Perf. 14	40.00	20.00
143	A26	2.50g rose lake	16.00	11.00
a.		Perf. 14	16.00	11.00
		Nos. 127-143 (17)	50.50	34.15

See Nos. 147-151 in Scott Standard catalogue, Vol. 5. For surcharges see Nos. B1-B3 in Scott Vol. 5.

Queen
Wilhelmina — A27

		Perf. 12½x12		
1938, Aug. 27		Photo.	Wmk. 202	
144	A27	1½c dull purple	.25	.25
145	A27	6c red orange	.80	.25
146	A27	15c royal blue	1.50	1.25
		Nos. 144-146 (3)	2.55	2.25

Reign of Queen Wilhelmina, 40th anniv.

AIR POST STAMPS

Regular Issues of
1915-22 Surcharged in
Black

		Perf. 12½		
1929, July 6		Typo.	Unwmk.	
C1	A13	50c on 12½c red	13.00	13.00
C2	A13	1g on 20c blue	13.00	13.00
C3	A13	2g on 15c ol grn	42.50	47.50
		Nos. C1-C3 (3)	68.50	73.50

Excellent forgeries exist.

Allegory,
"Flight" — AP1

1931-39			Engr.	
C4	AP1	10c Prus grn ('34)	.25	.25
C5	AP1	15c dull blue ('38)	.25	.25
C6	AP1	20c red	.75	.25
C7	AP1	25c gray ('38)	.75	.60
C8	AP1	30c yellow ('39)	.30	.30
C9	AP1	35c dull blue	.80	.90
C10	AP1	40c green	.60	.40
C11	AP1	45c orange	2.25	2.25
C12	AP1	50c lake ('38)	.75	.50
C13	AP1	60c brown vio	.60	.35
C14	AP1	70c black	6.50	2.50
C15	AP1	1.40g brown	4.25	5.25
C16	AP1	2.80g bister	5.00	5.50
		Nos. C4-C16 (13)	23.05	19.30

No. C6 Surcharged
in Black

1934, Aug. 25				
C17	AP1	10c on 20c red	19.00	17.00

POSTAGE DUE STAMPS

D1

Type I — 34 loops. "T" of "BETALEN" over center of loop, top branch of "E" of "TE" shorter than lower branch.
Type II — 33 loops. "T" of "BETALEN" over center of two loops.
Type III — 32 loops. "T" of "BETALEN" slightly to the left of loop, top of first "E" of "BETALEN" shorter than lower branch.

Value in Black

1889		Unwmk.	Typo.	Perf. 12½
			Type III	
J1	D1	2½c green	3.00	3.25
J2	D1	5c green	2.00	1.75
J3	D1	10c red	32.50	27.50
J4	D1	12½c green	375.00	200.00
J5	D1	15c green	20.00	17.00
J6	D1	20c green	9.00	9.00
J7	D1	25c green	190.00	150.00
J8	D1	30c green	10.00	9.00
J9	D1	40c green	10.00	9.00
J10	D1	50c green	40.00	37.50

Nos. J1-J10 were issued without gum.

			Type I	
J1a	D1	2½c	3.00	4.00
J2a	D1	5c	40.00	35.00
J3a	D1	10c	35.00	35.00
J4a	D1	12½c	375.00	200.00
J5a	D1	15c	21.00	19.00
J6a	D1	20c	65.00	65.00
J7a	D1	25c	600.00	350.00
J8a	D1	30c	75.00	75.00
J9a	D1	40c	75.00	75.00
J10a	D1	50c	45.00	40.00

			Type II	
J1b	D1	2½c	5.00	4.75
J2b	D1	5c	200.00	150.00
J3b	D1	10c	40.00	37.50
J4b	D1	12½c	400.00	250.00
J5b	D1	15c	25.00	20.00
J6b	D1	20c	425.00	425.00
J7b	D1	25c	1,600.	1,600.
J8b	D1	30c	400.00	400.00
J9b	D1	40c	400.00	400.00
10b	D1	50c	47.50	45.00

D2

1892-98		Value in Black	Perf. 12½	
J11	D2	2½c green (III)	.25	.25
J12	D2	5c green (III)	.60	.45
J13	D2	10c green (III)	1.50	.40
J14	D2	12½c green (III)	1.60	.60
J15	D2	15c green (III) ('95)	2.50	1.10
J17	D2	25c green (III)	1.25	.95
		Nos. J11-J17 (6)	7.70	3.75

		Type I		
J11a	D2	2½c	.50	.50
J12a	D2	5c	2.50	2.50
J13a	D2	10c	2.75	2.00
J14a	D2	12½c	2.00	1.40
J16	D2	20c green ('95)	3.50	1.40
J17a	D2	25c	1.50	1.50
J18	D2	30c green ('95)	25.00	13.00
J19	D2	40c green ('95)	25.00	15.00
J20	D2	50c green ('95)	30.00	15.00

		Type II		
J11b	D2	2½c	20.00	20.00
J12b	D2	5c	1.00	1.00
J13b	D2	10c	1.75	1.10
J14b	D2	12½c	9.00	8.00
J17b	D2	25c	12.50	12.50
		Nos. J11b-J17b (5)	44.25	42.60

Type I
On Yellowish or White Paper
Value in Color of Stamp

1915		Perf. 12½, 13½x12½		
J21	D2	2½c green	1.00	.95
J22	D2	5c green	1.00	.95
J23	D2	10c green	.90	.80
J24	D2	12½c green	1.25	1.10
J25	D2	15c green	1.90	2.00
J26	D2	20c green	1.00	1.75
J27	D2	25c green	.35	.25
J28	D2	30c green	3.00	3.25
J29	D2	40c green	3.00	3.25
J30	D2	50c green	2.50	3.00
		Nos. J21-J30 (10)	15.90	17.30

1944			Perf. 11½	
J23a	D2	10c yellow green	20.00	18.00
J24a	D2	12½c yellow green	20.00	10.00
J27a	D2	25c yellow green	40.00	1.00
		Nos. J23a-J27a (3)	80.00	29.00

NETHERLANDS INDIES

'ne-thər-lənd͜z 'in-dēs

(Dutch Indies)

LOCATION — East Indies
GOVT. — Dutch colony
AREA — 735,268 sq. mi.
POP. — 76,000,000 (estimated 1949)
CAPITAL — Jakarta (formerly Batavia)

Netherlands Indies consisted of the islands of Sumatra, Java, the Lesser Sundas, Madura, two thirds of Borneo, Celebes, the Moluccas, western New Guinea and many small islands.

100 Cents = 1 Gulden

Values for unused stamps are for examples with original gum as defined in the catalogue introduction. Very fine examples of No. 2 will have perforations touching the frameline on one or more sides due to the narrow spacing of the stamps on the plates. Stamps with perfs clear of the framelines on all four sides are scarce and will command higher prices.

Watermarks

Wmk. 202 —
Circles

Wmk. 228 —
Small Crown and
C of A Multiple

King William III — A1

		Unwmk.		
1864, Apr. 1		Engr.	Imperf.	
1	A1	10c lake	450.00	100.00

1868			Perf. 12½x12	
2	A1	10c lake	1,250.	150.00

Privately perforated examples of No. 1 sometimes are mistaken for No. 2.

King William III — A2

ONE CENT:
Type I — "CENT" 6mm long.
Type II — "CENT" 7½mm long.

		Perf. 11½x12, 12½, 12½x12, 13x14, 13½, 14, 13½x14		
1870-88			Typo.	
3	A2	1c sl grn, type I	6.00	4.50
a.		Perf. 13x14, small holes	10.00	8.00
4	A2	1c sl grn, type II	2.75	1.75
5	A2	2c red brown	6.00	4.00
a.		2c fawn	6.00	4.00
6	A2	2c violet brn	110.00	95.00
7	A2	2½c orange	35.00	20.00
8	A2	5c pale green	50.00	3.50
a.		Perf. 14, small holes	60.00	4.00
b.		Perf. 13x14, small holes	50.00	5.00
9	A2	10c orange brn	13.00	.25
a.		Perf. 14, small holes	24.00	.80
b.		Perf. 13x14, small holes	35.00	.80
10	A2	12½c gray	3.50	1.50
a.		Perf. 12½x12		1,000.
11	A2	15c bister	17.00	1.50
a.		Perf. 13x14, small holes	27.50	1.75
12	A2	20c ultra	100.00	5.00
a.		Perf. 14, small holes	100.00	5.00
b.		Perf. 13x14, small holes	100.00	5.25
13	A2	25c dk violet	14.00	.55
b.		Perf. 13x14, small holes	25.00	2.50
c.		Perf. 14, small holes	450.00	3.00
14	A2	30c green	27.50	3.25
15	A2	50c carmine	17.00	1.50
a.		Perf. 13x14, small holes	22.50	1.50
b.		Perf. 14, small holes	17.00	1.50
c.		Perf. 14, large holes	25.00	2.50
16	A2	2.50g green & vio	100.00	17.50
b.		Perf. 14, small holes	100.00	17.50
c.		Perf. 14, large holes	110.00	17.50
		Nos. 3-16 (14)	501.75	159.80

Imperforate examples of Nos. 3-16 are proofs. The 1c red brown and 2c yellow are believed to be bogus.
"Small hole" varieties have the spaces between the holes wider than the diameter of the holes.

Numeral of Value — A3

1883-90			Perf. 12½	
17	A3	1c slate grn ('88)	.75	.25
a.		Perf. 12½x12	1.10	.65
18	A3	2c brown ('84)	.75	.25
a.		Perf. 12½x12	.75	.30
b.		Perf. 11½x12	65.00	22.50
19	A3	2½c yellow	.75	.65
a.		Perf. 12½x12	1.25	.75
b.		Perf. 11½x12	20.00	7.50
20	A3	3c lilac ('90)	.85	.25
21	A3	5c green ('87)	45.00	27.50
22	A3	5c ultra ('90)	9.00	2.50
		Nos. 17-22 (6)	57.10	29.15

For surcharges and overprint see Nos. 46-47, O4.

Queen
Wilhelmina — A4

1892-97   *Perf. 12½*

23	A4	10c orange brn ('95)	5.00	.30
24	A4	12½c gray ('97)	9.00	12.50
25	A4	15c bister ('95)	15.00	1.75
26	A4	20c ultra ('93)	35.00	1.60
27	A4	25c violet	35.00	1.60
28	A4	30c green ('94)	42.50	2.00
29	A4	50c carmine ('93)	30.00	1.40
30	A4	2.50g org brn & ultra	165.00	40.00
		Nos. 23-30 (8)	336.50	61.15

For overprints see Nos. O21-O27.

Netherlands Nos. 67-69, 74, 77, 80, 84 Surcharged in Black

1900, July 1

31	A11	10c on 10c gray lil	1.40	.25
32	A11	12½c on 12½c blue	2.25	.55
33	A11	15c on 15c yel brn	2.50	.30
34	A11	20c on 20c yel grn	13.00	.60
35	A11	25c on 25c car & bl	13.00	.70
36	A11	50c on 50c brnz grn & red brn	22.50	.90

1902   *Perf. 11½x11*

37	A12	2.50g on 2½g brn lil	45.00	11.00
a.		Perf. 11	50.00	12.50
		Nos. 31-37 (7)	99.65	14.30

A6

1902-09   *Perf. 12½*

38	A6	½c violet	.35	.25
39	A6	1c olive grn	.35	.25
a.		Booklet pane of 6		
40	A6	2c yellow brn	2.75	.25
41	A6	2½c green	1.75	.25
a.		Booklet pane of 6		
42	A6	3c orange	1.75	1.10
43	A6	4c ultra ('09)	11.00	9.00
44	A6	5c rose red	4.25	.25
a.		Booklet pane of 6		
45	A6	7½c gray ('08)	2.25	.30
		Nos. 38-45 (8)	24.45	11.65

For overprints see Nos. 63-69, 81-87, O1-O9.

Nos. 18, 20 Surcharged

1902

46	A3	½c on 2c yel brn	.25	.25
a.		Double surcharge	175.00	150.00
47	A3	2½c on 3c violet	.25	.25

Queen
Wilhelmina — A9

1903-08

48	A9	10c slate	1.00	.25
a.		Booklet pane of 6		
49	A9	12½c deep blue ('06)	1.50	.25
a.		Booklet pane of 6		

50	A9	15c chocolate ('06)	7.25	2.00
a.		Ovptd. with 2 horiz. bars	2.50	1.50
51	A9	17½c bister ('08)	3.00	.25
52	A9	20c grnsh slate	1.50	1.50
53	A9	20c olive grn ('05)	30.00	.25
54	A9	22½c brn & ol grn ('08)	3.75	.25
55	A9	25c violet ('04)	12.50	.25
56	A9	30c orange brn	32.50	.30
57	A9	50c red brown ('04)	25.00	.30
		Nos. 48-57 (10)	118.00	5.60

For overprints and surcharges see Nos. 58, 70-78, 88-96, 139, O10-O18.

No. 52 Surcharged in
Black

1905, July 6

58	A9	10c on 20c grnsh slate	3.75	1.90

Queen
Wilhelmina — A10

1905-12   Engr.   *Perf. 11x11½*

59	A10	1g dull lilac ('06)	60.00	.40
a.		Perf. 11½x11	60.00	.50
b.		Perf. 11	70.00	11.00
60	A10	1g dl lil, bl ('12)	60.00	6.50
		Perf. 11	70.00	75.00
61	A10	2½g slate bl ('05)	82.50	3.00
a.		Perf. 11½	82.50	3.50
b.		Perf. 11½x11	90.00	3.50
c.		Perf. 11	675.00	
62	A10	2½g sl bl, bl ('12)	90.00	40.00
a.		Perf. 11	100.00	100.00
		Nos. 59-62 (4)	292.50	49.90

Sheets of Nos. 60 & 62 were soaked in an indigo solution.
For overprints and surcharge see Nos. 79-80, 97-98, 140, O19-O20.

Previous Issues
Overprinted

1908, July 1

63	A6	½c violet	.25	.25
64	A6	1c olive brn	.35	.25
65	A6	2c yellow brn	1.50	2.00
66	A6	2½c green	.75	.25
67	A6	3c orange	.65	1.10
68	A6	5c rose red	2.25	.40
69	A6	7½c gray	2.50	2.25
70	A9	10c slate	.55	.25
71	A9	12½c dp blue	12.00	3.50
72	A9	15c choc (#50a)	3.75	2.00
73	A9	17½c bister	1.40	.95
74	A9	20c olive grn	7.50	1.40
75	A9	22½c brn & ol grn	5.75	3.50
76	A9	25c violet	5.75	.30
77	A9	30c orange brn	20.00	3.25
78	A9	50c red brown	10.00	1.00
79	A10	1g dull lilac	90.00	4.50
80	A10	2½g slate blue	100.00	65.00
		Nos. 63-80 (18)	264.95	92.15

The above stamps were overprinted for use in the territory outside of Java and Madura, stamps overprinted "Java" being used in these latter places.
The 15c is overprinted, in addition, with two horizontal lines, 2½mm apart.
The overprint also exists on Nos. 59a-59b. Same values.

Overprint Reading Down

63a	A6	½c	.55	3.25
64a	A6	1c	.55	2.50
65a	A6	2c	2.25	4.50
66a	A6	2½c	.95	3.00
67a	A6	3c	15.00	40.00
68a	A6	5c	2.25	2.50
70a	A9	10c	.65	1.90
71a	A9	12½c	4.50	8.00
72a	A9	15c	32.50	75.00
74a	A9	20c	7.25	8.00
75a	A9	22½c	1,400.	1,400.
76a	A9	25c	5.50	7.25
77a	A9	30c	11.00	15.00
78a	A9	50c	7.50	9.00
79a	A10	1g	175.00	225.00
80a	A10	2½g	2,250.	2,500.

Overprinted   JAVA.

1908, July 1

81	A6	½c violet	.25	.25
b.		Double overprint	550.00	
82	A6	1c olive grn	.30	.30
83	A6	2c yellow brn	2.10	2.10
84	A6	2½c green	1.10	.25
85	A6	3c orange	.90	.90
86	A6	5c rose red	2.75	.25
87	A6	7½c gray	2.25	2.10
88	A9	10c slate	.75	.25
89	A9	12½c deep blue	2.50	.70
b.		Dbl. ovpt., one inverted	150.00	150.00
90	A9	15c choc (on No. 50a)	3.50	3.00
91	A9	17½c bister	1.90	.80
92	A9	20c olive grn	11.00	.90
93	A9	22½c brn & ol grn	4.75	2.50
94	A9	25c violet	4.75	.40
95	A9	30c orange brn	29.00	2.50
96	A9	50c red brown	18.00	.70
97	A10	1g dull lilac	45.00	3.00
b.		Perf. 11	57.50	5.00
98	A10	2½g slate blue	70.00	47.50
		Nos. 81-98 (18)	200.80	68.40

Inverted Overprint

81a	A6	½c	1.00	2.75
82a	A6	1c	1.00	3.25
83a	A6	2c	3.50	7.25
84a	A6	2½c	3.00	4.00
85a	A6	3c	20.00	27.50
86a	A6	5c	3.00	3.75
88a	A9	10c	2.00	2.50
89a	A9	12½c	3.25	5.75
90a	A9	15c	3.50	11.00
92a	A9	20c	11.00	12.00
94a	A9	25c	6.00	11.00
95a	A9	30c	29.00	29.00
96a	A9	50c	18.00	22.50
97a	A10	1g	180.00	180.00
98a	A10	2½g	2,750.	3,000.

A11

Queen Wilhelmina
A12   A13

Typo., Litho. (#114A)

1912-40   *Perf. 12½*

101	A11	½c lt vio	.25	.25
102	A11	1c olive grn	.25	.25
103	A11	2c yellow brn	.50	.25
104	A11	2c gray blk ('30)	.50	.25
105	A11	2½c green	1.40	.25
106	A11	2½c lt red ('22)	.30	.25
107	A11	3c yellow	.50	.25
108	A11	3c green ('29)	.80	.25
109	A11	4c ultra	.75	.30
110	A11	4c dp grn ('28)	1.40	.25
111	A11	4c yellow ('30)	10.00	4.50
112	A11	5c rose	1.25	.25
113	A11	5c green ('22)	1.05	.25
114	A11	5c chlky bl ('28)	.65	.25
114A	A11	5c ultra ('40)	1.00	.25
115	A11	7½c bister	.45	.25
116	A11	10c lilac ('22)	1.10	.25
117	A12	10c car rose ('14)	.85	.25
118	A12	12½c dull bl ('14)	1.10	.25
119	A12	12½c red ('22)	1.10	.25
120	A12	15c blue ('29)	10.00	.30
121	A12	17½c red brn ('15)	1.10	.30
122	A12	20c green ('15)	2.00	.30
123	A12	20c blue ('22)	2.00	.30
124	A12	20c orange ('32)	17.00	.30
125	A12	22½c orange ('15)	2.00	.50
126	A12	25c red vio ('15)	2.00	.25
127	A12	30c slate ('15)	2.25	.25
128	A12	32½c vio & red ('22)	2.25	.25
129	A12	35c org brn ('29)	10.00	.70
130	A12	40c green ('22)	2.25	.25

     Perf. 11½
     Engr.

131	A13	50c green ('13)	4.75	.25
a.		Perf. 11x11½	5.00	.35
b.		Perf. 12½	5.00	.35
132	A13	60c dp blue ('22)	5.50	.25
133	A13	80c green ('22)	4.75	.25
134	A13	1g brown ('13)	3.50	.25
a.		Perf. 11x11½	4.00	.25
135	A13	1.75g dk vio, p. 12½ ('31)	17.50	2.40
136	A13	2½g carmine ('13)	14.50	.50
a.		Perf. 11x11½	15.00	.75
b.		Perf. 12½	16.00	.75
		Nos. 101-136 (37)	128.55	16.90

For surcharges and overprints see Nos. 137-138, 144-150, 102a-123a, 158, 194-195, B1-B3, C1-C5.

Water Soluble Ink
Some values of types A11 and A12 and late printings of types A6 and A9 are in soluble ink. The design disappears when immersed in water.

Nos. 105, 109, 54, 59 Surcharged

1917-18   Typo.   *Perf. 12½*

137	A11	½c on 2½c	.30	.30
138	A11	1c on 4c ('18)	.55	.55
139	A9	17½c on 22½c 12½ ('18)	1.25	.55
a.		Inverted surcharge	350.00	425.00

     Perf. 11x11½

140	A10	30c on 1g ('18)	10.00	2.25
a.		Perf. 11½x11	140.00	55.00
		Nos. 137-140 (4)	12.10	3.65

Nos. 121, 125, 131, 134 Surcharged in Red or Blue

On A12   On A13

Two types of 32½c on 50c:
I — Surcharge bars spaced as in illustration.
II — Bars more closely spaced.

1922, Jan.   *Perf. 12½*

144	A12	12½c on 17½c (R)	.30	.25
145	A12	12½c on 22½c (R)	.40	.25
146	A12	20c on 22½c (Bl)	.40	.25

     Perf. 11½, 11x11½

147	A13	32½c on 50c (Bl) (I, perf. 11½)	1.25	.25
a.		Type II, perf. 11½	10.00	1.00
b.		Type I, perf. 11x11½	1,000.	6.00
c.		Type II, perf. 11x11½	19.00	3.00
148	A13	40c on 50c (R)	3.75	.45
149	A13	60c on 1g (Bl)	6.00	.40
150	A13	80c on 1g (R)	6.75	.90
		Nos. 144-150 (7)	18.85	2.75

Stamps of 1912-22 Overprinted in Red, Blue, Green or Black

a   b

No. 145a

1922, Sept. 18   Typo.   *Perf. 12½*

102a	A11(a)	1c ol grn (R)	7.00	5.75
103a	A11(a)	2c yel brn (Bl)	7.00	5.75
106a	A11(a)	2½c lt red (G)	65.00	72.50
107a	A11(a)	3c yellow (R)	7.00	7.00
109a	A11(a)	4c ultra (R)	38.50	36.00
113a	A11(a)	5c green (R)	13.00	10.00

115a	A11(a)	7½c drab (Bl)	9.00	5.75
116a	A11(a)	10c lilac (Bk)	70.00	80.00
145a	A12(b)	12½c on 22½c	7.00	7.00
121a	A12(b)	17½c red brn (Bk)	7.00	5.75
123a	A12(b)	20c blue (Bk)	7.00	5.75
		Nos. 102a-123a (11)	237.50	241.25

Issued to publicize the 3rd Netherlands Indies Industrial Fair at Bandoeng, Java.

Nos. 102a-123a were sold at a premium for 3, 4, 5, 6, 8, 9, 10, 12½, 15, 20 and 22½ cents respectively.

Queen Wilhelmina — A15

1923, Aug. 31   Engr.   Perf. 11½

151	A15	5c myrtle green	.25	.25
a.		Perf. 11½x11	400.00	140.00
b.		Perf. 11x11½	4.50	.55
152	A15	12½c rose	.25	.25
a.		Perf. 11½x11	1.25	.25
b.		Perf. 11½x11	1.75	.25
153	A15	20c dark blue	.35	.25
a.		Perf. 11½x11	3.25	.40
154	A15	50c red orange	1.40	.60
a.		Perf. 11½x11	6.50	1.25
b.		Perf. 11½x11	2.00	.90
c.		Perf. 11	4.50	.85
155	A15	1g brown vio	2.75	.40
a.		Perf. 11½x11	7.50	.80
156	A15	2½g gray black	35.00	12.00
157	A15	5g orange brown	135.00	125.00
		Nos. 151-157 (7)	175.00	138.75

25th anniversary of the assumption of the government of the Netherlands by Queen Wilhelmina, at the age of 18.

No. 123 Surcharged

1930, Dec. 13   Typo.   Perf. 12½

158	A12	12½c on 20c bl (R)	.30	.25
a.		Inverted surcharge	375.00	475.00

Prince William I, Portrait by Van Key — A16

1933, Apr. 18   Photo.

163	A16	12½c deep orange	1.25	.25

400th anniv. of the birth of Prince William I, Count of Nassau and Prince of Orange, frequently referred to as William the Silent.

Rice Field Scene A17   Queen Wilhelmina A18

Queen Wilhelmina A19

1933-37   Unwmk.   Perf. 11½x12½

164	A17	1c lilac gray ('34)	.25	.25
165	A17	2c plum ('34)	.25	.25
166	A17	2½c bister ('34)	.25	.25
167	A17	3c yellow grn	.25	.25
168	A17	3½c dark gray ('37)	.25	.25
169	A17	4c dk olive ('34)	1.00	.25
170	A17	5c ultra ('34)	.25	.25
171	A17	7½c violet ('34)	1.50	.25
172	A17	10c ver ('34)	2.10	.25
173	A18	10c ver ('37)	.30	.25
174	A18	12½c dp org ('34)	.30	.25
a.		12½c light orange, perf. 12½ ('33)	7.50	.40
175	A18	15c ultra ('34)	.30	.25
176	A18	20c plum ('34)	.50	.25
177	A18	25c blue grn ('34)	2.10	.25
178	A18	30c lilac gray ('34)	3.25	.25
179	A18	32½c bister ('34)	9.00	10.00
180	A18	35c violet ('34)	5.00	1.25
181	A18	40c yel grn ('34)	3.00	.25
182	A18	42½c yellow ('34)	3.00	.25

1934, Jan. 16   Perf. 12½

183	A19	50c lilac gray	5.00	.25
184	A19	60c ultra	6.00	.50
185	A19	80c vermilion	6.00	.60
186	A19	1g violet	6.25	.40
187	A19	1.75g yellow grn	20.00	15.00
188	A19	2.50g plum	22.50	2.00
		Nos. 164-188 (25)	98.60	34.25

See Nos. 200-225. For overprints and surcharges see Nos. 271-275 (in Scott Standard catalogue, Vol. 5), B48, B57 (in Scott Vol. 5).

Water Soluble Ink

Nos. 164-188 and the first printing of No. 163 have soluble ink and the design disappears when immersed in water.

Nos. C6-C7, C14, C9-C10 Surcharged in Black

a

b

1934   Typo.   Perf. 12½x11½, 12½

189	AP1(a)	2c on 10c	.30	.45
190	AP1(a)	2c on 20c	.25	.25
191	AP3(b)	2c on 30c	.40	.60
192	AP1(a)	42½c on 75c	4.25	.25
193	AP1(a)	42½c on 1.50g	4.25	.40
		Nos. 189-193 (5)	9.45	1.95

Nos. 127-128 Surcharged with New Value in Red or Black

1937, Sept.   Perf. 12½

194	A12	10c on 30c (R)	2.50	.25
a.		Double surcharge	675.00	
195	A12	10c on 32½c (Bk)	2.75	.30

Wilhelmina — A20

Perf. 12½x12

1938, Aug. 30   Photo.   Wmk. 202

196	A20	2c dull purple	.25	.25
197	A20	10c car lake	.25	.25
198	A20	15c royal blue	1.25	.75
199	A20	20c red orange	.50	.30
		Nos. 196-199 (4)	2.25	1.55

40th anniv. of the reign of Queen Wilhelmina.

Types of 1933-37

1938-40   Photo.   Perf. 12½x12

200	A17	1c lilac gray ('39)	.30	.80
201	A17	2c plum ('39)	.25	.25
202	A17	2½c bister ('39)	.50	.50
203	A17	3c yellow grn ('39)	1.50	1.05
205	A17	4c gray ol ('39)	1.50	1.25
206	A17	5c ultra ('39)	.25	.25
a.		Perf. 12x12½	1.25	
207	A17	7½c violet ('39)	2.50	1.00
208	A18	10c ver ('39)	.25	.25
210	A18	15c ultra ('39)	.25	.25
211	A18	20c plum ('39)	.25	.25
a.		Perf. 12x12½	1.25	
212	A18	25c blue grn ('39)	25.00	24.00
213	A18	30c lilac gray ('39)	6.50	.80
215	A18	35c violet ('39)	2.75	.65
216	A18	40c dp yel grn ('40)	5.00	.25

Perf. 12½

218	A19	50c lilac gray ('40)	275.00	
219	A19	60c ultra ('39)	10.50	1.25
220	A19	80c ver ('39)	62.50	26.00
221	A19	1g violet ('39)	27.50	.85
223	A19	2g Prus green	27.50	14.00
225	A19	5g yellow brn	25.00	6.00
		Nos. 200-216,219-225 (19)	199.80	79.85

The note following No. 188 applies also to this issue.

The 50c was sold only at the philatelic window in Amsterdam.

SEMI-POSTAL STAMPS

Regular Issue of 1912-14 Surcharged in Carmine

1915, June 10   Unwmk.   Perf. 12½

B1	A11	1c + 5c ol grn	4.50	4.50
B2	A11	5c + 5c rose	4.50	4.50
B3	A12	10c + 5c rose	7.25	7.25
		Nos. B1-B3 (3)	16.25	16.25

Surtax for the Red Cross.

Bali Temple SP1   Watchtower SP2

Menangkabau Compound — SP3

Borobudur Temple, Java SP4

Perf. 11½x11, 11x11½

1930, Dec. 1   Photo.

B4	SP1	2c (+ 1c) vio & brn	1.00	.80
B5	SP2	5c (+ 2½c) dk grn & brn	4.75	2.50
B6	SP3	12½c (+ 2½c) dp red & brn	3.25	.50
B7	SP4	15c (+ 5c) ultra & brn	5.75	5.75
		Nos. B4-B7 (4)	14.75	9.55

Surtax for youth care.

Farmer and Carabao SP5

5c, Fishermen. 12½c, Dancers. 15c, Musicians.

1931, Dec. 1   Engr.   Perf. 12½

B8	SP5	2c (+ 1c) olive bis	3.00	2.00
B9	SP5	5c (+ 2½c) bl grn	4.25	3.75
B10	SP5	12½c (+ 2½c) dp red	3.25	.55
B11	SP5	15c (+ 5c) dl bl	8.25	7.00
		Nos. B8-B11 (4)	18.75	13.30

The surtax was for the aid of the Leper Colony at Salatiga.

Weaving SP9

5c, Plaiting rattan. 12½c, Woman batik dyer. 15c, Coppersmith.

1932, Dec. 1   Photo.   Perf. 12½

B12	SP9	2c (+ 2½c) dp vio & bis	.40	.40
B13	SP9	5c (+ 2½c) dp grn & bis	2.50	2.00
B14	SP9	12½c (+ 2½c) brt rose & bis	.85	.30
B15	SP9	15c (+ 5c) bl & bis	3.25	3.00
		Nos. B12-B15 (4)	7.00	5.70

The surtax was donated to the Salvation Army.

Woman and Lotus — SP13

Designs: 5c, "The Light that Shows the Way." 12½c, YMCA emblem. 15c, Jobless man.

1933, Dec. 1   Perf. 12½

B16	SP13	2c (+ 1c) red vio & ol bis	.65	.30
B17	SP13	5c (+ 2½c) grn & ol bis	2.25	1.90
B18	SP13	12½c (+ 2½c) ver & ol bis	2.50	.30
B19	SP13	15c (+ 5c) bl & ol bis	2.75	2.00
		Nos. B16-B19 (4)	8.15	4.50

The surtax was for the Amsterdam Young Men's Society for Relief of the Poor in Netherlands Indies.

Dowager Queen Emma — SP17

1934, Sept. 15   Perf. 13x14

B20	SP17	12½c (+ 2½c) blk brn	1.25	.45

Issued in memory of the late Dowager Queen Emma of Netherlands. The surtax was for the Anti-Tuberculosis Society.

A Pioneer at Work — SP18

Designs: 5c, Cavalryman rescuing wounded native. 12½c, Artilleryman under fire. 15c, Bugler.

1935   Perf. 12½

B21	SP18	2c (+ 1c) plum & ol bis	1.25	1.00
B22	SP18	5c (+ 2½c) grn & ol bis	3.25	2.25
B23	SP18	12½c (+ 2½c) red org & ol bis	3.25	.25

B24 SP18 15c (+ 5c) brt bl &
ol bis 4.50 4.50
Nos. B21-B24 (4) 12.25 8.00

The surtax was for the Indies Committee of the Christian Military Association for the East and West Indies.

Child Welfare Work — SP22

1936, Dec. 1 Size: 23x20mm
B25 SP22 2c (+ 1c) plum 1.00 .60
Size: 30x26½mm
B26 SP22 5c (+ 2½c) gray vio 1.25 1.10
B27 SP22 7½c (+ 2½c) dk vio 1.25 1.25
B28 SP22 12½c (+ 2½c) red org 1.25 .30
B29 SP22 15c (+5c) brt bl 2.00 1.75
Nos. B25-B29 (5) 6.75 5.00

Surtax for Salvation Army.

Boy Scouts — SP23

1937, May 1
B30 SP23 7½c + 2½c dk ol brn 1.25 1.00
B31 SP23 12½c + 2½c rose car 1.25 .50

Fifth Boy Scout World Jamboree, Vogelenzang, Netherlands, July 31-Aug. 13, 1937. Surtax for Netherlands Indies Scout Association.

Sifting Rice — SP24

Designs: 3½c, Mother and children. 7½c, Plowing with carabao team. 10c, Carabao team and cart. 20c, Native couple.

1937, Dec. 1
B32 SP24 2c (+ 1c) dk brn & org 1.10 .80
B33 SP24 3½c (+ 1½c) gray 1.10 .80
B34 SP24 7½c (+ 2½c) Prus grn & org 2.25 .95
B35 SP24 10c (+ 2½c) car & org 1.25 .25
B36 SP24 20c (+ 5c) brt bl 1.25 1.10
Nos. B32-B36 (5) 5.95 3.90

Surtax for the Public Relief Fund for indigenous poor.

Modern Plane — SP28

Design: 20c, Plane nose facing left.

Wmk. 202
1938, Oct. 15 Photo. Perf. 12½
B36A SP28 17½c (+5c) olive brn .85 .85
B36B SP28 20c (+5c) slate .85 .55

10th anniversary of the Dutch East Indies Royal Air Lines (K. N. I. L. M.).
Surtax for the Aviation Fund in the Netherlands Indies.

Nun and Child
SP29 SP30

Designs: 7½c, Nurse examining child's arm. 10c, Nurse bathing baby. 20c, Nun bandaging child's head.

1938, Dec. 1 Wmk. 202 Perf. 12½
B37 SP29 2c (+ 1c) vio .60 .45
Perf. 11½x12
B38 SP30 3½c (+ 1½c) brt grn 1.00 .90
Perf. 12x11½
B39 SP30 7½c (+ 2½c) cop red .80 .85
B40 SP30 10c (+ 2½c) ver .90 .25
B41 SP30 20c (+ 5c) brt ultra 1.00 .95
Nos. B37-B41 (5) 4.30 3.40

The surtax was for the Central Mission Bureau in Batavia.

Social Workers SP34 / Indonesian Nurse Tending Patient SP35

European Nurse Tending Patient — SP36

Perf. 13x11½, 11½x13
1939, Dec. 1 Photo.
B42 SP34 2c (+ 1c) purple .25 .25
B43 SP35 3½c (+ 1½c) bl grn & pale bl grn .30 .25
B44 SP34 7½c (+ 2½c) cop brn .25 .25
B45 SP35 10c (+ 2½c) scar & pink 1.40 .80
B46 SP36 10c (+ 2½c) scar 1.40 .80
B47 SP36 20c (+ 5c) dk bl .40 .35
Nos. B42-B47 (6) 4.00 2.70

No. B44 shows native social workers. Nos. B45 and B46 were issued se-tenant vertically and horizontally. The surtax was used for the Bureau of Social Service.

No. 174 Surcharged in Brown

1940, Dec. 2 Unwmk. Perf. 12x12½
B48 A18 10c + 5c on 12½c dp org 1.10 .40

AIR POST STAMPS

Regular Issues of 1913-1923 Surcharged and New Values in Black or Blue

Perf. 12½, 11½
1928, Sept. 20 Unwmk.
C1 A12 10c on 12½c red 1.00 1.00
C2 A12 20c on 25c red vio 2.25 2.25
C3 A13 40c on 80c org 1.90 1.50

C4 A13 75c on 1g brn (Bl) .90 .55
C5 A13 1½g on 2½g car 6.25 5.50
Nos. C1-C5 (5) 12.30 10.80

On Nos. C4 and C5 there are stars over the original values and the airplane is of different shape. On No. C3 there are no bars under "OST."

Planes over Temple AP1

1928, Dec. 1 Litho. Perf. 12½x11½
C6 AP1 10c red violet .30 .25
C7 AP1 20c brown .85 .55
C8 AP1 40c rose 1.00 .55
C9 AP1 75c green 2.25 .25
C10 AP1 1.50g orange 4.00 .50
Nos. C6-C10 (5) 8.40 2.10

For surcharges see Nos. 189-190, 192-193, C11-C12, C17.

No. C8 Surcharged in Black or Green

1930-32
C11 AP1 30c on 40c rose .90 .25
C12 AP1 30c on 40c rose (G) ('32) 1.25 .25

Pilot at Controls of Plane AP2

1931, Apr. 1 Photo. Perf. 12½
C13 AP2 1g blue & brown 11.00 11.00

Issued for the first air mail flight from Java to Australia.

Landscape and Garudas AP3

1931, May
C14 AP3 30c red violet 2.25 .25
C15 AP3 4½g bright blue 8.00 3.00
C16 AP3 7½g yellow green 10.00 3.25
Nos. C14-C16 (3) 20.25 6.50

For surcharge see No. 191.

No. C10 Surcharged in Blue

1932, July 21 Perf. 12½x11½
C17 AP1 50c on 1.50g org 2.50 .40
a. Inverted surcharge 1,800. 2,000.

Airplane AP4

1933, Oct. 18 Photo. Perf. 12½
C18 AP4 30c deep blue 2.10 1.75

MARINE INSURANCE STAMPS

Floating Safe Attracting Gulls — MI1 / Floating Safe with Night Flare — MI2

Artistic Fantasy of Floating Safe — MI3

Perf. 11½
1921, Nov. 1 Unwmk. Engr.
GY1 MI1 15c slate green 2.25 40.00
GY2 MI1 60c rose 4.00 50.00
GY3 MI1 75c gray brn 4.00 55.00
GY4 MI2 1.50g dark blue 25.00 250.00
GY5 MI2 2.25g org brn 32.50 350.00
GY6 MI3 4½g black 65.00 600.00
GY7 MI3 7½g red 80.00 700.00
Nos. GY1-GY7 (7) 212.75 2,045.

POSTAGE DUE STAMPS

D1

D2

1845-46 Unwmk. Typeset Imperf.
Bluish Paper
J1 D1 black ('46) 1,650.
J2 D2 black 2,000.
a. "Maill" instead of "Mail" 3,200.

D3

Perf. 12½x12, 13x14, 10½x12
1874 Typo.
J3 D3 5c ocher 300.00 275.00
J4 D3 10c green, yel 120.00 100.00
J5 D3 15c ocher, org 25.00 20.00
a. Perf. 11½x12 40.00 40.00
J6 D3 20c green, blue 40.00 17.50
a. Perf. 11½x12 80.00 25.00
Nos. J3-J6 (4) 485.00 412.50

D4

Type I — 34 loops. "T" of "Betalen" over center of loop, top branch of "E" of "Te" shorter than lower branch.
Type II — 33 loops. "T" of "Betalen" over center of two loops.
Type III — 32 loops. "T" of "Betalen" slightly to the left of loop, top branch of first "E" of "Betalen" shorter than lower branch.
Type IV — 37 loops and letters of "PORT" larger than in the other three types.

Value in Black

Perf. 11½x12, 12½, 12½x12, 13½

1882-88				Type III
J7	D4	2½c carmine	.40	1.10
J8	D4	5c carmine	.25	.40
J9	D4	10c carmine	2.50	3.00
J10	D4	15c carmine	3.00	3.00
J11	D4	20c carmine	100.00	1.00
J12	D4	30c carmine	1.75	2.50
J13	D4	40c carmine	1.25	2.00
J14	D4	50c deep salmon	.75	.60
J15	D4	75c carmine	.45	.50
	Nos. J7-J15 (9)		145.35	14.10

Type I

J7a	D4	2½c carmine	.40	1.10
J8a	D4	5c carmine	.25	.45
J9a	D4	10c carmine	3.25	4.00
J10a	D4	15c carmine	3.25	3.50
J11a	D4	20c carmine	95.00	.50
J12a	D4	30c carmine	3.25	4.00
J13a	D4	40c carmine	1.40	2.00
J14a	D4	50c deep salmon	.80	.60
J15a	D4	75c carmine	.50	.60
	Nos. J7a-J15a (9)		108.10	16.75

Type II

J7b	D4	2½c carmine	.50	1.40
J8b	D4	5c carmine	.25	.60
J9b	D4	10c carmine	3.50	4.50
J10b	D4	15c carmine	3.75	4.00
J11b	D4	20c carmine	165.00	.99
J12b	D4	30c carmine	7.00	7.50
J13b	D4	40c carmine	1.50	2.50
J14b	D4	50c deep salmon	.85	.75
J15b	D4	75c carmine	.65	.85
	Nos. J7b-J15b (9)		183.00	23.00

Type IV

J7c	D4	2½c carmine	2.25	3.00
J8c	D4	5c carmine	1.00	1.75
J9c	D4	10c carmine	20.00	24.00
J10c	D4	15c carmine	13.00	14.00
J11c	D4	20c carmine	250.00	9.00
J13c	D4	40c carmine	2.50	3.50
J14c	D4	50c deep salmon	15.00	20.00
J15c	D4	75c carmine	1.25	2.50
	Nos. J7c-J15c (8)		305.00	77.75

D5

1892-95		Type I	Perf. 12½
J16	D5	10c carmine	2.25	.30
J17	D5	15c carmine ('95)	12.00	1.75
J18	D5	20c carmine	2.00	.25
	Nos. J16-J18 (3)		16.25	2.30

Type III

J16a	D5	10c dull red	2.75	2.00
J18a	D5	20c dull red	3.75	1.40

Type II

J16b	D5	10c dull red	13.00	13.00
J18b	D5	20c dull red	18.00	6.50

1906-09			Type I
J19	D5	2½c carmine ('08)	.50	.30
J20	D5	5c carmine ('09)	2.25	.25
J21	D5	30c carmine	17.50	5.75
J22	D5	40c carmine ('09)	12.50	1.50
J23	D5	50c carmine ('09)	8.50	.90
J24	D5	75c carmine ('09)	17.00	4.00
	Nos. J19-J24 (6)		58.25	12.70

Value in Color of Stamp

1913-39			Perf. 12½
J25	D5	1c salmon ('39)	.25	1.25
J26	D5	2½c salmon	.25	.25
J27	D5	3½c salmon ('39)	.25	1.25
J28	D5	5c salmon	.25	.25
J29	D5	7½c salmon ('22)	.25	.25
J30	D5	10c salmon	.25	.25
J31	D5	12½c salmon ('22)	2.75	.25
J32	D5	15c salmon	2.75	.25
J33	D5	20c salmon ('22)	.25	.25
J34	D5	25c salmon ('22)	.25	.25
J35	D5	30c salmon	.25	.25
J36	D5	37½c salmon ('30)	22.50	22.50
J37	D5	40c salmon	.25	.25
J38	D5	50c salmon	1.40	.25
J39	D5	75c salmon	2.50	.25
	Nos. J25-J39 (15)		34.40	28.00

Thick White Paper
Invisible Gum
Numerals Slightly Larger

1941		Litho.	Perf. 12½
J25a	D5	1c light red	.60	2.00
J28a	D5	5c light red	.65	1.00
J30a	D5	10c light red	10.50	10.00
J32a	D5	15c light red	1.00	1.00
J33a	D5	20c light red	.80	.80
J35a	D5	30c light red	1.25	1.00
J37a	D5	75c light red	.25	.25
	Nos. J25a-J37a (7)		15.80	16.60

No. J36 Surcharged with New Value

1937, Oct. 1		Unwmk.	Perf. 12½
J40	D5	20c on 37½c salmon	.25	.30

D6

1939-40				
J41	D6	1g salmon		5.00	7.50
J42	D6	1g blue ('40)		.30	4.50
a.	1g lt bl, thick paper, invisible gum			.90	1.00

OFFICIAL STAMPS

Regular Issues of
1883-1909
Overprinted

Perf. 12½

1911, Oct. 1		Typo.	Unwmk.
O1	A6	½c violet	.25	.30
O2	A6	1c olive grn	.25	.25
O3	A6	2c yellow brn	.25	.25
O4	A3	2½c yellow	.75	.75
O5	A6	2½c blue grn	1.40	1.25
O6	A6	3c orange	.40	.40
O7	A6	4c ultra	.25	.25
O8	A6	5c rose red	.80	.80
b.	Double overprint			325.00
O9	A6	7½c gray	2.75	2.75
O10	A9	10c slate	.25	.25
O11	A9	12½c deep blue	2.00	2.25
O12	A9	15c chocolate	.65	.65
a.	Overprinted with two bars			32.50
b.	As "a," "Dienst" inverted			52.50
O13	A9	17½c bister	2.75	2.50
O14	A9	20c olive grn	.60	.50
O15	A9	22½c brn & ol grn	3.50	3.00
O16	A9	25c violet	2.00	2.00
O17	A9	30c orange brn	.90	.60
O18	A9	50c red brown	12.00	7.00
O19	A10	1g dull lilac	3.00	1.25
O20	A10	2½g slate blue	27.50	30.00
	Nos. O1-O20 (20)		62.25	57.00

The overprint reads diagonally downward on Nos. O1-O3 and O5-O9.

Overprint Inverted

O1a	A6	½c	45.00	125.00
O2a	A6	1c	3.00	19.00
O3a	A6	2c	3.00	20.00
O5a	A6	2½c	9.00	30.00
O6a	A6	3c	110.00	40.00
O8a	A6	5c	3.00	20.00
O10a	A9	10c	3.00	7.00
O11a	A9	12½c	32.50	55.00
O14a	A9	20c	175.00	70.00
O16a	A9	25c	1,250.	1,000.
O17a	A9	30c	225.00	140.00
O18a	A9	50c	32.50	32.50
O19a	A10	1g	525.00	850.00
O20a	A10	2½g	225.00	625.00

Regular Issue of 1892-1894 Overprinted

1911, Oct. 1				
O21	A4	10c orange brn	1.25	.60
O22	A4	12½c gray	3.00	5.50
O23	A4	15c bister	3.00	3.00
O24	A4	20c blue	3.00	1.00
O25	A4	25c lilac	12.00	10.00
O26	A4	50c carmine	2.50	1.25
O27	A4	2.50g org brn & bl	55.00	55.00
	Nos. O21-O27 (7)		79.75	76.35

Inverted Overprints

O21a	A4	10c	15.00	50.00
O22a	A4	12½c	425.00	400.00
O23a	A4	15c	425.00	325.00
O24a	A4	20c	165.00	175.00
O25a	A4	25c	800.00	900.00
O26a	A4	50c	15.00	75.00
O27a	A4	2.50g	1,150.	1,450.

NEVIS

ˈnē-vəs

LOCATION — West Indies, southeast of Puerto Rico
GOVT. — Presidency of the Leeward Islands Colony (British)
AREA — 50 sq. mi.

POP. — 9,800 (1990)
CAPITAL — Charlestown

Nevis stamps were discontinued in 1890 and replaced by those of the Leeward Islands. From 1903 to 1956 stamps of St. Kitts-Nevis and Leeward Islands were used concurrently. See Leeward Islands and St. Kitts-Nevis.

12 Pence = 1 Shilling

PRE-STAMP POSTAL MARKINGS

Crowned Circle handstamp type VI is pictured in the Crowned Circle Handstamps and Great Britain Used Abroad section.

Charlestown

1852			
A1	VI	"Nevis" crowned circle handstamp in red, on cover	6,500.

The handstamp was used, in black, as a provisional to 1886.

STAMPS OF GREAT BRITAIN USED IN NEVIS

Numeral cancellation type A is pictured in the Crowned Circle Handstamps and Great Britain Used Abroad section.

1858-60			
		A09 (Charlestown)	
A2	A	1p rose red (#20)	700.00
A3	A	2p blue (#29, P7, 8)	2,250.
A4	A	4p rose (#26)	500.00
A5	A	6p lilac (#27)	350.00
A6	A	1sh green (#28)	2,750.

Issued under British Administration

Unused examples of Nos. 1-8 almost always have no original gum, and they are valued without gum. These stamps with original gum are worth more. Other issues are valued with original gum as defined in the catalogue introduction. Very fine examples of Nos. 1-8, will have perforations touching the design on at least one side due to the narrow spacing of the stamps on the plates. Stamps with perfs clear of the design on all four sides are scarce and will command higher prices.

Medicinal Spring
A1   A2

A3   A4

1861		Unwmk.	Engr.	Perf. 13
		Bluish Wove Paper		
1	A1	1p lake rose	325.00	140.00
2	A2	4p dull rose	950.00	200.00
3	A3	6p gray	775.00	260.00
4	A4	1sh green	1,100.	250.00

		Grayish Wove Paper		
5	A1	1p lake rose	110.00	60.00
6	A2	4p dull rose	175.00	80.00
7	A3	6p lilac gray	175.00	65.00
8	A4	1sh green	400.00	95.00

1867		White Wove Paper		Perf. 15
9	A1	1p red	65.00	55.00
10	A2	4p orange	155.00	25.00
11	A4	1sh yellow green	925.00	125.00
a.	Imperf.			7,500.
12	A4	1sh blue green	325.00	45.00

Laid Paper

13	A4	1sh yel green	25,000.	6,750.
	Manuscript cancel			3,000.

No. 13 values are for stamps with design cut into on one or two sides.

1876		Wove Paper	Litho.
14	A1	1p rose	32.50	25.00
14A	A1	1p red	45.00	30.00
b.	1p vermilion		45.00	45.00
c.	Imperf., pair		1,900.	
d.	Half used as ½p on cover			4,500.
15	A2	4p orange	190.00	45.00
a.	Imperf.			
b.	Vert. pair, imperf. between		12,750.	
16	A3	6p olive gray	250.00	250.00
17	A4	1sh gray green	100.00	125.00
a.	1sh dark green		135.00	175.00
b.	Horiz. strip of 3, perf. all around & imperf. btwn.		20,000.	

Perf. 11½

18	A1	1p vermilion	65.00	60.00
a.	Horiz. pair, imperf. btwn.			
b.	Half used as ½p on cover			4,500.
c.	Imperf., pair		1,000.	
	Nos. 14-18 (6)		682.50	535.00

Queen Victoria — A5

1879-80		Typo.	Wmk. 1	Perf. 14
19	A5	1p violet ('80)	90.00	55.00
a.	Diagonal half used as ½p on cover			1,500.
20	A5	2½p red brown	175.00	100.00

1882-90		Wmk. Crown and CA (2)	
21	A5	½p green ('83)	13.00	25.00
22	A5	1p violet	125.00	45.00
a.	Half used as ½p on cover			900.00
23	A5	1p rose ('83)	42.50	30.00
a.	1p carmine ('84)		20.00	20.00
24	A5	2½p red brown	140.00	55.00
25	A5	2½p ultra ('84)	24.00	27.50
26	A5	4p blue	400.00	55.00
27	A5	4p gray ('84)	25.00	10.00
28	A5	6p green ('83)	500.00	400.00
29	A5	6p brown org ('86)	27.50	77.50
30	A5	1sh violet ('90)	125.00	225.00
	Nos. 21-30 (10)		1,422.	950.00

Half of No. 22 Surcharged in Black or Violet

1883				
31	A5	½p on half of 1p	1,100.	60.00
a.	Double surcharge			450.00
b.	Unsevered pair		7,500.	
c.	Surcharged on half of 1p revenue stamp			600.00
32	A5	½p on half of 1p (V)	1,250.	55.00
a.	Double surcharge			450.00
b.	Unsevered pair		7,500.	850.00
c.	Surcharged on half of 1p revenue stamp			600.00

Surcharge reads up or down.

NEW BRITAIN

'nü 'bri-tᵊn

LOCATION — South Pacific Ocean, northeast of New Guinea
GOVT. — Australian military government
AREA — 13,000 sq. mi. (approx.)
POP. — 50,600 (approx.)
CAPITAL — Rabaul

The island Neu-Pommern, a part of former German New Guinea, was captured during World War I by Australian troops and named New Britain. Following the war it was mandated to Australia and designated a part of the Mandated Territory of New Guinea. See German New Guinea, North West Pacific Islands and New Guinea.

12 Pence = 1 Shilling

Stamps of German New Guinea, 1900, Surcharged

Kaiser's Yacht "The Hohenzollern"
A3   A4

First Setting
Surcharge lines spaced 6mm on 1p-8p, 4mm on 1sh-5sh

Perf. 14, 14½

1914, Oct. 17		Unwmk.
1 A3 1p on 3pf brown	750.00	875.00
a. "1" for "I"	2,200.	2,500.
b. Short "1"	2,200.	
c. "1" with straight top serif	2,200.	
d. "I" for "1" (setting 12)	3,800.	
2 A3 1p on 5pf green	95.00	110.00
a. "1" for "I"	385.00	475.00
b. Short "1"	385.00	465.00
c. "1" with straight top serif (settings 6 & 9)	525.00	600.00
3 A3 2p on 10pf car	100.00	135.00
a. "1" for "I"	440.00	550.00
4 A3 2p on 20pf ultra	100.00	110.00
a. "2d." dbl., "G.R.I." omitted	6,000.	
b. Inverted surcharge	16,500.	
c. "1" for "I"	425.00	475.00
5 A3 2½p on 10pf car	105.00	220.00
a. Fraction bar omitted (setting 9)	3,800.	3,850.
6 A3 2½p on 20pf ultra	120.00	250.00
a. Inverted surcharge		
b. Fraction bar omitted (setting 9)		10,500.
7 A3 3p on 25pf org & blk, *yel*	350.00	475.00
a. "1" for "I"	1,200.	1,400.
8 A3 3p on 30pf org & blk, *sal*	475.00	525.00
a. Double surcharge	15,000.	15,000.
b. Triple surcharge		
c. "1" for "I"	1,400.	1,650.
9 A3 4p on 40pf lake & black	475.00	550.00
a. Double surcharge	4,100.	5,000.
b. Inverted surcharge	16,250.	
c. "4d." omitted		
d. "1" for "I"	1,625.	
10 A3 5p on 50pf pur & blk, *sal*	825.00	1,100.
a. Double surcharge	16,250.	
b. "1" for "I"	2,500.	3,250.
11 A3 8p on 80pf lake & blk, *rose*	1,050.	1,650.
a. No period after "8d"	4,600.	
b. Surcharged "G.R.I. 4d" (error)	15,250.	
c. "1" for "I"	3,500.	4,600.
12 A4 1sh on 1m car	3,500.	4,750.
a. Large "s"	13,000.	13,000.
13 A4 2sh on 2m blue	3,250.	4,500.
a. Surcharged "G.R.I. 5s" (error)	45,000.	
b. Surcharged "G.R.I. 2d" corrected by hand-stamped "R"	55,000.	
c. Large "s"	12,500.	15,000.
14 A4 3sh on 3m blk vio	5,500.	7,750.
a. No period after "I"	14,000.	14,000.
b. Large "s"	16,500.	
15 A4 5sh on 5m slate & car	14,000.	16,500.
a. No period after "I"	18,500.	21,000.
b. Surcharged "G.R.I. 1s" (error)	87,500.	
c. Large "s"	30,000.	

"G.R.I." stands for Georgius Rex Imperator.

Second Setting
Surcharge lines spaced 5mm on 1p-8p, 5½mm on 1sh-5sh

1914, Dec. 16		
16 A3 1p on 3pf brown	75.00	95.00
a. Double surcharge	1,400.	1,850.
b. "I" for "1"	825.00	
c. "1" with straight top serif	135.00	165.00
d. Inverted surcharge	5,500.	
e. "4" for "1"	17,500.	
f. Small "1"	350.00	
g. Double surcharge, one inverted	7,750.	
17 A3 1p on 5pf green	30.00	55.00
a. Double surcharge	5,250.	
b. "G. I. R."	13,000.	14,000.
c. "d" inverted		3,500.
d. No periods after "G R I"		11,000.
e. Small "1"	140.00	210.00
f. "1d" double		—
g. No period after "1d"		
h. Triple surcharge		
i. No periods or spaces in "GRI"		11,000.
j. "1" with straight top serif	55.00	90.00
k. "1d" inverted		11,000.
18 A3 2p on 10pf car	45.00	65.00
a. Double surcharge	16,250.	16,250.
b. Dbl. surch., one inverted		13,000.
c. Surcharged "G. I. R., 3d"	13,000.	
d. Surcharged "1d"	12,000.	11,000.
e. Period before "G"	11,000.	
f. No period after "2d"	200.00	275.00
g. Inverted surcharge		
h. "2d" double, one inverted		
j. Pair, #18, 20	30,000.	
k. Vertical pair, #18, 20	22,000.	
19 A3 2p on 20pf ultra	50.00	75.00
a. Double surcharge	3,500.	4,750.
b. Double surch., one inverted	5,000.	6,500.
c. "R" inverted		9,250.
d. Surcharged "1d"	13,000.	14,000.
f. Inverted surcharge	10,500.	
h. Pair, one without surcharge	25,000.	
i. Vertical pair, #19, 21	20,000.	23,000.
j. No period after "d"	140.00	210.00
k. No period after "I"	1,650.	
20 A3 2½p on 10pf car	250.00	375.00
21 A3 2½p on 20pf ultra	2,100.	2,100.
a. Double surcharge, one invtd.		
b. "2½" triple		
c. Surcharged "3d" in pair with normal	42,500.	
22 A3 3p on 25pf org & blk, *yel*	185.00	275.00
a. Double surcharge	11,000.	13,000.
b. Inverted surcharge	11,000.	13,000.
c. "G. R. I." only		
d. "G. I. R."		
e. Pair, one without surcharge	15,000.	
f. Surcharged "G. I. R., 5d"		
g. Surcharged "1d"	22,000.	
h. Thick "3"	650.00	825.00
23 A3 3p on 30pf org & blk, *sal*	175.00	220.00
a. Double surcharge	4,000.	4,600.
b. Double surcharge, one invtd.	4,400.	5,000.
c. "d" inverted		
d. Surcharged "1d"	12,000.	14,000.
e. Triple surcharge		
g. Double inverted surcharge	13,000.	14,000.
h. Pair, one without surcharge	14,000.	
i. No period after "3d"	875.00	
j. Thick "3"	600.00	
k. Inverted surcharge	10,000.	
24 A3 4p on 40pf lake & blk	185.00	300.00
a. Double surcharge	3,500.	
b. Double surcharge, both invtd.	13,000.	
c. Double surcharge, one invtd.	5,250.	
d. Inverted surcharge	9,250.	
e. Surcharged "1d"	8,750.	
f. "1" on "4"		
g. As "e," inverted	20,000.	
h. Surcharge "G.R.I. 3d," double (error)	27,500.	
i. No period after "I"	3,500.	
25 A3 5p on 50pf pur & blk, *sal*	350.00	385.00
a. Double surcharge	4,400.	
b. Double surcharge, one invtd.	10,500.	10,500.
c. "5" omitted		
d. Inverted surcharge	9,750.	9,750.
e. Double inverted surcharge	13,000.	14,000.
f. "G. I. R."		
g. Surcharge "G.R.I. 3d" (error)	23,000.	
h. Thin "5"	1,200.	2,750.
26 A3 8p on 80pf lake & blk, *rose*	475.00	650.00
a. Double surcharge	7,000.	8,250.
b. Double surcharge, one invtd.	7,000.	8,250.
c. Triple surcharge	8,750.	9,250.
d. No period after "8d"	14,000.	14,000.
e. Inverted surcharge	18,500.	18,500.
f. Surcharged "3d"	18,500.	
27 A4 1sh on 1m car	5,250.	7,750.
a. No period after "I"	12,000.	
28 A4 2sh on 2m bl	5,500.	8,750.
a. Surcharged "5s"		
b. Double surcharge		
c. No period after "I"	13,000.	
29 A4 3sh on 3m blk vio	9,750.	16,250.
a. No periods after "R I"		
b. "G.R.I." double	45,000.	
29C A4 5sh on 5m sl & car	42,500.	45,000.
d. No period after "R I"		
e. Surcharged "1s"		

Nos. 18-19 Surcharged with Large "1"

1915, Jan.		
29F A3 1(p) on 2p on 10pf carmine	32,500.	30,000.
29G A3 1(p) on 2p on 20pf ultramarine	30,000.	17,500.

Same Surcharge on Stamps of Marshall Islands

1914		
30 A3 1p on 3pf brown	95.00	150.00
a. Inverted surcharge	9,250.	
b. "1" with straight top serif	185.00	325.00
c. ".G.R.I." and "1" with straight top serif		14,000.
31 A3 1p on 5pf green	90.00	95.00
a. Double surcharge	3,800.	5,000.
b. No period after "d"		
c. Inverted surcharge	5,250.	
d. "1" with straight top serif	155.00	175.00
e. "I" for "1"	1,300.	
f. Space between "1" and "d"	325.00	350.00
32 A3 2p on 10pf car	27.50	40.00
a. Double surcharge	3,800.	
b. Double surcharge, one invtd.	5,000.	
d. Surcharge sideways	10,500.	
e. No period after "2d"	875.00	
f. No period after "G"	875.00	
g. Inverted surcharge	7,000.	
33 A3 2p on 20 pf ultra	30.00	50.00
a. No period after "d"	80.00	125.00
b. Double surcharge	4,000.	5,250.
c. Double surcharge, one invtd.	9,750.	10,500.
d. Inverted surcharge	10,500.	10,500.
e. "I" omitted		
34 A3 3p on 25pf org & blk, *yel*	475.00	600.00
a. Double surcharge	4,100.	5,000.
b. Double surcharge, one invtd.	4,250.	
c. No period after "d"	925.00	1,250.
d. Inverted surcharge	13,000.	
e. Thick "3"	1,250.	1,500.
35 A3 3p on 30pf org & blk, *sal*	475.00	600.00
a. No period after "d"	925.00	1,200.
b. Inverted surcharge	8,750.	9,250.
c. Double surcharge	7,000.	
d. Double surcharge, one invtd.		
e. Thick "3"	1,250.	
36 A3 4p on 40pf lake & blk	175.00	250.00
a. No period after "d"	475.00	700.00
b. Double surcharge	7,000.	8,000.
c. "4d" omitted		
d. "1d" on "4d"		
e. No period after "R"		
f. Inverted surcharge	9,750.	
g. Surcharged "1d"	17,500.	
h. Surcharged "G.R.I. 3d" double		
i. "d" omitted		7,750.
j. Triple surcharge	14,000.	
k. Surcharged "3d"	17,500.	
37 A3 5p on 50pf pur & blk, *sal*	275.00	375.00
a. "d" omitted	4,000.	
b. Double surcharge	10,500.	
c. "5d" double		
d. Inverted surcharge	16,500.	
e. Thin "5"	4,000.	
38 A3 8p on 80pf lake & blk, *rose*	525.00	775.00
a. Inverted surcharge	10,500.	
b. Double surcharge	10,000.	
c. Double surcharge, one invtd.		
d. Triple surcharge	16,500.	
e. Double surcharge, both inverted	13,250.	14,000.
39 A4 1sh on 1m car	4,100.	5,500.
a. Double surcharge	45,000.	
b. Dbl. surch., one with "s1" for "1s"		
c. No period after "I"	6,500.	9,250.
d. Additional surcharge	50,000.	
40 A4 2sh on 2m blue	2,000.	4,500.
a. Double surcharge, one invtd.	45,000.	45,000.
b. Double surcharge	45,000.	
c. Large "S"		
d. No period after "I"	3,750.	6,500.
41 A4 3sh on 3m blk vio	6,500.	9,750.
a. Double surcharge	42,500.	45,000.
b. No period after "I"	8,750.	
c. No period after "R I"		
d. Inverted surcharge		
42 A4 5sh on 5m sl & car	14,000.	15,000.
a. Double surcharge, one invtd.		75,000.

See Nos. 44-45.

R.I. Käwieng
Deutsch Neu-Guinea
R
3d
№ 192

A5

Surcharged in Black on Registration Label
Town Name in Sans-Serif Letters

1914		*Perf. 12*
43 A5 3p black & red (Rabaul)	300.00	350.00
a. Double surcharge (Rabaul)	5,500.	7,000.
b. "(Deutsch-Neuguinea)"	475.00	600.00
c. No bracket before "Deutsch"	1,000.	1,400.
d. No bracket after "Neuguinea"	1,500.	2,250.
e. No bracket and double surcharge	16,500.	
f. "G.R.I. 3d" double	16,500.	16,500.
g. "G.R.I. 3d" inverted	16,500.	
h. No period after "I"	1,000.	
44 A5 3p black & red (Friedrich Wilhelms-haven)	275.00	875.00
a. No period after "d"	475.00	
b. "G" omitted	8,000.	
c. Inverted surcharge	16,500.	
d. "(Deutsch-Neuguinea)"	300.00	875.00
e. As "d", no period after "d"	525.00	
45 A5 3p black & red (Herbert-shohe)	300.00	825.00
a. No period after "d"	525.00	
b. No period after "I"	1,000.	2,000.
c. "G" omitted	8,750.	
d. Surcharge omitted (in horiz. pair with normal)	18,500.	
e. "(Deutsch Neu-Guinea)"	550.00	1,100.
f. "(Deutsch-Neuguinea)"		
46 A5 3p black & red (Kawieng)	350.00	700.00
a. No period after "d"		
b. No period after "d"	600.00	
c. "G.R.I." double	8,000.	
d. "3d" double	8,250.	
e. "G" omitted	8,750.	
f. "(Deutsch-Neuguinea)"	1,100.	
g. As "f", no bracket after "Neuguinea"	4,100.	
47 A5 3p black & red (Kieta)	500.00	875.00
a. Pair, one without surcharge	16,500.	
b. No bracket before "Deutsch"	1,750.	3,000.
c. No period after "d"	925.00	
d. No period after "I"	1,400.	
e. "G" omitted	8,250.	
48 A5 3p black & red (Manus)	325.00	925.00
a. Double surcharge	9,250.	
b. No bracket before "Deutsch"	1,300.	2,500.
49 A5 3p black & red (Deulon)	27,500.	30,000.
50 A5 3p black & red (Stephan-sort)		4,500.
a. No period after "d"		8,750.

Town Name in Letters with Serifs

44f Friedrich Wilhelmshafen "(Deutsch-Newguinea)"	300.00	825.00
g. As (f), no period after "d"	500.00	1,200.
h. As (f), no period after "d"	925.00	1,750.
i. As (f), no bracket before "Deutsch"	1,500.	2,500.
j. As (f), no bracket after "Neuguinea"	1,500.	2,500.
46h Kawieng "(Deutsch Newguinea)"	300.00	725.00
i. As (h), no period after "d"	500.00	
j. As (h), no period after "I"		
48c Manus "(Deutsch-Newguinea)"	4,500.	5,500.
d. As (c), no period after "I"	8,750.	8,250.

Nos. 32-33 Surcharged with Large "1"

1915		
51 A3 1p on 2p on 10pf	210.00	300.00
a. "1" double	16,500.	
b. "1" inverted	20,000.	20,000.
c. Small "1"	650.00	
52 A3 1p on 2p on 20pf	4,000.	2,750.
a. "1" inverted	20,000.	20,000.
b. On #33a	10,000.	4,500.

The stamps of Marshall Islands surcharged "G. R. I." and new values in British currency were all used in New Britain and are therefore listed here.

Stamps of Marshall Islands Surcharged
Surcharge lines spaced 6mm apart

53 A3 1p on 3pf brown		3,750.
a. Inverted surcharge		16,000.
54 A3 1p on 5pf green		3,750.
a. Inverted surcharge		16,500.

55	A3	2p on 10pf car	4,750.
56	A3	2p on 20pf ultra	4,250.
a.		Inverted surcharge	17,000.
57	A3	2½p on 10pf car	30,000.
58	A3	2½p on 20pf ultra	45,000.
59	A3	3p on 25pf org & blk, yel	7,000.
60	A3	3p on 30pf org & blk, sal	7,000.
61	A3	4p on 40pf lake & blk	7,000.
a.		Inverted surcharge	18,000.
62	A3	5p on 50pf pur & blk, sal	6,500.
63	A3	8p on 80pf lake & blk, rose	7,500.
a.		Inverted surcharge	20,000.

Surcharge lines spaced 6mm apart

64	A4	1sh on 1m car	17,000.
a.		Large "S"	22,500.
65	A4	2sh on 2m bl	14,500.
a.		Large "S"	20,000.
66	A4	3sh on 3m blk vi-ol	30,000.
a.		Large "S"	40,000.
67	A4	5sh on 5m sl & car	45,000.
a.		Large "S"	52,500.

OFFICIAL STAMPS

O1

German New Guinea Nos. 7-8 Surcharged

1915   Unwmk.   Perf. 14

O1	O1	1p on 3pf brown	35.00	80.00
a.		Double surcharge	5,500.	
b.		"1" and "d" spaced	100.00	190.00
O2	O1	1p on 5pf green	110.00	150.00
a.		"1" and "d" spaced	210.00	325.00

NEW CALEDONIA

'nü ,ka-lə-'dō-nyə

LOCATION — Island in the South Pacific Ocean, east of Queensland, Australia
GOVT. — French Overseas Territory
AREA — 7,375 sq. mi.
POP. — 147,200 (est. 1984)
CAPITAL — Noumea

Dependencies of New Caledonia are the Loyalty Islands, Isle of Pines, Huon Islands and Chesterfield Islands.

100 Centimes = 1 Franc

STAMPS OF FRENCH COLONIES USED IN NEW CALEDONIA

1859-65   Typo.   Unwmk.   Imperf.
Eagle and Crown Type A1

A4	1c olive green, *pale blue* ('62) (#1)		60.00
	Noumea c.d.s.		110.00
	On cover, from		
A5	5c yel grn, *grnsh* ('62) (#2)		55.00
	Noumea c.d.s.		90.00
	On cover, from		2,850.
A6	10c bister, *yel* (#3)		45.00
	Noumea c.d.s.		90.00
	On cover, from		1,750.
A7	20c bl, *bluish* ('65) (#4)		42.50
	Noumea c.d.s.		85.00
	On cover, from		1,150.
A8	40c org, *yelsh* (#5)		50.00
	Noumea c.d.s.		90.00
	On cover, from		1,650.
A9	80c car rose, *pnksh* ('65) (#6)		90.00
	Noumea c.d.s.		150.00
	On cover, from		

Values are for stamps cancelled with the losange of dots.
Rare stamps and covers of the French Colonies General Issues should be accompanied by certificates of authenticity issued by competent authorities and committees.

1871-72   Imperf.
Ceres Type A4, Napoleon III Types A2, A3, A5

A10	1c ol grn, *pale bl* ('72) (#7)		225.00
	On cover		

A11	5c yel grn, *grnsh* ('72) (#8)		800.00
A12	10c bis, *yelsh* (#9)		325.00
	On cover		2,750.
A13	15c bis, *yelsh* ('72) (#10)		225.00
A14	20c blue, *bluish* (#11)		92.50
A15	25c blue, *bluish* ('72) (#12)		8.00
A16	30c brn, *yelsh* (#13)		32.50
A17	40c org, *yelsh* (I) (#14)		10.00
A18	80c rose, *pinksh* (#15)		85.00
	On cover		

1872-77   Imperf.
Ceres Types A6, A7

A19	1c ol grn, *pale bl* ('72) (#16)		100.00
A20	5c grn, *pale bl* (#19)		25.00
A21	10c bis, *rosel* ('76) (#20)		80.00
	On cover, from		1,250.
A22	15c bister ('77) (#21)		340.00
A23	30c brn, *yelsh* (#22)		275.00
	On cover, from		650.00
A24	80c rose, *pnksh* ('73) (#23)		350.00
	On cover, from		

1877-78   Imperf.
Peace & Commerce Type A8 - Type I

A25	1c grn, *grnsh* (#24)		250.00
A26	4c grn, *grnsh* (#25)		225.00
A27	30c brn, *yelsh* ('78) (#26)		45.00
	On cover		200.00
A28	40c ver, *straw* (#27)		30.00
	On cover		125.00
A29	75c rose, *rose* ('78) (#28)		80.00
	On cover		500.00
a.	75c carmine, *rose* (#28a)		210.00
	On cover, from		1,900.
A30	1fr brnz grn, *straw* (#29)		135.00

Peace & Commerce - Type II

A31	2c grn, *grnsh* (#30)		250.00
A32	5c grn, *grnsh* (#31)		20.00
	On cover		
A33	10c grn, *grnsh* (#32)		40.00
	On cover		
A34	15c gray, *grnsh* (#33)		100.00
	On cover		
A35	20c red brn, *straw* (#34)		27.50
A36	25c ultra, *bluish* (#35)		90.00
a.	25c bl, *bluish* ('78) (#35a)		200.00
	On cover, from		1,000.
A37	35c vio blk, *org* (') (#36)		90.00

1878-80   Imperf.
Peace & Commerce Type A8 - Type II

A38	1c blk, *lil bl* (#38)		225.00
	On cover		
A39	2c brn, *buff* (#39)		175.00
	On cover, from		1,200.
A40	4c claret, *lav* (#40)		160.00
	On cover, from		1,600.
A41	10c blk, *lav* ('79) (#41)		21.00
	On cover, from		150.00
A42	15c blue ('79) (#42)		25.00
	On cover, from		1,350.
A43	20c red, *grn* ('79) (#43)		80.00
	On cover, from		1,450.
A44	25c blk, *red* ('79) (#44)		250.00
	On cover, from		1,350.
A45	25c yel, *straw* ('80) (#45)		45.00
	On cover		

No. 44 was used at Mayott, Nossi-Be and New Caledonia only. Beware of forgeries.

1881-86   Perf. 14x13½
Commerce Type A9

A46	1c blk, *lil bl* (#46)		150.00
	On cover		1,750.
A47	2c brn, *buff* (#47)		150.00
	On cover, from		
A48	4c claret, *lav* (#48)		125.00
	On cover, from		
A49	5c grn, *grnsh* (#49)		65.00
	On cover, from		200.00
A50	10c blk, *lav* (#50)		40.00
	On cover, from		
A51	15c blue (#41)		45.00
	On cover, from		600.00
A52	20c red, *yel grn* (#52)		60.00
	On cover		
A53	25c yel, *straw* (#53)		60.00
	On cover, from		1,100.
A54	25c blk, *rose* ('86) (#54)		75.00
	On cover, from		1,250.
A55	30c brn, *bister* (#55)		60.00
	On cover		
A56	35c vio blk, *yel org* (#56)		60.00
a.	35c vio blk, *yel* (#56a)		100.00
	On cover, from		
A57	40c ver, *straw* (#57)		90.00
	On cover		
A58	75c car, *rose* (#58)		90.00
	On cover, from		1,500.
A59	1fr brnz grn, *straw* (#59)		110.00
	On cover		

Napoleon III — A1

1859   Unwmk.   Litho.   Imperf.
Without Gum

1	A1	10c black	250.00	250.00
		On cover, with New South Wales postage		30,000.
		On philatelic cover		2,500.

Fifty varieties. Counterfeits abound.
See No. 315 in Scott Standard catalogue, Vol. 5.

Covers exist addressed to Australia, franked with No. 1, which might have paid local postage, and New South Wales stamps paying the maritime rate. Philatelic covers franked with No. 1 were made in the 1890s.

Covers addressed to Australia bearing stamps of Australian States canceled in Port-de-France or Noumea, from $30,000.

Covers addressed to Australia bearing stamps of Australian States in combination with stamps of French Colonies General issues, New Caledonia, canceled at Noumea, from $5,000.

Covers addressed to Australia bearing stamps of Australian States in combination with stamps of New Caledonia, canceled at Noumea, from $4,250.

Type of French Colonies, 1877 Surcharged in Black

Nos. 2-5   Nos. 6-7

1881-83

2	A8	5c on 40c red, *straw* ('82)	425.00	425.00
a.		Inverted surcharge	1,600.	1,600.
b.		Double surcharge	1,350.	
c.		Double surcharge, both inverted	1,900.	1,900.
3	A8	05c on 40c red, *straw* ('83)	40.00	40.00
		On cover		700.00
4	A8	25c on 35c dp vio, *yel*	300.00	300.00
		On cover		925.00
a.		Inverted surcharge	950.00	950.00
		On cover		2,500.
5	A8	25c on 75c rose car, *rose* ('82)	400.00	400.00
		On cover		1,100.
a.		Inverted surcharge	1,250.	1,250.

1883-84

6	A8	5c on 40c red, *straw* ('84)	26.50	26.50
		Never hinged	52.50	
		On cover		600.00
a.		Inverted surcharge	26.50	26.50
		Never hinged	55.00	
7	A8	5c on 75c rose car, *rose* ('83)	52.50	52.50
		On cover		600.00
a.		Inverted surcharge	75.00	75.00
		On cover		110.00

In type "a" surcharge, the narrower-spaced letters measure 14½mm, and an early printing of No. 4 measures 13½mm. Type "b" letters measure 18mm.

French Colonies No. 59 Surcharged in Black

No. 8   Nos. 9-10

1886   Perf. 14x13½

8	A9	5c on 1fr	32.50	26.50
		Never hinged	52.50	
		On cover		475.00
a.		Inverted surcharge	45.00	45.00
		Never hinged	100.00	
b.		Double surcharge	200.00	200.00
c.		Double surcharge, one inverted	225.00	225.00
9	A9	5c on 1fr	32.50	30.00
		Never hinged	60.00	
		On cover		475.00
a.		Inverted surcharge	60.00	60.00
		Never hinged	125.00	
b.		Double surcharge	200.00	200.00
c.		Double surcharge, one inverted	225.00	225.00

French Colonies No. 29 Surcharged
Imperf

10	A8	5c on 1fr	10,000.	11,500.
		On cover		

Types of French Colonies, 1877-86, Surcharged in Black

Nos. 11, 13   No. 12

1891-92   Imperf.

11	A8	10c on 40c red, *straw* ('92)	45.00	40.00
		Never hinged	82.50	
		On cover		165.00
a.		Inverted surcharge	42.50	37.50
		Never hinged	82.50	
b.		Double surcharge	100.00	100.00
c.		Double surcharge, one inverted	190.00	190.00
d.		No period after "10c"	125.00	125.00

Perf. 14x13½

12	A9	10c on 30c brn, *bis*	25.00	22.50
		Never hinged	45.00	
		On cover		300.00
a.		Inverted surcharge	25.00	22.50
		Never hinged	45.00	
b.		Double surcharge	67.50	67.50
c.		Double surcharge, inverted	60.00	60.00
d.		Double surcharge, one inverted	100.00	100.00
13	A9	10c on 40c red, *straw* ('92)	26.00	26.00
		Never hinged	52.50	
		On cover		300.00
a.		Inverted surcharge	26.00	26.00
b.		No period after "10c"	60.00	60.00
c.		Double surcharge	67.50	67.50
d.		Double surcharge, one inverted	110.00	100.00
		Nos. 11-13 (3)	96.00	88.50

Variety "double surcharge, one inverted" exists on Nos. 11-13. Value slightly higher than for "double surcharge."

Types of French Colonies, 1877-86, Handstamped in Black — g

1892   Imperf.

16	A8	20c red, *grn*	350.00	400.00
		On cover		675.00
a.		Inverted overprint	850.00	900.00
17	A8	35c violet, *org*	75.00	75.00
a.		Pair, one stamp without surcharge	950.00	
		On cover		500.00
18	A8	40c red, *straw*	1,500.	
		On cover		
19	A8	1fr bronz grn, *straw*	300.00	300.00
		On cover		525.00

The 1c, 2c, 4c and 75c of type A8 are believed not to have been officially made or actually used.

1892   Perf. 14x13½

23	A9	5c green, *grnsh*	19.00	15.00
		Never hinged	30.00	
		On cover		300.00
a.		Pair, one stamp without overprint	600.00	
		Never hinged	1,000.	
24	A9	10c blk, *lavender*	140.00	82.50
		Never hinged	210.00	
		On cover		300.00
25	A9	15c blue	110.00	60.00
		Never hinged	190.00	
		On cover		375.00
a.		Pair, one stamp without overprint	825.00	
26	A9	20c red, *grn*	110.00	60.00
		Never hinged	190.00	
		On cover		300.00
27	A9	25c yellow, *straw*	30.00	22.50
		Never hinged	50.00	
		On cover		250.00
28	A9	25c black, *rose*	110.00	37.50
		Never hinged	190.00	
		On cover		325.00
29	A9	30c brown, *bis*	90.00	75.00
		Never hinged	175.00	
		On cover		400.00
30	A9	35c violet, *org*	240.00	190.00
		Never hinged		725.00
a.		Inverted overprint	650.00	
b.		Pair, one stamp without overprint	1,350.	
32	A9	75c carmine, *rose*	225.00	190.00
		On cover		700.00
a.		Pair, one stamp without overprint	1,350.	
33	A9	1fr bronz grn, *straw*	190.00	175.00
		Nos. 23-33 (10)	1,264.	907.50

The note following No. 19 also applies to the 1c, 2c, 4c and 40c of type A9.

Surcharged in Blue or Black — h

1892-93   *Imperf.*
34   A8   10c on 1fr brnz grn,
      straw (Bl)   5,250.   4,500.
      On cover   6,000.

Perf. 14x13½
35   A9   5c on 20c red, *grn*
      (Bk)   27.50   22.50
      Never hinged   55.00
      On cover   375.00
  a.   Inverted surcharge   125.00   125.00
      Never hinged   225.00
  b.   Double surcharge   82.50   100.00
      Never hinged   160.00
36   A9   5c on 75c car,
      rose (Bk)   22.50   16.50
      Never hinged   45.00
      On cover   300.00
  a.   Inverted surcharge   125.00   125.00
      Never hinged   225.00
  b.   Double surcharge   82.50   82.50
      Never hinged   150.00
37   A9   5c on 75c car,
      rose (Bl)   18.50   15.00
      Never hinged   37.50
      On cover   300.00
  a.   Inverted surcharge   125.00   125.00
      Never hinged   225.00
  b.   Double surcharge   82.50   82.50
      Never hinged   150.00
38   A9   10c on 1fr brnz grn,
      straw (Bk)   21.00   15.00
      Never hinged   42.50
      On cover   300.00
  a.   Inverted surcharge   600.00   600.00
39   A9   10c on 1fr brnz grn,
      straw (Bl)   22.50   21.00
      Never hinged   45.00
      On cover   300.00
  a.   Inverted surcharge   125.00   125.00
      Never hinged   225.00
  b.   Double surcharge   85.00   85.00
      Never hinged   150.00
      Nos. 35-39 (5)   112.00   90.00

Navigation and
Commerce — A12

1892-1904   *Typo.*   *Perf. 14x13½*
Name of Colony in Blue or Carmine
40   A12   1c black, *blue*   1.10   1.10
      Never hinged   1.90
      On cover or postcard   200.00
41   A12   2c brown, *buff*   1.90   1.90
      Never hinged   3.00
      On cover or postcard   200.00
42   A12   4c claret, *lav*   2.50   2.25
      Never hinged   4.25
      On cover or postcard   175.00
      On cover, single franking   275.00
43   A12   5c green, *grnsh*   4.00   1.90
      Never hinged   7.25
      On cover   62.50
44   A12   5c yellow green
      ('00)   2.25   1.50
      Never hinged   3.75
      On cover   50.00
45   A12   10c blk, *lavender*   9.00   5.25
      Never hinged   15.00
      On cover   55.00
46   A12   10c rose red ('00)   11.00   1.50
      Never hinged   17.50
      On cover   50.00
47   A12   15c bl, quadrille pa-
      per   30.00   3.50
      Never hinged   57.50
      On cover   62.50
48   A12   15c gray ('00)   20.00   1.50
      Never hinged   27.50
      On cover   45.00
49   A12   20c red, *grn*   20.00   10.50
      Never hinged   35.00
      On cover   140.00
50   A12   25c black, *rose*   25.00   6.75
      Never hinged   45.00
      On cover   125.00
      On cover, single franking   225.00
51   A12   25c blue ('00)   22.00   10.50
      Never hinged   45.00
      On cover   175.00
      On cover, single franking   275.00
52   A12   30c brown, *bis*   25.00   13.50
      Never hinged   45.00
      On cover   125.00
      On cover, single franking   175.00
53   A12   40c red, *straw*   26.00   13.50
      Never hinged   45.00
      On cover   160.00
      On cover, single franking   190.00
54   A12   50c carmine, *rose*   67.50   37.50
      Never hinged   135.00
      On cover   275.00
      On cover, single franking   450.00
55   A12   50c brn, *az* (name
      in car) ('00)   125.00   85.00
      Never hinged   225.00
      On cover   875.00
      On cover, single franking   1,550.

---

56   A12   50c brn, *az* (name
      in bl) ('04)   65.00   42.50
      Never hinged   125.00
      On cover   550.00
      On cover, single franking   875.00
57   A12   75c violet, *org*   37.50   26.50
      Never hinged   75.00
      On cover   375.00
      On cover, single franking   625.00
58   A12   1fr bronz grn,
      straw   45.00   26.50
      Never hinged   110.00
      On cover   450.00
      On cover, single franking   700.00
      Nos. 40-58 (19)   539.75   293.15

Perf. 13½x14 stamps are counterfeits.
For overprints and surcharges see Nos. 59-87, 117-121.
Covers: Values for Nos. 40-42 are for covers or postcards with more than one stamp used to make the rate. This also applies to Nos. 66-68, 81-84, 88-90.

**Nos. 41-42, 52, 57-58, 53
Surcharged in Black**

     j   k

1900-01
59   A12 (h)   5c on 2c ('01)   22.50   19.00
      Never hinged   37.50
      On cover   225.00
  a.   Double surcharge   140.00   140.00
      Never hinged   240.00
  b.   Inverted surcharge   125.00   125.00
      Never hinged   210.00
60   A12 (h)   5c on 4c   4.50   4.50
      Never hinged   9.00
      On cover   125.00
  a.   Inverted surcharge   82.50   82.50
      Never hinged   150.00
  b.   Double surcharge   87.50   87.50
      Never hinged   160.00
61   A12 (j)   15c on 30c   5.00   4.50
      Never hinged   10.50
      On cover   125.00
  a.   Inverted surcharge   75.00   75.00
      Never hinged   140.00
  b.   Double surcharge   67.50   67.50
      Never hinged   125.00
  c.   "N.C.E." omitted from
      overprint   500.00   340.00
62   A12 (j)   15c on 75c ('01)   20.00   17.50
      Never hinged   37.50
      On cover   225.00
  a.   Pair, one without
      surcharge   —
  b.   Inverted surcharge   130.00   130.00
      Never hinged   225.00
  c.   Double surcharge   140.00   140.00
      Never hinged   240.00
63   A12 (j)   15c on 1fr ('01)   26.50   26.50
      Never hinged   45.00
      On cover   300.00
  a.   Double surcharge   175.00   175.00
      Never hinged   300.00
  b.   Inverted surcharge   175.00   175.00
      Never hinged   300.00
      Nos. 59-63 (5)   78.75   72.00

1902
64   A12 (k)   5c on 30c   10.50   9.00
      Never hinged   17.50
      On cover   125.00
  a.   Inverted surcharge   52.50   52.50
      Never hinged   100.00
65   A12 (k)   15c on 40c   10.50   8.25
      Never hinged   17.50
      On cover   125.00
  a.   Inverted surcharge   52.50   52.50
      Never hinged   100.00

Jubilee Issue

Stamps of 1892-1900
Overprinted in Blue,
Red, Black or Gold

1903
66   A12   1c blk, *lil bl* (Bl)   3.00   3.00
      Never hinged   5.25
      On cover or postcard   300.00
  a.   Inverted overprint   290.00   290.00
  b.   "I" in "TENAIRE" omitted   30.00   30.00
      Never hinged   57.50
67   A12   2c brown, *buff* (Bl)   5.25   4.50
      Never hinged   9.00
      On cover or postcard   300.00
  a.   "I" in "TENAIRE" omitted   32.50   32.50
      Never hinged   67.50
68   A12   4c claret, *lav* (Bl)   7.50   6.00
      Never hinged   13.50
      On cover or postcard   300.00
  a.   Double overprint   375.00   375.00
  b.   "I" in "TENAIRE" omitted   37.50   37.50
      Never hinged   75.00
69   A12   5c dk grn, *grnsh*
      (R)   7.50   4.50
      Never hinged   13.50
      On cover   225.00
  a.   "I" in "TENAIRE" omitted   52.50   52.50
      Never hinged   110.00

---

70   A12   5c yellow green
      (R)   10.00   9.00
      Never hinged   19.00
      On cover   225.00
  a.   "I" in "TENAIRE" omitted   60.00   60.00
      Never hinged   130.00
71   A12   10c blk, *lav* (R)   19.00   16.00
      Never hinged   35.00
      On cover   275.00
  a.   "I" in "TENAIRE" omitted   110.00   110.00
      Never hinged   225.00
72   A12   10c blk, *lav* (double
      G & Bk)   11.50   9.00
      Never hinged   19.00
      On cover   225.00
  a.   "I" in "TENAIRE" omitted   120.00   120.00
      Never hinged   240.00
73   A12   15c gray (R)   15.00   11.50
      Never hinged   26.00
      On cover   210.00
  a.   "I" in "TENAIRE" omitted   125.00   125.00
      Never hinged   245.00
74   A12   20c red, *grn* (Bl)   22.00   19.00
      Never hinged   37.50
      On cover   300.00
  a.   "I" in "TENAIRE" omitted   140.00   140.00
      Never hinged   280.00
75   A12   25c blk, *rose* (Bl)   19.50   15.00
      Never hinged   35.00
      On cover   350.00
  a.   Double overprint   325.00
  b.   "I" in "TENAIRE" omitted   170.00   170.00
      Never hinged   360.00
76   A12   30c brown, *bis* (R)   26.50   22.50
      Never hinged   45.00
      On cover   375.00
  a.   "I" in "TENAIRE" omitted   215.00   215.00
77   A12   40c red, *straw* (Bl)   34.00   30.00
      Never hinged   55.00
      On cover   450.00
  a.   "I" in "TENAIRE" omitted   260.00   260.00
78   A12   50c car, *rose* (Bl)   60.00   52.50
      Never hinged   110.00
      On cover   725.00
  a.   Pair, one without overprint   300.00
  b.   "I" in "TENAIRE" omitted   280.00   280.00
79   A12   75c vio, *org* (Bk)   77.50   72.50
      Never hinged   160.00
      On cover   950.00
  a.   Dbl. ovpt. in blk and red   500.00
  a.   "I" in "TENAIRE" omitted   280.00   280.00
80   A12   1fr brnz grn, *straw*
      (Bl)   120.00   115.00
      Never hinged   240.00
      On cover   1,100.
  a.   Dbl. ovpt., one in red   525.00   525.00
  b.   "I" in "TENAIRE" omitted   450.00   450.00
      Nos. 66-80 (15)   438.25   394.00

**With Additional Surcharge of New
Value in Blue**

    (a)   (b)

        (c)

81   A12 (a)   1c on 2c #67   1.90   1.90
      Never hinged   3.00
      On cover or postcard   300.00
  a.   Numeral double   115.00   115.00
      Never hinged   210.00
  b.   Numeral only   400.00
  c.   "I" in "TENAIRE" omitted   35.00   35.00
      Never hinged   67.50
82   A12 (b)   2c on 4c #68   3.50   3.50
      Never hinged   5.25
      On cover or postcard   300.00
  a.   "I" in "TENAIRE" omitted   35.00   35.00
83   A12 (a)   4c on 5c #69   2.25   2.25
      Never hinged   3.75
      On cover or postcard   275.00
  a.   Small "4"   650.00   650.00
  b.   "I" in "TENAIRE" omitted   35.00   35.00
      Never hinged   67.50
84   A12 (c)   4c on 5c #70   3.00   3.00
      Never hinged   5.25
      On cover or postcard   950.00
  a.   Pair, one without numeral
  b.   "I" in "TENAIRE" omitted   35.00   35.00
      Never hinged   67.50
85   A12 (b)   10c on 15c #73   3.00   3.00
      Never hinged   5.25
      On cover   250.00
  a.   "I" in "TENAIRE" omitted   35.00   35.00
      Never hinged   67.50
86   A12 (b)   15c on 20c #74   3.75   3.75
      Never hinged   6.00
      On cover   250.00
  a.   "I" in "TENAIRE" omitted   35.00   35.00
      Never hinged   67.50
87   A12 (b)   20c on 25c #75   9.00   9.00
      Never hinged   16.50
      On cover   375.00
  a.   "I" in "TENAIRE" omitted   110.00   110.00
      Never hinged   205.00
      Nos. 81-87 (7)   26.40   26.40

50 years of French occupation.
Surcharge on Nos. 81-83, 85-86 is horizontal, reading down.
There are three types of numeral on No. 83. The numeral on No. 84 is identical with that of No. 83a except that its position is upright.

Kagu
A16

Landscape
A17

Ship — A18

1905-28   *Typo.*   *Perf. 14x13½*
88   A16   1c blk, *green*   .30   .30
      Never hinged   .45
      On cover or postcard   95.00
89   A16   2c red brown   .30   .30
      Never hinged   .45
      On cover or postcard   95.00
90   A16   4c bl, *org*   .45   .45
      Never hinged   .60
      On cover or postcard   95.00
91   A16   5c pale green   .55   .55
      Never hinged   .75
      On cover   45.00
92   A16   5c dl bl ('21)   .40   .40
      Never hinged   .75
      On cover   95.00
93   A16   10c carmine   1.90   1.25
      Never hinged   2.60
      On cover   32.50
94   A16   10c green ('21)   .75   .75
      Never hinged   1.10
      On cover   37.50
95   A16   10c red, *pink* ('25)   .85   .85
      Never hinged   1.20
      On cover   32.50
96   A16   15c violet   .90   .85
      Never hinged   1.40
      On cover   45.00
97   A17   20c brown   .55   .55
      Never hinged   .75
      On cover   45.00
98   A17   25c blue, *grn*   1.05   .60
      Never hinged   1.60
      On cover   55.00
      On cover, single franking   160.00
99   A17   25c red, *yel* ('21)   .75   .75
      Never hinged   1.10
      On cover   32.50
100   A17   30c brn, *org*   1.40   .85
      Never hinged   1.90
      On cover   62.50
      On cover, single franking   190.00
101   A17   30c dp rose ('21)   2.50   2.50
      Never hinged   4.25
      On cover   50.00
102   A17   30c org ('25)   .60   .60
      Never hinged   1.00
      On cover   45.00
103   A17   35c blk, *yellow*   .75   .75
      Never hinged   1.10
      On cover   80.00
      On cover, single franking   250.00
104   A17   40c car, *grn*   1.25   1.05
      Never hinged   1.75
      On cover   62.50
      On cover, single franking   125.00
105   A17   45c vio brn, *lav*   .75   .75
      Never hinged   1.10
      On cover   62.50
      On cover, single franking   125.00
106   A17   50c car, *org*   3.25   3.00
      Never hinged   5.25
      On cover   75.00
      On cover, single franking   190.00
107   A17   50c dk bl ('21)   1.75   1.75
      Never hinged   2.40
      On cover   50.00
      On cover, single franking   145.00
108   A17   50c gray ('25)   1.05   1.05
      Never hinged   1.50
      On cover   70.00
      On cover, single franking   170.00
109   A17   65c dp bl ('28)   .90   .90
      Never hinged   1.50
      On cover   75.00
      On cover, single franking   190.00
110   A17   75c ol grn, *straw*   .85   .70
      Never hinged   1.20
      On cover   95.00
      On cover, single franking   250.00
111   A17   75c bl, *bluish* ('25)   .90   .90
      Never hinged   1.20
      On cover   62.50
      On cover, single franking   160.00
112   A17   75c violet ('27)   1.15   1.15
      Never hinged   1.90
      On cover   75.00
      On cover, single franking   225.00
113   A18   1fr bl, *yel grn*   1.30   1.05
      Never hinged   1.75
      On cover   95.00
      On cover, single franking   250.00
114   A18   1fr dp bl ('25)   1.90   1.90
      Never hinged   3.25
      On cover   95.00
      On cover, single franking   145.00
115   A18   2fr car, *bl*   3.50   2.25
      Never hinged   5.00
      On cover   105.00
      On cover, single franking   275.00
116   A18   5fr blk, *straw*   6.75   6.75
      Never hinged   12.00
      On cover   130.00
      On cover, single franking   350.00
      Nos. 88-116 (29)   39.30   35.50

See Nos. 311, 317a in Scott Standard catalogue, Vol. 5. For surcharges see Nos. 122-135, B1-B3, Q1-Q3.

Nos. 96, 98, 103, 106, 113 and 115, pasted on cardboard and handstamped "TRESORIER PAYEUR DE LA NOUVELLE CALEDONIE" were used as emergency currency in 1914.

Stamps of 1892-1904 Surcharged in Carmine or Black

Spacing between figures of surcharge 1.5mm (5c), 2mm (10c)

1912
117	A12	5c on 15c gray (C)	1.50	*1.90*
	Never hinged		2.25	
	On cover			105.00
a.	Inverted surcharge		210.00	210.00
	Never hinged		325.00	
118	A12	5c on 20c red, *grn*	1.50	*1.90*
	Never hinged		2.25	
	On cover			80.00
119	A12	5c on 30c brn, *bis* (C)	2.25	*3.00*
	Never hinged		3.75	
	On cover			105.00
120	A12	10c on 40c red, *straw*	3.25	*3.25*
	Never hinged		4.00	
	On cover			125.00
121	A12	10c on 50c brn, *az* (C)	3.25	*4.25*
	Never hinged		4.00	
	On cover			145.00
	Nos. 117-121 (5)		11.75	14.30

Spacing between figures of surcharge 2.25mm (5c), 2.75mm (10c)

117b	A12	5c on 15c gray (C)	200.00	200.00
	Never hinged		325.00	
c.	Inverted surcharge		4,000.	4,000.
	Never hinged		5,750.	
d.	In pair with No. 117		210.00	210.00
	Never hinged		340.00	
118a	A12	5c on 20c red, *grn*	130.00	130.00
	Never hinged		200.00	
d.	In pair with No. 118		150.00	150.00
	Never hinged		225.00	
119a	A12	5c on 30c brn, *bis* (C)	290.00	290.00
	Never hinged		450.00	
d.	In pair with No. 119		300.00	300.00
	Never hinged		500.00	
120a	A12	10c on 40c red, *straw*	200.00	200.00
	Never hinged		325.00	
d.	In pair with No. 120		210.00	210.00
	Never hinged		350.00	
121a	A12	10c on 50c brn, *az* (C)	240.00	240.00
	Never hinged		400.00	
d.	In pair with No. 121		250.00	250.00
	Never hinged		425.00	
	Nos. 117b-121a (5)		1,060.	1,060.

No. 96 Surcharged in Brown

1918
122	A16	5c on 15c violet	1.90	1.90
	Never hinged		3.00	
	On cover			160.00
a.	Double surcharge		75.00	75.00
	Never hinged		140.00	
b.	Inverted surcharge		45.00	45.00
	Never hinged		75.00	

The color of the surcharge on No. 122 varies from red to dark brown.

No. 96 Surcharged

1922
123	A16	5c on 15c vio (R)	.60	.60
	Never hinged		1.00	
	On cover			80.00
a.	Double surcharge		75.00	75.00
	Never hinged		120.00	

Stamps and Types of 1905-28 Surcharged New Value and Bars in Red or Black

1924-27
124	A16	25c on 15c vio	.75	.75
	Never hinged		1.20	
	On cover			45.00
a.	Double surcharge		75.00	
	Never hinged		120.00	
b.	Double surcharge, one inverted		110.00	
	Never hinged		190.00	
125	A18	25c on 2fr car, *bl*	.85	.85
	Never hinged		1.20	
	On cover			45.00
126	A18	25c on 5fr blk, *straw*	.90	.90
	Never hinged		1.40	
	On cover			45.00
a.	Double surcharge		125.00	125.00
	Never hinged		300.00	
b.	Triple surcharge		225.00	210.00
	Never hinged		425.00	
127	A17	60c on 75c bl grn (R)	.75	.75
	Never hinged		1.20	
	On cover			55.00
	On cover, single franking			190.00
128	A17	65c on 45c red brn	2.00	2.00
	Never hinged		3.25	
	On cover			62.50
	On cover, single franking			190.00
129	A17	85c on 45c red brn	2.00	2.00
	Never hinged		3.50	
	On cover			70.00
	On cover, single franking			200.00
130	A17	90c on 75c dp rose	1.05	1.05
	Never hinged		1.60	
	On cover			55.00
	On cover, single franking			190.00
131	A18	1.25fr on 1fr dp bl (R)	.90	.90
	Never hinged		1.40	
	On cover			80.00
	On cover, single franking			170.00
132	A18	1.50fr on 1fr dp bl, *bl*	1.60	1.60
	Never hinged		3.25	
	On cover			80.00
	On cover, single franking			170.00
133	A18	3fr on 5fr red vio	2.10	2.10
	Never hinged		3.50	
	On cover			95.00
	On cover, single franking			190.00
134	A18	10fr on 5fr ol, *lav* (R)	7.50	7.50
	Never hinged		12.00	
	On cover			105.00
	On cover, single franking			250.00
135	A18	20fr on 5fr vio rose, *org*	14.50	14.50
	Never hinged		25.00	
	On cover			120.00
	On cover, single franking			275.00
a.	Period after "F" omitted		52.50	52.50
	Never hinged		82.50	
	Nos. 124-135 (12)		34.90	34.90

Issue years: Nos. 125-127, 1924. Nos. 124, 128-129, 1925. Nos. 131, 134, 1926. Nos. 130, 132-133, 135, 1927.

Bay of Palétuviers Point A19

Landscape with Chief's House A20

Admiral de Bougainville and Count de La Pérouse — A21

1928-40   **Typo.**
136	A19	1c brn vio & ind	.25	.25
	Never hinged		.40	
	On cover			87.50
137	A19	2c dk brn & yel grn	.25	.25
	Never hinged		.40	
	On cover			75.00
137B	A19	3c brn vio & ind	.30	.30
	Never hinged		.45	
	On cover			80.00

138	A19	4c org & Prus grn	.25	.25
	Never hinged		.40	
	On cover			75.00
139	A19	5c Prus bl & dp ol	.45	.45
	Never hinged			
	On cover			70.00
140	A19	10c gray lil & dk brn	.30	.30
	Never hinged		.45	
	On cover			62.50
141	A19	15c yel brn & dp bl	.55	.55
	Never hinged		.85	
	On cover			62.50
142	A19	20c brn red & dk brn	.55	.55
	Never hinged		.85	
	On cover			50.00
143	A19	25c dk grn & dk brn	.70	.55
	Never hinged		1.00	
	On cover			30.00
144	A20	30c gray grn & bl grn	.60	.60
	Never hinged		.90	
	On cover			50.00
145	A20	35c blk & brt vio	.90	.90
	Never hinged		1.40	
	On cover			50.00
146	A20	40c brt red & olvn	.55	.55
	Never hinged		.85	
	On cover			30.00
147	A20	45c dp bl & red org	1.60	1.30
	Never hinged		.85	
	On cover			30.00
147A	A20	45c bl grn & dl grn	1.05	1.05
	Never hinged		1.40	
	On cover			62.50
148	A20	50c vio & brn	.85	.85
	Never hinged		1.20	
	On cover			25.00
149	A20	55c vio bl & car	3.50	2.25
	Never hinged		5.00	
	On cover			62.50
150	A20	60c vio bl & car	.75	.75
	Never hinged		1.00	
	On cover			50.00
151	A20	65c org brn & bl	1.30	1.15
	Never hinged		1.90	
	On cover			55.00
152	A20	70c dp rose & brn	.60	.60
	Never hinged		.90	
	On cover			55.00
153	A20	75c Prus bl & ol gray	1.40	1.15
	Never hinged		2.10	
	On cover			37.50
154	A20	80c red brn & grn	1.15	1.00
	Never hinged		1.60	
	On cover			55.00
155	A20	85c grn & brn	2.00	1.30
	Never hinged		2.90	
	On cover			55.00
156	A20	90c dp red & brt red	1.30	.90
	Never hinged		1.90	
	On cover			62.50
	On cover, single franking			140.00
157	A20	90c ol grn & rose red	1.05	1.05
	Never hinged		1.40	
	On cover			25.00
158	A21	1fr dp ol & sal red	7.25	4.25
	Never hinged		11.00	
	On cover			95.00
	On cover, single franking			170.00
159	A21	1fr rose red & dk car	2.25	1.75
	Never hinged		3.25	
	On cover			70.00
	On cover, single franking			125.00
160	A21	1fr brn red & grn	1.05	1.05
	Never hinged		1.50	
	On cover			30.00
161	A21	1.10fr dp grn & brn	12.00	12.00
	Never hinged		16.50	
	On cover			105.00
	On cover, single franking			175.00
162	A21	1.25fr brn red & grn	1.20	1.20
	Never hinged		1.90	
	On cover			50.00
	On cover, single franking			110.00
163	A21	1.25fr rose red & dk car	1.15	1.15
	Never hinged		1.50	
	On cover			45.00
	On cover, single franking			160.00
164	A21	1.40fr dk bl & red org	1.20	1.20
	Never hinged		1.60	
	On cover			50.00
	On cover, single franking			110.00
165	A21	1.50fr dp bl & bl	.90	.90
	Never hinged		1.25	
	On cover			62.50
	On cover, single franking			125.00
166	A21	1.60fr dp grn & brn	1.35	1.35
	Never hinged		1.90	
	On cover			55.00
	On cover, single franking			125.00
167	A21	1.75fr dk bl & red org	1.05	1.05
	Never hinged		1.50	
	On cover			62.50
	On cover, single franking			110.00

168	A21	1.75fr violet bl	1.50	1.05
	Never hinged		1.50	
	On cover			62.50
	On cover, single franking			110.00
169	A21	2fr red org & brn	1.25	.70
	Never hinged			
	On cover			75.00
	On cover, single franking			160.00
170	A21	2.25fr vio bl	1.20	1.20
	Never hinged		1.60	
	On cover			62.50
	On cover, single franking			140.00
171	A21	2.50fr brn & lt brn	1.75	1.75
	Never hinged		2.60	
	On cover			70.00
	On cover, single franking			190.00
172	A21	3fr mag & brn	.75	.75
	Never hinged		1.10	
	On cover			80.00
	On cover, single franking			200.00
173	A21	5fr dk bl & brn	1.15	1.15
	Never hinged		1.75	
	On cover			80.00
	On cover, single franking			160.00
174	A21	10fr vio & brn, *pnksh*	1.30	1.30
	Never hinged		1.90	
	On cover			95.00
	On cover, single franking			190.00
175	A21	20fr red & brn, *yel*	2.75	2.75
	Never hinged		4.25	
	On cover			105.00
	On cover, single franking			250.00
	Nos. 136-175 (42)		62.90	55.45

The 35c in Prussian green and dark green without overprint is listed as Wallis and Futuna No. 53a.

Issue years: 35c, 70c, 85c, #162, 167, 1933; 55c, 80c, #159, 168, 1938; #157, 163, 2.25fr, 1939; 3c, 60c, 1.40fr, 1.60fr, 2.50fr, 147A, 160, 1940; others, 1928.

Compare with Nos. 265A-265B.

For overprints see #180-207, 217-251 (in Scott Standard catalogue, Vol. 5), Q4-Q6.

Common Design Types pictured following the introduction.

Colonial Exposition Issue
Common Design Types

1931   **Engr.**   *Perf. 12½*
Country Name Typo. in Black
176	CD70	40c dp green	6.00	6.00
	Never hinged		10.50	
	On cover			105.00
177	CD71	50c violet	6.00	6.00
	Never hinged		10.50	
	On cover			87.50
178	CD72	90c red orange	6.00	6.00
	Never hinged		10.50	
	On cover			160.00
	On cover, single franking			225.00
179	CD73	1.50fr dull blue	6.00	6.00
	Never hinged		10.50	
	On cover			140.00
	On cover, single franking			190.00
	Nos. 176-179 (4)		24.00	24.00

Paris-Nouméa Flight Issue
Regular Issue of 1928 Overprinted

1932   *Perf. 14x13½*
180	A20	40c brt red & olvn	475.00	*500.00*
	Never hinged		700.00	
	On cover			1,250.
181	A20	50c vio & brn	475.00	*500.00*
	Never hinged		700.00	
	On cover			1,250.

Arrival on Apr. 5, 1932 at Nouméa, of the French aviators, Verneilh, Dévé and Munch. Excellent forgeries exist of #180-181.

Types of 1928-33 Overprinted in Black or Red

1933
182	A19	1c red vio & dl bl	6.50	*7.00*
	Never hinged		9.75	
	On cover			125.00
183	A19	2c dk brn & yel grn	6.50	*7.00*
	Never hinged		9.75	
	On cover			125.00

184	A19	4c dl org & Prus bl	6.50	7.00
		Never hinged	9.75	
		On cover		125.00
185	A19	5c Prus grn & ol (R)	6.50	7.00
		Never hinged	9.75	
		On cover		125.00
186	A19	10c gray lil & dk brn (R)	6.50	7.00
		Never hinged	9.75	
		On cover		125.00
187	A19	15c yel brn & dp bl (R)	6.50	7.00
		Never hinged	9.75	
		On cover		125.00
188	A19	20c brn red & dk brn	6.50	7.00
		Never hinged	9.75	
		On cover		125.00
189	A19	25c dk grn & dk brn (R)	6.50	7.00
		Never hinged	9.75	
		On cover		125.00
190	A20	30c gray grn & bl grn (R)	6.75	7.50
		Never hinged	10.50	
		On cover		125.00
191	A20	35c blk & lt vio	6.75	7.50
		Never hinged	10.50	
		On cover		125.00
192	A20	40c brt red & olvn	6.75	7.00
		Never hinged	10.50	
		On cover		125.00
193	A20	45c dp bl & red org	6.75	7.50
		Never hinged	10.50	
		On cover		125.00
194	A20	50c vio & brn	6.75	7.00
		Never hinged	10.50	
		On cover		125.00
195	A20	70c dp rose & brn	7.50	8.00
		Never hinged	11.00	
		On cover		140.00
196	A20	75c Prus bl & ol gray (R)	7.50	8.00
		Never hinged	11.00	
		On cover		125.00
197	A20	85c grn & brn	7.50	8.00
		Never hinged	11.00	
		On cover		125.00
198	A20	90c dp red & brt red	9.50	10.00
		Never hinged	13.00	
		On cover		160.00
199	A21	1fr dp ol & sal red	9.50	10.00
		Never hinged	13.00	
		On cover		160.00
200	A21	1.25fr brn red & grn	9.50	10.00
		Never hinged	13.50	
		On cover		165.00
201	A21	1.50fr dp bl & bl (R)	9.50	10.00
		Never hinged	13.50	
		On cover		165.00
202	A21	1.75fr dk bl & red org	9.50	10.00
		Never hinged	13.50	
		On cover		170.00
203	A21	2fr red org & brn	9.50	10.00
		Never hinged	13.50	
		On cover		190.00
204	A21	3fr mag & brn	9.50	10.00
		Never hinged	13.50	
		On cover		190.00
205	A21	5fr dk bl & brn (R)	9.50	10.00
		Never hinged	13.50	
		On cover		200.00
206	A21	10fr vio & brn, pnksh	10.00	11.00
		Never hinged	14.00	
		On cover		225.00
207	A21	20fr red & brn, yel	10.00	11.00
		Never hinged	14.00	
		On cover		230.00
		Nos. 182-207 (26)	204.25	218.50

1st anniv., Paris-Noumea flight. Plane centered on Nos. 190-207.

Paris International Exposition Issue
Common Design Types

			1937	**Engr.**	**Perf. 13**
208	CD74	20c dp vio		2.75	2.75
		Never hinged		4.00	
		On cover			105.00
209	CD75	30c dk grn		2.75	2.75
		Never hinged		4.00	
		On cover			87.50
210	CD76	40c car rose		2.75	2.75
		Never hinged		4.00	
		On cover			80.00
211	CD77	50c dk brn & bl		2.75	2.75
		Never hinged		4.00	
		On cover			75.00
212	CD78	90c red		2.75	2.75
		Never hinged		4.00	
		On cover			105.00
		On cover, single franking			190.00
213	CD79	1.50fr ultra		2.75	2.75
		Never hinged		4.00	
		On cover			95.00
		On cover, single franking			160.00
		Nos. 208-213 (6)		16.50	16.50

Colonial Arts Exhibition Issue
Souvenir Sheet
Common Design Type

			1937		**Imperf.**
214	CD78	3fr sepia		22.50	34.00
		Never hinged		35.00	
		On cover			190.00
		On cover, single franking			250.00

New York World's Fair Issue
Common Design Type

			1939		**Perf. 12½x12**
215	CD82	1.25fr car lake		1.60	1.60
		Never hinged		2.50	
		On cover			80.00
		On cover, single franking			160.00
216	CD82	2.25fr ultra		1.75	1.75
		Never hinged		2.50	
		On cover			80.00
		On cover, single franking			145.00

SEMI-POSTAL STAMPS

No. 93 Surcharged

			1915	**Unwmk.**	**Perf. 14x13½**
B1	A16	10c + 5c carmine		1.50	1.50
		Never hinged		2.25	
		On cover			75.00
a.		Inverted surcharge		75.00	75.00
		Never hinged		140.00	
b.		Cross omitted		100.00	
		Never hinged		300.00	
c.		Double surcharge		160.00	160.00
		Never hinged		275.00	

Regular Issue of 1905 Surcharged

			1917		
B2	A16	10c + 5c rose		1.50	1.30
		Never hinged		2.25	
		On cover			100.00
a.		Double surcharge		130.00	
		Never hinged		225.00	
B3	A16	15c + 5c violet		1.50	1.40
		Never hinged		2.25	
		On cover			95.00

Curie Issue
Common Design Type

			1938, Oct. 24		**Perf. 13**
B4	CD80	1.75fr + 50c brt ultra		16.50	17.50
		Never hinged		25.00	
		On cover			105.00
		On cover, single franking			190.00

French Revolution Issue
Common Design Type

1939, July 5   **Photo.**
Name and Value Typo. in Black

B5	CD83	45c + 25c green		13.50	13.50
		Never hinged		22.50	
		On cover			140.00
B6	CD83	70c + 30c brown		13.50	13.50
		Never hinged		22.50	
		On cover			105.00
B7	CD83	90c + 35c red org		13.50	13.50
		Never hinged		22.50	
		On cover			95.00
B8	CD83	1.25fr + 1fr rose pink		13.50	13.50
		Never hinged		22.50	
		On cover			160.00
		On cover, single franking			225.00
B9	CD83	2.25fr + 2fr blue		13.50	13.50
		Never hinged		22.50	
		On cover			140.00
		On cover, single franking			200.00
		Nos. B5-B9 (5)		67.50	67.50

AIR POST STAMPS

Seaplane Over Pacific Ocean AP1

			1938-40	**Unwmk.**	**Engr.**	**Perf. 13**
C1	AP1	65c deep violet			1.00	1.00
		Never hinged			1.50	
		On cover				80.00
		"65c" omitted			225.00	
C2	AP1	4.50fr red			1.60	1.60
		Never hinged			2.60	
		On cover				70.00
C3	AP1	7fr dk bl grn ('40)			1.15	.85
		Never hinged			1.50	
		On cover				75.00
C4	AP1	9fr ultra			3.00	2.60
		Never hinged			4.50	
		On cover				95.00
C5	AP1	20fr dk orange ('40)			2.25	2.25
		Never hinged			3.50	
		On cover				105.00
C6	AP1	50fr black ('40)			3.75	3.25
		Never hinged			5.00	
		On cover				125.00
		Nos. C1-C6 (6)			12.75	11.55

AIR POST SEMI-POSTAL STAMP

French Revolution Issue
Common Design Type
Unwmk.
1939, July 5   **Photo.**   **Perf. 13**
Name and Value Typo. in Orange

CB1	CD83	4.50fr + 4fr brn blk		34.00	34.00
		Never hinged		52.50	
		On cover			190.00
		On cover, single franking			300.00

POSTAGE DUE STAMPS

For a short time in 1894, 5, 10, 15, 20, 25 and 30c postage stamps (Nos. 43, 45, 47, 49, 50 and 52) were overprinted with a "T" in an inverted triangle and used as Postage Due stamps.

French Colonies Postage Due Stamps Overprinted in Carmine, Blue or Silver

			1903	**Unwmk.**		**Imperf.**
J1	D1	5c blue (C)			3.75	3.75
		Never hinged			6.75	
		On cover				300.00
a.		"I" in "TENAIRE" omitted			37.50	37.50
		Never hinged			67.50	
J2	D1	10c brown (C)			11.50	11.50
		Never hinged			20.00	
		On cover				375.00
a.		"I" in "TENAIRE" omitted			50.00	50.00
		Never hinged			95.00	
J3	D1	15c yel grn (C)			22.50	11.50
		Never hinged			45.00	
		On cover				375.00
a.		"I" in "TENAIRE" omitted			100.00	100.00
		Never hinged			200.00	
J4	D1	30c carmine (Bl)			19.00	15.00
		Never hinged			37.50	
		On cover				375.00
a.		"I" in "TENAIRE" omitted			97.50	97.50
		Never hinged			200.00	
J5	D1	50c violet (Bl)			65.00	22.50
		Never hinged			125.00	
		On cover				440.00
a.		"I" in "TENAIRE" omitted			260.00	260.00
J6	D1	60c brn, buff (Bl)			260.00	95.00
		On cover				800.00
a.		"I" in "TENAIRE" omitted			1,200.	1,200.
J7	D1	1fr rose, buff (S)			42.50	26.00
		Never hinged			75.00	
		On cover				500.00
a.		"I" in "TENAIRE" omitted			225.00	225.00
b.		Double overprint			225.00	225.00
J8	D1	2fr red brn (Bl)			1,300.	1,300.
a.		"I" in "TENAIRE" omitted			6,500.	
		Nos. J1-J8 (8)			1,724.	1,485.

Fifty years of French occupation.

Men Poling Boat — D2

			1906	**Typo.**		**Perf. 13½x14**
J9	D2	5c ultra, azure			.70	.75
		Never hinged			1.20	
		On cover				105.00
J10	D2	10c vio brn, buff			.70	.75
		Never hinged			1.20	
		On cover				100.00
J11	D2	15c grn, greenish			1.00	1.10
		Never hinged			1.60	
		On cover				105.00
J12	D2	20c blk, yellow			1.00	1.10
		Never hinged			1.60	
		On cover				125.00
J13	D2	30c carmine			1.35	1.50
		Never hinged			2.25	
		On cover				140.00
J14	D2	50c ultra, buff			2.25	2.25
		Never hinged			3.75	
		On cover				145.00
J15	D2	60c brn, azure			1.50	1.90
		Never hinged			2.40	
		On cover				160.00
J16	D2	1fr dk grn, straw			2.25	2.75
		Never hinged			4.00	
		On cover				190.00
		Nos. J9-J16 (8)			10.75	12.10

Type of 1906 Issue Surcharged

			1926-27		
J17	D2	2fr on 1fr vio		5.75	6.25
		Never hinged		8.25	
		On cover			250.00
J18	D2	3fr on 1fr org brn		5.75	6.25
		Never hinged		8.25	
		On cover			275.00

Malayan Sambar — D3

			1928		**Typo.**
J19	D3	2c sl bl & dp brn		.25	.40
		Never hinged		.40	
		On cover			125.00
J20	D3	4c brn red & bl grn		.45	.60
		Never hinged		.75	
		On cover			125.00
J21	D3	5c red org & bl blk		.60	.75
		Never hinged		1.00	
		On cover			95.00
J22	D3	10c mag & Prus bl		.60	.75
		Never hinged		1.00	
		On cover			80.00
J23	D3	15c dl grn & scar		.60	.75
		Never hinged		1.00	
		On cover			80.00
J24	D3	20c mar & ol grn		1.05	1.10
		Never hinged		1.50	
		On cover			95.00
J25	D3	25c bis brn & sl bl		.75	.90
		Never hinged		1.20	
		On cover			95.00
J26	D3	30c bl grn & ol grn		1.05	1.10
		Never hinged		1.50	
		On cover			95.00
J27	D3	50c lt brn & dk red		1.35	1.50
		Never hinged		1.90	
		On cover			105.00
J28	D3	60c mag & brt rose		1.35	1.50
		Never hinged		1.90	
		On cover			125.00
J29	D3	1fr dl bl & Prus grn		1.75	1.90
		Never hinged		2.60	
		On cover			140.00
J30	D3	2fr dk red & ol grn		1.90	2.25
		Never hinged		2.90	
		On cover			170.00
J31	D3	3fr violet & brn		2.75	3.00
		Never hinged		4.25	
		On cover			190.00
		Nos. J19-J31 (13)		14.45	16.50

PARCEL POST STAMPS

Type of Regular Issue of 1905-28 Srchd. or Ovptd.

			1926	**Unwmk.**	**Perf. 14x13½**
Q1	A18	50c on 5fr olive, lav		1.30	1.90
		Never hinged		2.25	
Q2	A18	1fr deep blue		1.75	2.75
		Never hinged		3.25	
Q3	A18	2fr car, bluish		2.10	3.00
		Never hinged		3.75	
		Nos. Q1-Q3 (3)		5.15	7.65

Regular
Issue of
1928
Overprinted

Colis Postaux

1930
Q4 A20 50c violet & brown 1.30 1.90
　　Never hinged 2.25
Q5 A21 1fr dp ol & sal red 1.75 2.75
　　Never hinged 3.25
Q6 A21 2fr red org & brn 2.10 3.00
　　Never hinged 3.75
　　　Nos. Q4-Q6 (3) 5.15 7.65

NEW GUINEA

ˈnü ˈgi-nē

LOCATION — On an island of the same name in the South Pacific Ocean, north of Australia.
GOVT. — Mandate administered by Australia
AREA — 93,000 sq. mi.
POP. — 675,369 (1940)
CAPITAL — Rabaul

The territory occupies the northeastern part of the island and includes New Britain and other nearby islands. It was formerly a German possession and should not be confused with British New Guinea (Papua) which is in the southeastern part of the same island, nor Netherlands New Guinea. For previous issues see German New Guinea, New Britain, North West Pacific Islands.

12 Pence = 1 Shilling
20 Shillings = 1 Pound

Native
Huts — A1

1925-28　　**Engr.**　　**Perf. 11**
1 A1 ½p orange 2.75 8.00
2 A1 1p yellow green 2.75 6.25
3 A1 1½p vermilion ('26) 3.75 3.00
4 A1 2p claret 5.50 5.00
5 A1 3p deep blue 6.00 4.50
6 A1 4p olive green 15.00 24.00
7 A1 6p yel bister ('28) 6.50 55.00
　a. 6p light brown 22.50 55.00
　b. 6p olive bister ('27) 11.00 52.50
8 A1 9p deep violet 15.00 40.00
9 A1 1sh gray green 17.50 30.00
10 A1 2sh red brown 35.00 40.00
11 A1 5sh olive bister 55.00 75.00
12 A1 10sh dull rose 120.00 100.00
13 A1 £1 grnsh gray 210.00 325.00
　　　Nos. 1-13 (13) 494.75 840.75

For overprints see Nos. C1-C13, O1-O9.

Bird of
Paradise — A2

1931, Aug. 2
18 A2 1p light green 4.50 4.00
19 A2 1½p red 5.75 11.50
20 A2 2p violet brown 5.75 2.50
21 A2 3p deep blue 5.75 5.50
22 A2 4p olive green 7.50 27.50
23 A2 5p slate green 7.00 22.50
24 A2 6p bister 8.00 25.00
25 A2 9p dull violet 9.50 21.00
26 A2 1sh bluish gray 7.00 17.00
27 A2 2sh red brown 11.50 47.50
28 A2 5sh olive brown 47.50 62.50
29 A2 10sh rose red 120.00 150.00
30 A2 £1 gray 250.00 300.00
　　　Nos. 18-30 (13) 489.75 696.50

10th anniversary of Australian Mandate.
For overprints see #C14-C27, O12-O22.

Type of 1931 without date scrolls
1932-34　　　　　　**Perf. 11**
31 A2 1p light green 5.50 .25
32 A2 1½p violet brown 5.50 16.00
33 A2 2p red 5.50 .25
34 A2 2½p dp grn ('34) 7.50 26.00
35 A2 3p gray blue 6.00 1.10
36 A2 3½p magenta ('34) 15.00 18.00
37 A2 4p olive green 6.00 7.00
38 A2 5p slate green 6.50 .80
39 A2 6p bister 7.00 3.75
40 A2 9p dull violet 11.00 25.00
41 A2 1sh bluish gray 6.00 11.50
42 A2 2sh red brown 5.00 19.00
43 A2 5sh olive brown 30.00 50.00
44 A2 10sh rose red 60.00 80.00
45 A2 £1 gray 120.00 110.00
　　　Nos. 31-45 (15) 296.50 368.65

For overprints see #46-47, C28-C43, O23-O35. See footnote following C43.

Silver Jubilee Issue

Stamps of 1932-34
Overprinted

1935, June 27
Glazed Paper
46 A2 1p light green 1.10 .85
47 A2 2p red 3.00 .85
　　Set, never hinged 6.50

King George VI — A3

1937, May 18　　　　**Engr.**
48 A3 2p salmon rose .30 1.60
49 A3 3p blue .30 1.90
50 A3 5p green .35 1.90
51 A3 1sh brown violet .45 2.50
　　　Nos. 48-51 (4) 1.40 7.90
　　Set, never hinged 2.50

AIR POST STAMPS

Regular
Issues of
1925-28
Overprinted

1931, June　　　　**Perf. 11**
C1 A1 ½p orange 1.75 8.50
C2 A1 1p yellow green 1.75 5.75
C3 A1 1½p vermilion 1.40 7.00
C4 A1 2p claret 1.40 8.00
C5 A1 3p deep blue 2.00 15.00
C6 A1 4p olive green 1.40 10.00
C7 A1 6p light brown 2.00 16.00
C8 A1 9p deep violet 3.50 19.00
C9 A1 1sh gray green 3.50 19.00
C10 A1 2sh red brown 8.00 47.50
C11 A1 5sh ol bister 22.50 75.00
C12 A1 10sh light red 92.50 120.00
C13 A1 £1 grnsh gray 170.00 290.00
　　　Nos. C1-C13 (13) 311.70 640.75

Type of Regular
Issue of 1931 and
Nos. 18-30
Overprinted

1931, Aug.
C14 A2 ½p orange 3.75 3.75
C15 A2 1p light green 4.50 6.00
C16 A2 1½p red 4.25 11.50
C17 A2 2p violet brown 4.25 3.50
C18 A2 3p deep blue 7.00 7.00
C19 A2 4p olive green 7.00 7.00

C20 A2 5p slate green 7.00 12.50
C21 A2 6p bister 8.00 30.00
C22 A2 9p dull violet 9.00 17.00
C23 A2 1sh bluish gray 8.50 17.00
C24 A2 2sh red brown 18.00 55.00
C25 A2 5sh olive brown 17.00 32.50
C26 A2 10sh rose red 87.50 140.00
C27 A2 £1 gray 150.00 290.00
　　　Nos. C14-C27 (14) 366.25 680.25

10th anniversary of Australian Mandate.

**Same Overprint on Type of Regular
Issue of 1932-34 and Nos. 31-45**
1932-34　　　　　　**Perf. 11**
C28 A2 ½p orange .65 1.75
C29 A2 1p light green 1.40 2.50
C30 A2 1½p violet brown 2.00 9.50
C31 A2 2p red 2.00 .35
C32 A2 2½p dp grn ('34) 8.75 2.75
C33 A2 3p gray blue 3.75 3.50
C34 A2 3½p mag ('34) 5.25 3.75
C35 A2 4p olive green 5.00 11.50
C36 A2 5p slate green 8.00 8.50
C37 A2 6p bister 5.00 17.00
C38 A2 9p dull violet 7.00 10.00
C39 A2 1sh bluish gray 7.00 10.00
C40 A2 2sh red brown 11.50 55.00
C41 A2 5sh olive brown 55.00 65.00
C42 A2 10sh rose red 100.00 92.50
C43 A2 £1 gray 87.50 62.50
　　　Nos. C28-C43 (16) 309.80 356.10

No. C28 exists without overprint, but is believed not to have been issued in this condition. Value $200.

Plane
over
Bulolo
Goldfield
AP1

1935, May 1　**Engr.**　**Unwmk.**
C44 AP1 £2 violet 350.00 160.00
C45 AP1 £5 green 750.00 550.00

AP2

1939, Mar. 1
C46 AP2 ½p orange 2.50 8.00
C47 AP2 1p green 2.00 5.00
C48 AP2 1½p vio brown 2.25 15.00
C49 AP2 2p red orange 5.00 4.00
C50 AP2 3p dark blue 8.50 21.00
C51 AP2 4p ol bister 9.00 9.75
C52 AP2 5p slate grn 8.00 4.50
C53 AP2 6p bister brn 20.00 26.00
C54 AP2 9p dl violet 20.00 32.50
C55 AP2 1sh sage green 20.00 27.50
C56 AP2 2sh car lake 45.00 65.00
C57 AP2 5sh ol brown 85.00 130.00
C58 AP2 10sh rose red 325.00 350.00
C59 AP2 £1 grnsh gray 95.00 130.00
　　　Nos. C46-C59 (14) 647.25 828.25
　　Set, never hinged 1,100.

OFFICIAL STAMPS

Regular
Issue of
1925
Overprinted

1925-29　　**Unwmk.**　　**Perf. 11**
O1 A1 1p yellow green 3.50 5.00
O2 A1 1½p vermilion ('29) 6.25 19.00
O3 A1 2p claret 2.50 4.25
O4 A1 3p deep blue 6.00 10.00
O5 A1 4p olive green 5.00 9.75
O6 A1 6p yel bister ('29) 8.00 40.00
　a. 6p olive bister 22.50 40.00
O7 A1 9p deep violet 4.50 40.00
O8 A1 1sh gray green 6.25 40.00
O9 A1 2sh red brown 35.00 70.00
　　　Nos. O1-O9 (9) 77.00 238.00

Nos. 18-28
Overprinted

1931, Aug. 2
O12 A2 1p light green 11.00 14.00
O13 A2 1½p red 11.00 13.50
O14 A2 2p violet brown 11.50 8.00
O15 A2 3p deep blue 7.50 7.00
O16 A2 4p olive green 7.00 9.75
O17 A2 5p slate green 11.50 13.50
O18 A2 6p bister 16.00 19.00
O19 A2 9p dull violet 18.00 32.50
O20 A2 1sh bluish gray 18.00 32.50
O21 A2 2sh red brown 45.00 80.00
O22 A2 5sh olive brown 110.00 200.00
　　　Nos. O12-O22 (11) 266.50 429.75

10th anniversary of Australian Mandate.

Same Overprint on Nos. 31-43
1932-34
O23 A2 1p light green 14.50 15.00
O24 A2 1½p violet brown 15.00 16.00
O25 A2 2p red 15.00 3.75
O26 A2 2½p dp green ('34) 6.75 8.25
O27 A2 3p gray blue 11.00 35.00
O28 A2 3½p magenta ('34) 6.50 10.00
O29 A2 4p olive green 15.00 27.50
O30 A2 5p slate green 10.00 27.50
O31 A2 6p bister 21.00 52.50
O32 A2 9p dull violet 16.00 47.50
O33 A2 1sh bluish gray 17.50 32.50
O34 A2 2sh red brown 40.00 85.00
O35 A2 5sh olive brown 140.00 190.00
　　　Nos. O23-O35 (13) 328.25 550.50

NEW HEBRIDES, BRITISH

'nü 'he-brə-ˌdēz

LOCATION — A group of islands in the South Pacific Ocean northeast of New Caledonia

GOVT. — Condominium under the joint administration of Great Britain and France

AREA — 5,790 sq. mi.

POP. — 100,000 (est. 1976)

CAPITAL — Vila (Port-Vila)

See French New Hebrides.

12 Pence = 1 Shilling
100 Centimes = 1 Franc

Catalogue values for unused stamps in this country are for Never Hinged items, beginning with Scott 62 in the regular postage section, Scott J11 in the postage due section.

British Issues

Stamps of Fiji, 1903-06, Overprinted

1908-09   **Wmk. 2**   *Perf. 14*
Colored Bar Covers "FIJI" on #2-6, 9

1	A22	½p gray grn ('09)	60.00	92.50
2	A22	2p vio & orange	2.25	2.50
3	A22	2½p vio & ultra, *bl*	2.00	2.50
4	A22	5p vio & green	3.50	4.00
5	A22	6p vio & car rose	3.50	3.50
6	A22	1sh grn & car rose	145.00	300.00
		Nos. 1-6 (6)	216.25	405.00

Wmk. Multiple Crown and CA (3)

7	A22	½p gray green	1.00	8.00
8	A22	1p carmine	.60	1.00
a.		Pair, one without overprint	10,000.	
9	A22	1sh grn & car rose ('09)	23.00	4.25
		Nos. 7-9 (3)	24.60	13.25

Nos. 2-6, 9 are on chalk-surfaced paper.

Stamps of Fiji, 1904-11, Overprinted in Black or Red

1910, Dec. 15

10	A22	½p green	4.00	27.50
11	A22	1p carmine	11.00	9.75
12	A22	2p gray	.80	3.50
13	A22	2½p ultra	1.00	4.75
14	A22	5p violet & ol grn	1.60	6.25
15	A22	6p violet	4.00	5.75
16	A22	1sh black, *grn* (R)	6.00	8.50
		Nos. 10-16 (7)	28.40	66.00

Nos. 14-16 are on chalk-surfaced paper.

Native Idols — A1

1911, July 25   **Engr.**   **Wmk. 3**

17	A1	½p pale green	1.00	2.00
18	A1	1p red	5.00	2.25
19	A1	2p gray	9.25	4.50
20	A1	2½p ultramarine	4.25	6.25
21	A1	5p olive green	5.00	8.00
22	A1	6p claret	3.50	5.75
23	A1	1sh black, *green*	3.00	15.00
24	A1	2sh violet, *blue*	40.00	25.00
25	A1	5sh green, *yel*	50.00	55.00
		Nos. 17-25 (9)	121.00	123.75

See Nos. 33-37. For surcharges see Nos. 26-29, 38-39, French Issues No. 36.

Surcharged

1d.

1920-21

26	A1	1p on 5p ol green	10.00	70.00
a.		Inverted surcharge	3,000.	
27	A1	1p on 1sh black, *grn*	3.75	15.00
28	A1	1p on 2sh violet, *blue*	1.75	11.50
29	A1	1p on 5sh green, *yel*	1.75	11.50

On French Issue No. 16

30	A2	2p on 40c red, *yel* ('21)	2.00	22.00
		Nos. 26-30 (5)	19.25	130.00

French Issue No. 27

2d.

Wmk. R F in Sheet

31	A2	2p on 40c red, *yel* ('21)	145.00	700.00

The letters "R.F." are the initials of "Republique Francaise." They are large double-lined Roman capitals, about 120mm high. About one-fourth of the stamps in each sheet show portions of the watermark, the other stamps are without watermark.

No. 26a is considered by some to be printers' waste.

Type of 1911 Issue

1921, Oct.   **Wmk. 4**

33	A1	1p rose red	2.90	16.00
34	A1	2p gray	5.00	42.50
37	A1	6p claret	16.00	85.00
		Nos. 33-37 (3)	23.90	143.50

For surcharge see No. 40.

Stamps of 1911-21 Surcharged with New Values as in 1920-21

1924, May 1   **Wmk. 3**

38	A1	1p on ½p pale green	4.50	25.00
39	A1	5p on 2½p ultra	8.50	26.00
a.		Inverted surcharge	3,250.	

Wmk. 4

40	A1	3p on 1p rose red	4.50	12.50
		Nos. 38-40 (3)	17.50	63.50

No. 39a is considered by some to be printers' waste.

A3

The values at the lower right denote the currency and amount for which the stamps were to be sold. The English stamps could be bought at the French post office in French money.

1925   **Engr.**

41	A3	½p (5c) black	1.40	19.00
42	A3	1p (10c) green	1.10	17.00
43	A3	2p (20c) grnsh gray	2.00	3.00
44	A3	2½p (25c) brown	1.10	15.00
45	A3	5p (50c) ultra	3.50	3.00
46	A3	6p (60c) claret	4.00	16.00
47	A3	1sh (1.25fr) black, *grn*	3.75	21.00
48	A3	2sh (2.50fr) vio, *bl*	7.00	25.00
49	A3	5sh (6.25fr) grn, *yel*	7.00	29.00
		Nos. 41-49 (9)	30.85	148.00

Beach Scene A5

1938, June 1   **Wmk. 4**   *Perf. 12*

50	A5	5c green	2.90	4.50
51	A5	10c dark orange	2.00	2.25
52	A5	15c violet	4.00	4.50
53	A5	20c rose red	2.50	3.00
54	A5	25c brown	1.90	3.00
55	A5	30c dark blue	2.50	3.00
56	A5	40c olive green	5.00	7.00
57	A5	50c brown vio	1.90	3.00
58	A5	1fr car, *emerald*	4.50	9.75
59	A5	2fr dk blue, *emer*	35.00	22.50
60	A5	5fr red, *yellow*	80.00	55.00
61	A5	10fr violet, *blue*	225.00	85.00
		Nos. 50-61 (12)	367.20	202.50
		Set, never hinged	500.00	

Catalogue values for unused stamps in this section, from this point to the end of the section, are for Never Hinged items.

Common Design Types pictured following the introduction.

UPU Issue
Common Design Type

1949, Oct. 10   **Engr.**   *Perf. 13½*

62	CD309	10c red orange	.30	1.00
63	CD309	15c violet	.30	1.00
64	CD309	30c violet blue	.40	1.00
65	CD309	50c rose violet	.60	1.10
		Nos. 62-65 (4)	1.60	4.10

Outrigger Canoes with Sails — A6

Designs: 25c, 30c, 40c and 50c, Native Carving. 1fr, 2fr and 5fr, Island couple.

1953, Apr. 30   *Perf. 12½*

66	A6	5c green	1.00	1.00
67	A6	10c red	1.00	.35
68	A6	15c yellow	1.00	.25
69	A6	20c ultramarine	1.00	.30
70	A6	25c olive	1.00	.40
71	A6	30c light brown	1.00	.50
72	A6	40c black brown	1.00	.80
73	A6	50c violet	1.25	.90
74	A6	1fr deep orange	6.25	1.75
75	A6	2fr red violet	6.25	9.00
76	A6	5fr scarlet	10.00	22.50
		Nos. 66-76 (11)	30.75	37.75

POSTAGE DUE STAMPS

British Issues
Type of 1925 Overprinted

1925, June   **Engr.**   **Wmk. 4**   *Perf. 14*

J1	A3	1p (10c) green	37.50	1.25
J2	A3	2p (20c) gray	40.00	1.25
J3	A3	3p (30c) carmine	40.00	3.25
J4	A3	5p (50c) ultra	45.00	5.50
J5	A3	10p (1fr) car, *blue*	52.50	6.50
		Nos. J1-J5 (5)	215.00	17.75

Values for Nos. J1-J5 are for toned stamps.

Regular Stamps of 1938 Overprinted in Black

1938, June 1   *Perf. 12*

J6	A5	5c green	20.00	32.50
J7	A5	10c dark orange	20.00	32.50
J8	A5	20c rose red	22.50	50.00

J9	A5	40c olive green	27.50	57.50
J10	A5	1fr car, *emerald*	35.00	67.50
		Nos. J6-J10 (5)	125.00	240.00

Catalogue values for unused stamps in this section, from this point to the end of the section, are for Never Hinged items.

Regular Stamps of 1953 Overprinted in Black

1953, Apr. 30   *Perf. 12½*

J11	A6	5c green	4.75	13.50
J12	A6	10c red	2.25	11.00
J13	A6	20c ultramarine	6.00	20.00
J14	A6	40c black brown	8.50	37.50
J15	A6	1fr deep orange	5.50	45.00
		Nos. J11-J15 (5)	27.00	127.00

NEW HEBRIDES, FRENCH

'nü 'he-bra-dēz

LOCATION — A group of islands in the South Pacific Ocean lying north of New Caledonia

GOVT. — Condominium under the joint administration of Great Britain and France

AREA — 5,790 sq. mi.

POP. — 100,000 (est. 1976)

CAPITAL — Port-Vila (Vila)

Postage stamps are issued by both Great Britain and France. In 1911 a joint issue was made bearing the coats of arms of both countries. The British stamps bore the coat of arms of Great Britain and the value in British currency on the right and the French coat of arms and values at the left. On the French stamps the positions were reversed. This resulted in some confusion when the value of the French franc decreased following World War II but the situation was corrected by arranging that both series of stamps be sold for their value as expressed in French currency.

See British New Hebrides.

12 Pence = 1 Shilling
100 Centimes = 1 Franc

Covers
Values are for commercial covers paying correct rates. Philatelic covers sell for less.

French Issues
Stamps of New Caledonia, 1905, Overprinted in Black or Red

Nos. 1-4

No. 5

1908   Unwmk.   Perf. 14x13½

1	A16	5c green	9.00	5.50
		On cover		—
2	A16	10c rose	9.50	6.75
		On cover		—
3	A17	25c blue, grnsh (R)	9.50	11.00
4	A17	50c carmine, org	8.50	12.00
		On cover		—
5	A18	1fr bl, yel grn (R)	22.50	24.00
		On cover		—
		Nos. 1-5 (5)	59.00	59.25

For overprints and surcharges see #6-10, 33-35.

Stamps of 1908 with Additional Overprint

1910

6	A16	5c green	6.50	3.00
		On cover		—
7	A16	10c rose	6.50	3.00
		On cover		—
8	A17	25c blue, grnsh (R)	3.50	6.00
		On cover		200.00
9	A17	50c car, orange	9.00	11.00
		On cover		—
10	A18	1fr bl, yel grn (R)	25.00	22.50
		On cover		—
		Nos. 6-10 (5)	50.50	45.50

A2

Perf. 14

1911, July 12   Engr.   Wmk. 3

11	A2	5c pale green	.90	2.50
		On cover		200.00
12	A2	10c red	.55	1.10
		On cover		—
13	A2	20c gray	2.00	4.00
		On cover		150.00
14	A2	25c ultramarine	2.75	7.00
		On cover		—
15	A2	30c vio, yellow	6.00	8.00
		On cover		—
16	A2	40c red, yellow	4.00	8.00
		On cover		—
17	A2	50c olive green	4.00	8.00
		On cover		—
18	A2	75c brn orange	7.00	20.00
		On cover		150.00
19	A2	1fr brn red, bl	4.50	7.00
		On cover		—
20	A2	2fr violet	12.00	22.50
		On cover		150.00
21	A2	5fr brn red, grn	14.00	40.00
		Nos. 11-21 (11)	57.70	128.10

For surcharges see Nos. 36-37, 43 and British issue No. 30.

1912   Wmk. R F in Sheet

22	A2	5c pale green	1.75	5.00
		On cover		—
23	A2	10c red	1.75	5.50
		On cover		—
24	A2	20c gray	2.10	2.10
		On cover		—
25	A2	25c ultramarine	2.50	3.00
		On cover		—
26	A2	30c vio, yellow	2.50	8.00
		On cover		125.00
27	A2	40c red, yellow	24.00	80.00
		On cover		150.00
28	A2	50c olive green	16.00	30.00
		On cover		150.00
29	A2	75c brn orange	9.00	42.50
		On cover		150.00
30	A2	1fr brn red, bl	7.00	10.00
		On cover		—
31	A2	2fr violet	9.25	50.00
		On cover		—
32	A2	5fr brn red, grn	27.50	60.00
		On cover		—
		Nos. 22-32 (11)	103.35	295.10

In the watermark, "R F" (République Française initials) are large double-lined Roman capitals, about 120mm high. About one-fourth of the stamps in each sheet show parts of the watermark. The other stamps are without watermark.

For surcharges see Nos. 38-42 and British issue No. 31.

Nos. 9 and 8 Surcharged

1920   Unwmk.   Perf. 14x13½

33	A17	5c on 50c red, org	2.50	5.00
		On cover		110.00
34	A17	10c on 25c bl, grnsh	1.00	1.50
		On cover		—

Same Surcharge on No. 4

35	A17	5c on 50c red, org	900.00	1,100.

British Issue No. 21 and French Issue No. 15 Surcharged

1921   Wmk. 3   Perf. 14

36	A1	10c on 5p ol grn	15.00	25.00
		On cover		—
37	A2	20c on 30c vio, yel	15.00	22.50
		On cover		—

Nos. 27 and 26 Surcharged

1921   Wmk. R F in Sheet

38	A2	5c on 40c red, yel	27.50	40.00
		On cover		120.00
39	A2	20c on 30c vio, yel	11.50	30.00

Stamps of 1910-12 Surcharged with New Values as in 1920-21

1924

40	A2	10c on 5c pale grn	2.75	2.75
		On cover		—
41	A2	30c on 10c red	2.75	2.75
		On cover		—
42	A2	50c on 25c ultra	4.50	4.50
		On cover		100.00

Wmk. 3

43	A2	50c on 25c ultra	40.00	60.00
		Nos. 40-43 (4)	50.00	70.00

A4

The values at the lower right denote the currency and amount for which the stamps were to be sold. The stamps could be purchased at the French post office and used to pay postage at the English rates.

1925   Engr.   Wmk. R F in Sheet

44	A4	5c (½p) black	.90	8.00
		On cover		100.00
45	A4	10c (1p) green	1.00	7.00
		On cover		100.00
46	A4	20c (2p) grnsh gray	2.50	3.75
		On cover		100.00
47	A4	25c (2½p) brown	1.00	8.00
		On cover		100.00
48	A4	30c (3p) carmine	1.75	11.00
		On cover		100.00
49	A4	40c (4p) car, org	2.00	6.00
50	A4	50c (5p) ultra	2.00	11.00
51	A4	75c (7½p) bis brn	1.75	17.50
52	A4	1fr (10p) car, blue	3.00	14.50
53	A4	2fr (1sh 8p) gray vio	3.50	22.50
54	A4	5fr (4sh) car, grnsh	7.00	30.00
		Nos. 44-54 (11)	26.40	140.25

For overprints see Nos. J1-J5.

Beach Scene
A6

1938   Perf. 12

55	A6	5c green	2.00	9.00
56	A6	10c dark orange	2.00	3.25
57	A6	15c violet	2.00	8.00
58	A6	20c rose red	2.00	5.50
59	A6	25c brown	4.00	8.00
60	A6	30c dark blue	4.00	8.00
61	A6	40c olive grn	2.75	15.00
62	A6	50c brown violet	2.75	5.00
63	A6	1fr dk car, grn	3.75	9.00
64	A6	2fr blue, grn	22.50	47.50
65	A6	5fr red, yellow	45.00	75.00
66	A6	10fr vio, blue	85.00	160.00
		Nos. 55-66 (12)	177.75	353.25
		Set, never hinged	350.00	

For overprints see Nos. 67-78 (in Scott Standard catalogue, Vol. 5), J6-J15 (J11-J15 in Scott Vol. 5).

POSTAGE DUE STAMPS

French Issues

1903. 43 46, 10, 50, 58 Overprinted

1925   Wmk. R F in Sheet   Perf. 14

J1	A4	10c green	50.00	4.75
J2	A4	20c greenish gray	50.00	4.75
J3	A4	30c carmine	50.00	4.75
J4	A4	50c ultramarine	50.00	4.75
J5	A4	1fr carmine, blue	50.00	4.75
		Nos. J1-J5 (5)	250.00	23.75

Nos. 55-56, 58, 61, 63 Overprinted

1938   Perf. 12

J6	A6	5c green	9.00	65.00
J7	A6	10c dark orange	12.50	65.00
J8	A6	20c rose red	16.00	70.00
J9	A6	40c olive green	25.00	140.00
J10	A6	1fr dark car, green	42.50	175.00
		Nos. J6-J10 (5)	105.00	515.00

NEW REPUBLIC

'nü ri-'pə-blik

LOCATION — In South Africa, located in the northern part of the present province of Natal
GOVT. — Republic
CAPITAL — Vryheid

New Republic was created in 1884 by Boer adventurers from Transvaal who proclaimed Dinizulu king of Zululand and claimed as their reward a large tract of country as their own, which they called New Republic. This area was excepted when Great Britain annexed Zululand in 1887, but New Republic became a part of Transvaal in 1888 and was included in the Union of South Africa.

12 Pence = 1 Shilling
20 Shillings = 1 Pound

New Republic stamps were individually handstamped on gummed and perforated sheets of paper. Naturally many of the impressions are misaligned and touch or intersect the perforations. Values are for stamps with good color and, for Nos. 37-64, sharp embossing. The alignment does not materially alter the value of the stamp.

A1

Handstamped

1886		**Unwmk.**	**Perf. 11½**	
1	A1	1p violet, yel	20.00	22.50
a.	"d" omitted, in pair with normal		2,750.	
1A	A1	1p black, yel		3,250.
2	A1	2p violet, yel	22.50	27.50
a.	"d" omitterd		4,750.	
b.	As "a," without date		—	
c.	tete-beche pair		—	
3	A1	3p violet, yel	50.00	60.00
a.	Double impression		—	
b.	"d" omitted (Oct. 13 '86)		4,750.	
c.	Tete-beche pair		—	
4	A1	4p violet, yel	85.00	
a.	Without date		—	
b.	"4d" omitted, in pair with normal		3,000.	
5	A1	6p violet, yel	65.00	70.00
a.	Double impression		—	
b.	"6d" omitted in pair with normal		—	
6	A1	9p violet, yel	125.00	
7	A1	1sh violet, yel	125.00	
a.	"1/S"		800.00	
b.	"1s" omitted in pair with normal		—	
8	A1	1/6 violet, yel	120.00	
a.	Without date		—	
b.	"1s6d"		600.00	
c.	as "b," tete-beche pair		—	
d.	as "b," "d" omitted		150.00	
9	A1	2sh violet, yel	75.00	
a.	tete-beche pair		875.00	
10	A1	2sh6p violet, yel	190.00	
a.	Without date		—	
b.	"2/6"		190.00	
11	A1	4sh violet, yel	825.00	
a.	"4/s"			
12	A1	5sh violet, yel	55.00	65.00
a.	Without date		—	
b.	"s" omitted in pair with normal		3,500.	
13	A1	5/6 violet, yel	300.00	
a.	"5s6d"		550.00	
14	A1	7sh6p violet, yel	175.00	
a.	"7/6"		250.00	
15	A1	10sh violet, yel	225.00	275.00
a.	Tete-beche pair		—	
16	A1	10sh6p violet, yel	250.00	
b.	"d" omitted		225.00	
16A	A1	13sh violet, yel	600.00	
17	A1	£1 violet, yel	150.00	
a.	Tete-beche pair		650.00	
18	A1	30sh violet, yel	150.00	
a.	tete-beche pair		750.00	

Granite Paper

19	A1	1p violet, gray	30.00	35.00
a.	"d" omitted		750.00	
b.	"1" omitted in pair with normal		—	
20	A1	2p violet, gray	22.50	25.00
a.	"ZUID AFRIKA" omitted		—	
b.	"d" omitted		1,350.	
c.	"2d." omitted in pair with normal		—	

21	A1	3p violet, gray	40.00	37.50
a.	tete-beche pair		375.00	
22	A1	4p violet, gray	55.00	60.00
23	A1	6p violet, gray	95.00	95.00
a.	"6" omitted in pair with normal		2,750.	
24	A1	9p violet, gray	150.00	
25	A1	1sh violet, gray	45.00	50.00
a.	tete-beche pair		425.00	
b.	"1s." omitted in pair with normal		2,750.	
26	A1	1sh6p violet, gray	125.00	
a.	tete-beche pair		750.00	
b.	"1/6"		190.00	
c.	"d" omitted		—	
27	A1	2sh violet, gray	150.00	
a.	"2s." omitted in pair with normal		3,250.	
28	A1	2/6 violet, gray	3,500.	
a.	"2/6"		250.00	
29	A1	4sh violet, gray	525.00	
30	A1	5sh6p violet, gray	425.00	
a.	"5/6"		325.00	
b.	As "a," "/" omitted		—	
c.	As "a," "6" omitted		4,500.	
31	A1	7/6 violet, gray	325.00	
a.	7s. 6d violet gray		450.00	
32	A1	10sh violet, gray	225.00	225.00
a.	tete-beche pair		525.00	
f.	"s" omitted		—	
32B	A1	10sh 6p vio, gray	275.00	
c.	Without date		—	
d.	tete-beche pair		—	
e.	"d" omitted		600.00	
33	A1	12sh violet, gray	450.00	
34	A1	13sh violet, gray	550.00	
35	A1	£1 violet, gray	375.00	
36	A1	30sh violet, gray	375.00	

Same with Embossed Arms

37	A1	1p violet, yel	22.50	25.00
a.	Arms inverted	30.00	35.00	
b.	Arms tete-beche, pair	125.00	135.00	
c.	tete-beche pair	950.00		
38	A1	2p violet, yel	27.50	30.00
a.	Arms inverted	30.00	35.00	
39	A1	4p violet, yel	80.00	85.00
b.	Arms tete-beche, pair	125.00	87.50	
40	A1	6p violet, yel	375.00	

Granite Paper

41	A1	1p violet, gray	30.00	30.00
a.	Imperf. vert., pair		—	
b.	Arms inverted	40.00	45.00	
c.	Arms tete-beche, pair	550.00		
42	A1	2p violet, gray	30.00	30.00
a.	Imperf. horiz., pair		—	
b.	Arms inverted	55.00	65.00	
c.	Arms tete-beche, pair	550.00		

There were several printings of the above stamps and the date upon them varies from "JAN 86" and "7 JAN 86" to "20 JAN 87."
Nos. 7, 8, 10, 13, 14, 26, 28 and 30 have the denomination expressed in two ways. Example: "1s 6d" or "1/6."

A2

1887		**Arms Embossed**		
43	A2	3p violet, yel	27.50	27.50
a.	Arms inverted	30.00	32.50	
b.	tete-beche pair	375.00	450.00	
c.	Imperf. vert., pair		—	
d.	Arms omitted		—	
e.	Arms tete-beche, pair	225.00		
f.	Arms sideways	375.00		
44	A2	4p violet, yel	20.00	20.00
a.	Arms inverted	25.00	25.00	
45	A2	6p violet, yel	17.50	17.50
a.	Arms inverted	50.00	50.00	
b.	Arms omitted	95.00		
c.	Arms tete-beche, pair	375.00		
46	A2	9p violet, yel	17.50	20.00
a.	Arms inverted	250.00		
b.	Arms tete-beche, pair	425.00		
47	A2	1sh violet, yel	20.00	20.00
a.	Arms inverted	75.00		
b.	Arms omitted		—	
48	A2	1sh6p violet, yel	50.00	42.50
49	A2	2sh violet, yel	42.50	45.00
a.	Arms inverted	65.00	60.00	
b.	Arms omitted	150.00		
50	A2	2sh6p violet, yel	40.00	40.00
a.	Arms inverted	45.00	45.00	
50B	A2	3sh violet, yel	65.00	65.00
c.	Arms inverted	80.00	80.00	
d.	Arms tete-beche, pair	600.00		
51	A2	4sh violet, yel	650.00	
a.	Arms omitted		—	
b.	"4/s"	65.00	65.00	
c.	As "b," arms omitted	275.00		
51B	A2	4/s violet, yel		
52	A2	5sh violet, yel	60.00	60.00
a.	Imperf. vert., pair		—	
b.	Arms inverted		175.00	
53	A2	6sh violet, yel	30.00	35.00
54	A2	7sh6p violet, yel	35.00	35.00
a.	Arms inverted	125.00		
b.	Arms tete-beche, pair		—	
55	A2	10sh violet, yel	30.00	35.00
a.	Arms inverted	40.00		
b.	Arms omitted	135.00	90.00	
c.	Imperf. vert., pair		—	
d.	Arms tete-beche, pair	150.00		

56	A2	10sh6p violet, yel	27.50	30.00
a.	Imperf. vert., pair		—	
b.	Arms omitted	55.00		
57	A2	£1 violet, yel	75.00	85.00
a.	Arms inverted	80.00		
b.	tete-beche pair	650.00	750.00	
58	A2	30sh violet, yel	225.00	

Granite Paper

59	A2	1p violet, gray	32.50	20.00
a.	Arms inverted	150.00	150.00	
b.	Arms inverted	30.00	30.00	
c.	Imperf. vert., pair		—	
d.	tete-beche pair	650.00		
e.	Arms tete-beche, pair		—	
f.	Arms sideways		—	
60	A2	2p violet, gray	20.00	20.00
a.	Arms inverted	135.00	125.00	
b.	Arms omitted	55.00	55.00	
c.	tete-beche pair	425.00		
d.	Arms tete-beche, pair		—	
61	A2	3p violet, gray	35.00	35.00
a.	Arms inverted	65.00	65.00	
b.	tete-beche pair	450.00		
c.	Arms tete-beche, pair		—	
62	A2	4p violet, gray	30.00	27.50
a.	Arms inverted	110.00		
b.	Tete-beche, pair	375.00		
c.	Arms tete-beche, pair	300.00		
63	A2	6p violet, gray	35.00	35.00
a.	Arms inverted	110.00		
64	A2	1sh6p violet, gray	50.00	42.50
a.	Arms inverted	175.00		
b.	Arms tete-beche, pair	475.00		
65	A2	2/6 violet, gray		1,150.
		Nos. 59-64 (6)	202.50	180.00

These stamps were valid only in New Republic.
All these stamps may have been valid for postage but bona-fide canceled examples of any but the 1p and 2p stamps are quite rare.

NEW ZEALAND

'nü 'zē-lənd

LOCATION — Group of islands in the south Pacific Ocean, southeast of Australia
GOVT. — Self-governing dominion of the British Commonwealth
AREA — 107,241 sq. mi.
POP. — 3,230,000 (est. 1983)
CAPITAL — Wellington

12 Pence = 1 Shilling
20 Shillings = 1 Pound

Catalogue values for unused stamps in this country are for Never Hinged items, beginning with Scott 246 in the regular postage section, Scott B9 in the semipostal section, Scott J21 in the postage due section, Scott O92 in the officials section, Scott OY29 in the Life Insurance Department section.

Watermarks

Wmk. 6 — Large Star   Wmk. 59 — N Z

Wmk. 60 — Lozenges

Wmk. 61 — N Z and Star Close Together   Wmk. 62 — N Z and Small Star Wide Apart

Wmk. 63 — Double-lined N Z and Star   Wmk. 64 — Small Star

Wmk. 253 — Multiple N Z and Star

PRE-STAMP POSTAL MARKINGS

Crowned Circle handstamp types I and III are pictured in the Crowned Circle Handstamps and Great Britain Used Abroad section.

Auckland

1846			
A1	I	"Auckland New Zealand" crowned circle handstamp in red, on cover	325.

Nelson

1846			
A2	I	"Nelson New Zealand" crowned circle handstamp in red, on cover	1,200.

New Plymouth

1846-54			
A3	I	"New Plymouth New Zealand" crowned circle handstamp in red, on cover	3,000.
A4	I	"New Plymouth New Zealand" crowned circle handstamp in black, on cover	3,000.

Similar to type I, "PAID/AT" straight

A5		"New Plymouth New Zealand" crowned circle handstamp in red, on cover ('54)	3,500.

A6 "New Plymouth New Zealand" crowned circle handstamp in black, on cover ('54) 3,500.

The device used for Nos. A5-A6 was made locally.

Otago
1851
A7 III "Otago New Zealand" crowned circle handstamp in red, on cover 2,100.

Petre
1846
A8 I "Petre New Zealand" crowned circle handstamp in red, on cover 1,500.

Port Victoria
1851
A9 III "Port Victoria New Zealand" crowned circle handstamp in red, on cover 1,300.

Russell
1846
A10 I "Russell New Zealand" crowned circle handstamp in red, on cover 7,500.

Wellington
1846
A11 I "Wellington New Zealand" crowned circle handstamp in red, on cover 375.

Issued under British Administration

Values for unused stamps are for examples with original gum as defined in the catalogue introduction.

Very fine examples of the perforated issues between Nos. 7a-69, AR1-AR30, J1-J11, OY1-OY9 and P1-P4 will have perforations touching the framelines or design on one or more sides due to the narrow spacing of the stamps on the plates and imperfect perforating methods.

The rouletted and serrate rouletted stamps of the same period rarely have complete roulettes and are valued as sound and showing partial roulettes. Stamps with complete roulettes range from very scarce to very rare, are seldom traded, and command great premiums.

Victoria — A1

London Print
Wmk. 6

1855, July 20   Engr.   Imperf.
White Paper
1 A1 1p dull carmine 75,000. 21,500.
   On cover —
  a. 1p orange ('57) 35,000.

Blued Paper
2 A1 2p deep blue 40,000. 750.
   On cover, single franking 1,750.
3 A1 1sh yellow green 52,500. 6,000.
   On cover 45,000.
  a. Half used as 6p on cover 45,000.

The blueing of Nos. 2 and 3 was caused by chemical action in the printing process.

Auckland Print
1855-58   Blue Paper   Unwmk.
4 A1 1p orange red 13,000. 2,150.
   On cover 7,250.
  a. A1 1p orange 35,000.
5 A1 2p blue ('56) 3,250. 325.
   On cover 1,250.
6 A1 1sh green ('58) 45,000. 4,750.
   On cover 10,000.
  a. Half used as 6p on cover 29,000.

Nos. 4-6 may be found with parts of the papermaker's name in double-lined letters.

1857-61   Unwmk.
Thin Hard or Thick Soft White Paper
7 A1 1p orange ('58) 3,500. 825.
  c. 1p vermilion Wmk 0 55,000.
   On cover, pair 65,000.
8 A1 2p blue ('58) 1,300. 200.
  e. 2p pale blue ('57) 1,300. 195.
  f. 2p deep dull blue 1,725. 300.
  g. 2p deep ultra ('58) 3,000. 1,000.
9 A1 6p brown ('59) 3,000. 325.
  e. 6p bister brown ('59) 4,100. 550.
  f. 6p chestnut ('59) 5,000. 650.
  h. 6p pale brown 2,700. 325.
10 A1 1sh blue green ('61) 18,500. 2,000.
  e. 1sh emerald ('58) 22,000. 2,000.

No. 7e is identical to a shade of No. 7. The only currently known example is a pair on a cover front. To qualify as No. 7e, a stamp must be on piece or on cover with a cancellation dated prior to 1862.

1859   Pin Rouletted 9-10
7a A1 1p dull orange 6,000.
8a A1 2p blue 3,800.
9a A1 6p brown 4,600.
10a A1 1sh greenish blue 8,250.

1859   Serrate Rouletted 16, 18
7b A1 1p dull orange 5,500.
8b A1 2p blue 4,100.
9b A1 6p brown 3,800.
  g. 6p chestnut 7,750.
10b A1 1sh greenish blue 7,000.

Value for No. 10b is for a damaged stamp.

1859   Rouletted 7
7c A1 1p dull orange 9,750. 5,500.
  f. Pair, imperf between
8c A1 2p blue 8,250. 3,500.
9c A1 6p brown 7,750. 3,000.
  l. Pair, imperf. between 27,500. 13,000.
10c A1 1sh greenish blue 5,250.
10d A1 1sh emerald green 5,250.

Roulettes are seldom complete or intact. Values for Nos. 7c to 10d are for stamps with partial roulettes.

1862   Perf. 13
7d A1 1p orange vermilion 8,000.
8d A1 2p blue 8,250. 3,800.
9d A1 6p brown 7,000.

See No. 26.

"H" Rouletted 16
8i A1 2p blue 5,000.
9i A1 6p brown 5,000.

"Y" Rouletted 18
7j A1 1p orange 6,000.
8j A1 2p blue 4,000.
9j A1 6p brown 5,000.
  k. 6d chesnut 5,000.
10j A1 1sh blue green 8,250.

Oblique Rouletted 13
7k A1 1p dull orange 6,500.

1862-63   Wmk. 6   Imperf.
11 A1 1p orange ver 1,100. 300.00
  d. 1p carmine vermilion ('63) 500.00 325.00
  e. 1p vermilion 775.00 300.00
  f. 1p carmine 850.00 400.00
12 A1 2p deep blue 1,000. 105.00
  d. 2p slate blue 2,100. 215.00
  e. Double impression 4,500.
  f. 2p milky blue, worn plate — 260.00
  g. 2p blue, worn plate 775.00 100.00
13 A1 3p brown lilac ('63) 950.00 175.00
14 A1 6p red brown ('63) 1,750. 125.00
  d. 6p black brown 2,100. 140.00
  e. 6p brown ('63) 2,200. 130.00
  f. 6p pale red brown 1,950. 150.00
  g. 6p gray brown 1,950. 165.00
15 A1 1sh yellow green 2,750. 390.00
  d. 1sh deep green 2,900. 410.00
  f. 1sh bronze green 2,100. 400.00
  g. 1sh olive green 2,250. 425.00

See No. 7e.

1862   Pin Rouletted 9-10
12a A1 2p deep blue — 3,250.
14a A1 6p black brown — 4,500.

1862   Serrate Rouletted 16, 18
11b A1 1p orange vermilion 11,000. 2,500.
12b A1 2p blue 1,300.
13b A1 3p brown lilac 6,250. 1,950.
14b A1 6p black brown 2,000.
  f. 6d brown 2,400.
15b A1 1sh yellow green 4,750.

1862   Rouletted 7
11c A1 1p vermilion 5,000. 875.
  g. 1p vermilion 3,500. 900.00
  h. 1p carmine vermilion 3,500. 900.
12c A1 2p blue 3,800. 525.
  h. 2p slate blue 4,600. 925.
  i. 2p pale blue 3,000. 650.
13c A1 3p brown lilac 3,800. 875.
14c A1 6p red brown 3,500. 550.
  h. 6p brown 4,000. 650.
  i. 6p black brown 4,000. 525.
  j. 6p gray brown 3,600. 525.

15c A1 1sh green 4,000. 1,000.
  h. 1sh green 4,100. 975.
  i. 1sh deep green 5,250. 1,200.
  j. 1sh bluish green 5,250. 1,200.

The 1p, 3p, 6p and 1sh come in two or more shades.

"H" Rouletted 16
12n A1 2p deep blue 2,200.
14n A1 6p black brown 2,200.
15n A1 1sh deep green 4,400.
  o. 1sh bluish green 4,400.

"Y" Rouletted 18
11p A1 1p orange vermilion 2,750.
12p A1 2p deep blue 2,100.
  t. 2p slate blue 2,200.
13p A1 3p brown-lilac 2,750.
14p A1 6p black brown 2,100.
  t. 6p brown 2,100.
15p A1 1sh yellowish green 4,400.

Oblique Rouletted 13
12q A1 2p deep blue 2,450.
  u. 2p slate blue —
13q A1 3p brown-lilac 3,250.
14q A1 6p black brown 2,450.

Square Rouletted 14
11r A1 1p orange vermilion 2,750.
12r A1 2p deep blue 2,200.
13r A1 3p brown lilac 3,250.
14r A1 6p black brown 2,750.

Serrate Rouletted 13
11s A1 1p orange vermilion 3,250.
12s A1 2p deep blue 2,100.
13s A1 3p brown lilac 4,750. 1,950.
14s A1 6p black brown 2,150.
15s A1 1sh black brown 4,400.

1863   Perf. 13
16 A1 1p carmine ver 3,000. 440.00
  a. 1p orange vermilion 3,500. 425.00
  b. 1p vermilion 3,500. 400.00
  c. As "a.," pair, imperf between 10,000.
17 A1 2p blue, no plate wear 3,000. 500.00
  a. 2p deep blue, no plate wear 825.00 110.00
  b. 2p slate blue, slight plate wear 700.00
  c. 2p milky blue, slight plate wear — 550.00
18 A1 3p brown lilac 2,750. 550.00
19 A1 6p red brown 1,500. 130.00
  b. 6p black brown 1,600. 260.00
  c. As "b.," horiz. pair, imperf. btwn. —
20 A1 1sh green 3,000. 400.00
  a. 1sh deep green 3,250. 475.00
  b. 1sh yellow green 3,250. 450.00
  c. 1sh bluish green 3,250. 450.00
  d. 1sh bronze green 3,250. 450.00

This issue was made at Dunedin by perforating stamps of the previous issue. Most of the shades known imperf also are known perf. 13.

1862   Unwmk.   Imperf.
Pelure Paper
21 A1 1p vermilion 12,000. 2,750.
  b. Rouletted 7 6,500.
  c. Serrate rouletted 13 10,500.
22 A1 2p pale dull ultra 5,500. 1,100.
  c. 2p gray blue 6,000. 1,100.
23 A1 3p brown lilac 55,000.
24 A1 6p black brown 3,500. 450.
  b. Rouletted 7 4,000. 550.
  c. Serrate rouletted 15 6,250.
  d. Serrate rouletted 13 6,500.
25 A1 1sh deep yel green 15,000. 1,250.
  b. 1sh deep green 15,000. 1,250.
  c. Rouletted 7 16,000. 2,000.
  d. Serrate rouletted 15 5,250.
  e. "Y" rouletted 18 5,250.

No. 23 was never placed in use.

1863   Perf. 13
21a A1 1p vermilion 16,000. 3,750.
22a A1 2p gray blue 9,250. 1,175.
  b. 2p pale dull ultramarine 8,250. 1,175.
24a A1 6p black brown 8,250. 450.
25a A1 1sh deep green 15,000. 2,250.

1863   Unwmk.   Perf. 13
Thick White Paper
26 A1 2p dull dark blue 3,750. 1,100.
  a. Imperf 2,150. 1,100.
  b. Pin roulette 9-10 1,100.

Nos. 26 and 26a differ from 8 and 8d by a white patch of wear at right of head.

1864   Wmk. 59   Imperf.
27 A1 1p carmine ver 1,000. 400.
28 A1 2p blue 1,750. 300.
29 A1 6p red brown 5,500. 800.
30 A1 1sh green 1,750. 340.

1864   Rouletted 7
27a A1 1p carmine vermilion 6,500. 3,250.
28a A1 2p blue 2,750. 825.
29a A1 6p deep red brown 7,500. 3,250.
30a A1 1sh green 5,000. 1,200.

1864   Perf. 12½
27B A1 1p carmine ver 12,500. 5,250.
28B A1 2p blue 475.00 85.00
29B A1 6p red brown 650.00 75.00
30B A1 1sh dp yel green 8,250. 3,250.

1864   Perf. 13
27C A1 1p carmine ver 12,500. 4,250.
  d. "Y" roulette 18 7,500.
28C A1 2p blue 1,100. 250.
30C A1 1sh yellow green 2,500. 900.
  d. Horiz. pair, imperf. btwn. 45,000.
  e. Perf. 6½x13 5,000.

1864-71   Wmk. 6   Perf. 12½
31 A1 1p vermilion 250.00 45.00
  a. 1p orange ('71) 650.00 100.00
32 A1 2p blue 250.00 24.00
  a. 2p blue, worn plate 350.00 32.50
  b. Horiz. pair, imperf. btwn. (#32) 5,500.
  c. Perf. 10x12½ 20,000.
  d. Imperf., pair (#32) 2,750. 2,000.
33 A1 3p lilac 175.00 37.50
  a. 3p mauve 875.00 100.00
  b. Imperf., pair (#33) 4,750. 2,100.
  c. As "a", imperf., pair 5,250. 2,100.
  d. 3p brown lilac 2,750. 900.00
34 A1 4p deep rose ('65) 3,500. 300.00
35 A1 4p yellow ('65) 275.00 145.00
  a. 4p orange yellow 2,500. 1,100.
36 A1 6p red brown 350.00 30.00
  a. 6p brown 400.00 45.00
  b. Horiz. pair, imperf. btwn. 3,000. 3,000.
37 A1 1sh pale yel green 350.00 135.00
  a. 1sh yellow green 700.00 150.00
  b. 1sh green 3,000. 900.00

The 1p, 2p and 6p come in two or more shades.

The 2p plate used for No. 32 was damaged and retouched in the bottom quarter of the plate. This is found also on all subsequent 2p issues.

Imperforate examples of the 1p pale orange, worn plate; 2p dull blue and 6p dull chocolate brown are reprints. Value, each $100.

1871   Wmk. 6   Perf. 10
38 A1 1p deep brown 1,000. 140.00

1871   Perf. 12½
39 A1 1p brown 275.00 55.00
  a. Imperf. 3,750. 2,250.
40 A1 2p orange 200.00 32.50
  a. 2p vermilion 225.00 35.00
  b. Imperf., pair 2,750. —
41 A1 6p blue 400.00 80.00
  Nos. 39-41 (3) 875.00 167.50

Shades exist.

1871   Perf. 10x12½
42 A1 1p brown 450.00 60.00
43 A1 2p orange 325.00 45.00
44 A1 6p blue 2,500. 600.00
  Nos. 42-44 (3) 3,275. 705.00

The 6p usually has only one side perf. 10, the 1p and 2p more rarely so. Shades exist.

1873   Wmk. 59   Perf. 12½
45 A1 1p brown 8,750.
46 A1 2p vermilion 1,300. 375.00

1873   Unwmk.   Perf. 12½
47 A1 1p brown 1,200. 275.00
48 A1 2p vermilion 175.00 60.00
49 A1 4p yellow orange 225.00 925.00

The watermark "T.H. SAUNDERS" in double-line capitals falls on 32 of the 240 stamps in a sheet. The 1p and 2p also are known with script "WT & CO" watermark.

1873   Wmk. 60
50 A1 2p vermilion 3,500. 750.

A2

A3

A4

A5

A6

A7

Perf. 10x12½, 11½, 12, 12½
1874		Typo.		Wmk. 62
51	A2	1p violet	125.00	15.50
a.		Bluish paper	250.00	45.00
b.		Imperf.	750.00	1,650.
52	A3	2p rose	130.00	9.00
a.		Bluish paper	250.00	45.00
53	A4	3p brown	225.00	90.00
a.		Bluish paper	425.00	120.00
54	A5	4p claret	325.00	75.00
a.		Bluish paper	650.00	130.00
55	A6	6p blue	300.00	13.50
a.		Bluish paper	500.00	60.00
56	A7	1sh green	650.00	40.00
a.		Bluish paper	1,200.	210.00
		Nos. 51-56 (6)	1,755.	243.00

1875		Wmk. 6		Perf. 12½
57	A2	1p violet	2,000.	325.00
58	A3	2p rose	825.00	45.00

A8

1878		Wmk. 62		Perf. 12x11½
59	A8	2sh deep rose	750.00	450.00
60	A8	5sh gray	800.00	500.00

No. 60 has numeral "5" in each of the four spandrels.
Beware of cleaned fiscally used examples of Nos. 59-60.

A9

A10

A11

A12

A13

A14

A15

Perf. 10, 11, 11½, 12, 12½ and Compound
1882				
61	A9	1p rose	12.00	.70
a.		Vert. pair, imperf. horiz.	900.00	
b.		Perf. 12x11½	50.00	7.00
c.		Perf. 12½	300.00	175.00
62	A10	2p violet	13.50	.35
a.		Vert. pair, imperf. btwn.	900.00	
b.		Perf. 12½	200.00	110.00
63	A11	3p orange	60.00	9.50
a.		3p yellow	62.50	14.00
64	A12	4p blue green	62.50	4.50
a.		Perf. 10x11	95.00	13.00
65	A13	6p brown	80.00	8.00
66	A14	8p blue	80.00	60.00
67	A15	1sh red brown	125.00	15.00
		Nos. 61-67 (7)	433.00	98.05

See #87. For overprints see #O1-O2, O5, O7-O8.

A15a

A16

A17

1891-95
67A	A15a	½p black ('95)	4.25	.25
a.		Perf. 12x11½	37.50	90.00
68	A16	2½p ultramarine	57.50	5.00
a.		Perf. 12½	375.00	200.00
69	A17	5p olive gray	70.00	25.00
		Nos. 67A-69 (3)	131.75	30.25

In 1893 advertisements were printed on the backs of Nos. 61-67, 68-69.
See #86C. For overprints see #O3-O4, O9.

Mt. Cook — A18

Lake Taupo — A19

Pembroke Peak — A20

Mt. Earnslaw, Lake Wakatipu — A21

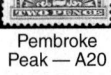

Mt. Earnslaw, Lake Wakatipu — A22

Huia, Sacred Birds — A23

White Terrace, Rotomahana A24

Otira Gorge and Mt. Ruapehu A25

Kiwi A26

Maori Canoe A27

Pink Terrace, Rotomahana A28

Kea & Kaka (Hawk-billed Parrots) A29

Milford Sound — A30

Mt. Cook — A31

Perf. 12 to 16
1898, Apr. 5		Engr.		Unwmk.
70	A18	½p lilac gray	9.25	1.75
a.		Horiz. or vert. pair, imperf. btwn.	1,750.	1,450.
b.		½p purple brown	9.50	1.75
c.		½p purple black	9.50	1.75
71	A19	1p yel brn & bl	6.50	.75
a.		Horiz. or vert. pair, imperf. btwn.	1,300.	
b.		Imperf. pair	950.00	1,000.
c.		1p brown & blue	7.25	1.00
d.		As "c," horiz. or vert. pair, imperf. btwn.	1,300.	
72	A20	2p rose brown	57.50	.30
a.		Horiz. pair, imperf. vert.	650.00	
b.		Vert. pair, imperf. btwn.	1,300.	
c.		2p lake	45.00	.30
d.		As "c," horiz. pair, imperf. btwn.	650.00	
73	A21	2½p bl (Wakitipu)	18.00	47.50
a.		2½p sky bl (Wakitipu)	15.00	50.00
74	A22	2½p bl (Wakatipu)	50.00	10.00
a.		2½p deep bl (Wakatipu)	50.00	10.00
75	A23	3p orange brn	37.50	10.00
76	A24	4p rose	18.00	22.00
a.		4p bright rose	18.00	22.00
b.		4p lake rose	25.00	27.50
77	A25	5p red brown	100.00	225.00
a.		5p violet brown	70.00	25.00
78	A26	6p green	90.00	55.00
a.		6p grass green	220.00	250.00
79	A27	8p dull blue	70.00	47.50
a.		8p indigo	70.00	50.00
b.		8p Prussian blue	70.00	50.00

A32

A33

A34

80	A28	9p lilac	65.00	42.50
81	A29	1sh dull red	110.00	29.00
a.		Pair, imperf. between	5,000.	
b.		1sh vermilion	110.00	30.00
82	A30	2sh blue green	300.00	160.00
a.		Vert. pair, imperf. btwn.	5,000.	5,000.
83	A31	5sh vermilion	400.00	550.00
		Nos. 70-83 (14)	1,331.	1,201.

The 5sh stamps are often found with revenue cancellations that are embossed or show a crown on the top of a circle. These are worth much less.
See Nos. 84, 88-89, 91-98, 99B, 102, 104, 106-107, 111-112, 114-121, 126-128, 1508-1521 (in Scott Standard catalogue, Vol. 5). For overprint see No. O10.

1900		Wmk. 63		Perf. 11
		Thick Soft Wove Paper		
84	A18	½p green	8.75	1.75
a.		½p yellow-green	9.50	2.00
b.		½p pale yellow-green ('00)	16.00	5.50
c.		½p deep green	9.00	1.75
d.		As "c," pair, imperf. btwn.	550.00	
85	A32	1p carmine rose	15.00	.25
a.		1p lake	42.50	4.50
b.		1p crimson	15.00	.25
c.		As "b," pair, imperf. btwn.	1,650.	1,550.
d.		As "c," horiz. pair, imperf. vert.	650.00	
86	A33	2p red violet	14.00	.90
a.		Pair, imperf. btwn.	1,450.	
b.		2p dull violet ('00)	16.50	.75
d.		Pair, imperf. btwn.	1,550.	
e.		2p mauve	20.00	1.75
		Nos. 84-86 (3)	37.75	2.90

Nos. 84 and 86 are re-engravings of Nos. 70 and 72 and are slightly smaller.
See No. 110.

1899-1900				Wmk. 63
86C	A15a	½p black ('00)	9.50	17.50
87	A10	2p violet ('00)	30.00	17.50
		Unwmk.		
88	A22	2½p blue	30.00	3.75
a.		Horiz. pair, imperf. vert.	1,450.	
b.		Vert. pair, imperf. btwn.	650.00	—
c.		2½p deep blue	16.50	4.00
89	A23	3p org brown	35.00	2.50
a.		Horiz. pair, imperf. vert.	650.00	
b.		Horiz. pair, imperf. btwn.	1,525.	
c.		3p deep brown	26.00	2.50
d.		As "c," pair, imperf. btwn.	1,550.	2.50
90	A34	4p yel brn & bl ('00)	15.00	4.00
c.		4p chestnut & bright blue	6.00	4.00
d.		4p bister-brown & deep blue	6.00	4.00
91	A25	5p red brown	50.00	10.00
a.		5p violet brown	42.50	5.00
92	A26	6p green	150.00	82.50
a.		6p yellow-green	110.00	140.00
93	A26	6p rose ('00)	50.00	7.00
a.		6p carmine	50.00	7.00
b.		6p scarlet	87.50	27.50
c.		As "b," double impression	875.00	925.00
d.		As #93, horiz. pair, imperf. vert.	600.00	
e.		As "a," horiz. pair, imperf. vert.	500.00	
f.		As "b," horiz. pair, imperf. vert.	825.00	
g.		As #93, horiz. pair, imperf. btwn.	1,300.	
h.		As "a," vert. pair, imperf. btwn.	1,550.	

94	A27	8p dark blue	45.00	16.50
a.		8p Prussian blue	50.00	17.50
95	A28	9p red lilac	52.50	30.00
a.		9p rosy purple	45.00	13.00
96	A29	1sh red	100.00	10.00
a.		1sh dull orange-red	65.00	8.00
b.		1sh dull brown-red	65.00	14.00
c.		1sh bright red	70.00	40.00
97	A30	2sh blue green	250.00	60.00
a.		2sh, "laid paper"	225.00	250.00
b.		2sh gray-green	150.00	70.00
98	A31	5sh vermilion	400.00	410.00
		Revenue cancel		25.00
a.		5sh carmine red	325.00	475.00
		Nos. 86C-98 (13)	1,217.	671.25

See #113. For overprints see #O11-O15.
The 5sh stamps are often found with revenue cancellations that are embossed or show a crown on the top of a circle. These are worth much less.

"Commerce" — A35

1901, Jan. 1   Unwmk.   Perf. 12 to 16

99	A35	1p carmine	8.00	4.50

Universal Penny Postage.
See Nos. 100, 103, 105, 108, 129. For overprint see No. O16. Compare design A35 with A42.

Boer War Contingent A36

Perf. 14, 11x14, 14x11

1901   Wmk. 63
Thick Soft Paper

99B	A18	½p green	15.00	5.50

Perf. 11, 14 and Compound

100	A35	1p carmine	18.00	.25
a.		Horiz. pair, imperf. vert.	325.00	325.00
101	A36	1½p brown org	35.00	20.00
a.		Vert. pair, imperf. horiz.	1,100.	
b.		Imperf., pair	1,200.	
		Nos. 99B-101 (3)	68.00	25.75

No. 101 was issued to honor the New Zealand forces in the South African War.
See No. 109.

Thin Hard Paper

102	A18	½p green	29.00	27.50
103	A35	1p carmine	16.00	4.75
a.		Horiz. pair, imperf. vert.	300.00	

1902   Unwmk.

104	A18	½p green	14.00	5.75
105	A35	1p carmine	14.00	3.25

1902   Perf. 11
Thin White Wove Paper

106	A26	6p rose red	45.00	7.00
a.		Watermarked letters	100.00	100.00

The sheets of No. 106 are watermarked with the words "LISBON SUPERFINE" in two lines, covering ten stamps.

Perf. 11, 14, 11x14, 14x11

1902-07   Wmk. 61

107	A18	½p green	8.00	1.35
a.		Horiz. pair, imperf. vert.	300.00	
108	A35	1p carmine	4.50	.25
a.		1p rose carmine	4.50	.25
b.		Imperf., pair		
c.		Imperf. x serrate perf.	200.00	
d.		Imperf. horiz. or vert. pair	200.00	
f.		Booklet pane of 6	300.00	
109	A36	1½p brown org ('07)	27.50	60.00
110	A33	2p dull vio ('03)	13.50	2.75
a.		Horiz. pair, imperf. vert.	550.00	875.00
b.		Vert. pair, imperf. horiz.	775.00	
111	A22	2½p blue	32.00	7.00
112	A23	3p org brown	35.00	2.50
113	A34	4p yel brn & bl	11.00	4.00
a.		Horiz. pair, imperf. vert.	650.00	
114	A25	5p red brown	50.00	15.00
		5p violet brown	65.00	32.50
115	A26	6p rose red	45.00	8.50
a.		6p rose	45.00	8.50
b.		6p pink	65.00	8.75
c.		6p brick red	80.00	20.00
d.		Horiz. pair, imperf. vert.	850.00	
116	A27	8p deep blue	45.00	13.00
117	A28	9p red violet	50.00	9.25
118	A31	1sh scarlet	80.00	16.50
a.		1sh orange red	85.00	8.00
b.		1sh brown red	90.00	15.50

119	A30	2sh blue green	225.00	45.00
120	A31	5sh vermilion	500.00	360.00
		Nos. 107-120 (14)	1,126.	545.10

Wmk. 61 is normally sideways on 3p, 5p, 8p, 9p and 1sh. The 6p exists with wmk. upright. The 1sh exists with wmk. upright and inverted.
The unique example of No. 113 with inverted center is used and is in the New Zealand National Philatelic Collection.
See No. 129. For overprints see Nos. O17-O22.
The 5sh stamps are often found with revenue cancellations that are embossed or show a crown on the top of a circle. These are worth much less.
In 1908 a quantity of the 1p carmine was overprinted "King Edward VII Land" and taken on a Shackleton expedition to the Antarctic. Because of the weather Shackleton landed at Victoria Land instead. The stamp was never sold to the public at face value. See No. 121a.
Similar conditions prevailed for the 1909-12 ½p green and 1p carmine overprinted "VICTORIA LAND." See Nos. 130d-131d.

1903   Unwmk.   Perf. 11
Laid Paper

121	A30	2sh blue green	325.00	250.00

No. 108a Overprinted in Green:
"King Edward VII Land"
in Two Lines Reading Up

1908, Jan. 15   Perf. 14

121a	A35	1p rose carmine	800.00	65.00

See note after No. 120.

Christchurch Exhibition Issue

Arrival of the Maoris A37

Maori Art — A38

Landing of Capt. Cook — A39

Annexation of New Zealand A40

Wmk. 61

1906, Nov.   Typo.   Perf. 14

122	A37	½p emerald	35.00	37.50
123	A38	1p vermilion	18.00	27.50
a.		1p claret	14,500.	25,000.
124	A39	3p blue & brown	60.00	115.00
125	A40	6p gray grn & rose	220.00	425.00
		Nos. 122-125 (4)	333.00	605.00

Value for No. 123a is for a fine example.

Designs of 1902-07 Issue, but smaller

Perf. 14, 14x13, 14x15

1907-08   Engr.

126	A23	3p orange brown	55.00	17.50
127	A26	6p carmine rose	62.50	11.50
128	A29	1sh orange red	225.00	35.00
		Nos. 126-128 (3)	342.50	64.00

The small stamps are about 21mm high, those of 1898-1902 about 23mm.

Type of 1902 Redrawn

1908   Typo.   Perf. 14x14½

129	A35	1p carmine	40.00	3.00

REDRAWN, 1p: The lines of shading in the globe are diagonal and the other lines of the design are generally thicker than on No. 108.

Edward VII A41

"Commerce" A42

1909-12   Perf. 14x14½

130	A41	½p yellow green	7.25	.55
a.		Booklet pane of 6	225.00	
b.		Booklet pane 5 + label	775.00	
c.		Imperf., pair	250.00	
131	A42	1p carmine	2.00	.25
a.		Imperf., pair	410.00	
b.		Booklet pane of 6	225.00	

Perf. 14x14½, 14x13½, 14
Engr.
Various Frames

132	A41	2p mauve	25.00	7.25
133	A41	3p orange brown	27.50	1.40
134	A41	4p red orange	32.50	27.50
135	A41	4p yellow ('12)	22.50	13.50
136	A41	5p red brown	22.00	5.00
137	A41	6p carmine rose	50.00	1.75
138	A41	8p deep blue	20.00	3.25
139	A41	1sh vermilion	75.00	6.75
		Nos. 130-139 (10)	283.75	67.20

Nos. 133, 136-138 exist in vert. pairs with perf. 14x13½ on top and perf. 14x14½ on the bottom. These sell for a premium.
See #177. For overprint see Cook Islands #49.

Nos. 130-131 Overprinted in Black:
"VICTORIA LAND" in Two Lines

1911-13

130d	A41	½p yellow green	1,100.	950.00
131d	A42	1p carmine	70.00	150.00

See note after No. 120.
Issue dates: 1p, Feb. 9; ½p, Jan. 18, 1913.

Stamps of 1909 Overprinted in Black

1913

130e	A41	½p yellow green	25.00	55.00
131e	A42	1p carmine	35.00	45.00
133e	A41	3p orange brown	250.00	400.00
137e	A41	6p carmine rose	300.00	500.00
		Nos. 130e-137e (4)	610.00	1,000.

This issue was valid only within New Zealand and to Australia from Dec. 1, 1913, to Feb. 28, 1914. The Auckland Stamp Collectors Club inspired this issue.

King George V — A43

1915   Typo.   Perf. 14x15

144	A43	½p yellow green	2.00	.25
b.		Booklet pane of 6	150.00	

See Nos. 163-164, 176, 178. For overprints see No. MR1, Cook Islands No. 40.

A44   A45

Perf. 14x14½, 14x13½

1915-22   Engr.

145	A44	1½p gray	4.25	2.00
146	A44	2p purple	14.50	45.00
147	A45	2p org yel ('16)	9.50	35.00
148	A44	2½p dull blue	9.00	5.75
149	A45	3p violet brown	16.50	1.40
150	A45	4p orange yellow	9.50	57.50
151	A45	4p purple ('16)	22.50	.55
c.		4p blackish violet	10.00	
d.		Vert. pair, top stamp imperf. bottom stamp perf 3 sides	1,200.	
152	A44	4½p dark green	25.00	26.00
153	A45	5p light blue ('21)	19.00	1.10
a.		Imperf., pair	250.00	200.00

154	A45	6p carmine rose	13.00	.55
a.		Horiz. pair, imperf. vert.		
155	A44	7½p red brown	22.50	26.00
156	A45	8p blue ('21)	25.00	50.00
157	A45	8p red brown ('22)	35.00	4.00
158	A45	9p olive green	30.00	5.00
a.		Imperf., pair	1,500.	
159	A45	1sh vermilion	30.00	.60
a.		Imperf., pair	450.00	
		Nos. 145-159 (15)	285.25	260.45

Nos. 145-156, 158-159 exist in vert. pairs with perf 14x13½ on top and perf 14x14½ on the bottom. These sell for a premium. The 5p and No. 151c exist with the perf varieties reversed. These are rare. No. 157 only comes perf 14x13½.
The former Nos. 151a and 151b probably were listed from sheets with No. 151d. They probably do not exist.
For overprints see Cook Islands Nos. 53-60.

A46   A47

1916-19   Typo.   Perf. 14x15, 14

160	A46	1½p gray black	9.00	1.40
161	A47	1½p gray black	11.00	.60
162	A47	1½p brown orange ('18)	3.50	.60
163	A43	2p yellow	2.60	.25
164	A43	3p chocolate ('19)	12.00	1.50
		Nos. 160-164 (5)	38.10	4.35

The engr. stamps have a background of geometric lathe-work; the typo. stamps have a background of crossed dotted lines.
Type A43 has three diamonds at each side of the crown, type A46 has two, and type A47 has one.
In 1916 the 1½, 2, 3 and 6p of the 1915-16 issue and the 8p of the 1909 issue were printed on paper intended for the long rectangular stamps of the 1902-07 issue. In this paper the watermarks are set wide apart, so that the smaller stamps often show only a small part of the watermark or miss it altogether.
For overprints see Cook Islands #50-52.

Victory Issue

"Peace" and British Lion — A48

Peace and Lion — A49

Maori Chief — A50

British Lion — A51

"Victory" — A52

King George V, Lion and Maori Fern at Sides — A53

1920, Jan. 27 — Perf. 14

165	A48	½p yellow green	3.25	2.75
166	A49	1p carmine	4.50	.65
167	A50	1½p brown orange	3.50	.55
168	A51	3p black brown	15.00	16.00
169	A52	6p purple	17.00	19.00
170	A53	1sh vermilion	25.00	55.00
		Nos. 165-170 (6)	68.25	93.95

No. 165
Surcharged in
Red

1922, Mar.

174	A48	2p on ½p yellow green	6.00	1.50

Map of New
Zealand — A54

1923 — Typo. — Perf. 14x15

175	A54	1p carmine rose	3.50	.70

Restoration of Penny Postage. The paper
varies from thin to thick.

Types of 1909-15
N Z and Star 'watermark' printed on
back, usually in blue

1925 — Unwmk. — Perf. 14x14½

176	A43	½p yellow green	3.50	3.50
177	A42	1p carmine	3.50	.90
178	A43	2p yellow	20.00	62.50
		Nos. 176-178 (3)	27.00	66.90

Exhibition
Buildings
A55

1925, Nov. 17 — Wmk. 61
Surface Tinted Paper

179	A55	½p yel green, grnsh	3.50	14.00
180	A55	1p car rose, pink	4.25	6.25
181	A55	4p red violet, lilac	37.50	80.00
		Nos. 179-181 (3)	45.25	100.25

Dunedin Exhibition.

George V in
Admiral's
Uniform
A56

In Field
Marshal's
Uniform
A57

1926 — Perf. 14, 14½x14

182	A56	2sh blue	70.00	35.00
a.		2sh dark blue	65.00	67.50
183	A56	3sh violet	130.00	175.00
a.		3sh deep violet	110.00	190.00

Perf. 14, 14x14½

184	A57	1p rose red	1.25	.25
a.		Booklet pane of 6	150.00	
b.		Imperf., pair	250.00	
		Nos. 182-184 (3)	201.25	210.25

For overprints see Cook Islands Nos. 74-75.

Pied Fantail
and Clematis
A58

Kiwi and
Cabbage
Palm
A59

Maori Woman
Cooking in
Boiling Spring
A60

Maori
Council
House
(Whare)
A61

Mt. Cook and Mountain Lilies — A62

Maori Girl
Wearing
Tiki — A63

Mitre
Peak — A64

Striped
Marlin
A65

Harvesting — A66

Tuatara
Lizard — A67

Maori Panel
from
Door — A68

Tui or Parson
Bird — A69

Capt. Cook
Landing at
Poverty
Bay — A70

Mt.
Egmont,
North
Island
A71

Perf. 14x14½, 14x13½, 13½x14, 13½

1935, May 1 — Engr. — Wmk. 61

185	A58	½p bright green	2.50	1.00
186	A59	1p copper red	2.50	1.00
186A	A59	1p copper red, re-engraved	9.00	4.00
b.		Booklet pane of 6 + ad labels	80.00	
187	A60	1½p red brown	6.50	10.00
188	A61	2p red orange	4.00	2.50
189	A62	2½p dk gray & dk brown	8.00	22.50
190	A63	3p chocolate	13.50	3.25
191	A64	4p blk brn & blk	4.25	3.25
192	A65	5p violet blue	26.00	35.00
193	A66	6p red	9.00	11.00
194	A67	8p dark brown	12.00	15.00

Litho.
Size: 18x21½mm

195	A68	9p black & scarlet	16.00	6.00

Engr.

196	A69	1sh dk sl green	22.50	15.00
197	A70	2sh olive green	50.00	50.00
198	A71	3sh yel brn & brn black	25.00	47.50
		Nos. 185-198 (15)	210.75	227.00
		Set, never hinged	500.00	

On No. 186A, the horizontal lines in the sky
are much darker.

The 2½p, 5p, 2sh and 3sh are perf. 13½
vertically; perf. 13-14 horizontally on each
stamp.

See Nos. 203-216, 244-245.

Silver Jubilee Issue

Queen
Mary and
King
George V
A72

1935, May 7 — Perf. 11x11½

199	A72	½p blue green	.75	1.00
200	A72	1p dark car rose	1.00	.75
201	A72	6p vermilion	20.00	30.00
		Nos. 199-201 (3)	21.75	31.75
		Set, never hinged	29.00	

25th anniv. of the reign of King George V.

Types of 1935
Perf. 12½ to 15 and Compound

1936-42 — Wmk. 253

203	A58	½p bright green	2.00	.25
204	A59	1p copper red	2.00	.25
205	A60	1½p red brown	9.50	6.00
206	A61	2p red orange	.25	.25
a.		Perf. 14	16.50	.90
b.		Perf. 14x15	21.00	25.00
c.		Perf. 12½	4.00	.25
207	A62	2½p dk gray & dk brn	1.50	6.00
208	A63	3p chocolate	20.00	1.50
209	A64	4p black brn & blk	1.50	.25
a.		Perf. 12½	22.50	17.50
210	A65	5p violet blue	2.50	1.25
a.		Perf. 12½	11.00	3.50
211	A66	6p red	1.25	.25
a.		Perf. 12½	1.75	5.00
212	A67	8p dark brown	2.00	.25
a.		Perf. 12½	2.25	1.60

Litho.
Size: 18x21½mm

213	A68	9p gray & scarlet	30.00	4.00
a.		9p black & scarlet	32.50	4.25

Engr.

214	A69	1sh dark slate grn	3.50	1.25
a.		Perf. 12½	35.00	25.00
215	A70	2sh olive green	6.50	1.50
a.		Perf. 13½x14	175.00	4.00
b.		Perf. 12½	12.50	9.50
216	A71	3sh yel brn & blk brn	5.50	3.25
a.		Perf. 12½ ('41)	45.00	50.00
		Nos. 203-216 (14)	88.00	27.50
		Set, never hinged	180.00	

Wool
Industry
A73

Butter
Industry
A74

Sheep
Farming
A75

Apple
Industry
A76

Shipping
A77

1936, Oct. 1 — Wmk. 61 — Perf. 11

218	A73	½p deep green	.25	.30
219	A74	1p red	.25	.25
220	A75	2½p deep blue	1.25	4.00
221	A76	4p dark purple	1.00	3.00
222	A77	6p red brown	2.00	3.50
		Nos. 218-222 (5)	4.75	11.05
		Set, never hinged	6.50	

Congress of the Chambers of Commerce of
the British Empire held in New Zealand.

Queen
Elizabeth
and King
George VI
A78

Perf. 13½x13

1937, May 13 — Wmk. 253

223	A78	1p rose carmine	.25	.25
224	A78	2½p dark blue	.50	1.25
225	A78	6p vermilion	.65	1.25
		Nos. 223-225 (3)	1.40	2.75
		Set, never hinged	2.25	

Coronation of George VI and Elizabeth.

A79

A80

1938-44 — Engr. — Perf. 13½

226	A79	½p emerald	4.75	.25
226B	A79	½p brown org ('41)	.25	.30
227	A79	1p rose red	3.75	.25
227A	A79	1p lt blue grn ('41)	.25	.25
228	A80	1½p violet brown	19.00	3.25
228B	A80	1½p red ('44)	.25	.35
228C	A80	3p blue ('41)	.25	.25
		Nos. 226-228C (7)	28.50	4.90
		Set, never hinged	40.00	

See Nos. 258-264. For surcharges see Nos.
242-243, 279, 285 (in Scott Standard catalogue, Vol. 5).

Landing of
the Maoris
in 1350
A81

Captain Cook, His Map of New
Zealand, 1769, H.M.S. Endeavour
A82

Victoria,
Edward
VII, George
V, Edward
VIII and
George
VI — A83

Abel Tasman, Ship, and Chart of West
Coast of New Zealand
A84

Treaty of Waitangi,
1840 — A85

Pioneer
Settlers
Landing on
Petone
Beach,
1840
A86

The
Progress of
Transport
A87

H.M.S. "Britomart"
at Akaroa — A88

Route of Ship Carrying First Shipment
of Frozen Mutton to England — A89

Maori
Council
A90

Gold
Mining in
1861 and
Modern
Gold
Dredge
A91

Giant Kauri — A92

Perf. 13½x13, 13x13½, 14x13½

			Wmk.	253
1940, Jan. 2		**Engr.**		
229	A81	½p dk blue green	.30	.25
230	A82	1p scarlet & sepia	2.25	.25
231	A83	1½p brt vio & ultra	.25	.60
232	A84	2p black brown &		
		Prussian green	1.10	.25
233	A85	2½p dk bl & myr grn	1.50	1.00
234	A86	3p dp plum & dk vio	2.75	1.00
235	A87	4p dk red vio & vio		
		brn	10.00	1.60
236	A88	5p brown & lt bl	6.00	4.00
237	A89	6p vio & brt grn	8.00	1.50
238	A90	7p org red & black	1.25	4.50
239	A90	8p org red & black	8.00	5.00
240	A91	9p dp org & olive	5.50	2.25
241	A92	1sh dk sl grn & ol	10.00	4.00
		Nos. 229-241 (13)	56.90	26.20
		Set, never hinged	95.00	

Centenary of British sovereignty established
by the treaty of Waitangi.
Imperfs of #229-241 exist. These probably
are plate proofs.
For surcharge see No. 246.

**Stamps of 1938 Surcharged with
New Values in Black**

		Wmk. 253		Perf. 13½
1941				
242	A79	1p on ½p emerald	1.00	.25
243	A80	2p on 1½p violet brn	1.00	.25
		Set, never hinged	3.50	

Type of 1935 Redrawn
1941   Typo.   Wmk. 61   *Perf. 14x15*
Size: 17½x20½mm

~~244 A68 9p int black & scarlet 70.00 30.00~~

245 A68 9p int black & scarlet 4.00 3.50
    Set, never hinged   140.00

> **Catalogue values for unused
> stamps in this section, from this
> point to the end of the section, are
> for Never Hinged items.**

No 231
Srchd. in
Black

1944   ***Perf. 13½x13***
246 A83 10p on 1½p brt vio & ul-
         tra   .45 .45

Peace Issue

Lake
Matheson
A93

Parliament House,
Wellington — A94

St. Paul's
Cathedral,
London — A95

The Royal
Family — A96

Badge of
Royal New
Zealand Air
Force
A97

New
Zealand
Army
Overseas
Badge
A98

Badge of
Royal Navy
A99

New
Zealand
Coat of
Arms
A100

Knight, Window
of Wellington
Boys' College
A101

Natl. Memorial
Campanile,
Wellington
A103

Southern
Alps and
Chapel
Altar
A102

Engr.; Photo. (1½p, 1sh)
Perf. 13x13½, 13½x13

			Wmk.	253
1946, Apr. 1				
247	A93	½p choc & dk bl grn	.25	.60
248	A94	1p emerald	.25	.25
249	A95	1½p scarlet	.25	.25
250	A96	2p rose violet	.25	.25
251	A97	3p dk grn & ultra	.25	.25
252	A98	4p brn org & ol grn	.25	.25
253	A99	5p ultra & blue grn	.80	.80
254	A100	6p org red & red brn	.25	.25
255	A101	8p brown lake & blk	.30	.30
256	A102	9p black & brt bl	.30	.30
257	A103	1sh gray black	.80	.40
		Nos. 247-257 (11)	3.95	3.90

Return to peace at the close of WWII.
Imperfs exist from the printer's archives.

George VI Type of 1938 and

King
George VI — A104

1947		**Engr.**	***Perf. 13½***	
258	A80	2p orange	.30	.25
260	A80	4p rose lilac	.75	.50
261	A80	5p gray	1.00	.50
262	A80	6p rose carmine	1.00	.25
263	A80	8p deep violet	1.00	1.00
264	A80	9p chocolate	2.00	.40

		Perf. 14		
265	A104	1sh dk car rose &		
		chnt	.75	.50
266	A104	1sh3p ultra & chnt	2.50	1.00
267	A104	2sh dk grn & brn		
		org	6.25	2.00
268	A104	3sh gray blk & chnt	5.00	3.00
		Nos. 258-268 (10)	20.55	9.40

Nos. 265-267 have watermark either upright
or sideways. On No. 268 watermark is always
sideways.

"John
Wickliffe"
and "Philip
Laing"
A105

Cromwell,
Otago
A106

First Church,
Dunedin — A107

University
of Otago
A108

1948, Feb. 23			***Perf. 13½***	
269	A105	1p green & blue	.25	.25
270	A106	2p brown & green	.25	.25
271	A107	3p violet	.35	.35
272	A108	6p lilac rose & gray blk	.35	.35
		Nos. 269-272 (4)	1.20	1.20

Otago Province settlement, cent.

> **A Royal Visit set of four was pre-
> pared but not issued. Examples of
> the 3p have appeared in the stamp
> market.**

A109

Black Surcharge
Wmk. 253

1950, July 28		**Typo.**	***Perf. 14***	
273	A109	1½p rose red	.40	.40

See No. 367 in Scott Standard catalogue,
Vol. 5.

Cathedral at
Christchurch — A110

"They
Passed this
Way"
A111

3p, John Robert Godley. 6p, Canterbury
University College. 1sh, View of Timaru.

1950, Nov. 20		**Engr.**	***Perf. 13x13½***	
274	A110	1p blue grn & blue	.50	.50
275	A111	2p car & red org	.50	.50
276	A110	3p indigo & blue	.50	.50
277	A111	6p brown & blue	.70	.70
278	A111	1sh claret & blue	.70	.70
		Nos. 274-278 (5)	2.90	2.90

Centenary of the founding of Canterbury
Provincial District.
Imperfs of #274-278 exist.

No. 227A Surcharged in Black

1952, Dec.			***Perf. 13½***	
279	A79	3p on 1p lt blue green	.30	.25

POSTAL-FISCAL STAMPS

In 1881 fiscal stamps of New Zealand
of denominations over one shilling were
made acceptable for postal duty. Values
for canceled stamps are for postal cancellations. Denominations above £5
appear to have been used primarily for
fiscal purposes.

Queen Victoria
PF1   PF2

Perf. 11, 12, 12½

1882		Typo.		**Wmk. 62**
AR1	PF1	2sh blue	125.00	20.00
AR2	PF1	2sh6p dk brown	125.00	20.00
AR3	PF1	3sh violet	225.00	25.00
AR4	PF1	4sh brown vio	325.00	40.00
AR5	PF1	4sh red brown	275.00	40.00
AR6	PF1	5sh green	325.00	40.00
AR7	PF1	6sh rose	500.00	65.00
AR8	PF1	7sh ultra	550.00	150.00
AR9	PF1	7sh6p ol gray	1,500.	500.00
AR10	PF1	8sh dull blue	525.00	125.00
AR11	PF1	9sh org red	900.00	300.00
AR12	PF1	10sh red brown	350.00	75.00

1882-90

AR13	PF2	15sh dk grn	1,500.	400.00
AR15	PF2	£1 rose	700.00	150.00
AR16	PF2	25sh blue		—
AR17	PF2	30sh brown		—
AR18	PF2	£1 15sh yellow		—
AR19	PF2	£2 purple		—

PF3   PF4

AR20	PF3	£2 10sh red brown	—
AR21	PF3	£3 yel green	—
AR22	PF3	£3 10sh rose	—
AR23	PF3	£4 ultramarine	—
AR24	PF3	£4 10sh olive brown	—
AR25	PF3	£5 dark blue	—
AR26	PF4	£6 orange red	—
AR27	PF4	£7 brown red	—
AR28	PF4	£8 green	—
AR29	PF4	£9 rose	—
AR30	PF4	£10 blue	—
AR30A	PF4	£20 yellow	—

No. AR31

With "COUNTERPART" at Bottom

1901				
AR31	PF1	2sh6p brown	300.00	400.00

Perf. 11, 14, 14½x14

1903-15				**Wmk. 61**
AR32	PF1	2sh blue ('07)	80.00	12.00
AR33	PF1	2sh6p blue ('07)	80.00	12.00
AR34	PF1	3sh violet	175.00	14.00
AR35	PF1	4sh brown red	200.00	30.00
AR36	PF1	5sh green ('06)	225.00	30.00
AR37	PF1	6sh rose	375.00	50.00
AR38	PF1	7sh dull blue	400.00	80.00
AR39	PF1	7sh6p ol gray ('06)	1,500.	400.00
AR40	PF1	8sh dark blue	450.00	75.00
AR41	PF1	9sh dl org ('06)	600.00	200.00
AR42	PF1	10sh dp claret	250.00	50.00

AR43	PF2	15sh blue grn	1,350.	350.00
AR44	PF2	£1 rose	500.00	150.00

Perf. 14½

AR45	PF2	£2 deep vio ('25)	600.00	150.00
a.		Perf. 14	700.00	150.00
Nos. AR32-AR45 (14)			*6,785.*	*1,603.*

For overprints see Cook Islands Nos. 67-71.

Coat of Arms — PF5

1931-39		**Wmk. 61**	**Perf. 14**

Type PF5 (Various Frames)

AR46	1sh3p lemon	30.00	40.00
AR47	1sh3p orange ('32)	8.00	9.00
AR48	2sh6p brown	16.00	5.25
AR49	4sh dull red ('32)	17.00	7.50
AR50	5sh green	21.00	12.50
AR51	6sh brt rose ('32)	37.50	15.00
AR52	7sh gray blue	32.50	25.00
AR53	7sh6p olive gray ('32)	75.00	92.50
AR54	8sh dark blue	50.00	37.50
AR55	9sh brn org	52.50	32.50
AR56	10sh dark car	27.50	10.50
AR57	12sh6p brn vio ('35)	250.00	250.00
AR58	15sh ol grn ('32)	70.00	42.50
AR59	£1 pink ('32)	75.00	22.50
AR60	25sh turq bl ('38)	550.00	600.00
AR61	30sh dk brn ('36)	300.00	200.00
AR62	35sh yellow ('37)	6,000.	7,500.
AR63	£2 violet ('33)	400.00	70.00
AR64	£2 10sh dark red ('36)	400.00	550.00
AR65	£3 light grn ('32)	400.00	210.00
AR66	£3 10sh rose ('39)	2,250.	2,250.
AR67	£4 light blue	400.00	175.00
AR68	£4 10sh dk ol gray ('39)	2,500.	2,500.
AR69	£5 dk blue ('32)	400.00	100.00

For overprints see Cook Islands Nos. 80-83.

No. AR62 Surcharged in Black

35/-

1939		**Perf. 14**
AR70	PF5 35sh on 35sh yel	500.00 350.00

Type PF5 Surcharged in Black

1940			
AR71	3sh6p on 3sh6p dl green	28.50	21.00
AR72	5sh6p on 5sh6p rose lilac	60.00	57.50
AR73	11sh on 11sh pale yellow	125.00	150.00
AR74	22sh on 22sh scar	275.00	350.00
Nos. AR71-AR74 (4)		*488.50*	*578.50*

Type of 1931

1940-58		**Wmk. 253**	**Perf. 14**

Type PF5 (Various Frames)

AR75	1sh3p orange	5.75	.60
AR76	2sh6p brown	5.75	.60
AR77	4sh dull red	6.75	.60
AR78	5sh green	11.50	.90
AR79	6sh brt rose	20.00	4.00
AR80	7sh gray bl	20.00	6.75
AR81	7sh6p ol gray ('50)	70.00	70.00
AR82	8sh dk blue	45.00	25.00
AR83	9sh orange ('46)	50.00	30.00
AR84	10sh dk carmine	25.00	3.25
AR85	15sh olive ('45)	55.00	20.00
AR86	£1 pink('45)	29.00	8.50
a.	Perf. 14x13½ ('58)	32.50	15.00
AR87	25sh blue ('46)	500.00	550.00
AR88	30sh choc ('46)	250.00	200.00
AR89	£2 violet ('46)	100.00	60.00
AR90	£2 10sh dk red ('51)	400.00	525.00
AR91	£3 lt grn ('46)	150.00	125.00
AR92	£3 10sh rose ('48)	2,250.	2,500.

AR93	£4 lt blue ('52)	150.00	160.00
AR94	£5 dk blue ('40)	175.00	150.00

Type PF5 Surcharged in Black

1942-45		**Wmk. 253**	
AR95	3sh6p on 3sh6p grn	12.50	8.00
AR96	5sh6p on 5sh6p rose lil ('44)	26.00	8.50
AR97	11sh on 11sh yel	67.50	52.50
AR98	22sh on 22sh car ('45)	325.00	275.00
Nos. AR95-AR98 (4)		*431.00*	*344.00*

SEMI-POSTAL STAMPS

Nurse
SP1   SP2

Inscribed: "Help Stamp out Tuberculosis, 1929"

Wmk. 61

1929, Dec. 11	Typo.	**Perf. 14**
B1	SP1 1p + 1p scarlet	12.50 20.00

Inscribed: "Help Promote Health, 1930"

1930, Oct. 29		
B2	SP2 1p + 1p scarlet	30.00 *45.00*

Boy — SP3

1931, Oct. 31		**Perf. 14½x14**
B3	SP3 1p + 1p scarlet	100.00 90.00
B4	SP3 2p + 1p dark blue	100.00 75.00

Hygeia, Goddess of Health — SP4

1932, Nov. 18	Engr.	**Perf. 14**
B5	SP4 1p + 1p carmine	22.50 *30.00*
	Never hinged	55.00

Road to Health — SP5

1933, Nov. 8		
B6	SP5 1p + 1p carmine	15.00 *20.00*
	Never hinged	35.00

Crusader — SP6

1934, Oct. 25		**Perf. 14x13½**
B7	SP6 1p + 1p dark carmine	12.50 *20.00*
	Never hinged	25.00

Child at Bathing Beach — SP7

1935, Sept. 30		**Perf. 11**
B8	SP7 1p + 1p scarlet	3.00 3.25
	Never hinged	5.00

> **Catalogue values for unused stamps in this section, from this point to the end of the section, are for Never Hinged items.**

Anzac — SP8

1936, Apr. 27		
B9	SP8 ½p + ½p green	.70 *2.00*
B10	SP8 1p + 1p red	.70 *1.60*

21st anniv. of Anzac landing at Gallipoli.

"Health" SP9

1936, Nov. 2		
B11	SP9 1p + 1p red	2.00 *4.25*

Boy Hiker — SP10

1937, Oct. 1		
B12	SP10 1p + 1p red	3.00 *4.00*

Children at Play — SP11

Perf. 14x13½

1938, Oct. 1		**Wmk. 253**
B13	SP11 1p + 1p red	6.25 3.25

Children at Play — SP12

1939, Oct. 16   Wmk. 61   *Perf. 11½*
Black Surcharge
B14 SP12 1p on ½p + ½p grn   5.00 5.00
~~B15 SP12 6p on 1p + 1p brown   8.00 8.00~~

1940, Oct. 1
B16 SP12 1p + ½p green   16.00 17.50
B17 SP12 2p + 1p org brown   16.00 17.50

The surtax was used to help maintain children's health camps.

Semi-Postal Stamps of 1940, Overprinted in Black "1941"
1941, Oct. 4   *Perf. 11½*
B18 SP12 1p + ½p green   3.00 3.50
B19 SP12 2p + 1p org brown   3.00 3.50

Children in Swing — SP13

1942, Oct. 1   *Engr.*
B20 SP13 1p + ½p green   .35 1.10
B21 SP13 2p + 1p dp org brown   .35 1.10

Imperf plate proofs on card exist for #B22-B27, B32-B33, B38-B39, B46-B48, B59-B60. Imperfs exist for B44-B45, B49-B51. These are from the printer's archives. See Scott Standard catalogue, Vol. 5, for listings after 1940.

Princess Elizabeth — SP14

Design: 1p+½p, Princess Margaret Rose.

1943, Oct. 1   Wmk. 253   *Perf. 12*
B22 SP14 1p + ½p dark green   .25   .40
  a. Vert. pair, imperf. between
B23 SP14 2p + 1p red brown   .25   .40
  a. Vert. pair, imperf. between

Princesses Margaret Rose and Elizabeth SP16

1944, Oct. 9   *Perf. 13½*
B24 SP16 1p + ½p blue green   .35   .45
B25 SP16 2p + 1p chalky blue   .35   .35

Peter Pan Statue, London — SP17

1945, Oct. 1
B26 SP17 1p + ½p gray green & bister brown   .25 .35
B27 SP17 2p + 1p car & olive bis   .25 .35

Soldier Helping Child over Stile SP18

1946, Oct. 24   *Perf. 13½x13*
B28 SP18 1p + ½p dk grn & org brn   .25 .35
~~B29 SP18 2p + 1p dk brn & org brn .25 .35~~

Statue of Eros, London — SP19

1947, Oct. 1   Engr.   *Perf. 13x13½*
B30 SP19 1p + ½p deep green   .25   .35
B31 SP19 2p + 1p deep carmine .25   .35

Children's Health Camp SP20

1948, Oct. 1   *Perf. 13½x13*
B32 SP20 1p + ½p blue grn & ultra   .25 .35
B33 SP20 2p + 1p red & dk brn   .25 .35

Nurse and Child — SP21

1949, Oct. 3   Photo.   *Perf. 14x14½*
B34 SP21 1p + ½p deep green   .30   .35
B35 SP21 2p + 1p ultramarine   .30   .35

Princess Elizabeth and Prince Charles — SP22

1950, Oct. 2
B36 SP22 1p + ½p green   .25   .35
B37 SP22 2p + 1p violet brown .25   .35

Racing Yachts SP23

Perf. 13½x13
1951, Nov. 1   Engr.   Wmk. 253
B38 SP23 1½p + ½p red & yel   .25   .35
B39 SP23 2p + 1p dp grn & yel .25   .35

Princess Anne SP24

Prince Charles SP25

Perf. 14x14½
1952, Oct. 1   Wmk. 253   Photo.
B40 SP24 1½p + ½p crimson   .25   .35
~~B41 SP25 2p + 1p crimson   .25 .35~~

AIR POST STAMPS

Plane over Lake Manapouri AP1

Perf. 14x14½
1931, Nov. 10   Typo.   Wmk. 61
C1 AP1 3p chocolate   27.50 22.50
  a. Perf. 14x15   150.00 500.00
C2 AP1 4p dark violet   27.50 27.50
C3 AP1 7p orange   30.00 27.50
  Nos. C1-C3 (3)   85.00 77.50

Most examples of No. C1a are poorly centered.

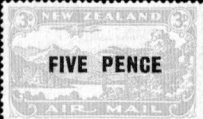

Type of 1931 Surcharged in Red

1931, Dec. 18   *Perf. 14x14½*
C4 AP1 5p on 3p yel green   20.00 25.00

Type of 1931 Overprinted in Dark Blue

1934, Jan. 17
C5 AP1 7p bright blue   50.00 55.00

1st official air mail flight between NZ and Australia.

Airplane over Landing Field AP2

1935, May 4   Engr.   *Perf. 14*
C6 AP2 1p rose carmine   1.10   .80
C7 AP2 3p dark violet   5.75   3.75
C8 AP2 6p gray blue   11.50 5.75
  Nos. C6-C8 (3)   18.35 10.30
  Set, never hinged 40.00

SPECIAL DELIVERY STAMPS

SD1

Perf. 14x½, 14x15
1903-26   Typo.   Wmk. 61
E1 SD1 6p purple & red ('26)   60.00 40.00
  a. 6p violet & red, perf. 11   70.00 50.00

Mail Car — SD2

1939, Aug. 16   Engr.   *Perf. 14*
E2 SD2 6p violet   1.75   6.00
  Never hinged   5.00

POSTAGE DUE STAMPS

D1

Wmk. 62
1899, Dec. 1   Typo.   *Perf. 11*
J1   D1 ½p green & red   8.00   19.00
  a. No period after "D" 75.00 60.00
J2   D1 1p green & red   12.50   2.10
J3   D1 2p green & red   40.00   6.25
J4   D1 3p green & red   20.00   6.00
J5   D1 4p green & red   42.50 25.00
J6   D1 5p green & red   45.00 60.00
J7   D1 6p green & red   45.00 60.00
J8   D1 8p green & red   110.00 150.00
J9   D1 10p green & red   175.00 225.00
J10 D1 1sh green & red   140.00 100.00
J11 D1 2sh green & red   225.00 300.00
  Nos. J1-J11 (11) 863.00 953.35

Nos. J1-J11 may be found with N. Z. and D. varying in size.

D2

1902, Feb. 28   Unwmk.
J12 D2 ½p gray grn & red   3.00   7.50
Wmk. 61
J13 D2 ½p gray grn & red   3.00   2.10
J14 D2 1p gray grn & red   12.00   4.00
J15 D2 2p gray grn & red   150.00 150.00

1904-28   *Perf. 14, 14x14½*
J16 D2 ½p green & car   3.75   4.25
J17 D2 1p green & car   7.00   1.00
J18 D2 2p green & car   9.00   3.50
J19 D2 3p grn & rose ('28)   50.00 25.00
  Nos. J16-J19 (4)   69.75 33.75

N Z and Star printed on the back in Blue

1925   Unwmk.   *Perf. 14x14½, 14x15*
J20 D2 ½p green & rose   4.00   26.00
J21 D2 2p green & rose   9.00   35.00

Catalogue values for unused stamps in this section, from this point to the end of the section, are for Never Hinged items.

D3

1939   Wmk. 61   Typo.   *Perf. 15x14*
J22 D3 ½p turquoise green   13.00   9.00
J23 D3 1p rose pink   5.00   .60
J24 D3 2p ultramarine   9.00   1.75
J25 D3 3p brown orange   26.00 29.00
  Nos. J22-J25 (4)   53.00 40.35

1945-49   Wmk. 253
J27 D3 1p rose pink ('49)   5.00   25.00
J28 D3 2p ultramarine ('47)   7.00   10.00
J29 D3 3p brown orange   15.00   5.75
  Nos. J27-J29 (3)   27.00 39.75

The use of postage due stamps was discontinued in Sept., 1951.

WAR TAX STAMP

No. 144 Overprinted in Black

Perf. 14x14½

1915, Sept. 24   Wmk. 61

MR1 A43 ½p green   2.10 .60

OFFICIAL STAMPS

Regular Issues of 1882-92 Overprinted & Handstamped

1892   Wmk. 62   *Perf as Before*
Rose or Magenta Handstamp

O1	A9	1p rose	600.
O2	A10	2p violet	800.
O3	A16	2½p ultramarine	700.
O4	A17	5p olive gray	1,000.
O5	A13	6p brown	1,200.

Violet Handstamp

O6	N1	½p rose	1,000.
O7	A9	1p rose	600.
O8	A10	2p violet	600.

Handstamped on No. 67A in Rose
1899   *Perf. 10, 10x11*

O9 A15a ½p black   600.

Handstamped on No. 79 in Violet
Unwmk.   *Perf. 14, 15*

O10 A27 8p dull blue   1,200.

Hstmpd. on Stamps of 1899-1900 in Violet

1902   *Perf. 11*

O11	A22	2½p blue	650.
O12	A23	3p org brown	1,000.
O13	A25	5p red brown	900.
O14	A27	8p dark blue	1,000.

Green Handstamp

O15 A25 5p red brown   900.

Handstamped on Stamp of 1901 in Violet
Wmk. 63   *Perf. 11*

O16 A35 1p carmine   600.

Handstamped on Stamps of 1902-07 in Violet or Magenta
1905-07   Wmk. 61   *Perf. 11, 14*

O17	A18	½p green	600.
O18	A35	1p carmine	600.
O19	A22	2½p blue	700.
O20	A25	5p red brown	
O21	A27	8p deep blue	
O22	A30	2sh blue green	5,000.

The "O. P. S. O." handstamp is usually struck diagonally, reading up, but on No. O19 it also occurs horizontally. The letters stand for "On Public Service Only."

Overprinted in Black

On Stamps of 1902-07
1907   *Perf. 14, 14x13, 14x14½*

O23	A18	½p green	12.00	2.00
O24	A35	1p carmine	12.00	1.00
a.		Booklet pane of 6	110.00	
O25	A33	2p violet	20.00	2.00
O26	A23	3p orange brn	60.00	6.00
O27	A26	6p carmine rose	250.00	40.00
a.		Horiz. pair, imperf. vert.	925.00	
O28	A29	1sh brown red	125.00	25.00
O29	A30	2sh blue green	175.00	50.00
a.		Horiz. pair, imperf. vert.	1,400.	
O30	A31	5sh vermilion	350.00	350.00
		Nos. O23-O30 (8)	1,004.	576.00

On No. 127
Perf. 14x13, 14x14½

O31 A26 6p carmine rose   325.00 65.00

On No. 129
1909   *Perf. 14x14½*

O32 A35 1p car (redrawn)   90.00 3.00

On Nos. 130-131, 133, 137, 139
1910   *Perf. 14, 14x13½, 14x14½*

O33	A41	½p yellow green	10.00	1.00
a.		Inverted overprint		1,600.
O34	A42	1p carmine	3.75	.25
O35	A41	3p orange brown	20.00	2.00
O36	A41	6p carmine rose	30.00	10.00
O37	A41	1sh vermilion	70.00	40.00
		Nos. O33-O37 (5)	133.75	53.25

For 3p see note on perf varieties following No. 139.

On Postal-Fiscal Stamps Nos. AR32, AR36, AR44

1911-14

O38	PF1	2sh blue ('14)	75.00	52.50
O39	PF1	5sh green ('13)	125.00	200.00
O40	PF2	£1 rose	1,000.	625.00
		Nos. O38-O40 (3)	1,200.	877.50

On Stamps of 1909-19
Perf. 14x13½, 14x14½

1915-19   Typo.

O41	A43	½p green	1.60	.25
O42	A46	1½p gray black ('16)	8.00	3.00
O43	A47	1½p gray black ('16)	5.75	1.00
O44	A47	1½p brown org ('19)	5.75	.60
O45	A43	2p yellow ('17)	5.75	.50
O46	A43	3p chocolate ('19)	16.00	1.50

Engr.

O47	A45	3p vio brn ('16)	8.00	1.50
O48	A45	6p car rose ('16)	12.00	1.00
O49	A41	8p dp bl (R) ('16)	20.00	30.00
O50	A45	1sh vermilion ('16)	7.50	2.25
a.		1sh orange	15.00	20.00
		Nos. O41-O50 (10)	90.35	41.60

For 8p see note on perf varieties following No. 139.

1922   On No. 157

O51 A45 8p red brown   125.00 200.00

1925   On Nos. 151, 158

O52	A45	4p purple	20.00	4.25
O53	A45	9p olive green	45.00	42.50

On No. 177
1925   *Perf. 14x14½*

O54 A42 1p carmine   5.00 5.00

On Nos. 184, 182
1927-28 Wmk. 61 *Perf. 14, 14½x14*

O55	A57	1p rose red	2.50	.25
O56	A56	2sh blue	125.00	140.00

On No. AR50
1933   *Perf. 14*

O57 PF5 5sh green   450.00 450.00

Nos. 186, 187, 196 Overprinted in Black

1936   *Perf. 14x13½, 13½x14, 14*

O58	A59	1p copper red	2.00	1.40
O59	A60	1½p red brown	14.00	30.00
O60	A61	1sh dark slate grn	30.00	52.50
		Nos. O58-O60 (3)	46.00	83.90
		Set, never hinged	80.00	

Same Overprint Horizontally in Black or Green on Stamps of 1936
Perf. 12½, 13½, 13x13½, 14x13½, 13½x14, 14

1936-42   Wmk. 253

O61	A58	½p brt grn ('37)	1.50	5.25
O62	A59	1p copper red	3.00	.60
O63	A60	1½p red brown	4.00	5.25

O64	A61	2p red org ('38)	1.00	.25
a.		Perf. 12½ ('42)	110.00	62.50
O65	A62	2½p dk gray & dk brown	8.00	24.00
O66	A63	3p choc ('38)	27.50	4.00
O67	A64	4p blk brn & blk	5.00	1.10
O68	A66	6p red ('37)	5.75	.35
O68B	A67	8p dp brn ('42)	8.50	20.00
O69	A68	9p black & scar (G) ('38)	80.00	45.00
O70	A69	1sh dk slate grn	14.00	1.60
a.		Perf. 12½ ('42)	27.50	1.75

Overprint Vertical

O71	A70	2sh ol grn ('37)	24.00	8.50
a.		Perf. 12½ ('42)	90.00	25.00
		Nos. O61-O71 (12)	182.25	115.90
		Set, never hinged	450.00	

Same Overprint Horizontally in Black on Nos. 226, 227, 228

1938

O72	A79	½p emerald	5.75	1.75
O73	A79	1p rose red	7.25	.30
O74	A80	1½p violet brn	37.50	10.50
		Nos. O72-O74 (3)	50.50	12.55
		Set, never hinged	95.00	

Same Overprint on No. AR50
1938   Wmk. 61   *Perf. 14*

O75 PF5 5sh green   75.00 47.50
     Never hinged   150.00

Nos. 229-235, 237, 239-241 Overprinted in Red or Black

Perf. 13½x13, 13x13½, 14x13½

1940   Wmk. 253

O76	A81	½p dk bl grn (R)	.60	.75
a.		"f" joined	29.00	70.00
O77	A82	1p scar & sepia	2.25	.30
a.		"f" joined	29.00	70.00
O78	A83	1½p brt vio & ultra	1.10	4.25
a.		"f" joined	29.00	70.00
O79	A84	2p black brn & Prus green	2.25	.30
a.		"f" joined	35.00	70.00
O80	A85	2½p dk bl & myr grn	1.40	4.50
a.		"f" joined	29.00	77.50
O81	A86	3p deep plum & dark vio (R)	5.75	.95
a.		"f" joined	24.00	55.00
O82	A87	4p dark red vio & violet brn	14.50	1.60
a.		"f" joined	70.00	92.50
O83	A89	6p vio & brt grn	14.50	1.60
a.		"f" joined	40.00	80.00
O84	A90	8p org red & blk	14.50	13.00
a.		"f" joined	40.00	110.00
O85	A91	9p org & olive	5.75	5.75
O86	A92	1sh dk sl grn & ol	35.00	5.25
		Nos. O76-O86 (11)	97.60	38.25
		Set, never hinged	190.00	

Nos. 227A, 228C Overprinted in Black

1941   Wmk. 253   *Perf. 13½*

O88	A79	1p light blue green	.30	.30
O89	A80	3p blue	.75	.30
		Set, never hinged	2.25	

Same Overprint on No. 245
1944   *Perf. 14x15*

Size: 17¼x20¼mm

O90 A68 9p int black & scar 20.00 17.00
     Never Hinged   60.00

Same Overprint on No. AR78
1944   *Perf. 14*

O91 PF5 5sh green   12.00 7.00
     Never Hinged   20.00

> **Catalogue values for unused stamps in this section, from this point to the end of the section, are for Never Hinged items.**

Same Ovpt. on Stamps of 1941-47
1946-51   *Perf. 13½, 14*

O92	A79	½p brn org ('46)	1.75	1.25
O92B	A80	1½p red	5.75	1.25
O93	A80	2p orange	.90	.30
O94	A80	4p rose lilac	4.00	1.25
O95	A80	6p rose carmine	5.75	1.25
O96	A80	8p deep violet	10.00	4.50
O97	A80	9p chocolate	11.50	5.75
O98	A104	1sh dk car rose & chestnut	11.50	1.75
O99	A104	2sh dk green & brown org	26.00	8.50
		Nos. O92-O99 (9)	77.15	25.80

LIFE INSURANCE

Lighthouses
LI1   LI2

Perf. 10, 11, 10x11, 12x11½
1891, Jan. 2   Typo.   Wmk. 62

OY1	LI1	½p purple	110.00	7.00
OY2	LI1	1p blue	80.00	2.00
OY3	LI1	2p red brown	150.00	4.25
OY4	LI1	3p chocolate	425.00	22.50
OY5	LI1	6p green	550.00	70.00
OY6	LI1	6p rose pink	800.00	140.00
		Nos. OY1-OY6 (6)	2,115.	245.75

Stamps from outside rows of the sheets sometimes lack watermark.

1903-04   Wmk. 61   *Perf. 11, 14x11*

OY7	LI1	½p purple	120.00	7.00
OY8	LI1	1p blue	75.00	1.10
OY9	LI1	2p red brown	200.00	10.00
		Nos. OY7-OY9 (3)	395.00	18.10

1905-32   *Perf. 11, 14, 14x14½*

OY10	LI2	½p yel grn ('13)	1.40	.90
OY11	LI2	½p green ('32)	5.75	2.75
OY12	LI2	1p blue ('06)	375.00	29.00
OY13	LI2	1p dp rose ('13)	9.75	1.10
OY14	LI2	1p scarlet ('31)	4.25	2.00
OY15	LI2	1½p gray ('17)	14.00	4.25
OY16	LI2	1½p brn org ('19)	1.75	1.40
OY17	LI2	2p red brown	2,750.	200.00
OY18	LI2	2p violet ('13)	20.00	17.00
OY19	LI2	2p yellow ('21)	6.00	6.00
OY20	LI2	3p ocher ('13)	29.00	20.00
OY21	LI2	3p choc ('31)	11.00	26.00
OY22	LI2	6p carmine rose ('13)	20.00	26.00
OY23	LI2	6p pink ('31)	20.00	45.00
		Nos. OY10-OY23 (14)	3,267.	381.40

#OY15, OY16 have "POSTAGE" at each side.
Stamps from outside rows of the sheets sometimes lack watermark.

1946-47   Wmk. 253   *Perf. 14x15*

OY24	LI2	½p yel grn ('47)	1.90	1.90
OY25	LI2	1p scarlet	1.40	1.25
OY26	LI2	2p yellow	2.25	15.00
OY27	LI2	3p chocolate	10.50	30.00
OY28	LI2	6p pink ('47)	8.50	25.00
		Nos. OY24-OY28 (5)	24.55	73.15
		Set, never hinged	42.50	

> **Catalogue values for unused stamps in this section, from this point to the end of the section, are for Never Hinged items.**

New Zealand Lighthouses

Castlepoint
LI3

Taiaroa — LI4

Cape Palliser
LI5

Cape
Campbell
LI6

Eddystone
(England)
LI7

Stephens
Island
LI8

The Brothers
LI9

Cape Brett — LI10

Perf. 13½x13, 13x13½

1947-65		Engr.	Wmk. 253	
OY29	LI3	½p dk grn & red orange	1.75	1.70
OY30	LI4	1p dk ol grn & blue	1.75	1.10
OY31	LI5	2p int bl & gray	.90	.90
OY32	LI6	2½p blk & blk ('63)	11.00	15.00
OY33	LI7	3p red vio & bl	3.50	.75
OY34	LI8	4p dk brn & org	4.50	1.75
a.		Wmkd. sideways ('65)	4.50	16.00
OY35	LI9	6p dk brn & bl	4.25	2.50
OY36	LI10	1sh red brn & bl	4.25	3.50
		Nos. OY29-OY36 (8)	31.90	27.20

Set first issued Aug. 1, 1947.
Exist imperf.

NEWSPAPER STAMPS

Queen Victoria — N1

Wmk. 59

1873, Jan. 1		Typo.	Perf. 10	
P1	N1	½p rose	140.00	47.50
a.		Perf. 12½x10	160.00	75.00
b.		Perf. 12½	210.00	75.00

The "N Z" watermark is widely spaced and intended for larger stamps. About a third of the stamps in each sheet are unwatermarked. They are worth a slight premium.
For overprint, see No. O6.

1875, Jan.		Wmk. 64	Perf. 12½	
P3	N1	½p rose	25.00	25.00
a.		Pair, imperf. between	800.00	500.00
b.		Perf. 12	70.00	12.50

1892		Wmk. 62	Perf. 12½	
P4	N1	½p bright rose	11.00	1.50
a.		Unwatermarked	20.00	10.00

NICARAGUA
,ni-kə-'rä-gwə

LOCATION — Central America, between Honduras and Costa Rica
GOVT. — Republic
AREA — 57,143 sq. mi.
POP. — 2,908,000 (est. 1984)
CAPITAL — Managua

100 Centavos = 1 Peso
100 Centavos = 1 Córdoba (1913)

GREAT BRITAIN POST OFFICE IN GREYTOWN

British influence on the Mosquito coast of Nicaragua dated from the mid-17th century, and the local Mosquito Indians were under British protection until 1860. A British postal agency existed in the port of Greytown as early as 1842, and British stamps were used from 1865 to May 1, 1882.

Values are for clear cancellations on sound, fault-free stamps, with average to fine centering. In many cases, very fine examples are rare or non-existent.

**Stamps of Great Britain
Canceled with barred oval "C57"
obliterator or with "GREYTOWN"
circular date stamp**

No. A22

1865-81

A1	½p rose red, plates 5, 10, 115 (#58), value from	85.00
A2	1p rose red, plates 180, 197, 210 (#33), value from	55.00
A3	1½p lake red, plate 3 (#32)	80.00
A4	2p blue, plate 9 (#29)	60.00
A5	2p blue, plates 14, 15 (#30), value from	60.00
A6	3p rose, plates 17-20 (#61), value from	60.00
A7	3p rose, plate 20 (#83)	—
A8	4p vermilion, plates 8, 10, 11, 13, 14 (#43), value from	60.00
A9	4p vermilion, plate 15 (#69)	325.00
A10	4p pale olive green, plate 15 (#70)	225.00
	Plate 16 (#70)	210.00
A11	4p gray brown, plate 17 (#71)	350.00
A12	4p gray brown, plate 17 (#84)	100.00
A13	6p gray, plates 14-17 (#62), value from	100.00
A14	8p orange (#73)	350.00
A15	1sh green, plate 4 (#48)	—
A16	1sh green, plates 6, 7 (#54), value from	—
A17	1sh green, plates 8, 10, 12, 13 (#64), value from	75.00
A18	1sh salmon, plate 13 (#65)	425.00
A19	1sh salmon, plate 13 (#87)	120.00
A20	2sh blue (#55)	175.00
A21	2sh brown (#56)	2,500.
A22	5sh rose, plate 1 (#57)	500.00
	Plate 2 (#57)	675.00
A23	5sh rose, plate 4 (#90a)	2,500.
A24	10shslate (#74)	4,000.

1880

A25	1p red brown (#79)	80.00
A26	1½p red brown (#80)	85.00

ISSUES OF THE REPUBLIC
Watermarks

Wmk. 117 — Liberty Cap

Wmk. 209 — Multiple Ovals

Liberty Cap on Mountain Peak; From Seal of Country — A1

A2   A3

Unwmk.

1862, Dec. 2		Engr.	Perf. 12	
Yellowish Paper				
1	A1	2c dark blue	75.00	20.00
		On cover		25,000.
2	A1	5c black	150.00	60.00
		On cover		10,000.

Designs of Nos. 1-2 measure 22½x18½mm. Perforations are invariably rough.
Values are for stamps without gum. Examples with gum sell for more. Nos. 1-2 were canceled only by pen.
There is one reported cover of No. 1, two of No. 2.
See No. C509 in Scott Standard catalogue, Vol. 5.

1869-71			White Paper	
3	A1	1c bister ('71)	3.00	1.25
		On cover		7,500.
4	A1	2c blue	3.00	1.25
		On cover		7,500.
5	A1	5c black	100.00	1.00
		On cover		6,000.
6	A2	10c vermilion	4.00	1.75
		On cover		5,000.
7	A3	25c green	7.50	4.00
		On cover		7,500.
		Nos. 3-7 (5)	117.50	9.25

Designs of Nos. 3-7 measure 22½x19mm. Perforations are clean cut.
There are two reported covers of No. 5, five of No. 7.

1878-80			Rouletted 8½	
8	A1	1c brown	2.00	1.25
		On cover		7,500.
9	A1	2c blue	2.00	1.25
		On cover		7,500.
10	A1	5c black	50.00	1.00
		On cover		6,000.
11	A2	10c ver ('80)	2.50	1.50
		On cover		5,000.
12	A3	25c green ('79)	2.50	4.00
		On cover		7,500.
		Nos. 8-12 (5)	59.00	9.00

Most values exist on thicker soft paper.
Stamps with letter/numeral cancellations other than "3 G," "6 M," "9 C" sell for more.
Nos. 3-12 were reprinted in 1892. The corresponding values of the two series are printed in the same shades which is not usually true of reprints. They are, however, similar to some of the original shades and the only certain test is comparison. Originals have thin white gum; reprints have rather thick yellowish gum. Value 50c each. Unused examples of Nos. 3-12 without gum should be presumed to be reprints. Nos. 5 and 10 unused are extremely scarce and should be purchased with original gum and should be expertized.

Seal of Nicaragua — A4

1882		Engr.	Perf. 12	
13	A4	1c green	.25	.25
14	A4	2c carmine	.25	.25
15	A4	5c blue	.25	.25
16	A4	10c dull violet	.25	.75
17	A4	15c yellow	.60	25.00
18	A4	20c slate gray	.90	5.00
19	A4	50c dull violet	1.25	25.00
		Nos. 13-19 (7)	3.75	56.50

Used Values

of Nos. 13-120 are for stamps with genuine cancellations applied while the stamps were valid. Various counterfeit cancellations exist.

Locomotive and Telegraph Key — A5

1890			Engr.	
20	A5	1c yellow brown	.25	.25
21	A5	2c vermilion	.25	.25
22	A5	5c deep blue	.25	.25
23	A5	10c lilac gray	.25	.25
24	A5	20c red	.25	1.75
25	A5	50c purple	.25	5.00
26	A5	1p brown	.25	8.50
27	A5	2p dark green	.25	9.00
28	A5	5p lake	.25	
29	A5	10p orange	.25	
		Nos. 20-29 (10)	2.50	

The issues of 1890-1899 were printed by the Hamilton Bank Note Co., New York, to the order of N. F. Seebeck who held a contract for stamps with the government of Nicaragua. Reprints were made, for sale to collectors, of the 1896, 1897 and 1898 issues, postage due and official stamps. See notes following those issues.
For overprints see Nos. O1-O10.

Perforation Varieties

Imperfs and part perfs of all the Seebeck issues, Nos. 20-120, exist for all except originals of the 1898 issue, Nos. 99-109M.

Goddess of Plenty — A6

1891			Engr.	
30	A6	1c yellow brn	.25	.35
31	A6	2c red	.25	.35
32	A6	5c dk blue	.25	.25
33	A6	10c slate	.25	.50
34	A6	20c plum	.25	2.00
35	A6	50c purple	.25	5.00
36	A6	1p black brn	.25	5.00
37	A6	2p green	.25	8.50
38	A6	5p brown red	.25	
39	A6	10p orange	.25	
		Nos. 30-39 (10)	2.50	

For overprints see Nos. O11-O20.

Columbus Sighting Land — A7

1892

			Engr.	
40	A7	1c yellow brn	.25	.25
41	A7	2c vermilion	.25	.25
42	A7	5c dk blue	.25	.25
43	A7	10c slate	.25	.25
44	A7	20c plum	.25	2.00
45	A7	50c purple	.25	7.00
46	A7	1p brown	.25	7.00
47	A7	2p blue grn	.25	8.50
48	A7	5p rose lake	.25	
49	A7	10p orange	.25	
		Nos. 40-49 (10)	2.50	

Commemorative of the 400th anniversary of the discovery of America by Columbus.

Stamps of the 1892 design were printed in other colors than those listed and overprinted "Telegrafos". The 1c blue, 10c orange, 20c slate, 50c plum and 2p vermilion are telegraph stamps which did not receive the overprint.

For overprints see Nos. O21-O30.

Arms — A8

1893

			Engr.	
51	A8	1c yellow brn	.25	.25
52	A8	2c vermilion	.25	.25
53	A8	5c dk blue	.25	.25
54	A8	10c slate	.25	.25
55	A8	20c dull red	.25	1.50
56	A8	50c violet	.25	4.00
57	A8	1p dk brown	.25	7.00
58	A8	2p blue green	.25	8.50
59	A8	5p rose lake	.25	
60	A8	10p orange	.25	
		Nos. 51-60 (10)	2.50	

The 1c blue and 2c dark brown are telegraph stamps which did not receive the "Telegrafos" overprint.

For overprints see Nos. O31-O41.

"Victory" — A9

1894

			Engr.	
61	A9	1c yellow brn	.25	.30
62	A9	2c vermilion	.25	.40
63	A9	5c dp blue	.25	.30
64	A9	10c slate	.25	.40
65	A9	20c lake	.25	2.00
66	A9	50c purple	.25	5.00
67	A9	1p brown	.25	9.50
68	A9	2p green	.25	17.50
69	A9	5p deep green red	.25	45.00
70	A9	10p orange	.25	45.00
		Nos. 61-70 (10)	2.50	125.40

There were three printings of this issue. Only the first is known postally used. Unused values are for the third printing.

Used values are for stamps with "DIRECCION" cancels in black that were removed from post office new year cards.

Specialists believe the 25c yellow green, type A9, is a telegraph denomination never issued for postal purposes. Stamps in other colors are telegraph stamps without the usual "Telegrafos" overprint.

For overprints see Nos. O42-O51.

Coat of Arms — A10

1895

			Engr.	
71	A10	1c yellow brn	.25	.30
72	A10	2c vermilion	.25	.30
73	A10	5c deep blue	.25	.25
74	A10	10c slate	.25	.25
75	A10	20c claret	.25	.75
76	A10	50c light violet	50.00	5.00
77	A10	1p dark brown	.25	5.00
78	A10	2p deep green	.25	8.00
79	A10	5p brown red	.25	11.00
80	A10	10p orange	.25	
		Nos. 71-80 (10)	52.25	

Frames of Nos. 71-80 differ for each denomination.

A 50c violet blue exists. Its status is questioned. Value 25c.

There was little proper use of No. 80. Canceled examples are almost always c-t-o or have faked cancels.

For overprints see Nos. O52-O71.

Map of Nicaragua — A11

1896

			Engr.	
81	A11	1c violet	.30	1.00
82	A11	2c blue grn	.30	.50
83	A11	5c brt rose	.30	.30
84	A11	10c blue	.50	.50
85	A11	20c bister brn	3.00	4.00
86	A11	50c blue gray	.60	8.00
87	A11	1p black	.75	11.00
88	A11	2p claret	.75	15.00
89	A11	5p deep blue	.75	15.00
		Nos. 81-89 (9)	7.25	55.30

There were two printings of this issue. Only the first is known postally used. Unused values are for the second printing.

See italic note after No. 109M.

For overprints see Nos. O82-O117.

Wmk. 117

89A	A11	1c violet	3.75	.90
89B	A11	2c bl grn	3.75	1.25
89C	A11	5c brt rose	15.00	.30
89D	A11	10c blue	25.00	.90
89E	A11	20c bis brn	22.50	4.25
89F	A11	50c bl gray	42.50	9.00
89G	A11	1p black	37.50	12.50
89H	A11	2p claret		18.00
89I	A11	5p dp bl		40.00

Same, dated 1897

			Engr.	Unwmk.
90	A11	1c violet	.50	.50
91	A11	2c bl grn	.50	.60
92	A11	5c brt rose	.50	.30
93	A11	10c blue	6.25	.75
94	A11	20c bis brn	2.50	3.75
95	A11	50c bl gray	9.00	9.50
96	A11	1p black	9.00	15.00
97	A11	2p claret	20.00	19.00
98	A11	5p dp bl	20.00	42.50
		Nos. 90-98 (9)	68.25	91.90

See italic note after No. 109M.

Wmk. 117

98A	A11	1c violet	14.00	.50
98B	A11	2c bl grn	14.00	.50
98C	A11	5c brt rose	20.00	.40
98D	A11	10c blue	22.50	.90
98E	A11	20c bis brn	22.50	4.25
98F	A11	50c bl gray	22.50	8.00
98G	A11	1p black	25.00	16.00
98H	A11	2p claret	25.00	25.00
98I	A11	5p dp bl	125.00	50.00
		Nos. 98A-98I (9)	290.50	105.55

Coat of Arms of "Republic of Central America" — A12

1898

			Engr.	Wmk. 117
99	A12	1c brown	.25	.40
100	A12	2c slate	.25	.40
101	A12	4c red brown	.25	.50
102	A12	5c olive green	40.00	22.50
103	A12	10c violet	15.00	.60
104	A12	15c ultra	.40	1.50
105	A12	20c blue	10.00	2.00
106	A12	50c yellow	10.00	9.50
107	A12	1p violet blue	.40	16.00
108	A12	2p brown	19.00	22.50
109	A12	5p orange	25.00	32.50
		Nos. 99-109 (11)	120.55	108.40

Unwmk.

109A	A12	1c brown	1.25	.30
109B	A12	2c slate	1.25	
109D	A12	4c red brown	2.25	.60
109E	A12	5c olive green	25.00	.25
109G	A12	10c violet	25.00	.60
109H	A12	15c ultra	25.00	
109I	A12	20c blue	25.00	
109J	A12	50c yellow	25.00	
109K	A12	1p deep ultra	25.00	
109L	A12	2p olive brown	25.00	
109M	A12	5p orange	25.00	
		Nos. 109A-109M (11)	204.75	

The paper of Nos. 109A to 109M is slightly thicker and more opaque than that of Nos. 81 to 89 and 90 to 98. The 5c and 10c also exist on very thin, semi-transparent paper.

Many reprints of Nos. 81-98, 98F-98H, 99-109M are on thick, porous paper, with and

---

without watermark. The watermark is sideways. Paper of the originals is thinner for Nos. 81-109 but thicker for Nos. 109A-109M. Value 25c each.

In addition, reprints of Nos. 81-89 and 90-98 exist on thin paper, but with shades differing slightly from those of originals.

For overprints see Nos. O118-O128.

"Justice" — A13

1899

			Litho.	
110	A13	1c gray grn	.25	.35
111	A13	2c brown	.25	.25
112	A13	4c dp rose	.35	.40
113	A13	5c dp bl	.25	.25
114	A13	10c buff	.25	.30
115	A13	15c chocolate	.25	.65
116	A13	20c dk grn	.35	.75
117	A13	50c brt rose	.25	3.00
118	A13	1p red	.25	8.50
119	A13	2p violet	.25	20.00
120	A13	5p lt bl	.25	25.00
		Nos. 110-120 (11)	2.95	59.45

Nos. 110-120 exist imperf. and in horizontal pairs imperf. between.

Nos. 110-111, 113 exist perf 6x12 due to defective perforating equipment.

For overprints see Nos. O129-O139.

Mt. Momotombo A14

Imprint: "American Bank Note Co. NY"

1900, Jan. 1

			Engr.	
121	A14	1c plum	.50	.25
122	A14	2c vermilion	.50	.25
123	A14	3c green	.75	.25
124	A14	4c ol grn	1.00	.25
125	A14	5c dk bl	4.00	.25
126	A14	6c car rose	14.00	5.00
127	A14	10c violet	7.00	.25
128	A14	15c ultra	8.00	.65
129	A14	20c brown	8.00	.65
130	A14	50c lake	7.00	1.10
131	A14	1p yellow	12.00	4.00
132	A14	2p salmon	10.00	2.25
133	A14	5p black	10.00	3.00
		Nos. 121-133 (13)	82.75	18.15

Used values for #123, 126, 130-133 are for canceled to order examples.

See Nos. 159-161. For overprints and surcharges see Nos. 134-136, 144-151, 162-163, 175-178, O150-O154, 1L1-1L13, 1L16-1L19, 1L20, 2L1-2L10, 2L16-2L24, 2L36-2L39.

Mt. Momotombo — A14a

1902

	White Wove Paper		*Imperf.*
	Size: 55x52mm		
133A	A14a	5c blue	
133B	A14a	10c red violet	
133C	A14a	20c brown	
133D	A14a	30c black green	
133E	A14a	50c red	

51x51mm

133F	A14a	2c dk red, *buff*	
133G	A14a	4c red brown, *buff*	

Nos. 133A-133G are documented on covers postmarked from 1902-04. Specimen pairs and blocks are from sheets of 35 (Nos. 133A-133E) or 28 (Nos. 133F-133G) sold in the 1990 American Bank Note Company archives sale. Nos. 133A-133G are not cutouts from similar postal envelopes issued in 1900.

Nos. 131-133 Surcharged in Black or Red

1901, Mar. 5

134	A14	2c on 1p yel	5.00	3.00
a.		Bar below date	14.00	9.00
b.		Inverted surcharge		35.00
c.		Double surcharge		50.00
135	A14	10c on 5p blk (R)	6.50	4.50
a.		Bar below date	14.00	8.00
136	A14	20c on 2p salmon	7.50	7.50
a.		Bar below date	14.00	10.00
		Nos. 134-136 (3)	19.00	15.00

A 2c surcharge on No. 121, the 1c plum, was not put on sale, though some are known used from a few sheets distributed by the post office to "government friends."

The 2c on 1p yellow without ornaments is a reprint.

Postage Due Stamps of 1900 Overprinted in Black or Gold

1901, Mar.

137	D3	1c plum	4.50	3.50
138	D3	2c vermilion	4.50	3.50
139	D3	5c dk bl	6.00	3.50
140	D3	10c pur (G)	8.50	5.00
a.		Double overprint	14.00	14.00
141	D3	20c dp grn	10.00	6.50
142	D3	30c dk grn	10.00	6.50
143	D3	50c lake	8.50	4.00
a.		"1091" for "1901"	35.00	35.00
b.		"Correo"	37.50	
		Nos. 137-143 (7)	52.00	32.50

In 1904 an imitation of this overprint was made to fill a dealer's order. The date is at top and "Correos" at bottom. The overprint is printed in black, sideways on the 1c and 2c and upright on the 5c and 10c. Some examples of the 2c were further surcharged "1 Centavo." None of these stamps was ever regularly used.

Nos. 126, 131-133 Surcharged

1901, Oct. 20 — Black Surcharge

144	A14	3c on 6c rose	6.00	5.00
a.		Bar below value	7.00	5.50
b.		Inverted surcharge	8.00	8.00
c.		Double surcharge	8.00	8.00
d.		Double surch., one inverted	25.00	25.00
145	A14	4c on 6c rose	5.00	4.00
a.		Bar below value	5.50	4.50
b.		"1 cent" instead of "4 cent"	8.00	8.00
c.		Double surcharge	20.00	20.00
146	A14	5c on 1p yellow	5.00	4.00
a.		Three bars below value	6.00	4.50
b.		Ornaments at each side of "1901"	6.00	4.50
c.		Double surcharge, one in red	15.00	15.00
147	A14	10c on 2p salmon	5.50	4.00
a.		Inverted surcharge	12.50	12.50
b.		Double surcharge		

Blue Surcharge

148	A14	3c on 6c rose	6.00	4.50
a.		Bar below value	7.00	5.50
b.		Double surcharge	8.00	8.00
149	A14	4c on 6c rose	6.50	5.00
a.		Bar below value	7.50	7.50
b.		"1 cent" instead of "4 cent"	10.00	10.00
c.		Inverted surcharge	20.00	20.00

Red Surcharge

150	A14	5c on 1p yellow	7.50	6.50
a.		Three bars below value	9.00	7.00
b.		Ornaments at each side of "1901"	9.00	7.00
c.		Inverted surcharge	12.00	12.00
d.		Double surcharge, inverted	17.50	17.50
151	A14	20c on 5p black	5.00	3.50
a.		Inverted surcharge	16.00	16.00
b.		Double surcharge	22.50	22.50
c.		Triple surcharge		
		Nos. 144-151 (8)	46.50	36.50

In 1904 a series was surcharged as above, but with "Centavos" spelled out. About the same time No. 122 was surcharged "1 cent" and "1901," "1902" or "1904." All of these surcharges were made to fill a dealer's order and none of the stamps was regularly issued or used.

Postage Due Stamps
of 1900 Overprinted
in Black

1901, Oct.

152	D3	1c red violet	1.00	.40
a.		Ornaments at each side of the stamp	1.10	.65
b.		Ornaments at each side of "1901"	1.10	.65
c.		"Correos" in italics	1.50	1.50
d.		Double overprint	14.00	14.00
153	D3	2c vermilion	.75	.40
a.		Double overprint	8.50	5.50
154	D3	5c dark blue	1.00	.60
a.		Double overprint, one inverted		
b.		Double overprint	7.00	7.00
155	D3	10c purple	1.00	.60
a.		Double overprint	10.00	10.00
c.		Double overprint, one inverted	12.00	12.00
156	D3	20c org brn	1.25	1.25
a.		Double overprint	7.00	7.00
157	D3	30c dk grn	1.00	1.10
a.		Double overprint	9.00	9.00
b.		Inverted overprint	19.00	19.00
158	D3	50c lake	1.00	1.10
a.		Triple overprint	25.00	25.00
b.		Double overprint	16.00	16.00
		Nos. 152-158 (7)	7.00	5.45

One stamp in each group of 25 has the 2nd "o" of "Correos" italic. Value twice normal.

Momotombo Type of 1900
Without Imprint

1902 **Litho.** **Perf. 14**

159	A14	5c blue	.50	.25
a.		Imperf., pair	3.75	
160	A14	5c carmine	.50	.25
a.		Imperf., pair	3.75	
161	A14	10c violet	1.50	.25
a.		Imperf., pair	3.75	
		Nos. 159-161 (3)	2.50	.75

No. 161 was privately surcharged 6c, 1p and 5p in black in 1903. Not fully authorized but known postally used. Value of c-t-o peso denominations, $5 each.

Nos. 121 and
122 Surcharged
in Black

1902, Oct. **Perf. 12**

162	A14	15c on 2c ver	2.00	.75
a.		Double surcharge	32.50	
b.		Blue surcharge	90.00	
163	A14	30c on 1c plum	1.00	2.25
a.		Double surcharge	9.00	
b.		Inverted surcharge	27.50	

Counterfeits of No. 163 exist in slightly smaller type.

President José
Santos Zelaya — A15

1903, Jan. **Engr.**

167	A15	1c emer & blk	.35	.50
168	A15	2c rose & blk	.70	.50
169	A15	5c ultra & blk	.35	.50
170	A15	10c yel & blk	.35	.85
171	A15	15c lake & blk	.60	2.00
172	A15	20c vio & blk	.60	2.00
173	A15	50c ol & blk	.60	5.00
174	A15	1p red brn & blk	.60	6.00
		Nos. 167-174 (8)	4.15	17.35

10th anniv. of 1st election of Pres. Zelaya.
The so-called color errors-1c orange yellow and black, 2c ultramarine and black, 5c lake and black and 10c emerald and black-were also delivered to postal authorities. They were intended for official use though not issued as such. Value, $4 each.

No. 161 Surcharged in Blue

Nos. 175-176

No. 177

1904-05

175	A14	5c on 10c vio ('05)	1.75	.25
a.		Inverted surcharge	2.00	1.40
b.		Without ornaments	2.00	.70
c.		Character for "cents" inverted	1.75	.40
d.		As "b," inverted		
e.		As "c," inverted	2.75	2.75
f.		Double surcharge	8.00	8.00
g.		"5" omitted	2.75	2.75
176	A14	15c on 10c vio ('05)	.30	.25
a.		Inverted surcharge	1.40	1.40
b.		Without ornaments	1.40	1.40
c.		Character for "cents" inverted	1.10	1.10
d.		As "b," inverted		
e.		As "c," inverted	1.75	1.75
f.		Imperf.	6.50	
h.		As "a," imperf.	9.00	9.00
i.		Double surcharge	14.00	14.00
177	A14	15c on 10c vio	4.50	2.75
a.		Inverted surcharge	6.00	6.00
b.		"Centcvos"	6.00	4.50
c.		"5" of "15" omitted	7.50	
d.		As "b," inverted	8.50	8.50
e.		Double surcharge	11.00	11.00
f.		Double surcharge, inverted	13.00	13.00
g.		Imperf., pair	9.00	9.00
		Nos. 175-177 (3)	6.55	3.30

There are two settings of the surcharge on No. 175. In the 1st the character for "cents" and the figure "5" are 2mm apart and in the 2nd 4mm.
The 2c vermilion, No. 122, with surcharge "1 cent. / 1904" was not issued.

No. 161
Surcharged in
Black

1905, June

178	A14	5c on 10c violet	.60	.35
a.		Inverted surcharge	2.75	2.75
b.		Double surcharge	4.50	4.50
c.		Surcharge in blue	75.00	

Coat of Arms — A18

Imprint: "American Bank Note Co. NY"

1905, July 25 **Engr.** **Perf. 12**

179	A18	1c green	.30	.25
180	A18	2c car rose	.30	.25
181	A18	3c violet	.45	.25
182	A18	4c org red	.45	.25
183	A18	5c blue	.45	.25
184	A18	6c slate	.60	.40
185	A18	10c yel brn	.85	.25
186	A18	15c brn olive	.75	.35
187	A18	20c lake	.60	.40
188	A18	50c orange	3.00	1.50
189	A18	1p black	1.50	1.50
190	A18	2p dk grn	1.50	2.00
191	A18	5p violet	1.75	2.50
		Nos. 179-191 (13)	12.50	10.15

See Nos. 202-208, 237-248. For overprints and surcharges see Nos. 193-201, 212-216, 235-236, 249-265, O187-O198, O210-O222, 1L21-1L62, 1L73-1L95, 1LO1-1LO3, 2L26-2L35, 2L42-2L46, 2L48-2L72, 2LO1-2LO4.

Nos. 179-184 and
191 Surcharged in
Black or Red
Reading Up or Down

1906-08

193	A18	10c on 2c car rose (up)	7.00	4.00
a.		Surcharge reading down	13.00	13.00
194	A18	10c on 3c vio (up)	.40	.25
a.		"c" normal	2.75	1.35
b.		Double surcharge	4.50	4.50
c.		Double surch., up and down	7.00	5.00
d.		Pair, one without surcharge	9.50	
e.		Surcharge reading down	.30	.25
195	A18	10c on 4c org red (up) ('08)	35.00	20.00
a.		Surcharge reading down	32.50	22.50
196	A18	15c on 1c grn (up)	.60	.30
a.		Double surcharge	7.50	7.50
b.		Dbl. surch., one reading down	11.00	11.00
c.		Surcharge reading down	.40	.25
197	A18	20c on 2c car rose (down) ('07)	.50	.30
a.		Double surcharge	13.00	13.00
b.		Surcharge reading up	37.50	32.50
c.		"V" omitted	10.00	10.00
198	A18	20c on 5c bl (down)	.75	.50
a.		Surcharge reading up	35.00	
199	A18	50c on 6c sl (R) (down)	.60	.50
a.		Double surcharge		
b.		Surcharge reading up	30.00	30.00
c.		Yellow brown surcharge	.60	.40
200	A18	1p on 5p vio (down) ('07)	42.50	25.00
		Nos. 193-200 (8)	87.55	50.85

There are several settings of these surcharges and many varieties in the shapes of the figures, the spacing, etc.

Surcharged in Red
Vertically Reading
Up

1908, May

201	A18	35c on 6c slate	3.00	2.25
a.		Double surcharge (R)	25.00	
b.		Double surcharge (R + Bk)	65.00	
c.		Carmine surcharge	3.00	2.25

Arms Type of 1905
Imprint: "Waterlow & Sons, Ltd."

1907, Feb. **Perf. 14 to 15**

202	A18	1c green	.70	.40
203	A18	2c rose	.80	.25
204	A18	4c brn org	2.00	.30
205	A18	10c yel brn	3.00	.25
206	A18	15c brn olive	4.50	.90
207	A18	20c lake	8.00	1.25
208	A18	50c orange	20.00	4.25
		Nos. 202-208 (7)	39.00	7.60

Nos. 202-204, 207-208 Surcharged in
Black or Blue (Bl)
Reading Down

1907-08

212	A18	10c on 2c rose	1.50	.50
a.		Double surcharge		10.00
b.		"Vale" only		22.50
c.		Surcharge reading up	14.00	6.50
213	A18	10c on 4c brn org (up) ('08)	2.25	.85
a.		Double surcharge		10.00
b.		Surcharge reading down		5.50
214	A18	10c on 20c lake ('08)	3.25	1.40
b.		Surcharge reading up		80.00
215	A18	10c on 50c org (Bl) ('08)	2.00	.60
216	A18	10c on 1c grn ('08)	32.50	4.00
		Nos. 212-216 (5)	41.50	7.35

Several settings of this surcharge provide varieties of numeral font, spacing, etc.

Revenue Stamps
Overprinted "CORREO-1908" — A19

1908, June

217	A19	5c yel & blk	.60	.40
a.		"CORROE"	2.75	2.75
b.		Overprint reading down		7.00
c.		Double overprint		13.00

218	A19	10c lt bl & blk	.50	.25
a.		Double overprint	4.50	4.50
b.		Overprint reading down	.50	.25
c.		Double overprint, up and down	13.00	13.00
219	A19	1p yel brn & blk	.50	2.00
a.		"CORROE"	7.50	7.50
220	A19	2p pearl gray & blk	.50	2.50
a.		"CORROE"	10.00	10.00
		Nos. 217-220 (4)	2.10	5.15

The overprint exists on a 5p in green (value $200) and on a 50p in black (value $300).

Revenue Stamps
Surcharged Vertically
Reading Up in Red
(1c, 15c), Blue(2c),
Green (4c) or Orange
(35c)

221	A19	1c on 5c yel & blk	.40	.25
a.		"1008"	1.50	1.50
b.		"8908"	1.50	1.50
c.		Surcharge reading down	4.00	4.00
d.		Double surcharge	4.00	4.00
222	A19	2c on 5c yel & blk	.50	.30
b.		"ORREO"	1.75	1.75
c.		"1008"	1.75	1.75
d.		"8908"	1.75	1.75
f.		Double surcharge	7.00	7.00
g.		Double surcharge, one inverted	7.00	7.00
h.		Surcharge reading down	9.00	9.00
223	A19	4c on 5c yel & blk	.65	.35
a.		"ORREO"	2.50	2.50
b.		"1008"	2.00	2.00
c.		"8908"	2.00	2.00
224	A19	15c on 50c ol & blk	.60	.40
a.		"1008"	2.50	2.50
b.		"8908"	2.00	2.00
c.		Surcharge reading down	10.00	10.00
225	A19	35c on 50c ol & blk	4.00	1.00
a.		Double surcharge, one inverted	12.00	12.00
b.		Surcharge reading down	12.00	12.00
		Double surcharge, one in black		
		Nos. 221-225 (5)	6.15	2.30

For surcharges and overprints see Nos. 225D-225H, 230-234, 266-278, 1L63-1L72A, 1L96-1L106, 2L47.

Revenue Stamps
Surcharged Vertically
Reading Up in Blue,
Black or Orange

1908, Nov.

225D	A19	2c on 5c yel & blk (Bl)	20.00	12.50
e.		"9c" instead of "2c"	75.00	75.00
225F	A19	10c on 50c ol & blk (Bk)	850.00	325.00
g.		Double surcharge	425.00	
225H	A19	35c on 50c ol & blk (O)	17.50	10.00

In this setting there are three types of the character for "cents."

Revenue Stamps Overprinted or Surcharged in Various Colors

No. 226

No. 227

1908, Dec.

226		2c org (Bk)	3.50	2.00
a.		Double overprint	6.00	6.00
b.		Overprint reading up	5.00	5.00
227		4c on 2c org (Bk)	1.75	.90
a.		Surcharge reading up	5.00	5.00
b.		Blue surcharge	80.00	80.00
228		5c on 2c org (Bl)	1.50	.60
a.		Surcharge reading up	6.00	6.00
229		10c on 2c org (G)	1.50	.30
a.		"1988" for "1908"	4.00	3.00
b.		Surcharge reading up	5.00	5.00

c. "c" inverted 4.00 4.00
d. Double surcharge 7.50
Nos. 226-229 (4) 8.25 3.80

Two printings of No. 229 exist. In the first, the initial of "VALE" is a small capital, and in the second a large capital.

The overprint "Correos-1908." 35mm long, handstamped on 1c blue revenue stamp of type A20, is private and fraudulent.

Revenue Stamps Surcharged in Various Colors

1909, Feb.   **Color: Olive & Black**
230 A19 1c on 50c (V) 4.00 1.60
231 A19 2c on 50c (Br) 7.00 3.00
232 A19 4c on 50c (G) 7.00 3.00
233 A19 5c on 50c (C) 4.00 1.75
  a. Double surcharge 12.50 12.50
234 A19 10c on 50c (Bk) 1.10 .75
Nos. 230-234 (5) 23.10 10.10

Nos. 230 to 234 are found with three types of the character for "cents."

Nos. 190 and 191 Surcharged in Black

1909, Mar.   **Perf. 12**
235 A18 10c on 2p dk grn 20.00 12.00
236 A18 10c on 5p vio *100.00 70.00*

There are three types of the character for "cents."

Arms Type of 1905
Imprint: "American Bank Note Co. NY"
1909, Mar.
237 A18 1c yel grn .35 .25
238 A18 2c vermilion .35 .25
239 A18 3c red org .35 .25
240 A18 4c violet .35 .25
241 A18 5c dp bl .35 .25
242 A18 6c gray brn 3.00 1.50
243 A18 10c lake .85 .25
244 A18 15c black .85 .25
245 A18 20c brn olive .85 .25
246 A18 50c dp grn 1.25 .40
247 A18 1p yellow 1.25 .40
248 A18 2p car rose 1.00 .40
Nos. 237-248 (12) 10.80 4.70

Nos. 239 and 244, Surcharged in Black or Red

1910, July
249 A18 2c on 3c red org 2.75 1.10
250 A18 10c on 15c blk (R) 1.25 .30
  a. "VLEA" 3.50 2.00
  b. Double surcharge 17.50 17.50

There are two types of the character for "cents."

Nos. 239, 244, 245 Surcharged in Black or Red

1910
252 A18 2c on 3c (Bk) 1.50 1.25
  a. Double surcharge 6.00 6.00
  b. Pair, one without surcharge
  c. "Vale" omitted 10.00 10.00
254 A18 5c on 20c (R) .40 .30
  a. Double surcharge (R) 6.00 5.00
  b. Inverted surcharge (R) 3.50 2.50
  c. Black surcharge 100.00
  d. Double surcharge (Bk) 140.00
  e. Inverted surcharge (Bk) 110.00

255 A18 10c on 15c (Bk) .90 .30
  a. "c" omitted 2.00 1.10
  b. "10c" omitted 2.50 1.50
  c. Inverted surcharge 4.00 4.00
  d. Double surcharge 6.00 6.00
  e. Double surch., one inverted 12.00
Nos. 252-255 (3) 2.80 1.85

There are several minor varieties in this setting, such as italic "L" and "E" and fancy "V" in "VALE," small italic "C," and italic "I" for "1" in "10."

Nos. 239, 244, 246 and 247, Surcharged in Black

1910, Dec. 10
256 A18 2c on 3c red org .85 .45
  a. Without period 1.00 .75
  b. Inverted surcharge 6.00 6.00
  c. Double surcharge 6.00 6.00
257 A18 10c on 15c blk 2.00 .75
  a. Without period 3.50 1.25
  b. Double surcharge 3.50 3.00
  c. Inverted surcharge 5.00 5.00
258 A18 10c on 50c dp grn 1.25 .40
  a. Without period 1.50 .75
  b. Double surcharge 3.00 3.00
  c. Inverted surcharge 3.00 3.00
259 A18 10c on 1p yel .90 .40
  a. Without period 1.25 .75
  b. Double surcharge 3.00 3.00
Nos. 256-259 (4) 5.00 2.00

The 15c on 50c deep green is a telegraph stamp from which the "Telegrafos" overprint was omitted. It appears to have been pressed into postal service, as all examples are used with postal cancels. Value $450.

Nos. 240, 244-248 Surcharged in Black

Surcharge as on Nos. 256-259 but lines wider apart.

1911, Mar.
260 A18 2c on 4c vio .30 .25
  a. "c" omitted .35 .30
  b. Double surcharge 3.50 3.00
  c. Double surcharge, inverted 4.00 4.00
  d. Double surcharge, one invtd. 3.50 3.50
  e. Inverted surcharge 7.50 7.50
261 A18 5c on 20c brn ol .30 .25
  a. Without period .60 .50
  b. Double surcharge 2.50 2.50
  c. Inverted surcharge 2.50 2.00
  d. Double surcharge, one invtd. 6.00 6.00
262 A18 10c on 15c blk .40 .25
  a. Without period 1.00 .50
  b. "Yale" 12.00 12.00
  c. Double surcharge 3.00 3.00
  d. Inverted surcharge 3.00 3.00
  e. Double surch., one inverted 5.00 4.00
  f. Double surch., both inverted 12.00 12.00
263 A18 10c on 50c dp grn .25 .25
  a. Without period 1.00 .50
  b. Double surcharge 3.00 2.50
  c. Double surcharge, one invtd. 5.00 4.00
  d. Inverted surcharge 5.00 5.00
264 A18 10c on 1p yel 1.50 .40
  a. Without period 2.00 1.50
  b. Double surcharge 4.00 4.00
  c. Double surcharge, one invtd. 7.50
265 A18 10c on 2p car rose .60 .50
  a. Without period 2.00 1.50
  b. Double surcharge 2.50 2.50
  c. Double surcharge, one invtd. 6.00 6.00
  d. Inverted surcharge 6.00 6.00
Nos. 260-265 (6) 3.35 1.90

Revenue Stamps Surcharged in Black

1911, Apr. 10   **Perf. 14 to 15**
266 A19 2c on 5p dl bl 1.00 1.25
  a. Without period 1.25 *1.50*
  b. Double surcharge 2.50 2.00
267 A19 2c on 5p ultra .35 *.40*
  a. Without period .75 1.25
  b. Double surcharge *3.50*
268 A19 5c on 10p pink .75 .40
  a. Without period 1.50 1.50
  b. "cte" for "cts" 1.50 1.00
  c. Double surcharge 4.00 4.00
  d. Inverted surcharge 2.50 2.50

269 A19 10c on 25c lilac .40 .25
  a. Without period 1.00 .75
  b. "cte" for "cts" 1.25 1.00
  c. Inverted surcharge 4.00 4.00
  d. Double surcharge 2.50 2.50
  e. Double surcharge, one inverted 4.00 4.00
270 A19 10c on 2p gray .40 .25
  a. Without period 1.00 .75
  b. "cte" for "cts" 1.25 1.00
  c. Double surcharge 5.00 5.00
  d. Double surcharge, one inverted 4.00 3.00
271 A19 35c on 1p brown .40 .30
  a. Without period 1.00 .75
  b. "cte" for "cts" 1.25 1.00
  c. "Corre" 1.50 1.50
  d. Double surcharge 2.50 2.50
  e. Double surcharge, one inverted 2.50 2.50
  f. Double surcharge inverted 3.00 3.00
  g. Inverted surcharge 5.00
Nos. 266-271 (6) 3.30 2.85

These surcharges are in settings of twenty-five. One stamp in each setting has a large square period after "cts" and two have no period. One of the 2c has no space between "02" and "cts" and one 5c has a small thin "s" in "Correos."

Surcharged in Black

1911, June
272 A19 5c on 2p gray 1.50 1.00
  a. Inverted surcharge 6.00 5.00

In this setting one stamp has a large square period and another has a thick up-right "c" in "cts."

Surcharged in Black

1911, June 12
273 A19 5c on 25c lilac 1.50 1.25
274 A19 5c on 50c ol grn 5.00 5.00
275 A19 5c on 5p blue 7.00 7.00
276 A19 5c on 5p ultra 6.00 6.00
  a. Inverted surcharge 45.00
277 A19 5c on 50p ver 5.00 5.00
278 A19 10c on 50c ol grn 1.50 1.00
Nos. 273-278 (6) 26.00 24.75

This setting has the large square period and the thick "c" in "cts." Many of the stamps have no period after "cts." Owing to broken type and defective impressions letters sometimes appear to be omitted.

A21

Revenue Stamps Surcharged on the Back in Black

a   b

Railroad coupon tax stamps (1st class red and 2nd class blue) are the basic stamps of Nos. 279-294. They were first surcharged for revenue use in 1903 in two types: I — "Timbre Fiscal" and "ctvs." II — "TIMBRE FISCAL" and "cents" (originally intended for use in Bluefields).

1911, July
279 A21 (a) 2c on 5c on 2 bl .25 .30
  a. New value in yellow on face 6.00 6.00
  b. New value in black on face 10.00 5.00
  c. New value in red on face 100.00

d. Inverted surcharge .75
e. Double surch., one inverted 7.50 7.50
f. "TIMBRE FISCAL" in black .75 .75
280 A21 (b) 2c on 5c on 2 bl .25 .30
  a. New value in yellow on face 3.00 3.00
  b. New value in black on face 9.00 4.00
  c. New value in red on face 100.00
  d. Inverted surcharge .90 1.00
  e. Double surch., one inverted 7.50 7.50
  f. "TIMBRE FISCAL" in black 1.00 1.00
281 A21 (a) 5c on 5c on 2 bl .25 .25
  a. Inverted surcharge .50 .35
  b. "TIMBRE FISCAL" in black 1.00 1.00
  c. New value in yellow on face
282 A21 (b) 5c on 5c on 2 bl .25 .25
  a. Inverted surcharge .40 .35
  b. "TIMBRE FISCAL" in black 1.00 1.00
  c. New value in yellow on face
283 A21 (a) 10c on 5c on 2 bl .25 .25
  a. Inverted surcharge .75 .50
  b. "TIMBRE FISCAL" in black 1.00 1.00
  c. New value in yellow on face *100.00*
  d. Double surcharge 6.00 6.00
284 A21 (b) 10c on 5c on 2 bl .25 .25
  a. Inverted surcharge .75 .50
  b. "TIMBRE FISCAL" in black 1.00 1.00
  c. Double surcharge 6.00 6.00
  d. New value in yellow on face *110.00*
285 A21 (a) 15c on 10c on 1 red .25 .25
  a. Inverted surcharge 1.00 1.25
  b. "Timbre Fiscal" double 5.00
286 A21 (b) 15c on 10c on 1 red .40 .35
  a. Inverted surcharge 1.00 1.00
  b. "Timbre Fiscal" double 5.00
Nos. 279-286 (8) 2.15 2.20

These surcharges are in settings of 20. For listing, they are separated into small and large figures, but there are many other varieties due to type and arrangement.

The colored surcharges on the face of the stamps were trial printings. These were then surcharged in black on the reverse. The olive yellow surcharge on the face of the 2c was later applied to prevent use as a 5c revenue stamps. Other colors known on the face are orange and green. Forgeries exist.

For overprints and surcharges see Nos. 287-294, O223-O244, 1L107-1L108.

Surcharged on the Face in Black

1911, Oct.
287 A21 2c on 10c on 1 red 6.50 6.50
  a. Inverted surcharge 1.40 1.40
  b. Double surcharge 10.00 10.00
288 A21 20c on 10c on 1 red 4.50 4.50
  a. Inverted surcharge 5.25 5.00
289 A21 50c on 10c on 1 red 5.25 4.50
  a. Inverted surcharge 10.00 10.00
Nos. 287-289 (3) 16.25 15.50

There are two varieties of the figures "2" and "5" in this setting.

Surcharged on the Back in Black

1911, Nov.
289B A21 5c on 10c on 1 red 37.50
  c. Inverted surcharge 20.00
289D A21 10c on 10c on 1 red 12.50
  e. Inverted surcharge 24.00

Surcharged on the Face

1911, Dec.
Dark Blue Postal Surcharge
290 A21 2c on 10c on 1 red .25 .25
  a. Inverted surcharge 2.50 2.50
  b. Double surcharge 5.00 5.00
291 A21 5c on 10c on 1 red .30 .25
  a. Double surcharge 2.50 2.50
  b. Inverted surcharge 2.50 2.50

292	A21	10c on 10c on 1 red	.35 .25
a.		Inverted surcharge	2.50 2.50
b.		Double surcharge	2.50 2.50
c.		"TIMBRE FISCAL" on back	3.50 3.50

Black Postal Surcharge

293	A21	10c on 10c on 1 red	1.50 1.00
a.		Inverted surcharge	7.00 7.00
b.		New value surch. on back	12.00 12.00

Red Postal Surcharge

293C	A21	5c on 5c on 2 blue	1.40 1.25
d.		"TIMBRE FISCAL" in black	2.50 1.75
e.		"5" omitted	3.75 3.75
f.		Inverted surcharge	4.75 4.75
		Nos. 290-293C (5)	3.80 3.00

Bar Overprinted on
No. O234 in Dark Blue

294	A21	10c on 10c on 1 red	1.25 1.00
a.		Inverted surcharge	2.50 2.50
b.		Bar at foot of stamp	5.00 5.00

Nos. 290-294 each have three varieties of the numerals in the surcharge.

"Liberty" — A22   Coat of Arms — A23

1912, Jan.   Engr.   Perf. 14, 15

295	A22	1c yel grn	.30 .25
296	A22	2c carmine	.40 .25
297	A22	3c yel brn	.30 .25
298	A22	4c brn vio	.30 .25
299	A22	5c blue & blk	.25 .25
300	A22	6c olive bister	.30 .80
301	A22	10c red brn	.25 .25
302	A22	15c vio	.25 .25
303	A22	20c red	.25 .25
304	A22	25c blue grn & blk	.30 .25
305	A23	35c grn & chnt	2.00 1.50
306	A22	50c lt blue	1.00 .40
307	A22	1p org	1.40 2.00
308	A22	2p dark blue grn	1.50 2.25
309	A22	5p blk	3.50 3.50
		Nos. 295-309 (15)	12.30 12.70

For overprints and surcharges see Nos. 310-324, 337A-348, 395-396, O245-O259.

No. 305 Surcharged in Violet

Vale 15 cts.
Correos-1913

1913, Mar.

310	A23	15c on 35c	.40 .25
a.		"ats" for "cts"	6.00 6.00

Stamps of 1912 Surcharged in Red or Black

VALE
medio
centavo
de córdoba
1913

1913-14

311	A22	½c on 3c yel brn (R)	.40 .35
a.		"Corooba"	2.50 2.50
b.		"do" for "de"	2.50 2.50
c.		Inverted surcharge	22.50
312	A22	½c on 15c vio (R)	.25 .25
a.		"Coroaba"	1.00 1.00
b.		"do" for "de"	1.25 1.25
313	A22	½c on 1p org	.25 .25
a.		"VALB"	1.50 1.00
b.		"ALE"	4.00 3.50
c.		"LE"	6.00 5.00
d.		"VALE" omitted	3.50 3.50
314	A22	1c on 3c yel brn	.75 .60
315	A22	1c on 4c brn vio	.25 .25
316	A22	1c on 50c lt blue	.25 .25
317	A22	1c on 5p blk	.25 .25
318	A22	2c on 4c brn vio	.35 .25
a.		"do" for "de"	1.25 1.25
319	A22	2c on 20c red	3.50 4.50
a.		"do" for "de"	17.50 12.50
320	A22	2c on 25c blue grn & blk	.35 .25
a.		"do" for "de"	3.50 2.50

321	A23	2c on 35c grn & chnt	.25 .40
a.		"9131"	3.00 2.00
b.		"do" for "de"	2.50 2.00
322	A22	2c on 50c lt blue	.25 .25
a.		"do" for "de"	1.25 1.25
323	A22	2c on 2p dark blue grn	.25 .25
a.		"VALB"	1.25 .75
b.		"ALE"	2.50 1.25
c.		"VALE" omitted	6.00
d.		"VALE" and "dos" omitted	6.00
324	A22	3c on 6c olive bis	.25 .25
a.		"VALB"	35.00
		Nos. 311-324 (14)	7.60 8.35

Nos. 311, 312 surcharged in black were not regularly issued.

Surcharged on Zelaya Issue of 1912

325	Z2	½c on 2c ver	.60 .45
a.		"Corooba"	1.25 1.25
b.		"do" for "de"	1.25 1.25
326	Z2	1c on 3c org brn	.50 .25
327	Z2	1c on 4c car	.50 .25
328	Z2	1c on 6c red brn	.40 .25
329	Z2	1c on 20c dark vio	.50 .25
330	Z2	1c on 25c grn & blk	.50 .25
331	Z2	2c on 1c yel grn ('14)	6.75 1.25
a.		"Centavos"	7.50 1.50
332	Z2	2c on 25c grn & blk	2.25 3.00
333	Z2	5c on 35c brn & blk	.40 .25
334	Z2	5c on 50c ol grn	.40 .25
a.		Double surcharge	22.50
335	Z2	6c on 1p org	.40 .25
336	Z2	10c on 2p org brn	.40 .25
337	Z2	1p on 5p dk bl grn	.40 .40
		Nos. 325-337 (13)	14.00 7.35

On No. 331 the surcharge has a space of 2½mm between "Vale" and "dos."

Space between "Vale" and "dos" 2½mm instead of 1mm, "de Córdoba" in different type.

1914, Feb.

337A	A22	2c on 4c brn vio	27.50 4.00
b.		"Ccntavos"	12.00
337C	A22	2c on 20c red	13.00 1.25
d.		"Ccntavos"	4.00
337E	A22	2c on 25c bl grn & blk	6.00
f.		"Ccntavos"	12.00
337G	A23	2c on 35c grn & chnt	8.50
h.		"Ccntavos"	15.00
337I	A22	2c on 50c lt bl	22.50 4.00
j.		"Ccntavos"	10.00

No. 310 with Additional Surcharge

medio
cvo. Córdoba

1913, Dec.

337K	A23	½c on 15c on 35c	300.00

The word "Medio" is usually in heavy-faced, shaded letters. It is also in thinner, unshaded letters and in letters from both fonts mixed.

No. 310 Surcharged in Black and Violet

¼ ct. Córdoba
Correos-1913.

338	A23	½c on 15c on 35c	.25 .25
a.		Double surcharge	3.50
b.		Inverted surcharge	3.50
c.		Surcharged on No. 305	12.00
339	A23	1c on 15c on 35c	.25 .25
a.		Double surcharge	4.00

Official Stamps of 1912 Surcharged

VALE
¢ 0.01

1914, Feb.

340	A22	1c on 25c lt bl	.40 .25
a.		Double surcharge	9.00
341	A23	1c on 35c lt bl	.40 .25
a.		"0.10" for "0.01"	10.00 10.00
341B	A22	1c on 50c lt bl	200.00
342	A22	1c on 1p lt bl	.25 .25
342A	A22	2c on 20c lt bl	200.00 150.00
b.		"0.12" for "0.02"	
343	A22	2c on 50c lt bl	.40 .25
a.		"0.12" for "0.02"	150.00
344	A22	2c on 2p lt bl	.40 .25
345	A22	2c on 5p lt bl	250.00
346	A22	5c on 5c lt bl	.25 .25

Red Surcharge

347	A22	5c on 1p lt bl	75.00
348	A22	5c on 5p lt bl	500.00

National Palace, Managua — A24

León Cathedral — A25

Various Frames

1914, May 13   Engr.   Perf. 12

349	A24	½c lt blue	.85 .25
350	A24	1c dk green	.85 .25
351	A25	2c red orange	.85 .25
352	A24	3c red brown	1.25 .30
353	A24	4c scarlet	1.25 .40
354	A24	5c gray black	.45 .25
355	A25	6c black brn	9.00 5.50
356	A25	10c orange yel	.85 .25
357	A24	15c dp violet	5.75 2.00
358	A25	20c slate	11.00 5.50
359	A25	25c orange	1.50 .45
360	A25	50c pale blue	1.40 .40
		Nos. 349-360 (12)	35.00 15.80

In 1924 the 5c, 10c, 25c, 50c were issued in slightly larger size, 27x22¾mm. The original set was 26x22½mm.

No. 356 with overprint "Union Panamericana 1890-1940" in green is of private origin. See Nos. 408-415, 483-495, 513-523, 652-664. For overprints and surcharges see Nos. 361-394, 397-400, 416-419, 427-479, 500, 540-548, 580-586, 600-648, 671-673, 684-685, C1-C3, C9-C13, C49-C66, C92-C105, C121-C134, C147-C149, C155-C163, C174-C185, CO1-CO24, O260-O294, O296-O319, O332-O376, RA1-RA5, RA10-RA11, RA26-RA35, RA39-RA40, RA44, RA47, RA52.

No. 355 Surcharged in Black

VALE
5 cts.
de Córdoba
1915

1915, Sept.

361	A25	5c on 6c blk brn	1.50 .40
a.		Double surcharge	7.00 7.00

Stamps of 1914 Surcharged in Black or Red

Vale
dos centavos
de córdoba

1918-19   New Value in Figures

362	A24	1c on 3c red brn	6.50 2.25
a.		Double surch., one invtd.	12.50
363	A25	2c on 4c scarlet	32.50 22.50
364	A24	5c on 15c dp vio (R)	7.50 1.50
a.		Double surcharge	12.00
364C	A24	5c on 15c dp vio	350.00

Surcharged in Black

VALE
por 2 centavos
de Córdoba

365	A25	2c on 20c slate	110.00 55.00
a.		"ppr" for "por"	500.00 300.00
b.		Double surcharge	300.00
c.		"Cordobo"	500.00 300.00
365D	A25	5c on 20c slate	— 200.00
e.		Double surcharge (Bk + R)	300.00
f.		"Cordobo"	300.00

The surcharge on No. 365 is in blue black, and that on No. 365D usually has an admixture of red.

Used only at Bluefields and Rama.

Surcharged in Black, Red or Violet

Vale
medio centavo
de córdoba

New Value in Words

366	A25	½c on 6c blk brn	4.00 1.50
a.		"Meio"	15.00
b.		Double surcharge	12.00
367	A25	½c on 10c yellow	2.50 .30
a.		"Val" for "Vale"	3.00
b.		"Codoba"	5.00
c.		Inverted surcharge	5.00
d.		Double surch., one inverted	10.00
368	A24	½c on 15c dp vio	2.50 .60
a.		Double surcharge	7.50
b.		"Codoba"	4.00
c.		"Meio"	6.00
369	A24	½c on 25c orange	5.00 2.00
a.		Double surcharge	8.00
b.		Double surch., one inverted	6.00
370	A25	½c on 50c pale bl	2.50 .30
a.		"Meio"	6.00
b.		Double surcharge	5.00
c.		Double surch., one inverted	7.00
371	A25	½c on 50c pale bl (R)	4.50 1.50
a.		Double surcharge	10.00
372	A24	1c on 3c red brown	3.00 .30
a.		Double surcharge	3.50
373	A25	1c on 6c blk brn	12.50 3.50
a.		Double surcharge	9.00
374	A25	1c on 10c yellow	24.00 8.00
a.		"nu" for "un"	22.50
375	A24	1c on 15c dp vio	4.50 .75
a.		Double surcharge	10.00
b.		"Codoba"	6.00
376	A25	1c on 20c slate	200.00 100.00
a.		Black surch. normal and red surch. invtd.	150.00
b.		Double surch., red & black	150.00
c.		Blue surcharge	200.00
377	A25	1c on 20c sl (V)	110.00 70.00
a.		Double surcharge (V + Bk)	150.00
378	A25	1c on 20c sl (R)	2.50 .30
a.		Double surch., one inverted	
b.		"Val" for "Vale"	3.50 3.00
379	A25	1c on 25c orange	4.50 1.00
a.		Double surcharge	11.00
380	A25	1c on 50c pale bl	14.00 4.50
a.		Double surcharge	17.50
381	A25	2c on 4c scarlet	3.50 .30
a.		"centavo"	10.00
b.		"Val" for "Vale"	5.00
382	A25	2c on 6c blk brn	24.00 8.00
a.		"Centavoss"	
b.		"Cordobas"	
383	A25	2c on 10c yellow	24.00 4.50
a.		"centavo"	
384	A25	2c on 20c sl (R)	13.00 3.25
a.		"pe" for "de"	15.00
b.		Double surch., red & blk	27.50
c.		"centavo"	12.00
d.		Double surcharge (R)	17.50
385	A24	2c on 25c orange	5.50 .40
a.		"Vle" for "Vale"	7.50
b.		"Codoba"	7.50
c.		Inverted surcharge	10.00
386	A25	5c on 6c blk brn	10.00 4.25
a.		Double surcharge	13.50
387	A24	5c on 15c dp vio	3.50 .60
a.		"cincoun" for "cinco"	15.00
b.		"Vle" for "Vale"	12.50
c.		"Codoba"	12.50
		Nos. 366-387 (22)	479.50 215.85

No. 378 is surcharged in light red and brown red: the latter color is frequently offered as the violet surcharge (No. 377).

Official Stamps of 1915 Surcharged in Black or Blue

Vale
diez centavos
de córdoba

1919-21

388	A24	1c on 25c lt blue	1.50 .25
a.		Double surcharge	10.00
b.		Inverted surcharge	12.00
389	A25	2c on 50c lt blue	1.50 .25
a.		"centavo"	4.00 4.00
b.		Double surcharge	12.00
390	A25	10c on 20c lt blue	1.40 .40
a.		"centovos"	5.00 5.00
b.		Double surcharge	8.00
390F	A25	10c on 20c lt bl (Bl)	65.00
		Nos. 388-390 (3)	4.40 .90

There are numerous varieties of omitted, inverted and italic letters in the foregoing surcharges.

No. 358 Surcharged in Black

VALE
5 Centavos

Types of the numerals

| I | II | III | IV |
| V | VI | VII | VIII |

| I | II | III | IV |

| V | VI | VII | VIII |

1919, May
391	A25	2c on 20c (I)	200.00	150.00
a.		Type II		
b.		Type III		
c.		Type IV		
d.		Type VI		
e.		Type VIII		
392	A25	5c on 20c (I)	110.00	40.00
a.		Type II	110.00	45.00
b.		Type III	125.00	50.00
c.		Type IV	125.00	50.00
d.		Type V	140.00	60.00
e.		Type VI	140.00	60.00
f.		Type VII	400.00	250.00
h.		Double surch., one inverted		

No. 358
Surcharged in
Black

393	A25	2 Cents on 20c		
		(I)	200.00	150.00
a.		Type II		
b.		Type III		
c.		Type IV		
d.		Type V		
e.		Type VI		
f.		Type VII		
393G	A25	5 Cents on 20c		
		sl, (VIII)	140.00	55.00

Nos. 391-393G used only at Bluefields and Rama.

No. 351
Surcharged in
Black

1920, Jan.
394	A25	1c on 2c red		
		org	1.50	.25
a.		Inverted surcharge		
b.		Double surcharge		

Official Stamps of
1912 Overprinted in
Carmine

1921, Mar.
395	A22	1c lt blue	1.50	.60
a.		"Parricular"	5.00	5.00
b.		Inverted overprint	10.00	
396	A22	5c lt blue	1.50	.40
a.		"Parricular"	5.00	5.00

Official Stamps of
1915 Surcharged
in Carmine

1921, May
397	A25	½c on 2c light blue	.50	.25
a.		"Mddio"	2.50	2.50
398	A25	½c on 4c light blue	1.25	.25
a.		"Mddio"	2.50	2.50
399	A24	1c on 3c light blue	1.25	.30
		Nos. 397-399 (3)	3.00	.80

No. 354
Surcharged in
Red

1921, Aug.
400	A24	½c on 5c gray blk	.75	.75

Trial printings of this stamp were surcharged in yellow, black and red, and yellow and red. Some of these were used for postage.

Gen. Manuel
José Arce — A26

José Cecilio del
Valle — A27

Miguel
Larreinaga
A28

Gen. Fernando
Chamorro
A29

Gen. Máximo
Jérez — A30

Gen. Pedro
Joaquín
Chamorro — A31

Rubén Darío — A32

1921, Sept.   Engr.
401	A26	½c lt bl & blk	1.00	1.00
402	A27	1c grn & blk	1.00	1.00
403	A28	2c rose red & blk	1.00	1.00
404	A29	5c ultra & blk	1.00	1.00
405	A30	10c org & blk	1.00	1.00
406	A31	25c yel & blk	1.00	1.00
407	A32	50c vio & blk	1.00	1.00
		Nos. 401-407 (7)	7.00	7.00

Centenary of independence.
For overprints and surcharges see Nos. 420-421, RA12-RA16, RA19-RA23.

Types of 1914 Issue
Various Frames

1922
408	A24	½c green	.25	.25
409	A24	1c violet	.25	.25
410	A25	2c car rose	.25	.25
411	A24	3c ol gray	.30	.25
411A	A25	4c vermilion	.35	.25
412	A25	6c red brn	.25	.25
413	A24	15c brown	.35	.25
414	A25	20c bis brn	.50	.25
415	A25	1cor blk brn	.90	.50
		Nos. 408-415 (9)	3.40	2.50

In 1924 Nos. 408-415 were issued in slightly larger size, 27x22¾mm. The original set was 26x22½mm.
Nos. 408, 410 exist with signature controls. See note before No. 600. Same values.

No. 356
Surcharged in
Black

1922, Nov.
416	A25	1c on 10c org yel	1.00	.35
417	A25	2c on 10c org yel	1.00	.25

Nos. 354 and 356
Surcharged in Red

1923, Jan.
418	A24	1c on 5c gray blk	1.25	.25
419	A25	2c on 10c org yel	1.25	.25
a.		Inverted surcharge		

Nos. 401 and 402
Overprinted in Red

1923
420	A26	½c lt blue & blk	7.50	7.50
421	A27	1c green & blk	2.50	.85
a.		Double overprint	7.50	

Francisco
Hernández de
Córdoba — A33

1924   Engr.
422	A33	1c deep green	1.50	.30
423	A33	2c carmine rose	1.50	.30
424	A33	5c deep blue	1.00	.30
425	A33	10c bister brn	1.00	.60
		Nos. 422-425 (4)	5.00	1.50

Founding of León & Granada, 400th anniv.
For overprint & surcharges see #499, 536, O295.

Stamps of 1914-22 Overprinted

Black, Red or Blue Overprint
1927, May 3
427	A24	½c green (Bk)	.25	.25
428	A24	1c violet (R)	.25	.25
a.		Double overprint	3.00	
428B	A24	1c violet (Bk)	85.00	55.00
429	A25	2c car rose (Bk)	.25	.25
a.		Inverted overprint	5.00	
b.		Double overprint	5.00	
430	A24	3c ol gray (Bk)	1.25	1.25
a.		Inverted overprint	5.00	
b.		Double overprint	5.00	
c.		Double ovpt., one invert-		
		ed	9.00	7.00
430D	A24	3c ol gray (Bl)	8.00	3.25
431	A25	4c ver (Bk)	16.00	13.00
a.		Inverted overprint		30.00
432	A24	5c gray blk (R)	1.25	.25
a.		Inverted overprint	7.50	
432B	A24	5c gray blk (Bk)	.75	.25
c.		Double ovpt., one invert-		
		ed	8.00	
d.		Double overprint	8.00	
433	A25	6c red brn (Bk)	13.00	11.00
a.		Inverted overprint	17.50	
b.		Double overprint		
c.		"1297" for "1927"		250.00
434	A25	10c yellow (Bl)	.65	.40
a.		Inverted overprint	12.50	
b.		Double ovpt., one invert-		
		ed	10.00	
435	A24	15c brown (Bk)	6.00	2.50
436	A25	20c bis brn (Bk)	6.00	2.50
a.		Double overprint	17.50	

437	A24	25c orange (Bk)	27.50	5.00
438	A25	50c pale bl (Bk)	7.50	3.00
439	A25	1cor blk brn (Bk)	15.00	9.00
		Nos. 427-439 (16)	188.65	107.15

Most stamps of this group exist with tall "1" in "1927." Counterfeits exist of normal stamps and errors of Nos. 427-478.

1927, May 19   Violet Overprint
440	A24	½c green	.25	.25
a.		Inverted overprint	2.00	2.00
b.		Double overprint	2.00	2.00
441	A24	1c violet	.25	.25
a.		Double overprint	2.00	2.00
442	A25	2c car rose	.25	.25
a.		Double overprint	2.00	2.00
b.		"1927" double	5.00	
d.		Double ovpt., one inverted	2.00	2.00
443	A24	3c ol gray	.25	.25
a.		Inverted overprint	6.00	
b.		Overprinted "1927" only	12.00	
c.		Double ovpt., one inverted	9.00	
444	A25	4c vermilion	37.50	27.50
a.		Inverted overprint	75.00	
445	A24	5c gray blk	1.00	.25
a.		Double overprint, one inverted	6.00	
446	A25	6c red brn	37.50	27.50
a.		Inverted overprint	75.00	
447	A25	10c yellow	.35	.25
a.		Double overprint	2.00	2.00
448	A24	15c brown	.75	.30
a.		Double overprint	5.00	
b.		Double overprint, one inverted	8.00	
449	A25	20c bis brn	.35	.25
a.		Double overprint		
450	A24	25c orange	.40	.25
451	A25	50c pale bl	.40	.25
a.		Double overprint	4.00	4.00
452	A25	1cor blk brn	.75	.25
a.		Double overprint	3.00	
b.		"1927" double	5.00	
c.		Double ovpt., one inverted	6.00	
		Nos. 440-452 (13)	80.00	57.80

Stamps of 1914-22 Overprinted in Violet

1928, Jan. 3
453	A24	½c green	.25	.25
a.		Double overprint	3.00	
b.		Double overprint, one inverted	4.00	
454	A24	1c violet	.25	.25
a.		Inverted overprint	2.00	
b.		Double overprint	2.00	
c.		Double overprint, one inverted	2.00	
d.		"928" for "1928"	2.50	
455	A25	2c car rose	.25	.25
a.		Inverted overprint	2.00	
b.		Double overprint	2.00	
c.		"1928" omitted	5.00	
d.		"928" for "1928"	2.50	
e.		As "d," inverted		
f.		"19" for "1928"		
456	A24	3c ol gray	.40	.25
457	A24	4c vermilion	.25	.25
458	A24	5c gray blk	.25	.25
a.		Double overprint	2.00	
b.		Double overprint, one inverted	5.00	
459	A25	6c red brn	.25	.25
460	A25	10c yellow	.25	.25
a.		Double overprint	2.50	
c.		Inverted overprint		
461	A24	15c brown	.35	.25
462	A25	20c bis brn	.50	.25
a.		Double overprint		
463	A24	25c orange	.75	.25
a.		Double overprint, one inverted	4.00	
464	A25	50c pale bl	1.25	.25
465	A25	1cor blk brn	1.25	.35
		Nos. 453-465 (13)	6.25	3.35

Stamps of 1914-22 Overprinted in Violet

1928, June 11
466	A24	½c green	.25	.25
467	A24	1c violet	.25	.25
a.		"928" omitted		
469	A24	3c ol gray	.75	.25
a.		Double overprint	6.00	
470	A24	4c vermilion	.35	.25
471	A24	5c gray blk	.25	.25
a.		Double overprint	4.00	
472	A25	6c red brn	.40	.25
a.		Double overprint	5.00	
473	A25	10c yellow	.50	.25
474	A24	15c brown	1.75	.25
a.		Double overprint		
475	A25	20c bis brn	2.00	.25
476	A24	25c orange	2.00	.25
a.		Double overprint, one inverted	6.00	
477	A25	50c pale bl	2.00	.25
478	A25	1cor blk brn	5.00	2.50
a.		Double overprint	10.00	
		Nos. 466-478 (12)	15.50	5.25

No. 410 with above overprint in black was not regularly issued.

No. 470 with
Additional
Surcharge in
Violet

1928
479 A25 2c on 4c ver   1.25   .35
  a. Double surcharge   9.00

A34

Inscribed: "Timbre Telegrafico"

1928   **Red Surcharge**
480 A34 1c on 5c bl & blk   .30   .25
  a. Double surcharge   5.00
  b. Double surcharge, one inverted
481 A34 2c on 5c bl & blk   .30   .25
  a. Double surcharge   5.00
482 A34 3c on 5c bl & blk   .30   .25
      Nos. 480-482 (3)   .90   .75

Stamps similar to Nos. 481-482, but with
surcharge in black and with basic stamp
inscribed "Timbre Fiscal," are of private origin.
See designs A36, A37, A44, PT1, PT4, PT6,
PT7.

Types of 1914 Issue
Various Frames

1928
483 A24 ½c org red   .40   .25
484 A24 1c orange   .40   .25
485 A24 2c green   .40   .25
486 A24 3c dp vio   .40   .25
487 A25 4c brown   .40   .25
488 A25 5c yellow   .40   .25
489 A24 6c lt bl   .40   .25
490 A24 10c dk bl   .90   .25
491 A24 15c car rose   1.40   .50
492 A24 20c dk grn   1.40   .50
493 A24 25c blk brn   27.50 6.00
494 A25 50c bis brn   3.25 1.00
495 A25 1cor dl vio   6.25 3.00
      Nos. 483-495 (13)   43.50 13.00

No. 425 Overprinted
in Violet

1929
499 A33 10c bis brn   .75 .60

No. 408
Overprinted in
Red

1929
500 A24 ½c green (R)   .25 .25
  a. Inverted overprint   2.50
  b. Double overprint   2.50
  c. Double overprint, one inverted 3.50

A36

**Ovptd. Horiz. in Black "R. de T."
Surcharged Vert. in Red**

1929
504 A36 1c on 5c bl & blk (R)   .25 .25
  a. Inverted surcharge   3.00
  b. Surcharged "0.10" for "0.01" 3.00
  c. "0.0" instead of "0.01"   5.00

---

509 A36 2c on 5c bl & blk (R)   .25 .25
  a. Double surcharge   2.50
  b. Double surcharge, one inverted 3.50
  c. Inverted surcharge   5.00

**Overprinted Horizontally in Black
"N. de O." Ourcharged Vertically in
Red**

510 A36 2c on 5c bl & blk (R)   22.50 1.25
  a. Dbl. surcharge, one inverted 25.00

A37

Surcharged in Red
511 A37 1c on 10c dk grn & blk
    (R)   .25 .25
  a. Double surcharge
512 A37 2c on 5c bl & blk (R)   .25 .25
      Nos. 504-512 (5)   23.50 2.25

The varieties tall "1" in "0.01" and "O$" for
"C$" are found in this surcharge.
Nos. 500, 504, 509-512 and RA38 were
surcharged in red and sold in large quantities
to the public. Surcharges in various other colors were distributed only to a favored few and
not regularly sold at the post offices.

Types of 1914 Issue
Various Frames

1929-31
513 A24 1c ol grn   .25   .25
514 A24 3c lt bl   .30   .25
515 A25 4c dk bl ('31)   .30   .25
516 A24 5c ol brn   .40   .25
517 A25 6c bis brn ('31)   .50   .30
518 A24 10c lt brn ('31)   .60   .25
519 A24 15c org red ('31)   .90   .25
520 A25 20c org ('31)   1.25   .35
521 A25 25c dk vio   .25   .25
522 A25 50c grn ('31)   .50   .25
523 A25 1cor yel ('31)   4.50 1.25
      Nos. 513-523 (11)   9.75 3.90

Nos. 513-523 exist with signature controls.
See note before No. 600. Same values.

New Post Office
at
Managua — A38

1930, Sept. 15   **Engr.**
525 A38 ½c olive gray   1.25 1.25
526 A38 1c carmine   1.25 1.25
527 A38 2c red org   .90   .90
528 A38 3c orange   1.75 1.75
529 A38 4c yellow   1.75 1.75
530 A38 5c ol grn   2.25 2.25
531 A38 6c bl grn   2.25 2.25
532 A38 10c black   2.75 2.75
533 A38 25c dp bl   5.50 5.50
534 A38 50c ultra   9.00 9.00
535 A38 1cor dp vio   25.00 25.00
      Nos. 525-535 (11)   53.65 53.65

Opening of the new general post office at
Managua. The stamps were on sale on day of
issuance and for an emergency in April, 1931.

No. 499 Surcharged
in Black and Red

1931, May 29
536 A33 2c on 10c bis brn   .50 1.60
  a. Red surcharge omitted   2.50
  b. Red surcharge double   5.00
  c. Red surcharge inverted   3.50
  d. Red surcharge double, one invtd.

Surcharge exists in brown.

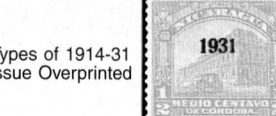

Types of 1914-31
Issue Overprinted

1931, June 11
540 A24 ½c green   .35 .25
  a. Double overprint   .80
  b. Double ovpt., one inverted   1.40
  c. Inverted overprint   .80
541 A24 1c ol grn   .35 .25
  a. Double overprint   .80
  b. Double ovpt., one inverted   1.40
542 A25 2c car rose   .35 .25
  a. Double overprint   .80
  b. Double ovpt., both inverted 2.50
  c. Inverted overprint   1.40
543 A24 3c lt bl   .35 .25
  a. Double overprint   .80
  b. Double ovpt., one inverted   1.40
  c. Inverted overprint   1.40
544 A24 5c yellow   3.50 2.25
545 A24 5c ol brn   1.00   .25
  a. Double overprint   4.50
  b. Inverted overprint   4.50
546 A24 15c org red   1.25   .40
  a. Double overprint   3.50
547 A24 25c blk brn   10.00 6.50
  a. Double overprint   11.00 7.00
  b. Inverted overprint   11.00 7.00
548 A24 25c dk vio   4.00 2.50
  a. Double overprint   6.50
      Nos. 540-548 (9)   21.15 12.90

Counterfeits exist of the scarcer values. The
4c brown and 6c light blue with this overprint
are bogus.

Managua P.O.
Before and
After
Earthquake
A40

1932, Jan. 1   Litho.   Perf. 11½
Soft porous paper, Without gum
556 A40 ½c emerald   1.50
557 A40 1c yel brn   1.90
558 A40 2c dp car   1.50
559 A40 3c ultra   1.50
560 A40 4c dp ultra   1.50
561 A40 5c yel brn   1.60
562 A40 6c gray brn   1.60
563 A40 10c yel brn   2.50
564 A40 15c dl rose   3.75
565 A40 20c orange   3.50
566 A40 25c dk vio   2.50
567 A40 50c emerald   2.50
568 A40 1cor yellow   6.25
      Nos. 556-568 (13)   32.10

Issued in commemoration of the earthquake
at Managua, Mar. 31, 1931. The stamps were
on sale on Jan. 1, 1932, only. The money
received from this sale was for the reconstruction of the Post Office building and for the
improvement of the postal service. Many
shades exist.
    Sheets of 10.
    *Reprints are on thin hard paper and do not
have the faint horiz. ribbing that is on the front
or back of the originals. Fake cancels abound.
Value 75 cents each.*
    See Nos. C20-C24. For overprints and
surcharges see Nos. C32-C43, C47-C48.

Rivas Railroad Issue

"Fill" at El Nacascolo — A41

1c, Wharf at San Jorge. 5c, Rivas Station.
10c, San Juan del Sur. 15c, Train at Rivas
Station.

1932, Dec. 17   Litho.   Perf. 12
Soft porous paper
570 A41 1c yellow   16.00
  a. 1c ocher   18.00
571 A41 2c carmine   16.00
572 A41 5c blk brn   16.00
573 A41 10c chocolate   16.00
574 A41 15c yellow   16.00
  a. 15c deep orange   18.00
      Nos. 570-574 (5)   80.00

Inauguration of the railroad from San Jorge
to San Juan del Sur. On sale only on Dec. 17,
1932.
    Sheets of 4, without gum. See #C67-C71.
    *Reprints exist on five different papers rang-
ing from thick soft light cream to thin very hard
paper and do not have the faint horiz. ribbing
that is normally on the front or back of the
originals. Originals are on very white paper.
Value of reprints, $5 each.*

Leon-Sauce Railroad Issue

Bridge No. 2 at Santa Lucia — A42

Designs: 1c, Environs of El Sauce. 5c,
Santa Lucia. 10c, Works at Km. 64. 15c, Rock
cut at Santa Lucia.

1932, Dec. 30   Perf. 12
Soft porous paper
575 A42 1c orange   16.00
576 A42 2c carmine   16.00
577 A42 5c blk brn   16.00
578 A42 10c brown   16.00
579 A42 15c orange   16.00
      Nos. 575-579 (5)   80.00

Inauguration of the railroad from Leon to El
Sauce. On sale only on Dec. 30, 1932.
    Sheets of 4, without gum. See #C72-C76.
    *Reprints exist on thin hard paper and do not
have the faint horiz. ribbing that is on the front
or back of the originals. Value $5 each.*

Nos. 514-515,
543 Surcharged
in Red

1932, Dec. 10
580 A24 1c on 3c lt bl (514)   .35 .25
  a. Double surcharge   3.50
581 A24 1c on 3c lt bl (543)   4.00 3.50
582 A25 2c on 4c dk bl (515)   .25 .25
  a. Double surcharge   2.50
      Nos. 580-582 (3)   4.60 4.00

Nos. 514, 516,
545 and 518
Surcharged in
Black or Red

1933
583 A24 1c on 3c lt bl (Bk)
    (514)   .25 .25
  a. "Censavo"   4.00 2.25
  b. Double surcharge, one inverted 4.00
584 A24 1c on 5c ol brn (R)
    (516)   .25 .25
  a. Inverted surcharge
  b. Double surcharge
585 A24 1c on 5c ol brn (R)
    (545)   6.50 5.00
  a. Red surcharge double   12.00
586 A25 2c on 10c lt brn (Bk)
    (518)   .25 .25
  a. Double surcharge   4.00 2.50
  b. Inverted surcharge   3.50 3.50
  c. Double surcharge, one inverted 4.50
      Nos. 583-586 (4)   7.25 5.75

On No. 586 "Vale Dos" measures 13mm
and 14mm.
No. 583 with green surcharge and No. 586
with red surcharge are bogus.

Flag of the Race Issue

Flag with Three
Crosses for
Three Ships of
Columbus
A43

1933, Aug. 3   Litho.   Rouletted 9
Without gum
587 A43 ½c emerald   1.75 1.75
588 A43 1c green   1.50 1.50
589 A43 2c red   1.50 1.50
590 A43 3c dp rose   1.50 1.50
591 A43 4c orange   1.50 1.50
592 A43 5c yellow   1.75 1.75
593 A43 10c dp brn   1.75 1.75
594 A43 15c dk brn   1.75 1.75
595 A43 20c vio bl   1.75 1.75
596 A43 25c dl bl   1.75 1.75
597 A43 30c violet   4.50 4.50

598 A43 50c red vio 4.50 4.50
599 A43 1cor ol brn 4.50 4.50
Nos. 587-599 (13) 30.00 30.00

Commemorating the raising of the symbolical "Flag of the Race"; also the 441st anniversary of the sailing of Columbus for the New World, Aug. 3, 1492. Printed in sheets of 10. See Nos. C77-C87, O320-O331.

In October, 1933, various postage, airmail and official stamps of current issues were overprinted with facsimile signatures of the Minister of Public Works and the Postmaster-General. These overprints are control marks.

Nos. 410 and 513 Overprinted in Black

1935 **Perf. 12**
600 A24 1c ol grn .25 .25
a. Inverted overprint 1.40 1.60
b. Double overprint 1.40 1.60
c. Double overprint, one inverted 1.60 1.60
601 A25 2c car rose .25 .25
a. Inverted overprint 1.60
b. Double overprint 1.60
c. Double overprint, one inverted 1.60
d. Double overprint, both inverted 2.50 2.25

No. 517 Surcharged in Red as in 1932

1936, June
602 A25 ½c on 6c bis brn .35 .25
a. "Ccentavo" .80 .80
b. Double surcharge 3.50 3.50

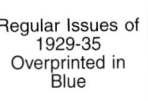

Regular Issues of 1929-35 Overprinted in Blue

1935, Dec.
603 A25 ½c on 6c bis brn .65 .25
604 A24 1c ol grn (#600) .80 .25
605 A25 2c car rose (#601) .80 .25
a. Black overprint inverted 6.00
606 A24 3c lt bl .80 .25
607 A24 5c ol brn 1.00 .25
608 A25 10c lt brn 1.60 .80
Nos. 603-608 (6) 5.65 2.05

Nos. 606-608 have signature control overprint. See note before No. 600.

Same Overprint in Red

1936, Jan.
609 A24 ½c dk grn .25 .25
610 A25 ½c on 6c bis brn (602) .25 .25
a. Double surch., one inverted 6.00 6.00
611 A24 1c ol grn (513) .25 .25
612 A24 1c ol grn (600) .25 .25
613 A25 2c car rose (410) .50 .25
614 A25 2c car rose (601) .25 .25
a. Black overprint inverted 2.50 2.50
b. Black ovpt. double, one invtd. 3.50 3.50
615 A24 3c lt bl .25 .25
616 A25 4c dk bl .25 .25
617 A24 5c ol brn .25 .25
618 A24 6c bis brn .25 .25
619 A24 10c lt brn .50 .25
620 A24 15c org red .25 .25
621 A25 20c orange .80 .25
622 A24 25c dk vio .25 .25
623 A25 50c green .35 .25
624 A25 1cor yellow .40 .25
Nos. 609-624 (16) 5.30 4.00

Red or blue "Resello 1935" overprint may be found inverted or double. Red and blue overprints on same stamp are bogus.
Nos. 615-624 have signature control overprint. See note before No. 600.

Regular Issues of 1922-29 Overprinted in Carmine

1936, May
625 A24 ½c green .25 .25
626 A24 1c olive green .25 .25
627 A25 2c carmine rose .50 .25
628 A24 3c light blue .25 .25
Nos. 625-628 (4) 1.25 1.00

No. 628 has signature control overprint. See note before No. 600.

Nos. 514, 516 Surcharged in Black

1936, June
629 A24 1c on 3c lt bl .25 .25
a. "1396" for "1936" 1.00 1.00
b. "Un" omitted 1.40 1.40
c. Inverted surcharge 1.60 1.60
d. Double surcharge 1.60 1.60
630 A24 2c on 5c ol brn .25 .25
a. "1396" for "1936" 1.40 1.40
b. Double surcharge 3.50 3.50

Regular Issues of 1929-31 Surcharged in Black or Red

1936
631 A24 ½c on 15c org red (R) .25 .25
a. Double surcharge 4.00
632 A25 1c on 4c dk bl (Bk) .25 .25
633 A24 1c on 5c ol brn (Bk) .25 .25
634 A25 1c on 6c bis brn (Bk) .40 .25
a. "1939" instead of "1936" 2.50 1.60
635 A24 1c on 15c org red (Bk) .25 .25
a. "1939" instead of "1936" 2.50 1.60
636 A25 1c on 20c org (Bk) .25 .25
a. "1939" instead of "1936" 2.50 1.60
b. Double surcharge 4.00
637 A25 1c on 20c org (R) .25 .25
638 A24 2c on 10c lt brn (Bk) .25 .25
639 A24 2c on 15c org red (Bk) 1.00 .80
640 A25 2c on 20c org (Bk) .50 .25
641 A24 2c on 25c dk vio (R) .35 .25
642 A24 2c on 25c dk vio (Bk) .35 .25
a. "1939" instead of "1936" 2.50 1.60
643 A25 2c on 50c org (Bk) .35 .25
a. "1939" instead of "1936" 2.50 1.60
644 A25 2c on 1 cor org (Bk) .35 .25
a. "1939" instead of "1936" 2.50 1.60
645 A25 3c on 4c dk bl (Bk) .65 .50
b. "s" of "Centavos" omitted and "r" of "Tres" inverted 2.50
Nos. 631-645 (15) 5.70 4.55

Nos. 634, 639, 643-644 exist with and without signature controls. Same values, except for No. 639, which is rare without the signature control. Nos. 635-636, 642, 645 do not have signature controls. Others have signature controls only. See note before No. 600.

Regular Issues of 1929-31 Overprinted in Black

1936, Aug.
646 A24 3c lt bl .35 .25
647 A24 5c ol brn .25 .25
648 A25 10c lt brn .50 .35
Nos. 646-648 (3) 1.10 .85

No. 648 bears script control mark.

A44

1936, Oct. 19 **Red Surcharge**
649 A44 1c on 5c grn & blk .25 .25
650 A44 2c on 5c grn & blk .25 .25

Types of 1914

1937, Jan. 1 **Engr.**
652 A24 ½c black .25 .25
653 A24 1c car rose .25 .25
654 A25 2c dp bl .25 .25
655 A24 3c chocolate .25 .25
656 A24 4c yellow .25 .25
657 A24 5c org red .25 .25
658 A25 6c dl vio .25 .25
659 A25 10c ol grn .25 .25
660 A24 15c green .25 .25
661 A25 20c red brn .25 .25
663 A25 50c brown .35 .25
664 A25 1cor ultra .60 .25
Nos. 652-664 (12) 3.45 3.00

See note after No. 360.

Mail Carrier — A45

Designs: 1c, Mule carrying mail. 2c, Mail coach. 3c, Sailboat. 5c, Steamship. 7½c, Train.

1937, Dec. **Litho.** **Perf. 11**
665 A45 ½c green .25 .25
666 A45 1c magenta .25 .25
667 A45 2c brown .25 .25
668 A45 3c purple .25 .25
669 A45 5c blue .25 .25
670 A45 7½c red org .55 .35
Nos. 665-670 (6) 1.80 1.60

75th anniv. of the postal service in Nicaragua.
Nos. 665-670 were also issued in sheets of 4, value, set of sheets, $7.
The miniature sheets are ungummed, and also exist imperf. and part-perf.

Nos. 662, 663 and 664 Surcharged in Red

1938 **Perf. 12**
671 A24 3c on 25c org .25 .25
672 A25 5c on 50c brn .25 .25
a. "e" of "Vale" omitted 1.60 1.00
673 A25 6c on 1cor ultra .25 .25
Nos. 671-673 (3) .75 .75

No. 672 has a script signature control and the surcharge is in three lines.

Dario Park A46

1939, Jan. **Engr.** **Perf. 12½**
674 A46 1½c yel grn .25 .25
675 A46 2c dp rose .25 .25
676 A46 3c brt bl .25 .25
677 A46 6c brn org .25 .25
678 A46 7½c dp grn .25 .25
679 A46 10c blk brn .25 .25
680 A46 15c orange .25 .25
681 A46 25c lt vio .25 .25
682 A46 50c brt yel grn .25 .25
683 A46 1cor yellow .65 .40
Nos. 674-683 (10) 2.90 2.65

Nos. 660 and 661 Surcharged in Red

1939 **Perf. 12**
684 A24 1c on 15c grn .25 .25
a. Inverted surcharge 2.00 2.00
685 A25 1c on 20c red brn .25 .25

AIR POST STAMPS

Counterfeits exist of almost all scarce surcharges among Nos. C1-C66.

Regular Issues of 1914-28 Overprinted in Red

1929, May 15 **Unwmk.** **Perf. 12**
C1 A24 25c orange 1.75 1.75
a. Double overprint, one inverted 50.00
b. Inverted overprint 50.00
c. Double overprint 50.00
C2 A24 25c blk brn 2.25 2.25
a. Double overprint, one inverted 50.00
b. Double overprint 50.00
c. Inverted overprint 50.00

There are numerous varieties in the setting of the overprint. The most important are: Large "1" in "1929" and large "A" in "Aereo" and "P. A. A."

Similar Overprint on Regular Issue of 1929 in Red

1929, June
C3 A24 25c dk vio 1.25 .75
a. Double overprint 50.00
b. Inverted overprint 50.00
c. Double overprint, one inverted 50.00
Nos. C1-C3 (3) 5.25 4.75

The stamps in the bottom row of the sheet have the letters "P. A. A." larger than usual.
Similar overprints, some including an airplane, have been applied to postage issues of 1914-20, officials of 1926 and Nos. 401-407. These are, at best, essays.

Airplanes over Mt. Momotombo — AP1

1929, Dec. 15 **Engr.**
C4 AP1 25c olive blk .50 .40
C5 AP1 50c blk brn .75 .75
C6 AP1 1cor org red 1.00 1.00
Nos. C4-C6 (3) 2.25 2.15

See Nos. C18-C19, C164-C168. For surcharges and overprints see Nos. C7-C8, C14-C17, C25-C31, C106-C120, C135-C146, C150-C154, C169-C173, CO25-CO29.

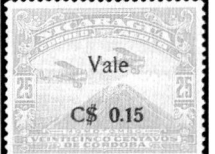

No. C4 Surcharged in Red or Black

1930, May 15
C7 AP1 15c on 25c ol blk (R) .50 .40
a. "$" inverted 3.50
b. Double surcharge (R + Bk) 7.00
c. As "b," red normal, blk invtd. 7.00
d. Double red surch., one inverted 7.00
C8 AP1 20c on 25c blk (Bk) .75 .60
a. "$" inverted 7.00
b. Inverted surcharge 15.00

Nos. C1, C2 and C3 Surcharged in Green

1931, June 7
C9 A24 15c on 25c org 50.00 50.00
C10 A24 15c on 25c blk 100.00 100.00
brn 100.00 100.00
C11 A24 15c on 25c dk vio 15.00 15.00
c. Inverted surcharge 30.00

C12	A24	20c on 25c dk vio	10.00	10.00
c.		Inverted surcharge	50.00	
d.		Double surcharge	50.00	
C13	A24	20c on 25c blk		
		brn	375.00	

No. C10 was not regularly issued.

"1391"

C9a	A24	15c on 25c		
C10a	A24	15c on 25c		
C11a	A24	15c on 25c	60.00	
d.		As "a," inverted	400.00	
C12a	A24	20c on 25c	25.00	
e.		As "a," inverted	400.00	
g.		As "a," double	400.00	
C13a	A24	20c on 25c		

"1921"

C9b	A24	15c on 25c		
C10b	A24	15c on 25c	400.00	
C11b	A24	15c on 25c	60.00	
e.		As "b," inverted	400.00	
C12b	A24	20c on 25c	25.00	
f.		As "b," inverted	400.00	
h.		As "b," double	400.00	
C13b	A24	20c on 25c		

Nos. C8,
C4-C6
Surcharged
in Blue

1931, June

C14	AP1	15c on 20c on 25c	9.00	9.00
b.		Blue surcharge inverted	25.00	
c.		"$" in blk, surch. invtd.	50.00	
d.		Blue surch. dbl., one invtd.	25.00	
C15	AP1	15c on 25c	5.50	5.50
b.		Blue surcharge inverted	25.00	
c.		Double surch., one invtd.	25.00	
C16	AP1	15c on 50c	40.00	40.00
C17	AP1	15c on 1cor	100.00	100.00
		Nos. C14-C17 (4)	154.50	154.50

"1391"

C14a	AP1	15c on 20c on 25c	50.00	
C15a	AP1	15c on 25c	30.00	
C16a	AP1	15c on 50c	80.00	
C17a	AP1	15c on 1cor	225.00	
		Nos. C14a-C17a (4)	385.00	

Momotombo Type of 1929

1931, July 8

C18	AP1	15c deep violet	.25	.25
C19	AP1	20c deep green	.40	.40

Managua Post
Office Before
and After
Earthquake
AP2

Without gum, Soft porous paper

1932, Jan. 1   Litho.   Perf. 11

C20	AP2	15c lilac	1.50	1.25
		15c violet	22.50	
b.		Vert. pair, imperf. btwn.	35.00	
C21	AP2	20c emerald	2.00	
b.		Horizontal pair, imperf. between	35.00	
C22	AP2	25c yel brn	6.50	
b.		Vertical pair, imperf. between	60.00	
C23	AP2	50c yel brn	8.00	
C24	AP2	1cor dp car	12.00	
a.		Vert. or horiz. pair, imperf. btwn.	80.00	
		Nos. C20-C24 (5)	30.00	

Sheets of 10. See note after No. 568.
For overprint and surcharges see #C44-C46.

Reprints: see note following No. 568. Value $1 each.

Nos. C5
and C6
Surcharged
in Red or
Black

1932, July 12   Perf. 12

C25	AP1	30c on 50c (Bk)	1.50	1.50
a.		"Valc"	25.00	
b.		Double surcharge	15.00	
c.		Double surch., one inverted	15.00	
d.		Period omitted after "O"	25.00	
e.		As "a," double	300.00	
C26	AP1	35c on 50c (R)	1.50	1.50
a.		"Valc"	30.00	
b.		Double surcharge	12.00	
c.		Double surch., one inverted	12.00	
d.		As "a," double	300.00	
C27	AP1	35c on 50c (Bk)	35.00	35.00
a.		"Valc"	250.00	

C28	AP1	40c on 1cor (Bk)	1.75	1.75
a.		"Valc"	25.00	
b.		Double surcharge	15.00	
c.		Double surch., one inverted	15.00	
d.		Inverted surcharge	15.00	
e.		As "a," inverted	300.00	
f.		As "a," double	300.00	
C29	AP1	55c on 1cor (R)	1.75	1.75
a.		"Valc"	25.00	
b.		Double surcharge	12.00	
c.		Double surch., one inverted	12.00	
d.		Inverted surcharge	12.00	
e.		As "a," inverted	300.00	
f.		As "a," double	300.00	
		Nos. C25-C29 (5)	41.50	41.50

No. C18
Overprinted
in Red

1932, Sept. 11

C30	AP1	15c dp vio	70.00	70.00
a.		"Aerreo"	150.00	150.00
b.		Invtd. "m" in "Septiembre"	150.00	

International Air Mail Week.

No. C6
Surcharged

1932, Oct. 12

C31	AP1	8c on 1 cor org red	20.00	20.00
a.		"1232"	30.00	30.00
b.		2nd "u" of "Inauguration" invtd.	30.00	30.00

Inauguration of airmail service to the interior.

Regular Issue
of 1932
Overprinted in
Red

1932, Oct. 24   Perf. 11½

Without Gum

C32	A40	1c yel brn	20.00	20.00
a.		Inverted overprint	125.00	125.00
C33	A40	2c carmine	20.00	20.00
a.		Inverted overprint	125.00	125.00
b.		Double overprint	100.00	100.00
C34	A40	3c ultra	9.50	9.50
a.		Inverted overprint	150.00	150.00
b.		As "a," vert. pair, imperf. btwn.	500.00	
C35	A40	4c dp ultra	9.50	9.50
a.		Inverted overprint	125.00	125.00
b.		Double overprint	100.00	100.00
c.		Vert. or horiz. pair, imperf. btwn.	300.00	
C36	A40	5c yel brn	9.50	9.50
a.		Inverted overprint	125.00	125.00
b.		Vert. pair, imperf. btwn.	75.00	
C37	A40	6c gray brn	9.50	9.50
a.		Inverted overprint	100.00	100.00
C38	A40	50c green	9.00	9.00
a.		Inverted overprint	125.00	125.00
C39	A40	1cor yellow	9.50	9.50
a.		Inverted overprint	125.00	125.00
b.		Horiz. pair, imperf. btwn.	200.00	
		Nos. C32-C39 (8)	96.50	96.50

Nos. 564, C20-C21 exist overprinted as C32-C39. The editors believe they were not regularly issued.

Surcharged in
Red

1932, Oct. 24

C40	A40	8c on 10c yel brn	9.00	9.00
a.		Inverted surcharge	125.00	125.00
C41	A40	16c on 20c org	9.00	9.00
a.		Inverted surcharge	125.00	125.00
C42	A40	24c on 25c dp vio	9.00	9.00
a.		Inverted surcharge	125.00	125.00
b.		Horiz. pair, imperf. vert.	500.00	

Surcharged in Red as No. C40 but without the word "Vale"

1932, Oct. 24

C43	A40	8c on 10c yel brn	45.00	45.00
a.		Inverted surcharge	125.00	125.00
b.		Horiz. pair, imperf. vert.	300.00	

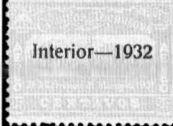

No. C22
Overprinted in
Red

1932, Oct. 24

C44	AP2	25c yel brn	8.00	8.00
a.		Inverted overprint	125.00	125.00

Nos. C23 and
C24
Surcharged in
Red

1932, Oct. 24

C45	AP2	32c on 50c yel brn	9.50	9.50
a.		Inverted surcharge	125.00	125.00
b.		"Interior-1932" inverted	150.00	150.00
c.		"Vale $0.32" inverted	150.00	150.00
d.		Horiz. pair, imperf. btwn.	200.00	
C46	AP2	40c on 1cor car	7.00	7.00
a.		Inverted surcharge	125.00	125.00
b.		"Vale $0.40" inverted	200.00	200.00

Nos. 557-558 Overprinted in Black like Nos. C32 to C39

1932, Nov. 16

C47	A40	1c yel brn	25.00	22.50
a.		"1232"	45.00	45.00
b.		Inverted overprint	125.00	125.00
c.		Double ovpt., one invtd.	125.00	125.00
d.		As "a," inverted	500.00	
C48	A40	2c dp car	20.00	17.50
a.		"1232"	45.00	45.00
b.		Inverted overprint	125.00	125.00
c.		As "a," inverted	125.00	125.00

Excellent counterfeits exist of Nos. C27, C30-C48. Forged overprints and surcharges as on Nos. C32-C48 exist on reprints of Nos. C20-C24.

Regular Issue of
1914-32
Surcharged in
Black

1932   Perf. 12

C49	A25	1c on 2c brt rose	.50	.30
C50	A24	2c on 3c lt bl	.50	.30
C51	A25	3c on 4c dk bl	.50	.30
C52	A24	4c on 5c gray brn	.50	.30
C53	A25	5c on 6c ol brn	.50	.30
C54	A25	6c on 10c lt brn	.50	.30
a.		Double surcharge	25.00	
C55	A24	8c on 15c org red	.50	.30
C56	A25	16c on 20c org	.50	.35
C57	A24	24c on 25c dk vio	2.00	1.00
C58	A24	25c on 25c dk vio	2.00	1.00
a.		Double surcharge	25.00	
C59	A25	32c on 50c grn	2.00	1.25
C60	A25	40c on 50c grn	2.25	1.40
C61	A25	50c on 1cor yel	3.50	2.25
C62	A25	1cor on 1cor yel	5.00	3.00
		Nos. C49-C62 (14)	20.75	12.35

Nos. C49-C62 exist with inverted surcharge.
In addition to C49 to C62, four other stamps, Type A25, exist with this surcharge:
40c on 50c bister brown, black surcharge.
1cor on 2c bright rose, black surcharge.
1cor on 1cor yellow, red surcharge.
1cor on 1cor dull violet, black surcharge.
The editors believe they were not regularly issued.

Surcharged on Nos. 548, 547

1932

C65	A24	24c on 25c dk vio	45.00	45.00
C66	A24	25c on 25c blk brn	50.00	50.00

Counterfeits of Nos. C65 and C66 are plentiful.

Rivas Railroad Issue

La Chocolata Cut — AP3

El Nacascola — AP4

Designs: 25c, Cuesta cut. 50c, Mole of San Juan del Sur. 1cor, View of El Estero.

1932, Dec.   Litho.

Soft porous paper

C67	AP3	15c dk vio	20.00
C68	AP4	20c bl grn	20.00
C69	AP4	25c dk brn	20.00
C70	AP4	50c blk brn	20.00
C71	AP4	1cor rose red	20.00
		Nos. C67-C71 (5)	100.00

Inauguration of the railroad from San Jorge to San Juan del Sur, Dec. 18, 1932. Printed in sheets of 4, without gum.

Reprints: see note following No. 574. Value, $6 each.

Leon-Sauce Railroad Issue

"Fill" at Santa Lucia River AP5

Designs: 15c, Bridge at Santa Lucia. 25c, Malpaicillo Station. 50c, Panoramic view. 1cor, San Andres.

1932, Dec. 30   Soft porous paper

C72	AP5	15c purple	20.00
C73	AP5	20c bl grn	20.00
C74	AP5	25c dk brn	20.00
C75	AP5	50c blk brn	20.00
C76	AP5	1cor rose red	20.00
		Nos. C72-C76 (5)	100.00

Inauguration of the railroad from Leon to El Sauce, 12/30/32. Sheets of 4, without gum.

Reprints: see note following No. 579. Value, $6 each.

Flag of the Race Issue

1933, Aug. 3   Litho.   Rouletted 9

Without gum

C77	A43	1c dk brn	1.50	1.50
C78	A43	2c red vio	1.50	1.50
C79	A43	4c violet	2.50	2.25
C80	A43	5c dl bl	2.25	2.25
C81	A43	6c vio bl	2.25	2.25
C82	A43	8c dp brn	.70	.70
C83	A43	15c ol brn	.70	.70
C84	A43	20c yellow	2.25	2.25
a.		Horiz. pair, imperf. btwn.	15.00	
b.		Horiz. pair, imperf. vert.	15.00	
C85	A43	25c orange	2.25	2.25
C86	A43	50c rose	2.25	2.25
C87	A43	1cor green	11.00	11.00
		Nos. C77-C87 (11)	29.15	28.90

See note after No. 599. Printed in sheets of 10.

Reprints exist, shades differ from postage and official stamps.

Imperf., Pairs

C78a	A43	2c	14.00
C79a	A43	4c	10.00
C81a	A43	6c	10.00
C82a	A43	8c	10.00
C83a	A43	15c	10.00
C87a	A43	1cor	30.00

AP7

1933, Nov.   *Perf. 12*
C88 AP7 10c bis brn   1.50   1.50
  a.   Vert. pair, imperf. between   35.00
C89 AP7 15c violet   1.25   1.25
  a.   Vert. pair, imperf. between   37.50
C90 AP7 25c red   1.40   1.40
  a.   Horiz. pair, imperf. between   22.50
C91 AP7 50c dp bl   1.50   1.50
      Nos. C88-C91 (4)   5.65   5.65

Intl. Air Post Week, Nov. 6-11, 1933. Printed in sheets of 4. Counterfeits exist.

Stamps and Types of 1928-31 Surcharged in Black

1933, Nov. 3
C92 A25 1c on 2c grn   .25   .25
C93 A24 2c on 3c ol gray   .25   .25
C94 A25 3c on 4c car rose   .25   .25
C95 A24 4c on 5c lt bl   .25   .25
C96 A25 5c on 6c dk bl   .25   .25
C97 A24 6c on 10c ol brn   .25   .25
C98 A24 8c on 15c bis brn   .25   .25
C99 A25 16c on 20c brn   .25   .25
C100 A24 24c on 25c ver   .25   .25
C101 A24 25c on 25c org   .25   .25
C102 A25 32c on 50c vio   .25   .25
C103 A24 40c on 50c grn   .25   .25
C104 A25 50c on 1cor yel   .25   .25
C105 A24 1cor on 1cor org red   .35   .25
      Nos. C92-C105 (14)   3.60   3.50

Nos. C100, C102-C105 exist without script control overprint. Value, each $1.50.

Type of Air Post Stamps of 1929 Surcharged in Black

1933, Oct. 28
C106 AP1 30c on 50c org red   .25   .25
C107 AP1 35c on 50c lt bl   .25   .25
C108 AP1 40c on 1cor yel   .40   .25
C109 AP1 55c on 1cor grn   .30   .25
      Nos. C106-C109 (4)   1.20   1.00

No. C19 Surcharged in Red

1934, Mar. 31
C110 AP1 10c on 20c grn   .30   .25
  a.   Inverted surcharge   15.00
  b.   Double surcharge, one invert-
      ed   15.00
  c.   "Ceutroamericano"   10.00

No. C110 with black surcharge is believed to be of private origin.

No. C4 Surcharged in Red

1935, Aug.
C111 AP1 10c on 25c ol blk   .25   .25
  a.   Small "v" in "vale" (R)   5.00
  b.   "centrvos" (R)   5.00
  c.   Double surcharge (R)   25.00

---

  d.   Inverted surcharge (R)   25.00
  g.   As "a," inverted   400.00
  h.   As "a," double   400.00

No. C111 with blue surcharge is believed to be private origin.

The editors do not recognize the Nicaraguan air post stamps overprinted in red "VALIDO 1935" in two lines with or without script control marks as having been issued primarily for postal purposes.

Nos C4-C6, C18-C19 Overprinted Vertically in Blue, Reading Up:

1935-36
C112 AP1 15c dp vio   1.00   1.00
C113 AP1 20c dp grn   1.75   1.75
C114 AP1 25c ol blk   2.25   2.25
C115 AP1 50c blk brn   5.00   5.00
C116 AP1 1cor org red   40.00   40.00
      Nos. C112-C116 (5)   50.00   50.00

Same Overprint on Nos. C106-C109 Reading Up or Down
C117 AP1 30c on 50c org red   1.50   1.40
C118 AP1 35c on 50c lt bl   6.50   6.50
C119 AP1 40c on 1cor yel   6.50   6.50
C120 AP1 55c on 1cor grn   6.50   6.50
      Nos. C117-C120 (4)   21.00   20.90
      Nos. C112-C120 (9)   71.00   70.90

Same Overprint in Red on Nos. C92-C105

1936
C121 A25 1c on 2c grn   .25   .25
C122 A24 2c on 3c ol gray   .25   .25
C123 A25 3c on 4c car rose   .25   .25
C124 A24 4c on 5c lt bl   .25   .25
C125 A25 5c on 6c dk bl   .25   .25
C126 A24 6c on 10c ol brn   .25   .25
C127 A24 8c on 15c bis brn   .25   .25
C128 A25 16c on 20c brn   .25   .25
C129 A24 24c on 25c ver   .35   .30
C130 A24 25c on 25c org   .25   .25
C131 A25 32c on 50c vio   .25   .25
C132 A25 40c on 50c grn   .55   .50
C133 A25 50c on 1cor yel   .40   .25
C134 A25 1cor on 1cor org
      red   1.40   .65
      Nos. C121-C134 (14)   5.20   4.20

Nos. C121 to C134 are handstamped with script control mark.

Overprint Reading Down on No. C110
C135 AP1 10c on 20c grn   *350.00*

This stamp has been extensively counterfeited.

Overprinted in Red on Nos. C4 to C6, C18 and C19
C136 AP1 15c dp vio   .55   .25
C137 AP1 20c dp grn   .65   .60
C138 AP1 25c ol blk   .65   .55
C139 AP1 50c blk brn   .55   .55
C140 AP1 1cor org red   1.10   .55

On Nos. C106 to C109
C141 AP1 30c on 50c org red   .65   .60
C142 AP1 35c on 50c lt bl   .65   .40
C143 AP1 40c on 1cor yel   .65   .55
C144 AP1 55c on 1cor grn   .65   .50

Same Overprint in Red or Blue on No. C111 Reading Up or Down
C145 AP1 10c on 25c, down   .55   .45
  a.   "Centrvos"   25.00
C146 AP1 10c on 25c (Bl), up   1.25   1.00
  a.   "Centrvos"   25.00
      Nos. C136-C146 (11)   7.90   6.00

Overprint on No. C145 is at right, on No. C146 in center.

Nos. C92, C93 and C98 Overprinted in Black

1936
C147 A25 1c on 2c grn   .25   .25
C148 A24 2c on 3c ol gray   .25   .25
  a.   "Resello 1936" dbl., one invtd.   2.50
C149 A24 8c on 15c bis brn   .25   .25
      Nos. C147-C149 (3)   .75   .75

With script control handstamp.

Nos. C5 and C6 Surcharged in Red

1936, Nov. 26
C150 AP1 15c on 50c blk brn   .25   .25
C151 AP1 15c on 1cor org red   .25   .25

Nos. C18 and C19 Overprinted in Carmine

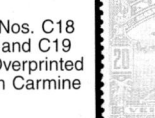

1936, July 2
C152 AP1 15c dp vio   .35   .25
C153 AP1 20c dp grn   .35   .25

Overprint reading up or down.

No. C4 Surcharged and Overprinted in Red

C154 AP1 10c on 25c olive blk   .30   .30
  a.   Surch. and ovpt. inverted   3.50

Same Overprint in Carmine on Nos. C92 to C99
C155 A25 1c on 2c green   .25   .25
C156 A24 2c on 3c olive gray   .65   .65
C157 A25 3c on 4c car rose   .25   .25
C158 A24 4c on 5c light blue   .25   .25
C159 A25 5c on 6c dark blue   .25   .25
C160 A25 6c on 10c olive brn   .25   .25
C161 A24 8c on 15c bister brn   .25   .25
C162 A25 16c on 20c brown   .25   .25
      Nos. C154-C162 (9)   2.70   2.70

No. 518 Overprinted in Black

C163 A25 10c lt brn   .25   .25
  a.   Overprint inverted   2.25
  b.   Double overprint   2.25

Two fonts are found in the sheet of #C163.

Momotombo Type of 1929

1937
C164 AP1 15c yel org   .25   .25
C165 AP1 20c org red   .25   .25
C166 AP1 25c black   .25   .25
C167 AP1 50c violet   .25   .25
C168 AP1 1cor orange   .55   .50
      Nos. C164-C168 (5)   1.55   1.25

Surcharged in Black

1937
C169 AP1 30c on 50c car rose   .25   .25
C170 AP1 35c on 50c olive grn   .25   .25
C171 AP1 40c on 1cor green   .25   .25
C172 AP1 55c on 1cor blue   .25   .25
      Nos. C169-C172 (4)   1.00   1.00

No. C168 Surcharged in Violet

1937   Unwmk.   *Perf. 12*
C173 AP1 10c on 1cor org   .25   .25
  a.   "Centauos"   10.00

No. C98 with Additional Overprint "1937"
C174 A24 8c on 15c bis brn   .45   .25
  a.   "1937" double   6.50

Nos. C92-C102 with Additional Overprint in Blue reading "HABILITADO 1937"
C175 A25 1c on 2c grn   .25   .25
  a.   Blue overprint double   2.50
C176 A24 2c on 3c ol gray   .25   .25
  a.   Double surch., one inverted   2.50
C177 A25 3c on 4c car rose   .25   .25
C178 A24 4c on 5c lt bl   .25   .25
C179 A24 5c on 6c dk bl   .25   .25
C180 A25 6c on 10c ol brn   .25   .25
C181 A24 8c on 15c bis brn   .25   .25
  a.   "Habilitado 1937" double   3.50
C182 A25 16c on 20c brn   .25   .25
  a.   Double surcharge   2.50
C183 A24 24c on 25c ver   .25   .25
C184 A24 25c on 25c org   .25   .25
C185 A25 32c on 50c vio   .25   .25
      Nos. C175-C185 (11)   2.75   2.75

Map of Nicaragua AP8

For Foreign Postage
1937, July 30   Engr.
C186 AP8 10c green   .25   .25
C187 AP8 15c dp bl   .25   .25
C188 AP8 20c yellow   .25   .25
C189 AP8 25c bl vio   .25   .25
C190 AP8 30c rose car   .25   .25
C191 AP8 50c org yel   .35   .25
C192 AP8 1cor ol grn   .70   .55
      Nos. C186-C192 (7)   2.30   2.05

Presidential Palace AP9

For Domestic Postage
C193 AP9 1c rose car   .25   .25
C194 AP9 2c dp bl   .25   .25
C195 AP9 3c ol grn   .25   .25
C196 AP9 4c black   .25   .25
C197 AP9 5c dk vio   .25   .25
C198 AP9 6c chocolate   .25   .25
C199 AP9 8c bl vio   .25   .25
C200 AP9 16c org yel   .25   .25
C201 AP9 24c yellow   .25   .25
C202 AP9 25c yel grn   .25   .25
      Nos. C193-C202 (10)   2.50   2.50

No. C201 with green overprint "Union Panamericana 1890-1940" is of private origin.

Managua AP10

Designs: 15c, Presidential Palace. 20c, Map of South America. 25c, Map of Central America. 30c, Map of North America. 35c, Lagoon of Tiscapa, Managua. 40c, Road Scene. 45c, Park. 50c, Another park. 55c, Scene in San Juan del Sur. 75c, Tipitapa River. 1cor, Landscape.

Wmk. 209
1937, Sept. 17   Typo.   *Perf. 11*
Center in Dark Blue
C203 AP10 10c yel grn   1.60   1.20
C204 AP10 15c orange   1.60   1.40
C205 AP10 20c red   1.00   1.00
C206 AP10 25c vio brn   1.00   1.00
  a.   Center, double impression
C207 AP10 30c bl grn   1.00   1.00
  a.   Great Lakes omitted   40.00   40.00

C208	AP10	35c lemon	.50 .45
C209	AP10	40c green	.40 .40
C210	AP10	45c brt vio	.40 .35
C211	AP10	50c rose lil	.40 .35
a.		Vert. pair, imperf. btwn.	140.00
C212	AP10	60c ll lil	.40 .35
C213	AP10	75c gray grn	.40 .35

Center in Brown Red

C214	AP10	1cor dk bl	1.00 .50
	Nos. C203-C214 (12)		9.70 8.35

150th anniv. of the Constitution of the US.

Diriangen — AP11

Designs: 4c, 10c, Nicarao. 5c, 15c, Bartolomé de Las Casas. 8c, 20c, Columbus.

For Domestic Postage
Without gum

1937, Oct. 12	**Unwmk.**		**Perf. 11**
C215	AP11	1c green	.25 .25
C216	AP11	4c brn car	.25 .25
C217	AP11	5c dk vio	.25 .25
a.		Without imprint	.40
C218	AP11	8c dp bl	.25 .25
a.		Without imprint	.50

For Foreign Postage
Wmk. 209
With Gum

C219	AP11	10c lt brn	.25 .25
C220	AP11	15c pale bl	.25 .25
a.		Without imprint	1.00
C221	AP11	20c pale rose	.25 .25
	Nos. C215-C221 (7)		1.75 1.75

Nos. C215-C221 printed in sheets of 4.

Imperf., Pairs

C215a	AP11	1c	.25 .25
C216a	AP11	4c	.25 .25
C217b	AP11	5c	.25 .25
C217c	AP11	5c Without imprint	
C218b	AP11	8c	.20
C218c	AP11	8c Without imprint	
C219a	AP11	10c	.25 .25
C220b	AP11	15c	.25 .25
C220c	AP11	15c Without imprint	
C221a	AP11	20c	.35 .35

Gen. Tomas Martinez — AP11a

Design: 10c-50c, Gen. Anastasio Somoza.

For Domestic Postage
Without gum
Perf. 11½, Imperf.

1938, Jan. 18	**Typo.**		**Unwmk.**
	Center in Black		
C221B	AP11a	1c orange	.25 .25
C221C	AP11a	5c red vio	.25 .25
C221D	AP11a	8c dk bl	.25 .25
C221E	AP11a	16c brown	.25 .25
f.		Sheet of 4, 1c, 5c, 8c, 16c	1.25 1.25

For Foreign Postage

C221G	AP11a	10c green	.25 .25
C221H	AP11a	15c dk bl	.25 .25
C221J	AP11a	25c violet	.40 .40
C221K	AP11a	50c carmine	.50 .45
m.		Sheet of 4, 10c, 15c, 25c, 50c	2.00 2.00
	Nos. C221B-C221K (8)		2.40 2.35

75th anniv. of postal service in Nicaragua. Printed in sheets of four.

Stamps of type AP11a exist in changed colors and with inverted centers, double centers and frames printed on the back. These varieties were private fabrications.

Lake Managua AP12

President Anastasio Somoza — AP13

For Domestic Postage

1939	**Unwmk.**	**Engr.**	**Perf. 12½**
C222	AP12	2c dp bl	.25 .25
C223	AP12	3c green	.25 .25
C224	AP12	8c pale lil	.25 .25
C225	AP12	16c orange	.25 .25
C226	AP12	24c yellow	.25 .25
C227	AP12	32c dk grn	.25 .25
C228	AP12	50c dp rose	.25 .25

For Foreign Postage

C229	AP13	10c dk brn	.25 .25
C230	AP13	15c dk bl	.25 .25
C231	AP13	20c org yel	.25 .25
C232	AP13	25c dk pur	.25 .25
C233	AP13	30c lake	.25 .25
C234	AP13	50c dp org	.25 .25
C235	AP13	1cor dk ol grn	.35 .40
	Nos. C222-C235 (14)		3.60 3.65

For Domestic Postage

Will Rogers and View of Managua AP14

Designs: 2c, Rogers standing beside plane. 3c, Leaving airport office. 4c, Rogers and US Marines. 5c, Managua after earthquake.

1939, Mar. 31	**Engr.**		**Perf. 12**
C236	AP14	1c brt grn	.25 .25
C237	AP14	2c org red	.25 .25
C238	AP14	3c lt ultra	.25 .25
C239	AP14	4c dk bl	.25 .25
C240	AP14	5c rose car	.25 .25
	Nos. C236-C240 (5)		1.25 1.25

Will Rogers' flight to Managua after the earthquake, Mar. 31, 1931.
For surcharges see Nos. 686, 688 in Scott Standard catalogue, Vol. 5.

Pres. Anastasio Somoza in US House of Representatives — AP19

President Somoza and US Capitol AP20

President Somoza, Tower of the Sun and Trylon and Perisphere AP21

For Domestic Postage

1940, Feb. 1			
C241	AP19	4c red brn	.25 .25
C242	AP20	8c blk brn	.25 .25
C243	AP19	16c grnsh bl	.25 .25
C244	AP20	20c brt plum	.50 .30
C245	AP21	32c scarlet	.25 .25

For Foreign Postage

C246	AP19	25c dp bl	.25 .25
C247	AP19	30c black	.25 .25
C248	AP20	50c rose pink	.45 .40
C249	AP21	60c green	.50 .30
C250	AP19	65c dk vio brn	.50 .25
C251	AP19	90c ol grn	.65 .30
C252	AP21	1cor violet	1.00 .55
	Nos. C241-C252 (12)		5.10 3.60

Visit of Pres. Somoza to US in 1939.

For surcharge see No. C636 in Scott Standard catalogue, Vol. 5.

L. S. Rowe, Statue of Liberty, Nicaraguan Coastline, Flags of 21 American Republics, US Shield and Arms of Nicaragua — AP22

1940, Aug. 2	**Engr.**		**Perf. 12½**
C253	AP22	1.25cor multi	.65 .60

50th anniversary of Pan American Union.
For overprint see No. C493 in Scott Standard catalogue, Vol. 5.

AIR POST OFFICIAL STAMPS

OA1

"Typewritten" Overprint on #O293

1929, Aug.	**Unwmk.**		**Perf. 12**
CO1	OA1	25c orange	50.00 45.00

Excellent counterfeits of No. CO1 are plentiful.

Official Stamps of 1926 Ovptd. in Dark Blue

1929, Sept. 15			
CO2	A24	25c orange	.50 .50
a.		Inverted overprint	25.00
b.		Double overprint	25.00
CO3	A25	50c pale bl	.75 .75
a.		Inverted overprint	25.00
b.		Double overprint	25.00
c.		Double overprint, one inverted	25.00

Nos. 519-523 Overprinted in Black

1932, Feb.			
CO4	A24	15c org red	.40 .40
a.		Inverted overprint	25.00
b.		Double overprint	25.00
c.		Double overprint, one invtd.	25.00
CO5	A25	20c orange	.45 .45
a.		Double overprint	25.00
CO6	A24	25c dk vio	.45 .45
CO7	A25	50c green	.55 .55
CO8	A25	1cor yellow	1.00 1.00
	Nos. CO4-CO8 (5)		2.85 2.85

Nos. CO4-CO5, CO7-CO8 exist with signature control overprint. Value, each, $2.50.

Overprinted on Stamp No. 547

CO9	A24	25c blk brn	42.50 42.50

The varieties "OFICAL", "OFIAIAL" and "CORROE" occur in the setting and are found on each stamp of the series.
Counterfeits of No. CO9 are plentiful.
Stamp No. CO4 with overprint "1931" in addition is believed to be of private origin.

Type of Regular Issue of 1914 Overprinted Like Nos. CO4-CO8

1933			
CO10	A24	25c olive	.25 .25
CO11	A25	50c ol grn	.25 .25
CO12	A25	1cor org red	.40 .40

On Stamps of 1914-28

CO13	A24	15c dp vio	.25 .25
CO14	A25	20c dp grn	.25 .25
	Nos. CO10-CO14 (5)		1.40 1.40

Nos. CO10-CO14 exist without signature control mark. Value, each $2.50.

Air Post Official Stamps of 1932-33 Ovptd. in Blue

1935			
CO15	A24	15c dp vio	1.00 .80
CO16	A25	20c dp grn	2.00 1.60
CO17	A24	25c olive	3.00 2.50
CO18	A25	50c ol grn	35.00 30.00
CO19	A25	1cor org red	40.00 37.50
	Nos. CO15-CO19 (5)		81.00 72.40

Overprinted in Red

CO20	A24	15c dp vio	.25 .25
CO21	A25	20c dp grn	.25 .25
CO22	A24	25c olive	.25 .25
CO23	A25	50c ol grn	.80 .80
CO24	A25	1cor org red	.80 .80
	Nos. CO20-CO24 (5)		2.35 2.35

Nos. CO15 to CO24 are handstamped with script control mark. Counterfeits of blue overprint are plentiful.

The editors do not recognize the Nicaraguan air post Official stamps overprinted in red "VALIDO 1935" in two lines and with or without script control marks as having been issued primarily for postal purposes.

Nos. C164-C168 Overprinted in Black

1937			
CO25	AP1	15c yel org	.80 .55
CO26	AP1	20c org red	.80 .60
CO27	AP1	25c black	.80 .70
CO28	AP1	50c violet	.80 .70
CO29	AP1	1cor orange	.80 .70
	Nos. CO25-CO29 (5)		4.00 3.25

Pres. Anastasio Somoza — OA2

1939, Feb. 7	**Engr.**		**Perf. 12½**
CO30	OA2	10c brown	.25 .25
CO31	OA2	15c dk bl	.25 .25
CO32	OA2	20c yellow	.25 .25
CO33	OA2	25c dk pur	.25 .25
CO34	OA2	30c lake	.25 .25
CO35	OA2	50c dp org	.65 .65
CO36	OA2	1cor dk ol grn	1.25 1.25
	Nos. CO30-CO36 (7)		3.15 3.15

POSTAGE DUE STAMPS

D1

1896	**Unwmk.**	**Engr.**	**Perf. 12**
J1	D1	1c orange	.50 1.25
J2	D1	2c orange	.50 1.25
J3	D1	5c orange	.50 1.25
J4	D1	10c orange	.50 1.25
J5	D1	20c orange	.50 1.25

J6	D1	30c orange	.50	1.25
J7	D1	50c orange	.50	1.50
		Nos. J1-J7 (7)	3.50	9.00

Wmk. 117

J8	D1	1c orange	1.00	1.50
J9	D1	2c orange	1.00	1.50
J10	D1	5c orange	1.00	1.50
J11	D1	10c orange	1.00	1.50
J12	D1	20c orange	1.25	2.00
J13	D1	30c orange	1.00	1.50
J14	D1	50c orange	1.00	1.50
		Nos. J8-J14 (7)	7.25	10.50

1897   Unwmk.

J15	D1	1c violet	.50	1.50
J16	D1	2c violet	.50	1.50
J17	D1	5c violet	.50	1.50
J18	D1	10c violet	.50	1.50
J19	D1	20c violet	1.25	2.00
J20	D1	30c violet	.50	1.50
J21	D1	50c violet	.50	1.50
		Nos. J15-J21 (7)	4.25	11.00

Wmk. 117

J22	D1	1c violet	.50	1.50
J23	D1	2c violet	.50	1.50
J24	D1	5c violet	.50	1.50
J25	D1	10c violet	.50	1.50
J26	D1	20c violet	1.00	2.00
J27	D1	30c violet	.50	1.50
J28	D1	50c violet	.50	1.50
		Nos. J22-J28 (7)	4.00	11.00

Reprints of Nos. J8-J28 are on thick, porous paper. Color of 1896 reprints, reddish orange; or 1897 reprints, reddish violet. On watermarked reprints, liberty cap is sideways. Value 25c each.

D2

1898   Litho.   Unwmk.

J29	D2	1c blue green	.25	2.00
J30	D2	2c blue green	.25	2.00
J31	D2	5c blue green	.25	2.00
J32	D2	10c blue green	.25	2.00
J33	D2	20c blue green	.25	2.00
J34	D2	30c blue green	.25	2.00
J35	D2	50c blue green	.25	2.00
		Nos. J29-J35 (7)	1.75	14.00

1899

J36	D2	1c carmine	.25	2.00
J37	D2	2c carmine	.25	2.00
J38	D2	5c carmine	.25	2.00
J39	D2	10c carmine	.25	2.00
J40	D2	20c carmine	.25	2.00
J41	D2	50c carmine	.25	2.00
		Nos. J36-J41 (6)	1.50	12.00

Some denominations are found in se-tenant pairs.
Various counterfeit cancellations exist on #J1-J41.

D3

1900   Engr.

J42	D3	1c plum	.75	
J43	D3	2c vermilion	.75	
J44	D3	5c dk bl	.75	
J45	D3	10c purple	.75	
J46	D3	20c org brn	.75	
J47	D3	30c dk grn	1.50	
J48	D3	50c lake	1.50	
		Nos. J42-J48 (7)	6.75	

Nos. J42-J48 were not placed in use as postage due stamps. They were only issued with "Postage" overprints. See Nos. 137-143, 152-158, O72-O81, 2L11-2L15, 2L25, 2L40-2L41.

OFFICIAL STAMPS

Types of Postage Stamps Overprinted in Red Diagonally Reading up

1890   Unwmk.   Engr.   Perf. 12

O1	A5	1c ultra	.25	.30
O2	A5	2c ultra	.25	.30
O3	A5	5c ultra	.25	.30
O4	A5	10c ultra	.25	.40
O5	A5	20c ultra	.25	.45
O6	A5	50c ultra	.25	.75
O7	A5	1p ultra	.25	1.25
O8	A5	2p ultra	.25	1.60
O9	A5	5p ultra	.25	2.40
O10	A5	10p ultra	.25	5.50
		Nos. O1-O10 (10)	2.50	11.75

All values of the 1890 issue are known without overprint and most of them with inverted or double overprint, or without overprint and imperforate. There is no evidence that they were issued in these forms.
Official stamps of 1890-1899 are scarce with genuine cancellations. Forged cancellations are plentiful.

Overprinted Vertically Reading Up

1891   Litho.

O11	A6	1c green	.25	.30
O12	A6	2c green	.25	.30
O13	A6	5c green	.25	.30
O14	A6	10c green	.25	.30
O15	A6	20c green	.25	.50
O16	A6	50c green	.25	1.10
O17	A6	1p green	.25	1.25
O18	A6	2p green	.25	1.30
O19	A6	5p green	.25	2.40
O20	A6	10p green	.25	4.00
		Nos. O11-O20 (10)	2.50	11.75

All values of this issue except the 2c and 5p exist without overprint and several with double overprint. They are not known to have been issued in this form.
Many of the denominations may be found in se-tenant pairs.

Overprinted in Dark Blue

1892   Engr.

O21	A7	1c yellow brown	.25	.30
O22	A7	2c yellow brown	.25	.30
O23	A7	5c yellow brown	.25	.30
O24	A7	10c yellow brown	.25	.30
O25	A7	20c yellow brown	.25	.50
O26	A7	50c yellow brown	.25	1.00
O27	A7	1p yellow brown	.25	1.25
O28	A7	2p yellow brown	.25	1.60
O29	A7	5p yellow brown	.25	2.40
O30	A7	10p yellow brown	.25	4.00
		Nos. O21-O30 (10)	2.50	11.95

The 2c and 1p are known without overprint and several values exist with double or inverted overprint. These probably were not regularly issued.
Commemorative of the 400th anniversary of the discovery of America by Christopher Columbus.

Overprinted in Red

1893   Engr.

O31	A8	1c slate	.25	.30
O32	A8	2c slate	.25	.30
O33	A8	5c slate	.25	.30
O34	A8	10c slate	.25	.30
O35	A8	20c slate	.25	.50
O36	A8	25c slate	.25	.75
O37	A8	50c slate	.25	.85
O38	A8	1p slate	.25	1.00
O39	A8	2p slate	.25	2.00
O40	A8	5p slate	.25	2.50
O41	A8	10p slate	.25	5.50
		Nos. O31-O41 (11)	2.75	14.30

The 2, 5, 10, 20, 25, 50c and 5p are known without overprint but probably were not regularly issued. Some values exist with double or inverted overprints.

Overprinted in Black

1894

O42	A9	1c orange	.30	.35
O43	A9	2c orange	.30	.35
O44	A9	5c orange	.30	.35
O45	A9	10c orange	.30	.35
O46	A9	20c orange	.30	.50
O47	A9	50c orange	.30	.75
O48	A9	1p orange	.30	1.50
O49	A9	2p orange	.30	2.00
O50	A9	5p orange	2.00	3.00
O51	A9	10p orange	2.00	4.00
		Nos. O42-O51 (10)	6.40	13.15

Reprints are yellow.

Overprinted in Dark Blue

1895

O52	A10	1c green	.25	.35
O53	A10	2c green	.25	.35
O54	A10	5c green	.25	.35
O55	A10	10c green	.25	.35
O56	A10	20c green	.25	.50
O57	A10	50c green	.25	1.00
O58	A10	1p green	.25	1.50
O59	A10	2p green	.25	2.00
O60	A10	5p green	.25	3.00
O61	A10	10p green	.25	4.00
		Nos. O52-O61 (10)	2.50	13.40

Wmk. 117

O62	A10	1c green	
O63	A10	2c green	
O64	A10	5c green	
O65	A10	10c green	
O66	A10	20c green	
O67	A10	50c green	
O68	A10	1p green	
O69	A10	2p green	
O70	A10	5p green	
O71	A10	10p green	

Nos. O62-O71 probably exist only as reprints. Value, each 15 cents.

Postage Due Stamps of Same Date Handstamped in Violet

1896   Unwmk.

O72	D1	1c orange	7.00
O73	D1	2c orange	7.00
O74	D1	5c orange	5.00
O75	D1	10c orange	5.00
O76	D1	20c orange	5.00
		Nos. O72-O76 (5)	29.00

Wmk. 117

O77	D1	1c orange	7.00
O78	D1	2c orange	7.00
O79	D1	5c orange	4.00
O80	D1	10c orange	4.00
O81	D1	20c orange	4.00
		Nos. O77-O81 (5)	26.00

Nos. O72-O81 were handstamped in rows of five. Several handstamps were used, one of which had the variety "Ofícial." Most varieties are known inverted and double.
Forgeries exist.

Types of Postage Stamps Overprinted in Red

1896   Unwmk.

O82	A11	1c red	2.50	3.00
O83	A11	2c red	2.50	3.00
O84	A11	5c red	2.50	3.00
O85	A11	10c red	2.50	3.00
O86	A11	20c red	3.00	3.00
O87	A11	50c red	5.00	5.00
O88	A11	1p red	12.00	12.00
O89	A11	2p red	12.00	12.00
O90	A11	5p red	16.00	16.00
		Nos. O82-O90 (9)	58.00	60.00

Wmk. 117

O91	A11	1c red	3.00	3.50
O92	A11	2c red	3.00	3.50
O93	A11	5c red	3.00	3.50
O94	A11	10c red	3.00	3.50
O95	A11	20c red	5.00	5.00
O96	A11	50c red	3.00	5.00
O97	A11	1p red	14.00	14.00
O98	A11	2p red	16.00	16.00
O99	A11	5p red	25.00	25.00
		Nos. O91-O99 (9)	75.00	79.00

Used values for Nos. O88-O90, O97-O99 are for CTO examples. Postally used examples are not known.

Same, Dated 1897

1897   Unwmk.

O100	A11	1c red	3.00	3.00
O101	A11	2c red	3.00	3.00
O102	A11	5c red	3.00	2.50
O103	A11	10c red	3.00	3.00
O104	A11	20c red	3.00	4.00
O105	A11	50c red	5.00	5.00
O106	A11	1p red	12.00	12.00
O107	A11	2p red	12.00	12.00
O108	A11	5p red	16.00	16.00
		Nos. O100-O108 (9)	60.00	60.50

Wmk. 117

O109	A11	1c red	5.00	5.00
O110	A11	2c red	5.00	5.00
O111	A11	5c red	5.00	5.00
O112	A11	10c red	10.00	10.00
O113	A11	20c red	10.00	10.00
O114	A11	50c red	12.00	12.00
O115	A11	1p red	20.00	20.00
O116	A11	2p red	20.00	20.00
O117	A11	5p red	20.00	20.00
		Nos. O109-O117 (9)	107.00	107.00

Reprints of Nos. O82-O117 are described in notes after No. 109M. Value 15c each.
Used values for Nos. O106-O108, O115-O117 are for CTO examples. Postally used examples are not known.

Overprinted in Blue

1898   Unwmk.

O118	A12	1c carmine	3.25	3.25
O119	A12	2c carmine	3.25	3.25
O120	A12	4c carmine	3.25	3.25
O121	A12	5c carmine	2.50	2.50
O122	A12	10c carmine	4.00	4.00
O123	A12	15c carmine	6.00	6.00
O124	A12	20c carmine	6.00	6.00
O125	A12	50c carmine	8.50	8.50
O126	A12	1p carmine	11.00	11.00
O127	A12	2p carmine	11.00	11.00
O128	A12	5p carmine	11.00	11.00
		Nos. O118-O128 (11)	69.75	69.75

Stamps of this set with sideways watermark 117 or with black overprint are reprints. Value 25c each.
Used values for Nos. O126-O128 are for CTO examples. Postally used examples are not known.

Overprinted in Dark Blue

1899

O129	A13	1c gray grn	.25	1.00
O130	A13	2c bis brn	.25	1.00
O131	A13	4c lake	.25	1.00
O132	A13	5c dk bl	.25	.50

O133 A13 10c buff .25 1.00
O134 A13 15c chocolate .25 2.00
O135 A13 20c dk grn .25 3.00
O136 A13 50c car rose .25 3.00
O137 A13 1p red .25 10.00
O138 A13 2p violet .25 10.00
O139 A13 5p lt bl .25 15.00
Nos. O129-O139 (11) 2.75 47.50

Counterfeit cancellations on Nos. O129-O139 are plentiful.

"Justice" — O5

1900 Engr.
O140 O5 1c plum .60 .60
O141 O5 2c vermilion .50 .50
O142 O5 4c ol grn .60 .60
O143 O5 5c dk bl 1.25 .45
O144 O5 10c purple 1.25 .35
O145 O5 20c brown .90 .35
O146 O5 50c lake 1.25 .50
O147 O5 1p ultra 3.50 2.50
O148 O5 2p brn org 4.00 4.00
O149 O5 5p grnsh blk 5.00 5.00
Nos. O140-O149 (10) 18.85 14.85

For surcharges see Nos. O155-O157.

Nos. 123, 161
Surcharged in
Black

1903 Perf. 12, 14
O150 A14 1c on 10c violet .25 .30
a. "Centovo" 1.00
b. "Contavo" 1.00
c. With ornaments .30
d. Inverted surcharge 1.00
e. "1" omitted at upper left 2.00
O151 A14 2c on 3c green .30 .40
a. "Centovos" 1.00
b. "Contavos" 1.00
c. With ornaments .35
d. Inverted surcharge 1.00
O152 A14 4c on 3c green 1.25 1.25
a. "Centovos" 2.50
b. "Contavos" 2.50
c. With ornaments 2.50
d. Inverted surcharge
O153 A14 4c on 10c violet 1.25 1.25
a. "Centovos" 2.50
b. "Contavos" 2.50
c. With ornaments 2.00
d. Inverted surcharge
O154 A14 5c on 3c green .25 .25
a. "Centovos" 1.00
b. "Contavos" 1.00
c. With ornaments .30
d. Double surcharge 2.00
e. Inverted surcharge
Nos. O150-O154 (5) 3.30 3.45

These surcharges are set up to cover 25 stamps. Some of the settings have bars or pieces of fancy border type below "OFICIAL." There are 5 varieties on #O150, 3 on #O151, 1 each on #O152, O153, O154.
In 1904 #O151 was reprinted to fill a dealer's order. This printing lacks the small figure at the upper right. It includes the variety "OFICILA." At the same time the same setting was printed in carmine on official stamps of 1900, 1c on 10c violet and 2c on 1p ultramarine. Also the 1, 2 and 5p official stamps of 1900 were surcharged with new values and the dates 1901 or 1902 in various colors, inverted, etc. It is doubtful if any of these varieties were ever in Nicaragua and certain that none of them ever did legitimate postal duty.

No. O145
Surcharged in Black

1904 Perf. 12
O155 O5 10c on 20c brn .25 .25
a. No period after "Ctvs" 1.00 .75
O156 O5 30c on 20c brn .25 .25
O157 O5 50c on 20c brn .50 .35
a. Lower "50" omitted 2.50 2.50
b. Upper figures omitted 2.50 2.50
c. Top left and lower figures omitted 3.50 3.50
Nos. O155-O157 (3) 1.00 .85

Coat of Arms — O6

1905, July 25 Engr.
O158 O6 1c green .25 .25
O159 O6 2c rose .25 .25
O160 O6 5c blue .25 .25
O161 O6 10c yel brn .25 .25
O162 O6 20c orange .25 .25
O163 O6 50c brn ol .25 .25
O164 O6 1p lake .25 .25
O165 O6 2p violet .25 .25
O166 O6 5p gray blk .25 .25
Nos. O158-O166 (9) 2.25 2.25

Surcharged
Vertically Up or
Down

1907
O167 O6 10c on 1c grn .75 .75
O168 O6 10c on 2c rose 25.00 22.50
O169 O6 50c on 1c grn 22.50 17.50
O170 O6 50c on 1c grn 1.50 1.50
O171 O6 50c on 2c rose 22.50 12.50

Surcharged

O172 O6 1p on 2c rose 1.50 1.50
O173 O6 2p on 2c rose 1.50 1.50
O174 O6 3p on 2c rose 1.50 1.50
O175 O6 4p on 2c rose
O176 O6 4p on 5c blue 2.25 2.25

The setting for this surcharge includes various letters from wrong fonts, the figure "1" for "I" in "Vale" and an "I" for "1" in "$1.00."

Surcharged

O177 O6 20c on 1c green 1.00 1.00
a. Double surcharge 5.00 5.00
Nos. O167-O174,O176-O177 (10) 80.00 62.50

The preceding surcharges are vertical, reading both up and down.

Revenue Stamps Surcharged

O7

1907 Perf. 14 to 15
O178 O7 10c on 2c org (Bk) .25 .25
O179 O7 35c on 1c bl (R) .25 .25
a. Inverted surcharge 3.00 3.00
O180 O7 70c on 1c bl (V) .25 .25
a. Inverted surcharge 3.00 3.00
O181 O7 70c on 1c bl (O) .25 .25
a. Inverted surcharge 3.00 3.00
O182 O7 1p on 2c org (G) .25 .25
a. Inverted surcharge 2.50 2.50
O183 O7 2p on 2c org (Br) .25 .25
O184 O7 3p on 5c brn (Bl) .25 .25
O185 O7 4p on 5c brn (G) .25 .25
a. Double surcharge 3.00 3.00

O186 O7 5p on 5c brn (G) .25 .25
a. Inverted surcharge 3.50 3.50
Nos. O178-O186 (9) 2.25 2.25

Letters and figures from several fonts were mixed in these surcharges.
See Nos. O199-O209.

No. 202 Surcharged

1907, Nov.
Black or Blue Black Surcharge
O187 A18 10c on 1c grn 15.00 13.00
O188 A18 15c on 1c grn 15.00 13.00
O189 A18 20c on 1c grn 15.00 13.00
O190 A18 50c on 1c grn 15.00 13.00
Red Surcharge
O191 A18 1(un)p on 1c grn 14.00 13.00
O192 A18 2(dos)p on 1c grn 14.00 13.00
Nos. O187-O192 (6) 88.00 78.00

No. 181 Surcharged

1908 Yellow Surcharge Perf. 12
O193 A18 10c on 3c vio 15.00 15.00
O194 A18 15c on 3c vio 15.00 15.00
O195 A18 20c on 3c vio 15.00 15.00
O196 A18 35c on 3c vio 15.00 15.00
O197 A18 50c on 3c vio 15.00 15.00
Nos. O193-O197 (5) 75.00 75.00

Black Surcharge
O198 A18 35c on 3c vio 100.00 100.00

**Revenue Stamps Surcharged like
1907 Issue
Dated "1908"**

1908 Perf. 14 to 15
O199 O7 10c on 1c bl (V) .75 .50
a. Inverted surcharge 3.50 3.50
O200 O7 35c on 1c bl (Bk) .75 .50
a. Inverted surcharge 3.50 3.50
b. Double surcharge 4.00 4.00
O201 O7 50c on 1c bl (R) .75 .50
O202 O7 1p on 1c bl (Br) 37.50 37.50
a. Inverted surcharge 65.00 65.00
O203 O7 2p on 1c bl (G) .90 .75
O204 O7 10c on 2c org (Bk) 1.10 .65
O205 O7 35c on 2c org (R) 1.10 .65
a. Double surcharge 3.50
O206 O7 50c on 2c org (Bk) 1.10 .65
O207 O7 70c on 2c org (Bl) 1.10 .65
O208 O7 1p on 2c org (G) 1.10 .65
O209 O7 2p on 2c org (Br) 1.10 .65
Nos. O199-O209 (11) 47.25 43.65

There are several minor varieties in the figures, etc., in these surcharges.

Nos. 243-248
Overprinted in Black

1909 Perf. 12
O210 A18 10c lake .25 .25
a. Double overprint 2.50 2.50
O211 A18 15c black .60 .50
O212 A18 20c brn ol 1.00 .75
O213 A18 50c dp grn 1.50 1.00
O214 A18 1p yellow 1.75 1.25
O215 A18 2p car rose 2.75 2.00
Nos. O210-O215 (6) 7.85 5.75

Overprinted in Black

1910
O216 A18 15c black 1.50 1.25
a. Double overprint 4.00 4.00
O217 A18 20c brn ol 2.50 2.00
O218 A18 50c dp grn 2.50 2.00
O219 A18 1p yellow 2.75 2.50
a. Inverted overprint 7.50 7.50
O220 A18 2p car rose 4.00 3.00
Nos. O216-O220 (5) 13.25 10.75

Nos. 239-240 Surcharged in Black

No. O221 No. O222

1911
O221 A18 5c on 3c red org 6.00 6.00
O222 A18 10c on 4c vio 5.00 5.00
a. Double surcharge 10.00 10.00
b. Pair, one without new value 20.00

Revenue Stamps
Surcharged in Black

1911, Nov. Perf. 14 to 15
O223 A21 10c on 10c on 1 red 3.00 3.00
a. Inverted surcharge 4.50
b. Double surcharge 4.50
O224 A21 15c on 10c on 1 red 3.00 3.00
a. Inverted surcharge 5.00
b. Double surcharge 4.50
O225 A21 20c on 10c on 1 red 3.00 3.00
a. Inverted surcharge 5.00
O226 A21 50c on 10c on 1 red 3.75 3.75
a. Inverted surcharge 4.50
O227 A21 1p on 10c on 1 red 5.00 7.00
a. Inverted surcharge 6.00
O228 A21 2p on 10c on 1 red 5.50 10.00
a. Inverted surcharge 7.50
b. Double surcharge 7.50
Nos. O223-O228 (6) 23.25 29.75

Surcharged in Black

1911, Nov.
O229 A21 10c on 10c on 1 red 22.50
O230 A21 15c on 10c on 1 red 22.50
O231 A21 20c on 10c on 1 red 22.50
O232 A21 50c on 10c on 1 red 16.00
Nos. O229-O232 (4) 83.50

Surcharged in Black

1911, Dec.
O233 A21 5c on 10c on 1 red 4.50 6.00
a. Double surcharge 7.50
b. Inverted surcharge 7.50
c. "5" omitted 6.00
O234 A21 10c on 10c on 1 red 5.50 7.00
O235 A21 15c on 10c on 1 red 6.00 7.50
O236 A21 20c on 10c on 1 red 6.50 8.50
O237 A21 50c on 10c on 1 red 7.50 10.00
Nos. O233-O237 (5) 30.00 39.00

Nos. O233 to O237 have a surcharge on the back like Nos. 285 and 286 with "15 cts" obliterated by a heavy horizontal bar.

Surcharged Vertically
in Black

1912
O238 A21 5c on 10c on 1 red 8.00 8.00
O239 A21 10c on 10c on 1 red 8.00 8.00
O240 A21 15c on 10c on 1 red 8.00 8.00

O241 A21 20c on 10c on 1 red 8.00 8.00
O242 A21 35c on 10c on 1 red 8.00 8.00
O243 A21 50c on 10c on 1 red 8.00 8.00
O244 A21 1p on 10c on 1 red 8.00 8.00
Nos. O238-O244 (7) 56.00 56.00

Nos. 238 to O244 are printed on Nos. 285 and 286 but the surcharge on the back is obliterated by a vertical bar.

Types of Regular Issue of 1912 Overprinted in Black

1912 Perf. 12
O245 A22 1c light blue .25 .25
O246 A22 2c light blue .25 .25
O247 A22 3c light blue .25 .25
O248 A22 4c light blue .25 .25
O249 A22 5c light blue .25 .25
O250 A22 6c light blue .25 .25
O251 A22 10c light blue .25 .25
O252 A22 15c light blue .25 .25
O253 A22 20c light blue .25 .25
O254 A22 25c light blue .25 .25
O255 A23 35c light blue .25 .25
O256 A22 50c light blue 1.50 1.50
O257 A22 1p light blue .30 .30
O258 A22 2p light blue .35 .35
O259 A22 5p light blue .50 .50
Nos. O245-O259 (15) 5.40 5.40

On the 35c the overprint is 15½mm wide, on the other values it is 13mm.

Types of Regular Issue of 1914 Overprinted in Black

1915, May
O260 A24 1c light blue .25 .25
O261 A25 2c light blue .25 .25
O262 A24 3c light blue .25 .25
O263 A25 4c light blue .25 .25
O264 A25 5c lt bl .25 .25
O265 A25 6c light blue .25 .25
O266 A25 10c light blue .25 .25
O267 A24 15c light blue .25 .25
O268 A25 20c light blue .25 .25
O269 A24 25c light blue .30 .30
O270 A25 50c light blue .60 .60
Nos. O260-O270 (11) 3.15 3.15

Regular Issues of 1914-22 Overprinted in Red

1925
O271 A24 ½c dp grn .25 .25
a. Double overprint 2.50 2.50
O272 A24 1c violet .25 .25
O273 A25 2c car rose .25 .25
O274 A24 3c ol grn .25 .25
O275 A24 4c vermilion .25 .25
a. Double overprint 2.50 2.50
O276 A24 5c black .25 .25
a. Double overprint 2.50 2.50
O277 A25 6c red brn .25 .25
O278 A25 10c yellow .30 .30
a. Double overprint 3.50 3.50
O279 A24 15c red brn .40 .40
O280 A25 20c bis brn .50 .50
O281 A25 25c orange .60 .60
a. Inverted overprint 4.00 4.00
O282 A25 50c pale bl .75 .75
a. Double overprint 5.00 5.00
Nos. O271-O282 (12) 4.30 4.30

Type II overprint has "f" and "i" separated. Comes on Nos. O272-O274 and O276.

Regular Issues of 1914-22 Overprinted in Black

1926
O283 A24 ½c dk grn .25 .25
O284 A24 1c dp vio .25 .25
O285 A25 2c car rose .25 .25
O286 A24 3c ol gray .25 .25
O287 A25 4c vermilion .25 .25

O288 A24 5c gray blk .25 .25
O289 A25 6c red brn .25 .25
O290 A25 10c yellow .25 .25
O291 A24 15c dp brn .25 .25
O292 A25 20c bis brn .25 .25
O293 A24 25c orange .25 .25
O294 A25 50c pale bl .25 .25
Nos. O283-O294 (12) 3.00 3.00

No. 499 Surcharged in Black

1931
O295 A33 5c on 10c bis brn .25 .25

Nos. 517-518 Overprinted in Red

1931
O296 A25 6c bis brn .25 .25
O297 A25 10c lt brn .25 .25

Nos. 541, 543, 545 With Additional Overprint in Red

O298 A24 1c ol grn .25 .25
O299 A24 3c lt bl .25 .25
a. "OFICIAL" inverted .80 .80
O300 A24 5c gray brn .25 .25
a. "1931" double .80 .80
Nos. O298-O300 (3) .75 .75

Regular Issues of 1914-31 Overprinted in Black

1932, Feb. 6
O301 A24 1c ol grn .25 .25
a. Double overprint 1.40 1.40
O302 A25 2c brt rose .25 .25
a. Double overprint 1.40 1.40
O303 A24 3c lt bl .25 .25
a. Double overprint .50 .50
O304 A25 4c dk bl .25 .25
O305 A24 5c ol brn .25 .25
O306 A25 6c bis brn .25 .25
a. Double overprint 2.00 2.00
O307 A24 10c lt brn .30 .30
O308 A24 15c org red .40 .40
a. Double overprint 2.25 2.25
O309 A25 20c orange .70 .70
O310 A25 25c dk vio 2.00 .50
O311 A25 50c green .25 .25
O312 A25 1cor yellow .25 .25
Nos. O301-O312 (12) 5.40 3.35

With Additional Overprint in Black

1932, Feb. 6
O313 A24 1c ol grn 5.50 5.50
O314 A24 2c brt rose 6.50 6.50
a. Double overprint 8.25 8.25
O315 A24 3c lt bl 5.00 5.00
O316 A24 5c ol brn 5.00 5.00
O317 A24 15c org red .65 .65
O318 A24 20c blk brn .65 .65
O319 A24 25c dk vio 1.50 1.50
Nos. O313-O319 (7) 24.80 24.80

The variety "OFIAIAL" occurs once in each sheet of Nos. O301 to O319 inclusive.
Despite the 1932 release date, the "1931" overprint on Nos. O313-O319 is correct.

Flag of the Race Issue
1933, Aug. 9 Litho. Rouletted 9
Without gum
O320 A43 1c orange 1.25 1.25
O321 A43 2c yellow 1.25 1.25
O322 A43 3c dk brn 1.25 1.25
O323 A43 4c dp brn 1.25 1.25
O324 A43 5c gray brn 1.25 1.25
O325 A43 6c dp ultra 1.50 1.50
O326 A43 10c dp vio 1.50 1.50
O327 A43 15c red vio 1.50 1.50
O328 A43 20c dp grn 1.50 1.50
O329 A43 25c green 2.50 2.50
O330 A43 50c carmine 3.00 3.00
O331 A43 1cor red 5.00 5.00
Nos. O320-O331 (12) 22.75 22.75

See note after No. 599.
Reprints of Nos. O320-O331 exist.
A 25c dull blue exists. Its status is questioned.

Regular Issue of 1914-31 Overprinted in Red

1933, Nov. Perf. 12
O332 A24 1c ol grn .25 .25
O333 A25 2c brt rose .25 .25
O334 A24 3c lt bl .25 .25
O335 A24 4c dk bl .25 .25
O336 A24 5c ol brn .25 .25
O337 A25 6c bis brn .25 .25
O338 A25 10c lt brn .25 .25
O339 A24 15c red org .25 .25
O340 A24 20c orange .25 .25
O341 A25 25c dk vio .25 .25
O342 A25 50c green .25 .25
O343 A25 1cor yellow .35 .35
Nos. O332-O343 (12) 3.10 3.00

Nos. O332-O343 exist with or without signature control overprint. Values are the same.

Official Stamps of 1933 Overprinted as Nos. CO15-CO19 in Blue
1935, Dec.
O344 A24 1c ol grn .65 .40
O345 A25 2c brt rose .65 .50
O346 A24 3c lt bl 1.60 .50
O347 A25 4c dk bl 1.60 1.60
O348 A24 5c ol brn 1.60 1.60
O349 A25 6c bis brn 2.00 2.00
O350 A25 10c lt brn 2.00 2.00
O351 A24 15c org red 27.50 27.50
O352 A25 20c orange 27.50 27.50
O353 A25 25c dk vio 27.50 27.50
O354 A25 50c green 27.50 27.50
O355 A25 1cor yellow 27.50 27.50
Nos. O344-O355 (12) 147.60 146.10

Nos. O344-O355 have signature control overprints. Counterfeits of overprint abound.

Same Overprinted in Red
1936, Jan.
O356 A24 1c ol grn .25 .25
O357 A24 2c brt rose .25 .25
O358 A24 3c lt bl .25 .25
a. Double overprint
O359 A24 4c dk bl .25 .25
O360 A24 5c ol brn .25 .25
O361 A25 6c bis brn .25 .25
O362 A25 10c lt brn .25 .25
O363 A24 15c org red .25 .25
O364 A25 20c orange .25 .25
O365 A25 25c dk vio .25 .25
O366 A25 50c green .25 .25
O367 A25 1cor yellow .35 .35
Nos. O356-O367 (12) 3.10 3.10

Nos. O356-O367 have signature control overprints.

Nos. 653 to 655, 657, 659 660, 662 to 664 Overprinted in Black

1937
O368 A24 1c car rose .25 .25
O369 A25 2c dp bl .25 .25
O370 A24 3c chocolate .25 .25
O371 A24 5c org red .35 .25
O372 A25 10c ol grn .65 .40
O373 A24 15c green .80 .50
O374 A24 25c orange 1.00 .65
O375 A25 50c brown 1.40 .80
O376 A25 1cor ultra 2.50 1.25
Nos. O368-O376 (9) 7.45 4.60

Islands of the Great Lake O9

1939, Jan. Engr. Perf. 12½
O377 O9 2c rose red .25 .25
O378 O9 3c lt bl .25 .25
O379 O9 6c brn org .25 .25
O380 O9 7½c brn org .25 .25
O381 O9 10c blk brn .25 .25
O382 O9 15c orange .25 .25
O383 O9 25c dk vio .25 .25
O384 O9 50c brt yel grn .45 .45
Nos. O377-O384 (8) 2.20 2.20

POSTAL TAX STAMPS

Official Stamps of 1915 Surcharged in Black

1921, July Unwmk. Perf. 12
RA1 A24 1c on 5c lt bl 1.50 .60
RA2 A25 1c on 6c lt bl .65 .25
a. Double surcharge, one inverted 1.00 1.00
RA3 A25 1c on 10c lt bl 1.00 1.00
a. Double surcharge 3.50 3.50
RA4 A24 1c on 15c lt bl 1.50 .25
a. Double surcharge, one inverted 5.00 5.00
Nos. RA1-RA4 (4) 4.65 1.35

"R de C" signifies "Reconstruccion de Comunicaciones." The stamps were intended to provide a fund for rebuilding the General Post Office which was burned in April, 1921. One stamp was required on each letter or parcel, in addition to the regular postage. In the setting of one hundred there are five stamps with antique "C" and twenty-one with "R" and "C" smaller than in the illustration. One or more stamps in the setting have a dotted bar, as illustrated over No. 388, instead of the double bar.
The use of the "R de C" stamps for the payment of regular postage was not permitted.

Official Stamp of 1915 Overprinted in Black

1921, July
RA5 A24 1c light blue 6.00 1.75

This stamp is known with the dotted bar as illustrated over No. 388, instead of the double bar.

Coat of Arms — PT1

1921, Sept. Red Surcharge
RA6 PT1 1c on 1c ver & blk .25 .25
RA7 PT1 1c on 2c grn & blk .25 .25
a. Double surcharge 3.00 3.00
b. Double surcharge, one inverted 4.00 4.00
RA8 PT1 1c on 4c org & blk .25 .25
a. Double surcharge 4.00 4.00
RA9 PT1 1c on 15c dk bl & blk .25 .25
a. Double surcharge 3.00 3.00
Nos. RA6-RA9 (4) 1.00 1.00

PT2

1922, Feb.   **Black Surcharge**
RA10 PT2 1c on 10c yellow   .25   .25
   a.   Period after "de"   .50   .40
   b.   Double surcharge   2.00   2.00
   c.   Double inverted surcharge   3.75   3.75
   d.   Inverted surcharge
   u.   Without period after "C"   1.00   1.00

No. 409
Overprinted in
Black

1922
RA11 A24 1c violet   .25   .25
   a.   Double overprint   2.00   2.00

This stamp with the overprint in red is a trial printing.

Nos. 402, 404-407
Surcharged in Black

1922, June
RA12 A27 1c on 1c grn & blk   .75   .75
RA13 A29 1c on 5c ultra & blk   .75   .75
RA14 A30 1c on 10c org & blk   .75   .40
RA15 A31 1c on 25c yel & blk   .75   .30
   a.   Inverted surcharge   5.00   5.00
RA16 A32 1c on 50c vio & blk   .30   .25
   a.   Double surcharge   4.00   4.00
   Nos. RA12-RA16 (5)   3.30   2.45

PT3

Surcharge in Red or Dark Blue

1922, Oct.   **Perf. 11½**
RA17 PT3 1c yellow (R)   .25   .25
   a.   No period after "C"   1.00   1.00
RA18 PT3 1c violet (DBl)   .25   .25
   a.   No period after "C"   1.00   1.00

Surcharge is inverted on 22 out of 50 of No. RA17, 23 out of 50 of No. RA18.

Nos. 403-407
Surcharged in Black

1923   **Perf. 12**
RA19 A28 1c on 2c rose red &
     black   .50   .45
RA20 A29 1c on 5c ultra & blk   .55   .25
RA21 A30 1c on 10c org & blk   .25   .25
RA22 A31 1c on 25c yel & blk   .35   .30
RA23 A32 1c on 50c vio & blk   .25   .25
   Nos. RA19-RA23 (5)   1.90   1.50

The variety no period after "R" occurs twice on each sheet.

Red Surcharge
Wmk. Coat of Arms in Sheet
Perf. 11½
RA24 PT3 1c pale blue   .25   .25

Unwmk.
Type of 1921 Issue
Without Surcharge of New Value
RA25 PT1 1c ver & blk   .25   .25
   a.   Double overprint, one inverted   3.00   3.00

No. 409
Overprinted in
Blue

1924
RA26 A24 1c violet   .25   .25
   a.   Double overprint   8.00   8.00

There are two settings of the overprint on No. RA26 with "1924" 6 if mm apart in one.

No. 409
Overprinted in
Blue

1925
RA27 A24 1c violet   .25   .25

No. 409
Overprinted in
Blue

1926
RA28 A24 1c violet   .25   .25

No. RA28
Overprinted in
Various Colors

1927
RA29 A24 1c vio (R)   .25   .25
   a.   Double overprint (R)   2.00   2.00
   b.   Inverted overprint (R)   3.00   3.00
RA30 A24 1c vio (V)   .25   .25
   a.   Double overprint   2.50   2.50
   b.   Inverted overprint   2.50   2.50
RA31 A24 1c vio (Bl)   .25   .25
   a.   Double overprint   5.00   5.00
RA32 A24 1c vio (Bk)   .25   .25
   a.   Double ovpt., one invtd.   4.25   4.25
   b.   Double overprint   4.25   4.25

Same Overprint on No. RA27
RA33 A24 1c vio (Bk)   15.00   10.00
   Nos. RA29-RA33 (5)   16.00   11.00

No. RA28
Overprinted in
Violet

1928
RA34 A24 1c violet   .25   .25
   a.   Double overprint   2.00   2.00
   b.   "928"   1.00   1.00

Similar to No. RA34 but 8mm space between "Resello" and "1928"
Black Overprint
RA35 A24 1c violet   .40   .25
   a.   "1828"   2.00   2.00

PT4

Inscribed "Timbre Telegrafico"
Horiz. Srch. in Black,
Vert. Srch. in Red
RA36 PT4 1c on 5c bl & blk   .60   .25
   a.   Comma after "R"   1.25   1.25
   b.   No period after "R"   1.25   1.25
   c.   No periods after "R" and "C"   1.25   1.25

("CORREOS" at
right) — PT5

1928   **Engr.**   **Perf. 12**
RA37 PT5 1c plum   .25   .25

See Nos. RA41-RA43. For overprints see Nos. RA45-RA46, RA48-RA51.

PT6

1929   **Red Surcharge**
RA38 PT6 1c on 5c bl & blk   .25   .25
   a.   Inverted surcharge   3.00   3.00
   b.   Double surcharge   2.00   2.00
   c.   Double surcharge, one inverted   2.00   2.00
   d.   Period after "de"   1.25   1.25
   e.   Comma after "R"   1.25   1.25

See note after No. 512.

Regular Issue of
1928 Overprinted
in Blue

RA39 A24 1c red orange   .25   .25

No. RA39 exists both with and without signature control overprint.

An additional overprint, "1929" in black or blue on No. RA39, is fraudulent.

No. 513
Overprinted in
Red

1929
RA40 A24 1c ol grn   .25   .25
   a.   Double overprint   .75   .75

No. RA40 is known with overprint in black, and with overprint inverted. These varieties were not regularly issued, but copies have been canceled by favor.

Type of 1928 Issue Inscribed at right "COMUNICACIONES"
1930-37
RA41 PT5 1c carmine   .25   .25
RA42 PT5 1c orange ('33)   .25   .25
RA43 PT5 1c green ('37)   .25   .25
   Nos. RA41-RA43 (3)   .75   .75

No. RA42 has signature control. See note before No. 600.

No. RA39
Overprinted in
Black

1931
RA44 A24 1c red orange   .25   .25
   a.   "1931" double overprint   .35   .35
   b.   "1931" double ovpt., one invtd.   .40   .40

No. RA44 exists with signature control overprint. See note before No. 600. Value is the same.

No. RA42
Overprinted
Vertically, up or
down, in Black

1935
RA45 PT5 1c orange   .25   .25
   a.   Double overprint   1.00   1.00
   b.   Double ovpt., one inverted

No. RA45 and
RA45a Overprinted
Vertically, Reading
Down, in Blue

RA46 PT5 1c orange   .50   .25
   a.   Black overprint double   2.00   2.00

Same Overprint in Red on Nos.
RA39, RA42 and RA45
RA47 A24 1c red org (#RA39)   50.00   50.00
RA48 PT5 1c org (#RA42)   .25   .25
RA49 PT5 1c org (#RA45)   .25   .25
   a.   Black overprint double   .80   .80

Overprint is horizontal on No. RA47 and vertical, reading down, on Nos. RA48-RA49.

No. RA48 exists with signature control overprint. See note before No. 600. Same values.

No. RA42
Overprinted
Vertically, Reading
Down, in Carmine

1935   **Unwmk.**   **Perf. 12**
RA50 PT5 1c orange   .25   .25

No. RA45 with Additional Overprint "1936", Vertically, Reading Down, in Red
1936
RA51 PT5 1c orange   .50   .25

No. RA39 with Additional Overprint "1936" in Red
RA52 A24 1c red orange   .50   .25

No. RA52 exists only with script control mark.

PT7

1936   **Vertical Surcharge in Red**
RA53 PT7 1c on 5c grn & blk   .25   .25
   a.   "Cenavo"   1.40   1.40
   b.   "Centavos"   1.40   1.40

Horizontal Surcharge in Red
RA54 PT7 1c on 5c grn & blk   .25   .25
   a.   Double surcharge   1.40   1.40

Baseball
Player
PT8

1937   **Typo.**   **Perf. 11**
RA55 PT8 1c carmine   .60   .25
RA56 PT8 1c yellow   .60   .25
RA57 PT8 1c blue   .60   .25
RA58 PT8 1c green   .60   .25
   b.   Sheet of 4, #RA55-RA58   6.00   3.00
   Nos. RA55-RA58 (4)   2.40   1.00

Issued for the benefit of the Central American Caribbean Games of 1937.

Control mark in red is variously placed. See dark oval below "OLIMPICO" in illustration.

Tête bêche Pairs

RA55a	PT8	1c	.75	.75
RA56a	PT8	1c	.75	.75
RA57a	PT8	1c	.75	.75
RA58a	PT8	1c	.75	.75
Nos. RA55a-RA58a (4)			3.00	3.00

PROVINCE OF ZELAYA

(Bluefields)

A province of Nicaragua lying along the eastern coast. Special postage stamps for this section were made necessary because for a period two currencies, which differed materially in value, were in use in Nicaragua. Silver money was used in Zelaya and Cabo Gracias a Dios while the rest of Nicaragua used paper money. Later the money of the entire country was placed on a gold basis.

Dangerous counterfeits exist of most of the Bluefields overprints.

Regular Issues of 1900-05 Handstamped in Black (4 or more types)

1904-05		**Unwmk.**	**Perf. 12, 14**	
On Engraved Stamps of 1900				
1L1	A14	1c plum	1.50	.75
1L2	A14	2c vermilion	1.50	.75
1L3	A14	3c green	1.90	1.50
1L4	A14	4c ol grn	11.00	9.00
1L5	A14	15c ultra	3.00	1.90
1L6	A14	20c brown	3.00	1.90
1L7	A14	50c lake	10.50	9.00
1L8	A14	1p yellow	21.00	
1L9	A14	2p salmon	30.00	
1L10	A14	5p black	37.50	
Nos. 1L1-1L10 (10)			120.90	
Nos. 1L1-1L7 (7)				24.80

On Lithographed Stamps of 1902

1L11	A14	5c blue	3.00	.75
1L12	A14	5c carmine	1.90	.90
1L13	A14	10c violet	1.50	.75
Nos. 1L11-1L13 (3)			6.40	2.40

On Postage Due Stamps Overprinted "1901 Correos"

1L14	D3	20c brn (No. 156)	4.50	1.90
1L15	D3	50c lake (No. 158)		

On Surcharged Stamps of 1904-05

1L16	A14	5c on 10c (#175)	1.50	1.10
1L17	A14	5c on 10c (#178)	3.00	1.50
1L18	A14	15c on 10c vio (#176)	1.50	1.50
1L19	A14	15c on 10c vio (#177)	14.00	4.50
Nos. 1L16-1L19 (4)			20.00	8.60

On Surcharged Stamp of 1901

1L20	A14	20c on 5p blk	18.00	3.00

On Regular Issue of 1905

1906-07			**Perf. 12**	
1L21	A18	1c green	.30	.30
1L22	A18	2c car rose	.30	.30
1L23	A18	3c violet	.30	.30
1L24	A18	4c org red	.45	.45
1L25	A18	5c blue	.25	.25
1L26	A18	10c yel brn	3.00	1.50
1L27	A18	15c brn ol	4.50	1.75
1L28	A18	20c lake	9.00	7.50
1L29	A18	50c orange	35.00	30.00
1L30	A18	1p black	30.00	27.50
1L31	A18	2p dk grn	37.50	
1L32	A18	5p violet	45.00	
Nos. 1L21-1L32 (12)			165.60	
Nos. 1L21-1L30 (10)				69.85

On Surcharged Stamps of 1906-08

1L33	A18	10c on 3c vio	.40	.40
1L34	A18	15c on 1c grn	.50	.50
1L35	A18	20c on 2c rose	3.50	3.50
1L36	A18	20c on 5c bl	1.50	1.50
1L37	A18	50c on 6c sl (R)	1.50	3.00
Nos. 1L33-1L37 (5)			7.40	8.90

Handstamped

Stamps with the above overprints were made to fill dealers' orders but were never regularly issued or used. Stamps with similar overprints handstamped are bogus.

Surcharged Stamps of 1906 Overprinted in Red, Black or Blue

1L38	A18	15c on 1c grn (R)	2.75	2.75
a.	Red overprint inverted			
1L39	A18	20c on 2c rose (Bk)	1.90	1.90
1L40	A18	20c on 5c bl (R)	3.00	3.00
1L41	A18	50c on 6c sl (Bl)	14.00	14.00
Nos. 1L38-1L41 (4)			21.65	21.65

Stamps of the 1905 issue overprinted as above No. 1L38 or similarly overprinted but with only 2¼mm space between "B" and "Dpto. Zelaya" were made to fill dealers' orders but not placed in use.

No. 205 Handstamped in Black

		Perf. 14 to 15		
1L42	A18	10c yel brn	24.00	24.00

Stamps of 1907 Overprinted in Red or Black

1L43	A18	15c brn ol (R)	3.00	3.00
1L44	A18	20c lake	.90	.90
a.	Inverted overprint		11.00	11.00

With Additional Surcharge

1L45	A18	5c brn org	.50	.45
a.	Inverted surcharge		7.50	7.50

With Additional Surcharge

1L46	A18	5c on 4c brn org	12.00	12.00

On Provisional Postage Stamps of 1907-08 in Black or Blue

1L47	A18	10c on 2c rose (Bl)	4.50	4.50
1L48	A18	10c on 2c rose		300.00
1L48A	A18	10c on 4c brn org		300.00
1L49	A18	10c on 20c lake	3.00	3.00
1L50	A18	10c on 50c org (Bl)	3.00	2.25

Arms Type of 1907 Overprinted in Black or Violet

1907				
1L51	A18	1c green	.30	.25
1L52	A18	2c rose	.30	.25
1L53	A18	3c violet	.40	.40
1L54	A18	4c brn org	.45	.45
1L55	A18	5c blue	4.50	2.25
1L56	A18	10c yel brn	.40	.30
1L57	A18	15c brn ol	.75	.50
1L58	A18	20c lake	.75	.45
1L59	A18	50c orange	2.25	1.50
1L60	A18	1p blk (V)	2.25	1.50
1L61	A18	2p dk grn	2.25	1.90
1L62	A18	5p violet	3.75	2.25
Nos. 1L51-1L62 (12)			18.35	11.90

Nos. 217-225 Overprinted in Green

1908				
1L63	A19	1c on 5c yel & blk (R)	.45	.40
1L64	A19	2c on 5c yel & blk (Bl)	.45	.40
1L65	A19	4c on 5c yel & blk (G)	.45	.40
a.	Overprint reading down		11.00	11.00
b.	Double overprint, reading up and down		18.00	18.00
1L66	A19	5c yel & blk	.45	.45
a.	"CORROE"		4.50	
b.	Double overprint		11.00	11.00
c.	Double overprint, reading up and down		19.00	19.00
d.	"CORREO 1908" double		15.00	15.00
1L67	A19	10c lt bl & blk	.45	.45
a.	Ovpt. reading down		.50	.50
b.	"CORREO 1908" triple		37.50	
1L68	A19	15c on 50c ol & blk (R)	.90	.90
a.	"1008"		4.50	
b.	"8908"		4.50	
1L69	A19	35c on 50c ol & blk	1.40	1.40
1L70	A19	1p yel brn & blk	1.90	1.90
a.	"CORROE"		12.00	12.00
1L71	A19	2p pearl gray & blk	2.25	2.25
a.	"CORROE"		15.00	15.00
Nos. 1L63-1L71 (9)			8.70	8.55

Overprinted Horizontally in Black or Green

1L72	A19	5c yel & blk	9.00	7.50
1L72A	A19	2p pearl gray & blk (G)		300.00

On Nos. 1L72-1L72A, space between "B" and "Dpto. Zelaya" is 13mm.

Nos. 237-248 Overprinted in Black

Imprint: "American Bank Note Co. NY"

1909			**Perf. 12**	
1L73	A18	1c yel grn	.25	.25
1L74	A18	2c vermilion	.25	.25
a.	Inverted overprint			
1L75	A18	3c red org	.25	.25
1L76	A18	4c violet	.25	.25
1L77	A18	5c dp bl	.30	.25
a.	Inverted overprint		9.00	9.00
b.	"B" inverted		7.50	7.50
c.	Double overprint		12.00	12.00
1L78	A18	6c gray brn	4.50	3.00
1L79	A18	10c lake	.30	.30
a.	"B" inverted		9.00	9.00
1L80	A18	15c black	.45	.40
a.	"B" inverted		11.00	11.00
b.	Inverted overprint		12.00	12.00
c.	Double overprint		14.00	14.00
1L81	A18	20c brn ol	.50	.50
a.	"B" inverted		19.00	19.00
1L82	A18	50c dp grn	1.50	1.50
1L83	A18	1p yellow	2.25	2.25
1L84	A18	2p car rose	3.00	3.00
a.	Double overprint		27.50	27.50
Nos. 1L73-1L84 (12)			13.80	12.20

One stamp in each sheet has the "o" of "Dpto." sideways.

Overprinted in Black

1910				
1L85	A18	3c red org	.40	.40
1L86	A18	4c violet	.40	.40
a.	Inverted overprint		14.00	14.00
1L87	A18	15c black	4.50	2.25
1L88	A18	20c brn ol	.25	.30
1L89	A18	50c dp grn	.30	.40
1L90	A18	1p yellow	.30	.45
a.	Inverted overprint		7.50	
1L91	A18	2p car rose	.40	.75
Nos. 1L85-1L91 (7)			6.55	4.95

Black Ovpt., Green Srch., Carmine Block-outs

Z1

1910				
1L92	Z1	5c on 10c lake	3.75	3.00

There are three types of the letter "B." It is stated that this stamp was used exclusively for postal purposes and not for telegrams.

No. 247 Surcharged in Black

1911				
1L93	A18	5c on 1p yellow	.75	.75
a.	Double surcharge			14.00
1L94	A18	10c on 1p yellow	1.50	1.50
1L95	A18	15c on 1p yellow	.75	.75
a.	Inverted surcharge		9.00	
b.	Double surcharge		9.00	
c.	Double surcharge, one invtd.		9.00	
Nos. 1L93-1L95 (3)			3.00	3.00

Revenue Stamps Surcharged in Black

		Perf. 14 to 15		
1L96	A19	5c on 25c lilac	.75	1.10
a.	Without period		1.50	1.50
b.	Inverted surcharge		9.00	9.00

1L97	A19	10c on 1p yel brn		1.10	.75
a.		Without period		1.90	1.90
b.		"01" for "10"		9.00	9.00
c.		Inverted surcharge		13.00	13.00

VALE
05 cts.
POSTAL B.
de 1911

Surcharged in Black

1L98	A19	5c on 1p yel brn		1.50	1.50
a.		Without period		2.25	
b.		"50" for "05"		14.00	14.00
c.		Inverted surcharge		15.00	15.00
1L99	A19	5c on 10p pink		1.50	1.50
a.		Without period		2.25	2.25
b.		"50" for "05"		11.00	11.00
1L100	A19	10c on 1p yel brn		82.50	82.50
a.		Without period		95.00	95.00
1L101	A19	10c on 25p grn		.75	.75
a.		Without period		2.25	2.25
b.		"1" for "10"		7.50	
1L102	A19	10c on 50p ver		11.00	11.00
a.		Without period		16.00	
b.		"1" for "10"		22.50	
		Nos. 1L98-1L102 (5)		97.25	97.25

With Additional Overprint "1904"

1L103	A19	5c on 10p pink		14.00	14.00
a.		Without period		24.00	24.00
b.		"50" for "05"		110.00	110.00
1L104	A19	10c on 2p gray		.75	.75
a.		Without period		1.90	
b.		"1" for "10"		7.50	
1L105	A19	10c on 25p grn		92.50	
a.		Without period		100.00	
1L106	A19	10c on 50p ver		7.50	7.50
a.		Without period		14.00	
b.		"1" for "10"		18.00	
c.		Inverted surcharge			

The surcharges on Nos. 1L96 to 1L106 are in settings of twenty-five. One stamp in each setting has a large square period after "cts" and another has a thick upright "c" in that word. There are two types of "1904".

B
Dpto. Zelaya

No. 293C Overprinted

1911

1L107	A21	5c on 5c on 2c bl (R)		32.50	
a.		"5" omitted		37.50	
b.		Red overprint inverted		40.00	
c.		As "a" and "b"		47.50	

**Same Overprint
On Nos. 290, 291, 292 and 289D
with
Lines of Surcharge spaced 2½mm
apart Reading Down**

1L107D	A21	2c on 10c on 1c red		250.00
e.		Overprint reading up		250.00
1L107F	A21	5c on 10c on 1c red		150.00
1L107G	A21	10c on 10c on 1c red (#292)		200.00
1L108	A21	10c on 10c on 1c red (#289D)		200.00

Locomotive — Z2

1912   Engr.   Perf. 14

1L109	Z2	1c yel grn		.75	.50
1L110	Z2	2c vermilion		.50	.25
1L111	Z2	3c org brn		.75	.45
1L112	Z2	4c carmine		.75	.30
1L113	Z2	5c dp bl		.75	.45
1L114	Z2	6c red brn		4.00	2.50
1L115	Z2	10c slate		.75	.30
1L116	Z2	15c dl lil		.75	.60
1L117	Z2	20c bl vio		.75	.60
1L118	Z2	25c grn & blk		1.00	.80
1L119	Z2	35c brn & blk		1.25	1.00
1L120	Z2	50c ol grn		1.25	1.00
1L121	Z2	1p orange		1.75	1.50

1L122	Z2	2p org brn		4.00	3.00
1L123	Z2	5p dk bl grn		7.00	6.50
		Nos. 1L109-1L123 (15)		26.00	19.75

The stamps of this issue were for use in all printing on the Atlantic Coast of Nicaragua where the currency was on a silver basis.
For surcharges see Nos. 325-337.

OFFICIAL STAMPS

Oficial
B

Regular Issue of 1909 Overprinted in Black

1909   Unwmk.   Perf. 12

1LO1	A18	20c brn ol		15.00	12.00
a.		Double overprint		30.00	

No. O216 Overprinted in Black

1LO2	A18	15c black		15.00	10.00

Same Overprint on Official Stamp of 1911

1911

1LO3	A18	5c on 3c red org		22.50	17.50

CABO GRACIAS A DIOS

A cape and seaport town in the extreme northeast of Nicaragua. The name was coined by Spanish explorers who had great difficulty finding a landing place along the Nicaraguan coast and when eventually locating this harbor expressed their relief by designating the point "Cape Thanks to God." Special postage stamps came into use for the same reasons as the Zelaya issues. See Zelaya.

Dangerous counterfeits exist of most of the Cabo Gracias a Dios overprints. Special caution should be taken with double and inverted handstamps of Nos. 2L1-2L25, as most are counterfeits. Expert opinion is required.

Regular Issues of 1900-04 Handstamped in Violet

On Engraved Stamps of 1900

1904-05   Unwmk.   Perf. 12, 14

2L1	A14	1c plum		2.25	1.10
2L2	A14	2c vermilion		4.50	1.25
2L3	A14	3c green		6.00	4.50
2L4	A14	4c ol grn		9.75	9.75
2L5	A14	15c ultra		35.00	22.50
2L6	A14	20c brown		3.00	2.25
		Nos. 2L1-2L6 (6)		60.50	41.35

On Lithographed Stamps of 1902

2L7	A14	5c blue		24.00	24.00
2L8	A14	10c violet		24.00	24.00

On Surcharged Stamps of 1904

2L9	A16	5c on 10c vio		22.50	22.50
2L10	A16	15c on 10c vio			

**On Postage Due Stamps
Violet Handstamp**

2L11	D3	20c org brn (#141)		5.00	1.25
2L12	D3	20c org brn (#156)		3.50	1.25
2L13	D3	30c dk grn (#157)		14.00	14.00
2L14	D3	50c lake (#158)		3.75	.75
		Nos. 2L11-2L14 (4)		26.25	17.25

Black Handstamp

2L15	D3	30c dk grn (#157)		24.00	24.00

Cabo

Stamps of 1900-05 Handstamped in Violet

On Engraved Stamps of 1900

2L16	A14	1c plum		2.75	2.25
2L17	A14	2c vermilion		27.50	24.00
2L18	A14	3c green		37.50	27.50
2L19	A14	4c ol grn		40.00	37.50
2L20	A14	15c ultra		45.00	45.00
		Nos. 2L16-2L20 (5)		152.75	136.25

On Lithographed Stamps of 1902

2L22	A14	5c dk bl		95.00	95.00
2L23	A14	10c violet		27.50	24.00

On Surcharged Stamp of 1904

2L24	A14	5c on 10c vio			

On Postage Due Stamp

2L25	D3	20c org brn (#141)			

Cabo

The editors have no evidence that stamps with this handstamp were issued. Examples were sent to the UPU and covers are known.

CABO

Stamps of 1900-08 Handstamped in Violet

1905   On Stamps of 1905

2L26	A18	1c green		1.10	1.10
2L27	A18	2c car rose		1.50	1.50
2L28	A18	3c violet		1.50	1.50
2L29	A18	4c org red		3.75	3.75
2L30	A18	5c blue		1.50	1.10
2L31	A18	6c slate		3.75	3.75
2L32	A18	10c yel brn		3.00	1.90
2L33	A18	15c brn ol		4.50	4.50
2L34	A18	1p black		20.00	20.00
2L35	A18	2p dk grn		35.00	35.00
		Nos. 2L26-2L35 (10)		75.60	74.10

Magenta Handstamp

2L26a	A18	1c		3.75	3.00
2L27a	A18	2c		3.00	2.75
2L28a	A18	3c		3.75	3.00
2L30a	A18	5c		7.50	6.00
2L33a	A18	15c		13.00	11.00
		Nos. 2L26a-2L33a (5)		31.50	25.75

On Stamps of 1900-04

2L36	A14	5c on 10c vio		14.00	14.00
2L37	A14	10c violet			
2L38	A14	20c brown		12.00	12.00
2L39	A14	20c on 5p blk			95.00

On Postage Due Stamps Overprinted "Correos"

2L40	D3	20c org brn (#141)		9.00	9.00
2L41	D3	20c org brn (#156)		5.00	4.50

On Surcharged Stamps of 1906-08

2L42	A18	10c on 3c vio			250.00
2L43	A18	10c on 5c blue		9.00	9.00
2L44	A18	50c on 6c slate		24.00	24.00

**On Stamps of 1907
Perf. 14 to 15**

2L44A	A18	2c rose			250.00
2L45	A18	10c yel brn		100.00	75.00
2L46	A18	15c brn ol		90.00	75.00

On Provisional Stamp of 1908 in Magenta

2L47	A19	5c yel & blk		7.50	7.50

Stamps with the above large handstamp in black instead of violet, are bogus. There are also excellent counterfeits in violet.
The foregoing overprints being handstamped are found in various positions, especially the last type.

"COSTA ATLANTICA"
C.

Stamps of 1907 Type A18, Overprinted in Black or Violet

1907

2L48	A18	1c green		.30	.30
a.		Vert. pair, imperf. btwn.			
2L49	A18	2c rose		.30	.30
2L50	A18	3c violet		.30	.30
a.		Vert. pair, imperf. btwn.		350.00	
2L51	A18	4c brn org		.40	.40
2L52	A18	5c blue		.50	.50
2L53	A18	10c yel brn		.40	.40
2L54	A18	15c brn ol		.75	.75
2L55	A18	20c lake		.75	.75
2L56	A18	50c orange		1.90	1.50
2L57	A18	1p blk (V)		2.25	1.90
2L58	A18	2p dk grn		3.00	2.25
2L59	A18	5p violet		4.50	3.75
		Nos. 2L48-2L59 (12)		15.35	13.10

C
Dpto. Zelaya

Nos. 237-248 Overprinted in Black

Imprint: American Bank Note Co.

1909   Perf. 12

2L60	A18	1c yel grn		.35	.40
2L61	A18	2c vermilion		.35	.40
2L62	A18	3c red org		.35	.40
2L63	A18	4c violet		.35	.40
2L64	A18	5c dp bl		.35	.60
2L65	A18	6c gray brn		6.00	6.00
2L66	A18	10c lake		.60	.75
2L67	A18	15c black		.90	.90
2L68	A18	20c brn ol		1.00	1.00
2L69	A18	50c dp grn		2.50	2.50
2L70	A18	1p yellow		4.00	4.00
2L71	A18	2p car rose		5.75	5.75
		Nos. 2L60-2L71 (12)		22.50	23.20

CABO

No. 199 Overprinted Vertically

2L72	A18	50c on 6c slate (R)		7.50	7.50

CABO GRACIAS A DIOS OFFICIAL STAMPS

CABO

Official Stamps of 1907 Overprinted in Red or Violet

1907

2LO1	A18	10c on 1c green		60.00
2LO2	A18	15c on 1c green		75.00
2LO3	A18	20c on 1c green		100.00
2LO4	A18	50c on 1c green		125.00

NIGER

ˈnī-jər

LOCATION — Northern Africa, directly north of Nigeria
GOVT. — Republic
AREA — 458,075 sq. mi.
POP. — 6,265,000 (est. 1984)
CAPITAL — Niamey

The colony, formed in 1922, was originally a military territory.

100 Centimes = 1 Franc

Stamps of Upper Senegal and Niger Type of 1914, Overprinted

Camel and Rider — A1

In the overprint, normal spacing between the words "DU" and "NIGER" is 2½mm. In one position (72) of all sheets in the first printing, the space between the two words is 3mm.

1921-26   Unwmk.   Perf. 13½x14

1	A1	1c brn vio & vio	.25	.40
		Never hinged	.40	
		On cover		87.50
a.		Wide spacing in ovpt.	13.50	13.50
		Never hinged	24.00	
2	A1	2c dk gray & dl vio	.25	.40
		Never hinged	.40	
		On cover		87.50
a.		Wide spacing in ovpt.	13.50	13.50
		Never hinged	24.00	
3	A1	4c black & blue	.30	.50
		Never hinged	.45	
		On cover		87.50
a.		Wide spacing in ovpt.	13.50	13.50
		Never hinged	24.00	
4	A1	5c ol brn & dk brn	.30	.50
		Never hinged	.45	
		On cover		42.50
a.		Wide spacing in ovpt.	13.50	13.50
		Never hinged	24.00	
5	A1	10c yel grn & bl grn	1.60	2.00
		Never hinged	2.75	
		On cover		95.00
a.		Wide spacing in ovpt.	21.00	21.00
		Never hinged	35.00	
6	A1	10c mag, bluish ('26)	.95	1.20
		Never hinged	1.25	
		On cover		27.50
7	A1	15c red brn & org	.40	.55
		Never hinged	.55	
		On cover		50.00
a.		Wide spacing in ovpt.	13.50	13.50
		Never hinged	24.00	
8	A1	20c brn vio & blk	.30	.50
		Never hinged	.45	
		On cover		42.50
a.		Wide spacing in ovpt.	13.50	13.50
		Never hinged	24.00	
9	A1	25c blk & bl grn	.80	.80
		Never hinged	1.25	
		On cover		35.00
a.		Wide spacing in ovpt.	14.50	14.50
		Never hinged	25.00	
10	A1	30c red org & rose	2.75	3.50
		Never hinged	4.75	
		On cover		62.50
		On cover, single franking		125.00
a.		Wide spacing in ovpt.	32.50	35.00
		Never hinged	55.00	
11	A1	30c bl grn & red org ('26)	.80	.80
		Never hinged	1.25	
		On cover		16.00
a.		Wide spacing in ovpt.	24.00	27.50
		Never hinged	40.00	
12	A1	35c rose & violet	.95	1.20
		Never hinged	1.50	
		On cover		50.00
		On cover, single franking		80.00
a.		Wide spacing in ovpt.	18.00	18.00
		Never hinged	30.00	
13	A1	40c gray & rose	.95	1.20
		Never hinged	1.60	
		On cover		45.00
		On cover, single franking		55.00
a.		Wide spacing in ovpt.	20.00	24.00
		Never hinged	32.50	
14	A1	45c blue & ol brn	1.30	1.60
		Never hinged	2.25	
		On cover		70.00
		On cover, single franking		110.00
a.		Wide spacing in ovpt.	20.00	24.00
		Never hinged	32.50	
15	A1	50c ultra & bl	.80	1.20
		Never hinged	1.40	
		On cover		50.00
		On cover, single franking		125.00
a.		Wide spacing in ovpt.	16.00	16.00
		Never hinged	26.00	
16	A1	50c dk gray & bl vio ('25)	1.60	1.60
		Never hinged	2.75	
		On cover		16.00
a.		Wide spacing in ovpt.	27.50	32.50
		Never hinged	47.50	

17	A1	60c org red ('26)	1.40	2.00
		Never hinged	2.00	
		On cover		42.50
		On cover, single franking		80.00
18	A1	75c yel & ol brn	1.40	1.60
		Never hinged	2.40	
		On cover		140.00
a.		Wide spacing in ovpt.	20.00	24.00
		Never hinged	32.50	
19	A1	1fr dk brn & dl vio	1.60	2.00
		Never hinged	2.75	
		On cover		75.00
		On cover, single franking		170.00
a.		Wide spacing in ovpt.	24.00	27.50
		Never hinged	40.00	
20	A1	2fr green & blue	1.60	2.00
		Never hinged	2.75	
		On cover		87.50
		On cover, single franking		190.00
a.		Wide spacing in ovpt.	24.00	27.50
		Never hinged	40.00	
21	A1	5fr violet & blk	2.75	4.00
		Never hinged	4.75	
		On cover		110.00
		On cover, single franking		210.00
a.		Wide spacing in ovpt.	32.50	35.00
		Never hinged	55.00	
		Nos. 1-21 (21)	23.05	29.55

Types of 1921 Surcharged in Black or Red

1922-26

22	A1	25c on 15c red brn & org ('25)	.95	.80
		Never hinged	1.20	
		On cover		20.00
a.		Multiple surcharge	260.00	
b.		"25c" inverted	140.00	
c.		Wide spacing in ovpt.	24.00	27.50
		Never hinged	45.00	
23	A1	25c on 2fr grn & bl (R) ('24)	.90	.80
		Never hinged	1.20	
		On cover		20.00
a.		Wide spacing in ovpt.	24.00	27.50
		Never hinged	45.00	
24	A1	25c on 5fr vio & blk (R) ('24)	.95	.80
		Never hinged	1.25	
		On cover		20.00
a.		Double surcharge	225.00	
		Never hinged	340.00	
b.		Wide spacing in ovpt.	32.50	35.00
		Never hinged	55.00	
25	A1	60c on 75c vio, pnksh	.90	1.20
		Never hinged	1.20	
		On cover		45.00
		On cover, single franking		70.00
a.		Wide spacing in ovpt.	27.50	32.50
		Never hinged	47.50	
26	A1	65c on 45c bl & ol brn ('25)	2.75	3.50
		On cover	4.75	
		On cover		87.50
		On cover, single franking		170.00
a.		Wide spacing in ovpt.	45.00	47.50
		Never hinged	72.50	
27	A1	85c on 75c yel & ol brn ('25)	2.75	3.50
		Never hinged	4.75	
		On cover		75.00
		On cover, single franking		140.00
a.		Wide spacing in ovpt.	45.00	47.50
		Never hinged	72.50	
28	A1	1.25fr on 1fr dp bl & lt bl (R) ('26)	1.10	1.20
		Never hinged	1.60	
		On cover		80.00
		On cover, single franking		140.00
a.		Surcharge omitted	260.00	
		Never hinged	400.00	
b.		As "a," in pair with unsurcharged stamp	1,700.	
		Nos. 22-28 (7)	10.30	11.80

Nos. 22-24 are surcharged "25c," No. 28, "1f25." Nos. 25-27 are surcharged like illustration.

Drawing Water from Well — A2

Zinder Fortress — A4

Boat on Niger River — A3

Perf. 13x14, 13½x14, 14x13, 14x13½
1926-40   Typo.

29	A2	1c lilac rose & olive	.25	.40
		Never hinged	.40	
		On cover		70.00
30	A2	2c dk gray & dl red	.25	.40
		Never hinged	.40	
		On cover		70.00
31	A2	3c red vio & ol gray ('40)	.25	.40
		Never hinged	.40	
		On cover		50.00
32	A2	4c amber & gray	.25	.40
		Never hinged	.40	
		On cover		70.00
33	A2	5c ver & yel grn	.25	.40
		Never hinged	.40	
		On cover		42.50
34	A2	10c dp bl & Prus bl	.25	.40
		Never hinged	.40	
		On cover		37.50
35	A2	15c gray grn & yel grn	.55	.80
		Never hinged	.80	
		On cover		25.00
36	A2	15c gray lil & lt red ('28)	.40	.40
		Never hinged	.80	
		On cover		22.50
37	A3	20c Prus grn & ol brn	.40	.55
		Never hinged	.55	
		On cover		27.50
38	A3	25c black & dl red	.40	.50
		Never hinged	.55	
		On cover		20.00
39	A3	30c bl grn & yel grn	.80	1.20
		Never hinged	1.20	
		On cover		37.50
40	A3	30c yel & red vio ('40)	.30	.50
		Never hinged	.45	
		On cover		22.50
41	A3	35c brn org & turq bl, bluish	.80	1.20
		Never hinged	1.20	
		On cover		37.50
42	A3	35c bl grn & dl grn ('38)	1.20	1.60
		Never hinged	1.60	
		On cover		42.50
43	A3	40c red brn & slate	.40	.50
		Never hinged	.55	
		On cover		14.00
44	A3	45c yel & red vio	1.60	1.90
		Never hinged	2.40	
		On cover		35.00
45	A3	45c bl grn & dl grn ('40)	.30	.50
		Never hinged	.50	
		On cover		27.50
46	A3	50c scar & grn, grnsh	.40	.40
		Never hinged	.55	
		On cover		14.00
47	A3	55c dk car & brn ('38)	2.00	2.00
		Never hinged	2.75	
		On cover		14.00
48	A3	60c dk car & brn ('40)	.55	.70
		Never hinged	.70	
		On cover		27.50
49	A3	65c ol grn & rose	.40	.55
		Never hinged	.55	
		On cover		50.00
50	A3	70c ol grn & rose ('40)	2.00	2.50
		Never hinged	2.40	
		On cover		37.50
51	A3	75c grn & vio, pink	2.00	2.25
		Never hinged	3.25	
		On cover		25.00
		On cover, single franking		35.00
a.		Center and value double	225.00	
		Never hinged	340.00	
52	A3	80c cl & ol grn ('38)	1.60	2.00
		Never hinged	2.40	
		On cover		70.00
		On cover, single franking		125.00
53	A3	90c brn red & ver	1.60	1.90
		Never hinged	2.40	
		On cover		37.50
		On cover, single franking		87.50
54	A3	90c brt rose & yel grn ('39)	2.00	2.40
		Never hinged	2.50	
		On cover		42.50
		On cover, single franking		95.00
55	A4	1fr rose & yel grn	8.00	8.75
		Never hinged	18.00	
		On cover		30.00
		On cover, single franking		50.00
56	A4	1fr dk red & red org ('38)	2.00	2.40
		Never hinged	2.75	
		On cover		87.50
57	A4	1fr red & red ('40)	.80	.80
		Never hinged	1.10	
		On cover		11.00
58	A4	1.10fr ol brn & grn	4.00	6.50
		Never hinged	6.50	
		On cover		225.00
		On cover, single franking		450.00
59	A4	1.25fr grn & red ('33)	2.40	2.40
		Never hinged	3.25	
		On cover		25.00
		On cover, single franking		70.00

60	A4	1.25fr dk red & red org ('39)	.80	1.20
		Never hinged	1.10	
		On cover		62.50
		On cover, single franking		125.00
61	A4	1.40fr red vio & dk brn ('40)	.80	1.50
		Never hinged	1.10	
		On cover		50.00
		On cover, single franking		105.00
62	A4	1.50fr dp bl & pale bl	.55	.70
		Never hinged	.70	
		On cover		37.50
		On cover, single franking		80.00
63	A4	1.60fr ol brn & grn ('40)	1.75	2.00
		Never hinged	2.00	
		On cover		45.00
		On cover, single franking		105.00
64	A4	1.75fr red vio & dk brn ('33)	1.60	2.40
		Never hinged	2.40	
		On cover		19.00
		On cover, single franking		25.00
65	A4	1.75fr bl & vio bl ('38)	1.25	1.60
		Never hinged	1.75	
		On cover		42.50
		On cover, single franking		80.00
66	A4	2fr red org & ol brn	.30	.50
		Never hinged	.50	
		On cover		35.00
		On cover, single franking		62.50
67	A4	2.25fr dk bl & vio bl ('39)	1.20	1.60
		Never hinged	1.60	
		On cover		55.00
		On cover, single franking		110.00
68	A4	2.50fr blk brn ('40)	1.20	1.60
		Never hinged	1.60	
		On cover		35.00
		On cover, single franking		70.00
69	A4	3fr dl vio & blk ('27)	.55	.80
		Never hinged	.80	
		On cover		42.50
		On cover, single franking		105.00
70	A4	5fr vio brn & blk, pink	.80	1.20
		Never hinged	1.20	
		On cover		50.00
		On cover, single franking		100.00
71	A4	10fr chlky bl & mag	1.60	2.00
		Never hinged	2.75	
		On cover		55.00
		On cover, single franking		105.00
72	A4	20fr yel grn & red org	1.60	2.00
		Never hinged	2.75	
		On cover		70.00
		On cover, single franking		125.00
		Nos. 29-72 (44)	52.40	66.70

For surcharges see Nos. B7-B10 in the *Scott Standard Postage Stamp Catalogue,* Vol. 5.

Common Design Types pictured following the introduction.

Colonial Exposition Issue
Common Design Types

1931   Typo.   Perf. 12½
Name of Country in Black

73	CD70	40c deep green	5.50	5.50
		Never hinged	9.00	
		On cover		105.00
74	CD71	50c violet	5.50	5.50
		Never hinged	9.00	
		On cover		87.50
75	CD72	90c red orange	5.75	5.75
		Never hinged	9.00	
		On cover		160.00
		On cover, single franking		225.00
76	CD73	1.50fr dull blue	5.75	5.75
		Never hinged	9.00	
		On cover		140.00
		On cover, single franking		190.00
		Nos. 73-76 (4)	22.50	22.50

Paris International Exposition Issue
Common Design Types

1937   Perf. 13

77	CD74	20c deep violet	2.00	2.00
		Never hinged	3.25	
		On cover		120.00
78	CD75	30c dark green	2.00	2.00
		Never hinged	3.25	
		On cover		100.00
79	CD76	40c carmine rose	2.00	2.00
		Never hinged	3.25	
		On cover		87.50
80	CD77	50c dark brown	1.60	1.60
		Never hinged	2.75	
		On cover		80.00
81	CD78	90c red	1.60	1.60
		Never hinged	2.75	
		On cover		110.00
		On cover, single franking		210.00
82	CD79	1.50fr ultra	2.00	2.00
		Never hinged	3.25	
		On cover		105.00
		On cover, single franking		190.00
		Nos. 77-82 (6)	11.20	11.20

Colonial Arts Exhibition Issue
Souvenir Sheet
Common Design Type

1937　　　　　　　　　*Imperf.*
83	CD74 3fr magenta	9.00	10.50
	Never hinged	13.00	
	On cover		140.00
	On cover, single franking		210.00

Caillie Issue
Common Design Type

1939　　　　　　　　　**Perf. 12½x12**
84	CD81 90c org brn & org	1.00	1.00
	Never hinged	1.25	
	On cover		14.00
85	CD81 2fr brt violet	1.10	1.10
	Never hinged	1.40	
	On cover		35.00
	On cover, single franking		55.00
86	CD81 2.25fr ultra & dk bl	1.10	1.10
	Never hinged	1.40	
	On cover		40.00
	On cover, single franking		70.00
	Nos. 84-86 (3)	3.20	3.20

New York World's Fair Issue
Common Design Type

1939, May 10
87	CD82 1.25fr carmine lake	1.10	1.10
	Never hinged	1.60	
	On cover		87.50
	On cover, single franking		170.00
88	CD82 2.25fr ultra	1.30	1.30
	Never hinged	1.90	
	On cover		87.50
	On cover, single franking		160.00

SEMI-POSTAL STAMPS

Curie Issue
Common Design Type

1938　Unwmk.　Engr.　Perf. 13
B1	CD80 1.75fr + 50c brt ultra	17.00	17.00
	Never hinged	27.50	
	On cover, single franking		125.00
	On cover, single franking		210.00

French Revolution Issue
Common Design Type

1939　Photo.　Perf. 13
Name and Value Typo. in Black
B2	CD83 45c + 25c grn	12.00	12.00
	Never hinged	20.00	
	On cover		160.00
B3	CD83 70c + 30c brn	12.00	12.00
	Never hinged	20.00	
	On cover		110.00
B4	CD83 90c + 35c red org	12.00	12.00
	Never hinged	20.00	
	On cover		100.00
B5	CD83 1.25fr + 1fr rose pink	12.00	12.00
	Never hinged	20.00	
	On cover		170.00
	On cover, single franking		250.00
B6	CD83 2.25fr + 2fr blue	12.00	12.00
	Never hinged	20.00	
	On cover		160.00
	On cover, single franking		225.00
	Nos. B2-B6 (5)	60.00	60.00

AIR POST STAMPS

Common Design Type

1940　Unwmk.　Engr.　Perf. 12½x12
C1	CD85 1.90fr ultra	.50	.50
	Never hinged	.70	
	On cover		50.00
C2	CD85 2.90fr dk red	.65	.65
	Never hinged	.95	
	On cover		50.00
C3	CD85 4.50fr dk gray grn	.95	.95
	Never hinged	1.40	
	On cover		55.00
C4	CD85 4.90fr yel bis	.95	.95
	Never hinged	1.40	
	On cover		67.50
C5	CD85 6.90fr dp org	.95	.95
	Never hinged	1.40	
	On cover		80.00
	Nos. C1-C5 (5)	4.00	4.00

POSTAGE DUE STAMPS

Postage Due Stamps of Upper Senegal and Niger, 1914, Overprinted

D1

1921　Unwmk.　Perf. 14x13½
J1	D1 5c green	.70	.95
	Never hinged	1.10	
	On cover		50.00
J2	D1 10c rose	.70	.95
	Never hinged	1.10	
	On cover		50.00
J3	D1 15c gray	.95	1.05
	Never hinged	1.25	
	On cover		50.00
J4	D1 20c brown	.95	1.05
	Never hinged	1.25	
	On cover		55.00
J5	D1 30c blue	1.05	1.20
	Never hinged	1.40	
	On cover		55.00
J6	D1 50c black	1.05	1.20
	Never hinged	1.40	
	On cover		62.50
J7	D1 60c orange	1.75	2.00
	Never hinged	2.25	
	On cover		75.00
J8	D1 1fr violet	1.75	2.00
	Never hinged	2.25	
	On cover		95.00
	Nos. J1-J8 (8)	8.90	10.40

Caravansary Near Timbuktu
D2

1927　　　　　　　　　**Typo.**
J9	D2 2c dk bl & red	.25	.40
	Never hinged	.40	
	On cover		50.00
J10	D2 4c ver & blk	.25	.40
	Never hinged	.40	
	On cover		50.00
J11	D2 5c org & vio	.30	.50
	Never hinged	.45	
	On cover		42.50
J12	D2 10c red brn & blk vio	.30	.50
	Never hinged	.45	
	On cover		42.50
J13	D2 15c grn & org	.40	.55
	Never hinged	.70	
	On cover		42.50
J14	D2 20c cer & ol brn	.55	.70
	Never hinged	.80	
	On cover		50.00
J15	D2 25c blk & ol brn	.55	.70
	Never hinged	.80	
	On cover		50.00
J16	D2 30c dl vio & blk	1.40	1.60
	Never hinged	2.00	
	On cover		55.00
J17	D2 50c dp red, *grnsh*	1.05	1.10
	Never hinged	1.50	
	On cover		62.50
J18	D2 60c gray vio & org, *bluish*	.70	.95
	Never hinged	1.10	
	On cover		67.50
J19	D2 1fr ind & ultra, *bluish*	1.00	1.10
	Never hinged	1.50	
	On cover		75.00
J20	D2 2fr rose red & vio	1.10	1.10
	Never hinged	1.75	
	On cover		95.00
J21	D2 3fr org brn & ultra	1.75	2.00
	Never hinged	2.50	
	On cover		100.00
	Nos. J9-J21 (13)	9.60	11.60

NIGER COAST PROTECTORATE

'nī-jər 'kōst prə-'tek-tə-rət

(Oil Rivers Protectorate)

LOCATION — West coast of Africa on Gulf of Guinea
GOVT. — British Protectorate

　　This territory was originally known as the Oil Rivers Protectorate, and its affairs were conducted by the British Royal Niger Company. The Company surrendered its charter to the Crown in 1899. In 1900 all of the territories formerly controlled by the Royal Niger Company were incorporated into the two protectorates of Northern and Southern Nigeria, the latter absorbing

the area formerly known as Niger Coast Protectorate. In 1914 Northern and Southern Nigeria joined to form the Crown Colony of Nigeria. (See Nigeria, Northern Nigeria, Southern Nigeria and Lagos.)

　　　　12 Pence = 1 Shilling

Stamps of Great Britain, 1881-87, Overprinted in Black

1892　　Wmk. 30　　Perf. 14
1	A54 ½p vermilion	22.50	13.00
2	A40 1p lilac	13.00	11.00
a.	"OIL RIVERS" at top	10,000.	
b.	Half used as ½p on cover		3,000.
3	A56 2p green & car	40.00	9.50
a.	Half used as 1p on cover		2,750.
4	A57 2½p violet, *bl*	10.00	2.75
5	A61 5p lilac & blue	20.00	7.25
6	A65 1sh green	77.50	100.00
	Nos. 1-6 (6)	183.00	143.50

For surcharges see Nos. 7-36, 50.

Dangerous forgeries exist of all surcharges.

No. 2 Surcharged in Red or Violet

1893
7	A40 ½p on half of 1p (R)	175.	160.
c.	Unsevered pair	550.	500.
d.	As "c," surcharge inverted and dividing line reversed		27,500.
e.	"½" omitted		
f.	Straight top to "1" in "½"	390.	400.
g.	Double surcharge in pair with normal		2,100.
7A	A40 ½p on half of 1p (V)	7,750.	5,500.
b.	Surcharge double	27,500.	
c.	Unsevered pair	20,000.	17,500.

Nos. 3-6 Handstamp Srchd. in Violet, Red, Carmine, Bluish Black, Deep Blue, Green or Black

1893　　Wmk. 30　　Perf. 14
8	A56 ½p on 2p (V)	525.	325.
a.	Surcharge inverted	19,000.	
b.	Surcharge diagonal, inverted	18,500.	
9	A57 ½p on 2½p (V)	13,500.	
10	A57 ½p on 2½p (R)	425.	275.
a.	Surcharge inverted	13,500.	
b.	Surcharge diagonal, inverted	15,500.	
11	A57 ½p on 2½p (C)	25,000.	24,500.
12	A57 ½p on 2½p (B)	40,000.	—
13	A57 ½p on 2½p (G)	550.	

14	A56 ½p on 2p (V)	450.	375.
15	A56 ½p on 2p (Bl)	2,200.	825.
16	A57 ½p on 2½p (V)	7,750.	
17	A57 ½p on 2½p (R)	650.	775.
18	A57 ½p on 2½p (Bl)	475.	450.
19	A57 ½p on 2½p (G)	500.	550.

20	A56 ½p on 2p (V)	550.	775.
21	A57 ½p on 2½p (R)	600.	475.
a.	Surcharge inverted	20,000.	
b.	Surcharge diagonal, inverted	8,250.	
22	A57 ½p on 2½p (C)	475.	500.
23	A57 ½p on 2½p (Bl Bk)	5,500.	
24	A57 ½p on 2½p (Bl)	475.	525.
25	A57 ½p on 2½p (G)	325.	275.
a.	Surcharge diagonal, inverted		
26	A57 ½p on 2½p (Bk)	4,750.	
a.	Surcharge inverted	16,500.	
b.	Surcharge diagonal, inverted	14,500.	

27	A57 ½p on 2½p (R)	10,000.	
28	A57 ½p on 2½p (G)	550.	500.

29	A56 1sh on 2p (V)	500.	425.
a.	Surcharge inverted	13,500.	
b.	Surcharge diagonal, inverted		
30	A56 1sh on 2p (R)	825.	4,500.
a.	Surcharge inverted	55,000.	
31	A56 1sh on 2p (Bk)	6,500.	
a.	Surcharge inverted	21,000.	

32	A56 5sh on 2d (V)	10,000.	12,500.
a.	Surcharge inverted	55,000.	
33	A61 10sh on 5p (R)	7,250.	11,000.
a.	Surcharge inverted	55,000.	
34	A65 20sh on 1sh (V)	155,000.	
a.	Surcharge inverted	21,000.	
35	A65 20sh on 1sh (R)	130,000.	
36	A65 20sh on 1sh (Bk)	135,000.	

The handstamped 1893 surcharges are known inverted, vertical, etc.

Queen Victoria
A8　　　　A9

A10　　　　A11

A12 A13

1893 **Unwmk.** **Perf. 12 to 15**
37	A8	½p vermilion	10.00	11.00
38	A9	1p light blue	6.75	5.25
a.		Half used as ½p on cover		825.00
39	A10	2p green	47.50	47.50
a.		Half used as 1p on cover		1,000.
b.		Horiz. pair, imperf. between		17,500.
40	A11	2½p car lake	17.50	4.50
41	A12	5p gray lilac	22.50	7.50
a.		5p lilac	16.50	24.00
42	A13	1sh black	15.50	16.00
		Nos. 37-42 (6)	119.75	91.75

For surcharge see No. 49.

A15 A16

A17 A18

A19 A20

1894 **Engr.**
43	A15	½p yel green	5.25	5.50
44	A16	1p vermilion	15.00	9.50
a.		1p orange vermilion	25.00	17.50
b.		Diagonal half, used as ½p on cover		875.00
45	A17	2p car lake	35.00	7.25
a.		Half used as 1p on cover		4.50
46	A18	2½p blue	18.50	
47	A19	5p dp violet	12.50	6.00
48	A20	1sh black	90.00	25.00
		Nos. 43-48 (6)	176.25	57.75

See #55-59, 61. For surcharges see #51-54.

Halves of Nos. 38, 3 & 44 Srchd. in Red, Blue, Violet or Black

No. 49

No. 50

Nos. 51-53

1894
49	A9	½p on half of 1p (R)	1,300.	425.
a.		Inverted surcharge	15,500.	

Perf. 14
Wmk. 30
50	A56	1p on half of 2p (R)	1,950.	425.
a.		Double surcharge	7,250.	1,350.
b.		Inverted surcharge		2,250.

Perf. 12 to 15
Unwmk.
51	A16	½p on half of 1p (Bl)	3,850.	550.
a.		Double surcharge		
52	A16	½p on half of 1p (V)	4,400.	775.
53	A16	½p on half of 1p (Bk)	6,000.	1,100.

This surcharge is found on both vertical and diagonal halves of the 1p.

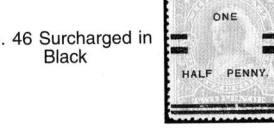

No. 46 Surcharged in Black

1894
54	A18	½p on 2½p blue	475.	275.
a.		Double surcharge	8,750.	2,500.

The surcharge is found in eight types. The "OIE" variety is broken type.

A27 A28

A29

1897-98 **Wmk. 2**
55	A15	½p yel green	5.00	1.75
56	A16	1p vermilion	6.50	1.60
57	A17	2p car lake	4.50	2.50
58	A18	2½p blue	15.00	3.25
a.		2½p slate blue	8.50	2.75
59	A19	5p dp violet	12.00	85.00
60	A27	6p yel brn ('98)	8.00	7.25
61	A20	1sh black	17.50	32.50
62	A28	2sh6p olive bister	25.00	100.00
63	A29	10sh dp pur ('98)	140.00	250.00
a.		10sh bright purple	135.00	225.00
		Nos. 55-63 (9)	233.50	483.85

The stamps of Niger Coast Protectorate were superseded in Jan. 1900, by those of Northern and Southern Nigeria.

NIGERIA

nī-'jir-ē-ə

LOCATION — West coast of Africa, bordering on the Gulf of Guinea
GOVT. — Republic
AREA — 356,669 sq. mi.
POP. — 82,390,000 (est. 1983)
CAPITAL — Lagos

The colony and protectorate were formed in 1914 by the union of Northern and Southern Nigeria. The mandated territory of Cameroons (British) was also attached for administrative purposes. See Niger Coast Protectorate,

---

Lagos, Northern Nigeria and Southern Nigeria.

12 Pence = 1 Shilling
20 Shillings = 1 Pound

Catalogue values for unused stamps in this country are for Never Hinged items, beginning with Scott 71 in the regular postage section.

King George V — A1

Numerals of 3p, 4p, 6p, 5sh and £1 of type A1 are in color on plain tablet.
Dies I and II are described at front of this volume.

Die I
Ordinary Paper
Wmk. Multiple Crown and CA (3)
1914-27 **Typo.** **Perf. 14**
1	A1	½p green	5.50	.70
a.		Booklet pane of 6		
2	A1	1p carmine	5.25	.25
a.		Booklet pane of 6		
b.		1p scarlet ('16)	10.00	.25
3	A1	2p gray	9.00	2.00
a.		2p slate gray ('18)	10.00	.85
4	A1	2½p ultramarine	10.00	4.75
a.		2½p dull blue ('15)	22.50	8.00

Chalky Paper
5	A1	3p violet, yel	1.60	3.00
6	A1	4p black & red, yel	1.10	4.75
7	A1	6p dull vio & red vio	10.00	11.00
8	A1	1sh black, green	1.10	10.00
a.		1sh black, emerald	1.40	15.00
b.		1sh black, bl grn, ol back	30.00	40.00
c.		As "a," olive back ('20)	9.00	47.50
9	A1	2sh6p blk & red, bl	17.50	7.25
10	A1	5sh grn & red, yel, white back	21.00	62.50
11	A1	10sh grn & red, grn	60.00	95.00
a.		10sh grn & red, emer	40.00	110.00
b.		10sh green & red, blue grn, olive back	1,000.	1,700.
c.		As "a," olive back	150.00	200.00
12	A1	£1 vio & blk, red	190.00	225.00
a.		Die II ('27)	225.00	325.00
		Nos. 1-12 (12)	332.05	426.20

Surface-colored Paper
13	A1	3p violet, yel	3.50	11.00
14	A1	4p black & red, yel	1.60	11.50
15	A1	1sh black, green	1.60	25.00
a.		1sh black, emerald	190.00	
16	A1	5sh grn & red, yel	18.00	55.00
17	A1	10sh grn & red, grn	50.00	170.00
		Nos. 13-17 (5)	74.70	272.50

Die II
1921-33 **Ordinary Paper** **Wmk. 4**
18	A1	½p green	6.00	.90
a.		Die I	1.25	.40
19	A1	1p carmine	1.75	.55
a.		Booklet pane of 6	27.50	
b.		Die I	3.25	.35
c.		Booklet pane of 6, Die I	37.50	
20	A1	1½p orange ('31)	7.00	.25
21	A1	2p gray	9.00	.50
a.		Die I	1.60	7.00
b.		Booklet pane of 6, Die I	55.00	
22	A1	2p red brown ('27)	5.00	1.00
a.		Booklet pane of 6	60.00	
23	A1	2p dk brown ('28)	2.50	.25
a.		Booklet pane of 6	50.00	
b.		Die I ('32)	6.00	.75
24	A1	2½p ultra (die I)	1.10	10.00
25	A1	3p dp violet	11.00	1.10
a.		Die I ('24)	6.00	3.50
26	A1	3p ultra ('31)	9.00	1.10

Chalky Paper
27	A1	4p blk & red, yel	.70	.60
a.		Die I ('32)	6.25	7.75
28	A1	6p dull vio & red vio	8.00	9.00
a.		Die I	14.00	32.50
29	A1	1sh black, emerald	3.50	2.25
30	A1	2sh6p blk & red, bl	7.25	42.50
a.		Die I ('32)	45.00	85.00
31	A1	5sh green & red, yel ('26)	16.00	75.00
a.		Die I ('32)	72.50	250.00
32	A1	10sh green & red, emer	67.50	225.00
a.		Die I ('32)	120.00	500.00
		Nos. 18-32 (15)	155.30	370.00

Silver Jubilee Issue
Common Design Type
1935, May 6 **Engr.** **Perf. 11x12**
34	CD301	1½p black & ultra	.80	1.50
35	CD301	2p indigo & green	1.75	1.75
36	CD301	3p ultra & brown	3.50	19.00
37	CD301	1sh brown vio & ind	6.50	37.50
		Nos. 34-37 (4)	12.55	59.75
		Set, never hinged	22.50	

Wharf at Apapa — A2

Picking Cacao Pods — A3

Dredging for Tin — A4

Timber — A5

Fishing Village — A6

Ginning Cotton — A7

Minaret at Habe — A8

Fulani Cattle — A9

Victoria-Buea Road — A10

Oil Palms A11

View of Niger at Jebba A12

Nigerian Canoe A13

1936, Feb. 1　　　　　**Perf. 11½x13**

38	A2	½p green	1.50	1.40
39	A3	1p rose car	.50	.40
40	A4	1½p brown	2.00	.40
a.		Perf. 12½x13½	80.00	4.50
41	A5	2p black	.50	.60
42	A6	3p dark blue	2.00	1.50
a.		Perf. 12½x13½	140.00	25.00
43	A7	4p red brown	2.00	2.00
44	A8	6p dull violet	.70	.60
45	A9	1sh olive green	2.25	10.00

Perf. 14

46	A10	2sh6p ultra & blk	5.50	27.50
47	A11	5sh ol grn & blk	16.00	47.50
48	A12	10sh slate & blk	75.00	110.00
49	A13	£1 orange & blk	100.00	170.00
		Nos. 38-49 (12)	207.95	372.10
		Set, never hinged	400.00	

Common Design Types
pictured following the introduction.

Coronation Issue
Common Design Type

1937, May 12　　　**Perf. 11x11½**

50	CD302	1p dark carmine	.50	2.00
51	CD302	1½p dark brown	1.25	2.50
52	CD302	3p deep ultra	1.50	4.00
		Nos. 50-52 (3)	3.25	8.50
		Set, never hinged	6.50	

George VI — A14

Victoria-Buea Road — A15

Niger at
Jebba
A16

1938-51　　**Wmk. 4**　　**Perf. 12**

53	A14	½p deep green	.25	.30
a.		Perf. 11½ ('50)	.80	1.25
54	A14	1p dk carmine	.25	.30
55	A14	1½p red brown	.25	.30
a.		Perf. 11½ ('50)	.25	.25
56	A14	2p black	.30	2.75
57	A14	2½p orange ('41)	.25	2.75
58	A14	3p deep blue	.25	.30
59	A14	4p orange	40.00	5.00
60	A14	6p brown violet	.25	.30
a.		Perf. 11½ ('51)	.70	.60
61	A14	1sh olive green	.35	.30
a.		Perf. 11½ ('50)	.40	.25
62	A14	1sh3p turq blue ('40)	.50	.30
a.		Perf. 11½ ('50)	1.10	.70
63	A15	2sh6p ultra & blk ('51)	4.50	4.75
a.		Perf. 13½ ('42)	1.90	5.50
b.		Perf. 14 ('42)	1.90	3.50
c.		Perf. 13x11½	42.50	9.50
64	A16	5sh org & blk, perf. 13½ ('42)	3.00	4.50
a.		Perf. 12 ('49)	5.00	4.00
b.		Perf. 14 ('48)	3.00	3.00
c.		Perf. 13x11½	75.00	9.00

1944, Dec. 1　　　　**Perf. 12**

65	A14	1p red violet	.25	.30
a.		Perf. 11½ ('50)	.25	.50
66	A14	2p deep red	.25	2.75
a.		Perf. 11½ ('50)	.25	.50
67	A14	3p black	.25	2.50
68	A14	4p dark green	.25	4.00
		Nos. 53-68 (16)	51.15	31.40
		Set, never hinged	75.00	

Issue date: Nos. 65a, 66a, Feb. 15.

Catalogue values for unused stamps in this section, from this point to the end of the section, are for Never Hinged items.

Peace Issue
Common Design Type

1946, Oct. 21　Engr.　Perf. 13½x14

71	CD303	1½p brown	.35	.25
72	CD303	4p deep blue	.35	2.00

Silver Wedding Issue
Common Design Types

1948, Dec. 20　Photo.　Perf. 14x14½

73	CD304	1p brt red violet	.35	.30

Perf. 11½x11
Engraved; Name Typographed

74	CD305	5sh brown orange	13.50	20.00

UPU Issue
Common Design Types
Engr.; Name Typo. on 3p, 6p
Perf. 13½, 11x11½

1949, Oct. 10　　　　**Wmk. 4**

75	CD306	1p red violet	.25	.25
76	CD307	3p indigo	.35	3.50
77	CD308	6p rose violet	.80	3.50
78	CD309	1sh olive	1.40	2.00
		Nos. 75-78 (4)	2.80	9.25

NIUE

nē-'ü-ͅͅā

LOCATION — Island in the south Pacific Ocean, northeast of New Zealand
AREA — 100 sq. mi.
POP. — 3,019 (est. 1984)
CAPITAL — Alofi

Niue, also known as Savage Island, was annexed to New Zealand in 1901 with the Cook Islands.

12 Pence = 1 Shilling
20 Shillings = 1 Pound

Catalogue values for unused stamps in this country are for Never Hinged items, beginning with Scott 90 in the regular postage section.

Watermarks

Wmk. 61 —
Single-lined NZ
and Star Close
Together

Wmk. 253 — NZ
and Star

New Zealand No. 100
Handstamped in Green

1902　　**Wmk. 63**　　**Perf. 11**
Thick Soft Paper

1	A35	1p carmine	375.00	375.00

Stamps of New Zealand Surcharged in Carmine, Vermilion or Blue

1/2p

1p

2 1/2p

Perf. 14
Thin Hard Paper

3	A18	½p green (C)	3.50	5.00
a.		Inverted surcharge	325.00	600.00
4	A35	1p carmine (R)	2.00	2.75
a.		No period after "PENI"	42.50	55.00
b.		Perf. 14	35.00	47.50
c.		As "a," perf. 14	475.00	500.00

Perf. 14
Wmk. 61

6	A18	½p green (V)	1.10	1.10
7	A35	1p carmine (R)	.85	1.10
a.		No period after "PENI"	9.00	16.00
b.		Double surcharge	1,800.	2,000.

Perf. 11
Unwmk.

8	A22	2½p blue (C)	4.00	4.50
a.		No period after "PENI"	45.00	47.50
9	A22	2½p blue (V)	1.75	2.00
a.		No period after "PENI"	20.00	25.00

The surcharge on the ½ & 1p stamps is printed in blocks of 60. Two stamps in each block have a space between the "U" and "E" of "NIUE" and one of the 1p stamps has a broken "E" like an "F."

Blue Surcharge on Stamps of New Zealand, Types of 1898

e

f

g

h

1903　　**Wmk. 61**　　**Perf. 11**

10	A23(e)	3p yellow brown	11.00	5.50
11	A26(f)	6p rose	14.00	12.50
13	A29(g)	1sh brown red	40.00	40.00
a.		1sh scarlet	40.00	45.00
b.		1sh orange red	50.00	52.50
c.		As "b," surcharge "h" (error)	750.00	
		Nos. 10-13 (3)	65.00	58.00

Surcharged in Carmine or Blue on Stamps of New Zealand — j

1911-12　　　　**Perf. 14, 14x14½**

14	A41(j)	½p yellow grn (C)	.60	.70
15	A41(f)	6p car rose (Bl)	2.50	7.50
16	A41(g)	1sh vermilion (Bl)	8.00	50.00
		Nos. 14-16 (3)	11.10	58.20

1915　　　　　　**Perf. 14**

18	A22(d)	2½p dark blue (C)	22.00	50.00

Surcharged in Brown or Dark Blue on Stamps of New Zealand

1917　　**Perf. 14x13½, 14x14½**

19	A42	1p carmine (Br)	19.00	6.25
a.		No period after "PENI"	800.00	
20	A45(e)	3p violet brn (Bl)	50.00	95.00
a.		No period after "Pene"	850.00	

New Zealand Stamps of 1909-19 Overprinted in Dark Blue or Red — k

1917-20　　　　　　**Typo.**

21	A43	½p yellow grn (R)	.80	2.75
22	A42	1p carmine (Bl)	11.00	10.00
23	A47	1½p gray black (R)	1.10	2.50
24	A47	1½p brown org (R)	1.00	6.50
25	A43	3p chocolate (Bl)	1.60	37.50

Engr.

26	A44	2½p dull blue (R)	3.00	11.00
27	A45	3p violet brown (Bl)	1.75	2.25
28	A45	6p car rose (Bl)	7.00	26.00
29	A45	1sh vermilion (R)	14.00	11.00
		Nos. 21-29 (9)	41.25	128.50

Same Overprint On Postal-Fiscal Stamps of New Zealand, 1906-15
Perf. 14, 14½ and Compound

1918-23

30	PF1	2sh blue (R)	18.00	35.00
31	PF1	2sh6p bn (Bl) ('23)	24.00	55.00
32	PF1	5sh green (R)	29.00	57.50
33	PF1	10sh red brn (Bl) ('23)	130.00	170.00
34	PF2	£1 rose (Bl) ('23)	170.00	250.00
		Nos. 30-34 (5)	371.00	567.50

Landing of
Captain Cook
A16

Avarua
Waterfront
A17

Capt. James
Cook — A18

Coconut
Palm — A19

Arorangi
Village — A20

Avarua
Harbor — A21

Unwmk.

1920, Aug. 23　Engr.　Perf. 14

35	A16	½p yel grn & blk	4.25	4.25
36	A17	1p car & black	2.25	1.40
37	A18	1½p red & black	2.75	14.00
38	A19	3p pale blue & blk	1.25	16.00
39	A20	6p dp grn & red brn	3.00	21.00
a.		Center inverted	1,000.	
40	A21	1sh blk brn & blk	3.00	21.00
		Nos. 35-40 (6)	16.50	77.65

See Nos. 41-42. For surcharge see No. 48.

Types of 1920 Issue and

Rarotongan
Chief (Te
Po) — A22

Avarua
Harbor — A23

1925-27　　　　　**Wmk. 61**

41	A16	½p yel grn & blk ('26)	1.60	9.00
42	A17	1p car & black	2.00	1.00
43	A22	2½p dk blue & blk ('27)	4.50	12.00
44	A23	4p dull vio & blk ('27)	8.00	22.50
		Nos. 41-44 (4)	16.10	44.50

New Zealand No. 182 Overprinted Type "k" in Red

1927

47	A56	2sh blue	18.00	35.00
a.		2sh dark blue	17.00	47.50

No. 37 Surcharged

1931   Unwmk.   Perf. 14
48 A18 2p on 1½p red & blk   4.25 1.10

New Zealand Postal-Fiscal Stamps of 1931-32 Overprinted Type "k" in Blue or Red

1931, Nov. 12   Wmk. 61
49 PF5 2sh6p deep brown   5.00 13.00
50 PF5 5sh green (R)   40.00 75.00
51 PF5 10sh dark car   40.00 110.00
52 PF5 £1 pink ('32)   75.00 160.00
    Nos. 49-52 (4)   160.00 358.00

See Nos. 86-89D, 116-119 (in Scott Standard catalogue, Vol. 5).

Landing of Captain Cook — A24

Capt. James Cook — A25

Polynesian Migratory Canoe — A26

Islanders Unloading Ship — A27

View of Avarua Harbor — A28

R.M.S. Monowai — A29

King George V — A30

Perf. 13, 14 (4p, 1sh)

1932, Mar. 16   Engr.   Unwmk.
53 A24 ½p yel grn & blk   10.00 25.00
  a. Perf. 14x13   275.00
54 A25 1p dp red & blk   1.10 .55
55 A26 2p org brn & blk   3.50 4.50
56 A27 2½p indigo & blk   8.50 80.00
57 A28 4p Prus blue & blk 16.00 60.00
  a. Perf. 13   15.00 65.00
58 A29 6p dp org & blk   2.75 2.25
59 A30 1sh dull vio & blk   2.50 5.50
    Nos. 53-59 (7)   44.35 177.80

For types overprinted see Nos. 67-69.

1933-36   Wmk. 61   Perf. 14
60 A24 ½p yel grn & blk   .50 3.50
61 A25 1p deep red & blk   .50 1.75
62 A26 2p brown & blk ('36) .50 1.75
63 A27 2½p indigo & blk   .50 4.75
64 A28 4p Prus blue & blk   2.00 4.25
65 A29 6p org & blk ('36)   .80 .90
66 A30 1sh dk vio & blk ('36) 9.00 25.00
    Nos. 60-66 (7)   13.80 41.90

See Nos. 77-82.

Silver Jubilee Issue

Types of 1932 Overprinted in Black or Red

1935, May 7   Perf. 14
67 A25 1p car & brown red   .80 3.50
68 A27 2½p indigo & bl (R)   3.50 12.00
  a. Vert. pair, imperf. horiz. 275.00
69 A29 6p dull org & grn   3.50 7.00
    Nos. 67-69 (3)   7.80 22.50
Set, never hinged   16.00

The vertical spacing of the overprint is wider on No. 69.

No. 68a is from proof sheets.

Coronation Issue

New Zealand Stamps of 1937 Overprinted in Black

Perf. 13½x13

1937, May 13   Wmk. 253
70 A78 1p rose carmine   .25 .25
71 A78 2½p dark blue   .25 1.50
72 A78 6p vermilion   .30 .30
    Nos. 70-72 (3)   .80 2.05
Set, never hinged   1.25

George VI — A31

Village Scene — A32

Coastal Scene with Canoe — A33

1938, May 2   Wmk. 61   Perf. 14
73 A31 1sh dp violet & blk   5.00 8.00
74 A32 2sh dk red brown & blk 6.50 17.00
75 A33 3sh yel green & blue 18.50 17.00
    Nos. 73-75 (3)   30.00 42.00
Set, never hinged   55.00

See Nos. 83-85.

Mt. Ikurangi behind Avarua — A34

Perf. 13½x14

1940, Sept. 2   Engr.   Wmk. 253
76 A34 3p on 1½p rose vio & blk .45 .25
    Never hinged   .75

Examples without surcharge are from printer's archives.

Types of 1932-38

1944-46   Wmk. 253   Perf. 14
77 A24 ½p yel grn & blk   .40 2.25
78 A25 1p dp red & blk ('45) .40 1.25
79 A26 2p org brn & blk ('46) 3.75 6.00
80 A27 2½p dk bl & blk ('45) .50 1.00
81 A28 4p Prus blue & blk   2.75 .90
82 A29 6p dp orange & blk   1.40 1.40
83 A31 1sh dp vio & blk   .85 1.00
84 A32 2sh brn car & blk ('45) 8.50 3.75
85 A33 3sh yel grn & bl ('45) 11.00 8.50
    Nos. 77-85 (9)   29.55 26.05
Set, never hinged   35.00

New Zealand Postal-Fiscal Stamps Overprinted Type "k" (narrow "E") in Blue or Red

1941-45   Wmk. 61   Perf. 14
86 PF5 2sh6p brown   55.00 60.00
87 PF5 5sh green (R)   225.00 150.00
88 PF5 10sh rose   95.00 150.00
89 PF5 £1 pink   150.00 225.00
    Nos. 86-89 (4)   525.00 585.00
Set, never hinged   775.00

Wmk. 253
89A PF5 2sh6p brown   2.50 11.00
89B PF5 5sh green (R)   5.25 12.50
  e. 5sh light yellow green, wmkd. sideways ('67) 35.00 95.00
89C PF5 10sh rose   37.50 110.00
89D PF5 £1 pink   30.00 67.50
    Nos. 89A-89D (4)   75.25 201.00
Set, never hinged   120.00

No. 89Be exists in both line and comb perf.

> **Catalogue values for unused stamps in this section, from this point to the end of the section, are for Never Hinged items.**

Peace Issue
New Zealand Nos. 248, 250, 254 and 255 Overprinted in Black or Blue

p   q

1946, June 4   Perf. 13x13½, 13½x13
90 A94 (p) 1p emerald   .40 .35
91 A96 (q) 2p rose violet (Bl) .40 .35
92 A100 (p) 6p org red & red brn .40 .75
93 A101 (p) 8p brn lake & blk (Bl) .50 .75
    Nos. 90-93 (4)   1.70 2.20

Map of Niue — A35

H.M.S. Resolution — A36

Designs: 2p, Alofi landing. 3p, Thatched Dwelling. 4p, Arch at Hikutavake. 6p, Alofi bay. 9p, Fisherman. 1sh, Cave at Makefu. 2sh, Gathering bananas. 3sh, Matapa Chasm.

Perf. 14x13½, 13½x14
1950, July 3   Engr.   Wmk. 253
94 A35 ½p red orange & bl   .25 1.25
95 A36 1p green & brown   2.50 2.50
96 A36 2p rose car & blk   1.10 2.00
97 A36 3p blue vio & blue   .25 .25
98 A36 4p brn vio & ol grn   .40 .40
99 A36 6p brn org & bl grn   .70 1.40
100 A35 9p dk brn & brn org   .85 1.40
101 A36 1sh black & purple   1.00 .60
102 A35 2sh dp grn & brn org 1.35 5.00
103 A35 3sh black & dp blue 4.00 5.00
    Nos. 94-103 (10)   12.40 19.80

For surcharges see Nos. 106-115 in Scott Standard catalogue, Vol. 5.

NORTH BORNEO

ˈnorth ˈbor-nē-ˌō

LOCATION — Northeast part of island of Borneo, Malay archipelago
AREA — 29,388 sq. mi.
POP. — 470,000 (est. 1962)
CAPITAL — Jesselton

The British North Borneo Company administered North Borneo, under a royal charter granted in 1881.

100 Cents = 1 Dollar

> Quantities of most North Borneo stamps through 1912 have been canceled to order with an oval of bars. Values given for used stamps beginning with No. 6 are for those with this form of cancellation. Stamps from No. 6 through Nos. 159 and J31 that do not exist cto have used values in italics. Stamps with dated town cancellations sell for much higher prices.

> **Catalogue values for unused stamps in this country are for Never Hinged items, beginning with Scott 238.**

North Borneo

Coat of Arms — A1

1883-84   Unwmk.   Litho.   Perf. 12
1 A1 2c brown   42.50 70.00
  a. Horiz. pair, imperf. btwn. 20,000.
2 A1 4c rose ('84)   55.00 60.00
3 A1 8c green ('84)   90.00 60.00
    Nos. 1-3 (3)   187.50 190.00

For surcharges see Nos. 4, 19-21.

No. 1 Surcharged in Black

EIGHT CENTS

4 A1 8c on 2c brown   500.00 210.00
  a. Double surcharge   5,000.

Coat of Arms with Supporters
A4   A5

Perf. 14
6 A4 50c violet   190.00 40.00
7 A5 $1 red   160.00 17.50

1886   Perf. 14
8 A1 ½c magenta   110.00 200.00
9 A1 1c orange   210.00 350.00
  a. Imperf., pair   300.00
  b. Vert. pair, imperf horiz. 1,500.
10 A1 2c brown   42.50 40.00
  a. Horiz. pair, imperf. between 675.00
11 A1 4c rose   20.00 50.00
12 A1 8c green   21.00 50.00
  a. Horiz. pair, imperf. between 900.00
13 A1 10c blue   50.00 60.00
  a. Imperf., pair   375.00
    Nos. 8-13 (6)   453.50 750.00

Nos. 8, 11, 12 and 13 Surcharged or Overprinted in Black

and Revenue

3 CENTS

b   c

3 CENTS

d

1886

14	A1 (b)	½c magenta	170.00	250.00
15	A1 (c)	3c on 4c rose	120.00	130.00
16	A1 (d)	3c on 4c rose	1,800.	
17	A1 (c)	5c on 8c green	130.00	130.00
		Double surcharge	*1,000.*	
18	A1 (b)	10c blue	225.00	275.00

On Nos. 2 and 3
Perf. 12

19	A1 (c)	3c on 4c rose	250.00	300.00
20	A1 (d)	3c on 4c rose	—	1,500.
a.		Double surcharge, both types of "3"		7,500.
21	A1 (c)	5c on 8c green	250.00	300.00

British North Borneo

A9

1886		Unwmk.	Litho.	Perf. 12
22	A9	½c lilac rose	250.00	425.00
23	A9	1c orange	200.00	275.00

Perf. 14

25	A9	½c rose	3.75	17.50
a.		½c lilac rose	17.50	50.00
b.		Imperf., pair	50.00	
26	A9	1c orange	2.25	12.00
a.		Imperf., pair	47.50	
27	A9	2c brown	2.25	10.00
a.		Imperf., pair	47.50	
b.		Horiz. pair, imperf. between	57.50	
28	A9	4c rose	4.50	17.50
a.		Cliché of 1c in plate of 4c	350.00	850.00
b.		Imperf., pair	50.00	
c.		As "a," imperf. in pair with #28	5,000.	
d.		Horiz. pair, imperf vert.	425.00	
29	A9	8c green	27.50	26.00
a.		Imperf., pair	50.00	
30	A9	10c blue	11.00	37.50
a.		Imperf., pair	50.00	
b.		Vert. pair, imperf btwn.	425.00	
		Nos. 25-30 (6)	*51.25*	*120.50*

For surcharges see Nos. 54-55.

A10   A11

A12   A13

31	A10	25c slate blue	350.00	20.00
a.		Imperf., pair	425.00	45.00
32	A11	50c violet	400.00	22.50
a.		Imperf., pair	475.00	45.00
33	A12	$1 red	375.00	21.00
a.		Imperf., pair	550.00	45.00
34	A13	$2 sage green	500.00	27.50
a.		Imperf., pair	450.00	47.50
		Nos. 31-34 (4)	*1,625.*	*91.00*
		Nos. 22-34 (12)	*2,121.*	*906.50*

See Nos. 44-47.

A14

1887-92				Perf. 14
35	A14	½c rose	1.50	.60
a.		½c magenta	4.00	3.00
36	A14	1c orange	4.50	.50
37	A14	2c red brown	6.00	.50
a.		2c brown	14.00	1.00
b.		As "a," horiz. pair imperf. between	425.00	
38	A14	3c violet	2.75	.50
39	A14	4c rose	9.00	.50
a.		Horiz. pair, imperf. vert.	250.00	
40	A14	5c slate	3.00	.50
41	A14	6c lake ('92)	15.00	.50

42	A14	8c green	25.00	1.00
a.		Horiz. pair, imperf. between		
43	A14	10c blue	7.25	.50
		Nos. 35-43 (9)	*74.00*	*5.10*

Exist imperf. Value $20 each, unused, $4.50 used. Forgeries exist, perf. 11½.

For surcharges see Nos. 52-53, 56-57.

Redrawn

25c. The letters of "BRITISH NORTH BORNEO" are 2mm high instead of 1½mm.

50c. The club of the native at left does not touch the frame. The 0's of "50" are flat at top and bottom instead of being oval.

$1.00. The spear of the native at right does not touch the frame. There are 14 pearls at each side of the frame instead of 13.

$2.00. "BRITISH" is 11mm long instead of 12mm. There are only six oars at the side of the dhow.

1888

44	A10	25c slate blue	80.00	.75
b.		Horiz. pair, imperf. between		275.00
c.		Imperf., pair	375.00	21.00
45	A11	50c violet	110.00	.75
a.		Imperf., pair	425.00	21.00
46	A12	$1 red	45.00	.75
a.		Imperf., pair	375.00	21.00
47	A13	$2 sage green	175.00	1.50
a.		Imperf., pair	500.00	24.00
		Nos. 44-47 (4)	*410.00*	*3.75*

For surcharges see Nos. 50-51, 58.

A15

A16

1889

48	A15	$5 red violet	350.00	9.00
a.		Imperf., pair	750.00	55.00
49	A16	$10 brown	350.00	12.50
b.		Imperf., pair	950.00	65.00

No. 44 Surcharged in Red — e

1890

50	A10	2c on 25c slate blue	75.00	100.00
a.		Inverted surcharge	450.00	450.00
b.		With additional surcharge "2 cents" in black		
51	A10	8c on 25c slate blue	105.00	125.00

Surcharged in Black On #42-43 — f

1891-92

52	A14	6c on 8c green	25.00	11.00
a.		"c" of "cents" inverted	550.00	650.00
b.		"cetns"	550.00	650.00
c.		Inverted surcharge	450.00	500.00
53	A14	6c on 10c blue	160.00	27.50

On Nos. 29 and 30

54	A9	6c on 8c green	9,000.	4,750.
55	A9	6c on 10c blue	67.50	22.50
a.		Inverted surcharge	300.00	300.00
b.		Double surcharge	1,000.	
c.		Triple surcharge	550.00	

Nos. 39, 40 and 44 Surcharged in Red

1892

56	A14	1c on 4c rose	25.00	15.00
a.		Double surcharge	1,500.	
b.		Surcharged on face & back		675.00
57	A14	1c on 5c slate	8.00	6.50
58	A10	8c on 25c blue	150.00	175.00
		Nos. 56-58 (3)	*183.00*	*196.50*

North Borneo

Dyak Chief — A21

Malayan Sambar — A22

Malay Dhow — A26

Sago Palm — A23

Saltwater Crocodile — A27

Argus Pheasant A24

Mt. Kinabalu A28

Coat of Arms — A25

Coat of Arms with Supporters — A29

A32

A33

A34

A35

Perf. 12 to 15 and Compound

1894		Engr.		Unwmk.
59	A21	1c bis brn & blk	1.40	.50
a.		Vert. pair, imperf. btwn.	950.00	
60	A22	2c rose & black	5.50	.75
a.		Horiz. pair, imperf. btwn.	950.00	950.00
b.		Vert. pair, imperf. btwn.	950.00	950.00
61	A23	3c vio & ol green	4.00	.55
a.		Horiz. pair, imperf. btwn.	—	850.00
62	A24	5c org red & blk	14.00	.75
a.		Horiz. pair, imperf. btwn.	850.00	
63	A25	6c brn ol & blk	4.50	.60
64	A26	8c lilac & black	6.50	.75
a.		Vert. pair, imperf. btwn.	550.00	350.00
b.		Horiz. pair, imperf. btwn.	750.00	
65	A27	12c ultra & black	47.50	3.00
		12c blue & black	30.00	2.75
66	A28	18c green & black	30.00	2.00
67	A29	24c claret & blue	25.00	2.00

		Litho.		Perf. 14
68	A30	25c slate blue	10.00	1.00
a.		Imperf., pair	60.00	12.00
69	A31	50c violet	42.50	2.00
a.		Imperf., pair		12.00
70	A32	$1 red	12.50	1.25
a.		Perf. 14x11	300.00	
b.		Imperf., pair	47.50	12.00
71	A33	$2 gray green	22.50	2.75
a.		Imperf., pair		18.00
72	A34	$5 red violet	275.00	16.00
a.		Imperf., pair	650.00	60.00
73	A35	$10 brown	300.00	16.00
a.		Imperf., pair	650.00	60.00
		Nos. 59-73 (15)	*800.90*	*49.90*

For #68-70 in other colors see Labuan #63a-65a.

For surcharges & overprints see #74-78, 91-94, 97-102, 115-119, 130-135, 115-119, 150-151, 158-159, J1-J8.

No. 70 Surcharged in Black

1895, June

74	A32	4c on $1 red	7.00	1.25
a.		Double surcharge	1,000.	
75	A32	10c on $1 red	26.00	.60
76	A32	20c on $1 red	47.50	.60
77	A32	30c on $1 red	40.00	1.25
78	A32	40c on $1 red	47.50	1.25
		Nos. 74-78 (5)	*168.00*	*4.95*

See No. 99.

A37

A38

A39

A40

A41

A42

A43

"Postal
Revenue" — A44

No "Postal
Revenue" — A45

Perf. 13 to 16 and Compound
1897-1900   **Engr.**

79	A37	1c bis brn & blk	12.00	.55
a.		Horiz. pair, imperf. btwn.		600.00
80	A38	2c dp rose & blk	25.00	.55
81	A38	2c grn & blk ('00)	60.00	.60
82	A39	3c lilac & ol green	24.00	.55
83	A40	5c orange & black	110.00	.75
84	A41	6c ol brown & blk	45.00	.50
85	A42	8c brn lilac & blk	13.00	.75
86	A43	12c blue & black	140.00	1.50
87	A44	18c green & black	27.50	3.00
a.		Vert. pair, imperf. btwn.		350.00
b.		Horiz. pair, imperf. vert.		95.00
c.		Imperf. pair		200.00
88	A45	24c claret & blue	26.00	3.00
		Nos. 79-88 (10)	482.50	11.75

For overprints and surcharges see Nos.
105-107, 109-112, 124-127, J9-J17, J20-J22,
J24-J26, J28.

"Postage & Revenue"
A46   A47

1897

89	A46	18c green & black	100.00	1.75
90	A47	24c claret & blue	50.00	2.10

For surcharges & overprints see #95-96,
128-129, 113-114, J18-J19, J30-J31.

Stamps of 1894-97
Surcharged in Black

1899

91	A40	4c on 5c org & blk	40.00	12.50
92	A41	4c on 6c ol brn & blk	20.00	25.00
93	A42	4c on 8c brn lil & blk	16.00	13.00
94	A43	4c on 12c bl & blk	29.00	15.00
a.		Horiz. pair, imperf. btwn.	850.00	
b.		Vert. pair, imperf. btwn.		950.00
95	A46	4c on 18c grn & blk	16.00	18.00
96	A47	4c on 24c cl & blue	25.00	20.00
a.		Perf. 16	55.00	55.00
97	A30	4c on 25c sl blue	6.00	10.00
98	A31	4c on 50c violet	18.00	18.00
99	A32	4c on $1 red	6.25	14.00
100	A33	4c on $2 gray grn	6.25	19.00

"CENTS" 8½mm below "4"

101	A34	4c on $5 red vio	7.25	18.00
a.		Normal spacing	170.00	250.00
102	A35	4c on $10 brown	7.25	18.00
a.		Normal spacing	130.00	250.00
		Nos. 91-102 (12)	197.00	200.50

No. 99 differs from No. 74 in the distance
between "4" and "cents" which is 4¾mm on
No. 99 and 3¾mm on No. 74.

Orangutan — A48

1899-1900   **Engr.**

103	A48	4c green & black	10.00	1.75
104	A48	4c dp rose & blk ('00)	40.00	.75

For overprints see Nos. 108, J23.

Stamps of 1894-
1900 Overprinted in
Red, Black, Green
or Blue — m

1901-05

105	A37	1c bis brn & blk (R)	4.00	.35
106	A38	2c grn & blk (R)	3.50	.35
107	A39	3c lil & ol grn (Bk)	2.00	.35
108	A48	4c dp rose & blk (G)	10.00	.35
109	A40	5c org & blk (G)	16.00	.35
110	A41	6c ol brn & blk (R)	4.50	.75
111	A42	8c brn & blk (Bl)	4.25	.55
a.		Vert. pair, imperf. btwn.		425.00
112	A43	12c blue & blk (R)	60.00	1.50
113	A46	18c grn & blk (R)	15.00	1.40
114	A47	24c red & blue (Bk)	18.00	1.75
115	A30	25c slate blue (R)	3.00	.60
a.		Inverted overprint	700.00	
116	A31	50c violet (R)	3.00	.70
117	A32	$1 red (R)	20.00	3.75
118	A32	$1 red (Bk)	10.00	2.75
a.		Double overprint		425.00
119	A33	$2 gray green (R)	37.50	4.00
a.		Double overprint	1,600.	
		Nos. 105-119 (15)	210.75	19.50

Nos. 110, 111 and 122 are known without
period after "PROTECTORATE."
See Nos. 122-123, 150-151.

Bruang (Sun
Bear) — A49

Railroad
Train — A50

1902   **Engr.**

120	A49	10c slate & dk brn	130.00	3.25
a.		Vertical pair, imperf. between		575.00
121	A50	16c yel brn & grn	150.00	3.75

Overprinted type "m" in Red or Black

122	A49	10c sl & dk brn (R)	75.00	1.10
a.		Double overprint	900.00	350.00
123	A50	16c yel brn & grn (Bk)	150.00	2.50
		Nos. 120-123 (4)	505.00	10.60

For overprints see Nos. J27, J29.

Stamps of 1894-97
Surcharged in Black

1904

124	A40	4c on 5c org & blk	50.00	14.00
125	A41	4c on 6c ol brn & blk	8.00	14.00
a.		Inverted surcharge	350.00	
126	A42	4c on 8c brn lil & blk	15.00	14.00
a.		Inverted surcharge	350.00	
127	A43	4c on 12c blue & blk	40.00	14.00
128	A46	4c on 18c grn & blk	16.00	14.00
129	A47	4c on 24c cl & bl	20.00	14.00
130	A30	4c on 25c sl blue	5.00	14.00
131	A31	4c on 50c violet	5.50	14.00
132	A32	4c on $1 red	7.00	14.00
133	A33	4c on $2 gray grn	10.50	14.00
134	A34	4c on $5 red vio	14.00	14.00
135	A35	4c on $10 brown	14.00	14.00
a.		Inverted surcharge	2,750.	
		Nos. 124-135 (12)	205.00	168.00

Malayan
Tapir — A51

Traveler's
Palm — A52

Railroad
Station — A53

Meeting of the
Assembly — A54

Elephant and
Mahout
A55

Sumatran
Rhinoceros
A56

Natives
Plowing — A57

Wild
Boar — A58

Palm Cockatoo
A59

Rhinoceros
Hornbill
A60

Banteng (Wild Ox)
A61   A62

Cassowary
A63

1909-22   Unwmk.   Engr.   Perf. 14
Center in Black

136	A51	1c chocolate	7.00	.30
b.		Perf. 13½	47.50	.40
c.		Perf. 15	3.25	.30
137	A52	2c green	1.00	.30
b.		Perf. 15	42.50	.55
138	A53	3c deep rose	3.25	.30
139	A53	3c green ('22)	42.50	.40
140	A54	4c dull red	2.75	.30
b.		Perf. 13½	11.00	10.50
c.		Perf. 15	21.00	.40
141	A55	5c yellow brn	16.00	.40
b.		Perf. 15		
142	A56	6c olive green	13.00	.30
b.		Perf. 15	80.00	1.00
143	A57	8c rose	4.00	.60
b.		Perf 15		12.00
144	A58	10c blue	45.00	2.00
b.		Perf. 13½	70.00	6.50
c.		Perf. 15		
145	A59	12c deep blue	42.50	1.00
c.		Perf. 15		12.00
146	A60	16c red brown	26.00	1.25
b.		Perf. 13½	30.00	6.50
147	A61	18c blue green	120.00	1.25
148	A62	20c on 18c bl grn (R)	7.00	.55
b.		Perf. 15	250.00	75.00
149	A63	24c violet	28.00	1.75
		Nos. 136-149 (14)	358.00	10.70

Issued: #139, 1922; others, July 1, 1909.
See #167-178. #136a-149a follow #162.
For surcharges and overprints see #160-
162, 166, B1-B12, B14-B24, B31-B41, J32-
J49.

Nos. 72-73 Overprinted type "m" in Red

1910

150	A34	$5 red violet	325.00	9.00
151	A35	$10 brown	550.00	11.00
a.		Double overprint		
b.		Inverted overprint	2,700.	450.00

A64

A65

1911   Engr.   Perf. 14
Center in Black

152	A64	25c yellow green	18.00	2.00
a.		Perf. 15	19.00	
b.		Imperf., pair	55.00	
153	A64	50c slate blue	18.00	2.25
a.		Perf. 15	24.00	22.50
b.		Imperf., pair	90.00	
154	A64	$1 brown	18.00	4.00
a.		Perf. 15	60.00	8.00
c.		Imperf., pair	180.00	
155	A64	$2 dk violet	75.00	5.00
156	A65	$5 claret	150.00	32.50
a.		Perf. 13½	150.00	
b.		Imperf., pair	200.00	
157	A65	$10 vermilion	500.00	90.00
a.		Imperf., pair	475.00	
		Nos. 152-157 (6)	779.00	135.75

See #179-184. #152c-153c follow #162.
For overprint and surcharges see Nos. B13,
B25-B30, B42-B47.

Nos. 72-73
Overprinted
in Red

1912
158	A34	$5 red violet	1,500.	9.25
159	A35	$10 brown	1,800.	9.25

Nos. 158 and 159 were prepared for use but
not regularly issued.

Nos. 138, 142
and 145
Surcharged in
Black or Red

1916   Center in Black   Perf. 14
160	A53	2c on 3c dp rose	30.00	15.00
a.		Inverted "S"	110.00	95.00
161	A56	4c on 6c ol grn (R)	30.00	20.00
a.		Inverted "S"	110.00	100.00
162	A59	10c on 12c bl (R)	60.00	70.00
a.		Inverted "S"	180.00	190.00
		Nos. 160-162 (3)	120.00	105.00

Stamps and Types of
1909-11 Overprinted
in Red or Blue

1922   Center in Black
136a	A51	1c brown	20.00	70.00
137a	A52	2c green	2.50	25.00
138a	A53	3c deep rose (B)	16.00	45.00
140a	A54	4c dull red (B)	3.75	45.00
141a	A55	5c yel brown (B)	9.50	65.00
142a	A56	6c olive green	9.50	70.00
143a	A57	8c rose (B)	8.50	42.50
144a	A58	10c gray blue	20.00	65.00
145a	A59	12c deep blue	12.00	45.00
146a	A60	16c red brown (B)	26.00	75.00
148a	A62	20c on 18c bl grn	27.50	90.00
149a	A63	24c violet	50.00	75.00
152c	A64	25c yel green	12.00	65.00
153c	A64	50c slate blue	17.50	70.00
		Nos. 136a-153c (14)	234.75	867.50

Industrial fair, Singapore, 3/31-4/15/22.

No. 140
Surcharged in
Black

1923
166	A54	3c on 4c dull red & blk	2.75	6.00
a.		Double surcharge	1,300.	

Types of 1909-22 Issues
1926-28   Engr.   Perf. 12½
Center in Black

167	A51	1c chocolate	1.00	.70
168	A52	2c lake	.85	.60
169	A53	3c green	3.00	.75
170	A54	4c dull red	.50	.25
171	A55	5c yellow brown	6.00	3.50
172	A56	6c yellow green	10.00	.90
173	A57	8c rose	4.75	.50
174	A58	10c bright blue	4.25	.90
175	A59	12c deep blue	24.00	.80
176	A60	16c orange brn	37.50	225.00
177	A62	20c on 18c bl grn (R)	6.00	4.00
178	A63	24c dull violet	60.00	170.00
179	A64	25c yellow grn	16.00	5.50
180	A64	50c slate blue	25.00	14.00
181	A64	$1 brown	25.00	500.00
182	A64	$2 dark violet	85.00	650.00
183	A65	$5 deep rose	200.00	1,300.
184	A65	$10 dull vermilion	550.00	1,500.
		Nos. 167-184 (18)	1,068.	4,377.

Murut — A66   Orangutan — A67

Dyak — A68

Mt.
Kinabalu
A69

Clouded
Leopard
A70

Coat of
Arms — A71

Arms with
Supporters
and Motto
A72

Arms with
Supporters — A73

1931, Jan. 1   Engr.   Perf. 12½
Center in Black

185	A66	3c blue green	1.50	1.50
186	A67	6c orange red	17.50	4.75
187	A68	10c carmine	4.50	13.00
188	A69	12c ultra	4.75	8.00
189	A70	25c deep violet	40.00	35.00
190	A71	$1 yellow green	27.50	110.00
191	A72	$2 red brown	47.50	110.00
192	A73	$5 red violet	160.00	500.00
		Nos. 185-192 (8)	303.25	782.25

50th anniv. of the North Borneo Co.

Buffalo
Transport
A74

Palm
Cockatoo — A75   Murut — A76

Proboscis
Monkey — A77   Bajaus — A78

 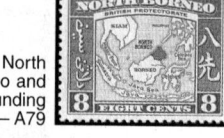

Map of North
Borneo and
Surrounding
Lands — A79

Orangutan — A80

Murut with
Blowgun — A81

Dyak — A82

River
Scene — A83

Proa — A84

Mt.
Kinabalu — A85

Coat of
Arms — A86

Arms with
Supporters
A87

1939, Jan. 1   Perf. 12½
193	A74	1c red brn & dk grn	2.75	2.25
194	A75	2c Prus bl & red vio	3.25	2.25
195	A76	3c dk grn & sl blue	3.50	2.50
196	A77	4c rose vio & ol grn	8.50	.50
197	A78	6c dp cl & dk blue	7.75	14.00
198	A79	8c red	11.00	2.00
199	A80	10c olive grn & vio	26.00	7.00
200	A81	12c ultra & grn	27.50	8.00
201	A82	15c bis brn & brt bl grn	21.00	13.00
202	A83	20c ind & rose vio	14.50	7.00
203	A84	25c dk brn & bl grn	21.00	15.00
204	A85	50c purple & brn	22.50	14.00
205	A86	$1 car & brown	72.50	22.50
206	A86	$2 ol grn & pur	120.00	150.00
207	A87	$5 blue & indigo	350.00	375.00
		Nos. 193-207 (15)	711.75	635.00
		Set, never hinged	1,200.	

For overprints see #208-237, MR1-MR2,
N1-N15, N16-N31.

Nos. 193 to
207
Overprinted
in
Black

1945, Dec. 17   Unwmk.   Perf. 12½
208	A74	1c red brn & dk grn	9.50	2.25
209	A75	2c Prus bl & red vio	10.00	2.00
210	A76	3c dk grn & sl bl	.90	1.25
211	A77	4c rose vio & ol grn	12.00	16.00
212	A78	6c dp cl & dk bl	.90	1.25
213	A79	8c red	2.10	.75
214	A80	10c ol green & vio	2.10	.40
215	A81	12c ultra & green	4.25	3.50
216	A82	15c bis brn & brt bl grn	1.20	1.10
217	A83	20c ind & rose vio	4.25	2.50
218	A84	25c dk brn & bl grn	4.75	1.50
219	A85	50c purple & brn	3.00	2.50
220	A86	$1 carmine & brn	35.00	40.00
221	A86	$2 ol green & pur	35.00	42.50
a.		Double overprint	4,000.	
222	A87	$5 blue & indigo	18.00	18.00
		Nos. 208-222 (15)	142.95	135.50
		Set, never hinged	235.00	

"BMA" stands for British Military
Administration.

Nos. 193 to 207
Ovptd. in Black or
Carmine

1947

223	A74	1c red brn & dk grn	.25	1.00
224	A75	2c Prus bl & red vio	1.25	.80
225	A76	3c dk grn & sl bl (C)	.25	.80
226	A77	4c rose vio & ol grn	.50	.80
227	A78	6c dp cl & dk bl (C)	.25	.25
228	A79	8c red	.25	.25
229	A80	10c olive grn & vio	1.10	.35
230	A81	12c ultra & grn	2.40	2.75
231	A82	15c bis brn & brt bl grn	1.75	.30
232	A83	20c ind & rose vio	2.40	.85
233	A84	25c dk brn & bl grn	2.40	.50
234	A85	50c purple & brn	2.00	.85
235	A86	$1 carmine & brn	8.50	1.75
236	A86	$2 ol green & pur	11.50	18.00
237	A87	$5 blue & ind (C)	19.00	25.00
		Nos. 223-237 (15)	53.80	54.25
		Set, never hinged	80.00	

The bars obliterate "The State of" and "British Protectorate."

Catalogue values for unused stamps in this section, from this point to the end of the section, are for Never Hinged items.

Silver Wedding Issue
Common Design Types
Perf. 14x14½
1948, Nov. 1   Wmk. 4   Photo.

238	CD304	8c scarlet	.30	.75

Perf. 11½x11
Engraved; Name Typographed

239	CD305	$10 purple	35.00	45.00

Common Design Types
pictured following the introduction.

UPU Issue
Common Design Types
Engr.; Name Typo. on 10c and 30c
1949, Oct. 10   Perf. 13½, 11x11½

240	CD306	8c rose carmine	.65	.25
241	CD307	10c chocolate	3.25	1.75
242	CD308	30c deep orange	1.50	1.75
243	CD309	55c blue	1.75	2.75
		Nos. 240-243 (4)	7.15	6.50

Mount Kinabalu — A88

Coconut Grove — A89

Designs: 2c, Musician. 4c, Hemp drying. 5c, Cattle at Kota Belud. 8c, Map. 10c, Logging. 15c, Proa at Sandakan. 20c, Bajau Chief. 30c, Suluk Craft. 50c, Clock tower. $1, Bajau horsemen. $2, Murut with blowgun. $5, Net fishing. $10, Arms.

Perf. 13½x14½, 14½x13½
1950, July 1   Photo.

244	A88	1c red brown	.25	1.25
245	A88	2c blue	.25	.50
246	A89	3c green	.25	.25
247	A89	4c red violet	.25	.25
248	A89	5c purple	.25	.25
249	A88	8c red	1.25	.85
250	A89	10c violet brn	1.75	.25
251	A88	15c brt ultra	2.00	.65
252	A88	20c dk brown	2.25	.25
253	A89	30c brown	5.50	.25
254	A89	50c cer (Jesselton)	1.75	4.75
255	A89	$1 red orange	6.00	1.25
256	A88	$2 dark green	15.00	20.00

257	A88	$5 emerald	25.00	30.00
258	A88	$10 gray blue	65.00	90.00
		Nos. 244-258 (15)	126.75	151.25

Redrawn
1952, May 1   Perf. 14½x13½

259	A89	50c cerise (Jesselton)	16.00	3.25

SEMI-POSTAL STAMPS

Nos. 136-138, 140-146, 148-149, 152 Ovptd. in Carmine or Vermilion

1916   Unwmk.   Perf. 14
Center in Black

B1	A51	1c chocolate	7.50	35.00
B2	A52	2c green	30.00	80.00
a.		Perf. 15	35.00	80.00
B3	A53	3c deep rose	27.50	50.00
B4	A54	4c dull red	7.25	32.50
a.		Perf. 15	275.00	180.00
B5	A55	5c yellow brown	50.00	55.00
B6	A56	6c olive green	70.00	75.00
a.		Perf. 15	225.00	225.00
B7	A57	8c rose	24.00	60.00
B8	A58	10c brt blue	55.00	70.00
B9	A59	12c deep blue	100.00	100.00
B10	A60	16c red brown	110.00	110.00
B11	A62	20c on 18c bl grn	55.00	100.00
B12	A63	24c violet	130.00	130.00
		Perf. 15		
B13	A64	25c yellow green	375.00	425.00
		Nos. B1-B13 (13)	1,041.	1,322.

All values exist with the vermilion overprint and all but the 4c with the carmine.

Of the total overprinting, a third was given to the National Philatelic War Fund Committee in London to be auctioned for the benefit of the wounded and veterans' survivors. The balance was lost en route from London to Sandakan when a submarine sank the ship. Very few were postally used.

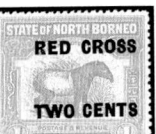

Nos. 136-138, 140-146, 149, 152-157 Surcharged

RED CROSS
TWO CENTS

1918   Center in Black   Perf. 14

B14	A51	1c + 2c choc	3.50	14.00
B15	A52	2c + 2c green	1.00	8.50
B16	A53	3c + 2c dp rose	14.00	19.00
a.		Perf. 15	30.00	65.00
B17	A54	4c + 2c dull red	.70	5.00
a.		Inverted surcharge	450.00	
B18	A55	5c + 2c yel brn	8.00	29.00
B19	A56	6c + 2c olive grn	5.00	29.00
a.		Perf. 15	225.00	250.00
B20	A57	8c + 2c rose	5.50	11.00
B21	A58	10c + 2c brt blue	8.00	27.50
B22	A59	12c + 2c deep bl	21.00	55.00
a.		Inverted surcharge	700.00	
B23	A60	16c + 2c red brn	22.50	45.00
B24	A63	24c + 2c violet	22.50	45.00
B25	A64	25c + 2c yel grn	12.00	42.50
B26	A64	50c + 2c sl blue	14.00	42.50
B27	A64	$1 + 2c brown	50.00	55.00
B28	A64	$2 + 2c dk vio	75.00	95.00
B29	A65	$5 + 2c claret	425.00	650.00
B30	A65	$10 + 2c ver	475.00	700.00
		Nos. B14-B30 (17)	1,162.	1,873.

On Nos. B14-B24 the surcharge is 15mm high, on Nos. B25-B30 it is 19mm high.

Nos. 136-138, 140-146, 149, 152-157 Surcharged in Red

FOUR CENTS

1918   Center in Black

B31	A51	1c + 4c choc	.60	5.00
B32	A52	2c + 4c green	.65	8.00
B33	A53	3c + 4c dp rose	1.00	3.75
B34	A54	4c + 4c dull red	.40	4.75
B35	A55	5c + 4c yel brn	2.00	22.50
B36	A56	6c + 4c olive grn	2.00	12.00
a.		Vert. pair, imperf. btwn.	2,500.	
B37	A57	8c + 4c rose	1.25	9.50
B38	A58	10c + 4c brt blue	3.75	12.00
B39	A59	12c + 4c dp blue	14.00	14.00

B40	A60	16c + 4c red brn	8.00	16.00
B41	A63	24c + 4c violet	11.00	20.00
B42	A64	25c + 4c yel grn	9.00	50.00
B43	A64	50c + 4c sl blue	15.00	45.00
a.		Perf. 15	60.00	
B44	A64	$1 + 4c brown	22.50	60.00
a.		Perf. 15	180.00	
B45	A64	$2 + 4c dk vio	55.00	80.00
B46	A65	$5 + 4c claret	300.00	400.00
B47	A65	$10 + 4c ver	375.00	450.00
		Nos. B31-B47 (17)	821.15	1,212.

POSTAGE DUE STAMPS

Regular Issues Overprinted

POSTAGE DUE

On Nos. 60 to 67
Reading Up Vert. (V), or Horiz. (H)
1895, Aug. 1   Unwmk.   Perf. 14, 15

J1	A22	2c rose & blk (V)	30.00	2.50
J2	A23	3c vio & ol grn (V)	6.00	1.25
J3	A24	5c org red & blk (V)	60.00	3.25
a.		Period after "DUE" (V)	275.00	
J4	A25	6c ol brn & blk (V)	20.00	2.75
J5	A26	8c lilac & blk (H)	50.00	3.00
a.		Double ovpt. (H)		400.00
J6	A27	12c blue & blk (H)	70.00	3.00
a.		Double overprint (H)		325.00
J7	A28	18c green & blk (V)	70.00	4.25
a.		Ovpt. reading down	600.00	350.00
b.		Overprinted horizontally	70.00	4.25
c.		Same as "b" inverted	375.00	400.00
J8	A29	24c claret & bl (H)	40.00	4.00
		Nos. J1-J8 (8)	346.00	24.00

1897   On Nos. 80 and 85

J9	A38	2c dp rose & blk (V)	8.50	1.50
a.		Overprinted horizontally	23.00	15.00
J10	A42	8c brn lil & blk (H)	65.00	80.00
a.		Period after "DUE"	30.00	75.00

On Nos. 81-88 and 104 Vertically reading up
1901

J11	A38	2c green & blk	75.00	.70
a.		Overprinted horizontally	225.00	
J12	A39	3c lilac & ol grn	32.00	.50
a.		Period after "DUE"	70.00	70.00
J13	A40	4c dp rose & blk	70.00	.50
J14	A40	5c orange & blk	28.00	.90
a.		Period after "DUE"	90.00	
J15	A41	6c olive brn & blk	7.00	.50
J16	A42	8c brown & blk	9.00	.50
a.		Overprinted horizontally	30.00	
b.		Period after "DUE" (H)	23.00	75.00
J17	A43	12c blue & blk	150.00	4.00
J18	A46	18c green & blk	80.00	4.00
J19	A47	24c red & blue	50.00	2.50
		Nos. J11-J19 (9)	501.00	14.10

On Nos. 105-114, 122-123 Horizontally
1903-11   Perf. 14

J20	A37	1c bis brn & blk, period after "DUE"	4.50	55.00
a.		Period omitted		
J21	A38	2c green & blk	27.50	.30
a.		Ovpt. vert., perf. 16	550.00	275.00
b.		Perf 15 (ovpt. horiz.)	55.00	55.00
J22	A39	3c lilac & ol grn	7.00	.35
a.		Ovpt. vert.	140.00	140.00
b.		Perf. 15 (ovpt. horiz.)	50.00	45.00
J23	A48	4c dp rose & blk, perf. 15	11.00	2.00
a.		"Postage Due" double	550.00	170.00
b.		Perf. 14	21.00	1.00
J24	A40	5c orange & blk	45.00	.45
a.		Ovpt. vert., perf. 15	250.00	160.00
b.		Perf. 13½ (ovpt. horiz.)		
c.		Perf. 16	85.00	35.00
J25	A41	6c olive brn & blk	24.00	.40
a.		"Postage Due" double	750.00	
b.		"Postage Due" inverted	500.00	125.00
c.		Perf. 16	90.00	37.50
J26	A42	8c brown & blk	27.50	.50
a.		Overprint vertical	200.00	125.00
J27	A49	10c slate & brn	130.00	1.60
J28	A43	12c blue & blk	42.50	3.75
J29	A50	16c yel brn & grn	85.00	3.75
J30	A46	18c green & blk	17.50	1.50
a.		"Postage Due" double	500.00	100.00
J31	A47	24c claret & blue	17.50	3.75
a.		"Postage Due" double	350.00	125.00
b.		Overprint vertical	325.00	140.00
		Nos. J20-J31 (12)	439.00	73.35

On Nos. 137 and 139-146
1921-31   Perf. 14, 15

J32	A52	2c green & blk	27.50	80.00
a.		Perf. 13½	11.00	75.00
J33	A53	3c green & blk	5.25	50.00
J34	A54	4c dull red & blk	1.25	1.25
J35	A55	5c yel brn & blk	9.50	30.00

J36	A56	6c olive grn & blk	17.00	17.00
J37	A57	8c rose & blk	2.00	2.00
J38	A58	10c blue & blk	16.00	19.00
a.		Perf. 15	200.00	200.00
J39	A59	12c dp vio & blk	70.00	55.00
J40	A60	16c red brn & blk	26.00	65.00
		Nos. J32-J40 (9)	174.50	319.00

On Nos. 168 to 176
1926-28   Perf. 12½

J41	A52	2c lake & blk	.75	2.00
J42	A53	3c green & blk	10.00	32.50
J43	A54	4c dull red & blk	3.25	2.00
J44	A55	5c yel brown & blk	8.50	90.00
J45	A56	6c yel green & blk	14.00	3.00
J46	A57	8c rose & black	11.00	22.50
J47	A58	10c brt blue & blk	12.00	90.00
J48	A59	12c dp blue & blk	32.50	160.00
J49	A60	16c org brn & blk	75.00	225.00
		Nos. J41-J49 (9)	167.00	627.00

Crest of British North Borneo Company — D1

1939, Jan. 1   Engr.   Perf. 12½

J50	D1	2c brown	4.25	80.00
J51	D1	4c carmine	4.75	110.00
J52	D1	6c dp rose violet	17.50	150.00
J53	D1	8c dk blue green	22.50	300.00
J54	D1	10c deep ultra	50.00	450.00
		Nos. J50-J54 (5)	99.00	1,090.
		Set, never hinged	160.00	

WAR TAX STAMPS

Nos. 193-194 Overprinted

No. MR1

WAR TAX

No. MR2

WAR TAX

1941, Feb. 24   Unwmk.   Perf. 12½

MR1	A74	1c red brown & dk green	2.75	4.50
MR2	A75	2c Prus blue & red violet	11.00	4.75

For overprints see Nos. N15A-N15B.

OCCUPATION STAMPS

Issued under Japanese Occupation

Nos. 193-207 Handstamped in Violet or Black

On Nos. N1-N15B, the violet overprint is attributed to Jesselton, the black to Sandakan. Nos. N1-N15 are generally found with violet overprint, Nos. N15A-N15B with black.

1942   Unwmk.   Perf. 12½

N1	A74	1c	200.00	250.00
N2	A75	2c	220.00	275.00
N3	A76	3c	175.00	300.00
N4	A77	4c	325.00	390.00
N5	A78	5c	200.00	355.00
N6	A79	8c	275.00	210.00
N7	A80	10c	250.00	360.00
N8	A81	12c	275.00	525.00
N9	A82	15c	220.00	525.00
N10	A83	20c	300.00	650.00
N11	A84	25c	300.00	700.00

N12	A85	50c	400.00	775.00
N13	A86	$1	440.00	925.00
N14	A86	$2	650.00	1,250.
N15	A87	$5	775.00	1,350.
	Nos. N1-N15 (15)		5,005.	8,840.

For overprints see Nos. N22a, N31a.

Same Overprint on Nos. MR1-MR2 in Black or Violet

1942

N15A	A74	1c	775.00	325.00
N15B	A75	2c	2,100.	650.00

Nos. 193 to 207 Overprinted in Black

1944, Sept. 30   Unwmk.   Perf. 12½

N16	A74	1c	8.25	13.00
N17	A75	2c	8.25	10.00
N18	A76	3c	8.25	11.00
N19	A77	4c	16.50	25.00
N20	A78	6c	12.00	7.00
N21	A79	8c	11.00	18.50
N22	A80	10c	9.25	14.50
a.	On No. N7		500.00	
N23	A81	12c	17.50	14.50
N24	A82	15c	17.50	17.50
N25	A83	20c	35.00	55.00
N26	A84	25c	35.00	55.00
N27	A85	50c	87.50	130.00
N28	A86	$1	105.00	165.00
	Nos. N16-N28 (13)		371.00	536.00

Nos. N1 and 205 Surcharged in Black

No. N30

No. N31

1944, May

N30	A74	$2 on 1c	5,500.	4,750.
N31	A86	$5 on $1	5,000.	3,750.
a.	On No. N13		10,000.	6,000.

Mt. Kinabalu OS1   Boat and Traveler's Palm OS2

1943, Apr. 29   Litho.

N32	OS1	4c dull rose red	30.00	60.00
N33	OS2	8c dark blue	25.00	55.00

Stamps of Japan, 1938-43, Overprinted in Black

1s, War factory girl. 2s, Gen. Maresuke Nogi. 3s, Power plant. 4s, Hyuga Monument and Mt. Fuji. 5s, Adm. Heihachiro Togo. 6s, Garambi Lighthouse, Formosa. 8s, Meiji Shrine, Tokyo. 10s, Palms and map of "Greater East Asia." 15s, Aviator saluting and Japanese flag. 20s, Mt. Fuji and cherry blossoms. 25s, Horyu Temple, Nara. 30s, Miyajima Torii, Itsukushima shrine. 50s, Golden Pavilion, Kyoto. 1y, Great Buddha, Kamakura. See Burma, Vol. 1, for illustrations of 2s, 3s, 5s, 8s, 20s and watermark. For others, see Japan.

Wmk. Curved Wavy Lines (257)

1944, Sept. 30   Perf. 13

N34	A144	1s orange brown	10.00	35.00
N35	A84	2s vermilion	8.25	30.00
N36	A85	3s green	10.00	05.00
N37	A146	4s emerald	18.50	27.50
N38	A86	5s brown lake	15.50	30.00
N39	A88	6s orange	24.00	32.50
N40	A90	8s dk purple & pale vio	7.00	32.50
N41	A148	10s crim & dull rose	15.00	35.00
N42	A150	15s dull blue	14.00	32.50
N43	A94	20s ultra	95.00	100.00
N44	A95	25s brown	65.00	95.00
N45	A96	30s peacock blue	195.00	105.00
N46	A97	50s olive	87.50	87.50
N47	A98	1y lt brown	95.00	120.00
	Nos. N34-N47 (14)		659.75	797.50

The overprint translates "North Borneo."

OCCUPATION POSTAGE DUE STAMPS

Nos. J50-J51, J53 Handstamped in Black

1942, Sept. 30

NJ1	D1	2c brown	—	5,000.
NJ2	D1	4c carmine	—	5,000.
NJ3	D1	8c dk blue green	—	5,000.

NORTHERN NIGERIA

'nor-<u>th</u>ə͏ r̩ n nĭ-'jir-ē-ə

LOCATION — Western Africa
GOVT. — A former British Protectorate
AREA — 281,703 sq. mi.
POP. — 11,866,250
CAPITAL — Zungeru

In 1914 Northern Nigeria united with Southern Nigeria to form the Colony and Protectorate of Nigeria.

12 Pence = 1 Shilling
20 Shillings = 1 Pound

Victoria — A1

Numerals of 5p and 6p, types A1 and A2, are in color on plain tablet.

Wmk. Crown and C A (2)

1900, Mar. Typo. *Perf. 14*
1	A1	½p lilac & grn	6.50	18.00
2	A1	1p lilac & rose	4.00	4.50
3	A1	2p lilac & yel	16.00	60.00
4	A1	2½p lilac & blue	13.00	37.50
5	A1	5p lilac & brn	27.50	60.00
6	A1	6p lilac & vio	29.00	50.00
7	A1	1sh green & blk	29.00	85.00
8	A1	2sh6p green & blue	180.00	550.00
9	A1	10sh green & brn	325.00	850.00
		Nos. 1-9 (9)	630.00	1,715.
		Set, ovptd. "SPECIMEN"	225.00	

Edward VII — A2

1902, July 1
10	A2	½p violet & green	2.00	1.00
11	A2	1p vio & car rose	4.00	.75
12	A2	2p violet & org	2.25	3.00
13	A2	2½p violet & ultra	2.00	9.50
14	A2	5p vio & org brn	6.50	6.50
15	A2	6p violet & pur	16.00	6.00
16	A2	1sh green & black	6.50	6.50
17	A2	2sh6p green & ultra	14.00	70.00
18	A2	10sh green & brown	55.00	60.00
		Nos. 10-18 (9)	108.25	163.25
		Set, ovptd. "SPECIMEN"	175.00	

1904, Apr. Wmk. 3
18A	A2	£25 green & car	50,000.

No. 18A was available for postage but probably was used only for fiscal purposes.

1905 Ordinary Paper
19	A2	½p violet & grn	27.50	8.50
20	A2	1p violet & car rose	22.50	1.25
21	A2	2p violet & org	19.00	32.50
22	A2	2½p violet & ultra	7.25	8.00
23	A2	5p violet & org brn	30.00	80.00
24	A2	6p violet & pur	29.00	65.00
25	A2	1sh green & black	65.00	100.00
26	A2	2sh6p green & ultra	50.00	60.00
		Nos. 19-26 (8)	250.25	355.25

1906-07 Chalky Paper
19a	A2	½p violet & grn	6.00	5.50
20a	A2	1p violet & car rose	6.00	1.25
21a	A2	2p violet & org	20.00	30.00
23a	A2	5p violet & org brn	35.00	75.00
24a	A2	6p violet & pur	45.00	45.00
25a	A2	1sh green & black	24.00	55.00
26a	A2	2sh6p green & ultra	37.50	60.00
		Nos. 19a-26a (7)	173.50	271.75

1910-11 Ordinary Paper
28	A2	½p green	2.25	1.25
29	A2	1p carmine	4.00	1.25
30	A2	2p gray	7.50	3.00
31	A2	2½p ultra	2.50	7.00

Chalky Paper
32	A2	3p violet, yel	4.50	.75
33	A2	5p vio & ol grn	5.50	13.00
34	A2	6p vio & red vio ('11)	5.50	6.00
a.		6p violet & deep violet	7.50	17.50
35	A2	1sh black, green	3.25	.75
36	A2	2sh6p blk & red, bl	16.00	40.00

37	A2	5sh grn & red, yel	27.50	75.00
38	A2	10sh grn & red, grn	55.00	50.00
		Nos. 28-38 (11)	133.50	198.00
		Set, ovptd. "SPECIMEN"	325.00	

George V — A3

For description of dies I and II, see A pages in front section of catalogue.

Die I

1912 Ordinary Paper
40	A3	½p green	3.25	.60
41	A3	1p carmine	3.25	.60
42	A3	2p gray	5.00	12.00

Chalky Paper
43	A3	3p violet, yel	2.25	1.25
44	A3	4p blk & red, yel	1.25	2.25
45	A3	5p vio & ol grn	4.00	15.00
46	A3	6p vio & red vio	4.25	4.50
47	A3	9p violet & scar	2.25	12.00
48	A3	1sh blk, green	5.00	2.25
49	A3	2sh6p blk & red, bl	8.75	55.00
50	A3	5sh grn & red, yel	25.00	90.00
51	A3	10sh grn & red, grn	45.00	50.00
52	A3	£1 vio & blk, red	200.00	120.00
		Nos. 40-52 (13)	309.25	365.45
		Set, ovptd. "SPECIMEN"	225.00	

Numerals of 3p, 4p, 5p and 6p, type A3, are in color on plain tablet.
Stamps of Northern Nigeria were replaced in 1914 by those of Nigeria.

NORTHERN RHODESIA

'nor-<u>th</u>ə͏ r̩ n rō-'dē-zh͏ ē-ə

LOCATION — In southern Africa, east of Angola and separated from Southern Rhodesia by the Zambezi River.
GOVT. — British Protectorate
AREA — 287,640 sq. mi.
POP. — 2,550,000 (est. 1962)
CAPITAL — Lusaka

Prior to April 1, 1924, Northern Rhodesia was administered by the British South Africa Company. See Rhodesia and Southern Rhodesia.

12 Pence = 1 Shilling
20 Shillings = 1 Pound

Catalogue values for unused stamps in this country are for Never Hinged items, beginning with Scott 46 in the regular postage section.

King George V
A1   A2

1925-29 Engr. Wmk. 4 *Perf. 12½*
1	A1	½p dk green	1.75	.80
2	A1	1p dk brown	1.75	.25
3	A1	1½p carmine	3.75	.30
4	A1	2p brown org	4.00	.25
5	A1	3p ultra	4.00	1.30
6	A1	4p dk violet	6.50	.50
7	A1	6p gray	7.00	.40
8	A1	8p rose lilac	7.00	60.00
9	A1	10p olive grn	7.00	50.00
10	A1	1sh black & org	4.00	2.25
11	A2	2sh ultra & brn	25.00	35.00
12	A2	2sh6p green & blk	24.00	15.00
13	A2	3sh indigo & vio	35.00	25.00
14	A2	5sh dk vio & gray	47.50	22.50
15	A2	7sh6p blk & lil rose	140.00	250.00
16	A2	10sh black & green	100.00	100.00
17	A2	20sh rose lil & red	225.00	275.00
		Nos. 1-17 (17)	643.25	838.55

High values with revenue cancellations are inexpensive.

Issue dates: 3sh, 1929; others, Apr. 1.

Common Design Types pictured following the introduction.

Silver Jubilee Issue
Common Design Type
1935, May 6 *Perf. 13½x14*
18	CD301	1p olive grn & ultra	1.50	1.50
19	CD301	2p indigo & grn	2.25	2.25
20	CD301	3p blue & brown	4.00	9.00
21	CD301	6p brt vio & indigo	8.00	3.50
		Nos. 18-21 (4)	15.75	16.25

Coronation Issue
Common Design Type
1937, May 12 *Perf. 11x11½*
22	CD302	1½p dark carmine	.25	.25
23	CD302	2p yellow brown	.45	.50
24	CD302	3p deep ultra	.65	1.25
		Nos. 22-24 (3)	1.35	2.00

King George VI — A3

1938-52 Wmk. 4 *Perf. 12½*
Size: 19x24mm
25	A3	½p green	.25	.25
26	A3	½p dk brown ('51)	1.40	1.50
a.		Perf. 12½x14	1.50	6.00
27	A3	1p dk brown	.25	.25
28	A3	1p green ('51)	.75	2.00
29	A3	1½p carmine	35.00	.75
a.		Horiz. pair, imperf. between	20,000.	
30	A3	1½p brown org ('41)	.30	.25
31	A3	2p brown org	45.00	1.75
32	A3	2p carmine ('41)	.85	.50
33	A3	2p rose lilac ('51)	.45	1.50
34	A3	3p ultra	.50	.30
35	A3	3p red ('51)	.45	3.00
36	A3	4p dk violet	.30	.40
37	A3	4½p dp blue ('52)	1.50	10.00
38	A3	6p dark gray	.30	.25
39	A3	9p violet ('52)	1.50	10.00
		Size: 21½x26¾mm		
40	A3	1sh blk & brn org	2.50	.60
41	A3	2sh6p green & blk	5.50	6.00
42	A3	3sh ind & dk vio	12.50	17.50
43	A3	5sh violet & gray	14.00	17.50
44	A3	10sh black & green	16.00	29.00
45	A3	20sh rose lil & red	37.50	75.00
		Nos. 25-45 (21)	176.80	178.30

Catalogue values for unused stamps in this section, from this point to the end of the section, are for Never Hinged items.

Peace Issue
Common Design Type
1946, Nov. 26 Engr. *Perf. 13½x14*
46	CD303	1½p deep orange	1.00	1.50
a.		Perf. 13½	14.00	13.00
47	CD303	2p carmine	.25	.50

Silver Wedding Issue
Common Design Types
1948, Dec. 1 Photo. *Perf. 14x14½*
48	CD304	1½p orange	.30	.25
		Perf. 11½x11		
		Engr.		
49	CD305	20sh rose brown	92.50	80.00

UPU Issue
Common Design Types
Engr.; Name Typo. on 3p, 6p
Perf. 13½, 11x11½
1949, Oct. 10 Wmk. 4
50	CD306	2p rose carmine	.50	.50
51	CD307	3p indigo	2.00	3.00
52	CD308	6p gray	1.50	1.50
53	CD309	1sh red orange	1.00	1.50
		Nos. 50-53 (4)	5.00	6.50

POSTAGE DUE STAMPS

D1

1929 Typo. Wmk. 4 *Perf. 14*
J1	D1	1p black	3.00	2.75
		On cover		150.00
a.		Wmk. 4a (error)	5,000.	
J2	D1	2p black	6.00	3.50
		On cover		180.00
a.		Bisected, used as 1d, on cover		850.00
J3	D1	3p black	3.50	27.50
		On cover		350.00
a.		Crown in watermark missing	600.00	
b.		Wmk. 4a (error)	375.00	
J4	D1	4p black	10.00	40.00
		On cover		400.00
		Nos. J1-J4 (4)	22.50	73.75

NORTH INGERMANLAND

'north 'iŋ-gər-mən-ˌland

LOCATION — In Northern Russia lying between the River Neva and Finland
CAPITAL — Kirjasalo

In 1920 the residents of this territory revolted from Russian rule and set up a provisional government. The new State existed only a short period as the revolution was quickly quelled by Soviet troops.

100 Pennia = 1 Markka

Arms — A1

Perf. 11½

1920, Mar. 21 Unwmk. Litho.

1 A1 5p green 2.50 *3.50*
2 A1 10p rose red 2.50 *3.50*
3 A1 25p bister 2.50 *3.50*
4 A1 50p dark blue 2.50 *3.50*
5 A1 1m car & black 30.00 *42.50*
6 A1 5m lilac & black 175.00 *175.00*
7 A1 10m brown & blk 225.00 *250.00*
Nos. 1-7 (7) 440.00 *481.50*

Well centered examples sell for twice the values shown.

Imperf., Pairs

1a A1 5p 40.00
2a A1 10p 40.00
3a A1 25p 50.00
4a A1 50p 50.00
5a A1 1m 65.00
6a A1 5m 200.00
7a A1 10m 350.00

Arms — A2

Peasant — A3

Plowing — A4

Milking — A5

Planting A6

Ruins of Church A7

Peasants Playing Zithers A8

1920, Aug. 2

8 A2 10p gray grn & ultra 3.00 *7.00*
9 A3 30p buff & gray grn 3.00 *7.00*
10 A4 50p ultra & red brn 3.00 *7.00*
11 A5 80p claret & slate 3.00 *7.00*
12 A6 1m red & slate 22.50 *45.00*
13 A7 5m dk vio & dl rose 9.00 *18.00*
14 A8 10m brn & violet 9.00 *18.00*
a. Center inverted 1,000.
Nos. 8-14 (7) 52.50 *109.00*

Counterfeits abound.

Nos. 8-14 exist imperf. Value for set in pairs, $200.

NORTH WEST PACIFIC ISLANDS

'north 'west pə-'si-fik 'ī-lənds

LOCATION — Group of islands in the West Pacific Ocean including a part of New Guinea and adjacent islands of the Bismarck Archipelago
GOVT. — Australian military government
AREA — 96,160 sq. mi.
POP. — 636,563

Stamps of Australia were overprinted for use in the former German possessions of Nauru and German New Guinea which Australian troops had captured. Following the League of Nations' decision which placed these territories under mandate to Australia, these provisional issues were discontinued. See German New Guinea, New Britain, Nauru and New Guinea.

12 Pence = 1 Shilling
20 Shillings = 1 Pound

Stamps of Australia Overprinted — a

Type a: "P" of "PACIFIC" above "S" of "ISLANDS."

There are two varieties of the letter "S" in the Type "a" overprint. These occur in three combinations: a, both normal "S"; b, 1st "S" with small head and long bottom stroke, 2nd "S" normal; c, both "S" with small head and long bottom stroke.

DESIGN A1
Die I — The inside frameline has a break at left, even with the top of the letters of the denomination.
Die II — The frameline does not show a break.

Die IV — As Die III, with a break in the top outside frameline above the "ST" of "AUSTRALIA." The upper right inside frameline has an incomplete corner.
Dies are only indicated when there are more than one for any denomination.

1915-16 Wmk. 8 *Perf. 12*

1 A1 2p gray 25.00 *75.00*
2 A1 2½p dark blue 5.00 *22.50*
3 A1 3p ol bis, die I 25.00 *65.00*
a. Die II 385.00 *600.00*
b. Pair, #3, 3a 825.00 *1,200.*
c. Pair, die I and die II 2,500.
d. 3p grnish olive (I) 210.00 300.00
e. As "c.," die II 120.00 150.00
4 A1 6p ultra 120.00 *130.00*
5 A1 9p violet 60.00 *72.50*
6 A1 1sh blue green 75.00 *77.50*
8 A1 5sh yel & gray ('16) 2,7500. *3,850.*
9 A1 10sh pink & gray 170.00 *200.00*
Revenue cancel
10 A1 £1 ultra & brown *600.00 775.00*
Nos. 1-6,8-10 (9) 28,580. 5,267.

For surcharge see No. 27.

Wmk. Wide Crown and Narrow A (9)
Perf. 12, 14

ONE PENNY
Die I — Normal die, having outside the oval band with "AUSTRALIA" a white line and a heavy colored line.
Die Ia — As die I with a small white spur below the right serif at foot of the "1" in left tablet.
Dies are only indicated when there are more than one for any denomination.

11 A4 ½p emerald 3.25 *10.00*
a. Double overprint
b. ½p bright green 3.25 11.00
12 A4 1p car (Die I) 7.75 7.25
a. 1p carmine rose (Die I) 120.00 *150.00*
b. 1p carmine (Die Ia) 110.00 *120.00*
13 A1 2p gray 20.00 *45.00*
14 A1 2½p dk bl ('16) *30,000. 30,000.*
16 A4 4p orange 4.50 *17.50*
17 A4 5p org brown 2.75 *19.00*
18 A1 6p ultra 11.00 *13.00*
19 A1 9p violet 17.50 *24.00*
20 A1 1sh blue green 12.50 *27.50*
21 A1 2sh brown 110.00 *130.00*
22 A1 5sh yellow & gray 82.50 *120.00*
Nos. 11-13,16-22 (10) 271.75 *413.25*

For surcharge see No. 28.

1915-16 Wmk. 10 *Perf. 12*

23 A1 2p gray, die I 9.00 *28.00*
24 A1 3p ol bis, die I 7.00 *15.00*
a. Die II 125.00 *190.00*
b. Pair, #24, 24a 250.00
25 A1 2sh brown ('16) 45.00 *65.00*
26 A1 £1 ultra & brn ('16) 400.00 *525.00*
Nos. 23-26 (4) 461.00 *633.00*

Nos. 6 and 17 Surcharged

1918, May 23 Wmk. 8 *Perf. 12*

27 A1 1p on 1sh bl grn 125.00 100.00

Wmk. 9 *Perf. 14*

28 A4 1p on 5p org brn 110.00 100.00

Stamps of Australia Overprinted — b

Type "b": "P" of "PACIFIC" above space between "I" and "S" of "ISLANDS."

1918-23 Wmk. 10 *Perf. 12*

29 A1 2p gray 8.50 *30.00*
a. Die II 13.50 *57.50*
30 A1 2½p dk bl ('19) 6.50 *19.00*
a. "1" of fraction omitted *13,000. 16,500.*
31 A1 3p ol bis, die I 27.50 *30.00*
a. Die II 80.00 *100.00*
b. Pair, #31, 31a 500.00 *650.00*
32 A1 6p ultra ('19) 7.50 *16.50*
a. 6p chalky blue 50.00 *75.00*
33 A1 9p violet ('19) 11.50 *60.00*
34 A1 1sh bl grn ('18) 16.50 *37.50*
a. 1sh emerald green 7.00 *32.50*
35 A1 2sh brown 25.00 *42.50*
36 A1 5sh yel & gray ('19) 75.00 *80.00*
37 A1 10sh pink & gray ('19) 200.00 *275.00*
38 A1 £1 ultra & brn 4,250. *5,500.*
Nos. 29-37 (9) 378.00 *590.50*

1919 Wmk. 11 *Perf. 14*

39 A4 ½p emerald 5.00 *6.00*

1918-23 Wmk. 9

40 A4 ½p emerald 2.00 *4.00*
41 A4 1p car red, die 1 4.25 1.75
a. 1p carmine red, die Ia 125.00 90.00
42 A4 1p scar, die I, rough paper 1,000. 675.00
a. 1p rose red, die Ia, rough paper 1,000. 675.00
43 A4 1p violet ('22) 2.75 *7.25*
44 A4 2p orange 8.75 2.75
45 A4 2p red ('22) 10.50 2.25
46 A4 4p yel org 4.00 *17.50*
47 A4 4p violet ('22) 22.50 *45.00*
a. "Four Penc" in thinner letters 900.00 *1,550.*
48 A4 4p light ultra ('22) 12.50 *65.00*
a. "Four Penc" in thinner letters 1,000. *2,000.*
49 A4 5p brown 4.25 *13.50*
Nos. 40-41,43-49 (9) 71.50 *159.00*

North West Pacific Islands stamps were largely used in New Britain. Some were used in Nauru. They were intended to serve the Bismarck Archipelago and other places.

NORWAY

'nor-ˌwā

LOCATION — Western half of the Scandinavian Peninsula in northern Europe
GOVT. — Kingdom
AREA — 125,051 sq. mi.
POP. — 4,134,353 (1984)
CAPITAL — Oslo

120 Skilling = 1 Specie Daler
100 Ore = 1 Krone (1877)

Watermarks

Wmk. 159 — Lion

Wmk. 160 — Post Horn

Coat of Arms — A1

Wmk. 159

1855, Jan. 1		**Typo.**		**Imperf.**
1	A1	4s blue	4,250.	175.
	On cover			375.
a.	Double foot on right hind leg of lion		3,000.	

Full margins = 1¾mm.

Values for multiples

Pair	—	600.
Strip of 3		2,000.
Strip of 4		7,500.
Strip of 5		12,000.
Strip of 6		17,500.
Block of 4		22,500.

Only a few genuine unused examples of No. 1 exist. Stamps often offered have had penmarkings removed. The unused catalogue value is for a stamp without gum. Stamps with original gum sell for much more.
No. 1 was reprinted in 1914 and 1924 unwatermarked. Lowest value reprint, $75.

ROULETTED REPRINTS

The various reprints of the early issues were never valid for postage and are not known canceled.
1963: No. 1, value $25; Nos. 2-5, 15, value each $15.
1966: Nos. 57, 70a, 100, 152, J1, O1. Value each $12.
1969: Nos. 69, 92, 107, 114, 128, J12. Value each $12.

King Oscar I — A2

1856-57		**Unwmk.**		**Perf. 13**
2	A2	2s yellow ('57)	800.00	160.00
	On cover			375.00
a.	2s orange		800.00	200.00
	On cover			600.00
3	A2	3s lilac ('57)	550.00	120.00
	On cover			925.00
4	A2	4s blue	450.00	20.00
a.	Imperf.			32.50
b.	Half used as 2s on cover			10,000.
c.	4s blackish blue	600.00	35.00
	On cover			100.00
d.	4s greenish blue	450.00	17.50
	On cover			40.00
e.	4s pale greenish blue	1,500.	60.00
	On cover			125.00

5	A2	8s dull lake	1,450.	65.00
	On cover			300.00
a.	8s lilac red		1,900.	90.00
	On cover			500.00

Nos. 2-5 were reprinted in 1914 and 1924, perf. 13½. Lowest valued reprint, $50 each.

A3

A4

1863		**Litho.**		**Perf. 14½x13½**
6	A3	2s yellow	1,250.	300.00
	On cover			500.00
7	A3	3s gray lilac	850.00	600.00
	On cover			925.00
8	A3	4s blue	275.00	18.00
	On cover			25.00
a.	4s greenish blue	400.00	26.00
	On cover			40.00
b.	4s dark blue	700.00	75.00
	On cover			—
	Half used as 2s on cover			
9	A3	8s rose	1,200.	80.00
	On cover			250.00
10	A3	24s brown	55.00	65.00
	On cover			1,450.
	On cover, single franking			1,900.
a.	24s dark brown		60.00	150.00
b.	24s reddish brown		72.50	180.00
	Nos. 6-10 (5)		3,630.	1,063.

There are four types of the 2, 3, 8 and 24 skilling and eight types of the 4 skilling. See note on used value of No. 10 following No. 21.
No. 8 exists imperf. Value, unused $900.

1867-68				**Typo.**
11	A4	1s black, coarse impression ('68)	100.00	70.00
	On cover			140.00
	1s dark gray, fine impression ('68)		175.00	120.00
	On cover			
12	A4	2s orange	35.00	30.00
	On cover			175.00
a.	2s brt yellow orange		90.00	110.00
	On cover			—
b.	Vert. pair, imperf between		1,750.	
13	A4	3s dl lil, coarse impression ('68)	600.00	160.00
	On cover			250.00
a.	3s reddish violet, fine impression		1,200.	275.00
	On cover			500.00
14	A4	4s blue, thin paper	175.00	15.00
	On cover			25.00
a.	4s greenish blue, thick paper		250.00	12.00
	On cover			25.00
15	A4	8s car rose	750.00	70.00
	On cover			250.00
a.	8s rose, clear impression		1,900.	550.00
	On cover			1,750.
	Nos. 11-15 (5)		1,660.	345.00

See note on used value of #12 following #21.
For surcharges see Nos. 59-61, 149.
No. 15 was reprinted in 1914 and 1924, perf. 13½. Lowest valued reprint, $50.

Post Horn and Crown — A5

1872-75				**Wmk. 160**
16	A5	1s yel grn ('75)	13.50	25.00
	On cover			35.00
a.	1s deep green ('73)	375.00	100.00
	On cover			150.00
b.	"E.EN"	25.00	75.00
c.	1s blue green, fine impression ('73)	350.00	105.00
	On cover			175.00
d.	Vert. pair, imperf between	—	
17	A5	2s ultra ('74)	20.00	40.00
	On cover			50.00
a.	2s Prussian blue ('74)	17,000.	5,000.
b.	2s gray blue	15.00	30.00
	On cover			350.00
18	A5	3s rose	85.00	35.00
	On cover			17.50
a.	3s carmine	95.00	16.00
	On cover			17.50
b.	3s carmine, *bluish* paper	450.00	50.00
	On cover			42.50
19	A5	4s lilac, thin paper ('73)	19.00	30.00
	On cover			50.00
a.	4s dark violet, *bluish*, thin paper ('73)	700.00	200.00
	On cover			350.00
b.	4s brown violet, *bluish* thin paper ('73)	700.00	250.00
	On cover			350.00
c.	4s violet, *white*, thick paper ('73)	140.00	60.00
	On cover			200.00
20	A5	6s org brn ('75)	675.00	90.00
	On cover			425.00

21	A5	7s red brn ('73)	75.00	65.00
	On cover			100.00
	Nos. 16-21 (6)		887.50	285.00

In this issue there are 12 types each of Nos. 16, 17, 18 and 19; 12 types of No. 20 and 20 types of No. 21. The differences are in the words of value.
Nos. 10, 12, 16, 17, 19 and 21 were re-released in 1888 and used until March 31, 1908. Used values of these stamps are for examples canceled in this later period, usually with a two-ring cancellation. Examples bearing clear dated cancellations before 1888 are worth considerably more, as follows: No. 10 $165, No. 12 $70, No. 16 $60, No. 17 $100, No. 17b $450, No. 19 $90, No. 21 $100.
No. 21 exists imperf. Value, unused without gum $800.
No. 19 comes on thin and thick paper.
For surcharges see Nos. 62-63.

Post Horn — A6   King Oscar II — A7

"NORGE" in Sans-serif Capitals, Ring of Post Horn Shaded

1877-78				
22	A6	1o drab	12.00	14.00
	On cover			60.00
23	A6	3o orange	125.00	45.00
	On cover			50.00
24	A6	5o ultra	40.00	18.00
	On cover			42.50
a.	5o dull blue	800.00	125.00
	On cover			175.00
b.	5o bright blue	300.00	70.00
	On cover			120.00
c.	No period after "Postfrim"	57.50	30.00
d.	Retouched plate	200.00	25.00
	On cover			60.00
e.	As "c," retouched plate	225.00	27.50
f.	5o Prussian blue	120.00	24.00
				72.50
g.	As "f," retouched plate	150.00	18.00
				75.00
25	A6	10o rose	120.00	4.50
	On cover			9.00
b.	Retouched plate	120.00	5.50
	On cover			9.50
26	A6	12o lt green	150.00	30.00
	On cover			90.00
27	A6	20o orange brn	450.00	20.00
	On cover			90.00
28	A6	25o lilac	600.00	150.00
	On cover			300.00
29	A6	35o bl grn ('78)	30.00	20.00
	On cover			60.00
	On cover, single franking			300.00
a.	Retouched plate	250.00	110.00
b.	35o dark blue green, coarse impression	30.00	18.00
c.	35o pale blue green	2,400.	310.00
30	A6	50o maroon	65.00	12.50
	On cover			110.00
	On cover, single franking			200.00
31	A6	60o dk bl ('78)	70.00	12.50
	On cover			110.00
	On cover, single franking			425.00
a.	60o pale steel blue	175.00	60.00
32	A7	1k gray grn & grn ('78)	45.00	12.50
				350.00
33	A7	1.50k ultra & bl ('78)	100.00	50.00
	On cover			540.00
34	A7	2k rose & mar ('78)	55.00	25.00
	On cover			540.00
	Nos. 22-34 (13)		1,862.	414.00

In this issue there are 12 types each of Nos. 16, 17, 18 and 19; 12 types of No. 20 and 20 types of No. 21. The differences are in the words of value. There are 6 types each of Nos. 22, 26 and 28 to 34; 12 types each of Nos. 23, 24, 25 and 27. The differences are in the numerals.
A 2nd plate of the 5o ultramarine has 100 types, the 10o, 200 types.
The retouch on 5o, 10o and 35o shows as a thin white line between crown and post horn.
Philatelic covers exist, especially for Nos. 29-34. They sell for much less.

Post Horn — A8

"NORGE" in Sans-serif Capitals, Ring of Horn Unshaded

1882-93		**Wmk. 160**		**Perf. 14½x13½**
35	A8	1o black brn ('86)	25.00	30.00
				90.00
a.	No period after "Postfrim"	60.00	60.00
b.	Small "N" in "NORGE"	60.00	60.00

36	A8	1o gray ('93)	15.00	15.00
	On cover			90.00
37	A8	2o brown ('90)	8.00	10.00
	On cover			30.00
	On cover, single franking			100.00
38	A8	3o yellow ('89)	100.00	12.50
	On cover			35.00
a.	3o orange ('83)	300.00	25.00
	On cover			55.00
b.	Perf. 13½x12½ ('93)	12,000.	4,000.
39	A8	5o bl grn ('89)	95.00	4.00
	On cover			15.00
a.	5o gray green ('86)	120.00	6.00
	On cover			27.50
b.	5o emerald ('88)	300.00	12.50
	On cover			35.00
c.	5o yellow green ('91)	100.00	4.50
	On cover			15.00
d.	Perf. 13½x12½ ('93)	5,000.	1,200.
40	A8	10o rose	80.00	2.00
	On cover			7.00
a.	10o rose red ('86)	80.00	2.00
	On cover			7.50
b.	10o carmine ('91)	80.00	2.00
	On cover			7.50
c.	As "b," imperf. ('91)	3,000.	2,750.
41	A8	12o green ('84)	1,800.	500.00
	On cover			3,000.
42	A8	12o orange brn ('84)	50.00	35.00
	On cover			1,450.
a.	12o bister brown ('83)	100.00	70.00
43	A8	20o brown	200.00	25.00
	On cover			210.00
44	A8	20o blue ('86)	125.00	3.50
	On cover			35.00
a.	20o ultramarine ('83)	500.00	25.00
	On cover			175.00
b.	No period after "Postfrim" ('85)	700.00	30.00
	On cover			175.00
c.	As "a," imperf. ('90)	2,500.	3,000.
d.	20o Prussian blue	350.00	30.00
45	A8	25o dull vio ('84)	25.00	30.00
	On cover			350.00
	On cover, single franking			600.00

Dies vary from 20 to 21mm high. Numerous types exist due to different production methods, including separate handmade dies for value figures. Many shades exist.
Philatelic covers bearing No. 45 sell for less.

No. 42 and 42a
Surcharged in Black

1888				**Perf. 14½x13½**
46	A8	2o on 12o org brn	3.50	4.50
	On cover			65.00
	On cover, single franking			175.00
a.	2o on 12o bister brown	7.00	5.50

Post Horn — A10

"NORGE" in Roman instead of Sans-serif capitals

Perf. 14½x13½

1893-1908				**Wmk. 160**
		Size: 16x20mm		
47	A10	1o gray ('99)	4.50	5.00
				7.00
48	A10	2o pale brn ('99)	3.25	3.00
	On cover, single franking			27.50
49	A10	3o orange yel	2.75	.40
				2.50
50	A10	5o dp green ('98)	7.00	.30
				1.75
b.	Booklet pane of 6	800.00	
51	A10	10o carmine ('98)	16.00	.30
				1.75
b.	Booklet pane of 6	1,100.	
d.	10o rose ('94)	350.00	4.00
e.	Imperf		4,000.
52	A10	15o brown ('08)	65.00	16.00
	On cover			35.00
53	A10	20o dp ultra	30.00	.40
				3.00
b.	Booklet pane of 6		
54	A10	25o red vio ('01)	85.00	5.00
				24.00
55	A10	30o sl gray ('07)	65.00	5.50
				30.00
56	A10	35o dk bl grn ('98)	18.00	12.50
				47.50
57	A10	50o maroon ('94)	75.00	3.00
				35.00
58	A10	60o dk blue ('00)	85.00	16.00
				120.00
	Nos. 47-58 (12)		456.50	67.40

Two dies exist of 3, 10 and 20o.
See Nos. 74-95, 162-166, 187-191, 193, 307-309, 325-326, 416-419, 606, 709-714, 960-968, 1141-1145. For overprints and surcharge see Nos. 99, 207-211, 220-224, 226, 329, 1282A-91. Post 1940 listings are in Scott Standard catalogue, Vol. 5.

Philatelic covers exist, especially for Nos. 54-58. They sell for less than values shown.

1893-98   Wmk. 160   Perf. 13½x12½

47a	A10	1o gray ('95)	25.00	15.00
		On cover		42.50
49a	A10	3o orange ('95)	50.00	12.00
		On cover		17.50
50a	A10	5o green	35.00	1.75
		On cover		9.00
51a	A10	10o carmine ('96)	35.00	1.50
		On cover		7.00
c.		10o rose ('95)	100.00	3.25
		On cover		7.00
53a	A10	20o dull ultra ('95)	110.00	7.50
		On cover		30.00
54a	A10	25o red violet ('98)	140.00	55.00
		On cover		125.00
56a	A10	35o dark blue green ('95)	100.00	30.00
		On cover		140.00
57a	A10	50o maroon ('97)	350.00	25.00
		On cover		120.00
		Nos. 47a-57a (8)	845.00	177.75

Two dies exist of each except 25 and 35o.

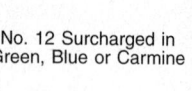

No. 12 Surcharged in Green, Blue or Carmine

1905   Unwmk.   Perf. 14½x13½

59	A4	1k on 2s org (G)	57.50	50.00
		On cover		150.00
60	A4	1.50k on 2s org (Bl)	100.00	85.00
		On cover		225.00
61	A4	2k on 2s org (C)	110.00	100.00
		On cover		175.00
		Nos. 59-61 (3)	267.50	235.00

Used values are for stamps canceled after 1910. Stamps used before that sell for twice as much.
Philatelic covers sell for less.

Nos. 19 and 21 Surcharged in Black

1906-08   Wmk. 160   Perf. 14½x13½

62	A5	15o on 4s lilac ('08)	8.50	8.50
		On cover		55.00
a.		15o on 4s violet ('08)	20.00	17.50
		On cover		60.00
63	A5	30o on 7s red brown	16.00	12.00
		On cover		95.00
a.		Inverted overprint		10,000.

Used values are for stamps canceled after 1914. Stamps used before that sell for twice as much.
Philatelic covers sell for less.

King Haakon VII — A11

Die B

Die C

Die A — Background of ruled lines. The coils at the sides are ornamented with fine cross-lines and small dots. Stamps 20¼mm high.
Die B — Background of ruled lines. The coils are ornamented with large white dots and dashes. Stamps 21¼mm high.
Die C — Solid background. The coils are without ornamental marks. Stamps 20¾mm high.

Die A

1907   Typo.   Perf. 14½x13½

64	A11	1k yellow grn	70.00	40.00
		On cover		425.00
65	A11	1.50k ultra	120.00	90.00
		On cover		500.00

66	A11	2k rose	185.00	125.00
		On cover		600.00
		Nos. 64-66 (3)	375.00	255.00

Used values are for stamps postmarked after 1910. Stamps postmarked before that sell for twice as much. Stamps postmarked after 1914 sell for one-half the values listed. See note after No. 180.

1909-10   Die B

67	A11	1k green	225.00	130.00
		On cover		600.00
68	A11	1.50k ultra	260.00	375.00
		On cover		1,500.
69	A11	2k rose	200.00	200.00
		On cover		300.00
		Nos. 67-69 (3)	685.00	513.00

Used values are for stamps canceled after 1914. Stamps used before that sell for twice as much.

1911-18   Die C

70	A11	1k light green	.90	.25
		On cover		12.00
a.		1k dark green	90.00	3.50
		On cover		50.00
71	A11	1.50k ultra	3.50	1.00
		On cover		30.00
72	A11	2k rose ('15)	4.50	1.50
		On cover		47.50
73	A11	5k dk violet ('18)	6.00	6.00
		On cover		120.00
		Nos. 70-73 (4)	14.90	8.75
		Set, never hinged	40.00	

See note following No. 180.
Philatelic covers sell for less.

Post Horn Type Redrawn

Original   Redrawn

In the redrawn stamps the white ring of the post horn is continuous instead of being broken by a spot of color below the crown. On the 3 and 30 ore the top of the figure "3" in the oval band is rounded instead of flattened.

1910-29   Perf. 14½x13½

74	A10	1o pale olive	.40	.75
75	A10	2o pale brown	.40	.50
76	A10	3o orange	.40	.50
77	A10	5o green	4.50	.25
a.		Booklet pane of 6	175.00	
		Complete booklet, 4 #77a	3,200.	
78	A10	5o magenta ('22)	.80	.25
79	A10	7o green ('29)	.80	.25
80	A10	10o car rose	6.50	.25
a.		Booklet pane of 6	100.00	
		Complete booklet, 2 #80a	500.00	
81	A10	10o green ('22)	8.00	.50
82	A10	12o purple ('17)	1.00	1.50
83	A10	15o brown	8.00	.50
a.		Booklet pane of 6	25.00	
		Complete booklet, 2 #83a	90.00	
84	A10	15o indigo ('20)	9.00	.25
85	A10	20o deep ultra	9.00	.25
a.		Booklet pane of 6	400.00	
		Complete booklet, 2 #85a	4,000.	
86	A10	20o ol grn ('21)	11.00	.30
87	A10	25o red lilac	55.00	.50
88	A10	25o car rose ('22)	9.00	.80
89	A10	30o slate gray	12.00	.50
90	A10	30o lt blue ('27)	10.00	8.00
91	A10	35o dk olive ('20)	15.00	.50
92	A10	40o ol grn ('17)	6.00	.50
93	A10	40o dp ultra ('22)	30.00	.30
94	A10	50o claret	25.00	.50
95	A10	60o deep blue	30.00	.50
		Nos. 74-95 (22)	251.80	18.15
		Set, never hinged	1,500.	

Constitutional Assembly of 1814 — A12

1914, May 10   Engr.   Perf. 13½

96	A12	5o green	1.25	.75
97	A12	10o car rose	3.00	.75
98	A12	20o deep blue	10.00	12.00
		Nos. 96-98 (3)	14.25	13.50
		Set, never hinged	80.00	

Norway's Constitution of May 17, 1814.

No. 87 Surcharged

1922, Mar. 1   Perf. 14½x13½

99	A10	5o on 25o red lilac	1.00	1.50
		Never hinged	2.00	

Lion Rampant — A13

"NORGE" in Roman capitals, Line below "Ore"

1922-24   Typo.   Perf. 14½x13½

100	A13	10o dp grn ('24)	10.00	.60
101	A13	20o dp vio	16.00	.25
102	A13	25o scarlet ('24)	27.50	.75
103	A13	45o blue ('24)	2.00	1.50
		Nos. 100-103 (4)	55.50	3.10
		Set, never hinged	250.00	

For surcharge see No. 129.

Polar Bear and Airplane — A14

1925, Apr. 1

104	A14	2o yellow brn	2.25	3.50
105	A14	3o orange	4.50	6.00
106	A14	5o magenta	12.00	22.50
107	A14	10o yellow grn	16.00	35.00
108	A14	15o dark blue	15.00	32.50
109	A14	20o plum	25.00	40.00
110	A14	25o scarlet	6.00	8.00
		Nos. 104-110 (7)	80.75	147.50
		Set, never hinged	180.00	

Issued to help finance Roald Amundsen's attempted flight to the North Pole.

A15

1925, Aug. 19

111	A15	10o yellow green	7.00	15.00
112	A15	15o indigo	5.00	9.00
113	A15	20o plum	7.00	2.50
114	A15	45o dark blue	6.00	9.00
		Nos. 111-114 (4)	25.00	35.50
		Set, never hinged	100.00	

Annexation of Spitsbergen (Svalbard).
For surcharge see No. 130.

A16

"NORGE" in Sans-serif Capitals, No Line below "Ore"

1926-34   Wmk. 160

Size: 16x19½mm

115	A16	10o yel grn	.70	.25
116	A16	14o dp org ('29)	2.25	3.00
117	A16	15o olive gray	.85	.25
118	A16	20o plum	30.00	.40
119	A16	20o scar ('27)	1.00	.25
a.		Booklet pane of 6	80.00	
		Complete booklet, 2 #119a	375.00	
120	A16	25o red	12.00	3.00
121	A16	25o org brn ('27)	1.25	.25
122	A16	30o dull bl ('28)	1.25	.25
123	A16	35o ol brn ('27)	75.00	.25
124	A16	35o red vio ('34)	2.00	.25
125	A16	40o dull blue	5.00	1.50
126	A16	40o slate ('27)	2.00	.25
127	A16	50o claret ('27)	2.00	.25
128	A16	60o Prus bl ('27)	2.00	.25
		Nos. 115-128 (14)	137.30	10.40
		Set, never hinged	675.00	

See Nos. 167-176, 192, 194-202A. For overprints and surcharges see Nos. 131, 212-

---

219, 225, 227-234, 302-303. Post 1940 listings are in Scott Standard catalogue, Vol. 5.

Nos. 103 and 114 Surcharged

1927, June 13

129	A13	30o on 45o blue	13.00	3.00
130	A15	30o on 45o dk blue	7.00	10.00
		Set, never hinged	60.00	

No. 120 Surcharged

1928

131	A16	20o on 25o red	2.50	2.50
		Never hinged	15.00	

See Nos. 302-303 in Scott Standard catalogue, Vol. 5.

Henrik Ibsen — A17

1928, Mar. 20   Litho.

132	A17	10o yellow grn	10.00	5.00
133	A17	15o chnt brown	4.00	4.50
134	A17	20o carmine	3.50	.90
135	A17	30o dp ultra	7.00	5.00
		Nos. 132-135 (4)	24.50	15.40
		Set, never hinged	85.00	

Ibsen (1828-1906), dramatist.

Postage Due Stamps of 1889-1923 Overprinted

a   b

1929, Jan.

136	D1 (a)	1o gray	.90	1.75
137	D1 (a)	4o lilac rose	.60	.60
138	D1 (a)	10o green	2.50	5.00
139	D1 (a)	15o brown	3.50	8.00
140	D1 (b)	20o dull vio	1.25	1.00
141	D1 (b)	40o deep ultra	2.00	1.00
142	D1 (b)	50o maroon	10.00	10.00
143	D1 (a)	100o orange yel	4.25	4.25
144	D1 (b)	200o dk violet	5.50	5.00
		Nos. 136-144 (9)	30.50	36.60
		Set, never hinged	75.00	

Niels Henrik Abel — A18

1929, Apr. 6   Litho.   Perf. 14½x13½

145	A18	10o green	3.50	1.00
146	A18	15o red brown	3.50	2.50
147	A18	20o rose red	1.25	.50
148	A18	30o deep ultra	3.25	3.00
		Nos. 145-148 (4)	11.50	7.00
		Set, never hinged	50.00	

Abel (1802-1829), mathematician.

No. 12 Surcharged

Perf. 14½x13½

1929, July 1   **Unwmk.**
149   A4   14o on 2s orange   3.50   *8.00*
   Never hinged   7.00

Saint Olaf
A19

Trondheim
Cathedral
A20

Death of Olaf
in Battle of
Stiklestad
A21

Typo.; Litho. (15o)
Perf. 14½x13½

1930, Apr. 1   **Wmk. 160**
150   A19   10o yellow grn   14.00   .70
151   A20   15o brn & blk   1.75   1.00
152   A19   20o scarlet   1.25   .50

Engr.
Perf. 13½
153   A21   30o deep blue   4.50   5.00
   Nos. 150-153 (4)   21.50   7.20
   Set, never hinged   90.00

King Olaf Haraldsson (995-1030), patron saint of Norway.

Björnson — A22

1932, Dec. 8   **Perf. 14½x13½**
154   A22   10o yellow grn   10.00   .75
155   A22   15o black brn   1.50   1.50
156   A22   20o rose red   1.00   .50
157   A22   30o ultra   3.50   *4.50*
   Nos. 154-157 (4)   16.00   7.25
   Set, never hinged   60.00

Björnstjerne Björnson (1832-1910), novelist, poet and dramatist.

Holberg — A23

1934, Nov. 23
158   A23   10o yellow grn   4.50   .90
159   A23   15o brown   1.00   1.25
160   A23   20o rose red   18.00   .50
161   A23   30o ultra   4.00   4.50
   Nos. 158-161 (4)   27.50   7.15
   Set, never hinged   90.00

Ludvig Holberg (1684-1754), Danish man of letters.

Types of 1893-1900, 1926-34
Second Redrawing
Perf. 13x13½

1937		Wmk. 160		Photo.

Size: 17x21mm
162   A10   1o olive   .70   2.00
163   A10   2o yellow brn   .70   1.75
164   A10   3o deep orange   1.75   *4.00*
165   A10   5o rose lilac   .55   .40
166   A10   7o brt green   .70   .40
167   A16   10o brt green   .45   .30
   Complete booklet, 2 panes
   of 6 #167   675.00
168   A16   14o dp orange   3.00   6.00
169   A16   15o olive bis   1.75   .25
170   A16   20o scarlet   1.25   .25
   Complete booklet, 2 panes
   of 6 #170   1,250.
   Complete booklet, panes of
   6 ea of #165, 167, 170   500.00
171   A16   25o dk org brn   6.00   .50
172   A16   30o ultra   3.50   .50
173   A16   35o brt vio   2.50   .25
174   A16   40o dk slate grn   3.50   .25

175   A16   50o deep claret   3.50   .75
176   A16   60o Prussian bl   2.50   .25
   Nos. 162-176 (15)   32.35   17.85
   Set, never hinged   125.00

Nos. 162 to 166 have a solid background inside oval. Nos. 74, 75, 76, 78, 79 have background of vertical lines.

King Haakon VII — A24

1937-38
177   A24   1k dark green   .25   .25
178   A24   1.50k sapphire ('38)   1.00   2.00
179   A24   2k rose red ('38)   1.00   1.25
180   A24   5k dl vio ('38)   9.00   10.00
   Nos. 177-180 (4)   11.25   13.50
   Set, never hinged   25.00

Nos. 64-66, 67-69, 70-73, 177-180 and B11-B14 were demonitized and banned on Sept. 30, 1940. Nos. 267, B19, B32-B34 and B38-B41 were demonitized on May 15, 1945. All of these stamps became valid again Sept. 1, 1981. Nos. 64-66, 67-69 and 70-73 rarely were used after 1981, and values represent stamps used in the earlier period. Values for Nos. B11-B14 used are for stamps used in the earlier period, and used examples in the later period are worth the same as mint stamps. Values for the other stamps used are for examples used in the later period, and stamps with dated cancellations prior to May 15, 1945 sell for more. False cancellations exist.

Reindeer — A25

Borgund
Church — A26

Jolster in
Sunnfiord
A27

Perf. 13x13½, 13½x13
1938, Apr. 20   **Wmk. 160**
181   A25   15o olive brn   1.25   1.25
182   A26   20o copper red   4.00   .55
183   A27   30o brt ultra   4.00   2.50
   Nos. 181-183 (3)   9.25   4.30
   Set, never hinged   40.00

1939, Jan. 16   **Unwmk.**
184   A25   15o olive brn   .50   .75
185   A26   20o copper red   .50   .25
186   A27   30o brt ultra   .50   .50
   Nos. 184-186 (3)   1.50   1.50
   Set, never hinged   3.00

Types of 1937
Perf. 13x13½
1940-49		Unwmk.		Photo.

Size: 17x21mm
187   A10   1o olive grn ('41)   .25   .25
188   A10   2o yellow brn
     ('41)   .25   .25
189   A10   3o dp orange
     ('41)   .25   .25
190   A10   5o rose lilac ('41)   .35   .25
191   A10   7o brt green ('41)   .40   .25
192   A16   10o brt green   .35   .25
   Complete booklet, 2 panes
   of 6 #192   50.00
193   A10   12o brt vio   .80   2.00
194   A16   14o dp org ('41)   1.50   4.00
195   A16   15o olive bister   .50   .25
196   A16   20o red   .45   .25
   Complete booklet, 2 panes
   of 6 #196   60.00
   Complete booklet, pane of
   6 ea of #190, 192, 196   200.00
   Complete booklet, pane of
   10 ea of #190, 192, 196   125.00

197   A16   25o dk org brn   1.25   .25
197A   A16   25o scarlet ('46)   .50   .25
   Complete booklet, pane of
   10 ea of #190, 192,
   197A   110.00
   Complete booklet, pane of
   10 ea of #192, 195,
   197A   100.00
198   A16   30o brt ultra ('41)   1.75   .40
198A   A16   30o gray ('49)   6.00   .25
199   A16   35o brt vio ('41)   1.75   .25
200   A16   40o dk sl grn ('41)   1.00   .25
200A   A16   40o dp ultra ('46)   3.75   .40
201   A16   50o dp claret ('41)   1.00   .25
201A   A16   55o dp org ('46)   15.00   .40
202   A16   60o Prus bl ('41)   1.25   .25
202A   A16   80o dk org brn
     ('46)   14.00   .40
   Nos. 187-202A (21)   52.35   11.35
   Set, never hinged   150.00

Lion Rampant — A28

1940   **Unwmk.**   **Photo.**   **Perf. 13x13½**
203   A28   1k brt green   1.00   .25
204   A28   1½k deep blue   1.75   .30
205   A28   2k bright red   2.50   1.25
206   A28   5k dull purple   7.00   *7.00*
   Nos. 203-206 (4)   12.25   8.80
   Set, never hinged   40.00

For overprints see Nos. 235-238 in Scott Standard catalogue, Vol. 5.

SEMI-POSTAL STAMPS

North Cape Issue

North
Cape — SP1

Perf. 13½x14
1930, June 28   **Wmk. 160**   **Photo.**
Size: 33¼x21½mm
B1   SP1   15o + 25o blk brn   2.00   *6.00*
B2   SP1   20o + 25o car   35.00   *80.00*
B3   SP1   30o + 25o ultra   90.00   *110.00*
   Nos. B1-B3 (3)   127.00   196.00
   Set, never hinged   275.00

The surtax was given to the Tourist Association. See No. B9-B10; Nos. B28-B30, B54-B56, B59-B61 in Scott Standard catalogue, Vol. 5.

Radium
Hospital
SP2

1931, Apr. 1   **Perf. 14½x13½**
B4   SP2   20o + 10o carmine   16.00   10.00
   Never hinged   65.00

The surtax aided the Norwegian Radium Hospital.

Fridtjof
Nansen — SP3

1935, Dec. 13   **Perf. 13½**
B5   SP3   10o + 10o green   3.50   *7.00*
B6   SP3   15o + 10o red brn   10.00   *15.00*
B7   SP3   20o + 10o crimson   5.00   4.50
B8   SP3   30o + 10o brt ultra   12.00   *16.00*
   Nos. B5-B8 (4)   30.50   42.50
   Set, never hinged   55.00

The surtax aided the International Nansen Office for Refugees.

North Cape Type of 1930
1938, June 20   **Perf. 13x13½**
Size: 27x21mm
B9   SP1   20o + 25o brn car   3.50   *9.00*
B10   SP1   30o + 25o dp ultra   13.50   32.50
   Set, never hinged   27.50

Surtax given to the Tourist Assoc.

Queen Maud — SP4

Perf. 13x13½
1939, July 24   **Photo.**   **Unwmk.**
B11   SP4   10o + 5o brt grn   .40   10.00
B12   SP4   15o + 5o red brn   .40   10.00
B13   SP4   20o + 5o blue   .50   7.50
B14   SP4   30o + 5o brt ultra   .40   12.00
   Nos. B11-B14 (4)   1.70   39.50
   Set, never hinged   4.00

The surtax was used for charities.

Fridtjof
Nansen — SP5   SP6

1940, Oct. 21
B15   SP5   10o + 10o dk grn   3.50   4.50
B16   SP5   15o + 10o henna brn   4.00   6.00
B17   SP5   20o + 10o dark red   .75   1.50
B18   SP5   30o + 10o ultra   2.50   4.50
   Nos. B15-B18 (4)   10.75   16.50
   Set, never hinged   16.00

The surtax was used for war relief work.

AIR POST STAMPS

Airplane over Akershus Castle
AP1   AP2

Perf. 13½x14½
1927-34   **Typo.**   **Wmk. 160**
C1   AP1   45o lt bl, strong frame
     line ('34)   4.50   *5.00*
   Never hinged   20.00
  a.   Faint or broken frame line   25.00   9.00
   Never hinged   150.00

1937, Aug. 18   **Photo.**   **Perf. 13**
C2   AP2   45o Prussian blue   .90   .70
   Never hinged   4.50

POSTAGE DUE STAMPS

Numeral of Value — D1

Inscribed "at betale"
Perf. 14½x13½
1889-1914   **Typo.**   **Wmk. 160**
J1   D1   1o olive green ('15)   1.25   *2.50*
   Never hinged   2.40
  a.   1o olive olive ('20)   7.00   18.00
   Never hinged   24.00
  b.   1o brownish gray ('89)   3.50   3.50
   Never hinged   16.00
  c.   1o gray ('93)   3.50   3.50
   Never hinged   16.00
J2   D1   4o magenta ('11)   2.00   2.00
   Never hinged   12.00
  a.   4o brown lilac ('08)   15.00   6.00
   Never hinged   75.00

b.		4o bluish violet ('93)		47.50	11.00
		Never hinged		210.00	
J3	D1	10o carmine rose ('99)		5.00	.90
		Never hinged		15.00	
a.		10o rose red ('89)		90.00	25.00
		Never hinged		425.00	
J4	D1	15o brown ('14)		4.50	1.75
		Never hinged		13.00	
J5	D1	20o ultra ('99)		3.50	.65
		Never hinged		15.00	
a.		Perf. 13⅙x12½ ('95)		250.00	115.00
		Never hinged		1,300.	
J6	D1	50o maroon ('89)		6.50	4.00
		Never hinged		30.00	
		Nos. J1-J6 (6)		22.75	11.80

See #J7-J12. For overprint see #136-144.

1922-23   Inscribed "a betale"

J7	D1	4o lilac rose	11.00	18.00
		Never hinged	35.00	
J8	D1	10o green	5.00	3.50
		Never hinged	22.50	
J9	D1	20o dull violet	8.00	8.00
		Never hinged	30.00	
J10	D1	40o deep ultra	12.00	1.50
		Never hinged	40.00	
J11	D1	100o orange yol	35.00	17.00
		Never hinged	150.00	
J12	D1	200o dark violet	75.00	30.00
		Never hinged	160.00	
		Nos. J7-J12 (6)	146.00	78.00

OFFICIAL STAMPS

Coat of Arms — O1

Perf. 14½x13½

1926   Typo.   Wmk. 160

O1	O1	5o rose lilac	.75	1.50
O2	O1	10o yellow green	.50	.50
O3	O1	15o indigo	2.00	4.50
O4	O1	20o plum	.50	.25
O5	O1	30o slate	4.50	10.00
O6	O1	40o deep blue	2.50	2.00
O7	O1	60o Prussian blue	5.00	10.00
		Nos. O1-O7 (7)	15.75	28.75
		Set, never hinged	40.00	

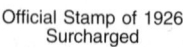

Official Stamp of 1926 Surcharged

1929, July 1

O8	O1	2o on 5o magenta	.60	1.75
		Never hinged	2.00	

Coat of Arms — O2

Perf. 14½x13½

1933-34   Litho.   Wmk. 160
Size: 35x19¼mm

O9	O2	2o ocher	.60	1.75
O10	O2	5o rose lilac	4.50	7.00
O11	O2	7o orange	4.50	10.00
O12	O2	10o green	30.00	1.25
O13	O2	15o olive	.60	1.25
O14	O2	20o vermilion	30.00	.60
O15	O2	25o yellow brn	.60	1.00
O16	O2	30o ultra	.90	1.25
O18	O2	40o slate	30.00	1.25
O19	O2	60o blue	18.00	2.00
O20	O2	70o olive brn	1.50	4.00
O21	O2	100o violet	2.00	3.50
		Nos. O9-O16,O18-O21 (12)	123.20	34.85
		Same, never hinged	600.00	

On the lithographed stamps, the lion's left leg is shaded.

Typo.
Size: 34x18¾mm

O10a	O2	5o rose lilac	1.50	4.00
O11a	O2	7o orange	8.00	22.50
O12a	O2	10o green	.70	.60
O13a	O2	15o olive	6.00	20.00
O14a	O2	20o vermilion	.70	.50
O17	O2	35o red violet ('34)	.90	.90
O18a	O2	40o slate	1.00	.90
O19a	O2	60o blue	1.25	1.25
		Nos. O10a-O14a,O17,O18a-O19a (8)	20.05	50.65
		Same, never hinged	60.00	

Coat of Arms — O3

1937-38   Photo.   Perf. 13½x13

O22	O3	5o rose lilac ('38)	.75	1.50
O23	O3	7o dp orange	.75	4.00
O24	O3	10o brt green	.40	.50
O25	O3	15o olive bister	.55	1.00
O26	O3	20o carmine ('38)	2.50	5.00
O27	O3	25o red brown ('38)	1.00	1.00
O28	O3	30o ultra	1.00	1.00
O29	O3	35o red vio ('38)	1.75	.60
O30	O3	40o Prus grn ('38)	1.00	.60
O31	O3	60o Prus bl ('38)	1.25	.60
O32	O3	100o dk vio ('38)	2.00	1.50
		Nos. O22-O32 (11)	12.95	17.30
		Set, never hinged	35.00	

See Nos. O33-O43, O55-O56. For surcharge see No. O57. Post 1940 listings are in Scott Standard catalogue, Vol. 5.

1939-47   Unwmk.

O33	O3	5o dp red lil ('41)	.25	.25
O34	O3	7o dp orange ('41)	.30	1.50
O35	O3	10o brt green ('41)	.25	.25
O36	O3	15o olive ('45)	.25	.25
O37	O3	20o carmine	.25	.25
O38	O3	25o red brown	3.00	20.00
O38A	O3	25o scarlet ('46)	.25	.25
O39	O3	30o ultra	2.75	2.75
O39A	O3	30o dk gray ('47)	.65	.55
O40	O3	35o brt lilac ('41)	.60	.50
O41	O3	40o grnsh blk ('41)	.55	.25
O41A	O3	40o dp ultra ('46)	3.00	.25
O42	O3	60o Prus blue ('41)	.65	.50
O43	O3	100o dk violet ('41)	1.00	.25
		Nos. O33-O43 (14)	13.75	27.80
		Set, never hinged	40.00	

NOSSI-BE

ˌno-sē-'bā

LOCATION — Island in the Indian Ocean, off the northwest coast of Madagascar
GOVT. — French Protectorate
AREA — 130 sq. mi.
POP. — 9,000 (approx. 1900)
CAPITAL — Hellville

In 1896 the island was placed under the authority of the Governor-General of Madagascar and postage stamps of Madagascar were placed in use.

100 Centimes = 1 Franc

Covers
Values are for commercial covers paying correct rates. Philatelic covers sell for less.

Stamps of French Colonies Surcharged in Blue

  a   b   c

On the following issues the colors of the French Colonies stamps, type A9, are: 5c, green, greenish; 10c, black, lavender; 15c, blue; 20c, red, green; 30c, brown, bister; 40c, vermilion, straw; 75c, carmine, rose; 1fr, bronze green, straw.

1889   Unwmk.   Imperf.

1	A8(a)	25 on 40c red, straw		2,600.	1,100.
		On cover			2,400.
a.		Double surcharge			3,400.
b.		Inverted surcharge		3,750.	1,600.
2	A8(b)	25c on 40c red, straw		3,100.	2,000.
		On cover			4,100.
a.		Double surcharge		5,500.	2,800.
b.		Inverted surcharge		5,500.	2,800.
c.		Pair, "a" and "c"			

Perf. 14x13½

3	A9(b)	5c on 10c		3,750.	1,450.
		On cover			3,250.
a.		Double surcharge			3,500.
b.		Inverted surcharge		5,000.	3,100.

4	A9(b)	5c on 20c		4,000.	1,600.
		On cover			3,250.
a.		Inverted surcharge		5,000.	3,100.
5	A9(c)	5c on 10c		3,100.	1,100.
		On cover			2,400.
a.		Inverted surcharge		5,600.	
6	A9(c)	5c on 20c		3,600.	2,400.
7	A9(a)	15 on 20c		2,800.	1,100.
		On cover			2,400.
a.		Double surcharge			2,400.
b.		Inverted surcharge		4,250.	1,750.
c.		15 on 30c (error)		32,000.	28,000.
8	A9(a)	25 on 30c		2,800.	950.
		On cover			2,500.
a.		Double surcharge			2,200.
b.		Inverted surcharge		3,600.	1,600.
9	A9(a)	25 on 40c		2,400.	1,100.
		On cover			2,500.
a.		Double surcharge			2,000.
b.		Inverted surcharge		3,600.	1,600.

d

e

f

1890   Black Surcharge

10	A9(d)	25c on 20c		425.00	300.00
		On cover			1,200.
11	A9(e)	0.25 on 20c		425.00	300.00
		On cover			1,200.
12	A9(f)	25 on 20c		1,000.	675.00
		On cover			2,100.
a.		In vert. pair with #10		1,800.	1,350.
b.		In vert. pair with #11		1,800.	1,350.
c.		Vert. strip of 3, #10-12		4,200.	4,200.
13	A9(d)	25c on 75c		425.00	300.00
		On cover			1,200.
14	A9(e)	0.25 on 75c		425.00	300.00
		On cover			1,200.
15	A9(f)	25 on 75c		1,000.	675.00
a.		In vert. pair with #13		1,800.	1,350.
b.		In vert. pair with #14		1,800.	1,350.
c.		Vert. strip of 3, #13-15		4,200.	4,200.
16	A9(d)	25c on 1fr		425.00	300.00
		On cover			1,200.
17	A9(e)	0.25 on 1fr		425.00	300.00
		On cover			1,200.
18	A9(f)	25 on 1fr		1,000.	675.00
a.		In vert. pair with #16		1,800.	1,350.
b.		In vert. pair with #17		1,800.	1,350.
c.		Vert. strip of 3, #16-18		4,200.	4,200.

Nos. 10-18 were overprinted in forms of 25 (5x5), with five rows of types d, e, f, d, e, making possible the various setenant multiples listed above.

The 25c on 20c with surcharge composed of "25 c." as in "d," "N S B" as in "e," and frame as in "f" is an essay.

Surcharged or Overprinted in Black, Carmine, Vermilion or Blue

j

k

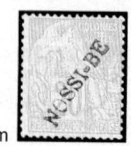

m

1893

23	A9(j)	25 on 20c (Bk)		52.50	45.00
		No gum		40.00	
		On cover			450.00
24	A9(j)	50 on 10c (Bk)		67.50	47.50
		No gum		52.50	
		On cover			550.00
a.		Inverted surcharge		400.00	260.00
		No gum		325.00	
25	A9(j)	75 on 15c (Bk)		300.00	240.00
		No gum		240.00	
		On cover			550.00
26	A9(j)	1fr on 5c (Bk)		150.00	110.00
		No gum		110.00	
		On cover			625.00
a.		Inverted surcharge		400.00	275.00
		No gum		325.00	

27	A9(k)	10c (C)		28.00	24.00
		Never hinged		45.00	
		On cover			450.00
a.		Inverted overprint		130.00	120.00
28	A9(k)	10c (V)		27.50	24.00
		Never hinged		45.00	
		On cover			450.00
29	A9(k)	15c (Bk)		32.50	32.50
		Never hinged		55.00	
		On cover			450.00
a.		Inverted overprint		140.00	130.00
b.		As "a," in pair with normal stamp		225.00	225.00
30	A9(k)	20c (Bk)		500.00	75.00
		Never hinged			600.00
		On cover			400.00
31	A9(m)	20c (Bl)		130.00	67.50
		Never hinged		240.00	
		On cover			400.00
a.		Inverted overprint		190.00	180.00
b.		As "a," in pair with normal stamp		450.00	450.00

Counterfeits exist of surcharges and overprints of Nos. 1-31.

Navigation and Commerce — A14

1894   Typo.   Perf. 14x13½
Name of Colony in Blue or Carmine

32	A14	1c blk, lil bl		1.60	1.60
		Never hinged		2.75	
		On cover			150.00
a.		No accent on "E" of "NOS-SI BE"		3.25	3.25
		Never hinged		5.50	
33	A14	2c brn, buff		2.00	2.00
		Never hinged		3.25	
		On cover			150.00
a.		No accent on "E" of "NOS-SI BE"		4.00	4.00
		Never hinged		7.25	
34	A14	4c claret, lav		2.75	2.00
		Never hinged		4.50	
		On cover			150.00
a.		No accent on "E" of "NOS-SI BE"		4.75	4.75
		Never hinged		8.75	
35	A14	5c grn, greenish		4.00	3.25
		Never hinged		7.25	
		On cover			100.00
a.		No accent on "E" of "NOS-SI BE"		7.25	6.50
		Never hinged		13.50	
36	A14	10c blk, lav		9.50	6.50
		Never hinged		17.50	
		On cover			100.00
a.		No accent on "E" of "NOS-SI BE"		20.00	16.00
		Never hinged		32.50	
37	A14	15c blue, quadrille paper		13.50	6.50
		Never hinged		24.00	
		On cover			125.00
a.		No accent on "E" of "NOS-SI BE"		27.50	20.00
		Never hinged		55.00	
38	A14	20c red, grn		9.50	6.50
		Never hinged		17.50	
		On cover			125.00
a.		No accent on "E" of "NOS-SI BE"		20.00	16.00
		Never hinged		32.50	
39	A14	25c blk, rose		16.00	9.50
		Never hinged		32.50	
		On cover			125.00
a.		No accent on "E" of "NOS-SI BE"		30.00	24.00
		Never hinged		60.00	
40	A14	30c brn, bister		16.00	14.50
		Never hinged		32.50	
		On cover			125.00
a.		No accent on "E" of "NOS-SI BE"		30.00	27.50
		Never hinged		60.00	
41	A14	40c red, straw		22.50	16.00
		Never hinged		45.00	
		On cover			300.00
a.		No accent on "E" of "NOS-SI BE"		40.00	32.50
		Never hinged		80.00	
42	A14	50c carmine, rose		22.50	16.00
		Never hinged		45.00	
		On cover			300.00
a.		No accent on "E" of "NOS-SI BE"		40.00	32.50
		Never hinged		80.00	
43	A14	75c dp vio, orange		37.50	37.50
		Never hinged		75.00	
		On cover			450.00
a.		No accent on "E" of "NOS-SI BE"		67.50	67.50
		Never hinged		140.00	
44	A14	1fr brnz grn, straw		27.50	27.50
		Never hinged		55.00	
		On cover			450.00
a.		No accent on "E" of "NOS-SI BE"		55.00	55.00
		Never hinged		125.00	
		Nos. 32-44 (13)		184.85	149.35

Perf. 13½x14 stamps are counterfeits.

POSTAGE DUE STAMPS

Stamps of French Colonies Surcharged in Black

n	o
Nossi-Bé chiffre-taxe 0.30 A PERCEVOIR	Nossi-Bé chiffre-taxe 0.35 A PERCEVOIR

1891   **Unwmk.**   **Perf. 14x13½**

J1	A9(n)	20 on 1c blk, lil bl	425.00	300.00
		On cover		1,500.
a.		Inverted surcharge	925.00	675.00
b.		Surcharged vertically	1,200.	1,400.
c.		Surcharge on back	1,050.	1,050.
J2	A9(n)	30 on 2c brn, buff	400.00	300.00
		On cover		1,500.
a.		Inverted surcharge	875.00	675.00
b.		Surcharge on back	1,000.	1,200.
J3	A9(n)	50 on 30c brn, bister	120.00	105.00
		On cover		900.00
a.		Inverted surcharge	925.00	675.00
b.		Surcharge on back	1,050.	1,300.
J4	A9(o)	35 on 4c cl, lav	450.00	325.00
		On cover		1,500.
a.		Inverted surcharge	925.00	675.00
b.		Surcharge on back	1,100.	1,300.
c.		Pair, one without surcharge		
J5	A9(o)	35 on 20c red, green	450.00	325.00
		On cover		1,500.
a.		Inverted surcharge	925.00	675.00
b.		Surcharge on back	1,050.	1,200.
J6	A9(o)	1fr on 35c vio, orange	325.00	240.00
		On cover		1,500.
a.		Inverted surcharge	925.00	625.00
b.		Surcharge on back	1,000.	1,100.

p	q
Nossi-Bé 5 C. A PERCEVOIR	Nossi-Bé 5 C. A PERCEVOIR

r

Nossi-Bé 0.10 A PERCEVOIR

1891

J7	A9(p)	5c on 20c	225.00	225.00
		On cover		1,250.
J8	A9(q)	5c on 20c	275.00	275.00
		On cover		1,250.
b.		In se-tenant pair with #J7	725.00	
J9	A9(r)	0.10c on 5c	27.50	24.00
		Never hinged	52.50	
		On cover		850.00
J10	A9(p)	10c on 15c	225.00	225.00
		On cover		1,250.
J11	A9(q)	10c on 15c	275.00	275.00
		On cover		1,500.
b.		In se-tenant pair with #J10	725.00	
J12	A9(p)	15c on 10c	200.00	200.00
		On cover		1,500.
J13	A9(q)	15c on 10c	210.00	210.00
		On cover		1,500.
b.		In se-tenant pair with #J12	725.00	
J14	A9(r)	0.15c on 20c	32.50	32.50
		Never hinged	65.00	
		On cover		1,250.
a.		25c on 20c (error)	40,000.	35,000.
J15	A9(p)	25c on 5c	180.00	180.00
		On cover		1,500.
J16	A9(q)	25c on 5c	200.00	200.00
		On cover		1,500.
b.		In se-tenant pair with #J15	700.00	
J17	A9(r)	0.25c on 75c	650.00	575.00
		On cover		3,000.

Inverted Surcharge

J7a	A9(p)	5c on 20c	425.00	425.00
J8a	A9(q)	5c on 20c	425.00	425.00
J10a	A9(p)	10c on 15c	425.00	425.00
J11a	A9(q)	10c on 15c	425.00	425.00
J12a	A9(p)	15c on 10c	425.00	425.00
J13a	A9(q)	15c on 10c	425.00	425.00
J15a	A9(p)	25c on 5c	425.00	425.00
J16a	A9(q)	25c on 5c	425.00	425.00
J17a	A9(r)	0.25c on 75c	1,800.	1,500.

Stamps of Nossi-Be were superseded by those of Madagascar.
Counterfeits exist of surcharges on #J1-J17.

NYASALAND PROTECTORATE

nī-ˈa-sə-ˌland prə-ˈtek-t̬ə-ˌrət

LOCATION — In southern Africa, bordering on Lake Nyasa
GOVT. — British Protectorate
AREA — 49,000 sq. mi.
POP. — 2,950,000 (est. 1962)
CAPITAL — Zomba

For previous issues, see British Central Africa.

12 Pence = 1 Shilling
20 Shillings = 1 Pound

> Catalogue values for unused stamps in this country are for Never Hinged items, beginning with Scott 68 in the regular postage section and Scott J1 in the postage due section.

A1

King Edward VII — A2

Wmk. Crown and C A (2)
1908, July 22   **Typo.**   **Perf. 14**

Chalky Paper

1	A1	1sh black, green	4.00	17.00

Wmk. Multiple Crown and C A (3)

Ordinary Paper

2	A1	½p green	2.00	2.25
3	A1	1p carmine	7.00	1.10

Chalky Paper

4	A1	3p violet, yel	1.75	4.75
5	A1	4p scar & blk, yel	1.75	1.75
6	A1	6p red vio & vio	4.25	12.50
7	A2	2sh 6p car & blk, bl	70.00	100.00
8	A2	4sh black & car	100.00	160.00
9	A2	10sh red & grn, grn	190.00	300.00
10	A2	£1 blk & vio, red	600.00	700.00
11	A2	£10 ultra & lilac	11,000.	7,000.
		Nos. 1-10 (10)	980.75	1,299.

A3   King George V — A4

1913-19   **Ordinary Paper**

12	A3	½p green	1.25	2.25
13	A3	1p scarlet	2.75	1.00
a.		1p carmine	4.00	2.00
14	A3	2p gray	6.00	1.00
15	A3	2½p ultra	2.25	7.00

Chalky Paper

16	A3	3p violet, yel	5.50	4.50
17	A3	4p scar & blk, yel	2.00	2.50
18	A3	6p red vio & dull vio	4.50	10.00
19	A3	1sh black, green	1.90	9.00
a.		1sh black, emerald	4.50	7.00
b.		1sh blk, bl grn, olive back	6.00	1.60
20	A4	2sh6p red & blk, bl ('18)	12.50	20.00
21	A4	4sh blk & red ('18)	35.00	75.00
22	A4	10sh red & grn, grn	110.00	140.00
23	A4	£1 blk & vio, red ('18)	200.00	170.00
24	A4	£10 brt ultra & slate vio ('19)	3,750.	2,000.
		Revenue cancel		275.00
a.		£10 pale ultra & dull vio ('14)	7,000.	
		Revenue cancel		300.00
		Nos. 12-23 (12)	383.65	442.25

Stamps of Nyasaland Protectorate overprinted "N. F." are listed under German East Africa.

1921-30   **Wmk. 4**   **Ordinary Paper**

25	A3	½p green	2.75	.50
26	A3	1p rose red	2.75	.50
27	A3	1½p orange	7.00	17.50
28	A3	2p gray	2.50	.50

Chalky Paper

29	A3	3p violet, yel	16.00	3.25
30	A3	4p scar & blk, yel	4.50	11.00
31	A3	6p red vio & dl vio	4.00	3.00
32	A3	1sh blk, grn ('30)	11.00	4.50
33	A4	2sh ultra & dl vio, bl	20.00	15.00
34	A4	2sh6p red & blk, bl ('24)	24.00	17.50
35	A4	4sh black & car	22.50	40.00
36	A4	5sh red & grn, yel ('29)	50.00	85.00
37	A4	10sh red & grn, emer	120.00	120.00
		Nos. 25-37 (13)	287.00	318.25

George V and Leopard A5

1934-35   **Engr.**   **Perf. 12½**

38	A5	½p green	.75	1.25
39	A5	1p dark brown	.75	.75
40	A5	1½p rose	.75	3.50
41	A5	2p gray	.90	1.25
42	A5	3p dark blue	3.00	1.50
43	A5	4p rose lilac ('35)	4.50	4.00
44	A5	6p dk violet	3.50	2.00
45	A5	9p olive bis ('35)	8.00	10.00
46	A5	1sh orange & blk	20.00	15.00
		Nos. 38-46 (9)	42.15	39.25

Common Design Types pictured following the introduction.

Silver Jubilee Issue
Common Design Type

1935, May 6   **Perf. 11x12**

47	CD301	1p gray blk & ultra	1.00	2.50
48	CD301	2p indigo & grn	2.75	2.75
49	CD301	3p ultra & brn	8.50	20.00
50	CD301	1sh brown vio & ind	25.00	55.00
		Nos. 47-50 (4)	37.25	80.25
		Set, never hinged	60.00	

Coronation Issue
Common Design Type

1937, May 12   **Perf. 11x11½**

51	CD302	½p deep green	.25	.30
52	CD302	1p dark brown	.40	.40
53	CD302	2p gray black	.40	.60
		Nos. 51-53 (3)	1.05	1.30
		Set, never hinged	1.75	

King George VI — A7

1938-44   **Engr.**   **Perf. 12½**

54	A6	½p green	.25	2.00
54A	A6	½p dk brown ('42)	.25	2.25
55	A6	1p dark brown	2.50	.35
55A	A6	1p green ('42)	.25	1.75
56	A6	1½p dark carmine	4.00	6.00
56A	A6	1½p gray ('42)	.25	5.75
57	A6	2p gray	5.00	1.25
57A	A6	2p dark car ('42)	.25	2.00
58	A6	3p blue	.60	1.00
59	A6	4p rose lilac	1.60	2.00
60	A6	6p dark violet	2.00	2.00
61	A6	9p olive bister	2.00	4.75
62	A6	1sh orange & blk	2.10	3.25

Typo.
Perf. 14

Chalky Paper

63	A7	2sh ultra & dl vio, bl	7.00	17.50
64	A7	2sh6p red & blk, bl	8.00	19.50

65	A7	5sh red & grn, yel	35.00	30.00
a.		5sh dk red & dp grn, yel ('44)	55.00	140.00
66	A7	10sh red & grn, grn	35.00	70.00

Wmk. 3

67	A7	£1 blk & vio, red	30.00	45.00
		Nos. 54-67 (18)	136.05	216.35
		Set, never hinged	220.00	

> Catalogue values for unused stamps in this section, from this point to the end of the section, are for Never Hinged items.

Canoe on Lake Nyasa — A8

Soldier of King's African Rifles — A9

Tea Estate, Mlanje Mountain A10

Map and Coat of Arms — A11

Fishing Village, Lake Nyasa — A12

Tobacco Estate — A13

Arms of Nyasaland and George VI A14

1945, Sept. 1   **Engr.**   **Perf. 12**

68	A8	½p brn vio & blk	.50	.25
69	A9	1p dp green & blk	.25	.75
70	A11	1½p gray grn & blk	.35	.45
71	A11	2p scarlet & blk	1.50	.80
72	A12	3p blue & blk	.45	.30
73	A10	4p rose vio & blk	2.00	.80
74	A10	6p violet & blk	3.00	.90
75	A8	9p ol grn & blk	3.50	3.00
76	A11	1sh myr grn & ind	3.75	.55
77	A12	2sh dl red brn & grn	9.50	5.50
78	A13	2sh6p ultra & green	9.50	4.00
79	A14	5sh ultra & lt vio	7.00	6.50
80	A11	10sh green & lake	20.00	18.00
81	A14	20sh black & scar	29.00	35.00
		Nos. 68-81 (14)	90.30	79.80

Peace Issue
Common Design Type
Perf. 13½x14

1946, Dec. 16			Wmk. 4	
82	CD302	1p bright green	~~.25~~	~~.25~~
83	CD303	2p red orange	.25	.25

A15

1947, Oct. 20			Perf. 12	
84	A15	1p emerald & org brn	.65	.50

Silver Wedding Issue
Common Design Types
1948, Dec. 15 Photo. Perf. 14x14½

85	CD304	1p dark green	.25	.25

Engr.; Name Typo.
Perf. 11½x11

86	CD305	10sh purple	19.00	32.50

UPU Issue
Common Design Types
Engr.; Name Typo. on 3p, 6p
Perf. 13½, 11x11½

1949, Nov. 21			Wmk. 4	
87	CD306	1p blue green	.35	.35
88	CD307	3p Prus blue	2.50	2.50
89	CD308	6p rose violet	.85	.85
90	CD309	1sh violet blue	.35	.35
	Nos. 87-90 (4)		4.05	4.05

Arms of British Central Africa and Nyasaland Protectorate — A16

1951, May 15		Engr.	Perf. 11x12	
Arms in Black				
91	A16	2p rose	1.50	1.50
92	A16	3p blue	1.50	1.50
93	A16	6p purple	1.50	2.25
94	A16	5sh deep blue	5.00	8.00
	Nos. 91-94 (4)		9.50	13.25

60th anniv. of the Protectorate, originally British Central Africa.

POSTAGE DUE STAMPS

Catalogue values for unused stamps in this section are for Never Hinged items.

D1

Perf. 14

1950, July 1		Wmk. 4	Typo.	
J1	D1	1p rose red	4.50	32.50
		On cover		300.00
J2	D1	2p ultramarine	17.50	32.50
		On cover		300.00
J3	D1	3p green	16.00	8.00
		On cover		300.00
J4	D1	4p claret	30.00	60.00
		On cover		500.00
J5	D1	6p ocher	42.50	160.00
		On cover		750.00
	Nos. J1-J5 (5)		110.50	293.00

Covers: Cover values are for properly franked commercial items. Philatelic usages sell for less.

NYASSA
nī-'a-sə

LOCATION — In the northern part of Mozambique in southeast Africa
GOVT. — Part of Portuguese East Africa Colony
AREA — 73,292 sq. mi.
POP. — 3,000,000 (estimated)
CAPITAL — Porto Amelia

The district formerly administered by the Nyassa Company is now a part of Mozambique. Postage stamps of Mozambique are used.

1000 Reis = 1 Milreis
100 Centavos = 1 Escudo (1919)

Mozambique Nos. 24-35 Overprinted in Black

1898		Unwmk.	Perf. 11½, 12½	
1	A3	5r yellow	2.50	1.50
2	A3	10r redsh violet	2.50	1.50
3	A3	15r chocolate	2.50	1.50
4	A3	20r gray violet	2.50	1.50
5	A3	25r blue green	2.50	1.50
6	A3	50r light blue	2.50	1.50
a.	Inverted overprint			
b.	Perf. 12½		6.00	3.50
7	A3	75r rose	3.00	2.00
8	A3	80r yellow grn	3.00	2.00
9	A3	100r brown, *buff*	3.00	2.00
10	A3	150r car, *rose*	6.50	4.00
11	A3	200r dk blue, *blue*	5.00	3.00
12	A3	300r dk blue, *salmon*	5.00	3.00
	Nos. 1-12 (12)		40.50	25.00

Reprints of Nos. 1, 5, 8, 9, 10 and 12 have white gum and clean-cut perforation 13½. Value of No. 9, $15; others $3 each.

Same Overprint on Mozambique Issue of 1898

1898			Perf. 11½	
13	A4	2½r gray	2.00	.80
14	A4	5r orange	2.00	.80
15	A4	10r light green	2.00	.80
16	A4	15r brown	2.50	1.00
17	A4	20r gray violet	2.50	1.00
18	A4	25r sea green	2.50	1.00
19	A4	50r blue	2.50	1.00
20	A4	75r rose	2.10	1.00
21	A4	80r violet	3.00	.80
22	A4	100r dk bl, *bl*	3.00	.80
23	A4	150r brown, *straw*	3.00	.80
24	A4	200r red lilac, *pnksh*	3.50	1.00
25	A4	300r dk blue, *rose*	4.00	1.00
	Nos. 13-25 (13)		34.60	11.80

Giraffe — A5

Camels — A6

1901		Engr.	Perf. 14	
26	A5	2½r blk & red brn	1.60	.55
27	A5	5r blk & violet	1.60	.55
28	A5	10r blk & dp grn	1.60	.55
29	A5	15r blk & org brn	1.60	.55
30	A5	20r blk & org red	1.60	.70
31	A5	25r blk & orange	1.60	.70
32	A5	50r blk & dl bl	1.60	.70
33	A5	75r blk & car lake	1.75	.70
34	A6	80r blk & lilac	1.75	.90
35	A6	100r blk & brn bis	1.75	.90
36	A6	150r blk & dp org	1.90	1.00
37	A6	200r blk & grnsh bl	2.00	1.00
38	A6	300r blk & yel grn	2.00	1.00
	Nos. 26-38 (13)		22.35	9.80

Nos. 26 to 38 are known with inverted centers but are believed to be purely speculative and never regularly issued. Value $80 each.
Perf. 13½, 14½, 15½ & compound also exist. For overprints and surcharges see Nos. 39-50, 63-80.

Nos. 34, 36, 38 Surcharged

1903				
39	A6	65r on 80r	1.00	.75
40	A6	115r on 150r	1.00	.75
41	A6	130r on 300r	1.00	.75
	Nos. 39-41 (3)		3.00	2.25

Nos. 29, 31 Overprinted

1903				
42	A5	15r black & org brn	1.00	.75
43	A5	25r black & orange	1.00	.75

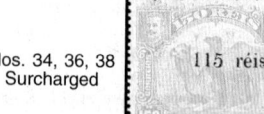

Nos. 34, 36, 38 Surcharged

1903				
44	A6	65r on 80r	32.50	15.00
45	A6	115r on 150r	32.50	15.00
46	A6	130r on 300r	32.50	15.00
	Nos. 44-46 (3)		97.50	45.00

Nos. 29, 31 Overprinted

1903				
47	A5	15r black & org brn	400.00	100.00
48	A5	25r black & orange	150.00	100.00

Forgeries exist of Nos. 44-48.

Nos. 26, 35 Surcharged

1910				
49	A5	5r on 2½r	1.00	.75
50	A6	50r on 100r	1.00	.75
a.	"50 REIS" omitted		300.00	

Reprints of Nos. 49-50, made in 1921, have 2mm space between surcharge lines, instead of 1½mm. Value, each 25 cents.

Zebra — A7

Vasco da Gama's Flagship "San Gabriel" — A8

Designs: Nos. 51-53, Camels. Nos. 57-59, Giraffe and palms.

1911			Red Overprint	
51	A7	2½r blk & dl vio	1.00	.55
52	A7	5r black	1.00	.55
53	A7	10r blk & gray grn	1.00	.55
54	A7	20r blk & car lake	1.00	.55
55	A7	25r blk & vio brn	1.00	.55
56	A7	50r blk & dp bl	1.00	.55
57	A8	75r blk & brn	1.00	.55
58	A8	100r blk & brn, *grn*	1.00	.55
59	A8	200r blk & dp grn, *sal*	1.10	1.00
60	A8	300r blk, *blue*	2.40	1.60
61	A8	400r blk & dk brn	3.00	2.00
a.	Pair, one without overprint			
62	A8	500r ol & vio brn	4.00	3.00
	Nos. 51-62 (12)		18.50	12.00

Nos. 51-62 exist without overprint but were not issued in that condition. Value $7.50 each.
For surcharges see Nos. 81-105.

Stamps of 1901-03 Surcharged

1918			On Nos. 26-38	
63	A5	¼c on 2½r	140.00	95.00
64	A5	½c on 5r	140.00	95.00
65	A5	1c on 10r	140.00	95.00
66	A5	1½c on 15r	2.10	1.10
67	A5	2c on 20r	1.25	1.00
68	A5	3½c on 25r	1.50	1.00
69	A5	5c on 50r	1.25	1.00
70	A6	7½c on 75r	1.25	1.00
71	A6	8c on 80r	1.25	1.00
72	A6	10c on 100r	1.25	1.00
73	A6	15c on 150r	2.10	2.00
74	A6	20c on 200r	2.00	2.00
75	A6	30c on 300r	3.25	2.40
			On Nos. 39-41	
76	A6	40c on 65r on 80r	18.00	16.50
77	A6	50c on 115r on 150r	3.00	2.00
78	A6	1e on 130r on 300r	5.00	2.00
			On Nos. 42-43	
79	A5	1½c on 15r	7.00	3.00
80	A5	3½c on 25r	2.00	1.00
	Nos. 63-80 (18)		472.20	323.00

On Nos. 70-78 there is less space between "REPUBLICA" and the new value than on the other stamps of this issue.
On Nos. 76-78 the 1903 surcharge is canceled by a bar.
The surcharge exists inverted on #64, 66-70, 72, 76, 78-80, and double on #64, 67, 69.

Nos. 51-62 Surcharged in Black or Red

Numerals: The "1" (large or small) is thin, sharp-pointed, and has thin serifs. The "2" is italic, with the tail thin and only slightly wavy. The "3" has a flat top. The "4" is open at the top. The "7" has thin strokes.
Centavos: The letters are shaded, i.e., they are thicker in some parts than in others. The "t" has a thin cross bar ending in a downward stroke at the right. The "s" is flat at the bottom and wider than in the next group.

1921			Lisbon Surcharges	
81	A7	¼c on 2½r	4.00	2.75
83	A7	½c on 5r (R)	4.00	2.75
a.	½c on 2½r (R) (error)		275.00	250.00
84	A7	1c on 10r	4.00	2.75
a.	Pair, one without surcharge			
85	A8	1½c on 300r (R)	4.00	2.75
86	A7	2c on 20r	4.00	2.75
87	A7	2½c on 25r	4.00	2.75
88	A8	3c on 400r	4.00	2.75
a.	"Republica" omitted			

89	A7	5c on 50r	4.00	2.75
90	A7	7½c on 75r	4.00	2.75
91	A8	10c on 100r	4.00	2.75
92	A8	12c on 500r	4.00	2.75
93	A8	20c on 200r	4.00	2.75
		Nos. 81-93 (12)	48.00	33.00

The surcharge exists inverted on Nos. 83-85, 87-88 and 92, and double on Nos. 81, 83 and 86.

Forgeries exist of Nos. 81-93.

London Surcharges

Numerals: The "1" has the vertical stroke and serifs thicker than in the Lisbon printing. The "2" is upright and has a strong wave in the tail. The small "2" is heavily shaded. The "3" has a rounded top. The "4" is closed at the top. The "7" has thick strokes. Centavos: The letters are heavier than in the Lisbon printing and are of even thickness throughout. The "t" has a thick cross bar with scarcely any down stroke at the end. The "s" is rounded at the bottom and narrower than in the Lisbon printing.

94	A7	¼c on 2½r	1.50	1.25
95	A7	½c on 5r (R)	1.50	1.25
96	A7	1c on 10r	1.50	1.25
97	A8	1½c on 300r (R)	1.50	1.25
98	A7	2c on 20r	1.50	1.25
99	A7	2½c on 25r	1.50	1.25
100	A8	3c on 400r	1.50	1.25
101	A7	5c on 50r	1.50	1.25
102	A8	7½c on 75r	1.50	1.25
	a.	Inverted surcharge		
103	A8	10c on 100r	1.50	1.25
104	A8	12c on 500r	1.50	1.25
105	A8	20c on 200r	1.50	1.25
		Nos. 94-105 (12)	18.00	15.00

A9

Zebra and
Warrior — A10

Designs: 2c-6c, Vasco da Gama. 7½c-20c, "San Gabriel." 2e-5e, Dhow and warrior.

Perf. 12½, 13½-15 & Compound
1921-23 Engr.

106	A9	¼c claret	1.00	.70
107	A9	½c steel blue	1.00	.70
108	A9	1c grn & blk	1.00	.70
109	A9	1½c blk & ocher	1.00	.70
110	A9	2c red & blk	1.00	.70
111	A9	2½c blk & ol grn	1.00	.70
112	A9	4c blk & org	1.00	.70
113	A9	5c ultra & blk	1.00	.70
114	A9	6c blk & vio	1.00	.70
115	A9	7½c blk & blk brn	1.00	.70
116	A9	8c blk & ol grn	1.00	.70
117	A9	10c blk & red brn	1.00	.70
118	A9	15c blk & carmine	1.00	.70
119	A9	20c blk & pale bl	1.00	.70
120	A10	30c blk & bister	1.00	.70
121	A10	40c blk & gray bl	1.00	.70
122	A10	50c blk & green	1.00	.70
123	A10	1e blk & red brn	1.00	.70
124	A10	2e red brn & blk ('23)	3.25	2.50
125	A10	5e ultra & red brn ('23)	3.00	2.25
		Nos. 106-125 (20)	24.25	17.35

POSTAGE DUE STAMPS

Giraffe — D1

½c, 1c, Giraffe. 2c, 3c, Zebra. 5c, 6c, 10c, "San Gabriel." 20c, 50c, Vasco da Gama.

1924 Unwmk. Engr. *Perf. 14*

J1	D1	½c deep green	1.00	1.75
J2	D1	1c gray	1.00	1.75
J3	D1	2c red	1.00	1.75
J4	D1	3c red orange	1.00	1.75
J5	D1	5c dark brown	1.00	1.75
J6	D1	6c orange brown	1.00	1.75
J7	D1	10c brown violet	1.00	1.75
J8	D1	20c carmine	1.00	1.75
J9	D1	50c lilac gray	1.00	1.75
		Nos. J1-J9 (9)	9.00	15.75

Used values are for c-t-o copies.

NEWSPAPER STAMP

Mozambique No. P6
Ovptd. Like Nos. 1-25
in Black

1898 Unwmk. *Perf. 13½*

P1	N3	2½r brown	2.00	1.00

Reprints have white gum and clean-cut perf. 13½. Value $1.

POSTAL TAX STAMPS

Pombal Issue
Mozambique Nos. RA1-RA3
Overprinted "NYASSA" in Red

1925 Unwmk. *Perf. 12½*

RA1	CD28	15c brown & blk	5.00	5.00
RA2	CD29	15c brown & blk	5.00	5.00
RA3	CD30	15c brown & blk	5.00	5.00
		Nos. RA1-RA3 (3)	15.00	15.00

POSTAL TAX DUE STAMPS

Pombal Issue
Mozambique Nos. RAJ1-RAJ3
Overprinted "NYASSA" in Red

1925 Unwmk. *Perf. 12½*

RAJ1	CD28	30c brown & blk	12.50	7.75
RAJ2	CD29	30c brown & blk	12.50	7.75
RAJ3	CD30	30c brown & blk	12.50	7.75
		Nos. RAJ1-RAJ3 (3)	37.50	23.25

OBOCK

'ō-,bäk

LOCATION — A seaport in eastern Africa on the Gulf of Aden, directly opposite Aden.

Obock was the point of entrance from which French Somaliland was formed. The port was acquired by the French in 1862 but was not actively occupied until 1884 when Sagallo and Tadjoura were ceded to France. In 1888 Djibouti was made into a port and the seat of government moved from Obock to the latter city. In 1902 the name Somali Coast was adopted on the postage stamps of Djibouti, these stamps superseding the individual issues of Obock.

100 Centimes = 1 Franc

Covers
Values are for commercial covers paying correct rates. Philatelic covers sell for less.

Counterfeits exist of Nos. 1-31.

Stamps of French Colonies Handstamped in Black

#1-11, J1-J4   #12-20, J5-J18

1892 Unwmk. *Perf. 14x13½*

1	A9	1c blk, *lil bl*	45.00	45.00
		On cover		—
2	A9	2c brn, *buff*	45.00	45.00
		On cover		—
3	A9	4c claret, *lav*	450.00	475.00
		On cover		—
4	A9	5c grn, *grnsh*	40.00	32.50
		On cover		—
5	A9	10c blk, *lavender*	80.00	47.50
		On cover		700.00
6	A9	15c blue	72.50	50.00
		On cover		700.00
7	A9	25c blk, *rose*	110.00	80.00
		On cover		700.00
8	A9	35c vio, *org*	450.00	450.00
9	A9	40c red, *straw*	400.00	425.00
10	A9	75c car, *rose*	450.00	475.00
11	A9	1fr brnz grn, *straw*	500.00	550.00
		On cover		—
		Nos. 1-11 (11)	2,642.	2,675.

No. 3 has been reprinted. On the reprints the second "O" of "OBOCK" is 4mm high instead of 3½mm. Value $32.50.

1892

12	A9	4c claret, *lav*	27.50	27.50
		On cover		—
13	A9	5c grn, *grnsh*	27.50	27.50
		On cover		—
14	A9	10c blk, *lavender*	27.50	27.50
		On cover		700.00
15	A9	15c blue	27.50	27.50
		On cover		700.00
16	A9	20c red, *grn*	47.50	45.00
		On cover		—
17	A9	25c blk, *rose*	35.00	27.50
		On cover		700.00
18	A9	40c red, *straw*	60.00	52.50
		On cover		—
19	A9	75c car, *rose*	325.00	275.00
20	A9	1fr brnz grn, *straw*	87.50	80.00
		Nos. 12-20 (9)	665.00	590.00

Exists inverted or double on all denominations.

Nos. 14, 15, 17, 20 with Additional Surcharge Handstamped in Red, Blue or Black

Nos. 21-30   No. 31

1892

21	A9	1c on 25c blk, *rose*	20.00	20.00
		On cover		—
22	A9	2c on 10c blk, *lav*	72.50	60.00
		On cover		—
23	A9	2c on 15c blue	20.00	20.00
		On cover		—
24	A9	4c on 15c bl (Bk)	20.00	20.00
		On cover		—
25	A9	4c on 25c blk, *rose* (Bk)	20.00	20.00
		On cover		—
26	A9	5c on 25c blk, *rose*	27.50	27.50
		On cover		—
27	A9	20c on 10c blk, *lav*	95.00	95.00
		On cover		—
28	A9	30c on 10c blk, *lav*	120.00	110.00
		On cover		—
29	A9	35c on 25c blk, *rose*	100.00	92.50
	a.	"3" instead of "35"	950.00	950.00
30	A9	75c on 1fr brnz grn, *straw*	110.00	110.00
	b.	"57" instead of "75"	8,750.	9,250.
	c.	"55" instead of "75"	8,750.	9,250.
31	A9	5fr on 1fr brnz grn, *straw* (Bl)	775.00	700.00
		On cover		—
		Nos. 21-31 (11)	1,380.	1,275.

Exists inverted on most denominations.

Navigation and
Commerce — A4

Obock in Red (1c, 5c, 15c, 25c, 75c, 1fr) or Blue

1892 Typo. *Perf. 14x13½*

32	A4	1c blk, *lil bl*	2.75	2.75
		On cover		190.00
33	A4	2c brn, *buff*	2.00	2.00
		On cover		190.00
34	A4	4c claret, *lav*	2.75	2.75
		On cover		170.00
35	A4	5c grn, *grnsh*	5.25	4.00
		On cover		95.00
36	A4	10c blk, *lavender*	8.00	5.25
		On cover		90.00
37	A4	15c bl, quadrille paper	19.50	11.50
		On cover		125.00
38	A4	20c red, *grn*	27.50	27.50
39	A4	25c blk, *rose*	27.50	24.00
		On cover		100.00
40	A4	30c brn, *bis*	24.00	20.00
41	A4	40c red, *straw*	24.00	20.00
		On cover		225.00
42	A4	50c car, *rose*	28.00	24.00
		On cover		190.00
43	A4	75c vio, *org*	32.50	24.00
		On cover		500.00
	a.	Name double	350.00	350.00
	b.	Name inverted	5,500.	5,500.
44	A4	1fr brnz grn, *straw*	47.50	40.00
		On cover		500.00
		Nos. 32-44 (13)	251.25	207.75

Perf. 13½x14 stamps are counterfeits.

Camel and
Rider — A5

Quadrille Lines Printed on Paper

1893 Size: 32mm at base *Imperf.*

44A	A5	2fr brnz grn	60.00	55.00

Size: 45mm at base

45	A5	5fr red	140.00	125.00

Somali
Warriors
A7

A8

1894 *Imperf.*
Quadrille Lines Printed on Paper

46	A7	1c blk & rose	2.75	2.75
		On cover		425.00
47	A7	2c vio brn & grn	2.75	2.75
		On cover		425.00
48	A7	4c brn vio & org	2.75	2.75
		On cover		425.00
49	A7	5c bl grn & brn	3.50	3.50
		On cover		300.00
50	A7	10c blk & grn	9.50	8.00
		On cover		300.00
	a.	Half used as 5c on cover		350.00
51	A7	15c bl & rose	9.50	7.25
		On cover		110.00
52	A7	20c brn org & mar	9.50	8.00
		On cover		250.00
	a.	Half used as 10c on cover ('01)		325.00
53	A7	25c blk & bl	10.50	6.50
		On cover		175.00
	a.	Right half used as 5c on cover ('01)		300.00
	b.	Left half used as 2c on cover ('03)		300.00
54	A7	30c bis & yel grn	20.00	14.50
		On cover		225.00
	a.	Half used as 15c on cover ('01)		2,200.

55	A7	40c red & bl grn	17.00	13.00
		On cover		210.00
56	A7	50c rose & bl	15.00	12.00
		On cover		250.00
a.		Half used as 25c on cover		3,400.
57	A7	75c gray lil & org	20.00	13.00
		On cover		—
58	A7	1fr ol grn & mar	17.00	10.50
		On cover		650.00

Size: 37mm at base

60	A8	2fr vio & org	115.00	115.00
		On cover		—

Size: 42mm at base

61	A8	5fr rose & bl	95.00	95.00
		On cover		—

Size: 46mm at base

62	A8	10fr org & red vio	150.00	150.00
		On cover		—
63	A8	25fr brn & bl	875.00	875.00
		On cover		—
64	A8	50fr red vio & grn	1,000.	1,000.
		On cover		—

Counterfeits exist of Nos. 63-64.
Stamps of Obock were replaced in 1901 by those of Somali Coast. The 5c on 75c, 5c on 25fr and 10c on 50fr of 1902 are listed under Somali Coast.

POSTAGE DUE STAMPS

Postage Due Stamps of French Colonies Handstamped Like #1-20

 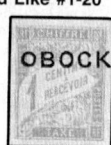

1892		**Unwmk.**		**Imperf.**
J1	D1	5c black	11,000.	
J2	D1	10c black	240.00	275.00
J3	D1	30c black	375.00	450.00
J4	D1	60c black	475.00	550.00
J5	D1	1c black	55.00	55.00
		Never hinged	120.00	
		On cover		350.00
J6	D1	2c black	45.00	45.00
		Never hinged	95.00	
		On cover		300.00
J7	D1	3c black	52.50	52.50
		Never hinged	110.00	
		On cover		350.00
J8	D1	4c black	45.00	45.00
		Never hinged	95.00	
		On cover		300.00
J9	D1	5c black	16.00	16.00
		Never hinged	35.00	
		On cover		200.00
J10	D1	10c black	35.00	35.00
		Never hinged	70.00	
		On cover		200.00
J11	D1	15c black	24.00	24.00
		Never hinged	45.00	
		On cover		225.00
J12	D1	20c black	32.50	32.50
		Never hinged	60.00	
		On cover		250.00
J13	D1	30c black	32.50	32.50
		Never hinged	60.00	
		On cover		250.00
J14	D1	40c black	60.00	60.00
		Never hinged	75.00	
		On cover		400.00
J15	D1	60c black	80.00	80.00
				500.00
J16	D1	1fr brown	225.00	225.00
J17	D1	2fr brown	240.00	240.00
J18	D1	5fr brown	525.00	525.00
		Nos. J2-J18 (17)	2,557.	2,742.

Overprint Inverted

J5a	D1	1c black	200.00	200.00
J6a	D1	2c black	200.00	200.00
J7a	D1	3c black	200.00	200.00
J8a	D1	4c black	200.00	200.00
J9a	D1	5c black	200.00	200.00
J10a	D1	10c black	250.00	250.00
J11a	D1	15c black	200.00	200.00
J15a	D1	60c black	275.00	275.00
J16a	D1	1fr brown	550.00	550.00
J17a	D1	2fr brown	550.00	550.00

Double Overprint

J5b	D1	1c black	200.00	200.00
J6b	D1	2c black	200.00	200.00
J9b	D1	5c black	250.00	250.00
J10b	D1	10c black	300.00	300.00
J11b	D1	15c black	250.00	250.00
J12b	D1	20c black	250.00	250.00
J13b	D1	30c black	250.00	250.00

These handstamped overprints may be found double on some values. Counterfeits exist of Nos. J1-J18.

No. J1 has been reprinted. The overprint on the original measures 12½x3¾mm and on the reprint 12x3¼mm. Value, $325.

OLTRE GIUBA

ˌōl-trä-ˈjü-bə

(Italian Jubaland)

LOCATION — A strip of land, 50 to 100 miles in width, west of and parallel to the Juba River in East Africa
GOVT. — Italian Protectorate
AREA — 33,000 sq. mi.
POP. — 12,000
CAPITAL — Kismayu

Oltre Giuba was ceded to Italy by Great Britain in 1924 and in 1926 was incorporated with Italian Somaliland. In 1936 it became part of Italian East Africa.

100 Centesimi = 1 Lira

Watermark

Wmk. 140 — Crown

Italian Stamps of 1901-26 Overprinted

On #1-15 On #16-20

1925, July 29		**Wmk. 140**		**Perf. 14**
1	A42	1c brown	4.75	30.00
		Never hinged	12.00	
		On cover		350.00
a.		Inverted overprint	475.00	
2	A43	2c yel brown	4.00	30.00
		Never hinged	10.00	
		On cover		350.00
3	A48	5c green	4.00	12.50
		Never hinged	10.00	
		On cover		350.00
4	A48	10c claret	4.00	12.50
		Never hinged	10.00	
		On cover		300.00
5	A48	15c slate	4.00	17.50
		Never hinged	10.00	
		On cover		340.00
6	A50	20c brn orange	4.00	17.50
		Never hinged	10.00	
		On cover		350.00
7	A49	25c blue	4.00	17.50
		Never hinged	10.00	
		On cover		350.00
8	A49	30c org brown	4.75	22.50
		Never hinged	12.00	
		On cover		350.00
9	A49	40c brown	9.50	17.50
		Never hinged	24.00	
		On cover		475.00
10	A49	50c violet	9.50	17.50
		Never hinged	24.00	
		On cover		350.00
11	A49	60c carmine	9.50	22.50
		Never hinged	24.00	
		On cover		725.00
12	A46	1 l brn & green	16.00	30.00
		Never hinged	40.00	
		On cover		650.00
13	A46	2 l dk grn & org	80.00	60.00
		Never hinged	200.00	
		On cover		—
14	A46	5 l blue & rose	110.00	87.50
		Never hinged	275.00	
		On cover		—
15	A51	10 l gray grn & red	20.00	95.00
		Never hinged	50.00	
		On cover		—
		Nos. 1-15 (15)	288.00	490.00

1925-26				
16	A49	20c green	6.50	17.50
		Never hinged	16.00	
		On cover		400.00
17	A49	30c gray	9.50	22.50
		Never hinged	22.50	
		On cover		525.00
18	A46	75c dk red & rose	40.00	95.00
		Never hinged	100.00	
		On cover		600.00
19	A46	1.25 l bl & ultra	87.50	160.00
		Never hinged	210.00	
		On cover		1,050.

20	A46	2.50 l dk grn & org	120.00	275.00
		Never hinged	300.00	
		On cover		1,750.
		Nos. 16-20 (5)	263.50	570.00

Issue years: #1-20, 1926; others 1925

Victor Emmanuel Issue

Italian Stamps of 1925 Overprinted

1925-26		**Unwmk.**		**Perf. 11**
21	A78	60c brown car	1.60	16.00
		Never hinged	4.00	
		On cover		650.00
a.		Perf. 13½	12,000.	
		Never hinged	18,000.	
		On cover		—
22	A78	1 l dark blue	1.60	25.00
		Never hinged	4.00	
		On cover		875.00
a.		Perf. 13½	650.00	2,400.
		Never hinged	1,600.	
		On cover		—
23	A78	1.25 l dk bl ('26)	6.50	40.00
		Never hinged	16.00	
		On cover		1,300.
a.		Perf. 13½	6.50	40.00
		Never hinged	16.00	
		On cover		1,300.
		Nos. 21-23 (3)	9.70	81.00

Saint Francis of Assisi Issue
Italian Stamps and Type of 1926 Overprinted

1926, Apr. 12		**Wmk. 140**		**Perf. 14**
24	A79	20c gray green	2.50	45.00
		Never hinged	6.25	
		On cover		725.00
25	A80	40c dark violet	2.50	45.00
		Never hinged	6.25	
		On cover		725.00
26	A81	60c red brown	2.50	65.00
		Never hinged	6.25	
		On cover		725.00

Overprinted in Red

		Unwmk.		
27	A82	1.25 l dk bl, perf. 11	2.50	87.50
		Never hinged	6.25	
		On cover		1,200.
28	A83	5 l + 2.50 l ol grn, perf. 13½	8.00	135.00
		Never hinged	20.00	
		On cover		—
		Nos. 24-28 (5)	18.00	377.50
		Set on overfranked philatelic cover		725.00

Map of Oltre Giuba — A1

1926, Apr. 21		**Typo.**		**Wmk. 140**
29	A1	5c yellow brown	1.60	35.00
		Never hinged	4.00	
		On cover		475.00
30	A1	20c blue green	1.60	35.00
		Never hinged	4.00	
		On cover		450.00
31	A1	25c olive brown	1.60	35.00
		Never hinged	4.00	
		On cover		450.00

32	A1	40c dull red	1.60	35.00
		Never hinged	4.00	
		On cover		450.00
33	A1	60c brown violet	1.60	35.00
		Never hinged	4.00	
		On cover		550.00
34	A1	1 l blue	1.60	35.00
		Never hinged	4.00	
		On cover		600.00
35	A1	2 l dark green	1.60	35.00
		Never hinged	4.00	
		Nos. 29-35 (7)	11.20	245.00
		Set on overfranked philatelic cover		260.00

Oltre Giuba was incorporated with Italian Somaliland on July 1, 1926, and stamps inscribed "Oltre Giuba" were discontinued.

SEMI-POSTAL STAMPS

Note preceding Italy semi-postals applies to No. 28.

Colonial Institute Issue

"Peace" Substituting Spade for Sword — SP1

		Wmk. 140		
1926, June 1		**Typo.**		**Perf. 14**
B1	SP1	5c + 5c brown	1.20	9.50
		Never hinged	3.00	
		On cover		475.00
B2	SP1	10c + 5c olive green	1.20	9.50
		Never hinged	3.00	
		On cover		400.00
B3	SP1	20c + 5c blue green	1.20	9.50
		Never hinged	3.00	
		On cover		450.00
B4	SP1	40c + 5c brown red	1.20	9.50
		Never hinged	3.00	
		On cover		475.00
B5	SP1	60c + 5c orange	1.20	9.50
		Never hinged	3.00	
		On cover		600.00
B6	SP1	1 l + 5c blue	1.20	20.00
		Never hinged	3.00	
		On cover		650.00
		Nos. B1-B6 (6)	7.20	67.50
		Set on overfranked philatelic cover		260.00

Surtax for Italian Colonial Institute.

SPECIAL DELIVERY STAMPS

Special Delivery Stamps of Italy Ovptd.

1926		**Wmk. 140**		**Perf. 14**
E1	SD1	70c dull red	32.50	65.00
		Never hinged	80.00	
E2	SD2	2.50 l blue & red	67.50	180.00
		Never hinged	160.00	

POSTAGE DUE STAMPS

Italian Postage Due Stamps of 1870-1903 Overprinted Like Nos. E1-E2

1925, July 29		**Wmk. 140**		**Perf. 14**
J1	D3	5c buff & magenta	24.00	24.00
		Never hinged	47.50	
J2	D3	10c buff & magenta	24.00	24.00
		Never hinged	47.50	
J3	D3	20c buff & magenta	24.00	40.00
		Never hinged	47.50	
J4	D3	30c buff & magenta	24.00	40.00
		Never hinged	47.50	
J5	D3	40c buff & magenta	24.00	45.00
		Never hinged	47.50	
J6	D3	50c buff & magenta	32.50	55.00
		Never hinged	65.00	
J7	D3	60c buff & brown	32.50	65.00
		Never hinged	65.00	
J8	D3	1 l blue & magenta	35.00	80.00
		Never hinged	65.00	
J9	D3	2 l blue & magenta	175.00	275.00
		Never hinged	350.00	

J10	D3	5 l blue & magenta	225.00 275.00
	Never hinged		450.00
	Nos. J1-J10 (10)		620.00 923.00

PARCEL POST STAMPS

These stamps were used by affixing them to the waybill so that one half remained on it following the parcel, the other half staying on the receipt given the sender. Most used halves are right halves. Complete stamps were obtainable canceled, probably to order. Both unused and used values are for complete stamps.

Italian Parcel Post Stamps of 1914-22 Overprinted

1925, July 29 Wmk. 140 Perf. 13½

Q1	PP2	5c brown	19.00 45.00
	Never hinged		37.50
Q2	PP2	10c blue	14.50 45.00
	Never hinged		29.00
Q3	PP2	20c black	14.50 45.00
	Never hinged		29.00
Q4	PP2	25c red	14.50 45.00
	Never hinged		29.00
Q5	PP2	50c orange	19.00 45.00
	Never hinged		37.50
Q6	PP2	1 l violet	14.50 100.00
	Never hinged		29.00
a.	Double overprint		550.00
Q7	PP2	2 l green	28.00 100.00
	Never hinged		56.00
Q8	PP2	3 l bister	65.00 130.00
	Never hinged		130.00
Q9	PP2	4 l slate	29.00 130.00
	Never hinged		57.50
Q10	PP2	10 l rose lilac	95.00 225.00
	Never hinged		190.00
Q11	PP2	12 l red brown	175.00 350.00
	Never hinged		350.00
Q12	PP2	15 l olive green	160.00 350.00
	Never hinged		325.00
Q13	PP2	20 l brown violet	160.00 350.00
	Never hinged		325.00
	Nos. Q1-Q13 (13)		808.00 1,960.

Halves Used

Q1-Q4	1.75
Q5-Q7	3.00
Q8-Q9	4.75
Q10	9.25
Q11	15.00
Q12-Q13	10.00

OMAN

'ō-ˌmän

Muscat and Oman

LOCATION — Southeastern corner of the Arabian Peninsula
GOVT. — Sultanate
AREA — 105,000 sq. mi.
POP. — 1,500,000 (est. 1982)
CAPITAL — Muscat

Nos. 16-93, the stamps with "value only" surcharges, were used not only in Muscat, but also in Dubai (Apr. 1, 1948 - Jan. 6, 1961), Qatar (Aug. 1950 - Mar. 31, 1957), and Abu Dhabi (Mar. 30, 1963 - Mar. 29, 1964). Occasionally they were also used in Bahrain and Kuwait.

12 Pies = 1 Anna
16 Annas = 1 Rupee

Catalogue values for all unused stamps in this country are for Never Hinged items.

Muscat

Stamps of India 1937-43 Overprinted in Black

On #1-13 the overprint is smaller — 13x6mm.

Wmk. Multiple Stars (196)
1944, Nov. 20 Perf. 13½x14

1	A83	3p slate	.75	8.00
	Never hinged		1.50	
2	A83	½a rose violet	.75	8.00
	Never hinged		1.50	
3	A83	9p lt green	.75	8.00
	Never hinged		1.50	
4	A83	1a carmine rose	.75	8.00
	Never hinged		1.50	
5	A84	1½a dark purple	.75	8.00
	Never hinged		1.50	
a.	Double overprint		400.00	
6	A84	2a scarlet	.85	8.00
	Never hinged		1.75	
7	A84	3a violet	1.75	8.00
	Never hinged		3.50	
8	A84	3½a ultra	1.75	8.00
	Never hinged		3.50	
9	A85	4a chocolate	2.00	8.00
	Never hinged		4.00	
10	A85	6a pck blue	2.25	8.00
	Never hinged		4.50	
11	A85	8a blue violet	2.75	8.50
	Never hinged		5.50	
12	A85	12a car lake	3.00	8.50
	Never hinged		6.00	
13	A81	14a rose violet	5.50	13.50
	Never hinged		11.00	
14	A82	1r brown & slate	3.25	12.50
	Never hinged		6.50	
15	A82	2r dk brn & dk vio	9.50	20.00
	Never hinged		20.00	
	Nos. 1-15 (15)		36.35	143.00

200th anniv. of Al Busaid Dynasty.

Great Britain, Nos. 258 to 263, 243, 248, 249A Surcharged
Perf. 14½x14
1948, Apr. 1 Wmk. 251

16	A101	½a on ½p green	3.00	8.00
	Never hinged		5.50	
17	A101	1a on 1p vermilion	3.25	.30
	Never hinged		6.00	
18	A101	1½a on 1½p lt red brn	15.00	4.25
	Never hinged		26.00	
19	A101	2a on 2p lt org	2.25	3.50
	Never hinged		4.00	
20	A101	2½a on 2½p ultra	4.25	8.50
	Never hinged		7.50	
21	A101	3a on 3p violet	4.00	.25
	Never hinged		7.00	
22	A102	6a on 6p rose lilac	4.50	.25
	Never hinged		8.00	
23	A103	1r on 1sh brown	5.00	.75
	Never hinged		9.00	
		Wmk. 259 Perf. 14		
24	A104	2r on 2sh6p yel grn	14.00	52.50
	Never hinged		25.00	
	Nos. 16-24 (9)		55.25	78.30

Silver Wedding Issue
Great Britain, Nos. 267 and 268, Surcharged with New Value in Black
Perf. 14½x14, 14x14½
1948, Apr. 26 Wmk. 251

25	A109	2½a on 2½p brt ultra	3.50	5.00
26	A110	15r on £1 dp chlky bl	42.50	42.50

Three bars obliterate the original denomination on No. 26.

Olympic Games Issue
Great Britain, Nos. 271 to 274, Surcharged with New Value in Black
1948, July 29 Perf. 14½x14

27	A113	2½a on 2½p brt ultra	.75	2.75
28	A114	3a on 3p dp violet	.85	2.75
29	A115	6a on 6p red violet	.95	3.00
30	A116	1r on 1sh dk brown	2.25	4.25
a.	Double surcharge	1,500.		
	Nos. 27-30 (4)		4.80	12.75

A square of dots obliterates the original denomination on Nos. 28-30.

UPU Issue
Great Britain Nos. 276 to 279 Surcharged with New Value and Square of Dots in Black
1949, Oct. 10 Photo.

31	A117	2½a on 2½p brt ultra	.75	3.75
32	A118	3a on 3p brt violet	.95	3.75
33	A119	6a on 6p red violet	1.10	2.50
34	A120	1r on 1sh brown	2.75	6.75
	Nos. 31-34 (4)		5.55	15.75

Great Britain Nos. 280-286 Surcharged with New Value in Black
1951

35	A101	½a on ½p lt org	1.00	9.00
36	A101	1a on 1p ultra	.60	7.50
37	A101	1½a on 1½p grn	17.00	35.00
38	A101	2a on 2p lt red brn	.85	8.00
39	A101	2½a on 2½p vermilion	1.50	16.00
40	A102	4a on 4p ultra	1.25	3.25

Perf. 11x12
Wmk. 259

41	A121	2r on 2sh6p green	45.00	7.00
	Nos. 35-41 (7)	67.20	85.75

Two types of surcharge on No. 41.

Stamps of Great Britain, 1952-54, Srchd. with New Value in Black and Dark Blue
1952-54 Wmk. 298 Perf. 14½x14

42	A126	½a on ½p red org ('53)	.35	2.00
43	A126	1a on 1p ultra ('53)	.35	2.00
44	A126	1½a on 1½p green ('52)	.40	2.00
45	A126	2a on 2p red brn ('53)	.50	.25
46	A127	2½a on 2½p scar ('52)	.35	.25
47	A127	3a on 3p dk pur (Dk Bl)	.50	1.00
48	A128	4a on 4p ultra ('53)	2.25	3.75
49	A129	6a on 6p lilac rose	.60	.45
50	A132	12a on 1sh3p dk grn ('53)	8.00	.90
51	A131	1r on 1sh6p dk bl ('53)	3.00	.75
	Nos. 42-51 (10)		16.30	13.35

OFFICIAL STAMPS

Official Stamps of India 1938-43 Overprinted in Black

Perf. 13½x14
1944, Nov. 20 Wmk. 196

O1	O8	3p slate	1.25	15.00
	Never hinged		1.75	
O2	O8	½a dk rose violet	1.25	15.00
	Never hinged		1.75	
O3	O8	9p green	1.25	15.00
	Never hinged		1.75	
O4	O8	1a carmine rose	1.25	15.00
	Never hinged		1.75	
O5	O8	1½a dull purple	1.25	15.00
	Never hinged		1.75	
O6	O8	2a scarlet	1.25	15.00
	Never hinged		2.50	
O7	O8	2½a purple	8.00	15.00
	Never hinged		12.00	
O8	O8	4a dark brown	3.00	15.00
	Never hinged		4.25	
O9	O8	8a blue violet	5.00	17.50
	Never hinged		13.00	
O10	A82	1r brown & slate	8.50	27.50
	Never hinged		13.00	
	Nos. O1-O10 (10)		32.00	165.00

Al Busaid Dynasty, 200th anniv. On Nos. O1-O9 the overprint is smaller — 13x6mm.

ORANGE RIVER COLONY

'är-inj 'ri-vər 'kä-lə-nē

(Orange Free State)

LOCATION — South Africa, north of the Cape of Good Hope between the Orange and Vaal Rivers
GOVT. — British Crown Colony
AREA — 49,647 sq. mi.
POP. — 528,174 (1911)
CAPITAL — Bloemfontein

Orange Free State was an independent republic, 1854-1900. Orange River Colony existed from May, 1900, to June, 1910, when it united with Cape of Good Hope, Natal and the Transvaal to form the Union of South Africa.

12 Pence = 1 Shilling

Values for unused stamps are for examples with original gum as defined in the catalogue introduction. Very fine examples of Nos. 1-60c will have perforations touching the design on one or more sides due to the narrow spacing of the stamps on the plates. Stamps with perfs clear of the design on all four sides are scarce and will command higher prices.

Een = 1
Twee = 2
Drie = 3
Vier = 4

Issues of the Republic

Orange Tree — A1

1868-1900 Unwmk. Typo. Perf. 14

1	A1	½p red brown ('83)	7.00	.75
2	A1	½p orange ('97)	3.00	.60
a.	½p yellow ('97)		3.00	.40
3	A1	1p red brown	22.50	.50
a.	1p pale brown		32.50	2.25
b.	1p deep brown		32.50	.60
4	A1	1p violet ('94)	5.00	.35
5	A1	1p ultra ('83)	20.00	1.40
a.	2p pale mauve ('83-'84)		23.00	.50
6	A1	3p ultra ('83)	7.75	2.25
7	A1	4p ultra ('78)	5.00	4.50
a.	4p pale blue ('78)		26.00	5.25
8	A1	6p car rose ('90)	30.00	13.00
a.	6p rose ('71)		32.50	8.00
b.	6p pale rose ('68)		72.50	8.75
c.	6p bright carmine ('94)		18.50	2.25
9	A1	6p ultramarine ('00)	80.00	
10	A1	1sh orange	65.00	1.75
a.	1sh orange buff		110.00	7.25
11	A1	1sh brown ('97)	32.50	1.75
12	A1	5sh green ('78)	12.00	18.50
	Nos. 1-8,10-12 (11)		209.75	45.35

No. 8b was not placed in use without surcharge.
For surcharges see #13-53, 44j-53c, 57-60.

No. 13

No. 8a Surcharged in Four Different Types

4	4	4	4
a	b	c	d

1877

13	(a) 4p on 6p rose	450.00	65.00
a.	Inverted surcharge	—	600.00
b.	Double surcharge, one inverted ("a" + "c" in-verted)		4,250.
c.	Double surcharge, one inverted ("a" inverted + "c")		6,000.
14	(b) 4p on 6p rose	1,450.	225.00
a.	Double surcharge, one inverted ("b" and "d")	—	1,250.
15	(c) 4p on 6p rose	220.00	42.50
a.	Inverted surcharge	—	400.00
16	(d) 4p on 6p rose	325.00	50.00
a.	Inverted surcharge	1,500.	500.00
b.	Double surcharge, one inverted ("d" and "c" in-verted)		4,250.
c.	Double surcharge, one inverted ("d" inverted and "c")		6,500.

No. 17

No. 12 Surcharged with Bar and

1d.	1d.	1d.
f	g	h

1d.	1d.	1d.
i	k	l

1881

First Printing

17	(f) 1p on 5sh green	120.00	32.50

Second Printing

18	(g) 1p on 5sh green	65.00	32.50
a.	Inverted surcharge	—	1,250.
b.	Double surcharge		1,450.

19	(h)	1p on 5sh green	300.00	95.00
	a.	Inverted surcharge	—	1,450.
	b.	Double surcharge	—	1,650.
20	(i)	1p on 5sh green	100.00	32.50
	a.	Inverted surcharge	2,000.	1,325.
	b.	Inverted surcharge	2,000.	1,000.
21	(h)	1p on 5sh green	300.00	275.00
	a.	Inverted surcharge		2,500.
	b.	Double surcharge		2,500.

Third Printing

21C	(l)	1p on 5sh green	95.00	32.50
	d.	Inverted surcharge	—	875.00
	e.	Double surcharge		900.00
		Nos. 17-21C (6)	1,280.	500.00

No. 12 Surcharged

1882

22	A1	½p on 5sh green	25.00	5.50
	a.	Double surcharge	550.00	400.00
	b.	Inverted surcharge	1,500.	1,000.

No. 7 Surcharged with Thin Line and

m n o p q

1882

23	(m)	3p on 4p ultra	100.00	35.00
	a.	Double surcharge		1,400.
24	(n)	3p on 4p ultra	100.00	20.00
	a.	Double surcharge		1,400.
25	(o)	3p on 4p ultra	55.00	25.00
	a.	Double surcharge		1,400.
26	(p)	3p on 4p ultra	275.00	80.00
	a.	Double surcharge		3,500.
27	(q)	3p on 4p ultra	100.00	24.00
	a.	Double surcharge		1,400.
		Nos. 23-27 (5)	630.00	184.00

No. 6 Surcharged

1888

28	A1	2p on 3p ultra	60.00	2.25
	a.	Wide "2" at top	77.50	10.00
	b.	As No. 28, invtd. surch.		350.00
	c.	As No. 28a, invtd. surch.		825.00
	d.	Curved base on "2"	1,450.	650.00

Nos. 6 and 7 Surcharged

r s

t

1890-91

29	(r)	1p on 3p ultra	9.50	.85
		('91)		
	a.	Double surcharge	100.00	77.50
	b.	"1" and "d" wide apart	170.00	135.00
30	(r)	1p on 4p ultra	45.00	40.50
	a.	Double surcharge	170.00	135.00
	b.	Triple surcharge		3,250.
31	(s)	1p on 3p ultra	25.00	3.00
		('91)		
	a.	Double surcharge	325.00	300.00
32	(s)	1p on 4p ultra	95.00	60.00
	a.	Double surcharge	475.00	375.00
33	(t)	1p on 4p ultra	2,500.	675.00

No. 6 Surcharged

1892

34	A1	2½p on 3p ultra	21.00	.80
	a.	Without period	92.50	55.00

No. 6 Surcharged

v w x y z

1896

35	(v)	½p on 3p ultra	8.50	12.00
	a.	Double surcharge "v" and "y"	15.50	15.50
36	(w)	½p on 3p ultra	14.50	3.00
	a.	Double surcharge "w" and "y"	15.00	11.00
37	(x)	½p on 3p ultra	14.50	2.50
38	(y)	½p on 3p ultra	9.00	5.50
	a.	Double surcharge	14.50	11.00
	b.	Triple surcharge	77.50	77.50
39	(z)	½p on 3p ultra	14.50	2.50

Surcharged as "v" but "1" with Straight Serif

40	A1	½p on 3p ultra	15.50	16.50
	a.	Double surcharge, one type "y"	75.00	75.00

Surcharged as "z" but "1" with Straight Serif

41	A1	½p on 3p ultra	15.50	15.50
	a.	Double surcharge, one type "y"	75.00	75.00
		Nos. 35-41 (7)	92.00	57.50

No. 6 Surcharged

1896

42	A1	½p on 3p ultra	1.10	.65
	a.	No period after "Penny"	22.50	35.00
	b.	"Peuny"	22.50	35.00
	c.	Inverted surcharge	65.00	72.50
	d.	Double surch., one inverted	200.00	225.00
	e.	Without bar	10.00	
	f.	With additional surcharge as on Nos. 35-41	37.50	
	g.	As "a," inverted surcharge	2,250.	
	h.	As "b," inverted surcharge	1,750.	

No. 6 Surcharged

1897

43	A1	2½p on 3p ultra	10.50	.90
	a.	Roman "I" instead of "1" in "½"	185.00	100.00

Issued under British Occupation

Nos. 2-8, 8a, 10-12
Surcharged or
Overprinted

Periods in "V.R.I." Level with Bottoms of Letters

1900, Mar.-Apr.　Unwmk.　Perf. 14

44	A1	½p on ½p org	5.00	6.50
	a.	No period after "V"	25.00	35.00
	b.	No period after "I"	175.00	175.00
	c.	"I" and period after "R" omitted	300.00	275.00
	f.	"½" omitted	210.00	210.00
	g.	Small "½"	65.00	65.00
	h.	Double surcharge	200.00	
	i.	As "g," double surcharge	575.00	
45	A1	1p on 1p violet	3.00	1.60
	a.	No period after "V"	20.00	18.50
	b.	"I" and period after "R" omitted	300.00	300.00
	d.	"1" of "1d" omitted	225.00	225.00
	e.	"d" omitted	425.00	425.00
	f.	"1d" omitted, "V.R.I." at top	475.00	
45O	A1	1p on 1p brown	675.00	450.00
	y.	No period after "V"	4,000.	
46	A1	2p on 2p violet	4.75	2.50
	a.	No period after "V"	20.00	24.00
	b.	No period after "R"	360.00	360.00
	c.	No period after "I"	360.00	360.00
47	A1	'2½' on 3p ultra	21.00	22.50
	a.	No period after "V"	105.00	105.00
	b.	Roman "I" in "½"	276.00	275.00
48	A1	3p on 3p ultra	3.25	4.75
	a.	No period after "V"	25.00	30.00
	b.	Dbl. surch. one diagonal	600.00	
	c.	Pair, one with surcharge omitted	725.00	
	j.	"3d" omitted	275.00	275.00
	k.	"V.R.I." omitted	275.00	275.00
49	A1	4p on 4p ultra	11.00	18.50
	a.	No period after "V"	72.50	82.50
50	A1	6p on 6p car rose	50.00	45.00
	a.	No period after "V"	275.00	300.00
	b.	"6" omitted	340.00	325.00
51	A1	6p on 6p ultra	14.50	6.50
	a.	No period after "V"	55.00	55.00
	c.	"6" omitted	95.00	100.00
	d.	"V.R.I." omitted	550.00	425.00
52	A1	1sh on 1sh brown	8.00	3.00
	a.	No period after "V"	55.00	35.00
	c.	"1" of "1s" omitted	165.00	155.00
	j.	"1s" omitted	225.00	220.00
	k.	"V.R.I." omitted	225.00	220.00
52G	A1	1sh on 1sh org	4,100.	2,750.
53	A1	5sh on 5sh green	32.50	60.00
	a.	No period after "V"	300.00	360.00
	b.	"5" omitted	1,100.	1,100.

#47, 47c overprinted "V.R.I." on #43.
No. 45f ("1d" omitted) with "V.R.I." at bottom is a shift which sells for a fifth of the value of the listed item. Varieties such as "V.R.I." omitted, denomination omitted and pair, one without surcharge are also the result of shifts.
For surcharges see Nos. 57, 60.

Nos. 2, 4-12
Surcharged or
Overprinted

Periods in "V.R.I." Raised Above Bottoms of Letters

1900-01

44j	A1	½p on ½p orange	.35	.25
	k.	Mixed periods	3.25	3.25
	l.	Pair, one with level periods	15.50	20.00
	m.	No period after "V"	4.00	4.25
	n.	No period after "I"	42.50	42.50
	o.	"V" omitted	675.00	
	p.	Small "½"	20.00	22.50
	q.	"1" for "I" in "V.R.I."	10.00	
	r.	Thick "V"	6.00	4.00
45i	A1	1p on 1p violet	.35	.25
	k.	Mixed periods	2.00	2.50
	l.	Pair, one with level periods	25.00	25.00
	m.	No period after "V"	6.00	7.00
	n.	No period after "R"	19.00	19.00
	o.	No period after "I"	19.00	19.00
	p.	Double surcharge	120.00	120.00
	q.	Inverted surcharge	425.00	
	s.	Small "1" in "1d"	120.00	120.00
	t.	"1" for "I" in "V.R.I."	13.00	
	u.	Thick "V"	7.50	.40
	v.	As "u," invtd. "1" for "I" in "V.R.I."	24.00	24.00
	w.	As "u," double surcharge	375.00	360.00
	z.	As "u," no period after "R"	50.00	55.00
	za.	Pair, one without surcharge		
	zb.	Stamp double impression, one inverted	2,750.	
	zc.	Stamp double impression, one inverted, thick "V"	7,500.	

46e	A1	2p on 2p violet	2.25	.35
	f.	Mixed periods	6.00	5.25
	g.	Pair, one with level periods	10.00	10.50
	h.	Inverted surcharge	360.00	360.00
	i.	Thick "V"	16.50	15.50
	j.	As "i," invtd. "1" for "I" in "V.R.I."	32.50	35.00
47c	A1	'2½' on 3p ultra	250.00	250.00
	d.	Thick "V"	4,250.	
	f.	As "d," Roman "I" on "½"		
48d	A1	3p on 3p ultra	1.60	.35
	f.	Mixed periods	9.50	9.50
	g.	Pair, one with level periods	25.00	25.00
	h.	Double surcharge	440.00	
	i.	Thick "V"	7.50	17.50
	l.	Double surcharge, one diagonal	450.00	
	m.	As "i," thick "V"	600.00	
	n.	As "i," mixed periods	7,500.	
	o.	As "n," thick "V"		
49b	A1	4p on 4p ultra	3.25	3.75
	d.	Mixed periods	11.00	16.00
	f.	Pair, one with level periods	24.00	35.00
50c	A1	6p on 6p car rose	45.00	55.00
	d.	Mixed periods	160.00	175.00
	f.	Pair, one with level periods	300.00	350.00
	g.	Thick "V"	500.00	525.00
51d	A1	6p on 6p ultra	1.10	.45
	e.	Mixed periods	10.50	11.00
	f.	Pair, one with level periods	25.00	30.00
	g.	Thick "V"	25.00	35.00
	i.	"6d" omitted	500.00	
52e	A1	1sh on 1sh brown	10.00	.50
	f.	Mixed periods	27.50	25.00
	g.	Pair, one with level periods	50.00	55.00
	i.	Thick "V"	32.50	11.00
52j	A1	1sh on 1sh orange	1,500.	1,500.
53c	A1	5sh on 5sh green	10.50	15.00
	d.	Mixed periods	400.00	400.00
	e.	Pair, one with level periods	1,600.	
	f.	"5" with short flag	65.00	77.50
	g.	Thick "V"	72.50	60.00
		Handstamped "SPECIMEN"	60.00	
		Handstamped "SPECIMEN", thick "V"	170.00	

Stamps with mixed periods have one or two periods level with the bottoms of letters. One stamp in each pane had all periods level. Later settings had several stamps with thick "V." Forgeries of the scarcer varieties exist.
"V.R.I." stands for Victoria Regina Imperatrix. On No. 59, "E.R.I." stands for Edward Rex Imperator.

Cape of Good Hope
Stamps of 1893-98
Overprinted

1900　　　　Wmk. 16

54	A15	½p green	.55	.25
	a.	No period after "COLONY"	12.00	25.00
	b.	Double overprint	900.00	775.00
55	A13	2½p ultramarine	3.50	.40
	a.	No period after "COLONY"	82.50	82.50

Overprinted as in 1900

1902, May

56	A15	1p carmine rose	2.25	.25
	a.	No period after "COLONY"	25.00	30.00

Nos. 51d, 53c, Surcharged and No. 8b Surcharged like No. 51 but Reading "E.R.I."

Carmine or Vermilion and Black Surcharges

1902　　　　Unwmk.

57	A1	4p on 6p on 6p ultra	1.60	2.25
	a.	Thick "V"	2.75	8.25
	b.	As "a," invtd. "1" instead of "I"	7.25	18.50
	c.	No period after "R"	42.50	55.00

Black Surcharge

59	A1	6p on 6p ultra	6.00	19.00
	a.	Double surcharge, one invtd.	—	—

Orange Surcharge

60	A1	1sh on 5sh on 5sh grn	10.50	25.00
a.		Thick "V"	17.50	55.00
b.		"5" with short flag	80.00	95.00
c.		Double surcharge	1,100.	
		Nos. 57-60 (3)	18.10	46.25

"E.R.I." stands for Edward Rex Imperator.

King Edward VII — A8

ORANGE RIVER COLONY (continued)

1903-04		**Wmk. 2**		**Typo.**
61	A8	½p yellow green	10.00	2.50
		Never hinged	16.00	
62	A8	1p carmine	8.25	.25
		Never hinged	10.50	
63	A8	2p chocolate	10.00	.85
		Never hinged	14.00	
64	A8	2½p ultra	5.50	1.10
		Never hinged	5.75	
65	A8	3p violet	10.50	1.10
		Never hinged	16.00	
66	A8	4p olive grn & car	42.50	5.50
		Never hinged	15.00	
a.		"IOSTAGE" for "POSTAGE"	1,000.	500.00
		Never hinged	1,600.	
67	A8	6p violet & car	9.25	1.10
		Never hinged	15.00	
68	A8	1sh bister & car	50.00	3.00
		Never hinged	67.50	
69	A8	5sh red brn & bl ('04)	160.00	30.00
		Never hinged	170.00	
		Nos. 61-69 (9)	306.00	45.40

Some of the above stamps are found with the overprint "C. S. A. R." for use by the Central South African Railway.

The "IOSTAGE" variety on the 4p is the result of filled in type.

Issue dates: 1p, Feb. 3. ½p, 2p, 2½p, 3p, 4p, 6p, 1sh, July 6. 5sh, Oct. 31.

1907-08				**Wmk. 3**
70	A8	½p yellow green	16.50	1.10
		Never hinged	21.00	
71	A8	1p carmine	10.50	.35
		Never hinged	17.00	
72	A8	4p olive grn & car	5.00	5.25
		Never hinged	8.00	
a.		"IOSTAGE" for "POSTAGE"	200.00	160.00
		Never hinged	350.00	
73	A8	1sh bister & car	85.00	25.00
		Never hinged	125.00	
		Nos. 70-73 (4)	117.00	31.70

The "IOSTAGE" variety on the 4p is the result of filled-in type.

Stamps of Orange River Colony were replaced by those of Union of South Africa.

MILITARY STAMP

M1

No. M1 was provided to members of the Orange Free State army on active service during the Second Boer War. Soldiers' mail carried free was required to bear either No. M1 or be signed by the sender's unit commander. The stamps were used extensively from Oct. 1899 until the fall of Kroonstad in May 1900.

No. M1 was typeset and printed by Curling & Co., Bloemfontein, in sheets of 20 (5x4), with each row of five containing slightly different types.

Forgeries exist. The most common counterfeits either have 17 pearls, rather than 16, in the top and bottom frames, or omit the periods after "BRIEF" and "FRANKO."

1899, Oct. 15		**Unwmk.**		**Perf. 12**
M1	M1	black, *bister yellow*	50.00	60.00
		Never hinged	90.00	
		On cover, *from*		1,200.

PAKISTAN

ˈpa-ki-ˌstan

LOCATION — In southern, central Asia
GOVT. — Republic
AREA — 307,293 sq. mi.
POP. — 88,000,000 (est. 1983)
CAPITAL — Islamabad

Pakistan was formed August 15, 1947, when India was divided into the Dominions of the Union of India and Pakistan, with some princely states remaining independent.

Pakistan had two areas made up of all or part of several predominantly Moslem provinces in the northwest and northeast corners of pre-1947 India. Western Pakistan consists of the entire provinces of Baluchistan, Sind (Scinde) and "Northwest Frontier," and 15 districts of the Punjab. Eastern Pakistan, consisting of the Sylhet district in

---

Assam and 14 districts in Bengal Province, became independent as Bangladesh in December 1971.

The state of Las Bela was incorporated into Pakistan.

12 Pies = 1 Anna
16 Annas = 1 Rupee

> **Catalogue values for all unused stamps in this country are for Never Hinged items.**

Stamps of India, 1937-43, Overprinted in Black

Nos. 1-12

Nos. 13-19

				Perf. 13½x14
1947, Oct. 1				**Wmk. 196**
1	A83	3p slate	.25	.25
		On cover		5.00
2	A83	½a rose violet	.25	.25
		On cover		5.00
3	A83	9p lt green	.25	.25
		On cover		5.00
4	A83	1a carmine rose	.25	.25
		On cover		5.00
4A	A84	1a3p bister ('49)	4.75	5.75
		Postally used		10.00
		On cover		24.00
5	A84	1½a dk purple	.25	.25
		On cover		5.00
6	A84	2a scarlet	.25	.40
		On cover		5.00
7	A84	3a violet	.25	.40
		On cover		5.00
8	A84	3½a ultra	1.25	3.00
		On cover		10.00
9	A85	4a chocolate	.55	.30
		On cover		5.00
10	A85	6a peacock blue	2.10	1.25
		On cover		5.00
11	A85	8a blue violet	.65	.85
		On cover		5.00
12	A85	12a carmine lake	2.10	.40
		On cover		5.00
13	A81	14a rose violet	5.75	3.50
		On cover		12.00
14	A82	1r brn & slate	3.50	1.50
		On cover		5.00
a.		Inverted overprint	310.00	
b.		Pair, one without ovpt.	900.00	
15	A82	2r dk brn & dk vio	6.50	3.25
		On cover		9.00
16	A82	5r dp ultra & dk grn	8.00	5.00
		On cover		17.00
17	A82	10r rose car & dk vio	10.00	6.50
		On cover		32.50
18	A82	15r dk grn & dk brn	65.00	100.00
		On cover		750.00
19	A82	25r dk vio & bl vio	87.50	77.50
		On cover		650.00
		Nos. 1-19 (20)	199.40	210.85
		Set, hinged	125.00	

Provisional use of stamps of India with handstamped or printed "PAKISTAN" was authorized in 1947-49. Nos. 4A, 14a 14b exist only as provisional issues.

Constituent Assembly Building, Karachi — A1

Crescent and Urdu Inscription — A2

Designs: 2½a, Karachi Airport entrance. 3a, Lahore Fort gateway.

			Unwmk.	
1948, July 9		**Engr.**		**Perf. 14**
20	A1	1½a bright ultra	1.25	2.00
21	A1	2½a green	1.25	.25
22	A1	3a chocolate	1.25	.30
			Perf. 12	
23	A2	1r red	1.25	.85
a.		Perf. 14	4.75	10.00
		Nos. 20-23 (4)	5.00	3.40

Pakistan's independence, Aug. 15, 1947. Examples of No. 23a used on cover are unknown. Used examples of No. 23a are cto.

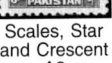

Scales, Star and Crescent A3

Star and Crescent A4

Karachi Airport Building A5

Karachi Port Authority Building — A6

Khyber Pass — A7

2½a, 3½a, 4a, Ghulan Muhammed Dam, Indus River, Sind. 1r, 2r, 5r, Salimullah Hostel.

Perf. 12½, 14 (3a, 10a), 14x13½ (2½a, 3½a, 6a, 12a)

			Unwmk.	
1948-57				
24	A3	3p org red, perf. 12½	.25	.25
a.		Perf. 13½ ('54)	2.00	1.00
25	A3	6p pur, perf. 12½	1.25	.25
a.		Perf. 13½ ('54)	4.00	3.50
26	A3	9p dk grn, perf. 12½	.55	.25
a.		Perf. 13½ ('54)	3.50	1.75
27	A4	1a dark blue	.25	.50
28	A4	1½a gray green	.25	.25
29	A4	2a orange red	2.75	.70
30	A6	2½a green	4.25	5.00
31	A4	3a olive green	8.00	1.00
32	A6	3½a violet blue	4.25	5.50
33	A6	4a chocolate	1.00	.25
34	A6	6a deep blue	2.00	.55
35	A6	8a black	1.00	1.50
36	A6	10a red	6.00	7.50
37	A6	12a red	7.50	1.25
			Perf. 14	
38	A5	1r ultra	12.00	.55
a.		Perf. 13½ ('54)	18.00	7.00
39	A5	2r dark brown	20.00	.80
a.		Perf. 13½ ('54)	30.00	3.00
			Perf. 13½	
40	A5	5r car ('54)	13.00	.40
a.		Perf. 13½x14	17.00	2.25
			Perf. 13	
41	A7	10r rose lilac ('51)	18.00	2.50
a.		Perf. 14	14.00	26.00
b.		Perf. 12	110.00	8.50
42	A7	15r blue green ('57)	22.50	20.00
a.		Perf. 14		65.00

---

b.		Perf. 12	32.50	20.00
		Perf. 14		
43	A7	25r purple	55.00	67.50
a.		Perf. 13 ('54)	40.00	27.50
b.		Perf. 12	32.50	37.50
		Nos. 24-43 (20)	179.80	116.50
		Set, hinged	100.00	

Many compound perforations exist. See No. 259, types A9-A11. For surcharges and overprints see Nos. 124, O14-O26, O35-O37, O41-O43A, O52, O63, O68.

Imperfs of Nos. 24-43 are from proof sheets improperly removed from the printer's archives.

"Quaid-i-Azam" (Great Leader), "Mohammed Ali Jinnah" — A8

			Perf. 13½x14	
1949, Sept. 11		**Engr.**		
44	A8	1½a brown	2.25	1.50
45	A8	3a dark green	2.25	1.50
46	A8	10a blk (English inscriptions)	7.75	9.00
		Nos. 44-46 (3)	12.25	12.00

1st anniv. of the death of Mohammed Ali Jinnah (1876-1948), Moslem lawyer, president of All-India Moslem League and first Governor General of Pakistan.

Re-engraved (Crescents Reversed)

A9

A10

A11

Perf. 12½, 13½x14 (3a, 10a), 14x13½ (6a, 12a)

1949-53				
47	A10	1a dk blue ('50)	5.25	.85
a.		Perf. 13 ('52)	7.00	.25
48	A10	1½a gray green	4.25	.85
a.		Perf. 13 ('53)	3.50	.25
49	A10	2a orange red	4.50	.25
a.		Perf. 13 ('53)	4.50	.25
b.		As "a," printed on gum side	55.00	
50	A9	3a olive green	10.00	1.00
51	A11	6a deep blue ('50)	12.50	2.50
52	A11	8a black ('50)	14.00	2.50
53	A9	10a red	22.50	3.75
54	A11	12a red ('50)	26.00	1.00
		Nos. 47-54 (8)	99.00	12.70

For overprints see #O27-O31, O38-O40.

Vase and Plate — A12

Star and Crescent, Plane and Hour Glass — A13

Moslem Leaf Pattern — A14

Arch and Lamp of Learning A15

1951, Aug. 14   Engr.   Perf. 13
55	A12	2½a dark red	1.90	1.25
56	A13	3a dk rose lako	1.00	.25
57	A12	3½a dp ultra (Urdu "⅓3")	1.25	2.75
57A	A12	3½a dp ultra (Urdu "3½") ('56)	3.50	2.50
58	A14	4a deep green	1.00	.25
59	A14	6a red orange	1.25	.25
60	A15	8a brown	5.50	.30
61	A15	10a purple	2.25	1.25
62	A13	12a dk slate blue	2.50	.25

Nos. 55-62 (9)   20.15   9.05

Fourth anniversary of independence.
On No. 57, the characters of the Urdu denomination at right appears as "⅓3." On the reengraved No. 57A, they read "3½."
Issue date: Dec. 1956.
See Nos. 88, O32-O34.
For surcharges see Nos. 255, 257.

OFFICIAL STAMPS

Official Stamps of India, 1939-43, Overprinted in Black

1947-49   Wmk. 196   Perf. 13½x14
O1	O8	3p slate	2.75	2.50
		On cover		5.00
O2	O8	½a dk rose vio	.60	.25
		On cover		5.00
O3	O8	9p green	5.50	4.25
		On cover		5.00
O4	O8	1a carmine rose	.60	.25
		On cover		5.00
O4A	O8	1a3p bister ('49)	9.00	25.00
		Postally used		15.00
		On cover		40.00
O5	O8	1½a dull purple	.60	.25
		On cover		5.00
O6	O8	2a scarlet	.60	.40
		On cover		5.00
O7	O8	2½a purple	7.00	11.00
		On cover		24.00
O8	O8	4a dk brown	1.40	1.75
		On cover		5.00
O9	O8	8a blue violet	2.00	4.00
		On cover		16.00

Nos. O1-O9 (10)   30.05   49.65

India Nos. O100-O103 Overprinted in Black

O10	A82	1r brown & slate	1.00	3.00
		On cover		8.00
O11	A82	2r dk brn & dk vio	7.50	7.00
		On cover		25.00
O12	A82	5r dp ultra & dk grn	30.00	65.00
		On cover		550.00
		Telegraph cancel		7.50
O13	A82	10r rose car & dk vio	75.00	130.00
		On cover		600.00
		Telegraph cancel		5.00

Nos. O1-O13 (14)   143.55 254.50
Set, hinged   90.00

Regular Issue of 1948 Overprinted in Black or Carmine—a

SERVICE

"C" in "SERVICE" is nearly round.

Perf. 12½, 13, 13½x14, 14x13½
1948, Aug. 14   Unwmk.
O14	A3	3p orange red	.25	.25
O15	A3	6p purple (C)	.25	.25
O16	A3	9p dk green (C)	.25	.25
O17	A4	1a dk blue (C)	4.25	.25
O18	A4	1½a gray grn (C)	4.00	.25
O19	A4	2a orange red	1.75	.25
O20	A5	3a olive green	29.00	14.00
O21	A6	4a chocolate	1.25	.25
O22	A6	8a black (C)	2.50	10.00
O23	A5	1r ultra	1.25	.30
O24	A5	2r dark brown	17.50	10.00
O25	A5	5r carmine	50.00	20.00
O26	A7	10r rose lil, perf.	22.50	60.00
		14x13½		
a.		Perf. 12	25.00	65.00
b.		Perf. 13	22.50	70.00

Nos. O14-O26 (13)   134.75 116.05
Set, hinged   72.50

Issued: No. O26a, 10/10/51; No. O26b, 1954(?).

Nos. 47-50 and 52 Overprinted Type "a" in Black or Carmine
1949-50   Perf. 12½, 13½x14
O27	A10	1a dark blue (C)	2.10	.25
O28	A10	1½a gray green (C)	.65	.25
a.		Inverted ovpt.	275.00	45.00
O29	A10	2a orange red	2.10	.25
O30	A0	3a olive grn ('49)	37.50	6.00
O31	A11	8a black (C)	57.50	20.00

Nos. O27-O31 (5)   99.85 26.75

Unwmk.
1951, Aug. 14   Engr.   Perf. 13
O32	A13	3a dark rose lake	9.25	10.00
O33	A14	4a deep green	2.40	.40
O34	A15	8a brown	12.00	5.00

Nos. O32-O34 (3)   23.65 15.40

BAHAWALPUR

LOCATION — A State of Pakistan.
AREA — 17,494 sq. mi.
POP. — 1,341,209 (1941)
CAPITAL — Bahawalpur

Bahawalpur was an Indian princely state that was autonomous from Aug. 15-Oct. 3, 1947, when it united with Pakistan. These stamps had franking power solely within Bahawalpur.

Used values are for c-t-o or favor cancels.

India George VI stamps of 1937-40 and 1941-43 were overprinted for use in Bahawalpur during the brief period of that state's independence, following the creation of the separate dominions of India and Pakistan on Aug. 15, 1947. These stamps were withdrawn when Bahawalpur united with Pakistan on Oct. 3, 1947. Until 1953, Pakistan stamps were valid for use in Bahawalpur.

Stamps of India Used in Bahawalpur

Overprinted in Red or Black

1947, Aug. 15
A1	A83	3p slate (R)	30.00
A2	A83	½a rose vio	30.00
A3	A83	9p light grn (R)	30.00
A4	A83	1a car rose	30.00
A5	A84	1½a dark pur (R)	30.00
A6	A84	2a scarlet	30.00
a.		Double overprint	3,500.
A7	A84	3a violet (R)	30.00
A8	A84	3½a ultramarine (R)	30.00
A9	A85	4a chocolate	30.00
A10	A85	6a peacock bl (R)	30.00
a.		Double overprint	3,500.

A11	A85	8a blue vio (R)		30.00
A12	A85	12a carm lake		30.00
A13	A81	14a rose vio		75.00
A14	A82	1r brn & slate		35.00
a.		Double overprint, one albino		400.00
A15	A82	2r dk brn & dk vio (R)		2,250.
A16	A82	5r dp ultra & dk grn (R)		2,250.
A17	A82	10r rose car & dk vio		2,250.

Covers: Commercial covers of Nos. A1-A17 are very rare, with perhaps one to three covers known for each.

Amir Muhammad Bahawal Khan I Abbasi — A1

Perf. 12½x12
1947, Dec. 1   Wmk. 274   Engr.
1   A1   ½a brt car rose & blk   4.00   8.00

Bicentenary of the ruling family.

Nawab Sadiq Muhammad Khan V Abbasi Bahadur — A2

Tombs of the Amirs — A3

Mosque, Sadiq Garh — A4

Fort Dirawar A5

Nur-Mahal Palace — A6

Palace, Sadiq Garh — A7

Nawab Sadiq Muhammad Khan V Abbasi Bahadur — A8

A9

Perf. 12½ (A2), 12x12½ (A3, A5, A6, A7), 12½x12 (A4, A8), 13x13½ (A9)
1948, Apr. 1   Engr.   Wmk. 274
2	A2	3p dp blue & blk	2.00	7.00
3	A2	½a lake & blk	2.00	7.00
4	A2	9p dk green & blk	2.00	7.00
5	A2	1a dp car & blk	2.00	7.00
6	A2	1½a violet & blk	3.00	7.00
7	A3	2a car & dp grn	3.00	7.00
8	A4	4a brn & org red	3.00	7.00
9	A5	6a dp bl & vio brn	3.50	7.00
10	A6	8a brt pur & car	3.75	7.00
11	A7	12a dp car & dk bl	4.50	7.00
12	A8	1r chocolate & vio	30.00	24.00
13	A8	2r dp mag & dk grn	57.50	40.00
14	A8	5r purple & black	57.50	50.00
15	A9	10r black & car	47.50	62.50

Nos. 2-15 (14)   221.25 246.50

See #18-21. For overprints see #O17-O24.

Soldiers of 1848 and 1948 — A10

1948, Oct. 15   Engr.   Perf. 11½
16   A10   1½a dp car & blk   1.75   8.00

Centenary of the Multan Campaign.

Amir Khan V and Mohammed Ali Jinnah — A11

1948, Oct. 3   Perf. 13x12½
17   A11   1½a grn & car rose   2.50   8.75

1st anniv. of the union of Bahawalpur with Pakistan.

Types of 1948
1948   Perf. 12x11½
18	A8	1r orange & dp grn	1.75	8.50
19	A8	2r carmine & blk	1.90	8.50
20	A8	5r ultra & red brn	2.25	8.50

Perf. 13½
21	A9	10r green & red brn	2.75	8.50

Nos. 18-21 (4)   8.65 34.00

Panjnad Weir — A12

1949, Mar. 3   *Perf. 14*

22	A12	3p shown	.25	6.00
23	A12	½a Wheat	.25	6.00
24	A12	9p Cotton	.25	6.00
25	A12	1a Sahiwal Bull	.25	6.00
		Nos. 22-25 (4)	1.00	24.00

25th anniv. of the acquisition of full ruling powers by Amir Khan V.

UPU Monument, Bern — A13

1949, Oct. 10   *Perf. 13*

Center in Black

26	A13	9p green	.25	3.00
27	A13	1a red violet	.25	3.00
28	A13	1½a brown orange	.25	3.00
29	A13	2½a blue	.25	3.00
		Nos. 26-29 (4)	1.00	12.00

UPU, 75th anniv. Exist perf 17½x17; value, each $2. Exist imperf.
For overprints see Nos. O25-O28.

OFFICIAL STAMPS

Two printings of Nos. O1-O10 exist. The first printing has brownish, streaky gum, and the second printing has clear, even gum.

Panjnad Weir — O1

Camel and Colt — O2

Antelopes O3

Pelicans O4

Juma Masjid Palace, Fort Derawar O5

Temple at Pattan Munara O6

Red Overprint

Wmk. 274

1945, Jan. 1   *Engr.*   *Perf. 14*

O1	O1	½a brt grn & blk	4.50	12.50
O2	O2	1a carmine & blk	5.75	12.50
O3	O3	2a violet & blk	5.00	12.50
O4	O4	4a olive & blk	12.50	16.00
O5	O5	8a brown & blk	29.00	21.00
O6	O6	1r orange & blk	29.00	21.00
		Nos. O1-O6 (6)	85.75	95.50

For types overprinted see Nos. O7-O9, O11-O13.

Types of 1945, Without Red Overprint, Srchd. in Black

1945   *Unwmk.*

O7	O5	½a on 8a lake & blk	6.00	4.75
O8	O6	1½a on 1r org & blk	50.00	16.00
O9	O1	1½a on 2r ultra & blk	200.00	20.00
		Nos. O7-O9 (3)	256.00	40.75

Camels — O7

1945, Mar. 10   *Red Overprint*

O10	O7	1a brown & black	80.00	75.00

Types of 1945, Without Red Overprint, Ovptd. in Black

1945

O11	O1	½a carmine & black	1.75	7.00
O12	O2	1a carmine & black	3.00	7.00
O13	O3	2a orange & black	5.25	7.00
		Nos. O11-O13 (3)	10.00	21.00

Nawab Sadiq Muhammad Khan V Abbasi Bahadur — O8

1945

O14	O8	3p dp blue & blk	4.50	8.00
O15	O8	1½a dp violet & blk	27.50	17.00

Flags of Allied Nations O9

1946, May 1

O16	O9	1½a emerald & gray	5.50	7.00

Victory of Allied Nations in World War II.

Stamps of 1948 Overprinted in Carmine or Black

Perf. 12½, 12½x12, 12x11½, 13½

1948   *Wmk. 274*

O17	A2	3p dp bl & blk (C)	1.10	7.00
O18	A2	1a dp carmine & blk	1.10	7.00
O19	A3	2a car & dp grn	1.10	7.00
O20	A4	4a brown & org red	1.10	7.00
O21	A8	1r org & blk (C)	1.10	7.00
O22	A8	2r car & blk (C)	1.10	7.00
O23	A8	5r ultra & red brn (C)	1.10	7.00
O24	A9	10r grn & red brn (C)	1.10	7.00
		Nos. O17-O24 (8)	8.80	56.00

Same Ovpt. in Carmine on #26-29

1949   *Perf. 13, 18*

Center in Black

O25	A13	9p green	.25	7.50
O26	A13	1a red violet	.25	7.50
O27	A13	1½a brown orange	.25	7.50
O28	A13	2½a blue	.25	7.50
		Nos. O25-O28 (4)	1.00	30.00

75th anniv. of the UPU. Exist perf 17½x17; value, each $2. Exist imperf.

PALESTINE

ˈpa-lə-ˌstin

LOCATION — Western Asia bordering on the Mediterranean Sea
GOVT. — British Mandate
AREA — 10,429 sq. mi.
POP. — 1,605,816 (estimated)
CAPITAL — Jerusalem

Formerly a part of Turkey, Palestine was occupied by the Egyptian Expeditionary Forces of the British Army in World War I and was mandated to Great Britain in 1923.

10 Milliemes = 1 Piaster
1000 Milliemes = 1 Egyptian Pound
1000 Mils = 1 Palestine Pound (1928)

Watermark

Wmk. 33

Issued under British Military Occupation

For use in Palestine, Transjordan, Lebanon, Syria and in parts of Cilicia and northeastern Egypt

A1

Wmk. Crown and "GvR" (33)

1918, Feb. 10   *Litho.*   *Rouletted 20*

1	A1	1pi deep blue	190.00	105.00
2	A1	1pi ultra	2.50	2.50

Nos. 2 & 1 Surcharged in Black

1918, Feb. 16

3	A1	5m on 1pi ultra	7.50	4.25
a.		5m on 1pi gray blue	110.00	600.00

Nos. 1 and 3a were issued without gum. No. 3a is on paper with a surface sheen.

1918   *Typo.*   *Perf. 15x14*

4	A1	1m dark brown	.35	.45
5	A1	2m blue green	.35	.50
6	A1	3m light brown	.40	.40
7	A1	4m scarlet	.40	.45
8	A1	5m orange	.75	.35
9	A1	1pi indigo	.50	.30
10	A1	2pi olive green	3.00	1.00
11	A1	5pi plum	3.25	2.50
12	A1	9pi bister	11.00	7.50
13	A1	10pi ultramarine	12.00	4.50
14	A1	20pi gray	16.00	20.00
		Nos. 4-14 (11)	48.00	37.95

Many shades exist.
Nos. 4-11 exist with rough perforation.
Issued: 1m, 2m, 4m, 2pi, 5pi, 7/16; 5m, 9/25; 1pi, 11/9; 3m, 9pi, 10pi, 12/17; 20pi, 12/27.
Nos. 4-11 with overprint "O. P. D. A." (Ottoman Public Debt Administration) or "H.J.Z." (Hejaz-Jemen Railway) are revenue stamps; they exist postally used.
For overprints on stamps and types see #15-62 & Jordan #1-63, 73-90, 92-102, 130-144, J12-J23.

Issued under British Administration
Overprinted at Jerusalem

Stamps and Type of 1918 Overprinted in Black or Silver

1920, Sept. 1   *Wmk. 33*   *Perf. 15x14*

Arabic Overprint 8mm long

15	A1	1m dark brown	9.00	2.25
16	A1	2m blu grn, perf 14	2.00	1.60
d.		Perf 15x14	9.50	5.00
17	A1	3m lt brown	15.00	6.00
d.		Perf 14	65.00	62.50
e.		Inverted overprint	525.00	700.00
18	A1	4m scarlet	4.50	1.50
19	A1	5m org, perf 14	4.75	1.00
e.		Perf 15x14	22.00	5.00
20	A1	1pi indigo (S)	4.75	.90
21	A1	2pi olive green	6.00	2.25
22	A1	5pi plum	27.50	27.50
23	A1	9pi bister	13.00	23.00
24	A1	10pi ultra	12.50	19.50
25	A1	20pi gray	35.00	50.00
		Nos. 15-25 (11)	134.00	135.50

Forgeries exist of No. 17e.

Similar Ovpt., with Arabic Line 10mm Long, Arabic "S" and "T" Joined, ".." at Left Extends Above Other Letters

1920-21   *Perf. 15x14*

15a	A1	1m dark brown	2.25	1.20
e.		Perf. 14	700.00	850.00
g.		As "a," invtd. ovpt.	450.00	
16a	A1	2m blue green	10.00	3.50
e.		"PALESTINE" omitted	2,500.	1,500.
f.		Perf. 14	4.75	4.50
17a	A1	3m light brown	3.75	1.20
18a	A1	4m scarlet	5.50	1.40
b.		Perf. 14	70.00	87.50
19a	A1	5m orange	2.60	.90
f.		Perf. 14	9.50	1.25
20a	A1	1pi indigo, perf. 14 (S) ('21)	57.50	1.40
d.		Perf. 15x14	525.00	32.50
21a	A1	2pi olive green ('21)	75.00	30.00
22a	A1	5pi plum ('21)	52.50	11.00
d.		Perf. 14	225.00	525.00
		Nos. 15a-22a (8)	209.10	51.60

This overprint often looks grayish to grayish black. In the English line the letters are frequently uneven and damaged.

Similar Ovpt., with Arabic Line 10mm Long, Arabic "S" and "T" Separated and 6mm Between English and Hebrew Lines

1920, Dec. 6

15b	A1	1m dk brn, perf 14	57.50	37.50
17b	A1	3m lt brn, perf 15x14	60.00	37.50
19b	A1	5m orange, perf 14	400.00	37.50
d.		Perf. 15x14	16,000.	13,750.
		Nos. 15b-19b (3)	517.50	112.50

Overprinted as Before, 7½mm Between English and Hebrew Lines, ".." at Left Even With Other Letters

1921   *Perf. 15x14*

15c	A1	1m dark brown	15.00	4.00
f.		1m dull brown, perf 14		2,300.

16c	A1	2m blue green	25.00	6.25
17c	A1	3m light brown	35.00	3.50
18c	A1	4m scarlet	35.00	4.00
19c	A1	5m orange	70.00	1.10
20c	A1	1pi indigo (S)	21.00	.90
21c	A1	2pi olive green	26.50	7.00
22c	A1	5pi plum	29.00	9.25
23c	A1	9pi bister	57.50	100.00
24c	A1	10pi ultra	70.00	16.00
25c	A1	20pi pale gray	100.00	57.50
d.		Perf. 14	13,750.	2,900.
		Nos. 15c-25c (11)	484.00	209.50

Overprinted at London

Stamps of 1918
Overprinted

1921   **Perf. 15x14**

37	A1	1m dark brown	1.50	.35
38	A1	2m blue green	2.50	.35
39	A1	3m light brown	2.75	.35
40	A1	4m scarlet	3.25	.70
41	A1	5m orange	3.00	.35
42	A1	1pi bright blue	2.25	.40
43	A1	2pi olive green	3.75	.45
44	A1	5pi plum	10.00	5.75
45	A1	9pi bister	20.00	16.00
46	A1	10pi ultra	26.00	600.00
47	A1	20pi gray	65.00	1,600.
		Nos. 37-47 (11)	140.00	
		Nos. 37-45 (9)		24.70

The 2nd character from left on bottom line that looks like quotation marks consists of long thin lines.
Deformed or damaged letters exist in all three lines of the overprint.

Similar Overprint on Type of 1921

1922   **Wmk. 4**   **Perf. 14**

48	A1	1m dark brown	1.75	.35
a.		Inverted overprint	—	13,750.
b.		Double overprint	260.00	500.00
49	A1	2m yellow	2.50	.35
50	A1	3m Prus blue	2.75	.25
51	A1	4m rose	2.75	.25
52	A1	5m orange	3.25	.35
53	A1	6m blue green	2.50	.35
54	A1	7m yellow brown	2.50	.35
55	A1	8m red	2.50	.35
56	A1	1pi gray	3.00	.35
57	A1	13m ultra	3.50	.25
58	A1	2pi olive green	3.50	.40
a.		Inverted overprint	350.00	575.00
b.		2pi yellow bister	140.00	14.00
59	A1	5pi plum	5.50	1.40
a.		Perf. 15x14	62.50	4.50

Perf. 15x14

60	A1	9pi bister	10.00	10.00
a.		Perf. 14	1,050.	225.00
61	A1	10pi light blue	8.50	3.00
a.		Perf. 14	75.00	15.00
62	A1	20pi violet	10.50	6.25
a.		Perf. 14	180.00	120.00
		Nos. 48-62 (15)	65.00	24.25

The 2nd character from left on bottom line that looks like quotation marks consists of short thick lines.
The "E. F. F." for "E. E. F." on No. 61 is caused by damaged type.

Rachel's Tomb — A3   Mosque of Omar (Dome of the Rock) — A4

Citadel at Jerusalem A5   Tiberias and Sea of Galilee A6

1927-42   **Typo.**   **Perf. 13½x14½**

63	A3	2m Prus blue	2.75	.25
		Never hinged	4.25	
64	A3	3m yellow green	1.75	.25
		Never hinged	2.75	
65	A4	4m rose red	9.00	1.40
		Never hinged	13.50	
66	A4	4m violet brn ('32)	2.50	.25
		Never hinged	3.75	
67	A5	5m brown org	4.25	.25
		Never hinged	6.50	
c.		Perf. 14 1½x14 (coil stamp) ('36)	16.00	21.00
		Never hinged	24.00	
68	A4	6m deep green	1.25	.25
		Never hinged	1.90	
69	A5	7m deep red	10.00	.70
		Never hinged	15.00	
70	A5	7m dk violet ('32)	1.00	.25
		Never hinged	1.50	
71	A4	8m yellow brown	17.50	7.00
		Never hinged	27.00	
72	A4	8m scarlet ('32)	1.50	.25
		Never hinged	2.25	
73	A3	10m deep gray	1.75	.25
		Never hinged	2.75	
a.		Perf. 14 1½x14 (coil stamp) ('38)	23.50	27.50
74	A4	13m ultra	17.50	.40
		Never hinged	27.00	
75	A4	13m olive bister ('32)	2.75	.25
		Never hinged	4.25	
76	A4	15m ultra ('32)	4.75	.50
		Never hinged	7.25	
77	A5	20m olive green	1.75	.25
		Never hinged	2.75	

Perf. 14

78	A6	50m violet brown	2.75	.40
		Never hinged	4.25	
79	A6	90m bister	70.00	60.00
		Never hinged	105.00	
80	A6	100m bright blue	2.60	.80
		Never hinged	4.00	
81	A6	200m dk violet	9.25	5.75
		Never hinged	14.00	
82	A6	250m dp brown ('42)	7.50	3.50
		Never hinged	11.00	
83	A6	500m red ('42)	7.50	3.50
		Never hinged	11.00	
84	A6	£1 gray black ('42)	10.00	4.00
		Never hinged	17.50	
		Nos. 63-84 (22)	189.60	90.45

Issued: 3m, #74, 6/1; 2m, 5m, 6m, 10m, #65, 69, 71, 77-81, 8/14; #70, 72, 6/1/32; #75, 15m, 8/1/32; #66, 11/1/32; #82-84, 1/15/42.

POSTAGE DUE STAMPS

D1

1923   **Unwmk.**   **Typo.**   **Perf. 11**

J1	D1	1m bister brown	20.00	29.00
		Never hinged	30.00	
b.		Horiz. pair, imperf. btwn.	1,300.	750.00
J2	D1	2m green	16.00	11.50
		Never hinged	24.00	
J3	D1	4m red	12.00	12.00
		Never hinged	18.00	
J4	D1	8m violet	8.50	8.50
		Never hinged	13.00	
b.		Horiz. pair, imperf. btwn.		2,300.
J5	D1	13m dark blue	7.50	7.50
		Never hinged	11.50	
b.		Horiz. pair, imperf. btwn.	1,050.	
		Nos. J1-J5 (5)	64.00	68.50

Imperfs. of 1m, 2m, 8m, are from proof sheets.
Values for Nos. J1-J5 are for fine centered copies.

D2   D3

1924, Dec. 1   **Wmk. 4**

J6	D2	1m brown	1.10	2.00
		Never hinged	1.60	
J7	D2	2m yellow	1.75	1.75
		Never hinged	6.00	
J8	D2	4m green	2.00	1.50
		Never hinged	3.00	
J9	D2	8m red	3.00	1.00
		Never hinged	4.50	
J10	D2	13m ultramarine	2.75	2.50
		Never hinged	4.25	
J11	D2	5pi violet	13.00	1.75
		Never hinged	19.50	
		Nos. J6-J11 (6)	25.85	10.50

1928-45   **Perf. 14**

J12	D3	1m lt brown	2.25	1.00
		Never hinged	3.50	
a.		Perf. 15x14 ('45)	42.50	80.00
J13	D3	2m yellow	3.00	.70
		Never hinged	4.75	
J14	D3	4m green	3.50	1.60
		Never hinged	5.50	
a.		4m bluish grn, perf. 15x14 ('45)	75.00	97.50
J15	D3	6m brown org ('33)	17.50	5.00
		Never hinged	27.00	
J16	D3	8m red	2.75	1.25
		Never hinged	4.25	
J17	D3	10m light gray	2.00	.70
		Never hinged	3.00	
J18	D3	13m ultra	4.50	2.25
		Never hinged	7.00	
J19	D3	20m olive green	4.50	1.25
		Never hinged	7.00	
J20	D3	50m violet	4.50	1.50
		Never hinged	7.00	
		Nos. J12-J20 (9)	44.50	15.25

The Hebrew word for "mil" appears below the numeral on all values but the 1m.
Issued: 6m, Oct. 1933; others, Feb. 1, 1928.

PANAMA

ˈpa-nə-ˌmä

LOCATION — Central America between Costa Rica and Colombia
GOVT. — Republic
AREA — 30,134 sq. mi.
POP. — 1,970,000 (est. 1983)
CAPITAL — Panama

Formerly a department of the Republic of Colombia, Panama gained its independence in 1903. Dividing the country at its center is the Panama Canal.

100 Centavos = 1 Peso
100 Centesimos = 1 Balboa (1904)

Watermark

Wmk. 229 — Wavy Lines

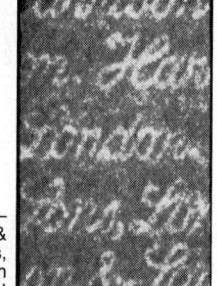

Wmk. 233 — "Harrison & Sons, London." in Script

GREAT BRITAIN USED in PANAMA
Stamps of Great Britain cancelled "C35" were used in Panama. Listings appear in the "Stamps of Great Britain Used in Colombia" section, at the beginning of Colombian listings.

Issues of the Sovereign State of Panama Under Colombian Dominion
Valid only for domestic mail.

Coat of Arms
A1   A2

1878   **Unwmk.**   **Litho.**   **Imperf.**
Thin Wove Paper

1	A1	5c gray green	25.00	30.00
a.		5c yellow green	25.00	30.00
2	A1	10c blue	60.00	60.00
3	A1	20c rose red	40.00	32.50
		Nos. 1-3 (3)	125.00	122.50

Very Thin Wove Paper

4	A2	50c buff		1,500.

All values of this issue are known rouletted unofficially.

Medium Thick Paper

5	A1	5c blue green	25.00	30.00
6	A1	10c blue	65.00	70.00
7	A2	50c orange	13.00	
		Nos. 5-7 (3)	103.00	100.00

Nos. 5-7 were printed before Nos. 1-4, according to Panamanian archives.
Values for used Nos. 1-5 are for hand-stamped postal cancellations.
These stamps have been reprinted in a number of shades, on thin to moderately thick, white or yellowish paper. They are without gum or with white, crackly gum. All values have been reprinted from new stones made from retouched dies. The marks of retouching are plainly to be seen in the sea and clouds. On the original 10c the shield in the upper left corner has two blank sections; on the reprints the design of this shield is completed. The impression of these reprints is frequently blurred.
Reprints of the 50c are rare. Beware of remainders of the 50c offered as reprints.

Issues of Colombia for use in the Department of Panama
Issued because of the use of different currency.

Map of Panama
A3   A4

1887-88   **Perf. 13½**

8	A3	1c black, *green*	.90	.80
9	A3	2c black, *pink* ('88)	1.60	1.25
a.		2c black, *salmon*	1.60	
10	A3	5c black, *blue*	.90	.35
11	A3	10c black, *yellow*	.90	.40
a.		Imperf., pair		
12	A3	20c black, *lilac*	1.00	.50
13	A3	50c brown ('88)	2.00	1.00
a.		Imperf.		
		Nos. 8-13 (6)	7.30	4.30

See No. 14. For surcharges and overprints see Nos. 24-30, 107-108, 115-116, 137-138.

1892   **Pelure Paper**

14	A3	50c brown	2.50	1.10

The stamps of this issue have been reprinted on papers of slightly different colors from those of the originals.
These are: 1c yellow green, 2c deep rose, 5c bright blue, 10c straw, 20c violet.
The 50c is printed from a very worn stone, in a lighter brown than the originals. The series includes a 10c on lilac paper.
All these stamps are to be found perforated, imperforate, imperforate horizontally or imperforate vertically. At the same time that they were made, impressions were struck upon a variety of glazed and surface-colored papers.

Wove Paper
1892-96   **Engr.**   **Perf. 12**

15	A4	1c green	.25	.25
16	A4	2c rose	.40	.25
17	A4	5c blue	1.50	.50
18	A4	10c orange	.35	.25
19	A4	20c violet ('95)	.50	.35
20	A4	50c bister brn ('96)	.50	.40
21	A4	1p lake ('96)	6.50	4.00
		Nos. 15-21 (7)	10.00	6.00

In 1903 Nos. 15-21 were used in Cauca and three other southern Colombia towns. Stamps canceled in these towns are worth much more.
For surcharges and overprints see Nos. 22-23, 51-106, 109-114, 129-136, 139, 151-162, 181-184, F12-F15, H4-H5.

Nos. 16, 12-14 Surcharged

a   b

c   d

e   f

g

1894   Black Surcharge
22 (a) 1c on 2c rose   .50   .40
  a. Inverted surcharge   2.50   2.50
  b. Double surcharge
23 (a) 1c on 2c rose   .40   .50
  a. "CCNTAVO"   2.50   2.50
  b. Inverted surcharge   2.50   2.50
  c. Double surcharge

Red Surcharge
24 (c) 5c on 20c black, *lil*   2.50   1.50
  a. Inverted surcharge   12.50   12.50
  b. Double surcharge
  c. Without "HABILITADO"
25 (d) 5c on 20c black, *lil*   3.50   3.00
  a. "CCNTAVOS"   7.50   7.50
  b. Inverted surcharge   12.50   12.50
  c. Double surcharge
  d. Without "HABILITADO"
26 (e) 5c on 20c black, *lil*   6.00   5.00
  a. Inverted surcharge   12.50   12.50
  b. Double surcharge
27 (f) 10c on 50c brown   3.00   3.00
  a. "1894" omitted   7.50
  b. "CCNTAVOS"   15.00
  c. Inverted surcharge   12.50   12.50
28 (g) 10c on 50c brown   12.50   12.50
  a. "CCNTAVOS"   32.50
  b. Inverted surcharge

Pelure Paper
29 (f) 10c on 50c brown   4.00   3.00
  a. "1894" omitted   7.50
  b. Inverted surcharge   12.50   12.50
  c. Double surcharge
30 (g) 10c on 50c brown   10.00   10.00
  a. "CCNTAVOS"
  b. Without "HABILITADO"
  c. Inverted surcharge   25.00   25.00
  d. Double surcharge
    Nos. 22-30 (9)   42.40   38.90

There are several settings of these surcharges. Usually the surcharge is about 15½mm high, but in one setting, it is only 13mm. All the types are to be found with a comma after "CENTAVOS." Nos. 24, 25, 26, 29 and 30 exist with the surcharge printed sideways. Nos. 23, 24 and 29 may be found with an inverted "A" instead of "V" in "CENTAVOS." There are also varieties caused by dropped or broken letters.

Issues of the Republic
Issued in the City of Panama

Stamps of 1892-96
Overprinted

1903, Nov. 16   Rose Handstamp
51 A4 1c green   2.00   1.50
52 A4 2c rose   5.00   3.00
53 A4 5c blue   2.00   1.25
54 A4 10c yellow   2.00   2.00
55 A4 20c violet   4.00   3.50
56 A4 50c bister brn   10.00   7.00
57 A4 1p lake   50.00   40.00
    Nos. 51-57 (7)   75.00   58.25

Blue Black Handstamp
58 A4 1c green   2.00   1.25
59 A4 2c rose   1.00   1.00
60 A4 5c blue   7.00   6.00
61 A4 10c yellow   5.00   3.50
62 A4 20c violet   10.00   7.50
63 A4 50c bister brn   10.00   7.50
64 A4 1p lake   50.00   42.50
    Nos. 58-64 (7)   85.00   69.25

The stamps of this issue are to be found with the handstamp placed horizontally, vertically or diagonally; inverted; double; double, one inverted; double, both inverted; in pairs, one without handstamp; etc.

This handstamp is known in brown rose on the 1, 5, 20 and 50c, in purple on the 1, 2, 50c

and 1p, and in magenta on the 5, 10, 20 and 50c.

Reprints were made in rose, black and other colors when the handstamp was nearly worn out, so that the "R" of "REPUBLICA" appears to be shorter than usual, and the bottom part of "LI" has been broken off. The "P" of "PAN-AMA" leans to the left and the tops of "NA" are broken. Many of these varieties are found inverted, double, etc.

Overprinted

Bar in Similar Color to Stamp

1903, Dec. 3   Black Overprint
65 A4 2c rose   2.50   2.50
  a. "PANAMA" 15mm long   3.50
  b. Violet bar   5.00
66 A4 5c blue   100.00
  a. "PANAMA" 15mm long   100.00
67 A4 10c yellow   2.50   2.50
  a. "PANAMA" 15mm long   6.00
  b. Horizontal overprint   17.50

Gray Black Overprint
68 A4 2c rose   2.00   2.00
  a. "PANAMA" 15mm long   2.50

Carmine Overprint
69 A4 5c blue   2.50   2.50
  a. "PANAMA" 15mm long   3.50
  b. Bar only   75.00   75.00
  c. Double overprint
70 A4 20c violet   7.50   6.50
  a. "PANAMA" 15mm long   10.00
  b. Double overprint, one in black 150.00
    Nos. 65,67-70 (5)   17.00   16.00

This overprint was set up to cover fifty stamps. "PANAMA" is normally 13mm long and 1¾mm high but, in two rows in each sheet, it measures 15 to 16mm.

This word may be found with one or more of the letters taller than usual; with one, two or three inverted "V's" instead of "A's"; with an inverted "Y" instead of "A"; an inverted "N"; an "A" with accent; and a fancy "P."

Owing to misplaced impressions, stamps exist with "PANAMA" once only, twice on one side, or three times.

Overprinted in Red

1903, Dec.
71 A4 1c green   .75   .60
  a. "PANAMA" 15mm long   1.25
  b. "PANAMA" reading down   3.00   .75
  c. "PANAMA" reading up and
      down   3.00
  d. Double overprint   8.00
72 A4 2c rose   .50   .40
  a. "PANAMA" 15mm long   1.00
  b. "PANAMA" reading down   .75   .50
  c. "PANAMA" reading up and
      down   4.00
  d. Double overprint   8.00
73 A4 20c violet   1.50   1.00
  a. "PANAMA" 15mm long   2.25
  b. "PANAMA" reading down
  c. "PANAMA" reading up and
      down   8.00   8.00
  d. Double overprint   18.00   18.00
74 A4 50c bister brn   3.00   2.50
  a. "PANAMA" 15mm long   5.00
  b. "PANAMA" reading up and
      down   12.00   12.00
  c. Double overprint   6.00   6.00
75 A4 1p lake   6.00   4.50
  a. "PANAMA" 15mm long   6.25
  b. "PANAMA" reading up and
      down   15.00   15.00
  c. Double overprint   15.00
  d. Inverted overprint   25.00
    Nos. 71-75 (5)   11.75   9.00

This setting appears to be a re-arrangement (or two very similar re-arrangements) of the previous overprint. The overprint covers fifty stamps. "PANAMA" usually reads upward but sheets of the 1, 2 and 20c exist with the word reading upward on one half the sheet and downward on the other half.

In one re-arrangement one stamp in fifty has the word reading in both directions. Nearly all the varieties of the previous overprint are repeated in this setting excepting the inverted "Y" and fancy "P." There are also additional varieties of large letters and "PANAMA" occasionally has an "A" missing or inverted. There are misplaced impressions, as the previous setting.

Overprinted in Red

1904-05
76 A4 1c green   .25   .25
  a. Both words reading up   1.50
  b. Both words reading down   2.75
  c. Double overprint
  d. Pair, one without overprint   15.00
  e. "PANAAM"   20.00
  f. Inverted "M" in "PANAMA"   5.00
77 A4 2c rose   .25   .25
  a. Both words reading up   2.50
  b. Both words reading down   2.50
  c. Double overprint   10.00
  d. Double overprint, one inverted 14.00
  e. Inverted "M" in "PANAMA"   5.00
78 A4 5c blue   .30   .25
  a. Both words reading up   3.00
  b. Both words reading down   4.25
  c. Inverted overprint   12.50
  d. "PANAAM"   25.00
  e. "PANANA"   8.00
  f. "PAMAMA"   5.00
  g. Inverted "M" in "PANAMA"   5.00
  h. Double overprint   20.00
79 A4 10c yellow   .30   .25
  a. Both words reading up   5.00
  b. Both words reading down   5.00
  c. Double overprint   15.00
  d. Inverted overprint   6.75
  e. "PANANA"   8.00
  f. Inverted "M" in "PANAMA"   15.00
  g. Red brown overprint   7.50   3.50
80 A4 20c violet   2.00   1.00
  a. Both words reading up   5.00
  b. Both words reading down   10.00
81 A4 50c bister brn   2.00   1.60
  a. Both words reading up   10.50
  b. Both words reading down   10.00
  c. Double overprint
82 A4 1p lake   5.00   5.00
  a. Both words reading up   12.50
  b. Both words reading down   12.50
  c. Double overprint
  d. Double overprint, one inverted 20.00
  e. Inverted "M" in "PANAMA"   45.00
    Nos. 76-82 (7)   10.10   8.60

This overprint is also set up to cover fifty stamps. One stamp in each fifty has "PAN-AMA" reading upward at both sides. Another has the word reading downward at both sides, a third has an inverted "V" in place of the last "A" and a fourth has a small thick "N." In a resetting all these varieties are corrected except the inverted "V." There are misplaced overprints as before.

Later printings show other varieties and have the bar 2½mm instead of 2mm wide. The colors of the various printings of Nos. 76-82 range from carmine to almost pink.

Experts consider the black overprint on the 5c to be speculative.

The 20c violet and 50c bister brown exist with bar 2½mm wide, including the error "PAMANA," but are not known to have been issued. Some examples have been canceled "to oblige."

Issued in Colon

Handstamped in
Magenta or Violet

On Stamps of 1892-96
1903-04
101 A4 1c green   .75   .75
102 A4 2c rose   .75   .75
103 A4 5c blue   1.00   1.00
104 A4 10c yellow   3.50   3.00
105 A4 20c violet   8.00   6.50
106 A4 1p lake   80.00   70.00

On Stamps of 1887-92
Ordinary Wove Paper
107 A3 50c brown   25.00   20.00
    Nos. 101-107 (7)   119.00 102.00

Pelure Paper
108 A3 50c brown   70.00

Handstamped in
Magenta, Violet or
Red

On Stamps of 1892-96
109 A4 1c green   5.00   5.00
110 A4 2c rose   5.50   5.00
111 A4 5c blue   5.50   5.00
112 A4 10c yellow   8.25   7.00
113 A4 20c violet   12.00   9.00
114 A4 1p lake   70.00   60.00

On Stamps of 1887-92
Ordinary Wove Paper
115 A3 50c brown   35.00   25.00
    Nos. 109-115 (7)   141.75 116.00

Pelure Paper
116 A3 50c brown   50.00   37.50

The first note after No. 64 applies also to Nos. 101-116.

The handstamps on Nos. 109-116 have been counterfeited.

Stamps with this overprint were a private speculation. They exist on cover. The overprint was to be used on postal cards.

Overprinted On
Stamps Of 1892-96

On Stamps of 1892-96
Carmine Overprint
129 A4 1c green   .40   .40
  a. Inverted overprint   6.00
  b. Double overprint   2.25
  c. Double overprint, one inverted 6.00
130 A4 5c blue   .50   .50

Brown Overprint
131 A4 1c green   12.00
  a. Double overprint, one inverted

Black Overprint
132 A4 1c green   60.00   30.00
  a. Vertical overprint   42.50
  b. Inverted overprint   42.50
  c. Double overprint, one inverted 42.50
133 A4 2c rose   .50   .50
  a. Inverted overprint
134 A4 10c yellow   .50   .50
  a. Inverted overprint   4.00
  b. Double overprint   16.00
  c. Double overprint, one inverted 6.00
135 A4 20c violet   .50   .50
  a. Inverted overprint   4.00
  b. Double overprint   5.50
136 A4 1p lake   16.00   14.00

On Stamps of 1887-88
Blue Overprint
Ordinary Wove Paper
137 A3 50c brown   3.00   3.00

Pelure Paper
138 A3 50c brown   3.00   3.00
  a. Double overprint   14.00

This overprint is set up to cover fifty stamps. In each fifty there are four stamps without accent on the last "a" of "Panama," one with accent on the "a" of "Republica" and one with a thick, upright "i."

Overprinted in
Carmine

On Stamp of 1892-96
139 A4 20c violet   *200.00*
  a. Double overprint

Unknown with genuine cancels.

Issued in Bocas del Toro

Stamps of 1892-96
Overprinted
Handstamped in
Violet

1903-04
151 A4 1c green   20.00   14.00
152 A4 2c rose   20.00   14.00
153 A4 5c blue   25.00   16.00
154 A4 10c yellow   15.00   8.25

155	A4	20c violet	50.00	30.00
156	A4	50c bister brn	100.00	55.00
157	A4	1p lake	140.00	110.00
		Nos. 151-157 (7)	370.00	247.25

The handstamp is known double and inverted. Counterfeits exist.

Handstamped in Violet

158	A4	1c green	100.00
159	A4	2c rose	70.00
160	A4	5c blue	80.00
161	A4	10c yellow	100.00
		Nos. 158-161 (4)	350.00

This handstamp was applied to these 4 stamps only by favor, experts state. Counterfeits are numerous. The 1p exists only as a counterfeit.

General Issues

A5

1905, Feb. 4   Engr.   Perf. 12

179	A5	1c green	.60	.40
180	A5	2c rose	.80	.50

Panama's Declaration of Independence from the Colombian Republic, Nov. 3, 1903.

Surcharged in Vermilion on Stamps of 1892-96 Issue

1906

181	A4	1c on 20c violet	.25	.25
a.		"Panrma"	2.25	2.25
b.		"Pnnama"	2.25	2.25
c.		"Pauama"	2.25	2.25
d.		Inverted surcharge	4.00	4.00
e.		Double surcharge	3.50	3.50
f.		Double surcharge, one inverted		

Stamps of 1892-96 Surcharged in Vermilion

182	A4	2c on 50c bister brn	.25	.25
a.		3rd "A" of "PANAMA" inverted	2.25	2.25
b.		Both "PANAMA" reading down	4.00	4.00
c.		Double surcharge		
d.		Inverted surcharge		2.50

The 2c on 20c violet was never issued to the public. All examples are inverted. Value, 75c.

Carmine Surcharge

183	A4	5c on 1p lake	.60	.40
a.		Both "PANAMA" reading down	6.00	6.00
b.		"5" omitted		
c.		Double surcharge		
d.		Inverted surcharge		
e.		3rd "A" of "PANAMA" inverted	5.50	5.50

On Stamp of 1903-04, No. 75

184	A4	5c on 1p lake	.60	.40
a.		"PANAMA" 15mm long		
b.		"PANAMA" reading up and down		
c.		Both "PANAMA" reading down		
d.		Inverted surcharge		
e.		Double surcharge		
f.		3rd "A" of "PANAMA" inverted		
		Nos. 181-184 (4)	1.70	1.30

National Flag — A6   Vasco Núñez de Balboa — A7

Fernández de Córdoba — A8   Coat of Arms — A9

Justo Arosemena A10   Manuel J. Hurtado A11

José de Obaldía — A12   Tomás Herrera — A13

José de Fábrega — A14

1906-07   Engr.   Perf. 11½

185	A6	½c orange & multi	.70	.35
186	A7	1c dk green & blk ('07)	.70	.35
187	A8	2c scarlet & blk	1.00	.35
188	A9	2½c red orange	1.00	.35
189	A10	5c blue & black	1.75	.35
a.		5c ultramarine & black	2.00	.50
190	A11	8c purple & blk	1.50	.65
191	A12	10c violet & blk	1.50	.50
192	A13	25c brown & blk	3.50	1.10
193	A14	50c black	9.00	3.50
		Nos. 185-193 (9)	20.65	7.50

Inverted centers exist of Nos. 185-187, 189, 189a, 190-193, Value, each $25. Nos. 185-193 exist imperf.
For surcharge see No. F29.
Issued: Nos. 185, 188-193, 11/20; No. 187, 9/1.

Map — A17   Balboa — A18

Córdoba — A19   Arms — A20

Arosemena A21   Obaldía A23

1909-16   Perf. 12

195	A17	½c orange ('11)	1.00	.30
196	A17	½c rose ('15)	.70	.60

197	A18	1c dk grn & blk	1.00	.50
a.		Inverted center	7,500.	7,500.
b.		Booklet pane of 6 ('16)	160.00	
		Complete booklet, 4 #197b		
198	A19	2c ver & blk	1.00	.30
a.		Booklet pane of 6	160.00	
199	A20	2½c red orange	1.50	.30
200	A21	5c blue & blk	2.00	.30
a.		Booklet pane of 6 ('16)	175.00	
201	A23	10c violet & blk	3.75	1.10
		Complete booklet, panes of 6 (3x2) of #195 (3), 197 (3), 199 (2), 200, 201 ('11)	—	
		Nos. 195-201 (7)	10.95	3.40

Value for No. 197a used is for an off-center example with faults.
The panes contained in the booklet listed following No. 201 are marginal blocks of 6 (3x2), without gum, stapled within the booklet cover, with advertising paper interleaving. The complete booklet was sold for B1.50.
Nos. 197b and 198a are gummed panes of 6 (2x3), imperf on outside edges.
For overprints and surcharges see #H23, I4-I7.

Balboa Sighting Pacific Ocean, His Dog "Leoncico" at His Feet — A24

1913, Sept. 1

202	A24	2½c dk grn & yel grn	1.75	.65

400th anniv. of Balboa's discovery of the Pacific Ocean.

Panama-Pacific Exposition Issue

Chorrera Falls — A25

Map of Panama Canal — A26

Balboa Taking Possession of the Pacific A27   Ruins of Cathedral of Old Panama A28

Palace of Arts — A29

Gatun Locks — A30

Culebra Cut — A31

Santo Domingo Monastery's Flat Arch — A32

1915, Mar. 1   Perf. 12

204	A25	½c ol grn & blk	.40	.30
205	A26	1c dk green & blk	.95	.30
206	A27	2c carmine & blk	.75	.30
a.		2c ver & blk ('16)	.75	.30
208	A28	2½c scarlet & blk	.95	.35
209	A29	3c violet & blk	1.60	.55
210	A30	5c blue & blk	2.10	.35
a.		Center inverted	1,500.	650.00
211	A31	10c orange & blk	2.10	.70
212	A32	20c brown & blk	10.50	3.25
a.		Center inverted	300.00	—
		Nos. 204-212 (8)	19.35	6.10

For surcharges and overprints see Nos. 217, 233, E1-E2.

Manuel J. Hurtado — A33

1916

213	A33	8c violet & blk	9.00	4.25

For surcharge see No. F30.

S. S. Panama in Culebra Cut Aug. 11, 1914 A34

S. S. Panama in Culebra Cut Aug. 11, 1914 A35

S. S. Cristobal in Gatun Lock — A36

1918, Aug. 23

214	A34	12c purple & blk	15.00	5.75
215	A35	15c brt blue & blk	10.00	3.50
216	A36	24c yellow brn & blk	15.00	3.50
		Nos. 214-216 (3)	40.00	12.75

No. 208 Surcharged in Dark Blue

1919, Aug. 15

217	A28	2c on 2½c scar & blk	.35	.35
a.		Inverted surcharge	11.00	5.00
b.		Double surcharge	15.00	6.00

City of Panama, 400th anniversary.

Dry Dock at Balboa A38

Ship in Pedro Miguel Lock — A39

1920, Sept. 1 Engr.
218 A38 50c orange & blk 30.00 22.50
219 A39 1b dk violet & blk 40.00 27.50

For overprint and surcharge see Nos. C6, C37.

Arms of Panama City — A40

José Vallarino — A41

"Land Gate" — A42

Simón Bolívar — A43

Statue of Cervantes — A44

Bolívar's Tribute — A45

Carlos de Ycaza — A46

Municipal Building in 1821 and 1921 — A47

Statue of Balboa — A48

Villa de Los Santos Church — A49

Herrera — A50

Fábrega — A51

1921, Nov.
220 A40 ½c orange .80 .25
221 A41 1c green 1.00 .25
222 A42 2c carmine 1.25 .25
223 A43 2½c red 2.75 1.10
224 A44 3c dull violet 2.75 1.10
225 A45 5c blue 2.75 .35
226 A46 8c olive green 10.00 3.50

227 A47 10c violet 6.75 1.50
228 A48 15c lt blue 8.00 2.00
229 A49 20c olive brown 14.50 3.50
230 A50 24c black brown 14.50 4.25
231 A51 50c black 25.00 8.00
Nos. 220-231 (12) 90.05 26.05

Centenary of independence.
For overprints and surcharges see Nos. 264, 275-276, 299, 304, 308-310, C35.

Hurtado — A52

1921, Nov. 28
232 A52 2c dark green .65 .65

Manuel José Hurtado (1821-1887), president and folklore writer.
For overprints see Nos. 258, 301.

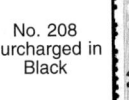
No. 208 Surcharged in Black

1923
233 A28 2c on 2½c scar & blk .45 .45
  a. "1923" omitted 4.00
  b. Bar over "CENTESIMOS" 4.00
  c. Inverted surcharge 4.00
  d. Double surcharge 4.00
  e. Pair, one without surcharge 4.00

Two stamps in each sheet have a bar above "CENTESIMOS" (No. 233b).

Arms — A53

1924, May Engr.
234 A53 ½c orange .25 .25
235 A53 1c dark green .25 .25
236 A53 2c carmine .25 .25
237 A53 5c dark blue .45 .25
238 A53 10c dark violet .60 .25
239 A53 12c olive green .75 .40
240 A53 15c ultra .95 .40
241 A53 24c yellow brown 1.90 .60
242 A53 50c orange 4.50 1.10
243 A53 1b black 6.75 2.50
  Nos. 234-243 (10) 16.65 6.25

For overprints & surcharges see Nos. 277, 321A, 331-338, 352, C19-C20, C68, RA5, RA10-RA22. Post 1940 listings in Scott Standard catalogue, Vol. 5.

Bolívar — A54

Statue of Bolívar — A55

Bolívar Hall — A56

1926, June 10 Perf. 12½
244 A54 ½c orange .55 .25
245 A54 1c dark green .55 .25
246 A54 2c scarlet .70 .30
247 A54 4c gray .90 .35
248 A54 5c dark blue 1.40 .50
249 A54 8c lilac 2.25 .80
250 A55 10c dull violet 1.60 .80
251 A55 12c olive green 2.50 1.00
252 A55 15c ultra 3.25 1.25
253 A55 20c brown 6.75 1.60

254 A56 24c black violet 8.00 2.00
255 A56 50c black 13.50 5.00
  Nos. 244-255 (12) 41.95 14.10

Bolívar Congress centennial.
For surcharges and overprints see Nos. 259-263, 266-267, 274, 298, 300, 302-303, 305-307, C33-C34, C36, C38-C39.

Lindbergh's Airplane, "The Spirit of St. Louis" — A57

Lindbergh's Airplane and Map of Panama — A58

1928, Jan. 9 Typo. Rouletted 7
256 A57 2c dk red & blk, salmon .40 .25
257 A58 5c dk blue, grn .60 .40

Visit of Colonel Charles A. Lindbergh to Central America by airplane.
No. 256 has black overprint.

No. 232 Overprinted in Red

1928, Nov. 1 Perf. 12
258 A52 2c dark green .25 .25
25th anniversary of the Republic.

No. 247 Surcharged in Black

1930, Dec. 17 Perf. 12½, 13
259 A54 1c on 4c gray .25 .25

Centenary of the death of Simón Bolívar, the Liberator.

Nos. 244-246 Overprinted in Red or Blue

1932 Perf. 12½
260 A54 ½c orange (R) .25 .25
261 A54 1c dark green (R) .35 .25
  a. Double overprint 18.00
262 A54 2c scarlet (Bl) .35 .25

No. 252 Surcharged in Red

263 A55 10c on 15c ultra 1.00 .50
  a. " 55.00
  Nos. 260-263 (4) 1.95 1.25

No. 220 Overprinted as in 1932 in Black

1933, May 25 Perf. 12
Overprint 19mm Long
264 A40 ½c orange .35 .25
  a. Overprint 17mm long —

Dr. Manuel Amador Guerrero — A60

1933, June 30 Engr. Perf. 12½
265 A60 2c dark red .50 .25

Centenary of the birth of Dr. Manuel Amador Guerrero, founder of the Republic of Panama and its first President.

No. 251 Surcharged in Red

1933
266 A55 10c on 12c olive grn 1.25 .65

No. 253 Overprinted in Red

267 A55 20c brown 2.25 1.75

José Domingo de Obaldía — A61

Quotation from Emerson — A63

National Institute — A64

Designs: 2c, Eusebio A. Morales. 12c, Justo A. Facio. 15c, Pablo Arosemena.

1934, July 24 Engr. Perf. 14
268 A61 1c dark green 1.00 .50
269 A61 2c scarlet 1.00 .45
270 A63 5c dark blue 1.25 .80
271 A64 10c brown 3.25 1.60
272 A61 12c yellow green 6.50 2.00
273 A61 15c Prus blue 8.50 2.50
  Nos. 268-273 (6) 21.50 7.75

25th anniv. of the Natl. Institute.

Nos. 248, 227 Overprinted in Black or Red

1935-36 — Perf. 12½, 12
274	A54	5c dark blue	.90 .30
275	A47	10c violet (R) ('36)	1.25 .60

No. 225
Surcharged in
Red

1936. Sept. 19 — Perf. 11½
276	A45	1c on 5c blue	.40 .40
a.		Lines of surcharge 1½mm btwn.	6.50

No. 241 Surcharged in
Blue

1936, Sept. 24 — Perf. 12
277	A53	2c on 24c yellow brn	.60 .50
a.		Double surcharge	20.00

Centenary of the birth of Pablo Arosemena, president of Panama in 1910-12. See Nos. C19-C20.

Panama
Cathedral
A67

Designs: ½c, Ruins of Custom House, Portobelo. 1c, Panama Tree. 2c, "La Pollera." 5c, Simon Bolivar. 10c, Cathedral Tower Ruins. Old Panama. 15c, Francisco Garcia y Santos. 20c, Madden Dam, Panama Canal. 25c, Columbus. 50c, Gaillard Cut. 1b, Panama Cathedral.

1936, Dec. 1 — Engr. — Perf. 11½
278	A67	½c yellow org	.55 .25
279	A67	1c blue green	.55 .25
280	A67	2c carmine rose	.55 .25
281	A67	5c blue	.80 .50
282	A67	10c dk violet	1.75 .75
283	A67	15c turq blue	1.75 .75
284	A67	20c red	2.00 1.50
285	A67	25c black brn	3.50 2.00
286	A67	50c orange	7.75 5.00
287	A67	1b black	18.00 12.00
	Nos. 278-287,C21-C26 (16)		62.70 40.00

4th Postal Congress of the Americas and Spain.

Stamps of
1936
Overprinted
in Red or
Blue

1937, Mar. 9
288	A67	½c yellow org (R)	.35 .30
a.		Inverted overprint	25.00
289	A67	1c blue green (R)	.45 .25
290	A67	2c car rose (Bl)	.45 .25
291	A67	5c blue (R)	.70 .25
292	A67	10c dk vio (R)	1.10 .35
293	A67	15c turq bl (R)	5.25 3.25
294	A67	20c red (Bl)	2.00 1.25
295	A67	25c black brn (R)	2.75 1.25
296	A67	50c orange (Bl)	9.00 6.00
297	A67	1b black (R)	14.50 10.00
	Nos. 288-297,C27-C32 (16)		84.60 54.15

Stamps of 1921-26
Overprinted in Red
or Blue

1937, July — Perf. 12, 12½
298	A54	½c orange (R)	1.10 .80
a.		Inverted overprint	30.00
299	A41	1c green (R)	.35 .25
a.		Inverted overprint	30.00
300	A54	1c dk green (R)	.35 .25
301	A52	2c dk green (R)	.45 .35
302	A54	2c scarlet (Bl)	.55 .35

Stamps of 1921-26
Surcharged in Red

303	A54	2c on 4c gray	.70 .45
304	A46	2c on 8c ol grn	.70 .60
305	A55	2c on 8c lilac	.70 .45
306	A55	2c on 10c dl vio	.70 .50
307	A55	2c on 12c ol grn	.70 .45
308	A48	2c on 15c lt blue	.70 .60
309	A50	2c on 24c blk brn	.70 .75
310	A51	2c on 50c black	.70 .35
	Nos. 298-310 (13)		8.40 6.15

Ricardo
Arango
A77

Juan A.
Guizado
A78

La
Concordia
Fire — A79

Modern
Fire
Fighting
Equipment
A80

Firemen's
Monument
A81

David H.
Brandon
A82

Perf. 14x14½, 14½x14
1937, Nov. 25 — Photo. — Wmk. 233
311	A77	½c orange red	2.10 .35
312	A78	1c green	2.10 .35
313	A79	2c red	2.10 .25
314	A80	5c brt blue	4.00 .50
315	A81	10c purple	7.25 1.25
316	A82	12c yellow grn	11.50 2.00
	Nos. 311-316,C40-C42 (9)		44.80 7.05

50th anniversary of the Fire Department.

Old Panama Cathedral Tower and Statue of Liberty Enlightening the World, Flags of Panama and US — A83

Engr. & Litho.
1938, Dec. 7 — Unwmk. — Perf. 12½
Center in Black; Flags in Red and Ultramarine
317	A83	1c deep green	.35 .25
318	A83	2c carmine	.55 .25
319	A83	5c blue	.80 .30
320	A83	12c olive	1.40 .75
321	A83	15c brt ultra	1.75 1.25
	Nos. 317-321,C49-C53 (10)		22.45 15.35

150th anniv. of the US Constitution.

No. 236 Overprinted in
Black

1938, June 5 — Perf. 12
321A	A53	2c carmine	.45 .25
b.		Inverted overprint	22.50
	Nos. 321A,C53A-C53B (3)		1.25 1.05

Opening of the Normal School at Santiago, Veraguas Province, June 5, 1938.

Gatun
Lake — A84

Designs: 1c, Pedro Miguel Locks. 2c, Allegory. 5c, Culebra Cut. 10c, Ferryboat. 12c, Aerial View of Canal. 15c, Gen. William C. Gorgas. 50c, Dr. Manuel A. Guerrero. 1b, Woodrow Wilson.

1939, Aug. 15 — Engr. — Perf. 12½
322	A84	½c yellow	.35 .25
323	A84	1c dp blue grn	.55 .25
324	A84	2c dull rose	.65 .25
325	A84	5c dull blue	1.00 .25
326	A84	10c dk violet	1.10 .35
327	A84	12c olive green	1.10 .50
328	A84	15c ultra	1.10 .80
329	A84	50c orange	2.75 1.60
330	A84	1b dk brown	5.75 3.00
	Nos. 322-330,C54-C61 (17)		34.35 14.45

25th anniversary of the opening of the Panama Canal. For surcharges see Nos. C64, G2 (in Scott Standard catalogue, Vol. 5).

AIR POST STAMPS

Special
Delivery
Stamp No.
E3 Srchd. in
Dark Blue

1929, Feb. 8 — Unwmk. — Perf. 12½
C1	SD1	25c on 10c org	1.00 .80
a.		Inverted surcharge	22.50 22.50

Nos. E3-E4
Overprinted
in Blue

1929, May 22
C2	SD1	10c orange	.50 .50
a.		Inverted overprint	20.00 17.50
b.		Double overprint	20.00 17.50

Some specialists claim the red overprint is a proof impression.

With Additional Surcharge of New Value
C3	SD1	15c on 10c org	.50 .50
C4	SD1	25c on 20c dk brn	1.10 .45
a.		Double surcharge	20.00 20.00
	Nos. C2-C4 (3)		2.10 2.00

No. E3
Surcharged
in Blue

1930, Jan. 25
C5	SD1	5c on 10c org	.50 .50

No. 219
Overprinted in
Red

1930, Feb. 28 — Perf. 12
C6	A39	1b dk vio & blk	16.00 12.50

AP5

1930-41 — Engr. — Perf. 12
C6A	AP5	5c blue ('41)	.25 .25
C6B	AP5	7c rose car ('41)	.25 .25
C6C	AP5	8c gray blk ('41)	.25 .25
C7	AP5	15c dp grn	.30 .25
C8	AP5	20c rose	.35 .25
C9	AP5	25c deep blue	.65 .65
	Nos. C6A-C9 (6)		2.05 1.90

Issued: Nos. C7-C9, 1/20; Nos. C6A-C6C, 7/1/41. See No. C112. For surcharges and overprints see Nos. 353, C16-C16A, C53B, C69, C82-C83, C109, C122, C124. Post 1940 listings are in Scott Standard catalogue, Vol. 5.

Airplane over
Map of
Panama — AP6

1930, Aug. 4 — Perf. 12½
C10	AP6	5c ultra	.25 .25
C11	AP6	10c orange	.30 .25
C12	AP6	30c dp vio	5.50 4.00
C13	AP6	50c dp red	1.50 .50
C14	AP6	1b black	5.50 4.00
	Nos. C10-C14 (5)		13.05 9.00

For surcharge and overprints see Nos. C53A, C70-C71, C115. Post 1940 listings are in Scott Standard catalogue, Vol. 5.

Amphibian
AP7

1931, Nov. 28 — Typo.
Without Gum
C15	AP7	5c deep blue	.80 1.00
a.		5c gray blue	.80 1.00
b.		Horiz. pair, imperf. btwn.	50.00

For the start of regular airmail service between Panama City and the western provinces, but valid only on Nov. 28-29 on mail carried by hydroplane "3 Noviembre."
Many sheets have a papermaker's watermark "DOLPHIN BOND" in double-lined capitals.

No. C9 Surcharged
in Red 19mm long

1932, Dec. 14 — Perf. 12
C16	AP5	20c on 25c dp bl	6.25 .70

Surcharge 17mm long
C16A	AP5	20c on 25c dp bl	200.00 2.50

Special Delivery Stamp No. E4 Overprinted in Red or Black

1934   *Perf. 12½*
C17   SD1 20c dk brn   1.00   .50
C17A SD1 20c dk brn (Bk)   100.00 55.00

Issued: No. C17, 7/31.

Surcharged In Black

1935, June
C18   SD1 10c on 20c dk brn   .80   .50
Same Surcharge with Small "10"
C18A SD1 10c on 20c dk brn   40.00   5.00
   b.   Horiz. pair, imperf. vert. 100.00

Nos. 234 and 242 Surcharged in Blue

1936, Oct. 8
C19   A53 5c on ½c org   400.00 250.00
C20   A53 5c on 50c org   1.00   .80
   a.   Double surcharge   60.00 60.00

Centenary of the birth of President Pablo Arosemena.
It is claimed that No. C19 was not regularly issued. Counterfeits of No. C19 exist.

Urracá Monument AP8

Palace of Justice AP9

10c, Human Genius Uniting the Oceans. 20c, Panama City. 30c, Balboa Monument. 50c, Pedro Miguel Locks.

1936, Dec. 1   Engr.   Perf. 12
C21   AP8 5c blue   .65   .40
C22   AP9 10c yel org   .85   .60
C23   AP9 20c red   3.00   1.50
C24   AP8 30c dk vio   3.50   2.50
C25   AP9 50c car rose   8.00   5.75
C26   AP9 1b black   9.50   6.00
      Nos. C21-C26 (6)   25.50 16.75

4th Postal Congress of the Americas and Spain.

Nos. C21-C26 Overprinted in Red or Blue

1937, Mar. 9
C27   AP8 5c blue (R)   .55   .30
   a.   Inverted overprint   50.00
C28   AP9 10c yel org (Bl)   .75   .45
C29   AP9 20c red (Bl)   1.75   1.00
   a.   Double overprint   50.00
C30   AP8 30c dk vio (R)   4.50   3.25
C31   AP8 50c car rose (Bl)   18.00 13.00
   a.   Double overprint   175.00
C32   AP9 1b black (R)   22.50 13.00
      Nos. C27-C32 (6)   48.05 31.00

Regular Stamps of 1921-26 Surcharged in Red

1937, June 30   Perf. 12, 12½
C33   A55 5c on 15c ultra   .75   .75
C34   A55 5c on 20c brn   .75   .75
C35   A47 10c on 10c vio   1.75   1.50

Regular Stamps of 1920-26 Surcharged in Red

C36   A56 5c on 24c blk vio   .75   .75
C37   A39 5c on 1b dk vio & blk   .75   .50
C38   A56 10c on 50c blk   2.25   2.00
   a.   Inverted surcharge   30.00

No. 248 Overprinted in Red

C39   A54 5c dark blue   .75   .75
   a.   Double overprint   18.00
      Nos. C33-C39 (7)   7.75   7.00

Fire Dept. Badge AP14

Florencio Arosemena AP15

José Gabriel Duque — AP16

Perf. 14x14½
1937, Nov. 25   Photo.   Wmk. 233
C40   AP14 5c blue   3.50   .60
C41   AP15 10c orange   5.00   1.00
C42   AP16 20c crimson   7.25   .75
      Nos. C40-C42 (3)   15.75   2.35

50th anniversary of the Fire Department.

Basketball — AP17

Baseball AP18

1938, Feb. 12   Perf. 14x14½, 14½x14
C43   AP17 1c shown   2.25   .25
C44   AP18 2c shown   2.25   .25
C45   AP18 7c Swimming   3.00   .25
C46   AP18 8c Boxing   3.00   .25
C47   AP17 15c Soccer   5.00   1.25
   a.   Souv. sheet of 5, #C43-C47 18.00 18.00
   b.   As "a," No. C43 omitted 3,500.
      Nos. C43-C47 (5)   15.50   2.25

4th Central American Caribbean Games.

US Constitution Type
Engr. & Litho.
1938, Dec. 7   Unwmk.   Perf. 12½
Center in Black, Flags in Red and Ultramarine
C49   A83 7c gray   .35   .25
C50   A83 8c brt ultra   .55   .35
C51   A83 15c red brn   .70   .45
C52   A83 50c orange   8.00   5.75
C53   A83 1b black   8.00   5.75
      Nos. C49-C53 (5)   17.60 12.55

Nos. C12 and C7 Surcharged in Red

1938, June 5   Perf. 12½, 12
C53A AP6 7c on 30c dp vio   .40   .40
   c.   Double surcharge   27.50
   d.   Inverted surcharge   27.50
C53B AP5 8c on 15c dp grn   .40   .40
   e.   Inverted surcharge   22.50

Opening of the Normal School at Santiago, Veraguas Province, June 5, 1938. The 8c surcharge has no bars.

Belisario Porras AP23

Designs: 2c, William Howard Taft. 5c, Pedro J. Sosa. 10c, Lucien Bonaparte Wise. 15c, Armando Reclus. 20c, Gen. George W. Goethals. 50c, Ferdinand de Lesseps. 1b, Theodore Roosevelt.

1939, Aug. 15   Engr.
C54   AP23 1c dl rose   .40   .25
C55   AP23 2c dp bl grn   .40   .25
C56   AP23 5c indigo   .65   .25
C57   AP23 10c dk vio   .70   .25
C58   AP23 15c ultra   1.60   .35
C59   AP23 20c rose pink   4.00   1.40
C60   AP23 50c dk brn   5.00   .70
C61   AP23 1b black   7.25   3.75
      Nos. C54-C61 (8)   20.00   7.00

Opening of Panama Canal, 25th anniv.
For surcharges see Nos. C63, C65; Nos. G1, G3 in Scott Standard catalogue, Vol. 5.

Flags of the 21 American Republics AP31

1940, Apr. 15   Unwmk.
C62   AP31 15c blue   .40   .35

Pan American Union, 50th anniversary. For surcharge see No. C66.

Stamps of 1939-40 Surcharged in Black

a

b

c

d

1940, Aug. 12
C63   AP23 (a) 5c on 15c lt ultra   .25   .25
   a.   "7 AÉREO 7" on 15c   60.00 60.00
C64   A84 (b) 7c on 15c ultra   .40   .25
C65   AP23 (c) 7c on 20c rose pink .40   .25
C66   AP31 (d) 8c on 15c blue   .40   .25
      Nos. C63-C66 (4)   1.45 1.00

SPECIAL DELIVERY STAMPS

Nos. 211-212 Overprinted in Red

1926   Unwmk.   Perf. 12
E1   A31 10c org & blk   7.50   3.25
   a.   "EXPRESO"   40.00
E2   A32 20c brn & blk   10.00   3.25
   a.   "EXPRESO"   40.00
   b.   Double overprint   35.00 35.00

Bicycle Messenger SD1

1929, Feb. 8   Engr.   Perf. 12½
E3   SD1 10c orange   1.25   1.00
E4   SD1 20c dk brn   4.75   2.50

For surcharges and overprints see Nos. C1-C5, C17-C18A, C67 (in Scott Standard catalogue, Vol. 5).

REGISTRATION STAMPS

Issued under Colombian Dominion

R1

1888   Unwmk.   Engr.   Perf. 13½
F1   R1 10c black, *gray*   8.00   5.25

Imperforate and part-perforate copies without gum and those on surface-colored paper are reprints.

Magenta, Violet or
Blue Black
Handstamped
Overprint — R2

1898　　　　　　　　　　*Perf. 12*
F2　R2 10c yellow　　　　7.00　6.50
The handstamp on No. F2 was also used as
a postmark.

R3

1900　　　Litho.　　　*Perf. 11*
F3　R3 10c blk, *lt bl*　　4.00　3.50

1901
F4　R3 10c brown red　　30.00　20.00

R4

1902　　　**Blue Black Surcharge**
F5　R4 20c on 10c brn red　20.00　16.00

**Issues of the Republic
Issued in the City of Panama**
Registration Stamps of Colombia
Handstamped in Blue Black or Rose

1903-04　　　　　　　　*Imperf.*
F6　R9 20c red brn, *bl*　　45.00　42.50
F7　R9 20c blue, *blue* (R)　45.00　42.50
For surcharges and overprints see Nos. F8-
F11, F16-F26.
*Reprints exist of Nos. F6 and F7; see note
after No. 64.*

With Additional Surcharge in Rose

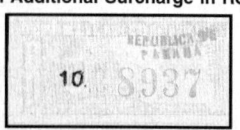

F8　R9 10c on 20c red brn, *bl*　60.00　55.00
　b.　"10" in blue black　　60.00　55.00
F9　R9 10c on 20c bl, *bl*　60.00　45.00

Handstamped in Rose

F10　R9 10c on 20c red brn, *bl*　60.00　55.00
F11　R9 10c on 20c blue, *blue*　45.00　42.50

Issued in Colon
Regular Issues Handstamped
"R/COLON" in Circle (as on F2)
Together with Other Overprints and
Surcharges

Handstamped

1903-04　　　　　　　　*Perf. 12*
F12　A4 10c yellow　　　　3.00　2.50

Handstamped

F13　A4 10c yellow　　　　22.50

Overprinted in Red

F14　A4 10c yellow　　　　3.00　2.50

Overprinted in
Black

F15　A4 10c yellow　　　　7.50　5.00
The handstamps on Nos. F12 to F15 are in
magenta, violet or red; various combinations
of these colors are to be found. They are
struck in various positions, including double,
inverted, one handstamp omitted, etc.

**Colombia No. F13 Handstamped
Like No. F12 in Violet**
　　　　　　　　　　　Imperf
F16　R9 20c red brn, *bl*　　60.00　55.00
Overprinted Like No. F15 in Black

F17　R9 20c red brn, *bl*　　6.00　5.75
No. F17 Surcharged in Manuscript
F18　R9 10c on 20c red brn, *bl*　60.00　55.00

No. F17 Surcharged in Purple **10**

F19　R9 10c on 20c　　　　82.50　80.00

No. F17 Surcharged in Violet

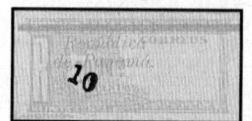

F20　R9 10c on 20c　　　　82.50　80.00
The varieties of the overprint which are
described after No. 138 are also to be found
on the Registration and Acknowledgment of
Receipt stamps. It is probable that Nos. F17
to F20 inclusive owe their existence more to
speculation than to postal necessity.

Issued in Bocas del Toro
Colombia Nos. F17 and F13
Handstamped in Violet

R DE PANAMA

1903-04
F21　R9 20c blue, *blue*　　125.00　125.00
F22　R9 20c red brn, *bl*　125.00　125.00
**No. F21 Surcharged in Manuscript
in Violet or Red**
F23　R9 10c on 20c bl, *bl*　150.00　140.00
**Colombia Nos. F13, F17 Hand-
stamped in Violet**

**Surcharged in Manuscript (a) "10"
(b) "10cs" in Red**
F25　R9　10 on 20c red
　　　　brn, *bl*　　　　70.00　65.00
F26　R9 10cs on 20c bl, *bl*　55.00　50.00
　　Nos. F21-F26 (5)　　525.00　505.00
No. F25 without surcharge is bogus, accord-
ing to leading experts.

General Issue

R5

1904, Aug. 1　　Engr.　　*Perf. 12*
F27　R5 10c green　　　　1.00　.50

**Nos. 190 and 213 Surcharged in
Red**

#F29-F30　　　　　#F29b

1916-17
F29　A11 5c on 8c pur & blk　3.00　2.25
　a.　"5" inverted　　　　75.00
　b.　Large, round "5"　　50.00
　c.　Inverted surcharge　12.50　11.00
　d.　Tête bêche surcharge
　e.　Pair, one without surcharge　10.00
F30　A33 5c on 8c vio & blk　3.50　.80
　a.　Inverted surcharge　13.00　8.25
　b.　Tête bêche surcharge
　c.　Double surcharge　　60.00
Issued: No. F29, 1/1/16; No. F30, 1/28/17.
Stamps similar to No. F30, overprinted in
green were unauthorized.

**ACKNOWLEDGMENT OF RECEIPT
STAMPS**

Issued under Colombian Dominion

Experts consider this handstamp-
"A.R. / COLON / COLOMBIA"-to be a
cancellation or a marking intended for a
letter to receive special handling. It was
applied at Colon to various stamps in
1897-1904 in different colored inks for
philatelic sale. It exists on cover, usually with the bottom line removed by
masking the handstamp.

Nos. 17-18
Handstamped in
Rose

1902
H4　A4　5c blue　　　　5.00　5.00
H5　A4 10c yellow　　　10.00　10.00
This handstamp was also used as a
postmark.

**Issues of the Republic
Issued in the City of Panama**

Colombia No. H3
Handstamped in
Rose

1903-04　　Unwmk.　　*Imperf.*
H9　AR2 10c blue, *blue*　10.00　8.00
Reprints exist of No. H9, see note after No.
64.

No. H9 Surcharged with New Value
H10　AR2　5c on 10c bl, *bl*　5.00　5.00

Colombia No. H3　**Panamá**
Handstamped in
Rose　　　　　 ▬▬▬▬▬▬

H11　AR2 10c blue, *blue*　17.50　14.00

Issued in Colon

Handstamped in　**REPUBLICA DE**
Magenta or Violet　**PANAMA**

　　　　　　　　Imperf
H17　AR2 10c blue, *blue*　15.00　15.00

Handstamped

H18　AR2 10c blue, *blue*　82.50　70.00

Overprinted in Black

H19　AR2 10c blue, *blue*　11.00　8.00
No. H19 Surcharged in Manuscript
H20　AR2 10c on 5c on 10c　100.00　82.50

Issued in Bocas del Toro
Colombia No. H3 Handstamped in
Violet and Surcharged in Manuscript in
Red Like Nos. F25-F26

1904
H21　AR2 5c on 10c blue, *blue*
No. H21, unused, without surcharge is
bogus.

General Issue

AR3

1904, Aug. 1　　Engr.　　*Perf. 12*
H22　AR3 5c blue　　　　1.00　.80

No. 199 Overprinted
in Violet

1916, Jan. 1

H23	A20	2½c red orange		1.00	.80
a.	"R.A." for "A.R."			50.00	
b.	Double overprint			8.00	
c.	Inverted overprint			8.00	

LATE FEE STAMPS

**Issues of the Republic
Issued in the City of Panama**
Colombia No. I4 Handstamped in
Rose or Blue Black

LF3

REPUBLICA DE
PANAMA

1903-04   Unwmk.   Imperf.

I1	LF3 5c pur, *rose*	12.50	9.00
I2	LF3 5c pur, *rose* (Bl Blk)	17.50	12.50

Reprints exist of #I1-I2; see note after #64.

General Issue

LF4

1904   Engr.   Perf. 12

I3	LF4	2½c lake	1.00	.65

No. 199 Overprinted
with Typewriter

Retardo

1910, Aug. 12

I4	A20	2½c red orange	125.00	100.00

Used only on Aug. 12-13.
Counterfeits abound.

Handstamped

RETARDO

1910

I5	A20	2½c red orange	60.00	50.00

Counterfeits abound.

No. 195
Surcharged in
Green

RETARDO

Un Centésimo

1917, Jan. 1

I6	A17	1c on ½c orange	.80	.80
a.	"UN CENTESIMO" inverted		50.00	
b.	Double surcharge		10.00	
c.	Inverted surcharge		6.50	6.50

No. 196
Surcharged in
Green

RETARDO

Un Centésimo

1921

I7	A17	1c on ½c rose	25.00	20.00

POSTAGE DUE STAMPS

San Lorenzo Castle
Gate, Mouth of
Chagres River
D1

Statue of
Columbus
D2

Pedro J.
Sosa — D4

D5

Design: 4c, Capitol, Panama City.

Unwmk.

1915, Mar. 25   Engr.   Perf. 12

J1	D1	1c olive brown	3.50	.75
J2	D2	2c olive brown	5.25	.65
J3	D1	4c olive brown	7.25	1.25
J4	D4	10c olive brown	5.25	1.75
		Nos. J1-J4 (4)	21.25	4.40

Type D1 was intended to show a gate of San
Lorenzo Castle, Chagres, and is so inscribed.

1930, Dec. 30   Perf. 12½

J5	D5	1c emerald	1.00	.60
J6	D5	2c dark red	1.00	.60
J7	D5	4c dark blue	1.60	.80
J8	D5	10c violet	1.60	.80
		Nos. J5-J8 (4)	5.20	2.80

POSTAL TAX STAMPS

Pierre and
Marie
Curie — PT1

Unwmk.

1939, June 15   Engr.   Perf. 12

RA1	PT1	1c rose carmine	.65	.25
RA2	PT1	1c green	.65	.25
RA3	PT1	1c orange	.65	.25
RA4	PT1	1c blue	.65	.25
		Nos. RA1-RA4 (4)	2.60	1.00

See Nos. RA6-RA18, RA24-RA27, RA30.
Post 1940 listings are in Scott Standard catalogue, Vol. 5.

Stamp of 1924
Overprinted in Black

1940, Dec. 20

RA5	A53	1c dark green	1.40	.75

PAPUA

ˈpa-pyə-wə

LOCATION — The southeastern por-
tion of the island of New Guinea,
north of Australia
AREA — 90,540 sq. mi.
POP. — 276,488 (1940)
CAPITAL — Port Moresby

In 1884 a British Protectorate was
proclaimed over this part of the island,
called "British New Guinea." In 1905 the

administration was transferred to Aus-
tralia and in 1906 the name was
changed to Territory of Papua.

12 Pence = 1 Shilling
20 Shillings = 1 Pound

Watermarks

Wmk. 13 —
Crown and
Double-Lined A

Wmk. 47 —
Multiple Rosette

Wmk. 74 —
Crown and
Single-Lined A
Sideways

Wmk. 228 —
Small Crown
and C of A
Multiple

British New Guinea

Lakatoi — A1

Wmk. 47

1901, July 1   Engr.   Perf. 14
Center in Black

1	A1	½p yellow green	21.00	6.00
2	A1	1p carmine	9.00	5.50
3	A1	2p violet	13.50	7.50
4	A1	2½p ultra	27.50	12.00
5	A1	4p black brown	40.00	40.00
a.	Deformed "d" at left (pl.3, pos.4 right pane)		310.00	260.00
6	A1	6p dark green	60.00	40.00
7	A1	1sh orange	65.00	75.00
8	A1	2sh6p brown ('05)	700.00	700.00
		Nos. 1-8 (8)	936.00	886.00

The paper varies in thickness and the watermark is found in two positions, with the greater
width of the rosette either horizontal or
vertical.
For overprints see Nos. 11-26.

Papua

Stamps of
British New
Guinea,
Overprinted

Large Overprint

1906, Nov. 8   Wmk. 47   Perf. 14
Center in Black

11	A1	½p yellow green	10.00	25.00
12	A1	1p carmine	20.00	22.50
13	A1	2p violet	15.00	10.00
14	A1	2½p ultra	8.00	18.00
15	A1	4p black brown	250.00	160.00
e.	Deformed "d" at left		260.00	350.00

16	A1	6p dark green	55.00	65.00
17	A1	1sh orange	30.00	50.00
18	A1	2sh6p brown	225.00	240.00
		Nos. 11-18 (8)	613.00	585.50

Small Overprint

1907   Center in Black

19	A1	½p yellow green	15.00	18.00
a.	Double overprint		3,500.	
20	A1	1p carmine	8.50	7.50
a.	Vertical overprint, up		6,500.	4,500.
21	A1	2p violet	7.00	4.00
a.	Double overprint		3,750.	
22	A1	2½p ultra	16.00	24.00
a.	Double overprint		3,750.	
b.	2½p dull blue & blk		175.00	190.00
23	A1	4p black brown	50.00	70.00
a.	Deformed "d" at left		600.00	
24	A1	6p dark green	47.50	55.00
a.	Double overprint		6,000.	11,000.
25	A1	1sh orange	55.00	60.00
a.	Double overprint		19,000.	13,000.
26	A1	2sh6p brown	60.00	75.00
b.	Vert. ovpt., down		8,500.	
d.	Double horiz. ovpt.			4,250.
e.	Triple horiz. ovpt.			3,100.
		Nos. 19-26 (8)	259.00	313.50

A2

Small "PAPUA"

Perf. 11, 12½

1907-08   Litho.   Wmk. 13
Center in Black

28	A2	1p carmine ('08)	7.50	5.75
29	A2	2p violet ('08)	17.00	6.00
30	A2	2½p ultra ('08)	8.00	9.00
31	A2	4p black brown	9.00	12.00
b.	Deformed "d" at left		35.00	62.50
32	A2	6p dk green ('08)	17.50	18.50
33	A2	1sh orange ('08)	37.50	32.50
		Nos. 28-33 (6)	96.50	83.75

Perf. 12½

30a	A2	2½p	150.00	175.00
31a	A2	4p	13.00	13.00
c.	Deformed "d" at left		62.50	62.50
33a	A2	1sh	77.50	77.50
		Nos. 30a-33a (3)	240.50	285.50

1909-10   Wmk. Sideways
Center in Black

34	A2	½p yellow green	5.50	6.50
a.	Perf. 11x12½		3,500.	3,500.
b.	Perf. 11		6.00	7.50
35	A2	1p carmine	10.00	14.00
a.	Perf. 11		11.00	9.25
36	A2	2p violet ('10)	7.50	15.00
a.	Perf. 11x12½		1,300.	
b.	Perf. 11		.1750	10.50
37	A2	2½p ultra ('10)	9.00	25.00
a.	Perf. 12½		13.00	45.00
38	A2	4p black brn ('10)	8.50	12.00
a.	Perf. 11x12½		12,000.	
b.	As "#38, deformed "d" at left		32.50	52.50
39	A2	6p dark green	19.00	22.50
a.	Perf. 12½		3,750.	10,000.
40	A2	1sh orange ('10)	30.00	45.00
a.	Perf. 11		85.00	95.00
		Nos. 34-40 (7)	89.50	140.00

One stamp in each sheet has a white line
across the upper part of the picture which is
termed the "rift in the clouds."

Large "PAPUA"

2sh6p:
Type I — The numerals are thin and irregular. The body of the "6" encloses a large spot
of color. The dividing stroke is thick and
uneven.

Type II — The numerals are thick and well
formed. The "6" encloses a narrow oval of
color. The dividing stroke is thin and sharp.

1910 — Wmk. 13
Center in Black

41	A2	½p yellow green	7.00	13.00
42	A2	1p carmine	15.00	12.00
43	A2	2p violet	12.50	9.00
44	A2	2½p blue violet	8.50	22.50
45	A2	4p black brown	13.50	14.00
46	A2	6p dark green	11.00	11.00
47	A2	1sh orange	18.00	22.50
48	A2	2sh6p brown, type II	50.00	60.00
a.		Type I	65.00	70.00
		Nos. 41-48 (8)	135.50	164.00

Wmk. Sideways

49	A2	2sh6p choc, type I	85.00	100.00

1911 — Typo. Wmk. 74 — Perf. 12½

50	A2	½p yellow green	1.25	4.00
51	A2	1p lt red	1.50	2.00
52	A2	2p lt violet	2.00	2.00
53	A2	2½p ultra	6.50	11.00
a.		2½p dull ultra	6.25	9.50
54	A2	4p olive green	4.75	18.00
55	A2	6p orange brown	5.00	6.50
56	A2	1sh yellow	14.00	20.00
57	A2	2sh6p rose	46.00	50.00
		Nos. 50-57 (8)	81.00	113.50

For surcharges see Nos. 74-79.

1915, June — Perf. 14

59	A2	1p light red	16.00	3.00

A3

1916-31

60	A3	½p pale yel grn & myr grn ('19)	1.50	2.00
61	A3	1p rose red & blk	3.50	1.50
62	A3	1½p yel brn & gray bl ('25)	2.50	1.00
63	A3	2p red vio & vio brn ('19)	3.75	1.50
64	A3	2p red brn & vio brn ('31)	4.00	1.50
a.		2p cop red & vio blk ('31)	29.00	2.25
65	A3	2½p ultra & dk grn ('19)	6.25	17.50
66	A3	3p emerald & blk	4.75	4.00
a.		3p dp bl grn & blk	5.75	9.25
67	A3	4p org & lt brn ('19)	5.75	7.00
68	A3	5p ol brn & sl ('31)	6.25	20.00
69	A3	6p vio & dl vio ('23)	6.00	12.00
70	A3	1sh ol grn & dk brn ('19)	10.00	12.00
71	A3	2sh6p rose & red brn ('19)	27.50	47.50
72	A3	5sh dp grn & blk	55.00	60.00
73	A3	10sh gray bl & grn ('25)	175.00	200.00
		Nos. 60-73 (14)	311.75	387.50

Type A3 is a redrawing of type A2.
The lines of the picture have been strengthened, making it much darker, especially the sky and water.
See Nos. 92-93. For surcharges & overprints see Nos. 88-91, O1-O10.

Stamps of
1911
Surcharged

1917 — Perf. 12½

74	A2	1p on ½p yellow grn	1.75	1.90
75	A2	1p on 2p lt violet	14.50	17.50
76	A2	1p on 2½p ultra	1.50	4.50
77	A2	1p on 4p olive green	2.10	5.25
78	A2	1p on 6p org brn	10.00	20.00
79	A2	1p on 2sh6p rose	2.25	7.00
		Nos. 74-79 (6)	32.10	56.15

No. 62
Surcharged

1931, Jan. 1 — Perf. 14

88	A3	2p on 1½p yellow brn & gray blue	1.75 2.75

Nos. 70, 71
and 72
Surcharged in
Black

1931

89	A3	5p on 1sh #70	2.50	4.25
90	A3	9p on 2sh6p #71	10.00	18.00
91	A3	1sh3p on 5sh #72	6.00	10.50
		Nos. 89-91 (3)	18.50	32.75

Type of 1916 Issue

1932 — Wmk. 228 — Perf. 11

92	A3	9p dp violet & gray	9.50	37.50
93	A3	1sh3p pale bluish green & grayish violet	14.50	37.50

For overprints see Nos. O11-O12.

Motuan Girl — A5

Bird of Paradise
and Boar's
Tusk — A6

Mother and
Child — A7

Papuan
Motherhood — A8

Dubu (Ceremonial
Platform) — A9

Fire
Maker — A10

Designs: 1p, Steve, son of Oala. 1½p, Tree houses. 3p, Papuan dandy. 5p, Masked dancer. 9p, Shooting fish. 1sh3p, Lakatoi. 2sh, Delta art. 2sh6p, Pottery making. 5sh, Sgt.-Major Simoi. £1, Delta house.

Unwmk.

1932, Nov. 14 — Engr. — Perf. 11

94	A5	½p orange & blk	2.50	3.75
a.		½p orange brown & black	15.00	26.00
95	A5	1p yel grn & blk	2.50	.70
96	A5	1½p red brn & blk	2.50	9.25
97	A6	2p light red	12.50	.35
98	A5	3p blue & blk	3.75	7.50
99	A7	4p olive green	9.00	11.00
100	A5	5p grnsh sl & blk	4.50	3.50
101	A8	6p bister brown	8.50	6.25
102	A5	9p lilac & blk	11.50	24.00
103	A9	1sh bluish gray	5.50	9.75

104	A5	1sh3p brown & blk	19.00	29.00
105	A5	2sh bluish slate & blk	19.00	26.00
106	A5	2sh6p rose lilac & blk	29.00	42.50
107	A5	5sh olive & blk	62.50	62.50
108	A10	10sh gray lilac	110.00	110.00
109	A5	£1 lt gray & black	225.00	175.00
		Nos. 94-109 (16)	527.25	521.05

For overprints see Nos. 114-117.

Hoisting
Union Jack at
Port Moresby
A21

H. M. S.
"Nelson" at
Port Moresby
A22

1934, Nov. 6

110	A21	1p dull green	1.10	3.50
111	A22	2p red brown	2.00	3.00
112	A21	3p blue	2.00	3.00
113	A22	5p violet brown	12.00	18.00
		Nos. 110-113 (4)	17.10	27.50
		Set, never hinged	27.50	

Declaration of British Protection, 50th anniv.

Silver Jubilee Issue
Stamps of 1932 Issue Overprinted in
Black

a   b

1935, July 9 — Glazed Paper

114	A5(a)	1p yellow grn & blk	1.20	4.00
115	A6(b)	2p light red	3.50	5.00
116	A5(a)	3p lt blue & blk	2.25	4.00
117	A5(a)	5p grnsh slate & blk	2.25	4.00
		Nos. 114-117 (4)	9.20	17.00
		Set, never hinged	16.50	

25th anniv. of the reign of George V.

Coronation Issue

King George
VI — A22a

Unwmk.

1937, May 14 — Engr. — Perf. 11

118	A22a	1p green	.40	.25
119	A22a	2p salmon rose	.40	1.50
120	A22a	3p blue	.40	1.50
121	A22a	5p brown violet	.40	2.00
		Nos. 118-121 (4)	1.60	5.25
		Set, never hinged	2.50	

AIR POST STAMPS

Regular Issue
of 1916
Overprinted

1929 — Wmk. 74 — Perf. 14

C1	A3	3p blue grn & dk gray	2.00	12.50
b.		Vert. pair, one without ovpt.	6,000.	
c.		Horiz. pair, one without ovpt.	6,500.	
d.		3p blue grn & sepia blk	57.50	75.00
e.		Overprint on back, vert.	5,000.	

No. C1 exists on white and on yellowish paper, No. C1d on yellowish paper only.

Regular Issues
of 1916-23
Overprinted in
Red

1930, Sept. 15 — Wmk. 74

C2	A3	3p blue grn & blk	2.00	7.00
a.		Yellowish paper	2,200.	3,750.
b.		Double overprint	1,500.	
C3	A3	6p violet & dull vio	8.00	12.00
a.		Yellowish paper	5.00	19.00
C4	A3	1sh ol green & ol brn	6.00	17.50
a.		Inverted overprint	11,000.	
b.		Yellowish paper	10.00	26.00
		Nos. C2-C4 (3)	16.00	36.50

Port Moresby
AP1

Unwmk.

1938, Sept. 6 — Engr. — Perf. 11

C5	AP1	2p carmine	2.75	3.25
C6	AP1	3p ultra	2.75	2.50
C7	AP1	5p dark green	2.75	3.50
C8	AP1	8p red brown	6.50	21.00
C9	AP1	1sh violet	17.50	22.50
		Nos. C5-C9 (5)	32.25	52.75
		Set, never hinged	65.00	

Papua as a British possession, 50th anniv.

Papuans
Poling
Rafts — AP2

1939-41

C10	AP2	2p carmine	3.00	6.00
C11	AP2	3p ultra	3.00	11.00
C12	AP2	5p dark green	3.00	2.25
C13	AP2	8p red brown	7.50	3.25
C14	AP2	1sh violet	9.00	9.00
C15	AP2	1sh6p lt olive ('41)	27.50	40.00
		Nos. C10-C15 (6)	53.00	71.50
		Set, never hinged	90.00	

OFFICIAL STAMPS

Nos. 60-63,
66-71, 92-93
Overprinted

1931 — Wmk. 74 — Perf. 14½

O1	A3	½p #60	2.50	5.50
O2	A3	1p #61	5.00	13.00
O3	A3	1½p #62	2.00	14.00
O4	A3	2p #63	4.50	14.00
O5	A3	3p #66	3.00	25.00
O6	A3	4p #67	3.00	21.00
O7	A3	5p #68	7.00	42.50
O8	A3	6p #69	5.00	9.75
O9	A3	1sh #70	11.00	35.00
O10	A3	2sh6p #71	47.50	97.50

1932 — Wmk. 228 — Perf. 11½

O11	A3	9p #92	37.50	55.00
O12	A3	1sh3p #93	37.50	55.00
		Nos. O1-O12 (12)	165.50	387.25

PARAGUAY

ˈpar-ə-ˌgwī

LOCATION — South America, bounded by Bolivia, Brazil and Argentina
GOVT. — Republic
AREA — 157,042 sq. mi.
POP. — 3,477,000 (1983)
CAPITAL — Asuncion

10 Reales = 100 Centavos = 1 Peso

Vigilant Lion Supporting Liberty Cap
A1   A2

A3

1870, Aug. Unwmk. Litho. Imperf.

1	A1 1r rose	9.00	16.50
	On cover		2,000.
	On cover, pen canceled		1,000.
a.	1r bright rose	4.50	9.
	On cover		2,100.
	On cover, pen canceled		1,100.
2	A2 2r blue	100.00	150.00
	On cover		4,000.
a.	2r dark blue		125.
	On cover		5,000.
3	A3 3r black	225.00	225.00
	On cover		8,000.
	On cover, pen canceled		1,000.
	Nos. 1-3 (3)	334.00	391.50

Counterfeits of 2r in blue and other colors are on thicker paper than originals. They show a colored dot in upper part of "S" of "DOS" in upper right corner.
For surcharges see Nos. 4-9, 19.

Handstamp Surcharged

1878 Black Surcharge

4	A1 5c on 1r rose	80.	110.
	On cover (see footnote)		10,000.
5	A2 5c on 2r blue	325.	300.
	On cover		13,000.
5E	A3 5c on 3r black	450.	450.
	On cover		15,000.
	Nos. 4-5E (3)	855.00	860.00

Blue Surcharge

5F	A1 5c on 1r rose	80.	110.
	On cover (see footnote)		10,000.
5H	A2 5c on 2r blue	1,000.	1,000.
	On cover		13,000.
6	A3 5c on 3r black	425.	425.
	On cover		15,000.
	Nos. 5F-6 (3)	1,505.	1,535.

The surcharge may be found inverted, double, sideways and omitted.
Remainders of Nos. 4 and 5F were placed on sale at Post Offices during 1892. Covers dated 1892 are worth about $7,500.
The originals are surcharged in dull black or dull blue. The reprints are in intense black and bright blue. The reprint surcharges are over-inked and show numerous breaks in the handstamp.

Handstamp Surcharged

Black Surcharge
|7|A2 5c on 2r blue|500.00|425.00|
| |On cover| |13,000.|

|8|A3 5c on 3r black|425.00|425.00|
| |On cover| |15,000.|

Blue Surcharge
9	A3 5c on 3r black	250.00	250.00
	On cover		15,000.
a.	Dbl. surch., large & small "5"	—
	Nos. 7-9 (3)	1,175.	1,100.

The surcharge on Nos. 7, 8 and 9 is usually placed sideways. It may be found double or inverted on Nos. 8 and 9.
Nos. 4 to 9 have been extensively counterfeited.
Two examples recorded of No. 9a, one without gum, the other with full but disturbed original gum.

A4   A4a

1879 Litho. Perf. 12½
Thin Paper
10	A4 5r orange		1.25
11	A4 10r red brown		1.50
a.	Imperf.		
b.	Horiz. pair, imperf. vert.		60.00

Nos. 10 and 11 were never placed in use.
For surcharges see Nos. 17-18.

1879-81 Thin Paper
12	A4a 5c orange brown	2.50	2.00
	On cover		500.00
a.	5c reddish brown	2.00	2.00
	On cover		525.00
13	A4a 10c blue grn ('81)	3.50	3.00
	On cover		700.00
a.	Imperf., pair	10.00	12.00

Reprints of Nos. 10-13 are imperf., perf. 11½, 12, 12½ or 14. They have yellowish gum and the 10c is deep green.

A5   A6

A7

1881, Aug. Litho. Perf. 11½-13½
14	A5 1c blue	.80	.70
	On cover		
a.	Imperf., pair		
b.	Horiz. pair, imperf. btwn.		
15	A6 2c rose red	.80	.70
	On cover		300.00
a.	2c dull orange red	1.00	.90
	On cover		300.00
b.	Imperf., pair	—	
c.	Horiz. pair, imperf. vert.	25.00	25.00
d.	Vert. pair, imperf. horiz.	25.00	25.00
16	A7 4c brown	.80	.70
	On cover		650.00
a.	Imperf., pair	—	
b.	Horiz. pair, imperf. vert.	25.00	25.00
c.	Vert. pair, imperf. horiz.	25.00	25.00

No. 11 Handstamped Surcharge in Black or Gray

1881, July Perf. 12½
17	A4 1c on 10c blue grn	15.00	10.00
	On cover		400.00
18	A4 2c on 10c blue grn	15.00	10.00
	On cover		450.00

Gray handstamps sell for 10 times more than black as many specialists consider the black to be reprints.

No. 1 Handstamped Surcharge in Black

1884, May 8 Imperf.
|19|A1 1c on 1r rose|10.00|8.00|
| |On cover| |1,750.|

The surcharges on Nos. 17-19 exist double, inverted and in pairs with one omitted. Counterfeits exist.

Seal of the Treasury
A11   A12

1884, Aug. 3 Litho. Perf. 12½
20	A11 1c green	1.00	.80
	On cover		35.00
21	A11 2c rose pink, thin paper	1.00	.80
b.	2c rose red, thin paper	.85	.85
c.	2c red, thick paper, perf. 11½	.70	.85

Perf. 11½
22	A11 5c pale blue, yellowish paper	1.00	.80
b.	5c blue, thin paper, perf. 12½	.65	.65
c.	5c pale blue, thin paper, perf. 12½	.65	.65
d.	5c blue, thin paper	3.75	3.75
e.	5c pale blue, thin paper	2.50	2.50
f.	5c blue, thick paper	11.50	9.00
	Nos. 20-22 (3)	3.00	2.40

There are two types of each value differing mostly in the shape of the numerals. In addition, there are numerous small flaws in the lithographic transfers.
For overprints see Nos. O1, O8, O15.

Imperf., Pairs
20a	A11 1c green	12.50
21a	A11 2c rose red	16.00
d.	2c red, thick paper	10.00
22a	A11 5c blue	16.00
	Nos. 20a-22a (3)	44.50

Perf. 11½, 11½x12, 12½x11½
1887 Typo.
23	A12 1c green	.30	.25
24	A12 2c rose	.30	.25
25	A12 5c blue	.50	.35
26	A12 7c brown	.90	.50
27	A12 10c lilac	.60	.35
28	A12 15c orange	.60	.35
29	A12 20c pink	.60	.35
	Nos. 23-29 (7)	3.80	2.40

See #42-45. For surcharges & overprints see #46, 49-50, 71-72, 167-170A, O20-O41, O49.

Symbols of Liberty from Coat of Arms — A13

1889, Feb. Litho. Perf. 11½
|30|A13 15c red violet|2.50|2.00|
|a.|Imperf., pair|10.00|8.00|

For overprints see Nos. O16-O19.

Overprint Handstamped in Violet

1892, Oct. 12 Perf. 12x12½
|31|A15 10c violet blue|10.00|5.00|

Discovery of America by Columbus, 400th anniversary. Overprint reads: "1492 / 12 DE OCTUBRE / 1892." Sold only on day of issue.

Cirilo A. Rivarola — A15

Designs: 2c, Salvador Jovellanos. 4c, Juan B. Gil. 5c, Higinio Uriarte. 10c, Cándido Bareiro. 14c, Gen. Bernardino Caballero. 20c, Gen. Patricio Escobar. 30c, Juan G. González.

1892-96 Litho. Perf. 12x12½
32	A15 1c gray (centavos)	.25	.25
33	A15 1c gray (centavo) ('96)	.25	.25
34	A15 2c green	.25	.25
a.	Chalky paper ('96)	.25	.25
35	A15 4c carmine	.25	.25
a.	Chalky paper ('96)	.25	.25
36	A15 5c violet ('93)	.25	.25
a.	Chalky paper ('96)	.25	.25
37	A15 10c vio bl (punched) ('93)	.25	.25
	Unpunched ('96)	5.00	
38	A15 10c dull blue ('96)	.25	.25
39	A15 14c yellow brown	.75	.50
40	A15 20c red ('93)	1.25	.50
41	A15 30c light green	2.00	.80
	Nos. 32-41 (10)	5.75	3.55

The 10c violet blue (No. 37) was, until 1896, issued punched with a circular hole in order to prevent it being fraudulently overprinted as No. 31.
Nos. 33 and 38 are on chalky paper.
For surcharge see No. 70.

Seal Type of 1887
1892 Typo.
42	A12 40c slate blue	3.00	1.25
43	A12 60c yellow	1.50	.50
44	A12 80c light blue	1.40	.50
45	A12 1p olive green	1.40	.50
	Nos. 42-45 (4)	7.30	2.75

For surcharges see Nos. 71-72.

No. 26 Surcharged in Black

1895, Aug. 1 Perf. 11½x12
|46|A12 5c on 7c brown|.75|.75|

Telegraph Stamps Surcharged

1896, Apr. Engr. Perf. 11½
Denomination in Black
47	5c on 2c brown & gray	.90	.60
a.	Inverted surcharge	10.00	10.00
48	5c on 4c yellow & gray	.90	.60
a.	Inverted surcharge	7.50	7.50

Nos. 28, 42 Surcharged

1898-99 Typo.
49	A12 10c on 15c org ('99)	.75	.45
a.	Inverted surcharge	17.50	17.50
b.	Double surcharge	11.00	11.00
50	A12 10c on 40c slate bl	.35	.25

Surcharge on No. 49 has small "c."

Telegraph Stamps Surcharged
1900, May 14 Engr. Perf. 11½
|50A|5c on 30c grn, gray & blk|2.75|1.50|
|50B|10c on 50c dl vio, gray & blk|6.00|3.75|

The basic telegraph stamps are like those used for Nos. 47-48, but the surcharges on Nos. 50A-50B consist of "5 5" and "10 10" above a blackout rectangle covering the engraved denominations.

A 40c red, bluish gray and black telegraph stamp (basic type of A24) was used provisionally in August, 1900, for postage. Value, postally used, $5.

Seal of the Treasury — A25

1900, Sept.　Engr.　Perf. 11½, 12

51	A25	2c gray	.40	.30
52	A25	3c orange brown	.40	.30
53	A25	5c dark green	.40	.30
54	A25	8c dark brown	.40	.30
55	A25	10c carmine rose	1.00	.30
56	A25	24c deep blue	1.20	.30
		Nos. 51-56 (6)	3.80	1.80

See Nos. 57-67. For surcharges see Nos. 69, 74, 76, 156-157.

Small Figures

1901, Apr.　Litho.　Perf. 11½

57	A25	2c rose	.25	.25
58	A25	5c violet brown	.25	.25
59	A25	40c blue	.85	.30
		Nos. 57-59 (3)	1.35	.80

1901-02　　　　Larger Figures

60	A25	1c gray green ('02)	.30	.30
61	A25	2c gray	.30	.30
a.		Half used as 1c on cover		10.00
62	A25	4c pale blue	.30	.30
63	A25	5c violet	.30	.30
64	A25	8c gray brown ('02)	.30	.30
65	A25	10c rose red ('02)	.75	.30
66	A25	28c orange ('02)	1.50	.30
67	A25	40c blue	.75	.30
		Nos. 60-67 (8)	4.50	2.40

For surcharges see Nos. 74, 76.

J. B. Eguszquiza — A26

Chalky Paper

1901, Sept. 24　Typo.　Perf. 12x12½

68	A26	1p slate	.30	.25

For surcharge see No. 73.

No. 56 Surcharged in Red

1902, Aug.

69	A25	20c on 24c dp blue	.50	.40
a.		Inverted surcharge	6.25	

Counterfeit surcharges exist.

Nos. 39, 43-44 Surcharged

1902, Dec. 22　　　　Perf. 12x12½

70	A15	1c on 14c yellow brn	.25	.25
a.		No period after "cent"	.90	.75
b.		Comma after "cent"	.65	.50
c.		Accent over "Un"	.65	.50

1903　　　　　　　　Perf. 11½

71	A12	5c on 60c yellow	.35	.30
72	A12	5c on 80c lt blue	.30	.30

Nos. 68, 64, 66 Surcharged

#73　　　　　　　　　#74

#76

1902-03　　　　　　Perf. 12

73	A26	1c on 1p slate ('03)	.40	.40
a.		No period after "cent"	3.25	3.00

Perf. 11½

74	A25	5c on 8c gray brown	.50	.40
a.		No period after "cent"	1.75	1.50
b.		Double surcharge	7.00	6.00
76	A25	5c on 28c orange	.50	.40
a.		No period after "cent"	1.75	1.50
b.		Comma after "cent"	.80	.60
		Nos. 73-76 (3)	1.40	1.20

The surcharge on Nos. 73 and 74 is found reading both upward and downward.

Sentinel Lion with Right Paw Ready to Strike for "Peace and Justice"

A32　　　　　　　A33

Perf. 11½

1903, Feb. 28　Litho.　Unwmk.

77	A32	1c gray	.30	.30
78	A32	2c blue green	.45	.30
79	A32	5c blue	.60	.30
80	A32	10c orange brown	.75	.30
81	A32	20c carmine	.75	.30
82	A32	30c deep blue	.90	.30
83	A32	60c purple	2.10	1.00
		Nos. 77-83 (7)	5.85	2.80

For surcharges and overprints see Nos. 139-140, 166, O50-O56.

1903, Sept.

84	A33	1c yellow green	.30	.30
85	A33	2c red orange	.30	.30
86	A33	5c dark blue	.45	.30
87	A33	10c purple	.45	.30
88	A33	20c dark green	5.00	.45
89	A33	30c ultramarine	1.50	.30
90	A33	60c ocher	1.75	.75
		Nos. 84-90 (7)	9.75	2.70

Nos. 84-90 exist imperf. Value for pairs, $3 each for 1c-20c, $4 for 30c, $5 for 60c.

The three-line overprint "Gobierno provisorio Ago. 1904" is fraudulent.

Sentinel Lion at Rest

A35　　　　　　　A36

Perf. 11½, 12, 11½x12

1905-10　　　　　　　　Engr.

Dated "1904"

91	A35	1c orange	.30	.25
92	A35	1c vermilion ('07)	.30	.25
93	A35	1c grnsh bl ('07)	.30	.25
94	A35	2c vermilion ('06)	.30	.25
95	A35	2c olive grn ('07)	60.00	
96	A35	2c car rose ('08)	.45	.25
97	A35	5c dark blue	.30	.25
98	A35	5c slate blue ('06)	.30	.25
99	A35	5c yellow ('06)	.30	.25
100	A35	10c bister ('06)	.30	.25
101	A35	10c emerald ('07)	.30	.25
102	A35	10c dp ultra ('08)	.30	.25
103	A35	20c violet ('06)	.45	.25
104	A35	20c bister ('07)	.45	.25

105	A35	20c apple grn ('07)	.45	.25
106	A35	30c turq bl ('06)	.65	.25
107	A35	30c blue gray ('07)	.65	.25
108	A35	30c dull lilac ('08)	.90	.25
109	A35	60c chocolate ('07)	.60	.25
110	A35	60c org brn ('07)	5.25	1.60
111	A35	60c salmon pink ('10)	5.25	1.60
		Nos. 91-111 (21)	78.10	
		Nos. 91-94,96-111 (20)	18.10	7.70

All but Nos. 92 and 104 exist imperf. Value for pair, $10 each, except No. 95 at $35.00 and Nos. 109-111 at $15.00 each pair.

For surcharges and overprints see Nos. 129-130, 146-155, 174-190, 266.

1904, Aug.　Litho.　Perf. 11½

112	A36	10c light blue	.50	.40
a.		Imperf., pair	6.00	

No. 112 Surcharged in Black

1904, Dec.

113	A36	30c on 10c light blue	.80	.50

Peace between a successful revolutionary party and the government previously in power.

Governmental Palace, Asunción — A37

Center in Black

Dated "1904"

1906-10　Engr.　Perf. 11½, 12

114	A37	1p bright rose	2.50	1.50
115	A37	1p brown org ('07)	1.00	.50
116	A37	1p ol gray ('07)	1.00	.50
117	A37	2p turquoise ('07)	.50	.40
118	A37	2p lake ('09)	.50	.40
119	A37	2p brn org ('10)	.60	.40
120	A37	5p red ('07)	1.50	1.00
121	A37	5p ol grn ('10)	1.50	1.00
122	A37	5p dull bl ('10)	1.50	1.00
123	A37	10p brown org ('07)	1.40	1.00
124	A37	10p dp blue ('10)	1.40	1.00
125	A37	10p choc ('10)	1.50	1.00
126	A37	20p olive grn ('10)	3.50	3.25
127	A37	20p violet ('10)	3.50	3.25
128	A37	20p yellow ('10)	3.50	3.25
		Nos. 114-128 (15)	25.40	19.45

Nos. 94 and 95 Surcharged

1907

129	A35	5c on 2c vermilion	.45	.30
a.		"5" omitted	1.50	1.50
b.		Inverted surcharge	5.25	5.25
c.		Double surcharge		
d.		Double surcharge, one inverted	1.50	1.50
e.		Double surcharge, both invtd.	9.00	9.00
130	A35	5c on 2c olive grn	.60	.30
a.		"5" omitted	1.50	1.50
b.		Inverted surcharge	1.50	1.50
c.		Double surcharge	3.00	3.00
d.		Bar omitted	3.00	3.00

Official Stamps of 1906-08 Surcharged

1908

131	O17	5c on 10c bister	.45	.30
a.		Double surcharge	4.50	4.50
132	O17	5c on 10c violet	.45	.30
a.		Inverted surcharge	3.50	3.50
133	O17	5c on 20c emerald	.45	.30
134	O17	5c on 20c violet	.45	.30
a.		Inverted surcharge	3.50	3.50

135	O17	5c on 30c slate bl	1.50	1.00
136	O17	5c on 30c turq bl	1.50	1.00
a.		Double surcharge		
b.		Double surcharge	9.00	9.00
137	O17	5c on 60c choc	.45	.30
a.		Double surcharge	9.00	9.00
138	O17	5c on 60c red brown	.90	.30
a.		Inverted surcharge	1.60	1.60
		Nos. 131-138 (8)	6.15	3.80

Same Surcharge on Official Stamps of 1903

139	A32	5c on 30c dp blue	3.75	3.25
140	A32	5c on 60c purple	1.50	.90
a.		Double surcharge	7.50	7.50

Official Stamps of 1906-08 Overprinted

141	O17	5c deep blue	.40	.40
a.		Inverted overprint	3.00	3.00
b.		Bar omitted	9.00	9.00
c.		Double overprint	4.00	4.00
142	O17	5c slate blue	.50	.40
a.		Inverted overprint	4.00	4.00
b.		Double overprint	3.50	3.50
c.		Bar omitted	9.00	9.00
143	O17	5c greenish blue	.40	.40
a.		Inverted overprint	2.50	2.50
b.		Bar omitted	7.50	7.50
144	O18	1p brown org & blk	.50	.50
a.		Double overprint	2.00	2.00
b.		Double overprint, one inverted	2.50	2.50
c.		Triple overprint, two inverted	4.50	4.50
145	O18	1p brt rose & blk	.90	.70
a.		Bar omitted		
		Nos. 141-145 (5)	2.70	2.40

Regular Issues of 1906-08 Surcharged

1908

146	A35	5c on 1c grnsh bl	.30	.30
a.		Inverted surcharge	1.50	1.50
b.		Double surcharge	2.25	2.25
c.		"5" omitted	2.25	2.25
147	A35	5c on 2c car rose	.30	.30
a.		Inverted surcharge	2.50	2.50
b.		"5" omitted	3.00	3.00
c.		Double surcharge	5.25	5.25
d.		Double surcharge, one invtd.		
148	A35	5c on 60c org brn	.30	.30
a.		Inverted surcharge	3.75	3.75
b.		"5" omitted	1.50	1.50
149	A35	5c on 60c sal pink	.30	.30
a.		Double surcharge	.75	.75
b.		Double surcharge, one invtd.	5.25	5.25
150	A35	5c on 60c choc	.30	.30
a.		Inverted surcharge	7.50	7.50
151	A35	20c on 1c grnsh bl	.30	.30
a.		Inverted surcharge	2.25	2.25
152	A35	20c on 2c ver	9.00	7.50
153	A35	20c on 2c car rose	5.25	4.50
a.		Inverted surcharge	19.00	
154	A35	20c on 30c dl lil	.30	.30
a.		Inverted surcharge	2.25	2.25
b.		Double surcharge		
155	A35	20c on 30c turq bl	2.25	2.25
		Nos. 146-155 (10)	18.60	16.35

Same Surcharge on Regular Issue of 1901-02

156	A25	5c on 28c org	1.90	1.60
157	A25	5c on 40c dk bl	.60	.45
a.		Inverted surcharge	6.00	6.00

Same Surcharge on Official Stamps of 1908

158	O17	5c on 10c emer	.40	.40
a.		Double surcharge	14.00	
159	O17	5c on 10c red lil	.40	.40
a.		Double surcharge	4.00	4.00
b.		"5" omitted	3.00	3.00
160	O17	5c on 20c bis	.80	.60
a.		Double surcharge	2.50	2.50
161	O17	5c on 20c sal pink	.80	.60
a.		"5" omitted	3.50	3.50
162	O17	5c on 30c bl gray	.40	.40
163	O17	5c on 30c yel	.40	.40
a.		"5" omitted	3.00	3.00
b.		Inverted surcharge	2.50	2.50
164	O17	5c on 60c org brn	.40	.40
a.		Double surcharge	12.00	12.00
165	O17	5c on 60c dp ultra	.40	.40
a.		Inverted surcharge	5.00	5.00
b.		"5" omitted	3.00	
		Nos. 158-165 (8)	4.00	3.60

Same Surcharge on No. O52

166	A32	20c on 5c blue	2.50	2.00
a.		Inverted surcharge	6.00	7.50

Stamp of 1887
Surcharged

1908 **On Stamp of 1887**
167 A12 20c on 2c car 6.50 3.00
a. Inverted surcharge 22.50

On Official Stamps of 1892
168 A12 5c on 15c org 7.50 5.25
169 A12 5c on 20c pink 120.00 95.00
170 A12 5c on 50c gray 52.50 37.50
170A A12 20c on 5c blue 4.50 3.75
b. Inverted surcharge 25.00 25.00
Nos. 167-170A (5) 191.00 144.50

Nos. 151, 152, 153, 155, 167, 170A, while duly authorized, all appear to have been sold to a single individual, and although they paid postage, it is doubtful whether they can be considered as ever having been placed on sale to the public.

Nos. O82-O84
Surcharged
(Date in Red)

1908-09
171 O18 1c on 1p brt rose & blk .50 .50
172 O18 1c on 1p lake & blk .50 .50
173 O18 1c on 1p brn org & blk ('09) 5.00 5.00
Nos. 171-173 (3) 6.00 6.00

Varieties of surcharge on Nos. 171-173 include: "CETTAVO"; date omitted, double or inverted; third line double or omitted.

Types of 1905-1910
Overprinted

1908, Mar. 5 **Perf. 11½**
174 A35 1c emerald .30 .30
175 A35 5c yellow .30 .30
176 A35 10c lilac brown .30 .30
177 A35 20c yellow orange .30 .30
178 A35 30c red .40 .30
179 A35 60c magenta .30 .30
180 A37 1p light blue .30 .30
Nos. 174-180 (7) 2.20 2.10

Overprinted

1909, Sept.
181 A35 1c blue gray .40 .40
182 A35 1c scarlet .40 .40
183 A35 5c dark green .40 .40
184 A35 5c deep orange .40 .40
185 A35 10c rose .40 .40
186 A35 10c bister brown .40 .40
187 A35 20c yellow .40 .40
188 A35 20c violet .40 .40
189 A35 30c orange brown .60 .40
190 A35 30c dull blue .60 .40
Nos. 181-190 (10) 4.40 4.00

Counterfeits exist.

Coat of Arms
above Numeral
of Value
A38

"The Republic"
A39

1910-21 **Litho.** **Perf. 11½**
191 A38 1c brown .40 .25
192 A38 5c bright violet .40 .25
a. Pair, imperf. between 2.00 2.00
193 A38 5c blue grn ('19) .40 .25
194 A38 5c lt blue ('21) .40 .25
195 A38 10c yellow green .40 .25
196 A38 10c dp vio ('19) .40 .25
197 A38 10c red ('21) .40 .25
198 A38 20c red .40 .25
199 A38 50c car rose .60 .25
200 A38 75c deep blue .40 .25
a. Diag. half perforated ('11) .40 .25
Nos. 191-200 (10) 4.20 2.50

Nos. 191-200 exist imperforate.
No. 200a was authorized for use as 20c.
For surcharges see Nos. 208, 241, 261, 265.

1911 **Engr.**
201 A39 1c olive grn & blk .30 .30
202 A39 2c dk blue & blk .45 .30
203 A39 5c carmine & indigo .45 .30
204 A39 10c dp blue & brn .45 .30
205 A39 20c olive grn & ind .60 .30
206 A39 50c lilac & indigo .75 .30
207 A39 75c ol grn & red lil .75 .30
Nos. 201-207 (7) 3.75 2.10

Centenary of National Independence.
The 1c, 2c, 10c and 50c exist imperf. Value for pairs, $2.25 each.

No. 199 Surcharged

1912
208 A38 20c on 50c car rose .30 .30
a. Inverted surcharge 1.90 1.90
b. Double surcharge 1.90 1.90
c. Bar omitted 2.50 2.50

National Coat of
Arms — A40

1913 **Engr.** **Perf. 11½**
209 A40 1c gray .30 .25
210 A40 2c orange .30 .25
211 A40 5c lilac .30 .25
212 A40 10c green .30 .25
213 A40 20c dull red .30 .25
214 A40 40c rose .30 .25
215 A40 75c deep blue .30 .25
216 A40 80c yellow .30 .25
217 A40 1p light blue .45 .25
218 A40 1.25p pale blue .45 .25
219 A40 3p greenish blue .45 .25
Nos. 209-219 (11) 3.75 2.75

For surcharges see Nos. 225, 230-231, 237, 242, 253, 262-263, L3-L4.

Nos. J7-J10
Overprinted

1918
220 D2 5c yellow brown .25 .25
221 D2 10c yellow brown .25 .25
222 D2 20c yellow brown .25 .25
223 D2 40c yellow brown .25 .25

Nos. J10 and 214
Surcharged

224 D2 5c on 40c yellow brn .25 .25
225 A40 30c on 40c rose .25 .25
Nos. 220-225 (6) 1.50 1.50

Nos. 220-225 exist with surcharge inverted, double and double with one inverted.
The surcharge "Habilitado-1918-5 cents 5" on the 1c gray official stamps of 1914, is bogus.

No. J11 Overprinted

1920
229 D2 1p yellow brown .25 .25
a. Inverted overprint .65 .65
e. As "g," "AABILITADO" .75 .75
f. As "g," "1929" for "1920" .75 .75
g. Overprint lines 8mm apart .25 .25

Nos. 216 and 219
Surcharged

230 A40 50c on 80c yellow .25 .25
231 A40 1.75p on 3p grnsh bl .75 .65

Same Surcharge on No. J12
232 D2 1p on 1.50p yel brn .25 .25
Nos. 229-232 (4) 1.50 1.40

Nos. 229-232 exist with various surcharge errors, including inverted, double, double inverted and double with one inverted. Those that were issued are listed.

Parliament
Building
A41

1920 **Litho.** **Perf. 11½**
233 A41 50c red & black .35 .30
a. "CORRLOS" 5.00 5.00
234 A41 1p lt blue & blk 1.00 .45
235 A41 1.75p dk blue & blk .30 .30
236 A41 3p orange & blk 1.50 .30
Nos. 233-236 (4) 3.15 1.35

50th anniv. of the Constitution.
All values exist imperforate and Nos. 233, 235 and 236 with center inverted. It is doubtful that any of these varieties were regularly issued.

No. 215 Surcharged

1920
237 A40 50c on 75c deep blue .60 .40

Nos. 200, 215
Surcharged

1921
241 A38 50c on 75c deep blue .40 .40
242 A40 50c on 75c deep blue .40 .40

A42

1922, Feb. 8 **Litho.** **Perf. 11½**
243 A42 50c car & dk blue .40 .40
a. Imperf. pair 1.00
b. Center inverted 20.00 20.00
244 A42 1p dk blue & brn .40 .40
a. Imperf. pair 1.00
b. Center inverted 25.00 25.00

For overprints see Nos. L1-L2.

Rendezvous
of
Conspirators
A43

1922-23
245 A43 1p deep blue .40 .40
246 A43 1p scar & dk bl ('23) .40 .40
247 A43 1p red vio & gray ('23) .40 .40
248 A43 1p org & gray ('23) .40 .40
249 A43 5p dark violet 1.20 .40
250 A43 5p dk bl & org brn ('23) 1.20 .40
251 A43 5p dl red & lt bl ('23) 1.20 .40
252 A43 5p emer & blk ('23) 1.20 .40
Nos. 245-252 (8) 6.40 3.20

National Independence.

No. 218 Surcharged "Habilitado en $1:-1924" in Red

1924
253 A40 1p on 1.25p pale blue .40 .40

This stamp was for use in Asunción. Nos. L3 to L5 were for use in the interior, as is indicated by the "C" in the surcharge.

Map of
Paraguay — A44

1924 **Litho.** **Perf. 11½**
254 A44 1p dark blue .40 .40
255 A44 2p carmine rose .40 .40
256 A44 4p light blue .40 .40
a. Perf. 12 .80 .40
Nos. 254-256 (3) 1.20 1.20

#254-256 exist imperf. Value $3 each pair.
For surcharges and overprint see Nos. 267, C5, C15-C16, C54-C55, L7.

Gen. José E.
Díaz — A45

1925-26 **Perf. 11½, 12**
257 A45 50c red .25 .25
258 A45 1p dark blue .25 .25
259 A45 1p emerald ('26) .25 .25
Nos. 257-259 (3) .75 .75

#257-258 exist imperf. Value $1 each pair.
For overprints see Nos. L6, L8, L10.

Columbus — A46

1925 **Perf. 11½**
260 A46 1p blue .50 .40
a. Imperf., pair 3.00

For overprint see No. L9.

Nos. 194, 214-215, J12
Surcharged in Black or
Red

1926
261 A38 1c on 5c lt blue .25 .25
262 A40 7c on 40c rose .25 .25
263 A40 15c on 75c dp bl (R) .25 .25
264 D2 1.50p on 1.50p yel brn .25 .25
Nos. 261-264 (4) 1.00 1.00

Nos. 194, 179 and 256 Surcharged "Habilitado" and New Values

1927
265	A38	2c on 5c lt blue	.25	.25
266	A35	50c on 60c magenta	.25	.25
a.		Inverted surcharge	2.00	
267	A44	1.50p on 4p lt blue	.25	.25

Official Stamp of 1914 Surcharged "Habilitado" and New Value

268	O19	50c on 75c dp bl	.25	.25
		Nos. 265-268 (4)	1.00	1.00

National Emblem — A47

Pedro Juan Caballero — A48

Map of Paraguay — A49

Fulgencio Yegros — A50

Ignacio Iturbe — A51

Oratory of the Virgin, Asunción — A52

Perf. 12, 11, 11½, 11x12

1927-38   **Typo.**
269	A47	1c lt red ('31)	.25	.25
270	A47	2c org red ('30)	.25	.25
271	A47	7c lilac	.25	.25
272	A47	7c emerald ('29)	.25	.25
273	A47	10c gray grn ('28)	.25	.25
a.		10c light green ('31)	.25	.25
274	A47	10c lil rose ('30)	.25	.25
275	A47	10c light bl ('35)	.25	.25
276	A47	20c dull bl ('28)	.25	.25
277	A47	20c lil brn ('30)	.25	.25
278	A47	20c lt vio ('31)	.25	.25
279	A47	20c rose ('35)	.25	.25
280	A47	50c ultramarine	.25	.25
281	A47	50c dl red ('28)	.25	.25
282	A47	50c orange ('30)	.25	.25
283	A47	50c gray ('31)	.25	.25
284	A47	50c brn vio ('34)	.25	.25
285	A47	50c rose ('36)	.25	.25
286	A47	70c ultra ('28)	.25	.25
287	A48	1p emerald	.25	.25
288	A48	1p org red ('30)	.25	.25
289	A48	1p brn org ('34)	.25	.25
290	A49	1.50p brown	.25	.25
291	A49	1.50p lilac ('28)	.25	.25
292	A49	1.50p rose red ('32)	.25	.25
293	A50	2.50p bister	.25	.25
294	A51	3p gray	.25	.25
295	A51	3p rose red ('36)	.25	.25
296	A51	3p brt vio ('36)	.25	.25
297	A52	5p chocolate	.25	.25
298	A52	5p violet ('36)	.25	.25
299	A52	5p pale org ('38)	.25	.25
300	A49	20p red ('29)	7.00	5.50
301	A49	20p emerald ('29)	7.00	5.50
302	A49	20p vio brn ('29)	7.00	5.50
		Nos. 269-302 (34)	28.75	24.25

No. 281 is also known perf. 10½x11½.
Papermaker's watermarks are sometimes found on No. 271 ("GLORIA BOND" in double-lined circle) and No. 280 ("Extra Vencedor Bond" or "ADBANCE/M M C").
For surcharges and overprints see Nos. 312, C4, C6, C13-C14, C17-C18, C25-C32, C34-C35, L11-L30, O94-O96, O98.

Arms of Juan de Salazar de Espinosa A53

Columbus A54

1928, Aug. 15   *Perf. 12*
303	A53	10p violet brown	3.00	2.00

Juan de Salazar de Espinosa, founder of Asunción.
A papermaker's watermark ("INDIAN BOND EXTRA STRONG S.&C") is sometimes found on Nos 303, 305-307.

1928   **Litho.**
304	A54	10p ultra	2.40	1.50
305	A54	10p vermilion	2.40	1.50
306	A54	10p deep red	2.40	1.50
		Nos. 304-306 (3)	7.20	4.50

For surcharge and overprint see Nos. C33, L37.

President Rutherford B. Hayes of US and Villa Occidental — A55

1928, Nov. 20   *Perf. 12*
307	A55	10p gray brown	10.00	3.50
308	A55	10p red brown	10.00	3.50

50th anniv. of the Hayes' Chaco decision.

Portraits of Archbishop Bogarin — A56

1930, Aug. 15
309	A56	1.50p lake	2.00	1.50
310	A56	1.50p turq blue	2.00	1.50
311	A56	1.50p dull vio	2.00	1.50
		Nos. 309-311 (3)	6.00	4.50

Archbishop Juan Sinforiano Bogarin, first archbishop of Paraguay.
For overprints see Nos. 321-322.

No. 272 Surcharged

1930
312	A47	5c on 7c emer	.25	.25

A57

1930-39   **Typo.**   *Perf. 11½, 12*
313	A57	10p brown	1.00	.40
314	A57	10p brn red, *bl* ('31)	1.00	.40
315	A57	10p dk bl, *pink* ('32)	1.00	.40

316	A57	10p gray brn ('36)	.80	.40
317	A57	10p gray ('37)	.80	.40
318	A57	10p blue ('39)	.40	.40
		Nos. 313-318 (6)	5.00	2.40

1st Paraguayan postage stamp, 60th anniv.
For overprint see No. L31.

Gunboat "Humaitá" — A58

1931   *Perf. 12*
319	A58	1.50p purple	.80	.50
		Nos. 319,C39-C53 (16)	25.75	18.05

Constitution, 60th anniv.
For overprint see No. L33.

View of San Bernardino — A59

1931, Aug.
320	A59	1p light green	.50	.40

Founding of San Bernardino, 50th anniv.
For overprint see No. L32.

Nos. 309-310 Overprinted in Blue or Red

1931, Dec. 31
321	A56	1.50p lake (Bl)	3.00	3.00
322	A56	1.50p turq blue (R)	3.00	3.00

Map of the Gran Chaco — A60

1932-35   **Typo.**   *Perf. 12*
323	A60	1.50p deep violet	.40	.40
324	A60	1.50p rose ('35)	.40	.40

For overprints see Nos. L34-L36, O97.

Nos. C74-C78 Surcharged

1933   **Litho.**
325	AP18	50c on 4p ultra	.50	.40
326	AP18	1p on 8p red	1.00	.80
327	AP18	1.50p on 12p bl grn	1.00	.80
328	AP18	2p on 16p dk vio	1.00	.80
329	AP18	5p on 20p org brn	2.25	1.75
		Nos. 325-329 (5)	5.75	4.55

Flag of the Race Issue

Flag with Three Crosses: Caravels of Columbus — A61

1933, Oct. 10   **Litho.**   *Perf. 11*
330	A61	10c multicolored	.60	.40
331	A61	20c multicolored	.60	.40
332	A61	50c multicolored	.60	.40
333	A61	1p multicolored	.60	.40
334	A61	1.50p multicolored	.60	.40
335	A61	2p multicolored	1.25	.50
336	A61	5p multicolored	1.25	1.00
337	A61	10p multicolored	1.25	1.00
		Nos. 330-337 (8)	6.75	4.50

441st anniv. of the sailing of Christopher Columbus from the port of Palos, Aug. 3, 1492, on his first voyage to the New World.
Nos. 332, 334 and 335 exist with Maltese crosses omitted.

Monstrance A62

Arms of Asunción A63

1937, Aug.   **Unwmk.**   *Perf. 11½*
338	A62	1p dk blue, yel & red	.40	.40
339	A62	3p dk blue, yel & red	.40	.40
340	A62	10p dk blue, yel & red	.40	.40
		Nos. 338-340 (3)	1.20	1.20

1st Natl. Eucharistic Congress, Asuncion.

1937, Aug.
341	A63	50c violet & buff	.60	.40
342	A63	1p bis & lt grn	.60	.40
343	A63	3p red & lt bl	.60	.40
344	A63	10p car rose & buff	.60	.40
345	A63	20p blue & drab	.60	.40
		Nos. 341-345 (5)	3.00	2.00

Founding of Asuncion, 400th anniv.

Oratory of the Virgin, Asunción — A64

1938-39   **Typo.**   *Perf. 11, 12*
346	A64	5p olive green	.60	.40
347	A64	5p pale rose ('39)	.60	.40
348	A64	11p violet brown	.80	.50
		Nos. 346-348 (3)	2.00	1.30

Founding of Asuncion, 400th anniv.

Carlos Antonio Lopez — A65

José Eduvigis Diaz — A66

1939

349	A65	2p lt ultra & pale brn	.90	.60
350	A66	2p lt ultra & brn	.90	.60

Reburial of ashes of Pres. Carlos Antonio Lopez (1790-1862) and Gen. José Eduvigis Diaz in the National Pantheon, Asuncion.

Pres. Patricio Escobar and Ramon Zubizarreta A67

Design: 5p, Pres. Bernardino Caballero and Senator José S. Decoud.

1939-40 Litho. Perf. 11½
Heads in Black

351	A67	50c dull org ('40)	.60	.60
352	A67	1p lt violet ('40)	.60	.60
353	A67	2p red brown ('40)	.60	.60
354	A67	5p lt ultra	.75	.60
		Nos. 351-354,C122-C123,O99-O104 (12)	27.55	26.20

Founding of the University of Asuncion, 50th anniv.

Varieties of this issue include inverted heads (50c, 1p, 2p); doubled heads; Caballero and Decoud heads in 50c frame: imperforates and part-perforates. Examples with inverted heads were not officially issued.

Coats of Arms — A69

Flags of Paraguay, United States — A70

Designs: 1p, Pres. Baldomir, flags of Paraguay, Uruguay. 2p, Pres. Benavides, flags of Paraguay, Peru. 5p, Pres. Alessandri, flags of Paraguay, Chile. 6p, Pres. Vargas, flags of Paraguay, Brazil. 10p, Pres. Ortiz, flags of Paraguay, Argentina.

1939 Engr.; Flags Litho. Perf. 12
Flags in National Colors

355	A69	50c violet blue	.30	.30
356	A70	1p olive	.30	.30
357	A70	2p blue green	.30	.30
358	A70	3p sepia	.35	.35
359	A70	5p orange	.30	.30
360	A70	6p dull violet	.75	.60
361	A70	10p bister brn	.60	.60
		Nos. 355-361,C113-C121 (16)	42.30	28.25

First Buenos Aires Peace Conference.
For overprint and surcharge, see Nos. 387, B10.

Coats of Arms of New York and Asunción A76

1939, Nov. 30

362	A76	5p scarlet	.80	.80
363	A76	10p deep blue	1.20	.80
364	A76	11p dk blue grn	1.20	1.20
365	A76	22p olive blk	2.00	1.60
		Nos. 362-365,C124-C126 (7)	33.95	31.40

New York World's Fair.

Paraguayan Soldier — A77

Paraguayan Woman — A78

Cowboys — A79

Plowing — A80

View of Paraguay River — A81

Oxcart A82

Pasture A83

Pirareta Falls — A84

1940, Jan. 1 Photo. Perf. 12½

366	A77	50c deep orange	.40	.25
367	A78	1p brt red violet	.40	.25
368	A79	3p bright green	.40	.25
369	A80	5p chestnut	.40	.25
370	A81	10p magenta	.40	.25
371	A82	20p violet	1.00	.30
372	A83	50p cobalt blue	2.00	.45
373	A84	100p black	4.00	1.40
		Nos. 366-373 (8)	9.00	3.40

Second Buenos Aires Peace Conference.
For surcharge see No. 386.

Map of the Americas — A85

1940, May Engr. Perf. 12

374	A85	50c red orange	.30	.25
375	A85	1p green	.30	.25
376	A85	5p dark blue	.50	.25
377	A85	10p brown	1.00	.50
		Nos. 374-377,C127-C130 (8)	12.20	9.20

Pan American Union, 50th anniversary.

Reproduction of Type A1 — A86

Sir Rowland Hill — A87

Designs: 6p, Type A2. 10p, Type A3.

1940, Aug. 15 Photo. Perf. 13½

378	A86	1p aqua & brt red vio	.50	.25
379	A87	5p dp yel grn & red brn	.65	.30
380	A86	6p org brn & ultra	1.50	.65
381	A86	10p ver & black	1.50	1.00
		Nos. 378-381 (4)	4.15	2.20

Postage stamp centenary.

Dr. José Francia
A90   A91

1940, Sept. 20 Engr. Perf. 12

382	A90	50c carmine rose	.30	.25
383	A91	50c plum	.30	.25
384	A90	1p bright green	.30	.25
385	A91	5p deep blue	.30	.25
		Nos. 382-385 (4)	1.20	1.00

Centenary of the death of Dr. Jose Francia (1766-1840), dictator of Paraguay, 1814-1840.

No. 366 Surcharged in Black

1940, Sept. 7 Perf. 12½

386	A77	5p on 50c dp org	.40	.25

In honor of Pres. Jose F. Estigarribia who died in a plane crash Sept. 7, 1940.

SEMI-POSTAL STAMPS

Red Cross Nurse SP1

Unwmk.
1930, July 22 Typo. Perf. 12

B1	SP1	1.50p + 50c gray violet	2.00	1.20
B2	SP1	1.50p + 50c deep rose	2.00	1.20
B3	SP1	1.50p + 50c dark blue	2.00	1.20
		Nos. B1-B3 (3)	6.00	3.60

The surtax was for the benefit of the Red Cross Society of Paraguay.

College of Agriculture — SP2

1930

B4	SP2	1.50p + 50c blue, pink	.60	.50

Surtax for the Agricultural Institute.
The sheet of No. B4 has a papermaker's watermark: "Vencedor Bond."
A 1.50p+50c red on yellow was prepared but not regularly issued. Value, 40 cents.

Red Cross Headquarters SP3

1932

B5	SP3	50c + 50c rose	.60	.60

AIR POST STAMPS

Official Stamps of 1913 Surcharged

1929, Jan. 1 Unwmk. Perf. 11½

C1	O19	2.85p on 5c lilac	2.25	1.50
C2	O19	5.65p on 10c grn	1.25	1.50
C3	O19	11.30p on 50c rose	2.00	1.25
		Nos. C1-C3 (3)	5.50	4.25

Counterfeits of surcharge exist.

Regular Issues of 1924-27 Surcharged

1929, Feb. 26 Perf. 12

C4	A51	3.40p on 3p gray	4.50	4.00
a.		Surch. "Correo / en $3.40 / Habilitado / Aereo"	8.75	
b.		Double surcharge	8.75	
c.		"Aéro" instead of "Aéreo"		
C5	A44	6.80p on 4p lt bl	4.50	3.25
a.		Surch. "Correo / Aereo / en $6.80 / Habilitado"	8.75	
C6	A52	17p on 5p choc	4.50	3.25
a.		Surch. "Correo / Habilitado / Habilitado / en 17p"	4.50	
b.		Double surcharge	25.00	25.00
		Nos. C4-C6 (3)	13.50	10.50

Wings AP1

Pigeon with Letter AP2

Airplanes — AP3

1929-31   Typo.   Perf. 12
C7 AP1 2.85p gray green   1.75 1.25
  a. Imperf., pair   37.50
C8 AP1 2.85p turq grn ('31)   .50 .50
C9 AP2 5.65p brown   2.00 1.25
C10 AP2 5.65p scar ('31)   1.00 .50
C11 AP3 11.30p chocolate   1.75 1.25
  a. Imperf., pair   37.50
C12 AP3 11.30p dp blue ('31)   .50 .50
  Nos. C7-C12 (6)   7.50 5.25

Sheets of these stamps sometimes show
portions of a papermaker's watermark "Indian
Bond C. Extra Strong."
Excellent counterfeits are plentiful.

Regular Issues of
1924-28 Surcharged
in Black or Red

1929   Perf. 11½, 12
C13 A47 95c on 7c lilac   .35 .30
C14 A47 1.90p on 20c dull bl   .35 .30
C15 A44 3.40p on 4p lt bl (R)   .45 .30
  a. Double surcharge   3.00
C16 A44 1.75p on 4p lt bl (R)   .90 .75
  a. Double surcharge   3.00
C17 A51 6.80p on 3p gray   1.00 .90
  a. Double surcharge   4.50
C18 A52 17p on 5p choc   3.00 3.00
  a. Horiz. pair, imperf. between   37.50
  Nos. C13-C18 (6)   6.05 5.55

Six stamps in the sheet of No. C17 have the
"$" and numerals thinner and narrower than
the normal type.

Airplane and
Arms — AP4

Cathedral of
Asunción
AP5

Airplane and
Globe — AP6

1930   Perf. 12
C19 AP4 95c dp red, *pink*   1.50 .90
C20 AP4 95c dk bl, *blue*   1.50 .90
C21 AP5 1.90p lt red, *pink*   1.50 .90
C22 AP5 1.90p violet, *blue*   1.50 .90
C23 AP6 6.80p blk, *lt bl*   1.50 .90
C24 AP6 6.80p green, *pink*   1.50 .90
  Nos. C19-C24 (6)   9.00 5.40

Sheets of Nos. C19-C24 have a
papermaker's watermark: "Extra Vencedor
Bond."
Counterfeits exist.

Stamps and Types
of 1927-28
Overprinted in Red

1930
C25 A47 10c olive green   .60 .40
  a. Double overprint   6.00
C26 A47 20c dull blue   .60 .40
  a. "CORREO CORREO" instead of
    "CORREO AEREO"   5.00
  b. "AEREO AEREO" instead of
    "CORREO AEREO"   5.00
C27 A48 1p emerald   1.40 1.40
C28 A51 3p gray   1.40 1.40
  Nos. C25-C28 (4)   4.00 3.60

Counterfeits of Nos. C26a and C26b exist.

**Nos. 273, 282, 286, 288, 300, 302,
305 Surcharged in Red or Black**

#C29-C30, C32   #C31

#C33   #C34-C35

1930   Red or Black Surcharge
C29 A47 5c on 10c gray grn
    (R)   .50 .50
  a. "AEREO" omitted   30.00
C30 A47 5c on 70c ultra (R)   .50 .50
  a. Vert. pair, imperf. between   40.00
C31 A48 20c on 1p org red   .60 .50
  a. "CORREO" double   6.00 6.00
  b. "AEREO" double   6.00 6.00
C32 A47 40c on 50c org (R)   .60 .50
  a. "AEREO" omitted   9.00 9.00
  b. "CORREO" double   6.00 6.00
  c. "AEREO" double   6.00 6.00
C33 A54 6p on 10p red   2.50 2.00
C34 A49 10p on 20p red   10.00 10.00
C35 A49 10p on 20p vio brn   10.00 10.00
  Nos. C29-C35 (7)   24.70 24.00

Declaration of
Independence
AP11

1930, May 14   Typo.
C36 AP11 2.85p dark blue   .70 .50
C37 AP11 3.40p dark green   .70 .40
C38 AP11 4.75p deep lake   .70 .40
  Nos. C36-C38 (3)   2.10 1.30

Natl. Independence Day, May 14, 1811.

Gunboat Type
Gunboat "Paraguay."

1931-39   Perf. 11½, 12
C39 A58 1p claret   .60 .60
C40 A58 1p dk blue ('36)   .60 .60
C41 A58 2p orange   .60 .60
C42 A58 2p dk brn ('36)   .60 .60
C43 A58 3p turq green   .75 .75
C44 A58 3p lt ultra ('36)   .90 .75
C45 A58 3p brt rose ('39)   .60 .60
C46 A58 6p dk green   1.20 .90
C47 A58 6p violet ('36)   1.40 .90
C48 A58 6p dull bl ('39)   1.20 .75
C49 A58 10p vermilion   3.00 1.75
C50 A58 10p bluish grn ('35)   4.50 3.00
C51 A58 10p yel brn ('36)   3.25 2.25
C52 A58 10p dk blue ('36)   2.75 1.50
C53 A58 10p lt pink ('39)   3.00 2.00
  Nos. C39-C53 (15)   24.95 17.55

1st constitution of Paraguay as a Republic
and the arrival of the "Paraguay" and
"Humaita."

Counterfeits of #C39-C53 are plentiful.

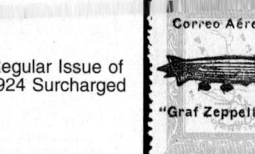

Regular Issue of
1924 Surcharged

1931, Aug. 22
C54 A44 3p on 4p lt bl   17.50 17.50

Overprinted

C55 A44 4p lt blue   15.00 15.00

On Nos. C54-C55 the Zeppelin is handstamped. The rest of the surcharge or overprint is typographed.

War Memorial
AP13

Orange Tree
and Yerba
Mate — AP14

Yerba
Mate — AP15

Palms — AP16

Eagle — AP17

1931-36   Litho.
C56 AP13 5c lt blue   .25 .40
  a. Horiz. pair, imperf. btwn.   6.25
C57 AP13 5c dp grn ('33)   .25 .40
C58 AP13 5c lt red ('33)   .30 .40
C59 AP13 5c violet ('35)   .25 .40
C60 AP14 10c dp violet   .25 .40
C61 AP14 10c brn lake ('33)   .25 .40
C62 AP14 10c yel brn ('33)   .25 .40
C63 AP14 10c ultra ('35)   .25 .40
  a. Imperf., pair   5.50
C64 AP15 20c red   .25 .40
C65 AP15 20c dl blue ('33)   .30 .40
C66 AP15 20c emer ('33)   .25 .40
C67 AP15 20c brn ('35)   .25 .40
  a. Imperf., pair   3.75
C68 AP16 40c dp green   .25 .40
C69 AP16 40c slate bl ('35)   .25 .40
C70 AP16 40c red ('36)   .30 .40
C71 AP17 80c dull blue   .25 .40
C72 AP17 80c dl grn ('33)   .50 .40
C73 AP17 80c scar ('33)   .30 .40
  Nos. C56-C73 (18)   4.95 7.20

Airship "Graf Zeppelin" — AP18

1932, Apr.   Litho.
C74 AP18 4p ultra   3.75 3.75
  a. Imperf., pair   19.00
C75 AP18 8p red   6.25 5.00
C76 AP18 12p blue grn   5.00 5.00
C77 AP18 16p dk violet   8.75 6.25
C78 AP18 20p orange brn   8.75 6.25
  Nos. C74-C78 (5)   32.50 26.25

For surcharges see Nos. 325-329.

"Graf
Zeppelin"
over
Brazilian
Terrain
AP19

"Graf Zeppelin" over Atlantic — AP20

1933, May 5
C79 AP19 4.50p dp blue   4.00 3.00
C80 AP19 9p dp rose   7.00 5.00
  a. Horiz. pair, imperf. between   150.00
C81 AP19 13.50p blue grn   8.00 6.00
C82 AP20 22.50p bis brn   18.00 14.00
C83 AP20 45p dull vio   24.00 24.00
  Nos. C79-C83 (5)   61.00 52.00

Excellent counterfeits are plentiful.
For overprints see Nos. C88-C97.

Posts and Telegraph Building,
Asunción — AP21

1934-37   Perf. 11½
C84 AP21 33.75p ultra   6.00 5.25
C85 AP21 33.75p car ('35)   6.00 5.25
  a. 33.75p rose ('37)   5.25 4.50
C86 AP21 33.75p emerald
    ('36)   7.50 6.00
C87 AP21 33.75p bis brn ('36)   2.25 2.25
  Nos. C84-C87 (4)   21.75 18.75

Excellent counterfeits exist.
For surcharge see No. C107.

Nos. C79-
C83
Overprinted
in Black

1934, May 26
C88 AP19 4.50p deep bl   3.00 2.25
C89 AP19 9p dp rose   3.75 3.00
C90 AP19 13.50p blue grn   10.50 7.50
C91 AP20 22.50p bis brn   9.00 6.00
C92 AP20 45p dull vio   13.50 10.50
  Nos. C88-C92 (5)   39.75 29.25

Types of
1933 Issue
Overprinted
in Black

1935
C93	AP19	4.50p rose red	3.50	2.50
C94	AP19	9p lt green	4.50	3.00
C95	AP19	13.50p brown	9.50	7.00
C96	AP20	22.50p violet	7.50	5.50
C97	AP20	45p blue	22.50	13.00
	Nos. C93-C97 (5)		47.50	31.00

Tobacco Plant — AP22

1935-39   Typo.
C98	AP22	17p lt brown	12.50	12.50
C99	AP22	17p carmine	21.00	21.00
C100	AP22	17p dark blue	15.00	15.00
C101	AP22	17p pale yel grn ('39)	8.00	8.00
	Nos. C98-C101 (4)		56.50	56.50

Excellent counterfeits are plentiful.

Church of Incarnation AP23

1935-38
C102	AP23	102p carmine	7.50	5.00
C103	AP23	102p blue	7.50	5.00
C103A	AP23	102p indigo ('36)	4.50	4.50
C104	AP23	102p yellow brn	5.50	4.75
a.		Imperf., pair	30.00	
C105	AP23	102p violet ('37)	2.50	2.50
C106	AP23	102p brn org ('38)	2.25	2.25
	Nos. C102-C106 (6)		29.75	24.00

Excellent counterfeits are plentiful.
For surcharges see Nos. C108-C109.

Types of 1934-35 Surcharged in Red

1937, Aug. 1
C107	AP21	24p on 33.75p sl bl	1.00	.70
C108	AP23	65p on 102p ol bis	2.50	1.75
C109	AP23	84p on 102p bl grn	2.50	1.50
	Nos. C107-C109 (3)		6.00	3.95

Plane over Asunción AP24

1939, Aug. 3   Typo.   Perf. 10½, 11½
C110	AP24	3.40p yel green	1.00	1.00
C111	AP24	3.40p orange brn	.60	.50
C112	AP24	3.40p indigo	.60	.50
	Nos. C110-C112 (3)		2.20	2.00

Buenos Aires Peace Conference Type and

Map of Paraguay with New Chaco Boundary AP28

Designs: 1p, Flags of Paraguay and Bolivia. 3p, Coats of Arms. 5p, Pres. Ortiz of Argentina, flags of Paraguay, Argentina. 10p, Pres. Vargas, Brazil. 30p, Pres. Alessandri, Chile. 50p, US Eagle and Shield. 100p, Pres. Benavides, Peru. 200p, Pres. Baldomir, Uruguay.

Engr.; Flags Litho.
1939, Nov.   Perf. 12½
Flags in National Colors
C113	A69	1p red brown	.60	.60
C114	A69	3p dark blue	.60	.60
C115	A70	5p olive blk	.60	.60
C116	A70	10p violet	.60	.60
C117	A70	30p orange	.60	.60
C118	A70	50p black brn	.90	.60
C119	A70	100p brt green	1.25	.90
C120	A70	200p green	6.75	3.75
C121	AP28	500p black	27.50	17.50
	Nos. C113-C121 (9)		39.40	25.75

For overprints see Nos. 388-390 in Scott Standard catalogue, Vol. 5.

University of Asuncion Type
Pres. Bernardino Caballero and Senator José S. Decoud.

1939, Sept.   Litho.   Perf. 12
C122	A67	28p rose & blk	10.00	10.00
C123	A67	90p yel grn & blk	12.00	12.00

Map with Asunción to New York Air Route — AP35

1939, Nov. 30   Engr.
C124	AP35	30p brown	7.75	6.00
C125	AP35	80p orange	9.00	9.00
C126	AP35	90p purple	12.00	12.00
	Nos. C124-C126 (3)		28.75	27.00

New York World's Fair.

Pan American Union Type
1940, May   Perf. 12
C127	A85	20p rose car	.60	.60
C128	A85	70p violet bl	1.25	.60
C129	A85	100p Prus blue	1.50	1.50
C130	A85	500p dk violet	6.75	5.25
	Nos. C127-C130 (4)		10.10	7.95

POSTAGE DUE STAMPS

D1

D2

1904   Unwmk.   Litho.   Perf. 11½
J1	D1	2c green	1.00	2.00
J2	D1	4c green	1.00	2.00
J3	D1	10c green	1.00	2.00
J4	D1	20c green	1.00	2.00
	Nos. J1-J4 (4)		4.00	8.00

1913   Engr.
J5	D2	1c yellow brown	1.00	1.00
J6	D2	2c yellow brown	1.00	1.00
J7	D2	5c yellow brown	1.00	1.00
J8	D2	10c yellow brown	1.00	1.00
J9	D2	20c yellow brown	1.00	1.00
J10	D2	40c yellow brown	1.00	1.00
J11	D2	1p yellow brown	1.00	1.00
J12	D2	1.50p yellow brown	1.00	1.00
	Nos. J5-J12 (8)		8.00	8.00

For overprints and surcharges see Nos. 220-224, 229, 232, 264, L5.

INTERIOR OFFICE ISSUES

The "C" signifies "Campana" (rural). These stamps were sold by Postal Agents in country districts, who received a commission on their sales. These stamps were available for postage in the interior but not in Asunción or abroad.

Nos. 243-244 Overprinted in Red

1922
L1	A42	50c car & dk bl	.50	.50
L2	A42	50c dk bl & brn	.50	.50

The overprint on Nos. L2 exists double or inverted. Counterfeits exist. Double or inverted overprints on No. L1 and all overprints in black are counterfeit.

Nos. 215, 218, J12 Surcharged

1924
L3	A40	50c on 75c deep bl	.50	.50
L4	A40	1p on 1.25p pale bl	.50	.50
L5	D2	1p on 1.50p yel brn	.50	.50
	Nos. L3-L5 (3)		1.50	1.50

Nos. L3-L4 exist imperf.

Nos. 254, 257-260 Overprinted in Black or Red

1924-26
L6	A45	50c red ('25)	1.00	1.00
L7	A44	1p dk blue (R)	1.00	1.00
L8	A45	1p dk bl (R) ('25)	1.00	1.00
L9	A46	1p blue (R) ('25)	1.00	1.00
L10	A45	1p emerald ('26)	2.00	.75
	Nos. L6-L10 (5)		6.00	4.75

Nos. L6, L8-L9 exist imperf. Value $2.50 each pair.

Same Overprint on Stamps and Type of 1927-36 in Red or Black
1927-39
L11	A47	50c ultra (R)	.50	.50
L12	A47	50c dl red ('28)	.50	.50
L13	A47	50c orange ('29)	.50	.50
L14	A47	50c lt bl ('30)	.50	.50
L15	A47	50c gray (R) ('31)	.50	.50
L16	A47	50c bluish grn (R) ('33)	.50	.50
L17	A47	50c vio (R) ('34)	.50	.50
L18	A48	1p emerald	.50	.50
L19	A48	1p org red ('29)	.50	.50
L20	A48	1p lil brn ('31)	.50	.50
L21	A48	1p dk bl (R) ('33)	.50	.50
L22	A48	1p brt vio (R) ('35)	.50	.50
L23	A49	1.50p brown	.50	.50
a.		Double overprint	3.00	
L24	A49	1.50p lilac ('28)	.50	.50
L25	A49	1.50p dull bl (R)	.50	.50
L26	A50	2.50p bister ('28)	.50	.50
L27	A50	2.50p vio (R) ('36)	.50	.50
L28	A51	3p gray (R)	.50	.50
L29	A51	3p rose red ('39)	.50	.50
L30	A52	5p vio (R) ('36)	.50	.50
L31	A57	10p gray brn (R) ('36)	5.00	3.00
	Nos. L11-L31 (21)		15.00	13.00

Types of 1931-35 and No. 305 Overprinted in Black or Red

1931-36
L32	A59	1p light red	2.00	1.00
L33	A58	1.50p dp bl (R)	1.00	.75
L34	A60	1.50p bis brn ('32)	2.00	1.00
L35	A60	1.50p grn (R) ('34)	2.00	1.00
L36	A60	1.50p bl (R) ('36)	2.00	1.00
L37	A54	10p vermilion	8.00	2.50
	Nos. L32-L37 (6)		17.00	7.25

The "C" signifies "Campana" (rural). These stamps were sold by Postal Agents in country districts, who received a commission on their sales. These stamps were available for postage in the interior but not in Asunción or abroad.

OFFICIAL STAMPS

O1

O2

O3

O4

O5

O6

O7

Unwmk.
1886, Aug. 20   Litho.   Imperf.
O1	O1	1c orange	4.50	4.50
O2	O2	2c violet	4.50	4.50
O3	O3	5c red	4.50	4.50
O4	O4	7c green	4.50	4.50
O5	O5	10c brown	4.50	4.50
O6	O6	15c slate blue	4.50	4.50
a.		Wavy lines on face of stamp		
b.		"OFICIAL" omitted	1.25	
O7	O7	20c claret	4.50	4.50
	Nos. O1-O7 (7)		31.50	31.50

Nos. O1 to O7 have the date and various control marks and letters printed on the back of each stamp in blue and black.
The overprints exist inverted on all values.
Nos. O1 to O7 have been reprinted from new stones made from slightly retouched dies.

Types of 1886 With Overprint

PARAGUAY (continued)

1886   *Perf. 11½*

O8	O1	1c dark green	1.00	1.00
O9	O2	2c scarlet	1.00	1.00
O10	O3	5c dull blue	1.00	1.00
O11	O4	7c orange	1.00	1.00
O12	O5	10c lake	1.00	1.00
O13	O6	15c brown	1.00	1.00
O14	O7	20c blue	1.00	1.00
		Nos. O8-O14 (7)	7.00	7.00

The overprint exists inverted on all values. Value, each $1.50.

No. 20 Overprinted

1886, Sept. 1

O15	A11	1c dark green	3.00	3.00

Types of 1889 Regular Issue Surcharged

Handstamped Surcharge in Black

1889   *Imperf.*

O16	A13	3c on 15c violet	2.25	1.50
O17	A13	5c on 15c red brn	2.25	1.50

Perf. 11½

O18	A13	1c on 15c maroon	2.25	1.50
O19	A13	2c on 15c maroon	2.25	1.50
		Nos. O16-O19 (4)	9.00	6.00

Counterfeits of Nos. O16-O19 abound.

Regular Issue of 1887 Handstamp Overprinted in Violet

Perf. 11½-12½ & Compounds

1890   *Typo.*

O20	A12	1c green	.35	.30
O21	A12	2c rose red	.35	.30
O22	A12	5c blue	.35	.30
O23	A12	7c brown	6.50	3.75
O24	A12	10c lilac	.35	.35
O25	A12	15c orange	.75	.45
O26	A12	20c pink	.65	.45
		Nos. O20-O26 (7)	9.30	5.90

Nos. O20-O26 exist with double overprint and all but the 20c with inverted overprint.
Nos. O20-O22, O24-O26 exist with blue overprint. The status is questioned. Value, set $15.

Stamps and Type of 1887 Regular Issue Overprinted in Black

1892

O33	A12	1c green	.30	.30
O34	A12	2c rose red	.30	.30
O35	A12	5c blue	.30	.30
O36	A12	7c brown	4.00	1.75
O37	A12	10c lilac	1.25	.55
O38	A12	15c orange	.35	.30
O39	A12	20c pink	.65	.35
O40	A12	50c gray	.75	.35
		Nos. O33-O40 (8)	7.90	4.20

No. 26 Overprinted

1893

O41	A12	7c brown	17.50	8.00

Counterfeits of No. O41 exist.

O16

1901, Feb.   *Engr.*   *Perf. 11½, 12½*

O42	O16	1c dull blue	.75	.50
O43	O16	2c rose red	.75	.50
O44	O16	4c dark brown	.75	.50
O45	O16	5c dark green	.75	.50
O46	O16	8c orange brn	.75	.50
O47	O16	10c car rose	2.50	1.00
O48	O16	20c deep blue	2.50	1.00
		Nos. O42-O48 (7)	8.75	4.50

A 12c deep green, type O16, was prepared but not issued.

No. 45 Overprinted

1902   *Perf. 12x12½*

O49	A12	1p olive grn	2.00	2.00
a.		Inverted overprint	10.00	

Counterfeits of No. O49a exist.

Regular Issue of 1903 Overprinted

1903   *Perf. 11½*

O50	A32	1c gray	.90	.35
O51	A32	2c blue green	.90	.35
O52	A32	5c blue	.90	.35
O53	A32	10c orange brn	.90	.35
O54	A32	20c carmine	.90	.35
O55	A32	30c deep blue	.90	.35
O56	A32	60c purple	.90	.35
		Nos. O50-O56 (7)	6.30	2.45

O17   O18

1905-08   *Engr.*   *Perf. 11½, 12*

O57	O17	1c gray grn	.50	.30
O58	O17	1c ol grn ('05)	.90	.30
O59	O17	1c brn org ('06)	.80	.30
O60	O17	1c ver ('08)	.50	.30
O61	O17	2c brown org	.35	.30
O62	O17	2c gray grn ('05)	.35	.30
O63	O17	2c red ('06)	2.00	.75
O64	O17	2c gray ('08)	1.00	.50
O65	O17	5c deep bl ('06)	.50	.35
O66	O17	5c gray bl ('08)	4.00	2.00
O67	O17	5c grnsh bl ('08)	2.00	1.50
O68	O17	10c violet ('06)	.35	.30
O69	O17	20c violet ('08)	2.00	1.25
		Nos. O57-O69 (13)	15.25	8.65

1908

O70	O17	10c bister	10.50
O71	O17	10c emerald	10.50
O72	O17	10c red lilac	13.50
O73	O17	20c bister	9.00
O74	O17	20c salmon pink	10.50
O75	O17	20c green	10.50
O76	O17	30c turquoise bl	10.50
O77	O17	30c blue gray	10.50
O78	O17	30c yellow	4.50
O79	O17	60c chocolate	12.00
O80	O17	60c orange brn	15.00
O81	O17	60c deep ultra	12.00
O82	O18	1p brt rose & blk	72.50
O83	O18	1p lake & blk	72.50
O84	O18	1p brn org & blk	75.00
		Nos. O70-O84 (15)	349.00

Nos. O70-O84 were not issued, but were surcharged or overprinted for use as regular postage stamps. See Nos. 131-138, 141-145, 158-165, 171-173.

O19

1913   *Perf. 11½*

O85	O19	1c gray	.30	.35
O86	O19	2c orange	.30	.35
O87	O19	5c lilac	.30	.35
O88	O19	10c green	.30	.35
O89	O19	20c dull red	.30	.35
O90	O19	50c rose	.30	.35
O91	O19	75c deep blue	.30	.35
O92	O19	1p dull blue	1.00	.50
O93	O19	2p yellow	1.00	.50
		Nos. O85-O93 (9)	4.10	3.45

For surcharges see Nos. 268, C1-C3.

Type of Regular Issue of 1927-38 Overprinted in Red

1935

O94	A47	10c light ultra	.35	.30
O95	A47	50c violet	.35	.30
O96	A48	1p orange	.35	.30
O97	A60	1.50p green	.35	.30
O98	A50	2.50p violet	.35	.30
		Nos. O94-O98 (5)	1.75	1.50

Overprint is diagonal on 1.50p.

University of Asunción Type

1940   *Litho.*   *Perf. 12*

O99	A67	50c red brn & blk	.50	.30
O100	A67	1p rose pink & blk	.50	.30
O101	A67	2p lt bl grn & blk	.50	.30
O102	A67	5p ultra & blk	.50	.30
O103	A67	10p lt vio & blk	.50	.30
O104	A67	50p dp org & blk	.50	.30
		Nos. O99-O104 (6)	3.00	1.80

PENRHYN ISLAND

pen-'rin 'ī-lənd

(Tongareva)

AREA — 3 sq. mi.
POP. — 395 (1926)

Stamps of Cook Islands were used in Penrhyn from 1932 until 1973.

12 Pence = 1 Shilling

Watermarks

Wmk. 61 — N Z and Star Close Together	Wmk. 63 — Double-lined N Z and Star

On watermark 61 the margins of the sheets are watermarked "NEW ZEALAND POST-AGE" and parts of the double-lined letters of these words are frequently found on the stamps. It occasionally happens that a stamp shows no watermark whatever.

Stamps of New Zealand Surcharged in Carmine, Vermilion, Brown or Blue

½ pence	1 pence

2½ pence

1902   *Wmk. 63*   *Perf. 14*

1	A18	½p green (C)	.90	11.00
a.		No period after "ISLAND"	175.00	300.00
2	A35	1p carmine (Br)	3.75	24.00
a.		Perf. 11	1,000.	1,200.
b.		Perf. 11x14	1,200.	1,400.

     Wmk. 61   *Perf. 14*

5	A18	½p green (V)	2.75	10.00
a.		No period after "ISLAND"	175.00	350.00
6	A35	1p carmine (Bl)	1.50	7.50
a.		No period after "ISLAND"	60.00	160.00
b.		Perf. 11x14	15,000.	8,500.

     Unwmk.   *Perf. 11*

8	A22	2½p blue (C)	8.00	9.00
a.		"½" and "PENI" 2mm apart	22.00	35.00
9	A22	2½p blue (V)	8.00	9.00
a.		"½" and "PENI" 2mm apart	22.00	35.00
		Nos. 1-9 (6)	24.90	70.50

Stamps with compound perfs. also exist perf. 11 or 14 on one or more sides.

d	e

f

1903   *Wmk. 61*

10	A23(d)	3p yel brn (Bl)	11.50	32.50
11	A26(e)	6p rose (Bl)	17.50	47.50
12	A29(f)	1sh org red (Bl)	62.50	62.50
a.		1sh bright red (Bl)	47.50	47.50
b.		1sh brown red (Bl)	65.00	65.00
		Nos. 10-12 (3)	91.50	142.50

1914-15   *Perf. 14, 14x14½*

13	A41(a)	½p yel grn (C)	.90	9.50
a.		No period after "ISLAND"	29.00	95.00
b.		No period after "PENI"	110.00	300.00
14	A41(a)	½p yel grn (V) ('15)	.90	9.25
a.		No period after "ISLAND"	11.50	65.00
b.		No period after "PENI"	55.00	180.00
15	A41(e)	6p car rose (Bl)	27.50	82.50
16	A41(f)	1sh ver (Bl)	50.00	110.00
		Nos. 13-16 (4)	79.30	211.25

New Zealand Stamps of 1915-19 Overprinted in Red or Dark Blue

Perf. 14x13½, 14x14½

1917-20   *Typo.*

17	A43	½p yel grn (R) ('20)	1.10	2.25
18	A47	1½p gray black (R)	7.50	24.00
19	A47	1½p brn org (R) ('19)	.70	24.00
20	A43	3p choc (Bl) ('19)	4.00	35.00

     Engr.

21	A44	2½p dull bl (R) ('20)	2.25	9.00
22	A45	3p vio brn (Bl) ('18)	11.00	80.00
23	A45	6p car rose (Bl) ('18)	5.75	21.00
24	A45	1sh vermilion (Bl)	14.00	37.50
		Nos. 17-24 (8)	46.30	232.75

Landing of
Capt. Cook
A10

Avarua
Waterfront
A11

Capt. James
Cook — A12

Coconut
Palm — A13

Arorangi Village,
Rarotonga — A14

Avarua
Harbor — A15

1920		Unwmk.		Perf. 14	
25	A10	½p emerald & blk		1.25	22.00
a.		Center inverted		625.00	
26	A11	1p red & black		2.00	19.00
a.		Center inverted		850.00	
27	A12	1½p violet & blk		7.75	24.00
28	A13	3p red org & blk		3.25	12.00
29	A14	6p dk brn & red brn		4.00	24.00
30	A15	1sh dull bl & blk		12.00	32.50
		Nos. 25-30 (6)		30.25	133.50

Rarotongan Chief (Te Po) — A16

1927		Engr.		Wmk. 61	
31	A16	2½p blue & red brn		10.00	37.50

Types of 1920 Issue

1928-29					
33	A10	½p yellow grn & blk		6.50	25.00
34	A11	1p carmine rose & blk		6.50	22.50

PERU

pə-'rü

LOCATION — West coast of South America
GOVT. — Republic
AREA — 496,093 sq. mi.
POP. — 18,300,000 (est. 1982)
CAPITAL — Lima

8 Reales = 1 Peso (1857)
100 Centimos = 8 Dineros = 4 Pesetas = 1 Peso (1858)
100 Centavos = 1 Sol (1874)

GREAT BRITAIN POST OFFICES IN PERU

British postal agencies operated in a number of Peruvian cities from 1846: Arica (1846-79), Callao (1846-79), Paita (1848-79), Pisco (1868-70), Iquique (1869-79), Islay (1869-77), and Mollendo (1877-79). British stamps were in use at these offices from 1865.

Values are for clear cancellations on sound, fault-free stamps, with average to fine centering. In many cases, very fine examples are rare or non-existent.

ARICA
Pre-Stamp Postmark

1850
Crowned Circle Handstamp Type I

A1	Inscribed "PAID AT ARICA" in red, on cover	5,000.

Earliest known use 11/5/50.

Stamps of Great Britain
Cancelled with "C36"

1865-79

A2	½p rose red, plates 5, 6, 10, 11, 13 (#58), value from	85.00
A3	1p rose red, plates 102, 139, 140, 163, 167 (#33), value from	62.50
A4	1½p lake red, plate 3 (#32)	—
A5	2p blue, plate 14 (#30)	85.00
A6	3p rose, plates 5, 9 (#49)	—
A7	3p rose, plates 11, 12, 17-19 (#61), value from	62.50
A8	4p vermilion, plates 10-14 (#43), value from	62.50
A9	4p vermilion, plate 15 (#69)	—
A10	4p pale olive green, plates 15, 16 (#70)	250.00
A11	6p lilac, plate 3 (#39)	—
a.	6p lilac, plate 4 (#39b)	—
A12	6p lilac, plate 5 (#45)	—
A13	6p dull violet, plate 6 (#50)	—
A14	6p violet, plates 8, 9 (#51)	90.00
A15	6p brown plate 11 (#59)	115.00
a.	6p pale buff, plate 11 (#59b)	110.00
A16	6p gray, plate 12 (#60)	240.00
A17	6p gray, plates 13-16 (#62), value from	62.50
A18	8p orange (#73)	—
A19	9p straw (#40)	—
A20	9p straw (#46)	—
A21	9p bister, plate 4 (#52)	250.00
A22	10p red brown (#53)	—
A23	1sh green (#42)	—
A24	1sh green, plate 4 (#48)	—
A25	1sh green, plates 4-7 (#54)	62.50
A26	1sh green, plates 8-13 (#64), value from	80.00
A27	2sh blue (#55)	200.00
A28	5sh rose, plate 1 (#57)	600.00
	Plate 2 (#57)	800.00

CALLAO
Pre-Stamp Postmark

1846
Crowned Circle Handstamp Type I

A32	Inscribed "PAID AT CALLAO" in red, straight-line "CALLAO", on cover	1,250.
a.	Used in 1865 or after on cover with stamps of Peru, value from	350.00
A33	Inscribed "PAID AT CALLAO" in red, curved "CALLAO", on cover	725.00
a.	Used in 1865 or after on cover with stamps of Peru, value from	350.00

Earliest known use 7/16/46.

Stamps of Great Britain
Cancelled with barred oval "C38" obliterator, either single or in duplex

No. A63

1865-79

A34	½p rose red, plates 5, 6, 10-14 (#58), value from	50.00
A35	1p rose red, plates 74, 88, 89, 93, 94, 97, 108, 123, 127, 128, 130, 134, 137, 139-141, 143-146, 148, 149, 157, 160, 163, 167, 171-173, 175, 176, 180-183, 185, 187, 190, 193, 195, 198-201, 204, 206, 209, 210, 212, 213, 215 (#33), value from	37.50
A36	1½p lake red, plate 3 (#32)	37.50
A37	2p blue, plates 9, 12 (#29)	37.50
A38	2p blue, plates 13-15 (#30)	37.50
A39	3p rose (#37)	—
A40	3p rose, plate 4 (#44)	110.00
A41	3p rose, plates 5-10 (#49), value from	50.00
A42	3p rose, plates 11, 12, 14-19 (#61), value from	50.00
A43	4p vermilion, plate 3 (#34)	—
a.	4p vermilion, plate 4 (#34a)	—
A44	4p vermilion, plates 8, 10-14 (#43), value from	42.50
A45	4p vermilion, plate 15 (#69)	350.00
A46	4p pale olive green, plates 15, 16 (#70)	225.00
A47	6p lilac, plate 3 (#39)	—
a.	6p lilac, plate 4 (#39b)	—
A48	6p lilac, plates 5, 6 (#45)	—
A49	6p dull violet, plate 6 (#50)	—
A50	6p violet, plates 8, 9 (#51), value from	80.00
A51	6p brown plate 11 (#59)	55.00
a.	6p pale buff, plates 11, 12 (#59b), value from	80.00
A52	6p gray, plate 12 (#60)	240.00
A53	6p gray, plates 13-16 (#62), value from	55.00
A54	8p orange (#73)	300.00
A55	9p straw (#40)	—
A56	9p straw, plate 4 (#46)	450.00
A57	9p bister, plate 4 (#52)	350.00
A58	10p red brown (#53)	300.00
A59	1sh green, plate 4 (#48)	—
A60	1sh green, plates 4-7 (#54), value from	42.50
A61	1sh green, plates 8-13 (#64), value from	62.50
A62	2sh blue (#55)	140.00
A63	5sh rose, plate 1 (#57)	525.00
	Plate 2 (#57)	675.00

IQUIQUE
Stamps of Great Britain
Cancelled with "D87" Type B obliterator

1865-79

A69	½p rose red, plates 5, 6, 13, 14 (#58), value from	85.00
A70	1p rose red, plates 76, 179, 185, 205 (#33), value from	55.00
A71	2p blue, plates 9, 12 (#29)	—
A72	2p blue, plates 13-15 (#30)	55.00
A73	3p rose, plates 5-9 (#49), value from	67.50
A74	3p rose, plates 12, 18, 19 (#61), value from	85.00
A75	4p vermilion, plates 12-14 (#43), value from	75.00
A76	4p vermilion, plate 15 (#69)	350.00
A77	4p pale olive green, plates 15, 16 (#70)	225.00
A78	6p violet, plates 8, 9 (#51)	—
A79	6p brown plate 11 (#59)	—
a.	6p pale buff, plates 11, 12 (#59b), value from	125.00
A80	6p gray, plate 12 (#60)	250.00
A81	6p gray, plates 13-16 (#62)	90.00
A82	8p orange (#73)	375.00
A83	9p bister, plate 4 (#52)	225.00
A84	10p red brown (#53)	—
A85	1sh green, plates 4, 6, 7 (#54)	67.50
A86	1sh green, plates 8-13 (#64), value from	90.00
A87	2sh blue (#55)	250.00

ISLAY / MOLLENDO
Pre-Stamp Postmark

1850
Crowned Circle Handstamp Type I

A90	Inscribed "PAID AT ISLAY" in red, curved "ISLAY", on cover	6,000.

Earliest known use 10/23/50.

Stamps of Great Britain
Cancelled with Type A barred oval "C42" obliterator or with circular date stamp

1865-79

A91	1p rose red, plates 78, 84, 87, 88, 96, 103, 125, 134 (#33), value from	62.50
A92	1½p lake red, plate 3 (#32)	—
A93	2p blue, plate 9 (#29)	62.50
A94	2p blue, plates 13, 15 (#30), value from	—
A95	3p rose (#37)	—
A96	3p rose, plate 4 (#44)	125.00
A97	3p rose, plates 4-6, 10 (#49), value from	67.50
A98	4p vermilion, plate 3 (#34)	150.00
a.	4p vermilion, plate 4 (#34a)	175.00
A99	4p vermilion, plates 9-13 (#43), value from	67.50
A100	4p vermilion, plate 15 (#69)	—
A101	4p pale olive green, plates 15, 16 (#70), value from	225.00
A102	6p lilac, plate 3 (#39)	100.00
a.	6p lilac, plate 4 (#39b)	150.00
A103	6p lilac, plate 5 (#45)	90.00
A104	6p bright violet, plate 6 (#50a)	100.00
A105	6p violet, plates 8, 9 (#51), value from	90.00
A106	6p brown plate 11 (#59)	—
a.	6p pale buff, plate 12 (#59b)	—
A107	6p gray, plate 12 (#60)	—
A108	6p gray, plates 13-16 (#62), value from	75.00
A109	9p straw (#46)	425.00
A110	9p bister, plate 4 (#52)	225.00
A111	10p red brown (#53)	325.00
A112	1sh green, plate 4 (#48)	—
A113	1sh green, plates 4-7 (#54), value from	67.50
A114	1sh green, plates 8, 10, 12, 13 (#64), value from	90.00
A115	2sh blue (#55)	—
A116	5sh rose, plate 1 (#57)	—
	Plate 2 (#57)	

PAITA
Pre-Stamp Postmarks

1850
Crowned Circle Handstamp Type I

A122	Inscribed "PAID AT PAITA" in black, curved "ISLAY", on cover	7,500.
A123	Inscribed "PAID AT PAITA" in red, curved "ISLAY", on cover	7,500.

Earliest known use 11/5/50.

Stamps of Great Britain
Cancelled with Type A barred oval "C43" obliterator or with circular date stamp

1865-79

A121	1p rose red, plates 127, 147 (#33)	75.00
A122	2p blue, plate 9 (#29)	75.00
A123	2p blue, plate 14 (#30)	75.00
A124	3p rose, plates 5, 6 (#49)	85.00
A125	3p rose, plates 17-19 (#61)	85.00
A126	4p vermilion, plates 10-14 (#43), value from	85.00
A127	4p pale olive green, plate 15 (#70)	—
A128	6p lilac, plate 3 (#39)	125.00
A129	6p lilac, plate 5 (#45)	110.00
a.	6p deep lilac, plate 6 (#50a)	190.00
A130	6p bright violet, plate 6 (#50a)	190.00
A131	6p red violet, plates 8, 9 (#51), value from	100.00
A132	6p brown plate 11 (#59)	200.00
a.	6p pale buff, plates 11, 12 (#59b)	200.00
A133	6p gray, plate 12 (#60)	—
A134	6p gray, plates 13-15 (#62)	—
A135	9p straw (#40)	—
A136	10p red brown (#53)	425.00
A137	1sh green, plate 4 (#48)	—
A138	1sh green, plate 4 (#54)	85.00
A139	1sh green, plates 8-10, 13 (#64)	100.00
A140	2sh blue (#55)	350.00
A141	5sh rose, plate 1 (#57)	750.00

PISAGUA
Stamps of Great Britain
Cancelled with Type B barred oval "D65" obliterator

1867

A150	1p rose red (#33)	—
A151	2p blue (#30)	—
A152	2sh blue (#55)	—

PISCO AND CHINCHA ISLANDS
Stamps of Great Britain
Cancelled with Type B barred oval "D74" obliterator

1865-70

A160	2p blue, plate 6 (#29)		—
A161	4p vermilion, plates 10, 12 (#43)		1,000.
A162	6p bright violet, plate 6 (#50a)		1,750.
A163	1sh green, plate 4 (#54)		—
A164	2sh blue (#55)		2,500.

ISSUES OF THE REPUBLIC

Sail and
Steamship — A1

Design: 2r, Ship sails eastward.

Unwmk.

1857, Dec. 1		**Engr.**	**Imperf.**
1	A1 1r blue, *blue*	1,700.	2,250.
2	A1 2r brn red, *blue*	1,900.	3,000.

The Pacific Steam Navigation Co. gave a quantity of these stamps to the Peruvian government so that a trial of prepayment of postage by stamps might be made.

Stamps of 1 and 2 reales, printed in various colors on white paper, laid and wove, were prepared for the Pacific Steam Navigation Co. but never put in use. Value $50 each on wove paper, $400 each on laid paper.

Coat of Arms
A2   A3

A4

Wavy Lines in Spandrels

1858, Mar. 1			**Litho.**
3	A2	1d deep blue	275.00	47.50
4	A3	1p rose red	1,100.	160.00
5	A4	½ pe- rose red		
		so	6,500.	4,750.
6	A4	½ pe- buff		
		so	2,750.	375.00
a.	½ peso orange yellow	2,750.	375.00

A5   A6

Large Letters

1858, Dec.		**Double-lined Frame**
7	A5 1d slate blue	450.00	45.00
8	A6 1p red	450.00	65.00

A7   A8

1860-61
Zigzag Lines in Spandrels

9	A7	1d blue	175.00	10.50
a.		1d Prussian blue	175.00	20.00
b.		Cornucopia on white ground	375.00	80.00
c.		Zigzag lines broken at angles	225.00	22.50
10	A8	1p rose	450.00	42.50
a.		1p brick red	450.00	42.50
b.		Cornucopia on white ground	450.00	42.50

Retouched, 10 lines instead of 9 in left label

11	A8 1p rose	250.00	27.50
a.	Pelure paper	1,100.	32.50
	Nos. 9-11 (3)	875.00	80.50

A9   A10

1862-63   **Embossed**

12	A9 1d red	14.50	4.50
a.	Arms embossed sideways	550.00	150.00
b.	Thick paper	120.00	37.50
c.	Diag. half used on cover		350.00
13	A10 1p brown ('63)	120.00	37.50
a.	Diag. half used on cover		1,000.

Counterfeits of Nos. 13 and 15 exist.

A11

1868-72

14	A11 1d green	19.00	3.75
a.	Arms embossed inverted	2,250.	1,200.
b.	Diag. half used on cover		2,000.
15	A10 1p orange ('72)	150.00	55.00
a.	Diag. half used on cover		1,100.

Nos. 12-15, 19 and 20 were printed in horizontal strips. Stamps may be found printed on two strips of paper where the strips were joined by overlapping.

Llamas — A12   A13

A14

1866-67   **Engr.**   **Perf. 12**

16	A12 5c green	10.50	.95
17	A13 10c vermilion	10.50	2.25
18	A14 20c brown	35.00	7.00
a.	Diagonal half used on cover		675.00
	Nos. 16-18 (3)	56.00	10.20

See Nos. 109, 111, 113.

Locomotive and
Arms — A15   Llama — A16

1871, Apr.   Embossed   *Imperf.*

19	A15 5c scarlet	125.00	42.50
a.	5c pale red	125.00	42.50

20th anniv. of the first railway in South America, linking Lima and Callao.

The so-called varieties "ALLAO" and "CALLA" are due to over-inking.

1873, Mar.   *Rouletted Horiz.*

20	A16 2c dk ultra	50.00	*325.00*

Counterfeits are plentiful.

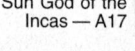

Sun God of the
Incas — A17

Coat of Arms
A18   A19

A20   A21

A22   A23

Embossed with Grill

1874-84		**Engr.**	**Perf. 12**
21	A17 1c orange ('79)	.90	.65
22	A18 2c dk violet	1.25	.95
23	A19 5c blue ('77)	1.40	.45
24	A19 5c ultra ('79)	13.00	3.25
25	A20 10c green ('76)	.45	.30
a.	Imperf., pair	35.00	
26	A20 10c slate ('84)	2.00	.45
a.	Diag. half used as 5c on cover		
27	A21 20c brown red	3.50	1.10
28	A22 50c green	15.00	4.25
29	A23 1s rose	2.40	2.40
	Nos. 21-29 (9)	39.90	13.80

No. 25a lacks the grill.

No. 26 with overprint "DE OFICIO" is said to have been used to frank mail of Gen. A. A. Caceres during the civil war against Gen. Miguel Iglesias, provisional president. Experts question its status.

1880

30	A17 1c green	2.50
31	A18 2c rose	2.50

Nos. 30 and 31 were prepared for use but not issued without overprint.

See Nos. 104-108, 110, 112, 114-115.

For overprints see Nos. 32-103, 116-128, J32-J33, O2-O22, N11-N23, 1N1-1N9, 3N11-3N20, 5N1, 6N1-6N2, 7N1-7N2, 8N7, 8N10-8N11, 9N1-9N3, 10N3-10N8, 10N10-10N11, 11N1-11N5, 12N1-12N3, 13N1, 14N1-14N16, 15N5-15N8, 15N13-15N18, 16N1-16N22.

Stamps of 1874-80
Overprinted in Red, Blue or Black

1880, Jan. 5

32	A17 1c green (R)	.90	.65
a.	Inverted overprint	10.00	10.00
b.	Double overprint	13.50	13.50
33	A18 2c rose (Bl)	1.75	1.10
a.	Inverted overprint	10.00	10.00
b.	Double overprint	14.00	12.00
34	A18 2c rose (Bk)	75.00	60.00
a.	Inverted overprint		
b.	Double overprint		
35	A19 5c ultra (R)	3.50	1.75
a.	Inverted overprint	10.00	10.00
b.	Double overprint	14.00	14.00
36	A22 50c green (R)	45.00	27.50
a.	Inverted overprint	45.00	45.00
b.	Double overprint	55.00	55.00
37	A23 1s rose (Bl)	70.00	50.00
a.	Inverted overprint	110.00	110.00
b.	Double overprint	110.00	110.00
	Nos. 32-37 (6)	196.15	141.00

Stamps of 1874-80
Overprinted in Red or Blue

1881, Jan. 28

38	A17 1c green (R)	1.25	.95
a.	Inverted overprint	8.25	8.25
b.	Double overprint	14.00	14.00
39	A18 2c rose (Bl)	24.00	15.00
a.	Inverted overprint	17.50	15.00
b.	Double overprint	25.00	20.00
40	A19 5c ultra (R)	2.75	1.25
a.	Inverted overprint	14.00	14.00
b.	Double overprint	20.00	20.00
41	A22 50c green (R)	750.00	425.00
a.	Inverted overprint	850.00	
42	A23 1s rose (Bl)	140.00	90.00
a.	Inverted overprint	175.00	

Reprints of Nos. 38 to 42 were made in 1884. In the overprint the word "PLATA" is 3mm high instead of 2½mm. The cross bars of the letters "A" of that word are set higher than on the original stamps. The 5c is printed in blue instead of ultramarine.

For stamps of 1874-80 overprinted with Chilean arms or small UPU "horseshoe," see Nos. N11-N23.

Stamps of 1874-79
Handstamped in Black or Blue

1883

65	A17 1c orange (Bk)	1.25	1.10
66	A17 1c orange (Bl)	50.00	50.00
68	A19 5c ultra (Bk)	13.00	8.00
69	A20 10c green (Bk)	1.25	1.10
70	A20 10c green (Bl)	5.00	4.00
71	A22 50c green (Bk)	7.00	4.25
73	A23 1s rose (Bk)	10.00	8.00
	Nos. 65-73 (7)	87.50	75.45
	Nos. 65,68-73 (6)	37.50	25.45

This overprint is found in 11 types.

The 1c green, 2c dark violet and 20c brown red, overprinted with triangle, are fancy varieties made for sale to collectors and never placed in regular use.

Overprinted Triangle and "Union Postal Universal Peru" in Oval

1883

77	A22 50c grn (R & Bk)	210.00	110.00
78	A23 1s rose (Bl & Bk)	250.00	160.00

The 1c green, 2c rose and 5c ultramarine, over printed with triangle and "U. P. U. Peru" oval, were never placed in regular use.

Overprinted Triangle and "Union Postal Universal Lima" in Oval

1883

79	A17 1c grn (R & Bl)	70.00	70.00
80	A17 1c grn (R & Bk)	7.00	7.00
a.	Oval overprint inverted		
b.	Double overprint of oval		
81	A18 2c rose (Bl & Bk)	7.00	7.00
82	A19 5c ultra (R & Bk)	11.00	10.00
83	A19 5c ultra (R & Bl)	17.00	10.00
84	A22 50c grn (R & Bk)	250.00	150.00
85	A23 1s rose (Bl & Bk)	275.00	275.00
	Nos. 79-85 (7)	637.00	529.00

Some authorities question the status of No. 79.

Nos. 80, 81, 84, and 85 were reprinted in 1884. They have the second type of oval overprint with "PLATA" 3mm high.

Overprinted Triangle and

1883

86	A17 1c grn (Bk & Bk)	1.75	1.25
a.	Horseshoe inverted	10.00	
87	A17 1c grn (Bl & Bk)	5.00	3.50
88	A18 2c ver (Bk & Bk)	1.75	1.25
89	A19 5c bl (Bk & Bk)	2.25	1.60
90	A19 5c bl (Bl & Bk)	12.00	10.50
91	A19 5c bl (R & Bk)	1,500.	1,100.

Overprinted Horseshoe Alone

1883, Oct. 23

95	A17	1c green	2.25	2.25
96	A18	2c vermilion	2.25	6.50
a.		Double overprint		
97	A19	5c blue	3.50	3.50
98	A19	5c ultra	20.00	15.00
99	A22	50c rose	57.50	57.50
100	A23	1s ultra	55.00	22.50
		Nos. 95-100 (6)	140.50	107.25

The 2c violet overprinted with the above design in red and triangle in black also the 1c green overprinted with the same combination plus the horseshoe in black, are fancy varieties made for sale to collectors.

No. 23 Overprinted in Black

1884, Apr. 28

103	A19	5c blue	.65	.40
a.		Double overprint	5.00	5.00

Stamps of 1c and 2c with the above overprint, also with the above and "U. P. U. LIMA" oval in blue or "CORREOS LIMA" in a double-lined circle in red, were made to sell to collectors and were never placed in use.

Without Overprint or Grill

1886-95

104	A17	1c dull violet	.90	.30
105	A17	1c vermilion ('95)	.65	.30
106	A18	2c green	1.25	.30
107	A18	2c dp ultra ('95)	.55	.30
108	A19	5c orange	1.00	.45
109	A12	5c claret ('95)	2.25	.85
110	A20	10c slate	.65	.30
111	A13	10c orange ('95)	1.00	.55
112	A21	20c blue	8.75	1.10
113	A14	20c dp ultra ('95)	10.50	2.25
114	A22	50c red	2.75	1.10
115	A23	1s brown	2.25	.85
		Nos. 104-115 (12)	32.50	8.65

Overprinted Horseshoe in Black and Triangle in Rose Red

1889

116	A17	1c green	.75	.75
a.		Horseshoe inverted	7.50	

Nos. 30 and 25 Overprinted "Union Postal Universal Lima" in Oval in Red

1889, Sept. 1

117	A17	1c green	2.00	1.60
117A	A20	10c green	2.00	2.00

The overprint on Nos. 117 and 117A is of the second type with "PLATA" 3mm high.

Stamps of 1874-80 Overprinted in Black

Pres. Remigio Morales Bermúdez

1894, Oct. 23

118	A17	1c orange	1.00	.65
a.		Inverted overprint	7.00	7.00
b.		Double overprint	7.00	7.00
119	A17	1c green	.65	.55
a.		Inverted overprint	3.50	3.50
b.		Dbl. inverted ovpt.	5.00	5.00
120	A18	2c violet	.65	.55
a.		Diagonal half used as 1c		
b.		Inverted overprint	7.00	7.00
c.		Double overprint	7.00	7.00
121	A18	2c rose	.65	.55
a.		Double overprint	7.00	7.00
b.		Inverted overprint	9.75	7.00
122	A19	5c blue	4.50	2.75
122A	A19	5c ultra	7.25	3.50
b.		Inverted overprint	10.00	10.00

123	A20	10c green	.65	.55
a.		Inverted overprint	7.00	7.00
124	A22	50c green	2.40	2.00
a.		Inverted overprint	10.00	10.00
		Nos. 118-124 (8)	17.75	11.10

Same, with Additional Ovpt. of Horseshoe

125	A18	2c vermilion	.55	.45
a.		Head inverted	2.50	2.50
b.		Head double	5.00	5.00
126	A19	5c blue	1.75	.85
a.		Head inverted	7.00	7.00
127	A22	50c rose	70.00	42.50
a.		Head double	55.00	45.00
b.		Head inverted	75.00	60.00
128	A23	1s ultra	175.00	150.00
a.		Both overprints inverted	200.00	110.00
b.		Head double	200.00	110.00
		Nos. 125-128 (4)	247.30	193.80

A23a

Vermilion Surcharge

1895 **Perf. 11½**

129	A23a	5c on 5c grn	18.00	13.00
130	A23a	10c on 10c ver	14.00	10.00
131	A23a	20c on 20c brn	14.00	13.00
132	A23a	50c on 50c ultra	18.00	13.00
133	A23a	1s on 1s red brn	18.00	13.00
		Nos. 129-133 (5)	81.00	59.00

Nos 129-133 were used only in Tumbes. The basic stamps were prepared by revolutionaries in northern Peru.

A23b

"Liberty" — A23c

1895, Sept. 8 **Engr.**

134	A23b	1c gray violet	1.90	1.10
135	A23b	2c green	1.90	1.10
136	A23b	5c yellow	1.90	1.10
137	A23b	10c ultra	1.90	1.10
138	A23c	20c orange	1.90	1.25
139	A23c	50c dark blue	10.00	7.00
140	A23c	1s car lake	55.00	35.00
		Nos. 134-140 (7)	74.50	47.65

Success of the revolution against the government of General Caceres and of the election of President Pierola.

Manco Capac, Founder of Inca Dynasty — A24

Francisco Pizarro Conqueror of the Inca Empire — A25

General José de La Mar — A26

1896-1900

141	A24	1c ultra	.90	.30
a.		1c blue (error)	70.00	60.00
142	A24	1c yel grn ('98)	.90	.30
143	A24	2c blue	.90	.30
144	A24	2c scar ('99)	.90	.30
145	A25	5c indigo	1.25	.30
146	A25	5c green ('97)	1.25	.30
147	A25	5c grnsh bl ('99)	.90	.55
148	A25	10c yellow	1.75	.45
149	A25	10c gray blk ('00)	1.75	.30
150	A25	20c orange	3.50	1.00
151	A26	50c car rose	8.75	1.60
152	A26	1s orange red	13.00	1.60
153	A26	2s claret	3.50	1.25
		Nos. 141-153 (13)	39.25	8.00

The 5c in black is a chemical changeling. For surcharges and overprints see Nos. 187-188, E1, O23-O26.

Paucartambo Bridge A27

Post and Telegraph Building, Lima — A28

Pres. Nicolás de Piérola — A29

1897, Dec. 31

154	A27	1c dp ultra	1.25	.60
155	A28	2c brown	1.25	.40
156	A29	5c bright rose	1.75	.60
		Nos. 154-156 (3)	4.25	1.60

Opening of new P.O. in Lima.

No. J1 Overprinted in Black

1897, Nov. 8

157	D1	1c bister	.90	.75
a.		Inverted overprint	4.50	4.50
b.		Double overprint	17.50	17.50

A31

1899

158	A31	5s orange red	2.75	2.75
159	A31	10s blue green	850.00	600.00

For surcharge see No. J36.

Pres. Eduardo de Romaña — A32

Admiral Miguel L. Grau — A33

1900 **Frame Litho., Center Engr.**

160	A32	22c yel grn & blk	13.00	1.40

1901, Jan.

2c, Col. Francisco Bolognes. 5c, Pres. Romaña.

161	A33	1c green & blk	1.75	.75
162	A33	2c red & black	1.75	.75
163	A33	5c dull vio & blk	1.75	.75
		Nos. 161-163 (3)	5.25	2.25

Advent of 20th century.

A34

1902 **Engr.**

164	A34	22c green	.55	.30

Municipal Hygiene Institute Lima — A35

1905

165	A35	12c dp blue & blk	1.75	.50

For surcharges see Nos. 166-167, 186, 189.

Same Surcharged in Red or Violet

1907

166	A35	1c on 12c (R)	.35	.30
a.		Inverted surcharge	8.00	8.00
b.		Double surcharge	8.00	8.00
167	A35	2c on 12c (V)	.65	.45
a.		Double surcharge	8.00	8.00
b.		Inverted surcharge	8.00	8.00

Monument of Bolognesi — A36

Admiral Grau — A37

Llama — A38

Statue of Bolivar — A39

City Hall, Lima, formerly an Exhibition Building — A40

School of Medicine, Lima — A41

Post and Telegraph Building, Lima — A42

Grandstand at Santa Beatrix Race Track — A43

Columbus Monument — A44

1907

168	A36	1c yel grn & blk	.55	.30
169	A37	2c red & violet	.55	.30
170	A38	4c olive green	9.25	1.25
171	A39	5c blue & blk	1.00	.30
172	A40	10c red brn & blk	1.75	.45
173	A41	20c dk grn & blk	40.00	.75
174	A42	50c black	40.00	1.60
175	A43	1s purple & grn	200.00	3.75
176	A44	2s dp bl & blk	200.00	160.00
		Nos. 168-176 (9)	493.10	168.70

For surcharges and overprint see #190-195, E2.

Manco Capac A45

Columbus A46

Pizarro A47

San Martin A48

Bolívar A49

La Mar A50

Ramón Castilla A51

Grau A52

Bolognesi — A53

1909

177	A45	1c gray	.35	.25
178	A46	2c green	.35	.25
179	A47	4c vermilion	.45	.30
180	A48	5c violet	.35	.25
181	A49	10c deep blue	.75	.30
182	A50	12c pale blue	1.75	.30
183	A51	20c brown red	1.90	.45
184	A52	50c yellow	8.25	.55
185	A53	1s brn red & blk	17.00	.65
		Nos. 177-185 (9)	31.15	3.30

See types A54, A78-A80, A81-A89.
For surcharges and overprint see Nos. 196-200, 208, E3.

No. 165 Surcharged in Red

1913, Jan.

186	A35	8c on 12c dp bl & blk	.90	.35

Stamps of 1899-1908 Surcharged in Magenta

a

b

c

1915

	On Nos. 142, 149			
187	A24(a)	1c on 1c	27.50	27.50
a.	Inverted surcharge		32.50	37.50
188	A25(a)	1c on 10c	1.75	1.25
a.	Inverted surcharge		4.50	4.50

	On No. 165			
189	A35(c)	2c on 12c	.45	.30
a.	Inverted surcharge		7.75	7.75

	On Nos. 168-170, 172-174			
190	A36(a)	1c on 1c	1.10	1.10
a.	Inverted surcharge		3.50	3.50
191	A37(a)	1c on 2c	1.75	1.60
a.	Inverted surcharge		4.50	4.50
192	A38(b)	1c on 4c	3.25	2.75
a.	Inverted surcharge		10.50	10.50
193	A40(b)	1c on 10c	1.75	1.25
a.	Inverted surcharge		3.75	3.75
193C	A40(c)	2c on 10c	175.00	125.00
b.	Inverted surcharge		175.00	
194	A41(c)	2c on 20c	22.50	21.00
a.	Inverted surcharge		45.00	45.00
195	A42(c)	2c on 50c	3.25	3.25
a.	Inverted surcharge		13.00	13.00
		Nos. 187-195 (10)	238.30	180.00

Nos. 182-184, 179, 185 Surcharged in Red, Green or Violet

d

e

f

1916

196	A50(d)	1c on 12c (R)	.35	.25
a.	Double surcharge		5.00	5.00
b.	Green surcharge		7.50	7.50
197	A51(d)	1c on 20c (G)	.35	.25
198	A50(f)	1c on 50c (G)	.35	.25
a.	Inverted surcharge		5.00	5.00
199	A47(e)	2c on 4c (V)	.35	.25
a.	Green surcharge		1.60	1.25
200	A53(f)	10c on 1s (G)	1.10	.25
a.	"VALF"		10.50	10.50
		Nos. 196-200 (5)	2.50	1.25

Official Stamps of 1909-14 Ovptd. or Srchd. in Green or Red

g

h

1916

201	O1(g)	1c red (G)	.25	.25
202	O1(h)	2c on 50c ol grn (R)	.35	.25
203	O1(g)	10c bis brn (G)	.25	.25

Postage Due Stamps of 1909 Surcharged in Violet-Black

204	D7	2c on 1c brown	.65	.65
205	D7	2c on 5c brown	.25	.25
206	D7	2c on 10c brown	.25	.25
207	D7	2c on 50c brown	.25	.25
		Nos. 201-207 (7)	2.35	2.15

Many copies of Nos. 187 to 207 have a number of pin holes. It is stated that these holes were made at the time the surcharges were printed.

The varieties which we list of the 1915 and 1916 issues were sold to the public at post offices. Many other varieties which were previously listed are now known to have been delivered to one speculator or to have been privately printed by him from the surcharging plates which he had acquired.

No. 179 Surcharged in Black

1917

208	A47	1c on 4c ver	.55	.55
a.	Double surcharge		8.25	8.25
b.	Inverted surcharge		8.25	8.25

San Martin — A54

Columbus at Salamanca — A62

Funeral of Atahualpa — A63

Battle of Arica, "Arica, the Last Cartridge" A64

Designs: 2c, Bolívar. 4c, José Gálvez. 5c, Manuel Pardo. 8c, Grau. 10c, Bolognesi. 12c, Castilla. 20c, General Cáceres.

1918 | **Centers in Black** | **Engr.**

209	A54	1c orange	.35	.25
210	A54	2c green	.35	.25
211	A54	4c lake	.45	.30
212	A54	5c dp ultra	.45	.30
213	A54	8c red brn	1.25	.45
214	A54	10c grnsh bl	.55	.30
215	A54	12c dl vio	1.75	.30
216	A54	20c ol grn	2.10	.30
217	A62	50c vio brn	8.25	.55

218	A63	1s greenish bl	21.00	.75
219	A64	2s deep ultra	35.00	1.10
		Nos. 209-219 (11)	71.50	4.85

For surcharges see Nos. 232, 233, 255-264.

Augusto B. Leguía — A65

1919, Dec. | | **Litho.**

220	A65	5c bl & blk	.35	.30
a.	Imperf.		.35	.35
b.	Center inverted		15.00	15.00
221	A65	5c brn & blk	.35	.30
a.	Imperf.		.35	.35
b.	Center inverted		15.00	15.00

Constitution of 1919.

San Martín — A66

Thomas Cochrane — A70

Oath of Independence — A69

Designs: 2c, Field Marshal Arenales. 4c, Field Marshal Las Heras. 10c, Martin Jorge Guisse. 12c, Vidal. 20c, Leguia. 50c, San Martin monument. 1s, San Martin and Leguia.

1921, July 28 | | **Engr.; 7c Litho.**

222	A66	1c ol brn & red brn	.45	.25
a.	Center inverted		600.00	600.00
223	A66	2c green	.55	.30
224	A66	4c car rose	1.90	.90
225	A69	5c ol brn	.60	.25
226	A70	7c violet	1.90	.65
227	A66	10c ultra	1.90	.65
228	A66	12c blk & slate	4.50	.90
229	A66	20c car & gray blk	4.50	1.10
230	A66	50c vio brn & dl vio	13.00	3.75
231	A69	1s car rose & yel grn	19.00	8.00
		Nos. 222-231 (10)	48.30	16.75

Centenary of Independence.

Nos. 213, 212 Surcharged in Black or Red Brown

1923-24

232	A54	5c on 8c No. 213	.75	.55
233	A54	4c on 5c (RB) ('24)	.55	.25
a.	Inverted surcharge		5.00	5.00
b.	Double surcharge, one inverted		6.00	6.00

A78

A79

Simón Bolívar — A80

Perf. 14, 14x14½, 14½, 13½
1924   Engr.; Photo. (4c, 5c)
234 A78 2c olive grn   .40 .25
235 A79 4c yellow grn   .65 .25
236 A79 5c black   2.25 .25
237 A80 10c carmine   .80 .25
238 A78 20c ultra   2.25 .30
239 A78 50c dull violet   5.50 1.10
240 A78 1s yellow brn   13.00 4.25
241 A78 2s dull blue   35.00 18.00
    Nos. 234-241 (8)   59.85 24.65
Centenary of the Battle of Ayacucho which ended Spanish power in South America.
No. 237 exists imperf.

José Tejada Rivadeneyra A81

Mariano Melgar A82

Iturregui A83

Leguía A84

José de La Mar — A85

Monument of José Olaya — A86

Statue of María Bellido — A87

De Saco — A88

José Leguía — A89

1924-29   Engr.   Perf. 12
Size: 18½x23mm
242 A81 2c olive gray   .35 .25
243 A82 4c dk grn   .35 .25
244 A83 8c black   3.25 3.25
245 A84 10c org red   .35 .25
245A A85 15c dp bl ('28)   1.00 .30
246 A86 20c blue   1.75 .30
247 A86 20c yel ('29)   2.75 .30
248 A87 50c violet   8.25 .45
249 A88 1s bis brn   15.00 1.60
250 A89 2s ultra   40.00 8.00
    Nos. 242-250 (10)   73.05 14.95

See Nos. 258, 260, 276-282.
For surcharges and overprint see Nos. 251-253, 257-260, 262, 268-271, C1.

No. 246 Surcharged in Red

a   b

1925
251 A86(a) 2c on 20c blue   550.00 550.00
252 A86(b) 2c on 20c blue   1.75 1.10
  a. Inverted surcharge   50.00 50.00
  b. Double surch., one inverted 50.00 50.00

No. 245 Overprinted

1925
253 A84 10c org red   1.75 1.75
  a. Inverted overprint   21.00 21.00
This stamp was for exclusive use on letters from the plebiscite provinces of Tacna and Arica, and posted on the Peruvian transport "Ucayali" anchored in the port of Arica.

No. 213 Surcharged

a   b

1929
255 A54(a) 2c on 8c   1.25 1.25
256 A54(b) 2c on 8c   1.25 1.25

No. 247 Surcharged

257 A86 15c on 20c yellow   1.25 1.25
  a. Inverted surcharge   13.00 13.00
    Nos. 255-257 (3)   3.75 3.75

Types of 1924 Coil Stamps
1929   Perf. 14 Horizontally
258 A81 2c olive gray   65.00 40.00
260 A84 10c orange red   70.00 37.50

Postal Tax Stamp of 1928 Overprinted

1930   Perf. 12
261 PT6 2c dark violet   .55 .55
  a. Inverted overprint   3.25 3.25

No. 247 Surcharged

262 A86 2c on 20c yellow   .55 .55

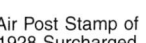

Air Post Stamp of 1928 Surcharged

263 AP1 2c on 50c dk grn   .55 .55
  a. "Habitada"   2.10 2.10

Coat of Arms — A91

Lima Cathedral A92

10c, Children's Hospital. 50c, Madonna & Child.

Perf. 12x11½, 11½x12
1930, July 5   Litho.
264 A91 2c green   1.75 .95
265 A92 5c scarlet   3.75 2.10
266 A92 10c dark blue   2.25 1.60
267 A91 50c bister brown 30.00 19.00
    Nos. 264-267 (4)   37.75 23.65
6th Pan American Congress for Child Welfare. By error the stamps are inscribed "Seventh Congress."

Type of 1924 Overprinted in Black, Green or Blue

1930, Dec. 22 Photo. Perf. 15x14
Size: 18¼x22mm
268 A84 10c orange red (Bk) 1.00 .80
  a. Inverted overprint   14.00 14.00
  b. Without overprint   8.50 8.50
  c. Double surcharge   7.00 7.00
Same with Additional Surcharge of Numerals in Each Corner
269 A84 2c on 10c org red (G) .35 .25
  a. Inverted surcharge   17.00
270 A84 4c on 10c org red (G) .35 .25
  a. Double surcharge   12.50 12.50
Engr.
Perf. 12
Size: 19x23½mm
271 A84 15c on 10c org red (Bl) .35 .25
  a. Inverted surcharge   14.00 14.00
  b. Double surcharge   14.00 14.00
    Nos. 268-271 (4)   2.05 1.55

Bolívar — A95

1930, Dec. 16   Litho.
272 A95 2c buff   .55 .55
273 A95 4c red   .90 .75
274 A95 10c blue green   .45 .30
275 A95 15c slate gray   .90 .90
    Nos. 272-275 (4)   2.80 2.50
Death cent. of General Simón Bolívar.
For surcharges see Nos. RA14-RA16.

Types of 1924-29 Issues
Size: 18x22mm
1931   Photo.   Perf. 15x14
276 A81 2c olive green   .45 .30
277 A82 4c dark green   .45 .30
279 A85 15c deep blue   1.25 .30
280 A86 20c yellow   2.10 .30
281 A87 50c violet   2.10 .45
282 A88 1s olive brown   3.25 .55
    Nos. 276-282 (6)   9.60 2.20

Pizarro — A96

Old Stone Bridge, Lima — A97

1931, July 28   Litho.   Perf. 11
283 A96 2c slate blue   2.10 1.75
284 A96 4c deep brown   2.10 1.75
285 A96 15c dark green   2.10 1.75
286 A97 10c rose red   2.10 1.75
287 A97 10c mag & lt grn   2.10 1.75
288 A97 15c yel & bl gray 2.10 1.75
289 A97 15c dk slate & red 2.10 1.75
    Nos. 283-289 (7)   14.70 12.25
1st Peruvian Phil. Exhib., Lima, July, 1931.

Manco Capac A99

Oil Refinery A100

Sugar Cane Field A102

Picking Cotton A103

Guano Deposits A104

Mining A105

Llamas A106

Arms of Piura A107

1931-32   Perf. 11, 11x11½
292 A99 2c olive black   .35 .25
293 A100 4c dark green   .65 .30
295 A102 10c red orange   1.75 .25
  a. Vertical pair, imperf. between 30.00
296 A103 15c turq blue   2.00 .30
297 A104 20c yellow   8.25 .30
298 A105 50c gray lilac   8.25 .30
299 A106 1s brown olive 20.00 1.40
    Nos. 292-299 (7)   41.25 3.10

1932, July 28   **Perf. 11½x12**
300　A107　10c dark blue　　8.25　8.00
301　A107　15c deep violet　8.25　8.00
　　　Nos. 300-301,C3 (3)　42.50　38.50

400th anniv. of the founding of the city of Piura. On sale one day. Counterfeits exist.

Parakas
A108

Chimu
A109

Inca — A110

1932, Oct. 15   **Perf. 11½, 12, 11½x12**
302　A108　10c dk vio　　.35　.25
303　A109　15c brn red　.65　.30
304　A110　50c dk brn　1.50　.30
　　　Nos. 302-304 (3)　2.50　.85

4th cent. of the Spanish conquest of Peru.

Arequipa and El Misti — A111

President Luis M. Sánchez Cerro — A112

Monument to Simón Bolívar at Lima — A115

1932-34   **Photo.**   **Perf. 13½**
305　A111　2c black　　　.25　.25
306　A111　2c blue blk　.25　.25
307　A111　2c grn ('34)　.25　.25
308　A111　4c dk brn　　.25　.25
309　A111　4c org ('34)　.25　.25
310　A112　10c vermilion　27.50　16.00
311　A115　15c ultra　　.60　.25
312　A115　15c mag ('34)　.60　.25
313　A115　20c red brn　1.25　.25
314　A115　20c vio ('34)　1.25　.25
315　A115　50c dk grn ('33)　1.25　.25
316　A115　1s dp org　11.00　1.60
317　A115　1s org brn　12.00　1.10
　　　Nos. 305-317 (13)　56.70　21.20

For overprint see No. RA24.

Statue of Liberty — A116

1934
318　A116　10c rose　　.75　.25

Pizarro — A117

The Inca — A119

Coronation of Huascar — A118

1934-35   **Perf. 13**
319　A117　10c crimson　　.40　.25
320　A117　15c ultra　　1.10　.25
321　A118　20c deep bl ('35)　2.00　.25
322　A118　50c dp red brn　1.60　.25
323　A119　1s dark vio　11.00　1.10
　　　Nos. 319-323 (5)　16.10　2.10

For surcharges and overprint see Nos. 354-355, J54, O32.

Pizarro and the Thirteen A120

Belle of Lima — A122

Francisco Pizarro — A123

4c, Lima Cathedral. 1s, Veiled woman of Lima.

1935, Jan. 18   **Perf. 13½**
324　A120　2c brown　　.55　.30
325　A120　4c violet　　.60　.45
326　A122　10c rose red　.60　.30
327　A123　15c ultra　　1.10　.75
328　A120　20c slate gray　2.25　.95
329　A122　50c olive grn　3.25　1.90
330　A122　1s Prus bl　6.00　3.75
331　A123　2s org brn　14.50　10.00
　　　Nos. 324-331,C6-C12 (15)　91.05　60.50

Founding of Lima, 4th cent.

View of Ica — A125

Lake Huacachina, Health Resort — A126

Grapes — A127

Cotton Boll — A128

Zuniga y Velazco and Philip IV — A129

Supreme God of the Nazcas — A130

Engr.; Photo. (10c)
1935, Jan. 17   **Perf. 12½**
332　A125　4c gray blue　.45　1.25
333　A126　5c dark car　.45　1.25
334　A127　10c magenta　6.50　3.25
335　A126　20c green　　2.25　2.25
336　A128　35c dark car　11.00　8.00
337　A129　50c org & brn　7.75　7.00
338　A130　1s pur & red　22.50　17.00
　　　Nos. 332-338 (7)　50.90　40.00

Founding of the City of Ica, 300th anniv.

Pizarro and the Thirteen — A131

1935-36   **Photo.**   **Perf. 13½**
339　A131　2c dp claret　.25　.25
340　A131　4c bl grn ('36)　.25　.25

For surcharge and overprints see Nos. 353, J53, RA25-RA26.

"San Cristóbal," First Peruvian Warship — A132

Naval College at Punta A133

Aerial View of Callao A135

Plan of Walls of Callao in 1746 A137

Grand Marshal José de La Mar — A138

Packetboat "Sacramento" — A139

Viceroy José Antonio Manso de Velasco — A140

Fort Maipú — A141

Plan of Fort Real Felipe A142

Independence Square, Callao — A134

Design: 15c, Docks and Custom House.

1936, Aug. 27   **Photo.**   **Perf. 12½**
341　A132　2c black　　.75　.30
342　A133　4c bl grn　　.75　.30
343　A134　5c yel brn　.75　.30
344　A135　10c bl gray　.75　.30
345　A135　15c green　　.75　.30
346　A137　20c dk brn　1.00　.30
347　A138　50c purple　1.90　.55
348　A139　1s olive grn　12.00　1.75

Engr.
349　A140　2s violet　20.00　9.00
350　A141　5s carmine　27.50　19.00
351　A142　10s red org & brn　65.00　55.00
　　　Nos. 341-351,C13 (12)　134.40　88.85

Province of Callao founding, cent.

PERU 973

Nos. 340, 321
and 323
Surcharged in
Black

1936 **Perf. 13½, 13**
353 A131 2c on 4c bl grn .35 .25
a. "0.20" for "0.02" 4.25 4.25
354 A118 10c on 20c dp bl .35 .25
a. Double surcharge 4.25 4.25
b. Inverted surcharge 4.25 4.25
355 A119 10c on 1s dk vio .55 .55
Nos. 353-355 (3) 1.25 1.05

Many varieties of the surcharge are found on these stamps: no period after "S," no period after "Cts," period after "2," "S" omitted, various broken letters, etc.
The surcharge on No. 355 is horizontal.

Peruvian
Cormorants
(Guano
Deposits) — A143

Oil Well at
Talara — A144

Avenue of
the
Republic,
Lima
A146

San Marcos
University
at Lima
A148

Post Office,
Lima — A149

Viceroy Manuel
de Amat y
Junyent — A150

Designs: 10c, "El Chasqui" (Inca Courier). 20c, Municipal Palace and Museum of Natural History. 5s, Joseph A. de Pando y Riva. 10s, Dr. José Dávila Condemarin.

1936-37 **Photo.** **Perf. 12½**
356 A143 2c lt brn .75 .30
357 A143 2c grn ('37) 1.00 .30
358 A144 4c blk brn .75 .30
359 A144 4c int blk ('37) .45 .30
360 A143 10c crimson .45 .30

361 A143 10c ver ('37) .35 .30
362 A146 15c ultra .90 .30
363 A146 15c brt bl ('37) .45 .30
364 A146 20c black .90 .30
365 A146 20c blk brn ('37) .35 .30
366 A148 50c org yel 3.25 .85
367 A148 50c dk gray vio
('37) 1.00 .30
368 A149 1s brn vio 6.50 1.10
369 A149 1s ultra ('37) 1.90 .30
Engr.
370 A150 2s ultra 13.00 2.75
371 A150 2s dk vio ('37) 4.50 .85
372 A150 5s slate bl 13.00 2.75
373 A150 10s dk vio & brn 75.00 37.50
Nos. 356-373 (18) 124.50 49.40

No. 370
Surcharged in
Black

1937
374 A150 1s on 2s ultra 3.25 3.25

 Children's Holiday Center, Ancón — A153

 Chavin Pottery — A154

 Highway Map of Peru — A155

 Archaeological Museum, Lima — A156

 Industrial Bank of Peru — A157

 Worker's Houses, Lima — A158

 Toribio de Luzuriaga A159

 Historic Fig Tree A160

 Idol from Temple of Chavin — A161

 Mt. Huascarán — A162

Imprint: "Waterlow & Sons Limited, Londres"

1938, July 1 **Photo.** **Perf. 12½, 13**
375 A153 2c emerald .25 .25
376 A154 4c org brn .25 .25
377 A155 10c scarlet .35 .25

378 A156 15c ultra .40 .25
379 A157 20c magenta .25 .25
380 A158 50c greenish blue .50 .25
381 A159 1s dp claret 1.60 .25
382 A160 2s green 6.50 .25
Engr.
383 A161 5s dl vio & brn 13.00 .75
384 A162 10s blk & ultra 27.50 1.25
Nos. 375-384 (10) 50.60 4.00

See Nos. 410-418, 426-433, 438-441. For surcharges see Nos. 388, 406, 419, 445-446A, 456, 758. Post 1940 listings are in Scott Standard catalogue, Vol. 5.

 Palace Square A163

 Lima Coat of Arms A164

 Government Palace — A165

1938, Dec. 9 **Photo.** **Perf. 12½**
385 A163 10c slate green .65 .45
Engraved and Lithographed
386 A164 15c blk, gold, red & bl 1.10 .55
Photo.
387 A165 1s olive 2.75 1.60
Nos. 385-387,C62-C64 (6) 9.30 5.90

8th Pan-American Conf., Lima, Dec. 1938.

 No. 377 Surcharged in Black

1940 **Perf. 13**
388 A155 5c on 10c scarlet .25 .25
a. Inverted surcharge

AIR POST STAMPS

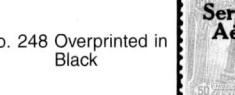 No. 248 Overprinted in Black

1927, Dec. 10 **Unwmk.** **Perf. 12**
C1 A87 50c violet 50.00 26.00
a. Inverted overprint 500.00 —

Two types of overprint: first printing, dull black ink; second printing, shiny black ink. Values are the same. No. C1a occurs in the first printing.
Counterfeits exist.

 President Augusto Bernardino Leguía — AP1

1928, Jan. 12 **Engr.**
C2 AP1 50c dark green 1.10 .55
For surcharge see No. 263.

Coat of Arms of Piura Type
1932, July 28 **Litho.**
C3 A107 50c scarlet 26.00 22.50
Counterfeits exist.

 Airplane in Flight — AP3

1934, Feb. **Engr.** **Perf. 12½**
C4 AP3 2s blue 6.50 .60
C5 AP3 5s brown 15.00 1.25

 Funeral of Atahualpa AP4

 Palace of Torre-Tagle AP7

Designs: 35c, Mt. San Cristobal. 50c, Avenue of Barefoot Friars. 10s, Pizarro and the Thirteen.

1935, Jan. 18 **Photo.** **Perf. 13½**
C6 AP4 5c emerald .35 .25
C7 AP4 35c brown .45 .45
C8 AP4 50c orange yel .90 .75
C9 AP4 1s plum 1.75 1.25
C10 AP7 2s red orange 2.75 2.40
C11 AP4 5s dp claret 11.00 7.00
C12 AP4 10s dk blue 45.00 30.00
Nos. C6-C12 (7) 62.20 42.05

4th centenary of founding of Lima.
Nos. C6-C12 overprinted "Radio Nacional" are revenue stamps.

 "La Callao," First Locomotive in South America AP9

1936, Aug. 27 **Perf. 12½**
C13 AP9 35c gray black 3.25 1.75
Founding of the Province of Callao, cent.

Nos. C4-C5 Surcharged "Habilitado" and New Value, like Nos. 353-355
1936, Nov. 4
C14 AP3 5c on 2s blue .55 .30
C15 AP3 25c on 5s brown 1.10 .55
a. Double surcharge 14.00 14.00
b. No period btwn. "O" & "25 Cts" 1.60 1.60
c. Inverted surcharge 21.00

There are many broken letters in this setting.

Mines of Peru AP10

Jorge Chávez AP14

Aerial View of Peruvian Coast AP16

View of the "Sierra" — AP17

St. Rosa of Lima — AP22

Designs: 5c, La Mar Park, Lima. 15c, Mail Steamer "Inca" on Lake Titicaca. 20c, Native Queña (flute) Player and Llama. 30c, Ram at Model Farm, Puno. 1s, Train in Mountains. 1.50s, Jorge Chavez Aviation School. 2s, Transport Plane. 5s, Aerial View of Virgin Forests.

1936-37   **Photo.**   *Perf. 12½*

C16	AP10	5c brt green	.35	.25
C17	AP10	5c emer ('37)	.35	.25
C18	AP10	15c lt ultra	.55	.25
C19	AP10	15c blue ('37)	.35	.25
C20	AP10	20c gray blk	1.50	.25
C21	AP10	20c pale ol grn ('37)	1.00	.30
C22	AP14	25c mag ('37)	.45	.25
C23	AP10	30c henna brn	4.75	1.10
C24	AP10	30c dk ol brn ('37)	1.50	.25
C25	AP14	35c brown	2.75	2.25
C26	AP10	50c yellow	.45	.30
C27	AP10	50c brn vio ('37)	.65	.25
C28	AP16	70c Prus grn	5.50	5.00
C29	AP16	70c pck grn ('37)	1.00	.85
C30	AP17	80c brn blk	6.50	5.00
C31	AP17	80c ol blk ('37)	1.25	.55
C32	AP10	1s ultra	4.75	.45
C33	AP10	1s red brn ('37)	2.40	.30
C34	AP14	1.50s red brn	7.75	6.00
C35	AP14	1.50s org yel ('37)	4.75	.45

Engr.

C36	AP10	2s deep blue	13.00	7.75
C37	AP10	2s yel grn ('37)	9.25	.80
C38	AP16	5s green	17.00	3.75
C39	AP22	10s car & brn	125.00	110.00
		Nos. C16-C39 (24)	212.80	146.85

Nos. C23, C25, C28, C30, C36 Surcharged in Black or Red

1936, June 26

C40	AP10	15c on 30c hn brn	.65	.45
C41	AP14	15c on 35c brown	.65	.45
C42	AP16	15c on 70c Prus grn	4.50	3.50
C43	AP17	25c on 80c brn blk (□)	1.00	0.00
C44	AP10	1s on 2s dp bl	7.75	6.50
		Nos. C40-C44 (5)	18.05	14.40

Surcharge on No. C43 is vertical, reading down.

First Flight in Peru, 1911 — AP23

Jorge Chávez — AP24

Airport of Limatambo at Lima — AP25

Map of Aviation Lines from Peru — AP26

Designs: 10c, Juan Bielovucic (1889-?) flying over Lima race course, Jan. 14, 1911. 15c, Jorge Chavez-Dartnell (1887-1910), French-born Peruvian aviator who flew from Brixen to Domodossola in the Alps and died of plane-crash injuries.

1937, Sept. 15   **Engr.**   *Perf. 12*

C45	AP23	10c violet	.65	.25
C46	AP24	15c dk green	.90	.25
C47	AP25	25c gray brn	.65	.25
C48	AP26	1s black	3.00	2.10
		Nos. C45-C48 (4)	5.20	2.85

Inter-American Technical Conference of Aviation, Sept. 1937.

Government Restaurant at Callao — AP27

Monument on the Plains of Junin — AP28

Rear Admiral Manuel Villar — AP29

View of Tarma — AP30

Dam, Ica River — AP31

View of Iquitos AP32

Highway and Railroad Passing AP33

Mountain Road — AP34

Plaza San Martín, Lima — AP35

National Radio of Peru AP36

Stele from Chavin Temple AP37

Ministry of Public Works, Lima — AP38

Crypt of the Heroes, Lima — AP39

Imprint: "Waterlow & Sons Limited, Londres."

1938, July 1   **Photo.**   *Perf. 12½, 13*

C49	AP27	5c violet brn	.25	.25
C50	AP28	15c dk brown	.25	.25
C51	AP29	20c dp magenta	.55	.30
C52	AP30	25c dp green	.25	.25
C53	AP31	30c orange	.25	.25
C54	AP32	50c green	.45	.30
C55	AP33	70c slate bl	.65	.30
C56	AP34	80c olive	1.25	.30
C57	AP35	1s slate grn	10.00	4.25
C58	AP36	1.50s purple	2.25	.30

Engr.

C59	AP37	2s ind & org brn	3.75	.95
C60	AP38	5s brown	18.00	1.75
C61	AP39	10s ol grn & ind	70.00	37.50
		Nos. C49-C61 (13)	107.90	46.95

See Nos. C73-C75, C89-C93, C103 in Scott Standard catalogue, Vol. 5.
For surcharges see Nos. C65, C76-C77, C82-C88, C108 in Scott Vol. 5.

Torre-Tagle Palace — AP40

National Congress Building — AP41

Manuel Ferreyros, José Gregorio Paz Soldán and Antonio Arenas — AP42

1938, Dec. 9   **Photo.**   *Perf. 12½*

C62	AP40	25c brt ultra	.90	.65
C63	AP41	1.50s brown vio	2.40	1.90
C64	AP42	2s black	1.50	.75
		Nos. C62-C64 (3)	4.80	3.30

8th Pan-American Conference at Lima.

SPECIAL DELIVERY STAMPS

No. 149 Overprinted in Black

1908   **Unwmk.**   *Perf. 12*

E1	A25	10c gray black	25.00	19.00

No. 172 Overprinted in Violet

1909

E2	A40	10c red brn & blk	40.00	22.50

No. 181 Handstamped in Violet

1910

E3	A49	10c deep blue	24.00	20.00

Two handstamps were used to make No. E2. Impressions from them measure 22½x6½mm and 24x6½mm.
Counterfeits exist of Nos. E1-3.

POSTAGE DUE STAMPS

Coat of Arms — D1

Steamship and Llama
D2   D3

D4   D5

With Grill

1874-79		Unwmk.	Engr.	Perf. 12	
J1	D1	1c bister ('79)		.45	.30
		On cover, postage due usage			1,000.
		On cover, postage usage			500.
J2	D2	5c vermilion		.55	.30
		On cover, postage due usage			350.
		On cover, postage usage			500.
J3	D3	10c orange		.65	.30
		On cover, postage due usage			350.
		On cover, postage usage			500.
J4	D4	20c blue		1.10	.55
		On cover, postage due usage			750.
J5	D5	50c brown		17.00	6.50
		On cover, postage due usage			1,000.
		On cover, postage usage			149.50
		Nos. J1-J5 (5)		19.75	7.95

A 2c green exists, but was not regularly issued.

For overprints and surcharges see Nos. 157, J6-J31, J37-J38, 8N14-8N15, 14N18.

1902-07			Without Grill	
J1a	D1	1c bister		.35
		On cover, postage due usage		250.00
		On cover, postage usage		250.00
J2a	D2	5c vermilion		.55
		On cover, postage due usage		250.00
		On cover, postage usage		250.00
J3a	D3	10c orange		.55
		On cover, postage due usage		500.00
		On cover, postage usage		250.00
J4a	D4	20c blue		.65
		On cover, postage usage		500.00
		Nos. J1a-J4a (4)		2.10

Nos. J1-J5 Overprinted in Blue or Red

1881			"PLATA" 2½mm High	
J6	D1	1c bis (Bl)		6.00	5.00
J7	D2	5c ver (Bl)		12.00	11.00
a.		Double overprint		24.00	24.00
b.		Inverted overprint		24.00	24.00
J8	D3	10c org (Bl)		12.00	11.00
a.		Inverted overprint		24.00	24.00
J9	D4	20c bl (R)		45.00	32.50
J10	D5	50c brn (Bl)		100.00	90.00
		Nos. J6-J10 (5)		175.00	149.50

In the reprints of this overprint "PLATA" is 3mm high instead of 2½mm. Besides being struck in the regular colors it was also applied to the 1, 5, 10 and 50c in red and the 20c in blue.

Overprinted in Red

1896-97				
J28	D1	1c bister		.65	.55
		On cover, postage due usage		500.00	
		On cover, postage usage			—
J29	D2	5c vermilion		.75	.45
		On cover, postage due usage		500.00	
		On cover, postage usage		150.00	
a.		Double overprint			
b.		Inverted overprint			
J30	D3	10c orange		1.00	.65
		On cover, postage due usage		500.00	
		On cover, postage usage		300.00	
a.		Inverted overprint			
J31	D4	20c blue		1.25	.85
		On cover, postage due usage		500.00	
		On cover, postage usage		300.00	
a.		Double overprint			

1881				
J11	D1	1c bister	9.00	9.00
J12	D2	5c vermilion	11.00	10.00
J13	D3	10c orange	13.00	13.00
J14	D4	20c blue	55.00	37.50
J15	D5	50c brown	125.00	125.00
		Nos. J11-J15 (5)	213.00	194.50

Originals of Nos. J11 to J15 are overprinted in brick-red, oily ink; reprints in thicker, bright red ink. The 5c exists with reprinted overprint in blue.

Overprinted "Union Postal Universal Lima Plata" in Oval in first named color and Triangle in second named color

1883				
J16	D1	1c bis (Bl & Bk)	9.00	6.50
J17	D1	1c bis (Bk & Bl)	13.00	13.00
J18	D2	5c ver (Bl & Bk)	13.00	13.00
		On cover, postage due usage		—
		On cover, postage usage		500.00
J19	D3	10c org (Bl & Bk)	13.00	13.00
		On cover, postage due usage		—
		On cover, postage usage		500.00
J20	D4	20c bl (R & Bk)	850.00	850.00
		On cover, postage due usage		—
		On cover, postage usage		500.00
J21	D5	50c brn (Bl & Bk)	60.00	60.00

Reprints of Nos. J16 to J21 have the oval overprint with "PLATA" 3mm. high. The 1c also exists with the oval overprint in red.

Overprinted in Black

1884				
J22	D1	1c bister	.90	.90
		On cover, postage due usage		500.00
		On cover, postage usage		500.00
J23	D2	5c vermilion	.90	.90
		On cover, postage due usage		250.00
		On cover, postage usage		250.00
J24	D3	10c orange	.90	.90
		On cover, postage due usage		250.00
		On cover, postage usage		350.00
J25	D4	20c blue	1.90	.90
		On cover, postage due usage		500.00
		On cover, postage usage		500.00
J26	D5	50c brown	5.50	1.75
		On cover, postage usage		500.00
		Nos. J22-J26 (5)	10.10	5.35

The triangular overprint is found in 11 types.

Overprinted "Lima Correos" in Circle in Red and Triangle in Black

1884				
J27	D1	1c bister	42.50	42.50

Reprints of No. J27 have the overprint in bright red. At the time they were made the overprint was also printed on the 5, 10, 20 and 50c Postage Due stamps.

Postage Due stamps overprinted with Sun and "CORREOS LIMA" (as shown above No. 103), alone or in combination with the "U. P. U. LIMA" oval or "LIMA CORREOS" in double-lined circle, are fancy varieties made to sell to collectors and never placed in use.

Overprinted

J32	A22	50c red ('97)	1.25	.85
		On cover, postage usage		750.00
J33	A23	1s brown ('97)	1.90	1.25
		On cover, postage usage		750.00
a.		Double overprint		
b.		Inverted overprint		
		Nos. J28-J33 (6)	6.80	4.60

Liberty — D6

1899				Engr.
J34	D6	5s yel grn	1.90	10.50
J35	D6	10s dl vio	1,700.	1,700.

For surcharge see No. J39.

DEFICIT CINCO CENTAVOS — No. J36   DÉFICIT UN CENTAVO — No. J37

1902			**On No. 159**	
J36	A31	5c on 10s bl grn	1.90	1.50
a.		Double surcharge	20.00	20.00

			On No. J4	
J37	D4	1c on 20c blue	1.10	.75
		On cover, postage due usage		750.00
		On cover, postage usage		—
a.		"DEFICIT" omitted	15.00	3.50
b.		"DÉFICIT" double	15.00	3.50
c.		"UN CENTAVO" double	15.00	3.50
d.		"UN CENTAVO" omitted	18.00	10.00

Surcharged Vertically

J38	D4	5c on 20c blue	2.75	1.75

			On No. J35	
J39	D6	1c on 10s dull vio	.75	.75
		Nos. J36-J39 (4)	6.50	4.75

D7

1909			Engr.	Perf. 12
J40	D7	1c red brown	.90	.30
		On cover, postage due usage		100.00
		On cover, postage usage		20.00
J41	D7	5c red brown	.90	.30
		On cover, postage due usage		50.00
		On cover, postage usage		10.00
J42	D7	10c red brown	1.10	.45
		On cover, postage due usage		50.00
		On cover, postage usage		10.00
J43	D7	50c red brown	1.75	.45
		On cover, postage due usage		200.00
		On cover, postage usage		30.00
		Nos. J40-J43 (4)	4.65	1.50

1921			Size: 18¼x22mm	
J44	D7	1c violet brown	.45	.30
		On cover, postage due usage		100.00
		On cover, postage usage		20.00
J45	D7	2c violet brown	.45	.30
		On cover, postage due usage		50.00
		On cover, postage usage		10.00
J46	D7	5c violet brown	.65	.30
		On cover, postage due usage		50.00
		On cover, postage usage		10.00
J47	D7	10c violet brown	.90	.45
		On cover, postage due usage		50.00
		On cover, postage usage		10.00
J48	D7	50c violet brown	2.75	1.25
		On cover, postage due usage		200.00
		On cover, postage usage		30.00
J49	D7	1s violet brown	13.00	5.25
		On cover, postage usage		30.00
J50	D7	2s violet brown	22.50	6.50
		On cover, postage usage		30.00
		Nos. J44-J50 (7)	40.70	14.35

Nos. J49 and J50 have the circle at the center replaced by a shield containing "S/.", in addition to the numeral.

In 1929 during a shortage of regular postage stamps, some of the Postage Due stamps of 1921 were used instead.

See Nos. J50A-J52, J55-J56. For surcharges see Nos. 204-207, 757 (in Scott Standard catalogue, Vol. 5).

Type of 1909-22
Size: 18¾x23mm

J50A	D7	2c violet brown	1.25	.30
		On cover, postage due usage		50.00
		On cover, postage usage		10.00
J50B	D7	10c violet brown	1.75	.45
		On cover, postage due usage		50.00
		On cover, postage usage		10.00

Type of 1909-22 Issues

1932		Photo.	Perf. 14½x14	
J51	D7	2c violet brown	1.25	.45
		On cover, postage due usage		50.00
		On cover, postage usage		10.00
J52	D7	10c violet brown	1.25	.45
		On cover, postage due usage		50.00
		On cover, postage usage		10.00

Regular Stamps of 1934-35 Overprinted in Black

1935			Perf. 13	
J53	A131	2c deep claret	1.25	.50
		On cover, postage due usage		100.00
		On cover, postage usage		100.00
J54	A117	10c crimson	1.25	.50
		On cover, postage due usage		100.00
		On cover, postage usage		100.00

Type of 1909-32
Size: 19x23mm
Imprint: "Waterlow & Sons, Limited, Londres."

1936		Engr.	Perf. 12½	
J55	D7	2c light brown	.45	.45
		On cover, postage due usage		50.00
		On cover, postage usage		100.00
J56	D7	10c gray green	.90	.90
		On cover, postage due usage		50.00
		On cover, postage usage		100.00

OFFICIAL STAMPS

Regular Issue of 1886 Overprinted in Red

1890, Feb. 2				
O2	A17	1c dl vio	2.40	2.40
		On cover		150.00
a.		Double overprint	14.00	14.00
O3	A18	2c green	2.40	2.40
		On cover		150.00
a.		Double overprint	14.00	14.00
b.		Inverted overprint	14.00	14.00
O4	A19	5c orange	3.50	2.75
		On cover		150.00
a.		Inverted overprint	14.00	14.00
b.		Double overprint	14.00	14.00
O5	A20	10c slate	2.00	1.25
		On cover		150.00
a.		Double overprint	14.00	14.00
b.		Inverted overprint	14.00	14.00
O6	A21	20c blue	5.50	3.50
		On cover		200.00
a.		Double overprint	14.00	14.00
b.		Inverted overprint	14.00	14.00
O7	A22	50c red	7.25	3.25
a.		Inverted overprint	20.00	
b.		Double overprint		
O8	A23	1s brown	9.00	8.00
a.		Double overprint	27.50	27.50
b.		Inverted overprint	27.50	27.50
		Nos. O2-O8 (7)	32.05	23.55

Nos. 118-124 (Bermudez Ovpt.) Overprinted Type "a" in Red

1894, Oct.				
O9	A17	1c green	2.40	2.40
		On cover		300.00
a.		"Gobierno" and head invtd.	11.00	9.25
b.		Dbl. ovpt. of "Gobierno"		
O10	A17	1c orange	40.00	32.50
		On cover		300.00
O11	A18	2c rose	2.40	2.40
		On cover		300.00
a.		Overprinted head inverted	17.00	17.00
b.		Both overprints inverted		
O12	A18	2c violet	2.40	2.40
		On cover		300.00
a.		"Gobierno" double		
O13	A19	5c ultra	40.00	32.50
		On cover		300.00
a.		Both overprints inverted		
O14	A19	5c blue	19.00	16.00
		On cover		300.00

O15 A20 10c green 6.00 6.00
On cover 300.00
O16 A22 50c green 9.00 9.00
Nos. O9-O16 (8) 121.20 103.20

Nos. 125-126 ("Horseshoe" Ovpt.)
Overprinted Type "a" in Red
O17 A18 2c vermilion 3.50 3.50
O18 A19 5c blue 3.50 3.50

Nos. 105, 107, 109, 113 Overprinted
Type "a" in Red

1895, May
O19 A17 1c vermilion 13.00 13.00
On cover 300.00
O20 A18 2c dp ultra 13.00 13.00
On cover 300.00
O21 A12 5c claret 11.00 11.00
On cover 300.00
O22 A14 20c dp ultra 11.00 11.00
On cover 300.00
Nos. O19-O22 (4) 48.00 48.00
Nos. O2-O22 have been extensively
counterfeited.

Nos. 141, 148, 149,
151 Overprinted in
Black

1896-1901
O23 A24 1c ultra .35 .30
On cover 30.00
O24 A25 10c yellow 1.00 .50
On cover 30.00
a. Double overprint 22.50
O25 A25 10c gray blk ('01) .35 .30
On cover 30.00
O26 A26 50c brt rose 5.00 5.00
On cover 60.00
Nos. O23-O26 (4) 6.70 6.10

O1

1909-14 Engr. Perf. 12
Size: 18½x22mm
O27 O1 1c red .55 .30
On cover 30.00
a. 1c brown red .55 .30
On cover 30.00
O28 O1 1c orange ('14) .90 .65
On cover 30.00
O29 O1 10c bis brn ('14) .35 .30
On cover 30.00
a. 10c violet brown .90 .45
On cover 30.00
O30 O1 50c ol grn ('14) 1.25 .65
On cover 60.00
a. 50c blue green 2.00 .65
On cover 60.00

Size: 18¾x23½mm
O30B O1 10c vio brn .90 .30
On cover 30.00
Nos. O27-O30B (5) 3.95 2.20

See Nos. O31, O33-O34. For parcel post and
surcharge see Nos. 201-203, 760 (in Scott
Standard catalogue, Vol. 5).

1933 Photo. Perf. 15x14
O31 O1 10c violet brown 1.25 .45
On cover 40.00

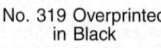

No. 319 Overprinted
in Black

1935 Unwmk. Perf. 13
O32 A117 10c crimson .35 .25
On cover 40.00

Type of 1909-33
Imprint: "Waterlow & Sons, Limited,
Londres."
1936 Engr. Perf. 12½
Size: 19x23mm
O33 O1 10c light brown .25 .25
On cover 60.00
O34 O1 50c gray green .65 .65
On cover 60.00

PARCEL POST STAMPS

PP1

PP2

PP3

1897 Typeset Unwmk. Perf. 12
Q1 PP1 1c dull lilac 4.00 3.50
Q2 PP2 2c bister 5.50 3.75
a. 2c olive 5.50 3.75
b. 2c yellow 5.50 3.75
c. Laid paper 65.00 65.00
Q3 PP3 5c dk bl 19.00 10.50
a. Tête bêche pair 375.00
Q4 PP3 10c vio brn 24.00 18.00
Q5 PP3 20c rose red 29.00 22.50
Q6 PP3 50c bl grn 85.00 75.00
Nos. Q1-Q6 (6) 166.50 133.25

Surcharged
in Black

1903-04
Q7 PP3 1c on 20c rose red 12.00 10.00
Q8 PP3 1c on 50c bl grn 12.00 10.00
Q9 PP3 5c on 10c vio brn 80.00 65.00
a. Inverted surcharge 125.00 110.00
b. Double surcharge
Nos. Q7-Q9 (3) 104.00 85.00

POSTAL TAX STAMPS

Plebiscite Issues

These stamps were not used in Tacna and
Arica (which were under Chilean occupation)
but were used in Peru to pay a supplementary
tax on letters, etc.
It was intended that the money derived from
the sale of these stamps should be used to
help defray the expenses of the plebiscite.

Morro
Arica — PT1

Adm. Grau and Col. Bolognesi
Reviewing Troops — PT2

Bolognesi
Monument
PT3

1925-26 Unwmk. Litho. Perf. 12
RA1 PT1 5c dp bl 2.75 .75
RA2 PT1 5c rose red 1.40 .55
RA3 PT1 5c yel grn 1.25 .55
RA4 PT2 10c brown 5.50 22.50
RA5 PT3 50c bl grn 35.00 17.00
Nos. RA1-RA5 (5) 45.90 41.35

PT4

1926
RA6 PT4 2c orange 1.10 .30

PT5

1927-28
RA7 PT5 2c dp org 1.10 .30
RA8 PT5 2c red brn 1.10 .30
RA9 PT5 2c dk bl 1.10 .30
RA10 PT5 2c gray vio 1.10 .30
RA11 PT5 2c bl grn ('28) 1.10 .30
RA12 PT5 20c red 5.50 1.75
Nos. RA7-RA12 (6) 11.00 3.25

PT6

1928 Engr.
RA13 PT6 2c dk vio .55 .25

The use of the Plebiscite stamps was discontinued July 26, 1929, after the settlement
of the Tacna-Arica controversy with Chile.
For overprint see No. 261.

Unemployment Fund Issues

These stamps were required in addition to
the ordinary postage, on every letter or piece
of postal matter. The money obtained by their
sale was to assist the unemployed.

Nos. 273-275
Surcharged

1931
RA14 A95 2c on 4c red 1.75 .75
a. Inverted surcharge 4.25 4.25
RA15 A95 2c on 10c bl grn .75 .75
a. Inverted surcharge 4.25 4.25
RA16 A95 2c on 15c sl gray .75 .75
a. Inverted surcharge 4.25 4.25
Nos. RA14-RA16 (3) 3.25 2.25

"Labor" Blacksmith
PT7 PT8

Two types of Nos. RA17-RA18:
I — Imprint 15mm.
II — Imprint 13¾mm.

Perf. 12x11½, 11½x12
1931-32 Litho.
RA17 PT7 2c emer (I) .25 .25
a. Type II .25
RA18 PT7 2c rose car (I) ('32) .25 .25
a. Type II .25

1932-34
RA19 PT8 2c dp gray .25 .25
RA20 PT8 2c pur ('34) .35 .25

Monument of 2nd of
May — PT9

Perf. 13, 13½, 13x13½
1933-35 Photo.
RA21 PT9 2c bl vio .25 .25
RA22 PT9 2c org ('34) .25 .25
RA23 PT9 2c brn vio ('35) .25 .25
Nos. RA21-RA23 (3) .75 .75

For overprint see No. RA27.

No. 307
Overprinted in
Black

1934 Perf. 13½
RA24 A111 2c green .25 .25
a. Inverted overprint 2.25 2.00

No. 339
Overprinted in
Black

1935
RA25 A131 2c deep claret .25 .25

No. 339 Overprinted Type "a" in Black
1936 Unwmk. Perf. 13½
RA26 A131 2c deep claret .25 .25

No. RA23
Overprinted in Black

1936 *Perf. 13x13½*
RA27 PT9 2c brn vio .25 .25
a. Double overprint 3.50
b. Overprint reading down 3.50
c. Overprint double, reading down 3.50

St. Rosa of Lima — PT10 | "Protection" by John Q. A. Ward — PT11

1937 **Engr.** *Perf. 12*
RA28 PT10 2c car rose .25 .25

Nos. RA27 and RA28 represented a tax to help erect a church.

Imprint: "American Bank Note Company"

1938 *Litho.*
RA29 PT11 2c brown .35 .25

The tax was to help the unemployed. See Nos. RA30, RA34, RA40 in Scott Standard catalogue, Vol. 5.

OCCUPATION STAMPS

Issued under Chilean Occupation

Stamps formerly listed as Nos. N1-N10 are regular issues of Chile canceled in Peru.

Stamps of Peru, 1874-80, Overprinted in Red, Blue or Black

1881-82 *Perf. 12*
N11 A17 1c org (Bl) .50 1.00
a. Inverted overprint
N12 A18 2c dk vio (Bk) .50 4.00
a. Inverted overprint 16.50
b. Double overprint 22.50
N13 A18 2c rose (Bk) 1.60 *18.00*
a. Inverted overprint
N14 A19 5c bl (R) 55.00 62.50
a. Inverted overprint
N15 A19 5c ultra (R) 90.00 100.00
N16 A20 10c grn (R) .50 *1.60*
a. Inverted overprint 6.50 6.50
b. Double overprint 12.00 12.00
N17 A21 20c brn red (Bl) 80.00 125.00
Nos. N11-N17 (7) 228.10 312.10

Reprints of No. N17 have the overprint in bright blue; on the originals it is in dull ultramarine. Nos. N11 and N12 exist with reprinted overprint in red or yellow. There are numerous counterfeits with the overprint in both correct and fancy colors.

Same, with Additional Overprint in Black

1882
N19 A17 1c grn (R) .50 .80
a. Arms inverted 8.25 10.00
b. Arms double 5.50 6.50
c. Horseshoe inverted 12.00 13.50
N20 A19 5c bl (R) .80 .80
a. Arms inverted 13.50 15.00
b. Arms double 13.50 15.00
N21 A22 50c rose (Bk) 1.60 2.00
a. Arms inverted 10.00

N22 A22 50c rose (Bl) 1.60 2.75
N23 A23 1s ultra (R) 3.25 4.50
a. Arms inverted 13.50
b. Horseshoe inverted 16.50
c. Arms and horseshoe inverted 20.00
d. Arms double 13.50
Nos. N19-N23 (5) 7.75 10.85

PROVISIONAL ISSUES

Stamps Issued in Various Cities of Peru during the Chilean Occupation of Lima and Callao

During the Chilean-Peruvian War which took place in 1879 to 1882, the Chilean forces occupied the two largest cities in Peru, Lima & Callao. As these cities were the source of supply of postage stamps, Peruvians in other sections of the country were left without stamps and were forced to the expedient of making provisional issues from whatever material was at hand. Many of these were former canceling devices made over for this purpose. Counterfeits exist of many of the overprinted stamps.

ANCACHS

(See Note under "Provisional Issues")

Regular Issue of Peru, Overprinted in Manuscript in Black

1884 **Unwmk.** *Perf. 12*
1N1 A19 5c blue 57.50 55.00

Regular Issues of Peru, Overprinted in Black

1N2 A19 5c blue 18.00 16.50

Regular Issues of Peru, Overprinted in Black

1N3 A19 5c blue 90.00 82.50
1N4 A20 10c green 55.00 40.00
1N5 A20 10c slate 55.00 35.00

Same, with Additional Overprint "FRANCA"

1N6 A20 10c green 82.50 42.50

Overprinted

1N7 A19 5c blue 30.00 25.00
1N8 A20 10c green 30.00 25.00

Same, with Additional Overprint "FRANCA"

1N9 A20 10c green

Revenue Stamp of Peru, 1878-79, Ovptd. in Black "CORREO Y FISCAL" & "FRANCA" — A1

1N10 A1 10c yellow 37.50 37.50

APURIMAC

(See Note under "Provisional Issues")
Provisional Issue of Arequipa Overprinted in Black

Overprint Covers Two Stamps

1885 **Unwmk.** *Imperf.*
2N1 A6 10c gray 100.00 90.00

Some experts question the status of No. 2N1.

AREQUIPA

(See Note under "Provisional Issues")

Coat of Arms
A1 A2
Overprint ("PROVISIONAL 1881-1882") in Black

1881, Jan. **Unwmk.** *Imperf.*
3N1 A1 10c blue 2.50 3.50
a. 10c ultramarine 2.50 4.00
b. Double overprint 12.00 13.50
c. Overprint on back of stamp 8.25 10.00
3N2 A2 25c rose 2.50 6.00
a. "2" in upper left corner invtd. 8.25
b. "Cevtavos" 8.25 10.00
c. Double overprint 12.00 13.50

The overprint also exists on 5s yellow.
The overprints "1883" in large figures or "Habilitado 1883" are fraudulent.
For overprints see Nos. 3N3, 4N1, 8N1, 10N1, 15N1-15N3.

With Additional Overprint Handstamped in Red

1881, Feb.
3N3 A1 10c blue 3.50 3.50
a. 10c ultramarine 13.50 11.50

A4

1883 *Litho.*
3N7 A4 10c dull rose 3.50 5.00
a. 10c vermilion 3.50 5.00

Overprinted in Blue like No. 3N3

3N9 A4 10c vermilion 5.00 4.00
a. 10c dull rose 3.50 5.00

See No. 3N10. For overprints see Nos. 8N2, 8N9, 10N2, 15N4.
Reprints of No. 3N9 are in different colors from the originals, orange, bright red, etc. They are printed in sheets of 20 instead of 25.

Redrawn
3N10 A4 10c brick red (Bl) 160.00

The redrawn stamp has small triangles without arabesques in the lower spandrels. The palm branch at left of the shield and other parts of the design have been redrawn.

Same Overprint in Black, Violet or Magenta On Regular Issues of Peru

1884 **Embossed with Grill** *Perf. 12*
3N11 A17 1c org (Bk, V or M) 6.50 6.50
3N12 A18 2c dk vio (Bk) 6.50 6.50
3N13 A19 5c bl (Bk, V or M) 2.00 1.40
a. 5c ultramarine (Bk or M) 8.25 6.50
3N15 A20 10c sl (Bk) 3.50 2.50
3N16 A21 20c brn red (Bk, V or M) 25.00 25.00
3N18 A22 50c grn (Bk or V) 25.00 25.00
3N20 A23 1s rose (Bk or V) 35.00 35.00
Nos. 3N11-3N20 (7) 103.50 101.90

A5 | A6 | A7 | A8

Rear Admiral M. L. Grau A7 | Col. Francisco Bolognesi A8

Same Overprint as on Previous Issues

1885 *Imperf.*
3N22 A5 5c olive (Bk) 5.25 5.25
3N23 A6 10c gray (Bk) 5.25 4.75
3N25 A7 5c blue (Bk) 5.25 4.75
3N26 A8 10c olive (Bk) 5.25 3.25
Nos. 3N22-3N26 (4) 21.00 18.00

For overprints see Nos. 2N1, 8N5-8N6, 8N12-8N13, 10N9, 10N12, 15N10-15N12.
These stamps have been reprinted without overprint; they exist however with forged overprint. Originals are on thicker paper with distinct mesh, reprints on paper without mesh.

Without Overprint

3N22a A5 5c olive 5.25 5.25
3N23a A6 10c gray 4.00 3.25
3N25a A7 5c blue 4.00 3.25
3N26a A8 10c olive 4.00 3.25
Nos. 3N22a-3N26a (4) 17.25 15.00

AYACUCHO

(See Note under "Provisional Issues")

Provisional Issue of Arequipa Overprinted in Black

1881 **Unwmk.** *Imperf.*
4N1 A1 10c blue 150.00 125.00
a. 10c ultramarine 150.00 125.00

CHACHAPOYAS

(See Note under "Provisional Issues")

Regular Issue of Peru Overprinted in Black

1884 **Unwmk.** *Perf. 12*
5N1 A19 5c ultra 190.00 160.00

CHALA

(See Note under "Provisional Issues")

Regular Issues of Peru Overprinted in Black

1884	**Unwmk.**	**Perf. 12**	
6N1	A19	5c blue	17.00 13.00
6N2	A20	10c slate	22.50 16.00

CHICLAYO

(See Note under "Provisional Issues")

Regular Issue of Peru Overprinted in Black

1884	**Unwmk.**	**Perf. 12**	
7N1	A19	5c blue	29.00 18.00

Same, Overprinted **FRANCA**

7N2	A19	5c blue	65.00 37.50

CUZCO

(See Note under "Provisional Issues")

Provisional Issues of Arequipa Overprinted in Black

1881-85	**Unwmk.**	**Imperf.**	
8N1	A1	10c blue	125.00 110.00
8N2	A4	10c red	125.00 110.00

Overprinted "CUZCO" in an oval of dots

8N5	A5	5c olive	200.00 175.00
8N6	A6	10c gray	200.00 175.00

Regular Issue of Peru Overprinted in Black "CUZCO" in a Circle
Perf. 12

8N7	A19	5c blue	50.00 50.00

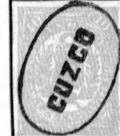

Provisional Issues of Arequipa Overprinted in Black

1883		**Imperf.**	
8N9	A4	10c red	18.00 18.00

Same Overprint in Black on Regular Issues of Peru

1884		**Perf. 12**	
8N10	A19	5c blue	29.00 18.00
8N11	A20	10c slate	29.00 18.00

Same Overprint in Black on Provisional Issues of Arequipa
Imperf

8N12	A5	5c olive	27.50 27.50
8N13	A6	10c gray	8.00 8.00

Postage Due Stamps of Peru Surcharged in Black

Perf. 12

8N14	D1	10c on 1c bis	200.00 175.00
8N15	D3	10c on 10c org	200.00 175.00

HUACHO

(See Note under "Provisional Issues")

Regular Issues of Peru Overprinted in Black

1884	**Unwmk.**	**Perf. 12**	
9N1	A19	5c blue	16.00 16.00
9N2	A20	10c green	13.00 13.00
9N3	A20	10c slate	27.50 27.50
	Nos. 9N1-9N3 (3)		56.50 56.50

MOQUEGUA

(See Note under "Provisional Issues")

Provisional Issues of Arequipa Overprinted in Violet

Overprint 27mm wide.

1881-83	**Unwmk.**	**Imperf.**	
10N1	A1	10c blue	75.00 70.00
10N2	A4	10c red ('83)	75.00 70.00

Same Overprint on Regular Issues of Peru in Violet

1884		**Perf. 12**	
10N3	A17	1c orange	75.00 70.00
10N4	A19	5c blue	55.00 35.00

Red Overprint

10N5	A19	5c blue	65.00 55.00

Same Overprint in Violet on Provisional Issues of Peru of 1880
Perf. 12

10N6	A17	1c grn (R)	12.00 9.75
10N7	A18	2c rose (Bl)	15.00 15.00
10N8	A19	5c bl (R)	30.00 30.00

Same Overprint in Violet on Provisional Issue of Arequipa

1885		**Imperf.**	
10N9	A6	10c gray	85.00 42.50

Regular Issues of Peru Overprinted in Violet

10N10	A19	5c blue	200.00 125.00
10N11	A20	10c slate	85.00 42.50

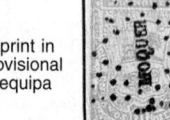

Same Overprint in Violet on Provisional Issue of Arequipa

Imperf

10N12	A6	10c gray	125.00 110.00

PAITA

(See Note under "Provisional Issues")

Regular Issues of Peru Overprinted

Black Overprint

1884	**Unwmk.**	**Perf. 12**	
11N1	A19	5c blue	40.00 40.00
a.		5c ultramarine	40.00 40.00
11N2	A20	10c green	27.50 27.50
11N3	A20	10c slate	40.00 40.00

Red Overprint

11N4	A19	5c blue	40.00 40.00

Overprint lacks ornaments on #11N4-11N5.

Violet Overprint Letters 5½mm High

11N5	A19	5c ultra	40.00 40.00
a.		5c blue	

PASCO

(See Note under "Provisional Issues")

Regular Issues of Peru Overprinted in Magenta or Black

1884	**Unwmk.**	**Perf. 12**	
12N1	A19	5c blue (M)	27.50 12.50
a.		5c ultramarine (M)	42.50 22.50
12N2	A20	10c green (Bk)	65.00 55.00
12N3	A20	10c slate (Bk)	125.00 90.00
	Nos. 12N1-12N3 (3)		217.50 157.50

PISCO

(See Note under "Provisional Issues")

Regular Issue of Peru Overprinted in Black

1884	**Unwmk.**	**Perf. 12**	
13N1	A19	5c blue	350.00 275.00

PIURA

(See Note under "Provisional Issues")

Regular Issues of Peru Overprinted in Black

1884	**Unwmk.**	**Perf. 12**	
14N1	A19	5c blue	35.00 21.00
a.		5c ultramarine	45.00 27.50
14N2	A21	20c brn red	150.00 150.00
14N3	A22	50c green	350.00 350.00

Same Overprint in Black on Provisional Issues of Peru of 1881

14N4	A17	1c grn (R)	35.00 35.00
14N5	A18	2c rose (Bl)	55.00 55.00
14N6	A19	5c ultra (R)	70.00 70.00

Regular Issues of Peru Overprinted in Violet, Black or Blue **PIURA**

14N7	A19	5c bl (V)	27.50 18.00
a.		5c ultramarine (V)	27.50 18.00
b.		5c ultramarine (Bk)	27.50 18.00
14N8	A21	20c brn red (Bk)	150.00 150.00
14N9	A21	20c brn red (Bl)	150.00 150.00

Same Overprint in Black on Provisional Issues of Peru of 1881

14N10	A17	1c grn (R)	35.00 35.00
14N11	A19	5c bl (R)	42.50 42.50
a.		5c ultramarine (R)	70.00 70.00

Regular Issues of Peru Overprinted in Black

14N13	A19	5c blue	7.25 6.50
14N14	A21	20c brn red	150.00 150.00

Regular Issues of Peru Overprinted in Black

14N15	A19	5c ultra	110.00 100.00
14N16	A21	20c brn red	250.00 225.00

Same Overprint on Postage Due Stamp of Peru

14N18	D3	10c orange	125.00 125.00

PUNO

(See Note under "Provisional Issues")

Provisional Issue of Arequipa Overprinted in Violet or Blue

Diameter of outer circle 20½mm, PUNO 11½mm wide, M 3½mm wide. Other types of this overprint are fraudulent.

1882-83	**Unwmk.**	**Imperf.**	
15N1	A1	10c blue (V)	29.00 29.00
a.		10c ultramarine (V)	35.00 35.00
15N3	A2	25c red (V)	45.00 35.00
15N4	A4	10c dl rose (Bl)	29.00 29.00
a.		10c vermilion (Bl)	29.00 29.00

The overprint also exists on 5s yellow of Arequipa.

Same Overprint in Magenta on Regular Issues of Peru

1884		**Perf. 12**	
15N5	A17	1c orange	19.00 15.00
15N6	A18	2c violet	65.00 65.00
15N7	A19	5c blue	10.00 10.00

Violet Overprint

15N8	A19	5c blue	10.00 10.00
a.		5c ultramarine	20.00 20.00

Same Overprint in Black on Provisional Issues of Arequipa

1885		**Imperf.**	
15N10	A5	5c olive	16.00 13.50
15N11	A6	10c gray	10.00 10.00
15N12	A8	10c olive	19.00 19.00

Regular Issues of Peru Overprinted in Magenta

1884		**Perf. 12**	
15N13	A17	1c orange	21.00 21.00
15N14	A18	2c violet	24.00 21.00
15N15	A19	5c blue	10.00 10.00
a.		5c ultramarine	20.00 20.00
15N16	A20	10c green	29.00 22.50
15N17	A21	20c brn red	150.00 150.00
15N18	A22	50c green	

YCA

(See Note under "Provisional Issues")

Regular Issues of Peru
Overprinted in Violet

1884		Unwmk.	Perf. 12	
16N1	A17	1c orange	70.00	70.00
16N3	A19	5c blue	22.50	18.00

Black Overprint

16N5	A19	5c blue	19.00	9.00

Magenta Overprint

16N6	A19	5c blue	19.00	9.00
16N7	A20	10c slate	55.00	55.00

Regular Issues of
Peru Overprinted in
Black

16N12	A19	5c blue	275.00	225.00
16N13	A21	20c brown	350.00	275.00

Regular Issues of Peru
Overprinted in Carmine

16N14	A19	5c blue	275.00	225.00
16N15	A20	10c slate	350.00	275.00

Same, with
Additional Overprint

16N21	A19	5c blue	275.00	275.00
16N22	A21	20c brn red	475.00	450.00

Various other stamps exist with the overprints "YCA" and "YCA VAPOR" but they are not known to have been issued. Some of them were made to fill a dealer's order and others are reprints or merely cancellations.

PHILIPPINES

ˌfi-lə-ˈpēnz

LOCATION — Group of about 7,100 islands and islets in the Malay Archipelago, north of Borneo, in the North Pacific Ocean
AREA — 115,830 sq. mi.
POP. — 53,350,000 (est. 1984)
CAPITAL — Quezon City

The islands were ceded to the United States by Spain in 1898. On November 15, 1935, they were given their independence, subject to a transition period which ended July 4, 1946.

20 Cuartos = 1 Real

100 Centavos de Peso = 1 Peso (1864)

100 Centimos de Escudo = 1 Escudo (1871)

100 Centimos de Peseta = 1 Peseta (1872)

1000 Milesimas de Peso = 100 Centimos or Centavos = 1 Peso (1878)

100 Cents = 1 Dollar (1899)

100 Centavos = 1 Peso (1906)

Watermarks

Wmk. 104 —
Loops

Wmk. 257 —
Curved Wavy
Lines

Watermark 104: loops from different watermark rows may or may not be directly opposite each other.

Wmk. 190PI —
Single-lined PIPS

Wmk. 191PI —
Double-lined PIPS

Watermark 191 has double-lined USPS.

Wmk. 233 —
"Harrison &
Sons,
London." in
Script

Issued under Spanish Dominion

The stamps of Philippine Islands punched with a round hole were used on telegraph receipts or had been withdrawn from use and punched to indicate that they were no longer available for postage. In this condition they sell for less, as compared to postally used copies.

Many color varieties exist of Nos. 1-88. Only major varieties are listed.

Queen Isabella II
A1   A2

1854		Unwmk.	Engr.	Imperf.
1	A1	5c orange	5,000.	350.
		On cover		3,000.
2	A1	10c carmine	850.	250.
		On cover		25,000.
d.		Half used as 5c on cover		50,000.
4	A2	1r blue	900.	300.
a.		1r slate blue	800.	300.
		On cover		
c.		"CORROS" (#4, pos. 26)	4,500.	4,000.
d.		"CORROS" (#4a, pos. 26)	4,500.	4,000.
5	A2	2r slate green	775.	250.

Forty varieties of each value.
A 10c black exists. This is a proof or an unissued trial color. Value about $10,000.
For overprints see Nos. 24A-25A.
Covers: There are two covers recorded with No. 2; two with No. 2a; seven with No. 4 and shades; five with No. 5 and shades.

Values for pairs

1	A1	5c orange	5,000.	650.
2	A1	10c carmine	1,550.	525.
a.		10c pale rose	2,100.	875.
4	A2	1r blue	1,500.	600.
a.		1r slate blue	1,900.	825.
c.		"CORROS"(#4, pos. 26)	7,250.	2,750.
5	A2	2r yellow green	2,300.	440.

Values for blocks of 4

1	A1	5c orange	16,500.	2,200.
2	A1	10c carmine	4,000.	1,550.
a.		10c pale rose	5,000.	2,200.
4	A2	1r blue	4,200.	1,650.
a.		1r slate blue	5,100.	2,100.
c.		"CORROS"(#4, pos. 26)	—	—
5	A2	2r yellow green	6,500.	1,550.

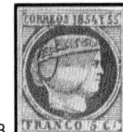

A3

1855			Litho.	
6	A3	5c pale red	1,500.	500.
		On cover		8,000.

Four varieties.

A3a

Redrawn

7	A3a	5c vermilion	8,500.	1,100.
		On cover		45,000.

In the redrawn stamp the inner circle is smaller and is not broken by the labels at top and bottom. Only one variety.
Covers: There are 10 covers recorded with singles of No. 6, two with pairs; four covers with No. 7, including one with a pair.

Values for pairs

6	A3	5c red	4,200.	1,600.
7	A3	5c vermilion	22,000.	—

Values for blocks of 4

6	A3	5c pale red	21,000.	7,000.
7	A3	5c vermilion	—	—

Queen Isabella II — A4

Blue Paper

1856		Typo.	Wmk. 104	
8	A4	1r gray green	100.00	75.00
		On cover		300.00
9	A4	2r carmine	400.00	200.00
		On cover		700.00

Nos. 8 and 9 used can be distinguished from Cuba Nos. 2 and 3 only by the cancellations.
For overprints, see Nos. 26-27.

Queen Isabella II — A5

Dot After "CORREOS"

1859, Jan. 1		Litho.	Unwmk.	
10	A5	5c vermilion	17.50	9.00
		On cover		600.00
a.		5c scarlet	24.00	12.00
		On cover		750.00

b.		5c orange	32.50	17.50
		On cover		1,000.
11	A5	10c lilac rose	17.00	27.50
		On cover		2,000.

Four varieties of each value, repeated in the sheet.
For overprint see No. 28.
Covers: Only two covers recorded bearing No. 11a.

Values for pairs

10	A5	5c vermilion	42.50	22.00
a.		5c scarlet	57.50	22.00
b.		5c orange	77.50	42.50
11	A5	10c lilac rose	40.00	62.50

Values for blocks of 4

10	A5	5c vermilion	87.50	47.50
a.		5c scarlet	120.00	65.00
b.		5c orange	160.00	95.00
11	A5	10c lilac rose	85.00	150.00
a.		10c rose	90.00	125.00
b.		10c pale rose	90.00	125.00

Covers
Values are for commercial covers paying correct rates. Philatelic covers sell for less.

Dot after CORREOS
A6   A7

1861-62				
12	A6	5c vermilion	37.50	42.50
		On cover		4,000.
13	A7	5c dull red ('62)	190.00	95.00
		On cover		3,000.

No. 12, one variety only, repeated in the sheet.
For overprint see No. 29.
Covers: There are about seven covers recorded with No. 12; 15 with No. 13.

Values for pairs

12	A6	5c vermilion	85.00	92.50
13	A7	5c dull red	475.00	240.00

Values for blocks of 4

12	A6	5c vermilion	190.00	210.00
13	A7	5c dull red	1,150.	600.00

Colon after
CORREOS — A8

A8a   A9

1863

14	A8	5c vermilion	13.50	8.25
		On cover		3,000.
	a.	10c carmine vermilion	14.00	11.00
		On cover		3,000.
15	A8	10c carmine	37.50	250.00
16	A8	1r violet	850.00	3,000.
17	A8	2r blue	650.00	1,000.
	a.	2r dark blue	625.00	350.00
18	A8a	1r gray grn	400.00	140.00
	a.	1r deep gray green	350.00	175.00
		On cover		3,500.
20	A9	1r green	200.00	60.00
		On cover		2,000.
		Nos. 14-20 (6)	*2,151.*	*4,458.*

No. 18 has "CORREOS" 10½mm long, the point of the bust is rounded and is about 1mm from the circle which contains 94 pearls.

No. 20 has "CORREOS" 11mm long, and the bust ends in a sharp point which nearly touches the circle of 76 pearls.

For overprints see Nos. 30-34.

Values for pairs

14	A8	5c vermilion	55.00	15.00
	a.	10c carmine vermilion	40.00	32.50
	b.	10c scarlet vermilion	40.00	32.50
15	A8	10ccarmine	105.00	—
16	A8	1r violet	1,700.	—
17	A8	2r blue	1,450.	—
18	A8a	1r gray grn	700.00	300.00
	a.	1r deep gray green	750.00	375.00
20	A9	1r green	375.00	110.00

Values for blocks of 4

14	A8	5c vermilion	80.00	60.00
	a.	10c carmine vermilion	85.00	80.00
	b.	10c scarlet vermilion	85.00	80.00
15	A8	10ccarmine	225.00	400.00
16	A8	1r violet	3,750.	3,900.
17	A8	2r blue	3,250.	3,000.
	a.	2r dark blue	3,100.	2,500.
18	A8a	1r gray grn	1,600.	775.00
	a.	1r deep gray green	1,750.	1,000.
20	A9	1r green	875.00	300.00

A10

1864 Typo.

21	A10	3⅛c blk, *yellow*	4.75	2.00
		On cover		400.00
	a.	3⅛c blk, *buff*	7.00	3.75
		On cover		400.00
22	A10	6⅜c grn, *rose*	6.75	2.00
		On cover		500.00
23	A10	12⅜c blue, *sal*	9.00	1.75
		On cover		600.00
24	A10	25c red, *buff*	12.00	3.75
		On cover		700.00
	a.	25c red, *rose*	17.50	4.75
		On cover		800.00
		Nos. 21-24 (4)	*32.50*	*9.50*

For overprints see Nos. 35-38.

Values for pairs

21	A10	3⅛c blk, *yellow*	9.50	6.50
	a.	3⅛c blk, *buff*	18.50	11.00
22	A10	6⅜c grn, *rose*	16.00	7.00
23	A10	12⅜c blue, *sal*	18.50	6.00
24	A10	25c red, *buff*	25.00	11.00
	a.	25c red, *rose*	45.00	21.00

Values for blocks of 4

21	A10	3⅛c blk, *yellow*	22.50	16.00
	a.	3⅛c blk, *buff*	42.50	27.50
22	A10	6⅜c grn, *rose*	35.00	15.00
23	A10	12⅜c blue, *sal*	42.50	13.50
24	A10	25c red, *buff*	55.00	26.00
	a.	25c red, *rose*	100.00	50.00

Preceding Issues
Handstamped

1868-74

24A	A1	5c orange ('74)	*8,000.*	*6,750.*
25	A2	1r sl bl ('74)	*2,400.*	*1,050.*
	b.	"CORROS" (pos. 26)	*4,500.*	*3,100.*
25A	A2	2r grn ('74)	*3,900.*	*8,000.*
26	A4	1r grn, *bl* ('73)	180.00	80.00
27	A4	2r car, *bl* ('73)	325.00	225.00
27A	A5	5c vermilion ('74)	*6,000.*	*12,000.*
28	A5	10c rose ('74)	80.00	45.00
29	A7	5c dull red ('73)	250.00	175.00

30	A8	5c ver ('72)	115.00	35.00
		On cover		3,500.
30A	A8	10c car ('72)	*6,000.*	
31	A8	1r vio ('72)	700.00	600.00
		On cover		20,000.
32	A8	2r bl ('72)	525.00	425.00
33	A8a	1r grn grn ('71)	175.00	85.00
34	A9	1r grn ('71)	50.00	30.00
		On cover		800.00
35	A10	3⅛c blk, *yellow*	9.50	4.75
		On cover		400.00
36	A10	6⅜c grn, *rose*	9.50	4.75
		On cover		400.00
37	A10	12⅜c bl, *salmon*	31.00	16.00
		On cover		500.00
38	A10	25c red, *buff*	29.00	15.00
		On cover		1,500.

Covers: There is one cover recorded with No. 31.

Reprints exist of #24A-38. These have crisp, sharp letters and usually have a broken first "A" of "HABILITADO."

Imperforates
Imperforates of designs A11-A16 probably are from proof or trial sheets.

"Spain"
A11

King Amadeo
A12

1871 Typo. Perf. 14

39	A11	5c blue	95.00	9.25
		On cover		1,000.
40	A11	10c deep green	15.00	6.00
		On cover		1,000.
41	A11	20c brown	110.00	50.00
42	A11	40c rose	170.00	60.00
		Nos. 39-42 (4)	*390.00*	*125.25*

1872

43	A12	12c rose	20.00	5.50
		On cover		400.00
44	A12	16c blue	200.00	37.50
		On cover		5,000.
45	A12	25c gray lilac	13.50	5.50
		On cover		400.00
46	A12	62c violet	40.00	9.75
		On cover		500.00
47	A12	1p25c yellow brn	85.00	42.50
		On cover		3,000.
		Nos. 43-47 (5)	*358.50*	*100.75*

A 12c in deep blue and a 62c in rose exist but were not issued. Value $30 each.
Covers: There are two covers recorded with No. 47.

"Peace"
A13

King Alfonso
XII
A14

1874

48	A13	12c gray lilac	22.50	5.50
		On cover		600.00
49	A13	25c ultra	8.25	2.75
		On cover		600.00
50	A13	62c rose	65.00	5.50
		On cover		600.00
51	A13	1p25c brown	300.00	82.50
		On cover		4,000.
		Nos. 48-51 (4)	*395.75*	*96.25*

1875-77

52	A14	2c rose	3.50	.95
		On cover		400.00
53	A14	2c dk blue ('77)	260.00	100.00
		On cover		2,500.
54	A14	6c orange ('77)	14.00	16.00
		On cover		1,000.
55	A14	10c blue ('77)	4.50	.85
		On cover		400.00
56	A14	12c lilac ('76)	4.50	.85
		On cover		300.00
57	A14	20c vio brn ('76	20.00	5.00
		On cover		3,000.
58	A14	25c dp green ('76	25.00	5.00
		On cover		3,000.
		Nos. 52-58 (7)	*331.50*	*128.65*

Imperforates of type A14 are from proof or trial sheets.

Nos. 52, 63
Handstamp
Surcharged in Black or
Blue

1877-79

59	A14	12c on 2c rose (Bk)	85.00	22.50
		On cover		3,000.
	a.	Surcharge inverted	*600.00*	*375.00*
	b.	Surcharge double	*475.00*	*350.00*
60	A16	12c on 25m blk (Bk) ('79)	105.00	47.50
		On cover		4,000.
	a.	Surcharge inverted	*875.00*	*650.00*
61	A16	12c on 25m blk (Bl) ('79)	350.00	225.00
		On cover		
		Nos. 59-61 (3)	*540.00*	*295.00*

A16

1878-79 Typo.

62	A16	25m black	3.50	.45
		On cover		300.00
63	A16	25m green ('79)	67.50	62.50
64	A16	50m dull lilac	34.00	10.00
		On cover		400.00
65	A16	0.0625 (62½m) gray	65.00	15.00
66	A16	100m car ('79)	110.00	37.50
67	A16	100m yel grn ('79)	10.00	2.75
		On cover		350.00
68	A16	125m blue	6.00	.50
		On cover		250.00
69	A16	200m rose ('79)	37.50	5.75
		On cover		400.00
70	A16	200m vio rose ('79)	350.00	900.00
		On cover		5,000.
71	A16	250m bister ('79)	13.00	2.75
		Nos. 62-71 (10)	*696.50*	*1,037.*

Imperforates of type A16 are from proof or trial sheets.
For surcharges see Nos. 60-61, 72-75.
Covers: There is one cover recorded with No. 70.

Stamps of 1878-79 Surcharged

a   b

1879

72	A16 (a)	2c on 25m grn	55.00	11.00
	b.	Inverted surcharge	*425.00*	*325.00*
73	A16 (a)	8c on 100m car	52.50	6.50
		On cover		2,000.
	a.	"COREROS"	*150.00*	*80.00*
	b.	Surcharge double		
74	A16 (b)	2c on 25m grn	300.00	57.50
75	A16 (b)	8c on 100m car	300.00	57.50
		Nos. 72-75 (4)	*707.50*	*132.50*

Covers: There are four covers recorded with No. 73.

A19

Original state: The medallion is surrounded by a heavy line of color of nearly even thickness, touching the line below "Filipinas"; the opening in the hair above the temple is narrow and pointed.

1st retouch: The line around the medallion is thin, except at the upper right, and does not touch the horizontal line above it; the opening in the hair is slightly wider and rounded; the lock of hair above the forehead is shaped like a broad "V" and ends in a point; there is a faint white line below it, which is not found on the original. The shape of the hair and the width of the white line vary.

2nd retouch: The lock of hair is less pointed; the white line is much broader.

1880-86 Typo.

76	A19	2c carmine	.90	.80
		On cover		200.00
77	A19	2½c brown	8.00	1.90
		On cover		350.00
78	A19	2⅝c ultra ('82)	1.25	2.25
		On cover		350.00
79	A19	2⅝c ultra, 1st retouch ('83)	.90	1.90
		On cover		350.00
80	A19	2⅝c ultra, 2nd retouch ('86)	10.50	4.25
		On cover		300.00
81	A19	5c gray blue ('82)	.90	1.90
		On cover		350.00
82	A19	6⅝c dp grn ('82)	7.00	11.00
		On cover		1,000.
83	A19	8c yellow brn	36.00	6.25
		On cover		300.00
84	A19	10c green	525.00	525.00
85	A19	10c brn lil ('82)	3.75	4.25
		On cover		350.00
86	A19	12⅝c brt rose ('82)	1.90	1.90
		On cover		250.00
87	A19	20c bis brn ('82)	3.50	1.75
		On cover		600.00
88	A19	25c dk brn ('82)	4.75	1.90
		On cover		800.00
		Nos. 76-88 (13)	*604.35*	*565.05*

See #137-139. For surcharges see #89-108, 110-111.

Surcharges exist double or inverted on many of Nos. 89-136.

Stamps and Type of 1880-86 Handstamp Surcharged in Black, Green or Red

c   d

e   f

Design A19

1881-88 Black Surcharge

89	(c)	2c on 2½c	4.25	2.25
		On cover		400.00
91	(f)	10c on 2⅝c (#80) ('87)	6.25	2.10
92	(d)	20c on 8c brn ('83)	10.00	3.25
93	(d)	1r on 2c ('83)	190.00	325.00
94	(d)	2r on 2⅝c (#78; '83)	6.25	2.10
		On cover		300.00
	a.	On No. 79	57.50	100.00
	b.	On No. 80	110.00	200.00

Most used examples of No. 93 are hole punched. Postally used examples are rare.

Green Surcharge

95	(e)	8c on 2c ('83)	11.00	2.25
95A	(d+e)	8c on 1r on 2c ('83)	200.00	275.00
96	(d)	10c on 2c ('83)	5.50	2.25
97	(d)	1r on 2c ('83)	190.00	150.00
98	(d)	1r on 5c gray bl ('83)	8.00	3.25
99	(d)	1r on 8c brn ('83)	10.00	3.25

Red Surcharge

100	(f)	1c on 2⅝c (#79; '87)	1.25	2.00
101	(f)	1c on 2⅝c (#80; '87)	3.50	3.00
102	(d)	16c on 2⅝c		
103	(d)	1r on 2c ('83)	6.25	3.25
		On cover		550.00
104	(d)	1r on 5c bl gray ('83)	12.00	5.25

Handstamp Surcharged in Magenta

g   h

1887

105	A19 (g)	8c on 2⅝c (#79)	1.25	.90
		On cover		300.00
106	A19 (g)	8c on 2⅝c (#80)	3.50	2.00
		On cover		500.00

1888

107	A19 (h)	2⅝c on 1c gray grn	1.75	1.00
108	A19 (h)	2⅝c on 5c bl gray	1.90	.90
109	N1 (h)	2⅝c on ⅛c grn	1.90	1.40
110	A19 (h)	2⅝c on 50m bis	1.90	.80
111	A19 (h)	2⅝c on 10c grn	1.75	.65
		Nos. 107-111 (5)	9.20	4.75

No. 109 is surcharged on a newspaper stamp of 1886-89 and has the inscriptions shown on cut N1.

On Revenue Stamps

R1   R2

R3(d)

Handstamp Surcharged in Black, Yellow, Green, Red, Blue or Magenta

j   k

m

1881-88   Black Surcharge

112	R1(c)	2c on 10c bis	50.00	12.50
113	R1(j)	2⅝c on 10c bis	12.00	1.75
		On cover		500.00
114	R1(j)	2⅝c on 2r bl	200.00	140.00
		On cover		2,000.
115	R1(j)	8c on 10c bis	450.00	6,000.
		On cover		30,000.
116	R1(j)	8c on 2r bl	8.50	2.10
		On cover		500.00
118	R1(d)	1r on 12⅝c gray bl ('83)	7.75	3.75
		On cover		600.00
119	R1(d)	1r on 10c bis ('82)	11.50	4.00

One example of No. 115 on cover is reported.

Yellow Surcharge

120	R2(e)	2c on 200m grn ('82)	6.25	8.00
121	R1(d)	16c on 2r bl ('83)	6.00	7.00

Green Surcharge

122	R1(d)	1r on 10c bis ('83)	11.50	4.00

Red Surcharge

123	R1(d+e)	2r on 8c on 2r blue	55.00	35.00
a.		On 8c on 2r blue (d+d)	80.00	75.00
124	R1(d)	1r on 12⅝c gray bl ('83)	16.50	13.00
125	R1(k)	6⅝c on 12⅝c gray bl ('85)	5.00	24.00
126	R3(d)	1r on 10p bis ('83)	95.00	23.00
127	R1(m)	1r green	350.00	700.00
127A	R1(m)	2r blue	900.00	1,150.
127B	R1(d)	1r on 1r grn ('83)	700.00	800.00
128	R2(d)	1r on 1p grn ('83)	150.00	65.00
129	R2(d)	1r on 200m grn ('83)	125.00	150.00
129A	R1(d)	2r on 2r blue	900.00	800.00

The surcharge on No. 129A is pale red.

Blue Surcharge

129B	R1(m)	10c bister ('81)	700.00	1,000.

Magenta Surcharge

130	R2(h)	2⅝c on 200m grn ('88)	4.25	2.10
131	R2(h)	2⅝c on 20c brn ('88)	12.50	5.75

On Telegraph Stamps

T1   T2

Surcharged in Red, or Black

1883-88

132	T1(d)	2r on 250m ultra (R)	7.75	3.75
133	T1(d)	20c on 250m ultra	750.00	375.00
134	T1(d)	2r on 250m ultra	10.00	4.75
135	T1(d)	1r on 20c on 250m ultra (R & Bk)	9.25	4.75

Magenta Surcharge

136	T2(h)	2⅝c on 1c bis ('88)	.95	.90

Most, if not all, used stamps of No. 133 are hole-punched. Used value is for examples with hole punches.

Type of 1880-86 Redrawn

1887-89

137	A19	50m bister	.65	6.00
		On cover		6.00
138	A19	1c gray grn ('88)	.65	5.00
		On cover		500.00
a.		1c yellow green ('89)	.70	6.00
		On cover		600.00
139	A19	6c yellow brn ('88)	10.00	47.50
		On cover		—
		Nos. 137-139 (3)	11.30	58.50

King Alfonso
XIII — A36

1890-97   Typo.

140	A36	1c violet ('92)	1.00	.75
		On cover		500.00
141	A36	1c rose ('94)	17.50	11.00
		On cover		600.00
142	A36	1c bl grn ('96)	2.25	1.00
		On cover		600.00
143	A36	1c claret ('97)	16.00	10.00
144	A36	2c claret ('94)	.25	.25
		On cover		200.00
145	A36	2c violet ('92)	.25	.25
		On cover		100.00
146	A36	2c dk brn ('94)	.25	3.50
		On cover		200.00
147	A36	2c ultra ('96)	.35	.35
		On cover		200.00
148	A36	2c gray brn ('96)	.85	2.25
		On cover		400.00
149	A36	2⅝c dull blue	.55	.30
		On cover		400.00
150	A36	2⅝c ol gray ('92)	.30	1.40
		On cover		400.00
151	A36	5c dark blue	.50	1.40
		On cover		300.00
152	A36	5c slate green	.85	1.40
		On cover		500.00
153	A36	5c green ('92)	.80	.55
		On cover		500.00
155	A36	5c vio brn ('96)	9.50	4.00
		On cover		500.00
a.		5c dk vio	750.00	300.00
156	A36	5c blue grn ('96)	6.00	3.00
157	A36	6c brown vio ('92)	.30	1.40
158	A36	6c red orange ('94)	.95	2.25
159	A36	6c car rose ('94)	6.00	4.00
160	A36	8c yellow grn	.30	.30
		On cover		600.00
161	A36	8c ultra ('92)	.75	.30
		On cover		400.00
162	A36	8c red brn ('94)	.85	.30
		On cover		500.00
163	A36	10c blue grn	1.75	1.25
		On cover		400.00
164	A36	10c pale cl ('91)	1.60	.40
		On cover		400.00
165	A36	10c claret ('94)	.75	.40
		On cover		300.00
166	A36	10c yel brn ('96)	.85	.30
		On cover		200.00
167	A36	12⅝c yellow grn	.30	.25
		On cover		500.00
168	A36	12⅝c org ('92)	.85	.25
		On cover		500.00
169	A36	15c red brn ('92)	.85	.30
		On cover		300.00
170	A36	15c rose ('94)	2.10	.75
		On cover		400.00
171	A36	15c bl grn ('96)	2.60	2.10
		On cover		800.00
172	A36	20c pale vermilion	30.00	40.00
173	A36	20c salmon	40.00	65.00

174	A36	20c gray brn ('92)	2.75	.45
		On cover		700.00
175	A36	20c dk vio ('94)	20.00	10.00
		On cover		600.00
176	A36	20c org ('96)	5.50	2.25
		On cover		500.00
177	A36	25c brown	9.50	2.00
		On cover		700.00
178	A36	25c dull bl ('91)	2.50	.50
		On cover		700.00
179	A36	40c dk vio ('97)	17.50	6.00
		On cover		700.00
180	A36	80c claret ('97)	30.00	40.00
		Nos. 140-180 (40)	235.75	222.15

Many of Nos. 140-180 exist imperf and in different colors. These are considered to be proofs.

Stamps of Previous Issues Handstamp Surcharged in Blue, Red, Black or Violet

1897   Blue Surcharge

181	A36	5c on 5c green	3.00	5.00
		On cover		2,000.
182	A36	15c on 15c red brn	5.50	3.00
		On cover		2,000.
183	A36	20c on 20c gray brn	12.00	12.00

Red Surcharge

185	A36	5c on 5c green	4.50	4.75
		On cover		2,500.

Black Surcharge

187	A36	5c on 5c green	100.00	300.00
188	A36	15c on 15c rose	5.50	3.00
		On cover		2,000.
189	A36	20c on 20c dk vio	35.00	18.00
190	A36	20c on 25c brown	25.00	40.00

Violet Surcharge

191	A36	15c on 15c rose	15.00	30.00
		On cover		3,000.
		Nos. 181-191 (9)	205.50	415.75

Inverted, double and other variations of this surcharge exist.

The 5c on 5c blue gray (#81a) was released during US Administration. The surcharge is a mixture of red and black inks.

Impressions in violet black are believed to be reprints. The following varieties are known: 5c on 2⅝c olive gray, 5c on 5c blue green, 5c on 25c brown, 15c on 15c rose, 15c on 15c red brown, 15c on 25c brown, 20c on 20c gray brown, 20c on 20c dark violet, 20c on 25c brown. Value: each $40. These surcharges are to be found double, inverted, etc.

King Alfonso
XIII — A39

1898   Typo.

192	A39	1m orange brown	.25	1.25
		On cover		500.00
193	A39	2m orange brown	.25	1.75
		On cover		600.00
194	A39	3m orange brown	.25	1.75
		On cover		600.00
195	A39	4m orange brown	13.00	40.00
		On cover		2,000.
196	A39	5m orange brown	.25	2.75
		On cover		500.00
197	A39	1c black violet	.25	.60
		On cover		500.00
198	A39	2c dk bl grn	.25	.60
		On cover		400.00
199	A39	3c dk brown	.25	.60
		On cover		300.00
200	A39	4c orange	20.00	47.50
201	A39	5c car rose	.25	.60
		On cover		500.00
202	A39	6c dk blue	1.15	1.75
203	A39	8c gray brown	.60	.35
		On cover		200.00
204	A39	10c vermilion	2.75	1.25
		On cover		300.00
205	A39	15c dull ol grn	2.25	1.10
		On cover		400.00
206	A39	20c maroon	2.50	1.60
		On cover		600.00
207	A39	40c violet	1.25	1.75
208	A39	60c black	6.00	4.00
209	A39	80c red brown	8.00	5.50
210	A39	1p yellow green	30.00	10.00
211	A39	2p slate blue	50.00	12.00
		Nos. 192-211 (20)	139.50	136.70

One cliche of No. 197 was included in error within the sheet of Puerto Rico No. 140. Pairs showing this error se-tenant are known. See Puerto Rico No. 140b.

Nos. 192-211 exist imperf. Value, set $2,000.

The Spanish surrendered in May 1898. Some Filipinos continued to fight until 1901. During this period provisional stamps were created in several areas. Some of these stamps may have been totally philatelic. See the *Scott Specialized Catalogue of U. S. Stamps* for stamps issued by Gen. Aguinaldo's Filipino Revolutionary Government.

Issued under U.S. Administration

Regular Issues of the United States Overprinted in Black

1899-1901   Unwmk.   Perf. 12

On U.S. Stamp No. 260

212	A96	50c orange	300.	225.
		Never hinged	775.	
		On cover		—

On U.S. Stamps Nos. 279, 279B, 279Bd, 279Be, 279Bf, 279Bc, 268, 281, 282C, 283, 284, 275, 275a

Wmk. Double-lined USPS (191)

213	A87	1c yellow green	4.00	.60
		Never hinged	10.00	
		On cover		10.00
214	A88	2c red, type IV	1.75	.60
		Never hinged	4.25	
		On cover		10.00
a.		2c orange red, type IV, ('01)	1.75	.60
		Never hinged	4.25	
b.		Bklt. pane of 6, red, type IV ('00)	250.00	300.00
		Never hinged	600.00	
c.		2c reddish carmine, type IV	2.50	1.00
		Never hinged	6.00	
		On cover		12.50
d.		2c rose carmine, type IV	3.00	1.10
		Never hinged	7.25	
		On cover		15.00
215	A89	3c purple	9.00	1.25
		Never hinged	21.50	
		On cover		50.00
216	A91	5c blue	9.00	1.00
		Never hinged	21.50	
		On cover		20.00
a.		Inverted overprint		6,500.

No. 216a is valued in the grade of fine.

217	A94	10c brown, type I	35.00	4.00
		Never hinged	80.00	
		On cover		100.00
217A	A94	10c orange brown, type II	125.00	27.50
		Never hinged	325.00	
		On cover		250.00

No. 217A was overprinted on U.S. No. 283a, vertical watermark.

218	A95	15c olive green	40.00	8.00
		Never hinged	95.00	
		On cover		110.00
219	A96	50c orange	125.00	37.50
		Never hinged	300.00	
		On cover		400.00
a.		50c red orange	250.00	55.00
		Never hinged	600.00	
		Nos. 213-219 (8)	348.75	80.45

Regular Issue

Same Overprint in Black On U.S. Stamps Nos. 280b, 282 and 272

1901, Aug. 30

220	A90	4c orange brown	35.00	5.00
		Never hinged	80.00	
		On cover		50.00
221	A92	6c lake	40.00	7.00
		Never hinged	95.00	
		On cover		65.00
222	A93	8c violet brown	40.00	7.50
		Never hinged	95.00	
		On cover		50.00
		Nos. 220-222 (3)	115.00	19.50

Same Overprint in Red On U.S. Stamps Nos. 276, 276A, 277a and 278

223	A97	$1 black, type I	300.00	200.00
		Never hinged	1,000.	
		On cover		800.00
223A	A97	$1 black, type II	2,000.	750.00
		Never hinged	5,000.	
		On cover		—
224	A98	$2 dark blue	350.00	325.00
		Never hinged	1,150.	
		On cover		3,250.

225	A99 $5 dark green	650.00	875.00	
	Never hinged	1,600.		
	On cover		12,500.	

Regular Issue
Same Overprint in Black On U.S.
Stamps Nos. 300 to 310 and Shades
1903-04

226	A115 1c blue green	7.00	.40	
	Never hinged	15.50		
	On cover		8.25	
227	A116 2c carmine	9.00	1.10	
	Never hinged	20.00		
	On cover		10.00	
228	A117 3c bright violet	67.50	12.50	
	Never hinged	150.00		
	On cover		55.00	
229	A118 4c brown	80.00	22.50	
	Never hinged	175.00		
a.	4c orange brown	80.00	20.00	
	Never hinged	175.00		
	On cover		40.00	
230	A119 5c blue	17.50	1.00	
	Never hinged	40.00		
	On cover		22.50	
231	A120 6c brownish lake	85.00	22.50	
	Never hinged	190.00		
	On cover		65.00	
232	A121 8c violet black	50.00	15.00	
	Never hinged	125.00		
	On cover		300.00	
233	A122 10c pale red brown	35.00	2.25	
	Never hinged	80.00		
	On cover		27.50	
a.	10c red brown	35.00	3.00	
	Never hinged	80.00		
	On cover		35.00	
b.	Pair, one without overprint	1,500.		
234	A123 13c purple black	35.00	17.50	
	Never hinged	80.00		
	13c brown violet	35.00	17.50	
	Never hinged	80.00		
	On cover		55.00	
235	A124 15c olive green	60.00	15.00	
	Never hinged	135.00		
	On cover		100.00	
236	A125 50c orange	125.00	35.00	
	Never hinged	275.00		
	On cover		300.00	
	Nos. 226-236 (11)	571.00	144.75	
	Set, never hinged	1,285.		

Same Overprint in Red On U.S.
Stamps Nos. 311, 312 and 313

237	A126 $1 black	300.00	200.00	
	Never hinged	800.00		
	On cover		1,000.	
238	A127 $2 dark blue	650.00	800.00	
	Never hinged	1,500.		
239	A128 $5 dark green	900.00	2,750.	
	Never hinged	1,800.		
240	A129 2c carmine	8.00	2.25	
	Never hinged	17.50		
	On cover		3.50	
a.	Booklet pane of 6	2,000.		
b.	2c scarlet	8.00	2.75	
	Never hinged	19.00		
	On cover		4.00	
c.	As "b," booklet pane of 6	—		

José Rizal — A40

Designs: 4c, McKinley. 6c, Ferdinand Magellan. 8c, Miguel Lopez de Legaspi. 10c, Gen. Henry W. Lawton. 12c, Lincoln. 16c, Adm. William T. Sampson. 20c, Washington. 26c, Francisco Carriedo. 30c, Franklin. 1p-10p, Arms of City of Manila.

Wmk. Double-lined PIPS (191)
1906, Sept. 8   Perf. 12

241	A40 2c deep green	.40	.25	
	Never hinged	1.00		
a.	2c yellow green ('10)	.60	.25	
	Never hinged	1.50		
b.	Booklet pane of 6	750.00	800.00	
	Never hinged	1,500.		
242	A40 4c carmine	.50	.25	
	Never hinged	1.25		
a.	4c carmine lake ('10)	1.00	.25	
	Never hinged	2.50		
b.	Booklet pane of 6	650.00	700.00	
	Never hinged	1,250.		
243	A40 6c violet	2.50	.25	
	Never hinged	6.25		
244	A40 8c brown	4.50	.90	
	Never hinged	11.00		
245	A40 10c blue	3.50	.30	
	Never hinged	8.75		
a.	10c dark blue	3.50	.30	
	Never hinged	8.75		
246	A40 12c brown lake	9.00	2.50	
	Never hinged	22.50		
247	A40 16c violet black	6.00	.35	
	Never hinged	15.00		
248	A40 20c orange brown	7.00	.35	
	Never hinged	17.50		
249	A40 26c violet brown	11.00	3.00	
	Never hinged	27.50		
250	A40 30c olive green	6.50	1.75	
	Never hinged	16.00		
251	A40 1p orange	50.00	7.50	
	Never hinged	120.00		

252	A40 2p black	50.00	1.75	
	Never hinged	130.00		
253	A40 4p dark blue	160.00	20.00	
	Never hinged	375.00		
254	A40 10p dark green	225.00	80.00	
	Never hinged	575.00		
	Nos. 241-254 (14)	535.90	119.15	
	Set, never hinged	1,316.		

1909-13   Change of Colors

255	A40 12c red orange	11.00	3.00	
	Never hinged	27.50		
256	A40 16c olive green	6.00	.75	
	Never hinged	15.00		
257	A40 20c yellow	9.00	1.25	
	Never hinged	22.50		
258	A40 26c blue green	3.50	1.25	
	Never hinged	8.75		
259	A40 30c ultramarine	13.00	3.50	
	Never hinged	32.50		
260	A40 1p pale violet	45.00	5.00	
	Never hinged	110.00		
260A	A40 2p violet brown ('13)	100.00	12.00	
	Never hinged	250.00		
	Nos. 255-260A (7)	187.50	26.75	
	Set, never hinged	466.25		

Wmk. Single-lined PIPS (190)
1911

261	A40 2c green	.75	.25	
	Never hinged	1.80		
	On cover		4.00	
a.	Booklet pane of 6	800.00	900.00	
	Never hinged	1,400.		
262	A40 4c carmine lake	3.00	.25	
	Never hinged	6.75		
	On cover		6.00	
a.	4c carmine	—	—	
b.	Booklet pane of 6	600.00	700.00	
	Never hinged	1,100.		
263	A40 6c deep violet	3.00	.25	
	Never hinged	6.75		
264	A40 8c brown	9.50	.50	
	Never hinged	21.50		
265	A40 10c blue	4.00	.25	
	Never hinged	9.00		
266	A40 12c orange	4.00	.45	
	Never hinged	9.00		
267	A40 16c olive green	4.50	.40	
	Never hinged	10.00		
a.	16c pale olive green	4.50	.50	
	Never hinged	10.00		
268	A40 20c yellow	3.50	.25	
	Never hinged	7.75		
a.	20c orange	4.00	.30	
	Never hinged	9.00		
269	A40 26c blue green	6.00	.30	
	Never hinged	13.50		
270	A40 30c ultramarine	6.00	.50	
	Never hinged	13.50		
271	A40 1p pale violet	27.50	.60	
	Never hinged	62.50		
272	A40 2p violet brown	45.00	1.00	
	Never hinged	100.00		
273	A40 4p deep blue	550.00	110.00	
	Never hinged	1,100.		
274	A40 10p deep green	200.00	30.00	
	Never hinged	400.00		
	Nos. 261-274 (14)	866.75	145.00	
	Set, never hinged	1,862.		

1914

275	A40 30c gray	12.00	.50	
	Never hinged	27.50		

1914   Perf. 10

276	A40 2c green	3.00	.25	
	Never hinged	7.00		
a.	Booklet pane of 6	750.00	800.00	
	Never hinged	1,250.		
277	A40 4c carmine	4.00	.30	
	Never hinged	9.00		
a.	Booklet pane of 6	750.00		
	Never hinged	1,300.		
278	A40 6c light violet	45.00	9.50	
	Never hinged	100.00		
a.	6c deep violet	50.00	6.25	
	Never hinged	110.00		
279	A40 8c brown	55.00	10.50	
	Never hinged	125.00		
280	A40 10c dark blue	30.00	.25	
	Never hinged	67.50		
281	A40 16c olive green	100.00	5.00	
	Never hinged	225.00		
282	A40 20c orange	40.00	1.00	
	Never hinged	85.00		
283	A40 30c gray	60.00	4.50	
	Never hinged	130.00		
284	A40 1p pale violet	150.00	3.75	
	Never hinged	350.00		
	Nos. 276-284 (9)	487.00	35.05	
	Set, never hinged	1,020.		

1918   Perf. 11

285	A40 2c green	21.00	4.25	
	Never hinged	40.00		
a.	Booklet pane of 6	750.00	800.00	
	Never hinged	1,300.		
286	A40 4c carmine	26.00	6.00	
	Never hinged	55.00		
a.	Booklet pane of 6	1,350.	2,000.	
287	A40 6c deep violet	40.00	6.00	
	Never hinged	90.00		
287A	A40 8c light brown	220.00	25.00	
	Never hinged	400.00		
288	A40 10c dark blue	60.00	3.00	
	Never hinged	140.00		
289	A40 16c olive green	110.00	10.00	
	Never hinged	250.00		
289A	A40 20c orange	175.00	12.00	
	Never hinged	400.00		
289C	A40 30c gray	95.00	18.00	
	Never hinged	215.00		

289D	A40 1p pale violet	100.00	25.00	
	Never hinged	225.00		
	Nos. 285-289D (9)	847.00	109.25	
	Set, never hinged	1,815.		

1917   Unwmk.   Perf. 11

290	A40 2c yellow green	.25	.25	
	Never hinged	.55		
	On cover		4.00	
a.	2c dark green	.30	.25	
	Never hinged	.65		
b.	Vert. pair, imperf. horiz.	2,000.		
c.	Horiz. pair, imperf. between	1,500.		
d.	Vertical pair, imperf. btwn.	1,750.	1,000.	
e.	Booklet pane of 6	27.50	30.00	
	Never hinged	60.00		
291	A40 4c carmine	.30	.25	
	Never hinged	.65		
	On cover		6.00	
a.	4c light rose	.30	.25	
	Never hinged	.65		
b.	Booklet pane of 6	20.00	22.50	
	Never hinged	35.00		
292	A40 6c deep violet	.35	.25	
	Never hinged	.70		
a.	6c lilac	.40	.25	
	Never hinged	.80		
b.	6c red violet	.40	.25	
	Never hinged	.70		
c.	Booklet pane of 6	550.00	800.00	
	Never hinged	900.00		
293	A40 8c yellow brown	.30	.25	
	Never hinged	.50		
a.	8c orange brown	.30	.25	
	Never hinged	.50		
294	A40 10c deep blue	.30	.25	
	Never hinged	.65		
295	A40 12c red orange	.35	.25	
	Never hinged	.75		
296	A40 16c light olive green	65.00	.25	
	Never hinged	130.00		
a.	16c olive bister	65.00	.50	
	Never hinged	130.00		
297	A40 20c orange yellow	.35	.25	
	Never hinged	.75		
298	A40 26c green	.50	.45	
	Never hinged	1.10		
a.	26c blue green	.60	.25	
	Never hinged	1.35		
299	A40 30c gray	.55	.25	
	Never hinged	1.35		
300	A40 1p pale violet	40.00	1.00	
	Never hinged	90.00		
a.	1p red lilac	40.00	1.00	
	Never hinged	90.00		
b.	1p pale rose lilac	40.00	1.10	
	Never hinged	90.00		
301	A40 2p violet brown	35.00	1.00	
	Never hinged	77.50		
302	A40 4p blue	32.50	.50	
	Never hinged	72.50		
a.	4p dark blue	35.00	.55	
	Never hinged	77.50		
	Nos. 290-302 (13)	175.75	5.20	
	Set, never hinged	377.00		

1923-26

Design: 16c, Adm. George Dewey.

303	A40 16c olive bister	1.00	.25	
	Never hinged	2.25		
a.	16c olive green	1.25	.25	
	Never hinged	2.75		
304	A40 10p deep green ('26)	50.00	20.00	
	Never hinged	110.00		

Legislative Palace A42

1926, Dec. 20   Perf. 12

319	A42 2c green & black	.50	.25	
	Never hinged	1.25		
a.	Horiz. pair, imperf. between	300.00		
b.	Vert. pair, imperf. between	575.00		
320	A42 4c carmine & black	.55	.40	
	Never hinged	1.20		
a.	Horiz. pair, imperf. between	325.00		
b.	Vert. pair, imperf. between	600.00		
321	A42 16c olive green & black	1.00	.65	
	Never hinged	2.25		
a.	Horiz. pair, imperf. between	350.00		
b.	Vert. pair, imperf. between	625.00		
c.	Double impression of center	675.00		
322	A42 18c light brown & black	1.10	.50	
	Never hinged	2.50		
a.	Double impression of center	1,250.		
b.	Vertical pair, imperf. between	675.00		
323	A42 20c orange & black	2.00	1.00	
	Never hinged	4.50		
a.	20c orange & brown	600.00		
b.	As No. 323, imperf., pair	575.00	575.00	
c.	As "a," imperf., pair	1,750.		
d.	Vert. pair, imperf. between	700.00		
324	A42 24c gray & black	1.00	.55	
	Never hinged	2.25		
a.	Vert. pair, imperf. between	700.00		
325	A42 1p rose lilac & black	47.50	50.00	
	Never hinged	100.00		
a.	Vert. pair, imperf. between	700.00		
	Nos. 319-325 (7)	53.65	53.35	
	Set, never hinged	83.95		

Opening of the Legislative Palace.

No. 322a is valued in the grade of fine.
For overprints, see Nos. O1-O4.

Rizal Type of 1906
Coil Stamp
1928   Perf. 11 Vertically

326	A40 2c green	7.50	12.50	
	Never hinged	18.75		
	On cover		100.00	

Types of 1906-1923
1925-31   Imperf.

340	A40 2c yel green ('31)	.50	.50	
	Never hinged	.90		
a.	2c green ('25)	.80	.75	
	Never hinged	1.80		
	P# block of 10, never hinged	800.00		
341	A40 4c car rose ('31)	.50	1.00	
	Never hinged	1.00		
a.	4c carmine ('25)	1.20	1.00	
	Never hinged	2.75		
342	A40 6c violet ('31)	3.00	3.75	
	Never hinged	5.00		
a.	6c deep violet ('25)	12.00	8.00	
	Never hinged	26.00		
343	A40 8c brown ('31)	2.00	5.00	
	Never hinged	4.00		
a.	8c yellow brown ('25)	13.00	8.00	
	Never hinged	26.00		
344	A40 10c blue ('31)	5.00	7.50	
	Never hinged	12.00		
a.	10c deep blue ('25)	45.00	20.00	
	Never hinged	100.00		
345	A40 12c dp orange ('31)	8.00	10.00	
	Never hinged	15.00		
a.	12c red orange ('25)	60.00	35.00	
	Never hinged	135.00		
346	A40 16c olive green ('31)	6.00	7.50	
	Never hinged	11.00		
a.	16c bister green ('25)	42.50	18.00	
	Never hinged	100.00		
347	A40 20c dp yel orange ('31)	5.00	7.50	
	Never hinged	11.00		
a.	20c yellow orange ('25)	45.00	20.00	
	Never hinged	100.00		
348	A40 26c green ('31)	6.00	9.00	
	Never hinged	11.00		
a.	26c blue green ('25)	45.00	25.00	
	Never hinged	110.00		
349	A40 30c light gray ('31)	8.00	10.00	
	Never hinged	16.00		
a.	30c gray ('25)	45.00	25.00	
	Never hinged	110.00		
350	A40 1p light violet ('31)	10.00	15.00	
	Never hinged	20.00		
a.	1p violet ('25)	200.00	100.00	
	Never hinged	425.00		
351	A40 2p brn vio ('31)	30.00	45.00	
	Never hinged	80.00		
a.	2p violet brown ('25)	400.00	400.00	
	Never hinged	675.00		
352	A40 4p blue ('31)	80.00	90.00	
	Never hinged	150.00		
a.	4p deep blue ('25)	2,200.	1,100.	
	Never hinged	3,500.		
353	A40 10p green ('31)	175.00	225.00	
	Never hinged	300.00		
a.	10p deep green ('25)	3,000.	2,950.	
	Never hinged	5,000.		
	Nos. 340-353 (14)	339.00	436.75	
	Set, never hinged	636.90		
	Nos. 340a-353a (14)	6,109.	4,710.	

Nos. 340a-353a were the original post office issue. These were reprinted twice in 1931 for sale to collectors (Nos. 340-353).

Mount Mayon, Luzon A43

Post Office, Manila A44

Pier No. 7, Manila Bay — A45

(See footnote) — A46

Rice
Planting
A47

Rice
Terraces
A48

Baguio
Zigzag
A49

1932, May 3 .... *Perf. 11*
354 A43 2c yellow green .... .75 .30
   Never hinged 1.25
355 A44 4c rose carmine .... .75 .30
   Never hinged 1.25
356 A45 12c orange .... 1.00 .75
   Never hinged 1.25
357 A46 18c red orange 50.00 15.00
   Never hinged 80.00
358 A47 20c yellow .... 1.10 .75
   Never hinged 1.75
359 A48 24c deep violet 1.75 1.00
   Never hinged 3.00
360 A49 32c olive brown 1.75 1.00
   Never hinged 3.00 6.50
   Nos. 354-360 (7) 57.10 19.10
   Set, never hinged 91.50

The 18c vignette was intended to show Pagsanjan Falls in Laguna, central Luzon, and is so labeled. Through error the stamp pictures Vernal Falls in Yosemite National Park, California.

For overprints see #C29-C35, C47-C51, C63 (in Scott Standard catalogue, Vol. 5).

Nos. 302, 302a
Surcharged in Orange
or Red

1932
368 A40 1p on 4p blue (O) 7.50 1.00
   Never hinged 12.00
   On cover 1.00
  a. 1p on 4p dark blue (O) ... 7.50 1.00
   Never hinged 12.00
369 A40 2p on 4p dark blue (R) .. 10.00 1.50
   Never hinged 17.00
  a. 2p on 4p blue (R) 10.00 1.00
   Never hinged 17.00
   On cover 2.00

Far Eastern Championship
Issued in commemoration of the Tenth Far Eastern Championship Games.

Baseball
Players
A50

Tennis
Player — A51

Basketball
Players — A52

1934, Apr. 14 .... *Perf. 11½*
380 A50 2c yellow brown .... 1.50 .80
   Never hinged 2.25
381 A51 6c ultramarine .... .25 .25
   Never hinged .... .30
382 A52 16c violet brown ...... .50 .50
   Never hinged .... .75
  a. Vertical pair, imperf. between 700.00
  a. Vert. pair, imperf. horiz. ... 950.00
   Nos. 380-382 (3) 2.25 1.55
   Set, never hinged 3.30

José Rizal — A53

Woman and
Carabao
A54

La Filipina — A55

Pearl Fishing
A56

Fort
Santiago
A57

Salt
Spring — A58

Magellan's
Landing,
1521 — A59

"Juan de la
Cruz" — A60

Rice Terraces
A61

"Blood
Compact,"
1565 — A62

Barasoain
Church,
Malolos
A63

Battle of
Manila
Bay, 1898
A64

Montalban
Gorge
A65

George
Washington
A66

1935, Feb. 15 .... *Perf. 11*
383 A53 2c rose .... .25 .25
   Never hinged .... .25
384 A54 4c yellow green .... .25 .25
   Never hinged .... .25
385 A55 6c dark brown .... .25 .25
   Never hinged .... .35
386 A56 8c violet .... .25 .25
   Never hinged .... .35
387 A57 10c rose carmine ...... .30 .25
   Never hinged .... .45
388 A58 12c black .... .35 .25
   Never hinged .... .50
389 A59 16c dark blue .... .35 .25
   Never hinged .... .55
390 A60 20c light olive green . .35 .25
   Never hinged .... .45
391 A61 26c indigo .... .40 .40
   Never hinged .... .60
392 A62 30c orange red .... .40 .40
   Never hinged .... .60
393 A63 1p red orange &
        black 2.00 1.25
   Never hinged 3.00
394 A64 2p bister brown &
        black 12.00 2.00
   Never hinged 16.00
395 A65 4p blue & black 12.00 4.00
   Never hinged 16.00
396 A66 5p green & black 25.00 5.00
   Never hinged 50.00
   Nos. 383-396 (14) 54.15 15.05
   Set, never hinged 74.45

For overprints & surcharges see Nos. 411-424, 433-446, 449, 463-466, 468, 472-474, 478-484, 485-494, C52-C53, O15-O36, O38, O40-O43, N2-N9, N28, NO2-NO6. Post 1940 listings are in Scott Standard catalogue, Vol. 5.

Issues of the Commonwealth
Issued to commemorate the inauguration of the Philippine Commonwealth, Nov. 15, 1935.

The Temples of Human
Progress — A67

1935, Nov. 15
397 A67 2c carmine rose .... .25 .25
   Never hinged .... .30
398 A67 6c deep violet .... .25 .25
   Never hinged .... .30
399 A67 16c blue .... .25 .25
   Never hinged .... .35
400 A67 36c yellow green ...... .40 .30
   Never hinged .... .60
401 A67 50c brown .... .60 .55
   Never hinged .... .90
   Nos. 397-401 (5) 1.75 1.60
   Set, never hinged 2.45

Jose Rizal Issue
75th anniversary of the birth of Jose Rizal (1861-1896), national hero of the Filipinos.

Jose Rizal — A68

1936, June 19 .... *Perf. 12*
402 A68 2c yellow brown .... .25 .25
   Never hinged .... .25
403 A68 6c slate blue .... .25 .25
   Never hinged .... .25
  a. Imperf. vertically, pair .... 1,000.
   Never hinged .... 1,500.
404 A68 36c red brown .... .50 .70
   Never hinged .... .75
   Nos. 402-404 (3) 1.00 1.20
   Set, never hinged 1.25

Commonwealth Anniversary Issue
Issued in commemoration of the first anniversary of the Commonwealth.

President
Manuel L.
Quezon — A69

1936, Nov. 15 .... *Perf. 11*
408 A69 2c orange brown .... .25 .25
   Never hinged .... .30
409 A69 6c yellow green .... .25 .25
   Never hinged .... .30
410 A69 12c ultramarine .... .25 .25
   Never hinged .... .30
   Nos. 408-410 (3) .... .75 .75
   Set, never hinged .... .90

Stamps of 1935 Overprinted in Black

a

COMMON-
WEALTH

b

COMMONWEALTH

1936-37
411 A53(a) 2c rose .... .25 .25
   Never hinged .... .25
  a. Bklt. pane of 6 ('37) ... 2.50 2.00
   Never hinged 4.00
  b. Hyphen omitted 125.00 100.00
412 A54(b) 4c yel grn ('37) .... .50 *4.00*
   Never hinged .... .75
413 A55(a) 6c dark brown ...... .25 .25
   Never hinged .... .25
414 A56(b) 8c violet ('37) .... .25 .25
   Never hinged .... .35
   On cover .... .25
415 A57(b) 10c rose carmine ... .25 .25
   Never hinged .... .25
  a. "COMMONWEALT" ...... 20.00 —
   Never hinged 30.00
416 A58(b) 12c black ('37) .... .25 .25
   Never hinged .... .30
   On cover .... .25
417 A59(b) 16c dark blue ...... .30 .25
   Never hinged .... .45
   On cover .... .25
418 A60(a) 20c lt ol grn ('37) . 1.00 .40
   Never hinged 1.60
   On cover .... .45
419 A61(b) 26c indigo ('37) ... .90 .35
   Never hinged 1.50
   On cover .... .40
420 A62(b) 30c orange red ..... .50 .25
   Never hinged .... .80
   On cover .... .40
421 A63(b) 1p red org & blk ... 1.00 .25
   Never hinged 1.60
   On cover .... .40
422 A64(b) 2p bis brn & blk
        ('37) 15.00 4.00
   Never hinged 25.00
   On cover 4.50
423 A65(b) 4p bl & blk ('37) .. 50.00 8.00
   Never hinged 80.00
   On cover *50.00*

424	A66(b)	5p grn & blk ('37)	15.00 *30.00*
	Never hinged		25.00
	On cover		*40.00*
	Nos. 411-424 (14)		85.45 48.75
	Set, never hinged		110.75

Eucharistic Congress Issue

Issued to commemorate the 33rd International Eucharistic Congress held at Manila, Feb. 3-7, 1937.

Map of Philippines — A70

1937, Feb. 3

425	A70	2c yellow green	.25	.25
	Never hinged		.25	
426	A70	6c light brown	.25	.25
	Never hinged		.25	
427	A70	12c sapphire	.25	.25
	Never hinged		.25	
428	A70	20c deep orange	.30	.25
	Never hinged		.50	
429	A70	36c deep violet	.55	.40
	Never hinged		.80	
430	A70	50c carmine	.70	.35
	Never hinged		1.10	
	Nos. 425-430 (6)		2.30	1.75
	Set, never hinged		3.15	

Arms of Manila — A71

1937, Aug. 27

431	A71	10p gray	6.00	2.00
	Never hinged		8.50	
432	A71	20p henna brown	5.00	1.40
	Never hinged		8.00	

Stamps of 1935 Overprinted in Black

 a

 b

1938-40

433	A53(a)	2c rose ('39)	.25	.25
	Never hinged		.25	
a.	Booklet pane of 6		3.50	3.50
	Never hinged		5.50	
b.	As "a," lower left-hand stamp overprinted "WEALTH COMMON-"		2,500.	
c.	Hyphen omitted		100.00	50.00
434	A54(b)	4c yel grn ('40)	3.00	*30.00*
	Never hinged		4.75	
435	A55(b)	6c dk brn ('39)	.25	.25
	Never hinged		.40	
a.	6c golden brown		.25	.25
	Never hinged		.40	
436	A56(b)	8c violet ('39)	.25	.25
	Never hinged		.25	
a.	"COMMONWEALT" (LR 31)		90.00	
	Never hinged		140.00	
437	A57(b)	10c rose car ('39)	.25	.25
	Never hinged		.25	
a.	"COMMONWEALT" (LR 31)		65.00	—
	Never hinged		100.00	
438	A58(b)	12c black ('40)	.25	.25
	Never hinged		.25	
439	A59(b)	16c dark blue	.25	.25
	Never hinged		.25	
440	A60(a)	20c lt ol grn ('39)	.25	.25
	Never hinged		.25	
441	A61(b)	26c indigo ('40)	1.00	1.00
	Never hinged		1.50	
442	A62(b)	30c org red ('39)	3.00	.70
	Never hinged		5.00	
443	A63(b)	1p red org & blk	.60	
	Never hinged		1.00	
444	A64(b)	2p bis brn & blk ('39)	10.00	1.00
	Never hinged		15.00	

445	A65(b)	4p bl & blk ('40)	175.00	250.00
	Never hinged		350.00	
	On cover			500.00
446	A66(b)	5p grn & blk ('40)	20.00	6.00
	Never hinged		35.00	
	Nos. 433-446 (14)		214.35	290.70
	Set, never hinged		414.15	

Overprint "b" measures 18½x1¾mm.
No. 433b occurs in booklet pane, No. 433a, position 5; all examples are straight-edged, left and bottom.

First Foreign Trade Week Issue
Nos. 384, 298a and 432 Surcharged in Red, Violet or Black

 a

 b   c

1939, July 5

449	A54(a)	2c on 4c yellow green (R)	.25	.25
	Never hinged		.35	
450	A40(b)	6c on 26c blue green (V)	.25	.50
	Never hinged		.35	
a.	6c on 26c green		3.00	1.00
	Never hinged		5.00	
451	A71(c)	50c on 20p henna brown (Bk)	1.25	1.00
	Never hinged		2.00	5.00
	Nos. 449-451 (3)		1.75	1.75
	Set, never hinged		2.70	

Commonwealth 4th Anniversary Issue (#452-460)

Triumphal Arch — A72

1939, Nov. 15

452	A72	2c yellow green	.25	.25
	Never hinged		.25	
453	A72	6c carmine	.25	.25
	Never hinged		.25	
454	A72	12c bright blue	.25	.25
	Never hinged		.25	
	Nos. 452-454 (3)		.75	.75
	Set, never hinged		.75	

For overprints see Nos. 469, 476 in Scott Standard catalogue, Vol. 5.

Malacañan Palace A73

1939, Nov. 15

455	A73	2c green	.25	.25
	Never hinged		.25	
456	A73	6c orange	.25	.25
	Never hinged		.25	
457	A73	12c carmine	.25	.25
	Never hinged		.25	
	Nos. 455-457 (3)		.75	.75
	Set, never hinged		.75	

For overprint, see No. 470 in Scott Standard catalogue, Vol. 5.

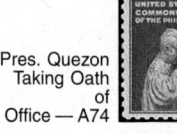

Pres. Quezon Taking Oath of Office — A74

1940, Feb. 8

458	A74	2c dark orange	.25	.25
	Never hinged		.25	

459	A74	6c dark green	.25	.25
	Never hinged		.25	
460	A74	12c purple	.25	.25
	Never hinged		.30	
	Nos. 458-460 (3)		.75	.75
	Set, never hinged		.00	

For overprints, see Nos. 471, 477 in Scott Standard catalogue, Vol. 5.

AIR POST STAMPS

Madrid-Manila Flight Issue

Issued to commemorate the flight of Spanish aviators Gallarza and Loriga from Madrid to Manila.

Regular Issue of 1917-26 Overprinted in Red or Violet

Designs: Nos. C7-C8, Adm. William T. Sampson. No. C9, Adm. George Dewey.

1926, May 13   Unwmk.   *Perf. 11*

C1	A40	2c green (R)	20.00	17.50
	Never hinged		45.00	
C2	A40	4c carmine (V)	30.00	20.00
	Never hinged		55.00	
a.	Inverted overprint		*4,000.*	—
C3	A40	6c lilac (R)	75.00	75.00
	Never hinged		125.00	
C4	A40	8c orange brown (V)	75.00	60.00
	Never hinged		125.00	
C5	A40	10c deep blue (R)	75.00	60.00
	Never hinged		140.00	
C6	A40	12c red orange (V)	80.00	65.00
	Never hinged		150.00	
C7	A40	16c light olive green (V)	*3,250.*	*3,250.*
C8	A40	16c olive bister (R)	*5,000.*	*5,000.*
C9	A40	16c olive green (V)	100.00	70.00
	Never hinged		160.00	
C10	A40	20c org yel (V)	100.00	80.00
	Never hinged		160.00	
C11	A40	26c blue green (V)	100.00	80.00
	Never hinged		160.00	
C12	A40	30c gray (V)	100.00	80.00
	Never hinged		160.00	
C13	A40	2p vio brn (R)	600.00	600.00
	Never hinged		1,100.	
	On cover			350.00
C14	A40	4p dark blue (R)	750.00	750.00
	Never hinged		1,300.	
	On cover			*575.00*
C15	A40	10p deep green (V)	1,350.	1,350.
	On cover			*775.00*

Same Overprint on No. 269
Wmk. Single-lined PIPS (190)
Perf. 12

C16	A40	26c blue green (V)	6,250.	

Same Overprint on No. 284
Perf. 10

C17	A40	1p pale violet (V)	300.00	225.00
	Never hinged		450.00	
	On cover			200.00

Flight of Spanish aviators Gallarza and Loriga from Madrid to Manila.

London-Orient Flight Issue

Issued Nov. 9, 1928, to celebrate the arrival of a British squadron of hydroplanes.

Regular Issue of 1917-25 Overprinted in Red

1928, Nov. 9   *Perf. 11*

C18	A40	2c green	1.00	1.00
	Never hinged		2.00	
C19	A40	4c carmine	1.25	1.50
	Never hinged		2.00	
C20	A40	6c violet	5.00	3.00
	Never hinged		10.00	
	On cover			2.50
C21	A40	8c orange brown	5.00	3.00
	Never hinged		10.00	
	On cover			3.00
C22	A40	10c deep blue	5.00	3.00
	Never hinged		10.00	
	On cover			3.00

C23	A40	12c red orange	8.00	4.00
	Never hinged		12.00	
	On cover			3.75
C24	A40	16c olive green (Dewey)	8.00	4.00
	Never hinged		12.00	
	On cover			3.00
C25	A40	20c orange yellow	8.00	4.00
	Never hinged		12.00	
	On cover			4.00
C26	A40	26c blue green	20.00	8.00
	Never hinged		35.00	
	On cover			9.25
C27	A40	30c gray	20.00	8.00
	Never hinged		35.00	
	On cover			9.25

Same Overprint on No. 271
Wmk. Single-lined PIPS (190)
Perf. 12

C28	A40	1p pale violet	55.00	30.00
	Never hinged		90.00	
	On cover			34.00
	Nos. C18-C28 (11)		136.25	69.50
	Set, never hinged		230.00	

Von Gronau Issue

Commemorating the visit of Capt. Wolfgang von Gronau's airplane on its round-the-world flight.

Nos. 354-360 Overprinted

1932, Sept. 27   Unwmk.   *Perf. 11*

C29	A43	2c yellow green	.90	.60
	Never hinged		1.40	
C30	A44	4c rose carmine	.90	.40
	Never hinged		1.40	
C31	A45	12c orange	1.25	.65
	Never hinged		2.00	
C32	A46	18c red orange	5.00	5.00
	Never hinged		8.00	
	On cover			3.50
C33	A47	20c yellow	4.00	4.00
	Never hinged		6.50	
	On cover			2.25
C34	A48	24c deep violet	4.00	4.00
	Never hinged		6.50	
	On cover			2.25
C35	A49	32c olive brown	3.50	3.00
	Never hinged		5.75	
	On cover			2.25
	Nos. C29-C35 (7)		19.55	17.65
	Set, never hinged		31.55	

Rein Issue

Commemorating the flight from Madrid to Manila of the Spanish aviator Fernando Rein y Loring.

Regular Issue of 1917-25 Overprinted

1933, Apr. 11

C36	A40	2c green	.75	.45
			1.10	
C37	A40	4c carmine	.90	.45
			1.40	
C38	A40	6c deep violet	1.10	.80
			1.75	
C39	A40	8c orange brown	3.75	2.00
			5.75	
C40	A40	10c dark blue	3.75	2.25
			5.75	
C41	A40	12c orange	3.75	2.00
			5.75	
C42	A40	16c ol grn (Dewey)	3.50	2.00
			5.25	
C43	A40	20c yellow	3.75	2.00
			5.75	
C44	A40	26c green	3.75	2.75
			5.75	
a.	26c blue green		4.00	2.00
			6.00	
C45	A40	30c gray	4.00	3.00
	Never hinged		6.00	
	Nos. C36-C45 (10)		29.00	17.70
	Set, never hinged		44.25	

No. 290a Overprinted

1933, May 26

C46	A40 2c green	.65	.40
	Never hinged	1.00	

Regular
Issue of
1932
Overprinted

C47	A44 4c rose carmine	.30	.25
	Never hinged	.45	
C48	A45 12c orange	.60	.25
	Never hinged	.90	
C49	A47 20c yellow	.60	.25
	Never hinged	.90	
C50	A48 24c deep violet	.65	.25
	Never hinged	1.00	
C51	A49 32c olive brown	.85	.35
	Never hinged	1.40	
	Nos. C46-C51 (6)	3.65	1.75
	Set, never hinged	5.65	

Transpacific Issue

Issued to commemorate the China
Clipper flight from Manila to San
Francisco, Dec. 2-5, 1935.

Nos. 387,
392
Overprinted
in Gold

1935, Dec. 2

C52	A57 10c rose carmine	.40	.25
	Never hinged	.60	
C53	A62 30c orange red	.60	.35
	Never hinged	.90	

Manila-Madrid Flight Issue

Issued to commemorate the Manila-
Madrid flight by aviators Antonio
Arnaiz and Juan Calvo.

Regular Issue of 1917-
25 Surcharged in
Various Colors

1936, Sept. 6

C54	A40 2c on 4c carmine (Bl)	.25	.25
		.25	
C55	A40 6c on 12c red orange (V)	.25	.25
		.30	
C56	A40 16c on 26c blue green (Bk)	.25	.25
	Never hinged	.40	
a.	16c on 26c green	2.00	.70
	Never hinged	3.00	
	Nos. C54-C56 (3)	.75	.95
	Set, never hinged	.95	

Air Mail Exhibition Issue

Issued to commemorate the first Air
Mail Exhibition, held Feb. 17-19, 1939.

Regular Issue of 1917-
37 Surcharged in
Black or Red

1939, Feb. 17

C57	A40 8c on 26c blue green (Bk)	2.00	2.00
	Never hinged	4.00	
a.	8c on 26c green (Bk)	10.00	4.00
	Never hinged	16.00	
C58	A71 1p on 10p gray (R)	8.00	4.00
	Never hinged	12.00	

SPECIAL DELIVERY STAMPS

United
States No.
E5
Overprinted
in Red

Wmk. Double-lined USPS (191)
1901, Oct. 15   *Perf. 12*

E1	SD3 10c dark blue	100.	80.
	Never hinged	185.	
	On cover		350.
a.	Dots in curved frame above messenger (Pl. 882)	175.	160.

Special
Delivery
Messenger
SD2

1906, Sept. 8

E2	SD2 20c deep ultra	45.00	8.00
	Never hinged	90.00	
	On cover		17.50
b.	20c pale ultramarine	35.00	8.00
	Never hinged	70.00	
	On cover		17.50

See Nos. E3-E6. For overprints see Nos.
E7-E10, EO1. Post 1940 listings are in Scott
Standard catalogue, Vol. 5.

SPECIAL PRINTING

U.S. No. E6
Overprinted
in Red

Wmk. Double-lined USPS (191)
1907

E2A	SD4 10c ultramarine		*2,750.*

Wmk. Single-lined PIPS (190)
1911, Apr.

E3	SD2 20c deep ultra	22.00	1.75
	Never hinged	42.00	
	On cover		12.50

1916   *Perf. 10*

E4	SD2 20c deep ultra	175.00	90.00
	Never hinged	275.00	
	On cover		100.00

1919   Unwmk.   *Perf. 11*

E5	SD2 20c ultramarine	.60	.25
	Never hinged	.90	
	On cover		5.00
a.	20c pale blue	.75	.25
	Never hinged	1.00	
	On cover		5.25
b.	20c dull violet	.60	.25
	Never hinged	.90	
	On cover		5.00

Type of 1906 Issue
1925-31   *Imperf.*

E6	SD2 20c dull violet ('31)	30.00	75.00
	Never hinged	45.00	
	On cover		250.00
a.	20c violet blue ('25)	50.00	
	Never hinged	80.00	
	On cover		—

Type of
1919
Overprinted
in Black

1939, Apr. 27   *Perf. 11*

E7	SD2 20c blue violet	.25	.25
	Never hinged	.40	
	On Cover		5.00

SPECIAL DELIVERY OFFICIAL STAMP

Type of
1906 Issue
Overprinted

1931   Unwmk.   *Perf. 11*

EO1	SD2 20c dull violet	3.00	75.00
	Never hinged	4.50	
a.	No period after "B"	50.00	250.00
	Never hinged	75.00	
b.	Double overprint	75.00	—

It is strongly recommended that expert opinion be acquired for No. EO1 used.

POSTAGE DUE STAMPS

U.S. Nos. J38-J44
Overprinted in Black

Wmk. Double-lined USPS (191)
1899, Aug. 16   *Perf. 12*

J1	D2 1c deep claret	7.50	2.50
	Never hinged	15.00	
	On cover		30.00
J2	D2 2c deep claret	7.50	2.50
	Never hinged	15.00	
	On cover		37.50
J3	D2 5c deep claret	15.00	2.50
	Never hinged	30.00	
	On cover		70.00
J4	D2 10c deep claret	19.00	5.50
	Never hinged	37.50	
	On cover		100.00
J5	D2 50c deep claret	200.00	100.00
	Never hinged	335.00	
	On cover		—

No. J1 was used to pay regular postage
Sept. 5-19, 1902.

1901, Aug. 31

J6	D2 3c deep claret	17.50	7.00
	Never hinged	35.00	
	On cover		60.00
J7	D2 30c deep claret	250.00	110.00
	Never hinged	415.00	
	On cover		—
	Nos. J1-J7 (7)	516.50	230.00
	Set, never hinged	882.50	

Post Office
Clerk — D3

1928, Aug. 21   Unwmk.   *Perf. 11*

J8	D3 4c brown red	.25	.25
	Never hinged	.25	
J9	D3 6c brown red	.30	.75
	Never hinged	.45	
J10	D3 8c brown red	.25	.75
	Never hinged	.35	
J11	D3 10c brown red	.30	.75
	Never hinged	.45	
J12	D3 12c brown red	.25	.75
	Never hinged	.35	
J13	D3 16c brown red	.30	.75
	Never hinged	.45	
J14	D3 20c brown red	.30	.75
	Never hinged	.45	
	Nos. J8-J14 (7)	1.95	4.75
	Set, never hinged	2.75	

No. J8 Surcharged in
Blue

1937, July 29   Unwmk.   *Perf. 11*

J15	D3 3c on 4c brown red	.25	.25
	Never hinged	.35	

See note after No. NJ1 in Scott Standard
catalogue, Vol. 5.

OFFICIAL STAMPS

Official Handstamped Overprints

"Officers purchasing stamps for government business may, if they so desire, surcharge them with the letters O.B. either in writing with black ink or by rubber stamps but in such a manner as not to obliterate the stamp that postmasters will be unable to determine whether the stamps have been previously used." C.M. Cotterman, Director of Posts, December 26, 1905.

Beginning January 1, 1906, all branches of the Insular Government used postage stamps to prepay postage instead of franking them as before. Some officials used manuscript, some utilized the typewriting machines but by far the larger number provided themselves with rubber stamps. The majority of these read "O.B." but other forms were: "OFFICIAL BUSINESS" or "OFFICIAL MAIL" in two lines, with variations on many of these.

These "O.B." overprints are known on U.S. 1899-1901 stamps; on 1903-06 stamps in red and blue; on 1906 stamps in red, blue, black, yellow and green.

"O.B." overprints were also made on the centavo and peso stamps of the Philippines, per order of May 25, 1907.

Beginning in 1926 the Bureau of Posts issued press-printed official stamps, but many government offices continued to handstamp ordinary postage stamps "O.B." The press-printed "O.B." overprints are listed below.

During the Japanese occupation period 1942-45, the same system of handstamped official overprints prevailed, but the handstamp usually consisted of the Tagalog words, "Kagamitang Pampamahalaan" (Official Business), and the two Japanese characters used in the printed overprint on Nos. NO1 to NO4.

Regular
Issue of
1926
Ovptd. in
Red

1926, Dec. 20   Unwmk.   *Perf. 12*

O1	A42 2c green & black	3.00	1.00
	Never hinged	4.50	
	On cover		2.00
O2	A42 4c car & blk	3.00	1.25
	Never hinged	4.50	
	On cover		2.00
a.	Vertical pair, imperf. between	750.00	
O3	A42 18c lt brn & blk	8.00	4.00
	Never hinged	12.00	
	On cover		6.50
O4	A42 20c org & blk	7.75	1.75
	Never hinged	11.50	
	On cover		2.25
	Nos. O1-O4 (4)	21.75	8.00
	Set, never hinged	32.50	

Opening of the Legislative Palace.

Regular Issue of 1917-
26 Overprinted

1931   *Perf. 11*

O5	A40 2c green	.40	.25
	Never hinged	.65	
a.	No period after "B"	17.50	17.50
	Never hinged	27.50	
b.	No period after "O"	40.00	30.00
	Never hinged	60.00	
O6	A40 4c carmine	.45	.25
	Never hinged	.70	
a.	No period after "B"	40.00	20.00
	Never hinged	60.00	
O7	A40 6c deep violet	.75	.25
	Never hinged	1.25	
O8	A40 8c yellow brown	.75	.25
	Never hinged	1.25	
O9	A40 10c deep blue	1.20	.25
	Never hinged	1.90	
O10	A40 12c red orange	2.00	.25
	Never hinged	3.00	
a.	No period after "B"	80.00	80.00
	Never hinged	120.00	
O11	A40 16c light olive green (Dewey)	1.00	.25
	Never hinged	1.50	
a.	16c olive bister	2.00	.25
	Never hinged	3.00	
O12	A40 20c orange yellow	1.25	.25
	Never hinged	1.90	
a.	No period after "B"	80.00	80.00
	Never hinged	120.00	
O13	A40 26c green	2.00	1.00
	Never hinged	2.50	
a.	26c blue green	2.50	1.50
	Never hinged	4.00	
O14	A40 30c gray	2.00	.25
	Never hinged	3.25	
	Nos. O5-O14 (10)	11.80	3.25
	Set, never hinged	18.65	

Overprinted on Nos.
383-392

1935

O15	A53	2c rose	.25	.25
		Never hinged	.30	
a.		No period after "B"	15.00	10.00
		Never hinged	22.50	
b.		No period after "O"	22.50	—
O16	A54	4c yellow green	.25	.25
		Never hinged	.30	
a.		No period after "B"	15.00	40.00
		Never hinged	22.50	
O17	A55	6c dark brown	.25	.25
		Never hinged	.40	
		No period after "B"	35.00	35.00
		Never hinged	52.50	
O18	A56	8c violet	.30	.25
		Never hinged	.45	
O19	A57	10c rose carmine	.30	.25
		Never hinged	.45	
O20	A58	12c black	.75	.25
		Never hinged	1.10	
O21	A59	16c dark blue	.55	.25
		Never hinged	.85	
O22	A60	20c light olive green	.60	.25
		Never hinged	.90	
O23	A61	26c indigo	.90	.25
		Never hinged	1.50	
O24	A62	30c orange red	.80	.25
		Never hinged	1.20	
		Nos. O15-O24 (10)	4.95	2.50
		Set, never hinged	7.40	

Nos. 411 and 418 with Additional Overprint in Black

1937-38

O25	A53	2c rose	.25	.25
		Never hinged	.30	
a.		No period after "B"	25.00	25.00
		Never hinged	45.00	
b.		Period after "B" raised (UL 4)	150.00	
O26	A60	20c lt ol grn ('38)	.70	.50
		Never hinged	1.10	

Regular Issue of 1935 Overprinted In Black

a

b

1938-40

O27	A53(a)	2c rose	.25	.25
		Never hinged	.30	
a.		Hyphen omitted	10.00	10.00
		Never hinged	15.00	
b.		No period after "B"	20.00	30.00
		Never hinged	30.00	
O28	A54(b)	4c yellow green	.75	1.00
		Never hinged	1.10	
O29	A55(a)	6c dark brown	.30	.25
		Never hinged	.45	
O30	A56(b)	8c violet	.75	.85
		Never hinged	1.10	
O31	A57(b)	10c rose carmine	.25	.25
		Never hinged	.30	
a.		No period after "O"	50.00	40.00
		Never hinged	75.00	
O32	A58(b)	12c black	.30	.25
		Never hinged	.45	
O33	A59(b)	16c dark blue	.30	.25
		Never hinged	.45	
O34	A60(a)	20c light olive green ('40)	.55	.85
		Never hinged	.85	
O35	A61(b)	26c indigo	1.50	2.00
		Never hinged	2.25	
O36	A62(b)	30c orange red	.75	.85
		Never hinged	1.10	
		Nos. O27-O36 (10)	5.70	6.80
		Set, never hinged	8.25	

NEWSPAPER STAMPS

N1   N2

1886-89   Unwmk.   Typo.   *Perf. 14*

P1	N1	⅛c yellow green	.30	7.50
		On cover or wrapper		500.00
P2	N1	1m rose ('89)	.30	21.00
		On cover or wrapper		500.00
P3	N1	2m blue ('89)	.30	21.00
		On cover or wrapper		500.00
P4	N1	5m dk brown ('89)	.30	21.00
		On cover or wrapper		1,000.
		Nos. P1-P4 (4)	1.20	70.50

1890-96

P5	N2	⅛c dark violet	.25	.25
		On cover or wrapper		400.00
P6	N2	⅛c green ('92)	6.75	10.00
		On cover or wrapper		600.00
P7	N2	⅛c orange brn ('94)	.25	.25
		On cover or wrapper		200.00
P8	N2	⅛c dull blue ('96)	.85	.60
		On cover or wrapper		200.00
P9	N2	1m dark violet	.25	.25
		On cover or wrapper		200.00
P10	N2	1m green ('92)	2.25	5.50
		On cover or wrapper		400.00
P11	N2	1m olive gray ('94)	.25	.45
		On cover or wrapper		200.00
P12	N2	1m ultra ('96)	.35	.25
		On cover or wrapper		200.00
P13	N2	2m dark violet	.25	.45
		On cover or wrapper		200.00
P14	N2	2m green ('92)	2.50	13.00
		On cover or wrapper		500.00
P15	N2	2m olive gray ('94)	.25	.45
		On cover or wrapper		200.00
P16	N2	2m brown ('96)	.30	.25
		On cover or wrapper		200.00
P17	N2	5m dark violet	.25	1.10
		On cover or wrapper		500.00
P18	N2	5m green ('92)	150.00	55.00
P19	N2	5m olive gray ('94)	.25	.45
		On cover or wrapper		500.00
P20	N2	5m dp blue grn ('96)	2.50	1.40
		On cover or wrapper		600.00
		Nos. P5-P20 (16)	167.50	89.65

Imperfs. exist of Nos. P8, P9, P11, P12, P16, P17 and P20.

FILIPINO REVOLUTIONARY GOVERNMENT

The Filipino Republic was instituted by Gen. Emilio Aguinaldo on June 23, 1899. At the same time he assumed the office of President. Aguinaldo dominated the greater part of the island of Luzon and some of the smaller islands until late in 1899. He was taken prisoner by United States troops on March 23, 1901.

The devices composing the National Arms, adopted by the Filipino Revolutionary Government, are emblems of the Katipunan political secret society or of Katipunan origin. The letters "K K K" on these stamps are the initials of this society whose complete name is "Kataas-taasang, Kagalang-galang Katipunan nang Mañga Anak nang Bayan," meaning "Sovereign Worshipful Association of the Sons of the Country."

The regular postage and telegraph stamps were in use on Luzon as early as Nov. 10, 1898. Owing to the fact that stamps for the different purposes were not always available together with a lack of proper instructions, any of the adhesives were permitted to be used in the place of the other. Hence telegraph and revenue stamps were accepted for postage and postage stamps for revenue or telegraph charges. In addition to the regular postal emission, there are a number of provisional stamps, issues of local governments of islands and towns.

POSTAGE ISSUES

A1   A2

Coat of Arms — A3

1898-99   Unwmk.   *Perf. 11½*

Y1	A1	2c red	175.00	125.00
		On cover		1,500.
a.		Double impression	325.00	
Y2	A2	2c red	.30	4.00
		On cover		450.00
b.		Double impression	—	
d.		Horiz. pair, imperf. between	—	
e.		Vert. pair, imperf. between	225.00	
Y3	A3	2c red	150.00	200.00
		On cover		2,000.

Imperf pairs and pairs, imperf horizontally, have been created from No. Y2e.

REGISTRATION STAMP

RS1

YF1	RS1	8c green	5.00	30.00
		On cover with #Y2		3,500.
a.		Imperf., pair	400.00	
b.		Imperf. vertically, pair	—	

NEWSPAPER STAMP

N1

YP1	N1	1m black	2.00	20.00
a.		Imperf., pair	5.00	20.00

PITCAIRN ISLANDS

ˈpit-ˌkärn ˈī-ləns

LOCATION — South Pacific Ocean, nearly equidistant from Australia and South America
GOVT. — British colony under the British High Commissioner in New Zealand
AREA — 1.75 sq. mi.
POP. — 57 (1984)

The district of Pitcairn also includes the uninhabited islands of Ducie, Henderson and Oeno.

Postal affairs are administered by Fiji.

12 Pence = 1 Shilling

Catalogue values for all unused stamps in this country are for **Never Hinged items.**

Cluster of Oranges
A1

Fletcher Christian with Crew and View of Pitcairn Island — A2

John Adams and His House A3

William Bligh and H. M. Armed Vessel "Bounty" A4

Map of Pitcairn and Pacific Ocean — A5

Bounty Bible — A6

H.M. Armed Vessel "Bounty" A7

Pitcairn School, 1949 — A8

Fletcher Christian and View of Pitcairn Island — A9

Fletcher Christian with Crew and Coast of Pitcairn A10

Perf. 12½, 11½x11

1940-51   Engr.   Wmk. 4

1	A1	½p blue grn & org	.50	.60
2	A2	1p red lil & rose vio	.70	.80
3	A3	1½p rose car & blk	.70	.50
4	A4	2p dk brn & brt grn	2.25	1.40
5	A5	3p dk blue & yel grn	1.50	1.40
5A	A6	4p dk blue grn & blk	22.50	11.00
6	A7	6p sl grn & dp brn	6.00	1.50
6A	A8	8p lil rose & grn	24.00	7.00
7	A9	1sh slate & vio	5.25	4.00
8	A10	2sh6p dk brn & brt grn	15.00	3.75
		Nos. 1-8 (10)	78.40	30.20

Nos. 1-5, 6 and 7-8 exist in a booklet of eight panes of one. Value $2,750.
Issued: 4p, 8p, 9/1/51; others, 10/15/40.

Common Design Types pictured following the introduction.

Peace Issue
Common Design Type

1946, Dec. 2   *Perf. 13½x14*
9	CD303	2p brown	.65 .65
10	CD303	3p deep blue	.75 .75

Silver Wedding Issue
Common Design Types

1949, Aug. 1   **Photo.**   *Perf. 14x14½*
11	CD304	1½p scarlet	1.75 1.00

Perf. 11½x11

Engraved; Name Typographed
12	CD305	10sh purple	55.00 52.50

UPU Issue
Common Design Types

Engr.; Name Typo. on 3p & 6p

1949, Oct. 10   *Perf. 13½, 11x11½*
13	CD306	2½p red brown	3.00 4.25
14	CD307	3p indigo	8.00 4.25
15	CD308	6p green	6.50 4.25
16	CD309	1sh rose violet	6.50 6.00
		Nos. 13-16 (4)	24.00 18.75

POLAND
ˈpō-lənd

LOCATION — Europe between Russia and Germany
GOVT. — Republic
AREA — 120,628 sq. mi.
POP. — 36,399,000 (est. 1983)
CAPITAL — Warsaw

100 Kopecks = 1 Ruble
100 Fenigi = 1 Marka (1918)
100 Halerzy = 1 Korona (1918)
100 Groszy = 1 Zloty (1924)

Watermarks

Wmk. 145 — Wavy Lines

Wmk. 234 — Multiple Post Horns

Issued under Russian Dominion

Coat of Arms — A1

Perf. 11½ to 12½

1860   **Typo.**   **Unwmk.**
1	A1 10k blue & rose	2,400.	250.
	On cover		1,000.
a.	10k blue & carmine	2,500.	325.
b.	10k dark blue & rose	3,000.	350.
c.	Added blue frame for inner oval	6,000.	850.
d.	Imperf.	—	7,500.

Used for letters within the Polish territory and to Russia. Postage on all foreign letters was paid in cash.
These stamps were superseded by those of Russia in 1865.
Counterfeits exist.

Issues of the Republic

Local issues were made in various Polish cities during the German occupation.

In the early months of the Republic many issues were made by overprinting the German occupation stamps with the words "Poczta Polska" and an eagle or bars often with the name of the city.
These issues were not authorized by the Government but were made by the local authorities and restricted to local use. In 1914 two stamps were issued for the Polish Legion and in 1918 the Polish Expeditionary Force used surcharged Russian stamps. The regularity of these issues is questioned.
Numerous counterfeits of these issues abound.

Warsaw Issues
Stamps of the Warsaw Local Post Surcharged

Statue of Sigismund III — A2

Coat of Arms of Warsaw — A3

Polish Eagle A4

Sobieski Monument A5

1918, Nov. 17   **Wmk. 145**   *Perf. 11½*
11	A2 5f on 2gr brn & buff	1.40	1.00
a.	Inverted surcharge	200.00	200.00
12	A3 10f on 6gr grn & buff	.70	.70
a.	Inverted surcharge	15.00	15.00
13	A4 25f on 10gr rose & buff	7.00	3.50
a.	Inverted surcharge	27.50	27.50
14	A5 50f on 20gr bl & buff	8.50	7.00
a.	Inverted surcharge	350.00	350.00
	Nos. 11-14 (4)	17.60	12.20

Counterfeits exist.

Occupation Stamps Nos. N6-N16 Overprinted or Surcharged

a

b

1918-19   **Wmk. 125**   *Perf. 14, 14½*
15	A16 3pf brown ('19)	35.00	27.50
16	A22 5pf on 2½pf gray	1.40	.70
17	A16 5pf on 3pf brown	5.00	3.50
18	A16 5pf green	1.75	.70
19	A16 10pf carmine	1.40	.50
20	A22 15pf dark violet	1.00	.50
21	A16 20pf blue	1.40	.50
a.	20pf ultramarine	775.00	2,250.
23	A22 25pf on 7½pf org	1.00	.50
24	A16 30pf org & blk, buff	1.00	.50
25	A16 40pf lake & black	1.75	1.25
26	A16 60pf magenta	1.40	.50
	Nos. 15-26 (11)	52.10	36.65

There are two settings of this overprint. The first printing, issued Dec. 5, 1918, has space of 3½mm between the middle two bars. The second printing, issued Jan. 15, 1919, has space of 4mm. No. 15 comes only in the second setting; all others in both. The German overprint on No. 21a is very glossy.
Varieties of this overprint and surcharge are numerous: double, inverted; misspellings (Pocata, Poczto, Pelska); letters omitted, inverted or wrong font; 3 bars instead of 4, etc.
No. 21a requires competent expertization. A number of shades of the blue No. 21 exist. Counterfeits exist.

Lublin Issue

Austrian Military Semi-Postal Stamps of 1918 Overprinted

1918, Dec. 5   **Unwmk.**   *Perf. 12½x13*
27	MSP7 10h gray green	8.50	7.50
a.	Inverted overprint	80.00	80.00
b.	Double overprint	1,750.	700.00
c.	Double ovpt., one inverted	2,100.	850.00
28	MSP8 20h magenta	6.50	7.50
a.	Inverted overprint	50.00	50.00
b.	Double overprint	1,750.	500.00
29	MSP7 45h blue	6.50	7.50
a.	Inverted overprint	50.00	50.00
b.	Double ovpt., one inverted	1,750.	500.00
	Nos. 27-29 (3)	21.50	22.50

Austrian Military Stamps of 1917 Surcharged

1918-19   *Perf. 12½*
30	M3 3hal on 3h ol gray	27.50	20.00
a.	Inverted surcharge	3,500.	3,500.
b.	Perf. 11½	50.00	27.50
c.	Perf. 11½x12½	30.00	27.50
31	M3 3hal on 15h brt rose	7.00	7.00
a.	Inverted surcharge	22.50	30.00

Surcharged in Black

32	M3 10hal on 30h sl grn	7.00	7.00
a.	Inverted surcharge	22.50	30.00
b.	Brown surcharge (error)	75.00	65.00
34	M3 25hal on 40h ol bis	15.00	12.00
a.	Inverted surcharge	37.50	42.50
b.	Perf. 11½	50.00	27.50
c.	As "b," inverted surcharge	175.00	175.00
35	M3 45hal on 60h rose	7.00	7.00
a.	Inverted surcharge	25.00	27.50
36	M3 45hal on 80h dl blue	8.50	8.50
a.	Inverted surcharge	35.00	35.00
37	M3 50hal on 60h rose	14.00	14.00
a.	Inverted surcharge	50.00	35.00

Similar surcharge with bars instead of stars over original value
38	M3 45hal on 80h dl blue	12.00	10.00
a.	Inverted surcharge	40.00	35.00
b.	Double srch., one inverted	1,350.	—

Overprinted

39	M3 50h deep green	27.50	27.50
a.	Inverted overprint	100.00	100.00
40	M3 90h dark violet	7.00	7.00
a.	Inverted overprint	100.00	100.00
	Nos. 30-40 (10)	132.50	120.00

Counterfeits
All Cracow issues, Nos. 41-60, J1-J12 and P1-P5, have been extensively counterfeited. Competent expertization is necessary. Prices apply only for authenticated stamps with identified plating position. Cost of certificate is not included in the catalogue value.

Cracow Issues

Austrian Stamps of 1916-18 Overprinted

1919, Jan. 17   **Typo.**
41	A37 3h brt violet	500.00	450.00
42	A37 5h lt green	625.00	475.00
43	A37 6h deep orange	70.00	65.00
a.	Inverted overprint	50,000.	
44	A37 10h magenta	500.00	450.00
45	A37 12h lt blue	70.00	70.00
46	A39 40h olive green	35.00	30.00
a.	Inverted overprint	350.00	—
b.	Double overprint	2,000.	
47	A39 50h blue green	20.00	14.00
a.	Inverted overprint	35,000.	
48	A39 60h deep blue	17.50	14.00
a.	Inverted overprint	350.00	—
49	A39 80h orange brown	14.00	14.00
a.	Inverted overprint.	300.00	250.00
b.	Double overprint	1,750.	
50	A39 90h red violet	1,200.	1,000.
51	A39 1k carmine, yel	30.00	27.50

Engr.
52	A40 2k blue	12.00	14.00
53	A40 3k carmine rose	190.00	175.00
54	A40 4k yellow green	200.00	175.00
55	A40 10k deep violet	12,000.	13,000.

The 3k is on granite paper.
The overprint on Nos. 52-55 is litho. and slightly larger than illustration with different ornament between lines of type.

Same Overprint on Nos. 168-171

1919   **Typo.**
56	A42 15h dull red	67.50	35.00
57	A42 20h dark green	300.00	140.00
58	A42 25h blue	1,900.	1,900.
59	A42 30h dull violet	550.00	350.00

Austria No. 157 Surcharged

1919, Jan. 24
60	A39 25h on 80h org brn	10.00	10.00
a.	Inverted overprint	240.00	150.00

Excellent counterfeits of Nos. 27 to 60 exist.

Polish Eagle — A9

1919, Feb. 25   **Litho.**   *Imperf.*
Without gum
Yellowish Paper
61	A9 2h gray	1.75	1.40
62	A9 3h dull violet	1.00	1.00
63	A9 5h green	1.00	.70
64	A9 6h orange	17.50	20.00
65	A9 10h lake	1.00	.70
66	A9 15h brown	1.00	.70
67	A9 20h olive green	1.00	1.00

Bluish Paper
68	A9 25h carmine	.70	.70
69	A9 50h indigo	1.00	1.00
70	A9 70h deep blue	1.75	1.40
71	A9 1k ol gray & car	1.75	1.75
	Nos. 61-71 (11)	29.45	30.35

Nos. 61-71 exist with privately applied perforations.
Counterfeits exist.
For surcharges see Nos. J35-J39.

Posen (Poznan) Issue
Germany Nos. 84-85, 87, 96, 98 Overprinted in Black

Perf. 14, 14½

1919, Aug. 5   **Wmk. 125**
72	A22 5pf on 2pf gray	30.00	24.00
73	A22 5pf on 7½pf org	2.00	1.40
a.	Double surcharge	1,000.	

74	A16	5pf on 20pf bl vio	2.00	1.25
75	A16	10pf on 25pf org & blk, *yel*	6.00	3.50
76	A16	10pf on 40pf lake & blk	3.50	1.40
		Nos. 72-76 (5)	43.50	31.55

Counterfeits exist.

Germany Nos. 96 and 98 Surcharged in Red or Green

a   b

1919, Sept. 15

77	A22	5pf on 2pf (R)	275.00	175.00
a.		Inverted surcharge	27,500.	
78	A22	10pf on 7½pf (G)	400.00	125.00

Nos. 77-78 are a provisional issue for use in Gniezno. Counterfeit surcharges abound.

Eagle and Fasces, Symbolical of United Poland
A10   A11

"Agriculture" A12

"Peace" — A13

Polish Cavalryman A14

For Northern Poland
Denominations as "F" or "M"

1919, Jan. 27   *Imperf.*
Wove or Ribbed Paper

81	A10	3f bister brn	.25	.35
82	A10	5f green	.25	.35
83	A10	10f red violet	.25	.35
84	A10	15f deep rose	.25	.25
85	A11	20f deep blue	.25	.50
86	A11	25f olive green	.25	.50
87	A11	50f blue green	.25	.50
88	A12	1m violet	2.50	3.75
89	A12	1.50m deep green	4.25	7.00
90	A12	2m dark brown	4.25	8.50
91	A13	2.50m orange brn	8.50	22.50
92	A14	5m red violet	17.50	40.00
		Nos. 81-92 (12)	38.75	84.55

Perf. 10, 11, 11½, 10x11½, 11½x10
1919-20

93	A10	3f bister brn	.25	.25
94	A10	5f green	.25	.25
95	A10	10f red violet	.25	.25
96	A10	10f brown ('20)	.25	.25
97	A10	15f deep rose	.25	.25
98	A10	15f vermilion ('20)	.25	.25
99	A11	20f deep blue	.25	.25
100	A11	25f olive green	.25	.25
101	A11	40f brt violet ('20)	.25	.25
102	A11	50f blue green	.25	.25
103	A12	1m violet	.70	.25
105	A12	1.50m deep green	.70	.35
106	A12	2m dark brown	1.75	.50
107	A13	2.50m orange brn	1.00	.70
108	A14	5m red violet	2.00	1.50
		Nos. 93-108 (15)	8.65	5.80

No. 108 exists in various shades of brown and violet.

Several denominations among Nos. 81-132 are found with double impression or in pairs

imperf. between. See Nos. 109-132, 140-152C, 170-175. For surcharges & overprints, see Nos. 153, 199-200, B1-B14, 2K1-2K12, Eastern Silesia 41-50.

For Southern Poland
Denominations as "H" or "K"

1919, Jan. 27   *Imperf.*

109	A10	3h red brown	.35	.35
110	A10	5h emerald	.35	.25
111	A10	10h orange	.35	.25
112	A10	15h vermilion	.35	.25
113	A11	20h gray brown	.35	.25
114	A11	25h light blue	.35	.25
115	A11	50h orange brn	.35	.70
116	A12	1k dark green	.35	1.40
117	A12	1.50k red brown	1.50	4.00
118	A12	2k dark blue	1.50	3.50
119	A13	2.50k dark violet	6.50	10.00
120	A14	5k slate blue	15.00	20.00
		Nos. 109-120 (12)	27.30	41.20

Perf. 10, 11½, 10x11½, 11½x10

121	A10	3h red brown	.25	.25
122	A10	5h emerald	.25	.25
123	A10	10h orange	.25	.25
124	A10	15h vermilion	.25	.25
125	A11	20h gray brown	.25	.25
126	A11	25h light blue	.25	.25
127	A11	50h orange brn	.25	.25
128	A12	1k dark green	.25	.25
129	A12	1.50k red brown	.35	.25
130	A12	2k dark blue	.70	.25
131	A13	2.50k dark violet	1.40	.70
132	A14	5k slate blue	1.40	1.10
		Nos. 121-132 (12)	5.85	4.30

National Assembly Issue

A20

Ignacy Jan Paderewski — A21

Adalbert Trampczynski — A22

Eagle Watching Ship — A24

25f, Gen. Josef Pilsudski. 1m, Griffin.

1919-20   *Perf. 11½*
Wove or Ribbed Paper

133	A20	10f red violet	.35	.25
134	A21	15f brown red	.35	.25
a.		Imperf., pair	25.00	
135	A22	20f dp brown (21x25mm)	.35	.25
136	A22	20f dp brown (17x20mm) ('20)	.75	1.60
137	A21	25f olive green	.35	.25
138	A24	50f Prus blue	.35	.25
139	A24	1m purple	1.00	.35
		Nos. 133-139 (7)	3.50	3.20

First National Assembly of Poland.

General Issue

1919   *Perf. 9 to 14½ and Compound*
Thin Laid Paper

140	A11	25f olive green	.25	.25
141	A11	50f blue green	.25	.25
142	A12	1m dark gray	.25	.25
143	A12	2m bister brn	.25	.25
144	A13	3m red brown	2.00	.35
a.		Pair, imperf. vert.	8.00	8.00
145	A14	5m red violet	1.25	.25
146	A14	6m deep rose	1.40	.25
a.		Pair, imperf. vert.	8.00	8.00
147	A14	10m brown red	.50	.30
a.		Horizontal pair, imperf.	8.00	8.00
148	A14	20m gray green	1.40	.50
		Nos. 140-148 (9)	7.55	2.65

Type of 1919 Redrawn
Perf. 9 to 14½ and Compound
1920-22   **Thin Laid or Wove Paper**

149	A10	1m red	.25	.25
150	A10	2m gray green	.25	.25
151	A10	3m light blue	.50	.35
152	A10	4m rose red	.25	.25
152A	A10	5m dark violet	.25	.25
b.		Horiz. pair, imperf. vert.	8.00	8.00
152C	A10	8m gray brown ('22)	.50	.50
		Nos. 149-152C (6)	2.00	1.85

The word "POCZTA" is in smaller letters and the numerals have been enlarged.

The color of No. 152A varies from dark violet to red brown.

No. 101 Surcharged

Perf. 10, 11½, 10x11½, 11½x10
1921, Jan. 25   **Thick Wove Paper**

153	A11	3m on 40f brt vio	.30	.25
a.		Double surcharge	25.00	25.00
b.		Inverted surcharge	—	—

Sower and Rainbow of Hope — A27

Thin Laid or Wove Paper
Perf. 9 to 14½ and Compound
1921   **Size: 28x22mm**   **Litho.**

154	A27	10m slate blue	.50	.25
155	A27	15m light brown	.25	.25
155A	A27	20m red	.80	.25
		Nos. 154-155A (3)	1.55	.75

Signing of peace treaty with Russia.
Nos. 154-155A exist imperf. Value, unused, each $6.

See No. 191. For surcharges see Nos. 196-198.

"Peace" and "Agriculture" A29

"Peace" A30

Sun (Peace) Breaking into Darkness (Despair) — A28

Perf. 11, 11½, 12, 12½, 13 and Compound
1921, May 2

156	A28	2m green	.40	9.50
157	A28	3m blue	1.50	10.00
158	A28	4m red	.35	.70
a.		4m carmine rose (error)	600.00	
159	A29	6m carmine rose	.35	1.50
160	A29	10m slate blue	1.25	.80
161	A30	25m dk violet	2.00	.70
162	A30	50m slate bl & buff	1.25	.25
		Nos. 156-162 (7)	7.10	23.90

Issued to commemorate the Constitution.

Polish Eagle — A31

Perf. 9 to 14½ and Compound
1921-23

163	A31	25m violet & buff	.80	.25
164	A31	50m vermilio & buff	.80	.25
a.		Vert. pair, imperf. horiz.		
165	A31	100m blk brn & org	.80	.25
166	A31	200m black & rose ('23)	.80	.25
167	A31	300m olive grn ('23)	.40	.25
168	A31	400m brown ('23)	.55	.25
169	A31	500m brn vio ('23)	.70	.25
169A	A31	1000m orange ('23)	1.25	.25
169B	A31	2000m dull blue ('23)	.35	.25
		Nos. 163-169B (9)	6.45	2.25

For surcharge see No. 195.

Type of 1919 and

Miner — A32

Perf. 9 to 14½ and Compound
1922-23

170	A10	5f blue	.25	1.00
171	A10	10f lt violet	.25	1.00
172	A11	20f pale red	.25	2.00
173	A11	40f violet brn	.25	2.00
174	A11	50f orange	.25	2.00
175	A11	75f blue green	.25	3.00
176	A32	1m black	.25	2.00
177	A32	1.25m dark green	.25	4.50
178	A32	2m deep rose	.25	2.00
179	A32	3m emerald	.25	2.00
180	A32	4m deep ultra	.25	4.00
181	A32	5m yellow brn	.25	2.00
182	A32	6m red orange	.25	8.50
183	A32	10m lilac brn	.25	3.50
184	A32	20m deep violet	.25	4.00
185	A32	50m olive green	.25	3.50
187	A32	80m vermilion ('23)	1.00	27.50
188	A32	100m violet ('23)	.60	40.00
189	A32	200m orange ('23)	2.50	40.00
190	A32	300m pale blue ('23)	6.00	60.00
		Nos. 170-190 (20)	14.10	214.50

Union of Upper Silesia with Poland.

There were 2 printings of Nos. 176 to 190, the 1st being from flat plates, the 2nd from rotary press on thin paper, perf. 12½.

Nos. 173 and 175 are printed from new plates showing larger value numerals and a single "f."

Sower Type Redrawn
Size: 25x21mm
1922   **Thick or Thin Wove Paper**

191	A27	20m carmine	.75	.25

In this stamp the design has been strengthened and made more distinct, especially the ground and the numerals in the upper corners.

Nicolaus Copernicus A33

Father Stanislaus Konarski — A34

1923   *Perf. 10 to 12½*

192	A33	1000m indigo	.35	.35
193	A34	3000m brown	.35	.70
a.		"Konapski"	17.00	19.00
194	A33	5000m rose	.35	.25
		Nos. 192-194 (3)	1.05	1.40

Nicolaus Copernicus (1473-1543), astronomer (Nos. 192, 194); Stanislaus Konarski (1700-1773), educator, and the creation by the Polish Parliament of the Commission of Public Instruction (No. 193).

No. 163 Surcharged

1923 *Perf. 9 to 14½ and Compound*

195	A31	10000m on 25m	.50 .25
a.		Double surcharge	60.00
b.		Inverted surcharge	35.00

Stamps of 1921
Surcharged

196	A27	25000m on 20m red	2.00 1.00
a.		Double surcharge	60.00
b.		Inverted surcharge	35.00
197	A27	50000m on 10m grnsh bl	.80 .25
a.		Double surcharge	60.00
b.		Inverted surcharge	35.00 —

No. 191
Surcharged

198	A27	25000m on 20m car	.60 .25
a.		Double surcharge	60.00
b.		Inverted surcharge	35.00

No. 150 Surcharged with New Value
1924
199	A10	20000m on 2m gray grn	.80 .25
a.		Inverted surcharge	35.00 —
b.		Double surcharge	60.00 —

Type of 1919 Issue Surcharged with New Value
200	A10	100000m on 5m red brn	.80 .25
a.		Double surcharge	60.00 —
b.		Inverted surcharge	35.00 —
		Nos. 195-200 (6)	5.50 2.25

Arms of
Poland — A35

Perf. 10 to 14½ and Compound
1924		**Thin Paper**	**Litho.**
205	A35	10,000m lilac brn	1.10 .50
206	A35	20,000m ol grn	.70 .35
207	A35	30,000m scarlet	1.25 .25
208	A35	50,000m apple grn	2.75 .25
209	A35	100,000m brn org	1.00 .25
210	A35	200,000m lt blue	1.10 .25
211	A35	300,000m red vio	2.75 1.00
212	A35	500,000m brn	2.50 1.00
213	A35	1,000,000m ple rose	.35 35.00
214	A35	2,000,000m dk grn	.35 225.00
		Nos. 205-214 (10)	13.85 263.85
		Set, never hinged	50.00

Arms of Poland A36	President Stanislaus Wojciechowski A37

Perf. 10 to 13½ and Compound
1924			
215	A36	1g orange brown	.35 .50
216	A36	2g dark brown	.35 .25
217	A36	3g orange	.35 .25
218	A36	5g olive green	.35 .25
219	A36	10g blue green	.75 .25
220	A36	15g red	.75 .25
221	A36	20g blue	2.50 .25
222	A36	25g red brown	6.50 .25
a.		25g indigo	12,000. 6,000.
223	A36	30g deep violet	10.00 .25
a.		30g gray blue	250.00 125.00
224	A36	40g indigo	2.50 .70
225	A36	50g magenta	.25 .25

Perf. 11½, 12
226	A37	1z scarlet	17.50 1.40
		Nos. 215-226 (12)	42.40 4.85
		Set, never hinged	265.00

For overprints see Nos. 1K1-1K11.

Holy Gate of Wilno (Vilnius) — A38	Poznan Town Hall — A39

Sigismund
Monument,
Warsaw — A40

Wawel Castle at
Cracow — A41

Sobieski Statue at Lwow — A42	Ship of State — A43

1925-27 *Perf. 10 to 13*
227	A38	1g bister brown	.55 .25
228	A42	2g brown olive	.65 .50
229	A40	3g blue	2.00 .25
230	A39	5g yellow green	2.75 .25
231	A40	10g violet	2.00 .25
232	A41	15g rose red	3.00 .25
233	A43	20g dull red	13.00 .25
234	A38	24g gray blue	5.50 .75
235	A42	30g dark blue	1.60 .25
236	A41	40g lt blue ('27)	1.60 .25
237	A43	45g dark violet	11.00 .25
		Nos. 227-237 (11)	43.65 3.50
		Set, never hinged	110.00

For overprints see Nos. 1K11A-1K17.

1926-27 **Redrawn**
238	A40	3g blue	.65 .25
239	A39	5g yellow green	1.00 .25
240	A40	10g violet	.85 .25
241	A41	15g rose red	.85 .25
		Nos. 238-241 (4)	3.35 1.00
		Set, never hinged	7.50

On Nos. 229-232 the lines representing clouds touch the numerals. On the redrawn stamps the numerals have white outlines, separating them from the cloud lines.

Marshal Pilsudski — A44	Frederic Chopin — A45

1927 **Typo.** *Perf. 12½, 11½*
242	A44	20g red brown	2.00 .25
243	A45	40g deep ultra	8.50 .75
		Set, never hinged	35.00

See No. 250. For overprint see No. 1K18.

President Ignacy
Moscicki — A46

1927, May 4 *Perf. 11½*
245	A46	20g red	3.00 1.00
		Never hinged	10.00

Dr. Karol
Kaczkowski — A47

1927, May 27 *Perf. 11½, 12½*
246	A47	10g gray green	3.00 3.50
247	A47	25g carmine	4.50 3.50
248	A47	40g dark blue	6.00 1.75
		Nos. 246-248 (3)	13.50 8.75
		Set, never hinged	50.00

4th Intl. Congress of Millitary Medicine and Pharmacy, Warsaw, May 30-June 4.

Juliusz
Slowacki — A48

1927, June 28 *Perf. 12½*
249	A48	20g rose	2.75 .70
		Never hinged	12.00

Transfer from Paris to Cracow of the remains of Julius Slowacki, poet.

Pilsudski Type of 1927
Design Redrawn
1928		*Perf. 11½, 12x11½, 12½x13*	
250	A44	25g yellow brown	2.00 .25
		Never hinged	8.50

Souvenir Sheet

A49

1928, May 3 **Engr.** *Perf. 12½*
251	A49	Sheet of 2	250.00 325.00
		Never hinged	475.00
a.		50g black brown	25.00 85.00
b.		1z black brown	25.00 85.00

1st Natl. Phil. Exhib., Warsaw, May 3-13. Sold to each purchaser of a 1.50z ticket to the Warsaw Philatelic Exhibition.
Counterfeits exist.

Marshal Pilsudski —
A49a

Perf. 10½ to 14 and Compound
1928-31		**Wove Paper**	
253	A49a	50g bluish slate	3.00 .25
254	A49a	50g blue grn ('31)	20.00 .35
		Set, never hinged	24.00

See No. 315.

Pres.
Moscicki — A50

Perf. 12x12½, 11½ to 13½ and Compound
1928			**Laid Paper**
255	A50	1z black, *cream*	15.00 .70
		Never hinged	50.00
a.		Horizontally laid paper ('30)	25.00 1.75
		Never hinged	70.00

See Nos. 305, 316. For surcharges and overprints see Nos. J92-J94, 1K19, 1K24.

General Josef
Bem — A51

Wove Paper
1928, May		**Typo.**	*Perf. 12½*
256	A51	25g rose red	2.00 .35
		Never hinged	8.50

Return from Syria to Poland of the ashes of General Josef Bem.

Henryk
Sienkiewicz — A52

1928, Oct.
257	A52	15g ultra	.75 .25
		Never hinged	3.25

For overprint see No. 1K23.

Eagle Arms — A53

1928-29 *Perf. 12x12½*
258	A53	5g dark violet	.25 .25
259	A53	10g green	.25 .25
260	A53	25g red brown	.25 .25
		Nos. 258-260 (3)	.75 .75
		Set, never hinged	4.00

See design A58. For overprints see Nos. 1K20-1K22.

"Swiatowid," Ancient
Slav God — A54

1928, Dec. 15 *Perf. 12½x12*
261	A54	25g brown	.50 .25
		Never hinged	3.50

Poznan Agricultural Exhibition.

King John III
Sobieski — A55

1930, July *Perf. 12x12½*
262	A55	75g claret	1.50 .25
		Never hinged	6.00

Stylized Soldiers — A56

1930, Nov. 1   **Perf. 12½**
263 A56 5g violet brown   .35 .25
264 A56 15g dark blue   2.75 .25
265 A56 25g red brown   .25 .25
266 A56 30g dull red   5.00 2.25
    Nos. 263-266 (4)   8.35 3.00
    Set, never hinged   25.00

Centenary of insurrection of 1830.

Kosciuszko, Washington, Pulaski — A57

Laid Paper

1932, May 3   **Perf. 11½**
267 A57 30g brown   1.00 .35
    Never hinged   3.50

200th birth anniv. of George Washington.

A58

Perf. 12x12½

1932-33   **Typo.**   **Wmk. 234**
268 A58 5g dull vio ('33)   .35 .25
269 A58 10g green   .35 .25
270 A58 15g red brown ('33)   .35 .25
271 A58 20g gray   .75 .25
272 A58 25g buff   .75 .25
273 A58 30g deep rose   .85 .25
274 A58 60g blue   3.75 .50
    Nos. 268-274 (7)   7.15 2.00
    Set, never hinged   27.50

For overprints and surcharge see Nos. 280-281, 284, 292, 1K25-1K27.

Torun City Hall — A59

1933, Jan. 2   **Engr.**   **Perf. 11½**
275 A59 60g blue   27.50 1.00
    Never hinged   90.00

700th anniversary of the founding of the City of Torun by the Grand Master of the Knights of the Teutonic Order.
See No. B28.

Altar Panel of St. Mary's Church, Cracow — A60

Perf. 11½-12½ & Compound
1933, July 10   **Laid Paper**   **Unwmk.**
277 A60 80g red brown   8.50 .70
    Never hinged   30.00

400th death anniv. of Veit Stoss, sculptor and woodcarver.
For surcharge see No. 285.

John III Sobieski and Allies before Vienna, painted by Jan Matejko — A61

1933, Sept. 12   **Laid Paper**
278 A61 1.20z indigo   20.00 2.00
    Never hinged   70.00

250th anniv. of the deliverance of Vienna by the Polish and allied forces under command of John III Sobieski, King of Poland, when besieged by the Turks in 1683.
For surcharge see No. 286.

Cross of Independence A62

Wmk. 234
1933, Nov. 11   **Typo.**   **Perf. 12½**
279 A62 30g scarlet   1.75 .30
    Never hinged   6.25

15th anniversary of independence.

Type of 1932 Overprinted in Red or Black

Wyst. Filat. 1934 Katowice

1934, May 5   **Perf. 12**
280 A58 20g gray (R)   20.00 40.00
281 A58 30g deep rose   30.00 45.00
    Set, never hinged   175.00

Katowice Philatelic Exhibition. Counterfeits exist.

Josef Pilsudski — A63

Perf. 11½ to 12½ and Compound
1934, Aug. 6   **Engr.**   **Unwmk.**
282 A63 25g gray blue   1.25 .70
283 A63 30g black brown   1.75 .70
    Set, never hinged   17.50

Polish Legion, 20th anniversary.
For overprint see No. 293.

Nos. 274, 277-278 Surcharged in Black or Red

1934   **Wmk. 234**   **Perf. 12x12½**
284 A58 55g on 60g blue   1.75 .25
    Perf. 11½-12½ & Compound
    Unwmk.
285 A60 25g on 80g red brn   2.50 .25
286 A61 1z on 1.20z ind (R)   9.50 4.25
   a. Figure "1" in surcharge 5mm
     high instead of 4 ½mm   9.50 4.25
     Never hinged   50.00
    Nos. 284-286 (3)   13.75 4.75
    Set, never hinged   75.00

Surcharge of No. 286 includes bars.

Marshal Pilsudski — A64

1935   **Perf. 11 to 13 and Compound**
287 A64 5g black   .35 .25
288 A64 15g black   .35 .25
289 A64 25g black   .45 .25
290 A64 45g black   2.75 .50
291 A64 1z black   5.00 3.50
    Nos. 287-291 (5)   8.90 4.75
    Set, never hinged   30.00

Pilsudski mourning issue.
Nos. 287-288 are typo., Nos. 290-291 litho.
No. 289 exists both typo. and litho.
See No. B35b.

Nos. 270, 282 Overprinted in Blue or Red

Kopiec Marszalka Pilsudskiego

1935   **Wmk. 234**   **Perf. 12x12½**
292 A58 15g red brown   .75 .25
    Perf. 11½, 11½x12½
    Unwmk.
293 A63 25g gray blue (R)   2.00 .85
    Set, never hinged   12.00

Issued in connection with the proposed memorial to Marshal Pilsudski, the stamps were sold at Cracow exclusively.

"The Dog Cliff" — A65   President Ignacy Moscicki — A75

Designs: 10g, "Eye of the Sea." 15g, M. S. "Pilsudski." 20g, View of Pieniny. 25g, Belvedere Palace. 30g, Castle in Mira. 45g, Castle at Podhorce. 50g, Cloth Hall, Cracow. 55g, Raczynski Library, Poznan. 1z, Cathedral, Wilno.

1935-36   **Typo.**   **Perf. 12½x13**
294 A65 5g violet blue   .25 .25
295 A65 10g yellow green   .40 .25
296 A65 15g Prus green   1.90 .25
297 A65 20g violet black   .95 .25
    Engr.
298 A65 25g myrtle green   .30 .30
299 A65 30g rose red   .75 .25
300 A65 45g plum ('36)   .25 .25
301 A65 50g black ('36)   .25 .25
302 A65 55g blue ('36)   1.25 .25
303 A65 1z brown ('36)   3.50 3.50
304 A75 3z black brown   1.00 5.25
    Nos. 294-304 (11)   10.80 11.05
    Set, never hinged   40.00

See Nos. 308-311. For overprints see Nos. 306-307, 1K28-1K32.

Type of 1928 inscribed "1926. 3. VI. 1936" on Bottom Margin

1936, June 3
305 A50 1z ultra   2.00 4.00
    Never hinged   6.50

Presidency of Ignacy Moscicki, 10th anniv.

Nos. 299, 302 Overprinted in Blue or Red

1936, Aug. 15
306 A65 30g rose red   3.50 3.50
307 A65 55g blue (Π)   5.50 2.25
    Set, never hinged   30.00

Gordon-Bennett Intl. Balloon Race. Counterfeits exist.

Scenic Type of 1935-36

Designs: 5g, Church at Czestochowa. 10g, Maritime Terminal, Gdynia. 15g, University, Lwow. 20g, Municipal Building, Katowice.

1937   **Engr.**   **Perf. 12½**
308 A65 5g violet blue   .25 .25
309 A65 10g green   .40 .25
310 A65 15g red brown   .35 .25
311 A65 20g orange brown   .35 .25
    Nos. 308-311 (4)   1.35 1.00
    Set, never hinged   2.00

For overprints see Nos. 1K31-1K32.

Marshal Smigly-Rydz — A80

1937   **Perf. 12½x13**
312 A80 25g slate green   .25 .25
313 A80 55g blue   .25 .25
    Set, never hinged   2.00

For surcharges see Nos. N30, N32.

Types of 1928-37

1937   **Souvenir Sheets**
314   Sheet of 4   14.00 20.00
  a. A80 25g, dark brown   1.75 2.75
315   Sheet of 4   14.00 20.00
  a. A49a 50g, deep blue   1.75 2.75
316   Sheet of 4   12.50 20.00
  a. A50 1z, gray black   1.75 2.75
    Set, never hinged   120.00

Visit of King Carol of Romania to Poland, June 26-July 1.
See No. B35c.

President Moscicki — A81

1938, Feb. 1   **Perf. 12½**
317 A81 15g slate green   .70 .25
318 A81 30g rose violet   .35 .25
    Set, never hinged   1.25

71st birthday of President Moscicki.
For surcharge see No. N31.

Kosciuszko, Paine and Washington and View of New York City — A82

1938, Mar. 17   **Perf. 12½x12½**
319 A82 1z gray blue   1.40 .70
    Never hinged   5.00

150th anniv. of the US Constitution.

Boleslaus I and Emperor Otto III at Gnesen — A83   Marshal Pilsudski — A95

Designs: 10g, King Casimir III. 15g, King Ladislas II Jagello and Queen Hedwig. 20g, King Casimir IV. 25g, Treaty of Lublin. 30g, King Stephen Bathory commending Wielock, the peasant. 45g, Stanislas Zolkiewski and Jan Chodkiewicz. 50g, John III Sobieski entering Vienna. 55g, Union of nobles, commoners and peasants. 75g, Dabrowski, Kosciuszko and Poniatowski. 1z, Polish soldiers. 2z, Romuald Traugutt.

1938, Nov. 11 Engr. Perf. 12½

320	A83	5g red orange	.25	.25
321	A83	10g green	.25	.25
322	A83	15g fawn	.25	.25
323	A83	20g peacock blue	.25	.25
324	A83	25g dull violet	.35	.25
325	A83	30g rose red	.35	.25
326	A83	45g black	.45	.25
327	A83	50g brt red vio	.35	.25
328	A83	55g ultra	.35	.25
329	A83	75g dull green	1.40	1.00
330	A83	1z orange	1.60	1.75
331	A83	2z carmine rose	6.50	15.00
332	A95	3z gray black	3.00	10.00
		Nos. 320-332 (13)	15.35	30.00
		Set, never hinged	57.50	

20th anniv. of Poland's independence. See No. 339. For surcharges see Nos. N33-N47.

Souvenir Sheet

Marshal Pilsudski, Gabriel Narutowicz, President Moscicki, Marshal Smigly-Rydz — A96

1938, Nov. 11 Perf. 12½

333	A96	Sheet of 4	10.00	18.00
		Never hinged	35.00	
a.		25g dull violet (Pilsudski)	1.10	1.75
b.		25g dull violet (Narutowicz)	1.10	1.75
c.		25g dull violet (Moscicki)	1.10	1.75
d.		25g dull violet (Smigly-Rydz)	1.10	1.75

20th anniv. of Poland's independence.

Poland Welcoming Teschen People — A97

1938, Nov. 11

334	A97	25g dull violet	1.75	.50
		Never hinged	5.00	

Restoration of the Teschen territory ceded by Czechoslovakia.

Skier — A98

1939, Feb. 6

335	A98	15g orange brown	.50	.70
336	A98	25g dull violet	.50	.70
337	A98	30g rose red	1.40	.70
338	A98	55g brt ultra	3.25	1.25
		Nos. 335-338 (4)	5.65	3.35
		Set, never hinged	20.00	

Intl. Ski Meet, Zakopane, Feb. 11-19.

Type of 1938

15g, King Ladislas II Jagello, Queen Hedwig.

Re-engraved

1939, Mar. 2 Perf. 12½

339	A83	15g redsh brown	.25	.25
		Never hinged		.70

No. 322 with crossed swords and helmet at lower left. No. 339, swords and helmet have been removed.

Marshal Pilsudski Reviewing Troops — A99

1939, Aug. 1 Engr.

340	A99	25g dull rose violet	.25	.90
		Never hinged		1.00

Polish Legion, 25th anniv. See No. B35a.

SEMI-POSTAL STAMPS

Regular Issue of 1919 Surcharged in Violet

a   b

1919, May 3 Unwmk. Imperf.

B1	A10(a)	5f + 5f grn	.35	.35
B2	A10(a)	10f + 5f red vio	.35	.50
B3	A10(a)	15f + 5f dp red	.35	.50
B4	A11(b)	25f + 5f ol grn	.35	.35
B5	A11(b)	50f + 5f bl grn	.35	.70

Perf. 11½

B6	A10(a)	5f + 5f grn	.25	.25
B7	A10(a)	10f + 5f red vio	.50	.50
B8	A10(a)	15f + 5f dp red	.25	.25
B9	A11(b)	25f + 5f ol grn	.25	.25
B10	A11(b)	50f + 5f bl grn	.35	.35
		Nos. B1-B10 (10)	3.35	4.00
		Set, never hinged	15.00	

First Polish Philatelic Exhibition. The surtax benefited the Polish White Cross Society.

Regular Issue of 1920 Surcharged in Carmine

1921, Mar. 5 Perf. 9
Thin Laid Paper

B11	A14	5m + 30m red vio	1.50	8.50
B12	A14	6m + 30m dp rose	1.50	8.50
B13	A14	10m + 30m lt red	3.00	8.50
B14	A14	20m + 30m gray grn	45.00	140.00
		Nos. B11-B14 (4)	51.00	165.50
		Set, never hinged	125.00	

Counterfeits, differently perforated, exist of Nos. B11-B14.

SP1

1925, Jan. 1 Typo. Perf. 12½

B15	SP1	1g orange brn	4.50	35.00
B16	SP1	2g dk brown	4.50	35.00
B17	SP1	3g orange	4.50	35.00
B18	SP1	5g olive grn	4.50	35.00
B19	SP1	10g blue grn	4.50	35.00
B20	SP1	15g red	4.50	35.00
B21	SP1	20g blue	4.50	35.00
B22	SP1	25g red brown	4.50	35.00
B23	SP1	30g dp violet	4.50	35.00

B24	SP1	40g indigo	110.00	35.00
B25	SP1	50g magenta	4.50	35.00
		Nos. B15-B25 (11)	155.00	385.00
		Set, never hinged	350.00	

"Na Skarb" means "National Funds." These stamps were sold at a premium of 50 groszy each, for charity.

Light of Knowledge — SP2

1927, May 3 Perf. 11½

B26	SP2	10g + 5g choc & grn	6.25	7.00
B27	SP2	20g + 5g dk bl & buff	7.50	12.00
		Set, never hinged	37.50	

"NA OSWIATE" means "For Public Instruction." The surtax aided an Association of Educational Societies.

Torun Type of 1933

1933, May 21 Engr.

B28	A59	60g (+40g) red brn, buff	8.50	10.00
		Never hinged	30.00	

Philatelic Exhibition at Torun, May 21-28, 1933, and sold at a premium of 40g to aid the exhibition funds.

Souvenir Sheet

Stagecoach and Wayside Inn — SP3

1938, May 3 Engr. Imperf.

B29	SP3	Sheet of 4	52.50	100.00
		Never hinged	125.00	
a.		45g green	5.25	7.00
b.		55g blue	5.25	7.00

Perf. 12

B29C	SP3	Sheet of 4	67.50	120.00
		Never hinged	150.00	
d.		45g green	6.50	8.50
e.		55g blue	6.50	8.50

5th Phil. Exhib., Warsaw, May 3-8. The sheets each contain two 45g and two 55g stamps. Sold for 3z.

Souvenir Sheet

Stratosphere Balloon over Mountains — SP4

1938, Sept. 15 Perf. 12½

B31	SP4	75g dp vio, sheet	40.00	65.00
		Never hinged	120.00	

Issued in advance of a proposed Polish stratosphere flight. Sold for 2z.

Winterhelp Issue

SP5

1938-39

B32	SP5	5g + 5g red org	.45	.25
B33	SP5	25g + 10g dk vio ('39)	.90	.25
B34	SP5	55g + 15g brt ultra ('39)	1.10	3.00
		Nos. B32-B34 (3)	2.45	3.50
		Set, never hinged	9.50	

For surcharges see Nos. N48-N50.

Souvenir Sheet

SP6

1939, Aug. 1

B35	SP6	Sheet of 3, dark blue gray	15.00	24.00
		Never hinged	40.00	
a.		25g Marshal Pilsudski Reviewing Troops	3.50	2.75
b.		25g Marshal Pilsudski	3.50	2.75
c.		25g Marshal Smigly-Rydz	3.50	2.75

25th anniv. of the founding of the Polish Legion. The sheets sold for 1.75z, the surtax going to the National Defense fund.
See types A64, A80, A99.

AIR POST STAMPS

Biplane — AP1

Perf. 12½

1925, Sept. 10 Typo. Unwmk.

C1	AP1	1g lt blue	.65	10.00
C2	AP1	2g orange	.65	10.00
C3	AP1	3g yellow brn	.65	10.00
C4	AP1	5g dk brown	.65	.85
C5	AP1	10g dk green	.65	.85
C6	AP1	15g red violet	3.25	.85
C7	AP1	20g olive grn	7.50	4.50
C8	AP1	30g dull rose	7.50	2.50
C9	AP1	45g dk violet	8.50	4.25
		Nos. C1-C9 (9)	30.00	43.80
		Set, never hinged	95.00	

Counterfeits exist.
Nos. C1-C9 exist imperf. Value, set $125.
For overprint see No. C11.

Capt. Franciszek Zwirko and Stanislaus Wigura — AP2

Perf. 11½ to 12½ and Compound

1933, Apr. 15   Engr.   Wmk. 234

C10 AP2 30g gray green   14.00 1.00
    Never hinged   42.50

Winning of the circuit of Europe flight by two Polish aviators in 1932. The stamp was available for both air mail and ordinary postage.
For overprint see No. O12.

Nos. C7 and C10 Ovptd. in Red

Challenge
1934

1934, Aug. 28   Unwmk.   Perf. 12½

C11 AP1 20g olive green   5.00 7.00

Wmk. 234
Perf. 11½

C12 AP2 30g gray green   6.00 2.00
    Set, never hinged   50.00

POSTAGE DUE STAMPS

Cracow Issues

Postage Due Stamps of Austria, 1916, Overprinted in Black or Red

1919, Jan. 10   Unwmk.   Perf. 12½

J1	D4	5h rose red	17.50	20.00
J2	D4	10h rose red	5,250.	8,500.
J3	D4	15h rose red	12.00	10.00
a.		Inverted overprint	3,500.	3,000.
J4	D4	20h rose red	825.00	3,500.
J5	D4	25h rose red	40.00	40.00
J6	D4	30h rose red	1,900.	1,500.
J7	D4	40h rose red	400.00	400.00
J8	D5	1k ultra (R)	5,500.	6,250.
J9	D5	5k ultra (R)	5,500.	6,250.
J10	D5	10k ultra (R)	22,500.	25,000.
a.		Black overprint	85,000.	100,000.

Overprint on Nos. J1-J7, J10a is type. Overprint on Nos. J8-J10 is slightly larger than illustration, has a different ornament between lines of type and is litho.

Type of Austria, 1916-18, Surcharged in Black

D6

1919, Jan. 10

J11 D6 15h on 36h vio   525.00 425.00
J12 D6 50h on 42h choc   70.00 50.00
  a. Double surcharge   3,500. 5,500.

See note above No. 41.
Counterfeits exist of Nos. J1-J12.

Regular Issues

Numerals of
Value — D7

1919   Typo.   Perf. 11½
For Northern Poland

J13	D7	2f red orange	.25	.25
J14	D7	4f red orange	.25	.25
J15	D7	5f red orange	.25	.25
J16	D7	10f red orange	.25	.25
J17	D7	20f red orange	.25	.25
J18	D7	30f red orange	.25	.25
J19	D7	50f red orange	.25	.25
J20	D7	100f red orange	.50	.35
J21	D7	500f red orange	2.50	2.40

For Southern Poland

J22	D7	2h dark blue	.25	.25
J23	D7	4h dark blue	.25	.25
J24	D7	5h dark blue	.25	.25
J25	D7	10h dark blue	.25	.25
J26	D7	20h dark blue	.25	.25
J27	D7	30h dark blue	.25	.25
J28	D7	50h dark blue	.35	.25
J29	D7	100h dark blue	.45	.80
J30	D7	500h dark blue	1.40	1.60
		Nos. J13-J30 (18)	8.45	8.65

Counterfeits exist.
Nos. J13-J30 never hinged valued at 4x hinged value.

1920   Perf. 9, 10, 11½
Thin Laid Paper

J31	D7	20f dark blue	.25	.25
J32	D7	100f dark blue	.25	.25
J33	D7	200f dark blue	.35	.25
J34	D7	500f dark blue	.35	.25
		Nos. J31-J34 (4)	1.20	1.00

Nos. J31-J34 never hinged valued at 3.5x hinged values.

Regular Issue of
1919 Surcharged

6 Mk.
dopłata

1921, Jan. 25   Imperf.
Wove Paper

J35	A9	6m on 15h brown	.75	.75
J36	A9	6m on 25h car	.75	.75
J37	A9	20m on 10h lake	5.00	7.00
J38	A9	20m on 50h indigo	4.00	3.75
J39	A9	35m on 70h dp bl	7.00	9.00
		Nos. J35-J39 (5)	17.50	21.25

Counterfeits exist.

8

DOPŁATA

Numerals of
Value — D8

Thin Laid or Wove Paper
Size: 17x22mm

Perf. 9 to 14½ and Compound
1921-22   Typo.

J40	D8	1m indigo	.25	.25
J41	D8	2m indigo	.25	.25
J42	D8	4m indigo	.25	.25
J43	D8	6m indigo	.45	.25
J44	D8	8m indigo	.45	.25
J45	D8	20m indigo	.45	.25
J46	D8	50m indigo	.45	.25
J47	D8	100m indigo	.70	.35
		Nos. J40-J47 (8)	3.25	2.10

Nos. J40-J47 never hinged valued at 4x hinged values.

Nos. J44-J45, J41 Surcharged
Perf. 9 to 14½ and Compound
1923, Nov.

J48	D8	10,000(m) on 8m indigo	.35	.25
J49	D8	20,000(m) on 20m indigo	.35	.25
J50	D8	50,000(m) on 2m indigo	.45	.45
		Nos. J48-J50 (3)	1.15	.95

Nos. J48-J50 never hinged valued at 5x hinged values.

Type of 1921-22 Issue
Size: 19x24mm

1923   Typo.   Perf. 12½

J51	D8	50m indigo	.25	.25
J52	D8	100m indigo	.25	.25
J53	D8	200m indigo	.25	.25
J54	D8	500m indigo	.60	.25
J55	D8	1000m indigo	.35	.25
J56	D8	2000m indigo	.40	.30
J57	D8	10,000m indigo	.25	.25
J58	D8	20,000m indigo	.25	.25
J59	D8	30,000m indigo	.25	.25
J60	D8	50,000m indigo	.25	.25
J61	D8	100,000m indigo	.40	.25
J62	D8	200,000m indigo	.25	.25
J63	D8	300,000m indigo	5.00	.35
J64	D8	500,000m indigo	1.75	.25
J65	D8	1,000,000m indigo	1.00	.30

J66	D8	2,000,000m indigo	1.75	.35
J67	D8	3,000,000m indigo	3.00	1.40
		Nos. J51-J67 (17)	16.70	5.70
		Set, never hinged	60.00	

POCZTA POLSKA
2 GROSZE
DOPŁATA

D9

Perf. 10 to 13½ and Compound
1924   Size: 20x25½mm

J68	D9	1g brown	.25	.25
J69	D9	2g brown	.25	.25
J70	D9	4g brown	.30	.25
J71	D9	6g brown	.30	.25
J72	D9	10g brown	1.25	.25
J73	D9	15g brown	4.50	.25
J74	D9	20g brown	3.25	.25
J75	D9	25g brown	6.25	.25
J76	D9	30g brown	.75	.25
J77	D9	40g brown	1.00	.25
J78	D9	50g brown	1.00	.25
J79	D9	1z brown	.45	.25
J80	D9	2z brown	.45	.25
J81	D9	3z brown	.75	1.50
J82	D9	5z brown	.40	.60
		Nos. J68-J82 (15)	21.15	5.35
		Set, never hinged	92.50	

Nos. J68-J69 and J72-J75 exist measuring 19½x24½mm.
For surcharges see Nos. J84-J91.

POCZTA POLSKA
5
DOPŁATA

D10

1930, July   Perf. 12½

J83 D10 5g olive brown   .70 .25
    Never hinged   1.00

POCZTA POLSKA
50 groszy
DOPŁATA

Postage Due
Stamps of 1924
Surcharged

Perf. 10 to 13½ and Compound
1934-38

J84	D9	10g on 2z brown ('38)	.25	.25
J85	D9	15g on 2z brown	.25	.25
J86	D9	20g on 1z brown	.40	.25
J87	D9	20g on 5z brown	6.00	.25
J88	D9	25g on 40g brown	.85	.25
J89	D9	30g on 40g brown	1.40	.25
J90	D9	50g on 40g brown	1.40	.50
J91	D9	50g on 3z brown ('35)	.85	.35
		Nos. J84-J91 (8)	11.40	2.35
		Set, never hinged	12.00	

DOPŁATA
25 GR.

No. 255a
Surcharged in Red
or Indigo

1934-36   Laid Paper

J92	A50	10g on 1z (R) ('36)	.80	.75
a.		Vertically laid paper (No. 255)	25.00	18.00
J93	A50	20g on 1z (R) ('36)	2.50	.80
J94	A50	25g on 1z (I)	.80	.30
a.		Vertically laid paper (No. 255)	30.00	18.00
		Nos. J92-J94 (3)	4.10	1.35
		Set, never hinged	10.00	

POCZTA POLSKA
5
GR   DOPŁATA   GR

D11

1938-39   Typo.   Perf. 12½x12

J95	D11	5g dark blue green	.25	.25
J96	D11	10g dark blue green	.25	.25
J97	D11	15g dark blue green	.25	.25
J98	D11	20g dark blue green	.35	.25
J99	D11	25g dark blue green	.35	.25
J100	D11	30g dark blue green	.60	.25
J101	D11	50g dark blue green	.95	.25
J102	D11	1z dark blue green	5.00	1.65
		Nos. J95-J102 (8)	8.00	3.40
		Set, never hinged	14.00	

For surcharges see Nos. N51-N55.

OFFICIAL STAMPS

POCZTA POLSKA
3
O1

Perf. 10, 11½, 10x11½, 11½x10
1920, Feb. 1   Litho.   Unwmk.

O1	O1	3f vermilion	.25	.25
O2	O1	5f vermilion	.25	.25
O3	O1	10f vermilion	.25	.25
O4	O1	15f vermilion	.25	.25
O5	O1	25f vermilion	.25	.25
O6	O1	50f vermilion	.25	.25
O7	O1	100f vermilion	.25	.25
O8	O1	150f vermilion	.25	.25
O9	O1	200f vermilion	.65	.45
O10	O1	300f vermilion	.75	.50
O11	O1	600f vermilion	1.40	1.75
		Nos. O1-O11 (11)	4.80	4.70
		Set, never hinged	14.00	

The stars on either side of the denomination do not appear on Nos. O7-O11.

Numerals Larger
Stars inclined outward

1920, Nov. 20   Perf. 11½
Thin Laid Paper

O12	O1	5f red	.25	.25
O13	O1	10f red	.25	.25
O14	O1	15f red	.25	.25
O15	O1	25f red	.60	.25
O16	O1	50f red	.35	.25
		Nos. O12-O16 (5)	1.70	1.25
		Set, never hinged	5.25	

POCZTA POLSKA   POCZTA POLSKA
PRZESYŁKA URZĘDOWA ZWYCZAJNA   PRZESYŁKA URZĘDOWA ZWYCZAJNA

Polish Eagle
O3   O4

Perf. 12x12½

1933, Aug. 1   Typo.   Wmk. 234

O17 O3 (30g) vio (Zwyczajna)   .35 .25
O18 O3 (80g) red (Polecona)   .35 .25
    Set, never hinged   3.00

1935, Apr. 1

O19 O4 (25g) bl vio (Zwyczajna)   .25 .25
O20 O4 (55g) car (Polecona)   .25 .25
    Set, never hinged

Stamps inscribed "Zwyczajna" or "Zwykła" were for ordinary official mail. Those with "Polecona" were for registered official mail.

NEWSPAPER STAMPS

POCZTA POLSKA

Austrian Newspaper
Stamps of 1916
Overprinted

1919, Jan. 10   Unwmk.   Imperf.

P1	N9	2h brown	17.50	35.00
P2	N9	4h green	14.00	27.50
P3	N9	6h dark blue	14.00	27.50
P4	N9	10h orange	275.00	550.00
P5	N9	30h claret	17.50	35.00
		Nos. P1-P5 (5)	338.00	675.00

OCCUPATION STAMPS

Issued under German Occupation

German Stamps of 1905 Overprinted

Perf. 14, 14½

1915, May 12   Wmk. 125
N1	A16	3pf brown	.60	.50
N2	A16	5pf green	1.25	.50
N3	A16	10pf carmine	1.25	.50
N4	A16	20pf ultra	2.50	3.75
N5	A16	40pf lake & blk	7.50	3.75
	Nos. N1-N5 (5)		13.10	6.00
	Set, never hinged		40.00	

German Stamps of 1905-17 Overprinted

1916-17
N6	A22	2½pf gray	1.25	2.50
N7	A16	3pf brown	1.25	2.50
N8	A16	5pf green	1.25	2.50
N9	A22	7½pf orange	1.25	2.50
N10	A16	10pf carmine	1.25	2.50
N11	A22	15pf yel brn	3.50	3.50
N12	A22	15pf dk vio ('17)	1.25	2.50
N13	A16	20pf ultra	1.75	2.50
N14	A16	30pf org & blk, *buff*	7.00	15.00
N15	A16	40pf lake & blk	2.50	2.50
N16	A16	60pf magenta	3.00	3.50
	Nos. N6-N16 (11)		25.25	42.00
	Set, never hinged		70.00	

For overprints and surcharges see #15-26.

German Stamps of 1934 Surcharged in Black

1939, Dec. 1   Wmk. 237   *Perf. 14*
N17	A64	6g on 3pf bister	.25	.40
N18	A64	8g on 4pf dl bl	.25	.40
N19	A64	12g on 6pf dk grn	.25	.40
N20	A64	16g on 8pf vermilion	.40	1.00
N21	A64	20g on 10pf choc	.25	.40
N22	A64	24g on 12pf dp car	.25	.25
N23	A64	30g on 15pf maroon	.50	.90
N24	A64	40g on 20pf brt bl	.40	.40
N25	A64	50g on 25pf ultra	.40	.75
N26	A64	60g on 30pf ol grn	.40	.40
N27	A64	80g on 40pf red vio	.50	.80
N28	A64	1z on 50pf dk grn & blk	1.00	1.25
N29	A64	2z on 100(pf) org & blk	2.00	3.50
	Nos. N17-N29 (13)		6.85	10.85
	Set, never hinged		25.00	

Stamps of Poland 1937, Surcharged in Black or Brown

1940   Unwmk.   *Perf. 12½, 12½x13*
N30	A80	24g on 25g sl grn	1.25	3.25
N31	A81	40g on 30g rose vio	.40	1.25
N32	A80	50g on 55g blue	.25	.65

Similar Surcharge on Stamps of 1938-39
N33	A83	2g on 5g red org	.25	.40
N34	A83	4g on 5g red org	.25	.40
N35	A83	6(g) on 10g grn	.25	.40

N36	A83	8(g) on 10g grn (Br)	.25	.40
N37	A83	10(g) on 10g grn	.25	.40
N38	A83	12(g) on 15g redsh brn (#339)	.25	.40
N39	A83	16(g) on 15g redsh brn (#339)	.25	.40
N40	A83	24g on 25g dl vio	.25	.40
N41	A83	30(g) on 30g rose red	.25	.40
N42	A83	50(g) on 50g brt red vio	.25	.65
N43	A83	60(g) on 55g ultra	6.00	17.00
N44	A83	80(g) on 75g dl grn	6.00	17.00
N45	A83	1z on 1z org	6.00	17.00
N46	A83	2z on 2z car rose	3.00	7.50
N47	A95	3z on 3z gray blk	4.00	10.00

Similar Surcharge on Nos. B32-B34
N48	SP5	30g on 5g+5g	.25	.65
N49	SP5	40g on 25g+10g	.25	.65
N50	SP5	1z on 55g+15g	4.00	10.00

Similar Surcharge on Nos. J98-J102

Perf. 12½x12
N51	D11	50(g) on 20g	1.25	3.25
N52	D11	50(g) on 25g	6.00	17.50
N53	D11	50(g) on 30g	14.00	37.50
N54	D11	50(g) on 50g	.75	2.40
N55	D11	50(g) on 1z	1.75	4.75
	Nos. N30-N55 (26)		57.65	154.60
	Set, never hinged		160.00	

The surcharge on Nos. N30 to N55 is arranged to fit the shape of the stamp and obliterate the original denomination. On some values, "General Gouvernement" appears at the bottom. Counterfeits exist.

St. Florian's Gate, Cracow — OS1   Palace, Warsaw — OS13

Designs: 8g, Watch Tower, Cracow. 10g, Cracow Gate, Lublin. 12g, Courtyard and statue of Copernicus. 20g, Dominican Church, Cracow. 24g, Wawel Castle, Cracow. 30g, Church, Lublin. 40g, Arcade, Cloth Hall, Cracow. 48g, City Hall, Sandomierz. 50g, Court House, Cracow. 60g, Courtyard, Cracow. 80g, St. Mary's Church, Cracow.

1940-41   Unwmk.   Photo.   *Perf. 14*
N56	OS1	6g brown	.25	.75
N57	OS1	8g brn org	.25	.75
N58	OS1	8g bl blk ('41)	.25	.50
N59	OS1	10g emerald	.25	.25
N60	OS1	12g dk grn	1.75	.70
N61	OS1	12g dp vio ('41)	.25	.25
N62	OS1	20g dk ol brn	.25	.25
N63	OS1	24g henna brn	.25	.25
N64	OS1	30g purple	.25	.25
N65	OS1	30g vio brn ('41)	.25	.25
N66	OS1	40g slate blk	.25	.25
N67	OS1	48g chnt brn ('41)	.50	1.50
N68	OS1	50g brt bl	.25	.25
N69	OS1	60g slate grn	.25	.25
N70	OS1	80g dull pur	.25	.50
N71	OS13	1z rose lake	1.25	1.25
N72	OS13	1z Prus grn ('41)	.55	1.00
	Nos. N56-N72 (17)		7.30	9.20
	Set, never hinged		14.50	

For surcharges see Nos. NB1-NB4.

OCCUPATION SEMI-POSTAL STAMPS

Issued under German Occupation

Types of 1940 Occupation Postage Stamps Surcharged in Red

Unwmk.

1940, Aug. 17   Photo.   *Perf. 14*
NB1	OS1	12g + 8g olive gray	1.25	3.50
NB2	OS1	24g + 16g olive gray	1.25	3.50
NB3	OS1	50g + 50g olive gray	1.50	4.00
NB4	OS1	80g + 80g olive gray	1.50	4.00
	Nos. NB1-NB4 (4)		5.50	15.00
	Set, never hinged		15.00	

German Peasant Girl in Poland OSP1

Designs: 24g+26g, Woman wearing scarf. 30g+20g, Similar to type OSP4.

1940, Oct. 26   Engr.   *Perf. 14½*
Thick Paper
NB5	OSP1	12g + 38g dk sl grn	.85	2.75
NB6	OSP1	24g + 26g cop red	.85	2.75
NB7	OSP1	30g + 20g dk pur	1.50	5.00
	Nos. NB5-NB7 (3)		3.20	10.50
	Set, never hinged		8.50	

1st anniversary of the General Government.

German Peasant OSP4

1940, Dec. 1   *Perf. 12*
NB8	OSP4	12g + 8g dk grn	.35	.90
NB9	OSP4	24g + 16g rose red	.40	1.75
NB10	OSP4	30g + 30g vio brn	1.00	2.50
NB11	OSP4	50g + 50g ultra	1.00	3.00
	Nos. NB8-NB11 (4)		2.75	8.15
	Set, never hinged		7.00	

The surtax was for war relief.

OCCUPATION RURAL DELIVERY STAMPS

Issued under German Occupation

OSD1

Perf. 13½

1940, Dec. 1   Photo.   Unwmk.
NL1	OSD1	10g red orange	.45	1.00
NL2	OSD1	20g red orange	.45	1.25
NL3	OSD1	30g red orange	.45	1.25
NL4	OSD1	50g red orange	1.10	3.00
	Nos. NL1-NL4 (4)		2.45	6.50
	Set, never hinged		6.00	

OCCUPATION OFFICIAL STAMPS

Issued under German Occupation

Eagle and Swastika OOS1

Perf. 12, 13½x14

1940, Apr.   Photo.   Unwmk.
Size: 31x23mm
NO1	OOS1	6g lt brown	.50	2.00
NO2	OOS1	8g gray	.50	2.00
NO3	OOS1	10g green	.50	2.00
NO4	OOS1	12g dk green	.50	1.75
NO5	OOS1	20g dk brown	.50	2.50
NO6	OOS1	24g henna brn	8.00	1.75
NO7	OOS1	30g rose lake	.60	2.00
NO8	OOS1	40g dl violet	.60	5.00
NO9	OOS1	48g dl olive	6.50	5.00
NO10	OOS1	50g royal bl	.50	2.75
NO11	OOS1	60g dk ol grn	.50	2.00
NO12	OOS1	80g rose vio	.50	2.00

Size: 35x26mm
NO13	OOS1	1z gray blk & brn vio	1.25	4.75
NO14	OOS1	3z gray blk & chnt	1.25	4.75
NO15	OOS1	5z gray blk & org brn	2.00	5.50
	Nos. NO1-NO15 (15)		24.20	46.50
	Set, never hinged		70.00	

1940   Size: 21¼x16¼mm   *Perf. 12*
NO16	OOS1	6g brown	.35	1.10
NO17	OOS1	8g slate	.50	1.75
NO18	OOS1	10g dp grn	.85	2.00
NO19	OOS1	12g slate grn	.85	2.00
NO20	OOS1	20g blk brn	.50	1.10
NO21	OOS1	24g cop brn	.35	1.10
NO22	OOS1	30g rose lake	.50	1.75
NO23	OOS1	40g dl pur	.85	2.00
NO24	OOS1	50g royal blue	.85	2.00
	Nos. NO16-NO24 (9)		5.60	14.80
	Set, never hinged		20.00	

POLISH OFFICES ABROAD

OFFICES IN DANZIG

Poland Nos. 215-225 Overprinted

1925, Jan. 5   Unwmk.   *Perf. 11½x12*
1K1	A36	1g orange brn	.25	3.50
1K2	A36	2g dk brown	.25	1.75
1K3	A36	3g orange	.35	1.40
1K4	A36	5g olive grn	7.00	1.75
1K5	A36	10g blue grn	5.25	1.25
1K6	A36	15g red	22.50	1.75
1K7	A36	20g blue	1.10	.70
1K8	A36	25g red brown	3.50	.70
1K9	A36	30g dp violet	1.40	.70
1K10	A36	40g indigo	1.40	.70
1K11	A36	50g magenta	1.75	.70
	Nos. 1K1-1K11 (11)		44.75	14.90
	Set, never hinged		210.00	

Same Ovpt. on Poland Nos. 230-231

1926   *Perf. 11½, 12*
1K11A	A39	5g yellow grn	30.00	35.00
1K12	A40	10g violet	12.50	15.00
	Set, never hinged		100.00	

Counterfeit overprints are known on Nos. 1K1-1K32.

No. 232 Overprinted

1926-27
1K13	A41	15g rose red	20.00	40.00
	Never hinged		75.00	

Same Overprint on Redrawn Stamps of 1926-27
Perf. 13
1K14	A39	5g yellow grn	1.10	1.10
1K15	A40	10g violet	2.00	1.10
1K16	A41	15g rose red	1.10	1.10
1K17	A43	20g dull red	1.50	2.25
	Nos. 1K14-1K17 (4)		5.70	5.55
	Set, never hinged		24.00	

Same Ovpt. on Poland Nos. 250, 255a

1928-30   *Perf. 12½*
1K18	A44	25g yellow brn	3.50	1.75
	Never hinged		14.00	

Laid Paper
Perf. 11½x12, 12½x11½
1K19	A50	1z blk, *cr* ('30)	15.00	20.00
	Never hinged		30.00	

See note above No. 41.
Counterfeits exist of Nos. P1-P5.

Poland Nos. 258-260
Overprinted

1929-30   *Perf. 12x12½*
1K20 A53   5g dk violet   .75   .75
1K21 A53   10g green ('30)   .75   .75
1K22 A53   25g red brown   1.50   .75
    Nos. 1K20-1K22 (3)   3.00   2.25
    Set, never hinged   10.00

Same Overprint on Poland No. 257
1931, Jan. 5   *Perf. 12½*
1K23 A52   15g ultra   2.75   1.40
    Never hinged   10.00

Poland No. 255
Overprinted in Dark
Blue

1933, July 1   Laid Paper   Perf. 11½
1K24 A50   1z black, *cream*   45.00   150.00
    Never hinged   125.00

Poland Nos. 268-270
Overprinted in Black

1934-36   Wmk. 234   Perf. 12x12½
1K25 A58   5g dl violet   .35   .70
1K26 A58   10g green ('36)   17.50   85.00
1K27 A58   15g red brown   .35   .70
    Nos. 1K25-1K27 (3)   18.20   86.40
    Set, never hinged   55.00

Poland Nos. 294,
296, 298
Overprinted in
Black in one or
two lines

1935-36   Unwmk.   Perf. 12½x13
1K28 A65   5g violet blue   1.75   2.00
1K29 A65   15g Prus green   2.00   3.00
1K30 A65   25g myrtle green   3.00   2.50
    Nos. 1K28-1K30 (3)   6.75   7.50
    Set, never hinged   17.50

Same Overprint in Black on Poland Nos. 308, 310
1937, June 5
1K31 A65   5g violet blue   1.10   1.75
1K32 A65   15g red brown   1.10   1.75
    Set, never hinged   7.00

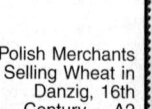

Polish Merchants
Selling Wheat in
Danzig, 16th
Century — A2

1938, Nov. 11   Engr.   Perf. 12½
1K33 A2   5g red orange   .25   1.40
1K34 A2   15g red brown   .25   1.40
1K35 A2   25g dull violet   .70   1.40
1K36 A2   55g brt ultra   1.00   1.40
    Nos. 1K33-1K36 (4)   2.20   5.60
    Set, never hinged   5.25

OFFICES IN THE TURKISH EMPIRE

Stamps of Poland
1919, Overprinted in
Carmine

1919, May   Unwmk.   Perf. 11½
    Wove Paper
2K1 A10   3f bister brn   55.00   100.00
2K2 A10   5f green   55.00   100.00
2K3 A10   10f red vio   55.00   100.00
2K4 A10   15f red   55.00   100.00
2K5 A11   20f dp blue   55.00   100.00
2K6 A11   25f olive grn   55.00   100.00
2K7 A11   50f blue grn   55.00   100.00

Overprinted

2K8   A12   1m violet   140.00   120.00
2K9   A12   1.50m dp green   140.00   120.00
2K10 A12   2m dk brown   140.00   140.00
2K11 A13   2.50m orange brn   140.00   120.00
2K12 A14   5m red violet   140.00   140.00
    Nos. 2K1-2K12 (12)   1,085.   1,340.

Counterfeit cancellations are plentiful.
Counterfeits exist of Nos. 2K1-2K12.
Reissues are lighter, shiny red. Value, set $15.
Polish stamps with "P.P.C." overprint (Poste Polonaise Constantinople) were used on consular mail for a time.

Seven stamps with these overprints were not issued. Value, set: unused $10, never hinged $35.

PONTA DELGADA

ˌpän-tə del-ˈgä-də

LOCATION — Administrative district of the Azores comprising the islands of Sao Miguel and Santa Maria
GOVT. — A district of Portugal
AREA — 342 sq. mi.
POP. — 124,000 (approx.)
CAPITAL — Ponta Delgada

    1000 Reis = 1 Milreis

STAMPS OF PORTUGAL USED IN PONTA DELGADA

    Barred Numeral "50"
1853   **Queen Maria II**
A1   5r org brn (#1)   1,300.
A2   25r blue (#2)   75.
A3   50r dp yel grn (#3)   1,350.
   a. 50r blue grn (#3a)   2,000.
A4   100r lilac (#4)   2,750.

1855   King Pedro V (Straight Hair)
A5   5r red brn (#5)   1,400.
A6   25r blue, type II (#6)   70.00
   a. Type I (#6a)   70.00
A7   50r green (#7)   110.00
A8   100r lilac (#8)   140.00

1856-58   King Pedro V (Curled Hair)
A9   5r red brn (#9)   150.00
A10   25r blue, type II (#10)   110.00
   a. Type I (#10a)   80.00
A11   25r rose, type II (#11; '58)   24.00

1862-64   **King Luiz**
A12   5r brown (#12)   77.50
A13   10r orange (#13)   85.00
A14   25r rose (#14)   15.00
A15   50r yel green (#15)   110.00
A16   100r lilac (#16; '64)   125.00

1866-67   **King Luiz**
      Imperf.
A17   5r black (#17)   75.00
A18   10r yellow (#18)   160.00
A19   20r bister (#19)   150.00
A20   25r rose (#20)   50.00
A21   50r green (#21)   150.00
A22   80r orange (#22)   150.00
A23   100r dk lilac (#23; '67)   190.00
A24   120r blue (#24)   140.00
      Perf. 12½
A28   25r rose (#28)   130.00

Issued under Portuguese Administration

King Carlos — A1

1892-93   Typo.   Unwmk.
   Enamel Surfaced Paper
      Perf. 12½
1   A1   5r yellow   2.75   1.60
    Never hinged   3.75
  c.   Diagonal half used as 2½r
     on piece   17.50
2   A1   10r reddish vio   2.75   1.60
    Never hinged   3.75
3   A1   15r chocolate   3.50   2.25
    Never hinged   4.75
4   A1   20r lavender   3.50   2.25
    Never hinged   4.75
5a   A1   25r deep green   7.50   1.60
    Never hinged   11.00
6   A1   50r ultra   9.00   3.25
    Never hinged   13.00
7a   A1   75r carmine   7.75   5.25
    Never hinged   11.00
8   A1   80r yellow grn   11.00   9.00
    Never hinged   15.00
9   A1 100r brn, *yel*   11.00   5.50
    Never hinged   15.00
11   A1 200r dk bl, *bl*   50.00   30.00
    Never hinged   80.00
12   A1 300r dk bl, *salmon*   50.00   30.00
    Never hinged   80.00
    Nos. 1-12 (11)   158.75   92.30
      Perf. 13½
1a   A1   5r yellow   3.00   1.60
    Never hinged   4.00
2a   A1   10r reddish vio   4.00   2.25
    Never hinged   5.25
3a   A1   15r chocolate   3.75   2.25
    Never hinged   5.25
4a   A1   20r lavender   6.00   2.00
    Never hinged   7.75
6a   A1   50r blue   11.00   5.50
    Never hinged   16.50
7   A1   75r carmine   9.00   5.50
    Never hinged   13.00
8a   A1   80r yellow grn   15.50   8.75
    Never hinged   22.50
9a   A1 100r brn, *yel*   15.50   7.50
    Never hinged   22.50
10   A1 150r car, *rose*   30.00   30.00
    Never hinged   87.50
      Perf. 11½
1b   A1   5r yellow   8.50   5.50
    Never hinged   14.50
5   A1   25r green   7.50   1.60
    Never hinged   12.00
6b   A1   50r blue   10.50   3.00
    Never hinged   17.50
      Chalky Paper
      Perf. 11½
1d   A1   5r yellow   5.00   1.50
    Never hinged   6.75
5b   A1   25r green   12.50   3.25
    Never hinged   17.50
      Perf. 12½
5c   A1   25r green   10.00   4.75
    Never hinged   13.00
      Perf. 13½
1e   A1   5r yellow   3.00   .80
    Never hinged   4.00
5d   A1   25r green   7.50   1.10
    Never hinged   9.50

The 5r and 25r values were issued on two types of paper: enamel surfaced, which is white, with a uniform low gloss; and chalky, which bears a low-gloss application in a pattern of tiny lozenges, producing a somewhat duller appearance.
    Nos. 1, 4 and 9-12 were reprinted in 1900 (perf. 11½). Value, each $50. All values were reprinted in 1905 (perf. 13½). Value, each $25. The reprints are on paper slightly thinner than that of the originals, and unsurfaced. They have white gum and clean-cut perfs.

King Carlos — A2

Name and Value in Black except Nos. 25 and 34
1897-1905   *Perf. 11½*
13   A2   2½r gray   .60   .35
    Never hinged   .95
14   A2   5r orange   .60   .35
    Never hinged   .95
15   A2   10r lt green   .60   .35
    Never hinged   .95
16   A2   15r brown   4.00   2.00
    Never hinged   10.50
17   A2   15r gray grn ('99)   2.25   1.10
    Never hinged   2.75
18   A2   20r dull violet   2.25   1.25
    Never hinged   2.75
19   A2   25r sea green   3.00   1.25
    Never hinged   3.75
20   A2   25r rose red ('99)   2.25   .40
    Never hinged   2.75
21   A2   50r blue   3.00   1.25
    Never hinged   3.75
22   A2   50r ultra ('05)   20.00   11.00
    Never hinged   24.00
23   A2   65r slate blue ('98)   2.00   .45
    Never hinged   2.50
24   A2   75r rose   7.00   1.25
    Never hinged   8.75
25   A2   75r brn & car, *yel* ('05)   15.00   8.75
    Never hinged   17.50
26   A2   80r violet   2.00   1.25
    Never hinged   2.40
27   A2 100r dk bl, *bl*   4.25   1.25
    Never hinged   5.25
28   A2 115r org brn, *rose* ('98)   5.00   1.60
    Never hinged   5.75
29   A2 130r gray brn, *buff* ('98)   5.00   1.60
    Never hinged   6.00
30   A2 150r lt brn, *buff*   5.00   2.25
    Never hinged   6.00
31   A2 180r sl, *pnksh* ('98)   5.00   2.25
    Never hinged   6.00
32   A2 200r red vio, *pnksh*   7.75   5.50
    Never hinged   9.25
33   A2 300r blue, *rose*   9.00   5.50
    Never hinged   9.25
  a.   Perf. 12½   45.00   30.00
    Never hinged   55.00
34   A2 500r blk & red, *bl*   19.00   10.00
    Never hinged   19.00
  a.   Perf. 12½   30.00   13.00
    Never hinged   35.00
    Nos. 13-34 (22)   124.55   60.95
      Yellowish Paper
14a   A2   5r orange   .55   .30
    Never hinged   .75
15a   A2   10r lt green   .55   .30
    Never hinged   .75
23a   A2   65r slate blue ('98)   1.25   .45
    Never hinged   1.60

    Imperfs are proofs.

The stamps of Ponta Delgada were superseded by those of the Azores, which in 1931 were replaced by those of Portugal.

PORTUGAL

'pōr-chi-gəl

LOCATION — Southern Europe, on the western coast of the Iberian Peninsula
GOVT. — Republic
AREA — 35,516 sq. mi.
POP. — 9,930,000 (est. 1983)
CAPITAL — Lisbon

Figures for area and population include the Azores and Madeira, which are integral parts of the republic. The republic was established in 1910. See Azores, Funchal, Madeira.

1000 Reis = 1 Milreis
10 Reis = 1 Centimo
100 Centavos = 1 Escudo (1912)

Queen Maria II
A1   A2

A3   A4

Typo. & Embossed
1853   Unwmk.   Imperf.

1	A1	5r reddish brown	2,850.	850.00
		On newspaper or wrapper		3,500.
a.		5r orange brown	3,250.	1,000.
		On newspaper or wrapper		3,900.
b.		Double impression		4,250.
		On cover		24,000.
2	A2	25r blue	925.	19.00
		On cover		75.00
a.		25r greenish blue	1,600.	32.50
		On cover		125.00
b.		Double impression	4,750.	1,500.
		On cover		6,200.
3	A3	50r dp yellow grn	3,400.	875.00
		On cover		3,500.
a.		50r blue green	6,750.	1,650.
		On cover		6,500.
b.		50r green	3,400.	875.00
		On cover		3,500.
c.		Double impression	14,000.	6,000.
		On cover		24,000.
4	A4	100r lilac	31,000.	1,900.
		On cover		9,000.

Full margins = 2mm.

Values for pairs

1	A1	5r reddish brown	2,600.
1a	A1	5r orange brown	2,900.
2	A2	25r blue	57.50
2a	A2	25r greenish blue	100.00
3	A3	50r deep yellow green	2,650.
3a	A3	50r blue green	4,800.
3b	A3	50r green	2,650.
4	A4	100r lilac	5,750.

Values for blocks of 4

1	A1	5r reddish brown	6,900.
1a	A1	5r orange brown	7,750.
2	A2	25r blue	150.00
2a	A2	25r greenish blue	275.00
3	A3	50r deep yellow green	7,000.

3a	A3	50r blue green	13,000.
3b	A3	50r green	7,000.
4	A4	100r lilac	15,000.

The stamps of the 1853 issue were reprinted in 1864, 1885, 1905 and 1953. Many stamps of subsequent issues were reprinted in 1885 and 1905. The reprints of 1864 are on thin white paper with white gum. The originals have brownish gum which often stains the paper. The reprints of 1885 are on a stout, very white paper. They are usually ungummed, but occasionally have a white gum with yellowish spots. The reprints of 1905 are on creamy white paper of ordinary quality with shiny white gum.

When perforated the reprints of 1885 have a rather rough perforation 13½ with small holes; those of 1905 have a clean-cut perforation 13½ with large holes making sharp pointed teeth.

The colors of the reprints usually differ from those of the originals, but actual comparison is necessary.

The reprints are often from new dies which differ slightly from those used for the originals.

5 reis: There is a defect in the neck which makes the Adam's apple appear very large in the first reprint. The later ones can be distinguished by the paper and the shades and by the absence of the pendant curl.

25 reis: The burelage of the ground work in the original is sharp and clear, while in the 1864 reprint it is blurred in several places; the upper and lower right hand corners are very thick and blurred. The central oval is less than ½mm from the frame at the sides in the originals and fully ¾mm in the 1885 and 1905 reprints.

50 reis: In the reprints of 1864 and 1885 there is a small break in the upper right hand diagonal line of the frame, and the initials of the engraver (F. B. F.), which in the originals are plainly discernible in the lower part of the bust, do not show. The reprints of 1905 have not the break in the frame and the initials are distinct.

100 reis: The small vertical lines at top and bottom at each side of the frame are heavier in the reprints of 1864 than in the originals. The reprints of 1885 and 1905 can be distinguished only by the paper, gum and shades.

Reprints of 1953 have thick paper, no gum and dates "1853/1953" on back. Value $55 each.

Values of lowest-cost earlier reprints (1905) of Nos. 1, $100; No. 2, $120; Nos. 3, 4, $150.

King Pedro V
A5   A6

1855   With Straight Hair

TWENTY-FIVE REIS:
Type I — Pearls mostly touch each other and oval outer line.
Type II — Pearls are separate from each other and oval outer line.

5	A5	5r red brown	8,250.	900.00
		On newspaper or wrapper		3,500.
6	A6	25r blue, type II	950.00	25.00
		On cover		100.00
a.		25r blue, type I	1,150.	30.00
		On cover		125.00

A7   A8

7	A7	50r green	500.00	70.00
		On cover		275.00
a.		50r blue green	825.00	100.00
		On cover		400.00
b.		Double impression	1,900.	725.00
8	A8	100r lilac	750.00	90.00
		On cover		375.00
		On cover, single franking		600.00

Full margins = 2mm.

Values for pairs

5	A5	5r red brown	2,650.
6	A6	25r blue, type II	72.50
6a	A6	25r blue, type I	87.50
7	A7	50r green	210.00
7a	A7	50r blue green	300.00
8	A8	100r lilac	275.00

Values for blocks of 4

5	A5	5r red brown	7,000.
6	A6	25r blue, type II	200.00
6a	A6	25r blue, type I	250.00
7	A7	50r green	550.00
7a	A7	50r ble green	800.00
8	A8	100r lilac	725.00

Several types of No. 5 exist, differing in number of pearls encircling head (74 to 89) and other details.

All values were reprinted in 1885 and 1905. Value for lowest-cost, $60 each.
See note after No. 4.

1856   With Curled Hair

TWENTY-FIVE REIS:
Type I — The network is fine (single lines).
Type II — The network is coarse (double lines).

9	A5	5r brown	400.00	70.00
		On cover		275.00
		On newspaper or wrapper		550.00
a.		5r yellow brown	525.00	140.00
		On cover		575.00
b.		5r red brown	475.00	92.50
		On cover		375.00
c.		5r rose brown	475.00	92.50
		On cover		375.00
d.		5r bister brown	475.00	92.50
		On cover		375.00
e.		5r gray brown	475.00	92.50
		On cover		375.00
f.		5r dark brown	475.00	92.50
		On cover		375.00
g.		Double impression	1,400.	375.00
		On cover		1,500.
10	A6	25r blue, type II	400.00	13.50
		On cover		52.50
a.		25r blue, type I	9,500.	55.00
		On cover		225.00

Full margins = 2mm.

Values for pairs

9	A5	5r brown	400.00
9a	A5	5r yellow brown	275.00
9b	A5	5r red brown	275.00
9c	A5	5r rose brown	275.00
9d	A5	5r bister brown	275.00
9e	A5	5r gray brown	275.00
9f	A5	5r dark brown	275.00
10	A6	25r blue, type II	40.00
10a	A6	25r blue, type I	175.00

Values for blocks of 4

9	A5	5r brown	1,100.
9a	A5	5r yellow brown	750.00
9b	A5	5r red brown	750.00
9c	A5	5r rose brown	750.00
9d	A5	5r bister brown	750.00
9e	A5	5r gray brown	750.00
9f	A5	5r dark brown	750.00
10	A6	25r blue, type II	100.00
10a	A6	25r blue, type I	450.00

1858

11	A6	25r rose, type II	275.00	6.50
		On cover		19.00
		Pair		13.50
		Block of 4		42.50
a.		Double impression	525.00	275.00
		On cover		1,100.

Full margins = 2mm.

The 5r dark brown, formerly listed and sold at about $1, is now believed by the best authorities to be a reprint made before 1866. It is printed on thin yellowish white paper with yellowish white gum and is known only unused. The same remarks will apply to a 25r blue which is common unused but not known used. It is printed from a die which was not

used for the issued stamps but the differences are slight and can only be told by expert comparison.

Nos. 9 and 10, also 10a in rose, were reprinted in 1885 and Nos. 9, 10, 10a and 11 in 1905. Value of lowest-cost reprints, $40 each.
See note after No. 4.

King Luiz
A9   A10

A11   A12

A13

FIVE REIS:
Type I — The distance between "5" and "reis" is 3mm.
Type II — The distance between "5" and "reis" is 2mm.

1862-64

12	A9	5r brown, type I	125.00	10.00
		On cover		40.00
		On newspaper or wrapper		325.00
a.		5r brown, type II	160.00	25.00
		On cover		110.00
		On newspaper or wrapper		410.00
b.		Double impression, type II	650.00	350.00
		On cover		1,300.
c.		5r reddish brown	—	125.00
		On cover		500.00
d.		Double embossing, type I	—	275.00
		On cover		1,100.
13	A10	10r orange	125.00	40.00
		On cover		275.00
14	A11	25r rose	100.00	4.75
		On cover		17.50
a.		Double impression	1,350.	375.00
		On cover		1,400.
b.		Double embossing, type I	1,350.	375.00
		On cover		1,400.
15	A12	50r yellow green	725.00	77.50
		On cover		360.00
a.		50r blue green	850.00	100.00
		On cover		450.00
16	A13	100r lilac ('64)	825.00	90.00
		On cover		400.00
		Nos. 12-16 (5)	1,900.	222.25

Full margins = 2mm.

Values for pairs

12	A9	5r brown, type I	30.00
12a	A9	5r brown, type II	75.00
12c	A9	5r reddish brown	375.00
13	A10	10r orange	140.00
14	A11	25r rose	14.00
15	A12	50r yellow green	225.00
15a	A12	50r blue green	300.00
16	A13	100r lilac ('64)	275.00

Values for blocks of 4

No.	Type	Description	Value
12	A9	5r brown, type I	80.00
12a	A9	5r brown, type II	210.00
12c	A9	5r reddish brown	1,000.
13	A10	10r orange	375.00
14	A11	25r rose	37.50
15	A12	50r yellow green	600.00
15a	A12	50r blue green	800.00
16	A13	100r lilac ('64)	375.00

All values were reprinted in 1885 and all except the 25r in 1905. Value of lowest-cost reprints, $10 each.
See note after No. 4.

King Luiz
A14　　　A15

1866-67　　　Imperf.

No.	Type	Description	Unused	Used
17	A14	5r black	100.00	10.00
		On cover		40.00
a.		Double impression	275.00	190.00
		On cover		750.00
18	A14	10r yellow	225.00	140.00
		On cover		575.00
19	A14	20r bister	175.00	67.50
		On cover		260.00
		On cover, single franking		550.00
20	A14	25r rose ('67)	200.00	6.00
		On cover		32.50
a.		Double impression		225.00
		On cover		800.00
21	A14	50r green	250.00	50.00
		On cover		260.00
		On cover, single franking		550.00
22	A14	80r orange	250.00	50.00
		On cover		260.00
23	A14	100r dk lilac ('67)	300.00	75.00
		On cover		500.00
24	A14	120r blue	325.00	70.00
		On cover		275.00
a.		Double impression	725.00	450.00
		On cover		1,800.
		Nos. 17-24 (8)	1,825.	468.50

Full margins = 1¾mm.

Some values with unofficial percé en croix (diamond) perforation were used in Madeira.
All values were reprinted in 1885 and 1905. Value: Nos. 17-23, each $30-$40; No. 24, $100.
See note after No. 4.

Typographed & Embossed
1867-70　　　Perf. 12½

No.	Type	Description	Unused	Used
25	A14	5r black	125.00	42.50
		On cover		225.00
a.		Double impression	225.00	110.00
		On cover		425.00
26	A14	10r yellow	250.00	110.00
		On cover		425.00
27	A14	20r bister ('69)	300.00	110.00
		On cover		425.00
28	A14	25r rose	65.00	5.00
		On cover		425.00
a.		Double impression	550.00	200.00
		On cover		800.00
29	A14	50r green ('68)	250.00	100.00
		On cover		425.00
30	A14	80r orange ('69)	350.00	100.00
		On cover		425.00
31	A14	100r lilac ('69)	250.00	100.00
		On cover		425.00
32	A14	120r blue	300.00	67.50
		On cover		260.00
a.		Double impression	625.00	160.00
		On cover		650.00
33	A14	240r pale violet ('70)	1,000.	475.00
		On cover		1,900.
		Nos. 25-33 (9)	2,890.	1,110.

Nos. 25-33 frequently were separated with scissors. Slightly blunted perfs on one or two sides are to be expected for stamps of this issue.

Two types each of 5r and 100r differ in the position of the "5" at upper right and the "100" at lower right in relation to the end of the label.
Nos. 25-33 were reprinted in 1885 and 1905. Some of the 1885 reprints were perforated 12½ as well as 13½. Value of the lowest-cost reprints, $40 each.
See note after No. 4.

Typographed & Embossed
1870-84　　　Perf. 12½
Plain Paper

No.	Type	Description	Unused	Used
34	A15	5r black	55.00	5.00
		On newspaper or wrapper		55.00
f.		Double impression	275.00	67.50
		On cover		260.00
35	A15	10r yellow ('71)	77.50	27.50
		On cover		150.00
f.		Double impression	300.00	125.00
		On cover		500.00
36	A15	10r blue grn ('79)	375.00	175.00
		On cover		1,000.
37	A15	10r yellow grn ('80)	110.00	24.00
		On newspaper or wrapper		125.00
		On post card		160.00
d.		Double impression	250.00	130.00
		On cover		575.00
38	A15	15r lilac brn ('75)	100.00	29.00
		On cover		110.00
39	A15	20r bister	72.50	25.00
		On cover		150.00
g.		Double impression	—	175.00
40	A15	20r rose ('84)	325.00	55.00
		On cover		400.00
41	A15	25r rose	30.00	3.75
		On cover		15.00
f.		Double impression	240.00	30.00
		On cover		120.00
42	A15	50r pale green	140.00	40.00
		On cover		150.00
43	A15	50r blue ('79)	350.00	50.00
		On cover		210.00
44	A15	80r orange	140.00	30.00
		On cover		120.00
45	A15	100r pale lilac ('71)	110.00	21.00
		On cover		85.00
46	A15	120r blue ('71)	300.00	62.50
		On cover		275.00
47	A15	150r pale bl ('76)	375.00	110.00
		On cover		460.00
d.		Double impression	1,050.	390.00
		On cover		1,550.
48	A15	150r yellow ('80)	140.00	40.00
		On cover		500.00
49	A15	240r pale violet ('73)	1,700.	1,050.
		On cover		4,100.
50	A15	300r dull violet ('76)	110.00	27.50
		On cover		410.00
		On cover, single franking		1,100.
51	A15	1000r black ('84)	275.00	77.50
		On cover		325.00
		On cover, single franking		1,350.

Perf. 13½

No.	Type	Description	Unused	Used
34d	A15	5r black	65.00	8.25
		On newspaper or wrapper		32.50
35d	A15	10r yellow	95.00	35.00
		On cover		150.00
36a	A15	10r blue green	675.00	300.00
		On cover		1,250.
37a	A15	10r yellow grn ('80)	125.00	27.50
		On newspaper or wrapper		110.00
		On post card		165.00
38a	A15	15r lilac brown	140.00	57.50
		On cover		225.00
39c	A15	20r bister	110.00	27.50
		On cover		160.00
40a	A15	20r rose ('84)	350.00	85.00
		On cover		425.00
b.		Double impression	—	1,050.
		On cover		—
41d	A15	25r rose	30.00	4.00
		On cover		16.00
g.		Double impression	—	32.50
42a	A15	50r pale green	160.00	40.00
		On cover		160.00
43a	A15	50r blue ('79)	325.00	52.50
		On cover		210.00
44c	A15	80r orange	165.00	40.00
		On cover		160.00
45b	A15	100r pale lilac	165.00	50.00
		On cover		200.00
46a	A15	120r blue		3,500.
		On cover		—
47b	A15	150r blue	750.00	300.00
		On cover		1,200.
48a	A15	150r yellow ('80)	175.00	77.50
		On cover		300.00
50a	A15	300r dull violet ('76)	110.00	27.50
		On cover		360.00
51a	A15	1000r black ('84)	275.00	77.50
		On cover		325.00
		On cover, single franking		1,350.

Perf. 11

No.	Type	Description	Unused	Used
34b	A15	5r black	—	550.00
		On newspaper or wrapper		550.00
35b	A15	10r yellow	—	550.00
		On cover		—
39b	A15	20r bister	—	550.00
		On cover		—
41b	A15	25r rose	—	3,500.
		On cover		—
42b	A15	50r pale green	—	550.00
		On cover		—
44b	A15	80r orange	—	550.00
		On cover		—
49b	A15	240r pale violet	—	—
		On cover		—

Perf. 14¼

No.	Type	Description	Unused	Used
34c	A15	5r black	225.00	125.00
		On newspaper or wrapper		600.00
35c	A15	10r yellow	425.00	275.00
		On cover		1,600.
41c	A15	25r rose	425.00	25.00
		On cover		125.00
44c	A15	80r orange	1,050.	800.00
		On cover		3,200.
45a	A15	100r pale lilac	1,300.	800.00
		On cover		3,200.

Imperforate

No.	Type	Description	Value
34a	A15	5r black	550.00
35a	A15	10r yellow	550.00
39a	A15	20r bister	550.00
41a	A15	25r rose	550.00

Ribbed Paper
Perf. 12½

No.	Type	Description	Unused	Used
34e	A15	5r black	150.00	22.50
		On cover		92.50
35e	A15	10r yellow	210.00	110.00
		On cover		450.00
39d	A15	20r bister	300.00	100.00
		On cover		400.00
41e	A15	25r rose	125.00	21.00
		On cover		85.00
42c	A15	50r pale green	400.00	90.00
		On cover		350.00
44d	A15	80r orange	400.00	100.00
		On cover		425.00
45c	A15	100r pale lilac	400.00	100.00
		On cover		400.00
46b	A15	120r blue	950.00	225.00
		On cover		950.00
49c	A15	240r pale violet	3,250.	2,100.
		On cover		8,750.

Enamel Surfaced Paper
Perf. 12½

No.	Type	Description	Unused	Used
37b	A15	10r yellow grn ('80)	110.00	24.00
		On cover		125.00
		On post card		175.00
38b	A15	15r lilac brown	110.00	30.00
		On cover		125.00
d.		Double impression	500.00	260.00
		On cover		1,050.
39e	A15	20r bister	100.00	25.00
		On cover		110.00
44e	A15	80r orange	125.00	19.00
		On cover		75.00
45e	A15	100r pale lilac ('71)	65.00	12.00
		On cover		75.00
48b	A15	150r yellow ('80)	125.00	13.50
		On cover		55.00
50b	A15	300r dull violet ('76)	110.00	30.00
		On cover		225.00

Perf. 13½

No.	Type	Description	Unused	Used
37c	A15	10r yellow grn ('80)	140.00	45.00
		On cover		175.00
		On post card		190.00
38c	A15	15r lilac brown	110.00	30.00
		On cover		125.00
39f	A15	20r bister	140.00	30.00
		On cover		125.00
44f	A15	80r orange	140.00	30.00
		On cover		120.00
45f	A15	100r pale lilac	160.00	42.50
		On cover		175.00
48c	A15	150r yellow ('80)	150.00	35.00
		On cover		250.00
50c	A15	300r dull violet ('76)	150.00	40.00
		On cover		250.00

Two types each of 15r, 20r and 80r differ in the distance between the figures of value.
Imperfs probably are proofs.
For overprints and surcharges see Nos. 86-87, 94-96.
All values of the issues of 1870-84 were reprinted in 1885 and 1905. Value of the lowest-cost reprints, $30 each.
See note after No. 4.

King Luiz
A16　　　A17

A18　　　A19

1880-81　　Typo.　　Perf. 12½, 13½

No.	Type	Description	Unused	Used
52	A16	5r black	30.00	4.00
		On newspaper or wrapper		32.50
a.		Enamel surfaced paper, perf 12½	150.00	50.00
		On cover		200.00
b.		Enamel surfaced paper, perf 13½	140.00	50.00
		On cover		200.00
53	A17	25r bluish gray	300.00	29.00
		On cover		110.00
54	A18	25r gray	40.00	3.50
		On cover		15.00
55	A18	25r brown vio ('81)	40.00	3.50
		On cover		15.00
56	A19	50r blue ('81)	300.00	15.00
		On cover		75.00
		Nos. 52-56 (5)	710.00	55.00

All values were reprinted in 1885 and 1905. Value of the lowest-cost reprints, $15 each.
See note after No. 4.

A20　　　A21

King Luiz
A22　　　A23

A24　　　A24a

1882-87　　　Perf. 12½
Plain Paper

No.	Type	Description	Unused	Used
57	A20	2r black ('84)	20.00	15.00
		On cover		110.00
60a	A23	25r brown	42.50	3.00
		On cover		13.50
61a	A23	50r blue	52.50	3.00
		On cover		25.00
62	A24a	500r black ('84)	500.00	300.00
		On cover		1,200.
63	A24a	500r violet ('87)	275.00	52.50
		On cover		500.00
		Nos. 57-63 (5)	890.00	373.50

Perf. 13½

No.	Type	Description	Unused	Used
57a	A20	2r black ('84)	25.00	16.00
		On cover		110.00
60b	A23	25r brown	37.50	3.60
		On cover		15.00
61b	A23	50r blue	52.50	4.00
		On cover		27.50
62a	A24a	500r black ('84)	900.00	725.00
		On cover		2,900.
63a	A24a	500r violet ('87)	825.00	275.00
		On cover		1,800.

Perf. 11½

No.	Type	Description	Unused	Used
57b	A20	2r black ('84)	—	—
58c	A21	5r black	32.50	3.25
		On newspaper or wrapper		27.50
60	A23	25r brown	27.50	2.25
		On cover		10.00

Enamel Surfaced Paper
Perf. 12½

No.	Type	Description	Unused	Used
58a	A21	5r black ('84)	30.00	3.00
		On newspaper or wrapper		22.50
58d	A21	5r gray ('83)	32.50	3.50
		On newspaper or wrapper		27.50
59a	A22	10r green ('84)	50.00	4.00
		On cover		55.00
60c	A23	25r brown	32.50	2.60
		On cover		10.00
61c	A23	50r blue	52.50	3.25
		On cover		25.00

Perf. 13½

No.	Type	Description	Unused	Used
58b	A21	5r black ('84)	35.00	7.25
		On newspaper or wrapper		45.00
58e	A21	5r gray ('83)	37.50	7.25
		On newspaper or wrapper		45.00
59b	A22	10r green ('84)	62.50	7.25
		On newspaper or wrapper		100.00
60d	A23	25r brown	37.50	3.50
		On cover		13.50
61d	A23	50r blue	50.00	10.00
		On cover		42.50

Perf. 11½

No.	Type	Description	Unused	Used
58	A21	5r black ('84)	32.50	3.50
		On newspaper or wrapper		11.00
58f	A21	5r gray ('83)	50.00	11.00
		On newspaper or wrapper		55.00
59	A22	10r green ('84)	35.00	4.00
		On newspaper or wrapper		55.00
60e	A23	25r brown	32.50	2.25
		On cover		10.00
61	A24	50r blue	45.00	3.00
		On cover		22.50

For overprints see Nos. 79-82, 85, 88-89, 93.
The stamps of the 1882-87 issues were reprinted in 1885, 1893 and 1905. Value of the lowest-cost reprints, $20 each.
See note after No. 4.
Covers: The values for Nos. 57, 57a and 57b are for philatelic covers or post cards.

A25　　　A26

1887　　　Perf. 11½

No.	Type	Description	Unused	Used
64	A25	20r rose	45.00	17.00
		On cover		65.00
65	A26	25r violet	30.00	3.00
		On cover		12.00
66	A26	25r lilac rose	27.50	3.00
		On cover		11.00
		Nos. 64-66 (3)	102.50	23.00

For overprints see Nos. 83-84, 90-92.
Nos. 64-66 were reprinted in 1905. Value $22.50 each. See note after No. 4.

King Carlos — A27

1892-93 — Perf. 12½
Enamel Surfaced Paper

68	A27 10r redsh violet	30.00	4.00
	On cover		55.00
69	A27 15r chocolate	27.50	6.00
	On cover		55.00
70	A27 20r lavender	35.00	9.25
	On cover		55.00
72	A27 50r blue	35.00	9.25
	On cover		65.00
73	A27 75r carmine ('93)	67.50	8.00
	On cover		82.50
74	A27 80r yellow grn	100.00	52.50
	On cover		325.00
75	A27 100r brn, *buff* ('93)	65.00	6.25
	On cover		110.00
76a	A27 150r car, *rose* ('93)	250.00	100.00
	On cover		400.00
77	A27 200r dk bl, *bl* ('93)	160.00	35.00
	On cover		550.00
78	A27 300r dk bl, *sal* ('93)	175.00	57.50
	On cover		550.00
	Nos. 67-78 (10)	945.00	287.75

Perf. 13½

68b	A27 10r reddish violet	30.00	6.50
	On cover		65.00
69a	A27 15r chocolate	32.50	8.50
	On cover		70.00
70a	A27 20r lavender	50.00	11.50
	On cover		65.00
72b	A27 50r blue	100.00	12.00
	On cover		72.50
73a	A27 75r carmine ('93)	175.00	30.00
	On cover		225.00
74a	A27 80r yellow green	85.00	42.50
	On cover		325.00
75b	A27 100r brown, *buff* ('93)	100.00	12.50
	On cover		175.00
76	A27 150r car, *rose* ('93)	160.00	42.50
	On cover		225.00
77a	A27 200r dk blue, *blue* ('93)	175.00	65.00
	On cover		650.00

Perf. 11½

67	A27 5r orange	11.00	2.00
	On newspaper or wrapper		11.00
68a	A27 10r reddish violet	1,700.	45.00
	On cover		275.00
71	A27 25r dark green	37.50	2.50
	On cover		10.00
72a	A27 50r blue	52.50	6.00
	On cover		55.00
73b	A27 75r carmine ('93)	350.00	13.00
	On cover		110.00
75a	A27 100r brown, *buff* ('93)	400.00	16.00
	On cover		200.00

Chalky Paper
Perf. 12½

68d	A27 10r reddish violet	275.00	42.50
	On cover		325.00
70b	A27 20r lavender	1,100.	550.00
	On cover		2,250.
73c	A27 75r carmine ('93)	225.00	37.50
	On cover		275.00

Perf. 13½

68e	A27 10r reddish violet	37.50	8.00
	On cover		65.00
69b	A27 15r chocolate	27.50	5.00
	On cover		55.00
73d	A27 75r carmine ('93)	225.00	18.00
	On cover		140.00

Perf. 11½

67a	A27 5r orange	13.00	2.00
	On newspaper or wrapper		11.00
68c	A27 10r reddish violet	35.00	2.00
	On cover		55.00
71a	A27 25r dark green	27.50	2.00
	On cover		8.25

Nos. 67-78 were issued on two types of paper: enamel surfaced, which is white, with a uniform low gloss; and chalky, which bears a low-gloss application in a pattern of tiny lozenges, producing a somewhat duller appearance.
Nos. 76-78 were reprinted in 1900 (perf. 11½). Value, each $100. All values were reprinted in 1905 (perf. 13½). Value, each $50.
See note after No. 4.

Stamps and Types of Previous Issues Overprinted in Black or Red

a   b

c

1892

79	A21 (a) 5r gray blk	16.00	8.75
	On newspaper or wrapper		45.00
a.	Double overprint	650.00	450.00
80	A22 (b) 10r green	16.00	8.75
	On newspaper or wrapper		110.00
a.	Inverted overprint	—	—
b.	Double overprint	650.00	450.00

1892-93

81	A21 (c) 5r gray blk (R)	13.50	6.75
	On newspaper or wrapper		55.00
82	A22 (c) 10r green (R)	16.00	9.25
	On newspaper or wrapper		110.00
a.	Inverted overprint	160.00	160.00
83	A25 (c) 20r rose	42.50	22.50
	On cover		160.00
a.	Inverted overprint	225.00	225.00
84	A26 (c) 25r rose lilac, perf. 11½	14.50	5.25
	On cover		160.00
a.	Perf. 12½	475.00	70.00
	On cover		275.00
85	A24 (c) 50r blue (R) ('93)	77.50	62.50
	On cover		375.00
	Nos. 81-85 (5)	164.00	106.25

1893

86	A15 (c) 15r bister brn, plain paper, perf 12½ (R)	20.00	12.00
	On cover		120.00
a.	Perf 13½	550.00	310.00
	On cover		1,250.
b.	Surfaced paper, perf 12½	20.00	11.50
	On cover		110.00
c.	Surfaced paper, perf 13½	27.50	22.50
	On cover		175.00
87	A15 (c) 80r yellow	110.00	87.50
	On cover		275.00

Nos. 86-87 are found in two types each. See note below No. 51.
Some of Nos. 79-87 were reprinted in 1900 and all values in 1905. Value of lowest-cost reprint, $10.
See note after No. 4.

Stamps and Types of Previous Issues Overprinted or Surcharged in Black or Red

d   e

1893 — Perf. 11½, 12½

88	A21 (d) 5r gray blk (R)	26.00	22.50
	On cover		160.00
89	A22 (d) 10r green, perf. 11½ (R)	24.00	20.00
	On cover		160.00
a.	"1938"	300.00	300.00
	On cover		3,250.
b.	"1863"	300.00	300.00
	On cover		3,250.
c.	"1838"	300.00	300.00
	On cover		3,250.
d.	Perf. 12½	1,650.	1,100.
90	A25 (d) 20r rose	40.00	32.50
	On cover		160.00
a.	Inverted overprint	125.00	100.00
b.	"1938"	300.00	300.00
	On cover		3,250.
91	A26 (e) 20r on 25r lil rose	52.50	47.50
	On cover		190.00
92	A26 (d) 25r lilac rose	110.00	100.00
	On cover		350.00
a.	Inverted overprint	275.00	275.00
93	A24 (d) 50r blue (R)	110.00	110.00
	On cover		450.00

Perf. 12½

94	A15 (e) 50r on 80r yel	150.00	100.00
	On cover		275.00
95	A15 (e) 75r on 80r yel	75.00	72.50
	On cover		375.00
a.	"1893" and "50rs" double	350.00	200.00
	On cover		
96	A15 (d) 80r yellow	125.00	95.00
	On cover		375.00
a.	"1893" double	450.00	450.00
	Nos. 88-96 (9)	712.50	600.00

Nos. 94-96 are found in two types each. See note below No. 51.
Some of Nos. 88-96 were reprinted in 1900 and all values in 1905. Value of lowest-cost reprint, $45 each.
See note after No. 4.
Covers: Values for Nos. 89a and 89b are for philatelic covers.

Prince Henry on his Ship — A46

Prince Henry Directing Fleet Maneuvers A47

Symbolic of Prince Henry's Studies — A48

1894 — Litho. — Perf. 14

97	A46 5r orange	3.75	.65
	Never hinged	15.00	
	On cover or post card		82.50
98	A46 10r magenta	3.75	.65
	Never hinged	15.00	
	On cover or post card		82.50
99	A46 15r red brown	11.00	3.25
	Never hinged	45.00	
	On cover		225.00
100	A46 20r dull violet	11.00	4.00
	Never hinged	45.00	
	On cover		225.00
101	A47 25r gray green	9.75	1.40
	Never hinged	—	
	On cover		110.00
102	A47 50r blue	27.50	6.00
	Never hinged	—	
	On cover		110.00
103	A47 75r car rose	52.50	11.50
	Never hinged	—	
	On cover		225.00
104	A47 80r yellow grn	52.50	14.00
	Never hinged	—	
	On cover		225.00
105	A47 100r lt brn, *pale buff*	40.00	10.00
	Never hinged	—	
	On cover		110.00

Engr.

106	A48 150r lt car, *pale rose*	150.00	32.50
	Never hinged	—	
	On cover		225.00
107	A48 300r dk bl, *sal buff*	175.00	37.50
	Never hinged	—	
	On cover		225.00
108	A48 500r dp vio, *pale lil*	400.00	77.50
	Never hinged	—	
	On cover		300.00
109	A48 1000r gray blk, *grysh*	600.00	110.00
	Never hinged	—	
	On cover		300.00
	Nos. 97-109 (13)	1,536.	308.95

5th centenary of the birth of Prince Henry the Navigator.
Covers: Values for Nos. 99-100, 103-104, 106-109 are for overfranked covers, usually philatelic.

King Carlos — A49

1895-1905 — Typo. — Perf. 11½
Value in Black or Red (#122, 500r)

110	A49 2½r gray	.25	.25
	Never hinged	.50	
	On newspaper or wrapper		5.50
111	A49 5r orange	.25	.25
	Never hinged	.80	
	On newspaper or wrapper		5.50
112	A49 10r lt green	.50	.25
	Never hinged	1.10	
	On postcard		5.50
113	A49 15r brown	90.00	3.50
	Never hinged	160.00	
	On cover		110.00
114	A49 15r gray grn ('99)	47.50	2.40
	Never hinged	85.00	
	On cover		11.00
115	A49 20r gray violet	.85	.35
	Never hinged	1.40	
	On cover or postcard		5.50
116	A49 25r sea green	65.00	.25
	Never hinged	120.00	
	On cover		5.50
117	A49 25r car rose ('99)	.40	.25
	Never hinged	.70	
	On cover		4.50
118	A49 50r blue	82.50	.40
	Never hinged	150.00	
	On cover		22.50
119	A49 50r ultra ('05)	.55	.25
	Never hinged	1.10	
	On cover		11.00
120	A49 65r slate bl ('98)	.55	.25
	Never hinged	1.10	
	On cover		11.00
121	A49 75r rose	110.00	4.50
	Never hinged	225.00	
	On cover		110.00
122	A49 75r brn, *yel* ('05)	1.75	.65
	Never hinged	3.00	
	On cover		55.00
123	A49 80r violet	2.10	1.25
	Never hinged	4.50	
	On cover		110.00
124	A49 100r dk bl, *bl*	1.00	.40
	Never hinged	2.00	
	On cover		55.00
125	A49 115r org brn, *pink* ('98)	4.75	2.75
	Never hinged	9.50	
	On cover		110.00
126	A49 130r gray brn, *straw* ('98)	3.75	1.40
	Never hinged	7.25	
	On cover		160.00
127	A49 150r lt brn, *straw*	140.00	22.50
	Never hinged	275.00	
	On cover		325.00
128	A49 180r sl, *pnksh* ('98)	15.00	9.00
	Never hinged	30.00	
	On cover		225.00
129	A49 200r red lil, *pnksh*	5.00	1.25
	Never hinged	10.00	
	On cover		110.00
a.	200r brown violet, *rose*	16.00	2.25
	Never hinged	32.50	
	On cover		190.00
130	A49 300r blue, *rose*	3.75	2.00
	Never hinged	7.50	
	On cover		275.00
131	A49 500r blk, *bl* ('96)	9.75	4.50
	Never hinged	19.00	
	On cover		275.00
a.	Perf. 12½	110.00	26.00
	Never hinged	225.00	
	On cover		550.00
	Nos. 110-131 (22)	585.20	58.60

Several values of the above type exist without figures of value, also with figures inverted or otherwise misplaced but they were not regularly issued.

St. Anthony and his Vision — A50

St. Anthony Preaching to Fishes — A51

St. Anthony Ascends to Heaven — A52   St. Anthony, from Portrait — A53

Perf. 11½, 12½ and Compound
1895 — Typo.

132	A50 2½r black	4.00	1.10
	Never hinged	16.00	
	On newspaper or wrapper		225.00

Litho.

133	A51 5r brown org	4.00	1.10
	Never hinged	16.00	
	On newspaper or wrapper		160.00
134	A51 10r red lilac	13.50	8.25
	Never hinged	55.00	
	On newspaper or wrapper		160.00
135	A51 15r chocolate	14.50	8.25
	Never hinged	60.00	
	On cover		225.00
136	A51 20r gray violet	14.50	8.25
	Never hinged	60.00	
	On cover		225.00
137	A51 25r green & vio	13.00	1.00
	Never hinged	52.50	
	On cover		225.00
138	A52 50r blue & brn	32.50	22.50
	Never hinged	125.00	
	On cover		225.00
139	A52 75r rose & brn	50.00	40.00
	Never hinged	200.00	
	On cover		225.00
140	A52 80r lt grn & brn	62.50	60.00
	Never hinged	225.00	
	On cover		225.00
141	A52 100r choc & blk	55.00	30.00
	Never hinged	225.00	
	On cover		225.00
142	A53 150r carmine & bis	160.00	100.00
	Never hinged	225.00	
	On cover		225.00
143	A53 200r blue & bis	150.00	125.00
	Never hinged	450.00	
	On cover		450.00
144	A53 300r slate & bis	250.00	140.00
	Never hinged	550.00	
	On cover		550.00

No.	Type	Description		
145	A53	500r vio brn & grn	450.00	300.00
		Never hinged	300.00	
		On cover		1,100.
146	A53	1000r violet & grn	800.00	375.00
		Never hinged	300.00	
		On cover		1,300.
		Nos. 132-146 (15)	3,070	1,640.

7th centenary of the birth of Saint Anthony of Padua. Stamps have eulogy in Latin printed on the back.

Covers: Values for Nos. 135-136, 139-140, 142 are for overfranked covers, usually philatelic.

Vasco da Gama Issue
Common Design Types
1898   Engr.   Perf. 12½ to 16

No.	Type	Description		
147	CD20	2½r blue green	1.40	.35
		On newspaper or wrapper	55.00	
148	CD21	5r red	1.40	.35
		On cover	55.00	
149	CD22	10r red violet	8.50	1.25
		On cover or postcard	55.00	
150	CD23	25r yellow green	5.00	.50
		On cover	55.00	
151	CD24	50r dark blue	10.50	3.00
		On cover	110.00	
152	CD25	75r violet brown	45.00	9.00
		On cover	82.50	
153	CD26	100r bister brown	30.00	9.00
		On cover	110.00	
154	CD27	150r bister	67.50	20.00
		On cover	160.00	
		Nos. 147-154 (8)	169.30	43.45

For overprints and surcharges see Nos. 185-192, 199-206.

King Manuel II
A62   A63

1910   Typo.   Perf. 14½x15

No.	Type	Description		
156	A62	2½r violet	.25	.25
157	A62	5r black	.25	.25
158	A62	10r gray green	.25	.25
159	A62	15r lilac brown	2.75	1.40
160	A62	20r carmine	.80	.65
161	A62	25r violet brn	.60	.25
162	A62	50r dark blue	1.50	.65
163	A62	75r bister brn	9.25	5.00
164	A62	80r slate	2.50	2.25
165	A62	100r brn, *lt grn*	10.00	3.00
166	A62	200r dk grn, *sal*	6.00	4.25
167	A62	300r blk, *azure*	6.75	5.00
168	A63	500r ol grn & vio brn	13.50	11.50
169	A63	1000r dk bl & blk	30.00	24.00
		Nos. 156-169 (14)	84.40	58.70

For overprint see No. RA1.

Preceding Issue
Overprinted in
Carmine or Green

1910

No.	Type	Description		
170	A62	2½r violet	.25	.25
171	A62	5r black	.25	.25
172	A62	10r gray green	3.50	1.25
173	A62	15r lilac brn	1.25	.85
174	A62	20r carmine (G)	4.25	1.50
175	A62	25r violet brn	.80	.25
176	A62	50r dk blue	6.00	2.00
177	A62	75r bister brn	9.00	3.75
178	A62	80r slate	3.25	2.40
179	A62	100r brn, *lt grn*	2.00	.75
180	A62	200r dk grn, *sal*	2.50	1.60
181	A62	300r blk, *azure*	3.75	2.75
182	A63	500r ol grn & vio brn	9.50	8.25
183	A63	1000r dk bl & blk	24.00	24.00
		Nos. 170-183 (14)	70.30	49.85

The numerous inverted and double overprints on this issue were unofficially and fraudulently made.
The 50r with blue overprint is a fraud.

Vasco da Gama Issue Overprinted or Surcharged

a

b

c

1911   Perf. 12½ to 16

No.	Type	Description		
185	CD20(a)	2½r blue green	.45	.25
a.		Inverted overprint	14.00	12.00
186	CD21(b)	15r on 5r red	.80	.35
a.		Inverted surcharge	10.50	9.00
187	CD23(a)	25r yellow grn	.45	.25
188	CD24(a)	50r dark blue	3.25	1.60
189	CD25(a)	75r violet brn	42.50	32.50
190	CD27(b)	80r on 150r bis	8.00	4.75
191	CD26(a)	100r bister brn	8.00	3.00
a.		Inverted overprint	29.00	24.00
192	CD22(c)	1000r on 10r red vio	62.50	37.50
		Nos. 185-192 (8)	125.95	80.20

Postage Due Stamps of 1898 Overprinted or Surcharged for Regular Postage

d

e

1911   Perf. 12

No.	Type	Description		
193	D1(d)	5r black	.85	.35
a.		Double ovpt., one inverted	40.00	20.00
194	D1(d)	10r magenta	1.50	.65
195	D1(d)	20r orange	5.75	3.00
196	D1(d)	200r brn, *buff*	125.00	67.50
197	D1(e)	300r on 50r slate	90.00	42.50
198	D1(e)	500r on 100r car, *pink*	60.00	24.00
a.		Inverted surcharge	125.00	87.50
		Nos. 193-198 (6)	283.10	138.00

Vasco da Gama Issue of Madeira Ovptd. or Srchd. Types "a," "b" and "c"

1911   Perf. 12½ to 16

No.	Type	Description		
199	CD20(a)	2½r blue grn	11.50	8.25
a.		Double overprint		
200	CD21(b)	15r on 5r red	2.50	2.00
a.		Inverted surcharge	12.50	11.00
201	CD23(a)	25r yellow grn	5.75	4.75
202	CD24(a)	50r dk blue	11.00	8.25
a.		Inverted overprint		
203	CD25(a)	75r violet brn	11.00	5.50
a.		Inverted overprint	35.00	30.00
204	CD27(b)	80r on 150r bis	12.50	11.00
a.		Inverted surcharge	47.50	40.00
205	CD26(a)	100r bister brn	37.50	8.25
a.		Inverted overprint	125.00	100.00
206	CD22(c)	1000r on 10r red vio	37.50	50.00
		Nos. 199-206 (8)	129.25	98.00

Ceres — A64

**Chalky Paper
With Imprint**

1912-20   Typo.   Perf. 15x14

No.	Type	Description		
207	A64	¼c dark olive	8.00	5.00
		Never hinged	16.00	
208	A64	½c black	8.00	5.00
		Never hinged	16.00	
209	A64	1c deep green	6.50	2.50
		Never hinged	13.00	
210	A64	1½c chocolate	20.00	9.00
		Never hinged	40.00	
211	A64	2c carmine	20.00	9.00
		Never hinged	40.00	
212	A64	2½c violet	9.50	9.50
		Never hinged	20.00	
213	A64	5c dp blue	5.50	.55
		Never hinged	11.00	
214	A64	7½c yellow brn	65.00	13.50
		Never hinged	130.00	
215	A64	8c slate	3.00	3.00
		Never hinged	6.00	
216	A64	10c org brn	45.00	25.00
		Never hinged	90.00	
217	A64	15c plum	300.00	75.00
		Never hinged	600.00	
218	A64	20c vio brn, *grn*	13.00	1.50
		Never hinged	26.00	
219	A64	20c brn, *buff* ('20)	15.00	3.50
		Never hinged	30.00	
220	A64	30c brn, *pink*	100.00	9.50
		Never hinged	200.00	
221	A64	30c lt brn, *yel* ('17)	8.75	1.60
		Never hinged	17.50	
222	A64	50c org, *sal* ('18)	12.00	1.10
		Never hinged	24.00	
a.		50c orange, *yellow*	15.00	1.10
		Never hinged	30.00	
223	A64	1e dp grn, *bl*	19.00	1.40
		Never hinged	38.00	
		Nos. 207-223 (17)	658.25	175.65

1920   Typo.   Perf. 12x11½

No.	Type	Description		
224	A64	14c dk bl, *yel*	3.25	1.25
		Never hinged	5.00	
225	A64	20c chocolate, *buff*	800.00	200.00
		Never hinged	1,300.	
226	A64	50c orange, *salmon*	225.00	30.00
		Never hinged	450.00	
		Nos. 224-226 (3)	1,028.	231.25

1917-26   Typo.   Perf. 15x14
Ordinary Paper

No.	Type	Description		
227	A64	¼c dark olive ('18)	.65	.25
		Never hinged	1.00	
a.		Thick carton paper	35.00	7.25
		Never hinged	52.50	
228	A64	½c black ('18)	.40	.25
a.		Thick carton paper	35.00	7.25
		Never hinged	52.50	
b.		Bluish paper	.95	.55
		Never hinged	1.40	
229	A64	1c deep green	.65	.25
		Never hinged	1.00	
a.		"CORREIC" for "CORREIO"	700.00	700.00
230	A64	1c chocolate	.25	.25
		Never hinged	.40	
a.		Thick carton paper	30.00	7.50
		Never hinged	45.00	
231	A64	1½c chocolate	5.50	2.50
		Never hinged	8.75	
232	A64	1½c dp grn ('18)	.30	.25
		Never hinged	.50	
233	A64	2c carmine	5.50	2.50
		Never hinged	8.75	
234	A64	2c orange ('18)	.25	.25
		Never hinged	.40	
235	A64	2½c violet	.25	.25
		Never hinged	.40	
236	A64	3c car rose	.25	.25
		Never hinged	.40	
237	A64	3c ultra ('21)	200.00	80.00
		Never hinged	400.00	
238	A64	3½c lt grn ('18)	.25	.25
		Never hinged	.40	
239	A64	4c lt grn ('19)	.40	.30
		Never hinged	.65	
a.		Thick carton paper	30.00	7.50
		Never hinged	50.00	
240	A64	5c yel brn	.50	.30
		Never hinged	.80	
240A	A64	5c deep blue	2.40	.25
		Never hinged	4.00	
241	A64	6c pale rose ('20)	.25	.25
		Never hinged	.40	
a.		Thick carton paper	1.75	.95
		Never hinged	2.75	
242	A64	7½c dp blue	.50	.45
		Never hinged	.80	
243	A64	7½c yellow brn	12.00	2.50
		Never hinged	20.00	
244	A64	8c slate	5.50	.75
		Never hinged	8.75	
245	A64	10c org brn	25.00	1.50
		Never hinged	40.00	
246	A64	12c bl gray ('20)	1.25	.65
		Never hinged	2.00	
247	A64	15c plum	3.25	.85
		Never hinged	5.25	
248	A64	20c chocolate ('20)	60.00	5.00
		Never hinged	95.00	
249	A64	30c gray brown	120.00	21.00
		Never hinged	240.00	
250	A64	36c red ('21)	4.50	1.25
		Never hinged	7.00	
251	A64	60c blue ('21)	4.00	1.90
		Never hinged	6.50	
252	A64	80c brn rose ('21)	1.40	1.10
		Never hinged	2.25	
253	A64	90c blue ('21)	5.50	4.75
		Never hinged	8.75	

No.	Type	Description		
254	A64	1e violet ('21)	185.00	65.00
		Never hinged	300.00	
		Nos. 227-254 (29)	645.70	195.05

1920-26   Perf. 12x11½
Ordinary Paper

No.	Type	Description		
255	A64	¼c dark olive	.40	.25
		Never hinged	.65	
256	A64	½c black	.40	.25
		Never hinged	.65	
a.		Thick carton paper	13.50	2.00
		Never hinged	22.00	
257	A64	1c chocolate	.25	.25
		Never hinged	.40	
a.		Thick carton paper	70.00	21.00
		Never hinged	140.00	
258	A64	1½c dp grn	.25	.25
		Never hinged	.40	
259	A64	2c orange	.70	.40
		Never hinged	1.10	
a.		Thick carton paper	110.00	14.50
		Never hinged	225.00	
b.		2c orange yellow	1.50	.30
		Never hinged	1.50	
c.		As "b." thick carton paper	110.00	14.50
		Never hinged	225.00	
260	A64	2c yellow	.55	.25
		Never hinged	.90	
261	A64	2c choc ('26)	1.40	*5.00*
		Never hinged	2.25	
262	A64	2½c violet	4.00	2.25
		Never hinged	6.25	
263	A64	3c car rose	.30	.30
		Never hinged	.50	
264	A64	3c ultra ('21)	.50	.25
		Never hinged	.80	
265	A64	4c lt grn ('19)	.25	.25
		Never hinged	.40	
a.		Thick carton paper	150.00	90.00
		Never hinged	240.00	
266	A64	4c orange ('26)	1.40	1.60
		Never hinged	2.25	
267	A64	5c yel brn	1.00	.40
		Never hinged	2.25	
268	A64	5c ol brn ('23)	.25	.25
		Never hinged	.40	
269	A64	6c pale rose	.40	.40
		Never hinged	.65	
a.		Thick carton paper	1.60	.90
		Never hinged	2.50	
270	A64	6c brown ('24)	.55	.25
		Never hinged	.90	
271	A64	7½c dp blue	.25	.25
		Never hinged	.40	
272	A64	8c slate	.25	.25
		Never hinged	.40	
273	A64	8c bl grn ('22)	.45	.25
		Never hinged	.70	
274	A64	8c org ('24)	.45	.45
		Never hinged	.70	
275	A64	10c org brn	.45	.25
		Never hinged	.70	
a.		Thick carton paper	42.50	3.50
		Never hinged	65.00	
276	A64	12c dp grn ('21)	.45	.40
		Never hinged	.70	
277	A64	13½c chlky bl	1.40	.45
		Never hinged	2.25	
278	A64	14c brt vio ('21)	1.10	.55
		Never hinged	1.75	
a.		Thick carton paper	250.00	175.00
		Never hinged	400.00	
279	A64	15c black ('23)	.40	.25
		Never hinged	.65	
280	A64	16c brt ultra ('24)	.90	.65
		Never hinged	1.45	
a.		16c pale blue ('26)	.90	.65
		Never hinged	1.45	
281	A64	20c dk brn	.50	.25
		Never hinged	.80	
a.		Thick carton paper	60.00	10.00
		Never hinged	100.00	
282	A64	20c dp grn ('23)	.45	.25
		Never hinged	.70	
283	A64	20c gray ('24)	.25	.25
		Never hinged	.40	
284	A64	24c grnsh bl ('21)	.45	.25
		Never hinged	.70	
285	A64	25c salmon pink ('23)	.45	.25
		Never hinged	.70	
286	A64	25c lt gray ('26)	.45	.25
		Never hinged	.70	
287	A64	30c gray brn ('21)	.50	.25
		Never hinged	.80	
288	A64	30c dk brn ('24)	20.00	4.00
		Never hinged	30.00	
289	A64	32c dp grn ('24)	1.10	.40
		Never hinged	1.75	
290	A64	36c red ('21)	1.75	.45
		Never hinged	2.75	
291	A64	40c dk bl ('23)	.90	.55
		Never hinged	1.45	
a.		"CORREIC" for "CORREIO"	225.00	140.00
292	A64	40c choc ('24)	.45	.45
		Never hinged	.70	
a.		"CORREIC" for "CORREIO"	32.50	57.50
293	A64	40c green ('26)	.25	.25
		Never hinged	.40	
294	A64	48c rose ('24)	7.50	4.00
		Never hinged	12.00	
295	A64	50c yellow ('21)	1.90	.70
		Never hinged	2.75	
296	A64	60c blue ('21)	1.40	.60
		Never hinged	2.25	
297	A64	64c pale ultra ('24)	9.50	5.50
		Never hinged	14.50	
298	A64	75c dull rose ('23)	15.00	7.50
		Never hinged	27.00	
298A	A64	80c brn rose ('21)	32.50	9.50
		Never hinged	45.00	

298B	A64	80c violet ('24)	1.00	.55
		Never hinged	1.60	
298C	A64	90c chalky bl ('21)	1.60	.85
		Never hinged	2.50	
298D	A64	96c dp rose ('26)	42.50	27.50
		Never hinged	70.00	
298E	A64	1e violet ('21)	4.50	1.90
		Never hinged	7.00	
298F	A64	1.10e yel brn ('21)	4.50	1.60
		Never hinged	7.00	
298G	A64	1.20e yel grn ('21)	2.50	1.40
		Never hinged	4.00	
298H	A64	2e sl grn ('21)	45.00	5.50
		Never hinged	100.00	
		Nos. 255-298H (52)	198.30	85.40

1923-26 — *Perf. 12x11½*
Glazed Paper

298I	A64	1e dk blue	5.00	2.25
		Never hinged	9.00	
298J	A64	1e gray vio ('24)	1.50	1.10
		Never hinged	2.75	
298K	A64	1.20e buff ('24)	50.00	32.50
		Never hinged	90.00	
298L	A64	1.50e blk vio	17.50	3.25
		Never hinged	30.00	
298M	A64	1.50e lilac ('24)	30.00	5.00
		Never hinged	55.00	
298N	A64	1.60e dp bl ('24)	19.00	5.00
		Never hinged	35.00	
298O	A64	2e sl grn ('24)	37.50	5.50
		Never hinged	145.00	
298P	A64	2.40e ap grn ('26)	160.00	110.00
		Never hinged	190.00	
298Q	A64	3e pink ('26)	160.00	100.00
		Never hinged	190.00	
298R	A64	3.20e gray grn ('24)	32.50	12.00
		Never hinged	57.50	
298S	A64	5e emer ('24)	35.00	9.00
		Never hinged	65.00	
298T	A64	10e pink ('24)	150.00	50.00
		Never hinged	250.00	
298U	A64	20e pale turq ('24)	300.00	160.00
		Never hinged	500.00	
		Nos. 298I-298U (13)	958.50	495.60

See design A85. For surcharges & overprints see Nos. 453-495, RA2.
See 496A-496R.

Presidents of Portugal and Brazil and Aviators Cabral and Coutinho A65

1923 — **Litho.** — *Perf. 14*

299	A65	1c brown	.25	.65
300	A65	2c orange	.25	.65
301	A65	3c ultra	.25	.65
302	A65	4c yellow grn	.25	.65
303	A65	5c bister brn	.25	.65
304	A65	10c brown org	.25	.65
305	A65	15c black	.25	.65
306	A65	20c blue grn	.25	.65
307	A65	25c rose	.25	.65
308	A65	30c olive brn	.60	1.90
309	A65	40c chocolate	.25	.65
310	A65	50c yellow	.50	.85
311	A65	75c violet	.50	1.00
312	A65	1e dp blue	.50	2.00
313	A65	1.50e olive grn	.75	2.50
314	A65	2e myrtle grn	1.00	6.00
		Nos. 299-314 (16)	6.35	20.75

Flight of Sacadura Cabral and Gago Coutinho from Portugal to Brazil.

Camoens at Ceuta A66

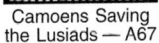

Camoens Saving the Lusiads — A67

Luis de Camoens — A68

First Edition of the Lusiads — A69

Camoens Dying — A70

Tomb of Camoens A71

Monument to Camoens — A72

Engr.; Values Typo. in Black
1924, Nov. 11 — *Perf. 14, 14½*

315	A66	2c lt blue	.25	.25
316	A66	3c orange	.25	.25
317	A66	4c dk gray	.25	.25
318	A66	5c yellow grn	.25	.25
319	A66	6c lake	.25	.25
320	A67	8c orange brn	.25	.25
321	A67	10c gray vio	.25	.25
322	A67	15c olive grn	.25	.25
323	A67	16c violet brn	.25	.25
324	A67	20c dp orange	.30	.25
325	A68	25c lilac	.30	.25
326	A68	30c dk brown	.30	.25
327	A68	32c dk green	.90	1.00
328	A68	40c ultra	.30	.25
329	A68	48c red brown	1.25	1.25
330	A69	50c red orange	1.40	.90
331	A69	64c green	1.40	.90
332	A69	75c dk violet	1.40	.90
333	A69	80c bister	1.10	.90
334	A69	96c lake	1.10	.90
335	A70	1e slate	1.10	.80
336	A70	1.20e lt brown	5.25	4.75
337	A70	1.50e red	1.25	.90
338	A70	1.60e dk blue	1.25	.90
339	A70	2e apple grn	5.25	4.75
340	A71	2.40e green, *grn*	3.75	2.75
341	A71	3e dk bl, *bl*	1.60	1.00
a.		Value double	125.00	125.00
b.		Value omitted		
342	A71	3.20e blk, *green*	1.60	1.00
343	A71	4.50e blk, *orange*	4.25	2.75
344	A71	10e dk brn, *pnksh*	9.25	8.00
345	A72	20e dk vio, *lil*	9.25	7.00
		Nos. 315-345 (31)	55.80	44.60

Birth of Luis de Camoens, poet, 400th anniv.
For overprints see Nos. 1S6-1S71.

Castello-Branco's House at Sao Miguel de Seide — A73

Castello-Branco's Study — A74

Camillo Castello-Branco A75

Teresa de Albuquerque A76

Mariana and Joao de Cruz — A77

Simao de Botelho — A78

1925, Mar. 26 — *Perf. 12½*

346	A73	2c orange	.25	.25
347	A73	3c green	.25	.25
348	A73	4c ultra	.25	.25
349	A73	5c scarlet	.25	.25
350	A73	6c brown vio	.25	.25
a.		"6" and "C" omitted		
351	A73	8c black brn	.25	.25
352	A74	10c pale blue	.25	.25
353	A73	15c olive grn	.25	.25
354	A74	16c red orange	.30	.30
355	A74	20c dk violet	.30	.30
356	A75	25c car rose	.30	.30
357	A74	30c bister brn	.30	.30
358	A75	32c green	1.10	1.00
359	A75	40c green & blk	.65	.65
360	A74	48c red brn	3.00	3.00
361	A75	50c blue green	.65	.65
362	A76	64c orange brn	3.00	3.00
363	A76	75c gray blk	.60	.60
364	A75	80c brown	.60	.60
365	A76	96c car rose	1.50	1.50
366	A76	1e gray vio	1.50	1.50
367	A76	1.20e yellow grn	1.50	1.50
368	A77	1.50e dk bl, *bl*	25.00	13.50
369	A76	1.60e indigo	4.75	3.75
370	A77	2e dk grn, *grn*	6.25	4.25
371	A77	2.40e red, *org*	52.50	32.50
372	A77	3e lake, *bl*	67.50	40.00
373	A77	3.20e *green*	32.50	32.50
374	A75	4.50e red & blk	12.50	3.00
375	A77	10e brn, *yel*	13.00	3.00
376	A78	20e *orange*	13.50	3.00
		Nos. 346-376 (31)	244.80	152.70
		Set, never hinged	400.00	

Centenary of the birth of Camillo Castello-Branco, novelist.

First Independence Issue

Alfonso the Conqueror, First King of Portugal — A79

Batalha Monastery and King John I — A80

Battle of Aljubarrota A81

Filipa de Vilhena Arming her Sons A82

King John IV (The Duke of Braganza) A83

Independence Monument, Lisbon — A84

Center in Black
1926, Aug. 13 — *Perf. 14, 14½*

377	A79	2c orange	.25	.25
378	A80	3c ultra	.25	.25
379	A79	4c yellow grn	.25	.25
380	A80	5c black brn	.25	.25
381	A79	6c ocher	.25	.25
382	A80	15c dk green	.25	.25
383	A79	16c dp blue	.70	.65
384	A81	20c dull violet	.70	.65
385	A82	25c scarlet	.70	.65
386	A81	32c dp green	.90	.90
387	A82	40c yellow brn	.55	.55
388	A80	46c carmine	3.25	3.25
389	A82	50c olive bis	3.25	3.25
390	A83	64c blue green	4.50	4.50
391	A82	75c red brown	4.50	4.50
392	A84	80c dull red	6.75	6.75
393	A83	1e black vio	7.00	7.00
394	A81	1.60e myrtle grn	9.25	9.25
395	A84	3e plum	27.50	27.50
396	A84	4.50e olive grn	35.00	35.00
397	A81	10e carmine	55.00	55.00
		Nos. 377-397 (21)	161.05	160.90
		Set, never hinged	275.00	

The use of these stamps instead of the regular issue was obligatory on Aug. 13th and 14th, Nov. 30th and Dec. 1st, 1926.

Stamps of 1926 Surcharged in Black

1926 Center in Black — *Perf. 13½x14*

397A	A80	2c on 5c blk brn	1.50	1.10
		Never hinged	1.90	
397B	A80	2c on 46c car	1.50	1.10
		Never hinged	1.90	
397C	A83	2c on 64c bl grn	2.00	1.50
		Never hinged	2.50	
397D	A82	2c on 75c red brn	2.00	1.50
		Never hinged	2.50	
397E	A84	3c on 96c dull red	2.00	2.00
		Never hinged	2.50	
397F	A83	3c on 1e blk vio	2.00	1.60
		Never hinged	2.50	
397G	A81	4c on 1.60e myr grn	11.50	11.50
		Never hinged	14.00	
397H	A84	4c on 3e plum	6.00	4.00
		Never hinged	7.50	
397J	A84	6c on 4.50e ol grn	6.00	4.00
		Never hinged	7.50	
397K	A81	6c on 10e carmine	6.00	4.00
		Never hinged	7.50	
		Nos. 397A-397K (10)	40.50	32.30
		Set, never hinged	47.50	

There are two styles of the ornaments in these surcharges.

Ceres — A85

Without Imprint
1926, Dec. 2 — **Typo.** — *Perf. 13½x14*

398	A85	2c chocolate	.25	.25
		Never hinged	.50	
399	A85	3c brt blue	.25	.25
		Never hinged	.50	
400	A85	4c dp orange	.25	.25
		Never hinged	.50	

401	A85	5c dp brown	.25	.25
		Never hinged	.50	
402	A85	6c orange brn	.25	.25
		Never hinged	.50	
403	A85	10c orange red	.25	.25
		Never hinged	.50	
404	A85	15c black	.25	.25
		Never hinged	.50	
405	A85	16c ultra	.25	.25
		Never hinged	.50	
406	A85	25c gray	.25	.25
		Never hinged	.50	
407	A85	32c dp green	.55	.35
		Never hinged	1.10	
408	A85	40c blue green	.35	.25
		Never hinged	.70	
409	A85	48c rose	1.10	.90
		Never hinged	2.25	
410	A85	50c ocher	2.00	1.60
		Never hinged	4.00	
411	A85	64c deep blue	2.00	1.60
		Never hinged	4.00	
412	A85	80c violet	3.75	.55
		Never hinged	7.50	
413	A85	96c car rose	2.10	1.10
		Never hinged	4.25	
414	A85	1e red brown	10.00	1.00
		Never hinged	20.00	
415	A85	1.20e yellow brn	10.00	1.00
		Never hinged	20.00	
416	A85	1.60e dark blue	2.40	.55
		Never hinged	4.75	
417	A85	2e green	14.50	1.00
		Never hinged	32.50	
418	A85	3.20e olive grn	5.50	1.00
		Never hinged	11.00	
419	A85	4.50e yellow	5.50	1.00
		Never hinged	11.00	
420	A85	5e brown olive	60.00	3.75
		Never hinged	130.00	
421	A85	10e red	8.75	2.00
		Never hinged	17.50	
		Nos. 398-421 (24)	130.75	19.90
		Set, never hinged	275.00	

See design A64.

Second Independence Issue

Gonçalo Mendes da Maia — A86
Dr. Joao das Regras — A88

Guimaraes Castle — A87

Battle of Montijo — A89

Brites de Almeida — A90
Joao Pinto Ribeiro — A91

Center in Black

		1927, Nov. 29 Engr.	Perf. 14	
422	A86	2c brown	.25	.25
423	A87	3c ultra	.25	.25
424	A86	4c orange	.25	.25
425	A88	5c olive brn	.25	.25
426	A89	6c orange brn	.25	.25
427	A87	15c black brn	.45	.35
428	A88	16c deep blue	1.00	.35
429	A86	25c gray	1.25	1.10
430	A89	32c blue grn	2.50	1.60
431	A90	40c yellow grn	.65	.50
432	A86	48c brown red	11.50	10.00
433	A87	80c dk violet	8.25	7.00
434	A90	96c dull red	14.50	13.50
435	A88	1.60e myrtle grn	15.00	14.50
436	A91	4.50e bister	22.50	22.50
		Nos. 422-436 (15)	78.85	72.65
		Set, never hinged	140.00	

The use of these stamps instead of the regular issue was compulsory on Nov. 29-30, Dec. 1-2, 1927. The money derived from their sale was used for the purchase of a palace for a war museum, the organization of an international exposition in Lisbon, in 1940, and for fêtes to be held in that year in commemoration of the 8th cent. of the founding of Portugal and the 3rd cent. of its restoration.

Third Independence Issue

Gualdim Paes — A93
The Siege of Santarem — A94

Battle of Rolica — A95

Battle of Atoleiros A96

Joana de Gouveia A97
Matias de Albuquerque A98

		1928, Nov. 28	Center in Black	
437	A93	2c lt blue	.25	.25
438	A94	3c lt green	.25	.25
439	A95	4c lake	.25	.25
440	A96	5c olive grn	.25	.25
441	A97	6c orange brn	.25	.25
442	A94	15c slate	.75	.75
443	A95	16c dk violet	.75	.75
444	A93	25c ultra	.75	.75
445	A97	32c dk green	3.75	3.75
446	A96	40c olive brn	.75	.75
447	A95	50c red orange	9.25	5.75
448	A94	80c lt gray	9.75	7.00
449	A97	96c carmine	17.50	15.00
450	A96	1e claret	27.50	27.50
451	A93	1.60e dk blue	13.00	11.50
452	A98	4.50e yellow	14.00	13.50
		Nos. 437-452 (16)	99.00	88.25
		Set, never hinged	150.00	

Obligatory Nov. 27-30. See note after No. 436.

Type and Stamps of 1912-28 Surcharged in Black

		1928-29	Perf. 12x11½, 15x14	
453	A64	4c on 8c orange	.40	.35
		Never hinged	.50	
454	A64	4c on 30c dk brn	.40	.35
		Never hinged	.50	
455	A64	10c on ¼c dk ol	.40	.35
		Never hinged	.50	
a.		Inverted surcharge	110.00	100.00
		Never hinged	230.00	
456	A64	10c on ½c blk (R)	.60	.45
		Never hinged	1.10	
a.		Perf. 15x14	17.50	12.50
		Never hinged	37.50	
457	A64	10c on 1c choc	.60	.45
		Never hinged	1.10	
a.		Perf. 15x14	75.00	55.00
		Never hinged	150.00	
458	A64	10c on 4c grn	.45	.35
		Never hinged	.90	
a.		Perf. 15x14	87.50	67.50
		Never hinged	180.00	
459	A64	10c on 4c orange	.45	.35
		Never hinged	.90	
460	A64	10c on 5c ol brn	.45	.35
		Never hinged	.90	
461	A64	15c on 16c blue	1.10	.80
		Never hinged	2.00	
462	A64	15c on 16c ultra	1.10	.80
		Never hinged	2.00	
463	A64	15c on 20c brown	32.50	32.50
		Never hinged	65.00	
464	A64	15c on 20c gray	.45	.35
		Never hinged	.90	
465	A64	15c on 24c grnsh bl	2.10	1.60
		Never hinged	4.00	
466	A64	15c on 25c gray	.45	.35
		Never hinged	.90	
467	A64	15c on 25c sal pink	.45	.35
		Never hinged	.90	
468	A64	16c on 32c dp grn	.90	.80
		Never hinged	1.90	
469	A64	40c on 2c orange	.45	.35
		Never hinged	.90	
a.		Thick carton paper	165.00	32.50
			265.00	
470	A64	40c on 2c yellow	4.50	3.25
		Never hinged	9.50	
471	A64	40c on 2c choc	.40	.35
		Never hinged	.80	
472	A64	40c on 3c ultra	.45	.35
		Never hinged	.90	
473	A64	40c on 50c yellow	.40	.25
		Never hinged	.80	
474	A64	40c on 60c dull bl	.90	.65
		Never hinged	1.90	
a.		Perf. 15x14	10.00	8.00
		Never hinged	20.00	
475	A64	40c on 64c pale ultra	.90	.80
		Never hinged	1.90	
476	A64	40c on 75c dl rose	.90	.90
		Never hinged	1.90	
477	A64	40c on 80c violet	.65	.55
		Never hinged	1.40	
478	A64	40c on 90c chlky bl	4.50	3.25
		Never hinged	9.50	
a.		Perf. 15x14	11.50	8.75
		Never hinged	24.00	
479	A64	40c on 1e gray vio	.85	.85
		Never hinged	1.75	
480	A64	40c on 1.10e yel brn	.90	.80
		Never hinged	1.90	
481	A64	80c on 6c pale rose	.85	.70
		Never hinged	1.60	
a.		Thick carton paper	5.75	5.00
		Never hinged	12.00	
482	A64	80c on 6c choc	.85	.70
		Never hinged	1.75	
483	A64	80c on 48c rose	1.25	1.10
		Never hinged	2.00	
484	A64	80c on 1.50e lilac	3.00	1.25
		Never hinged	6.00	
485	A64	96c on 1.20e yel grn	3.50	2.40
		Never hinged	7.00	
486	A64	96c on 1.20e buff	3.50	2.75
		Never hinged	7.00	
487	A64	1.60e on 2e slate grn	35.00	27.50
		Never hinged	70.00	
487A	A64	1.60e on 2e slate green, glazed paper	37.50	25.00
		Never hinged	80.00	
488	A64	1.60e on 3.20e gray grn	15.00	7.25
		Never hinged	30.00	
489	A64	1.60e on 20e pale turq	18.00	10.00
		Never hinged	37.50	
		Nos. 453-489 (37)	139.55	106.55
		Set, never hinged	360.00	

Stamps of 1912-26 Overprinted in Black or Red

		1929	Perf. 12x11½	
490	A64	10c orange brn	.45	
		Never hinged	.65	
a.		Perf. 15x14	275.00	275.00
		Never hinged	425.00	
491	A64	15c black (R)	.40	.35
		Never hinged	.60	
492	A64	40c lt green	.65	.55
		Never hinged	.95	
493	A64	40c chocolate	.55	.45
		Never hinged	.80	
494	A64	96c dp rose	5.50	4.50
		Never hinged	8.00	
495	A64	1.60e brt blue	22.50	15.00
		Never hinged	32.50	
a.		Double overprint	110.00	100.00
		Never hinged	160.00	
		Nos. 490-495 (6)	30.05	20.85
		Set, never hinged	45.00	

Liberty — A100

		1929, May	Perf. 12x11½	
496	A100	1.60e on 5c red brn	11.50	7.00

Types of 1912-20 Issues
With Imprint
Perf. 12x11½

		1930-31 Typo.	Wove Paper	
496A	A64	4c orange	.25	.25
		Never hinged	.45	
496B	A64	5c blk brn ('31)	.25	.25
		Never hinged	.45	
496C	A64	6c red brn	.25	.25
		Never hinged	.45	
496D	A64	10c red ('31)	.45	.25
		Never hinged	.75	
496E	A64	15c black	2.50	.50
		Never hinged	4.25	
496F	A64	25c lt gray	.90	.25
		Never hinged	1.50	
496G	A64	25c blue grn	.90	.25
		Never hinged	1.50	
496H	A85	32c dp green	.90	.45
		Never hinged	1.50	
496I	A64	40c green	3.50	1.25
		Never hinged	6.00	
496J	A64	50c bister	2.25	1.40
		Never hinged	3.75	
496K	A64	50c red brn ('30)	2.25	1.40
		Never hinged	3.75	
496L	A64	75c car rose	2.25	1.40
		Never hinged	3.75	
496M	A64	80c dk grn	2.25	1.40
		Never hinged	3.75	
496N	A64	1e brn lake	6.50	1.10
		Never hinged	11.00	
496O	A64	1.20e pur brn ('31)	4.50	1.10
		Never hinged	7.50	
496P	A64	1.25e dk bl ('31)	4.50	1.10
		Never hinged	7.50	
496Q	A64	2e red vio ('31)	19.00	6.50
		Never hinged	32.50	
496R	A64	4.50e org ('31)	65.00	45.00
		Never hinged	110.00	
		Nos. 496A-496R (18)	118.40	64.50
		Set, never hinged	200.00	

Nos. 496A-496R were printed at the Lisbon Mint from new plates produced from the original dies. The paper is whiter than the paper used for earlier Ceres stamps. The gum is white.

"Portugal" Holding Volume of "Lusiads" — A101

		1931-38 Typo.	Perf. 14	
497	A101	4c bister brn	.25	.25
498	A101	5c olive gray	.25	.25
499	A101	6c lt gray	.25	.25
500	A101	10c dk violet	.25	.25
501	A101	15c gray blk	.25	.25
502	A101	16c brt blue	1.25	.65
503	A101	25c deep green	3.00	.35
504	A101	25c brt bl ('33)	3.50	.40
505	A101	30c dk grn ('33)	1.90	.40
506	A101	40c orange red	6.25	.25
507	A101	48c fawn	1.25	.95
508	A101	50c lt brown	.30	.25
509	A101	75c car rose	5.00	1.10
510	A101	80c emerald	.40	.25
511	A101	95c car rose ('33)	16.00	6.75
512	A101	1e claret	30.00	.25
513	A101	1.20e olive grn	2.10	.95
514	A101	1.25e dk blue	1.90	.25
515	A101	1.60e dk blue ('33)	32.50	4.25
516	A101	1.75e dk blue ('38)	.65	.25
517	A101	2e dull violet	.75	.25
518	A101	4.50e orange	1.50	.25
519	A101	5e yellow grn	1.50	.25
		Nos. 497-519 (23)	111.00	19.30
		Set, never hinged	175.00	

Birthplace of St. Anthony A102

Font where St. Anthony was Baptized
A103

Lisbon Cathedral
A104

St. Anthony with Infant Jesus
A105

Santa Cruz Cathedral
A106

St. Anthony's Tomb at Padua
A107

1931, June   **Typo.**   *Perf. 12*
528 A102 15c plum   .65   .25

Litho.
529 A103 25c gray & pale grn   1.00   .25
530 A104 40c gray brn & buff   .65   .25
531 A105 75c dl rose & pale rose   22.50   14.00
532 A106 1.25e gray & pale bl   52.50   30.00
533 A107 4.50e gray vio & lil   25.00   3.50
    Nos. 528-533 (6)   102.30   48.25
    Set, never hinged   190.00

7th centenary of the death of St. Anthony of Padua and Lisbon.
For surcharges see Nos. 543-548.

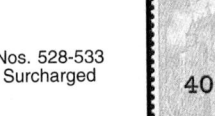

Nuno Alvares Pereira (1360-1431), Portuguese Warrior and Statesman — A108

1931, Nov. 1   **Typo.**   *Perf. 12x11½*
534 A108 15c black   1.00   1.10
535 A108 25c gray grn & blk   10.50   1.10
536 A108 40c orange   2.75   .50
   a.   Value omitted   150.00   150.00
537 A108 75c car rose   21.00   21.00
538 A108 1.25e dk bl & pale bl   26.00   20.00
539 A108 4.50e choc & lt grn   125.00   52.50
   a.   Value omitted   350.00   350.00
    Nos. 534-539 (6)   186.25   96.20
    Set, never hinged   325.00

For surcharges see Nos. 549-554.

Nos. 528-533 Surcharged

1933   *Perf. 12*
543 A104 15c on 40c   1.00   .35
544 A102 40c on 15c   3.00   1.25
545 A103 40c on 25c   2.00   .25
546 A105 40c on 75c   14.00   5.25

547 A106 40c on 1.25e   14.00   5.25
548 A107 40c on 4.50e   14.00   5.25
    Nos. 543-548 (6)   48.00   17.70
    Set, never hinged   80.00

Nos. 534-539 Surcharged

1933   *Perf. 12x11½*
549 A108 15c on 40c   .65   .35
550 A108 40c on 15c   3.75   2.40
551 A108 40c on 25c   1.00   .80
552 A108 40c on 75c   10.00   4.00
553 A108 40c on 1.25e   10.00   4.00
554 A108 40c on 4.50e   10.00   4.00
    Nos. 549-554 (6)   35.40   15.55
    Set, never hinged   80.00

President Carmona
A109

Head of a Colonial
A110

1934, May 28   **Typo.**   *Perf. 11½*
556 A109 40c brt violet   18.00   .35
   Never hinged   32.50

1934, July   *Perf. 11½x12*
558 A110 25c dk brown   3.00   1.60
559 A110 40c scarlet   19.00   .40
560 A110 1.60e dk blue   29.00   2.00
    Nos. 558-560 (3)   51.00   4.00
    Set, never hinged   125.00

Colonial Exposition.

Roman Temple, Evora
A111

Prince Henry the Navigator
A112

"All for the Nation"
A113

Coimbra Cathedral
A114

1935-41   *Perf. 11½x12*
561 A111 4c black   .45   .25
562 A111 5c blue   .50   .25
563 A111 6c choc ('36)   .75   .35
    Perf. 11½, 12x11½ (1.75e)
564 A112 10c turq grn   .65   .25
565 A112 15c red brown   .35   .25
   a.   Booklet pane of 4
566 A113 25c dp blue   6.00   .45
   a.   Booklet pane of 4
567 A113 40c brown   2.00   .25
   a.   Booklet pane of 4
568 A113 1e rose red   9.25   .50
568A A114 1.75e blue   85.00   1.25
568B A113 10e gray blk ('41)   50.00   2.50
569 A113 20e turq grn ('41)   70.00   2.10
    Nos. 561-569 (11)   224.95   8.40
    Set, never hinged   400.00

For overprint see No. O1.

Queen Maria
A115

Rod and Bowl of Aesculapius
A116

Typographed, Head Embossed
1935, June 1   *Perf. 11½*
570 A115 40c scarlet   1.40   .25
   Never hinged   2.10

First Portuguese Philatelic Exhibition.

1937, July 24   **Typo.**   *Perf. 11½x12*
571 A116 25c blue   8.00   .85
   Never hinged   15.00

Centenary of the establishment of the School of Medicine in Lisbon and Oporto.

Gil Vicente
A117

Grapes
A118

1937
572 A117 40c dark brown   10.00   .25
573 A117 1e rose red   2.00   .25
    Set, never hinged   32.50

400th anniversary of the death of Gil Vicente (1465-1536), Portuguese playwright. Design shows him in cowherd role in his play, "Auto do Vaqueiro."

1938   *Perf. 11½*
575 A118 15c brt purple   1.40   .55
576 A118 25c brown   3.00   1.60
577 A118 40c dp red lilac   10.00   .35
578 A118 1.75e dp blue   30.00   5.00
    Nos. 575-578 (4)   44.40   7.50
    Set, never hinged   70.00

International Vineyard and Wine Congress.

Emblem of Portuguese Legion — A119

1940, Jan. 27   **Unwmk.**   *Perf. 11½*
579 A119 5c dull yellow   .35   .25
580 A119 10c violet   .35   .25
581 A119 15c brt blue   .35   .25
582 A119 25c brown   22.50   1.10
583 A119 40c dk green   37.50   .40
584 A119 80c yellow grn   2.40   .55
585 A119 1e brt red   57.50   3.50
586 A119 1.75e dark blue   8.00   2.75
   a.   Souv. sheet of 8, #579-586   250.00   250.00
    Never hinged   600.00
    Nos. 579-586 (8)   128.95   9.05
    Set, never hinged   190.00

Issued in honor of the Portuguese Legion.
No. 586a sold for 5.50e, the proceeds going to various charities.

Portuguese World Exhibition
A120

King John IV — A121

Discoveries Monument, Belém — A122

King Alfonso I — A123

1940   **Engr.**   *Perf. 12x11½, 11½x12*
587 A120 10c brown violet   .25   .25
588 A121 15c dk grnsh bl   .25   .25
589 A122 25c dk slate grn   1.40   .25
590 A121 35c yellow green   1.10   .25
591 A123 40c olive bister   2.75   .25
592 A120 80c dk violet   5.25   .35
593 A122 1e dark red   12.00   1.60
594 A123 1.75e ultra   7.00   2.75
   a.   Souv. sheet of 8, #587-594 ('41)   140.00   110.00
    Never hinged   275.00
    Nos. 587-594 (8)   30.00   6.05
    Set, never hinged   50.00

Portuguese Intl. Exhibition, Lisbon (10c, 80c); restoration of the monarchy, 300th anniv (15c, 35c); Portuguese independence, 800th anniv (40c, 1.75e).
No. 594a sold for 10e.

Sir Rowland Hill — A124

1940, Aug. 12   **Typo.**   *Perf. 11½x12*
595 A124 15c dk violet brn   .25   .25
596 A124 25c dp org brn   .30   .25
597 A124 35c green   .30   .25
598 A124 40c brown violet   .50   .25
599 A124 50c turq green   18.00   4.25
600 A124 80c lt blue   2.10   1.10
601 A124 1e crimson   21.00   3.50
602 A124 1.75e dk blue   6.75   3.50
   a.   Souv. sheet of 8, #595-602 ('41)   75.00   75.00
    Never hinged   125.00
    Nos. 595-602 (8)   49.20   13.35
    Set, never hinged   75.00

Postage stamp centenary.
No. 602a sold for 10e.

AIR POST STAMPS

Symbol of Aviation
AP1

Perf. 12x11½

1936-41		Unwmk.	Typo.
C1	AP1	1.50e dark blue	.45	.30
C2	AP1	1.75e red orange	.75	.35
C3	AP1	2.50e rose red	.85	.35
C4	AP1	3e brt blue ('41)	14.00	12.00
C5	AP1	4e dp yel grn		
		('41)	10.91	10.00
C6	AP1	5e car lake	1.75	1.25
C7	AP1	10e brown lake	3.00	1.25
C8	AP1	15e orange ('41)	11.50	7.00
C9	AP1	20e black brn	9.00	2.75
C10	AP1	50e brn vio ('41)	160.00	75.00
		Nos. C1-C10 (10)	219.30	118.25
		Set, never hinged	390.00	

Nos. C1-C10 exist imperf.

POSTAGE DUE STAMPS

Vasco da Gama Issue

The Zamorin of Calicut Receiving Vasco da Gama — D1

		Unwmk.		
1898, May 1		Typo.	**Perf. 12**	
		Denomination in Black		
J1	D1	5r black	2.40	1.25
		On cover		—
a.		Value and "Continente" omitted	20.00	5.00
J2	D1	10r lilac & blk	4.00	1.75
		On cover		1,100.
J3	D1	20r orange & blk	6.50	2.50
		On cover		550.00
J4	D1	50r slate & blk	50.00	11.00
		On cover		1,100.
J5	D1	100r car & blk, *pink*	87.50	40.00
		On cover		1,100.
J6	D1	200r brn & blk, *buff*	92.50	60.00
		On cover		1,100.

For overprints and surcharges see Nos. 193-198.

D2

1904			**Perf. 11½x12**	
J7	D2	5r brown	.45	.40
J8	D2	10r orange	2.75	.90
a.		Imperf.		—
J9	D2	20r lilac	8.00	3.75
J10	D2	30r gray green	5.75	2.75
J11	D2	40r gray violet	7.00	2.75
J12	D2	50r carmine	52.50	4.50
a.		Imperf.		—
J13	D2	100r dull blue	8.75	6.50
a.		Imperf.		—
		Nos. J7-J13 (7)	85.20	21.55

Preceding Issue Overprinted in Carmine or Green

1910				
J14	D2	5r brown	.40	.25
J15	D2	10r orange	.40	.25
J16	D2	20r lilac	1.40	1.00
J17	D2	30r gray green	1.25	.25
J18	D2	40r gray violet	1.40	.25
J19	D2	50r carmine (G)	6.00	4.50
J20	D2	100r dull blue	6.50	5.25
		Nos. J14-J20 (7)	17.35	11.75

See note after No. 183.

D3

1915, Mar. 18			Typo.	
J21	D3	½c brown	.60	.60
J22	D3	1c orange	.60	.60
J23	D3	2c claret	.60	.60
J24	D3	3c green	.60	.60
J25	D3	4c gray violet	.60	.60
J26	D3	5c carmine	.60	.60
J27	D3	10c dark blue	.60	.60
		Nos. J21-J27 (7)	4.20	4.20

1921-27				
J28	D3	½c gray green ('22)	.35	.35
J29	D3	4c gray green ('27)	.35	.35
J30	D3	8c gray green ('23)	.35	.35
J31	D3	10c gray green ('22)	.35	.35
J32	D3	12c gray green	.50	.50
J33	D3	16c gray green ('23)	.50	.50
J34	D3	20c gray green	.50	.50
J35	D3	24c gray green	.50	.50
J36	D3	32c gray green ('23)	.50	.50
J37	D3	36c gray green	1.50	.75
J38	D3	40c gray green ('23)	1.50	.75
J39	D3	48c gray green ('23)	.65	.65
J40	D3	50c gray green	.65	.65
J41	D3	60c gray green	.65	.65
J42	D3	72c gray green	.65	.65
J43	D3	80c gray green ('23)	7.50	7.50
J44	D3	1.20e gray green	3.00	3.00
		Nos. J28-J44 (17)	20.00	18.50

D4

1932-33				
J45	D4	5c buff	.50	.45
J46	D4	10c lt blue	.50	.45
J47	D4	20c pink	1.25	1.00
J48	D4	30c blue green	1.50	1.00
J49	D4	40c lt green	1.50	1.00
a.		Figure of value inverted		—
J50	D4	50c gray	1.60	1.00
J51	D4	60c rose	4.25	2.00
J52	D4	80c violet brn	10.00	4.00
J53	D4	1.20e gray ol ('33)	13.00	12.00
		Nos. J45-J53 (9)	34.10	22.90

D5

1940, Feb. 1		Unwmk.	**Perf. 12½**	
J54	D5	5c bister, perf. 14	.50	.35
J55	D5	10c rose lilac	.30	.25
J56	D5	20c dk car rose	.30	.25
J57	D5	30c purple	.30	.25
J58	D5	40c cerise	.30	.25
J59	D5	50c brt blue	.30	.25
J60	D5	60c yellow grn	.30	.25
J61	D5	80c scarlet	.30	.25
J62	D5	1e brown	.30	.25
J63	D5	2e dk rose vio	.55	.45
J64	D5	5e org yel, perf. 14	11.00	9.00
a.		Perf. 12½	175.00	125.00
		Nos. J54-J64 (11)	14.45	11.80

Nos. J54-J64 were first issued perf. 14. In 1955 all but the 5c were reissued in perf. 12½.

OFFICIAL STAMPS

No. 567 Overprinted in Black

1938		Unwmk.	**Perf. 11½**	
O1	A113	40c brown	.45	.25

NEWSPAPER STAMPS

N1

Perf. 11½, 12½, 13½

1876		Typo.	Unwmk.	
P1	N1	2½r bister	9.50	1.40
		On newspaper or wrapper		5.00
a.		2½r olive green	9.00	1.40
		On newspaper or wrapper		5.00

Various shades.

PARCEL POST STAMPS

Mercury and Commerce PP1

1920-22		Unwmk.	Typo.	**Perf. 12**
Q1	PP1	1c lilac brown	.25	.25
Q2	PP1	2c orange	.25	.25
Q3	PP1	5c lt brown	.25	.25
Q4	PP1	10c red brown	.25	.25
Q5	PP1	20c gray blue	.30	.25
Q6	PP1	40c carmine rose	.35	.25
Q7	PP1	50c black	.50	.45
Q8	PP1	60c dk blue ('21)	.50	.45
Q9	PP1	70c gray brn ('21)	3.00	2.00
Q10	PP1	80c ultra ('21)	3.50	3.25
Q11	PP1	90c lt vio ('21)	3.50	2.25
Q12	PP1	1e lt green	4.00	2.25
Q13	PP1	2e pale lilac ('22)	11.00	3.50
Q14	PP1	3e olive ('22)	21.00	4.00
Q15	PP1	4e ultra ('22)	42.50	7.00
Q16	PP1	5e gray ('22)	55.00	4.75
Q17	PP1	10e chocolate ('22)	82.50	9.25
		Nos. Q1-Q17 (17)	228.65	40.65

Parcel Post Package PP2

1936			**Perf. 11½**	
Q18	PP2	50c olive brown	.65	.50
Q19	PP2	1e bister brown	.65	.50
Q20	PP2	1.50e purple	.65	.50
Q21	PP2	2e carmine lake	2.75	.60
Q22	PP2	2.50e olive green	2.75	.60
Q23	PP2	4.50e brown lake	5.75	.65
Q24	PP2	5e violet	9.00	.75
Q25	PP2	10e orange	12.00	1.75
		Nos. Q18-Q25 (8)	34.20	5.85

POSTAL TAX STAMPS

These stamps represent a special fee for the delivery of postal matter on certain days in each year. The money derived from their sale is applied to works of public charity.

Regular Issues Overprinted in Carmine

1911, Oct. 4		Unwmk.	**Perf. 14½x15**	
RA1	A62	10r gray green	8.50	2.25

The 20r carmine of this type was for use on telegrams.

1912, Oct. 4			**Perf. 15x14½**	
RA2	A64	1c deep green	6.00	1.75

The 2c carmine of this type was for use on telegrams.

"Lisbon" — PT1

1913, June 8		Litho.	**Perf. 12x11½**	
RA3	PT1	1c dark green	.95	.70

The 2c dark brown of this type was for use on telegrams.

"Charity" — PT2

1915, Oct. 4			Typo.	
RA4	PT2	1c carmine	.35	.30

The 2c plum of this type was for use on telegrams. See No. RA6.

No. RA4 Surcharged

1924, Oct. 4				
RA5	PT2	15c on 1c dull red	1.25	.70

The 30c on 2c claret of this type was for use on telegrams.

Charity Type of 1915 Issue

1925, Oct. 4			**Perf. 12½**	
RA6	PT2	15c carmine	.35	.35

The 30c brown violet of this type was for use on telegrams.

Comrades of the Great War Issue

Muse of History with Tablet — PT3

1925, Apr. 8		Litho.	**Perf. 11**	
RA7	PT3	10c brown	1.10	1.10
RA8	PT3	10c green	1.10	1.10
RA9	PT3	10c rose	1.10	1.10
RA10	PT3	10c ultra	1.10	1.10
		Nos. RA7-RA10 (4)	4.40	4.40

The use of these stamps, in addition to the regular postage, was obligatory on certain days of the year. If the tax represented by these stamps was not prepaid, it was collected by means of Postal Tax Due Stamp No. RAJ1.

Pombal Issue

Common Design Types

Engraved; Value and "Continente" Typographed in Black

1925, May 8			**Perf. 12½**	
RA11	CD28	15c ultra	.50	.40
RA12	CD29	15c ultra	1.00	.75
RA13	CD30	15c ultra	1.00	.75
		Nos. RA11-RA13 (3)	2.50	1.90

Olympic Games Issue

Hurdler — PT7

1928 **Litho.** **Perf. 12**
RA14 PT7 15c dull red & blk 6.00 2.75

The use of this stamp, in addition to the regular postage, was obligatory on May 22-24, 1928. 10% of the money thus obtained was retained by the Postal Administration; the balance was given to a Committee in charge of Portuguese participation in the Olympic games at Amsterdam.

POSTAL TAX DUE STAMPS

Comrades of the Great War Issue

PTD1

1925 Unwmk. Typo. Perf. 11x11½
RAJ1 PTD1 20c brown orange .55 .45
See Note after No. RA10.

Pombal Issue
Common Design Types

1925 **Perf. 12½**
RAJ2 CD28 30c ultra 1.10 1.10
RAJ3 CD29 30c ultra 1.10 1.10
RAJ4 CD30 30c ultra 1.10 1.10
Nos. RAJ2-RAJ4 (3) 3.30 3.30

When the compulsory tax was not paid by the use of stamps #RA11-RA13, double the amount was collected by means of #RAJ2-RAJ4.

Olympic Games Issue

PTD2

1928 **Litho.** **Perf. 11½**
RAJ5 PTD2 30c lt red & blk 7.00 1.75

FRANCHISE STAMPS

These stamps are supplied by the Government to various charitable, scientific and military organizations for franking their correspondence. This franking privilege was withdrawn in 1938.

FOR THE RED CROSS SOCIETY

F1

Perf. 11½
1889-1915 **Unwmk.** **Typo.**
1S1 F1 rose & blk ('15) .45 .40
  On cover or postcard 82.50
 a. Vermilion & black ('08) 5.75 1.25
  On cover or postcard 82.50
 b. Red & black, perf. 12½ 65.00 6.25
  On cover or postcard 190.00

No. 1S1 Overprinted in Green

1917
1S3 F1 rose & black 80.00 77.50
 a. Inverted overprint 150.00 150.00

"Charity" Extending Hope to Invalid — F1a

1926 **Litho.** **Perf. 14**
Inscribed "LISBOA"
1S4 F1a black & red 7.00 7.00
Inscribed "DELEGACOES"
1S5 F1a black & red 7.00 7.00
No. 1S4 was for use in Lisbon. No. 1S5 was for the Red Cross chapters outside Lisbon. For overprints see Nos. 1S72-1S73.

Camoens Issue of 1924 Overprinted in Black or Red

1927
1S6 A68 40c ultra 1.10 1.00
1S7 A68 48c red brown 1.10 1.00
1S8 A69 64c green 1.10 1.00
1S9 A69 75c dk violet 1.10 1.00
1S10 A71 4.50e blk, *org* (R) 1.10 1.00
1S11 A71 10e dk brn, *pnksh* 1.10 1.00
Nos. 1S6-1S11 (6) 6.60 6.00

Camoens Issue of 1924 Overprinted in Red

1928
1S12 A67 15c olive grn 1.10 1.00
1S13 A67 16c violet brn 1.10 1.00
1S14 A68 25c lilac 1.10 1.00
1S15 A68 40c ultra 1.10 1.00
1S16 A70 1.20e lt brown 1.10 1.00
1S17 A70 2e apple green 1.10 1.00
Nos. 1S12-1S17 (6) 6.60 6.00

Camoens Issue of 1924 Overprinted in Red

1929
1S18 A68 30c dk brown 1.10 1.00
1S19 A68 40c ultra 1.10 1.00
1S20 A69 80c bister 1.10 1.00
1S21 A70 1.50e red 1.10 1.00
1S22 A70 1.60e dark blue 1.10 1.00
1S23 A71 2.40e green, *grn* 1.10 1.00
Nos. 1S18-1S23 (6) 6.60 6.00

Same Overprint Dated "1930"
1930
1S24 A68 40c ultra 1.10 1.00
1S25 A69 50c red orange 1.10 1.00
1S26 A69 96c lake 1.10 1.00
1S27 A70 1.60e dk blue 1.10 1.00
1S28 A71 3e dk blue, *bl* 1.10 1.00
1S29 A72 20e dk violet, *lil* 1.10 1.00
Nos. 1S24-1S29 (6) 6.60 6.00

Camoens Issue of 1924 Overprinted in Red

1931
1S30 A68 25c lilac 1.25 1.10
1S31 A68 32c dk green 1.25 1.10
1S32 A68 40c ultra 1.25 1.10
1S33 A69 96c lake 1.25 1.10
1S34 A70 1.60e dark blue 1.25 1.10
1S35 A71 3.20e black, *green* 1.25 1.10
Nos. 1S30-1S35 (6) 7.50 6.60

Same Overprint Dated "1932"
1931
1S36 A67 20c dp orange 1.75 1.75
1S37 A68 40c ultra 1.75 1.75
1S38 A68 48c red brown 1.75 1.75
1S39 A69 64c green 1.75 1.75
1S40 A70 1.60e dark blue 1.75 1.75
1S41 A71 10e dk brown, *pnksh* 1.75 1.75
Nos. 1S36-1S41 (6) 10.50 10.50

Nos. 1S6-1S11 Overprinted in Red

1932
1S42 A68 40c ultra 1.75 1.75
1S43 A68 48c red brown 1.75 1.75
1S44 A69 64c green 1.75 1.75
1S45 A69 75c dk violet 1.75 1.75
1S46 A71 4.50e blk, *orange* 1.75 1.75
1S47 A71 10e dk brn, *pnksh* 1.75 1.75
Nos. 1S42-1S47 (6) 10.50 10.50

1933 **Dated "1934"**
1S48 A68 40c ultra 2.25 2.25
1S49 A68 48c red brown 2.25 2.25
1S50 A69 64c green 2.25 2.25
1S51 A69 75c dark violet 2.25 2.25
1S52 A71 4.50e blk, *orange* 2.25 2.25
1S53 A71 10e dk brown, *pnksh* 2.25 2.25
Nos. 1S48-1S53 (6) 13.50 13.50

1935 **Dated "1935"**
1S54 A68 40c ultra 2.60 2.60
1S55 A68 48c red brown 2.60 2.60
1S56 A69 64c green 2.60 2.60
1S57 A69 75c dk violet 2.60 2.60
1S58 A71 4.50e black, *orange* 2.60 2.60
1S59 A71 10e dk brn, *pnksh* 2.60 2.60
Nos. 1S54-1S59 (6) 15.60 15.60

Camoens Issue of 1924 Overprinted in Black or Red

1935
1S60 A68 25c lilac 1.10 1.00
1S61 A68 40c ultra (R) 1.10 1.00
1S62 A69 50c red orange 1.10 1.00
1S63 A70 1e slate 1.10 1.00
1S64 A70 2e apple green 1.10 1.00
1S65 A72 20e dk violet, *lilac* 1.10 1.00
Nos. 1S60-1S65 (6) 6.60 6.00

Camoens Issue of 1924 Overprinted in Red

1936
1S66 A68 30c dk brown 1.10 1.10
1S67 A68 32c dk green 1.10 1.10
1S68 A69 80c bister 1.10 1.10
1S69 A70 1.20e lt brown 1.10 1.10
1S70 A71 3e dk blue, *bl* 1.10 1.10
1S71 A71 4.50e black, *yel* 1.10 1.10
Nos. 1S66-1S71 (6) 6.60 6.60

No. 1S4 Overprinted "1935"
1936 **Unwmk.** **Perf. 14**
1S72 F1a black & red 8.25 8.25

Same Stamp with Additional Overprint "Delegacoes"
1S73 F1a black & red 8.25 8.25

After the government withdrew the franking privilege in 1938, the Portuguese Red Cross Society distributed charity labels which lacked postal validity.

FOR CIVILIAN RIFLE CLUBS

Rifle Club Emblem — F2

Perf. 11½x12
1899-1910 **Typo.** **Unwmk.**
2S1 F2 bl grn & car ('99) 10.00 10.00
2S2 F2 brn & yel grn ('00) 10.00 10.00
2S3 F2 car & buff ('01) 1.00 1.00
2S4 F2 bl & org ('02) 1.00 1.00
2S5 F2 grn & org ('03) 1.00 1.00
2S6 F2 lt brn & car ('04) 1.60 1.60
2S7 F2 mar & ultra ('05) 4.25 4.25
2S8 F2 ultra & buff ('06) 1.00 1.00
2S9 F2 choc & yel ('07) 1.00 1.00
2S10 F2 car & ultra ('08) 1.60 1.60
2S11 F2 bl & yel grn ('09) 1.00 1.00
2S12 F2 bl grn & brn, *pink* ('10) 4.00 4.00
Nos. 2S1-2S12 (12) 37.45 37.45

FOR THE GEOGRAPHICAL SOCIETY OF LISBON

Coat of Arms
F3   F4

1903-34 **Unwmk. Litho.** **Perf. 11½**
3S1 F3 blk, rose, bl & red 9.00 5.00
3S2 F3 bl, yel, red & grn ('09) 12.00 5.00
3S3 F4 blk, org, bl & red ('11) 5.50 4.00
3S4 F4 blk & brn org ('22) 6.75 4.75
3S5 F4 blk & bl ('24) 15.00 8.50
3S6 F4 blk & rose ('26) 6.75 4.75
3S7 F4 blk & grn ('27) 6.75 4.75
3S8 F4 bl, yel & red ('29) 4.75 3.50
3S9 F4 bl, red & vio ('30) 4.75 3.50
3S10 F4 dp bl, lil & red ('31) 4.75 3.50
3S11 F4 bis brn & red ('32) 4.75 3.50
3S12 F4 lt grn & red ('33) 4.75 3.50
3S13 F4 blue & red ('34) 4.75 3.50
Nos. 3S1-3S13 (13) 90.25 57.75

No. 3S12 with three-line overprint, "C.I.C.I. Portugal 1933," was not valid for postage and was sold only to collectors.
No. 3S2 was reprinted in 1933. Green vertical lines behind "Porte Franco" omitted. Value $7.50.

F5

1934 **Litho.** **Perf. 11½**
3S15 F5 blue & red 5.00 3.50

1935-38 **Perf. 11**
3S16 F5 blue 12.00 5.25
3S17 F5 dk bl & red ('36) 4.75 4.25
3S18 F5 lil & red ('37) 3.50 2.75
3S19 F5 blk, grn & car ('38) 3.50 2.75
Nos. 3S16-3S19 (4) 23.75 15.00

The inscription in the inner circle is omitted on No. 3S16.

FOR THE NATIONAL AID SOCIETY FOR CONSUMPTIVES

F10

Perf. 11½x12
1904, July **Typo.** **Unwmk.**
4S1 F10 brown & green 5.00 5.00
4S2 F10 carmine & yellow 5.00 5.00

PORTUGUESE AFRICA

'pōr-chə-ˌgēz 'a-fri-kə

For use in any of the Portuguese possessions in Africa.

1000 Reis = 1 Milreis
100 Centavos = 1 Escudo

Common Design Types pictured following the introduction.

Vasco da Gama Issue
Common Design Types
Inscribed "Africa - Correios"
Perf. 13½ to 15½
1898, Apr. 1 **Engr.** **Unwmk.**
1 CD20 2½r blue green .90 .90
Never hinged 1.15
2 CD21 5r red .90 .90
Never hinged 1.15
3 CD22 10r red violet .90 .90
Never hinged 1.15
4 CD23 25r yellow green .90 .90
Never hinged 1.15
5 CD24 50r dark blue 1.10 1.10
Never hinged 1.30
6 CD25 75r violet brown 6.25 6.25
Never hinged 7.50
7 CD26 100r bister brown 5.00 4.50
Never hinged 7.00
8 CD27 150r bister 8.00 6.25
Never hinged 10.50
Nos. 1-8 (8) 23.95 21.70
Set, never hinged 32.50
Vasco da Gama's voyage to India.

WAR TAX STAMPS

Liberty
WT1

Overprinted in Black, Orange or Carmine

Perf. 12x11½, 15x14
1919 **Typo.** **Unwmk.**
MR1 WT1 1c green (Bk) .75 .75
a. Figures of value omitted 40.00
MR2 WT1 4c green (O) 1.00
MR3 WT1 5c green (C) .75 .75
Nos. MR1-MR3 (D) 2.50 1.50

Values the same for either perf.
No. MR2 used is known only with fiscal cancelation. Some authorities consider No. MR2 a revenue stamp.

PORTUGUESE CONGO

'pōr-chi-gēz 'käŋˌgō

LOCATION — The northernmost district of the Portuguese Angola Colony on the southwest coast of Africa
CAPITAL — Cabinda

Stamps of Angola replaced those of Portuguese Congo.

1000 Reis = 1 Milreis
100 Centavos = 1 Escudo (1913)

King Carlos — A1

Perf. 12½
1894, Aug. 5 **Typo.** **Unwmk.**
1 A1 5r yellow 1.25 .75
a. 5r orange yellow .90 .75
b. As "a," Perf. 13½ 17.00 12.50
2 A1 10r redsh violet 2.00 .80
a. Perf. 13½ 17.50 12.50
3 A1 15r chocolate 3.00 2.00
a. Perf. 11½ 5.00 2.10
4 A1 20r lavender, ordinary paper 2.50 2.00
a. Paper with enamel lozenges 2.50 1.75
b. Perf. 11½ 5.00 2.10
5 A1 25r green 2.00 .80
a. Paper with enamel lozenges 3.50 .85
b. Perf. 11½ 3.25 .85
Perf. 13½
6 A1 50r light blue 2.75 2.00
a. Perf. 11½ 13.00 4.50
Perf. 11½
7 A1 75r rose 5.00 3.75
a. Perf. 12½ 20.00 15.00
8 A1 80r yellow green 7.00 6.00
a. Perf. 12½ 60.00 37.50
9 A1 100r brown, yel 5.50 3.75
a. Perf. 13½ 32.50 19.00
Perf. 12½
10 A1 150r carmine, rose 12.00 9.00
11 A1 200r dk blue, bl 12.00 9.00
12 A1 300r dk blue, salmon 15.00 11.00
Nos. 1-12 (12) 70.00 50.85

For surcharges and overprints see Nos. 36-47, 127-131.

King Carlos — A2

Name & Value in Black except 500r
1898-1903 **Perf. 11½**
13 A2 2½r gray .35 .30
14 A2 5r orange .35 .30
15 A2 10r lt green .55 .30
16 A2 15r brown 1.50 1.25
17 A2 15r gray grn ('03) 1.00 .55
18 A2 20r gray violet 1.00 .70
19 A2 25r sea green 1.40 .90
20 A2 25r car rose ('03) .90 .45
21 A2 50r deep blue 1.60 1.25
22 A2 50r brown ('03) 2.75 1.75
23 A2 65r dull blue ('03) 20.00 6.50
24 A2 75r rose 4.00 2.25
25 A2 75r red lilac ('03) 2.75 2.25
26 A2 80r violet 3.00 2.50
27 A2 100r dk bl, bl 2.40 1.75
28 A2 115r org brn, pink ('03) 6.50 5.00
29 A2 130r brn, straw ('03) 24.00 11.00
30 A2 150r brown, buff 4.00 2.50
31 A2 200r red lilac, pnksh 5.00 3.00
32 A2 300r dk blue, rose 6.00 3.25
33 A2 400r dl bl, straw ('03) 12.00 9.50

34 A2 500r blk & red, bl ('01) 16.00 9.00
35 A2 700r vio, yelsh ('01) 25.00 17.50
Nos. 13-35 (23) 142.05 83.75

For overprints and surcharges see Nos. 49-53, 60-74, 112-126, 136-138.

Surcharged in Black

Perf. 12½, 11½ (#41, 43), 13½ (#44)
1902 **On Issue of 1894**
36 A1 65r on 15r choc 3.50 3.00
a. Perf. 11½ 17.00 9.00
37 A1 65r on 20r lav (#4) 4.00 3.00
a. Lozenge paper (#4a) 13.50 11.00
38 A1 65r on 25r green (#5) 4.00 3.00
a. Perf. 11½ 17.00 12.50
b. Lozenge paper (#5a) 4.75 4.50
39 A1 65r on 300r bl, sal 5.00 4.50
40 A1 115r on 70r red vio 4.00 3.00
41 A1 115r on 50r lt bl 4.00 2.50
a. Perf. 13½ 4.00 2.75
42 A1 130r on 5r yellow 5.00 2.75
a. Inverted surcharge 27.50 27.50
b. Perf. 13½ 4.00 2.75
43 A1 130r on 75r rose 4.00 3.00
a. Perf. 12½ 7.00 6.00
44 A1 130r on 100r brn, yel 4.00 3.75
a. Inverted surcharge 40.00 35.00
b. Perf. 11½ 20.00 12.50
45 A1 400r on 80r yel grn 1.75 1.25
a. Perf. 12½ 5.00 3.50
46 A1 400r on 150r car, rose 2.25 1.90
47 A1 400r on 200r bl, bl 2.25 1.90

On Newspaper Stamps of 1894
48 N1 115r on 2½r brn 3.75 2.50
a. Inverted surcharge 25.00 25.00
b. Perf. 13½ 3.75 3.25
Nos. 36-48 (13) 47.50 36.05

Nos. 16, 19, 21 and 24 Overprinted in Black

1902 **Perf. 11½**
49 A2 15r brown 3.00 1.25
50 A2 25r sea green 3.00 1.40
51 A2 50r blue 3.00 1.40
a. Double overprint 20.00 18.00
52 A2 75r rose 4.00 2.75
a. Double ovpt, one albino 10.00 6.00
Nos. 49-52 (4) 13.00 6.80

No. 23 Surcharged

1905
53 A2 50r on 65r dull blue 6.00 2.50

Angola Stamps of 1898-1903 (Port. Congo type A2) Overprinted or Surcharged

a b

1911
54 (a) 2½r gray 1.10 .90
55 (a) 5r orange 1.60 1.25
56 (a) 10r lt green 1.60 1.25
a. "REPUBLICA" inverted 17.50 17.50
57 (a) 15r gray green 1.60 1.25
a. "REPUBLICA" inverted 17.50 17.50
58 (b) 25r on 200r red vio, pnksh 2.50 2.00
a. "REPUBLICA" inverted 17.50 17.50
b. "CONGO" double 17.50 17.50

Thin Bar and "CONGO" as Type "b"
59 (a) 2½r gray 1.10 .90
Nos. 54-59 (6) 9.50 7.55

Issue of 1898-1903
Overprinted in Carmine or Green —
c

1911
60 A2 2½r gray .25 .25
61 A2 5r orange .25 .25
62 A2 10r lt green .25 .25
63 A2 15r gray grn .25 .25
64 A2 20r gray vio .45 .25
65 A2 25r car rose (G) 2.00 .90
66 A2 50r brown .65 .35
67 A2 75r red lilac 1.10 .55
68 A2 100r dk bl, bl 1.00 .60
69 A2 115r org brn, pink 2.10 1.40
70 A2 130r brown, straw 2.10 1.40
71 A2 200r red vio, pnksh 3.00 1.90
72 A2 400r dull bl, straw 5.25 2.50
73 A2 500r blk & red, bl 5.75 2.25
74 A2 700r violet, yelsh 5.75 2.25
Nos. 60-74 (15) 30.15 15.35

Numerous inverts and doubles exist. These are printer's waste or made to order.

Common Design Types pictured following the introduction.

Vasco da Gama Issue of Various Portuguese Colonies Surcharged

1913 **On Stamps of Macao**
75 CD20 ¼c on ½a bl grn 1.25 1.25
76 CD21 ½c on 1a red 1.25 1.25
77 CD22 1c on 2a red vio 1.25 1.25
78 CD23 2½c on 4a yel grn 1.25 1.25
79 CD24 5c on 8a dk blue 1.25 1.25
80 CD25 7½c on 12a vio brn 2.50 2.50
81 CD26 10c on 16a bis brn 1.75 1.75
82 CD27 15c on 24a bister 1.75 1.75
Nos. 75-82 (8) 12.25 12.25

On Stamps of Portuguese Africa
83 CD20 ¼c on 2½r bl grn 1.00 .80
84 CD21 ½c on 5r red 1.00 .80
85 CD22 1c on 10r red vio 1.00 .80
86 CD23 2½c on 25r yel grn 1.00 .80
87 CD24 5c on 50r dk blue 1.10 1.10
88 CD25 7½c on 75r vio brn 1.90 1.90
89 CD26 10c on 100r bis brn 1.25 1.25
a. Inverted surcharge 25.00 25.00
90 CD27 15c on 150r bister 1.50 1.50
Nos. 83-90 (8) 9.75 8.95

On Stamps of Timor
91 CD20 ¼c on ½a bl grn 1.25 1.25
92 CD21 ½c on 1a red 1.25 1.25
93 CD22 1c on 2a red vio 1.25 1.25
94 CD23 2½c on 4a yel grn 1.25 1.25
95 CD24 5c on 8a dk blue 1.25 1.25
a. Double surcharge 25.00 25.00
96 CD25 7½c on 12a vio brn 2.50 2.50
97 CD26 10c on 16a bis brn 2.25 2.25
98 CD27 15c on 24a bister 2.25 2.25
Nos. 91-98 (8) 13.25 13.25
Nos. 75-98 (24) 34.45 34.45

Ceres — A3

Name and Value in Black Chalky Paper
1914 **Typo.** **Perf. 15x14**
99 A3 ¼c olive brn .35 .50
Never hinged .55
a. Inscriptions inverted
100 A3 ½c black .75 1.00
Never hinged 1.20
101 A3 1c blue grn 3.00 4.25
Never hinged 4.75
102 A3 1½c lilac brn 2.00 1.40
Never hinged 3.25
103 A3 2c carmine 2.00 1.40
Never hinged 3.25
104 A3 2½c lt violet .75 .90
Never hinged 1.20
105 A3 5c dp blue 1.00 1.40
Never hinged 1.40
106 A3 7½c yellow brn 1.50 1.40
Never hinged 2.40
107 A3 8c slate 2.00 3.25
Never hinged 3.25
108 A3 10c orange brn 2.00 3.25
Never hinged 3.25

109	A3	15c plum	2.00	3.25
		Never hinged	3.25	
110	A3	20c yellow grn	2.25	3.25
		Never hinged	3.50	
111	A3	30c brown, *grn*	2.75	5.00
		Never hinged	4.50	
112	A3	40c brown, *pink*	5.00	6.50
		Never hinged	8.00	
113	A3	50c orange, *salmon*	6.00	6.50
		Never hinged	9.50	
114	A3	1e green, *blue*	8.00	8.75
		Never hinged	13.00	
		Nos. 99-114 (16)	41.35	52.00

1920   **Ordinary Paper**

115	A3	¼c olive brn	.40	.55
		Never hinged	.65	
116	A3	2c carmine	.75	1.15
		Never hinged	1.20	

Issue of 1898-1903
Overprinted Locally
in Green or Red

1914-18   **Perf. 11½**

117	A2	50r brown (G)	1.00	.65
118	A2	75r rose (G)	450.00	
119	A2	75r red lilac (G)	3.00	1.50
120	A2	100r blue, *bl* (R)	1.00	.80
121	A2	200r red vio, *pink* (G)	2.00	1.25
122	A2	400r dl bl, *straw* (R) ('18)	80.00	55.00
123	A2	500r blk & red, *bl* (R)	65.00	42.50

Same on Nos. 51-52

124	A2	50r blue (R)	1.00	.70
125	A2	75r rose (G)	1.50	1.10

Same on No. 53

126	A2	50r on 65r dl bl (R)	1.25	1.10
		Nos. 117,119-126 (9)	155.75	104.60

No. 118 was not regularly issued.

Provisional Issue of 1902
Overprinted Type "c" in Red

1915   **Perf. 11½, 12½, 13½**

127	A1	115r on 10r red vio	.75	.25
a.		Perf. 13½	17.00	14.00
128	A1	115r on 50r lt bl	2.00	.25
a.		Perf. 11½	2.00	.65
129	A1	130r on 5r yellow	1.00	.25
130	A1	130r on 75r rose	2.00	.65
131	A1	130r on 100r brn, *buff*	1.00	.40
135	N1	115r on 2½r brn	.80	.40

Nos. 49, 51 Overprinted Type "c"

136	A2	15r brown	.85	.55
137	A2	50r blue	.85	.40

No. 53 Overprinted Type "c"

138	A2	50r on 65r dull blue	1.25	.40
		Nos. 127-138 (9)	10.50	3.55

NEWSPAPER STAMP

N1

Perf. 12½

1894, Aug. 5   **Typo.**   **Unwmk.**

P1	N1	2½r brown	1.50	.60
a.		Perf. 13½	1.50	.60

For surcharge and overprint see Nos. 48, 135.

PORTUGUESE GUINEA

'pōr-chi-gēz 'gi-nē

LOCATION — On the west coast of Africa between Senegal and Guinea
GOVT. — Portuguese Overseas Territory
AREA — 13,944 sq. mi.
POP. — 560,000 (est. 1970)
CAPITAL — Bissau

1000 Reis = 1 Milreis
100 Centavos = 1 Escudo (1913)

STAMPS OF CAPE VERDE USED IN PORTUGUESE GUINEA

Before Mar. 19, 1879, Portuguese Guinea was an administrative dependency of Cape Verde. Cape Verde stamps Nos. 1-4, 4a, 5-7 and 14 were used in Portuguese Guinea in 1877-1881, overlapping slightly with the issues of Portuguese Guinea.

Use in Portuguese Guinea can be distinguished by the cancellations composed of several concentric rings, with or without a heavy dot at the center. There are several types of these canceling devices, and some similar ones were also at Cape Verde. Identification of the cancellations by experts is advised.

1877-81

A1	A1	5r black (#1)	
A2	A1	10r yellow (#2)	
A3	A1	20r bister (#3)	
A4	A1	25r rose, perf 12½ (#4)	
	A1	25r rose, perf 13½ (#4a)	
A5	A1	40r blue, perf 12½ (#5)	
A6	A1	50r green (#6)	
A7	A1	50r blue (#14)	
A8	A1	100r lilac (#7)	

Issued under Portuguese Administration

Nos. 1-7 are valued with small faults such as short perfs or small thins. Completely fault-free examples of any of these stamps are very scarce and are worth more than the values given.

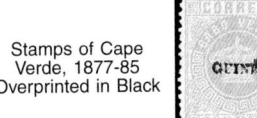

Stamps of Cape Verde, 1877-85 Overprinted in Black

1881   **Unwmk.**   **Perf. 12½**
Without Gum (Nos. 1-7)

1	A1	5r black	1,000.	800.
1A	A1	10r yellow	2,000.	800.
2	A1	20r bister	500.	250.
3	A1	25r rose	1,400.	775.
4	A1	40r blue	1,250.	800.
a.		Cliché of Mozambique in Cape Verde plate	16,500.	15,250.
4B	A1	50r green	2,000.	725.
5	A1	100r lilac	300.	175.
6	A1	200r orange	600.	475.
7	A1	300r brown	600.	475.

Excellent forgeries exist of Nos. 1-7.

Overprinted in Red or Black

1881-85   **Perf. 12½**

8	A1	5r black (R)	4.00	2.75
10	A1	10r green ('85)	6.00	5.50
11	A1	20r bister	3.00	2.25
12	A1	20r rose ('85)	6.75	5.00
a.		Double overprint		
13	A1	25r carmine	2.40	1.75
14	A1	25r violet ('85)	3.00	1.90
a.		Double overprint		
15b	A1	40r blue	180.00	115.00
c.		Cliché of Mozambique in Cape Verde plate	1,350.	900.00
16	A1	40r yellow ('85)	1.90	1.60
a.		Cliché of Mozambique in Cape Verde plate	50.00	45.00
b.		Imperf.		
c.		As "a," imperf.		
g.		Double overprint		
17a	A1	50r green	180.00	115.00
18	A1	50r blue ('85)	5.75	2.75
a.		Imperf.		
b.		Double overprint		
19	A1	100r lilac	7.75	6.00
a.		Inverted overprint	7.75	6.00
b.		100r lilac		
20	A1	200r orange	11.50	9.00
21	A1	300r yellow brn	14.00	11.00
		300r lake brown	16.00	12.50

Perf. 13½

8a	A1	5r black (R)	4.00	3.00
9	A1	10r yellow	160.00	160.00
10a	A1	10r green ('85)	6.75	5.00
11a	A1	20r bister	3.25	2.25
12b	A1	20r rose ('85)	6.75	5.50

13a	A1	25r rose	67.50	37.50
15	A1	40r blue	175.00	110.00
a.		Cliché of Mozambique in Cape Verde plate	1,500.	875.00
16d	A1	40r yellow ('85)	4.00	3.00
e.		Cliché of Mozambique in Cape Verde plate	50.00	45.00
f.		Imperf.		
17	A1	50r green	175.00	110.00
18c	A1	50r blue ('85)	10.50	10.00
19c	A1	50r pale lilac	9.00	5.50
d.		100r gray lilac	9.00	5.50

Varieties of this overprint may be found without accent on "E" of "GUINE," or with grave instead of acute accent.

Stamps of the 1881-85 issues were reprinted on a smooth white chalky paper, ungummed, and on thin white paper with shiny white gum and clean-cut perforation 13½.

King Luiz — A3

1886   **Typo.**   **Perf. 12½, 13½**

22	A3	5r gray black	6.00	5.50
a.		Imperf.		
23	A3	10r green	7.25	4.00
a.		Perf. 13½	8.25	6.75
b.		Imperf.		
24	A3	20r carmine	10.50	4.00
25	A3	25r red lilac	10.50	6.25
a.		Imperf.		
26	A3	40r chocolate	8.50	6.25
a.		Perf. 12½	82.50	60.00
27	A3	50r blue	17.00	6.25
a.		Imperf.		
28	A3	80r gray	16.00	10.00
a.		Perf. 12½	82.50	60.00
29	A3	100r brown	16.00	10.00
a.		Perf. 12½	37.50	22.50
30	A3	200r gray lilac	37.50	20.00
31	A3	300r orange	47.50	30.00
a.		Perf. 13½	210.00	210.00
		Nos. 22-31 (10)	176.75	102.25

For surcharges and overprints see Nos. 67-76, 180-183.

Reprinted in 1905 on thin white paper with shiny white gum and clean-cut perforation 13½.

King Carlos
A4   A5

1893-94   **Perf. 11½**

32	A4	5r yellow	1.90	1.10
a.		Perf. 12½	2.00	1.25
33	A4	10r red violet	1.90	1.10
34	A4	15r chocolate	2.40	1.60
35	A4	20r lavender	2.40	1.60
36	A4	25r blue green	2.40	1.60
37	A4	50r lt blue	5.00	3.75
a.		Perf. 12½	17.00	12.50
b.		Perf. 11½, lozenge paper	175.00	125.00
38	A4	75r rose	12.00	7.50
39	A4	80r lt green	12.00	7.50
40	A4	100r brn, *buff*	12.00	7.50
41	A4	150r car, *rose*	12.00	8.00
42	A4	200r dk bl, *bl*	20.00	15.00
43	A4	300r dk bl, *sal*	20.00	15.00
		Nos. 32-43 (12)	104.00	71.25

Almost all of Nos. 32-43 were issued without gum.

For surcharges and overprints see #77-88, 184-188, 203-205.

1898-1903   **Perf. 11½**
Name & Value in Black except 500r

44	A5	2½r gray	.40	.35
45	A5	5r orange	.40	.35
46	A5	10r lt green	.40	.35
47	A5	15r brown	3.25	2.25
48	A5	15r gray grn ('03)	1.75	1.25
49	A5	20r gray violet	1.40	1.10
50	A5	25r sea green	1.75	.90
51	A5	25r carmine ('03)	1.00	.55
52	A5	50r dark blue	2.75	1.40
53	A5	50r brown ('03)	3.25	2.25
54	A5	65r dl blue ('03)	15.00	8.75
55	A5	75r rose	20.00	8.00
56	A5	75r lilac ('03)	4.00	2.25
57	A5	80r brt violet	3.00	1.90
58	A5	100r dk bl, *bl*	2.75	1.90
a.		Perf. 12½	52.50	22.50
59	A5	115r org brn, *pink* ('03)	8.50	6.00
a.		115r orange brown, *yellowish*	8.25	5.00
60	A5	130r brn, *straw* ('03)	10.00	7.50
61	A5	150r lt brn, *buff*	11.00	3.25
62	A5	200r red lilac, *pnksh*	10.00	3.25

63	A5	300r blue, *rose*	11.00	4.25
64	A5	400r dl bl, *straw* ('03)	13.00	10.00
65	A5	500r blk & red, *bl* ('01)	14.50	7.75
66	A5	700r vio, *yelsh* ('01)	20.00	10.00
		Nos. 44-66 (23)	159.10	85.55

Stamps issued in 1903 were without gum.
For overprints and surcharges see Nos. 90-115, 190-194, 197.

Issue of 1886
Surcharged in Black or Red

1902, Oct. 20   **Perf. 12½**

67	A3	65r on 10r green	6.50	5.50
a.		Inverted surcharge	30.00	25.00
68	A3	65r on 20r car	6.50	5.00
69	A3	65r on 25r red lilac	6.50	5.00
70	A3	115r on 40r choc	5.75	4.50
a.		Perf. 13½	13.00	9.50
71	A3	115r on 50r blue	5.75	4.50
a.		Inverted surcharge	30.00	25.00
72	A3	115r on 300r orange	7.25	5.75
73	A3	130r on 80r gray	7.25	5.00
a.		Perf. 13½	14.00	5.75
74	A3	130r on 100r brown	7.75	5.75
a.		Perf. 13½	20.00	14.00
75	A3	400r on 200r gray lil	13.00	8.75
76	A3	400r on 5r gray blk (R)	32.50	24.00
		Nos. 67-76 (10)	98.75	73.75

Reprints of No. 76 are in black and have clean-cut perforation 13½.

Same Surcharge on Issue of 1893-94

Perf. 11½, 12½ (#80)

77	A4	65r on 10r red vio	5.75	3.50
78	A4	65r on 15r choc	5.75	3.50
79	A4	65r on 20r lav	5.75	3.50
80	A4	65r on 50r lt bl	3.00	1.75
a.		Perf. 13½	3.25	2.50
81	A4	115r on 5r yel	5.50	3.00
a.		Inverted surcharge	45.00	45.00
b.		Perf. 12½	55.00	40.00
82	A4	115r on 25r bl grn	6.00	3.25
83	A4	130r on 150r car, *rose*	6.00	3.25
84	A4	130r on 200r dk bl, *bl*	6.50	4.50
85	A4	130r on 300r dk bl, *sal*	6.50	4.50
86	A4	400r on 75r rose	4.50	3.00
87	A4	400r on 80r lt grn	3.00	1.60
88	A4	400r on 100r brn, *buff*	4.00	1.60

Same Surcharge on No. P1

Perf. 13½

89	N1	115r on 2½r brn	4.50	3.25
a.		Inverted surcharge	30.00	25.00
b.		Perf. 12½	4.75	3.50
c.		As "b," inverted surcharge	30.00	25.00
		Nos. 77-89 (13)	66.75	40.70

Issue of 1898
Overprinted in Black

1902, Oct. 20   **Perf. 11½**

90	A5	15r brown	2.50	1.25
91	A5	25r sea green	2.50	1.60
92	A5	50r dark blue	3.00	1.60
93	A5	75r rose	5.75	4.00
		Nos. 90-93 (4)	13.75	8.45

No. 54 Surcharged in Black

1905

94	A5	50r on 65r dull blue	5.00	2.50

Issue of 1898-1903
Overprinted in Carmine or Green

1911   **Perf. 11½**

95	A5	2½r gray	.40	.35
a.		Inverted overprint	19.00	19.00

96	A5	5r orange	.40	.35
97	A5	10r lt green	.70	.50
98	A5	15r gray green	.70	.50
99	A5	20r gray violet	.70	.50
100	A5	25r carmine (G)	.70	.50
a.		Double overprint	15.00	15.00
101	A5	50r brown	.45	.40
102	A5	75c lilac	.45	.40
103	A5	100r dk bl, bl	1.30	.75
104	A5	115r blg brn, pink	1.50	1.00
105	A5	130r brn, straw	1.50	1.00
106	A5	200r red lil, pink	6.50	3.25
107	A5	400r dl bl, straw	2.50	1.50
108	A5	500r blk & red, bl	2.75	1.50
109	A5	700r vio, yelsh	4.25	2.25
		Nos. 95-109 (15)	25.00	14.75

Issued without gum: #101-102, 104-105, 107.

Issue of 1898-1903
Overprinted in Red

1913   *Perf. 11½*

Without Gum (Nos. 110-115)

110	A5	15r gray grn	12.00	6.50
111	A5	75r lilac	12.00	6.50
a.		Inverted overprint	35.00	35.00
112	A5	100r bl, bl	6.00	4.50
a.		Inverted overprint	35.00	35.00
113	A5	200r red lil, pnksh	40.00	25.00
a.		Inverted overprint	82.50	82.50

Same Overprint on Nos. 90, 93 in Red

114	A5	15r brown	11.00	7.25
a.		"REPUBLICA" double	35.00	35.00
b.		"REPUBLICA" inverted	30.00	30.00
115	A5	75r rose	11.00	7.25
a.		"REPUBLICA" inverted	35.00	35.00
		Nos. 110-115 (6)	92.00	57.00

Vasco da Gama Issue of Various Portuguese Colonies Surcharged

1913   **On Stamps of Macao**

116	CD20	¼c on ½a bl grn	1.60	1.60
117	CD21	½c on 1a red	1.60	1.60
118	CD22	1c on 2a red vio	1.60	1.60
119	CD23	2½c on 4a yel grn	1.60	1.60
120	CD24	5c on 8a dk bl	1.60	1.60
121	CD25	7½c on 12a vio brn	3.25	3.25
122	CD26	10c on 16a bis brn	1.60	1.60
a.		Inverted surcharge	30.00	30.00
123	CD27	15c on 24a brn	2.75	2.75
		Nos. 116-123 (8)	15.60	15.60

On Stamps of Portuguese Africa

124	CD20	¼c on 2½c bl grn	1.40	1.40
125	CD21	½c on 5r red	1.40	1.40
126	CD22	1c on 10r red vio	1.40	1.40
127	CD23	2½c on 25r yel grn	1.40	1.40
128	CD24	5c on 50r dk bl	1.40	1.40
129	CD25	7½c on 75r vio brn	3.00	3.00
130	CD26	10c on 100r bis brn	1.40	1.40
131	CD27	15c on 150r bis	4.00	4.00
		Nos. 124-131 (8)	15.40	15.40

On Stamps of Timor

132	CD20	¼c on ½a bl grn	1.60	1.60
133	CD21	½c on 1a red	1.60	1.60
134	CD22	1c on 2a red vio	1.60	1.60
135	CD23	2½c on 4a yel grn	1.60	1.60
136	CD24	5c on 8a dk blue	1.60	1.60
137	CD25	7½c on 12a vio brn	3.00	3.00
138	CD26	10c on 16a bis brn	1.60	1.60
139	CD27	15c on 24a bister	3.00	3.00
		Nos. 132-139 (8)	15.60	15.60
		Nos. 116-139 (24)	46.60	46.60

Ceres — A6

Name and Value in Black
Chalky Paper

1914   *Perf. 15x14*

140	A6	¼c olive brown	.25	.25
		Never hinged	.40	
141	A6	½c black	.40	.30
		Never hinged	.65	
142	A6	1c blue green	1.40	1.40
		Never hinged	2.25	
143	A6	1½c lilac brn	.60	.60
		Never hinged	.95	

144	A6	2c carmine	.65	.65
		Never hinged	1.05	
145	A6	2½c lt violet	1.00	1.00
		Never hinged	1.60	
146	A6	5c deep blue	.65	.55
		Never hinged	1.05	
147	A6	7½c yellow brn	1.00	.40
		Never hinged	1.50	
148	A6	8c slate	.65	.55
		Never hinged	1.05	
149	A6	10c orange brn	.80	.65
		Never hinged	1.30	
150	A6	15c plum	8.25	7.25
		Never hinged	13.00	
151	A6	20c yellow grn	1.15	.85
		Never hinged	1.75	
152	A6	30c brown, grn	7.00	6.00
		Never hinged	11.00	
153	A6	40c brown, pink	3.50	3.25
		Never hinged	5.50	
154	A6	50c orange, salmon	3.50	3.25
		Never hinged	5.50	
155	A6	1e green, blue	4.00	3.50
		Never hinged	6.50	
		Nos. 140-155 (16)	34.75	30.45

1919-20

Ordinary Paper

156	A6	¼c olive brown	.40	.35
		Never hinged	.65	
157	A6	½c black ('20)	.25	.25
		Never hinged	.40	
158	A6	1c blue green	2.75	2.50
		Never hinged	4.50	
159	A6	2c carmine	.65	.65
		Never hinged	1.05	
		Nos. 156-159 (4)	4.05	3.75

1921-26   *Perf. 12x11½*

160	A6	¼c olive brown	3.00	2.25
		Never hinged	4.75	
161	A6	½c black	.25	.25
		Never hinged	.40	
162	A6	1c yellow green ('22)	.25	.25
		Never hinged	.40	
163	A6	1½c lilac brn	.25	.25
		Never hinged	.40	
164	A6	2c carmine	.25	.25
		Never hinged	.40	
165	A6	2c gray ('25)	.25	*1.60*
		Never hinged	.40	
166	A6	2½c lt violet	.25	.25
		Never hinged	.40	
167	A6	3c orange ('22)	.25	*1.60*
		Never hinged	.40	
168	A6	4c deep red ('22)	.25	*1.60*
		Never hinged	.40	
169	A6	4½c gray ('22)	.25	*1.60*
		Never hinged	.40	
170	A6	5c brt blue ('22)	.25	.25
		Never hinged	.40	
171	A6	6c lilac ('22)	.25	*1.60*
		Never hinged	.40	
172	A6	7c ultra ('22)	.30	*1.60*
		Never hinged	.50	
173	A6	7½c yellow brn	.25	.25
		Never hinged	.40	
174	A6	8c slate	.25	.25
		Never hinged	.40	
175	A6	10c orange brn	.25	.25
		Never hinged	.40	
176	A6	12c blue grn ('22)	.65	.50
		Never hinged	1.05	
177	A6	15c brn rose ('22)	.50	.35
		Never hinged	.80	
178	A6	20c yellow grn	.25	.25
		Never hinged	.40	
179	A6	24c ultra ('25)	1.90	1.60
		Never hinged	3.00	
179A	A6	25c brown ('25)	2.50	2.25
		Never hinged	4.00	
179B	A6	30c gray grn ('22)	.90	.25
		Never hinged	1.45	
179C	A6	40c turq bl ('22)	.90	.40
		Never hinged	1.45	
179D	A6	50c violet ('25)	1.90	.90
		Never hinged	3.00	
179E	A6	60c dk blue ('22)	1.90	.95
		Never hinged	3.00	
179F	A6	60c dp rose ('26)	2.50	1.75
		Never hinged	4.00	
179G	A6	80c brt rose ('22)	1.60	1.00
		Never hinged	2.50	
179H	A6	1e indigo ('26)	3.50	2.75
		Never hinged	5.50	
		Nos. 160-179H (28)	25.80	27.05

1922-25

Glazed Paper

179I	A6	1e pale rose	2.75	1.50
		Never hinged	4.00	
179J	A6	2e dk violet	3.00	1.50
		Never hinged	4.75	
179K	A6	5e buff ('25)	13.00	10.50
		Never hinged	21.00	
179L	A6	10e pink ('25)	30.00	17.50
		Never hinged	47.50	
179M	A6	20e pale turq ('25)	80.00	35.00
		Never hinged	125.00	
		Nos. 179I-179M (5)	128.75	66.00

For surcharges see Nos. 195-196, 211-213.

Provisional Issue of 1902 Overprinted in Carmine

1915   *Perf. 11½, 12½, 13½*

180	A3	115r on 40r choc	1.10	.65
a.		Perf. 13½	13.00	8.50
181	A3	115r on 50r blue	1.40	.75
a.		Perf. 12½	27.50	22.50
182	A3	130r on 80r gray	4.50	1.90
a.		Perf. 13½	14.50	11.00
183	A3	130r on 100r brn	3.50	1.90
184	A4	115r on 5r yellow	.80	.65
a.		Perf. 11½	5.00	4.50
185	A4	115r on 25r bl grn	.75	.65
186	A4	130r on 150r car, rose	1.25	.80
187	A4	130r on 200r bl, bl	.80	.70
188	A4	130r on 300r dk bl, sal	1.10	.80
189	N1	115r on 2½r brn	1.25	.90
a.		Perf. 13½	13.00	11.00
b.		Inverted overprint	22.50	22.50

On Nos. 90, 92, 94

Perf. 11½

190	A5	15r brown	.80	.70
191	A5	50r dark blue	.80	.70
192	A5	50r on 65r dl bl	.80	.70
		Nos. 180-192 (13)	18.85	11.80

Nos. 64, 66
Overprinted

1919   **Without Gum**   *Perf. 11½*

193	A5	400r dl bl, straw	90.00	21.00
194	A5	700r vio, yelsh	13.50	10.00

Nos. 140, 141 and 59 Surcharged

a   b

1920, Sept.   *Perf. 15x14, 11½*

Without Gum

195	A6(a)	4c on ¼c	3.25	2.75
		Never hinged	5.25	
196	A6(a)	6c on ½c	4.00	2.75
		Never hinged	6.50	
197	A5(b)	12c on 115r	8.00	5.50
		Never hinged	13.00	
		Nos. 195-197 (3)	15.25	11.00

Nos. 86-88
Surcharged

1925   *Perf. 11½*

203	A4	40c on 400r on 75r	.95	.80
204	A4	40c on 400r on 80r	.95	.80
205	A4	40c on 400r on 100r	.95	.80
		Nos. 203-205 (3)	2.85	2.40

Nos. 179F-179G, 179J
Surcharged

1931   *Perf. 12x11½*

211	A6	50c on 60c dp rose	3.25	1.60
		Never hinged	5.25	
212	A6	70c on 80c pink	3.25	1.90
		Never hinged	5.25	
213	A6	1.40e on 2e dk vio	6.50	4.00
		Never hinged	10.50	
213A	A6	1.40e on 2e dk vio (glazed paper)	6.50	4.00
		Never hinged	10.50	
		Nos. 211-213 (3)	13.00	7.50

Ceres — A7

1933   **Wmk. 232**

214	A7	1c bister	.25	.25
		Never hinged	.40	
215	A7	5c olive brn	.25	.25
		Never hinged	.40	
216	A7	10c violet	.25	.25
		Never hinged	.40	
217	A7	15c black	.25	.25
		Never hinged	.40	
218	A7	20c gray	.25	.25
		Never hinged	.40	
219	A7	30c dk green	.25	.25
		Never hinged	.40	
220	A7	40c red orange	.45	.25
		Never hinged	.70	
221	A7	45c lt blue	1.10	.80
		Never hinged	1.75	
222	A7	50c lt brown	1.10	.55
		Never hinged	1.75	
223	A7	60c olive grn	1.40	.55
		Never hinged	2.25	
224	A7	70c orange brn	2.75	.65
		Never hinged	4.50	
225	A7	80c emerald	1.50	.80
		Never hinged	2.40	
226	A7	85c deep rose	3.00	1.40
		Never hinged	4.75	
227	A7	1e red brown	1.40	.90
		Never hinged	2.25	
228	A7	1.40e dk blue	6.50	2.25
		Never hinged	10.50	
229	A7	2e red violet	4.50	1.90
		Never hinged	7.25	
230	A7	5e apple green	10.00	5.75
		Never hinged	16.00	
231	A7	10e olive bister	17.50	9.50
		Never hinged	28.00	
232	A7	20e orange	55.00	25.00
		Never hinged	87.50	
		Nos. 214-232 (19)	107.70	51.80

Common Design Types pictured following the introduction.

Common Design Types

Engr.; Name & Value Typo. in Black

1938   Unwmk.   *Perf. 13½x13*

233	CD34	1c gray grn	.25	.25
234	CD34	5c orange brn	.25	.25
235	CD34	10c dk carmine	.25	.25
236	CD34	15c dk vio brn	.25	.25
237	CD34	20c slate	.40	.25
238	CD35	30c rose violet	.60	.25
239	CD35	35c brt green	.65	.25
240	CD35	40c brown	1.10	.35
241	CD35	50c brt red vio	1.10	.35
242	CD36	60c gray black	1.60	.35
243	CD36	70c brown vio	1.60	.35
244	CD36	80c orange	1.90	.70
245	CD36	1e red	1.50	.50
246	CD37	1.75e blue	2.10	1.00
247	CD37	2e brown car	5.00	1.40
248	CD37	5e olive grn	5.50	2.25
249	CD38	10e blue vio	7.50	2.75
250	CD38	20e red brown	22.50	4.50
		Nos. 233-250 (18)	54.05	16.35

AIR POST STAMPS

Common Design Type

Perf. 13½x13

1938, Sept. 19   **Engr.**   **Unwmk.**

Name and Value in Black

C1	CD39	10c red orange	.60	.45
C2	CD39	20c purple	.60	.45
C3	CD39	50c orange	.65	.45
C4	CD39	1e ultra	.65	.50
C5	CD39	2e lilac brown	6.00	3.50
C6	CD39	3e dark green	2.00	1.25
C7	CD39	5e red brown	5.00	1.25
C8	CD39	9e rose carmine	7.00	3.00
C9	CD39	10e magenta	11.50	3.50
		Nos. C1-C9 (9)	34.00	14.35

No. C7 exists with overprint "Exposicao Internacional de Nova York, 1939-1940" and Trylon and Perisphere.

POSTAGE DUE STAMPS

D1

Without Gum

		1904	Unwmk.	Typo.	Perf. 12
J1	D1	5r yellow green		.60	.45
J2	D1	10r slate		.60	.45
J3	D1	20r yellow brown		.65	.55
J4	D1	30r red orange		1.90	1.60
J5	D1	50r gray brown		1.90	1.60
J6	D1	60r red brown		4.25	2.75
J7	D1	100r lilac		4.25	2.75
J8	D1	130r dull blue		3.25	2.10
J9	D1	200r carmine		6.50	5.25
J10	D1	500r violet		11.00	6.00
		Nos. J1-J10 (10)		34.90	23.50

Same Overprinted in Carmine or Green

		1911		Without Gum
J11	D1	5r yellow green	.25	.25
J12	D1	10r slate	.25	.25
J13	D1	20r yellow brown	.35	.35
J14	D1	30r red orange	.35	.35
J15	D1	50r gray brown	.35	.35
J16	D1	60r red brown	1.00	.80
J17	D1	100r lilac	1.90	1.40
J18	D1	130r dull blue	1.90	1.00
J19	D1	200r carmine (G)	1.90	1.50
J20	D1	500r violet	1.10	1.00
		Nos. J11-J20 (10)	9.35	7.25

Nos. J2-J10 Overprinted

		1919		Without Gum
J21	D1	10r slate	8.25	8.25
J22	D1	20r yellow brown	9.00	9.00
J23	D1	30r red orange	6.50	5.75
J24	D1	50r gray brown	2.50	2.10
J25	D1	60r red brown	600.00	500.00
J26	D1	100r lilac	2.25	1.90
J27	D1	130r dull blue	22.50	19.00
J28	D1	200r carmine	2.75	2.50
J29	D1	500r violet	24.00	20.00
		Nos. J21-J24,J26-J29 (8)	77.75	68.50

No. J25 was not regularly issued but exists on genuine covers.

D2

		1921		
J30	D2	½c yellow green	.25	.25
J31	D2	1c slate	.25	.25
J32	D2	2c orange brown	.25	.25
J33	D2	3c orange	.25	.25
J34	D2	5c gray brown	.25	.25
J35	D2	6c light brown	.25	.25
J36	D2	10c red violet	.60	.60
J37	D2	13c dull blue	.60	.60
J38	D2	20c carmine	.60	.60
J39	D2	50c gray	.60	.60
		Nos. J30-J39 (10)	3.90	3.90

WAR TAX STAMPS

WT1

Perf. 11½x12

		1919, May 20	Typo.	Unwmk.
MR1	WT1	10r brn, buff & blk	45.00	27.50
MR2	WT1	40r brn, buff & blk	40.00	22.50
MR3	WT1	50r brn, buff & blk	42.50	25.00
		Nos. MR1-MR3 (3)	127.50	75.00

The 40r is not overprinted "REPUBLICA." Some authorities consider Nos. MR2-MR3 to be revenue stamps.

NEWSPAPER STAMP

N1

		1893	Typo.	Unwmk.	Perf. 12½
P1	N1	2½r brown		1.25	.75
a.		Perf. 13½		1.25	.90

For surcharge and overprint see Nos. 89, 189.

POSTAL TAX STAMPS

Pombal Issue
Common Design Types

		1925	Unwmk.	Engr.	Perf. 12½
RA1	CD28	15c red & black		.55	.45
RA2	CD29	15c red & black		.55	.45
RA3	CD30	15c red & black		.55	.45
		Nos. RA1-RA3 (3)		1.65	1.35

Coat of Arms — PT7

Without Gum

		1934, Apr. 1	Typo.	Perf. 11½
RA4	PT7	50c red brn & grn	7.50	5.00
a.		Tête beche pair		450.00

Coat of Arms — PT8

		1938-40		Without Gum
RA5	PT8	50c ol bis & citron	6.50	3.25
RA6	PT8	50c lt grn & ol brn ('40)	6.50	3.25

POSTAL TAX DUE STAMPS

Pombal Issue
Common Design Types

		1925	Unwmk.	Perf. 12½
RAJ1	CD28	30c red & black	.55	.45
RAJ2	CD29	30c red & black	.55	.45
RAJ3	CD30	30c red & black	.55	.45
		Nos. RAJ1-RAJ3 (3)	1.65	1.35

PORTUGUESE INDIA

ˈpȯr-chi-gēz ˈin-dē-ə

LOCATION — West coast of the Indian peninsula
GOVT. — Portuguese colony
AREA — 1,537 sq. mi.
POP. — 649,000 (1958)
CAPITAL — Panjim (Nova-Goa)

1000 Reis = 1 Milreis
12 Reis = 1 Tanga (1881-82)
(Real = singular of Reis)
16 Tangas = 1 Rupia

Expect Nos. 1-55, 70-112 to have rough perforations. Stamps frequently were cut apart because of the irregular and missing perforations. Scissor separations that do not remove perfs do not negatively affect value.

Numeral of Value	
A1	A2

A1: Large figures of value. "REIS" in Roman capitals. "S" and "R" of "SERVICO" smaller and "E" larger than the other letters. 33 lines in background. Side ornaments of four dashes.
A2: Large figures of value. "REIS" in block capitals. "S," "E" and "R" same size as other letters of "SERVICO." 44 lines in background. Side ornaments of five dots.

Handstamped from a Single Die
Perf. 13 to 18 & Compound

		1871, Oct. 1		Unwmk.
		Thin Transparent Brittle Paper		
1	A1	10r black	625.00	325.00
2	A1	20r dk carmine	1,350	300.00
a.		20r orange vermilion	1,350.	300.00
3	A1	40r Prus blue	475.00	325.00
4	A1	100r yellow grn	550.00	375.00
5	A1	200r ocher yel	850.00	450.00

		1872		**Thick Soft Wove Paper**
5A	A1	10r black	1,500.	350.00
6	A1	20r dk carmine	1,650.	400.00
7	A1	20r orange ver	1,800.	400.00
7A	A1	100r yellow grn		
8	A1	200r ocher yel	1,700.	1,000.
9	A1	300r dp red violet		3,000.

The 600r and 900r of type A1 are bogus.
See Nos. 24-28. For surcharges see Nos. 70-71, 73, 83, 94, 99, 104, 108.

Perf. 12½ to 14½ & Compound
1872

10	A2	10r black	260.00	100.00
11	A2	20r vermilion	225.00	85.00
a.		"20" omitted		1,000.
12	A2	40r blue	70.00	60.00
a.		Tête beche pair	5,750.	5,750.
b.		40r dark blue	85.00	60.00
13	A2	100r deep green	70.00	60.00
14	A2	200r yellow	275.00	250.00
15	A2	300r red violet	275.00	225.00
a.		Imperf.		
16	A2	600r red violet	175.00	140.00
a.		"600" double		700.00
17	A2	900r red violet	200.00	175.00
		Nos. 10-17 (8)	1,550.	1,095.

An unused 100r blue green exists with watermark of lozenges and gray burelage on back. Experts believe it to be a proof.

White Laid Paper

18	A2	10r black	37.50	32.50
a.		Tête beche pair	14,000.	8,500.
b.		10r brownish black	37.50	30.00

19	A2	20r vermilion	35.00	27.50
20	A2	40r blue	70.00	57.50
a.		"40" double	—	—
b.		Tête beche pair	—	—
21	A2	100r green	62.50	45.00
a.		"100" double	450.00	
22	A2	200r yellow	175.00	175.00
		Nos. 18-22 (5)	380.00	337.50

See No. 23. For surcharges see Nos. 72, 82, 95-96, 100-101, 105-106, 109-110.

Re-issues

		1873	**Thin Bluish Toned Paper**	
23	A2	20r vermilion	200.00	160.00
24	A1	10r black	14.00	8.50
a.		"1" inverted	125.00	100.00
b.		"10" inverted	400.00	
25	A1	20r vermilion	17.00	11.50
a.		"20" double	400.00	
b.		"20" inverted		
26	A1	300r dp violet	110.00	85.00
a.		"300" double	475.00	
27	A1	600r dp violet	140.00	100.00
a.		"600" double	575.00	
b.		"600" inverted	575.00	
28	A1	900r dp violet	140.00	100.00
a.		"900" double	675.00	
b.		"900" triple	1,000.	
		Nos. 23-28 (6)	621.00	465.00

Nos. 23 to 26 are re-issues of Nos. 11, 5A, 7, and 9. The paper is thinner and harder than that of the 1871-72 stamps and slightly transparent. It was originally bluish white but is frequently stained yellow by the gum.
Nos. 23 to 26 may be found with part of the papermaker's watermark "ORIGINAL TURKISH MILL KENT."

A3   A4

A3: Same as A1 with small figures.
A4: Same as A2 with small figures.

		1874	**Thin Bluish Toned Paper**	
29	A3	10r black	35.00	27.50
a.		"10" and "20" superimposed	475.00	450.00
30	A3	20r vermilion	550.00	350.00
a.		"20" double		625.00

For surcharge see No. 84.
Nos. 29 and 30 may be found with part of the papermaker's watermark "ORIGINAL TURKISH MILL KENT."

		1875		
31	A4	10r black	37.50	22.50
a.		Value sideways		550.00
32	A4	15r rose	12.50	9.00
a.		"15" inverted	475.00	
b.		"15" double		
c.		Value omitted	1,150.	
33	A4	20r vermilion	70.00	42.50
a.		"0" missing	850.00	575.00
b.		"20" sideways	850.00	
c.		"20" double		
		Nos. 31-33 (3)	120.00	74.00

For surcharges see Nos. 74, 78, 85.
Nos. 31 to 33 may be found with part of the papermaker's watermark "HODGKINSON & CO."

A5   A6

A5: Re-cutting of A1.
Small figures. "REIS" in Roman capitals. Letters larger. "V" of "SERVICO" barred. 33 lines in background. Side ornaments of five dots.
A6: First re-cutting of A2.
Small figures. "REIS" in block capitals. Letters re-cut. "V" of "SERVICO" barred. 41 lines above and 43 below "REIS." Side ornaments of five dots.

Perf. 12½ to 13½ & Compound
1876

34	A5	10r black	20.00	14.00
35	A5	20r vermilion	16.00	11.50
a.		"20" double		
36	A6	10r black	6.25	4.25
a.		Double impression	525.00	
b.		"10" double	525.00	
37	A6	15r rose	425.00	325.00
a.		"15" omitted	—	1,000.
38	A6	20r vermilion	22.50	17.00
39	A6	40r blue	110.00	85.00

40	A6	100r green	160.00	150.00
a.		Imperf.		
41	A6	200r yellow	1,000.	675.00
42	A6	300r violet	550.00	450.00
a.		"300" omitted		
43	A6	600r violet	800.00	675.00
44	A6	900r violet	1,200.	750.00
a.		"900" omitted		

For surcharges see 10, 10C-80, 86-87, 91-92, 98, 102, 107, 111.

Nos. 34 to 44 may be found with part of the papermaker's watermark "SPICER BROTHERS."

A7   A8

A9

A7: Same as A5 with addition of a star above and a bar below the value.

A8: Second re-cutting of A2. Same as A6 but 41 lines both above and below "REIS." Star above and bar below value.

A9: Third re-cutting of A2. 41 lines above and 38 below "REIS." Star above and bar below value. White line around central oval.

1877

45	A7	10r black	30.00	25.00
46	A8	10r black	42.50	37.50
47	A9	10r black	29.00	25.00
a.		"10" omitted		
48	A9	15r rose	32.50	27.50
49	A9	20r vermilion	8.50	8.00
50	A9	40r blue	17.00	16.00
a.		"40" omitted	42.50	35.00
51	A9	100r green	70.00	60.00
a.		"100" omitted		
52	A9	200r yellow	75.00	70.00
53	A9	300r violet	100.00	85.00
54	A9	600r violet	100.00	85.00
55	A9	900r violet	100.00	85.00
		Nos. 45-55 (11)	604.50	524.00

For surcharges see Nos. 77, 81, 88-90, 93, 112.

No. 47, 20r, 40r and 200r exist imperf.

Nos. 45 to 55 may be found with part of the papermaker's watermark "SPICER BROTHERS."

Portuguese Crown — A10

Perf. 12½, Thin paper

1877, July 15				**Typo.**
56	A10	5r black	5.00	3.50
57	A10	10r yellow	9.00	7.25
a.		Imperf.		
58	A10	20r bister	9.50	7.00
59	A10	25r rose	10.00	8.00
60a	A10	40r blue	175.00	140.00
61	A10	50r yellow grn	32.50	20.00
62	A10	100r lilac	16.00	11.50
63	A10	200r orange	22.50	17.50

Perf. 13½, Thin paper

56a	A10	5r black	5.00	3.50
57b	A10	10r yellow	10.00	8.50
58a	A10	20r bister	9.50	6.00
59a	A10	25r rose	10.00	8.00
60	A10	40r blue	14.00	11.00
61a	A10	50r yellow grn	32.50	20.00
62a	A10	100r lilac	15.00	11.50
64	A10	300r yel brn	29.00	25.00

Perf. 13½, Medium paper

56b	A10	5r black	5.00	3.50
57c	A10	10r yellow	9.00	7.25
58b	A10	20r bister	9.50	6.00
59b	A10	25r rose	10.00	8.00
60b	A10	40r blue	13.50	11.00
63a	A10	200r orange	22.50	17.00
63b	A10	200r pale orange	22.50	17.00
64a	A10	300r yel brn	29.00	25.00

1880-81

Perf 12½, Thin Paper

65	A10	10r green	17.00	13.50
66a	A10	25r slate	72.50	55.00
67	A10	25r violet	37.50	25.00
68	A10	40r yellow	37.50	25.00
69	A10	50r dk blue	37.50	25.00

Perf 13½, Thin Paper

65a	A10	10r green	10.00	8.50
66	A10	25r slate	37.50	27.50
67a	A10	25r violet	27.50	20.00
68a	A10	40r yellow	35.00	27.50
69a	A10	50r dk blue	17.50	16.00
		Nos. 65a-69a (5)	127.50	99.50

Perf 13½, Medium Paper

65b	A10	10r green	10.00	8.50
66b	A10	25r slate	37.50	27.50
67b	A10	25r violet	27.50	20.00
68b	A10	40r yellow	32.50	25.00
69b	A10	50r blue	17.50	15.00
c.		50c dark blue	19.00	16.00

For surcharges see Nos. 113-161.

The stamps of the 1877-81 issues were reprinted in 1885, on stout very white paper, ungummed and with rough perforation 13½. They were again reprinted in 1905 on thin white paper with shiny white gum and clean-cut perforation 13½ with large holes. Value of the lowest-cost reprint, $3 each.

Stamps of 1871-77 Surcharged with New Values

1881   **Black Surcharge**

70	A1	1½r on 20r (#2)		1,500.
71	A1	1½r on 20r (#7)		1,000.
72	A2	1½r on 20r (#11)		800.00
73	A1	1½r on 20r (#25)	225.00	200.00
74	A4	1½r on 20r (#33)	140.00	125.00
a.		Inverted surcharge		250.00
75	A5	1½r on 20r (#35)	110.00	85.00
76	A6	1½r on 20r (#38)	125.00	110.00
77	A9	1½r on 20r (#49)	200.00	140.00
78	A4	5r on 15r (#32)	2.50	2.50
a.		Double surcharge	10.00	
b.		Inverted surcharge	10.00	
78C	A6	5r on 15r (#37)	2.50	2.50
79	A5	5r on 20r (#35)	2.50	
a.		Double surcharge	14.00	
b.		Inverted surcharge	—	
80	A6	5r on 20r (#38)	2.75	2.50
a.		Double surcharge	—	
b.		Inverted surcharge	—	
81	A9	5r on 20r (#49)	5.00	4.00
a.		Double surcharge	—	
b.		Invtd. surcharge	—	

Red Surcharge

82	A2	5r on 10r (#18)	600.00	350.00
83	A1	5r on 10r (#24)	600.00	300.00
84	A3	5r on 10r (#29)	1,750.	
85	A4	5r on 10r (#31)	125.00	125.00
86	A5	5r on 10r (#34)	6.00	6.00
a.		Double surcharge	17.00	
87	A6	5r on 10r (#36)	9.50	7.75
a.		Inverted surcharge		
88	A7	5r on 10r (#45)	90.00	50.00
a.		Inverted surcharge	175.00	
89	A8	5r on 10r (#46)	190.00	82.50
90	A9	5r on 10r (#47)	40.00	35.00
a.		Inverted surcharge	82.50	
b.		Double surcharge	82.50	

Similar Surcharge, Handstamped Black Surcharge

1883				
91	A5	1½r on 10r (#34)	1,650.	825.00
92	A6	1½r on 10r (#36)	1,100.	825.00
93	A9	1½r on 10r (#47)	825.00	600.00
94	A1	4½r on 40r (#3)	2,500.	775.00
95	A2	4½r on 40r (#12)	35.00	35.00
96	A2	4½r on 40r (#20)	35.00	35.00
98	A6	4½r on 40r (#39)	35.00	35.00
99	A1	4½r on 100r (#4)	2,500.	775.00
100	A2	4½r on 100r (#13)	45.00	42.50
101	A2	4½r on 100r (#21)	45.00	42.50
102	A6	4½r on 100r (#40)	40.00	42.50
104	A1	6r on 100r (#4)	2,200.	1,200.
105	A2	6r on 100r (#13)	375.00	275.00
106	A2	6r on 100r (#21)	275.00	225.00
107	A6	6r on 100r (#40)	350.00	275.00
108	A1	6r on 200r (#5)	825.00	600.00
109	A2	6r on 200r (#14)		275.00
110	A2	6r on 200r (#22)	275.00	275.00
111	A6	6r on 200r (#41)		450.00
112	A9	6r on 200r (#52)	550.00	500.00

Stamps of 1877-81 Surcharged in Black

1881-82

113	A10	1½r on 5r blk	1.40	1.10
a.		With additional surcharge "4½" in blue	150.00	125.00
114	A10	1½r on 10r grn	1.40	1.10
a.		With additional surch. "6"	160.00	110.00
115	A10	1½r on ...	11.90	8.75
a.		Inverted surcharge	27.50	
b.		Double surcharge	27.50	
c.		Pair, one without surcharge	—	
116	A10	1½r on 25r slate	40.00	35.00
117	A10	1½r on 100r lil	60.00	47.50
118	A10	4½r on 10r grn	190.00	160.00
119	A10	4½r on 20r bis	4.00	2.75
a.		Inverted surcharge	82.50	65.00
120	A10	4½r on 25r vio	11.50	11.00
121	A10	4½r on 100r lil	225.00	160.00
122	A10	6r on 10r yel	47.50	45.00
123	A10	6r on 10r grn	10.00	8.00
124	A10	6r on 20r bis	17.00	15.00
125	A10	6r on 25r slate	35.00	27.50
126	A10	6r on 25r vio	2.25	1.75
127	A10	6r on 40r blue	82.50	70.00
128	A10	6r on 40r yel	42.50	35.00
129	A10	6r on 50r grn	47.50	38.50
130	A10	6r on 50r blue	110.00	90.00
		Nos. 113-130 (18)	939.05	757.95

Surcharged in Black

131	A10	1t on 10r grn	450.00	325.00
a.		With additional surch. "6"	900.00	775.00
132	A10	1t on 20r bis	47.50	42.50
133	A10	1t on 25r slate	35.00	30.00
134	A10	1t on 25r vio	13.00	9.00
135	A10	1t on 40r blue	19.00	17.50
136	A10	1t on 50r grn	55.00	47.50
137	A10	1t on 50r blue	25.00	19.00
138	A10	1t on 100r lil	24.00	13.00
139	A10	1t on 200r org	47.50	42.50
140	A10	2t on 25r slate	35.00	35.00
a.		Small "T"	55.00	40.00
141	A10	2t on 25r vio	14.00	11.50
142	A10	2t on 40r blue	42.50	35.00
143	A10	2t on 40r yel	52.50	42.50
144	A10	2t on 50r grn	15.00	13.00
a.		Inverted surcharge	110.00	100.00
145	A10	2t on 50r blue	90.00	75.00
146	A10	2t on 100r lil	11.50	9.25
147	A10	2t on 200r org	40.00	35.00
148	A10	2t on 300r brn	35.00	30.00
149	A10	4t on 10r grn	14.00	11.50
a.		Inverted surcharge	45.00	45.00
150	A10	4t on 50r grn	13.00	10.00
a.		With additional surch. "2"	160.00	110.00
151	A10	4t on 200r org	40.00	35.00
152	A10	8t on 20r bis	35.00	24.00
153	A10	8t on 25r rose	190.00	160.00
154	A10	8t on 40r blue	47.50	40.00
155	A10	8t on 100r lil	40.00	35.00
156	A10	8t on 200r org	35.00	30.00
157	A10	8t on 300r brn	47.50	40.00
		Nos. 131-157 (27)	1,513.	1,217.

1882   **Blue Surcharge**

158	A10	4½r on 5r black	12.00	10.50

Similar Surcharge, Handstamped

1883				
159	A10	1½r on 5r black	55.00	35.00
160	A10	1½r on 10r grn	82.50	45.00
161	A10	1½r on 100r lil	400.00	325.00

The "2" in "½" is 3mm high, instead of 2mm as on Nos. 113, 114 and 121.

The handstamp is known double on #159-161.

A12

With or Without Accent on "E" of "REIS"

1882-83				**Typo.**
162	A12	1½r black	.55	.45
a.		"½" for "1½"		
163	A12	4½r olive bister	.95	.45
164	A12	6r green	.80	.45
165	A12	1t rose	.80	.45
166	A12	2t blue	.80	.45
167	A12	4t lilac	3.25	2.75
168	A12	8t orange	3.25	2.75
		Nos. 162-168 (7)	10.40	7.75

There were three printings of the 1882-83 issue. The first had "REIS" in thick letters with acute accent on the "E." The second had "REIS" in thin letters with accent on the "E." The third had the "E" without accent. In the first printing the "E" sometimes had a grave or circumflex accent.

The third printing may be divided into two sets, with or without a small circle in the cross of the crown.

The stamps doubly printed or with value omitted, double, inverted or misplaced are printed.

Nos. 162-168 were reprinted on thin white paper, with shiny white gum and clean-cut perforation 13½. Value of lowest-cost reprint, $1 each.

"REIS" no serifs — A13   "REIS" with serifs — A14

1883   **Litho.**   **Imperf.**

169	A13	1½r black	1.40	1.10
a.		Tête bêche pair	425.00	325.00
b.		"1½" double		
170	A13	4½r olive grn	14.00	11.00
a.		"4½" omitted	350.00	275.00
171	A13	6r green	14.00	11.00
a.		Tête bêche pair	1,200.	
b.		"6" omitted	400.00	300.00
172	A14	1½r black	125.00	55.00
a.		"1½" omitted	350.00	325.00
173	A14	6r green	62.50	47.50
a.		"6" omitted	425.00	350.00
		Nos. 169-173 (5)	216.90	125.60

Nos. 169-171 exist with unofficial perf. 12.

King Luiz — A15   King Carlos — A16

Perf. 12½, 13½

1886, Apr. 29			**Embossed**	
174	A15	1½r black	2.50	1.40
a.		Perf. 13½	150.00	87.50
175	A15	4½r bister	3.25	1.50
a.		Perf. 13½	30.00	14.00
176	A15	6r dp green	4.50	1.75
a.		Perf. 13½	35.00	16.00
177	A15	1t brt rose	6.50	3.00
178	A15	2t deep blue	8.75	4.50
179	A15	4t gray vio	11.00	4.50
180	A15	8t orange	10.00	4.75
		Nos. 174-180 (7)	46.50	21.40

For surcharges and overprints see Nos. 224-230, 277-278, 282, 317-323, 354, 397.

Nos. 178-179 were reprinted. Originals have yellow gum. Reprints have white gum and clean-cut perforation 13½. Value, $4 each.

1895-96 Typo.   Perf. 11½, 12½, 13½

181	A16	1½r black	2.00	.65
182	A16	4½r pale orange	2.00	.65
a.		Perf. 13½	8.00	1.60
183	A16	6r green	2.00	.65
a.		Perf. 12½	3.00	1.10
184	A16	9r gray lilac	5.00	3.00
185	A16	1t lt blue	2.00	.55
a.		Perf. 12½	5.50	2.50
186	A16	2t rose	1.50	.65
a.		Perf. 12½	4.25	2.25
187	A16	4t dk blue	2.00	.80
a.		Perf. 12½	5.25	3.25
188	A16	8t brt violet	5.00	2.75
		Nos. 181-188 (8)	21.50	9.70

For surcharges and overprints see Nos. 231-238, 275-276, 279-281, 324-331, 352.

No. 184 was reprinted. Reprints have white gum, and clean-cut perforation 13½. Value $10.

Common Design Types pictured following the introduction.

Vasco da Gama Issue
Common Design Types

1898, May 1		**Engr.**	**Perf. 14 to 15**	
189	CD20	1½r blue green	1.00	.90
190	CD21	4½r red	1.00	.90
191	CD22	6r red violet	1.25	.75
192	CD23	9r yellow green	1.50	1.00
193	CD24	1t dk blue	3.00	1.60
194	CD25	2t violet brn	3.75	1.90
195	CD26	4t bister brn	3.75	1.90
196	CD27	8t bister	5.00	2.00
		Nos. 189-196 (8)	20.25	12.95

For overprints and surcharges see Nos. 290-297, 384-389.

King Carlos — A17

Name and Value in Black
except No. 219

1898-1903		Typo.	Perf. 11½	
197	A17	1r gray ('02)	.35	.25
198	A17	1½r orange	.35	.25
199	A17	1½r slate ('02)	.45	.25
200	A17	2r orange ('02)	.35	.25
201	A17	2½r yel brn ('02)	.45	.25
202	A17	3r dp blue ('02)	.45	.25
203	A17	4½r lt green	.70	.55
204	A17	6r brown	.70	.55
205	A17	6r gray grn ('02)	.45	.25
206	A17	9r dull vio	.80	.55
a.		9r gray lilac	1.75	1.75
208	A17	1t sea green	.80	.50
209	A17	1t car rose ('02)	.60	.25
210	A17	2t blue	1.40	.55
a.		Perf. 13½	30.00	7.75
211	A17	2t brown ('02)	3.25	2.10
212	A17	2½t dull bl ('02)	15.00	6.50
213	A17	4t blue, blue	3.25	2.25
214	A17	5t brn, straw ('02)	4.50	2.10
215	A17	8t red lil, pnksh	5.50	1.40
216	A17	8t red vio, pink ('02)	5.00	3.00
217	A17	12t blue, pink	10.00	2.25
218	A17	12t grn, pink ('02)	9.00	3.25
219	A17	1rp blk & red, bl	10.00	6.50
220	A17	1rp dl bl, straw ('02)	15.00	7.25
221	A17	2rp vio, yelsh	18.00	8.25
222	A17	2rp gray blk, straw ('03)	20.00	12.00
		Nos. 197-222 (25)	126.35	61.55

Several stamps of this issue exist without value or with value inverted but they are not known to have been issued in this condition. The 1r and 6r in carmine rose are believed to be color trials.

For surcharges and overprints see Nos. 223, 239-259, 260C-274, 283-289, 300-316, 334-350, 376-383, 390-396, 398-399.

No. 210 Surcharged
in Black

1900				
223	A17	1½r on 2t blue	4.50	1.10
a.		Inverted surcharge	35.00	22.50
b.		Perf. 13½		

Stamps of 1885-96
Surcharged in Black
or Red

On Stamps of 1886

1902			Perf. 12½, 13½	
224	A15	1r on 2t blue	1.10	.50
225	A15	2r on 4½r bis	.65	.50
a.		Inverted surcharge	22.50	22.50
b.		Double surcharge		
226	A15	2½t on 6r green	.55	.25
227	A15	3r on 1t rose	.55	.25
228	A15	2½t on 1½r blk (R)	3.00	1.40
229	A15	2½t on 4t gray vio	5.00	2.75
230	A15	5t on 8t orange	3.00	.65
a.		Perf. 12½	27.50	17.00

On Stamps of 1895-96
Perf. 11½, 12½, 13½

231	A16	1r on 6r green	.50	.25
232	A16	2r on 8t brt vio	.35	.25
233	A16	2½r on 9r gray vio	.35	.35
234	A16	3r on 4½r yel	2.00	1.00
a.		Inverted surcharge	24.00	24.00
235	A16	3r on 1t lt bl	2.00	.90
236	A16	2½t on 1½r blk (R)	3.00	.80
237	A16	5t on 6r green	3.00	.80
a.		Perf. 12½	35.00	22.50
238	A16	5t on 4t dk bl	3.00	.80
a.		Perf. 12½	35.00	22.50
		Nos. 224-238 (15)	28.05	11.45

Nos. 224, 229, 231, 233, 234, 235 and 238 were reprinted in 1905. They have whiter gum than the originals and very clean-cut perf. 13½. Value $2.50 each.

Nos. 204, 208, 210
Overprinted

1902			Perf. 11½	
239	A17	6r brown	3.00	1.40
a.		Inverted overprint		
240	A17	1t sea green	4.00	1.40
241	A17	2t blue	3.00	1.40
a.		Perf. 13½	150.00	100.00
		Nos. 239-241 (3)	10.00	4.20

No. 212 Surcharged
in Black

1905				
243	A17	2t on 2½t dull blue	2.25	1.60

Stamps of 1898-1903
Overprinted in Lisbon
in Carmine or Green

1911				
244	A17	1r gray	.25	.25
a.		Inverted overprint	11.00	11.00
245	A17	1½r slate	.25	.25
a.		Double overprint	11.00	11.00
246	A17	2r orange	.25	.25
a.		Double overprint	15.00	15.00
b.		Inverted overprint	11.00	11.00
247	A17	2½r yellow brn	.25	.25
248	A17	3r deep blue	.25	.25
249	A17	4½r light green	.35	.25
250	A17	6r gray green	.25	.25
251	A17	9r gray lilac	.35	.25
252	A17	1t car rose (G)	.50	.25
253	A17	2t brown	.50	.25
254	A17	4t blue, blue	1.40	1.00
255	A17	5t brn, straw	1.40	1.00
256	A17	8t vio, pink	4.25	2.50
257	A17	12t grn, pink	4.50	2.50
258	A17	1rp dl bl, straw	7.00	4.75
259	A17	2rp gray blk, straw	8.75	7.50
		Nos. 244-259 (16)	30.50	21.75

A18

Values are for pairs, both halves.

1911		Perforated Diagonally		
260	A18	1r on 2r orange	.80	.70
a.		Without diagonal perf.	4.50	4.00
b.		Cut diagonally instead of perf.	3.50	3.25

Stamps of Preceding Issues
Perforated Vertically through the
Middle and Each Half Surcharged

a   b

Values are for pairs, both halves of the stamp.

1912-13		On Issue of 1898-1903		
260C	A17(a)	1r on 2r org	.25	.25
261	A17(a)	1r on 1t car	.25	.25
262	A17(a)	1r on 5t brn, straw	275.00	225.00
263	A17(b)	1r on 5t brn, straw	7.75	6.00
264	A17(a)	1½r on 2½r yel brn	.75	.65
264C	A17(a)	1½r on 4½r lt grn	12.00	7.75
265	A17(a)	1½r on 9r gray lil	.55	.45

266	A17(a)	1½r on 4t bl, bl	.55	.45
267	A17(a)	2r on 2½r yel brn	.70	.45
268	A17(a)	2r on 4t bl, bl	1.00	.70
269	A17(a)	3r on 2½r yel brn	.70	.45
270	A17(a)	3r on 2t brown	.70	.45
271	A17(a)	6r on 4½r lt grn	.70	.60
272	A17(a)	6r on 9r gray lil	.70	.55
273	A17(a)	6r on 9r dull vio	4.50	3.50
274	A17(b)	6r on 8t red vio, pink	1.60	1.00

On Nos. 237-238, 230, 226, 233

275	A16(b)	1r on 5t on 2t	20.00	17.00
276	A16(b)	1r on 5t on 4t	10.00	9.25
277	A15(b)	1r on 5t on 8t	5.00	3.25
278	A15(a)	2r on 2½r on 6r	4.25	3.25
279	A16(a)	2r on 2½r on 9r	25.00	24.00
280	A16(b)	3r on 5t on 2t	7.75	6.25
281	A16(b)	3r on 5t on 4t	7.75	6.25
282	A15(b)	3r on 5t on 8t	2.50	1.60

On Issue of 1911

283	A17(a)	1r on 1r gray	.25	.25
283B	A17(a)	1r on 2r org	.25	.25
284	A17(a)	1r on 1t car	.35	.25
285	A17(a)	1r on 5t brn, straw	.35	.25
285A	A17(b)	1r on 5t brn, straw	825.00	550.00
285B	A17(a)	1½r on 4½r lt grn	.65	.50
286	A17(a)	3r on 2t brn	11.50	8.50
289	A17(a)	6r on 9r gray lil	.55	.45

There are several settings of these surcharges and many minor varieties of the letters and figures, notably a small "6." Nos. 260-289 were issued mostly without gum.

More than half of Nos. 260C-289 exist with inverted or double surcharge, or with bisecting perforation omitted. The legitimacy of these varieties is questioned. Price of inverted surcharges, $3-$15; double surcharges, $1-$4; perf. omitted, $1.50-$15.

Similar surcharges made without official authorization on stamps of type A17 are: 2r on 2½r, 3r on 2½r, 3r on 5t, and 6r on 4½r.

Vasco da
Gama Issue
Overprinted

1913				
290	CD20	1½r blue green	.35	.25
291	CD21	4½r red	.35	.25
a.		Double overprint	22.50	
292	CD22	6r red violet	.45	.40
a.		Double overprint	22.50	
293	CD23	9r yellow grn	.45	.40
294	CD24	1t dark blue	1.00	.55
295	CD25	2t violet brown	2.25	1.25
296	CD26	4t orange brn	1.25	1.00
297	CD27	8t bister	2.25	1.40
		Nos. 290-297 (8)	8.35	5.50

Issues of 1898-1913
Overprinted Locally
in Red

1913-15		On Issues of 1898-1903		
300	A17	2r orange	10.00	10.00
301	A17	2½r yellow brn	.95	.80
302	A17	3r dp blue	19.00	17.00
303	A17	4½r lt green	1.90	1.60
304	A17	6r gray grn	25.00	20.00
305	A17	9r gray lilac	1.90	1.40
306	A17	1t sea green	45.00	30.00
307	A17	2t blue	50.00	35.00
309	A17	4t blue, blue	40.00	27.50
310	A17	5t brn, straw	55.00	45.00
311	A17	8t red vio, pink	65.00	45.00
312	A17	12t grn, pink	3.50	2.50
313	A17	1rp blk & red, bl	100.00	82.50
314	A17	1rp dl bl, straw	65.00	45.00
315	A17	2rp gray blk, straw	82.50	55.00
316	A17	2rp vio, yelsh	77.50	45.00
		Nos. 300-316 (16)	642.25	458.30

Inverted or double overprints exist on 2½r, 4½r, 9r, 1rp and 2rp.

Nos. 300-316 were issued without gum except 4½r and 9r.

Nos. 302, 304, 306, 307, 310, 311 and 313 were not regularly issued. Nor were the 1½r, 2t brown and 12t blue on pink with preceding overprint.

Same Overprint in Red or Green on
Provisional Issue of 1902

317	A15	1r on 2t blue	45.00	27.50
a.		"REPUBLICA" inverted	140.00	

318	A15	2r on 4½r bis	45.00	27.50
a.		"REPUBLICA" inverted	140.00	
319	A15	2½r on 6r grn	.75	.65
a.		"REPUBLICA" inverted	19.00	19.00
320	A15	3r on 1t rose (R)	11.00	8.75
321	A15	2½t on 4t gray vio	110.00	45.00
323	A15	5t on 8t org (G)	15.00	8.25
a.		Red overprint	27.50	22.50
324	A16	1r on 6r grn	35.00	22.50
325	A16	2r on 8t vio	35.00	22.50
a.		Inverted surcharge	110.00	
327	A16	3r on 4½r bl	82.50	55.00
328	A16	3r on 1t lt bl	82.50	55.00
329	A16	5t on 2t rose (G)	10.00	3.00
330	A16	5t on 4t bl (G)	10.00	3.00
331	A16	5t on 4t bl (R)	10.00	4.25
a.		"REPUBLICA" inverted	55.00	
b.		"REPUBLICA" double	55.00	
		Nos. 317-331 (15)	491.75	282.90

The 2½r on 1½r of types A15 and A16, the 3r on 1t (A15) and 2½r on 9r (A16) were clandestinely printed.

Some authorities question the status of No. 317-318, 320-321, 324, 327-328.

Same Overprint on Nos. 240-241

1913-15				
334	A17	1t sea green	15.00	5.00
335	A17	2t blue	15.00	6.00

This overprint was applied to No. 239 without official authorization. Value $35.

On Issue of 1912-13 Perforated
through the Middle

Values are for pairs, both halves of the stamp.

336	A17(a)	1r on 2r org	17.00	11.00
340	A17(a)	1½r on 4½r lt grn	17.00	11.00
341	A17(a)	1½r on 9r gray lil	20.00	
342	A17(a)	1½r on 4t bl, bl	27.50	
343	A17(a)	2r on 2½r yel brn	27.50	7.25
344	A17(a)	2r on 4t bl, bl	27.50	7.25
345	A17(a)	3r on 2½r yel brn	22.50	
346	A17(a)	3r on 2t brn	17.00	5.25
347	A17(a)	6r on 4½r lt grn	1.10	.90
348	A17(a)	6r on 9r gray lil	1.60	1.60
350	A17(b)	6r on 8t red vio, pink	1.60	1.60
352	A16(b)	1r on 5t on 4t bl	110.00	
354	A15(a)	2r on 2½r on 6r grn	13.00	
		Nos. 334-354 (15)	325.80	

The 1r on 5t (A15), 1r on 1t (A17), 1½r on 2½r (A17), 3r on 5t on 8t (A15), and 6r on 9r (A17) were clandestinely printed.

Nos. 336, 347 exist with inverted surcharge.

Some authorities question the status of Nos. 341-345, 352 and 354.

Ceres — A21

Name and Value in Black
Chalky Paper

1914		Typo.	Perf. 15x14	
357	A21	1r olive brn	.35	.55
		Never hinged	.55	
358	A21	1½r yellow grn	.35	.55
		Never hinged	.55	
359	A21	2r black	.70	.40
		Never hinged	1.10	
360	A21	2½r olive grn	.70	.40
		Never hinged	1.10	
361	A21	3r lilac	.70	.40
		Never hinged	1.10	
362	A21	4½r orange brn	.70	.40
		Never hinged	1.10	
363	A21	5r blue green	.70	.50
		Never hinged	1.10	
364	A21	6r lilac brown	.70	.40
		Never hinged	1.10	
365	A21	9r ultra	.70	.40
		Never hinged	1.10	
366	A21	10r carmine	.95	.55
		Never hinged	1.50	
367	A21	1t violet	1.25	.55
		Never hinged	2.00	
368	A21	2t deep blue	1.25	.55
		Never hinged	2.00	
369	A21	3t yellow brown	1.90	.95
		Never hinged	3.00	
370	A21	4t slate	2.25	1.25
		Never hinged	3.50	
371	A21	8t plum	4.50	4.00
		Never hinged	7.25	
372	A21	12t brown, green	4.00	3.25
		Never hinged	6.50	
373	A21	1rp brown, pink	40.00	50.00
		Never hinged	65.00	
374	A21	2rp org, salmon	30.00	60.00
		Never hinged	47.50	
375	A21	3rp green, blue	40.00	60.00
		Never hinged	65.00	
		Nos. 357-375 (19)	131.70	185.10

The 1r, 2r, 2½r, 3r, 4½r, 5r, 6r and 10r, 1t and 3t exist on glazed paper.

1919-20
Ordinary Paper

375A	A21	1r olive brn	.80	*1.25*
		Never hinged	1.30	
375B	A21	1½r yellow grn	.80	*1.25*
		Never hinged	1.30	
	b.	Imperf.		
375C	A21	2r black ('19)	.11	*1.80*
375D	A21	2½r olive grn ('19)	.80	*1.25*
		Never hinged	1.30	
375E	A21	3r lilac ('16)	.80	*1.25*
		Never hinged	1.30	
375F	A21	4½r orange brn ('19)	.80	*1.25*
		Never hinged	1.30	
375G	A21	6r lilac brown ('16)	.80	*1.25*
		Never hinged	1.30	
375H	A21	1t lt violet ('16)	.80	*1.25*
		Never hinged	1.30	
375I	A21	2t deep blue ('16)	.80	*1.25*
		Never hinged	1.30	
		Nos. 375A-375I (9)	7.20	11.25

1921-23   *Perf. 12x11½*

375J	A21	1r olive brn	.80	*1.25*
		Never hinged	1.30	
375K	A21	1½r yellow grn	.80	*1.25*
		Never hinged	1.30	
375L	A21	2r black	1.50	*1.50*
		Never hinged	2.40	
375M	A21	3r lilac ('22)	.80	*1.25*
		Never hinged	1.30	
375N	A21	4r blue ('22)	1.40	1.25
		Never hinged	2.25	
375O	A21	4½r orange brn	2.75	1.60
		Never hinged	4.50	
375P	A21	5r blue green	10.00	6.00
		Never hinged	16.00	
375Q	A21	6r lilac brown	.80	.70
		Never hinged	1.30	
375R	A21	9r ultra	1.60	.95
		Never hinged	2.50	
375S	A21	10r carmine	2.50	1.45
		Never hinged	4.00	
375T	A21	1t lt violet	2.75	1.25
		Never hinged	4.00	
375U	A21	1½t gray green ('22)	1.40	.95
		Never hinged	2.25	
375V	A21	2t deep blue	2.75	1.25
		Never hinged	4.50	
375W	A21	2½t turquoise blue ('22)	1.50	1.25
		Never hinged	2.40	
375X	A21	3t4r yellow brown ('23)	5.50	4.50
		Never hinged	8.75	
375Y	A21	4t slate	2.25	1.25
		Never hinged	3.50	
375Z	A21	8t plum	7.75	5.50
		Never hinged	12.50	
		Nos. 375J-375Z (17)	46.85	33.15

The 1, 2, 2½, 3, 4½r, 1, 2, and 4t exist with the black inscriptions inverted and the 2½r with them double, one inverted, but it is not known that any of these were regularly issued. For surcharges see Nos. 400, 400A, 420, 421, 423.

Nos. 249, 251-253, 256-259 Surcharged in Black

1914

376	A17	1½r on 4½r grn	.35	.25
377	A17	1½r on 9r gray lil	.45	.35
378	A17	1½r on 12t grn, *pink*	.55	.50
379	A17	3r on 1t car rose	.45	.40
380	A17	3r on 2t brn	3.25	2.75
381	A17	3r on 8t red vio, *pink*	2.50	2.25
382	A17	3r on 1rp dl bl, *straw*	1.00	.60
383	A17	3r on 2rp gray blk, straw	1.10	.80

There are 3 varieties of the "2" in "1½."
Nos. 376-377 exist with inverted surcharge.

Vasco da Gama Issue Surcharged in Black

1925, Jan. 30   **Without Gum**   Litho.

384	CD21	1½r on 4½r red	.40	.35
385	CD23	1½r on 9r yel grn	.50	.35
386	CD24	3r on 1t dk bl	.40	.35
387	CD25	3r on 2t vio brn	.60	.50
388	CD26	3r on 4t org brn	.35	.25
389	CD27	3r on 8t bister	1.40	1.25
		Nos. 376-389 (14)	13.30	10.95

Double, inverted and other surcharge varieties exist on Nos. 384-386, 389.

Nos. 303, 305, 312 and 315 Surcharged in Black

1915

390	A17	1½r on 4½r grn	45.00	22.50
	a.	"REPUBLICA" omitted	77.50	47.50
	b.	"REPUBLICA" inverted	82.50	
391	A17	1½r on 9r gray lil	14.00	8.25
	a.	"REPUBLICA" omitted	35.00	
392	A17	1½r on 12t grn, *pink*	1.40	1.10
396	A17	3r on 2rp gray blk, straw	55.00	22.50
		Nos. 390-396 (4)	115.40	54.35

Nos. 390, 390a, 390b, 391, and 391a were not regularly issued. The 3r on 2½r (A17) was surcharged without official authorization.

Preceding Issues Overprinted in Carmine

1915   **On No. 230**

397	A15	5t on 8t org	2.75	1.50

On Nos. 241, 243

398	A17	2t blue	2.25	1.40
399	A17	2t on 2½t dl bl	2.75	1.40
		Nos. 397-399 (3)	7.75	4.30

Nos. 375, 359 Surcharged in Carmine

1922

400	A21	1½r on 2r black (ordinary paper)	.75	.60
		Never hinged	1.25	
400A	A21	1½r on 2r black (chalky paper)	.50	.40
		Never hinged	.80	

No. 400 also exists on glazed paper.

Ceres Type of 1913-23
Name and Value in Black

1922   **Typo.**   *Perf. 12x11½*
Glazed Paper

407	A21	1rp gray brn	17.50	17.00
		Never hinged	28.00	
408	A21	2rp yellow	30.00	*90.00*
		Never hinged	47.50	
409	A21	3rp bluish grn	40.00	*100.00*
		Never hinged	65.00	
410	A21	5rp carmine rose	50.00	*150.00*
		Never hinged	80.00	
		Nos. 407-410 (4)	137.50	357.00

Vasco da Gama and Flagship A22

1925, Jan. 30   **Without Gum**   Litho.

411	A22	6r brown	5.00	3.25
412	A22	1t red violet	7.00	5.00

400th anniv. of the death of Vasco da Gama (1469?-1524), Portuguese navigator.

Monument to St. Francis — A23   Image of St. Francis — A25

Autograph of St. Francis A24

Image of St. Francis — A26   Tomb of St. Francis — A28

Church of Bom Jesus at Goa — A27

1931, Dec. 3   *Perf. 14*

414	A23	1r gray green	.95	.80
415	A24	2r brown	.95	.80
416	A25	6r red violet	1.60	.80
417	A26	1½t yellow brn	7.00	3.50
418	A27	2t deep blue	9.00	4.75
419	A28	2½t light red	12.00	5.50
		Nos. 414-419 (6)	31.50	16.15

Exposition of St. Francis Xavier at Goa, in December, 1931.

Nos. 371 and 375X Surcharged

1931-32   *Perf. 15x14*
Chalky Paper

420	A21	1½r on 8t plum ('32)	2.25	1.60

Ordinary Paper
Perf. 12x11½

421	A21	1½r on 8t plum ('32)	1.50	1.10
423	A21	2½t on 3t4r yel brn	80.00	50.00

"Portugal" and Vasco da Gama's Flagship "San Gabriel" — A29

Perf. 11½x12

1933   **Typo.**   **Wmk. 232**

424	A29	1r bister	.25	.25
425	A29	2r olive brn	.25	.25
426	A29	4r violet	.25	.25
427	A29	6r dk green	.25	.25
428	A29	8r black	.40	.30
429	A29	1t gray	.40	.30
430	A29	1½t dp rose	.40	.30
431	A29	2t brown	.40	.30
432	A29	2½t dk blue	2.25	.55
433	A29	3t brt blue	2.50	.55
434	A29	5t red orange	2.50	.55
435	A29	1rp olive grn	11.00	3.25
436	A29	2rp maroon	27.50	7.50

437	A29	3rp orange	40.00	8.75
438	A29	5rp apple grn	55.00	25.00
		Nos. 424-438 (15)	143.35	48.35

For surcharges see Nos. 454-463, 472-474, J34-J36 in Scott Standard catalogue, Vol. 5.

Common Design Types
Perf. 13½x13

1938, Sept. 1   **Engr.**   Unwmk.
Name and Value in Black

439	CD34	1r gray brn	.30	.25
440	CD34	2r orange brn	.30	.25
441	CD34	3r dk vio brn	.30	.25
442	CD34	6r brt green	.30	.25
443	CD35	10r dk carmine	.40	.30
444	CD35	1t brt red vio	.55	.30
445	CD35	1½t red	.90	.30
446	CD37	2t orange	.90	.30
447	CD37	2½t blue	.90	.30
448	CD37	3t slate	1.75	.35
449	CD36	5t rose vio	2.75	.50
450	CD36	1rp brown car	4.50	.90
451	CD36	2rp olive grn	7.75	2.75
452	CD38	3rp blue vio	13.00	6.50
453	CD38	5rp red brown	22.50	6.50
		Nos. 439-453 (15)	57.10	20.00

For surcharges see Nos. 492-495, 504-505 in Scott Standard catalogue, Vol. 5.

AIR POST STAMPS

Common Design Type
Perf. 13½x13

1938, Sept. 1   **Engr.**   Unwmk.
Name and Value in Black

C1	CD39	1t red orange	.70	.40
C2	CD39	2½t purple	.80	.40
C3	CD39	3½t orange	.80	.40
C4	CD39	4½t ultra	1.60	.45
C5	CD39	7t lilac brown	1.75	.55
C6	CD39	7½t dark green	2.50	.80
C7	CD39	9t red brown	4.50	1.25
C8	CD39	11t magenta	5.00	1.25
		Nos. C1-C8 (8)	17.65	5.50

No. C4 exists with overprint "Exposicao Internacional de Nova York, 1939-1940" and Trylon and Perisphere. Value, unused $90, never hinged $125.

POSTAGE DUE STAMPS

D1

1904   **Unwmk.**   **Typo.**   *Perf. 11½*
Name and Value in Black

J1	D1	2r gray green	.50	.35
J2	D1	3r yellow grn	.50	.35
J3	D1	4r orange	.50	.45
J4	D1	5r slate	.50	.50
J5	D1	6r gray	.50	.50
J6	D1	9r yellow brn	.60	.60
J7	D1	1t red orange	2.25	.80
J8	D1	2t gray brown	3.25	1.60
J9	D1	5t dull blue	4.50	3.00
J10	D1	10t carmine	7.75	3.50
J11	D1	1rp dull vio	13.00	7.50
		Nos. J1-J11 (11)	33.85	19.15

Nos. J1-J11 Overprinted in Carmine or Green

1911

J12	D1	2r gray grn	.25	.25
J13	D1	3r yellow grn	.25	.25
J14	D1	4r orange	.25	.25
J15	D1	5r slate	.25	.25
J16	D1	6r gray	.45	.25
J17	D1	9r yellow brn	.55	.35
J18	D1	1t red org	.65	.35
J19	D1	2t gray brn	.90	.55
J20	D1	5t dull blue	2.25	1.40
J21	D1	10t carmine (G)	3.25	1.90
J22	D1	1rp dull violet	7.75	3.25
		Nos. J12-J22 (11)	16.80	9.05

Nos. J1-J11
Overprinted

1914

J23	D1	2r gray grn	1.50	1.10
J24	D1	3r yellow grn	1.50	1.10
J25	D1	4r orange	1.50	1.10
J26	D1	5r slate	1.50	1.10
J27	D1	6r gray	1.60	1.10
J28	D1	9r yellow brn	1.60	1.10
J29	D1	1t red org	3.25	1.10
J30	D1	2t gray brn	20.00	3.25
J31	D1	5t dull blue	21.00	4.50
J32	D1	10t carmine	25.00	6.50
J33	D1	1rp dull violet	45.00	8.75
		Nos. J23-J33 (11)	123.45	30.70

WAR TAX STAMPS

Overprinted in Black or Carmine

WT1

Denomination in Black

Perf. 15x14

1919, Apr. 15   Typo.   Unwmk.

MR1	WT1	0:00:05,48rp grn	2.25	1.50
MR2	WT1	0:01:09,94rp grn	4.75	3.00
MR3	WT1	0:02:03,43rp grn		
		(C)	4.75	3.00
		Nos. MR1-MR3 (3)	11.75	7.50

Some authorities consider No. MR2 a revenue stamp.

POSTAL TAX STAMPS

Pombal Issue
Common Design Types

1925   Unwmk.   Perf. 12½

RA1	CD28	6r rose & black	.50	.50
RA2	CD29	6r rose & black	.50	.50
RA3	CD30	6r rose & black	.50	.50
		Nos. RA1-RA3 (3)	1.50	1.50

POSTAL TAX DUE STAMPS

Pombal Issue
Common Design Types

1925   Unwmk.   Perf. 12½

RAJ1	CD28	1t rose & black	.65	.65
RAJ2	CD29	1t rose & black	.65	.65
RAJ3	CD30	1t rose & black	.65	.65
		Nos. RAJ1-RAJ3 (3)	1.95	1.95

See note after Portugal No. RAJ4.

PUERTO RICO

ˌpwer-tə-'rē-ˌkō

(Porto Rico)

LOCATION — A large island in the West Indies, east of Hispaniola
GOVT. — Former Spanish Colony
AREA — 3,435 sq. mi.
POP. — 953,243 (1899)
CAPITAL — San Juan

The island was ceded to the United States by the Treaty of 1898.

100 Centimes = 1 Peseta
1000 Milesimas = 100 Centavos = 1 Peso (1881)
100 Cents = 1 Dollar (1898)

Puerto Rican stamps of 1855-73, a part of the Spanish colonial period, were also used in Cuba. They are listed as Cuba Nos. 1-4, 9-14, 18-21, 31-34, 39-41, 47-49, 51-53, 55-57.

STAMPS OF CUBA USED IN PUERTO RICO

Values for Stamps on Cover

1855-73

A1	½ p blue green (#1)	100.00
A2	1r p gray green (#2)	200.00
A3	2r p carmine (#3)	500.00
A4	½r p yel grn (#9)	50.00
a.	½r p greenish blue (#9a)	60.00
A5	2r p orange (#10)	75.00
A6	2r p orange red (#11)	300.00
A7	½r p blue (#12)	25.00
a.	½r p milky blue (#12a)	30.00
A8	1r p gray green (#13)	25.00
c.	1r p pale green (#13c)	30.00
A9	2r p dull rose (#14)	150.00
A10	½r p blue (#18)	10.00
A11	½r p green, pale rose (#19)	15.00
a.	½r p green, rose lilac (#19a)	15.00
A12	1r p blue, salmon (#20)	50.00
A13	2r p vermilion, buff (#21)	150.00
a.	2r p red, buff (#21a)	175.00
A14	5c dull violet (#31)	300.00
A15	10c blue (#32)	20.00
A16	20c green (#33)	30.00
A17	40c rose (#34)	200.00
A18	5c rose (#38)	—
A18A	10c red brown (#39)	15.00
A19	20c orange (#40)	25.00
A20	40c dull violet (#41)	150.00
A21	10c green (#47)	15.00
A22	20c red brown (#48)	25.00
A23	40c rose (#49)	150.00
A24	25c ultramarine (#51)	15.00
A25	50c gray green (#52)	40.00
A26	1p pale brown (#53)	150.00
A27	25c gray (#55)	20.00
a.	25c lilac (#55b)	30.00
A28	50c brown (#56)	50.00
A29	1p red brown (#57)	200.00

Most local inland covers of this period (1855-73) are official fronts of covers only. The values stated above for lower denominations are for such fronts. Complete covers with the same stamps are worth at least double these values.

OFFICIAL STAMPS OF SPAIN USED IN PUERTO RICO

1858

A30	½o black, yellow, (#O5)	30.00
	On cover or wrapper	200.00
	On cover in combination with Cuba #18 (A10) or #19 (A11)	300.00
a.	½o black, straw, (#O5a)	30.00
	On cover or wrapper	200.00
A31	1o black, rose, (#O6)	30.00
	On cover or wrapper	300.00
a.	1o black, salmon rose, (#O6a)	30.00
	On cover or wrapper	300.00
A32	1o black, blue green, (#O7)	175.00
	On cover or wrapper	500.00
a.	4o black, green, (#O7a)	150.00
	On cover or wrapper	500.00
A33	1 l black, blue, (#O8)	375.00
	On wrapper	1,000.

Values are for stamps with clear readable or identifiable cancellations of Puerto Rico.

Values for Pairs

A30	½o black, yellow,	75.00
A30a	½o black, straw, (#O5a)	75.00
A31	1o black, rose, (#O6)	75.00
A31a	1o black, salmon rose, (#O6a)	75.00
A32	4o black, blue green (#O7)	375.00
A32a	4o black, blue, (#O8)	775.00
A33	1 l black, blue, (O8)	775.00

Values for Blocks of 4

A30	½o black, yellow, (#O5)	150.00
A30a	½o black, straw, (#O5a)	150.00
A31	1o black, rose, (#O6)	150.00
A31a	1o black, salmon rose, (#O6a)	225.00
A32	4o black, blue green, (#O7)	850.00
A32a	4o black, blue, (#O7a)	900.00
A33	1l black, blue, (#O8)	1,050.

STAMPS OF GREAT BRITAIN USED IN PUERTO RICO

Aguadilla
Stamps of Great Britain Cancelled Type B "F84"

1873-77

A34	½p rose red (#58, plate 6)	115.00
A35	1p rose red (#33, plates 119, 122, 139, 149, 156, 160)	72.50
A36	2p blue (#30, plate 14)	—
A37	3p rose (#49, plates 7-9)	—
A38	3p rose (#61, plate 12)	—
A39	4p pale green (#13c)	85.00
A40	4p vermilion (#69, plate 15)	400.00
A41	6p buff (#59b, plate 11)	—
A42	6p gray (#62, plates 13, 14)	—
A43	9p bister (#52, plate 4)	450.00
A44	10p red brown (#53)	450.00
A45	1sh green (#54, plates 4-7)	77.50
A46	1sh green (#64, plates 8-12)	90.00
A47	2sh blue (#55, plate 55)	350.00

Nos. A34-A47 on cover are valued from $1,500.

Arroyo
Stamps of Great Britain Cancelled Type B "F83" in black or red or with circular date stamp

1873-77

A48	½p rose red (#58, plate 5)	77.50
A49	1p rose red (#33, plates 149-151, 156, 164, 174, 175)	72.50
A50	1½p lake red (#32, plates 1, 3)	—
A51	2p blue (#30, plate 14)	—
A52	3p rose (#49, plates 5, 7, 10)	77.50
A53	3p rose (#61, plates 11, 12, 14, 16, 18)	72.50
A54	4p vermilion (#43, plates 12-14)	72.50
A55	4p vermilion (#69, plate 15)	400.00
A56	6p brown (#59, plate 11)	85.00
A57	6p buff (#59b, plate 11)	105.00
A58	6p gray (#60, plate 12)	—
A59	6p gray (#62, plates 13-15)	77.50
A60	9p bister (#52, plate 4)	400.00
A61	10p red brown (#53)	400.00
A62	1sh green (#48, plate 4)	—
A63	1sh green (#54, plates 4-7)	77.50
A64	1sh green (#64, plates 8-13)	92.50
A65	2sh blue (#55)	300.00
A66	5sh rose (#57, plate 2)	—

Nos. A48-A66 on cover are valued from $2,000.

Mayaguez
Stamps of Great Britain Cancelled Type B "F85" in black or blue

1873-77

A67	½p rose red (#58, plates 4-6, 8, 10, 11)	72.50
A68	1p rose red (#33, plates 76, 120-124, 134, 137, 140, 146, 149-151, 154-157, 160, 167, 170, 174-176, 178, 180, 182, 185, 186, 189)	50.00
A69	1½p lake red (#32, plates 1, 3)	65.00
A70	2p blue (#30, plates 13-15)	65.00
A71	3p rose (#49, plates 7-10)	72.50
A72	3p rose (#61, plates 11, 12, 14, 16-19)	65.00
A73	4p vermilion (#43, plates 11-14)	65.00
A74	4p vermilion (#69, plate 15)	400.00
A75	4p pale olive green (#70, plate 15)	—
A76	6p bright violet (#51, plate 9)	—
A77	6p buff (#59b, plate 11)	105.00
A78	6p brown (#59, plate 11)	92.50
A79	6p gray (#60, plate 12)	260.00
A80	6p gray (#62, plates 13-16)	65.00

(Ponce column continued)

A81	8p orange (#73)	400.00
A82	9p bister (#52, plate 4)	300.00
A83	10p red brown (#53)	400.00
A84	1sh green (#54, plates 4-7)	57.50
A85	1sh green (#64, plates 8-13)	240.00
A86	1sh blue (#88)	—
A87	5sh rose (#57, plate 1)	—
A88	5sh rose (#57, plate 2)	—

Nos. A67-A88 on cover are valued from $500.

Naguabo
Stamps of Great Britain Cancelled Type B "582"

1875-77

A89	½p rose red (#58, plates 2, 12, 14)	—
A90	1p rose red (#33, plates 159, 165)	450.00
A91	3p rose (#61, plates 17, 18)	725.00
A92	4p vermilion (#43, plates 13, 14)	650.00
A93	4p vermilion (#69, plate 15)	—
A94	6p gray (#62, plates 14, 15)	—
A95	9p bister (#52, plate 4)	—
A96	10p red brown (#53)	1,250.
A97	1sh green (#64, plates 11, 12)	—
A98	2sh blue (#55)	1,000.

Only two covers bearing British stamps canceled "582" are known. Values from $10,000.

Ponce
Stamps of Great Britain Cancelled Type B "F88"

1873-77

A99	½p rose red (#58, plates 5, 10, 12)	72.50
A100	1p rose red (#33, plates 120-124, 146, 148, 154, 156-158, 160, 167, 171, 174, 175, 179, 186, 187)	57.50
A101	1½p lake red (#32, plate 3)	145.00
A102	2p blue (#30, plates 13, 14)	72.50
A103	3p rose (#49, plates 7-9)	—
A104	3p rose (#61, plates 12, 16-19)	65.00
A105	4p vermilion (#43, plates 8, 9, 12-14)	72.50
A106	4p vermilion (#69, plate 15)	400.00
A107	4p pale olive green (#70, plates 15, 16)	275.00
A108	6p buff (#59b, plates 11, 12)	97.50
A109	6p brown (#59, plate 11)	85.00
A110	6p gray (#60, plate 12)	—
A111	6p gray (#62, plates 13-15)	72.50
A112	9p bister (#52, plate 4)	350.00
A113	10p red brown (#53)	400.00
A114	1sh green (#54, plates 4, 6, 7)	65.00
A115	1sh green (#64, plates 8-13)	77.50
A116	2sh blue (#55)	—
A117	5sh rose (#57, plate 1)	500.00
A118	5sh rose (#57, plate 2)	700.00

Nos. A99-A118 on cover are valued from $1,000.

San Juan
Crowned Circle Type I

1844

A119	I	Crowned circle handstamp "Paid at San Juan," double circle curved "PAID" in black, on cover	1,000.
		As #A119, with additional local postage, cover	1,200.
A120	I	Crowned circle handstamp "Paid at San Juan," double circle curved "PAID" in red, on cover	1,000.
		As #A120, with additional local postage, cover	1,500.

Stamps of Great Britain Cancelled Type A or B "C61"

1865-77

A121	½p rose red (#58, plates 5, 10, 15)	65.00
A122	1p rose red (#33, plates 73, 73, 81, 84, 90, 94, 100-102, 107, 117, 122, 124, 125, 127, 130, 137-140, 145, 146, 149, 153, 156, 159, 160, 162, 163, 169, 171-175, 179, 180, 182, 186)	50.00

A123	1½p lake red (#32, plates 1, 3)	85.00
A124	2p blue (#29, plate 9)	50.00
A125	2p blue (#30, plates 13, 14)	45.00
A126	3p rose (#44, plate 1)	120.00
A127	3p rose (#61, plates 11, 12, 14-18)	65.00
A128	3p rose (#61, plates 11, 12, 14-18)	60.00
A129	4p vermilion (#43, plates 7-14)	65.00
A130	4p vermilion (#69, plate 15)	400.00
A131	6p lilac (#45, plates 5, 6)	97.50
A132	6p lilac (#50, plate 6)	92.50
A133	6p bright violet (#50a, plate 6)	100.00
A134	6p bright violet (#51, plates 8, 9)	92.50
A135	6p buff (#59b, plates 11, 12)	97.50
A136	6p brown (#59, plate 11)	65.00
A137	6p gray (#60, plate 12)	—
A138	6p gray (#62, plates 13-15)	65.00
A139	9p straw (#40)	400.00
A140	9p straw (#46, plate 4)	500.00
A141	9p bister (#52, plate 4)	275.00
A142	10p red brown (#53)	350.00
A143	1sh green (#48, plate 4)	185.00
A144	1sh green (#54, plates 4-7)	57.50
A145	1sh green (#64, plates 8-13)	77.50
A146	2sh blue (#55)	175.00
A147	5sh rose (#57, plate 1)	600.00
A148	5sh rose (#57, plate 2)	750.00

Nos. A121-A148 on cover are valued from $300.

Issued under Spanish Dominion

Values for unused stamps are for examples with original gum as defined in the catalogue introduction. Very fine examples of Nos. 1-170, MR1-MR13 will have perforations clear of the design but will be noticeably poorly centered. Extremely fine examples will be well centered; these are scarce and command substantial premiums.

Stamps of Cuba Overprinted in Black

a

b

c

d

1873 Unwmk. Perf. 14

1	A10	(a) 25c gray	62.50	2.10
		On cover		50.00
a.		25c lilac	67.50	3.25
		On cover		75.00
2	A10	(a) 50c brown	140.00	6.25
3	A10	(a) 1p red brown	550.00	21.00
		On cover		500.00
		Nos. 1-3 (3)	752.50	29.35

1874

4	A11	(b) 25c ultra	47.50	10.00
		On cover		50.00
a.		Double overprint	275.00	
b.		Inverted overprint	275.00	

1875

5	A12	(b) 25c ultra	37.50	3.25
		On cover		50.00
a.		Inverted overprint	95.00	55.00
6	A12	(b) 50c green	45.00	3.50
		On cover		200.00
a.		Inverted overprint	210.00	55.00
7	A12	(b) 1p brown	160.00	17.50
		On cover		500.00
		Nos. 5-7 (3)	242.50	24.25

1876

8	A13	(c) 25c pale violet	4.25	1.90
		On cover		50.00
a.		25c bluish gray	5.50	2.75
		On cover		60.00
9	A13	(c) 50c ultra	10.50	3.25
		On cover		200.00
10	A13	(c) 1p black	75.00	12.00
		On cover		700.00

11 A13 (d) 25c pale violet   35.00   1.40
On cover   100.00
12 A13 (d) 1p black   75.00   11.00
On cover   500.00
Nos. 8-12 (5)   199.75   29.55

Varieties of overprint on Nos. 8-11 include: inverted, double, partly omitted and sideways. Counterfeit overprints exist.

King Alfonso XII
A5   A6

1877   **Typo.**
13 A5 5c yellow brown   10.00   2.75
On cover   100.00
  a. 5c carmine (error)   300.00   —
14 A5 10c carmine   40.00   7.50
On cover   100.00
  a. 10c brown (error)   300.00   —
15 A5 15c deep green   60.00   15.50
On cover   200.00
16 A5 25c ultra   25.00   2.60
On cover   50.00
17 A5 50c bister   40.00   6.50
On cover   300.00
Nos. 13-17 (5)   175.00   34.85

Imperf. examples of Nos. 13-17 are from proof or trial sheets. Value, set $400.

1878   **Dated "1878"**
18 A5 5c ol bister   22.00   22.00
On cover   300.00
19 A5 10c red brown   350.00   120.00
On cover   500.00
20 A5 25c deep green   2.75   1.75
On cover   50.00
21 A5 50c ultra   9.00   3.50
On cover   200.00
22 A5 1p bister   18.00   8.50
On cover   500.00
Nos. 18-22 (5)   401.75   155.75

Imperf. examples of Nos. 18-22 are from proof or trial sheets. Value, set $600.

1879   **Dated "1879"**
23 A5 5c lake   20.00   6.50
On cover   200.00
24 A5 10c dark brown   20.00   6.50
On cover   300.00
25 A5 15c dk olive grn   20.00   6.50
On cover   300.00
26 A5 25c blue   5.00   2.25
On cover   50.00
27 A5 50c dark green   20.00   6.50
On cover   200.00
28 A5 1p gray   110.00   30.00
On cover   500.00
Nos. 23-28 (6)   195.00   58.25

Imperf. examples of Nos. 23-28 are from proof or trial sheets.

1880
29 A6 ¼c deep green   37.50   25.00
On cover   400.00
30 A6 ½c brt rose   9.00   3.25
On cover   300.00
31 A6 1c brown lilac   16.50   13.00
On cover   300.00
32 A6 2c gray lilac   8.50   5.50
On cover   300.00
33 A6 3c buff   9.50   6.00
On cover   300.00
34 A6 4c black   9.50   6.00
On cover   300.00
35 A6 5c gray green   4.75   2.50
On cover   200.00
36 A6 10c rose   5.25   3.00
On cover   200.00
37 A6 15c yellow brn   9.50   4.50
On cover   200.00
38 A6 25c gray blue   4.75   2.10
On cover   50.00
39 A6 40c gray   18.00   22.00
On cover   100.00
40 A6 50c dark brown   40.00   20.00
On cover   400.00
41 A6 1p olive bister   140.00   26.50
On cover   700.00
Nos. 29-41 (13)   312.75   139.35

1881   **Dated "1881"**
42 A6 ½m lake   .55   .50
On cover   300.00
  a. ½m carmine rose   .55   .50
On cover   300.00
43 A6 1m violet   .55   .30
On cover   200.00
  a. 1m reddish violet   .70   .45
On cover   200.00
44 A6 2m pale rose   .75   .50
On cover   200.00
  a. 2m deep rose   .70   .50
On cover   200.00
45 A6 4m brt yellowish green   1.30   .30
On cover   200.00
  a. 4m emerald green   3.50   1.40
On cover   200.00

46 A6 6m brown lilac   1.30   .70
On cover   200.00
  a. 6m pale lilac   3.50   1.40
On cover   200.00
47 A6 8m ultra   3.25   1.75
On cover   200.00
  a. 8m steel blue   5.50   2.10
On cover   200.00
48 A6 1c gray green   4.25   1.50
On cover   100.00
49 A6 2c lake   5.75   4.75
On cover   75.00
50 A6 3c dark brown   12.50   7.75
On cover   100.00
  a. 3c chestnut brown   14.50   7.75
On cover   100.00
  b. Double impression of top inscriptions   30.00   15.00
51 A6 5c grayish ultra   4.75   .55
On cover   50.00
  a. 5c blue   6.50   2.25
On cover   60.00
52 A6 8c brown   4.75   2.25
On cover   100.00
53 A6 10c slate   75.00   11.50
On cover   400.00
54 A6 20c olive bister   90.00   21.00
On cover   700.00
Nos. 42-54 (13)   204.70   53.35

Alfonso XII   Alfonso XIII
A7   A8

1882-86
55 A7 ½m rose   .30   .25
On cover   200.00
  a. ½m salmon rose   .55   .35
On cover   200.00
56 A7 ½m lake ('84)   .90   .40
On cover   200.00
57 A7 1m pale lake   .90   1.10
On cover   200.00
58 A7 1m brt rose ('84)   .30   .25
On cover   200.00
59 A7 2m violet   .30   .25
On cover   200.00
60 A7 4m brown lilac   .30   .25
On cover   150.00
61 A7 6m brown   .45   .25
On cover   150.00
62 A7 8m yellow green   .45   .25
On cover   300.00
63 A7 1c gray green   .30   .25
On cover   100.00
64 A7 2c rose   1.15   .25
On cover   100.00
65 A7 3c yellow   4.25   2.25
On cover   100.00
  a. Cliché of 8c in plate of 3c   120.00
66 A7 3c yellow brn ('84)   4.25   .90
On cover   100.00
  a. Cliché of 8c in plate of 3c   25.00
67 A7 5c gray blue   15.00   1.25
On cover   50.00
68 A7 5c gray bl, 1st retouch ('84)   15.00   3.00
On cover   *75.00*
69 A7 5c gray bl, 2nd retouch ('86)   115.00   5.75
On cover   *75.00*
70 A7 8c gray brown   3.75   .25
On cover   *75.00*
71 A7 10c dark green   3.75   .30
On cover   200.00
72 A7 20c gray lilac   5.50   .30
On cover   500.00
  a. 20c olive brown (error)   *120.00*
73 A7 40c blue   65.00   15.00
On cover   —
74 A7 80c olive bister   70.00   21.00
On cover   —
Nos. 55-74 (20)   306.85   53.50

For differences between the original and the retouched stamps see note on the 1883-86 issue of Cuba.

1890-97
75 A8 ½m black   .30   .25
On cover   150.00
  a. ½m jet black   .25   .25
On cover   150.00
76 A8 ½m olive gray ('92)   .25   .25
On cover   150.00
  a. ½m bronze green   .25   .25
On cover   150.00
77 A8 ½m red brn ('94)   .25   .25
On cover   150.00
78 A8 ½m dull vio ('96)   .25   .25
On cover   150.00
79 A8 1m emerald   .25   .25
On cover   150.00
80 A8 1m dk violet ('92)   .25   .25
On cover   150.00
81 A8 1m ultra ('94)   .25   .25
On cover   100.00
82 A8 1m dp brown ('96)   .25   .25
On cover   100.00
83 A8 2m lilac rose   .25   .25
On cover   100.00
84 A8 2m violet brn ('92)   .25   .25
On cover   100.00
85 A8 2m red orange ('94)   .25   .25
On cover   100.00

86 A8 2m yellow grn ('96)   .25   .25
On cover   100.00
87 A8 4m dk olive grn   11.50   5.75
On cover   200.00
88 A8 4m ultra ('92)   .25   .25
On cover   150.00
89 A8 4m yellow brn ('94)   .25   .25
On cover   100.00
90 A8 4m blue grn ('96)   1.00   .35
On cover   100.00
91 A8 6m dk brown   50.00   15.00
On cover   200.00
92 A8 6m pale rose ('92)   .25   .25
On cover   150.00
93 A8 8m olive bister   35.00   22.00
On cover   200.00
94 A8 8m yellow grn ('92)   .25   .25
On cover   150.00
95 A8 1c yellow brown   .30   .25
On cover   100.00
96 A8 1c blue grn ('91)   .55   .25
On cover   100.00
97 A8 1c violet brn ('94)   6.00   .45
On cover   100.00
98 A8 1c claret ('96)   .65   .25
On cover   100.00
99 A8 2c brownish violet   1.00   .85
On cover   150.00
  a. 2c blackish violet   1.40   1.10
On cover   150.00
100 A8 2c red brown ('92)   .95   .25
On cover   100.00
101 A8 2c lilac ('94)   2.25   .45
On cover   75.00
102 A8 2c orange brn ('96)   .65   .25
On cover   50.00
103 A8 3c slate blue   7.50   1.00
On cover   150.00
104 A8 3c orange ('92)   .90   .25
On cover   100.00
105 A8 3c ol gray ('94)   6.00   .45
On cover   100.00
106 A8 3c blue ('96)   22.00   .35
On cover   100.00
107 A8 3c claret brn ('97)   .30   .25
On cover   100.00
108 A8 4c slate bl ('94)   1.50   .45
On cover   75.00
109 A8 4c gray brn ('96)   .70   .25
On cover   75.00
110 A8 5c brown violet   13.00   .45
On cover   50.00
111 A8 5c yellow grn ('94)   5.75   1.10
On cover   50.00
112 A8 5c blue green ('92)   .90   .25
On cover   50.00
113 A8 5c blue ('96)   .30   .25
On cover   50.00
114 A8 6c orange ('94)   .45   .25
On cover   100.00
115 A8 6c violet ('96)   .35   .25
On cover   100.00
116 A8 8c ultra   16.00   1.75
On cover   150.00
117 A8 8c gray brown ('92)   .25   .25
On cover   75.00
118 A8 8c dull vio ('94)   13.00   5.00
On cover   75.00
119 A8 8c car rose ('96)   3.00   1.50
On cover   75.00
120 A8 10c rose   4.75   1.10
On cover   150.00
  a. 10c salmon rose   11.50   2.75
On cover   150.00
  b. 10c carmine rose   6.00   1.20
On cover   150.00
121 A8 10c lilac rose ('92)   1.50   .35
On cover   150.00
122 A8 20c red orange   5.25   4.75
On cover   400.00
123 A8 20c lilac ('92)   2.50   .55
On cover   400.00
  a. 20c violet   2.50   .55
On cover   400.00
124 A8 20c car rose ('94)   1.50   .45
On cover   400.00
125 A8 20c olive gray ('96)   6.75   1.50
On cover   300.00
126 A8 40c orange   200.00   57.50
On cover   —
127 A8 40c slate blue ('92)   5.75   4.00
On cover   —
128 A8 40c claret ('94)   7.50   13.50
On cover   800.00
129 A8 40c salmon ('96)   7.00   1.60
On cover   500.00
130 A8 80c yellow green   750.00   240.00
On cover   5,000.
131 A8 80c orange ('92)   14.50   11.50
132 A8 80c black ('97)   27.50   23.50

Imperforates of type A8 were not issued and are variously considered to be proofs or printer's waste.
For overprints see Nos. 154A-170, MR1-MR13.

Landing of Columbus on Puerto Rico — A9

1893   **Litho.**   *Perf. 12*
133 A9 3c dark green   250.00   60.00
On cover, philatelic   200.00
On cover, commercial   500.00

400th anniversary, landing of Columbus on Puerto Rico. Counterfeits exist.

Alfonso XIII — A10

1898   **Typo.**
135 A10 1m orange brown   .25   .25
On cover   100.00
136 A10 2m orange brown   .25   .25
On cover   100.00
137 A10 3m orange brown   .25   .25
On cover   150.00
138 A10 4m orange brown   2.40   .75
On cover   150.00
139 A10 5m orange brown   .25   .25
On cover   150.00
140 A10 1c black violet   .25   .25
On cover   100.00
  a. Tête bêche pair   *1,700.*
  b. Pair, #140 & Philippines #197 (cliche error)   *1,500.*
141 A10 2c dk blue green   .25   .25
On cover   100.00
142 A10 3c dk brown   .25   .25
On cover   75.00
143 A10 4c orange   2.40   1.60
On cover   100.00
144 A10 5c brt rose   .30   .25
On cover   75.00
145 A10 6c dark blue   .85   .25
On cover   100.00
146 A10 8c gray brown   .30   .25
On cover   100.00
147 A10 10c vermilion   .30   .25
On cover   150.00
148 A10 15c dull olive grn   .30   .25
On cover   200.00
149 A10 20c maroon   3.00   .75
On cover   200.00
150 A10 40c violet   2.25   2.00
On cover   500.00
151 A10 60c black   2.25   2.00
152 A10 80c red brown   8.50   7.25
153 A10 1p yellow green   18.00   14.50
154 A10 2p slate blue   50.00   22.00
Nos. 135-154 (20)   92.60   53.85

Nos. 135-154 exist imperf. Value, set $1,300.

Stamps of 1890-97 Handstamped in Rose or Violet

1898
154A A8 ½m dull violet   19.50   11.00
On cover   300.00
155 A8 1m deep brown   1.75   1.75
On cover   300.00
156 A8 2m yellow green   .50   .50
On cover   200.00
157 A8 4m blue green   .50   .50
On cover   300.00
158 A8 1c claret   5.00   5.00
On cover   300.00
159 A8 2c orange brown   .70   *1.00*
On cover   300.00
160 A8 3c blue   42.50   18.00
161 A8 3c claret brn   3.25   3.25
On cover   300.00
162 A8 4c gray brn   .80   .80
On cover   300.00
163 A8 4c slate blue   23.00   16.50
164 A8 5c yellow grn   11.00   8.50
165 A8 5c blue   .80   .80
On cover   300.00
166 A8 6c violet   .80   .55
On cover   300.00
  a. Inverted Ovpt., on cover   —
167 A8 8c car rose (V)   1.40   1.00
On cover   200.00
  a. Rose overprint   21.00   21.00
On cover   1,000.
168 A8 20c olive gray   1.40   1.40
On cover   —
169 A8 40c salmon   3.25   3.25
On cover   —

170	A8	80c black	45.00	27.50
	On cover			2,000.
	Nos. 154A-170 (17)		161.15	101.30

As usual with handstamps there are many inverted, double and similar varieties. Counterfeits of Nos. 154A-170 abound.

Issued under U.S. Administration
PROVISIONAL ISSUES
Ponce Issue

A11

Handstamped

1898		Unwmk.		Imperf.
200	A11	5c violet, yellowish	7,500.	

The only way No. 200 is known used is handstamped on envelopes. Unused stamps always have a violet control mark. Used envelopes do not have the control mark. The same handstamp used to prepare No. 200 also is known handstamped on an unused envelope, also without the control mark. Research into whether the envelopes represent prepaid postmaster provisional usage is ongoing.

Uses on 2c U.S. stamps on cover were strictly as a cancellation, not as provisional postage.

Dangerous forgeries exist.

Coamo Issue

A12

Types of "5":
I — Curved flag. Pos. 2, 3, 4, 5.
II — Flag turns down at right. Pos. 1, 9, 10.
III — Fancy outlined "5." Pos. 6, 7.
IV — Flag curls into ball at right. Pos. 8.

Coamo Issue
Typeset, setting of 10

1898, Aug.		Unwmk.		Imperf.
201	A12	5c black	650.	1,050.
	On cover			27,500.

See the Scott U.S. Specialized Catalogue for more detailed listings.

The stamps bear the control mark "F. Santiago" in violet. About 500 were issued.

Dangerous forgeries exist.

Regular Issue

United States Nos. 279, 279Bf, 281, 272 and 282C Overprinted in Black at 36 degree angle

1899		Wmk. 191		Perf. 12
210	A87	1c yellow green	6.00	1.40
a.	Overprint at 25 degree angle		8.00	2.25
211	A88	2c redsh car, type IV	5.00	1.25
a.	Overprint at 25 degree angle, Mar. 15		6.50	2.25
212	A91	5c blue	12.50	2.50
213	A93	8c violet brown	40.00	17.50
a.	Overprint at 25 degree angle		45.00	19.00
c.	"PORTO RIC"		150.00	110.00
214	A94	10c brown, type I	24.00	6.00
	Nos. 210-214 (5)		87.50	28.65

Misspellings of the overprint on Nos. 210-214 (PORTO RICU, PORTU RICO, FORTO RICO) are actually broken letters.

United States Nos. 279 and 279B Overprinted Diagonally in Black

1900				
215	A87	1c yellow green	7.50	1.40
	On cover			50.00

216	A88	2c red, type IV	5.50	2.00
	On cover			50.00
b.	Inverted overprint			12,500.

No. 216b is unique.
Stamps of Puerto Rico were replaced by those of the United States.

POSTAGE DUE STAMPS

United States Nos. J38, J39 and J42 Overprinted in Black at 36 degree angle

1899		Wmk. 191		Perf. 12
J1	D2	1c deep claret	22.50	5.50
	On cover			125.00
a.	Overprint at 25 degree angle		22.50	7.50
J2	D2	2c deep claret	20.00	6.00
	On cover			250.00
a.	Overprint at 25 degree angle		20.00	7.00
J3	D2	10c deep claret	180.00	55.00
	On cover			—
a.	Overprint at 25 degree angle		160.00	75.00
	Nos. J1-J3 (3)		222.50	66.50

WAR TAX STAMPS

Stamps of 1890-94 Overprinted or Surcharged by Handstamp

1898		Unwmk.		Perf. 14
		Purple Overprint or Surcharge		
MR1	A8	1c yellow brn	8.00	5.75
	On cover			
MR2	A8	2c on 2m orange	3.75	3.00
	On cover			300.00
MR3	A8	2c on 5c blue grn	5.00	3.50
	On cover			
MR4	A8	2c dark violet	.95	.95
	On cover			300.00
MR5	A8	2c lilac	.90	.90
	On cover			300.00
MR6	A8	2c red brown	.50	.30
	On cover			200.00
MR7	A8	5c blue green	1.90	1.90
	On cover			300.00
MR8	A8	5c on 5c bl grn	8.75	6.00
	On cover			300.00
		Rose Surcharge		
MR9	A8	2c on 2m orange	1.90	1.90
	On cover			300.00
MR10	A8	5c on 1m dk vio	.30	.30
	On cover			300.00
MR11	A8	5c on 1m dl bl	.85	.85
	On cover			300.00
		Magenta Surcharge		
MR12	A8	5c on 1m dk vio	.50	.30
	On cover			300.00
MR13	A8	5c on 1m dl bl	3.00	3.00
	On cover			300.00
	Nos. MR1-MR13 (13)		36.30	28.65

Nos. MR2-MR13 were issued as War Tax Stamps (2c on letters or sealed mail; 5c on telegrams) but, during the early days of the American occupation, they were accepted for ordinary postage.

Double, inverted and similar varieties of overprints are numerous in this issue.

Counterfeit overprints exist.

QUELIMANE

ˌkel-ə-ˈmän-ə

LOCATION — A district of the Mozambique Province in Portuguese East Africa
GOVT. — Part of the Portuguese East Africa Colony
AREA — 39,800 sq. mi.
POP. — 877,000 (approx.)
CAPITAL — Quelimane

This district was formerly a part of Zambezia. Quelimane stamps were replaced by those of Mozambique.

100 Centavos = 1 Escudo

Vasco da Gama Issue

Various Portuguese Colonies Surcharged

1913		Unwmk.	Perf. 12½ to 16	
		On Stamps of Macao		
1	CD20	¼c on ½a bl grn	4.00	4.00
2	CD21	½c on 1a red	3.00	3.00
3	CD22	1c on 2a red vio	3.00	3.00
4	CD23	2½c on 4a yel grn	3.00	3.00
5	CD24	5c on 8a dk bl	3.00	3.00
6	CD25	7½c on 12a vio brn	5.00	5.00
7	CD26	10c on 16a bis brn	3.00	3.00
a.	Inverted surcharge		45.00	
8	CD27	15c on 24a bister	3.00	3.00
	Nos. 1-8 (8)		27.00	27.00
		On Stamps of Portuguese Africa		
9	CD20	¼c on 2½r bl grn	2.50	3.00
10	CD21	½c on 5r red	2.50	3.00
11	CD22	1c on 10r red vio	2.50	3.00
12	CD23	2½c on 25r yel grn	2.50	3.00
13	CD24	5c on 50r dk bl	2.50	3.00
14	CD25	7½c on 75r vio brn	4.00	4.50
15	CD26	10c on 100r bister	2.75	3.00
16	CD27	15c on 150r bister	2.75	3.00
	Nos. 9-16 (8)		22.00	25.50
		On Stamps of Timor		
17	CD20	¼c on ½a bl grn	2.50	3.00
18	CD21	½c on 1a red	2.50	3.00
19	CD22	1c on 2a red vio	2.50	3.00
20	CD23	2½c on 4a yel grn	2.50	3.00
21	CD24	5c on 8a dk bl	2.50	3.00
22	CD25	7½c on 12a vio brn	4.00	4.50
23	CD26	10c on 16a bis brn	2.75	3.00
24	CD27	15c on 24a bister	2.75	3.00
	Nos. 17-24 (8)		22.00	25.50
	Nos. 1-24 (24)		66.00	80.00

Ceres — A1

1914		Typo.	Perf. 15x14	
		Name and Value in Black		
		Chalky Paper		
25	A1	¼c olive brown	1.50	2.75
	Never hinged		2.25	
26	A1	½c black	1.75	2.75
	Never hinged		2.50	
27	A1	1c blue green	1.75	2.75
	Never hinged		2.50	
a.	Imperf.			
28	A1	1½c lilac brown	2.00	3.00
	Never hinged		3.00	
29	A1	2c carmine	2.10	3.00
	Never hinged		3.25	
30	A1	2½c light violet	1.25	1.50
	Never hinged		1.90	
31	A1	5c deep blue	2.00	3.00
	Never hinged		3.75	
32	A1	7½c yellow brown	3.00	3.00
	Never hinged		4.50	
33	A1	8c slate	3.00	3.00
	Never hinged		4.50	
34	A1	10c orange brown	3.00	3.00
	Never hinged		4.50	
35	A1	15c plum	3.50	4.50
	Never hinged		5.25	
36	A1	20c yellow green	3.00	2.50
	Never hinged		4.50	
37	A1	30c brown, green	6.00	8.00
	Never hinged		9.00	
38	A1	40c brown, pink	7.00	9.00
	Never hinged		10.50	
39	A1	50c orange, salmon	9.00	10.00
	Never hinged		13.50	
40	A1	1e green, blue	12.50	11.00
	Never hinged		19.00	
	Nos. 25-40 (16)		62.35	72.75
		Ordinary Paper		
25B	A1	¼c olive brown	1.75	2.75
	Never hinged		2.50	
27B	A1	1c blue green	2.50	2.75
	Never hinged		3.75	
32B	A1	7½c yellow brown	3.50	3.00
	Never hinged		5.25	
34B	A1	10c orange brown	2.00	3.00
	Never hinged		5.25	
36B	A1	20c yellow green	4.50	2.50
	Never hinged		6.75	
	Nos. 25B-36B (5)		14.25	14.00

REUNION

LOCATION — An island in the Indian Ocean about 400 miles east of Madagascar
GOVT. — French Colony
AREA — 970 sq. mi.

POP. — 490,000 (est. 1974)
CAPITAL — St. Denis

100 Centimes = 1 Franc

A1　　　　　　　A2

1852		Unwmk.	Typo.	Imperf.
1	A1	15c black, blue	39,000.	25,000.
	On cover			45,000.
2	A2	30c black, blue	39,000.	25,000.
	On cover			35,000.

Four varieties of each value.
The reprints are printed on a more bluish paper than the originals. They have a frame of a thick and a thin line, instead of one thick and two thin lines. Value, $62.50 each.

Stamps of French Colonies
Surcharged or Overprinted in Black

a　　　　　　　b

1885				
3	A1(a)	5c on 40c org, yelsh	450.00	375.00
	On cover			1,200.
a.	Inverted surcharge		2,250.	2,100.
b.	Double surcharge		2,250.	2,100.
4	A1(a)	25c on 40c org, yelsh	70.00	55.00
	On cover			950.00
a.	Inverted surcharge		1,000.	900.00
b.	Double surcharge		1,000.	900.00
5	A5(a)	5c on 30c brn, yelsh	70.00	57.50
	On cover			950.00
a.	"5" inverted		3,500.	3,000.
b.	Double surcharge		1,100.	900.00
c.	Inverted surcharge		1,000.	900.00
6	A4(a)	5c on 40c org, yelsh (I)	62.50	45.00
	On cover			950.00
a.	5c on 40c org, yelsh (II)		2,500.	2,500.
b.	Inverted surcharge (I)		1,100.	900.00
c.	Double surcharge (I)		1,100.	900.00
7	A8(a)	5c on 40c org, yelsh	22.50	18.00
	On cover			950.00
8	A8(a)	5c on 40c ver, straw	135.00	115.00
	On cover			950.00
a.	Inverted surcharge		950.00	850.00
b.	Double surcharge		925.00	850.00
9	A8(a)	10c on 40c ver, straw	27.50	22.50
	On cover			950.00
a.	Inverted surcharge		950.00	850.00
b.	Double surcharge		950.00	850.00
10	A8(a)	20c on 30c brn, yelsh	90.00	75.00
	On cover			1,050.

Overprint Type "b"
With or Without Accent on "E"

1891				
11	A4	40c org, yelsh (I)	575.00	550.00
	On cover			1,750.
a.	40c orange, yelsh (II)		6,750.	6,750.
b.	Double overprint		750.00	750.00
12	A7	80c car, pnksh	80.00	62.50
	Never hinged		150.00	
	On cover			400.00
13	A8	30c brn, yelsh	52.50	52.50
	Never hinged		100.00	
	On cover			325.00
14	A8	40c ver, straw	42.50	42.50
	Never hinged		80.00	
	On cover			825.00
a.	With accent on "E"		260.00	210.00
15	A8	75c car, rose	475.00	475.00
a.	With accent on "E"		1,200.	1,200.
16	A8	1fr brnz grn, straw	62.50	52.50
	Never hinged		110.00	
	On cover			325.00
a.	With accent on "E"		425.00	425.00
		Perf. 14x13½		
17	A9	1c blk, lil bl	4.75	4.00
	Never hinged		10.50	
	On cover			475.00
a.	Inverted overprint		60.00	60.00
	Never hinged		125.00	
b.	Double overprint		52.50	52.50
	Never hinged		110.00	
18	A9	2c brn, buff	6.50	5.00
	Never hinged		13.50	
	On cover			475.00
a.	Inverted overprint		40.00	40.00
	Never hinged		85.00	
19	A9	4c claret, lav	10.00	8.00
	On cover			21.00
				475.00

a.	Inverted overprint		72.50	72.50
	Never hinged		150.00	
20	A9 5c grn, *grnsh*		11.50	9.00
	Never hinged		22.50	
	On cover			300.00
a.	Inverted overprint		60.00	60.00
	Never hinged		125.00	
b.	Double overprint		60.00	57.50
	Never hinged		125.00	
21	A9 10c blk, *lav*		40.00	8.00
	Never hinged		80.00	
	On cover			300.00
a.	Inverted overprint		90.00	80.00
	Never hinged		180.00	
b.	Double overprint		100.00	80.00
	Never hinged		200.00	
22	A9 15c blue		57.50	9.00
	On cover			300.00
a.	Inverted overprint		120.00	110.00
	Never hinged			
23	A9 20c red, *grn*		45.00	30.00
	Never hinged		85.00	
	On cover			190.00
a.	Inverted overprint		175.00	150.00
b.	Double overprint		175.00	150.00
24	A9 25c blk, *rose*		50.00	7.25
	Never hinged		92.50	
	On cover			240.00
a.	Inverted overprint		125.00	120.00
25	A9 35c dp vio, *yel*		45.00	35.00
	Never hinged		85.00	
	On cover			300.00
b.	Inverted overprint		180.00	175.00
26	A9 40c red, *straw*		72.50	62.50
	Never hinged		150.00	
	On cover			475.00
a.	Inverted overprint		240.00	225.00
27	A9 75c car, *rose*		675.00	575.00
	On cover			1,100.
a.	Inverted overprint		1,600.	1,400.
28	A9 1fr brnz grn, *straw*		575.00	500.00
	On cover			1,500.
a.	Inverted overprint		1,600.	1,500.
b.	Double overprint		1,500.	1,500.

For surcharges see Nos. 29-33, 53-55.

Overprinted "RUNION"

17c	A9 1c blk, *lil bl*		27.50	27.50
	Never hinged		57.50	
18c	A9 2c brn, *buff*		32.50	32.50
	Never hinged		70.00	
19c	A9 4c claret, *lav*		37.50	37.50
	Never hinged		80.00	
20c	A9 5c grn, *grnsh*		37.50	32.50
	Never hinged		80.00	
21c	A9 10c blk, *lav*		72.50	70.00
	Never hinged		150.00	
22c	A9 15c blue		90.00	85.00
	Never hinged		180.00	
23c	A9 20c red, *grn*		100.00	100.00
24c	A9 25c blk, *rose*		80.00	70.00
	Never hinged		160.00	
25c	A9 35c dp vio, *yel*		72.50	72.50
	Never hinged		150.00	
26c	A9 40c red, *straw*		240.00	240.00
27c	A9 75c car, *rose*		1,600.	1,500.
28c	A9 1fr brnz grn, *straw*		1,600.	1,500.

Overprinted "REUNIONR"

13d	A8 30c brn, *yelsh*		525.00	525.00
14d	A8 40c ver, *straw*		500.00	500.00
15d	A8 75c car, *rose*		1,600.	1,600.
16d	A8 1fr brnz grn, *straw*		1,000.	1,000.
17d	A9 1c blk, *lil bl*		32.50	32.50
	Never hinged		70.00	
18d	A9 2c brn, *buff*		32.50	32.50
	Never hinged		70.00	
19d	A9 4c claret, *lav*		37.50	37.50
	Never hinged		80.00	
20d	A9 5c grn, *grnsh*		37.50	32.50
	Never hinged		80.00	
21d	A9 10c blk, *lav*		72.50	70.00
	Never hinged		150.00	
22d	A9 15c blue		90.00	85.00
	Never hinged		190.00	
23d	A9 20c red, *grn*		100.00	100.00
24d	A9 25c blk, *rose*		80.00	70.00
	Never hinged		160.00	
25d	A9 35c dp vio, *yel*		72.50	72.50
	Never hinged		150.00	
26d	A9 40c red, *straw*		200.00	200.00
27d	A9 75c car, *rose*		1,600.	1,500.
28d	A9 1fr brnz grn, *straw*		1,600.	1,500.

Overprinted "REUNIOU"

17e	A9 1c blk, *lil bl*		35.00	35.00
	Never hinged		72.50	
20e	A9 5c grn, *grnsh*		35.00	35.00
	Never hinged		80.00	
24e	A9 25c blk, *rose*		97.50	90.00
	Never hinged		190.00	
27e	A9 75c car, *rose*		1,700.	1,500.
28e	A9 1fr brnz grn, *straw*		1,750.	1,500.

Overprinted "REUNOIN"

17f	A9 1c blk, *lil bl*		32.50	15.00
	Never hinged		70.00	
18f	A9 2c brn, *buff*		32.50	15.00
	Never hinged		70.00	
19f	A9 4c claret, *lav*		35.00	20.00
	Never hinged		80.00	
20f	A9 5c grn, *grnsh*		40.00	17.50
	Never hinged		85.00	
21f	A9 10c blk, *lav*		72.50	45.00
	Never hinged		150.00	
22f	A9 15c blue		90.00	50.00
	Never hinged		180.00	
23f	A9 20c red, *grn*		100.00	60.00
24f	A9 25c blk, *rose*		100.00	45.00
	Never hinged		200.00	
25f	A9 35c dp vio, *yel*		90.00	45.00
	Never hinged		190.00	
26f	A9 40c red, *straw*		225.00	225.00
27f	A9 75c car, *rose*		1,750.	1,500.

28f	A9 1fr brnz grn, *straw*		1,750.	1,500.

Overprinted "RUENION"

15g	A8 75c car, *rose*		2,350.	2,350.
17g	A9 1c blk, *lil bl*		27.50	27.50
	Never hinged		55.00	
18g	A9 2c brn, *buff*		45.00	45.00
	Never hinged		92.50	
19g	A9 4c claret, *lav*		45.00	45.00
	Never hinged		92.50	
20g	A9 5c grn, *grnsh*		72.50	65.00
	Never hinged		150.00	
21g	A9 10c blk, *lav*		80.00	72.50
	Never hinged		160.00	
22g	A9 15c blue		110.00	100.00
26g	A9 40c red, *straw*		200.00	200.00

Overprinted "EUNION"

11h	A4 40c org, *yelsh* (I)		4,500.	4,500.
12h	A7 80c car, *pnksh*		650.00	450.00
14h	A8 40c ver, *straw*		190.00	125.00
15h	A8 75c car, *rose*		2,400.	1,750.
17h	A9 1c blk, *lil bl*		27.50	15.00
	Never hinged		55.00	
18h	A9 2c brn, *buff*		37.50	15.00
	Never hinged		80.00	
19h	A9 4c claret, *lav*		52.50	27.50
	Never hinged		110.00	
20h	A9 5c grn, *grnsh*		60.00	27.50
	Never hinged		125.00	
21h	A9 10c blk, *lav*		80.00	72.50
	Never hinged		160.00	
22h	A9 15c blue		90.00	50.00
	Never hinged		180.00	
23h	A9 20c red, *grn*		90.00	50.00
	Never hinged		180.00	
24h	A9 25c blk, *rose*		110.00	55.00
25h	A9 35c dp vio, *yel*		90.00	50.00
	Never hinged		180.00	
26h	A9 40c red, *straw*		200.00	110.00
27h	A9 75c car, *rose*		1,750.	1,500.
28h	A9 1fr brnz grn, *straw*		1,750.	1,500.

Overprinted "ERUNION"

17i	A9 1c blk, *lil bl*		27.50	27.50
	Never hinged		55.00	
18i	A9 2c brn, *buff*		32.50	32.50
	Never hinged		70.00	
19i	A9 4c claret, *lav*		52.50	52.50
	Never hinged		110.00	
20i	A9 5c grn, *grnsh*		60.00	57.50
	Never hinged		125.00	
21i	A9 10c blk, *lav*		72.50	72.50
	Never hinged		150.00	
22i	A9 15c blue		90.00	72.50
	Never hinged		180.00	
23i	A9 20c red, *grn*		110.00	100.00
24i	A9 25c blk, *rose*		110.00	90.00
	Never hinged		225.00	
25i	A9 35c dp vio, *yel*		90.00	90.00
	Never hinged		180.00	
26i	A9 40c red, *straw*		200.00	200.00
27i	A9 75c car, *rose*		1,750.	1,500.
28i	A9 1fr brnz grn, *straw*		1,750.	1,500.

Overprinted "REUNIN"

18j	A9 2c brn, *buff*		32.50	32.50
	Never hinged		70.00	
23j	A9 20c red, *grn*		87.50	80.00
	Never hinged		70.00	

For surcharges see Nos. 29-33, 53-55.

No. 23 with Additional Surcharge in Black

c   d

e   f

1891

29	A9(c) 02c on 20c red, *grn*		14.50	14.50
	Never hinged		27.50	
	On cover			300.00
a.	Inverted surcharge		90.00	90.00
	Never hinged		140.00	
b.	No "c" after "02"		57.50	57.50
	Never hinged		100.00	
c.	Overprinted "RUNION"		90.00	90.00
	Never hinged		180.00	
30	A9(c) 15c on 20c red, *grn*		18.00	18.00
	Never hinged		35.00	
	On cover			300.00
a.	Inverted surcharge		70.00	70.00
	Never hinged		125.00	
b.	No "c" after "15"		60.00	60.00
	Never hinged		120.00	
c.	Overprinted "RUNION"		140.00	140.00
31	A9(d) 2c on 20c red, *grn*		5.00	5.00
	Never hinged		10.00	
	On cover			300.00

32	A9(e) 2c on 20c red, *grn*		6.00	5.75
	Never hinged		11.50	
	On cover			300.00
a.	Overprinted "RUENION"		52.50	52.50
	Never hinged		110.00	
b.	Overprinted "RUNOIN"		52.50	52.50
	Never hinged		110.00	
33	A9(f) 2c on 20c red, *grn*		10.00	10.00
	On cover			300.00
	Nos. 29-33 (5)		53.50	53.25

Navigation and Commerce — A14

1892-1905   Typo.   Perf. 14x13½
Name of Colony in Blue or Carmine

34	A14 1c blk, *lil bl*		2.00	1.25
	Never hinged		3.25	
	On cover			125.00
35	A14 2c brn, *buff*		2.00	1.25
	Never hinged		3.25	
	On cover			125.00
36	A14 4c claret, *lav*		3.25	2.25
	Never hinged		4.50	
	On cover			125.00
37	A14 5c grn, *grnsh*		7.25	2.25
	Never hinged		12.50	
	On cover			105.00
38	A14 5c yel grn ('00)		1.75	1.75
	Never hinged		2.40	
	On cover			12.50
39	A14 10c blk, *lav*		9.50	3.50
	Never hinged		17.50	
	On cover			92.50
40	A14 10c red ('00)		4.50	4.50
	Never hinged		5.50	
	On cover			25.00
41	A14 15c bl, quadrille paper		30.00	3.50
	Never hinged		60.00	
	On cover			80.00
42	A14 15c gray ('00)		10.00	3.50
	Never hinged		15.00	
	On cover			25.00
43	A14 20c red, *grn*		20.00	9.00
	Never hinged		40.00	
	On cover			225.00
	On cover, single franking			340.00
44	A14 25c blk, *rose*		22.50	3.50
	Never hinged		42.50	
	On cover			190.00
	On cover, single franking			310.00
a.	"Reunion" double		425.00	450.00
	Never hinged		675.00	
45	A14 25c blue ('00)		29.00	27.50
	Never hinged		45.00	
	On cover			250.00
	On cover, single franking			400.00
46	A14 30c brn, *bis*		23.00	12.00
	Never hinged		47.50	
	On cover			160.00
	On cover, single franking			250.00
47	A14 40c red, *straw*		32.50	19.00
	Never hinged		60.00	
	On cover			225.00
	On cover, single franking			300.00
48	A14 50c car, *rose*		80.00	42.50
	Never hinged		150.00	
	On cover			225.00
	On cover, single franking			280.00
a.	"Reunion" in red and blue		500.00	500.00
49	A14 50c brn, *az* ("Reunion" in car) ('00)		57.50	50.00
	Never hinged		105.00	
	On cover			425.00
	On cover, single franking			550.00
50	A14 50c brn, *az* ("Reunion" in bl) ('05)		57.50	50.00
	Never hinged		105.00	
	On cover			440.00
	On cover, single franking			625.00
51	A14 75c dp vio, *org*		62.50	45.00
	Never hinged		125.00	
	On cover			290.00
	On cover, single franking			375.00
a.	"Reunion" double		375.00	375.00
52	A14 1fr brnz grn, *straw*		50.00	35.00
	Never hinged		105.00	
	On cover			260.00
	On cover, single franking			350.00
a.	"Reunion" double		360.00	375.00
	Nos. 34-52 (19)		504.75	317.25

Perf. 13½x14 stamps are counterfeits.
For surcharges and overprint see Nos. 56-59, 99-106, Q1.

French Colonies No. 52 Surcharged in Black

g   h

j

1893

53	A9(g) 2c on 20c red, *grn*		3.25	3.25
	Never hinged		5.50	
	On cover			250.00
54	A9(h) 2c on 20c red, *grn*		6.00	6.00
	Never hinged		9.50	
	On cover			250.00
55	A9(j) 2c on 20c red, *grn*		22.50	22.50
	Never hinged		45.00	
	On cover			250.00
	Nos. 53-55 (3)		31.75	31.75

Reunion Nos. 47-48, 51-52 Surcharged in Black

1901

56	A14 5c on 40c red, *straw*		7.00	7.00
	Never hinged		11.00	
	On cover			60.00
a.	Inverted surcharge		47.50	47.50
	Never hinged		92.50	
b.	No bar		240.00	240.00
c.	Thin "5"		—	
d.	"5" inverted		1,400.	1,200.
57	A14 5c on 50c car, *rose*		7.75	7.25
	Never hinged		13.50	
	On cover			80.00
a.	Inverted surcharge		47.50	47.50
	Never hinged		92.50	
b.	No bar		240.00	240.00
c.	Thin "5"		—	
58	A14 15c on 75c vio, *org*		22.50	22.50
	Never hinged		37.50	
	On cover			150.00
a.	Inverted surcharge		57.50	57.50
	Never hinged		105.00	
b.	No bar		240.00	240.00
c.	Thin "5" and small "1"		47.50	47.50
	Never hinged		87.50	
d.	As "c," inverted		800.00	800.00
59	A14 15c on 1fr brnz grn, *straw*		19.00	19.00
	Never hinged		35.00	
	On cover			150.00
a.	Inverted surcharge		57.50	57.50
	Never hinged		105.00	
b.	No bar		240.00	240.00
c.	Thin "5" and small "1"		47.50	47.50
	Never hinged		85.00	
d.	As "c," inverted		—	
	Nos. 56-59 (4)		56.25	55.75

Map of Réunion A19

Coat of Arms and View of St. Denis A20

View of St. Pierre A21

1907-30   Typo.

60	A19 1c vio & lt rose		.30	.30
	Never hinged		.45	
	On cover			42.50
a.	1c violet & dark rose		.45	.45
	Never hinged		.70	
	On cover			42.50
61	A19 2c brn & ultra		.30	.30
	Never hinged		.45	
	On cover, single franking			400.00
62	A19 4c brn & red		.40	.40
	Never hinged		.65	
	On cover			42.50
a.	Center double		225.00	
	Never hinged		350.00	
63	A19 5c grn & red		1.35	.40
	Never hinged		2.00	
	On cover			50.00

64	A19	5c org & vio ('22)	.30	.30
		Never hinged	.55	
		On cover		12.50
65	A19	10c car & grn	2.75	.40
		Never hinged	4.00	
		On cover		19.00
66	A19	10c grn ('22)	.30	.30
		Never hinged	.55	
		On cover		10.00
a.		10c green & blue green	14.00	14.00
		Never hinged	21.00	
67	A19	10c brn red & org red, *bluish* ('26)	.70	.70
		Never hinged	1.00	
		On cover		12.50
68	A19	15c blk & ultra ('17)	.55	.40
		Never hinged	.80	
		On cover		12.50
a.		Center double	250.00	250.00
		Never hinged	400.00	
69	A19	15c gray grn & bl grn ('26)	.40	.40
		Never hinged	.70	
		On cover		8.75
70	A19	15c bl & lt red ('28)	.55	.45
		Never hinged	.70	
		On cover		10.00
71	A20	20c gray grn & bl grn	.45	.45
		Never hinged	.70	
		On cover		15.00
a.		Center omitted	1,100.	1,100.
72	A20	25c dp bl & vio brn	7.00	4.00
		Never hinged	11.00	
		On cover		29.00
		On cover, single franking		80.00
73	A20	25c lt brn & bl ('22)	.55	.55
		Never hinged	.85	
		On cover		8.75
74	A20	30c yel brn & grn	1.50	1.00
		Never hinged	2.10	
		On cover		30.00
		On cover, single franking		92.50
75	A20	30c rose & pale rose ('22)	1.50	1.50
		Never hinged	2.25	
		On cover		22.50
		On cover, single franking		80.00
76	A20	30c gray & car rose ('26)	.55	.55
		Never hinged	.70	
		On cover		10.00
77	A20	30c dp grn & yel grn ('28)	1.20	1.20
		Never hinged	1.75	
		On cover		10.00
78	A20	35c ol grn & bl	1.75	1.10
		Never hinged	2.50	
		On cover		37.50
		On cover, single franking		105.00
79	A20	40c gray grn & brn ('25)	.70	.70
		Never hinged	1.00	
		On cover		19.00
80	A20	45c vio & car rose	1.90	1.10
		Never hinged	2.75	
		On cover		25.00
		On cover, single franking		62.50
81	A20	45c red brn & ver ('25)	.90	.90
		Never hinged	1.25	
		On cover		22.50
82	A20	45c vio & red org ('28)	3.00	2.75
		Never hinged	4.50	
		On cover		12.50
83	A20	50c red brn & ultra	5.00	1.75
		Never hinged	6.50	
		On cover		37.50
		On cover, single franking		80.00
84	A20	50c bl & ultra ('22)	1.40	1.40
		Never hinged	2.10	
		On cover		32.50
		On cover, single franking		80.00
85	A20	50c yel & vio ('26)	1.10	1.10
		Never hinged	1.75	
		On cover		30.00
86	A20	60c dk bl & yel brn ('25)	1.10	1.10
		Never hinged	1.75	
		On cover		32.50
		On cover, single franking		92.50
87	A20	65c vio & lt bl ('28)	1.60	1.40
		Never hinged	2.00	
		On cover		15.00
88	A20	75c red & car rose	.80	.70
		Never hinged	1.25	
		On cover		42.50
		On cover, single franking		92.50
89	A20	75c ol brn & red vio ('28)	2.50	2.25
		Never hinged	3.25	
		On cover		12.50
90	A20	90c brn red & brt red ('30)	9.00	8.25
		Never hinged	12.00	
		On cover		50.00
		On cover, single franking		92.50
91	A21	1fr ol grn & bl	1.50	1.40
		Never hinged	2.00	
		On cover		50.00
		On cover, single franking		105.00

92	A21	1fr blue ('25)	.95	.95
		Never hinged	1.60	
		On cover		25.00
		On cover, single franking		62.50
93	A21	1fr yel brn & red ('26)	1.60	1.40
		Never hinged	2.40	
		On cover		32.50
		On cover, single franking		62.50
94	A21	1.10fr org brn & rose lil ('28)	1.50	1.40
		Never hinged	2.00	
		On cover		62.50
		On cover, single franking		190.00
95	A21	1.50fr dk bl & ultra ('30)	16.00	16.00
		Never hinged	19.00	
		On cover		75.00
		On cover, single franking		110.00
96	A21	2fr red & grn	6.75	4.25
		Never hinged	7.25	
		On cover		55.00
		On cover, single franking		92.50
97	A21	3fr red vio ('30)	14.50	9.50
		Never hinged	17.50	
		On cover		67.50
		On cover, single franking		110.00
98	A21	5fr car & vio brn	11.50	6.75
		Never hinged	14.50	
		On cover		87.50
		On cover, single franking		160.00
		Nos. 60-98 (39)	105.60	79.05

For surcharges see Nos. 107-121, 178-180 (in Scott Standard catalogue, Vol. 5), B1-B3.

Stamps of 1892-1900 Surcharged in Black or Carmine

1912
Spacing between figures of surcharge 1.5mm (5c), 2mm (10c)

99	A14	5c on 2c brn, *buff*	1.60	1.60
		Never hinged	2.25	
		On cover		42.50
100	A14	5c on 15c gray (C)	1.40	1.40
		Never hinged	2.25	
		On cover		42.50
a.		Inverted surcharge	210.00	210.00
101	A14	5c on 20c red, grn	2.40	2.40
		Never hinged	4.00	
		On cover		105.00
102	A14	5c on 25c blk, rose (C)	1.60	1.60
		Never hinged	2.50	
		On cover		92.50
103	A14	5c on 30c brn, bis (C)	1.40	1.40
		Never hinged	2.40	
		On cover		80.00
104	A14	10c on 40c red, straw	1.40	1.40
		Never hinged	2.40	
		On cover		80.00
105	A14	10c on 50c brn, az (C)	5.75	5.75
		Never hinged	9.50	
		On cover		105.00
106	A14	10c on 75c dp vio, org	9.50	9.50
		Never hinged	14.50	
		On cover		110.00
		Nos. 99-106 (8)	25.05	25.05

Spacing between figures of surcharge 2.25mm (5c), 2.75mm (10c)

99a	A14	5c on 2c brn, *buff*	30.00	30.00
		Never hinged	55.00	
100b	A14	5c on 15c gray (C)	30.00	30.00
		Never hinged	55.00	
101a	A14	5c on 20c red, grn	325.00	325.00
		Never hinged	550.00	
102a	A14	5c on 25c blk, rose (C)	105.00	105.00
		Never hinged	190.00	
103a	A14	5c on 30c brn, bis (C)	105.00	105.00
		Never hinged	190.00	
104a	A14	10c on 40c red, straw	65.00	65.00
		Never hinged	120.00	
105a	A14	10c on 50c brn, az (C)	105.00	105.00
		Never hinged	190.00	
106a	A14	10c on 75c dp vio, org	275.00	275.00
		Never hinged	450.00	
		Nos. 99a-106a (8)	1,040.	1,040.

Se-tenant Pairs, Both Ovpt. Settings

99b	A4	5c on 2c, #59 + #59a	35.00	35.00
100c	A14	5c on 15c, #100 + #100a	35.00	35.00
		Never hinged	65.00	
101b	A14	5c on 20c, #101 + #101a	375.00	375.00
		Never hinged	600.00	
102b	A14	5c on 25c, #102 + #102a	140.00	140.00
		Never hinged	225.00	
103b	A14	5c on 30c, #103 + #103a	140.00	140.00
		Never hinged	225.00	
104b	A14	10c on 40c, #104 + #104a	72.50	72.50
		Never hinged	130.00	
105b	A14	10c on 50c, #105 + #105a	140.00	140.00
		Never hinged	225.00	
106b	A14	10c on 75c, #106 + #106a	300.00	300.00
		Never hinged	475.00	
		Nos. 99b-106b (8)	1,237.	1,237.

No. 62 Surcharged

1917

107	A19	1c on 4c ol grn & red	2.00	2.00
		Never hinged	2.75	
		On cover		62.50
a.		Inverted surcharge	80.00	80.00
		Never hinged	140.00	
		On cover		275.00
b.		Double surcharge	70.00	70.00
		Never hinged	100.00	
c.		In pair with unsurcharged #62	625.00	625.00

Stamps and Types of 1907-30 Surcharged in Black or Red

1922-33

108	A20	40c on 20c grn & yel	.80	.80
		Never hinged	1.10	
		On cover		10.00
a.		Double surcharge, one inverted	175.00	175.00
		Never hinged	300.00	
b.		Center double	175.00	175.00
		Never hinged	300.00	
c.		Surcharge omitted	1,200.	1,200.
109	A20	50c on 45c red brn & ver ('33)	1.20	1.20
		Never hinged	2.005	
		On cover		8.75
109A	A20	50c on 45c vio & red org ('33)	325.00	275.00
		Never hinged	500.00	
b.		Double surcharge	1,750.	
		Never hinged	2,500.	
110	A20	50c on 65c vio & lt bl ('33)	1.20	1.20
		Never hinged	2.00	
		On cover		10.00
111	A20	60c on 75c red & rose	.85	.85
		Never hinged	1.25	
		On cover		25.00
		On cover, single franking		62.50
a.		Double surcharge	225.00	225.00
		Never hinged	350.00	
112	A19	65c on 15c blk & ultra (R) ('25)	2.00	2.00
		Never hinged	2.90	
		On cover, single franking		42.50
		On cover		80.00
113	A19	85c on 15c blk & ultra (R) ('25)	2.00	2.00
		Never hinged	2.90	
		On cover, single franking		42.50
		On cover		92.50
114	A20	85c on 75c red & cer ('25)	2.25	2.25
		Never hinged	3.00	
		On cover, single franking		42.50
		On cover		92.50

115	A20	90c on 75 brn red & rose red ('27)	2.25	2.25
		Never hinged	2.90	
		On cover		61.00
		On cover, single franking		92.50
		Nos. 108-109,110-115 (8)	12.55	12.55

Stamps and Type of 1907-30 Srchd. in Black or Red

1924-27

116	A21	25c on 5fr car & brn	1.10	1.10
		Never hinged	1.50	
		On cover		8.75
a.		Double surcharge	110.00	
		Never hinged	160.00	
117	A21	1.25fr on 1fr bl (R) ('26)	1.10	1.10
		Never hinged	1.50	
		On cover		32.50
		On cover, single franking		80.00
a.		Double surcharge	125.00	
		Never hinged	180.00	
118	A21	1.50fr on 1fr ind & ultra, *bluish* ('27)	1.50	1.50
		Never hinged	2.10	
		On cover		30.00
		On cover, single franking		50.00
a.		Double surcharge	140.00	
		Never hinged	210.00	
b.		Surcharge omitted	200.00	
		Never hinged	300.00	
119	A21	3fr on 5fr dl red & lt bl ('27)	4.25	3.00
		Never hinged	5.25	
		On cover		40.00
		On cover, single franking		105.00
a.		No period after "F"	14.50	14.50
		Never hinged	24.00	
120	A21	10fr on 5fr bl grn & brn red ('27)	19.50	17.00
		Never hinged	25.00	
		On cover		62.50
		On cover, single franking		140.00
121	A21	20fr on 5fr blk brn & rose ('27)	24.00	19.00
		Never hinged	30.00	
		On cover		75.00
		On cover, single franking		170.00
		Nos. 116-121 (6)	51.45	42.70

Colonial Exposition Issue
Common Design Types

1931　　Engr.　　Perf. 12½
Name of Country Typo. in Black

122	CD70	40c dp green	5.50	5.50
		Never hinged	7.50	
		On cover		50.00
123	CD71	50c violet	5.50	5.50
		Never hinged	7.50	
		On cover		42.50
124	CD72	90c red orange	5.50	5.50
		Never hinged	7.50	
		On cover		80.00
		On cover, single franking		125.00
125	CD73	1.50fr dull blue	5.50	5.50
		Never hinged	7.50	
		On cover		75.00
		On cover, single franking		110.00
		Nos. 122-125 (4)	22.00	22.00

Cascade of Salazie — A22

Waterfowl Lake and Anchain Peak — A23

Léon Dierx Museum, St. Denis — A24

Perf. 12, 12½ and Compound

1933-40   **Engr.**

126	A22	1c violet	.25	.25
		Never hinged	.40	
		On cover		30.00
127	A22	2c dark brown	.25	.25
		Never hinged	.40	
		On cover		30.00
128	A22	3c rose vio ('40)	.25	.25
		Never hinged	.40	
		On cover		37.50
129	A22	4c olive green	.25	.25
		Never hinged	.40	
		On cover		30.00
130	A22	5c red orange	.25	.25
		Never hinged	.40	
		On cover		25.00
131	A22	10c ultramarine	.25	.25
		Never hinged	.40	
		On cover		22.50
132	A22	15c black	.25	.25
		Never hinged	.40	
		On cover		21.00
133	A22	20c indigo	.30	.25
		Never hinged	.45	
		On cover		10.00
134	A22	25c red brown	.40	.30
		Never hinged	.55	
		On cover		19.00
135	A22	30c dark green	.40	.40
		Never hinged	.55	
		On cover		19.00
136	A23	35c green ('38)	.55	.55
		Never hinged	.80	
		On cover		25.00
137	A23	40c ultramarine	.55	.55
		Never hinged	.80	
		On cover		5.00
138	A23	40c brn blk ('40)	.40	.40
		Never hinged	.55	
		On cover		30.00
139	A23	45c red violet	1.00	1.00
		Never hinged	1.20	
		On cover		12.50
140	A23	45c green ('40)	.45	.45
		Never hinged	.65	
		On cover		30.00
141	A23	50c red	.30	.25
		Never hinged	.45	
		On cover		5.00
142	A23	55c brn org ('38)	1.50	1.00
		Never hinged	1.80	
		On cover		5.00
143	A23	60c dull bl ('40)	.45	.45
		Never hinged	.65	
		On cover		25.00
144	A23	65c olive green	1.10	.80
		Never hinged	1.25	
		On cover		7.50
145	A23	70c ol grn ('40)	.65	.65
		Never hinged	.85	
		On cover		10.00
146	A23	75c dark brown	5.00	4.25
		Never hinged	6.00	
		On cover		15.00
147	A23	80c black ('38)	1.00	.80
		Never hinged	1.25	
		On cover		10.00
148	A23	90c carmine	2.50	2.10
		Never hinged	3.50	
		On cover		22.50
		On cover, single franking		62.50
149	A23	90c dl rose vio ('39)	1.00	1.00
		Never hinged	1.20	
		On cover		8.75
150	A23	1fr green	2.00	.70
		Never hinged	2.50	
		On cover		15.00
		On cover, single franking		37.50
151	A23	1fr dk car ('38)	2.50	.70
		Never hinged	3.50	
		On cover		16.00
		On cover, single franking		37.50
152	A23	1fr black ('40)	.70	.70
		Never hinged	1.10	
		On cover		12.50
153	A24	1.25fr orange brown	.70	.55
		Never hinged	1.10	
		On cover		10.00
		On cover, single franking		25.00
154	A24	1.25fr brt car rose ('39)	1.00	1.00
		Never hinged	1.20	
		On cover		42.50
		On cover, single franking		62.50
155	A22	1.40fr pck bl ('40)	1.00	1.00
		Never hinged	1.20	
		On cover		37.50
		On cover, single franking		62.50
156	A24	1.50fr ultramarine	.40	.40
		Never hinged	.55	
		On cover		12.50
		On cover, single franking		30.00
157	A22	1.60fr dk car rose ('40)	1.40	1.40
		Never hinged	1.65	
		On cover		42.50
		On cover, single franking		75.00
158	A24	1.75fr olive green	1.00	.65
		Never hinged	1.25	
		On cover		19.00
		On cover, single franking		42.50
159	A22	1.75fr dk bl ('38)	1.40	.85
		Never hinged	2.10	
		On cover		19.00
		On cover, single franking		42.50
160	A24	2fr vermilion	.55	.55
		Never hinged	.80	
		On cover		25.00
		On cover, single franking		62.50
161	A22	2.25fr brt ultra ('39)	2.00	2.00
		Never hinged	2.40	
		On cover		42.50
		On cover, single franking		80.00
162	A22	2.50fr chnt ('40)	1.40	1.40
		Never hinged	1.65	
		On cover		50.00
		On cover, single franking		75.00
163	A24	3fr purple	.55	.55
		Never hinged	.80	
		On cover		30.00
		On cover, single franking		62.50

164	A24	5fr magenta	.55	.55
		Never hinged	.80	
		On cover		37.50
		On cover, single franking		67.50
165	A24	10fr dark blue	1.10	1.10
		Never hinged	1.40	
		On cover		50.00
		On cover, single franking		92.50
166	A24	20fr red brown	1.50	1.50
		Never hinged	2.25	
		On cover		60.00
		On cover, single franking		105.00
		Nos. 126-166 (41)	39.05	32.55

For overprints and surcharges see Nos. 177A, 181-220, 223 in Scott Standard catalogue, Vol. 5; C1.

Paris International Exposition Issue
Common Design Types

1937   **Perf. 13**

167	CD74	20c dp vio	2.25	2.25
		Never hinged	3.50	
		On cover		62.50
168	CD75	30c dk grn	2.25	2.25
		Never hinged	3.50	
		On cover		50.00
169	CD76	40c car rose	2.25	2.25
		Never hinged	3.50	
		On cover		42.50
170	CD77	50c dk brn & blk	2.10	2.10
		Never hinged	3.25	
		On cover		42.50
171	CD78	90c red	2.10	2.10
		Never hinged	3.25	
		On cover		67.50
		On cover, single franking		125.00
172	CD79	1.50fr ultra	2.25	2.25
		Never hinged	3.25	
		On cover		62.50
		On cover, single franking		110.00
		Nos. 167-172 (6)	13.20	13.20
		Set, never hinged	20.00	

Colonial Arts Exhibition Issue
Souvenir Sheet
Common Design Type

1937   **Imperf.**

173	CD74	3fr ultra	8.50	*10.00*
		Never hinged	16.00	
		On cover		105.00
		On cover, single franking		165.00

New York World's Fair Issue
Common Design Type

1939   **Engr.**   **Perf. 12½x12**

174	CD82	1.25fr car lake	1.40	1.40
		Never hinged	2.25	
		On cover		50.00
		On cover, single franking		110.00
175	CD82	2.25fr ultra	1.40	1.40
		Never hinged	2.25	
		On cover		50.00
		On cover, single franking		110.00
		Set, never hinged	4.50	

For overprints, see Nos. 221-222 in Scott Standard catalogue, Vol. 5.

SEMI-POSTAL STAMPS

No. 65 Surcharged in Black or Red

1915   **Unwmk.**   **Perf. 14x13½**

B1	A19	10c + 5c (Bk)	160.00	120.00
		Never hinged	250.00	
		On cover		200.00
a.		Inverted surcharge	450.00	350.00
B2	A19	10c + 5c (R)	1.75	1.75
		Never hinged	6.75	
		On cover		35.00
a.		Inverted surcharge	77.50	77.50
		Never hinged	175.00	
b.		Double surcharge, both inverted	675.00	675.00

No. 65 Surcharged in Red

1916

B3	A19	10c + 5c	1.90	1.90
		Never hinged	2.40	
		On cover		27.50

Curie Issue
Common Design Type

1938   **Perf. 13**

B4	CD80	1.75fr + 50c brt ultra	14.00	14.00
		Never hinged	24.00	
		On cover		52.50
		On cover, single franking		80.00

French Revolution Issue
Common Design Type

1939   **Photo.**   **Unwmk.**
Name and Value Typo. in Black

B5	CD83	45c + 25c grn	12.50	12.50
		Never hinged	21.00	
		On cover		67.50
B6	CD83	70c + 30c brn	12.50	12.50
		Never hinged	21.00	
		On cover		52.50
B7	CD83	90c + 35c red org	12.50	12.50
		Never hinged	21.00	
		On cover		40.00
B8	CD83	1.25fr + 1fr rose pink	12.50	12.50
		Never hinged	21.00	
		On cover		67.50
B9	CD83	2.25fr + 2fr blue	12.50	12.50
		Never hinged	21.00	
		On cover		60.00
		Nos. B5-B9 (5)	62.50	62.50
		Set, never hinged	110.00	

See CB1.

AIR POST STAMPS

No. 141 Ovptd. in Blue

1937, Jan. 23   **Unwmk.**   **Perf. 12½**

C1	A23	50c red	290.00	250.00
		Never hinged	500.00	
		On cover		600.00
a.		Vert. pair, one without overprint	1,800.	1,800.
b.		Inverted overprint	6,000.	
c.		As "b," in pair with unoverprinted stamp	26,000.	

Flight of the "Roland Garros" from Reunion to France by aviators Laurent, Lenier and Touge in Jan.-Feb., 1937.

Airplane and Landscape — AP2

1938, Mar. 1   **Engr.**   **Perf. 12½**

C2	AP2	3.65fr slate blue & car	1.00	.90
		Never hinged	1.40	
		On cover		55.00
C3	AP2	6.65fr brown & org red	1.00	.90
		Never hinged	1.40	
		On cover		55.00
C4	AP2	9.65fr car & ultra	1.00	.90
		Never hinged	1.40	
		On cover		62.50
C5	AP2	12.65fr brown & green	2.00	1.50
		Never hinged	2.90	
		On cover		75.00
		Nos. C2-C5 (4)	5.00	4.20
		Set, never hinged	7.00	

For overprints see Nos. C14-C17 in Scott Standard catalogue, Vol. 5.

AIR POST SEMI-POSTAL STAMP

French Revolution Issue
Common Design Type

1939   **Unwmk.**   **Perf. 13**
Name and Value Typo. in Orange

CB1	CD83	3.65fr + 4fr brn blk	25.00	25.00
		Never hinged	37.50	
		On cover		92.50
		On cover, single franking		165.00

POSTAGE DUE STAMPS

D1   D2

1889-92   Unwmk.   Type-set   Imperf.
Without Gum

J1	D1	5c black	29.00	16.00
		On cover		800.00
a.		Missing "ti" of "Centimes" and "à"	190.00	190.00
b.		Double impression	150.00	150.00
J2	D1	10c black	35.00	16.00
		On cover		700.00
a.		Double impression	150.00	150.00
b.		Triple impression	300.00	300.00
J3	D1	15c black ('92)	67.50	42.50
a.		Missing "ti" of "Centimes"	225.00	225.00
b.		Missing "ti" of "Centimes" and "à"	225.00	225.00
c.		Double impression	210.00	210.00
J4	D1	20c black	50.00	27.50
a.		Double impression	210.00	210.00
J5	D1	30c black	45.00	27.50
a.		Double impression	150.00	150.00
		Nos. J1-J5 (5)	226.50	129.50

Ten varieties of each value.

Nos. J1-J2, J4-J5 issued on yellowish paper in 1889; Nos. J1-J3, J5 on bluish white paper in 1892.

Many small printing varieties exist, as well as intermediate stages of the plate deterioration that resulted in Nos. J1a and J3a, Which appear in one position in the second printing of the 5c and 15c values.

1907   **Typo.**   **Perf. 14x13½**

J6	D2	5c carmine, *yel*	.90	.90
		Never hinged	1.60	
		On cover		150.00
J7	D2	10c blue, *bl*	.90	.90
		Never hinged	1.60	
		On cover		150.00
J8	D2	15c black, *bluish*	1.50	1.50
		Never hinged	2.40	
		On cover		150.00
J9	D2	20c carmine	1.50	1.50
		Never hinged	2.40	
		On cover		150.00
J10	D2	30c green, *grnsh*	2.25	2.25
		Never hinged	3.50	
		On cover		*175.00*
J11	D2	50c red, *green*	2.60	2.60
		Never hinged	4.00	
		On cover		*210.00*
J12	D2	60c carmine, *bl*	2.60	2.60
		Never hinged	4.00	
		On cover		*210.00*
J13	D2	1fr violet	3.00	3.00
		Never hinged	5.25	
		On cover		*300.00*
		Nos. J6-J13 (8)	15.25	15.25
		Set, never hinged	27.50	

Type of 1907 Issue Surcharged

1927

J14	D2	2fr on 1fr org red	12.50	12.50
		Never hinged	19.00	
		On cover		190.00
J15	D2	3fr on 1fr org brn	12.50	12.50
		Never hinged	19.00	
		On cover		190.00
a.		No period after "F"	52.50	52.50
		Never hinged	87.50	
		Set, never hinged	40.00	

Arms of Réunion — D3

1933   **Engr.**   **Perf. 13x13½**

J16	D3	5c deep violet	.25	.25
		Never hinged	.40	
J17	D3	10c dark green	.25	.25
		Never hinged	.40	
J18	D3	15c orange brown	.25	.25
		Never hinged	.40	
J19	D3	20c light red	.35	.35
		Never hinged	.55	
J20	D3	30c olive green	.35	.35
		Never hinged	.55	
J21	D3	50c ultramarine	.80	.80
		Never hinged	1.20	
J22	D3	60c black brown	.80	.80
		Never hinged	1.20	
J23	D3	1fr light violet	.80	.80
		Never hinged	1.20	

J24	D3	2fr deep blue	.80	.80
		Never hinged	1.25	
J25	D3	3fr carmine	1.00	1.00
		Never hinged	1.60	
		Nos. J16-J25 (10)	5.65	5.65
		Set, never hinged	8.75	

PARCEL POST STAMP

No. 40 Overprinted

1906　　Unwmk.　　Perf. 14x13½

Q1	A14	10c red	22.50	22.50
		Never hinged	47.50	

RHODESIA
rō-'dē-zhē-ə

(British South Africa)

LOCATION — Southeastern Africa
GOVT. — Administered by the British South Africa Company
AREA — 440,653 sq. mi.
POP. — 1,738,000 (estimated 1921)
CAPITAL — Salisbury

In 1923 the area was divided and the portion south of the Zambezi River became the British Crown Colony of Southern Rhodesia. In the following year the remaining territory was formed into the Protectorate of Northern Rhodesia.

12 Pence = 1 Shilling
20 Shillings = 1 Pound

A1　　　　　　A2

Coat of Arms — A3

Thin Paper
Engr. (A1, A3); Engr., Typo. (A2)
1890-94　　Unwmk.　　Perf. 14, 14½

1	A2	½p blue & ver ('91)	3.50	5.25
a.		½p dp blue & ver ('93)	4.00	7.75
2	A1	1p black	16.50	3.75
3	A2	2p gray grn & ver ('91)	24.00	6.50
4	A2	3p gray & grn ('91)	22.00	4.50
5	A2	4p red brn & blk ('91)	42.50	5.00
6	A1	6p ultra	72.50	28.00
7	A1	6p deep blue	46.00	4.25
8	A2	8p rose & bl ('91)	21.00	24.00
a.		8p red & ultramarine ('92)	16.50	24.00
9	A1	1sh gray brown	55.00	15.00
10	A1	2sh vermilion	77.50	38.00
11	A1	2sh6p dull lilac	47.50	55.00
		Revenue cancellation		1.00
a.		2sh6p lilac ('93)	65.00	60.00
		Revenue cancellation		1.50
12	A2	3sh brn & grn ('94)	195.00	100.00
		Revenue cancellation		2.50
13	A2	4sh gray & ver ('93)	45.00	60.00
		Revenue cancellation		1.00
14	A1	5sh yellow	92.50	65.00
		Revenue cancellation		1.50
15	A1	10sh deep green	120.00	110.00
		Revenue cancellation		1.25
16	A3	£1 dark blue	300.00	175.00
		Revenue cancellation		6.75

17	A3	£2 rose	550.00	200.00
		Revenue cancellation		22.50
18	A3	£5 yellow grn	1,775.	500.00
		Revenue cancellation		50.00
19	A3	£10 orange brn	3,000.	800.00
		Revenue cancellation		75.00
		Nos. 1-16 (16)	1,180.	699.25

The paper of the 1891 issue has the trademark and initials of the makers in a monogram watermarked in each sheet. Some of the lower values were also printed on a slightly thicker paper without watermark.
Examples of #16-19 with cancellations removed are frequently offered as unused specimens.
See #24-25, 58.
For surcharges see #20-23, 40-42. For overprints see British Central Africa #1-20.

Nos. 6 and 9 Surcharged in Black

1891, Mar.

20	A1	½p on 6p ultra	150.00	525.00
21	A1	2p on 6p ultra	195.00	700.00
22	A1	4p on 6p ultra	210.00	825.00
23	A1	8p on 1sh brown	225.00	925.00
		Nos. 20-23 (4)	780.00	2,975.

Beware of forged surcharges.

1895　　Thick Soft Paper　　Perf. 12½

24	A2	2p green & red	30.00	19.00
25	A2	4p ocher & black	30.00	21.00
a.		Imperf., pair	2,250.	

A4

Die I — Small dot at the right of the tail of the supporter at the right of the shield, and the body of the lion is not fully shaded.
Die II — No dot and the lion is heavily shaded.

1896　　Engraved, Typo.　　Perf. 14

26	A4	½p slate & violet	5.00	3.75
27	A4	1p scar & emer	11.00	5.50
a.		1p scarlet & emerald (I)	27.50	5.00
b.		1p car red & emerald green (I)	—	
28	A4	2p brown & rose lil (II)	25.00	9.50
a.		2p brown & rose lilac (I)	32.50	5.75
29	A4	3p red brn & ultra	11.00	2.50
30	A4	4p blue & red lil	20.00	.60
a.		4p ultra & red lilac (II)	85.00	14.00
b.		4p blue & red lilac (I)	42.50	24.00
c.		4p ultra & red lilac (I)	62.50	
d.		Horiz. pair, imperf. btwn. (I)		
31	A4	6p vio & pale rose (II)	16.50	.85
a.		6p violet & pink (I)	87.50	26.00
32	A4	8p dp grn & vio, buff (I)	16.00	.70
a.		Imperf. pair	4,500.	
b.		Horiz. pair, imperf. btwn.		
33	A4	1sh brt grn & ultra	24.00	4.00
34	A4	2sh dk bl & grn, buff	50.00	12.00
35	A4	2sh6p brn & vio, yel	92.50	60.00
36	A4	3sh grn & red vio, bl	87.50	47.50
a.		Imperf. pair	12,500.	
37	A4	4sh red & bl, grn	65.00	4.00
38	A4	5sh org red & grn	65.00	12.50
39	A4	10sh sl & car, rose	140.00	72.50
		Nos. 26-39 (14)	628.50	235.90

See type A7.

Nos. 4, 13-14 Surcharged in Black

1896, Apr.　　Perf. 14

40	A2	1p on 3p	650.00	850.00
a.		"P" of "Penny" inverted	50,000.	
b.		"y" of "Penny" inverted		
c.		Double surcharge		
41	A2	1p on 4sh	325.00	350.00
a.		"P" of "Penny" inverted	37,500.	
b.		Single bar in surch.	1,250.	1,400.
c.		"y" of "Penny" inverted	37,500.	
42	A1	3p on 5s yellow	225.00	275.00
a.		"T" of "THREE" inverted	50,000.	
b.		"R" of "THREE" inverted	37,500.	
		Nos. 40-42 (3)	1,200.	1,475.

Cape of Good Hope Stamps Overprinted in Black

1896, May 22　　Wmk. 16

43	A6	½p slate	17.50	25.00
44	A15	1p carmine	18.50	26.00
45	A6	2p bister brown	26.00	15.00
46	A6	4p deep blue	30.00	27.50
a.		"COMPANY" omitted	11,000.	
47	A3	6p violet	77.50	90.00
48	A6	1sh yellow buff	175.00	165.00
		Wmk. 2		
49	A6	3p claret	60.00	85.00
		Nos. 43-49 (7)	404.50	433.50

Nos. 42-49 were used at Bulawayo during the Matabele Rebellion.
Forgeries are known.

Remainders
Rhodesian authorities made available remainders in large quantities of all stamps in 1897, 1898-1908, 1905, 1909 and 1910 issues, CTO. Some varieties exist only as remainders. See notes following Nos. 100 and 118.

A7

Type A7 differs from type A4 in having the ends of the scroll which is below the shield curved between the hind legs of the supporters instead of passing behind one leg of each. There are other minor differences.

Perf. 13½ to 16
1897　　Unwmk.　　Engr.

50	A7	½p slate & violet	6.00	9.50
51	A7	1p ver & gray grn	8.00	8.75
52	A7	2p brown & lil rose	19.00	4.25
53	A7	3p red brn & gray bl	7.00	.55
a.		Vert. pair, imperf. btwn.	5,000.	
54	A7	4p ultra & red lilac	25.00	4.50
a.		Horiz. pair, imperf. btwn.	18,000.	17,500.
55	A7	6p violet & salmon	15.00	4.00
56	A7	8p dk grn & vio, buff	25.00	.55
a.		Vert. pair, imperf. btwn.	—	4,000.
57	A7	£1 black & red, grn	450.00	250.00
		Revenue cancellation		12.00
		Nos. 50-56 (7)	105.00	32.10

Thick Paper
Perf. 15

58	A3	£2 bright red	1,900.	500.00
		Revenue cancellation		65.00

See note on remainders following No. 49.

A8　　　　　　A9

A10

1898-1908　　Perf. 13½ to 16

59	A8	½p yellow green ('04)	6.00	3.25
a.		Imperf. pair	1,000.	
b.		Horiz. pair, imperf. vert.	975.00	
c.		Vert. pair, imperf between	1,675.	
d.		½p dull blue green	15.00	3.25
e.		½p deep green (shades) ('08)	35.00	3.75
60	A8	1p rose (shades)	12.00	.60
a.		Horiz. pair, imperf. btwn.		1,150.
b.		Vert. pair, imperf between	825.00	
c.		Imperf. pair	1,000.	900.00
d.		1p red (shades) ('05)	10.50	.55
e.		As "d," horiz. pair, imperf vert.	450.00	500.00
f.		As "d," vert. pair, imperf horiz.	1,100.	
g.		As "d," imperf. pair	675.00	650.00
h.		As "d," horiz. pair, imperf between	900.00	550.00
i.		As "d," vert. strip of 4, imperf between	3,000.	
61	A8	2p brown	9.00	2.00
62	A8	2½p dull blue (shades)	20.00	2.00
a.		Horiz. pair, imperf vert.	1,100.	1,300.
b.		2½p gray blue (shades) ('03)	19.00	1.90
63	A8	3p claret ('08)	16.00	.90
a.		Vert. pair, imperf between	800.00	
64	A8	4p olive green	15.00	.35
a.		Vert. pair, imperf. btwn.	800.00	
65	A8	6p lilac	23.00	3.00
a.		6p reddish mauve ('02)	26.00	7.00
66	A9	1sh bister	30.00	4.50
a.		Vert. pair, imperf. btwn.	3,500.	3,500.
b.		Horiz. pair, imperf between	4,000.	4,000.
c.		1sh deep olive bister ('07)	400.00	375.00
d.		As "c," imperf., pair	3,500.	
e.		As "c," horiz. pair, imperf between	4,750.	
f.		1sh bister brown ('08)	75.00	17.50
g.		1sh brownish yellow ('08)	30.00	12.50
67	A9	2sh6p bluish gray ('06)	72.50	2.25
a.		Vert. pair, imperf. between	1,300.	575.00
68	A9	3sh purple ('02)	30.00	4.00
a.		2sh6p deep blue violet ('08)	82.50	16.00
69	A9	5sh orange ('01)	65.00	22.50
70	A9	7sh6p black ('01)	105.00	30.00
71	A9	10sh bluish grn ('08)	60.00	2.25
72	A10	£1 gray violet, perf 15½	425.00	165.00
		Revenue cancellation		17.50
a.		£1 blackish purple, perf 14 ('01)	725.00	150.00
		Revenue cancellation		9.50
73	A10	£2 red brown ('08)	130.00	7.50
		Revenue cancellation		135.00
74	A10	£5 dk brown ('01)	3,750.	3,000.
		Revenue cancellation		125.00
75	A10	£10 blue lil ('01)	3,750.	3,000.
		Revenue cancellation		125.00
75A	A10	£20 bister ('01?)	22,500.	
		Revenue cancellation		175.00
75B	A10	£100 cherry red ('01)	185,000.	
		Revenue cancellation		900.00
		Nos. 59-73 (15)	1,018.	250.10

For overprints and surcharges see #82-100.
See note on remainders following #49.

Victoria
Falls — A11

Perf. 14, 14½x15 (#78)

1905, July 13

76	A11	1p rose red	8.50	10.00
a.		Perf 14½x15	19.00	20.00
77	A11	2½p ultra	18.00	12.00
a.		Perf 14½x15	30.00	20.00
78	A11	5p magenta	35.00	60.00
a.		Perf 14	70.00	90.00
79	A11	1sh blue green	42.50	57.50
a.		Imperf., pair	35,000.	
b.		Horiz. pair, imperf. vert.	37,500.	
c.		Horiz. pair, imperf. btwn.	45,000.	
d.		Vert. pair, imperf. btn.	45,000.	
e.		Perf 14½x15		425.00
80	A11	2sh6p black	135.00	180.00
81	A11	5sh violet	125.00	50.00
a.		Perf 14½x15	475.00	
		Nos. 76-81 (6)	364.00	369.50
		Nos. 76-81 overprinted "SPECIMEN"	400.00	

Opening of the Victoria Falls bridge across the Zambezi River.
See note on remainders following No. 49.

Stamps of 1898-1908 Overprinted or Surcharged

1909   **Perf. 14, 15**

82	A8	½p green (shades)	5.00	3.00
a.		No period after "RHODESIA"	90.00	45.00
b.		½p yellow green ('11)	45.00	30.00
83	A8	1p carmine rose	10.00	1.75
a.		Horiz. pair, imperf between	525.00	
b.		No period after "RHODESIA"	95.00	35.00
c.		1p deep carmine rose	10.00	1.75
d.		As "c," horiz. pair, imperf between	525.00	
84	A8	2p brown	4.50	7.25
a.		No period after "RHODESIA"	155.00	100.00
85	A8	2½p cobalt blue	3.00	.90
a.		No period after "RHODESIA"	60.00	32.50
86	A8	3p claret	3.00	3.00
a.		Double overprint	1,600.	1,600.
b.		Inverted overprint	20.00	20.00
c.		No period after "RHODESIA"	180.00	85.00
87	A8	4p olive green	12.00	3.75
a.		Inverted overprint		16.50
b.		No period after "RHODESIA"	100.00	75.00
88	A8	5p on 6p lilac	12.50	20.00
a.		Violet surcharge	100.00	
b.		5p on 6p dull purple	24.00	20.00
89	A8	6p lilac	8.00	9.00
a.		No period after "RHODESIA"	90.00	
b.		6p dull purple	25.00	9.00
c.		As "b," no period after "RHODESIA"	110.00	65.00
90	A9	7½p on 2sh6p	4.50	4.25
a.		Violet surcharge	25.00	11.00
b.		Double surcharge	10,000.	
91	A9	10p on 3sh pur, violet surch.	7.75	4.50
a.		Black surcharge	16.50	20.00
92	A9	1sh dp brnsh bister	14.00	9.00
a.		No period after "RHODESIA"	110.00	60.00
b.		1sh bister	30.00	
c.		As "b," no period after "RHODESIA"	200.00	
93	A9	2sh on 5sh org	14.00	8.50
94	A9	2sh6p bluish gray	30.00	12.00
a.		No period after "RHODESIA"	135.00	75.00
b.		Inverted overprint		25.00
95	A9	3sh purple	25.00	12.50
96	A9	5sh orange	50.00	80.00
a.		No period after "RHODESIA"	225.00	225.00

97	A9	7sh6p black	110.00	30.00
98	A9	10sh bluish grn	70.00	22.50
a.		No period after "RHODESIA"	400.00	250.00
99	A10	£1 gray violet	220.00	110.00
a.		Vert. pair, lower stamp without overprint	47,500.	
b.		Violet overprint	425.00	220.00
100	A10	£2 red brown, bluish, perf 14½x15 ('12)	4,500.	330.00
a.		£2 brown	4,750.	375.00
100B	A10	£5 deep blue, bluish	9,000.	5,000.
		Nos. 82-99 (18)	603.25	341.90

See note on remainders following No. 49.
Nos. 86b, 87a and 94b are from the remainders.

Queen Mary
and King
George
V — A12

1910 Engr. Perf. 14, 15x14, 14x15

101	A12	½p green	15.00	2.00
a.		½p olive green	45.00	5.50
b.		Perf. 15	350.00	14.50
c.		Imperf., pair	16,000.	8,000.
d.		Perf. 13½	350.00	55.00
102	A12	1p rose car	32.50	4.50
a.		Vertical pair, imperf. btwn.	22,500.	14,500.
b.		Perf. 15	350.00	10.00
c.		Perf. 13½	2,250.	55.00
103	A12	2p gray & blk	60.00	12.50
b.		Perf. 15	1,000.	47.50
104	A12	2½p ultramarine	27.50	10.00
a.		2½p light blue	29.00	24.00
b.		Perf. 15	82.50	45.00
c.		Perf. 13½	45.00	77.50
105	A12	3p ol yel & vio	50.00	52.00
a.		Perf. 15	3,650.	82.50
b.		Perf. 14x15	7,750.	325.00
106	A12	4p org & blk	55.00	27.50
a.		4p orange & violet black	95.00	72.50
b.		Perf. 15x14	550.00	
c.		Perf. 15	65.00	82.50
107	A12	5p ol grn & brn	60.00	60.00
a.		5p olive yel & brn (error)	725.00	165.00
b.		Perf. 15	875.00	115.00
108	A12	6p claret & brn	72.50	25.00
a.		Perf. 15	1,000.	67.50
109	A12	8p brn vio & gray blk	190.00	110.00
a.		Perf. 13½	67.50	275.00
110	A12	10p plum & rose red	55.00	55.00
111	A12	1sh turq grn & black	72.50	24.00
a.		Perf. 14x15	32,500.	3,250.
b.		Perf. 15	1,325.	62.50
112	A12	2sh gray bl & black	125.00	82.50
a.		Perf. 15	2,500.	400.00
113	A12	2sh6p car rose & blk	400.00	450.00
114	A12	3sh vio & bl grn	250.00	210.00
115	A12	5sh yel grn & brn red	325.00	225.00
116	A12	7sh6p brt bl & car	725.00	500.00
117	A12	10sh red org & bl grn	475.00	550.00
a.		10sh red org & myrtle grn	725.00	325.00
118	A12	£1 bluish sl & car	1,650.	775.00
a.		£1 black & red	1,550.	425.00
c.		Perf. 15	19,000.	4,750.
d.		As "a," carmine and reddish mauve (error)	14,500.	
		Nos. 101-118 (18)	4,640.	3,175.

See note on remainders following No. 49.
The £1 in plum and red is from the remainders.

King George V — A13

Three dies were used for Nos. 122, 124-138: I, Outline at top of cap absent or very faint

and broken. Left ear not shaded or outlined and appears white; II, Outline at top of cap faint and broken. Ear shaded all over, with no outline; III, Outline at top of cap continuous. Ear shaded all over, with continuous outline. Die types are noted in parentheses.

1913-23   **Perf. 14**

119	A13	½p deep green	9.25	2.50
a.		Vert. pair, imperf horiz.	925.00	
b.		Vert. strip of 5, imperf between	4,250.	
c.		½p blue green	12.00	2.50
d.		As "c," perf 15	9.50	30.00
e.		½p yellow green	24.00	2.50
f.		Horiz. pair, imperf between	1,000.	
g.		½p dull green	13.50	2.50
h.		As "g," horiz. pair, imperf vert.	1,000.	1,000.
i.		As "g," horiz. pair, imperf vert	1,300.	
j.		½p bright green	28.00	2.50
k.		As "j," vert. pair, imperf between	1,750.	
l.		½p green, perf 15	16.00	24.00
m.		As "l," perf 14x15	7,750.	225.00
n.		As "l," perf 15x14	7,750.	400.00
120	A13	1p brown rose	4.50	4.00
a.		Perf. 15	7.50	10.00
b.		1p bright rose	7.25	2.50
c.		As "b," horiz. pair, imperf btwn.	1,100.	950.00
d.		1p carmine red (shades)	12.50	4.00
e.		As "d," pair, imperf between	1,650.	
f.		1p red	8.00	2.50
g.		As "f," horiz. pair, imperf btwn.	1,250.	
h.		As "f," perf. 13½		600.00
i.		1p scarlet	24.00	3.00
j.		As "i," horiz. pair, imperf btwn.	1,350.	
k.		1p rose red	12.50	2.50
l.		As "k," horiz. pair, imperf btwn.	1,000.	1,000.
m.		As "k," vert. pair, imperf btwn.	3,000.	
n.		As "k," perf. 15	675.00	24.50
o.		As "n," horiz. pair, imperf between	19,000.	
p.		1p bright rose red (rosine)	550.00	22.50
q.		1p cherry red	—	
121	A13	1½p bister brown ('17)	6.00	2.50
a.		Horiz. pair, imperf between	900.00	900.00
b.		Perf. 15 ('19)	50.00	8.00
c.		As "b," horiz. pair, imperf between	26,500.	
d.		1½p brown ocher ('19)	5.50	2.50
e.		As "d," horiz. pair, imperf between	875.00	900.00
f.		As "d," perf 15 ('17)	55.00	16.00
g.		1½p drab brown ('19)	7.25	2.50
h.		As "g," horiz. pair, imperf between	875.00	
i.		As "g," vert. pair, imperf between	2,500.	
122	A13	2p vio blk & blk (III) '22	13.50	9.00
a.		2p gray & black (III)	11.50	4.00
b.		Perf. 15 (II)	13.50	25.00
c.		Horiz. pair, imperf. btwn. (III)	6,750.	
d.		2p gray & brnish blk (III), perf 15	6,500.	
123	A13	2½p ultra	8.25	40.00
a.		Perf. 15	17.50	65.00
124	A13	3p org yel & blk (III)	20.00	4.75
a.		3p yellow & black (III)	17.50	4.25
b.		Perf. 15 (I)	9.00	27.50
125	A13	4p org red & blk (I)	12.00	42.50
a.		Perf. 15 (I)	175.00	32.50
126	A13	5p yel grn & blk (I)	7.25	22.50
127	A13	6p lilac & blk (III)	16.50	8.75
a.		Perf. 15 (I)	10.50	12.00
128	A13	8p gray grn & violet (II)	19.00	82.50
a.		Perf. 15 (III)	77.50	
b.		8p green & violet (II)	225.00	190.00
129	A13	10p car rose & bl, perf. 15 (II)	16.50	50.00
a.		Perf. 14 (III) '22	18.50	75.00
130	A13	1sh turq bl & blk (III) '22	15.00	22.50
a.		1sh lt grn & blk (III) ('19)	95.00	60.00
b.		Perf. 15 (II)	77.50	22.50
132	A13	2sh brn & blk, perf. 14 (III)('19)	22.50	20.00
a.		Perf. 15 (II)	17.50	55.00
133	A13	2sh6p ol gray & vio bl (III) '22	65.00	110.00
a.		2sh6p gray & blue (II)	82.50	60.00
b.		Perf. 15 (II)	55.00	105.00
134	A13	3sh brt blue & red brown (II)	130.00	165.00
a.		Perf. 15 (III) '23	195.00	
b.		3sh blue & chocolate (II)	775.00	325.00

135	A13	5sh grn & bl (II)	95.00	100.00
a.		Perf. 15 (II)	210.00	225.00
136	A13	7sh6p black & vio, perf. 15 (II)	175.00	300.00
a.		Perf. 14 (III) '22	250.00	425.00
137	A13	10sh yel grn & car (III) '23	275.00	360.00
a.		Perf. 15 (III) '23	250.00	425.00
138	A13	£1 violet & blk (II)	450.00	675.00
a.		£1 magenta & black (III) '23	950.00	1,250.
b.		Perf. 15 (III) '23	1,100.	
c.		Perf. 15, black & purple (II)	1,750.	1,750.
		Nos. 119-138 (19)	1,360.	2,021.

No. 120 Surcharged in Dark Violet

No. 139   No. 140

1917

139	A13	½p on 1p	2.75	10.50
a.		Inverted surcharge	1,600.	1,650.
140	A13	½p on 1p	2.00	10.00

RIO DE ORO

ˌrē-ō dē 'or-ˌō

LOCATION — On the northwest coast of Africa, bordering on the Atlantic Ocean
GOVT. — Spanish Colony
AREA — 71,600 sq. mi.
POP. — 24,000
CAPITAL — Villa Cisneros

Prior to the issuance of Rio de Oro stamps, Spanish stamps were used 1901-1904, canceled "Rio de Oro."
Rio de Oro became part of Spanish Sahara in 1924.

100 Centimos = 1 Peseta

King Alfonso XIII — A1

Control Numbers on Back in Blue

1905   Unwmk.   Typo.   *Perf. 14*

1	A1	1c blue green	4.00	3.00
2	A1	2c claret	5.00	3.00
3	A1	3c bronze green	5.00	3.00
4	A1	4c dark brown	5.00	3.00
5	A1	5c orange red	5.00	3.00
6	A1	10c dk gray brown	5.00	3.00
7	A1	15c red brown	5.00	3.00
8	A1	25c dark blue	95.00	32.50
9	A1	50c dark green	45.00	13.50
10	A1	75c dark violet	45.00	19.00
11	A1	1p orange brown	32.50	8.00
12	A1	2p buff	100.00	57.50
13	A1	3p dull violet	70.00	20.00
14	A1	4p blue green	70.00	20.00
15	A1	5p dull blue	100.00	45.00
16	A1	10p pale red	250.00	150.00
		Nos. 1-16 (16)	841.50	386.50
		Set, never hinged	1,700.	

For surcharges see Nos. 17, 34-36, 60-66.

No. 8 Handstamp Surcharged in Rose — a

1907

17	A1	15c on 25c dk blue	250.00	60.00
		Never hinged	400.00	

The surcharge exists inverted, double and in violet, normally positioned. Value for each, $450.

King Alfonso XIII — A2

Control Numbers on Back in Blue

1907   Typo.

18	A2	1c claret	3.00	2.75
19	A2	2c black	3.50	2.75
20	A2	3c dark brown	3.50	2.75
21	A2	4c red	3.50	2.75
22	A2	5c black brown	3.50	2.75
23	A2	10c chocolate	3.50	2.75
24	A2	15c dark blue	3.50	2.75
25	A2	25c deep green	9.50	2.75
26	A2	50c black violet	9.50	2.75
27	A2	75c orange brown	9.50	2.75
28	A2	1p orange	16.00	2.75
29	A2	2p dull violet	5.50	2.75
30	A2	3p blue green	5.50	2.75
a.		Cliché of 4p in plate of 3p	400.00	260.00
31	A2	4p dark blue	9.00	5.00
32	A2	5p red	9.00	5.25
33	A2	10p deep green	9.00	12.00
		Nos. 18-33 (16)	106.50	58.00
		Set, never hinged	250.00	

For surcharges see Nos. 38-43, 67-70.

Nos. 9-10 Handstamp Surcharged in Red

1907

34	A1	10c on 50c dk green	100.00	30.00
		Never hinged	175.00	
a.		"10" omitted	175.00	100.00
		Never hinged	250.00	
35	A1	10c on 75c dk violet	100.00	32.00
		Never hinged	175.00	

No. 12 Handstamp Surcharged in Violet

1908

36	A1	2c on 2p buff	52.50	24.00
		Never hinged	100.00	

No. 36 is found with "1908" measuring 11mm and 12mm.

Same Surcharge in Red on No. 26

1908

38	A2	10c on 50c blk vio	22.50	3.75
		Never hinged	37.50	

A 5c on 10c (No. 23) was not officially issued.

Nos. 25, 27-28 Handstamp Surcharged Type "a" in Red, Violet or Green

1908

39	A2	15c on 25c dp grn (R)	25.00	3.75
40	A2	15c on 75c org brn (V)	32.50	17.50
a.		Green surcharge	50.00	6.75
		Never hinged	72.50	
41	A2	15c on 1p org (V)	37.50	15.00
42	A2	15c on 1p org (R)	35.00	15.00
43	A2	15c on 1p org (G)	25.00	12.00
		Nos. 39-43 (5)	155.00	63.25
		Set, never hinged	325.00	

As this surcharge is handstamped, it exists in several varieties: double, inverted, in pairs with one surcharge omitted, etc.

A3

Revenue stamps overprinted and surcharged

1908   *Imperf.*

44	A3	5c on 50c green (C)	90.00	30.00
		Never hinged	160.00	
45	A3	5c on 50c green (V)	130.00	52.50
		Never hinged	225.00	

The surcharge, which is handstamped, exists in many variations.
Nos. 44-45 are found with and without control numbers on back. Stamps with control numbers sell at about double the above values. Counterfeits exist.

King Alfonso XIII — A4

Control Numbers on Back in Blue

1909   Typo.   *Perf. 14½*

46	A4	1c red	.85	.50
47	A4	2c orange	.85	.50
48	A4	5c dark green	.85	.50
49	A4	10c orange red	.85	.50
50	A4	15c blue green	.85	.50
51	A4	20c dark violet	2.10	.70
52	A4	25c deep blue	2.10	.70
53	A4	30c claret	2.10	.70
54	A4	40c chocolate	2.10	.70
55	A4	50c red violet	4.00	.70
56	A4	1p dark brown	5.25	3.25

57	A4	4p carmine rose	6.25	4.75
58	A4	10p claret	14.00	7.75
		Nos. 46-58 (13)	42.15	21.75
		Set, never hinged	80.00	

Stamps of 1905 Handstamped in Black

1910

60	A1	10c on 5p dull bl	21.00	8.50
a.		Red surcharge	90.00	55.00
		Never hinged	145.00	
62	A1	10c on 10p pale red	21.00	8.50
a.		Violet surcharge	145.00	62.50
		Never hinged	210.00	
b.		Green surcharge	145.00	62.50
		Never hinged	210.00	
65	A1	15c on 3p dull vio	21.00	8.50
a.		Imperf.	110.00	
		Never hinged	190.00	
66	A1	15c on 4p blue grn	21.00	8.50
a.		10c on 4p bl grn	925.00	275.00
		Never hinged	1,300.	
		Nos. 60-66 (4)	84.00	34.00
		Set, never hinged	160.00	

See note after No. 43.

Nos. 31 and 33 Surcharged in Red or Violet

1911-13

67	A2	2c on 4p dk blue (R)	12.50	9.00
68	A2	5c on 10p dp grn (V)	37.50	9.00

Nos. 29-30 Surcharged in Black

69	A2	10c on 2p dull vio	19.00	8.25
69A	A2	10c on 3p bl grn ('13)	225.00	50.00

Nos. 30, 32 Handstamped Type "a"

69B	A2	15c on 3p bl grn ('13)	200.00	24.00
70	A2	15c on 5p red	13.50	9.00
		Nos. 67-70 (6)	507.50	109.25
		Set, never hinged	650.00	

King Alfonso XIII
A5   A6

Control Numbers on Back in Blue

1912   Typo.   *Perf. 13½*

71	A5	1c carmine rose	.40	.35
72	A5	2c lilac	.40	.35
73	A5	5c deep green	.40	.35
74	A5	10c red	.40	.35
75	A5	15c brown orange	.40	.35
76	A5	20c brown	.40	.35
77	A5	25c dull blue	.40	.35
78	A5	30c dark violet	.40	.35
79	A5	40c blue green	.40	.35
80	A5	50c lake	.40	.35
81	A5	1p red	4.00	.80
82	A5	4p claret	7.50	4.00
83	A5	10p dark brown	11.00	6.00
		Nos. 71-83 (13)	26.50	14.30
		Set, never hinged	60.00	

For overprints see Nos. 97-109.

Control Numbers on Back in Blue

1914   *Perf. 13*

84	A6	1c olive black	.40	.35
85	A6	2c maroon	.40	.35
86	A6	5c deep green	.40	.35
87	A6	10c orange red	.40	.35
88	A6	15c orange red	.40	.35
89	A6	20c deep claret	.40	.35
90	A6	25c dark blue	.40	.35
91	A6	30c blue green	.40	.35
92	A6	40c brown orange	.40	.35
93	A6	50c dark brown	.40	.35
94	A6	1p dull lilac	3.00	2.40

95	A6	4p carmine rose	7.25	6.25
96	A6	10p dull violet	7.50	6.25
		Nos. 84-96 (13)	21.75	18.40
		Set, never hinged	50.00	

Nos. 71-83 Overprinted in Black

1917   *Perf. 13½*

97	A5	1c carmine rose	17.50	1.40
98	A5	2c lilac	17.50	1.40
99	A5	5c deep green	3.50	1.40
100	A5	10c red	3.50	1.40
101	A5	15c orange brn	3.50	1.40
102	A5	20c brown	3.50	1.40
103	A5	25c dull blue	3.50	1.40
104	A5	30c dark violet	3.50	1.40
105	A5	40c blue green	3.50	1.40
106	A5	50c lake	3.50	1.40
107	A5	1p red	19.00	1.40
108	A5	4p claret	22.50	6.25
109	A5	10p dark brown	42.50	9.25
		Nos. 97-109 (13)	147.00	34.25
		Set, never hinged	300.00	

Nos. 97-109 exist with overprint inverted or double (value 50 percent over normal) and in dark blue (value twice normal). Forgeries exist.

King Alfonso XIII — A7

Control Numbers on Back in Blue

1919   Typo.   *Perf. 13*

114	A7	1c brown	1.25	.55
115	A7	2c claret	1.25	.55
116	A7	5c light green	1.25	.55
117	A7	10c carmine	1.25	.55
118	A7	15c orange	4.00	2.00
119	A7	20c orange	1.25	.55
120	A7	25c blue	1.25	.55
121	A7	30c green	1.25	.55
122	A7	40c vermilion	1.25	.55
123	A7	50c brown	1.25	.55
124	A7	1p lilac	8.00	4.50
125	A7	4p rose	14.50	7.50
126	A7	10p violet	25.00	10.00
		Nos. 114-126 (13)	62.75	28.95
		Set, never hinged	100.00	

A8   A9

Control Numbers on Back in Blue

1920   *Perf. 13*

127	A8	1c gray lilac	1.10	.55
128	A8	2c rose	1.10	.55
129	A8	5c light red	1.10	.55
130	A8	10c blue	1.10	.55
131	A8	15c light brown	1.10	.55
132	A8	20c greenish blue	1.10	.55
133	A8	25c yellow	1.10	.55
134	A8	30c dull blue	6.25	4.50
135	A8	40c orange	3.75	2.10
136	A8	50c dull rose	3.75	2.10
137	A8	1p gray green	5.25	2.10
138	A8	4p lilac rose	7.00	4.25
139	A8	10p brown	25.00	10.00
		Nos. 127-139 (13)	58.70	28.90
		Set, never hinged	100.00	

Control Numbers on Back in Blue

1922

140	A9	1c yellow	1.00	.60
141	A9	2c red brown	1.00	.60
142	A9	5c blue green	1.00	.60
143	A9	10c pale red	1.00	.60
144	A9	15c myrtle green	1.00	.60
145	A9	20c turq blue	1.00	.65
146	A9	25c deep blue	1.00	.65
147	A9	30c deep rose	1.75	1.25
148	A9	40c violet	1.75	1.25
149	A9	50c orange	1.75	1.25
150	A9	1p lilac	5.50	1.75
151	A9	4p claret	12.00	4.00
152	A9	10p dark brown	20.00	8.25
		Nos. 140-152 (13)	49.75	22.05
		Set, never hinged	100.00	

For subsequent issues see Spanish Sahara.

ROMANIA

rō-'mā-nēə

(Rumania, Roumania)

LOCATION — Southeastern Europe, bordering on the Black Sea
GOVT. — Kingdom
AREA — 91,699 sq. mi.
POP. — 22,600,000 (est. 1984)
CAPITAL — Bucharest

Romania was formed in 1861 from the union of the principalities of Moldavia and Walachia in 1859. It became a kingdom in 1881. Following World War I, the original territory was considerably enlarged by the addition of Bessarabia, Bukovina, Transylvania, Crisana, Maramures and Banat.

40 Parale = 1 Piaster
100 Bani = 1 Leu (plural "Lei") (1868)

Catalogue values for unused stamps in this country are for Never Hinged items, beginning with Scott 475 in the regular postage section, Scott B82 in the semipostal section, Scott CB1 in the airpost semi-postal section, Scott J82 in the postage due section, Scott O1 in the official section, Scott RA16 in the postal tax section, and Scott RAJ1 in the postal tax postage due section.

Watermarks

Wmk. 95 — Wavy Lines

Wmk. 163 — Coat of Arms

Wmk. 164 — PR

Wmk. 165 — PR Interlaced

Wmk. 167 — Coat of Arms Covering 25 Stamps

Wmk. 200 — PR

Wmk. 225 — Crown over PTT, Multiple

Wmk. 230 — Crowns and Monograms

Values for unused stamps are for examples with original gum as defined in the catalogue introduction except for Nos. 1-4 which are valued without gum.

Moldavia

Coat of Arms
A1   A2

Laid Paper

Handstamped

1858, July   Unwmk.   Imperf.

1	A1	27pa blk, *rose*	60,000.	25,000.
a.		Tête bêche pair		
2	A1	54pa blue, *grn*	15,500.	10,000.
3	A1	108pa blue, *rose*	35,000.	16,000.

Wove Paper

4	A1	81pa blue, *bl*	50,000.	55,000.

Full margins = 3mm.

Cut to shape or octagonally, Nos. 1-4 sell for one-fourth to one-third of these values.

1858   Bluish Wove Paper

5	A2	5pa black	15,000.	15,000.
a.		Tête bêche pair		
6	A2	40pa blue	275.	225.
a.		Tête bêche pair	1,300.	2,650.
7	A2	80pa red	7,750.	875.
a.		Tête bêche pair		

Full margins = 3mm.

1859   White Wove Paper

8	A2	5pa black	15,000.	10,000.
a.		Tête bêche pair		
b.		Frame broken at bottom	175.	
c.		As "b," tête bêche pair	600.	
9	A2	40pa blue	175.	190.
b.		Tête bêche pair	650.	1,500.
10	A2	80pa red	475.	300.
b.		Tête bêche pair	1,750.	3,250.

Full margins = 3mm.

No. 8b has a break in the frame at bottom below "A." It was never placed in use.

Moldavia-Walachia

Coat of Arms — A3

Printed by Hand from Single Dies

1862   White Laid Paper

11	A3	3pa orange	300.00	2,250.
a.		3pa yellow	300.00	2,250.
12	A3	6pa carmine	300.00	475.00
13	A3	6pa red	300.00	475.00
14	A3	30pa blue	87.50	115.00
		Nos. 11-14 (4)	987.50	3,315.

White Wove Paper

15	A3	3pa orange yel	85.00	275.00
a.		3pa lemon	85.00	275.00
16	A3	6pa carmine	95.00	275.00
17	A3	6pa vermilion	77.50	225.00
18	A3	30pa blue	60.00	65.00
		Nos. 15-18 (4)	317.50	840.00

Greenish-Blue Paper

15C	A3	3pa orange yel	—	2,500.
		On cover		109,000.

Only one cover is known with No. 15C: 10 examples prepaying the single letter rate of 30pa. On cover value is based on 2011 Swiss auction price realized.

Tête bêche pairs

11b	A3	3pa orange	1,550.	
12a	A3	6pa carmine	1,000.	1,250.
14a	A3	30pa blue	190.00	1,550.
15b	A3	3pa orange yellow	210.00	1,600.
16a	A3	6pa carmine	275.00	1,750.
17a	A3	6pa vermilion	190.00	1,600.
18a	A3	30pa blue	175.00	1,600.

Full margins = 2mm.

Nos. 11-18 were printed with a hand press, one at a time, from single dies. The impressions were very irregularly placed and occasionally overlapped. Sheets of 32 (4x8). The 3rd and 4th rows were printed inverted, making the second and third rows tête bêche. All values come in distinct shades, frequently even on the same sheet. The paper of this and the following issues through No. 52 often shows a bluish, grayish or yellowish tint.

White Wove Paper

1864   Typographed from Plates

19	A3	3pa yellow	60.00	1,500.
a.		Tête bêche pair	350.00	
b.		Pair, one sideways	150.00	
20	A3	6pa deep rose	22.50	
a.		Tête bêche pair	52.50	
b.		Pair, one sideways	52.50	
21	A3	30pa deep blue	17.50	100.00
a.		Tête bêche pair	57.50	
b.		Pair, one sideways	57.50	2,650.
c.		Bluish wove paper	150.00	
		Nos. 19-21 (3)	100.00	

Full margins = 1¼mm.

Stamps of 1862 issue range from very clear to blurred impressions but rarely have broken or deformed characteristics. The 1864 issue, though rarely blurred, usually have various imperfections in the letters and numbers. These include breaks, malformations, occasional dots at left of the crown or above the "R" of "PAR," a dot on the middle stroke of the "F," and many other bulges, breaks and spots of color.

The 1864 issue were printed in sheets of 40 (5x8). The first and second rows were inverted. Clichés in the third row were placed sideways, 4 with head to right and 4 with head to left, making one tête bêche pair. The fourth and fifth rows were normally placed.

No. 20 was never placed in use.

All values exist in shades, light to dark.

Counterfeit cancellations exist on #11-21.

Three stamps in this design- 2pa, 5pa, 20pa- were printed on white wove paper in 1864, but never placed in use. Value, set $9.

Romania

Prince Alexandru Ioan Cuza — A4

TWENTY PARALES:
Type I — The central oval does not touch the inner frame. The "I" of "DECI" extends above and below the other letters.

Type II — The central oval touches the frame at the bottom. The "I" of the "DECI" is the same height as the other letters.

1865, Jan.   Unwmk.   Litho.   Imperf.

22	A4	2pa orange	70.00	250.00
a.		2pa yellow	77.50	325.00
b.		2pa ocher	325.00	325.00
23	A4	5pa blue	45.00	275.00
24	A4	20pa red, type I	35.00	47.50
a.		Bluish paper	350.00	
25	A4	20pa red, type II	35.00	40.00
a.		Bluish paper	350.00	
		Nos. 22-25 (4)	185.00	612.50

Full margins = 1¼mm.

The 20pa types are found se-tenant.

White Laid Paper

26	A4	2pa orange	60.00	275.00
a.		2pa ocher	125.00	
27	A4	5pa blue	95.00	450.00

Full margins = 1¼mm.

Prince Carol — A5   Type I — A6

Type II — A7

TWENTY PARALES:
Type I — A6. The Greek border at the upper right goes from right to left.
Type II — A7. The Greek border at the upper right goes from left to right.

1866-67   Thin Wove Paper

29	A5	2pa blk, *yellow*	35.00	95.00
a.		Thick paper	65.00	400.00
30	A5	5pa blk, *dk bl*	60.00	575.00
a.		5pa black, *indigo*	100.00	—
b.		Thick paper	70.00	525.00
31	A6	20pa blk, *rose*	30.00	26.50
a.		Dot in Greek border, thin paper	400.00	150.00
b.		Thick paper	175.00	87.50
c.		Dot in Greek border, thick paper	125.00	72.50
32	A7	20pa blk, *rose*, (II)	30.00	26.50
a.		Thick paper	175.00	87.50
		Nos. 29-32 (4)	155.00	723.00

Full margins = 1¼mm.

The 20pa types are found se-tenant.
Faked cancellations are known on Nos. 22-27, 29-32.
The white dot of Nos. 31a and 31c occurs in extreme upper right border.
Thick paper was used in 1866, thin in 1867.

Prince Carol
A8   A9

1868-70

33	A8	2b orange	42.50	40.00
a.		2b yellow	45.00	40.00
34	A8	3b violet ('70)	42.50	40.00
35	A8	4b dk blue	55.00	47.50
36	A8	18b scarlet	225.00	30.00
a.		18b rose	225.00	30.00
		Nos. 33-36 (4)	365.00	157.50

Full margins = 1¼mm.

1869

37	A9	5b orange yel	72.50	42.50
a.		5b deep orange	75.00	42.50
38	A9	10b blue	40.00	35.00
a.		10b ultramarine	77.50	52.50
b.		10b indigo	85.00	40.00
40	A9	15b vermilion	40.00	35.00
41	A9	25b orange & blue	40.00	26.50
42	A9	50b blue & red	150.00	52.50
a.		50b indigo & red	175.00	55.00
		Nos. 37-42 (5)	342.50	191.50

Full margins = 1mm.

No. 40 on vertically laid paper was not issued. Value $1,250.

Prince Carol
A10　　　　A11

1871-72　　　　　　　**Imperf.**

43	A10	5b rose	42.50	35.00
a.		5b vermilion	45.00	45.00
44	A10	10b orange yel	55.00	35.00
a.		Vertically laid paper	450.00	450.00
45	A10	10b blue	125.00	70.00
46	A10	15b red	210.00	210.00
47	A10	25b olive brown	47.50	47.50
		Nos. 43-47 (5)	480.00	397.50

Full margins = 1mm.

1872

48	A10	10b ultra	42.50	52.50
a.		Vertically laid paper	175.00	300.00
b.		10b greenish blue	150.00	175.00
49	A10	50b blue & red	225.00	240.00

Full margins = 1mm.

No. 48 is a provisional issue printed from a new plate in which the head is placed further right.

Faked cancellations are found on No. 49.

1872　Wove Paper　Perf. 12½

50	A10	5b rose	65.00	52.50
a.		5b vermilion	1,300.	700.00
51	A10	10b blue	57.50	52.50
a.		10b ultramarine	60.00	25.00
52	A10	25b dark brown	47.50	47.50
		Nos. 50-52 (3)	170.00	152.50

No. 43a with faked perforation is frequently offered as No. 50a.

Paris Print, Fine Impression
Tinted Paper

1872　Typo.　Perf. 14x13½

53	A11	1½b brnz grn, *bluish*	25.00	5.00
54	A11	3b green, *bluish*	32.50	5.00
55	A11	5b bis, *pale buff*	21.00	4.50
56	A11	10b blue	21.00	5.00
57	A11	15b red brn, *pale buff*	140.00	15.00
58	A11	25b org, *pale buff*	145.00	18.50
59	A11	50b rose, *pale rose*	150.00	42.50
		Nos. 53-59 (7)	534.50	95.50

Nos. 53-59 exist imperf.

Bucharest Print, Rough Impression
Perf. 11, 11½, 13½, and Compound
1876-79

60	A11	1½b brnz grn, *bluish*	6.50	4.25
61	A11	5b bis, *yelsh*	17.00	3.25
b.		Printed on both sides		75.00
62	A11	10b bl, *yelsh* ('77)	27.50	5.00
a.		10b pale bl, *yelsh*	25.00	5.00
b.		10b dark blue, *yelsh*	42.50	5.00
d.		Cliché of 5b in plate of 10b ('79)	425.00	425.00
63	A11	10b ultra, *yelsh* ('77)	47.50	5.00
64	A11	15b red brn, *yelsh*	72.50	9.25
a.		Printed on both sides		100.00
65	A11	30b org red, *yelsh* ('78)	190.00	50.00
a.		Printed on both sides		210.00
		Nos. 60-65 (6)	361.00	76.75

#60-65 are valued in the grade of fine.
#62d has been reprinted in dark blue. The originals are in dull blue. Value of reprint, $175.

Perf. 11, 11½, 13½ and Compound
1879

66	A11	1½b blk, *yelsh*	6.25	4.25
b.		Imperf.		12.00
67	A11	3b ol grn, *bluish*	17.50	12.50
a.		Diagonal half used as 1½b on cover		
68	A11	5b green, *bluish*	6.75	4.25
69	A11	10b rose, *yelsh*	13.50	2.50
b.		Cliché of 5b in plate of 10b	3.75.00	475.00
70	A11	15b brown red, *yelsh*	50.00	12.50
71	A11	25b blue, *yelsh*	140.00	25.00
72	A11	50b bister, *yelsh*	120.00	35.00
		Nos. 66-72 (7)	354.00	96.00

#66-72 are valued in the grade of fine.
There are two varieties of the numerals on the 15b and 50b.

No. 69b has been reprinted in dark rose. Originals are in pale rose. Value of reprint, $40.

King Carol I
A12　　　　A13

1880　　　　White Paper

73	A12	15b brown	12.50	2.50
74	A12	25b blue	23.50	3.25

#73-74 are valued in the grade of fine.
No. 74 exists imperf.

Perf. 13½, 11½ & Compound
1885-89

75	A13	1½b black	3.50	1.75
a.		Printed on both sides		
76	A13	3b violet	5.00	1.75
a.		Half used as 1½b on cover		21.00
77	A13	5b green	75.00	1.75
78	A13	15b red brown	14.50	2.50
79	A13	25b blue	17.00	6.00
		Nos. 75-79 (5)	115.00	13.75

Tinted Paper

80	A13	1½b blk, *bluish*	5.00	1.75
81	A13	3b vio, *bluish*	5.00	1.75
82	A13	3b ol grn, *bluish*	5.00	1.75
83	A13	5b bl grn, *bluish*	5.00	1.75
84	A13	10b rose, *pale buff*	5.00	2.50
85	A13	15b red brn, *pale buff*	18.50	2.75
86	A13	25b bl, *pale buff*	18.50	6.00
87	A13	50b bis, *pale buff*	75.00	12.50
		Nos. 80-87 (8)	137.00	39.25

Thin Pale Yellowish Paper

1889　　　　Wmk. 163

88	A13	1½b black	30.00	6.00
89	A13	3b violet	21.00	6.00
90	A13	5b green	21.00	6.00
91	A13	10b rose	21.00	6.00
92	A13	15b red brown	72.50	13.00
93	A13	25b dark blue	47.50	10.00
		Nos. 88-93 (6)	213.00	47.00

King Carol I
A14　　　　A15

1890　Perf. 13½, 11½ & Compound

94	A14	1½b maroon	5.00	3.50
95	A14	3b violet	25.00	3.50
96	A14	5b emerald	12.00	3.50
97	A14	10b red	13.00	5.00
a.		10b rose	17.00	6.75
98	A14	15b dk brown	30.00	3.50
99	A14	25b gray blue	25.00	3.50
100	A14	50b orange	65.00	32.50
		Nos. 94-100 (7)	175.00	55.00

1891　　　　Unwmk.

101	A14	1½b lilac rose	1.75	1.25
b.		Printed on both sides		65.00
102	A14	3b lilac	2.00	1.75
a.		3b violet	2.25	2.25
b.		Printed on both sides		
c.		Impressions of 5b on back	100.00	75.00
103	A14	5b emerald	3.50	1.75
104	A14	10b pale red	21.00	1.75
a.		Printed on both sides	140.00	110.00
105	A14	15b gray brown	13.00	1.25
106	A14	25b gray blue	13.00	1.75
107	A14	50b orange	85.00	13.00
		Nos. 101-107 (7)	139.25	22.50

Nos. 101-107 exist imperf.

1891

108	A15	1½b claret	6.00	7.00
109	A15	3b lilac	6.00	7.00
110	A15	5b emerald	7.50	8.50
111	A15	10b red	7.50	8.50
112	A15	15b gray brown	7.50	8.50
		Nos. 108-112 (5)	34.50	39.50

25th year of the reign of King Carol I.

1894　　　　Wmk. 164

113	A14	3b lilac	9.25	5.00
114	A14	5b pale green	9.25	5.00
115	A14	25b gray blue	13.50	6.25
116	A14	50b orange	27.50	12.50
		Nos. 113-116 (4)	59.50	28.75

King Carol I
A17　　　　A18

A19　　　　A20

A21　　　　A23

1893-98　　　　Wmk. 164 & 200

117	A17	1b pale brown	1.25	1.25
118	A17	1½b black	.85	1.25
119	A18	3b chocolate	1.25	.85
120	A19	5b blue	1.75	.85
a.		Cliché of the 25b in the plate of 5b	185.00	200.00
121	A19	5b yel grn ('98)	5.00	3.00
a.		5b emerald	5.00	3.00
122	A20	10b emerald	2.50	1.75
123	A20	10b rose ('98)	6.00	2.50
124	A21	15b rose	2.50	.85
125	A21	15b black ('98)	6.00	2.00
126	A19	25b violet	3.75	1.25
127	A19	25b indigo ('98)	9.25	3.25
128	A19	40b gray grn	21.00	3.50
129	A19	50b orange	12.50	2.00
130	A23	1 l bis & rose	30.00	2.00
131	A23	2 l orange & brn	35.00	3.25
		Nos. 117-131 (15)	138.60	29.55

This watermark may be found in four versions (Wmks. 164, 200 and variations). The paper also varies in thickness.

A 3b orange of type A18; 10b brown, type A20; 15b rose, type A21, and 25b bright green with similar but different border, all watermarked "P R," were prepared but never issued. Value, each $15.

See Nos. 132-157, 224-229. For overprints and surcharges see Romanian Post Offices in the Turkish Empire Nos. 1-6, 10-11.

King Carol I — A24

Thin Paper, Tinted Rose on Back

Perf. 11½, 13½ and Compound
1900-03　　　　Unwmk.

132	A17	1b pale brown	1.75	1.75
133	A24	1b brown ('01)	1.75	1.25
134	A24	1b black ('03)	1.75	1.25
135	A18	3b red brown	1.75	.85
136	A19	5b emerald	2.50	.85
137	A20	10b rose	3.00	1.25
138	A21	15b black	2.50	.85
139	A21	15b lil gray ('01)	2.50	.85
140	A21	15b dk vio ('03)	2.50	1.25
141	A19	25b blue	4.25	1.75
142	A19	40b gray grn	8.50	1.75
143	A19	50b orange	17.00	1.75
144	A23	1 l bis & rose ('01)	34.00	3.00
145	A23	1 l grn & blk ('03)	30.00	3.50
146	A23	2 l org & brn ('01)	30.00	3.50
147	A23	2 l red brn & blk ('03)	25.00	4.25
		Nos. 132-147 (16)	168.75	29.65

#132 inscribed BANI; #133-134 BAN.

1900, July　　　　Wmk. 167

148	A17	1b pale brown	12.00	5.00
149	A18	3b red brown	12.00	5.50
150	A19	5b emerald	10.00	5.00
151	A20	10b rose	15.00	6.00
152	A21	15b black	17.00	7.25
153	A19	25b blue	19.00	12.50
154	A19	40b gray grn	30.00	12.50
155	A19	50b orange	30.00	12.50
156	A23	1 l bis & rose	34.00	17.00
157	A23	2 l orange & brn	42.50	21.00
		Nos. 148-157 (10)	221.50	104.25

Mail Coach Leaving PO — A25

Thin Paper, Tinted Rose on Face

1903　Unwmk.　Perf. 14x13½

158	A25	1b gray brown	2.00	1.75
159	A25	3b brown violet	3.75	2.00
160	A25	5b pale green	7.50	2.50
161	A25	10b rose	6.00	3.00
162	A25	15b black	6.00	4.00
163	A25	25b blue	20.00	11.00
164	A25	40b dull green	27.50	13.50
165	A25	50b orange	35.00	19.00
		Nos. 158-165 (8)	107.75	56.75

Counterfeits are plentiful. See note after No. 172. See No. 428.

King Carol I and Façade of New Post Office — A26

Thick Toned Paper

1903　Engr.　Perf. 13½x14

166	A26	15b black	5.00	3.75
167	A26	25b blue	11.00	6.50
168	A26	40b gray grn	19.00	9.00
169	A26	50b orange	21.00	11.00
170	A26	1 l dk brown	16.00	9.00
171	A26	2 l dull red	130.00	65.00
a.		2 l orange (error)	180.00	150.00
172	A26	5 l dull violet	160.00	110.00
a.		5 l red violet	80.00	32.50
		Nos. 166-172 (7)	362.00	214.25

Opening of the new PO in Bucharest (Nos. 158-172).
Counterfeits exist.

Prince Carol Taking Oath of Allegiance, 1866 — A27

Prince in Royal Carriage A28

Prince Carol at Calafat in 1877 — A29

Prince Carol Shaking Hands with His Captive, Osman Pasha — A30

Carol I as Prince in 1866 and King in 1906 — A31

Romanian Army Crossing Danube — A32

Romanian Troops Return to Bucharest in 1878 — A33

Prince Carol at Head of His Command in 1877 — A34

King Carol I at the Cathedral in 1896 — A35

King Carol I at Shrine of St. Nicholas, 1904 — A36

1906   **Engr.**   **Perf. 12**

176	A27	1b bister & blk	.65 .45
177	A28	3b red brn & blk	1.40 .45
178	A29	5b dp grn & blk	1.75 .45
179	A30	10b carmine & blk	1.10 .45
180	A31	15b dull vio & blk	1.10 .45
181	A32	25b ultra & blk	7.00 5.25
a.		25b olive green & black	9.00 5.25
182	A33	40b dk brn & blk	1.90 1.60
183	A34	50b bis brn & blk	2.00 1.60
184	A35	1 l vermilion & blk	2.25 1.90
185	A36	2 l orange & blk	2.50 2.40
		Nos. 176-185 (10)	21.65 15.00

40 years' rule of Carol I as Prince & King. No. 181a was never placed in use. Cancellations were by favor.

King Carol I — A37

1906

186	A37	1b bister & blk	.90 .45
187	A37	3b red brn & blk	2.25 .85
188	A37	5b dp grn & blk	1.50 .75
189	A37	10b carmine & blk	1.50 .75
190	A37	15b dl vio & blk	1.50 .75
191	A37	25b ultra & blk	13.50 7.00
192	A37	40b dk brn & blk	6.00 1.50
193	A37	50b bis brn & blk	6.00 1.50
194	A37	1 l red & blk	6.00 1.50
195	A37	2 l orange & blk	6.00 1.50
		Nos. 186-195 (10)	45.15 16.55

25th anniversary of the Kingdom.

Plowman and Angel — A38

Exposition Building — A39

Exposition Buildings
A40   A41

King Carol I — A42   Queen Elizabeth (Carmen Sylva) — A43

1906   **Typo.**   **Perf. 11½, 13½**

196	A38	5b yel grn & blk	4.50 1.40
197	A38	10b carmine & blk	4.50 1.40
198	A39	15b violet & blk	6.50 2.25
199	A39	25b blue & blk	6.50 2.25
200	A40	30b red & blk brn	8.75 2.25
201	A40	40b green & blk brn	9.50 2.75
202	A41	50b orange & blk	8.75 3.25
203	A41	75b lt brn & dk brn	7.75 3.25
204	A42	1.50 l red lil & blk brn	97.50 45.00
a.		Center inverted	
205	A42	2.50 l yellow & brn	37.50 26.00
a.		Center inverted	
206	A43	3 l brn org & brn	28.00 26.00
		Nos. 196-206 (11)	219.75 115.80

General Exposition. They were sold at post offices July 29-31, 1906, and were valid only for those three days. Those sold at the exposition are overprinted "S E" in black. Remainders were sold privately, both unused and canceled to order, by the Exposition promoters. Value for set, unused or used, $450.

A44   A45

King Carol I — A46

Perf. 11½, 13½ & Compound

1908-18   **Engr.**

207	A44	5b pale yel grn	2.50 .25
208	A44	10b carmine	.70 .25
209	A45	15b purple	11.50 2.25
210	A44	25b deep blue	1.75 .25
211	A44	40b brt green	.85 .25
212	A44	40b dk brn ('18)	5.25 2.25
213	A44	50b orange	.65 .25
214	A44	50b lt red ('18)	2.00 .70
215	A44	1 l brown	2.00 .40
216	A44	2 l red	10.00 2.50
		Nos. 207-216 (10)	37.20 9.35

Perf. 13½x14, 11½, 13½ & Compound

1909-18   **Typo.**

217	A46	1b black	.60 .25
218	A46	3b red brown	1.25 .25
219	A46	5b yellow grn	.60 .25
220	A46	10b rose	1.25 .25
221	A46	15b dull violet	21.00 12.50

222	A46	15b olive green	1.25 .25
223	A46	15b red brn ('18)	1.10 .65
		Nos. 217-223 (7)	27.05 14.40

Nos. 217-219, 222 exist imperf.
No. 219 in black is a chemical changeling. For surcharge and overprints see Nos. 240-242, 245-247, J50-J51, RA1-RA2, RA11-RA12, Romanian Post Offices in the Turkish Empire 7-9.

Types of 1893-99

1911-19   **White Paper**   **Unwmk.**

224	A17	1½b straw	1.75 .45
225	A19	25b deep blue ('18)	1.00 .85
226	A19	40b gray brn ('19)	1.25 .85
227	A19	50b dull red ('19)	1.75 .85
228	A23	1 l gray grn ('18)	2.25 .50
229	A23	2 l orange ('18)	2.25 .85
		Nos. 224-229 (6)	10.25 4.35

For overprints see Romanian Post Offices in the Turkish Empire Nos. 10-11.

Romania Holding Flag — A47   Romanian Crown and Old Fort on Danube — A48

Troops Crossing Danube — A49

View of Turtucaia — A50

Mircea the Great and Carol I — A51

View of Silistra — A52

Perf. 11½x13½, 13½x11½

1913, Dec. 25

230	A47	1b black	.85 .40
231	A48	3b ol gray & choc	2.25 .85
232	A49	5b yel grn & blk brn	1.75 .40
233	A50	10b org & gray	.85 .40
234	A51	15b bister & vio	2.25 .85
235	A52	25b blue & choc	3.00 1.25
236	A49	40b bis & red vio	6.00 4.75
237	A48	50b yellow & bl	16.00 6.50
238	A48	1 l bl & ol bis	25.00 14.50
239	A48	2 l org red & rose	40.00 20.00
		Nos. 230-239 (10)	97.95 49.90

Romania's annexation of Silistra.

No. 217 Handstamped in Red

Perf. 13½x14, 11½, 13½ & Compound

1918, May 1

240	A46	25b on 1b black	2.25 2.25

This handstamp is found inverted.

No. 219 and 220 Overprinted in Black

1918

241	A46	5b yellow green	.60 .55
a.		Inverted overprint	3.25 3.25
b.		Double overprint	3.25 3.25
242	A46	10b rose	.60 .55
a.		Inverted overprint	3.25 3.25
b.		Double overprint	3.25 3.25

Nos. 217, 219 and 220 Overprinted in Red or Black

1919, Nov. 8

245	A46	1b black (R)	.40 .25
a.		Inverted overprint	6.75
b.		Double overprint	10.00 2.25
246	A46	5b yel grn (Bk)	.40 .25
a.		Double overprint	10.00 3.25
b.		Inverted overprint	6.75 2.00
247	A46	10b rose (Bk)	.40 .25
a.		Inverted overprint	6.75 2.00
b.		Double overprint	10.00 3.00
		Nos. 245-247 (3)	1.20 .75

Recovery of Transylvania and the return of the King to Bucharest.

King Ferdinand
A53   A54

1920-22   **Typo.**

248	A53	1b black	.25 .25
249	A53	5b yellow grn	.25 .25
250	A53	10b rose	.25 .25
251	A53	15b red brown	.75 .25
252	A53	25b deep blue	1.50 .40
253	A53	25b brown	.75 .25
254	A53	40b gray brown	1.25 .35
255	A53	50b salmon	.35 .25
256	A53	1 l gray grn	1.25 .25
257	A53	1 l rose	.75 .25
258	A53	2 l orange	1.25 .25
259	A53	2 l dp blue	1.25 .25
260	A53	2 l rose ('22)	3.00 1.75
		Nos. 248-260 (13)	12.85 5.00

Nos. 248-260 are printed on two papers: coarse, grayish paper with bits of colored fiber, and thinner white paper of better quality. Nos. 248-251, 253 exist imperf.

Type I   Type II   Type III
Type I   Type II   Type I   Type II

TWO LEI:
Type I — The "2" is thin, with tail 2½mm wide. Top of "2" forms a hook.
Type II — The "2" is thick, with tail 3mm wide. Top of "2" forms a ball.
Type III — The "2" is similar to type II. The "E" of "LEI" is larger and about 2mm wide.

THREE LEI:
Type I — Top of "3" begins in a point. Top and middle bars of "E" of "LEI" are without serifs.
Type II — Top of "3" begins in a ball. Top and middle bars of "E" of "LEI" have serifs.

FIVE LEI:
Type I — The "5" is 2½mm wide. The end of the final stroke of the "L" of "LEI" almost touches the vertical stroke.
Type II — The "5" is 2mm wide and are broader than in type I. The end of the final stroke of the "L" of "LEI" is separated from the vertical by a narrow space.

Perf. 13½x14, 11½, 13½ & Compound

1920-26

261	A54	3b black	.25	.25
262	A54	5b black	.25	.25
263	A54	10b yel grn ('25)	.25	.25
a.		10b olive green ('25)	.40	
264	A54	25b bister brn	.25	.25
265	A54	25b salmon	.25	.25
266	A54	30b violet	.25	.25
267	A54	50b orange	.25	.25
268	A54	60b gray grn	1.00	.55
269	A54	1 l violet	.25	.25
270	A54	2 l rose (I)	1.25	.25
a.		2 l claret (I)	47.50	
271	A54	2 l lt green (II)	.70	.25
a.		2 l light green (I)	.95	.40
b.		2 l light green (III)	.80	.25
272	A54	3 l blue (I)	2.60	.80
273	A54	3 l buff (II)	2.60	.80
a.		3 l buff (I)	12.50	2.25
274	A54	3 l salmon (II)	.25	.25
a.		3 l salmon (I)	1.60	1.25
275	A54	3 l car rose (II)	.65	.25
276	A54	5 l emer (II)	2.10	.50
277	A54	5 l lt brn (II)	.45	.25
a.		5 l light brown (I)	1.60	.80
278	A54	6 l blue	2.60	1.25
279	A54	6 l carmine	5.75	3.25
280	A54	6 l ol grn ('26)	2.50	.80
281	A54	7½ l pale bl	2.10	.45
282	A54	10 l deep blue	2.10	.45
		Nos. 261-282 (22)	28.65	12.10

#273 and 273a, 274 and 274a, exist se-tenant. The 50b exists in three types.
For surcharge see No. Q7.

Alba Iulia
Cathedral
A55

King
Ferdinand
A56

Coat of
Arms — A57

Queen Marie
as
Nurse — A58

Michael the Brave and
King Ferdinand
A59

King
Ferdinand
A60

Queen Marie — A61

Perf. 13½x14, 13½, 11½ & Compound

1922, Oct. 15　　Photo.　　Wmk. 95

283	A55	5b black	.40	.30
a.		Engraver's name omitted	.40	.30
284	A56	25b chocolate	1.25	.40
285	A57	50b dp green	1.25	.60
286	A58	1 l olive grn	1.50	.85
287	A59	2 l carmine	1.50	.85

288	A60	3 l blue	4.00	1.25
289	A61	6 l violet	11.50	8.00
		Nos. 283-289 (7)	21.40	12.25

Coronation of King Ferdinand I and Queen Marie on Oct. 15, 1922, at Alba Iulia. All values exist imperforate. Value, set $150, unused or used.

King Ferdinand
A62　　　　A63

1926, July 1　　Unwmk.　　Perf. 11

291	A62	10b yellow grn	.40	.35
292	A62	25b orange	.40	.35
293	A62	50b orange brn	.40	.35
294	A63	1 l dk violet	.40	.35
295	A63	2 l dk green	.40	.35
296	A63	3 l brown car	.40	.75
297	A63	5 l black brn	.40	.75
298	A63	6 l dk olive	.40	.75
a.		6 l bright blue (error)	80.00	80.00
300	A63	9 l slate	.40	.75
301	A63	10 l brt blue	.40	.75
b.		10 l brown carmine (error)	80.00	80.00
		Nos. 291-301 (10)	4.00	5.50

60th birthday of King Ferdinand.
Exist imperf. Value, set $110, unused or used. Imperf. examples with watermark 95 are proofs.

King Carol
I and King
Ferdinand
A69

King
Ferdinand
A70

A71

1927, Aug. 1　　　　Perf. 13½

308	A69	25b brown vio	.25	.25
309	A70	30b gray blk	.25	.25
310	A71	50b dk green	.25	.25
311	A69	1 l bluish slate	.25	.25
312	A70	2 l dp green	.25	.30
313	A70	3 l violet	.35	.35
314	A71	4 l dk brown	.50	.45
315	A71	4.50 l henna brn	1.50	1.10
316	A70	5 l red brown	.35	.35
317	A71	6 l carmine	.85	.75
318	A69	7.50 l grnsh bl	.45	.35
319	A69	10 l brt blue	1.50	.75
		Nos. 308-319 (12)	6.75	5.40

50th anniversary of Romania's independence from Turkish suzerainty.
Some values exist imperf. All exist imperf. and with value numerals omitted.

King Michael
A72　　　　A73

Perf. 13½x14 (25b, 50b); 13½

1928-29　　Typo.　　Unwmk.

Size: 19x25mm

320	A72	25b black	.25	.25
321	A72	30b fawn ('29)	.40	.25

322	A72	50b olive grn	.25	.25

Photo.
Size: 18½x24½mm

323	A73	1 l violet	.45	.25
324	A73	2 l dp green	.45	.25
325	A73	3 l brt rose	.90	.25
326	A73	5 l red brown	1.40	.25
327	A73	7.50 l ultra	6.25	.90
328	A73	10 l blue	5.25	.35
		Nos. 320-328 (9)	15.60	3.00

See Nos. 343-345, 353-357. For overprints see Nos. 359-368A.

Parliament House, Bessarabia — A74

Designs: 1 l, 2 l, Parliament House, Bessarabia. 3 l, 5 l, 20 l, Hotin Fortress. 7.50 l, 10 l, Fortress Cetatea Alba.

1928, Apr. 29　　Wmk. 95　　Perf. 13½

329	A74	1 l deep green	2.00	.80
330	A74	2 l deep brown	2.00	.80
331	A74	3 l black brown	2.00	.80
332	A74	5 l carmine lake	2.50	1.00
333	A74	7.50 l ultra	2.50	1.00
334	A74	10 l Prus blue	5.75	2.25
335	A74	20 l black vio	8.50	3.50
		Nos. 329-335 (7)	25.25	10.15

Reunion of Bessarabia with Romania, 10th anniv.

King Carol
I and King
Michael
A77

View of
Constanta
Harbor
A78

Trajan's
Monument
at Adam
Clisi
A79

Cernavoda Bridge — A80

1928, Oct. 25

336	A77	1 l blue green	1.10	.45
337	A78	2 l red brown	1.10	.45
338	A77	3 l gray black	1.40	.50
339	A79	5 l dull lilac	1.75	.60
340	A79	7.50 l ultra	2.10	.80
341	A80	10 l blue	3.25	1.90
342	A80	20 l carmine rose	5.50	3.25
		Nos. 336-342 (7)	16.20	7.95

Union of Dobruja with Romania, 50th anniv.

Michael Types of 1928-29
Perf. 13½x14

1928, Sept. 1　　Typo.　　Wmk. 95

343	A72	25b black	.60	.25

Photo.

344	A73	7.50 l ultra	2.00	.75
345	A73	10 l blue	4.00	.60
		Nos. 343-345 (3)	6.60	1.60

Ferdinand I; Stephen the Great;
Michael the Brave; Corvin and
Constantine Brancoveanu — A81

Union with
Transylvania
A82

Avram
Jancu — A83

Prince Michael
the Brave — A84

Castle Bran — A85

King
Ferdinand
I — A86

1929, May 10　　Photo.　　Wmk. 95

347	A81	1 l dark violet	2.25	1.75
348	A82	2 l olive green	2.25	1.75
349	A83	3 l violet brown	2.50	1.75
350	A84	4 l cerise	2.75	2.25
351	A85	5 l orange	4.50	2.25
352	A86	10 l brt blue	7.50	4.25
		Nos. 347-352 (6)	21.75	14.00

Union of Transylvania and Romania.

Michael Type of 1928

1930　　Unwmk.　　Perf. 14½x14

Size: 18x23mm

353	A73	1 l deep violet	.80	.25
354	A73	2 l deep green	1.25	.25
355	A73	3 l carmine rose	2.40	.25
356	A73	7.50 l ultra	5.00	1.10
357	A73	10 l deep blue	16.00	7.00
		Nos. 353-357 (5)	25.45	8.85

Stamps of 1928-30
Overprinted

On Nos. 320-322, 326, 328
Perf. 13½x14, 13½

1930, June 8　　　　Typo.

359	A72	25b black	.40	.25
360	A72	30b fawn	.80	.25
361	A72	50b olive green	.80	.25

Photo.
Size: 18½x24½mm

362	A73	5 l red brown	1.60	.25

362A	A73	10 l brt blue	8.25	1.50

On Nos. 353-357
Perf. 14½x14
Size: 18x23mm

363	A73	1 l deep violet	.80	.25
364	A73	2 l deep green	.80	.25
365	A73	3 l carmine rose	1.60	.25
366	A73	7.50 l ultra	4.00	.75
367	A73	10 l deep blue	3.25	.75

On Nos. 343-344
Perf. 13½x14, 13½
Typo.   **Wmk. 95**

368	A72	25b black	1.25	.35

Photo.
Size: 18½x24½mm

368A	A73	7.50 l ultra	5.00	1.50
		Nos. 359-368A (12)	28.55	6.60

Accession to the throne by King Carol II.
This overprint exists on Nos. 323, 345.

A87   A88

King Carol II — A89

Perf. 13½, 14, 14x13½
1930   **Wmk. 225**

369	A87	25b black	1.10	.25
370	A87	50b chocolate	3.25	.45
371	A87	1 l dk violet	2.25	.25
372	A87	2 l gray green	2.75	.25
373	A88	3 l carmine rose	2.25	.25
374	A88	4 l orange red	3.25	.25
375	A88	6 l carmine brn	4.25	.25
376	A88	7.50 l ultra	4.25	.30
377	A89	10 l deep blue	2.25	.25
378	A89	16 l peacock grn	4.75	.25
379	A89	20 l orange	1.40	.60
		Nos. 369-379 (11)	31.75	3.35

Exist imperf. Value, unused or used, $250.
See Nos. 405-414.

A90   A91

1930, Dec. 24   **Unwmk.**   *Perf. 13½*

380	A90	1 l dull violet	1.25	.45
381	A91	2 l green	2.25	.50
382	A91	4 l vermilion	2.50	.50
383	A91	6 l brown carmine	6.50	.45
		Nos. 380-383 (4)	12.50	1.75

First census in Romania.

King Carol
II — A92

King Carol   King
I — A93   Ferdinand — A96

King Carol
II — A94

King Carol II, King
Ferdinand and
King Carol
I — A95

1931, May 10   **Photo.**   **Wmk. 225**

384	A92	1 l gray violet	2.50	1.75
385	A93	2 l green	4.25	2.00
386	A94	6 l red brown	11.00	3.25
387	A95	10 l blue	16.00	6.00
388	A96	20 l orange	22.50	8.50
		Nos. 384-388 (5)	56.25	21.50

50th anniversary of Romanian Kingdom.

Using   Romanian
Bayonet — A97   Infantryman
             1870 — A98

Romanian Infantry
1830 — A99

King Carol I   Infantry
A100   Advance
              A101

King Ferdinand   King Carol II
A102   A103

1931, May 10

389	A97	25b gray black	1.40	.75
390	A98	50b dk red brn	2.10	1.10
391	A99	1 l gray violet	2.75	1.10
392	A100	2 l deep green	4.25	1.50
393	A101	4 l carmine rose	10.00	3.50
394	A102	7.50 l ultra	13.00	9.00
395	A103	16 l blue green	16.00	4.00
		Nos. 389-395 (7)	49.50	20.95

Centenary of the Romanian Army.

Naval Cadet
Ship "Mircea"
A104

10 l, Ironclad. 16 l, Light cruiser. 20 l,
Destroyer.

1931, May 10

396	A104	6 l red brown	7.00	4.00
397	A104	10 l blue	9.50	4.50
398	A104	16 l blue green	40.00	6.00
399	A104	20 l orange	17.50	10.00
		Nos. 396-399 (4)	74.00	24.50

50th anniversary of the Romanian Navy.

King Carol II — A108

1931   **Unwmk.**   **Engr.**   *Perf. 12*

400	A108	30 l ol bis & dk bl	1.00	.60
401	A108	50 l red & dk bl	2.00	1.00
402	A108	100 l dk grn & dk bl	5.00	2.10
		Nos. 400-402 (3)	8.00	3.70

Exist imperf. Value, unused or used, $150.

Carol II,
Ferdinand,
Carol
I — A109

Wmk. 230
1931, Nov. 1   **Photo.**   *Perf. 13½*

403	A109	16 l Prus green	12.00	.90

Exists imperf. Value, unused or used, $300.

Carol II Types of 1930
Perf. 13½, 14, 14½ and Compound
1932   **Wmk. 230**

405	A87	25b black	.50	.25
406	A87	50b dark brown	1.00	.25
407	A87	1 l dark violet	1.40	.25
408	A87	2 l gray green	1.75	.25
409	A88	3 l carmine rose	2.25	.25
410	A88	4 l orange red	5.25	.25
411	A88	6 l carmine brn	12.50	.25
412	A88	7.50 l ultra	21.50	.75
413	A89	10 l deep blue	125.00	.90
414	A89	20 l orange	110.00	9.00
		Nos. 405-414 (10)	281.15	12.40

Alexander the   King Carol
Good — A110   II — A111

1932, May   *Perf. 13½*

415	A110	6 l carmine brown	12.00	6.00

500th death anniv. of Alexander the Good,
Prince of Moldavia, 1400-1432.

1932, June

416	A111	10 l brt blue	12.00	.45

Exists imperf. Value, unused or used, $200.

Cantacuzino and Gregory Ghika,
Founders of Coltea and Pantelimon
Hospitals — A112

Session of
the
Congress
A113

Aesculapius and Hygeia — A114

1932, Sept.   *Perf. 13½*

417	A112	1 l carmine rose	7.50	7.50
418	A113	6 l deep orange	20.00	11.00
419	A114	10 l brt blue	34.00	18.50
		Nos. 417-419 (3)	61.50	37.00

9th Intl. History of Medicine Congress,
Bucharest.

Bull's Head   Lion
and Post   Rampant and
Horn   Bridge
A116   A117

 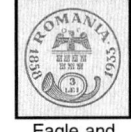

Dolphins   Eagle and
A118   Castles
            A119

Coat of   Eagle and
Arms — A120   Post
             Horn — A121

Bull's Head and Post
Horn — A122

1932, Nov. 20   **Typo.**   *Imperf.*

421	A116	25b black	.85	.40
422	A117	1 l violet	2.00	.70
423	A118	2 l green	2.50	.90
424	A119	3 l car rose	2.80	1.10
425	A120	6 l red brown	3.50	1.25
426	A121	7.50 l lt blue	4.25	1.75
427	A122	10 l dk blue	8.00	3.00
		Nos. 421-427 (7)	23.90	9.10

75th anniv. of the first Moldavian stamps.

Mail Coach Type of 1903
1932, Nov. 20   *Perf. 13½*

428	A25	16 l blue green	11.00	5.50

30th anniv. of the opening of the new post
office, Bucharest, in 1903.

Arms of City of Turnu-Severin, Ruins
of Tower of Emperor Severus — A123

Inauguration of Trajan's
Bridge — A124

Prince Carol Landing at Turnu-
Severin — A125

Bridge
over the
Danube
A126

1933, June 2   Photo.   Perf. 14½x14
429 A123 25b gray green   .75   .30
430 A124 50b dull blue   1.10   .45
431 A125 1 l black brn   1.75   .75
432 A126 2 l olive blk   3.25 1.10
    Nos. 429-432 (4)   6.85 2.60
  Centenary of the incorporation in Walachia
of the old Roman City of Turnu-Severin.
  Exist imperf. Value, unused or used, $150.

Queen
Elizabeth
and King
Carol
I — A127

Profiles of
Kings
Carol I,
Ferdinand
and Carol
II — A128

Castle
Peles,
Sinaia
A129

1933, Aug.
433 A127 1 l dark violet   2.50 2.00
434 A128 3 l olive brown   3.00 2.75
435 A129 6 l vermilion   4.25 3.25
    Nos. 433-435 (3)   9.75 8.00
  50th anniversary of the erection of Castle
Peles, the royal summer residence at Sinaia.
  Exist imperf. Value, unused or used, $125.

A130   A131

King Carol
II — A132

1934, Aug.   Perf. 13½
436 A130 50b brown   1.00   .40
437 A131 2 l gray green   2.00   .40
438 A131 4 l red   3.50   .55
439 A132 6 l deep claret   8.00   .40
    Nos. 436-439 (4)   14.50 1.75
  See Nos. 446-460 for stamps inscribed
"Posta." Nos. 436, 439 exist imperf. Value for
both, unused or used, $100.

Child and
Grapes — A133

Woman and
Fruit — A134

1934, Sept. 14
440 A133 1 l dull green   5.00 2.25
441 A134 2 l violet brown   5.00 2.25
  Natl. Fruit Week, Sept. 14-21. Exist imperf.
Value, unused or used, $125.

Crisan,
Horia and
Closca
A135

1935, Feb. 28
442 A135 1 l shown   .65   .50
443 A135 2 l Crisan   .90   .60
444 A135 6 l Closca   2.25 1.00
445 A135 10 l Horia   5.00 2.25
    Nos. 442-445 (4)   8.80 4.35
  150th anniversary of the death of three
Romanian martyrs. Exist imperf. Value,
unused or used, $110.

A139   A140

A141   A142

King Carol
II — A143

Wmk. 230
1935-40   Photo.   Perf. 13½
446 A139 25b black brn   .25   .25
447 A142 50b brown   .25   .25
448 A140 1 l purple   .25   .25
449 A141 2 l green   .45   .25
449A A141 2 l dk bl grn ('40)   .65   .25
450 A142 3 l deep rose   .70   .25
450A A142 3 l grnsh bl ('40)   .85   .30
451 A141 4 l vermilion   1.25   .25
452 A140 5 l rose car ('40)   1.25   .80
453 A142 6 l maroon   1.25   .80
454 A140 7.50 l ultra   1.90   .30
454A A142 8 l magenta ('40)   1.90   .70
455 A141 9 l brt ultra ('40) 2.50   .80
456 A142 10 l brt blue   1.00   .25
456A A143 12 l slate bl ('40) 1.60 1.25
457 A139 15 l dk brn ('40)   1.60   .95
458 A143 16 l Prus blue   2.10   .35
459 A143 20 l orange   1.25   .35
460 A143 24 l dk car ('40)   2.10   .95
    Nos. 446-460 (19)   23.45 8.90
  Exist imperf. Value, unused or used, $240.

Nos. 454, 456
Overprinted in Red

1936, Dec. 5
461 A140 7.50 l ultra   4.25 4.25
462 A142 10 l brt blue   4.25 4.25
  16th anniversary of the Little Entente.
Overprints in silver or gold are fraudulent.

Birthplace
of Ion
Creanga
A144

Ion
Creanga
A145

1937, May 15
463 A144 2 l green   1.25   .80
464 A145 3 l carmine rose   1.75   .90
465 A144 4 l dp violet   2.00 1.10
466 A145 6 l red brown   5.00 2.50
    Nos. 463-466 (4)   10.00 5.30
  Creanga (1837-89), writer. Exist imperf.
Value, unused or used, $125.

Cathedral at
Curtea de
Arges — A146

1937, July 1
467 A146 7.50 l ultra   2.50 1.10
468 A146 10 l blue   3.25   .80
  The Little Entente (Romania, Czechoslovakia, Yugoslavia). Exist imperf. Value, unused
or used, $125.

Souvenir Sheet

A146a

**Surcharged in Black with New
Values**
1937, Oct. 25   Unwmk.   Perf. 13½
469 A146a   Sheet of 4   9.00 9.00
  a.   2 l on 20 l orange   .35   .35
  b.   6 l on 10 l bright blue .35   .35
  c.   10 l on 6 l maroon   .45   .45
  d.   20 l on 2 l green   1.00 1.00
  Promotion of the Crown Prince Michael to
the rank of Lieutenant on his 17th birthday.

Arms of
Romania,
Greece, Turkey
and Yugoslavia
A147

Perf. 13x13½
1938, Feb. 10   Wmk. 230
470 A147 7.50 l ultra   1.50   .90
471 A147 10 l blue   2.00   .80
  The Balkan Entente.
  Exist imperf. Value, unused or used, $100.

A148

King Carol II
A149   A150

1938, May 10   Perf. 13½
472 A148 3 l dk carmine   .75   .50
473 A149 6 l violet brn   1.25   .50
474 A150 10 l blue   2.00   .90
    Nos. 472-474 (3)   4.00 1.90
  New Constitution of Feb. 27, 1938.
  Exist imperf. Value, unused or used, $100.

**Catalogue values for unused
stamps in this section, from this
point to the end of the section, are
for Never Hinged items.**

Prince
Carol at
Calatorie,
1866
A151

Examining Plans
for a Monastery
A153

Prince Carol and
Carmen Sylva
(Queen Elizabeth)
A155

Sigmaringen and Peles
Castles — A154

Prince Carol, Age
6 — A156

Equestrian Statue — A159

Battle of Plevna — A160

On Horseback A161

Cathedral of Curtea de Arges A164

King Carol I and Queen Elizabeth A163

Designs: 50b, At Calafat. 4 l, In 1866. 5 l, In 1877. 12 l, in 1914.

Perf. 14, 13½

1939, Apr. 10 Wmk. 230

475	A151	25b olive blk	.25	.25
476	A151	50b violet brn	.25	.25
477	A153	1 l dk purple	.25	.25
478	A154	1.50 l green	.25	.25
479	A155	2 l myrtle grn	.25	.25
480	A156	3 l red orange	.25	.25
481	A156	4 l rose lake	.25	.25
482	A156	5 l black	.25	.25
483	A159	7 l olive blk	.25	.25
484	A160	8 l dark blue	.25	.25
485	A161	10 l deep mag	.25	.25
486	A161	12 l dull blue	.30	.25
487	A163	15 l ultra	.35	.25
488	A164	16 l Prus green	.75	.40
	Nos. 475-488 (14)		4.15	3.65

Centenary of the birth of King Carol I.
Nos. 475-488 exist imperf. Value, unused or used, $150.

Souvenir Sheets

1939 **Perf. 14x13½**

488A	Sheet of 3, #475-476, 478	3.50	3.50
d.	Imperf. ('40)	7.00	7.00

Perf. 14x15½

488B	Sheet of 4, #480-482, 486	3.50	3.50
e.	Imperf. ('40)	7.00	7.00
488C	Sheet of 4, #479, 483-485	3.50	3.50
f.	Imperf. ('40)	7.00	7.00

No. 488A sold for 20 l, Nos. 488B-488C for 50 l, the surtax for national defense.

Nos. 488A-488C and 488Ad-488Cf were overprinted "PRO-PATRIA 1940" to aid the armament fund. Value, set of 6, $100.

Nos. 488A-488C exist with overprint of "ROMA BERLIN 1940" and bars, but these are not recognized as having been officially issued.

Romanian Pavilion A165

Romanian Pavilion A166

1939, May 8 **Perf. 14x13½, 13½**

489	A165	6 l brown carmine	1.25	.60
490	A166	12 l brt blue	1.25	.60

New York World's Fair.
Nos. 489-490 exist imperf. Value, unused or used, $250.

Mihail Eminescu
A167   A168

1939, May 22 **Perf. 13½**

491	A167	5 l olive gray	1.25	.60
492	A168	7 l brown carmine	1.25	.60

Mihail Eminescu, poet, 50th death anniv.
Nos. 491-492 exist imperf. Value, unused or used, $300.

Three Types of Locomotives — A169

Modern Train A170

Wood-burning Locomotive A171

Streamlined Locomotive A172

Railroad Terminal A173

1939, June 10 **Typo.** **Perf. 14**

493	A169	1 l red violet	1.75	.60
494	A170	4 l deep rose	1.75	.60
495	A171	5 l gray lilac	1.75	.60
496	A171	7 l claret	1.75	.60
497	A172	12 l blue	3.50	1.75
498	A173	15 l green	3.50	2.40
	Nos. 493-498 (6)		14.00	6.55

Romanian Railways, 70th anniversary.
Nos. 493-498 exist imperf. Value, unused or used, $200.

Arms of Romania, Greece, Turkey and Yugoslavia — A174

Wmk. 230

1940, May 27 **Photo.** **Perf. 13½**

504	A174	12 l lt ultra	1.25	.75
505	A174	16 l dull blue	1.25	.75

The Balkan Entente.
Nos 504-505 exist imperf. Value, unused or used, $125.

King Michael — A175

1940-42 **Wmk. 230** **Perf. 14**

506	A175	25b Prus green	.25	.25
506A	A175	50b dk grn ('42)	.25	.25
507	A175	1 l purple	.25	.25
508	A175	2 l red orange	.25	.25
508A	A175	4 l slate ('42)	.25	.25
509	A175	5 l rose pink	.25	.25
509A	A175	7 l dp blue ('42)	.25	.25
510	A175	10 l dp magenta	.40	.25
511	A175	12 l dull blue	.25	.25
511A	A175	13 l dk vio ('42)	.25	.25
512	A175	16 l Prus blue	.55	.25
513	A175	20 l brown	1.60	.25
514	A175	30 l yellow grn	.25	.25
515	A175	50 l olive brn	.25	.25
516	A175	100 l rose brown	.75	.25
	Nos. 506-516 (15)		6.05	3.75

See Nos. 535A-553 in Scott Standard catalogue, Vol. 5.

SEMI-POSTAL STAMPS

Queen Elizabeth Spinning — SP1

Perf. 11½, 11½x13½

1906, Jan. 14 **Typo.** **Unwmk.**

B1	SP1	3b (+ 7b) brown	6.00	3.75
B2	SP1	5b (+ 10b) lt grn	6.00	3.75
B3	SP1	10b (+ 10b) rose red	29.00	11.00
B4	SP1	15b (+ 10b) violet	20.00	7.50
	Nos. B1-B4 (4)		61.00	26.00

The Queen Weaving — SP2

1906, Mar. 18

B5	SP2	3b (+ 7b) org brn	6.00	3.75
B6	SP2	5b (+ 10b) bl grn	6.00	3.75
B7	SP2	10b (+ 10b) car	29.00	11.00
B8	SP2	15b (+ 10b) red vio	20.00	7.50
	Nos. B5-B8 (4)		61.00	26.00

Queen as War Nurse SP3

1906, Mar. 23 **Perf. 11½, 13½x11½**

B9	SP3	3b (+ 7b) org brn	6.00	3.75
B10	SP3	5b (+ 10b) bl grn	6.00	3.75
B11	SP3	10b (+ 10b) car	29.00	11.00
B12	SP3	15b (+ 10b) red vio	20.00	7.50
	Nos. B9-B12 (4)		61.00	26.00
	Nos. B1-B12 (12)		183.00	78.00

Booklet panes of 4 exist of Nos. B1-B3, B5-B7, B9-B12.

Counterfeits of Nos. B1-B12 are plentiful. Examples of Nos. B1-B12 with smooth, even gum are counterfeits.

SP4

1906, Aug. 4 **Perf. 12**

B13	SP4	3b (+ 7b) ol brn, buff & bl	3.25	1.50
B14	SP4	5b (+ 10b) grn, rose & buff	3.25	1.50
B15	SP4	10b (+ 10b) rose red, buff & bl	5.00	3.00
B16	SP4	15b (+ 10b) vio, buff & bl	13.00	3.75
	Nos. B13-B16 (4)		24.50	9.75

Guardian Angel Bringing Poor to Crown Princess Marie SP5

1907, Feb. **Engr.** **Perf. 11**
Center in Brown

B17	SP5	3b (+ 7b) org brn	4.00	1.50
B18	SP5	5b (+ 10b) dk grn	4.00	1.50
B19	SP5	10b (+ 10b) dk car	4.00	1.50
B20	SP5	15b (+ 10b) dl vio	4.00	1.50
	Nos. B17-B20 (4)		16.00	6.00

Nos. B1-B20 were sold for more than face value. The surtax, shown in parenthesis, was for charitable purposes.

Map of Romania SP9

Stephen the Great SP10

Michael the Brave SP11

Kings Carol I and Ferdinand SP12

Adam Clisi Monument — SP13

1927, Mar. 15 **Typo.** **Perf. 13½**

B21	SP9	1 l + 9 l lt vio	4.25	1.60
B22	SP10	2 l + 8 l Prus grn	4.25	1.60
B23	SP11	3 l + 7 l dp rose	4.25	1.60
B24	SP12	5 l + 5 l dp bl	4.25	1.60
B25	SP13	6 l + 4 l ol grn	6.25	2.50
	Nos. B21-B25 (5)		23.25	8.90

50th anniv. of the Royal Geographical Society. The surtax was for the benefit of that society. The stamps were valid for postage only from 3/15-4/14.

Boy Scouts in Camp — SP15   The Rescue — SP16

Designs: 3 l+3 l, Swearing in a Tenderfoot. 4 l+4 l, Prince Nicholas Chief Scout. 6 l+6 l, King Carol II in Scout's Uniform.

1931, July 15   Photo.   Wmk. 225

B26	SP15	1 l + 1 l car rose	3.75	2.50
B27	SP16	2 l + 2 l dp grn	5.00	3.00
B28	SP15	3 l + 3 l ultra	6.00	3.00
B29	SP16	4 l + 4 l ol gray	7.50	8.00
B30	SP16	6 l + 6 l red brn	10.00	8.00
	Nos. B26-B30 (5)		32.25	24.50

The surtax was for the benefit of the Boy Scout organization.

Boy Scout Jamboree Issue

Scouts in Camp SP20   Semaphore Signaling SP21

Trailing — SP22   Camp Fire — SP23

King Carol II — SP24   King Carol II and Prince Michael — SP25

1932, June 8   Wmk. 230

B31	SP20	25b + 25b pck grn	3.00	1.10
B32	SP21	50b + 50b brt bl	4.00	2.25
B33	SP22	1 l + 1 l ol grn	4.50	3.25
B34	SP23	2 l + 2 l org red	7.50	4.50
B35	SP24	3 l + 3 l Prus bl	14.00	9.00
B36	SP25	6 l + 6 l blk brn	16.00	11.50
	Nos. B31-B36 (6)		49.00	31.60

For overprints see Nos. B44-B49.

Tuberculosis Sanatorium — SP26

Memorial Tablet to Postal Employees Who Died in World War I — SP27

Carmen Sylva Convalescent Home — SP28

1932, Nov. 1

B37	SP26	4 l + 1 l dk grn	5.00	4.00
B38	SP27	6 l + 1 l chocolate	5.50	4.75
B39	SP28	10 l + 1 l dp bl	10.00	8.00
	Nos. B37-B39 (3)		20.50	16.75

The surtax was given to a fund for the employees of the postal and telegraph services.

Philatelic Exhibition Issue
Souvenir Sheet

King Carol II — SP29

1932, Nov. 20   Unwmk.   Imperf.
B40   SP29   6 l + 5 l dk ol grn   50.00   50.00

Intl. Phil. Exhib. at Bucharest, Nov. 20-24, 1932. Each holder of a ticket of admission to the exhibition could buy an example of No. B40. The ticket cost 20 lei.

Roadside Shrine — SP31   Woman Spinning — SP33

Woman Weaving SP32

1934, Apr. 16   Wmk. 230   Perf. 13½

B41	SP31	1 l + 1 l dk brn	1.00	.90
B42	SP32	2 l + 1 l blue	1.25	1.10
B43	SP33	3 l + 1 l slate grn	1.75	1.50
	Nos. B41-B43 (3)		4.00	3.50

Weaving Exposition.

Boy Scout Mamaia Jamboree Issue

Semi-Postal Stamps of 1932 Overprinted in Black or Gold

1934, July 8

B44	SP20	25b + 25b pck grn	3.75	2.50
B45	SP21	50b + 50b brt bl (G)	5.00	3.00
B46	SP22	1 l + 1 l ol grn	6.00	4.75
B47	SP23	2 l + 2 l org red	7.50	5.50
B48	SP24	3 l + 3 l Prus bl (G)	16.00	7.00
B49	SP25	6 l + 6 l blk brn (G)	18.00	9.50
	Nos. B44-B49 (6)		56.25	32.25

Sea Scout Saluting SP34   Scout Bugler SP35

Sea and Land Scouts SP36

King Carol II — SP37   Sea, Land and Girl Scouts — SP38

1935, June 8

B50	SP34	25b ol blk	1.25	1.00
B51	SP35	1 l violet	2.75	2.25
B52	SP36	2 l green	3.50	3.00
B53	SP37	6 l + 1 l red brn	5.00	4.50
B54	SP38	10 l + 2 l dk ultra	14.00	13.00
	Nos. B50-B54 (5)		26.50	23.75

Fifth anniversary of accession of King Carol II, and a national sports meeting held June 8. Surtax aided the Boy Scouts.
Nos. B50-B54 exist imperf. Value $250.

King Carol II — SP39

1936, May
B55   SP39   6 l + 1 l rose car   .75   .55

Bucharest Exhibition and 70th anniversary of the dynasty. Exists imperf. Value $125

Girl of Oltenia — SP40

Girl of Saliste — SP42

Youth from Gorj — SP44

Designs: 1 l+1 l, Girl of Banat. 3 l+1 l, Girl of Hateg. 6 l+3 l, Girl of Neamt. 10 l+5 l, Youth and girl of Bucovina.

1936, June 8

B56	SP40	50b + 50b brown	.60	.40
B57	SP40	1 l + 1 l violet	.60	.40
B58	SP42	2 l + 1 l Prus grn	.60	.40
B59	SP42	3 l + 1 l car rose	.60	.40
B60	SP44	4 l + 2 l red org	1.00	.75
B61	SP40	6 l + 3 l ol gray	1.00	.90
B62	SP42	10 l + 5 l brt bl	2.25	2.00
	Nos. B56-B62 (7)		6.65	5.25

6th anniv. of accession of King Carol II. The surtax was for child welfare. Exist imperf. Value $300, unused or used.

Insignia of Boy Scouts
SP47   SP48

Jamboree Emblem — SP49

1936, Aug. 20

B63	SP47	1 l + 1 l brt bl	5.75	6.25
B64	SP48	3 l + 3 l ol gray	9.75	6.50
B65	SP49	6 l + 6 l car rose	13.00	6.50
	Nos. B63-B65 (3)		28.50	19.25

Boy Scout Jamboree at Brasov (Kronstadt). Exist imperf. Value $350, unused or used.

Submarine "Delfinul" SP50

Designs: 3 l+2 l, Training ship "Mircea." 6 l+3 l, Steamship "S.M.R."

1936, Oct.

B66	SP50	1 l + 1 l pur	2.75	2.50
B67	SP50	3 l + 2 l ultra	2.50	2.25
B68	SP50	6 l + 3 l car rose	3.50	2.25
	Nos. B66-B68 (3)		8.75	7.00

Marine Exhibition at Bucharest. Exist imperf. Value $325, unused or used.

Soccer SP53

Swimming
SP54

Throwing the
Javelin — SP55

Skiing — SP56

King Carol II
Hunting — SP57

Rowing
SP58

Horsemanship
SP59

Founding of
the U.F.S.R.
SP60

1937, June 8   Wmk. 230   Perf. 13½

B69	SP53	25b + 25b ol blk	.75	.25
B70	SP54	50b + 50b brown	.75	.40
B71	SP55	1 l + 50b violet	.95	.55
B72	SP56	2 l + 1 l slate grn	1.25	.60
B73	SP57	3 l + 1 l rose lake	1.90	.75
B74	SP58	4 l + 1 l red org	3.00	.80
B75	SP59	6 l + 2 l dp claret	3.75	1.25
B76	SP60	10 l + 4 l brt blue	4.50	1.90
	Nos. B69-B76 (8)		16.85	6.50

25th anniversary of the Federation of Romanian Sports Clubs (U.F.S.R.); 7th anniversary of the accession of King Carol II.
Exist imperf. Value $200, unused or used.

Start of
Race — SP61

Javelin
Thrower — SP62

Designs: 4 l+1 l, Hurdling. 6 l+1 l, Finish of race. 10 l+1 l, High jump.

1937, Sept. 1   Wmk. 230   Perf. 13½

B77	SP61	1 l + 1 l purple	.75	.90
B78	SP62	2 l + 1 l green	.95	1.25
B79	SP61	4 l + 1 l vermilion	1.25	1.75
B80	SP62	6 l + 1 l maroon	1.40	1.90
B81	SP61	10 l + 1 l brt bl	4.25	3.50
	Nos. B77-B81 (5)		8.60	9.30

8th Balkan Games, Bucharest. Exist imperf. Value $200, unused or used.

Catalogue values for unused stamps in this section, from this point to the end of the section, are for Never Hinged items.

King Carol
II — SP66

1938, May 24

B82 SP66 6 l + 1 l deep magenta 1.50 .45

Bucharest Exhibition (for local products), May 19-June 19, celebrating 20th anniversary of the union of Rumanian provinces.
Exists imperf. Value $200, unused or used.

Dimitrie
Cantemir — SP67

Maria
Doamna — SP68

Mircea the Great
SP69

Constantine
Brancoveanu
SP70

Stephen the
Great — SP71

Prince
Cuza — SP72

Michael the
Brave — SP73

Queen
Elizabeth — SP74

King Carol
II — SP75

King Ferdinand
I — SP76

King Carol
I — SP77

1938, June 8   Perf. 13½

B83	SP67	25b + 25b ol blk	.80	.50
B84	SP68	50b + 50b brn	1.25	.50
B85	SP69	1 l + 1 l blk vio	1.25	.50
B86	SP70	2 l + 2 l dk yel grn	1.40	.50
B87	SP71	3 l + 2 l dp mag	1.40	.50
B88	SP72	4 l + 2 l scarlet	1.40	.50
B89	SP73	6 l + 2 l vio brn	1.50	.80

B90	SP74	7.50 l gray bl	1.75	.80
B91	SP75	10 l brt bl	2.25	1.00
B92	SP76	16 l dk slate grn	3.50	2.00
B93	SP77	20 l vermilion	4.75	2.50
	Nos. B83-B93 (11)		21.25	10.10

8th anniv. of accession of King Carol II. Surtax was for Straja Tarii, a natl. org. for boys. Exist imperf. Value $175, unused or used.

"The
Spring" — SP78

"Escorting
Prisoners"
SP79

"Rodica, the
Water Carrier"
SP81

Nicolae
Grigorescu
SP82

Design: 4 l+1 l, "Returning from Market."

1938, June 23   Perf. 13½

B94	SP78	1 l + 1 l brt bl	2.25	.70
B95	SP79	2 l + 1 l yel grn	2.25	1.25
B96	SP79	4 l + 1 l vermilion	2.25	1.25
B97	SP81	6 l + 1 l lake	3.00	2.25
B98	SP82	10 l + 1 l brt bl	6.75	2.50
	Nos. B94-B98 (5)		16.50	7.95

Birth centenary of Nicolae Grigorescu, Romanian painter.
Exist imperf. Value $200, unused or used.

St. George and the
Dragon — SP83

1939, June 8   Photo.

B99	SP83	25b + 25b ol gray	.60	.45
B100	SP83	50b + 50b brn	.60	.45
B101	SP83	1 l + 1 l pale vio	.60	.45
B102	SP83	2 l + 2 l lt grn	.60	.45
B103	SP83	3 l + 2 l red vio	1.00	.45
B104	SP83	4 l + 2 l red org	1.40	.55
B105	SP83	6 l + 2 l car rose	1.50	.55
B106	SP83	8 l gray vio	1.75	.55
B107	SP83	10 l brt bl	1.90	.70
B108	SP83	12 l brt ultra	2.10	1.40
B109	SP83	16 l bl grn	2.25	1.75
	Nos. B99-B109 (11)		14.30	7.75

9th anniv. of accession of King Carol II. Exist imperf. Value $175, unused or used.

King Carol II
SP87   SP88

SP89

SP90

SP91

Wmk. 230

1940, June 8   Photo.   Perf. 13½

B113	SP87	1 l + 50b dl pur	.75	.30
B114	SP88	4 l + 1 l fawn	.75	.45
B115	SP89	6 l + 1 l blue	.75	.45
B116	SP90	8 l rose brn	1.10	.65
B117	SP89	16 l ultra	1.25	.90
B118	SP91	32 l dk vio brn	2.00	1.25
	Nos. B113-B118 (6)		6.60	4.00

10th anniv. of accession of King Carol II. Exist imperf. Value $200, unused or used.

King Carol II
SP92   SP93

1940, June 1

B119	SP92	1 l + 50b dk grn	.25	.25
B120	SP92	2.50 l + 50b Prus grn	.25	.25
B121	SP92	3 l + 1 l rose car	.35	.25
B122	SP92	3.50 l + 50b choc	.35	.35
B123	SP93	4 l + 1 l org brn	.50	.35
B124	SP93	6 l + 1 l sapphire	.75	.25
B125	SP93	9 l + 1 l brt bl	.85	.70
B126	SP93	14 l + 1 l dk bl grn	1.10	.90
	Nos. B119-B126 (8)		4.40	3.30

Surtax was for Romania's air force. Exist imperf. Value $200, unused or used.

View of
Danube
SP94

Greco-Roman
Ruins — SP95

Designs: 3 l+1 l, Hotin Castle. 4 l+1 l, Hurez Monastery. 5 l+1 l, Church in Bucovina. 8 l+1 l, Tower. 12 l+2 l, Village church, Transylvania. 16 l+2 l, Arch in Bucharest.

Inscribed: "Straja Tarii 8 Junie 1940"

1940, June 8   Perf. 14½x14, 14x14½

B127	SP94	1 l + 1 l dp vio	.40	.25
B128	SP95	2 l + 1 l red brn	.45	.30
B129	SP94	3 l + 1 l yel grn	.50	.35
B130	SP94	4 l + 1 l grnsh blk	.55	.40
B131	SP95	5 l + 1 l org ver	.60	.45
B132	SP95	8 l + 1 l brn car	.85	.60
B133	SP95	12 l + 2 l ultra	1.75	1.10
B134	SP95	16 l + 2 l dk bl gray	3.00	2.00
	Nos. B127-B134 (8)		8.10	5.45

Issued to honor Straja Tarii, a national organization for boys. Exist imperf. Value $140, unused or used.

King Michael — SP102

1940-42 Photo. Wmk. 230

B138	SP102	1 l + 50b yel grn		.25	.25
B138A	SP102	2 l + 50b yel grn		.25	.25
B139	SP102	2.50 l + 50b dk bl grn		.25	.25
B140	SP102	3 l + 1 l pur		.25	.25
B141	SP102	3.50 l + 50b rose pink		.25	.25
B141A	SP102	4 l + 50b org ver		.25	.25
B142	SP102	4 l + 1 l brn		.25	.25
B142A	SP102	5 l + 1 l dp plum		.75	.40
B143	SP102	6 l + 1 l lt ultra		.25	.25
B143A	SP102	7 l + 1 l sl grn		.40	.25
B143B	SP102	8 l + 1 l dp vio		.25	.25
B143C	SP102	12 l + 1 l brn vio		.40	.25
B144	SP102	14 l + 1 l brt bl		.40	.25
B144A	SP102	19 l + 1 l lil rose		.60	.40
		Nos. B138-B144A (14)		4.80	3.80

Issue years: Nos. B138A, B141A, B142A, B143A, B143B, B143C, B144A, 1942; others, 1940.

Corneliu Codreanu — SP103

1940, Nov. 8   Unwmk.   Perf. 13½
B145	SP103	7 l + 30 l dk grn		6.00	5.00

13th anniv. of the founding of the Iron Guard by Corneliu Codreanu.

AIR POST STAMPS

Capt. C. G. Craiu's Airplane AP1

Wmk. 95 Vertical
1928   Photo.   Perf. 13½
C1	AP1	1 l red brown	3.00	2.50
C2	AP1	2 l brt blue	3.00	2.50
C3	AP1	5 l carmine rose	3.00	2.50

Wmk. 95 Horizontal
C4	AP1	1 l red brown	4.00	3.25
C5	AP1	2 l brt blue	4.00	3.25
C6	AP1	5 l carmine rose	4.00	3.25
		Nos. C1-C6 (6)	21.00	17.25

Nos. C4-C6 also come with white gum.

Nos. C4-C6 Overprinted

1930
C7	AP1	1 l red brown	8.00	6.75
C8	AP1	2 l brt blue	8.00	6.75
a.		Vert. pair, imperf. btwn.		175.00
C9	AP1	5 l carmine rose	8.00	6.75
		Nos. C7-C9 (3)	24.00	20.25

Same Overprint on Nos. C1-C3
Wmk. 95 Vertical
C10	AP1	1 l red brown	50.00	50.00
C11	AP1	2 l brt blue	50.00	50.00
C12	AP1	5 l carmine rose	50.00	50.00
		Nos. C10-C12 (3)	150.00	150.00
		Nos. C7-C12 (6)	174.00	170.25

Nos. C7-C12 for the accession of King Carol II.

Excellent connterfeits are known of Nos. C10-C12.

King Carol II — AP2

Bluish Paper
1930, Oct. 4   Unwmk.
C13	AP2	1 l dk violet	2.00	2.25
C14	AP2	2 l gray green	2.50	2.50
C15	AP2	5 l red brown	5.00	5.00
C16	AP2	10 l brt blue	9.00	7.00
		Nos. C13-C16 (4)	18.50	14.75
		Set, never hinged	36.50	

Junkers Monoplane AP3

Monoplanes AP7

Designs: 3 l, Monoplane with biplane behind. 5 l, Biplane. 10 l, Monoplane flying leftward.

1931, Nov. 4   Wmk. 230
C17	AP3	2 l dull green	1.50	1.25
C18	AP3	3 l carmine	2.00	1.75
C19	AP3	5 l red brown	2.50	2.00
C20	AP3	10 l blue	6.00	4.50
C21	AP7	20 l dk violet	15.00	6.00
		Nos. C17-C21 (5)	27.00	15.50
		Set, never hinged	40.00	

Exist imperforate. Value $350, unused or used.

AIR POST SEMI-POSTAL STAMPS

> Catalogue values for unused stamps in this section are for Never Hinged items.

Corneliu Codreanu SPAP1

Unwmk.
1940, Dec. 1   Photo.   Perf. 14
CB1	SPAP1	20 l + 5 l Prus grn	3.00	1.50

Propaganda for the Rome-Berlin Axis. No. CB1 exists with overprint "1 Mai 1941 Jamboreea Nationala."

POSTAGE DUE STAMPS

D1

Regular Issue of 1908 Overprinted

TAXA DE PLATĂ

Perf. 11, 11½, 13½ and Compound
1881   Typo.   Unwmk.
J1	D1	2b brown	4.00	1.25
J2	D1	5b brown	4.00	1.00
a.		Tête bêche pair	190.00	75.00
J3	D1	10b brown	30.00	1.25
J4	D1	30b brown	32.50	1.25
J5	D1	50b brown	26.00	2.50
J6	D1	60b brown	21.00	3.00
		Nos. J1-J6 (6)	136.00	11.25

1885
J7	D1	10b pale red brown	8.00	.50
J8	D1	30b pale red brown	8.00	.50

1887-90
J9	D1	2b gray green	4.00	.75
J10	D1	5b gray green	8.00	3.00
J11	D1	10b gray green	8.00	3.00
J12	D1	30b gray green	8.00	.75
		Nos. J9-J12 (4)	28.00	7.50

1888
J14	D1	2b green, yellowish	.90	.75
J15	D1	5b green, yellowish	2.25	2.25
J16	D1	10b green, yellowish	32.50	2.75
J17	D1	30b green, yellowish	17.50	1.25
		Nos. J14-J17 (4)	53.15	7.00

1890-96   Wmk. 163
J18	D1	2b emerald	1.60	.45
J19	D1	5b emerald	.80	.45
J20	D1	10b emerald	1.25	.45
J21	D1	30b emerald	2.00	.45
J22	D1	50b emerald	6.50	.95
J23	D1	60b emerald	8.75	3.25
		Nos. J18-J23 (6)	20.90	6.00

1898   Wmk. 200
J24	D1	2b blue green	.70	.45
J25	D1	5b blue green	.90	.30
J26	D1	10b blue green	1.40	.30
J27	D1	30b blue green	1.90	.30
J28	D1	50b blue green	4.75	.90
J29	D1	60b blue green	5.50	1.75
		Nos. J24-J29 (6)	15.15	4.00

1902-10   Unwmk.
Thin Paper, Tinted Rose on Back
J30	D1	2b green	.85	.25
J31	D1	5b green	.50	.25
J32	D1	10b green	.40	.25
J33	D1	30b green	.50	.25
J34	D1	50b green	2.50	.90
J35	D1	60b green	5.25	2.25
		Nos. J30-J35 (6)	10.00	4.15

1908-11   White Paper
J36	D1	2b green	.80	.50
J37	D1	5b green	.60	.50
a.		Tête bêche pair	12.00	12.00
J38	D1	10b green	.40	.30
a.		Tête bêche pair	12.00	12.00
J39	D1	30b green	.50	.30
a.		Tête bêche pair	12.00	12.00
J40	D1	50b green	2.00	1.25
		Nos. J36-J40 (5)	4.30	2.85

D2

1911   Wmk. 165
J41	D2	2b dark blue, green	.25	.25
J42	D2	5b dark blue, green	.25	.25
J43	D2	10b dark blue, green	.25	.25
J44	D2	15b dark blue, green	.25	.25
J45	D2	20b dark blue, green	.25	.25
J46	D2	30b dark blue, green	.25	.25
J47	D2	50b dark blue, green	.50	.30
J48	D2	60b dark blue, green	.60	.40
J49	D2	2 l dark blue, green	1.00	.80
		Nos. J41-J49 (9)	3.60	3.00

The letters "P.R." appear to be embossed instead of watermarked. They are often faint or entirely invisible.

The 20b, type D2, has two types, differing in the width of the head of the "2." This affects Nos. J45, J54, J58, and J63.

See Nos. J52-J77, J82, J87-J88 (in Scott Standard catalogue, Vol. 5). For overprints see Nos. J78-J81, RAJ1-RAJ2, RAJ20-RAJ21, 3NJ1-3NJ7.

1918   Unwmk.
J50	A46	5b yellow green	1.25	.40
a.		Inverted overprint	5.00	5.00
J51	A46	10b black	3.75	3.75
a.		Inverted overprint	3.75	3.75

Postage Due Type of 1911
1920   Wmk. 165
J52	D2	5b black, green	.25	.25
J53	D2	10b black, green	.25	.25
J54	D2	20b black, green	4.00	.60
J55	D2	30b black, green	1.10	.40
J55A	D2	50b black, green	3.00	.90
		Nos. J52-J55A (5)	8.60	2.40

Perf. 11½, 13½ and Compound
1919   Unwmk.
J56	D2	5b black, green	.30	.25
J57	D2	10b black, green	.30	.25
J58	D2	20b black, green	1.00	.25
J59	D2	30b black, green	.90	.25
J60	D2	50b black, green	2.25	.40
		Nos. J56-J60 (5)	4.75	1.40

1920-26   White Paper
J61	D2	5b black	.25	.25
J62	D2	10b black	.25	.25
J63	D2	20b black	.25	.25
J64	D2	30b black	.25	.25
J65	D2	50b black	.40	.40
J66	D2	60b black	.25	.25
J67	D2	1 l black	.30	.30
J68	D2	2 l black	.25	.25
J69	D2	3 l black ('26)	.25	.25
J70	D2	6 l black ('26)	.30	.30
		Nos. J61-J70 (10)	2.75	2.75

1923-24
J74	D2	1 l black, pale green	.25	.25
J75	D2	2 l black, pale green	.45	.25
J76	D2	3 l black, pale green ('24)	1.25	.60
J77	D2	6 l blk, pale green ('24)	1.75	.60
		Nos. J74-J77 (4)	3.70	1.70

Postage Due Stamps of 1920-26 Overprinted

1930   Perf. 13½
J78	D2	1 l black	.25	.25
J79	D2	2 l black	.25	.25
J80	D2	3 l black	.35	.25
J81	D2	6 l black	.60	.30
		Nos. J78-J81 (4)	1.45	1.05

Accession of King Carol II.

> Catalogue values for unused stamps in this section, from this point to the end of the section, are for Never Hinged items.

Type of 1911 Issue
1931   Wmk. 225
J82	D2	2 l black	.90	.35

D3

1932-37   Wmk. 230
J83	D3	1 l black	.25	.25
J84	D3	2 l black	.25	.25
J85	D3	3 l black ('37)	.25	.25
J86	D3	6 l black ('37)	.25	.25
		Nos. J83-J86 (4)	1.00	1.00

See Nos. J89-J98 in Scott Standard catalogue, Vol. 5.

OFFICIAL STAMPS

> Catalogue values for unused stamps in this section are for Never Hinged items.

Eagle Carrying National Emblem — O1

1929   Photo.   Wmk. 95   Perf. 13½
O1	O1	25b red orange	.25	.25
O2	O1	50b dk brown	.25	.25
O3	O1	1 l dk violet	.30	.25
O4	O1	2 l olive grn	.30	.25
O5	O1	3 l rose car	.45	.25
O6	O1	4 l dk olive	.45	.25
O7	O1	6 l Prus blue	2.50	.25
O8	O1	10 l deep blue	.80	.25
O9	O1	25 l carmine brn	1.60	1.25
O10	O1	50 l purple	4.75	3.50
		Nos. O1-O10 (10)	11.65	6.75

Type of Official Stamps of 1929 Overprinted

1930   Unwmk.
O11	O1	25b red orange	.25	.25
O12	O1	50b dk brown	.25	.25
O13	O1	1 l dk violet	.35	.25
O14	O1	3 l rose carmine	.50	.25
		Nos. O11-O14 (4)	1.35	1.00

Nos. O11-O14 were not placed in use without overprint.

Same Overprint on Nos. O1-O10
Wmk. 95
O15	O1	25b red orange	.25	.25
O16	O1	50b dk brown	.25	.25
O17	O1	1 l dk violet	.25	.25
O18	O1	2 l dp green	.25	.25
O19	O1	3 l rose carmine	.60	.25
O20	O1	4 l olive black	.75	.25
O21	O1	6 l Prus blue	2.00	.25
O22	O1	10 l deep blue	.80	.25
O23	O1	25 l carmine brown	3.00	2.50
O24	O1	50 l purple	4.00	3.50
		Nos. O15-O24 (10)	12.15	8.00

Accession of King Carol II to the throne of Romania (Nos O11-O24).

Coat of Arms — O2

Perf. 13½, 13½x14½
1931-32		**Typo.**	**Wmk. 225**
O25	O2	25b black	.30	.25
O26	O2	1 l lilac	.30	.25
O27	O2	2 l emerald	.60	.40
O28	O2	3 l rose	1.00	.70
		Nos. O25-O28 (4)	2.20	1.60

1932   Wmk. 230   Perf. 13½
O29	O2	25b black	.30	.25
O30	O2	1 l violet	.40	.35
O31	O2	2 l emerald	.65	.55
O32	O2	3 l rose	.80	.65
O33	O2	6 l red brown	1.25	1.00
		Nos. O29-O33 (5)	3.40	2.80

PARCEL POST STAMPS

PP1

Perf. 11½, 13½ and Compound
1895		**Wmk. 163**	**Typo.**
Q1	PP1	25b brown red	12.50	2.25

1896
Q2	PP1	25b vermilion	10.00	1.25

Perf. 13½ and 11½x13½
1898		**Wmk. 200**
Q3	PP1	25b brown red	7.00	1.25
a.		Tête bêche pair	
Q4	PP1	25b vermilion	7.00	.90

Thin Paper
Tinted Rose on Back
1905		**Unwmk.**	**Perf. 11½**
Q5	PP1	25b vermilion	7.50	1.25

1911   White Paper
Q6	PP1	25b pale red	7.50	1.25

No. 263 Surcharged in Carmine

1928   Perf. 13½
Q7	A54	5 l on 10b yellow green	1.50	.30

POSTAL TAX STAMPS

Regular Issue of 1908 Overprinted

Perf. 11½, 13½, 11½x13½
1915			**Unwmk.**
RA1	A46	5b green	.25	.25
RA2	A46	10b rose	.40	.25

The "Timbru de Ajutor" stamps represent a tax on postal matter. The money obtained from their sale was turned into a fund for the assistance of soldiers' families.

Until 1923 the only "Timbru de Ajutor" stamps used for postal purposes were the 5b and 10b. Stamps of higher values with this inscription were used to pay the taxes on railway and theater tickets and other fiscal taxes. In 1923 the postal rate was advanced to 25b.

The Queen Weaving — PT1

1916-18   Typo.
RA3	PT1	5b gray blk	.25	.25
RA4	PT1	5b green ('18)	.70	.25
RA5	PT1	10b brown	.40	.25
RA6	PT1	10b gray blk ('18)	1.00	.45
		Nos. RA3-RA6 (4)	2.35	1.35

For overprints see Nos. RA7-RA8, RAJ7-RAJ9, 3NRA1-3NRA8.

Stamps of 1916 Overprinted in Red or Black

1918   Perf. 13½
RA7	PT1	5b gray blk (R)	.70	.25
a.		Double overprint	5.00
c.		Black overprint	5.00
RA8	PT1	10b brn (Bk)	.70	.25
a.		Double overprint	5.00
b.		Double overprint, one inverted	5.00
c.		Inverted overprint	5.00

Same Overprint on RA1 and RA2
1919
RA11	A46	5b yel grn (R)	19.00	12.50
RA12	A46	10b rose (Bk)	19.00	12.50

Charity — PT3

Perf. 13½, 11½, 13½x11½
1921-24		**Typo.**	**Unwmk.**
RA13	PT3	10b green	.25	.25
RA14	PT3	25b blk ('24)	.25	.25

Type of 1921-24 Issue
1928			**Wmk. 95**
RA15	PT3	25b black	1.00	.45

Nos. RA13, RA14 and RA15 are the only stamps of type PT3 issued for postal purposes. Other denominations were used fiscally.

> Catalogue values for unused stamps in this section, from this point to the end of the section, are for Never Hinged items.

Airplane PT4   Head of Aviator PT5

1931   Photo.   Unwmk.
RA16	PT4	50b Prus bl	.45	.25
a.		Double impression	15.00
RA17	PT4	1 l dk red brn	.75	.25
RA18	PT4	2 l ultra	1.00	.25
		Nos. RA16-RA18 (3)	2.20	.75

The use of these stamps, in addition to the regular postage, was obligatory on all postal matter for the interior of the country. The money thus obtained was to augment the National Fund for Aviation. When the stamps were not used to prepay the special tax, it was collected by means of Postal Tax Due stamps Nos. RAJ20 and RAJ21.

Nos. RA17 and RA18 were also used for other than postal tax.

1932   Wmk. 230   Perf. 14 x 13½
RA19	PT5	50b Prus bl	.30	.25
RA20	PT5	1 l red brn	.45	.25
RA21	PT5	2 l ultra	.70	.25
		Nos. RA19-RA21 (3)	1.45	.75

See notes after No. RA18.

After 1937 use of Nos. RA20-RA21 was limited to other than postal matter.

Nos. RA19-RA21 exist imperf.

Four stamps similar to type PT5, but inscribed "Fondul Aviatiei," were issued in 1936: 10b sepia, 20b violet, 3 l green and 5 l red. These were used for purposes other than postal tax.

Aviator — PT6

1937   Perf. 13½
RA22	PT6	50b Prus grn	.25	.25
RA23	PT6	1 l red brn	.35	.25
RA24	PT6	2 l ultra	.45	.25
		Nos. RA22-RA24 (3)	1.05	.75

Stamps overprinted or inscribed "Fondul Aviatiei" other than Nos. RA22, RA23 or RA24 were used to pay taxes on other than postal matters.

POSTAL TAX DUE STAMPS

> Catalogue values for unused stamps in this section are for Never Hinged items.

Postage Due Stamps of 1911 Overprinted

PTD1

Perf. 11½, 13½, 11½x13½
1915			**Unwmk.**
RAJ1	D2	5b dk bl, *grn*	.75	.25
RAJ2	D2	10b dk bl, *grn*	.75	.25
a.		Wmk. 165	10.00	1.00

1916   Typo.   Unwmk.
RAJ3	PTD1	5b brn, *grn*	.40	.25
RAJ4	PTD1	10b red, *grn*	.40	.25

See Nos. RAJ5-RAJ6, RAJ10-RAJ11. For overprint see No. 3NRAJ1.

1918
RAJ5	PTD1	5b red, *grn*	.25	.25
a.		Wmk. 165	1.00	.25
RAJ6	PTD1	10b brn, *grn*	.25	.25
a.		Wmk. 165	1.75	.25

Postal Tax Stamps of 1916, Overprinted in Red, Black or Blue

RAJ7	PT1	5b gray blk (R)	.40	.25
a.		Inverted overprint	7.50
RAJ8	PT1	10b brn (Bk)	.80	.25
a.		Inverted overprint	7.50
RAJ9	PT1	10b brn (Bl)	5.00	5.00
a.		Vertical overprint	20.00	15.00
		Nos. RAJ7-RAJ9 (3)	6.20	5.50

Type of 1916
1921
RAJ10	PTD1	5b red	.50	.25
RAJ11	PTD1	10b brown	.50	.25

PTD2

1922-25   Greenish Paper   Typo.
RAJ12	PTD2	10b brown	.25	.25
RAJ13	PTD2	20b brown	.25	.25
RAJ14	PTD2	25b brown	.25	.25
RAJ15	PTD2	50b brown	.25	.25
		Nos. RAJ12-RAJ15 (4)	1.00	1.00

1923-26
RAJ16	PTD2	10b lt brn	.25	.25
RAJ17	PTD2	20b lt brn	.25	.25
RAJ18	PTD2	25b brown ('26)	.25	.25
RAJ19	PTD2	50b brown ('26)	.25	.25
		Nos. RAJ16-RAJ19 (4)	1.00	1.00

J82 and Type of 1911 Postage Due Stamps Overprinted in Red

1931   Wmk. 225   Perf. 13½
RAJ20	D2	1 l black	.25	.25
RAJ21	D2	2 l black	.25	.25

When the Postal Tax stamps for the Aviation Fund issue (Nos. RA16 to RA18) were not used to prepay the obligatory tax on letters, etc., it was collected by affixing Nos. RAJ20 and RAJ21.

OCCUPATION STAMPS

ISSUED UNDER AUSTRIAN OCCUPATION

Emperor Karl of Austria
OS1   OS2

1917	Unwmk.	Engr.	Perf. 12½	
1N1	OS1	3b ol gray	2.00	3.00
1N2	OS1	5b ol grn	2.00	3.00
1N3	OS1	6b violet	2.00	3.00
1N4	OS1	10b org brn	.40	.70
1N5	OS1	12b dp bl	1.50	2.50
1N6	OS1	15b brt rose	1.50	2.50
1N7	OS1	20b red brn	.40	.70
1N8	OS1	25b ultra	.40	.70
1N9	OS1	30b slate	.70	1.00
1N10	OS1	40b olive bis	.70	1.00
a.	Perf. 11½		100.00	175.00
b.	Perf. 11½x12½		100.00	175.00
1N11	OS1	50b dp grn	.40	.70
1N12	OS1	60b rose	.40	.70
1N13	OS1	80b dl bl	.35	.65
1N14	OS1	90b dk vio	.70	1.00
1N15	OS2	2 l rose, straw	1.10	1.60
1N16	OS2	3 l grn, bl	1.10	2.00
1N17	OS2	4 l rose, grn	1.50	2.50
	Nos. 1N1-1N17 (17)		17.15	27.25

Nos. 1N1-1N14 have "BANI" surcharged in red.
Nos. 1N1-1N17 also exist imperforate. Value, set $125.

OS3   OS4

1918				
1N18	OS3	3b ol gray	.35	.85
1N19	OS3	5b ol grn	.35	.85
1N20	OS3	6b violet	.35	.85
1N21	OS3	10b org brn	.35	.85
1N22	OS3	12b dp bl	.35	.85
1N23	OS3	15b brt rose	.35	.85
1N24	OS3	20b red brn	.35	.85
1N25	OS3	25b ultra	.35	.85
1N26	OS3	30b slate	.35	.85
1N27	OS3	40b ol bis	.35	.85
1N28	OS3	50b dp grn	.35	.85
1N29	OS3	60b rose	.35	.85
1N30	OS3	80b dl bl	.35	.85
1N31	OS3	90b dk vio	.35	.85
1N32	OS4	2 l rose, straw	.35	.85
1N33	OS4	3 l grn, bl	.75	2.25
1N34	OS4	4 l rose, grn	1.00	2.25
	Nos. 1N18-1N34 (17)		7.00	17.25

Exist. imperf. Value, set $80.00.
The complete series exists with "BANI" or "LEI" inverted, also with those words and the numerals of value inverted. Neither of these sets was regularly issued.

Austrian Nos. M69-M82 Overprinted In Black

1918	Typo.		Perf. 12½	
1N35	M5	1h grnsh blue	40.00	
	Never hinged		87.50	
1N36	M5	2h orange	25.00	
	Never hinged		50.00	
1N37	M5	3h olive gray	47.50	
	Never hinged		87.50	
1N38	M5	5h yellow green	25.00	
	Never hinged		50.00	
1N39	M5	10h dark brown	70.00	
	Never hinged		140.00	
1N40	M5	20h red	70.00	
	Never hinged		140.00	
1N41	M5	25h blue	27.50	
	Never hinged		55.00	
1N42	M5	30h bister	47.50	
	Never hinged		95.00	
1N43	M5	45h dark slate	52.50	
	Never hinged		105.00	
1N44	M5	50h deep green	60.00	
	Never hinged		120.00	
1N45	M5	60h violet	80.00	
	Never hinged		160.00	
1N46	M5	80h rose	1,000.	
	Never hinged		2,000.	
1N47	M5	90h brown violet	80.00	
	Never hinged		160.00	
	Nos. 1N35-1N47 (13)		1,625.	

Nos. 1N35-1N47 were on sale at the Vienna post office for a few days before the Armistice signing. They were never issued at the Army Post Offices.

ISSUED UNDER BULGARIAN OCCUPATION

Dobruja District

Bulgarian Stamps of 1915-16 Overprinted in Red or Blue

1916	Unwmk.		Perf. 11½, 14	
2N1	A20	1s dk blue grn (R)	.25	.25
2N2	A23	5s grn & vio brn (R)	3.00	1.75
2N3	A24	10s brn & brnsh blk (Bl)	.30	.25
2N4	A26	25s indigo & blk (Bl)	.30	.25
	Nos. 2N1-2N4 (4)		3.85	2.50

Many varieties of overprint exist.

ISSUED UNDER GERMAN OCCUPATION

German Stamps of 1905-17 Surcharged

1917	Wmk. 125		Perf. 14	
3N1	A22	15b on 15pf dk vio (R)	1.00	1.00
3N2	A16	25b on 20pf ultra (Bk)	1.00	1.00
3N3	A16	40b on 30pf org & blk, buff (R)	17.50	17.50
	Nos. 3N1-3N3 (3)		19.50	19.50

"M.V.iR." are the initials of "Militär Verwaltung in Rumänien" (Military Administration of Romania).

German Stamps of 1905-17 Surcharged

1917-18				
3N4	A16	10b on 10pf car	1.10	1.40
3N5	A22	15b on 15pf dk vio	5.50	4.50
3N6	A16	25b on 20pf ultra	3.00	4.00
3N7	A16	40b on 30pf org & blk, buff	1.00	1.40
a.	"40" omitted		90.00	350.00
	Nos. 3N4-3N7 (4)		10.60	11.30

German Stamps of 1905-17 Surcharged

1918				
3N8	A16	5b on 5pf grn	.60	1.75
3N9	A16	10b on 10pf car	.60	1.50
3N10	A22	15b on 15pf dk vio	.25	.40
3N11	A16	25b on 20pf bl vio	.60	1.50
a.	25b on 20pf blue		2.50	8.00
3N12	A16	40b on 30pf org & blk, buff	.30	.35
	Nos. 3N8-3N12 (5)		2.35	5.50

German Stamps of 1905-17 Overprinted

1918				
3N13	A16	10pf carmine	8.75	40.00
3N14	A22	15pf dk vio	13.00	35.00
3N15	A16	20pf blue	1.25	1.75
3N16	A16	30pf org & blk, buff	13.00	22.50
	Nos. 3N13-3N16 (4)		36.00	99.25

POSTAGE DUE STAMPS ISSUED UNDER GERMAN OCCUPATION

Postage Due Stamps and Type of Romania Overprinted in Red

1918	Perf. 11½, 13½ and Compound		Wmk. 165	
3NJ1	D2	5b dk bl, grn	20.00	60.00
3NJ2	D2	10b dk bl, grn	20.00	60.00

The 20b, 30b and 50b with this overprint are fraudulent.

	Unwmk.			
3NJ3	D2	5b dk bl, grn	8.00	10.50
3NJ4	D2	10b dk bl, grn	8.00	10.50
3NJ5	D2	20b dk bl, grn	3.00	2.75
3NJ6	D2	30b dk bl, grn	3.00	2.75
3NJ7	D2	50b dk bl, grn	3.00	2.75
	Nos. 3NJ1-3NJ7 (7)		65.00	149.25

POSTAL TAX STAMPS ISSUED UNDER GERMAN OCCUPATION

Romanian Postal Tax Stamps and Type of 1916

Overprinted in Red or Black

1917	Perf. 11½, 13½ and Compound		Unwmk.	
3NRA1	PT1	5b gray blk (R)	.80	2.75
3NRA2	PT1	10b brown (Bk)	.80	2.75

Same, Overprinted

1917-18				
3NRA3	PT1	5b gray blk (R)	1.50	3.50
a.	Black overprint		57.00	750.00
3NRA4	PT1	10b brown (Bk)	9.00	19.00
3NRA5	PT1	10b violet (Bk)	1.50	5.00
	Nos. 3NRA3-3NRA5 (3)		12.00	27.50

Same, Overprinted in Red or Black

1918				
3NRA6	PT1	5b gray blk (R)	45.00	30.00
3NRA7	PT1	10b brown (Bk)	45.00	30.00

Same, Overprinted

1918				
3NRA8	PT1	10b violet (Bk)	.80	2.75

POSTAL TAX DUE STAMP ISSUED UNDER GERMAN OCCUPATION

Type of Romanian Postal Tax Due Stamp of 1916 Overprinted

1918	Perf. 11½, 13½, and Compound		Wmk. 165	
3NRAJ1	PTD1	10b red, green	2.50	3.00

ROMANIAN POST OFFICES IN THE TURKISH EMPIRE

40 Paras = 1 Piaster

King Carol I
A1   A2

1896	Perf. 11½, 13½ and Compound			
	Wmk. 200	Black Surcharge		
1	A1	10pa on 5b blue	32.50	30.00
2	A2	20pa on 10b emer	24.00	22.50
3	A1	1pa on 25b violet	24.00	22.50
	Nos. 1-3 (3)		80.50	75.00
	Violet Surcharge			
4	A1	10pa on 5b blue	17.00	15.00
5	A2	20pa on 10b emer	17.00	15.00
6	A1	1pa on 25b violet	17.00	15.00
	Nos. 4-6 (3)		51.00	45.00

Romanian Stamps of 1908-18 Overprinted in Black or Red

1919	Typo.		Unwmk.	
7	A46	5b yellow grn	.50	.50
8	A46	10b rose	.65	.65
9	A46	15b red brown	.75	.75
10	A19	25b dp blue (R)	.85	.85
11	A19	40b gray brn (R)	2.75	2.75
	Nos. 7-11 (5)		5.50	5.50

All values exist with inverted overprint.

ROMANIAN POST OFFICES IN THE TURKISH EMPIRE POSTAL TAX STAMP

Romanian Postal Tax Stamp of 1918 Overprinted

1919	Unwmk.	Perf. 11½, 11½x13½		
RA1	PT1	5b green	1.75	1.75

ROUAD, ILE

ēl-ru-ad

(Arwad)

LOCATION — An island in the Mediterranean, off the coast of Latakia, Syria
GOVT. — French Mandate

In 1916, while a French post office was maintained on Ile Rouad, stamps were issued by France.

25 Centimes = 1 Piaster

French Offices in the Levant 1902-06 Stamps Ovptd.

Perf. 14x13½

1916, Jan. 12			Unwmk.
1	A2	5c green	550.00 260.00
		On cover	1,250.
2	A3	10c rose red	550.00 260.00
		On cover	1,250.
3	A5	1pi on 25c blue	550.00 260.00
		On cover	1,250.

Dangerous counterfeits exist.

A 40c and 2pi-on-50c exist but were not regularly issued. Most examples have favor cancels. Value so canceled, $700 each.

Stamps of French Offices in the Levant, 1902-06, Overprinted Horizontally

1916, Dec.

4	A2	1c gray	1.40	1.40
		Never hinged	2.25	
		On cover		55.00
a.		Grayish paper (GC) ('18)	3.00	2.75
		Never hinged	5.00	
b.		1c slate ('20)	3.00	2.75
		Never hinged	5.00	
5	A2	2c lilac brown	1.50	1.50
		Never hinged	2.25	
		On cover		55.00
a.		Grayish paper (GC) ('18)	3.00	3.00
		Never hinged	5.00	
b.		2c violet brown ('20)	3.00	3.00
		Never hinged	5.00	
6	A2	3c red orange	1.60	1.60
		Never hinged	2.25	
		On cover		55.00
a.		Double overprint	210.00	
b.		Grayish paper (GC) ('19)	1.75	1.75
		Never hinged	3.00	
7	A2	5c green	1.75	1.75
		Never hinged	3.00	
		On cover		45.00
8	A3	10c rose	2.00	2.00
		Never hinged	3.25	
		On cover		37.50
9	A3	15c pale red	2.00	2.00
		Never hinged	3.25	
		On cover		30.00
10	A3	20c brown violet	3.75	3.75
		Never hinged	6.25	
		On cover		50.00
		On cover, single franking		95.00
a.		Grayish paper (GC) ('19)	5.00	5.00
		Never hinged	8.25	
		On cover		62.50
		On cover, single franking		105.00
11	A5	1pi on 25c blue	2.75	2.75
		Never hinged	4.50	
		On cover		45.00
		On cover, single franking		62.50
12	A3	30c violet	2.50	2.50
		Never hinged	4.00	
		On cover		50.00
		On cover, single franking		67.50
13	A4	40c red & pale bl	6.00	6.00
		Never hinged	9.00	
		On cover		62.50
		On cover, single franking		80.00
14	A6	2pi on 50c bis brn & lavender	9.00	9.00
		Never hinged	14.50	
		On cover		105.00
		On cover, single franking		170.00
15	A6	4pi on 1fr cl & ol grn	16.00	16.00
		Never hinged	27.00	
		On cover		170.00
		On cover, single franking		275.00
16	A6	20pi on 5fr dk bl & buff	40.00	40.00
		Never hinged	67.50	
		On cover		440.00
		On cover, single franking		1,100.
		Nos. 4-16 (13)	90.25	90.25

There is a wide space between the two words of the overprint on Nos. 13 to 16 inclusive.

(Note on G. C. paper follows France No. 184.)

RUANDA-URUNDI

rü-ˌän-də ü'rün-dē

(Belgian East Africa)

LOCATION — In central Africa, bounded by Congo, Uganda and Tanganyika
AREA — 20,540 sq. mi.
POP. — 4,700,000 (est. 1958)
CAPITAL — Usumbura

See German East Africa for stamps issued under Belgian occupation.

100 Centimes = 1 Franc

Stamps of Belgian Congo, 1923-26, Overprinted

1924-26			Perf. 12	
6	A32	5c orange yel	.25	.25
		Never hinged	.40	
7	A32	10c green	.25	.25
		Never hinged	.55	
		On cover		2.75
a.		Double overprint	70.00	70.00
		Never hinged	125.00	
8	A32	15c olive brn	.25	.25
		Never hinged	.55	
		On cover		2.75
9	A32	20c olive grn	.25	.25
		Never hinged	.55	
		On cover		23.00
10	A44	20c green ('26)	.25	.25
		Never hinged	.35	
		On cover		27.50
11	A44	25c red brown	.40	.25
		Never hinged	.80	
		On cover		30.00
12	A44	30c rose red	.35	.35
		Never hinged	1.50	
		On cover		30.00
13	A44	30c olive grn ('25)	.25	.25
		Never hinged	.35	
		On cover		23.00
14	A32	40c violet ('25)	.35	.35
		Never hinged	.75	
		On cover		30.00
a.		Inverted overprint	95.00	95.00
		Never hinged	170.00	
15	A44	50c gray blue	.35	.35
		Never hinged	1.50	
		On cover		2.75
16	A44	50c buff ('25)	.40	.35
		Never hinged	.75	
		On cover		17.00
17	A44	75c red org	.65	.60
		Never hinged	1.90	
		On cover		2.75
18	A44	75c gray blue ('25)	.60	.45
		Never hinged	1.00	
		On cover		27.50
19	A44	1fr bister brown	.70	.60
		Never hinged	1.50	
		On cover		47.50
20	A44	1fr dull blue ('26)	.75	.50
		Never hinged	1.00	
		On cover		30.00
21	A44	3fr gray brown	6.00	2.50
		Never hinged	16.50	
		On cover		110.00
22	A44	5fr gray	12.00	9.00
		Never hinged	30.00	
		On cover		62.50
23	A44	10fr gray black	22.50	20.00
		Never hinged	82.50	
		Nos. 6-23 (18)	46.55	36.80
		Set, never hinged	140.00	

Belgian Congo Nos. 112-113 Overprinted in Red or Black

1925-27			Perf. 12½	
24	A44	45c dk vio (R) ('27)	.35	.35
		Never hinged	.75	
		On cover		23.00
25	A44	60c car rose (Bk)	.60	.50
		Never hinged	1.00	
		On cover		15.00
		Set, never hinged	1.75	

Stamps of Belgian Congo, 1923-1927, Overprinted

1927-29				
26	A32	10c green ('29)	.65	.65
		Never hinged	1.60	
		On cover		19.00
27	A32	15c ol brn ('29)	1.75	1.75
		Never hinged	3.25	
		On cover		19.00
28	A44	35c green	.35	.35
		Never hinged	.70	
		On cover		30.00
29	A44	75c salmon red	.50	.45
		Never hinged	.90	
		On cover		27.50
30	A44	1fr rose red	.60	.50
		Never hinged	1.50	
		On cover		30.00
31	A32	1.25fr dull blue	.95	.70
		Never hinged	3.00	
		On cover		40.00
32	A32	1.50fr dull blue	.95	.65
		Never hinged	3.00	
		On cover		47.50
33	A32	1.75fr dull blue	2.50	1.60
		Never hinged	6.25	
		On cover		47.50

No. 32 Surcharged

34	A32	1.75fr on 1.50fr dl bl	.95	.70
		Never hinged	3.00	
		On cover		47.50
		Nos. 26-34 (9)	9.20	7.35
		Set, never hinged	23.50	

Nos. 30 and 33 Surcharged

1931				
35	A44	1.25fr on 1fr rose red	3.50	2.00
		Never hinged	7.50	
		On cover		47.50
36	A32	2fr on 1.75fr dl bl	5.50	3.00
		Never hinged	12.50	
		On cover		75.00
		Set, never hinged	20.00	

Porter — A1

Mountain Scene — A2

Designs: 5c, 60c, Porter. 15c, Warrior. 25c, Kraal. 40c, Cattle herders. 50c, Cape buffalo. 75c, Bahutu greeting. 1fr, Barundi women. 1.25fr, Bahutu mother. 1.50fr, 2fr, Making wooden vessel. 2.50fr, 3.25fr, Preparing hides. 4fr, Watuba potter. 5fr, Mututsi dancer. 10fr, Watusi warriors. 20fr, Urundi prince.

1931-38		Engr.		Perf. 11½	
37	A1	5c dp lil rose ('38)	.25	.25
		Never hinged	.40	
		On cover		30.00
38	A2	10c gray	.25	.25
		Never hinged	.40	
		On cover		22.50
39	A2	15c pale red	.25	.25
		Never hinged	.40	
		On cover		25.00
40	A2	25c brown vio	.25	.25
		Never hinged	.40	
		On cover		22.50

41	A1	40c green	.50	.50
		Never hinged	1.00	
		On cover		19.00
42	A2	50c gray lilac	.25	.25
		Never hinged	.40	
		On cover		19.00
43	A1	60c lilac rose	.25	.25
		Never hinged	.40	
		On cover		12.50
44	A1	75c gray black	.25	.25
		Never hinged	.65	
		On cover		12.50
45	A2	1fr rose red	.40	.25
		Never hinged	.90	
		On cover		12.50
46	A1	1.25fr red brown	.40	.25
		Never hinged	.90	
		On cover		15.00
47	A2	1.50fr brown vio ('37)	.25	.25
		Never hinged	.40	
		On cover		30.00
48	A2	2fr deep blue	.50	.25
		Never hinged	.90	
		On cover		19.00
49	A2	2.50fr dp blue ('37)	.60	.60
		Never hinged	1.75	
		On cover		37.50
50	A2	3.25fr brown vio	.65	.30
		Never hinged	1.75	
		On cover		27.50
51	A2	4fr rose	.65	.45
		Never hinged	1.75	
		On cover		27.50
52	A1	5fr gray	.65	.50
		Never hinged	1.75	
		On cover		55.00
53	A1	10fr brown violet	.90	.90
		Never hinged	2.75	
		On cover		62.50
54	A1	20fr brown	3.25	3.00
		Never hinged	7.75	
		Nos. 37-54 (18)	10.50	9.00
		Set, never hinged	25.00	

King Albert Memorial Issue

King Albert — A16

1934			Photo.	
55	A16	1.50fr black	.65	.65
		Never hinged	2.50	
		On cover		12.50

SEMI-POSTAL STAMPS

Belgian Congo Nos. B10-B11 Overprinted

1925		Unwmk.		Perf. 12½	
B1	SP1	25c + 25c car & blk	.75	.50
		Never hinged	1.90	
B2	SP1	25c + 25c car & blk	.75	.50
		Never hinged	1.90	
		Set, never hinged	3.75	

No. B2 inscribed "BELGISCH CONGO." Commemorative of the Colonial Campaigns in 1914-1918. Nos. B1 and B2 alternate in the sheet.

Belgian Congo Nos. B12-B20 Overprinted in Blue or Red

1930			Perf. 11½	
B3	SP3	10c + 5c ver	1.00	1.00
		Never hinged	1.35	
B4	SP3	20c + 10c dk brn	1.50	1.50
		Never hinged	4.50	
B5	SP5	35c + 15c dp grn	2.00	2.00
		Never hinged	1.25	
B6	SP5	60c + 30c dl vio	2.25	2.25
		Never hinged	10.00	
B7	SP3	1fr + 50c dk car	3.75	3.75
		Never hinged	19.00	
B8	SP5	1.75fr + 75c dp bl (R)	9.75	9.75
		Never hinged	25.00	

B9	SP5	3.50fr + 1.50fr rose lake	15.00	15.00
		Never hinged	47.50	
B10	SP5	5fr + 2.50fr red brn	15.00	15.00
		Never hinged	30.00	
B11	SP5	10fr + 5fr grn blk	10.00	10.00
		Never hinged	32.50	
		Nos. B3-B11 (9)	66.25	66.25
		Set, never hinged	170.00	

On Nos. B3, B4 and B7 there is a space of 26mm between the two words of the overprint. The surtax was for native welfare.

Queen Astrid with Native Children — SP1

1936			**Photo.**	
B12	SP1	1.25fr + 5c dk brn	.75	.75
		Never hinged	2.25	
		On cover		30.00
B13	SP1	1.50fr + 10c dl rose	.75	.75
		Never hinged	2.25	
		On cover		30.00
B14	SP1	2.50fr + 25c dk bl	1.50	1.50
		Never hinged	4.50	
		On cover		37.50
		Nos. B12-B14 (3)	3.00	3.00
		Set, never hinged	9.00	

Issued in memory of Queen Astrid. The surtax was for the National League for Protection of Native Children.

POSTAGE DUE STAMPS

Belgian Congo Nos. J1-J7 Overprinted

1924-27		**Unwmk.**	**Perf. 14**	
J1	D1	5c black brn	.25	.25
		Never hinged	.30	
a.		Double overprint	60.00	60.00
J2	D1	10c deep rose	.25	.25
		Never hinged	.30	
J3	D1	15c violet	.30	.25
		Never hinged	.55	
a.		Double overprint	60.00	60.00
J4	D1	30c green	.50	.30
		Never hinged	.70	
J5	D1	50c ultra	.50	.40
		Never hinged	.70	
J6	D1	50c brt blue ('27)	.80	.45
		Never hinged	1.05	
J7	D1	1fr gray	.70	.55
		Never hinged	.90	
		Nos. J1-J7 (7)	3.30	2.45
		Set, never hinged	4.50	

RUSSIA

'rəsh-ə

(Union of Soviet Socialist Republics)

LOCATION — Eastern Europe and Northern Asia
GOVT. — Republic
AREA — 8,650,000 sq. mi.
POP. — 276,300,000 (est. 1985)
CAPITAL — Moscow

An empire until 1917, the government was overthrown in that year and a socialist union of republics was formed under the name of the Union of Soviet Socialist Republics. The USSR includes the following autonomous republics which have issued their own stamps: Armenia, Azerbaijan, Georgia and Ukraine.

100 Kopecks = 1 Ruble

Watermarks

Wmk. 166 — Colorless Numerals ("1" for Nos. 1-2, "2" for No. 3, "3" for No. 4)

Wmk. 168 — Cyrillic EZGB & Wavy Lines

Initials are those of the State Printing Plant.

Wmk. 169 — Lozenges   Wmk. 171 — Diamonds

Wmk. 170 — Greek Border and Rosettes

Wmk. 226 — Diamonds Enclosing Four Dots

Empire

A1

A2

Coat of Arms — A3

				Wmk. 166	
1857, Dec. 10			**Typo.**		**Imperf.**
1	A1	10k brown & blue		25,000.	850.
		Pen cancellation			675.
		Penmark & postmark			700.
		Pair			2,500.
		On cover, postal cancellation only			3,500.
		On cover, pen cancellation			1,750.
		On cover, pen & postal cancellations			3,500.

Full margins = ¾mm.

Genuine unused examples of No. 1 are exceedingly rare. Most of those offered are used with pen cancellation removed. The unused value is for an example without gum. The very few known stamps with original gum sell for much more.

See Poland for similar stamp inscribed "ZALOT KOP. 10."

1858, Jan. 10			**Perf. 14½, 15**	
2	A1	10k brown & blue	18,000.	150.
		On cover		400.
3	A1	20k blue & orange	10,000.	1,750.
		On cover		15,000.
4	A1	30k carmine & green	12,500.	3,000.
		On cover		5,000.

No. 3 exists in green & violet. It is an essay, value with or without watermark, about $1,000.

Wove Paper

1858-64		**Unwmk.**	**Perf. 12½**	
5	A2	1k black & yel ('64)	150.00	75.00
		On cover		175.00
		On cover, single franking		750.00
a.		1k black & orange	200.00	75.00
		On cover		175.00
		On cover, single franking		750.00
6	A2	3k black & green ('64)	475.00	80.00
		On cover		525.00
7	A2	5k black & lilac ('64)	300.00	100.00
		On cover		700.00
8	A1	10k brown & blue	800.00	10.00
		On cover		115.00
		Half used as 5k on cover		70.00
9	A1	20k blue & orange	1,000.	90.00
		On cover		500.00
a.		Half used as 10k on cover		—
10	A1	30k carmine & green	1,000.	100.00
		On cover		850.00
		Nos. 5-10 (6)	3,725.	455.00

1863				
11	A3	5k black & blue	25.00	175.00
		On cover, local use, dated 1863-July 1864		4,500.
		On cover, dated after July 1864		1,250.

No. 11 was issued to pay local postage in St. Petersburg and Moscow. It is known to have been used in other cities. In Aug. 1864 it was authorized for use on mail addressed to other destinations. No. 11 was withdrawn from use 12/21/84.

1865, June 2			**Perf. 14½, 15**	
12	A2	1k black & yellow	200.00	20.00
		On cover		35.00
		On cover, single franking		110.00
a.		1k black & orange	200.00	30.00
		On cover		45.00
		On cover, single franking		135.00
13	A2	3k black & green	250.00	15.00
		On cover		35.00
14	A2	5k black & lilac	275.00	20.00
		On cover		40.00
15	A1	10k brown & blue	200.00	3.00
		On cover		15.00
a.		Thick paper	250.00	7.50
		On cover		35.00
17	A1	20k blue & orange	1,200.	40.00
		On cover		90.00
18	A1	30k carmine & green	1,200.	50.00
		On cover		175.00
		Nos. 12-18 (6)	3,325.	148.00

Horizontally Laid Paper

1866-70			**Wmk. 168**	
19	A2	1k black & yellow	6.50	1.00
		On cover		3.00
		On cover, single franking		27.50
a.		1k black & orange	6.50	1.25
		On cover		3.00
		On cover, single franking		30.00
b.		Imperf.		75,000.
c.		Vertically laid	225.00	50.00
		On cover		100.00
		On cover, single franking		200.00

d.		Groundwork inverted	6,250.	6,000.
e.		Thick paper	75.00	60.00
f.		As "c," imperf.	8,500.	8,000.
g.		As "b," "c" & "d"		
		blk & org, vert. laid paper	275.00	40.00
		On cover		100.00
		On cover, single franking		200.00
20	A2	3k black & dp green	10.00	1.00
		On cover		3.00
a.		3k black & yellow green	10.00	1.00
		On cover		3.00
b.		Imperf.		2,500.
c.		Vertically laid	375.00	55.00
		On cover		100.00
d.		V's in groundwork (error) ('70)	1,000.	150.00
		On cover		450.00
e.		3k black & blue green	5.00	.60
		On cover		3.00
22	A2	5k black & lilac	10.00	2.00
		On cover		3.00
a.		5k black & gray	125.00	20.00
		On cover		175.00
b.		Imperf.	3,500.	2,000.
c.		Vertically laid	10,000.	175.00
		On cover		275.00
d.		As "c," imperf.		25,000.
23	A1	10k brown & blue	50.00	1.50
		On cover		2.50
a.		Vertically laid	250.00	11.00
		On cover		60.00
b.		Center inverted		60,000.
c.		Imperf.		25,000.
24	A1	20k blue & orange	100.00	15.00
		On cover		30.00
a.		Vertically laid	5,000.	150.00
		On cover		175.00
25	A1	30k carmine & green	110.00	35.00
		On cover		225.00
		On cover, single franking		450.00
a.		Vertically laid	750.00	52.50
		On cover		225.00
		On cover, single franking		525.00
		Nos. 19-25 (6)	286.50	55.50

Arms — A4

1875-82			**Horizontally Laid Paper**	
26	A2	2k black & red	20.00	.75
		On cover		4.00
		On cover, single franking		37.50
a.		Vertically laid	7,500.	125.00
		On cover		275.00
		On cover, single franking		2,250.
b.		Groundwork inverted		65,000.
27	A4	7k gray & rose ('79)	25.00	1.00
		On cover		3.00
a.		Imperf.		25,000.
b.		Vertically laid	2,000.	65.00
		On cover		300.00
c.		Wmkd. hexagons ('79)		110,000.
d.		Center inverted		50,000.
e.		Center omitted	10,000.	3,000.
f.		7k black & carmine ('80)	5.75	.60
		On cover		3.50
g.		7k pale gray & carmine ('82)	6.25	.60
		On cover		2.50
28	A4	8k gray & rose	10.00	1.00
		On cover		2.50
a.		Vertically laid	2,250.	70.00
		On cover		475.00
b.		Imperf.		25,000.
c.		"C" instead of "B" in "Bocem"	200.00	275.00
29	A4	10k brown & blue	100.00	6.50
		On cover		20.00
a.		Center inverted		65,000.
30	A4	20k blue & orange	100.00	11.00
		On cover		20.00
a.		Cross-shaped "T" in bottom word	125.00	30.00
b.		Center inverted		85,000.
c.		Center double		100,000.
		Nos. 26-30 (5)	255.00	20.25

The hexagon watermark of No. 27c is that of revenue stamps. Four examples of No. 27c are recorded, all used at Perm. One example of No. 27d is recorded.

See Finland for stamps similar to designs A4-A15, which have "dot in circle" devices or are inscribed "Markka," "Markkaa," "Pen.," or "Pennia."

Imperial Eagle and Post
Horns
A5   A6

Perf. 14 to 15 and Compound
1883-88   **Wmk. 168**
Horizontally Laid Paper

31	A5	1k orange	8.00	.50
a.		Imperf.	70,000.	
b.		Groundwork inverted	10,000.	
c.		1k yellow	6.00	.55
32	A5	2k dark green	10.00	.65
a.		2k yellow green ('88)	8.00	.55
b.		Imperf.	700.00	700.00
c.		Wove paper	700.00	500.00
d.		Groundwork inverted		35,000.
33	A5	3k carmine	12.50	.45
a.		Imperf.	3,000.	3,000.
b.		Groundwork inverted		35,000.
c.		Wove paper	500.00	425.00
34	A5	5k red violet	15.00	.45
a.		Groundwork inverted		7,000.
35	A5	7k blue	12.50	.45
a.		Imperf.	750.00	500.00
b.		Groundwork inverted	1,600.	1,600.
c.		Double impression of frame and center		25,000.
36	A6	14k blue & rose	30.00	.75
a.		Imperf.	800.00	800.00
b.		Center inverted	7,000.	6,250.
c.		Diagonal half surcharge "7" in red, on cover ('84)		10,000.
37	A6	35k violet & green	60.00	6.00
38	A6	70k brown & orange	75.00	7.00
		Nos. 31-38 (8)	223.00	16.25

Before 1882 the 1, 2, 3 and 5 kopecks had small numerals in the background; beginning with No. 31 these denominations have a background of network, like the higher values.

No. 36c is handstamped. It is known with cancellations of Tiflis and Kutais, both in Georgia. It is believed to be of philatelic origin.

A7

1884   **Perf. 13½, 13½x11½**
Vertically Laid Paper

39	A7	3.50r black & gray	1,000.	700.
a.		Horiz. laid	100,000.	15,000.
40	A7	7r black & orange	1,100.	750.

Forgeries exist, both unused and used.

A8

Imperial Eagle and
Post Horns with
Thunderbolts — A9

**With Thunderbolts Across Post
Horns**
Perf. 14 to 15 and Compound
1889, May 14
Horizontally Laid Paper

41	A8	4k rose	1.80	.30
a.		Groundwork inverted	20,000.	
b.		Double impression	5,000.	
42	A8	10k dark blue	2.00	.25
43	A8	20k blue & carmine	6.00	.75
a.		Groundwork inverted	20,000.	
44	A8	50k violet & green	16.00	1.00

Perf. 13½

45	A9	1r lt brn, brn & org	50.00	3.00
a.		Pair, imperf. between	750.00	750.00
b.		Center omitted	500.00	500.00
		Nos. 41-45 (5)	75.80	5.30

See #57C, 60, 63, 66, 68, 82, 85, 87, 126, 129, 131. For surcharges see #216, 219, 223, 226.

A10   A11

A12

**With Thunderbolts Across Post
Horns**
1889-92   **Perf. 14½x15**
Horizontally Laid Paper

46	A10	1k orange	3.50	.50
a.		Imperf.	—	—
47	A10	2k green	3.50	.50
a.		Imperf.	650.00	500.00
b.		Groundwork inverted		18,500.
48	A10	3k carmine	3.50	.50
a.		Imperf.	350.00	350.00
49	A10	5k red violet	4.75	.60
b.		Groundwork omitted	725.00	725.00
50	A10	7k dark blue	3.50	.50
a.		Imperf.		10,000.
b.		Groundwork inverted	17,500.	12,500.
c.		Groundwork omitted	200.00	200.00
51	A11	14k blue & rose	12.00	.50
a.		Center inverted	7,500.	5,000.
52	A11	35k violet & green	29.00	1.90

Perf. 13½

53	A12	3.50r black & gray	25.00	9.00
54	A12	7r black & yellow	200.00	12.00
a.		Dbl. impression of black		50,000.
		Nos. 46-54 (9)	284.75	26.00

Perf. 14 to 15 and Compound
1902-05   **Vertically Laid Paper**

55	A10	1k orange	3.00	.35
a.		Imperf.	1,100.	1,100.
b.		Groundwork inverted	850.00	850.00
c.		Groundwork omitted	200.00	200.00
56	A10	2k yellow green	3.00	.35
a.		2k deep green	9.00	.70
b.		Groundwork omitted	600.00	300.00
c.		Groundwork inverted	850.00	850.00
d.		Groundwork double	425.00	425.00
57	A10	3k rose red	5.00	.35
a.		Groundwork omitted	350.00	175.00
b.		Double impression	275.00	165.00
d.		Imperf.	1,500.	500.00
e.		Groundwork inverted	210.00	210.00
f.		Groundwork double	300.00	
57C	A8	4k rose red ('04)	10.00	.50
f.		Double impression	200.00	200.00
g.		Groundwork inverted	6,000.	6,000.
58	A10	5k red violet	10.00	.60
a.		5k dull violet	14.00	2.50
b.		Groundwork inverted	—	16,250.
c.		Imperf.	250.00	250.00
d.		Groundwork omitted	250.00	165.00
e.		Groundwork double	1,500.	
59	A10	7k dark blue	8.00	.35
a.		Groundwork omitted	350.00	300.00
b.		Imperf.	550.00	375.00
c.		Groundwork inverted	1,000.	1,000.
60	A8	10k dark blue ('04)	3.00	.35
a.		Groundwork inverted	12.50	5.00
b.		Groundwork omitted	165.00	35.00
c.		Groundwork double	165.00	35.00
61	A11	14k blue & rose	25.00	.35
a.		Center inverted	5,000.	3,750.
b.		Center omitted	1,100.	700.00
62	A11	15k brown vio & blue ('05)	50.00	1.25
a.		Center omitted		
b.		Center inverted	5,000.	4,000.
63	A8	20k blue & car ('04)	25.00	.75

64	A11	25k dull grn & lil ('05)	30.00	1.25
a.		Center inverted	8,000.	6,500.
b.		Center omitted	1,500.	1,500.
65	A11	35k dk vio & grn	40.00	2.00
a.		Center inverted		115,000.
b.		Center omitted	1,500.	
66	A8	50k vio & grn ('05)	45.00	1.00
67	A11	70k brown & org	55.00	1.25

Perf. 13½

68	A9	1r lt brown, brn & orange	100.00	1.00
a.		Perf. 11½	750.00	50.00
b.		Perf. 13½x11½, 11½x13½	675.00	575.00
c.		Imperf.	600.00	
d.		Center inverted	250.00	250.00
e.		Center omitted	250.00	150.00
f.		Pair, imperf. btwn.	1,200.	250.00
69	A12	3.50r black & gray	30.00	3.00
a.		Center inverted		14,000.
b.		Imperf., pair	2,000.	2,000.
70	A12	7r black & yel	10.00	4.00
a.		Center inverted	7,500.	15,000.
b.		Horiz. pair, imperf. btwn.	3,250.	1,600.
c.		Imperf., pair	5,000.	5,000.

A13

1906   **Perf. 13½**

71	A13	5r dk blue, grn & pale blue	50.00	5.00
a.		Perf. 11½	500.00	300.00

72	A13	10r car rose, yel & gray	350.00	11.50
		Nos. 55-72 (19)	852.00	35.20

The design of No. 72 differs in many details from the illustration. Nos. 71-72 were printed in sheets of 25.

See Nos. 80-81, 83-84, 86, 108-109, 125, 127-128, 130, 132-135, 137-138. For surcharges see Nos. 217-218, 220-222, 224-225, 227-229.

A14   A15

**Vertical Lozenges of Varnish on
Face**
1909-12   **Unwmk.**   **Perf. 14x14½**
Wove Paper

73	A14	1k dull orange yellow	.25	.25
a.		1k orange yellow ('09)	.25	.25
c.		Double impression	100.00	100.00
74	A14	2k dull green	.25	.25
a.		2k green ('09)	.25	.25
b.		Double impression	100.00	100.00
75	A14	3k carmine	.25	.25
a.		3k rose red ('09)	.25	.25
76	A15	4k carmine	.25	.25
a.		4k carmine rose ('09)	.25	.25
77	A14	5k claret	.25	.25
a.		5k lilac ('12)	.75	.65
b.		Double impressions	100.00	100.00
78	A14	7k blue	.25	.25
a.		7k light blue ('09)	1.75	.65
b.		Imperf.	1,000.	250.00
79	A15	10k dark blue	.25	.25
a.		10k light blue ('09)	500.00	85.00
b.		10k pale blue	8.00	2.00

80	A11	14k dk blue & car	.25	.25
a.		14k blue & rose ('09)	.25	.25
81	A11	15k red brown & dp blue	.25	.25
a.		15k dull violet & blue ('09)	.95	.40
c.		Center	115.00	85.00
d.		Center double	50.00	50.00
82	A8	20k dull bl & dk car	.25	.25
a.		20k blue & carmine ('10)	.95	.55
b.		Groundwork omitted	30.00	30.00
c.		Center double	30.00	30.00
d.		Center and value omitted	85.00	85.00
83	A11	25k dl grn & dk vio	.25	.25
a.		25k green & violet ('09)	.35	.30
b.		Center omitted	115.00	115.00
c.		Center double	25.00	25.00
84	A11	35k red brn & grn	.25	.25
a.		35k brown vio & yel green	.60	.40
b.		35k violet & green ('09)	.60	.40
c.		Center double	25.00	25.00
85	A8	50k red brn & grn	.25	.25
a.		50k violet & green ('09)	.60	.40
b.		Groundwork omitted	30.00	30.00
c.		Center double	32.50	32.50
d.		Center and value omitted	115.00	115.00
86	A11	70k brn & red org	.25	.25
a.		70k lt brown & orange ('09)	.35	.25
b.		Center double	40.00	40.00
c.		Center omitted	115.00	115.00

Perf. 13½

87	A9	1r pale brown, dk brn & orange	.25	.25
a.		1r pale brn, brn & org ('10)	.30	.25
b.		Perf. 12½	.30	.25
c.		Groundwork inverted	100.00	100.00
d.		Pair, imperf. between	22.50	22.50
e.		Center inverted	40.00	40.00
f.		Center double	25.00	16.00
		Nos. 73-87 (15)	3.75	3.75

See Nos. 119-124. For surcharges see Nos. 117-118, B24-B29.

No. 87a was issued in sheets of 40 stamps, while Nos. 87 and 87b came in sheets of 50. Nos. 87g-87k are listed below No. 138a.

Nearly all values of this issue are known without the lines of varnish.

The 7k has two types:

I — The scroll bearing the top inscription ends at left with three short lines of shading beside the first letter. Four pearls extend at lower left between the leaves and denomination panel.

II — Inner lines of scroll at top left end in two curls; three pearls at lower left.

Three clichés of type II (an essay) were included by mistake in the plate used for the first printing. Value of pair, type I with type II, unused $2,500.

SURCHARGES

Russian stamps of types A6-A15 with various surcharges may be found listed under Armenia, Batum, Far Eastern Republic, Georgia, Latvia, Siberia, South Russia, Transcaucasian Federated Republics, Ukraine, Russian Offices in China, Russian Offices in the Turkish Empire and Army of the Northwest.

Peter I — A16

Alexander II — A17

Alexander III — A18

Peter I — A19

Nicholas II A20

A21

Catherine II — A22

Nicholas I — A23

Alexander I — A24

Alexis Mikhailovich A25

Paul I A26

Elizabeth Petrovna A27

Michael Feodorovich A28

The Kremlin — A29

Winter Palace — A30

Romanov Castle — A31

Nicholas II — A32

Without Lozenges of Varnish

1913, Jan. 2		**Typo.**	**Perf. 13½**	
88	A16	1k brown orange	.45	.25
89	A17	2k yellow green	.55	.25
90	A18	3k rose red	.75	.25
b.		Double impression	700.00	
91	A19	4k dull red	.90	.25
92	A20	7k brown	1.25	.25
b.		Double impression	900.00	350.00
93	A21	10k deep blue	1.50	.30
94	A22	14k blue green	2.00	.45
95	A23	15k yellow brown	3.50	.65
96	A24	20k olive green	4.50	.75
97	A25	25k red violet	4.00	1.20
98	A26	35k gray vio & dk grn	3.75	.80
99	A27	50k brown & slate	4.25	1.20
100	A28	70k yel grn & brn	4.50	1.60

Engr.

101	A29	1r deep green	25.00	5.50
102	A30	2r red brown	30.00	8.75
103	A31	3r dark violet	35.00	16.50
104	A32	5r black brown	30.00	22.50
		Nos. 88-104 (17)	151.90	61.45
		Set, never hinged	650.00	

Imperf

88a	A16	1k brown orange	*1,000.*	
90a	A18	3k rose red	*1,000.*	
92a	A20	7k brown	*1,000.*	
93a	A21	10k deep blue	*1,000.*	
102a	A30	2r red brown	*1,000.*	
103b	A31	3r dark violet	*1,000.*	

Tercentenary of the founding of the Romanov dynasty.
See Nos. 105-107, 112-116, 139-141. For surcharges see Nos. 110-111, Russian Offices in the Turkish Empire 213-227.

Arms and 5-line Inscription on Back
Thin Cardboard
Without Gum

1915, Oct.		**Typo.**	**Perf. 13½**	
105	A21	10k blue	1.65	4.25
106	A23	15k brown	1.65	4.25
107	A24	20k olive green	1.65	4.25
		Nos. 105-107 (3)	4.95	12.75

Imperf

105a	A21	10k	125.00	
106a	A23	15k	125.00	125.00
107a	A24	20k	125.00	

Nos. 105-107, 112-116 and 139-141 were issued for use as paper money, but contrary to

regulations were often used for postal purposes. Back inscription means: "Having circulation on par with silver subsidiary coin."

Types of 1906 Issue
Vertical Lozenges of Varnish on Face

1915			**Perf. 13½, 13½x13**	
108	A13	5r ind, grn & lt blue	.50	.50
a.		5r dk bl, grn & pale bl ('15)	2.50	.70
b.		Perf. 12½	3.25	1.00
c.		Center double		
d.		Pair, imperf. between	200.00	
109	A13	10r car lake, yel & gray	.50	.50
a.		10r carmine, yel & light gray	.65	.50
b.		10r rose red, yel & gray ('15)	1.10	.65
c.		10r car, yel & gray blue (error)	3,000.	
d.		Groundwork inverted	500.00	
e.		Center double	50.00	50.00

Nos. 108a and 109b were issued in sheets of 25. Nos. 108, 108b, 109 and 109a came in sheets of 50. Chemical forgeries of No. 109c exist. Genuine examples usually are centered to upper right.

Nos. 92, 94 Surcharged

1916				
110	A20	10k on 7k brown	.50	.50
a.		Inverted surcharge	150.00	150.00
111	A22	20k on 14k bl grn	.50	.50

Types of 1913 Issue
Arms, Value & 4-line inscription on Back
Surcharged Large Numerals on Nos. 112-113
Thin Cardboard

1916-17			**Without Gum**	
112	A16	1 on 1k brn org ('17)	2.50	5.00
113	A17	2 on 2k yel green ('17)	2.50	5.00

Without Surcharge

114	A16	1k brown orange	25.00	32.50
115	A17	2k yellow green	35.00	55.00
116	A18	3k rose red	.75	4.50

See note after No. 107.

Nos. 78a, 80a Surcharged

a

b

1917			**Perf. 14x14½**	
117	A14	10k on 7k lt blue	.50	.25
a.		Inverted surcharge	75.00	75.00
b.		Double surcharge	90.00	
118	A11	20k on 14k bl & rose	.50	.25
a.		Inverted surcharge	50.00	50.00

Provisional Government
Civil War
Type of 1889-1912 Issues
Vertical Lozenges of Varnish on Face

Two types of 7r:
Type I — Single outer frame line.
Type II — Double outer frame line.

Wove Paper

1917		**Typo.**	**Imperf.**	
119	A14	1k orange	.25	.25
120	A14	2k gray green	.25	.25
121	A14	3k red	.25	.25
122	A15	4k carmine	.25	.25
123	A14	5k claret	.25	.25
124	A15	10k dark blue	25.00	25.00
125	A11	15k red brn & dp blue	.25	.25
a.		Center omitted	65.00	
126	A8	20k blue & car	.25	.35
a.		Groundwork omitted	25.00	25.00
127	A11	25k grn & gray vio	1.00	1.00
128	A11	35k red brn & grn	.25	.35
129	A8	50k brn vio & grn	.25	.25
a.		Groundwork omitted	25.00	25.00

130 A11	70k brn & orange		.25	.40
a.	Center omitted	115.00		
131 A9	1r pale brn, brn & red org		.25	.25
a.	Center inverted	25.00	50.00	
b.	Center omitted	25.00	25.00	
c.	Center double	25.00	25.00	
d.	Groundwork double	200.00	200.00	
e.	Groundwork inverted	75.00	75.00	
f.	Groundwork omitted	75.00	75.00	
g.	Frame double	25.00	25.00	
132 A12	3.50r mar & lt green		.25	.25
133 A13	5r dk blue, grn & pale blue		.35	.35
a.	5r dk bl, grn & red (error)	1,000.		
b.	Groundwork inverted	4,000.		
134 A12	7r dk green & pink (I)		1.00	1.00
a.	Center inverted	7,250.		
135 A13	10r scarlet, yel & gray		50.00	45.00
a.	10r scarlet, green & gray (error)	1,250.		
	Nos. 119-135 (17)		80.35	75.70

Beware of trimmed examples of No. 109 offered as No. 135.

Vertical Lozenges of Varnish on Face

1917   **Perf. 13½, 13½x13**

137 A12	3.50r mar & lt grn		.25	.25
138 A12	7r dark green & pink (II)		.25	.25
d.	Type I	2.00	2.00	

Perf. 12½

137a A12	3.50r maroon & lt grn		.25	.25
138a A12	7r dk grn & pink (II)		1.00	1.00

Horizontal Lozenges of Varnish on Face

Perf. 13½x13

87g A9	1r pale brown, brn & red orange		.25	.25
h.	Imperf.	12.50		
i.	As "h," center omitted	25.00		
j.	As "h," center inverted	25.00		
k.	As "h," center double	25.00		
137b A12	3.50r mar & lt green		.65	.25
d.	Imperf.	2,000.		
138b A12	7r dk grn & pink (II)		.65	.25
c.	Imperf.	1,500.		

Nos. 87g, 137b and 138b often show the eagle with little or no embossing.

Types of 1913 Issue
Surcharge & 4-line Inscription on Back
Surcharged Large Numerals

1917

Thin Cardboard, Without Gum

139 A16	1 on 1k brown org		1.50	6.00
a.	Imperf.	200.00	30.00	
140 A17	2 on 2k yel green		1.50	6.00
a.	Imperf.	200.00	30.00	
b.	Surch. omitted, imperf.	225.00	45.00	

Without Surcharge

141 A18	3k rose red		2.00	6.00
a.	Imperf.			
	Nos. 139-141 (3)	5.00	18.00	

See note after No. 107.

Stamps overprinted with a Liberty Cap on Crossed Swords with reduced facsimiles of pages of newspapers were a private speculation and without official sanction.

RUSSIAN TURKESTAN

Russian stamps of 1917-18 surcharged as above are frauds.

Russian Soviet Federated Socialist Republic

Severing Chain of Bondage — A33

1918   **Typo.**   **Perf. 13½**

149 A33	35k blue		.35	7.00
a.	Imperf., pair	1,750.		
150 A33	70k brown		.40	8.00
a.	Imperf., pair	12,000.		

For surcharges see Nos. B18-B23, J1-J9 and note following No. B17.

A 15k stamp exists but was not regularly issued. Value, $30,000.

During 1918-22, the chaotic conditions of revolution and civil war brought the printing of stamps by the central government to a halt. Stocks of old tsarist Arms type stamps and postal stationery remained in use, and postal savings and various revenue stamps were authorized for postage use. During this period, stamps were sold and used at different rates at different times: 1918-20, sold at face value; from March, 1920, sold at 100 times face value; from Aug. 15, 1921, sold at 250r each, regardless of face value; from April, 1922, sold at 10,000r per 1k or 1r. In Oct. 1922, these issues were superseded by gold currency stamps.

See Nos. AR1-AR25 for fiscal stamps used as postage stamps during this period.

Symbols of Agriculture — A40   Symbols of Industry — A41

Soviet Symbols of Agriculture and Industry — A42

Science and Arts — A43

1921   **Unwmk.**   **Litho.**   **Imperf.**

177 A40	1r orange		1.75	10.00
178 A40	2r lt brown		1.25	10.00
a.	Double impression	100.00		
179 A41	5r dull ultra		1.50	10.00
a.	Double impression	100.00		
180 A42	20r blue		1.50	7.50
a.	Double impression	200.00		
b.	Pelure paper	3.25	8.00	
c.	As "b," double impression	200.00		
181 A40	100r orange		.25	.25
a.	Double impression	200.00		
b.	Pelure paper	.25	.25	
c.	As "b," double impression	150.00		
182 A40	200r lt brown		.25	.35
a.	Double impression	200.00		
b.	Triple impression	150.00		
c.	200r gray brown	15.00	15.00	
183 A43	250r dull violet		.25	.25
a.	Tête bêche pair	25.00	250.00	
b.	Double impression	100.00		
c.	Pelure paper	.25	.60	
d.	As "c," tête bêche pair	35.00	250.00	
e.	As "c," double impression	100.00		
f.	Chalk surfaced paper	12.50	25.00	
184 A40	300r green		.25	1.25
a.	Double impression	150.00		
b.	Pelure paper	12.50	25.00	
185 A41	500r blue		.25	2.25
a.	Double impression	200.00		
186 A41	1000r carmine		.25	.30
a.	Double impression	150.00		
b.	Triple impression	150.00		
c.	Pelure paper	.30	.60	
d.	As "c," double impression	150.00		
e.	Thick paper	5.00	7.50	
f.	Chalk surfaced paper	1.00	2.00	
	Nos. 177-186 (10)	7.50	42.15	

Nos. 177-180 were on sale only in Petrograd, Moscow and Kharkov. Used values are for cancelled-to-order stamps. Postally used examples are worth substantially more.

Nos. 183a and 183d are from printings in which one of the two panes of 25 in the sheet

were inverted. Thus, they are horizontal pairs, with a vertical gutter.

See Nos. 203, 205. For surcharges see Nos. 191-194, 196-199, 201, 210, B40, B43-B47, J10.

New Russia Triumphant A44

Type I — 37½mm by 23½mm.
Type II — 38½mm by 23¼mm.

1921, Aug. 10   **Wmk. 169**   **Engr.**

187 A44	40r slate, type II		.60	1.00
a.	Type I	2.00	1.25	

The types are caused by paper shrinkage. One type has the watermark sideways in relation to the other.

For surcharges see Nos. 195, 200.

Initials Stand for Russian Soviet Federated Socialist Republic — A45

1921   **Litho.**   **Unwmk.**

188 A45	100r orange		.50	.55
189 A45	250r violet		.50	.55
190 A45	1000r carmine rose		1.00	1.40
	Nos. 188-190 (3)		2.00	2.50

4th anniversary of Soviet Government.
A 200r was not regularly issued. Value $60.

Nos. 177-179 Surcharged in Black

1922

191 A40	5000r on 1r orange		3.50	.80
a.	Inverted surcharge	200.00	22.50	
b.	Double surch., red & blk	400.00	22.50	
c.	Pair, one without surcharge	250.00		
192 A40	5000r on 2r lt brown		3.50	1.25
a.	Inverted surcharge	100.00	100.00	
b.	Double surcharge	70.00		
193 A41	5000r on 5r ultra		3.50	2.00
a.	Inverted surcharge	100.00	100.00	
b.	Double surcharge	75.00		

Beware of digitally created forgeries of the errors of Nos. 191-193 and 196-199.

No. 180 Surcharged

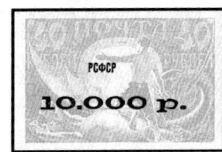

194 A42	5000r on 20r blue		2.00	2.50
a.	Pelure paper	5.00	2.25	
b.	Pair, one without surcharge	100.00		

Nos. 177-180, 187-187a Surcharged in Black or Red

195 A44	10,000r on 40r, type I		5.00	5.00
a.	Inverted surcharge	225.00	150.00	
b.	Type II	6.00	2.50	

Wmk. Lozenges (169)

c.	"1.0000" instead of "10.000"	2,750.		
d.	Double surcharge	150.00		

Red Surcharge
Unwmk.

196 A40	5000r on 1r org		6.50	6.50
a.	Inverted surcharge	150.00	150.00	
197 A40	5000r on 2r lt brn		6.50	6.50
a.	Inverted surcharge	150.00	150.00	
198 A41	5000r on 5r ultra		6.50	6.50
199 A42	5000r on 20r blue		3.00	2.25
a.	Inverted surcharge	250.00	250.00	
b.	Pelure paper	5.00	5.00	

Wmk. Lozenges (169)

200 A44	10,000r on 40r, type I (R)		2.00	1.00
a.	Inverted surcharge	250.00	250.00	
b.	Double surcharge	150.00	150.00	
c.	With periods after Russian letters	300.00	35.00	
d.	Type II	2.00	3.00	
e.	As "a," type II	150.00	150.00	
f.	As "c," type II	225.00	45.00	

No. 183
Surcharged in
Black or Blue
Black

1922, Mar.   **Unwmk.**

201 A43	7500r on 250r (Bk)		.25	.25
a.	Pelure paper	1.00	1.00	
b.	Chalk surfaced paper	1.00	1.00	
c.	Blue black surcharge	1.00	1.00	
	Nos. 191-201 (11)		42.25	34.55

Nos. 201, 201a and 201b exist with surcharge inverted (value about $20 each), and double (about $25 each).

The horizontal surcharge was prepared but not issued.

Type of 1921 and

"Workers of the World Unite" A46

1922		Litho.	Wmk. 171	
202	A46	5000r dark violet	.75	3.25
203	A42	7500r blue	.25	.35
204	A46	10,000r blue	19.00	15.00
		Unwmk.		
205	A42	7500r blue, *buff*	.25	.40
a.		Double impression	250.00	
206	A46	22,500r dk violet, *buff*	.50	.60
		Nos. 202-206 (5)	20.75	19.60

For surcharges see Nos. B41-B42.

No. 183 Surcharged Diagonally

1922		**Unwmk.**		*Imperf.*
210	A43	100,000r on 250r	.50	.50
a.		Inverted surcharge	60.00	60.00
b.		Pelure paper	1.00	1.00
c.		Chalk surfaced paper	1.00	1.00
d.		As "b," inverted surcharge	150.00	150.00

Marking 5th Anniversary of October Revolution — A48

1922				Typo.
211	A48	5r ocher & black	.60	.25
212	A48	10r brown & black	.60	.25
213	A48	25r violet & black	1.75	.60
214	A48	27r rose & black	6.00	1.00
215	A48	45r blue & black	4.00	.75
		Nos. 211-215 (5)	12.95	2.85
		Pelure Paper		
213a	A48	25r violet & black	60.00	
214a	A48	27r rose & black	60.00	
215a	A48	45r blue & black	65.00	

5th anniv. of the October Revolution. Sold in the currency of 1922 which was valued at 10,000 times that of the preceding years.
For surcharges see Nos. B38-B39.

Nos. 81, 82a, 85-86, 125-126, 129-130 Surcharged

1922-23				Perf. 14½x15
216	A8	5r on 20k	1.00	2.00
a.		Inverted surcharge	100.00	100.00
b.		Double surcharge	100.00	100.00
217	A11	20r on 15k	1.75	2.00
a.		Inverted surcharge	100.00	100.00
218	A11	20r on 70k	1.00	.35
a.		Inverted surcharge	75.00	50.00
b.		Double surcharge	50.00	50.00
219	A8	30r on 50k	1.75	.50
c.		Inverted surcharge	75.00	75.00
c.		Groundwork omitted	50.00	50.00
d.		Double surcharge	50.00	50.00
220	A11	40r on 15k	1.10	.35
a.		Inverted surcharge	75.00	50.00
b.		Double surcharge	100.00	100.00
221	A11	100r on 15k	1.10	.35
a.		Inverted surcharge	100.00	75.00
b.		Double surcharge	100.00	75.00
222	A11	200r on 15k	1.10	.35
a.		Inverted surcharge	50.00	50.00
b.		Double surcharge	75.00	50.00

Nos. 218-220, 222 exist in pairs, one without surcharge; Nos. 221-222 with triple surcharge; No. 221 with double surcharge, one inverted. Value, each $100.

				Imperf
223	A8	5r on 20k	35.00	25.00
224	A11	20r on 15k	7,500.	
225	A11	20r on 70k	1.00	1.00
a.		Inverted surcharge	25.00	25.00
226	A8	30r on 50k brn vio & green	5.00	4.50

227	A11	40r on 15k	.30	.60
a.		Inverted surcharge	100.00	100.00
b.		Double surcharge	100.00	100.00
228	A11	100r on 15k	2.25	2.00
a.		Inverted surcharge	125.00	125.00
229	A11	200r on 15k	1.00	1.00
a.		Inverted surcharge	125.00	125.00
b.		Double surcharge	100.00	100.00
		Nos. 216-223,225-229 (13)	54.60	41.00

Forgeries of No. 223-229 exist, including a dangerous digital forgery of No. 224.

Worker   Soldier
A49   A50

1922-23		Typo.		*Imperf.*
230	A49	10r blue	.25	.25
231	A50	50r brown	.25	.25
232	A50	70r brown violet	.25	.25
233	A50	100r red	.25	.25
		Nos. 230-233 (4)	1.00	1.00

1923				Perf. 14x14½
234	A49	10r dp bl, perf. 13½	.75	.25
a.		Perf. 14	15.00	16.00
b.		Perf. 12½	3.00	3.00
235	A50	50r brown	.75	.25
a.		Perf. 12½	7.50	6.00
b.		Perf. 13½	1.50	2.00
236	A50	70r brown violet	.75	.25
a.		Perf. 12½	2.00	2.00
237	A50	100r red	.75	.40
a.		Cliché of 70r in plate of 100r	40.00	35.00
b.		Corrected cliché	150.00	175.00
		Nos. 234-237 (4)	3.00	1.15

No. 237b has extra broken line at right.
Nos. 230-233 were surcharged for use in Far Eastern Republic. See Far Eastern Republic Nos. 66-70.

Soldier — Worker — Peasant
A51   A52   A53

1923				Perf. 14½x15
238	A51	3r rose	.25	.25
239	A52	4r brown	.25	.25
240	A53	5r light blue	.25	.25
a.		Double impression	125.00	125.00
241	A51	10r gray	.25	.25
e.		Double impression	150.00	
241A	A51	20r brown violet	.35	.35
b.		Double impression	150.00	150.00
		Nos. 238-241A (5)	1.35	1.35
		Imperf		
238a	A51	3r rose	25.00	25.00
239a	A52	4r brown	25.00	25.00
b.		As "a," double impression	150.00	
240b	A53	5r light blue	8.00	10.00
241d	A51	10r gray	10.00	10.00
f.		As "d," double impression	200.00	
241c	A51	20r brown violet	450.00	100.00

Stamps of 1r buff, type A52, and 2r green, type A53, perf. 12 and imperf. were prepared but not put in use. Value $1 each.
The imperfs of Nos. 238-241A were sold only by the philatelic bureau in Moscow.
Stamps of 20r, type A51, printed in gray black or dull violet are essays. Value, $200 each.
The stamps of this and the following issues were sold for the currency of 1923, one ruble of which was equal to 100 rubles of 1922 and 1,000,000 rubles of 1921.

Union of Soviet Socialist Republics

Reaping — A54

Sowing — A55

Fordson Tractor A56

Symbolical of the Exhibition — A57

1923, Aug. 19		Litho.		*Imperf.*
242	A54	1r brown & orange	5.00	5.00
243	A55	2r dp grn & pale grn	5.00	5.00
244	A56	5r dp bl & pale blue	5.00	5.00
245	A57	7r rose & pink	5.00	5.00
		Perf. 12½, 13½		
246	A54	1r brown & orange	5.00	7.50
a.		Perf. 12½	35.00	75.00
247	A55	2r dp grn & pale grn, perf. 12½	5.00	7.50
a.		Perf. 13½	16.00	16.00
248	A56	5r dp bl & pale bl	5.00	7.50
a.		Perf. 12½	16.00	16.00
249	A57	7r rose & pink	5.00	7.50
a.		Perf. 12½	16.00	25.00
		Nos. 242-249 (8)	40.00	50.00

1st Agriculture and Craftsmanship Exhibition, Moscow.

Worker — Soldier — Peasant
A58   A59   A60

1923		**Unwmk.**	Litho.	*Imperf.*
250	A58	1k orange	.90	.25
251	A60	2k green	1.40	.40
252	A59	3k red brown	1.20	.40
253	A58	4k deep rose	2.60	.65
254	A59	5k lilac	1.40	.65
255	A60	6k light blue	2.75	.30
256	A59	10k dark blue	2.75	.30
257	A58	20k yellow green	4.25	.55
258	A60	50k dark brown	6.00	1.90
259	A59	1r red & brown	25.00	5.00
		Nos. 250-259 (10)	48.25	10.40

1924				Perf. 14½x15
261	A58	4k deep rose	100.00	150.00
262	A59	10k dark blue	100.00	100.00
263	A60	30k violet	25.00	8.00
264	A60	40k slate gray	25.00	8.00
		Nos. 261-264 (4)	250.00	266.00

See Nos. 273-290, 304-321. For surcharges see Nos. 349-350.

Vladimir Ilyich Ulyanov (Lenin) — A61

1924				*Imperf.*
265	A61	3k red & black	5.00	2.00
266	A61	6k red & black	5.00	2.00
267	A61	12k red & black	5.00	2.00
268	A61	20k red & black	5.00	2.00
		Nos. 265-268 (4)	20.00	8.00

Three printings of Nos. 265-268 differ in size of red frame.

		Perf. 13½		
269	A61	3k red & black	5.00	2.00
270	A61	6k red & black	5.00	2.00
271	A61	12k red & black	5.00	2.75
272	A61	20k red & black	5.00	3.25
		Nos. 269-272 (4)	20.00	10.00
		Nos. 265-272 (8)	40.00	18.00

Death of Lenin (1870-1924).
Forgeries of Nos. 265-272 exist.

Types of 1923 and

Worker — A62

There are small differences between the lithographed stamps of 1923 and the typographed of 1924-25. On a few values this may be seen in the numerals.

Type A58: Lithographed. The two white lines forming the outline of the ear are continued across the cheek. Typographed. The outer lines of the ear are broken where they touch the cheek.

Type A59: Lithographed. At the top of the right shoulder a white line touches the frame at the left. Counting from the edge of the visor of the cap, lines 5, 6 and sometimes 7 touch at their upper ends. Typographed. The top line of the shoulder does not reach the frame. On the cap lines 5, 6 and 7 run together and form a white spot.

Type A60: In the angle above the first letter "C" there is a fan-shaped ornament enclosing four white dashes. On the lithographed stamps these dashes reach nearly to the point of the angle. On the typographed stamps the dashes are shorter and often only three are visible.

On unused examples of the typographed stamps the raised outlines of the designs can be seen on the backs of the stamps.

1924-25		Typo.		*Imperf.*
273	A59	3k red brown	3.00	1.25
274	A58	4k deep rose	3.00	1.25
275	A59	10k dark blue	4.00	1.25
275A	A60	50k brown	3,000.	25.00

Other typographed and imperf. values include: 2k green, 5k lilac, 6k light blue, 20k green and 1r red and brown. Value, unused: $150, $100, $150, $200 and $1,000, respectively.

Nos. 273-275A were regularly issued. The 7k, 8k, 9k, 30k, 40k, 2r, 3r, and 5r also exist imperf. Value, set of 8, $275.

		Perf. 14½x15		
		Typo.		
276	A58	1k orange	75.00	5.50
277	A60	2k green	2.00	.50
278	A59	3k red brown	2.00	.50
279	A58	4k deep rose	2.00	.50
280	A58	5k lilac	50.00	10.00
281	A60	6k lt blue	2.00	.50
282	A59	7k chocolate	2.00	.50
283	A58	8k brown olive	2.00	.50
284	A60	9k orange red	5.00	1.00
285	A59	10k dark blue	2.00	.50
286	A58	14k slate blue	250.00	5.00
287	A60	15k yellow	27,500.	150.00
288	A58	20k gray green	5.00	.50
288A	A60	30k violet	350.00	8.00
288B	A60	40k slate gray	400.00	8.00
289	A60	50k brown	125.00	20.00
290	A59	1r red & brown	10.00	2.00
291	A62	2r green & rose	15.00	4.00
		Nos. 276-286,288-291 (17)	1,299.	67.50

See No. 323. Forgeries of No. 287 exist.

1925				Perf. 12
276a	A58	1k orange	2.00	1.00
277a	A60	2k green	10.00	2.00
278a	A59	3k red brown	7.00	2.00
279a	A58	4k deep rose	100.00	50.00
280a	A58	5k lilac	5.00	1.00
282a	A59	7k chocolate	20.00	1.00
283a	A58	8k brown olive	100.00	5.00
284a	A60	9k orange red	40.00	5.00
285a	A59	10k dark blue	50.00	2.00
286a	A58	14k slate blue	5.00	1.00
287a	A60	15k yellow	2.00	1.00
288c	A58	20k gray green	25.00	5.00
288d	A60	30k violet	25.00	3.00
288e	A59	40k slate gray	100.00	5.00
289a	A60	50k brown	10.00	2.00
290a	A59	1r red & brown	2,500.	600.00
		Nos. 276a-290a (16)	3,001.	682.00

Soldier — A63   Worker — A64

1924-25   **Perf. 13½**
292 A63 3r blk brn & grn   10.00   4.00
   a.   Perf. 10   3,250.   50.00
   b.   Perf. 13½x10   1,500.   325.00
293 A64 5r dk bl & gray
         brn   100.00   10.00
   a.   Perf. 10½   50.00   65.00

See Nos. 324-325.

Lenin
Mausoleum,
Moscow — A65

Wmk. 170
1925, Jan.   **Photo.**   **Imperf.**
294 A65   7k deep blue   10.00   5.00
295 A65 14k dark green   40.00   8.00
296 A65 20k carmine rose   22.00   5.50
297 A65 40k red brown   28.00   6.50
    Nos. 294-297 (4)   100.00   25.00

        Perf. 13½x14
298 A65   7k deep blue   11.00   5.00
299 A65 14k dark green   37.50   7.50
300 A65 20k carmine rose   22.50   5.75
301 A65 40k red brown   29.00   7.00
    Nos. 298-301 (4)   100.00   25.25
    Nos. 294-301 (8)   100.00   50.25

First anniversary of Lenin's death.
Nos. 294-301 are found on both ordinary
and thick paper. Those on thick paper sell for
twice as much, except for No. 301, which is
scarcer on ordinary paper.

Lenin — A66

Wmk. 170
1925, July   **Engr.**   **Perf. 13½**
302 A66   5r red brown   37.50   6.00
   a.   Perf. 12½   40.00   11.00
   b.   Perf. 10½ ('26)   37.50   8.00
303 A66 10r indigo   37.50   11.00
   a.   Perf. 12½   190.00   90.00
   b.   Perf. 10½ ('26)   27.50   11.00

Imperfs. exist. Value, set $75.
See Nos. 407-408, 621-622.

Types of 1923 Issue
1925-27   **Wmk. 170**   **Typo.**   **Perf. 12**
304 A58   1k orange   .40   .35
305 A60   2k green   .40   .35
306 A59   3k red brown   .40   .35
307 A58   4k deep rose   .40   .35
308 A58   5k lilac   .75   .35
309 A59   6k lt blue   1.90   .75
310 A59   7k chocolate   1.90   .35
311 A58   8k brown olive   1.90   .35
   a.   Perf. 14½x15   100.00   50.00
312 A60   9k red   3.00   .75
313 A59 10k dark blue   3.00   .75
   a.   10k pale blue ('27)   10.00   5.00
314 A58 14k slate blue   4.50   .75
315 A60 15k yellow   6.00   1.50
316 A59 18k violet   5.25   .75
317 A58 20k gray green   5.25   .75
318 A60 30k violet   7.50   .75
319 A59 40k slate gray   11.00   .75
320 A60 50k brown   19.00   1.50
321 A59   1r red & brown   15.00   2.25
   a.   Perf. 14½x15   200.00   100.00
323 A62   2r green & rose
         red   75.00   11.00
   a.   Perf. 14½x15   20.00   5.00

        Perf. 13½
324 A63   3r blk brn & green   20.00   5.00
   a.   Perf. 12½   300.00   25.00

---

325 A64   5r dark blue &
         gray brown   25.00   5.00
    Nos. 304-325 (21)   207.55   34.70

Nos. 304-315, 317-325 exist imperf. Value,
set $125.

Mikhail V. Lomonosov and Academy
of Sciences — A67

1925, Sept. Photo.   **Perf. 12½, 13½**
326 A67   3k orange brown   7.50   4.00
   a.   Perf. 12½x12   15.00   7.50
   b.   Perf. 13½x12½   850.00   850.00
   c.   Perf. 13½   20.00   10.00
327 A67 15k dk olive green   12.50   4.50
   a.   Perf. 12½   20.00   7.50

Russian Academy of Sciences, 200th anniv.
Exist unwatermarked, on thick paper with yellow gum, perf. 13½. These are essays, later
perforated and gummed. Value, each $50.

Prof. Aleksandr S.
Popov (1859-1905),
Radio Pioneer — A68

1925, Oct.   **Perf. 13½**
328 A68   7k deep blue   7.00   2.00
329 A68 14k green   13.00   3.00

For surcharge see No. 353.

Decembrist   Street Rioting in St.
Exiles — A69   Petersburg — A70

Revolutionist
Leaders — A71

1925, Dec. 28   **Imperf.**
330 A69   3k olive green   10.00   3.00
331 A70   7k brown   15.00   4.50
332 A71 14k carmine lake   15.00   6.00

         Perf. 13½
333 A69   3k olive green   5.00   2.25
   a.   Perf. 12½   200.00   100.00
334 A70   7k brown   15.00   3.00
335 A71 14k carmine lake   15.00   4.00
    Nos. 330-335 (6)   75.00   22.75

Centenary of Decembrist revolution.
For surcharges see Nos. 354, 357.

Revolters   Speaker
Parading — A72   Haranguing
            Mob — A73

Street Barricade, Moscow — A74

1925, Dec. 20   **Imperf.**
336 A72   3k olive green   15.00   15.00
337 A73   7k brown   17.50   17.50
338 A74 14k carmine lake   24.00   3.50

      Perf. 12½, 12x12½
339 A72   3k olive green   4.50   4.50
   a.   Perf. 13½   8.00   8.00
340 A73   7k brown   10.00   10.00
   a.   Perf. 13½   15.00   10.50
   b.   Horiz. pair, imperf. btwn.   55.00   50.00
341 A74 14k carmine lake   7.50   7.50
   a.   Perf. 13½   40.00   15.00
    Nos. 336-341 (6)   78.50   58.00

20th anniversary of Revolution of 1905.
For surcharges see Nos. 355, 358.

Lenin — A75   Liberty
            Monument,
          Moscow — A76

1926   Wmk. 170   Engr.   Perf. 10½
342 A75   1r dark brown   12.00   3.25
343 A75   2r black violet   16.00   5.75
   a.   Perf. 12½   250.00   100.00
344 A75   3r dark green   22.50   5.75
    Nos. 342-344 (3)   50.50   14.75

Nos. 342-343 exist imperf.
See Nos. 406, 620.

1926, July   Litho.   Perf. 12x12½
347 A76   7k blue green & red   6.50   2.50
348 A76 14k blue green & violet   10.00   2.50

6th International Esperanto Congress at
Leningrad. Exist perf. 11½. Value, set $8,500.
For surcharge see No. 356.

Nos. 282, 282a and 310
Surcharged in Black

1927, June   Unwmk.   Perf. 14½x15
349 A59 8k on 7k chocolate   12.00   1.50
   a.   Perf. 12   9.00   7.50
   b.   Inverted surcharge   125.00   110.00

        Perf. 12
       Wmk. 170
350 A59 8k on 7k chocolate   8.00   1.50
   a.   Inverted surcharge   525.00   35.00

The surcharge on Nos. 349-350 comes in
two types: With space of 2mm between lines,
and with space of ¾mm. The latter is much
scarcer.

**Same Surcharge on Stamps of
1925-26 in Black or Red**
    Perf. 13½, 12½, 12x12½
353 A68 8k on 7k dp bl (R)   6.00   4.50
   a.   Inverted "8"   75.00   100.00
354 A70 8k on 7k brown   17.50   9.25
355 A73 8k on 7k brown   22.50   12.25
356 A76 8k on 7k blue
         green & red   17.50   11.00

        Imperf
357 A70 8k on 7k brown   7.50   5.25
358 A73 8k on 7k brown   7.50   5.25
    Nos. 349-350,353-358 (8)   98.50   50.50

Postage Due Stamps
of 1925 Surcharged

Two settings: A's aligned (shown), bottom A
to left.

Lithographed or Typographed
1927, June   **Perf. 12**
359 D1 8k on 1k red, typo.   3.00   4.00
   a.   Litho.   1,000.   250.00
360 D1 8k on 2k violet   4.00   4.00

     Perf. 12, 14½x14
361 D1 8k on 3k lt blue   4.25   3.00
362 D1 8k on 7k brown   4.75   2.50
363 D1 8k on 8k green   3.75   4.00
364 D1 8k on 10k dk blue   4.50   2.50
365 D1 8k on 14k brown   3.75   4.00
    Nos. 359-365 (7)   28.00   24.00

Exist with inverted surcharge. Value each,
$100.

Wmk. 170
1927, June   **Typo.**   **Perf. 12**
366 D1 8k on 1k red   2.10   2.10
367 D1 8k on 2k violet   2.10   2.10
368 D1 8k on 3k lt blue   4.25   4.25
369 D1 8k on 7k orange   4.25   4.25
370 D1 8k on 8k green   2.10   2.10
371 D1 8k on 10k dk blue   2.10   2.10
372 D1 8k on 14k brown   3.25   3.25
    Nos. 366-372 (7)   20.15   20.15

Nos. 366, 368-372 exist inverted surcharge. Value each, $100.

Dr. L. L.
Zamenhof
A77

1927   **Photo.**   **Perf. 10½**
373 A77 14k yel green & brown   5.00   2.50

        Unwmk.
374 A77 14k yel green & brown   5.00   2.50

40th anniversary of creation of Esperanto.
No. 374 exists perf. 10, 10x10½ and imperf.
Value, imperf. pair $2,400.

Worker, Soldier, Peasant — A78

Worker and Sailor — A81

Lenin in Car Guarded by Soldiers A79

Smolny Institute, Leningrad A80

Map of the USSR A82

Men of Various Soviet Republics — A83

Workers of Different Races; Kremlin in Background — A84

Typo. (3k, 8k, 18k), Engr. (7k), Litho. (14k), Photo. (5k, 28k)
Perf. 13½, 12½x12, 11
1927, Oct.   **Unwmk.**

375	A78	3k bright rose	2.50	.80
a.		Imperf., pair	5,000.	
376	A79	5k deep brown	6.75	2.25
a.		Imperf.	1,000.	500.00
b.		Perf. 12½	200.00	125.00
c.		Perf. 12½x10½	40.00	27.50
377	A80	7k myrtle green	13.00	3.00
a.		Perf. 11½	150.00	75.00
b.		Imperf., pair	4,000.	
378	A81	8k brown & black	6.00	1.50
a.		Perf. 10½x12½	40.00	27.50
379	A82	14k dull blue & red	6.75	1.65
380	A83	18k blue	5.25	1.25
a.		Imperf.	1,500.	
381	A84	28k olive brown	20.00	8.00
a.		Perf. 10	40.00	35.00
		Nos. 375-381 (7)	60.25	18.45

10th anniversary of October Revolution.

The paper of No. 375 has an overprint of pale yellow wavy lines.

No. 377b exists with watermark 170. Value, $1,000.

Worker — A85   Peasant — A86

Lenin — A87

1927-28   **Typo.**   **Perf. 13½**
Chalk Surfaced Paper

382	A85	1k orange	.90	.85
383	A86	2k apple green	.90	.55
385	A85	4k bright blue	.90	.55
386	A86	5k brown	.90	.55
388	A86	7k dark red ('28)	4.75	1.00
389	A85	8k green	2.50	.75
391	A85	10k light brown	2.25	.75
392	A87	14k dark green ('28)	2.50	.95
393	A87	18k olive green	5.00	1.60
394	A87	18k dark blue ('28)	4.50	1.90
395	A86	20k dark gray green	3.00	1.25
396	A86	40k rose red	12.00	7.00
397	A86	50k bright blue	7.00	2.25
399	A85	70k gray green	12.00	4.00
400	A86	80k orange	18.00	3.50
		Nos. 382-400 (15)	77.10	27.45

The 1k, 2k and 10k exist imperf. Value, each $1,000.

Soldier and Kremlin — A88   Sailor and Flag — A89

Cavalryman A90   Aviator A91

1928, Feb. 6
Chalk Surfaced Paper

402	A88	8k light brown	4.50	.40
a.		Imperf.	1,200.	200.00
403	A89	14k deep blue	7.00	.90
404	A90	18k carmine rose	7.00	1.75
a.		Imperf.	7,000.	
405	A91	28k yellow green	25.00	4.00
		Nos. 402-405 (4)	43.50	7.05

10th anniversary of the Soviet Army.

Lenin Types of 1925-26
Perf. 10, 10½
1928-29   **Engr.**   **Wmk. 169**

406	A75	3r dark green ('29)	19.00	3.50
407	A66	5r red brown	22.50	7.50
408	A66	10r indigo	32.50	9.00
		Nos. 406-408 (3)	74.00	20.00

No. 406 exists imperf. Value, $1,000.

Bugler Sounding Assembly
A92   A93

Perf. 12½x12
1929, Aug. 18   **Photo.**   **Wmk. 170**

411	A92	10k olive brown	25.00	7.00
a.		Perf. 10½	65.00	25.00
b.		Perf. 12½x12x10½x12	125.00	75.00
412	A93	14k slate	7.00	3.00
a.		Perf. 12½x12x10½x10½x12	150.00	75.00

First All-Soviet Assembly of Pioneers.

Factory Worker A95

Peasant A96

Farm Worker A97

Soldier A98

Worker, Soldier, Peasant A100

Worker A103

Lenin A104

Peasant A107

Factory Worker A109

Farm Worker A111

Perf. 12x12½
1929-31   **Typo.**   **Wmk. 170**

413	A103	1k orange	.40	.25
a.		Perf. 10½	30.00	13.00
b.		Perf. 14x14½	50.00	35.00
414	A95	2k yellow green	.50	.25
415	A96	3k blue	.65	.25
a.		Perf. 14x14½	50.00	50.00
416	A97	4k claret	.85	.25
417	A98	5k orange brown	1.00	.25
a.		Perf. 10½	75.00	75.00
418	A100	7k scarlet	1.25	.90
419	A103	10k olive green	1.60	.25
a.		Perf. 10½	40.00	22.50

Unwmk.

420	A104	14k indigo	1.10	1.00
a.		Perf. 10½	7.50	3.25

Wmk. 170

421	A100	15k dk ol grn ('30)	1.75	.25
422	A107	20k green	1.75	.25
a.		Imperf.	200.00	100.00
423	A109	30k dk violet	2.75	.85
424	A111	50k dp brown	3.50	1.75
425	A98	70k dk red ('30)	4.25	1.90
426	A107	80k red brown ('31)	5.50	1.90
		Nos. 413-426 (14)	26.85	10.30

Nos. 422, 423, 424 and 426 have a background of fine wavy lines in pale shades of the colors of the stamps.

See Nos. 456-466, 613A-619A. For surcharge see No. 743.

Symbolical of Industry A112

Tractors Issuing from Assembly Line — A113

Iron Furnace (Inscription reads, "More Metal More Machines") A114

Blast Furnace and Chart of Anticipated Iron Production A115

1929-30   **Perf. 12x12½**

427	A112	5k orange brown	2.00	1.50
428	A113	10k olive green	2.00	2.00

Perf. 12½x12

429	A114	20k dull brown	5.00	3.50
430	A115	28k violet black	3.50	2.25
		Nos. 427-430 (4)	12.50	9.25

Publicity for greater industrial production. No. 429 exists perf. 10½. Value $4,000.

Red Cavalry in Polish Town after Battle A116

Cavalry Charge A117

Staff Officers of 1st Cavalry Army A118

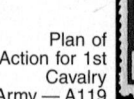

Plan of Action for 1st Cavalry Army — A119

1930, Feb.   **Perf. 12x12½**

431	A116	2k yellow green	3.00	2.00
432	A117	5k light brown	3.00	2.00
433	A118	10k olive gray	5.50	3.25
434	A119	14k indigo & red	3.50	2.75
		Nos. 431-434 (4)	15.00	10.00

1st Red Cavalry Army, 10th anniversary.

Students Preparing a Poster Newspaper A120

1930, Aug. 15

435	A120	10k olive green	2.50	2.00

Educational Exhibition, Leningrad, 7/1-8/15/30.

Telegraph Office, Moscow A121

Lenin Hydroelectric Power Station on Volkhov River A122

1930 Photo. Wmk. 169 Perf. 10½
436 A121 1r deep blue   10.00 10.00

Wmk. 170
437 A122 3r yel green & blk brn   11.50 10.00

See Nos. 467, 469.

Battleship Potemkin A123

Inside Presnya Barricade A124

Moscow Barricades in 1905 — A125

1930 Typo. Perf. 12x12½, 12½x12
438 A123 3k red   1.75 .55
439 A124 5k blue   1.75 .70
440 A125 10k dk green & red   3.50 1.00
    Nos. 438-440 (3)   7.00 2.25

1931 Imperf.
452 A123 3k red   10.00 10.00
453 A124 5k deep blue   18.00 18.00
454 A125 10k dk green & red   35.00 35.00
    Nos. 452-454 (3)   63.00 63.00
    Nos. 438-454 (6)   70.00 65.25

Revolution of 1905, 25th anniversary.

Types of 1929-31 Regular Issue
1931-32 Imperf.
456 A103 1k orange   2.00 1.00
457 A95 2k yellow green   1.00 1.25
458 A96 3k blue   1.00 1.25
459 A97 4k claret   75.00 12.50
460 A98 5k orange brown   2.00 1.00
462 A103 10k olive green   55.00 25.00
464 A100 15k dk olive green   35.00 35.00
466 A109 30k dull violet   75.00 50.00
467 A121 1r dark blue   200.00 175.00
    Nos. 456-467 (9)   446.00 302.00

Nos. 459, 462-467 were sold only by the philatelic bureau.

Type of 1930 Issue
1931 Wmk. 170 Perf. 12x12½
469 A121 1r dark blue   2.00 .50
    Never hinged   5.00

Maxim Gorki — A133

1932-33 Photo.
470 A133 15k dark brown   3.00 2.50
    a. Imperf.   200.00 200.00
471 A133 35k dp ultra ('33)   47.50 12.00
    Set, never hinged   100.00

40th anniversary of Gorki's literary activity.

Lenin Addressing the People A134

Revolution in Petrograd (Leningrad) A135

Dnieper Hydroelectric Power Station A136

Asiatics Saluting the Soviet Flag — A139

Breaking Prison Bars — A140

Designs (dated 1917 1932): 15k, Collective farm. 20k, Magnitogorsk metallurgical plant in Urals. 30k, Radio tower and heads of 4 men.

1932-33 Perf. 12½x12; 12½ (30k)
472 A134 3k dark violet   1.80 1.25
473 A135 5k dark brown   1.80 1.25
474 A136 10k ultra   4.25 2.50
475 A136 15k dark green   2.60 1.50
476 A136 20k lake ('33)   3.25 2.00
477 A136 30k dark gray ('33)   65.00 30.00
478 A139 35k gray black   95.00 110.00
    Nos. 472-478 (7)   173.70 148.50
    Set, never hinged   350.00

October Revolution, 15th anniversary.

1932, Nov. Litho. Perf. 12½x12
479 A140 50k dark red   20.00 8.00
    Never hinged   50.00

Intl. Revolutionaries' Aid Assoc., 10th anniv.

Trier, Birthplace of Marx — A141

Grave, Highgate Cemetery, London — A142

35k, Portrait & signature of Karl Marx (1818-83).

Perf. 12x12½, 12½x12
1933, Mar. Photo.
480 A141 3k dull green   7.00 1.80
481 A142 10k black brown   8.50 3.50
482 A142 35k brown violet   35.00 14.50
    Nos. 480-482 (3)   50.50 19.80
    Set, never hinged   150.00

Fine Arts Museum, Moscow — A145

1932, Dec. Perf. 12½
485 A145 15k black brown   17.50 13.00
486 A145 35k ultra   40.00 45.00
    a. Perf. 10½   75.00 40.00
    Set, never hinged   200.00

Moscow Philatelic Exhibition, 1932. Nos. 485 and 486 were also issued in imperf. sheets of 4 containing 2 of each value, on thick paper for presentation purposes. They were not valid for postage. Value, from $25,000. Replicas of the sheet were made for Moscow 97 by the Canadian Society of Russian Philately.

Nos. 485 and 486a Surcharged

1933, Mar. Perf. 12½
487 A145 30k on 15k black brn   35.00 25.00

Perf. 10½
488 A145 70k on 35k ultra   350.00 175.00
    Set, never hinged   650.00

Leningrad Philatelic Exhibition, 1933.

Peoples of the Soviet Union

Kazaks A146

Lezghians A147

Tungus A150

Crimean Tartars A148

Jews, Birobidzhan A149

Buryats — A151

Yakuts — A156

Chechens A152

Abkhas A153

Georgians A154

Nientzians A155

Great Russians — A157

Tadzhiks — A158

Transcaucasians — A159

Turkmen — A160

Ukrainians — A161

Uzbeks — A162

Byelorussians — A163

Koryaks
A164

Bashkirs
A165

Chuvashes
A166

**Perf. 12, 12x12½, 12½x12, 11x12,
12x11**

1933, Apr.			Photo.	
489	A146	1k black brown	14.00	2.00
490	A147	2k ultra	10.00	2.00
491	A148	3k gray green	17.00	3.00
492	A149	4k gray black	10.00	2.00
493	A150	5k brown violet	6.75	1.00
494	A151	6k indigo	14.00	2.00
495	A152	7k black brown	14.00	2.00
496	A153	8k rose red	14.00	2.00
497	A154	9k ultra	14.00	2.00
498	A155	10k black brown	10.00	2.00
499	A156	14k olive green	10.00	2.00
500	A157	15k orange	10.00	2.00
501	A158	15k ultra	10.00	2.00
502	A159	15k dark brown	10.00	2.00
503	A160	15k rose red	10.00	2.00
504	A161	15k violet brown	10.00	2.00
505	A162	15k gray black	10.00	2.00
506	A163	15k dull green	10.00	2.00
507	A164	20k dull blue	14.00	3.00
508	A165	30k brown violet	24.00	5.00
509	A166	35k black	42.50	6.00
	Nos. 489-509 (21)		284.25	50.00
	Set, never hinged		750.00	

V. V.
Vorovsky
A169

3k, V. M. Volodarsky. 5k, M. S. Uritzky.

1933, Oct.			Perf. 12x12½	
514	A169	1k dull green	2.00	.55
515	A169	3k blue black	2.00	.75
516	A169	5k olive brown	6.00	1.25
	Nos. 514-516 (3)		10.00	2.55
	Set, never hinged		50.00	

10th anniv. of the murder of Soviet Representative Vorovsky; 15th anniv. of the murder of the Revolutionists Volodarsky and Uritzky.
See Nos. 531-532, 580-582.

Order of the Red
Banner, 15th
Anniv. — A173

1933, Nov. 17		Unwmk.	Perf. 14	
518	A173	20k black, red & yel	10.00	3.00
		Never hinged	30.00	

No. 518, perf. 9½, is a proof. Value $950.

Commissar
Schaumyan
A174

Commissar
Prokofii A.
Dzhaparidze
A175

Commissars Awaiting
Execution — A176

Designs: 35k, Monument to the 26 Commissars. 40k, Worker, peasant and soldier dipping flags in salute.

1933, Dec. 1				
519	A174	4k brown	37.50	2.00
520	A175	5k dark gray	37.50	2.00
521	A176	20k purple	42.50	2.00
522	A176	35k ultra	75.00	15.00
523	A176	40k carmine	57.50	10.00
	Nos. 519-523 (5)		250.00	31.00
	Set, never hinged		750.00	

15th anniv. of the execution of 26 commissars at Baku. No. 521 exists imperf. Many part-perf varieties exist on all values of this issue, including imperf between pairs of several values.

Lenin's
Mausoleum
A179

1934, Feb. 7		Engr.	Perf. 14	
524	A179	5k brown	3.00	3.00
a.		Imperf.	1,200.	100.00
525	A179	10k slate blue	25.00	10.00
a.		Imperf.	1,200.	100.00
526	A179	15k dk carmine	25.00	5.50
527	A179	20k green	2.50	1.50
528	A179	35k dark brown	45.00	10.00
	Nos. 524-528 (5)		100.50	30.00
	Set, never hinged		300.00	

10th anniversary of Lenin's death.

Ivan Fedorov
A180

1934, Mar. 5				
529	A180	20k carmine rose	42.50	7.50
a.		Imperf.	500.00	250.00
530	A180	40k indigo	17.50	7.50
a.		Imperf.	500.00	250.00
	Set, never hinged		150.00	

350th anniv. of the death of Ivan Fedorov, founder of printing in Russia.

Portrait Type of 1933

Designs: 10k, Yakov M. Sverdlov. 15k, Victor Pavlovich Nogin.

1934, Mar.		Photo.	Wmk. 170	
531	A169	10k ultra	100.00	10.50
532	A169	15k red	150.00	24.50
	Set, never hinged		600.00	

Deaths of Yakov M. Sverdlov, chairman of the All-Russian Central Executive Committee of the Soviets, 15th anniv., Victor Pavlovich Nogin, chairman Russian State Textile Syndicate, 10th anniv.

A184

Dmitri
Ivanovich
Mendeleev
A185

1934, Sept. 15		Wmk. 170	Perf. 14	
536	A184	5k emerald	40.00	3.00
537	A185	10k black brown	100.00	9.00
538	A185	15k vermilion	90.00	7.50
539	A184	20k ultra	70.00	5.50
	Nos. 536-539 (4)		300.00	25.00
	Set, never hinged		650.00	

Prof. D. I. Mendeleev (1834-1907), chemist who discovered the Periodic Law of Classification of the Elements.
Imperfs. exist of 5k (value $400) and 15k (value $400).

Lenin as Child and Youth
A186   A187

Demonstration before Lenin
Mausoleum — A190

Designs: 5k, Lenin in middle age. 10k, Lenin the orator. 30k, Lenin and Stalin.

1934, Nov. 23		Unwmk.	Perf. 14	
540	A186	1k indigo & black	15.00	2.25
541	A187	3k indigo & black	15.00	2.50
542	A187	5k indigo & black	30.00	3.75
543	A187	10k indigo & black	22.50	3.75
544	A190	20k brn org & ultra	50.00	7.50
545	A190	30k brn org & car	160.00	15.00
	Nos. 540-545 (6)		292.50	34.75
	Set, never hinged		650.00	

First decade without Lenin.
See Nos. 931-935, 937 in Scott Standard catalogue, Vol. 5.

Bombs Falling
on City
A192

"Before War and
Afterwards"
A194

Designs: 10k, Refugees from burning town. 20k, "Plowing with the sword." 35k, "Comradeship."

1935, Jan. 1		Wmk. 170	Perf. 14	
546	A192	5k violet black	22.50	5.00
547	A192	10k ultra	75.00	0.00
548	A194	15k green	225.00	12.00
549	A194	20k dark brown	37.50	7.50
550	A194	35k carmine	290.00	25.00
	Nos. 546-550 (5)		650.00	57.50
	Set, never hinged		1,250.	

Anti-war propaganda, the designs symbolize the horrors of modern warfare.

Subway
Tunnel
A197

Subway
Station Cross
Section
A198

Subway
Station
A199

Train in Station — A200

1935, Feb. 25		Wmk. 170	Perf. 14	
551	A197	5k orange	60.00	2.50
552	A198	10k dark ultra	60.00	1.50
553	A199	15k rose carmine	425.00	30.00
554	A200	20k emerald	60.00	15.00
	Nos. 551-554 (4)		605.00	49.00
	Set, never hinged		1,250.	

Completion of Moscow subway.

Friedrich Engels
(1820-1895),
German Socialist
and Collaborator
of Marx — A201

1935, May		Wmk. 170	Perf. 14	
555	A201	5k carmine	10.00	2.50
556	A201	10k dark green	40.00	6.00
557	A201	15k dark blue	140.00	10.00
558	A201	20k brown black	10.00	3.00
	Nos. 555-558 (4)		200.00	21.50
	Set, never hinged		350.00	

Running — A202

Designs: 2k, Diving. 3k, Rowing. 4k, Soccer. 5k, Skiing. 10k, Bicycling. 15k, Tennis. 20k, Skating. 35k, Hurdling. 40k, Parade of athletes.

1935, Apr. 22   **Unwmk.**   *Perf. 14*
559	A202	1k orange & ultra	30.00	2.00
560	A202	2k black & ultra	30.00	2.00
561	A202	3k grn & blk brn	30.00	6.00
562	A202	4k rose red & ultra	30.00	2.00
563	A202	5k pur & blk brn	30.00	2.00
564	A202	10k rose red & vio	30.00	4.00
565	A202	15k black & blk brn	140.00	25.00
566	A202	20k blk brn & ultra	30.00	8.00
567	A202	35k ultra & blk brn	100.00	15.00
568	A202	40k black brn & car	50.00	10.00
		Nos. 559-568 (10)	500.00	76.00
		Set, never hinged	1,250.	

International Spartacist Games, Moscow. The games never took place.

Silver Plate of Sassanian Dynasty A212

1935, Sept. 10   **Wmk. 170**
569	A212	5k orange red	22.50	3.00
570	A212	10k dk yellow green	22.50	5.00
571	A212	15k dark violet	22.50	8.00
572	A212	35k black brown	52.50	14.00
		Nos. 569-572 (4)	120.00	30.00
		Set, never hinged	350.00	

3rd International Congress of Persian Art, Leningrad, Sept. 12-18, 1935.

Kalinin, the Worker — A213   Mikhail Kalinin — A216

Kalinin as: 5k, farmer. 10k, orator.

1935, Nov. 20   **Unwmk.**   *Perf. 14*
573	A213	3k rose lilac	1.25	1.00
574	A213	5k green	2.50	1.00
575	A213	10k blue slate	5.25	2.00
576	A216	20k brown black	11.00	3.00
		Nos. 573-576 (4)	20.00	7.00
		Set, never hinged	100.00	

60th birthday of Mikhail Kalinin, chairman of the Central Executive Committee of the USSR. The 20k exists imperf. Value $1,400.

A217

Leo Tolstoy — A218

Design: 20k, Statue of Tolstoy.

1935, Dec. 4   *Perf. 14*
577	A217	3k ol black & vio	3.50	2.00
578	A218	10k vio blk & blk brn	10.00	3.00

579	A217	20k dk grn & blk brn	20.00	5.00
		Nos. 577-579 (3)	33.50	10.00
		Set, never hinged	100.00	

Perf. 11
577a	A217	3k	4.00	1.50
578a	A218	10k	9.00	2.50
579a	A217	20k	22.00	5.00
		Nos. 577a-579a (3)	35.00	9.00
		Set, never hinged	100.00	

25th anniv. of the death of Count Leo N. Tolstoy (1828-1910).

Portrait Type of 1933

Designs: 2k, Mikhail V. Frunze. 4k, N. E. Bauman. 40k, Sergei M. Kirov.

1935, Nov.   **Wmk. 170**   *Perf. 11*
580	A169	2k purple	4.50	2.75
581	A169	4k brown violet	6.50	6.00
582	A169	40k black brown	14.00	10.00
		Nos. 580-582 (3)	25.00	18.75
		Set, never hinged	75.00	

Perf. 14
580a	A169	2k	10.00	1.50
581a	A169	4k	20.00	3.00
582a	A169	40k	30.00	4.00
		Nos. 580a-582a (3)	60.00	8.50
		Set, never hinged	100.00	

Death of three revolutionary heroes. Nos. 580-582 exist imperf. but were not regularly issued. Value, set $3,000.

Pioneers Preventing Theft from Mailbox A223

Designs: 3k, 5k, Pioneers preventing destruction of property. 10k, Helping recover kite. 15k, Girl Pioneer saluting.

1936, Apr.   **Unwmk.**   *Perf. 14*
583	A223	1k yellow green	2.25	.35
584	A223	2k copper red	3.25	.45
585	A223	3k slate blue	5.50	1.00
586	A223	5k rose lake	6.00	1.00
587	A223	10k gray blue	13.50	3.25
588	A223	15k brown olive	18.00	6.00
		Nos. 583-588 (6)	48.50	12.05
		Set, never hinged	200.00	

Perf. 11
583a	A223	1k	1.50	.55
584a	A223	2k	2.50	.60
585a	A223	3k	4.50	1.25
586a	A223	5k	6.50	1.50
587a	A223	10k	22.50	4.00
588a	A223	15k	12.50	2.25
		Nos. 583a-588a (6)	50.00	10.15
		Set, never hinged	200.00	

Nikolai A. Dobrolyubov, Writer and Critic, Birth Cent. — A227

1936, Aug. 13   **Typo.**   *Perf. 11½*
589	A227	10k rose lake	5.00	2.00
		Never hinged	12.50	
a.		Perf. 14	5.00	2.50
		Never hinged	15.00	

Aleksander Sergeyevich Pushkin — A228   Statue of Pushkin, Moscow — A229

Chalky or Ordinary Paper

Perf. 11 to 14 and Compound

1937, Feb. 1
590	A228	10k yellow brown	1.25	.50
591	A228	20k Prus green	1.75	.50
592	A228	40k rose lake	3.00	.50
593	A229	50k blue	7.00	1.00
594	A229	80k carmine rose	7.00	.75
595	A229	1r green	30.00	1.75
		Nos. 590-595 (6)	50.00	5.00
		Set, never hinged	150.00	

Souvenir Sheet
Imperf
596		Sheet of 2	25.00	*150.00*
		Never hinged	65.00	
a.		A228 10k brown	4.00	*20.00*
b.		A229 50k brown	4.00	*27.50*

Pushkin (1799-1837), writer and poet.

Tchaikovsky Concert Hall — A230

Designs: 5k, 15k, Telegraph Agency House. 10k, Tchaikovsky Concert Hall. 20k, 50k, Red Army Theater. 30k, Hotel Moscow. 40k, Palace of the Soviets.

Unwmk.

1937, June   **Photo.**   *Perf. 12*
597	A230	3k brown violet	2.25	.40
598	A230	5k henna brown	2.50	.40
599	A230	10k dark brown	3.50	.40
600	A230	15k black	9.00	.40
601	A230	20k olive green	2.50	1.00
602	A230	30k gray black	3.00	1.00
a.		Perf. 11	100.00	100.00
603	A230	40k violet	3.25	2.00
a.		Souv. sheet of 4, imperf.	25.00	*50.00*
604	A230	50k dark brown	5.00	2.00
		Nos. 597-604 (8)	31.00	7.60
		Set, never hinged	90.00	

First Congress of Soviet Architects. The 30k is watermarked Greek Border and Rosettes (170).
Nos. 597-601, 603-604 exist imperf. Value, each $500.

Feliks E. Dzerzhinski A235   Shota Rustaveli A236

1937, July 27   **Typo.**   *Perf. 12*
606	A235	10k yellow brown	3.00	.35
607	A235	20k Prus green	5.00	.75
608	A235	40k rose lake	16.00	1.10
609	A235	80k carmine	26.00	1.75
		Nos. 606-609 (4)	50.00	3.95
		Set, never hinged	125.00	

Dzerzhinski, organizer of Soviet secret police, 10th death anniv. Exist imperf. Value, each $500.

Line Perf 12¼

1938, Feb.   **Unwmk.**   **Photo.**
610	A236	20k deep green	3.00	1.00
		Never hinged	12.00	
a.		Comb perf. 12½x12	2,000.	125.00

750th anniversary of the publication of the poem "Knight in the Tiger Skin," by Shota Rustaveli, Georgian poet.
Exists imperf. Value $4,000.

Statue Surmounting Pavilion A237   Soviet Pavilion at Paris Exposition A238

1938   **Typo.**
611	A237	5k red	1.50	.60
a.		Imperf.	600.00	
612	A238	20k rose	3.50	1.25
613	A237	50k dark blue	2.00	3.00
		Nos. 611-613 (3)	7.00	4.85
		Set, never hinged	35.00	

USSR participation in the 1937 International Exposition at Paris.

Types of 1929-32 and Lenin Types of 1925-26

1937-52   **Unwmk.**   *Perf. 11½x12, 12*
613A	A103	1k dull org ('40)	15.00	5.00
614	A95	2k yel grn ('39)	5.00	2.00
615	A97	4k claret ('40)	30.00	5.00
615A	A98	5k org brn ('46)	75.00	20.00
616	A109	10k blue ('38)	2.00	1.00
616A	A103	10k olive ('40)	125.00	25.00
616B	A109	10k black ('52)	.50	.50
617	A97	20k dull green	1.00	.50
617A	A107	20k green ('39)	100.00	12.50
618	A109	30k claret ('39)	20.00	2.00
619	A104	40k indigo ('38)	10.00	1.00
619A	A111	50k dp brn ('40)	1.00	.50

Engr.
620	A75	3r dk grn ('39)	1.50	.50
621	A66	5r red brn ('39)	10.00	5.00
622	A66	10r indigo ('39)	5.00	3.00
		Nos. 613A-622 (15)	401.00	83.50
		Set, never hinged	825.00	

#615-619 exist imperf but were not regularly issued.
No. 616B was re-issued in 1954-56 in slightly smaller format, 14½x21mm, and in gray black. See note after No. 738.

Airplane Route from Moscow to North Pole — A239   Soviet Flag and Airplanes at North Pole — A240

1938, Feb. 25   **Litho.**   *Perf. 12*
625	A239	10k brn & black	2.50	.45
626	A239	20k blue gray & blk	4.25	.65

Typo.
627	A240	40k dull green & car	19.00	2.50
a.		Imperf.	2,750.	
628	A240	80k rose car & car	5.00	1.75
a.		Imperf.	1,500.	
		Nos. 625-628 (4)	30.75	5.35
		Set, never hinged	75.00	

Soviet flight to the North Pole.

Infantryman A241   Soldier A242

Stalin Reviewing Cavalry A246

Chapayev and Boy — A247

Designs: 30k, Sailor, 40k, Aviator. 50k, Antiaircraft soldier.

Unwmk.

1938, Mar.   Photo.   Perf. 12

629	A241	10k gray blk & dk red	7.00 .50
630	A242	20k gray blk & dk red	7.00 .80
631	A242	30k gray blk & dk red	7.00 1.00
632	A242	40k gray blk & dk red	7.00 1.75
633	A242	50k gray blk & dk red	7.00 1.50
634	A246	80k gray blk & dk red	7.00 1.75

Typo.   Perf. 12x12½

635	A247	1r black & carmine	7.00 2.00
		Nos. 629-635 (7)	49.00 9.30
		Set, never hinged	150.00

Workers' & Peasants' Red Army, 20th anniv. No. 635 exists imperf. Value $2,000.

Aviators Chkalov, Baidukov, Beliakov and Flight Route — A248

Aviators Gromov, Danilin, Yumashev and Flight Route — A249

1938, Apr. 10   Photo.

636	A248	10k black & red	4.25 .60
637	A248	20k brn blk & red	4.25 .90
638	A248	40k brown & red	8.50 2.00
639	A248	50k brown vio & red	12.50 2.00
		Nos. 636-639 (4)	29.50 5.50
		Set, never hinged	75.00

First Trans-Polar flight, June 18-20, 1937, from Moscow to Vancouver, Wash. Nos. 636-639 exist imperf. Value $250 each.

1938, Apr. 13

640	A249	10k claret	10.00 .75
641	A249	20k brown black	8.00 2.50
642	A249	50k dull violet	17.00 3.00
		Nos. 640-642 (3)	35.00 6.25
		Set, never hinged	100.00

First Trans-Polar flight, July 12-14, 1937, from Moscow to San Jacinto, Calif. Nos. 640-642 exist imperf. Value, each $500.

Arrival of the Rescuing Ice-breakers Taimyr and Murmansk A250

Ivan Papanin and His Men Aboard Ice-breaker Yermak — A251

1938, June 21   Typo.   Perf. 12, 12½

643	A250	10k violet brown	5.00 1.25
644	A250	20k dark blue	5.00 1.50

Photo.

645	A251	30k olive brown	17.50 3.00
646	A251	50k ultra	22.50 4.00
a.		Imperf.	1,200.
		Nos. 643-646 (4)	50.00 9.75
		Set, never hinged	135.00

Rescue of Papanin's North Pole Expedition.

Arms of Armenia — A252

Arms of USSR A253

ГРУЗИНСКАЯ ССР   #650

КАЗАХСКАЯ ССР   #651

Р.С.Ф.С.Р.   #654

ТАДЖИКСКАЯ ССР   #655

ТУРКМЕНСКАЯ ССР   #656

Designs: Different arms on each stamp.

Perf. 12, 12½

1937-38   Unwmk.   Typo.

647	A252	20k dp bl (Armenia)	6.00 2.75
648	A252	20k dull violet (Azerbaijan)	6.00 2.75
649	A252	20k brown orange (Byelorussia)	6.00 2.75
650	A252	20k carmine rose (Georgia)	6.00 2.75
651	A252	20k bl grn (Kazakh)	6.00 2.75
652	A252	20k emer (Kirghiz)	6.00 2.75
653	A252	20k yel org (Uzbek)	6.00 2.75
654	A252	20k bl (R.S.F.S.R.)	6.00 2.75
655	A252	20k claret (Tadzhik)	6.00 2.75
656	A252	20k car (Turkmen)	6.00 2.75
657	A252	20k red (Ukraine)	6.00 2.75

Engr.

658	A253	40k brown red	9.00 4.00
		Nos. 647-658 (12)	75.00 34.25
		Set, never hinged	300.00

Constitution of USSR. No. 649 has inscriptions in Yiddish, Polish, Byelorussian and Russian.

Issue dates: 40k, 1937. Others, 1938. See Nos. 841-842 in Scott Standard catalogue, Vol. 5.

Nurse Weighing Child — A264

Children at Lenin's Statue — A265

Biology Lesson A266

Health Camp A267

Young Model Builders A268

1938, Sept. 15   Unwmk.   Perf. 12

659	A264	10k dk blue green	6.00 1.50
660	A265	15k dk blue green	6.00 1.50
661	A266	20k violet brown	6.00 2.00
662	A267	30k claret	9.50 3.00
663	A266	40k light brown	9.50 3.00
664	A268	50k deep blue	24.00 10.00
665	A268	80k light green	24.00 9.00
		Nos. 659-665 (7)	85.00 30.00
		Set, never hinged	200.00

Child welfare.

View of Yalta A269

Crimean Shoreline — A272

Designs: No. 667, View along Crimean shore. No. 668, Georgian military highway. No, 670, View near Yalta. No. 671, "Swallows' Nest" Castle. 20k, Dzerzhinski Rest House for workers. 30k, Sunset in Crimea. 40k, Alupka. 50k, Gursuf. 80k, Crimean Gardens. 1r, "Swallows' Nest" Castle, horiz.

Unwmk.

1938, Sept. 21   Photo.   Perf. 12

666	A269	5k brown	2.90 2.00
667	A269	5k black brown	2.90 2.00
668	A269	10k slate green	4.00 2.00
669	A272	10k brown	4.00 2.00
670	A269	15k black brown	8.00 2.00
671	A272	15k black brown	8.00 2.00
672	A269	20k dark brown	9.00 2.00
673	A272	30k black brown	10.00 2.75
674	A269	40k brown	11.00 2.75
675	A272	50k slate green	13.00 5.50
676	A269	80k brown	17.50 5.50
677	A269	1r slate green	35.00 ▓▓
		Set, never hinged (12)	125.30 39.25
			300.00

Children Flying Model Plane A281

Glider A282

Captive Balloon — A283

Dirigible over Kremlin — A284

Parachute Jumpers — A285

Hydroplane A286

Balloon in Flight — A287

Balloon Ascent — A288

Four-motor Plane A289

Unwmk.

1938, Oct. 7   Typo.   Perf. 12

678	A281	5k violet brown	5.00 3.00
679	A282	10k olive gray	5.00 3.00
680	A283	15k pink	8.00 2.25
681	A284	20k deep blue	8.00 2.25
682	A285	30k claret	10.00 4.50
683	A286	40k deep blue	15.00 4.50
684	A287	50k blue green	20.00 5.50
685	A288	80k brown	30.00 6.00
686	A289	1r blue green	50.00 6.50
		Nos. 678-686 (9)	151.00 37.50
		Set, never hinged	350.00

For overprints see Nos. C76-C76D.

Mayakovsky Station, Moscow Subway — A290

Sokol Terminal — A291

Kiev Station — A292

Dynamo Station A293

Train in Tunnel A294

Revolution Square Station A295

Unwmk.

1938, Nov. 7	Photo.		Perf. 12	
687	A290	10k deep red violet	2.25	.90
688	A291	15k dark brown	3.25	1.00
689	A292	20k black brown	4.50	1.50
690	A293	30k dark red violet	9.00	2.00
691	A294	40k black brown	12.00	3.00
692	A295	50k dark brown	20.00	6.50
	Nos. 687-692 (6)		51.00	14.90
	Set, never hinged		200.00	

Second line of the Moscow subway opening.

Girl with Parachute A296

Young Miner A297

Harvesting A298

Designs: 50k, Students returning from school. 80k, Aviator and sailor.

1938, Dec. 7	Typo.		Perf. 12	
693	A296	20k deep blue	5.00	3.00
694	A297	30k deep claret	8.00	3.00
695	A298	40k violet brown	10.00	3.00
696	A296	50k deep rose	30.00	6.00
697	A298	80k deep blue	50.00	10.00
	Nos. 693-697 (5)		103.00	25.00
	Set, never hinged		225.00	

20th anniv. of the Young Communist League (Komsomol).

Diving — A301

Discus Thrower — A302

Designs: 15k, Tennis. 20k, Acrobatic motorcyclists. 30k, Skier. 40k, Runners. 50k, Soccer. 80k, Physical culture.

Unwmk.

1938, Dec. 28	Photo.		Perf. 12	
698	A301	5k scarlet	2.00	.85
699	A302	10k black	4.00	1.00
700	A302	15k brown	6.00	1.25
701	A302	20k green	8.00	1.75
702	A302	30k dull violet	12.50	2.75
703	A302	40k deep green	15.00	3.25
704	A302	50k blue	40.00	4.00
705	A302	80k deep blue	65.00	4.75
	Nos. 698-705 (8)		152.50	19.60
	Set, never hinged		300.00	

Gorki Street, Moscow — A309

Dynamo Subway Station A315

Moscow scenes: 20k, Council House & Hotel Moscow. 30k, Lenin Library. 40k, Crimea Bridge. 50k, Bridge over Moscow River. 80k, Khimki River Terminal.

Paper with network as in parenthesis

1939, Mar.	Typo.		Perf. 12	
706	A309	10k brn (*red brown*)	3.50	1.00
707	A309	20k dk sl grn (*lt blue*)	6.25	3.00
708	A309	30k brn vio (*red brn*)	8.50	3.00
709	A309	40k blue (*lt blue*)	12.50	5.00
710	A309	50k rose lake (*red brn*)	12.50	6.00
711	A309	80k gray ol (*lt blue*)	25.00	8.00
712	A315	1r dk blue (*lt blue*)	25.00	10.00
	Nos. 706-712 (7)		93.25	36.00
	Set, never hinged		250.00	

"New Moscow." On 30k, denomination is at upper right.

Foundry-man — A316

1939, Mar.				
713	A316	15k dark blue	10.00	1.50
	Never hinged		25.00	
a.	Imperf.		1,250.	
	Never hinged		2,000.	

Statue on USSR Pavilion — A317

USSR Pavilion A318

1939, May			Photo.	
714	A317	30k indigo & red	2.50	.35
a.	Imperf. ('40)		1.00	.50
715	A318	50k blue & bister brn	2.50	.60
a.	Imperf. ('40)		1.00	.50
	Set, never hinged		20.00	
	Set, imperf., never hinged		20.00	

Russia's participation in the NY World's Fair.

Paulina Osipenko A318a

Marina Raskova A318b

Design: 60k, Valentina Grizodubova.

1939, Mar.				
718	A318a	15k green	6.50	3.00
719	A318b	30k brown violet	12.50	3.75
720	A318b	60k red	21.00	8.25
	Nos. 718-720 (3)		40.00	15.00
	Set, never hinged		95.00	

Non-stop record flight from Moscow to the Far East.
Exist imperf. Value, each $350.

Shevchenko, Early Portrait — A319

Monument at Kharkov — A321

30k, Shevchenko portrait in later years.

1939, Mar. 9				
721	A319	15k black brn & blk	6.00	1.50
722	A319	30k dark red & blk	6.00	2.50
723	A321	60k green & dk brn	15.00	6.00
	Nos. 721-723 (3)		27.00	10.00
	Set, never hinged		125.00	

Taras G. Shevchenko (1814-1861), Ukrainian poet and painter.

Milkmaid with Prize Cow — A322

Tractor-plow at Work on Abundant Harvest A323

Designs: 20k, Shepherd tending sheep. No. 727, Fair pavilion. No. 728, Fair emblem. 45k, Turkmen picking cotton. 50k, Drove of horses. 60k, Symbolizing agricultural wealth. 80k, Kolkhoz girl with sugar beets. 1r, Hunter with Polar foxes.

1939, Aug.				
724	A322	10k rose pink	1.90	.25
725	A323	15k red brown	1.90	.25
726	A323	20k slate black	4.90	1.10
727	A323	30k purple	3.00	.85
728	A322	30k red orange	3.00	.85
729	A322	45k dark green	4.90	1.10
730	A322	50k copper red	4.90	1.10
731	A322	60k bright purple	7.25	1.40
732	A322	80k dark violet	6.00	1.40
733	A322	1r dark blue	12.00	1.60
	Nos. 724-733 (10)		49.75	9.90
	Set, never hinged		125.00	

Soviet Agricultural Fair.

Worker A331

Soldier A332

Aviator — A333

Arms of USSR
A334   A335

1939-43	Unwmk.	Typo.	Perf. 12	
734	A331	5k red	.40	.25
735	A332	15k dark green	.50	.25
736	A333	30k deep blue	.75	.25
737	A334	60k fawn ('43)	5.00	.40
	Photo.			
738	A335	60k rose carmine	1.00	.40
	Nos. 734-738 (5)		7.65	1.55
	Set, never hinged		15.00	

No. 734 was re-issued in 1954-56 in slightly smaller format: 14x21½mm, instead of 14¾x22¼mm. Other values reissued in smaller format: 10k, 15k, 20k, 25k, 30k, 40k and 1r. (See notes following No. 622; Nos. 1260, 1347 and 1689 in Scott Standard catalogue, Vol. 5.)

No. 416 Surcharged with New Value in Black

1939			Wmk. 170	
743	A97	30k on 4k claret	30.00	25.00
	Never hinged		50.00	
a.	Unwmkd.		250.00	150.00

M.E. Saltykov (N. Shchedrin)
A336   A337

1939, Sept.   Typo.   Unwmk.

745 A336 15k claret	1.75	.35
746 A337 30k dark green	2.60	.75
747 A336 45k olive gray	4.40	1.00
748 A337 60k dark blue	6.25	1.25
Nos. 745-748 (4)	15.00	3.35
Set, never hinged	80.00	

Mikhail E. Saltykov (1826-89), writer & satirist who used pen name of N. Shchedrin.

Sanatorium of the State Bank — A338

Designs: 10k, 15k, Soviet Army sanatorium. 20k, Rest home, New Afyon. 30k, Clinical Institute. 50k, 80k, Sanatorium for workers in heavy industry. 60k, Rest home, Sukhumi.

1939, Nov.   Photo.   Perf. 12

749 A338 5k dull brown	3.25	.40
750 A338 10k carmine	3.25	.40
751 A338 15k yellow green	3.25	.40
752 A338 20k dk slate green	3.25	.40
753 A338 30k bluish black	4.50	.75
754 A338 50k gray black	7.50	1.25
755 A338 60k brown violet	10.50	1.50
756 A338 80k orange red	13.50	2.25
Nos. 749-756 (8)	49.00	7.35
Set, never hinged	125.00	

Mikhail Y. Lermontov (1814-1841), Poet and Novelist, in 1837 — A346

Portrait in 1838 — A347   Portrait in 1841 — A348

1939, Dec.

757 A346 15k indigo & sepia	7.50	1.75
758 A347 30k dk grn & dull blk	7.50	1.75
759 A348 45k brick red & indigo	15.00	6.50
Nos. 757-759 (3)	30.00	10.00
Set, never hinged	60.00	

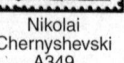

Nikolai Chernyshevski A349   Anton Chekhov A350

1939, Dec.   Photo.

760 A349 15k dark green	5.00	1.00
761 A349 30k dull violet	7.00	1.50
762 A349 60k Prus green	8.00	2.50
Nos. 760-762 (3)	20.00	5.00
Set, never hinged	50.00	

50th anniversary of the death of Nikolai Chernyshevski, scientist and critic.

1940, Feb.   Unwmk.   Perf. 12

Design: 20k, 30k, Portrait with hat.

763 A350 10k dark yellow green	3.00	.50
764 A350 15k ultra	3.00	.50
765 A350 20k violet	6.00	.50
766 A350 30k copper brown	8.00	3.50
Nos. 763-766 (4)	20.00	5.00
Set, never hinged	40.00	

Chekhov (1860-1904), playwright.

Welcome to Red Army by Western Ukraine and Western Byelorussia A352

Designs: 30k, Villagers welcoming tank crew. 50k, 60k, Soldier giving newspapers to crowd. 1r, Crowd waving to tank column.

1940, Apr.

767 A352 10k deep rose	1.50	.75
768 A352 30k myrtle green	2.10	1.25
769 A352 50k gray black	3.00	2.00
770 A352 60k indigo	4.25	2.00
771 A352 1r red	7.00	4.00
Nos. 767-771 (5)	17.85	10.00
Set, never hinged	50.00	

Liberation of the people of Western Ukraine and Western Byelorussia.

Ice-breaker "Josef Stalin," Captain Beloussov and Chief Ivan Papanin A356

Badigin and Papanin A358

Map of the Drift of the Sedov and Crew Members — A359

Design: 30k, Icebreaker Georgi Sedov, Captain Vadygin and First Mate Trofimov.

1940, Apr.

772 A356 15k dull yel green	1.90	.75
773 A356 30k dull purple	3.25	1.20
774 A358 50k copper brown	8.25	1.75
775 A359 1r dark ultra	16.50	3.25
Nos. 772-775 (4)	29.90	6.95
Set, never hinged	75.00	

Heroism of the Sedov crew which drifted in the Polar Basin for 812 days.

A360

Vladimir V. Mayakovsky — A361

1940, June

776 A360 15k deep red	1.50	.40
777 A360 30k copper brown	2.00	.50
778 A361 60k dark gray blue	4.00	.75
779 A361 80k bright ultra	6.00	1.50
Nos. 776-779 (4)	13.50	3.15
Set, never hinged	40.00	

Mayakovsky, poet (1893-1930).

K.A. Timiryazev and Academy of Agricultural Sciences A362

In the Laboratory of Moscow University A363

Last Portrait A364

Monument in Moscow — A365

1940, June

780 A362 10k indigo	1.50	.60
781 A363 15k purple	2.50	1.20
782 A364 30k dk violet brown	5.50	3.25
783 A365 60k dark green	10.50	5.00
Nos. 780-783 (4)	20.00	10.05
Set, never hinged	50.00	

20th anniversary of the death of K. A. Timiryasev, scientist and professor of agricultural and biological sciences.

Relay Race — A366

Sportswomen Marching A367

Children's Sport Badge — A368

Skier A369

Throwing the Grenade A370

1940, July 21

784 A366 15k carmine rose	2.50	.40
785 A367 30k sepia	4.50	.40
786 A368 50k dk violet blue	6.50	.70

787 A369 60k dk violet blue	8.50	.75
788 A370 1r grayish green	10.00	2.00
Nos. 784-788 (5)	35.00	5.00
Set, never hinged	100.00	

2nd All-Union Physical Culture Day.

Tchaikovsky Museum at Klin A371   Tchaikovsky & Passage from his Fourth Symphony A372

Peter Ilich Tchaikovsky and Excerpt from Eugene Onegin — A373

1940, Aug.   Unwmk.   Typo.   Perf. 12

789 A371 15k Prus green	4.50	3.00
790 A372 20k brown	4.50	3.00
791 A372 30k dark blue	5.25	3.00
792 A371 50k rose lake	8.75	4.00
793 A373 60k red	12.00	7.00
Nos. 789-793 (5)	35.00	20.00
Set, never hinged	100.00	

Tchaikovsky (1840-1893), composer.

Volga Provinces Pavilion A374

Northeast Provinces Pavilion — A376

ПАВИЛЬОН МОСКОВСКОЙ, РЯЗАНСКОЙ И ТУЛЬСКОЙ ОБЛ.
#797

ПАВИЛЬОН УКРАИНСКОЙ ССР
#798

ПАВИЛЬОН БЕЛОРУССКОЙ ССР
#799

ПАВИЛЬОН АЗЕРБАЙДЖАНСКОЙ ССР
#800

ПАВИЛЬОН ГРУЗИНСКОЙ ССР
#801

ПАВИЛЬОН АРМЯНСКОЙ ССР
#802

У ВХОДА В ПАВИЛЬОН УЗБЕКСКОЙ ССР
#803

ПАВИЛЬОН ТУРКМЕНСКОЙ ССР
#804

ПАВИЛЬОН ТАДЖИКСКОЙ ССР
#805

ПАВИЛЬОН КИРГИЗСКОЙ ССР
#806

ПАВИЛЬОН КАЗАХСКОЙ ССР
#807

ПАВИЛЬОН КАРЕЛО-ФИНСКОЙ ССР
#808

1940, Oct.				Photo.
794	A374	10k shown	2.25	1.10
795	A374	15k Far East Provinces	2.75	1.10
796	A376	30k shown	3.00	1.10
797	A376	30k Central Regions	3.00	1.10
798	A376	30k Ukrainian	3.00	1.10
799	A376	30k Byelorussian	3.00	1.10
800	A376	30k Azerbaijan	3.00	1.10
801	A374	30k Georgian	3.00	1.10
802	A376	30k Armenian	3.00	1.10
803	A374	30k Uzbek	3.00	1.10
804	A374	30k Turkmen	3.00	1.10
805	A374	30k Tadzhik	3.00	1.10
806	A376	30k Kirghiz	3.00	1.10
807	A374	30k Kazakh	3.00	1.10
808	A376	30k Karelian Finnish	3.00	1.10
809	A376	50k Main building	15.00	2.25
810	A376	60k Mechanizaton Pavilion, Stalin statue	15.00	2.50
		Nos. 794-810 (17)	74.00	21.25
		Set, never hinged	200.00	

All-Union Agricultural Fair.
Nos. 796-808 printed in three sheet formats with various vertical and horizontal se-tenant combinations.

Monument to Red Army Heroes — A391   Map of War Operations and M. V. Frunze — A393

Heroic Crossing of the Sivash A394

Designs: 15k, Grenade thrower. 60k, Frunze's headquarters, Stroganovka. 1r, Victorious soldier.

1940				Imperf.
811	A391	10k dark green	3.00	.50
812	A391	15k orange ver	3.00	.50
813	A393	30k dull brown & car	3.00	.50
814	A394	50k violet brn	3.00	1.00
815	A394	60k indigo	3.00	1.50
816	A391	1r gray black	5.00	1.50
		Nos. 811-816 (6)	20.00	5.50
		Set, never hinged	40.00	

				Perf. 12
811A	A391	10k dark green	1.50	.30
812A	A391	15k orange ver	1.50	.30
813A	A393	30k dull brown & car	1.50	1.00
814A	A394	50k violet brn	1.90	.70
815A	A394	60k indigo	1.90	.70
816A	A391	1r gray black	1.90	.70
		Nos. 811A-816A (6)	10.20	3.70
		Set, never hinged	20.00	

20th anniversary of battle of Perekop.

POSTAL-FISCAL STAMPS

During 1918-22, Postal Savings stamps and Control stamps were authorized for postal use. Because of hyper-inflation during 1920-22, Russian Arms stamps and these postal-fiscal stamps were sold and used at different rates at different times: 1918-20, sold at face value; from March, 1920, sold at 100 times face value; from Aug. 15, 1921, sold at 250r each, regardless of face value; from April, 1922, sold at 10,000r per 1k or 1r. In Oct. 1922, these issues were superseded by gold currency stamps.

Postal Savings Stamps

PF1

			Perf. 14½x14¾	
1918, Jan. 12		Wmk. 171		Typo.
AR1	PF1	1k dp red, buff	.25	1.90
		Never hinged	.40	
AR2	PF1	5k green, buff	.25	1.90
		Never hinged	.50	
AR3	PF1	10k chocolate, buff	.35	6.25
		Never hinged	.70	
		Nos. AR1-AR3 (3)	.85	10.05

Nos. AR1-AR14 have a faint burelé background, which is noted as the paper color in these listings.
For surcharges of Nos. AR1-AR3, see Armenia Nos. 250-253, Far Eastern Republic Nos. 35 and 36, South Russia Nos. 47-49 and numerous Ukraine issues beginning with Nos. 45e-47e.

Postal Savings Stamps

PF2

PF3

1918, June 5		Litho.		Perf. 13
AR4	PF2	25k black, rose	19.00	75.00
		Never hinged	37.50	
AR5	PF2	50k brown, pale brown	25.00	100.00
		Never hinged	50.00	
AR6	PF3	50k brown, pale brown	62.50	125.00
		Never hinged	125.00	
		Nos. AR4-AR6 (3)	106.50	300.00

Control Stamps

PF4

PF5

PF6

PF7

PF8

1918, June 5		Litho.		Perf. 13
AR7	PF4	25k black, pale brn	19.00	62.50
		Never hinged	37.50	
AR8	PF4	50k brown, buff	25.00	100.00
		Never hinged	50.00	
AR9	PF5	1r orange, buff	3.00	6.25
		Never hinged	6.00	
AR10	PF5	3r green, buff	3.00	6.25
		Never hinged	6.00	
AR11	PF5	5r dp blue, buff	3.00	6.25
		Never hinged	6.00	
AR12	PF6	10r dp red, buff	3.00	6.25
		Never hinged	6.00	
AR13	PF7	25r dp brn, buff	10.00	25.00
		Never hinged	20.00	
AR14	PF8	100r black, blue & car	7.50	12.50
		Never hinged	15.00	
		Nos. AR7-AR14 (8)	73.50	225.00

General Revenue Stamps

PF9

1918		Litho.		Perf. 12x12½
AR15	PF9	5k lilac brn, buff	.60	6.25
		Never hinged	1.25	
AR16	PF9	10k olive brn, lt blue	.60	6.25
		Never hinged	1.25	
AR17	PF9	15k dp blue, pink	5.00	15.00
		Never hinged	10.00	
AR18	PF9	20k reddish brn, buff	3.00	12.50
		Never hinged	6.00	
AR19	PF9	50k org red, gray	4.25	19.00
		Never hinged	8.50	
AR20	PF9	75k olive grn, buff	6.25	25.00
		Never hinged	12.50	
AR21	PF9	1r red, pale blue	12.50	30.00
		Never hinged	25.00	
AR22	PF9	1.25r dk brn, redsh brn	6.25	30.00
		Never hinged	12.50	
AR23	PF9	2r violet, dk grn	67.50	150.00
		Never hinged	140.00	
AR24	PF9	3r dp vio blue, rose lilac	9.00	37.50
		Never hinged	18.00	
AR25	PF9	5r dp blue grn, lt grn	12.50	62.50
		Never hinged	25.00	
		Nos. AR15-AR25 (11)	127.45	394.00

SEMI-POSTAL STAMPS

Empire

Admiral Kornilov Monument, Sevastopol SP1   Pozharski and Minin Monument, Moscow SP2

Statue of Peter the Great, Leningrad SP3   Alexander II Memorial and Kremlin, Moscow SP4

			Perf. 11½ to 13½ and Compound	
1905		Typo.		Unwmk.
B1	SP1	3k red, brn & grn	8.00	3.25
a.		Perf. 13½x 11½	350.00	250.00
b.		Perf. 13½	40.00	40.00
c.		Perf. 11½x13½	300.00	225.00
B2	SP2	5k lilac, vio & straw	6.25	2.00
B3	SP3	7k lt bl, dk bl & pink	9.25	2.00
a.		Perf. 13½	65.00	65.00
B4	SP4	10k lt blue, dk bl & yel	16.50	3.50
		Nos. B1-B4 (4)	40.00	10.75

These stamps were sold for 3 kopecks over face value. The surtax was donated to a fund for the orphans of soldiers killed in the Russo-Japanese war.

Ilya Murometz Legendary Russian Hero — SP5

Designs: 3k, Don Cossack Bidding Farewell to His Sweetheart. 7k, Symbolical of Charity. 10k, St. George Slaying the Dragon.

1914				Perf. 11½, 12½
B5	SP5	1k red brn & dk grn, straw	1.25	1.25
B6	SP5	3k mar & gray grn, pink	1.25	1.25
B7	SP5	7k dk brn & dk grn, buff	1.25	1.25
B8	SP5	10k dk blue & brn, blue	6.25	6.25
		Nos. B5-B8 (4)	10.00	10.00

			Perf. 13½	
B5a	SP5	1k	1.00	1.00
B6a	SP5	3k	125.00	125.00
B7a	SP5	7k	1.50	1.50
B8a	SP5	10k	22.50	22.50
		Nos. B5a-B8a (4)	150.00	150.00

			Perf. 11½, 12½, 13½	
1915				White Paper
B9	SP5	1k orange brn & gray	1.00	1.50
B10	SP5	3k car & gray black	1.00	1.50
a.		Horiz. pair, imperf btwn.	150.00	
B12	SP5	7k dk brn & dk grn	6.50	
B13	SP5	10k dk blue & brown	1.00	1.50
		Nos. B9-B13 (4)	9.50	

These stamps were sold for 1 kopeck over face value. The surtax was donated to charities connected with the war of 1914-17.
No. B12 not regularly issued. It exists only perf 11½ (with Specimen overprint) and 12½.
Nos. B5-B13 exist imperf. Value each, unused or used, $400.
For surcharges of Nos. B5-B13, see Armenia Nos. 255-265 and Siberia No. 64.

Russian Soviet Federated Socialist Republic
Volga Famine Relief Issue

Relief Work on Volga River — SP9

Administering Aid to Famine Victim — SP10

1921   **Litho.**   **Imperf.**
B14 SP9 2250r green   3.75   10.00
  a.   Pelure paper   125.00   85.00
B15 SP9 2250r deep red   3.25   6.50
  a.   Pelure paper   19.00   18.00
B16 SP9 2250r brown   3.25   16.00
B17 SP10 2250r dark blue   7.75   21.00
    Nos. B14-B17 (4)   18.00   53.50

Forged cancels and counterfeits of Nos. B14-B17 are plentiful.

Stamps of type A33 with this overprint were not charity stamps nor did they pay postage in any form.

They represent taxes paid on stamps exported from or imported into Russia. In 1925 the semi-postal stamps of 1914-15 were surcharged for the same purpose. Stamps of the regular issues 1918 and 1921 have also been surcharged with inscriptions and new values, to pay the importation and exportation taxes.

Nos. 149-150 Surcharged in Black, Red, Blue or Orange

1922, Feb.   **Perf. 13½**
B18 A33 100r + 100r on 70k   .75   2.50
  a.   "100 p. + p. 100"   140.00 140.00
B19 A33 100r + 100r on 70k
        (R)   1.00   2.50
B20 A33 100r + 100r on 70k
        (Bl)   1.00   1.25
B21 A33 250r + 250r on 35k   .65   1.25
B22 A33 250r + 250r on 35k
        (R)   2.50   2.50
B23 A33 250r + 250r on 35k
        (O)   2.50   5.00
    Nos. B18-B23 (6)   8.40   15.00

Issued to raise funds for Volga famine relief. Nos. B18-B22 exist with surcharge inverted and with surcharge doubled. Values $25 to $50.

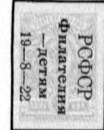

Regular Issues of 1909-18 Overprinted

1922, Aug. 19   **Perf. 14**
B24 A14 1k orange   400.00 350.00
B25 A14 2k green   20.00   35.00
B26 A14 3k red   20.00   35.00
B27 A14 5k claret   20.00   35.00
B28 A15 10k dark blue   20.00   35.00

          Imperf
B29 A14 1k orange   350.00 350.00
    Nos. B24-B29 (6)   830.00 840.00

The overprint means "Philately for the Children". The stamps were sold at five million times their face values and 80% of the amount was devoted to child welfare. The stamps were sold only at Moscow and for one day.

Exist with overprint reading up. Counterfeits exist including those with overprint reading up. Reprints exist.

Worker and Peasant (Industry and Agriculture) — SP11

Allegory: Agriculture Will Help End Distress SP12

Star of Hope, Wheat and Worker-Peasant Handclasp — SP13

Sower — SP14

1922   **Litho.**   **Imperf.**
          Without Gum
B30 SP11 2t (2000r) green   15.00 250.00
B31 SP12 2t (2000r) rose   20.00 250.00
B32 SP13 4t (4000r) rose   20.00 250.00
B33 SP14 6t (6000r) green   20.00 250.00
    Nos. B30-B33 (4)   75.00 1,000.

Nos. B30-B33 exist with double impression.

Counterfeits of Nos. B30-B33 exist; beware also of forged cancellations.

Miniature examples of Nos. B30-B33 exist, taken from the 1933 Soviet catalogue.

Automobile SP15

Steamship SP16

Railroad Train SP17

Airplane SP18

1922   **Imperf.**
B34 SP15 (20r+5r) light violet   .35   .50
B35 SP16 (20r+5r) violet   .35   .50
B36 SP17 (20r+5r) gray blue   .35   .50
B37 SP18 (20r+5r) blue gray   2.00   3.50
    Nos. B34-B37 (4)   3.05   5.00

Inscribed "For the Hungry." Each stamp was sold for 200,000r postage and 50,000r charity. Counterfeits of Nos. B34-B37 exist.

Nos. 212, 183, 202 Surcharged in Bronze, Gold or Silver

1923   **Imperf.**
B38 A48 1r +1r on 10r   500.00 500.00
  a.   Inverted surcharge   3,500. 3,500.
B39 A48 1r +1r on 10r
        (G)   50.00   30.00
  a.   Inverted surcharge   350.00 350.00
B40 A43 2r +2r on 250r   50.00   45.00
  a.   Pelure paper   30.00   30.00
  b.   Inverted surcharge   300.00 300.00
  c.   Double surcharge
          Wmk. 171
B41 A46 4r +4r on 5000r   30.00   25.00
  a.   Date spaced "1 923"   250.00 250.00
  b.   Inverted surcharge   400.00 400.00
B42 A46 4r +4r on 5000r
        (S)   1,000. 675.00
  a.   Inverted surcharge   1,500. 1,250.
  b.   Date spaced "1 923"   1,500. 1,250.
  c.   As "b," inverted surch. 5,000.
    Nos. B38-B42 (5)   1,630. 1,275.

The inscriptions mean "Philately's Contribution to Labor." The stamps were on sale only at Moscow and for one day. The surtax was for charitable purposes.

Counterfeits of No. B42 exist.

Leningrad Flood Issue

Nos. 181-182, 184-186 Surcharged

1924   **Unwmk.**   **Imperf.**
B43 A40 3k + 10k on 100r   1.00   1.50
  a.   Pelure paper   6.00   8.00
  b.   Inverted surcharge   500.00 250.00
B44 A40 7k + 20k on 200r   1.00   1.50
  a.   Inverted surcharge   500.00 250.00
B45 A40 14k + 30k on 300r   1.25   1.75
  a.   Inverted surcharge   500.00 250.00
      Similar Surcharge in Red or Black
B46 A41 12k + 40k on 500r
        (R)   2.25   3.25
  a.   Double surcharge   500.00 500.00
  b.   Inverted surcharge   500.00 500.00
B47 A41 20k + 50k on
          1000r   1.60   2.25
  a.   Thick paper   22.50   22.50
  b.   Pelure paper   40.00   40.00
  c.   Chalk surface paper   20.00   20.00
    Nos. B43-B47 (5)   7.10   10.25

The surcharge on Nos. B43 to B45 reads: "S.S.S.R. For the sufferers by the inundation at Leningrad." That on Nos. B46 and B47 reads: "S.S.S.R. For the Leningrad Proletariat, 23, IX, 1924."

No. B46 is surcharged vertically, reading down, with the value as the top line.

Orphans SP19

Lenin as a Child SP20

1926   **Typo.**   **Perf. 13½**
B48 SP19 10k brown   12.00   17.50
B49 SP20 20k deep blue   13.00   22.50
          Wmk. 170
B50 SP19 10k brown   6.00   3.00
B51 SP20 20k deep blue   14.00   7.00
    Nos. B48-B51 (4)   45.00   50.00

Two kopecks of the price of each of these stamps was donated to organizations for the care of indigent children.

Types of 1926 Issue

1927
B52 SP19 8k + 2k yel green   2.25   .50
B53 SP20 18k + 2k deep rose 5.25   1.50

Surtax was for child welfare.

Industrial Training SP21

Agricultural Training SP22

Perf. 10, 10½, 12½
1929-30   **Photo.**   **Unwmk.**
B54 SP21 10k +2k ol brn &
          org brn   5.00   2.50
  a.   Perf. 10½   200.00 110.00
B55 SP21 10k +2k ol grn
          ('30)   2.50   2.00
B56 SP22 20k +2k blk brn &
          bl, perf. 10½   5.00   4.00
  a.   Perf. 12½   75.00   55.00
  b.   Perf. 10   25.00   15.00
B57 SP22 20k +2k bl grn
          ('30)   3.00   4.50
    Nos. B54-B57 (4)   15.50   13.00

Surtax was for child welfare.

AIR POST STAMPS

AP1

Plane Overprint in Red
1922   **Unwmk.**   **Imperf.**
C1 AP1 45r green & black   10.00   50.00

5th anniversary of October Revolution.

No. C1 was on sale only at the Moscow General Post Office. Counterfeits exist.

Fokker F-111 — AP2

1923   **Photo.**
C2 AP2 1r red brown   11.00
C3 AP2 3r deep blue   15.00
C4 AP2 5r green   14.00
  a.   Wide "5"   27,500.
C5 AP2 10r carmine   10.00
    Nos. C2-C5 (4)   50.00

Nos. C2-C5 were not placed in use.

Nos. C2-C5
Surcharged

1924
C6	AP2	5k on 3r dp blue		5.00	1.25
C7	AP2	10k on 5r green		5.00	1.25
	a.	Wide "5"		1,400.	1,000.
	b.	Inverted surcharge		12,000.	1,200.
C8	AP2	15k on 1r red brown		5.00	1.25
	a.	Inverted surcharge		3,000.	1,000.
C9	AP2	20k on 10r car		5.00	1.25
	a.	Inverted surcharge		22,000.	500.00
		Nos. C6-C9 (4)		20.00	5.00

Airplane over Map of World AP3

1927, Sept. 1   Litho.   Perf. 13x12
C10	AP3	10k dk bl & yel brn	30.00	15.00
C11	AP3	15k dp red & ol grn	45.00	20.00

1st Intl. Air Post Cong. at The Hague, initiated by the USSR.

Graf Zeppelin and "Call to Complete 5-Year Plan in 4 Years" — AP4

1930   Photo.   Wmk. 226   Perf. 12½
C12	AP4	40k dark blue	35.00	17.50
	a.	Perf. 10½	35.00	17.50
	b.	Imperf.	2,750.	700.00
C13	AP4	80k carmine	45.00	22.50
	a.	Perf. 10½	45.00	22.50
	b.	Imperf.	2,750.	700.00

Flight of the Graf Zeppelin from Friedrichshafen to Moscow and return.

Symbolical of Airship Communication from the Tundra to the Steppes — AP5

Airship over Dneprostroi Dam — AP6

Airship over Lenin Mausoleum — AP7

Airship Exploring Arctic Regions — AP8

Constructing an Airship AP9

1931-32   Wmk. 170   Photo.   Imperf.
C15	AP5	10k dark violet	60.00	40.00
		Litho.		
C16	AP6	15k gray blue	60.00	40.00
		Typo.		
C17	AP7	20k dk carmine	60.00	40.00
		Photo.		
C18	AP8	50k black brown	60.00	40.00
C19	AP9	1r dark green	60.00	40.00
		Nos. C15-C19 (5)	300.00	200.00

Perf. 10½, 12, 12½ and Compound
C20	AP5	10k dark violet	12.00	3.50
		Litho.		
C21	AP6	15k gray blue	21.00	5.50
		Typo.		
C22	AP7	20k dk carmine	15.00	3.00
	a.	20k light red	11.00	4.50
		Photo.		
C23	AP8	50k black brown	12.00	3.00
	a.	50k gray blue (error)	950.00	600.00
C24	AP9	1r dark green	13.00	3.00

Perf. 12½
			Unwmk.	Engr.
C25	AP6	15k gray blk ('32)	3.00	.75
	a.	Perf. 10½	600.00	200.00
	b.	Perf. 14	60.00	45.00
	c.	Imperf.	5,750.	
		Nos. C20-C25 (6)	76.00	18.75

The 11½ perforation on Nos. C20-C25 is of private origin; beware also of bogus perforation "errors."

North Pole Issue

Graf Zeppelin and Icebreaker "Malygin" Transferring Mail — AP10

1931   Wmk. 170   Imperf.
C26	AP10	30k dark violet	20.00	8.50
C27	AP10	35k dark green	14.50	8.50
C28	AP10	1r gray black	22.50	25.00
C29	AP10	2r deep ultra	20.00	8.50
		Nos. C26-C29 (4)	77.00	50.50

Perf. 12x12½
C30	AP10	30k dark violet	40.00	30.00
C31	AP10	35k dark green	35.00	25.00
C32	AP10	1r gray black	40.00	30.00
C33	AP10	2r deep ultra	40.00	30.00
		Nos. C30-C33 (4)	155.00	115.00

Map of Polar Region, Airplane and Icebreaker "Sibiryakov" — AP11

Perf. 12, 10½
1932, Aug. 26   Wmk. 170
C34	AP11	50k carmine rose	75.00	22.50
	a.	Perf. 10½	27,500.	2,750.
	b.	Perf. 10½x12		23,000.
C35	AP11	1r green	75.00	22.50
	a.	Perf. 12	125.00	75.00

2nd International Polar Year in connection with proposed flight from Franz-Josef Land to Archangel which, being impossible, actually went from Archangel to Moscow to destinations.

Stratostat "U.S.S.R." — AP12

1933   Photo.   Perf. 14
C37	AP12	5k ultra	150.00	10.00
	a.	Vert. pair, imperf. btwn.		2,300.
C38	AP12	10k carmine	75.00	10.00
	a.	Horiz. pair, imperf. btwn.		2,250.
C39	AP12	20k violet	75.00	10.00
		Nos. C37-C39 (3)	300.00	30.00

Ascent into the stratosphere by Soviet aeronauts, Sept. 30th, 1933.

Furnaces of Kuznetsk AP13

Designs: 10k, Oil wells. 20k, Collective farm. 50k, Map of Moscow-Volga Canal project. 80k, Arctic cargo ship.

1933   Wmk. 170   Perf. 14
C40	AP13	5k ultra	55.00	10.00
C41	AP13	10k green	55.00	10.00
C42	AP13	20k carmine	120.00	15.00
C43	AP13	50k dull blue	150.00	15.00
C44	AP13	80k purple	120.00	15.00
		Nos. C40-C44 (5)	500.00	65.00

Unwmk.
C45	AP13	5k ultra	45.00	6.50
C46	AP13	10k green	45.00	6.50
	a.	Horiz. pair, imperf. btwn.	2,800.	1,800.
C47	AP13	20k carmine	60.00	12.00
C48	AP13	50k dull blue	160.00	22.50
C49	AP13	80k purple	90.00	12.00
		Nos. C45-C49 (5)	400.00	59.50

10th anniversary of Soviet civil aviation and airmail service. Counterfeits exist, perf 11½.

I. D. Usyskin AP18

10k, A. B. Vasenko. 20k, P. F. Fedoseinko.

1934   Wmk. 170   Perf. 11
C50	AP18	5k vio brown	40.00	5.00
C51	AP18	10k brown	70.00	5.00
C52	AP18	20k ultra	40.00	5.00
		Nos. C50-C52 (3)	150.00	15.00

Perf. 14
C50a	AP18	5k	110.	225.
C51a	AP18	10k	10,000.	8,500.
C52a	AP18	20k	20,000.	8,500.
		Nos. C50a-C52a (3)	30,110.	17,225.

Honoring victims of the stratosphere disaster. See Nos. C77-C79 in Scott Standard catalogue, Vol. 5.

Beware of examples of Nos. C50-C52 reperforated to resemble Nos. C50a-C52a.

Airship "Pravda" — AP19

Airship Landing — AP20

Airship "Voroshilov" — AP21

Sideview of Airship — AP22

Airship "Lenin" — AP23

1934   Perf. 14
C53	AP19	5k red orange	65.00	4.75
C54	AP20	10k claret	65.00	7.25
C55	AP21	15k brown	50.00	10.00
C56	AP22	20k black	125.00	15.00
C57	AP23	30k ultra	200.00	15.00
		Nos. C53-C57 (5)	505.00	52.00

Capt. V. Voronin and "Chelyuskin" — AP24

Prof. Otto Y. Schmidt — AP25

A. V. Lapidevsky AP26

S. A. Levanevsky
AP27

"Schmidt Camp" — AP28

Designs: 15k, M. G. Slepnev. 20k, I. V.
Doronin. 25k, M. V. Vodopianov. 30k, V. S.
Molokov. 40k, N. P. Kamanin.

1935			Perf. 14	
C58	AP24	1k red orange	45.00	4.25
C59	AP25	3k rose car-		
		mine	57.50	4.25
C60	AP26	5k emerald	45.00	4.25
C61	AP27	10k dark brown	57.50	4.25
C62	AP27	15k black	65.00	4.25
C63	AP27	20k deep claret	75.00	8.50
C64	AP27	25k indigo	225.00	17.50
C65	AP27	30k dull green	325.00	20.00
C66	AP27	40k purple	225.00	13.00
C67	AP28	50k dark ultra	225.00	17.50
		Nos. C58-C67 (10)	1,345.	97.75

Aerial rescue of ice-breaker Chelyuskin
crew and scientific expedition.

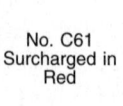

No. C61
Surcharged in
Red

1935, Aug.				
C68	AP27	1r on 10k dk		
		brn	650.00	925.00
	Never hinged		3,250.	
a.	Inverted surcharge		100,000.	100,000.
b.	Lower case Cyrillic "Ь"		1,800.	2,000.
c.	As "b," inverted surcharge		600,000.	

Moscow-San Francisco flight. Counterfeits
exist.

Single-Engined Monoplane — AP34

Five-Engined Transport — AP35

20k, Twin-engined cabin plane. 30k, 4r-
motored transport. 40k, Single-engined
amphibian. 50k, Twin-motored transport. 80k,
8-motored transport.

1937			Unwmk.	Perf. 12	
C69	AP34	10k yel brn & blk		2.50	1.00
a.	Imperf.			250.00	
C70	AP34	20k gray grn & blk		4.25	1.00

C71	AP34	30k red brn & blk	6.50	1.00
C72	AP34	40k vio brn & blk	8.25	1.25
C73	AP34	50k dk vio & blk	12.50	2.00
C74	AP35	80k bl vio & brn	40.00	2.00
C75	AP35	1r black brown & buff	25.00	4.00
a.	Sheet of 4, imperf.		200.00	300.00
	Never hinged		400.00	
	Nos. C69-C75 (7)		99.00	12.25
	Set, never hinged		400.00	

Jubilee Aviation Exhib., Moscow, Nov. 15-20.
Vertical pairs, imperf. between, exist for No.
C71, value $4,000; No. C72, value $5,750; No.
C73, value $2,300.

Types of
1938 Regular
Issue
Overprinted
in Various
Colors

1939			Typo.	
C76	A282	10k red (C)	5.25	1.00
C76A	A285	30k blue (R)	5.25	1.00
C76B	A286	40k dull green (Br)	5.25	1.00
C76C	A287	50k dull violet (R)	8.25	2.00
C76D	A289	1r brown (Bl)	11.00	5.00
a.	Double overprint		1,000.	
	Nos. C76-C76D (5)		35.00	10.00
	Set, never hinged		100.00	

Soviet Aviation Day, Aug. 18, 1939.

AIR POST OFFICIAL STAMPS

Used on mail from Russian embassy
in Berlin to Moscow. Surcharged on
Consular Fee stamps. Currency: the
German mark.

OA1

Surcharge in Carmine
Bicolored Burelage

1922, July		Litho.	Perf. 13½	
CO1	OA1	12m on 2.25r	175.00	150.00
CO2	OA1	24m on 3r	175.00	225.00
CO3	OA1	120m on 2.25r	225.00	
CO4	OA1	600m on 3r	250.00	
CO5	OA1	1200m on 10k	1,000.	
CO6	OA1	1200m on 50k	43,000.	
CO7	OA1	1200m on 2.25r	2,500.	
CO8	OA1	1200m on 3r	3,000.	

Three types of each denomination, distinguished by shape of "C" in surcharge and
length of second line of surcharge. Used
stamps have pen or crayon cancel. Forgeries
exist.

SPECIAL DELIVERY STAMPS

Motorcycle
Courier — SD1

Express
Truck — SD2

Design: 80k, Locomotive.

Perf. 12½x12, 12x12½

1932		Photo.	Wmk 170	
E1	SD1	5k dull brown	6.00	1.75
E2	SD2	10k violet brown	18.00	4.75
E3	SD2	80k dull green	26.00	8.50
		Nos. E1-E3 (3)	50.00	15.00
		Set, never hinged	150.00	

Used values are for c-t-o.

POSTAGE DUE STAMPS

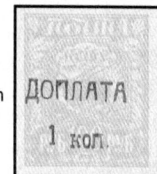

Regular Issue of 1918
Surcharged in Red or
Carmine

1924-25		Unwmk.	Perf. 13½	
J1	A33	1k on 35k blue	.25	.90
J2	A33	3k on 35k blue	.25	.90
J3	A33	5k on 35k blue	.25	.90
a.	Imperf.		300.00	
J4	A33	8k on 35k blue ('25)	.50	.90
a.	Imperf.		250.00	
J5	A33	10k on 35k blue	.50	1.40
a.	Pair, one without surcharge		400.00	
J6	A33	12k on 70k brown	.30	1.10
J7	A33	14k on 35k blue ('25)	.30	1.10
a.	Imperf.		250.00	
J8	A33	32k on 35k blue	.35	3.00
J9	A33	40k on 35k blue	.35	3.00
a.	Imperf.		300.00	
		Nos. J1-J9 (9)	3.05	13.20

Surcharge is found inverted on Nos. J1-J2,
J4, J6-J9, value $25-$50. Double on Nos. J2,
J4-J6; value, $40-$50.

Regular Issue of
1921 Surcharged in
Violet

1924			Imperf.	
J10	A40	1k on 100r orange	2.50	5.00
a.	1k on 100r yellow		7.00	20.00
b.	Pelure paper		7.00	20.00
c.	Inverted surcharge		100.00	

D1

Lithographed or Typographed

1925			Perf. 12	
J11	D1	1k red	3.00	1.50
J12	D1	2k violet	1.50	2.25
J13	D1	3k light blue	1.50	2.25
J14	D1	7k orange	1.50	2.25
J15	D1	8k green	1.50	3.00
J16	D1	10k dark blue	2.50	4.50
J17	D1	14k brown	3.50	4.50
		Nos. J11-J17 (7)	15.00	20.25

		Perf. 14½x14		
J13a	D1	3k	5.00	6.00
J14a	D1	7k	8.25	12.50
J16a	D1	10k	21,500.	40.00
J17a	D1	14k	2.25	3.50
		Nos. J13a-J17a (4)	21,515.	62.00

Value of No. J16a unused is based on 2012
auction realization.

1925		Wmk. 170	Typo.	Perf. 12	
J18	D1	1k red		.85	.85
J19	D1	2k violet		.85	.85
J20	D1	3k light blue		1.10	1.10
J21	D1	7k orange		1.20	1.10
J22	D1	8k green		1.20	1.10
J23	D1	10k dark blue		1.60	2.00
J24	D1	14k brown		2.50	2.50
		Nos. J18-J24 (7)		9.30	9.50

For surcharges see Nos. 359-372.

WENDEN (LIVONIA)

A former district of Livonia, a province
of the Russian Empire, which became

part of Latvia under the name of
Vidzeme.

Used values for Nos. L2-L12 are for
pen-canceled stamps. Postmarked
examples sell for considerably more.

A1

1862		Unwmk.	Imperf.
L1	A1	(2k) blue	30.00
a.	Tête bêche pair		350.00

No. L1 may have been used for a short
period of time but withdrawn because of small
size. Some consider it an essay.

A2

A3

1863				
L2	A2	(2k) rose & black	240.00	240.00
a.	Background inverted		600.00	600.00
L3	A3	(4k) blue grn & blk	175.00	250.00
a.	(4k) yellow green & black		300.00	300.00
b.	Half used as 2k on cover			2,500.
c.	Background inverted		950.00	500.00
d.	As "a," background inverted		650.00	400.00

The official imitations of Nos. L2 and L3
have a single instead of a double hyphen after
"WENDEN." Value, each $20.

Coat of Arms
A4   A5   A6

1863-71				
L4	A4	(2k) rose & green	90.00	90.00
a.	Yellowish paper			
b.	Green frame around central oval		95.00	60.00
c.	Tête bêche pair		2,500.	
L5	A5	(2k) rose & grn ('64)	100.00	75.00
L6	A6	(2k) rose & green	75.00	75.00
		Nos. L4-L6 (3)	265.00	240.00

Official imitations of Nos. L4b and L5 have a
rose instead of a green line around the central
oval. The first official imitation of No. L6 has
the central oval 5½mm instead of 6¼mm wide;
the second imitation is less clearly printed
than the original and the top of the "f" of
"Briefmarke" is too much hooked. Value, each
$20.

Coat of Arms
A7   A8

1872-75			Perf. 12½	
L7	A7	(2k) red & green	75.00	75.00
L8	A8	2k yel grn & red ('75)	8.50	11.00
a.	Numeral in upper right corner resembles an inverted "3"		30.00	30.00

Reprints of No. L8 have no horizontal lines
in the background. Those of No. L8a have the
impression blurred and only traces of the horizontal lines.

A9

1878-80
L9	A9	2k green & red	8.50	10.00
a.		Imperf.		
L10	A9	2k blk, grn & red ('80)	10.00	10.00
a.		Imperf., pair	35.00	

No. L9 has been reprinted in blue green and yellow green with perforation 11½ and in gray green with perforation 12½ or imperforate.

1884 | **Perf. 11½**

L11	A9	2k black, green & red	10.00	3.00
a.		Green arm omitted	21.00	
b.		Arm inverted	21.00	
c.		Arm double	27.50	
d.		Imperf., pair	150.00	

Wenden
Castle — A10

1901 | **Litho.**

L12	A10	2k dk green & brown	12.00	10.00
a.		Tête bêche pair	45.00	
b.		Imperf., pair	120.00	

OCCUPATION STAMPS

ISSUED UNDER GERMAN OCCUPATION

German Stamps
Overprinted in Black

On Stamps of 1905-17

1916-17 | **Wmk. 125** | **Perf. 14, 14½**

N1	A22	2½pf gray	.65	1.00
N2	A16	3pf brown	.25	.25
N3	A16	5pf green	.65	1.00
N4	A22	7½pf orange	.65	1.00
N5	A16	10pf carmine	.65	1.00
N6	A22	15pf yel brn	3.00	2.00
N7	A22	15pf dk vio ('17)	.65	1.00
N8	A16	20pf ultra	1.00	1.00
N9	A16	25pf org & blk, *yel*	.50	.50
N10	A16	40pf lake & blk	1.00	3.75
N11	A16	50pf vio & blk, *buff*	1.00	1.50
N12	A17	1m car rose	12.00	3.50
		Nos. 1N1-1N12 (12)	22.00	17.50
		Set, never hinged	40.00	

These stamps were used in the former Russian provinces of Suvalki, Vilnius, Kaunas, Kurland, Estland and Lifland.

ISSUED UNDER FINNISH OCCUPATION

Finnish Stamps of 1917-18 Overprinted

1919 | **Unwmk.** | **Perf. 14**

N13	A19	5p green	12.50	15.00
N14	A19	10p rose	12.50	15.00
N15	A19	20p buff	12.50	15.00
N16	A19	40p red violet	12.50	15.00
N17	A19	50p orange brn	150.00	150.00
N18	A19	1m dl rose & blk	140.00	140.00
N19	A19	5m violet & blk	425.00	425.00
N20	A19	10m brown & blk	725.00	725.00
		Nos. N13-N20 (8)	1,490.	1,500.

"Aunus" is the Finnish name for Olonets, a town of Russia.

Counterfeits overprints exist.

ARMY OF THE NORTHWEST

(Gen. Nicolai N. Yudenich)

Russian Stamps of 1909-18 Overprinted in Black or Red

On Stamps of 1909-12

Perf. 14 to 15 and Compound

1919, Aug. 1

1	A14	2k green	5.00	10.00
2	A14	5k claret	5.00	10.00
3	A15	10k dk blue (R)	10.00	15.00
4	A11	15k red brn & bl	5.00	8.00
5	A8	20k blue & car	8.00	15.00
6	A11	25k grn & gray violet	15.00	20.00
7	A8	50k brn vio & grn	10.00	15.00

Perf. 13½

8	A9	1r pale brn, dk brn & org	25.00	50.00
9	A13	10r scar, yel & gray	75.00	125.00

On Stamps of 1917

Imperf

10	A14	3k red	5.00	10.00
11	A12	3.50r mar & lt grn	17.50	35.00
12	A13	5r dk blue, grn & pale bl	17.50	30.00
13	A12	7r dk green & pink	150.00	200.00

No. 2 Surcharged
Perf. 14, 14½x15

14	A14	10k on 5k claret	12.00	24.00
		Nos. 1-14 (14)	360.00	567.00

Nos. 1-14 exist with inverted overprint or surcharge. The 1, 3½, 5, 7 and 10 rubles with red overprint are trial printings (value $150 each). The 20k on 14k, perforated, and the 1, 2, 5, 15, 70k and 1r imperforate were overprinted but never placed in use. Value: $300, $30, $45, $45, $45 and $65.

These stamps were in use from Aug. 1 to Oct. 15, 1919.

Counterfeits of Nos. 1-14 abound.

ARMY OF THE NORTH

A1 | A2

A3 | A4

A5

1919, Sept. | **Typo.** | **Imperf.**

1	A1	5k brown violet	.60	1.00
2	A2	10k blue	.60	1.00
3	A3	15k yellow	.60	1.00
4	A4	20k rose	.60	1.00
5	A5	50k green	.60	1.00
		Nos. 1-5 (5)	3.00	5.00

The letters OKCA are the initials of Russian words meaning "Special Corps, Army of the North." The stamps were in use from about the end of September to the end of December, 1919.

Used values are for c-t-o stamps.

(General Miller)

A set of seven stamps of this design was prepared in 1919, but not issued. Value, set $35. Counterfeits exist.

RUSSIA OFFICES ABROAD

For various reasons the Russian Empire maintained Post Offices to handle its correspondence in several foreign countries. These were similar to the Post Offices in foreign countries maintained by other world powers.

OFFICES IN CHINA

100 Kopecks = 1 Ruble
100 Cents = 1 Dollar (1917)

Russian Stamps Overprinted in Blue or Red

On Issues of 1889-92
Horizontally Laid Paper

1899-1904 | **Wmk. 168** | **Perf. 14½x15**

1	A10	1k orange (Bl)	.75	1.00
2	A10	2k yel green (R)	.75	1.00
3	A10	3k carmine (Bl)	.75	1.00
4	A10	5k red violet (Bl)	.75	1.00
5	A10	7k dk blue (R)	1.50	2.50
a.		Inverted overprint	500.00	
6	A8	10k dk blue (R)	1.50	2.50
7	A8	50k vio & grn (Bl) ('04)	12.00	8.50

Perf. 13½

8	A9	1r lt brn, brn & org (Bl) ('04)	150.00	150.00
		Nos. 1-8 (8)	168.00	167.50

On Issues of 1902-05
Overprinted in Black, Red or Blue
Perf. 14½ to 15 and Compound

1904-08 | **Vertically Laid Paper**

9	A8	4k rose red (Bl)	6.00	3.50
10	A10	7k dk blue (R)	15.00	15.00
11	A8	10k dk blue (R)	1,500.	1,300.
a.		Groundwork inverted	14,500.	
12	A11	14k bl & rose (R)	10.00	10.00
13	A11	15k brn vio & blue (Bl) ('08)	35.00	30.00
14	A8	20k blue & car (Bl)	5.00	5.00
15	A11	25k dull grn & lil (R) ('08)	50.00	50.00
16	A11	35k dk vio & grn (R)	10.00	10.00
17	A8	50k vio & grn (Bl)	100.00	125.00
18	A11	70k brn & org (Bl)	15.00	13.00

Perf. 13½

19	A9	1r lt brn, brn & org (Bl)	25.00	25.00
20	A12	3.50r blk & gray (R)	5.00	5.00
21	A13	5r dk bl, grn & pale bl (R) ('07)	8.50	12.00
a.		Inverted overprint	2,500.	
22	A12	7r blk & yel (Bl)	25.00	12.00
23	A13	10r scar, yel & gray (Bl) ('07)	100.00	100.00
		Nos. 9-10,12-23 (14)	409.50	415.50

On Issues of 1909-12
Wove Paper
Lozenges of Varnish on Face

1910-16 | **Unwmk.** | **Perf. 14x14½**

24	A14	1k orange yel (Bl)	.50	.50
25	A14	1k org yel (Bl Bk)	6.00	5.00

26	A14	2k green (Bk)	1.00	1.00
27	A14	2k green (Bl)	7.50	15.00
a.		Double ovpt. (Bk and Bl)		
28	A14	3k rose red (Bl)	2.00	2.00
29	A14	3k rose red (Bk)	12.00	12.00
30	A15	4k carmine (Bl)	1.00	2.00
31	A15	4k carmine (Bk)	10.00	10.00
32	A14	7k lt blue (Bl)	1.00	1.00
33	A15	10k blue (Bk)	1.00	1.00
34	A11	14k blue & rose (Bk)	10.00	5.00
35	A11	14k blue & rose (Bl)		
36	A11	15k dl vio & bl (Bk)	1.00	1.25
37	A8	20k blue & car (Bk)	5.00	7.00
38	A11	25k green & vio (Bl)	3.50	6.00
39	A11	25k grn & vio (Bk)	1.00	1.60
40	A11	35k vio & grn (Bk)	1.00	1.00
42	A8	50k vio & grn (Bk)	2.00	2.00
43	A8	50k brn vio & grn (Bl)	18.00	20.00
44	A11	70k lt brn & org (Bl)	1.00	2.00

Perf. 13½

45	A9	1r pale brn, brn & org (Bl)	1.25	2.40
47	A13	5r dk bl, grn & pale bl (R)	25.00	15.00
		Nos. 24-34,36-47 (21)	110.75	115.75

The existence of #35 is questioned.

Russian Stamps of 1902-12
Surcharged

a | b

c

On Stamps of 1909-12

1917 | **Perf. 11½, 13½, 14, 14½x15**

50	A14(a)	1c on 1k dl org yel	.60	5.50
51	A14(a)	2c on 2k dull grn	.60	5.50
a.		Inverted surcharge	100.00	
52	A14(a)	3c on 3k car	.60	5.50
a.		Inverted surcharge	100.00	
b.		Double surcharge	150.00	
53	A15(a)	4c on 4k car	1.25	4.25
54	A14(a)	5c on 5k claret	1.25	15.00
55	A15(b)	10c on 10k dk blue	1.25	15.00
a.		Inverted surcharge	100.00	100.00
b.		Double surcharge	115.00	
56	A11(b)	14c on 14k dk blue & carmine	1.25	10.00
a.		Imperf.	6.00	
b.		Inverted surcharge	100.00	
57	A11(a)	15c on 15k brn lilac & dp blue	1.25	15.00
a.		Inverted surcharge	50.00	
58	A8(b)	20c on 20k bl & car	1.25	15.00
59	A11(a)	25c on 25k grn & violet	1.25	15.00
60	A11(a)	35c on 35k brn vio & green	1.50	15.00
a.		Inverted surcharge	50.00	
61	A8(a)	50c on 50k brn vio & green	1.25	15.00
62	A11(a)	70c on 70k brn & red orange	1.25	15.00
63	A9(c)	$1 on 1r pale brn, brn & org	1.25	15.00
		Nos. 50-63 (14)	15.80	

On Stamps of 1902-05
Vertically Laid Paper
Perf. 11½, 13, 13½, 13½x11½
Wmk. Wavy Lines (168)

64	A12	$3.50 on 3.50r blk & gray	20.00	40.00
65	A13	$5 on 5r dk bl, grn & pale blue	20.00	40.00
66	A12	$7 on 7r blk & yel	10.00	32.50

On Stamps of 1915
Wove Paper
Unwmk. | **Perf. 13½**

68	A13	$5 on 5r ind, grn & lt blue	25.00	50.00
a.		Inverted surcharge	500.00	
70	A13	$10 on 10r car lake, yel & gray	50.00	100.00
		Nos. 64-70 (5)	125.00	262.50

The surcharge on Nos. 64-70 is in larger type than on the $1.

Russian Stamps of 1909-18 Surcharged in Black or Red

On Stamps of 1909-12

1920   **Perf. 14, 14½x15**

72	A14	1c on 1k dull org yellow	175.00	275.00
73	A14	2c on 2k dull grn (R)	16.00	27.50
74	A14	3c on 3k car	16.00	37.50
75	A15	4c on 4k car	18.00	22.50
a.		Inverted surcharge	130.00	150.00
76	A14	5c on 5k claret	60.00	90.00
77	A15	10c on 10k dk bl (R)	150.00	225.00
78	A14	10c on 10k on 7k blue (R)	125.00	190.00

On Stamps of 1917-18
Imperf

79	A14	1c on 1k orange	42.50	37.50
a.		Inverted surcharge	125.00	150.00
80	A14	5c on 5k claret	35.00	55.00
a.		Inverted surcharge	150.00	
b.		Double surcharge	250.00	
c.		Surcharged "Cent" only	95.00	
		Nos. 72-80 (9)	637.50	960.00

OFFICES IN THE TURKISH EMPIRE

Various powers maintained post offices in the Turkish Empire before World War I by authority of treaties which ended with the signing of the Treaty of Lausanne in 1923. The foreign post offices were closed Oct. 27, 1923.

100 Kopecks = 1 Ruble
40 Paras = 1 Piaster (1900)

Coat of Arms
A1

1863   **Unwmk.**   **Typo.**   **Imperf.**

1	A1	6k blue	375.00	1,000.
a.		6k light blue, thin paper	350.00	1,350.
b.		6k light blue, medium paper	350.00	1,350.
c.		6k dark blue, chalky paper	200.00	

Forgeries exist.

A2   A3

1865   **Litho.**

2	A2	(2k) brown & blue	800.00	750.00
3	A3	(20k) blue & red	900.00	850.00

Twenty-eight varieties of each.

A4   A5   A6

1866   **Horizontal Network**

4	A4	(2k) rose & pale bl	25.00	30.00
a.		(2k) pale rose & blue	50.00	75.00
5	A5	(20k) deep blue & rose	40.00	50.00
a.		(20k) pale blue & rose	67.50	70.00

1867   **Vertical Network**

6	A4	(2k) rose & pale bl	75.00	100.00
a.		(2k) pale rose & deep blue	80.00	95.00
7	A5	(20k) dp blue & rose	200.00	100.00

The initials inscribed on Nos. 2 to 7 are those of the Russian Company of Navigation and Trade.

The official imitations of Nos. 2 to 7 are on yellowish white paper. The colors are usually paler than those of the originals and there are minor differences in the designs.

Horizontally Laid Paper

1868   **Typo.**   **Wmk. 168**   **Perf. 11½**

8	A6	1k brown	50.00	20.00
9	A6	3k green	60.00	25.00
10	A6	5k blue	60.00	25.00
11	A6	10k car & green	75.00	25.00
		Nos. 8-11 (4)	245.00	95.00

Colors of Nos. 8-11 dissolve in water.

1872-90   **Perf. 14½x15**

12	A6	1k brown	10.00	2.00
13	A6	3k green	25.00	3.00
14	A6	5k blue	5.00	1.00
15	A6	10k pale red & grn ('90)	1.25	.60
b.		10k carmine & green	24.00	3.75
		Nos. 12-15 (4)	41.25	6.60

Vertically Laid Paper

12a	A6	1k	75.00	18.00
13a	A6	3k	75.00	18.00
14a	A6	5k	75.00	18.00
15a	A6	10k	190.00	47.50
		Nos. 12a-15a (4)	415.00	101.50

Nos. 12-15 exist imperf.

No. 15 Surcharged in Black or Blue

a   b

c

1876

16	A6(a)	8k on 10k (Bk)	75.00	45.00
a.		Vertically laid		2,750.
b.		Inverted surcharge	400.00	
17	A6(a)	8k on 10k (Bl)	90.00	75.00
a.		Vertically laid		
b.		Inverted surcharge		

1879

18	A6(b)	7k on 10k (Bk)	80.00	65.00
a.		Vertically laid	750.00	750.00
b.		Inverted surcharge		
19	A6(b)	7k on 10k (Bl)	125.00	85.00
a.		Vertically laid	1,750.	1,750.
b.		Inverted surcharge	500.00	
19C	A6(c)	7k on 10k (Bl)	1,250.	1,250.
19D	A6(c)	7k on 10k (Bk)	1,250.	1,250.

Nos. 16-19D have been extensively counterfeited.

1879   **Perf. 14½x15**

20	A6	1k black & yellow	3.00	1.00
a.		Vertically laid	10.00	5.00
21	A6	2k black & rose	5.00	3.00
a.		Vertically laid	10.00	5.00
22	A6	7k carmine & gray	9.00	1.00
a.		Vertically laid	42.50	15.00
		Nos. 20-22 (3)	17.00	5.00

1884

23	A6	1k orange	.75	.50
24	A6	2k green	1.00	.75
25	A6	5k pale red violet	4.00	2.00
26	A6	7k blue	2.00	1.50
		Nos. 23-26 (4)	7.75	4.75

Nos. 23-26 imperforate are believed to be proofs

No. 23 surcharged "40 PARAS" is bogus, though some examples were postally used.

Russian Company of Navigation and Trade

This overprint, in two sizes, was privately applied in various colors to Russian Offices in the Turkish Empire stamps of 1900-1910.

A7   A8   A9

A10   A11

Surcharged in Blue, Black or Red

1900   **Horizontally Laid Paper**

27	A7	4pa on 1k orange (Bl)	1.25	1.25
a.		Inverted surcharge	30.00	30.00
28	A7	4pa on 1k orange (Bk)	1.25	1.25
a.		Inverted surcharge	30.00	30.00
29	A7	10pa on 2k green	.25	.25
a.		Inverted surcharge		
30	A8	1pi on 10k dk blue	.50	.60
a.		Inverted surcharge		
		Nos. 27-30 (4)	3.25	3.35

1903-05   **Vertically Laid Paper**

31	A7	10pa on 2k yel green	.60	.40
a.		Inverted surcharge	75.00	
32	A8	20pa on 4k rose red (Bl)	.60	.40
a.		Inverted surcharge	95.00	
33	A8	1pi on 10k dk blue	.60	.40
a.		Groundwork inverted	50.00	15.00
34	A8	2pi on 20k blue & car (Bk)	1.40	.75
35	A8	5pi on 50k brn vio & grn	3.50	1.25
36	A9	7pi on 70k brn & org (Bl)	4.00	2.00

Perf. 13½

37	A10	10pi on 1r lt brn, brn & org (Bl)	6.50	4.00
38	A11	35pi on 3.50r blk & gray	20.00	10.00
39	A11	70pi on 7r blk & yel	24.00	12.50
		Nos. 31-39 (9)	61.20	31.70

A12   A13

A14

Wove Paper
Lozenges of Varnish on Face

1909   **Unwmk.**   **Perf. 14½x15**

40	A12	5pa on 1k orange	.30	.40
41	A12	10pa on 2k green	.35	.65
a.		Inverted surcharge	30.00	30.00
42	A12	20pa on 4k carmine	70	1.00
43	A12	1pi on 10k blue	.75	1.20
44	A12	5pi on 50k vio & grn	1.40	1.60
45	A12	7pi on 70k brn & org	2.00	2.75

Perf. 13½

46	A13	10pi on 1r brn & org	3.00	5.00
47	A14	35pi on 3.50r mar & lt grn	12.00	14.00
48	A14	70pi on 7r dk grn & pink	20.00	25.00
		Nos. 40-48 (9)	40.50	51.60

50th anniv. of the establishing of the Russian Post Offices in the Levant.

Nos. 40-48 Overprinted with Names of Various Cities Overprinted "Constantinople" in Black

1909-10   **Perf. 14½x15**

61	A12	5pa on 1k	.40	.40
c.		Inverted overprint	50.00	
62	A12	10pa on 2k	.40	.40
c.		Inverted overprint	30.00	
63	A12	20pa on 4k	.75	.75
c.		Inverted overprint	30.00	
64	A12	1pi on 10k	.75	.75
65	A12	5pi on 50k	1.50	1.50
66	A12	7pi on 70k	3.00	3.00

Perf. 13½

67	A13	10pi on 1r	15.00	15.00
a.		"Constanttinople"	100.00	100.00
68	A14	35pi on 3.50r	50.00	30.00
c.		"Constautinople"	100.00	100.00
d.		"Constantjnople"	100.00	100.00
69	A14	70pi on 7r	45.00	42.50
c.		"Constanjinople"	100.00	100.00
d.		"Constantjnople"	100.00	100.00

Blue Overprint
Perf. 14½x15

70	A12	5pa on 1k	8.00	8.00
		Nos. 61-70 (10)	124.80	102.30

"Consnantinople"

61a	A12	5pa on 1k	10.00	
62a	A12	10pa on 2k	10.00	
63a	A12	20pa on 4k	10.00	
64a	A12	1pi on 10k	10.00	
65a	A12	5pi on 50k	10.00	
66a	A12	7pi on 70k	12.00	
68a	A14	35pi on 3.50r	50.00	
69a	A14	70pi on 7r	90.00	
70a	A12	5pa on 1k	10.00	
		Nos. 61a-70a (9)	212.00	

"Constantinopie"

61b	A12	5pa on 1k	25.00	
d.		Inverted overprint	50.00	
62b	A12	10pa on 2k	25.00	
d.		Inverted overprint	50.00	
63b	A12	20pa on 4k	30.00	
d.		Inverted overprint	60.00	
64b	A12	1pi on 10k	30.00	
65b	A12	5pi on 50k	30.00	
66b	A12	7pi on 70k	30.00	
68b	A14	35pi on 3.50r	60.00	
69b	A14	70pi on 7r	90.00	
		Nos. 61b-69b (8)	320.00	

Overprinted "Jaffa"
Black Overprint

71	A12	5pa on 1k	2.10	3.75
a.		Inverted overprint	75.00	
72	A12	10pa on 2k	2.50	4.00
a.		Inverted overprint	50.00	
73	A12	20pa on 4k	3.00	5.25
a.		Inverted overprint	60.00	
74	A12	1pi on 10k	3.75	5.25
a.		Double overprint	95.00	
75	A12	5pi on 50k	9.00	10.50
76	A12	7pi on 70k	11.00	14.00

Perf. 13½

77	A13	10pi on 1r	50.00	50.00
78	A14	35pi on 3.50r	100.00	100.00
79	A14	70pi on 7r	125.00	150.00

Blue Overprint
Perf. 14½x15

80	A12	5pa on 1k	12.00	12.00
		Nos. 71-80 (10)	318.35	354.75

Overprinted "Ierusalem" in Black
Black Overprint

81	A12	5pa on 1k	2.10	2.75
a.		Inverted overprint	60.00	
b.		"erusalem"	25.00	
c.		As "b," overprint inverted	50.00	
82	A12	10pa on 2k	2.75	4.25
a.		Inverted overprint	30.00	
b.		"erusalem"	25.00	
c.		As "b," overprint inverted	50.00	
83	A12	20pa on 4k	4.25	5.50
a.		Inverted overprint	30.00	
b.		"erusalem"	25.00	
c.		As "b," overprint inverted	50.00	
84	A12	1pi on 10k	4.25	5.50
a.		"erusalem"	30.00	
85	A12	5pi on 50k	7.25	11.00
a.		"erusalem"	35.00	
86	A12	7pi on 70k	14.00	17.50
a.		"erusalem"	35.00	

Perf. 13½

87	A13	10pi on 1r	50.00	50.00
88	A14	35pi on 3.50r	125.00	125.00
89	A14	70pi on 7r	125.00	150.00

Blue Overprint
Perf. 14½x15

90	A12	5pa on 1k	15.00	25.00
		Nos. 81-90 (10)	349.60	396.50

Overprinted "Kerassunde"
Black Overprint

91	A12	5pa on 1k	.60	.80
a.		Inverted overprint	50.00	
92	A12	10pa on 2k	.60	.80
a.		Inverted overprint	50.00	
93	A12	20pa on 4k	1.00	1.10
a.		Inverted overprint	50.00	
94	A12	1pi on 10k	1.25	1.25
95	A12	5pi on 50k	2.25	2.50
96	A12	7pi on 70k	3.50	4.00

Perf. 13½
97 A13 10pi on 1r — 13.00 / 15.00
98 A14 35pi on 3.50r — 42.50 / 42.50
99 A14 70pi on 7r — 65.00 / 52.50

Blue Overprint
Perf. 14½x15
100 A12 5pa on 1k — 15.00 / 15.00
Nos. 91-100 (10) — 144.70 / 135.45

Overprinted "Mont Athos"
Black Overprint
101 A12 5pa on 1k — 1.00 / 1.50
  b. Inverted overprint — 50.00
102 A12 10pa on 2k — 1.00 / 1.50
  b. Inverted overprint — 50.00
103 A12 20pa on 4k — 1.50 / 3.00
  b. Inverted overprint — 50.00
104 A12 1pi on 10k — 2.00 / 4.00
  b. Double overprint — 60.00
105 A12 5pi on 50k — 6.50 / 7.00
106 A12 7pi on 70k — 8.00 / 8.00
  b. Pair, one without "Mont Athos" — 60.00

Perf. 13½
107 A13 10pi on 1r — 30.00 / 35.00
108 A14 35pi on 3.50r — 70.00 / 80.00
109 A14 70pi on 7r — 130.00 / 145.00

Blue Overprint
Perf. 14½x15
110 A12 5pa on 1k — 10.00 / 15.00
Nos. 101-110 (10) — 260.00 / 300.00

"Mont Atho"
101a A12 5pa on 1k — 25.00
102a A12 10pa on 2k — 25.00
103a A12 20pa on 4k — 25.00
  c. Inverted overprint — 100.00
104a A12 1pi on 10k — 25.00
  c. As "a," double overprint — 125.00
105a A12 5pi on 50k — 25.00
106a A12 7pi on 70k — 25.00
110a A12 5pa on 1k — 30.00

"M nt Athos"
101d A12 5pa on 1k — 25.00
102d A12 10pa on 2k — 25.00
103d A12 20pa on 4k — 25.00
105d A12 5pi on 50k — 50.00
106d A12 7pi on 70k — 75.00

Overprinted

111 A12 5pa on 1k — 1.50 / 2.00
  a. Pair, one without overprint — 50.00
112 A12 10pa on 2k — 1.50 / 2.00
  a. Pair, one without overprint — 65.00
113 A12 20pa on 4k — 2.50 / 3.50
  a. Pair, one without overprint — 65.00
114 A12 1pi on 10k — 4.50 / 6.00
  a. Pair, one without overprint — 75.00
115 A12 5pi on 50k — 7.00 / 9.50
  a. Pair, one without overprint — 100.00
116 A12 7pi on 70k — 13.00 / 17.50
  a. Pair, one without overprint — 125.00

Perf. 13½
117 A13 10pi on 1r — 80.00 / 80.00
Nos. 111-117 (7) — 110.00 / 120.50
The overprint is larger on No. 117.

Overprinted "Salonique"
Black Overprint
Perf. 14½x15
131 A12 5pa on 1k — 1.50 / 2.00
  a. Inverted overprint — 55.00
  b. Pair, one without overprint — 60.00
132 A12 10pa on 2k — 2.00 / 4.00
  a. Inverted overprint — 55.00
  b. Pair, one without overprint — 60.00
133 A12 20pa on 4k — 2.50 / 5.00
  a. Inverted overprint — 55.00
  b. Pair, one without overprint — 60.00
134 A12 1pi on 10k — 3.00 / 6.00
  a. Pair, one without overprint — 75.00
135 A12 5pi on 50k — 3.50 / 6.00
136 A12 7pi on 70k — 5.00 / 8.00

Perf. 13½
137 A13 10pi on 1r — 32.50 / 40.00
138 A14 35pi on 3.50r — 80.00 / 85.00
139 A14 70pi on 7r — 100.00 / 115.00

Blue Overprint
Perf. 14½x15
140 A12 5pa on 1k — 15.00 / 15.00
Nos. 131-140 (10) — 245.00 / 286.00

Overprinted "Smyrne"
Black Overprint
141 A12 5pa on 1k — .65 / 1.25
  a. Double overprint — 10.00
  b. Inverted overprint — 10.00
142 A12 10pa on 2k — .65 / 1.25
  a. Inverted overprint — 25.00
143 A12 20pa on 4k — 1.40 / 1.60
  a. Inverted overprint — 17.50
144 A12 1pi on 10k — 1.40 / 1.75
145 A12 5pi on 50k — 3.00 / 3.00
146 A12 7pi on 70k — 4.50 / 6.00

Perf. 13½
147 A13 10pi on 1r — 18.00 / 22.50
148 A14 35pi on 3.50r — 37.50 / 40.00
149 A14 70pi on 7r — 55.00 / 62.50

Blue Overprint
Perf. 14½x15
150 A12 5pa on 1k — 11.00 / 11.00
Nos. 141-150 (10) — 133.10 / 150.85

"Smyrn"
141c A12 5pa on 1k — 18.00 / 20.00
142b A12 10pa on 2k — 18.00 / 20.00
143b A12 20pa on 4k — 18.00 / 20.00
144a A12 1pi on 10k — 20.00 / 25.00
145a A12 5pi on 50k — 20.00 / 25.00
146a A12 7pi on 70k — 20.00 / 25.00
Nos. 141c-146a (6) — 114.00 / 135.00

Overprinted "Trebizonde"
Black Overprint
151 A12 5pa on 1k — .80 / 1.00
  a. Inverted overprint — 25.00
  b. Pair, one without overprint — 60.00
152 A12 10pa on 2k — .80 / 1.00
  a. Inverted overprint — 25.00
  b. Pair, one without "Trebizonde" — 60.00
153 A12 20pa on 4k — .95 / .95
  a. Inverted overprint — 25.00
  b. Double overprint — 100.00
154 A12 1pi on 10k — .95 / 1.50
  a. Pair, one without "Trebizonde" — 35.00
155 A12 5pi on 50k — 2.10 / 2.50
156 A12 7pi on 70k — 4.25 / 5.50

Perf. 13½
157 A13 10pi on 1r — 19.00 / 20.00
158 A14 35pi on 3.50r — 37.50 / 37.50
159 A14 70pi on 7r — 52.50 / 55.00

Blue Overprint
Perf. 14½x15
160 A12 5pa on 1k — 6.25 / 7.50
Nos. 151-160 (10) — 125.10 / 132.45
On Nos. 158 and 159 the overprint is spelled "Trebisonde".

Overprinted "Beyrouth"
Black Overprint
1910
161 A12 5pa on 1k — .50 / .85
162 A12 10pa on 2k — .50 / .85
  a. Inverted overprint — 25.00
163 A12 20pa on 4k — .80 / 1.10
164 A12 1pi on 10k — .80 / 1.40
165 A12 5pi on 50k — 1.90 / 2.75
166 A12 7pi on 70k — 4.00 / 5.50

Perf. 13½
167 A13 10pi on 1r — 19.00 / 21.00
168 A14 35pi on 3.50r — 40.00 / 42.50
169 A14 70pi on 7r — 55.00 / 60.00
Nos. 161-169 (9) — 122.50 / 135.95

Overprinted "Dardanelles"
Perf. 14½x15
171 A12 5pa on 1k — 1.25 / 2.50
  a. Pair, one without overprint — 60.00
172 A12 10pa on 2k — 1.25 / 2.50
  a. Pair, one without overprint — 60.00
173 A12 20pa on 4k — 3.25 / 3.25
  a. Inverted overprint — 25.00
174 A12 1pi on 10k — 3.50 / 3.50
175 A12 5pi on 50k — 6.50 / 7.50
176 A12 7pi on 70k — 14.00 / 14.00

Perf. 13½
177 A13 10pi on 1r — 21.00 / 21.00
178 A14 35pi on 3.50r — 37.50 / 40.00
  a. Center and ovpt. inverted — 5,000. / 2,750.
179 A14 70pi on 7r — 60.00 / 65.00
Nos. 171-179 (9) — 148.25 / 159.25

Overprinted "Metelin"
Perf. 14½x15
181 A12 5pa on 1k — 1.00 / 2.00
  a. Inverted overprint — 50.00
182 A12 10pa on 2k — 1.00 / 2.00
  a. Inverted overprint — 50.00
183 A12 20pa on 4k — 2.00 / 5.00
  a. Inverted overprint — 50.00
184 A12 1pi on 10k — 3.00 / 6.00
185 A12 5pi on 50k — 5.00 / 8.00
186 A12 7pi on 70k — 8.00 / 10.00

Perf. 13½
187 A13 10pi on 1r — 20.00 / 30.00
188 A14 35pi on 3.50r — 70.00 / 70.00
189 A14 70pi on 7r — 80.00 / 85.00

Blue Overprint
Perf. 14½x15
190 A12 5pa on 1k — 10.00 / 15.00
Nos. 181-190 (10) — 200.00 / 233.00

Overprinted "Rizeh"
Perf. 14½x15
191 A12 5pa on 1k — .65 / 1.00
  a. Inverted overprint — 30.00
192 A12 10pa on 2k — .65 / 1.00
  a. Inverted overprint — 30.00
193 A12 20pa on 4k — 1.10 / 1.40
  a. Inverted overprint — 30.00

194 A12 1pi on 10k — 1.10 / 1.40
195 A12 5pi on 50k — 1.75 / 3.75
196 A12 7pi on 70k — 3.25 / 6.00

Perf. 13½
197 A13 10pi on 1r — 17.50 / 21.00
198 A14 35pi on 3.50r — 27.50 / 35.00
199 A14 70pi on 7r — 44.00 / 52.50
Nos. 191-199 (9) — 97.50 / 123.05
Nos. 61-199 for the establishing of Russian Post Offices in the Levant, 50th anniv.

A15   A16   A17

Vertically Laid Paper
1910 Wmk. 168 *Perf. 14½x15*
200 A15 20pa on 5k red violet (Bl) — .60 / .60

Wove Paper
Vertical Lozenges of Varnish on Face
1910 Unwmk. *Perf. 14x14½*
201 A16 5pa on 1k org yel (Bl) — .40 / .50
202 A16 10pa on 2k green (R) — .40 / .50
  a. Inverted overprint — 25.00
203 A17 20pa on 4k car rose (Bl) — .40 / .50
204 A17 1pi on 10k blue (R) — .40 / .50
  a. Inverted overprint — 25.00
205 A8 5pi on 50k vio & grn (Bl) — .75 / 1.20
206 A9 7pi on 70k lt brn & org (R) — 1.00 / 1.25

Perf. 13½
207 A10 10pi on 1r pale brn, brn & org (Bl) — 1.40 / 1.50
Nos. 201-207 (7) — 4.75 / 5.95

Russian Stamps of 1909-12 Surcharged in Black

No. 208   Nos. 209-212

1912 *Perf. 14x14½*
208 A14 20pa on 5k claret — .80 / .60
209 A11 1½pi on 15k dl vio & blue — .80 / .75
210 A8 2pi on 20k bl & car — .80 / .90
211 A12 2½pi on 25k grn & vio — 1.00 / 1.25
  a. Double surcharge — 150.00 / 150.00
212 A11 3½pi on 35k vio & grn — 1.60 / 1.60
Nos. 208-212 (5) — 5.00 / 5.10

Russia Nos. 88-91, 93, 95-104 Surcharged

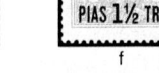

c   d
e   f
g

1913 *Perf. 13½*
213 A16(c) 5pa on 1k — .25 / .25
  Never hinged — .40
214 A17(d) 10pa on 2k — .25 / .25
  Never hinged — .40
215 A18(c) 15pa on 3k — .25 / .25
  Never hinged — .40
216 A19(c) 20pa on 4k — .25 / .25
  Never hinged — .40
217 A21(e) 1pi on 10k — .25 / .25
  Never hinged — .40
218 A23(f) 1½pi on 15k — .50 / .50
  Never hinged — .70
219 A24(f) 2pi on 20k — .50 / .50
  Never hinged — .70
220 A25(f) 2½pi on 25k — .75 / .75
  Never hinged — .90
221 A26(f) 3½pi on 35k — 1.60 / 1.60
  Never hinged — 2.25
222 A27(e) 5pi on 50k — 2.00 / 2.00
  Never hinged — 2.75
223 A28(f) 7pi on 70k — 8.00 / 15.00
  Never hinged — 10.50
224 A29(e) 10pi on 1r — 9.00 / 15.00
  Never hinged — 10.50
225 A30(e) 20pi on 2r — 1.60 / 8.00
  Never hinged — 2.25
226 A31(g) 30pi on 3r — 2.75 / 250.00
  Never hinged — 3.50
227 A32(e) 50pi on 5r — 150.00 / 500.00
  Never hinged — 225.00
Nos. 213-227 (15) — 177.95 / 794.60
Romanov dynasty tercentenary.
Forgeries exist of overprint on No. 227.

Russia Nos. 75, 71, 72 Surcharged

h   i

Perf. 14x14½
Wove Paper
228 A14(h) 15pa on 3k — .25 / .25
  Never hinged — .40

Perf. 13, 13½
230 A13(i) 50pi on 5r — 3.00 / 10.00
  Never hinged — 7.50

Vertically Laid Paper
Wmk. Wavy Lines (168)
231 A13(i) 100pi on 10r — 7.00 / 20.00
  Never hinged — 15.00
  a. Double surcharge — 750.00 / —
Nos. 228-231 (3) — 10.25 / 30.25
No. 228 has lozenges of varnish on face but No. 230 has not.

Wrangel Issues

For the Posts of Gen. Peter Wrangel's army and civilian refugees from South Russia, interned in Turkey, Serbia, etc.

Very few of the Wrangel overprints were actually sold to the public, and many of the covers were made up later with the original cancels. Reprints abound. Values probably are based on sales of reprints in most cases.

Russian Stamps of 1902-18 Surcharged in Blue, Red or Black

On Russia Nos. 69-70
Vertically Laid Paper
1921 Wmk. 168 *Perf. 13½*
232 A12 10,000r on 3.50r — 250.00 / 250.00
233 A12 10,000r on 7r — 250.00 / 250.00
234 A12 20,000r on 3.50r — 250.00 / 250.00
235 A12 20,000r on 7r — 250.00 / 250.00
Nos. 232-235 (4) — 1,000. / 1,000.

On Russia Nos. 71-86, 87a, 117-118, 137-138
Wove Paper
Perf. 14x14½, 13½
Unwmk.
236 A14 1000r on 1k — 3.25 / 3.25
237 A14 1000r on 2k (R) — 3.25 / 3.25
237A A14 1000r on 2k (Bk) — 47.50 / 47.50
238 A14 1000r on 3k — 1.10 / 1.10
  a. Inverted surcharge — 10.00 / 10.00
239 A15 1000r on 4k — 1.10 / 1.10
  a. Inverted surcharge — 10.00 / 10.00

240 A14 1000r on 5k 1.10 1.10
  a. Inverted surcharge 10.00 10.00
241 A14 1000r on 7k 1.10 1.10
  a. Inverted surcharge 10.00 10.00
242 A15 1000r on 10k 1.10 1.10
  a. Inverted surcharge 10.00 10.00
243 A14 1000r on 10k on 7k 1.10 1.10
244 A14 5000r on 3k 1.10 1.10
245 A14 5000r on 14k 10.00 10.00
246 A11 5000r on 15k 1.10 1.10
  a. "PYCCKIN" 12.00 12.00
247 A11 5000r on 20k 3.50 3.50
  a. "PYCCKIN" 12.00 12.00
248 A11 5000r on 20k on 14k 3.50 3.50
249 A11 5000r on 25k 1.10 1.10
250 A11 5000r on 35k 1.10 1.10
  a. Inverted surcharge 10.00 10.00
  b. New value omitted 10.00 10.00
251 A8 5000r on 50k 1.10 1.10
  a. Inverted surcharge 10.00 10.00
252 A11 5000r on 70k 1.10 1.10
  a. Inverted surcharge 10.00 10.00
253 A9 10,000r on 1r (Bl) 1.10 1.10
254 A9 10,000r on 1r (Bk) 8.25 8.25
255 A12 10,000r on 3.50r 3.50 3.50
256 A13 10,000r on 5r 45.00 45.00
257 A13 10,000r on 10r 4.25 4.25
258 A9 20,000r on 1r 2.50 2.50
259 A12 20,000r on 3.50r 2.50 2.50
  a. Inverted surcharge 10.00 10.00
  b. New value omitted 20.00 20.00
260 A12 20,000r on 7r 92.50 92.50
261 A13 20,000r on 10r 2.50 2.50
  Nos. 236-261 (27) 246.30 246.30

On Russia No. 104
261A A32 20,000r on 5r 950.00

On Russia Nos. 119-123, 125-135
Imperf
262 A14 1000r on 1k 1.20 1.20
263 A14 1000r on 2k (R) 1.20 1.20
263A A14 1000r on 2k (Bk) 1.50 1.50
264 A14 1000r on 3k 1.20 1.20
265 A15 1000r on 4k 40.00 40.00
266 A14 1000r on 5k 1.50 1.50
267 A14 5000r on 3k 1.20 1.20
268 A11 5000r on 15k 1.50 1.50
268A A8 5000r on 20k 60.00
268B A11 5000r on 25k 60.00
269 A11 5000r on 35k 3.00 3.00
270 A8 5000r on 50k 3.00 3.00
271 A11 5000r on 70k 1.20 1.20
272 A9 10,000r on 1r (Bl) 1.20 1.20
  a. Inverted surcharge 10.00 10.00
273 A9 10,000r on 1r (Bk) 1.20 1.20
274 A12 10,000r on 3.50r 1.20 1.20
275 A13 10,000r on 5r 10.00 10.00
276 A12 10,000r on 7r 60.00 60.00
276A A13 10,000r on 10r 200.00
277 A9 20,000r on 1r (Bl) 1.20 1.20
  a. Inverted surcharge 10.00 10.00
278 A9 20,000r on 1r (Bk) 1.20 1.20
279 A12 20,000r on 3.50r 10.00 10.00
280 A13 20,000r on 5r 1.20 1.20
281 A13 20,000r on 7r 47.50 47.50
281A A13 20,000r on 10r 275.00
  Nos. 262-268,269-276,277-281 (21) 191.20 191.20

A18   A19

On Russia AR1-AR3
Perf. 14½x15
Wmk. 171
282 A18 10,000r on 1k red, buff 6.50 6.50
283 A19 10,000r on 5k grn, buff 6.50 6.50
  a. Inverted surcharge 10.00
284 A19 10,000r on 10k brn, buff 6.50 6.50
  a. Inverted surcharge 10.00
  Nos. 282-284 (3) 19.50 19.50

On Stamps of Russian Offices in Turkey On No. 38-39
Vertically Laid Paper
Wmk. Wavy Lines (168)
284B A11 20,000r on 35pi on 3.50r 300.00
284C A11 20,000r on 70pi on 7r 400.00

On Nos. 200-207
Vertically Laid Paper
284D A15 1000r on 20pa on 5k 5.00 5.00

Wove Paper Unwmk.
285 A16 1000r on 5pa on 1k 2.50 2.50
286 A16 1000r on 10pa on 2k 0.50 0.50
287 A17 1000r on 20pa on 4k 2.50 2.50
288 A17 1000r on 1pi on 10k 2.50 2.50
289 A8 1000r on 5pi on 50k 2.50 2.50
290 A9 5000r on 7pi on 70k 2.50 2.50
291 A10 10,000r on 10pi on 1r 12.50 12.50
  a. Inverted surcharge 25.00 25.00
  b. Pair, one without surcharge 20.00 20.00
292 A10 20,000r on 10pi on 1r 2.50 2.50
  a. Inverted surcharge 25.00 25.00
  b. Pair, one without surcharge 25.00 25.00
  Nos. 284D-292 (9) 35.00 35.00

On Nos. 208-212
293 A14 1000r on 20pa on 5k 2.50 2.50
294 A11 5000r on 1½pi on 15k 2.50 2.50
295 A8 5000r on 2pi on 20k 2.50 2.50
296 A11 5000r on 2½pi on 25k 2.50 2.50
297 A11 5000r on 3½pi on 35k 2.50 2.50
  Nos. 293-297 (5) 12.50 12.50

On Nos. 228, 230-231
298 A14 1000r on 15pa on 3k 1.00 1.00
299 A13 10,000r on 50pi on 5r 65.00 65.00
300 A13 10,000r on 100pi on 10r 92.50 92.50
301 A13 20,000r on 50pi on 5r 1.00 1.00
302 A13 20,000r on 100pi on 10r 92.50 92.50
  Nos. 298-302 (5) 252.00 252.00

On Stamps of South Russia Denikin Issue
Imperf
303 A5 5000r on 5k org 1.00 1.00
  a. Inverted surcharge 10.00
304 A5 5000r on 10k green 1.00 1.00
305 A5 5000r on 15k red 1.00 1.00
306 A5 5000r on 35k lt bl 1.00 1.00
307 A5 5000r on 70k dk blue 1.00 1.00
307A A5 10,000r on 70k dk blue 50.00 50.00
308 A6 10,000r on 1r brn & red 1.00 1.00
309 A6 10,000r on 2r gray vio & yel 1.00 1.00
  a. Inverted surcharge 30.00 30.00
310 A6 10,000r on 3r dull rose & grn 3.50 3.50
311 A6 10,000r on 5r slate & vio 2.50 2.50
312 A6 10,000r on 7r gray grn & rose 100.00 100.00
313 A6 10,000r on 10r red & gray 2.00 2.00
314 A6 20,000r on 1r brn & red 1.00 1.00
315 A6 20,000r on 2r gray vio & yel (Bl) 35.00 35.00
  a. Inverted surcharge 30.00 30.00
315B A6 20,000r on 2r gray vio & yel (Bk) 1.00 1.00
316 A6 20,000r on 3r dull rose & grn (Bl) 50.00 50.00
316A A6 20,000r on 3r dull rose & grn (Bk) 30.00 30.00
317 A6 20,000r on 5r slate & vio 1.00 1.00
318 A6 20,000r on 7r gray grn & rose 60.00 60.00
319 A6 20,000r on 10r red & gray 1.00 1.00
  Nos. 303-319 (20) 344.00 344.00

Trident Stamps of Ukraine Surcharged in Blue, Red, Black or Brown

1921   Perf. 14, 14½x15
320 A14 10,000r on 1k org .45 .45
321 A14 10,000r on 2k grn 5.00 5.00
322 A14 10,000r on 3k red .45 .45
  a. Inverted surcharge 10.00 10.00
323 A15 10,000r on 4k car .45 .45
324 A14 10,000r on 5k cl .45 .45
325 A14 10,000r on 7k lt bl .45 .45
  a. Inverted surcharge 10.00 10.00
326 A15 10,000r on 10k dk bl .45 .45
  a. Inverted surcharge 10.00 10.00
327 A14 10,000r on 10k on 7k lt bl .45 .45
  a. Inverted surcharge 10.00 10.00

328 A8 20,000r on 20k bl & car (Br) .45 .45
  a. Inverted surcharge 10.00 10.00
329 A8 20,000r on 20k bl & buff (Dk) .45 .45
  a. Inverted surcharge 35.00 35.00
330 A11 20,000r on 20k on 14k bl & rose .45 .45
331 A11 20,000r on 35k red brn & grn 75.00 75.00
332 A8 20,000r on 50k brn vio & grn .45 .45
  a. Inverted surcharge 10.00 10.00
  Nos. 320-332 (13) 84.95 84.95

Imperf
333 A14 10,000r on 1k org .75 .75
  a. Inverted surcharge 10.00
334 A14 10,000r on 2k grn 2.00 2.00
335 A14 10,000r on 3k red .75 .75
336 A8 20,000r on 20k bl & car .75 .75
337 A11 20,000r on 35k red brn & grn 40.00 40.00
338 A8 20,000r on 50k brn vio & grn 2.00 2.00
  Nos. 333-338 (6) 46.25 46.25

There are several varieties of the trident surcharge on Nos. 320 to 338.

Same Surcharge on Russian Stamps
On Stamps of 1909-18
Perf. 14x14½
338A A14 10,000r on 1k dl org yel 2.50 2.50
339 A14 10,000r on 2k dl grn 2.50 2.50
340 A14 10,000r on 3k car .50 .50
341 A15 10,000r on 4k car .50 .50
342 A14 10,000r on 5k dk cl .50 .50
343 A14 10,000r on 7k blue .50 .50
344 A15 10,000r on 10k dk bl 2.50 2.50
344A A14 10,000r on 10k on 7k bl 3.75 3.75
344B A11 20,000r on 14k dk bl & car 35.00 35.00
345 A11 20,000r on 15k red brn & dp bl .50 .50
346 A8 20,000r on 20k dl bl & dk car .50 .50
347 A11 20,000r on 20k on 14k dk bl & car 3.50 3.50
348 A11 20,000r on 35k red brn & grn 2.00 2.00
349 A8 20,000r on 50k brn vio & grn .50 .50
349A A11 20,000r on 70k brn & red org 2.50 2.50
  Nos. 338A-349A (15) 57.75 57.75

On Stamps of 1917-18
Imperf
350 A14 10,000r on 1k org .75 .75
351 A14 10,000r on 2k gray grn .75 .75
352 A14 10,000r on 3k red .75 .75
353 A15 10,000r on 4k car 40.00 40.00
354 A14 10,000r on 5k claret .75 .75
355 A11 20,000r on 15k red brn & dp bl .75 .75
356 A8 20,000r on 50k brn vio & grn 2.00 2.00
357 A11 20,000r on 70k brn & org .75 .75
  Nos. 350-357 (8) 46.50 46.50

Same Surcharge on Stamps of Russian Offices in Turkey
On Nos. 40-45
Perf. 14½x15
358 A12 10,000r on 5pa on 1k 5.00 5.00
359 A12 10,000r on 10pa on 2k 5.00 5.00
360 A12 10,000r on 20pa on 4k 5.00 5.00
361 A12 10,000r on 1pi on 10k 5.00 5.00
362 A12 20,000r on 50k 5.00 5.00
363 A12 20,000r on 7pi on 70k 5.00 5.00
  Nos. 358-363 (6) 30.00 30.00

On Nos. 201-206
364 A16 10,000r on 5pa on 1k 6.00 6.00
365 A16 10,000r on 10pa on 2k 6.00 6.00
366 A17 10,000r on 20pa on 4k 6.00 6.00
367 A17 10,000r on 1pi on 10k 6.00 6.00
368 A8 20,000r on 5pi on 50k 6.00 6.00
369 A9 20,000r on 7pi on 70k 6.00 6.00
  Nos. 364-369 (6) 36.00 36.00

On Nos. 228, 208-212, Stamps of 1912-13
370 A11 10,000r on 15pa on 3k 5.00 5.00
371 A14 10,000r on 20pa on 5k 5.00 5.00
372 A11 20,000r on 15k 5.00 5.00
373 A8 20,000r on 2pi on 20k 5.00
374 A11 20,000r on 2½pi on 25k 5.00
375 A11 20,000r on 3½pi on 35k 5.00

Same Surcharge on Stamp of South Russia, Crimea Issue
376 A8 20,000r on 5r on 20k bl & car 750.00
  Nos. 370-376 (7) 780.00 15.00

SAAR

'sär

LOCATION — On the Franco-German border southeast of Luxembourg
GOVT. — A German state
POP. — 1,400,000 (1959)
AREA — 991 sq. mi.
CAPITAL — Saarbrücken

A former German territory, the Saar was administered by the League of Nations 1920-35. After a January 12, 1935, plebiscite, it returned to Germany, and the use of German stamps was resumed.

100 Pfennig = 1 Mark
100 Centimes = 1 Franc (1921)

German Stamps of
1906-19 Overprinted

Nos. 1-16 exist in three types. Type I: larger letters, "Sarre" 10.7mm wide, no control mark below bar. Type II: as Type I, control mark (a short, thin line) below bar. Type III: smaller letters, "Sarre" 10.5mm wide, control mark below bar.

Type I

Perf. 14, 14½

1920, Jan. 30   **Wmk. 125**

1	A22	2pf gray	1.60	4.50
		Never hinged	4.50	
		On cover		8.00
c.		Inverted overprint	325.00	550.00
		Never hinged	525.00	
		On cover		725.00
2	A22	2½pf gray	9.50	27.50
		Never hinged	24.00	
		On cover		35.00
c.		Inverted overprint	350.00	650.00
		Never hinged	600.00	
		On cover		800.00
d.		2½pf deep greenish gray or bronze	97.50	250.00
		Never hinged	200.00	
		On cover		325.00
3	A16	3pf brown	1.00	2.75
		Never hinged	2.25	
		On cover		4.00
c.		Inverted overprint	325.00	550.00
		Never hinged	525.00	
		On cover		725.00
4	A16	5pf deep green	.50	1.00
		Never hinged	.95	
		On cover		1.60
c.		Inverted overprint	600.00	
		Never hinged	1,050.	
d.		5pf dark bluish green	1.40	3.60
		Never hinged	2.60	
		On cover		5.00
5	A22	7½pf orange	.65	1.75
		Never hinged	1.10	
		On cover		3.00
c.		Inverted overprint	—	800.00
		Never hinged		
d.		7½pf red orange	3.40	11.00
		Never hinged	6.50	
		On cover		20.00
e.		7½pf pale reddish orange	2.00	6.25
		Never hinged	3.25	
		On cover		13.50
6	A16	10pf carmine	.55	1.25
		Never hinged	1.10	
		On cover		1.60
c.		Inverted overprint	550.00	1,050.
		Never hinged	975.00	
d.		Double overprint	725.00	1,200.
		Never hinged	1,200.	
		On cover		1,450.
e.		10pf rose red	2.00	4.50
		Never hinged	3.75	
		On cover		6.75
f.		As "e," double overprint	750.00	1,250.
		Never hinged	1,200.	
		On cover		1,450.
g.		10pf scarlet red	130.00	240.00
		Never hinged	240.00	
		On cover		280.00
7	A22	15pf dk violet	.50	1.00
		Never hinged	1.10	
		On cover		1.60
c.		Double overprint	800.00	1,450.
		Never hinged	1,350.	
		On cover		1,500.
d.		15pf blackish violet	7.25	17.00
		Never hinged	14.50	
		On cover		28.00
e.		15pf bluish violet	20.00	110.00
		Never hinged	40.00	
		On cover		170.00
8	A16	20pf blue violet	.50	1.00
		Never hinged	1.10	
		On cover		1.60
c.		Double overprint	600.00	950.00
		Never hinged	950.00	
		On cover		1,200.
9	A16	25pf red org & blk, *yellow*	9.50	20.00
		Never hinged	24.00	
		On cover		28.00
c.		Inverted overprint	800.00	2,400.
		Never hinged	1,350.	

d.		25pf yel org & blk, *yellow*	30.00	110.00
		Never hinged	57.50	
		On cover		135.00
10	A16	30pf org & blk, *yel buff*	17.50	35.00
		Never hinged	35.00	
		On cover		57.50
d.		30pf org & blk, *org buff*	240.00	500.00
		Never hinged	400.00	
		On cover		725.00
11	A22	35pf red brown	.55	1.25
		Never hinged	1.10	
		On cover		1.60
c.		Inverted overprint	475.00	1,050.
		Never hinged	900.00	
		On cover		1,200.
12	A16	40pf dp lake & blk	.55	1.25
		Never hinged	1.20	
		On cover		1.60
c.		Inverted overprint	475.00	1,050.
		Never hinged	900.00	
		On cover		1,200.
d.		40pf reddish lake & blk	5.50	8.50
		Never hinged	11.00	
		On cover		13.50
13	A16	50pf pur & blk, *yel buff*	.55	1.60
		Never hinged	1.45	
		On cover		1.75
c.		Inverted overprint	400.00	725.00
		Never hinged	725.00	
		On cover		800.00
d.		50pf pur & blk, *org buff*	22.00	75.00
		Never hinged	50.00	
		On cover		115.00
14	A16	60pf dp gray lilac	.55	1.25
		Never hinged	1.10	
		On cover		2.00
c.		60pf red lilac	300.00	750.00
		Never hinged	600.00	
		On cover		1,350.
15	A16	75pf green & blk	.55	1.25
		Never hinged	1.00	
		On cover		2.50
c.		Inverted overprint	240.00	400.00
		Never hinged	400.00	
		On cover		500.00
16	A16	80pf lake & blk, *rose*	190.00	275.00
		Never hinged	525.00	
		On cover		1,050.

Type II

1a	A22	2pf gray	160.00	450.00
		Never hinged	375.00	
		On cover		600.00
2a	A22	2½pf olive gray	525.00	975.00
		Never hinged	1,050.	
		On cover		2,500.
2e	A22	2½pf dp grnsh gray or bronze	1,600.	3,400.
		Never hinged	3,400.	—
3a	A16	3pf brown	175.00	360.00
		Never hinged	340.00	
		On cover		575.00
4a	A16	5pf deep green	11.00	65.00
		Never hinged	19.50	
		On cover		100.00
4e	A16	5pf dark bluish green	55.00	145.00
		Never hinged	115.00	
		On cover		200.00
5a	A22	7½pf yellow orange	50.00	180.00
		Never hinged	100.00	
		On cover		260.00
5f	A22	7½pf red orange	1,600.	3,400.
		On cover	3,400.	—
12a	A16	40pf deep lake & blk	1.80	6.00
		Never hinged	4.50	
		On cover		10.00
13a	A16	50pf pur & blk, *yel buff*	1.60	5.25
		Never hinged	3.75	
		On cover		11.00

Type III

1b	A22	2pf gray	5.00	20.00
		Never hinged	11.50	
		On cover		32.50
d.		Double overprint	2,000.	2,600.
		Never hinged	3,500.	
2b	A22	2½pf olive gray	1.60	5.75
		Never hinged	4.50	
		On cover		8.00
2f	A22	2½pf dp grnsh gray or bronze	52.50	115.00
		Never hinged	92.50	
		On cover		145.00
3b	A16	3pf brown	1.30	4.50
		Never hinged	2.60	
		On cover		6.50
4b	A16	5pf deep green	.50	1.00
		Never hinged	1.00	
		On cover		1.60
f.		Double overprint	800.00	1,450.
		Never hinged	1,450.	
4g	A16	5pf dk bluish green	1.30	3.75
		Never hinged	2.10	
		On cover		5.00
h.		Double overprint	1,000.	1,450.
		Never hinged	1,800.	
5b	A22	7½pf yellow orange	4.75	25.00
		Never hinged	10.00	
		On cover		40.00
5g	A22	7½pf red orange	24.00	65.00
		Never hinged	47.50	
		On cover		100.00
5h	A22	7½pf pale reddish org	16.00	2,400.
		Never hinged	32.50	
		On cover		3,600.
6b	A16	10pf carmine	.60	1.10
		Never hinged	1.10	
		On cover		1.50
6h	A16	10pf rose red	1.75	6.00
		Never hinged	3.50	
		On cover		9.00
6i	A16	10pf scarlet red	67.50	120.00
		Never hinged	130.00	
		On cover		200.00

7b	A22	15pf dk violet	.50	1.10
		Never hinged	1.10	
		On cover		1.50
7f	A22	15pf blackish violet	1.50	5.00
		Never hinged	3.00	
		On cover		8.00
8b	A16	20pf blue violet	.50	1.25
		Never hinged	1.10	
		On cover		2.00
9b	A16	25pf red org & blk, *yellow*	115.00	350.00
		Never hinged	260.00	
		On cover		575.00
9e	A16	25pf yel org & blk, *yel*	60.00	120.00
		Never hinged	120.00	
		On cover		180.00
10b	A16	30pf org & blk, *yel buff*	45.00	100.00
		Never hinged	90.00	
		On cover		120.00
10c	A16	30pf org & blk, *org buff*	210.00	500.00
		Never hinged	400.00	
		On cover		725.00
11b	A22	35pf red brown	16.00	47.50
		Never hinged	32.00	
		On cover		110.00
12b	A16	40pf deep lake & blk	2.50	8.00
		Never hinged	4.50	
		On cover		12.00
e.		Inverted overprint	575.00	975.00
		Never hinged	975.00	
		On cover		1,200.
13b	A16	50pf pur & blk, *yel buff*	.60	1.10
		Never hinged	1.45	
		On cover		2.00
14b	A16	60pf dp gray lilac	.50	1.10
		Never hinged	1.00	
		On cover		1.60
15b	A16	75pf green & blk	.65	1.20
		Never hinged	1.15	
		On cover		1.60
d.		Double overprint	2,000.	—
		Never hinged	3,500.	
16b	A16	80pf lake & blk, *rose*	200.00	300.00
		Never hinged	575.00	
		On cover		1,000.

Overprinted

Type I

17	A17	1m carmine rose (25x17 holes)	27.50	40.00
		Never hinged	57.50	
		On cover		115.00
a.		Inverted overprint	725.00	1,450.
		Never hinged	1,200.	
		On cover		1,800.
b.		Double overprint	800.00	1,450.
		Never hinged	1,350.	
		On cover		1,800.
c.		1m carmine rose (26x17 holes)	1,050.	1,550.
		Never hinged	2,800.	
		On cover		3,250.
d.		As "c," double overprint	8,000.	15,000.
		Never hinged	14,500.	

Type II

17f	A17	1m carmine rose	40.00	80.00
		Never hinged	100.00	
		On cover		160.00
17g	A17	1m Inverted overprint	975.00	1,800.
		Never hinged	1,600.	
		On cover		1,800.
17h	A17	1m Double overprint	1,050.	1,950.
		Never hinged	1,800.	
		On cover		
		Nos. 1-17 (17)	262.05	417.35

The 3m type A19 exists overprinted like No. 17, but was not issued. Value, $16,000 unused, $33,000 never hinged.
Overprint forgeries exist.

Bavarian Stamps of
1914-16 Overprinted

Perf. 14x14½

1920, Mar. 1   **Wmk. 95**

19	A10	2pf gray	900.00	4,750.
		Never hinged	2,000.	
		On cover		6,500.
20	A10	3pf brown	80.00	650.00
		Never hinged	225.00	
		On cover		975.00
21	A10	5pf yellow grn	.75	1.60
		Never hinged	1.60	
		On cover		5.00
a.		Double overprint	800.00	
b.		Pair, one stamp without ovpt.	—	—
22	A10	7½pf green	32.50	275.00
		Never hinged	72.50	
		On cover		450.00

23	A10	10pf carmine rose	.75	1.60
		Never hinged	1.60	
		On cover		4.00
a.		Double overprint	325.00	650.00
		Never hinged	500.00	
b.		Pair, one stamp without ovpt.	—	
		Never hinged		
24	A10	15pf vermilion	.95	1.90
		Never hinged	1.60	
		On cover		5.00
a.		Double overprint	400.00	800.00
		Never hinged	575.00	
25	A10	15pf carmine	7.25	16.00
		Never hinged	16.00	
		On cover		24.00
26	A10	20pf blue	.65	1.60
		Never hinged	1.60	
		On cover		4.00
a.		Double overprint	325.00	650.00
		Never hinged	500.00	
27	A10	25pf gray	11.00	16.00
		Never hinged	22.50	
		On cover		32.50
28	A10	30pf orange	6.50	11.00
		Never hinged	14.50	
		On cover		24.00
30	A10	40pf olive green	10.50	16.00
		Never hinged	21.00	
		On cover		32.50
31	A10	50pf red brown	2.00	4.50
		Never hinged	4.50	
		On cover		5.75
a.		Double overprint	350.00	650.00
		Never hinged	575.00	
32	A10	60pf dark green	3.25	8.00
		Never hinged	6.50	
		On cover		24.00
a.		60pf blackish green on thick paper	3.40	10.00
		Never hinged	7.25	
		On cover		28.00

Overprinted

Perf. 11½

35	A11	1m brown	24.00	35.00
		Never hinged	52.50	
		On cover		130.00
a.		1m dark brown	16.00	32.50
		Never hinged	40.00	
		On cover		120.00
36	A11	2m dk gray violet	60.00	140.00
		Never hinged	130.00	
		On cover		350.00
a.		2m dk purple violet	1,850.	2,900.
		Never hinged	3,250.	
		On cover		3,250.
37	A11	3m scarlet	120.00	160.00
		Never hinged	275.00	
		On cover		1,450.
		Nos. 35-37 (3)	204.00	335.00

Overprinted

38	A12	5m deep blue	800.00	875.00
		Never hinged	2,000.	
		On cover		3,200.
39	A12	10m yellow green	140.00	250.00
		Never hinged	360.00	
		On cover		1,000.
a.		Double overprint	3,400.	8,500.
		Never hinged	6,000.	

Nos. 19, 20 and 22 were not officially issued, but were available for postage. Examples are known legitimately used on cover. The 20m type A12 was also overprinted in small quantity. Values: unused $125,000; never hinged $200,000.
No. 21a is valued without gum.
Overprint forgeries exist.

German Stamps of
1906-20 Overprinted

Perf. 14, 14½

1920, Mar. 26   **Wmk. 125**

41	A16	5pf green	.25	.50
		Never hinged	.50	
		On cover		3.00
a.		Inverted overprint	16.00	160.00
		Never hinged	32.50	
		On cover		240.00

42	A16	5pf red brown	.50	.80
		Never hinged	1.10	
		On cover		2.40
b.		5pf brown	4.00	13.00
		Never hinged	10.00	
		On cover		20.00
43	A16	10pf carmine	.25	.50
		Never hinged		
		On cover		3.00
a.		Inverted overprint	47.50	325.00
		Never hinged	97.50	
		On cover		500.00
44	A16	10pf orange	.45	.50
		Never hinged	1.10	
		On cover		2.40
a.		Inverted overprint	16.00	
		Never hinged	28.00	
b.		Double ovpt., never hinged	80.00	
45	A22	15pf dk violet	.25	.50
		Never hinged	.65	
		On cover		3.00
a.		Inverted overprint	27.50	240.00
		Never hinged	55.00	
		On cover		325.00
46	A16	20pf blue violet	.25	.50
		Never hinged	.65	
		On cover		3.00
a.		Inverted overprint	35.00	—
		Never hinged	72.50	
47	A16	20pf green	.95	.50
		Never hinged	1.90	
		On cover		2.50
a.		Double overprint, never hinged	80.00	
48	A16	30pf org & blk, *buff*	.40	.50
		Never hinged	1.00	
		On cover		3.00
a.		Double overprint	65.00	
		Never hinged	120.00	
b.		Inverted overprint	—	
		Never hinged	—	
49	A16	30pf dull blue	.55	.75
		Never hinged	1.40	
		On cover		3.25
50	A16	40pf lake & blk	.30	.50
		Never hinged	.65	
		On cover		3.00
51	A16	40pf car rose	1.00	.75
		Never hinged	2.00	
		On cover		3.25
52	A16	50pf pur & blk, *buff*	.55	.50
		Never hinged	1.10	
		On cover		3.00
a.		Double overprint	65.00	400.00
		Never hinged	120.00	
c.		50pf pur & blk, *orange buff*	3.25	22.50
		Never hinged	6.50	
		On cover		40.00
53	A16	60pf red violet	.65	.50
		Never hinged	1.60	
		On cover		3.00
a.		Inverted overprint	80.00	325.00
		Never hinged	175.00	
		On cover		500.00
54	A16	75pf green & blk	.75	.50
		Never hinged	1.60	
		On cover		3.00
a.		Double overprint	110.00	400.00
		Never hinged	200.00	
b.		Inverted overprint	110.00	
		Never hinged	240.00	
55	A17	1.25m green	2.75	1.25
		Never hinged	5.75	
		On cover		7.25
a.		Inverted overprint	95.00	
		Never hinged	200.00	
56	A17	1.50m yellow brn	2.00	1.25
		Never hinged	4.50	
		On cover		7.25
a.		Inverted overprint	95.00	800.00
		Never hinged	200.00	
57	A21	2.50m lilac red	4.75	13.50
		Never hinged	9.50	
		On cover		24.00
a.		2.50m lilac rose	12.50	62.50
		Never hinged	27.50	
		On cover		80.00
b.		2.50m lilac	100.00	925.00
		Never hinged	200.00	
		On cover		1,200.
c.		2.50m brown lilac	10.00	55.00
		Never hinged	20.00	
		On cover		85.00
58	A16	4m black & rose	8.75	22.50
		Never hinged	20.00	
		On cover		72.50
a.		Double overprint, never hinged	110.00	
		Nos. 41-58 (18)	25.35	46.30

On No. 57 the overprint is placed vertically at each side of the stamp.

Counterfeit overprints exist.

Germany No. 90
Surcharged in Black

1921, Feb.

65	A16	20pf on 75pf grn & blk	.40	1.25
		Never hinged	1.20	
		On cover		4.00
a.		Inverted surcharge	24.00	72.50
		Never hinged	50.00	
		On cover		110.00
b.		Double surcharge	55.00	125.00
		Never hinged	100.00	
		On cover		160.00

Germany No. 120
Surcharged

66	A22	5m on 15pf vio brn	5.50	16.00
		Never hinged	20.00	
		On cover		80.00
67	A22	10m on 15pf vio brn	6.00	19.00
		Never hinged	20.00	
		On cover		100.00
		Nos. 65-67 (3)	11.90	36.25

Forgeries exist of Nos. 66-67.

Old Mill near Mettlach — A3

Miner at Work — A4

Entrance to Reden Mine — A5

Saar River Traffic — A6

Saar River near Mettlach — A7

Slag Pile at Völklingen — A8

Signal Bridge, Saarbrücken — A9

Church at Mettlach — A10

"Old Bridge," Saarbrücken A11

Cable Railway at Ferne — A12

Colliery Shafthead — A13

Saarbrücken City Hall — A14

Pottery at Mettlach — A15

St. Ludwig's Cathedral — A16

Presidential Residence, Saarbrücken A17

Burbach Steelworks, Dillingen A18

1921   Unwmk.   Typo.   Perf. 12½

68	A3	5pf ol grn & vio	.35	.50
		Never hinged	.65	
		On cover		5.00
a.		Tête bêche pair	3.50	20.00
		Never hinged	7.25	
		On cover		65.00
c.		Center inverted	100.00	340.00
		Never hinged	210.00	
d.		Center printed in green	85.00	300.00
		Never hinged	190.00	
		On cover		500.00
69	A4	10pf org & ultra	.35	.50
		Never hinged	.80	
		On cover		5.00
70	A5	20pf grn & slate	.35	1.00
		Never hinged	.65	
		On cover		11.50
a.		Tête bêche pair	6.50	40.00
		Never hinged	12.50	
		On cover		120.00
c.		Perf. 10½	22.50	225.00
		Never hinged	40.00	
		On cover		280.00
d.		As "c," tête bêche pair	140.00	675.00
		Never hinged	200.00	
		On cover		—
71	A6	25pf brn & dk bl	.40	.80
		Never hinged	.85	
		On cover		12.00
a.		Tête bêche pair	7.25	40.00
		Never hinged	14.50	
		On cover		125.00
72	A7	30pf gray grn & brn	.40	.75
		Never hinged	.85	
		On cover		7.50
a.		Tête bêche pair	12.00	60.00
		Never hinged	22.50	
		On cover		200.00
c.		30pf ol grn & blk	2.40	22.50
		Never hinged	5.00	
		On cover		00.00
d.		As "c," tête bêche pair	12.50	72.50
		Never hinged	24.00	
		On cover		225.00
e.		As "c," imperf., pair	120.00	
		Never hinged	250.00	
73	A8	40pf vermilion	.40	.50
		Never hinged	.85	
		On cover		5.00
a.		Tête bêche pair	19.00	80.00
		Never hinged	36.00	
		On cover		250.00
74	A9	50pf gray & blk	.95	4.00
		Never hinged	2.00	
		On cover		12.50
75	A10	60pf red & dk brn	1.60	3.50
		Never hinged	3.75	
		On cover		20.00
76	A11	80pf deep blue	.75	1.00
		Never hinged	1.40	
		On cover		12.00
a.		Tête bêche pair	21.00	110.00
		Never hinged	42.50	
		On cover		200.00
77	A12	1m lt red & blk	.80	1.60
		Never hinged	1.60	
		On cover		12.00

a.		1m grn & blk	450.00	
		Never hinged	1,000.	
78	A13	1.25m lt brn & blk	.95	2.00
		Never hinged	2.40	
		On cover		20.00
79	A14	2m red & black	2.40	4.00
		Never hinged	6.00	
		On cover		20.00
80	A15	3m brn & dk ol	3.25	9.50
		Never hinged	8.00	
		On cover		28.00
a.		Center inverted	125.00	
		Never hinged	300.00	
b.		3m orange brown & black	27.50	85.00
		Never hinged	55.00	
		On cover		125.00
81	A16	5m yellow & vio	12.00	24.00
		Never hinged	20.00	
		On cover		90.00
82	A17	10m grn & red brn	12.00	24.00
		Never hinged	25.00	
		On cover		115.00
83	A18	25m ultra, red & blk	32.50	80.00
		Never hinged	90.00	
		On cover		325.00
a.		25m deep gray blue, deep cinnamon & black	2,400.	3,750.
		Never hinged	3,750.	
		On cover		
		Nos. 68-83 (16)	69.45	157.65

Values are for tête bêche pairs. Horizontal pairs sell for about twice as much.

The ultramarine ink on No. 69 appears to be brown where it overlays the orange.

Exist imperf but were not regularly issued. Value $1,400.

Nos. 70-83 Surcharged in Red, Blue or Black

a

b

c

1921, May 1

85	A5(a)	3c on 20pf (R)	.40	.50
		Never hinged	.75	
		On cover		2.00
a.		Tête bêche pair	4.75	32.50
		Never hinged	10.00	
		On cover		100.00
b.		Inverted surcharge	95.00	
		Never hinged	180.00	
d.		Perf. 10½	4.75	160.00
		Never hinged	12.50	
		On cover		225.00
e.		As "d," tête bêche pair	21.00	—
		Never hinged	40.00	
86	A6(a)	5c on 25pf (R)	.40	.50
		Never hinged	.85	
		On cover		.85
a.		Tête bêche pair	95.00	400.00
		Never hinged	150.00	
		On cover		1,250.
87	A7(a)	10c on 30pf (Bl)	.40	.50
		Never hinged	.85	
		On cover		1.60
a.		Tête bêche pair	4.75	25.00
		Never hinged	9.75	
		On cover		72.50
b.		Inverted surcharge	95.00	450.00
		Never hinged	180.00	
c.		Double surcharge	95.00	475.00
		Never hinged	180.00	
		On cover		—
88	A8(a)	15c on 40pf (Bk)	.50	.50
		Never hinged	1.20	
		On cover		1.60
a.		Tête bêche pair	95.00	400.00
		Never hinged	160.00	
		On cover		1,200.
b.		Inverted surcharge	95.00	450.00
		Never hinged	180.00	

89	A9(a)	20c on 50pf		
		(R)	.40	.50
	Never hinged		.85	
	On cover			1.25
90	A10(a)	25c on 60pf		
		(Bl)	.50	.50
	Never hinged		1.10	
	On cover			1.25
91	A11(a)	30c on 80pf		
		(Bk)	1.60	1.00
	Never hinged		4.00	
	On cover			2.00
a.	Tête bêche pair		12.50	60.00
	Never hinged		25.00	
	On cover			225.00
c.	Inverted surcharge		140.00	600.00
	Never hinged		240.00	
d.	Double surcharge		140.00	600.00
	Never hinged		250.00	
92	A12(a)	40c on 1m		
		(Bl)	2.00	.50
	Never hinged		5.75	
	On cover			2.00
a.	Inverted surcharge		110.00	450.00
	Never hinged		180.00	
	On cover			—
b.	Double surcharge		140.00	600.00
	Never hinged		250.00	
93	A13(a)	50c on 1.25m		
		(Bk)	3.25	1.00
	Never hinged		10.00	
	On cover			3.00
a.	Double surcharge		275.00	950.00
	Never hinged		500.00	
b.	Perf. 10½		72.50	140.00
	Never hinged		145.00	
	On cover			325.00
94	A14(a)	75c on 2m		
		(Bl)	4.75	2.00
	Never hinged		16.00	
	On cover			6.50
a.	Inverted surcharge		110.00	
	Never hinged		200.00	
95	A15(b)	1fr on 3m		
		(Bl)	4.50	2.40
	Never hinged		16.00	
	On cover			5.75
a.	On No. 80b		22.50	125.00
	Never hinged		60.00	
	On cover			260.00
96	A16(b)	2fr on 5m		
		(Bl)	12.00	6.50
	Never hinged		36.00	
	On cover			16.00
97	A17(b)	3fr on 10m		
		(Bk)	17.50	25.00
	Never hinged		52.50	
	On cover			72.50
b.	Double surcharge		200.00	800.00
	Never hinged		325.00	
98	A18(c)	5fr on 25m		
		(Bl)	17.50	35.00
	Never hinged		52.50	
	On cover			250.00
	Nos. 85-98 (14)		65.70	76.40

In these surcharges the period is occasionally missing and there are various wrong font and defective letters.

Values for tête bêche pairs are for vertical pairs. Horizontal pairs sell for about twice as much.

Nos. 85-89, 91, 93, 97-98 exist imperforate but were not regularly issued.

Cable Railway, Ferne — A19

Miner at Work — A20

"Old Bridge," Saarbrücken A21

Saarbrücken City Hall — A22

Slag Pile at Völklingen A23

Pottery at Mettlach — A24

Saar River Traffic — A25

St. Ludwig's Cathedral A26

Colliery Shafthead A27

Mettlach Church — A28

Burbach Steelworks, Dillingen A29

Perf. 12½x13½, 13½x12½

1922-23				Typo.
99	A19	3c ol grn & straw	.40	.65
	Never hinged		.75	
	On cover			2.50
100	A20	5c orange & blk	.40	.40
	Never hinged		.75	
	On cover			1.25
101	A21	10c blue green	.40	.40
	Never hinged		.75	
	On cover			1.25
102	A19	15c deep brown	1.25	.40
	Never hinged		3.00	
	On cover			1.60
103	A19	15c orange ('23)	2.40	.40
	Never hinged		7.00	
	On cover			2.50
104	A22	20c dk bl & lem	13.50	.40
	Never hinged		40.00	
	On cover			2.50
105	A22	20c brt bl & straw		
		('23)	4.00	.40
	Never hinged		9.50	
	On cover			2.50
106	A22	25c red & yellow	6.50	2.25
	Never hinged		16.00	
	On cover			7.50
107	A22	25c mag & straw		
		('23)	2.40	.40
	Never hinged		7.00	
	On cover			1.25
108	A23	30c carmine & yel	2.00	2.10
	Never hinged		5.25	
	On cover			3.25
109	A24	40c brown & yel	1.60	.40
	Never hinged		4.00	
	On cover			1.60
110	A25	50c dk bl & straw	.95	.40
	Never hinged		2.00	
	On cover			1.60
111	A24	75c dp grn & straw	13.50	24.00
	Never hinged		40.00	
	On cover			65.00

112	A24	75c blk & straw		
		('23)	32.50	3.25
	Never hinged		77.50	
	On cover			7.25
113	A26	1fr brown red	2.40	.80
	Never hinged		10.00	
	On cover			2.50
114	A27	2fr deep violet	6.50	3.25
	Never hinged		16.00	
	On cover			5.00
115	A28	3fr org & dk grn	24.00	6.50
	Never hinged		65.00	
	On cover			8.50
116	A29	5fr brn & red brn	24.00	45.00
	Never hinged		65.00	
	On cover			100.00
	Nos. 99-116 (18)		138.70	91.40

Nos. 99-116 exist imperforate but were not regularly issued.
For overprints see Nos. O1-O15.

Madonna of Blieskastel — A30

1925, Apr. 9 Photo. Perf. 13½x12½
Size: 23x27mm

118	A30	45c lake brown	2.75	5.25
	Never hinged		7.00	
	On cover			20.00

Size: 31½x36mm
Perf. 12

119	A30	10fr black brown	16.00	24.00
	Never hinged		30.00	
	On cover			90.00

Nos. 118-119 exist imperforate but were not regularly issued.
For overprint see No. 154.

Market Fountain, St. Johann — A31

View of Saar Valley A32

Colliery Shafthead A35

Burbach Steelworks A36

Designs: 15c, 75c, View of Saar Valley. 20c, 40c, 90c, Scene from Saarlouis fortifications. 25c, 50c, Tholey Abbey.

1927-32				Perf. 13½
120	A31	10c deep brown	.75	.50
	Never hinged		1.40	
	On cover			1.60
121	A32	15c olive black	.40	1.10
	Never hinged		1.10	
	On cover			3.25
122	A32	20c brown orange	.40	.50
	Never hinged		1.10	
	On cover			1.60
123	A32	25c bluish slate	.75	.50
	Never hinged		1.25	
	On cover			3.25
124	A31	30c olive green	.95	.50
	Never hinged		1.60	
	On cover			1.60
125	A32	40c olive brown	.75	.50
	Never hinged		1.40	
	On cover			3.25
126	A32	50c magenta	.95	.50
	Never hinged		2.00	
	On cover			1.60

127	A35	60c red org ('30)	4.00	.55
	Never hinged		10.00	
	On cover			3.25
128	A32	75c brown violet	.75	.50
	Never hinged		1.30	
129	A35	80c red orange	2.40	8.75
	Never hinged		6.50	
	On cover			20.00
130	A32	90c deep red		
		('32)	12.00	17.50
	Never hinged		37.50	
	On cover			57.50
131	A35	1fr violet	2.40	.50
	Never hinged		5.75	
	On cover			2.50
132	A36	1.50fr sapphire	6.50	.50
	Never hinged		17.50	
	On cover			2.50
133	A36	2fr brown red	6.50	.50
	Never hinged		17.50	
	On cover			3.25
134	A36	3fr dk olive grn	14.50	1.25
	Never hinged		35.00	
	On cover			5.00
135	A36	5fr deep brown	14.50	7.25
	Never hinged		35.00	
	On cover			20.00
	Nos. 120-135 (16)		68.50	41.40

For surcharges and overprints see Nos. 136-153, O16-O26.

Nos. 126 and 129 Surcharged

1930-34

136	A32	40c on 50c mag ('34)	1.60	1.60
	Never hinged		4.00	
	On cover			10.00
137	A35	60c on 80c red orange	2.00	2.40
	Never hinged		5.00	
	On cover			8.00

Plebiscite Issue

Stamps of 1925-32 Ovptd. in Various Colors

Perf. 13½, 13½x13, 13x13½

1934, Nov. 1				
139	A31	10c brown (Br)	.40	.55
	Never hinged		1.25	
	On cover			2.10
140	A32	15c black grn (G)	.40	.55
	Never hinged		1.25	
	On cover			2.10
141	A32	20c brown org		
		(O)	.65	1.40
	Never hinged		1.60	
	On cover			3.00
142	A32	25c bluish sl (Bl)	.65	1.40
	Never hinged		1.60	
	On cover			3.00
143	A31	30c olive grn (G)	.40	.55
	Never hinged		1.25	
	On cover			1.25
144	A32	40c olive brn (Br)	.40	.75
	Never hinged		1.10	
	On cover			2.00
145	A32	50c magenta (R)	.75	1.40
	Never hinged		2.00	
	On cover			3.00
146	A35	60c red orge (O)	.65	.55
	Never hinged		1.10	
	On cover			1.60
147	A32	75c brown vio (V)	.75	1.25
	Never hinged		2.00	
	On cover			4.25
148	A32	90c deep red (R)	.75	1.40
	Never hinged		2.00	
	On cover			4.25
149	A35	1fr violet (V)	.75	1.60
	Never hinged		2.00	
	On cover			4.25
150	A36	1.50fr sapphire (Bl)	1.25	3.25
	Never hinged		4.25	
	On cover			10.00
151	A36	2fr brown red		
		(R)	2.00	4.75
	Never hinged		5.75	
	On cover			14.50
152	A36	3fr dk ol grn (G)	4.75	9.50
	Never hinged		12.00	
	On cover			25.00
153	A36	5fr dp brown		
		(Br)	20.00	32.50
	Never hinged		52.50	
	On cover			85.00

Size: 31½x36mm
Perf. 12

154	A30	10fr black brn		
		(Br)	24.00	60.00
	Never hinged		57.50	
	On cover			200.00
	Nos. 139-154 (16)		58.55	121.40

SEMI-POSTAL STAMPS

Red Cross Dog Leading Blind Man — SP1

Maternity Nurse with Child — SP4

Designs: #B2, Nurse and invalid. #B3, Children getting drink at spring.

Perf. 13½
1926, Oct. 25   Photo.   Unwmk.

B1	SP1	20c + 20c dk ol grn	8.00	20.00
		Never hinged	20.00	
		On cover		65.00
B2	SP1	40c + 40c dk brn	8.00	20.00
		Never hinged	20.00	
		On cover		65.00
B3	SP1	50c + 50c red org	8.00	20.00
		Never hinged	20.00	
		On cover		57.50
B4	SP4	1.50fr + 1.50fr brt bl	19.00	47.50
		Never hinged	45.00	
		On cover		160.00
		Nos. B1-B4 (4)	43.00	107.50

Nos. B1-B4 Overprinted

1927, Oct. 1

B5	SP1	20c + 20c dk ol grn	12.50	35.00
		Never hinged	32.50	
		On cover		110.00
B6	SP1	40c + 40c dk brn	12.50	35.00
		Never hinged	32.50	
		On cover		145.00
B7	SP1	50c + 50c red org	11.00	32.50
		Never hinged	24.00	
		On cover		110.00
B8	SP4	1.50fr + 1.50fr brt bl	17.50	72.50
		Never hinged	40.00	
		On cover		280.00
		Nos. B5-B8 (4)	53.50	175.00

"The Blind Beggar" by Dyckmans SP5

"Almsgiving" by Schiestl SP6

"Charity" by Raphael — SP7

1928, Dec. 23   Photo.

B9	SP5	40c (+40c) blk brn	12.00	72.50
		Never hinged	30.00	
		On cover		100.00
B10	SP5	50c (+50c) brn rose	12.00	72.50
		Never hinged	30.00	
		On cover		100.00
B11	SP5	1fr (+1fr) dl vio	12.00	72.50
		Never hinged	30.00	
		On cover		125.00
B12	SP6	1.50fr (+1.50fr) cob bl	12.00	72.50
		Never hinged	30.00	
		On cover		135.00
B13	SP6	2fr (+2fr) red brn	14.00	100.00
		Never hinged	32.50	
		On cover		200.00
B14	SP6	3fr (+3fr) dk ol grn	14.00	135.00
		Never hinged	32.50	
		On cover		375.00
B15	SP7	10fr (+10fr) dk brn	360.00	4,000.
		Never hinged	725.00	
		On cover		6,250.
		Nos. B9-B15 (7)	436.00	4,525.
		Set of first day covers (7)		8,500.
		Set of one first day cover		6,500.

"Orphaned" by Kaulbach SP8

"St. Ottilia" by Feuerstein SP9

"Madonna" by Ferruzzio — SP10

1929, Dec. 22

B16	SP8	40c (+15c) ol grn	2.00	5.50
		Never hinged	5.25	
		On cover		30.00
B17	SP8	50c (+20c) cop red	4.00	9.50
		Never hinged	10.00	
		On cover		45.00
B18	SP8	1fr (+50c) vio brn	4.00	11.00
		Never hinged	10.00	
		On cover		70.00
B19	SP9	1.50fr (+75c) Prus bl	4.00	11.00
		Never hinged	10.00	
		On cover		90.00
B20	SP9	2fr (+1fr) brn car	4.00	11.00
		Never hinged	10.00	
		On cover		110.00
B21	SP9	3fr (+2fr) sl grn	8.00	25.00
		Never hinged	16.00	
		On cover		145.00
B22	SP10	10fr (+8fr) blk brn	47.50	135.00
		Never hinged	110.00	
		On cover		575.00
		Nos. B16-B22 (7)	73.50	208.00

"The Safety-Man" SP11

"The Good Samaritan" SP12

"In the Window" — SP13

1931, Jan. 20

B23	SP11	40c (+15c)	8.00	24.00
		Never hinged	20.00	
		On cover		65.00
B24	SP11	60c (+20c)	9.00	21.00
		Never hinged	20.00	
		On cover		65.00
B25	SP12	1fr (+50c)	8.00	47.50
		Never hinged	20.00	
		On cover		145.00
B26	SP11	1.50fr (+75c)	8.00	47.50
		Never hinged	28.00	
		On cover		200.00
B27	SP12	2fr (+1fr)	8.00	47.50
		Never hinged	28.00	
		On cover		225.00
B28	SP12	3fr (+2fr)	20.00	47.50
		Never hinged	40.00	
		On cover		300.00
B29	SP13	10fr (+10fr)	95.00	290.00
		Never hinged	210.00	
		On cover		800.00
		Nos. B23-B29 (7)	155.00	528.00
		Set on first day cover		1,250.

St. Martin of Tours — SP14

#B33-B35, Charity. #B36, The Widow's Mite.

1931, Dec. 23

B30	SP14	40c (+15c)	12.50	35.00
		Never hinged	35.00	
		On cover		65.00
B31	SP14	60c (+20c)	12.50	35.00
		Never hinged	35.00	
		On cover		65.00
B32	SP14	1fr (+50c)	16.00	55.00
		Never hinged	40.00	
		On cover		130.00
B33	SP14	1.50fr (+75c)	19.00	55.00
		Never hinged	45.00	
		On cover		210.00
B34	SP14	2fr (+1fr)	22.50	55.00
		Never hinged	55.00	
		On cover		225.00
B35	SP14	3fr (+2fr)	27.50	95.00
		Never hinged	72.50	
		On cover		350.00
B36	SP14	5fr (+5fr)	95.00	325.00
		Never hinged	260.00	
		On cover		1,200.
		Nos. B30-B36 (7)	205.00	655.00
		Set on first day cover		2,000.

Ruins at Kirkel — SP17

Illingen Castle, Kerpen SP23

Designs: 60c, Church at Blie. 1fr, Castle Ottweiler. 1.50fr, Church of St. Michael, Saarbrucken. 2fr, Statue of St. Wendel. 3fr, Church of St. John, Saarbrucken.

1932, Dec. 20

B37	SP17	40c (+15c)	9.50	22.50
		Never hinged	32.50	
		On cover		80.00
B38	SP17	60c (+20c)	9.50	22.50
		Never hinged	32.50	
		On cover		100.00
B39	SP17	1fr (+50c)	14.00	40.00
		Never hinged	32.50	
		On cover		130.00
B40	SP17	1.50fr (+75c)	20.00	47.50
		Never hinged	60.00	
		On cover		160.00
B41	SP17	2fr (+1fr)	20.00	55.00
		Never hinged	60.00	
		On cover		180.00
B42	SP17	3fr (+2fr)	55.00	175.00
		Never hinged	130.00	
		On cover		575.00
B43	SP23	5fr (+5fr)	125.00	290.00
		Never hinged	260.00	
		On cover		1,000.
		Nos. B37-B43 (7)	253.00	652.50
		Set on first day cover		1,700.

Scene of Neunkirchen Disaster — SP24

1933, June 1

B44	SP24	60c (+ 60c) org red	16.00	20.00
		Never hinged	40.00	
		On cover		57.50
B45	SP24	3fr (+ 3fr) ol grn	35.00	72.50
		Never hinged	90.00	
		On cover		140.00
B46	SP24	5fr (+ 5fr) org brn	35.00	72.50
		Never hinged	90.00	
		On cover		250.00
		Nos. B44-B46 (3)	86.00	165.00
		Set on first day cover		525.00

The surtax was for the aid of victims of the explosion at Neunkirchen, Feb. 10.

"Love" — SP25

Designs: 60c, "Anxiety." 1fr, "Peace." 1.50fr, "Solace." 2fr, "Welfare." 3fr, "Truth." 5fr, Figure on Tomb of Duchess Elizabeth of Lorraine

1934, Mar. 15   Photo.

B47	SP25	40c (+15c) blk brn	5.50	16.00
		Never hinged	14.50	
		On cover		40.00
B48	SP25	60c (+20c) red org	5.50	16.00
		Never hinged	14.50	
		On cover		40.00
B49	SP25	1fr (+50c) dl vio	7.25	20.00
		Never hinged	20.00	
		On cover		60.00
B50	SP25	1.50fr (+75c) blue	14.00	35.00
		Never hinged	35.00	
		On cover		125.00
B51	SP25	2fr (+1fr) car rose	12.50	35.00
		Never hinged	32.50	
		On cover		120.00
B52	SP25	3fr (+2fr) ol grn	14.00	35.00
		Never hinged	35.00	
		On cover		135.00
B53	SP25	5fr (+5fr) red brn	32.50	87.50
		Never hinged	80.00	
		On cover		350.00
		Nos. B47-B53 (7)	91.25	244.50
		Set on first day cover		850.00

Nos. B47-B53 Overprinted like Nos. 139-154 in Various Colors Reading up

1934, Dec. 1   Perf. 13x13½

B54	SP25	40c (+15c) (Br)	3.50	14.00
		Never hinged	8.00	
		On cover		40.00
B55	SP25	60c (+20c) (R)	3.50	14.00
		Never hinged	8.00	
		On cover		40.00
B56	SP25	1fr (+50c) (V)	11.00	25.00
		Never hinged	21.00	
		On cover		72.50
B57	SP25	1.50fr (+75c) (Bl)	7.25	25.00
		Never hinged	18.00	
		On cover		80.00
B58	SP25	2fr (+1fr) (R)	11.00	35.00
		Never hinged	26.00	
		On cover		90.00
B59	SP25	3fr (+2fr) (G)	10.00	32.50
		Never hinged	25.00	
		On cover		100.00
B60	SP25	5fr (+5fr) (Br)	15.00	40.00
		Never hinged	40.00	
		On cover		130.00
		Nos. B54-B60 (7)	61.25	185.50

AIR POST STAMPS

Airplane over Saarbrücken — AP1

Perf. 13½

1928, Sept. 19   Unwmk.   Photo.

C1	AP1 50c brown red	4.00	4.00
	Never hinged	10.00	
	On cover		15.00
	On first day cover		3,000.
C2	AP1 1fr dark violet	6.50	4.75
	Never hinged	14.50	
	On cover		25.00
	On first day cover		2,000.

For overprints see Nos. C5, C7.

Saarbrücken Airport and Church of St. Arnual — AP2

1932, Apr. 30

C3	AP2 60c orange red	6.50	4.75
	Never hinged	16.00	
	On cover		20.00
	On first day cover		62.50
C4	AP2 5fr dark brown	45.00	95.00
	Never hinged	130.00	
	On cover		200.00
	On first day cover		240.00

For overprints see Nos. C6, C8.

Nos. C1-C4 Overprinted like Nos. 139-154 in Various Colors

1934, Nov. 1   Perf. 13½, 13½x13

C5	AP1 50c brn red (R)	4.00	7.25
	Never hinged	10.00	
	On cover		20.00
	On first day cover		40.00
C6	AP2 60c org red (O)	3.25	2.75
	Never hinged	7.50	
	On cover		8.00
	On first day cover		40.00
C7	AP1 1fr dk vio (V)	7.25	9.50
	Never hinged	16.00	
	On cover		32.50
	On first day cover		80.00
C8	AP2 5fr dk brn (Br)	9.50	14.00
	Never hinged	20.00	
	On cover		65.00
	On first day cover		100.00
	Nos. C5-C8 (4)	24.00	33.50
	Set on first day cover		250.00

OFFICIAL STAMPS

Regular Issue of 1922-1923 Ovptd. Diagonally in Red or Blue

Nos. O1-O15 have two types of overprint: Type I, center bar of "E" slightly above center, "S" has rounded bottom, "A" symetrical; Type 2, center bar of "E" centered, "S" has flat bottom, "A" slightly inclined to right. Overprints are Type I unless noted.

Perf. 12½x13½, 13½x12½

1922-23   Unwmk.

O1	A19 3c ol grn & straw (R)	.95	35.00
	Never hinged	2.75	
	On cover		120.00
O2	A20 5c org & blk (R)	.40	.40
	Never hinged	1.10	
	On cover		6.50
a.	Pair, one without overprint	275.00	
	Never hinged	575.00	
O3	A21 10c bl grn (R)	.40	.35
	Never hinged	1.10	
	On cover		6.50
a.	Inverted overprint	32.50	
	Never hinged	80.00	
O4	A19 15c dp brn (Bl)	.40	.35
	Never hinged	1.10	
	On cover		6.50
a.	Pair, one without overprint	290.00	
	Never hinged	600.00	
b.	Double overprint	65.00	
	Never hinged	180.00	
O5	A19 15c org (Bl) ('23)	2.40	.50
	Never hinged	5.75	
	On cover		10.00
O6	A22 20c dk bl & lem (R)	.40	.35
	Never hinged	1.10	
	On cover		6.50
a.	Inverted overprint	32.50	
	Never hinged	80.00	
b.	Double overprint	65.00	
	Never hinged	160.00	
O7	A22 20c brt bl & straw (R) ('23)	2.40	.50
	Never hinged	5.75	
	On cover		10.00

O8	A22 25c red & yel (Bl)	4.00	1.20
	Never hinged	11.50	
	On cover		20.00
O9	A22 25c mag & straw (Bl) ('23)	2.40	.50
	Never hinged	5.75	
	On cover		10.00
a.	Overprint Type II ('24)	16.00	2.50
	Never hinged	40.00	
	On cover		50.00
O10	A23 30c car & yel (Bl)	.40	.35
	Never hinged	1.20	
	On cover		8.00
a.	Inverted overprint	52.50	
	Never hinged	140.00	
O11	A24 40c brn & yel (Bl)	.55	.35
	Never hinged	1.60	
	On cover		8.50
O12	A25 50c dk bl & straw (R)	.55	.35
	Never hinged	1.70	
	On cover		6.50
a.	Inverted overprint	32.50	
	Never hinged	80.00	
O13	A24 75c dp grn & straw (R)	24.00	27.50
	Never hinged	80.00	
	On cover		150.00
O14	A24 75c blk & straw (R) ('23)	4.75	2.40
	Never hinged	12.00	
	On cover		20.00
O15	A26 1fr brn red (Bl)	47.50	16.00
	Never hinged	145.00	
	On cover		100.00
a.	Inverted overprint	150.00	
	Never hinged	400.00	
b.	Double overprint	150.00	
	Never hinged	400.00	
c.	Overprint Type II ('24)	12.00	2.40
	Never hinged	32.50	
	On cover		32.50
	Nos. O1-O15 (15)	91.50	86.10

The set (Type I) exists imperf. Value, hinged $1850. No. O15c (Type II) exists imperf. Value, hinged $325.

Regular Issue of 1927-30 Overprinted in Various Colors

Two types of overprint: Type I, overprint at 32 degree angle ('27-'32); Type II, overprint at 23 to 25 degree angle ('29-'34).

1927-34   Perf. 13½

O16	A31 10c dp brn (Bl) (II) ('34)	2.00	2.40
	Never hinged	8.00	
	On cover		17.00
O17	A32 15c ol blk (Bl) (II) ('34)	2.00	6.50
	Never hinged	8.00	
	On cover		50.00
O18	A32 20c brn org (Bk) (II) ('31)	2.00	1.60
	Never hinged	8.00	
	On cover		17.00
O19	A32 25c bluish sl (Bl) (II)	2.40	6.50
	Never hinged	8.50	
	On cover		17.00
O20	A31 30c ol grn (C) (I)	5.75	.80
	Never hinged	16.00	
	On cover		6.50
a.	Orange red ovpt. (II)	2.00	.50
	Never hinged	8.00	
	On cover		6.50
b.	Carmine ovpt. (II)	4.00	2.10
	Never hinged	11.50	
	On cover		12.50
O21	A32 40c ol brn (C) (I)	5.75	.80
	Never hinged	16.00	
	On cover		6.00
a.	Double overprint		80.00
b.	40c olive brown (C) (II)	2.00	.35
	Never hinged	8.00	
	On cover		6.75
c.	As "b," double overprint	100.00	
	Never hinged	240.00	
O22	A32 50c mag (Bl) (I)	20.00	.65
	Never hinged	65.00	
	On cover		6.50
a.	Double overprint		80.00
b.	50c magenta (Bl) (II)	4.00	.40
	Never hinged	13.00	
	On cover		6.50
c.	As "b," double overprint	55.00	
	Never hinged	100.00	
O23	A35 60c red org (Bk) (II) ('30)	1.20	.35
	Never hinged	4.00	
	On cover		6.50
a.	Double overprint	55.00	
	Never hinged	100.00	
O24	A32 75c brn vio (C) (I)	5.75	.85
	Never hinged	14.50	
	On cover		20.00
a.	Double overprint		85.00
b.	75c brown violet (C) (II)	2.40	.40
	Never hinged	8.00	
	On cover		16.00
O25	A35 1fr vio (RO) (I)	5.75	.85
	Never hinged	16.00	
	On cover		4.25
a.	Double overprint		85.00
b.	1fr violet (RO) (II)	2.40	.40
	Never hinged	16.00	
	On cover		8.50

c.	As "b," double overprint	85.00	
	Never hinged	160.00	
O26	A36 2fr brn red (Bl) (I)	14.50	1.60
	Never hinged	50.00	
	On cover		12.00
a.	Double overprint		80.00
b.	2fr brown red (Bl) (II)	2.40	.40
	Never hinged	16.00	
	On cover		8.00
c.	As "b," double overprint	75.00	
	Never hinged	125.00	
	Nos. O16-O26 (11)	67.10	22.90

The overprint on Nos. O16 and O20 is known only inverted.

ST. CHRISTOPHER

sänt ˈkris-tə-fər

LOCATION — Island in the West Indies, southeast of Puerto Rico
GOVT. — A Presidency of the Leeward Islands Colony
AREA — 68 sq. mi.
POP. — 18,578 (estimated)
CAPITAL — Basseterre

Stamps of St. Christopher were discontinued in 1890 and replaced by those of Leeward Islands. For later issues see St. Kitts-Nevis.

12 Pence = 1 Shilling

STAMPS OF GREAT BRITAIN USED IN ST. CHRISTOPHER

Numeral cancellation type A is pictured in the Crowned Circle Handstamps and Great Britain Used Abroad section.

1858-60

A12 (Basseterre)

A1	A 1p rose red (#20)		775.00
A2	A 2p blue (#29, P7)		2,000.
A3	A 4p rose (#26)		450.00
A4	A 6p lilac (#27)		300.00
A5	A 1sh green (#28)		2,500.

See footnote after No. 23.

Issued under British Administration

Queen Victoria — A1

Wmk. Crown and C C (1)

1870, Apr. 1   Typo.   Perf. 12½

1	A1 1p dull rose	95.00	52.50
2	A1 1p lilac rose	82.50	35.00
3	A1 6p green ('71)	140.00	8.75
a.	6p yellow green ('70)	140.00	21.00
	Nos. 1-3 (3)	317.50	96.25

1875-79   Perf. 14

4	A1 1p lilac rose	80.00	8.00
b.	Half used on cover (2½p rate)		2,500.
c.	Half used as ½p on newsprint (½p rate)		2,500.
5	A1 2½p red brown ('79)	200.00	275.00
6	A1 4p blue ('79)	225.00	16.00
7	A1 6p green	60.00	6.00
a.	Horiz. pair, imperf. vert.		—
	Nos. 4-7 (4)	565.00	305.00

The value for No. 4b is for covers dated between March and June, 1882.
For surcharges see Nos. 18-20.

1882-90   Wmk. Crown and C A (2)

8	A1 ½p green	5.00	3.00
9	A1 1p rose	2.50	2.25
a.	Half used as ½p on cover		
10	A1 1p lilac rose	600.00	77.50
a.	Diagonal half used as ½p on cover		6.50
11	A1 2½p red brown	200.00	67.50
a.	2½p deep red brown	210.00	72.50
12	A1 2½p ultra ('84)	4.50	2.00
13	A1 4p blue	550.00	27.50
14	A1 4p gray ('84)	1.60	1.10
15	A1 6p olive brn ('90)	95.00	425.00
16	A1 1sh violet ('87)	105.00	75.00
a.	1sh bright mauve ('90)	95.00	175.00
	Nos. 8-16 (9)	1,563.	680.85

For surcharges see Nos. 17, 21-23.

No. 9 Bisected and Handstamp Surcharged in Black

1885, Mar.

17	A1 ½p on half of 1p	29.00	45.00
b.	Inverted surcharge	250.00	125.00
c.	Unsevered pair	140.00	140.00
d.	As "c," one surcharge inverted	450.00	325.00
e.	Double surcharge		

No. 7 Surcharged in Black

No. 18   No. 19

No. 20

1884-86   Wmk. 1

18	A1 1p on 6p green ('86)	22.50	37.50
a.	Inverted surcharge	10,000.	
b.	Double surcharge		1,650.
19	A1 4p on 6p green	75.00	57.50
a.	Period after "PENCE"	75.00	57.50
b.	Double surcharge	—	3,000.
20	A1 4p on 6p green ('86)	60.00	105.00
a.	Without period after "d"	250.00	325.00
b.	Double surcharge	2,750.	3,000.
	Nos. 18-20 (3)	157.50	200.00

The line through original value on Nos. 18 and 20 was added by hand. Value for No. 18b is for stamp with pen cancellation or with violet handstamp (revenue cancels).

Nos. 8 and 12 Surcharged in Black Like No. 18 or

No. 21   No. 22

1887-88   Wmk. 2

21	A1 1p on ½p green	50.00	60.00
22	A1 1p on 2½p green ('88)	72.50	72.50
a.	Inverted surcharge	27,500.	11,000.
23	A1 1p on 2½p, no line over original value ('88)	31,500.	15,000.

Nos. 18 and 21 have the same type of One Penny surcharge. The line through the original value on Nos. 21 and 22 were added by hand. No. 23 probably is a sheet that was meant to be No. 22 but was missed when the bars were added.

Antigua No. 18 was used in St. Christopher in 1890. It is canceled "A12" instead of "A02." Values: used $140, on cover $850.

POSTAL FISCAL ISSUES

Nevis Nos. 22 and 28 Overprinted "REVENUE" Horizontally and "Saint Christopher" Diagonally

1883

AR1	A5 1p violet	425.00	
AR2	A5 6p green	130.00	170.00

Stamps of St. Christopher Ovptd. "SAINT KITTS / NEVIS / REVENUE" in 3 Lines

1885

AR3	A1 1p rose	3.00	19.00
AR4	A1 3p violet	17.50	72.50
AR5	A1 6p orange brown	15.00	55.00
AR6	A1 1sh olive	3.25	47.50

Other values exist with the above overprints but were not available for postal purposes.

ST. HELENA

sānt ˈhe-lə-nə

LOCATION — Island in the Atlantic Ocean, 1,200 miles west of Angola
GOVT. — British Crown Colony
AREA — 47 sq. mi.
POP. — 5,499 (1982)
CAPITAL — Jamestown

12 Pence = 1 Shilling
20 Shillings = 1 Pound

> Catalogue values for unused stamps in this country are for Never Hinged items, beginning with Scott 128 in the regular postage section.

Values for unused stamps are for examples with original gum as defined in the catalogue introduction. Very fine examples of Nos. 2-7, 11-39a and 47-47b will have perforations touching the design on one or more sides due to the narrow spacing of the stamps on the plates. Stamps with perfs clear of the design on all four sides are scarce and will command higher prices.

Watermark

Wmk. 6 — Star

Queen Victoria — A1

1856, Jan. Wmk. 6 Engr. Imperf.
1   A1 6p blue   600.00 225.00
For types surcharged see Nos. 8-39, 47.

1861 Clean-Cut Perf. 14 to 15½
2   A1 6p blue   2,100. 325.00

1863 Rough Perf. 14 to 15½
2B A1 6p blue   525.00 160.00

1871-74 Wmk. 1 Perf. 12½
3   A1 6p dull blue   900.00 125.00
4   A1 6p ultra ('73)   500.00 97.50

1879 Perf. 14x12½
5   A1 6p gray blue   475.00 60.00

1889 Perf. 14
6   A1 6p gray blue   550.00 60.00

1889 Wmk. Crown and C A (2)
7   A1 6p gray   35.00   6.00

Type of 1856 Surcharged

a   b

Long Bar, 16, 17, 18 or 19mm

1863 Wmk. 1 Imperf.
8   A1(a) 1p on 6p brown red (surch. 17mm)   150.00 225.00
  a.   Double surcharge   9,788. 4,250.
  b.   Surcharge omitted   23,000.
9   A1(a) 1p on 6p brown red (surch. 19mm)   150.00 250.00
  a.   Vertical pair, #8, 9   11,500.
10 A1(b) 4p on 6p carmine   600.00 300.00
  b.   Double surcharge   16,000. 10,000.

1864-73 Perf. 12½
11 A1(a) 1p on 6p brn red   70.00 35.00
  a.   Double surcharge   12,000.
12 A1(b) 1p on 6p brn red ('71)   140.00 21.00
  a.   Blue black surcharge   1,200. 675.00
13 A1(b) 2p on 6p yel ('73)   150.00 50.00
  a.   Blue black surcharge   4,800. 2,700.
14 A1(b) 3p on 6p dk vio ('73)   140.00 72.50
15 A1(b) 4p on 6p car   175.00 60.00
  a.   Double surcharge   6,750.
16 A1(b) 1sh on 6p grn (bar 16 to 17mm)   450.00 35.00
  a.   Double surcharge   24,000.
17 A1(b) 1sh on 6p dp grn (bar 18mm) ('73)   750.00 20.00
  a.   Blue black surcharge

1868 Short Bar, 14 or 15mm
18 A1(a) 1p on 6p brn red   225.00 67.50
  a.   Imperf., pair   6,000.
  b.   Double surcharge
19 A1(b) 2p on 6p yellow   200.00 72.50
  a.   Imperf   12,000.
20 A1(b) 3p on 6p dk vio   120.00 60.00
  a.   Double surcharge   7,250.
  b.   Imperf., pair   2,000.
  c.   3p on 6p pale purple   3,300. 900.00
21 A1(b) 4p on 6p car (words 18mm)   140.00 72.50
  a.   Double surcharge   6,000.
  b.   Imperf, single   14,500.
22 A1(b) 4p on 6p car (words 19mm)   325.00 150.00
  a.   Words double, 18mm and 19mm   26,000. 11,000.
  b.   Imperf.
  c.   Surcharge omitted   6,000.
23 A1(a) 1sh on 6p yel grn   750.00 160.00
  a.   Double surcharge   19,500.
  b.   Pair, one without surcharge   19,500.
  c.   Imperf   17,000.
24 A1(a) 5sh on 6p org   67.50 77.50
  a.   5sh on 6p yellow   550.00 450.00

1882 Perf. 14x12½
25 A1(a) 1p on 6p brown red   90.00 18.00
26 A1(b) 2p on 6p yellow   140.00 60.00
27 A1(b) 3p on 6p violet   350.00 85.00
28 A1(b) 4p on 6p carmine (words 16½mm)   170.00 72.50

1883 Perf. 14
29 A1(a) 1p on 6p brown red   120.00 22.50
30 A1(b) 2p on 6p yellow   150.00 37.50
31 A1(a) 1sh on 6p yel grn   25.00 15.00

Long Bar, 18mm

1882 Perf. 14x12½
32 A1(b) 1sh on 6p dp green   900.00 30.00

Short Bar, 14 or 14½mm

1884-94 Wmk. 2 Perf. 14
33 A1(b) ½p on 6p grn (words 17mm)   12.00 20.00
  a.   ½p on 6p emer, blurred print (words 17mm) ('84)   16.00 23.00
  b.   Double surcharge   1,450. 1,575.
  c.   "N" and "Y" spaced .8mm (#33)   550.00 800.00
  d.   "N" and "Y" spaced .8mm (#33a)   1,300.
  e.   As "d," double surcharge   13,500.
34 A1(b) ½p on 6p grn (words 15mm) ('94)   3.25   3.50
  a.   "N" and "Y" spaced .8mm   1,800.
35 A1(a) 1p on 6p red ('87)   5.75   4.50
  a.   1p on 6p pale red   7.75   3.75
36 A1(b) 2p on 6p yel ('94)   3.25   9.50
37 A1(b) 3p on 6p dp vio ('87)   9.00 13.50
  a.   3p on 6p red violet   6.00   6.00
  b.   Double surcharge, #37a   11,500. 7,250.
  c.   Double surcharge, #37   11,000.

---

38 A1(b) 4p on 6p pale brn (words 16½mm; '90)   67.50 35.00
  a.   4p on 6p dk brn (words 17mm; '94)   30.00 21.00
  b.   With thin bar below thick one   850.00

The spacing between "N" and "Y" in surcharges on Nos. 33 and 34 is normally .5mm. Examples with .8mm spacing are from one position within the pane.

1894 Long Bar, 18mm
39 A1(b) 1sh on 6p yel grn   65.00 30.00
  a.   Double surcharge   5,750.

See note after No. 47.

Queen Victoria — A3

1890-97 Typo. Perf. 14
40 A3 ½p green ('97)   3.25   7.75
41 A3 1p rose ('96)   20.00   2.40
42 A3 1½p red brn & grn   5.50 10.00
43 A3 2p yellow ('96)   6.00 14.50
44 A3 2½p ultra ('96)   18.00 14.50
45 A3 5p violet ('96)   13.50 37.50
46 A3 10p brown ('96)   29.00 72.50
  Nos. 40-46 (7)   95.25 159.15
Set, ovptd. "SPECIMEN"   360.00

Type of 1856 Surcharged

1893 Engr. Wmk. 2
47 A1 2½p on 6p blue   3.75   6.75
  a.   Double surcharge   24,000.
  b.   Double impression   11,500.

In 1905 remainders of Nos. 34-47 were sold by the postal officials. They are canceled with bars, arranged in the shape of diamonds, in purple ink. No such cancellation was ever used on the island and the stamps so canceled are of slight value. With this cancellation removed, these remainders are sometimes offered as unused. Some have been recanceled with a false dated postmark.

King Edward VII — A5

1902 Typo. Wmk. 2
48 A5 ½p green   1.90   3.00
49 A5 1p carmine rose   13.00   .85
Nos. 48, 49, ovptd. "SPECIMEN"   90.00

Government House — A6

"The Wharf" — A7

1903, June Wmk. 1
50 A6 ½p gray grn & brn   2.40   4.00
51 A7 1p carmine & blk   1.90   .50
52 A6 2p ol grn & blk   9.00   1.50
53 A7 8p brown & blk   26.50 37.50

---

54 A6 1sh org buff & brn   27.50 47.50
55 A7 2sh violet & blk   65.00 100.00
  Nos. 50-55 (6)   132.30 191.00
Set, ovptd. "SPECIMEN"   275.00

A8

1908, May Wmk. 3
Ordinary Paper
56 A8 2½p ultra   2.00   1.90
57 A8 4p black & red, yel ('11)   4.00 21.00
  a.   Chalky paper   11.00 24.00
58 A8 6p dull violet ('11)   7.75 17.00
  a.   Chalky paper   20.00 37.50
  Nos. 56-58 (3)   13.75 39.90

Wmk. 2
Chalky Paper
60 A8 10sh grn & red, grn   250.00 325.00
Set, ovptd. "SPECIMEN"   300.00

Nos. 57 and 58 exist on both ordinary and chalky paper; No. 56 on ordinary and No. 60 on chalky paper.

Government House — A9

"The Wharf" — A10

1912-16 Ordinary Paper Wmk. 3
61 A9 ½p green & blk   3.25 12.00
62 A10 1p carmine & blk   5.75   2.00
  a.   1p scarlet & black ('16)   14.50 24.00
63 A10 1½p orange & blk   4.25   9.00
64 A9 2p gray & black   5.50   2.00
65 A10 2½p ultra & blk   4.25   7.25
66 A9 3p vio & blk, yel   4.25   6.00
67 A10 8p dull vio & blk   8.50 60.00
68 A9 1sh black, green   11.00 42.50
69 A10 2sh ultra & blk, bl   50.00 95.00
70 A10 3sh violet & blk   75.00 160.00
  Nos. 61-70 (10)   171.75 395.75
Set, ovptd. "SPECIMEN"   360.00

See Nos. 75-77.

A11   A12

Die I

For description of dies I and II see "Dies of British Colonial Stamps" in the front of the catalogue.

1912 Chalky Paper
71 A11 4p black & red, yel   15.00 30.00
72 A11 6p dull vio & red vio   4.75   6.00
Set, ovptd. "SPECIMEN"   110.00

1913 Ordinary Paper
73 A12 4p black & red, yel   10.00   3.25
74 A12 6p dull vio & red vio   16.00 35.00
Set, ovptd. "SPECIMEN"   110.00

1922 Wmk. 4
75 A10 1p green   2.75 47.50
76 A10 1½p rose red   12.00 45.00
77 A9 3p ultra   25.00 85.00
  Nos. 75-77 (3)   39.75 177.50
Set, ovptd. "SPECIMEN"   140.00

Badge of the Colony — A13

1922-27   Chalky Paper   Wmk. 4
79	A13	½p black & gray	4.00	4.00
80	A13	1p grn & blk	3.25	2.00
81	A13	1½p rose red	3.25	15.00
82	A13	2p pale gray & gray	4.50	2.40
83	A13	3p ultra	2.40	4.75
84	A13	5p red & grn, emer	3.75	6.75
85	A13	6p red vio & blk	5.50	9.75
86	A13	8p violet & blk	4.50	8.50
87	A13	1sh dk brn & blk	7.75	11.00
88	A13	1sh6p grn & blk, emer	18.00	60.00
89	A13	2sh ultra & vio, bl	22.50	55.00
90	A13	2sh6p car & blk, yel	17.00	77.50
91	A13	5sh grn & blk, yel	45.00	90.00
92	A13	7sh6p orange & blk	120.00	180.00
93	A13	10sh ol grn & blk	160.00	225.00
94	A13	15sh vio & blk, bl	1,075.	2,500.
		Nos. 79-93 (15)	421.40	751.65
		Set, ovptd. "SPECIMEN"	1,450.	

Nos. 88, 90, and 91 are on ordinary paper.

Wmk. 3   Chalky Paper
95	A13	4p black, yel	14.00	7.25
96	A13	1sh6p bl grn & blk, grn	26.50	72.50
97	A13	2sh6p car & blk, yel	30.00	77.50
98	A13	5sh grn & blk, yel	50.00	120.00
99	A13	£1 red vio & blk, red	475.00	650.00
		Nos. 95-99 (5)	595.50	927.25
		Set, ovptd. "SPECIMEN"	600.00	

Issue dates: ½p, 1½p, 2p, 3p, 4p, 8p, February, 1923; 5p, Nos. 88-91, 1927; others, June 1922.

Centenary Issue

Lot and Lot's Wife — A14

Plantation; Queen Victoria and Kings William IV, Edward VII, George V A15

Map of the Colony A16

Quay, Jamestown A17

View of James Valley — A18

View of Jamestown A19

View of Mundens A20

St. Helena — A21

View of High Knoll — A22

Badge of the Colony A23

Perf. 12
1934, Apr. 23   Engr.   Wmk. 4
101	A14	½p dk vio & blk	1.25	1.00
102	A15	1p green & blk	.80	1.00
103	A16	1½p red & blk	3.00	4.00
104	A17	2p orange & blk	3.50	1.50
105	A18	3p blue & blk	1.75	5.50
106	A19	6p lt blue & blk	4.00	3.75
107	A20	1sh dk brn & blk	8.00	22.50
108	A21	2sh6p car & blk	50.00	60.00
109	A22	5sh choc & blk	100.00	100.00
110	A23	10sh red vio & black	300.00	350.00
		Nos. 101-110 (10)	472.30	549.25
		Set, never hinged	725.00	
		Set, perf. "SPECIMEN"	450.00	

Common Design Types
For description of dies I and II see "Dies of British Colonial Stamps" in Table of Contents.

Silver Jubilee Issue
Common Design Type
1935, May 6   Perf. 13½x14
111	CD301	1½p car & dk blue	1.25	6.75
112	CD301	2p gray blk & ultra	2.40	1.25
113	CD301	6p indigo & grn	8.50	4.25
114	CD301	1sh brt vio & ind	19.00	21.00
		Nos. 111-114 (4)	31.15	33.25
		Set, never hinged	52.50	
		Set, perf. "SPECIMEN"	170.00	

Coronation Issue
Common Design Type
1937, May 19
115	CD302	1p deep green	.45	.90
116	CD302	2p deep orange	.40	.55
117	CD302	3p bright ultra	.60	.60
		Nos. 115-117 (3)	1.45	2.05
		Set, never hinged	2.00	
		Set, perf. "SPECIMEN"	100.00	

Badge of the Colony — A24

1938-40   Perf. 12½
118	A24	½p purple	.25	.75
119	A24	1p dp green	7.00	2.40
119A	A24	1p org yel ('40)	.25	.30
120	A24	1½p carmine	.30	.40
121	A24	2p orange	.25	.25
122	A24	3p ultra	55.00	18.00
122A	A24	3p gray ('40)	.35	.30
122B	A24	4p ultra ('40)	1.10	.85
123	A24	6p gray blue	1.10	1.40
123A	A24	8p olive ('40)	1.75	1.00
124	A24	1sh sepia	1.10	.35
125	A24	2sh6p deep claret	11.00	6.75
126	A24	5sh brown	11.00	12.50
127	A24	10sh violet	11.00	18.00
		Nos. 118-127 (14)	101.45	63.25
		Set, never hinged	160.00	
		Set, perf. "SPECIMEN"	450.00	

Issue dates: May 12, 1938, July 8, 1940.
See Nos. 136-138.

Catalogue values for unused stamps in this section, from this point to the end of the section, are for Never Hinged items.

Peace Issue
Common Design Type
Perf. 13½x14
1946, Oct. 21   Wmk. 4   Engr.
128	CD303	2p deep orange	.30	.40
129	CD303	4p deep blue	.35	.30
		Set, perf. "SPECIMEN"	100.00	

Silver Wedding Issue
Common Design Types
1948, Oct. 20   Photo.   Perf. 14x14½
130	CD304	3p black	.30	.30

Perf. 11½x11
Engr.; Name Typo.
131	CD305	10sh blue violet	32.50	42.50

UPU Issue
Common Design Types
Engr.; Name Typo. on 4p, 6p
1949, Oct. 10   Perf. 13½, 11x11½
132	CD306	3p rose carmine	.30	1.00
133	CD307	4p indigo	3.50	1.60
134	CD308	6p olive	.65	3.25
135	CD309	1sh slate	.40	1.25
		Nos. 132-135 (4)	4.85	7.10

George VI Type of 1938
1949, Nov. 1   Engr.   Perf. 12½
Center in Black
136	A24	1p blue green	1.35	1.60
137	A24	1½p carmine rose	1.35	1.60
138	A24	2p carmine	1.35	1.60
		Nos. 136-138 (3)	4.05	4.80

WAR TAX STAMPS

No. 62a Surcharged

1916   Wmk. 3   Perf. 14
MR1	A10	1p + 1p scarlet & blk	3.00	4.00
		Ovptd. "SPECIMEN"	67.50	
a.		Double surcharge	20,000.	

No. 62 Surcharged

1919
MR2	A10	1p + 1p carmine & blk	2.10	5.50
		Ovptd. "SPECIMEN"	67.50	

ST. KITTS-NEVIS

sānt ˈkits-ˈnē-vəs

LOCATION — West Indies southeast of Puerto Rico
GOVT. — Associated State in British Commonwealth
AREA — 153 sq. mi.
POP. — 48,000, excluding Anguilla (est. 1976)
CAPITAL — Basseterre, St. Kitts

A presidency of the Leeward Islands colony.

See "St. Christopher" for stamps used in St. Kitts before 1890. From 1890 until 1903, stamps of the Leeward Islands were used. From 1903 until 1956, stamps of St. Kitts-Nevis and Leeward Islands were used concurrently.

12 Pence = 1 Shilling
20 Shillings = 1 Pound
100 Cents = 1 Dollar (1951)

> Catalogue values for unused stamps in this country are for Never Hinged items, beginning with Scott 91 in the regular postage section.

Columbus Looking for Land — A1   Medicinal Spring — A2

Wmk. Crown and C A (2)

1903	Typo.		Perf. 14	
1	A1	½p grn & vio	2.00	.80
2	A2	1p car & black	5.25	.25
3	A1	2p brn & vio	3.00	12.00
4	A1	2½p ultra & black	20.00	4.75
5	A2	3p org & green	20.00	32.50
6	A1	6p red vio & blk	6.00	45.00
7	A1	1sh org & grn	7.75	12.00
8	A2	2sh blk & grn	13.50	22.50
9	A1	2sh6p violet & blk	20.00	47.50
10	A2	5sh ol grn & gray vio	65.00	62.50
		Nos. 1-10 (10)	162.50	239.80
		Set, ovptd. "SPECIMEN"	145.00	

1905-18			Wmk. 3	
11	A1	½p green & violet	13.00	6.50
12	A1	½p green ('07)	1.10	.65
a.		½p dull blue green ('16)	.70	3.00
13	A2	1p carmine & blk	7.00	.30
14	A2	1p carmine ('07)	2.50	.25
a.		1p scarlet ('16)	1.00	.25
15	A1	2p brn & vio, ordinary paper	11.00	9.00
a.		Chalky paper	7.25	9.00
16	A1	2½p ultra & blk	29.00	4.50
17	A2	2½p ultra	2.75	.60
18	A2	3p org & grn, chalky paper	3.25	3.00
a.		Ordinary paper	16.00	12.00
19	A1	6p red violet & gray blk ('16)	9.00	29.00
a.		6p purple & gray, chalky paper ('08)	23.00	32.50
b.		6p dp vio & gray blk, ordinary paper	27.50	55.00
20	A1	1sh org & grn, chalky paper ('09)	4.00	35.00
a.		Ordinary paper ('09)	32.50	50.00
21	A2	5sh ol grn & gray vio ('18)	37.50	100.00
		Nos. 11-21 (11)	120.10	188.80

Nos. 13, 19a and 21 are on chalky paper only and Nos. 15, 18 and 20 are on both ordinary and chalky paper.
For stamp and type overprinted see #MR1-MR2.

King George V — A3

A4

1920-22			Ordinary Paper	
24	A3	½p green	4.25	6.00
25	A4	1p carmine	2.50	6.75
26	A3	1½p orange	1.40	2.00
27	A4	2p gray	3.25	5.00
28	A3	2½p ultramarine	7.00	10.00
a.		"A" missing from watermark	600.00	

Chalky Paper

29	A3	4p vio & dull vio, yel	2.00	12.00
30	A3	6p red vio & dull vio	4.00	12.00
31	A4	1sh blk, gray grn	4.00	4.50
32	A3	2sh ultra & dull vio, bl	20.00	42.50
33	A4	2sh 6p red & blk, bl	5.50	40.00
34	A3	5sh red & grn, yel	5.50	45.00
35	A4	10sh red & grn, grn	14.50	52.50
36	A3	£1 blk & vio, red ('22)	300.00	375.00
		Nos. 24-36 (13)	373.90	613.25
		Set, ovptd. "SPECIMEN"	360.00	

1921-29		Ordinary Paper	Wmk. 4	
37	A3	½p yel green	2.50	1.50
a.		½p blue green	2.50	1.60
38	A4	1p rose red	.75	.25
39	A4	1p dp violet ('22)	7.50	1.10
a.		1p pale violet ('29)	7.75	1.75
40	A3	1½p rose red ('25)	6.00	2.00
41	A3	1½p fawn ('28)	1.25	.35
42	A4	2p gray	.75	.65
43	A3	2½p pale bright blue ('22)	1.75	2.50
44	A3	2½p brown ('22)	3.50	10.00

Chalky Paper

43a	A3	2½p ultra ('27)	1.75	2.00
45	A4	3p ultra ('22)	1.10	4.75
46	A4	3p dull vio, yel	.85	3.00
47	A3	6p red vio & dull vio ('24)	5.50	6.75
48	A4	1sh black, grn ('29)	4.50	5.00
49	A3	2sh ultra vio, bl ('22)	11.00	27.50
50	A4	2sh6p red & blk, bl ('27)	19.00	29.00
51	A3	5sh red & grn, yel ('29)	50.00	95.00
		Nos. 37-51 (16)	117.70	191.35

No. 43 exists on ordinary and chalky paper.

Caravel in Old Road Bay — A5

1923			Wmk. 4	
52	A5	½p green & blk	2.50	7.75
53	A5	1p violet & blk	5.00	1.75
54	A5	1½p carmine & blk	5.00	11.00
55	A5	2p dk gray & blk	4.25	1.75
56	A5	2½p brown & blk	6.50	35.00
57	A5	3p ultra & blk	4.25	16.00
58	A5	6p red vio & blk	10.50	35.00
59	A5	1sh ol grn & blk	15.00	35.00
60	A5	2sh ultra & blk, bl	52.50	77.50
61	A5	2sh6p red & blk, blue	55.00	92.50
62	A5	10sh red & blk, emer	300.00	500.00

Wmk. 3

63	A5	5sh red & blk, yel	92.50	210.00
64	A5	£1 vio & blk, red	825.00	1,775.
		Nos. 52-63 (12)	553.00	1,023.
		Set, ovptd. "SPECIMEN"	775.00	

Tercentenary of the founding of the colony of St. Kitts (or St. Christopher).

Common Design Types pictured following the introduction.

Silver Jubilee Issue
Common Design Type
Inscribed "St. Christopher and Nevis"

1935, May 6		Engr.		Wmk. 4	
				Perf. 11x12	
72	CD301	1p car & dk blue		1.10	.75
73	CD301	1½p gray blk & ultra		.85	.85
74	CD301	2½p ultra & brown		1.10	.90
75	CD301	1sh brn vio & ind		8.50	16.00
		Nos. 72-75 (4)		11.55	18.50
		Set, never hinged		19.50	
		Set, ovptd. "SPECIMEN"		105.00	

Coronation Issue
Common Design Type
Inscribed "St. Christopher and Nevis"

1937, May 12			Perf. 13½x14	
76	CD302	1p carmine	.25	.30
77	CD302	1½p brown	.30	.25
78	CD302	2½p bright ultra	.40	1.50
		Nos. 76-78 (3)	.95	2.05
		Set, never hinged	1.25	
		Set, ovptd. "SPECIMEN"	87.50	

George VI A6   Medicinal Spring A7

Columbus Looking for Land — A8

Map Showing Anguilla A9

		Perf. 13½x14 (A6, A9), 14 (A7, A8)		
1938-48			**Typo.**	
79	A6	½p green	.25	.25
80	A6	1p carmine	1.00	.55
81	A6	1½p orange	.25	.30
82	A7	2p gray & car	.90	1.40
83	A6	2½p ultra	.50	.35
84	A7	3p car & pale lilac	2.75	5.50
85	A8	6p rose lil & dull vio	5.00	1.60
86	A7	1sh green & gray blk	3.00	1.00
87	A7	2sh6p car & gray blk	8.50	4.50
88	A8	5sh car & dull grn	17.50	13.00

Typo., Center Litho.
Chalky Paper

89	A9	10sh brt ultra & blk	9.50	21.00
90	A9	£1 brown & blk	9.50	25.00
		Nos. 79-90 (12)	58.65	74.45
		Set, never hinged	85.00	
		Set, ovptd. "SPECIMEN"	250.00	

Issued: ½, 1, 1½, 2½p, 8/15/38; 2p, 1941; 3, 6p, 2sh6p, 5sh, 1942; 1sh, 1943; 10sh, £1, 9/1/48.
For types overprinted see Nos. 99-104.

1938, Aug. 15			Perf. 13x11½	
82a	A7	2p	18.00	3.00
84a	A7	3p	16.00	7.50
85a	A8	6p	6.50	3.00
86a	A7	1sh	8.50	1.50
87a	A7	2sh6p	22.50	10.00
88a	A8	5sh	47.50	23.00
		Nos. 82a-88a (6)	119.00	48.00

> Catalogue values for unused stamps in this section, from this point to the end of the section, are for Never Hinged items.

Peace Issue
Common Design Type
Inscribed "St. Kitts-Nevis"

1946, Nov. 1		Engr.	Perf. 13½x14	
91	CD303	1½p deep orange	.25	.25
92	CD303	3p carmine	.25	.25
		Set, perf "SPECIMEN"	82.50	

Silver Wedding Issue
Common Design Types
Inscribed: "St. Kitts-Nevis"

1949, Jan. 3	Photo.	Perf. 14x14½	
93	CD304	2½p bright ultra	.25	.50
		Perf. 11½x11		
	Engraved; Name Typographed			
94	CD305	5sh rose carmine	11.00	6.75

UPU Issue
Common Design Types
Inscribed: "St. Kitt's-Nevis"

	Engr.; Name Typo. on 3p, 6p			
1949, Oct. 10			**Perf. 13½, 11x11½**	
95	CD306	2½p ultra	.25	.35
96	CD307	3p deep carmine	2.50	2.50
97	CD308	6p red lilac	.25	1.40
98	CD309	1sh blue green	.35	.45
		Nos. 95-98 (4)	3.35	4.70

Types of 1938 Overprinted in Black or Carmine

On A6   On A7-A8

		Perf. 13½x14, 13x12½		
1950, Nov. 10			**Wmk. 4**	
99	A6	1p carmine	.25	.25
100	A6	1½p orange	.25	.55
a.		Wmk. 4a (error)	3,000.	
101	A6	2½p ultra	.25	.25
102	A7	3p car & pale lilac	.80	.85
103	A8	6p rose lil & dl grn	.45	.25
104	A7	1sh grn & gray blk (C)	1.50	.40
		Nos. 99-104 (6)	3.50	2.55

300th anniv. of the settlement of Anguilla.

University Issue
Common Design Types
Inscribed: "St. Kitts-Nevis"

			Perf. 14x14½	
1951, Feb. 16		Engr.	**Wmk. 4**	
105	CD310	3c org yel & gray blk	.45	.25
106	CD311	12c red violet & aqua	.45	1.25

St. Christopher-Nevis-Anguilla

Bath House and Spa, Nevis — A10

Map — A11

Designs: 2c, Warner Park, St. Kitts. 4c, Brimstone Hill, St. Kitts. 5c, Nevis. 6c, Pinney's Beach, Nevis. 12c, Sir Thomas Warner's Tomb. 24c, Old Road Bay, St. Kitts. 48c, Picking Cotton. 60c, Treasury, St. Kitts. $1.20, Salt Pond, Anguilla. $4.80, Sugar Mill, St. Kitts.

1952, June 14			Perf. 12½	
107	A10	1c ocher & dp grn	.25	1.75
108	A10	2c emerald	1.00	1.00
109	A11	3c purple & red	.40	1.25
110	A10	4c red	.25	.25
111	A10	5c gray & ultra	.40	.25
112	A10	6c deep ultra	.40	.25
113	A11	12c redsh brn & dp blue	1.25	.25
114	A10	24c car & gray blk	.40	.25
115	A10	48c vio brn & ol bister	3.00	4.75
116	A10	60c dp grn & och	2.25	4.50
117	A10	$1.20 dp ultra & dp green	8.00	4.75
118	A10	$4.80 car & emer	15.00	20.00
		Nos. 107-118 (12)	32.60	39.25

WAR TAX STAMPS

No. 12 Overprinted

1916		**Wmk. 3**		**Perf. 14**
MR1	A1	½p green	1.50	.65
	Overprinted "SPECIMEN"		45.00	

Type of 1905-18 Issue
Overprinted

1918				
MR2	A1	1½p orange	1.50	.95
	Overprinted "SPECIMEN"		50.00	

ST. LUCIA

sānt 'lü-shə

LOCATION — Island in the West Indies, one of the Windward group
GOVT. — British Colony
AREA — 240 sq. mi.
POP. — 126,800 (est. 1984)
CAPITAL — Castries

12 Pence = 1 Shilling
100 Cents = 1 Dollar (1949)

Catalogue values for unused stamps in this country are for Never Hinged items, beginning with Scott 127 in the regular postage section, Scott J3 in the postage due section.

Watermark

Wmk. 5 — Small Star

PRE-STAMP POSTAL MARKINGS

Crowned Circle handstamp type I is pictured in the Crowned Circle Handstamps and Great Britain Used Abroad section.

Castries

1844

A1	I	"St. Lucia" crowned circle handstamp in red, on cover	1,250.

The handstamp was used, in black, as a provisional in April and May 1904, due to a stamp shortage. Value, on cover $375.

STAMPS OF GREAT BRITAIN USED IN ST. LUCIA

Numeral cancellation type A is pictured in the Crowned Circle Handstamps and Great Britain Used Abroad section.

1858-60

A11 (Castries)

A2	A	1p rose red (#20)	1,250.
A3	A	2p blue (#29, P7, 8)	
A4	A	4p rose (#26)	500.00
A5	A	6p lilac (#27)	275.00
A6	A	1sh green (#28)	2,000.

Issued under British Administration

Values for unused stamps are for examples with original gum as defined in the catalogue introduction. Very fine examples of Nos. 1-26 will have perforations touching the design on at least one side due to the narrow spacing of the stamps on the plates. Stamps with perfs clear of the framelines on all four sides are very scarce and will command higher prices.

Queen Victoria — A1

		Perf. 14 to 16		
1860, Dec. 18		**Engr.**		**Wmk. 5**
1	A1	(1p) rose red	110.00	75.00
a.	Double impression		2,500.	
b.	Horiz. pair, imperf vert.		—	
2	A1	(4p) blue	250.00	175.00
a.	Horiz. pair, imperf vert.		—	
b.	4p deep blue		—	
3	A1	(6p) green	325.00	225.00
a.	Horiz. pair, imperf vert.		—	
b.	6p deep green		400.00	275.00
	Nos. 1-3 (3)		685.00	475.00

For types overprinted see #15, 17, 19-26.

1863		**Wmk. 1**		**Perf. 12½**
4	A1	(1p) lake	95.00	110.00
a.	(1p) brownish lake		110.00	110.00
5	A1	(4p) slate blue	140.00	150.00
6	A1	(6p) emerald	225.00	225.00
a.	Watermark inverted		—	
	Nos. 4-6 (3)		460.00	485.00

Nos. 4-6 exist imperforate on stamp paper, from proof sheets.

1864				
7	A1	(1p) black	27.00	14.00
a.	(1p) deep black		24.00	12.50
8	A1	(4p) yellow	190.00	50.00
a.	(4p) olive yellow		425.00	100.00
b.	(4p) lemon yellow		1,750.	
c.	(4p) chrome yellow		225.00	42.50
d.	Watermark reversed		250.00	50.00
9	A1	(6p) violet	140.00	42.50
a.	(6p) lilac		210.00	32.50
b.	(6p) deep lilac		160.00	42.50
10	A1	(1sh) red orange	250.00	32.50
a.	(1sh) orange		275.00	32.50
b.	(1sh) brown orange		360.00	32.50
c.	Horiz. pair, imperf between		—	
	Nos. 7-10 (4)		607.00	139.00

Nos. 7-10 exist imperforate on stamp paper, from proof sheets.

		Perf. 14		
11	A1	(1p) deep black	45.00	22.00
a.	Horiz. pair, imperf between		—	
12	A1	(4p) yellow	130.00	24.00
a.	(4p) olive yellow		325.00	105.00
13	A1	(6p) pale lilac	125.00	24.00
a.	(6p) deep lilac		125.00	45.00
b.	(6p) violet		275.00	77.50
14	A1	(1sh) deep orange	170.00	19.00
a.	(1sh) orange		250.00	25.00
	Nos. 11-14 (4)		470.00	89.00

Type of 1860 Surcharged in Black or Red

a   b

1881				
15	A1(a)	½p green	80.00	100.00
17	A1(b)	2½p scarlet	60.00	27.50

1883-84		**Wmk. Crown and CA (2)**		
19	A1(a)	½p green	29.00	42.50
20	A1(a)	1p black (R)	42.50	16.00
a.	Half used as ½p on cover			
21	A1(a)	4p yellow	325.00	24.00
22	A1(a)	6p violet	45.00	45.00
23	A1(a)	1sh orange	310.00	190.00
	Nos. 19-23 (5)		751.50	317.50

1884				**Perf. 12**
24	A1(a)	4p yellow	300.00	32.50

Nos. 5 & 6 Surcharged

1885		**Wmk. 1**		**Perf. 12½**
25	A1	½p emerald	77.50	
26	A1	6p slate blue	1,500.	

Nos. 25 and 26 were prepared for use but not issued.

A5

Die A

For explanation of dies A and B see "Dies of British Colonial Stamps..." in the catalogue Table of Contents.

1883-98		**Typo.**	**Wmk. 2**	**Perf. 14**
27a	A5	½p green	15.00	9.50
28	A5	1p rose	55.00	18.00
29a	A5	1p lilac ('86)	14.00	7.25
b.	Imperf., pair		900.00	
31a	A5	2½p ultra	70.00	3.00
32a	A5	3p lilac & grn ('86)	150.00	20.00
33a	A5	4p brown ('85)	50.00	1.50
b.	Imperf., pair		1,050.	
34	A5	6p violet ('86)	300.00	240.00
a.	Imperf., pair		2,000.	
35	A5	6p lilac & blue ('87)	7.00	17.50
36	A5	1sh brn org ('85)	450.00	175.00
37a	A5	1sh lil & red ('87)	150.00	37.50
	Nos. 27a-37a (10)		1,224.	515.50
	Nos. 27-39 (10)		812.00	450.50

Die B

27	A5	½p green ('91)	4.00	1.25
29	A5	1p lilac ('91)	7.00	.35
30	A5	2p ultra & brn org ('98)	6.00	1.25
31	A5	2½p ultra ('91)	9.50	1.25
32	A5	3p lilac & grn ('91)	7.50	6.50
33	A5	4p brown ('93)	7.00	2.75
35a	A5	6p lilac & blue ('91)	32.00	29.00
37	A5	1sh lil & red ('91)	11.00	6.00
38	A5	5sh lil & org ('91)	60.00	175.00
39	A5	10sh lil & blk ('91)	110.00	175.00
	Nos. 27-39 (10)		254.00	398.35

Nos. 32, 32a, 35a and 33a Surcharged in Black

No. 40   No. 41   No. 42

Die A

1892				
40a	A5	½p on 3p lil & grn	175.00	85.00
e.	Small "A" in "HALF"		425.00	180.00
f.	Small "O" in "ONE"		425.00	180.00
41	A5	½p on half of 6p lilac & blue	30.00	4.00
a.	Slanting serif		240.00	150.00
c.	Without the bar of "½"		325.00	160.00
d.	"2" of "½" omitted		575.00	600.00
e.	Surcharged sideways		1,700.	
f.	Double surcharge		725.00	725.00
g.	Triple surcharge		1,450.	
h.	Figure "1" used as fraction bar		575.00	325.00
42	A5	1p on 4p brown	8.00	4.25
b.	Double surcharge		275.00	
c.	Inverted surcharge		1,100.	950.00
d.	Thick diagonal stroke in first "N"		30.00	24.00
e.	Thick diagonal stroke in second "N"		30.00	24.00

Die B

40	A5	½p on 3p lil & grn	95.00	30.00
b.	Double surcharge		1,000.	800.00
c.	Inverted surcharge		2,450.	800.00
d.	Triple surcharge, one on back		1,350.	1,500.
g.	Small "O" in "ONE"		240.00	110.00
h.	Small "A" in "HALF"		240.00	110.00
i.	"O" over "H" shift		240.00	110.00
	Nos. 40-42 (3)		213.00	93.25

Edward VII   The Pitons
A9   A10

Numerals of 3p, 6p, 1sh and 5sh of type A9 are in color on plain tablet.

1902-03				**Typo.**
43	A9	½p violet & green	4.50	1.90
44	A9	1p violet & car rose	6.50	.90
46	A9	2½p violet & ultra	35.00	7.50
47	A9	3p violet & yellow	9.50	10.00
48	A9	1sh green & black	17.00	45.00
	Nos. 43-48 (5)		72.50	65.30
	Set, ovptd. "SPECIMEN"		120.00	

Wmk. 1 sideways

1902, Dec. 16				**Engr.**
49	A10	2p brown & green	14.00	2.50
	Overprinted "SPECIMEN"		67.50	

Fourth centenary of the discovery of the island by Columbus.

1904-05		**Typo.**		**Wmk. 3**
50	A9	½p violet & green	8.00	.65
51	A9	1p violet & car rose	8.00	1.40
52	A9	2½p violet & ultra	35.00	2.25
53	A9	3p violet & yellow	12.00	3.25
54	A9	6p vio & dp vio ('05)	25.00	28.00
55	A9	1sh green & blk ('05)	45.00	32.50
56	A9	5sh green & car ('05)	82.50	200.00
	Nos. 50-56 (7)		215.50	268.05

#50, 51, 52, 54 are on both ordinary and chalky paper. #55 is on chalky paper only.

1907-10				
57	A9	½p green	2.00	1.10
58	A9	1p carmine	4.75	.35
59	A9	2½p ultra	4.25	2.00

				Chalky Paper
60	A9	3p violet, yel ('09)	3.25	19.00
61	A9	6p violet & red violet	9.25	40.00
a.	6p violet & dull vio ('10)		75.00	90.00
62	A9	1sh black, grn ('09)	5.25	8.75
63	A9	5sh green & red, yel	67.50	77.50
	Nos. 57-63 (7)		96.25	148.70
	Set, ovptd. "SPECIMEN"		300.00	

King George V
A11   A12

Numerals of 3p, 6p, 1sh and 5sh of type A11 are in color on plain tablet.
For description of dies I and II see "Dies of British Colonial Stamps" in Table of Contents.

Die I

1912-19				**Ordinary Paper**
64	A11	½p deep green	.75	.50
65	A11	1p scarlet	8.00	.25
a.	1p carmine		2.00	.25
66	A12	2p gray ('13)	1.60	4.50
67	A11	2½p bright blue	3.75	3.00
a.	2½p ultra		4.00	3.00

		Chalky Paper		
		Numeral on White Tablet		
68	A11	3p violet, yel	1.40	2.50
a.	Die II		27.50	60.00
69	A11	6p vio & red vio	2.25	20.00
70	A11	1sh black, green	5.50	5.50
a.	1sh black, bl grn, ol back		14.00	16.00
71	A11	1sh fawn	19.00	50.00
72	A11	5sh green & red, yel	26.50	85.00
	Nos. 64-72 (9)		68.75	171.25

A13   A14

1913-14				**Chalky Paper**
73	A13	4p scar & blk, yel	1.00	2.25
74	A14	2sh6p black & red, bl	25.00	50.00

Nos. 64-74, ovptd. "SPECI-
MEN" 250.00

Surface-colored Paper

75	A13	4p scarlet & blk, *yel*	.75	*1.60*
	Overprinted "SPECIMEN"		32.50	

Die II

1921-24   Wmk. 4   Ordinary Paper

76	A11	½p green	1.00	.55
77	A11	1p carmine	14.50	19.00
78	A11	1p dk brn ('22)	1.60	.25
79	A13	1½p rose red ('22)	.85	2.75
80	A12	2p gray	.85	.25
81	A11	2½p ultra	7.50	3.00
82	A11	2½p orange ('24)	15.00	55.00
83	A11	3p dull blue ('24)	6.00	12.00
a.		3p bright blue ('22)	6.00	18.00

Chalky Paper

84	A11	3p violet, *yel*	2.75	13.50
85	A13	4p scar & blk, *yel* ('24)	1.40	2.75
86	A11	6p vio & red vio	2.25	5.25
87	A11	1sh fawn	6.00	3.50
88	A14	2sh6p blk & red, *bl* ('24)	20.00	30.00
89	A11	5sh grn & red, *yel*	60.00	95.00
		Nos. 76-89 (14)	139.70	242.80
		Set, ovptd. "SPECIMEN"	325.00	

Common Design Types
For description of dies I and II see "Dies of British Colonial Stamps" in Table of Contents.

Silver Jubilee Issue
Common Design Type

1935, May 6   Engr.   Perf. 13½x14

91	CD301	½p green & blk	.30	2.00
92	CD301	2p gray blk & ultra	.95	1.40
93	CD301	2½p blue & brn	1.25	1.40
94	CD301	1sh brt vio & ind	13.50	16.00
		Nos. 91-94 (4)	16.00	20.80
		Set, never hinged	26.00	
		Set, perforated "SPECIMEN"	100.00	

Port Castries
A15

Columbus Square, Castries
A16

Ventine Falls
A17

Soldiers' Monument
A19

Fort Rodney, Pigeon Island
A18

Government House
A20

Seal of the Colony
A21

Center in Black

1936, Mar. 1   Perf. 14

95	A15	½p light green	.35	.55
a.		Perf. 13x12	5.00	24.00
96	A16	1p dark brown	.45	.25
a.		Perf. 13x12	9.00	4.00
97	A17	1½p carmine	.70	.35
a.		Perf. 12x13	15.00	2.50
98	A15	2p gray	.60	.25
99	A16	2½p blue	.60	.25
100	A17	3p dull green	1.40	.75
101	A15	4p brown	1.00	1.00
102	A16	6p orange	1.75	.75
103	A18	1sh light blue, perf. 13x12	3.25	2.50
104	A19	2sh6p ultra	14.00	14.00
105	A20	5sh violet	18.00	25.00
106	A21	10sh car rose, perf. 13x12	60.00	90.00
		Nos. 95-106 (12)	102.10	136.15
		Set, never hinged	225.00	
		Set, perforated "SPECIMEN"	250.00	

Nos. 95a, 96a and 97a are coils.
Issue date: Nos. 95a, 96a, Apr. 8.

Coronation Issue
Common Design Type

1937, May 12   Perf. 11x11½

107	CD302	1p dark purple	.25	.40
108	CD302	1½p dark carmine	.40	.25
109	CD302	2½p deep blue	.40	1.40
		Nos. 107-109 (3)	1.05	2.05
		Set, never hinged	1.75	
		Set, perforated "SPECIMEN"	90.00	

King George VI — A22

Columbus Square, Castries
A23

Government House
A24

The Pitons
A25

Loading Bananas
A26

Arms of the Colony — A27

Perf. 12½ (#110-111, 1½p-3½p, 8p, 3sh, 5sh, £1), 12 (6p, 1sh, 2sh, 10sh)

1938-48

110	A22	½p green ('43)	.25	.25
a.		Perf. 14½x14	1.40	.25
111	A22	1p deep violet	.25	.25
a.		Perf. 14½x14	2.00	.85
112	A22	1p red, Perf. 14½x14 ('47)	.25	.25
a.		Perf. 12½	.65	.25
113	A22	1½p carmine ('43)	1.00	1.40
a.		Perf. 14½x14	1.40	.50
114	A22	2p gray ('43)	.25	.25
a.		Perf. 14½x14	2.25	1.75

115	A22	2½p ultra ('43)	.25	.25
a.		Perf. 14½x14	3.00	.25
116	A22	2½p violet ('47)	.85	.25
117	A22	3p red org ('43)	.25	.25
a.		Perf. 14½x14	1.00	.25
118	A22	3½p brt ultra ('47)	.85	.25
119	A23	6p magenta ('48)	6.50	1.75
a.		Perf. 13½	2.00	.50
120	A22	8p choc ('46)	2.75	.40
121	A24	1sh lt brn ('48)	.75	.40
a.		Perf. 13½	1.10	.40
122	A25	2sh red vio & sl bl	3.50	1.50
123	A22	3sh brt red vio ('46)	6.75	2.00
124	A26	5sh rose vio & blk	10.00	11.00
125	A27	10sh black, *yel*	7.50	9.00
126	A21	£1 sepia ('46)	9.00	8.00
		Nos. 110-126 (17)	50.95	37.45
		Set, never hinged	75.00	
		Set, perforated "SPECIMEN"	425.00	

See Nos. 135-148.

> Catalogue values for unused stamps in this section, from this point to the end of the section, are for Never Hinged items.

Peace Issue
Common Design Type

Perf. 13½x14

1946, Oct. 8   Wmk. 4   Engr.

127	CD303	1p lilac	.25	.30
128	CD303	3½p deep blue	.25	.30
		Set, perforated "SPECIMEN"	80.00	

Silver Wedding Issue
Common Design Types

1948, Nov. 26   Photo.   Perf. 14x14½

129	CD304	1p scarlet	.25	.25

Perf.   11½x11
Engraved; Name Typographed

130	CD305	£1 violet brown	22.00	45.00

UPU Issue
Common Design Types
Engr.; Name Typo. on 6c, 12c.
Perf. 13½, 11x11½

1949, Oct. 10   Wmk. 4

131	CD306	5c violet	.25	.85
132	CD307	6c deep orange	1.60	2.50
133	CD308	12c red lilac	.30	.25
134	CD309	24c blue green	.40	.25
		Nos. 131-134 (4)	2.55	3.85

Types of 1938
Values in Cents and Dollars

1949, Oct. 1   Engr.   Perf. 12½

135	A22	1c green	.35	.25
a.		Perf. 14	3.25	.50
136	A22	2c rose lilac	1.25	.25
a.		Perf. 14½x14	4.50	1.25
137	A22	3c red	1.60	2.50
138	A22	4c gray	.95	.25
a.		Perf. 14½x14		17,000.
139	A22	5c violet	1.75	.25
140	A22	6c red orange	1.25	3.50
141	A22	7c ultra	4.00	3.00
142	A22	12c rose lake	6.75	4.00
a.		Perf. 14½x14 ('50)	750.00	550.00
143	A22	16c brown	5.75	.65

Perf.   11½

144	A27	24c Prus blue	.75	.25
145	A27	48c olive green	1.75	1.60
146	A27	$1.20 purple	2.75	10.00
147	A27	$2.40 blue green	4.50	20.00
148	A27	$4.80 dark car rose	11.50	21.00
		Nos. 135-148 (14)	44.90	67.50

Nos. 144 to 148 are of a type similar to A27, but with the denomination in the top corners and "St. Lucia" at the bottom.
For overprints see Nos. 152-155.

University Issue
Common Design Types
Perf. 14x14½

1951, Feb. 16   Wmk. 4

149	CD310	3c red & gray black	.55	.75
150	CD311	12c brown carmine & blk	.85	.75

Phoenix Rising from Burning Buildings — A28

Engr. & Typo.

1951, June 19   Perf. 13½x13

151	A28	12c deep blue & carmine	.50	1.10

Reconstruction of Castries.

Nos. 136, 138, 139 and 142 Overprinted in Black

1951, Sept. 25   Perf. 12½

152	A22	2c rose lilac	.25	.85
153	A22	4c gray	.25	.60
154	A22	5c violet	.25	.85
155	A22	12c rose lilac	.45	.60
		Nos. 152-155 (4)	1.20	2.90

Adoption of a new constitution for the Windward Islands, 1951.

POSTAGE DUE STAMPS

D1

Type I — Nos. J1-J2) 3mm wide (shown).
Type II — Nos. J1a-J2a) 4mm wide.

Rough Perf. 12

1931   Unwmk.   Typeset

J1	D1	1p blk, *gray bl*, type I	10.00	20.00
a.		Type II	24.00	47.50
J2	D1	2p blk, *yel*, type I	22.00	47.50
a.		Type II	45.00	105.00
b.		Vertical pair, imperf. btwn.		7,500.

The serial numbers are handstamped. Type II has round "o" and period. Type I has tall "o" and square period.

> Catalogue values for unused stamps in this section, from this point to the end of the section, are for Never Hinged items.

D2

1933-47   Typo.   Wmk. 4   Perf. 14

J3	D2	1p black	15.00	8.00
J4	D2	2p black	40.00	10.00
J5	D2	4p black ('47)	11.00	50.00
J6	D2	8p black ('47)	11.00	60.00
		Nos. J3-J6 (4)	77.00	128.00
		Set, perforated "SPECIMEN"	160.00	

Issue date: June 28, 1947.

1949, Oct. 1   Values in Cents

J7	D2	2c black	.25	9.50
J8	D2	4c black	.60	13.00
J9	D2	8c black	3.50	47.50
J10	D2	16c black	5.00	65.00
		Nos. J7-J10 (4)	9.35	135.00

Values are for examples on chalky paper, which were issued in 1952. Regular paper examples are worth more.

Wmk. 4a (error)

J7a	D2	2c	40.00
J8a	D2	4c	55.00
J9a	D2	8c	350.00
J10a	D2	16c	475.00
		Nos. J7a-J10a (4)	920.00

WAR TAX STAMPS

No. 65 Overprinted

1916	**Wmk. 3**			**Perf. 14**
MR1	A11	1p scarlet	13.00	19.00
a.		Double overprint	550.00	650.00
b.		1p carmine	67.50	55.00

Overprinted

MR2	A11	1p scarlet	1.40	.35
a.		Overprinted "SPECIMEN"	47.50	

STE. MARIE DE MADAGASCAR

sānt-mə-rē-də-ˌmad-ə-ˈgas-kər

LOCATION — An island off the east coast of Madagascar
GOVT. — French Possession
AREA — 64 sq. mi.
POP. — 8,000 (approx.)

In 1896 Ste.-Marie de Madagascar was attached to the colony of Madagascar for administrative purposes.

100 Centimes = 1 Franc

Navigation and Commerce — A1

1894	**Unwmk.**	**Typo.**	**Perf. 14x13½**	
Name of Colony in Blue or Carmine				
1	A1	1c black, *lil bl*	1.75	1.75
		Never hinged	3.00	
		On cover		190.00
2	A1	2c brown, *buff*	2.75	2.75
		Never hinged	5.25	
		On cover		190.00
3	A1	4c claret, *lavender*	5.00	5.00
		Never hinged	9.25	
		On cover		190.00
4	A1	5c green, *grnsh*	12.00	11.00
		Never hinged	24.00	
		On cover		80.00
5	A1	10c black, *lavender*	13.50	10.50
		Never hinged	27.50	
		On cover		70.00
6	A1	15c blue	40.00	36.00
		Never hinged	80.00	
		On cover		110.00
7	A1	20c red, *green*	30.00	28.00
		Never hinged	62.50	
		On cover		150.00
		On cover, single franking		275.00
8	A1	25c black, *rose*	25.00	22.00
		Never hinged	52.50	
		On cover		80.00
		On cover, single franking		140.00
9	A1	30c brown, *bister*	17.50	16.00
		Never hinged	35.00	
		On cover		140.00
		On cover, single franking		190.00
10	A1	40c red, *straw*	17.50	16.00
		Never hinged	35.00	
		On cover		140.00
		On cover, single franking		250.00
11	A1	50c carmine, *rose*	52.50	52.50
		Never hinged	125.00	
		On cover		250.00
		On cover, single franking		350.00
12	A1	75c violet, *org*	100.00	72.50
		Never hinged	195.00	
		On cover		450.00
		On cover, single franking		550.00
13	A1	1fr brnz grn, *straw*	52.50	47.50
		Never hinged	110.00	
		On cover		425.00
		On cover, single franking		690.00
		Nos. 1-13 (13)	370.00	321.50

Perf. 13½x14 stamps are counterfeits.

Covers: Values are for usages on Ste. Marie de Madagascar. These stamps were also used on Madagascar.

Values are for commercial covers paying correct rates. Philatelic covers sell for less.

These stamps were replaced by those of Madagascar.

ST. PIERRE & MIQUELON

sānt-ˈpiˌər and ˈmik-ə-ˌlän

LOCATION — Two small groups of islands off the southern coast of Newfoundland
GOVT. — French Colony
AREA — 93 sq. mi.
POP. — 6,051 (est. 1984)
CAPITAL — St. Pierre

100 Centimes = 1 Franc

STAMPS OF FRENCH COLONIES GENERAL ISSUES USED IN ST. PIERRE & MIQUELON

Canceled SPM in Lozenge of Dots

On Eagle & Crown Type, #1-6

1859-65				
A1	A1	1c ol grn, *pale bl* ('62)	400.00	
		On cover		
A2	A1	5c yel grn, *grnsh* ('62)	390.00	
		On cover		5.00
A3	A1	10c bister, *yel*	175.00	
		On cover		3,500.
A4	A1	20c bl, *bluish* ('65)	190.00	
		On cover		3,500.
A5	A1	40c org, *yelsh*	170.00	
		On cover		3,500.
A6	A1	80c car rose, *pnksh* ('65)	140.00	
		On cover		925.00

On Ceres and Napoleon III Types, #7//15

1871-72				
A7	A2	1c ol grn, *pale bl* ('72)	325.00	
		On cover		
A10	A4	15c bis, *yelsh* ('72)	900.00	
		On cover		
A12	A4	25c bl, *bluish* ('72)	575.00	
		On cover		9,250.
a.		With circular date stamp		625.00
A13	A5	30c brn, *yelsh*	325.00	
		On cover		8,000.
A14	A4	40c org, *yelsh* (I)	140.00	
		On cover		2,000.
a.		With circular date stamp		190.00
A15	A5	80c rose, *pnksh*	325.00	
		On cover		9,250.

On Ceres Type, #16//23

1872-77				
A16	A6	1c ol grn, *pale bl* ('73)	325.00	
		On cover		
A19	A6	5c grn, *pale bl*	150.00	
		On cover		1,700.
a.		With circular date stamp		170.00
A20	A7	10c bis, *rose* ('76)	97.50	
		On cover		1,100.
a.		With circular date stamp		125.00
		On cover		1,350.
A22	A7	30c brn, *yelsh*	240.00	
		On cover		275.00
a.		With circular date stamp		
A23	A7	80c rose, *pnksh* ('73)	150.00	
		On cover		2,200.
a.		With circular date stamp		175.00

Cancelled with Circular Date Stamps
On Peace & Commerce Types, #24//59

1877-78				
Type I				
A24	A8	1c grn, *grnsh*	425.00	
A25	A8	4c grn, *grnsh*	425.00	
A26	A8	30c brn, *yelsh* ('78)	225.00	
A27	A8	40c ver, *straw*	125.00	

A28	A8	75c rose, *rose* ('78)	325.00	
		On cover		
A29	A8	1fr brnz grn, *straw*	325.00	
		On cover		
Type II				
A30	A8	2c grn, *grnsh*	375.00	
		On cover		
A31	A8	5c grn, *grnsh*	125.00	
		On cover		
A32	A8	10c grn, *grnsh*	160.00	
		On cover		
A33	A8	15c gray, *grnsh*	200.00	
		On cover		
A34	A8	20c red brn, *straw*	150.00	
		On cover		
A35	A8	25c ultra *bluish*	275.00	
		On cover		
A36	A8	35c vio blk, *org* ('78)	95.00	

On Peace & Commerce Type, #38//45

1878-80				
Type II				
A38	A8	1c blk, *lil bl*	290.00	
		On cover		
A40	A8	4c claret, *lav*	290.00	
		On cover		
A41	A8	10c blk, *lav* ('79)	250.00	
		On cover		
A42	A8	15c blue ('79)	90.00	
		On cover		
A43	A8	20c red, *grn* ('79)	225.00	
		On cover		
A45	A8	25c yel, *straw* ('80)	70.00	
		On cover		500.00

On Commerce Type, #46-59

1881-86				
A46	A9	1c blk, *lil bl*	275.00	
		On cover		
A47	A9	2c brn, *buff*	275.00	
		On cover		
A48	A9	4c claret, *lav*	225.00	
		On cover		
A49	A9	5c grn, *grnsh*	82.50	
		On cover		1,000.
A50	A9	10c blk, *lavender*	100.00	
		On cover		1,250.
A51	A9	15c blue	100.00	
		On cover		
A52	A9	20c red, *yel grn*	150.00	
		On cover		2,000.
A53	A9	25c yel, *straw*	40.00	
		On cover		
A54	A9	25c blk, *rose* ('86)	32.50	
		On cover		725.00
A55	A9	30c brn, *bis*	82.50	
		On cover		
A56	A9	35c vio blk, *yel org*	140.00	
a.		35c violet black, *yellow*	200.00	
		On cover		
A57	A9	40c ver, *straw*	200.00	
		On cover		
A58	A9	75c car, *rose*	100.00	
		On cover		
A59	A9	1fr brnz grn, *straw*	160.00	
		On cover		

Covers
Values are for commercial covers bearing correct frankings. Philatelic covers generally sell for less.

REGULAR ISSUES

Stamps of French Colonies Handstamp Surcharged in Black

1885	**Unwmk.**			**Imperf.**
1	A8	05c on 40c ver, *straw*	150.00	60.00
		On cover		1,000.
a.		Surcharge "05" missing		240.00
b.		Surcharge "05" double	375.00	325.00
2	A8	10c on 40c ver, *straw*	45.00	35.00
		On cover		850.00
a.		"M" inverted	375.00	350.00
b.		Surcharge "10" double	225.00	190.00
c.		As "b," one inverted	1,050.	
3	A8	15c on 40c ver, *straw*	45.00	35.00
		On cover		850.00
a.		Double surcharge	525.00	500.00
		Nos. 1-3 (3)	240.00	130.00

Nos. 2 and 3 exist with "SPM" 17mm wide instead of 15½mm.
Nos. 1-3 exist with surcharge inverted and with it doubled.

Handstamp Surcharged in Black

b

c

---

d

1885				
4	A8	(b) 05c on 35c blk, *yel*	160.00	110.00
		On cover		950.00
a.		Double surcharge	800.00	
5	A8	(b) 05c on 75c car, *rose*	375.00	300.00
		On cover		1,100.
a.		Double surcharge	1,400.	
6	A8	(b) 05c on 1fr brnz grn, *straw*	40.00	32.50
		On cover		850.00
a.		Double surcharge	360.00	325.00
b.		"SPM" omitted		260.00
7	A8	(c) 25c on 1fr brnz grn, *straw*	14,000.	2,800.
		On cover		4,000.
a.		"25" sideways		5,800.
b.		"25" reversed		5,250.
c.		Surcharge reversed		
8	A8	(d) 25c on 1fr brnz grn, *straw*	2,700.	1,925.
a.		Surcharge sideways	5,500.	2,900.
b.		"SPM" reversed	5,500.	

Nos. 7 and 8 exist with surcharge inverted, and with it vertical. No. 7 exists with "S P M" above "25" (the handstamping was done in two steps).

1885				**Perf. 14x13½**
9	A9	(c) 5c on 2c brn, *buff*	7,250.	2,700.
a.		Surcharge upright	16,500.	
10	A9	(d) 5c on 4c cl, *lav*	550.00	350.00
		On cover		
a.		Surcharge inverted	1,325.	1,100.
b.		"SPM" double	1,325.	1,100.
11	A9	(b) 5c on 20c red, *grn*	47.50	47.50
		On cover		850.00
a.		Double surcharge	360.00	325.00
b.		"SPM" in larger letters	240.00	200.00

A15

1886, Feb.	**Typo.**			**Imperf.**
Without Gum				
12	A15	5c black		1,500.
		On cover		5,000.
13	A15	10c black		1,600.
		On cover		5,000.
14	A15	15c black		1,400.
		On cover		3,000.
		Nos. 12-14 (3)		4,500.

Used values for Nos. 12-14 are for examples canceled with c.d.s. "St. Pierre et Miquelon." Stamps canceled at Langlade, Miquelon or Ile des Chiens sell for about double these values.
"P D" are the initials for "Payé a destination." Excellent forgeries exist.

Stamps of French Colonies Surcharged in Black

e

f

1891				**Perf. 14x13½**
15	A9	(e) 15c on 30c brn, *bis*	52.50	40.00
		On cover		700.00
a.		Inverted surcharge	310.00	260.00
b.		Double surcharge	260.00	210.00
16	A9	(e) 15c on 35c blk, *org*	725.00	575.00
		On cover		1,500.
a.		Inverted surcharge	875.00	700.00
17	A9	(f) 15c on 35c blk, *org*	2,000.	1,650.
		On cover		
a.		Inverted surcharge		2,100.
18	A9	(e) 15c on 40c red, *straw*	125.00	95.00
		On cover		700.00
a.		Inverted surcharge	300.00	250.00

Stamps of French Colonies Overprinted in Black or Red

1891, Oct. 15

19	A9	1c blk, *lil bl*		17.00	13.50
		Never hinged		30.00	
		On cover			450.00
a.		Inverted overprint		40.00	40.00
b.		"S" omitted in "ST"		100.00	100.00
20	A9	1c blk, *lil bl* (R)		17.00	15.00
		Never hinged		32.50	
		On cover			450.00
a.		Inverted overprint		40.00	40.00
		Never hinged		80.00	
21	A9	2c brn, *buff*		17.00	13.50
		Never hinged		32.50	
		On cover			450.00
a.		Inverted overprint		40.00	40.00
b.		"S" omitted in "ST"		110.00	110.00
22	A9	2c brn, *buff* (R)		32.50	30.00
		Never hinged		65.00	
		On cover			450.00
a.		Inverted overprint		82.50	82.50
		Never hinged		130.00	
23	A9	4c claret, *lav*		17.00	13.50
		Never hinged		32.50	
		On cover			450.00
a.		Inverted overprint		40.00	40.00
b.		"S" omitted in "ST"		110.00	110.00
24	A9	4c claret, *lav* (R)		32.50	30.00
		Never hinged		65.00	
		On cover			450.00
a.		Inverted overprint		65.00	65.00
		Never hinged		120.00	
25	A9	5c grn, *grnsh*		27.50	19.00
		Never hinged		45.00	
		On cover			400.00
a.		Double surcharge		260.00	
b.		"S" omitted in "ST"		130.00	130.00
26	A9	10c blk, *lav*		47.50	40.00
		Never hinged		80.00	
		On cover			400.00
a.		Inverted overprint		95.00	95.00
b.		"S" omitted in "ST"		160.00	160.00
27	A9	10c blk, *lav* (R)		32.50	30.00
		Never hinged		65.00	
		On cover			400.00
a.		Inverted overprint		65.00	65.00
		Never hinged		120.00	
28	A9	15c blue		45.00	32.50
		Never hinged		72.50	
a.		"S" omitted in "ST"		160.00	160.00
29	A9	20c red, *grn*		110.00	100.00
		On cover			400.00
a.		"S" omitted in "ST"		300.00	300.00
30	A9	25c blk, *rose*		40.00	27.50
		Never hinged		65.00	
		On cover			250.00
a.		"S" omitted in "ST"		160.00	160.00
31	A9	30c brn, *bis*		150.00	125.00
		On cover			450.00
a.		"S" omitted in "ST"		400.00	400.00
32	A9	35c vio, *org*		525.00	400.00
		Never hinged		—	
a.		"S" omitted in "ST"		925.00	
33	A9	40c red, *straw*		100.00	80.00
		On cover			450.00
a.		Double surcharge		500.00	
b.		"S" omitted in "ST"		340.00	340.00
34	A9	75c car, *rose*		140.00	130.00
		Never hinged		—	
		On cover			475.00
a.		Inverted overprint		240.00	225.00
b.		"S" omitted in "ST"		425.00	425.00
35	A9	1fr brnz grn, *straw*		120.00	105.00
		Never hinged		—	
		On cover			525.00
a.		Inverted overprint		220.00	220.00
b.		"S" omitted in "ST"		350.00	350.00
		Nos. 19-35 (17)		1,470.	1,204.

Numerous varieties of mislettering occur in the preceding overprint: "ST," "P," "M," "ON," or "-" missing; "-" instead of "ON"; "=" instead of "-" These varieties command values double or triple those of normal stamps.

Surcharged in Black

1891-92

36	A9	1c on 5c grn, *grnsh*		16.00	16.00
		Never hinged		22.50	
		On cover			450.00
37	A9	1c on 10c blk, *lav*		18.00	16.50
		Never hinged		26.00	
		On cover			450.00
a.		Double surcharge		175.00	175.00
38	A9	1c on 25c blk, *rose* ('92)		12.50	12.00
		Never hinged		19.00	
		On cover			450.00
39	A9	2c on 10c blk, *lav*		16.00	16.00
		Never hinged		22.50	
		On cover			450.00
a.		Double surcharge		170.00	170.00
b.		Triple surcharge		350.00	350.00
40	A9	2c on 15c bl		18.00	16.50
		Never hinged		26.00	
		On cover			450.00

41	A9	2c on 25c blk, *rose* ('92)		12.50	12.00
		Never hinged		19.00	
		On cover			450.00
42	A9	4c on 20c red, *grn*		16.00	16.00
		Never hinged		22.50	
		On cover			450.00
b.		"S" omitted in "ST"		120.00	120.00
43	A9	4c on 25c blk, *rose* ('92)		12.50	12.00
		Never hinged		19.00	
		On cover			450.00
a.		Double surcharge		160.00	160.00
b.		As "a," in pair with normal stamp		325.00	
44	A9	4c on 30c brn, *bis*		32.50	26.00
		Never hinged		52.50	
		On cover			450.00
a.		"S" omitted in "ST"		150.00	150.00
b.		"ST PIERRE M-on" double		275.00	
45	A9	4c on 40c red, *straw*		32.50	26.00
		Never hinged		52.50	
		On cover			450.00
		Nos. 36-45 (10)		186.50	169.00

See note after No. 35.

French Colonies 1881-86 Stamps Surcharged in Black

j   k

1892, Nov. 4

46	A9 (j)	1c on 5c grn, *grnsh*		16.00	14.00
		Never hinged		22.50	
		On cover			450.00
47	A9 (j)	2c on 5c grn, *grnsh*		16.00	14.00
		Never hinged		22.50	
		On cover			450.00
48	A9 (j)	4c on 5c grn, *grnsh*		16.00	14.00
		Never hinged		22.50	
		On cover			450.00
49	A9 (k)	1c on 25c blk, *rose*		12.50	12.00
		Never hinged		19.00	
		On cover			450.00
50	A9 (k)	2c on 25c blk, *rose*		12.50	12.00
		Never hinged		19.00	
		On cover			450.00
51	A9 (k)	4c on 25c blk, *rose*		12.50	12.00
		Never hinged		19.00	
		On cover			450.00
		Nos. 46-51 (6)		85.50	78.00

See note after No. 35.

Postage Due Stamps of French Colonies Overprinted in Red

1892, Dec. 1   *Imperf.*

52	D1	10c black		60.00	40.00
		Never hinged		75.00	
		On cover			450.00
53	D1	20c black		40.00	35.00
		Never hinged		62.50	
		On cover			450.00
54	D1	30c black		37.50	37.50
		Never hinged		62.50	
		On cover			500.00
55	D1	40c black		32.50	32.50
		Never hinged		47.50	
		On cover			500.00
56	D1	60c black		140.00	140.00
		Never hinged		—	
		On cover			—

Black Overprint

57	D1	1fr brown		190.00	190.00
		Never hinged		—	
		On cover			—
58	D1	2fr brown		325.00	325.00
		Never hinged		—	
		On cover			—
59	D1	5fr brown		500.00	475.00
		Never hinged		—	
		On cover			—
		Nos. 52-59 (8)		1,325.	1,275.

See note after No. 35. "T P" stands for "Timbre Poste."

Navigation and Commerce — A16

1892-1908   *Typo.*   *Perf. 14x13½*

60	A16	1c blk, *lil bl*		1.90	1.90
		Never hinged		3.00	
		On cover			290.00
61	A16	2c brown, *buff*		1.90	1.90
		Never hinged		3.00	
		On cover			290.00
62	A16	4c claret, *lav*		3.00	3.00
		Never hinged		5.25	
		On cover			250.00

63	A16	5c green, *grnsh*		4.50	3.75
		Never hinged		7.50	
		On cover			95.00
64	A16	5c yel grn ('08)		6.00	3.75
		Never hinged		10.50	
		On cover			62.50
65	A16	10c black, *lav*		8.25	6.75
		Never hinged		14.00	
		On cover			200.00
66	A16	10c red ('00)		6.00	3.75
		Never hinged		10.50	
		On cover			62.50
67	A16	15c bl, quadrille paper		19.00	6.00
		Never hinged		32.50	
		On cover			125.00
68	A16	15c gray, *lt gray* ('00)		100.00	65.00
		Never hinged		200.00	
		On cover			600.00
69	A16	20c red, *grn*		30.00	24.00
		Never hinged		55.00	
		On cover			425.00
		On cover, single franking			550.00
70	A16	25c black, *rose*		13.50	3.75
		Never hinged		25.00	
		On cover			95.00
		On cover, single franking			160.00
71	A16	25c blue ('00)		25.00	15.00
		Never hinged		35.00	
		On cover			125.00
		On cover, single franking			200.00
72	A16	30c brown, *bis*		13.50	9.00
		Never hinged		25.00	
		On cover			250.00
		On cover, single franking			340.00
73	A16	35c blk, *yel* ('06)		8.00	7.25
		Never hinged		13.50	
		On cover			150.00
		On cover, single franking			250.00
74	A16	40c red, *straw*		9.75	9.00
		Never hinged		15.00	
		On cover			250.00
		On cover, single franking			340.00
75	A16	50c car, *rose*		52.50	42.50
		Never hinged		95.00	
		On cover			440.00
		On cover, single franking			550.00
76	A16	50c brown, *az* ('00)		40.00	37.50
		Never hinged		75.00	
		On cover			500.00
		On cover, single franking			625.00
77	A16	75c violet, *org*		35.00	30.00
		Never hinged		60.00	
		On cover			500.00
		On cover, single franking			625.00
78	A16	1fr brnz grn, *straw*		35.00	26.00
		Never hinged		60.00	
		On cover			550.00
		On cover, single franking			675.00
		Nos. 60-78 (19)		412.80	299.80

Perf. 13½x14 stamps are counterfeits.
For surcharges and overprints see Nos. 110-120, Q1-Q2.

Fisherman A17

Fulmar Petrel A18

Fishing Schooner A19

1909-30

79	A17	1c orange red & ol		.40	.50
		Never hinged		.65	
		On cover			110.00
80	A17	2c olive & dp bl		.40	.50
		Never hinged		.65	
		On cover			105.00
81	A17	4c violet & ol		.55	.75
		Never hinged		.85	
a.		Perf 11		160.00	
		Never hinged		240.00	
82	A17	5c bl grn & ol grn		1.20	.75
		Never hinged		1.90	
		On cover			62.50
83	A17	5c blue & blk ('22)		.55	.75
		Never hinged		1.20	
		On cover			105.00
		On cover, single franking			190.00
84	A17	10c car rose & red		1.20	1.10
		Never hinged		2.00	
		On cover			62.50
85	A17	10c bl grn & ol grn ('22)		.75	.75
		Never hinged		1.40	
		On cover			95.00

86	A17	10c bister & mag ('25)		.55	.75
		Never hinged		1.20	
		On cover			62.50
86A	A17	15c dl vio & rose ('17)		.80	.75
		Never hinged		1.25	
		On cover			75.00
87	A17	20c bis brn & vio brn		1.25	1.10
		Never hinged		2.00	
		On cover			95.00
88	A18	25c dp blue & blue		4.50	3.00
		Never hinged		7.50	
		On cover			110.00
		On cover, single franking			225.00
a.		25c dp blue & dp blue		12.00	8.25
		Never hinged		22.50	
		On cover			190.00
b.		Perf 11		160.00	
		Never hinged		240.00	
89	A18	25c ol brn & bl grn ('22)		1.25	1.50
		Never hinged		2.00	
		On cover			62.50
90	A18	30c orange & vio brn		2.60	2.60
		Never hinged		4.00	
		On cover			105.00
		On cover, single franking			225.00
91	A18	30c rose & dull red ('22)		1.75	2.25
		Never hinged		2.60	
		On cover			110.00
92	A18	30c red brn & bl ('25)		1.00	1.00
		Never hinged		1.60	
		On cover			105.00
93	A18	30c gray grn & bl grn ('26)		1.50	2.25
		Never hinged		2.25	
		On cover			110.00
94	A18	35c ol grn & vio brn		.80	.80
		Never hinged		1.25	
		On cover, single franking			105.00
		On cover, single franking			250.00
95	A18	40c vio brn & ol grn		4.00	3.00
		Never hinged		6.00	
		On cover			80.00
		On cover, single franking			150.00
96	A18	45c violet & ol grn		1.10	1.50
		Never hinged		1.90	
		On cover			80.00
		On cover, single franking			150.00
97	A18	50c olive & ol grn		2.25	2.25
		Never hinged		3.75	
		On cover			125.00
		On cover, single franking			275.00
98	A18	50c bl & pale bl ('22)		1.75	2.25
		Never hinged		2.75	
		On cover			110.00
		On cover, single franking			200.00
99	A18	50c yel brn & mag ('25)		1.60	2.25
		Never hinged		2.40	
		On cover			62.50
		On cover, single franking			150.00
100	A18	60c dk bl & ver ('25)		1.40	1.90
		Never hinged		2.25	
		On cover			95.00
		On cover, single franking			200.00
101	A18	65c vio & org brn ('28)		2.50	3.00
		Never hinged		4.00	
		On cover			105.00
		On cover, single franking			225.00
102	A18	75c brown & ol-ive		1.90	2.25
		Never hinged		3.00	
		On cover			125.00
		On cover, single franking			275.00
103	A18	90c brn red & org red ('30)		35.00	37.50
		Never hinged		47.50	
		On cover			340.00
		On cover, single franking			475.00
104	A19	1fr ol grn & dp bl		5.00	3.75
		Never hinged		8.25	
		On cover			105.00
		On cover, single franking			200.00
a.		Perf 11		160.00	
		Never hinged		225.00	
105	A19	1.10fr bl grn & org red ('28)		5.50	7.50
		Never hinged		9.25	
		On cover			190.00
		On cover, single franking			375.00
106	A19	1.50fr bl & dp bl ('30)		15.00	15.00
		Never hinged		20.00	
		On cover			275.00
		On cover, single franking			375.00
107	A19	2fr violet & brn		6.00	4.50
		Never hinged		9.75	
		On cover			125.00
		On cover, single franking			225.00
108	A19	3fr red violet ('30)		18.00	22.50
		Never hinged		30.00	
		On cover			300.00
		On cover, single franking			400.00
109	A19	5fr vio brn & ol grn		13.50	12.50
		Never hinged		20.00	
		On cover			190.00
		On cover, single franking			300.00
a.		Perf 11		160.00	
		Never hinged		240.00	
		Nos. 79-109 (32)		135.55	142.75

For overprints and surcharges see Nos. 121-131, 206C-206D, B1-B2, Q3-Q5. Post

1940 listings are in Scott Standard catalogue, Vol. 5.

Stamps of 1892-1906 Surcharged in Carmine or Black

1912

Spacing between figures of surcharge 1.5mm (5c), 2mm (10c)

110	A16	5c on 2c brn, buff		3.75	4.00
		Never hinged		6.00	
		On cover			125.00
111	A16	5c on 4c claret, lav (C)		1.10	1.50
		Never hinged		1.90	
		On cover			80.00
112	A16	5c on 15c blue (C)		1.10	1.50
		Never hinged		1.90	
		On cover			95.00
113	A16	5c on 20c red, grn		.90	1.10
		Never hinged		1.50	
		On cover			67.50
114	A16	5c on 25c blk, rose (C)		.90	1.10
		Never hinged		1.40	
		On cover			55.00
115	A16	5c on 30c brn, bis (C)		1.10	1.50
		Never hinged		1.50	
		On cover			110.00
116	A16	5c on 35c blk, yel (C)		1.90	2.25
		Never hinged		3.00	
		On cover			110.00
117	A16	10c on 40c red, straw		1.50	1.90
		Never hinged		1.90	
		On cover			95.00
b.		Pair, one stamp without surcharge		625.00	
118	A16	10c on 50c car, rose		1.50	1.90
		Never hinged		2.75	
		On cover			105.00
119	A16	10c on 75c dp vio, org		3.75	4.50
		Never hinged		6.00	
		On cover			125.00
120	A16	10c on 1fr brnz grn, straw		5.25	6.25
		Never hinged		9.00	
		On cover			160.00
		Nos. 110-120 (11)		22.75	27.50

Spacing between figures of surcharge 2.25mm (5c), 2.75mm (10c)

110a	A16	5c on 2c brn, buff		400.00	400.00
		Never hinged		775.00	
111a	A16	5c on 4c claret, lav (C)		37.50	37.50
		Never hinged		75.00	
112a	A16	5c on 15c blue (C)		60.00	60.00
		Never hinged		125.00	
113a	A16	5c on 20c red, grn		26.00	26.00
		Never hinged		52.50	
114a	A16	5c on 25c blk, rose (C)		26.00	26.00
		Never hinged		52.50	
115a	A16	5c on 30c brn, bis (C)		55.00	55.00
		Never hinged		110.00	
116a	A16	5c on 35c blk, yel (C)		22.50	22.50
		Never hinged		40.00	
117a	A16	10c on 40c red, straw		26.00	26.00
		Never hinged		52.50	
118a	A16	10c on 50c car, rose		37.50	37.50
		Never hinged		75.00	
119a	A16	10c on 75c dp vio, org		95.00	95.00
		Never hinged		190.00	
120a	A16	10c on 1fr brnz grn, straw		95.00	95.00
		Never hinged		190.00	
		Nos. 110a-120a (11)		880.50	880.50

Se-tenant Pairs, Both Ovpt. Settings

110b	A16	5c on 2c, #110 + #110a		440.00	440.00
111b	A16	5c on 4c, #111 + #111a		40.00	40.00
		Never hinged		80.00	
112b	A16	5c on 15c, #112 + #112a		67.50	67.50
		Never hinged		150.00	
113b	A16	5c on 20c, #113 + #113a		30.00	30.00
		Never hinged		60.00	
114b	A16	5c on 25c, #114 + #114a		30.00	30.00
		Never hinged		60.00	

115b	A16	5c on 30c, #115 + #115a		62.50	62.50
		Never hinged		120.00	
116b	A16	5c on 35c, #116 + #116a		26.00	26.00
		Never hinged		50.00	
117c	A16	10c on 40c, #117 + #117a		30.00	30.00
		Never hinged		60.00	
118b	A16	10c on 50c, #118 + #118a		45.00	45.00
		Never hinged		85.00	
119b	A16	10c on 75c, #119 + #119a		100.00	100.00
		Never hinged		200.00	
120b	A16	10c on 1fr, #118 + #118a		100.00	100.00
		Never hinged		200.00	

Stamps and Types of 1909-17 Surcharged in Black, Blue (Bl) or Red

1924-27

121	A17	25c on 15c dl vio & rose ('25)		.55	.75
		Never hinged		1.20	
		On cover			62.50
a.		Double surcharge		190.00	
		Never hinged		240.00	
b.		Triple surcharge		210.00	
		Never hinged		260.00	
c.		In pair with unovpted. stamp		700.00	
		Never hinged		1,000.	
122	A19	25c on 2fr vio & lt brn (Bl)		.80	1.10
		Never hinged		1.25	
		On cover			62.50
123	A19	25c on 5fr brn & ol grn (Bl)		.90	1.10
		Never hinged		1.25	
		On cover			62.50
a.		Triple surcharge		210.00	
		Never hinged		250.00	
124	A18	65c on 45c vio & ol grn ('25)		2.25	3.00
		Never hinged		3.75	
		On cover			110.00
		On cover, single franking			210.00
125	A18	85c on 75c brn & ol ('25)		2.25	3.00
		Never hinged		3.75	
		On cover			140.00
		On cover, single franking			250.00
126	A18	90c on 75c brn red & dp org ('27)		3.00	3.75
		Never hinged		4.75	
		On cover			125.00
		On cover, single franking			225.00
127	A19	1.25fr on 1fr dk bl & ultra (R) ('26)		3.00	3.75
		Never hinged		4.75	
		On cover			75.00
		On cover, single franking			140.00
128	A19	1.50fr on 1fr ultra & dk bl ('27)		4.00	4.50
		Never hinged		6.00	
		On cover			87.50
		On cover, single franking			200.00
129	A19	3fr on 5fr ol brn & red vio ('27)		5.25	6.00
		Never hinged		8.25	
		On cover			105.00
		On cover, single franking			225.00
130	A19	10fr on 5fr ver & ol grn ('27)		25.00	29.00
		Never hinged		40.00	
		On cover			210.00
		On cover, single franking			375.00
131	A19	20fr on 5fr vio & ver ('27)		32.50	40.00
		Never hinged		52.50	
		On cover			260.00
		On cover, single franking			475.00
		Nos. 121-131 (11)		79.50	95.95

Common Design Types pictured following the introduction.

Colonial Exposition Issue
Common Design Types

1931, Apr. 13   Engr.   Perf. 12½
Name of Country in Black

132	CD70	40c deep green		6.00	6.00
		Never hinged		9.75	
		On cover			105.00
133	CD71	50c violet		6.00	6.00
		Never hinged		9.75	
		On cover			87.50
134	CD72	90c red orange		6.00	6.00
		Never hinged		9.75	
		On cover			150.00
		On cover, single franking			210.00
135	CD73	1.50fr dull blue		6.00	6.00
		Never hinged		9.75	
		On cover			150.00
		On cover, single franking			200.00
		Nos. 132-135 (4)		24.00	24.00

Map and Fishermen — A20

Lighthouse and Fish — A21

Fishing Steamer and Sea Gulls A22

Perf. 13½x14, 14x13½

1932-33   Typo.

136	A20	1c red brn & ultra		.25	.35
		Never hinged		.40	
		On cover			150.00
137	A21	2c blk & dk grn		.40	.50
		Never hinged		.65	
		On cover			150.00
138	A22	4c mag & ol brn		.40	.60
		Never hinged		.60	
		On cover			140.00
139	A22	5c vio & dk brn		.80	1.10
		Never hinged		1.20	
		On cover			125.00
140	A21	10c red brn & blk		.80	1.10
		Never hinged		1.20	
		On cover			105.00
141	A21	15c dk blue & vio		1.60	2.25
		Never hinged		2.60	
		On cover			95.00
142	A20	20c blk & red org		1.90	2.25
		Never hinged		3.00	
		On cover			75.00
143	A20	25c lt vio & lt grn		1.90	2.25
		Never hinged		3.00	
		On cover			62.50
144	A22	30c ol grn & bl grn		1.90	2.25
		Never hinged		3.00	
		On cover			62.50
145	A22	40c dp bl & dk brn		1.90	2.25
		Never hinged		3.00	
		On cover			62.50
146	A21	45c ver & dp grn		1.90	2.25
		Never hinged		3.00	
		On cover			62.50
147	A21	50c dk brn & dk grn		2.25	2.60
		Never hinged		3.25	
		On cover			55.00
148	A22	65c ol brn & org		2.60	3.00
		Never hinged		4.00	
		On cover			110.00
149	A20	75c grn & red org		2.25	2.60
		Never hinged		3.25	
		On cover			75.00
150	A20	90c dull red & red		2.75	3.75
		Never hinged		4.00	
		On cover			85.00
		On cover, single franking			150.00
151	A22	1fr org brn & org red		2.60	3.00
		Never hinged		3.75	
		On cover			75.00
		On cover, single franking			140.00
152	A20	1.25fr dp bl & lake ('33)		2.60	3.00
		Never hinged		4.00	
		On cover			95.00
		On cover, single franking			190.00
153	A20	1.50fr dp blue & blue		2.60	3.00
		Never hinged		4.00	
		On cover			105.00
		On cover, single franking			200.00
154	A22	1.75fr blk & dk brn ('33)		3.25	3.75
		Never hinged		4.75	
		On cover			110.00
		On cover, single franking			210.00
155	A22	2fr bl blk & Prus bl		12.00	13.50
		Never hinged		17.50	
		On cover			140.00
		On cover, single franking			250.00
156	A21	3fr dp grn & dk brn		15.00	19.00
		Never hinged		21.00	
		On cover			190.00
		On cover, single franking			300.00
157	A21	5fr brn red & dk brn		32.50	37.50
		Never hinged		42.50	
		On cover			340.00
		On cover, single franking			500.00
158	A22	10fr dk grn & vio		75.00	82.50
		Never hinged		120.00	
		On cover			500.00
		On cover, single franking			675.00

159	A20	20fr ver & dp grn		85.00	92.50
		Never hinged		125.00	
		On cover			550.00
		On cover, single franking			750.00
		Nos. 136-159 (24)		254.15	286.85

For overprints and surcharges see Nos. 160-164, 207-221 (in Scott Standard catalogue, Vol. 5).

Nos. 147, 149, 153-154, 157 Overprinted in Black, Red or Blue

p

q

1934, Oct. 18

160	A21(p)	50c (Bk)		6.50	7.50
		Never hinged		10.00	
		On cover			105.00
161	A20(q)	75c (Bk)		9.50	10.50
		Never hinged		13.50	
		On cover			125.00
162	A20(q)	1.50fr (Bk)		9.50	10.50
		Never hinged		16.00	
		On cover			170.00
		On cover, single franking			250.00
163	A22(p)	1.75fr (R)		10.00	12.50
		Never hinged		17.00	
		On cover			160.00
		On cover, single franking			225.00
164	A21(p)	5fr (Bl)		45.00	47.50
		Never hinged		75.00	
		On cover			300.00
		On cover, single franking			500.00
		Nos. 160-164 (5)		80.50	88.50

400th anniv. of the landing of Jacques Cartier.

Paris International Exposition Issue
Common Design Types

1937   Perf. 13

165	CD74	20c deep violet		2.40	2.75
		Never hinged		3.25	
		On cover			105.00
166	CD75	30c dark green		2.40	2.75
		Never hinged		3.25	
		On cover			87.50
167	CD76	40c carmine rose		2.40	2.75
		Never hinged		3.25	
		On cover			80.00
168	CD77	50c dk brown & blue		2.40	2.75
		Never hinged		3.25	
		On cover			75.00
169	CD78	90c red		2.50	2.75
		Never hinged		3.50	
		On cover			140.00
		On cover, single franking			225.00
170	CD79	1.50fr ultra		2.50	2.75
		Never hinged		3.50	
		On cover			125.00
		On cover, single franking			200.00
		Nos. 165-170 (6)		14.60	16.50

Colonial Arts Exhibition Issue
Souvenir Sheet
Common Design Type

1937   Imperf.

171	CD78	3fr dark ultra		35.00	47.50
		Never hinged		52.50	
		On cover			190.00
		On cover, single franking			250.00

Dog Team A23

Port St. Pierre A24

Tortue
Lighthouse
A25

Soldiers'
Bay at
Langlade
A26

1938-40   Photo.   Perf. 13½x13

172	A23	2c dk blue green	.25	.35
		Never hinged	.40	
		On cover		105.00
a.		Value omitted	425.00	
		Never hinged	540.00	
173	A23	3c brown violet	.25	.35
		Never hinged	.40	
		On cover		105.00
174	A23	4c dk red violet	.30	.40
		Never hinged	.45	
		On cover		105.00
175	A23	5c carmine lake	.30	.40
		Never hinged	.45	
		On cover		95.00
176	A23	10c bister brown	.30	.40
		Never hinged	.45	
		On cover		87.50
177	A23	15c red violet	.65	.80
		Never hinged	.95	
		On cover		85.00
178	A23	20c blue violet	.90	1.10
		Never hinged	1.25	
		On cover		75.00
179	A23	25c Prus blue	2.50	3.00
		Never hinged	3.40	
		On cover		62.50
180	A24	30c dk red violet	.65	.80
		Never hinged	.95	
		On cover		62.50
181	A24	35c deep green	.90	1.10
		Never hinged	1.25	
		On cover		62.50
182	A24	40c slate blue ('40)	.25	.35
		Never hinged	.40	
		On cover		62.50
183	A24	45c dp grn ('40)	.50	.60
		Never hinged	.65	
		On cover		67.50
a.		Value omitted	110.00	
		Never hinged	175.00	
184	A24	50c carmine rose	.90	1.10
		Never hinged	1.25	
		On cover		75.00
185	A24	55c Prus blue	4.25	4.50
		Never hinged	6.00	
		On cover		80.00
186	A24	60c violet ('39)	.65	.90
		Never hinged	1.00	
		On cover		62.50
187	A24	65c brown	6.50	6.75
		Never hinged	8.75	
		On cover		100.00
188	A24	70c org yel ('39)	.75	1.00
		Never hinged	1.10	
		On cover		55.00
189	A25	80c violet	1.60	1.90
		Never hinged	2.50	
		On cover		62.50
190	A25	90c ultra ('39)	1.00	1.25
		Never hinged	1.40	
		On cover		55.00
191	A25	1fr brt pink	13.00	14.00
		Never hinged	16.50	
		On cover		150.00
		On cover, single franking		250.00
192	A25	1fr pale ol grn ('40)	1.00	1.25
		Never hinged	1.40	
		On cover		55.00
193	A25	1.25fr brt rose ('39)	2.40	2.75
		Never hinged	3.00	
		On cover		105.00
		On cover, single franking		150.00
194	A25	1.40fr dk brown ('40)	1.25	1.50
		Never hinged	1.60	
		On cover		75.00
		On cover, single franking		110.00
195	A25	1.50fr blue green	1.25	1.50
		Never hinged	1.75	
		On cover		75.00
		On cover, single franking		150.00
196	A25	1.60fr rose violet ('40)	1.25	1.50
		Never hinged	1.60	
		On cover		75.00
		On cover, single franking		150.00
197	A25	1.75fr deep blue	3.50	4.50
		Never hinged	5.25	
		On cover		105.00
		On cover, single franking		190.00
198	A26	2fr rose violet	.90	1.10
		Never hinged	1.25	
		On cover		75.00
		On cover, single franking		125.00
199	A26	2.25fr brt blue ('39)	1.25	1.60
		Never hinged	1.75	
		On cover		95.00
		On cover, single franking		140.00
200	A26	2.50fr org yel ('40)	1.25	1.50
		Never hinged	1.90	
		On cover		100.00
		On cover, single franking		150.00
201	A26	3fr gray brown	1.10	1.50
		Never hinged	1.60	
		On cover		75.00
		On cover, single franking		125.00

202	A26	5fr henna brown	1.25	1.50
		Never hinged	1.60	
		On cover		85.00
		On cover, single franking		140.00
203	A26	10fr dk bl, bluish	1.90	2.25
		Never hinged	2.00	
		On cover		95.00
		On cover, single franking		150.00
204	A26	20fr slate green	2.50	3.00
		Never hinged	3.25	
		On cover		110.00
		On cover, single franking		190.00
		Nos. 172-204 (33)	57.20	66.50

For overprints and surcharges see Nos. 222-255, 260-299, B9-B10 in Scott Standard catalogue, Vol. 5.

New York World's Fair Issue
Common Design Type

1939, May 10   Engr.   Perf. 12½x12

205	CD82	1.25fr carmine lake	2.40	3.00
		Never hinged	3.40	
		On cover		100.00
		On cover, single franking		190.00
206	CD82	2.25fr ultra	2.40	3.00
		Never hinged	3.40	
		On cover		95.00
		On cover, single franking		140.00

For overprints and surcharges see Nos. 256-259 in Scott Standard catalogue, Vol. 5.

SEMI-POSTAL STAMPS

Regular
Issue of
1909-17
Surcharged
in Red

1915-17   Unwmk.   Perf. 14x13½

B1	A17	10c + 5c car rose & red	3.00	3.75
		Never hinged	4.50	
		On cover		95.00
B2	A17	15c + 5c dl vio & rose ('17)	3.00	3.75
		Never hinged	4.50	
		On cover		95.00

Curie Issue
Common Design Type

1938, Oct. 24   Engr.   Perf. 13

B3	CD80	1.75fr + 50c brt ultra	21.00	22.50
		Never hinged	29.00	
		On cover		140.00
		On cover, single franking		250.00

French Revolution Issue
Common Design Type

1939, July 5   Photo.
Name and Value Typo. in Black

B4	CD83	45c + 25c green	13.50	14.50
		Never hinged	19.00	
		On cover		140.00
B5	CD83	70c + 30c brown	13.50	14.50
		Never hinged	19.00	
		On cover		105.00
B6	CD83	90c + 35c red org	13.50	14.50
		Never hinged	19.00	
		On cover		95.00
B7	CD83	1.25fr + 1fr rose pink	13.50	14.50
		Never hinged	19.00	
		On cover		150.00
		On cover, single franking		225.00
B8	CD83	2.25fr + 2fr blue	13.50	14.50
		Never hinged	19.00	
		On cover		140.00
		On cover, single franking		200.00
		Nos. B4-B8 (5)	67.50	72.50

POSTAGE DUE STAMPS

Postage Due Stamps of
French Colonies
Overprinted in Red

1892   Unwmk.   Imperf.

J1	D1	5c black	85.00	85.00
		On cover		—
J2	D1	10c black	26.00	26.00
		Never hinged	55.00	
		On cover		1,000.
J3	D1	15c black	26.00	26.00
		Never hinged	55.00	
		On cover		1,000.
J4	D1	20c black	26.00	26.00
		Never hinged	55.00	
		On cover		1,000.

J5	D1	30c black	26.00	26.00
		Never hinged	55.00	
		On cover		1,000.
J6	D1	40c black	26.00	26.00
		Never hinged	55.00	
		On cover		1,000.
J7	D1	60c black	82.50	90.00
		On cover		1,200.

Black Overprint

J8	D1	1fr brown	200.00	200.00
J9	D1	2fr brown	200.00	200.00
		Nos. J1-J9 (9)	697.50	705.00

These stamps exist with and without hyphen. See note after No. 59.

Postage Due Stamps of
France, 1893-1924,
Overprinted

1925-27   Perf. 14x13½

J10	D2	5c blue	.75	1.10
		Never hinged	1.10	
		On cover		190.00
J11	D2	10c dark brown	.75	1.10
		Never hinged	1.10	
		On cover		200.00
J12	D2	20c olive green	.80	1.10
		Never hinged	1.10	
		On cover		210.00
J13	D2	25c rose	1.10	1.50
		Never hinged	1.50	
		On cover		210.00
J14	D2	30c red	1.90	2.25
		Never hinged	2.60	
		On cover		210.00
J15	D2	45c blue green	1.90	2.25
		Never hinged	2.60	
		On cover		240.00
J16	D2	50c brown vio	2.60	3.75
		Never hinged	4.50	
		On cover		275.00
J17	D2	1fr red brn, straw	3.50	4.00
		Never hinged	4.75	
		On cover		300.00
J18	D2	3fr magenta ('27)	12.00	15.00
		Never hinged	20.00	
		On cover		350.00

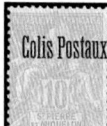

Surcharged

J19	D2	60c on 50c buff	2.75	3.75
		Never hinged	4.75	
		On cover		275.00
J20	D2	2fr on 1fr red	4.50	5.50
		Never hinged	8.25	
		On cover		300.00
		Nos. J10-J20 (11)	32.55	41.30

Newfoundland Dog — D3

1932, Dec. 5   Typo.

J21	D3	5c dk blue & blk	1.50	1.90
		Never hinged	2.25	
		On cover		125.00
J22	D3	10c green & blk	1.50	1.90
		Never hinged	2.25	
		On cover		125.00
J23	D3	20c red & blk	1.75	2.25
		Never hinged	2.75	
		On cover		140.00
J24	D3	25c red vio & blk	1.75	2.25
		Never hinged	2.75	
		On cover		140.00
J25	D3	30c orange & blk	3.50	4.50
		Never hinged	5.25	
		On cover		150.00
J26	D3	45c lt blue & blk	5.50	6.75
		Never hinged	8.75	
		On cover		170.00
J27	D3	50c blue grn & blk	8.50	10.50
		Never hinged	12.00	
		On cover		210.00
J28	D3	60c brt rose & blk	12.00	15.00
		Never hinged	16.00	
		On cover		210.00
J29	D3	1fr yellow brn & blk	22.50	30.00
		Never hinged	32.50	
		On cover		250.00
J30	D3	2fr dp violet & blk	32.50	37.50
		Never hinged	55.00	
		On cover		300.00
J31	D3	3fr dk brown & blk	45.00	55.00
		Never hinged	65.00	
		On cover		375.00
		Nos. J21-J31 (11)	136.00	167.55

For overprints and surcharge see Nos. J42-J46 in Scott Standard catalogue, Vol. 5.

Codfish — D4

1938, Nov. 17   Photo.   Perf. 13

J32	D4	5c gray black	.40	.50
		Never hinged	.65	
		On cover		80.00
J33	D4	10c dk red violet	.40	.50
		Never hinged	.65	
		On cover		80.00
J34	D4	15c slate green	.50	.75
		Never hinged	.70	
		On cover		95.00
J35	D4	20c deep blue	.55	.75
		Never hinged	.75	
		On cover		95.00
J36	D4	30c rose carmine	.55	.75
		Never hinged	.70	
		On cover		95.00
J37	D4	50c dk blue green	.70	.80
		Never hinged	.95	
		On cover		100.00
J38	D4	60c dk blue	.95	1.10
		Never hinged	1.25	
		On cover		110.00
J39	D4	1fr henna brown	1.90	2.25
		Never hinged	2.50	
		On cover		140.00
J40	D4	2fr gray brown	4.50	5.25
		Never hinged	6.00	
		On cover		175.00
J41	D4	3fr dull violet	4.75	6.00
		Never hinged	7.00	
		On cover		210.00
		Nos. J32-J41 (10)	15.20	18.65

For overprints see Nos. J48-J67 in Scott Standard catalogue, Vol. 5.

PARCEL POST STAMPS

No. 65 Overprinted

1901   Unwmk.   Perf. 14x13½

Q1	A16	10c black, lavender	140.00	140.00
		Never hinged	225.00	
a.		Inverted overprint	1,250.	1,250.
b.		Double overprint	600.00	600.00

No. 66 Overprinted

Q2	A16	10c red	30.00	32.50
		Never hinged	52.50	

Nos. 84
and 87
Overprinted

1917-25

Q3	A17	10c car rose & red	4.50	6.00
		Never hinged	6.75	
a.		Double overprint	300.00	
		Never hinged	360.00	
Q4	A17	20c bis brn & vio brn ('25)	3.75	5.25
		Never hinged	5.25	
a.		Double overprint	190.00	
		Never hinged	260.00	

ST. THOMAS & PRINCE ISLANDS

sänt-'täm-əs and 'prin̪t̪s 'ī-lənd

LOCATION — Two islands in the Gulf of Guinea, 125 miles off the west coast of Africa
GOVT. — Portuguese Colony
AREA — 372 sq. mi.
POP. — 102,000 (est. 1984)
CAPITAL — Sao Tome

1000 Reis = 1 Milreis
100 Centavos = 1 Escudo (1913)

Portuguese Crown — A1   King Luiz — A2

5, 25, 50 REIS:
Type I — "5" is upright.
Type II — "5" is slanting.

10 REIS:
Type I — "1" has short serif at top.
Type II — "1" has long serif at top.

40 REIS:
Type I — "4" is broad.
Type II — "4" is narrow.

Perf. 12½, 13½

			Unwmk.	Typo.
1	A1	5r black, I	2.00	1.90
a.		Type II	2.00	1.90
2	A1	10r yellow, I	14.00	8.50
a.		Type II	17.50	10.50
3	A1	20r bister	3.50	2.75
4	A1	25r rose, I	1.25	1.10
a.		25r red	4.50	1.50
5	A1	40r blue ('75), I	5.00	3.50
a.		Type II	5.50	4.50
6	A1	50r gray grn, II	9.00	7.00
a.		Type I	15.00	14.00
7	A1	100r gray lilac	6.00	5.50
8	A1	200r red orange ('75)	9.00	6.25
9	A1	300r chocolate ('75)	9.00	7.00
		Nos. 1-9 (9)	58.75	43.50

1881-85

10	A1	10r gray grn, I	8.00	6.75
a.		Type II	9.50	6.00
b.		Perf. 13½, I	11.00	8.00
11	A1	20r car rose ('85)	4.00	3.00
12	A1	25r vio ('85), II	2.25	1.75
13	A1	40r yel buff, II	5.00	4.00
a.		Perf. 13½	6.00	4.50
14	A1	50r dk blue, I	2.50	2.25
a.		Type II	2.50	2.25
		Nos. 10-14 (5)	21.75	17.75

For surcharges and overprints see Nos. 63-64, 129-129B, 154.

Nos. 1-14 have been reprinted on stout white paper, ungummed, with rough perforation 13½, also on ordinary paper with shiny white gum and clean-cut perforation 13½ with large holes.

Typo., Head Embossed

1887   Perf. 12½, 13½

15	A2	5r black	3.75	2.50
16	A2	10r green	4.25	2.50
17	A2	20r brt rose	4.25	3.00
a.		Perf. 12½	55.00	55.00
18	A2	25r violet	4.25	1.60
19	A2	40r brown	4.25	2.25
20	A2	50r blue	4.25	2.25
21	A2	100r yellow brn	4.25	2.00
22	A2	200r gray lilac	15.00	10.50
23	A2	300r orange	15.00	10.50
		Nos. 15-23 (9)	59.25	37.35

For surcharges and overprints see Nos. 24-26, 62, 65-72, 130-131, 155-158, 234-237.

Nos. 15, 16, 19, 21, 22, and 23 have been reprinted in paler colors than the originals, with white gum and cleancut perforation 13½. Value $1.50 each.

Nos. 16-17, 19 Surcharged

a   b

c

1889-91   Without Gum

24	A2(a)	5r on 10r	35.00	20.00
25	A2(b)	5r on 20r	25.00	20.00
26	A2(c)	50r on 40r ('91)	225.00	50.00
		Nos. 24-26 (3)	285.00	90.00

Varieties of Nos. 24-26, including inverted and double surcharges, "5" inverted, "Cinoc" and "Cinco," were deliberately made and unofficially issued.

King Carlos
A6   A7

1895   Typo.   Perf. 11½, 12½

27	A6	5r yellow	1.00	.60
28	A6	10r red lilac	1.50	1.00
29	A6	15r red brown	1.50	1.10
30	A6	20r lavender	2.00	1.10
31	A6	25r green	2.00	.75
32	A6	50r light blue	2.00	.70
a.		Perf. 13½	3.00	1.50
33	A6	75r rose	8.00	3.25
34	A6	80r yellow grn	8.00	6.25
35	A6	100r brn, yel	4.00	3.00
36	A6	150r car, rose	6.00	5.00
37	A6	200r dk bl, bl	7.75	6.50
38	A6	300r dk bl, sal	8.50	7.75
		Nos. 27-38 (12)	52.25	37.00

For surcharges and overprints see Nos. 73-84, 132-137, 159-165, 238-243, 262-264, 268-274.

1898-1903   Perf. 11½

Name and Value in Black except 500r

39	A7	2½r gray	.30	.25
40	A7	5r orange	.30	.25
41	A7	10r lt green	.40	.30
42	A7	15r brown	2.00	1.75
43	A7	15r gray grn ('03)	1.10	1.10
44	A7	20r gray violet	.90	.50
45	A7	25r sea green	.70	.25
46	A7	25r carmine ('03)	1.10	.30
47	A7	50r blue	1.00	.50
48	A7	50r brown ('03)	4.50	4.50
49	A7	65r dull blue ('03)	20.00	9.00
50	A7	75r rose	10.00	6.50
51	A7	75r red lilac ('03)	2.50	1.40
52	A7	80r brt violet	5.00	5.00
53	A7	100r dk blue, bl	3.00	2.00
54	A7	115r org brn, pink ('03)	10.00	8.00
55	A7	130r brn, straw ('03)	10.00	6.00
56	A7	150r brn, buff	5.00	2.25
57	A7	200r red lil, pnksh	6.00	2.75
58	A7	300r dk blue, rose	8.00	5.00
59	A7	400r dull bl, straw ('03)	15.00	8.50
60	A7	500r blk & red, bl ('01)	10.00	5.00
61	A7	700r vio, yelsh ('01)	16.00	12.00
		Nos. 39-61 (23)	132.80	83.10

For overprints and surcharges see Nos. 86-105, 116-128, 138-153, 167-169, 244-249, 255-261, 265-267.

Stamps of 1869-95
Surcharged in Red or Black

1902

62	A2	130r on 5r blk (R)	6.00	5.00
a.		Perf. 13½	32.50	32.50

On Stamps of 1869

63	A1	115r on 50r grn	10.00	7.50
64	A1	400r on 10r yel	25.00	12.00
a.		Double surcharge	75.00	50.00

On Stamps of 1887

65	A2	65r on 20r rose	6.25	4.50
a.		Perf. 13½	8.50	7.00
66	A2	65r on 25r violet	4.50	4.00
a.		Inverted surcharge	35.00	25.00
67	A2	65r on 100r yel brn	4.50	4.75
68	A2	115r on 10r blue grn	4.50	4.00
69	A2	115r on 300r orange	4.50	4.00
70	A2	130r on 200r gray lil	6.00	5.00
71	A2	400r on 40r brown	8.00	7.00
72	A2	400r on 50r blue	14.00	12.00
a.		Perf. 13½	110.00	90.00

On Stamps of 1895

73	A6	65r on 5r yellow	5.00	3.00
74	A6	65r on 10r red vio	5.00	3.00
75	A6	65r on 15r choc	5.00	3.00
76	A6	65r on 20r lav	5.00	3.00
77	A6	115r on 25r grn	5.00	3.00
78	A6	115r on 150r car, rose	5.00	3.00
79	A6	115r on 200r bl, bl	5.00	3.00
80	A6	130r on 75r rose	5.00	3.00
81	A6	130r on 100r brn, yel	5.00	3.50
a.		Double surcharge	30.00	20.00
82	A6	130r on 300r bl, sal	5.00	3.00
83	A6	400r on 50r lt blue	1.10	.95
a.		Perf. 13½	2.00	1.60
84	A6	400r on 80r yel grn	2.00	1.50

On Newspaper Stamp No. P12

85	N3	400r on 2½r brown	1.10	.95
a.		Double surcharge		
		Nos. 62-85 (24)	147.45	103.65

Reprints of Nos. 63, 64, 67, 71, and 72 have shiny white gum and clean-cut perf. 13½.

Stamps of 1898
Overprinted

1902

86	A7	15r brown	2.00	1.50
87	A7	25r sea green	2.00	1.25
88	A7	50r blue	2.25	1.25
89	A7	75r rose	5.00	3.50
		Nos. 86-89 (4)	11.25	7.50

No. 49 Surcharged in Black

1905

90	A7	50r on 65r dull blue	5.00	2.75

Stamps of 1898-1903
Overprinted in Carmine or Green

1911

91	A7	2½r gray	.25	.25
a.		Inverted overprint	15.00	11.00
92	A7	5r orange	.25	.25
93	A7	10r lt green	.25	.25
a.		Inverted overprint	15.00	12.00
94	A7	15r gray green	.25	.25
95	A7	20r gray violet	.25	.25
96	A7	25r carmine (G)	.60	.25
97	A7	50r brown	.30	.25
a.		Inverted overprint	15.00	12.00
98	A7	75r red lilac	.40	.25
99	A7	100r dk bl, bl	.75	.50
a.		Inverted overprint	17.50	14.00
100	A7	115r org brn, pink	1.50	.95
101	A7	130r brown, straw	1.50	.95
102	A7	200r red lil, pnksh	6.00	4.25
103	A7	400r dull blue, straw	2.00	1.00
104	A7	500r blk & red, bl	2.00	1.00
105	A7	700r violet, yelsh	2.00	1.00
		Nos. 91-105 (15)	18.30	11.65

King Manuel II — A8

Overprinted in Carmine or Green

1912   Perf. 11½, 12

106	A8	2½r violet	.25	.25
a.		Double overprint	16.00	16.00
b.		Double overprint, one inverted	25.00	
107	A8	5r black	.25	.25
108	A8	10r gray green	.25	.25
a.		Double overprint	14.00	14.00
109	A8	20r carmine (G)	1.00	.75
110	A8	25r violet brn	.60	.45
111	A8	50r dk blue	.60	.55
112	A8	75r bister brn	.90	.55
113	A8	100r brn, lt grn	1.10	.50
114	A8	200r dk grn, sal	2.00	1.40
115	A8	300r black, azure	2.00	2.00
		Nos. 106-115 (10)	8.95	6.95

Stamps of 1898-1905
Overprinted in Black

1913   On Stamps of 1898-1903

116	A7	2½r gray	2.00	1.00
a.		Inverted overprint	15.00	15.00
b.		Double overprint	12.00	12.00
117	A7	5r orange	1.50	1.00
118	A7	15r gray green	22.50	17.50
a.		Inverted overprint	75.00	
119	A7	20r gray violet	3.00	1.50
a.		Inverted overprint	15.00	
120	A7	25r carmine	9.00	4.50
a.		Inverted overprint	30.00	
b.		Double overprint	30.00	
121	A7	75r red lilac	6.00	5.00
122	A7	100r bl, bluish	10.00	7.50
123	A7	115r org brn, pink	37.50	35.00
a.		Double overprint	75.00	60.00
124	A7	130r brn, straw	13.00	13.00
125	A7	200r red lil, pnksh	20.00	13.00
126	A7	400r dl bl, straw	14.00	12.50
127	A7	500r blk & red, gray	35.00	42.50
128	A7	700r vio, yelsh	47.50	40.00
		Nos. 116-128 (13)	221.00	194.00

On Provisional Issue of 1902

129	A1	115r on 50r grn	110.00	85.00
a.		Inverted overprint		
129B	A1	400r on 10r yel	600.00	500.00
130	A2	115r on 10r blue grn	3.00	2.50
a.		Inverted overprint	25.00	
131	A2	400r on 50r blue	75.00	75.00
132	A6	115r on 25r grn	2.00	1.75
a.		Inverted overprint	20.00	
133	A6	115r on 150r car, rose	42.50	40.00
a.		Inverted overprint	20.00	
134	A6	115r on 200r bl, bl	3.00	2.00
a.		Inverted overprint	25.00	
135	A6	130r on 75r rose	3.00	2.00
a.		Inverted overprint	25.00	
136	A6	400r on 50r lt bl	4.00	4.00
a.		Perf. 13½	20.00	10.00
137	A6	400r on 80r yel grn	5.00	4.25

Same Overprint on Nos. 86, 88, 90

138	A7	15r brown	3.00	1.75
139	A7	50r blue	3.00	2.00
140	A7	50r on 65r dl bl	16.00	12.00
		Nos. 138-140 (3)	22.00	15.75

No. 123-125, 130-131 and 137 were issued without gum.

Stamps of 1898-1905
Overprinted in Black

On Stamps of 1898-1903

141	A7	2½r gray	.60	.50
a.		Inverted overprint	9.00	
b.		Double overprint	11.00	11.00
c.		Double overprint inverted	30.00	
142	A7	5r orange	27.50	22.50
143	A7	15r gray green	2.00	1.50
a.		Inverted overprint	25.00	
144	A7	20r gray violet	400.00	200.00
a.		Inverted overprint	500.00	
145	A7	25r carmine	40.00	27.50
a.		Inverted overprint	75.00	
146	A7	75r red lilac	3.00	2.25
a.		Inverted overprint	5.00	

147 A7 100r blue, *bl*   2.25   1.75
148 A7 115r org brn, *pink*   10.00   8.00
  a.   Inverted overprint   25.00
149 A7 130r brown, *straw*   8.00   7.00
  a.   Inverted overprint   25.00
150 A7 200r red lil, *pnksh*   2.50   1.75
  a.   Inverted overprint   10.00
151 A7 400r dull bl, *straw*   10.00   8.00
152 A7 500r blk & red,
                      gray   9.00   8.50
153 A7 700r violet, *yelsh*   9.00   8.50

On Provisional Issue of 1902

154 A1 115r on 50r green   200.00 150.00
155 A2 115r on 10r bl grn   2.50   2.25
156 A2 115r on 300r org   250.00 125.00
157 A2 130r on 5r black   300.00 125.00
158 A2 400r on 50r blue   200.00 90.00
159 A6 115r on 25r green   2.00   1.75
160 A6 115r on 15r car,
                      rose   2.50   2.25
  a.   "REPUBLICA" inverted   20.00
161 A6 115r on 200r bl, *bl*   2.50   2.25
162 A6 130r on 75r rose   2.25   2.00
  a.   Inverted surcharge   20.00
163 A6 130r on 100r brn,
                      yel   700.00 500.00
164 A6 400r on 50r lt bl   3.50   3.00
  a.   Perf. 13½   17.50   6.00
165 A6 400r on 80r yel grn   2.50   2.25
166 N3 400r on 2½r brn   2.00   1.75

Same Overprint on Nos. 86, 88, 90

167 A7 15r brown   1.50   1.25
  a.   Inverted overprint   20.00
168 A7 50r blue   1.50   1.25
  a.   Inverted overprint   20.00
169 A7 50r on 65r dull bl   2.25   1.50
        Nos. 167-169 (3)   5.25   4.00

Most of Nos. 141-169 were issued without gum.

Common Design Types pictured following the introduction.

Vasco da Gama Issue of Various Portuguese Colonies Surcharged

On Stamps of Macao

170 CD20 ¼c on ½a bl grn   1.60   1.40
171 CD21 ½c on 1a red   1.60   1.40
172 CD22 1c on 2a red vio   1.60   1.40
173 CD23 2½c on 4a yel grn   1.60   1.40
174 CD24 5c on 8a dk bl   1.90   1.60
175 CD25 7½c on 12a vio brn   3.00   3.00
176 CD26 10c on 16a bis brn   1.90   1.60
177 CD27 15c on 24a bister   1.90   1.60
          Nos. 170-177 (8)   15.10 13.40

On Stamps of Portuguese Africa

178 CD20 ¼c on 2½r bl grn   1.10   1.00
179 CD21 ½c on 5r red   1.10   1.00
180 CD22 1c on 10r red vio   1.10   1.00
181 CD23 2½c on 25r yel grn   1.10   1.00
182 CD24 5c on 50r dk bl   1.10   1.00
183 CD25 7½c on 75r vio brn   2.10   2.00
184 CD26 10c on 100r bis brn   1.10   1.00
185 CD27 15c on 150r bister   1.10   1.00
          Nos. 178-185 (8)   10.10   9.00

On Stamps of Timor

186 CD20 ¼c on ½a bl grn   1.40   1.25
187 CD21 ½c on 1a red   1.40   1.25
188 CD22 1c on 2a red vio   1.40   1.25
  a.   Double surcharge   30.00
189 CD23 2½c on 4a yel grn   1.40   1.25
190 CD24 5c on 8a dk bl   1.75   1.60
191 CD25 7½c on 12a vio brn   2.50   2.50
192 CD26 10c on 16a bis brn   1.40   1.40
193 CD27 15c on 24a bister   1.40   1.40
          Nos. 186-193 (8)   12.65 11.90
          Nos. 170-193 (24)   37.85 34.30

Ceres — A9

Name and Value in Black Chalky Paper

1914   Typo.   Perf. 15x14
194 A9 ¼c olive brown   .40   .40
        Never hinged   .60
195 A9 ½c black   .40   .40
        Never hinged   .60
196 A9 1c blue green   .50   .40
        Never hinged   .75
197 A9 1½c lilac brn   .30   .25
        Never hinged   .45
198 A9 2c carmine   .40   .40
        Never hinged   .60
199 A9 2½c lt violet   .40   .40
        Never hinged   .60

---

200 A9 5c deep blue   .45   .35
        Never hinged   .70
201 A9 7½c yellow brn   .65   .50
        Never hinged   1.00
202 A9 8c slate   .65   .50
        Never hinged   1.00
203 A9 10c orange brn   .65   .50
        Never hinged   1.00
204 A9 15c plum   2.00   1.25
        Never hinged   3.00
205 A9 20c yellow green   1.25   .75
        Never hinged   1.90
206 A9 30c brown, *grn*   2.00   1.40
        Never hinged   3.00
207 A9 40c brown, *pink*   1.75   1.40
        Never hinged   2.75
208 A9 50c orange, *sal*   4.00   3.00
        Never hinged   6.00
209 A9 1e green, *blue*   4.00   3.00
        Never hinged   6.00
        Nos. 194-209 (16)   19.80 14.90

For surcharges see Nos. 250-253, 281-282.

1920

Ordinary Paper

210 A9 ¼c olive brown   .25   .25
        Never hinged   .40
211 A9 1½c lilac brn   .75   .75
        Never hinged   1.15
212 A9 7½c yellow brn   1.25   1.25
        Never hinged   1.90
213 A9 10c orange brn   1.50   1.25
        Never hinged   2.25
        Nos. 210-213 (4)   3.75   3.50

1922-26   **Perf. 12x11½**

214 A9 ¼c olive brown   .25   .25
        Never hinged   .40
  a.   ¼c olive   .25   .25
        Never hinged   .40
215 A9 ½c black   .25   .25
        Never hinged   .40
216 A9 1c yellow grn
                ('22)   .25   .25
        Never hinged   .40
217 A9 1½c lilac brn   .30   .25
        Never hinged   .45
218 A9 2c carmine   .25   .25
        Never hinged   .40
219 A9 2c gray ('26)   .25   .25
        Never hinged   .40
220 A9 2½c lt violet   .25   .25
        Never hinged   .40
221 A9 3c orange ('22)   .25   .25
        Never hinged   .40
222 A9 4c rose ('22)   .25   .25
        Never hinged   .40
223 A9 4½c gray ('22)   .25   .25
        Never hinged   .40
224 A9 5c brt blue ('22)   .25   .25
        Never hinged   .40
225 A9 6c lilac ('22)   .25   .25
        Never hinged   .40
226 A9 7c ultra ('22)   .25   .25
        Never hinged   .40
227 A9 7½c yellow brn   .25   .25
        Never hinged   .40
228 A9 8c slate   .25   .25
        Never hinged   .40
229 A9 10c orange brn   .30   .25
        Never hinged   .45
230 A9 12c blue green
                ('22)   .40   .40
        Never hinged   .60
231 A9 15c brn rose
                ('22)   .25   .25
        Never hinged   .40
232 A9 20c yellow green   .45   .45
        Never hinged   .70
233 A9 24c ultra ('26)   3.00   2.00
        Never hinged   4.50
233A A9 25c choc ('26)   3.00   2.00
        Never hinged   4.50
233B A9 30c gray grn
                ('22)   .40   .30
        Never hinged   .60
233C A9 40c turq bl ('22)   .40   .30
        Never hinged   .60
233D A9 50c lt violet ('26)   .40   .30
        Never hinged   .60
233E A9 60c dk blue ('22)   2.00   .75
        Never hinged   3.00
233F A9 60c rose ('26)   2.00   .75
        Never hinged   3.00
233G A9 80c brt rose
                ('22)   1.60   .50
        Never hinged   2.40

Glazed Paper

233H A9 1e pale rose
                ('22)   2.50   1.40
        Never hinged   3.75
233I A9 1e blue ('26)   2.00   1.00
        Never hinged   3.00
233J A9 2e dk violet
                ('22)   2.75   1.50
        Never hinged   4.25
233K A9 5e buff ('26)   15.00   7.50
        Never hinged   22.50
233L A9 10e pink ('26)   25.00 14.00
        Never hinged   37.50
233M A9 20e pale turq
                ('26)   70.00 40.00
        Never hinged   105.00
        Nos. 214-233M (33) 135.25 77.40

Preceding issues Overprinted in Bt. Red

1915

On Provisional Issue of 1902

234 A2 115r on 10r green   1.75   1.60
235 A2 115r on 300r org   1.75   1.75
236 A2 130r on 5r black   4.00   2.75
237 A2 130r on 200r gray lil 1.40   1.25
238 A6 115r on 25r green   .60   .40
239 A6 115r on 150r car, *rose* .60 .40
240 A6 115r on 200r bl, *bl* .60   .40
241 A6 130r on 75r rose   .60   .40
242 A6 130r on 100r brn, *yel* 1.10 1.25
243 A6 130r on 300r bl, *sal* 1.00   .75

Same Overprint on Nos. 88 and 90

244 A7 50r blue   .70   .55
245 A7 50r on 65r dull bl   .70   .55
        Nos. 234-245 (12) 14.80 12.05

No. 86 Overprinted in Blue and Surcharged in Black

1919

246 A7 2½c on 15r brown   .60   .55

No. 91 Surcharged in Black

247 A7 ½c on 2½r gray   3.00   2.75
248 A7 1c on 2½r gray   2.25   2.00
249 A7 2½c on 2½r gray   1.10   .65

No. 194 Surcharged in Black

250 A9 ½c on ¼c ol brn   2.00   1.75
        Never hinged   3.00
251 A9 2c on ¼c ol brn   2.25   1.90
        Never hinged   3.50
252 A9 2½c on ¼c ol brn   6.00   5.00
        Never hinged   9.00

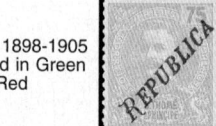

No. 199 Surcharged in Black

253 A9 4c on 2½c lt vio   .90   .75
        Nos. 246-253 (8)   18.10 15.35

Nos. 246-253 were issued without gum.

Stamps of 1898-1905 Overprinted in Green or Red

1920   On Stamps of 1898-1903

255 A7 75r red lilac (G)   .55   .50
256 A7 100r blue, *blue* (R) .80   .75
257 A7 115r org brn, *pink* (G) 2.00 1.40
258 A7 130r brn, *straw* (G) 90.00 50.00
259 A7 200r red lil, *pnksh* (G) 2.00 1.00
260 A7 500r blk, & red, *gray*
                      (G)   1.50   1.00
261 A7 700r vio, *yelsh* (G) 2.00   1.25

On Stamps of 1902

262 A6 115r on 25r grn (R)   1.00   .60
263 A6 115r on 200r bl, *bl* (R) 1.50 1.00
264 A6 130r on 75r rose (R) 1.50   1.50

On Nos. 88-89

265 A7 50r blue (R)   1.50   1.10

---

266 A7 75r rose (G)   15.00   7.00

On No. 90

267 A7 50r on 65r dl bl (R) 14.00   7.00
        Nos. 255-257,259-267 (12) 43.85 24.10

Nos. 238-243 Surcharged in Blue or Red

1923   **Without Gum**

268 A6 10c on 115r on 25r (Bl) .70   .50
269 A6 10c on 115r on 150r (Bl) .70   .50
270 A6 10c on 115r on 200r (R) .70   .50
271 A6 10c on 130r on 75r (Bl) .70   .50
272 A6 10c on 130r on 100r (Bl) .70   .50
273 A6 10c on 130r on 300r (R) .70   .50
        Nos. 268-273 (6)   4.20   3.00

Nos. 268-273 are usually stained and discolored.

Nos. 84-85 Surcharged

1925

274 A6 40c on 400r on 80r yel
                      grn   .90   .45
275 N3 40c on 400r on 2½r brn .90   .45

Nos. 233H and 233J Surcharged

1931

281 A9 70c on 1e pale rose   2.00   1.25
282 A9 1.40e on 2e dk vio   2.75   2.50
        Never hinged   4.00

Ceres — A11

Perf. 12x11½

1934   Typo.   Wmk. 232
283 A11 1c bister   .25   .25
        Never hinged   .40
284 A11 5c olive brown   .25   .25
        Never hinged   .40
285 A11 10c violet   .25   .25
        Never hinged   .40
286 A11 15c black   .25   .25
        Never hinged   .40
287 A11 20c gray   .25   .25
        Never hinged   .40
288 A11 30c dk green   .25   .25
        Never hinged   .40
289 A11 40c red orange   .25   .25
        Never hinged   .40
290 A11 45c brt blue   .50   .50
        Never hinged   .75
291 A11 50c brown   .25   .25
        Never hinged   .40
292 A11 60c olive grn   .50   .50
        Never hinged   .75
293 A11 70c brown org   .50   .50
        Never hinged   .75
294 A11 80c emerald   .50   .50
        Never hinged   .75
295 A11 85c deep rose   2.25   1.60
        Never hinged   3.50
296 A11 1e maroon   .95   .65
        Never hinged   1.45
297 A11 1.40e dk blue   2.50   2.10
        Never hinged   3.75
298 A11 2e dk violet   2.50   1.75
        Never hinged   3.75
299 A11 5e apple green   10.00   3.75
        Never hinged   15.00
300 A11 10e olive bister   18.00   6.00
        Never hinged   27.00
301 A11 20e orange   50.00 18.00
        Never hinged   75.00
        Nos. 283-301 (19) 90.20 37.85

Common Design Types
Inscribed "S. Tomé"

1938   Unwmk.   Perf. 13½x13
Name and Value in Black

302	CD34	1c gray green	.25	.25
303	CD34	5c orange brown	.25	.25
304	CD34	10c dk carmine	.25	.25
305	CD34	15c dk violet brn	.25	.25
306	CD34	20c slate	.25	.25
307	CD35	30c rose violet	.25	.25
308	CD35	35c brt green	.25	.25
309	CD35	40c brown	.25	.25
310	CD35	50c brt red vio	.25	.25
311	CD36	60c gray black	.25	.25
312	CD36	70c brown violet	.25	.25
313	CD36	80c orange	.45	.25
314	CD36	1e red	2.25	1.10
315	CD37	1.75e blue	2.00	1.50
316	CD37	2e brown car	15.00	5.50
317	CD37	5e olive green	15.00	5.50
318	CD38	10e blue violet	17.00	7.50
319	CD38	20e red brown	30.00	9.50
		Nos. 302-319 (18)	84.45	33.10

Marble Column and
Portuguese Arms
with Cross — A12

1938   Perf. 12½

320	A12	80c blue green	2.75	1.40
321	A12	1.75e deep blue	10.50	4.00
322	A12	20e brown	40.00	17.50
		Nos. 320-322 (3)	53.25	22.90

Visit of the President of Portugal in 1938.

Common Design Types
Inscribed "S. Tomé e Principe"

1939   Perf. 13½x13
Name and Value in Black

323	CD34	1c gray grn	.25	.25
324	CD34	5c orange brn	.25	.25
325	CD34	10c dk carmine	.25	.25
326	CD34	15c dk vio brn	.25	.25
327	CD34	20c slate	.45	.25
328	CD35	30c rose violet	.25	.25
329	CD35	35c brt green	.25	.25
330	CD35	40c brown	.45	.25
331	CD35	50c brt red vio	.45	.25
332	CD36	60c gray black	.45	.25
333	CD36	70c brown violet	.45	.25
334	CD36	80c orange	.45	.25
335	CD36	1e red	.90	.60
336	CD37	1.75e blue	1.50	.60
337	CD37	2e brown car	2.40	1.50
338	CD37	5e olive green	6.25	2.75
339	CD38	10e blue violet	9.00	4.00
340	CD38	20e red brown	15.00	5.50
		Nos. 323-340 (18)	39.25	17.95

AIR POST STAMPS

Common Design Type
Inscribed "S. Tomé"

1938   Perf. 13½x13
Name and Value in Black

C1	CD39	10c red orange	62.50	45.00
C2	CD39	20c purple	30.00	22.50
C3	CD39	50c orange	3.00	2.50
C4	CD39	1e ultra	5.25	4.00
C5	CD39	2e lilac brown	7.75	6.25
C6	CD39	3e dark green	12.00	8.00
C7	CD39	5e red brown	15.00	13.00
C8	CD39	9e rose carmine	17.50	13.00
C9	CD39	10e magenta	19.00	13.00
		Nos. C1-C9 (9)	172.00	127.25

Common Design Type
Inscribed "S. Tomé e Principe"

1939   Engr.   Unwmk.
Name and Value Typo. in Black

C10	CD39	10c scarlet	.60	.30
C11	CD39	20c purple	.60	.30
C12	CD39	50c orange	.60	.30
C13	CD39	1e deep ultra	.60	.30
C14	CD39	2e lilac brown	1.75	1.25
C15	CD39	3e dark green	2.40	1.50
C16	CD39	5e red brown	3.50	2.10
C17	CD39	9e rose carmine	6.25	3.00
C18	CD39	10e magenta	7.25	3.00
		Nos. C10-C18 (9)	23.55	12.05

No. C16 exists with overprint "Exposicao International de Nova York, 1939-1940" and Trylon and Perisphere.

POSTAGE DUE STAMPS

"S. Thomé" — D1

1904   Unwmk.   Typo.   Perf. 12

J1	D1	5r yellow green	.55	.55
J2	D1	10r slate	.65	.65
J3	D1	20r yellow brown	.65	.65
J4	D1	30r orange	1.00	.65
J5	D1	50r gray brown	1.75	1.40
J6	D1	60r red brown	2.50	1.60
J7	D1	100r red lilac	3.00	1.75
J8	D1	130r dull blue	4.00	3.25
J9	D1	200r carmine	4.50	3.50
J10	D1	500r gray violet	8.00	5.00
		Nos. J1-J10 (10)	26.60	19.00

Overprinted in
Carmine or Green

1911

J11	D1	5r yellow green	.30	.30
J12	D1	10r slate	.30	.30
J13	D1	20r yellow brown	.30	.30
J14	D1	30r orange	.30	.30
J15	D1	50r gray brown	.30	.30
J16	D1	60r red brown	.65	.65
J17	D1	100r red lilac	.80	.80
J18	D1	130r dull blue	.80	.80
J19	D1	200r carmine (G)	.80	.80
J20	D1	500r gray violet	1.25	1.25
		Nos. J11-J20 (10)	5.80	5.80

Nos. J1-J10
Overprinted in Black

1913   Without Gum

J21	D1	5r yellow green	4.00	3.75
J22	D1	10r slate	6.00	4.50
J23	D1	20r yellow brown	3.00	2.50
J24	D1	30r orange	3.00	2.50
J25	D1	50r gray brown	3.00	2.50
J26	D1	60r red brown	4.00	3.00
J27	D1	100r red lilac	5.00	4.00
J28	D1	130r dull blue	35.00	35.00
a.		Inverted overprint	70.00	70.00
J29	D1	200r carmine	50.00	50.00
J30	D1	500r gray violet	75.00	40.00
		Nos. J21-J30 (10)	188.00	147.75

Nos. J1-J10
Overprinted in Black

1913   Without Gum

J31	D1	5r yellow green	4.00	3.00
a.		Inverted overprint	40.00	40.00
J32	D1	10r slate	5.00	4.00
J33	D1	20r yellow brown	4.00	3.00
J34	D1	30r orange	4.00	3.00
a.		Inverted overprint	40.00	
J35	D1	50r gray brown	4.00	3.00
J36	D1	60r red brown	5.00	4.00
J37	D1	100r red lilac	5.00	4.00
J38	D1	130r dull blue	5.00	4.00
J39	D1	200r carmine	7.00	6.00
J40	D1	500r gray violet	17.00	15.00
		Nos. J31-J40 (10)	60.00	49.00

No. J5 Overprinted "Republica" in Italic Capitals like Regular Issue in Green

1920   Without Gum

J41	D1	50r gray brn	40.00	35.00

"S. Tomé" — D2

1921   Typo.   Perf. 11½

J42	D2	½c yellow green	.25	.25
J43	D2	1c slate	.25	.25
J44	D2	2c orange brown	.25	.25
J45	D2	3c orange	.25	.25
J46	D2	5c gray brown	.25	.25
J47	D2	6c lt brown	.25	.25
J48	D2	10c red violet	.25	.25
J49	D2	13c dull blue	.25	.25
J50	D2	20c carmine	.25	.25
J51	D2	50c gray	.35	.40
		Nos. J42-J51 (10)	2.60	2.65

In each sheet one stamp is inscribed "S. Thomé" instead of "S. Tomé." Value, set of 10, $60.

NEWSPAPER STAMPS

N1   N2

Perf. 11½, 12½ and 13½
1892   Without Gum   Unwmk.
Black Surcharge

P1	N1	2½r on 10r green	95.00	55.00
P2	N1	2½r on 20r rose	125.00	57.50
P3	N2	2½r on 10r rose	125.00	57.50
P4	N2	2½r on 20r rose	125.00	57.50
		Nos. P1-P4 (4)	470.00	227.50

Green Surcharge

P5	N1	2½r on 5r black	67.50	30.00
P6	N1	2½r on 20r rose	125.00	57.50
P8	N2	2½r on 5r black	125.00	60.00
P9	N2	2½r on 10r green	125.00	62.50
P10	N2	2½r on 20r rose	125.00	77.50
		Nos. P5-P10 (5)	567.50	287.50

Both surcharges exist on No. 18 in green.

N3   d

1893   Typo.   Perf. 11½, 13½

P12	N3	2½r brown	.45	.40

For surcharges and overprints see Nos. 85, 166, 275, P13.

No. P12 Overprinted Type "d" in Blue

1899   Without Gum

P13	N3	2½r brown	25.00	16.00

POSTAL TAX STAMPS

Pombal Issue
Common Design Types

1925   Unwmk.   Perf. 12½

RA1	CD28	15c orange & black	.45	.45
RA2	CD29	15c orange & black	.45	.45
RA3	CD30	15c orange & black	.45	.45
		Nos. RA1-RA3 (3)	1.35	1.35

Certain revenue stamps (5e, 6e, 7e, 8e and other denominations) were surcharged in 1946 "Assistencia," 2 bars and new values (1e or 1.50e) and used as postal tax stamps.

POSTAL TAX DUE STAMPS

Pombal Issue
Common Design Types

1925   Unwmk.   Perf. 12½

RAJ1	CD28	30c orange & black	.75	.75
RAJ2	CD29	30c orange & black	.75	.75
RAJ3	CD30	30c orange & black	.75	.75
		Nos. RAJ1-RAJ3 (3)	2.25	2.25

ST. VINCENT

sānt ˈvin̪t̪-sənt

LOCATION — Island in the West Indies
GOVT. — British Colony
AREA — 150 sq. mi.
POP. — 123,000 (est. 1984)
CAPITAL — Kingstown

12 Pence = 1 Shilling
20 Shillings = 1 Pound
100 Cents = 1 Dollar (1949)

Catalogue values for unused stamps in this country are for Never Hinged items, beginning with Scott 152 in the regular postage section.

PRE-STAMP POSTAL MARKINGS

Crowned Circle handstamp type I is pictured in the Crowned Circle Handstamps and Great Britain Used Abroad section.

1852

A1	I	"St. Vincent" crowned circle handstamp in red, on cover	1,150.

STAMPS OF GREAT BRITAIN USED IN ST. VINCENT

Numeral cancellation type A is pictured in the Crowned Circle Handstamps and Great Britain Used Abroad section.

1858-60   **A10**

A2	A	1p rose red (#20)	725.
A3	A	2p blue (#29, p7, 8)	—
A4	A	4p rose (#26)	440.
A5	A	6p lilac (#27)	325.
A6	A	1sh green (#28)	2,000.

Issued under British Administration

Values for unused stamps are for examples with original gum as defined in the catalogue introduction. Early stamps were spaced extremely narrowly on the plates, and the perforations were applied irregularly.

Therefore, very fine examples of Nos. 1-28, 30-39 will have perforations that cut into the design slightly on one or more sides. Also, very fine examples of Nos. 40-53, 55-60 will have perforations touching the design on at least one side. These stamps with perfs clear of the design on all four sides, especially Nos. 1-28, 30-39, are extremely scarce and command substantially higher prices.

Watermark

Wmk. 5 — Small Star

Queen Victoria — A1

1861   **Engr.**   **Unwmk.**   **Perf. 14 to 16**

1	A1	1p rose	*62.50*	20.00
a.	Imperf., pair		300.00	
c.	Horiz. pair, imperf. vert.		400.00	
1B	A1	6p yellow green	8,250.	250.00

Perfs on Nos. 1-1B are not clean cut. See Nos. 2-3 for rough perfs.

1862-66   **Rough Perf. 14 to 16**

2	A1	1p rose	55.00	15.50
a.	Horiz. pair, imperf. vert.		400.00	
3	A1	6p dark green	65.00	21.00
a.	Imperf., pair		1,250.	
b.	Horiz. pair, imperf. between		14,500.	15,500.
4	A1	1sh slate ('66)	425.00	160.00
	Nos. 2-4 (3)		545.00	196.50

1863-69   **Perf. 11 to 13**

5	A1	1p rose	45.00	22.50
6	A1	4p blue ('66)	300.00	125.00
a.	Horiz. pair, imperf. vert.			
7	A1	4p orange ('69)	400.00	175.00
8	A1	6p deep green	250.00	82.50
8A	A1	1sh slate ('66)	*2,750.*	1,000.
9	A1	1sh indigo ('69)	425.00	100.00
10	A1	1sh brown ('69)	550.00	175.00

Perf. 11 to 13x14 to 16

11	A1	1p rose	*6,500.*	1,250.
12	A1	1sh slate	300.00	140.00

Rough Perf. 14 to 16

1871-78   **Wmk. 5**

13	A1	1p black	65.00	15.50
a.	Vert. pair, imperf. btwn.		20,000.	
14	A1	6p dk blue green	350.00	77.50
a.	Watermark sideways		100.00	

Clean-Cut Perf. 14 to 16

14A	A1	1p black	65.00	15.50
14B	A1	6p dp bl grn	1,650.	55.00
c.	6p dull blue green		2,250.	55.00
15	A1	6p pale yel green ('78)	800.00	32.50
15A	A1	1sh vermilion ('77)	*50,000.*	

For surcharge see No. 30.

Perf. 11 to 13

16	A1	4p dk bl ('77)	600.00	110.00
17	A1	1sh deep rose ('72)		
			825.00	160.00
18	A1	1sh claret ('75)	675.00	300.00

Perf. 11 to 13x14 to 16

20	A1	1p black	95.00	16.50
a.	Horiz. pair, imperf. btwn.		25,000.	
21	A1	6p pale yel grn ('77)	725.00	55.00
22	A1	1sh lilac rose ('72)	*6,250.*	400.00
23	A1	1sh vermilion ('77)	1,100.	100.00
a.	Horiz. pair, imperf. vert.			

See Nos. 25-28A, 36-39, 42-53. For surcharges see Nos. 30, 32-33, 40, 55-60.

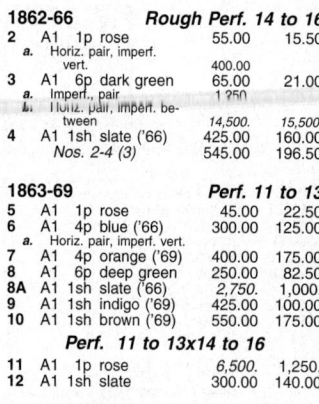

Victoria   Seal of Colony
A2   A3

1880-81   **Perf. 11 to 13**

24	A2	½p orange ('81)	8.00	8.75
25	A1	1p gray green	190.00	5.50
26	A1	1p drab ('81)	800.00	15.50
27	A1	4p ultra ('81)	1,350.	130.00
a.	Horiz. pair, imperf. btwn.			
28	A1	6p yellow green	550.00	77.50
a.	Horiz. pair, imperf. btwn.		27,500.	
28A	A1	1sh vermilion	900.00	65.00
29	A3	5sh rose	1,275.	*1,650.*
a.	Imperf		8,250.	

No. 29 is valued well centered with design well clear of the perfs.

See Nos. 35, 41, 54, 598 (in Scott Standard catalogue, Vol. 5). For surcharges see Nos. 31-33.

No. 14B Bisected and Surcharged in Red

1880, May   **Perf. 14 to 16**

30	A1	1p on half of 6p	600.00	425.00
a.	Unsevered pair		2,250.	1,350.

No. 28 Bisected and Surcharged in Red

1881, Sept. 1

31	A1	½p on half of 6p yel grn ('81)	75.	190.
a.	Unsevered pair		525.	550.
b.	"1" with straight top		1,100.	
c.	Without fraction bar, pair, #31, 31c		4,750.	5,500.

Nos. 28 and 28A Surcharged in Black

c   d

1881, Nov.   **Perf. 11 to 13**

32	A1(c)	1p on 6p yel green	500.	400.
33	A1(d)	4p on 1sh ver	1,850.	925.
a.	3 mm spacing between "4d" and bar		3,500.	2,500.

1883-84   **Wmk. 2**   **Perf. 12**

35	A2	½p green ('84)	110.00	40.00
36	A1	4p ultra	825.00	55.00
37	A1	4p dull blue ('84)	2,500.	275.00
38	A1	6p yellow grn	175.00	350.00
39	A1	1sh orange ver	175.00	65.00
a.	Imperf., pair			

The ½p orange, 1p rose red, 1p milky blue and 5sh carmine lake were never placed in use. Some authorities believe them to be color trials.

Nos. 35-60 may be found watermarked with single straight line. This is from the frame which encloses each group of 60 watermark designs.

Type of A1 Surcharged in Black — e

1883   **Perf. 14**

40	A1(e)	2½p on 1p lake	27.50	1.75

1883-97

41	A1	½p green ('85)	1.10	.65
a.	½p deep green		2.75	.65
42	A1	1p drab	80.00	3.50
43	A1	1p rose red ('85)	3.00	1.00
44	A1	1p pink ('86)	6.75	1.90
a.	1p carmine red ('89)		27.50	4.25
45	A1	2½p brt blue ('97)	10.00	2.25
46	A1	4p ultra	725.00	85.00
a.	4p dull ultramarine		1,100.	400.00
47	A1	4p red brown ('85)	1,100.	25.00
48	A1	4p lake brn ('86)	100.00	1.60
a.	4p purple brown ('86)		100.00	1.00
49	A1	4p yellow ('93)	2.00	15.00
		Ovptd. "SPECIMEN"	40.00	
a.	4p olive yellow		350.00	350.00
50	A1	5p gray brn ('97)	8.75	32.50
a.	5p black brown		10.00	30.00
51	A1	6p violet ('88)	225.00	225.00
52	A1	6p red violet ('91)	3.00	25.00
53	A1	1sh org ver ('91)	6.00	17.50
a.	1sh red orange		15.00	22.50
54	A3	5sh car lake ('88)	32.50	60.00
a.	5sh brown lake		35.00	60.00
b.	Printed on both sides		8,250.	

Grading footnote after No. 29 applies equally to Nos. 54-54a.

No. 40 Resurcharged in Black

1885, Mar.

55	A1	1p on 2½p on 1p lake	35.00	27.50

Examples with 3-bar cancel are proofs.

Stamps of Type A1 Surcharged in Black or Violet

g   h

j

1890-91

56	A1(e)	2½p on 1p brt blue	2.00	.40
a.	2½p on 1p milky blue		27.50	9.50
b.	2½p on 1p gray blue		27.50	.75
57	A1(g)	2½p on 4p vio brn ('90)	90.00	130.00
a.	Without fraction bar		475.00	575.00

1892-93

58	A1(h)	5p on 4p lake brn (V)	40.00	55.00
59	A1(j)	5p on 6p dp lake ('93)	2.00	1.90
a.	5p on 6p carmine lake		22.50	32.50
b.	Double surcharge		7,750.	4,500.

1897

60	A1(j)	3p on 1p lilac	6.00	26.50
a.	3p on 1p reddish lilac		15.50	52.50
		Ovptd. "SPECIMEN"	50.00	

Victoria   Edward VII
A13   A14

Numerals of 1sh and 5sh, type A13, and of 2p, 1sh, 5sh and £1, type A14, are in color on plain tablet.

1898   **Typo.**   **Perf. 14**

62	A13	½p lilac & grn	3.00	3.00
63	A13	1p lil & car rose	5.00	1.70
64	A13	2½p lilac & ultra	6.50	2.25
65	A13	3p lilac & ol grn	4.50	21.00
66	A13	4p lilac & org	7.25	25.00
67	A13	5p lilac & blk	8.25	21.00
68	A13	6p lilac & brn	14.50	55.00
69	A13	1sh grn & car rose	18.50	60.00
70	A13	5sh green & ultra	100.00	175.00
	Nos. 62-70 (9)		167.50	363.95
	Set, ovptd. "SPECIMEN"		200.00	

1902

71	A14	½p violet & green	4.75	.75
72	A14	1p vio & car rose	4.75	.35
73	A14	2p violet & black	6.50	6.00
74	A14	2½p violet & ultra	5.50	4.00
75	A14	3p violet & ol grn	5.50	7.25
76	A14	6p violet & brn	12.00	45.00
77	A14	1sh grn & car rose	28.00	70.00
78	A14	2sh green & violet	27.50	65.00
79	A14	5sh green & ultra	82.50	140.00
	Nos. 71-79 (9)		177.00	338.35
	Set, ovptd. "SPECIMEN"		175.00	

1904-11   **Wmk. 3**   **Chalky Paper**

82	A14	½p vio & grn	1.50	1.50
a.	Ordinary paper		9.00	5.50
83	A14	1p vio & car rose	26.00	1.75
a.	Ordinary paper		29.00	1.90
84	A14	2½p vio & ultra	19.00	52.50
85	A14	6p vio & brn	19.00	55.00
86	A14	1sh grn & car rose	15.50	17.50
a.	Ordinary paper		24.00	57.50
87	A14	2sh vio & bl, *bl*	25.00	52.50
88	A14	5sh grn & red, *yel*	19.00	55.00
89	A14	£1 vio & blk, *red*	300.00	400.00
	Nos. 82-88 (7)		125.00	235.75
	Nos. 87-89, ovptd. "SPECIMEN"		225.00	

Issued: 1p, 1904; ½p, 6p, 1905; 2½p, 1906; 1sh, 1908; 2sh, 5sh, 1909; £1, July 22, 1911.

"Peace and Justice"
A15   A16

1907   Engr.   Ordinary Paper

90	A15	½p yellow green	4.00	2.75
91	A15	1p carmine	4.25	.25
92	A15	2p orange	1.75	7.75
93	A15	2½p ultra	45.00	19.00
94	A15	3p dark violet	9.50	18.00
		Nos. 90-94 (5)	64.50	38.75
		Set, ovptd. "SPECIMEN"	145.00	

1909   Without Dot under "d"

95	A16	1p carmine	1.50	.35
96	A16	6p red violet	8.75	50.00
97	A16	1sh black, green	5.00	11.00
		Nos. 95-97 (3)	15.25	61.35
		Set, ovptd. "SPECIMEN"	90.00	

1909-11   With Dot under "d"

98	A16	½p yellow grn ('10)	2.50	.70
99	A16	1p carmine	4.00	.25
100	A16	2p gray ('11)	6.50	12.00
101	A16	2½p ultra	9.50	4.50
102	A16	3p violet, yel	3.00	14.50
103	A16	6p red violet	20.00	11.00
		Nos. 98-103 (6)	45.50	42.95

King George V — A17

1913-17   Perf. 14

104	A17	½p gray green	.45	.25
105	A17	1p carmine	1.00	.90
a.		1p rose red	1.10	.85
b.		1p scarlet	20.00	8.00
106	A17	2p slate	3.50	42.50
a.		2p gray	8.75	42.50
107	A17	2½p ultra	.60	.90
108	A17	3p violet, yellow	1.00	7.50
a.		3p violet, lemon	3.25	14.00
b.		3p violet, pale yellow	2.75	10.50
109	A17	4p red, yellow	1.00	2.40
110	A17	5p olive green	2.50	17.00
111	A17	6p claret	2.50	5.00
112	A17	1sh black, green	1.75	4.25
113	A17	1sh bister ('14)	4.75	35.00
114	A16	2sh vio & ultra	5.75	40.00
115	A16	5sh dk grn & car	15.00	60.00
116	A16	£1 black & vio	110.00	200.00
		Nos. 104-116 (13)	149.80	415.70
		Set, ovptd. "SPECIMEN"	300.00	

Issued: 5p, 11/7; #113, 5/1/14; others, 1/1/13.
For overprints see Nos. MR1-MR2.

No. 112 Surcharged in Carmine

1915

117	A17	1p on 1sh black, grn	11.00	45.00
a.		"PENNY" & bar double	750.00	725.00
b.		Without period	15.00	
c.		"ONE" omitted	1,550.	1,350.
d.		"ONE" double	750.00	
e.		"PENNY" & bar omitted	1,450.	

Space between surcharge lines varies from 8 to 10mm.

1921-32   Wmk. 4

118	A17	½p green	2.10	.35
119	A17	1p carmine ('21)	1.15	1.00
a.		1p red	2.75	.25
120	A17	1½p yel brn ('32)	4.00	.25
121	A17	2p gray	3.00	1.00
122	A17	2½p ultra ('26)	1.50	1.75
123	A17	3p ultra	1.15	7.25
124	A17	3p vio, yel ('27)	1.15	1.75
125	A17	4p red, yel ('30)	2.10	7.25
126	A17	5p olive green	1.15	7.75
127	A17	6p claret ('27)	1.75	4.25
128	A17	1sh ocher ('27)	4.00	20.00
a.		1sh bistre	7.50	30.00
129	A16	2sh brn vio & ultra	9.00	15.00
130	A16	5sh dk grn & car	21.00	37.50
131	A16	£1 blk & vio ('28)	110.00	150.00
		Nos. 118-131 (14)	163.05	255.10
		Set, ovptd. or perf "SPECIMEN"	360.00	

Common Design Types pictured following the introduction.

Silver Jubilee Issue
Common Design Type

1935, May 6   Perf. 11x12

134	CD301	1p car & dk blue	.55	4.75
135	CD301	1½p gray blk & ultra	1.40	4.50
136	CD301	2½p ultra & brn	2.50	5.00
137	CD301	1sh brn vio & ind	5.00	7.00
		Nos. 134-137 (4)	9.45	21.25
		Set, never hinged	16.00	
		Set, perforated "SPECIMEN"	110.00	

Coronation Issue
Common Design Type

1937, May 12   Perf. 11x11½

138	CD302	1p dark purple	.25	1.25
139	CD302	1½p dark carmine	.25	1.25
140	CD302	2½p deep ultra	.30	2.25
		Nos. 138-140 (3)	.80	4.75
		Set, never hinged	1.50	
		Set, perforated "SPECIMEN"	87.50	

Seal of the Colony — A18

Young's Island and Fort Duvernette — A19

Kingstown and Fort Charlotte — A20

Villa Beach — A21

Victoria Park, Kingstown — A22

1938-47   Wmk. 4   Perf. 12

141	A18	½p grn & brt bl	.25	.25
142	A19	1p claret & blue	.25	.25
143	A20	1½p scar & lt grn	.25	.25
144	A18	2p black & green	.30	.25
145	A21	2½p pck bl & ind	.25	.25
145A	A22	2½p choc & grn ('47)	.25	.25
146	A18	3p dk vio & org	.25	.25
146A	A21	3½p dp bl grn & ind ('47)	.40	2.25
147	A18	6p claret & blk	.70	.40
148	A22	1sh green & vio	.70	.75
149	A18	2sh dk vio & brt blue	5.25	1.00
149A	A18	2sh6p dp bl & org brn ('47)	.95	4.25
150	A18	5sh dk grn & car	8.75	3.00
150A	A18	10sh choc & dp vio ('47)	7.50	10.00
151	A18	£1 black & vio	22.50	18.00
		Nos. 141-151 (15)	48.55	41.40
		Set, never hinged	55.00	

Issue date: Mar. 11, 1938.
See Nos. 156-169, 180-184.

> Catalogue values for unused stamps in this section, from this point to the end of the section, are for Never Hinged items.

Peace Issue
Common Design Type

1946, Oct. 15   Engr.   Perf. 13½x14

| 152 | CD303 | 1½p carmine | .25 | .25 |
| 153 | CD303 | 3½p deep blue | .25 | .25 |

Silver Wedding Issue
Common Design Types

1948, Nov. 30   Photo.   Perf. 14x14½

| 154 | CD304 | 1½p scarlet | .25 | .25 |

Engraved; Name Typographed
Perf. 11½x11

| 155 | CD305 | £1 red violet | 27.50 | 30.00 |

Types of 1938

1949, Mar. 26   Engr.   Perf. 12

156	A18	1c grn & brt bl	.25	1.75
157	A19	2c claret & bl	.25	.50
158	A20	3c scar & lt grn	.55	1.00
159	A18	4c gray blk & grn	.40	.25
160	A22	5c choc & grn	.25	.25
161	A18	6c dk vio & org	.55	1.25
162	A21	7c pck blue & ind	5.50	1.50
163	A18	12c claret & blk	.50	.25
164	A22	24c green & vio	.50	.55
165	A18	48c dk vio & brt bl	4.50	6.00
166	A18	60c dp bl & org brn	2.00	5.50
167	A18	$1.20 dk grn & car	4.75	4.75
168	A18	$2.40 choc & dp vio	6.75	10.00
169	A18	$4.80 gray blk & vio	13.00	20.00
		Nos. 156-169 (14)	39.75	53.55

For overprints see Nos. 176-179.

UPU Issue
Common Design Types
Engr.; Name Typo. on 6c, 12c
Perf. 13½, 11x11½

1949, Oct. 10   Wmk. 4

170	CD306	5c blue	.25	.25
171	CD307	6c dp rose violet	.55	2.00
172	CD308	12c red lilac	.30	2.00
173	CD309	24c blue green	1.10	.80
		Nos. 170-173 (4)	2.20	5.05

University Issue
Common Design Types

1951, Feb. 16   Engr.   Perf. 14x14½

| 174 | CD310 | 3c red & blue green | .50 | .65 |
| 175 | CD311 | 12c rose lilac & blk | .50 | 1.50 |

Nos. 158-160 and 163 Overprinted in Black

1951, Sept. 21   Perf. 12

176	A20	3c scarlet & lt grn	.30	1.60
177	A18	4c gray blk & grn	.30	.60
178	A22	5c chocolate & grn	.30	.60
179	A18	12c claret & blk	.95	1.25
		Nos. 176-179 (4)	1.85	4.05

Adoption of a new constitution for the Windward Islands, 1951.

Type of 1938-47

1952

180	A18	1c gray black & green	.30	2.25
181	A18	3c dk violet & orange	.30	2.25
182	A18	4c green & brt blue	.30	.25
183	A20	6c scarlet & dp green	.30	2.00
184	A21	10c peacock blue & ind	.45	.35
		Nos. 180-184 (5)	1.65	7.10

WAR TAX STAMPS

No. 105 Overprinted

Type I — Words 2 to 2½mm apart.
Type II — Words 1½mm apart.
Type III — Words 3½mm apart.

1916   Wmk. 3   Perf. 14

MR1	A17	1p car, type III	3.25	25.00
a.		Double ovpt., type III	275.00	250.00
b.		1p carmine, type I	12.50	18.50
c.		Comma after "STAMP", type I	12.50	30.00
d.		Double ovpt., type I	200.00	200.00
e.		1p carmine, type II	135.00	87.50
f.		Double ovpt., type II	1,450.	

Overprinted

| MR2 | A17 | 1p carmine | 1.40 | 2.25 |
| | | Ovptd. "SPECIMEN" | 55.00 | |

SALVADOR, EL

'el 'sal-və-,dor

LOCATION — On the Pacific coast of Central America, between Guatemala, Honduras and the Gulf of Fonseca
GOVT. — Republic
AREA — 8,236 sq. mi.
POP. — 5,300,000 (est. 1984)
CAPITAL — San Salvador

8 Reales = 100 Centavos = 1 Peso
100 Centavos = 1 Colón

Watermarks

Wmk. 117 —
Liberty Cap

Position of wmk.
on reprints

Wmk. 172 — Honeycomb

Wmk. 173 — S

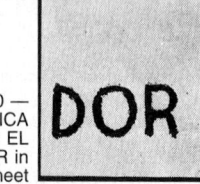
Wmk. 240 —
REPUBLICA
DE EL
SALVADOR in
Sheet

Volcano San
Miguel — A1

1867		Unwmk.	Engr.	Perf. 12
1	A1	½r blue	2.00	10.00
2	A1	1r red	2.00	2.00
3	A1	2r green	7.00	6.00
4	A1	4r bister	12.00	10.00
		Nos. 1-4 (4)	23.00	28.00

There were at least two printings of Nos. 1-4. Stamps from the second printing are lighter in color. Nos. 1-4 when overprinted "Contra Sello" and shield with 14 stars, are telegraph stamps. For similar overprint see Nos. 5-12. Counterfeits exist.

Nos. 1-4 Handstamped Either Type I or Type II in Black

Type I　　　　　Type II

Type II

1874

5	A1	½r blue	30.00	10.00
6	A1	1r red	20.00	10.00
7	A1	2r green	30.00	10.00
8	A1	4r bister	40.00	20.00
		Nos. 5-8 (4)	120.00	50.00

Nos. 1-4 Handstamped Type III in Black

Type III

9	A1	½r blue	8.00	6.00
10	A1	1r red	8.00	3.00
11	A1	2r green	10.00	3.00
12	A1	4r bister	12.00	10.00
		Nos. 9-12 (4)	38.00	22.00

The overprints on Nos. 5-12 exist double. Counterfeits are plentiful.

Coat of Arms
A2　　　　　　A3

A4　　　　　　A5

A6

1879		Litho.	Perf. 12½
13	A2	1c green	3.00 1.75
a.		Invtd. "V" for 2nd "A" in "SAL-VADOR"	6.00 3.00
b.		Invtd. "V" for "A" in "REPUBLI-CA"	6.00 3.00
c.		Invtd. "V" for "A" in "UNIVER-SAL"	6.00 3.00
d.		Thin paper	
14	A3	2c rose	4.25 2.25
a.		Invtd. scroll in upper left corner	12.00 7.50
15	A4	5c blue	7.50 1.90
a.		5c ultra	12.00 6.00
16	A5	10c black	15.00 5.25
17	A6	20c violet	24.00 15.00
		Nos. 13-17 (5)	53.75 26.15

There are fifteen varieties of the 1c and 2c, twenty-five of the 5c and five each of the 10 and 20c.
In 1881 the 1c, 2c and 5c were redrawn, the 1c in fifteen varieties and the 2c and 5c in five varieties each.
No. 15 comes in a number of shades from light to dark blue.
These stamps, when overprinted "Contra sello" and arms, are telegraph stamps.
Counterfeits of No. 14 exist.
For overprints see Nos. 25D-25E, 28A-28C.

Allegorical Figure of El Salvador — A7　　　Volcano — A8

1887		Engr.	Perf. 12
18	A7	3c brown	2.00 2.00
a.		Imperf., pair	10.00 10.00
19	A8	10c orange	30.00 3.00

For surcharges and overprints see Nos. 25, 26C-28, 30-32.

A9　　　　　　A10

1888			Rouletted
20	A9	5c deep blue	1.50 1.50

For overprints see Nos. 35-36.

1889			Perf. 12
21	A10	1c green	.40
22	A10	2c scarlet	.40

Nos. 21-22
Overprinted in Black

23	A10	1c green	.40 3.00
24	A10	2c scarlet	.40

Nos. 21, 22 and 24 were never placed in use.
For overprints see Nos. 26, 29.

No. 18 Surcharged

1 centavo　　　1 centavo
Type I　　　　　Type II

Type I — thick numerals, heavy serifs.
Type II — thin numerals, straight serifs.

25	A7	1c on 3c brn, type II	4.00 7.00
a.		Double surcharge	1.50
b.		Triple surcharge	3.50
c.		Type I	.65

The 1c on 2c scarlet is bogus.

Handstamped

1889			Violet Handstamp
25D	A2	1c green	19.00 19.00
25E	A6	20c violet	45.00 45.00
26	A10	1c green, #23	10.50 15.00
26C	A7	1c on 3c, #25	50.00 50.00
27	A7	3c brown	7.50 15.00
28	A8	10c orange	10.00 12.50

Black Handstamp

28A	A7	3c brown	22.50 21.00
28B	A3	2c rose	26.00 26.00
28C	A6	20c violet	45.00 45.00
29	A10	1c green, #23	10.50 15.00
30	A7	3c brown	10.50 15.00
31	A7	1c on 3c, #25	40.00 40.00
32	A8	10c orange	15.00 12.50

Rouletted
Black Handstamp

35	A9	5c deep blue	9.00 15.00

Violet Handstamp

36	A9	5c deep blue	9.00 15.00

The 1889 handstamps as usual, are found double, inverted, etc. Counterfeits are plentiful.

A13

1890		Engr.	Perf. 12
38	A13	1c green	.50 .50
39	A13	2c bister brown	.50 .50
40	A13	2c yellow	.50 .50
41	A13	5c blue	.50 .50
42	A13	10c violet	.50 .50
43	A13	20c orange	.75 3.00
44	A13	25c red	1.50 5.00
45	A13	50c claret	2.00 7.50
46	A13	1p carmine	5.00 30.00
		Nos. 38-46 (9)	11.75 48.00

The issues of 1890 to 1899 inclusive were printed by the Hamilton Bank Note Co., New York, to the order of N. F. Seebeck, who held a contract for stamps with the government of El Salvador. This contract gave the right to make reprints of the stamps and such were subsequently made in some instances, as will be found noted in italic type.

Used values of 1890-1899 issues are for stamps with genuine cancellations applied while the stamps were valid. Various counterfeit cancellations exist.

A14

1891			
47	A14	1c vermilion	.50 .50
48	A14	2c yellow green	.50 .50
49	A14	3c violet	.50 .50
50	A14	5c carmine lake	2.00 .50
51	A14	10c blue	.50 .50
52	A14	11c violet	.50 .50
53	A14	20c green	.50 .50
54	A14	25c yellow brown	.50 2.50
55	A14	50c dark blue	2.00 7.50
56	A14	1p dark brown	.75 25.00
		Nos. 47-56 (10)	8.25 38.50

For surcharges see Nos. 57-59.
Nos. 47 and 56 have been reprinted in thick toned paper with dark gum.

A15

Nos. 48, 49 Surcharged in Black or Violet

UN CENTAVO　　CENTAVOS
b　　　　　　　　c

1891			
57	A15	1c on 2c yellow grn	2.25 2.00
a.		Inverted surcharge	8.00
b.		Surcharge reading up	12.00
58	A14 (b)	1c on 2c yellow grn	1.60 1.40
59	A14 (c)	5c on 3c violet	4.00 3.25
		Nos. 57-59 (3)	7.85 6.65

Landing of Columbus — A18

1892			Engr.
60	A18	1c blue green	.50 .50
61	A18	2c orange brown	.50 .50
62	A18	3c ultra	.50 .50
63	A18	5c gray	.50 .50
64	A18	10c vermilion	.50 .50
65	A18	11c brown	.50 .50
66	A18	20c orange	.50 .75

67	A18	25c maroon	.50	2.00
68	A18	50c yellow	.50	7.00
69	A18	1p carmine lake	.50	25.00
		Nos. 60-69 (10)	5.00	37.75

400th anniversary of the discovery of America by Columbus.

Nos. 63, 66-67 Surcharged

Nos. 70, 72   Nos. 73-75

Surcharged in Black, Red or Yellow

1892

70	A18	1c on 5c gray (Bk) (down)	3.00	.75
a.		Surcharge reading up	5.00	2.00
72	A18	1c on 5c gray (R) (up)	1.00	3.00
a.		Surcharge reading down		
73	A18	1c on 20c org (Bk)	1.50	.75
a.		Inverted surcharge	3.50	2.50
b.		"V" of "CENTAVO" inverted	3.50	2.50
		Nos. 70-73 (3)	5.50	4.50

Similar Surcharge in Yellow or Blue, "centavo" in lower case letters

74	A18	1c on 25c mar (Y)	1.50	1.25
a.		Inverted surcharge	2.50	2.50
75	A18	1c on 25c mar (Bl)	250.00	250.00
a.		Double surcharge (Bl + Bk)	275.00	275.00

Counterfeits exist of Nos. 75 and 75a. Nos. 75, 75a have been questioned.

Pres. Carlos Ezeta — A21

1893   **Engr.**

76	A21	1c blue	.50	.50
77	A21	2c brown red	.50	.50
78	A21	3c purple	.50	.50
79	A21	5c deep brown	.50	.50
80	A21	10c orange brown	.50	.50
81	A21	11c vermilion	.50	.50
82	A21	20c green	.50	1.00
83	A21	25c dk olive gray	.50	2.25
84	A21	50c red orange	.50	5.00
85	A21	1p black	.50	20.00
		Nos. 76-85 (10)	5.00	31.25

For surcharge see No. 89.

Founding City of Isabela — A22

Columbus Statue, Genoa — A23

Departure from Palos — A24

1893

86	A22	2p green	.75	—
87	A23	5p violet	.75	
88	A24	10p orange	.75	
		Nos. 86-88 (3)	2.25	

Discoveries by Columbus. No. 86 is known on cover, but experts are not positive that Nos. 87 and 88 were postally used.

No. 77 Surcharged "UN CENTAVO"

1893

89	A21	1c on 2c brown red	1.00	1.25
a.		"CENTNVO"	6.00	5.00

Liberty — A26

Columbus before Council of Salamanca — A27

Columbus Protecting Indian Hostages A28

Columbus Received by Ferdinand and Isabella A29

1894, Jan.

91	A26	1c brown	.75	.50
92	A26	2c blue	.75	.50
93	A26	3c maroon	.75	.50
94	A26	5c orange brn	.75	.50
95	A26	10c violet	.75	.75
96	A26	11c vermilion	.75	.75
97	A26	20c dark blue	.75	1.00
98	A26	25c orange	.75	5.00
99	A26	50c black	.75	10.00
100	A26	1p slate blue	1.10	20.00
101	A27	2p deep blue	1.10	
102	A28	5p carmine lake	1.10	
103	A29	10p deep brown	1.10	
		Nos. 91-103 (13)	11.15	
		Nos. 91-100 (10)		39.50

Nos. 101-103 for the discoveries by Columbus. Experts are not positive that these were postally used.

No. 96 Surcharged

1894, Dec.

104	A26	1c on 11c vermilion	4.50	.65
a.		"Ccntavo"	40.00	40.00
b.		Double surcharge		

Coat of Arms
A31   A32

Arms Overprint in Second Color Various Frames

1895, Jan. 1

105	A31	1c olive & green	.50	.25
106	A31	2c dk green & bl	.25	—
a.		2c dark green & green	.50	.85
107	A31	3c brown & brown	.50	—
108	A31	5c blue & brown	.50	—
109	A31	10c orange & brn	.50	—
110	A31	12c magenta & brn	.50	—
111	A31	15c ver & ver	.50	—
112	A31	20c yellow & brn	.50	—
a.		Inverted overprint	2.00	

113	A31	24c violet & brn	.50	—
114	A31	30c dp blue & blue	.50	—
115	A31	50c carmine & brn	.50	—
116	A31	1p black & brn	.50	—
		Nos. 105-116 (12)	5.75	

As printed, Nos. 105-116 portrayed Gen. Antonio Ezeta, brother of Pres. Carlos Ezeta. Before issuance, Ezeta's overthrow caused the government to obliterate his features with the national arms overprint. The 3c, 10c, 30c exist without overprint. Value $1 each.

All values have been reprinted. Reprints of 2c are in dark yellow green on thick paper. Value, 25c each.

Various Frames

1895   **Engr.**   **Perf. 12**

117	A32	1c olive	7.25	.50
118	A32	2c dk blue grn	7.25	.50
119	A32	3c brown	10.00	.75
120	A32	5c blue	2.00	.75
121	A32	10c orange	5.00	.75
122	A32	12c claret	17.50	1.00
123	A32	15c vermilion	22.00	1.00
124	A32	20c deep green	30.00	2.00
125	A32	24c violet	22.50	4.00
126	A32	30c deep blue	30.00	5.00
127	A32	50c carmine lake	3.00	35.00
128	A32	1p gray black	10.00	35.00
		Nos. 117-128 (12)	166.50	86.25

The reprints are on thicker paper than the originals, and many of the shades differ. Value 25c each.

Nos. 122, 124-126 Surcharged in Black or Red

1895

129	A32	1c on 12c claret (Bk)	2.00	1.75
130	A32	1c on 24c violet	2.00	1.75
131	A32	1c on 30c dp blue	2.00	1.75
132	A32	2c on 20c dp green	2.00	1.75
133	A32	3c on 30c dp blue	3.00	2.75
a.		Double surcharge	9.00	
		Nos. 129-133 (5)	11.00	9.75

"Peace" — A45

1896, Jan. 1   **Engr.**   **Unwmk.**

134	A45	1c blue	2.00	.50
135	A45	2c dark brown	.50	.50
136	A45	3c blue green	.50	.50
137	A45	5c brown olive	2.00	.50
138	A45	10c yellow	.50	.50
139	A45	12c dark blue	4.00	1.00
140	A45	15c brt ultra	.25	—
a.		15c light violet	1.10	2.00
141	A45	20c magenta	4.00	3.00
142	A45	24c vermilion	1.50	5.00
143	A45	30c orange	1.50	5.00
144	A45	50c black brn	3.00	7.50
145	A45	1p rose lake	6.00	20.00
		Nos. 134-145 (12)	25.75	44.00

The frames of Nos. 134-145 differ slightly on each denomination.
For overprints see Nos. O1-O12, O37-O48.

Wmk. 117

145B	A45	2c dark brown	.25	.25

All values have been reprinted. The paper is thicker than that of the originals and the shades are different. The watermark is always upright on original stamps of Salvador, sideways on the reprints. Value 25c each.

Coat of Arms — A46   "White House" — A47

Locomotive
A48   Mt. San Miguel A49

Ocean Steamship
A50   A51

Post Office
A52   Lake Ilopango A53

Atehausillas Waterfall
A54   Coat of Arms A55

Coat of Arms
A56   Columbus A57

1896

146	A46	1c emerald	.50	1.50
147	A47	2c lake	.50	.90
148	A48	3c yellow brn	.75	.75
149	A49	5c deep blue	.90	.50
150	A50	10c brown	2.00	.90
151	A51	12c slate	2.00	.90
152	A52	15c blue green	1.75	.75
153	A53	20c carmine rose	2.00	1.25
154	A54	24c violet	8.00	1.25
155	A55	30c deep green	5.00	2.00
156	A56	50c orange	10.00	5.00
157	A57	100c dark blue	15.00	12.50
		Nos. 146-157 (12)	48.40	28.20

Nos. 146-157 exist imperf.

Unwmk.

157B	A46	1c emerald	3.75	.90
157C	A47	2c lake	3.75	.50
157D	A48	3c yellow brn	6.00	.50
157E	A49	5c deep blue	4.00	.75
157F	A50	10c brown	7.50	.75
157G	A51	12c slate	10.00	1.00
157I	A52	15c blue green	20.00	1.75
157J	A53	20c carmine rose	7.50	1.00
157K	A54	24c violet	10.00	1.25
157M	A55	30c deep green	10.00	2.50
157N	A56	50c orange	15.00	7.00
157O	A57	100c dark blue	20.00	15.00
		Nos. 157B-157O (12)	117.50	32.90

See Nos. 159-170L. For surcharges and overprints see Nos. 158, 158D, 171-174C, O13-O36, O49-O72, O79-O126.

All values have been reprinted, the 15c, 30c, 50c and 100c on watermarked and the 1c, 2c, 3c, 5c, 12c, 20c, 24c and 100c on unwatermarked paper. The papers of the reprints are thicker than those of the originals and the shades are different. Value, 25c each.

Black Surcharge on Nos. 154, 157K

1896			Wmk. 117
158	A54	15c on 24c violet	4.00 4.00
a.		Double surcharge	20.00 30.00
b.		Inverted surcharge	15.00

Unwmk.

158D	A54	15c on 24c violet	4.00 3.00

Exist spelled "Qnince."

Types of 1896

1897		Engr.	Wmk. 117
159	A46	1c scarlet	2.75 .90
160	A47	2c yellow grn	2.75 .50
161	A48	3c bister brn	2.50 .50
162	A49	5c orange	2.50 .75
163	A50	10c blue grn	3.00 .75
164	A51	12c blue	8.00 1.00
165	A52	15c black	20.00 10.00
166	A53	20c slate	8.00 2.00
167	A54	24c yellow	20.00 20.00
168	A55	30c rose	15.00 5.00
169	A56	50c violet	15.00 5.00
170	A57	100c brown lake	30.00 15.00
		Nos. 159-170 (12)	129.50 61.40

Unwmk.

170A	A46	1c scarlet	2.00 1.50
170B	A47	2c yellow grn	1.00 .90
170C	A48	3c bister brn	.75 .75
170D	A49	5c orange	.90 .50
170E	A50	10c blue grn	5.00 .90
170F	A51	12c blue	1.00 2.00
170G	A52	15c black	10.00 10.00
170H	A53	20c slate	10.00 10.00
170I	A54	24c yellow	20.00 10.00
170J	A55	30c rose	10.00 10.00
170K	A56	50c violet	9.50 10.00
170L	A57	100c brown lake	50.00 50.00
		Nos. 170A-170L (12)	120.15 116.55

All values have been have been reprinted. The papers of the reprints are thicker than those of the originals. Value, 25c each.

Surcharged in Red or Black

1897			Wmk. 117
171	A54	13c on 24c yel (R)	2.50 2.50
172	A55	13c on 30c rose (Bk)	2.50 2.50
173	A56	13c on 50c vio (Bk)	2.50 2.50
174	A57	13c on 100c brn lake (Bk)	2.50 2.50

Unwmk.

174A	A54	13c on 24c yel (R)	2.50 2.50
174B	A55	13c on 30c rose (Bk)	2.50 2.50
174C	A56	13c on 50c vio (Bk)	2.50 2.50
		Nos. 171-174C (7)	17.50 17.50

Coat of Arms of "Republic of Central America" — A59

ONE CENTAVO:
Originals: The mountains are outlined in red and blue. The sea is represented by short red and dark blue lines on a light blue background.
Reprints: The mountains are outlined in red only. The sea is printed in green and dark blue, much blurred.

FIVE CENTAVOS:
Originals: The sea is represented by horizontal and diagonal lines of dark blue on a light blue background.
Reprints: The sea is printed in green and dark blue, much blurred. The inscription in gold is in thicker letters.

1897			Litho.
175	A59	1c bl, gold, rose & grn	1.00 —
176	A59	5c rose, gold, bl & grn	2.00 —

Forming of the "Republic of Central America."
For overprints see Nos. O73-O76.
Stamps of type A59 formerly listed as "Type II" are now known to be reprints.

Allegory of Central American Union — A60

1898		Engr.	Wmk. 117
177	A60	1c orange ver	2.25 .50
178	A60	2c rose	2.25 .50
179	A60	3c pale yel grn	2.00 .50
180	A60	5c blue green	2.00 .75
181	A60	10c gray blue	7.50 .75
182	A60	12c violet	8.50 1.00
183	A60	13c brown lake	8.50 1.00
184	A60	20c deep blue	9.50 2.00
185	A60	24c deep ultra	7.50 5.25
186	A60	26c bister brn	10.00 5.00
187	A60	50c orange	10.00 5.00
188	A60	1p yellow	25.00 15.00
		Nos. 177-188 (12)	95.00 37.25

For overprints and surcharges see Nos. 189-198A, 224-241, 269A-269B, O129-O142. The entire set has been reprinted. The shades of the reprints are not the same as those of the originals, and the paper is thicker. Value, 25c each.

No. 180 Overprinted Vertically, up or down in Black, Violet, Red, Magenta and Yellow

1899			
189	A60	5c blue grn (Bk)	7.50 6.25
a.		Italic 3rd "r" in "Territorial"	12.50 12.50
b.		Double ovpt. (Bk + Y)	37.50 37.50
190	A60	5c blue grn (V)	82.50 82.50
191	A60	5c blue grn (R)	70.00 70.00
191A	A60	5c blue grn (M)	70.00 70.00
191B	A60	5c blue grn (Y)	75.00 75.00
		Nos. 189-191B (5)	305.00 303.75

Counterfeits exist.

Nos. 177-184 Overprinted in Black

1899			
192	A60	1c orange ver	2.00 .50
193	A60	2c rose	2.50 1.00
194	A60	3c pale yel grn	2.50 .50
195	A60	5c blue green	2.50 .50
196	A60	10c gray blue	4.00 1.25
197	A60	12c violet	6.50 2.50
198	A60	13c brown lake	6.50 2.00
198A	A60	20c deep blue	75.00 75.00
		Nos. 192-198 (7)	26.50 8.25

The overprint on No. 198A is only seen on the reprints.
Counterfeits exist of the "wheel" overprint used in 1899-1900.

Ceres ("Estado") — A61

Inscribed: "Estado de El Salvador"

1899		Unwmk. Litho.	Perf. 12
199	A61	1c brown	.25
200	A61	2c gray green	.25
201	A61	3c blue	.25
202	A61	5c brown org	.25
203	A61	10c chocolate	.25
204	A61	12c dark green	.25
205	A61	13c deep rose	.25
206	A61	24c light blue	.25
207	A61	26c carmine rose	.25
208	A61	50c orange red	.25
209	A61	100c violet	.25
		Nos. 199-209 (11)	2.75

#208-209 were probably not placed in use.
For overprints and surcharges see Nos. 210-223, 242-252D, O143-O185.

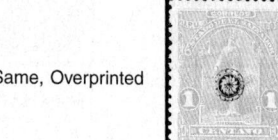

Same, Overprinted

Red Overprint

210	A61	1c brown	60.00 40.00

Blue Overprint

211	A61	1c brown	2.00 1.50
212	A61	5c brown org	2.00 1.50
212A	A61	10c chocolate	10.00 10.00

Black Overprint

213	A61	1c brown	1.50 .75
214	A61	2c gray grn	2.00 .40
215	A61	3c blue	2.25 1.00
216	A61	5c brown org	1.50 .65
217	A61	10c chocolate	1.50 .80
218	A61	12c dark green	4.00 4.00
219	A61	13c deep rose	3.50 3.50
220	A61	24c light blue	30.00 27.50
221	A61	26c car rose	7.50 5.00
222	A61	50c orange red	9.00 7.50
223	A61	100c violet	10.00 9.00
		Nos. 213-223 (11)	72.75 60.10

"Wheel" overprint exists double and triple.

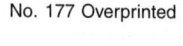

No. 177 Handstamped

1900			Wmk. 117
224	A60	1c orange ver	1.00 1.00

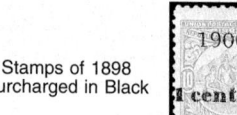

No. 177 Overprinted

225	A60	1c orange ver	15.00 15.00

Stamps of 1898 Surcharged in Black

1900			
226	A60	1c on 10c gray blue	15.00 15.00
a.		Inverted surcharge	15.00 15.00
227	A60	1c on 13c brn lake	100.00
228	A60	2c on 12c vio	50.00 50.00
b.		"eentavo"	
c.		"centavos"	90.00
d.		As "c," double surcharge	
e.		Vertical surcharge	
229	A60	2c on 13c brn lake	5.00 5.00
a.		"eentavo"	8.00 7.00
b.		Inverted surcharge	12.50 10.00
c.		"1900" omitted	7.50 7.50
230	A60	2c on 20c dp blue	5.00 5.00
a.		Inverted surcharge	8.00 8.00
230B	A60	2c on 26c bis brn	
231	A60	3c on 12c vio	90.00 —
a.		"eentavo"	—
b.		Inverted surcharge	—
c.		Double surcharge	
232	A60	3c on 50c org	35.00 35.00
a.		Inverted surcharge	35.00 35.00
233	A60	5c on 12c vio	
234	A60	5c on 24c ultra	50.00 50.00
a.		"eentavo"	
b.		"centavos"	70.00
235	A60	5c on 26c bis brn	150.00 150.00
a.		Inverted surcharge	35.00 35.00
236	A60	5c on 1p yel	50.00 35.00
a.		Inverted surcharge	60.00 60.00

With Additional Overprint in Black

237	A60	2c on 12c vio	2.50 2.50
a.		Inverted surcharge	2.50 2.50
b.		"eentavo"	8.00
c.		"centavos" (plural)	75.00
d.		"1900" omitted	
237H	A60	2c on 13c brn lake	
238	A60	3c on 12c vio	125.00 125.00
a.		"eentavo"	75.00 75.00
239	A60	5c on 26c bis brn	150.00 150.00
a.		Inverted surcharge	

Vertical Surcharge "Centavos" in the Plural

240	A60	2c on 12c vio	125.00 125.00
b.		Without wheel	
240A	A60	5c on 24c dp ultra	125.00 125.00

With Additional Overprint in Black

241	A60	5c on 12c vio	50.00 50.00
a.		Surcharge reading downward	

Counterfeits exist of the surcharges on Nos. 226-241 and the "wheel" overprint on Nos. 237-239, 241.

Same Surcharge on Stamps of 1899 Without Wheel

1900			Unwmk.
242	A61	1c on 13c dp rose	1.50 1.50
a.		Inverted surcharge	4.00 3.00
b.		"eentavo"	4.00 3.00
c.		"ecntavo"	5.00 3.00
d.		"1 centavo 1"	15.00 10.00
e.		Double surcharge	
243	A61	2c on 12c dk grn	8.00 8.00
a.		Inverted surcharge	15.00 15.00
b.		"eentavo"	
244	A61	2c on 13c dp rose	3.00 2.50
a.		"eentavo"	3.00 4.00
b.		"ecntavo"	6.00 2.50
c.		Inverted surcharge	9.00
245	A61	3c on 12c dk grn	3.00 3.00
a.		Inverted surcharge	9.00 5.00
b.		"eentavo"	12.00 12.00
c.		Double surcharge	9.00
		Nos. 242-245 (4)	15.50 14.50

With Additional Overprint in Black

246	A61	1c on 2c gray grn	1.00 1.00
a.		"eentavo"	4.00 3.00
b.		Inverted surcharge	10.00 9.00
247	A61	1c on 13c dp rose	4.00 4.00
a.		"eentavo"	15.00
b.		"1 centavo 1"	
248	A61	2c on 12c dk grn	5.00 4.00
a.		"eentavo"	15.00
b.		Inverted surcharge	4.00 4.00
c.		Double surcharge	8.00
249	A61	2c on 13c dp rose	100.00 100.00
a.		"eentavo"	
b.		Double surcharge	150.00 150.00
250	A61	3c on 12c dk grn	5.00 3.00
a.		Inverted surcharge	5.50 4.00
b.		"eentavo"	8.00 7.00
c.		Date double	15.00
251	A61	5c on 24c lt bl	12.00 5.00
a.		Inverted surcharge	20.00 20.00
252	A61	5c on 26c car rose	4.00 4.00
a.		Inverted surcharge	12.00 9.00
b.		"eentavo"	6.00 5.00
252D	A61	5c on 1c on 26c car rose	
		Nos. 246-248,250-252 (6)	31.00 21.00

Counterfeits exist of the surcharges on Nos. 242-252D and the "wheel" overprint on Nos. 246-252D.

Ceres ("Republica") — A63

There are two varieties of the 1c, type A63, one with the word "centavo" in the middle of the label (#253, 263, 270, 299, 305, 326), the other with "centavo" nearer the left end than the right (#270, 299, 305, 326).
The stamps of type A63 are found in a great variety of shades. Stamps of type A63 without handstamp were not regularly issued.

Handstamped in Violet or Black

Inscribed: "Republica de El Salvador"

1900			
253	A63	1c blue green	.90 .90
a.		1c yellow green	.90 .90
254	A63	2c rose	1.50 1.00
255	A63	3c gray black	1.25 1.00

256	A63	5c pale blue	1.00	.60
a.		5c deep blue	5.00	.60
257	A63	10c deep blue	2.00	.60
258	A63	12c yel green	5.00	3.50
259	A63	13c yel brown	4.00	3.00
260	A63	24c gray	15.00	15.00
261	A63	26c yel brown	7.00	7.00
262	A63	50c rose red	2.00	2.00
		Nos. 253-262 (10)	39.65	34.60

For overprints and surcharges see Nos. 263-269, 270-282, 293A-311B, 317, 326-335, O223-O242, O258-O262, O305-O312.

Handstamped in Violet or Black

263	A63	1c lt green	10.00	4.00
264	A63	2c pale rose	10.00	3.00
265	A63	3c gray black	10.00	3.00
266	A63	5c slate blue	14.00	3.00
267	A63	10c deep blue	—	—
268	A63	13c yellow brn	35.00	35.00
269	A63	50c dull rose	15.00	15.00
		Nos. 263-266,268-269 (6)	94.00	63.00

Handstamped on 1898 Stamps Wmk. 117

269A	A60	2c rose	30.00	30.00
269B	A60	10c gray blue	30.00	30.00

The overprints on Nos. 253 to 269B are handstamped and, as usual with that style of overprint, are to be found double, inverted, omitted, etc.

Specialists have questioned the existence of No. 267. The editors would like to see authenticated evidence of the existence of a genuine example.

Stamps of Type A63 Overprinted in Black

		1900		Unwmk.
270	A63	1c light green	1.50	1.00
271	A63	2c rose	7.50	2.00
272	A63	3c gray black	1.50	1.00
273	A63	5c pale blue	7.50	2.00
a.		5c dark blue	6.00	1.00
274	A63	10c deep blue	7.50	2.00
a.		10c pale blue	7.50	2.00
275	A63	12c light green	2.25	1.50
276	A63	13c yellow brown	1.50	1.00
277	A63	24c gray	1.75	1.25
278	A63	26c yellow brown	3.00	2.00
		Nos. 270-278 (9)	34.00	13.75

This overprint is known double, inverted, etc.

Nos. 271-273 Surcharged in Black

		1902		
280	A63	1c on 2c rose	8.25	6.75
281	A63	1c on 3c black	6.00	4.25
282	A63	1c on 5c blue	3.75	3.00
		Nos. 280-282 (3)	18.00	14.00

Morazán Monument — A64

		Perf. 14, 14½		
		1903 Engr.		Wmk. 173
283	A64	1c green	1.00	.60
284	A64	2c carmine	1.00	.60
285	A64	3c orange	10.00	2.00
286	A64	5c dark blue	1.00	.60
287	A64	10c dull violet	1.00	.60
288	A64	12c slate	1.25	.60
289	A64	13c red brown	1.25	.60
290	A64	24c scarlet	7.50	3.75
291	A64	26c yellow brn	7.50	3.75
292	A64	50c bister	3.75	2.25
293	A64	100c grnsh blue	11.00	7.50
		Nos. 283-293 (11)	46.25	22.85

For surcharges and overprint see Nos. 312-316, 318-325, O253.

Stamps of 1900 with Shield in Black Overprinted

(5¾x13½mm) — a | 1905 (5x14¾mm) — b

(4½x16mm) — c | 1905 (4½x13½mm) — d

(5x14½mm) — e | 1905

		1905-06 Unwmk.	Perf. 12	
		Blue Overprint		
293A	A63 (a)	2c rose	—	—
294	A63 (a)	3c gray blk	8.00	6.00
a.		Without shield	—	—
295	A63 (a)	5c blue	10.00	7.50
		Purple Overprint		
296	A63 (b)	3c gray blk (Shield in pur)	—	—
296A	A63 (b)	5c bl (Shield in pue)	—	—
297	A63 (b)	3c gray blk	—	—
298	A63 (b)	5c blue	—	—
		Black Overprint		
298A	A63 (b)	5c blue	—	—
		Blue Overprint		
299	A63 (c)	1c green	10.00	5.00
299B	A63 (c)	2c rose	.50	.40
c.		"1905" vert.	1.00	
300	A63 (c)	5c blue	6.00	4.00
301	A63 (c)	10c deep blue	2.00	1.00
		Black Overprint		
302	A63 (c)	2c rose	10.00	5.00
303	A63 (c)	5c blue	25.00	25.00
304	A63 (c)	10c deep blue	12.00	7.00
		Blue Overprint		
305	A63 (d)	1c green	15.00	10.00
306	A63 (d)	2c rose, ovpt. vert.	9.00	5.00
a.		Overprint horiz.		
306B	A63 (d)	3c gray black	8.00	4.00
307	A63 (d)	5c blue	3.00	1.50
		Blue Overprint		
311	A63 (e)	2c rose	10.00	8.00
a.		Without shield	15.00	12.00
		Black Overprint		
311B	A63 (e)	5c blue	30.00	20.00
		Nos. 294-295,299-311B (15)	158.50	109.40

These overprints are found double, inverted, omitted, etc. Counterfeits exist.

Regular Issue of 1903 Surcharged

UN CENTAVO — f | 5 CENTAVOS — g

h

		1905-06 Wmk. 173	Perf. 14, 14½	
		Black Surcharge		
312	A64 (f)	1c on 2c car	4.00	2.00
a.		Double surcharge	20.00	20.00
		Red Surcharge		
312B	A64 (g)	5c on 12c slate	5.00	4.00
c.		Double surcharge		
d.		Black surcharge	15.00	15.00
e.		As "d," double surcharge		
		Blue Handstamped Surcharge		
313	A64 (h)	1c on 2c car	2.00	2.00
314	A64 (h)	1c on 10c vio	2.00	2.00
315	A64 (h)	1c on 12c sl ('06)	2.00	2.00
316	A64 (h)	1c on 13c red brn	22.50	15.00

No. 271 with Handstamped Surcharge in Blue Unwmk.

317	A63 (h)	1c on 2c rose	—	—
		Nos. 312-316 (6)	37.50	27.00

The "h" is handstamped in strips of four stamps each differing from the others in the size of the upper figures of value and in the letters of the word "CENTAVO," particularly in the size of the "N" and the "O" of that word. The surcharge is known inverted, double, etc.

Regular Issue of 1903 with Handstamped Surcharge

i

j | k

Wmk. 173
Red Handstamped Surcharge

318	A64 (i)	5c on 12c slate	4.00	3.00
319	A64 (j)	5c on 12c slate	6.00	5.00
a.		Blue surcharge		
		Blue Handstamped Surcharge		
320	A64 (k)	5c on 12c slate	3.50	2.50
		Nos. 318-320 (3)	13.50	10.50

One or more of the numerals in the handstamped surcharges on Nos. 318, 319 and 320 are frequently omitted, inverted, etc.

Regular Issue of 1903 Surcharged

l | m

Blue Handstamped Surcharge

321	A64 (l)	6c on 12c slate	.75	.50
322	A64 (l)	6c on 13c red brn	1.50	.60
		Red Handstamped Surcharge		
323	A64 (l)	6c on 12c slate	27.50	15.00

Type "l" is handstamped in strips of four varieties, differing in the size of the numerals and letters. The surcharge is known double and inverted.

Black Surcharge

324	A64 (m)	1c on 13c red brn	2.25	1.50
a.		Double surcharge	6.00	4.50
b.		Right "1" & dot omitted		
c.		Both numerals omitted		
325	A64 (m)	3c on 13c red brn	.75	.60

Stamps of 1900, with Shield in Black, Overprinted — n

	01905		

		1905 Unwmk.	Perf. 12	
		Blue Overprint		
326	A63 (n)	1c green	9.00	6.00
a.		Inverted overprint		
327	A63 (n)	2c rose	5.00	5.00
a.		Vertical overprint	12.50	12.50
b.		Imperforate	9.00	6.00
327B	A63 (n)	3c black	50.00	30.00
327C	A63 (n)	5c blue	25.00	20.00
328	A63 (n)	10c deep blue	15.00	9.00
		Black Overprint		
328A	A63 (n)	10c deep blue	20.00	15.00
		Nos. 326-328A (6)	124.00	85.00

Counterfeits of Nos. 326-335 abound.

Stamps of 1900, with Shield in Black Surcharged or Overprinted

o | p

q

		1906 Blue and Black Surcharge		
329	A63 (o)	2c on 26c brn org	1.00	.80
a.		"2" & dot double	15.00	15.00
330	A63 (o)	3c on 26c brn org	8.00	6.50
a.		"3" & dot double		
		Black Surcharge or Overprint		
331	A63 (o)	3c on 26c brn org	9.00	7.00
a.		Disks & numerals omitted		
b.		"3" and disks double		
c.		"1906" omitted		
333	A63 (p)	10c deep blue	6.00	4.00
334	A63 (q)	10c ultra & blk	6.00	4.00
334A	A63 (q)	26c brown org	50.00	45.00
b.		"1906" in blue		
		No. 257 Overprinted in Black		
335	A63 (q)	10c dp bl (Shield in violet)	—	—
a.		Overprint type "p"		
		Nos. 329-334A (6)	80.00	67.30

There are numerous varieties of these surcharges and overprints.

Pres. Pedro José Escalón — A65

		1906 Engr.	Perf. 11½	
		Glazed Paper		
336	A65	1c green & blk	.25	.25
a.		Thin paper	.75	.25
337	A65	2c red & blk	.25	.25
338	A65	3c yellow & blk	.25	.25
339	A65	5c ultra & blk	.25	.25
a.		5c dark blue & black		
340	A65	6c carmine & blk	.25	.25
341	A65	10c violet & blk	.25	.25
342	A65	12c violet & blk	.25	.25
343	A65	13c dk brn & blk	.25	.25
345	A65	24c carmine & blk	.35	.35
346	A65	26c choc & blk	.35	.35
347	A65	50c yellow & blk	.35	.45
348	A65	100c blue & blk	3.00	3.00
		Nos. 336-348 (12)	6.05	6.15

All values of this set are known imperforate but are not believed to have been issued in this condition.

See Nos. O263-O272. For overprints and surcharges see Nos. 349-354.

The entire set has been reprinted, perforated 11.8. Value, set of 12, $1.20.

Nos. 336-338 Overprinted in Black

		1907		
349	A65	1c green & blk	.25	.25
a.		Shield in red	3.50	
350	A65	2c red & blk	.25	.25
a.		Shield in red	3.50	
351	A65	3c yellow & blk	.25	.25
		Nos. 349-351 (3)	.75	.75

Reprints of Nos. 349 to 351 have the same characteristics as the reprints of the preceding issue. Value, set of 3, 15c.

Stamps of 1906
Surcharged with
Shield and

352	A65	1c on 5c ultra & blk	.25	.25
a.		1c on 5c dark blue & black	.25	.25
b.		Inverted surcharge	.35	.35
c.		Double surcharge	.45	.45
352D	A65	1c on 6c rose & blk	.25	.25
e.		Double surcharge	1.25	1.25
353	A65	2c on 6c rose & blk	2.00	1.00
354	A65	10c on 6c rose & blk	.50	.35
		Nos. 352-354 (4)	3.00	1.85

The above surcharges are frequently found
with the shield double, inverted, or otherwise
misplaced.

National
Palace — A66

Overprinted with Shield in Black

1907   Engr.   Unwmk.
Paper with or without colored dots

355	A66	1c green & blk	.25	.25
356	A66	2c red & blk	.25	.25
357	A66	3c yellow & blk	.25	.25
358	A66	5c blue & blk	.25	.25
a.		5c ultramarine & black	.25	.25
359	A66	6c ver & blk	.25	.25
a.		Shield in red	3.25	
360	A66	10c violet & blk	.25	.25
361	A66	12c violet & blk	.25	.25
362	A66	13c sepia & blk	.25	.25
363	A66	24c rose & blk	.25	.25
364	A66	26c yel brn & blk	.30	.25
365	A66	50c orange & blk	.50	.35
a.		50c yellow & black	3.50	
366	A66	100c turq bl & blk	1.00	.50
		Nos. 355-366 (12)	4.05	3.35

Most values exist without shield, also with
shield inverted, double, and otherwise mis-
printed. Many of these were never sold to the
public.
    See 2nd footnote following No. 421.
    See Nos. 369-373, 397-401. For surcharges
and overprints see Nos. 367-368A, 374-77,
414-421, 443-444, J71-J74, J76-J80, O329-
O331.

No. 356 With
Additional
Surcharge in Black

1908
367	A66	1c on 2c red & blk	.25	.25
a.		Double surcharge	1.00	1.00
b.		Inverted surcharge	.50	.50
c.		Double surcharge, one inverted	.50	.50
d.		Red surcharge		

Same Surcharged in
Black or Red

368	A66	1c on 2c	19.00	17.50
368A	A66	1c on 2c (R)	27.50	25.00

Counterfeits exist of the surcharges on Nos.
368-368A.

Type of 1907
1909   Engr.   Wmk. 172
369	A66	1c green & blk	.25	.25
370	A66	2c rose & blk	.25	.25
371	A66	3c yellow & blk	.25	.25

372	A66	5c blue & blk	.25	.25
373	A66	10c violet & blk	.30	.25
		Nos. 369-373 (5)	1.30	1.25

The note after No. 366 will apply here also.

Nos. 355, 369
Overprinted in Red

1909, Sept.   Unwmk.
374	A66	1c green & blk	2.25	1.10
a.		Inverted overprint	10.00	

Wmk. 172
375	A66	1c green & blk	1.75	1.40
a.		Inverted overprint		

88th anniv. of El Salvador's independence.

Nos. 362, 364
Surcharged

1909   Unwmk.
376	A66	2c on 13c sep & blk	1.50	1.25
a.		Inverted surcharge		
377	A66	3c on 26c yel brn & blk	1.75	1.40
a.		Inverted surcharge		

A67   A68

Design: Pres. Fernando Figueroa.

1910   Engr.   Wmk. 172
378	A67	1c sepia & blk	.25	.25
379	A67	2c dk grn & blk	.25	.25
380	A67	3c orange & blk	.25	.25
381	A67	4c carmine & blk	.25	.25
a.		4c scarlet & black	.25	
382	A67	5c purple & blk	.25	.25
383	A67	6c scarlet & blk	.25	.25
384	A67	10c purple & blk	.25	.25
385	A67	12c dp bl & blk	.25	.25
386	A67	17c ol grn & blk	.25	.25
387	A67	19c brn red & blk	.25	.25
388	A67	29c choc & blk	.25	.25
389	A67	50c yellow & blk	.25	.25
390	A67	100c turq bl & blk	.25	.25
		Nos. 378-390 (13)	3.25	3.25

Paper with colored dots
1911   Unwmk.

5c, José Matías Delgado. 6c, Manuel José
Arce. 12c, Centenary Monument.

391	A68	5c dp blue & brn	.25	.25
392	A68	6c orange & brn	.25	.25
393	A68	12c violet & brn	.25	.25

Wmk. 172
394	A68	5c dp blue & brn	.25	.25
395	A68	6c orange & brn	.25	.25
396	A68	12c violet & brn	.25	.25
		Nos. 391-396 (6)	1.50	1.50

Centenary of the insurrection of 1811.

Palace Type of 1907 without Shield
1911
Paper without colored dots
397	A66	1c scarlet	.25	.25
398	A66	2c chocolate	.30	.30
a.		Paper with brown dots		
399	A66	13c deep green	.25	.25
400	A66	24c yellow	.25	.25
401	A66	50c dark brown	.25	.25
		Nos. 397-401 (5)	1.30	1.30

José Matías
Delgado — A71

Manuel José
Arce — A72

Francisco
Morazán — A73

Rafael
Campo — A74

Trinidad
Cabañas
A75

Monument of
Gerardo
Barrios
A76

Centenary
Monument
A77

National Palace
A78

Rosales
Hospital — A79

Coat of
Arms — A80

1912   Unwmk.   Perf. 12
402	A71	1c dp bl & blk	1.00	.25
403	A72	2c bis brn & blk	1.00	.25
404	A73	5c scarlet & blk	1.00	.25
405	A74	6c dk grn & blk	1.00	.25
406	A75	12c ol grn & blk	3.00	.25
407	A76	17c violet & slate	10.00	.25
408	A77	19c scar & slate	3.00	.30
409	A78	29c org & slate	5.00	.30
410	A79	50c blue & slate	5.00	.45
411	A80	1col black & slate	10.00	1.00
		Nos. 402-411 (10)	40.00	3.55

Juan Manuel
Rodríguez
A81

Pres. Manuel E.
Araujo
A82

1914   Perf. 11½
412	A81	10c orange & brn	5.00	1.50
413	A82	25c purple & brn	5.00	1.50

Type of 1907 without
Shield Overprinted in
Black

1915
Paper overlaid with colored dots
414	A66	1c gray green	.25	.25
415	A66	2c red	.25	.25
416	A66	5c ultra	.25	.25
417	A66	6c pale blue	.25	.25
418	A66	10c yellow	.60	.30
419	A66	12c brown	.50	.25
420	A66	50c violet	.25	.25
421	A66	100c black brn	1.40	1.40
		Nos. 414-421 (8)	3.75	3.20

Varieties such as center omitted, center
double, center inverted, imperforate exist with
or without date, date inverted, date double,
etc., but are believed to be entirely unofficial.
    Preceding the stamps with the "1915" over-
print a quantity of stamps of this type was
overprinted with the letter "S." Evidence is
lacking that they were ever placed in use. The
issue was demonetized in 1916.

National
Theater — A83

Various frames.

1916   Engr.   Perf. 12
431	A83	1c deep green	.25	.25
432	A83	2c vermilion	.25	.25
433	A83	5c deep blue	.25	.25
434	A83	6c gray violet	.25	.25
435	A83	10c black brn	.25	.25
436	A83	12c violet	2.50	.50
437	A83	17c orange	.35	.25
438	A83	25c dk brown	.80	.25
439	A83	29c black	5.00	.75
440	A83	50c slate	20.00	10.00
		Nos. 431-440 (10)	29.90	13.00

Watermarked letters which occasionally
appear are from the papermaker's name.
    For surcharges and overprints see Nos.
450-455, 457-466, O332-O341.

Nos. O324-O325 with "OFICIAL"
Barred out in Black

1917
441	O3	2c red	.90	.90
a.		Double bar		
442	O3	5c ultramarine	1.00	.70
a.		Double bar		

Regular Issue of
1915 Overprinted
"OFICIAL" and Re-
overprinted In Red

443	A66	6c pale blue	1.25	1.00
a.		Double bar		
444	A66	12c brown	1.75	1.25
a.		Double bar		
b.		"CORRIENTE" inverted		

Same Overprint in Red
On Nos. O323-O327
445	O3	1c gray green	3.50	2.50
a.		"CORRIENTE" inverted		
b.		Double bar		
c.		"CORRIENTE" omitted		
446	O3	2c red	3.50	2.50
a.		Double bar		
447	O3	5c ultra	18.00	12.00
a.		Double bar, both in black		
448	O3	10c yellow	2.00	1.00
a.		Double bar		
b.		"OFICIAL" and bar omitted		
449	O3	50c violet	1.00	1.00
a.		Double bar		
		Nos. 443-449 (7)	31.00	21.25

Nos. O334-O335 Overprinted or
Surcharged in Red

a   b

450	A83 (a)	5c deep blue	3.00	2.00
a.		"CORRIENTE" double		
451	A83 (b)	1c on 6c gray vio	2.00	1.50
a.		"CORRIERTE"		
b.		"CORRIENRE"	5.00	
c.		"CORRIENTE" double		

No. 434
Surcharged in
Black

1918
452 A83 1c on 6c gray vio 1.75 1.00
  a. Double surcharge
  b. Inverted surcharge

No. 434
Surcharged in
Black

1918
453 A83 1c on 6c gray vio 1.50 .75
  a. "Centado" 2.25 1.50
  b. Double surcharge 2.50 1.75
  c. Inverted surcharge

No. 434
Surcharged in
Black or Red

1918
454 A83 1c on 6c gray vio 10.00 6.00
  a. Double surcharge
  b. Inverted surcharge 5.00 5.00
455 A83 1c on 6c gray vio (R) 10.00 6.00
  a. Double surcharge
  b. Inverted surcharge 5.00 5.00
    Nos. 454-455 (2) 20.00 12.00

Counterfeits exist of Nos. 454-455.

Pres. Carlos
Meléndez — A85

1919   **Engr.**
456 A85 1col dk blue & blk .50 .50

For surcharge see No. 467.

No. 437
Surcharged in
Black

1919
457 A83 1c on 17c orange .25 .25
  a. Inverted surcharge 1.00 1.00
  b. Double surcharge 1.00 1.00

**Nos. 435-436, 438, 440 Surcharged
in Black or Blue**

1920-21
458 A83 1c on 12c violet .25 .25
  a. Double surcharge 1.00 1.00

459 A83 2c on 10c dk brn .25 .25
460 A83 5c on 50c slate ('21) .40 .25
461 A83 6c on 25c dk brn (Bl) 2.00 1.00
    ('21)
Same Surch. in Black on No. O337
462 A83 1c on 12c violet 1.00 1.00
  a. Double surcharge
    Nos. 458-462 (5) 3.90 2.75

No. 460 surcharged in yellow and 461
surcharged in red are essays.
No. 462 is due to some sheets of Official
Stamps being mixed with the ordinary 12c
stamps at the time of surcharging. The error
stamps were sold to the public and used for
ordinary postage.

Surcharged in Red, Blue or Black

15c Types:

  I   II   III   IV

463 A83 15c on 29c blk (III) ('21) 1.00 .40
  a. Double surcharge 2.00
  b. Type I 1.50 1.00
  c. Type II 1.00 .75
  d. Type IV 2.50
464 A83 26c on 29c blk (Bl) 1.00 .60
  a. Double surcharge
466 A83 35c on 50c slate (Bk) 1.00 .60
467 A85 60c on 1col dk bl & blk .30 .25
    (R)
    Nos. 463-467 (4) 3.30 1.85

Surcharge on No. 464 differs from 15c illustration in that bar at bottom extends across
stamp and denomination includes "cts." One
stamp in each row of ten of No. 464 has the "t"
of "cts" inverted and one stamp in each row of
No. 466 has the letters "c" in "cinco" larger
than the normal.
Setting for No. 467 includes three types of
numerals and "CENTAVOS" measuring from
16mm to 20mm wide.
No. 464 surcharged in green or yellow and
the 35c on 29c black are essays.

A93

1921
468 A93 1c on 1c ol grn .25 .25
  a. Double surcharge .75
469 A93 1c on 5c yellow .25 .25
  a. Inverted surcharge
  b. Double surcharge
470 A93 1c on 10c blue .25 .25
  a. Double surcharge .50
471 A93 1c on 25c green .25 .25
  a. Double surcharge
472 A93 1c on 50c olive .25 .25
  a. Double surcharge
473 A93 1c on 1p gray blk .25 .25
  a. Double surcharge
    Nos. 468-473 (6) 1.50 1.50

The frame of No. 473 differs slightly from the
illustration.
Setting includes many wrong font letters and
numerals.

Francisco   Manuel José
Menéndez   Arce
A94   A95

Confederation
Coin — A96

Delgado
Addressing
Crowd — A97

Coat of Arms   Francisco
of Confedera-   Morazán
tion   A99
A98

Independence   Columbus
Monument   A101
A100

1921   **Engr.**   **Perf. 12**
474 A94 1c green 2.50 .25
475 A95 2c black 5.00 .25
476 A96 5c orange 2.00 .25
477 A97 6c carmine rose 2.00 .25
478 A98 10c deep blue 2.00 .25
479 A99 25c olive grn 4.00 .25
480 A100 60c violet 9.00 .50
481 A101 1col black brn 15.00 .75
    Nos. 474-481 (8) 41.50 2.75

For overprints and surcharges see Nos.
481A-485, 487-494, 506, O342-O349.

**Nos. 474-477 Overprinted in Red,
Black or Blue**

a   b

1921
481A A94 (a) 1c green (R) 5.00 4.00
481B A95 (a) 2c black (R) 5.00 4.00
481C A96 (b) 5c orange (Bk) 5.00 4.00
481D A97 (b) 6c car rose (Bl) 5.00 4.00
    Nos. 481A-481D (4) 20.00 16.00

Centenary of independence.

No. 477 Surcharged

a

 b

1923
482 A97 (a) 5c on 6c 4.00 .25
483 A97 (b) 5c on 6c 4.00 .25
484 A97 (b) 20c on 6c 4.00 .25
    Nos. 482-484 (3) 12.00 .75

Nos. 482-484 exist with double surcharge.

No. 475 Surcharged
in Red

1923
485 A95 10c on 2c black 4.00 .25

José Simeón Cañas
y Villacorta — A102

1923
486 A102 5c blue .60 .30
Centenary of abolition of slavery.
For surcharge see No. 571.

Nos. 479, 481
Surcharged in Red or
Black

1924   **Perf. 12**
487 A99 1c on 25c ol grn (R) .30 .25
  a. Numeral at right inverted
  b. Double surcharge
488 A99 6c on 25c ol grn (R) .25 .25
489 A99 20c on 25c ol grn (R) .60 .25
490 A10120c on 1col blk brn (Bk) .75 .35
    Nos. 487-490 (4) 1.90 1.10

Nos. 476, 478 Surcharged

1924
491 A96 1c on 5c orange (Bk) .40 .25
492 A98 6c on 10c dp bl (R) .40 .25

Nos. 491-492 exist with double surcharge.
A stamp similar to No. 492 but with
surcharge "6 centavos 6" is an essay.

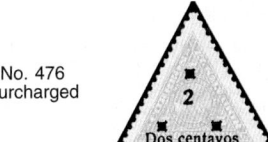

No. 476
Surcharged

1924
493 A96 2c on 5c orange .40 .40
  a. Top ornament omitted 2.00 2.00
    Nos. 491-493 (3) 1.20 .90

No. 480 Surcharged

1924   Red Surcharge
494 A100 5c on 60c violet   6.00   5.00
   a.   "1781" for "1874"   13.00   12.00
   b.   "1934" for "1924"   13.00   12.00

Universal Postal Union, 50th anniversary.
This stamp with black surcharge is an
essay. Examples have been passed through
the post.

Daniel Hernández Monument A106

National Gymnasium A107

Atlacatl — A108

Conspiracy of 1811 — A109

Bridge over Lempa River — A110

Map of Central America — A111

Balsam Tree — A112

Tulla Serra — A114

Columbus at La Rábida — A115

Coat of Arms — A116

Photogravure; Engraved (35c, 1col)
1924-25   Perf. 12½; 14 (35c, 1col)
495 A106   1c red violet   .25   .25
496 A107   2c dark red   .40   .25
497 A108   3c chocolate   .30   .25
498 A109   5c olive blk   .30   .25
499 A110   6c grnsh blue   .40   .25
500 A111   10c orange   .85   .90
   a.   "ATLANT CO"   8.00   8.00
501 A112   20c deep green   1.50   .40
502 A114   35c scar & grn   3.50   .50
503 A115   50c orange brown   2.75   .35
504 A116   1col grn & vio ('25)   3.50   .90
     Nos. 495-504 (10)   14.25   3.25

For overprints and surcharges see Nos.
510-511, 520-534, 585, C1-C10, C19, O350-
O361, RA1-RA4.

No. 480 Surcharged in Red

1925, Aug.   Perf. 12
506 A100 2c on 60c violet   1.50   1.25

City of San Salvador, 400th anniv.
The variety with dates in black is an essay.

View of San Salvador — A118

1925   Photo.   Perf. 12½
507 A118 1c blue   1.10   1.00
508 A118 2c deep green   1.10   1.00
509 A118 3c Mahogany red   1.10   1.00
     Nos. 507-509 (3)   3.30   3.00

#506-509 for the 4th centenary of the found-
ing of the City of San Salvador.

Black Surcharge

1928, July 17
510 A111 3c on 10c orange   1.25   .75
   a.   "ATLANT CO"   20.00   20.00

Industrial Exhibition, Santa Ana, July 1928.

Red Surcharge

1928
511 A109 1c on 5c olive black   .45   .25
   a.   Bar instead of top left "1"   .60   .25

Pres. Pío Romero Bosque, Salvador, and Pres. Lázaro Chacón, Guatemala A121

1929   Litho.   Perf. 11½
Portraits in Dark Brown
512 A121 1c dull violet   .60   .45
   a.   Center inverted   11.50   11.50
513 A121 3c bister brn   .60   .45
   a.   Center inverted   35.00   35.00
514 A121 5c gray grn   .60   .45
515 A121 10c orange   .60   .45
     Nos. 512-515 (4)   2.40   1.80

Opening of the international railroad connecting El Salvador and Guatemala.
Nos. 512-515 exist imperforate. No. 512 in
the colors of No. 515.

Tomb of Menéndez A122

1930, Dec. 3
516 A122 1c violet   4.50   3.50
517 A122 3c brown   4.50   3.50
518 A122 5c dark green   4.50   3.50
519 A122 10c yellow brn   4.50   3.50
     Nos. 516-519 (4)   18.00   14.00

Centenary of the birth of General Francisco
Menéndez.

Stamps of 1924-25 Issue Overprinted

1932   Perf. 12½, 14
520 A106 1c deep violet   .30   .25
521 A107 2c dark red   .30   .25
522 A108 3c chocolate   .45   .25
523 A109 5c olive blk   .45   .25
524 A110 6c deep blue   .60   .25
525 A111 10c orange   1.50   .25
   a.   "ATLANT CO"   12.00   9.00
526 A112 20c deep green   2.40   .75
527 A114 35c scar & grn   3.25   1.00
528 A115 50c orange brown   4.50   1.50
529 A116 1col green & vio   7.50   3.25
     Nos. 520-529 (10)   21.25   8.00

Values are for the overprint measuring
7½x3mm. It is found in two other sizes:
7½x3¼mm and 8x3mm.

Types of 1924-25
Surcharged with New Values in Red or Black

1934   Perf. 12½
530 A109 2(c) on 5c grnsh blk   .25   .25
   a.   Double surcharge
531 A111 3(c) on 10c org (Bk)   .45   .25
   a.   "ATLANT CO"   6.00   6.00

Nos. 503, 504, 502 Surcharged with New Values in Black
Perf. 12½, 14½
532 A115 2(c) on 50c   .45   .25
   a.   Double surcharge   3.00
533 A116 8(c) on 1col   .25   .25
534 A114 15(c) on 35c   .45   .45
     Nos. 530-534 (5)   1.85   1.45

Police Barracks, Type I — A123

Type II

Two types of the 2c:
Type I — The clouds have heavy lines of shading.
Type II — The lines of shading have been removed from the clouds.

Wmk. 240
1934-35   Litho.   Perf. 12½
535 A123 2c gray brn, type I   .25   .25
   a.   2c brown, type II   .25   .25
536 A123 5c car, type II   .25   .25
537 A123 8c lt ultra, type II   .25   .25
     Nos. 535-537,C33-C35 (6)   4.70   2.45

Discus Thrower A124

1935, Mar. 16   Engr.   Unwmk.
538 A124 5c carmine   3.00   2.25
539 A124 8c blue   3.25   2.75
540 A124 10c orange yel   4.50   3.00
541 A124 15c bister   4.50   3.25
542 A124 37c green   6.00   4.50
     Nos. 538-542,C36-C40 (10)   74.50   60.00

3rd Central American Games.

Same Overprinted in Black

1935, June 27
543 A124 5c carmine   5.00   3.00
544 A124 8c blue   7.00   3.00
545 A124 10c orange yel   7.00   3.50
546 A124 15c bister   7.00   3.50
547 A124 37c green   12.00   5.50
     Nos. 543-547,C41-C45 (10)   99.00   63.75

Flag of El Salvador A125

Tree of San Vicente A126

1935, Oct. 26   Litho.   Wmk. 240
548 A125 1c gray blue   .30   .25
549 A125 2c black brn   .30   .25
550 A125 3c plum   .30   .25
551 A125 5c rose carmine   .45   .25
552 A125 8c ultra   .45   .25
553 A125 15c fawn   .60   .45
     Nos. 548-553,C46 (7)   3.25   2.15

1935, Dec. 26
Numerals in Black, Tree in Yellow Green
554 A126 2c black brn   .85   .45
555 A126 3c dk blue grn   .85   .45
556 A126 5c rose red   .85   .45
557 A126 8c dark blue   .85   .55
558 A126 15c brown   .60   .45
     Nos. 554-558,C47-C51 (10)   10.25   7.35

Tercentenary of San Vicente.

Volcano of Izalco — A127

Wharf at Cutuco — A128

Doroteo Vasconcelos A129

Parade Ground A130

Dr. Tomás G. Palomo — A131

Sugar Mill — A132

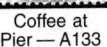
Coffee at
Pier — A133

Gathering
Balsam — A134

Pres. Manuel E.
Araujo — A135

1935, Dec.   Engr.   Unwmk.
559 A127 1c deep violet   .25   .25
560 A128 2c chestnut   .25   .25
561 A129 3c green   .25   .25
562 A130 5c carmine   .60   .25
563 A131 8c dull blue   .25   .25
564 A132 10c orange   .60   .25
565 A133 15c dk olive bis   .60   .25
566 A134 50c indigo   3.00   1.75
567 A135 1col black   7.50   4.50
  Nos. 559-567 (9)   13.30   8.00

Paper has faint imprint "El Salvador" on face.
For surcharges and overprint see Nos. 568-570, 573, 583-584, C52.

Stamps of 1935 Surcharged with New Value in Black
1938   Perf. 12½
568 A130 1c on 5c carmine   .25   .25
569 A132 3c on 10c orange   .25   .25
570 A133 8c on 15c dk ol bis   .30   .25
  Nos. 568-570 (3)   .80   .75

No. 486 Surcharged with New Value in Red
1938   Perf. 11½
571 A102 3c on 5c blue   .30   .25

Centenary of the death of José Simeón Cañas, liberator of slaves in Latin America.

Map and Flags of US and El
Salvador — A136

Engraved and Lithographed
1938, Apr. 21   Perf. 12
572 A136 8c multicolored   .95   .70
US Constitution, 150th anniv. See #C61.

No. 560 Surcharged with New Value in Black
1938   Perf. 12½
573 A128 1c on 2c chestnut   .25   .25

Indian Sugar
Mill — A137

Designs: 2c, Indian women washing. 3c, Indian girl at spring. 5c, Indian plowing. 8c, Izote flower. 10c, Champion cow. 20c, Extracting balsam. 50c, Maquilishuat in bloom. 1col, Post Office, San Salvador.

1938-39   Engr.   Perf. 12
574 A137 1c dark violet   .25   .25
575 A137 2c dark green   .25   .25
576 A137 3c dark brown   .30   .25
577 A137 5c scarlet   .30   .25
578 A137 8c dark blue   2.00   .25
579 A137 10c yel org ('39)   3.00   .25
580 A137 20c bis brn ('39)   2.75   .25

581 A137 50c dull blk ('39)   3.25   .70
582 A137 1col black ('39)   3.00   1.00
  Nos. 574-582 (9)   15.10   3.45

For surcharges & overprints see Nos. 591-592, C96 in Scott Standard catalogue, Vol. 5.

Nos. 566-567, 504
Surcharged in Red

1939, Sept. 25   Perf. 12½, 14
583 A134 8c on 50c indigo   .45   .25
584 A135 10c on 1col blk   .80   .25
585 A116 50c on 1col grn & vio   4.50   3.25
  Nos. 583-585 (3)   5.75   3.75

Battle of San Pedro Perulapán, 100th anniv.

Sir Rowland
Hill — A146

1940, Mar. 1   Perf. 12½
586 A146 8c dk bl, lt bl & blk   6.00   2.00
  Nos. 586,C69-C70 (3)   36.50   22.00

Postage stamp centenary.

AIR POST STAMPS

Regular Issue of
1924-25 Overprinted
in Black or Red

First Printing.
15c on 10c: "15 QUINCE 15" measures 22½mm.
20c: Shows on the back of the stamp an albino impression of the 50c surcharge.
25c on 35c: Original value canceled by a long and short bar.
40c on 10c: Only one printing.
50c on 1col: Surcharge in dull orange red.

Perf. 12½, 14
1929, Dec. 28   Unwmk.
C1 A112 20c dp green (Bk)   6.00   5.00
a. Red overprint   850.00   850.00

Counterfeits exist of No. C1a.

With Additional Surcharge of New Values and Bars in Black or Red
C3 A111 15c on 10c orange   1.10   1.10
a. "ALTANT CO"   37.50   35.00
C4 A114 25c on 35c scar & grn   2.50   2.25
a. Bars inverted   10.00   10.00
C5 A115 40c on 50c org brn   .85   .55
C6 A116 50c on 1col grn & vio (R)   15.00   10.00
  Nos. C1-C6 (5)   25.45   18.90

Second Printing.
15c on 10d: "15 QUINCE 15" measures 20½mm.
20c: Has not the albino impression on the back of the stamp.
25c on 35c: Original value cancelled by two bars of equal length.
50c on 1col: Surcharge in carmine rose.

1930, Jan. 10
C7 A112 20c deep green   1.00   1.00
C8 A111 15c on 10c org   .75   .75
a. "ATLANT CO"   37.50   35.00
b. Double surcharge   20.00
c. As "a," double surcharge   75.00
d. Pair, one without surcharge   175.00
C9 A114 25c on 35c scar & grn   .90   .90
C10 A116 50c on 1col grn & vio (C)   2.00   2.00
a. Without bars over "UN CO-LON"   4.50

b. As "a," without block over "1"   4.50
  Nos. C7-C10 (4)   4.65   4.65

Numerous wrong font and defective letters exist in both printings of the surcharges. No. C10 with black surcharge is bogus.

Mail Plane
over San
Salvador
AP1

1930, Sept. 15   Engr.   Perf. 12½
C11 AP1 15c deep red   .40   .25
C12 AP1 20c emerald   .40   .25
C13 AP1 25c brown violet   .40   .25
C14 AP1 40c ultra   .60   .25
  Nos. C11-C14 (4)   1.80   1.00

Simón
Bolivar — AP2

1930, Dec. 17   Litho.   Perf. 11½
C15 AP2 15c deep red   6.00   5.00
a. "15" double   82.50
C16 AP2 20c emerald   6.00   5.00
C17 AP2 25c brown violet   6.00   5.00
a. Vert. pair, imperf. btwn.   175.00
b. Imperf., pair
C18 AP2 40c dp ultra   6.00   5.00
  Nos. C15-C18 (4)   24.00   20.00

Centenary of death of Simón Bolivar. Counterfeits of Nos. C15-C18 exist.

Tower of La
Merced
Church — AP3

1931, June 29   Engr.   Perf. 14
C19 A116 1col green & vio   4.50   3.00

1931, Nov. 5   Litho.   Perf. 11½
C20 AP3 15c dark red   4.50   3.25
a. Imperf., pair   50.00
C21 AP3 20c blue green   4.50   3.25
C22 AP3 25c dull violet   4.50   3.25
a. Vert. pair, imperf. btwn.   110.00
C23 AP3 40c ultra   4.50   3.25
a. Imperf., pair   60.00
  Nos. C20-C23 (4)   18.00   13.00

120th anniv. of the 1st movement toward the political independence of El Salvador. In the tower of La Merced Church (AP3) hangs the bell which José Matias Delgado-called the Father of his Country-rang to initiate the movement for liberty.

José Matias
Delgado — AP4

1932, Nov. 12   Wmk. 271   Perf. 12½
C24 AP4 15c dull red & vio   1.25   1.10
C25 AP4 20c blue grn & bl   1.60   1.40
C26 AP4 25c dull vio & brn   1.60   1.40
C27 AP4 40c ultra & grn   1.90   1.75
  Nos. C24-C27 (4)   6.35   5.65

1st centenary of the death of Father José Matías Delgado, who is known as the Father of El Salvadoran Political Emancipation. Nos. C24-C27 show cheek without shading in the 72nd stamp of each sheet.

Airplane and
Caravels of
Columbus — AP5

1933, Oct. 12   Wmk. 240   Perf. 13
C28 AP5 15c red orange   2.00   1.75
C29 AP5 20c blue green   3.00   2.50
C30 AP5 25c lilac   3.00   2.50
C31 AP5 40c ultra   3.00   2.50
C32 AP5 1col black   3.00   2.50
  Nos. C28-C32 (5)   14.00   11.75

Sailing of Chistopher Columbus from Palos, Spain, for the New World, 441st anniv.

Police Barracks Type
1934, Dec. 16   Perf. 12½
C33 A123 25c lilac   .60   .25
C34 A123 30c brown   .95   .45
a. Imperf., pair   80.00
C35 A123 1col black   2.40   1.00
  Nos. C33-C35 (3)   3.95   1.70

Runner
AP7

1935, Mar. 16   Engr.   Unwmk.
C36 AP7 15c carmine   4.50   4.25
C37 AP7 25c violet   4.50   4.25
C38 AP7 30c brown   4.25   3.25
C39 AP7 55c blue   24.00   17.50
C40 AP7 1col black   16.00   15.00
  Nos. C36-C40 (5)   53.25   44.25

Third Central American Games. For overprints and surcharge see Nos. C41-C45, C53.

Nos. C36-C40 Overprinted in Black

1935, June 27
C41 AP7 15c carmine   4.50   2.75
C42 AP7 25c violet   4.50   2.75
C43 AP7 30c brown   4.50   2.75
C44 AP7 55c blue   32.50   25.00
C45 AP7 1col black   15.00   12.00
  Nos. C41-C45 (5)   61.00   45.25

Flag of El Salvador Type
1935, Oct. 26   Litho.   Wmk. 240
C46 A125 30c black brown   .85   .45

Tree of San Vicente Type
1935, Dec. 26   Perf. 12½
Numerals in Black, Tree in Yellow Green
C47 A126 10c orange   1.25   1.00
C48 A126 15c brown   1.25   1.00
C49 A126 20c dk blue grn   1.25   1.00
C50 A126 25c dark purple   1.25   1.00
C51 A126 30c black brown   1.25   1.00
  Nos. C47-C51 (5)   6.25   5.00

Tercentenary of San Vicente.

No. 565
Overprinted in Red

1937   Engr.   Unwmk.
C52 A133 15c dk olive bis   .60   .45
a.   Double overprint   25.00

No. C44
Surcharged
in Red

C53 AP7 30c on 55c blue   3.00 1.10

Panchimalco Church — AP10

1937, Dec. 3   Engr.   Perf. 12
C54 AP10 15c orange yel   .30   .25
C55 AP10 20c green   .30   .25
C56 AP10 25c violet   .30   .25
C57 AP10 30c brown   .30   .25
C58 AP10 40c blue   .30   .25
C59 AP10 1col black   1.40   .45
C60 AP10 5col rose carmine   4.50 3.25
      Nos. C54-C60 (7)   7.40 4.95

**US Constitution Type of Regular
Issue**
1938, Apr. 22   Engr. & Litho.
C61 A136 30c multicolored   .95   .70

José Simeón
Cañas y
Villacorta — AP12

1938, Aug. 18   Engr.
C62 AP12 15c orange   1.40 1.25
C63 AP12 20c brt green   1.75 1.25
C64 AP12 30c redsh brown   1.90 1.25
C65 AP12 1col black   6.00 4.50
      Nos. C62-C65 (4)   11.05 8.25

José Simeón Cañas y Villacorta (1767-
1838), liberator of slaves in Central America.

Golden Gate Bridge, San Francisco
Bay — AP13

1939, Apr. 14   Perf. 12½
C66 AP13 15c dull yel & blk   .45   .25
C67 AP13 30c dk brown & blk   .45   .25
C68 AP13 40c dk blue & blk   .60   .45
      Nos. C66-C68 (3)   1.50   .95

Golden Gate Intl. Exposition, San Francisco.
  For surcharges see Nos. C86-C91 in Scott
Standard catalogue, Vol. 5.

Sir Rowland Hill Type
1940, Mar. 1   Engr.
C69 A146 30c dk brn, buff &
            blk   8.00 2.50
C70 A146 80c org red & blk   30.50 17.50
  Centenary of the postage stamp. Covers
postmarked Feb. 29 were predated. Actual
first day was Mar. 1.

Map of the Americas, Figure of Peace,
Plane — AP15

1940, May 22   Perf. 12
C71 AP15 30c brown & blue   .45   .25
C72 AP15 80c dk rose & blk   .85   .55

Pan American Union, 50th anniversary.

Coffee Tree in
Bloom — AP16

Coffee Tree with
Ripe
Berries — AP17

1940, Nov. 27
C73 AP16 15c yellow orange   1.60   .45
C74 AP16 20c deep green   2.25   .45
C75 AP16 25c dark violet   2.50   .55
C76 AP17 30c copper brown   3.00   .25
C77 AP17 1col black   9.00   .70
      Nos. C73-C77 (5)   18.35 2.40

REGISTRATION STAMPS

Gen. Rafael Antonio
Gutiérrez — R1

1897   Engr.   Wmk. 117   Perf. 12
F1 R1 10c dark blue   125.00
F2 R1 10c brown lake   .25
                    Unwmk.
F3 R1 10c dark blue   .25
F4 R1 10c brown lake   .25
  Nos. F1 and F3 were probably not placed in
use without the overprint "FRANQUEO
OFICIAL" (Nos. O127-O128).
  The reprints are on thick unwatermarked
paper. Value, set of 2, 16c.

**ACKNOWLEDGMENT OF RECEIPT
STAMPS**

AR1

1897   Engr.   Wmk. 117   Perf. 12
H1 AR1 5c dark green   .25
                    Unwmk.
H2 AR1 5c dark green   .25
  No. H2 has been reprinted on thick paper.
Value 20c.

POSTAGE DUE STAMPS

D1

1895   Unwmk.   Engr.   Perf. 12
J1 D1 1c olive green   .40   —
J2 D1 2c olive green   .40   —
J3 D1 3c olive green   .40   —
J4 D1 5c olive green   .40   —
J5 D1 10c olive green   .40   —
J6 D1 15c olive green   .40   —
J7 D1 25c olive green   .40   —
J8 D1 50c olive green   .90   —
      Nos. J1-J8 (8)   3.70
  See Nos. J9-J56. For overprints see Nos.
J57-J64, O186-O214.

1896   Wmk. 117
J9 D1 1c red   .60   —
J10 D1 2c red   .60   —
J11 D1 3c red   .90   —
J12 D1 5c red   1.10   —
J13 D1 10c red   1.10   —
J14 D1 15c red   1.25   —
J15 D1 25c red   1.25   —
J16 D1 50c red   1.25   —
      Nos. J9-J16 (8)   8.05
                    Unwmk.
J17 D1 1c red   .40   —
J18 D1 2c red   .40   —
J19 D1 3c red   .40   —
J20 D1 5c red   .40   —
J21 D1 10c red   .40   —
J22 D1 15c red   .50   —
J23 D1 25c red   .50   —
J24 D1 50c red   .50   —
      Nos. J17-J24 (8)   3.50
  Nos. J17-J24 exist imperforate.

1897
J25 D1 1c deep blue   .40   —
J26 D1 2c deep blue   .40   —
J27 D1 3c deep blue   .40   —
J28 D1 5c deep blue   .40   —
J29 D1 10c deep blue   .50   —
J30 D1 15c deep blue   .50   —
J31 D1 25c deep blue   .40   —
J32 D1 50c deep blue   .40   —
      Nos. J25-J32 (8)   3.40

1898
J33 D1 1c violet   3.00
J34 D1 2c violet   1.00
J35 D1 3c violet   1.00
J36 D1 5c violet   5.00
J37 D1 10c violet   1.00
J38 D1 15c violet   1.00
J39 D1 25c violet   1.00
J40 D1 50c violet   1.00
      Nos. J33-J40 (8)   14.00
  Reprints of Nos. J1 to J40 are on thick
paper, often in the wrong shades and usually
with the impression somewhat blurred. Value,
set of 40, $2, watermarked or unwatermarked.

1899   Wmk. 117 Sideways
J41 D1 1c orange   .40
J42 D1 2c orange   .40
J43 D1 3c orange   .40
J44 D1 5c orange   .40
J45 D1 10c orange   .40
J46 D1 15c orange   .40
J47 D1 25c orange   .40
J48 D1 50c orange   .40
      Nos. J41-J48 (8)   3.20
                    Unwmk.
            Thick Porous Paper
J49 D1 1c orange   .40
J50 D1 2c orange   .40
J51 D1 3c orange   .40
J52 D1 5c orange   .40
J53 D1 10c orange   .40
J54 D1 15c orange   .40
J55 D1 25c orange   .40
J56 D1 50c orange   .40
      Nos. J49-J56 (8)   3.20
  Nos. J41-J56 were probably not put in use
without the wheel overprint.

Nos. J49-J56
Overprinted in Black

1900
J57 D1 1c orange   2.00
J58 D1 2c orange   2.00
J59 D1 3c orange   2.00
J60 D1 5c orange   3.00
J61 D1 10c orange   4.00
J62 D1 15c orange   4.00
J63 D1 25c orange   5.00
J64 D1 50c orange   6.00
      Nos. J57-J64 (8)   28.00
      See note after No. 198A.

Morazán
Monument — D2

Perf. 14, 14½
1903   Engr.   Wmk. 173
J65 D2 1c yellow green   1.75 1.25
J66 D2 2c carmine   2.75 1.75
J67 D2 3c orange   2.75 1.75
J68 D2 5c dark blue   2.75 1.75
J69 D2 10c dull violet   2.75 1.75
J70 D2 25c blue green   2.75 1.75
      Nos. J65-J70 (6)   15.50 10.00

Nos. 355, 356, 358
and 360 Overprinted

1908   Unwmk.   Perf. 11½
J71 A66 1c green & blk   .80   .70
J72 A66 2c red & blk   .60   .25
J73 A66 5c blue & blk   1.50 1.00
J74 A66 10c violet & blk   2.25 2.00

Same Overprint on No. O275
J75 O3 3c yellow & blk   1.50 1.25
      Nos. J71-J75 (5)   6.65 5.20

Nos. 355-358, 360
Overprinted

J76 A66 1c green & blk   .50   .50
J77 A66 2c red & blk   .60   .60
J78 A66 3c yellow & blk   .70   .70
J79 A66 5c blue & blk   1.00 1.00
J80 A66 10c violet & blk   2.00 2.00
      Nos. J76-J80 (5)   4.80 4.80

  It is now believed that stamps of type A66,
on paper with Honeycomb watermark, do not
exist with genuine overprints of the types used
for Nos. J71-J80.

Pres. Fernando
Figueroa — D3

			1910	**Engr.**	**Wmk. 172**

J81	D3	1c sepia & blk		.30	.30
J82	D3	2c dk grn & blk		.30	.30
J83	D3	3c orange & blk		.30	.30
J84	D3	4c scarlet & blk		.30	.30
J85	D3	5c purple & blk		.30	.30
J86	D3	12c deep blue & blk		.30	.30
J87	D3	24c brown red & blk		.30	.30
		Nos. J81-J87 (7)		2.10	2.10

OFFICIAL STAMPS

Nos. 134-157O
Overprinted — a

Type a

1896		**Unwmk.**	**Perf. 12**
O1	A45	1c blue	.25
O2	A45	2c dk brown	.25
a.		Double overprint	
O3	A45	3c blue grn	1.00
O4	A45	5c brown ol	.25
O5	A45	10c yellow	.25
O6	A45	12c dk blue	.30
O7	A45	15c blue vio	.25
O8	A45	20c magenta	1.00
O9	A45	24c vermilion	.25
O10	A45	30c orange	1.00
O11	A45	50c black brn	.45
O12	A45	1p rose lake	.30
		Nos. O1-O12 (12)	5.55

Nos. O1-O12 were not issued.
The 1c has been reprinted on thick unwatermarked paper. Value 25c.

		Wmk. 117		
O13	A46	1c emerald	4.75	3.00
O14	A47	2c lake	4.75	3.50
O15	A48	3c yellow brn	6.00	4.00
a.		Inverted overprint		
O16	A49	5c dp blue	5.00	5.00
O17	A50	10c brown	7.00	3.75
a.		Inverted overprint		
O18	A51	12c slate	10.50	8.00
O19	A52	15c blue grn	12.50	8.75
O20	A53	20c car rose	12.50	8.00
a.		Inverted overprint		
O21	A54	24c violet	12.50	9.00
O22	A55	30c dp green	15.00	12.50
O23	A56	50c orange	25.00	17.00
O24	A57	100c dk blue	40.00	25.00
		Nos. O13-O24 (12)	155.50	107.50

		Unwmk.		
O25	A46	1c emerald	2.50	3.50
a.		Double overprint		175.00
O26	A47	2c lake	2.75	
O27	A48	3c yellow brn	3.00	2.50
O28	A49	5c dp blue	3.00	.90
O29	A50	10c brown	2.50	2.50
a.		Inverted overprint		
O30	A51	12c slate	10.00	7.00
O31	A52	15c blue grn	12.00	7.75
O32	A53	20c car rose	20.00	11.00
a.		Inverted overprint		
O33	A54	24c violet	20.00	11.00
O34	A55	30c dp green	—	—
O35	A56	50c orange	—	—
O36	A57	100c dk blue	—	—
		Nos. O25-O36 (12)	75.75	221.15

All values have been reprinted. Value 25c each.

Nos. 134-145
Handstamped in Black
or Violet — b

Type b

1896			
O37	A45	1c blue	11.00
O38	A45	2c dk brown	11.00
O39	A45	3c blue green	11.00
O40	A45	5c brown olive	11.00
O41	A45	10c yellow	13.00
O42	A45	12c dk blue	16.00
O43	A45	15c blue violet	16.00
O44	A45	20c magenta	16.00
O45	A45	24c vermilion	16.00
O46	A45	30c orange	16.00
O47	A45	50c black brown	22.50
O48	A45	1p rose lake	22.50
		Nos. O37-O48 (12)	182.00

Reprints of the 1c and 2c on thick paper exist with this handstamp. Value, 25c each.
The legitimacy of the "De Officio" handstamp has been questioned. The editors would like to see evidence regarding the authorized use of this handstamp.

Forged overprints exist of Nos. O37-O76, O103-O126 and of the higher valued stamps of O141-O214.

Nos. 146-157F, 157I-157O, 158D
Handstamped Type b in Black or
Violet

1896			**Wmk. 117**
O49	A46	1c emerald	9.00
O50	A47	2c lake	9.00
O51	A48	3c yellow brn	9.00
O52	A49	5c deep blue	9.00
O53	A50	10c brown	9.00
O54	A51	12c slate	16.00
O55	A52	15c blue green	16.00
O56	A53	20c carmine rose	16.00
O57	A54	24c violet	16.00
O58	A55	30c deep green	16.00
O59	A56	50c orange	16.00
O60	A57	100c dark blue	16.00
		Nos. O49-O60 (12)	157.00

		Unwmk.	
O61	A46	1c emerald	9.00
O62	A47	2c lake	9.00
O63	A48	3c yellow brn	9.00
O64	A49	5c deep blue	9.00
O65	A50	10c brown	13.50
O66	A52	15c blue green	16.00
O67	A53	15c on 24c vio	11.50
O68	A53	20c carmine rose	16.00
O69	A54	24c violet	16.00
O70	A55	30c deep green	16.00
O71	A56	50c orange	19.00
O72	A57	100c dark blue	19.00
		Nos. O61-O72 (12)	163.00

Nos. 175-176 Overprinted Type a in
Black

1897			
O73	A59	1c bl, gold, rose & grn	.30
O74	A59	5c rose, gold, bl & grn	.30

These stamps were probably not officially issued.

Nos. 175-176 Handstamped Type b in
Black or Violet

1900			
O75	A59	1c bl, gold, rose & grn	22.50
O76	A59	5c rose, gold, bl & grn	22.50

Nos. 159-170L Overprinted Type a in
Black

1897			**Wmk. 117**
O79	A46	1c scarlet	8.00	8.00
O80	A47	2c yellow green	8.00	8.00
O81	A48	3c bister brown	7.00	7.00
O82	A49	5c orange	7.00	7.00
O83	A50	10c blue green	9.00	9.00
O84	A51	12c blue	20.00	20.00
O85	A52	15c black	40.00	40.00
O86	A53	20c slate	20.00	20.00
O87	A54	24c yellow	40.00	40.00
a.		Inverted overprint		
O88	A55	30c rose	40.00	40.00
O89	A56	50c violet	40.00	40.00
O90	A57	100c brown lake	100.00	100.00
		Nos. O79-O90 (12)	339.00	

		Unwmk.		
O91	A46	1c scarlet	5.00	5.00
O92	A47	2c yellow green	3.00	3.00
O93	A48	3c bister brown	2.00	2.00
O94	A49	5c orange	3.00	3.00
O95	A50	10c blue green	10.00	10.00
O96	A51	12c blue	3.00	3.00
O97	A52	15c black	30.00	30.00
O98	A53	20c slate	20.00	20.00
O99	A54	24c yellow	30.00	30.00
O100	A55	30c rose	30.00	30.00
O101	A56	50c violet	20.00	20.00
O102	A57	100c brown lake	50.00	50.00
		Nos. O91-O102 (12)	206.00	

All values have been reprinted. Value 25c each.

Nos. 159-170L Handstamped Type b
in Violet or Black

1897			**Wmk. 117**
O103	A46	1c scarlet	7.50
O104	A47	2c yellow green	7.50
O105	A48	3c bister brown	7.50
O106	A49	5c orange	7.50
O107	A50	10c blue green	8.75
O108	A51	12c blue	
O109	A52	15c black	
O110	A53	20c slate	15.00
O111	A54	24c yellow	17.50
O112	A55	30c rose	
O113	A56	50c violet	
O114	A57	100c brown lake	

		Unwmk.	
O115	A46	1c scarlet	7.50
O116	A47	2c yellow grn	7.50
O117	A48	3c bister brn	7.50
O118	A49	5c orange	7.50
O119	A50	10c blue green	7.50
O120	A51	12c blue	

O121	A52	15c black	
O122	A53	20c slate	
O123	A54	24c yellow	
O124	A55	30c rose	15.00
O125	A56	50c violet	
O126	A57	100c brown lake	17.50

Reprints of the 1 and 15c on thick watermarked paper and the 12, 30, 50 and 100c on thick unwatermarked paper are known with this overprint. Value, 25c each.

Nos. F1, F3 Overprinted Type a in
Red

		Wmk. 117	
O127	R1	10c dark blue	.30

		Unwmk.	
O128	R1	10c dark blue	.30

The reprints are on thick paper. Value 15c.
Originals of the 10c brown lake Registration Stamp and the 5c Acknowledgment of Receipt stamp are believed not to have been issued with the "FRANQUEO OFICIAL" overprint. They are believed to exist only as reprints.

Nos. 177-188 Overprinted Type a

1898			**Wmk. 117**	
O129	A60	1c orange ver	4.50	4.50
O130	A60	2c rose	4.50	4.50
O131	A60	3c pale yel grn	4.00	4.00
O132	A60	5c blue green	4.00	4.00
O133	A60	10c gray blue	15.00	15.00
O134	A60	12c violet	17.00	17.00
O135	A60	13c brown lake	17.00	17.00
O136	A60	20c deep blue	19.00	19.00
O137	A60	24c ultra	15.00	15.00
O138	A60	26c bister brn	20.00	20.00
O139	A60	50c orange	20.00	20.00
O140	A60	1p yellow	50.00	50.00
		Nos. O129-O140 (12)	190.00	190.00

Reprints of the above set are on thick paper. Value, 25c each.

No. 177 Handstamped Type b in Violet

O141	A60	1c orange ver	35.00	—

No. O141 with Additional Overprint Type c in Black

c

Type "c" is called the "wheel" overprint.

O142	A60	1c orange ver		

Counterfeits exist of the "wheel" overprint.

Nos. 204-205, 207
and 209 Overprinted

1899			**Unwmk.**	
O143	A61	12c dark green	—	50.00
O144	A61	13c deep rose	50.00	
O145	A61	26c carmine rose	50.00	—
O146	A61	100c violet	100.00	—

Nos. O143-O144 Punched With
Twelve Small Holes

O147	A61	12c dark green	
O148	A61	13c deep rose	

Official stamps punched with twelve small holes were issued and used for ordinary postage.

Nos. 199-209
Overprinted — d

1899			**Blue Overprint**	
O149	A61	1c brown	.30
O150	A61	2c gray green	.30
O151	A61	3c blue	.30
O152	A61	5c brown orange	.30
O153	A61	10c chocolate	.30
O154	A61	13c deep rose	.30
O155	A61	26c carmine rose	.30
O156	A61	50c orange red	.30
O157	A61	100c violet	.30

		Black Overprint		
O158	A61	3c blue	.30
O159	A61	12c dark green	.30
O160	A61	24c lt blue	.30
		Nos. O149-O160 (12)	3.60

Nos. O149-O160 were probably not placed in use.

With Additional Overprint Type c in
Black

O161	A61	1c brown	.60	.60
O162	A61	2c gray green	1.10	1.10
O163	A61	3c blue	.60	.60
O164	A61	5c brown org	.60	.60
O165	A61	10c chocolate	.75	.75
O166	A61	12c dark green	—	—
O167	A61	13c deep rose	1.50	1.50
O168	A61	24c lt blue	30.00	30.00
O169	A61	26c carmine rose	.75	.75
O170	A61	50c orange red	1.50	1.50
O171	A61	100c violet	1.50	1.50
		Nos. O161-O165,O167-O171 (10)	38.90	38.90

Nos. O149-O155,
O159-O160 Punched
With Twelve Small
Holes

		Blue Overprint		
O172	A61	1c brown	5.00	1.00
O173	A61	2c gray green	3.25	5.00
O174	A61	3c blue	8.00	3.75
O175	A61	5c brown org	10.00	3.00
O176	A61	10c chocolate	15.00	5.00
O177	A61	13c deep rose	7.50	7.00
O177A	A61	24c lt blue		
O178	A61	26c carmine rose	100.00	35.00

		Black Overprint		
O179	A61	12c dark green	6.00	4.50
		Nos. O172-O177,O178-O179 (8)	154.75	64.25

It is stated that Nos. O172-O214 inclusive were issued for ordinary postage and not for use as Official stamps.

Nos. O161-O167, O169 Overprinted
Type c in Black

O180	A61	1c brown	1.25	1.10
O180A	A61	2c gray green		
O181	A61	3c blue		
O182	A61	5c brown orange	1.25	
O182A	A61	10c chocolate		
O182B	A61	12c dark green		
O183	A61	13c deep rose	4.00	5.00
O184	A61	26c carmine rose		

No. 209 Ovptd. Types a and e in Black

e

O185	A61	100c violet		

Nos. J49-J56
Overprinted in Black

1900				
O186	D1	1c orange	27.50
O187	D1	2c orange	27.50
O188	D1	3c orange	27.50
O189	D1	5c orange	27.50
O190	D1	10c orange	27.50
O191	D1	15c orange	62.50
O192	D1	25c orange	62.50
O193	D1	50c orange	62.50
		Nos. O186-O193 (8)	325.00

Nos. O186-O189, O191-O193
Overprinted Type c in Black

O194	D1	1c orange		25.00
O195	D1	2c orange		25.00
O196	D1	3c orange		25.00
O197	D1	5c orange		25.00
O198	D1	15c orange	16.00	25.00
O199	D1	25c orange	19.00	25.00
O200	D1	50c orange	160.00	

Nos. O186-O189 Punched With Twelve Small Holes

O201	D1	1c orange	45.00
O202	D1	2c orange	45.00
O203	D1	3c orange	45.00
O204	D1	5c orange	45.00
Nos. O201-O204 (4)			*180.00*

Nos. O201-O204 Overprinted Type c in Black

O205	D1	1c orange	9.00	6.50
O206	D1	2c orange		6.50
O207	D1	3c orange		6.50
O208	D1	5c orange	20.00	6.50

Overprinted Type a in Violet and Type c in Black

O209	D1	2c orange	*25.00*
a.		Inverted overprint	*25.00*
O210	D1	3c orange	*25.00*
O211	D1	10c orange	3.00

Nos. O186-O188 Handstamped Type e in Violet

O212	D1	1c orange	9.00	7.50
O213	D1	2c orange	9.00	7.50
O214	D1	3c orange	9.00	9.00
Nos. O212-O214 (3)			*27.00*	*24.00*

See note after No. O48.

Type of Regular Issue of 1900 Overprinted Type a in Black

O223	A63	1c lt green	22.50	—
a.		Inverted overprint		—
O224	A63	2c rose	27.50	—
a.		Inverted overprint		—
O225	A63	3c gray black	17.50	—
a.		Overprint vertical		—
O226	A63	5c blue	17.50	—
O227	A63	10c blue	45.00	—
a.		Inverted overprint		—
O228	A63	12c yellow grn	45.00	—
O229	A63	13c yellow brn	45.00	—
O230	A63	24c gray black	32.50	—
O231	A63	26c yellow brn	30.00	—
O232	A63	50c dull rose		—
a.		Inverted overprint		—
Nos. O223-O231 (9)			*282.50*	

Nos. O223-O224, O231-O232 Overprinted in Violet — f

O233	A63	1c lt green	4.75	4.00
O234	A63	2c rose	25.00	
a.		"FRANQUEO OFICIAL" invtd.		
O235	A63	26c yellow brown	.50	.50
O236	A63	50c dull rose	.75	.55

Nos. O223, O225-O228, O232 Overprinted in Black — g

O237	A63	1c lt green	5.00	5.00
O238	A63	3c gray black		
O239	A63	5c blue	40.00	
O240	A63	10c blue		
O241	A63	12c yellow green		

Violet Overprint

O242	A63	50c dull rose	10.00

The shield overprinted on No. O242 is of the type on No. O212.

O1

1903		**Wmk. 173**	**Perf. 14, 14½**	
O243	O1	1c yellow green	.45	.25
O244	O1	2c carmine	.45	.25
O245	O1	3c orange	5.00	.85
O246	O1	5c dark blue	5.00	.25
O247	O1	10c dull violet	.70	.35
O248	O1	13c red brown	.70	.35
O249	O1	15c yellow brown	5.00	1.75
O250	O1	24c scarlet	.45	.35
O251	O1	50c bister	.70	.35
O252	O1	100c grnsh blue	.70	.75
Nos. O243-O252 (10)			*19.15*	*5.50*

For surcharges see Nos. O254-O257.

No. 285 Handstamped Type b in Black

1904

O253	A64	3c orange	35.00

Nos. O246-O248 Surcharged in Black

1905

O254	O1	2c on 5c dark blue	6.50	5.50
O255	O1	3c on 5c dark blue		
a.		Double surcharge		
O256	O1	3c on 10c dl vio	18.00	12.00
O257	O1	3c on 13c red brn	1.75	1.40

A 2c surcharge of this type exists on No. O247.

No. O225 Overprinted in Blue

a　　　　　　　b

1905　　　　　　**Unwmk.**

O258	A63(a)	3c gray black	4.00	3.50
O259	A63(b)	3c gray black	3.50	3.00

Nos. O224-O225 Overprinted in Blue

c　　　　　　　d

1906

O260	A63(c)	2c rose	22.50	20.00
O261	A63(c)	3c gray black	2.50	2.00
a.		Overprint "1906" in blk		
O262	A63(d)	3c gray black	2.75	2.50
Nos. O260-O262 (3)			*27.75*	*24.50*

Escalón — O2　　　National Palace — O3

1906		**Engr.**	**Perf. 11½**	
O263	O2	1c green & blk	.40	.25
O264	O2	2c carmine & blk	.40	.25
O265	O2	3c yellow & blk	.40	.25
O266	O2	5c blue & blk	.40	.75
O267	O2	10c violet & blk	.40	.25
O268	O2	13c dk brown & blk	.40	.25
O269	O2	15c red org & blk	.50	.25
O270	O2	24c carmine & blk	.60	.35
O271	O2	50c orange & blk	.60	1.50
O272	O2	100c dk blue & blk	.70	4.50
Nos. O263-O272 (10)			*4.80*	*8.60*

The centers of these stamps are also found in blue black.

Nos. O263 to O272 have been reprinted, perforated 11.8. Value, set of 10, $2.50.

1908

O273	O3	1c green & blk	.25	.25
O274	O3	2c red & blk	.25	.25
O275	O3	3c yellow & blk	.25	.25
O276	O3	5c blue & blk	.25	.25
O277	O3	10c violet & blk	.25	.25
O278	O3	13c violet & blk	.25	.25
O279	O3	15c pale brn & blk	.25	.25
O280	O3	24c rose & blk	.25	.25
O281	O3	50c yellow & blk	.25	.25
O282	O3	100c turq blue & blk	.35	.35
Nos. O273-O282 (10)			*2.60*	*2.60*

For overprints see Nos. 441-442, 445-449, J75, O283-O292, O323-O328.

Nos. O273-O282 Overprinted Type g in Black

O283	O3	1c green & blk	3.00	
O284	O3	2c red & blk	4.00	
O285	O3	3c yellow & blk		
O286	O3	5c blue & blk	5.00	
O287	O3	10c violet & blk	5.00	
O288	O3	13c violet & blk	6.00	
O289	O3	15c pale brn & blk	6.00	
O290	O3	24c rose & blk	8.00	
O291	O3	50c yellow & blk	9.00	
O292	O3	100c turq & blk	10.00	
Nos. O283-O292 (10)			*60.00*	

Pres. Figueroa — O4

1910		**Engr.**	**Wmk. 172**	
O293	O4	2c dk green & blk	.30	.25
O294	O4	3c orange & blk	.30	.25
O295	O4	4c scarlet & blk	.30	.25
a.		4c carmine & black		
O296	O4	5c purple & blk	.30	.25
O297	O4	6c scarlet & blk	.30	.25
O298	O4	10c purple & blk	.30	.25
O299	O4	12c dp blue & blk	.30	.25
O300	O4	17c olive grn & blk	.30	.25
O301	O4	19c brn red & blk	.30	.25
O302	O4	29c choc & blk	.30	.25
O303	O4	50c yellow & blk	.30	.25
O304	O4	100c turq & blk	.30	.25
Nos. O293-O304 (12)			*3.60*	*3.00*

Regular Issue, Type A63, Overprinted or Surcharged

a　　　　　　　b

c

1911			**Unwmk.**	
O305	A63(a)	1c lt green	.25	.25
O306	A63(b)	3c on 13c yel brn	.25	.25
O307	A63(b)	5c on 10c dp bl	.25	.25
O308	A63(a)	10c deep blue	.25	.25
O309	A63(a)	12c lt green	.25	.25
O310	A63(b)	13c yellow brn	.25	.25
O311	A63(b)	50c on 10c dp bl	.25	.25
O312	A63(c)	1col on 13c yel brn	.25	.25
Nos. O305-O312 (8)			*2.00*	*2.00*

O5　　　　　　　O6

1914		**Typo.**	**Perf. 12**	
Background in Green, Shield and "Provisional" in Black				
O313	O5	2c yellow brn	.50	.25
O314	O5	3c yellow	.50	.25
O315	O5	5c dark blue	.50	.25
O316	O5	10c red	.50	.25
O317	O5	12c green	.50	.25
O318	O5	17c violet	.50	.25
O319	O5	50c brown	.50	.25
O320	O5	100c dull rose	.50	.25
Nos. O313-O320 (8)			*4.00*	*2.00*

Stamps of this issue are known imperforate or with parts of the design omitted or misplaced. These varieties were not regularly issued.

1914			**Typo.**	
O321	O6	2c blue green	.50	.25
O322	O6	3c orange	.50	.25

Type of Official Stamps of 1908 With Two Overprints

1915

O323	O3	1c gray green	1.00	.60
a.		"1915" double		
b.		"OFICIAL" inverted		
O324	O3	2c red	1.00	.60
O325	O3	5c ultra	.35	.70
O326	O3	10c yellow	.35	.60
a.		Date omitted		
O327	O3	50c violet	.90	1.50
O328	O3	100c black brown	1.90	3.25
Nos. O323-O328 (6)			*5.50*	*7.25*

Same Overprint on #414, 417, 429

O329	A66	1c gray green	10.00	1.60
O330	A66	6c pale blue	1.00	.45
a.		6c ultramarine		
O331	A66	12c brown	1.00	.75
Nos. O329-O331 (3)			*12.00*	*2.80*

O323-O327, O329-O331 exist imperf. Nos. O329-O331 exist with "OFICIAL" inverted and double. See note after No. 421.

Nos. 431-440 Overprinted in Blue or Red

1916

O332	A83	1c deep green	.45	.75
O333	A83	2c vermilion	1.60	1.60
O334	A83	5c dp blue (R)	1.25	1.60
O335	A83	6c gray vio (R)	.45	.75
O336	A83	10c black brown	.45	.75
O337	A83	12c violet	2.00	3.25
O338	A83	17c orange	.45	.75
O339	A83	25c dark brown	.45	.75
O340	A83	29c black (R)	.45	.75
O341	A83	50c slate (R)	2.00	.75
Nos. O332-O341 (10)			*9.55*	*11.70*

Nos. 474-481 Overprinted

a　　　　　　　b

1921

O342	A94(a)	1c green	.25	.25
O343	A95(a)	2c black	.25	.25
a.		Inverted overprint		
O344	A96(b)	5c orange	.25	.25
O345	A97(a)	6c carmine rose	.25	.25
O346	A98(a)	10c deep blue	.30	.25
O347	A99(a)	25c olive green	.75	.35
O348	A100(a)	60c violet	1.00	.60
O349	A101(a)	1col black brown	1.10	.70
Nos. O342-O349 (8)			*4.15*	*2.90*

Nos. 498 and 500 Overprinted in Black or Red

1925

O350	A109	5c olive black	.45	.25
O351	A111	10c orange (R)	.85	.25
a.		"ATLANT CO"	13.00	11.00

Inverted overprints exist.

Regular Issue of 1924-25 Overprinted in Black or Red

1927

O352	A106	1c red violet	.25	.25
O353	A107	2c dark red	.45	.25
O354	A109	5c olive blk (R)	.45	.25
O355	A110	6c dp blue (R)	5.25	4.50
O356	A111	10c orange	.50	.30
a.		"ATLANT CO"	22.50	19.00
O357	A116	1col grn & vio (R)	2.25	1.40
		Nos. O352-O357 (6)	9.15	6.95

Inverted overprints exist on 1c, 2c, 5c, 10c.

Regular Issue of
1924-25 Overprinted
in Black

1932 Perf. 12½

O358	A106	1c deep violet	.25	.25
O359	A107	2c dark red	.45	.25
O360	A109	5c olive black	.25	.25
O361	A111	10c orange	.85	.35
a.		"ATLANT CO"	22.50	19.00
		Nos. O358-O361 (4)	1.80	1.10

PARCEL POST STAMPS

Mercury
PP1

1895 Unwmk. Engr. Perf. 12

Q1	PP1	5c brown orange	.45
Q2	PP1	10c dark blue	.45
Q3	PP1	15c red	.45
Q4	PP1	20c orange	.45
Q5	PP1	50c blue green	.45
		Nos. Q1-Q5 (5)	2.25

POSTAL TAX STAMPS

PT1

Overprinted "REVISADO" in Violet,
Black or Red

1900-04 Typo. Perf. 11½

RA1	PT1	1c black	
RA2	PT1	1c black, dated "1903"	
RA3	PT1	1c black, dated "1904"	

Use of these stamps was obligatory on all domestic letters. The funds raised were used to maintain the public schools.

Nos. 503, 501
Surcharged

1931 Unwmk. Perf. 12½

RA4	A115	1c on 50c org brn	.50	.40
a.		Double surcharge	5.00	5.00
RA5	A112	2c on 20c dp grn	.50	.40

Nos. 501, 503
Surcharged

RA6	A112	1c on 20c dp grn	.50	.40
RA7	A115	2c on 50c org brn	.50	.40
a.		Without period in "0.02"	3.00	

The use of these stamps was obligatory, in addition to the regular postage, on letters and other postal matter. The money obtained from their sale was to be used to erect a new post office in San Salvador.

SAMOA

sə-'mō-ə

(Western Samoa)

LOCATION — An archipelago in the South Pacific Ocean, east of Fiji
GOVT. — Monarchy and (partially) German possession
AREA — 1,130 sq. mi.
POP. — 39,000 (est. 1910)
CAPITAL — Apia

In 1861-99, Samoa was an independent kingdom under the influence of the US, to which the harbor of Pago Pago had been ceded, and that of Great Britain and Germany. In 1898 a disturbance arose, resulting in the withdrawal of Great Britain, and the partitioning of the islands between Germany and the US. Early in World War I the islands under German domination were occupied by New Zealand troops and in 1920 the League of Nations declared them a mandate to New Zealand.

12 Pence = 1 Shilling
20 Shillings = 1 Pound
100 Pfennig = 1 Mark (1900)

> Catalogue values for unused stamps in this country are for Never Hinged items, beginning with Scott 191 in the regular postage section.

Watermarks

Wmk. 61 — N Z and Star Close Together

Wmk. 62 — N Z and Star Wide Apart

On watermark 61 the margins of the sheets are watermarked "NEW ZEALAND POSTAGE" and parts of the double-lined letters of these words are frequently found on the stamps. It occasionally happens that a stamp shows no watermark whatever.

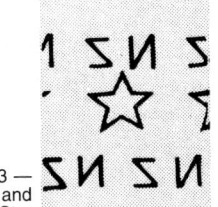

Wmk. 253 — Multiple N Z and Star

Issues of the Kingdom

A1

Type I   Type II

Type III   Type IV

Type I

Line above "X" is usually unbroken. Dots over "SAMOA" are uniform and evenly spaced. Upper right serif of "M" is horizontal.

Printed in sheets of 20 (5x4), imperf on outer edges. Only six stamps may be perforated all around. Eight stamps in each pane of the 1p have a stop after "PENNY."

1877 Litho. Unwmk. Perf. 12½

1c	A1	1p sky blue	300.00	400.00
3c	A1	3p vermilion	450.00	250.00
4b	A1	6p bright violet	300.00	350.00
4c	A1	6p pale lilac	400.00	350.00

No. 6a shows the line above "X" unbroken, but has the dot between "M" and "O" characteristic of type I.

Stamps were pen cancelled from October 1877 to March 1878, when the circular date stamp arrived.

Type II

Line above "X" is usually broken. Small dot near upper right serif of letter "M." Printed in sheets of 10 (5x2), imperf on outer edges, so that all stamps have at least one straight edge.

1878-79 Perf. 12½

1b	A1	1p sky blue	150.00	250.00
3b	A1	3p vermilion	400.00	750.00
4a	A1	6p violet	900.00	1,000.
6	A1	1sh orange yellow	325.00	135.00
6a	A1	1sh dull yellow	400.00	100.00
6b	A1	1sh lemon yellow	400.00	100.00
6c	A1	1sh golden yellow, Perf 11¾		
		('79)	110.00	260.00
7a	A1	2sh red brown	450.00	750.00
7b	A1	2sh chocolate	450.00	750.00
8b	A1	5sh gray green	4,000.	1,500.

Type III

Line above "X" roughly retouched. Upper right serif of letter "M" bends down (joined to dot).

Printed in sheets of 10 (5x2), except the 1p, which was printed in sheets of 20 (5x4).

1879 Perf. 12½

1a	A1	1p sky blue	260.00	125.00
3	A1	3p vermilion	550.00	300.00
4	A1	6p lilac	550.00	135.00
7	A1	2sh deep brown	370.00	500.00
7c	A1	2sh chocolate	450.00	500.00
8	A1	5sh emerald green	1,875.	850.00
8c	A1	5sh line above "X" not repaired (pos. 2/3)	—	

1879-82 Perf. 11¾

1	A1	1p blue	37.50	1,000.
1d	A1	1p ultramarine	75.00	
1e	A1	1p deep blue	35.00	
3a	A1	3p scarlet vermilion, clean-cut perfs	120.00	
3d	A1	3p vermilion, rough perfs	65.00	
4c	A1	6p dull lilac	55.00	100.00
4d	A1	6p bright violet	40.00	800.00
7d	A1	2sh deep brown	275.00	
8a	A1	5sh yellow green	725.00	
8d	A1	5sh deep green	1,000.	

8e	A1	5sh line above "X" not repaired (pos. 2/3)	—	

Nos. 1-8e are found with either clean-cut or rough-cut perforations.

Only the 6p and 1sh denominations of the type III, perf 11¾ issue are known used.

Type IV

Speck of color on curved line below center of "M."

1880-82 Perf. 11¾

2	A1	2p lilac rose ('82)	25.00	
5	A1	9p pale chestnut	80.00	425.00
5a	A1	9p pale org brown	100.00	800.00

The 2p was never placed in use since the Samoa Express service was discontinued late in 1881.

Some examples of Nos. 1-8 appear with portions of the papermaker's watermark.

Imperforates of this issue are proofs.

Reprints are of type IV and nearly always perforated on all sides. They have a spot of color at the edge of the panel below the "M." This spot is not on any originals except the 2p, which may be distinguished by its color, and the 9p which may be distinguished by having a rough blind perf. 12.

Forgeries abound.

Covers: Covers with Nos. 1-8 are rare. Last known date is Sept. 24, 1881, although the service officially ended Aug. 31st.

Palms
A2

King Malietoa
Laupepa
A3

Three forms of watermark 62 are found on stamps of type A2:
1 — Wide "N Z" and wide star, 6mm apart (used 1886-87).
2 — Wide "N Z" and narrow star, 4mm apart (1890).
3 — Narrow "NZ" and narrow star, 7mm apart (1890-1900).

Wmk. 62, Type 1 (6mm spacing)

1886 Typo. Perf. 12½

9	A2	½p purple brown	40.00	40.00
11	A2	1p yellow green	20.00	20.00
13	A2	2p brown orange	20.00	20.00
16	A2	4p blue	55.00	13.50
18	A2	1sh rose carmine	67.50	13.50
a.		Diagonal half canceled in blue, on cover (Apr-June '95)		375.00
19	A2	2sh6p violet	50.00	40.00

No. 18e was authorized for use between April 24 and June, 1895, after stocks of other values were destroyed in a fire, and was canceled in blue. No. 18a was used to pay various rates, most commonly 2½p. Value is for examples paying this rate.

No. 18 was later bisected for sale to collectors. These stamps were canceled in black, and most were bisected vertically. Value on piece $7.50.

Wmk. 62, Type 1 (6mm spacing)

1887 Perf. 12x11½

9a	A2	½p purple brown	40.00	100.00
11a	A2	1p yellow green	100.00	40.00
13a	A2	2p yellow	40.00	100.00
16a	A2	4p blue	100.00	100.00
17	A2	6p brown lake	20.00	20.00
18b	A2	1sh rose carmine		100.00
19a	A2	2sh6p violet	2,000.	

Wmk. 62, Type 2 (4 mm spacing)

1890, May Perf. 12x11½

9b	A2	½p dp pur brown	100.00	40.00
11b	A2	1p yellow green	20.00	20.00
13b	A2	2p orange brown	40.00	10.00
16b	A2	4p deep blue	100.00	10.00
17a	A2	6p maroon	325.00	12.50
18c	A2	1sh rose	200.00	20.00
19b	A2	2sh6p bright violet	100.00	10.00

Wmk. 62, Type 3 (7 mm spacing)

1890-92 Perf. 12x11½

9c	A2	½p purple brown	10.00	10.00
11c	A2	1p green ('91)	20.00	10.00
d.		1p blue green	20.00	10.00
13c	A2	2p orange	10.00	10.00
14	A3	2½p rose ('92)	80.00	6.00
16c	A2	4p blue	100.00	20.00
17b	A2	6p brown lake	40.00	10.00
18d	A2	1sh rose	100.00	10.00
19c	A2	2sh6p violet	100.00	10.00

Wmk. 62, Type 3 (7 mm spacing)

1891-92   *Perf. 12½*

13d	A2	2p orange yellow		750.00
14a	A3	2½p rose ('92)	10.00	20.00
16d	A2	4p blue		750.00
17c	A2	6p brown lake	3,000.	1,250.
18e	A2	1sh rose	£3,500.	1,500.
19d	A2	2sh6p violet		2,500.

½p and 1p values, perf 12½ with watermark 62 type 3, may exist. The editors would like to examine any documentation of certified examples.

Wmk. 62, Type 3 (7 mm spacing)

1895, May-1900   *Perf. 11*

9d	A2	½p purple brown	5.75	2.10
e.		½p deep purple brown ('00)	2.00	100.00
10	A2	½p dull bl grn ('99)	4.00	4.50
11e	A2	1p green	10.00	20.00
f.		1p bluish green ('97)	4.00	2.00
g.		1p deep green ('00)	2.00	100.00
12	A2	1p red brown	4.25	20.00
13e	A2	2p yellow	40.00	40.00
f.		2p orange yellow ('96)	20.00	20.00
g.		2p bright yellow ('97)	16.00	10.00
h.		2p pale ocher ('97)	2.00	20.00
i.		2p brown ocher ('00)	2.00	
14b	A3	2½p rose	4.25	10.50
c.		2½p dp rose carmine ('00)	2.00	100.00
15	A3	2½p black, perf 10x11 ('96)	2.25	3.25
a.		Perf 11 ('96)	150.00	100.00
b.		Mixed perfs, 10 and 11	100.00	—
16e	A2	4p blue	40.00	20.00
f.		4p deep blue ('00)	1.60	52.50
17d	A2	6p brown lake	20.00	20.00
e.		6p maroon ('00)	2.00	62.50
18f	A2	1sh rose	10.00	20.00
g.		1sh carmine ('00)	1.80	—
19e	A2	2sh6p reddish lilac	10.00	20.00
f.		2sh6p purple ('97)	10.00	
g.		2sh6p purple ('97)	40.00	
h.		2sh6p deep purple ('98)	5.00	10.00
i.		As "h," vert. pair, imperf. btw.	475.00	

Watermark is inverted on No. 19d and reversed on No. 19g.
The 1900 printings are on a coarse paper.

For surcharges or overprints on stamps or types of design A2 see Nos. 20-22, 24-38.

Nos. 16b and 16c Handstamp Surcharged in Black or Red

a   b

c

1893   *Perf. 12x11½*

20	A2(a)	5p on 4p blue (#16c)	55.00	100.00
a.		On 4p deep blue (#16b)	100.00	100.00
21	A2(b)	5p on 4p blue (#16c)	70.00	—
a.		On 4p deep blue (#16b)	100.00	110.00
22	A2(c)	5p on 4p blue (#16c) (R)	37.50	37.50
a.		On 4p deep blue (#16b)	42.50	50.00
		Nos. 20-22 (3)	162.50	137.50

As the surcharges on Nos. 20-21 were handstamped in two steps, with bars of differing lengths, and on No. 22 in three steps. Various varieties exist.

Flag Design — A7

1894-95   Typo.   *Perf. 11½x12*

23	A7	5p vermilion	30.00	7.50
a.		Perf. 11 ('95)	70.00	15.00
b.		As "a," deep red ('00)	5.00	20.00

Types of 1887-1895 Surcharged in Blue, Black, Red or Green

1½p, 2½p   3p

Handstamped Surcharges

1895   *Perf. 11*

24	A2	1½p on 2p orange (Bl)	7.50	10.00
a.		1½p on 2p brn org, perf 12x11½ (Bl)	27.50	20.00
b.		1½p on 2p yellow, "2" ends with vertical stroke	5.00	27.50
c.		As No. 24, pair, one without surcharge	650.00	
25	A2	3p on 2p orange (Bk)	10.00	15.00
a.		3p on 2p brn org, perf. 12x11½ (Bk)	60.00	25.00
b.		3p on 2p org yellow, narrow "R" (Bk)	6.00	50.00
c.		Vert. pair, imperf. btwn.	650.00	
d.		As "b," pair, one without surcharge		

Typographed Surcharges (#26 Handstamped)

1898-1900   *Perf. 11*

26	A2	2½p on 1sh rose (Bk), handstamped surcharge	50.00	50.00
a.		2½p, typo surcharge	12.00	15.00
b.		As "a," double surcharge	500.00	500.00
27	A2	2½p on 2sh6p vio (Bk)	12.00	20.00
28	A2	2½p on 1p bl grn (R)	1.75	5.00
a.		Inverted surcharge	850.00	425.00
29	A2	2½p on 1sh rose car (R)	8.50	20.00
a.		Double surcharge	400.00	
30	A2	3p on 2p dp red org (G)	5.00	130.00
		Nos. 26-30 (5)	77.25	225.00

No. 30 was a reissue, available for postage. The surcharge is not as tall as the 3p surcharge illustrated, which is the surcharge on No. 25. As Nos. 24-26 are handstamped, various varieties exist.

Stamps of 1886-99 Overprinted in Red or Blue

1899

31	A2	½p dull bl green (R)	3.50	8.00
32	A2	1p red brown (Bl)	4.25	20.00
33	A2	2p br orange (R)	2.50	20.00
a.		2p deep ocher	4.00	20.00
34	A2	4p blue (R)	1.00	20.00
35	A7	5p dp scarlet (Bl)	3.75	20.00
36	A2	6p maroon (Bl)	2.00	20.00
37	A2	1sh rose car (Bl)	2.00	25.00
38	A2	2sh6p mauve (R)	4.75	40.00
		Nos. 31-38 (8)	23.75	173.00

In 1900 the Samoan islands were partitioned between the US and Germany. The part which became American has since used US stamps.

Issued under German Dominion

Stamps of Germany Overprinted

1900   Unwmk.   *Perf. 13½x14½*

51	A9	3pf dark brown	11.00	15.00
		Never hinged	32.50	
		On cover		82.50
52	A9	5pf green	14.00	20.00
		Never hinged	45.00	
		On cover		82.50
53	A10	10pf carmine	11.00	20.00
		Never hinged	25.00	
		On cover		65.00
54	A10	20pf ultra	21.00	32.50
		Never hinged	57.50	
		On cover		125.00
55	A10	25pf orange	42.50	85.00
		Never hinged	115.00	
		On cover		400.00
56	A10	50pf red brown	42.50	80.00
		Never hinged	125.00	
		On cover		115.00
		On cover		142.00
		Nos. 51-56 (6)		252.50

Covers: Value for No. 56 on cover is for overfranked complete cover, usually philatelic.

Kaiser's Yacht "Hohenzollern"
A12   A13

1900   Typo.   *Perf. 14*

57	A12	3pf brown	1.25	1.40
		Never hinged	2.00	
		On cover		57.50
58	A12	5pf green	1.25	1.40
		Never hinged	2.00	
		On cover		25.00
59	A12	10pf carmine	1.25	1.40
		Never hinged	2.00	
		On cover		29.00
60	A12	20pf ultra	1.25	2.75
		Never hinged	1.80	
		On cover		52.50
61	A12	25pf org & blk, yel	1.40	14.00
		Never hinged	2.25	
		On cover		90.00
62	A12	30pf org & blk, sal	1.40	13.00
		Never hinged	2.90	
		On cover		90.00
63	A12	40pf lake & blk	1.50	14.00
		Never hinged	2.90	
		On cover		90.00
64	A12	50pf pur & blk, sal	1.50	15.00
		Never hinged	2.90	
		On cover		37.50
65	A12	80pf lake & blk, rose	3.50	37.50
		Never hinged	5.25	
		On cover		70.00

Perf. 14½x14
Engr.

66	A13	1m carmine	3.75	70.00
		Never hinged	15.00	
		On cover		100.00
67	A13	2m blue	5.00	120.00
		Never hinged	25.00	
		On cover		175.00
68	A13	3m black vio	9.00	175.00
		Never hinged	32.50	
		On cover		180.00
69	A13	5m slate & car	140.00	600.00
		Never hinged	500.00	
		On cover		800.00
		Nos. 57-69 (13)		172.05

Covers: Values for Nos. 64-69 on cover are for overfranked complete covers, usually philatelic.

1915   Wmk. 125   Typo.   *Perf. 14*

70	A12	3pf brown		1.25
		Never hinged		2.50
71	A12	5pf green		1.50
		Never hinged		2.90
72	A12	10pf carmine		1.50
		Never hinged		3.00

Perf. 14½x14
Engr.

73	A13	5m slate & car, 25x17 holes ('19)		32.50
		Never hinged		100.00
a.		26x17 holes ('15)		40.00
		Never hinged		160.00

Nos. 70-73 were never put in use.

Issued under British Dominion
Nos. 57-69 Surcharged

On A12

On A13

1914   Unwmk.   *Perf. 14*

101	A12	½p on 3pf brn	60.00	16.00
a.		Double surcharge	800.00	625.00
b.		Fraction bar omitted	90.00	42.50
c.		Comma after "I"	750.00	450.00
102	A12	½p on 5pf grn	65.00	20.00
a.		Double surcharge	800.00	625.00
b.		Fraction bar omitted	140.00	62.50
c.		Comma after "I"	190.00	
103	A12	1p on 10pf car	110.00	42.50
a.		Double surcharge	850.00	675.00
104	A12	2½p on 20pf ultra	62.50	14.00
a.		Fraction bar omitted	95.00	45.00
b.		Inverted surcharge	1,150.	1,050.
c.		Double surcharge	800.00	675.00
d.		Commas after "I"	575.00	375.00
105	A12	3p on 25pf org & blk, yel	80.00	42.50
a.		Double surcharge	1,150.	850.00
b.		Comma after "I"	5,250.	1,150.
106	A12	4p on 30pf org & blk, sal	135.00	62.50
107	A12	5p on 40pf lake & blk	135.00	75.00
108	A12	6p on 50pf pur & blk, sal	67.50	37.50
a.		Inverted "9" for "6"	190.00	110.00
b.		Double surcharge	1,250.	1,150.
109	A12	9p on 80pf lake & blk, rose	210.00	110.00

Perf. 14½x14

110	A13	1sh on 1m car ("1 Shillings")	3,500.	3,750.
a.		"1 Shilling."	11,500.	7,500.
111	A13	2sh on 2m blue	4,000.	3,500.
112	A13	3sh on 3m blk vio	1,600.	1,500.
a.		Double surcharge	10,500.	11,500.
113	A13	5sh on 5m slate & car	1,200.	1,100.
a.		Double surcharge	15,000.	15,000.

G.R.I. stands for Georgius Rex Imperator. The 3d on 30pf and 4d on 40pf were produced at a later time.
Unauthorized overprints, created as favors, exist on Nos. 101-113.

Stamps of New Zealand Overprinted in Red or Blue

k   m

1914, Sept. 29   *Perf. 14, 14x13½, 14x14½*   Wmk. 61

114	A41(k)	½p yel grn (R)	1.50	.35
115	A42(k)	1p carmine	1.40	.25
116	A41(k)	2p mauve (R)	1.40	1.10
117	A22(m)	2½p blue (R)	2.00	2.00
118	A41(k)	6p car rose, perf. 14x14½	2.25	2.00
a.		Perf. 14x13½	19.00	26.00
119	A41(k)	1sh vermilion	10.00	22.00
		Nos. 114-119 (6)	18.55	27.70

Overprinted Type "m"

1914-25   *Perf. 14, 14½x14*

120	PF1	2sh blue (R)	7.00	6.25
121	PF1	2sh6p brown (Bl)	6.25	14.00
122	PF1	3sh vio (R) ('22)	18.00	65.00
123	PF1	5sh green (R)	21.00	11.00
124	PF1	10sh red brn (Bl)	45.00	42.50
125	PF2	£1 rose (Bl)	100.00	85.00
126	PF2	£2 vio (R) ('25)	400.00	
		Nos. 120-126 (7)	597.25	
		Nos. 120-125 (6)		203.75

Postal use of the £2 is questioned.

Overprinted Type "k"

Perf. 14x13½, 14x14½

1916-19   Typo.

127	A43	½p yellow grn (R)	1.00	1.40
128	A47	1½p gray blk (R) ('17)	.55	.25
129	A47	1½p brn org (R) ('19)	.35	.50
130	A43	2p yellow (R) ('18)	2.00	.25
131	A43	3p chocolate (R)	3.25	20.00

Engr.

132	A44	2½p dull blue (R)	1.25	.60
133	A45	3p violet brn (Bl)	.65	1.10
134	A45	6p carmine rose (Bl)	2.25	2.50
135	A45	1sh vermilion (Bl)	4.25	1.75
		Nos. 127-135 (9)	15.55	28.35

New Zealand Victory Issue of 1919 Overprinted Type "k"

1920, June   *Perf. 14*

136	A48	½p yellow grn (R)	6.50	15.00
137	A49	1p carmine (Bl)	3.00	19.00
138	A50	1½p brown org (R)	2.00	10.50
139	A51	3p black brn (Bl)	9.25	10.50
140	A52	6p purple (R)	5.25	8.00
141	A53	1sh vermilion (Bl)	15.00	12.50
		Nos. 136-141 (6)	41.00	75.50

PROVISIONAL GOVT.

British Flag and
Samoan House — A22

1921, Dec. 23   Engr.   Perf. 14x13½
142	A22	½p green	5.50	2.00
a.		Perf. 14x14½	4.50	14.00
143	A22	1p lake	5.75	.25
a.		Perf. 14x14½	9.00	1.50
144	A22	1½p orange brn, perf. 14x14½	1.50	19.00
a.		Perf. 14x13½	19.00	12.00
145	A22	2p yel, perf. 14x14½	2.75	2.95
a.		Perf. 14x13½	15.00	.90
146	A22	2½sh dull blue	2.00	9.25
147	A22	3p dark brown	2.00	5.50
148	A22	4p violet	2.00	4.00
149	A22	5p brt blue	2.00	8.50
150	A22	6p carmine rose	2.00	7.50
151	A22	8p red brown	2.25	15.00
152	A22	9p olive green	2.50	37.50
153	A22	1sh vermilion	2.25	30.00
		Nos. 142-153 (12)	32.50	141.45

For overprints see Nos. 163-165.

New Zealand Nos. 182-183 Overprinted Type "m" in Red

1926-27   Perf. 14½x14
|154|A56|2sh dark blue|5.75|21.00|
|a.| |2sh blue ('27)|7.00|50.00|
|155|A56|3sh deep violet|24.00|50.00|
|a.| |3sh violet ('27)|62.50|110.00|

Issued: 2sh, Nov.; 3sh, Oct.; Nos. 154a, 155a, 11/10.

New Zealand Postal-Fiscal Stamps, Overprinted Type "m" in Blue or Red

1932, Aug.   Perf. 14
156	PF5	2sh6p brown	18.00	55.00
157	PF5	5sh green (R)	30.00	57.50
158	PF5	10sh lake	55.00	110.00
159	PF5	£1 pink	80.00	160.00
160	PF5	£2 violet (R)	950.00	
161	PF5	£5 dk bl (R)	2,600.	
		Nos. 156-159 (4)	183.00	382.50

See Nos. 175-180, 195-202, 216-219 (in Scott Standard catalogue, Vol. 5).

Silver Jubilee Issue

Stamps of 1921
Overprinted in Black

1935, May 7   Perf. 14x13½
|163|A22|1p lake|.40|.50|
|a.| |Perf. 14x14½|110.00|200.00|
164	A22	2½p dull blue	.75	1.00
165	A22	6p carmine rose	3.25	4.00
		Nos. 163-165 (3)	4.40	5.50
		Set, never hinged	9.00	

25th anniv. of the reign of George V.

Western Samoa

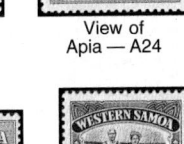

Samoan Girl and Kava Bowl — A23 · View of Apia — A24

River Scene — A25 · Samoan Chief and Wife — A26

Samoan Canoe and House — A27 · "Vailima," Stevenson's Home — A28

Stevenson's Tomb — A29 · Lake Lanuto'o — A30

Falefa Falls — A31

Perf. 14x13½, 13½x14
1935, Aug. 7   Engr.   Wmk. 61
166	A23	½p yellow grn	.25	.40
167	A24	1p car lake & blk	.25	.25
168	A25	2p red org & blk, perf. 14	4.00	4.00
a.		Perf. 13½x14	5.00	4.25
169	A26	2½p dp blue & blk	.25	.25
170	A27	4p blk brn & dk gray	.50	.35
171	A28	6p plum	.70	.35
172	A29	1sh brown & violet	.50	.50
173	A30	2sh red brn & yel grn	1.10	.80
174	A31	3sh org brn & brt bl	2.50	3.50
		Nos. 166-174 (9)	10.05	10.40
		Set, never hinged	20.00	

See Nos. 186-188.

Postal-Fiscal Stamps of New Zealand Overprinted in Blue or Carmine

1935   Perf. 14
175	PF5	2sh6p brown	11.00	18.00
176	PF5	5sh green	22.50	30.00
177	PF5	10sh dp carmine	70.00	85.00
178	PF5	£1 pink	62.50	110.00
179	PF5	£2 violet (C)	180.00	400.00
180	PF5	£5 dk bl (C)	260.00	525.00
		Nos. 175-180 (6)	606.00	1,168.

See Nos. 195-202, 216-219 (in Scott Standard catalogue, Vol. 5).

Samoan Coastal Village — A32 · Map of Western Samoa — A33

Samoan Dancing Party A34 · Robert Louis Stevenson A35

Perf. 13½x14
1939, Aug. 29   Engr.   Wmk. 253
181	A32	1p scar & olive	.60	.35
182	A33	1½p copper brn & bl	1.00	.90
183	A34	2½p dk blue & brn	1.10	1.00

Perf. 14x13½
184	A35	7p dp sl grn & vio	4.25	4.25
		Nos. 181-184 (4)	6.95	6.50
		Set, never hinged	12.00	

25th anniv. of New Zealand's control of the mandated territory of Western Samoa.

Samoan Chief — A36

1940, Sept. 2   Perf. 14x13½
|185|A36|3p on 1½p brown|.50|.35|
| | |Never hinged|.85| |

Issued only with surcharge. Examples without surcharge are from printer's archives.

Types of 1935 and

Apia Post Office — A37

1944-49   Wmk. 253   Perf. 14
186	A23	½p yellow green	.30	21.00
187	A25	2p red orange & blk	2.00	7.00
188	A26	2½p dp blue & blk ('48)	5.00	40.00

Perf. 13½x14
189	A37	5p dp ultra & ol brn ('49)	1.40	1.00
		Nos. 186-189 (4)	8.70	69.00
		Set, never hinged	14.50	

Issue date: 5p, June 8.

Catalogue values for unused stamps in this section, from this point to the end of the section, are for Never Hinged items.

Peace Issue
New Zealand Nos. 248, 250, 254, and 255 Overprinted in Black or Blue

p · q

1946, June 1   Perf. 13x13½, 13½x13
191	A94(p)	1p emerald	.40	.25
192	A96(q)	2p rose violet (Bl)	.40	.25
193	A100(p)	6p org red & red brn	.80	.25
194	A101(p)	8p brn lake & blk (Bl)	.45	.25
		Nos. 191-194 (4)	2.05	1.00

Stamps and Type of New Zealand, 1931-50 Overprinted Like Nos. 175-180 in Blue or Carmine

1945-50   Wmk. 253   Perf. 14
195	PF5	2sh6p brown	15.00	27.50
196	PF5	5sh green	21.00	18.00
197	PF5	10sh car ('48)	23.00	19.00
198	PF5	£1 pink ('48)	130.00	200.00
199	PF5	30sh choc ('48)	200.00	350.00
200	PF5	£2 violet (C)	210.00	310.00
201	PF5	£3 lt grn ('50)	300.00	425.00
202	PF5	£5 dk bl (C) ('50)	425.00	500.00

Making Siapo Cloth — A38

Western Samoa and New Zealand Flags, Village A39

Thatching Hut A40 · Samoan Chieftainess A41

Designs: 2p, Western Samoa seal. 3p, Aleisa Falls (actually Malifa Falls). 5p, Manumea (tooth-billed pigeon). 6p, Fishing canoe. 8p, Harvesting cacao. 2sh, Preparing copra.

Perf. 13, 13½x13
1952, Mar. 10   Engr.   Wmk. 253
203	A38	½p org brn & claret	.25	2.00
204	A39	1p green & olive	.25	.25
205	A38	2p deep carmine	.25	.25
206	A39	3p indigo & blue	.45	.25
207	A38	5p dk grn & org brn	9.00	.80
208	A39	6p dp rose pink & bl	1.00	.25
209	A39	8p rose carmine	.35	.30
210	A40	1sh blue & brown	.25	.25
211	A39	2sh yellow brown	1.10	.50
212	A41	3sh ol gray & vio brn	2.75	2.75
		Nos. 203-212 (10)	15.65	7.60

SAN MARINO

ˌsan məˈrē-ˌnō

LOCATION — Eastern Italy, about 20 miles inland from the Adriatic Sea
GOVT. — Republic
AREA — 24.1 sq. mi.
POP. — 21,622 (1981)
CAPITAL — San Marino

100 Centesimi = 1 Lira

Watermarks

Wmk. 140 — Crown

Wmk. 174 — Coat of Arms

Wmk. 217 — Three Plumes

Nos. 1-28 were spaced very narrowly on the plates, so that perforations often cut into the design on one or two sides. Values are for very fine stamps, with perforations clear of the design. Examples with perfs cutting in the design sell for less, while examples with four clear, full margins sell for substantially more than the values shown. Never hinged premiums do not apply to stamps with perforations cutting the design.

	A1 Numeral		A2 Coat of Arms	

1877-99　Typo.　Wmk. 140　Perf. 14

1	A1	2c green	37.50	19.00
	Never hinged		95.00	
	No gum		7.50	
	On cover			225.00
2	A1	2c blue ('94)	15.00	19.00
	Never hinged		42.50	
	No gum		3.40	
	On cover			225.00
3	A1	2c claret ('95)	13.50	19.00
	Never hinged		35.00	
	No gum		2.75	
	On cover			200.00
4	A2	5c orange ('90)	180.00	50.00
	Never hinged		475.00	
	No gum		37.50	
	On cover			350.00
5	A2	5c olive grn ('92)	9.00	9.25
	Never hinged		24.00	
	No gum		1.90	
	On cover			90.00
6	A2	5c green ('99)	9.25	14.00
	Never hinged		24.00	
	No gum		1.90	
	On cover			135.00
7	A2	10c ultra	350.00	115.00
	Never hinged		875.00	
	No gum		70.00	
	On cover			575.00
a.		10c blue ('90)	3,600.	300.00
	Never hinged		9,000.	
	No gum		190.00	
	On cover			3,100.
8	A2	10c dk green ('92)	9.25	11.00
	Never hinged		24.00	
	No gum		1.90	
	On cover			110.00
9	A2	10c claret ('99)	9.25	13.50
	Never hinged		24.00	
	No gum		1.90	
	On cover			140.00
10	A2	15c claret ('94)	170.00	120.00
	Never hinged		425.00	
	No gum		42.50	
	On cover			1,250.

11	A2	20c vermilion	45.00	19.00
	Never hinged		115.00	
	No gum		9.50	
	On cover			225.00
12	A2	20c lilac ('95)	9.25	19.00
	Never hinged		24.00	
	No gum		1.90	
	On cover			165.00
13	A2	25c maroon ('90)	150.00	90.00
	Never hinged		390.00	
	No gum		30.00	
	On cover			450.00
14	A2	25c blue ('99)	9.25	17.00
	Never hinged		24.00	
	No gum		1.90	
	On cover			165.00
15	A2	30c brown	925.00	125.00
	Never hinged		2,800.	
	No gum		185.00	
	On cover			1,250.
16	A2	30c org yel ('92)	9.25	19.00
	Never hinged		24.00	
	No gum		1.90	
a.		30c yellow ochre	10.50	21.50
	On cover			210.00
17	A2	40c violet	925.00	125.00
	Never hinged		2,800.	
	No gum		185.00	
	On cover			1,250.
18	A2	40c dk brown ('92)	9.25	19.00
	Never hinged		24.00	
	On cover			190.00
19	A2	45c gray grn ('92)	9.25	19.00
	Never hinged		24.00	
	No gum		1.90	
a.		45c deep olive green	9.25	19.00
	On cover			190.00
20	A2	65c red brown ('92)	9.25	19.00
	Never hinged		22.50	
	No gum		1.90	
	On cover			190.00
21	A2	1 l car & yel ('92)	1,825.	950.00
	Never hinged		4,750.	
	No gum		650.00	
	On cover			3,750.
22	A2	1 l lt blue ('95)	1,675.	750.00
	Never hinged		4,250.	
	No gum		550.00	
	On cover			3,000.
23	A2	2 l brn & yel ('94)	90.00	120.00
	Never hinged		240.00	
	No gum		22.50	
	On cover			1,250.
24	A2	5 l vio & grn ('94)	225.00	450.00
	Never hinged		575.00	
	No gum		55.00	
	On cover			3,750.

Cover values are for properly franked covers, paying correct postage rates. Overfranked covers and other philatelic covers sell for about one-half of the values quoted.
Values for never-hinged stamps are for examples with very fine centering. Premiums do not apply to stamps with perforations cutting the design.

Values for Blocks of 4
(2 stamps never hinged)
(Average to Fine Centering)

1	A1	2c green	275.00	90.00
2	A1	2c blue ('94)	135.00	135.00
3	A1	2c claret ('95)	120.00	110.00
4	A2	5c orange ('90)	1,500.	1,425.
5	A2	5c olive grn ('92)	75.00	90.00
6	A2	5c green ('99)	75.00	97.50
7	A2	10c ultra	2,500.	1,250.
a.		10c blue ('90)	12,000.	3,000.
8	A2	10c dk green ('92)	75.00	90.00
9	A2	10c claret ('99)	75.00	97.50
10	A2	15c claret ('94)	1,300.	925.00
11	A2	20c vermilion	350.00	110.00
12	A2	20c lilac ('95)	75.00	110.00
13	A2	25c maroon ('90)	1,250.	1,350.
14	A2	25c blue ('99)	75.00	110.00
15	A2	30c brown	8,250.	3,200.
16	A2	30c org yel ('92)	75.00	135.00
17	A2	40c violet	8,250.	3,200.
18	A2	40c dk brown ('92)	75.00	135.00
19	A2	45c gray grn ('92)	75.00	135.00
20	A2	65c red brown ('92)	75.00	135.00
21	A2	1 l car & yel ('92)	17,500.	19,000.
22	A2	1 l lt blue ('95)	16,000.	14,500.
23	A2	2 l brn & yel ('94)	725.00	925.00
24	A2	5 l vio & grn ('94)	1,800.	5,000.

See Nos. 911-915 in Scott Standard catalogue, Vol. 6.

Nos. 7a, 15, 11
Surcharged in Black

C mi. 10

1892

25	A2	5c on 10c blue	90.00	26.00
	Never hinged		225.00	
	No gum		22.50	
	On cover			265.00
a.		Inverted surcharge	110.00	34.00
	Never hinged		275.00	
	On cover			340.00
b.		5c on 10c ultramarine	50,000.	12,000.
	Never hinged		62,500.	
	On cover			13,750.
c.		As "b," inverted surch.	—	—
d.		Double surcharge, one inverted	—	—
	On cover			—
e.		Pair, one without surcharge		2,250.

f.		Pair, one without surcharge, surcharge inverted	4,500. 2,250.	
		surcharge inverted	4,500.	
26	A2	5c on 30c brown	300.00	135.00
	Never hinged		750.00	
	No gum		75.00	
	On cover			1,325.
a.		Inverted surcharge	375.00	170.00
	Never hinged		950.00	
	On cover			1,700.
b.		Double surch., one inverted	375.00	210.00
	Never hinged		950.00	
c.		Double invtd. surcharge	375.00	210.00
	Never hinged		950.00	
27	A2	10c on 20c ver	67.50	15.00
	Never hinged		175.00	
	No gum		17.00	
	On cover			150.00
a.		Inverted surcharge	75.00	22.50
	Never hinged		190.00	
	On cover			225.00
b.		Double surch., one inverted	82.50	30.00
	Never hinged		210.00	
	On cover			300.00
c.		Double surcharge	82.50	30.00
	Never hinged		210.00	
	On cover			300.00

Ten to twelve varieties of each surcharge.

10　　10

No. 11 Surcharged

28	A2	10c on 20c ver	300.00	19.00
	Never hinged		750.00	
	No gum		75.00	
	On cover			190.00
a.		Only one "10" in surcharge	600.00	
	Never hinged		1,500.	

Values for never-hinged stamps are for examples with very fine centering. Premiums do not apply to stamps with perforations cutting the design.

Values for Blocks of 4
(2 stamps never hinged)

25	A2	5c on 10c blue	685.00	120.00
b.		5c on 10c ultramarine		45,000.
26	A2	5c on 30c brown	2,250.	610.00
27	A2	10c on 20c ver	525.00	70.00
28	A2	10c on 20c ver	2,250.	85.00

Government Palace and Portraits of
Regents, Tonnini and Marcucci
A6　　　　　　A7

Portraits of
Regents and
View of Interior
of Palace — A8

Wmk. 174
1894, Sept. 30　Litho.　Perf. 15½

29	A6	25c blue & dk brn	7.50	3.00
	Never hinged		52.50	
	On cover			60.00
30	A7	50c dull red & dk brn	45.00	9.50
	Never hinged		320.00	
	On cover			190.00
31	A8	1 l green & dk brown	35.00	11.50
	Never hinged		240.00	
	On cover			225.00
	Nos. 29-31 (3)		87.50	24.00

Opening of the new Government Palace and the installation of the new Regents.

Statue of Liberty — A9

Wmk. 140
1899-1922　Typo.　Perf. 14

32	A9	2c brown	3.75	1.90
	Never hinged		9.50	
	On cover			37.50

33	A9	2c claret ('22)	.75	.75
	Never hinged		1.90	
	On cover			20.00
34	A9	5c brown org	7.50	1.50
	Never hinged		19.00	
	On cover			45.00
35	A9	5c olive grn ('22)	.75	.75
	Never hinged		1.90	
	On cover			4.00
36	A9	10c govt org ('22)	.75	.75
	Never hinged		1.90	
	On cover			15.00
37	A9	20c dp brown ('22)	.75	.75
	Never hinged		1.90	
	On cover			15.00
38	A9	25c ultra ('22)	1.50	1.50
	Never hinged		3.75	
	On cover			22.50
39	A9	45c red brown ('22)	3.00	3.00
	Never hinged		7.50	
	On cover			22.50
	Nos. 32-39 (8)		18.75	13.90

	Numeral of Value — A10		Mt. Titano — A11	

1903-25　　　　　Perf. 14, 14½x14

40	A10	2c violet	22.50	12.00
	Never hinged		55.00	
	On cover			75.00
41	A10	2c orange brn ('21)	1.50	1.10
	Never hinged		3.75	
	On cover			37.50
42	A11	5c blue grn	11.00	7.50
	Never hinged		28.00	
	On cover			37.50
43	A11	5c olive grn ('21)	1.50	1.10
	Never hinged		3.75	
	On cover			19.00
a.		Imperforate	85.00	
	Never hinged		175.00	
44	A11	5c red brn ('25)	.75	.75
	Never hinged		1.90	
	On cover			7.50
45	A11	10c claret	11.50	7.50
	Never hinged		29.00	
	On cover			37.50
46	A11	10c brown org ('21)	1.50	1.20
	Never hinged		3.75	
	On cover			18.00
a.		Imperforate	85.00	
	Never hinged		175.00	
47	A11	10c olive grn ('25)	.75	.75
	Never hinged		1.90	
	On cover			7.50
48	A11	15c blue grn ('22)	1.50	1.10
	Never hinged		3.75	
	On cover			18.00
49	A11	15c brown vio ('25)	.75	.75
	Never hinged		1.90	
	On cover			7.50
50	A11	20c brown orange	150.00	60.00
	Never hinged		375.00	
	On cover			600.00
51	A11	20c brown ('21)	1.50	1.20
	Never hinged		3.75	
	On cover			26.00
52	A11	20c blue grn ('25)	.75	.75
	Never hinged		1.90	
	On cover			11.00
53	A11	25c blue	27.50	12.00
	Never hinged		70.00	
	On cover			37.50
54	A11	25c gray ('21)	1.50	1.10
	Never hinged		3.75	
	On cover			26.00
55	A11	25c violet ('25)	.75	.75
	Never hinged		1.90	
	On cover			7.50
56	A11	30c brown red	12.00	18.50
	Never hinged		30.00	
	On cover			82.50
57	A11	30c claret ('21)	1.50	1.20
	Never hinged		3.75	
	On cover			75.00
58	A11	30c orange ('25)	22.50	3.75
	Never hinged		57.50	
	On cover			45.00
59	A11	40c orange red	22.50	18.50
	Never hinged		57.50	
	On cover			75.00
60	A11	40c dp rose ('21)	1.50	1.20
	Never hinged		3.75	
	On cover			26.00
61	A11	40c brown ('25)	.75	.75
	Never hinged		1.90	
	On cover			10.50
62	A11	45c yellow	16.50	18.50
	Never hinged		42.50	
	On cover			75.00
63	A11	50c brown vio ('23)	3.00	3.00
	Never hinged		7.50	
	On cover			67.50
64	A11	50c gray blk ('25)	.75	.75
	Never hinged		1.90	
	On cover			7.50
65	A11	60c brown red ('25)	.75	.75
	Never hinged		3.75	
	On cover			45.00
66	A11	65c chocolate	17.00	18.50
	Never hinged		42.50	
	On cover			75.00
67	A11	80c blue ('21)	6.00	6.00
	Never hinged		15.00	
	On cover			67.50
68	A11	90c brown ('23)	6.00	6.00
	Never hinged		15.00	
	On cover			67.50

69	A11	1 l olive green	60.00	30.00
		Never hinged	150.00	
		On cover		600.00
70	A11	1 l ultra ('21)	6.00	6.00
		Never hinged	15.00	
		On cover		67.50
71	A11	1 l lt blue ('25)	1.50	.75
		Never hinged	3.75	
		On cover		45.00
72	A11	2 l violet	1,000.	425.00
		Never hinged	2,000.	
		On cover		3,500.
73	A11	2 l orange ('21)	22.50	27.00
		Never hinged	55.00	
		On cover		375.00
74	A11	2 l lt green ('25)	7.50	7.50
		Never hinged	19.00	
		On cover		325.00
75	A11	5 l slate	275.00	300.00
		Never hinged	700.00	
		On cover		1,850.
76	A11	5 l ultra ('25)	16.50	19.00
		Never hinged	42.50	
		On cover		300.00
		Nos. 40-76 (37)	1,735.	1,022.

For overprints and surcharges see Nos. 77, 93-96, 103, 107, 188-189 (in Scott Standard catalogue, Vol. 6), B1-B2, E2, E4.

No. 50 Surcharged

1905, Sept. 1

77	A11	15c on 20c brown org	15.00	10.50
		Never hinged	37.50	
		On cover		52.50
a.		Large 5 in 1905 on level with 9	92.50	45.00

Coat of Arms
A12   A13

Two types:
I — Width 18½mm.
II — Width 19mm.

1907-10 Unwmk. Engr. *Perf. 12*

78	A12	1c brown, II ('10)	8.00	2.00
		Never hinged	20.00	
		On cover		45.00
a.		Type I	16.00	3.00
		Never hinged	40.00	
		On cover		45.00
79	A13	15c gray, I	37.50	6.00
		Never hinged	95.00	
		On cover		60.00
a.		Imperforate	140.00	140.00
		Never hinged	275.00	
b.		Type II ('10)	300.00	32.50
		Never hinged	725.00	
		On cover		225.00
c.		As "b," imperforate	600.00	600.00
		Never hinged	1,250.	
		Nos. 78a, 79 on over-franked philatelic cover		70.00
		Nos. 78, 79a on over-franked philatelic cover		275.00

No. 79a Surcharged in Brown

1918, Mar. 15

80	A13	20c on 15c gray	6.00	3.75
		Never hinged	16.00	
		On cover		32.50

St. Marinus — A14

Perf. 14½x14, 14x14½
1923, Aug. 11 Typo. Wmk. 140

81	A14	30c dark brown	.75	.75
		Never hinged	2.00	
		On cover		20.00

San Marino Intl. Exhib. of 1923. Proceeds from the sale of this stamp went to a mutual aid society.
Imperforate examples on chalky paper are proofs. Value, $175.

Italian Flag and Views of Arbe and Mt. Titano
A15

1923, Aug. 6

82	A15	50c olive green	.75	.75
		Never hinged	2.00	
		On cover		20.00
a.		Reverse printing omitted	215.00	
		Never hinged	425.00	
b.		Gummed on both sides	15.00	
		Never hinged	30.00	

Presentation to San Marino of the Italian flag which had flown over the island of Arbe, the birthplace of the founder of San Marino. Inscribed on back: "V. Moraldi dis. Blasi inc. Petiti impr.-Roma."
Imperfroate examples on chalky paper are proofs. Value, $175.

Mt. Titano and Sword — A16

1923, Sept. 29 *Perf. 14x14½*

83	A16	1 l dark brown	22.50	22.50
		Never hinged	60.00	
		On cover		100.00

In honor of the San Marino Volunteers who were killed or wounded in WWI.

Giuseppe Garibaldi   Allegory-San
A17   Marino
                         Sheltering
                         Garibaldi
                         A18

1924, Sept. 25 *Perf. 14*

84	A17	30c dark violet	3.75	4.00
		Never hinged	9.50	
		On cover		10.00
85	A17	50c olive brown	3.75	4.00
		Never hinged	9.00	
		On cover		10.00
86	A17	60c dull red	5.00	5.00
		Never hinged	12.00	
		On cover		12.00
87	A18	1 l deep blue	9.00	9.00
		Never hinged	22.50	
		On cover		22.50
88	A18	2 l gray green	11.00	11.00
		Never hinged	27.50	
		On cover		120.00
		Nos. 84-88 (5)	32.50	33.00
		Set on overfranked philatelic cover		90.00

75th anniv. of Garibaldi's taking refuge in San Marino.

No. B8 Surcharged in Black

1924, Oct. 9

89	SP1	30c on 45c yel brn & blk	3.00	3.00
		Never hinged	7.50	
		On cover		22.50
a.		Pair, one stamp without surcharge	1,100.	1,100.
		Never hinged	2,200.	

Nos. B9-B11 Surcharged

90	SP2	60c on 1 l bl grn & blk	10.50	10.50
		Never hinged	26.50	
		On cover		55.00
91	SP2	1 l on 2 l vio & blk	29.00	29.00
		Never hinged	72.50	
		On cover		95.00
92	SP2	2 l on 3 l claret & blk	22.00	22.00
		Never hinged	52.50	
		On cover		215.00
		Nos. 89-92 (4)	64.50	64.50
		Set on overfranked philatelic cover		245.00

Nos. 67 and 68 Surcharged in Black or Red

1926, July 1

93	A11	75c on 80c blue	2.25	2.50
		Never hinged	6.00	
		On cover		22.50
94	A11	1.20 l on 90c brown	2.25	2.50
		Never hinged	6.00	
		On cover		22.50
95	A11	1.25 l on 90c brn (R)	3.75	3.75
		Never hinged	9.50	
		On cover		40.00
96	A11	2.50 l on 80c blue (R)	8.00	8.00
		Never hinged	20.00	
		On cover		45.00
		Nos. 93-96 (4)	16.25	16.75
		Set on overfranked philatelic cover		67.50

Antonio Onofri — A19

Unwmk.
1926, July 29 Engr. *Perf. 11*

97	A19	10c dk blue & blk	.75	.75
		Never hinged	1.90	
		On cover		4.00
98	A19	20c olive grn & blk	1.50	1.50
		Never hinged	3.75	
		On cover		6.00
99	A19	45c dk vio & blk	.75	.75
		Never hinged	1.90	
		On cover		22.50
100	A19	65c green & blk	.75	.75
		Never hinged	1.90	
		On cover		22.50
101	A19	1 l orange & blk	5.50	5.50
		Never hinged	13.50	
		On cover		37.50
102	A19	2 l red vio & blk	5.50	5.50
		Never hinged	13.50	
		On cover		45.00
		Nos. 97-102 (6)	14.75	14.75
		Set on overfranked philatelic cover		75.00

For surcharges see Nos. 104-106, 181-182.

Special Delivery Stamp No. E2 Surcharged

A20

Perf. 14½x14
1926, Nov. 25 Wmk. 140

103	A20	1.85 l on 60c violet	.80	.80
		Never hinged	2.00	
		On cover		25.00

Nos. 101 and 102 Surcharged

13 Dots in Curved Row in Surcharge *Perf.* 11 Unwmk.

		1927, Mar. 10		**1927, Mar. 10**
104	A19	1.25 l on 1 l	9.50	9.50
		Never hinged	22.50	
		On cover		40.00
105	A19	2.50 l on 2 l	19.00	19.00
		Never hinged	45.00	
		On cover		75.00
106	A19	5 l on 2 l	55.00	55.00
		Never hinged	135.00	
		On cover		275.00
		Nos. 104-106 (3)	83.50	83.50
		Set on overfranked philatelic cover		250.00

14 Dots in Surcharge (Position 29)

104a	A19	1.25 l on 1 l	30.00	
		Never hinged	60.00	
105a	A19	2.50 l on 2 l	60.00	
		Never hinged	120.00	
106a	A19	5 l on 2 l	185.00	
		Never hinged	375.00	

12 Dots in Surcharge (Position 9, 22, 32)

104b	A19	1.25 l on 1 l	20.00	
		Never hinged	40.00	
105b	A19	2.50 l on 2 l	37.50	
		Never hinged	75.00	
106b	A19	5 l on 2 l	125.00	
		Never hinged	250..00	

11 Dots in Surcharge (Position 20)

| 104c | A19 | 1.25 l on 1 l | 30.00 | |
| | | Never hinged | 60.00 | |

9 Dots in Surcharge (Position 2)

| 106d | A19 | 5 l on 2 l | 225.00 | |
| | | Never hinged | 450.00 | |

Type of Special Delivery Stamp of 1923 Surcharged

1927, Sept. 15 Wmk. 140 *Perf. 14*

107	A11	1.75 l on 50c on 25c vio	1.25	1.25
		Never hinged	3.25	
		On cover		27.50

13 Dots in Curved Row in Surcharge

War Memorial
A21

Unwmk.
1927, Sept. 28 Engr. *Perf. 12*

108	A21	50c brown violet	2.25	2.25
		Never hinged	8.50	
109	A21	1.25 l blue	3.25	3.25
		Never hinged	8.50	

110 A21   10 l gray   30.00   30.00
   Never hinged   70.00
   Nos. 108-110 (3)   35.50   35.50
Set on overfranked philatel-
ic cover   150.00

Erection of a cenotaph in memory of the
San Marino volunteers in WWI

Capuchin
Church
and
Convent
A22

Design: 2.50 l, 5 l, Death of St. Francis.

1928, Jan. 2
111 A22   50c red   27.50   10.50
   Never hinged   65.00
112 A22   1.25 l dp blue   12.00   12.00
   Never hinged   30.00
113 A22   2.50 l dk brown   12.00   12.00
   Never hinged   30.00
114 A22   5 l dull violet   37.50   35.00
   Never hinged   90.00
   Nos. 111-114 (4)   89.00   69.50
Set on overfranked phila-
telic cover   225.00

7th centenary of the death of St. Francis of
Assisi.
For surcharges see Nos. 183-184.

The Rocca   Government
(State Prison)   Palace
A24   A25

Statue of Liberty — A26

1929-35   **Wmk. 217**
115 A24   5c vio brn & ul-
      tra   1.50   .75
   Never hinged   4.25
116 A24   10c grnsh blue &
      red vio   2.00   1.25
   Never hinged   5.25
117 A24   15c dp org & em-
      er   1.50   .75
   Never hinged   4.25
118 A24   20c dk bl & org
      red   1.50   .75
   Never hinged   4.25
119 A24   25c grn & gray
      blk   1.50   .75
   Never hinged   4.25
120 A24   30c gray brn &
      red   1.50   .75
   Never hinged   4.25
121 A24   50c red vio & ol
      gray   1.50   .75
   Never hinged   4.25
122 A24   75c dp red &
      gray blk   1.50   .75
   Never hinged   4.25
123 A25   1 l dk brn & em-
      er   1.50   .75
   Never hinged   4.25
124 A25   1.25 l dk blue & blk   1.50   .75
   Never hinged   4.25
125 A25   1.75 l green & org   4.00   2.00
   Never hinged   10.00
126 A25   2 l bl gray & red   2.00   1.25
   Never hinged   5.25
127 A25   2.50 l car rose &
      ultra   2.00   1.25
   Never hinged   5.25
128 A25   3 l dp org & bl   2.00   1.25
   Never hinged   5.25
129 A25   3.70 l ol blk & red
      brn ('35)   2.00   1.25
   Never hinged   5.25
130 A26   5 l dk vio & dk
      grn   4.00   3.75
   Never hinged   10.00
131 A26   10 l bis brn & dk
      bl   16.00   15.00
   Never hinged   40.00
132 A26   15 l green & red
      vio   75.00   90.00
   Never hinged   210.00
   On cover   375.00

133 A26   20 l dk bl & red   350.00 350.00
   Never hinged   950.00
   On cover   1,150.
   Nos. 115-133 (19)   472.50 473.75

General Post
Office — A27

1932, Feb. 4
134 A27   20c blue green   35.00   22.50
   Never hinged   87.50
135 A27   50c dark red   42.50   26.00
   Never hinged   105.00
136 A27   1.25 l dark blue   275.00 190.00
   Never hinged   675.00
137 A27   1.75 l dark brown   170.00 105.00
   Never hinged   425.00
138 A27   2.75 l dark violet   85.00   60.00
   Never hinged   210.00
   Nos. 134-138 (5)   607.50 403.50
Set on overfranked phila-
telic cover   675.00

Opening of new General Post Office.
For surcharges see Nos. 151-160.

San Marino-Rimini Electric
Railway — A28

1932, June 11
139 A28   20c deep green   4.50   4.50
   Never hinged   11.00
140 A28   50c dark red   7.50   7.50
   Never hinged   19.00
141 A28   1.25 l dark blue   19.00   19.00
   Never hinged   47.50
142 A28   5 l deep brown   105.00 105.00
   Never hinged   260.00
   Nos. 139-142 (4)   136.00 136.00
Set on overfranked phila-
telic cover   350.00

Opening of the new electric railway between
San Marino and Rimini.

Giuseppe Garibaldi — A29

Garibaldi's Arrival at San
Marino — A30

1932, July 30
143 A29   10c violet brown   12.50   5.00
   Never hinged   30.00
144 A29   20c violet   12.50   5.00
   Never hinged   30.00
145 A29   25c green   12.50   5.00
   Never hinged   30.00
146 A29   50c yellow brn   17.00   10.00
   Never hinged   42.50
147 A30   75c dark red   42.50   21.00
   Never hinged   105.00
148 A30   1.25 l dark blue   50.00   30.00
   Never hinged   125.00
149 A30   2.75 l brown org   100.00   60.00
   Never hinged   250.00
150 A30   5 l olive green   340.00 425.00
   Never hinged   850.00
   Nos. 143-150 (8)   587.00 561.00
Set on overfranked phila-
telic cover   650.00

Garibaldi (1807-1882), Italian patriot.

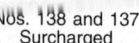

Nos. 138 and 137
Surcharged

1933, May 27
151 A27   25c on 2.75 l   16.00   16.00
   Never hinged   40.00
152 A27   50c on 1.75 l   32.50   32.50
   Never hinged   80.00
153 A27   75c on 2.75 l   65.00   65.00
   Never hinged   160.00
154 A27   1.25 l on 1.75 l   425.00 425.00
   Never hinged   1,050.
   Nos. 151-154 (4)   538.50 538.50
Set on overfranked phila-
telic cover   575.00

Convention of philatelists, San Marino, May
28.

Nos. 134-137
Surcharged in Black

1934, Apr. 12
155 A27   25c on 1.25 l   3.25   3.25
   Never hinged   8.00
156 A27   50c on 1.75 l   4.75   4.75
   Never hinged   11.50
157 A27   75c on 50c   11.00   11.00
   Never hinged   27.50
158 A27   1.25 l on 20c   40.00   40.00
   Never hinged   100.00
   Nos. 155-158 (4)   59.00   59.00
Set on overfranked phila-
telic cover   135.00

San Marino's participation (with a philatelic
pavilion) in the 15th annual Trade Fair at Milan,
Apr. 12-27.

**Nos. 136 and 138 Surcharged Wheel
and New Value**
1934, Apr. 12
159 A27   3.70 l on 1.25 l   67.50   67.50
   Never hinged   160.00
160 A27   3.70 l on 2.75 l   82.50   82.50
   Never hinged   200.00
Set on overfranked philatel-
ic cover   450.00

Ascent to
Mt.
Titano
A31

Unwmk.
1935, Feb. 7   Engr.   Perf. 14
161 A31   5c choc & blk   .75   .75
   Never hinged   1.90
162 A31   10c dk vio & blk   .75   .75
   Never hinged   1.90
163 A31   20c orange & blk   .75   .75
   Never hinged   1.90
164 A31   25c green & blk   .75   .75
   Never hinged   1.90
165 A31   50c olive bis & blk   .75   .75
   Never hinged   1.90
166 A31   75c brown red & blk   3.50   3.50
   Never hinged   8.75
167 A31   1.25 l blue & blk   7.00   7.00
   Never hinged   17.50
   Nos. 161-167 (7)   14.25   14.25
Set on overfranked philatelic
cover   42.50

12th anniv. of the founding of the Fascist
Movement.

Melchiorre   Statue of
Delfico — A32   Delfico — A33

1935, Apr. 15   Wmk. 217   Perf. 12
Center in Black
169 A32   5c brown lake   2.50   2.50
   Never hinged   6.25
170 A32   7½c lt brown   2.50   2.50
   Never hinged   6.25
171 A32   10c dk blue grn   2.50   2.50
   Never hinged   6.25
172 A32   15c rose carmine   50.00   25.00
   Never hinged   125.00
173 A32   20c orange   3.25   3.00
   Never hinged   8.00
174 A32   25c green   3.25   3.00
   Never hinged   8.00
175 A33   30c dull violet   3.25   3.00
   Never hinged   8.00
176 A33   50c olive green   5.00   5.00
   Never hinged   12.50
177 A33   75c red   15.00   15.00
   Never hinged   37.50
178 A33   1.25 l dark blue   4.25   4.25
179 A33   1.50 l dk brown   70.00   70.00
   Never hinged   175.00
180 A33   1.75 l brown org   100.00 105.00
   Never hinged   250.00
   Nos. 169-180 (12)   261.50 240.75
Set on overfranked phila-
telic cover   475.00

Melchiorre Delfico (1744-1835), historian.
For surcharges see Nos. 202, 277 in Scott
Standard catalogue, Vol. 6.

Nos. 99-100
Surcharged in Black

Nos. 112-113 Surcharged in Black

1936   Unwmk.   Perf. 11
181 A19   80c on 45c dk vio &
      blk   4.00   4.00
   Never hinged   10.00
182 A19   80c on 65c grn & blk   4.00   4.00
   Never hinged   10.00

Perf. 12
183 A22   2.05 l on 1.25 l   9.50   9.50
   Never hinged   24.00
184 A22   2.75 l on 2.50 l   25.00   25.00
   Never hinged   62.50
   Nos. 181-184 (4)   42.50   42.50
Nos. 181-182 on over-
franked philatelic cover   32.50
Nos. 183-184 on over-
franked philatelic cover   110.00

Issued: Nos. 181-182, 4/14; Nos. 183-184,
8/23.

Souvenir Sheet

Design from Base of Roman
Column — A34

1937, Aug. 23   Engr.   Wmk. 217
185 A34   5 l steel blue   15.00   12.50
   Never hinged   25.00
   On first day cover

Unveiling of the Roman Column at San
Marino. The date "1636 d. F. R." means the
1,636th year since the founding of the
republic.
No. 185 was privately surcharged "+ 10 L
1941."

Souvenir Sheets

Abraham Lincoln — A35

1938, Apr. 7   **Wmk. 217**   **Perf. 13**
186	A35	3 l dark blue	2.75	2.75
		Never hinged	3.75	
187	A35	5 l rose red	18.00	18.00
		Never hinged	37.50	
		Nos. 186-187 on first day cover		47.50

Dedication of a Lincoln bust, Sept. 3, 1937.

SEMI-POSTAL STAMPS

Regular Issue of 1903 Surcharged

a   b

1917, Dec. 15   **Wmk. 140**   **Perf. 14**
B1	A10(a)	25c on 2c violet	15.00	15.00
		Never hinged	37.50	
B2	A11(b)	50c on 2 l violet	60.00	60.00
		Never hinged	150.00	
		Nos. B1-B2 on overfranked philatelic cover		350.00

Statue of
Liberty — SP1

View of
San Marino
SP2

1918, June 1   **Typo.**
B3	SP1	2c dl vio & blk	3.75	3.75
		Never hinged	9.50	
B4	SP1	5c bl grn & blk	3.75	3.75
		Never hinged	9.50	
B5	SP1	10c lake & blk	3.75	3.75
		Never hinged	9.50	
B6	SP1	20c brn org & blk	3.75	3.75
		Never hinged	9.50	
B7	SP1	25c ultra & blk	3.75	3.75
		Never hinged	9.50	
B8	SP1	45c yel brn & blk	3.75	3.75
		Never hinged	9.50	
B9	SP2	1 l bl grn & blk	20.00	24.00
		Never hinged	50.00	
B10	SP2	2 l vio & blk	17.00	21.00
		Never hinged	42.50	
B11	SP2	3 l claret & blk	17.00	21.00
		Never hinged	42.50	
		Nos. B3-B11 (9)	76.50	88.50
		Set on overfranked philatelic cover		300.00

These stamps were sold at an advance of 5c each over face value, the receipts from that source being devoted to the support of a hospital for Italian soldiers.

For surcharges see Nos. 89-92.

Nos. B6-B8
Overprinted

1918, Dec. 12
B12	SP1	20c brn org & blk	6.00	6.00
		Never hinged	15.00	
B13	SP1	25c ultra & blk	6.00	6.00
		Never hinged	15.00	
B14	SP1	45c yel brn & blk	6.00	6.00
		Never hinged	15.00	

Nos. B9-
B11 Ovptd.

B15	SP2	1 l blue grn & blk	10.50	10.50
		Never hinged	25.00	
B16	SP2	2 l violet & blk	19.00	20.00
		Never hinged	47.50	
B17	SP2	3 l claret & blk	19.00	20.00
		Never hinged	47.50	
		Nos. B12-B17 (6)	66.50	68.50
		Set on overfranked philatelic cover		240.00

Celebration of Italian Victory over Austria.
Inverted overprints were privately produced.

Coat of   Liberty
Arms   SP4
SP3

1923, Sept. 20   **Engr.**
B18	SP3	5c + 5c olive grn	.80	.80
		Never hinged	2.00	
B19	SP3	10c + 5c orange	.80	.80
		Never hinged	2.00	
B20	SP3	15c + 5c dk green	.80	.80
		Never hinged	2.00	
B21	SP3	25c + 5c brn lake	.80	.80
		Never hinged	2.00	
B22	SP3	40c + 5c vio brn	4.00	4.00
		Never hinged	10.00	
B23	SP3	50c + 5c gray	2.40	.80
		Never hinged	6.00	
B24	SP4	1 l + 5c blk & bl	8.00	8.00
		Never hinged	20.00	
		Nos. B18-B24 (7)	17.60	16.00
		Set on overfranked philatelic cover		145.00

AIR POST STAMPS

View of
San
Marino
AP1

Wmk. 217
1931, June 11   **Engr.**   **Perf. 12**
C1	AP1	50c blue grn	32.50	22.50
		Never hinged	80.00	
C2	AP1	80c red	32.50	22.50
		Never hinged	80.00	
C3	AP1	1 l bister brn	9.50	11.00
		Never hinged	24.00	
C4	AP1	2 l brt violet	9.50	11.00
		Never hinged	24.00	
C5	AP1	2.60 l Prus bl	65.00	80.00
		Never hinged	160.00	
C6	AP1	3 l dk gray	55.00	62.50
		Never hinged	140.00	
C7	AP1	5 l olive grn	9.50	11.00
		Never hinged	24.00	
C8	AP1	7.70 l dk brown	19.00	22.50
		Never hinged	47.50	
C9	AP1	9 l dp orange	19.00	22.50
		Never hinged	47.50	
C10	AP1	10 l dk blue	400.00	525.00
		Never hinged	1,000.	
		Nos. C1-C10 (10)	651.50	790.50

Set, never hinged	1,625.	
Set on overfranked philatelic cover	2,150.	
Exist imperf.		

Graf Zeppelin Issue
Stamps of Type AP1 Surcharged in
Blue or Black

1933, Apr. 28
C11	AP1	3 l on 50c org	9.50	165.00
		Never hinged	24.00	
		On flown cover		300.00
C12	AP1	5 l on 80c ol grn	47.50	165.00
		Never hinged	110.00	
		On flown cover		350.00
C13	AP1	10 l on 1 l dk bl (Bk)	47.50	210.00
		Never hinged	110.00	
		On flown cover		700.00
C14	AP1	12 l on 2 l yel brn	47.50	260.00
		Never hinged	110.00	
		On flown cover		1,150.
C15	AP1	15 l on 2.60 l dl red (Bk)	47.50	280.00
		Never hinged	110.00	
		On flown cover		1,400.
C16	AP1	20 l on 3 l bl grn (Bk)	47.50	450.00
		Never hinged	110.00	
		On flown cover		1,400.
		Nos. C11-C16 (6)	247.00	1,530.
		Set, never hinged	600.00	
		Set, on single over-franked flight cover		4,500.

Exist imperf.

Nos. C1 and C2 Surcharged

1936, Apr. 14
C17	AP1	75c on 50c blue grn	2.40	2.40
		Never hinged	6.00	
C18	AP1	75c on 80c red	14.00	14.00
		Never hinged	35.00	
		Set, never hinged	40.00	
		Set, on single overfranked flight cover		65.00

SPECIAL DELIVERY STAMPS

SD1

Unwmk.
1907, Apr. 25   **Engr.**   **Perf. 12**
E1	SD1	25c carmine	35.00	17.50
		Never hinged	110.00	

For surcharges see Nos. E3, E5.

Type of Regular Issue
of 1903 Overprinted

Perf. 14½x14
1923, May 30   **Wmk. 140**
E2	A11	60c violet	1.75	1.25
		Never hinged	3.75	

For surcharge see No. 103.

Type of 1907 Issue Surcharged

1923, July 26   **Perf. 14**
E3	SD1	60c on 25c carmine	1.50	1.25
		Never hinged	3.75	
a.		Vert. pair, imperf. between	275.00	
		Never hinged	550.00	

No. E2 Surcharged

1926, Nov. 25   **Perf. 14½x14**
E4	A11	1.25 l on 60c violet	1.90	1.90
		Never hinged	5.00	

No. E3 Surcharged

1927, Sept. 15
E5	SD1	1.25 l on 60c on 25c	1.50	1.25
		Never hinged	3.75	
a.		Inverted surcharge	175.00	
		Never hinged	350.00	
b.		Vert. pair, imperf. between	800.00	
		Never hinged	1,600.	
c.		Double surcharge	190.00	
		Never hinged	380.00	

Statue of Liberty and View of San
Marino — SD2

Wmk. 217
1929, Aug. 29   **Engr.**   **Perf. 12**
E6	SD2	1.25 l green	.65	.50
		Never hinged	1.90	

Overprinted in Red

E7	SD2	2.50 l deep blue	1.00	1.00
		Never hinged	3.00	

SEMI-POSTAL SPECIAL DELIVERY
STAMP

SPSD1

Wmk. 140
1923, Sept. 20   **Engr.**   **Perf. 14**
EB1	SPSD1	60c + 5c brown red	1.75	1.75
		Never hinged	4.25	

POSTAGE DUE STAMPS

D1   D2

D3   D4

Wmk. 140

1897-1920   Typo.   *Perf. 14*

J1	D1	5c bl grn & dk brn	1.25	1.25
		Never hinged	3.25	
		On cover		12.00
J2	D2	10c bl grn & dk brn	1.25	1.25
		Never hinged	3.25	
		On cover		12.00
a.		Numerals inverted	375.00	—
J3	D2	30c grn & dk brn	3.25	3.00
		Never hinged	6.50	
		On cover		12.00
J4	D2	50c bl grn & dk brn	3.50	3.50
		Never hinged	8.00	
		On cover		27.50
a.		Numerals inverted	375.00	—
J5	D2	60c bl grn & dk brn	40.00	20.00
		Never hinged	95.00	
		On cover		100.00
J6	D3	1 l claret & dk brn	7.50	7.50
		Never hinged	19.00	
		On cover		47.50
J7	D4	3 l claret & brn ('20)	20.00	25.00
		Never hinged	65.00	
		On cover		160.00
J8	D4	5 l claret & dk brn	80.00	55.00
		Never hinged	190.00	
		On cover		275.00
J9	D2	10 l claret & dk brn	40.00	35.00
		Never hinged	80.00	
		On cover		225.00
		Nos. J1-J9 (9)	196.75	151.50

See Nos. J10-J36, J61. For surcharges see Nos. J37-J60, J64.

1924

J10	D1	5c rose & brown	1.75	1.75
		Never hinged	4.75	
		On cover		24.00
J11	D2	10c rose & brown	1.75	1.75
		Never hinged	4.75	
		On cover		16.00
J12	D2	30c rose & brown	3.00	3.00
		Never hinged	8.00	
		On cover		24.00
J13	D2	50c rose & brown	3.25	3.25
		Never hinged	9.50	
		On cover		27.50
J14	D2	60c rose & brown	12.00	12.00
		Never hinged	32.50	
		On cover		80.00
J15	D3	1 l green & brown	20.00	20.00
		Never hinged	47.50	
		On cover		120.00
J16	D4	3 l green & brown	55.00	55.00
		Never hinged	130.00	
		On cover		360.00
J17	D4	5 l green & brown	70.00	70.00
		Never hinged	160.00	
		On cover		440.00
J18	D2	10 l green & brown	325.00	325.00
		Never hinged	750.00	
		Nos. J10-J18 (9)	491.75	491.75

Postage Due Types of 1897 and

D5

1925-39   *Perf. 14*

J19	D1	5c blue & brn	1.50	.75
		Never hinged	3.50	
a.		Numerals inverted	300.00	—
J20	D2	10c blue & brn	1.50	.75
		Never hinged	3.50	
a.		Numerals inverted	300.00	—
J21	D2	15c blue & brn ('39)	1.00	.80
		Never hinged	3.50	
J22	D2	20c blue & brn ('39)	1.00	.80
		Never hinged	1.60	
J23	D2	25c blue & brn ('39)	1.50	1.25
		Never hinged	2.40	
J24	D2	30c blue & brn	1.50	.80
		Never hinged	3.25	
J25	D2	40c blue & brn ('39)	7.50	9.00
		Never hinged	19.00	
J26	D2	50c blue & brn	2.50	1.25
		Never hinged	5.00	
a.		Numerals inverted	300.00	—
J27	D2	60c blue & brn	6.50	1.60
		Never hinged	13.00	
J28	D3	1 l buff & brn	9.50	1.60
		Never hinged	19.00	

J29	D4	2 l buff & brn ('39)	4.00	3.00
		Never hinged	9.50	
J30	D4	3 l buff & brn	125.00	50.00
		Never hinged	250.00	
J31	D4	5 l buff & brn	35.00	7.50
		Never hinged	70.00	
J32	D2	10 l buff & brn	47.50	20.00
		Never hinged	95.00	
J33	D5	15 l buff & brn ('28)	5.50	2.00
		Never hinged	8.00	
J34	D5	25 l buff & brn ('28)	67.50	40.00
		Never hinged	135.00	
J35	D5	30 l buff & brn ('28)	11.50	18.00
		Never hinged	29.00	
J36	D5	50 l buff & brn ('28)	13.50	18.00
		Never hinged	32.50	
		Nos. J19-J36 (18)	343.50	177.10

Postage Due Stamps of 1925 Surcharged in Black and Silver

1931, May 18

J37	D1	15c on 5c bl & brn	1.50	1.50
		Never hinged	3.25	
J38	D2	15c on 10c bl & brn	1.50	1.50
		Never hinged	3.25	
J39	D2	15c on 30c bl & brn	1.50	1.50
		Never hinged	3.25	
J40	D1	20c on 5c bl & brn	1.50	1.50
		Never hinged	3.25	
J41	D2	20c on 5c bl & brn	1.50	1.50
		Never hinged	3.25	
J42	D2	20c on 20c bl & brn	1.50	1.50
		Never hinged	3.25	
J43	D1	25c on 5c bl & brn	4.50	3.00
		Never hinged	8.00	
J44	D2	25c on 5c bl & brn	4.50	3.00
		Never hinged	8.00	
J45	D2	25c on 25c bl & brn	25.00	20.00
		Never hinged	65.00	
J46	D1	40c on 5c bl & brn	4.50	1.50
		Never hinged	8.00	
J47	D2	40c on 10c bl & brn	5.50	1.50
		Never hinged	9.50	
J48	D2	40c on 30c bl & brn	5.50	1.50
		Never hinged	9.50	
J49	D1	2 l on 5c bl & brn	55.00	55.00
		Never hinged	130.00	
J50	D2	2 l on 10c bl & brn	140.00	100.00
		Never hinged	300.00	
J51	D2	2 l on 30c bl & brn	90.00	75.00
		Never hinged	190.00	
		Nos. J37-J51 (15)	343.50	269.50

Nos. J19, J24-J25, J30, J34, J33, J22 Surcharged in Black

Perf. 14, 14½x14

1936-40   **Wmk. 140**

J52	D1	10c on 5c ('38)	5.50	3.00
		Never hinged	9.50	
J53	D2	25c on 30c ('38)	17.50	16.00
		Never hinged	35.00	
J54	D1	50c on 5c ('37)	17.50	16.00
		Never hinged	35.00	
J55	D2	1 l on 30c	67.50	11.00
		Never hinged	160.00	
J56	D2	1 l on 40c ('40)	11.50	12.00
		Never hinged	27.50	
J57	D4	1 l on 3 l ('37)	67.50	4.75
		Never hinged	160.00	
J58	D5	1 l on 25 l ('39)	110.00	30.00
		Never hinged	250.00	
J59	D5	2 l on 15 l ('38)	55.00	35.00
		Never hinged	110.00	
J60	D2	3 l on 20c ('40)	35.00	35.00
		Never hinged	90.00	
		Nos. J52-J60 (9)	387.00	162.75

Postage Due Type of 1897

1939   Typo.   *Perf. 14*

J61	D2	5c blue & brown	1.25	.50
		Never hinged	1.60	

Nos. J61 and J36 Surcharged

1940-43

J62	D2	10c on 5c	.80	.40
		Never hinged	1.60	
J63	D2	50c on 5c	4.00	1.50
		Never hinged	6.50	

J64	D5	25 l on 50 l ('43)	3.50	3.50
		Never hinged	9.50	
		Nos. J62-J64 (3)	8.30	5.40

PARCEL POST STAMPS

These stamps were used by affixing them to the way bill so that one half remained on it following the parcel, the other half staying on the receipt given the sender. Most used halves are right halves. Complete stamps were and are obtainable canceled, probably to order. Both unused and used values are for complete stamps. Most exist imperf and are scarce to rare thus.

PP1

Engraved, Typographed
1928, Nov. 22   Unwmk.   *Perf. 12*
Pairs are imperforate between

Q1	PP1	5c blk brn & bl	.60	.60
		Never hinged	1.60	
a.		Imperf.	75.00	
Q2	PP1	10c dk bl & bl	.60	.60
		Never hinged	1.60	
Q3	PP1	20c gray blk & bl	.60	.60
		Never hinged	1.60	
a.		Imperf.	75.00	
Q4	PP1	25c car & blue	.60	.60
		Never hinged	1.60	
Q5	PP1	30c ultra & blue	.60	.60
		Never hinged	1.60	
Q6	PP1	50c orange & bl	.60	.60
		Never hinged	1.60	
Q7	PP1	60c rose & blue	.60	.60
		Never hinged	1.60	
Q8	PP1	1 l violet & brn	.60	.60
		Never hinged	1.60	
a.		Imperf.	75.00	
Q9	PP1	2 l green & brn	1.50	1.00
		Never hinged	3.25	
Q10	PP1	3 l bister & brn	1.75	1.25
		Never hinged	4.00	
Q11	PP1	4 l gray & brn	2.25	1.50
		Never hinged	4.75	
Q12	PP1	10 l rose lilac & brn	4.75	3.00
		Never hinged	9.50	
Q13	PP1	12 l red brn & brn	18.00	18.00
		Never hinged	35.00	
Q14	PP1	15 l olive grn & brn	27.50	27.50
		Never hinged	55.00	
a.		Imperf.	75.00	
Q15	PP1	20 l brn vio & brn	45.00	45.00
		Never hinged	90.00	
		Nos. Q1-Q15 (15)	105.55	102.05

Halves Used

Q1-Q8	.25
Q9-Q10	.25
Q11	.25
Q12	.35
Q13	.65
Q14	2.75
Q15	3.00

SARAWAK
sə-'rä-ˌwäˌ

LOCATION — Northwestern part of the island of Borneo, bordering on the South China Sea
GOVT. — British Crown Colony
AREA — 48,250 sq. mi. (approx.)
POP. — 975,918 (1970)
CAPITAL — Kuching

The last ruling Raja, who retired in 1946 when he ceded Sarawak to the British Crown, was Sir Charles Vyner Brooke, an Englishman. He inherited the title from his father, Sir Charles Johnson Brooke, who in turn received it from his uncle, Sir James Brooke. The title of Raja was conferred on Sir James by Raja Muda Hassim after Sir James had aided him in subduing a rebellion. The title and right of succession were

---

duly recognized by the Sultan of Brunei and by Great Britain.

100 Cents = 1 Dollar

> **Catalogue values for unused stamps in this country are for Never Hinged items, beginning with Scott 155.**

Watermarks

Wmk. 47 —   Wmk. 71 —
Multiple Rosettes   Rosette

Wmk. 231 —
Oriental Crown

Unused examples of Nos. 1-7, 25 and 32-35 are valued without gum. Stamps with original gum are worth more.

Sir James
Brooke — A1

Unwmk.
1869, Mar. 1   Litho.   *Perf. 11*

1	A1	3c brown, *yellow*	57.50	240.00
		On cover		

Covers: Only one authenticated cover is recorded with No. 1.

Sir Charles Johnson
Brooke — A2

1871, Jan.

2	A2	3c brown, *yellow*	3.00	4.00
		On cover		
a.		Vertical pair, imperf between	600.00	
b.		Horizontal pair, imperf between	1,000.	
c.		Period after "THREE"	70.00	85.00

No. 2 surcharged "TWO CENTS" is believed to be bogus.

There are a number of lithographic flaws, including narrow A, "period" after THREE, etc. Imperfs. of Nos. 1, 2 are proofs.

A papermaker's watermark, "LNL," usually appears once or twice in each pane. For surcharges see Nos. 25, 32.

Covers: Only one authenticated cover is recorded with No. 2.

1875, Jan. 1   *Perf. 12*

3	A2	2c gray lilac, *lilac*	24.00	22.00
4	A2	4c brown, *yellow*	6.50	4.00
b.		Vertical pair, imperf between	925.00	975.00
5	A2	6c green, *green*	5.25	4.50
6	A2	8c blue, *blue*	5.50	6.50
7	A2	12c red, *rose*	11.00	9.00
		Nos. 3-7 (5)	52.25	46.00

Nos. 3-7 have each five varieties of the words of value.

Imperfs are proofs.

A papermaker's watermark usually appears once or twice in each pane of No. on No. 5, "LNL" on N...

Some

For surcharges see Nos. 33-35.

Sir Charles Johnson
Brooke — A4

		1888-97	Typo.		Perf. 14	
8	A4	1c lilac & blk ('92)			5.25	1.60
9	A4	2c lilac & carmine			7.00	5.00
a.		2c pur & rose ('97)			17.50	6.00
10	A4	3c lilac & blue			9.25	5.50
11	A4	4c lilac & yellow			40.00	70.00
12	A4	5c lilac & grn ('91)			34.00	5.00
13	A4	6c lilac & brown			29.00	70.00
14	A4	8c green & car			19.50	6.00
a.		8c green & rose ('97)			34.00	17.50
15	A4	10c grn & vio ('91)			52.50	16.50
16	A4	12c green & blue			20.00	15.00
17	A4	16c gray grn & org ('97)			70.00	95.00
18	A4	25c green & brown ('97)			75.00	52.50
19	A4	32c gray grn & blk ('97)			60.00	75.00
20	A4	50c gray green ('97)			80.00	130.00
21	A4	$1 gray grn & blk ('97)			110.00	110.00
		Nos. 8-21 (14)			611.50	657.10

No. 21 shows the numeral on white tablet. Three higher values — $2, $5, $10 — were prepared but not issued. Value $950 each. For surcharges see Nos. 22-24, 26-27.

Nos. 14 and 16 Surcharged in Black

No. 22

No. 23

No. 24

		1889-91			
22	A4	2c on 8c		4.25	9.75
a.		Double surcharge		525.00	
b.		Pair, one without surcharge		8,500.	
c.		Inverted surcharge		4,500.	
23	A4	5c on 12c ('91)		35.00	60.00
a.		Double surcharge		1,400.	1,400.
b.		Pair, one without surcharge		13,000.	
c.		No period after "C"		45.00	70.00
d.		Without "C"		850.00	975.00
e.		Double surch., one vert.		4,250.	
24	A4	5c on 12c ('91)		350.00	375.00
a.		No period after "C"		190.00	200.00
b.		Double surcharge		1,500.	
c.		"C" omitted		1,200.	1,300.

No. 2 Surcharged in Black

		1892, May 23			Perf. 11	
25	A2	1c on 3c brown, yel			2.50	3.00
b.		Without bar			375.00	275.00
c.		Period after "THREE"			57.50	70.00
d.		Double surcharge			475.00	550.00
e.		Vertical pair, imperf between			800.00	
f.		Vertical pair, imperf horiz.			800.00	

Examples of No. 25b must be from the first printing, wherein the bar was applied after the

surcharge. Examples of No. 25 with parts of the surcharge and/or bar omitted are stamps that had gum on the face prior to the surcharging operation. The ink was removed when the gum was washed off.

No. 10 Surcharged in Black

e

f

		1892			Perf. 14	
26	A4(e)	1c on 3c lil & bl			3.75	3.75
a.		No period after "cent"			275.00	300.00
27	A4(f)	1c on 3c lil & bl			80.00	50.00
b.		Double surcharge			800.00	850.00

Issued: #26, Feb.; #27, Jan. 12.

Sir Charles Johnson Brooke
A11   A12

A13   A14

		1895, Jan. 1	Engr.	Perf. 11½, 12	
28	A11	2c red brn		17.50	9.75
a.		Perf. 12½		27.00	5.00
b.		Vertical pair, imperf between		650.00	
c.		Horizontal pair, imperf between		500.00	
d.		As "a," horiz. pair, imperf between		750.00	
29	A12	4c black		17.50	3.75
a.		Horizontal pair, imperf between		875.00	
30	A13	6c violet		20.00	9.75
31	A14	8c deep green		45.00	6.00
		Nos. 28-31 (4)		100.00	29.25

The 2c and 8c imperf are proofs. Perforated stamps of these designs in other colors are color trials, which exist surcharged with new values in pence. These surcharged varieties were used in trial printings of a British South African issue.

Stamps of 1871-75 Surcharged in Black or Red

		1899			Perf. 11	
32	A2	2c on 3c brown, yel			3.75	2.00
a.		Period after "THREE"			90.00	90.00
b.		Vertical pair, imperf between			1,000.	
					Perf. 12	
33	A2	2c on 12c red, rose			3.75	4.50
a.		Inverted surcharge			1,000.	1,400.
34	A2	4c on 6c green, grn (R)			60.00	110.00
35	A2	4c on 8c blue, bl (R)			9.25	14.00
		Nos. 32-35 (4)			76.75	130.50

Sir Charles J.
Brooke — A16

		1899-1908	Typo.	Perf. 14	
36	A16	1c blue & car ('01)		1.60	1.35
a.		1c ultra & pink		12.00	3.75
37	A16	2c gray green		2.25	1.00
38	A16	3c dull violet ('08)		22.50	.75
39	A16	4c aniline carmine		2.75	.25
a.		4c rose ('99)		17.00	2.90
40	A16	8c yellow & black		2.75	.90
41	A16	10c ultra		5.00	1.10
42	A16	12c light violet ('99)		7.00	5.00
a.		12c bright purple ('05)		50.00	13.00
43	A16	16c org brn & grn		8.50	1.90
44	A16	20c brn ol & vio ('00)		7.00	7.50
45	A16	25c brown & ultra		11.00	7.00
46	A16	50c ol grn & brn		30.00	40.00
47	A16	$1 rose & green		100.00	130.00
a.		$1 pink & pale green		100.00	140.00
		Nos. 36-47 (12)		200.35	196.75

A 5c was prepared but not issued. Value $15.

		1901		Wmk. 71	
48	A16	2c gray green		50.00	19.00

Sir Charles Vyner
Brooke — A17

		1918-23		Unwmk.	
50	A17	1c slate bl & rose		2.60	3.25
51	A17	2c deep green		3.00	1.75
52	A17	2c violet ('23)		2.25	3.00
53	A17	3c violet brown		3.75	3.00
54	A17	3c dp grn ('22)		3.25	1.40
55	A17	4c carmine rose		8.00	4.00
56	A17	4c purple brn ('23)		2.25	2.50
57	A17	5c orange ('23)		2.50	2.75
58	A17	6c lake brown ('22)		1.75	1.60
59	A17	8c yellow & blk		14.00	70.00
60	A17	8c car brown ('22)		5.25	35.00
61	A17	10c ultra		5.00	5.00
a.		10c blue		5.00	5.00
62	A17	10c black ('23)		3.50	4.75
63	A17	12c violet		19.00	45.00
64	A17	12c ultra ('22)		12.50	21.00
65	A17	16c brn & blue grn		7.00	8.50
66	A17	20c olive bis & vio		9.50	7.50
a.		20c olive green & violet		8.00	7.50
67	A17	25c brown & blue		4.75	22.00
68	A17	30c bis & gray ('22)		4.25	4.75
69	A17	50c olive grn & rose		11.50	17.00
70	A17	$1 car rose & grn		32.00	32.50
		Nos. 50-70 (21)		157.60	296.25

In 1918 a supply of the 1c (No. 50) had the value tablet printed, by error, in slate blue instead of rose. It is officially stated that this stamp was never issued and had no franking power. Value $22.

The $1 denomination shows numeral of value in color on white tablet.

Nos. 61 and 63 Surcharged

1st Printing — Bars 1¼mm apart.
2nd Printing — Bars ¾mm apart.

		1923, Jan.			
77	A17	1c on 10c ultra		16.50	62.50
a.		"cnet"		450.00	975.00
b.		Bars ¾mm apart		160.00	450.00
78	A17	2c on 12c violet		11.00	47.50
a.		Bars ¾mm apart		92.50	300.00

Type of 1918 Issue

		1928-29	Typo.	Wmk. 47	
79	A17	1c slate blue & rose		1.75	.40
80	A17	2c dull violet		2.75	1.40
81	A17	3c deep green		4.00	5.75
82	A17	4c purple brown		2.10	.25
83	A17	5c orange ('29)		14.00	5.75
84	A17	6c brown lake		1.50	.35
85	A17	8c carmine		4.00	27.50
86	A17	10c black		2.00	1.40
87	A17	12c ultra		4.00	37.50
88	A17	16c dp brn & bl grn		4.00	4.50
89	A17	20c dp olive & vio		4.00	8.00
90	A17	25c dk brown & ultra		6.50	9.75
91	A17	30c olive bis & gray		5.50	11.50
92	A17	50c olive grn & rose		13.00	24.00
93	A17	$1 car rose & grn		20.00	27.50
		Nos. 79-93 (15)		89.10	165.55
		Set, never hinged		170.00	

Sir Charles Vyner Brooke
A18   A19

		1932, Jan. 1	Engr.	Wmk. 231	Perf. 12½	
94	A18	1c indigo			1.00	1.10
95	A18	2c dark green			1.25	2.25
96	A18	3c deep violet			5.00	1.10
97	A18	4c deep orange			10.00	.85
98	A18	5c brown lake			8.50	1.40
99	A18	6c deep red			9.75	11.00
100	A18	8c orange yel			11.00	9.75
101	A18	10c black			2.75	3.75
102	A18	12c violet blue			5.00	11.00
103	A18	15c orange brown			8.25	11.00
104	A18	20c violet & org			8.00	9.00
105	A18	25c org brn & yel			15.00	25.00
106	A18	30c org red & ol brn			12.50	35.00
107	A18	50c olive grn & red			17.50	15.00
108	A18	$1 car & green			25.00	40.00
		Nos. 94-108 (15)			140.50	177.20

		1934-41		Unwmk.	Perf. 12	
109	A19	1c brown violet			1.50	.25
110	A19	2c blue green			1.75	.25
111	A19	2c black ('41)			4.75	1.75
112	A19	3c black			1.40	.25
113	A19	3c blue grn ('41)			8.00	5.00
114	A19	4c magenta			2.25	.25
115	A19	5c violet			2.25	.25
116	A19	6c deep rose			3.00	.70
117	A19	6c red brn ('41)			8.75	9.00
118	A19	8c red brown			2.50	.25
119	A19	8c dp rose ('41)			9.25	.25
120	A19	10c red			4.25	.45
121	A19	12c deep ultra			3.50	.30
122	A19	12c orange ('41)			7.50	6.25
123	A19	15c orange			7.50	12.00
124	A19	15c deep blue ('41)			9.75	20.00
125	A19	20c dp rose & olive			7.50	1.50
126	A19	25c orange & vio			7.50	2.00
127	A19	30c violet & red brn			7.75	3.25
128	A19	50c red & violet			9.00	1.00
129	A19	$1 dk brn & red			4.00	1.00
130	A19	$2 violet & mag			24.00	24.00
131	A19	$3 bl grn & rose			45.00	50.00
132	A19	$4 red & ultra			45.00	80.00
133	A19	$5 red brn & red			65.00	85.00
134	A19	$10 orange & blk			30.00	85.00
		Nos. 109-134 (26)			322.65	389.95

Issue dates: May 1, 1934, Mar. 1, 1941. For overprints see #135-154, 159-173, N1-N22.

Stamps of 1934-41
Overprinted in Black
or Red

1945, Dec. 17

135	A19	1c brown violet	.85	.70
136	A19	2c black (R)	2.00	1.40
137	A19	3c blue green	.85	1.75
138	A19	4c magenta	1.90	.35
139	A19	5c violet (R)	2.75	1.10
140	A19	6c red brown	2.40	.90
141	A19	8c deep rose	9.50	20.00
142	A19	10c red	1.10	.90
143	A19	12c orange	2.75	4.25
144	A19	15c deep blue	4.75	.45
145	A19	20c dp rose & ol	2.75	4.00
146	A19	25c org & vio (R)	3.00	3.00
147	A19	30c vio & red brn	5.50	3.00
148	A19	50c red & violet	1.00	.40
149	A19	$1 dk brn & red	1.90	3.75
150	A19	$2 violet & mag	6.75	17.50
151	A19	$3 bl grn & rose	20.00	90.00
152	A19	$4 red & ultra	26.00	60.00
153	A19	$5 red brn & red	140.00	250.00
154	A19	$10 org & blk (R)	125.00	250.00
		Nos. 135-154 (20)	360.75	713.35
		Set, never hinged	525.00	

> Catalogue values for unused
> stamps in this section, from this
> point to the end of the section, are
> for Never Hinged items.

Sir James Brooke, Sir Charles V.
Brooke and Sir Charles J. Brooke
A20

1946, May 18

155	A20	8c dark carmine	3.25	1.25
156	A20	15c dark blue	3.50	2.50
157	A20	50c red & black	3.75	3.50
158	A20	$1 sepia & black	4.00	32.50
		Nos. 155-158 (4)	14.50	39.75

Type of 1934-41
Overprinted in Blue or
Red

1947, Apr. 16   Wmk. 4   Perf. 12

159	A19	1c brown violet	.25	.30
160	A19	2c black (R)	.25	.25
161	A19	3c blue green (R)	.25	.25
162	A19	4c magenta	.25	.25
163	A19	6c red brown	.30	1.00
164	A19	8c deep rose	1.00	.25
165	A19	10c red	.35	.25
166	A19	12c orange	.70	1.10
167	A19	15c deep blue (R)	.50	.55
168	A19	20c dp rose & ol (R)	2.25	.65
169	A19	25c orange & vio (R)	.65	.55
170	A19	50c red & violet (R)	1.25	.90
171	A19	$1 dk brown & red	1.50	1.50
172	A19	$2 violet & magenta	3.75	4.25
173	A19	$5 red brown & red	4.50	4.00
		Nos. 159-173 (15)	17.75	16.05

Common Design Types
pictured following the introduction.

Silver Wedding Issue
Common Design Types

1948, Oct. 25   Photo.   Perf. 14x14½

174	CD304	8c scarlet	.40	.40

Perf. 11½x11

Engraved; Name Typographed

175	CD305	$5 light brown	52.50	55.00

UPU Issue
Common Design Types
Engr.; Name Typo. on 15c, 25c
Perf. 13½, 11x11½

1949, Oct. 10   Wmk. 4

176	CD306	10c rose car	1.00	2.00
177	CD307	15c indigo	3.50	2.50
178	CD308	25c green	2.00	1.50
179	CD309	50c violet	2.00	6.50
		Nos. 176-179 (4)	9.00	11.10

Troides
Brookiana
A21

Western
Tarsier — A22

Designs: 3c, Kayan tomb. 4c, Kayan girl and
boy. 6c, Bead work. 8c, Dyak dancer. 10c,
Scaly anteater. 12c, Kenyah boys. 15c, Fire
making. 20c, Kelemantan rice barn. 25c, Pepper vines. 50c, Iban woman. $1, Kelabit
smithy. $2, Map of Sarawak. $5, Arms of
Sarawak.

Perf. 11½x11, 11x11½

1950, Jan. 3   Engr.

180	A21	1c black	.75	.30
181	A22	2c orange red	.40	.50
182	A22	3c green	.40	.80
183	A22	4c brown	.65	.25
184	A22	6c aquamarine	.45	.25
185	A21	8c red	1.00	.30
186	A21	10c orange	2.50	6.00
187	A21	12c purple	4.50	1.75
188	A21	15c deep blue	3.50	.25
189	A21	20c red org & brn	2.75	.50
190	A21	25c carmine & grn	4.25	.60
191	A22	50c purple & brn	7.00	.45
192	A21	$1 dk brn & bl grn	26.00	5.00
193	A21	$2 rose car & blue	37.50	18.50

Engr. and Typo.

194	A21	$5 dp vio, blk, red & yel	30.00	18.50
		Nos. 180-194 (15)	121.65	53.95

1952, Feb. 1

195	A21	10c orange (Map)	2.75	.80

OCCUPATION STAMPS

Issued under Japanese Occupation

Stamps of 1934-41
Handstamped in Violet

1942   Unwmk.   Perf. 12

N1	A19	1c brown violet	45.00	85.00
N2	A19	2c blue green	125.00	200.00
N3	A19	2c black	150.00	160.00
N3A	A19	3c black	500.00	500.00
N4	A19	3c blue green	80.00	110.00
N5	A19	4c magenta	110.00	120.00
N6	A19	5c violet	130.00	140.00
N7	A19	6c deep rose	180.00	180.00
N8	A19	6c red brown	120.00	130.00
N8A	A19	8c red brown	450.00	450.00
N9	A19	8c deep rose	100.00	120.00
N10	A19	10c red	110.00	130.00
N11	A19	12c deep ultra	190.00	200.00
N12	A19	12c orange	190.00	200.00
N12A	A19	15c orange	550.00	550.00
N13	A19	15c deep blue	150.00	160.00
N14	A19	20c dp rose & ol	90.00	120.00
N15	A19	25c orange & vio	130.00	150.00
N16	A19	30c violet & red brn	90.00	120.00
N17	A19	50c red & violet	100.00	120.00
N18	A19	$1 dk brown & red	150.00	170.00
N19	A19	$2 violet & mag	325.00	400.00
N19A	A19	$3 blue grn & rose	2,750.	2,750.
N20	A19	$4 red & ultra	325.00	475.00
N21	A19	$5 red brown & red	325.00	475.00
N22	A19	$10 orange & blk	325.00	475.00
		Nos. N1-N22 (26)	7,790.	8,690.

Stamps overprinted with Japanese characters in oval frame or between 2 vertical black
lines were not for paying postage.

SASENO

ˌsə-ˈzä-ˌnō

LOCATION — An island in the Adriatic
Sea, lying at the entrance of Valona
Bay, Albania
GOVT. — Italian possession
AREA — 2 sq. mi.

Italy occupied this Albanian islet in
1914, and returned it to Albania in
1947.

100 Centesimi = 1 Lira

> Used values in italics are for pos-
> tally used stamps. CTO's sell for
> about the same as unused, hinged
> stamps.

Italian Stamps of 1901-
22 Overprinted

1923   Wmk. 140   Perf. 14

1	A48	10c claret	30.00	82.50
		Never hinged	72.50	
2	A48	15c slate	30.00	82.50
		Never hinged	72.50	
3	A50	20c brown orange	30.00	82.50
		Never hinged	72.50	
4	A49	25c blue	30.00	82.50
		Never hinged	72.50	
5	A49	30c yellow brown	30.00	82.50
		Never hinged	72.50	
6	A49	50c violet	30.00	82.50
		Never hinged	72.50	
7	A49	60c carmine	30.00	82.50
		Never hinged	72.50	
8	A46	1 l brown & green	30.00	82.50
		Never hinged	72.50	
a.		Double overprint	450.00	
		Nos. 1-8 (8)	240.00	660.00
		Set, never hinged	575.00	

Superseded by postage stamps of Italy.

SAUDI ARABIA

ˈsau-dē ə-ˈrā-bē-ə

LOCATION — Southwestern Asia, on
the Arabian Peninsula between the
Red Sea and the Persian Gulf
GOVT. — Kingdom
AREA — 927,000 sq. mi.
POP. — 8,400,000 (est. 1984)
CAPITAL — Riyadh

In 1916 the Grand Sherif of Mecca
declared the Sanjak of Hejaz independent of Turkish rule. In 1925, Ibn Saud,
then Sultan of the Nejd, captured the
Hejaz after a prolonged siege of Jedda,
the last Hejaz stronghold.

The resulting Kingdom of the Hejaz
and Nejd was renamed Saudi Arabia in
1932.

**40 Paras = 1 Piaster = 1 Guerche
(Garch, Qirsh)**

11 Guerche = 1 Riyal (1928)

110 Guerche = 1 Sovereign (1931)

HEJAZ

Sherifate of Mecca

Adapted from Carved Door Panels of
Mosque El Salih Talay, Cairo — A1

Taken from Page of Koran in Mosque
of El Sultan Barquq, Cairo — A2

Taken from Details of an Ancient
Prayer Niche in the Mosque of El Amri
at Qus in Upper Egypt — A3

Perf. 10, 12

1916, Oct.   Unwmk.   Typo.

L1	A1	¼pi green	50.00	32.50
L2	A2	½pi red	50.00	30.00
a.		Perf. 10	225.00	90.00
L3	A3	1pi blue	20.00	11.00
		On cover		150.00
a.		Perf. 12	160.00	140.00
b.		Perf. 10x12		1,200.
		Nos. L1-L3 (3)	120.00	73.50

Exist imperf. Forged perf. exist.
See Nos. L5-L7, L10-L12. For overprints
see Nos. L16-L18, L26-L28, L52-L54, L57-
L59, L61-L66, L67, L70-L72, L77-L81, 37.

Central Design Adapted from a Koran
Design for a Tomb. Background is
from Stone Carving on Entrance Arch
to the Ministry of Wakfs — A4

1916-17   Roulette 20

L4	A4	⅛pi orange ('17)	5.00	1.40
		Never hinged	6.00	
		On cover		150.00
L5	A1	¼pi green	6.00	1.40
		Never hinged	7.00	
		On cover		200.00
L6	A2	½pi red	9.00	1.40
		Never hinged	10.00	
L7	A3	1pi blue	9.50	1.40
		Never hinged	10.50	
		On cover, single franking		100.00
		Nos. L4-L7 (4)	29.50	5.60

See No. L9. For overprints & surcharge see
Nos. L15a, L16c, L17b, L18d, L25, L51, L56,
L69, 33.

Adapted from Stucco Work above
Entrance to Cairo R. R. Station
A5

Adapted
from First
Page of the
Koran of
Sultan
Farag — A6

1917   Serrate Roulette 13

L8	A5	1pa lilac brown	4.10	1.40
		Never hinged	5.00	
		On cover		75.00
L9	A4	⅛pi orange	4.75	1.40
		Never hinged	5.75	
		On cover		75.00
L10	A1	¼pi green	5.25	1.40
		Never hinged	6.25	
		On cover		75.00

L11	A2	½pi red	5.75	1.40
		Never hinged	6.75	
		On cover		150.00
L12	A3	1pi blue	6.00	1.40
		Never hinged	7.00	
		On cover, single franking		100.00
L13	A6	2pi magenta	10.00	9.00
		Never hinged	12.00	
		On cover, single franking		425.00
		Nos. L8-L13 (6)	35.85	16.00

Designs A1-A6 are inscribed "Hejaz Postage."

For overprints and surcharge see Nos. L14-L31, L55-60, L62, L65--L75, L79a-81.

Kingdom of the Hejaz
Stamps of 1917-18 Overprinted in Black, Red or Brown

1921, Dec. 21   Serrate Roulette 13

L14	A5	1pa lilac brown	65.00	14.00
a.		Date omitted at right	150.00	
b.		Date omitted at left	275.00	
L15	A4	⅛pi orange	35.00	16.00
a.		Inverted overprint	110.00	
b.		Double overprint	225.00	
c.		Roulette 20	800.00	
d.		As "c," invtd. overprint	1,750.	*1,400.*
e.		Double overprint, one inverted	500.00	
f.		Double overprint, both inverted	500.00	
g.		Date omitted at right	100.00	
g.		Date omitted at right	100.00	
L16	A1	¼pi green	35.00	5.50
		On cover		250.00
a.		Inverted overprint	110.00	
b.		Double overprint	225.00	
c.		Roulette 20	800.00	
d.		As "c," invtd. overprint	1,750.	
e.		Double overprint, one inverted	600.00	
f.		Double overprint, both inverted	200.00	
g.		Date omitted at right	100.00	
L17	A2	½pi red	35.00	6.75
		On cover		325.00
a.		Inverted overprint	200.00	77.50
b.		Roulette 20	800.00	
c.		Double overprint	500.00	
d.		Double overprint, both inverted	500.00	
e.		Date omitted at right	100.00	
L18	A3	1pi blue (R)	35.00	6.25
		On cover		325.00
a.		Brown overprint	30.00	18.00
b.		Black overprint	40.00	27.50
c.		As "b," invtd. overprint	400.00	
d.		Roulette 20	800.00	
e.		Date omitted at right	100.00	
L19	A6	2pi magenta	35.00	9.00
a.		Double overprint	*3,500.*	
b.		Date omitted at right	100.00	
c.		As "a," date omitted at right	12,500.	
		Nos. L14-L19 (6)	240.00	57.50

Nos. L15-L17, L18b and L19 exist with date (1340) omitted at left or right side.

All values except No. L15 exist with gold overprint.

No. L19c is unique.

No. L14 With Additional Surcharge

a

b

L22	A5(a)	½pi on 1pa	350.00	125.00
		Never hinged	450.00	
		No gum	50.00	
L23	A5(b)	1pi on 1pa	350.00	125.00
		Never hinged	450.00	
		No gum	50.00	

Forgeries of Nos. L14-L23 abound.

Stamps of 1917-18 Overprinted in Black

1922, Jan. 7

L24	A5	1pa lilac brown	12.50	2.75
a.		Inverted overprint	150.00	
b.		Double overprint	110.00	
c.		Double overprint, one inverted	225.00	
L25	A4	⅛pi orange	20.00	6.25
a.		Inverted overprint	110.00	
b.		Double ovpt., one inverted	225.00	
L26	A1	¼pi green	8.00	2.75
a.		Inverted overprint	110.00	
b.		Double ovpt., one inverted	225.00	
L27	A2	½pi red	10.00	1.75
a.		Inverted overprint	110.00	
b.		Double ovpt., one inverted	225.00	
L28	A3	1pi blue	5.00	.80
a.		Double overprint	95.00	
b.		Inverted overprint	175.00	
L29	A6	2pi magenta	9.00	5.50
a.		Double overprint	175.00	

With Additional Surcharge of New Value

L30	A5(a)	½pi on 1pa lil brn	40.00	14.00
L31	A5(b)	1pi on 1pa lil brn	4.00	.90
		On cover, single franking		325.00
a.		Inverted surcharge	105.00	
b.		Double surcharge	100.00	
c.		Dbl. surch., one invtd., ovpt. invtd.	300.00	
d.		Inverted overprint	115.00	
e.		Inverted overprint and surcharge	225.00	
f.		Inverted overprint, double surcharge	225.00	
g.		Words of surcharge transposed	225.00	
h.		Overprint and surcharge inverted, words of surcharge transposed	500.00	
i.		Right hand character of surcharge inverted	100.00	
		Nos. L24-L31 (8)	108.50	34.70

The 1921 and 1922 overprints read: "The Arab Hashemite Government, 1340."

The overprint on No. L28 in red is bogus. Forgeries abound.

Types A7 and A8
Very fine examples will be somewhat off center but perforations will be clear of the framelines.

Arms of Sherif of Mecca — A7

1922, Feb.   Typo.   Perf. 11½

L32	A7	⅛pi red brown	3.00	.45
		Never hinged	4.00	
L34	A7	½pi red	3.25	.45
		Never hinged	4.50	
		On cover		125.00
L35	A7	1pi dark blue	3.50	.45
		Never hinged	4.75	
		On cover		125.00
L36	A7	1½pi violet	4.00	.45
		Never hinged	5.00	
		On cover, single franking		200.00
L37	A7	2pi orange	5.00	.45
		Never hinged	6.00	
		On cover, single franking		75.00
L38	A7	3pi olive brown	4.00	.45
		Never hinged	5.00	
a.		3pi brown	3.00	.25
		Never hinged	5.00	
L39	A7	5pi olive green	4.25	.55
		Never hinged	5.25	
		Nos. L32-L39 (7)	27.00	3.25

Numerous shades exist. Some values were printed in other colors in 1925 for handstamping by the Nejdi authorities in Mecca. These exist without handstamps.

Exist imperf.

Forgeries exist, usually perf. 11.

Reprints of Nos. L32, L35 exist; paper and shades differ.

See Nos. L48A-L49. For surcharges and overprints see Nos. L40-L48, L76, L82-L159, 7-20, 38A-48, 55A-58A, LJ11-LJ16, LJ26-LJ39, J1-J8, J10-J11, P1-P3, Jordan 64-72, 91, 103-120, J1-J17, O1.

Stamps of 1922 Surcharged with New Values in Arabic

c

d

1923

L40	A7(c)	¼pi on ⅛pi org	40.00	32.50
		brn	60.00	
		On cover		300.00
a.		Double surcharge	150.00	
b.		Double inverted surcharge	375.00	
c.		No gum	40.00	
d.		Double surch., one invtd.	400.00	
		No gum	50.00	
L41	A7(d)	10pi on 5pi ol grn	45.00	27.50
		Never hinged	70.00	
a.		Double surch., one invtd.	200.00	
b.		Inverted surcharge	175.00	

Forgeries exist.

Caliphate Issue

Stamps of 1922 Overprinted in Gold

1924

L42	A7	⅛pi orange brown	5.50	
		Never hinged	6.50	
		On cover		700.00
L43	A7	½pi red	4.00	
		Never hinged	5.00	
L44	A7	1pi dark blue	6.00	—
		Never hinged	7.00	
		On cover		700.00
a.		Inverted overprint	225.00	
L45	A7	1½pi violet	5.75	
		Never hinged	6.75	
		On cover		1,250.
L46	A7	2pi orange	5.25	
		Never hinged	6.25	
		On cover		1,250.
a.		Inverted overprint	225.00	
L47	A7	3pi olive brown	6.00	
		Never hinged	7.00	
L48	A7	5pi olive green	7.00	
		Never hinged	8.00	
a.		Inverted overprint	225.00	
		Nos. L42-L48 (7)	39.50	

Assumption of the Caliphate by King Hussein in Mar., 1924. The overprint reads "In commemoration of the Caliphate, Shaaban, 1342."

The overprint was typographed in black and dusted with "gold" powder while wet. Inverted overprints on other values are forgeries. So-called black overprints are either forgeries or gold overprints with the gold rubbed off. No genuine black overprints are known.

The overprint is 18-20mm wide. The 1st setting of the ½pi is 16mm.

Forgeries exist.

Nos. L43-L44, L46 exist with postage due overprint as on Nos. LJ11-LJ13.

Type of 1922 and

Arms of Sherif of Mecca — A8

1924   Perf. 11½

L48A	A7	¼pi yellow green	7.50	5.75
		Never hinged	9.00	
b.		Tête bêche pair	50.00	
L49	A7	3pi brown red	11.00	9.00
		Never hinged	12.00	
a.		3pi dull red	3.50	4.50
L50	A8	10pi vio & dk brn	7.00	4.50
		Never hinged	8.00	
a.		Center inverted	60.00	55.00
c.		10pi purple & sepia	4.00	4.50
		Nos. L48A-L50 (3)	25.50	19.25

Nos. L48A, L50, L50a exist imperf.

Several printings of Nos. L48A-L50 exist; paper and shades differ.

A plate flaw in position 13 of No. L48A, which appears as a large white gash in the upper left portion of the stamp, exists. Values: unused single, $50; unused tête-bêche pair, $250.

Forgeries exist, usually perf. 11.

For overprint see Nos. L76A, Jordan 121.

Jedda Issues
Stamps of 1916-17 Overprinted

The Jedda overprints on Nos. L51-L159 read: "Al-hukuma al Hejaziyeh, 5 Rabi al'awwal 1343" (The Hejaz Government, October 4, 1924). This is the date of the accession of King Ali. Counterfeits exist of all Jedda overprints.

Jedda issues were also used in Medina and Yambo.

Used values for #L51-L186 and LJ17-LJ39 are for genuine cancels. Privately applied cancels exist for "Mekke" (Mecca, bilingual or all Arabic), Khartoum, Cairo, as well as for Jeddah. Many private cancels have wrong dates, some as early as 1916. These are worth half the used values.

Red Overprint

1925, Jan.   Roulette 20

L51	A4	⅛pi orange	40.00	14.00
a.		Inverted overprint	110.00	
b.		Ovptd. on face and back	225.00	
c.		Normal ovpt. on face, double ovpt. on back	325.00	
L52	A1	¼pi green	40.00	14.00
a.		Inverted overprint	75.00	
b.		Double overprint	125.00	
c.		Double overprint, one invtd.	175.00	
L53	A2	½pi red	90.00	67.50
a.		Inverted overprint	175.00	
L54	A3	1pi blue	40.00	32.50
a.		Inverted overprint	175.00	
b.		Double ovpt., one invtd.	175.00	
		Nos. L51-L53 (3)	170.00	95.50

Serrate Roulette 13

L55	A5	1pa lilac brown	30.00	12.50
a.		Inverted overprint	75.00	
b.		Double overprint	70.00	
c.		Ovptd. on face and back	200.00	
d.		Normal ovpt. on face, double ovpt. on back	150.00	
L56	A4	⅛pi orange	60.00	35.00
a.		Inverted overprint	100.00	
L57	A1	¼pi green	37.50	20.00
a.		Pair, one without overprint	2,000.	
b.		Inverted overprint	55.00	
c.		Double ovpt., one inverted	300.00	
L58	A2	½pi red	55.00	27.50
a.		Inverted overprint	175.00	
L59	A3	1pi blue	60.00	32.50
a.		Inverted overprint	125.00	
L60	A6	2pi magenta	45.00	35.00
a.		Inverted overprint	150.00	
		Nos. L55-L60 (6)	287.50	162.50

Gold Overprint
Roulette 20

L61	A1	¼pi green, gold on red ovpt.	2,250.	
		Never hinged	3,000.	
		No gum	1,000.	
a.		Gold on blue ovpt.	4,000.	7,000.
		On cover front		125,000.

Serrate Roulette 13

L62	A1	¼pi green, gold on red ovpt.	45.00	22.50
a.		Inverted overprint	300.00	

The overprint on No. L61 was typographed in red or blue (No. L62 only in red) and dusted with "gold" powder while wet.

Blue Overprint
Roulette 20

L63	A1	¼pi green	150.00	22.50
a.		Inverted overprint	175.00	
b.		Ovptd. on face and back	250.00	550.00
L64	A2	½pi red, invtd. ovpt.	150.00	80.00
a.		Upright overprint	200.00	

Serrate Roulette 13

L65	A1	¼pi green	35.00	16.00
a.		Inverted overprint	75.00	
b.		Vertical overprint	1,100.	
L66	A2	½pi red	55.00	27.50
a.		Inverted overprint	110.00	
L66B	A6	2pi mag, invtd. ovpt.	1,900.	

Blue overprint on Nos. L4, L8, L9 are bogus.

Same Overprint in Blue on Provisional Stamps of 1922
Overprinted on No. L17

L67	A2	½pi red	2,750.	
		No gum	425.00	

Overprinted on Nos. L24-L29

L68	A5	1pa lilac brn	225.00	160.00
L69	A4	⅛pi orange	2,500.	1,800.
		No gum	375.00	
a.		Inverted overprint	4,500.	
		No gum	120.00	
L70	A1	¼pi green	80.00	65.00
a.		Inverted overprint	800.00	
		No gum	120.00	

L71	A2	½pi red	100.00	*85.00*
a.		Inverted overprint	900.00	
		No gum	135.00	
L72	A3	1pi blue	125.00	*110.00*
L73	A6	2pi magenta	175.00	*160.00*
a.		Inverted overprint	1,500.	
		No gum	225.00	

Same Overprint on Nos. L30 and L31

L74	A5(a)	½pi on 1pa	105.00	*90.00*
L75	A5(b)	1pi on 1pa	90.00	*75.00*
a.		Inverted overprint	800.00	
		No gum	120.00	

Same Overprint in Blue Vertically, Reading Up or Down, on Stamps of 1922-24

Perf. 11½

L76	A7	½pi red	900.00	*900.00*
L76A	A8	10pi vio & dk brn	1,800.	*1,800.*

Nos. L5, L10 Overprinted Reading Up in Blue or Red

(Overprint reads up in illustration.)

Small three-line overprint. Top line 14mm long.

Roulette 20

L77a	*A1*	*¼pi green (Bl)*	*550.00*	*500.00*
L78	A1	¼pi green (R)	500.00	*450.00*

Serrate Roulette 13

L79a	*A1*	*¼pi green (Bl)*	*350.00*	*300.00*
L80	A1	¼pi green (R)	75.00	*60.00*

Overprint Reading Down

Roulette 20

L77	A1	¼pi green (Bl)	200.00	*175.00*

Serrate Roulette 13

L79	A1	¼pi green (Bl)	105.00	*90.00*
L80a	*A1*	*¼pi green (R)*	*225.00*	*200.00*
L80b	*A1*	*¼pi green (R), double ovpt.*	*450.00*	
L80c	*A1*	*¼pi green (R), double ovpt., 1 reading up and 1 reading down*	*500.00*	
L80d	*A1*	*¼pi green (R), triple ovpt., all reading up*	*600.00*	

Nos. L10, L32-L39, L48A, L49a, L50 Overprinted

Large three-line overprint. Top line 16mm long.

Serrate Roulette 13

Red Overprint (vertical, reading down)

L81	A1	¼pi green	1,350.	
a.		Overprint reading up	1,500.	
b.		Overprint horizontal	1,750.	
c.		As "b," overprint inverted	1,750.	

Perf. 11½

Blue Overprint

L82	A7	⅛pi red brown	13.00	*5.50*
a.		Inverted overprint	55.00	
L83	A7	½pi red	15.00	*7.25*
a.		Double overprint	75.00	
b.		Inverted overprint	50.00	*45.00*
c.		Double ovpt., one invtd.	100.00	
d.		Overprint reading up	175.00	
L84	A7	1pi dark blue	600.00	
a.		Inverted overprint	600.00	
L85	A7	1½pi violet	22.50	*11.00*
a.		Inverted overprint	50.00	*45.00*
L86	A7	2pi orange	22.50	*11.00*
		On cover, single franking		*200.00*
a.		Double ovpt., one invtd.	75.00	
b.		Inverted overprint	50.00	
c.		Double overprint	75.00	
L87	A7	3pi olive brown	20.00	*9.00*
a.		Inverted overprint	50.00	
b.		Double ovpt., one invtd.	75.00	
c.		Overprint reading up	180.00	
d.		Dbl. ovpt., both invtd.	105.00	
L88	A7	3pi dull red	24.00	*11.00*
a.		Inverted overprint	50.00	
b.		Double ovpt., one invtd.	75.00	
L89	A7	5pi olive green	21.00	*11.00*
a.		Inverted overprint	55.00	

Some values exist in pairs, one without overprint.

Black Overprint

L90	A7	⅛pi red brown	90.00	
a.		Inverted overprint	175.00	
L91	A7	½pi red	11.00	*4.50*
a.		Inverted overprint	75.00	
L92	A7	1pi dark blue	600.00	
a.		Inverted overprint	600.00	

L93	A7	1½pi violet	26.00	*12.00*
a.		Inverted overprint	75.00	
L94	A7	2pi orange	15.00	*7.25*
		On cover		*125.00*
a.		Inverted overprint	50.00	
L95	A7	3pi olive brown	12.00	*5.50*
a.		Inverted overprint	75.00	*67.50*
		Inverted overprint		
L96	A7	3pi dull red	15.00	*7.25*
a.		Inverted overprint	50.00	
L97	A7	5pi olive green	20.00	*9.00*
a.		Inverted overprint	50.00	

Red Overprint

L98	A7	⅛pi red brn, invtd.	950.00	
L99	A7	¼pi yellow grn	35.00	*16.00*
a.		Tête bêche pair	100.00	
b.		Inverted overprint	50.00	
c.		Tête bêche pair, one with inverted overprint	125.00	
L100	A7	½pi red	1,000.	*500.00*
a.		Inverted overprint	1,100.	*500.00*
L101	A7	1pi dark blue	20.00	*8.00*
a.		Inverted overprint	50.00	
b.		Double ovpt., one invtd.	40.00	
L102	A7	1½pi violet	11.00	*4.50*
a.		Inverted overprint	50.00	
L103	A7	2pi orange	27.50	*12.00*
a.		Inverted overprint	50.00	
b.		Overprint reading up	200.00	
L104	A7	3pi olive brown	27.50	*12.00*
a.		Inverted overprint	50.00	
L105	A7	3pi dull red, invtd.	1,700.	
L106	A7	5pi olive green	20.00	*7.25*
a.		Inverted overprint	50.00	
b.		Overprint reading up	175.00	
c.		Overprint reading down	175.00	
L107	A8	10pi vio & dk brn	35.00	*16.00*
a.		Inverted overprint	50.00	
b.		Center inverted	125.00	
c.		As "b," invtd. ovpt.	175.00	

Nos. L98, L105 with normal overprint are fakes.

Gold Overprint

L108	A7	⅛pi red brown	35.00	*27.50*
		Never hinged	52.50	
L109	A7	½pi red	35.00	*27.50*
		Never hinged	52.50	
L110	A7	1pi dark blue	40.00	*27.50*
		Never hinged	60.00	
L111	A7	1½pi violet	125.00	*110.00*
		Never hinged	190.00	
L112	A7	2pi orange	110.00	*90.00*
		Never hinged	170.00	
L113	A7	3pi olive brown	45.00	*35.00*
		Never hinged	67.50	
L114	A7	3pi dull red	130.00	*100.00*
		Never hinged	195.00	
L115	A7	5pi olive green	105.00	*85.00*
		Never hinged	160.00	
		Nos. L108-L115 (8)	625.00	*502.50*

Inverted overprints are forgeries.

Same Overprint on Nos. L42-L48

Blue Overprint

L116	A7	⅛pi red brown	50.00	*42.50*
a.		Double ovpt., one invtd.	300.00	
L117	A7	½pi red	95.00	*80.00*
L118	A7	1pi dark blue	80.00	*55.00*
L119	A7	1½pi violet	90.00	*65.00*
L120	A7	2pi orange	300.00	*275.00*
a.		Inverted overprint	500.00	
L121	A7	3pi olive brown	125.00	*110.00*
a.		Inverted overprint	225.00	
L122	A7	5pi olive green	50.00	*37.50*
a.		Inverted overprint	250.00	
		Nos. L116-L122 (7)	790.00	*665.00*

Black Overprint

L123	A7	⅛pi red brown	50.00	*42.50*
a.		Inverted overprint	275.00	
L125	A7	1½pi violet	150.00	*140.00*
a.		Inverted overprint	300.00	
L127	A7	3pi olive brown	125.00	*110.00*
a.		Inverted overprint	300.00	
L128	A7	5pi olive green	155.00	*140.00*
a.		Inverted overprint	300.00	
		Nos. L123-L128 (4)	480.00	*432.50*

Red Overprint

L129	A7	1pi dark blue	125.00	*90.00*
		Never hinged	190.00	
L130	A7	1½pi violet	135.00	*110.00*
		Never hinged	205.00	
L131	A7	2pi orange	150.00	*90.00*
		Never hinged	225.00	
		Nos. L129-L131 (3)	410.00	*290.00*

Overprints on stamps or in colors other than those listed are forgeries.

Stamps of 1922-24 Surcharged

a

and Handstamp Surcharged

b — ¼pi

b — 1pi   b — 10pi

1925   Litho.   Perf. 11½

L135	A7	¼pi on ¼pi on ½pi red brn	75.00	*47.50*
b.		1pi on ¼pi on ½pi red brown	225.00	
L136	A7	¼pi on ¼pi on ½pi red	50.00	*30.00*
c.		1pi on ¼pi on ½pi	125.00	*55.00*
L138	A7	1pi on 1pi on 2pi orange	50.00	*30.00*
a.		¼pi on 1pi on 2pi org	125.00	
b.		10pi on 1pi on 2pi org	105.00	
c.		1pi on 1pi on 2pi org	55.00	
d.		1pi on 1pi on 2pi org	105.00	
L139	A7	1pi on 1pi on 3pi ol brn	30.00	*22.50*
L140	A7	1pi on 1pi on 3pi dl red	45.00	*35.00*
b.		¼pi on 1pi on 3pi dl red	125.00	
L141	A7	10pi on 10pi on 5pi ol grn	25.00	*16.00*
b.		1pi on 10 pi on 5 pi	110.00	
		Nos. L135-L141 (6)	275.00	*181.00*

The printed surcharge (a) reads "The Hejaz Government. October 4, 1924." with new denomination in third line. This surcharge alone was used for the first issue (Nos. L135a-L141a). The new denomination was so small and indistinct that its equivalent in larger characters was soon added by handstamp (b) at bottom of each stamp for the second issue (Nos. L135-L141).

The handstamped surcharge (b) is found double, inverted, etc. It is also known in dark violet.

Without Handstamp "b"

L135a	*A7*	*¼pi on ⅛pi red brn*	*110.00*	
		Never hinged	*170.00*	
L136b	*A7*	*¼pi on ½pi red*	*110.00*	
		Never hinged	*170.00*	
L138e	*A7*	*1pi on 2pi orange*	*110.00*	
		Never hinged	*170.00*	
L139a	*A7*	*1pi on 3pi olive brn*	*110.00*	
		Never hinged	*170.00*	
L140a	*A7*	*1pi on 3pi dull red*	*110.00*	
		Never hinged	*170.00*	
L141a	*A7*	*10pi on 5pi olive grn*	*110.00*	
		Never hinged	*170.00*	
		Nos. L135a-L141a (6)	*660.00*	

Stamps of 1922-24 Surcharged

Black Surcharge

L142	A7	⅛pi on ½pi red	10.00	*7.25*
a.		Inverted surcharge	40.00	
L143	A7	¼pi on ½pi red	11.00	*7.25*
a.		Inverted surcharge	40.00	
L144	A7	1pi on ½pi red	12.50	*7.25*
a.		Inverted surcharge	40.00	
L145	A7	1pi on 1½pi vio	12.50	*7.25*
a.		Inverted surcharge	40.00	
L146	A7	1pi on 2pi org	10.00	*7.25*
a.		"10pi"	100.00	
b.		Inverted surcharge	50.00	
c.		As "a," inverted surcharge	150.00	
L147	A7	1pi on 3pi olive brn	12.50	*7.25*
a.		"10pi"	100.00	
b.		Inverted surcharge	55.00	
c.		As "a," inverted surcharge	150.00	

L148	A7	10pi on 5pi olive grn	20.00	*14.00*
a.		Inverted surcharge	75.00	
		Nos. L142-L148 (7)	88.50	*57.50*

Blue Surcharge

L149	A7	⅛pi on ½pi red	11.00	*11.00*
a.		Inverted surcharge	75.00	
b.		Double surcharge	225.00	
L150	A7	¼pi on ½pi red	15.00	*11.00*
a.		Inverted surcharge	75.00	
L151	A7	1pi on ½pi red	15.00	*11.00*
a.		Inverted surcharge	75.00	
b.		Double surcharge	125.00	
L152	A7	1pi on 1½pi vio	20.00	*11.00*
a.		Inverted surcharge	75.00	
L153	A7	1pi on 2pi org	17.50	*11.00*
a.		"10pi"	100.00	
b.		Inverted surcharge	90.00	
L154	A7	1pi on 3pi olive brn	30.00	*22.50*
a.		"10pi"	110.00	
b.		Inverted surcharge	75.00	
L155	A7	10pi on 5pi olive grn	35.00	*25.00*
a.		Inverted surcharge	75.00	
		Nos. L149-L155 (7)	150.00	*102.50*

Red Surcharge

L156	A7	1pi on 1½pi vio	30.00	*22.50*
a.		Inverted surcharge	90.00	
L157	A7	1pi on 2pi org	30.00	*22.50*
a.		"10pi"	100.00	
b.		Inverted surcharge	90.00	
L158	A7	1pi on 3pi olive brn	32.50	*22.50*
a.		"10pi"	125.00	
b.		Inverted surcharge	90.00	
L159	A7	10pi on 5pi olive grn	32.50	*22.50*
a.		Inverted surcharge	90.00	
		Nos. L156-L159 (4)	125.00	*90.00*
		Nos. L142-L159 (18)	363.50	*250.00*

The "10pi" surcharge is found inverted on Nos. L146a, L147a. The existence of genuine inverted "10pi" surcharges on Nos. L153a, L154a, L157a and L158a is in doubt. The 10pi on 1½pi is bogus.

King Ali Issue

A9

A10

A11

A12

1925, May-June   Perf. 11½

Black Overprint

L160	A9	⅛pi chocolate	2.25	*1.50*
L161	A9	¼pi ultra	2.25	*1.50*
L162	A9	½pi car rose	2.25	*1.50*
L163	A10	1pi yellow green	3.00	*1.75*
L164	A10	1½pi orange	3.00	*1.75*
L165	A10	2pi blue	3.50	*2.25*
L166	A11	3pi dark green	3.50	*2.25*
L167	A11	5pi orange brn	3.50	*2.25*
L168	A12	10pi red & green	6.00	*4.50*
a.		Center inverted	90.00	
		Nos. L160-L168 (9)	29.25	*19.25*

Red Overprint

L169	A9	⅛pi chocolate	4.00	*2.75*
L170	A9	¼pi ultra	2.50	*1.60*
L171	A10	1pi yellow green	3.00	*2.00*
L172	A10	1½pi orange	3.00	*2.00*
L173	A10	2pi deep blue	3.50	*2.00*
		On cover, single franking		*650.00*
L174	A11	3pi dark green	3.25	*2.75*
a.		Horiz. pair, imperf. vert.	75.00	
L175	A11	5pi org brn	4.00	*2.75*
L176	A12	10pi red & green	6.50	*5.50*
		Nos. L169-L176 (8)	29.75	*21.85*

Blue Overprint

L177	A9	⅛pi chocolate	2.75	*1.75*
L179	A9	½pi car rose	2.75	*1.75*
L180	A10	1pi yellow green	2.75	*1.75*

L181	A10	1½pi orange	2.75	1.75
L182	A11	3pi dark green	2.75	1.75
L183	A11	5pi orange brn	6.75	5.50
L184	A12	10pi red & green	9.00	7.25
L185	A12	10pi red & org	275.00	
		Nos. L177-L184 (7)	29.50	21.50

Without Overprint

L186	A12	10pi red & green	8.00	6.75
a.		Dbl. impression of center	90.00	

The overprint in the tablets on Nos. L160-L185 reads: "5 Rabi al'awwal, 1343" (Oct. 4, 1924), the date of the accession of King Ali.

The tablet overprints vary slightly in size. Each is found reading upward or downward and at either side of the stamp. These control overprints were first applied in Jedda by the government press.

They were later made from new plates by the stamp printer in Cairo. In the Jedda overprint, the bar over the "0" figure extends to the left.

Some values exist with 13m or 15mm instead of 18mm between tablets. They sell for more. The lines of the Cairo overprinting are generally wider, but more lightly printed, usually appearing slightly grayish and the bar is at center right. The Cairo overprints are believed not to have been placed in use.

Imperforates exist.

Nos. L160-L168 are known with the overprints spaced as on type D3 and aligned horizontally.

Examples of these stamps (perforated or imperforate) without the overprint, except No. L186 were not regularly issued and not available for postage.

No. L185 exists only with Cairo overprint. Imperfs of No. L185 sell for much less than No. L185. Fake perfs have been added to the imperfs.

The ¼pi with blue overprint is bogus.

No. L186 in other colors are color trials.

For overprints see #58B-58D, Jordan 122-129.

NEJDI ADMINISTRATION OF HEJAZ

Handstamped in Blue, Red, Black or Violet

The overprint reads: "1343. Barid al Sultanat an Nejdia" (1925. Post of the Sultanate of Nejd).

The overprints on this and succeeding issues are handstamped and, as usual, are found double, inverted, etc. These variations are scarce.

On Stamp of Turkey, 1915, With Crescent and Star in Red

1925, Mar.-Apr.   Unwmk.   *Perf. 12*

1	A22	5pa ocher (Bl)	30.00	27.50
		Never hinged	50.00	
2	A22	5pa ocher (R)	30.00	20.00
		Never hinged	50.00	
3	A22	5pa ocher (Bk)	30.00	22.50
		Never hinged	50.00	
4	A22	5pa ocher (V)	30.00	18.00
		Never hinged	50.00	

On Stamp of Turkey, 1913

5	A28	10pa green (Bl)	40.00	16.00
		Never hinged	60.00	
a.		Inverted overprint	500.00	
		Never hinged	1,000.	
6	A28	10pa green (R)	40.00	12.50
		Never hinged	60.00	

On Stamps of Hejaz, 1922-24
Perf. 11½

7	A7	⅛pi red brn (R)	70.00	24.00
		Never hinged	110.00	
8	A7	⅛pi red brn (Bk)	70.00	35.00
		Never hinged	110.00	
9	A7	⅛pi red brn (V)	50.00	24.00
		Never hinged	75.00	
10	A7	⅛pi car (R)	70.00	30.00
		Never hinged	110.00	
11	A7	⅛pi car (Bk)	70.00	35.00
		Never hinged	110.00	
12	A7	⅛pi car (V)	50.00	27.50
		Never hinged	75.00	
13	A7	½pi red (Bl)	40.00	22.50
		Never hinged	60.00	
14	A7	½pi red (V)	40.00	18.00
		Never hinged	60.00	
15	A7	1½pi vio (R)	60.00	24.00
		Never hinged	90.00	
16	A7	2pi yel buff (R)	85.00	57.50
		Never hinged	140.00	
a.		2pi orange (R)	110.00	
		Never hinged	160.00	
17	A7	2pi yel buff (V)	85.00	57.50
		Never hinged	140.00	
a.		2pi orange (V)	100.00	32.50
		Never hinged	150.00	
18	A7	3pi brn red (Bl)	70.00	30.00
		Never hinged	110.00	

19	A7	3pi brn red (R)	70.00	22.50
		Never hinged	110.00	
20	A7	3pi brn red (V)	70.00	25.00
		Never hinged	110.00	

Many Hejaz stamps of the 1922 type were especially printed for this and following issues. The re-impressions are usually more clearly printed, in lighter shades than the 1922 stamps, and some are in new colors. Counterfeits exist.

Arabic Inscriptions
R1   R2

On Hejaz Bill Stamp

22	R1	1pi violet (R)	40.00	15.00
		Never hinged	60.00	

On Hejaz Notarial Stamps

23	R2	1pi violet (R)	50.00	20.00
		Never hinged	75.00	
24	R2	2pi blue (R)	50.00	30.00
		Never hinged	75.00	
25	R2	2pi blue (V)	50.00	27.50
		Never hinged	75.00	

For overprint see No. 49.

On Hejaz Railway Tax Stamps

Locomotive — R3

Type I

Type II

Two design types appear on the basic revenue stamps. Type I depicts the cab's window and the band at the center of the boiler as a series of horizontal lines, the top of the cab does not touch the frame line above it, and the coupler at rear of car appears as a fine hook that does not touch the right frame. Type 2 depicts the cab's window and band on boiler as open vertical spaces, the top of the cab touches the frame line above it, and the coupler appears as a blob connected to the right frame line. Type 2 appears in position 12 in the sheet of 18 (6x3) of the 500pi value, and in position 30 in the 36-stamp (6x6) sheets in which the other values were printed.

Type 1

26	R3	1pi blue (R)	40.00	9.00
		Never hinged	60.00	
a.		Type 2	60.00	
		Never hinged	90.00	
27	R3	2pi ocher (R)	60.00	14.00
		Never hinged	90.00	
a.		Type 2	90.00	
		Never hinged	140.00	
28	R3	2pi ocher (V)	60.00	14.00
		Never hinged	90.00	
a.		Type 2	90.00	
		Never hinged	140.00	
29	R3	3pi lilac (R)	60.00	20.00
		Never hinged	90.00	
a.		Type 2	90.00	
		Never hinged	140.00	
		Nos. 1-20,22-29 (28)	1,510.	698.50

For overprints and surcharges see Nos. 34, 50-54, 55, 59-68, J12-J15.

Pilgrimage Issue
Various Stamps Handstamp Surcharged in Blue and Red in Types "a" and "b" and with Tablets with New Values

a

b

Surcharge "a" reads: "Tezkar al Hajj al Awwal Fi 'ahd al Sultanat al Nejdia, 1343" (Commemorating the first pilgrimage under the Nejdi Sultanate, 1925).
"b" reads: "Al Arba" (Wednesday).

On Stamps of Turkey, 1913

1925, July 1   *Perf. 12*

30	A28	1pi on 10pa grn (Bl & R)	100.00	55.00
		Never hinged	150.00	
31	A30	5pi on 1pi bl (Bl & R)	100.00	55.00
		Never hinged	150.00	

On Stamps of Hejaz, 1917-18
Serrate Roulette 13

32	A5	2pi on 1pa lil brn (R & Bl)	125.00	67.50
		Never hinged	175.00	
33	A4	4pi on ⅛pi org (R & Bl)	400.00	350.00
		Never hinged	500.00	

On Hejaz Railway Tax Stamp
Perf. 11½

34	R3	3pi lilac, type 1 (Bl & R)	200.00	40.00
		Never hinged	300.00	
		On cover		425.00
a.		Type 2	300.00	
		Never hinged	450.00	
		Nos. 30-34 (5)	925.00	567.50

No. 30 with handstamp "a" in black was a favor item. Nos. 30 and 33 with both handstamps in red are forgeries.

Handstamped in Blue, Red, Black or Violet

This overprint has practically the same meaning as that described over No. 1. The Mohammedan year (1343) is omitted.
This handstamp is said to be in private hands at this time. Extreme caution is advised before buying rare items.

1925, July-Aug.   *Perf. 12*
On Stamp of Turkey, 1915, with Crescent and Star in Red

35	A22	5pa ocher (Bl)	50.00	24.00
		Never hinged	75.00	

On Stamps of Turkey, 1913

36	A28	10pa green (Bl)	60.00	20.00
		Never hinged	90.00	
a.		Black overprint	120.00	
b.		As "a," overprint inverted	650.00	

On Stamps of Hejaz, 1922 (Nos. L28-L29)
Serrate Roulette 13

37	A3	1pi blue (R)	120.00	67.50
		Never hinged	180.00	
38	A6	2pi magenta (Bl)	120.00	67.50
		Never hinged	180.00	

On Stamps of Hejaz, 1922-24
Perf. 11½

38A	A7	⅛pi red brn (Bk)	4,500.	
		No gum	1,500.	
38B	A7	⅛pi red brn (Bl)	3,750.	
		No gum	1,000.	
39	A7	½pi red (Bl)	12.50	10.00
		On cover		75.00
a.		Imperf., pair	25.00	22.50
39B	A7	½pi red (Bk)	20.00	18.00
c.		Imperf., pair	50.00	37.50
40	A7	1pi gray vio (R)	50.00	29.00
		Never hinged	75.00	
		1pi black violet (R)	50.00	
		Never hinged	75.00	
41	A7	1½pi dk red (Bk)	50.00	30.00
		Never hinged	75.00	
		1½pi brick red (Bk)	50.00	
		Never hinged	75.00	

42	A7	2pi yel buff (Bl)	80.00	47.50
		Never hinged	120.00	
a.		2pi orange (Bl)	110.00	55.00
		Never hinged	160.00	
43	A7	2pi deep vio (Bl)	85.00	52.50
		Never hinged	125.00	
44	A7	3pi brown red (Bl)	50.00	30.00
		Never hinged	75.00	
45	A7	5pi scarlet (Bl)	70.00	37.50
		Never hinged	110.00	
		Nos. 35-38,39-45 (12)	767.50	433.50

Overprint on Nos. 38A, 39B, 39C is blue-black.
See note above No. 35.

With Additional Surcharge of New Value Typo. in Black

c   d

e

Color in parenthesis is that of overprint on basic stamp.

46	A7(c)	1pi on ½pi (Bl)	12.50	1.75
		On cover, single franking		75.00
a.		Imperf., pair	40.00	
b.		Ovpt. & surch. inverted	90.00	
47	A7(d)	1½pi on ½pi (Bl)	17.50	7.25
a.		Imperf., pair	30.00	
b.		Black overprint	20.00	
48	A7(e)	2pi on 3pi (Bl)	17.50	16.00
		Nos. 46-48 (3)	47.50	25.00

Several variations in type settings of "c," "d" and "e" exist, including inverted letters and values.

On Hejaz Notarial Stamp

49	R2	2pi blue (Bk)	50.00	20.00
		Never hinged	75.00	
		On cover		125.00
		On cover, single franking		425.00

On Hejaz Railway Tax Stamps

50	R3	1pi blue, type 1 (R)	40.00	25.00
		Never hinged	60.00	
		On cover		100.00
a.		Type 2	60.00	
		Never hinged	90.00	
51	R3	1pi blue, type 1 (Bk)	60.00	9.00
		Never hinged	90.00	
		On cover		125.00
a.		Type 2	90.00	
		Never hinged	140.00	
52	R3	2pi ocher, type 1 (Bl)	60.00	9.00
		Never hinged	90.00	
		On cover		125.00
a.		Type 2	90.00	
		Never hinged	140.00	
53	R3	3pi lilac, type 1 (Bl)	70.00	22.50
		Never hinged	110.00	
a.		Type 2	100.00	
		Never hinged	150.00	
54	R3	5pi green, type 1 (Bl)	60.00	20.00
		Never hinged	90.00	
a.		Type 2	90.00	
		Never hinged	140.00	
		Nos. 49-54 (6)	340.00	105.50

Hejaz Railway Tax Stamp Handstamped in Black

This overprint reads: "Al Saudia. — Al Sultanat al Nejdia." (The Saudi Sultanate of Nejd.)

Small Handstamp

1925-26

55	R3	1pi blue, type 1	—	200.00
b.		Type 2		400.00

On Nos. L34, L36-L37, L41

56	A7	1½pi violet	—	375.00
57	A7	2pi orange	—	375.00
57A	A7	10pi on 5pi ol green	—	375.00

On Nos. L95 and L97

58	A7	3pi olive brown	—	400.00
58A	A7	5pi olive green	—	400.00

On Nos. L162-L163, L173

Perf. 11½

58B	A9	½pi car rose	350.00	
58C	A10	1pi yel grn	—	225.00
58D	A10	2pi blue	—	350.00

Large Handstamp

58K	R3	1pi blue		7,000.
58L	A7	3pi brown (#L95b)		1,000.
a.		Overprint reading down		1,000.
58M	A10	1pi yel grn (#L163)	1,500.	1,000.

Nos. 55-58M were provisionally issued at Medina after its capitulation.

Only one example of No. 58K, a single stamp used on piece, is known.

This overprint exists on Nos. L160-L161, L164-L172, L174-L175, L180-L183. These 17 are known as bogus items, but may exist genuine.

Lithographed overprints are forgeries.

Medina Issue

Hejaz Railway Tax Stamps Handstamped

and Handstamp Surcharged in Various Colors

The large overprint reads: "The Nejdi Posts — 1344 — Commemorating Medina, the Illustrious." The tablet shows the new value.

1925

59	R3	1pi on 10pi vio, type 1 (Bk & V)	70.00	70.00
		Never hinged	95.00	
a.		Type 2	100.00	
		Never hinged	150.00	
60	R3	2pi on 50pi lt bl, type 1 (R & Bl)	70.00	70.00
		Never hinged	95.00	
a.		Type 2	100.00	
		Never hinged	150.00	
61	R3	3pi on 100pi red brn, type 1 (Bl & Bk)	70.00	70.00
		Never hinged	95.00	
a.		Type 2	100.00	
		Never hinged	150.00	
62	R3	4pi on 500pi dull red, type 1 (Bl & Bk)	70.00	70.00
		Never hinged	95.00	
a.		Type 2	100.00	
		Never hinged	150.00	

63	R3	5pi on 1000pi dp red, type 1 (Bl & Bk)	70.00	70.00
		Never hinged	95.00	
a.		Type 2	100.00	
		Never hinged	150.00	
		Nos. 59-63 (5)	350.00	350.00

JEDDA ISSUE

Hejaz Railway Tax Stamps Handstamped and Tablet with New Value in Various Colors

This handstamp reads: "Commemorating Jedda — 1344 — The Nejdi Posts."

1925

64	R3	1pi on 10pi vio, type 1 (Bk & Bl)	70.00	70.00
		Never hinged	95.00	
a.		Horiz. pair, imperf between	450.00	
b.		Type 2	100.00	
		Never hinged	150.00	
65	R3	2pi on 50pi lt bl, type 1 (R & Bk)	70.00	70.00
		Never hinged	95.00	
a.		Type 2	100.00	
		Never hinged	150.00	
66	R3	3pi on 100pi red brn, type 1 (R & Bl)	70.00	70.00
		Never hinged	95.00	
a.		Type 2	100.00	
		Never hinged	150.00	
67	R3	4pi on 500pi dl red, type 1 (Bk & Bl)	70.00	70.00
		Never hinged	95.00	
a.		Type 2	100.00	
		Never hinged	150.00	
68	R3	5pi on 1000pi dp red, type 1 (Bk & Bl)	70.00	70.00
		Never hinged	95.00	
a.		Type 2	100.00	
		Never hinged	150.00	
		Nos. 64-68 (5)	350.00	350.00

Nos. 59-63 and 64-68 were prepared in anticipation of the surrender of Medina and Jedda.

Kingdom of Hejaz-Nejd

Arabic Inscriptions and Value — A1

A2

Inscriptions in upper tablets: "Barid al Hejaz wa Nejd" (Posts of the Hejaz and Nejd)

1926, Feb.   Typo.   Unwmk.   Perf. 11

69	A1	¼pi violet	45.00	17.00
		Never hinged	60.00	
70	A1	½pi gray	45.00	17.00
		Never hinged	60.00	
71	A1	1pi deep blue	45.00	21.00
		Never hinged	60.00	
72	A2	2pi blue green	45.00	17.00
		Never hinged	60.00	
73	A2	3pi carmine	45.00	18.00
		Never hinged	60.00	
74	A2	5pi maroon	45.00	12.00
		Never hinged	60.00	
		Nos. 69-74 (6)	270.00	102.00

Nos. 69-72, 74 exist imperf. Value, each $40.
Used values are for favor cancels.

1926, Mar.   Perf. 11

75	A1	¼pi orange	12.00	10.00
		On cover		75.00
76	A1	½pi blue green	5.25	15.00
a.		Horiz. pair, imperf between	100.00	
b.		Vertz. pair, imperf between	100.00	
77	A1	1pi carmine	4.25	7.50
		On cover		125.00
a.		Horiz. pair, imperf between	100.00	
b.		Vert. pair, imperf between	100.00	

78	A2	2pi violet	5.25	12.50
a.		Horiz. pair, imperf between	100.00	
b.		Vert. pair, imperf between	100.00	
79	A2	3pi dark blue	5.25	7.50
a.		Horiz. pair, imperf between	100.00	
b.		Vert. pair, imperf between	100.00	
80	A2	5pi lt brown	10.00	20.00
a.		5pi olive brown		
b.		Horiz. pair, imperf between	100.00	
c.		Vert. pair, imperf between	100.00	
		Nos. 75-80 (6)	42.00	72.50

Nos. 75-80 also exist imperf. Value, twice the values shown above. Examples that are perforated 14, 14x11 and 11x14 were privately produced.

Counterfeits of types A1 and A2 are perf. 11½. They exist with and without overprints.

Types A1 and A2 in colors other than listed are proofs.

Pan-Islamic Congress Issue

Stamps of 1926 Hstmpd.

1926   Perf. 11

92	A1	¼pi orange	12.00	4.00
		Never hinged	24.00	
93	A1	½pi blue green	12.00	4.00
		Never hinged	24.00	
94	A1	1pi carmine	12.00	4.00
		Never hinged	24.00	
95	A2	2pi violet	12.00	4.00
		Never hinged	24.00	
		On cover		150.00
96	A2	3pi dark blue	12.00	4.00
		Never hinged	24.00	
		On cover, single franking		200.00
97	A2	5pi light brown	12.00	4.00
		Never hinged	24.00	
		Nos. 92-97 (6)	72.00	24.00

The overprint reads: "al Mootamar al Islami 20 Zilkada, Sanat 1344." (The Islamic Congress, June 1, 1926.)

See counterfeit note after No. 80.

Tughra of King Abdul Aziz — A3

1926-27   Typo.   Perf. 11½

98	A3	⅛pi ocher	5.00	.60
		Never hinged	7.50	
99	A3	¼pi gray green	6.00	1.50
		Never hinged	9.00	
100	A3	½pi dull red	6.00	1.50
		Never hinged	9.00	
		On paper wrapper		75.00
		On cover		100.00
		On cover, single franking		200.00
b.		Horiz. pair, imperf between	400.00	
101	A3	1pi deep violet	6.50	1.50
		Never hinged	10.00	
102	A3	1½pi gray blue	18.00	2.25
		Never hinged	27.00	
103	A3	3pi olive green	14.00	4.75
		Never hinged	21.00	
104	A3	5pi brown orange	27.50	5.00
		Never hinged	40.00	
105	A3	10pi dark brown	70.00	7.00
		Never hinged	105.00	
		Nos. 98-105 (8)	153.00	24.10

Inscription at top reads: "Al Hukumat al Arabia" (The Arabian Government). Inscription below tughra reads: "Barid al Hejaz wa Nejd" (Post of the Hejaz and Nejd).

Stamps of 1926-27 Handstamped in Black or Red

1927

107	A3	⅛pi ocher	13.00	4.75
108	A3	¼pi gray grn	13.00	4.75
109	A3	½pi dull red	13.00	4.75
110	A3	1pi deep violet	13.00	4.75
111	A3	1½pi gray bl (R)	13.00	4.75
112	A3	3pi olive green	13.00	4.75
113	A3	5pi brown orange	14.50	4.75

114	A3	10pi dark brown	16.00	4.75
		On cover		100.00
		Nos. 107-114 (8)	108.50	38.00
		Set, never hinged	175.00	

The overprint reads: "In commemoration of the Kingdom of Nejd and Dependencies, 25th Rajab 1345."

Inverted varieties have not been authenticated.

Turkey No. 258 Surcharged in Violet

1925   Perf. 12

115	A28	1g on 10pa green	175.00	
		Never hinged	225.00	
		No gum		50.00

Similar surcharges of 6g and 20g were made in red, but were not known to have been issued. Values: 6g, $350; 20g, $500.

A4   A5

1929-30   Typo.   Perf. 11½

117	A4	1¾g gray blue	40.00	4.50
		Cover, single franking		50.00
119	A4	20g violet	50.00	10.00
120	A4	30g green	80.00	22.50

1930   Perf. 11, 11½

125	A5	½g rose	19.00	3.25
126	A5	1½g violet	19.00	2.10
127	A5	1¾g ultra	19.00	2.75
128	A5	3½g emerald	19.00	4.25

Perf. 11

129	A5	5g black brown	30.00	6.50
		Nos. 125-129 (5)	106.00	18.85

Anniversary of King Ibn Saud's accession to the throne of the Hejaz, January 8, 1926.

A6   A7

1931-32   Perf. 11½

130	A6	⅛g ocher ('32)	22.50	3.25
131	A6	¼g blue green	22.50	2.50
133	A6	1¾g ultra	37.50	3.25
		On cover		50.00
		Nos. 130-133 (3)	82.50	9.00

1932   Perf. 11½

135	A7	¼g blue green	16.00	32.50
a.		Perf 11		
136	A7	½g scarlet	47.50	5.25
a.		Perf 11		
137	A7	2¼g ultra	90.00	8.50
a.		Perf 11		
		Nos. 135-137 (3)	153.50	46.25

Kingdom of Saudi Arabia

A8

1934, Jan.   Perf. 11½, Imperf.

138	A8	¼g yellow green	11.00	10.00
		Never hinged	15.00	
139	A8	½g red	11.00	10.00
		Never hinged	15.00	
140	A8	1½g light blue	21.00	19.00
		Never hinged	27.50	
141	A8	3g blue green	21.00	19.00
		Never hinged	27.50	
142	A8	3½g ultra	37.50	7.75
		Never hinged	47.50	

143 A8 5g yellow 50.00 37.50
Never hinged 65.00
144 A8 10g red orange 90.00
Never hinged 120.00
145 A8 20g bright violet 110.00
Never hinged 150.00
146 A8 ¼s claret 225.00
Never hinged 300.00
147 A8 30g dull violet 140.00
Never hinged 180.00
148 A8 ½s chocolate 475.00
Never hinged 700.00
149 A8 1s violet brown 1,075.
Never hinged 1,750.
Nos. 138-149 (12) 2,266.

Proclamation of Emir Saud as Heir Apparent of Arabia. Perf. and imperf. stamps were issued in equal quantities.
Favor cancels exist on Nos. 144-149.

Tughra of King Abdul Aziz — A9

1934-57 Perf. 11, 11½
159 A9 ⅛g yellow 5.25 .45
160 A9 ¼g yellow grn 5.25 .45
161 A9 ½g rose red ('43) 3.75 .25
a. ½g dark carmine 12.00 1.40
162 A9 ⅞g lt blue ('56) 6.50 .55
163 A9 1g blue green 5.25 .45
164 A9 2g olive grn ('57) 9.00 2.25
a. 2g olive bister ('57) 25.00 7.25
165 A9 2⅞g violet ('57) 6.50 .55
166 A9 3g ultra ('38) 6.50 .25
a. 3g light blue 20.00 1.75
167 A9 3½g lt ultra 35.00 2.25
168 A9 5g orange 6.50 .55
169 A9 10g red 19.00 1.75
170 A9 20g purple brn 32.50 1.10
a. 20g purple black 25.00 2.25
171 A9 100g red vio ('42) 90.00 5.25
172 A9 200g vio brn ('42) 115.00 7.00
Nos. 159-172 (14) 346.00 23.10
Set, never hinged 450.00

The ½g has two types differing in position of the tughra.
No. 162 measures 31x22mm. No. 164 30½x21½mm. No. 165, 30½x22mm. No. 166 30x21mm. No. 171, 31x22mm. No. 172, 30½x21½mm. Rest of set, 29x20½mm. Grayish paper was used in 1946-49 printings.
No. 168 exists with pin-perf 6.
For overprint see No. J24.

HEJAZ POSTAGE DUE STAMPS

From Old Door at El Ashraf Barsbai in Shari el Ashrafiya, Cairo — D1

Serrate Roulette 13
1917, June 27 Typo. Unwmk.
LJ1 D1 20pa red 3.25 2.00
Never hinged 4.00
LJ2 D1 1pi blue 3.50 2.00
Never hinged 4.25
LJ3 D1 2pi magenta 3.75 2.00
Never hinged 4.75
Nos. LJ1-LJ3 (3) 10.50 6.00

For overprints see Nos. LJ4-LJ10, LJ17-LJ25, J9.

Nos. LJ1-LJ3 Overprinted in Black or Red — a

1921, Dec. Type a
LJ4 D1 20pa red 20.00 2.75
Never hinged 30.00
a. Double overprint, one at left 140.00
b. Overprint at left 30.00 20.00
Never hinged 45.00
LJ5 D1 1pi blue (R) 7.00 3.50
Never hinged 11.00

LJ6 D1 1pi bl, ovpt. at left 30.00 18.00
Never hinged 45.00
a. Overprint at right 27.50 32.50
Never hinged 40.00
LJ7 D1 2pi magenta 12.50 7.25
Never hinged 19.00
a. Double overprint, one at left 62.50
Never hinged 27.50
b. Overprint at left 27.50
Never hinged 40.00
Nos. LJ4-LJ7 (4) 69.50 31.50

Nos. LJ1-LJ3 Overprinted in Black — b

1922, Jan. Type b
LJ8 D1 20pa red 25.00 27.50
Never hinged 37.50
a. Overprint at left 35.00
LJ9 D1 1pi blue 5.00 3.25
Never hinged 7.50
a. Overprint at left 45.00
LJ10 D1 2pi magenta 5.00 3.25
Never hinged 7.50
a. Overprint at left 32.50
Nos. LJ8-LJ10 (3) 35.00 34.00

Regular issue of 1922 Overprinted

1923 Black Overprint Perf. 11½
LJ11 A7 ½pi red 4.25 1.40
Never hinged 5.25
a. Inverted overprint 50.00
Never hinged 75.00
LJ12 A7 1pi dark blue 7.50 1.40
Never hinged 11.50
a. Inverted overprint 80.00
Never hinged 120.00
b. Double overprint 125.00
LJ13 A7 2pi orange 5.00 1.75
Never hinged 6.25
a. Inverted overprint 47.50
Never hinged 70.00
Nos. LJ11-LJ13 (3) 16.75 4.55

1924 Blue Overprint
LJ14 A7 ½pi red 17.50 2.75
Never hinged 26.00
a. Inverted overprint 80.00
LJ15 A7 1pi dark blue 37.50 2.75
Never hinged 57.50
a. Inverted overprint 100.00
LJ16 A7 2pi orange 27.50 4.50
Never hinged 57.50
a. Inverted overprint 40.00
Nos. LJ14-LJ16 (3) 82.50 10.00

This overprint reads "Mustahaq" (Due).

Jedda Issues

Nos. LJ1-LJ3 Overprinted in Red or Blue (Overprint reads up in illustration)

Jedda issues were also used in Medina and Yambo. **Used values for #L51-L186 and LJ17-LJ39 are for genuine cancels. Privately applied cancels exist for "Mekke" (Mecca, bilingual or all Arabic), Khartoum, Cairo, as well as for Jeddah. Many private cancels have wrong dates, some as early as 1916. These are worth half the used values.**

1925, Jan. Serrate Roulette 13
LJ17 D1 20pa red (R) 400.00 350.00
LJ18 D1 20pa red (Bl) 75.00
LJ19 D1 1pi blue (R) 20.00 18.00
LJ20 D1 1pi blue (Bl) 27.50 25.00
LJ21 D1 2pi mag (Bl) 15.00 14.00

Overprint Reading Down
LJ17a D1 20pa 550.00 550.00
LJ18a D1 20pa 450.00
LJ19a D1 1pi 18.00 18.00
LJ20a D1 1pi 67.50 80.00
LJ21a D1 2pi 60.00 60.00

Nos. LJ1-LJ3 Overprinted in Blue or Red

1925
LJ22 D1 20pa red (Bl) 475.00 425.00
a. Inverted overprint 325.00 325.00
LJ24 D1 1pi blue (R) 25.00 27.50
a. Inverted overprint 32.50 32.50
LJ25 D1 2pi magenta (Bl) 20.00 18.00
a. Inverted overprint 35.00 45.00
b. Double overprint 350.00
No. LJ2 with this overprint in blue is bogus.

Regular Issues of 1922-24 Overprinted

and Handstamped — b

1925 Perf. 11½
LJ26 A7 ⅛pi red brown 20.00 18.00
Never hinged 30.00
b. Pair, one without hand-stamp 100.00 —
c. Overprint inverted 60.00 —
d. Violet handstamp 75.00 —
LJ27 A7 ½pi red 27.50 25.00
Never hinged 42.50
b. Pair, one without hand-stamp 100.00 —
c. Overprint inverted 60.00 —
LJ28 A7 1pi dark blue 20.00 18.00
Never hinged 30.00
b. Pair, one without hand-stamp 100.00 —
c. Overprint inverted 60.00 —
LJ29 A7 1½pi violet 22.50 18.00
Never hinged 35.00
b. Pair, one without hand-stamp 100.00 —
c. Overprint inverted 60.00 —
d. Violet handstamp 75.00 —
LJ30 A7 2pi orange 25.00 20.00
Never hinged 37.50
b. Pair, one without hand-stamp 100.00 —
c. Overprint inverted 60.00 —
d. Violet handstamp 75.00 —
LJ31 A7 3pi olive brown 25.00 20.00
Never hinged 37.50
b. Pair, one without hand-stamp 100.00 —
c. Overprint inverted 60.00 —
d. Violet handstamp 75.00 —
LJ32 A7 3pi dull red 50.00 45.00
Never hinged 75.00
b. Pair, one without hand-stamp 100.00 —
c. Overprint inverted 60.00 —
d. Violet handstamp 75.00 —
LJ33 A7 5pi olive green 25.00 20.00
Never hinged 37.50
b. Pair, one without hand-stamp 100.00 —
c. Overprint inverted 60.00 —
LJ34 A7 10pi vio & dk brn 30.00 25.00
Never hinged 45.00
b. Pair, one without hand-stamp 100.00 —
c. Overprint inverted 60.00 —
d. Violet handstamp 75.00 —
Nos. LJ26-LJ34 (9) 245.00 209.00

The printed overprint (a), consisting of the three top lines of Arabic, was used alone for the first issue (Nos. LJ26a-LJ34a). The "postage due" box was so small and indistinct that its equivalent in larger characters was added by boxed handstamp (b) at bottom of each stamp for the second issue (Nos. LJ26-LJ34). The handstamped overprint (b) is found double, inverted, etc. It is also known in dark violet.
Counterfeits exist of both overprint and handstamp.

Without Boxed Handstamp "b"
LJ26a A7 ⅛pi red brown 42.50
LJ27a A7 ½pi red 42.50
LJ28a A7 1pi dark blue 42.50
LJ29a A7 1½pi violet 42.50
LJ30a A7 2pi orange 42.50

LJ31a A7 3pi olive brown 42.50
LJ32a A7 3pi dull red 42.50
LJ33a A7 5pi olive green 55.00
LJ34a A7 10pi vio & dk brn 55.00
Nos. LJ26a-LJ34a (9) 407.50

Regular Issue of 1922 Overprinted

and Handstamped

LJ35 A7 ½pi red 150.00 140.00
LJ36 A7 1½pi violet 150.00 140.00
a. Overprint in red, boxed handstamp violet 1,400.
LJ37 A7 2pi orange 200.00 175.00
LJ38 A7 3pi olive brown 150.00 140.00
LJ39 A7 5pi olive green 150.00 140.00
Nos. LJ35-LJ39 (5) 800.00 735.00
Set, never hinged 1,000.

Counterfeits exist of Nos. LJ4-LJ39.

Arabic Numeral of Value — D2

1925, May-June Perf. 11½
LJ40 D2 ½pi light blue 3.00
LJ41 D2 1pi orange 3.00
LJ42 D2 2pi lt brown 3.00
LJ43 D2 3pi pink 3.00
Nos. LJ40-LJ43 (4) 12.00

Nos. LJ40-LJ43 have no overprint and were not officially issued. No. LJ40 exists only on cover.
Nos. LJ40-LJ43 exist imperforate. Impressions in colors other than issued are trial color proofs.

Arabic Numeral of Value — D3

1925 Black Overprint
LJ44 D3 ½pi light blue 3.00
Never hinged 4.50
LJ45 D3 1pi orange 3.00
Never hinged 4.50
LJ46 D3 2pi light brown 3.00
Never hinged 4.50
LJ47 D3 3pi pink 3.75
Never hinged 6.00
Nos. LJ44-LJ47 (4) 12.75

Nos. LJ44-LJ47 exist with either Jedda or Cairo overprints and the tablets normally read upward. Values for Cairo overprints; Jedda overprints sell for more.

Red Overprint

LJ48	D3	½pi light blue	3.75
		Never hinged	6.00
LJ49	D3	1pi orange	3.75
		Never hinged	6.00
LJ50	D3	2pi light brown	3.75
		Never hinged	6.00
LJ51	D3	3pi pink	3.75
		Never hinged	6.00

Blue Overprint

LJ52	D3	½pi light blue	3.75
		Never hinged	6.00
LJ53	D3	1pi orange	3.75
		Never hinged	6.00
LJ54	D3	2pi light brown	3.75
		Never hinged	6.00
LJ55	D3	3pi pink	3.75
		Never hinged	6.00
		Nos. LJ40-LJ55 (16)	54.75

Red and blue overprints are from Cairo. Nos. LJ44-LJ55 exist imperf.

NEJDI ADMINISTRATION OF HEJAZ POSTAGE DUE STAMPS

Nos. LJ11-LJ16 Handstamped in Blue, Red or Black

1925, Apr.-June Unwmk. Perf. 11½

J1	A7	½pi red (Bl)	27.50	27.50
J2	A7	1pi lt blue (R)	55.00	55.00
a.		1pi dark blue (R)	35.00	35.00
J3	A7	2pi yel buff (Bl)	55.00	55.00
a.		2pi orange (Bl)	47.50	47.50
		Nos. J1-J3 (3)	137.50	137.50

The original boxed overprint is printed on Nos. J1, J2a and J3a. Nos. J2-J3 are overprinted on a new printing of the basic stamps with handstamped boxed overprints.

Same, with Postage Due Overprint in Blue

J4	A7	½pi red (Bl)	140.00
J5	A7	1pi dk blue (R)	550.00
J6	A7	2pi orange (Bl)	175.00

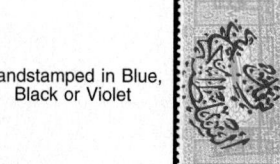

On Hejaz Stamps of 1922-24 Handstamped in Blue

J7	A7	½pi red (Bl & Bl)	16.00	16.00
J8	A7	3pi brn red (Bl & Bl)	19.00	19.00

Handstamped in Blue, Black or Violet

On Hejaz No. LJ9
Serrate Roulette 13½

J9	D1	1pi blue (V)	60.00	27.50

See note before No. 35.

Same Overprint on Hejaz Stamps of 1924 with additional Handstamp in Black, Blue or Red

Perf. 11½

J10	A7	3pi brn red (Bl & Bk)	11.00	11.00
J11	A7	3pi brn red (Bk & Bl)	11.00	11.00

Same Handstamps on Hejaz Railway Tax Stamps

J12	R3	1pi blue, type 1 (Bk & R)	12.00	12.00
a.		Type 2	40.00	
		Never hinged	60.00	
J13	R3	2pi ocher, type 1 (Bl & Bk)	12.00	12.00
a.		Type 2	40.00	
		Never hinged	60.00	
J14	R3	5pi green, type 1 (Bk & R)	20.00	20.00
a.		Type 2	60.00	
		Never hinged	90.00	
J15	R3	5pi green, type 1 (V & BK)	20.00	9.00
a.		Type 2	60.00	
		Never hinged	90.00	
		Nos. J10-J15 (6)	86.00	75.00

The second handstamp, which is struck on the lower part of the Postage Due Stamps, is the word Mustahaq (Due) in various forms. #J13 exists with 2nd handstamp in blue.

Hejaz-Nejd

1926 Typo. Perf. 11

J16	D1	½pi carmine	4.00	10.00
		On cover		200.00
J17	D1	2pi orange	4.00	10.00
		On cover		175.00
		On cover, single franking		425.00
J18	D1	6pi light brown	4.00	10.00
		Nos. J16-J18 (3)	12.00	30.00
		Set, never hinged	22.00	

Nos. J16-J18 exist with perf. 14, 14x11 and 11x14, and imperf. These sell for six times the values quoted.
Nos. J16-J18 in colors other than listed (both perf. and imperf.) are proofs.
Counterfeit note after No. 80 also applies to Nos. J16-J21.

Pan-Islamic Congress Issue
Postage Due Stamps of 1926
Handstamped like Regular Issue

J19	D1	½pi carmine	5.50	4.50
		Never hinged	8.00	
J20	D1	2pi orange	5.50	4.50
		Never hinged	8.00	
J21	D1	6pi light brown	5.50	4.50
		Never hinged	8.00	
		Nos. J19-J21 (3)	16.50	13.50

D2

1927 Perf. 11½

J22	D2	1pi slate	18.00	.45
		Never hinged	27.00	
a.		Inscription reads "2 piastres" in upper right circle	200.00	100.00
J23	D2	2pi dark violet	5.75	.45
		Never hinged	9.00	

Saudi Arabia

Saudi Arabia No. 161 Handstamped in Black

1935

J24	A9	½g dark carmine	350.00

Two types of overprint.

D3

1937-39 Unwmk.

J25	D3	½g org brn ('39)	20.00	20.00
		Never hinged	20.00	
J26	D3	1g light blue	20.00	20.00
		Never hinged	20.00	
J27	D3	2g rose vio ('39)	29.00	13.50
		Never hinged	25.00	
		Nos. J25-J27 (3)	69.00	53.50

OFFICIAL STAMPS

Official stamps were normally used only on external correspondence.

O1

1939 Unwmk. Typo. Perf. 11½

O1	O1	3g deep ultra	5.25	2.40
		On cover, single franking		15.00

Perf. 11, 11½

O2	O1	5g red violet	6.75	3.00
		On cover, single franking		10.00

Perf. 11

O3	O1	20g brown	14.00	6.25
O4	O1	50g blue green	27.50	13.00
O5	O1	100g olive grn	110.00	60.00
O6	O1	200g purple	90.00	40.00
		Nos. O1-O6 (6)	253.50	124.65

No. O1 on royal cover is valued at $50.

NEWSPAPER STAMPS

Nos. 8, 9 and 14 with Additional Overprint in Black

1925 Unwmk. Perf. 11½

P1	A7	⅛pi red brown (Bk)	1,800.	1,800.
P2	A7	⅛pi red brown (V)	1,400.	900.
P3	A7	½pi red (V)	2,750.	1,800.

Overprint reads: "Matbu'a" (Newspaper), but these stamps were normally used for regular postage. Counterfeits exist.
The status of this set in question. The government may have declared it to be unauthorized.

POSTAL TAX STAMPS

PT1

1934, May 15 Unwmk. Perf. 11½

RA1	PT1	⅛g scarlet	100.00	4.50
		Never hinged	190.00	
		On cover		75.00

No. RA1 collected a "war tax" to aid wounded of the 1934 Saudi-Yemen war.

Nos. RA2-RA8 raised funds for the Medical Aid Society. Nos. RA4-RA8 in Scott Standard catalogue, Vol. 6.

General Hospital, Mecca PT2

PT2a

1936, Oct. Size: 37x20mm

RA2	PT2	⅛g scarlet	400.00	9.00
		Never hinged	625.00	
		On cover		100.00

Type of 1936, Redrawn

1937-42 Size: 30½x18mm

RA3	PT2a	⅛g scarlet	35.00	.90
		Never hinged	75.00	
		On cover		10.00
a.		⅛g rose ('39)	60.00	1.75
		Never hinged	125.00	
		On cover		20.00
b.		⅛g rose car, perf. 11 ('42)	125.00	6.75
		Never hinged	225.00	

SCHLESWIG

'shles-ˌwig

LOCATION — In the northern part of the former Schleswig-Holstein Province, in northern Germany.

Schleswig was divided into North and South Schleswig after the Versailles Treaty, and plebiscites were held in 1920. North Schleswig (Zone 1) voted to join Denmark, South Schleswig to stay German.

100 Pfennig = 1 Mark
100 Ore = 1 Krone

Watermark

Wmk. 114 —
Multiple Crosses

Plebiscite Issue

Arms — A11

View of
Schleswig
A12

Perf. 14x15

			.25	.80
1920, Jan. 25	**Typo.**	**Wmk. 114**		
1	A11	2½pf gray	.25	.80
	Never hinged		.80	
	On cover			6.75
2	A11	5pf green	.25	.80
	Never hinged		.80	
	On cover			4.25
3	A11	7½pf yellow brown	.25	.80
	Never hinged		.80	
	On cover			6.75
4	A11	10pf deep rose	.25	.80
	Never hinged		.80	
	On cover			4.25
5	A11	15pf red violet	.25	.80
	Never hinged		.80	
	On cover			4.25
6	A11	20pf deep blue	.25	.80
	Never hinged		.80	
	On cover			4.25
7	A11	25pf orange	.35	.80
	Never hinged		1.60	
	On cover			8.50
8	A11	35pf brown	.45	1.00
	Never hinged		2.50	
	On cover			17.00
9	A11	40pf violet	.35	.80
	Never hinged		1.60	
	On cover			10.00
10	A11	75pf greenish blue	.45	.80
	Never hinged		2.50	
	On cover			21.00
11	A12	1m dark brown	.45	.80
	Never hinged		2.50	
	On cover			21.00
12	A12	2m deep blue	.70	1.20
	Never hinged		4.25	
	On cover			60.00
13	A12	5m green	1.50	1.60
	Never hinged		6.75	
	On cover			135.00
14	A12	10m red	2.75	3.25
	Never hinged		13.50	
	On cover			—
	Nos. 1-14 (14)		8.50	15.05
	Set, never hinged		40.00	

The colored areas of type A11 are white, and the white areas are colored, on Nos. 7-10.

Types of 1920
Overprinted in Blue

1920, May 20

15	A11	1o dark gray	.25	2.40
	Never hinged		.75	
	On cover			21.00

16	A11	5o green	.25	1.60
	Never hinged		.75	
	On cover			21.00
17	A11	7o yellow brn	.25	1.60
	Never hinged		.75	
	On cover			21.00
18	A11	10o rose red	.25	1.60
	Never hinged		.75	
	On cover			21.00
19	A11	15o lilac rose	.25	2.40
	Never hinged		.75	
	On cover			21.00
20	A11	20o dark blue	.25	2.75
	Never hinged		.75	
	On cover			30.00
21	A11	25o orange	.25	8.00
	Never hinged		1.20	
	On cover			67.50
22	A11	35o brown	.85	14.50
	Never hinged		6.00	
	On cover			85.00
23	A11	40o violet	.25	4.75
	Never hinged		2.60	
	On cover			85.00
24	A11	75o greenish blue	.45	8.00
	Never hinged		3.25	
	On cover			120.00
25	A12	1k dark brown	.65	13.00
	Never hinged		4.00	
	On cover			150.00
26	A12	2k deep blue	7.00	47.50
	Never hinged		40.00	
	On cover			—
27	A12	5k green	3.50	47.50
	Never hinged		30.00	
	On cover			—
28	A12	10k red	8.00	87.50
	Never hinged		40.00	
	On cover			—
	Nos. 15-28 (14)		22.45	243.10
	Set, never hinged		165.00	

OFFICIAL STAMPS

Nos. 1-14 Overprinted

1920	**Wmk. 114**		**Perf. 14x15**	
O1	A11	2½pf gray	65.00	92.50
	Never hinged		125.00	
	On cover			500.00
O2	A11	5pf green	65.00	110.00
	Never hinged		125.00	
	On cover			475.00
O3	A11	7½pf yellow brn	65.00	92.50
	Never hinged		125.00	
	On cover			600.00
O4	A11	10pf deep rose	65.00	120.00
	Never hinged		125.00	
	On cover			550.00
O5	A11	15pf red violet	42.50	60.00
	Never hinged		85.00	
	On cover			275.00
O6	A11	20pf dp blue	65.00	67.50
	Never hinged		125.00	
	On cover			275.00
a.	Double overprint		1,500.	
O7	A11	25pf orange	125.00	175.00
	Never hinged		290.00	
	On cover			625.00
a.	Inverted overprint		1,050.	
O8	A11	35pf brown	125.00	175.00
	Never hinged		290.00	
	On cover			725.00
O9	A11	40pf violet	110.00	100.00
	Never hinged		210.00	
	On cover			550.00
O10	A11	75pf grnsh blue	125.00	250.00
	Never hinged		250.00	
	On cover			850.00
O11	A12	1m dark brown	125.00	250.00
	Never hinged		250.00	
	On cover			850.00
O12	A12	2m deep blue	185.00	275.00
	Never hinged		375.00	
	On cover			1,100.
O13	A12	5m green	275.00	425.00
	Never hinged		550.00	
	On cover			—
O14	A12	10m red	500.00	625.00
	Never hinged		1,000.	
	Nos. O1-O14 (14)		1,937.	2,817.
	Set, never hinged		3,800.	

The letters "C.I.S." are the initials of "Commission Interalliée Slesvig," under whose auspices the plebiscites took place.
Counterfeit overprints exist.

SENEGAL

ˌse-ni-'gäl

LOCATION — West coast of Africa, bordering on the Atlantic Ocean
GOVT. — Republic
AREA — 76,000 sq. mi.
POP. — 6,300,000 (est. 1984)
CAPITAL — Dakar

The former French colony of Senegal became part of French West Africa in 1943. The Republic of Senegal was established Nov. 25, 1958. From Apr. 4, 1959, to June 20, 1960, the Republic of Senegal and the Sudanese Republic together formed the Mali Federation. After its breakup, Senegal resumed issuing its own stamps in 1960.

100 Centimes = 1 Franc

French Colonies Nos. 48, 49, 51, 52, 55, Type A9, Surcharged

1887	**Unwmk.**	**Perf. 14x13½**		
		Black Surcharge		
1	(a) 5c on 20c red, *grn*		210.00	210.00
	On cover			550.00
a.	Double surcharge		500.00	
2	(b) 5c on 20c red, *grn*		375.00	375.00
	On cover			600.00
3	(c) 5c on 20c red, *grn*		1,250.	1,250.
	On cover			2,000.
4	(d) 5c on 20c red, *grn*		260.00	260.00
	On cover			400.00
5	(e) 5c on 20c red, *grn*		475.00	475.00
	On cover			800.00
6	(a) 5c on 30c brn, *bis*		325.00	325.00
	On cover			750.00
7	(b) 5c on 30c brn, *bis*		1,400.	1,400.
	On cover			2,250.
8	(d) 5c on 30c brn, *bis*		475.00	475.00
	On cover			800.00
	Nos. 1-8 (8)		4,770.	4,770.

See Madagascar #6-7 for stamps with surcharge like "d" on 10c and 25c stamps.

9	(f) 10c on 4c cl, *lav*		160.00	160.00
	Never hinged		300.00	
	On cover			500.00
10	(g) 10c on 4c cl, *lav*		240.00	240.00
	On cover			500.00
11	(h) 10c on 4c cl, *lav*		120.00	120.00
	Never hinged		225.00	
	On cover			500.00

12	(i) 10c on 4c cl, *lav*		120.00	120.00
	On cover			600.00
a.	"1" without top stroke			
13	(f) 10c on 20c red, *grn*		725.00	725.00
	On cover			1,500.
14	(g) 10c on 20c red, *grn*		750.00	750.00
	On cover			1,500.
15	(h) 10c on 20c red, *grn*		650.00	650.00
	On cover			1,350.
16	(i) 10c on 20c red, *grn*		3,750.	3,750.
	On cover			7,500.
17	(j) 10c on 20c red, *grn*		750.00	750.00
	On cover			1,500.
18	(k) 10c on 20c red, *grn*		2,500.	2,500.
	On cover			5,000.
19	(l) 10c on 20c red, *grn*		750.00	750.00
	On cover			1,500.
20	(m) 10c on 20c red, *grn*		750.00	750.00
	On cover			1,500.

21	(n) 15c on 20c red, *grn*		130.00	130.00
	Never hinged		250.00	
	On cover			500.00
22	(o) 15c on 20c red, *grn*		110.00	110.00
	Never hinged		225.00	
	On cover			500.00
23	(p) 15c on 20c red, *grn*		87.50	87.50
	Never hinged		175.00	
	On cover			500.00
24	(q) 15c on 20c red, *grn*		160.00	160.00
	On cover			500.00
25	(r) 15c on 20c red, *grn*		100.00	100.00
	Never hinged		190.00	
	On cover			500.00
26	(s) 15c on 20c red, *grn*		100.00	100.00
	Never hinged		190.00	
	On cover			500.00
27	(t) 15c on 20c red, *grn*		260.00	260.00
	On cover			750.00
28	(u) 15c on 20c red, *grn*		87.50	87.50
	Never hinged		175.00	
	On cover			500.00
29	(v) 15c on 20c red, *grn*		120.00	120.00
	Never hinged		225.00	
	On cover			500.00
30	(w) 15c on 20c red, *grn*		425.00	425.00
	On cover			500.00
	Nos. 21-30 (10)		1,580.	1,580.

Counterfeits exist of Nos. 1-34.

French Colonies Stamps of 1881-86 Surcharged

1892		**Black Surcharge**		
31	A9 75c on 15c blue		450.00	200.00
	On cover			650.00
a.	"SENEGAL" double			950.00

32	A9	1fr on 5c grn, *grnsh*	450.00	200.00
		On cover		*650.00*
a.		"SENEGAL" double		14,750.
b.		"SENEGAL" omitted		2,800.
c.		"1F" double		325.00

"SENEGAL" in Red

33	A9	75c on 15c blue	15,250.	5,500.
		On cover		13,000.
34	A9	1fr on 5c grn, *grnsh*	6,500.	1,600.
		On cover		3,900.

Navigation and
Commerce — A24

Name of Colony in Blue or Carmine

1892-1900		**Typo.**	**Perf. 14x13½**	
35	A24	1c blk, *lil bl*	1.60	1.20
		Never hinged	2.40	
		On cover		95.00
36	A24	2c brn, *buff*	2.75	2.40
		Never hinged	4.75	
		On cover		95.00
37	A24	4c claret, *lav*	2.75	2.00
		Never hinged	4.75	
		On cover		95.00
38	A24	5c grn, *grnsh*	3.25	2.40
		Never hinged	5.50	
		On cover		50.00
39	A24	5c yel grn ('00)	2.75	1.60
		Never hinged	4.75	
		On cover		19.00
40	A24	10c blk, *lav*	8.00	6.50
		Never hinged	14.50	
		On cover		37.50
41	A24	10c red ('00)	6.00	2.00
		Never hinged	9.50	
		On cover		19.00
42	A24	15c bl, quadrille paper	15.00	2.40
		Never hinged	27.50	
		On cover		45.00
43	A24	15c gray ('00)	7.25	2.75
		Never hinged	13.50	
		On cover		19.00
44	A24	20c red, *grn*	12.00	6.50
		Never hinged	22.50	
		On cover		80.00
		On cover, single franking		140.00
45	A24	25c blk, *rose*	18.50	7.25
		Never hinged	35.00	
		On cover		37.50
46	A24	25c blue ('00)	45.00	37.50
		Never hinged	90.00	
		On cover		250.00
47	A24	30c brn, *bis*	20.00	9.50
		Never hinged	37.50	
		On cover		62.50
		On cover, single franking		105.00
48	A24	40c red, *straw*	28.00	24.00
		Never hinged	55.00	
		On cover		80.00
49	A24	50c car, *rose*	45.00	32.50
		Never hinged	92.50	
		On cover		100.00
		On cover, single franking		125.00
50	A24	50c brn, *az* ('00)	52.50	47.50
		Never hinged	100.00	
		On cover		300.00
		On cover, single franking		375.00
51	A24	75c vio, *org*	22.50	21.00
		Never hinged	45.00	
		On cover		125.00
		On cover, single franking		190.00
52	A24	1fr brnz grn, *straw*	26.00	23.00
		Never hinged	52.50	
		On cover		140.00
		On cover, single franking		225.00
		Nos. 35-52 (18)	318.85	232.00

Perf. 13½x14 stamps are counterfeits.
For surcharges see Nos. 53-56, 73-78.

Stamps of 1892 Surcharged

1903				
53	A24	5c on 40c red, *straw*	20.00	20.00
		Never hinged	32.50	
		On cover		95.00
54	A24	10c on 50c car, *rose*	28.00	28.00
		Never hinged	47.50	
		On cover		125.00
55	A24	10c on 75c vio, *org*	28.00	28.00
		Never hinged	47.50	
		On cover		110.00
56	A24	10c on 1fr brnz grn, *straw*	92.50	92.50
		Never hinged	175.00	
		On cover		300.00
		Nos. 53-56 (4)	168.50	168.50

General
Louis
Faidherbe
A25

Oil Palms — A26

Dr. Noel
Eugène
Ballay
A27

"SÉNÉGAL" in Red or Blue

1906				**Typo.**
57	A25	1c slate	1.60	1.60
		Never hinged	2.75	
		On cover		62.50
a.		"SENEGAL" omitted	160.00	160.00
58	A25	2c choc (R)	2.00	1.60
		Never hinged	3.50	
		On cover		62.50
58A	A25	2c choc (Bl)	3.25	2.40
		Never hinged	5.50	
		On cover		75.00
59	A25	4c choc, *gray bl*	2.75	2.40
		Never hinged	5.25	
		On cover		62.50
60	A25	5c green	3.25	1.20
		Never hinged	5.50	
		On cover		130.00
a.		"SENEGAL" omitted	13.50	1.20
61	A25	10c car (Bl)	27.50	
		Never hinged		
		On cover		21.00
a.		"SENEGAL" omitted	500.00	500.00
62	A25	15c violet	8.00	4.00
		Never hinged	16.00	
		On cover		50.00
63	A26	20c blk, *az*	9.50	4.75
		Never hinged	18.00	
		On cover		30.00
64	A26	25c bl, *pnksh*	4.00	3.25
		Never hinged	7.50	
		On cover		45.00
65	A26	30c choc, *pnksh*	9.50	6.50
		Never hinged	19.00	
		On cover		37.50
		On cover, single franking		70.00
66	A26	35c blk, *yellow*	32.50	3.25
		Never hinged	72.50	
		On cover		37.50
		On cover, single franking		55.00
a.		"SENEGAL" double	240.00	*260.00*
67	A26	40c car, *az* (Bl)	13.00	7.25
		Never hinged	25.00	
		On cover		62.50
		On cover, single franking		140.00
67A	A26	45c choc, *grnsh*	25.00	17.00
		Never hinged	60.00	
		On cover		80.00
		On cover, single franking		110.00
68	A26	50c dp violet	13.50	7.25
		Never hinged	27.50	
		On cover		62.50
		On cover, single franking		105.00
69	A26	75c bl, *org*	10.50	8.75
		Never hinged	20.00	
		On cover		95.00
		On cover, single franking		225.00
70	A27	1fr blk, *azure*	32.50	32.50
		Never hinged	67.50	
		On cover		140.00
		On cover, single franking		275.00
71	A27	2fr blue, *pink*	40.00	40.00
		Never hinged	90.00	
		On cover		175.00
		On cover, single franking		300.00
72	A27	5fr car, *straw* (Bl)	72.50	72.50
		Never hinged	150.00	
		On cover		250.00
		On cover, single franking		475.00
		Nos. 57-72 (18)	296.85	217.40

Stamps of 1892-1900 Surcharged in Carmine or Black

**Spacing between figures of
surcharge 1.5mm (5c), 2mm (10c)**

1912				
73	A24	5c on 15c gray (C)	1.20	1.20
		Never hinged	2.00	
		On cover		50.00
74	A24	5c on 20c red, *grn*	2.40	*2.40*
		Never hinged	4.00	
		On cover		100.00
75	A24	5c on 30c brn, *bis* (C)	1.60	1.60
		Never hinged	2.75	
		On cover		62.50
76	A24	10c on 40c red, *straw*	2.00	2.00
		Never hinged	3.25	
		On cover		75.00
77	A24	10c on 50c car, *rose*	4.75	5.50
		Never hinged	8.00	
		On cover		100.00
78	A24	10c on 75c vio, *org*	7.25	8.75
		Never hinged	12.00	
		Nos. 73-78 (6)	19.20	21.45

**Spacing between figures of
surcharge 2.25mm (5c), 2.75mm
(10c)**

73a	A24	5c on 15c gray (C)	22.50	22.50
		On cover		50.00
74a	A24	5c on 20c red, *grn*	250.00	250.00
75a	A24	5c on 30c brn, *bis* (C)	75.00	75.00
		On cover		200.00
76a	A24	10c on 40c red, *straw*	37.50	37.50
		On cover		90.00
77a	A24	10c on 50c car, *rose*	75.00	75.00
		On cover		200.00
78a	A24	10c on 75c vio, *org*	210.00	210.00
		Nos. 73a-78a (6)	670.00	670.00

Senegalese
Preparing
Food
A28

1914-33				**Typo.**
79	A28	1c ol brn & vio	.25	.25
		Never hinged	.40	
		On cover		62.50
a.		Chalky paper	.35	.25
		Never hinged	.40	
		On cover		62.50
80	A28	2c black & blue	.30	.30
		Never hinged	.55	
		On cover		62.50
81	A28	4c gray & brn	.30	.30
		Never hinged	.55	
		On cover		62.50
82	A28	5c yel grn & bl grn	.50	.25
		Never hinged	.80	
		On cover		21.00
a.		Chalky paper	1.10	.50
		Never hinged	2.00	
		On cover		25.00
83	A28	5c blk & rose ('22)	.25	.25
		Never hinged	.40	
		On cover		25.00
a.		Center double	340.00	
		Never hinged		450.00
84	A28	10c org red & rose	1.45	.25
		Never hinged	2.25	
		On cover		12.50
a.		Chalky paper	1.45	.25
		Never hinged	2.25	
		On cover		12.50
85	A28	10c yel grn & bl grn ('22)	.30	.30
		Never hinged	.50	
		On cover		37.50
86	A28	10c red brn & bl ('25)	.40	.40
		Never hinged	.80	
		On cover		40.00
87	A28	15c red org & brn vio ('17)	.40	.40
		Never hinged	.80	
		On cover		12.50
88	A28	20c choc & blk	.40	.30
		Never hinged	.70	
		On cover		21.00
89	A28	20c grn & bl grn ('26)	.55	.55
		Never hinged	.80	
		On cover		5.25
90	A28	20c db & lt bl ('27)	.80	.80
		Never hinged	1.20	
		On cover		16.50
91	A28	25c ultra & bl	1.20	.50
		Never hinged	2.00	
		On cover		22.50
		On cover, single franking		55.00
92	A28	25c red & blk ('22)	.65	.30
		Never hinged	1.00	
		On cover		6.25
93	A28	30c black & rose	.75	.30
		Never hinged	1.25	
		On cover		25.00
		On cover, single franking		70.00
94	A28	30c red org & rose ('22)	.65	.30
		Never hinged	1.00	
		On cover		25.00
		On cover, single franking		50.00
95	A28	30c gray & bl ('26)	.55	.30
		Never hinged	.80	
		On cover		9.00

96	A28	30c dl grn & dp grn ('28)	.80	.55
		Never hinged	1.20	
		On cover		37.50
97	A28	35c orange & vio	.70	.50
		Never hinged	1.30	
		On cover		30.00
		On cover, single franking		62.50
a.		Chalky paper	3.25	2.40
		Never hinged	5.50	
		On cover		45.00
98	A28	40c violet & grn	.90	.50
		Never hinged	1.35	
		On cover		37.50
		On cover, single franking		80.00
99	A28	45c bl & ol brn	1.90	1.25
		Never hinged	3.25	
		On cover		50.00
		On cover, single franking		110.00
100	A28	45c rose & bl ('22)	.95	.50
		Never hinged	1.50	
		On cover		50.00
		On cover, single franking		110.00
101	A28	45c rose & ver ('25)	.80	.80
		Never hinged	1.20	
		On cover		35.00
102	A28	45c ol brn & org ('28)	3.50	3.00
		Never hinged	5.50	
		On cover		35.00
		On cover, single franking		50.00
103	A28	50c vio brn & bl	1.90	1.20
		Never hinged	3.25	
		On cover		55.00
		On cover, single franking		125.00
104	A28	50c ultra & bl ('22)	2.40	2.10
		Never hinged	4.00	
		On cover		22.50
		On cover, single franking		50.00
105	A28	50c red org & grn ('26)	.65	.40
		Never hinged	.95	
		On cover		6.25
106	A28	60c vio, *pnksh* ('26)	.65	.40
		Never hinged	.95	
		On cover		25.00
		On cover, single franking		55.00
107	A28	65c rose red & dp grn ('28)	1.75	1.60
		Never hinged	2.75	
		On cover		40.00
		On cover, single franking		75.00
108	A28	75c gray & rose	1.20	.70
		Never hinged	2.00	
		On cover		37.50
		On cover, single franking		70.00
109	A28	75c dk bl & lt bl ('25)	1.20	1.20
		Never hinged	2.00	
		On cover		22.50
		On cover, single franking		45.00
110	A28	75c rose & gray bl ('26)	2.00	1.05
		Never hinged	3.25	
		On cover		11.00
111	A28	90c brn red & rose ('30)	5.50	5.50
		Never hinged	9.00	
		On cover		55.00
		On cover, single franking		140.00
112	A28	1fr violet & blk	1.20	.70
		Never hinged	2.00	
		On cover		55.00
		On cover, single franking		140.00
113	A28	1fr blue ('26)	1.05	1.05
		Never hinged	1.40	
		On cover		35.00
		On cover, single franking		87.50
114	A28	1fr blk & gray bl ('26)	1.75	1.05
		Never hinged	3.00	
		On cover		14.00
		On cover, single franking		20.00
115	A28	1.10fr bl grn & blk ('28)	4.25	*4.50*
		Never hinged	7.25	
		On cover		105.00
		On cover, single franking		275.00
116	A28	1.25fr dp grn & dp org ('33)	1.60	1.60
		Never hinged	2.40	
		On cover		19.00
		On cover, single franking		62.50
117	A28	1.50fr dk bl & bl ('30)	3.25	3.25
		Never hinged	4.75	
		On cover		50.00
		On cover, single franking		125.00
118	A28	1.75fr dk brn & Prus bl ('33)	7.25	1.60
		Never hinged	11.50	
		On cover		15.00
		On cover, single franking		21.00
119	A28	2fr carmine & bl	4.00	2.60
		Never hinged	7.25	
		On cover		70.00
		On cover, single franking		140.00
120	A28	2fr lt bl & brn ('22)	2.75	1.05
		Never hinged	4.50	
		On cover		42.50
		On cover, single franking		125.00
121	A28	3fr red vio ('30)	4.00	2.40
		Never hinged	7.25	
		On cover		67.50
		On cover, single franking		170.00
122	A28	5fr green & vio	5.50	2.00
		Never hinged	11.00	
		On cover		80.00
		On cover, single franking		150.00
		Nos. 79-122 (44)	73.10	49.10

For surcharges see Nos. 123-137, B1-B2.

No. 108
and Type of
1914
Srchd.

1922-25
123　A28　60c on 75c vio,
　　　pnksh　　　　　　1.10　1.10
　　Never hinged　　　　1.60
　　On cover　　　　　　　　15.00
　　On cover, single franking　　25.00
　a.　Double surcharge　140.00
　　Never hinged　　230.00
124　A28　65c on 15c red org
　　　& dl vio ('25)　　1.60　1.60
　　Never hinged　　　　2.40
　　On cover　　　　　　　　55.00
　　On cover, single franking　　125.00
125　A28　85c on 15c red org
　　　& dl vio ('25)　　1.60　1.60
　　Never hinged　　　　2.40
　　On cover　　　　　　　　37.50
　　On cover, single franking　　70.00
126　A28　85c on 75c ('25)　1.60　1.60
　　Never hinged　　　　2.40
　　On cover　　　　　　　　37.50
　　On cover, single franking　　70.00

No. 87
Srchd. in
Various
Colors

1922
127　A28　1c on 15c (Bk)　.80　.80
　　Never hinged　　　　1.20
　　On cover　　　　　　　　75.00
128　A28　2c on 15c (Bl)　.80　.80
　　Never hinged　　　　1.20
　　On cover　　　　　　　　75.00
129　A28　4c on 15c (G)　.80　.80
　　Never hinged　　　　1.20
　　On cover　　　　　　　　75.00
130　A28　5c on 15c (R)　.80　.80
　　Never hinged　　　　1.20
　　On cover　　　　　　　　30.00
　　Nos. 123-130 (8)　9.10　9.10

Stamps and Type of 1914 Surcharged
with New Value and Bars in Black or
Red
1924-27
131　A28　25c on 5fr grn &
　　　vio　　　　　　　.95　.95
　　Never hinged　　　　1.60
　　On cover　　　　　　　　6.25
132　A28　90c on 75c brn
　　　red & cer
　　　('27)　　　　　1.60　1.20
　　Never hinged　　　　2.40
　　On cover　　　　　　　　42.50
　　On cover, single franking　　75.00
　a.　Double surcharge　140.00　125.00
　　Never hinged　　230.00
133　A28　1.25fr on 1fr bl & lt
　　　bl (R) ('26)　　1.20　1.20
　　Never hinged　　　　2.00
　　On cover　　　　　　　　42.50
　　On cover, single franking　　87.50
134　A28　1.50fr on 1fr dk bl
　　　& ultra ('27)　1.60　1.20
　　Never hinged　　　　2.40
　　On cover　　　　　　　　37.50
　　On cover, single franking　　62.50
　a.　Surcharge omitted　160.00
　　Never hinged　　325.00
135　A28　3fr on 5fr mag &
　　　ol brn ('27)　　4.00　2.40
　　Never hinged　　　　6.75
　　On cover　　　　　　　　70.00
　　On cover, single franking　　140.00
　a.　Period after "F" omitted　16.00　12.50
　　Never hinged　　27.50
136　A28　10fr on 5fr dk bl
　　　& red org
　　　('27)　　　　8.75　4.00
　　Never hinged　　15.00
　　On cover　　　　　　　　87.50
　　On cover, single franking　　160.00
137　A28　20fr on 5fr vio &
　　　ol bis ('27)　8.75　8.00
　　Never hinged　　16.00
　　On cover　　　　　　　100.00
　　On cover, single franking　　200.00
　a.　Period after "F" omitted　27.50　26.00
　　Never hinged　　52.50
　　Nos. 131-137 (7)　26.85　18.95

Common Design Types
pictured following the introduction

Colonial Exposition Issue
Common Design Types
Name of Country Typographed in
Black
1931　　　Engr.　　Perf. 12½
138　CD70　40c deep green　4.50　4.50
　　Never hinged　　　　7.25
　　On cover　　　　　　　　80.00
139　CD71　50c violet　　4.50　4.50
　　Never hinged　　　　7.25
　　On cover　　　　　　　　70.00

140　CD72　90c red orange　4.50　4.50
　　Never hinged　　　　7.25
　　On cover　　　　　　　110.00
　a.　"SENEGAL" double　175.00
　　Never hinged　　250.00
141　CD73　1.50fr dull blue　4.50　4.50
　　Never hinged　　　　7.25
　　On cover　　　　　　　105.00
　　On cover, single franking　　165.00
　　Nos. 138-141 (4)　18.00　18.00

Faidherbe
Bridge, St.
Louis
A29

Diourbel
Mosque
A30

1935-40　　　Perf. 12½x12
142　A29　1c　violet blue　.25　.25
　　Never hinged　　　.40
　　On cover　　　　　　27.50
143　A29　2c　brown　　.25　.25
　　Never hinged　　　.40
　　On cover　　　　　　27.50
144　A29　3c　violet ('40)　.30　.30
　　Never hinged　　　.50
　　On cover　　　　　　27.50
145　A29　4c　gray blue　.25　.25
　　Never hinged　　　.40
　　On cover　　　　　　27.50
146　A29　5c　orange red　.25　.25
　　Never hinged　　　.40
　　On cover　　　　　　22.50
147　A29　10c　violet　　.25　.25
　　Never hinged　　　.40
　　On cover　　　　　　20.00
148　A29　15c　black　　.25　.25
　　Never hinged　　　.40
　　On cover　　　　　　16.00
149　A29　20c　dk carmine　.30　.25
　　Never hinged　　　.50
　　On cover　　　　　　16.00
150　A29　25c　black brn　.30　.25
　　Never hinged　　　.50
　　On cover　　　　　　12.50
151　A29　30c　green　　.30　.30
　　Never hinged　　　.50
　　On cover　　　　　　20.00
152　A29　40c　rose lake　.30　.30
　　Never hinged　　　.50
　　On cover　　　　　　8.75
153　A29　45c　dk blue grn　.30　.30
　　Never hinged　　　.50
　　On cover　　　　　　22.50
154　A30　50c　red orange　.30　.25
　　Never hinged　　　.50
　　On cover　　　　　　6.25
155　A30　60c　violet ('40)　.30　.30
　　Never hinged　　　.50
　　On cover　　　　　　20.00
156　A30　65c　dk violet　.30　.30
　　Never hinged　　　.50
　　On cover　　　　　　27.50
157　A30　70c　red brn ('40)　.80　.80
　　Never hinged　　　.95
　　On cover　　　　　　22.50
158　A30　75c　brown　　.80　.65
　　Never hinged　　1.00
　　On cover　　　　　　10.00
159　A30　90c　rose car　2.10　1.60
　　Never hinged　　2.75
　　On cover　　　　　　27.50
　　On cover, single franking　　70.00
160　A30　1fr　violet　10.50　2.60
　　Never hinged　14.50
　　On cover　　　　　　12.50
　　On cover, single franking　　19.00
161　A30　1.25fr redsh brn　1.35　.95
　　Never hinged　　1.90
　　On cover　　　　　　21.00
　　On cover, single franking　　42.50
162　A30　1.25fr rose car ('39)　.95　.95
　　Never hinged　　1.40
　　On cover　　　　　　55.00
　　On cover, single franking　　105.00
163　A30　1.40fr dk bl grn ('40)　.95　.95
　　Never hinged　　1.40
　　On cover　　　　　　32.50
　　On cover, single franking　　80.00
164　A30　1.50fr dk blue　.30　.30
　　Never hinged　　.50
　　On cover　　　　　　25.00
　　On cover, single franking　　62.50
165　A30　1.60fr pck bl ('40)　.95　.95
　　Never hinged　　1.20
　　On cover　　　　　　32.50
　　On cover, single franking　　92.50
166　A30　1.75fr dk blue grn　.40　.30
　　Never hinged　　.55
　　On cover　　　　　　8.25
　　On cover, single franking　　15.00
167　A30　2fr　blue　　.80　.30
　　Never hinged　　1.00
　　On cover　　　　　　14.00
　　On cover, single franking　　21.00
168　A30　3fr　green　　.75　.50
　　Never hinged　　.95
　　On cover　　　　　　32.50
　　On cover, single franking　　62.50
169　A30　5fr　black brn　.80　.75
　　Never hinged　　1.00
　　On cover　　　　　　40.00
　　On cover, single franking　　75.00

170　A30　10fr　rose lake　1.75　1.10
　　Never hinged　　2.25
　　On cover　　　　　　45.00
　　On cover, single franking　　87.50
171　A30　20fr　grnsh slate　1.75　1.10
　　Never hinged　　2.25
　　On cover　　　　　　62.50
　　On cover, single franking　　105.00
　　Nos. 142-171 (30)　29.15　17.85

Nos. 143, 148 and 156 surcharged with new
values are listed under French West Africa in
Scott Standard catalogue, Vol. 2.
For surcharges see Nos. B9, B11-B12 in
Scott Standard catalogue, Vol. 6.

Paris International Exposition Issue
Common Design Types
1937　　　　　　Perf. 13
172　CD74　20c deep violet　2.00　2.00
　　Never hinged　　3.25
　　On cover　　　　　　87.50
　a.　Sénégal omitted　100.00　110.00
　　Never hinged　　150.00
　　On cover　　　　　　300.00
173　CD75　30c dark green　2.00　2.00
　　Never hinged　　3.25
　　On cover　　　　　　70.00
174　CD76　40c car rose　2.00　2.00
　　Never hinged　　3.25
　　On cover　　　　　　55.00
175　CD77　50c dark brown　1.60　1.60
　　Never hinged　　2.50
　　On cover　　　　　　50.00
176　CD78　90c red　　1.60　1.60
　　Never hinged　　2.50
　　On cover　　　　　　95.00
　　On cover, single franking　　165.00
177　CD79　1.50fr ultra　2.00　2.00
　　Never hinged　　3.25
　　On cover　　　　　　80.00
　　On cover, single franking　　140.00
　　Nos. 172-177 (6)　11.20　11.20

Colonial Arts Exhibition Issue
Souvenir Sheet
Common Design Type
1937　　Unwmk.　　*Imperf.*
178　CD76　3fr rose violet　8.75　10.50
　　Never hinged　13.00
　　On cover　　　　　110.00
　　On cover, single franking　　165.00
　a.　Inscriptions inverted　1,600.
　　Never hinged　　2,100.

Senegalese
Woman — A31

1938-40　　Perf. 12x12½, 12½x12
179　A31　35c green　　.65　.65
　　Never hinged　　1.00
　　On cover　　　　　　27.50
180　A31　55c chocolate　.65　.65
　　Never hinged　　1.00
　　On cover　　　　　　7.50
181　A31　80c violet　1.10　.75
　　Never hinged　　1.60
　　On cover　　　　　　50.00
　　On cover, single franking　　70.00
182　A31　90c lt rose vio ('39)　.80　.80
　　Never hinged　　1.10
　　On cover　　　　　　37.50
　　On cover, single franking　　87.50
183　A31　1fr car lake　2.10　1.20
　　Never hinged　　2.75
　　On cover　　　　　　32.50
　　On cover, single franking　　62.50
184　A31　1fr cop brn ('40)　.70　.70
　　Never hinged　　.90
　　On cover　　　　　　7.00
185　A31　1.75fr ultra　1.10　.80
　　Never hinged　　1.60
　　On cover　　　　　　30.00
　　On cover, single franking　　55.00
186　A31　2.25fr ultra ('39)　1.05　1.05
　　Never hinged　　1.50
　　On cover　　　　　　37.50
　　On cover, single franking　　70.00
187　A31　2.50fr black ('40)　1.50　1.50
　　Never hinged　　2.00
　　On cover　　　　　　30.00
　　On cover, single franking　　55.00
　　Nos. 179-187 (9)　9.65　8.10

For surcharge see No. B10 in Scott Standard catalogue, Vol. 6.

Caillié Issue
Common Design Type
1939　　Engr.　　Perf. 12½x12
188　CD81　90c org brn & org　.80　.80
　　Never hinged　　.95
　　On cover　　　　　　3.75
189　CD81　2fr brt vio　1.20　1.20
　　Never hinged　　1.50
　　On cover　　　　　　22.50
　　On cover, single franking　　42.50

190　CD81　2.25fr ultra & dk bl　1.20　1.20
　　Never hinged　　1.50
　　On cover　　　　　　27.50
　　On cover, single franking　　50.00
　　Nos. 188-190 (3)　3.20　3.20

For No. 188 surcharged 20fr and 50fr, see
French West Africa in Scott Standard catalogue, Vol. 2.

New York World's Fair Issue
Common Design Type
1939　　　Perf. 12½x12
191　CD82　1.25fr car lake　.95　.95
　　Never hinged　　1.40
　　On cover　　　　　　62.50
　　On cover, single franking　　140.00
192　CD82　2.25fr ultra　1.05　1.05
　　Never hinged　　1.40
　　On cover　　　　　　62.50
　　On cover, single franking　　125.00

SEMI-POSTAL STAMPS

No. 84
Surcharged
in Red

1915　　Unwmk.　　Perf. 14x13½
B1　A28　10c + 5c org red &
　　　rose　　　　　2.00　2.00
　　Never hinged　　3.25
　　On cover　　　　　　37.50
　a.　Chalky paper　　2.00　2.00
　　Never hinged　　3.25
　　On cover　　　　　　37.50
　b.　Double surcharge　190.00
　　Never hinged　　340.00

No. B1 is on both ordinary and chalky paper.

Same Surcharge on No. 87
1918
B2　A28　15c + 5c red org &
　　　brn vio　　　2.00　2.00
　　Never hinged　　3.25
　　On cover　　　　　　37.50
　a.　Double surcharge　190.00
　　Never hinged　　340.00
　b.　Inverted surcharge　190.00
　　Never hinged　　340.00
　c.　Double surcharge, one in-
　　　verted　　　　　225.00

Curie Issue
Common Design Type
1938　　Engr.　　Perf. 13
B3　CD80　1.75fr + 50c brt ul-
　　　tra　　　　13.00　13.00
　　Never hinged　21.00
　　On cover　　　　　　80.00
　　On cover, single franking　　150.00

French Revolution Issue
Common Design Type
Photo., Name & Value Typo. in
Black
1939
B4　CD83　45c + 25c green　9.50　9.50
　　Never hinged　14.50
　　On cover　　　　　140.00
B5　CD83　70c + 30c brown　9.50　9.50
　　Never hinged　14.50
　　On cover　　　　　　95.00
B6　CD83　90c + 35c red
　　　org　　　　9.50　9.50
　　Never hinged　14.50
　　On cover　　　　　　80.00
B7　CD83　1.25fr + 1fr rose
　　　pink　　　9.50　9.50
　　Never hinged　14.50
　　On cover　　　　　140.00
　　On cover, single franking　　200.00
B8　CD83　2.25fr + 2fr blue　9.00　9.00
　　Never hinged　14.50
　　Nos. B4-B8 (5)　47.00　47.00

AIR POST STAMPS

Landscape
AP1

Caravan
AP2

Perf. 12½x12, 12x12½

1935	Engr.	Unwmk.	
C1	AP1	25c dk brown	.30	.30
	Never hinged	.50	
	On cover		19.00
C2	AP1	50c red orange	.65	.50
	Never hinged	.90	
	On cover		15.00
C3	AP1	1fr rose lilac	.30	.30
	Never hinged	.50	
	On cover		21.00
C4	AP1	1.25fr yellow grn	.30	.30
	Never hinged	.50	
	On cover		25.00
C5	AP1	2fr blue	.30	.30
	Never hinged	.50	
	On cover		30.00
C6	AP1	3fr olive grn	.50	.30
	Never hinged	.65	
	On cover		50.00
C7	AP2	3.50fr violet	.50	.30
	Never hinged	.65	
	On cover		45.00
C8	AP2	4.75fr orange	.95	.50
	Never hinged	1.40	
	On cover		55.00
C9	AP2	6.50fr dk blue	1.45	1.10
	Never hinged	1.75	
	On cover		62.50
C10	AP2	8fr black	1.75	1.75
	Never hinged	2.40	
	On cover		75.00
C11	AP2	15fr rose lake	1.75	1.40
	Never hinged	2.40	
	On cover		75.00
	Nos. C1-C11 (11)	8.75	7.05

No. C8 surcharged "ENTR' AIDE FRANCAIS + 95f 25" in green, red violet or blue, was never issued in this colony.

Common Design Type

1940	Engr.	Perf. 12½x12	
C12	CD85	1.90fr ultra	.55	.55
	Never hinged	.80	
	On cover		35.00
C13	CD85	2.90fr dk red	.55	.55
	Never hinged	.80	
	On cover		35.00
C14	CD85	4.50fr dk gray grn	.65	.65
	Never hinged	.90	
	On cover		40.00
C15	CD85	4.90fr yellow bis	.95	.95
	Never hinged	1.25	
	On cover		45.00
a.	"SENEGAL" double	350.00	
	Never hinged	500.00	
C16	CD85	6.90fr dp orange	1.30	1.30
	Never hinged	1.75	
	On cover		62.50
	Nos. C12-C16 (5)	4.00	4.00

AIR POST SEMI-POSTAL STAMPS

French Revolution Issue
Common Design Type

1939	Unwmk.	Photo.	Perf. 13	

Name and Value Typo. in Orange

CB1	CD83	4.75 + 4fr brn blk	16.00	16.00
	Never hinged	27.50	
	On cover		110.00
	On cover, single franking		200.00

Surtax used for the defense of the colonies.

POSTAGE DUE STAMPS

Postage Due Stamps of
French Colonies
Surcharged

1903	Unwmk.	Imperf.	
J1	D1	10c on 50c lilac	105.00	105.00
	Never hinged	220.00	
	On cover		450.00
J2	D1	10c on 60c brown, buff	105.00	105.00
	Never hinged	220.00	
	On cover		450.00
J3	D1	10c on 1fr rose, buff	475.00	475.00
	Nos. J1-J3 (3)	685.00	685.00

D2

1906	Typo.	Perf. 14x13½	
J4	D2	5c green, grnsh	6.50	4.75
	Never hinged	12.00	
	On cover		87.50
J5	D2	10c red brown	8.00	5.50
	Never hinged	16.00	
	On cover		87.50
J6	D2	15c dark blue	8.00	7.25
	Never hinged	16.00	
	On cover		100.00
J7	D2	20c black, yellow	10.50	7.25
	Never hinged	21.00	
	On cover		100.00
J8	D2	30c red, straw	11.00	11.00
	Never hinged	22.00	
	On cover		125.00
J9	D2	50c violet	13.50	13.50
	Never hinged	27.50	
	On cover		140.00
J10	D2	60c black, buff	17.00	17.00
	Never hinged	37.50	
	On cover		145.00
J11	D2	1fr black, pinkish	26.00	26.00
	Never hinged	55.00	
	On cover		175.00
	Nos. J4-J11 (8)	100.50	92.25

D3

1914			
J12	D3	5c green	.55	.55
	Never hinged	1.00	
	On cover		42.50
J13	D3	10c rose	.55	.55
	Never hinged	1.00	
	On cover		42.50
J14	D3	15c gray	.95	.80
	Never hinged	1.50	
	On cover		42.50
J15	D3	20c brown	1.20	1.10
	Never hinged	1.60	
	On cover		50.00
J16	D3	30c blue	1.60	1.40
	Never hinged	2.40	
	On cover		50.00
J17	D3	50c black	1.90	1.75
	Never hinged	2.75	
	On cover		55.00
J18	D3	60c orange	2.25	1.60
	Never hinged	3.50	
	On cover		62.50
J19	D3	1fr violet	2.25	1.90
	Never hinged	3.50	
	On cover		75.00
	Nos. J12-J19 (8)	11.25	9.65

Type of 1914 Issue
Surcharged

1927			
J20	D3	2fr on 1fr lilac rose	8.00	8.00
	Never hinged	14.50	
	On cover		95.00
a.	Period after "F" omitted	32.50	
	Never hinged	65.00	
J21	D3	3fr on 1fr orange brown	8.00	8.00
	Never hinged	14.50	
	On cover		105.00

D4

1935	Engr.	Perf. 12½x12	
J22	D4	5c yellow green	.30	.30
	Never hinged	.50	
	On cover		32.50
J23	D4	10c red orange	.30	.30
	Never hinged	.50	
	On cover		32.50
J24	D4	15c violet	.30	.30
	Never hinged	.50	
	On cover		32.50
J25	D4	20c olive green	.30	.30
	Never hinged	.50	
	On cover		32.50
J26	D4	30c reddish brown	.30	.30
	Never hinged	.50	
	On cover		32.50
J27	D4	50c rose lilac	1.10	1.10
	Never hinged	1.40	
	On cover		24.00
J28	D4	60c orange	1.50	1.50
	Never hinged	2.00	
	On cover		45.00
J29	D4	1fr black	1.10	1.10
	Never hinged	1.40	
	On cover		45.00
J00	D1	£fi dark blue	1.10	1.10
	Never hinged	1.40	
	On cover		75.00
J31	D4	3fr dark carmine	1.50	1.50
	Never hinged	2.00	
	Nos. J22-J31 (10)	7.80	7.80

SENEGAMBIA & NIGER

ˌse-nə-ˈgam-bē-ə and ˈnī-jər

A French Administrative unit for the Senegal and Niger possessions in Africa during the period when the French possessions in Africa were being definitively divided into colonies and protectorates. The name was dropped in 1904 when this territory was consolidated with part of French Sudan, under the name Upper Senegal and Niger.

100 Centimes = 1 Franc

Covers
Values are for commercial covers bearing correct frankings. Philatelic covers sell for less.

Navigation and
Commerce — A1

1903	Unwmk.	Typo.	Perf. 14x13½	

Name of Colony in Blue or Carmine

1	A1	1c black, lil bl	2.40	3.25
	Never hinged	4.00	
	On cover		340.00
a.	Accent omitted from first "e" of "Sénégambie"	14.50	20.00
	Never hinged	24.00	
2	A1	2c brown, buff	2.50	3.25
	Never hinged	4.00	
	On cover		340.00
a.	Accent omitted from first "e" of "Sénégambie"	14.50	20.00
	Never hinged	24.00	
3	A1	4c claret, lav	5.50	7.25
	Never hinged	10.00	
	On cover		310.00
a.	Accent omitted from first "e" of "Sénégambie"	32.50	45.00
	Never hinged	65.00	
4	A1	5c yel grn	6.75	8.50
	Never hinged	12.00	
	On cover		225.00
5	A1	10c red	7.50	9.00
	Never hinged	13.50	
	On cover		175.00
6	A1	15c gray	14.00	16.00
	Never hinged	25.00	
	On cover		275.00
7	A1	20c red, green	12.50	16.00
	Never hinged	24.00	
	On cover		400.00
	On cover, single franking		550.00
8	A1	25c blue	21.00	20.00
	Never hinged	40.00	
	On cover		250.00
9	A1	30c brn, bister	17.50	21.00
	Never hinged	35.00	
	On cover		325.00
	On cover, single franking		400.00
10	A1	40c red, straw	25.00	30.00
	Never hinged	45.00	
	On cover		340.00
	On cover, single franking		425.00
11	A1	50c brn, azure	50.00	55.00
	Never hinged	100.00	
	On cover		310.00
	On cover, single franking		425.00
12	A1	75c deep vio, org	55.00	62.50
	Never hinged	120.00	
	On cover		425.00
	On cover, single franking		675.00
13	A1	1fr brnz grn, straw	67.50	80.00
	Never hinged	140.00	
	On cover		550.00
	On cover, single franking		925.00
	Nos. 1-13 (13)	287.15	331.75

Perf. 13½x14 stamps are counterfeits.

SERBIA

ˈsər-bē-ə

LOCATION — In southeastern Europe, bounded by Romania and Bulgaria on the east, the former Austro-Hungarian Empire on the north, Greece on the south, and Albania and Montenegro on the west.

GOVT. Kingdom
AREA — 18,650 sq. mi.
POP. — 2,911,701 (1910)
CAPITAL — Belgrade

Following World War I, Serbia united with Montenegro, Bosnia and Herzegovina, Croatia, Dalmatia and Slovenia to form Yugoslavia.

100 Paras = 1 Dinar

Coat of
Arms — A1

Prince Michael
(Obrenovich
III) — A2

1866	Unwmk.	Typo.	Imperf.	

Paper colored Through

1	A1	1p dk green, dk vio rose		55.00

Surface Colored Paper, Thin or Thick

2	A1	1p dk green, lil rose		55.00
a.	1p olive green, rose		55.00
b.	1p yel grn, pale rose (thick paper)		375.00
3	A1	2p red brown, lilac		75.00
a.	2p red brn, lil gray (thick paper)		250.00
b.	2p dl grn, lil gray (thick paper)		800.00
	Nos. 1-3 (3)		185.00

Vienna Printing
Perf. 12

4	A2	10p orange	1,100.	675.00
5	A2	20p rose	750.00	30.00
6	A2	40p blue	750.00	125.00
a.	Half used as 20p on cover		
	Nos. 4-6 (3)	2,600.	830.00

Belgrade Printing
Perf. 9½

7	A2	1p green		22.50
8	A2	2p bister brn		32.50
9	A2	20p rose	15.00	22.50
a.	Pair, imperf. between		
10	A2	40p blue	240.00	275.00
a.	Half used as 20p on cover		
	Nos. 7-10 (4)		310.00

Pelure Paper

11	A2	10p orange	90.00	110.00
12	A2	20p rose	75.00	15.00
a.	Pair, imperf. between		
13	A2	40p ultra	55.00	37.50
a.	Pair, imperf. between		
b.	Half used as 20p on cover		
	Nos. 11-13 (3)	220.00	162.50

Nos. 1-3, 7-8, 14-16, 25-26 were used only as newspaper tax stamps.

1868-69	Ordinary Paper	Imperf.	
14	A2	1p green		37.50
a.	1p olive green ('69)		3,750.
15	A2	2p brown		75.00
a.	2p bister brown ('69)		260.00

Counterfeits of type A2 are common.

Prince Milan (Obrenovich IV)
A3   A4

Perf. 9½, 12 and Compound

1869-78			
16	A3	1p yellow	5.50	110.00
17	A3	10p red brown	9.00	4.75
a.	10p yellow brown	475.00	75.00
18	A3	10p orange ('78)	2.25	6.00
19	A3	15p orange	85.00	30.00
20	A3	20p gray blue	1.50	2.50
a.	20p ultramarine	4.50	2.25
b.	Half used as 10p on cover		
21	A3	25p rose	2.25	7.50
22	A3	35p lt green	4.50	4.50

23	A3	40p violet	2.25	3.00
a.		Half used as 20p on cover		
24	A3	50p blue green	11.00	7.50
		Nos. 16-24 (9)	123.25	175.75

The first setting, which included all values except No. 18, had the stamps 2-2 ½mm apart.

A new setting, introduced in 1878, had the stamps 3-4mm apart, providing wider margins. Only Nos. 17, 18, 20 and 21 exist in this new setting, which differs also in shades from the earlier setting.

The narrow-spaced Nos. 17, 20 and 21 are rarer, especially unused, as are the early shades of Nos. 23 and 24.

All values except Nos. 19 and 24 are known in various partly perforated varieties.

Counterfeits exist.

See No. 25.

1872-79 *Imperf.*

25	A3	1p yellow	6.75	19.00
a.		Tête bêche pair		
26	A4	2p blk, thin paper ('79)	.75	.75
a.		Thick paper ('73)	2.25	19.00

Used value of No. 26 is for canceled-to-order.

King Milan
I — A5

King Alexander
(Obrenovich V) — A6

1880 *Perf. 13x13½*

27	A5	5p green	1.90	.45
a.		5p olive green	550.00	3.75
28	A5	10p rose	2.25	.35
29	A5	20p orange	1.10	.75
a.		20p yellow	4.50	1.90
30	A5	25p ultra	1.50	1.10
a.		25p blue	1.90	1.10
31	A5	50p brown	1.50	5.50
a.		50p brown violet	210.00	4.50
32	A5	1d violet	6.75	6.00
		Nos. 27-32 (6)	15.00	14.05

1890

33	A6	5p green	.35	.25
34	A6	10p rose red	1.25	.25
35	A6	15p red violet	1.10	.25
36	A6	20p orange	.75	.25
37	A6	25p blue	.90	.35
38	A6	50p brown	2.25	2.25
39	A6	1d dull lilac	11.00	9.00
		Nos. 33-39 (7)	17.60	12.60

King Alexander — A7

1894-96 *Perf. 13x13½*
Granite Paper

40	A7	5p green	4.00	.45
a.		Perf. 11½	7.50	.40
41	A7	10p car rose	5.50	.25
b.		Perf. 11½	90.00	1.50
42	A7	15p violet	9.00	.25
43	A7	20p orange	67.50	.75
a.		Half used as 10p on cover		375.00
44	A7	25p blue	19.00	.35
45	A7	50p brown	22.50	.75
46	A7	1d dk green	1.50	3.00
47	A7	1d red brn, *bl* ('96)	19.00	3.75
		Nos. 40-47 (8)	148.00	9.35

1898-1900 *Perf. 13x13½, 11½*
Ordinary Paper

48	A7	1p dull red	.30	.25
49	A7	5p green	3.75	.25
50	A7	10p rose	60.00	.25
51	A7	15p violet	7.50	.25
52	A7	20p orange	6.25	.25
53	A7	25p deep blue	7.00	.25
54	A7	50p brown	15.00	3.00
		Nos. 48-54 (7)	99.80	4.60

Nos. 49-54 exist imperf.

Nos. 49-51, 53 and 56-57 exist with perf. 13x13½x11½x13½.

Type of 1900 Stamp
Surcharged

1900

56	A7	10p on 20p rose	5.50	.75

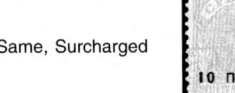

Same, Surcharged

1901

57	A7	10p on 20p rose	1.75	.25
58	A7	15p on 1d red brn,		
		bl	5.25	1.00
a.		Inverted surcharge	100.00	110.00

King Alexander
(Obrenovich V)
A8   A9

1901-03 *Typo.* *Perf. 11½*

59	A8	5p green	.35	.35
60	A8	10p rose	.35	.35
61	A8	15p red violet	.35	.35
62	A8	20p orange	.35	.35
63	A8	25p ultra	.35	.35
64	A8	50p bister	.75	.75
65	A9	1d brown	1.10	1.90
66	A9	3d brt rose	11.00	15.00
67	A9	5d deep violet	11.00	15.00
		Nos. 59-67 (9)	25.60	34.40

Counterfeits of Nos. 66-67 exist. Nos. 59-67 imperf. value of set of pairs, $100.

Arms of Serbia on
Head of King
Alexander — A10

Type I   Type II

Two Types of the Overprint

Type I — Overprint 12mm wide. Bottom of mantle defined by a single line. Wide crown above shield.

Type II — Overprint 10mm wide. Double line at bottom of mantle. Smaller crown above shield.

Arms Overprinted in Blue, Black, Red and Red Brown

1903-04 *Type I* *Perf. 13½*

68	A10	1p red lil & blk (Bl)	.90	1.10
a.		Inverted overprint		10.00
69	A10	5p yel grn & blk (Bl)	.75	.35
70	A10	10p car & blk (Bk)	.50	.35
a.		Double overprint		8.75
71	A10	15p ol gray & blk (Bk)	.50	.35
a.		Double overprint		8.75
72	A10	20p org & blk (Bk)	.75	.35
73	A10	25p bl & blk (Bk)	.75	.35
a.		Double overprint		10.00
74	A10	50p gray & blk (R)	4.50	1.10

There were two printings of the type I overprint on Nos. 68-74, one typographed and one lithographed.

Type II

75	A10	1d bl grn & blk (Bk)	11.00	4.50

#68-75 with overprint omitted, value, set $75.

Perf. 11½
Type I

75A	A10	5p (Bl)	.75	1.50
75B	A10	50p (R)	2.25	7.50
75C	A10	1d (Bk)	2.25	15.00

Type II

76	A10	3d vio & blk (R Br)	3.00	3.75
a.		Perf. 13½	110.00	110.00
77	A10	5d lt brn & blk (Bl)	3.00	3.75

Type I With Additional
Surcharge

78	A10	1p on 5d (R)	2.25	11.00
a.		Perf. 13½	750.00	750.00
		Nos. 68-78 (14)	33.15	50.95

Karageorge
and Peter
I — A11

Insurgents,
1804
A12

1904 *Typo.*

79	A11	5p yellow green	1.50	.75
80	A11	10p rose red	.75	.75
81	A11	15p red violet	.75	.75
82	A11	25p blue	1.50	1.50
83	A11	50p gray brown	1.50	1.50
84	A12	1d bister	2.25	5.25
85	A12	3d blue green	3.00	7.50
86	A12	5d violet	3.75	9.00
		Nos. 79-86 (8)	15.00	27.00

Centenary of the Karageorgevich dynasty and the coronation of King Peter. Counterfeits of Nos. 79-86 exist.

King Peter I Karageorgevich
A13   A14

Perf. 11½, 12x11½

1905 **Wove Paper**

87	A13	1p gray & blk	.25	.25
88	A13	5p yel grn & blk	.90	.25
89	A13	10p red & blk	2.50	.25
90	A13	15p red lil & blk	3.00	.25
91	A13	20p yellow & blk	5.25	.25
92	A13	25p ultra & blk	6.25	.25
93	A13	30p sl grn & blk	4.50	.25
94	A13	50p dk brown & blk	5.50	.50
95	A13	1d bister & blk	.90	.25
96	A13	3d blue grn & blk	.90	.90
97	A13	5d violet & blk	3.75	2.75
		Nos. 87-97 (11)	33.70	6.25

Counterfeits of Nos. 87-97 abound.

The stamps of this issue may be found on both thick and thin paper.

1908 **Laid Paper**

98	A13	1p gray & blk	.35	.25
99	A13	5p yel grn & blk	2.25	.25
100	A13	10p red & blk	6.75	.25
101	A13	15p red lilac & blk	9.00	.25
102	A13	20p yellow & blk	9.00	.35
103	A13	25p ultra & blk	6.75	.35
104	A13	30p gray grn & blk	10.00	.35
105	A13	50p dk brn & blk	13.00	.75
		Nos. 98-105 (8)	57.10	2.80

Nos. 90, 98-100, 102-104 are known imperforate but are not believed to have been issued in this condition.

Values of Nos. 98-105 are for horizontally laid paper. Four values also exist on vertically laid paper (1p, 5p, 10p, 30p).

1911-14 **Thick Wove Paper**

108	A14	1p slate green	.25	.25
109	A14	2p dark violet	.25	.25
110	A14	5p green	.25	.25
111	A14	5p pale yel grn ('14)	.25	.25
112	A14	10p carmine	.25	.25
113	A14	10p red ('14)	.25	.25
114	A14	15p red violet	.35	.25
115	A14	15p slate blk ('14)	.25	.25
a.		15p red (error)	900.00	—
116	A14	20p yellow	.30	.25
117	A14	20p brown ('14)	.50	.30
118	A14	25p deep blue	.45	.25
119	A14	25p indigo ('14)	.25	.25
120	A14	30p blue green	.30	.30
121	A14	30p olive grn ('14)	.25	.30
122	A14	50p dk brown	.50	.35
123	A14	50p brn red ('14)	.45	.35
124	A14	1d orange	22.50	45.00
125	A14	1d slate ('14)	3.75	7.50
126	A14	3d lake	30.00	90.00
127	A14	3d olive yel ('14)	150.00	1,100.
128	A14	5d violet	27.50	62.50
129	A14	5d dk violet ('14)	6.00	19.00
		Nos. 108-129 (22)	244.85	1,328.

Counterfeits exist.

King Peter
and Military
Staff — A15

1915 *Perf. 11½*

132	A15	5p yellow green	.35	—
133	A15	10p scarlet	.35	—
134	A15	15p slate	5.50	
135	A15	20p brown	1.50	
136	A15	25p blue	11.00	
137	A15	30p olive green	7.50	
138	A15	50p orange brown	30.00	
		Nos. 132-138 (7)	56.20	

Nos. 134-138 were prepared but not issued for postal use. Instead they were permitted to be used as wartime emergency currency. Some are known imperf. The 15p also exists in blue from an erroneous cliche in the 25p plate; value $325.

Stamps of France, 1900-1907, with this handstamped control were used in 1916-1918 by the Serbian Postal Bureau on the Island of Corfu. On the 1c to 35c, the handstamp covers 2 or 3 stamps. It was applied after the stamps were on the cover.

King Peter and
Prince
Alexander — A16

1918-20 *Typo.* *Perf. 11, 11½*

155	A16	1p black	.25	.25
156	A16	2p olive brown	.25	.25
157	A16	5p apple green	.25	.25
158	A16	10p red	.25	.25
159	A16	15p black brown	.25	.25
160	A16	20p red brown	.25	.25
161	A16	20p violet ('20)	1.60	.90
162	A16	25p deep blue	.25	.25
163	A16	30p olive green	.25	.25
164	A16	50p violet	.25	.25
165	A16	1d violet brown	1.10	.25
166	A16	3d slate green	1.50	.90
167	A16	5d red brown	1.90	1.10
		Nos. 155-167 (13)	8.35	5.40

Nos. 157-160, 164 exist imperf. Value each $9.

1920 **Pelure Paper** *Perf. 11½*

169	A16	1p black	.25	.25
170	A16	2p olive brown	.25	.25

POSTAGE DUE STAMPS

Coat of Arms
D1   D2

1895   Unwmk.   Typo.   Perf. 13x13½
Granite Paper

J1	D1	5p red lilac	6.00	1.00
J2	D1	10p blue	6.00	.40
J3	D1	20p orange brown	47.50	8.00
J4	D1	30p green	.40	.80
J5	D1	50p rose	.40	1.10
a.		Cliché of 5p in plate of 50p	80.00	100.00
		Nos. J1-J5 (5)	60.30	11.30

No. J1 exists imperf. Value $75.

1898-1904   Ordinary Paper

J6	D1	5p magenta ('04)	.70	.70
J7	D1	20p brown	6.00	1.00
a.		Tête bêche pair	150.00	150.00
J8	D1	20p dp brn ('04)	6.00	1.00
		Nos. J6-J8 (3)	12.70	2.70

1906   Granite Paper   Perf. 11½

J9	D1	5p magenta	5.25	1.00

1909   Laid Paper

J10	D1	5p magenta	.80	.60
J11	D1	10p pale blue	4.75	7.50
J12	D1	20p pale brown	.40	.80
		Nos. J10-J12 (3)	5.95	8.90

1914   White Wove Paper

J13	D1	5p rose	.40	2.00
J14	D1	10p deep blue	6.00	9.00

1918-20   Perf. 11

J15	D2	5p red	.40	.85
J16	D2	5p red brown ('20)	.40	.85
J17	D2	10p yellow green	.40	.85
J18	D2	20p olive brown	.40	.85
J19	D2	30p slate green	.40	.85
J20	D2	50p chocolate	.90	1.50
		Nos. J15-J20 (6)	2.90	5.75

NEWSPAPER STAMPS

N1

Overprinted with Crown-topped Shield in Black

1911   Unwmk.   Typo.   Perf. 11½

P1	N1	1p gray	.80	.80
P2	N1	5p green	.80	.80
P3	N1	10p orange	.80	.80
a.		Cliché of 1p in plate of 10p	225.00	
P4	N1	15p violet	.80	.80
P5	N1	20p yellow	.80	.80
a.		Cliché of 50p in plate of 20p	85.00	140.00
P6	N1	25p blue	.80	.80
P7	N1	30p slate	7.50	7.50
P8	N1	50p brown	6.25	6.25
P9	N1	1d bister	6.25	6.25
P10	N1	3d rose red	7.50	7.50
P11	N1	5d gray vio	6.25	6.25
		Nos. P1-P11 (11)	38.55	38.55

ISSUED UNDER AUSTRIAN OCCUPATION

100 Heller = 1 Krone

Stamps of Bosnia,
1912-14,
Overprinted

1916   Unwmk.   Perf. 12½

1N1	A23	1h olive green	2.25	5.25
1N2	A23	2h brt blue	2.25	5.25
1N3	A23	3h claret	2.25	5.25
1N4	A23	5h green	.40	.75
1N5	A23	6h dk gray	1.50	3.75
1N6	A23	10h rose carmine	.40	.75
1N7	A23	12h dp olive grn	.80	2.25
1N8	A23	20h orange brown	.80	1.40
1N9	A23	25h ultra	.80	2.25
1N10	A23	30h orange red	.80	2.25
1N11	A24	35h myrtle grn	.80	2.25
1N12	A24	40h dk violet	.80	2.25
1N13	A24	45h olive brown	.80	2.25
1N14	A24	50h slate blue	.80	2.25
1N15	A24	60h brown violet	.80	2.25
1N16	A24	72h dark blue	.80	2.25
1N17	A25	1k brn vio, *straw*	1.50	2.25
1N18	A25	2k dk gray, *bl*	1.50	2.25
1N19	A26	3k carmine, *grn*	1.50	2.25
1N20	A26	5k dk vio, *gray*	1.50	2.25
1N21	A26	10k dk ultra, *gray*	15.00	30.00
		Nos. 1N1-1N21 (21)	38.05	81.65

Stamps of Bosnia, 1912-14,
Overprinted "SERBIEN" Horizontally at
Bottom

1916

1N22	A23	1h olive green	8.00	19.00
1N23	A23	2h bright blue	8.00	19.00
1N24	A23	3h claret	8.00	19.00
1N25	A23	5h green	.50	3.00
1N26	A23	6h dark gray	8.00	19.00
1N27	A23	10h rose carmine	.50	3.00
1N28	A23	12h dp olive grn	8.00	19.00
1N29	A23	20h orange brn	8.00	19.00
1N30	A23	25h ultra	8.00	19.00
1N31	A23	30h orange red	8.00	19.00
1N32	A24	35h myrtle green	8.00	19.00
1N33	A24	40h dk violet	8.00	19.00
1N34	A24	45h olive brown	8.00	19.00
1N35	A24	50h slate blue	8.00	19.00
1N36	A24	60h brown violet	8.00	19.00
1N37	A24	72h dark blue	8.00	19.00
1N38	A25	1k brn vio, *straw*	19.00	40.00
1N39	A25	2k dk gray, *bl*	19.00	40.00
1N40	A26	3k carmine, *grn*	22.50	47.50
1N41	A26	5k dk vio, *gray*	27.50	60.00
1N42	A25	10k dk ultra, *gray*	52.50	100.00
		Nos. 1N22-1N42 (21)	253.50	559.50

Nos. 1N22-1N42 were prepared in 1914, at
the time of the 1st Austrian occupation of Serbia. They were not issued at that time because
of the retreat. The stamps were put on sale in
1916, at the same time as Nos. 1N1-1N21.

SEYCHELLES

sā-¹shelᶻ̗

LOCATION — A group of islands in the Indian Ocean, off the coast of Africa north of Madagascar.
GOVT. — British Colony
AREA — 156 sq. mi.
POP. — 64,718 (est. 1984)
CAPITAL — Victoria

The islands were attached to the British colony of Mauritius from 1810 to 1903, when they became a separate colony.

100 Cents = 1 Rupee

Catalogue values for unused stamps in this country are for Never Hinged items, beginning with Scott 149 in the regular postage section and Scott J1 in the postage due section.

STAMPS OF MAURITIUS USED IN SEYCHELLES

Various Issues Canceled B64

1861		**Post Paid**
A1	2p blue (#4b)	11,000.

1861	**Britannia**	**Imperf.**
A2	6p blue (#18)	975.00
A3	6p gray violet (#20)	2,500.
A4	1sh vermilion (#19)	1,600.

1861-63		**Perf. 14**
A5	1p brown lilac (#24)	260.00
A6	2p blue (#25)	300.00
A7	4p rose (#26)	260.00
A8	6p green (#27)	1,100.
A9	6p lilac (#28)	750.00
A10	9p dull lilac (#29)	140.00
A11	1sh buff (#30)	375.00
A12	1sh green (#31)	850.00

1862		**Perf. 14 to 16**
A13	6p slate (#22)	925.00

1863-72		**Wmk. 1**
A14	1p lilac brown (#32)	140.00
a.	1p bister brown (#32a)	125.00
b.	1p brown (#32b)	110.00
A15	2p pale blue (#33)	150.00
a.	2p bright blue (#33)	150.00
A16	3p vermilion (#34)	100.00
a.	3p deep red (#34a)	180.00
A17	4p rose (#35)	55.00
A18	6p lilac (#36)	275.00
A19	6p blue grn (#37)	85.00
a.	6p yellow green (#37a)	125.00
A20	9p green (#38)	1,800.
A21	10p claret (#42)	375.00
A22	1sh org yel (#39)	125.00
a.	1sh yellow (#39a)	120.00
A23	1sh blue (#40)	350.00
A24	5sh berl violet (#41)	1,000.
a.	5sh bright violet (#41a)	1,000.

1876-77		**Surcharges**
A25	½p on 9p (#43)	375.00
A26	½p on 10p claret (#46)	350.00
A27	½p on 10p claret (#47)	750.00
A28	1p on 4p rose (#48)	—
A29	1sh on 5sh red vio (#49)	—
a.	1sh on 5sh violet (#49a)	—

1878		**Decimal Surcharges**
A30	2c claret (#50)	110.00
A31	4c on 1p bister brn (#51)	425.00
A32	8c on 2p blue (#52)	47.50
A33	13c on 3p org red (#53)	140.00
A34	17c on 4p rose (#54)	47.50
A35	25c on 6p sl blue (#55)	125.00
A36	38c on 9p violet (#56)	575.00
A37	50c on 1sh green (#57)	125.00
A38	2r50c on 5sh violet (#58)	575.00

1879-80	**Wmk. 1**	**New Designs**
A39	2c red brown (#59)	150.00
A40	4c orange (#60)	150.00
A41	8c blue (#61)	47.50
A42	13c slate (#62)	1,500.
A43	17c rose (#63)	100.00
A44	25c bister (#64)	210.00
A45	38c violet (#65)	1,900.
A46	50c green (#66)	975.00
A47	2r50c brn vio (#67)	975.00

1882-93		**Wmk. 2**
A48	2c red brown (#69)	110.00
A49	2c green (#70)	200.00
A50	4c orange (#71)	75.00

A51	4c rose (#72)	110.00
A52	25c bister (#74)	125.00
A53	50c deep orange (#75)	1,000.

1883		**Surcharges**
A54	16c on 17c rose, "16 CENTS" (#76)	150.00
A55	16c on 17c rose, "SIXTEEN CENTS" (#79)	50.00

1885		
A56	16c orange brown (#82)	62.50

1885-87		**Wmk. 1**
A57	2c on 38c violet (#64)	—
A58	2c on 13c slate (R) (#84)	—

Issued under British Administration

Queen Victoria — A1

Die I

Die II

Two dies of 2c, 4c, 8c, 10c, 13c, 16c:

Die I — Shading lines at right of diamond in tiara band.
Die II — No shading lines in this rectangle.

				Perf. 14
1890-1900		**Typo.**	**Wmk. 2**	
1	A1	2c grn & rose (II)	3.50	1.25
a.		Die I	6.50	16.00
2	A1	2c org brn & grn ('00)	2.50	1.75
3	A1	3c dk vio & org ('93)	2.00	.75
4	A1	4c car rose & grn (II)	3.50	1.75
a.		Die I	45.00	17.00
5	A1	6c car rose ('00)	4.50	.75
6	A1	8c brn vio & ultra (II)	15.00	2.50
a.		8c brn vio & bl (I)	15.00	4.50
7	A1	10c ultra & brn (II)	15.00	4.25
a.		10c bl & brn (I)	13.00	32.00
8	A1	12c ol gray & grn ('93)	3.50	.85
9	A1	13c slate & blk (II)	5.00	2.50
a.		Die I	8.00	17.00
10	A1	15c ol grn & vio ('93)	6.00	2.75
11	A1	15c ultra ('00)	10.00	5.00
12	A1	16c org brn & bl (I)	12.00	5.50
a.		16c org brn & ultra (II)	52.50	14.50
13	A1	18c ultra ('97)	10.00	1.50
14	A1	36c brn & rose ('97)	40.00	6.00
15	A1	45c brn & rose ('93)	30.00	45.00
16	A1	48c ocher & green	25.00	15.00
17	A1	75c yel & pur ('00)	70.00	87.50
18	A1	96c violet & car	67.50	60.00
19	A1	1r vio & red ('97)	16.00	6.50

20	A1	1.50r blk & rose ('00)	90.00	110.00
21	A1	2.25r vio & grn ('00)	125.00	110.00
		Nos. 1-21 (21)	556.00	471.10

Numerals of 75c, 1r, 1.50r and 2.25r of type A1 are in color on plain tablet.
The 10c in ultramarine and orange brown, Die I, is known only with "SPECIMEN" overprint. Value $800.
For surcharges see Nos. 22-37.

Surcharged in Black

1893				
22	A1	3c on 4c car rose & green (II)	1.50	2.00
a.		Inverted surcharge	375.00	450.00
b.		Double surcharge	600.00	
d.		Pair, one without surcharge	14,000.	
23	A1	12c on 16c org brn & ultra (II)	20.00	3.50
a.		12c on 16c org brn & bl (I)	4.75	5.00
b.		Inverted surcharge (I)	575.00	
d.		Double surcharge (I)	15,750.	11,000.
e.		Double surcharge (II)	5,500.	5,500.
24	A1	15c on 16c org brn & ultra (II)	23.00	4.00
a.		15c on 16c org brn & bl (I)	12.00	17.50
b.		Inverted surcharge (II)	400.00	375.00
c.		Inverted surcharge (II)	1,100.	1,250.
d.		Double surcharge (II)	1,500.	1,500.
e.		Double surcharge (II)	825.00	875.00
f.		Triple surcharge (II)	5,000.	
25	A1	45c on 48c ocher & grn	35.00	7.00
26	A1	90c on 96c vio & car	70.00	45.00
		Nos. 22-26 (5)	149.50	61.50

No. 15 Surcharged in Black

1896				
27	A1	18c on 45c brn & rose	10.00	4.25
a.		Double surcharge	1,850.	1,850.
b.		Triple surcharge	2,750.	
28	A1	36c on 45c brn & rose	12.00	70.00
a.		Double surcharge	1,850.	
		Nos. 27-28, ovptd. "SPECIMEN"	75.00	

Surcharged in Black

1901				
29	A1	3c on 10c bl & brn (II)	2.25	.90
a.		Double surcharge	950.00	
b.		Triple surcharge	3,250.	
30	A1	3c on 16c org brn & ultra (II)	5.00	7.50
a.		"3 cents" omitted (II)	675.00	675.00
b.		Inverted surcharge (II)	800.00	800.00
c.		Double surcharge (II)	625.00	650.00
31	A1	3c on 36c brn & rose	1.00	1.10
a.		Without bars		
b.		Double surcharge	950.00	1,100.
c.		"3 cents" omitted	800.00	850.00
32	A1	6c on 8c brn vio & ultra (II)	4.50	4.00
a.		Inverted surcharge	800.00	925.00
		Nos. 29-32 (4)	12.75	13.50
		Set, ovptd. "SPECIMEN"	110.00	

Stamps of 1890-1900 Surcharged

1902, June				
33	A1	2c on 4c car rose & grn (II)	3.75	3.50
34	A1	30c on 75c yel & pur	2.25	5.50
a.		Narrow "0" in "30"	12.50	57.50
35	A1	30c on 1r vio & red	15.00	45.00
a.		Narrow "0" in "30"	35.00	110.00
b.		Double surcharge	1,750.	
36	A1	45c on 1r vio & red	8.50	60.00
37	A1	45c on 2.25r vio & grn	52.50	160.00
a.		Narrow "5" in "45"	250.00	450.00
		Nos. 33-37 (5)	82.00	274.00
		Set, opt. "SPECIMEN"	140.00	

King Edward VII — A6

Numerals of 75c, 1.50r and 2.25r of type A6 are in color on plain tablet.

				Wmk. 2
1903, May 26		**Typo.**		
38	A6	2c red brn & grn	2.25	2.50
39	A6	3c green	1.25	1.60
40	A6	6c carmine rose	3.50	1.60
41	A6	12c ol gray & grn	3.75	3.25
42	A6	15c ultra	5.00	3.25
43	A6	18c pale yel grn & rose	5.25	8.25
44	A6	30c purple & grn	8.75	15.00
45	A6	45c brown & rose	8.75	15.00
46	A6	75c yel & pur	12.50	35.00
47	A6	1.50r black & rose	55.00	87.50
48	A6	2.25r red vio & grn	45.00	110.00
		Nos. 38-48 (11)	151.00	282.95
		Set, ovptd. "SPECIMEN"	210.00	

Nos. 42-43, 45 Surcharged

1903				
49	A6	3c on 15c	1.40	4.25
50	A6	3c on 18c	4.00	52.50
51	A6	3c on 45c	4.25	4.25
		Nos. 49-51 (3)	9.65	61.00
		Set, ovptd. "SPECIMEN"	85.00	

		Type of 1903		
1906				**Wmk. 3**
52	A6	2c red brn & grn	1.90	5.50
53	A6	3c green	1.90	1.90
54	A6	6c car rose	2.50	1.00
55	A6	12c ol gray & grn	4.00	4.00
56	A6	15c ultra	4.00	2.50
57	A6	18c pale yel grn & rose	4.00	8.00
58	A6	30c purple & grn	7.75	10.00
59	A6	45c brown & rose	4.00	10.00
60	A6	75c yellow & pur	11.00	67.50
61	A6	1.50r black & rose	65.00	72.50
62	A6	2.25r red vio & grn	47.50	72.50
		Nos. 52-62 (11)	153.55	255.40

King George V — A7

Numerals of 75c, 1.50r and 2.25r of type A7 are in color on plain tablet.

				Perf. 14
1912				
63	A7	2c org brn & grn	1.00	7.50
64	A7	3c green	4.50	.70
65	A7	6c car rose	4.75	2.00
66	A7	12c ol gray & grn	1.50	5.00
67	A7	15c ultra	4.00	1.75
68	A7	18c pl yel grn & rose	3.50	9.00
69	A7	30c pur & grn	10.00	1.50
70	A7	45c brn & rose	3.00	50.00
71	A7	75c yell & pur	3.25	6.00
72	A7	1.50r blk & rose	9.50	1.10
73	A7	2.25r vio & grn	75.00	2.75
		Nos. 63-73 (11)	120.00	87.30
		Set, ovptd. "SPECIMEN"	240.00	

King George V — A8

For description of dies I and II see Dies of British Colonial Stamps in the Table of Contents.

The 5c of type A8 has a colorless numeral on solid-color tablet. Numerals of 9c, 20c, 25c, 50c, 75c, and 1r to 5r of type A8 are in color on plain tablet.

1917-20   **Die I**

74	A8	2c org brn & grn	.55	3.00
75	A8	3c green	2.25	1.40
76	A8	5c brown ('20)	3.00	10.00
77	A8	6c carmine rose	4.00	1.60
78	A8	12c gray	2.50	1.10
79	A8	15c ultra	1.90	1.60
80	A8	18c violet, *yel*	4.00	40.00
a.		Die II ('20)	2.75	24.00
81	A8	25c blk & red, *yel* ('20)	2.75	47.50
a.		Die II ('20)	3.50	43.00
82	A8	30c dull vio & ol grn	1.60	12.00
83	A8	45c dull vio & org	3.50	42.50
84	A8	50c dull vio & blk ('20)	9.00	45.00
85	A8	75c blk, *bl grn*, ol back	1.75	23.00
a.		75c blk, *emer* (Die II) ('20)	1.50	21.00
86	A8	1r dl vio & red ('20)	18.00	65.00
87	A8	1.50r vio & bl, *bl*	10.00	57.50
a.		Die II ('20)	20.00	35.00
88	A8	2.25r gray grn & dp vio	55.00	160.00
89	A8	5r gray grn & ultra ('20)	140.00	275.00
		Nos. 74-89 (16)	259.80	786.20
		Set, ovptd. "SPECIMEN"	325.00	

Die II

1921-32   **Ordinary Paper**   **Wmk. 4**

91	A8	2c org brn & grn	.30	.25
92	A8	3c green	1.90	.25
93	A8	3c black ('22)	1.10	.35
94	A8	4c green ('22)	1.10	2.75
95	A8	4c ol grn & rose red ('28)	7.25	19.00
96	A8	5c dk brown	1.25	6.00
97	A8	6c car rose	3.00	10.00
98	A8	6c violet ('22)	1.25	.25
99	A8	9c rose red ('27)	3.50	4.75
100	A8	12c gray	3.00	.25
a.		Die I ('32)	25.00	.65
101	A8	12c carmine ('22)	1.50	.35
102	A8	15c ultra	2.25	65.00
103	A8	15c yellow ('22)	1.10	3.00
104	A8	18c violet, *yel*	2.75	17.00
105	A8	20c ultra ('22)	1.60	.40

Chalky Paper

106	A8	25c blk & red, *yel* ('25)	3.00	25.00
107	A8	30c dull vio & ol grn	1.60	17.00
108	A8	45c dull vio & org	1.40	5.75
109	A8	50c dull vio & blk	2.75	2.50
110	A8	75c blk, *emer* ('24)	9.00	24.00
111	A8	1r dull vio & red	24.00	20.00
a.		Die I ('32)	12.00	37.50
112	A8	1.50r vio & bl, *bl* ('24)	14.00	25.00
113	A8	2.25r green & vio	17.00	16.00
114	A8	5r green & ultra	120.00	175.00
		Nos. 91-114 (24)	225.60	439.85
		Set, ovptd. "SPECIMEN"	425.00	

Common Design Types pictured following the introduction.

Silver Jubilee Issue
Common Design Type

1935, May 6   **Engr.**   **Perf. 11x12**

118	CD301	6c black & ultra	1.25	3.00
		Never hinged	2.75	
119	CD301	12c indigo & green	4.75	2.25
		Never hinged	7.50	
120	CD301	20c ultra & brown	3.50	3.75
		Never hinged	5.50	
121	CD301	1r brn vio & indigo	8.00	22.00
		Never hinged	15.00	
		Nos. 118-121 (4)	17.50	31.00
		Set, never hinged	30.00	
		Set, perf "SPECIMEN"	160.00	

Coronation Issue
Common Design Type

1937, May 12   **Perf. 11x11½**

122	CD302	6c olive green	.30	.25
		Never hinged	.45	
123	CD302	12c deep orange	.45	.55
		Never hinged	.70	
124	CD302	20c deep ultra	.45	1.10
		Never hinged	.75	
		Nos. 122-124 (3)	1.20	1.90
		Set, never hinged	2.00	
		Set, perf "SPECIMEN"	95.00	

Coco-de-mer Palm — A9   Seychelles Giant Tortoise — A10

Fishing Canoe — A11

Perf. 13½x14½, 14½x13½

1938-41   **Photo.**   **Wmk. 4**
Chalky Paper

125a	A9	2c pur brn	1.00	.40
		Never hinged	1.60	
126	A10	3c green	5.50	2.50
		Never hinged	9.00	
128	A11	6c orange	8.50	3.75
		Never hinged	14.00	
130	A9	9c rose red	9.50	3.25
		Never hinged	14.50	
132	A10	12c violet	30.00	1.75
		Never hinged	50.00	
134a	A9	18c rose lake	7.00	.65
		Never hinged	10.50	
135	A11	20c bright blue ('41)	25.00	6.50
		Never hinged	45.00	
137	A9	25c ocher	30.00	15.00
		Never hinged	52.50	
138	A10	30c rose lake	30.00	10.00
		Never hinged	52.50	
140a	A11	45c chocolate	15.00	2.75
		Never hinged	22.50	
141a	A9	50c dp reddish violet	9.00	.65
		Never hinged	15.00	
142	A10	75c gray blue	50.00	45.00
		Never hinged	87.50	
144	A11	1r yel grn	72.50	70.00
		Never hinged	125.00	
146a	A9	1.50r ultra	19.00	4.75
		Never hinged	27.50	
147a	A10	2.25r olive bister	35.00	11.50
		Never hinged	52.50	
148	A11	5r copper red	13.00	*11.00*
		Never hinged	17.50	

Issued: 3c, 6c, 12c, 20c, 25c, 30c-5r, 2/10/38; 18c. 8/8/41.

New Values and Color Changes

1941-49
Chalky Paper

127a	A10	3c orange	.90	*1.10*
		Never hinged	1.40	
129	A11	6c grayish grn	2.75	1.40
		Never hinged	4.25	
129a	A11	6c green ('49)	5.75	1.40
		Never hinged	8.25	
131a	A9	9c gray blue	10.75	.40
		Never hinged	20.00	
133a	A10	15c brn carmine	14.00	.45
		Never hinged	20.00	
134b	A9	18c rose carmine ('49)	15.00	12.50
		Never hinged	25.00	
136a	A11	20c brn ocher	10.00	.70
		Never hinged	15.00	
139a	A9	30c blue	10.50	.55
		Never hinged	21.00	
140b	A11	45c pur brn ('49)	17.00	13.50
		Never hinged	26.00	
141b	A9	50c br lilac ('49)	2.50	2.50
		Never hinged	4.25	
143a	A10	75c dp sla lilac	11.00	4.25
		Never hinged	16.50	
145a	A11	1r gray black	20.00	3.50
		Never hinged	37.50	

Issued: 3c, 6c (#129), 9c, 15c, 20c, 30c, 75c, 1r, 8/8/41; 6c (#129a), 45c, 4/5/49; 50c, 6/13/49.

1942-45
Ordinary Paper

125	A9	2c violet brown	.40	*1.75*
		Never hinged	.75	
127	A10	3c orange	.50	1.50
		Never hinged	.65	
129b	A11	6c green	.45	*2.40*
		Never hinged	.60	
131	A9	9c peacock blue ('45)	4.25	3.25
		Never hinged	6.75	
131b	A9	9c gray blue ('45)	11.00	1.60
		Never hinged	16.00	
133	A10	15c copper red	4.00	*4.25*
		Never hinged	6.75	
134	A9	18c rose lake	4.75	3.00
		Never hinged	7.25	
136	A11	20c ocher	1.90	*3.25*
		Never hinged	2.75	
139	A9	30c bright blue	1.90	*5.50*
140	A11	45c brown	2.25	2.50
		Never hinged	3.00	
141	A9	50c dull lilac ('49)	2.50	3.00
		Never hinged	3.00	
143	A10	75c dull lilac		
		Never hinged	2.75	
145	A11	1r gray	2.00	*5.00*
		Never hinged	2.50	
146	A9	1.50r ultra	3.75	13.00
		Never hinged	4.75	
147	A10	2.25r olive bister	16.00	29.00
		Never hinged	25.00	
148a	A11	5r copper red	17.50	35.00
		Never hinged	25.00	

Issued: all except #131, 11/18/42; #131, 11/19/45.

See Nos. 158-169, 174-188 (in Scott Standard catalogue, Vol. 6).

> **Catalogue values for unused stamps in this section, from this point to the end of the section, are for Never Hinged items.**

Peace Issue
Common Design Type
Perf. 13½x14

1946, Sept. 23   **Engr.**   **Wmk. 4**

149	CD303	9c light blue	.25	.25
150	CD303	30c dark blue	.30	.25

Silver Wedding Issue
Common Design Types

1948, Nov. 11   **Photo.**   **Perf. 14x14½**

151	CD304	9c bright ultra	.25	.75

Engraved; Name Typographed
Perf. 11½x11

152	CD305	5r rose carmine	16.00	45.00

UPU Issue
Common Design Types
Perf. 13½, 11x11½

1949, Oct. 10   **Engr.**

153	CD306	18c red violet	.25	.25
154	CD307	50c dp rose violet	2.00	2.25
155	CD308	1r gray	.55	.35
156	CD309	2.25r olive	.45	*1.25*
		Nos. 153-156 (4)	3.25	4.10

Types of 1938-41 Redrawn and

Sailfish — A12

Map — A13

Perf. 14½x13½, 13½x14½

1952, Mar. 3   **Photo.**   **Wmk. 4**

157	A12	2c violet	.75	.75
158	A10	3c orange	.75	.30
159	A9	9c peacock blue	.70	1.75
160	A11	15c yellow green	.60	1.00
161	A13	18c rose lake	1.75	.25
162	A11	20c ocher	2.00	1.50
163	A10	25c bright red	.80	2.25
164	A12	40c ultra	1.25	2.00
165	A11	45c violet brown	1.50	.35
166	A9	50c brt violet	1.40	1.75
167	A11	1r gray	4.75	4.25
168	A9	1.50r brt blue	11.00	16.00
169	A9	2.25r olive bister	17.50	18.00
170	A13	5r copper red	18.00	19.00
171	A12	10r green	25.00	45.00
		Nos. 157-171 (15)	87.75	114.15

Wmk. 4a (Error)

157a	A12	2c violet	140.00	200.00
b.		Crown omitted in wmk.	825.00	
158a	A10	3c orange	190.00	190.00
b.		Crown omitted in wmk.	600.00	600.00
159a	A9	9c peacock blue	325.00	400.00
b.		Crown omitted in wmk.	1,300.	
160a	A11	15c yellow green	275.00	325.00
b.		Crown omitted in wmk.	825.00	
161a	A13	18c rose lake	375.00	325.00
b.		Crown omitted in wmk.	1,200.	
162a	A11	20c ocher	450.00	450.00
b.		Crown omitted in wmk.	1,300.	1,100.
163a	A10	25c bright red	450.00	
b.		Crown omitted in wmk.	1,600.	
164a	A12	40c ultra	775.00	
b.		Crown omitted in wmk.	1,750.	
165a	A11	45c violet brown	525.00	525.00
b.		Crown omitted in wmk.	1,750.	
166a	A9	50c brt violet	600.00	725.00
b.		Crown omitted in wmk.	1,900.	1,750.
167a	A13	1r gray	1,450.	
168a	A9	1.50r brt blue	3,000.	
169a	A13	2.25r olive bister	1,500.	
b.		5r copper red	1,200.	

The redrawn design shows a new portrait of King George VI surmounted by crown, as on type A12.

POSTAGE DUE STAMPS

> **Catalogue values for unused stamps in this section are for Never Hinged items.**

D1

Engr.; Denomination Typo. in Carmine

1951, Mar. 1   **Wmk. 4**   *Perf. 11½*

J1	D1	2c carmine	1.50	*3.00*
J2	D1	3c blue green	2.25	3.00
J3	D1	6c ocher	2.25	*2.25*
J4	D1	9c brown orange	2.25	4.00
J5	D1	15c purple	2.10	12.50
J6	D1	18c deep blue	2.75	12.50
J7	D1	20c black brown	2.75	12.50
J8	D1	30c red brown	2.75	9.00
		Nos. J1-J8 (8)	18.60	58.75

SIBERIA

sī-'bir-ē-ə

LOCATION — A vast territory of Russia lying between the Ural Mountains and the Pacific Ocean.

The anti-Bolshevist provisional government set up at Omsk by Adm. Aleksandr V. Kolchak issued Nos. 1-10 in 1919. The monarchist, anti-Soviet government in Priamur province issued Nos. 51-118 in 1921-22.

(Stamps of the Czechoslovak Legion are listed under Czechoslovakia.)

100 Kopecks = 1 Ruble

Russian Stamps of 1909-18 Surcharged

a   b

On Stamps of 1909-12

1919		Unwmk.	Perf. 14x14½

Wove Paper
Lozenges of Varnish on Face

1	A14(a)	35k on 2k dull grn	.60	2.00
a.		Inverted surcharge	100.00	
b.		"5" omitted	150.00	
c.		Double surcharge		
2	A14(a)	50k on 3k car	.60	2.00
a.		Inverted surcharge	100.00	
3	A14(a)	70k on 1k dl org yel	1.00	4.50
a.		Inverted surcharge	100.00	
4	A15(b)	1r on 4k car	1.25	2.00
a.		Dbl. surch., one inverted	200.00	110.00
b.		Inverted surcharge	100.00	
c.		Double surcharge	200.00	
5	A14(b)	3r on 7k blue	7.00	9.50
a.		Double surcharge	100.00	30.00
b.		Inverted surcharge	100.00	25.00
c.		Pair, one without surcharge	400.00	—
d.		"3" omitted		
6	A11(b)	5r on 14k dk bl & car	9.50	20.00
a.		Double surcharge	100.00	40.00
b.		Inverted surcharge	100.00	40.00

On Stamps of 1917
Imperf

7	A14(a)	35k on 2k gray grn	1.25	4.50
a.		Inverted surcharge	100.00	
8	A14(a)	50k on 3k red	1.00	4.50
a.		Inverted surcharge	200.00	
b.		Double surcharge	100.00	
9	A14(a)	70k on 1k orange	.75	4.50
a.		Inverted surcharge	100.00	
b.		Dbl. surch., one inverted		—
10	A15(b)	1r on 4k car	9.50	16.00
		Nos. 1-10 (10)	32.45	69.50

Nos. 1-10 were first issued in Omsk during the regime of Admiral Kolchak. Later they were used along the line of the Trans-Siberian railway to Vladivostok.

Some experts question the postal use of most off-cover canceled examples of Nos. 1-10.

25 P 1-

Similar surcharges, handstamped as above are bogus.

Priamur Government Issues
Nikolaevsk Issue

A5   A6

A7

1909-17 Russian Stamps Handstamp Surcharged or Overprinted

1921		Unwmk.	Perf. 14x14½, 13½
51	A5	10k on 4k carmine	250.00
52	A5	10k on 10k dark blue	2,000.
53	A6	15k on 14k dark blue & carmine	200.00
54	A6	15k on 15k red brown & deep blue	80.00
55	A6	15k on 35k red brown & green	100.00
56	A6	15k on 50k brown violet & green	100.00
57	A6	15k on 70k brown & red orange	225.00
58	A7	20k on 1r brn & org	200.00
59	A5	on 20k dull blue & dark carmine	350.00
60	A5	on 20k on 14k dk blue & car (#118)	200.00
a.		15k on 20k on 14k dark blue & carmine (error)	1,100.
61	A7	20k on 3½r maroon & light green	250.00
62	A7	20k on 5r indigo, grn & lt blue	950.00
63	A7	20k on 7r dark green & pink	950.00

Nos. 59-60 are overprinted with initials but original denominations remain.

A 10k on 5k claret (Russia No. 77) and a 15k on 20k blue & carmine (Russia No. 82a) were not officially issued. Some authorities consider them bogus.

Reprints exist.

On Semi-Postal Stamp of 1914

64	SP6	20k on 3k mar & gray grn, pink	900.00

On Stamps of 1917

65	A5	10k on 1k orange	100.00
66	A5	10k on 2k gray green	100.00
67	A5	10k on 3k red	100.00
68	A5	10k on 5k claret	700.00
69	A6	15k on 1r pale brn, brn & red org	150.00
70	A7	20k on 1r pale brn, brn & red org	200.00
71	A7	20k on 3½r maroon & light green	350.00
72	A7	20k on 7r dark green & pink	950.00

The letters of the overprint are the initials of the Russian words for "Nikolaevsk on Amur Priamur Provisional Government."

As the surcharges on Nos. 51-72 are handstamped, a number exist inverted or double.

A 20k blue & carmine (Russia No. 126) with Priamur overprint and a 15k on 20k (Russia No. 126) were not officially issued. Some authorities consider them bogus.

No evidence found of genuine usage of Nos. 51-72.

Stamps of Far Eastern Republic Overprinted

1922				
78	A2	2k gray green	25.00	25.00
a.		Inverted overprint	200.00	
79	A2a	4k rose	25.00	25.00
a.		Inverted overprint	250.00	
80	A2	5k claret	25.00	25.00
81	A2a	10k blue	25.00	25.00
		Nos. 78-81 (4)	100.00	100.00

Anniv. of the overthrow of the Bolshevik power in the Priamur district.

The letters of the overprint are the initials of "Vremeno Priamurski Pravitel'stvo" i.e. Provisional Priamur Government, 26th May.

Russian Stamps of 1909-21 Overprinted in Dark Blue or Vermilion

---

On Stamps of 1909-18

1922			Perf. 14x14½
85	A14	1k dull org yel	75.00	100.00
86	A14	2k dull green	125.00	110.00
87	A14	3k carmine	35.00	50.00
88	A15	4k carmine	25.00	35.00
89	A15	5k dk claret	35.00	40.00
90	A14	7k blue (V)	100.00	45.00
91	A15	10k dark blue (V)	65.00	70.00
92	A11	14k dk bl & car	75.00	85.00
93	A11	15k red brn & dp bl	15.00	25.00
94	A8	20k dl bl & dk car	50.00	25.00
95	A11	20k on 14k dark blue & carmine	120.00	150.00
96	A11	25k dull green & dark violet (V)	50.00	50.00
97	A11	35k red brn & grn	10.00	15.00
a.		Inverted overprint	200.00	
98	A8	50k brn vio & grn	20.00	30.00
99	A11	70k brn & red org	55.00	55.00
		Nos. 85-99 (15)	855.00	885.00

On Stamps of 1917
Imperf

100	A14	1k orange	10.00	25.00
a.		Inverted overprint	250.00	100.00
101	A14	2k gray green	15.00	25.00
102	A14	3k red	20.00	25.00
103	A15	4k carmine	100.00	100.00
104	A14	5k claret	35.00	25.00
105	A11	15k red brn & dp bl	100.00	125.00
106	A8	20k blue & car	125.00	75.00
107	A9	1r pale brn, brn & red org	30.00	40.00
		Nos. 100-107 (8)	435.00	440.00

On Stamps of Siberia, 1919
Perf. 14½x15

108	A14	35k on 2k green	100.00	100.00

Imperf

109	A14	70k on 1k orange	110.00	120.00

On Stamps of Far Eastern Republic, 1921

110	A2	2k gray green	20.00	20.00
111	A2a	4k rose	20.00	7.00
112	A2	5k claret	20.00	25.00
a.		Inverted overprint	100.00	
113	A2a	10k blue (R)	20.00	30.00
		Nos. 109-113 (5)	190.00	202.00

Same, Surcharged with New Values

114	A2	1k on 2k gray grn	20.00	25.00
115	A2a	3k on 4k rose	20.00	25.00

The overprint is in a rectangular frame on stamps of 1k to 10k and 1r; on the other values the frame is omitted. It is larger on the 1 ruble than on the smaller stamps.

The overprint reads "Priamurski Zemski Krai," Priamur Rural Province.

Far Eastern Republic Nos. 30-32 Overprinted in Blue

Perf. 14½x15

116	A14	35k on 2k green	20.00	25.00

Imperf

117	A14	35k on 2k green	60.00	120.00
118	A14	70k on 1k orange	30.00	15.00
		Nos. 116-118 (3)	110.00	160.00

Counterfeits of Nos. 51-118 abound.

SIERRA LEONE

sē-ˌer-ə lē-'ōn

LOCATION — West coast of Africa, between Guinea and Liberia
GOVT. — British Colony
AREA — 27,925 sq. mi.
POP. — 3,354,000 (est. 1982)
CAPITAL — Freetown

Sierra Leone was a British colony and protectorate.

12 Pence = 1 Shilling
20 Shillings = 1 Pound

Queen Victoria
A1   A2

1859-74		Unwmk.	Typo.	Perf. 14
1	A1	6p bright violet	60.00	30.00
a.		6p dull violet ('59)	225.00	55.00
b.		6p gray lilac ('65)	300.00	45.00

1872				Perf. 12½
5	A1	6p violet	425.00	70.00

1872		Wmk. 1 Sideways	Perf. 12½
6	A2	1p rose	85.00	45.00
8	A2	3p yellow buff	160.00	42.50
9	A2	4p blue	200.00	45.00
10	A2	1sh yellow green	525.00	62.50

1873		Wmk. 1 Upright	
6a	A2	1p	140.00	35.00
7	A2	2p magenta	150.00	55.00
8a	A2	3p	550.00	95.00
9a	A2	4p	375.00	57.50
10a	A2	1sh	600.00	110.00

1876-96		Wmk. 1 Upright	Perf. 14
11	A2	½p bister	4.75	12.00
12	A2	1p rose	60.00	16.00
13	A2	1½p violet ('77)	55.00	10.00
14	A2	2p magenta	75.00	4.50
15	A2	3p yellow buff	65.00	6.50
16	A2	4p blue	225.00	7.25
17	A2	6p brt violet ('85)	67.50	27.50
a.		Half used as 3p on cover		2,750.
18	A1	6p violet brn ('90)	24.00	16.00
19	A1	6p brown vio ('96)	3.00	7.75
20	A2	1sh green	80.00	7.25
		Nos. 11-20 (10)	659.25	114.75

For surcharge see No. 32.

1883-93		Wmk. Crown and C A (2)	
21	A2	½p bister	37.50	57.50
22	A2	½p dull green ('84)	3.50	2.25
23	A2	1p carmine ('84)	11.00	1.10
a.		1p rose carmine	32.50	9.50
b.		1p rose	225.00	40.00
24	A2	1½p violet ('93)	3.25	7.25
25	A2	2p magenta	70.00	9.50
26	A2	2p slate ('84)	55.00	3.00
27	A2	2½p ultra ('91)	15.00	1.75
28	A2	3p org yel ('92)	4.00	11.00
29	A2	4p blue	1,000.	32.50
30	A2	4p bister ('84)	2.75	3.00
31	A2	1sh org brn ('88)	26.00	17.00
		Nos. 21-28,30-31 (10)	228.00	113.35

For surcharge see No. 33.

Nos. 13 and 24 Surcharged in Black

1893			Wmk. 1
32	A2	½p on 1½p violet	525.00	800.00
a.		"PFNNY"	3,750.	4,500.

			Wmk. 2
33	A2	½p on 1½p violet	7.50	3.50
a.		"PFNNY"	85.00	82.50
b.		Inverted surcharge	125.00	125.00
c.		Same as "a," inverted	8,000.	5,500.
d.		Double surcharge	1,200.	

A4

1896-97				
34	A4	½p lilac & grn ('97)	2.75	3.50
35	A4	1p lilac & car	4.75	2.00
36	A4	1½p lilac & blk ('97)	4.50	24.00
37	A4	2p lilac & org	2.75	5.50
38	A4	2½p lilac & ultra	2.75	1.40
39	A4	3p lilac & sl ('97)	9.50	7.75
40	A4	4p lilac & car ('97)	10.50	14.50
41	A4	5p lilac & blk	14.50	16.00
42	A4	6p lilac ('97)	9.00	27.50
43	A4	1sh green & blk	6.75	22.50
44	A4	2sh green & ultra	30.00	75.00
45	A4	5sh green & car	90.00	225.00
46	A4	£1 violet, red	275.00	500.00
		Nos. 34-46 (13)	462.75	924.65

Numerals of Nos. 39-46 of type A4 are in color on plain tablet.

A5

A6

a

b

c

d

e

f

1897   Wmk. C A over Crown (46)

47	A5	1p lilac & grn	6.50	4.25
a.		Double overprint	2,000.	2,000.
48	A6(a)	2 ½p on 3p lil & grn	13.50	19.00
a.		Double surcharge	40,000.	
b.		Double surcharge, types "a" and "b"	32,000.	
c.		Double surcharge, types "a" and "c"	55,000.	
49	A6(b)	2 ½p on 3p	67.50	85.00
50	A6(c)	2 ½p on 3p	200.00	225.00
51	A6(d)	2 ½p on 3p	400.00	525.00
52	A6(a)	2 ½p on 6p lil & grn	10.50	19.00
53	A6(b)	2 ½p on 6p	50.00	75.00
54	A6(c)	2 ½p on 6p	150.00	175.00
55	A6(d)	2 ½p on 6p	325.00	400.00
56	A6(b)	2 ½p on 1sh lilac	110.00	80.00
57	A6(c)	2 ½p on 1sh lilac	1,100.	1,100.
58	A6(c)	2 ½p on 1sh lilac	525.00	500.00
a.		Italic "N" in "REVENUE"	1,750.	1,400.
59	A6(e)	2 ½p on 1sh lilac	1,750.	2,000.
59A	A6(f)	2 ½p on 1sh lilac	1,800.	1,500.
60	A6(a)	2 ½p on 2sh lilac	4,000.	2,750.
61	A6(b)	2 ½p on 2sh lilac	20,000.	
62	A6(b)	2 ½p on 2sh lilac	11,500.	15,000.
a.		Italic "N" in "REVENUE"	50,000.	50,000.
63	A6(c)	2 ½p on 2sh lilac	47,500.	
63A	A6(f)	2 ½p on 2sh lilac	47,500.	50,000.

The words "POSTAGE AND REVENUE" on Nos. 56-63A are set in two lines and overprinted below instead of above "2½d."

The "d" in type "f" is 3½mm wide; that in type "a" is 3mm.

Very fine examples of Nos. 47-63A will have perforations touching the frameline on one or more sides.

Nos. 56-59A are often found discolored. Such stamps sell for about half the values quoted.

King Edward VII — A7

Numerals of 3p to £1 of type A7 are in color on plain tablet.

1903   Wmk. Crown and C A (2)

64	A7	½p violet & grn	3.25	6.50
65	A7	1p violet & car	2.25	1.10
66	A7	1 ½p violet & blk	1.50	19.00
67	A7	2p violet & brn org	4.50	17.50
68	A7	2 ½p violet & ultra	5.00	9.00
69	A7	3p violet & gray	13.00	15.00
70	A7	4p violet & car	8.00	19.00
71	A7	5p violet & blk	11.00	45.00
72	A7	6p violet & dull vio	12.50	28.00
73	A7	1sh green & blk	21.00	67.50
74	A7	2sh green & ultra	50.00	70.00
75	A7	5sh green & car	80.00	120.00
76	A7	£1 violet, red	260.00	275.00
		Nos. 64-76 (13)	472.00	692.60

1904-05   Wmk. 3   Chalky Paper

77	A7	½p violet & grn	5.75	5.25
78	A7	1p violet & car	6.00	1.75
a.		On ordinary paper	1.75	1.00
79	A7	1 ½p violet & blk	3.50	15.00
80	A7	2p violet & brn org	4.75	4.50
81	A7	2 ½p violet & ultra	6.50	2.25
82	A7	3p violet & gray	50.00	4.00
83	A7	4p violet & car	10.00	8.00
84	A7	5p violet & blk	13.00	32.00
85	A7	6p violet & dl vio	5.50	3.50
86	A7	1sh green & blk	8.50	10.00
87	A7	2sh green & ultra	28.00	30.00
88	A7	5sh green & car	45.00	60.00
89	A7	£1 violet, red	250.00	275.00
		Nos. 77-89 (13)	436.50	451.25

The 1p also exists on ordinary paper.

1907-10   Ordinary Paper

90	A7	½p green	1.00	.60
91	A7	1p carmine	17.00	.80
92	A7	1 ½p orange ('10)	2.50	2.25
93	A7	2p gray	2.25	1.75
94	A7	2 ½p ultra	4.00	3.25

Chalky Paper

95	A7	3p violet, yel	11.00	3.25
a.		On ordinary paper	12.50	15.00
96	A7	4p blk & red, yel	2.60	1.75
97	A7	5p vio & ol grn	19.00	5.75
98	A7	6p vio & red vio	17.00	9.00
99	A7	1sh black, green	6.25	5.75
100	A7	2sh vio & bl, bl	23.00	22.50
101	A7	5sh grn & red, yel	45.00	62.50
102	A7	£1 vio & blk, red	300.00	210.00
		Nos. 90-102 (13)	450.60	329.15

King George V and Seal of the Colony

A8   A9

Die I

For description of dies I and II see "Dies of British Colonial Stamps" in Table of Contents.

Numerals of 3p, 4p, 5p, 6p and 10p of type A8 are in color on plain tablet. Numerals of 7p and 9p are on solid-color tablet.

1912-24   Ordinary Paper   Wmk. 3

103	A8	½p green	3.75	3.50
104	A8	1p scarlet	8.50	1.00
a.		1p carmine	2.25	.45
105	A8	1 ½p orange	2.25	2.75
106	A8	2p gray	1.50	.25
107	A8	2 ½p ultra	1.25	1.00
a.		2 ½p deep blue	10.50	3.00

Chalky Paper

108	A9	3p violet, yel	4.25	3.75
109	A8	4p blk & red, yel	3.25	14.00
a.		Die II ('24)	5.00	6.00
110	A8	5p violet & ol grn	1.50	7.00
111	A8	6p vio & red vio	4.00	6.75
112	A8	7p violet & org	3.50	9.50
113	A8	9p violet & blk	5.75	14.00
114	A8	10p violet & red	3.50	20.00
115	A9	1sh black, green	7.50	5.25
a.		1sh black, emerald		190.00
116	A9	2sh vio & ultra, bl	22.00	6.25
117	A9	5sh grn & red, yel	20.00	30.00
118	A9	10sh grn & red, grn	90.00	150.00
119	A9	£1 vio & blk, red	225.00	275.00
120	A9	£2 violet & ultra	850.00	1,100.
121	A9	£5 gray grn & org	2,750.	3,500.
		Nos. 103-119 (17)	407.50	550.00

The status of #115a has been questioned.

Die II

1921-27   Ordinary Paper   Wmk. 4

122	A8	½p green	1.75	1.10
123	A8	1p violet ('26)	5.00	.25
a.		Die I ('24)	3.25	2.50
124	A8	1 ½p scarlet	2.00	1.50
125	A8	2p gray ('22)	1.25	.25

126	A8	2 ½p ultra	2.50	17.00
127	A8	3p ultra ('22)	1.75	1.40
128	A8	4p blk & red, yel	3.75	3.75
129	A8	5p vio & ol grn	1.50	1.40

Chalky Paper

130	A8	6p dp vio & red vio	1.50	2.75
131	A8	7p vio & org ('27)	3.25	27.00
132	A8	9p dl vio & blk ('22)	4.25	23.00
133	A8	10p violet & red	4.00	32.00
134	A9	1sh blk, emerald	12.00	8.00
135	A9	2sh vio & ultra, bl	10.00	11.50
136	A9	5sh grn & red, yel	10.00	57.50
137	A9	10sh grn & red, grn	140.00	250.00
138	A9	£2 violet & ultra	750.00	1,000.
139	A9	£5 gray grn & org	2,250.	3,500.
		Nos. 122-137 (16)	204.50	438.40

Rice Field — A10

Palms and Kola Tree — A11

1932, Mar. 1   Engr.   Perf. 12½

140	A10	½p green	.25	.50
141	A10	1p dk violet	.30	.30
142	A10	1 ½p rose car	.35	1.75
143	A10	2p yellow brn	.35	.30
144	A10	3p ultra	1.25	2.25
145	A10	4p orange	1.00	11.00
146	A10	5p olive green	2.00	6.50
147	A10	6p light blue	1.00	4.25
148	A10	1sh red brown	5.50	11.00

Perf. 12

149	A11	2sh dk brown	6.00	8.25
150	A11	5sh indigo	17.00	24.00
151	A11	10sh deep green	85.00	160.00
152	A11	£1 deep violet	160.00	275.00
		Nos. 140-152 (13)	280.00	505.10

Wilberforce Issue

Arms of Sierra Leone — A12

Slave Throwing Off Shackles — A13

Map of Sierra Leone — A14

Old Slave Market, Freetown A15

Fruit Seller — A16

Government Sanatorium — A17

Bullom Canoe — A18

Punting near Banana Islands — A19

Government Buildings, Freetown A20

Old Slavers' Resort, Bunce Island — A21

African Elephant — A22

George V A23

Freetown Harbor — A24

1933, Oct. 2

153	A12	½p deep green	1.00	1.25
154	A13	1p brown & blk	.85	.25
155	A14	1 ½p orange brn	6.50	4.75
156	A15	2p violet	3.50	.25
157	A16	3p ultra	5.50	1.75
158	A17	4p dk brown	7.00	10.00
159	A18	5p red brn & sl grn	7.50	11.00
160	A19	6p dp org & blk	10.00	7.00
161	A20	1sh dk violet	5.00	18.00
162	A21	2sh bl & dk brn	37.50	50.00
163	A22	5sh red vio & blk	160.00	200.00
164	A23	10sh green & blk	275.00	425.00
165	A24	£1 yel & dk vio	550.00	700.00
		Nos. 153-165 (13)	1,069.	1,429.

Abolition of slavery in the British colonies and cent. of the death of William Wilberforce, English philanthropist and agitator against the slave trade.

Common Design Types

For description of dies I and II see "Dies of British Colonial Stamps" in Table of Contents.

Silver Jubilee Issue
Common Design Type

1935, May 6   *Perf. 11x12*

166	CD301	1p black & ultra	1.25	*2.50*
167	CD301	3p ultra & brown	2.25	*8.50*
168	CD301	5p indigo & green	3.00	*25.00*
169	CD301	1sh brown vio & ind	12.00	*19.00*
		Nos. 166-169 (4)	18.50	*55.00*
		Set, never hinged	32.50	

Coronation Issue
Common Design Type

1937, May 12   *Perf. 11x11½*

170	CD302	1p deep orange	.40	.90
171	CD302	2p dark violet	.65	1.00
172	CD302	3p deep ultra	.90	3.75
		Nos. 170-172 (3)	1.95	5.65
		Set, never hinged	3.75	

Freetown Harbor A25

Rice Harvesting A26

1938-44   *Perf. 12½*

173	A25	½p green & blk	.25	.50
174	A25	1p dp cl & blk	.30	.70
175	A26	1½p rose red	12.50	1.25
175A	A26	1½p red vio ('41)	.25	.70
176	A26	2p red violet	30.00	3.00
176A	A26	2p dark red ('41)	.25	2.10
177	A25	3p ultra & blk	.30	.60
178	A25	4p red brn & blk	.55	4.50
179	A26	5p olive green	3.75	4.00
180	A26	6p gray	.55	.60
181	A25	1sh ol grn & blk	1.40	.90
181A	A26	1sh3p org yel ('44)	.30	.60
182	A25	2sh sepia & blk	2.75	2.75
183	A26	5sh red brown	6.00	14.00
184	A26	10sh emerald	15.00	16.00
185	A25	£1 dk blue	11.00	*30.00*
		Nos. 173-185 (16)	85.15	82.20
		Set, never hinged	150.00	

> Catalogue values for unused stamps in this section, from this point to the end of the section, are for Never Hinged items.

Peace Issue
Common Design Type
Perf. 13½x14

1946, Oct. 1   Engr.   Wmk. 4

186	CD303	1½p lilac	.25	.25
187	CD303	3p bright ultra	.25	.25

Silver Wedding Issue
Common Design Types

1948, Dec. 1   Photo.   *Perf. 14x14½*

188	CD304	1½p brt red violet	.25	.25

Engraved; Name Typographed
Perf. 11½x11

189	CD305	£1 dark blue	24.50	*26.00*

UPU Issue
Common Design Types
Engr.; Name Typo. on 3p, 6p

1949, Oct. 10   *Perf. 13½, 11x11½*

190	CD306	1½p rose violet	.25	.35
191	CD307	3p indigo	.50	1.75
192	CD308	6p gray	.85	2.00
193	CD309	1sh olive	1.40	1.00
		Nos. 190-193 (4)	3.00	5.10

SINGAPORE
ˈsiŋ-ə-ˌpor

LOCATION — An island just off the southern tip of the Malay Peninsula, south of Johore
GOVT. — British Colony
AREA — 239 sq. mi.
POP. — 2,529,100 (est. 1984)
CAPITAL — Singapore

Singapore, Malacca and Penang were the British settlements which, together with the Federated Malay States, composed the former colony of Straits Settlements. On April 1, 1946, Singapore became a separate colony when the Straits Settlements colony was dissolved. Malacca and Penang joined the Malayan Union, which was renamed the Federation of Malaya in 1948.

See Straits Settlements for stamps of India canceled Singapore.

100 Cents = 1 Dollar

> Catalogue values for all unused stamps in this country are for Never Hinged items.

King George VI — A1

1948   Wmk. 4   Typo.   *Perf. 14*

1	A1	1c black	.25	.50
2	A1	2c orange	.25	.50
3	A1	3c green	.75	.80
4	A1	4c chocolate	.50	.50
6	A1	6c gray	.60	.65
7	A1	8c rose red	.90	.95
9	A1	10c plum	.50	.25
11	A1	15c ultra	8.50	.40
12	A1	20c dk green & blk	5.00	.55
14	A1	25c org & rose lilac	6.00	.60
16	A1	40c dk vio & rose red	11.00	9.50
17	A1	50c ultra & black	5.50	.40
18	A1	$1 vio brn & ultra	22.50	4.50
19	A1	$2 rose red & emer	77.50	6.75
20	A1	$5 chocolate & emer	175.00	9.00
		Nos. 1-20 (15)	314.75	35.85
		Set, hinged	140.00	

1949-52   *Perf. 18*

1a	A1	1c black ('52)	.75	1.75
2a	A1	2c orange	1.50	1.50
4a	A1	4c chocolate	2.00	.25
5	A1	5c rose violet ('52)	4.75	1.00
6a	A1	6c gray ('52)	2.00	2.00
8	A1	8c green ('52)	9.00	3.00
9a	A1	10c plum ('52)	.70	.25
10	A1	12c rose red ('52)	14.00	9.50
11a	A1	15c ultra ('52)	22.50	.50
12a	A1	20c dark green & black	12.00	4.00
13	A1	20c ultra ('52)	10.00	.75
14a	A1	25c org & rose lil ('50)	4.00	.25
15	A1	35c dk vio & rose red ('52)	10.00	2.50
16a	A1	40c dk vio & rose red ('51)	50.00	20.00
17a	A1	50c ultra & black ('50)	8.50	.30
18a	A1	$1 violet brown & ultra	20.00	.90
b.		Wmk. 4a (error)	15,000.	
19a	A1	$2 rose red & emer ('51)	140.00	3.25
b.		Wmk. 4a (error)	18,000.	
20a	A1	$5 choc & emerald ('51)	300.00	4.00
		Nos. 1a-20a (18)	611.70	55.70
		Set, hinged	300.00	

Common Design Types pictured following the introduction.

Silver Wedding Issue
Common Design Types
Inscribed: "Singapore"

1948, Oct. 25   Photo.   *Perf. 14x14½*

21	CD304	10c purple	1.25	.40

Perf. 11½x11

Engraved; Name Typographed

22	CD305	$5 light brown	145.00	55.00

UPU Issue
Common Design Types
Inscribed: "Malaya-Singapore"
Engr.; Name Typo. on 15c, 25c
Perf. 13½, 11x11½

1949, Oct. 10   Wmk. 4

23	CD306	10c rose violet	1.00	.70
24	CD307	15c indigo	4.50	2.50
25	CD308	25c orange	7.75	4.50
26	CD309	50c slate	11.00	6.50
		Nos. 23-26 (4)	24.25	14.20

SLOVAKIA
slō-ˈvä-kē-ə

LOCATION — Central Europe
GOVT. — Independent republic
AREA — 18,932 sq. mi.
POP. — 5,296,768 (est. 1992)
CAPITAL — Bratislava

Formerly a province of Czechoslovakia, Slovakia declared its independence in Mar., 1939. A treaty was immediately concluded with Germany guaranteeing Slovakian independence but providing for German "protection" for 25 years.

100 Halierov = 1 Koruna

> Catalogue values for unused stamps in this country are for never hinged items, beginning with Scott 26 in the regular postage section, Scott B1 in the semipostal section, Scott C1 in the airmail section, Scott EX1 in the personal delivery section, Scott J1 in the postage due section, and Scott P10 in the newspaper section.

Watermark

Wmk. 263 — Double-Barred Cross Multiple

Stamps of Czechoslovakia, 1928-39, Overprinted in Red or Blue

1939   *Perf. 10, 12½, 12x12½*

2	A29	5h dk ultra	1.50	1.40
3	A29	10h brown	.25	.25
4	A29	20h red (Bl)	.25	.25
5	A29	25h green	6.00	5.00
6	A29	30h red violet (Bl)	.25	.25
7	A61a	40h dark blue	.25	.25
8	A73	50h deep green	.25	.25
9	A63	50h deep green	.25	.25
10	A63	60h dull violet	.25	.25
11	A63	60h dull blue	9.50	10.25
12	A60	1k rose lake (Bl) (On No. 212)	.25	.25

Overprinted Diagonally

13	A64	1.20k rose lilac (Bl)	1.25	1.25
14	A65	1.50k carmine (Bl)	1.25	1.25
15	A79	1.60k olive grn	2.00	2.75
16	A66	2k dk blue green	2.00	2.75
17	A67	2.50k dark blue	1.25	1.25
18	A68	3k brown	1.25	1.25
19	A69	3.50k dk violet	27.50	27.50
20	A69	3.50k dk violet (Bl)	40.00	40.00
21	A70	4k dk violet	17.50	17.50
22	A71	5k green	22.50	*22.50*
23	A72	10k blue	200.00	175.00
		Nos. 2-23 (22)	335.50	311.65

Excellent counterfeit overprints exist.

Stefánik Type of Czechoslovakia

Gen. Milan Stefánik

1939, Mar. 30   Engr.   *Perf. 12½*

23A	A63	60h dark blue	45.00	37.50

Prepared by Czechoslovakia prior to the German occupation March 15, 1939. Subsequently issued for use in Slovakia.

Andrej Hlinka — A1

Overprinted in Red or Blue
Perf. 12½

1939, Apr.   Unwmk.   Photo.

24	A1	50h dark green (R)	.70	.70
a.		Perf. 10½	5.00	2.50
b.		Perf. 10½x12½	25.00	12.50
25	A1	1k dk car rose (Bl)	.75	.65
a.		Perf. 10½	1,200.	*1,000.*
		Never hinged	1,800.	
b.		Perf. 10½x12½	30.00	17.50

> Catalogue values for unused stamps in this section, from this point to the end of the section, are for Never Hinged items.

Andrej Hlinka — A2

1939   Unwmk.   *Perf. 12½*

26	A2	5h brt ultra	.55	.45
27	A2	10h olive green	.90	.70
a.		Perf. 10½x12½	110.00	50.00
b.		Perf. 10½	600.00	80.00
28	A2	20h orange red	.90	.70
a.		Imperf.	.85	.80
29	A2	30h dp violet	.90	.70
a.		Imperf.	1.00	*1.25*
b.		Perf. 10½x12½	20.00	10.00
c.		Perf. 10½	50.00	12.00
30	A2	50h dk green	.90	.70
31	A2	1k dk carmine rose	1.25	.70
32	A2	2.50k brt blue	1.25	.70
a.		Perf. 10½x12½	150.00	70.00
33	A2	3k black brown	3.00	.50
a.		Perf. 10½x12½	15.00	5.00
b.		Perf. 10½	15.00	1.50
		Nos. 26-33 (8)	9.65	4.75

On Nos. 32 and 33 a pearl frame surrounds the medallion. See Nos. 55-57, 69 (in Scott Standard catalogue, Vol. 6).

General Stefánik and Memorial Tomb — A3

1939, May   *Perf. 12½*
Size: 25x20mm

34	A3	40h dark blue	1.10
35	A3	60h slate green	1.10
36	A3	1k gray violet	1.10

Size: 30x23¾mm

37	A3	2k bl vio & sepia	1.25
		Nos. 34-37 (4)	4.55

20th anniv. of the death of Gen. Milan Stefánik, but not issued.

Rev. Josef Murgas and Radio Towers — A4

1939   Unwmk.

38	A4	60h purple	.30	.30
39	A4	1.20k slate black	.75	.25

10th anniv. of the death of Rev. Josef Murgas. See No. 65 in Scott Standard catalogue, Vol. 6.

Girl
Embroidering
A5

Woodcutter
A6

Girl at
Spring — A7

1939-44   Wmk. 263   Perf. 12½
40	A5	2k dk blue green	6.25	.50
41	A6	4k copper brown	1.40	1.00
42	A7	5k orange red	1.00	.50
a.		Perf. 10 ('44)	1.25	1.00
		Nos. 40-42 (3)	8.65	2.00

Dr. Josef
Tiso — A8

Presidential
Residence — A9

1939-44   Wmk. 263   Perf. 12½
43	A8	50h slate green	.45	.30
43A	A8	70h dk red brn ('42)	.35	.25
b.		Perf. 10½ ('44)	.50	.35

See No. 88 in Scott Standard catalogue, Vol. 6.

1940, Mar. 14
44	A9	10k deep blue	1.00	.75

Tatra
Mountains
A10

Krivan Peak
A11

Edelweiss in
the Tatra
Mountains
A12

Chamois
A13

Church at
Javorina — A14

1940-43   Wmk. 263   Perf. 12½
Size: 17x21mm
45	A10	5h dk olive grn	.30	.25
46	A11	10h deep brown	.25	.25
47	A12	20h blue black	.25	.25
48	A13	25h olive brown	.55	.25
49	A14	30h chestnut brown	.35	.25
a.		Perf. 10½ ('43)	2.50	1.00
		Nos. 45-49 (5)	1.70	1.25

See Nos. 84-87, 103-107 in Scott Standard catalogue, Vol. 6.

Hlinka Type of 1939
1940-42   Wmk. 263   Perf. 12½
55	A2	1k dk car rose	.90	.60
56	A2	2.50k brt blue ('42)	1.25	.75
a.		Perf. 10½	.60	.60
57	A2	3k black brn ('41)	2.00	1.00
a.		Perf. 10½	2.00	.90

On Nos. 56 and 57 a pearl frame surrounds the medallion.

SEMI-POSTAL STAMPS

> Catalogue values for unused stamps in this section are for Never Hinged items.

Josef Tiso — SP1

Wmk. 263
1939, Nov. 6   Photo.   Perf. 12½
B1	SP1	2.50k + 2.50k royal blue	3.75	4.00

The surtax was used for Child Welfare.

AIR POST STAMPS

> Catalogue values for unused stamps in this section are for Never Hinged items.

Planes over Tatra Mountains
AP1   AP2

Perf. 12½
1939, Nov. 20   Photo.   Unwmk.
C1	AP1	30h violet	.40	.40
C2	AP1	50h dark green	.40	.40
C3	AP1	1k vermilion	.40	.40
C4	AP2	2k grnsh black	.65	.65
C5	AP2	3k dark brown	1.00	1.00
C6	AP2	4k slate blue	1.90	1.90
		Nos. C1-C6 (6)	4.75	4.75

See No. C10 in Scott Standard catalogue, Vol. 6.

Plane in
Flight — AP3

1940, Nov. 30   Wmk. 263   Perf. 12½
C7	AP3	5k dk violet brn	1.50	1.50
C8	AP3	10k gray black	1.75	1.75
C9	AP3	20k myrtle green	2.25	2.25
		Nos. C7-C9 (3)	5.50	5.50

PERSONAL DELIVERY STAMPS

> Catalogue values for unused stamps in this section are for Never Hinged items.

PD1

1940   Wmk. 263   Photo.   Imperf.
EX1	PD1	50h indigo & blue	1.00	1.75
EX2	PD1	50h carmine & rose	1.00	1.75

POSTAGE DUE STAMPS

> Catalogue values for unused stamps in this section are for Never Hinged items.

D1

1939   Unwmk.   Photo.   Perf. 12½
J1	D1	5h bright blue	1.00	.55
J2	D1	10h bright blue	.50	.55
J3	D1	20h bright blue	.50	.55
J4	D1	30h bright blue	3.00	1.00
J5	D1	40h bright blue	.70	.75
J6	D1	50h bright blue	2.50	.80
J7	D1	60h bright blue	2.00	.80
J8	D1	1k dark carmine	14.00	8.25
J9	D1	2k dark carmine	14.00	2.50
J10	D1	5k dark carmine	8.00	2.50
J11	D1	10k dark carmine	55.00	7.50
J12	D1	20k dark carmine	18.00	9.25
		Nos. J1-J12 (12)	119.20	35.00

1940-41   Wmk. 263
J13	D1	5h bright blue ('41)	.75	.55
J14	D1	10h bright blue ('41)	.30	.30
J15	D1	20h bright blue ('41)	.50	.30
J16	D1	30h bright blue ('41)	4.00	2.00
J17	D1	40h bright blue ('41)	.60	.55
J18	D1	50h bright blue ('41)	.75	.95
J19	D1	60h bright blue	.90	.95
J20	D1	1k dark carmine ('41)	.90	1.10
J21	D1	2k dark carmine ('41)	20.00	9.00
J22	D1	5k dark carmine ('41)	4.00	2.75
J23	D1	10k dark carmine ('41)	3.00	3.25
		Nos. J13-J23 (11)	35.70	21.70

NEWSPAPER STAMPS

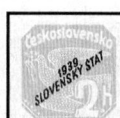
Newspaper Stamps of Czechoslovakia, 1937, Overprinted in Red or Blue

1939, Apr.   Unwmk.   Imperf.
P1	N2	2h bister brn (Bl)	.50	.40
P2	N2	5h dull blue (R)	.50	.40
P3	N2	7h red org (Bl)	.50	.40
P4	N2	9h emerald (R)	.50	.40
P5	N2	10h henna brn (Bl)	.50	.40
P6	N2	12h ultra (R)	.50	.40
P7	N2	20h dk green (R)	1.10	.95
P8	N2	50h dk brown (Bl)	3.00	2.50
P9	N2	1k grnsh gray (R)	11.00	10.00
		Nos. P1-P9 (9)	18.10	15.85

Excellent counterfeits exist of Nos. P1-P9.

> Catalogue values for unused stamps in this section, from this point to the end of the section, are for Never Hinged items.

Arms of
Slovakia — N1

1939   Typo.
P10	N1	2h ocher	.30	.25
P11	N1	5h ultra	.45	.40
P12	N1	7h red orange	.35	.30
P13	N1	9h emerald	.35	.30
P14	N1	10h henna brown	1.60	1.10
P15	N1	12h dk ultra	.40	.35
P16	N1	20h dark green	1.60	1.10
P17	N1	50h red brown	1.90	1.25
P18	N1	1k grnsh gray	1.60	1.10
		Nos. P10-P18 (9)	8.55	6.15

1940-41   Wmk. 263
P20	N1	5h ultra	.25	.25
P23	N1	10h henna brown	.25	.25
P24	N1	15h brt purple ('41)	.30	.25
P25	N1	20h dark green	.60	.50
P26	N1	25h lt blue ('41)	.60	.50
P27	N1	40h red org ('41)	.60	.50
P28	N1	50h chocolate	1.10	.75
P29	N1	1k grnsh gray ('41)	1.10	.75
P30	N1	2k emerald ('41)	2.25	1.60
		Nos. P20-P30 (9)	7.05	5.35

SOLOMON ISLANDS

ˈsä-lə-mən ˈī-lənds

British Solomon Islands

LOCATION — West Pacific Ocean, east of Papua
GOVT. — British Protectorate
AREA — 11,500 sq. mi.
POP. — 258,193 (1984)
CAPITAL — Honiara

The Solomons include 10 large islands and four groups of small islands extending over an area of 375,000 square miles.

12 Pence = 1 Shilling
20 Shillings = 1 Pound

Catalogue values for unused stamps in this country are for Never Hinged items, beginning with Scott 80 in the regular postage section.

War Canoe — A1

Unwmk.

1907, Feb. 14 — Litho. — Perf. 11

1	A1	½p ultra	11.00	16.00
2	A1	1p red	27.50	30.00
3	A1	2p dull blue	40.00	35.00
a.		Horiz. pair, imperf. btwn.	15,000.	
4	A1	2½p orange	38.50	50.00
a.		Vert. pair, imperf. btwn.	7,500.	
b.		Horiz. pair, imperf. btwn.	11,000.	7,000.
5	A1	5p yellow green	67.50	80.00
6	A1	6p chocolate	75.00	77.50
a.		Vertical pair, imperf. btwn.	7,000.	
7	A1	1sh violet	97.50	110.00
		Nos. 1-7 (7)	357.00	398.50

Imperf. between varieties should be accompanied by certificates of authenticity issued by competent authorities. Excellent counterfeits are plentiful.

War Canoe A2 — George V A3

Wmk. Multiple Crown and CA (3)

1908-11 — Engr. — Perf. 14

8	A2	½p green	1.75	1.25
9	A2	1p carmine	1.50	1.25
10	A2	2p gray	1.50	1.25
11	A2	2½p ultra	4.25	2.50
12	A2	4p red, yel ('11)	3.75	13.50
13	A2	5p olive green	10.50	8.75
14	A2	6p claret	11.50	8.25
15	A2	1sh black, green	9.75	9.25
16	A2	2sh vio, bl ('10)	50.00	70.00
17	A2	2sh6p red, bl ('10)	62.50	95.00
18	A2	5sh bl, yel ('10)	115.00	140.00
		Nos. 8-18 (11)	272.00	351.00
		Set, ovptd. "SPECIMEN"	325.00	

Inscribed "POSTAGE - POSTAGE"

1913-24 — Typo.

19	A3	½p green	.95	4.00
20	A3	1p carmine	3.50	16.50
21	A3	3p violet, yel	1.00	4.75
a.		3p violet, orange buff	9.25	27.50
22	A3	11p dull violet & red	5.75	14.00

Wmk. 4

23	A3	1½p scarlet ('24)	2.50	.80
		Nos. 19-23 (5)	13.70	40.05
		Nos. 19-22, ovptd. "SPECIMEN"	80.00	

Inscribed "POSTAGE - REVENUE"

1914-23 — Wmk. 3

28	A3	½p green	1.10	13.50
a.		½p yellow green ('17)	5.50	21.00
29	A3	1p carmine	1.75	1.50
a.		1p scarlet ('17)	5.50	7.50

30	A3	2p gray	3.75	10.50
31	A3	2½p ultra	4.25	5.75

Chalky Paper

32	A3	3p violet, yel ('23)	26.00	120.00
33	A3	4p blk & red, yel	2.25	3.00
34	A3	5p dull vio & ol grn	22.50	35.00
a.		5p brown purple & olive green	22.50	35.00
35	A3	6p dull vio & red vio	7.00	16.00
36	A3	1sh blk, green	5.50	8.00
a.		1sh blk, bl grn, ol back	8.50	27.50
37	A3	2sh dull vio & ultra, bl	8.00	11.50
38	A3	2sh6p blk & red, bl	11.00	22.50
39	A3	5sh grn & red, yel	45.00	55.00
a.		5sh green & red, orange buff	52.50	80.00
40	A3	10sh grn & red, grn	97.50	100.00
41	A3	£1 vio & blk, red	300.00	150.00
		Nos. 28-41 (14)	535.60	552.25
		Set, ovptd. "SPECIMEN"	450.00	

Inscribed "POSTAGE - REVENUE"

1922-31 — Wmk. 4

43	A3	½p green	.40	4.00
44	A3	1p carmine ('23)	12.50	12.50
45	A3	1p violet ('27)	1.10	8.50
46	A3	2p gray ('23)	5.25	17.00
47	A3	3p ultra ('23)	.85	5.25

Chalky Paper

48	A3	4p blk & red, yel ('27)	4.25	26.00
49	A3	4½p red brn ('31)	3.75	22.50
50	A3	5p dull vio & ol grn	3.75	32.50
51	A3	6p dull vio & red vio	4.50	32.50
52	A3	1sh black, emer	5.00	15.00
53	A3	2sh dull vio & ultra, bl ('27)	16.00	45.00
54	A3	2sh6p blk & red, bl	8.75	55.00
55	A3	5sh grn & red, yel	32.50	65.00
56	A3	10sh grn & red, emer ('25)	130.00	130.00
		Nos. 43-56 (14)	228.60	470.75

No. 49 is on ordinary paper.

Common Design Types pictured following the introduction.

Silver Jubilee Issue
Common Design Type

1935, May 6 — Engr. — Perf. 13½x14

60	CD301	1½p car & dk bl	1.50	1.50
61	CD301	3p blue & brown	5.00	7.50
62	CD301	6p ol grn & lt bl	13.50	12.00
63	CD301	1sh brt vio & ind	7.50	17.00
		Nos. 60-63 (4)	27.50	38.00
		Set, never hinged	45.00	
		Set, perforated "SPECIMEN"	140.00	

Coronation Issue
Common Design Type

1937, May 13 — Perf. 11x11½

64	CD302	1p dark purple	.25	1.00
65	CD302	1½p dark carmine	.25	.55
66	CD302	3p deep ultra	.40	.45
		Nos. 64-66 (3)	.90	2.00
		Set, never hinged	1.40	
		Set, perforated "SPECIMEN"	110.00	

Spears and Shield — A4

Policeman and Chief — A5

Artificial Island, Malaita — A6

Canoe House, New Georgia A7

Roviana War Canoe — A8

View of Munda Point — A9

Meeting House, Reef Islands A10 — Coconut Plantation A11

Breadfruit A12

Tinakula Volcano, Santa Cruz Islands A13

Scrub Fowl — A14

Malaita Canoe — A15

Perf. 12½, 13½ (A7, A13, A14)

1939-51 — Wmk. 4

67	A4	½p deep grn & ultra	.25	1.10
		Never hinged	.40	
68	A5	1p dk pur & choc	.25	1.75
		Never hinged	.40	
69	A6	1½p car & sl grn	.30	1.50
		Never hinged	.90	
70	A7	2p blk & org brn	.35	1.60
		Never hinged	.75	
a.		2p black & red brown ('43)	.35	1.75
		Never hinged	.70	
b.		Perf. 12 ('51)	.25	1.60
		Never hinged	.40	
71	A8	2½p ol grn & rose vio	1.25	2.75
		Never hinged	3.50	
a.		Vert. pair, imperf. horiz.	24,000.	
72	A9	3p ultra & blk, perf. 13½	.60	2.00
		Never hinged	1.50	
a.		Perf. 12 ('51)	.85	3.00
		Never hinged	2.00	

73	A10	4½p dk brn & yel grn	3.25	13.00
		Never hinged	5.50	
74	A11	6p rose lil & dk pur	.40	1.25
		Never hinged	1.25	
75	A12	1sh blk & grn	.80	1.25
		Never hinged	1.50	
76	A13	2sh dp org & blk	4.75	6.00
		Never hinged	13.00	
a.		2sh dp org & vio blk ('43)	4.75	6.50
		Never hinged	13.00	
77	A14	2sh6p dull vio & blk	17.50	5.00
		Never hinged	35.00	
78	A15	5sh red & brt bl grn	20.00	12.00
		Never hinged	35.00	
79	A10	10sh red lil & ol ('42)	4.00	8.00
		Never hinged	8.00	
		Nos. 67-79 (13)	53.70	57.20
		Set, never hinged	110.00	

Catalogue values for unused stamps in this section, from this point to the end of the section, are for Never Hinged items.

Peace Issue
Common Design Type

Perf. 13½x14

1946, Oct. 15 — Wmk. 4 — Engr.

80	CD303	1½p carmine	.25	1.00
81	CD303	3p deep blue	.25	.30
		Set, perforated "SPECIMEN"	92.50	

Silver Wedding Issue
Common Design Types

1949, Mar. 14 — Photo. — Perf. 14x14½

82	CD304	2p black	.40	.40

Perf. 11½x11

Engr.; Name Typo.

83	CD305	10sh red violet	13.00	13.00

UPU Issue
Common Design Types

Engr.; Name Typo. on 3p and 5p

Perf. 13½, 11x11½

1949, Oct. 10 — Wmk. 4

84	CD306	2p red brown	.75	.85
85	CD307	3p indigo	2.10	1.25
86	CD308	5p green	.75	1.40
87	CD309	1sh slate	.75	1.40
		Nos. 84-87 (4)	4.35	4.90

POSTAGE DUE STAMPS

D1

Perf. 12

1940, Sept. 1 — Typo. — Wmk. 4

J1	D1	1p emerald	4.50	8.00
J2	D1	2p dark red	4.75	8.00
J3	D1	3p chocolate	4.75	13.00
J4	D1	4p dark blue	7.25	13.00
J5	D1	5p deep green	8.00	27.50
J6	D1	6p brt red vio	8.00	20.00
J7	D1	1sh dull violet	10.00	32.50
J8	D1	1sh6p turq green	17.50	60.00
		Nos. J1-J8 (8)	64.75	182.00
		Set, never hinged	120.00	
		Set, perforated "SPECIMEN"	225.00	

SOMALIA

sō-'mä-lē-ə

(Italian Somaliland)

(Benadir)

LOCATION — Eastern Africa, bordering on the Indian Ocean and the Gulf of Aden
GOVT. — Italian Colony
AREA — 246,201 sq. mi.
POP. — 3,862,000 (est. 1982)
CAPITAL — Mogadiscio

The former Italian colony which included the territory west of the Juba River became known as Oltre Giuba (Trans-Juba), was absorbed into Italian East Africa in 1936.

4 Besas = 1 Anna
16 Annas = 1 Rupee
100 Besas = 1 Rupee (1922)
100 Centesimi = 1 Lira (1905, 1925)

Used values in italics are for postally used Italian Somalia stamps. CTO's sell for about the same as unused, hinged stamps.

Watermark

Wmk. 140 —
Crown

Italian Somaliland

Elephant — A1   Lion — A2

Wmk. 140

1903, Oct. 12	**Typo.**		**Perf. 14**	
1	A1	1b brown	140.00	26.00
	Never hinged		350.00	
	On cover			375.00
2	A1	2b blue green	1.60	15.00
	Never hinged		3.75	
	On cover			265.00
3	A2	1a claret	1.60	19.00
	Never hinged		3.75	
	On cover			340.00
4	A2	2a orange brown	2.00	37.50
	Never hinged		4.50	
	On cover			525.00
5	A2	2½a blue	1.60	37.50
	Never hinged		3.75	
	On cover			1,000.
6	A2	5a orange	2.00	75.00
	Never hinged		4.50	
	On cover			2,000.
7	A2	10a lilac	2.00	75.00
	Never hinged		4.50	
	On cover			—
	Nos. 1-7 (7)		150.80	285.00
	Set on overfranked cover			1,000.

Covers: Cover values are for properly franked and traveled covers. Overpaid and other philatelic souvenirs sell for much less.
For surcharges see Nos. 8-27, 40-50, 70-77.

Surcharged

1905, Dec. 29

8	A2	15c on 5a orange	3,500.	1,300.
	Never hinged		6,750.	
	On cover			5,000.
9	A2	40c on 10a lilac	1,100.	450.00
	Never hinged			
	On cover			2,800.

Covers: Cover values are for properly franked and traveled covers, generally abroad. Internal covers, normally overpaid and not traveled, and other philatelic souvenirs sell for much less.

Surcharged

1906-07

10	A1	2c on 1b brown	6.50	19.00
	Never hinged		15.00	
	On cover			240.00
11	A1	5c on 2b blue grn	6.50	14.00
	Never hinged		15.00	
	On cover			115.00
a.	Double surcharge		350.00	
b.	Double surcharge, one invtd.			5,250.
c.	Pair, one without surcharge		5,000.	

Surcharges on No. 11c are virtually on top of each other. Certificates are necessary.

Surcharged

12	A2	10c on 1a claret	6.50	14.00
	Never hinged		15.00	
	On cover			110.00
13	A2	15c on 2a brn org ('06)	6.50	14.00
	Never hinged		15.00	
	On cover			150.00
14	A2	25c on 2½a blue	16.00	14.00
	Never hinged		37.50	
	On cover			165.00
15	A2	50c on 5a yellow	32.50	35.00
	Never hinged		75.00	
	On cover			300.00

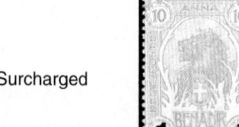

Surcharged

16	A2	1 l on 10a lilac	32.50	47.50
	Never hinged		75.00	
	On cover			825.00
	Nos. 10-16 (7)		107.00	157.50

Covers: Cover values are for properly franked and traveled covers. Overpaid and other philatelic souvenirs sell for much less.

Nos. 15 and 16 With Bars Over Former Surcharge and

1916, Apr.

18	A2	5c on 50c on 5a yel	47.50	52.50
	Never hinged		110.00	
	On cover			300.00
a.	Double surcharge, one invtd.		5,000.	
b.	Lower left bar of surcharge omitted		120.00	
19	A2	20c on 1 l on 10a dl lil	9.50	35.00
	Never hinged		22.50	
	On cover			210.00
a.	Bar of surcharge at top of stamp		125.00	125.00
b.	Bar of surcharge omitted		675.00	

No. 4 Surcharged

20	A2	20c on 2a org brn	24.00	16.00
	Never hinged		55.00	
	On cover			150.00
	Nos. 18-20 (3)		81.00	103.50

Nos. 11-16 Surcharged

a   b

1922, Feb. 1

22	A1(a)	3b on 5c on 2b	13.00	24.00
	Never hinged		30.00	
	On cover			165.00
23	A2(b)	6c on 10c on 1a	24.00	19.00
	Never hinged		55.00	
	On cover			180.00
24	A2(b)	9b on 15c on 2a	24.00	24.00
	Never hinged		55.00	
	On cover			180.00
25	A2(b)	15b on 25c on 2½a	24.00	18.00
	Never hinged		55.00	
	On cover			240.00
a.	"15" at left omitted		300.00	
26	A2(b)	30b on 50c on 5a	26.00	52.50
	Never hinged		60.00	
	On cover			300.00
27	A2(b)	60b on 1 l on 10a	26.00	87.50
	Never hinged		60.00	
	On cover			650.00
	Nos. 22-27 (6)		137.00	225.00

Victory Issue

Italy Nos. 136-139
Surcharged

1922, Apr.			**Perf. 14**	
28	A64	3b on 5c olive grn	2.00	7.25
	Never hinged		4.50	
	On cover			125.00
c.	Surcharge denomination omitted		750.00	
29	A64	6b on 10c red	2.00	7.25
	Never hinged		4.50	
	On cover			225.00
30	A64	9b on 15c slate grn	2.00	11.00
	Never hinged		4.50	
	On cover			240.00
31	A64	15b on 25c ultra	2.00	11.00
	Never hinged		4.50	
	On cover			275.00
	Nos. 28-31 (4)		8.00	36.50

			Perf. 14x13½	
28a	A64	3b on 5c olive grn	4.75	16.00
	Never hinged		9.00	
29a	A64	6b on 10c red	4.75	16.00
	Never hinged		9.00	
30a	A64	9b on 15c slate grn	4.75	24.00
	Never hinged		9.00	
31a	A64	15b on 25c ultra	4.75	24.00
	Never hinged		9.00	
	Nos. 28a-31a (4)		19.00	80.00

			Perf. 13½	
29b	A64	6b on 10c red	125.00	250.00
	Never hinged		250.00	
31b	A64	15b on 25c ultra	125.00	
	Never hinged		250.00	

Nos. 10-16 Surcharged with Bars and

c   d

1923, July 1

40	A1	1b brown	9.50	37.50
	Never hinged		25.00	
	On cover			250.00

41	A1(c)	2b on 2c on 1b	9.50	37.50
	Never hinged		25.00	
	On cover			175.00
42	A1(c)	3b on 2c on 1b	9.50	18.00
	Never hinged		25.00	
	On cover			175.00
43	A1(c)	4b on 5c on 2b	9.00	15.00
	Never hinged		25.00	
	On cover			125.00
44	A1(c)	6b on 5c on 2b	17.50	19.00
	Never hinged		40.00	
	On cover			145.00
45	A2(d)	18b on 10c on 1a	17.50	19.00
	Never hinged		40.00	
	On cover			190.00
46	A2(d)	20b on 15c on 2a	21.00	19.00
	Never hinged		45.00	
	On cover			250.00
47	A2(d)	25b on 15c on 2a	21.00	19.00
	Never hinged		45.00	
	On cover			250.00
48	A2(d)	30b on 25c on 2½a	24.00	24.00
	Never hinged		55.00	
	On cover			225.00
49	A2(d)	60b on 1 l on 10a	24.00	52.50
	Never hinged		55.00	
	On cover			475.00
50	A2(d)	1r on 1 l on 10a	65.00	65.00
	Never hinged		135.00	
	On cover			675.00
	Nos. 40-50 (11)		228.00	329.50

No. 40 is No. 10 with bars over the 1907 surcharge.

Propagation of the Faith Issue

Italy Nos. 143-146 Surcharged

1923, Oct. 24			**Wmk. 140**	
51	A68	6b on 20c ol grn & brn org	11.50	50.00
	Never hinged		25.00	
	On cover			—
52	A68	13b on 30c cl & brn org	11.50	50.00
	Never hinged		25.00	
	On cover			—
53	A68	20b on 50c vio & brn org	7.50	57.50
	Never hinged		14.50	
	On cover			—
54	A68	30b on 1 l bl & brn org	7.50	87.50
	Never hinged		14.50	
	On cover			—
	Nos. 51-54 (4)		38.00	245.00

Fascisti Issue

Italy Nos. 159-164 Surcharged in Red or Black

1923, Oct. 29		**Unwmk.**	**Perf. 14**	
55	A69	3b on 10c dk grn (R)	15.00	19.00
	Never hinged		37.50	
	On cover			300.00
56	A69	13b on 30c dk vio (R)	15.00	19.00
	Never hinged		37.50	
	On cover			300.00
57	A69	20b on 50c brn car	15.00	26.00
	Never hinged		37.50	
	On cover			300.00

			Wmk. 140	
58	A70	30b on 1 l blue	15.00	50.00
	Never hinged		37.50	
	On cover			575.00
59	A70	1r on 2 l brown	15.00	60.00
	Never hinged		37.50	
	On cover			825.00
60	A71	3r on 5 l blk & bl (R)	15.00	90.00
	Never hinged		37.50	
	On cover			300.00
	Nos. 55-60 (6)		90.00	264.00
	Set on overfranked philatelic cover			750.00

Manzoni Issue
Italy Nos. 165-170 Surcharged in Red

1924, Apr. 1

61	A72	6b on 10c brn red & blk		12.00	75.00
		Never hinged		30.00	
62	A72	9b on 15c bl grn & blk		12.00	75.00
		Never hinged		30.00	
63	A72	13b on 30c blk & sl		12.00	75.00
		Never hinged		30.00	
64	A72	20b on 50c org brn & blk		12.00	75.00
		Never hinged		30.00	

Surcharged in Red

65	A72	30b on 1 l bl & blk		72.50	450.00
		Never hinged		185.00	
66	A72	3r on 5 l vio & blk		475.00	3,000.
		Never hinged		1,200.	
		Nos. 61-66 (6)		595.50	3,750.

Covers bearing stamps of this issue are very scarce.

Victor Emmanuel Issue
Italy Nos. 175-177 Overprinted

1925-26   Unwmk.   Perf. 13½, 11

67	A78	60c brown car		2.25	13.50
		Never hinged		4.00	
		On cover			160.00
a.		Perf. 11		180.00	375.00
		Never hinged		350.00	
		On cover			475.00
68	A78	1 l dk bl, perf. 11		3.00	19.00
		Never hinged		6.00	
		On cover			240.00
a.		Perf. 13½		10.50	57.50
		Never hinged		24.00	
		On cover			475.00
69	A78	1.25 l dk blue ('26)		2.25	30.00
		Never hinged		4.00	
		On cover			325.00
a.		Perf. 11		1,050.	1,875.
		Never hinged		1,900.	
		On cover			2,800.
		Nos. 67-69 (3)		7.50	62.50

Stamps of 1907-16 with Bars over Original Values

1926, Mar. 1   Wmk. 140   Perf. 14

70	A1	2c on 1b brown		27.50	55.00
		Never hinged		75.00	
		On cover			275.00
71	A1	5c on 2b blue grn		19.00	27.50
		Never hinged		50.00	
		On cover			175.00
72	A2	10c on 1a rose red		13.00	11.00
		Never hinged		32.50	
		On cover			140.00
73	A2	15c on 2a org brn		13.00	14.50
		Never hinged		32.50	
		On cover			160.00
74	A2	20c on 2a org brn		14.50	14.50
		Never hinged		37.50	
		On cover			140.00
75	A2	25c on 2½a blue		14.50	19.00
		Never hinged		37.50	
		On cover			200.00
76	A2	50c on 5a yellow		19.00	35.00
		Never hinged		50.00	
		On cover			325.00
77	A2	1 l on 10a dull lil		27.50	47.50
		Never hinged		75.00	
		On cover			600.00
		Nos. 70-77 (8)		148.00	224.00

Saint Francis of Assisi Issue

Italy Nos. 178-180 Overprinted

1926, Apr. 12   Perf. 14

78	A79	20c gray green		2.40	13.50
		Never hinged		6.00	
		On cover			125.00
79	A80	40c dark violet		2.40	13.50
		Never hinged		6.00	
		On cover			140.00
80	A81	60c red brown		2.40	24.00
		Never hinged		6.00	
		On cover			140.00

Italy Nos. 182 and Type of 1926 Overprinted in Red

Unwmk.   Perf. 11

81	A82	1.25 l dark blue		2.40	35.00
		Never hinged		6.00	
		On cover			260.00

Perf. 14

82	A83	5 l + 2.50 l ol grn		6.50	67.50
		Never hinged		16.00	
		On cover			
		Nos. 78-82 (5)		16.10	153.50
		Set on overfranked philatelic cover			425.00

Italian Stamps of 1901-26 Overprinted

1926-30   Wmk. 140

83	A43	2c orange brown		7.50	6.50
		Never hinged		12.00	
		On cover			65.00
84	A48	5c green		7.50	6.50
		Never hinged		12.00	
		On cover			55.00
85	A48	10c claret		7.50	.40
		Never hinged		9.50	
		On cover			55.00
86	A49	20c violet brown		11.00	2.40
		Never hinged		9.50	
		On cover			100.00
87	A46	25c grn & pale grn		7.50	1.60
		Never hinged		9.50	
		On cover			72.50
88	A49	30c gray ('30)		20.00	50.00
		Never hinged		47.50	
		On cover			275.00
89	A49	60c brown orange		9.00	12.00
		Never hinged		14.50	
		On cover			325.00
a.		Double overprint			4,000.
90	A46	75c dk red & rose		160.00	50.00
		Never hinged		325.00	
		On cover			300.00
91	A46	1 l brown & grn		9.00	.80
		Never hinged		14.50	
		On cover			105.00
92	A46	1.25 l blue & ultra		19.00	2.40
		Never hinged		32.50	
		On cover			250.00
93	A46	2 l dk grn & org		42.50	16.00
		Never hinged		82.50	
		On cover			550.00
94	A46	2.50 l dk grn & org		42.50	24.00
		Never hinged		82.50	
		On cover			675.00
95	A46	5 l blue & rose		90.00	57.50
		Never hinged		215.00	
		On cover			2,800.
96	A51	10 l gray grn & red		90.00	97.50
		Never hinged		215.00	
		On cover			—
		Nos. 83-96 (14)		523.00	327.60

Volta Issue

Type of Italy, 1927, Overprinted

1927, Oct. 10

97	A84	20c purple		7.00	40.00
		Never hinged		12.00	
		On cover			240.00
98	A84	50c deep orange		12.00	30.00
		Never hinged		20.00	
		On cover			240.00
a.		Double overprint		175.00	
		Never hinged		375.00	
99	A84	1.25 l brt blue		17.00	77.50
		Never hinged		27.50	
		On cover			450.00
		Nos. 97-99 (3)		36.00	147.50
		Set on overfranked philatelic cover			350.00

Italian Stamps of 1927-28 Overprinted in Black or Red

1928-30

100	A86	7½c lt brown		34.00	75.00
		Never hinged		47.50	
		On cover			300.00
a.		Double overprint		550.00	
		Never hinged		1,000.	
101	A85	50c brn & sl (R)		34.00	10.00
		Never hinged		47.50	
		On cover			60.00
102	A86	50c brt violet ('30)		60.00	90.00
		Never hinged		100.00	
		On cover			160.00

Perf. 11
Unwmk.

103	A85	1.75 l deep brown		105.00	20.00
		Never hinged		190.00	
		On cover			95.00
		Nos. 100-103 (4)		233.00	195.00

Monte Cassino Issue

Monte Cassino Issue of Italy Overprinted in Red or Blue

1929, Oct. 14   Wmk. 140   Perf. 14

104	A96	20c dk green (R)		6.00	21.00
		Never hinged		16.00	
		On cover			240.00
105	A96	25c red org (Bl)		6.00	21.00
		Never hinged		16.00	
		On cover			175.00
106	A98	50c + 10c crim (Bl)		6.00	22.50
		Never hinged		16.00	
		On cover			125.00
107	A98	75c + 15c ol brn (R)		6.00	22.50
		Never hinged		16.00	
		On cover			240.00
108	A96	1.25 l + 25c dk vio (R)		13.50	42.50
		Never hinged		37.50	
		On cover			300.00
109	A98	5 l + 1 l saph (R)		13.50	45.00
		Never hinged		37.50	
		On cover			—

Overprinted in Red

Unwmk.

110	A100	10 l + 2 l gray brn		13.50	67.50
		Never hinged		37.50	
		On cover			
		Nos. 104-110 (7)		64.50	242.00

Royal Wedding Issue

Type of Italian Royal Wedding Stamps of 1930 Overprinted

1930, Mar. 17   Wmk. 140

111	A101	20c yellow green		3.00	9.00
		Never hinged		4.00	
		On cover			110.00
112	A101	50c + 10c dp org		2.25	9.00
		Never hinged		3.00	
		On cover			145.00

113	A101	1.25 l + 25c rose red		2.25	18.00
		Never hinged		3.00	
		On cover			240.00
		Nos. 111-113 (3)		7.50	36.00
		Set on overfranked philatelic cover			160.00

Ferrucci Issue

Types of Italian Stamps of 1930 Overprinted in Red or Blue

1930, July 26

114	A102	20c violet (R)		6.00	6.00
		Never hinged		13.00	
		On cover			120.00
115	A103	25c dark green (R)		6.00	6.00
		Never hinged		13.00	
		On cover			145.00
116	A103	50c black (R)		6.00	11.00
		Never hinged		13.00	
		On cover			120.00
117	A103	1.25 l deep blue (R)		6.00	21.00
		Never hinged		13.00	
		On cover			275.00
118	A104	5 l + 2 l dp car (bl)		13.50	45.00
		Never hinged		26.00	
		Nos. 114-118 (5)		37.50	89.00
		Set on overfranked philatelic cover			275.00

Virgil Issue

Types of Italian Stamps of 1930 Overprinted in Red or Blue

1930, Dec. 4   Photo.   Wmk. 140

119	A106	15c violet blue		1.20	11.00
		Never hinged		3.00	
		On cover			150.00
120	A106	20c orange brown		1.20	4.50
		Never hinged		3.00	
		On cover			90.00
121	A106	25c dark green		1.20	4.50
		Never hinged		3.00	
		On cover			82.50
122	A106	30c lt brown		1.20	4.50
		Never hinged		3.00	
		On cover			90.00
123	A106	50c dull violet		1.20	4.50
		Never hinged		3.00	
		On cover			75.00
124	A106	75c rose red		1.20	9.00
		Never hinged		3.00	
		On cover			175.00
125	A106	1.25 l gray blue		1.20	11.00
		Never hinged		3.00	
		On cover			275.00

Engr.
Unwmk.

126	A106	5 l + 1.50 l dk vio		4.50	45.00
		Never hinged		8.75	
		On cover			—
127	A106	10 l + 2.50 l ol brn		4.50	67.50
		Never hinged		8.75	
		On cover			—
		Nos. 119-127 (9)		17.40	161.50
		Set on overfranked philatelic cover			450.00

Saint Anthony of Padua Issue

Types of Italian Stamps of 1931 Overprinted in Blue or Red

1931, May 7   Photo.   Wmk. 140

129	A116	20c brown (Bl)		1.60	21.00
		Never hinged		4.00	
		On cover			110.00
130	A116	25c green (R)		1.60	7.50
		Never hinged		4.00	
		On cover			110.00
131	A118	30c gray brn (Bl)		1.60	7.50
		Never hinged		4.00	
		On cover			175.00
132	A118	50c dull vio (Bl)		1.60	7.50
		Never hinged		4.00	
		On cover			110.00
133	A120	1.25 l slate bl (R)		1.60	37.50
		Never hinged		4.00	
		On cover			360.00

Overprinted in Red or Black

			Engr.	Unwmk.
134	A121	75c black (R)	1.60	21.00
		Never hinged	4.00	
		On cover		300.00
135	A122	5 l + 2.50 l dk brn (Bk)	10.50	73.00
		Never hinged	19.00	—
		On cover		—
		Nos. 129-135 (7)	20.10	*175.00*
		Set on overfranked philatelic cover		*475.00*

Italy Nos. 218, 221 Overprinted in Red

			1931	Wmk. 140
136	A94	25c dk green (R)	15.00	25.00
		Never hinged	35.00	
		On cover		260.00
137	A95	50c purple (R)	15.00	4.50
		Never hinged	35.00	
		On cover		125.00

Lighthouse at Cape Guardafui — A3

Tower at Mnara Ciromo — A4

Governor's Palace at Mogadishu — A5

Termite Nest — A6

Ostrich — A7

Hippopotamus — A8

Greater Kudu — A9

Lion — A10

		1932	Wmk. 140	Photo.	Perf. 12
138	A3	5c deep brown	12.00	*15.00*
		Never hinged	32.50	
		On cover		65.00
139	A3	7½c violet	19.00	*37.50*
		Never hinged	45.00	
		On cover		200.00
140	A3	10c gray black	26.00	.40
		Never hinged	65.00	
		On cover		4.75
141	A3	15c olive green	9.50	1.20
		Never hinged	25.00	
		On cover		26.00

142	A4	20c carmine	400.00	.40
		Never hinged	935.00	
		On cover		2.40
143	A4	25c deep green	9.50	.40
		Never hinged	25.00	
		On cover		2.40
		brown	105.00	1.20
		Never hinged	190.00	
		On cover		7.25
145	A5	35c dark blue	11.00	*22.50*
		Never hinged	30.00	
		On cover		90.00
146	A5	50c violet	475.00	.40
		Never hinged	1,150.	
		On cover		2.40
147	A5	75c carmine	11.00	.80
		Never hinged	30.00	
		On cover		12.00
148	A6	1.25 l dark blue	37.50	.80
		Never hinged	92.50	
		On cover		12.00
149	A6	1.75 l red orange	26.00	.80
		Never hinged	60.00	
		On cover		12.00
150	A6	2 l carmine	11.00	.40
		Never hinged	30.00	
		On cover		14.50
151	A7	2.55 l indigo	60.00	*135.00*
		Never hinged	150.00	
		On cover		800.00
152	A7	5 l carmine	34.00	15.00
		Never hinged	87.50	
		On cover		400.00
153	A8	10 l violet	52.50	37.50
		Never hinged	125.00	
		On cover		1,750.
154	A9	20 l dark green	110.00	*150.00*
		Never hinged	290.00	
		On cover		—
155	A10	25 l dark blue	110.00	*290.00*
		Never hinged	290.00	
		On cover		—
		Nos. 138-155 (18)	*1,519.*	*709.30*
		Set, never hinged	*3,750.*	
		Set on overfranked philatelic cover		*2,600.*

		1934-37		Perf. 14
138a	A3	5c deep brown	3.75	.80
		Never hinged	7.50	
		On cover		8.00
139a	A3	7½c violet	3.75	*50.00*
		Never hinged	7.50	
		On cover		110.00
140a	A3	10c gray black	3.75	.40
		Never hinged	7.50	
		On cover		2.40
141a	A3	15c olive green	3.75	*2.40*
		Never hinged	7.50	
		On cover		26.00
142a	A4	20c carmine	3.75	.25
		Never hinged	7.50	
		On cover		5.50
143a	A4	25c deep green	3.75	.40
		Never hinged	7.50	
		On cover		4.00
144a	A4	30c dark brown	7.50	.40
		Never hinged	15.00	
		On cover		6.50
145a	A5	35c dark blue	19.00	*57.50*
		Never hinged	27.50	
		On cover		80.00
146a	A5	50c violet	50.00	.40
		Never hinged	92.50	
		On cover		2.40
147a	A5	75c carmine	67.50	.40
		Never hinged	150.00	
		On cover		12.50
148a	A6	1.25 l dark blue	135.00	1.20
		Never hinged	260.00	
		On cover		12.50
149a	A6	1.75 l red orange	340.00	42.50
		Never hinged	650.00	
		On cover		40.00
150a	A6	2 l carmine	82.50	.80
		Never hinged	165.00	
		On cover		20.00
151a	A7	2.55 l indigo	375.00	*975.00*
		Never hinged	750.00	
		On cover		3,000.
152a	A7	5 l carmine	37.50	3.25
		Never hinged	75.00	
		On cover		120.00
153a	A8	10 l violet	290.00	45.00
		Never hinged	500.00	
		On cover		675.00
154a	A9	20 l dark green	15,000.	*2,500.*
		Never hinged	20,000.	
		On cover		—
155a	A10	25 l dark blue	950.00	825.00
		Never hinged	2,250.	
		On cover		—
		Nos. 138a-153a,155a (17)	*2,376.*	*2,005.*
		Set, never hinged	*5,650.*	

Perf. 12x14 or 14x12 (20c, 25c, 75c-2 l)

		1932		
139b	A3	7½c violet	95.00	*160.00*
140b	A3	10c gray black	—	1,000.
142b	A4	20c carmine	2,000.	1,000.
143b	A4	25c deep green	160.00	65.00
145b	A5	35c dark blue	110.00	*140.00*
146b	A5	50c violet	80.00	40.00
		c. Perf 14x12		
147b	A5	75c carmine	120.00	95.00
148b	A6	1.25 l dark blue	—	1,200.
149b	A6	1.75 l red orange	525.00	525.00
150b	A6	2 l carmine	525.00	525.00
151b	A7	2.55 l indigo	2,700.	—
153b	A8	10 l violet	95.00	*120.00*

Perf 12 on 3 sides, Perf 14 on either top or bottom

140c	A3	15c olive green	—	675.00
142c	A4	20c carmine	1,200.	1,100.
143c	A4	25c deep green	160.00	160.00

Perf 12 on 3 sides, Perf 14 on left

147c	A5	75c carmine	2,400.	1,100.

Types of 1932 Issue Overprinted in Black or Red

		1934, May		Perf. 14
156	A3	10c brown (Bk)	21.00	*50.00*
		Never hinged	30.00	
		On cover		400.00
157	A4	25c green	21.00	*50.00*
		Never hinged	30.00	
		On cover		400.00
158	A5	50c dull vio (Bk)	21.00	*50.00*
		Never hinged	30.00	
		On cover		275.00
159	A6	1.25 l blue	21.00	*50.00*
		Never hinged	30.00	
		On cover		475.00
160	A7	5 l brown black	21.00	*50.00*
		Never hinged	30.00	
		On cover		—
161	A8	10 l car rose (Bk)	21.00	*97.50*
		Never hinged	30.00	
		On cover		—
162	A9	20 l dull blue	21.00	*97.50*
		Never hinged	30.00	
		On cover		—
163	A10	25 l dark green	21.00	*97.50*
		Never hinged	30.00	
		On cover		—
		Nos. 156-163 (8)	*168.00*	*542.50*
		Set, never hinged	*375.00*	
		Set on overfranked philatelic cover(s)		*725.00*

Duke of the Abruzzi (Luigi Amadeo, 1873-1933).

Mother and Child A11

		1934, Oct.		
164	A11	5c ol grn & brn	5.25	21.00
		Never hinged	10.00	
		On cover		325.00
165	A11	10c yel brn & blk	5.25	21.00
		Never hinged	10.00	
		On cover		275.00
166	A11	20c scarlet & blk	5.25	19.00
		Never hinged	10.00	
		On cover		275.00
167	A11	50c dk violet & brn	5.25	19.00
		Never hinged	10.00	
		On cover		250.00
168	A11	60c org brn & blk	5.25	26.00
		Never hinged	10.00	
		On cover		325.00
169	A11	1.25 l dk blue & grn	5.25	45.00
		Never hinged	10.00	
		On cover		400.00
		Nos. 164-169,C1-C6 (12)	*63.00*	*302.00*
		Nos. 164-169, never hinged	75.00	
		Nos. 164-169 on overfranked philatelic cover(s)		*325.00*

Second Colonial Arts Exhibition, Naples.

SEMI-POSTAL STAMPS

Italy Nos. B1-B4 Overprinted

		1916	Wmk. 140	Perf. 14
B1	SP1	10c + 5c rose	16.00	45.00
		Never hinged	50.00	
		On cover		175.00
B2	SP2	15c + 5c slate	67.50	57.50
		Never hinged	125.00	
		On cover		250.00
B3	SP2	20c + 5c orange	16.00	52.50
		Never hinged	50.00	
		On cover		275.00
B4	SP2	20c on 15c + 5c slate	67.50	95.00
		Never hinged	125.00	
		On cover		325.00
		Nos. B1-B4 (4)	*167.00*	*250.00*
		Set on overfranked philatelic cover(s)		*350.00*

Holy Year Issue
Italy Nos. B20-B25 Surcharged in Black or Red

		1925, June 1		Perf. 12
B5	SP4	6b + 3b on 20c + 10c	3.75	*22.50*
		Never hinged	8.00	
		On cover		200.00
B6	SP4	13b + 6b on 30c + 15c	3.75	*24.00*
		Never hinged	8.00	
		On cover		200.00
B7	SP4	15b + 8b on 50c + 25c	3.75	*22.50*
		Never hinged	8.00	
		On cover		200.00
B8	SP4	18b + 9b on 60c + 30c	3.75	*30.00*
		Never hinged	8.00	
		On cover		275.00
B9	SP8	30b + 15b on 1 l +50c (R)	3.75	*37.50*
		Never hinged	8.00	
		On cover		—
B10	SP8	1r + 50b on 5 l +2.50 l (R)	3.75	*57.50*
		Never hinged	8.00	
		On cover		—
		Nos. B5-B10 (6)	*22.50*	*194.00*
		Set on overfranked philatelic cover(s)		*450.00*

Colonial Institute Issue

"Peace" Substituting Spade for Sword — SP10

		1926, June 1	Typo.	Perf. 14
B11	SP10	5c + 5c brown	1.10	*9.50*
		Never hinged	2.40	
		On cover		175.00
B12	SP10	10c + 5c olive grn	1.10	*9.50*
		Never hinged	2.40	
		On cover		125.00
B13	SP10	20c + 5c blue grn	1.10	*9.50*
		Never hinged	2.40	
		On cover		100.00
B14	SP10	40c + 5c brown red	1.10	*9.50*
		Never hinged	2.40	
		On cover		100.00
B15	SP10	60c + 5c orange	1.10	*9.50*
		Never hinged	2.40	
		On cover		175.00
B16	SP10	1 l + 5c blue	1.10	*20.00*
		Never hinged	2.40	
		On cover		275.00
		Nos. B11-B16 (6)	*6.60*	*67.50*
		Set on overfranked philatelic cover(s)		*250.00*

The surtax was for the Italian Colonial Institute.

Italian Semi-Postal Stamps of 1926 Overprinted

		1927, Apr. 21	Unwmk.	Perf. 11½
B17	SP10	40c + 20c dk brn & blk	3.75	*42.50*
		Never hinged	6.00	
		On cover		175.00
B18	SP10	60c + 30c brn red & ol brn	3.75	*42.50*
		Never hinged	6.00	
		On cover		190.00
B19	SP10	1.25 l + 60c dp bl & blk	3.75	*60.00*
		Never hinged	6.00	
		On cover		350.00
B20	SP10	5 l + 2.50 l dk grn & blk	6.00	*92.50*
		Never hinged	10.00	
		On cover		—
		Nos. B17-B20 (4)	*17.25*	*237.50*
		Set on overfranked philatelic cover(s)		*500.00*

The surtax was for the charitable work of the Voluntary Militia for Italian National Defense.

Allegory of Fascism
and Victory — SP11

1928, Oct. 15   Wmk. 140   Perf. 14

B21	SP11	20c + 5c blue grn	3.25	13.50
	Never hinged		7.50	
	On cover			160.00
B22	SP11	30c + 5c red	3.25	13.50
	Never hinged		7.50	
	On cover			160.00
B23	SP11	50c + 10c purple	3.25	22.50
	Never hinged		7.50	
	On cover			150.00
B24	SP11	1.25 l + 20c dk blue	4.00	30.00
	Never hinged		9.25	
	On cover			400.00
	Nos. B21-B24 (4)		13.75	79.50
	Set on overfranked philatelic cover(s)			300.00

46th anniv. of the Societa Africana d'Italia. The surtax aided that society.

Italian
Semi-Postal
Stamps of
1928
Overprinted

1929, Mar. 4   Unwmk.   Perf. 11

B25	SP10	30c + 10c red & blk	4.50	26.00
	Never hinged		10.00	
	On cover			175.00
B26	SP10	50c + 20c vio & blk	4.50	28.00
	Never hinged		10.00	
	On cover			175.00
B27	SP10	1.25 l + 50c brn & bl	6.75	50.00
	Never hinged		12.00	
	On cover			450.00
B28	SP10	5 l + 2 l ol grn & blk	6.75	97.50
	Never hinged		12.00	
	Nos. B25-B28 (4)		22.50	201.50
	Set on overfranked philatelic cover(s)			475.00

The surtax was for the charitable work of the Voluntary Militia for Italian National Defense.

Italian Semi-Postal
Stamps of
1926 Ovptd.
in Black or
Red

1930, Oct. 20   Perf. 14

B29	SP10	30c + 10c dk grn & bl grn (Bk)	35.00	60.00
	Never hinged		62.50	
	On cover			275.00
B30	SP10	50c + 10c dk grn & vio (R)	35.00	97.50
	Never hinged		62.50	
	On cover			300.00
B31	SP10	1.25 l + 30c ol brn & red brn (R)	35.00	97.50
	Never hinged		62.50	
	On cover			500.00
B32	SP10	5 l + 1.50 l ind & grn (R)	110.00	260.00
	Never hinged		215.00	
	On cover			—
	Nos. B29-B32 (4)		215.00	515.00
	Set on overfranked philatelic cover(s)			800.00

The surtax was for the charitable work of the Voluntary Militia for Italian National Defense.

Irrigation
Canal
SP14

1930, Nov. 27   Photo.   Wmk. 140

B33	SP14	50c + 20c olive brn	4.00	24.00
	Never hinged		10.00	
	On cover			200.00

B34	S414	1.25 l + 20c dp blue	4.00	24.00
	Never hinged		10.00	
	On cover			275.00
B35	SP14	1.75 l + 20c green	4.00	26.00
	Never hinged		10.00	
	On cover			350.00
B36	SP14	2.55 l + 50c purple	9.00	42.50
	Never hinged		16.00	
	On cover			550.00
B37	SP14	5 l + 1 l dp car	9.00	65.00
	Never hinged		16.00	
	On cover			—
	Nos. B33-B37 (5)		30.00	181.50
	Set on overfranked philatelic cover(s)			325.00

25th anniv. of the Italian Colonial Agricultural Institute. The surtax was for the aid of that institution.

SP15

King Victor
Emmanuel
III — SP16

1935, Jan. 1

B38	SP15	5c + 5c blk brn	6.00	34.00
	Never hinged		12.50	
	On cover			300.00
B39	SP15	7 ½c + 7 ½c vio	6.00	34.00
	Never hinged		12.50	
	On cover			350.00
B40	SP15	15c + 10c ol blk	6.00	34.00
	Never hinged		12.50	
	On cover			260.00
B41	SP15	20c + 10c rose red	6.00	34.00
	Never hinged		12.50	
	On cover			260.00
B42	SP15	25c + 10c dp grn	6.00	34.00
	Never hinged		12.50	
	On cover			275.00
B43	SP15	30c + 10c brn	6.00	34.00
	Never hinged		12.50	
	On cover			300.00
B44	SP15	50c + 10c pur	6.00	34.00
	Never hinged		12.50	
	On cover			300.00
B45	SP15	75c + 15c rose car	6.00	34.00
	Never hinged		12.50	
	On cover			350.00
B46	SP15	1.25 l + 15c dp bl	6.00	34.00
	Never hinged		12.50	
	On cover			475.00
B47	SP15	1.75 l + 25c red org	6.00	34.00
	Never hinged		12.50	
	On cover			675.00
B48	SP15	2.75 l + 25c gray	37.50	135.00
	Never hinged		77.50	
	On cover			—
B49	SP15	5 l + 1 l dp cl	37.50	135.00
	Never hinged		77.50	
	On cover			—
B50	SP15	10 l + 1.80 l red brn	37.50	135.00
	Never hinged		77.50	
	On cover			—
B51	SP16	25 l + 2.75 l brn & red	200.00	500.00
	Never hinged		440.00	
	On cover			—
	Nos. B38-B51 (14)		372.50	1,245.
	Set, never hinged		850.00	
	Set on overfranked philatelic cover(s)			2,800.

Visit of King Victor Emmanuel III.

AIR POST STAMPS

View of
Coast
AP1

Cheetahs
AP2

Wmk. 140

1934, Oct.   Photo.   Perf. 14

C1	AP1	25c sl bl & red org	5.25	21.00
	Never hinged		10.00	
	On cover			250.00
C2	AP1	50c dk grn & blk	5.25	19.00
	Never hinged		10.00	
	On cover			200.00
C3	AP1	75c brn & red org	5.25	19.00
	Never hinged		10.00	
	On cover			275.00
a.	Imperf.		3,000.	
			3,000.	
C4	AP2	80c org brn & blk	5.25	21.00
	Never hinged		10.00	
	On cover			325.00
C5	AP2	1 l scar & blk	5.25	26.00
	Never hinged		10.00	
	On cover			350.00
C6	AP2	2 l dk bl & brn	5.25	45.00
	Never hinged		10.00	
	On cover			525.00
	Nos. C1-C6 (6)		24.00	136.00
	Set, never hinged		80.00	
	Set, on flown cover			400.00

2nd Colonial Arts Exhibition, Naples.
For overprint see No. CO1.

Banana
Tree and
Airplane
AP3

Designs: 25c, 1.50 l, Banana tree and plane. 50c, 2 l, Plane over cotton field. 60c, 5 l, Plane over orchard. 75c, 10 l, Plane over field workers. 1 l, 3 l, Small girl watching plane.

1936   Photo.

C7	AP3	25c slate green	3.50	9.00
	Never hinged		5.50	
				100.00
C8	AP3	50c brown	2.00	.25
	Never hinged		3.75	
				2.40
C9	AP3	60c red orange	4.00	13.50
	Never hinged		7.50	
				20.00
C10	AP3	75c orange brn	3.50	2.40
	Never hinged		5.50	
				20.00
C11	AP3	1 l deep blue	2.00	.25
	Never hinged		3.75	
				2.40
C12	AP3	1.50 l purple	3.50	.80
	Never hinged		5.50	
				20.00
C13	AP3	2 l slate blue	7.50	1.20
	Never hinged		20.00	
				160.00
C14	AP3	3 l copper red	26.00	15.00
	Never hinged		52.50	
				275.00
C15	AP3	5 l yellow green	30.00	18.00
	Never hinged		60.00	
				475.00
C16	AP3	10 l dp rose red	37.50	34.00
	Never hinged		75.00	
				950.00
	Nos. C7-C16 (10)		119.50	94.40
	Set, never hinged		260.00	
	Set, on flown cover			475.00

AIR POST SEMI-POSTAL STAMPS

King Victor
Emmanuel
III — SPAP1

Wmk. 140

1934, Nov. 5   Photo.   Perf. 14

CB1	SPAP1	25c + 10c gray grn	9.00	26.00
	Never hinged		16.00	
	On cover			300.00
CB2	SPAP1	50c + 10c brn	9.00	26.00
	Never hinged		16.00	
	On cover			300.00
CB3	SPAP1	75c + 15c rose red	9.00	26.00
	Never hinged		16.00	
	On cover			325.00
CB4	SPAP1	80c + 15c blk brn	9.00	26.00
	Never hinged		16.00	
	On cover			400.00
CB5	SPAP1	1 l + 20c red brn	9.00	26.00
	Never hinged		16.00	
	On cover			450.00
CB6	SPAP1	2 l + 20c brt bl	9.00	26.00
	Never hinged		16.00	
	On cover			—
CB7	SPAP1	3 l + 25c pur	26.00	120.00
	Never hinged		55.00	
	On cover			—
CB8	SPAP1	5 l + 25c org	26.00	120.00
	Never hinged		55.00	
	On cover			—
CB9	SPAP1	10 l + 30c rose vio	26.00	120.00
	Never hinged		55.00	
	On cover			—
CB10	SPAP1	25 l + 2 l dp grn	26.00	120.00
	Never hinged		55.00	
	On cover			—
	Nos. CB1-CB10 (10)		158.00	636.00
	Set, never hinged		375.00	
	Set, on flown cover			1,500.

65th birthday of King Victor Emmanuel III; non-stop flight from Rome to Mogadishu. For overprint see No. CBO1.

AIR POST OFFICIAL STAMP

No. C1
Overprinted

Wmk. 140

1934, Nov. 11   Photo.   Perf. 14

CO1	AP1	25c sl bl & red org	2,800.	5,250.
	Never hinged		4,900.	
	On flown cover			7,200.
	Pair on flown cover			14,500.

Forgeries of this overprint exist.

AIR POST SEMI-POSTAL OFFICIAL STAMP

Air Post
Semi-Postal
Stamps of
1934
Overprinted
in Black

1934, Nov. 5   **Wmk. 140**   *Perf. 14*
CBO1 SPAP1 25 l + 2 l cop red	2,950.	6,000.
Never hinged	5,250.	
On flown cover		8,000.

SPECIAL DELIVERY STAMPS

Italy No. E3 Surcharged

1923, July 16   **Wmk. 140**   *Perf. 14*
E1 SD1 30b on 60c dl red	32.50	30.00
Never hinged	62.50	
On cover		250.00

Italy, Type of 1908 Special Delivery Stamp Surcharged

E2 SD2 60b on 1.20 l bl & red	47.50	57.50
Never hinged	92.50	
On cover		600.00

"Italia" SD3

1924, June   **Engr.**   *Unwmk.*
E3 SD3 30b dk red & brn	13.00	24.00
Never hinged	25.00	
On cover		250.00
E4 SD3 60b dk blue & red	24.00	35.00
Never hinged	50.00	
On cover		550.00

Nos. E3-E4 Surcharged in Black or Red

1926, Oct.
E5 SD3 70c on 30b (Bk)	15.00	21.00
Never hinged	30.00	
On cover		325.00
E6 SD3 2.50 l on 60b (R)	17.00	29.00
Never hinged	45.00	
On cover		550.00
a. Imperf., pair	1,200.	

Same Surcharge on No. E3

1927   *Perf. 11*
E7 SD3 1.25 l on 30b	16.50	19.00
Never hinged	40.00	
On cover		160.00
a. Perf. 14	300.00	975.00
Never hinged	600.00	
On cover		4,000.
b. Imperf., pair	1,050.	
Never hinged	1,500.	

AUTHORIZED DELIVERY STAMP

Italy No. EY2 Overprinted in Black

1939   **Wmk. 140**   *Perf. 14*
EY1 AD2 10c brown	80.00	—
Never hinged	200.00	
On cover		600.00

No. EY1 has yellowish gum. A 1941 printing in grayish brown, with white gum, was not issued. The overprint on the 1939 printing is located between the "OS" and "AN" of POSTE ITALIANE, while the overprint on the 1941 printing is centered. Value: unused, 80 cents; never hinged, $2.00.

POSTAGE DUE STAMPS

Values for Nos. J1-J41 are for examples with perforations touching or cutting into the design on at least one side. Examples with perforations clear of the design on all four sides are scarce and command considerable premiums.

Postage Due Stamps of Italy Overprinted

1906-08   **Wmk. 140**   *Perf. 14*
J1 D3 5c buff & magenta	26.00	52.50
Never hinged	32.50	
On cover		750.00
J2 D3 10c buff & magenta	75.00	75.00
Never hinged	105.00	
On cover		550.00
J3 D3 20c org & magenta	52.50	90.00
Never hinged	77.50	
On cover		490.00
J4 D3 30c buff & magenta	52.50	105.00
Never hinged	62.50	
On cover		650.00
J5 D3 40c buff & magenta	375.00	105.00
Never hinged	435.00	
On cover		750.00
J6 D3 50c buff & magenta	82.50	120.00
Never hinged	115.00	
On cover		750.00
J7 D3 60c buff & mag ('08)	75.00	120.00
Never hinged	100.00	
On cover		—
J8 D3 1 l blue & magenta	1,500.	550.00
Never hinged	1,900.	
J9 D3 2 l blue & magenta	1,500.	550.00
Never hinged	1,900.	
J10 D3 5 l blue & magenta	1,500.	550.00
Never hinged	1,900.	
J11 D3 10 l blue & magenta	300.00	500.00
Never hinged	360.00	
On cover		—
Nos. J1-J11 (11)	5,538.	2,817.

Postage Due Stamps of Italy Overprinted at Top of Stamps

1909-19
J12 D3 5c buff & magenta	9.50	30.00
Never hinged	14.00	
On cover		550.00
c. Overprint at center of stamp	27.50	
Never hinged	42.50	
J13 D3 10c buff & magenta	9.50	30.00
Never hinged	14.00	
On cover		400.00
J14 D3 20c buff & magenta	20.00	60.00
Never hinged	30.00	
On cover		450.00
J15 D3 30c buff & magenta	60.00	60.00
Never hinged	82.50	
On cover		550.00
J16 D3 40c buff & magenta	60.00	82.50
Never hinged	82.50	
On cover		450.00
J17 D3 50c buff & magenta	60.00	105.00
Never hinged	82.50	
On cover		450.00
J18 D3 60c buff & mag ('19)	82.50	90.00
Never hinged	100.00	
On cover		—
J19 D3 1 l blue & magenta	170.00	105.00
Never hinged	250.00	
On cover		650.00
J20 D3 2 l blue & magenta	240.00	240.00
Never hinged	365.00	
J21 D3 5 l blue & magenta	275.00	325.00
Never hinged	415.00	
J22 D3 10 l blue & magenta	55.00	110.00
Never hinged	82.50	
Nos. J12-J22 (11)	1,041.	1,237.

Same with Overprint at Bottom of Stamps

1920
J12a D3 5c buff & magenta	150.00	225.00
Never hinged	260.00	
On cover		550.00
b. Double overprint	550.00	
Never hinged	850.00	
J13a D3 10c buff & magenta	150.00	225.00
Never hinged	260.00	
On cover		550.00
J14a D3 20c buff & magenta	210.00	150.00
Never hinged	390.00	
On cover		400.00
J15a D3 30c buff & magenta	210.00	150.00
Never hinged	425.00	
On cover		475.00
J16a D3 40c buff & magenta	210.00	225.00
Never hinged	425.00	
On cover		725.00
J17a D3 50c buff & magenta	210.00	210.00
Never hinged	425.00	
On cover		525.00
J18a D3 60c buff & magenta	210.00	210.00
Never hinged	425.00	
On cover		—
J19a D3 1 l blue & magenta	210.00	300.00
Never hinged	425.00	
On cover		950.00
b. Overprint at center of stamp	350.00	
Never hinged	850.00	
J20a D3 2 l blue & magenta	210.00	300.00
Never hinged	425.00	
On cover		—
J21a D3 5 l blue & magenta	210.00	375.00
Never hinged	425.00	
On cover		—
Nos. J12a-J21a (10)	1,980.	2,370.

D4

1923, July 1
J23 D4 1b buff & black	3.00	11.50
Never hinged	4.50	
On cover		525.00
J24 D4 2b buff & black	3.00	11.50
Never hinged	4.50	
On cover		400.00
a. Inverted numeral and ovpt.	550.00	
Never hinged	850.00	
J25 D4 3b buff & black	3.00	11.50
Never hinged	4.50	
On cover		400.00
J26 D4 5b buff & black	4.50	11.50
Never hinged	5.00	
On cover		400.00
J27 D4 10b buff & black	4.50	11.50
Never hinged	5.00	
On cover		550.00
J28 D4 20b buff & black	4.50	11.50
Never hinged	5.00	
On cover		550.00
J29 D4 40b buff & black	4.50	11.50
Never hinged	5.00	
On cover		900.00
J30 D4 1r blue & black	4.50	62.50
Never hinged	10.00	
On cover		—
Nos. J23-J30 (8)	31.50	143.00

Type of Postage Due Stamps of Italy Overprinted

1926, Mar. 1
J31 D3 5c buff & black	30.00	37.50
Never hinged	57.50	
On cover		550.00
J32 D3 10c buff & black	30.00	26.00
Never hinged	57.50	
On cover		350.00
J33 D3 20c buff & black	30.00	45.00
Never hinged	57.50	
On cover		325.00
J34 D3 30c buff & black	30.00	26.00
Never hinged	57.50	
On cover		400.00
J35 D3 40c buff & black	30.00	26.00
Never hinged	57.50	
On cover		475.00
J36 D3 50c buff & black	45.00	26.00
Never hinged	60.00	
On cover		325.00
J37 D3 60c buff & black	45.00	26.00
Never hinged	60.00	
On cover		650.00
J38 D3 1 l blue & black	67.50	45.00
Never hinged	125.00	
On cover		725.00
J39 D3 2 l blue & black	105.00	45.00
Never hinged	190.00	
J40 D3 5 l blue & black	115.00	60.00
Never hinged	225.00	
J41 D3 10 l blue & black	150.00	82.50
Never hinged	260.00	
Nos. J31-J41 (11)	677.50	445.00

Numerals and Ovpt. Invtd.
J32a D3 10c	260.00
Never hinged	350.00
J33a D3 20c	825.00
Never hinged	1,100.
J34a D3 30c	260.00
Never hinged	350.00
J35a D3 40c	260.00
Never hinged	350.00
J36a D3 50c	260.00
Never hinged	350.00
J37a D3 60c	260.00
Never hinged	350.00

Postage Due Stamps of Italy, 1934, Overprinted in Black

1934, May 12
J42 D6 5c brown	1.50	7.50
Never hinged	2.40	
On cover		550.00
J43 D6 10c blue	1.50	7.50
Never hinged	2.40	
On cover		350.00
J44 D6 20c rose red	4.00	15.00
Never hinged	9.50	
On cover		300.00
J45 D6 25c green	4.00	15.00
Never hinged	9.50	
On cover		250.00
J46 D6 30c red orange	12.00	19.00
Never hinged	20.00	
On cover		350.00
J47 D6 40c black brown	12.00	26.00
Never hinged	24.00	
On cover		550.00
J48 D6 50c violet	20.00	9.00
Never hinged	42.50	
On cover		250.00
J49 D6 60c black	20.00	45.00
Never hinged	50.00	
On cover		600.00
J50 D7 1 l red orange	27.50	22.50
Never hinged	65.00	
On cover		325.00
J51 D7 2 l green	50.00	45.00
Never hinged	125.00	
On cover		550.00
J52 D7 5 l violet	52.50	105.00
Never hinged	125.00	
On cover		—
J53 D7 10 l blue	52.50	110.00
Never hinged	125.00	
On cover		—
J54 D7 20 l carmine	60.00	170.00
Never hinged	140.00	
On cover		—
Nos. J42-J54 (13)	317.50	596.50

PARCEL POST STAMPS

These stamps were used by affixing them to the way bill so that one half remained on it following the parcel, the other half staying on the receipt given the sender. Most used halves are right halves. Complete stamps were and are obtainable canceled, probably to order. Both unused and used values are for complete stamps.

Parcel Post Stamps of Italy, 1914-17, Overprinted

1917-19   **Wmk. 140**   *Perf. 13½*
Q1 PP2 5c brown	8.00	67.50
Never hinged	16.00	
a. Double overprint	500.00	—
Never hinged	650.00	
Q2 PP2 10c blue	9.50	45.00
Never hinged	19.00	
Q3 PP2 20c black ('19)	375.00	225.00
Never hinged	700.00	
Q4 PP2 25c red	16.00	80.00
Never hinged	32.50	
a. Double overprint	—	
Never hinged	—	
Q5 PP2 50c orange	165.00	97.50
Never hinged	325.00	
Q6 PP2 1 l lilac	52.50	97.50
Never hinged	100.00	
Q7 PP2 2 l green	72.50	97.50
Never hinged	150.00	
Q8 PP2 3 l bister	80.00	170.00
Never hinged	160.00	
Q9 PP2 4 l slate	87.50	170.00
Never hinged	175.00	
Nos. Q1-Q9 (9)	866.00	1,050.

Halves Used
Q1	1.60
Q2	1.60
Q3	7.25
Q4	3.50
Q5	6.00
Q6	4.75
Q7	4.75
Q8	4.75
Q9	4.75

Nos. Q5-Q9 were overprinted in 1922 with a slightly different type in which the final "A" of SOMALIA is directly over the final "A" of ITALIANA. They were not regularly issued. Value for set: unused $1,600; never hinged $2,400.

Parcel Post Stamps of Italy, 1914-17, Overprinted

1923

Q10	PP2	25c red	75.00	*165.00*
		Never hinged	145.00	
Q11	PP2	50c orange	110.00	*165.00*
		Never hinged	225.00	
Q12	PP2	1 l violet	135.00	275.00
		Never hinged	250.00	
Q13	PP2	2 l green	135.00	275.00
		Never hinged	250.00	
Q14	PP2	3 l bister	210.00	275.00
		Never hinged	400.00	
Q15	PP2	4 l slate	210.00	275.00
		Never hinged	400.00	
	Nos. Q10-Q15 (6)		*875.00*	*1,430.*

Halves Used

Q10	4.75
Q11	4.75
Q12	3.00
Q13	3.00
Q14	4.75
Q15	5.50

Parcel Post Stamps of Italy, 1914-17, Surcharged

1923

Q16	PP2	3b on 5c brown	27.50	*37.50*
		Never hinged	55.00	
Q17	PP2	5b on 5c brown	27.50	*37.50*
		Never hinged	55.00	
Q18	PP2	10b on 10c blue	27.50	34.00
		Never hinged	55.00	
Q19	PP2	25b on 25c red	27.50	52.50
		Never hinged	55.00	
Q20	PP2	50b on 50c org	35.00	*75.00*
		Never hinged	70.00	
Q21	PP2	1r on 1 l lilac	47.50	75.00
		Never hinged	95.00	
Q22	PP2	2r on 2 l green	80.00	120.00
		Never hinged	160.00	
Q23	PP2	3r on 3 l bister	80.00	120.00
		Never hinged	160.00	
Q24	PP2	4r on 4 l slate	95.00	120.00
		Never hinged	190.00	
	Nos. Q16-Q24 (9)		*447.50*	*671.50*

Halves Used

Q16	1.60
Q17	1.60
Q18	1.60
Q19	3.25
Q20	3.25
Q21	3.25
Q22	3.25
Q23	3.25
Q24	3.25

No. Q16 has the numeral "3" at the left also.

Parcel Post Stamps of Italy, 1914-22 Overprinted

1926-31   **Red Overprint**

Q25	PP2	5c brown	34.00	*82.50*
		Never hinged	65.00	
Q26	PP2	10c blue	32.50	*82.50*
		Never hinged	65.00	
Q27	PP2	20c black	72.50	82.50
		Never hinged	145.00	
Q28	PP2	25c red	72.50	82.50
		Never hinged	145.00	
Q29	PP2	50c orange	72.50	82.50
		Never hinged	145.00	
Q30	PP2	1 l violet	97.50	82.50
		Never hinged	190.00	
Q31	PP2	2 l green	160.00	82.50
		Never hinged	325.00	
Q32	PP2	3 l yellow	30.00	82.50
		Never hinged	55.00	
Q33	PP2	4 l slate	30.00	82.50
		Never hinged	55.00	
Q34	PP2	10 l vio brn ('30)	55.00	*105.00*
		Never hinged	110.00	

Q35	PP2	12 l red brn '31)	55.00	*105.00*
		Never hinged	110.00	
Q36	PP2	15 l olive ('31)	55.00	*190.00*
		Never hinged	110.00	
Q37	PP2	20 l dull vio ('31)	55.00	*190.00*
		Never hinged	110.00	
	Nos. Q25-Q37 (13)		*821.50*	*1,332.*

Halves Used

Q25	2.00
Q26	2.00
Q27	3.25
Q28	3.25
Q29	3.25
Q30	3.25
Q31	3.25
Q32	3.25
Q33	4.00
Q34	4.00
Q35	4.00
Q36	4.00
Q37	4.00

Nos. Q25-Q31 come with two types of overprint: I — The first "I" and last "A" of ITALIANA extend slightly at both sides of SOMALIA. II — Only the "I" extends. These seven stamps with type I overprint were not regularly issued, and Nos. Q27-Q31 (type I) sell for less than with type II overprint.

Black Overprint

Q38	PP2	10 l violet brown	82.50	87.50
		Never hinged	160.00	
Q39	PP2	12 l red brown	55.00	87.50
		Never hinged	110.00	
Q40	PP2	15 l olive	55.00	87.50
		Never hinged	110.00	
Q41	PP2	20 l dull violet	55.00	87.50
		Never hinged	110.00	
	Nos. Q38-Q41 (4)		*247.50*	*350.00*

Halves Used

Q38	4.00
Q39	4.00
Q40	4.00
Q41	4.00

Same Overprint on Parcel Post Stamps of Italy, 1927-38

1928-39   **Black Overprint**

Q42	PP3	25c red, type I ('31)	45.00	52.50
		Never hinged	80.00	
a.		Type II	80.00	160.00
		Never hinged	160.00	
Q43	PP3	30c ultra	6.00	7.50
		Never hinged	6.50	
Q43A	PP3	50c orange	12,750.	
		Never hinged	18,000.	
Q44	PP3	60c red	6.00	8.00
		Never hinged	6.50	
Q45	PP3	1 l lilac brn, type II ('31)	40.00	52.50
		Never hinged	80.00	
a.		Type I	875.00	2,400.
		Never hinged	1,750.	
b.		1 l lilac, type I	2,250.	
		Never hinged	3,400.	
Q46	PP3	2 l green, type II ('31)	40.00	52.50
		Never hinged	80.00	
a.		Type I	800.00	3,250.
		Never hinged	1,600.	
Q47	PP3	3 l bister	15.00	20.00
		Never hinged	13.00	
Q48	PP3	4 l gray black	15.00	20.00
		Never hinged	13.00	
Q49	PP3	10 l rose lil ('34)	475.00	675.00
		Never hinged	900.00	
Q50	PP3	20 l lil brn ('34)	475.00	750.00
		Never hinged	900.00	
	Nos. Q42-Q43,Q44-Q50 (9)		*1,117.*	*1,638.*

Halves Used

Q42	8.75
Q43	.45
Q43A	160.00
Q44	.45
Q45	2.75
Q46	2.75
Q47	.80
Q48	.80
Q49	20.00
Q50	20.00

The 25c, 1 l and 2 l come with both types of overprint (see note below No. Q37). Both types were regularly issued. Values are for type I on 25c, type II on 1 l and 2 l.

Red Overprint

Q51	PP3	5c brown ('39)	16.00	
		Never hinged	24.00	
Q52	PP3	3 l bister ('30)	32.50	80.00
		Never hinged	47.50	
		Half stamp		2.00
Q53	PP3	4 l gray black ('30)	32.50	80.00
		Never hinged	47.50	
		Half stamp		2.00
	Nos. Q51-Q53 (3)		*81.00*	

Same Overprint in Black on Italy Nos. Q24-Q25

1940   **Perf. 13**

Q54	PP3	5c brown	6.00	13.50
		Never hinged	4.75	
		Half stamp		.50
Q55	PP3	10c deep blue	7.50	13.50
		Never hinged	6.00	
		Half stamp		.50

SOMALI COAST

sō-'mä-lē 'kōst

(Djibouti)

LOCATION — Eastern Africa, bordering on the Gulf of Aden
GOVT. — French Overseas Territory
AREA — 8,500 sq. mi.
POP. — 86,000 (est. 1963)
CAPITAL — Djibouti (Jibuti)

The port of Obock, which issued postage stamps in 1892-1894, was included in the territory and began to use stamps of Somali Coast in 1902.

100 Centimes = 1 Franc

Obock Nos. 32-33, 35, 45 with Overprint or Surcharge Handstamped in Black, Blue or Red

Navigation and Commerce
A1   A2

A3

Camel and Rider A4

1894   **Unwmk.**   **Perf. 14x13½**

1	A1	5c grn & red, *grnsh* (with bar)	190.00	160.00
		On cover		1,500.
a.		Without bar	1,400.	925.00
b.		Bar double	900.00	450.00
2	A2	25c on 2c brn & bl, *buff* (Bl & Bk)	400.00	250.00
		On cover		1,000.
a.		"25" omitted	1,150.	950.00
b.		"25" double	1,850.	
c.		"DJIBOUTI" omitted	1,150.	950.00

---

d.		"DJIBOUTI" inverted	1,300.	1,100.
e.		"DJIBOUTI" double	1,850.	1,400.
3	A3	50c on 1c blk & red, *bl* (R & Bl)	400.00	275.00
				1,250.
a.		"5" instead of "50"	1,800.	1,300.
b.		"0" instead of "50"	1,800.	1,300.
c.		"DJIBOUTI" omitted	1,800.	1,400.

Imperf

4	A4	1fr on 5fr car	725.00	575.00
a.		"DJIBOUTI" omitted	5,000.	
b.		"DJIBOUTI" double	2,200.	1,900.
c.		"1" double	2,200.	1,900.
5	A4	5fr carmine	2,200.	1,500.

Counterfeits exist of Nos. 4-5.

View of Djibouti, Somali Warriors — A5

French Gunboat A7

Crossing Desert (Size: 66mm wide, including simulated perfs.) — A8

Designs: 15c, 25c, 30c, 40c, 50c, 75c, Different views of Djibouti. 1fr, 2fr, Djibouti quay.

Imperf. (Simulated Perforations in Frame Color)

1894-1902   **Typo.**
Quadrille Lines Printed on Paper

6	A5	1c blk & claret	4.00	3.25
		Never hinged	7.25	
		On cover		150.00
a.		Thick paper	20.00	20.00
		Never hinged	32.50	
7	A5	2c claret & blk	4.00	3.25
		Never hinged	7.25	
		On cover		150.00
a.		Thick paper	20.00	20.00
		Never hinged	32.50	
8	A5	4c vio brn & bl	16.00	9.50
		Never hinged	32.50	
		On cover		190.00
a.		Thick paper	45.00	26.00
		Never hinged	95.00	
9	A5	5c bl grn & red	16.00	7.25
		Never hinged	32.50	
		On cover		110.00
10	A5	5c grn & yel grn ('02)	12.00	8.75
		Never hinged	24.00	
		On cover		110.00
11	A5	10c brown & grn	20.00	8.75
		Never hinged	40.00	
		On cover		105.00
a.		Half used as 5c on cover		200.00
12	A5	15c violet & grn	20.00	8.75
		Never hinged	40.00	
		On cover		105.00
13	A5	25c rose & blue	32.50	11.00
		Never hinged	65.00	
		On cover		300.00
14	A5	30c gray brn & rose	20.00	12.00
		Never hinged	40.00	
		On cover		250.00
a.		Half used as 15c on cover		600.00

15	A5	40c org & bl ('00)	60.00	40.00
		Never hinged	125.00	
		On cover		300.00
a.		Half used as 20c on cover		950.00
16	A5	50c blue & rose	32.50	20.00
		Never hinged	65.00	
		On cover		375.00
a.		Half used as 25c on cover		2,000.
17	A5	75c violet & org	55.00	45.00
		Never hinged	110.00	
		On cover		425.00
18	A5	1fr ol grn & blk	28.00	20.00
		Never hinged	55.00	
		On cover		500.00
19	A5	2fr gray brn & rose	105.00	80.00
		On cover		625.00
a.		Half used as 1fr on cover		2,400.
20	A7	5fr rose & blue	210.00	150.00
21	A8	25fr rose & blue	1,050.	1,100.
22	A8	50fr blue & rose	675.00	750.00
		Nos. 6-20 (15)	635.00	427.50

High values are found with the overprint "S" (Specimen) erased and, usually, a cancellation added.

Values for bisects are for complete covers, newspapers or other printed matter.

For surcharges see Nos. 24-27B.

A9

1899   **Black Surcharge**

23	A9	40c on 4c brn & bl	3,400.	35.00
		On cover		250.00
a.		Double surcharge	6,500.	1,600.
b.		Pair, one without surcharge		4,750.
c.		Inverted surcharge		1,800.
d.		Double surcharge, both inverted		3,400.

Nos. 17-20 Surcharged

1902   **Blue Surcharge**

24	A5	0.05c on 75c	80.00	47.50
		Never hinged	160.00	
		On cover		250.00
a.		Inverted surcharge	650.00	575.00
b.		Double surcharge	650.00	575.00
c.		Pair, one without surcharge		2,800.
d.		Comma instead of period in surcharge	110.00	50.00
		On cover		275.00
e.		As "d," double surcharge	575.00	525.00
25	A5	0.10c on 1fr	92.50	72.50
		Never hinged	190.00	
		On cover		300.00
a.		Inverted surcharge	575.00	450.00
b.		Double surcharge	575.00	450.00
26	A5	0.40c on 2fr	650.00	450.00
		On cover		1,500.
a.		Double surcharge	2,250.	2,100.

        Black Surcharge

27	A7	0.75c on 5fr	650.00	450.00
		On cover		1,900.
a.		Inverted surcharge	3,000.	2,400.
c.		Double surcharge	3,000.	2,400.

Obock No. 57 Surcharged in Blue

27B	A7	0.05c on 75c gray lil & org	1,700.	1,200.
		On cover		2,250.

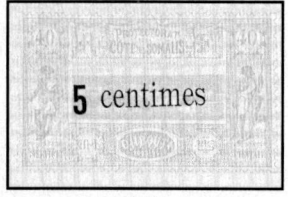

A10

Nos. 15-16 Surcharged in Black

28	A10	5c on 40c	8.75	5.50
		Never hinged	17.50	
		On cover		250.00
a.		Double surcharge	150.00	150.00

29	A10	10c on 50c	32.50	32.50
		Never hinged	65.00	
		On cover		375.00
a.		Inverted surcharge	575.00	550.00
b.		Double surcharge	675.00	

Stamps of Obock Surcharged

Group of Warriors
A11

        Black Surcharge

30	A11	5c on 30c bis & yel grn	20.00	12.00
		Never hinged	40.00	
		On cover		350.00
a.		Inverted surcharge	325.00	325.00
b.		Double surcharge	350.00	325.00
c.		Triple surcharge		1,700.

A12

        Red Surcharge

31	A12	10c on 25c blk & bl	20.00	14.50
		Never hinged	40.00	
		On cover		350.00
a.		Inverted surcharge	325.00	325.00
b.		Double surcharge	350.00	350.00
c.		Triple surcharge	1,850.	1,850.
d.		"Djibouti" omitted	1,000.	1,400.

A13

        Black Surcharge

32	A13	10c on 10fr org & red vio	45.00	35.00
		Never hinged	95.00	
		On cover		375.00
a.		Double surcharge	275.00	225.00
b.		Double surch., one invtd.	2,500.	2,400.
c.		Triple surcharge	1,700.	1,700.
d.		"Djibouti" omitted	130.00	92.50

A14

        Black Surcharge

33	A14	10c on 2fr dl vio & org	72.50	60.00
		Never hinged	150.00	
		On cover		450.00
a.		Double surcharge	525.00	500.00
b.		Double surcharge, one inverted	2,500.	2,500.
c.		Triplr surcharge, one inverted	3,100.	3,100.
d.		"DJIBOUTI" inverted	275.00	260.00
e.		Large "0" in "10"	160.00	130.00
f.		As "e," double surcharge	1,700.	1,300.
g.		As "e," inverted surcharge	1,800.	1,400.

Same Surcharge on Obock No. 53 in Red

33D	A7	10c on 25c blk & bl	35,000.	25,000.

A14a

Black Surcharge on Obock Nos. 63-64

33E	A14a	5c on 25fr brn & bl	67.50	60.00
		Never hinged	150.00	
		On cover		450.00
33F	A14a	10c on 50fr red vio & grn	92.50	67.50
		Never hinged	190.00	
		On cover		500.00
g.		"01" instead of "10"	260.00	240.00
h.		"CENTIMES" inverted	3,250.	3,250.
i.		Double surcharge	2,800.	2,400.
k.		Double surcharge, one inverted	2,800.	2,600.

Tadjoura Mosque
A15

Somalis on Camel
A16

Warriors — A17

1902   **Engr.**   **Perf. 11½**

34	A15	1c brn vio & org	1.20	1.20
		Never hinged	2.00	
		On cover		110.00
35	A15	2c yel brn & yel grn	1.60	1.60
		Never hinged	2.75	
		On cover		110.00
36	A15	4c bl & carmine	2.75	2.40
		Never hinged	5.00	
		On cover		110.00
37	A15	5c bl grn & yel grn	3.25	2.00
		Never hinged	5.50	
		On cover		95.00
38	A15	10c car & red org	7.25	4.75
		Never hinged	13.50	
		On cover		62.50
39	A15	15c brn org & bl	7.25	4.75
		Never hinged	13.50	
		On cover		60.00
40	A16	20c vio & green	17.00	8.75
		Never hinged	35.00	
		On cover		95.00
41	A16	25c blue	26.00	14.50
		Never hinged	52.50	
		On cover		62.50
a.		25c indigo & blue ('03)	28.00	16.00
42	A16	30c red & black	7.25	5.50
		Never hinged	13.50	
		On cover		105.00
		On cover, single franking		150.00
43	A16	40c orange & blue	17.50	10.50
		Never hinged	37.50	
		On cover		105.00
		On cover, single franking		150.00
44	A16	50c grn & red org	52.50	45.00
		Never hinged	110.00	
		On cover		190.00
		On cover, single franking		250.00
45	A16	75c orange & vio	12.00	7.25
		Never hinged	24.00	
		On cover		250.00
		On cover, single franking		375.00
46	A17	1fr red org & vio	32.50	20.00
		Never hinged	65.00	
		On cover		300.00
		On cover, single franking		475.00
47	A17	2fr yel grn & car	47.50	35.00
		Never hinged	110.00	
		On cover		375.00
		On cover, single franking		550.00
a.		Without names of designer and engraver at bottom	160.00	160.00
48	A17	5fr orange & blue	32.50	28.00
		Never hinged	65.00	
		On cover		425.00
		On cover, single franking		700.00
		Nos. 34-48 (15)	268.05	191.20

1903

49	A15	1c brn vio & blk	1.20	1.20
		Never hinged	2.00	
		On cover		95.00

50	A15	2c yel brn & blk	1.60	1.20
		Never hinged	2.75	
		On cover		95.00
51	A15	4c lake & blk	2.00	2.00
		Never hinged	3.50	
		On cover		95.00
a.		4c red & black	3.35	3.75
		On cover		100.00
52	A15	5c bl grn & blk	4.75	3.50
		Never hinged	7.50	
		On cover		60.00
53	A15	10c carmine & blk	9.50	4.50
		Never hinged	17.50	
		On cover		60.00
a.		10c red & black	9.50	4.50
		Never hinged	17.50	
		On cover		.60
54	A15	15c org brn & blk	21.00	11.00
		Never hinged	42.50	
		On cover		60.00
a.		15c brown & black	21.00	11.00
		Never hinged	42.50	
		On cover		60.00
55	A16	20c dl vio & blk	27.50	20.00
		Never hinged	55.00	
		On cover		85.00
56	A16	25c ultra & blk	16.00	11.00
		Never hinged	30.00	
		On cover		85.00
58	A16	40c orange & blk	12.00	12.00
		Never hinged	22.50	
		On cover		85.00
		On cover, single franking		110.00
a.		40c bister & black	26.00	26.00
		Never hinged	52.50	
		On cover		125.00
59	A16	50c green & blk	27.50	17.00
		Never hinged	55.00	
		On cover		85.00
		On cover, single franking		125.00
60	A16	75c buff & blk	14.50	13.00
		Never hinged	25.00	
		On cover		200.00
		On cover, single franking		350.00
a.		75c brown orange & black	87.50	87.50
		Never hinged	190.00	
		On cover		500.00
61	A17	1fr orange & blk	24.00	26.00
		Never hinged	50.00	
		On cover		275.00
		On cover, single franking		450.00
62	A17	2fr yel grn & blk	13.50	10.50
		Never hinged	24.00	
		On cover		300.00
		On cover, single franking		500.00
a.		Without names of designer and engraver at bottom	55.00	55.00
		Never hinged	125.00	
63	A17	5fr red org & blk	28.00	24.00
		Never hinged	55.00	
		On cover		375.00
		On cover, single franking		625.00
a.		5fr ocher & black	40.00	35.00
		Never hinged	80.00	
		On cover		450.00
		Nos. 49-63 (14)	203.05	156.90

Imperforates, transposed colors and inverted centers exist in the 1902 and 1903 issues. Most of these were issued from Paris and some are said to have been fraudulently printed.

Tadjoura Mosque
A18

Somalis on Camel — A19

Warriors — A20

1909   **Typo.**   **Perf. 14x13½**

64	A18	1c maroon & brn	1.20	1.20
		Never hinged	2.00	
		On cover		62.50
65	A18	2c vio & ol gray	1.20	1.20
		Never hinged	2.00	
		On cover		62.50
66	A18	4c ol gray & bl	1.60	1.20
		Never hinged	2.75	
		On cover		62.50
67	A18	5c grn & gray grn	2.00	1.20
		Never hinged	3.25	
		On cover		37.50
68	A18	10c car & ver	5.25	2.00
		Never hinged	8.50	
		On cover		20.00
69	A18	20c blk & red brn	8.00	6.50
		Never hinged	14.50	
		On cover		40.00
70	A19	25c bl & pale bl	5.50	4.50
		Never hinged	10.00	
		On cover		45.00
		On cover, single franking		95.00
71	A19	30c brn & scar	8.75	6.50
		Never hinged	14.50	
		On cover		70.00
		On cover, single franking		95.00

72	A19	35c vio & grn	11.00	8.00
		Never hinged	20.00	
		On cover		40.00
		On cover, single franking		60.00
73	A19	40c rose & vio	10.50	7.25
		Never hinged	18.50	
		On cover		62.50
		On cover, single franking		140.00
74	A19	45c brn & bl grn	10.50	7.25
		Never hinged	18.50	
		On cover		62.50
		On cover, single franking		110.00
75	A19	50c maroon & brn	10.50	8.00
		Never hinged	18.50	
		On cover		80.00
		On cover, single franking		160.00
76	A19	75c scarlet & grn	24.00	16.00
		Never hinged	47.50	
		On cover		100.00
		On cover, single franking		200.00
77	A20	1fr vio & brn	28.00	26.00
		Never hinged	55.00	
		On cover		125.00
		On cover, single franking		240.00
78	A20	2fr brn & rose	45.00	35.00
		Never hinged	92.50	
		On cover		140.00
		On cover, single franking		275.00
79	A20	5fr vio brn & bl grn	72.50	52.50
		Never hinged	140.00	
		On cover		190.00
		On cover, single franking		350.00
		Nos. 64-79 (16)	245.50	184.30

Drummer A21   Somali Girl A22

Djibouti-Addis Ababa Railroad Bridge — A23

1915-33   **Perf. 13½x14**

Chalky Paper

80	A21	1c brt vio & red brn	.25	.30
		Never hinged	.40	
		On cover		55.00
a.		Ordinary paper	.25	.30
		Never hinged	.40	
		On cover		55.00
81	A21	2c ocher & ind	.25	.25
		Never hinged	.40	
		On cover		55.00
a.		Ordinary paper	.25	.25
		Never hinged	.40	
		On cover		55.00
82	A21	4c dk brn & red	.30	.40
		Never hinged	.55	
		On cover		55.00
a.		Ordinary paper	.30	.30
		Never hinged	.55	
		On cover		55.00
83	A21	5c yel grn & grn	1.20	1.20
		Never hinged	2.00	
		On cover		21.00
a.		Ordinary paper	2.60	2.60
		Never hinged	4.50	
		On cover		25.00
84	A21	5c org & dl red ('22)	.80	.80
		Never hinged	1.25	
		On cover		30.00
85	A22	10c car & dk red	2.10	1.20
		Never hinged	3.25	
		On cover		12.50
a.		Ordinary paper	2.10	1.10
		Never hinged	3.25	
		On cover		12.50
86	A22	10c ap grn & grn ('22)	1.20	1.20
		Never hinged	2.00	
		On cover		30.00
87	A22	10c ver & grn ('25)	.50	.55
		Never hinged	.70	
		On cover		40.00
88	A22	15c brn vio & car ('18)	1.20	.80
		Never hinged	1.60	
		On cover		12.50
a.		Ordinary paper	1.20	.80
		Never hinged	1.60	
		On cover		12.50
89	A22	20c org & blk brn	.40	.40
		Never hinged	.65	
		On cover		21.00
a.		Ordinary paper	.40	.40
		Never hinged	.65	
		On cover		21.00
90	A22	20c dp grn & bl grn ('25)	.40	.40
		Never hinged	.80	
		On cover		9.00

91	A22	20c dk grn & red ('27)	.55	.55
		Never hinged	.80	
		On cover		25.00
92	A22	25c ultra & dl bl	1.20	.95
		Never hinged	2.00	
		On cover		21.00
		On cover, single franking		50.00
a.		Ordinary paper	1.20	.95
		Never hinged	2.00	
		On cover		21.00
93	A22	25c blk & bl grn ('22)	1.20	1.20
		Never hinged	2.00	
		On cover		6.25
94	A22	30c blk & bl grn	2.40	2.40
		Never hinged	4.00	
		On cover		25.00
		On cover, single franking		65.00
95	A22	30c rose & red brn ('22)	1.60	1.60
		Never hinged	2.50	
		On cover		30.00
		On cover, single franking		60.00
96	A22	30c vio & ol grn ('25)	.50	.55
		Never hinged	.70	
		On cover		9.00
97	A22	30c grn & dl grn ('27)	.55	.55
		Never hinged	.80	
		On cover		30.00
98	A22	35c lt grn & dl rose	.80	.80
		Never hinged	1.20	
		On cover		20.00
		On cover, single franking		30.00
99	A22	40c bl & brn vio	1.20	.80
		Never hinged	2.00	
		On cover		30.00
		On cover, single franking		50.00
100	A22	45c red brn & dk bl	1.20	.80
		Never hinged	2.00	
		On cover		40.00
		On cover, single franking		75.00
101	A22	50c car rose & blk	12.00	8.00
		Never hinged	20.00	
		On cover		55.00
		On cover, single franking		125.00
102	A22	50c ultra & ind ('24)	1.60	1.60
		Never hinged	2.60	
		On cover		30.00
		On cover, single franking		60.00
103	A22	50c dk brn & red vio ('25)	.90	.65
		Never hinged	1.25	
		On cover		6.00
104	A22	60c ol grn & red vio ('25)	.65	.65
		Never hinged	.95	
		On cover		21.00
		On cover, single franking		50.00
105	A22	65c car rose & ol grn ('25)	.80	.80
		Never hinged	1.20	
		On cover		20.00
		On cover, single franking		30.00
106	A22	75c dl vio & choc	.80	.80
		Never hinged	1.20	
		On cover		40.00
		On cover, single franking		100.00
a.		Ordinary paper	1.20	1.00
		Never hinged	2.00	
		On cover		45.00
107	A22	75c ind & ultra ('25)	.70	.80
		Never hinged	1.10	
		On cover		21.00
		On cover, single franking		50.00
108	A22	75c brt vio & ol brn ('27)	2.10	1.75
		Never hinged	2.75	
		On cover		11.00
109	A22	85c vio brn & bl grn ('25)	1.20	1.20
		Never hinged	2.00	
		On cover		40.00
		On cover, single franking		70.00
110	A22	90c brn red & brt red ('30)	8.75	6.50
		Never hinged	13.50	
		On cover		55.00
		On cover, single franking		125.00
111	A23	1fr bis brn & red	2.40	1.60
		Never hinged	4.00	
		On cover		55.00
		On cover, single franking		140.00
a.		Ordinary paper	2.40	1.60
		Never hinged	4.00	
		On cover		55.00
112	A23	1.10fr lt brn & ultra ('28)	4.75	6.50
		Never hinged	8.00	
		On cover		110.00
		On cover, single franking		300.00
113	A23	1.25fr dk bl & blk brn ('33)	10.50	8.75
		Never hinged	17.50	
		On cover		55.00
		On cover, single franking		140.00
114	A23	1.50fr lt bl & dk bl ('30)	1.60	1.60
		Never hinged	2.40	
		On cover		50.00
		On cover, single franking		110.00
115	A23	1.75fr gray grn & lt red ('33)	8.75	5.50
		Never hinged	14.50	
		On cover		35.00
		On cover, single franking		45.00
116	A23	2fr bl vio & blk	4.00	3.25
		Never hinged	6.75	
		On cover		70.00
		On cover, single franking		140.00
a.		Ordinary paper	4.00	3.25
		Never hinged	6.75	
		On cover		70.00
117	A23	3fr red vio ('30)	12.00	4.50
		Never hinged	20.00	
		On cover		80.00
		On cover, single franking		160.00

118	A23	5fr rose red & blk	7.25	4.75
		Never hinged	13.50	
		On cover		80.00
		On cover, single franking		160.00
a.		Ordinary paper	7.25	4.75
		Never hinged	13.50	
		On cover		80.00
		Nos. 80-118 (39)	100.55	76.90

No. 99 is on ordinary paper.
For surcharges and overprints see Nos. 119-134, 183-193 (in Scott Standard catalogue, Vol. 6).

Nos. 83, 92
Surcharged in Green or Blue

1922

119	A21	10c on 5c, ordinary paper (G)	.80	.80
		Never hinged	1.25	
		On cover		40.00
a.		Double surcharge	125.00	
		Never hinged	210.00	
b.		Chalky paper	1.20	1.20
		Never hinged	2.00	
		On cover		45.00
120	A22	50c on 25c (Bl)	.80	.80
		Never hinged	1.25	
		On cover		22.50
		On cover, single franking		45.00

Type of 1915
Surcharged in
Various Colors

1922

Ordinary Paper

121	A22	0,01c on 15c vio & rose (Bk)	.30	.50
		Never hinged	.45	
		On cover		70.00
a.		Chalky paper	5.50	4.50
		Never hinged	8.75	
		On cover		100.00
122	A22	0,02c on 15c vio & rose (Bl)	.50	.70
		Never hinged	.70	
		On cover		70.00
a.		Chalky paper	5.50	4.50
		Never hinged	8.75	
		On cover		100.00
123	A22	0,04c on 15c vio & rose (G)	.80	.80
		Never hinged	1.20	
		On cover		70.00
a.		Chalky paper	4.00	3.00
		Never hinged	6.50	
		On cover		90.00
124	A22	0,05c on 15c vio & rose (R)	.80	.80
		Never hinged	1.20	
		On cover		27.50
		Nos. 121-124 (4)	2.40	2.80

Nos. 88, 99 and Type
of 1915 Surcharged

1923-27

Ordinary Paper

125	A22	60c on 75c ol grn & vio	.80	.80
		Never hinged	1.20	
		On cover		16.00
		On cover, single franking		27.50
126	A22	65c on 15c ('25)	2.75	3.25
		Never hinged	4.00	
		On cover		55.00
		On cover, single franking		125.00
a.		Chalky paper	4.75	4.75
		Never hinged	8.00	
		On cover		125.00
127	A22	85c on 40c ('25)	2.00	2.40
		Never hinged	3.25	
		On cover		40.00
		On cover, single franking		75.00

128	A22	90c on 75c brn red & red ('27)	5.50	6.50
		Never hinged	8.75	
		On cover, single franking		105.00
a.		Double surcharge	92.50	
		Never hinged	150.00	
		Nos. 125-128 (4)	11.05	12.95

No. 118 and Type of 1915-17
Surcharged with New Value and Bars
in Black or Red

1924-27

129	A23	25c on 5fr	1.60	1.60
		Never hinged	2.40	
		On cover		6.25
a.		Chalky paper	8.75	8.75
		Never hinged	15.00	
		On cover		65.00
130	A23	1.25fr on 1fr dk bl & ultra (R) ('26)	1.20	1.20
		Never hinged	2.00	
		On cover		50.00
		On cover, single franking		95.00
131	A23	1.50fr on 1fr lt bl & dk bl ('27)	1.20	1.60
		Never hinged	2.00	
		On cover		40.00
		On cover, single franking		55.00
132	A23	3fr on 5fr ver & red vio ('27)	5.50	6.50
		Never hinged	8.75	
		On cover		70.00
		On cover, single franking		140.00
a.		Period after "F" omitted	32.50	32.50
		Never hinged	52.50	
133	A23	10fr on 5fr brn red & ol brn ('27)	9.50	11.00
		Never hinged	16.00	
		On cover		90.00
		On cover, single franking		175.00
134	A23	20fr on 5fr gray grn & lil rose ('27)	15.00	18.50
		Never hinged	27.50	
		On cover		110.00
		On cover, single franking		225.00
		Nos. 129-134 (6)	34.00	40.40

Common Design Types
pictured following the introduction.

Colonial Exposition Issue
Common Design Types
Engr., Name of Country Typo. in Black

1931			**Perf. 12½**	
135	CD70	40c deep green	6.50	6.50
		Never hinged	10.00	
		On cover		95.00
136	CD71	50c violet	6.50	6.50
		Never hinged	10.00	
		On cover		80.00
137	CD72	90c red orange	6.50	6.50
		Never hinged	10.00	
		On cover, single franking		125.00
		On cover, single franking		190.00
a.		Country name omitted, in pair with normal stamp		1,450.
138	CD73	1.50fr dull blue	6.50	6.50
		Never hinged	10.00	
		On cover		110.00
		On cover, single franking		165.00
		Nos. 135-138 (4)	26.00	26.00

Paris International Exposition Issue
Common Design Types

1937		**Engr.**	**Perf. 13**	
139	CD74	20c deep violet	2.10	2.10
		Never hinged	3.25	
		On cover		90.00
140	CD75	30c dark green	2.10	2.10
		Never hinged	3.25	
		On cover		70.00
141	CD76	40c carmine rose	2.10	2.10
		Never hinged	3.25	
		On cover		55.00
a.		Country name double	225.00	
		Never hinged	330.00	
142	CD77	50c dk brn & bl	2.25	2.25
		Never hinged	3.50	
		On cover		50.00
143	CD78	90c red	2.00	2.00
		Never hinged	3.25	
		On cover		95.00
		On cover, single franking		160.00
144	CD79	1.50fr ultra	2.40	2.40
		Never hinged	3.50	
		On cover		80.00
		On cover, single franking		140.00
a.		Country name inverted	140.00	150.00
		Never hinged	210.00	
		Nos. 139-144 (6)	12.95	12.95

Colonial Arts Exhibition Issue
Souvenir Sheet
Common Design Type

1937			**Imperf.**	
145	CD75	3fr dull violet	13.00	15.00
		Never hinged	18.00	
		On cover		140.00
		On cover, single franking		210.00

Mosque of Djibouti — A24　　Somali Warriors — A25

Governor Léonce Lagarde — A26

View of Djibouti — A27

1938-40   *Perf. 12x12½, 12½*

146	A24	2c dull red vio	.25	.25
	Never hinged		.40	
	On cover			25.00
147	A24	3c slate grn ('40)	.25	.25
	Never hinged		.40	
	On cover			30.00
148	A24	4c dull red brn	.25	.25
	Never hinged		.40	
	On cover			25.00
149	A24	5c carmine	.25	.25
	Never hinged		.40	
	On cover			21.00
150	A24	10c blue gray	.25	.25
	Never hinged		.40	
	On cover			19.00
151	A24	15c slate black	.30	.30
	Never hinged		.50	
	On cover			19.00
152	A24	20c dark orange	.30	.30
	Never hinged		.50	
	On cover			19.00
153	A25	25c dark brown	.90	.70
	Never hinged		1.10	
	On cover			15.00
154	A25	30c dark blue	.40	.40
	Never hinged		.55	
	On cover			15.00
155	A25	35c olive grn	1.05	.80
	Never hinged		1.25	
	On cover			25.00
156	A24	40c org brn ('40)	.25	.25
	Never hinged		.40	
	On cover			14.00
157	A24	45c dull grn ('40)	.35	.35
	Never hinged		.45	
	On cover			22.50
158	A25	50c red	.70	.55
	Never hinged		.95	
	On cover			12.50
159	A25	55c dull red vio	1.05	.80
	Never hinged		1.25	
	On cover			7.50
160	A25	60c black ('40)	.70	.70
	Never hinged		.95	
	On cover			20.00
161	A25	65c orange brown	1.10	.95
	Never hinged		1.40	
	On cover			12.50
162	A25	70c lt violet ('40)	1.45	1.45
	Never hinged		2.00	
	On cover			22.50
163	A26	80c gray blk	2.75	2.10
	Never hinged		4.00	
	On cover			45.00
	On cover, single franking			75.00
164	A25	90c rose vio ('39)	1.60	1.60
	Never hinged		2.40	
	On cover			55.00
	On cover, single franking			105.00
165	A26	1fr carmine	3.50	2.40
	Never hinged		5.25	
	On cover			30.00
	On cover, single franking			55.00
166	A26	1fr black ('40)	.55	.55
	Never hinged		.75	
	On cover			7.00
167	A26	1.25fr magenta ('39)	1.30	1.30
	Never hinged		1.75	
	On cover			55.00
	On cover, single franking			105.00
168	A26	1.40fr pck bl ('40)	1.20	1.20
	Never hinged		1.70	
	On cover			35.00
	On cover, single franking			80.00
169	A26	1.50fr dull green	1.20	1.20
	Never hinged		1.60	
	On cover			15.00
	On cover, single franking			25.00
170	A26	1.60fr brn car ('40)	1.20	1.20
	Never hinged		1.70	
	On cover			35.00
	On cover, single franking			95.00

171	A26	1.75fr ultra	1.60	1.20
	Never hinged		2.00	
	On cover			27.50
	On cover, single franking			50.00
172	A26	2fr dk orange	1.20	1.20
	Never hinged		1.60	
	On cover			19.00
	On cover, single franking			50.00
173	A26	2.25fr ultra ('39)	2.00	2.00
	Never hinged		2.60	
	On cover			50.00
	On cover, single franking			95.00
174	A26	2.50fr org brn ('40)	2.10	2.10
	Never hinged		2.75	
	On cover			30.00
	On cover, single franking			55.00
175	A26	3fr dull violet	1.20	1.20
	Never hinged		1.60	
	On cover			30.00
	On cover, single franking			55.00
176	A27	5fr brn & pale cl	2.40	2.40
	Never hinged		3.50	
	On cover			40.00
	On cover, single franking			70.00
177	A27	10fr ind & pale bl	2.75	2.75
	Never hinged		4.00	
	On cover			45.00
	On cover, single franking			90.00
178	A27	20fr car lake & gray	2.75	2.75
	Never hinged		4.00	
	On cover			55.00
	On cover, single franking			100.00
	Nos. 146-178 (33)		39.10	35.95

For overprints and surcharge see Nos. 194-223 in the Scott Standard Catalogue, Vol. 6.

New York World's Fair Issue
Common Design Type

1939	**Engr.**		*Perf. 12½x12*	
179	CD82	1.25fr car lake	1.40	1.40
	Never hinged		2.00	
	On cover			62.50
	On cover, single franking			125.00
180	CD82	2.25fr ultra	1.50	1.50
	Never hinged		2.00	
	On cover			62.50
	On cover, single franking			110.00

SEMI-POSTAL STAMPS

Somali Girl — SP1

1915	**Unwmk.**		*Perf. 13½x14*	
	Chalky Paper			
B1	SP1	10c + 5c car & dk red	10.50	9.50
	Never hinged		17.50	
	On cover			60.00

Curie Issue
Common Design Type

1938	**Engr.**		*Perf. 13*	
B2	CD80	1.75fr + 50c brt ul-tra	8.75	8.75
	Never hinged		14.50	
	On cover			90.00
	On cover, single franking			150.00

French Revolution Issue
Common Design Type
Photo., Name and Value Typo. in Black

1939				
B3	CD83	45c + 25c green	10.50	10.50
	Never hinged		17.50	
	On cover			140.00
B4	CD83	70c + 30c brown	10.50	10.50
	Never hinged		17.50	
	On cover			100.00
B5	CD83	90c + 35c red org	10.50	10.50
	Never hinged		17.50	
	On cover			90.00
B6	CD83	1.25fr + 1fr rose pink	10.50	10.50
	Never hinged		17.50	
	On cover			90.00
	On cover, single franking			225.00
B7	CD83	2.25fr + 2fr blue	10.50	10.50
	Never hinged		17.50	
	On cover			140.00
	On cover, single franking			200.00
	Nos. B3-B7 (5)		52.50	52.50

POSTAGE DUE STAMPS

D1

1915	**Unwmk. Typo.**		*Perf. 14x13½*	
	Chalky Paper			
J1	D1	5c deep ultra	.40	*.65*
	Never hinged		.65	
	On cover			45.00
a.	Ordinary paper		1.20	1.20
	Never hinged		2.00	
	On cover			50.00
J2	D1	10c brown red	.65	*.80*
	Never hinged		.95	
	On cover			45.00
a.	Ordinary paper		2.40	2.40
	Never hinged		4.00	
	On cover			55.00
J3	D1	15c black	.95	*1.40*
	Never hinged		1.60	
	On cover			45.00
a.	Ordinary paper		2.40	2.40
	Never hinged		4.00	
	On cover			55.00
J4	D1	20c purple	2.00	*2.40*
	Never hinged		2.75	
	On cover			50.00
J5	D1	30c orange	2.00	*2.40*
	Never hinged		2.75	
	On cover			50.00
J6	D1	50c maroon	3.25	*3.50*
	Never hinged		5.25	
	On cover			55.00
J7	D1	60c green	4.75	*5.50*
	Never hinged		7.50	
	On cover			62.50
J8	D1	1fr dark blue	6.00	*7.25*
	Never hinged		9.50	
	On cover			75.00
	Nos. J1-J8 (8)		20.00	23.90

See Nos. J11-J20.

Type of 1915 Issue Surcharged

2F.

1927				
J9	D1	2fr on 1fr light red	9.50	*10.50*
	Never hinged		15.00	
	On cover			90.00
J10	D1	3fr on 1fr lilac rose	9.50	*10.50*
	Never hinged		15.00	
	On cover			100.00

Type of 1915

1938	**Engr.**		*Perf. 12½x13*	
J11	D1	5c light ultra	.25	*.30*
	Never hinged		.40	
	On cover			35.00
J12	D1	10c dark carmine	.25	*.30*
	Never hinged		.40	
	On cover			35.00
J13	D1	15c brown black	.30	*.40*
	Never hinged		.50	
	On cover			35.00
J14	D1	20c violet	.30	*.40*
	Never hinged		.50	
	On cover			35.00
J15	D1	30c orange yellow	1.10	*1.20*
	Never hinged		1.50	
	On cover			35.00
J16	D1	50c brown	.70	*.80*
	Never hinged		.95	
	On cover			40.00
J17	D1	60c emerald	1.10	*1.20*
	Never hinged		1.50	
	On cover			45.00
J18	D1	1fr indigo	2.25	2.25
	Never hinged		3.25	
	On cover			45.00
J19	D1	2fr red	1.00	*1.10*
	Never hinged		1.50	
	On cover			55.00
J20	D1	3fr dark brown	1.40	*1.50*
	Never hinged		2.25	
	On cover			75.00
	Nos. J11-J20 (10)		8.65	9.45
	Set, never hinged		13.00	

Inscribed "Inst de Grav" below design.

SOMALILAND PROTECTORATE

sō-'mä-lē-ˌland
prə-'tek-tˌə-ˌrət

LOCATION — Eastern Africa, bordering on the Gulf of Aden
GOVT. — British Protectorate
AREA — 68,000 sq. mi.

POP. — 640,000 (estimated)
CAPITAL — Hargeisa

Formerly administered by the Indian Government, the territory was taken over by the British Foreign Office in 1898 and transferred to the Colonial Office in 1905.

16 Annas = 1 Rupee
100 Cents = 1 Shilling (1951)

> **Catalogue values for unused stamps in this country are for Never Hinged items, beginning with Scott 108.**

BRITISH SOMALILAND

Stamps of India, 1882-1900, Overprinted at Top of Stamp

1903		**Wmk. 39**	*Perf. 14*	
1	A17	½a light green	3.00	*4.50*
	Never hinged		5.25	
2	A19	1a carmine rose	3.00	*4.00*
	Never hinged		5.25	
3	A21	2a violet	2.50	1.60
	Never hinged		4.50	
a.	Double overprint		800.00	
4	A28	2½a ultra	2.25	*1.90*
	Never hinged		4.00	
5	A22	3a brown orange	3.50	3.50
	Never hinged		6.25	
6	A23	4a olive green	4.00	3.00
	Never hinged		7.00	
7	A25	8a red violet	4.25	5.50
	Never hinged		8.00	
8	A26	12a brown, *red*	4.50	8.00
	Never hinged		8.00	
a.	Inverted overprint			1,200.
9	A29	1r car rose & grn	7.50	*11.00*
	Never hinged		13.50	
10	A30	2r yel brn & car rose	38.00	*52.50*
	Never hinged		67.50	
11	A30	3r green & brown	36.00	*62.50*
	Never hinged		62.50	
12	A30	5r violet & blue	59.00	*72.50*
	Never hinged		105.00	
	Wmk. Elephant's Head (38)			
13	A14	6a bister	6.50	5.25
	Never hinged		11.50	
	Nos. 1-13 (13)		174.00	235.75

Nos. 1-5 exist without the 2nd "l" of "BRITISH."

"BRIT SH" for "BRITISH"

1b	A17	½a light green	180.00	*275.00*
2b	A19	1a carmine rose	225.00	*300.00*
3b	A21	2a violet	400.00	*500.00*
4b	A28	2½a ultra	600.00	
5b	A22	3a brown orange	800.00	

"BR1TISH" for "BRITISH"

1c	A17	½a light green	170.00	*275.00*
2c	A19	1a carmine rose	170.00	
3c	A21	2a violet	325.00	
4c	A28	2½a ultra	375.00	
5c	A22	3a brown orange	400.00	*425.00*
6c	A23	4a olive green	400.00	*425.00*
7c	A25	8a red violet	400.00	
8c	A26	12a brown, *red*	400.00	*500.00*
9c	A29	1r car rose & grn	500.00	
13c	A14	6a bister	300.00	

Curved Overprint

10d	A30	2r yel brn & car rose	500.00	
11d	A30	3r green & brown	550.00	
12d	A30	5r violet & blue	550.00	

"SOMAL.LAND"

13e	A14	6a bister	175.00	

Same, but Overprinted at Bottom of Stamp

1903			**Wmk. 39**	
14	A28	2½a ultra	5.00	*8.50*
	Never hinged		9.00	
15	A26	12a violet, *red*	13.00	*14.00*
	Never hinged		23.00	
16	A29	1r car rose & grn	8.00	*17.50*
	Never hinged		14.00	
17	A30	2r yel brn & car rose	130.00	*200.00*
	Never hinged		235.00	
18	A30	3r green & brn	140.00	*200.00*
	Never hinged		250.00	
a.	Double overprint, both inverted, one albino		1,000.	
19	A30	5r violet & blue	130.00	*180.00*
	Never hinged		225.00	
	Wmk. 38			
20	A14	6a bister	8.50	*8.00*
	Never hinged		15.00	
	Nos. 14-20 (7)		434.50	628.00

"BRIT SH" for "BRITISH"

14b	A28	2½a ultra	1,100.	

"BR1TISH" for "BRITISH"

14c	A28	2½a ultra	200.00	
15c	A26	12a violet, red	300.00	
16c	A29	1r car rose & grn	350.00	

Curved Overprint

17d	A30	2r yel brn & car rose	750.00	1,100.
18d	A30	3r green & brn	800.00	
19d	A30	5r violet & blue	700.00	

"SOMAL.LAND"

14e	A28	2½a ultra	275.00	
15e	A26	12a violet, red	350.00	
16e	A29	1r car rose & grn	450.00	
17e	A30	2r yel brn & car rose	750.00	
18e	A30	3r green & brn	800.00	
19e	A30	5r violet & blue	700.00	

"SUMALILAND"

14f	A28	2½a ultra	275.00	
15f	A26	12a violet, red	350.00	
16f	A29	1r car rose & grn	450.00	
17f	A30	2r yel brn & car rose	750.00	
18f	A30	3r green & brn	800.00	
19f	A30	5r violet & blue	700.00	

Stamps of India, 1902-03, Ovptd.

1903   **Wmk. 39**

21	A33	½a light green	3.25	.60
		Never hinged	5.75	
22	A34	1a car rose	1.40	.35
		Never hinged	2.50	
23	A35	2a violet	1.90	2.75
		Never hinged	2.85	
24	A37	3a brown orange	2.75	2.75
		Never hinged	5.00	
25	A38	4a olive green	1.60	4.50
		Never hinged	3.00	
26	A40	8a red violet	1.90	2.50
		Never hinged	3.50	
		Nos. 21-26 (6)	12.80	13.45

"BRIT SH" for "BRITISH"

21b	A33	½a light green	450.00	
22b	A34	1a car rose	300.00	
23b	A35	2a violet	1,200.	

"BR1TISH" for "BRITISH"

21c	A33	½a light green	120.00	
22c	A34	1a car rose	300.00	
23c	A35	2a violet	225.00	
24c	A37	3a brown orange	250.00	
25c	A38	4a olive green	200.00	
26c	A40	8a red violet	300.00	

"SOMAL.LAND"

21e	A33	½a light green	70.00	80.00
22e	A34	1a car rose	60.00	70.00
23e	A35	2a violet	120.00	
24e	A37	3a brown orange	130.00	50.00
25e	A38	4a olive green	130.00	
26e	A40	8a red violet	175.00	

"SUMALILAND"

21f	A33	½a light green	120.00	
22f	A34	1a car rose	120.00	
23f	A35	2a violet	225.00	
24f	A37	3a brown orange	225.00	
25f	A38	4a olive green	200.00	
26f	A40	8a red violet	350.00	

The above overprints vary in length, also in the relative positions of the letters.

A1

King Edward VII — A2

1904   **Wmk. 2**   **Typo.**

27	A1	½a dl grn & grn	2.25	4.50
28	A1	1a carmine & blk	18.00	3.50
29	A1	2a red vio & dull vio	2.25	2.40
30	A1	2½a ultramarine	8.50	4.00
31	A1	3a gray grn & vio brn	2.50	4.00
32	A1	4a black & gray grn	3.75	6.50
33	A1	6a vio & gray grn	8.50	18.00
34	A1	8a pale blue & blk	7.50	8.00
35	A1	12a ocher & blk	11.00	11.50

Wmk. Crown and C C (1)

36	A2	1r gray grn	16.00	47.50
37	A2	2r red vio & dull vio	60.00	90.00
38	A2	3r blk & gray grn	60.00	130.00
39	A2	5r carmine & blk	62.50	130.00
		Nos. 27-39 (13)	262.75	459.90
		Set, ovptd. "SPECIMEN"	225.00	

1905   **Wmk. 3**

Ordinary Paper

40	A1	½a dl grn & grn	2.00	8.00
41	A1	1a carmine & blk	17.50	1.75
42	A1	2a red vio & dull vio	8.25	15.00
43	A1	2½a ultramarine	4.50	11.00
44	A1	3a gray grn & vio brn	2.50	16.00
45	A1	4a black & gray grn	5.00	20.00
46	A1	6a violet & gray grn	6.00	27.50
47	A1	8a pale blue & blk	8.00	11.00
48	A1	12a ocher & black	7.25	11.00
		Nos. 40-48 (9)	61.00	121.25

Nos. 41, 42, 44-48 are on both ordinary and chalky paper.

Chalky Paper

41a	A1	1a carmine & black ('06)	15.00	1.75
42a	A1	2a red violet & dull violet ('09)	19.00	16.00
44a	A1	3a gray green & violet brown ('11)	12.50	42.50
45a	A1	4a black & gray green ('11)	19.00	50.00
46a	A1	6a violet & gray green ('11)	35.00	75.00
47a	A1	8a blue & black ('11)	30.00	80.00
48a	A1	12a orange brown & black ('11)	19.00	75.00

1909

49	A1	½a bluish green	37.50	37.50
50	A1	1a carmine	3.00	2.25
		Ovptd. "SPECIMEN"	35.00	

For overprints see Nos. O11-O16.

A3

King George V — A4

The ½, 1 and 2½a of type A3 are on ordinary paper, the other values of types A3 and A4 are on chalky paper.

1912-19

51	A3	½a green	.90	9.25
52	A3	1a carmine	3.00	.60
a.		1p scarlet ('17)	3.50	1.40
53	A3	2a red vio & dull vio	4.25	16.00
a.		2a violet purple & dull purple ('19)	27.50	47.50
54	A3	2½a ultramarine	1.25	9.75
55	A3	3a gray grn & vio brn	2.75	7.50
56	A3	4a blk & grn ('13)	3.00	11.50
57	A3	6a violet & green	3.00	7.00
58	A3	8a lt blue & blk	4.25	17.50
59	A3	12a ocher & blk	4.00	24.00
60	A4	1r dull grn & grn	17.50	22.00
61	A4	2r red vio & dull vio ('19)	28.00	80.00
62	A4	3r blk & gray grn ('19)	80.00	150.00
63	A4	5r car & blk ('19)	80.00	200.00
		Nos. 51-63 (13)	231.90	555.10
		Set, ovptd. "SPECIMEN"	300.00	

1921   **Wmk. 4**

64	A3	½a blue green	3.75	15.00
65	A3	1a scarlet	4.25	.80
66	A3	2a vio & dull vio	5.00	1.10
67	A3	2½a ultramarine	1.25	8.00
68	A3	3a gray grn & vio brown	3.00	8.50
69	A3	4a black & grn	3.00	10.00
70	A3	6a violet & grn	2.00	15.00
71	A3	8a lt blue & blk	2.50	8.00
72	A3	12a ocher & blk	11.00	17.50
73	A4	1r dull grn & grn	10.00	55.00
74	A4	2r vio & dull vio	30.00	62.50
75	A4	3r blk & gray grn	42.50	125.00
76	A4	5r scarlet & blk	90.00	200.00
		Nos. 64-76 (13)	208.25	526.40
		Set, ovptd. "SPECIMEN"	275.00	

Common Design Types

pictured following the introduction.

Silver Jubilee Issue
Common Design Type

1935, May 6   **Engr.**   **Perf. 11x12**

77	CD301	1a car & dk blue	2.75	4.00
78	CD301	2a black & ultra	3.25	4.00
79	CD301	3a ultra & brown	2.75	18.00

80	CD301	1r brown vio & ind	9.00	20.00
		Nos. 77-80 (4)	17.75	46.00
		Set, never hinged	32.50	
		Set, perf "SPECIMEN"	110.00	

Coronation Issue
Common Design Type

1937, May 13   **Perf. 13½x14**

81	CD302	1a carmine	.25	.40
82	CD302	2a black	.35	2.00
83	CD302	3a bright ultra	.50	1.00
		Nos. 81-83 (3)	1.10	3.40
		Set, never hinged	2.25	
		Set, perf "SPECIMEN"	95.00	

Blackhead Sheep — A5   Greater Kudu — A6

Map of Somaliland Protectorate A7

1938, May 10   **Wmk. 4**   **Perf. 12½**

84	A5	½a green	.80	5.75
		Never hinged	1.20	
85	A5	1a carmine	.60	1.75
		Never hinged	.90	
86	A5	2a deep claret	2.00	4.50
		Never hinged	3.00	
87	A5	3a ultra	10.00	17.50
		Never hinged	15.00	
88	A6	4a dark brown	4.00	12.00
		Never hinged	6.00	
89	A6	6a purple	8.50	13.00
		Never hinged	13.00	
90	A6	8a gray black	3.75	13.50
		Never hinged	5.75	
91	A6	12a orange	10.00	35.00
		Never hinged	15.00	
92	A7	1r green	8.75	85.00
		Never hinged	13.25	
93	A7	2r rose violet	16.00	85.00
		Never hinged	24.00	
94	A7	3r ultramarine	14.00	50.00
		Never hinged	21.00	
95	A7	5r black	20.00	50.00
		Never hinged	30.00	
a.		Horiz. pair, imperf. btwn.	25,000.	
		Nos. 84-95 (12)	98.40	373.00
		Set, never hinged	148.10	
		Set, perf "SPECIMEN"	275.00	

A8

A9

A10

1942, Apr. 22

96	A8	½a green	.25	.50
97	A8	1a carmine	.25	.25
98	A8	2a deep claret	.40	.25
99	A8	3a ultramarine	1.50	.25
100	A9	4a dark brown	2.00	.25
101	A9	6a purple	2.00	.25
102	A9	8a gray	2.50	.25
103	A9	12a orange	2.25	1.50
104	A10	1r green	1.75	2.75
105	A10	2r rose violet	2.75	9.50

106	A10	3r ultra	5.50	16.00
107	A10	5r black	9.00	11.00
		Nos. 96-107 (12)	30.15	42.75
		Set, never hinged	47.50	
		Set, perf "SPECIMEN"	250.00	

For surcharges see Nos. 116-126.

> Catalogue values for unused stamps in this section, from this point to the end of the section, are for Never Hinged items.

Peace Issue
Common Design Type

Perf. 13¾x14

1946, Oct. 15   **Engr.**   **Wmk. 4**

108	CD303	1a carmine	.25	.25
		Never hinged	.40	
a.		Perf. 13½	16.00	65.00
		Never hinged	24.00	
109	CD303	3a deep blue	.25	.25
		Never hinged	.40	
		Set, perf "SPECIMEN"	85.00	

Silver Wedding Issue
Common Design Types

1949, Jan. 28 Photo.   **Perf. 14x14½**

110	CD304	1a scarlet	.25	.25
		Never hinged	.40	

Perf. 11½x11

Engraved; Name Typographed

111	CD305	5r gray black	6.75	8.00
		Never hinged	10.00	

UPU Issue
Common Design Types
Surcharged in Black or Carmine with New Values in Annas

Engr.; Name Typo. on 3a, 6a

1949, Oct. 10   **Perf. 13½, 11x11½**

112	CD306	1a on 10c rose car	.25	.35
		Never hinged	.40	
113	CD307	3a on 30c ind (C)	1.25	4.00
		Never hinged	1.90	
114	CD308	6a on 50c rose vio	.35	3.00
		Never hinged	.55	
115	CD309	12a on 1sh red org	.60	.60
		Never hinged	.90	
		Nos. 112-115 (4)	2.45	7.95

Nos. 96 and 98 to 107 Surcharged with New Value in Black or Carmine

1951, Apr. 2   **Wmk. 4**   **Perf. 12½**

116	A8	5c on ½a green	.40	2.25
117	A8	10c on 2a deep claret	.40	.75
118	A8	15c on 3a ultramarine	1.75	2.25
119	A9	20c on 4a dark brown	2.40	.25
120	A9	30c on 6a purple	2.00	1.00
121	A9	50c on 8a gray	2.75	.25
122	A9	70c on 12a red	4.25	8.50
123	A10	1sh on 1r green	2.50	2.00
124	A10	2sh on 2r rose violet	5.50	22.50
125	A10	2sh on 3r ultra	12.00	9.50
126	A10	5sh on 5r black (C)	20.00	15.00
		Nos. 116-126 (11)	53.95	64.25

OFFICIAL STAMPS

Official Stamps of India, 1883-1900, Overprinted

1903, June 1   **Wmk. 39**   **Perf. 14**

O1	A17	½a light green	8.50	55.00
		Never hinged	15.00	
O2	A19	1a carmine rose	20.00	12.50
		Never hinged	35.00	
O3	A21	2a violet	14.00	55.00
		Never hinged	24.00	
O4	A25	8a red violet	17.50	450.00
		Never hinged	28.00	
a.		No period after "M" of "O.H.M.S."	3,250.	
O5	A29	1r car rose & grn	20.00	750.00
		Never hinged	30.00	
		Nos. O1-O5 (5)	80.00	1,322.

"BRITIS H" for "BRITISH"

O1b	A17	½a light green	325.00	750.00
O2b	A19	1a carmine rose	325.00	425.00
O3b	A21	2a violet	400.00	
O4b	A25	8a red violet	1,100.	
O5b	A29	1r car rose & grn	1,200.	

"BR1TISH" for "BRITISH"

O1c	A17	½a light green	450.00	
O2c	A19	1a carmine rose	450.00	500.00
O3c	A21	2a violet	500.00	
O4c	A25	8a red violet	1,400.	
O5c	A29	1r car rose & grn	3,000.	

India Nos. 61-63, 68, 49 Overprinted

1903

O6	A33	½a green	.85	
		Never hinged	1.50	
O7	A34	1a carmine rose	.85	
		Never hinged	1.50	
O8	A35	2a violet	1.50	
		Never hinged	2.50	
O9	A40	8a red violet	7.00	
		Never hinged	13.00	
O10	A29	1r car rose & grn	22.50	
		Never hinged	40.00	
		Nos. O6-O10 (5)	32.70	

Nos. O6-O10 were not regularly issued, although used examples are known.

"BRIT SH" for "BRITISH"

O6b	A33	½a green	75.00
O7b	A34	1a carmine rose	75.00
O8b	A35	2a violet	110.00
O9b	A40	8a red violet	2,250.
O10b	A29	1r car rose & grn	2,250.

"BR1TISH" for "BRITISH"

O6c	A33	½a green	70.00
O7c	A34	1a carmine rose	70.00
O8c	A35	2a violet	100.00
O9c	A40	8a red violet	1,800.
O10c	A29	1r car rose & grn	1,800.

"SOMAL.LAND"

O6e	A33	½a green	70.00
O7e	A34	1a carmine rose	70.00
O10e	A29	1r car rose & grn	1,800.

"SUMALILAND"

O6f	A33	½a green	70.00
O7f	A34	1a carmine rose	70.00
O8f	A35	2a violet	100.00
O9f	A40	8a red violet	1,800.
O10f	A29	1r car rose & grn	1,800.

Regular Issue of 1904 Overprinted

O.H.M.S.

1904   Wmk. Crown and C A (2)

O11	A1	½a gray green	8.00	55.00
		Never hinged	14.00	
a.		No period after "M"	300.00	
O12	A1	1a carmine & blk	4.00	8.00
		Never hinged	7.50	
a.		No period after "M"	250.00	325.00
O13	A1	2a red vio & dull vio	275.00	70.00
		Never hinged	500.00	
a.		No period after "M"	2,750.	800.00
O14	A1	8a pale blue & blk	80.00	150.00
		Never hinged	140.00	
a.		No period after "M"	650.00	850.00
		Nos. O11-O14 (4)	367.00	283.00

Wmk. Crown and C C (1)

O15	A2	1r gray green	275.00	1,000.

Same Overprint on No. 42

1905   Wmk. 3

O16	A1	2a red vio & dull vio	125.00	1,100.
a.		No period after "M"	2,250.	

The period after "M" may be found missing on Nos. O11-O14 and O16.

SOUTH AFRICA

sauth 'a-fri-kə

LOCATION — Southern Africa
GOVT. — Republic
AREA — 433,678 sq. mi.
POP. — 26,749,000 (est. 1984)
CAPITAL — Pretoria (administrative); Cape Town (legislative)

The union was formed on May 31, 1910, comprising the former British colonies of Cape of Good Hope, Natal, Transvaal and the Orange Free State, which became provinces.

For previous listings, see individual headings.

12 Pence = 1 Shilling
20 Shillings = 1 Pound

Catalogue values for unused stamps in this country are for Never Hinged items, beginning with Scott 74 in the regular postage section, Scott B1 in the semipostal section, Scott J22 in the postage due section, and Scott O21 in the officials section.

Watermarks

Wmk. 47 — Multiple Rosette   Wmk. 177 — Springbok's Head

Wmk. 201 — Multiple Springbok's Head

STAMPS OF GREAT BRITAIN USED IN SOUTH AFRICA

Stamps of Great Britain used in South Africa during the Boer War, 1899-1902, with circular or octagonal postmarks "British Army South Africa" or "Natal Field Force" in several types.

1881

A1	1p lilac (16 dots) (#89)	5.75

1883-84

A2	2sh6p lilac (#96)	300.00
A3	5sh rose (#108)	375.00
A4	10sh ultramarine (#109)	750.00

1887-92

A5	½p vermilion (#111)	7.00
A6	1½p violet & green (#112)	32.50
A7	2p green & carmine rose (#113)	18.00
A8	2½p violet, *blue* (#114)	7.50
A9	3p violet, *yellow* (#115)	14.00
A10	4p brown & green (#116)	22.50
A11	4½p carmine rose & green (#117)	85.00
A12	5p lilac blue, type II (#118)	17.50
A13	6p violet (#119)	14.00
A14	9p blue & lilac (#120)	85.00
A15	10p carmine rose & lilac (#121)	80.00
A16	1sh green (#122)	120.00
A17	£1 green (#142)	1,200.

1900

A18	½p blue green (#125)	7.50
A19	1sh carmine rose & green (#126)	200.00

1902

A20	½p blue green (#127a)	17.50
A21	1p scarlet (#128)	11.50
A22	1½p violet & green (#129)	70.00
A23	2p yellow green & carmine (#130)	50.00
A24	2½p ultramarine (#131)	22.50
A25	3p dull purple *orange yellow* (#132)	60.00
A26	4p gray brown & green (#133)	70.00

A27	5p dull purple & ultramarine (#134)	70.00
A28	6p pale violet (#135)	40.00
A29	9p ultramarine & dull violet (#136)	130.00
A30	10p carmine & dull purple (#137)	130.00
A31	1sh carmine & dull green (#138)	90.00

ARMY OFFICIAL STAMPS

1896-1901

AO1	½p vermilion (#O54)	110.00
AO2	½p blue green (#O57)	110.00
AO3	1p lilac (#O55)	100.00
AO4	6p purple, *rose red* (#O58)	—

From Aug. 19, 1910, through December 31, 1937, the stamps of the provinces (Cape of Good Hope, Natal, Orange River Colony and Transvaal) were valid for postage throughout South Africa. They were demonetized effective Jan. 1, 1938.

Union of South Africa

George V — A1

1910   Engr.   Wmk. 47   Perf. 14

1	A1	2½p blue	3.00	1.75
		Never hinged	6.50	
a.		2½ deep blue	3.00	2.75
		Never hinged	10.00	
		Handstamped "SPECIMEN"	400.00	

Union Parliament opening, Nov. 4, 1910.

Type A2 stamps have very small margins at top and bottom. Values are for examples with perfs close to, or touching the frame.

George V — A2

1913-24   Typo.   Wmk. 177

2	A2	½p green	1.50	.30
		Never hinged	2.25	
a.		Double impression	15,000.	
b.		½p blue green	2.00	.25
c.		½p yellow green	2.50	.50
d.		½p dark mossy green	500.00	190.00
e.		Printed on gummed side	825.00	
3	A2	1p rose red	1.75	.25
		Never hinged	2.00	
a.		1p scarlet	3.00	.75
b.		1p carmine red	2.25	.25
c.		1p deep carmine lake	12.50	4.50
d.		Printed on gummed side	925.00	
4	A2	1½p org brn ('20)	.80	.25
		Never hinged	2.00	
a.		Tête bêche pair	2.00	18.00
b.		1½p dark chestnut	4.50	15.00
c.		Printed on gummed side	1,000.	
5	A2	2p dull violet	2.25	.25
		Never hinged	4.50	
a.		2p deep purple	2.50	.25
b.		2p reddish purple	3.00	.65
c.		2p deep plum	385.00	190.00
d.		Printed on gummed side	1,000.	
6	A2	2½p ultra	5.50	1.60
		Never hinged	10.50	
a.		2½p deep blue	5.50	3.00
7	A2	3p brn org & blk	13.00	.55
		Never hinged	25.00	
a.		3p dull orange red & black	10.00	.70
8	A2	3p ultra ('22)	4.75	1.75
		Never hinged	10.00	
a.		3p dk ultramarine	6.50	2.50
9	A2	4p ol grn & org	11.00	.55
		Never hinged	20.00	
a.		4p sage green & orange	7.00	.55
10	A2	6p violet & black	9.50	.70
		Never hinged	20.00	
a.		6p bright violet & black	9.50	1.00
b.		6p reddish violet & black	10.00	1.00
c.		"Z" of "ZUID" missing	80.00	37.50
11	A2	1sh orange	20.00	.90
		Never hinged	32.50	
a.		1sh orange yellow	22.50	1.00
12	A2	1sh3p violet ('20)	17.50	11.00
		Never hinged	37.50	
a.		1sh3p deep violet	17.00	11.00
13	A2	2sh6p green & cl	70.00	5.50
		Never hinged	115.00	

14	A2	5sh blue & claret	140.00	9.00
		Never hinged	250.00	
a.		5sh light blue & reddish purple	110.00	10.00
15	A2	10sh ol grn & blue	350.00	14.50
		Never hinged	450.00	
16	A2	£1 red & dp grn ('16)	850.00	1,600.
		Never hinged	1,400.	
a.		£1 lt red & gray green ('24)	1,100.	1,600.
		Never hinged	1,650.	
		Nos. 2-16 (15)	1,497.	1,647.
		Set, ovptd. or handstamped "SPECIMEN"	1,400.	

The ½p, 1p and 1½p have the words "Revenue" and "Inkomst" on the stamps. On other stamps of this type these words are replaced by short vertical lines.

All values exist in many shades. No. 4a exists with and without gutter between.

Unwatermarked examples of the 1p are the result of misplaced watermarks.

All values except the 2sh6p and £1 exist with watermark inverted. No. 4 exists with watermark sideways.

Nos. 3, 7 and 8 exist bisected. These are philatelic creations and have little value.

For overprint see No. O1.

Coil Stamps
Perf. 14 Horizontally

17	A2	½p green	9.25	1.90
a.		½p blue green	11.00	2.50
b.		½p yellow green	11.00	2.50
18	A2	1p rose red ('14)	15.00	6.25
a.		1p scarlet	20.00	8.75
b.		1p carmine red	16.50	9.00
19	A2	1½p org brown ('20)	17.00	27.50
20	A2	2p dull violet ('21)	18.00	5.00
a.		2p deep purple	22.50	7.50
b.		2p reddish purple	22.50	7.50
		Nos. 17-20 (4)	59.25	40.65

"Hope" — A3

Design: No. 22, inscribed SUIDAFRIKA.

1926   Engr.   Wmk. 201   Imperf.

21	A3	4p blue gray	2.00	1.40
22	A3	4p blue gray	2.00	1.40

Nos. 21 and 22 were privately rouletted and perforated, but such varieties were not officially made.

No. 21 (English inscription) was printed in a separate sheet from No. 22 (Afrikaans inscription).

English-Afrikaans Se-Tenant

Stamps with English inscriptions and with Afrikaans inscriptions were printed alternately in the same sheets, starting with No. 23. Major-number listings and values are for horizontal pairs (vertical pairs sell for about one-third less) of such stamps consisting of one English and one Afrikaans-inscribed stamp, unless otherwise described.

Values are for pairs with no fold marks between stamps and no perf separations.

Beware of pairs that have been rejoined.

Springbok A5

Jan van Riebeek's Ship, Drommedaris — A6

Orange Tree — A7

1926   Typo.   Perf. 14½x14

23	A5	½p dk grn & blk, pair	3.00	4.00
a.		Single, English	.25	.25
b.		Single, Afrikaans	.25	.25
c.		Tete beche pair ('27)	1,500.	
d.		Center omitted	2,000.	
e.		Booklet pane of 6	225.00	
f.		As "e," perf. 14	350.00	
g.		Missing "1" in "1/2" (Afrikaans only)	2,000.	
h.		Perf 13½x14 ('27)	85.00	85.00
i.		As "h," single, English		4.00
j.		As "h," single, Afrikaans		4.00
24	A6	1p car & blk, pair	3.00	3.00
a.		Single, English	.25	.25
b.		Single, Afrikaans	.25	.25
c.		Imperf., pair	1,350.	
d.		Tete beche pair ('27)	1,750.	
f.		Booklet pane of 6	200.00	
g.		As "f," perf. 14	300.00	
h.		Imperf on three sides, vert. pair	700.00	800.00
i.		Perf 13½x14 ('27)	110.00	85.00
j.		As "h," single, English		4.00
k.		As "h," single, Afrikaans		4.00
25	A7	6p org & grn, pair	42.50	47.50
a.		Single, English	3.00	2.25
b.		Single, Afrikaans	3.00	2.25
		Nos. 23-25 (3)	48.50	54.50

Nos. 23c and 24d are from uncut sheets printed for the perf. 14 booklet panes of 1928, Nos. 23f and 24g.

See Nos. 33-35, 42, 45-50, 59-61, 98-99. For overprints see Nos. O2-O4, O6-O9, O12-O15, O18, O21-O25, O30-O32, O42-O45, O48.

Government Buildings, Pretoria — A8

"Groote Schuur," Rhodes's Home — A9

Native Kraal — A10

Gnu — A11

Trekking — A12

Ox Wagon — A13

Cape Town and Table Mountain — A14

Perf. 14, 14x13½

1927-28   Engr.   Wmk. 201

26	A8	2p vio brn & gray, pair	13.50	26.00
a.		Single, English	2.50	1.40
b.		Single, Afrikaans	2.50	1.40
c.		Perf. 14x13½, pair	32.50	32.50
d.		As "c," single, English	6.00	.75
e.		As "c," single, Afrikaans	6.00	.75
27	A9	3p red & blk, pair	24.00	37.50
a.		Single, English	2.10	1.40
b.		Single, Afrikaans	2.10	1.40
c.		Perf. 14x13½, pair	67.50	82.50
d.		As "c," single, English	3.25	2.75
e.		As "c," single, Afrikaans	3.25	2.75
28	A10	4p brown, pair ('28)	32.50	67.50
a.		Single, English	3.25	1.90
b.		Single, Afrikaans	3.25	1.90
c.		Perf. 14x13½, pair	67.50	82.50
d.		As "c," single, English	3.25	2.75
e.		As "c," single, Afrikaans	3.25	2.75
29	A11	1sh dp bl & bis brn, pair	47.50	87.50
a.		Single, English	7.50	2.75
b.		Single, Afrikaans	7.50	2.75
c.		Perf. 14x13½, pair ('30)	50.00	60.00
d.		As "c," single, English	7.50	1.25
e.		As "c," single, Afrikaans	7.50	1.25
30	A12	2sh6p brn & bl grn, pair	140.00	400.00
a.		Single, English	20.00	24.00
b.		Single, Afrikaans	20.00	24.00
c.		Perf. 14x13½, pair	475.00	675.00
d.		As "c," single, English	32.50	37.50
e.		As "c," single, Afrikaans	32.50	37.50
31	A13	5sh dp grn & blk, pair	275.00	650.00
a.		Single, English	30.00	40.00
b.		Single, Afrikaans	30.00	40.00
c.		Perf. 14x13½, pair	525.00	850.00
d.		As "c," single, English	47.50	52.50
e.		As "c," single, Afrikaans	47.50	52.50
32	A14	10sh ol brn & bl, pair	200.00	200.00
a.		Single, English	20.00	16.00
b.		Single, Afrikaans	20.00	16.00
c.		Perf. 14x13½, pair	275.00	375.00
d.		As "c," single, English	25.00	20.00
e.		As "c," single, Afrikaans	25.00	20.00
f.		Center inverted, single, English ('28)	12,500.	
g.		Center inverted, single, Afrikaans ('28)	12,500.	
h.		As "c," center inverted	57,500.	
		Nos. 26-32 (7)	732.50	1,468.
		Set, handstamped "SPECIMEN"	925.00	

See Nos. 36-41, 43-44, 53-54, 58, 62-66. For overprints see Nos. O5, O10-O111, O16-O17, O19-O20, O28, O33-O35, O39, O41, O49-O53.

Types of 1926-28 Redrawn
"SUIDAFRIKA" (No Hyphen) on Afrikaans Stamps

The photogravure, unhyphenated stamps of 1930-45 are distinguished from the 1926-28 typographed or engraved stamps (also unhyphenated) by the following characteristics:

½p, 1p, 6p. Leg of "R" in AFRICA or AFRIKA ends in a straight line in the photogravure set; in a curved line in the typographed.

No. 35 differs from No. 34, having 2mm space between POSSEEL—INKOMSTE instead of 1mm.

2p. A memorial statue has been added just above and leftward of the "2" in value tablet on Nos. 36-37 (photogravure).

3p. Top frame on No. 38 consists of 3 heavy lines. On No. 27 it has 3 heavy and 2 very thin lines.

4p. On Nos. 40-41 the background in upper corners is solid. On No. 28 it consists of horizontal and vertical lines. No. 41 has pretzel-shaped scroll endings at bottom. On No. 40 these scroll endings enclose a solid mass of color.

1sh. No. 43 has no fine shading lines projecting from the curved top of the left inner frame, as No. 29 has. On No. 43 the shading of the last "A" of the country name partly covers the flower below it.

2sh6p. On No. 44 the shading below the country name is solid or shows signs of wear. On No. 30 it is composed of fine lines.

The engraved pictorials are much more finely executed and show details more clearly than the photogravure.

Perf. 15x14 (½p, 1p, 6p), 14

1930-45   Photo.   Wmk. 201

33	A5	½p bl grn & blk, pair	3.75	3.50
		Never hinged	6.50	
a.		Single, English	.25	.25
b.		Single, Afrikaans	.25	.25
c.		Tete-beche pair	1,250.	
d.		As "c," gutter between	1,750.	

e.		Booklet pane of 6	50.00	50.00
f.		Vert. pair, monolingual	40.00	—
34	A6	1p car & blk, pair	4.75	3.50
		Never hinged	10.00	
a.		Single, English	.25	.25
b.		Single, Afrikaans	.25	.25
c.		Center omitted	4,500.	
d.		Frame omitted	2,500.	
e.		Tete-beche pair	1,800.	
f.		As "e," gutter between	1,500.	
g.		Booklet pane of 6	20.00	20.00
35	A6	1p rose & blk, pair ('32)	47.50	4.50
		Never hinged	95.00	
a.		Single, English	1.00	.25
b.		Single, Afrikaans	1.00	.25
c.		Center omitted	750.00	
36	A8	2p vio & gray, pair ('31)	24.00	22.50
		Never hinged	55.00	
a.		Single, English	2.00	.40
b.		Single, Afrikaans	2.00	.40
c.		Frame omitted, single stamp (English)	3,000.	
d.		Frame omitted, single stamp (Afrikaans)	3,000.	
e.		Tete-beche pair	6,500.	
f.		Booklet pane of 4	240.00	240.00
37	A8	2p vio & ind, pair ('38)	250.00	100.00
		Never hinged	325.00	
a.		Single, English	12.50	7.25
b.		Single, Afrikaans	12.50	7.25
38	A9	3p red & blk, pair ('31)	72.50	95.00
		Never hinged	150.00	
a.		Single, English	6.75	6.75
b.		Single, Afrikaans	6.75	6.75
39	A9	3p ultra & bl, pair ('33)	22.50	10.00
		Never hinged	45.00	
a.		Single, English	2.00	1.00
b.		Single, Afrikaans	2.00	1.00
c.		Center omitted	30,000.	
40	A10	4p redsh brn, pair ('32)	250.00	210.00
		Never hinged	500.00	
a.		Single, English	25.00	11.00
b.		Single, Afrikaans	25.00	11.00
41	A10	4p brn, pair ('36)	6.50	5.00
		Never hinged	14.00	
a.		Single, English	1.10	.45
b.		Single, Afrikaans	1.10	.45
42	A7	6p org & grn, pair ('31)	20.00	6.50
		Never hinged	57.50	
a.		Single, English	1.10	.45
b.		Single, Afrikaans	1.10	.45
43	A11	1sh dl bl & yel brn, pair	140.00	57.50
		Never hinged	250.00	
a.		Single, English	9.00	2.00
b.		Single, Afrikaans	9.00	2.00
c.		1sh dp bl & brn, pair ('32)	72.50	32.50
		Never hinged	115.00	
d.		As "c," single, English	5.25	.40
e.		As "c," single, Afrikaans	5.25	.40
44	A12	2sh 6p brn & bl, pair ('45)	29.00	19.00
		Never hinged	55.00	
a.		Single, English	1.75	.70
b.		Single, Afrikaans	1.75	.70
c.		2sh6p brn & sl grn ('36), pair	250.00	300.00
d.		As "c," single, English	18.00	8.00
e.		As "c," single, Afrikaans	18.00	8.00
f.		2sh6p choc & dp grn ('37), pair	205.00	190.00
		Never hinged	500.00	
g.		As "f," single, English	14.00	6.50
h.		As "f," single, Afrikaans	14.00	6.50
i.		2sh6p red brn & grn, pair ('32)	210.00	200.00
		Never hinged	400.00	
j.		As "i," single, English	17.50	6.50
k.		As "i," single, Afrikaans	17.50	6.50
		Nos. 33-44 (12)	870.50	537.00

No. 34 unwatermarked, or watermarked multiple clover leaf, is a proof.

Types of 1926-28 with "SUID-AFRIKA" Hyphenated on Afrikaans Stamps, and

Gold Mine — A15

Government Buildings, Pretoria — A16

Government Buildings, Pretoria — A16a

Groote Schuur — A17

Groot Constantia — A18

½p. No. 45 shading in leaves and ornaments strengthened; 40 lines in center background. Size: 18½x22½mm.

No. 46 has 28 heavy horizontal shading lines in center background and similar thicker lines in frame. Top and bottom green bars are scored by a white horizontal line. Size: 18½x22½mm.

No. 47 is smaller, 18x22mm.

1p. No. 48, size 18½x22½mm.

No. 49, size 18x22mm.

No. 50. Size: 17½x21½mm.

2p. On Nos. 53-54, S's in SOUTH and POSTAGE are narrower than on Nos. 36-37.

5sh. On No. 64, Die I, U and A in SOUTH AFRICA have projections. Lines are contained within the design. Size 27x21¾mm.

5sh. On No. 65, Die I, dots are contained within the design, instead of lines. Size 27x21½mm.

5sh. On No. 66, Die II, U and A in SOUTH AFRICA have been redrawn to eliminate projections. Dots are contained within the design. Size 26¾x21½mm.

6p. Die I, "SUID-AFRIKA" 16½mm. Shading in leaves framing oval very faint and broken. Size: 18½x22½mm.

Die II, "SUID-AFRIKA" 17mm. Leaves strongly shaded. Heavy lines of shading in background of tree. Size: 18½x22½mm.

Die III, "question mark" scrolls below top panel are cleanly defined without intrusion of background shading. Size: 18x22mm.

Nos. 45-67 were printed in many shades. Some denominations in some printings were partly or wholly screened. Except for No. 47, the screened stamps were issued after 1947.

5sh. No. 65. Type I, letters "U" and "A" in SOUTH AFRICA have projections. Size: 27x21½mm.

No. 66. Type II, letters "U" and "A" redrawn to eliminate projections. Size: 26½x21½mm.

Perf. 15x14 (½p, 1p, 6p), 14

1933-54   Photo.   Wmk. 201

45	A5	½p grn & gray, pair ('36)	4.00	2.00
		Never hinged	4.50	
a.		Single, English	.25	.25
b.		Single, Afrikaans	.25	.25
c.		Bklt. pane of 6, marginal ads	30.00	30.00
d.		Perf. 13½x14 (coil), pair	40.00	65.00
		Never hinged	80.00	
e.		As "d," single, English	1.75	1.25
f.		As "d," single, Afrikaans	1.75	1.25
46	A5	½p grn & gray, redrawn, pair ('37)	10.00	.40
		Never hinged	20.00	
a.		Single, English	.25	.25
b.		Single, Afrikaans	.25	.25
c.		Booklet pane of 6	45.00	36.00
d.		Booklet pane of 2	10.00	1.25
e.		As "c," 4 blank margins	42.50	42.50
f.		Perf. 14x14 (coil), pair	12.50	7.25
g.		As "f," single, English	2.25	.80
h.		As "f," single, Afrikaans	2.25	.80
47	A5	½p grn & gray, pair ('47)	1.50	4.00
		Never hinged	2.00	
a.		Single, English	.25	.25
b.		Single, Afrikaans	.25	.25
c.		Bklt. pane of 6, marginal ads	4.75	4.25
d.		As "c," no horiz. margins	6.00	3.50
48	A6	1p car & gray, pair ('34)	1.75	2.00
		Never hinged	3.50	
a.		Single, English	.25	.25
b.		Single, Afrikaans	.25	.25
c.		Booklet pane of 6	45.00	45.00
d.		Booklet pane of 2	3.50	1.50
e.		Perf. 13½x14 (coil), pair	85.00	125.00
		Never hinged	170.00	
f.		As "e," single, English	1.40	2.75
g.		As "e," single, Afrikaans	1.40	2.75
h.		Center omitted, pair	325.00	
j.		Bklt. pane of 6, marginal ads	32.50	32.50
k.		As "j," 4 blank margins	36.00	36.00
m.		Perf. 14½x14 (coil), pair	11.00	11.00
n.		As "m," single, English	1.40	1.40
p.		As "m," single, Afrikaans	1.40	1.40
49	A6	1p rose car & gray blk, pair ('40)	1.50	.30
a.		Single, English	.25	.25
b.		Single, Afrikaans	.25	.25
c.		Unwmkd., pair	325.00	325.00
d.		Booklet pane of 6	4.50	3.25
e.		Perf. 14½x14 (coil), pair	4.00	6.00
f.		As "e," single, English	1.40	.90
g.		As "e," single, Afrikaans	1.40	.90
h.		As "d," marginal ads	6.00	5.00

50	A6	1p car & blk, pair ('51)	1.50	4.00
		Never hinged	2.25	
a.		Single, English	.25	.25
		Single, Afrikaans	.25	.25
51	A15	1½p dk grn & gold, 27x21½mm, pair ('55)	2.25	2.25
		Never hinged	3.50	
a.		Single, English	.25	.25
b.		Single, Afrikaans	.25	.25
c.		Booklet pane of 4	11.00	9.50
d.		Center omitted, pair	1,000.	
52	A15	1½p sl grn & och, 22x18mm, pair ('41)	2.25	1.50
		Never hinged	3.50	
a.		Single, English	.25	.25
b.		Single, Afrikaans	.25	.25
c.		Center omitted, pair	7,500.	5,500.
d.		Booklet pane of 6	8.00	5.50
53	A16	2p bl vio & dl bl, pair ('38)	55.00	37.50
		Never hinged	75.00	
a.		Single, English	3.00	1.25
b.		Single, Afrikaans	3.00	1.25
54	A16	2p dl vio & gray, pair ('41)	45.00	85.00
		Never hinged	60.00	
a.		Single, English	1.00	1.50
b.		Single, Afrikaans	1.00	1.50
55	A16a	2p dp reddish vio & sl, 27x21½mm, pair ('45)	1.50	4.00
a.		Single, English	.25	.25
b.		Single, Afrikaans	.25	.25
56	A16a	2p pur & sl bl, 21½ x 17¼mm, pair ('50)	2.75	11.00
		Never hinged	4.00	
a.		Single, English	.25	.25
b.		Single, Afrikaans	.25	.25
c.		Booklet pane of 6 ('51)	4.50	4.50
57	A17	3p ultra, pair ('40)	9.50	3.25
		Never hinged	13.00	
a.		Single, English	.25	.25
b.		Single, Afrikaans	.25	.25
c.		3p bl, pair ('49)	2.00	6.00
		Never hinged	3.00	
d.		As "c," single, English	.25	.25
e.		As "c," single, Afrikaans	.25	.25
58	A10	4p choc brn, pair ('52)	3.50	11.00
		Never hinged	5.00	
a.		Single, English	.25	.25
b.		Single, Afrikaans	.25	.25
59	A7	6p org & bl grn, I, pair ('37)	55.00	35.00
		Never hinged	70.00	
a.		Single, English	3.75	1.10
b.		Single, Afrikaans	3.75	1.10
60	A7	6p org & grn, II, pair ('38)	29.00	3.00
		Never hinged	40.00	
a.		Single, English	1.50	.25
b.		Single, Afrikaans	1.50	.25
61	A7	6p red org & bl grn, III ('50), pair	2.50	1.00
		Never hinged	3.75	
a.		Single, English	.25	.25
b.		Single, Afrikaans	.25	.25
c.		6p org & grn, III, pair ('46)	14.50	1.90
		Never hinged	20.00	
d.		As "c," single, English	1.00	.25
e.		As "c," single, Afrikaans	1.00	.25
62	A11	1sh chlky bl & lt brn ('50), pair	9.00	10.00
		Never hinged	10.00	
a.		As "f," single, English	.55	.25
b.		As "f," single, Afrikaans	.55	.25
c.		1sh lt bl & ol brn, pair ('39)	40.00	15.00
		Never hinged	50.00	
d.		As "c," single, English	1.00	.25
e.		As "c," single, Afrikaans	1.00	.25
f.		1sh vio bl & brnsh blk, pair	16.00	15.00
		Never hinged	18.00	
g.		Single, English	.50	.30
h.		Single, Afrikaans	.50	.30
63	A12	2sh6p brn & brt grn, pair ('49)	7.50	30.00
		Never hinged	10.00	
a.		Single, English	1.25	1.00
b.		Single, Afrikaans	1.25	1.00
64	A13	5sh grn & blk, I, pair	45.00	75.00
		Never hinged	55.00	
a.		Single, English	2.50	2.00
b.		Single, Afrikaans	2.50	2.00
65	A13	5sh bl grn & blk, I, pair ('49)	42.50	75.00
		Never hinged	45.00	
a.		Single, English	4.00	3.50
b.		Single, Afrikaans	4.00	3.50
66	A13	5sh dp yel grn & blk, II, pair ('54)	40.00	95.00
		Never hinged	50.00	
a.		Single, English	4.00	4.00
b.		Single, Afrikaans	4.00	4.00
67	A18	10sh ol blk & bl, pair ('39)	50.00	17.50
		Never hinged	65.00	
a.		Single, English	3.00	1.00
b.		Single, Afrikaans	3.00	1.00
		Nos. 45-67 (23)	422.50	509.70

See Nos. 98-99. For overprints see Nos. O26-O27, O29, O36-O38, O40, O46-O47, O54.

George V and Springboks — A19

1935, May 1   Wmk. 201   Perf. 15x14

68	A19	½p Prus grn & blk, pair	5.00	12.00
		Never hinged	9.00	
a.		Single, English top	.25	.25
b.		Single, Afrikaans top	.25	.25
69	A19	1p car rose & blk, pair	5.00	10.00
		Never hinged	9.00	
a.		Single, English top	.25	.25
b.		Single, Afrikaans top	.25	.25
70	A19	3p bl & dk bl, pair	17.50	55.00
		Never hinged	40.00	
a.		Single, English top	1.40	2.75
b.		Single, Afrikaans top	1.40	2.75
71	A19	6p org & grn, pair	35.00	90.00
		Never hinged	75.00	
a.		Single, English top	2.10	3.25
b.		Single, Afrikaans top	2.10	3.25
		Nos. 68-71 (4)	62.50	167.00
		Set, never hinged	105.00	

25th anniv. of the reign of George V.

English and Afrikaans inscriptions are transposed on alternate stamps. On the ½p, 3p and 6p with "SOUTH AFRICA" at top, "SILWER JUBILEUM" is at left of medallion, but on 1p with English at top, it is at the right.

Johannesburg International Philatelic Exhibition Issue
Souvenir Sheets

A20

A21

Black Overprint, "JIPEX 1936"

1936, Nov. 2   Perf. 15x14

72	A20	Sheet of 6 (½p)	6.00	9.50
		Never hinged	10.00	
73	A21	Sheet of 6 (1p)	5.75	6.50
		Never hinged	11.00	
		Set, never hinged	25.00	

Sheets made by overprinting booklet panes Nos. 45c and 48j. Sheets exist with and without horizontal perforations through right margin. Sheet size: 81x72.

> **Catalogue values for unused stamps in this section, from this point to the end of the section, are for Never Hinged items.**

George VI — A22

"KRONING SUID-AFRIKA" on alternate stamps.

1937, May 12   Perf. 14

74	A22	½p grn & ol blk, pair	.80	1.25
a.		Single, English	.25	.25
b.		Single, Afrikaans	.25	.25
75	A22	1p car & ol blk, pair	.85	1.00
a.		Single, English	.25	.25
b.		Single, Afrikaans	.25	.25
76	A22	1½p Prus grn & org, pair	.85	.80
a.		Single, English	.25	.25
b.		Single, Afrikaans	.25	.25
77	A22	3p bl & ultra, pair	1.75	3.00
a.		Single, English	.25	.25
b.		Single, Afrikaans	.25	.25
78	A22	1sh Prus bl & org brn, pair	5.00	5.00
a.		Single, English	.50	.25
b.		Single, Afrikaans	.50	.25
		Nos. 74-78 (5)	9.25	11.05

Coronation of George VI and Queen Elizabeth.

Wagon Wheel — A23

Voortrekker Family — A24

Alternate stamps inscribed "SOUTH AFRICA," "SUID-AFRIKA."

1938, Dec. 14   Perf. 15x14

79	A23	1p rose & slate, pair	7.00	5.50
a.		Single, English	.30	.30
b.		Single, Afrikaans	.30	.30
80	A24	1½p red brn & Prus bl, pair	8.00	6.50
a.		Single, English	.30	.35
b.		Single, Afrikaans	.30	.35

Issued to commemorate the Voortrekkers.

Infantry A25

Nurse and Ambulance A26

Airman and Spitfires (Flight Lt. Robert Kershaw) A27

Sailor A28

Women's Services A29

Artillery — A30

Welder — A31

Tank Corps A32

Signal Corps — A33

Bilingual inscriptions on 2p and 1sh.

Perf. 14 (2p, 4p, 6p), 15x14

1941-43   Photo.   Wmk. 201

81	A25	½p dp bl grn, pair	1.50	3.25
a.		Single, English	.25	.25
b.		Single, Afrikaans	.25	.25
82	A26	1p brt rose, pair	2.00	3.25
a.		Single, English	.25	.25
b.		Single, Afrikaans	.25	.25
83	A27	1½p Prus grn, pair ('42)	1.50	3.00
a.		Single, English	.25	.25
b.		Single, Afrikaans	.25	.25
84	A28	2p dk violet	1.00	.75
85	A29	3p dp blue, pair	22.50	40.00
a.		Single, English	1.00	.75
b.		Single, Afrikaans	1.00	.75
86	A30	4p org brn, pair	22.50	25.00
a.		Single, English	1.00	.25
b.		Single, Afrikaans	1.00	.25
c.		4p red brown, pair	35.00	37.50
d.		As "c," single, English	1.50	1.25
e.		As "c," single, Afrikaans	1.50	1.25
87	A31	6p brt red org, pair	11.75	14.00
a.		Single, English	.50	.25
b.		Single, Afrikaans	.50	.25
88	A32	1sh dark brown	2.25	1.00
89	A33	1sh3p dk ol brn, pair ('43)	13.00	11.00
a.		Single, English	.50	.30
b.		Single, Afrikaans	.50	.30
c.		1sh3p dark brown, pair	6.00	8.00
d.		As "c," single, English	.50	.30
e.		As "c," single, Afrikaans	.50	.30
		Nos. 81-89 (9)	78.00	101.25

Infantry A34

Nurse A35

Airman — A36

Sailor — A37

Women's Services — A38

Welder — A40

Artillery — A39

Tank Corps — A41

Bilingual inscriptions on 4p and 1sh.

Pairs: Perf. 14, Roul. 6½ btwn.
Strips of 3: Perf. 15x14, Roul. 6½ btwn.

1942-43			**Photo.**	**Wmk. 201**	
90	A34	½p Horiz. strip of 3		2.00	1.50
a.		Single, English		.25	.25
b.		Single, Afrikaans		.25	.25
c.		As #90, imperf. between		900.00	650.00
91	A35	1p Horiz. strip of 3 ('43)		1.50	1.50
a.		Single, English		.25	.25
b.		Single, Afrikaans		.25	.25
c.		As #91, imperf. between		725.00	725.00
92	A36	1½p Horiz. pair		.70	2.50
a.		Single, English		.25	.25
b.		Single, Afrikaans		.25	.25
c.		As #92, roul. 13		4.50	4.50
d.		As #92, imperf. btwn.		350.00	375.00
93	A37	2p Horiz. pair ('43)		1.00	2.50
a.		Single, English		.25	.25
b.		Single, Afrikaans		.25	.25
c.		As #93, imperf. btwn.		800.00	675.00
94	A38	3p Vert strip of 3		7.00	18.00
a.		Single, English		.25	.25
b.		Single, Afrikaans		.25	.25
95	A39	4p Vert. strip of 3		18.00	11.00
a.		Single		.25	.25
96	A40	6p Horiz. pair		3.00	2.75
a.		Single, English		.25	.25
b.		Single, Afrikaans		.25	.25
97	A41	1sh Vert. pair		15.00	4.00
a.		Single		.25	.25
		Nos. 90-97 (8)		48.20	43.75

Because of the rouletting these are collected as pairs or strips of three, even on the bilingual stamps.

Types of 1926 Redrawn "SUID-AFRIKA" Hyphenated Coil Stamps

1943			**Photo.**	**Perf. 15x14**	
98	A5	½p myrtle grn, vert. pair		3.00	5.00
a.		Single, English		.25	.25
b.		Single, Afrikaans		.25	.25
99	A6	1p rose pink, vert. pair		3.50	4.00
a.		Single, English		.25	.25
b.		Single, Afrikaans		.25	.25

"Victory" — A42

"Peace" — A43

Design: 3p, Profiles of couple ("Hope").

1945, Dec. 3			**Photo.**	**Perf. 14**	
100	A42	1p rose pink & choc, pair		.35	1.25
a.		Single, English		.25	.25
b.		Single, Afrikaans		.25	.25
101	A43	2p vio & sl bl, pair		.35	1.25
a.		Single, English		.25	.25
b.		Single, Afrikaans		.25	.25
102	A43	3p ultra & dp ultra, pair		.50	1.50
a.		Single, English		.25	.25
b.		Single, Afrikaans		.25	.25
		Nos. 100-102 (3)		1.20	4.00

World War II victory of the Allies.

George VI — A44

King George VI and Queen Elizabeth A45

Princesses Margaret Rose and Elizabeth A46

Perf. 15x14			
1947, Feb. 17			**Wmk. 201**
103	A44	1p cer & gray, pair	.30 .40
a.	Single, English		.25 .25
b.	Single, Afrikaans		.25 .25
104	A45	2p purple, pair	.30 .60
a.	Single, English		.25 .25
b.	Single, Afrikaans		.25 .25
105	A46	3p dk blue, pair	.40 .75
a.	Single, English		.25 .25
b.	Single, Afrikaans		.25 .25
		Nos. 103-105 (3)	1.00 1.75

Visit of the British Royal Family, Mar.-Apr., 1947.

George VI, Elizabeth — A47

1948, Apr. 26		**Photo.**	**Perf. 14**
106	A47	3p dp chlky bl & sil, pair	.70 1.25
a.	Single, English		.25 .25
b.	Single, Afrikaans		.25 .25

25th anniv. of the marriage of George VI and Queen Elizabeth.

Gold Mine — A48

Vertical Pairs Perf. 14 all around, Rouletted 6½ between

1948, Apr.			
107	A48	1½p sl & och, vert. pair	3.25 5.00
a.	Single, English		.25 .25
b.	Single, Afrikaans		.25 .25

"Wanderer" in Port Natal A49

1949, May 2		**Photo.**	**Perf. 15x14**
108	A49	1½p red brown, pair	.60 .60
a.	Single, English		.25 .25
b.	Single, Afrikaans		.25 .25

Mercury and Globe — A50

1949, Oct. 1			**Perf. 14x15**
109	A50	½p dk green, pair	.60 .60
a.	Single, English		.25 .25
b.	Single, Afrikaans		.25 .25
110	A50	1½p dk red, pair	.90 .90
a.	Single, English		.25 .25
b.	Single, Afrikaans		.25 .25
111	A50	3p ultra, pair	1.50 1.50
a.	Single, English		.25 .25
b.	Single, Afrikaans		.25 .25
		Nos. 109-111 (3)	3.00 3.00

75th anniv. of the UPU.

Except for Nos. 216, 310-313, 518a, 669a listed in Scott Standard catalogue, Vol. 6, this is the end of bi-lingual multiples in the postage section.

Voortrekkers en Route to Natal — A51

Voortrekker Monument, Pretoria A52

Voortrekkers Looking Toward Natal, and Open Bible — A53

1949, Dec. 1			**Perf. 15x14**
112	A51	1p magenta	.25 .25
113	A52	1½p dull green	.25 .25
114	A53	3p dark blue	.25 .25
		Nos. 112-114 (3)	.75 .75

Inauguration of the Voortrekker Monument at Pretoria.

Riebeeck's Seal and Dutch East India Company Monogram A54

Maria de la Quellerie — A55

2p, van Riebeeck's Ships. 4½p, Jan van Riebeeck. 1sh, Landing of van Riebeeck.

Perf. 15x14, 14x15			
1952, Mar. 14			**Wmk. 201**
115	A54	½p dk brn & red vio	.25 .25
116	A55	1p dark green	.25 .25
117	A54	2p dark purple	.25 .25
118	A55	4½p dark blue	.25 .25
119	A54	1sh brown	.55 .50
		Nos. 115-119 (5)	1.55 1.50

300th anniv. of the landing of Jan van Riebeeck at the Cape of Good Hope.

Nos. 116-117 Overprinted "SATISE" (1p) and "SADIPU" (2p)

1952, Mar. 26			
120	A55	1p dark green	.30 .55
121	A54	2p dark purple	.35 .70

South African Tercentenary Intl. Stamp Exhib., Cape Town, Mar. 26-Apr. 5, 1952.

SEMI-POSTAL STAMPS

Catalogue values for unused stamps in this section are for Never Hinged items.

English-Afrikaans Se-Tenant Stamps with English inscriptions and with Afrikaans inscriptions of Nos. B1-B11 were printed alternately in the same sheets. Major-number listings and values are for pairs consisting of one English and one Afrikaans-inscribed stamp.

Church of the Vow — SP1

Cradock's Pass — SP2

Voortrekker — SP3

Voortrekker Woman — SP4

1933-36		**Photo.**	**Wmk. 201**	**Perf. 14**
B1	SP1	½p + ½p grn & blk, pair ('36)	11.00	5.50
a.		Single, English	.55	.55
b.		Single, Afrikaans	.55	.55
B2	SP2	1p + ½p rose & blk, pair	7.25	3.75
a.		Single, English	.45	.45
b.		Single, Afrikaans	.45	.35
B3	SP3	2p + 1p dull vio & gray, pair	12.00	6.00
a.		Single, English	.55	.55
b.		Single, Afrikaans	.55	.60
B4	SP4	3p + 1½p dp blue & gray, pair	18.00	9.50
a.		Single, English	1.50	1.10
b.		Single, Afrikaans	1.50	1.10
		Nos. B1-B4 (4)	48.25	24.75

Issued to commemorate the Voortrekkers. Surtax went to the National Memorial Fund for a national Voortrekker monument.

Voortrekker Plowing — SP5

Crossing the Drakensberg — SP6

Signing Dingaan-Retief Treaty — SP7

Proposed Monument — SP8

1938, Dec. 14			**Perf. 14**
B5	SP5	½p + ½p dl grn & ind, pair	7.00 6.75
a.		Single, English	1.00 .60
b.		Single, Afrikaans	1.00 .60
B6	SP6	1p + 1p rose & sl, pair	17.00 7.75
a.		Single, English	1.00 .70
b.		Single, Afrikaans	1.00 .70
		Perf. 15x14	
B7	SP7	1½p + ½p Prus grn & choc, pair	22.50 13.50
a.		Single, English	1.40 1.40
b.		Single, Afrikaans	1.40 1.40

B8	SP8	3p + 3p chlky bl,		
		pair	26.00	16.00
a.		Single, English	1.75	2.00
b.		Single, Afrikaans	1.75	2.00
		Nos. B5-B8 (4)	72.50	44.00

Voortrekker centenary. Surtax went to the Natl Memorial Fund for a Voortrekker monument.

"The Old Vicarage," Huguenot Museum — SP9

Rising Sun and Cross — SP10

Huguenot Dwelling, Drakenstein Mountain Valley — SP11

1939, July 17   Photo.   Perf. 14

B9	SP9	½p + ½p Prus grn & gray brn, pair	11.00	8.00
a.		Single, English	1.00	.85
b.		Single, Afrikaans	1.00	.85
B10	SP10	1p + 1p rose car & Prus grn, pair	13.00	10.00
a.		Single, English	1.00	1.00
b.		Single, Afrikaans	1.00	1.00

Perf. 15x14

B11	SP11	1½p + 1½p, pair	27.50	15.00
a.		Single, English	1.60	1.60
b.		Single, Afrikaans	1.60	1.60
		Nos. B9-B11 (3)	51.50	33.00

250th anniv. of the landing of the Huguenots in South Africa. Surtax went to a fund to build a Huguenot memorial at Paarl.

AIR POST STAMPS

Mail Plane — AP1

Biplane in Flight — AP2

Unwmk.

1925, Feb. 26   Litho.   Perf. 12

C1	AP1	1p red	4.50	10.00
C2	AP1	3p ultramarine	10.00	13.00
C3	AP1	6p violet	17.50	24.00
C4	AP1	9p gray green	29.00	32.50
		Nos. C1-C4 (4)	61.00	79.50
		Set, never hinged	150.00	

Forgeries exist.

1929, Aug. 16   Typo.   Perf. 14x13½

C5	AP2	4p blue green	8.50	2.75
C6	AP2	1sh orange	27.50	21.00
		Set, never hinged	75.00	

POSTAGE DUE STAMPS

On cover values are for properly franked commercial covers. Philatelic usages also exist and sell for less.

D1

Wmk. Springbok's Head (177)

1914-15   Typo.   Perf. 14

J1	D1	½p green & blk	2.50	4.25
		On cover		70.00
J2	D1	1p red & blk	2.50	.25
		On cover		20.00
J3	D1	2p vio & blk ('14)	7.50	.80
		On cover		20.00
J4	D1	3p ultra & blk	2.50	.80
		On cover		35.00
J5	D1	5p brown & blk	4.50	30.00
		On cover		600.00
J6	D1	6p gray & blk	11.00	30.00
		On cover		650.00
J7	D1	1sh black & red	77.50	160.00
		On cover		2,000.
		Nos. J1-J7 (7)	108.00	226.10

1922   Unwmk.   Litho.   Rouletted 7-8

J8	D1	½p blue grn & blk	1.60	15.00
		On cover		60.00
J9	D1	1p dull red & blk	1.75	1.25
		On cover		30.00
J10	D1	1½p yellow brn & blk	2.00	2.40
		On cover		40.00
		Nos. J8-J10 (3)	5.35	18.65

1922-26   Perf. 14

J11	D1	½p blue grn & blk	.85	1.75
		On cover		20.00
J12	D1	1p rose & blk ('23)	.90	.25
		On cover		15.00
J13	D1	1½p yel brn & blk ('24)	1.60	1.25
		On cover		40.00
J14	D1	2p vio & blk ('23)	1.40	.80
		On cover		20.00
a.		Imperf. pair	300.00	400.00
J15	D1	3p blue & blk ('26)	8.00	22.50
		On cover		35.00
J16	D1	6p gray & blue ('23)	16.00	8.00
		On cover		20.00
		Nos. J11-J16 (6)	28.75	34.55

D2

1927-28   Typo.

J17	D2	½p blue green & blk	1.00	3.50
		On cover		20.00
J18	D2	1p rose & black	1.40	.80
		On cover		15.00
J19	D2	2p violet & black	1.40	1.25
		On cover		20.00
J20	D2	3p ultra & black	13.00	25.00
		On cover		35.00
J21	D2	6p gray & black	24.00	20.00
		On cover		90.00
		Nos. J17-J21 (5)	40.80	50.55

Type of 1927-28 Redrawn

Perf. 15x14

1932-40   Photo.   Wmk. 201

J22	D2	½p blue grn & blk ('34)	2.75	1.75
		On cover		20.00
J23	D2	1p rose car & blk ('34)	2.50	.95
		On cover		15.00
J24	D2	2p blk violet & blk	15.00	2.50
		On cover		15.00
a.		2p dark purple & black ('40)	32.50	.25
J25	D2	3p dp blue & blk	27.50	14.00
		On cover		100.00
J26	D2	3p ultra & dk bl ('35)	8.00	.40
		On cover		20.00
J27	D2	3p blue & dk bl ('40)	85.00	3.50
		On cover		50.00
J28	D2	6p brn org & grn ('33)	25.00	6.00
		On cover		70.00
J29	D2	6p brn org & grn ('38)	15.00	3.50
		On cover		70.00
		Nos. J22-J29 (8)	180.75	32.60

The ½p No. J22 photogravure has larger but thinner numeral and the "d" is taller and thinner than on No. J17.

The 1p No. J23 photogravure has numeral with parallel sides. The "d" is taller and thicker than on No. J18.

On Nos. J25 and J27 the numeral is followed by a large "d" with thick lines and a large round period below it.

Nos. J22, J24 and J25 have frame in photogravure, value typographed.

> **Catalogue values for unused stamps in this section, from this point to the end of the section, are for Never Hinged items.**

See "English-Afrikaans Se-tenant" note preceding No. 23.

D3

Horiz. strips of Three, Perf. 15x14 All Around, Rouletted 6½ Between

1943-44   Photo.   Wmk. 201

J30	D3	½p Prus green ('44)	15.00	50.00
		On cover		400.00
a.		Single	.25	.25
J31	D3	1p brt carmine	11.00	5.50
		On cover		400.00
a.		Single	.25	.25
J32	D3	2p dark purple	9.00	12.00
		On cover		650.00
a.		Single	.25	.25
J33	D3	3p dark blue	55.00	85.00
		On cover		800.00
a.		Single	.25	1.25
		Nos. J30-J33 (4)	90.00	152.50

Catalogued as strips of 3 because of the perforations.

Type of 1932-38 Redrawn
Thick Numerals, Capital "D"

1948-49   Perf. 15x14

J34	D2	½p blue green & blk	9.00	13.50
		On cover		40.00
J35	D2	1p deep rose & blk	16.00	6.00
		On cover		30.00
J36	D2	2p dk pur & blk ('49)	17.50	9.00
		On cover		30.00
J37	D2	3p ultra & dk blue	16.00	17.50
		On cover		60.00
J38	D2	6p dp org & grn ('49)	37.50	8.00
		On cover		80.00
		Nos. J34-J38 (5)	96.00	54.00

Redrawn Type of 1948-49
Hyphen between Suid-Afrika

1950-58   Perf. 15x14

J40	D2	1p car rose & blk	1.25	.45
		On cover		20.00
J41	D2	2p dk pur & blk ('51)	.85	.30
		On cover		15.00
J42	D2	3p ultra & dk blue	6.25	2.50
		On cover		25.00
J43	D2	4p emer & dk grn ('58)	14.50	15.00
		On cover		60.00
J44	D2	6p dp org & grn ('52)	11.50	11.50
		On cover		60.00
J45	D2	1sh brn red & dk brn ('58)	17.50	16.00
		On cover		100.00
		Nos. J40-J45 (6)	51.85	45.75

OFFICIAL STAMPS

Type A2 stamps have very small margins at top and bottom. Values are for examples with perfs close to, or touching the frame.

No. 5 Overprinted in Black, Periods in Overprint

1926   Wmk. 177   Perf. 14

O1	A2	2p dull violet	22.50	2.00

See "English-Afrikaans Se-tenant" note preceding No. 23.

On Nos. 23-25
Perf. 14½x14
Wmk. 201

O2	A5	½p dk grn & blk, pair	8.00	18.00
a.		Single, English	.75	1.50
b.		Single, Afrikaans	.75	1.50
O3	A6	1p car & blk, pair	4.00	8.50
a.		Single, English	.25	.50
b.		Single, Afrikaans	.25	.50
O4	A7	6p org & grn, pair	550.00	80.00
a.		Single, English	25.00	11.00
b.		Single, Afrikaans	25.00	11.00

Nos. 26 and 25 Overprinted, No Periods in Overprint — b

(Reading Up)

1928-29   Perf. 14, 14½x14
Space between words 19mm

O5	A8	2p vio brn & gray, pair ('29)	7.50	20.00
a.		Single, English	.50	1.50
b.		Single, Afrikaans	.50	1.50
c.		Space 17½mm, pair	6.00	24.00
d.		As "c," single, English	.50	2.00
e.		As "c," single, Afrikaans	.50	2.00

Space between words 11½mm

O6	A7	6p org & grn, pair	22.50	47.50
a.		Single, English	2.75	2.75
b.		Single, Afrikaans	2.75	2.75

#23-25 Ovptd. type "b" Reading Down
Space between words 13½-14mm

1929   Perf. 14½x14

O7	A5	½p grn & blk, pair	2.50	4.75
a.		Single, English	.25	.35
b.		Single, Afrikaans	.25	.35
c.		Period after "OFFISIEEL" on English stamp	5.00	5.00
d.		Pair, "c" + normal ½p	45.00	45.00
e.		Period after "OFFISIEEL." on Afrikaans stamp	5.00	5.00
f.		Pair, "e" + normal 1sh	55.00	65.00
O8	A6	1p car & blk, pair	3.00	6.00
a.		Single, English	.30	.50
b.		Single, Afrikaans	.30	.50
O9	A7	6p org & grn, pair	8.00	40.00
a.		Single, English	1.25	3.50
b.		Single, Afrikaans	1.25	3.50
c.		Period after "OFFISIEEL" on English stamp	10.00	10.00
d.		Pair, "c" + normal 6p	75.00	150.00
e.		Period after "OFFISIEEL." on Afrikaans stamp	12.00	12.00
f.		Pair, "e" + normal 6p	90.00	160.00
		Nos. O7-O9 (3)	13.50	50.75

#29-30 Ovptd. type "b" Reading Down
Space between words 17½-19mm

1931   Engr.   Perf. 14, 14x13½

O10	A11	1sh dp bl & bis brn, pair	40.00	90.00
a.		Single, English	3.00	10.00
b.		Single, Afrikaans	3.00	10.00
c.		Period after "OFFICIAL." on Afrikaans stamp	50.00	50.00
d.		Pair, "c" + normal 1sh	115.00	240.00
O11	A12	2sh6p brn & bl grn, pair	65.00	150.00
a.		Single, English	10.00	19.00
b.		Single, Afrikaans	10.00	19.00
c.		Period after "OFFICIAL." on Afrikaans stamp	72.50	100.00
d.		Pair, "c" + normal 2sh6p	300.00	550.00

Regular Issues of 1930-45 Overprinted type "b" Reading Down ("SUIDAFRIKA" on Afrikaans stamps)

Perf. 15x14 (½p, 1p, 6p), 14

1930-47   Photo.   Wmk. 201
Space between words 9½-12mm
(Various spacings occur in same setting)

O12	A5	½p bl grn & blk (#33), pair ('31)	2.25	5.00
a.		Single, English	.25	.40
b.		Single, Afrikaans	.25	.40
c.		Period after "OFFISIEEL." on English stamp	5.00	5.00
d.		Pair, "c" + normal ½p	37.50	60.00
e.		Period after "OFFISIEEL." on Afrikaans stamp	5.00	5.00
f.		Pair, "e" + normal ½p	27.50	50.00

Space between words 12½-13½mm

O13	A5	½p bl grn & blk, pair (#33)	3.00	4.00
a.		Single, English	.25	.50
b.		Single, Afrikaans	.25	.50
O14	A6	1p car & blk, pair (#34)	6.00	6.00
a.		Single, English	.50	.60
b.		Single, Afrikaans	.50	.60
c.		Period after "OFFISIEEL." on English stamp	5.00	5.00
d.		Pair, "c" + normal 1p	50.00	75.00

e.	Period after "OFFISIEEL."			
	on Afrikaans stamp	5.00	5.00	
f.	Pair, "e" + normal 1p	35.00	55.00	
O15	A6	1p rose & blk,		
		pair (#35)		
		('33)	15.00	9.00
a.	Single, English	1.00	1.00	
b.	Single, Afrikaans	1.00	1.00	
c.	Double ovpt., pair	275.00	400.00	
d.	As "c," English	—	—	
e.	As "c," Afrikaans			

Space between words 20½-22mm

O16	A8	2p vio & gray,		
		pair (#36)		
		('31)	8.00	11.00
a.	Single, English	.80	1.50	
b.	Single, Afrikaans	.80	1.50	
O17	A8	2p vio & ind,		
		pair (#37)	150.00	100.00
a.	Single, English	10.00	10.00	
b.	Single, Afrikaans	10.00	10.00	

Space between words 12½-13½mm

O18	A7	6p org & grn,		
		pair (#42)	8.50	8.50
a.	Single, English	.75	1.00	
b.	Single, Afrikaans	.75	1.00	
c.	Period after "OFFISIEEL."			
	on English stamp	7.00	7.00	
d.	Pair, "c" + normal 6p	90.00	100.00	
e.	Period after "OFFISIEEL."			
	on Afrikaans stamp	5.50	5.50	
f.	Pair, "e" + normal 6p	75.00	90.00	

Space between words 21mm

O19	A11	1sh dp bl & brn,		
		pair (#43c)		
		('32)	60.00	90.00
a.	Single, Afrikaans	7.50	7.50	
c.	1sh dk bl & yel brn (#43),			
	19mm, pair	50.00	90.00	
d.	As "c," single, English	8.50	7.50	
e.	As "c," single, Afrikaans	8.50	7.50	
f.	As "c," spaced 21mm, pair	42.50	65.00	
g.	As "f," single, English	6.00	7.50	
h.	As "f," single, Afrikaans	6.00	7.50	

Space between words 17½-18½mm

O20	A12	2sh6p brn & sl grn		
		(#44c)		
		('37), pair	80.00	140.00
a.	Single, English	15.00	15.00	
b.	Single, Afrikaans	15.00	15.00	
c.	Spaced 21mm, pair	75.00	75.00	
d.	As "c," single, English	4.50	8.00	
e.	As "c," single, Afrikaans	4.50	8.00	
f.	2sh6p red brn & grn, pair			
	(#44i) ('33)	50.00	90.00	
g.	As "f," single, English	5.00	8.50	
h.	As "f," single, Afrikaans	5.00	8.50	
j.	2sh6p brn & bl, 19-20mm			
	(#44) ('47), pair	30.00	60.00	
k.	As "j," single, English	3.00	5.00	
m.	As "j," single, Afrikaans	3.00	5.00	
	Nos. O12-O20 (9)	*332.75*	*373.50*	

> **Catalogue values for unused stamps in this section, from this point to the end of the section, are for Never Hinged items.**

Regular Issue of 1933-54
Overprinted type "b" Reading Down
("SUID-AFRIKA" Hyphenated)
1935-50   Photo.   Perf. 15x14, 14
Space between words given with each listing

O21	A5	½p grn & gray (#45),		
		12½-13mm, pair		
		('36)	7.00	30.00
a.	Single, English	.25	1.75	
b.	Single, Afrikaans	.25	1.75	
O22	A5	½p grn & gray, (#46),		
		11½-13mm, pair		
		('38)	12.00	12.50
a.	Single, English	.50	1.25	
b.	Single, Afrikaans	.50	1.25	
O23	A5	½p grn & gray (#47),		
		11½mm, pair		
		('48)	1.25	5.00
a.	Single, English	.25	.70	
b.	Single, Afrikaans	.25	.70	
O24	A6	1p car & gray (#48),		
		11-13mm, pair	4.00	3.00
a.	Single, English	.25	.25	
b.	Single, Afrikaans	.25	.25	
O25	A6	1p rose car & gray		
		blk (#49), 11½-		
		12mm, pair ('41)	1.00	.50
a.	Single, English	.25	.25	
b.	Single, Afrikaans	.25	.25	
O26	A15	1½p dk grn &		
		gold (#51),		
		19-21mm,		
		pair ('37)	30.00	25.00
a.	Single, English	2.25	1.75	
b.	Single, Afrikaans	2.25	1.75	
O27	A15	1½p sl grn &		
		ocher		
		(#52),		
		16mm, pair		
		('44)	50.00	11.50
a.	Single, English	1.25	1.25	
b.	Single, Afrikaans	1.25	1.25	
c.	Ovpt. spaced 14-14½mm,			
	pair	3.00	10.00	
d.	As "c," single, English	.25	.80	
e.	As "c," single, Afrikaans	.25	.80	
O28	A8	2p bl vio & dl bl		
		(#53), 20-		
		21mm, pair		
		('39)	150.00	40.00
a.	Single, English	7.50	2.50	
b.	Single, Afrikaans	7.50	2.50	

O29	A16	2p pur & sl		
		(#55), 19-		
		21mm, pair		
		('48)	5.75	25.00
a.	Single, English	.25	2.00	
b.	Single, Afrikaans	.25	2.00	
O30	A7	6p org & bl grn,		
		I (#59), 12-		
		13mm, pair		
		('38)	80.00	45.00
a.	Single, English	6.50	3.75	
b.	Single, Afrikaans	6.50	3.75	
O31	A7	6p org & grn, II		
		(#60), 12-		
		13mm, pair		
		('39)	14.00	10.00
a.	Single, English	1.25	1.25	
b.	Single, Afrikaans	1.25	1.25	
O32	A7	6p org & grn III		
		(#61), 11½-		
		12mm, pair		
		('47)	5.00	11.00
a.	Single, English	.85	1.25	
b.	Single, Afrikaans	.85	1.25	
O33	A11	1sh lt bl & ol brn		
		(#62c), 19-		
		21mm, pair		
		('40)	80.00	50.00
a.	Single, English	4.50	2.50	
b.	Single, Afrikaans	4.50	2.50	
c.	"OFFICIAL" on both sides	3,000.		
d.	"OFFISIEEL" on both sides	3,000.		
e.	1sh chlky bl & lt brn (#62)			
	('50), pair	11.00	30.00	
f.	As "e," single, English	2.00	2.50	
g.	As "e," single, Afrikaans	2.00	2.50	
h.	1sh vio bl & brnsh blk			
	(#62f), 18-19mm, pair	65.00	27.50	
j.	As "h," single, English	4.50	2.00	
k.	As "h," single, Afrikaans	4.50	2.00	
O34	A13	5sh grn & blk		
		(#64) 19-		
		20mm, pair	65.00	160.00
a.	Single, English	3.50	13.50	
b.	Single, Afrikaans	3.50	13.50	
O35	A13	5sh bl grn & blk		
		(#65),		
		20mm, pair	40.00	110.00
a.	Single, English	3.50	12.50	
b.	Single, Afrikaans	3.50	12.50	
O36	A18	10sh ol blk & bl		
		(#67), 19½-		
		20mm, pair		
		('48)	100.00	275.00
a.	Single, English	10.00	24.00	
b.	Single, Afrikaans	10.00	24.00	
	Nos. O21-O36 (16)	*645.00*	*813.50*	

Nos. 52 and 56 Overprinted type "b"
Space between words 16mm
1949-50   Size: 22x18mm   Perf. 14

O37	A15	1½p sl grn &		
		ocher, pair	85.00	85.00
a.	Single, English	5.00	4.00	
b.	Single, Afrikaans	5.00	4.00	

Size: 21½x17½mm

O38	A16	2p pur & sl bl,		
		pair ('50)	3,250.	3,750.
a.	Single, English	200.	275.	
b.	Single, Afrikaans	200.	275.	

Nos. 64, 67 Overprinted

c

Space between words 18-19mm
1940   Perf. 14

O39	A13	5sh grn & blk,		
		pair	125.00	140.00
a.	Single, English	12.00	12.50	
b.	Single, Afrikaans	12.00	12.50	
O40	A18	10sh ol brn & bl,		
		pair	500.00	525.00
a.	Single, English	32.50	37.50	
b.	Single, Afrikaans	32.50	37.50	

No. 54 Overprinted type "c"
Reading Up
Space between words 19mm
1945   Perf. 14

O41	A8	2p dl vio & gray, pair	11.00	32.50
a.	Single, English	1.00	2.25	
b.	Single, Afrikaans	1.00	2.25	

No. 47 Overprinted

1947   Perf. 15x14

O42	A5	½p grn & gray, pair	22.50	20.00
a.	Single, English	1.00	2.00	
b.	Single, Afrikaans	1.00	2.00	

Stamps of 1937-54 Overprinted

1950-54   Perf. 15x14, 14
Space between words 10mm

O43	A5	½p grn & gray,		
		pair (#47)	.90	1.50
a.	Single, English	.25	.25	
b.	Single, Afrikaans	.25	.25	
O44	A6	1p rose car &		
		gray blk,		
		pair (#49)	1.00	6.00
a.	Single, English	.25	.25	
b.	Single, Afrikaans	.25	.25	
O45	A6	1p car & blk,		
		pair (#50)	1.00	3.50
a.	Single, English	.25	.25	
b.	Single, Afrikaans	.25	.25	

Space between words 14½mm

O46	A15	1½p sl grn &		
		ocher, pair		
		(#52)	2.00	5.00
a.	Single, English	.25	.35	
b.	Single, Afrikaans	.25	.35	
O47	A16	2p pur & sl bl,		
		pair (#56)	1.00	2.00
a.	Single, English	.25	.25	
b.	Single, Afrikaans	.25	.25	
c.	Ovpt. reading up, pair			

Space between words 10mm

O48	A7	6p red org & bl		
		grn, III,		
		pair (#61c)	2.00	4.00
a.	Single, English	.35	.35	
b.	Single, Afrikaans	.35	.35	

Space between words 19mm

O49	A11	1sh chlky bl & lt		
		brn, pair		
		(#62)	6.75	18.00
a.	Single, English	.50	2.00	
b.	Single, Afrikaans	.50	2.00	
c.	1sh vio bl & brnsh blk			
	(#62f), pair	175.00	200.00	
d.	As "c," single, English	12.50	17.50	
e.	As "c," single, Afrikaans	12.50	17.50	
O50	A12	2sh6p brn & brt		
		grn, pair		
		(#63)	10.00	37.50
a.	Single, English	1.00	3.50	
b.	Single, Afrikaans	1.00	3.50	
O51	A13	5sh bl grn & blk,		
		pair (#64)	190.00	125.00
a.	Single, English	10.00	10.00	
b.	Single, Afrikaans	10.00	10.00	
O52	A13	5sh pale bl grn		
		& blk, I,		
		pair (#65)	65.00	85.00
a.	Single, English	5.00	6.50	
b.	Single, Afrikaans	5.00	6.50	
O53	A13	5sh dp yel grn &		
		blk, II, pair		
		(#66)	80.00	100.00
a.	Single, English	8.00	9.00	
b.	Single, Afrikaans	8.00	9.00	
O54	A18	10sh ol blk & bl,		
		pair (#67)	80.00	250.00
a.	Single, English	9.00	22.50	
b.	Single, Afrikaans	9.00	22.50	
	Nos. O43-O54 (12)	*439.65*	*637.50*	

SOUTHERN NIGERIA

ˈsə-<u>th</u>ərn nī-ˈjir-ē-ə

LOCATION — In western Africa bordering on the Gulf of Guinea

GOVT. — British Crown Colony and Protectorate

AREA — 90,896 sq. mi.

POP. — 8,590,545

CAPITAL — Lagos

The Protectorate of Southern Nigeria, formed in 1900, absorbed in that year the Niger Coast Protectorate. In 1906 it united with Lagos and became the Colony and Protectorate of Southern Nigeria. An amalgamation was effected in 1914 between Northern and Southern Nigeria to form the Colony and Protectorate of Nigeria. See Nigeria, Northern Nigeria, Niger Coast Protectorate and Lagos.

12 Pence = 1 Shilling
20 Shillings = 1 Pound

Victoria — A1

Wmk. Crown and C A (2)

		Typo.		Perf. 14
1901, Mar.				
1	A1	½p yel grn & blk	2.00	2.75
a.	A1	½p yel grn & sepia ('02)	2.50	3.00
2	A1	1p car rose & blk	1.75	1.75
a.		1p carmine rose & sepia		
		('02)	3.00	2.00
3	A1	2p org brn & blk	3.75	5.00
4	A1	4p ol grn & blk	3.25	24.00
5	A1	6p red vio & blk	4.25	8.50
6	A1	1sh blk & gray		
		grn	9.75	30.00
7	A1	2sh6p brn & blk	57.50	92.50
8	A1	5sh yellow & blk	60.00	120.00
9	A1	10sh vio & blk, *yel*	130.00	250.00
		Nos. 1-9 (9)	*272.25*	*534.50*

Edward VII — A2

1903-04

10	A2	½p yel grn & blk	1.10	.35
11	A2	1p car rose &		
		blk	1.50	.80
12	A2	2p org brn &		
		blk	12.00	1.75
13	A2	2½p ultra & blk		
		('04)	2.25	1.00
14	A2	4p ol grn & blk	3.25	6.25
15	A2	6p red vio & blk	8.00	9.25
16	A2	1sh blk & gray		
		grn	40.00	22.50
17	A2	2sh6p brown & blk	40.00	75.00
18	A2	5sh yellow & blk	90.00	200.00
19	A2	10sh vio & blk, *yel*	45.00	140.00
20	A2	£1 pur & gray		
		grn	450.00	950.00
		Nos. 10-20 (11)	*693.10*	*1,406.*

1904-07		**Chalky Paper**	**Wmk. 3**	
21	A2	½p yel grn & blk	.75	.25
22	A2	1p carmine & blk	14.00	.50
23	A2	2p org brn & blk	3.00	.50
24	A2	2½p ultra & blk	1.25	1.10
24A	A2	3p vio & org brn		
		('07)	11.00	1.50
25	A2	4p ol grn & blk		
		('05)	16.00	29.00
26	A2	6p red vio & blk	14.50	5.00
27	A2	1sh blk & gray grn	3.75	4.00
28	A2	2sh6p brn & blk		
		('05)	27.50	21.00
29	A2	5sh yellow & blk	50.00	85.00
30	A2	10sh vio & blk, *yel*		
		('08)	160.00	210.00
31	A2	£1 pur & gray		
		grn ('05)	325.00	400.00
		Nos. 21-31 (12)	*626.75*	*757.60*

#23 and 24 are on ordinary paper, #24A and 25 on chalky, and the other values on both papers.

1907-10			**Ordinary Paper**	
32	A2	½p green ('08)	2.25	.25
33	A2	1p carmine	4.00	.70
34	A2	2p gray	3.00	.80
35	A2	2½p ultra	5.00	4.25

			Chalky Paper	
36	A2	3p violet, *yel*	2.25	.35
37	A2	4p scar & blk, *yel*	2.50	.90
38	A2	6p red vio & dl		
		vio	29.00	3.75
39	A2	1sh black & grn	8.00	.50
40	A2	2sh6p car & blk, *bl*	11.00	1.75
41	A2	5sh scar & grn,		
		yel	45.00	55.00
42	A2	10sh red & grn, *grn*	90.00	130.00
43	A2	£1 blk & vio, *red*	250.00	498.25
		Nos. 32-43 (12)	*452.00*	*498.25*

1910		**Ordinary Paper**	**Redrawn**	
44	A2	1p carmine	1.10	.25

In the redrawn stamp the "1" of "1d" is not as thick as in No. 33 but the "d" is taller and broader.

King George V — A3

1912

45	A3	½p green	3.00	.25
46	A3	1p carmine	3.00	.25
47	A3	2p gray	1.00	.95
48	A3	2½p ultra	4.50	3.25
49	A3	3p violet, *vel*	1.25	.35
50	A3	4p scar & blk, *yel*	1.60	2.40
51	A3	6p red vio & dl vio	3.00	1.50
52	A3	1sh black, *green*	3.50	1.00
53	A3	2sh6p red & blk, *bl*	10.00	42.50
54	A3	5sh red & blk, *yel*	26.00	87.50
55	A3	10sh red & grn, *grn*	60.00	110.00
56	A3	£1 blk & vio, *red*	225.00	275.00
		Nos. 45-56 (12)	341.85	524.95

Stamps of Southern Nigeria were replaced in 1914 by those of Nigeria.

SOUTHERN RHODESIA

ˈsə-<u>th</u>ərn rō-ˈdē-zhē̠-ə

LOCATION — Southeastern Africa between Northern Rhodesia and Mozambique
GOVT. — British Colony
AREA — 150,333 sq. mi.
POP. — 4,010,000 (est. 1963)
CAPITAL — Salisbury

Prior to 1923 this territory was administered by the British South Africa Company. The colony was created in that year by the British Government at the request of the inhabitants.

12 Pence = 1 Shilling
20 Shillings = 1 Pound

Catalogue values for unused stamps in this country are for Never Hinged items, beginning with Scott 56 in the regular postage section and Scott J1 in the postage due section.

King George V — A1

1924-30 Unwmk. Engr. Perf. 14

1	A1	½p dark green	5.00	.25
a.		Vert. pair, imperf. btwn.	1,100.	1,200.
b.		Horiz. pair, imperf. btwn.	1,100.	1,200.
c.		Horiz. pair, imperf. vert.	1,200.	
2	A1	1p scarlet	2.00	.25
a.		Horiz. pair, imperf. btwn.	900.00	1,000.
b.		Perf. 12½ (coil) ('30)	3.25	92.50
c.		Vert. pair, imperf. btwn.	1,600.	
d.		Vert. pair, imperf. horiz.	950.00	
3	A1	1½p bister brown	2.25	.90
a.		Horiz. pair, imperf. btwn.	12,000.	
b.		Vert. pair, imperf. btwn.	7,000.	
4	A1	2p vio blk & blk	4.50	1.50
a.		Horiz. pair, imperf. btwn.	14,000.	
5	A1	3p deep blue	3.50	4.00
6	A1	4p org red & blk	3.25	3.25
7	A1	6p lilac & blk	2.50	6.00
a.		Horiz. pair, imperf. btwn.	40,000.	
8	A1	8p gray grn & vio	12.50	50.00
9	A1	10p rose red & bl	17.00	57.50
10	A1	1sh turq bl & blk	7.00	9.00
11	A1	1sh6p yellow & blk	22.50	37.50
12	A1	2sh brown & blk	20.00	20.00
13	A1	2sh6p blk brn & bl	35.00	70.00
14	A1	5sh bl grn & bl	75.00	175.00
		Nos. 1-14 (14)	214.75	435.15

Values for imperf between pairs are for stamps from the same pane. Stamps separated by wide margins are cross-gutter pairs and sell for much lower prices.

George V Victoria Falls
A2 A3

1931-37 Perf. 11½, 14 (1p)

16	A2	½p dp green ('33)	1.00	.25
a.		Bklt. pane of 6 ('32)	150.00	
b.		Perf. 12	1.50	1.10
c.		Perf. 14 ('35)	1.90	.35

17	A2	1p scarlet ('35)	.60	.25
a.		Bklt. pane of 6 ('32)	150.00	
b.		Perf. 11½ ('33)	2.25	.25
c.		Perf. 12	1.10	.80
18	A2	1½p dp brown ('32)	3.00	.90
a.		Bklt. pane of 6 ('32)	600.00	
b.		Perf. 12 ('33)	62.50	47.50

Typo. Perf. 14½x14

19	A3	2p blk brn & blk	6.50	1.75
20	A3	3p dark blue	11.50	12.50

Perf. 12, 11½ (2sh6p)
Engr.

21	A2	4p org red & blk	1.50	1.75
a.		Perf. 14 ('37)	37.50	60.00
b.		Perf. 11½ ('35)	20.00	5.75
22	A2	6p rose lilac & blk	2.50	3.50
a.		Perf. 14 ('36)	8.00	1.00
b.		Perf. 11½ ('33)	17.50	1.75
23	A2	8p green & violet	2.00	3.75
a.		Perf. 14 ('34)	20.00	37.50
24	A2	9p gray grn & ver ('34)	7.25	10.50
25	A2	10p car & ultra	8.50	2.75
a.		Perf. 11½ ('33)	7.50	15.00
26	A2	1sh turq bl & blk	2.25	3.00
a.		Perf. 11½ ('36)	125.00	70.00
b.		Perf. 14 ('37)	250.00	160.00
27	A2	1sh6p ocher & blk	12.00	22.50
a.		Perf. 11½ ('36)	65.00	130.00
28	A2	2sh dk brn & blk	25.00	7.50
a.		Perf. 11½ ('33)	42.50	35.00
29	A2	2sh6p ol brn & ultra ('33)	45.00	35.00
a.		Perf. 12	40.00	42.50
30	A2	5sh brn & ultra	50.00	57.50
		Nos. 16-30 (15)	178.60	163.40

Victoria Falls — A4

1932, May Perf. 12½

31	A4	2p dark brn & grn	8.50	1.50
32	A4	3p dark blue	8.50	2.25
a.		Vert. pair, imperf. horiz.	11,000.	13,000.
b.		Vert. pair, imperf. btwn.	30,000.	
		Set, never hinged	22.50	

See Nos. 37-37A.

Silver Jubilee Issue

Victoria Falls and George V
A5

1935, May 6 Perf. 11x12

33	A5	1p car rose & olive	4.25	3.25
34	A5	2p blk brn & lt grn	7.50	8.50
35	A5	3p blue & violet	6.25	11.00
36	A5	6p dp violet & blk	11.00	22.50
		Nos. 33-36 (4)	29.00	45.25
		Set, never hinged	42.50	

25th anniv. of the reign of George V.

"Postage and Revenue"
A6

1935-41 Perf. 14

37	A6	2p dk brn & grn ('41)	2.50	.25
b.		Perf. 12½	6.50	16.00
		Never hinged	5.00	
37A	A6	3p deep blue ('38)	4.00	1.25
		Set, never hinged	17.00	

Queen Elizabeth, George VI — A7

King George VI — A8

1937, May 12 Perf. 12½

38	A7	1p carmine & gray grn	.45	1.00
39	A7	2p brown & green	.45	1.75
40	A7	3p lt blue & violet	2.00	9.50
41	A7	6p red violet & blk	1.10	4.00
		Nos. 38-41 (4)	4.00	16.25
		Set, never hinged	7.50	

Coronation of George VI & Elizabeth.

1937, Nov. 25 Perf. 14

42	A8	½p yellow green	.40	.25
43	A8	1p red	.40	.25
44	A8	1½p red brown	.75	.35
45	A8	4p orange red	1.00	.25
46	A8	6p dark gray	1.00	.60
47	A8	8p blue green	1.50	4.00
48	A8	9p blue	1.25	1.10
49	A8	10p violet	1.75	3.50
50	A8	1sh green & blk	1.50	.25
51	A8	1sh6p ocher & blk	9.50	3.00
52	A8	2sh brown & blk	16.00	.70
53	A8	2sh6p violet & blue	8.00	8.00
54	A8	5sh green & blue	15.00	3.50
		Nos. 42-54 (13)	58.05	25.75
		Set, never hinged	85.00	

Catalogue values for unused stamps in this section, from this point to the end of the section, are for Never Hinged items.

Seal of British South Africa Co. — A9

Fort Salisbury, 1890 — A10

Cecil John Rhodes — A11

Pioneer Fort and Mail Coach
A12

Rhodes Makes Peace, 1896 — A13

Victoria Falls Bridge — A14

Sir Charles Coghlan — A15

Queen Victoria, George VI, Lobengula's Kraal and Government House
A16

Unwmk.

1940, June 3 Engr. Perf. 14

56	A9	½p dp grn & dull vio	.25	.65
57	A10	1p red & vio blue	.25	.25
58	A11	1½p cop brn & blk	.25	.80
59	A12	2p pur & brt grn	.50	.40
60	A13	3p dk blue & blk	.80	1.00
61	A14	4p brn & bl grn	2.00	3.00
62	A15	6p sepia & dull grn	1.50	3.00
63	A16	1sh dk bl & brt grn	1.50	2.00
		Nos. 56-63 (8)	7.05	11.10

50th anniv. of the founding of Southern Rhodesia by Cecil John Rhodes.

Pioneer — A17

1943, Nov. 1 Photo. Wmk. 201

64	A17	2p Prus grn & choc	.35	.50

50th anniv. of Matabeleland under British control.

Princess Elizabeth and Princess Margaret Rose
A18

King George VI and Queen Elizabeth
A19

Unwmk.

1947, Apr. 1 Engr. Perf. 14

65	A18	½p dk green & blk	.30	.60
66	A19	1p carmine & blk	.30	.60

Visit of the British Royal Family, Apr., 1947.

Victory Issue

Queen Elizabeth George VI
A20 A21

Princess Elizabeth Princess Margaret Rose
A22 A23

1947, May 8

67	A20	1p deep carmine	.25	.25
68	A21	2p slate black	.25	.25
69	A22	3p deep blue	.60	.50
70	A23	6p red orange	.30	.75
		Nos. 67-70 (4)	1.40	1.75

Victory of the Allied Nations in WW II.

Common Design Types pictured following the introduction.

UPU Issue
Common Design Types
Engr.; Name Typo.

1949, Oct. 10   Wmk. 4   Perf. 11x11½

71	CD307	2p slate black	.70	.50
72	CD308	3p slate blue	1.25	1.75

75th anniv. of the UPU.

Queen Victoria and King George VI A24

Unwmk.

1950, Sept. 12   Engr.   Perf. 14

73	A24	2p choc & blue grn	.90	1.10

60th anniversary of Rhodesia.

POSTAGE DUE STAMPS

Catalogue values for unused stamps in this section are for Never Hinged items.

Great Britain Postage Due Stamps of 1938-51 Overprinted in Black

1951   Wmk. 251   Perf. 14x14½

J1	D1	½p emerald	3.75	17.50
		On cover		500.00
J2	D1	1p violet blue	3.50	2.75
		On cover		175.00
J3	D1	2p black brown	3.00	2.25
		On cover		125.00
J4	D1	3p violet	3.25	3.00
		On cover		200.00
J5	D1	4p brt blue	2.25	4.00
		On cover		250.00
a.		4p slate green	275.00	600.00
		On cover		1,200.
J6	D1	1sh blue	3.00	4.50
		On cover		250.00
		Nos. J1-J6 (6)	18.75	34.00

Covers are for properly franked commercial items. Philatelic usages sell for less.

SOUTH RUSSIA
sauth 'rəsh-ə

LOCATION — An area in southern Russia bordering on the Caspian and Black Seas.

A provisional government set up and maintained by General Denikin in opposition to the Bolshevik forces in Russia following the downfall of the Empire. The stamps were used in the field postal service established for carrying on communication between the various armies united in the revolt. These armies included the Don Cossacks, the Kuban Cossacks, and also the neighboring southern Russian people in favor of the counter-revolution against the Bolsheviks.

100 Kopecks = 1 Ruble

Values for used stamps are for canceled to order examples. Postally used stamps sell for considerably more.

Watermark

Wmk. 171 — Diamonds

Don Government (Novocherkassk) Rostov Issue
Russian Stamps of 1909-17 Surcharged

1918   Unwmk.   Perf. 14x14½

1	A14	25k on 1k dl org yel	2.00	1.90
a.		Inverted surcharge	100.00	100.00
2	A14	25k on 2k dl grn	.50	.60
a.		Inverted surcharge	100.00	75.00
3	A14	25k on 3k car	.75	.75
a.		Double surcharge	75.00	75.00
b.		Inverted surcharge	75.00	
4	A15	25k on 4k car	2.50	3.50
a.		Inverted surcharge	100.00	100.00
5	A14	50k on 7k blue	5.00	6.50

Imperf

6	A14	25k on 1k orange	.60	1.25
a.		Inverted surcharge	75.00	100.00
7	A14	25k on 2k gray grn	7.50	12.50
8	A14	25k on 3k red	4.75	3.00
a.		Inverted surcharge	100.00	
		Nos. 1-8 (8)	23.60	30.00

Counterfeits exist of Nos. 1-8.

Ermak, Cossack Leader — A1

Inscription on Back

1919   Perf. 11½

10	A1	20k green	50.00	85.00

This stamp was available for both postage and currency.

Novocherkassk Issue

Russian stamps with these surcharges are bogus.

Kuban Government Ekaterinodar Issues
Russian Stamps of 1909-17 Surcharged

d   e

f   g

1919   Wmk. 171   Perf. 14½x15

47	A2	10r on 1k red, *buff*	50.00	60.00
a.		Inverted surcharge	75.00	

h   i

1918-20   Unwmk.   Perf. 14x14½

20	A14(d)	25k on 1k dl org yel	.50	.65
a.		Inverted surcharge	75.00	27.50
b.		Dbl. surch., one inverted	75.00	25.00
21	A14(d)	50k on 2k dl grn	6.00	6.00
a.		Inverted surcharge	50.00	27.50
b.		Double surcharge	100.00	20.00
c.		Dbl. surcharge inverted	75.00	20.00
22	A14(e)	70k on 5k dk cl	2.00	6.00
23	A14(f)	1r on 3k car	5.00	5.00
a.		Inverted surcharge	50.00	20.00
b.		Double surcharge	100.00	15.00
c.		Pair, one without surch.	50.00	15.00
24	A14(g)	1r on 3k car	.65	1.00
a.		Inverted surcharge	50.00	20.00
b.		Double surcharge	100.00	20.00
c.		Pair, one without surcharge	100.00	20.00
25	A15(h)	3r on 4k rose	10.00	15.00
a.		Inverted surcharge	100.00	50.00
b.		Double surcharge	100.00	20.00
c.		Double surcharge	100.00	60.00
d.		Dbl. surcharge inverted	100.00	60.00
26	A15(i)	10r on 4k rose	15.00	5.00
a.		10r on 4k carmine	12.00	13.00
b.		Inverted surcharge	75.00	55.00
27	A11(i)	10r on 15k red brn & dp bl	1.25	2.00
a.		Surchd. on face & back	40.00	15.00
b.		Dbl. surch., one inverted	75.00	60.00
28	A14(d)	25r on 3k car	10.00	3.00
a.		Inverted surcharge	100.00	20.00
29	A14(i)	25r on 7k bl	25.00	50.00
a.		Inverted surcharge	100.00	100.00
30	A11(i)	25r on 14k bl & car	75.00	80.00
a.		Inverted surcharge	100.00	100.00
31	A11(i)	25r on 25k dl grn & dk vio	30.00	60.00
a.		Inverted surcharge	100.00	70.00
		Nos. 20-31 (12)	180.40	233.65

Imperf

35	A14(d)	25d on 1k org	5.00	2.50
36	A14(d)	50k on 2k gray grn	2.00	.60
a.		Inverted surcharge	50.00	50.00
b.		Double surcharge	50.00	25.00
c.		Pair, one without surch.	50.00	30.00
37	A14(e)	70k on 5k claret	2.50	3.25
38	A14(f)	1r on 3k red	1.40	2.00
a.		Inverted surcharge	40.00	20.00
b.		Double surcharge	30.00	15.00
c.		Pair, one without surch.	30.00	15.00
d.		Double surcharge, both inverted	100.00	
39	A14(g)	1r on 3k red	1.00	1.00
a.		Double surcharge	20.00	20.00
b.		Pair, one without surch.	20.00	20.00
c.		As "a," inverted	40.00	45.00
d.		Inverted surcharge	100.00	
40	A11(i)	10r on 15k red brn & dp bl	4.75	6.00
41	A14(i)	25r on 3k red	6.00	10.00
a.		Inverted surcharge	100.00	
		Nos. 35-41 (7)	22.65	25.35

Russian Stamps of 1909-17 Surcharged

1919   Perf. 14, 14½x15

45	A14	70k on 1k dl org yel	1.25	1.00
a.		Inverted surcharge	100.00	

Imperf

46	A14	70k on 1k orange	1.25	2.40
a.		Inverted surcharge	100.00	20.00
b.		Double surch., one inverted	100.00	25.00

The 1k postal savings stamp with this surcharge inverted is a proof. Value, $500.
Counterfeits exist of Nos. 20-46.

On Russia Nos. AR1-AR3

A2

1919   Wmk. 171   Perf. 14½x15

47	A2	10r on 1k red, *buff*	50.00	60.00
a.		Inverted surcharge	75.00	

48	A2	10r on 5k grn, *buff*	50.00	60.00
a.		Double surcharge	250.00	
49	A2	10r on 10k brn, *buff*	120.00	150.00
		Nos. 47-49 (3)	220.00	270.00

Counterfeits exist of Nos. 47-49.

Crimea
Russian Stamp of 1917 Surcharged

1919   Unwmk.   Imperf.

51	A14	35k on 1k orange	2.00	3.00
a.		Comma, instead of period in surcharge	2.00	

A3

Paper with Buff Network; Inscription on Back

1919   Imperf.

52	A3	50k brown	40.00	85.00

Available for both postage and currency.

Russia Nos. 77, 82, 123, 73, 119 Surcharged

Nos. 53-57   Nos. 58-59

1920   Perf. 14x14½

53	A14	5r on 5k dk claret	1.25	2.40
a.		Inverted surcharge	100.00	
b.		Double surcharge	100.00	
54	A8	5r on 20k dl bl & dk car	1.25	2.40
a.		Inverted surcharge	100.00	
b.		Double surcharge	100.00	
c.		"5" omitted	75.00	

Imperf

55	A14	5r on 5k claret	1.25	2.40
a.		Double surcharge	25.00	

Same Surcharge on Stamp of Denikin Issue, No. 64

57	A5	5r on 35k lt bl	12.00	14.00
a.		Double surcharge	80.00	
		Nos. 53-57 (4)	15.75	21.20

1920   Perf. 14x14½

58	A14	100r on 1k dl org yel	5.00	
a.		"10" in place of "100"	100.00	
b.		Inverted surcharge	150.00	
c.		Double surcharge	150.00	

Imperf

59	A14	100r on 1k orange	2.75	

Nos. 53-57 were issued at Sevastopol during the occupation by General Wrangel's army. Nos. 58-59 were prepared but not used.

Denikin Issue

A5   St. George — A6

1919   Unwmk.   Imperf.

61	A5	5k orange	.25	.25
62	A5	10k green	.25	.25
63	A5	15k red	.25	.35
64	A5	35k light blue	.25	.25
65	A5	70k dark blue	.25	.35
a.		Tête bêche pair	90.00	
66	A6	1r brown & red	.90	.90
67	A6	2r gray vio & yellow	1.50	1.60
68	A6	3r dl rose & green	1.00	1.25

69	A6	5r slate & violet	1.25	1.40
70	A6	7r gray grn & rose	2.25	3.25
71	A6	10r red & gray	2.00	2.50
		Nos. 61-71 (11)	10.15	12.35

Perf 11½

68a	A6	3r dull rose & green	3.00	10.00
69a	A6	5r slate & violet	4.00	10.00
71a	A6	10r red & gray	3.00	10.00
		Nos. 68a-71a (3)	10.00	30.00

Nos. 61-71 were issued at Ekaterinodar and used in all parts of South Russia that were occupied by the People's Volunteer Army under Gen. Anton Ivanovich Denikin. The inscription on the stamps reads "United Russia."

Stamps of type A6 with rosettes instead of numerals in the small circles at the sides may be essays. Perforated examples of Nos. 61-67 and 70 are of private origin.

For surcharges see Russia, Offices in Turkish Empire Nos. 303-319.

SOUTH WEST AFRICA

sauth 'west 'a-fri-kə

LOCATION — Southwestern Africa between Angola and Cape of Good Hope, bordering on the Atlantic Ocean
GOVT. — Administered by the Republic of South Africa under a mandate of the League of Nations
AREA — 318,261 sq. mi.
POP. — 1,039,800 (1982)
CAPITAL — Windhoek

Formerly a German possession, South West Africa was occupied by South African forces in 1915 and by the Treaty of Versailles was mandated to the Union of South Africa.

12 Pence = 1 Shilling
20 Shillings = 1 Pound

Catalogue values for unused stamps in this country are for Never Hinged items, beginning with Scott 125 in the regular postage section, Scott B1 in the semipostal section, Scott J86 in the postage due section, and Scott O13 in the officials section.

Watermarks
Watermarks 177 and 201 can be found at the beginning of South Africa.

Major-number listings and values of Nos. 1-40 and 85-93 are for pairs with both overprints.

Stamps of South Africa, Nos. 2-3, 5 and 9-16, Overprinted in English or Afrikaans alternately throughout the sheets.

Setting I

"South West" 14½mm wide
"Zuid-West" 13mm wide
Overprint Spaced 14mm

1923, Jan. 2   Wmk. 177   Perf. 14

1	A2	½p green, pair	3.00	10.50
a.		Single, Dutch	1.10	1.10
2	A2	1p red, pair	4.00	10.50
a.		Single, Dutch	1.10	1.10
b.		Inverted overprint, pair	550.00	
c.		As "b," single, English	125.00	
d.		As "b," single, Dutch	125.00	
e.		As #2, English "Af.rica"	175.00	275.00
f.		Double overprint, pair	1,000.	
g.		As "f," single, English	500.00	
h.		As "f," single, Dutch	500.00	

3	A2	2p dull vio, pair	6.50	14.00
a.		Single, Dutch	1.75	1.75
b.		Inverted overprint, pair	700.00	800.00
c.		As "b," single, English	150.00	
d.		As "b," single, Dutch	150.00	
4	A2	3p ultra, pair	6.00	10.00
a.		Single, English	3.25	3.25
5	A2	4p ol grn & org, pair	15.00	52.50
a.		Single, Dutch	4.50	4.50
6	A2	6p vio & blk, pair	9.25	50.00
a.		Single, Dutch	4.75	4.75
7	A2	1sh orange, pair	27.50	55.00
a.		Single, Dutch	5.75	5.75
b.		As #7, without period after "Afrika"	7,500.	
8	A2	1sh3p violet, pair	37.50	62.50
a.		Single, Dutch	6.50	6.50
b.		Inverted overprint, pair	400.00	
c.		As "b," single, English	75.00	
d.		As "b," single, Dutch	75.00	
9	A2	2sh6p grn & cl, pair	70.00	150.00
a.		Single, Dutch	22.50	22.50
10	A2	5sh blue & cl, pair	200.00	375.00
a.		Single, Dutch	57.50	57.50
11	A2	10sh ol grn & bl, pair	1,500.	2,900.
a.		Single, Dutch	475.00	500.00
12	A2	£1 red & dp grn, pair	800.00	2,000.
a.		Single, Dutch	300.00	300.00
		Nos. 1-12 (12)	2,681.	5,699.

Most values exist with "t" of "West" partly or totally missing. Vertical displacement in overprinting accounts for the stamps with only one line of overprint.
The English overprint of Setting I is the same as that of Setting III. See Nos. 16a-27a.

Setting II

Words Same Width as Setting I
Overprint Spaced 9½-10mm

1923, Apr.

13	A2	5sh blue & cl, pair	160.00	300.00
a.		Single, English	52.50	52.50
b.		Single, Dutch	52.50	52.50
c.		As #13, without period after "Afrika"	1,200.	1,400.
d.		As "b," without period after "Afrika"	225.00	225.00
14	A2	10sh ol grn & bl, pair	575.00	1,000.
a.		Single, English	160.00	160.00
b.		Single, Dutch	160.00	160.00
c.		As #14, without period after "Afrika"	2,600.	3,250.
d.		As "b," without period after "Afrika"	550.00	550.00
15	A2	£1 red & green, pair	1,150.	1,700.
a.		Single, English	225.00	225.00
b.		Single, Dutch	225.00	225.00
c.		As #15, without period after "Afrika"	6,000.	5,750.
d.		As "b," without period after "Afrika"	1,000.	1,000.

Setting III

"South West" 14½mm wide
"Zuidwest" 13mm wide

English as in Setting I
"Zuidwest" 11mm wide, No Hyphen
Overprint Spaced 14mm

1923-24

16	A2	½p grn, pair (24)	9.00	40.00
a.		Single, English	1.10	4.25
b.		Single, Dutch	.75	4.25
17	A2	1p red, pair	6.25	10.50
a.		Single, English	1.10	1.60
b.		Single, Dutch	.30	1.60
18	A2	2p dull vio, pair	9.00	11.00
a.		Single, English	.50	1.50
b.		Single, Dutch	.50	1.50
c.		Dbl. ovpt., pair	1,200.	
d.		As "c," single, English	150.00	
e.		As "c," single, Dutch	150.00	
19	A2	3p ultra, pair	5.75	11.50
a.		Single, English	.70	1.50
b.		Single, Dutch	.70	1.50
20	A2	4p ol grn & org, pair	7.00	24.00
a.		Single, English	.75	3.25
b.		Single, Dutch	.75	3.25
21	A2	6p vio & blk, pair	14.00	47.50
a.		Single, English	1.00	5.50
b.		Single, Dutch	1.00	5.50
22	A2	1sh orange, pair	16.00	52.50
a.		Single, English	1.50	5.75
b.		Single, Dutch	1.50	5.75
23	A2	1sh3p violet, pair	32.50	52.50
a.		Single, English	2.25	6.25
b.		Single, Dutch	2.25	6.25
24	A2	2sh6p grn & cl, pair	52.50	92.50
a.		Single, English	7.00	11.50
b.		Single, Dutch	7.00	11.50
25	A2	5sh blue & cl, pair	70.00	150.00
a.		Single, English	11.00	21.00
b.		Single, Dutch	11.00	21.00
26	A2	10sh ol grn & bl, pair	190.00	300.00
a.		Single, English	35.00	47.50
b.		Single, Dutch	35.00	47.50
27	A2	£1 red & green, pair	350.00	450.00
a.		Single, English	55.00	70.00
b.		Single, Dutch	55.00	70.00
		Nos. 16-27 (12)	762.00	1,242.

Setting IV

Type g (on left), Type h (on right)

"South West" 16mm wide
"Zuidwest" 12mm wide
Overprint Spaced 14mm

1924, July

28	A2	2sh6p grn & cl, pair	92.50	175.00
a.		Single, English	15.00	32.50
b.		Single, Dutch	15.00	32.50

Setting VI

k   l

"South West" 16, 16½mm wide
"Zuidwest" 12½mm wide
Overprint Spaced 9½mm

1924, Dec.

29	A2	½p green, pair	8.00	45.00
a.		Single, English	.50	5.75
b.		Single, Dutch	.50	5.75
30	A2	1p red, pair	3.75	11.50
a.		Single, English	.25	1.60
b.		Single, Dutch	.25	1.60
31	A2	2p dull vio, pair	5.75	25.00
a.		Single, English	.30	2.00
b.		Single, Dutch	.30	2.00
32	A2	3p ultra, pair	5.25	32.50
a.		Single, English	.50	3.25
b.		Single, Dutch	.50	3.25
33	A2	4p ol grn & org, pair	7.50	52.50
a.		Single, English	.70	4.50
b.		Single, Dutch	.70	4.50
34	A2	6p vio & blk, pair	10.50	55.00
a.		Single, English	.75	5.75
b.		Single, Dutch	.75	5.75
35	A2	1sh orange, pair	12.50	55.00
a.		Single, English	.90	5.75
b.		Single, Dutch	.90	5.75
36	A2	1sh3p violet, pair	17.50	55.00
a.		Single, English	1.25	5.75
b.		Single, Dutch	1.25	5.75
37	A2	2sh6p grn & cl, pair	37.50	80.00
a.		Single, English	5.00	11.50
b.		Single, Dutch	5.00	11.50
38	A2	5sh blue & cl, pair	52.50	140.00
a.		Single, English	8.50	16.00
b.		Single, Dutch	8.50	16.00
39	A2	10sh ol grn & bl, pair	92.50	180.00
a.		Single, English	13.00	22.50
b.		Single, Dutch	13.00	22.50

40	A2	£1 red & grn, pair	290.00	475.00
a.		Single, English	50.00	75.00
b.		Single, Dutch	50.00	75.00
		Nos. 29-40 (12)	543.25	1,206.

Setting VII
South Africa Nos. 21-22 Overprinted

m

n

o

1926-27   Wmk. 201   Imperf.

81	A3 (m)	4p blue gray	.85	3.50
82	A3 (n)	4p blue gray	.85	3.50
83	A3 (o)	4p blue gray ('27)	7.00	22.50
		Nos. 81-83 (3)	8.70	29.50

Nos. 81-83 were not officially perforated, but firms and individuals applied various forms of perforation and rouletting for their own convenience. Perf. 11 examples of Nos. 81-82 were made by John Meinert, Ltd., Windhoek, same values.

Setting VIII
South Africa Nos. 23-25 Overprinted Alternately with type "p" on English-inscribed Stamps and type "q" on Afrikaans-inscribed Stamps

p   q

"South West" 16½mm wide
"Suidwes" 11mm wide
Overprint Spaced 11½mm

1926   Typo.   Perf. 14½x14

85	A5	½p dk grn & blk, pair	4.25	9.00
a.		Single, English	.75	1.00
b.		Single, Afrikaans	.75	1.00
c.		Ovpt. "q" on English stamp	.75	1.00
d.		Ovpt. "p" on Afrikaans stamp	.75	1.00
e.		Pair, "c" + "d"	2.25	9.00
f.		As "e," without period after "Africa"	175.00	
86	A6	1p car & blk, pair	3.50	8.00
a.		Single, English	.50	.80
b.		Single, Afrikaans	.50	.80
c.		Ovpt. "q" on English stamp	.50	.50
d.		Ovpt. "p" on Afrikaans stamp	.50	.50
e.		Pair, "c" + "d"	3.50	3.50
f.		As "e," without period after "Africa"	350.00	
87	A7	6p org & grn, pair	24.00	50.00
a.		Single, English	7.00	8.50
b.		Single, Afrikaans	7.00	8.50
c.		Ovpt. "q" on English stamp	3.00	3.50
d.		Ovpt. "p" on Afrikaans stamp	3.00	3.50
e.		Pair, "c" + "d"	10.00	35.00
f.		As "e," without period after "Africa"	210.00	
		Nos. 85-87 (3)	31.75	67.00

For overprints see Nos. O1-O3.

Setting IX
South Africa Nos. 26-27, 29-32
Overprinted in Blue with types "p" and
"q" Spaced 16mm

1927		Engr.	Perf. 14	
88	A8	2p vio brn & gray, pair	5.50	17.50
a.		Single, English	.60	2.00
b.		Single, Afrikaans	.60	2.00
89	A9	3p red & blk, pair	5.50	32.50
a.		Single, English	.75	3.00
b.		Single, Afrikaans	.75	3.00
90	A11	1sh dp bl & bis brn, pair	17.50	37.50
a.		Single, English	1.75	4.50
b.		Single, Afrikaans	1.75	4.50
91	A12	2sh6p brn & bl grn, pair	40.00	110.00
a.		Single, English	8.00	15.00
b.		Single, Afrikaans	8.00	15.00
92	A13	5sh dp grn & blk, pair	85.00	225.00
a.		Single, English	17.50	22.50
b.		Single, Afrikaans	17.50	22.50
93	A14	10sh ol brn & bl, pair	75.00	180.00
a.		Single, English	12.00	22.50
b.		Single, Afrikaans	12.00	22.50
		Nos. 88-93 (6)	228.50	602.50

South Africa Nos. 12
and 16a Overprinted at
Foot

1927		Typo.	Wmk. 177	
94	A2	1sh3p violet	1.50	7.50
a.		Without period after "A"	110.00	
95	A2	£1 lt red & gray grn	110.00	190.00
a.		Without period after "A"	1,750.	2,600.

South Africa Nos. 23-25 Overprinted
type "r" at Foot

1927		Wmk. 201	Perf. 14½x14	
96	A5	½p green & blk, pair	2.75	8.00
a.		Single, English	.25	.90
b.		Single, Afrikaans	.25	.90
c.		As #96, without period after "A" on one stamp	47.50	85.00
97	A6	1p car & blk, pair	1.50	3.75
a.		Single, English	.25	.65
b.		Single, Afrikaans	.25	.65
c.		As #97, without period after "A" on one stamp	47.50	85.00
d.		Ovpt. at top, pair ('30)	2.00	16.00
e.		As "d," single, English	.35	1.90
f.		As "d," single, Afrikaans	.35	1.90
98	A7	6p org & grn, pair	11.00	28.00
a.		Single, English	1.75	3.25
b.		Single, Afrikaans	1.75	3.25
c.		As #98, without period after "A" on one stamp	125.00	
		Nos. 96-98 (3)	15.25	39.75

For overprints see Nos. O5-O7.

South Africa Nos. 26-32 Overprinted
type "r" at Top

1927-28		Engr.	Perf. 14	
99	A8	2p vio brn & gray, pair	10.50	32.50
a.		Single, English	1.25	1.75
b.		Single, Afrikaans	1.25	1.75
c.		As #99, without period after "A" on one stamp	85.00	140.00
d.		Double ovpt., one inverted	800.00	1,050.
100	A9	3p red & blk, pair	7.00	26.00
a.		Single, English	1.00	3.75
b.		Single, Afrikaans	1.00	3.75
c.		As #100, without period after "A" on one stamp	92.50	150.00
101	A10	4p brn, pair ('28)	17.50	45.00
a.		Single, English	1.75	8.00
b.		Single, Afrikaans	1.75	8.00
c.		As #101, without period after "A" on one stamp	97.50	150.00
102	A11	1sh dp bl & bis brn, pair	22.50	55.00
a.		Single, English	1.75	5.75
b.		Single, Afrikaans	1.75	5.75
c.		As #102, without period after "A" on one stamp	1,500.	1,800.
103	A12	2sh6p brn & bl grn, pair	47.50	97.50
a.		Single, English	6.50	14.00
b.		Single, Afrikaans	6.50	14.00
c.		As #103, without period after "A" on one stamp	250.00	400.00
104	A13	5sh dp grn & blk, pair	70.00	140.00
a.		Single, English	9.50	21.00
b.		Single, Afrikaans	9.50	21.00

c.	As #104, without period after "A" on one stamp	325.00	475.00
105 A14	10sh ol brn & bl, pair	110.00	225.00
a.	Single, English	20.00	32.50
b.	Single, Afrikaans	20.00	32.50
c.	As #105, without period after "A" on one stamp	425.00	675.00
	Nos. 99-105 (7)	285.00	621.00

Nos. 99-102 exist perf 14x13½. Values
about two times those shown.
For overprint see No. O8.

South Africa Nos. 33-34 Overprinted
type "r" at Foot

1930		Photo.	Perf. 15x14	
106	A5	½p bl grn & blk, pair	15.00	37.50
a.		Single, English	1.50	3.25
b.		Single, Afrikaans	1.50	3.25
107	A6	1p car rose & blk, pair	10.00	30.00
a.		Single, English	1.25	3.25
b.		Single, Afrikaans	1.25	3.25

Kori
Bustard — A15

Cape
Cross — A16

Mail
Transport — A17

Bogenfels — A18

Windhoek — A19

Waterberg — A20

Lüderitz
Bay — A21

Bush
Scene — A22

Elands — A23

Zebras and
Brindled
Gnus — A24

			.25
			.35
			.35
b.			.35
111	A18		6.50
a.	Single, E...	.25	.25
b.	Single, Afrika...	.25	.25
112	A19	3p dp b... blk, pair	.80	5.00
a.	Single, English	.25	.25
b.	Single, Afrikaans	.25	.25
113	A20	4p brn vio & grn, pair	2.10	8.00
a.	Single, English	.30	.25
b.	Single, Afrikaans	.30	.25
114	A21	6p ol brn & bl, pair	1.75	11.00
a.	Single, English	.30	.25
b.	Single, Afrikaans	.30	.25
115	A22	1sh bl & vio brn, pair	3.00	15.00
a.	Single, English	.50	.30
b.	Single, Afrikaans	.50	.30
116	A23	1sh3p ocher & pur, pair	8.75	12.50
a.	Single, English	.60	.60
b.	Single, Afrikaans	.60	.60
117	A24	2sh6p dk gray & rose, pair	24.00	27.50
a.	Single, English	2.75	2.00
b.	Single, Afrikaans	2.75	2.00
118	A25	5sh vio brn & ol grn, pair	19.00	45.00
a.	Single, English	3.50	3.25
b.	Single, Afrikaans	3.50	3.25
119	A26	10sh grn & brn, pair	52.50	57.50
a.	Single, English	9.50	7.00
b.	Single, Afrikaans	9.50	7.00
120	A27	20sh bl grn & mar, pair	85.00	95.00
a.	Single, English	12.50	12.50
b.	Single, Afrikaans	12.50	12.50
		Nos. 108-120 (13)	231.20	293.25

For overprints see Nos. O13-O27.

George V — A28

1935, May 6			Perf. 14x13½	
121	A28	1p carmine & blk	1.25	.30
122	A28	2p dk brown & blk	1.25	.30
123	A28	3p blue & blk	8.00	22.50
124	A28	6p violet & blk	4.00	13.00
		Nos. 121-124 (4)	14.50	36.10
		Set, never hinged	30.00	

25th anniv. of the reign of George V.

> Catalogue values for unused
> stamps in this section, from this
> point to the end of the section, are
> for Never Hinged items.

Herero
Houses — A25

A29

			Perf. 13½x14	
		...blk, pair	.45	.25
			.25	.25
			.25	.25
		...& blk, pair	.45	.25
		...ish	.25	.25
			.25	.25
		...org & blk, pair	.45	.25
		...English	.25	.25
		...Afrikaans	.25	.25
		...2p dk brn & blk, pair	.45	.30
		...e, English	.25	.25
		...gle, Afrikaans	.25	.25
	A29	3p brt bl & blk, pair	.55	.30
		Single, English	.25	.25
		Single, Afrikaans	.25	.25
	A29	4p dk vio & blk, pair	.55	.35
a.		Single, English	.25	.25
b.		Single, Afrikaans	.25	.25
131	A29	6p yel & blk, pair	.60	3.25
a.		Single, English	.25	.25
b.		Single, Afrikaans	.25	.30
132	A29	1sh gray & blk, pair	2.00	3.50
a.		Single, English	.25	.75
b.		Single, Afrikaans	.25	.75
		Nos. 125-132 (8)	5.50	8.45

George VI & Queen Elizabeth coronation.

Voortrekker Issue
South Africa Nos. 79-80 Overprinted
type "r"

1938, Dec. 14		Photo.	Perf. 15x14	
133	A23	1p rose & sl, pair	14.00	22.50
a.		Single, English	1.50	1.75
b.		Single, Afrikaans	1.50	1.75
134	A24	1½p red brn & Prus bl, pair	21.00	27.50
a.		Single, English	2.00	2.25
b.		Single, Afrikaans	2.00	2.25

Issued to commemorate the Voortrekkers.

South Africa Nos. 81-89
Overprinted — s

Perf. 14 (2p, 4p, 6p); 15x14

1941-43			Wmk. 201	
135	A25	½p dp blue grn, pair	1.75	2.75
a.		Single, English	.25	.25
b.		Single, Afrikaans	.25	.25
136	A26	1p brt rose, pair	2.00	3.75
a.		Single, English	.25	.25
b.		Single, Afrikaans	.25	.25
137	A27	1½p Prus grn, pair ('42)	3.00	4.00
a.		Single, English	.25	.25
b.		Single, Afrikaans	.25	.25
138	A28	2p dk violet	.60	1.75
139	A29	3p dp blue, pair	24.50	26.00
a.		Single, English	1.00	1.25
b.		Single, Afrikaans	1.00	1.25
140	A30	4p brown, pair	7.50	20.00
a.		Single, English	.80	1.00
b.		Single, Afrikaans	.80	1.00
141	A31	6p brt red org, pair	8.00	9.00
a.		Single, English	.75	1.00
b.		Single, Afrikaans	.75	1.00
142	A32	1sh dk brown	1.60	2.00
143	A33	1sh3p dk ol brn, pair ('43)	15.00	24.50
a.		Single, English	1.25	1.50
b.		Single, Afrikaans	1.25	1.50
		Nos. 135-143 (9)	63.95	93.75

South Africa Nos. 90-97 Overprinted

t   u

Pairs or Strips of 3 Perf. 14 or 15x14 all around, Rouletted 6½ or 13 btwn.

1942-45   **Wmk. 201**

144	A34(t)	½p dp grn, horiz.	
		strip of 3	.75 7.00
a.		Single, English	.25 .25
b.		Single, Afrikaans	.25 .25
c.		½p dp bl grn, horiz. strip of 3	4.25 7.50
d.		As "c," single, English	.25 .25
e.		As "c," single, Afrikaans	.25 .25
145	A35(t)	1p brt car, horiz.	
		strip of 3	3.50 7.00
a.		Single, English	.25 .25
b.		Single, Afrikaans	.25 .25
c.		1p rose car, horiz. strip of 3	4.00 7.00
d.		As "c," single, English	.25 .25
e.		As "c," single, Afrikaans	.25 .25
146	A36(u)	1½p cop brn, horiz.	
		pair	.75 1.75
a.		Single, English	.25 .25
b.		Single, Afrikaans	.25 .25
147	A37(t)	2p dk vio, horiz.	
		pair	8.50 5.50
a.		Single, English	.25 .25
b.		Single, Afrikaans	.25 .25
148	A38(t)	3p dp bl, vert.	
		strip of 3	4.00 22.50
a.		Single, English	.25 .65
b.		Single, Afrikaans	.25 .65
149	A39(t)	4p sl grn, vert.	
		strip of 3	5.00 22.50
a.		Single	.30 .35
b.		As "c," single	55.00 60.00
c.		Invtd. ovpt., strip of 3	850.00 550.00
150	A40(t)	6p brt red org, horiz. pair	7.00 3.00
a.		Single, English	.30 .35
b.		Single, Afrikaans	.30 .35
c.		Inverted overprint, pair	650.00
d.		As "c," single, English	60.00 60.00
e.		As "c," single, Afrikaans	60.00 60.00
151	A41(u)	1sh dk brn, vert. pair	15.00 29.00
a.		Single	1.25 2.00
b.		As "c," single	85.00
c.		Inverted overprint, pair	700.00 375.00
152	A41(u)	1sh dk brn, vert. pair	5.00 6.50
a.		Single	.30 .35
b.		As "c," single	55.00 40.00
c.		Invtd. ovpt., vert. pair	600.00 350.00
		Nos. 144-152 (9)	49.50 104.75

Issue years: #144-145, 147-151, 1943; #152, 1944; #144c, 145c, 149c, 1945.

Peace Issue
South Africa Nos. 100-102 Overprinted Type "w"

1945, Dec. 3   **Wmk. 201**   *Perf. 14*

153	A42	1p rose pink & choc, pair	.40 .75
a.		Single, English	.25 .25
b.		Single, Afrikaans	.25 .25
c.		Inverted overprint, pair	400.00 425.00
d.		As "c," single, English	40.00
e.		As "c," single, Afrikaans	40.00
154	A43	2p vio & sl bl, pair	.40 .75
a.		Single, English	.25 .25
b.		Single, Afrikaans	.25 .25
155	A43	3p ultra & dp ultra, pair	1.75 2.00
a.		Single, English	.30 .25
b.		Single, Afrikaans	.30 .25
		Nos. 153-155 (3)	2.55 3.50

WW II victory of the Allies.

Royal Visit Issue

South Africa Nos. 103-105 Overprinted

1947, Feb. 17   *Perf. 15x14*

156	A44	1p cerise & gray, pair	.30 .25
a.		Single, English	.25 .25
b.		Single, Afrikaans	.25 .25
157	A45	2p purple, pair	.30 .60
a.		Single, English	.25 .25
b.		Single, Afrikaans	.25 .25
158	A46	3p dk blue, pair	.40 .45
a.		Single, English	.25 .25
b.		Single, Afrikaans	.25 .25
		Nos. 156-158 (3)	1.00 1.30

Visit of the British Royal Family, Mar.-Apr., 1947.

South Africa No. 106 Overprinted

1948, Apr. 26   *Perf. 14*

159	A47	3p dp chalky bl & sil, pair	1.25 .35
a.		Single, English	.25 .25
b.		Single, Afrikaans	.25 .25

25th anniv. of the marriage of George VI and Queen Elizabeth.

UPU Issue
South Africa Nos. 109-111 Overprinted type "w" 13mm wide

1949, Oct. 1   *Perf. 14x15*

160	A50	½p dk green, pair	1.10 2.25
a.		Single, English	.25 .30
b.		Single, Afrikaans	.25 .30
161	A50	1½p dk red, pair	1.10 1.75
a.		Single, English	.25 .25
b.		Single, Afrikaans	.25 .25
162	A50	3p ultra, pair	1.75 2.00
a.		Single, English	.25 .30
b.		Single, Afrikaans	.25 .30
		Nos. 160-162 (3)	3.95 6.00

75th anniv. of the UPU.

This ends the bi-lingual multiples in the postage section.

Voortrekker Monument Issue

South Africa Nos. 112-114 Ovptd.

1949, Dec. 1   *Perf. 15x14*

163	A51	1p magenta	.25 .25
164	A52	1½p dull green	.25 .25
165	A53	3p dark blue	.30 .30
		Nos. 163-165 (3)	.80 .80

Inauguration of the Voortrekker Monument at Pretoria.

South Africa Nos. 115-119 Overprinted

1952, Mar. 14   *Perf. 15x14, 14x15*

166	A54(w)	½p dk brown & red vio	.40 .50
167	A55(x)	1p dark green	.40 .40
168	A54(w)	2p dark purple	.85 .40
169	A55(x)	4½p dark blue	.85 2.00
170	A54(w)	1sh brown	1.75 1.00
		Nos. 166-170 (5)	4.25 4.30

300th anniv. of the landing of Jan van Riebeeck at the Cape of Good Hope.

SEMI-POSTAL STAMPS

> Catalogue values for unused stamps in this section are for Never Hinged items.

Voortrekker Monument Issue

South Africa Nos. B1-B4 Overprinted

1935-36   **Wmk. 201**   *Perf. 14*

B1	SP1	½p + ½p grn & blk, pair	3.00 7.00
a.		Single, English	.40 .85
b.		Single, Afrikaans	.40 .85
B2	SP2	1p + 1p rose & blk, pair	4.00 4.00
a.		Single, English	.45 .45
b.		Single, Afrikaans	.45 .45
B3	SP3	2p + 1p dl vio & gray, pair	17.50 10.00
a.		Single, English	1.75 1.25
b.		Single, Afrikaans	1.75 1.25
B4	SP4	3p + 1½p dp bl & gray, pair	30.00 40.00
a.		Single, English	3.25 4.50
b.		Single, Afrikaans	3.25 4.50
		Nos. B1-B4 (4)	54.50 61.00

Voortrekker Centenary Issue
South Africa Nos. B5-B8 Overprinted

1938, Dec. 14   *Perf. 14*

B5	SP5	½p + ½p dl grn & indigo, pair	11.00 25.00
a.		Single, English	1.00 2.25
b.		Single, Afrikaans	1.00 2.25

Perf. 15x14

B6	SP6	1p + 1p rose & sl, pair	27.50 20.00
a.		Single, English	1.50 1.50
b.		Single, Afrikaans	1.50 1.50
B7	SP7	1½p + 1½p Prus grn & choc, pair	29.00 35.00
a.		Single, English	2.00 3.25
b.		Single, Afrikaans	2.00 3.25
B8	SP8	3p + 3p chlky bl, pair	55.00 85.00
a.		Single, English	4.50 8.50
b.		Single, Afrikaans	4.50 8.50
		Nos. B5-B8 (4)	122.50 165.00

Same Overprint on South Africa Nos. B9-B11

1939, July 17   *Perf. 14*

B9	SP9	½p + ½p Prus grn & gray brn, pair	14.00 16.00
a.		Single, English	1.00 1.25
b.		Single, Afrikaans	1.00 1.25
B10	SP10	1p + 1p rose car & Prus grn, pair	21.00 16.00
a.		Single, English	1.25 1.25
b.		Single, Afrikaans	1.25 1.25

Perf. 15x14

B11	SP11	1½p + 1½p rose vio, dk vio & Prus grn, pair	34.00 20.00
a.		Single, English	2.00 1.75
b.		Single, Afrikaans	2.00 1.75
		Nos. B9-B11 (3)	69.00 52.00

250th anniv. of the landing of the Huguenots in South Africa. Surtax went to a fund to build a Huguenot memorial at Paarl.

AIR POST STAMPS

South Africa Nos. C5-C6 Overprinted

1930   **Unwmk.**   *Perf. 14x13½*

C1	AP2	4p blue green	10.00 32.50
a.		Without period after "A"	80.00 150.00
C2	AP2	1sh orange	16.00 57.50
a.		Without period after "A"	500.00 750.00

Overprinted

C3	AP2	4p blue green	1.50 7.00
a.		Double overprint	200.00
b.		Inverted overprint	200.00
c.		Small "I" in "AIR"	6.00
C4	AP2	1sh orange	4.25 17.50
a.		Double overprint	575.00

Monoplane over Windhoek — AP3

Biplane over Windhoek — AP4

Wmk. 201

1931, Mar. 5   **Engr.**   *Perf. 14*

C5	AP3	3p blue & dk brn, pair	40.00 45.00
a.		Single, English	3.00 3.00
b.		Single, Afrikaans	3.00 3.00
C6	AP4	10p brn vio & blk, pair	85.00 85.00
a.		Single, English	7.00 7.00
b.		Single, Afrikaans	7.00 7.00

POSTAGE DUE STAMPS

STAMPS OF TRANSVAAL USED IN SOUTH WEST AFRICA
Prior to the issue of Nos. J1-J9, postage due stamps of South Africa and Transvaal were used in South West Africa.

1915-23

AJ7		6p Transvaal #J6, on cover	500.00
AJ8		1sh Transvaal #J7, on cover	700.00

Values are for covers commercially used in South West Africa during 1915-1923.

REGULAR ISSUES
Postage Due Stamps of South Africa and Transvaal Overprinted like Regular Issues.
Setting I
On South Africa Nos. J11, J14

1923   **Unwmk.**   *Perf. 14*

J1	D1	½p blue grn & blk, pair	6.75 30.00
a.		Single, English	.75 5.50
b.		Single, Dutch	.75 5.50
c.		As #J1, without period after "Afrika"	130.00
d.		Inverted ovpt., pair	600.00
J2	D1	2p violet & blk, pair	4.00 28.00
a.		Single, English	.50 5.00
b.		Single, Dutch	.50 5.00
c.		As #J2, without period after "Afrika"	170.00 170.00

On South Africa Nos. J9-J10

Rouletted 7-8

J3	D1	1p dull red & blk, pair	8.00 30.00
a.		Single, English	.90 5.50
b.		Single, Dutch	.90 5.50
c.		As #J3, without period after "Afrika"	150.00 150.00
d.		Pair, imperf. between	1,800.
J4	D1	1½p yel brn & blk, pair	1.50 16.00
a.		Single, English	.25 2.75
b.		Single, Dutch	.25 2.75
c.		As #J4, without period after "Afrika"	110.00 110.00

On South Africa Nos. J3-J4, J6

Perf. 14

Wmk. 177

J5	D1	2p violet & blk, pair	42.50 55.00
a.		Single, English	3.00 10.00
b.		Single, Dutch	3.00 10.00
c.		As #J5, without period after "Afrika"	275.00
d.		"Wes" for "West"	325.00
J6	D1	3p ultra & blk, pair	21.00 55.00
a.		Single, English	1.50 10.00
b.		Single, Dutch	1.50 10.00
J7	D1	6p gray & blk, pair	40.00 65.00
a.		Single, English	4.00 13.00
b.		Single, Dutch	4.00 13.00
		Nos. J5-J7 (3)	103.50 175.00

On Transvaal Nos. J5-J6
Wmk. Multiple Crown and C A (3)

J8	D1	5p violet & blk, pair	4.50 55.00
a.		Single, English	.75 11.00
b.		Single, Dutch	.75 11.00
c.		As #J8, without period after "Afrika"	130.00 130.00

J9	D1	6p red brn & blk, pair	19.00	55.00
a.		Single, Dutch	2.50	11.00
b.		As #J9, without period after "Afrika"	275.00	

For No. J9 single in English see No. J17a and note after No. 27.

The "t" of "West" may be found partly or entirely missing on Nos. J1, J3-J6, J8-J9.

Setting II
On South Africa No. J9
Rouletted
Unwmk.

J10	D1	1p dull red & blk, pair	14,000.	
a.		Single, English	800.00	1,600.
b.		Single, Dutch	800.00	1,600.

On South Africa Nos. J3-J4
Perf. 14
Wmk. 177

J11	D1	2p violet & blk, pair	19.00	50.00
a.		Single, English	1.75	9.00
b.		Single, Dutch	1.75	9.00
c.		As #J11, without period after "Afrika"	275.00	250.00
J12	D1	3p ultra & blk, pair	8.50	32.50
a.		Single, English	1.00	5.50
b.		Single, Dutch	1.00	5.50
c.		As #J12, without period after "Afrika"	130.00	150.00

On Transvaal No. J5
Wmk. Multiple Crown and C A (3)

J13	D1	5p violet & blk, pair	75.00	200.00
a.		Single, English	15.00	20.00
b.		Single, Dutch	15.00	20.00

Setting III
On South Africa Nos. J11, J12, J9
Unwmk.

J14	D1	½p blue grn & blk, pair	17.50	37.50
a.		Single, Dutch	1.50	5.50
J15	D1	1p rose & black, pair	27.50	37.50
a.		Single, English	1.50	6.00
b.		Single, Dutch	1.50	6.00

Rouletted 7

J16	D1	1p dull red & blk, pair	9.50	37.50
a.		Single, Dutch	1.00	6.00

For Nos. J14 and J16 singles in English see Nos. J1a and J3a and note after No. 27.

On Transvaal No. J6
Perf. 14
Wmk. 3

J17	D1	6p red brown & blk, pair	23.50	100.00
a.		Single, English	2.50	20.00
b.		Single, Dutch	2.50	20.00

See note below No. 27.

Setting IV
On South Africa Nos. J11-J12, J16
1924   Unwmk.

J18	D1	½p blue grn & blk, pair	8.50	35.00
a.		Single, English	.75	5.50
b.		Single, Dutch	.75	5.50
J19	D1	1p rose & blk, pair	8.50	32.50
a.		Single, English	.60	5.50
b.		Single, Dutch	.60	5.50
J20	D1	6p gray & blk, pair	3.00	45.00
a.		Single, English	.30	9.00
b.		Single, Dutch	.30	9.00

On Transvaal No. J5
Wmk. Multiple Crown and C A (3)

J21	D1	5p violet & blk, pair	800.00	1,200.
a.		Single, English	140.00	175.00
b.		Single, Dutch	140.00	175.00

Setting V

South West	Zuidwest
1½d	1½d
Africa.	Afrika.
i	j

"South West" 16mm wide
"Zuidwest" 12mm wide
Overprint Spaced 12mm

On South Africa Nos. J4, J11, J13
1924   Unwmk.

J22	D1	½p green & blk, pair	3.50	32.50
a.		Single, English	.25	6.50
b.		Single, Dutch	.25	6.50

J23	D1	1½p yel brown & blk	5.75	47.50
a.		Single, English	.50	7.50
b.		Single, Dutch	.50	7.50

Wmk. Springbok's Head (177)

On Transvaal No. J5
Wmk. Multiple Crown and C A (3)

J24	D1	3p ultra & black, pair	16.00	60.00
a.		Single, English	1.75	11.00
b.		Single, Dutch	1.75	11.00
J25	D1	5p violet & blk, pair	3.00	25.00
a.		Single, English	.40	7.50
b.		Single, Dutch	.40	7.50

Setting VI
On South Africa Nos. J4, J11-J16
1924, Dec.   Unwmk.

J26	D1	½p blue grn & blk, pair	14.00	40.00
a.		Single, English	1.00	7.50
b.		Single, Dutch	1.00	7.50
J27	D1	1p rose & black, pair	2.25	14.00
a.		Single, English	.25	1.75
b.		Single, Dutch	.25	1.75
c.		As #J27, without period after "Afrika"	100.00	
J28	D1	1½p yel brown & blk, pair	5.00	35.00
a.		Single, English	.30	6.50
b.		Single, Dutch	.30	6.50
c.		As #J28, without period after "Africa"	110.00	
J29	D1	2p violet & blk, pair	3.00	19.00
a.		Single, English	.35	3.50
b.		Single, Dutch	.35	3.50
c.		As #J29, without period after "Africa"	85.00	
J30	D1	3p blue & black, pair	5.25	20.00
a.		Single, English	.85	3.75
b.		Single, Dutch	.85	3.75
c.		As #J30, without period after "Africa"	92.50	
J31	D1	6p gray & black, pair	16.00	57.50
a.		Single, English	2.00	14.00
b.		Single, Dutch	2.00	14.00
c.		As #J31, without period after "Africa"	180.00	
		Nos. J26-J31 (6)	45.50	185.50

Wmk. Springbok's Head (177)

J32	D1	3p ultra & black, pair	10.00	65.00
a.		Single, English	1.75	11.00
b.		Single, Dutch	1.75	11.00

On Transvaal No. J5
Wmk. 3

J33	D1	5p violet & blk, pair	3.25	22.50
a.		Single, English	.25	3.50
b.		Single, Dutch	.25	3.50
c.		As #J33, without period after "Africa"	92.50	75.00

Setting VIII
On South Africa Nos. J18, J13-J16
1927   Unwmk.

J34	D2	1p rose & black, pair	1.25	13.00
a.		Single, English	.25	2.25
b.		Single, Afrikaans	.25	2.25
c.		As #J34, without period after "Africa"	10.50	17.50
J35	D1	1½p yel brown & blk, pair	1.25	22.50
a.		Single, English	.25	3.50
b.		Single, Afrikaans	.25	3.50
c.		As #J35, without period after "Africa"	50.00	60.00
J36	D1	2p violet & blk, pair	6.00	18.00
a.		Single, English	.30	3.25
b.		Single, Afrikaans	.30	3.25
c.		As #J36, without period after "Africa"	50.00	60.00
J37	D1	3p blue & black, pair	16.00	50.00
a.		Single, English	1.75	11.00
b.		Single, Afrikaans	1.75	11.00
c.		As #J37, without period after "Africa"	70.00	70.00
J38	D1	6p gray & black, pair	12.00	40.00
a.		Single, English	1.50	8.50
b.		Single, Afrikaans	1.50	8.50
c.		As #J38, without period after "Africa"	100.00	115.00
		Nos. J34-J38 (5)	36.50	143.50

On Transvaal No. J5
Wmk. Multiple Crown and C A (3)

J39	D1	5p violet & blk, pair	22.50	97.50
a.		Single, English	3.00	22.50
b.		Single, Afrikaans	3.00	22.50

S.W.A. 3d

South Africa Nos. J15-J16 Overprinted

1928			Unwmk.	
J79	D1	3p blue & black	1.65	12.00
J80	D1	6p gray & black	7.50	32.50

Same Overprint on South Africa Nos. J17-J21

J81	D2	½p blue grn & blk	.65	9.50
a.		Without period after "A"	45.00	50.00
J82	D2	1p rose & black	.65	4.00
a.		Without period after "A"	45.00	50.00
J83	D2	2p violet & black	.65	5.00
a.		Without period after "A"	62.50	
J84	D2	3p ultra & black	2.75	30.00
a.		Without period after "A"	62.50	
J85	D2	6p gray & black	1.75	22.50
a.		Without period after "A"	62.50	225.00
		Nos. J81-J85 (5)	6.45	71.00

> Catalogue values for unused stamps in this section, from this point to the end of the section, are for Never Hinged items.

D3

Wmk. 201
1931, Feb. 23   Litho.   Perf. 12
Size: 19x22mm

J86	D3	½p yel green & blk	2.00	8.50
		On cover		120.00
J87	D3	1p rose & black	2.00	1.65
		On cover		90.00
J88	D3	2p violet & black	2.50	3.25
		On cover		90.00
J89	D3	3p blue & black	5.00	15.00
		On cover		130.00
J90	D3	6p gray & black	17.50	30.00
		On cover		275.00
		Nos. J86-J90 (5)	29.00	58.40

Cover values are for properly franked commercial items. Philatelic usages also exist and sell for less.

OFFICIAL STAMPS

Nos. 85-87 (Setting VIII) Overprinted at top with type "c" on English-inscribed Stamps and type "d" on Afrikaans-inscribed Stamps

OFFICIAL   OFFISIEEL

c   d

Without Periods after Words

1927		Wmk. 201	Perf. 14½x14	
O1	A5	½p dk green & blk, pair	95.00	200.00
a.		Single, English	12.50	30.00
b.		Single, Afrikaans	12.50	30.00
O2	A6	1p car & blk, pair	95.00	200.00
a.		Single, English	12.50	30.00
b.		Single, Afrikaans	12.50	30.00
O3	A7	6p org & grn, pair	120.00	225.00
a.		Single, English	15.00	30.00
b.		Single, Afrikaans	15.00	30.00

South Africa No. 5 Overprinted As Nos. 85-87 plus "c" and "d"
Perf. 14
Wmk. 177

O4	A2	2p dull violet	225.00	375.00
a.		Single, English	35.00	45.00
b.		Single, Afrikaans	35.00	45.00

Nos. 96-98 Overprinted like Nos. J79-J85 at foot, Overprinted Types "c" and "d" at Top

1929		Wmk. 201	Perf. 14½x14	
O5	A5	½p green & blk, pair	1.25	17.50
a.		Single, English	.25	2.75
b.		Single, Afrikaans	.25	2.75
O6	A6	1p car & blk, pair	2.00	23.00
a.		Single, English	.25	3.25
b.		Single, Afrikaans	.25	3.25
O7	A7	6p org & grn, pair	4.50	23.00
a.		Single, English	.75	3.75
b.		Single, Afrikaans	.75	3.75
		Nos. O5-O7 (3)	7.75	63.50

No. 99 Overprinted in Black

OFFICIAL / OFFISIEEL — S.W.A. / S.W.A.

With Periods after Words
Perf. 14

O8	A8	2p vio brn & gray, pair	2.50	22.50
a.		Single, English	.35	3.75
b.		Single, Afrikaans	.35	3.75
c.		Without period after "OFFICIAL"	7.00	50.00
d.		Pair, "c" + normal 2p	17.00	95.00
e.		Without period after "OFFISIEEL"	7.00	50.00
f.		Pair, "e" + normal 2p	17.00	95.00
g.		Pair, "c" + "e"	22.00	95.00

In each sheet of 120 stamps there were 12 No. O8c and 10 No. O8e.

South Africa Nos. 23-25 Overprinted

OFFICIAL / OFFISIEEL — S.W.A. / S.W.A.

Without Periods after Words

1929		Wmk. 201	Perf. 14½x14	
O9	A5	½p green & blk, pair	.85	16.00
a.		Single, English	.25	2.75
b.		Single, Afrikaans	.25	2.75
O10	A6	1p car & blk, pair	1.25	17.50
a.		Single, English	.25	3.25
b.		Single, Afrikaans	.25	3.25
O11	A7	6p org & grn, pair	3.00	27.50
a.		Single, English	.40	6.50
b.		Single, Afrikaans	.40	6.50
		Nos. O9-O11 (3)	5.10	61.00

South Africa No. 26 Overprinted

OFFICIAL S.W.A. / OFFISIEEL S.W.A.

With Periods after Words
Perf. 14

O12	A8	2p vio brn & gray, pair	1.50	22.00
a.		Single, English	.25	3.50
b.		Single, Afrikaans	.25	3.50
c.		Without period after "OFFICIAL"	3.75	45.00
d.		Pair, "c" + normal 2p	17.00	95.00
e.		Without period after "OFFISIEEL"	6.50	50.00
f.		Pair, "e" + normal 2p	17.00	95.00
g.		Pair, "c" + "e"	22.00	95.00

> Catalogue values for unused stamps in this section, from this point to the end of the section, are for Never Hinged items.

Nos. 108-109, 111 and 114 Overprinted in Red

OFFICIAL

1931

O13	A15	½p green & blk, pair	15.00	22.00
a.		Single, English	1.25	3.75
b.		Single, Afrikaans	1.25	3.75
O14	A16	1p red & indigo, pair	1.50	19.00
a.		Single, English	.25	3.50
b.		Single, Afrikaans	.25	3.50
O15	A18	2p dk brn & dk bl, pair	3.75	11.00
a.		Single, English	.40	2.25
b.		Single, Afrikaans	.40	2.25
O16	A21	6p ol brn & bl, pair	5.75	15.00
a.		Single, English	.50	3.25
b.		Single, Afrikaans	.50	3.25
		Nos. O13-O16 (4)	26.00	67.00

No. 110 Overprinted in Red

1938, July 1   **Wmk. 201**

O17	A17	1½p violet brn, pair	36.50	50.00
a.		Single, English	3.50	6.00
b.		Single, Afrikaans	3.50	6.00

Nos. 108-111, 114 Ovptd. in Red

1945-50   **Wmk. 201**   *Perf. 14x13½*

O18	A15	½p green & blk, pair	14.00	35.00
a.		Single, English	1.50	5.00
b.		Single, Afrikaans	1.50	5.00
O19	A16	1p red & ind, pair ('50)	14.00	20.00
a.		Single, English	.85	3.25
b.		Single, Afrikaans	.85	3.25
O20	A17	1½p vio brown, pair	40.00	55.00
a.		Single, English	5.00	7.00
b.		Single, Afrikaans	5.00	7.00
O21	A18	2p dk brn & dk bl, pair ('47)	675.00	875.00
a.		Single, English	100.00	100.00
b.		Single, Afrikaans	100.00	100.00
O22	A21	6p ol brn & bl, pair	30.00	70.00
a.		Single, English	2.00	8.00
b.		Single, Afrikaans	2.00	8.00
		Nos. O18-O20,O22 (4)	98.00	180.00

Nos. 108-111, 114 Ovptd. in Red

1951-52

O23	A15	½p grn & blk, pair ('52)	19.00	25.00
a.		Single, English	2.00	4.50
b.		Single, Afrikaans	2.00	4.50
O24	A16	1p red & ind, pair	6.00	22.50
a.		Single, English	.40	2.00
b.		Single, Afrikaans	.40	2.00
c.		Ovpt. transposed, pair	110.00	250.00
d.		As "c," single, English ovpt.	10.00	
e.		As "c," single, Afrikaans ovpt.	10.00	
O25	A17	1½p violet brn, pair	30.00	32.50
a.		Single, English	3.00	5.00
b.		Single, Afrikaans	3.00	5.00
c.		Ovpt. transposed, pair	80.00	95.00
d.		As "c," single, English ovpt.	7.50	
e.		As "c," single, Afrikaans ovpt.	7.50	
O26	A18	2p dk brn & dk bl, pair	4.00	26.00
a.		Single, English	.45	3.50
b.		Single, Afrikaans	.45	3.50
c.		Ovpt. transposed, pair	75.00	250.00
d.		As "c," single, English ovpt.	4.50	
e.		As "c," single, Afrikaans ovpt.	4.50	
O27	A21	6p ol brn & blue, pair	4.00	55.00
a.		Single, English	.50	7.50
b.		Single, Afrikaans	.50	7.50
c.		Ovpt. transposed, pair	28.00	170.00
d.		As "c," single, English ovpt.	4.00	
e.		As "c," single, Afrikaans ovpt.	4.00	
		Nos. O23-O27 (5)	63.00	161.00

"Overprint transposed" means English inscription on Afrikaans stamp, or vice versa. Use of official stamps ceased in Jan. 1955.

SPAIN

'spān

LOCATION — Southwestern Europe, Iberian Peninsula
GOVT. — Monarchy
AREA — 194,884 sq. mi.
POP. — 38,219,534 (est. 1983)
CAPITAL — Madrid

Spain was a monarchy until about 1931, when a republic was established. After the Civil War (1936-39), the Spanish State of Gen. Francisco Franco was recognized.

32 Maravedis = 8 Cuartos = 1 Real
1000 Milesimas = 100 Centimos = 1 Escudo (1866)
100 Milesimas = 1 Real
4 Reales = 1 Peseta
100 Centimos = 1 Peseta (1872)

Watermarks

Wmk. 104 — Loops

Wmk. 105 — Crossed Lines

Wmk. 116 — Crosses and Circles

Wmk. 178 — Castle

6 CUARTOS:
Type I — "T" and "O" of CUARTOS separated.
Type II — "T" and "O" joined.

Unwmk.
1850, Jan. 1   **Litho.**   *Imperf.*

1	A1	6c blk, thin paper (II)	650.00	17.00
		On cover		90.00
a.		Thick paper (II)	650.00	25.00
		On cover		125.00
b.		Thick paper (I)	850.00	20.00
		On cover		100.00
c.		Thin paper (I)	850.00	32.50
		On cover		150.00
d.		6c intense black (II)	850.00	32.50
e.		6c intense black (I)	850.00	25.00
2	A2	12c lilac	3,000.	250.00
		On cover		1,575.
a.		Thin paper	4,500.	325.00
		On cover		1,675.
b.		12c violet	4,400.	275.00
		On cover		2,100.
3	A2a	5r red	3,000.	250.00
		On cover		3,100.
		On cover, single franking		9,500.

Stamps punched with a small round hole have done telegraph service. In this condition most of these sell for 20 cents to $20 apiece.
Stamps of 1851 to 1882 cancelled with three parallel horizontal bars or two thin lines are remainders. Most of these are valued through No. 101.

CANCELLATIONS

"Spider"   Town (c-d-s)

Grid   Cartwheel

Several types of cancellations were used on early Spanish issues. Most common are the so-called "Spider" cancels, applied in red, blue or black. Circular date stamp (c-d-s) cancellations and grid cancellations were also generally used. In addition, a variety of pre-philatelic cancels may be found. These sell for more than the other types.

Kingdom

Queen Isabella II
A1   A2

A2a   A2b

A2c

Type I

Type II

6 CUARTOS:
Type I — "T" and "O" of CUARTOS separated.
Type II — "T" and "O" joined.

a.		5r pale red	3,800.	450.00
b.		5r deep dark red	4,800.	500.00
4	A2b	6r blue	3,750.	800.00
		On cover		4,800.
		On cover, single franking		14,500.
		6r deep dark blue	5,850.	900.00
5	A2c	10r green	6,000.	1,700.
		On cover		6,400.
		On cover, single franking		
a.		10r dark green	8,200.	2,900.
b.		10r pale green	6,900.	2,400.

Full margins = ¾mm.

Stamps of types A2, A3, A4, A6, A7a and A8 are inscribed "FRANCO" on the cuarto values and "CERTIFICADO," "CERTIFO" or "CERT DO" on the reales values.

Values for Singles and Covers

Black Spider Cancellations

1		16.50
	On cover	100.00
b.		21.50
	On cover	120.00
2		300.00
	On cover	1,575.
b.		
3		300.00
	On cover	3,100.
4		850.00
	On cover	4,800.
5		2,400.
	On cover	6,400.

Blue Spider Cancellations

1		145.00
	On cover	350.00
b.		100.00
	On cover	350.00
2		1,100.
b.		
3		900.00
	On cover	
4		2,200.
5		6,000.
	On cover	

Red Spider Cancellations

1		135.00
	On cover	300.00
b.		92.50
	On cover	300.00
2		850.00
b.		
3		1,450.
4		1,650.
5		6,250.
	On cover	

Red Circular Date Cancellations

1		32.50
	On cover	145.00
b.		55.00
	On cover	160.00
2		3,750.
b.		
3		475.00
	On cover	2,000.
4		1,350.
5		8,500.
	On cover	

Blue Circular Date Cancellations

1		
	On cover	—
b.		
	On cover	1,575.
2		5,250.
	On cover	
b.		
3		
4		
5		
	On cover	

Black Circular Date Cancellations

1		
	On cover	—
b.		1,100.
2		
b.		
3		
4		
5		
	On cover	

Values for pairs

1	A1	6c blk, thin paper (II)	1,750.	82.50
a.		Thick paper (II)	2,350.	125.00
b.		Thick paper (I)	2,100.	72.00
c.		Thin paper (I)	2,800.	170.00
d.		6c intense black (II)	2,150.	110.00
e.		6c intense black (I)	2,450.	100.00
2	A2	12c lilac	10,000.	900.00
a.		Thin paper		1,000.
b.		12c violet	10,000.	900.00
3	A2a	5r red	8,100.	900.00
a.		5r pale red	8,100.	1,350.
b.		5r deep dark red	9,600.	1,500.
4	A2b	6r blue	10,500.	2,500.
a.		6r deep dark blue	12,000.	3,250.
5	A2c	10r green		6,000.
a.		10r dark green		7,500.

b. 10r pale green — 6,000.

Values for strips of 3
1 A1 6c blk, thin paper (II) 2,700. 160.00
a. Thick paper (II) 3,500. 200.00
b. Thick paper (I) 3,200. 150.00
c. Thin paper (I) 4,000. 340.00
d. 6c intense black (II) 3,400. 190.00
e. 6c intense black (I) 3,750. 200.00
2 A2 12c lilac 1,600. —
a. Thin paper 2,000.
b. 12c violet 1,900.
3 A2a 5r red 2,250.
a. 5r pale red 2,350.
b. 5r deep dark red 4,250.
4 A2b 6r blue 5,000.
a. 6r deep dark blue — 11,500.
5 A2c 10r green — 12,500.
a. 10r dark green 11,500.
b. 10r pale green 11,500.

Values for blocks of 4
1 A1 6c blk, thin paper (II) 5,200. 675.00
a. Thick paper (II) 5,900. 800.00
b. Thick paper (I) 6,500. 600.00
c. Thin paper (I) 7,500. 1,350.
d. 6c intense black (II) 6,400. 750.00
e. 6c intense black (I) 7,000. 800.00
2 A2 12c lilac 1,900.
a. Thin paper 3,000.
b. 12c violet 2,900.
3 A2a 5r red 3,750.
a. 5r pale red 4,500.
b. 5r deep dark red 4,600.
4 A2b 6r blue 22,000. 8,500.
a. 6r deep dark blue 30,000. 9,000.
5 A2c 10r green 23,000.
a. 10r dark green 25,000.
b. 10r pale green 23,000.

A3

A4

1851, Jan. 1   Thin Paper   Typo.
6 A3 6c black 375.00 3.50
On cover, single franking 32.50
On cover, in combination with other stamps 375.00
a. Thick paper 825.00 20.00
On cover 65.00
b. 6c gray black 400.00 4.00
c. 6c intense black 675.00 6.50
7 A3 12c lilac 7,000. 200.00
On cover 1,000.
On cover, single franking 1,000.
a. 12c violet 7,500. 210.00
b. 12c gray 6,500. 375.00
c. 12c dark lilac 6,250. 225.00
8 A3 2r red 24,000. 7,000.
On cover 47,500.
a. 2r deep orange red 30,000. 15,000.
On cover 50,000.
9 A3 5r rose 3,000. 225.00
On cover 2,275.
On cover, single franking 8,800.
a. 5r red brown (error) 22,000. —
b. 5r rose carmine 4,200. 360.00
10 A3 6r blue 5,250. 750.00
On cover 4,100.
On cover, single franking 16,000.
a. Cliche of 2r in plate of 6r — 125,000.
b. Pair, #10, 10a 175,000.
c. 6r deep blue 6,250. 1,450.
d. 6r pale blue 5,750. 1,100.
11 A3 10r green 3,750. 550.00
On cover 2,675.
On cover, single franking 13,000.
a. 10r deep green 4,600. 675.00
b. 10r pale green 4,250. 550.00

Full margins = ¾mm.

Values for Singles and Covers
Black Spider Cancellations
6 ... 3.75
On cover 37.50
7 ... 225.00
On cover 1,150.
8 ... 13,500.
On cover 47,500.
9 ... 325.00
On cover 2,650.
10 ... 1,275.
On cover 4,750.

11 ... 625.00
On cover 3,150.

Blue Spider Cancellations
6 ... 42.50
On cover 190.00
7 ... 475.00
On cover 3,150.
8 ... 26,500.
9 ... 1,125.
10 ... 3,500.
11 ... 2,350.

Red Spider Cancellations
6 ... 22.50
On cover 160.00
7 ... 425.00
8 ... 26,500.
9 ... 725.00
10 ... 2,750.
11 ... 1,350.

Red Circular Date Stamp Cancellations
6 ... 250.00
7 ... 575.00
8 ... 26,500.
9 ... 1,250.

Black Grid Cancellations
6 ... 375.00
7 ...

Blue Grid Cancellations
6 ... 300.00
7 ... 1,625.

Red Grid Cancellations
6 ... 525.00
7 ...

Values for pairs
6 A3 6c black 775.00 24.50
a. Thick paper 2,000. 140.00
b. 6c gray black 1,000. 27.50
c. 6c intense black 1,650. 45.00
7 A3 12c lilac 500.00
a. 12c violet 525.00
b. 12c gray 875.00
c. 12c dark lilac 575.00
8 A3 2r red 33,000.
a. 2r deep orange red 39,000.
9 A3 5r rose 6,900. 675.00
b. 5r rose carmine 8,600. 900.00
10 A3 6r blue 2,750.
c. 6r deep blue 3,500.
d. 6r pale blue 2,750.
11 A3 10r green 1,375.
a. 10r deep green 11,500. 1,575.
b. 10r pale green 1,375.

Values for strips of 3
6 A3 6c black 1,300. 80.00
a. Thick paper 3,300. 400.00
b. 6c gray black 1,600. 80.00
c. 6c intense black 2,700. 130.00
7 A3 12c lilac 750.00
a. 12c violet 850.00
b. 12c gray 1,500.
c. 12c dark lilac 925.00
8 A3 2r red —
a. 2r deep orange red —
9 A3 5r rose 1,100.
b. 5r rose carmine 1,500.
10 A3 6r blue 4,400.
c. 6r deep blue 5,750.
d. 6r pale blue 4,400.
11 A3 10r green 2,250.
a. 10r deep green 2,750.
b. 10r pale green 2,250.

Values for blocks of 4
6 A3 6c black 2,000. 350.00
a. Thick paper —
b. 6c gray black 5,000. 450.00
c. 6c intense black 5,450. 700.00
7 A3 12c lilac 36,000. 1,250.
a. 12c violet 44,000. 1,350.
b. 12c gray 38,500. 2,450.
c. 12c dark lilac 38,000. 1,500.
8 A3 2r red —
a. 2r deep orange red —
9 A3 5r rose 21,000. 1,800.
b. 5r rose carmine 27,500. 2,350.
10 A3 6r blue 7,250.
c. 6r deep blue 9,500.
d. 6r pale blue 7,250.
11 A3 10r green 25,500. 3,750.
a. 10r deep green 30,000. 4,500.
b. 10r pale green 28,500. 3,750.

1852, Jan. 1   Thick Paper
12 A4 6c rose 400.00 3.50
On cover, single franking 20.00
On cover, in combination with other values 425.00

a. Thin paper 625.00 5.50
On cover 27.50
b. 6c deep rose 625.00 5.50
On cover 27.50
c. 6c carmine lake 900.00 9.00
On cover 75.00
13 A4 12c lilac 2,600. 150.00
On cover, single franking 875.00
On cover, in combination with other values 1,100.
a. 12c gray lilac 3,600. 225.00
On cover 1,250.
b. 12c dark lilac 3,500. 210.00
On cover 1,100.
14 A4 2r pale red 18,000. 4,500.
On cover, single franking 22,500.
a. 2r orange red 24,500. 6,600.
On cover 27,500.
15 A4 5r yellowish green 2,950. 125.00
On cover 3,600.
On cover, single franking 7,250.
a. 5r green 2,950. 125.00
On cover 3,600.
b. 5r deep green 3,800. 160.00
On cover 4,500.
16 A4 6r grnsh blue 4,600. 525.00
On cover 6,000.
On cover, single franking 7,250.
a. 6r blue 4,600. 525.00
On cover 6,000.
b. 6r dark bluish grn 5,500. 650.00
On cover 7,250.

Full margins = ¾mm.

Values for pairs
12 A4 6c rose 1,400. 11.00
b. 6c deep rose 1,600. 42.50
c. 6c carmine lake 2,250. 52.50
13 A4 12c lilac 7,100. 400.00
a. 12c gray lilac 11,500. 550.00
b. 12c dark lilac 11,500. 600.00
14 A4 2r pale red 55,000. 15,250.
a. 2r orange red 67,500. 16,750.
15 A4 5r yellowish green 5,000. 225.00
a. 5r green 5,000. 350.00
b. 5r deep green 8,100. 250.00
16 A4 6r greenish blue 1,500.
a. 6r blue 1,500.
b. 6r dark bluish green 1,850.

Values for strips of 3
12 A4 6c rose 2,500. 45.00
b. 6c deep rose 4,400. 135.00
c. 6c carmine lake 4,500. 190.00
13 A4 12c lilac 600.00
a. 12c gray lilac 900.00
b. 12c dark lilac 850.00
14 A4 2r pale red 22,500.
a. 2r orange red 27,500.
15 A4 5r yellowish green 525.00
a. 5r green 525.00
b. 5r deep green 675.00
16 A4 6r greenish blue 2,100.
a. 6r blue 2,100.
b. 6r dark bluish green 2,600.

Values for blocks of 4
12 A4 6c rose 3,500. 300.00
b. 6c deep rose 4,400. 600.00
c. 6c carmine lake 6,300. 1,400.
13 A4 12c lilac 900.00
a. 12c gray lilac 1,375.
b. 12c dark lilac 1,300.
14 A4 2r pale red 45,000.
a. 2r orange red 55,000.
15 A4 5r yellowish green 750.00
a. 5r green 750.00
b. 5r deep green 1,000.
16 A4 6r greenish blue 3,150.
a. 6r blue 3,250.
b. 6r dark bluish green 3,900.

Arms of Madrid — A5

Isabella II — A6

1853, Jan. 1   Thin Paper
17 A5 1c bronze 3,000. 400.00
On cover 1,600.
a. 1c golden bronze 4,500. 900.00
18 A5 3c bronze 18,000. 7,000.
On cover 12,000.
a. 3c golden bronze 23,500. 10,000.
19 A6 6c carmine rose 750.00 2.25
On cover 15.00
a. Thick paper 975.00 16.00
b. Thick bluish paper 1,300. 22.50
c. 6c rose red, thin paper 675.00 7.50

20 A6 12c reddish purple 2,750. 135.00
On cover 850.00
a. 12c dark violet 3,500. 165.00
b. Thick paper 3,750. 475.00
21 A6 2r vermilion 15,000. 2,500.
On cover 21,500.
On cover, single franking 150,000.
a. 2r bright vermilion 17,000. 3,750.
22 A6 5r lt green 2,500. 130.00
On cover 3,600.
On cover, single franking 11,000.
a. 5r deep green 3,800. 165.00
23 A6 6r deep blue 3,900. 450.00
On cover 6,000.
On cover, single franking 27,500.
a. 6r blackish blue 4,900. 575.00

Full margins = ¾mm.

Nos. 17-18 were issued for use on Madrid city mail only. *They were reprinted on this white paper in duller colors.*

Values for Singles and Covers
Black Grid Cancellations
17 ... 650.00
On cover 1,850.
18 ... 9,250.
19 ... 13,750.
... 2.75
... 17.00
20 ... 145.00
On cover 1,000.
21 ... 4,000.
22 ... 25,000.
... 145.00
23 ... 4,200.
On cover 525.00
... 7,000.

Red Grid Cancellations
17 ... 2,100.
19 ... 100.00
On cover ...
20 ... 575.00
22 ... 600.00
23 ... 1,500.

Blue Grid Cancellations
17 ... 1,275.
On cover
19 ... 45.00
On cover 160.00
20 ... 400.00
On cover
21 ... 8,000.
22 ... 550.00
On cover
23 ... 1,200.

Red Circular Date Stamp Cancellations
17 ... 1,700.
19 ... 500.00
20 ... 1,000.

Black Circular Date Stamp Cancellations
17 ... 1,700.
19 ... 500.00
20 ... 9.00
23 ... 1,275.

Values for pairs
17 A5 1c bronze 15,500.
17a A5 1c golden bronze 20,500.
19 A6 6c carmine rose 1,600. 8.00
19c A6 6c rose lake 1,700. 27.50
20 A6 12c red violet 325.00
20a A6 12c dark violet — 425.00
21 A6 2r vermilion 10,500.
21a A6 2r bright vermilion 11,750.
22 A6 5r light green 7,500. 325.00
22a A6 5r deep green 9,500. 425.00
23 A6 6r deep blue 10,500. 1,350.
23a A6 6r blackish blue 10,000. 1,500.

Values for strips of 3
17 A5 1c bronze 23,000.
17a A5 1c golden bronze 31,000.
19 A6 6c carmine rose 2,900. 16.00
19c A6 6c rose lake 3,000. 50.00
20 A6 12c red violet 500.00
20a A6 12c dark violet — 675.00
21 A6 2r vermilion 17,500.
21a A6 2r bright vermilion 18,750.
22 A6 5r light green 600.00
22a A6 5r deep green 800.00
23 A6 6r deep blue 2,250.
23a A6 6r blackish blue 2,750.

Values for blocks of 4

17	A5	1c bronze			33,000.
17a	A5	1c golden bronze			45,000.
19	A6	6c carmine rose		3,800.	210.00
19c	A6	6c rose lake		4,000.	675.00
20	A6	12c red violet		—	750.00
20a	A6	12c dark violet		—	1,000.
21	A6	2r vermilion			28,000.
21a	A6	2r bright vermilion			28,000.
22	A6	5r light green		21,000.	900.00
22a	A6	5r deep green		28,000.	1,200.
23	A6	6r deep blue			3,000.
23a	A6	6r blackish blue			4,750.

A7

A7a

Coat of Arms of
Spain — A8

1854　　　　　　**Thin White Paper**

24	A7	2c green		2,650.	525.00
		On cover, single franking			1,100.
		On cover, in combination with other values			4,500.
a.		2c dark green		3,350.	675.00
		On cover, single franking			1,450.
25	A7a	4c carmine		450.00	2.10
		On cover, single franking			12.00
		On cover, in combination with other values			100.00
b.		4c dark carmine lake		675.00	3.50
		On cover			18.00
		Bar cancellation			4.00
26	A8	6c carmine		400.00	1.60
		On cover			18.00
		Pair, on cover			45.00
		On cover, in combination with other values			400.00
c.		6c dark carmine		525.00	2.25
		On cover			30.00
d.		6c pale red		525.00	5.00
		Bar cancellation			3.00
		On cover			35.00
27	A7a	1r indigo		4,000.	350.00
		On cover			2,250.
		On cover, single franking			4,500.
a.		1r blue black		5,250.	425.00
		Bar cancellation			21.00
		On cover			2,750.

28	A8	2r scarlet		2,100.	120.00
		On cover			1,350.
		On cover, single franking			
a.		2r vermilion		2,400.	150.00
		On cover			2,000.
b.		2r pale red		3,250.	160.00
		On cover			2,000.
		Bar cancellation #28			16.00
29	A8	5r green		2,000.	110.00
		Bar cancellation			16.00
		On cover			1,350.
		On cover, single franking			5,400.
a.		5r dark green		2,500.	125.00
		Bar cancellation			16.00
		On cover			1,500.
30	A8	6r blue		4,500.	325.00
		Bar cancellation			25.00
		On cover			4,150.
		On cover, single franking			12,500.
a.		6r dark blue		4,100.	400.00
		Bar cancellation			25.00
		On cover			5,000.

Full margins = ¾mm.

Thick White Paper

24c	A7	2c green		3,650.	525.00
25a	A7a	4c carmine		675.00	17.50
		Bar cancellation			4.75
28c	A8	2r scarlet		—	250.00

See boxed note on bar cancellation before #1.

Thick Bluish Paper

31	A7	2c green		17,500.	2,100.
		On cover, single franking			6,000.
a.		2c dark green		20,000.	2,700.
		On cover, single franking			7,500.
32	A7a	4c carmine		525.00	5.50
		On cover, single franking			37.50
		On cover, in combination with other values			110.00
b.		4c dark carmine lake		700.00	9.00
		On cover, single franking			45.00
32A	A8	6c carmine		1,050.	19.00
		Bar cancellation			2.00
33	A7a	1r pale blue		7,500.	
		Bar cancellation			150.00
		On cover, single franking			27,500.
34	A8	2r dull red		7,500.	700.00
		On cover			2,250.

Full margins = ¾mm.

The 2c with watermark 104 is a proof.

Thin Bluish Paper

31b	A7	2c green		18,500.	2,400.
32c	A7a	4c carmine		600.00	17.50
32Ad	A8	6c carmine		—	100.00
33a	A7a	1r pale blue		—	9,500.
34a	A8	2r dull red		7,500.	700.00

**Values for Singles and Covers
Black Grid Cancellations**

24		625.00
	On cover	1,250.
25		2.50
	On cover	14.00
26		1.90
	On cover	21.00
27		415.00
	On cover	2,600.
28		130.00
	On cover	1,500.
29		125.00
	On cover	1,500.
30		375.00
	On cover	4,750.
31		2,400.
	On cover	6,750.
32		6.75
	On cover	42.50
33		9,500.
	On cover	30,000.
34		750.00
	On cover	3,750.

Red Grid Cancellations

24		5.25
	On cover	10.00
25		60.00
	On cover	450.00
26		47.50
	On cover	290.00
27		3.50
28		600.00
	On cover	—
29		600.00
	On cover	—
30		1,000.
	On cover	—
31		20.00
32		57.50
	On cover	60.00
33		450.00
	On cover	80.00
	On cover	275.00

Blue Grid Cancellations

24		950.00
25		35.00
	On cover	100.00
26		13.00
	On cover	52.50
27		850.00
28		275.00
29		350.00
	On cover	—
30		1,000.
32		35.00
33		100.00
		10,000.

**Black Circular Date Stamp
Cancellations**

24		2,000.
25		45.00
	On cover	240.00
26		75.00
	On cover	11.00
27		1,000.
28		525.00
29		550.00
32		50.00
	On cover	375.00

**Red Circular Date Stamp
Cancellations**

24		18.00
26		100.00
	On cover	1,250.

**Blue Circular Date Stamp
Cancellations**

24		14,000.
25		95.00
	On cover	
32		115.00
	On cover	

Values for pairs

24	A7	2c green		6,500.	1,650.
24a	A7	2c dark green		7,500.	2,100.
25	A7a	4c carmine		1,500.	7.50
25b	A7a	4c dk carmine lake		1,900.	11.50
26	A8	6c carmine		1,400.	6.00
		On cover			50.00
26c	A8	6c dark carmine		1,650.	9.00
26d	A8	6c pale red		1,650.	11.00
27	A7a	1r indigo			1,100.
27a	A7a	1r blue black			1,250.
28	A8	2r scarlet		5,600.	350.00
		On cover			2,000.
28a	A8	2r vermilion		5,300.	450.00
28b	A8	2r pale red		9,100.	450.00
29	A8	5r green			350.00
29a	A8	5r dark green			400.00
30	A8	6r blue			1,000.
30a	A8	6r dark blue			1,375.
31	A7	2c green			7,000.
32	A7a	4c carmine		1,350.	17.50
32b	A7a	4c dk carmine lake		1,700.	24.00

Values for strips of 3

24	A7	2c green			3,400.
24a	A7	4c carmine			4,200.
25	A7a	4c carmine			28.00
25b	A7a	4c dk carmine lake			42.50
26	A8	6c carmine		2,350.	26.00
26c	A8	6c dark carmine		2,750.	37.50
26d	A8	6c pale red		2,750.	47.50
27	A7a	1r indigo			1,675.
27a	A7a	1r blue black			2,000.
32	A7a	4c carmine			32.50
32b	A7a	4c dk carmine lake			42.50
33	A7a	1r pale blue			35,000.

Values for blocks of 4

24	A7	2c green		12,500.	7,000.
24a	A7	2c dark green		19,500.	9,000.
25	A7a	4c carmine			55.00
25b	A7a	4c dk carmine lake			850.00
26	A8	6c carmine		1,850.	45.00
26c	A8	6c dark carmine		3,950.	70.00
26d	A8	6c pale red		3,950.	90.00
27	A7a	1r indigo			2,600.
27a	A7a	1r blue black			3,150.
28	A8	2r scarlet			800.00
28a	A8	2r vermilion			1,000.
28b	A8	2r pale red			1,000.
29	A8	5r green			800.00
29a	A8	5r dark green			900.00
30	A8	6r blue			2,500.
30a	A8	6r dark blue			3,200.
32	A7a	4c carmine			80.00
32b	A7a	4c dk carmine lake			115.00
33	A7a	1r pale blue			65,000.

Isabella II — A9

Blue Paper

1855, Apr. 1					**Wmk. 104**
36	A9	2c green		3,400.	140.00
		On cover, single franking			400.00
a.		2c yellow green		4,000.	175.00
		On cover, single franking			500.00
		Bar cancellation, #36 or 36a			10.00
37	A9	4c brown red		300.00	1.00
		On cover, single franking			10.00
a.		4c carmine		440.00	2.50
		On cover, single franking			25.00
b.		4c lake		350.00	.90
		On cover, single franking			10.00
		Bar cancellation, #37, 37a or 37b			2.50
c.		4c brown red, white to grayish paper			5.75
d.		4c lake red, white to grayish paper		475.00	9.25
		Bar cancellation		525.00	2.50
38	A9	1r green blue		1,300.	15.00
		On cover, single franking			110.00
a.		1r blue		1,600.	20.00
		On cover, single franking			140.00
		Bar cancellation, #38 or 38a			5.00
b.		Cliché of 2r in plate of 1r		25,000.	3,250.
		Bar cancellation, #38b			850.00

39	A9	2r reddish pur- ple		900.00	15.00
		On cover, single franking			110.00
a.		2r deep violet		1,450.	20.00
		On cover, single franking			
b.		2r grayish violet		1,450.	20.00
		On cover, single franking			95.00
		Bar cancellation, #39, 39a or 39b			13.50

Full margins = ¾mm.

**Values for Singles and Covers
Black Grid Cancellations**

36		150.00
	On cover	425.00
37		.90
38		5.00
	On cover	17.00
		120.00
39		17.00
	On cover	120.00

Red Grid Cancellations

36		425.00
37		28.50
	On cover	150.00
38		92.50
	On cover	—
39		14.00

Blue Grid Cancellations

36		150.00
	On cover	
37		3.00
	On cover	40.00
38		30.00
	On cover	250.00
39		32.50
	On cover	300.00

**Black Circular Date Stamp
Cancellations**

36		800.00
	On cover	1,150.
37		27.50
	On cover	95.00
38		85.00
	On cover	200.00
39		60.00
	On cover	175.00

**Blue Circular Date Stamp
Cancellations**

37		57.50
	On cover	145.00
38		150.00
39		150.00

Cartwheel Cancellation

36		375.00
	On cover	700.00
37		37.50
	On cover	95.00
38		85.00
	On cover	145.00
39		85.00
	On cover	145.00

Values for pairs

36	A9	2c green		9,500.	525.00
36a	A9	2c yellow green		12,000.	675.00
37	A9	4c brown red		950.00	3.75
37a	A9	4c carmine		1,300.	7.75
37b	A9	4c lake red		950.00	6.25
38	A9	1r green blue		4,000.	50.00
38a	A9	1r blue		4,000.	60.00
38b	A9	2r green blue with #38		50,000.	5,000.
39	A9	2r reddish violet		3,400.	42.50
39a	A9	2r deep violet		4,250.	52.50
39b	A9	2r grayish violet		4,250.	52.50

Values for strips of 3

36	A9	2c green		14,000.	1,850.
36a	A9	2c yellow green		17,000.	2,400.
37	A9	4c brown red		1,250.	5.50
37a	A9	4c carmine		1,750.	1,200.
37b	A9	4c lake red		1,250.	10.00
38	A9	1r green blue		5,800.	85.00
38a	A9	1r blue		6,000.	100.00
39	A9	2r reddish violet		4,600.	65.00
39a	A9	2r deep violet		5,900.	80.00
39b	A9	2r grayish violet		5,900.	80.00

Values for blocks of 4

36	A9	2c green			4,000.
36a	A9	2c yellow green			5,000.
37	A9	4c brown red		2,200.	11.50
37a	A9	4c carmine		3,000.	24.00
37b	A9	4c lake red		2,200.	19.00
38	A9	1r green blue		9,500.	110.00
38a	A9	1r blue		9,500.	130.00
39	A9	2r reddish violet		6,400.	95.00
39a	A9	2r deep violet		8,300.	115.00
39b	A9	2r grayish violet		8,300.	115.00

Rough Yellowish Paper

1856, Jan. 1					**Wmk. 105**
40	A9	2c green		4,000.	250.00
		On cover, single franking			875.00
a.		2c pale green		4,000.	300.00
		On cover, single franking			375.00
		Bar cancellation, #40 or 40a			15.00
41	A9	4c rose		13.50	2.25
		On cover, single franking			20.00
a.		4c deep rose		14.00	3.00
		On cover, single franking			25.00
		Bar cancellation, #41 or 41a			2.50
42	A9	1r grnsh blue		5,500.	200.00
		On cover			800.00
a.		1r dull blue		5,750.	275.00
		On cover			1,200.
		Bar cancellation, #42 or 42a			8.50
43	A9	2r brown purple		600.00	25.00
		On cover, single franking			140.00
a.		2r dark reddish purple		775.00	45.00
		On cover, single franking			175.00
b.		2r grayish purple		650.00	45.00

On cover, single franking 175.00
Bar cancellation, #43, 43a or 43b 7.50

Full margins = ¾mm.

White Smooth Paper

1856, Apr. 11 Unwmk.
44 A9 2c blue green 700.00 42.50
  On cover, single franking 115.00
  On cover with other values, from 160.00
a. 2c yellow green 825.00 50.00
  On cover, single franking 140.00
  Bar cancellation, #44 or 44a 7.50
45 A9 4c rose 5.75 .35
  On cover, single franking 5.25
  On cover with other values, from 32.50
a. 4c carmine ('59) 9.25 20.00
  On cover, single franking 67.50
  On cover with other values, from 115.00
46 A9 1r blue 27.50 25.00
  On cover, single franking 110.00
  On cover with other values, from 160.00
a. 1r pale greenish blue 40.00 32.50
  On cover, single franking 125.00
  Bar cancellation, #46 or 46a 4.00
47 A9 2r brown lilac 90.00 29.00
  On cover, single franking 100.00
  On cover with other values, from 160.00
a. 2r dull lilac 100.00 35.00
  On cover, single franking 140.00
  Bar cancellation, #47 or 47a 10.00

Full margins = ¾mm.

Three types of No. 45.

1859
48 A9 12c dark orange 200.00 55.00
  Bar cancellation
a. Tete-beche pair (#48) 5,750.
b. 12c light orange 1,550.
  Bar cancellation 150.00

Full margins = ¾mm.

Nos. 48-48b were never put in use. All canceled examples have the bar cancellation. Stamps of the 1st printing (#48b) may be distinguished by shade and by a break at lower left, which is not on the 2nd printing (#48).
Reprints exist.

A10   A11

1860-61 Tinted Paper
49 A10 2c green, *grn* 400.00 19.00
  Bar cancellation 2.50
  On cover, single franking 85.00
  On cover with other values, from 115.00
50 A10 4c orange, *grn* 55.00 .80
  On cover, single franking 5.50
  On cover with other values, from 27.50
51 A10 12c car, *buff* 350.00 14.00
  Bar cancellation 8.75
  On cover, single franking 47.50
  On cover with other values, from 140.00
52 A10 19c brn, *buff* ('61) 2,500. 1,200.
  On cover, single franking 9,000.
53 A10 1r blue, *grn* 325.00 12.50
  Bar cancellation 4.50
  On cover, single franking 145.00
  On cover with other values, from 160.00
a. 1r dark blue, *green* 525.00 18.00
b. 1r pale blue, *green* 600.00 18.00
54 A10 2r lilac, *lil* 400.00 11.00
  Bar cancellation 4.50
  On cover, single franking 72.50
  On cover with other values, from 140.00
a. 2r dark violet, *mauve* 550.00 15.00
b. 2r lilac, *blue,* thick paper 750.00 52.50

Full margins = ¾mm.

1862, July 16
55 A11 2c dp bl, *yel* 37.50 11.00
  On cover, single franking 82.50
  On cover with other values, from 130.00
56 A11 4c dk brn, *redsh buff* 2.40 .70
  On cover, single franking 5.00
  On cover with other values, from 26.00
a. 4c brown, *white* 24.00 7.00
  Bar cancellation 2.50
  On cover, single franking 50.00
57 A11 12c blue, *pnksh* 42.50 8.50
  Bar cancellation 3.25
  On cover, single franking 37.50
  On cover with other values, from 125.00
58 A11 19c car, *lil* 200.00 225.00
  On cover, single franking 3,600.
a. 19c carmine, *white* 300.00 275.00
  On cover, single franking 4,000.

Bar cancellation, #58 or 58a 175.00
59 A11 1r brown, *yel* 57.50 17.50
  Bar cancellation 3.50
  On cover, single franking 140.00
  On cover with other values, from 140.00
a. 1r brown, *yellow gold* 300.00 60.00
60 A11 2r green, *pnksh* 37.50 11.00
  Bar cancellation 3.25
  On cover, single franking 72.50
  On cover with other values, from 85.00
a. 2r yellow green, *rose* 45.00 14.00
b. 2r dark yellow green, *rose* 70.00 21.00
Nos. 55-60 (6) 377.40 273.70

Full margins = ¾mm.

A12   A13

1864, Jan. 1
61 A12 2c dk bl, *lil* 50.00 20.00
  On cover, single franking 82.50
  On cover with other values, from 160.00
62 A12 4c rose, *redsh buff* 2.50 1.00
  On cover, single franking 5.75
  On cover with other values, from 24.00
a. 4c carmine, *reddish buff* 22.50 7.50
  Bar cancellation, #62 or 62a 2.50
63 A12 12c green, *pnksh* 42.50 14.50
  On cover, single franking 55.00
  On cover with other values, from 125.00
a. 12c dark green, *pnksh* 67.50 17.50
64 A12 19c violet, *pnksh* 210.00 190.00
  On cover, single franking 4,500.
65 A12 1r brown, *grn* 190.00 75.00
  Bar cancellation 5.00
  On cover, single franking 375.00
  On cover with other values, from 350.00
66 A12 2r blue, *pnksh* 45.00 12.00
  On cover, single franking 72.50
  On cover with other values, from 130.00
a. 2r deep blue, *pnksh* 65.00 17.50
  Bar cancellation, #66 or 66a 5.00
Nos. 61-66 (6) 540.00 312.50

Full margins = 1mm.

1865, Jan. 1 Litho. Imperf.
67 A13 2c rose 325.00 35.00
  On cover, single franking 150.00
  On cover with other values, from 150.00
68 A13 4c blue 2,750.
69 A13 12c blue & rose 425.00 19.00
  Bar cancellation 5.25
  On cover, single franking 80.00
  On cover with other values, from 140.00
a. Frame inverted 13,500. 800.00
  Bar cancellation 100.00
b. Pair, #69, 69a 2,750.
70 A13 19c brown & rose 1,300. 600.00
  On cover, single franking 100.00
  On cover with other values, from 6,400.
71 A13 1r yellow grn 425.00 65.00
  Bar cancellation 17.50
  On cover, single franking 275.00
  On cover with other values, from 275.00
72 A13 2r red lilac 425.00 35.00
  Bar cancellation 16.00
  On cover, single franking 175.00
  On cover with other values, from 175.00
73 A13 2r rose 550.00 65.00
  Bar cancellation 17.50
  On cover, single franking 250.00
  On cover with other values, from 250.00
a. 2r salmon 475.00 70.00
  Bar cancellation 12.50
  On cover, single franking 350.00
  On cover with other values, from 325.00
b. 2r orange 575.00 100.00
c. 2r yellow brown 600.00 110.00

Full margins = 1mm.

No. 68 is without gum and was never put in use.

A majority of the perforated stamps from 1865 to about 1950 are rather poorly centered. The very fine examples that are valued will be fairly well centered. Poorly centered stamps sell for less. Stamps of some issues are almost always badly centered, and our values will be for examples with fine centering. Such issues will be noted.

1865, Jan. 1 *Perf. 14*
74 A13 2c rose red 600.00 130.00
  Bar cancellation 13.50
  On cover, single franking 300.00
  On cover with other values, from 425.00
75 A13 4c blue 60.00 1.00
  On cover, single franking 5.75
  On cover with other values, from 30.00
76 A13 12c blue & rose 750.00 60.00
  Bar cancellation 10.50
  On cover, single franking 100.00
  On cover with other values, from 190.00
a. Frame inverted 20,000. 2,650.
  As "a," bar cancel 50.00
b. Pair, #76, 76a 30,000. 4,000.
77 A13 19c brown & rose 4,000. 2,500.
  On cover, single franking 13,500.
78 A13 1r yellow grn 2,000. 525.00
  Bar cancellation 26.50
  On cover, single franking 1,000.
  On cover with other values, from 1,225.
a. 1r dark green 2,400. 600.00
  Bar cancellation 26.50
  On cover, single franking 1,250.
79 A13 2r violet 1,700. 250.00
  Bar cancellation 24.00
  On cover, single franking 925.00
  On cover with other values, from 1,425.
80 A13 2r rose 1,400. 350.00
  On cover, single franking 1,100.
  On cover with other values, from 1,850.
a. 2r salmon 1,400. 350.00
  On cover, single franking 1,100.
  On cover with other values, from 1,850.
b. 2r dull orange 1,400. 350.00
  On cover, single franking 1,100.
  On cover with other values, from 1,850.
  Bar cancellation, #80, 80a or 80b 35.00

Values for Nos. 74-80 are for stamps with perforations touching the frame on at least one side.

A14   A14a

1866, Jan. 1
81 A14 2c rose 250.00 32.50
  On cover, single franking 82.50
  On cover with other values, from 125.00
a. 2c dark carmine 375.00 35.00
  On cover, single franking 90.00
  On cover with other values, from 140.00
  Bar cancellation, #81 or 81a 5.50
82 A14 4c blue 42.50 .80
  On cover, single franking 7.75
  On cover with other values, from 30.00
83 A14 12c orange 260.00 12.75
  On cover, single franking 47.50
  On cover with other values, from 62.50
a. 12c orange yellow 350.00 25.00
  On cover, single franking 85.00
  On cover with other values, from 125.00
84 A14 19c brown 1,250. 525.00
  Bar cancellation 50.00
  On cover, single franking 1,575.
  On cover with other values, from 2,125.
Nos. 81-84 (4) 1,802. 571.05

1866
85 A14 10c green 300.00 27.50
  Bar cancellation 4.00
  On cover, single franking 125.00
  On cover with other values, from 150.00
86 A14 20c lilac 200.00 21.00
  Bar cancellation 4.00
  On cover, single franking 110.00
  On cover with other values, from 150.00

87 A14a 20c dull lilac 1,250. 75.00
  Ori cover, single franking 225.00
  On cover with other values, from 275.00
a. 20c dark lilac 1,250. 100.00
  Bar cancellation, #87 or 87a 3.00
Nos. 85-87 (3) 1,750. 123.50

For the Type A14a 20c in green, see Cuba No. 25.

A15   A15a

A15b   A15c

1867-68
88 A15 2c yell brn 450.00 47.50
  On cover, single franking 110.00
  On cover with other values, from 150.00
89 A15a 4c blue 27.50 1.00
  On cover, single franking 8.00
  On cover with other values, from 30.00
90 A15b 12c org yell 250.00 8.00
  On cover, single franking 42.50
  On cover with other values, from 62.50
a. 12c dark orange 300.00 12.00
  On cover, single franking 57.50
  On cover with other values, from 87.50
b. 12c red orange ('68) 925.00 40.00
  On cover, single franking 125.00
  On cover with other values, from 300.00
91 A15c 19c rose 1,450. 425.00
  Bar cancellation 40.00
  On cover, single franking 1,250.

See Nos. 100-102. For overprints see Nos. 114a-115a, 124-128, 124a-128a, 124c-124c, 124e-126e.

A15d   A15e

92 A15d 10c blue green 275.00 24.50
  Bar cancellation 2.50
  On cover, single franking 110.00
  On cover with other values, from 110.00
a. 10c dark green 300.00 30.00
93 A15e 20c lilac 130.00 10.50
  On cover, single franking 47.50
  On cover with other values, from 62.50
a. 20c dark lilac 160.00 15.00
b. 20c gray lilac 160.00 15.00
  Bar cancellation, #93, 93a or 93b 2.50

For overprints see Nos. 116-117, 116a-117a, 116c-117c, 117d, 117e, 117f.

A16   A17

A18   A19

94 A16 5m green 47.50 17.50
  On cover or newsprint, single franking 72.50
  On cover with other values, from 150.00

a.		5m bluish green	60.00	27.50
		Bar cancellation, #94 or 94a		2.50
95	A17	10m brown	47.50	17.50
		On cover or newsprint, single franking		90.00
		On cover with other		100.00
a.		Tête bêche pair	20,000.	
b.		10m yellow brown	45.00	17.50
c.		10m dark brown	60.00	27.50
96	A18	25m blue & rose	225.00	24.00
		Bar cancellation		5.00
		On cover, single franking		100.00
		On cover with other values, from		125.00
a.		Frame inverted		50,000.
b.		25m blue & carmine	250.00	29.00
97	A18	50m bister brown	22.00	.80
		On cover, single franking		7.75
		On cover with other values, from		32.50
a.		50m dark brown	24.00	1.25
		Bar cancellation, #97 or 97a		2.50
		Nos. 94-97 (4)	342.00	59.80

See No. 98. For overprints see Nos. 118-122, 118a-122a, 120c-122c, 122d, 120e, 122e, 119f, 122f.

1868-69

98	A18	25m blue	275.00	17.00
		Bar cancellation		3.50
		On cover, single franking		85.00
		On cover with other values, from		125.00
99	A19	50m violet	29.00	.60
		On cover, single franking		8.00
		On cover with other values, from		30.00
a.		50m blackish violet	37.50	1.25
		Bar cancellation, #99 or 99a		2.50
100	A15b	100m brown	550.00	75.00
		Bar cancellation		2.50
		On cover, single franking		225.00
		On cover with other values, from		250.00
101	A15c	200m green	210.00	14.00
		Bar cancellation		2.50
		On cover, single franking		85.00
		On cover with other values, from		65.00
102	A15c	19c brown	2,700.	525.00
		ing		3,650.
		On cover with other values, from		6,500.

For overprints see #123, 123a, 123c, 123e.

Provisional Government

Excellent counterfeits exist of the provisional and provincial overprints.

For Madrid

Regular Issues
Handstamped in Black

1868-69

116	A15d	10c green	30.00	16.00
117	A15e	20c lilac	25.00	12.00
118	A16	5m green	20.00	5.50
119	A17	10m brown	15.00	5.50
120	A18	25m blue & rose	40.00	14.50
g.		Frame inverted	15,000.	
121	A18	25m blue	40.00	12.00
g.		Double overprint (black & red)		75.00
122	A18	50m bister brn	10.00	5.00
123	A19	50m violet	10.00	5.00
124	A15b	100m brown	100.00	28.50
125	A15c	200m green	37.50	9.00
126	A15b	12c orange yellow (#90)	40.00	11.00
g.		12c dark orange (#90a)	40.00	14.00
h.		12c red orange (#90b)	75.00	18.00
127	A15c	19c rose	400.00	140.00
128	A15c	19c brown	850.00	165.00
		Nos. 116-128 (13)	1,617.	429.00

Nos. 116-128 exist with handstamp in blue, a few in red. These sell for more.
No. 120g was for use exclusively in Salamanca.

For Andalusian Provinces

Regular Issues
Handstamped in Blue

114a	A15	2c brown	87.50	36.00
115a	A15a	4c blue	45.00	25.00
116a	A15d	10c green	45.00	15.00
117a	A15e	20c lilac	32.50	16.00
118a	A16	5m green	22.50	8.25
119a	A17	10m brown	16.50	6.00
120a	A18	25m blue & rose	50.00	15.00
b.		Frame inverted	22,000.	
121a	A18	25m blue	50.00	15.50
122a	A18	50m bister brown	11.00	5.50
123a	A19	50m violet	11.00	5.50
124a	A15b	100m brown	110.00	32.50
125a	A15c	200m green	35.00	12.00
126a	A15b	12c org yel (#90)	37.50	13.50
b.		12c dark org (#90a)	60.00	18.00
127a	A15c	19c rose	475.00	210.00
128a	A15c	19c brown	950.00	275.00
		Nos. 114a-128a (15)	1,978.	690.75

For Valladolid Province

Regular Issues
Handstamped in Black

(Two types of overprint)

116c	A15d	10c green	45.00	16.50
117c	A15e	20c lilac	42.50	19.00
118c	A16	5m green (#94)	20.00	
119c	A17	10m brown (#95)	20.00	
120c	A18	25m blue & rose	65.00	15.00
121c	A18	25m blue	65.00	21.00
122c	A18	50m bister brown	18.00	9.25
123c	A19	50m violet	18.00	7.75
124c	A15b	100m brown	130.00	38.00
125c	A15c	200m green	45.00	15.00
126c	A15b	12c orange	45.00	12.50
127c	A15c	19c rose	450.00	175.00
128c	A15c	19c brown	1,150.	240.00
		Nos. 116c-126c (11)	513.50	154.00

For Asturias Province Llanes (Oviedo)

Regular Issues
Handstamped in Black

117d	A15e	20c lilac	210.00	125.00
122d	A18	50m bister brown	230.00	125.00

For Teruel Province

Regular Issues
Handstamped in Black

117e	A15e	20c lilac	90.00	55.00
120e	A18	25m blue & rose	110.00	55.00
122e	A18	50m bister brown	85.00	32.50
123e	A19	50m violet	85.00	32.50
124e	A15b	100m brown	185.00	75.00
125e	A15c	200m green	135.00	45.00
126e	A15b	12c orange	110.00	60.00
		Nos. 117e-126e (7)	800.00	355.00

For Salamanca Province

Regular Issues
Handstamped in Blue

117f	A15e	20c lilac	90.00	55.00
119f	A17	10m brown	80.00	42.00
122f	A18	50m bister brown	90.00	50.00
		Nos. 117f-122f (3)	260.00	147.00

Duke de la Torre Regency

"España" — A20

1870, Jan. 1

				Typo.
159	A20	1m brn lil, *buff*	6.50	6.50
		Bar cancellation		2.00
		On cover, single franking		110.00
		On cover with other values, from		125.00
a.		1m brn lil, *buff*	7.00	7.75
161	A20	2m blk, *pinkish*	7.75	8.00
		On cover with other values, from		110.00
a.		2m black, *buff*	8.75	9.00
		On cover, single franking		125.00
163	A20	4m bister brn	16.00	13.50
		On cover, single franking		160.00
164	A20	10m rose	19.00	6.00
		On cover, single franking		165.00
		On cover with other values, from		95.00
a.		10m carmine	21.00	7.50
		On cover, single franking		110.00
165	A20	25m lilac	52.50	6.50
		Bar cancellation		2.00
		On cover, single franking		35.00
a.		25m gray lilac	55.00	6.50
		On cover, single franking		30.00
		On cover with other values, from		27.50
b.		25m aniline violet	85.00	8.25
		On cover, single franking		35.00
166	A20	50m ultra	11.50	.35
		On cover, single franking		3.50
		On cover with other values, from		7.50
a.		50m dull blue	125.00	5.00
		On cover, single franking		75.00
167	A20	100m red brown	35.00	5.25
		Bar cancellation		1.40
		On cover, single franking		27.50
		On cover with other values, from		19.00
a.		100m claret	35.00	6.25
		On cover, single franking		32.50
b.		100m orange brown	35.00	5.50
		On cover, single franking		27.50
168	A20	200m pale brown	32.50	5.25
		Bar cancellation		2.00
		On cover, single franking		22.50
		On cover with other values, from		19.00
169	A20	400m green	350.00	25.00
		Bar cancellation		3.00
		On cover, single franking		110.00
		On cover with other values, from		85.00
170	A20	1e600m dull lilac	1,700.	850.00
		Bar cancellation		27.50
		On cover, single franking		7,000.
171	A20	2e blue	1,400.	525.00
		Bar cancellation		27.50
		On cover		—
172	A20	12c red brown	325.00	7.25
		On cover, single franking		30.00
		On cover with other values, from		40.00
a.		12c deep brown	260.00	7.00
		On cover, single franking		35.00
173	A20	19c yellow green	450.00	225.00
		On cover, single franking		1,750.
a.		19c bright green	310.00	210.00
		On cover, single franking		2,100.

The 12c carmine rose and 12c blue on pink paper were not put in use. Value $1,000. and $1,250., respectively.

Kingdom

A21

1872, Oct. 1   *Imperf.*

174	A21	¼c ultra	2.25	2.25
		On cover, pair of ¼c only		60.00
a.		Complete 1c (block of 4 ¼c)	120.00	90.00
		Bar cancellation		5.00
		On cover		110.00
b.		As "a," one cliche inverted	1,800.	1,750.

See No. 221A.

A22

King Amadeo
A23   A24

1872-73   *Perf.* 14

176	A22	2c gray lilac	20.00	8.00
		On cover or newsprint		75.00
		On cover with other values, from		70.00
a.		2c violet	90.00	10.00
		On cover or newsprint, single franking		110.00
b.		Imperf.		75.00
177	A22	5c green	150.00	62.50
		On cover with other values, from		175.00
a.		Imperf.	170.00	175.00
178	A23	5c rose ('73)	27.50	5.75
		On cover, single franking		42.50
		On cover with other values, from		40.00
179	A23	6c blue	160.00	39.00
		On cover, single franking		110.00
		On cover with other values, from		140.00
180	A23	10c brown lilac	400.00	240.00
		On cover, single franking		450.00
		On cover with other values, from		425.00
181	A23	10c ultra ('73)	10.00	.55
		On cover, single franking		2.50
		On cover with other values, from		6.50
182	A23	12c gray lilac	27.50	3.00
		Bar cancellation		3.10
		On cover, single franking		11.00
		On cover with other values, from		27.50
183	A23	20c gray vio ('73)	140.00	80.00
		Bar cancellation		5.25
		On cover, single franking		175.00
		On cover with other values, from		160.00
184	A23	25c brown	90.00	12.00
		Bar cancellation		2.10
		On cover, single franking		32.50
185	A23	40c pale red brn	65.00	10.50
		Bar cancellation		2.10
		On cover, single franking		27.50
186	A23	50c deep green	105.00	11.00
		Bar cancellation		2.10
		On cover, single franking		65.00
		On cover with other values, from		47.50
187	A24	1p lilac	115.00	55.00
		Bar cancellation		3.50
		On cover, single franking		200.00
		On cover with other values, from		140.00
188	A24	4p red brown	750.00	625.00
		Bar cancellation		8.00
		On cover		
189	A24	10p deep green	2,300.	2,400.
		Bar cancellation		260.00
		On cover		15,000.

First Republic

Mural Crown
A25

"España"
A26

1873, July 1   *Imperf.*

190	A25	¼c green	1.00	1.00
a.		Complete 1c (block of 4 ¼c)	37.50	20.00
		As "a," bar cancellation		2.50
		As "a," on cover		85.00
b.		As "a," deep green	45.00	35.00
c.		As "a," bluish green	52.50	25.00
d.		As "a," ultra (error)	210.00	160.00

1873, July 1   *Perf.* 14

191	A26	2c orange	13.50	6.00
		On cover, single franking		75.00
		On cover with other values, from		50.00
192	A26	5c claret	30.00	6.00
		Bar cancellation		2.00
		On cover, single franking		50.00
		On cover with other values, from		27.50
193	A26	10c green	6.75	.35
		Bar cancellation		2.00
		On cover, single franking		3.25
		On cover with other values, from		13.00
a.		Tête bêche pair		32,500.
194	A26	20c black	110.00	25.00
		Bar cancellation		3.75
		On cover, single franking		150.00
		On cover with other values, from		150.00
195	A26	25c deep brown	35.00	6.00
		Bar cancellation		2.00
		On cover, single franking		40.00

	On cover with other values, from			30.00
196	A26 40c brown vio	42.50	6.00	
	Bar cancellation			2.00
	On cover, single franking			32.50
	On cover with other values, from			30.00
197	A26 50c ultra	21.00	6.75	
	Bar cancellation			2.00
	On cover, single franking			32.50
	On cover with other values, from			30.00
198	A26 1p lilac	72.50	32.50	
	Bar cancellation			2.00
	On cover, single franking			190.00
	On cover with other values, from			110.00
a.	1p deep lilac	47.50	32.50	
b.	1p gray	55.00	45.00	
199	A26 4p red brown	800.00	475.00	
	Bar cancellation			12.50
	On cover			—
200	A26 10p violet brn	2,100.	1,750.	
	Bar cancellation			17.50

Only one example of No. 193a is known, and it is in a block of six stamps.

"Justice"
A27

Coat of Arms
A28

1874, July 1

201	A27 2c yellow	22.50	8.50	
	Bar cancellation			2.10
	On cover, single franking			70.00
	On cover with other values, from			40.00
202	A27 5c violet	45.00	10.00	
	Bar cancellation			2.10
	On cover, single franking			35.00
	On cover with other values, from			32.50
a.	5c red violet	32.50	10.00	
	On cover, single franking			45.00
203	A27 10c ultra	12.50	.40	
	On cover, single franking			3.25
	On cover with other values, from			13.00
a.	Imperf.	13.50		
204	A27 20c dark green	225.00	45.00	
	Bar cancellation			4.00
	On cover, single franking			225.00
	On cover with other values, from			150.00
205	A27 25c red brown	50.00	6.75	
	Bar cancellation			2.10
	On cover, single franking			32.50
	On cover with other values, from			27.50
a.	25c lilac (error)	325.00		
	As "a," bar cancellation			30.00
b.	Imperf.			57.50
206	A27 40c violet	450.00	8.00	
	Bar cancellation			2.10
	On cover, single franking			30.00
	On cover with other values, from			27.50
a.	40c brown (error)	250.00		
b.	Imperf.	190.00		
207	A27 50c yellow	105.00	8.25	
	Bar cancellation			2.10
	On cover, single franking			32.50
	On cover with other values, from			30.00
a.	Imperf.	120.00		
b.	50c orange	100.00	9.00	
208	A27 1p yellow green	100.00	34.00	
	Bar cancellation			2.10
	On cover, single franking			190.00
	On cover with other values, from			—
a.	1p emerald	92.50	47.50	
	On cover, single franking			250.00
b.	Imperf.	175.00		
209	A27 4p rose	800.00	410.00	
	Bar cancellation			8.00
	On cover			—
	On cover with other values, from			1,900.
a.	4p carmine	800.00	600.00	
	On cover, single franking			—
210	A27 10p black	3,200.	1,900.	
	Bar cancellation			10.50
	On cover, single franking			—
	On cover with other values, from			4,000.

1874, Oct. 1

211	A28 10c red brown	25.00	.70	
	Bar cancellation			1.60
	On cover			3.75
a.	10c brown	42.50	3.50	
b.	Imperf.	90.00		

Kingdom

Nos. 212-221 are almost always badly centered and are often irregularly perforated. Values are for stamps with complete perforations and fine centering. Sound stamps with average centering are worth about 50% of these values. Stamps with very fine centering sell for more.

King
Alfonso XII — A29

1875, Aug. 1
Blue Framed Numbers on Back, 1-100 on Each Sheet

212	A29 2c orange brown	22.50	11.00	
	On cover, single franking			60.00
	On cover with other values, from			55.00
a.	2c chocolate brown	30.00	15.00	
	On cover, single franking			85.00
b.	Imperf.	45.00	45.00	
213	A29 5c lilac	95.00	13.00	
	On cover, single franking			45.00
	On cover with other values, from			37.50
	Imperf.	95.00	87.50	
214	A29 10c blue	8.25	.40	
	Bar cancellation			2.00
	On cover, single franking			3.75
	On cover with other values, from			13.00
a.	Imperf.	22.50	22.50	
215	A29 20c brown orange	300.00	125.00	
	On cover, single franking			300.00
	On cover with other values, from			275.00
216	A29 25c rose	72.50	8.00	
	Bar cancellation			2.00
	On cover, single franking			30.00
	On cover with other values, from			25.00
217	A29 40c deep brown	125.00	37.50	
	Bar cancellation			4.50
	On cover, single franking			65.00
	On cover with other values, from			50.00
a.	Imperf.	140.00	140.00	
218	A29 50c gray lilac	175.00	42.50	
	Bar cancellation			5.25
	On cover, single franking			65.00
	On cover with other values, from			65.00
219	A29 1p black	225.00	80.00	
	Bar cancellation			3.00
	On cover, single franking			140.00
	On cover with other values, from			130.00
220	A29 4p dark green	600.00	525.00	
	On cover, single franking			—
	On cover, with other values, from			1,000.
221	A29 10p ultra	1,800.	1,750.	
	On cover, single franking			—
	On cover, with other values, from			3,500.

1876, June 1 — Imperf.

221A	A21 ¼c green		.25	.25
	On cover			9.00
	Complete 1c (block 4 ¼c)	1.10	.30	
a.	As "b," on cover			30.00
c.	As "b," two ¼c sideways, one invtd.	110.00	110.00	
d.	As "b," both upper ¼c invtd.	140.00	140.00	
e.	As "b," upper left ¼c invtd.	1,000.	500.00	
f.	As "b," both lower ¼c invtd.	140.00	140.00	

No. 221Ac has one stamp upright, one inverted, one facing right and one facing left.

Nos. 222-230 are almost always badly centered. Values are for stamps with fine centering, fresh color and, in the case of mint stamps, full original gum. Sound stamps with average centering are worth about 50% of these values. Stamps with very fine centering sell for more.

King Alfonso XII
A30　　A31

Type I

Type II

ONE PESETA:

Type I — Thin figures of value and "PESETA" in thick letters.
Type II — Thick figures of value and "PESETA" in thin letters.

Wmk. 178
1876, June 1 — Engr. — Perf. 14

222	A30 5c yellow brown	15.50	3.75	
	On cover, single franking			35.00
	On cover with other values, from			25.00
223	A30 10c blue	3.75	.45	
	Bar cancellation			50.00
	On cover with other values, from			2.75
				13.00
224	A30 20c bronze green	19.00	13.00	
	On cover, single franking			50.00
	On cover with other values, from			40.00
a.	20c dark green	19.00	15.00	
	On cover			65.00
225	A30 25c brown	8.50	5.50	
	On cover, single franking			15.00
	On cover with other values, from			19.00
226	A30 40c black brown	80.00	100.00	
	On cover, single franking			—
	On cover with other values, from			290.00
227	A30 50c green	15.00	6.75	
	On cover, single franking			42.50
	On cover with other values, from			27.50
228	A30 1p dp blue, I	20.00	9.00	
	On cover, single franking			37.50
	On cover with other values, from			45.00
a.	1p ultra, II	27.50	13.00	
229	A30 4p brown violet	55.00	57.50	
	On cover, single franking			—
	On cover with other values, from			1,500.
230	A30 10p vermilion	150.00	125.00	
	On cover, single franking			—
	On cover with other values, from			2,600.
	Nos. 222-230 (9)	366.75	320.95	

Imperf

222a	A30 5c		11.50
223a	A30 10c		5.75
225a	A30 25c		12.50
227a	A30 50c		18.00
228b	A30 1p		26.00
229a	A30 4p		92.50
230a	A30 10p		200.00

Two plates each were used for the 5c, 10c, 25c, 50c, 1p and 10p. The 1p plates are most easily distinguished.

The 20c value also exists imperf. Value $500.

Unwmk.
1878, July 1 — Typo. — Perf. 14

232	A31 2c mauve	32.50	11.00	
	On cover, single franking			35.00
a.	Imperf.	60.00		
b.	2c lilac	35.00	13.00	
233	A31 5c orange	45.00	14.00	
	On cover			30.00
	On cover, single franking			45.00
a.	5c yellow gold	50.00	10.00	
234	A31 10c brown	8.25	.50	
	Bar cancellation			3.00
	On cover			3.00
235	A31 20c black	175.00	125.00	
	On cover			290.00
a.	Imperf.	275.00		
236	A31 25c olive bister	25.00	2.75	
	Bar cancellation			6.25
	On cover			8.50
237	A31 40c red brown	190.00	140.00	
	On cover			375.00
238	A31 50c blue green	120.00	11.00	
	On cover			32.50
239	A31 1p gray	100.00	21.00	
	Bar cancellation			2.00
	On cover			80.00
	On cover, single franking			100.00
240	A31 4p violet	225.00	125.00	
	On cover			1,200.
241	A31 10p blue	450.00	350.00	
	On cover			1,900.
a.	Imperf.	475.00		
	Nos. 232-241 (10)	1,370.	800.25	

A32

A33

1879, May 1

242	A32 2c black	9.50	4.50	
	Bar cancellation			3.00
	On cover			22.50
243	A32 5c gray green	15.00	1.10	
	Bar cancellation			3.00
	On cover			14.00
	On cover, single franking			17.50
244	A32 10c rose	15.00	.45	
	Bar cancellation			2.00
	On cover			2.50
245	A32 20c red brown	175.00	15.00	
	Bar cancellation			2.00
	On cover			45.00
246	A32 25c bluish gray	15.50	.45	
	Bar cancellation			2.00
	On cover			13.50

247	A32 40c brown	29.00	5.50	
	Bar cancellation			2.00
	On cover			22.50
248	A32 50c dull buff	130.00	5.00	
	Bar cancellation			2.00
	On cover			22.50
	On cover, single franking			27.50
a.	50c yellow	190.00	7.00	
	On cover			32.50
	On cover, single franking			37.50
249	A32 1p brt rose	150.00	2.25	
	Bar cancellation			2.00
	On cover			32.50
	On cover, single franking			90.00
250	A32 4p lilac gray	750.00	32.50	
	Bar cancellation			3.00
	On cover			1,200.
251	A32 10p olive bister	2,200.	175.00	
	Bar cancellation			6.25
	On cover			5,000.

1882, Jan. 1

252	A33 15c salmon	10.50	.25	
	Bar cancellation			2.00
	On cover			1.75
a.	15c reddish orange	35.00	.45	
	On cover			5.50
b.	15c yellow	40.00	.85	
	On cover			11.00
253	A33 30c red lilac	310.00	5.25	
	Bar cancellation			2.00
	On cover			60.00
	On cover, single franking			65.00
254	A33 75c gray lilac	210.00	4.75	
	Bar cancellation			2.00
	On cover			55.00
a.	Imperf.	300.00		
b.	75c gray	250.00	5.75	
	On cover			140.00

Nos. 255-270 are usually poorly centered and often exhibit defective perforations. Values are for fine to very fine examples, well centered but not very fine, fresh and without perforation faults. Average examples sell for about half these values.

King Alfonso XIII — A34

1889-99

255	A34 2c blue green	6.00	.45	
	On cover			7.00
	On cover, single franking			13.00
256	A34 2c black ('99)	35.00	7.25	
	On cover			30.00
	On cover, single franking			65.00
257	A34 5c blue	12.50	.25	
	On cover			3.25
	On cover, single franking			6.50
258	A34 5c blue grn ('99)	145.00	1.40	
	On cover			7.75
	On cover, single franking			19.00
259	A34 10c yellow brown	16.50	.25	
	On cover			2.75
a.	10c red brown	17.50	.45	
	On cover			5.50
260	A34 10c red ('99)	240.00	4.50	
	On cover			22.50
261	A34 15c violet brown	4.75	.25	
	On cover			1.00
262	A34 20c yellow green	50.00	4.75	
	On cover			25.00
	On cover, single franking			27.50
263	A34 25c blue	20.00	.25	
	On cover			3.25
264	A34 30c olive gray	82.50	5.25	
	On cover			35.00
	On cover, single franking			45.00
265	A34 40c brown	87.50	3.00	
	On cover			22.50
	On cover, single franking			32.50
266	A34 50c rose	80.00	2.10	
	On cover			15.00
267	A34 75c orange	210.00	4.25	
	On cover			30.00
	On cover, single franking			32.50
268	A34 1p dark violet	55.00	.45	
	On cover			45.00
	On cover, single franking			65.00
a.	1p carmine rose (error)			350.00
269	A34 4p carmine rose	650.00	47.50	
	On cover			725.00
270	A34 10p orange red	1,200.	110.00	
	On cover			1,750.

The 15c yellow, type A34 is an official stamp listed as No. O9.
No. 270 exists perf 10. Value, unused $1,000.
Several values exist imperf.

Nos. 272-286 are almost always badly centered. Values are for stamps with fine centering, fresh color and, if unused, full original gum. Sound stamps with average centering sell for about half these values. Very fine stamps sell more more.

King Alfonso XIII — A35

Control Number on Back

1901-05	Engr.		Unwmk.
272 A35	2c bister brown	3.25	.25
	Never hinged	5.50	
	On cover		3.25
273 A35	5c dark green	5.75	.25
	Never hinged	8.75	
	On cover		3.25
274 A35	10c rose red	9.50	.25
	Never hinged	13.00	
	On cover		3.25
275 A35	15c blue black	17.00	.25
	Never hinged	20.00	
	On cover		3.25
276 A35	15c dull lilac ('02)	13.00	.25
	Never hinged	16.00	
	On cover		3.25
277 A35	15c purple ('05)	6.25	.25
	Never hinged	8.75	
	On cover		1.75
278 A35	20c grnsh black	32.50	2.75
	Never hinged	47.50	
	On cover, single franking		30.00
279 A35	25c blue	6.25	.40
	Never hinged	10.00	
	On cover		3.25
b.	25c green (error)	4,000.	
280 A35	30c deep green	42.50	.35
	Never hinged	45.00	
	On cover		3.50
a.	30c pale bluish green	35.00	.40
	Never hinged	55.00	
	On cover		3.50
c.	30c yellow green	32.50	.30
	Never hinged	45.00	
	On cover		3.50
281 A35	40c olive bister	150.00	5.00
	Never hinged	150.00	
	On cover		22.50
	On cover, single franking		70.00
282 A35	40c rose ('05)	300.00	4.50
	Never hinged	375.00	
	On cover		22.50
	On cover, single franking		450.00
283 A35	50c slate blue	32.50	.55
	Never hinged	45.00	
	On cover		4.50
b.	50c blue green (error)	2,250.	1,100.
c.	50c pale greenish blue	35.00	.60
	Never hinged	50.00	
	On cover		5.00
284 A35	1p lake	30.00	.80
	Never hinged	45.00	
	On cover		4.50
285 A35	4p dk violet	250.00	22.50
	Never hinged	325.00	
	On cover		300.00
286 A35	10p brown orange	225.00	72.50
	Never hinged	325.00	
	On cover		450.00
	Nos. 272-286 (15)	1,123.	110.85
	Set, never hinged	2,000.	

There are numerous shades and unissued colors for this issue.

Imperf

272a	A35	2c	57.50
273a	A35	5c	25.00
274a	A35	10c	25.00
275a	A35	15c	110.00
276a	A35	15c	22.50
277a	A35	15c	17.00
278a	A35	20c	90.00
279a	A35	25c	17.00
280b	A35	30c	110.00
282a	A35	40c	300.00
283a	A35	50c	125.00
284a	A35	1p	57.50
285a	A35	4p	200.00
286a	A35	10p	190.00

The 15c in red brown (value $850), 30c blue ($950), 1p olive ($1,000), 1p blue green ($900) and 1p dark violet ($900) were prepared but not issued.

Nos. 287-296 are almost always badly centered. Values are for stamps with fine centering, fresh color and, if unused, full original gum. Sound stamps with average centering sell for about half these values. Very fine stamps sell for more.

Don Quixote Starts Forth A36

10c, Don Quixote attacks windmill. 15c, Meets country girls. 25c, Sancho Panza tossed in blanket. 30c, Don Quixote knighted. 40c, Tilting at sheep. 50c, On Wooden horse. 1p, Adventure with lions. 4p, In bullock cart, 10p, The Enchanted Lady.

Control Number on Back

1905, May 1			Typo.
287 A36	5c dark green	1.25	1.10
	Never hinged	3.75	
	On cover		25.00
a.	Imperf.	50.00	
288 A36	10c orange red	2.50	1.75
	Never hinged		
	On cover		35.00
a.	10c pale red	6.75	
	Never hinged	13.50	
	On cover		70.00
289 A36	15c violet	2.50	1.75
	Never hinged	6.00	
	On cover		37.50
a.	Imperf.	80.00	
b.	15c pale violet	6.75	3.75
	Never hinged	13.00	
	On cover		75.00
290 A36	25c dark blue	7.00	3.50
	Never hinged	18.00	
	On cover		26.00
291 A36	30c dk blue green	50.00	10.00
	Never hinged	115.00	
	On cover		100.00
a.	30c pale blue green	62.50	40.00
	Never hinged	150.00	
	On cover		200.00
292 A36	40c bright rose	70.00	32.50
	Never hinged	225.00	
	On cover		200.00
293 A36	50c slate	22.50	7.00
	Never hinged	49.00	
	On cover		90.00
294 A36	1p rose red	200.00	90.00
	Never hinged	750.00	
	On cover		500.00
295 A36	4p dk violet	110.00	90.00
	Never hinged	225.00	
	On cover		250.00
296 A36	10p brown orange	160.00	135.00
	Never hinged	390.00	
	On cover		300.00
	Nos. 287-296 (10)	625.75	372.60
	Set, never hinged	2,300.	

300th anniversary of the publication of Cervantes' "Don Quixote."
Counterfeits exist of Nos. 287-296.
For surcharges see Nos. 586-588, C91.

Six stamps picturing King Alfonso XIII and Queen Victoria Eugenia were put on sale Oct. 1, 1907, at the Madrid Industrial Exhibition. They were not valid for postage. Value, unused $40, mint never hinged $60.

The original labels were engraved and perf 11½. Examples printed by other methods or with other perfs are reprints. Value $2.

Alfonso XIII — A46

Blue Control Number on Back
Perf. 13x12½, 13, 13½x13, 14

1909-22			Engr.
297 A46	2c dark brown	.55	.55
	Never hinged	2.00	
a.	No control number	.55	.25
	Never hinged	2.00	
298 A46	5c green	2.00	.25
	Never hinged	5.00	
299 A46	10c carmine	3.00	.25
	Never hinged	6.50	
300 A46	15c violet	9.50	.25
	Never hinged	32.50	
301 A46	20c olive green	50.00	.90
	Never hinged	160.00	
302 A46	25c deep blue	4.75	.25
	Never hinged	17.00	
303 A46	30c blue green	9.75	.25
	Never hinged	29.00	
304 A46	40c rose	15.50	.65
	Never hinged	52.50	
305 A46	50c blue ('22)	11.50	.40
	Never hinged	42.50	
a.	50c slate blue	12.50	.40
	Never hinged	24.00	
306 A46	1p lake	32.50	.40
	Never hinged	100.00	
307 A46	4p deep violet	80.00	12.00
	Never hinged	325.00	
309 A46	10p orange	100.00	26.00
	Never hinged	420.00	
	Nos. 297-309 (12)	319.05	42.15
	Set, never hinged	1,200.	

Nos. 297-309 exist imperforate. Value $500.
The 5c exists in carmine; the 10c in yellow orange (value $400); the 15c in blue (value $400); the 4p in lake (value $1,000). The 5c and 15c are unissued trial colors, privately perforated and back-numbered. The 4p lake is known only with perfin "B.H.A." (Banco Hispano-Americano). 100 examples of the 4p exist, most poorly centered.
See Nos. 310, 315-317. For overprints see Nos. C1-C5, C58-C61.
Counterfeits exist.

Control Number on Back in Red or Orange

1917			
310 A46	15c yellow ocher	3.50	.35
	Never hinged	6.00	
a.	Control number in blue	14.50	1.10
	Never hinged	22.50	

Control Number on Back in Blue

1918			
313 A46	40c light red	82.50	5.75
	Never hinged	150.00	

A47

1920		Typo.	Imperf.
314 A47	1c blue green	.25	.25
	Never hinged		.30

Perf. 13x12½, Litho.

315 A46	2c bister	5.00	.25
	Never hinged	15.00	
316 A46	20c violet	42.50	.25
	Never hinged	110.00	
	Nos. 314-316 (3)	47.75	.75
	Set, Never Hinged	145.00	

Nos. 314-315 have no control number on back.
For overprints and surcharge see Nos. 358, 449, 457, 468, 10L1, 11LB1.

1921			Engr.
317 A46	20c violet	30.00	.25
	Never hinged	52.50	

King Alfonso XIII
A49   A49a

Type I   Type II

FIFTEEN CENTIMOS:
Type I — Narrow "5."
Type II — Wide "5."

Type I   Type II

TWENTY FIVE CENTIMOS:
Type I — "25" is 2¾mm high. Vertical stroke of "5" is 1mm long.
Type II — "25" is 3mm high. Vertical stroke of "5" is 1½mm long.

Perf. 11 to 14, Compound

1922-26	Engr.		Unwmk.
331 A49	2c olive green	.85	.25
	Never hinged	3.00	
a.	2c deep orange (error)	87.50	210.00
	Never hinged	125.00	
b.	2c bronze green	1.10	.25
	Never hinged	3.00	

Control Number on Back

332 A49	5c red violet	4.00	.25
	Never hinged	12.00	
333 A49	5c claret	1.60	.25
	Never hinged	6.00	
334 A49	10c carmine	1.60	1.10
	Never hinged	6.00	
335 A49	10c yellow green	1.50	.25
	Never hinged	9.25	
a.	10c blue green ('23)	2.25	.25
	Never hinged	7.50	
336 A49	15c slate bl (I)	8.00	.25
	Never hinged	25.00	
a.	15c black green (II)	27.50	2.25
	Never hinged	65.00	
b.	15c dk slate grn (I)	55.00	19.00
	Never hinged	150.00	
337 A49	20c violet	3.50	.25
	Never hinged	14.00	
a.	20c lilac	5.00	.25
	Never hinged	15.00	
338 A49	25c carmine (I)	3.50	.25
	Never hinged	14.00	
a.	25c rose red (II)	5.50	1.00
	Never hinged	15.00	
b.	25c lilac rose (error)	100.00	160.00
	Never hinged	225.00	
339 A49	30c black brn ('26)	15.00	.25
	Never hinged	42.50	
340 A49	40c deep blue	4.00	.25
	Never hinged	15.00	
341 A49	50c orange	19.50	.25
	Never hinged	60.00	
a.	50c orange red	77.50	1.90
	Never hinged	150.00	
342 A49a	1p blue black	18.00	.25
	Never hinged	70.00	
343 A49a	4p lake	85.00	4.00
	Never hinged	250.00	
344 A49a	10p brown	40.00	13.50
	Never hinged	125.00	
	Nos. 331-344 (14)	206.05	21.35
	Set, never hinged	650.00	

Nos. 331, 334, 336-344 exist imperf. The 5c exists in vermilion (value $110); the 25c in dark blue (value $200). The 50c exists in red brown, the 4p in brown and 10p in lake; value, each $90. These five were not regularly issued.
For overprints see Nos. 359-370, 467.
Nos. 331-344 are almost always found poorly centered.

"Santa Maria" and View of Seville A50

Madrid Post Office — A48

1920, Oct. 1	Typo.	Perf. 13½	
Center and Portrait in Black			
318 A48	1c blue green	.25	.25
	Never hinged	.45	
319 A48	2c olive bister	.25	.25
	Never hinged	.45	

Control Number on Back

320 A48	5c green	1.00	1.10
	Never hinged	2.50	
321 A48	10c red	1.00	1.10
	Never hinged	2.50	
322 A48	15c yellow	1.60	1.40
	Never hinged	3.25	
323 A48	20c violet	1.90	1.75
	Never hinged	5.50	
324 A48	25c gray blue	3.00	3.00
	Never hinged	5.75	
325 A48	30c dark green	7.00	5.50
	Never hinged	17.50	
326 A48	40c rose	29.00	7.25
	Never hinged	72.50	
327 A48	50c brt blue	32.50	20.00
	Never hinged	82.50	
328 A48	1p brown red	32.50	16.50
	Never hinged	82.50	
329 A48	4p brown violet	100.00	70.00
	Never hinged	250.00	
330 A48	10p orange	200.00	145.00
	Never hinged	520.00	
	Nos. 318-330 (13)	410.00	273.10
	Set, never hinged	1,200.	

Perf. 14

318a A48	1c blue green	.25	.25
	Never hinged	.45	
320a A48	5c green	.85	.90
	Never hinged	2.40	
322a A48	15c yellow	1.75	1.40
	Never hinged	4.00	
323a A48	20c violet	2.50	1.50
	Never hinged	7.75	
324a A48	25c gray blue	2.60	2.50
	Never hinged	7.75	
325a A48	30c dark green	5.75	4.25
	Never hinged	15.00	
326a A48	40c rose	30.00	7.25
	Never hinged	100.00	
330a A48	10p orange	350.00	250.00
	Never hinged	1,000.	

Universal Postal Union Congress, Madrid, Oct. 10-Nov. 30.
Nos. 318-330 exist imperforate. Value, $2,500.

Herald of Barcelona — A51

Exposition Buildings — A52

King Alfonso XIII and View of Barcelona A53

1929, Feb. 15   **Perf. 11**

345	A50	1c grnsh blue	2.50	2.50
		Never hinged	4.75	
346	A51	2c pale yel grn	.30	.30
		Never hinged	.65	
347	A52	5c rose lake	.50	.50
		Never hinged	.95	

Control Number on Back

348	A53	10c green	.50	.50
		Never hinged	1.25	
349	A50	15c Prus blue	.85	.85
		Never hinged	1.90	
350	A51	20c purple	.55	.55
		Never hinged	1.10	
351	A50	25c brt rose	.55	.55
		Never hinged	1.10	
352	A52	30c black brn	4.00	4.75
		Never hinged	12.00	
353	A53	40c dark blue	7.75	7.75
		Never hinged	20.00	
354	A51	50c deep orange	7.75	4.75
		Never hinged	11.50	
355	A52	1p blue black	11.50	12.00
		Never hinged	32.50	
356	A53	4p deep rose	25.00	25.00
		Never hinged	62.50	
357	A53	10p brown	65.00	70.00
		Never hinged	115.00	
		Nos. 345-357,E2 (14)	146.25	152.50
		Set, never hinged	340.00	

Perf. 14

345a	A50	1c greenish blue	.70	.70
		Never hinged	1.10	
348a	A53	10c green	20.00	37.50
		Never hinged	32.50	
349a	A50	15c Prus blue	22.50	22.50
		Never hinged	32.50	
350a	A51	20c purple	26.00	37.50
		Never hinged	45.00	
351a	A50	25c bright rose	32.50	37.50
		Never hinged	45.00	
352a	A52	30c black brown	32.50	37.50
		Never hinged	45.00	
353a	A53	40c dark blue	70.00	90.00
		Never hinged	100.00	
354a	A51	50c deep orange	32.50	37.50
		Never hinged	45.00	
355a	A52	1p blue black	32.50	37.50
		Never hinged	45.00	
356a	A53	4p deep rose	25.00	25.00
		Never hinged	55.00	
357a	A53	10p brown	110.00	140.00
		Never hinged	225.00	
		Nos. 345a-357a,E2a (12)	436.70	540.70
		Set, never hinged	725.00	

Seville and Barcelona Exhibitions.
Nos. 345-357 exist imperf. Value, set $2,500. See note after No. 432.

Nos. 314, 331, 333, 335-344 Overprinted in Red or Blue

1929, June 10   **Imperf.**

358	A47	1c blue green	.50	.80
		Never hinged	1.75	

Perf. 13½x12½

359	A49	2c olive green	.55	1.00
		Never hinged	1.75	
360	A49	5c claret (Bl)	.55	1.00
		Never hinged	1.75	
361	A49	10c yellow green	.55	1.00
		Never hinged	1.75	
362	A49	15c slate blue	.55	1.00
		Never hinged	1.75	
363	A49	20c violet	.55	1.00
		Never hinged	1.75	
364	A49	25c carmine (Bl)	.55	1.00
		Never hinged	1.75	
365	A49	30c black brown	2.25	4.00
		Never hinged	7.25	
366	A49	40c deep blue	2.25	4.00
		Never hinged	7.25	
367	A49	50c orange (Bl)	2.25	4.00
		Never hinged	7.25	
368	A49a	1p blue black	11.00	19.00
		Never hinged	32.50	
369	A49a	4p lake (Bl)	11.00	21.00
		Never hinged	32.50	
370	A49a	10p brown (Bl)	40.00	70.00
		Never hinged	120.00	
		Nos. 358-370,E4 (14)	84.55	153.80
		Set, never hinged	250.00	

55th assembly of League of Nations at Madrid June 10-16. The stamps were available for postal use only on those days.
Nos. 359-370 values are for off-center stamps.

Exposition Building — A54

1930   **Litho.**   **Perf. 11**

371	A54	5c dk blue & salmon	6.25	5.00
		Never hinged	9.75	
372	A54	5c dk violet & blue	6.25	5.00
		Never hinged	22.50	

Barcelona Philatelic Congress and Exhibition. "C. F. y E. F." are the initials of "Congreso Filatelico y Exposicion Filatelica." For each admission ticket, costing 2.75 pesetas, the holder was allowed to buy one of each of these stamps.

A55

Locomotives A56

1930, May 10   **Perf. 14**

373	A55	1c light blue	.95	.95
		Never hinged	2.40	
374	A55	2c apple green	.95	.95
		Never hinged	2.40	

Control Number on Back

375	A55	5c lake	1.10	1.10
		Never hinged	2.75	
376	A55	10c yellow green	1.10	1.10
		Never hinged	2.75	
377	A55	15c bluish gray	1.10	1.10
		Never hinged	2.75	
378	A55	20c purple	1.10	1.10
		Never hinged	2.75	
379	A55	25c brt rose	1.10	1.00
		Never hinged	2.75	
380	A55	30c olive gray	3.50	3.50
		Never hinged	8.75	
381	A55	40c dark blue	3.50	3.50
		Never hinged	8.75	
382	A55	50c dk orange	8.00	8.00
		Never hinged	20.00	
383	A56	1p dark gray	8.00	8.00
		Never hinged	20.00	
384	A56	4p deep rose	80.00	100.00
		Never hinged	290.00	
385	A56	10p bister brn	300.00	375.00
		Never hinged	950.00	
		Nos. 373-385,C12-C17,E6 (20)	565.90	652.80
		Set, never hinged	1,800.	

11th Intl. Railway Congress, Madrid, 1930. These stamps were on sale May 10-21, 1930, exclusively at the Palace of the Senate in Madrid and at the Barcelona and Seville expositions.
Forgeries are plentiful.

Francisco de Goya at Age 80 ("1746 1828") ("1828 1928") A57   A59

"La Maja Desnuda" — A58

1930, June 15   **Litho.**   **Perf. 12½**
Inscribed "Correos Espana"

386	A57	1c yellow	.25	.25
		Never hinged	.25	
387	A57	2c bister brn	.25	.25
		Never hinged	.25	
388	A57	5c lilac rose	.25	.25
		Never hinged	.25	
389	A57	10c green	.25	.25
		Never hinged	.25	

Engr.

390	A57	15c lt blue	.30	.25
		Never hinged	.40	
391	A57	20c brown violet	.30	.25
		Never hinged	.40	
392	A57	25c red	.30	.25
		Never hinged	.40	
393	A57	30c brown	4.25	4.00
		Never hinged	5.75	
394	A57	40c dark blue	4.25	4.00
		Never hinged	5.75	
395	A57	50c vermilion	4.25	4.00
		Never hinged	5.75	
396	A57	1p black	5.00	4.75
		Never hinged	6.50	
397	A58	1p dark violet	1.25	.75
		Never hinged	1.75	
398	A58	4p slate gray	.90	.55
		Never hinged	1.20	
399	A58	10p red brown	12.50	7.00
		Never hinged	17.00	

Inscribed "1828 Goya 1928"
Litho.

400	A59	2c olive green	.25	.25
		Never hinged	.25	
401	A59	5c gray violet	.25	.25
		Never hinged	.25	

Engr.

402	A59	25c rose carmine	.40	.35
		Never hinged	.55	
		Nos. 386-402,C18-C30,CE1,E7 (32)	49.40	41.90
		Set, never hinged	66.00	

To commemorate the death of Francisco de Goya y Lucientes, painter and engraver.
Nos. 386-399 were issued in connection with the Spanish-American Exposition at Seville.
Nos. 386-402 exist imperf. Value, set $300. See note after No. 432.

King Alfonso XIII — A61

Two types of the 40c

Type I   Type II

1930   **Perf. 11½, 12x11½**

406	A61	2c red brown	.25	.25
		Never hinged	.25	

Control Number on Back

407	A61	5c black brown	.70	.25
		Never hinged	1.60	
408	A61	10c green	3.25	.25
		Never hinged	9.75	
409	A61	15c slate green	11.00	.25
		Never hinged	45.00	
410	A61	20c dark violet	6.00	.70
		Never hinged	20.00	
411	A61	25c carmine	.70	.25
		Never hinged	1.60	
412	A61	30c brown lake	15.50	1.75
		Never hinged	45.00	
413	A61	40c dk blue (I)	21.00	1.10
		Never hinged	52.50	
a.		Type II	27.50	1.10
		Never hinged	60.00	
414	A61	50c orange	19.00	1.90
		Never hinged	65.00	
		Nos. 406-414 (9)	77.40	6.70
		Set, never hinged	240.00	

Nos. 406-414 exist imperf. Value for set, $350.
For overprints see #450-455, 458-466, 469-487.

Bow of "Santa Maria" — A63

Stern of "Santa Maria" — A64

"Santa Maria," "Niña," "Pinta" — A65

Columbus Leaving Palos — A66

Columbus Arriving in America — A67

1930, Sept. 29   **Litho.**   **Perf. 12½**

418	A63	1c olive gray	.25	.25
		Never hinged	.60	
419	A64	2c olive green	.25	.25
		Never hinged	.60	
420	A63	2c olive green	.25	.25
		Never hinged	.60	
421	A64	5c red brown	.25	.25
		Never hinged	.60	
422	A63	5c red brown	.25	.25
		Never hinged	.60	
423	A64	10c blue green	.85	.70
		Never hinged	1.50	
424	A63	15c ultra	.85	.90
		Never hinged	1.50	
425	A64	20c violet	1.25	1.10
		Never hinged	1.90	

Engr.

426	A65	25c dark red	1.25	1.10
		Never hinged	1.90	
427	A66	30c bis brn, bl & blk brn	5.00	5.50
		Never hinged	14.00	
428	A65	40c ultra	4.50	5.00
		Never hinged	14.00	
429	A66	50c dk vio, bl & vio brn	6.50	5.75
		Never hinged	14.00	

430	A65	1p black	6.50	5.75
		Never hinged	14.00	
431	A67	4p blk & dk blue	8.00	6.50
		Never hinged	14.00	
432	A67	10p red brn & dk brn	25.00	25.00
		Never hinged	70.00	
		Nos. 418-432,E8 (16)	62.85	60.45
		Set, never hinged	107.00	

Christopher Columbus tribute.

Nos. 418 to 432 were privately produced. Their promoters presented a certain quantity of these labels to the Spanish Postal Authorities, who placed them on sale and allowed them to be used for three days, retaining the money obtained from the sale.

This note will also apply to Nos. 345-357, 386-402, 433-448, 557-571, B1-B105, C18-C57, C73-C87, CB1-CB5, CE1, E2, E7-E9, E15 and EB1.

Many so-called "errors" of color and perforation are known.

Nos. 418-432 exist imperf. Value, set $450.

See Nos. 2671, B194 in Scott Standard catalogue, Vol. 6.

Arms of Spain, Bolivia, Paraguay — A68

Pavilion and Map of Central America — A69

Exhibition Pavilion of Ecuador — A70

Colombia Pavilion — A71

Dominican Republic Pavilion A72

Uruguay Pavilion A73

Argentina Pavilion A74

Chile Pavilion A75

Brazil Pavilion A76

Mexico Pavilion A77

Cuba Pavilion A78

Peru Pavilion A79

U.S. Pavilion A80

Exhibition Pavilion of Portugal — A81

King Alfonso XIII and Queen Victoria — A82

Unwmk.

	1930, Oct. 10	Photo.	Perf. 14	
433	A68	1c blue green	.25	.25
		Never hinged	.35	
434	A69	2c bister brown	.25	.25
		Never hinged	.35	
435	A70	5c olive brown	.25	.25
		Never hinged	.35	
436	A71	10c dark green	.35	.35
		Never hinged	1.00	
437	A72	15c indigo	.35	.35
		Never hinged	1.00	
438	A73	20c violet	.35	.35
		Never hinged	1.00	
439	A74	25c car rose	.35	.35
		Never hinged	1.00	
440	A75	25c car rose	.35	.35
		Never hinged	1.00	
441	A76	30c rose lilac	1.75	1.75
		Never hinged	4.00	
442	A77	40c slate blue	1.00	1.00
		Never hinged	1.60	
443	A78	40c slate blue	1.00	1.00
		Never hinged		
444	A79	50c brown org	1.75	1.75
		Never hinged	4.00	
445	A80	1p ultra	2.50	2.50
		Never hinged	5.25	
446	A81	4p brown violet	30.00	27.50
		Never hinged	100.00	
447	A82	10p brown	2.10	2.10
		Never hinged	5.25	

Perf. 11, 14
Engr.

448	A82	10p dk reddish brn	47.50	47.50
		Never hinged	110.00	
		Nos. 433-448,C50-C57,E9 (25)	112.30	103.85
		Set, never hinged	325.00	

Spanish-American Union Exhibition, Seville. The note after No. 432 will also apply to Nos. 433-448. All values exist imperforate. Value, set: hinged $250; never hinged $350.

Reprints of Nos. 433-448 have blurred colors, yellowish paper and an inferior, almost invisible gum. They sell for about one-tenth the value of originals.

Revolutionary Issues
Madrid Issue

Regular Issues of 1920-30 Overprinted in Black, Green or Red

	1931	On No. 314	Imperf.	
449	A47	1c blue green	.25	.25
		Never hinged	.30	

On Nos. 406-411
Perf. 11½

450	A61	2c red brown (G)	.30	.25
		Never hinged	.60	
451	A61	5c black brn (R)	.40	.40
		Never hinged	.70	
452	A61	10c green	.70	.70
		Never hinged	1.25	
453	A61	15c slate grn (R)	1.40	1.50
		Never hinged	2.50	
454	A61	20c dk violet (R)	1.40	1.50
		Never hinged	2.50	
455	A61	25c carmine (G)	1.90	2.25
		Never hinged	3.50	
		Nos. 449-455,E10 (8)	11.35	11.85
		Set, never hinged	22.50	

The status of Nos. 449-455, E10 has been questioned.

First Barcelona Issue

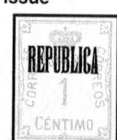

Regular Issues of 1920-30 Overprinted in Black or Red

	1931	On No. 314	Imperf.	
457	A47	1c blue green	.25	.25
		Never hinged	.30	

On Nos. 406-414
Perf. 11½

458	A61	2c red brown	.25	.25
		Never hinged	.30	
459	A61	5c black brown	.25	.25
		Never hinged	.30	
460	A61	10c green	.55	.55
		Never hinged	1.00	
461	A61	15c slate grn (R)	.60	.60
		Never hinged	1.25	
462	A61	20c dk violet (R)	.60	.60
		Never hinged	1.25	
463	A61	25c carmine	.60	.60
		Never hinged	1.25	
464	A61	30c brown lake	4.50	4.50
		Never hinged	10.00	
465	A61	40c dk blue (R)	1.25	1.25
		Never hinged	2.50	
466	A61	50c orange	1.25	1.25
		Never hinged	2.50	

On Stamp of 1922-26

467	A49a	1p blue blk (R)	7.50	6.25
		Never hinged	16.00	
		Nos. 457-467,E11 (12)	23.10	21.85
		Set, never hinged	45.00	

Nos. 457-467 are known both with and without accent over "U."

The status of Nos. 457-467, E11 has been questioned.

Second Barcelona Issue

Regular Issues of 1920- [...] or Red

		On No. 314	Imperf.	
468	A47	1c blue green	.25	.25
		Never hinged	.30	

On Nos. 406-414
Perf. 11½

469	A61	2c red brown	.25	.25
		Never hinged	.30	
470	A61	5c black brown (R)	.25	.25
		Never hinged	.30	
471	A61	10c green	.25	.25
		Never hinged	.40	
472	A61	15c slate grn (R)	1.40	1.25
		Never hinged	2.50	
473	A61	20c dark violet (R)	.40	.45
		Never hinged	.70	
474	A61	25c carmine	.40	.45
		Never hinged	.70	
475	A61	30c brown lake	5.75	5.75
		Never hinged	11.00	
476	A61	40c dark blue (R)	1.25	1.25
		Never hinged	2.25	
477	A61	50c orange	4.50	3.50
		Never hinged	10.00	
		Nos. 468-477 (10)	14.70	13.65
		Set, never hinged	27.50	

The status of Nos. 469-477, C58-C61 has been questioned.

General Issue of the Republic

Nos. 406-414, 342 Overprinted in Blue or Red

	1931, May 27			
478	A61	2c red brown	.25	.25
		Never hinged	.25	
479	A61	5c black brn (R)	.25	.25
		Never hinged	.70	
480	A61	10c green (R)	.30	.25
		Never hinged	.95	
481	A61	15c slate grn (R)	3.50	.25
		Never hinged	6.25	
482	A61	20c dk violet (R)	1.50	1.00
		Never hinged	3.50	
483	A61	25c carmine	.50	.25
		Never hinged	.95	
484	A61	30c brown lake	4.50	1.00
		Never hinged	9.75	
485	A61	40c dk blue (R)	4.50	.55
		Never hinged	9.75	
486	A61	50c orange	7.75	.55
		Never hinged	21.00	
487	A49a	1p blue blk (R)	57.50	1.00
		Never hinged	130.00	
		Nos. 478-487,E12 (11)	87.05	6.60
		Set, never hinged	230.00	

The setting contained 18 repetitions of "Republica Espanola" for each vertical row of 10 stamps. According to its sheet position, a stamp received different parts of the overprinted words.

Overprint position varieties include: reading down on 25c, 30c, 40c and 50c; double on 1p; double, both reading down, on 25c, 40c and 50c.

"Republica Espanola"

Stamps of various Spanish colonies overprinted "Republica Espanola" are listed with the colonies.

Fountain of Lions, The Alhambra, Granada A84

Interior of Mosque, Córdoba — A85

Alcántara Bridge and Alcazar, Toledo A86

Francisco García y Santos A87

Puerta del Sol, Madrid, on April 14, 1931 as Republic Was Proclaimed A88

Perf. 12½

			Unwmk.	**Engr.**
1931, Oct. 10				
491	A84	5c violet brown	.25	.25
		Never hinged	.25	
492	A85	10c blue green	.35	.35
		Never hinged	1.00	
493	A86	15c dark violet	.35	.35
		Never hinged	1.00	
494	A85	25c deep red	.35	.35
		Never hinged	1.00	
495	A87	30c olive green	.35	.35
		Never hinged	1.00	
496	A84	40c indigo	.90	.90
		Never hinged	2.50	
497	A85	50c orange red	.90	.90
		Never hinged	2.50	
498	A86	1p black	1.60	1.60
		Never hinged	5.00	
499	A88	4p red violet	8.00	8.00
		Never hinged	25.00	
500	A88	10p red brown	25.00	25.00
		Never hinged	77.50	
	Nos. 491-500,C62-C67,CO1-			
	CO6,O20-O29 (32)		100.25	99.35
	Set, never hinged		170.00	

3rd Pan-American Postal Union Cong., Madrid.
Nos. 491-500 exist imperforate. Value, set: hinged $150; never hinged $250.

Symbolical of Montserrat Cut With a Saw — A89

Abbott Oliva and Monastery Workman — A90

"Black Virgin"
A91   A92

Montserrat Monastery — A93

				Perf. 11, 14
1931, Dec. 9				
501	A89	1c myrtle green	1.25	1.50
		Never hinged	2.50	
a.		Perf. 14	21.00	21.00
		Never hinged	40.00	
502	A89	2c red brown	.70	1.10
		Never hinged	1.40	
a.		Perf. 14	15.00	16.00
		Never hinged	30.00	

Control Number on Back

503	A89	5c black brown	.85	1.40
		Never hinged	1.75	
a.		Perf. 14	15.00	16.00
		Never hinged	30.00	
504	A89	10c yellow green	.95	1.40
		Never hinged	1.75	
a.		Perf. 14	15.00	19.00
		Never hinged	30.00	
505	A90	15c myrtle green	1.25	1.75
		Never hinged	2.25	
a.		Perf. 14	21.00	25.00
		Never hinged	40.00	
506	A91	20c dark violet	2.50	2.50
		Never hinged	4.50	
a.		Perf. 11	110.00	150.00
		Never hinged	210.00	
507	A92	25c lake	3.50	3.50
		Never hinged	6.50	
a.		Perf. 14	6.25	7.25
		Never hinged	12.50	
508	A91	30c deep red	35.00	32.50
		Never hinged	62.50	
a.		Perf. 14	45.00	45.00
		Never hinged	87.50	
509	A93	40c dull blue	20.00	18.00
		Never hinged	32.50	
a.		Perf. 11	150.00	175.00
		Never hinged	310.00	
510	A90	50c dark orange	45.00	40.00
		Never hinged	90.00	
a.		Perf. 14	70.00	80.00
		Never hinged	140.00	
511	A92	1p gray black	45.00	40.00
		Never hinged	90.00	
a.		Perf. 11	87.50	110.00
		Never hinged	175.00	
512	A93	4p lilac rose	425.00	400.00
		Never hinged	850.00	
a.		Perf. 14	575.00	900.00
		Never hinged	1,000.	
513	A92	10p deep brown	325.00	275.00
		Never hinged	720.00	
a.		Perf. 14	800.00	950.00
		Never hinged	1,500.	
	Nos. 501-511,C68-C72,E13			
	(17)		270.55	262.20
	Set, never hinged		410.00	
	Nos. 501-513,C68-C72,E13			
	(19)		978.00	903.65
	Set, never hinged		2,000.	

Commemorative of the building of the old Monastery at Montserrat, started in 1031, and of the image of the Black Virgin (said to have been carved by St. Luke) which was crowned by Pope Leo XIII in 1881.
Nos. 501-513 exist imperforate. Value, set $4,000.
For surcharges see Nos. 589, C92-C96.

Francisco Pi y Margall — A95

Joaquín Costa — A96

Nicolás Salmerón A97

Pablo Iglesias A99

 Emilio Castelar — A100

Without Control Number

				Perf. 11½
1931-34				
526	A103	2c red brown ('32)	.25	.25
		Never hinged	.40	
528	A103	5c chocolate ('34)	.25	.25
		Never hinged	.40	
532	A95	20c dark violet	.25	.25
		Never hinged	.50	
534	A104	25c lake ('34)	.45	.25
		Never hinged	.80	
538	A100	60c apple green ('32)	.25	.25
		Never hinged	.50	
	Nos. 526-538 (5)		1.45	1.25
	Set, never hinged		2.50	

Imperf

526a	A103	2c	14.00	
		Never hinged	27.50	
528a	A103	5c	2.75	
		Never hinged	5.50	
532a	A95	20c	6.25	
		Never hinged	13.00	
534a	A104	25c	5.25	
		Never hinged	10.50	
538a	A100	60c	6.25	
		Never hinged	13.00	
	Nos. 526a-538a (5)		34.50	
	Set, never hinged		70.00	

For overprints and surcharges see Nos. 8LB3, 8LB7, 9LC3, 9LC8-9LC9, 9LC14, 10L6, 10L13, 11L4, 11L8, 11LB5, 11LB9, 12L5, 12L9, 13L5, 13L7, 14L3, 14L7, 14L15, 14L19.

				Perf. 11½
1931-32				
Control Number on Back				
516	A95	5c brnsh black	3.00	.30
		Never hinged	6.50	
517	A96	10c yellow green	7.25	.30
		Never hinged	18.00	
518	A97	15c slate green	4.75	.25
		Never hinged	21.00	
520	A99	25c lake	22.50	.70
		Never hinged	60.00	
b.		Imperf.	175.00	
		Never hinged	225.00	
521	A99	30c carmine rose	7.25	.25
		Never hinged	18.00	
c.		Imperf.	82.50	
		Never hinged	125.00	
522	A100	40c dark blue	42.50	4.50
		Never hinged	130.00	
523	A97	50c orange	52.50	7.75
		Never hinged	165.00	
	Nos. 516-523 (7)		139.75	14.05
	Set, never hinged		425.00	

Without Control Number

516a	A95	5c brownish blk ('32)	4.50	.25
		Never hinged	7.75	
517a	A96	10c yellow green ('32)	4.00	.25
		Never hinged	7.75	
518a	A97	15c slate green ('32)	.60	.25
		Never hinged	1.10	
520a	A99	25c lake	32.50	.25
		Never hinged	72.50	
521a	A99	30c carmine rose	1.90	.25
		Never hinged	3.25	
522a	A100	40c dark blue ('32)	.25	.25
		Never hinged	.25	
523a	A97	50c orange ('32)	26.00	.50
		Never hinged	57.50	
	Nos. 516a-523a (7)		69.75	2.00
	Set, never hinged		150.00	

Without Control Number, Imperf.

516b	A95	5c	6.50	
		Never hinged	13.00	
517b	A96	10c	11.00	
		Never hinged	22.50	
518b	A97	15c	6.25	
		Never hinged	12.50	
520c	A99	25c	110.00	
		Never hinged	210.00	
521b	A99	30c	5.50	
		Never hinged	11.00	
522b	A100	40c	14.00	
		Never hinged	25.00	
523b	A97	50c	125.00	
		Never hinged	250.00	
	Nos. 516b-523b (7)		278.25	
	Set, Never Hinged		550.00	

See Nos. 532, 538, 550, 579, 579a.
For overprints and surcharges see Nos. 7LC12-7LC13, 7LC15-7LC16, 7LC18, 7LE4, 8LB6, 8LB9-8LB10, 9LC17-9LC18, 10L7, 10L10-10L12, 10L16-10L18, 10L22-10L23, 11L7, 11L10-11L12, 11LB8, 12L4, 12L8, 12L11-12L12, 13L8, 14L6, 14L10-14L12, 14L18, 14L22-14L24.

Blasco Ibáñez A103

Manuel Ruiz-Zorrilla A104

Cliff Houses, Cuenca — A105

Alcázar of Segovia — A106

Gate of the Sun at Toledo — A107

				Perf. 10
1932-38				
539	A105	1p gray black ('38)	.25	.25
		Never hinged	.40	
540	A106	4p magenta ('38)	.30	.40
		Never hinged	.60	
541	A107	10p deep brown ('38)	.65	.70
		Never hinged	1.75	
	Nos. 539-541 (3)		1.20	1.35
	Set, never hinged		2.75	

Imperf

539a	A105	1p	5.25	2.75
		Never hinged	11.50	
540a	A106	4p	9.00	6.50
		Never hinged	20.00	
541a	A107	10p	6.50	6.00
		Never hinged	14.00	
	Nos. 539a-541a (3)		20.75	15.25
	Set, never hinged		45.00	

Perf. 11½

539b	A105	1p	.25	.25
		Never hinged	.40	
540b	A106	4p	.70	.85
		Never hinged	1.40	
541b	A107	10p	1.90	3.00
		Never hinged	3.50	
	Nos. 539b-541b (3)		2.85	4.10
	Set, never hinged		5.00	

For overprints and surcharge see Nos. 9LC19, 10L19, 13L9, 14L25, 14L27-14L28.

Numeral A108

Santiago Ramón y Cajal A109

			Unwmk. Typo.	**Imperf.**
1933				
542	A108	1c blue green	.25	.25
		Never hinged	.40	

Perf. 11½

543	A108	2c buff	.25	.25
		Never hinged	.40	
a.		Perf. 13½x13	.65	.25
		Never hinged	1.40	
	Set, never hinged		.65	

See Nos. 592-597. For surcharges and overprints see Nos. 590-590A, 634A-634D, 8LB1-8LB2, 9LC1-9LC2, 9LC4-9LC7, 9LC11-9LC12, 9LC20, 9LC26, 10L2-10L4, 11L1-11L2, 11LB2-11LB3, 12L1-12L2, 13L1-13L3, 14L1, 14L13.

		Engr.		**Perf. 11½x11**
1934				
545	A109	30c black brown	6.00	1.10
		Never hinged	16.00	
a.		Perf. 14	22.50	30.00
		Never hinged	42.50	
b.		Imperf.	32.50	
		Never hinged	55.00	

Type of 1931 and

Mariana Pineda A110

Concepción Arenal A111

...

Gumersindo
de Azcarate
A112

Gaspar
Melchor de
Jovellanos
A113

1935

546	A110	10c green	.25	.25
		Never hinged	.35	
b.		10c blue green ('36)	.25	.25
		Never hinged	.35	
547	A111	15c green	.25	.25
		Never hinged	.35	
b.		15c yellow green ('36)	.25	.25
		Never hinged	.35	
548	A112	30c carmine rose	7.25	.25
		Never hinged	19.00	
549	A113	30c rose red	.25	.25
		Never hinged	.35	
550	A97	50c dark blue	1.00	.30
		Never hinged	2.50	
		Nos. 546-550 (5)	9.00	1.30
		Set, never hinged	22.00	

Imperf

546a	A110	10c	1.60	
		Never hinged	3.00	
547a	A111	15c	5.25	
		Never hinged	9.50	
548a	A112	30c	26.00	
		Never hinged	47.50	
549a	A113	30c	1.90	
		Never hinged	3.50	
550a	A97	50c	225.00	
		Never hinged	450.00	
		Nos. 546a-550a (5)	259.75	
		Set, never hinged	500.00	

Shades exist.
For overprints and surcharges see Nos.
7LE3, 8LB4-8LB5, 8LB8, 10L8-10L9, 10L14,
10L20-10L21, 11L5-11L6, 11L9, 11LB6-
11LB7, 11LB10, 12L6-12L7, 12L10, 13L6,
14L4-14L5, 14L8, 14L16-14L17, 14L20.

Lope's
Bookplate
A116

Lope de
Vega
A117

Alcántara
and Alcázar,
Toledo
A118

1935, Oct. 12   *Perf. 11½x11, 11x11½*

552	A116	15c myrtle green	6.25	.30
		Never hinged	12.50	
553	A117	30c rose red	2.75	.30
		Never hinged	5.00	
554	A117	50c dark blue	12.00	3.00
		Never hinged	42.50	
555	A118	1p blue black	23.00	2.00
		Never hinged	60.00	
		Nos. 552-555 (4)	44.00	5.60
		Set, never hinged	100.00	

Imperf

552a	A116	15c	450.00	
		Never hinged	625.00	
553a	A117	30c	16.00	
		Never hinged	20.00	
554a	A117	50c	70.00	
		Never hinged	110.00	
555a	A118	1p	65.00	
		Never hinged	90.00	
		Nos. 552a-555a (4)	601.00	
		Set, never hinged	1,100.	

Perf. 14

553b	A117	30c	6.50	14.50
		Never hinged	14.00	
554b	A117	50c	29.00	45.00
		Never hinged	62.50	
555b	A118	1p	32.50	50.00
		Never hinged	75.00	
		Nos. 553b-555b (3)	68.00	109.50
		Set, never hinged	150.00	

Lope Felix de Vega Carpio (1562-1635),
Spanish dramatist and poet.
For surcharge see No. 11LB11.

Map of Amazon
by Bartolomeo
Oliva, 16th
Century
A119

1935, Oct. 12   *Perf. 11½*

556	A119	30c rose red	2.10	.95
		Never hinged	5.50	
a.		Perf. 14	26.00	
		Never hinged	54.00	
b.		Imperf.	37.50	
		Never hinged	72.50	

Proposed Iglesias Amazon Expedition.

Miguel
Moya — A120

Torcuato Luca
de Tena — A121

José Francos
Rodríguez
A122

Alejandro
Lerroux
A123

Nazareth School and Rotary
Press — A124

1936, Feb. 14   *Photo.*   *Perf. 12½*
Size: 22x26mm

557	A120	1c crimson	.25	.25
		Never hinged	.25	
558	A121	2c orange brown	.25	.25
		Never hinged	.25	
559	A122	5c black brown	.25	.25
		Never hinged	.25	
560	A123	10c emerald	.25	.25
		Never hinged	.25	

Size: 24x28½mm

561	A120	15c blue green	.25	.25
		Never hinged	.25	
562	A121	20c violet	.25	.25
		Never hinged	.25	
563	A122	25c red violet	.25	.25
		Never hinged	.25	
564	A123	30c crimson	.25	.25
		Never hinged	.25	

Size: 25½x30½mm

565	A120	40c orange	.55	.40
		Never hinged	.90	
566	A121	50c ultra	.25	.25
		Never hinged	.50	
567	A122	60c olive green	.55	.40
		Never hinged	.90	
568	A123	1p gray black	.55	.40
		Never hinged	.95	
569	A124	2p lt blue	7.25	3.25
		Never hinged	14.00	
570	A124	4p lilac rose	7.25	6.50
		Never hinged	15.00	
571	A124	10p red brown	18.50	15.50
		Never hinged	35.00	
		Nos. 557-571,E15 (16)	37.15	29.00
		Set, never hinged	70.00	
		Nos. 557-571,C73-C87,E15 (31)	68.30	47.90
		Set, never hinged	130.00	

Madrid Press Association, 40th anniversary.
Nos. 557-571 exist imperf. Values about 7
times those of perf. stamps.
See note after No. 432. See Nos. C73-C87.

Arms of
Madrid — A125

1936, Apr. 2   *Engr.*   *Imperf.*

572	A125	10c brown black	47.50	47.50
		Never hinged	55.00	
573	A125	15c dark green	47.50	47.50
		Never hinged	55.00	
		Set, never hinged	135.00	

1st National Philatelic Exhibition which
opened in Madrid, Apr. 2, 1936.
For overprints see Nos. C88-C89.

"Republica
Espanola" — A126

1936   *Litho.*   *Perf. 11½, 13½x13*

574	A126	2c orange brown	.25	.25
		Never hinged	.35	

For surcharges & overprints see #591,
9LC24, 10L5, 11L3, 11LB4, 12L3, 13L4, 14L2,
14L14.

Gregorio
Fernández — A127

1936, Mar. 10   *Engr.*   *Perf. 11½*

576	A127	30c carmine	1.10	.85
		Never hinged	2.25	
a.		Perf. 14	9.00	8.25
		Never hinged	17.50	
b.		Imperf.	15.00	
		Never hinged	22.50	

Tercentenary of the death of Gregorio Fernandez, sculptor.
For overprints see Nos. 7LC20-7LC21.

Type of 1931 and

Pablo Iglesias
A128   A129

Velázquez
A130

Fermín
Salvoechea
A131

1936-38   *Perf. 11, 11½, 11½x11*

577	A128	30c rose red	.25	.25
		Never hinged	.25	
578	A129	30c car rose	1.10	.50
		Never hinged	3.00	
579	A100	40c car rose ('37)	1.10	.50
		Never hinged	3.00	
580	A129	45c carmine ('37)	.25	.25
		Never hinged	.25	
581	A130	50c dark blue	.25	.25
		Never hinged	.25	
582	A131	60c indigo ('37)	.75	.90
		Never hinged	2.00	
583	A131	60c dp orange ('38)	6.00	5.00
		Never hinged	15.00	
		Nos. 577-583 (7)	9.70	7.65
		Set, never hinged	26.00	

Perf. 14

577a	A128	30c rose red	6.50	
		Never hinged	13.00	
578a	A129	30c carmine rose	6.75	
		Never hinged	13.50	
579a	A100	40c carmine rose	6.50	
		Never hinged	13.50	
580a	A129	45c carmine	6.00	
		Never hinged	12.00	
582a	A131	60c indigo	6.00	
		Never hinged	12.00	
583a	A131	60c deep orange	9.50	
		Never hinged	19.00	
		Nos. 577a-583a (6)	41.25	
		Set, never hinged	90.00	

Nos. 577-583 exist imperf. Value, set $70,
never hinged $150.
For overprints see Nos. C90, 7LC17,
7LC22-7LC23, 10L15, 14L21.

Statue of Liberty, Spanish and US
Flags — A132

1938, June 1   *Photo.*   *Perf. 11½*

585	A132	1p multicolored	16.50	17.50
		Never hinged	32.50	
a.		Imperf., pair	82.50	55.00
		Never hinged	110.00	
b.		Horiz. pair, imperf. vert.	62.50	82.50
		Never hinged	92.50	
c.		Souvenir sheet of 1	27.50	32.50
		Never hinged	44.00	
d.		As "c," imperf.	350.00	250.00
		Never hinged	600.00	

150th anniv. of the US Constitution.
For surcharge see No. C97.

No. 289 Surcharged in Black

1938   *Perf. 14*

586	A36	45c on 15c violet	15.50	15.50
		Never hinged	19.00	

7th anniversary of the Republic.
Values are for examples with perforations
nearly touching the design on one or two
sides.

No. 289 Surcharged in Black

a

b

1938, May 1

587	A36	45c on 15c violet	3.00	3.00
		Never hinged	4.00	
588	A36	1p on 15c violet	5.25	5.25
		Never hinged	7.00	
		Set, never hinged	12.00	

Issued to commemorate Labor Day.
Values are for examples with perforations
nearly touching the design on one or two
sides.

No. 507
Surcharged in
Black

1938, Nov. 10 — Perf. 11½
589 A92 2.50p on 25c lake — .25 .25
  Never hinged — .25
  b. Perf. 14 — 3.50 6.00
    Never hinged — 6.00

Types of 1933-36
Surcharged in Blue or
Red

1938 — Perf. 10, 11, 13½x13, 13x14
590 A108 45c on 1c grn (R) — .40 .25
  Never hinged — .90
  b. Imperf. — 6.00 5.00
    Never hinged — 10.00
590A A108 45c on 2c buff (Bl) — 17.00 14.00
  Never hinged — 27.50
591 A126 45c on 2c org brn (Bl) — .25 .25
  Never hinged — .60
  Nos. 590-591 (3) — 17.65 14.50
  Set, never hinged — 29.00

Many overprint varieties exist.

Numeral Type of 1933
1938-39 — Litho. — Perf. 11½, 13
White or Gray Paper
592 A108 5c gray brown — .25 .25
  Never hinged — .25
593 A108 10c yellow green — .25 .25
  Never hinged — .25
594 A108 15c slate green — .25 .25
  Never hinged — .25
595 A108 20c vio, gray paper — .25 .25
  Never hinged — .25
596 A108 25c red violet — .25 .25
  Never hinged — .25
597 A108 30c scarlet — .25 .25
  Never hinged — .25
  Nos. 592-597 (6) — 1.50 1.50
  Set, never hinged — 1.75

"Republic" — A133

1938 — Perf. 11½
598 A133 40c rose red — .25 .25
  Never hinged — .25
599 A133 45c car rose — .25 .25
  Never hinged — .25
  a. Printed on both sides — 11.00 11.00
    Never hinged — 27.50
600 A133 50c ultra — .25 .25
  Never hinged — .25
601 A133 60c dp ultra — .50 .30
  Never hinged — .60
  Nos. 598-601 (4) — 1.05
  Set, never hinged — 1.10

Nos. 598-601 exist imperf. Value for set $22.50

Machine
Gunners
A134

Infantry — A135

Perf. 11½x11, 11x11½, Imperf.
1938, Sept. 1 — Photo.
602 A134 25c dark green — 12.00 9.25
  Never hinged — 30.00
603 A135 45c red brown — 12.00 9.25
  Never hinged — 30.00
  Set, never hinged — 60.00

43rd Division of the Republican Army. Sold only at the Philatelic Agency and for foreign exchange.
Nos. 602-603 exist imperf. Value, set $60.

Blast Furnace
A136

Steel Mill and
Sculpture,
"Defenders of
Numantia"
A137

1938, Aug. 9 — Perf. 16
604 A136 45c black — .25 .25
  Never hinged — .30
605 A137 1.25p dark blue — .25 .25
  Never hinged — .30
  Set, never hinged — 2.00

Issued in honor of the workers of Sagunto.

Submarine — A137a

Designs: 1p, 15p, U-Boat D1. 2p, 6p, U-Boat A1. 4p, 10p, U-Boat B2.

1938, Aug. 11 — Perf. 16
605A A137a 1p blue — 5.50 5.50
605B A137a 2p red brown — 10.00 10.00
605C A137a 4p red orange — 12.00 12.00
605D A137a 6p deep blue — 25.00 25.00
605E A137a 10p magenta — 40.00 40.00
605F A137a 15p dp gray green — 350.00 350.00
  Nos. 605A-605F (6) — 442.50 442.50
  Set, never hinged — 700.00

Souvenir Sheet
Perf. 10½
605G A137a Sheet of 3 — 500.00 500.00
  Never hinged — 775.00
  a. 4p carmine & gray black — 100.00 100.00
  b. 6p dull blue & gray black — 100.00 100.00
  c. 15p green & gray black — 100.00 100.00

Nos. 605A-605G were issued for use on a proposed submarine mail service between Barcelona and Mahon, Minorca. One voyage was made on this mail route, carrying 300 agency-prepared covers. The stamps were also valid for ordinary mail.
Nos. 605A-605G were sold only at the Philatelic Agency in Barcelona, for double their face value.
Nos. 605A-605G exist imperf. Value: set of 6 stamps, $775 unused, $1,000 never hinged; souvenir sheet, $2,250 unused, $2,900, never hinged.

Riflemen
A138

Machine
Gunners
A139

Bomb
Throwing — A140

1938, Nov. 25 — Engr. — Perf. 10
606 A138 5c sepia — 3.50 3.50
  Never hinged — 7.00
607 A138 10c dp violet — 3.50 3.50
  Never hinged — 7.00
608 A138 25c blue green — 3.50 3.50
  Never hinged — 7.00
609 A139 45c rose red — 3.50 3.50
  Never hinged — 7.00
610 A139 60c dark blue — 6.25 6.25
  Never hinged — 10.00
611 A139 1.20p black — 125.00 125.00
  Never hinged — 225.00
612 A140 2p orange — 37.50 37.50
  Never hinged — 75.00
613 A140 5p dark brown — 200.00 200.00
  Never hinged — 390.00
614 A140 10p dk blue grn — 40.00 40.00
  Never hinged — 72.50
  Nos. 606-614 (9) — 422.75 422.75
  Set, never hinged — 800.00

Honoring the Militia. Sold only at the Philatelic Agency and for foreign exchange. Exist imperf. Value unused $1,200, never hinged $1,800.

Spanish State

Arms of Spain — A141

1936 — Litho. — Imperf.
Thin Transparent Paper
615 A141 30c blue — 250.00
  Never hinged — 345.00
616 A141 30c pale green — 250.00
  Never hinged — 345.00

Perf. 11
Thick Wove Paper
617 A141 30c dark blue — 550.00 150.00
  Never hinged — 810.00
  Set, never hinged — 1,500.

Issued in Granada during siege. After the city was liberated, these stamps were used throughout the province of Granada.

A143

Cathedral of
Burgos — A145

University of
Salamanca
A146

Cathedral del Pilar,
Zaragoza — A147

"La Giralda,"
Seville — A148

Xavier Castle,
Navarre — A149

Court of Lions,
Alhambra at
Granada
A150

Mosque,
Córdoba
A151

Alcántara Bridge
and Alcázar,
Toledo — A152

Soldier
Carrying
Flag — A153

Troops Landing
at Algeciras
A154

Type II

Two types of 30c:
Type I — Imprint 12mm long; "3" does not touch frame.
Type II — Imprint 8mm long; "3" touches frame.

1936 — Unwmk. — Litho. — Imperf.
623 A143 1c green — 6.00 4.50
  Never hinged — 9.50
Perf. 11½
624 A143 2c orange brown — .60 .45
  Never hinged — 1.15
625 A145 5c gray brown — .60 .55
  Never hinged — 1.15
626 A146 10c green — .60 .45
  Never hinged — 1.15
627 A147 15c dull green — .60 .45
  Never hinged — 1.15
628 A148 25c rose lake — .85 .45
  Never hinged — 2.00
629 A149 30c carmine (I) — .60 .45
  Never hinged — 1.15
  a. Type II — .70 .55
    Never hinged — 1.70
630 A150 50c deep blue — 14.00 8.75
  Never hinged — 29.00
631 A151 60c yellow green — .95 .70
  Never hinged — 1.70
632 A152 1p black — 5.25 3.75
  Never hinged — 12.00
633 A153 4p rose vio, red & yel — 52.50 29.00
  Never hinged — 135.00
634 A154 10p light brown — 52.50 29.00
  Never hinged — 135.00
  Nos. 623-634 (12) — 135.05 78.50
  Set, never hinged — 310.00

Nos. 624-634 exist imperf. Value, set $275.
Numerous forgeries exist for Nos. 623-634.
Nos. 625-631, 633-634 were privately overprinted "VIA AEREA" and plane, supposedly for use in Ifni.
For surcharges see Nos. 9LC21, 9LC23.

Nos. 542-543
Surcharged in Two
Lines

Habilitado
0'05 ptas.

1936 — Imperf., Perf. 11½
634A A108 5c on 1c bl grn — 2.25 3.00
  Never hinged — 3.75
634B A108 5c on 2c buff — 2.25 3.00
  Never hinged — 3.75
634C A108 10c on 1c bl grn — 2.25 3.00
  Never hinged — 3.75
634D A108 15c on 2c buff — 2.25 3.00
  Never hinged — 3.75
  Nos. 634A-634D (4) — 9.00 12.00
  Set, never hinged — 15.00

Issued in the Balearic Islands to meet a shortage of these values. Nos. 634A and 634C are imperf., Nos. 634B and 634D are perf. 11½.

St. James of
Compostela — A155

St. James
Cathedral
A156

Pórtico de
la Gloria
A157

Type I　　　　Type II

Two types of 30c:
I — No dots in "1937."
II — Dot before and after "1937."

1937   *Perf. 11½, 11x11½*

635	A155	15c violet brown	.95	1.25
	Never hinged		3.50	
636	A156	30c rose red (I)	5.00	.55
	Never hinged		14.00	
a.	Type II		17.50	14.00
	Never hinged		37.50	
637	A157	1p blue & orange	14.50	3.25
	Never hinged		42.50	
a.	Center inverted		350.00	250.00
	Never hinged		500.00	
	Nos. 635-637 (3)		20.45	5.05
	Set, never hinged		60.00	

Holy Year of Compostela. Nos. 635-637
exist imperf. Value for set $175.

"Estado Espanol"
A159　　　　A160

"El Cid" — A161　　Isabella
I — A162

Two types of 5c, 30c and 10p.
5 Centimos: Type I Imprint 9½mm long.
Type II Imprint 14mm long.
30 Centimos: Type I Imprint, "Hija De B.
Fournier Burgos." Type II Imprint, "Fournier
Burgos."
10 Pesetas: Type I "10" 2½mm high. Type II
"10" 3mm high.

With Imprint

1936-40   *Imperf.*

638	A159	1c green	.25	.25
	Never hinged		.30	

         Perf. 11

640	A160	2c brown	.25	.25
	Never hinged		.30	

Perf. 11, 11½, 11½x11, 11½x10½

641	A161	5c brown (I)	.45	
	Never hinged		1.00	
642	A161	5c brown (II)	.25	.25
	Never hinged		.30	
643	A161	10c green	.25	.25
	Never hinged		.30	

         Perf. 11, 11x11½

644	A162	15c gray black	.25	.25
	Never hinged		.30	

645	A162	20c dark violet	.40	.25
	Never hinged		.70	
646	A162	25c brown lake	.25	.25
	Never hinged		.40	
647	A162	30c rose (I)	.50	.25
	Never hinged		.95	
648	A162	30c rose (II)	17.50	2.10
	Never hinged			
649	A162	40c orange	1.60	.25
	Never hinged		4.00	
650	A162	50c dark blue	1.60	.25
	Never hinged		4.00	
651	A162	60c yellow	.30	.25
	Never hinged		.70	
652	A162	1p blue	16.50	.50
	Never hinged		32.50	
653	A162	4p magenta	21.00	5.25
	Never hinged		40.00	
654	A161	10p dk bl (I) ('37)	75.00	40.00
	Never hinged		130.00	
655	A161	10p dp bl (II) ('40)	32.50	15.00
	Never hinged		65.00	
	Nos. 638-655 (17)		168.85	65.85
	Set, never hinged		375.00	

No. 638 was privately perforated. See Nos.
662-667. For overprint and surcharges see
Nos. E18, 9LC10, 9LC13, 9LC15-9LC16,
9LC22, 9LC25, 9LC27-9LC30, 9LC34-9LC53.

Ferdinand the
Catholic — A163

1938   *Perf. 10½, 11½x11*

Imprint: "Lit Fournier Vitoria"

656	A163	15c deep green	1.75	.25
	Never hinged		6.75	
657	A163	30c deep red	5.75	.25
	Never hinged		16.00	

Imprint: "Fournier Vitoria"

         Perf. 10

658	A163	15c deep green	1.75	.25
	Never hinged		8.50	
659	A163	20c purple	13.00	1.40
	Never hinged		37.50	
660	A163	25c brown car	.90	.25
	Never hinged		2.00	
661	A163	30c deep red	6.50	.25
	Never hinged		40.00	
	Nos. 656-661 (6)		29.65	2.65
	Set, never hinged		110.00	

Nos. 656-661 exist imperf.; value for set,
$150. Part-perf. varieties exist.
For overprints see Nos. C98-C99.

Type I　　Type II

Without Imprint

Two types of the 15 Centimos:
Type I — Medieval style numerals with diagonal line through "5."
Type II — Modern numerals. Narrower "5"
without diagonal line.

Without Imprint

1938-50   *Perf. 11, 13½*

662	A159	1c green, imperf.	.25	.25
			.30	
663	A160	2c brn (18½x22mm; '40)	.25	.25
	Never hinged		.30	
a.	2c bis brn (17½x21mm; '48)		.25	.25
	Never hinged		.30	
664	A161	5c gray brn ('39)	.25	.25
	Never hinged		.30	
a.	Perf. 13½x13¼ ('49)		.25	.25
	Never hinged		.30	
665	A161	10c dk carmine	.25	.25
	Never hinged		.30	
a.	10c rose		.35	
	Never hinged		.75	
b.	Perf. 13½x13¼ ('49)		.25	.25
	Never hinged		.30	
666	A161	15c dk green (I)	.90	.25
	Never hinged		1.40	
666A	A161	15c dk green (II)	.60	.25
	Never hinged		1.40	
b.	Perf 13½x13¼ ('50)		.65	.25
	Never hinged		.85	
667	A162	70c dk blue ('39)	.75	.25
	Never hinged		1.40	
	Nos. 662-667 (7)		3.25	1.75
	Set, never hinged		4.85	

Emblem of the
Falange — A164

1938, July 17   *Perf. 10*

668	A164	15c bl grn & lt grn	4.25	3.75
	Never hinged		9.00	
669	A164	25c rose red & rose	4.25	3.75
	Never hinged		9.00	
670	A164	60c dk bl & lt bl		3.60
	Never hinged			3.75
671	A164	1p brown & yellow	90.00	80.00
	Never hinged		200.00	
	Nos. 668-671 (4)		100.75	90.00
	Set, never hinged		250.00	

Second anniversary of the Civil War.
Imperforate 4-value set also exists, value
$725, $950 never hinged.

Isabella I
A165　　　　Gen. Francisco
Franco
A166

1938-39   *Litho.*   *Perf. 10*

672	A165	20c brt violet ('39)	.60	.25
	Never hinged		3.50	
673	A165	25c brown carmine	6.00	.60
	Never hinged		16.50	
674	A165	30c rose red	.25	.25
	Never hinged		.40	
675	A165	40c dull violet	.30	.25
	Never hinged		.50	
676	A165	50c indigo ('39)	27.50	2.50
	Never hinged		62.50	
677	A165	1p deep blue	9.00	.90
	Never hinged		22.50	
	Nos. 672-677 (6)		43.65	4.75
	Set, never hinged		120.00	

Nos. 672-677 exist imperf. Value set, $225
hinged, $350 never hinged.

Imprint: "Sanchez Toda"

1939-40   *Perf. 10*

678	A166	20c brt violet	.35	.25
	Never hinged		.50	
679	A166	25c rose lake	.35	.25
	Never hinged		.50	
680	A166	30c rose carmine	.30	.25
	Never hinged		.50	
681	A166	40c slate green	.25	.25
	Never hinged		.50	
682	A166	45c vermilion ('40)	1.75	1.75
	Never hinged		4.00	
683	A166	50c indigo	.30	.25
	Never hinged		.50	
684	A166	60c orange	2.75	2.75
	Never hinged		5.00	
685	A166	70c blue	.40	.25
	Never hinged		.50	
686	A166	1p black	11.00	.25
	Never hinged		20.00	
687	A166	2p dark brown	15.00	1.25
	Never hinged		30.00	
688	A166	4p dark violet	85.00	17.50
	Never hinged		200.00	
689	A166	10p light brown	40.00	44.00
	Never hinged		90.00	
	Nos. 678-689 (12)		157.45	69.00
	Set, never hinged		300.00	

#686-689 have value & "Pta." on 1 line while
#702-705 have value & "Pta." on 2 lines.
Nos. 678-689 exist imperf. Value set, $525
hinged, $700 never hinged.

Without Imprint

1939-47   *Litho.*   *Perf. 9½x10½*

				Unwmk.
690	A166	5c dull brn vio	.50	.25
	Never hinged		.95	
691	A166	10c brown orange	2.25	.65
	Never hinged		4.50	
692	A166	15c lt green	.55	.25
	Never hinged		1.05	
693	A166	20c brt violet ('40)	.55	.25
	Never hinged		1.05	
694	A166	25c dp claret ('40)	.55	.25
	Never hinged		1.05	
695	A166	30c blue ('40)	.55	.25
	Never hinged		1.05	
697	A166	40c Prus grn ('40)	.55	.25
	Never hinged		1.05	
a.	40c greenish black		.60	
	Never hinged		1.10	
698	A166	45c ultra ('41)	.55	.25
	Never hinged		1.05	
699	A166	50c indigo ('40)	.50	.25
	Never hinged		1.05	
a.	Perf. 11½ ('47)		32.50	3.00
	Never hinged		55.00	
700	A166	60c dull org ('40)	.70	.25
	Never hinged		1.25	
701	A166	70c blue ('40)	.55	.25
	Never hinged		1.60	
702	A166	1p gray blk ('40)	7.50	.25
	Never hinged		15.00	
703	A166	2p dull brn ('41)	8.75	.25
	Never hinged		17.50	
704	A166	4p dull rose ('40)	32.50	.25
	Never hinged		70.00	

705	A166	10p lt brown ('40)	160.00	2.75
	Never hinged		330.00	
	Nos. 690-705 (15)		216.85	6.65
	Set, never hinged		425.00	

The 40c exists in three types, with variations
in the value tablet. I. "CTO" does not touch
bottom line. II. Light background in tablet.
"CTS" touches bottom line. III. As type I, but
with well defined lines of white and color
around rectangle.
The 60c exists in two types: I. Top and left
side of value tablet touch rest of design. II.
Tablet separated from rest of design by white
lines.
Five values exist with perf. 10: 5c, 10c, 45c,
4p and 10p.
Nos. 690-704 exist imperf. Values, set: mint,
never hinged, $1,600; unused, $1,200.
The imperforate 10c dull claret, type A166,
without imprint, is a postal tax stamp, RA14.

SEMI-POSTAL STAMPS

Red Cross Issue

Princesses
María
Cristina and
Beatrice
SP1

Queen as a
Nurse — SP2　　Queen Victoria
Eugénia — SP3

Prince of
Asturias — SP4　　King Alfonso
XIII — SP5

         Perf. 12½

1926, Sept. 15			*Unwmk.*	*Engr.*
B1	SP1	1c black	2.50	2.25
B2	SP2	2c ultra	2.50	2.25
B3	SP3	5c violet brn	5.50	4.00
B4	SP4	10c green	4.50	4.00
B5	SP1	15c indigo	1.75	1.50
B6	SP4	20c dull violet	1.75	1.50
a.	20c violet brown (error)		600.00	375.00
B7	SP5	25c rose red	.30	.30
B8	SP1	30c blue green	42.50	40.00
B9	SP3	40c dark blue	24.00	21.00
B10	SP2	50c red orange	24.00	21.00
B11	SP4	1p slate	1.75	1.10
B12	SP3	4p magenta	1.40	.80
B13	SP5	10p brown	1.40	1.10
	Nos. B1-B13,EB1 (14)		122.60	109.55
	Set, never hinged		260.00	

The 20c was printed in violet brown for use
in the colonies (Cape Juby, Spanish Guinea,
Spanish Morocco and Spanish Sahara). No.
B6a, the missing overprint error, is listed here
because it is not known to which colony it
belongs.
For overprints see Nos. B19-B46.

Airplane and Map of Madrid-Manila
Flight — SP6

1926, Sept. 15

B14	SP6	15c dp ultra & org	.40	.40
B15	SP6	20c car & yel grn	.40	.40
B16	SP6	30c dk brn & ultra	.40	.40

B17	SP6	40c dk grn & brn org	.40	.40
B18	SP6	4p magenta & yel	100.00	100.00
		Nos. B14-B18,CB1-CB5 (10)	109.10	109.10
		Set, never hinged	250.00	

Madrid to Manila flight of Captains Eduardo G. Gallarza and Joaquim Loriga y Taboada. Nos. B1-B18, CB1-CB5 and EB1 were used for regular postage on Sept. 15, 16, 17, 1926. Subsequently the unsold stamps were given to the Spanish Red Cross Society, by which they were sold uncanceled but they then had no franking power.

For overprints see Nos. B47-B53.

Coronation Silver Jubilee Issue
Red Cross Stamps of 1926 Overprinted "ALFONSO XIII," Dates and Ornaments in Various Colors

1927, May 27

B19	SP1	1c black (R)	6.00	6.00
B20	SP1	2c ultra (Bl)	11.00	11.00
B21	SP3	5c vio brn (R)	2.75	2.75
a.		Double overprint	37.50	
B22	SP4	10c green (Bl)	75.00	75.00
B23	SP1	15c indigo (R)	2.25	2.25
B24	SP4	20c dull vio (R)	4.00	4.00
B25	SP5	25c rose red (Bl)	.50	.50
B26	SP1	30c blue grn (Bl)	1.00	1.00
B27	SP3	40c dk blue (R)	1.00	1.00
B28	SP2	50c red org (Bl)	1.00	1.00
B29	SP4	1p slate (R)	2.25	2.25
B30	SP3	4p magenta (Bl)	11.00	11.00
B31	SP5	10p brown (G)	42.50	42.50
		Nos. B19-B31 (13)	160.25	160.25
		Set, never hinged	375.00	

Same with Additional Surcharges of New Values

B32	SP2	3c on 2c (G)	9.50	9.50
B33	SP2	4c on 2c (Bk)	9.50	9.50
B34	SP5	10c on 25c (Bk)	.55	.55
B35	SP5	25c on 25c (Bl)	.55	.55
B36	SP2	55c on 2c (R)	1.00	1.00
B37	SP4	55c on 10c (Bk)	55.00	55.00
B38	SP4	55c on 20c (Bk)	55.00	55.00
B39	SP1	75c on 15c (R)	.70	.70
B40	SP1	75c on 30c (R)	140.00	140.00
B41	SP3	80c on 40c (R)	52.50	50.00
B42	SP3	2p on 40c (R)	1.00	1.00
B43	SP1	2p on 1p (R)	1.00	1.00
B44	SP2	5p on 50c (G)	1.90	1.90
B45	SP3	5p on 4p (Bk)	3.25	3.25
B46	SP5	10p on 10p (R)	27.50	27.50
		Nos. B32-B46 (15)	358.95	356.45
		Set, never hinged	800.00	

Nos. B14-B18 Overprinted

B47	SP6	15c (Br)	.50	.40
a.		Double overprint	30.00	
B48	SP6	20c (Bl)	.50	.40
a.		Brown overprint (error)	65.00	
b.		Inverted overprint	30.00	
B50	SP6	30c (R)	.50	.40
a.		Blue overprint (error)	65.00	
b.		Double overprint	30.00	
B52	SP6	40c (Br)	.50	.40
a.		Inverted overprint	30.00	
b.		Double ovpt. (Bl + Br)	95.00	
B53	SP6	4p (Bl)	100.00	95.00
a.		Inverted overprint	160.00	

Semi-Postal Special Delivery Stamp
Overprinted "ALFONSO XIII," Dates and Ornaments in Violet

B54	SPSD1	20c	5.50	5.50
		Nos. B47-B54 (6)	107.50	102.10

Nos. CB1-CB5 Overprinted in Various Colors

B55	SPAP1	5c (R)	2.25	1.60
a.		Inverted overprint	30.00	
B56	SPAP1	10c (R)	2.50	2.25
a.		Inverted overprint	30.00	
B57	SPAP1	25c (Bl)	.40	.40
B58	SPAP1	50c (Bl)	.40	.40
a.		Double ovpt., one invtd.	72.50	
B59	SPAP1	1p (R)	3.00	2.50
a.		Inverted overprint	95.00	

Same with Additional Surcharges of New Values

B60	SPAP1	75c on 5c (R)	5.00	3.25
a.		Inverted surcharge	30.00	

B61	SPAP1	75c on 10c (R)	22.50	13.00
a.		Inverted surcharge	30.00	
B62	SPAP1	75c on 25c (Bl)	47.50	27.50
a.		Double surcharge	55.00	
B63	SPAP1	75c on 50c (Bl)	18.00	13.00
		Nos. B55-B63 (9)	101.55	63.90
		Set, never hinged	300.00	

Nos. B54-B63 were available for ordinary postage.

Stamps of Spanish Offices in Morocco and Spanish Colonies, 1926 (Spain Types SP3, SP5) Surcharged in Various Colors

On Spanish Morocco

B64	SP3	55c on 4p bis (Bl)	25.00	21.00
B65	SP5	80c on 10p vio (Br)	25.00	21.00

On Spanish Tangier

B66	SP5	1p on 10p vio (Br)	135.00	110.00
B67	SP3	4p bis (G)	45.00	40.00

On Cape Juby

B68	SP3	5p on 4p bis (R)	85.00	70.00
B69	SP5	10p on 10p vio (R)	45.00	40.00

On Spanish Guinea

B70	SP5	1p on 10p vio (Bl)	25.00	21.00
B71	SP3	2p on 4p bis (G)	25.00	21.00

On Spanish Sahara

B72	SP5	80c on 10p vio (R)	40.00	32.50
B73	SP3	2p on 4p bis (R)	25.00	21.00
		Nos. B64-B73 (10)	475.00	397.50
		Set, never hinged	1,300.	

Nos. B64-B73 were available for postage in Spain only.
Nos. B19-B73 were for the 25th year of the reign of King Alfonso XIII.
Counterfeits of Nos. B64-B73 abound.

Catacombs Restoration Issues

Pope Pius XI and King Alfonso XIII — SP7

1928, Dec. 23   Engr.   Perf. 12½

Santiago Issue

B74	SP7	2c violet & blk	.30	.30
B75	SP7	2c lake & blk	.35	.35
B76	SP7	3c bl blk & vio	.30	.30
B77	SP7	3c dl bl & vio	.35	.35
B78	SP7	5c ol grn & vio	.65	.65
B79	SP7	10c yel grn & blk	1.25	1.25
B80	SP7	15c bl grn & vio	3.25	3.25
B81	SP7	25c dp rose & vio	3.25	3.25
B82	SP7	40c ultra & blk	.30	.30
B83	SP7	55c ol brn & vio	.30	.30
B84	SP7	80c red & blk	.30	.30
B85	SP7	1p gray blk & vio	.30	.30
B86	SP7	2p red brn & blk	4.25	4.25
B87	SP7	3p pale rose & vio	4.25	4.25
B88	SP7	4p vio brn & blk	4.25	4.25
B89	SP7	5p grnsh blk & vio	4.25	4.25

Toledo Issue

B90	SP7	2c bl blk & car	.30	.30
B91	SP7	2c ultra & car	.35	.35
B92	SP7	3c bis brn & ultra	.30	.30
B93	SP7	3c ol grn & ultra	.35	.35
B94	SP7	5c red vio & car	.65	.65
B95	SP7	10c yel grn & ultra	1.25	1.25
B96	SP7	15c slate bl & car	3.25	3.25
B97	SP7	25c red brn & ultra	3.25	3.25
B98	SP7	40c ultra & car	.30	.30
B99	SP7	55c dk brn & ultra	.30	.30
B100	SP7	80c black & car	.30	.30
B101	SP7	1p yellow & car	.30	.30
B102	SP7	2p dk gray & ultra	4.25	4.25
B103	SP7	3p violet & car	4.25	4.25
B104	SP7	4p vio brn & car	4.25	4.25
B105	SP7	5p bister & ultra	4.25	4.25
		Nos. B74-B105 (32)	55.80	55.80
		Set, never hinged	140.00	

Nos. B74-B105 replaced regular stamps from Dec. 23, 1928 to Jan. 6, 1929. The proceeds from their sale were given to a fund to restore the catacombs of Saint Damasus and Saint Praetextatus at Rome.

Nos. B74-B105 exist imperf. Value set, $325 hinged, $400 never hinged.

Issues of the Republic

SP13

1938, Apr. 15   Perf. 11½

B106	SP13	45c + 2p bl & grnsh bl	.90	.75
a.		Imperf., pair	17.50	14.50
b.		Souv. sheet of 1	26.00	26.00
c.		Souv. sheet of 1, imperf.	725.00	650.00
		Never hinged	1,000.	

Surtax for the defenders of Madrid.
For overprint and surcharge see Nos. B108, CB6.

Nurse and Orderly Carrying Wounded Soldier — SP14

1938, June 1   Engr.   Perf. 10

B107	SP14	45c + 5p cop red	.55	.55
a.		Imperf., pair	220.00	

For surcharge see No. CB7.

No. B106 Overprinted in Black

1938, Nov. 7   Perf. 11½

B108	SP13	45c + 2p	3.25	3.25
		Never hinged	5.00	

Defense of Madrid, 2nd anniversary.
A similar but larger overprint was applied to cover blocks of four. Value, $15 hinged, $30 never hinged.

Values for souvenir sheets of 1937-38 are for examples with some faults. Undamaged sheets are very hard to find.

Spanish State
Souvenir Sheets

Alcazar, Toledo SP15

Design: No. B108C, A patio of Alcazar after Civil War fighting.

1937   Unwmk.   Photo.   Perf. 11½
Control Numbers on Back

B108A	SP15	2p org brn	22.00	22.00
a.		Imperf.	450.00	450.00
B108C	SP15	2p dark green	22.00	22.00
d.		Imperf.	450.00	450.00
		Never hinged	95.00	
		Set, never hinged	125.00	
		Set, B108Ab, B108Cd, never hinged	1,300.	

Nos. B108A-B108C sold for 4p each.

SP16

Designs: 20c, Covadonga Cathedral. 30c, Palma Cathedral, Majorca. 50c, Alcazar of Segovia. 1p, Leon Cathedral.

1938   Unwmk.   Photo.   Perf. 12½
Control Numbers on Back

B108E	SP16	Sheet of 4	42.50	42.50
f.		20c dull violet	5.00	5.00
g.		30c rose red	5.00	5.00
h.		50c bright blue	5.00	5.00
i.		1p greenish gray	5.00	5.00
j.		Imperf. sheet	72.50	65.00
		Never hinged	125.00	

Each sheet sold for 4p.

SP17

Designs, alternating in sheet: Flag bearer. Battleship "Admiral Cervera." Soldiers in trenches. Moorish guard.

1938, July 1   Unwmk.   Perf. 13
Control Numbers on Back

B108K	SP17	Sheet of 20	40.00	40.00
		Never hinged	52.50	
l.		Imperf. sheet	185.00	185.00
		Never hinged	240.00	

Sheet measures 175x132mm. Consists of five vertical rows of four 2c violet, 3c deep blue, 5c olive gray, 10c deep green and 30c red orange, with each denomination appearing in two different designs. Marginal inscription: "Homenaje al Ejercito y a la Marina" (Honoring the Army and Navy). Sold for 4p, or double face value.

Souvenir Sheets

Don Juan of Austria — SP18

Battle of Lepanto SP19

Perf. 12½
1938, Dec. 15   Unwmk.   Engr.
Control Numbers on Back

B108M	SP18	30c dk car	22.50	22.50
B108N	SP19	50c blue black	22.50	22.50
		Nos. B108M-B108N (2)	45.00	45.00
		Set, never hinged	77.50	

Imperf

B108O	SP18	30c black vio	400.00	*550.00*
B108P	SP19	50c dk sl grn	400.00	*550.00*
		Nos. B108O-B108P (2)	800.00	*1,100.*
		Set, never hinged	1,300.	

Victory over the Turks in the Battle of Lepanto, 1571.
Nos. B108M-B108P contain one stamp. The dates "1571-1938" appear in the lower sheet margin. Size: 89x74mm. Sold for 10p a pair.

LOCAL CHARITY STAMPS

Hundreds of different charity stamps were issued by local organizations and cities during the Civil War, 1936-39. Some had limited franking value, but most were simply charity labels. They are of three kinds: 1. Local semipostals. 2. Obligatory surtax stamps. 3. Propaganda or charity labels.

Ruins of Belchite SP20

Miracle of Calanda — SP21

Designs: 10c+5c, 70c+20c, Ruins of Belchite. 15c+10c, 80c+20c, The Rosary. 20c+10c, 1.50p+50c, El Pilar Cathedral. 25c+10c, 1p+30c, Mother Raffols praying. 40c+10c, 2.50p+50c, The Little Chamber. 45c+15c, 1.40p+40c, Oath of the Besieged. 10p+4p, The Apparition.

Perf. 10½, 11½x10½, 11½

1940, Jan. 29   Litho.   Unwmk.
Design SP20

B109	10c + 5c dp bl & vio brn	.25	.25
B110	15c + 10c rose vio & dk grn	.25	.25
B111	20c + 10c vio & dp bl	.25	.25
B112	25c + 10c dp rose & vio brn	.25	.25
B113	40c + 10c sl grn & rose vio	.25	.25
B114	45c + 15c vio & dp rose	.30	.30
B115	70c + 20c multi	.30	.30
B116	80c + 20c dp rose & vio	.40	.40
B117	1p + 30c dk sl grn & pur	.40	.40
B118	1.40p + 40c pur & gray blk	40.00	40.00
B119	1.50p + 50c lt bl & brn vio	.50	.50
B120	2.50p + 50c choc & bl	.50	.50

Design SP21

B121	4p + 1p rose lil & sl grn	12.00	12.00
B122	10p + 4p ultra & chnt	190.00	190.00
	Nos. B109-B122,CB8-CB17,EB2 (25)	464.70	464.60
	Set, never hinged		1,100.

19th centenary of the Virgin of the Pillar. The surtax was used to help restore the Cathedral at Zaragoza, damaged during the Civil War.

No. B121 exists in violet & slate green, No. B122 in ultramarine & brown violet. Value, $42.50 each.

Nos. B109-B122 exist imperf. Value, $750.

See No. 743 (in Scott Standard catalogue, Vol. 6), CB8-CB17.

General Franco — SP23

Knight and Lorraine Cross — SP24

1940, Dec. 23	**Unwmk.**		**Perf. 10**
B123	SP23 20c + 5c dk grn & red	.65	.65
B124	SP23 40c + 10c dk bl & red	.90	.40
	Set, never hinged		3.50

The surtax was for the tuberculosis fund.

AIR POST STAMPS

Regular Issue of 1909-10 Overprinted in Red or Black

Perf. 13x12½, 14

1920, Apr. 4   Unwmk.

C1	A46	5c green (R)	1.50	1.00
a.	Imperf., pair		105.00	105.00
b.	Double overprint		35.00	35.00
c.	Inverted overprint		90.00	90.00
d.	Double ovpt., one invtd.		35.00	35.00
e.	Triple overprint		35.00	35.00
C2	A46	10c car (Bk)	1.75	1.25
a.	Imperf., pair		105.00	105.00
b.	Double overprint		35.00	35.00
d.	Double ovpt., one invtd.		35.00	35.00
C3	A46	25c dp blue (R)	3.25	1.75
a.	Inverted overprint		90.00	90.00
b.	Double overprint		35.00	35.00
C4	A46	50c sl blue (R)	13.00	6.00
a.	Imperf., pair		105.00	105.00
C5	A46	1p lake (Bk)	42.50	22.50
a.	Imperf., pair		385.00	385.00
		Nos. C1-C5 (5)	62.00	32.50
		Set, never hinged	170.00	

Dangerous counterfeits are plentiful.

A 30c green was authorized, but not issued. Value: hinged $550; never hinged $900. For overprints see Nos. C58-C61.

"Spirit of St. Louis" over Coast of Europe — AP1

Seville-Barcelona Exposition Issue
Control Numbers on Back

1929, Feb. 15   Engr.   Perf. 11

C6	AP1	5c brown	6.00	5.00
C7	AP1	10c rose	6.00	5.00
C8	AP1	25c dark blue	7.00	5.50
C9	AP1	50c purple	8.00	5.75
C10	AP1	1p green	37.50	25.00
C11	AP1	4p black	25.00	20.00
		Nos. C6-C11 (6)	89.50	66.25
		Set, never hinged	300.00	

Nos. C6 to C11 exist imperforate. Value set, $800.

The so-called errors of color of Nos. C10, C18-C21, C23-C24, C28-C31, C37, C40, C42, C44, C46, C48, C50, C52, C55, C62-C67 are believed to have been irregularly produced.

Plane and Congress Seal — AP2

Railway Congress Issue
Control Numbers on Back

1930, May 10   Litho.   Perf. 14

C12	AP2	5c bister brn	6.00	7.50
	Never hinged		8.25	
C13	AP2	10c rose	6.00	7.50
	Never hinged		8.25	
C14	AP2	25c dark blue	6.00	7.50
	Never hinged		8.25	
C15	AP2	50c purple	17.50	15.00
	Never hinged		26.00	
a.	Vert. pair, imperf. between		300.00	
	Never hinged		600.00	

C16	AP2	1p yellow green	35.00	30.00
	Never hinged		52.50	
C17	AP2	4p black	35.00	30.00
	Never hinged		52.50	
		Nos. C12-C17 (6)	92.25	92.25
		Set, never hinged	400.00	

Dangerous counterfeits exist.

Goya Issue

Fantasy of Flight AP3

Asmodeus and Cleofas — AP4

Fantasy of Flight AP5

Fantasy of Flight — AP6

1930, June 15   Engr.   Perf. 12½

C18	AP3	5c brn red & yel	.25	.25
	Never hinged		.30	
C19	AP3	15c blk & red org	.25	.25
	Never hinged		.30	
C20	AP3	25c brn car & dp red	.25	.25
	Never hinged		.30	
C21	AP4	5c ol grn & grnsh bl	.25	.25
	Never hinged		.30	
C22	AP4	10c sl grn & yel grn	.25	.25
	Never hinged		.20	
C23	AP4	20c ultra & rose red	.25	.25
	Never hinged		.20	
C24	AP4	40c vio bl & lt bl	.30	.30
	Never hinged		.35	
C25	AP5	30c brown & vio	.30	.30
	Never hinged		.35	
C26	AP5	50c ver & grn	.30	.30
	Never hinged		.35	
C27	AP5	4p brn car & blk	2.00	2.00
	Never hinged		2.65	
C28	AP6	1p vio brn & vio	.30	.30
	Never hinged		.35	
C29	AP6	4p bl blk & sl grn	2.00	2.00
	Never hinged		2.50	
C30	AP6	10p blk brn & bis brn	7.00	7.00
	Never hinged		10.00	
		Nos. C18-C30,CE1 (14)	13.95	13.95
		Set, never hinged	18.75	

Nos. C18-C30 exist imperf. Value for set, $150.

Christopher Columbus Issue

La Rábida Monastery — AP7

Martín Alonso Pinzón — AP8

Vicente Yanez Pinzón — AP9

Columbus in His Cabin — AP10

1930, Sept. 29   Litho.

C31	AP7	5c lt red brn	.25	.25
	Never hinged		.30	
C32	AP7	5c olive bister	.25	.25
	Never hinged		.30	
C33	AP7	10c blue green	.25	.25
	Never hinged		.50	
C34	AP7	15c dark violet	.25	.25
	Never hinged		.50	
C35	AP7	20c ultra	.25	.25
	Never hinged		.50	

Engr.

C36	AP8	25c carmine rose	.25	.25
	Never hinged		.50	
C37	AP9	30c dp red brn	2.00	2.00
	Never hinged		2.75	
C38	AP8	40c indigo	2.00	2.00
	Never hinged		2.75	
C39	AP9	50c orange	2.00	2.00
	Never hinged		2.75	
C40	AP8	1p dull violet	2.00	2.00
	Never hinged		2.75	
C41	AP10	4p olive green	2.00	2.00
	Never hinged		2.75	
C42	AP10	10p light brown	11.00	12.00
	Never hinged		16.50	
		Nos. C31-C42 (12)	22.50	23.50
		Set, never hinged	35.00	

Nos. C31-C42 exist imperf. Value for set, $190.

Spanish-American Issue

AP11

Columbus AP12

Columbus and Pinzón Brothers AP13

1930, Sept. 29   Litho.

C43	AP11	5c lt red	.25	.25
	Never hinged		.25	
C44	AP11	10c dull green	.25	.25
	Never hinged		.30	

Engr.

C45 AP12 25c scarlet .25 .25
Never hinged .40
C46 AP12 50c slate gray 2.50 2.10
Never hinged 4.00
C47 AP12 1p fawn 2.50 2.10
Never hinged 4.00
C48 AP13 4p slate blue 2.50 2.10
Never hinged 4.00
C49 AP13 10p brown violet 11.00 10.00
Never hinged 18.00
Nos. C43-C49 (7) 19.25 17.05
Set, never hinged 35.00

Nos. C43-C49 exist imperf. Value for set, $250.

Spanish-American Exhibition Issue

Santos-Dumont and First Flight of His Airplane — AP14

Teodoro Fels and His Airplane AP15

Dagoberto Godoy and Pass over Andes — AP16

Sacadura Cabral and Gago Coutinho and Their Airplane AP17

Sidar of Mexico and Map of South America — AP18

Ignacio Jiménez and Francisco Iglesias — AP19

Charles A. Lindbergh, Statue of Liberty, Spirit of St. Louis and Cat AP20

Santa Maria, Plane and Torre del Oro, Seville AP21

1930, Oct. 10 Photo. Perf. 14
C50 AP14 5c gray black .90 .55
Never hinged 4.50
C51 AP15 10c dk olive grn .90 .55
Never hinged 4.50
C52 AP16 25c ultra .90 .55
Never hinged 4.50
C53 AP17 50c blue gray 1.90 1.40
Never hinged 7.50
C54 AP18 50c black 1.90 1.40
Never hinged 7.50
C55 AP19 1p car lake 4.00 3.00
Never hinged 11.00
a. 1p brown violet 75.00 75.00
Never hinged 175.00
C56 AP20 1p deep green 4.00 3.00
Never hinged 9.50
C57 AP21 4p slate blue 7.25 5.50
Never hinged 40.00
Nos. C50-C57 (8) 21.75 15.95
Set, never hinged 90.00

Exist imperf. Value, set $110.
Note after No. 432 also applies to Nos. C31-C57.

Reprints of Nos. C50-C57 have blurred impressions, yellowish paper. Value: one-tenth of originals. Examples of No. C56 exist with portrait of Lindbergh inverted, doubled with one inverted and missing.

Nos. C1-C4 Overprinted in Red or Black

1931 Perf. 13x12½
C58 A46 5c green (R) 12.50 11.50
Never hinged 26.00
C59 A46 10c carmine (Bk) 12.50 11.50
Never hinged 26.00
C60 A46 25c deep blue (R) 17.50 16.50
Never hinged 37.50
C61 A46 50c slate blue (R) 35.00 26.00
Never hinged 70.00
Nos. C58-C61 (4) 77.50 65.50
Set, never hinged 160.00

Counterfeits of overprint exist.
The status of Nos. C58-C61 has been questioned.

Plane and Royal Palace, Madrid AP22

Madrid Post Office and Cibeles Fountain AP23

Plane over Calle de Alcalá, Madrid AP24

1931, Oct. 10 Engr. Perf. 12
C62 AP22 5c brown violet .25 .30
Never hinged .25
C63 AP22 10c deep green .25 .30
Never hinged .25
C64 AP22 25c dull red .25 .30
Never hinged .25
C65 AP23 50c deep blue .45 .50
Never hinged .80
C66 AP23 1p deep violet .65 .60
Never hinged 1.40

C67 AP24 4p black 9.00 9.00
Never hinged 16.50
Nos. C62-C67 (6) 10.85 11.00
Set, never hinged 15.00

3rd Pan-American Postal Union Congress, Madrid.
Exist imperf. Value, set $45.
For overprints see Nos. CO1-CO6.

Montserrat Issue

Plane over Montserrat Pass — AP25

1931, Dec. 9 Perf. 11½
Control Number on Back
C68 AP25 5c black brown .50 .50
Never hinged .85
C69 AP25 10c yellow green 2.00 2.00
Never hinged 3.50
C70 AP25 25c deep rose 7.00 7.50
Never hinged 13.00
C71 AP25 50c orange 22.50 30.00
Never hinged 47.50
C72 AP25 1p gray black 15.00 20.00
Never hinged 35.00
Nos. C68-C72 (5) 74.05 74.05
Set, never hinged 100.00

Perf. 14
C68a AP25 5c 7.50 *14.50*
Never hinged 10.00
C69a AP25 10c 40.00 *45.00*
Never hinged 50.00
C70a AP25 25c 72.50 *72.50*
Never hinged 82.50
C71a AP25 50c 72.50 *72.50*
Never hinged 82.50
C72f AP25 1p 72.50 *72.50*
Never hinged 82.50
Nos. C68a-C72f (5) 265.00 277.00
Set, never hinged 275.00

900th anniv. of Montserrat Monastery.
Nos. C68-C72 exist imperf. Value set, $525.

Autogiro over Seville — AP26

1935-39 Perf. 11½
C72A AP26 2p gray blue 22.50 4.50
Never hinged 37.50
g. Imperf., pair 450.00

Re-engraved
C72B AP26 2p dk blue ('38) .75 .25
Never hinged 2.50
c. Imperf., pair 20.00
d. Perf. 10 ('39) 1.50 1.10
Never hinged 3.00
Set, #C72A-C72B, never hinged 45.00

The sky has heavy horizontal lines of shading. Entire design is more heavily shaded than No. C72A.
No. C72B exists privately perforated 14. Value, $9 unused, $9 used.
For overprints see Nos. 7LC14, 7LC19, 14L26.

Eagle and Newspapers — AP27

Press Building, Madrid — AP28

Don Quixote and Sancho Panza Flying on the Wooden Horse — AP29

Design: 15c, 30c, 50c, 1p, Autogiro over House of Nazareth.

1936, Mar. 11 Photo. Perf. 12½
C73 AP27 1c rose car .25 .25
Never hinged .25
C74 AP28 2c dark brown .25 .25
Never hinged .25
C75 AP27 5c black brown .25 .25
Never hinged .25
C76 AP28 10c dk yellow grn .25 .25
Never hinged .25
C77 AP28 15c Prus blue .25 .25
Never hinged .25
C78 AP27 20c violet .25 .25
Never hinged .25
C79 AP28 25c magenta .25 .25
Never hinged .25
C80 AP28 30c red orange .25 .25
Never hinged .25
C81 AP27 40c orange .50 .25
Never hinged .75
C82 AP28 50c light blue .30 .25
Never hinged .50
C83 AP28 60c olive green .65 .40
Never hinged 1.25
C84 AP28 1p brnsh black .65 .45
Never hinged 1.25
C85 AP29 2p brt ultra 5.75 2.25
Never hinged 8.50
C86 AP29 4p lilac rose 5.75 2.75
Never hinged 8.50
C87 AP29 10p violet brown 16.00 11.00
Never hinged 24.00
Nos. C73-C87 (15) 31.20 18.85
Set, never hinged 46.75

Madrid Press Association, 40th anniv.
Exist imperf. Value, set $250 hinged, and $325 never hinged.
See note after No. 432.

Types of Regular Postage of 1936 Overprinted in Blue or Red

1936 Imperf.
C88 A125 10c dk red (Bl) 150.00 150.00
Never hinged 250.00
C89 A125 15c dk blue (R) 150.00 150.00
Never hinged 250.00
Set, never hinged 450.00

1st National Philatelic Exhibition which opened in Madrid, Apr. 2, 1936.

No. 577 Overprinted in Black

1936, Aug. 1 Perf. 11½
C90 A128 30c rose red 3.00 3.75
Never hinged 7.75
b. Imperf., pair 140.00

Issued in commemoration of the flight of aviators Antonio Arnaiz and Juan Calvo from Manila to Spain.
Counterfeit overprints exist.
Exists privately perforated 14. Value, $50 unused, $50 used.

No. 288 Surcharged in Black

1938, Apr. 13   *Perf. 14*
C91 A36 2.50p on 10c   90.00   80.00
    Never hinged   175.00

7th anniversary of the Republic.
Values are for examples with perforations nearly touching the design on one or two sides.

No. 507
Surcharged in
Various Colors

1938, Aug.   *Perf. 11½*
C92 A92   50c on 25c (Bk)   29.00   29.00
    Never hinged   50.00
C93 A92   1p on 25c (G)   2.25   1.50
    Never hinged   3.00
C94 A92   1.25p on 25c (R)   2.25   1.50
    Never hinged   3.00
C95 A92   1.50p on 25c (Bl)   2.25   1.50
    Never hinged   3.00
C96 A92   2p on 25c (Bk &   40.00   34.00
              R)
    Never hinged   52.50
    Nos. C92-C96 (5)   75.75   67.50
    Set, never hinged   150.00

No. 585 Surcharged

1938, June 1   *Perf. 11*
C97 A132 5p on 1p multi   275.   275.
    Never hinged   500.
a.   Imperf., pair   600.   550.
b.   Inverted surcharge   350.   350.
c.   Souvenir sheet   1,700.   1,700.
    Never hinged   2,500.
d.   As "c," imperf.   6,500.   6,500.
e.   As "c," inverted
      surcharge   6,000.   6,000.

Counterfeit surcharges exist.

Type of 1938-39
Overprinted in Red or
Carmine

1938, May   *Perf. 10, 10½*
C98 A163 50c indigo (R)   .70   .55
    Never hinged   1.25
C99 A163 1p dk blue (C)   3.00   .70
    Never hinged   3.25
    Set, never hinged   4.50

Exist imperf. Value, each $100.
Examples without overprint are proofs.

Juan de
la Cierva
and his
Autogiro
over
Madrid
AP30

1939, Jan. Unwmk. Litho.   *Perf. 11*
C100 AP30 20c red orange   .60   .40
    Never hinged   .70
C101 AP30 25c dk carmine   .45   .25
    Never hinged   .55
C102 AP30 35c brt violet   .65   .40
    Never hinged   .75
C103 AP30 50c dk brown   .65   .25
    Never hinged   .75
C105 AP30 1p blue   .65   .25
    Never hinged   .75
C107 AP30 2p green   3.25   1.75
    Never hinged   5.00

C108 AP30 4p dull blue   5.00   2.75
    Never hinged   9.00
    Nos. C100-C108 (7)   11.25   6.05
    Set, never hinged   19.00

Exist imperf. Value, set $325.

AIR POST SEMI-POSTAL STAMPS

Red Cross Issue

Ramon
Franco's
Plane Plus
Ultra
SPAP1

Perf. 12½, 13
1926, Sept. 15   **Engr.**   *Unwmk.*
CB1 SPAP1 5c black & vio   1.40   1.40
CB2 SPAP1 10c ultra & blk   3.00   3.00
CB3 SPAP1 25c carmine & blk   .30   .30
CB4 SPAP1 50c red org & blk   .30   .30
CB5 SPAP1 1p black & green   2.50   2.50
    Nos. CB1-CB5 (5)   7.50   7.50
    Set, never hinged   10.00

For overprints and surcharges see Nos. B55-B63.

No. B106 Surcharged in Black

1938, Apr. 15   *Perf. 11½*
CB6 SP13 45c + 2p + 5p   250.   225.
    Never hinged   650.
a.   Imperf., pair   1,150.   900.
b.   Souvenir sheet of 1   3,000.   4,500.
    Never hinged   6,000.
c.   Souvenir sheet, imperf.   6,000.   6,000.
d.   Souv. sheet, surch. invtd.   6,500.   5,750.

The surtax was used to benefit the defenders of Madrid.
This issue has been extensively counterfeited.

No. B107
Surcharged

1938, June 1   *Perf. 10*
CB7 SP14 45c + 5p + 3p   10.00   9.75
    Never hinged   17.50

Monument
SPAP2

Dome
Fresco by
Goya,
Cathedral of
Zaragoza
SPAP3

#CB9, CB14, Caravel Santa Maria. #CB10, CB12, The Ascension. #CB13, The Coronation. #CB17, Bombardment of Cathedral of Zaragoza.

Perf. 10½, 11½x10½, 11½
1940, Jan. 29   **Litho.**   *Unwmk.*
Bicolored
CB8 SPAP2   25c + 5c   .40   .40
CB9 SPAP2   50c + 5c   .40   .40
CB10 SPAP2   65c + 15c   .40   .40
CB11 SPAP2   70c + 15c   .40   .40
CB12 SPAP2   90c + 20c   .40   .40
CB13 SPAP2   1.20p + 30c   .40   .40
CB14 SPAP2   1.40p + 40c   .50   .50
CB15 SPAP2   2p + 50c   .75   .75
CB16 SPAP3   4p + 1p sl
              grn &
              rose lil   15.00   15.00
CB17 SPAP3   10p + 4p
              chnt &
              ultra   200.00   200.00
    Nos. CB8-CB17 (10)   218.65   218.65
    Set, never hinged   550.00

19th centenary of the Pillar Virgin. The surtax was used to help restore the Cathedral at Zaragoza, damaged during the Civil War.
No. CB16 exists in slate green & violet, No. CB17 in red violet & ultramarine. Value, $32.50 each.
Nos. CB8-CB17 exist imperf. Value, set $400.

AIR POST SPECIAL DELIVERY STAMP

Goya Commemorative Issue

Type of Air Post
Stamp of 1930
Overprinted

1930   **Unwmk.**   *Perf. 12½*
CE1 AP4 20c bl blk & lt brn
            (Bk)   .25   .25
    Never hinged   .25
a.   Blue overprint   15.00   7.75
    Never hinged   21.00
b.   Overprint omitted   15.00   22.50
    Never hinged   25.00

See note after No. 432.

AIR POST OFFICIAL STAMPS

Pan-American Postal Union Congress Issue
Types of Air Post Stamps of 1931
Overprinted in Red or Blue

1931   **Unwmk.**   *Perf. 12*
CO1 AP22 5c red brown (R)   .25   .25
CO2 AP22 10c blue grn (Bl)   .25   .25
CO3 AP22 25c rose (Bl)   .25   .25
CO4 AP23 50c lt blue (R)   .25   .25

CO5 AP23 1p violet (R)   .25   .25
CO6 AP24 4p gray blk (R)   3.50   3.50
    Nos. CO1-CO6 (6)   4.75   4.75
    Set, never hinged   7.00

Shades exist.

Nos. CO1-CO6 exist imperf. Value, set $22.50

SPECIAL DELIVERY STAMPS

Pegasus and Coat of Arms — SD1

1905-25 Unwmk. Typo.   *Perf. 14*
Control Number on Back
E1 SD1 20c deep red   45.00   .30
    Never hinged   100.00
a.   20c rose red, litho. ('25)   38.00   .30
    Never hinged   70.00
b.   Imperf., pair   300.00
c.   As "a," imperf., pair   300.00

Gazelle
SD2

1929   **Engr.**   *Perf. 11*
Control Number on Back
E2 SD2 20c dull red   19.50   22.50
    Never hinged   37.50
a.   Perf. 14   32.50   37.50
    Never hinged   60.00

Seville and Barcelona Exhibitions. See note after No. 432.

Pegasus — SD3

1929-32   *Perf. 13½x12½, 11½*
Control Number on Back
E3 SD3 20c red   21.00   4.00
    Never hinged   40.00
a.   Imperf., pair   400.00
b.   Without control number, perf.
      11½ ('32)   60.00   1.50
    Never hinged   97.50
c.   As "b," imperf., pair   950.00

No. E3 Overprinted like Nos. 358-370
E4 SD3 20c red (Bl)   12.00   25.00
    Never hinged   30.00

League of Nations 55th assembly.
For overprints see Nos. E5, E10-E12.

No. E3 Overprinted in
Blue

1930   *Perf. 13½x12½, 11½*
E5 SD3 20c red   13.50   .75
    Never hinged   40.00

Railway Congress Issue

Electric Locomotive — SD4

1930, May 10   Litho.   *Perf. 14*
Control Number on Back
E6   SD4   20c brown orange   50.00 50.00
    Never hinged   105.00
      See note after No. 385.

Goya Issue

Type of Regular
Issue of 1930
Overprinted

1930   *Perf. 12½*
E7   A57   20c lilac rose   .25   .30
    Never hinged   .45

Christopher Columbus Issue

Type of Regular
Issue of 1930
Overprinted

1930 Sept. 29
E8   A64   20c brown violet   1.90   1.90
    Never hinged   3.00
      See note after No. 432.

Spanish-American Exhibition Issue

View of Seville Exhibition — SD5

1930, Oct. 10   Photo.   *Perf. 14*
E9   SD5   20c orange   .45   .30
    Never hinged   .60
      See note after No. 432.

Madrid Issue

No. E5 Overprinted in
Green

1931   *Perf. 11½*
E10   SD3   20c red   5.00   5.00
    Never hinged   8.00
The status of No. E10 has been questioned.

Barcelona Issue

No. E3 Overprinted

E11   SD3   20c red   5.50   5.50
    Never hinged   12.00
No. E11 also exists with accent over "U."
The status of No. E11 has been questioned.

No. E3 Overprinted in
Blue

E12   SD3   20c red   6.50   1.25
    Never hinged   21.00

Montserrat Issue

Pegasus — SD6

1931   Engr.   *Perf. 11*
Control Number on Back
E13   SD6   20c vermilion   25.00 25.00
    Never hinged   38.00
    a.   Perf. 14   55.00 60.00

SD7

1934   *Perf. 10*
E14   SD7   20c vermilion   .25   .25
    Never hinged   .20
    a.   Imperf., pair   32.50
For overprints see #10LE1, 11LE1-11LE4,
14LE1.

Newsboy — SD8

1936   Photo.   *Perf. 12½*
E15   SD8   20c rose carmine   .25   .30
    Never hinged   .50
40th anniversary of the Madrid Press
Association.
      See note after No. 432.

Pegasus
SD9

Spanish State
1937-38   Unwmk.   Litho.   *Perf. 11*
With imprint "Hija. deB Fournier-
Burgos"
E16   SD9   20c violet brn   7.75   4.50
    Never hinged   11.00
    a.   Imperf., pair   77.50

Without Imprint
E17   SD9   20c dk vio brn ('38) 1.50   .30
    Never hinged   3.00
    a.   Imperf., pair   50.00

1931
ER2   D1   5c black   1.25   1.40
    Never hinged   2.25
    No. ER2 also exists with accent over "U."

No. 645 Overprinted
in Black

1937
E18   A162   20c dark violet   11.00 11.00
    Never hinged   14.50

Pegasus
SD10

1939-42   *Perf. 10½*
Imprint: "SANCHEZ TODA"
E19   SD10   25c carmine   4.50   .70
    Never hinged   6.25
    a.   Imperf., pair   50.00

Without Imprint
Perf. 10
E20   SD10   25c carmine ('42)   .25   .25
    Never hinged   .30
    a.   Imperf., pair   8.50

SEMI-POSTAL SPECIAL DELIVERY
STAMPS

Red Cross Issue

Royal Family
Group
SPSD1

1926   Unwmk.   Engr.   *Perf. 12½, 13*
EB1   SPSD1   20c red vio & vio
            brn   8.75   8.75
    Never hinged   17.00
    See notes after Nos. 432 and B18.
    For overprint see No. B54.

Motorcyclist
and
Zaragoza
Cathedral
SPSD2

1940   Litho.   *Perf. 11½*
EB2   SPSD2   25c + 5c rose red &
            buff   .40   .30
    19th cent. of the Pillar Virgin. The surtax
was used to help restore the Cathedral at
Zaragoza, damaged during the Civil War.

DELIVERY TAX STAMPS

D1

1931   Unwmk.   Litho.   *Perf. 11½*
ER1   D1   5c black   7.25   .25
    Never hinged   12.00
    For overprints see Nos. ER2-ER3, 7LE5-
7LE6.

No. ER1 Overprinted in
Red

No. ER1 Overprinted in
Red

ER3   D1   5c black   3.00   3.00
    Never hinged   5.50
    These stamps were originally issued for
Postage Due purpose but were later used as
regular postage stamps.

WAR TAX STAMPS

    These stamps did not pay postage
but represented a fiscal tax on mail matter in addition to the postal fees. Their
use was obligatory.

Coat of Arms
WT1   WT2
Unwmk.
1874, Jan. 1   Typo.   *Perf. 14*
MR1   WT1   5c black   11.00   .95
    On cover   6.50
    a.   Imperf. pair   14.00
MR2   WT1   10c pale blue   12.00   1.60
    On cover   9.00
    a.   Imperf., pair   62.50

1875, Jan. 1
MR3   WT2   5c green   6.00   .60
    On cover   4.00
    a.   Imperf., pair   27.50
MR4   WT2   10c lilac   12.00   2.75
    On cover   10.00
    a.   Imperf., pair   55.00

King Alfonso XII
WT3   WT4

1876, June 1
MR5   WT3   5c pale green   7.50   1.00
    On cover   5.50
MR6   WT3   10c blue   7.50   1.00
    On cover   5.50
    a.   Cliche of 5c in plate of
        10c   125.00
MR7   WT3   25c black   50.00 17.00
MR8   WT3   1p lilac   475.00 110.00
MR9   WT3   5p rose   900.00 300.00
    Nos. MR5-MR9 exist imperforate. Value,
$1,100.

1877, Sept. 1
MR10   WT4   15c claret   27.50   1.00
    On cover   5.00
    a.   Imperf., pair   100.00
MR11   WT4   50c yellow   900.00 110.00

WT5

1879
MR12   WT5   5c blue   65.00
MR13   WT5   10c rose   37.50
MR14   WT5   15c violet   25.00
MR15   WT5   25c brown   40.00
MR16   WT5   50c olive green   25.00
MR17   WT5   1p bister   40.00
MR18   WT5   5p gray   150.00
    Nos. MR12-MR18 (7)   382.50

    Nos. MR12-MR18 were never placed in use.
Nos. MR17 and MR18 exist imperforate.
Value, $225.

WT6

Inscribed "1897 A 1898"

1897 *Perf. 14*

MR19	WT6 5c green	3.25	2.10
	On cover		3.25
MR20	WT6 10c green	3.25	2.10
	On cover		3.25
MR21	WT6 15c green	750.00	250.00
MR22	WT6 20c green	8.25	3.25
	On cover		7.00

Nos. MR19-MR22 exist imperf. Value for set $825.

Inscribed

1898

MR23	WT6 5c black	2.25	1.75
	On cover		3.75
MR24	WT6 10c black	2.25	1.75
	On cover		3.75
MR25	WT6 15c black	50.00	9.50
MR26	WT6 20c black	3.50	3.00
	Nos. MR23-MR26 (4)	58.00	16.00

Nos. MR23-MR26 exist imperf. Value about $275 a pair.

King Alfonso XIII — WT7

1898

MR27	WT7 5c black	9.00	.60
	On cover		3.00
a.	Imperf., pair	85.00	

OFFICIAL STAMPS

Coat of Arms
O1 O2

Unwmk.

1854, July 1 **Typo.** *Imperf.*

O1	O1 ½o blk, *yellow*	2.10	2.75
	On cover		20.00
O2	O1 1o blk, *rose*	2.75	3.25
	On cover		22.50
a.	1o black, *blue*	29.00	
O3	O1 4o blk, *green*	7.50	9.25
	On cover		35.00
O4	O1 1 l blk, *blue*	52.50	60.00
	On cover		300.00
	Nos. O1-O4 (4)	64.85	75.25
	Set, never hinged	100.00	

1855-63

O5	O2 ½o blk, *yellow*	1.50	1.75
	On cover		10.50
a.	½o black, *straw* ('63)	1.75	1.90
	On cover		12.00
O6	O2 1o blk, *rose*	1.50	1.75
	On cover		10.50
a.	1o black, *salmon rose*	3.25	1.90
	On cover		12.00
O7	O2 4o blk, *green*	3.25	1.90
	On cover		17.50
a.	4o black, *yellow green*	8.75	1.90
	On cover		17.50
O8	O2 1 l blk, *gray blue*	14.50	17.50
	On cover		70.00
	Nos. O5-O8 (4)	20.75	22.90
	Set, never hinged	25.00	

Full margins of Nos. O1-O8 = ¾mm.

The "value indication" on Nos. O1-O8 actually is the weight of the mail in onzas (ounces, "o") and libras (pounds, "l") for which they were valid.

Type of Regular Issue of 1889

1895 *Perf. 14*

O9	A34 15c yellow	11.00	6.00
	Never hinged	15.00	
	On cover		17.50
a.	Imperf., pair	250.00	

Coat of Arms — O5

1896-98

O10	O5 rose	5.25	1.75
	On cover		20.00
a.	Imperf., pair	87.50	
O11	O5 dk blue ('98)	19.00	6.00
	On cover		32.50

Cervantes Issue

Chamber of Deputies O6

Statue of Cervantes — O7

Cervantes — O9

National Library O8

1916, Apr. 22 **Engr.** *Perf. 12*

For the Senate

O12	O6 green & blk	1.10	.90
O13	O7 brown & blk	1.10	.90
O14	O8 carmine & blk	1.10	.90
O15	O9 brown & blk	1.10	.90

For the Chamber of Deputies

O16	O6 violet & blk	1.10	.90
O17	O7 carmine & blk	1.10	.90
O18	O8 green & blk	1.10	.90
O19	O9 violet & blk	1.10	.90
	Nos. O12-O19 (8)	8.80	7.20

Exist imperf. Value set of pairs, $110.
Exist with centers inverted. Value for set, $87.50

Pan-American Postal Union Congress Issue

Types of Regular Issue of 1931 Overprinted in Red or Blue

1931 *Perf. 12½*

O20	A84 5c dk brown (R)	.50	.25
O21	A85 10c brt green (Bl)	.50	.25
O22	A86 15c dull violet (R)	.50	.25
O23	A85 25c deep rose (Bl)	.50	.25
O24	A87 30c olive green (Bl)	.50	.25
O25	A84 40c ultra (R)	.70	.60
O26	A85 50c deep orange (Bl)	.70	.60
O27	A86 1p blue black (R)	.70	.60
O28	A88 4p magenta (Bl)	14.00	14.00
O29	A88 10p lt brown (R)	25.00	25.00
	Nos. O20-O29 (10)	43.60	42.05
	Set, never hinged	70.00	

Nos. O22-O29 exist imperf. Values about 3 times those quoted.

POSTAL TAX STAMPS

PT5

PT6

Perf. 10½x11½

1937, Dec. 23 **Litho.**

RA11	PT5 10c blk, pale bl & red	8.00	5.00
	Never hinged	21.00	
a.	Imperf. pair	80.00	
	Never hinged	120.00	

The tax was for the tuberculosis fund.

1938, Dec. 23 *Perf. 11½*

RA12	PT6 10c multicolored	4.50	1.75
	Never hinged	10.00	
a.	Imperf. pair	45.00	
	Never hinged	55.00	

The tax was for the tuberculosis fund.

"Spain" Holding Wreath of Peace over Marching Soldiers PT7

1939, July 18 *Perf. 11*

RA13	PT7 10c blue	.25	.25
	Never hinged	.25	
a.	Imperf. pair	65.00	
	Never hinged	82.50	

Type of Regular Issue, 1939

Without Imprint

Unwmk.

1939, Dec. 23 **Litho.** *Imperf.*

RA14	A166 10c dull claret	.25	.25
	Never hinged	.25	

Tuberculosis Fund Issue

Types of Corresponding Semi-Postal Stamps

1940, Dec. 23 *Perf. 10*

RA15	SP23 10c violet & red	.25	.25
	Never hinged	.25	

POSTAL TAX AIR POST STAMPS

Tuberculosis Fund Issues

Franco Type of Semi-Postal Stamps

Unwmk.

1940, Dec. 23 **Litho.** *Perf. 10*

RAC1	SP23 10c bright pink & red	.90	.90
	Never hinged	2.50	

FRANCHISE STAMPS

F1

F2

1869 **Unwmk.** **Litho.** *Imperf.*

S1	F1 blue	52.50	38.00
a.	Tête bêche pair	135.00	120.00

The franchise of No. S1 was granted to Diego Castell to use in illustrating his publications on Spanish postal history.

1881

S2	F2 black, *buff*	36.00	15.50

The franchise of No. S2 was granted to Antonio Fernandez Duro for his book, "Resena histórico-descriptiva de los sellos correos de Espana."

Reprints of No. S2 have been made on carmine, blue, gray, fawn and yellow paper.

CARLIST STAMPS

From the beginning of the Civil War (April 21, 1872) until separate stamps were issued on July 1, 1873, stamps of France were used on all mail from the provinces under Carlist rule.

King Carlos VII — A1

Tilde on N — A1a

Unwmk.

1873, July 1 **Litho.** *Imperf.*

X1	A1 1r blue	650.00	
X2	A1a 1r blue	550.00	350.00

These stamps were reprinted three times in 1881 and once in 1887. The originals have 23 white lines and dots in the lower right spandrel. They are thin and of even width and spacing. The first reprint has 17 to 20 lines in the spandrel, most of them thick and of irregular width and length. The second and third reprints have 21 very thin lines, the second from the bottom being almost invisible. In the fourth reprint the lower right spandrel is an almost solid spot of color.

Originals of type A1 have the curved line above "ESPANA" broken at the left of the "E." All reprints of this type have the curved line continuous.

The reprints exist in various shades of blue, rose, violet and black.

King Carlos VII
A2 A3

A4

A5

1874

X3	A2 1r violet	325.00	325.00
X4	A3 16m rose	5.50	*72.50*
X5	A4 ½r rose	150.00	100.00

Nos. X3 and X6-X7 were for use in the Basque Provinces and Navarra; No. X4 in Catalonia, and No. X5 in Valencia.

Two types of No. X5, alternating in each sheet.

No. X4 with favor cancellation (lozenge of dots) sells for same price as unused.

1875 **White Paper**

X6	A5 50c green	8.00	*82.50*
a.	50c blue green	25.00	*100.00*
b.	Bluish paper	50.00	
X7	A5 1r brown	8.00	*82.50*
a.	Bluish paper	50.00	
	Set, #X6-X7, never hinged	24.00	

Fake cancellations exist on Nos. X1-X7.

REVOLUTIONARY OVERPRINTS

Issued by the Nationalist (Revolutionary) Forces

Many districts or cities made use of the stamps of the Republic overprinted in various forms. Most such overprinting was authorized by military or postal officials but some were without official sanction. These overprints were applied in patriotic celebration and partly as a protection from the use of unoverprinted stamps seized or stolen by soldiers.

BURGOS AIR POST STAMPS

Revenue Stamps Overprinted in Red, Blue or Black

RAP1

1936, Dec. 1   Unwmk.   Perf. 11½
Control Number on Face of Stamp

7LC1	RAP1	25c gray grn & blk (R)	47.50	47.50
a.		Blue overprint	47.50	47.50
7LC2	RAP1	1.50p bl & blk (R)	6.00	6.00
7LC3	RAP1	3p rose & blk (Bl)	6.00	6.00
		Nos. 7LC1-7LC3 (3)	59.50	59.50
		Set, never hinged	105.00	

RAP2   RAP4

Perf. 13½
Blue Control Number on Back

7LC4	RAP2	15c green (R)	3.75	3.75
7LC5	RAP2	25c blue (R)	27.50	27.50
		Set, never hinged	45.00	

Perf. 11½
Without Control Number
Overprint in Black

7LC6	RAP4	1.50p dk blue	6.50	6.50
7LC7	RAP4	3p carmine	6.50	6.50
		Set, never hinged	21.00	

RAP5   RAP6

Overprint in Black
Perf. 13½, 11½

7LC8	RAP5	1.20p green	25.00	25.00
		Never hinged	37.50	

Perf. 14
Control Number on Back

7LC9	RAP6	1.20p green	25.00	25.00
7LC10	RAP6	2.40p green	25.00	25.00
		Set #7LC9-7LC10, never hinged	70.00	

No. 7LC9 is inscribed "CLASE 8a."

RAP7

1937   Unwmk.   Perf. 11½
Control Number on Back

7LC11	RAP7	25c ultra (R)	225.00	225.00

Stamps of Spain, 1931-36, Overprinted in Red or Black (10p)

Perf. 11, 11½, 11x11½
1937   Unwmk.
Overprint 13mm high

7LC12	A100	40c blue	1.10	1.10
a.		Ovpt. 15mm high	1.10	1.10
7LC13	A97	50c dark blue	1.40	1.40
a.		Ovpt. 15mm high	1.40	1.40
7LC14	A130	50c dark blue	1.75	1.75
a.		Ovpt. 15mm high	1.75	1.75
7LC15	A100	60c apple green	2.50	2.50
a.		Ovpt. 15mm high	2.50	2.50
7LC16	AP26	2p gray blue	32.50	32.50
a.		Ovpt. 15mm high	32.50	32.50
7LC17	A49a	10p brown	82.50	82.50
a.		Ovpt. 15mm high	82.50	82.50
		Nos. 7LC12-7LC17 (6)	121.75	121.75

Issue dates: Nos. 7LC12-7LC17, 4/1. Nos. 7LC12a-7LC17a, 5/1.

Spain Nos. 576, 578 and 541b overprinted in Blue or Black

Nos. 7LC18, 7LC19   Nos. 7LC20, 7LC21

Perfs as on Basic Stamps
1937, May

7LC18	A127	30c carmine (Bk)	1.40	1.40
7LC19	A127	30c carmine (Bl)	.70	.70
7LC20	A129	30c car rose (Bk)	1.40	1.40
7LC21	A129	30c car rose (Bl)	.70	.70
7LC22	A107	10p dp brn (Bk)	11.00	11.00
		Nos. 7LC18-7LC22 (5)	15.20	15.20

Spain Nos. 539b and 540b, the 1p and 4p values, were prepared with this overprint in January, 1938, but were not issued. Value, each $4.50.

BURGOS ISSUE SPECIAL DELIVERY STAMPS

Pair of Spain No. 546 Overprinted in Black

1936   Unwmk.   Perf. 11½x11

7LE3	A110	20c (10c+10c) emer	4.50	4.50
		Never hinged	9.00	
a.		Overprint inverted	14.00	

Type of Regular Stamp of 1931 Overprinted in Red

7LE4	A95	20c dark violet	10.00	10.00

Type of Delivery Tax Stamp of 1931 Overprinted in Red on Block of 4

Perf. 11½

7LE5	D1	20c black	8.75	8.00
		Never hinged	13.50	

Same Overprinted in Red on Block of 4

7LE6	D1	20c black	30.00	25.00
		Never hinged	50.00	

SD1

1936   Unwmk.   Perf. 11½

7LE7	SD1	20c green & blk	7.25	5.50
7LE8	SD1	20c green & red	7.25	5.50
		Set, never hinged	25.00	

Nos. 7LE7-7LE8 exist with control number on back. Value $42.50 each.

CADIZ ISSUE SEMI-POSTAL STAMPS

Stamps of Spain, 1931-36, Surcharged in Black or Red

1936   Unwmk.   Imperf.

8LB1	A108	1c + 5c blue grn	.25	.25

Perf. 11½x11, 11½

8LB2	A108	2c + 5c orange brn	.25	.25
8LB3	A103	5c + 5c choc (R)	.45	.45
8LB4	A110	10c + 5c green	.45	.45
8LB5	A111	15c + 5c Prus grn (R)	2.75	2.75
8LB6	A95	20c + 5c dk vio (R)	3.25	3.25
8LB7	A104	25c + 5c lake	2.50	2.50
8LB8	A113	30c + 5c rose red	1.40	1.40
8LB9	A100	40c + 5c dk blue (R)	3.25	3.25

8LB10	A97	50c + 5c dk blue (R)	6.50	6.50
		Nos. 8LB1-8LB10 (10)	21.05	21.05

CANARY ISLANDS AIR POST STAMPS

Issued for Use via the Lufthansa Service

Stamps of Spain, 1932-34, Surcharged in Blue

1936, Oct. 27   Unwmk.   Imperf.

9LC1	A108	50c on 1c bl grn	27.50	17.50

Perf. 11½x11

9LC2	A108	80c on 2c buff	14.50	6.50
9LC3	A103	1.25p on 5c choc	30.00	17.50
		Nos. 9LC1-9LC3 (3)	72.00	41.50
		Set, never hinged	82.50	

The date July 18, 1936, in the overprints of Nos. 9LC1-9LC22 marks the beginning of the Franco insurrection.

Spain Nos. 542, 543, 528 and 641 Surcharged in Black, Red or Green

The surcharge on Nos. 9LC4 and 9LC6 exists in two types: Type I, 2½-3mm space between numerals and "Cts.". Type II, 1½-2mm space between numerals and "Cts.".

1936-37   Imperf.

9LC4	A108	50c on 1c bl grn (I)	4.50	2.75
a.		Overprint type II	11.00	7.75
9LC5	A108	50c on 1c bl grn (R) ('37)	4.50	2.75

Perf. 11, 11½x11

9LC6	A108	80c on 2c buff (I)	2.25	1.60
a.		Overprint type II	5.50	3.25
9LC7	A108	80c on 2c buff (G) ('37)	3.25	1.60
9LC8	A103	1.25 Pts on 5c choc (R)	6.25	4.50
9LC9	A103	Pts 1.25 on 5c choc (R) ('37)	17.00	11.00
9LC10	A161	1.25p on 5c brn (G) ('37)	3.25	1.40
		Nos. 9LC4-9LC10 (7)	41.00	25.60
		Set, never hinged		

Issued: Nos. 9LC4, 9LC6, 11/28/36; No. 9LC8, 1/7/37; Nos. 9LC4a, 9LC6a, 9LC9, 2/12/37; Nos. 9LC5, 9LC7, 9LC10, 3/2/37.

Spain Nos. 542, 543 and 641 Surcharged in Blue

The surcharge on Nos. 9LC11-9LC13 exists in two types: Type I, 18mm tall. Type II, 20mm tall.

1937, Mar. 31   Imperf.

9LC11	A108	50c on 1c bl grn (I)	11.00	5.50
a.		Overprint type II	4.50	2.25

Perf. 11

9LC12	A108	80c on 2c buff (I)	11.00	4.50
a.		Overprint type II	2.75	1.10
9LC13	A161	1.25p on 5c brown (I)	3.25	1.10
		Nos. 9LC11-9LC13 (3)	25.25	11.10
		Set, never hinged	40.00	

Type II overprints issued 4/17/37.

Stamps of Spain, 1931-1936, Surcharged in Blue or Red (#9LC17, 9LC19)

The surcharge on Nos. 9LC15 and 9LC18 exists in two types: Type I, 2mm space between "+" and denomination. Type II, "+" abuts surcharged denomination. Other values are Type I.

1937

9LC14	A104	25c + 50c lake	55.00	10.00
9LC15	A162	30c + 80c rose	19.50	7.75
a.		Overprint type II	19.50	7.75
9LC16	A162	30c + 1.25p rose	25.00	8.25
9LC17	A97	50c + 1.25p dp bl	32.50	11.00
9LC18	A100	60c + 80c ap grn	25.00	8.75
a.		Overprint type II	27.50	10.00
9LC19	A105	1p + 1.25p bl blk	80.00	22.50
		Nos. 9LC14-9LC19 (6)	237.00	68.25
		Set, never hinged	350.00	

The surcharge represents the airmail rate and the basic stamp the postage rate.
Issued: 9LC15a, 9LC18a, 4/15. 9LC14-9LC19, 5/5.

Spain Nos. 542, 624 and 641 Surcharged in Black

1937, May 25　　Unwmk.　　Imperf.

9LC20	A108	50c on 1c bl grn	7.75	4.50

Perf. 11½, 11½x11

9LC21	A143	80c on 2c org brn	6.50	2.25
9LC22	A161	1.25p on 5c gray brn	6.50	2.25
		Nos. 9LC20-9LC22 (3)	20.75	9.00
		Set, never hinged	30.00	

Stamps and Type of Spain, 1933-36, Surcharged in Black

1937, July　　Perf. 13½x13, 11, 11½

9LC23	A143	50c on 2c org brn	3.50	2.25
9LC24	A126	80c on 2c org brn	300.00	180.00
9LC25	A161	80c on 5c gray brn	3.50	2.25
9LC26	A108	1.25p on 1c bl grn	4.25	2.25
9LC27	A161	2.50p on 10c grn	16.00	8.75

Spain Nos. 647, 650 and 652 Surcharged in Black or Red

Perf. 11

9LC28	A162	30c + 80c rose	3.00	1.40
9LC29	A162	50c + 1.25p dk bl (R)	10.50	5.00
9LC30	A162	1p + 1.25p bl (R)	16.00	8.75
		Nos. 9LC23-9LC30 (8)	356.75	210.65
		Set, never hinged	550.00	

See note after No. 9LC19.

AP1

Perf. 14x13½
1937, July 16　　Wmk. 116
Surcharge in Various Colors

9LC31	AP1	50c on 5c ultra (Br)	2.75	2.50
9LC32	AP1	80c on 5c ultra (V)	1.50	1.75
9LC33	AP1	1.25p on 5c ultra (V)	2.25	2.25
		Nos. 9LC31-9LC33 (3)	6.90	6.50
		Set, never hinged	10.00	

Spain Nos. 641, 643 and 640 Surcharged in Green or Orange

1937, Oct. 29　　Unwmk.　　Perf. 11

9LC34	A161	50c on 5c (G)	9.25	3.75
9LC35	A161	80c on 10c (O)	5.75	2.75
9LC36	A160	1.25p on 2c (G)	10.50	7.25
		Nos. 9LC34-9LC36 (3)	25.50	13.75
		Set, never hinged	40.00	

Spain Nos. 638, 640 and 643 Surcharged in Red, Blue or Violet

1937, Dec. 23　　Imperf.

9LC37	A159	50c on 1c (R)	10.50	4.50

Perf. 11, 11x11½

9LC38	A160	80c on 2c (Bl)	4.25	2.75
9LC39	A161	1.25p on 10c (V)	9.25	3.50
		Nos. 9LC37-9LC39 (3)	24.00	10.75
		Set, never hinged	37.50	

Spain Nos. 647, 650 to 652 Surcharged in Black, Green or Brown

1937, Dec. 29

9LC40	A162	30c + 30c rose	4.50	3.75
9LC41	A162	50c + 2.50p dk bl (G)	29.00	21.00
9LC42	A162	60c + 2.30p yel (G)	29.00	21.00
9LC43	A162	1p + 5p bl (R)	35.00	21.00
		Nos. 9LC40-9LC43 (4)	97.50	66.75
		Set, never hinged	110.00	

See note after No. 9LC19.

Stamps of Spain, 1936, Surcharged in Black, Green, Blue or Red

1938, Feb. 2　　Perf. 11, 11½, 11x11½

9LC44	A160	50c on 2c brn	5.00	3.75
9LC45	A161	80c on 5c brn (G)	3.75	3.25
9LC46	A162	80c on 30c rose (Bl)	4.50	2.50
9LC47	A161	1.25p on 10c grn (Bl)	4.50	3.25
9LC48	A162	1.25p on 50c dk bl (R)	4.50	2.50
		Nos. 9LC44-9LC48 (5)	22.25	15.50
		Set, never hinged	27.50	

Spain Nos. 645, 646 and 649 Surcharged in Brown, Green or Violet

1938, Feb. 14

9LC51	A162	2.50p on 20c (Br)	50.00	25.00
9LC52	A162	5p on 25c (G)	50.00	25.00
9LC53	A162	10p on 40c (V)	50.00	25.00
		Nos. 9LC51-9LC53 (3)	150.00	75.00
		Set, never hinged	175.00	

MALAGA ISSUE

Stamps of 1900-08 Overprinted in Black or Red

1937　　Unwmk.　　Imperf.

10L1	A47	1c blue green	.25	.25
10L2	A108	1c blue green	.25	.25
10L3	A108	1c lt green (R)	.25	.25

Perf. 13½, 13½x13, 11, 11½x11

10L4	A108	2c orange brn	14.50	14.50
10L5	A126	2c orange brn	.25	.25
10L6	A103	5c chocolate (R)	.25	.25
10L7	A96	10c yellow green	12.00	12.00
10L8	A110	10c emerald	.30	.30
10L9	A111	15c Prus grn (R)	.55	.55
10L10	A97	15c blue grn (R)	.55	.55
10L11	A95	20c dk violet (R)	.50	.50
10L12	A99	25c lake	1.50	1.50
10L13	A104	25c lake	.50	.50
10L14	A113	30c carmine	.50	.50
10L15	A129	30c carmine rose	2.50	2.50
10L16	A100	40c blue (R)	.45	.45
10L17	A97	50c dk blue (R)	2.50	2.50
10L18	A100	60c apple green	1.40	1.40
10L19	A105	1p black (R)	2.75	2.75
		Nos. 10L1-10L19 (19)	41.75	41.75

Stamps of 1932-35 Overprinted in Red or Black in panes of 25, reading down. "8.2.37" and "¡Arriba Espana!" form the lower half of all overprints. The upper half varies.

Overprint a (1st and 2nd rows): "MALAGA AGRADECIDA A TRANQUILLO-BIANCHI"
Overprint b (3rd row): "MALAGA A SU SALVADOR QUEIPO DE LLANO"
Overprint c (4th and 5th rows): "MALAGA A SU CAUDILLO FRANCO"

Values are for vertical strips of 3 containing examples of each overprint type.

1937　　　　　　Perf. 11½

10L20	A111	15c Prus grn (R)	5.50	5.50
a.		15c single stamp, ovpt. a	.85	.85
b.		15c single stamp, ovpt. b	1.60	1.60
c.		15c single stamp, ovpt. c	.85	.85
10L21	A113	30c rose red (Bk)	5.50	5.50
a.		30c single stamp, ovpt. a	.85	.85
b.		30c single stamp, ovpt. b	1.60	1.60
c.		30c single stamp, ovpt. c	.85	.85
10L22	A97	50c dk blue (R)	8.75	8.75
a.		50c single stamp, ovpt. a	1.60	1.60
b.		50c single stamp, ovpt. b	3.25	3.25
c.		50c single stamp, ovpt. c	1.60	1.60
10L23	A100	60c apple grn (Bk)	11.00	11.00
a.		60c single stamp, ovpt. a	1.60	1.60
b.		60c single stamp, ovpt. b	3.25	3.25
c.		60c single stamp, ovpt. c	1.60	1.60
		Nos. 10L20-10L23 (4)	30.75	30.75

SPECIAL DELIVERY STAMP

Overprinted like Nos. 10L1-10L19 on Type of Special Delivery Stamp of 1934

1937　　　　　　Perf. 10

10LE1	SD7	20c rose red (Bk)	.45	.45

ORENSE ISSUE

Stamps of 1931-36 Overprinted in Red, Blue or Black

1936　　　　　　Imperf.

11L1	A108	1c blue grn (Bl)	.45	.45
a.		Red overprint	1.10	1.10

Perf. 11½, 13½x13

11L2	A108	2c org brn (Bk)	3.50	3.25
11L3	A126	2c org brn (Bk)	.65	.65
11L4	A103	5c brown (R)	1.50	1.50
11L5	A110	10c lt green (Bl)	2.25	2.25
a.		Red overprint	11.00	11.00
11L6	A111	15c Prus grn (R)	3.25	3.25
11L7	A95	20c violet (Bl)	3.25	3.25
11L8	A104	25c lake (Bk)	3.75	3.75
11L9	A113	30c rose red (Bl)	2.75	2.75
a.		Black overprint	5.50	5.50
11L10	A100	40c blue (R)	3.75	3.75
a.		Imperf, pair	50.00	
11L11	A97	50c dark blue (R)	6.50	6.50
11L12	A100	60c apple grn (Bk)	4.75	4.75
a.		Red overprint	17.00	17.00
b.		As "a," Imperf, pair	50.00	
		Nos. 11L1-11L12 (12)	36.35	36.10

SEMI-POSTAL STAMPS

Stamps of Spain, 1931-36, Surcharged in Blue on front and on back of stamp

1936-37　　Unwmk.　　Imperf.

11LB1	A47	1c + 5c bl grn	2.25	2.25
11LB2	A108	1c + 5c green	.40	.40

Perf. 13½x13, 11½, 11½x11

11LB3	A108	2c + 5c org brn	.45	.45
11LB4	A126	2c + 5c red brn	.45	.45
11LB5	A103	5c + 5c choc	.65	.65
11LB6	A110	10c + 5c emer	.65	.65
11LB7	A111	15c + 5c Prus grn	.95	.95
11LB8	A95	20c + 5c violet	.65	.65
11LB9	A104	25c + 5c lake	.95	.95
11LB10	A113	30c + 5c rose red	2.75	2.75
11LB11	A117	30c + 5c rose red	42.50	42.50
11LB12	A100	60c + 5c apple grn	250.00	190.00
		Nos. 11LB1-11LB12 (12)	302.65	242.65

SPECIAL DELIVERY STAMPS

Type of Special Delivery Stamp of 1934 Overprinted "!VIVA ESPANA!" in Blue or Black

1936　　　　　　Perf. 10

11LE1	SD7	20c rose red (Bl)	1.90	1.90
11LE2	SD7	20c rose red (Bk)	4.25	4.25

Same with Surcharge "+ 5 cts."

11LE3	SD7	20c + 5c rose red	1.00	1.00

Same Surcharge, Overprint Repeated at Right

11LE4	SD7	20c + 5c rose red	1.10	1.10
		Nos. 11LE1-11LE4 (4)	8.25	8.25

SAN SEBASTIAN ISSUE

For Use in Province of Guipuzcoa

Stamps of 1931-36 Overprinted in Red or Blue

1937　　Unwmk.　　Imperf.

12L1	A108	1c bl grn (R)	.65	.65

Perf. 11, 13½

12L2	A108	2c buff (Bl)	1.00	1.50
12L3	A126	2c org brn (Bl)	2.10	2.10
12L4	A95	5c chocolate (R)	5.00	5.00
12L5	A103	5c chocolate (R)	1.75	1.75
12L6	A110	10c emerald (R)	1.75	1.75
12L7	A111	15c Prus grn (R)	2.10	2.10
12L8	A95	20c dk violet (R)	2.75	2.75
12L9	A104	25c car lake (Bl)	2.75	2.75
12L10	A113	30c rose red (Bl)	2.75	2.75
12L11	A100	40c blue (R)	5.50	5.50
12L12	A97	50c dark blue (R)	5.50	5.50
		Nos. 12L1-12L12 (12)	33.60	34.10

SANTA CRUZ DE TENERIFE ISSUE

Stamps of Spain, 1931-36 Overprinted in Black or Red

1936　　Unwmk.　　Imperf.

13L1	A108	1c bl grn (R)	.75	.75

13L2	A108	1c bl grn (Bk)	2.75	2.75

Perf. 11, 13½

13L3	A108	2c buff (Bk)	5.50	5.50
13L4	A126	2c org brn (Bk)	.95	.95
13L5	A103	5c choc (R)	3.00	3.00
13L6	A110	10c green (R)	3.00	3.00
13L7	A104	25c lake (Bk)	11.00	11.00
13L8	A100	40c dk blue (R)	3.25	3.25
13L9	A107	10p dp brn (Bk)	300.00	225.00
		Nos. 13L1-13L9 (9)	330.20	255.20

Many forgeries of #13L9 exist.

SEVILLE ISSUE

Stamps of Spain, 1931-36, Overprinted in Black or Red

Sevilla
"VIVA
ESPAÑA"
Julio-1936

1936   **Imperf.**

14L1	A108	1c blue grn (Bk)	.30	.30

Perf. 13½x13, 11, 11½x11

14L2	A126	2c org brn (Bk)	.35	.35
14L3	A103	5c chocolate (R)	.45	.45
14L4	A110	10c emerald (Bk)	.55	.55
14L5	A111	15c Prus grn (R)	1.40	1.40
14L6	A95	20c violet (R)	1.40	1.40
14L7	A104	25c lake (Bk)	1.40	1.40
14L8	A113	30c carmine (Bk)	1.40	1.40
14L9	A128	30c rose red (Bk)	8.25	8.25
14L10	A100	40c blue (R)	5.50	5.50
14L11	A97	50c dk blue (R)	5.50	5.50
14L12	A100	60c apple grn (Bk)	6.75	6.75
		Nos. 14L1-14L12 (12)	33.25	33.25

Stamps of Spain, 1931-36, Handstamped in Black

SEVILLA
"VIVA
ESPAÑA"
JULIO-1936

Imperf

14L13	A108	1c blue grn	.30	.30

Perf. 13½x13, 11, 11x11½, 11½x13

14L14	A126	2c orange brn	.45	.45
14L15	A103	5c chocolate	.45	.45
14L16	A110	10c emerald	.45	.45
14L17	A111	15c Prus green	.55	.55
14L18	A95	20c violet	.55	.55
14L19	A104	25c lake	.55	.55
14L20	A113	30c carmine	.55	.55
14L21	A128	30c rose red	3.00	3.00
14L22	A100	40c blue	1.10	1.10
14L23	A97	50c dk blue	3.00	3.00
14L24	A100	60c apple grn	1.00	1.00
14L25	A105	1p black	3.00	3.00
14L26	AP26	2p gray blue	13.50	13.50
14L27	A106	4p magenta	7.25	7.25
14L28	A107	10p deep brown	47.95	47.95
		Nos. 14L13-14L28,14LE1 (17)	47.95	47.95

The date "Julio-1936" in the overprints of Nos. 14L1-14L28 and 14LE1 marks the beginning of the Franco insurrection.

SPECIAL DELIVERY STAMP

Overprinted like Nos. 14L13-14L25 on Type of Special Delivery Stamp of 1934

1936			**Perf. 10**
14LE1	SD7	20c rose red	1.75 1.75

SPANISH GUINEA

ˈspa-nish ˈgi-nē

LOCATION — In western Africa, bordering on the Gulf of Guinea
GOVT. — Spanish Colony
AREA — 10,852 sq. mi.
POP. — 212,000 (est. 1957)
CAPITAL — Santa Isabel

Spanish Guinea Nos. 1-84 were issued for and used only in the continental area later called Rio Muni. From 1909 to 1960, Spanish Guinea also included Fernando Po, Elobey, Annobon and Corisco.

100 Centimos = 1 Peseta

King Alfonso XIII — A1

Blue Control Numbers on Back

1902		**Unwmk.** **Typo.**		**Perf. 14**
1	A1	5c dark green	12.50	6.25
2	A1	10c indigo	12.50	6.25
3	A1	25c claret	92.50	47.50
4	A1	50c deep brown	92.50	47.50
5	A1	75c violet	92.50	47.50
6	A1	1p carmine rose	140.00	47.50
7	A1	2p olive green	180.00	100.00
8	A1	5p dull red	275.00	175.00
		Nos. 1-8 (8)	897.50	477.50
		Set, never hinged	1,800.	

Exists imperf, value set $3,500.

Revenue Stamps Surcharged

HABILITADO
PARA
CORREOS
10 cen de peseta

Blue or Black Control Numbers on Back

1903				**Imperf.**
8A		10c on 25c blk (R)	550.00	240.00
8B		10c on 50c org (Bl)	140.00	40.00
8D		10c on 1p 25c car (Bk)	750.00	400.00
8F		10c on 2p cl (Bk)	800.00	600.00
g.		Blue surcharge	1,450.	800.00
8H		10c on 2p 50c red brn (Bl)	1,100.	725.00
8J		10c on 5p ol blk (R)	1,500.	525.00

Nos. 8A-8J are surcharged on stamps inscribed "Posesiones Espanolas de Africa Occidental" and "1903," with arms at left.
This surcharge was also applied to revenue stamps of 10, 15, 25, 50, 75 and 100 pesetas and in other colors.
See Nos. 98-101C.

King Alfonso XIII — A2

Blue Control Numbers on Back

1903		**Typo.**		**Perf. 14**
9	A2	¼c black	1.50	.85
10	A2	½c blue green	1.50	.85
11	A2	1c claret	1.50	.70
12	A2	2c dark olive	1.50	.70
13	A2	3c dark brown	1.50	.70
14	A2	4c vermilion	1.50	.70
15	A2	5c black brown	1.50	.70
16	A2	10c red brown	2.50	.85
17	A2	15c dark blue	8.50	6.25
18	A2	25c orange buff	8.50	6.25
19	A2	50c carmine lake	16.00	14.00
20	A2	75c violet	21.00	14.00
21	A2	1p blue green	35.00	22.00
22	A2	2p dark green	35.00	22.00
23	A2	3p scarlet	95.00	28.50
24	A2	4p dull blue	110.00	50.00
25	A2	5p dark violet	210.00	72.50
26	A2	10p carmine rose	300.00	100.00
		Nos. 9-26 (18)	852.00	341.55
		Set, never hinged	1,700.	

Blue Control Numbers on Back

1905			**Same, Dated "1905"**	
27	A2	1c black	.30	.25
28	A2	2c blue grn	.30	.25
29	A2	3c claret	.30	.25
30	A2	4c bronze grn	.30	.25
31	A2	5c dark brown	.30	.25
32	A2	10c red	1.60	.85
33	A2	15c black brown	4.50	2.75
34	A2	25c chocolate	4.50	2.75
35	A2	50c dark blue	9.75	6.25
36	A2	75c orange buff	11.00	6.25
37	A2	1p carmine rose	11.00	6.25
38	A2	2p violet	26.00	13.00
39	A2	3p blue green	67.50	27.50
40	A2	4p dark green	67.50	39.00
40A	A2	5p vermilion	110.00	42.00
41	A2	10p dull blue	200.00	130.00
		Nos. 27-41 (16)	514.85	277.85
		Set, never hinged	950.00	

Stamps of Elobey, 1905, Overprinted in Violet or Blue

1906				
42	A1	1c rose	4.00	2.25
43	A1	2c deep violet	4.00	2.25
44	A1	3c black	4.00	2.25
45	A1	4c orange red	4.00	2.25
46	A1	5c deep green	4.00	2.25
47	A1	10c blue green	9.25	5.25
48	A1	15c violet	16.00	9.00
49	A1	25c rose lake	16.00	9.00
50	A1	50c orange buff	22.50	13.00
51	A1	75c dark blue	26.00	15.00
52	A1	1p red brown	47.50	25.00
53	A1	2p black brown	67.50	37.50
54	A1	3p vermilion	97.50	55.00
55	A1	4p dark brown	475.00	250.00
56	A1	5p bronze green	475.00	250.00
57	A1	10p claret	2,000.	1,100.
		Nos. 42-54 (13)	322.25	180.00

King Alfonso XIII
A3   A4

Blue Control Numbers on Back

1907				**Typo.**
58	A3	1c dark green	.75	.25
59	A3	2c dull blue	.75	.25
60	A3	3c violet	.75	.25
61	A3	4c yellow grn	.75	.25
62	A3	5c carmine lake	.75	.25
63	A3	10c orange	4.00	1.25
64	A3	15c brown	3.00	.80
65	A3	25c dark blue	3.00	.80
66	A3	50c black brown	3.00	.80
67	A3	75c blue green	3.00	.80
68	A3	1p red	6.00	1.40
69	A3	2p dark brown	9.00	6.25
70	A3	3p olive gray	9.00	6.25
71	A3	4p maroon	13.00	6.25
72	A3	5p green	13.50	9.50
73	A3	10p red violet	20.00	12.00
		Nos. 58-73 (16)	90.25	47.35
		Set, never hinged	210.00	

Issue of 1907 Surcharged in Black or Red

HABILITADO
PARA
05 CTMS

1908-09				
74	A3	05c on 1c dk grn (R)	3.00	1.50
75	A3	05c on 2c dk blue (R)	3.00	1.50
76	A3	05c on 3c violet	3.00	1.50
77	A3	05c on 4c yel grn	3.00	1.50
78	A3	05c on 10c orange	3.00	1.50
a.		Red surcharge	5.25	2.75
84	A3	15c on 10c orange	14.00	9.00
		Nos. 74-84 (6)	29.00	16.50

Many stamps of this issue are found with the surcharge inverted, sideways, double and in both black and red. Other stamps of the 1907 issue are known with this surcharge but are not believed to have been put in use. Value, each $17.

Blue Control Numbers on Back

1909		**Typo.**		**Perf. 14½**
85	A4	1c orange brown	.25	.25
86	A4	2c rose	.25	.25
87	A4	5c dark green	1.40	.25
88	A4	10c vermilion	.40	.25
89	A4	15c dark brown	.40	.25
90	A4	20c violet	.65	.35
91	A4	25c dull blue	.65	.35
92	A4	30c chocolate	.85	.30
93	A4	40c lake	.50	.30
94	A4	50c dark violet	.50	.30
95	A4	1p blue green	13.50	7.00
96	A4	4p orange	3.50	4.25
97	A4	10p red	3.50	4.25
		Nos. 85-97 (13)	26.35	18.35
		Set, never hinged	50.00	

For overprints see Nos. 102-114.

Revenue Stamps Surcharged like Nos. 8A-8J in Black

1909				**Imperf.**

With or Without Control Numbers on Back

98		10c on 50c bl grn	87.50	57.50
a.		Red or violet surcharge	110.00	80.00
99		10c on 1p 25c violet	150.00	80.00
100		10c on 2p dk brn	600.00	350.00
100A		10c on 5p dk vio	600.00	350.00
101		10c on 25p red brn	800.00	575.00
101A		10c on 50p brn lil	2,750.	1,600.
101B		10c on 75p carmine	2,750.	1,600.
101C		10c on 100p orange	2,750.	1,600.

Nos. 98-101C are surcharged on undated stamps, arms centered. Stamps inscribed: "Territorios Espanoles del Africa Occidental." Basic revenue stamps similar to Rio de Oro type A3.

Stamps of 1909 Overprinted with Handstamp in Black, Blue, Green or Red

1911				
102	A4	1c orange brn (Bl)	.40	.35
103	A4	2c rose (G)	.40	.35
104	A4	5c dk green (R)	2.00	.35
105	A4	10c vermilion	1.15	.45
106	A4	15c dk brown (R)	2.00	.75
107	A4	20c violet	2.50	1.15
108	A4	25c dull blue (R)	3.00	2.40
109	A4	30c choc (R)	3.75	3.50
110	A4	40c lake (Bl)	4.00	3.50
111	A4	50c dark violet	6.75	5.00
112	A4	1p blue grn (R)	55.00	40.00
113	A4	4p orange (R)	29.00	23.00
114	A4	10p red (G)	37.50	40.00
		Nos. 102-114 (13)	147.45	120.80
		Set, never hinged	300.00	

The date "1911" is missing from the overprint on the first stamp in each row, or ten times in each sheet of 100 stamps. This variety occurs on all stamps of the series. Value, set $550.

King Alfonso XIII
A5   A6

Blue Control Numbers on Back

1912		**Typo.**		**Perf. 13½**
115	A5	1c black	.30	.30
116	A5	2c dark brown	.30	.30
117	A5	5c deep green	.30	.30
118	A5	10c red	.30	.30
119	A5	15c claret	.30	.30
120	A5	20c red	.30	.30
121	A5	25c dull blue	.30	.30
122	A5	30c lake	3.50	2.00
123	A5	40c car rose	2.10	1.00
124	A5	50c brown org	2.00	.35
125	A5	1p dark violet	2.25	1.25
126	A5	4p lilac	5.00	2.50
127	A5	10p blue green	10.50	9.50
		Nos. 115-127 (13)	27.45	18.70
		Set, never hinged	50.00	

For overprints and surcharges see Nos. 141-157.

Blue Control Numbers on Back

1914				**Perf. 13**
128	A6	1c dull violet	.35	.30
129	A6	2c car rose	.35	.30
130	A6	5c deep green	.35	.30
131	A6	10c vermilion	.35	.30
132	A6	15c dark violet	.35	.30
133	A6	20c dark brown	1.05	.55
134	A6	25c dark blue	.45	.35
135	A6	30c brown orange	1.60	.55
136	A6	40c blue green	1.60	.55
137	A6	50c dp claret	.75	.35
138	A6	1p vermilion	2.00	2.25
139	A6	4p maroon	7.00	4.50
140	A6	10p olive black	7.75	8.50
		Nos. 128-140 (13)	23.95	19.10
		Set, never hinged	60.00	

Stamps with these or similar overprints are unauthorized and fraudulent.

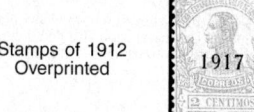

Stamps of 1912
Overprinted

1917   *Perf. 13½*

141	A5	1c black	125.00	85.00
142	A5	2c dark brown	125.00	85.00
143	A5	5c deep green	.40	.35
144	A5	10c red	.40	.35
145	A5	15c claret	.40	.35
146	A5	20c red	.40	.35
147	A5	25c dull blue	.40	.35
148	A5	30c lake	.40	.35
149	A5	40c carmine rose	.75	.40
150	A5	50c brown orange	.40	.35
151	A5	1p dark violet	.75	.40
152	A5	4p lilac	8.25	4.00
153	A5	10p blue green	8.25	4.00
		Nos. 141-153 (13)	270.80	181.25
		Set, never hinged	550.00	

Nos. 143-153 exist with overprint double, inverted, in dark blue, reading "9117" and in pairs one without overprint.

Stamps of 1917
Surcharged

1918

154	A5	5c on 40c car rose	36.00	14.50
155	A5	10c on 4p lilac	36.00	14.50
156	A5	15c on 20c red	65.00	25.00
157	A5	25c on 10p bl grn	65.00	25.00
a.		"52" for "25"	500.00	425.00
		Nos. 154-157 (4)	202.00	79.00
		Set, never hinged	345.00	

The varieties "Gents" and "Censt" occur on Nos. 154-157. Values 50 percent more.

King Alfonso XIII
A7   A8

1919   *Typo.*   *Perf. 13*
Blue Control Numbers on Back

158	A7	1c lilac	1.00	.30
159	A7	2c rose	1.00	.30
160	A7	5c vermilion	1.00	.30
161	A7	10c violet	1.75	.30
162	A7	15c brown	1.75	.55
163	A7	20c blue	1.75	.80
164	A7	25c green	1.75	.80
a.		25c blue (error)	62.50	
165	A7	30c orange	2.25	.80
166	A7	40c orange	4.50	.80
167	A7	50c red	4.50	.80
168	A7	1p light green	4.50	2.75
169	A7	4p claret	10.00	10.50
170	A7	10p brown	20.00	19.00
		Nos. 158-170 (13)	55.75	38.00
		Set, never hinged	90.00	

1920
Blue Control Numbers on Back

171	A8	1c brown	.35	.30
172	A8	2c dull rose	.35	.30
173	A8	5c gray green	.35	.30
174	A8	10c dull rose	.35	.30
175	A8	15c orange	.35	.30
176	A8	20c yellow	.35	.35
177	A8	25c dull blue	1.15	.35
178	A8	30c greenish blue	42.50	25.00
179	A8	40c lt brown	2.00	.35
180	A8	50c lilac	2.40	.35
181	A8	1p light red	2.40	.35

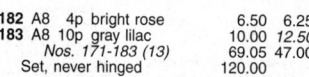

182	A8	4p bright rose	6.50	6.25
183	A8	10p gray lilac	10.00	*12.50*
		Nos. 171-183 (13)	69.05	47.00
		Set, never hinged	120.00	

A9   Nipa
House — A10

1922
Blue Control Numbers on Back

184	A9	1c dark brown	.70	.25
185	A9	2c claret	.70	.25
186	A9	5c blue green	.70	.25
187	A9	10c pale red	4.75	1.15
188	A9	15c orange	.70	.30
189	A9	20c lilac	3.00	1.05
190	A9	25c dark blue	4.75	1.40
191	A9	30c violet	4.50	1.50
192	A9	40c turq blue	3.25	.75
193	A9	50c deep rose	3.25	.75
194	A9	1p myrtle green	3.25	.75
195	A9	4p red brown	13.00	13.00
196	A9	10p yellow	26.00	25.00
		Nos. 184-196 (13)	68.55	46.40
		Set, never hinged	130.00	

1924
Blue Control Numbers on Back

197	A10	5c choc & bl	.25	.25
198	A10	10c gray grn & bl	.25	.25
199	A10	15c rose & blk	.25	.25
200	A10	20c violet & blk	.25	.25
201	A10	25c org red & blk	.40	.25
202	A10	30c orange & blk	.40	.25
203	A10	40c dl bl & blk	.40	.25
204	A10	50c claret & blk	.40	.25
205	A10	60c red brn & blk	.40	.25
206	A10	1p dk vio & blk	1.60	.25
a.		Center inverted	600.00	140.00
207	A10	4p brt bl & blk	3.75	2.25
208	A10	10p bl grn & blk	8.75	4.50
		Nos. 197-208 (12)	17.10	9.25
		Set, never hinged	25.00	

Seville-Barcelona
Issue of Spain,
1929, Overprinted
in Red or Blue

1929   *Perf. 11*

209	A52	5c rose lake	.35	.40
210	A53	10c green (R)	.35	.40
211	A50	15c Prus bl (R)	.35	.40
212	A51	20c purple (R)	.35	.40
213	A50	25c brt rose	.35	.40
214	A52	30c black brn	.35	.40
215	A53	40c dk blue (R)	.70	.65
216	A51	50c dp orange	.70	.65
217	A52	1p blue blk (R)	11.50	6.00
218	A53	4p deep rose	22.00	11.50
219	A53	10p brown	42.50	23.00
		Nos. 209-219 (11)	79.50	44.20
		Set, never hinged	160.00	

Porter   Drummers
A11   A12

King Alfonso XIII
and Queen
Victoria — A13

1931   *Engr.*   *Perf. 14*

220	A11	1c blue green	.30	.25
221	A11	2c red brown	.30	.25

Blue Control Numbers on Back

222	A11	5c brown black	.30	.25
223	A11	10c light green	.30	.25
224	A11	15c dark green	.30	.25
225	A11	20c deep violet	.30	.25
226	A12	25c carmine	.00	.00
227	A12	30c lake	.40	.25
228	A12	40c dark blue	.90	.65
229	A12	50c red orange	1.75	1.25
230	A13	80c blue violet	3.25	1.90
231	A13	1p black	5.75	5.25
232	A13	4p violet rose	37.50	20.00
233	A13	5p dark brown	17.50	14.00
		Nos. 220-233 (14)	69.15	45.05
		Set, never hinged	175.00	

Exist imperf. Value for set, $300.

See Nos. 262-271. For overprints and surcharges see Nos. 234-277, 282-283, 298 (in Scott Standard catalogue, Vol. 6).

Stamps of 1931
Overprinted

1931

234	A11	1c blue green	.30	.30
235	A11	2c red brown	.30	.30
236	A11	5c brown black	.30	.30
237	A11	10c light green	.30	.30
238	A11	15c dark green	.30	.30
239	A11	20c deep violet	.30	.30
240	A12	25c carmine	.30	.30
241	A12	30c lake	.30	.30
242	A12	40c dark blue	2.25	.65
243	A12	50c red orange	14.50	7.75
244	A13	80c blue violet	4.50	2.50
245	A13	1p black	14.50	5.00
246	A13	4p violet rose	25.00	14.50
247	A13	5p dark brown	25.00	14.50
		Nos. 234-247 (14)	88.15	47.30
		Set, never hinged	200.00	

Stamps of 1931
Overprinted in Red
or Blue

1933

248	A11	1c blue grn (R)	.30	.25
249	A11	2c red brown (Bl)	.30	.25
250	A11	5c brown blk (R)	.30	.25
251	A11	10c lt green (Bl)	.30	.25
252	A11	15c dk green (R)	.30	.25
253	A11	20c dp violet (R)	.30	.25
254	A12	25c carmine (Bl)	.30	.25
255	A12	30c lake (Bl)	.30	.25
256	A12	40c dk blue (R)	3.50	.95
257	A12	50c red orange (Bl)	22.00	4.75
258	A13	80c blue vio (R)	7.25	4.25
259	A13	1p black (R)	25.00	4.50
260	A13	4p violet rose (Bl)	47.50	20.00
261	A13	5p dk brown (Bl)	47.50	20.00
		Nos. 248-261 (14)	155.15	56.45
		Set, never hinged	250.00	

**Types of 1931
Without Control Number**

1934-35   *Engr.*   *Perf. 10*

262	A11	1c blue green ('35)	11.50	.25
263	A11	2c red brown ('35)	11.50	.25
264	A11	5c black brn	2.25	.25
265	A11	10c light green	2.25	.25
266	A11	15c dark green	3.50	.25
267	A12	30c rose red	4.50	.35
268	A12	50c indigo ('35)	9.75	1.10
		Nos. 262-268 (7)	45.25	2.70
		Set, never hinged	70.00	

Stamps of 1931-33
Surcharged in Black

1936-37   *Perf. 10, 14*

272	A12	30c on 40c (#228)	5.50	3.50
273	A12	30c on 40c (#242)	22.00	5.25
274	A12	30c on 40c (#256)	80.00	25.00
		Nos. 272-274 (3)	107.50	33.75
		Set, never hinged	170.00	

The surcharge on Nos. 272-274 exists in two types, differing in the "3" which is scarcer in italic.

No. 268 Surcharged
in Red

275	A12	1p on 50c indigo	30.00
276	A12	4p on 50c indigo	90.00
277	A12	5p on 50c indigo	55.00
		Nos. 275-277 (3)	175.00

Nos. 275-277 were not issued.

Stamps of Spain,
1936, Overprinted in
Black or Carmine

1938   *Perf. 11*

278	A161	10c gray green	1.75	.55
279	A162	15c gray black (C)	1.75	.55
280	A162	20c dark violet	4.25	1.75
281	A162	25c brown lake	4.25	1.75
		Nos. 278-281 (4)	12.00	4.60
		Set, never hinged	16.00	

Nos. 278-281 exist imperf. Value $175.

Stamps of 1931-33,
Surcharged in Black

1939

282	A13	40c on 80c (#244)	12.00	8.00
283	A13	40c on 80c (#258)	12.00	5.00
		Set, never hinged	32.50	

A14   A15

**Revenue Stamps Surcharged in
Black**

1940-41   *Perf. 11½*

284	A14	5c on 35c pale grn	6.00	2.10
285	A14	25c on 60c org brn	6.25	2.50
286	A14	50c on 75c blk brn	8.75	2.75
		Nos. 284-286 (3)	21.00	7.35

Red Surcharge

287	A15	10c on 75c blk brn	8.75	2.75
288	A15	15c on 1.50p lt vio	6.25	2.50
289	A15	25c on 60c org brn	11.00	3.50
		Nos. 287-289 (3)	26.00	8.75

A16   A17

Black or Carmine Surcharge
Perf. 11

290	A16	1p on 17p deep red	52.50	15.50
291	A17	1p on 40p yel grn (C)	12.50	4.00

See No. C1 in Scott Standard catalogue, Vol. 6.

A18 A19

Black Surcharge
Perf. 11, 13x12½

292	A18	5c carmine	5.25	1.40
293	A19	1p yellow	87.50	32.50

A20

Black Surcharge

294	A20	1p on 15c gray grn	9.50	3.25

General Francisco
Franco — A21

1940 *Perf. 11½, 13½*

295	A21	5c olive brown	3.75	.50
296	A21	40c blue	5.50	.50
297	A21	50c green	6.75	.50
a.		50c greenish gray	40.00	9.00
		Nos. 295-297 (3)	16.00	1.50
		Set, never hinged	75.00	

Nos. 295-297 exist imperf. Values $50.

SEMI-POSTAL STAMPS

Red Cross Issue

Types of Semi-Postal Stamps of Spain, 1926, Ovptd. in Black or Blue

1926 Unwmk. *Perf. 12½, 13*

B1	SP3	5c black brown	11.00	7.00
B2	SP4	10c dark green	11.00	7.00
B3	SP1	15c dark vio (Bl)	2.50	1.75
B4	SP4	20c violet brown	2.50	1.75
B5	SP5	25c deep carmine	2.50	1.75
B6	SP1	30c olive green	2.50	1.75
B7	SP3	40c ultra	.55	.25
B8	SP2	50c red brown	.55	.25
B9	SP5	60c myrtle green	.55	.25
B10	SP3	1p vermilion	.55	.25
B11	SP3	4p bister	2.25	1.50
B12	SP5	10p light violet	7.50	5.00
		Nos. B1-B12 (12)	43.95	28.50
		Set, never hinged	60.00	

See Spain No. B6a for No. B4 without overprint. For surcharges see Spain Nos. B70-B71.

SPANISH MOROCCO

'spa-nish mə-'rä-ˌkō

LOCATION — Northwest coast of Africa
GOVT. — Spanish Protectorate
AREA — 17,398 sq. mi. (approx.)
POP. — 1,010,117 (1950)
CAPITAL — Tetuán

100 Centimos = 1 Peseta

Spanish authority in northern Morocco was established after Spain's invasion of the area in 1859. Unoverprinted Spanish stamps were used in Spanish Morocco from 1860 until the appearance of separate issues for the territory in 1903. Spain No. E1 was used as a regular postage stamp in April 1914.

Spanish Offices in Morocco

Spain No. 221A Overprinted in Carmine

1903-09 Unwmk. *Imperf.*

1	A21	¼c blue green	.55	.25
a.		Complete 1c (block 4 ¼c)	2.25	1.50

See Nos. 26, 39, 52, Tetuan 1, 7.

Stamps of Spain Overprinted in Carmine or Blue — a

On Stamps of 1900
Perf. 14

2	A35	2c bister brown	1.75	1.40
3	A35	5c green	2.10	.80
4	A35	10c rose red (Bl)	2.25	.35
5	A35	15c brt violet	3.25	.80
6	A35	20c grnsh black	13.00	3.50
7	A35	25c blue	1.00	.85
8	A35	30c blue green	7.50	3.50
9	A35	40c rose (Bl)	13.00	6.00
10	A35	50c slate grn	7.75	5.75
11	A35	1p lake (Bl)	16.00	8.00
12	A35	4p dull violet	42.50	14.00
13	A35	10p brown org (Bl)	42.50	35.00
		Nos. 1-13 (13)	153.15	80.20
		Set, never hinged	375.00	

Many varieties of overprint exist. Nos. 7-13 exist imperf. Value, $500.
See Tetuan Nos. 2-6, 8-15.

On Stamps of 1909-10

1909-10 *Perf. 13x12½, 14*

14	A46	2c dark brown	.75	.25
15	A46	5c green	3.75	.30
16	A46	10c carmine (Bl)	4.25	.30
17	A46	15c violet	10.50	.65
18	A46	20c olive green	26.00	1.25
19	A46	25c deep blue	95.00	
20	A46	30c blue green	8.50	.65
21	A46	40c rose (Bl)	8.50	.65
22	A46	50c slate blue	14.50	14.00
23	A46	1p lake (Bl)	34.50	29.00
24	A46	4p deep violet	95.00	
25	A46	10p orange (Bl)	95.00	
		Nos. 14-18,20-23 (9)	111.25	47.05
		Set, never hinged	200.00	
		Nos. 14-25 (12)	396.25	

The stamps overprinted "Correo Espanol Marruecos" were used in all Morocco until the year 1914. After the issue of special stamps for the Protectorate the "Correo Espanol" stamps were continued in use solely in the city of Tangier.
Many varieties of overprint exist.
Nos. 19, 24 and 25 were not regularly issued.
See Nos. 27-38, 40-51, 53-67, 75-76, 78.

Spanish Morocco

Spain No. 221A Overprinted in Carmine

1914 *Imperf.*

26	A21	¼c green	.25	.25
a.		Complete 1c (block 4 ¼c)	1.25	.90

Stamps of Spain 1909-10 Overprinted in Carmine or Blue

Perf. 13x12½, 14

27	A46	2c dark brown (C)	.35	.25
28	A46	5c green (C)	.35	.25
29	A46	10c carmine (Bl)	.35	.25
30	A46	15c violet (C)	1.50	.90
31	A46	20c olive grn (C)	3.00	1.90
32	A46	25c deep blue (C)	3.00	1.50
33	A46	30c blue grn (C)	5.75	2.75
34	A46	40c rose (Bl)	13.00	3.75
35	A46	50c slate blue (C)	6.50	2.75
36	A46	1p lake (Bl)	6.50	3.75
37	A46	4p dp violet (C)	33.00	24.00
38	A46	10p orange (Bl)	50.00	32.00
		Nos. 26-38,E1 (14)	129.30	76.90
		Set, never hinged	350.00	

Many varieties of overprint exist, including inverted.
#27-38 exist imperf. Value for set, $525.

Stamps of Spain 1876 and 1909-10 Overprinted in Red or Blue

1915 *Imperf.*

39	A21	¼c blue grn (R)	.25	.25
a.		Complete 1c (block 4 ¼c)	1.50	1.50

Perf. 13x12½, 14

40	A46	2c dk brown (R)	.30	.30
41	A46	5c green (R)	.35	.35
42	A46	10c carmine (Bl)	.35	.35
43	A46	15c violet (R)	.35	.35
44	A46	20c olive grn (R)	1.25	.35
45	A46	25c deep blue (R)	1.25	.55
46	A46	30c blue grn (R)	1.40	.60
47	A46	40c rose (Bl)	3.75	.60
48	A46	50c slate blue (R)	6.25	.55
49	A46	1p lake (Bl)	6.25	.60
50	A46	4p deep violet (R)	42.50	26.00
51	A46	10p orange (Bl)	60.00	29.00
		Nos. 39-51,E2 (14)	127.25	61.45
		Set, never hinged	350.00	

One stamp in the setting on Nos. 39-51 has the first "R" of "PROTECTORADO" inverted. Many other varieties of overprint exist, including double and inverted.
Nos. 40-51 exist imperf. Value, set $650.

Stamps of Spain 1877 and 1909-10 Overprinted in Red or Blue — b

ZONA DE PROTECTORADO ESPAÑOL EN MARRUECOS

1916-18 *Imperf.*

52	A21	¼c blue grn (R)	1.25	.25
a.		Complete 1c (block 4 ¼c)	2.00	1.40

Perf. 13x12½, 14

53	A46	2c dk brown (R)	1.25	.25
54	A46	5c green (R)	5.50	.25
55	A46	10c carmine (Bl)	6.00	.25
56	A46	15c violet (R)	140.00	
57	A46	20c olive grn (R)	140.00	
58	A46	25c dp blue (R)	21.00	3.25
59	A46	30c blue grn (R)	27.50	22.00
60	A46	40c rose (Bl)	28.50	.50
61	A46	50c slate blue (R)	13.50	.25
62	A46	1p lake (Bl)	33.00	2.40
63	A46	4p dp violet (R)	55.00	32.50
64	A46	10p orange (R)	110.00	72.50
		Nos. 52-55,58-64 (11)	302.50	134.40
		Set, never hinged	440.00	
		Nos. 52-64 (13)	582.50	
		Set, never hinged	1,100.	

Nos. 56-57 were not regularly issued.
Varieties of overprint, including double and inverted, exist for several denominations.
The 5c exists in olive brown. Value $525.

Same Overprint on Spain No. 310

1920

65	A46	15c ocher (Bl)	5.50	.30

Exists imperf.; also with overprint inverted.

Nos. 44, 46 Perforated through the middle and each half Surcharged "10 céntimos" in Red

1920

66	A46	10c on half of 20c	5.00	1.90
67	A46	15c on half of 30c	11.00	7.25

No. E1 Divided and Surcharged in Black

68	SD1	10c on half of 20c	12.00	7.75
a.		"10/cts." surcharge added	160.00	50.00
		Nos. 66-68 (3)	28.00	16.90

Values of Nos. 66-68 are for pairs, both halves of the stamp. Varieties were probably made deliberately.

"Justice" — A1

Revenue Stamps Perforated through the Middle and each half Surcharged in Red or Green

1920 *Perf. 11½*

69	A1	5c on 5p lt bl	11.50	2.40
70	A1	5c on 10p green	.50	.50
71	A1	10c on 25p dk grn	.50	.50
a.		Inverted surcharge	13.50	12.00
72	A1	10c on 50p indigo	.55	.40
73	A1	15c on 100p red (G)	.55	.40
74	A1	15c on 500p cl (G)	15.50	8.00
		Nos. 69-74 (6)	29.10	11.70
		Set, never hinged	55.00	

Values of Nos. 69-74 are for pairs, both halves of the stamp.

Stamps of Spain 1917-20 Overprinted Type "a" in Blue or Red
1921-24 *Perf. 13*

75	A46	15c ocher (Bl)	1.50	.25
76	A46	20c violet (R)	2.25	.25

Stamps of Spain 1920-21 Overprinted Type "b" in Red
Imperf.

77	A47	1c blue green	1.50	.25

Engr.
Perf. 13

78	A46	20c violet	11.00	.25

See No. 92.

Stamps of Spain, 1922 Overprinted Type "a" in Red or Blue
1923-28 *Perf. 13½x12½*

79	A49	2c olive green	4.25	.25
80	A49	5c red violet (Bl)	4.25	.25
81	A49	10c yellow green (R)	5.00	.25
82	A49	20c violet (R)	7.00	1.10
		Nos. 79-82 (4)	20.50	1.85

Same Overprinted Type "b"
1923-25

83	A49	2c olive green (R)	.75	.25
84	A49	5c red violet (Bl)	.75	.25
85	A49	10c yellow grn (R)	3.00	.25
86	A49	15c blue (R)	3.00	.25
87	A49	20c violet (R)	6.50	.25
88	A49	25c carmine (Bl)	13.00	1.50
89	A49	40c deep blue (R)	13.50	5.00
90	A49	50c orange (Bl)	35.00	8.50
91	A49a	1p blue black (R)	55.00	5.00
		Nos. 83-91,E3 (10)	142.50	31.00
		Set, never hinged	350.00	

Spain No. 314 Overprinted Type "a" in Red

1927 *Imperf.*

92	A47	1c blue green	.25	.25

Mosque of Alcazarquivir
A2

Moorish Gateway at Larache
A3

Well at
Alhucemas
A4

View of
Xauen — A5

View of
Tetuan — A6

1928-32   Engr.   Perf. 14, 14½

93	A2	1c red ("Cs")	.25	.25
94	A2	1c car rose ("Ct")		
		('32)	.50	.40
95	A2	2c dark violet	.30	.25
96	A2	5c deep blue	.35	.25
97	A2	10c dark green	.35	.25
98	A2	15c orange brown	.75	.35
99	A3	20c olive green	.75	.35
100	A3	25c copper red	.80	.35
102	A3	30c black brown	2.60	.40
103	A3	40c dull blue	3.25	.40
104	A3	50c brown violet	6.75	.40
105	A4	1p yellow green	8.25	.45
106	A5	2.50p red violet	32.50	10.00
107	A6	4p ultra	24.00	7.50
		Nos. 93-107,E4 (15)	86.40	23.20
		Set, never hinged	225.00	

Seville-Barcelona Issue of Spain, 1929, Ovptd. in Red or Blue

1929   Perf. 11, 14

108	A50	1c greenish blue	.40	.30
109	A51	2c pale yel grn	.40	.30
110	A52	5c rose lake (Bl)	.40	.30
111	A51	10c green	.40	.30
112	A50	15c Prussian blue	.40	.30
113	A51	20c purple	.40	.30
114	A50	25c bright rose (Bl)	.40	.30
115	A52	30c black brown (bl)	1.00	.75
116	A53	40c dark blue	1.00	.75
117	A51	50c deep orange		
		(Bl)	1.00	.75
118	A52	1p blue black	8.00	5.75
119	A53	4p deep rose (Bl)	18.00	12.50
120	A53	10p brown (Bl)	40.00	29.00
		Nos. 108-120 (13)	71.80	51.60
		Set, never hinged	115.00	

See Nos. L1-L11.

Stamps of Spain, 1922-31, Overprinted Type "a" in Black, Blue or Red

1929-34   Perf. 11½, 13x12½

121	A49	5c claret (Bk)	3.50	.25
122	A61	10c green (R)	3.00	.45
123	A61	15c slate grn (R)	110.00	1.10
124	A61	20c violet (R)	3.00	.50
125	A61	30c brown lake (Bl)	3.25	1.10
126	A61	40c dark blue (R)	12.00	5.50
127	A49	50c orange (Bl)	30.00	5.25
128	A49a	10p brown (Bl)	3.00	5.75
		Nos. 121-128 (8)	167.75	19.90
		Set, never hinged	300.00	

Stamps of Spain, 1922-26, overprinted diagonally as above, and with no control number, or with "A000,000" on back, were not issued but were presented to the delegates at the 1929 UPU Congress in London. Value of complete set of 16, $3,250.

Stamps of Spain 1931-
32, Overprinted in Black

1933-34   Imperf.

130	A108	1c blue green	.25	.25
		Perf. 11½		
131	A108	2c buff	.25	.25
132	A95	5c brnsh black	.25	.25
133	A97	15c slate green	.25	.25
135	A95	20c dark violet	.30	.25
136	A104	25c lake	.30	.25
137	A99	30c carmine rose	60.00	6.00
138	A100	40c dark blue	.65	.35
139	A97	50c orange	1.25	.30
140	A100	60c apple green	1.25	.30
141	A105	1p blue black	1.25	.50
142	A106	4p magenta	2.75	2.50
143	A107	10p deep brown	3.50	5.50
		Nos. 130-143,E7 (15)	74.00	17.35
		Set, never hinged	130.00	

Street Scene in
Tangier — A7

View of
Xauen
A8

Gate in
Town Wall,
Arzila — A9

Street Scene in
Tangier
A10

Mosque of
Alcazarquivir
A11

Caliph and
His Guard
A12

View of
Tangier
A13

Green Control Numbers Printed on Gum

1933-35   Photo.   Perf. 14, 13½

144	A7	1c brt rose	.35	.25
145	A8	2c green ('35)	.35	.25
146	A9	5c magenta ('35)	.35	.25
147	A10	10c dark green	.45	.25
148	A11	15c yellow ('35)	3.00	.30
149	A7	20c slate green	1.25	.30
150	A12	25c crimson ('35)	29.00	.30
151	A10	30c red brown	8.00	.35
152	A13	40c deep blue	12.50	.35
153	A13	50c red orange	42.50	5.00
154	A8	1p slate blk ('35)	18.00	.35
155	A9	2.50p brown ('35)	32.50	5.00
156	A11	4p yel grn ('35)	42.50	5.00
157	A13	5p black ('35)	42.50	5.25
		Nos. 144-157,E5 (15)	234.40	23.45
		Set, never hinged	400.00	

For surcharge see No. CB1.

Mosque — A14

Landscape
A15

Green Control Numbers Printed on Gum

1935

158	A14	25c violet	1.25	.25
159	A14	30c crimson	16.50	.25
160	A14	40c orange	8.50	.25
161	A14	50c bright blue	8.50	.30
162	A14	60c dk blue green	8.50	.35
163	A15	2p brown lake	42.50	6.00
		Nos. 158-163 (6)	85.75	7.40
		Set, never hinged	160.00	

See No. 174.

Regular Issue and Special Delivery Stamp of 1928, Surcharged in Blue, Green or Red with New Values and Ornaments

1936

164	A6	1c on 4p ultra (Bl)	.35	.25
165	A5	2c on 2.50p red vio (G)	.35	.25
166	A3	5c on 25c cop red (R)	.35	.25
167	A4	10c on 1p yel grn (G)	10.00	4.00
168	SD2	15c on 20c blk (Bl)	7.75	2.10
		Nos. 164-168 (5)	18.80	6.85
		Set, never hinged	24.50	

Caliph and
Viziers — A16

View of
Bokoia
A17

View of Alcazarquivir — A18

Sidi Saida
Mosque
A19

Caliph and
Procession
A20

Without Control Numbers

1937   Photo.   Perf. 13½

169	A16	1c green	.30	.25
170	A17	2c red violet	.30	.25
171	A18	5c orange	.30	.25
172	A16	15c violet	.30	.25

173	A19	30c red	.85	.25
a.		Souvenir sheet of 4, #170-173	22.00	12.00
174	A14	1p ultra	7.50	.30
a.		Souv. sheet of 4, #169-171, 174	33.00	13.00
		Nos. 169-175 (7)	69.55	19.05
		Set, never hinged	150.00	

Nos. 173a, 174a for 1st year of the Spanish Civil War.

Nos. 173a, 174a were privately overprinted "TANGER" in black on each stamp in the sheet for "use" in the International City of Tangier, and "GUINEA" for "use" in Spanish Guinea.

Harkeno
Rifleman — A21

Troops
Marching
A22

Designs: 2c, Legionnaires. 5c, Cavalryman leading his mount. 10c, Moroccan phalanx. 15c, Legion flag-bearer. 20c, Colonial soldier. 25c, Ifni sharpshooters. 30c, Mounted trumpeters. 40c, Cape Juby Dromedary Corps. 50c, Regular infantry. 60c, Caliphate guards. 1p, Orderly on guard. 2p, Sentry. 2.50p, Regular cavalry. 4p, Orderly.

1937   Perf. 13½

176	A21	1c dull blue	.35	.25
177	A21	2c orange brn	.35	.25
178	A21	5c cerise	.35	.25
179	A21	10c emerald	.35	.25
180	A21	15c brt blue	.35	.25
181	A21	20c red brown	.35	.25
182	A21	25c magenta	.35	.30
183	A21	30c red orange	.35	.30
184	A21	40c violet	.35	.35
185	A21	50c ultra	.35	.35
186	A21	60c yellow grn	.35	.35
187	A21	1p blue violet	.35	.35
188	A21	2p Prus blue	11.50	5.00
189	A21	2.50p gray black	11.50	5.00
190	A21	4p dark brown	11.50	5.00
191	A22	10p black	11.50	5.00
		Nos. 176-191,E6 (17)	50.45	23.75
		Set, never hinged	120.00	

First Year of Spanish Civil War.
Exists imperf. Value, set $250.
For overprints see Nos. 214-229.

Spanish
Quarter — A25

Designs: 10c, Moroccan quarter. 15c, Street scene, Larache. 20c, Tetuan.

1939   Unwmk.   Photo.   Perf. 13½

194	A25	5c orange	.30	.25
195	A25	10c brt blue grn	.30	.25
196	A25	15c golden brown	.50	.30
197	A25	20c brt ultra	.50	.30
		Nos. 194-197 (4)	1.60	1.10

Postman — A26

Mail Box — A27

Landscape
A28

Street Scene,
Alcazarquivir
A29

Cavalry — A40

Day of
Court — A41

1940 Unwmk. Photo. Perf. 11½x11

198	A26	1c dark brown	.35	.30
199	A27	2c olive grn	.35	.30
200	A28	5c dk blue	.35	.30
201	A29	10c dk red lilac	.35	.30
202	A30	15c dk green	.45	.35
203	A31	20c purple	.35	.35
204	A32	25c black brown	.35	.35
205	A33	30c brt green	.35	.35
206	A34	40c slate green	2.75	.35
207	A35	45c orange ver	1.10	.35
208	A36	50c brown orange	1.10	.35
209	A37	70c sapphire	1.10	.35
210	A38	1p indigo & brn	3.25	.35
211	A39	2.50p choc & dk grn	18.00	4.75
212	A40	5p dk cerise & sep	3.50	.45
213	A41	10p dk ol grn & brn org	32.50	8.00

Nos. 198-213,E8 (17) 67.05 17.90
Set, never hinged 120.00

"ZONA" printed in black on back.
Exists imperf. Value, set $325.

Mosque de Baja and
Plane — AP1

Stamps of 1937
Overprinted in
Various Colors

1940 Unwmk. Perf. 13½

214	A21	1c dull blue (Bk)	.95	.70
215	A21	2c org brn (Bk)	.95	.70
216	A21	5c cerise (Bk)	.95	.70
217	A21	10c emerald (Bk)	.95	.70
218	A21	15c brt blue (Bk)	.95	.70
219	A21	20c red brn (Bk)	.95	.70
220	A21	25c mag (Bk)	.95	.70
221	A21	30c red org (V)	.95	.70
222	A21	40c orange (V)	1.60	1.40
223	A21	50c ultra (Bk)	1.60	1.40
224	A21	60c yel grn (Bk)	1.60	1.40
225	A21	1p blue vio (V)	1.60	1.40
226	A21	2p Prus bl (Bl)	50.00	50.00
227	A21	2.50p gray blk (V)	50.00	50.00
228	A21	4p dk brn (Bl)	50.00	50.00
229	A22	10p black (R)	50.00	50.00

Nos. 214-229,E10 (17) 226.00 220.70
Set, never hinged 500.00

4th anniversary of Spanish Civil War.

SEMI-POSTAL STAMPS

Types of
Semi-Postal
Stamps of
Spain, 1926,
Ovptd. in
Black or Blue

1926 Unwmk. Perf. 12½, 13

B1	SP1	1c orange	8.50	5.50
B2	SP2	2c rose	12.00	10.00
B3	SP3	5c black brn	4.50	3.50
B4	SP4	10c dark grn	4.50	3.50
B5	SP1	15c dk violet (Bl)	.80	.65
B6	SP2	20c violet brn	.80	.65
B7	SP5	25c deep carmine	.80	.65
B8	SP1	30c olive grn	.80	.65
B9	SP3	40c ultra	.25	.25
B10	SP2	50c red brown	.25	.25
B11	SP4	1p vermilion	.25	.25

View of
Xauen — A30

Sentry
Guarding
Palace at
Sat — A31

The
Chieftain — A32

Market Place,
Larache — A33

Tetuán — A34

Ancient
Gateway at
Xauen — A35

Scene in
Alcazarquivir
A36

Post Office
A37

Spanish War
Veterans — A38

Victory Flag
Bearers — A39

B12	SP3	4p bister	.80	.65
B13	SP5	10p light violet	3.50	2.75

Nos. B1-B13,EB1 (14) 40.50 31.65
Set, never hinged 70.00

See Spain No. B6a for No. B6 without overprint. For surcharges see Spain Nos. B64-B65.

AIR POST STAMPS

View of
Tetuán and
Plane
AP2

10c, Stork of Alcazar. 25c, Shore scene, plane. 40c, Desert tribesmen watching plane. 75c, View of shoreline at Larache. 1p, Arab mailman, plane above. 1.50p, Arab farmers, stork. 2p, Plane at twilight. 3p, Shadow of plane over city.

1938 Unwmk. Photo. Perf. 13½

C1	AP1	5c red brown	.25	.25
C2	AP1	10c emerald	.25	.25
C3	AP1	25c crimson	.25	.25
C4	AP1	40c dull blue	2.00	.50
C5	AP2	50c cerise	.25	.25
C6	AP2	75c ultra	.25	.25
C7	AP1	1p dark brown	.25	.25
C8	AP1	1.50p purple	.65	.35
C9	AP1	2p brown lake	.40	.25
C10	AP1	3p gray black	1.75	.25

Nos. C1-C10 (10) 6.30 2.85
Set, Never Hinged 11.00

Nos. C1-C10 exist imperf. Value of set, $100.
For surcharge see No. C32 in Scott Standard catalogue, Vol. 6.

AIR POST SEMI-POSTAL STAMPS

No. 150
Surcharged
in Black

1936 Unwmk. Perf. 14

CB1	A12	25c + 2p on 25c	14.00	5.75
		Never hinged	50.00	
a.		Bars at right omitted	57.50	42.50
b.		Blue surcharge	45.00	15.00

25c was for postage, 2p for air post.

Nos. C1-C10 surcharged "Lucha Antituberculosa," a Lorraine cross and surtax are stated to be bogus.

SPECIAL DELIVERY STAMPS

**Special Delivery Stamp of Spain
Overprinted in Blue**

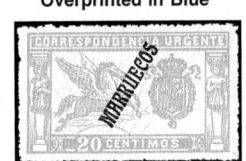

1914 Unwmk. Perf. 14
E1 SD1 20c red 5.75 2.60

**Special Delivery Stamp of Spain
Overprinted in Blue**

1915
E2 SD1 20c red 3.00 1.60
For bisected surcharge see No. 68.

**Special Delivery Stamp of Spain
Overprinted in Blue**

1923
E3 SD1 20c red 12.00 9.75

Mounted
Courier
SD2

1928 Engr. Perf. 14, 14½
E4 SD2 20c black 5.00 1.60
For surcharge see No. 168.

Moorish
Postman — SD3

1935 Photo. Perf. 14
Green Control Number on Back
E5 SD3 20c vermilion 1.15 .25
See No. E9.

Mounted
Courier — SD4

1937 Perf. 13½
E6 SD4 20c bright carmine .25 .25
1st Year of the Spanish Civil War.
For surcharge see No. E10.

Spain No. E14 Overprinted in Black

1938 Perf. 10
E7 SD7 20c vermilion 1.50 .25

Arab
Postman — SD5

1940   **Photo.**   **Perf. 11½x11**
E8   SD5 25c scarlet   .85   .35
"ZONA" printed on back in black.

Type of 1935
1940   **Litho.**   **Perf. 10**
E9   SD3 20c black brown   2.60
No. E9 was prepared but not issued.
Exists imperf. Value, $10.

No. E6 Surcharged
with New Value, Bars
and

1940   **Perf. 13½**
E10   SD4 25c on 20c brt car   12.00   9.50
4th anniversary of Spanish Civil War.

SEMI-POSTAL SPECIAL DELIVERY STAMP

**Type of Semi-Postal Special
Delivery Stamp of Spain, 1926,
Overprinted like #B1-B13**
1926   **Unwmk.**   **Perf. 12½, 13**
EB1   SPSD1 20c ultra & black   2.75 2.40

POSTAL TAX STAMPS

General Francisco
Franco — PT1

1937-39   Unwmk.   Photo.   Perf. 12½
RA1   PT1 10c sepia   .50   .25
   a.   Sheet of 4, imperf.   4.50   1.75
RA2   PT1 10c copper brn ('38)   .50   .25
   a.   Sheet of 4, imperf.   4.50   1.75
RA3   PT1 10c blue ('39)   .50   .25
   a.   Sheet of 4, imperf.   4.50   1.75
     Nos. RA1-RA3 (3)   1.50   .75
   Set, never hinged   3.50
   Set, RA1a-RA3a   13.50

The tax was used for the disabled soldiers in
North Africa.

TANGIER

For the International City of Tangier
Seville-Barcelona Issue of Spain,
1929, Ovptd. in Blue or Red

1929   **Perf. 11**
L1   A52   5c rose lake   .30   .30
L2   A53   10c green (R)   .30   .30
L3   A50   15c Prus blue (R)   .30   .30
L4   A51   20c purple (R)   .30   .30
L5   A50   25c brt rose   .30   .30
L6   A52   30c black brown   .30   .30
L7   A53   40c dk blue (R)   .75   .75
L8   A51   50c deep org   .75   .75
L9   A52   1p blue blk (R)   7.75   7.75
L10   A53   4p deep rose   21.00 21.00
L11   A53   10p brown   30.00 30.00
     Nos. L1-L11 (11)   62.05 62.05
   Set, never hinged   105.00

Overprints of 1937-39
The following overprints on stamps
of Spain exist in black or in red:
"TANGER" vertically on Nos. 517-
518, 522-523, 528, 532, 534, 539-
543, 549.
"Correo Espanol Tanger" horizontally or vertically in three lines on
Nos. 540, 592-597 (gray paper), 598-
601.
"Tanger" horizontally on Nos. 539-
541, 592-601.
"Correo Tanger" horizontally in two
lines on five consular stamps.

TANGIER SEMI-POSTAL STAMPS

Types of
Semi-Postal
Stamps of
Spain, 1926,
Overprinted

1926   **Perf. 12½, 13**
LB1   SP1   1c orange   7.50   8.00
LB2   SP2   2c rose   7.50   8.00
LB3   SP3   5c black brn   3.75   3.75
LB4   SP4   10c dk green   3.75   3.75
LB5   SP1   15c dk violet   1.25   1.60
LB6   SP4   20c violet brn   1.25   1.60
LB7   SP5   25c dp carmine   1.25   1.60
LB8   SP1   30c olive grn   1.25   1.60
LB9   SP3   40c ultra   .35   .35
LB10   SP2   50c red brn   .35   .35
LB11   SP4   1p vermilion   .75   .75
LB12   SP3   4p bister   .75   .75
LB13   SP5   10p lt violet   3.25   3.25
    Nos. LB1-LB13,LEB1 (14)   35.95 38.35
   Set, never hinged   65.00

For overprints & surcharges see Spain Nos.
B66-B67.

TANGIER SEMI-POSTAL SPECIAL DELIVERY STAMP

**Types of Semi-Postal Special
Delivery Stamp of Spain, 1926,
Overprinted like #LB1-LB13**
1926   **Unwmk.**   **Perf. 12½, 13**
LEB1   SPSD1 20c ultra & black   3.00 3.00
     Never hinged   5.00

TETUAN

Stamps of Spanish
Offices in Morocco,
1903-09, Handstamped
in Black, Blue or Violet

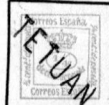

1908   **Unwmk.**   **Imperf.**
1   A21   ¼c blue green   13.00 10.00
           Perf. 14
2   A35   2c bister brown   175.00   60.00
3   A35   5c green   165.00   35.00
4   A35   10c rose red   165.00   35.00
5   A35   20c grnsh black   325.00 125.00
6   A35   25c blue   125.00   35.00
     Nos. 1-6 (6)   968.00 300.00

**Same Handstamp On Stamps of
Spain, 1876 and 1900-05, in Black,
Blue or Violet**
1908   **Imperf.**
7   A21   ¼c deep green   7.50   3.25

            Perf. 14
8   A35   2c bister brn   55.00   13.00
9   A35   5c dark green   70.00   22.50
10   A35   10c rose red   77.50   22.50
11   A35   15c purple   77.50   25.00
12   A35   20c grnsh black   175.00   60.00
13   A35   25c blue   95.00   35.00
14   A35   30c blue green   200.00   60.00
15   A35   40c olive bister   250.00 110.00
     Nos. 7-15 (9)   1,007. 401.25
Counterfeits of this overprint are plentiful.

SPANISH SAHARA

ˈspa-nish sə-ˈhar-ə

(Spanish Western Sahara)

LOCATION — Northwest Africa, bor-
dering on the Atlantic Ocean.
GOVT. — Spanish possession.
AREA — 102,703 sq. mi.
POP. — 32,000 (1940)
CAPITAL — Aaiún.

Spanish Sahara was a subdivision of
Spanish West Africa. It included the colony of Rio de Oro and the territory of
Saguiet el Hamra. Spanish Sahara was
formerly known as Spanish Western
Sahara, which superseded the older
title of Rio de Oro.

100 Centimos = 1 Peseta

Tuareg and
Camel — A1

1924   **Unwmk.**   **Typo.**   **Perf. 13**
     Control Number on Back
1   A1   5c blue green   3.00   .90
2   A1   10c gray green   3.00   .90
3   A1   15c turq blue   3.00   .90
4   A1   20c dark violet   3.00   1.25
5   A1   25c red   3.00   1.25
6   A1   30c red brown   3.00   1.25
7   A1   40c dark blue   3.00   1.25
8   A1   50c orange   3.00   1.25
9   A1   60c violet   3.00   1.25
10   A1   1p rose   16.00   6.50
11   A1   4p chocolate   70.00   33.00
12   A1   10p claret   170.00 105.00
     Nos. 1-12 (12)   283.00 154.70
   Set, never hinged   450.00

Nos. 1-12 were for use in La Aguera & Rio
de Oro.
   An unissued set of 10, similar to Nos. 3-12,
exists perf. 10 or imperf, and no control num-
ber except on 50c. The set also exists perf. 14.
Value, $200.
   Nos. 1-12 also exist perf 14. Value, unused
$300.
   For overprints see Nos. 24-35.

Seville-Barcelona
Issue of Spain,
1929 Overprinted
in Blue or Red

1929   **Perf. 11**
13   A52   5c rose lake   .30   .30
14   A53   10c green (R)   .30   .30
15   A50   15c Prus blue (R)   .30   .30
16   A51   20c purple (R)   .40   .30
17   A50   25c bright rose   .40   .30
18   A52   30c black brown   .40   .30
19   A53   40c dark blue (R)   .90   .45
20   A51   50c deep orange   .90   .45
21   A52   1p blue black (R)   3.50   1.90
22   A53   4p deep rose   27.50 17.50
23   A53   10p brown   52.50 35.00
     Nos. 13-23 (11)   87.40 57.10
   Set, never hinged   125.00

Stamps of 1924
Overprinted in Red or
Blue

1931   **Perf. 13**
24   A1   5c blue grn (R)   .95   .65
25   A1   10c gray grn (R)   .95   .65
26   A1   15c turq blue (R)   .95   .65
27   A1   20c dark violet (R)   .95   .65
28   A1   25c red   .95   .65
29   A1   30c red brown   .95   .65
30   A1   40c dark blue (R)   4.50   .90
31   A1   50c orange   4.50   2.25
32   A1   60c violet   4.50   2.25
33   A1   1p rose   4.50   2.25
34   A1   4p chocolate   45.00 22.00
35   A1   10p claret   92.50 50.00
     Nos. 24-35 (12)   161.20 83.55
   Set, never hinged   240.00

The stamps of the 1931 issue exist with the
overprint reading upward, downward, or horizontally. Some values also exist with double
overprint, double overprint, one inverted and
diagonal overprint.

SEMI-POSTAL STAMPS

Red Cross Issue

Types of Semi-
Postal Stamps of
Spain, 1926,
Overprinted

1926   **Unwmk.**   **Perf. 12½, 13**
B1   SP3   5c black brown   8.75   8.75
B2   SP4   10c dark green   8.75   8.75
B3   SP1   15c dark violet   2.75   2.75
B4   SP4   20c violet brown   2.75   2.75
B5   SP5   25c deep carmine   2.75   2.75
B6   SP1   30c olive green   2.75   2.75
B7   SP3   40c ultra   .25   .25
B8   SP2   50c red brown   .25   .25
B9   SP5   60c myrtle green   .25   .25
B10   SP4   1p vermilion   .25   .25
B11   SP3   4p bister   2.75   2.10
B12   SP5   10p light violet   7.25   6.00
     Nos. B1-B12 (12)   39.50 37.60
   Set, never hinged   57.50

See Spain No. B6a for No. B4 without overprint. For surcharges see Spain Nos. B72-
B73.

STELLALAND

ˈste-lə-ˌland

LOCATION — South Africa
GOVT. — Republic
AREA — 5,000 sq. mi. (approx.)
CAPITAL — Vryburg

This short-lived republic was set up by the Boers in an effort to annex territory ruled by the Bechuana chiefs. Great Britain refused to recognize it and in 1885 sent an expeditionary force which ended the political career of the country.

Stellaland was annexed by Great Britain in 1885 and became a part of British Bechuanaland.

12 Pence = 1 Shilling

Coat of
Arms — A1

1884, Feb. Unwmk. Litho. Perf. 12

1	A1	1p red	225.00	375.00
a.		Horiz. pair, imperf. vert.	4,250.	
b.		Vert. pair, imperf. horiz.	4,600.	
2	A1	3p orange	30.00	375.00
a.		Horiz. pair, imperf. vert.	850.00	
b.		Vert. pair, imperf. horiz.	1,700.	
3	A1	4p gray	27.00	400.00
a.		Horiz. pair, imperf. vert.	750.00	
b.		Vert. pair, imperf. horiz.	2,100.	
4	A1	6p lilac	30.00	400.00
a.		Horiz. pair, imperf. vert.	1,500.	
b.		Vert. pair, imperf. horiz.	1,750.	
5	A1	1sh green	70.00	750.00
		Nos. 1-5 (5)	382.00	2,300.

Imperf. varieties are believed to be proofs.

No. 3
Handstamped in
Blackish Violet

1885

6	A1	2p on 4p gray	4,000.

The status of No. 6 has long been questioned.

STRAITS SETTLEMENTS

'sträts 'se-t³l-mənts

LOCATION — Malay Peninsula in southeastern Asia
GOVT. — British Colony
AREA — 1,356 sq. mi.
POP. — 1,435,895 (estimated)
CAPITAL — Singapore

The colony comprised the settlements of Malacca, Singapore and Penang, which were incorporated under one government in 1826 and the administration transferred from India to the Secretary of State for the Colonies in 1867.

Stamps of India were used in Malacca, Penang and Singapore, 1854-67.

The colony was dissolved in 1946 when Singapore became a separate crown colony. Malacca and Penang were incorporated into the Malayan Union, which became the Federation of Malaya in 1948.

See Malaya for stamps of the Federated Malay States, Johore, Kedah, Kelantan, Negri Sembilan, Pahang, Penang, Perak, Selangor, Sungei Ujong and Trengganu.

100 Cents = 1 Dollar

STAMPS OF INDIA USED IN STRAITS SETTLEMENTS

SINGAPORE

Stamps of India canceled with the Octagonal postmark "B/172"

	1854	Wmk. 37	Imperf.
A1	½a blue (#2)		290.
A2	1a red (#4)		200.
A4	1a red (#7)		2,200.
A5	2a green (#5)		100.
a.	Half used as 1a on cover		250,000.
A6	4a red & blue (#6)		1,275.

	1855-64	Unwmk. Typo.	Perf. 14
	Blue Glazed Paper		
A9	4a black (#9)		52.50
a.	Half used as 2a on cover (#9b, '59)		20,000.
A10	8a rose (#10)		52.50
a.	Half used as 4a on cover (#10b, '59)		120,000.

	1855-64		White Paper
A11	½a blue (#11)		70.00
A12	1a brown (#12)		35.00
a.	Half used as ½a on cover (#12c, '59)		130,000.
A13	2a dull rose (#13)		65.00
A14	2a buff (#15)		52.50
a.	2a orange (#15a)		65.00
A16	4a black (#16)		35.00
a.	Diagonal half used as 2a on cover (#16b, '59)		60,000.
A17	4a green ('64) (#17)		180.00
A18	8a rose (#18)		47.50
a.	Half used as 4a on cover (#18a, '59)		120,000.

	1860-64	Unwmk.	Perf. 14
A19	8p lilac (#19)		95.00
a.	Diagonal half used as 4p on cover (#19a)		130,000.
A20	8p lilac, bluish (#)		850.00

	1865-67	Wmk. 38 (Elephant)	
A22	½a blue (#20)		80.00
A23	8p lilac (#21)		190.00
A24	1a brown (#22)		65.00
A25	2a orange (#23)		70.00
a.	2a yellow (#23a)		70.00
A26	4a green (#24)		150.00
A27	8a rose (#25)		325.00

	1866-67		
A28	4a green, type I (#26)		200.00
A29	6a8p slate (#27)		500.00

	1866		Official Stamps
A30	½a blue (#O5)		800.00
A31	2a yellow (#O8)		950.00

Stamps of India canceled with the Singapore Duplex Town Datestamp and Numeral "172" in adjacent diamond-shaped canceler

	1855-64		White Paper
A32	1a brown (#12)		400.00
A33	2a orange (#15a)		525.00
A34	4a black (#16)		525.00
A35	8a rose (#18)		525.00

	1860-64	Unwmk.	Perf. 14
A36	8p lilac (#19)		600.00

	1865-67		
A37	2a orange (#23)		500.00
	2a yellow (#23a)		500.00
A38	4a green (#24)		650.00

PENANG

Stamps of India canceled with the Octagonal postmark "B/147"

	1854	Wmk. 37	Imperf.
A50	½a blue (#2)		750.00
A51	1a red (#4)		275.00
A52	2a green (#5)		400.00
A53	4a red & blue (#6)		1,750.

	1855-64	Unwmk.	Perf. 14
	Blue Glazed Paper		
A56	4a black (#9)		140.00
A57	8a rose (#10)		125.00
a.	Half used as 4a on cover (#10b)		120,000.

	1855-64		White Paper
A58	½a blue (#11)		140.00
A59	1a brown (#12)		80.00
A60	2a dull rose (#13)		120.00
A61	2a buff (#15)		105.00
a.	2a orange (#15a)		110.00
A63	4a black (#16)		80.00
A64	8a rose (#18)		100.00

	1860-64	Unwmk.	Perf. 14
A65	8p lilac (#19)		275.00

Stamps of India canceled with the Penang Duplex Town Datestamp and Numeral "147" in adjacent diamond-shaped canceler

	1854	Wmk. 37	Imperf.
A66	1a red (#4)		4,250.

	1855-64		White Paper
A67	½a blue (#2)		350.00
A68	1a brown (#12)		90.00
A69	2a orange (#15a)		100.00
A70	4a black (#16)		90.00
A71	4a green (#17)		300.00
A72	8a rose (#18)		95.00

	1860-64	Unwmk.	Perf. 14
A73	8p lilac (#19)		150.00

	1865-67		Wmk. 38
A75	8p lilac (#21)		—
A76	1a brown (#22)		90.00
A77	2a yellow (#23a)		100.00
A78	4a green (#24)		325.00
A79	8a rose (#25)		—

	1866-67		
A80	4a green (#26)		350.00

MALACCA

Stamps of India canceled with the Octagonal postmark "B/109"

	1854	Wmk. 37	Imperf.
A90	½a blue (#2)		2,200.
A91	1a red (#4)		1,900.
A93	2a green (#5)		2,400.
A94	4a red & blue, cut to shape (#6)		2,400.

	1855-64	Unwmk.	Perf. 14
	Blue Glazed Paper		
A97	8a rose (#10)		850.00

	1855-64		White Paper
A98	½a blue (#11)		525.00
A99	1a brown (#12)		425.00
A100	2a dull rose (#13)		600.00
A101	2a buff (#15)		450.00
a.	2a orange (#15a)		475.00
A103	4a green (#17)		800.00
A104	8a rose (#18)		525.00

	1860-64	Unwmk.	Perf. 14
A105	8p lilac (#19)		750.00
A106	8p lilac, bluish (#19C)		1,400.

	1865-67		Wmk. 38
A107	4a green (#24)		850.00

Issued under British Administration

Stamps of India Surcharged in Red, Blue, Black Violet or Green

Nos. 1-7

Nos. 8-9

	1867, Sept. 1	Wmk. 38	Perf. 14	
1	A7	1½c on ½a bl (R)	110.00	200.00
	Postal cancel, no company chop			235.00
2	A7	2c on 1a brn (R)	180.00	85.00
	Postal cancel, no company chop			97.50
3	A7	3c on 1a brn (Bl)	175.00	90.00
	Postal cancel, no company chop			100.00
4	A7	4c on 1a brn (Bk)	300.00	275.00
	Postal cancel, no company chop			300.00
5	A7	6c on 2a yel (V)	750.00	250.00
	Postal cancel, no company chop			290.00
6	A7	8c on 2a yel (G)	275.00	42.50
	Postal cancel, no company chop			52.50
7	A9	12c on 4a grn (R)	1,175.	325.00
a.	Double surcharge		4,500.	
	Postal cancel, no company chop			365.00
8	A7	24c on 8a rose (Bl)	600.00	90.00
	Postal cancel, no company chop			100.00
9	A7	32c on 2a yel (Bk)	425.00	95.00
	Postal cancel, no company chop			110.00

Manuscript Surcharge, Pen Bar Across "THREE HALF" of No. 1

9A	A7	2(c) on 1½c on ½a	20,000.	6,500.

Values for Nos. 1-9A are for stamps with perforations touching the frame line on one or two sides. Used values for Nos. 1-9 are for stamps with company chops in addition to postal cancellations.

Covers: Covers of this issue are very rare and seldom offered. Values start at about $1,500.

A2

A3

A4

A5

	1867-72	Typo.	Wmk. 1	Perf. 14	
10	A2	2c bister brown		47.50	7.50
a.	2c yellow brown		55.00	7.25
b.	2c deep brown		140.00	20.00
11	A2	4c rose		80.00	12.50
a.	4c deep rose		110.00	17.00
12	A2	6c violet		125.00	22.50
a.	6c bright lilac		160.00	24.00
13	A3	8c yellow		210.00	18.00
a.	8c orange		240.00	20.00
14	A3	12c blue		180.00	10.00
a.	12c ultra		210.00	13.50
15	A3	24c green		160.00	8.00
a.	24c yellow green		410.00	32.50
16	A3	30c claret ('72)		425.00	17.50
17	A5	32c pale red		600.00	70.00
18	A5	96c olive gray		425.00	55.00
	Nos. 10-18 (9)			2,252.	221.00

Corner ornaments of types A2, A3 and A5 differ for each value.

See Nos. 19, 40-44, 48-50, 52-57. For surcharges see Nos. 20-35, 58-59, 61-66, 73-82, 91. For overprints see Malaya, Johore No. 1, Perak Nos. 1, O1-O2, Selangor Nos. 1-2, Sungei Ujong Nos. 2-3.

Stamps of Straits Settlements, 1867-82, overprinted "B" are listed under Bangkok.

	1871		Perf. 12½	
19	A5	96c olive gray	2,750.	275.00

Stamps of 1867-72 Surcharged

	1879, May		Perf. 14	
20	A3	5c on 8c yellow	125.00	190.00
a.	No period after "CENTS"	1,100.	1,275.
21	A5	7c on 32c pale red	160.00	200.00
a.	No period after "CENTS"	1,750.	2,200.

No. 16 Surcharged

e   f

     g   k

     m

1010
j   h

	1880				
22	A4(e)	10c on 30c		325.00	55.00
23	A4(f)	10c on 30c		850.00	125.00
24	A4(g)	10c on 30c		325.00	55.00
25	A4(h)	10c on 30c		—	22,500.
25A	A4(j)	10c on 30c		6,500.	1,000.
25B	A4(k)	10c on 30c		6,500.	1,000.
25C	A4(m)	10c on 30c		6,500.	1,000.

Surcharges e & f and g, h, j & m are virtually identical. These must have an expert certificate identifying them. Values can be suspect because of misidentifications.

Unused examples are valued without gum.

With Additional Surcharge

26	A4(e)	10c on 30c		600.	100.
27	A4(f)	10c on 30c		9,750.	1,000.
27A	A4(g)	10c on 30c		6,000.	600.
28	A4(h)	10c on 30c		16,000.	2,000.
28A	A4(j)	10c on 30c		16,000.	2,000.
28B	A4(k)	10c on 30c		16,000.	2,000.
28C	A4(m)	10c on 30c		16,000.	2,000.

Unused examples are valued without gum.

No. 13 Surcharged

n   o   p

	1880				
29	A3(n)	5c on 8c yellow		170.00	200.00
30	A3(o)	5c on 8c yellow		650.00	800.00
31	A3(p)	5c on 8c yellow		180.00	220.00

No. 11 Surcharged

1882, Jan.
32 A2 5c on 4c rose ... 325.00 400.00

Nos. 12, 14a, 16
Surcharged

1880-81
33 A2 10c on 6c violet ('81) ... 80.00 7.50
  a. Double surcharge ... — 3,250.
34 A3 10c on 12c blue ('81) ... 65.00 12.00
  a. 10c on 12c ultra ('81) ... 82.50 20.00
35 A4 10c on 30c claret ... 475.00 100.00
  Nos. 33-35 (3) ... 620.00 119.50

A6   A7

1882, Jan.   Typo.   Perf. 14
38 A6 5c violet brown ... 120.00 125.00
39 A7 10c slate ... 500.00 80.00

See Nos. 45-47, 51. For surcharges see Nos. 60, 67-72, 89-92.

1882-99   Wmk. Crown and C A (2)
40 A2 2c bister brown ... 350.00 52.50
41 A2 2c car rose ('83) ... 13.00 1.00
  a. 2c rose ... 47.50 4.75
42 A2 4c rose ... 150.00 10.50
43 A2 4c car rose ('99) ... 13.00 1.40
44 A2 4c bister brn ('83) ... 52.50 4.25
45 A6 5c ultra ('83) ... 19.00 1.10
46 A6 5c brown ('94) ... 14.00 1.10
47 A6 5c magenta ('99) ... 2.75 2.40
48 A2 6c violet ... 2.75 11.00
  a. 6c lilac ('84) ... 27.50 18.00
49 A3 8c orange ... 4.75 1.10
50 A3 8c ultra ('94) ... 5.25 .60
  a. 8c bright blue ... 7.75 .95
51 A7 10c slate ... 12.00 1.50
52 A3 12c vio brn ('83) ... 80.00 17.00
53 A3 12c claret ('94) ... 26.00 12.00
54 A3 24c blue grn ('83) ... 9.00 6.00
  a. 24c yellow green ('84) ... 85.00 11.00
55 A4 30c claret ('91) ... 20.00 21.00
56 A5 32c red org ('87) ... 14.00 4.50
57 A5 96c olive gray ('88) ... 80.00 80.00
  Nos. 40-57 (18) ... 868.00 228.95

For overprints see Malaya, Perak Nos. O3-O9, Selangor Nos. 3-4, Sungei Ujong Nos. 6-7, 11.

Preceding Issues Surcharged

Surcharged Vertically

1883-84   Wmk. 2, 1
58 A3 2c on 8c orange ... 175.00 90.00
  a. Double surcharge ... 3,750. 1,275.
59 A5 2c on 32c pale red ... 900.00 900.00
  a. Double surcharge
60 A6 2c on 5c ultra ('84) ... 175.00 180.00
  a. Pair, one without surcharge
  b. Double surcharge
  Nos. 58-60 (3) ... 1,250. 1,170.

Five types of surcharge on No. 58, two types on No. 59 and three types on No. 60.

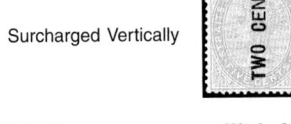

Surcharged in Black

1883   Wmk. 2
61 A2 2c on 4c rose ... 90.00 100.00
  b. "s" of "Cents." inverted ... 1,700. 1,900.

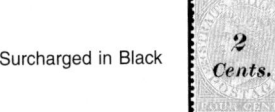

Wmk. 1
62 A3 2c on 12c blue ... 425.00 180.00
  a. "s" of "Cents." inverted ... 7,000. 3,750.

Surcharged in Black or Blue

1884
63 A3 8c on 12c blue ... 950.00 175.00

Wmk. 2
64 A3 8c on 12c vio brn ... 600.00 175.00

With Additional Surcharge Handstamped in Red

65 A3 8c on 8c on 12c vio brn (R + Bk) ... 475.00 500.00
66 A3 8c on 8c on 12c vio brn (R + Bl) ... 10,000.

Surcharged in Black or Red

1884
67 A6 4c on 5c ultra (Bk) ... 3,500. 4,250.
68 A6 4c on 5c ultra (R) ... 160.00 125.00

No. 68 Surcharged in Red

69 A6 4c on 4c on 5c ultra ... 37,500.

No. 69 may be a trial printing. "Usage" seems to been restricted to less than 10 letters known sent from the Postmaster General to his wife.

Surcharged in Black

1885-87
70 A6 3c on 5c ultra ... 160.00 250.00
  a. Double surcharge ... 3,500.

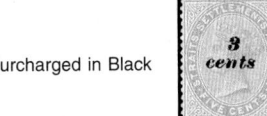

Surcharged in Black

71 A6 3c on 5c vio brn ('86) ... 275.00 290.00

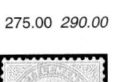

Surcharged

72 A6 2c on 5c ultra ('87) ... 42.50 90.00
  a. Double surcharge ... 1,700. 1,600.
  b. "C" omitted ... 4,500.

In the surcharged issues of 1883 to 1887, Nos. 59, 62, 63 and 71 are on stamps watermarked Crown and C C, the others are watermarked Crown and C A.

Surcharged

1885-94   Wmk. Crown and C A (2)
73 A5 3c on 32c magenta ... 2.25 1.10
  a. 3c on 32c pale magenta ... 6.00 4.50
    Ovptd. "SPECIMEN" ... 300.00
74 A5 3c on 32c rose ('94) ... 2.75 .85
  a. Without surcharge ... 4,500.
    Ovptd. "SPECIMEN" ... 65.00

No. 74a value is for a stamp with perfs touching frame line.

Surcharged

1891
75 A3 10c on 24c green ... 7.00 1.40
  a. Narrow "0" in "10" ... 32.50 37.50

Surcharged

76 A5 30c on 32c red orange ... 14.00 4.25

Surcharged

Surcharged

1892
77 A2 1c on 2c rose ... 2.25 4.25
78 A2 1c on 4c bister brn ... 7.00 6.25
  a. Double surcharge ... 1,800.
79 A2 1c on 6c violet ... 1.75 9.50
  a. Dbl. surch., one invtd. ... 2,150. 1,900.
80 A3 1c on 8c orange ... 1.25 3.25
81 A3 1c on 12c vio brown ... 5.75 10.50
  Nos. 77-81 (5) ... 18.00 33.75

Surcharged

82 A3 1c on 8c gray green ... 1.10 1.75

Queen Victoria — A13

1892-99   Typo.
83 A13 1c gray green ... 7.50 .80
84 A13 3c car rose ('95) ... 13.00 .55
85 A13 3c brown ('99) ... 14.00 .70
  a. 3c yellow brown ... 13.00 .80
86 A13 25c dk vio & grn ... 37.50 7.50
  a. 25c purple brown & green ... 42.50 7.50
87 A13 50c ol grn & car ... 25.00 3.00
88 A13 $5 org & car ('98) ... 500.00 275.00
  Nos. 83-88 (6) ... 597.00 287.55
  Set ovptd. "SPECIMEN" ... 240.00

Denomination of $5, is in color on plain tablet.

Stamps of 1883-94 Surcharged

1899
89 A6 4c on 5c ultra ... 9.50 24.00
  a. Double surcharge ... — 3,750.

90 A6 4c on 5c brown ... 3.25 5.25
91 A3 4c on 8c brt blue ... 2.25 1.40
  a. 4c on 8c ultra ... 2.75 3.25
  b. Double surcharge ... 1,600. 1,500.
  Nos. 89-91 (3) ... 15.00 30.65

Type of 1882 Issue Surcharged

92 A6 4c on 5c rose ... 1.10 .40
  a. Without surcharge ... 40,000.
    Ovptd. "SPECIMEN" ... 60.00

King Edward VII — A14

Numerals of 5c, 8c, 10c, 30c, $1 and $5, type A14, are in color on plain tablet.

1902   Wmk. 2   Typo.
93 A14 1c green ... 3.00 4.00
  a. 1c pale green ... 5.00 4.25
94 A14 3c vio & org ... 3.75 .25
95 A14 4c violet, red ... 5.00 .35
96 A14 5c violet ... 6.00 2.00
97 A14 8c violet, blue ... 4.75 .30
98 A14 10c vio & blk, yel ... 29.00 1.60
99 A14 25c violet & grn ... 16.00 9.00
100 A14 30c gray & car rose ... 22.00 8.50
101 A14 50c grn & car rose ... 22.50 22.50
  a. 50c dull green & carmine ... 24.50 25.00
102 A14 $1 green & blk ... 25.00 80.00
103 A14 $2 violet & blk ... 80.00 80.00
104 A14 $5 grn & brn ... 215.00 180.00
104A A14 $100 dl vio & grn, yel ... 16,000.
  Nos. 93-104 (12) ... 432.00 388.50
  Nos. 93-104 ovptd. "SPECIMEN" ... 500.00

High values of the 1902 and 1904 issues with revenue cancellations are of minimal value. No. 104A is inscribed "Postage & Revenue" but the limit of weight probably precluded its use postally.

See Nos. 113, 115-128B, 133.

A15   A16

A17   A18

1903-04
105 A15 1c gray green ... 3.50 8.50
106 A16 3c dull violet ... 12.00 4.75
107 A17 4c violet, red ... 11.00 .35
108 A18 8c violet, blue ... 52.50 1.50
  Nos. 105-108 (4) ... 79.00 15.10

See Nos. 109-112, 114, 129-132, 134.

1904-11   Chalky Paper   Wmk. 3
109 A15 1c gray green ... 5.25 .25
110 A16 3c dull violet ... 3.00 .35
111 A17 4c violet, red ... 24.00 .80
112 A17 4c dull vio ('08) ... 6.50 .25
113 A14 5c violet ('06) ... 24.00 25.00
114 A18 8c violet, bl ... 52.50 1.60
115 A14 10c vio & blk, yel ... 9.00 .85
116 A14 10c vio & yel ('08) ... 15.00 1.10
117 A14 25c vio & grn ... 60.00 40.00
118 A14 25c violet ('09) ... 22.50 9.00
119 A14 30c gray & car rose ... 55.00 3.25

120	A14	30c vio & org ('09)	60.00	4.50
121	A14	50c grn & car rose	65.00	22.00
122	A14	50c blk, grn ('10)	9.50	5.25
123	A14	$1 green & blk	75.00	37.50
124	A14	$1 blk & red, bl ('11)	16.00	6.50
125	A14	$2 violet & blk	120.00	95.00
		Revenue cancel		15.00
126	A14	$2 grn & red, yel ('09)	27.50	25.00
127	A14	$5 grn & brn org	325.00	210.00
128	A14	$5 grn & red, grn ('10)	150.00	80.00
		Revenue cancel		6.50
128A	A14	$25 green & blk	2,750.	2,750.
		Revenue cancel		55.00
128B	A14	$100 dl vio & grn, yel	17,500.	
		Revenue cancel		200.00
		Nos. 109-128 (20)	1,124.	545.95

Nos. 125, 128A and 128B are on chalky
paper, the other values are on both ordinary
and chalky. The note about No. 104A will
apply to No. 128B.

1906-11		**Ordinary Paper**		
129	A15	1c blue grn ('10)	25.00	1.25
130	A16	3c carmine ('08)	7.50	.25
131	A17	4c carmine ('07)	8.50	3.00
132	A17	4c lake ('11)	3.50	.95
133	A14	5c orange ('09)	3.00	2.75
134	A18	8c ultra ('06)	4.50	.65
		Nos. 129-134 (6)	52.00	8.85

Stamps of Labuan 1902-03, Overprinted or Surcharged in Red or Black

a

b

c

Perf. 12½ to 16 and Compound

1907				Unwmk.
134A	A38(a)	1c violet & blk	75.00	190.00
135	A38(a)	2c grn & blk	425.00	500.00
136	A38(a)	3c brn & blk	25.00	95.00
137	A38(c)	4c on 12c yel & blk	3.00	10.00
a.		No period after "CENTS"	650.00	—
138	A38(c)	4c on 16c org brn & grn (Bk)	9.00	11.00
a.		With additional name in red	700.00	800.00
139	A38(c)	4c on 18c bis & blk	3.00	10.00
a.		No period after "CENTS"	425.00	525.00
b.		"FOUR CENTS." & bar double	12,000.	
140	A38(a)	8c orange & blk	5.25	9.00
141	A38(b)	10c sl bl & brn	9.50	12.00
a.		No period after "Settlements"	650.00	
142	A38(a)	25c grnsh bl & grn	35.00	47.50
143	A38(a)	50c gray lil & vio	25.00	75.00
144	A38(a)	$1 org & red brn	50.00	125.00
		Nos. 134A-144 (11)	664.75	1,084.

A19

A20

1908-11	**Typo.**	**Wmk. 3**	*Perf. 14*	
		Chalky Paper		
145	A19	$25 bl & vio, bl ('11)	3,000.	2,150.
146	A19	$500 violet & org	135,000.	
		Revenue cancel		100.

No. 146 is inscribed "Postage-Revenue" but
was probably used only for revenue.
Excellent forgeries of No. 146 exist.

1910		**Chalky Paper**		
147	A20	21c maroon & vio	7.00	40.00
148	A20	45c black, green	3.75	4.50

King George V

A21　　　　　A22

A23

A24

A25　　　　　A26

Die I (Type A24)

For description of dies I and II see front
section of the Catalogue.
The 25c, 50c and $2 denominations of type
A24 show the numeral on horizontally-lined
tablet.

1912-18		**Chalky Paper**	**Wmk. 3**	
149	A21	1c green	12.00	1.60
150	A21	1c black ('18)	3.00	1.90
151	A25	2c dp green ('18)	2.25	.55
152	A22	3c scarlet	2.75	.25
a.		3c carmine	3.50	1.35
153	A23	4c gray violet	2.75	.65
154	A23	4c scarlet ('18)	3.00	.25
a.		Booklet pane of 1		
b.		Booklet pane of 12		
c.		4c carmine ('18)	2.00	.25
155	A24	5c orange	2.25	1.10
156	A25	6c claret ('18)	2.25	.55
157	A25	8c ultra	3.75	.85
158	A24	10c violet, yel	1.60	1.10
159	A24	10c ultra ('18)	10.00	1.60
160	A26	21c maroon & vio	12.00	13.00
161	A24	25c vio & red vio	17.00	15.00
162	A24	30c vio & org ('14)	8.50	5.25
163	A26	45c blk, bl grn, ol back ('14)	7.50	27.50
a.		45c black, emerald ('17)	4.00	13.75
164	A24	50c black, grn ('14)	6.50	4.50
a.		50c black, bl grn, olive back	25.00	10.00
b.		50c black, emerald	13.00	10.50
c.		Die II	3.25	4.50
165	A24	$1 blk & red, bl ('14)	17.00	16.00
166	A24	$2 grn & red, yel ('15)	17.00	52.50
167	A24	$5 grn & red, grn ('15)	120.00	85.00
a.		$5 grn & red, bl grn, ol back	190.00	115.00
b.		$5 grn & red, emer ('15)	240.00	140.00
c.		Die II	125.00	90.00
		Nos. 149-167 (19)	251.10	229.15

The 1c, 3c, 5c and 8c are on ordinary paper.

Surface-colored Paper

168	A24	10c violet, grn	1.75	1.25
169	A26	45c black, grn ('14)	7.50	19.00
170	A24	$2 grn & red, yel ('14)	16.00	52.50
171	A24	$5 grn & red, grn	120.00	60.00
		Nos. 168-171 (4)	145.25	132.75

See Nos. 179-201. For surcharges see Nos.
B1-B2.

A27

1915				
172	A27	$25 bl & vio, bl	2,150.	650.00
		Revenue cancel		5.75
173	A27	$100 red & blk, bl	8,500.	
		Revenue cancel		90.00
174	A27	$500 grn & dl vio	90,000.	
		Revenue cancel		200.00

Although Nos. 173 and 174 were available
for postage, it is probable that they were used
only for fiscal purposes.
See Nos. 202-204, AR1.

Die II (Type A24)

1921-32		**Ordinary Paper**	**Wmk. 4**	
179	A21	1c black	.65	.25
180	A25	2c green	.65	.25
181	A25	2c brown	8.00	3.75
182	A22	3c green	1.75	.90
183	A23	4c scarlet	2.25	5.00
184	A23	4c dp violet ('25)	.70	.25
185	A23	4c orange ('29)	1.10	.25
186	A24	5c orange ('23)	2.75	1.50
a.		Die I	3.75	.25
187	A24	5c dk brown ('32)	3.25	.25
a.		Die I ('32)	5.75	.25
188	A25	6c claret	2.50	.25
189	A25	6c scarlet ('27)	3.00	.25
a.		6c rose red ('25)	30.00	11.00
190	A24	10c ultra (I)	2.00	4.25

		Chalky Paper		
191	A24	10c vio, yel ('27)	3.25	.35
a.		Die I ('25)	3.00	14.00
192	A24	12c ultra	1.35	.25
193	A26	21c maroon & vio	7.00	60.00
194	A24	25c vio & red vio	5.75	2.00
a.		Die I	35.00	90.00
195	A24	30c violet & org	2.25	1.50
a.		Die I	29.00	60.00
196	A26	35c orange & vio	14.00	7.00
197	A26	35c vio & car ('31)	11.50	8.00
198	A24	50c blk, emerald	2.00	.45
199	A24	$1 blk & red, bl	7.00	1.40
200	A24	$2 grn & red, yel	11.50	9.25
201	A24	$5 grn & red, grn	100.00	37.50
202	A27	$25 bl & vio, bl	1,200.	200.00
203	A27	$100 red & blk, bl	8,000.	2,750.
204	A27	$500 org & dl vio	65,000.	
		Nos. 179-201 (23)	194.20	144.85

No. 192 is on ordinary paper.
Nos. 203 and 204 were probably used only
for fiscal purposes.

Stamps of 1912-21
Overprinted in Black

1922			**Wmk. 3**	
151d	A25	2c deep green	40.00	95.00
154d	A23	4c scarlet	10.00	26.00
155d	A24	5c orange	8.00	22.50
157d	A25	8c ultra	2.25	10.00
161d	A24	25c vio & red vio	4.25	47.50
163d	A26	45c blk, bl grn, ol back	3.75	42.50
165d	A24	$1 blk & red, bl	475.00	1,500.
166d	A24	$2 grn & red, yel	30.00	160.00
167d	A24	$5 grn & red, grn	425.00	750.00

		Wmk. 4		
179d	A21	1c black	3.50	22.50
180d	A25	2c green	2.75	16.00
183d	A23	4c scarlet	4.00	52.50
186d	A24	5c orange (II)	3.25	52.50
190d	A24	10c ultra	2.75	29.00
199d	A24	$1 blk & red, bl	22.50	160.00
		Nos. 151d-199d (15)	1,037.	2,986.

Industrial fair at Singapore, Mar. 31-Apr. 15,
1922.

Common Design Types

pictured following the introduction.

Silver Jubilee Issue
Common Design Type

1935, May 6	**Engr.**		*Perf. 11x12*	
213	CD301	5c black & ultra	3.50	.35
214	CD301	8c indigo & green	3.75	3.50
215	CD301	12c ultra & brown	3.75	8.50
216	CD301	25c brown vio & ind	4.00	12.75
		Nos. 213-216 (4)	15.00	25.10
		Set, never hinged	25.00	

George V — A28

1936-37		**Typo.**	*Perf. 14*	
		Chalky Paper		
217	A28	1c black ('37)	1.60	.25
218	A28	2c green	1.60	.80
220	A28	4c orange brn	2.40	.80
221	A28	5c brown	1.10	.35
222	A28	6c rose red	1.35	1.25
223	A28	8c gray	3.75	.80
224	A28	10c dull vio	2.40	.70
225	A28	12c ultra	2.25	3.00
226	A28	25c rose red & vio	1.60	.60
227	A28	30c org & dk vio	1.40	3.50
229	A28	40c dk vio & car	1.40	2.75
230	A28	50c blk, emerald	4.75	1.40
232	A28	$1 red & blk, blue	20.00	1.90
233	A28	$2 rose red & gray grn	57.50	11.50
234	A28	$5 grn & red, grn ('37)	140.00	11.50
		Nos. 217-234 (15)	243.10	41.10
		Set, never hinged	325.00	

Coronation Issue
Common Design Type

1937, May 12	**Engr.**		*Perf. 13½x14*	
235	CD302	4c deep orange	.65	.25
236	CD302	8c gray black	.80	.25
237	CD302	12c bright ultra	1.80	1.10
		Nos. 235-237 (3)	3.25	1.60
		Set, never hinged	6.00	

George VI — A29

Die I　　　　　Die II

Two Dies

Die I. Printed in two operations. Lines of
background touch outside of central oval. Foliage of palms touches outer frame line. Palm
frond in front of King's eye has two points.
Die II. Printed from a single plate. Lines of
background separated from central oval by a
white line. Foliage of palms does not touch
outer frame line. Palm frond in front of King's
eye has one point.

1937-41		**Typo.**	*Perf. 14*	
238	A29	1c black (I)	6.00	.25
239	A29	2c green (I)	11.00	.25
c.		Die II ('38)	35.00	.45
239A	A29	2c brown org ('41) (II)	1.25	20.00
239B	A29	3c green ('41) (II)	5.00	4.25
240	A29	4c brown org (I)	13.50	.25
a.		Die II ('38)	50.00	.25
241	A29	5c brown (I)	12.00	.35
a.		Die II ('39)	20.00	.25
242	A29	6c rose red ('38) (I)	5.50	.65
243	A29	8c gray ('38) (I)	19.00	.25
244	A29	10c dull vio (I)	6.00	.25
245	A29	12c ultra ('38) (I)	6.00	.35
245A	A29	15c ultra ('41) (II)	5.00	10.50
246	A29	25c rose red & vio (I)	25.00	1.10
247	A29	30c org & vio (I)	11.00	2.00
248	A29	40c dk vio & rose red (I)	10.00	2.50
249	A29	50c blk, emer ('38) (I)	10.00	.45
250	A29	$1 red & blk, bl ('38) (I)	15.00	.40
251	A29	$2 rose red & gray grn ('38) (I)	30.00	12.50
252	A29	$5 grn & red, grn ('38) (I)	15.00	7.50
		Nos. 238-252 (18)	206.25	63.80
		Set, never hinged	375.00	

For overprints see Nos. 256-271, N1-N29
and Malaya, Malacca Nos. N1-N14, Penang
Nos. N1-N26.

Stamps and Type of
1937-41 Overprinted in
Red or Black

1945-48

256	A29	1c black (R)	.25	.25
257	A29	2c brown org (II)	.25	.25
a.		Die I ('46)	7.50	3.75
258	A29	3c green	.25	.25
259	A29	5c brown	.75	.60
260	A29	6c gray	.25	.25
261	A29	8c rose red	.25	.25
262	A29	10c dull vio (I)	.30	.25
a.		10c claret (II) ('48)	10.00	1.25
263	A29	12c ultra	1.75	3.25
264	A29	15c ultra (Bk)	2.25	4.75
265	A29	15c ultra (R)	.25	.25
266	A29	25c rose red & vio	1.40	.25
a.		Double overprint	400.00	
267	A29	50c blk, *emer* (R)	.60	.25
268	A29	$1 rose red & blk	.25	.25
269	A29	$2 rose red & gray grn	2.50	.65
270	A29	$5 grn & red, *grn*	72.50	72.50
271	A29	$5 brn org & vio	3.75	2.75
		Nos. 256-271 (16)	89.30	87.00
		Set, never hinged	140.00	

The letters "B M A" are initials of "British Military Administration".

An 8c gray with BMA overprint was prepared but not issued. Value $5.

The 6c gray, 8c rose red and $5 brown orange & violet exist without BMA overprint, but were issued only with it.

No. 262a does not exist without overprint.

No. 262 exists in at least three shades.

POSTAL-FISCAL STAMP

**Type of 1915 with head George VI
Inscribed "REVENUE" at each side**

1938

AR1	A27	$25 Blue & purple, *blue*	4,250.	600.00

Although documentation authorizing its postal use has not been found, No. AR1 was frequently used as a postage stamp throughout 1941.

SEMI-POSTAL STAMPS

Nos. 152-153
Surcharged

1917   Wmk. 3   Perf. 14

B1	A22	3c + 2c scarlet	3.00	32.50
a.		No period after "C"	475.00	900.00
B2	A23	4c + 2c gray violet	4.00	35.00
a.		No period after "C"	525.00	900.00

POSTAGE DUE STAMPS

D1

1924-26   Typo.   Wmk. 4   Perf. 14

J1	D1	1c violet	8.50	5.50
		On cover		110.00
J2	D1	2c black	3.50	1.25
		On cover		25.00
J3	D1	4c green ('26)	2.25	5.00
		On cover		75.00
J4	D1	8c red	4.75	.60
		On cover		40.00
J5	D1	10c orange	6.50	.90
		On cover		40.00
J6	D1	12c ultramarine	7.50	.75
		On cover		50.00
		Nos. J1-J6 (6)	33.00	14.00
		Set never hinged	55.00	

Cover values are for properly franked commercial covers. Philatelic usages also exist and sell for less.

OCCUPATION STAMPS

Issued Under Japanese Occupation

Nos. 238, 239A-B, 243
and 245A Hstmpd. in
Red

1942, Mar. 16   Wmk. 4   Perf. 14

N1	A29	1c black	22.50	22.50
N2	A29	2c brown orange	16.00	16.00
N3	A29	3c green	70.00	85.00
N4	A29	8c gray	27.50	22.50
N5	A29	15c ultra	21.00	20.00
		Nos. N1-N5 (5)	157.00	166.00
		Set, never hinged	200.00	

Other denominations with this handstamp are believed to be proofs.

The handstamp reads: "Seal of Post Office of Malayan Military Department."

Stamps of 1937-41,
Handstamped in Red,
Black, Violet or Brown

1942, Apr. 3

N6	A29	1c black	4.00	4.00
N6A	A29	2c green (V)	3,750.	2,750.
N7	A29	2c brown org	3.50	3.50
N8	A29	3c green	3.50	3.50
N9	A29	5c brown	30.00	32.50
N10	A29	8c gray	8.50	8.50
N11	A29	10c dull violet	70.00	50.00
N12	A29	12c ultra	100.00	160.00
N13	A29	15c ultra		45.00
N14	A29	30c orange & vio	4,250.	4,250.
N15	A29	40c dk vio & rose red	150.00	125.00
N16	A29	50c blk, *emerald*	80.00	60.00
N17	A29	$1 red & blk, *bl*	105.00	80.00
N18	A29	$2 rose red & gray grn	180.00	225.00
N19	A29	$5 grn & red, *grn*	240.00	300.00

Nos. N6-N7, N9, N11-N12, N15-N19 with red handstamp were used in Sumatra. The 2c green with red handstamp was not regularly issued.

Straits Settlements Nos.
239A, 239B, 243 and
245A Ovptd. in Black

1942

N20	A29	2c brown orange	4.00	1.00
a.		Inverted overprint	17.50	27.50
b.		Dbl. ovpt., one invtd.	60.00	70.00
N21	A29	3c green	62.50	75.00
N22	A29	8c gray	11.00	4.75
a.		Inverted overprint	22.50	45.00
N23	A29	15c ultra	26.00	16.00
		Nos. N20-N23 (4)	103.50	96.75
		Set never hinged	100.00	

Straits Settlements Nos.
239A and 243
Overprinted in Black

1942, Nov. 3

N24	A29	2c brown orange	14.00	25.00
a.		Inverted overprint	375.00	425.00
N25	A29	8c gray	15.00	25.00
a.		Inverted overprint	375.00	425.00

Agricultural-Horticultural Exhibition held at Kuala Lumpur, Selangor, Nov. 1-2, 1942. Sold only at a temporary post office at the exhibition.

Straits Settlements Nos.
243, 245 and 248
Ovptd. in Black or Red

1943

N26	A29	8c gray (Bk)	1.60	1.00
a.		Inverted overprint	60.00	75.00
N27	A29	8c gray (R)	2.75	4.00
N28	A29	12c ultramarine	2.00	16.00
N29	A29	40c dk vio & rose red	4.25	8.00
		Nos. N26-N29 (4)	10.60	29.00
		Set never hinged	10.00	

The Japanese characters read: "Japanese Postal Service."

SUDAN

sü-'dan

LOCATION — Northeastern Africa, south of Egypt
GOVT. — Administered jointly by Egypt and Great Britain
AREA — 967,500 sq. mi.
POP. — 20,564,364 (1983)
CAPITAL — Khartoum

10 Milliemes = 1 Piaster
100 Piasters = 1 Pound

Watermarks

Wmk. 71 —
Rosette

Wmk. 179 —
Multiple Crescent
and Star

Wmk. 214 —
Multiple S G

Egyptian Stamps of
1884-93 Overprinted
in Black

1897, Mar. 1   Wmk. 119   Perf. 14

1	A18	1m brown	4.25	2.50
		Never hinged	5.25	
a.		Inverted overprint	325.00	
2	A19	2m green	3.00	2.75
		Never hinged	3.75	
3	A20	3m orange	2.25	2.10
		Never hinged	2.75	
4	A22	5m carmine rose	3.00	2.00
		Never hinged	3.75	
a.		Inverted overprint	325.00	275.00
5	A14	1p ultra	10.00	2.50
		Never hinged	13.50	
6	A15	2p orange brown	85.00	19.00
		Never hinged	110.00	
7	A16	5p gray	87.50	22.50
		Never hinged	105.00	
a.		Double overprint	6,000.	
8	A23	10p violet	55.00	60.00
		Never hinged	60.00	
		Nos. 1-8 (8)	250.00	113.35

Counterfeits of Nos. 1-8 are plentiful.

Camel Post — A1

1898, Mar. 1   Typo.   Wmk. 71

9	A1	1m rose & brn	2.25	3.00
		Never hinged	3.00	

10	A1	2m brown & grn	4.00	3.00
		Never hinged	5.75	
11	A1	3m green & vio	4.50	2.75
		Never hinged	6.00	
12	A1	5m black & rose	4.00	2.00
		Never hinged	5.25	
13	A1	1p yel brn & ultra	16.00	4.75
		Never hinged	22.50	
14	A1	2p ultra & blk	45.00	4.00
		Never hinged	47.50	
15	A1	5p grn & org brn	50.00	21.00
		Never hinged	57.50	
16	A1	10p dp vio & blk	40.00	3.00
		Never hinged	55.00	
		Nos. 9-16 (8)	165.75	43.50

See Nos. 17-27, 43-50. For overprints see Nos. C3, MO1-MO15, O1-O9, O17-O24. For surcharges see Nos. 28, 62, C16.

1902-21   Wmk. 179

17	A1	1m car rose & brn ('05)	1.60	.90
		Never hinged	2.50	
18	A1	2m brown & grn	2.25	.25
		Never hinged	3.50	
19	A1	3m grn & vio ('03)	3.00	.35
		Never hinged	4.50	
20	A1	4m ol brn & bl ('07)	2.00	3.50
		Never hinged	3.00	
21	A1	4m brn & red ('07)	2.00	1.00
		Never hinged	3.00	
22	A1	5m blk & rose red ('03)	2.50	.25
		Never hinged	3.75	
23	A1	1p brn & ultra ('03)	3.00	.40
		Never hinged	4.50	
24	A1	2p ultra & blk ('08)	37.50	2.50
		Never hinged	52.50	
25	A1	2p org & vio brn, chalky paper ('21)	9.00	11.00
		Never hinged	10.50	
26	A1	5p grn & org brn ('08)	35.00	.45
		Never hinged	52.50	
a.		On chalky paper	37.50	4.50
27	A1	10p dp vio & blk ('11)	35.00	4.75
		Never hinged	52.50	
a.		On chalky paper	32.50	10.00
		Nos. 17-27 (11)	132.85	25.35

No. 15 Surcharged
in Black

1903, Sept.   Wmk. 71

28	A1	5m on 5p	10.00	12.00
		Never hinged	15.00	
a.		Inverted surcharge	325.00	275.00

A2

1921-22   Typo.   Wmk. 179

29	A2	1m orange & blk ('22)	1.25	5.25
30	A2	2m dk brn & org ('22)	11.00	13.50
a.		2m dark brown & yellow ('23)	12.00	12.00
31	A2	3m green & vio ('22)	3.00	11.00
32	A2	4m brown & vio ('22)	8.00	9.00
33	A2	5m blk & ol brn ('22)	3.00	.25
34	A2	10m black & car ('22)	6.00	.25
35	A2	15m org brn & ultra	4.00	1.25
		Nos. 29-35 (7)	36.25	40.50

See Nos. 36-42. For overprints see Nos. C1-C2, O10-O16. For surcharges see Nos. 60-61.

1927-40   Wmk. 214
Chalky Paper

36	A2	1m org yel & blk	1.00	.25
37	A2	2m dk brn & org	1.00	.25
38	A2	3m green & violet	1.00	.25
39	A2	4m brown & green	.90	.25
40	A2	5m blk & ol brn	.75	.25
a.		Booklet pane of 4		
41	A2	10m black & car	2.00	.25
42	A2	15m org brn & ultra	2.25	.25
43	A1	2p orange & vio brn	4.50	.25
44	A1	3p dk bl & red brn ('40)	8.50	.25
45	A1	4p black & ultra ('36)	4.75	.25
46	A1	5p dk grn & org brn ('36)	1.75	.25
47	A1	6p blk & pale bl ('36)	13.00	2.75
48	A1	8p blk & pck grn ('36)	13.00	4.50
49	A1	10p dp vio & blk	9.00	.25
50	A1	20p bl & lt bl ('35)	11.00	.25
		Nos. 36-50 (15)	74.40	10.50

Thick, Smooth, Unsurfaced Paper ('41)

36a	A2	1m org yel & blk	1.00	.25
37a	A2	2m dk brn & org	1.60	.25
38a	A2	3m green & violet	3.00	.35
39a	A2	4m brown & green	3.75	.25
41a	A2	10m black & car	3.25	.25
42a	A2	15m org brn & ultra	4.00	.25
43a	A1	2p orange & vio brn	4.25	.25
44a	A1	3p dk bl & red brn	18.00	.25
46a	A1	5p dk grn & org brn	5.50	2.25
47a	A1	6p blk & pale blue	37.50	2.25
48a	A1	8p blk & pck grn	50.00	4.50
49a	A1	10p bright mauve & blk	9.50	.75
50a	A1	20p bl & lt blue	9.00	.25
		Nos. 36a-50a (14)	153.10	12.45

Charles George
Gordon — A3

Gordon
Memorial
College
A4

Memorial Service at Khartoum — A5

1935, Jan. 1   Engr.   Perf. 13½x14

51	A3	5m deep green	.75	.25
52	A3	10m brown	1.50	.30
53	A3	13m ultra	1.75	13.50
54	A3	15m carmine	3.00	.30
55	A4	2p deep blue	2.75	.25
56	A4	5p orange	3.00	.50
57	A4	10p dull violet	11.00	10.00
58	A5	20p black	32.50	72.50
59	A5	50p red brown	125.00	155.00
		Nos. 51-59 (9)	181.25	252.60
		Set, never hinged	325.00	

50th anniv. of the death of Gen. Charles George ("Chinese") Gordon (1833-85).

No. 41 Surcharged in Black

5 Mills.

Wmk. Multiple S G (214)
1940, Feb. 25   Typo.   Perf. 14

60	A2	5m on 10m black & car	1.50	1.50

Nos. 40 and 48 Surcharged in Black

a   b

1940-41

61	A2(a)	4½p on 5m ('41)	65.00	12.00
62	A1(b)	4½p on 8p	57.50	14.00

AIR POST STAMPS

Nos. 40-41, 43 Overprinted in Black

AIR MAIL

Nos. C1-C2   No. C3

1931   Wmk. 214   Perf. 11½x12½, 14

C1	A2	5m blk & olive brown	1.00	1.00
		Never hinged	2.00	
C2	A2	10m blk & carmine	1.75	4.00
		Never hinged	3.50	
C3	A1	2p org & vio brown	2.50	3.50
		Never hinged	5.00	
		Nos. C1-C3 (3)	5.25	8.50

Statue of
Gen.
C. G. Gordon
AP3

1931-35   Engr.   Perf. 14

C4	AP3	3m dk brn & grn ('33)	3.50	7.25
		Never hinged	7.00	
C5	AP3	5m grn & blk	1.50	.25
		Never hinged	3.00	
C6	AP3	10m car rose & blk	1.50	.25
		Never hinged	3.00	
C7	AP3	15m dk brn & brn	.75	.25
		Never hinged	1.50	
C8	AP3	2p org & blk	.65	.25
		Never hinged	1.50	
C9	AP3	2½p bl & red vio ('33)	4.75	.25
		Never hinged	9.50	
C10	AP3	3p gray & blk	1.00	.25
		Never hinged	2.00	
C11	AP3	3½p dl vio & blk	2.25	.90
		Never hinged	4.50	
C12	AP3	4½p gray & brn	12.50	16.50
		Never hinged	25.00	
C13	AP3	5p ultra & blk	1.75	.35
		Never hinged	3.50	
C14	AP3	7½p pck grn & dk grn ('35)	12.00	6.00
		Never hinged	24.00	
C15	AP3	10p peacock bl & sep ('35)	11.50	2.00
		Never hinged	23.00	
		Nos. C4-C15 (12)	53.65	34.50

See Nos. C23-C30. For surcharges see Nos. C17-C22, C31-C34.

No. 43 Surcharged
in Black

AIR MAIL

1932, July 18   Typo.

C16	A1	2½p on 2p	2.50	4.00
		Never hinged	5.00	

Nos. C6, C4-
C5, C12
Surcharged

2½ PIASTRES

1935   Engr.   Perf. 14

C17	AP3	15m on 10m	.60	.25
		Never hinged	1.25	
a.		Double surcharge	950.00	1,100.
b.		Arabic characters omitted	750.00	
C18	AP3	2½p on 3m	1.25	6.00
		Never hinged	2.50	
a.		"½" 2¼mm high instead of 3mm	4.50	20.00
b.		Second Arabic character of surcharge omitted	65.00	125.00
C19	AP3	2½p on 5m	.85	1.75
		Never hinged	1.75	
a.		"½" 2¼mm high instead of 3mm	4.75	9.00
b.		Second Arabic character of surcharge omitted	40.00	60.00
c.		Inverted surcharge	1,000.	1,200.
d.		As "a," inverted	2,500.	20,000.

e.		As "b," inverted	1,500.	1,600.
f.		Pair, C19c and C19d	37,500.	
C20	AP3	3p on 4½p	2.50	18.50
		Never hinged	5.00	
C21	AP3	7½p on 4½p	9.00	52.50
		Never hinged	18.00	
C22	AP3	10p on 4½p	9.00	52.50
		Never hinged	18.00	
		Nos. C17-C22 (6)	23.20	131.50

Type of 1931-35
1936-37   Perf. 11½x12½

C23	AP3	15m dk brn & brn ('37)	4.75	.25
		Never hinged	9.50	
C24	AP3	2p org & blk ('37)	5.25	18.00
		Never hinged	11.00	
C25	AP3	2½p bl & red vio	3.00	.25
		Never hinged	6.00	
C26	AP3	3p gray & blk ('37)	1.00	.40
		Never hinged	2.00	
C27	AP3	3½p dl vio & blk ('37)	2.50	15.00
		Never hinged	5.00	
C28	AP3	5p ultra & blk ('37)	4.25	.40
		Never hinged	8.50	
C29	AP3	7½p pck grn & dk grn ('37)	4.75	11.00
		Never hinged	9.50	
C30	AP3	10p pck bl & sep ('37)	7.00	27.50
		Never hinged	14.00	
		Nos. C23-C30 (8)	32.50	72.80

Nos. C25,
C11, C14
and C15
Srchd. as in
1935

5 MILLIEMES

1938   Wmk. 214   Perf. 11½x12½, 14

C31	AP3	5m on 2½p	3.50	.25
		Never hinged	7.00	
C32	AP3	3p on 3½p	42.50	60.00
		Never hinged	85.00	
a.		On No. C27	700.00	750.00
C33	AP3	3p on 7½p	7.50	7.25
		Never hinged	15.00	
a.		On No. C29	700.00	750.00
C34	AP3	5p on 10p	1.75	5.50
		Never hinged	3.50	
a.		On No. C30	700.00	750.00
		Nos. C31-C34 (4)	55.25	73.00

POSTAGE DUE STAMPS

Postage Due Stamps
of Egypt, 1889,
Overprinted in Black

1897   Wmk. 119   Perf. 14

J1	D3	2m green	2.50	6.00
J2	D3	4m maroon	2.50	6.00
J3	D3	1p ultra	14.00	5.00
J4	D3	2p orange	14.00	10.00
		Nos. J1-J4 (4)	33.00	27.00

Steamboat on Nile
River — D1

1901   Typo.   Wmk. 179

J5	D1	2m orange brn & blk	1.00	.85
J6	D1	4m blue green & brn	3.25	1.25
J7	D1	10m blue vio & blue grn	8.00	5.00
J8	D1	20m car rose & ultra	4.75	4.75
		Nos. J5-J8 (4)	17.00	11.85

1927-30   Wmk. Multiple S G (214)

J9	D1	2m org brn & blk ('30)	4.50	3.00
J10	D1	4m blue grn & brn	1.75	1.00
J11	D1	10m violet & blue grn	2.75	2.00
		Nos. J9-J11 (3)	9.00	6.00

ARMY OFFICIAL STAMPS

Regular Issues of 1898 and 1902-08 Overprinted in Black

Nos. MO1, MO3 and MO2, MO4

1905   Wmk. 71   Perf. 14

MO1	A1	1m rose & brown	190.00	200.00
a.		"OFF!CIAL"	4,750.	3,250.
b.		Pair, #MO1 and #MO2	4,500.	
MO2	A1	1m rose & brown	3,000.	3,000.
		Wmk. 179		
MO3	A1	1m car rose & brn	6.50	3.00
a.		"OFF!CIAL"	80.00	47.50
b.		Inverted overprint	70.00	60.00
c.		Horizontal overprint	450.00	
MO4	A1	1m car rose & brn	60.00	30.00
a.		Inverted overprint	350.00	375.00

Army Service

Regular Issues of
1902-11
Overprinted in
Black

1906-11

MO5	A1	1m car rose & brn	2.50	.30
a.		"Army" and "Service" 14mm apart	550.00	400.00
b.		Inverted overprint	650.00	700.00
c.		Pair, one without ovpt.		7,000.
d.		Double overprint		1,750.
e.		"Service" omitted		4,500.
MO6	A1	2m brn & grn	22.50	1.25
a.		Pair, one without ovpt.	4,000.	
b.		"Army" omitted	4,200.	4,200.
MO7	A1	3m green & violet	22.50	.50
a.		Inverted overprint	2,200.	
MO8	A1	5m blk & rose red	3.50	.25
a.		Inverted overprint		375.00
b.		Double overprint	325.00	250.00
c.		Double ovpt., one invtd.	1,500.	550.00
MO9	A1	1p yel brn & ultra	22.50	.40
a.		"Army" omitted	3,250.	3,250.
MO10	A1	2p ultra & blk ('09)	85.00	15.00
a.		Double overprint		3,400.
MO11	A1	5p grn & org brn ('08)	175.00	75.00
MO12	A1	10p dp vio & blk ('11)	625.00	750.00
		Nos. MO5-MO12 (8)	958.50	842.70

Same Overprint On Regular Issue of 1898
Wmk. 71

MO13	A1	2p ultra & black	90.00	11.50
a.		Inverted overprint		
MO14	A1	5p grn & org brn	130.00	250.00
MO15	A1	10p dp vio & blk	175.00	475.00

There are two types of this overprint which may be distinguished by the size and shape of the "y."

PERFORATED ARMY OFFICIAL STAMPS

Stamps of Sudan punched with "AS" (Army Service) replaced the overprinted Army Official stamps Jan. 1, 1912.

These perforated Official stamps were used on internal military mail until the return of the Egyptian Army to Egypt in 1924. They continued to be used on mail to foreign destinations until supplies of individual denominations were exhausted or until 1936, when remaining stocks were destroyed. They were replaced by stamps overprinted or punched "SG."

Catalogue numbers are "MOA" plus Scott No. of basic, unoverprinted stamps.

1912-22
On Second Large Camel Post Issue
23 holes: 12 in "A," 11 in "S"

MOA17	A1	1m car rose & brn	65.00	7.25
MOA18	A1	2m brn & grn	9.25	.75
MOA19	A1	3m grn & vio	57.50	3.50
MOA22	A1	5m blk & rose red	15.00	.55
MOA23	A1	1p brn & ultra	29.00	.85
MOA24	A1	2p ultra & blk	70.00	5.50
MOA25	A1	2p org & vio brn ('22)	75.00	62.50
MOA26	A1	5p grn & org brn	80.00	35.00
a.		Chalky paper (#26a)	80.00	35.00
MOA27	A1	10p dp vio & blk	550.00	300.00
		Nos. MOA17-MOA27 (9)	950.75	415.90

1922-24
On Small Camel Post Issue
17 holes: 8 in "A," 9 in "S"

MOA30	A2	2m dk brn & org	85.00	50.00
MOA33	A2	5m blk & ol brn	16.00	4.50
MOA34	A2	10m black & car	22.50	7.00
		Nos. MOA30-MOA34 (3)	123.50	61.50

OFFICIAL STAMPS

PERFORATED OFFICIAL STAMPS

Stamps of Sudan punched with "SG" (Sudan Government) were issued for franking official mail in 1900-1901 and again in 1913-30. They were used on internal correspondence until 1932 and for foreign correspondence until 1936.

The perforated initials can appear upright, inverted, reversed, and inverted and reversed on the 1900-01 stamps, but upright only on later issues.

Values are for very fine examples, well-centered and free of encroaching perfin holes.

Catalogue numbers are "OA" plus Scott No. of basic, unoverprinted stamps.

1900, Feb. 8
On 1897 Ovpt. on Egypt
26 holes: 14 in "S," 12 in "G"

OA4	A22	5m carmine rose	55.00	17.50

1901, Jan.
On First Large Camel Post
26 holes: 14 in "S," 12 in "G"

OA9	A1	1m rose & brown	50.00	32.50

Regular Issue of 1898 Overprinted in Black

1902-06   **Wmk. 71**   **Perf. 14**

O1	A1	1m rose & brown	3.50	11.00
		Never hinged	7.00	
a.		Inverted overprint	325.00	450.00
b.		Round periods	8.00	45.00
c.		Double overprint	650.00	
d.		Oval "O" in overprint	90.00	
e.		As "d," inverted overprint	5,500.	
O2	A1	10p dp vio & blk ('06)	16.00	27.50
		Never hinged	32.50	

Same Ovpt. on Stamps of 1902-11

1903-12   **Wmk. 179**

O3	A1	1m car rose & brn ('04)	.60	.25
		Never hinged	1.20	
a.		Double overprint		
O4	A1	3m grn & vio ('04)	3.25	.25
		Never hinged	6.50	
a.		Double overprint		
O5	A1	5m blk & rose red	3.25	.25
		Never hinged	6.50	
O6	A1	1p yel brn & ultra	6.00	.25
		Never hinged	12.00	
O7	A1	2p ultra & blk	30.00	.25
		Never hinged	60.00	
O8	A1	5p grn & org brn	2.75	.40
		Never hinged	5.50	
O9	A1	10p dp vio & blk	5.25	70.00
		Never hinged	11.00	
		Nos. O3-O9 (7)	51.10	71.65

1913-22
On Second Large Camel Post
25 holes: 12 in "S," 13 in "G"

OA17	A1	1m car rose & brn	12.50	.30
		Never hinged	25.00	
OA18	A1	2m brown & grn ('15)	12.00	8.50
		Never hinged	24.00	
OA19	A1	3m grn & vio	20.00	.80
		Never hinged	40.00	
OA22	A1	5m blk & rose red	6.75	.25
		Never hinged	13.50	
OA23	A1	1p brn & ultra	9.25	.40
		Never hinged	18.50	
OA24	A1	2p ultra & blk	20.00	.75
		Never hinged	40.00	
OA25	A1	2p org & vio brn ('22)	55.00	8.00
		Never hinged	110.00	
OA26	A1	5p grn & org brn	40.00	1.75
		Never hinged	80.00	
a.		On chalky paper	40.00	5.00
		Never hinged	80.00	
OA27	A1	10p dp vio & blk ('14)	50.00	35.00
		Never hinged	100.00	
a.		On chalky paper	50.00	35.00
		Never hinged	100.00	
		Nos. OA17-OA27 (9)	225.50	55.75

1922
On First Small Camel Post Issue
19 holes: 9 in "S," 10 in "G"

OA31	A2	3m green & vio	19.00	16.00
OA32	A2	4m brown & grn	26.00	10.00
OA33	A2	5m blk & ol brn	5.00	1.75
OA34	A2	10m black & car	5.00	1.75
		Nos. OA31-OA34 (4)	55.00	29.50

1927-30
19 holes: 9 in "S," 10 in "G"

OA38	A2	3m org yel & blk ('28)	18.00	4.00
OA39	A2	4m brown & grn ('30)	90.00	55.00
OA40	A2	5m blk & ol brn	7.50	.25
OA41	A2	10m black & car	2.00	.40

25 holes: 12 in "S," 13 in "G"

OA43	A1	2p orange & vio brn	25.00	1.10
OA46	A1	5p dk grn & org brn	22.00	4.00
OA49	A1	10p dp vio & blk	47.50	11.00
		Nos. OA38-OA49 (7)	232.00	75.75

Regular Issue of 1927-40 Overprinted in Black

Perf. 14, 13½x14

1936-46   **Wmk. 214**

O10	A2	1m dk org & int blk ('46)	2.25	12.50
O11	A2	2m dk brn & dk org ('45)	2.25	8.00
O12	A2	3m green & vio ('37)	2.00	.25
O13	A2	4m brown & green	3.25	4.00
O14	A2	5m blk & ol brn ('40)	3.00	.25
O15	A2	10m blk & car ('46)	.90	.25
O16	A2	15m org brn & ultra ('37)	7.50	.35

Regular Issue of 1927-40 Overprinted in Black

O17	A1	2p org & vio brn ('37)	11.50	.25
O18	A1	3p dk bl & red brn ('46)	5.25	3.00
O19	A1	4p blk & ultra ('46)	22.00	5.50
O20	A1	5p dk grn & org brn	8.50	9.00
O21	A1	6p blk & pale bl ('46)	6.00	7.00
O22	A1	8p blk & pck grn ('46)	4.00	22.50
O23	A1	10p dp vio & blk ('37)	37.50	6.50
O24	A1	20p bl & lt bl ('46)	25.00	32.50
		Nos. O10-O24 (15)	140.90	111.85

SURINAM

ˈsur-ə-ˌnam

(Dutch Guiana)

LOCATION — On the northeast coast of South America, bordering on the Atlantic Ocean
GOVT. — Dutch Colony
AREA — 70,087 sq. mi.
POP. — 370,000 (est. 1984)
CAPITAL — Paramaribo

100 Cents = 1 Gulden (Florin)

Watermark

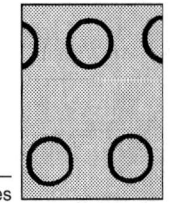

Wmk. 202 — Circles

Early issues of Surinam were sent to the colony without gum. Many of these were subsequently gummed locally.

King William III — A1   Numeral of Value — A2

Perf. 11½, 11½x12, 12½x12, 13½, 14
1873-89   **Typo.**   **Unwmk.**
Without Gum

1	A1	1c lil gray ('85)	2.50	3.00
2	A1	2c yellow ('85)	1.75	1.75
3	A1	2½c rose	1.75	1.75
4	A1	3c green	21.00	18.50
5	A1	5c dull violet	20.00	7.00
6	A1	10c bister	4.00	2.75
7	A1	12½c sl bl ('85)	21.00	8.25
8	A1	15c gray ('89)	25.00	8.25
9	A1	20c green ('89)	37.50	35.00
10	A1	25c grnsh blue	85.00	10.00
11	A1	25c ultra	300.00	25.00
12	A1	30c red brn ('88)	35.00	37.50
13	A1	40c dk brn ('89)	32.50	32.50
14	A1	50c brown org	32.50	21.00
15	A1	1g red brn & gray ('89)	52.50	52.50
16	A1	2.50g grn & org ('79)	80.00	70.00
		Nos. 1-16 (16)	752.00	334.75

Perf. 14, Small Holes

3b	A1	2½c rose	12.00	14.00
4b	A1	3c green	22.00	29.00
5b	A1	5c dull violet	22.00	18.00
6b	A1	10c bister	21.00	25.00
11b	A1	25c ultra	300.00	72.50
14b	A1	50c brown org	57.50	50.00
		Nos. 3b-14b (6)	434.50	208.50

The paper of Nos. 3-6, 11 and 14 sometimes has an accidental bluish tinge of varying strength. During its manufacture a chemical whitener (bluing agent) was added in varying quantities. No particular printing was made on bluish paper.

"Small hole" varieties have the spaces between the holes wider than the diameter of the holes.

Nos. 1-16 and 3b-14b exist with gum.
For surcharges see Nos. 23, 31-35, 39-42.

1890   **Perf. 11½x11, 12½**
Without Gum

17	A2	1c gray	1.90	1.40
18	A2	2c yellow brn	3.00	2.50
19	A2	2½c carmine	2.50	2.00
20	A2	3c green	5.75	4.00
21	A2	5c ultra	27.50	1.50
		Nos. 17-21 (5)	40.65	11.40

Nos. 17-21 exist with gum.
For surcharges see Nos. 63-64.

A3

1892, Aug. 11   **Perf. 10½**
Without Gum

22	A3	2½c black & org	1.90	1.25
a.		First and fifth vertical words have fancy "F"	27.50	17.50
b.		Imperf.	2.50	
c.		As "a," imperf.	32.50	

No. 14 Surcharged in Black

1892, Aug. 1   **Perf. 14**
Without Gum

23	A1	2½c on 50c	250.00	12.00
a.		Perf. 12½x12	375.00	12.00
b.		Perf. 11½x12	425.00	17.50
c.		Double surcharge	375.00	275.00
d.		Perf. 14, small holes	275.00	12.00

Nos. 23-23c were issued without gum.

Queen Wilhelmina — A5

1892-93   **Typo.**   **Perf. 12½**
Without Gum

25	A5	10c bister	42.50	3.25
26	A5	12½c rose lilac	50.00	5.75
27	A5	15c gray	4.00	2.75
28	A5	20c green	4.50	3.25
29	A5	25c blue	10.00	5.75
30	A5	30c red brown	5.75	5.00
		Nos. 25-30 (6)	116.75	25.75

Nos. 25-30 exist with gum.
For surcharges see Nos. 65-66.

Nos. 7-12 Surcharged

1898   **Perf. 11½x12, 12½x12, 13½**
Without Gum

31	A1	10c on 12½c sl bl	27.50	4.00
32	A1	10c on 15c gray	65.00	55.00
33	A1	10c on 20c green	5.25	5.00
34	A1	10c on 25c grnsh bl	11.00	6.25
c.		Perf. 11½x12	12.00	12.00
34A	A1	10c on 25c ultra	575.00	500.00
b.		Perf. 11½x12	675.00	600.00
35	A1	10c on 30c red brn	4.25	4.25
a.		Double surcharge	325.00	

Dangerous counterfeits exist.

Netherlands Nos. 80, 83-84 Surcharged

No. 36   Nos. 37-38

1900, Jan. 8   **Perf. 12½**
Without Gum

36	A11	50c on 50c	27.50	9.00

Engr.
Perf. 11½x11

37	A12	100c on 1g dk grn	25.00	14.00
38	A12	2.50g on 2½g brn lil	25.00	12.50
		Nos. 36-38 (3)	77.50	35.50

For surcharge see No. 67.

Nos. 13-16 Surcharged

Perf. 11½, 11½x12, 12½x12, 14
1900   **Typo.**
Without Gum

39	A1	25c on 40c	5.00	3.50
40	A1	25c on 50c	5.00	3.50
a.		Perf. 14, small holes	130.00	140.00
b.		Perf. 11½x12	3.75	3.75

41	A1	50c on 1g	40.00	35.00
42	A1	50c on 2.50g	150.00	175.00
		Nos. 39-42 (4)	200.00	217.00

Counterfeits of No. 42 exist.

A9

A10

Queen Wilhelmina — A11

1902-08   **Typo.**   **Perf. 12½**
Without Gum

44	A9	½c violet	1.00	.90
45	A9	1c olive grn	2.10	1.25
46	A9	2c yellow brn	11.50	4.50
47	A9	2½c blue grn	5.00	.45
48	A9	3c orange	8.25	5.25
49	A9	5c red	8.25	.45
50	A9	7½c gray ('08)	18.00	8.25
51	A10	10c slate	12.00	.95
52	A10	12½c deep blue	4.50	.45
53	A10	15c dp brown	30.00	10.50
54	A10	20c olive grn	27.50	5.25
55	A10	22½c brn & ol grn	24.00	13.00
56	A10	25c violet	20.00	1.25
57	A10	30c orange brn	47.50	15.00
58	A10	50c lake brown	37.50	9.25

Engr.
Perf. 11

59	A11	1g violet	60.00	20.00
60	A11	2½g slate blue	60.00	65.00
		Nos. 44-60 (17)	377.10	161.70

Nos. 44-60 exist with gum.

A12

1909   **Typeset**   *Serrate Roulette 13½*
Without Gum

61	A12	5c red	13.50	11.50
a.		Tête bêche pair	190.00	175.00

Perf. 11½x10½

62	A12	5c red	14.50	12.00
a.		Tête bêche pair	140.00	140.00

Nos. 17-18, 29-30, 38 Surcharged in Red

Nos. 63-64   Nos. 65-66

No. 67

1911, July 15   **Typo.**   **Perf. 12½**
Without Gum

63	A2	½c on 1c	1.75	1.10
64	A2	½c on 2c	12.25	9.00
65	A5	15c on 25c	75.00	57.50
66	A5	20c on 30c	14.00	9.50

Engr.
Perf. 11½x11

67	A12	30c on 2.50g on 2½g	125.00	110.00
		Nos. 62-67 (5)	660.00	507.10

A13

1912, July   **Typeset**   **Perf. 11½**
Without Gum

70	A13	½c lilac	.95	.95
a.		Horiz. pair, imperf. btwn.	200.00	
71	A13	2½c dk green	.95	.95
a.		Vert. pair, imperf. btwn.	240.00	
72	A13	5c pale red	8.75	8.75
73	A13	12½c deep blue	11.00	11.00
		Nos. 70-73 (4)	21.65	21.65

Numeral of Value — A14

Queen Wilhelmina
A15   A16

1913-31   **Typo.**   **Perf. 12½**

74	A14	½c violet	.40	.25
75	A14	1c olive green	.40	.25
76	A14	1½c blue, perf 11½ ('21)	.40	.25
a.		Perf. 12½ ('32)	1.10	.85
77	A14	2c yellow brn	1.60	1.10
78	A14	2½c green	.95	.25
79	A14	3c yellow	.80	.65
80	A14	3c green ('26)	3.25	2.50
81	A14	4c chlky bl ('26)	8.25	5.00
82	A14	5c rose	1.60	.25
83	A14	5c green ('22)	2.00	1.00
84	A14	5c lilac ('26)	1.60	.25
85	A14	6c bister ('26)	2.75	2.50
86	A14	6c red org ('31)	2.25	.50
87	A14	7½c drab	1.00	.40
a.		Perf. 11x11½	1.40	.65
88	A14	7½c orange ('27)	1.40	.40
89	A14	7½c yellow ('31)	9.25	9.25
90	A14	10c violet ('22)	5.00	5.00
91	A14	10c rose ('26)	4.00	.55
92	A14	10c car rose	1.40	.65
93	A15	12½c blue	1.90	.65
94	A15	12½c red ('22)	2.00	2.25
95	A15	15c olive grn	.55	.70
96	A15	15c lt blue ('26)	7.75	4.75
97	A15	20c green	3.50	3.25
98	A15	20c blue ('22)	2.40	2.00
99	A15	20c ol grn ('26)	3.50	2.75
100	A15	22½c orange	2.50	2.50
101	A15	25c red violet	4.00	.40
102	A15	30c slate	5.00	1.10
103	A15	32½c vio & org ('22)	15.00	17.50
104	A15	35c sl & red ('26)	5.00	5.00

Perf. 11, 11½, 11½x11, 12½
Engr.

105	A16	50c green	4.00	.85
a.		Perf. 12½ ('32)	14.00	1.60
106	A16	1g brown	5.00	.50
a.		Perf. 12½ ('32)	15.00	1.00
107	A16	1½g dp vio ('26)	35.00	35.00
108	A16	2½g carmine ('23)	30.00	26.00
a.		Perf. 11½x11	35.00	32.50
		Nos. 74-108 (35)	175.90	136.20

Nos. 74, 75, 77-79, 82, 87, 105, 106 and 108 were issued both with and without gum. Early printings of Nos. 74-104 had water soluble ink.
For surcharges see Nos. 116-120, 139.

Engr.
Perf. 11½x11

67	A12	30c on 2.50g on 2½g	125.00	110.00

Queen Wilhelmina — A17

1923, Oct. 5   **Perf. 11, 11x11½, 11½**

109	A17	5c green	1.10	.70
110	A17	10c car rose	1.75	1.50
111	A17	20c indigo	3.50	3.00
112	A17	50c brown org	19.00	19.00
113	A17	1g brown vio	26.00	17.00
114	A17	2½g gray blk	75.00	200.00
115	A17	5g brown	100.00	240.00
		Nos. 109-115 (7)	226.35	481.20

25th anniv. of the assumption of the government of the Netherlands by Queen Wilhelmina, at age 18.
Values for Nos. 114-115 used are for stamps with postmarks clearly dated before July 15, 1924.

Nos. 83, 93-94, 98 Surcharged in Black or Red

j   k

m

1925, Dec. 19   **Typo.**   **Perf. 12½**

116	A14	3c on 5c green	1.10	1.10
117	A15	10c on 12½c red	2.25	2.25
118	A15	15c on 12½c blue (R)	1.60	1.60
119	A15	15c on 20c blue	1.60	1.60
		Nos. 116-119 (4)	6.55	6.55

No. 100 Surcharged in Blue

1926, Jan. 1

120	A15	12½c on 22½c org	27.50	27.50

Postage Due Stamps Nos. J14 and J29 Surcharged in Blue or Black

o   p

121	D2(o)	12½c on 40c (Bl)	3.25	3.25
122	D2(p)	12½c on 40c (Bk)	30.00	30.00
		Nos. 120-122 (3)	60.75	60.75

No. 121 issued without gum.

Queen Wilhelmina — A21

1927-30   **Engr.**   **Perf. 11½**

123	A21	10c carmine	1.00	.40
124	A21	12½c red orange	1.75	1.90
125	A21	15c dark blue	2.00	.60
126	A21	20c indigo	2.00	.80
127	A21	21c dk brown ('30)	19.00	19.00
128	A21	22½c brown ('28)	8.00	9.75

129	A21	25c dk violet	3.00	.70
130	A21	30c dk green	3.00	1.10
131	A21	35c black brown	3.00	3.00
		Nos. 123-131 (9)	42.75	37.25

Types of Netherlands Marine Insurance Stamps Inscribed "SURINAME" and Surcharged

1927, Oct. 26

132	MI1	3c on 15c dk grn	.65	.65
133	MI1	10c on 60c car rose	.65	.65
134	MI1	12½c on 75c gray brn	.65	.65
135	MI2	15c on 1.50 dk blue	2.75	2.75
136	MI2	25c on 2.25g org brn	7.25	7.25
137	MI3	30c on 4½g black	9.00	7.25
138	MI3	50c on 7½g red	7.25	7.25
		Nos. 132-138 (7)	28.20	26.45

Nos. 135-137 have "FRANKEERZEGEL" in small capitals in one line. Nos. 135 and 136 have a heavy bar across the top of the stamp.

No. 88 Surcharged

1930, Mar. 1 Typo. Perf. 12½

139	A14	6c on 7½c orange	1.90	1.00

Prince William I (Portrait by Van Key) — A22

1933, Apr. 24 Photo.

141	A22	6c deep orange	6.75	1.90

400th birth anniv. of Prince William I, Count of Nassau and Prince of Orange, frequently referred to as William the Silent.

Van Walbeeck's Ship A23

Queen Wilhelmina A24

1936-41 Litho. Perf. 13½x12½

142	A23	½c yellow brn	.30	.30
143	A23	1c lt yellow grn	.40	.25
144	A23	1½c brt blue	.55	.40
145	A23	2c black brown	.60	.25
146	A23	2½c green	.25	.25
a.		Perf. 13 ('41)	9.00	3.25
147	A23	3c dark ultra	.60	.40
148	A23	4c orange	.60	.75
149	A23	5c gray	.60	.25
150	A23	6c red	2.50	2.00
151	A23	7½c red violet	.25	.25
a.		7½c plum, perf. 13 ('41)	3.00	.25

Engr.
Perf. 14, 12½
Size: 20x30mm

152	A24	10c vermilion	.85	.25
a.		Perf. 12½ ('39)	60.00	11.50
153	A24	12½c dull green	3.50	1.25
154	A24	15c dark blue	1.25	.60
155	A24	20c yellow org	2.10	.60
156	A24	21c dk gray	3.25	3.00
a.		Perf. 12½ ('39)	3.75	3.75
157	A24	25c brown lake	2.40	1.00
158	A24	30c brown vio	3.75	1.00
159	A24	35c olive brown	4.00	4.00

Perf. 12½x14
Size: 22x33mm

160	A24	50c dull yel grn	4.00	2.00
161	A24	1g dull blue	8.25	3.00
162	A24	1.50g black brown	22.50	18.00
163	A24	2.50g rose lake	13.50	9.50
		Nos. 142-163 (22)	76.00	49.30

For surcharges see Nos. 181-183, B37-B40 in Scott Standard catalogue, Vol. 6.

Queen Wilhelmina — A25

Perf. 12½x12
1938, Aug. 30 Photo. Wmk. 202

164	A25	2c dull purple	.50	.30
165	A25	7½c red orange	1.50	1.25
166	A25	15c royal blue	3.00	3.00
		Nos. 164-166 (3)	5.00	4.55

Reign of Queen Wilhelmina, 40th anniv.

SEMI-POSTAL STAMPS

SP1   SP2
Green Cross — SP3

Perf. 12½
1927, Aug. 1 Unwmk. Photo.

B1	SP1	2c (+ 2c) bl blk & grn	1.10	1.00
B2	SP2	5c (+ 3c) vio & grn	1.10	1.00
B3	SP3	10c (+ 3c) ver & grn	2.00	1.75
		Nos. B1-B3 (3)	4.20	3.75
		Set, never hinged		10.50

Surtax was given to the Green Cross Society, which promotes public health services.

Nurse and Patient SP4

Good Samaritan SP5

1928, Dec. 1 Perf. 11½

B4	SP4	1½c (+ 1½c) ultra	4.50	4.50
B5	SP4	2c (+ 2c) bl green	4.50	4.50
B6	SP4	5c (+ 3c) vio	4.50	4.50
B7	SP4	7½c (+ 2½c) ver	4.50	4.50
		Nos. B4-B7 (4)	18.00	18.00
		Set, never hinged		67.50

The surtax on these stamps was for a fund to combat indigenous diseases.

1929, Dec. 1 Perf. 12½

B8	SP5	1½c (+ 1½c) grn	6.75	6.75
B9	SP5	2c (+ 2c) scar	6.75	6.75
B10	SP5	5c (+ 3c) ultra	6.75	6.75
B11	SP5	6c (+ 4c) blk	6.75	6.75
		Nos. B8-B11 (4)	27.00	27.00
		Set, never hinged		72.50

Surtax for the Green Cross Society.

Surinam Mother and Child — SP6

1931, Dec. 14

B12	SP6	1½c (+ 1½c) blk	4.75	4.75
B13	SP6	2c (+ 2c) car rose	4.75	4.75
B14	SP6	5c (+ 3c) ultra	4.75	4.75
B15	SP6	6c (+ 4c) dp grn	4.75	4.75
		Nos. B12-B15 (4)	19.00	19.00
		Set, never hinged		45.00

The surtax was for Child Welfare Societies.

Designs Symbolical of the Creed of the Moravians
SP7   SP8

1935, Aug. 1 Perf. 13x14

B16	SP7	1c (+ ½c) dk brn	6.00	6.00
B17	SP7	2c (+ 1c) dp ultra	6.00	6.00
B18	SP8	3c (+ 1½c) grn	7.50	7.50
B19	SP8	4c (+ 2c) red org	7.50	7.50
B20	SP8	5c (+ 2½c) blk brn	9.00	9.00
B21	SP7	10c (+ 5c) car	9.00	9.00
		Nos. B16-B21 (6)	45.00	45.00
		Set, never hinged		90.00

200th anniv. of the founding of the Moravian Mission in Surinam.

Surinam Child — SP9

1936, Dec. 14 Perf. 12½

B22	SP9	2c (+ 1c) dk grn	2.75	2.75
B23	SP9	3c (+ 1½c) dk bl	2.75	2.75
B24	SP9	5c (+ 2½c) brn blk	4.00	4.00
B25	SP9	10c (+ 5c) lake	4.00	4.00
		Nos. B22-B25 (4)	13.50	13.50
		Set, never hinged		26.50

Surtax for baby food and the Green Cross Society.

"Emancipation" SP10

Surinam Girl SP11

1938, June 1 Litho. Perf. 12½x12

B26	SP10	2½c (+ 2c) dk bl grn	2.40	1.90

Photo.

B27	SP11	3c (+ 2c) vio blk	2.40	1.90
B28	SP11	5c (+ 3c) dk brn	2.60	2.25
B29	SP11	6c (+ 5c) indigo	2.60	2.25
		Nos. B26-B29 (4)	10.00	8.30
		Set, never hinged		20.00

75th anniv. of the abolition of slavery in Surinam. Surtax to Slavery Remembrance Committee.

Creole Woman — SP12
Javanese Woman — SP13

Hindustani Woman — SP14
American Indian Woman — SP15

1940, Jan. 8 Engr. Perf. 13x14

B30	SP12	2½c (+ 2c) dk grn	3.00	3.00
B31	SP13	3c (+ 2c) red org	3.00	3.00
B32	SP14	40c dp bl	3.00	3.00
B33	SP15	7½c (+ 5c) henna brn	3.00	3.00
		Nos. B30-B33 (4)	12.00	12.00
		Set, never hinged		25.00

Surtax to leper care and baby food.

AIR POST STAMPS

Allegory of Flight — AP1

Perf. 12½
1930, Sept. 3 Unwmk. Engr.

C1	AP1	10c dull red	3.75	.50
C2	AP1	15c ultra	3.75	.75
C3	AP1	20c dull green	.25	.25
C4	AP1	40c orange	.25	.35
C5	AP1	60c brown violet	.55	.40
C6	AP1	1g gray black	1.60	1.75
C7	AP1	1½g deep brown	1.75	1.90
		Nos. C1-C7 (7)	11.90	5.90

Nos. C1-C7 Overprinted in Black or Red

1931, Aug. 8

C8	AP1	10c red (Bk)	19.00	15.00
a.		Double overprint	425.00	
C9	AP1	15c ultra (Bk)	19.00	15.00
C10	AP1	20c dull grn (R)	19.00	15.00
C11	AP1	40c orange (Bk)	29.00	22.50
a.		Double overprint	425.00	
C12	AP1	60c brn vio (R)	62.50	52.50
C13	AP1	1g gray blk (R)	72.50	65.00
C14	AP1	1½g deep brn (Bk)	72.50	67.50
		Nos. C8-C14 (7)	293.50	252.50

The variety with period omitted after "Do" occurs twice on each sheet.
Warning: The red overprint may dissolve in water.

POSTAGE DUE STAMPS

D1   D2

Type I — 34 loops. "T" of "BETALEN" over center of loop; top branch of "E" of "TE" shorter than lower branch.
Type II — 33 loops. "T" of "BETALEN" over space between two loops.
Type III — 32 loops. "T" of "BETALEN" over slightly to the left of center of loop; top branch of first "E" of "BETALEN" shorter than lower branch.
Type IV — 37 loops and letters of "PORT" larger than in the other 3 types.

Value in Black
Perf. 12½x12

1886-88		**Typo.**		**Unwmk.**
		Type III		
J1	D1	2½c lilac	3.00	3.00
J2	D1	5c lilac	9.00	9.00
J3	D1	10c lilac	100.00	65.00
J4	D1	20c lilac	9.00	9.00
J5	D1	25c lilac	12.50	12.50
J6	D1	30c lilac ('88)	2.50	2.50
J7	D1	40c lilac	6.00	6.00
J8	D1	50c lilac ('88)	3.00	3.00
	Nos. J1-J8 (8)		145.00	110.00
		Type I		
J1a	D1	2½c	6.00	6.00
J2a	D1	5c	11.00	11.00
J3a	D1	10c	125.00	90.00
J4a	D1	20c	22.50	22.50
J5a	D1	25c	19.00	19.00
J6a	D1	30c	22.50	22.50
J7a	D1	40c	12.50	12.50
J8a	D1	50c	4.00	4.00
	Nos. J1a-J8a (8)		222.50	187.50
		Type II		
J1b	D1	2½c	5.00	5.00
J2b	D1	5c	10.00	10.00
J3b	D1	10c	1,250.	1,250.
J4b	D1	20c	9.00	9.00
J5b	D1	25c	300.00	300.00
J6b	D1	30c	75.00	75.00
J7b	D1	40c	350.00	350.00
J8b	D1	50c	5.00	5.00
		Type IV		
J3c	D1	10c	350.00	250.00
J5c	D1	25c	160.00	150.00
J7c	D1	40c	150.00	150.00
	Nos. J3c-J7c (3)		660.00	550.00

Nos. J1-J16 were issued without gum. For surcharges, see Nos. J15-J16.

1892-96	**Value in Black**		**Perf. 12½**	
		Type III		
J9	D2	2½c lilac	.40	.40
J10	D2	5c lilac	1.25	1.00
J11	D2	10c lilac	24.00	22.50
J12	D2	20c lilac	2.50	2.25
J13	D2	25c lilac	10.00	10.00
		Type I		
J9a	D2	2½c	.40	.40
J10a	D2	5c	2.00	2.00
J11a	D2	10c	24.00	20.00
J12a	D2	20c	5.00	5.00
J13a	D2	25c	13.00	12.50
J14	D2	40c ('96)	3.25	4.50
		Type II		
J9b	D2	2½c	.80	.80
J10b	D2	5c	3.00	3.00
J11b	D2	10c	40.00	42.50
J12b	D2	20c	90.00	90.00
J13b	D2	25c	100.00	100.00

For surcharges, see Nos. 121-122.

Stamps of 1888
Surcharged in Red

1911, July 15				
J15	D1	10c on 30c lil (III)	80.00	80.00
a.	10c on 30c lilac (I)		200.00	225.00
b.	10c on 30c lilac (II)		1,800.	1,800.
J16	D1	10c on 50c lil (III)	110.00	110.00
a.	10c on 50c lilac (I)		115.00	115.00
b.	10c on 50c lilac (II)		115.00	115.00

D3

Type I
Value in Color of Stamp

1913-31		**Perf. 12½, 13½x12½**		
J17	D2	½c lilac ('30)	.25	.25
J18	D2	1c lilac ('31)	.25	.35
J19	D2	2c lilac ('31)	.25	.25
J20	D2	2½c lilac	.25	.25
J21	D2	5c lilac	.25	.25
J22	D2	10c lilac	.25	.25

J23	D2	12c lilac ('31)	.25	.25
J24	D2	12½c lilac ('22)	.25	.25
J25	D2	15c lilac ('26)	.55	.45
J26	D2	20c lilac	.85	.45
J27	D2	25c lilac	.45	.25
J28	D2	30c lilac ('26)	.45	.60
J29	D2	40c lilac ('26)		
J30	D2	50c lilac ('26)	1.25	1.25
J31	D2	75c lilac ('26)	1.50	1.50
J32	D3	1g lilac ('26)	1.75	1.50
	Nos. J17-J32 (16)		23.30	22.10

SWAZILAND

ˈswä-zē-ˌland

LOCATION — Southeast Africa bordered by the Transvaal and Zululand in South Africa and by Mozambique
GOVT. — Constitutional monarchy
AREA — 6,705 sq. mi.
POP. — 626,000 (est. 1984)
CAPITAL — Mbabane

An independent state in the 19th century, Swaziland was administered by Transvaal from 1894 to 1906, when the administration was transferred to the British High Commissioner for South Africa. In 1934 Swaziland and Bechuanaland Protectorate came under the administration of the British High Commissioner for Basutoland. The issuing of individual postage stamps had been resumed in 1933.

12 Pence = 1 Shilling
20 Shillings = 1 Pound

> **Catalogue values for unused stamps in this country are for Never Hinged items, beginning with Scott 38 in the regular postage section.**

Coat of Arms — A1   George V — A2

Black Overprint

1889	**Unwmk.**	**Perf. 12½, 12½x12**		
1	A1	½p gray	10.50	24.00
a.	Inverted overprint		1,250.	750.00
b.	"Swazielan"		1,800.	1,000.
c.	As "b," inverted overprint			7,500.
2	A1	1p rose	24.00	24.00
a.	Inverted overprint		800.00	750.00
3	A1	2p olive bister	32.50	18.00
a.	Inverted overprint		950.00	750.00
b.	"Swazielan"		550.00	475.00
c.	Perf. 12½x12		100.00	37.50
d.	As "c," "Swazielan"		1,250.	725.00
e.	As "d," inverted overprint			1,400.
f.	As "b," inverted overprint		7,500.	5,000.
g.	Double overprint		2,600.	
4	A1	6p gray blue	40.00	55.00
a.	Inverted overprint		1,100.	525.00
5	A1	1sh green	17.00	16.00
a.	Inverted overprint		1,100.	525.00
6	A1	2sh6p yellow	325.00	450.00
7	A1	5sh slate	175.00	275.00
a.	Inverted overprint		1,900.	3,000.
b.	"Swazielan"		5,250.	
c.	As "b," inverted overprint		5,750.	
8	A1	10sh lt brown	6,500.	4,000.

1892		**Red Overprint**		
9	A1	½p gray	8.50	19.00
a.	Inverted overprint		575.00	
b.	Double overprint		525.00	525.00
c.	Pair, one without overprint		2,000.	

Beware of counterfeits.
Reprints have a period after "Swazieland."

Stamps of Swaziland were replaced by those of Transvaal in 1895. Swaziland issues were resumed in 1933.

		Perf. 14		
1933, Jan. 2		**Engr.**		**Wmk. 4**
10	A2	½p green	.40	.35
11	A2	1p carmine	.40	.25
12	A2	2p lt brown	.40	.50
13	A2	3p ultra	.55	3.00
14	A2	4p orange	3.50	3.50
15	A2	6p rose violet	1.60	1.10
16	A2	1sh olive green	1.90	3.25

17	A2	2sh6p violet	19.00	25.00
18	A2	5sh gray	37.50	57.50
19	A2	10sh black brown	100.00	140.00
	Nos. 10-19 (10)		165.25	234.45
	Set, never hinged		475.00	

Common Design Types
pictured following the introduction.

Silver Jubilee Issue
Common Design Type

1935, May 4		**Perf. 11x12**		
20	CD301	1p carmine & blue	.55	2.00
21	CD301	2p black & ultra	1.75	2.00
22	CD301	3p ultra & brown	1.00	6.00
23	CD301	6p brown, vio & ind	2.75	3.00
	Nos. 20-23 (4)		6.05	13.00
	Set, never hinged		8.75	

Coronation Issue
Common Design Type

1937, May 12		**Perf. 11x11½**		
24	CD302	1p dark carmine	.35	.95
25	CD302	2p brown	.35	.25
26	CD302	3p deep ultra	.35	.55
	Nos. 24-26 (3)		1.05	1.75
	Set, never hinged		1.75	

George VI — A3

1938, Apr. 1		**Perf. 13, 13x13½**		
27	A3	½p green	.25	1.25
28	A3	1p rose carmine	.60	1.25
29	A3	1½p light blue	.30	.85
a.	Perf. 14 ('42)		1.60	1.25
	Never hinged		3.25	
30	A3	2p brown	.30	.45
31	A3	3p ultra	4.50	1.75
32	A3	4p red orange	.60	1.40
33	A3	6p rose violet	2.75	1.50
34	A3	1sh olive green	.75	.75
35	A3	2sh6p dark violet	12.50	4.00
36	A3	5sh gray	25.00	19.00
37	A3	10sh black brown	5.50	7.00
	Nos. 27-37 (11)		53.05	39.20
	Set, never hinged		85.00	

> **Catalogue values for unused stamps in this section, from this point to the end of the section, are for Never Hinged items.**

Peace Issue

South Africa,
Nos. 100-102
Overprinted

Basic stamps inscribed alternately in English and Afrikaans.

1945, Dec. 3		**Wmk. 201**	**Perf. 14**	
38	A42	1p rose pink & choc, pair	.80	1.25
a.	Single, English		.25	.25
b.	Single, Afrikaans		.25	.25
39	A43	2p vio & sl blue, pair	.80	1.25
a.	Single, English		.25	.25
b.	Single, Afrikaans		.25	.25
40	A43	3p ultra & dp ultra, pair	.80	3.00
a.	Single, English		.25	.25
b.	Single, Afrikaans		.25	.25
	Nos. 38-40 (3)		2.40	5.50

World War II victory of the Allies.

Royal Visit Issue
Type of Basutoland, 1947
Perf. 12½

1947, Feb. 17		**Wmk. 4**	**Engr.**	
44	A3	1p red	.25	.25
45	A4	2p green	.25	.25
46	A5	3p ultramarine	.25	.25
47	A6	1sh dark violet	.25	.25
	Nos. 44-47 (4)		1.00	1.00

Visit of the British Royal Family, 3/25/47.

Silver Wedding Issue
Common Design Types

1948, Dec. 1		**Photo.**	**Perf. 14x14½**	
48	CD304	1½p bright ultra	.30	.25

Perf. 11½x11
Engraved; Name Typographed

49	CD305	10sh violet brown	40.00	47.50

UPU Issue
Common Design Types
Engr.; Name Typo. on 3p, 6p
Perf. 13½, 11x11½

1949, Oct. 10			**Wmk. 4**	
50	CD306	1½p blue	.30	.25
51	CD307	3p indigo	1.60	2.00
52	CD308	6p red lilac	.40	1.75
53	CD309	1sh olive	.50	.65
	Nos. 50-53 (4)		2.80	4.65

POSTAGE DUE STAMPS

> **Catalogue values for unused stamps in this section are for Never Hinged items.**

D1

1933		**Typo.** **Wmk. 4**	**Perf. 14**	
J1	D1	1p carmine rose	4.00	17.50
	On cover			175.00
a.	Wmk. 4a (error)		275.00	
J2	D1	2p violet	12.00	35.00
	On cover			225.00

Value, Nos. J1-J2 hinged $6.
On cover values are for properly franked commercial covers. Philatelic usages sell for less.

SWEDEN

'swē-dᵊn

LOCATION — Northern Europe, occupying the eastern half of the Scandinavian Peninsula
GOVT. — Constitutional Monarchy
AREA — 173,341 sq. mi.
POP. — 8,330,577 (est. 1983)
CAPITAL — Stockholm

48 skilling banco = 1 rixdaler banco (until 1858)
100 öre = 1 rixdaler (1858 to 1874)
100 öre = 1 krona (since 1874)

Watermarks

Wmk. 180 — Crown

Wmk. 181 — Wavy Lines

Values for unused stamps are for examples with original gum as defined in the catalogue introduction except Nos. 1-5, excluding reprints, and LX1 which are valued without gum.

Coat of Arms
A1   A2

1855   Unwmk.   Typo.   Perf. 14

1	A1	3s blue green, thin paper		10,000.	5,000.
		On cover			35,000.
a.		3s orange (error)			3,000,000.
b.		3s pale bluish green, thin paper		8,000.	4,000.
		On cover			35,000.
2	A1	4s lt blue, thin paper		1,600.	110.00
		On cover			110.00
a.		4s blue, thin paper		1,550.	80.00
		On cover			90.00
b.		4s bright blue, dense background, thin paper		2,250.	180.00
		On cover			350.00
c.		4s dull blue, dense background, thick paper		5,350.	200.00
		On cover			400.00
d.		4s bright blue, dense background, thick paper ('56)		—	250.00
		On cover			400.00
e.		4s grayish ultramarine, thick paper ('57)		—	300.00
		On cover			450.00
f.		4s dark grayish ultramarine, thick paper ('57)		1,200.	700.00
		On cover			3,000.
g.		4s turquoise, blurred print, thick paper ('57)		1,200.	1,500.
		On cover			6,000.
h.		4s greenish blue, thick paper ('57)		1,550.	120.00
		On cover			130.00
i.		4s blue, clear print, thick paper ('58)		1,550.	80.00
		On cover			100.00
3	A1	6s gray, thin paper		10,000.	1,600.
		On cover			9,700.
a.		6s gray black, thin paper			4,450.
b.		6s pale gray, thin paper		9,450.	1,450.
		On cover			9,850.
c.		6s gray brown ('56)		2,200.	2,650.
		On cover			11,000.

d.		6s brownish gray, thick paper ('58)		10,000.	1,350.
		On cover			—
e.		6s gray brown, thick paper ('58)			1,450.
		On cover			10,000.
f.		Imperf.			
4	A1	8s red orange, thin paper		5,500.	650.00
		On cover			1,000.
a.		8s brownish orange, thin paper ('56)		5,200.	700.00
		On cover			1,150.
b.		8s lemon yellow, greenish, thin paper ('56)		1,150.	2,300.
		On cover			2,300.
c.		8s bright yellow, thin paper ('56)		2,300.	1,150.
		On cover			2,300.
d.		8s dull olive yellow, thin paper ('56)		—	1,050.
		On cover			—
e.		8s yellow orange, thick paper ('57)		5,200.	575.00
		On cover			1,350.
f.		8s orange yellow, blurred print, thick paper ('57)		1,150.	925.00
		On cover			1,700.
g.		8s orange yellow, clear print, thick paper ('58)			650.00
		On cover			—
h.		Imperf.			5,750.
5	A1	24s dull red, thin paper		8,750.	2,200.
		On cover			10,000.
a.		24s orange red, thin paper ('56)		8,000.	2,100.
		On cover			10,000.
b.		24s brick red, thick paper ('57)		1,150.	2,000.
		On cover			10,000.
c.		24s light orange red, thick paper ('57)		2,350.	2,200.
		On cover			10,000.
d.		24s brownish red, blurred print, thick paper ('58)			2,900.
		On cover			10,500.

Nos. 1-5 were reprinted from new blocks in 1868 (twice), 1871 (No. 1 only) and 1885. These later printings were made after Nos. 1-5 were withdrawn, but before being demonetized, and were valid for postal use until 1910. The post office did not distinguish between these re-issues and earlier printings, although most saw little, if any, postal use.

Distinguishing characteristics of Reprints: 3s, a white dot or short white line right of the "I" in "SKILLING": a short colored line between the "F" and "R" of left "FRIMARKE." **4s**, "E" in left "FRIMARKE." broken at bottom, so that letter resembles an "F"; **6s**, most reprints have a small white dot in front of "S" in "SEX"; all reprints differ in shade of color, having a lilac cast that does not appear in the original printings; **8s**, no distinguishing characteristic, but most reprints reveal small defects in the plate, when compared to original printings; **24s**, "E" in right "FRIMARKE" broken at bottom.

Re-issue

1868   Perf. 14

First Printing

1p	A1	3s yel grn, thin background		525.00
		Never Hinged		925.00
2p	A1	4s blue, thin background		525.00
		Never Hinged		925.00
3p	A1	6s br gray, thin background		525.00
		Never Hinged		925.00
4p	A1	8s orange, dense background		525.00
		Never Hinged		925.00
5p	A1	24s dark red, thin background		525.00
		Never Hinged		925.00

Second Printing

1q	A1	3s green, dense background		460.00	925.00
		Never Hinged		925.00	
2q	A1	4s lt blue, thin background		460.00	925.00
		Never Hinged		925.00	
3q	A1	6s lilac, dense background		460.00	925.00
		Never Hinged		925.00	
4q	A1	8s yellow orange, dense background		460.00	925.00
		Never Hinged		925.00	
5q	A1	24s orange red, dense background		460.00	925.00
		Never Hinged		925.00	

1871   Perf. 14

1r	A1	3s lt yel green, dense background		800.00
		Never Hinged		1,400.

1885   Perf. 13

1s	A1	3s green		300.00
		Never Hinged		460.00
2s	A1	4s blue		300.00
		Never Hinged		460.00

3s	A1	6s gray		300.00
		Never Hinged		460.00
4s	A1	8s orange		300.00
		Never Hinged		460.00
5s	A1	24s red		300.00
		Never Hinged		460.00

1858-62   Perf. 14

6	A2	5o green		210.00	20.00
		On cover			200.00
a.		5o deep green		575.00	250.00
		On cover			575.00
7	A2	9o violet		425.00	275.00
		On cover			900.00
a.		9o red lilac		625.00	325.00
		On cover			1,200.
b.		9o bluish lilac		425.00	310.00
		On cover			900.00
c.		9o blue violet ('64-'72)		425.00	275.00
		On cover			900.00
8	A2	12o blue		225.00	2.00
		On cover			6.00
a.		12o greenish dark blue		790.00	35.00
		On cover			100.00
9	A2	12o ultra ('61)		450.00	12.50
		On cover			19.00
10	A2	24o orange		500.00	35.00
		On cover			70.00
a.		24o yellow		750.00	62.50
		On cover			85.00
b.		24o dark orange ('58-'60)		525.00	57.50
		On cover			175.00
11	A2	30o brown		500.00	35.00
		On cover			225.00
a.		30o dark red brown		750.00	87.50
		On cover			350.00
b.		30o rose red brown ('60-'62)		2,350.	72.50
		On cover			375.00
12	A2	50o rose		600.00	110.00
		On cover			550.00
a.		50o carmine		750.00	110.00
		On cover			625.00
b.		50o bright dark carmine ('61-'64)		750.00	110.00
		On cover			660.00
		Nos. 6-12 (7)		2,910.	489.50

Nos. 6 and 8 exist with double impressions. No. 8 is known printed on both sides. No. 11 exists imperf.

Re-issue

1885   Perf. 13

6s	A2	5o green		110.00
		Never Hinged		175.00
7s	A2	9o violet		110.00
		Never Hinged		175.00
8s	A2	12o blue		110.00
		Never Hinged		175.00
10s	A2	24o orange		110.00
		Never Hinged		175.00
11s	A2	30o brown		110.00
		Never Hinged		175.00
12s	A2	50o rose		110.00
		Never Hinged		175.00

Nos. 6s-12s were reprinted from new blocks. The post office did not distinguish between this re-issue and original printings, which were valid for postage until Dec. 30, 1910, but used examples of the re-issue are not known.

These values were also reprinted in 1963, perf. 13½, with lines in stamp color crossing denominations, and affixed to book page. Value $12.50 each.

Lion and Arms
A3   A4

Type I   Type II

1862-69

3 Ore:
Type I — The horizontal inner frameline in the upper right corner extends beyond the curved spiral.
Type II — The horizontal inner frameline in the upper right corner does not extend beyond the curved spiral.

13	A3	3o bister brown, type II ('63)		275.00	16.00
		On cover			35.00
a.		Printed on both sides, type II			3,700.
b.		3o brown, type I		925.00	675.00
		On cover			725.00
c.		3o orange brown, type I ('62)		975.00	725.00
		On cover			850.00
d.		3o olive gray brown, type II ('63)		500.00	200.00
		On cover			450.00

14	A4	17o red violet ('66)		800.00	160.00
		On cover			600.00
a.		17o bluish red lilac ('66)		800.00	130.00
		On cover			500.00
15	A4	17o gray ('69)		850.00	800.00
		On cover			16,000.
16	A4	20o vermilion ('66)		300.00	20.00
		On cover			180.00
a.		20o brownish orange red ('66)		310.00	35.00
		On cover			475.00
		Nos. 13-16 (4)		2,225.	996.00

Re-issue

1885   Perf. 13

13s	A3	3o bister brown, type II		97.50
		Never Hinged		175.00
14s	A4	17o red violet		125.00
		Never Hinged		225.00
16s	A4	20o red		95.00
		Never Hinged		165.00

Nos. 13s-16s were reprinted from new blocks. The post office did not distinguish between this re-issue and original printings, which were valid for postage until Dec. 30, 1910, but used examples of the re-issue are not known.

Numeral of Value — A5   Coat of Arms — A6

1872-77   Perf. 14

17	A5	3o bister brown		80.00	10.00
		On cover			32.50
18	A5	4o gray ('76)		525.00	170.00
		On cover			700.00
19	A5	5o blue green		400.00	5.00
		On cover			200.00
a.		5o emerald		500.00	25.00
		On cover			450.00
20	A5	6o violet		400.00	50.00
		On cover			55.00
a.		6o dark violet		1,250.	310.00
		On cover			55.00
21	A5	6o gray ('74)		1,100.	95.00
		On cover			140.00
22	A5	12o blue		250.00	1.00
		On cover			5.00
23	A5	20o vermilion		1,000.	1.00
		On cover			67.50
a.		20o pale org ('75)		3,500.	55.00
		On cover			675.00
b.		Double impression, dull yel & ver ('76)		4,000.	55.00
		On cover			350.00
24	A5	24o orange		1,000.	42.50
		On cover			72.50
a.		24o yellow		1,000.	42.50
		On cover			72.50
25	A5	30o pale brown		875.00	11.00
		On cover			115.00
a.		30o black brown		875.00	14.00
		On cover			120.00
26	A5	50o rose		925.00	50.00
		On cover			400.00
a.		50o carmine		1,000.	50.00
		On cover			400.00
27	A6	1rd bister & blue		1,150.	95.00
		On cover			2,850.
a.		1rd bister & ultra		1,150.	95.00
		On cover			2,850.
		Nos. 17-27 (11)		7,705.	538.50

1877-79   Perf. 13

28	A5	3o yellow brown		125.00	6.00
		On cover			19.00
29	A5	4o gray ('79)		240.00	3.50
		On cover			19.00
30	A5	5o dark green		150.00	1.00
		On cover			22.50
31	A5	6o lilac		175.00	5.00
		On cover			32.50
a.		6o red lilac		375.00	14.00
		On cover			37.50
32	A5	12o blue		35.00	1.00
		On cover			4.00
33	A5	20o vermilion		275.00	1.00
		On cover			30.00
a.		"TRETIO" instead of "TJUGO" ('79)		12,000.	7,500.
		On cover			18,000.
34	A5	24o orange ('78)		75.00	30.00
		On cover			80.00
a.		24o lemon yellow ('83)		625.00	55.00
		On cover			300.00
35	A5	30o pale brown		450.00	2.00
		On cover			26.00
a.		30o black brown		875.00	3.00
		On cover			37.50
36	A5	50o carmine ('78)		325.00	9.00
		On cover			82.50
37	A6	1rd bister & blue		2,400.	500.00
		On cover			8,000.
s.		1rd yel brn & dk blue ('85)		400.00	
		Never Hinged		625.00	
38	A6	1k bister & bl ('78)		625.00	20.00
		On cover			310.00
		Nos. 28-36,38 (10)		2,475.	78.50

Imperf., Pairs

28a	A5	3o		1,000.
29a	A5	4o		1,000.
30a	A5	5o		1,000.

31b	A5	6o	1,000.	
32a	A5	12o	1,000.	
33b	A5	20o	1,000.	
34b	A5	24o	1,000.	
35b	A5	30o	1,000.	4,000.
36a	A5	50o	1,000.	
38a	A6	1k	1,000.	

See Nos. 40,41,46,49. For surcharge see Nos. B1-B10, B22-B31.

No. 37s was a postally valid re-issue, printed from new blocks. It is not known used.

King Oscar II — A7

1885   **Typo.**

39	A7	10o dull rose	225.00	1.00
		On cover		7.50
a.		Imperf., pair	2,500.	

Numeral Type with Post Horn on Back

1886-91

40	A5	2o orange ('91)	2.50	8.00
		On cover		42.50
a.		Period before "FRIMARKE"	12.00	22.50
b.		Imperf., pair	725.00	
41	A5	3o yellow brn ('87)	15.00	25.00
		On cover		100.00
42	A5	4o gray	30.00	2.00
		On cover		12.50
43	A5	5o green	62.50	1.00
		On cover		9.50
44	A5	6o red lilac ('88)	30.00	62.50
		On cover		125.00
a.		6o violet	35.00	62.50
		On cover		125.00
45	A7	10o pink	87.50	.50
		On cover		3.75
a.		10o rose	87.50	.25
		On cover		3.75
b.		Imperf.		3,250.
46	A5	20o vermilion	125.00	1.00
		On cover		9.50
47	A5	30o pale brown	210.00	2.00
		On cover		9.50
48	A5	50o rose	190.00	5.00
		On cover		75.00
49	A6	1k bister & dk bl	100.00	3.00
		On cover		50.00
a.		Imperf., pair	700.00	
		Nos. 40-49 (10)	852.50	110.00

Nos. 32, 34 with Blue Surcharge

1889, Oct. 1

50	A5	10o on 12o blue	3.75	5.00
		On cover		32.50
51	A5	10o on 24o orange	11.00	50.00
		On cover		90.00

A9

King Oscar II
A10   A11

Wmk. 180

1891-1904   **Typo.**   **Perf. 13**

52	A9	1o brown & ultra ('92)	1.40	.65
		On cover		2.50
53	A9	2o blue & yellow org	3.25	.40
		On cover		2.00
54	A9	3o brown & orange ('92)	.60	1.75
		On cover		3.50
55	A9	4o carmine & ultra ('92)	4.75	.50
		On cover		1.20

Engr.

56	A10	5o yellow green	2.75	.30
		On cover		.50
a.		5o blue green	11.50	.30
		On cover		.50
d.		5o brown (error)	7,500.	—
e.		Booklet pane of 6	140.00	

57	A10	8o red violet ('03)	3.25	1.25
		On cover		12.50
58	A10	10o carmine	4.50	.30
		On cover		.50
c.		Booklet pane of 6	240.00	
59	A10	15o red brown ('00)	27.50	.50
		On cover		3.00
60	A10	20o blue	28.00	.40
		On cover		3.00
b.		20o ultramarine	37.50	.50
		On cover		6.00
61	A10	25o red orange ('96)	37.50	.50
		On cover		4.00
62	A10	30o brown	55.00	.40
		On cover		3.00
63	A10	50o slate	125.00	.85
		On cover		5.50
64	A10	50o olive gray ('04)	100.00	.85
		On cover		5.50
65	A11	1k car & sl ('00)	175.00	2.25
		On cover		25.00
		Nos. 52-65 (14)	568.50	10.90

Imperf., Pairs

52a	A9	1o	87.50
53a	A9	2o	325.00
54a	A9	3o	325.00
55a	A9	4o	325.00
56b		No. 56	85.00
c.		No. 56a	300.00
57a	A10	8o	500.00
58a	A10	10o	52.50
59a	A10	15o	500.00
60a	A10	20o	150.00
61a	A10	25o	600.00
62a	A10	30o	600.00
63a	A10	50o	650.00
64a	A10	50o	500.00
65a	A11	1k	625.00

No. 56d may be a color proof.

A booklet pane of 6 invalid stamps similar to No. 56 but with engraved lines through the denominations was released in 2004 to commemorate the 100th anniversary of the first Swedish booklet. This booklet pane is unwatermarked.

See Nos. 75-76.

Stockholm Post Office — A12

1903, Oct. 26

66	A12	5k blue	240.00	27.50
a.		Imperf., pair	3,000.	

Opening of the new General Post Office at Stockholm.
For surcharge see No. B11.

Arms — A13   Gustaf V — A14

Perf. 13, 13x13½

1910-14   **Typo.**   **Wmk. 180**

67	A13	1o black ('11)	.65	1.50
68	A13	2o orange	1.75	4.00
69	A13	4o violet	2.50	1.10

Engr.

70	A14	5o green ('11)	14.00	29.00
71	A14	10o carmine	10.00	.50
72	A14	1k black, yel ('11)	95.00	.50
73	A14	5k claret, yel ('14)	2.00	3.00
		Nos. 67-73 (7)	125.90	39.60

See #77-98. For surcharges see #99-104, Q1-Q2.

1911   **Unwmk.**

75	A10	20o blue	22.50	15.00
76	A10	25o red orange	27.50	4.00

1910-19

77	A14	5o green ('11)	3.00	.30
a.		Booklet pane of 10	225.00	
b.		Booklet pane of 4	125.00	
78	A14	7o gray grn ('18)	.30	.30
a.		Booklet pane of 10	8.75	
79	A14	8o magenta ('12)	.30	.30

80	A14	10o carmine ('10)	2.50	.30
a.		Booklet pane of 10	225.00	
b.		Booklet pane of 4	125.00	
81	A14	12o rose lake ('18)	.30	.30
a.		Booklet pane of 10	6.70	
82	A14	15o red brown ('11)	6.50	.30
a.		Booklet pane of 10	325.00	
83	A14	20o deep blue ('11)	9.50	.30
a.		Booklet pane of 10	350.00	
84	A14	25o orange red ('11)	.30	.30
85	A14	27o pale blue ('18)	.40	.90
86	A14	30o claret brn ('11)	20.00	.30
87	A14	35o dk violet ('11)	17.00	.30
88	A14	40o olive green ('17)	25.00	.30
89	A14	50o gray ('12)	50.00	.30
90	A14	55o pale blue ('18)	2,100.	6,500.
91	A14	65o pale ol grn ('18)	.65	2.00
92	A14	80o black ('18)	2,100.	6,500.
93	A14	90o gray green ('18)	.60	.65
94	A14	1k black, yel ('19)	92.50	.30
		Nos. 77-89,91,93-94 (16)	228.85	7.45

Excellent forgeries of Nos. 90 and 92 exist.

1911-19   **Typo.**   **Wmk. 181**   **Perf. 13**

95	A13	1o black	.30	.30
96	A13	2o orange	.30	.30
97	A13	3o pale brown ('19)	.30	.30
98	A13	4o pale violet	.30	.30
		Nos. 95-98 (4)	1.20	1.20

Remainders of Nos. 95-98 received various private overprints, mostly as publicity for stamp exhibitions. They were not postally valid.

Unwatermarked Stamps with Watermarks

Stamps of these and later issues through the UPU Congress issue of 1924, are frequently found with watermark showing parts of the words "Kungl Postverket" in double-lined capitals. This watermark is normally located in the margins of the sheets of unwatermarked paper or paper watermarked wavy lines or crown.

Nos. 80, 84, 91, 90, 92 Surcharged

a   b

1918   **Unwmk.**

99	A14(a)	7o on 10o	.30	.40
100	A14(b)	12o on 25o	1.90	.40
a.		Inverted surcharge	625.00	1,200.
101	A14(a)	12o on 65o	.85	1.40
102	A14(a)	27o on 55o	.75	1.60
103	A14(a)	27o on 65o	1.40	3.50
104	A14(a)	27o on 80o	.85	1.60
		Nos. 99-104 (6)	6.05	8.90

Arms A15   Heraldic Lion Supporting Arms of Sweden A16

Two types each of 5o green, 5o copper red and 10o violet, type A16.

Perf. 10 Vertically

1920-25   **Engr.**   **Unwmk.**

115	A15	3o copper red	.30	.40
116	A16	5o green ('25)	4.00	.40
117	A16	5o copper red ('21)	5.00	.40
118	A16	10o green ('21)	21.00	.40
a.		Tête bêche pair	1,650.	3,250.
119	A16	10o violet ('25)	5.25	.40
120	A16	25o orange ('21)	13.00	.40
121	A16	30o brown	.45	.45

Wmk. 181

122	A16	5o green	2.50	1.30
123	A16	5o copper red ('21)	8.25	1.00
124	A16	10o green ('21)	2.50	1.30
		Nos. 115-125 (11)	70.50	24.45

Coil Stamps

Unless part of a booklet pane any stamp perforated only horizontally or vertically is a coil stamp.

1920-26   **Unwmk.**   **Perf. 10**

126	A16	5o green	4.00	1.00
a.		Booklet pane of 10	80.00	
127	A16	10o green ('21)	11.50	3.50
a.		Booklet pane of 10	225.00	
128	A16	10o violet ('25)	6.50	.85
a.		Booklet pane of 10	180.00	
129	A16	30o brown	32.50	4.00

Wmk. 181

130	A16	5o green	11.50	30.00
131	A16	10o green ('21)	45.00	100.00
a.		Booklet pane of 10	425.00	

Perf. 13 Vertically

Unwmk.

132	A16	5o green ('25)	4.00	1.50
133	A16	5o copper red ('21)	325.00	160.00
134	A16	10o violet ('26)	25.00	37.50

Wmk. 181

135	A16	5o green ('25)	2.00	8.00
136	A16	5o copper red ('22)	2.00	7.00
137	A16	10o green ('24)	9.00	40.00
138	A16	10o violet ('25)	8.00	25.00
		Nos. 126-138 (13)	486.00	418.35

The paper used for the earlier printings of types A16, A17, A18, A18a and A20 is usually tinted by the color of the stamp. Printings of 1934 and later are on white paper in slightly different shades.

King Gustaf V — A17

1920-21   **Unwmk.**   **Perf. 10 Vertically**

139	A17	10o rose	30.00	.40
140	A17	15o claret	.30	.45
141	A17	20o blue	35.00	.50

Perf. 10

142	A17	10o rose	12.50	6.00
143	A17	20o blue ('21)	29.00	11.00
a.		Booklet pane of 10	550.00	
		Nos. 139-143 (5)	106.80	18.35

Wmk. 181

144	A17	20o blue	4,000.	

A18

Crown and Post Horn — A18a

See note after No. 138 regarding paper. There are 2 types of the 35, 40, 45 and 60o.

1920-34   **Unwmk.**   **Perf. 10 Vert.**

145	A18	35o yellow ('22)	42.50	.75
146	A18	40o olive green	32.50	.75
147	A18	45o brown ('22)	1.25	.55
148	A18	60o claret	19.00	.60
149	A18	70o red brn ('22)	.60	2.50
150	A18	80o deep green	.40	.40
151	A18	85o myrtle grn ('29)	4.50	.45
152	A18	90o lt blue ('25)	60.00	.40
153	A18a	1kr dp org ('21)	7.75	.40
154	A18	110o ultra	.40	.40
155	A18	110o red brn ('29)	9.00	.45
156	A18	120o gray blk ('25)	60.00	.60
157	A18	120o lil rose ('33)	14.00	.60
158	A18	140o gray black	.90	.30
159	A18	145o brt grn ('30)	8.50	.55

Wmk. 181

160	A18	35o yellow ('23)	50.00	7.50
161	A18	60o red violet	80.00	*150.00*
162	A18	80o blue green	8.25	15.00
163	A18	110o ultra	3.50	4.50
		Nos. 145-163 (19)	403.15	186.40

The value for #147 is for the 2nd type, issued in 1925.

Gustavus Adolphus — A19

Perf. 10 Vertically

1920, July 28   Unwmk.

164	A19	20o deep blue	2.25	.40

Wmk. 181

165	A19	20o blue	160.00	35.00

Unwmk.
Perf. 10

166	A19	20o blue	6.25	2.25
a.		Booklet pane of 10	130.00	
		Nos. 164-166 (3)	168.50	37.65

Tercentenary of Swedish post which first ran between Stockholm and Hamburg.

King Gustaf V — A20

See note after No. 138 regarding paper.
There are two types each of the 15o rose and 40o olive green.

1921-36   Unwmk.   *Perf. 10 Vert.*

167	A20	15o violet ('22)	17.00	.40
168	A20	15o rose ('28)	5.50	.45
169	A20	15o brown ('36)	4.75	.45
170	A20	20o violet	.25	.30
171	A20	20o rose ('22)	22.50	.60
172	A20	20o orange ('25)	.25	.45
174	A20	25o rose red ('22)	.55	1.50
175	A20	25o dk bl ('25)	17.00	.40
176	A20	25o ultra ('34)	17.00	.80
177	A20	25o yel org ('36)	27.50	.45
178	A20	30o blue ('23)	19.00	.45
179	A20	30o brown ('25)	20.00	.35
180	A20	30o lt ultra ('36)	6.00	.70
181	A20	35o red vio ('30)	24.00	.45
182	A20	40o blue	.45	.70
183	A20	40o ol grn ('29)	40.00	2.00
184	A20	45o brown ('29)	5.00	.90
185	A20	50o gray	1.75	1.00
186	A20	85o myrtle grn ('25)	17.00	2.00
187	A20	115o brn red ('25)	11.00	2.00
188	A20	145o apple grn ('25)	8.25	2.00
		Nos. 167-188 (21)	264.75	18.35

Wmk. 181

189	A20	15o violet ('22)	3,500.	1,050.
189A	A20	20o violet		*4,750.*

1922-36   Unwmk.   *Perf. 10*

190	A20	15o violet	17.50	.70
a.		Booklet pane of 10	400.00	
191	A20	15o rose red ('25)	22.50	.90
a.		Booklet pane of 10	600.00	
192	A20	15o brown ('36)	5.75	1.25
a.		Booklet pane of 10	175.00	
193	A20	20o violet ('22)	.50	*1.50*
a.		Booklet pane of 10	10.00	
		Nos. 190-193 (4)	46.25	4.35

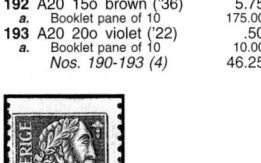

Gustavus Vasa — A21

1921, June   *Perf. 10 Vertically*

194	A21	20o violet	14.00	*30.00*
195	A21	110o ultra	55.00	8.00
196	A21	140o gray black	30.00	8.00
		Nos. 194-196 (3)	99.00	46.00

400th anniversary of Gustavus Vasa's war of independence from the Danes.

Universal Postal Union Congress

Composite View of Stockholm's Skyline A22

King Gustaf V — A23

1924, July 4   Unwmk.   *Perf. 10*

197	A22	5o red brown	1.60	*3.25*
198	A22	10o green	1.60	*3.25*
199	A22	15o dk violet	1.60	*2.50*
200	A22	20o rose red	12.50	*21.00*
201	A22	25o dp orange	15.00	*21.00*
202	A22	30o deep blue	15.00	*21.00*
a.		30o greenish blue	87.50	125.00
203	A22	35o black	20.00	*28.00*
204	A22	40o olive green	29.00	*32.50*
205	A22	45o deep brown	32.50	32.50
206	A22	50o gray	32.50	32.50
207	A22	60o violet brn	47.50	*55.00*
208	A22	80o myrtle grn	37.50	37.50
209	A23	1k green	57.50	*87.50*
210	A23	2k rose red	125.00	*250.00*
211	A23	5k deep blue	275.00	*450.00*

Wmk. 181

212	A22	10o green	26.00	*65.00*
		Nos. 197-212 (16)	729.80	*1,142.*
		Set, never hinged	1,400.	

Postrider Watching Airplane A24

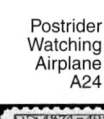

Carrier Pigeon and Globe — A25

1924, Aug. 16   Engr.   Unwmk.

213	A24	5o red brown	2.75	4.50
214	A24	10o green	2.75	5.75
215	A24	15o dk violet	3.00	3.00
216	A24	20o rose red	21.00	32.50
217	A24	25o deep orange	26.00	32.50
218	A24	30o deep blue	26.00	32.50
a.		30o greenish blue	90.00	52.50
219	A24	35o black	32.50	47.50
220	A24	40o olive green	32.50	32.50
221	A24	45o deep brown	37.50	35.00
222	A24	50o gray	50.00	62.50
223	A24	60o violet brown	50.00	77.50
224	A24	80o myrtle green	37.50	37.50
225	A25	1k green	75.00	87.50
226	A25	2k rose red	125.00	75.00
227	A25	5k deep blue	250.00	225.00

Wmk. 181

228	A24	10o green	35.00	*65.00*
		Nos. 213-228 (16)	806.50	855.75
		Set, never hinged	1,800.	

Universal Postal Union issue.

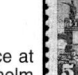

Royal Palace at Stockholm A26

1931, Nov. 26   Unwmk.   *Perf. 10*

229	A26	5k dark green	100.00	12.50
		Never hinged	325.00	
a.		Booklet pane of 10	3,100.	

Death of Gustavus Adolphus — A27

1932, Nov. 1

230	A27	10o dark violet	2.50	5.50
a.		Booklet pane of 10	40.00	
231	A27	15o dark red	4.50	2.00
a.		Booklet pane of 10	110.00	

Perf. 10 Vertically

232	A27	10o dark violet	1.90	.40
233	A27	15o dark red	2.50	.40
234	A27	25o dark blue	6.00	.95
235	A27	90o dark green	22.50	2.25
		Nos. 230-235 (6)	39.90	11.50
		Set, never hinged	85.00	

300th anniv. of the death of King Gustavus Adolphus II who was killed on the battlefield of Lützen, Nov. 6, 1632.

Catching Sunlight in Bowl — A28

1933, Dec. 6   *Perf. 10*

236	A28	5o green	2.50	2.00
a.		Booklet pane of 10	60.00	

There are two types of No. 236.

Perf. 10 Vertically

237	A28	5o green	2.50	.40

Perf. 13 Vertically

238	A28	5o green	3.50	7.25
		Nos. 236-238 (3)	8.50	9.65
		Set, never hinged	17.50	

50th anniv. of the Swedish Postal Savings Bank.

The Old Law Courts — A29

The "Four Estates" and Arms of Engelbrekt A34

Designs: 10o, Stock exchange. 15o, Parish church (Storkyrkan). 25o, House of the Nobility. 35o, House of Parliament.

1935, Jan. 10   *Perf. 10*

239	A29	5o green	2.25	1.40
a.		Booklet pane of 10	55.00	
240	A29	10o dull violet	4.25	*5.75*
a.		Booklet pane of 10	60.00	
241	A29	15o carmine	4.75	1.10
a.		Booklet pane of 10	125.00	

Perf. 10 Vertically

242	A29	5o green	1.25	.40
243	A29	10o dull violet	5.75	.40
244	A29	15o carmine	2.25	.40
245	A29	25o ultra	6.00	.60
246	A29	35o deep claret	12.00	2.25
247	A34	60o deep claret	17.50	2.50
		Nos. 239-247 (9)	56.00	14.80
		Set, never hinged	125.00	

500th anniv. of the Swedish Parliament.

Chancellor Axel Oxenstierna A35

Post Runner — A36

Mounted Courier — A37

Old Sailing Packet — A38

Mail Paddle Steamship A39

Mail Coach — A40

1855 Stamp Model — A41

Mail Train — A42

Postmaster General A. W. Roos — A43

Mail Truck and Trailer — A44

Modern Swedish Liner — A45

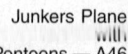

Junkers Plane
with
Pontoons — A46

1936, Feb. 20   Engr.   Perf. 10
248	A35	5o green	1.75	.85
a.		Booklet pane of 18	72.50	
249	A36	10o dk violet	2.10	3.00
a.		Booklet pane of 18	95.00	
250	A37	15o dk carmine	3.00	.55
a.		Booklet pane of 18	250.00	

Perf. 10 Vertically
251	A35	5o green	1.75	.25
252	A36	10o dk violet	1.75	.25
253	A37	15o dk carmine	3.25	.25
254	A38	20o lt blue	8.25	5.00
255	A39	25o lt ultra	5.25	.50
256	A40	30o yellow brn	16.00	3.25
257	A41	35o plum	5.50	1.25
258	A42	40o olive grn	5.75	2.75
259	A43	45o myrtle grn	7.75	1.50
260	A44	50o gray	20.00	2.75
261	A45	60o maroon	25.00	.70
262	A46	1k deep blue	8.25	8.50
		Nos. 248-262 (15)	115.35	31.35
		Set, never hinged	320.00	

300th anniv. of the Swedish Postal Service.
See Nos. 946-950, B55-B56 in Scott Standard catalogue, Vol. 6.

Airplane
over
Bromma
Airport
A47

Design Size: 33.25mm x 25.5mm

1936, May 23   Perf. 10 Vert.
263	A47	50o ultra	4.00	8.50
		Never hinged	10.50	

Opening of Bromma Airport near Stockholm.

Swedish Booklets

Before 1940, booklets were handmade and usually held two panes of 10 stamps (2x5). About every third booklet contained one row of stamps with straight edges at right or left side. Setenant pairs may be obtained with one stamp perforated on 4 sides and one perforated on 3 sides.

Starting in 1940, booklet stamps have one or more straight edges.

Some combination booklets containing multiple face-different stamps may exist with different configurations of those stamps. The most common configuration has been valued.

Emanuel
Swedenborg — A48

1938, Jan. 29   Perf. 12½
264	A48	10o violet	1.00	.35
a.		Perf. on 3 sides	8.00	4.00
		Never hinged	17.00	
b.		Booklet pane of 10	30.00	

Perf. 12½ Vertically
266	A48	10o violet	.90	.25
267	A48	100o green	2.00	1.40
		Nos. 264-267 (3)	3.90	2.00
		Set, never hinged	14.00	

250th anniv. of the birth of Swedenborg, scientist, philosopher and religious writer.

Johann Printz
and Indian
Chief — A49

"Kalmar Nyckel"
Sailing from
Gothenburg
A50

Symbolizing the
Settlement of
New
Sweden — A51

Holy Trinity
Church,
Wilmington,
Del. — A52

Queen
Christina — A53

1938, Apr. 8   Perf. 12½ Vert.
268	A49	5o green	.40	.30
269	A50	15o brown	.50	.30
270	A51	20o red	.90	.70
271	A52	30o ultra	2.00	.85
272	A53	60o brown lake	2.50	.35

Perf. 12½
273	A49	5o green	1.00	1.00
a.		Perf. on 3 sides	5.00	7.50
		Never hinged	17.00	
b.		Booklet pane of 18	67.50	
274	A50	15o brown	1.50	.70
a.		Perf. on 3 sides	10.00	4.75
		Never hinged	29.00	
b.		Booklet pane of 18	115.00	
		Nos. 268-274 (7)	8.80	4.20
		Set, never hinged	39.00	

Tercentenary of the Swedish settlement at Wilmington, Del. See No. B54 in Scott Standard catalogue, Vol. 6.

King Gustaf V — A54

1938, June 16   Perf. 12½ Vert.
275	A54	5o green	.40	.30
276	A54	15(o) brown	.45	.30
277	A54	30(o) ultra	5.00	.75

Perf. 12½
278	A54	5o green	.85	.40
a.		Perf. on 3 sides	5.00	5.50
		Never hinged	22.50	
b.		Booklet pane of 10	45.00	
279	A54	15(o) brown	1.00	.40
a.		Perf. on 3 sides	7.00	1.40
		Never hinged	35.00	
b.		Booklet pane of 10	37.50	
		Nos. 275-279 (5)	7.70	2.15
		Set, never hinged	37.00	

80th birthday of King Gustaf V.

King Gustaf
V — A55

Three
Crowns — A56

1939   Perf. 12½ Vertically
280	A55	10o violet	.40	.40
281	A55	20o carmine	1.00	.60
282	A56	60o lake	.40	.30
283	A56	85o dk green	.30	.30
284	A56	90o peacock blue	.30	.30
285	A56	1k orange	.30	.30
286	A56	1.15k henna brn	.30	.30
287	A56	1.20k brt rose vio	.80	.30
288	A56	1.45k lt yel grn	.85	.80

Perf. 12½
289	A55	10o violet	1.00	4.00
a.		Perf. on 3 sides	25.00	65.00
		Never hinged	80.00	
b.		Bklt. pane of 10, perf. on 4 sides	30.00	
		Nos. 280-289 (10)	6.65	7.60
		Set, never hinged	20.00	

See Nos. 394-398, 416-417, 425-426, 431, 439-441, 473, 588-591, 656-664 in Scott Standard catalogue, Vol. 6.

Per Henrik Ling — A57

1939, Feb. 25   Perf. 12½ Vert.
290	A57	5o green	.25	.25
291	A57	25(o) brown	.40	.40

Perf. 12½
292	A57	5o green	.40	.40
a.		Perf. on 3 sides	6.00	6.00
		Never hinged	29.00	
b.		Booklet pane of 10	37.50	
		Nos. 290-292 (3)	1.05	1.05
		Set, never hinged	4.00	

Centenary of the death of P. H. Ling, father of Swedish gymnastics.

J. J. Berzelius
A58

Carl von Linné
A59

Perf. 12½ Vertically

1939, June 2   Engr.
293	A58	10o violet	1.00	.40
294	A59	15o fawn	.25	.30
295	A58	30o ultra	6.00	.45
296	A59	50o gray	6.50	1.00

Perf. 12½
297	A58	10o violet	.90	.65
a.		Perf. on 3 sides	25.00	19.00
		Never hinged	135.00	
b.		Booklet pane of 10	65.00	
298	A59	15o fawn	1.00	.50
a.		Perf. on 3 sides	5.00	.45
		Never hinged	20.00	
b.		Booklet pane of 10	100.00	
c.		As "a," bklt. pane of 20	450.00	
		Nos. 293-298 (6)	15.65	3.30
		Set, never hinged	70.00	

200th anniv. of the founding of the Royal Academy of Science at Stockholm.

King Gustaf V — A60

Type A55 Re-engraved

1939-46   Perf. 12½
299	A60	5o dp green ('46)	.30	.30
b.		Perf. on 3 sides ('41)	.30	.30
		Never hinged	.50	
c.		As "b," bklt. pane of 20	12.00	
300	A60	10(o) violet ('46)	.30	.30
a.		Bklt. pane of 10, perf. on 4 sides	55.00	
		Never hinged	.50	
c.		Perf. on 3 sides	2.00	.30
i.		As "c," booklet pane of 20	50.00	
300D	A60	15(o) chestnut ('46)	.30	.30
f.		Perf. on 3 sides	.30	.30
		Never hinged	.65	
j.		As "f," booklet pane of 20	7.75	
300G	A60	20(o) red ('42)	.30	.25
h.		Booklet pane of 20	6.50	
		Nos. 299-300G (4)	1.20	1.15
		Set, never hinged	1.50	

No. 300 differs slightly from the original due to deeper engraving. No. 300G was issued only in booklets; all examples have one straight edge. Nos. 299, 300, 300D exist in booklet panes of 20 made from sheets of stamps. These can be collected as booklets.

1940-42   Perf. 12½ Vertically
301	A60	5o dp green ('41)	.25	.30
302	A60	10(o) violet	.25	.30
302A	A60	15(o) chestnut ('42)	.25	.30
303	A60	20(o) red	.25	.30
304	A60	25(o) orange	.40	.30
305	A60	30(o) ultra	.40	.30
306	A60	35(o) red vio ('41)	.40	.30
307	A60	40(o) olive grn	.40	.30
308	A60	45(o) dk brown	.40	.30
309	A60	50(o) gray blk ('41)	2.75	.30
		Nos. 301-309 (10)	5.75	3.00
		Set, never hinged	10.00	

Numerals measure 4½mm high. Less shading around head gives a lighter effect. Horizontal lines only as background for "SVERIGE."
See Nos. 391-393, 399 in Scott Standard catalogue, Vol. 6.

Carl Michael
Bellman — A61

1940, Feb. 4   Engr.   Perf. 12½ Vert.
310	A61	5o green	.25	.25
311	A61	35(o) rose red	.40	.40

Perf. 12½
312	A61	5o green	.50	.60
a.		Perf. on 3 sides	2.25	.75
		Never hinged	21.00	
b.		Booklet pane of 10	50.00	
c.		As "a," bklt. pane of 20	425.00	
		Nos. 310-312 (3)	1.15	1.25
		Set, never hinged	3.75	

Bellman (1740-95), lyric poet.

Tobias Sergel — A62

1940, Sept. 5   Perf. 12½ on 3 Sides
313	A62	15o lt brown	3.00	.50
a.		Booklet pane of 20	275.00	

Perf. 12½ Vertically
314	A62	15o lt brown	.75	.40
315	A62	50o gray black	5.00	1.40
		Nos. 313-315 (3)	8.75	2.30
		Set, never hinged	70.00	

Bicentenary of birth of Johan Tobias von Sergel (1740-1814), sculptor.

SEMI-POSTAL STAMPS

Type of 1872-91 Issues
Surcharged in Dark
Blue

Perf. 13x13½

1916, Dec. 21   Wmk. 181
B1	A5	5o + 5o on 2o org	4.75	7.25
B2	A5	5o + 5o on 3o yel brn	4.75	7.25
B3	A5	5o + 5o on 4o gray	4.75	7.25
B4	A5	5o + 5o on 6o lilac	4.75	7.25
B5	A5	5o + 5o on 6o lilac	4.75	7.25
B6	A5	10o + 10o on 12o pale bl	4.75	7.25
B7	A5	10o + 10o on 20o red org	4.75	7.25
B8	A5	10o + 10o on 24o yel	4.75	7.25
B9	A5	10o + 10o on 30o brn	4.75	7.25
B10	A5	10o + 10o on 50o rose red	4.75	7.25
		Nos. B1-B10 (10)	47.50	72.50

The surtax on Nos. B1-B31 was for the militia. See note after No. B21.
For surcharges see Nos. B22-B31.

No. 66
Surcharged in
Dark Blue

1916, Dec. 21   Wmk. 180   Perf. 13
B11	A12	10o + 4.90k on 5k	150.00	375.00

Nos. J12-J22 Surcharged in Dark Blue

1916, Dec. 21   Unwmk.   Perf. 13

B12	D1	5o + 5o on 1o	25.00	18.00
B13	D1	5o + 5o on 3o	5.00	7.00
B14	D1	5o + 5o on 5o	18.00	7.00
B15	D1	5o + 10o on 6o	5.00	8.00
B16	D1	5o + 15o on 12o	42.50	32.50
B17	D1	10o + 20o on 20o	15.00	25.00
B18	D1	10o + 40o on 24o	55.00	100.00
B19	D1	10o + 20o on 30o	6.50	6.00
B20	D1	10o + 40o on 50o	20.00	42.50
B21	D1	10o + 90o on 1kr	150.00	375.00
		Nos. B12-B21 (10)	342.00	621.00

The surtax on Nos. B12-B21 is indicated not in figures, but in words at bottom of surcharge: Fem, 5; Tio, 10; Femton, 15; Tjugo, 20; Fyrtio, 40; Nittio, 90.

Nos. B1-B10 Surcharged

1918, Dec. 18   Wmk. 181

B22	A5	7o + 3o on #B1	8.00	9.00
B23	A5	7o + 3o on #B2	2.75	1.25
B24	A5	7o + 3o on #B3	2.75	1.25
B25	A5	7o + 3o on #B4	2.75	1.25
B26	A5	7o + 3o on #B5	2.75	1.25
B27	A5	12o + 8o on #B6	2.75	1.25
B28	A5	12o + 8o on #B7	2.75	1.25
B29	A5	12o + 8o on #B8	2.75	1.25
B30	A5	12o + 8o on #B9	2.75	1.25
B31	A5	12o + 8o on #B10	2.75	1.25
		Nos. B22-B31 (10)	32.75	20.25

The 12o+8o surcharge exists on Nos. B1-B5 and the 7o+3o surcharge exists on Nos. B6-B10. Value, each $72.50.

Nos. B24, B26, B28 and B30 exist with surcharge inverted. Value unused, each $140.

King Gustaf V — SP1

Unwmk.

1928, June 16   Engr.   Perf. 10

B32	SP1	5o (+ 5o) yel grn	2.75	6.00
B33	SP1	10o (+ 5o) dk vio	2.75	6.00
B34	SP1	15o (+ 5o) car	2.75	4.50
		Complete booklet, pane of 8 ea. #B32, B33, B34	275.00	
B35	SP1	20o (+ 5o) org	4.75	2.75
B36	SP1	25o (+ 5o) dk bl	4.75	3.25
		Nos. B32-B36 (5)	17.75	22.50
		Set, never hinged	27.50	

70th birthday of King Gustaf V. The surtax was used for anti-cancer work.

AIR POST STAMPS

Official Stamps Surcharged in Dark Blue

1920, Sept. 17   Wmk. 181   Perf. 13

C1	O3	10o on 3o brn	2.25	7.75
a.		Inverted surcharge	375.00	1,350.
C2	O3	20o on 2o org	3.50	11.00
a.		Inverted surcharge	375.00	1,100.
C3	O3	50o on 4o vio	19.00	25.00
a.		Inverted surcharge	375.00	1,350.
		Nos. C1-C3 (3)	24.75	43.75
		Set, never hinged	62.50	

Wmk. 180

C4	O3	20o on 2o org	3,250.	
C5	O3	50o on 4o vio	190.00	600.00

Airplane over Stockholm AP2

Perf. 10 Vertically

1930, May 9   Engr.   Unwmk.

C6	AP2	10o deep blue	.25	.60
C7	AP2	50o dark violet	.65	1.75
		Set, never hinged	1.50	

POSTAGE DUE STAMPS

D1

1874   Unwmk.   Typo.   Perf. 14

J1	D1	1o black	75.00	40.00
J2	D1	3o rose	75.00	40.00
J3	D1	5o brown	75.00	35.00
J4	D1	6o yellow	150.00	95.00
J5	D1	12o pale red	7.75	6.00
J6	D1	20o blue	80.00	37.50
J7	D1	24o violet	625.00	375.00
J8	D1	24o gray	75.00	52.50
J9	D1	30o dk grn	87.50	40.00
J10	D1	50o brown	275.00	60.00
J11	D1	1k blue & bister	300.00	75.00
		Nos. J1-J11 (11)	1,825.	856.00

1877-86   Perf. 13

J12	D1	1o black ('80)	2.75	4.00
J13	D1	3o rose	6.25	7.25
J14	D1	5o brown	4.50	4.50
J15	D1	6o yellow	4.50	4.50
a.		Printed on both sides	1,600.	
J16	D1	12o pale red ('82)	14.50	17.00
J17	D1	20o pale blue ('78)	5.25	4.50
J18	D1	24o red lilac ('86)	26.00	29.00
a.		24o violet ('84)	26.00	29.00
J19	D1	24o gray lil ('82)	190.00	240.00
J20	D1	30o yellow green	6.50	4.50
J21	D1	50o yellow brown	10.50	5.75
J22	D1	1k blue & bister	30.00	17.50
		Nos. J12-J22 (11)	300.75	338.50

Nos. J12-J17, J19-J22 exist imperf. Value, pairs, each $400.

For surcharges see Nos. B12-B21.

STAMPS FOR CITY POSTAGE

S1

1856-62   Typo.   Unwmk.   Perf. 14

LX1	S1	(1sk) (3o) blk, medium thick paper ('58)	1,100.	550.00
		On cover		600.00
		On cover, before July 1, 1858		750.00
a.		(1sk) gray black, thin paper ('56)	5,000.	900.00
		On cover		2,750.
LX2	S1	(3o) bis brn ('62)	600.00	575.00
		On cover		675.00
a.		(3o) olive brown ('62)	675.00	525.00
		On cover		675.00

From 1856 to 1858 Nos. LX1, LX1a were sold at 1sk, from 1858 to 1862 No. LX1 was sold for 3o.

Issued: No. LX1, 7/1/58; LX1a, 5/22/56; LX2, 1/1/62.

REPRINTS AND RE-ISSUES

No. LX1 was reprinted twice in 1868 from new blocks. Nos. LX1 and LX2 were reprinted in 1871 and 1885 from an original plate. These re-issues and reprints were valid for postage until 1910, but only the 1871 issue is known used.

No. LX1 Original Printing

No. LX1 1868 Re-Issue

Distinguishing characteristics: #LX1p, **LX1q,** a white line runs from the pearl at right of "LOKALBREF" to the right frame line; the two pearls above the "M" of "FRIMÄRKE" are damaged and run together; there is a black spot over the pearl adjacent to the space between the "E" of "FRIMÄRKE" and the "F" of "LOKALBREF." On No. LX1p, the white ring surrounding this spot is clear and relatively strong; on No. LX1q, it is weak and sometimes barely discernible.

No. LX1r: as original, except perforation is straighter and often has wider corner perfs.

No. LX2r: yellowish brown; perfs are straighter than originals, with somewhat thicker teeth.

No. LX1s: perf 13; black is sharper and more intense than on other printings.

No. LX2s: perf 13; printed in an orange brown shade.

1868   Perf. 14

LX1p	S1	(3o) black (1st ptg.)	525.00	
		Never hinged	925.00	
LX1q	S1	(3o) black (2nd ptg.)	350.00	
		Never hinged	575.00	

1871   Perf. 14

LX1r	S1	(3o) black	290.00	525.00
		Never hinged	460.00	
LX2r	S1	(3o) yellow brown	250.00	400.00
		Never hinged	400.00	

1885   Perf. 13

LX1s	S1	(3o) black	190.00	
		Never hinged	290.00	
LX2s	S1	(3o) orange brown	160.00	
		Never hinged	250.00	

OFFICIAL STAMPS

O1

1874-77   Unwmk.   Typo.   Perf. 14

O1	O1	3o bister	90.00	42.50
		On cover		45.00
O2	O1	4o gray ('77)	300.00	75.00
		On cover		80.00
O3	O1	5o yel green	140.00	52.50
		On cover		130.00
O4	O1	6o lilac	275.00	65.00
		On cover		75.00
O5	O1	6o gray	525.00	175.00
		On cover		200.00
O6	O1	12o blue	200.00	3.00
		On cover		15.00
O7	O1	20o pale red	1,050.	90.00
		On cover		300.00
O8	O1	24o yellow	1,050.	20.00
		On cover		55.00
a.		24o orange	1,050.	22.50
		On cover		60.00
O9	O1	30o pale brn	425.00	37.50
		On cover		210.00
O10	O1	50o rose	600.00	125.00
		On cover		425.00
O11	O1	1k bl & bis	1,700.	65.00
		On cover		750.00
		Nos. O1-O11 (11)	6,355.	750.50

Imperf., Pairs

O1a	O1	3o		1,500.
O2a	O1	4o		1,500.
O3a	O1	5o		1,500.
O4a	O1	6o		1,500.
O6a	O1	12o		1,500.
O7a	O1	20o		1,500.
O8b	O1	24o		1,500.
O9a	O1	30o		1,500.
O10a	O1	50o		1,500.
O11a	O1	1k		2,500.

1881-95   Perf. 13

O12	O1	2o org ('91)	1.40	2.00
		On cover		22.50
O13	O1	3o bis brn	1.40	2.25
		On cover		17.00
O14	O1	4o gray blk ('93)	2.50	.70
		On cover		8.00
a.		4o gray ('82)	20.00	8.00
		On cover		8.00
O15	O1	5o grn ('84)	5.25	.60
		On cover		9.00

O16	O1	6o red lil ('82)	40.00	60.00
		On cover		62.50
a.		6o lilac ('81)	45.00	65.00
		On cover		75.00
O17	O1	10o car ('95)	3.00	.25
		On cover		4.00
b.		10o rose ('85)	45.00	1.25
		On cover		14.00
O18	O1	12o blue	57.50	22.50
		On cover		24.00
O19	O1	20o ver ('82)	200.00	2.50
		On cover		55.00
O20	O1	20o dk bl ('91)	5.75	.60
		On cover		12.00
O21	O1	24o yellow	72.50	20.00
		On cover		65.00
a.		24o orange	65.00	25.00
		On cover		125.00
O22	O1	30o brown	26.00	.70
		On cover		12.50
O23	O1	50o pale rose	140.00	25.00
		On cover		110.00
O24	O1	50o pale gray ('93)	18.00	3.00
		On cover		17.50
O25	O1	1k dk bl & yel brn	9.00	3.00
		On cover		32.50
		Nos. O12-O25 (14)	582.30	148.10

Imperf., Pairs

O12a	O1	2o		400.00
O17a	O1	10o No. O17		400.00
c.		No. O17b		400.00
O20a	O1	20o		50.00
O24a	O1	50o		400.00

Surcharged in Dark Blue

1889

O26	O1	10o on 12o blue	13.00	18.00
		On cover		525.00
a.		Inverted surcharge	2,100.	5,000.
b.		Perf. 14	5,500.	5,500.
O27	O1	10o on 24o yel	16.00	25.00
		On cover		2,000.
a.		Inverted surcharge	7,000.	5,500.
b.		Perf. 14	5,500.	5,500.

O3

1910-12   Wmk. 180   Typo.

O28	O3	1o black	.30	.45
		Never hinged	.50	
		On cover		16.00
O29	O3	2o orange	1.40	4.50
		Never hinged	2.50	
		On cover		24.00
O30	O3	4o pale violet	1.75	4.00
		Never hinged	3.75	
		On cover		16.00
O31	O3	5o green	.50	1.10
		Never hinged	1.25	
		On cover		12.00
O32	O3	8o claret	.40	1.10
		Never hinged	1.20	
		On cover		32.50
O33	O3	10o red	11.00	.70
		Never hinged	27.50	
		On cover		17.00
O34	O3	15o red brown	.80	.80
		Never hinged	2.00	
		On cover		27.50
O35	O3	20o deep blue	7.00	1.75
		Never hinged	20.00	
		On cover		37.50
O36	O3	25o red orange	7.00	2.50
		Never hinged	20.00	
		On cover		40.00
O37	O3	30o chocolate	7.00	3.50
		Never hinged	20.00	
		On cover		55.00
O38	O3	50o gray	7.00	3.50
		Never hinged	20.00	
		On cover		27.50
O39	O3	1k black, *yellow*	7.75	7.75
		Never hinged	20.00	
		On cover		35.00
O40	O3	5k claret, *yellow*	10.00	4.00
		Never hinged	25.00	
		On cover		45.00
		Nos. O28-O40 (13)	61.90	35.65

1910-19   Wmk. Wavy Lines (181)

O41	O3	1o black	2.00	3.75
		Never hinged	5.00	
		On cover		17.00
O42	O3	2o orange	.30	.40
		Never hinged	.40	
		On cover		6.00
O43	O3	3o pale brown	.40	1.00
		Never hinged	.80	
		On cover		9.00
O44	O3	4o pale violet	.30	.40
		Never hinged	.50	
		On cover		5.00
O45	O3	5o green	.30	.40
		Never hinged	.50	
		On cover		3.00
O46	O3	7o gray green	.40	1.25
		Never hinged	.80	
		On cover		15.00

O47	O3 8o rose	18.00	27.50
	Never hinged	35.00	
	On cover		100.00
O48	O3 10o red	.30	.25
	Never hinged	.40	
	On cover		5.00
O49	O3 12o rose red	.30	.40
	Never hinged	.60	
	On cover		5.50
O50	O3 15o org brown	.30	.30
	Never hinged	.60	
	On cover		8.00
O51	O3 20o deep blue	.45	.40
	Never hinged	.70	
	On cover		8.00
O52	O3 25o orange	.80	.50
	Never hinged	2.00	
	On cover		12.00
O53	O3 30o chocolate	.55	.55
	Never hinged	1.25	
	On cover		12.00
O54	O3 35o dark violet	.85	1.00
	Never hinged	1.75	
	On cover		12.00
O55	O3 50o gray	3.25	2.25
	Never hinged	6.50	
	On cover		14.00
	Nos. O41-O55 (15)	28.50	40.25

For surcharges see Nos. C1-C5.

Use of official stamps ceased on July 1, 1920.

PARCEL POST STAMPS

Regular Issue of 1914
Surcharged

1917	**Wmk. 180**		**Perf. 13**
Q1	A14 1.98k on 5k claret, *yel*	1.40	6.00
Q2	A14 2.12k on 5k claret, *yel*	1.40	6.00

SWITZERLAND

ˈswit-sər-lənd

(Helvetia)

LOCATION — Central Europe, between France, Germany and Italy
GOVT. — Republic
AREA — 15,943 sq. mi.
POP. — 6,423,100 (est. 1983)
CAPITAL — Bern

100 Rappen or Centimes = 1 Franc

Watermarks

Type I   Type II
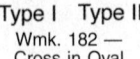
Wmk. 182 —
Cross in Oval

Wmk. 183 —
Swiss Cross

Watermark 182 is not a true watermark, having been impressed after the paper was manufactured. There are two types: I- width just under 9mm; heighth just under 11mm; double oval lines nearly 1mm apart; cross has short, thick arms; II- width just under 8½mm; double oval lines very close together; cross has longer, thinner arms than Type I.

CANTONAL ADMINISTRATION

Unused values of Nos. 1L1-3L1 are for stamps without gum. Counterfeit and repaired examples of Nos. 1L1-3L1 abound.

Zurich

A1   A2
Numerals of Value

1843	**Unwmk. Litho.**		**Imperf.**
	Red Vertical Lines		
1L1	A1 4r black	20,000.	16,500.
	On cover		40,000.
1L2	A2 6r black	7,000.	1,750.
	On cover		3,750.
1846	**Red Horizontal Lines**		
1L3	A1 4r black	17,500.	22,000.
	On cover		50,000.
1L4	A2 6r black	2,150.	1,650.
	On cover		3,500.

Full margins = ½mm. There are dividing lines between stamps.

Five varieties of each value.
Reprints of the Zurich stamps show signs of wear and lack the red lines. Values 4r, $7,000; 6r, $2,350.

Coat of Arms — A3

1850	**Unwmk.**		**Imperf.**
1L5	A3 2½r black & red	6,000.	3,500.
	On cover, single franking		42,500.
	Pair	29,000.	10,000.
	On cover, pair		27,500.

Full margins = 1¼mm.

No. 1L5 has separation designs in the margins between stamps as shown. Values are for

stamps showing part of the separation design on all four sides.

Geneva

Coat of Arms —
A4

1843	**Unwmk. Litho.**		**Imperf.**
2L1	A4 10c blk, *yel grn*	62,500.	40,000.
	On cover		62,500.
a.	Either half	23,500.	9,250.
	On cover		14,000.
b.	Stamp composed of right half at left & left half at right	77,500.	60,000.
	On cover		100,000.

Full margins = ¾mm. There are dividing lines between stamps.

A5   A6

1845-48			
2L2	A5 5c blk, *yel grn*	3,200.	1,675.
	On cover		3,400.
2L3	A6 5c blk, *yel grn* ('46)	2,200.	1,750.
	On cover		3,500.
2L4	A6 5c blk, *dk grn* ('48)	4,500.	2,750.
	On cover		4,500.

Full margins: No. 2L2 = ¼mm; Nos. 2L3-2L4 = ½mm.

Values for pairs

2L2	A5 5c blk, *yel grn*	20,000.	25,000.
	On cover		47,500.

2L3	A6 5c blk, *yel grn*	16,000.	19,000.
	On cover		27,500.
2L4	A6 5c blk, *dk grn*	20,000.	20,000.
	On cover		27,500.

A7   Coat of
Arms — A8

1849-50			
2L5	A7 4c black & red	40,000.	20,000.
	On cover		40,000.
2L6	A7 5c blk & red ('50)	2,750.	1,750.
	On cover		3,250.

Full margins = 1mm. There are dividing lines between stamps.

Values for pairs

2L5	A7 4c black & red	125,000.	125,000.
	On cover		200,000.
2L6	A7 5c black & red	20,000.	22,000.
	On cover		32,500.

1851			
2L7	A8 5c black & red	9,000.	3,800.
	On cover		7,000.
	Pair	125,000.	125,000.
	On cover		195,000.

Full margins = 1mm. There are dividing lines between stamps.

ENVELOPE STAMP USED AS ADHESIVE

E1

1847	**Unwmk.**		**Imperf.**
2LU1	E1 5c yel grn, see footnote		23,500.

Value is for cut-out stamp used on folded letters. This use was authorized and is known from Feb. 19, 1847. Value of unused envelope cut-out, $550. Value of used cut-out off cover, $3,000.

Basel

Dove of Basel — A9

	Typo. & Embossed		
1845	**Unwmk.**		**Imperf.**
3L1	A1 2½r blk, crim & bl	14,000.	13,500.
	On cover		25,000.
	Pair	120,000.	120,000.
	On cover		195,000.
a.	2½r blk, crim & brt blue	18,000.	15,000.
	On cover		27,500.

Full margins = 1¼mm.

Proofs are black, vermilion and green. Value, $6,000.

FEDERAL ADMINISTRATION

Due to its tendency to damage the paper and/or the color of the stamps, the gum on Nos. 1-40 very often is removed. Unused values for Nos. 1-40 are for stamps without gum. Stamps with original gum sell for about the same prices.

A10   A11

1850 Unwmk. Litho. Imperf.
Full Black Frame Around Cross

1	A10	2½r black & red	3,000.	1,500.
		On cover, single franking		6,500.
		On cover, pair		6,000.
2	A11	2½r black & red	2,500.	1,400.
		On cover, single franking		4,750.
		On cover, pair		5,000.

Without Frame Around Cross

3	A10	2½r black & red	6,000.	2,750.
		On cover, single franking		7,900.
		On cover, pair		11,750.
4	A11	2½r blk & red	52,500.	25,000.
		On cover		67,500.
		On cover, pair		120,000.

Full margins = ¾mm. There are dividing lines between stamps.

Forty types of each.

A12   A13

1850
Full Black Frame Around Cross

5	A12	5r dk bl, blk & red	5,250.	1,250.
		On cover		3,250.
a.		5r dk grayish bl, blk & red	5,750.	1,250.
		On cover		3,500.
6	A13	10r yel, blk & red		115,000.
		On cover		200,000.

Full margins = ¾mm. There are dividing lines between stamps.

No. 6 used, with only parts of frame around cross showing, value $175 to $900. Beware of examples of Nos. 7-8 with faked frame added.

Without Frame Around Cross

7	A12	5r lt bl, blk & red	1,750.	450.
		On cover		1,200.
a.		5r dp bl, blk & red	1,550.	450.
		On cover		1,250.
b.		5r pur bl, blk & red	—	5,500.
		On cover		10,500.
c.		5r grnsh bl, blk & red	2,000.	450.
		On cover		1,325.
d.		5r grayish vio, blk & red	2,350.	575.
		On cover		1,400.
8	A13	10r yel, blk & red	1,000.	125.
		On cover		250.
a.		10r buff, blk & red	1,275.	225.
		On cover		340.
b.		10r org yel, blk & red	1,250.	250.
		On cover		500.
c.		10r dark org, blk & red		9,750.
		On cover		600.
d.		Half used as 5r on cover, 5r rate		16,000.
		As "d," 15r rate		15,000.
		As "d," 25r rate		18,500.

		As "d," 30r rate		—
e.		Very thin paper	2,500.	325.00
f.		Thick carton paper	2,500.	400.00

Full margins = ¾mm. There are dividing lines between stamps.

1851
Full Blue Frame Around Cross

9	A12	5r light blue & red		210,000.
		On cover		400,000.

Full margins = ¾mm. There are dividing lines between stamps.

No. 9 used, with only parts of frame around cross showing, value $180 to $3,750. Beware of examples of No. 10 with faked frame added.

Without Frame Around Cross

10	A12	5r lt blue & red	650.	125.00
		On cover		325.00
a.		Thin paper	1,200.	350.00
		On cover		475.00

Full margins = ¾mm. There are dividing lines between stamps.

Forty types of each.

A14   A15

A16

1852
Vermilion Frame Around Cross

11	A14	15r vermilion	15,000.	700.
				1,700.
12	A15	15r vermilion	2,500.	125.
		On cover		325.
13	A16	15c vermilion	14,000.	1,000.
				2,550.

Full margins = ¾mm. There are dividing lines between stamps.

Ten types of each.

On October 1st, 1854, all stamps of the preceding issues were declared obsolete.

The Sitting Helvetia type (Scott Nos. 14-40) are valued with three margins clear of frame lines, with the fourth margin touching or lightly cutting into the frame line. Stamps with four margins clear of all frame lines are rare and command sustantial premiums.

Helvetia — A17

1854 Embossed. Unwmk.
Thin Paper, Fine Impressions
Emerald Silk Threads

14	A17	5r orange brn	7,500.	1,700.
		On cover		3,750.
15	A17	5r red brown	625.00	160.00
		On cover		275.00
16	A17	10r blue	825.00	80.00
		On cover		140.00

17	A17	15r carmine rose	1,200.	175.00
		On cover		375.00
a.		15r pale rose	1,350.	190.00
		On cover		400.00
18	A17	40r pale yel grn	9,500.	1,300.
				3,350.
19	A17	40r yellow grn	1,250.	325.00
		On cover		650.00

Full margins = ¼mm.

1854-55
Emerald Silk Threads
Medium Thick Paper
Fine Impressions

20	A17	5r pale yel brn	650.00	160.00
		On cover		300.00
21	A17	10r blue	1,600.	125.00
		On cover		275.00
22	A17	15r rose	925.00	110.00
		On cover		210.00
23	A17	20r pale orange	1,400.	190.00
		On cover		325.00

Full margins = ¼mm.

1855-57
Colored ( ) Silk Threads
Medium Thick Paper
Fine to Rough Impressions

24	A17	5r yel brn (yel)	550.00	115.00
		On cover		225.00
25	A17	5r dk brown (blk)	325.00	40.00
		On cover		80.00
26	A17	10r mlky bl (red)	1,000.	200.00
		On cover		350.00
27	A17	10r blue (car)	300.00	50.00
		On cover		80.00
a.		Thin paper	5,000.	475.00
		On cover		1,000.
28	A17	15r rose (bl)	550.00	75.00
		On cover		130.00
29	A17	40r yel grn (mar)	1,000.	110.00
		On cover		210.00
30	A17	1fr lav (blk)	1,400.	1,000.
		On cover		2,000.
31	A17	1fr lav (yel)	1,350.	1,000.
		On cover		2,000.
a.		Thin paper	19,000.	7,500.
		On cover		18,500.

Full margins = ¼mm.

1857
Thin (Emergency) Paper
Rough Impressions
Green Silk Threads

32	A17	5r pale gray brn	4,500.	1,000.
		On cover		2,250.
32A	A17	10r blue	6,500.	950.
		On cover		1,750.
33	A17	15r pale dl rose	3,250.	350.
		On cover		650.
34	A17	20r pale dl org	3,400.	275.
		On cover		525.

Full margins = ¼mm.

1858-62
Thick Ordinary Paper
Rough Impressions
Green Silk Threads

35	A17	2r gray	275.00	575.00
		On newspaper or wrapper, single franking		1,100.
a.		One and one-half used as 3r on newspaper or wrapper		15,000.
c.		Half used as 1r on cover		
36	A17	5r brown	225.00	24.00
		On cover		42.50
a.		5r black brown	275.00	47.50
		On cover		75.00
b.		5r gray brown	240.00	27.50
		On cover		47.50
c.		Half used as 2r on cover		1,550.
37	A17	10r blue	240.00	27.50
		On cover		42.50
a.		Half used as 5r on cover		7,250.

b.		10r pale blue	260.00	27.50
		On cover		50.00
c.		10r dark blue	250.00	24.00
		On cover		42.50
d.		10r greenish blue	310.00	45.00
		On cover		75.00
38	A17	15r dark rose	375.00	65.00
		On cover		130.00
a.		15r pale rose	400.00	72.50
		On cover		145.00
39	A17	20r dark orange	475.00	75.00
		On cover		160.00
a.		Half used as 10r on cover		17,500.
b.		20r yel orange	500.00	80.00
		On cover		175.00
40	A17	40r green (to dp grn)	450.00	100.00
		On cover		175.00
a.		Half used as 20r on cover		27,500.
b.		40r yellow green	475.00	100.00
		On cover		190.00
		Nos. 35-40 (6)	2,040.	866.50

Full margins = ¼mm.

Most examples of No. 35a are on pieces of newsprint, rather than on complete newspapers or wrappers. Value for single and bisected single on piece, $4,000.

Helvetia — A18

Double transfer errors, Nos. 43c, 44a, 55b, 60a, 61a, 61b, 67b, have the design impressed twice. These do not refer to the "embossed" watermark.

1862-64 Wmk. 182 Perf. 11½
White Wove Paper

41	A18	2c gray	125.00	4.75
		Never hinged	250.00	
		On cover		14.00
42	A18	3c black	14.50	115.00
		Never hinged	21.00	
		On cover		400.00
		On cover, single franking		575.00
		On newspaper		210.00
43	A18	5c dark brown	3.50	1.00
		Never hinged	6.50	
		On cover		4.00
a.		5c bister brown	115.00	4.00
		Never hinged	240.00	
		On cover		10.00
b.		5c gray brown	110.00	32.50
		On cover		45.00
c.		Dbl. transfer, one invtd.	4,250.	500.00
		On cover		1,000.
d.		Dbl. transfer of lower left "5"		1,500.
		On cover		3,500.
44	A18	10c blue	625.00	1.00
		Never hinged	1,100.	
		On cover		4.00
a.		Dbl. transfer, one invtd.		9,000.
		On cover		15,000.
45	A18	20c orange	2.50	2.75
		Never hinged	5.00	
		On cover		13.00
a.		20c yellow orange	400.00	4.00
		Never hinged	800.00	
		On cover		14.00
46	A18	30c vermilion	1,500.	47.50
		Never hinged	3,000.	
		On cover		80.00
47	A18	40c green	1,400.	65.00
		Never hinged	2,800.	
		On cover		135.00
48	A18	60c bronze	1,400.	180.00
		Never hinged	2,800.	
		On cover		375.00
50	A18	1fr gold	25.00	120.00
		Never hinged	47.50	
		On cover		400.00
a.		1fr yellowish bronze ('64)	1,600.	550.00
		Never hinged	3,200.	
		On cover		950.00
b.		1fr reddish bronze	1,700.	475.00
		Never hinged	3,500.	
		On cover		950.00

1867-78

52	A18	2c bister brown	3.25	1.80
		Never hinged	6.25	
		On cover		4.00
a.		2c red brown	700.00	275.00
		Never hinged	1,400.	
		On cover		400.00

53	A18 10c carmine	4.75	1.00
	Never hinged	9.25	
	On cover		3.25
54	A18 15c lemon	3.25	45.00
	Never hinged	6.50	
	On cover		85.00
55	A18 25c blue green	1.60	4.00
	Never hinged	9.25	
	On cover		16.50
a.	25c yellow green	60.00	40.00
	On cover		125.00
b.	Dbl. transfer, one invtd.		600.00
	On cover		1,100.
56	A18 30c ultra	475.00	9.50
	Never hinged	950.00	
	On cover		24.00
a.	30c blue	2,200.	275.00
	Never hinged	5,400.	
	On cover		550.00
58	A18 40c gray	1.60	160.00
	Never hinged	3.25	
	On cover		425.00
59	A18 50c violet	55.00	55.00
	Never hinged	110.00	
	On cover		225.00
	Nos. 52-59 (7)	544.45	276.30

1881 Granite Paper

60	A18 2c bister	.80	22.50
	Never hinged	1.60	
	On cover		42.50
a.	Dbl. transfer, one invtd.	300.00	
	On cover	575.00	
61	A18 5c brown	.45	10.00
	Never hinged	.80	
	On cover		20.00
a.	Dbl. transfer, one invtd.	40.00	450.00
	Never hinged	80.00	
	On cover		1,050.
b.	Double transfer of lower left "5"		1,250.
	On cover		2,500.
62	A18 10c rose	8.00	10.00
	Never hinged	16.00	
	On cover		20.00
63	A18 15c lemon	10.00	450.00
	Never hinged	20.00	
	On cover		625.00
64	A18 20c orange	.80	135.00
	Never hinged	1.60	
	On cover		250.00
65	A18 25c green	.60	100.00
	Never hinged	1.25	
	On cover		190.00
66	A18 40c gray	1.00	3,400.
	Never hinged	2.00	
	On cover		15,000.
67	A18 50c deep violet	16.00	475.00
	Never hinged	32.50	
	On cover		1,150.
b.	Dbl. transfer, one invtd.	325.00	4,500.
	Never hinged	625.00	
	On cover		11,000.
68	A18 1fr gold	20.00	1,100.
	Never hinged	40.00	
	On cover		5,000.

The granite paper contains fragments of blue and red silk threads.

Forged or backdated cancellations are found frequently on Nos. 42, 50, 54, 58 and 60-68.

All stamps of the preceding issues were declared obsolete on October 1st, 1883. Some of the remainders of Nos. 41-68 were overprinted "AUSSER KURS" (Obsolete) diagonally in black.

Numeral — A19

Wmk. 182 (Type II)
1882-89 Typo. Perf. 11½
Granite Paper

69	A19 2c bister	2.50	1.25
	Never hinged	5.00	
	On cover		5.00
70	A19 3c gray brown	3.25	16.00
	Never hinged	6.50	
	On cover		25.00
a.	3c gray	65.00	72.50
	On cover		6.00
71	A19 5c maroon	25.00	.80
	Never hinged	50.00	
	On cover		6.00
a.	Tête bêche pair	—	
72	A19 5c deep grn ('99)	12.00	.80
	Never hinged	24.50	
	On cover		2.50
73	A19 10c red	9.75	.80
	Never hinged	20.00	
	On cover		4.00
74	A19 12c ultra	12.00	1.25
	Never hinged	25.00	
	On cover		10.00
a.	12c dull blue	400.00	45.00
	Never hinged	800.00	
	On cover		120.00
76	A19 15c lilac ('89)	80.00	4.00
	Never hinged	160.00	
	On cover		37.50
a.	15c brownish red-lilac	120.00	18.00
	Never hinged	240.00	
	On cover		105.00
	Nos. 69-76 (7)	144.50	24.90
	Set, never hinged	291.00	

Wmk. 182 (Type I)

69a	A19 2c olive brown	40.00	6.00
	Never hinged	80.00	
	On cover		20.00

70b	A19 3c gray	65.00	75.00
	Never hinged	145.00	
	On cover		100.00
71b	A19 5c brownish lilac	97.50	3.25
	Never hinged	210.00	
	On cover		6.50
73a	A19 10c carmine	115.00	2.00
	Never hinged	250.00	
	On cover		0.50
73b	A19 10c light rose	700.00	12.50
	Never hinged	1,250.	
	On cover		25.00
74c	A19 12c ultramarine	165.00	6.50
	Never hinged	325.00	
	On cover		15.00
75	A19 15c yellow	200.00	40.00
	Never hinged	500.00	
	On cover		70.00
75a	A19 15c yellow-orange	20,000.	5,750.
b.	Tête bêche pair		16,500.
76b	A19 15c dull purple	500.00	32.50
	Never hinged	1,000.	
	On cover		80.00

Wmk. 182 (Type II)
1882 White Paper

77	A19 2c olive brown	525.00	450.00
	Never hinged	1,000.	
	On cover		650.00
78	A19 5c brownish lilac	1,425.	120.00
	Never hinged	3,650.	
	On cover		250.00
79	A19 10c pale rose	2,850.	77.50
	Never hinged	7,500.	
	On cover		150.00
80	A19 12c grayish ultra	300.00	32.50
	Never hinged	525.00	
	On cover		55.00
81	A19 15c yellow	400.00	400.00
	Never hinged	800.00	
	On cover		575.00

Nos. 77-81 were the first stamps issued in the Numeral series.
See Nos. 113-118.

Helvetia
(Large numerals)
A20

Helvetia
(Small numerals)
A21

Wmk. 182 (Type I)
1882-1904 Engr. Perf. 11½ - 11¾

82	A20 20c orange	200.00	6.25
	Never hinged	400.00	
	On cover		25.00
83	A20 25c green	105.00	3.25
	Never hinged	210.00	
	On cover		20.00
95b	A20 30c brown	—	22,500.
84	A20 40c gray	160.00	50.00
	Never hinged	310.00	
	On cover		135.00
86	A20 50c blue	160.00	25.00
	Never hinged	310.00	
	On cover		95.00
87	A20 1fr claret	275.00	7.00
	Never hinged	550.00	
	On cover		325.00
	On cover, single franking		400.00
88	A20 3fr yellow brn ('91)	240.00	22.50
	Never hinged	475.00	
	On cover		1,200.
	On cover, single franking		1,750.

Wmk. 182 (Type II)

85	A21 40c gray ('04)	47.50	27.50
	Never hinged	100.00	
	On cover		160.00
88d	A20 3fr yellow brown ('04)		4,250.

1888 Wmk. 182 (Type I) Perf. 9½

89	A20 20c orange	1,000.	125.00
	Never hinged	2,100.	
	On cover		200.00
90	A20 25c yellow grn	160.00	20.00
	Never hinged	340.00	
	On cover		67.50
91	A20 40c gray	950.00	700.00
	Never hinged	2,000.	
	On cover		2,000.
92	A20 50c blue	1,350.	375.00
	Never hinged	3,000.	
	On cover		1,000.
93	A20 1fr claret	975.00	100.00
	Never hinged	2,150.	
	On cover		700.00
	On cover, single franking		800.00

Values for Nos. 89-93 are for well-centered stamps with slightly uneven perforations. Stamps missing perforations sell for much less.

Wmk. 182 (Type I)
1891-1903 Perf. 11½x11

82c	A20 20c orange	600.00	8.25
	On cover		55.00
83b	A20 25c green	275.00	6.00
	On cover		30.00
95b	A20 30c red brown ('92)	500.00	52.50
	On cover		135.00
84c	A20 40c gray	1,100.	135.00
	On cover		400.00

86b	A20 50c blue	450.00	27.50
	On cover		95.00
87c	A20 1fr claret	825.00	22.50
	On cover		375.00
88c	A20 1fr claret		17,500.

Wmk. 182 (Type II)

90	A20 25c green		22.00
	Never hinged	150.00	
83a	A20 25c green	12.50	1.60
	Never hinged	25.00	
	On cover		22.00
94	A20 25c blue ('99)	14.00	2.40
	Never hinged	28.00	
	On cover		22.00
95	A20 30c red brn ('92)	40.00	2.40
	Never hinged	80.00	
	On cover		35.00
84a	A20 40c gray	85.00	6.25
	Never hinged	170.00	
	On cover		80.00
86a	A20 50c blue	50.00	14.00
	Never hinged	100.00	
	On cover		70.00
96	A20 50c green ('99)	55.00	27.50
	Never hinged	110.00	
	On cover		100.00
87a	A20 1fr claret	47.50	4.75
	Never hinged	100.00	
	On cover		200.00
	On cover, single franking		240.00
97	A20 1fr carmine ('03)	100.00	10.00
	Never hinged	200.00	
	On cover		240.00
	On cover, single franking		300.00
88a	A20 3fr yellow brown	175.00	30.00
	Never hinged	350.00	
	On cover		900.00
	On cover, single franking		1,100.

Wmk. 182 (Type II)
1901-03 Perf. 11½x12

82b	A20 20c orange	32.50	2.00
	Never hinged	65.00	
	On cover		16.00
94a	A20 25c blue	15.50	1.35
	Never hinged	32.50	
	On cover		16.00
95a	A20 30c red brown	47.50	2.25
	Never hinged	100.00	
	On cover		32.50
84b	A20 40c gray	100.00	40.00
	Never hinged	200.00	
	On cover		135.00
96a	A20 50c green	77.50	8.00
	Never hinged	150.00	
	On cover		60.00
87b	A20 1fr claret	2,200.	310.00
	Never hinged	4,400.	
	On cover, single franking		850.00
	On cover, single franking		1,000.
97a	A20 1fr carmine ('03)	475.00	42.50
	Never hinged	950.00	
	On cover		550.00
88b	A20 3fr yellow brown	240.00	24.00
	Never hinged	475.00	
	On cover		975.00
	On cover, single franking		1,100.

Numerous retouches and plate flaws exist on all values of this issue.
Nos. 82-88 are ½mm taller (paper size) than Nos. 82b-88b.
See Nos. 105-112, 119-125.

UPU Allegory — A22

1900 Perf. 11½

98	A22 5c gray green	40.00	2.00
	Never hinged	80.00	
	On cover		4.75
99	A22 10c carmine rose	12.50	2.00
	Never hinged	25.00	
	On cover		4.75
100	A22 25c blue	32.00	35.00
	Never hinged	62.50	
	On cover		95.00
	Nos. 98-100 (3)	84.50	39.00

Re-engraved

101	A22 5c gray green	4.00	1.75
	Never hinged	8.00	
	On cover		4.00
102	A22 10c carmine rose	57.50	47.50
	Never hinged	115.00	
	On cover		90.00
a.	10c red purple	1,000.	8,000.
103	A22 25c blue	800.00	12,500.
	Never hinged	1,600.	
	On cover		15,000.

Universal Postal Union, 25th anniv.

The impression of the re-engraved stamps is much clearer, especially the horizontally lined background. The figures of value are lined instead of being solid.

Helvetia Types of 1882-1904
1905 Wmk. 183 Perf. 11½x11
White Paper

105	A20 20c orange	4.75	2.40
	Never hinged	9.50	
	On cover		22.00

106	A20 25c blue	6.25	10.00
	Never hinged	12.50	
	On cover		57.50
107	A20 30c brown	6.25	2.40
	Never hinged	12.50	
	On cover		25.00
108a	A21 40c gray	230.00	110.00
	Never hinged		
	On cover		425.00
109	A20 50c green	40.00	9.25
	Never hinged	80.00	
	On cover		95.00
110	A20 1fr carmine	100.00	4.00
	Never hinged	200.00	
	On cover		65.00
	On cover, single franking		240.00
111	A20 3fr yellow brn	250.00	145.00
	Never hinged	500.00	
	On cover		190.00
	On cover, single franking		1,200.

Some clichés in the plates of the 20c, 25c, 30c, 50c and 3fr have been retouched.

1906 Re-engraved Perf. 11½x11

112	A20 25c pale blue	7.75	2.75
	Never hinged	16.00	
	On cover		27.50

In the re-engraved stamp the stars are larger and the background below "FRANCO" is of horiz. or horiz. and vert. crossed lines, instead of horiz. and curved lines.

1906 Perf. 11½

112a	A20 25c pale blue	110.00	9.50
	Never hinged	220.00	
	On cover		25.00
108	A21 40c gray	35.00	14.00
	Never hinged	70.00	
	On cover		135.00

1907 Perf. 11½x12

105a	A20 20c orange	8.00	8.00
	Never hinged	16.00	
	On cover		77.50
109a	A20 50c green	47.50	16.00
	Never hinged	95.00	
	On cover		120.00
110a	A20 1fr carmine	125.00	12.00
	Never hinged	250.00	
	On cover		325.00
	On cover, single franking		
111a	A20 3fr yellow brown	310.00	225.00
	Never hinged	625.00	
	On cover		450.00
	On cover, single franking		1,750.

Numeral Type of 1882-99
1905 Typo. Perf. 11½
Granite Paper

113	A19 2c dull bister	5.50	2.40
	Never hinged	11.00	
	On cover		11.00
114	A19 3c gray brown	5.50	80.00
	Never hinged	11.00	
	On cover		11.00
115	A19 5c green	5.50	.80
	Never hinged	11.00	
	On cover		4.00
116	A19 10c scarlet	5.50	.80
	Never hinged	11.00	
	On cover		4.00
117	A19 12c ultra	7.00	2.25
	Never hinged	14.00	
	On cover		11.00
118	A19 15c brown vio	80.00	17.00
	Never hinged	160.00	
	On cover		95.00
a.	15c red lilac	325.00	140.00
	Never hinged	650.00	190.00
	On cover		275.00
	Nos. 113-118 (6)	109.00	103.25

Helvetia Types of 1882-1904
1907 Engr. Perf. 11½x12
Granite Paper

119	A20 20c orange	4.00	4.00
	Never hinged	8.00	
	On cover		20.00
120	A20 25c blue	12.50	14.00
	Never hinged	25.00	
	On cover		30.00
121	A20 30c red brown	7.75	20.00
	Never hinged	16.00	
	On cover		65.00
122	A21 40c gray	32.50	57.50
	Never hinged	65.00	
	On cover		135.00
a.	Helvetia without diadem	375.00	1,350.
	Never hinged	750.00	
123	A20 50c gray green	8.50	15.50
	Never hinged	17.00	
	On cover		75.00
124	A20 1fr carmine	32.50	7.75
	Never hinged	65.00	
	On cover		190.00
125a	A20 3fr yellow brown		14,500.

There are retouches and plate flaws on all values.

Perf. 11½x11

120a	A20 25c deep blue	12.00	7.75
	Never hinged	24.00	
	On cover		25.00
121a	A20 30c red brown	250.00	475.00
	Never hinged	500.00	
	On cover		1,000.
122b	A20 40c gray		17,500.
124a	A20 1fr carmine	16,000.	6,500.
125	A20 3fr yel brn	130.00	80.00
	Never hinged	275.00	
	On cover		1,200.

William Tell's Son — A23

Helvetia
A24   A25

1907-25 Typo. Perf. 11½
Granite Paper

126	A23	2c pale bister	.30	.55
127	A23	3c lilac brn	.25	10.00
128	A23	5c yellow grn	2.25	.50
129	A24	10c rose red	1.50	.50
130	A24	12c ocher	.30	3.50
131	A24	15c red vio	3.00	13.00
132	A25	20c red & yel ('08)	2.25	1.00
133	A25	25c dp blue ('08)	1.90	.65
a.		Tête bêche pair	17.00	55.00
134	A25	30c yel brn & pale grn ('08)	1.60	.50
135	A25	35c yel grn & yel ('08)	1.90	1.40
136	A25	40c red vio & yel ('08)	12.50	1.00
a.		Designer's name in full on the rock ('08)	6.00	82.50
137	A25	40c deep blue ('22)	1.75	.50
a.		40c light blue ('21)	5.50	1.90
138	A25	40c red vio & grn ('25)	25.00	.50
139	A25	50c dp grn & pale grn ('08)	11.00	.50
140	A25	60c brn org & buff ('18)	9.25	.65
141	A25	70c dk brn & buff ('08)	55.00	17.00
142	A25	70c vio & buff ('24)	14.50	2.25
143	A25	80c slate & buff ('15)	9.75	1.10
144	A25	1fr dp cl & pale grn ('08)	7.00	.55
145	A25	3fr bis & yel ('08)	275.00	2.10
		Nos. 126-145 (20)	436.00	57.75

No. 136 has two leaves and "CL" below sword hilt. No. 136a has three leaves and designer's full name below hilt.

For surcharges and overprints see Nos. 189, 199, O10-O13, O15, 1O6-1O8, 1O14-1O16, 2O18-2O26, 3O14-3O22.

1933 With Grilled Gum

135a	A25	35c yel grn & yel	1.40	12.50
138a	A25	40c red vio & grn	32.50	1.50
139a	A25	50c dp grn & pale grn	9.00	1.50
140a	A25	60c brn org & buff	12.00	1.50
142a	A25	70c vio & buff	17.50	3.75
143a	A25	80c slate & buff	4.25	6.50
144a	A25	1fr dp cl & pale grn	19.00	6.50
		Nos. 146-144a (7)	104.40	31.50

"Grilled" Gum

In 1930-44 many Swiss stamps were treated with a light grilling process, applied with the gumming to counteract the tendency to curl. It resembles a faint grill of vertical and horizontal ribs covering the entire back of the stamp, and can be seen after the gum has been removed. Listings of the grilled gum varieties begin with No. 135a.

William Tell's Son — A26

Bow-string in front of stock

1909 Perf. 11½, 12
Granite Paper

146	A26	2c bister	.25	1.40
a.		Tête bêche pair	3.25	17.50
147	A26	3c dark violet	.25	14.00
148	A26	5c green	3.75	.25
a.		Tête bêche pair	14.00	50.00
		Nos. 146-148 (3)	4.25	15.65

See Nos. 149-163. For surcharges and overprints see Nos. 186, 193-195, 207-208, 1O1-1O3, 1O9-1O11, 2O1-2O7, 3O1-3O5.

First Redrawing

Bow-string behind stock. Thin loop above crossbow. Letters of "HELVETIA" without serifs.

1910-17 Granite Paper

149	A26	2c bister ('10)	8.75	8.00
150	A26	3c dk violet ('10)	.25	.25
a.		Tête bêche pair	2.75	2.75
b.		Booklet pane of 6	12.50	
151	A26	3c brown org ('17)	.25	.25
a.		Tête bêche pair	8.25	11.00
152	A26	5c green ('10)	21.00	6.50
a.		Tête bêche pair	92.50	175.00
		Nos. 149-152 (4)	30.25	15.00

Second Redrawing

Bow-string behind stock. Thick loop above crossbow. Letters of "HELVETIA" with serifs.
7½ CENTIMES:
Type I — Top of "7" is ½mm thick. The "1" of "½" has only traces of serifs. The two base plates of the statue are of even thickness.
Type II — Top of "7" is 1mm thick. The "1" of "½" has distinct serifs. The upper base plate is thinner than the lower.

1911-30 Granite Paper

153	A26	2c bister ('11)	.25	.25
a.		Tête bêche pair	3.25	1.60
154	A26	2½c claret ('18)	.25	1.10
155	A26	2½c ol, buff ('28)	.55	2.10
156	A26	3c ultra, buff ('30)	2.75	6.00
157	A26	5c green ('11)	1.75	.25
a.		Tête bêche pair	5.50	10.00
158	A26	5c org, buff ('21)	.25	.25
a.		Bklt. pane of 6 (5 #158, 168)	14.00	47.50
159	A26	5c gray vio, buff ('24)	.25	.25
a.		Bklt. pane of 6 (5 #159, 168)	6.50	19.00
160	A26	5c red vio, buff ('27)	.25	.25
a.		Bklt. pane 6 (5 #160, 168)	30.00	65.00
161	A26	5c dk grn, buff ('30)	.30	.25
a.		Bklt. pane 6 (5 #161, 169)	27.50	70.00
162	A26	7½c gray (I) ('18)	1.10	.25
b.		Tête bêche pair	13.00	45.00
c.		7½c slate (II)	4.50	2.75
163	A26	7½c dp grn, buff (I) ('28)	.30	3.25
		Nos. 153-163 (11)	8.00	14.20

1933 With Grilled Gum

156a	A26	3c ultra, buff	4.75	17.50
161b	A26	5c dark green, buff	.55	5.00

Helvetia   William Tell
A27   A28

1909 Granite Paper

164	A27	10c carmine	.60	.40
a.		Tête bêche pair	2.25	6.00
165	A27	12c bister brn	.85	.40
166	A27	15c red violet	26.00	1.10
		Nos. 164-166 (3)	27.45	1.90

For surcharge see No. 187.

1914-30 Granite Paper Perf. 11½

TEN CENTIMES:
Type I — Bust 16½mm high. "HELVETIA" 15½mm wide. Cross bar of "H" at middle of the letter.
Type II — Bust 15mm high. "HELVETIA" 15mm wide. Cross bar of "H" above middle of the letter.

167	A28	10c red, buff (type II)	.75	.25
a.		10c red, buff (type I)	2.50	26.00
b.		Tête bêche pair (II)	3.25	4.25
d.		Bklt. pane 6 (5 #167, 172)	50.00	160.00
168	A28	10c grn, buff (type II) ('21)	.25	.25
a.		Tête bêche pair	1.10	1.40
168C	A28	10c bl grn, buff (type II) ('28)	.25	.25
d.		Tête bêche pair	2.50	2.50
169	A28	10c vio, buff (type II) ('30)	2.25	.25
a.		Tête bêche pair	9.25	1.40
170	A28	12c brn, buff	.25	3.25
171	A28	13c ol grn, buff ('15)	1.40	.50

172	A28	15c vio, buff	3.50	.25
b.		15c dk vio, buff	32.50	4.25
c.		Tête bêche pair	87.50	125.00
173	A28	15c brn red, buff ('28)	2.50	2.75
174	A28	20c red vio, buff ('21)	3.25	.25
a.		Tête bêche pair	6.50	7.50
175	A28	20c ver, buff ('24)	1.00	.50
a.		Tête bêche pair	5.75	9.25
176	A28	20c car, buff ('25)	.25	.25
a.		Tête bêche pair	2.50	.55
177	A28	25c ver, buff ('21)	2.25	1.60
178	A28	25c car, buff ('22)	1.10	.85
179	A28	25c brn, buff ('25)	3.25	1.25
180	A28	30c dp bl, buff ('24)	9.25	.50
		Nos. 167-180 (15)	31.50	12.95

1932-33 With Grilled Gum

169c	A28	10c violet, buff	4.50	1.50
173a	A28	15c brn red, buff ('33)	50.00	52.50
176c	A28	20c carmine, buff	7.25	1.50
179a	A28	25c brown, buff ('33)	125.00	35.00
180a	A28	30c deep blue, buff	72.50	2.50
		Nos. 169c-180a (5)	259.25	93.00

For surcharges and overprints see Nos. 188, 196-198, 1O4-1O5, 1O12-1O13, 2O8-2O17, 3O6-3O13.

The Mythen
A29

The Rütli — A30

The Jungfrau
A31

1914-30 Engr. Granite Paper

181	A29	3fr dk green	650.00	6.50
182	A29	3fr red ('18)	87.50	1.40
183	A30	5fr dp ultra	35.00	3.00
184	A31	10fr dull violet	100.00	3.25
185	A31	10fr gray grn ('30)	225.00	37.50
		Nos. 181-185 (5)	1,097.	51.65

See No. 206. For overprints see Nos. 2O27-2O30, 3O23-3O26.

Stamps of 1909-14 Surcharged

a   b

c

1915

186	A26(a)	1c on 2c bister	.25	1.25
187	A27(b)	13c on 12c bis brn	.25	9.25
188	A28(c)	13c on 12c brn, buff	.30	.90
		Nos. 186-188 (3)	.80	11.40

No. 141 Surcharged

189	A25	80c on 70c	25.00	17.50

Significant of Peace
A32

"Peace"
A33

"Dawn of Peace"
A34

Perf. 11½
1919, Aug. 1 Typo. Unwmk.

190	A32	7½c olive drab & blk	.80	2.25
191	A33	10c red & yel	1.10	8.75
192	A34	15c violet & yel	1.90	2.75
		Nos. 190-192 (3)	3.80	13.75

Commemorating Peace after World War I.

Nos. 151, 149, 162, 171-172, 133 Surcharged in Black, Red or Dark Blue

a   b

c

1921 Wmk. 183

193	A26(a)	2½c on 3c (Bl)	.25	1.10
a.		Tête bêche pair	1.10	1.25
b.		Inverted surcharge	800.00	1,550.
c.		Double surcharge	550.00	775.00
194	A26(a)	5c on 2c (R)	.25	4.50
a.		Double surcharge	450.00	450.00
195	A26(a)	5c on 7½c (R)	.25	.55
a.		Tête bêche pair	6.50	55.00
b.		Double surcharge	550.00	550.00
c.		5c on 7½c slate (II)	2,200.	4,500.
196	A28(b)	10c on 13c (R)	.25	2.25
a.		Double surcharge	550.00	550.00
197	A28(c)	20c on 15c (Bk)	.55	2.75
a.		Tête bêche pair	2.50	55.00
b.		Double surcharge	875.00	875.00
198	A28(c)	20c on 15c (Bl)	2.25	5.50
b.		Double surcharge	875.00	875.00
199	A25(c)	20c on 25c dp bl (R)	.25	.55
a.		Tête bêche pair	1.50	4.50
		Nos. 193-199 (7)	4.05	17.20

A36

1924 Typo. Perf. 11½
Granite Paper, Surface Colored

200	A36	90c grn & red, grn	15.00	2.75
		Never hinged	45.00	
201	A36	1.20fr brn rose & red, rose	5.25	5.25
		Never hinged	16.00	
202	A36	1.50fr bl & red, bl	37.50	6.50
		Never hinged	115.00	
203	A36	2fr gray blk & red, gray	47.50	6.75
		Never hinged	150.00	
		Nos. 200-203 (4)	105.25	21.25
		Set, never hinged	325.00	

1933 With Grilled Gum

200a	A36	90c	17.50	3.25
		Never hinged	45.00	
201a	A36	1.20fr	47.50	5.50
		Never hinged	125.00	
202a	A36	1.50fr	32.50	6.50
		Never hinged	82.50	

203a	A36	2fr	27.50	8.25
		Never hinged	70.00	
	Nos. 200a-203a (4)		125.00	23.50
	Set, never hinged		325.00	

For overprints see Nos. O16-O18, 2O31-2O34, 3O27-3O30.

1940   With Smooth Gum
Ordinary Paper

200b	A36	90c	16.00	80.00
		Never hinged	40.00	
201b	A36	1.20fr	16.00	80.00
		Never hinged	40.00	
202b	A36	1.50fr	16.00	650.00
		Never hinged	40.00	
	Nos. 200b-202b (3)		48.00	810.00

Building in Bern, Location of 1st UPU Congress, 1874
A37   A38

1924, Oct. 9   Engr.   Wmk. 183
Granite Paper

204	A37	20c vermilion	.55	1.60
205	A38	30c dull blue	1.10	6.25
	Set, never hinged		3.25	

50th anniv. of the UPU.

Type of 1914 Issue

The Rütli — A39

1928   Re-engraved   Perf. 11½

206	A39	5fr blue	110.00	9.75
		Never hinged	300.00	
a.		Imperf., pair, never hinged	10,000.	

In the re-engraved stamp the picture is clearer and lighter than on No. 183. "HELVETIA" is in smaller letters. The names at foot of the stamp are "Grasset-J. Sprenger" instead of "E. GRASSET-A. BURKHARD."
For overprints see Nos. 2O35, 3O31.

Nos. 155 and 163 Surcharged

1930, June   Perf. 11½

207	A26	3c on 2½c ol grn, *buff*	.25	2.75
208	A26	5c on 7½c dp grn, *buff*	.25	8.00
	Set, never hinged		1.10	

The Mythen A40

1931   Engr.   Granite Paper

209	A40	3fr orange brown	65.00	5.25
		Never hinged	150.00	

For overprints see Nos. 2O56, 3O47.

Dove on Broken Sword — A41

Peace A42

1932, Feb. 2   Typo.   Perf. 11½
Granite Paper

210	A41	5c peacock blue	.25	.25
211	A41	10c orange	.25	.25
212	A41	20c cerise	.25	.25
213	A41	30c ultra	2.25	1.60
214	A41	60c olive brown	17.50	8.75

Unwmk.
Photo.

215	A42	1fr olive gray & bl	17.50	8.75
	Nos. 210-215 (6)		38.00	19.85
	Set, never hinged		95.00	

Intl. Disarmament Conf., Geneva, Feb. 1932.
For overprints see #2O36-2O41, 3O32-3O37.

Louis Favre — A43   Alfred Escher — A44

Design: 30c, Emil Welti.

Wmk. 183
1932, May 31   Engr.   Perf. 11½
Granite Paper

216	A43	10c red brown	.25	.25
217	A44	20c vermilion	.25	.25
218	A44	30c deep ultra	.55	2.10
	Nos. 216-218 (3)		1.05	2.60
	Set, never hinged		3.00	

Completion of the St. Gotthard tunnel, 50th anniv.
Nos. 216-218 exist imperforate.

Staubbach Falls A46   Mt. Pilatus A47

Chillon Castle A48   Rhone Glacier A49

St. Gotthard Railroad A50   Via Mala Gorge A51

Rhine Falls — A52

1934, July 2   Typo.   Perf. 11½
Granite Paper

219	A46	3c olive	.25	3.00
220	A47	5c emerald	.25	.25
221	A48	10c brt violet	.40	.25
222	A49	15c orange	.50	3.25
223	A50	20c red	.60	.60

224	A51	25c brown	7.75	8.25
225	A52	30c ultra	25.00	2.10
	Nos. 219-225 (7)		34.75	17.70
	Set, never hinged		100.00	

Tête bêche Pairs

...II		00	1.60	1.60
221a	A48	10c	1.50	.85
222a	A49	15c	1.75	3.00
223a	A50	20c	3.50	2.25

1934, Sept. 29   Souvenir Sheet

226	Sheet of 4		500.00	550.00
	Never hinged		825.00	

No. 226 was issued in connection with the Swiss National Philatelic Exhibition at Zurich, Sept. 29 to Oct. 7, 1934. It contains one each of Nos. 220-223. Size: 62x72mm.
For overprints see Nos. 2O42-2O46, 3O48.

Staubbach Falls A53   Mt. Pilatus A54

Chillon Castle A55   Rhone Glacier A56

St. Gotthard Railroad A57   Via Mala Gorge A58

Rhine Falls — A59   Balsthal Pass — A60

Alpine Lake of Säntis — A61

Type I   Type II

Two types of 10c red violet:
I — Shading inside "0" of 10 has only vertical lines.
II — Shading in "0" includes two diagonal lines.

1936-42   Unwmk.   Engr.   Perf. 11½

227	A53	3c olive	.25	.25
228	A54	5c blue green	.25	.25
229	A55	10c red vio (II)	.85	.25
b.		Type I	.85	.25
230	A55	10c dk red brn ('39)	.25	.25
230B	A55	10c org brn ('42)	.25	.25
231	A56	15c orange	.40	1.10
232	A57	20c carmine	4.75	.25
233	A58	25c lt brown	.50	1.10
234	A59	30c ultra	.90	.25
235	A60	35c yellow grn	1.10	1.25
236	A61	40c gray	6.00	.25
	Nos. 227-236 (11)		15.50	5.45
	Set, never hinged		37.50	

Two types of the 20c. See Nos. 316-321 in Scott Standard catalogue, Vol. 6.
For overprints see Nos. O1-O4, O6-O9, O19-O19-O22, O24-O27, 2O47-2O55, 2O68-

2O68A, 2O70-2O73, 2O75-2O78, 3O38-3O46, 3O60-3O60A, 3O62-3O65, 3O67-3O70, 4O1-4O4, 4O6-4O9, 4O23-4O24, 4O27-4O28, 5O1-5O2, 5O5. Post 1940 listings are in Scott Standard catalogue, Vol. 6.

Tête bêche Pairs

228a	A54	5c blue green	.45	.30
229a	A55	10c red violet (II)	4.50	5.50
230a	A55	10c dark red brown	1.75	1.10
230d	A55	10c orange brown	.50	.60
232a	A57	20c carmine	25.00	35.00

1936-40   With Grilled Gum

227a	A53	3c olive	.65	6.25
228d	A54	5c blue green	.30	.25
229d	A55	10c red violet (II)	.30	.25
e.		Type I	1.00	.25
230e	A55	10c dark red brown ('40)	1.90	25.00
231a	A56	15c orange	.30	1.10
232c	A57	20c carmine	6.75	.25
233a	A58	25c light brown	1.00	5.00
234a	A59	30c ultra	.95	.25
235a	A60	35c yellow green	1.40	3.25
236a	A61	40c gray	9.25	.25
	Nos. 227a-236a (10)		22.80	42.10
	Set, never hinged		47.50	

Mobile Post Office A62

1937, Sept. 5   Photo.
Granite Paper

237	A62	10c black & yellow	.25	.50
		Never hinged	.55	

No. 237 was sold exclusively by the traveling post office. It exists on two kinds of granite paper, black and red fibers or blue and red fibers. See No. 307 for type A62 redrawn.

View of Labor Building from Lake Geneva A63

Palace of League of Nations A64

Main Building, Palace of League of Nations A65

Labor Building and Albert Thomas Monument A66

1938, May 2   Perf. 11½
Granite Paper

238	A63	20c red & buff	.25	.25
239	A64	30c blue & lt blue	.45	.25
240	A65	60c brown & buff	1.75	2.25
241	A66	1fr black & buff	7.50	17.00
	Nos. 238-241 (4)		9.95	19.75
	Set, never hinged		25.00	

Opening of Assembly Hall of the Palace of the League of Nations.
For overprints see Nos. 2O57-2O64, 3O49-3O56.

Souvenir Sheet

A67

Engraved and Typographed
1938, Sept. 17   Unwmk.   Perf. 11½
Granite Paper

242	A67	Sheet of 3	37.50	32.50
		Never hinged	70.00	
a.		AP4 10c on 65c gray bl & dp	19.00	25.00
b.		A68 20c red	1.10	2.50

Natl. Phil. Exhib. at Aarau, Sept. 17-25, and 25th anniv. of Swiss air mail. No. 242 contains 2 No. 243, but on granite paper, and a 10c on 65c similar to No. C22 but redrawn, with wing tips 1½mm from side frame lines; overall size 37x20½mm; no watermark.

On No. C22, wing tips touch frame lines; size is 36x21½mm; Wmk. 183.

Lake Lugano — A68

First Federal Pact, 1291
A69

Diet of Stans, 1481
A70

Citizens Voting
A71

1938, Sept. 17   Engr.   Perf. 11½

243	A68	20c red	.25	.25
a.		"c," tête bêche pair	.50	.85
c.		Grilled gum	.40	.40
d.		As "c," tête bêche pair	1.40	15.00

Granite Paper

244	A69	3fr brn car, grnsh	11.00	8.75
245	A70	5fr slate bl, grnsh	7.50	6.00
246	A71	10fr grn, grnsh	47.50	35.00
		Nos. 243-246 (4)	66.25	50.00
		Set, never hinged	190.00	

No. 243 is printed on ordinary paper. Nos. 244-246 are on granite surface-colored paper. The greenish surface coating has faded on most examples.

For type A68 in orange brown, see No. 318 in Scott Standard catalogue, Vol. 6.

See Nos. 242b, 284-286 (in Scott Standard catalogue, Vol. 6). For overprints see Nos. O5, O23, 2O65-2O67, 2O69, 2O74, 2O88-2O90, 3O57-3O59, 3O61, 3O66, 3O80-3O82, 4O5, 4O19-4O21, O4O25, 5O3, 5O23-5O25, 7O18-7O20. Post 1940 listings are in Scott Standard catalogue, Vol. 6.

Deputation of Trades and Professions — A72

Swiss Family A73

Alpine Scenery A74

Engr., Photo. (30c)
1939, Feb. 1   Perf. 11½
Inscribed in French

247	A72	10c dl pur & red	.25	.25
248	A73	20c lake & red	.50	.25
249	A74	30c dp blue & red	2.50	3.00

Inscribed in German

250	A72	10c dl pur & red	.25	.25
251	A73	20c lake & red	.40	.25
252	A74	30c dp blue & red	2.50	8.25

Inscribed in Italian

253	A72	10c dl pur & red	.25	.25
254	A73	20c lake & red	1.90	.25
255	A74	30c dp blue & red	2.50	9.25
		Nos. 247-255 (9)	11.05	22.00
		Set, never hinged	35.00	

National Exposition of 1939, Zurich.

Tree and Crossbow — A75

1939, May 6   Photo.   Perf. 11½
Granite Paper
Inscribed in French

256	A75	5c deep green	.55	1.60
257	A75	10c gray brown	.55	1.90
258	A75	20c brt carmine	1.10	1.60
259	A75	30c violet blue	3.00	8.00

Inscribed in German

260	A75	5c deep green	.55	2.50
261	A75	10c gray brown	.55	2.50
262	A75	20c brt carmine	1.10	3.50
263	A75	30c violet blue	8.75	9.50

Inscribed in Italian

264	A75	5c deep green	.85	4.50
265	A75	10c gray brown	.55	3.50
266	A75	20c brt carmine	1.10	4.25
267	A75	30c violet blue	3.25	11.00
		Nos. 256-267 (12)	21.90	54.35
		Set, never hinged	32.50	

National Exposition of 1939.

The 5c, 10c and 20c stamps in the three languages exist se-tenant in coils. On the 10c coil stamp, the inscription "COURVOISIER S.A." beneath is design is smaller, with the "A" just left of the point on the "V" of "HELVETIA". On the sheet stamp, the "A" is just right of the "V". Value about three times that of the sheet stamp.

1939   With Grilled Gum

256a	A75	5c deep green	.75	2.25
257a	A75	10c gray brown	.75	2.25
258a	A75	20c bright carmine	1.90	3.00
260a	A75	5c deep green	.75	1.60
262a	A75	20c bright carmine	1.90	1.60
264a	A75	5c deep green	1.10	3.75
265a	A75	10c gray brown	1.00	3.00
266a	A75	20c bright carmine	1.90	3.25
		Nos. 256a-266a (8)	10.05	20.70

View of Geneva A76

Perf. 11½
1939, Aug. 22   Photo.   Unwmk.
Granite Paper

268	A76	20c red, car & buff	.25	.25
269	A76	30c blue, car & gray	.30	2.75
		Set, never hinged	1.40	

75th anniv. of the founding of the Intl. Red Cross Society.

SEMI-POSTAL STAMPS

Nos. B1-B76, B81-B84 were sold at premiums of 2c for 3c stamps, 5c for 5c-20c stamps and 10c for 30c-40c stamps.

Helvetia and Matterhorn — SP2

Perf. 11½, 12
1913, Dec. 1   Typo.   Wmk. 183
Granite Paper

B1	SP2	5c green	2.75	8.25
		Never hinged	7.75	

Boy (Appenzell) SP3   Girl (Lucerne) SP4

1915, Dec. 1   Perf. 11½

B2	SP3	5c green, buff	3.25	8.25
a.		Tête bêche pair	82.50	875.00
		Never hinged	160.00	
B3	SP4	10c red, buff	100.00	87.50
		Set, never hinged	225.00	

Girl (Fribourg) SP5   Dairy Boy (Bern) SP6

Girl (Vaud) — SP7

1916, Dec. 1

B4	SP5	3c vio, buff	5.00	37.50
B5	SP6	5c grn, buff	11.00	9.25
B6	SP7	10c brn red, buff	47.50	77.50
		Nos. B4-B6 (3)	63.50	124.25
		Set, never hinged	175.00	

Girl (Valais) SP8   Girl (Unterwalden) SP9

Girl (Ticino) — SP10

1917, Dec. 1

B7	SP8	3c vio, buff	3.25	50.00
B8	SP9	5c green, buff	7.75	5.50
B9	SP10	10c red, buff	19.00	22.50
		Nos. B7-B9 (3)	30.00	78.00
		Set, never hinged	87.50	

Uri SP11   Geneva SP12

Straw-Surfaced Paper

1918, Dec. 1

B10	SP11	10c red, org & blk	7.75	25.00
B11	SP12	15c vio, red, org & blk	9.25	11.00
		Set, never hinged	52.50	

Nidwalden SP13   Vaud SP14

Obwalden — SP15

Cream-Surfaced Paper

1919, Dec. 1

B12	SP13	7½c gray, red & blk	2.50	14.00
B13	SP14	10c lake, grn & blk	2.50	14.00
B14	SP15	15c pur, red & blk	5.00	7.25
		Nos. B12-B14 (3)	10.00	35.25
		Set, never hinged	22.50	

Schwyz SP16   Zürich SP17

Ticino — SP18

Cream-Surfaced Paper

1920, Dec. 1

B15	SP16	7½c gray & red	3.75	11.50
B16	SP17	10c red & lt bl	5.00	12.50
B17	SP18	15c violet, red & bl	2.75	6.00
		Nos. B15-B17 (3)	11.50	30.00
		Set, never hinged	25.00	

Valais SP19   Bern SP20

Switzerland — SP21

1184   SWITZERLAND

Cream-Surfaced Paper

1921, Dec. 1
B18 SP19 10c grn, red & blk   .65   3.00
B19 SP20 20c vio, red, org &
           blk   1.90   3.50
B20 SP21 40c blue & red   7.25 47.50
     Nos. B18-B20 (3)   9.80 54.33
     Set, never hinged   25.00

Zug
SP22

Fribourg
SP23

Lucerne
SP24

Switzerland
SP25

Cream-Surfaced Paper

1922, Dec. 1
B21 SP22 5c org, pale bl &
           blk   .50   5.50
B22 SP23 10c ol grn & blk   .60   2.50
B23 SP24 20c vio, pale bl &
           blk   1.00   2.50
B24 SP25 40c bl & red   8.75 47.50
     Nos. B21-B24 (4)   10.85 58.00
     Set, never hinged   26.00

Basel
SP26

Glarus (St.
Fridolin)
SP27

Neuchâtel
SP28

Switzerland
SP29

Cream-Surfaced Paper

1923, Dec. 1
B25 SP26 5c org & blk   .40   3.50
B26 SP27 10c multi   .40   1.90
B27 SP28 20c multi   .45   1.90
B28 SP29 40c dk bl & red   7.75 37.50
     Nos. B25-B28 (4)   9.00 44.80
     Set, never hinged   21.00

Appenzell
SP30

Solothurn
SP31

Schaffhausen
SP32

Switzerland
SP33

Cream-Surfaced Paper

1924, Dec. 1
B29 SP30 5c dk vio & blk   .25   1.60
B30 SP31 10c grn, red & blk   .40   1.00
B31 SP32 20c car, yel & blk   .65   1.00
B32 SP33 30c bl, red & blk   1.40 11.00
     Nos. B29-B32 (4)   2.70 14.60
     Set, never hinged   6.50

St. Gallen
(Canton)
SP34

Appenzell-
Ausser-
Rhoden
SP35

Grisons
SP36

Switzerland
SP37

Cream-Surfaced Paper

1925, Dec. 1
B33 SP34 5c vio, grn & blk   .25   1.10
B34 SP35 10c grn & blk   .25   .85
B35 SP36 20c multi   .25   .85
B36 SP37 30c dk bl, red & blk   1.10   8.25
     Nos. B33-B36 (4)   1.85 11.05
     Set, never hinged   4.50

Thurgau
SP38

Basel
SP39

Aargau
SP40

Switzerland
SP41

Cream-Surfaced Paper

1926, Dec. 1
B37 SP38 5c vio, bis & grn   .25   1.40
B38 SP39 10c gray grn, red &
           blk   .25   1.40
B39 SP40 20c red, blk & bl   .25   1.40
B40 SP41 30c dk bl & red   1.10 12.50
     Nos. B37-B40 (4)   1.85 16.70
     Set, never hinged   4.50

Orphan
SP42

Orphan at
Pestalozzi
School
SP43

SP44

J. H.
Pestalozzi
SP45

1927, Dec. 1   Typo.   Wmk. 183
Granite Paper
B41 SP42 5c red vio & yel,
           grysh   .25   1.60
B42 SP43 10c grn & fawn, grnsh   .25   .60
Engr.
B43 SP44 20c red   .25   .60

Unwmk.
Photo.
B44 SP45 30c gray bl & blk   1.10   6.50
     Nos. B41-B44 (4)   1.85   9.30
     Set, never hinged   3.25

Nos. B41-B44 for the centenary of the death
of Johann Heinrich Pestalozzi, the Swiss educational reformer.

Lausanne
SP46

Winterthur
SP47

St. Gallen
(City) — SP48

J. H.
Dunant
SP49

1928, Dec. 1   Typo.   Wmk. 183
Cream-Surfaced Paper.
B45 SP46 5c dk vio, red & blk   .25   1.60
B46 SP47 10c bl grn, org red &
           blk   .25   .90
B47 SP48 20c brn red, blk & yel   .25   .90
Unwmk.
Photo.
Thick White Paper
B48 SP49 30c dl bl & red   1.10   7.00
     Nos. B45-B48 (4)   1.85 10.40
     Set, never hinged   3.50

No. B48 for the centenary of the birth of
Jean Henri Dunant, Swiss author, philanthropist and founder of the Red Cross Society.

Lake
Lugano and
Mt.
Salvatore
SP50

Lake
Engstlen
and Mt.
Titlis
SP51

Mt.
Lyskamm
SP52

Nicholas
von der
Flüe
SP53

1929, Dec. 1   Perf. 11x11½
B49 SP50 5c dk vio & red org   .25   1.40
B50 SP51 10c ol brn & gray bl   .25   1.10
B51 SP52 20c brn garnet & bl   .25   1.10
B52 SP53 30c dk blue   1.25 12.50
     Nos. B49-B52 (4)   2.00 16.10
     Set, never hinged   4.50

No. B52 for Nicholas von der Flüe, the
Swiss patriot. By his advice the Swiss Confederation was continued and Swiss independence was saved.

Fribourg
SP54

Altdorf
SP55

Schaffhausen
SP56

Jeremias
Gotthelf
SP57

Wmk. 183
1930, Dec. 1   Typo.   Perf. 11½
Cream-Surfaced Paper
B53 SP54 5c dp grn, dl bl & blk   .25   1.40
B54 SP55 10c multicolored   .25   .90
B55 SP56 20c multicolored   .30   .90
Engr.
White Paper
B56 SP57 30c slate blue   1.25   6.00
     Nos. B53-B56 (4)   2.05   9.20
     Set, never hinged   4.00

No. B56 for Jeremias Gotthelf, pen name of
Albrecht Bitzius, pastor and author.

Lakes
Silvaplana
and Sils
SP58

Wetterhorn
SP59

Lake
Geneva
SP60

Alexandre
Vinet
SP61

1931, Dec. 1   Photo.   Unwmk.
Granite Paper
B57 SP58 5c dp grn   .45   1.60
B58 SP59 10c dk vio   .40   .85
B59 SP60 20c brn red   .55   1.10
Wmk. 183
Engr.
B60 SP61 30c ultra   4.50 19.00
     Nos. B57-B60 (4)   5.90 22.55
     Set, never hinged   14.00

No. B60 for Alexandre Rudolph Vinet, critic
and theologian.

Flag Swinger
SP62

Putting the
Stone
SP63

Wrestling
SP64

Eugen Huber
SP65

1932, Dec. 1   Typo.   Unwmk.
Granite Paper
B61	SP62	5c dk grn & red	.30	1.90
B62	SP63	10c orange	.45	2.25
B63	SP64	20c scarlet	.55	1.90

Wmk. 183
Engr.
B64	SP65	30c ultra	2.25	8.75
	Nos. B61-B64 (4)		3.55	*14.80*
	Set, never hinged		9.50	

No. B64 for Eugen Huber, jurist and author of the Swiss Civil Law Book.

Girl of
Vaud — SP66

Girl of
Bern — SP67

Girl of Ticino
SP68

Jean Baptiste
Girard (Le Père
Grégoire)
SP69

1933, Dec. 1   Photo.   Unwmk.
Granite Paper
B65	SP66	5c grn & buff	.30	1.50
B66	SP67	10c vio & buff	.30	1.10
B67	SP68	20c red & buff	.45	2.10

Wmk. 183
Engr.
B68	SP69	30c ultra	2.50	8.50
	Nos. B65-B68 (4)		3.55	*13.20*
	Set, never hinged		8.25	

Girl of
Appenzell
SP70

Girl of Valais
SP71

Girl of Grisons
SP72

Albrecht von
Haller
SP73

1934, Dec. 1   Photo.   Unwmk.
B69	SP70	5c grn & buff	.30	1.60
B70	SP71	10c vio & buff	.45	1.10
B71	SP72	20c red & buff	.45	1.60

Wmk. 183
Engr.
B72	SP73	30c ultra	2.50	8.75
	Nos. B69-B72 (4)		3.70	*13.05*
	Set, never hinged		8.25	

Girl of Basel
SP74

Girl of Lucerne
SP75

Girl of Geneva
SP76

Stefano
Franscini
SP77

1935, Dec. 1   Photo.   Unwmk.
Granite Paper
B73	SP74	5c grn & buff	.25	1.75
B74	SP75	10c vio & buff	.45	1.10
B75	SP76	20c red & buff	.45	2.75

Wmk. 183
Engr.
B76	SP77	30c ultra	2.50	8.75
	Nos. B73-B76 (4)		3.65	*14.35*
	Set, never hinged		8.25	

No. B76 honors Stefano Franscini (1796-1857), political economist and educator.

Alpine
Herdsman — SP78

Perf. 11½
1936, Oct. 1   Photo.   Unwmk.
Granite Paper
B77	SP78	10c + 5c vio	.55	1.00
B78	SP78	20c + 10c dk red	.85	4.25
B79	SP78	30c + 10c ultra	3.75	20.00
	Nos. B77-B79 (3)		5.15	*25.25*
	Set, never hinged		11.00	

Souvenir Sheet
B80	SP78	Sheet of 3	35.00	125.00
	Never hinged		70.00	
a.	Block of 4 sheets		190.00	*875.00*
	Never hinged		300.00	

Swiss National Defense Fund Drive.
No. B80 contains stamps similar to Nos. B77-B79, but on grilled granite paper with blue and red fibers instead of black and red. Sold for 2fr. Size: 120x130mm.

Johann Georg
Nägeli
SP79

Girl of
Neuchâtel
SP80

Girl of Schwyz
SP81

Girl of Zurich
SP82

Wmk. 183
1936, Dec. 1   Engr.   Perf. 11½
Granite Paper
B81	SP79	5c grn	.55	.70

Unwmk.
Photo.
B82	SP80	10c vio & buff	.55	.70
B83	SP81	20c red & buff	.25	1.90
B84	SP82	30c ultra & buff	3.50	30.00
	Nos. B81-B84 (4)		4.85	*33.30*
	Set, never hinged		11.00	

Gen. Henri
Dufour — SP83

Nicholas von
der
Flüe — SP84

Boy
SP85

Girl
SP86

Perf. 11½
1937, Dec. 1   Unwmk.   Engr.
B85	SP83	5c + 5c bl grn	.25	.55
B86	SP84	10c + 5c red vio	.25	.55

Photo.
Granite Paper
B87	SP85	20c + 5c red & silver	.30	.55
B88	SP86	30c + 10c ultra & sil	1.25	5.50
	Nos. B85-B88 (4)		2.05	*7.15*
	Set, never hinged		3.50	

25th anniv. of the Pro Juventute (child welfare) stamps.

Souvenir Sheet
1937, Dec. 20   Imperf.
B89		Sheet of 2	6.50	57.50
a.	SP85 20c + 5c red & silver		1.60	17.00
b.	SP86 30c + 10c ultra & silver		1.60	17.00
	Never hinged		7.50	

Simulated perforation in silver. Sheet sold for 1fr.

Tell
Chapel,
Lake
Lucerne
SP87

1938, June 15   Perf. 11½
Granite Paper
B90	SP87	10c + 10c brt vio & yel	.45	1.10
	Never hinged		1.10	
a.	Grilled gum		22.50	77.50
	Never hinged		32.50	

National Fête Day.

Salomon
Gessner
SP88

Girl of St.
Gallen
SP89

Girl of
Uri — SP90

Girl of
Aargau — SP91

1938, Dec. 1   Engr.   Perf. 11½
B91	SP88	5c + 5c dp bl grn	.25	.50

Photo.
Granite Paper
B92	SP89	10c + 5c pur & buff	.25	.55
B93	SP90	20c + 5c red & buff	.25	.55
B94	SP91	30c + 10c ultra	1.60	6.50
	Nos. B91-B94 (4)		2.35	*8.10*
	Set, never hinged		4.50	

Castle at
Laupen
SP92

1939, June 15
B95	SP92	10c + 10c brn, gray & red	.30	1.10
	Never hinged			

600th anniversary of the Battle of Laupen. The surtax was used to aid needy mothers.

Hans Herzog
SP93

Girl of Fribourg
SP94

Girl of
Nidwalden
SP95

Girl of Basel
SP96

Perf. 11½
1939, Dec. 1   Unwmk.   Engr.
B96	SP93	5c + 5c dk grn	.25	.45

Photo.
Granite Paper
B97	SP94	10c + 5c rose vio & buff	.25	.45
B98	SP95	20c + 5c org red	.30	1.40
B99	SP96	30c + 10c ultra & buff	1.60	11.50
	Nos. B96-B99 (4)		2.40	*13.80*
	Set, never hinged		5.00	

Sempach,
1386 — SP97

Giornico,
1478 — SP98

Calven, 1499
SP99

WWI Ranger
SP100

1940, Mar. 20 — Photo.
Granite Paper
B100	SP97	5c + 5c emer, blk & red	.30	1.25
B101	SP98	10c + 5c brn org, blk & car	.30	.55
B102	SP99	20c + 5c brn red, blk & car	2.25	.95
a.		20c + 5c lt red, blk & car	1.60	32.50
B103	SP100	30c + 5c brt bl, brn blk & red	1.60	8.25

National Fête Day. The surtax was for the National Fund and the Red Cross.

Redrawn
B104	SP99	20c + 5c brn red, blk & car	9.75	6.50
	Nos. B100-B104 (5)		14.20	17.50
	Set, never hinged		26.00	

The base of statue has been heavily shaded. "Calven 1499" moved nearer to bottom line of base. Top line of base removed.

Souvenir Sheet
Unwmk.
1940, July 16 — Photo. Imperf.
Granite Paper
B105	Sheet of 4		250.00	575.00
	Never hinged		425.00	
a.	SP97 5c+5c yel grn, blk & red		11.00	26.00
b.	SP98 10c+5c org yel, blk & red		47.50	210.00
c.	SP99 20c+5c brn red, blk & red (redrawn)		47.50	210.00
d.	SP100 30c+10c chlky bl, blk & red		11.00	26.00

National Fete Day. Sheets measure 125x65mm and sold for 5fr.

Gottfried Keller
SP102

Girl of Thurgau
SP103

Girl of Solothurn
SP104

Girl of Zug
SP105

1940, Dec. 1 — Engr. Perf. 11½
B106	SP102	5c + 5c dk bl grn	.25	.40

Photo.
B107	SP103	10c + 5c brn & buff	.25	.30
B108	SP104	20c + 5c org red & buff	.25	.40
B109	SP105	30c + 10c dp ultra & buff	1.40	9.50
	Nos. B106-B109 (4)		2.15	10.60
	Set, never hinged		4.00	

AIR POST STAMPS

Nos. 134 and 139 Overprinted in Carmine

1919-20 Wmk. 183 Perf. 11½
Granite Paper
C1	A25	30c yel brn & pale grn ('20)	110.00	1,250.
C2	A25	50c dp & pale grn	32.50	110.00
	Set, never hinged		350.00	

Counterfeits of overprint and fraudulent cancellations exist.

Airplane
AP1

Pilot at Controls of Airplane
AP2

Biplane against Sky — AP3

Allegorical Figure of Flight
AP4

Perf. 11½, 12 and Compound
1923-25 Typo.
C3	AP1	15c brn red & ap grn	2.25	8.25
C4	AP1	20c grn & lt grn ('25)	.90	6.00
C5	AP1	25c dk bl & bl	7.75	22.50
C6	AP2	35c brn & buff	11.00	42.50
C7	AP2	40c vio & gray vio	14.50	45.00
C8	AP3	45c red & ind	1.60	7.25
C9	AP3	50c blk & red	12.50	17.00

Perf. 11½
C10	AP4	65c gray bl & dp bl ('24)	3.25	16.00
C11	AP4	75c org & brn red ('24)	15.00	55.00
C12	AP4	1fr vio & dp vio ('24)	42.50	32.50
	Nos. C3-C12 (10)		111.25	252.00
	Set, never hinged		275.00	

For surcharges see Nos. C19, C22, C26.

1933-37 With Grilled Gum
C4a	AP1	20c grn & lt grn ('37)	.30	.40
C5a	AP1	25c dk bl & bl ('34)	5.00	50.00
C8a	AP3	45c red & indigo ('37)	2.50	52.50
C9a	AP3	50c gray grn & scar ('35)	1.10	1.60
C10a	AP4	65c gray bl & dp bl ('37)	2.75	8.50
C11a	AP4	75c org & brn red ('36)	27.50	175.00
C12a	AP4	1fr vio & deep vio	2.10	3.25
	Nos. C4a-C12a (7)		41.25	291.25
	Set, never hinged		65.00	

See Grilled Gum note after No. 145.

Allegory of Air Mail — AP5

Bird Carrying Letter
AP6

1929-30 Granite Paper
C13	AP5	35c red brn, bis & claret	15.00	42.50
C14	AP5	40c dl grn, yel grn & bl	57.50	82.50

C15	AP6	2fr blk brn & red brn, gray ('30)	85.00	85.00
	Nos. C13-C15 (3)		157.50	210.00
	Set, never hinged		425.00	

Front View of Airplane
AP7

1932, Feb. 2 Granite Paper
C16	AP7	15c dp grn & lt grn	.55	1.60
C17	AP7	20c dk red & buff	1.10	2.50
C18	AP7	90c dp bl & gray	7.25	30.00
	Nos. C16-C18 (3)		8.90	34.10
	Set, never hinged		22.50	

Intl. Disarmament Conf., Geneva, Feb. 1932. For surcharges see Nos. C20-C21, C23-C25.

Nos. C3, C10, C16-C18 Surcharged with New Values and Bars in Black or Red
1935-38
C19	AP1	10c on 15c	4.75	37.50
C20	AP7	10c on 15c	.40	.55
a.		Inverted surcharge	6,500.	12,000.
C21	AP7	10c on 20c ('36)	.45	2.25
C22	AP4	10c on 65c ('38)	.25	.40
C23	AP7	30c on 90c ('36)	3.00	14.00
C24	AP7	40c on 20c ('37)	3.75	15.00
C25	AP7	40c on 90c ('36) (R)	3.25	14.50
a.		Vermilion surcharge	92.50	800.00
	Never hinged, #C25a	150.00	
	Nos. C19-C25 (7)		15.85	84.20
	Set, never hinged		40.00	

Stamp similar to No. C22, but from souvenir sheet, is listed as No. 242a.

Type of Air Post Stamp of 1923 Srchd. in Black

1938, May 22 Wmk. 183 Perf. 11½
C26	AP3	75c on 50c gray & scar	6.50	

"Pro Aero" Meeting, May 21-22. No. C26 was not sold to the public in the ordinary way, but affixed to air mail letters by postal officials. It was not regularly obtainable unused.

POSTAGE DUE STAMPS

D1

D2

Type I Frame Normal - UR Ornament

Type I Frame Normal - UL Triangle

Type I Frame Normal: Ornament at UR is undamaged. UL triangle tip and star tip align horizontally. LR triangle tip aligns horizontally with the center of the star.

Wmk. 182 Typo. Perf. 11½
Type I Frame Normal
J1	D1	1c ultra	2.75	2.50
	On cover			40.00
J2	D2	2c ultra	2.75	2.50
	On cover			35.00
J3	D2	3c ultra	22.50	25.00
	On cover			90.00
J4	D2	5c ultra	25.00	12.50
	On cover			52.50
J5	D2	10c ultra	275.00	10.50
	On cover			62.50
J6	D2	20c ultra	300.00	9.00
	On cover			62.50
J7	D2	50c ultra	575.00	27.50
	On cover			130.00
J8	D2	100c ultra	750.00	25.00
	On cover			500.00
J9	D2	500c ultra	700.00	40.00
	On cover			3,500.
	Nos. J1-J9 (9)		2,653.	154.50

A 5c in design D1 exists.

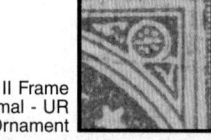
Type I Frame Inverted - UL Triangle

Type I Frame Inverted: Ornament at LL is undamaged. UL triangle tip aligns horizontally with star center. LR triangle tip and star tip align horizontally.

Wmk. 182
1878-80 Typo. Perf. 11½
Type I Frame Inverted
J1a	1c ultra	18.00	20.00
J2a	2c ultra	2.75	2.75
J3a	3c ultra	22.50	23.00
J4a	5c ultra	27.00	11.00
J5a	10c ultra	275.00	18.00
J6a	20c ultra	300.00	11.00
J7a	50c ultra	600.00	35.00
J8a	100c ultra	750.00	25.00
J9a	500c ultra	700.00	40.00
Nos. J1a-J9a (9)		2,695.	185.75

Type II Frame Normal - UR Ornament

Type II Frame Normal: Ornament at UR is broken with a white gap in center. UL triangle tip and star tip align horizontally. LR triangle tip aligns horizontally with the center of the star.

Wmk. 182
1878-80 Typo. Perf. 11½
Type II Frame Normal
J3b	3c ultra	18.00	17.00
J4b	5c ultra	25.00	22.50
J5b	10c ultra	250.00	10.00
J6b	20c ultra	300.00	8.00
J7b	50c ultra	600.00	30.00
J8b	100c ultra	1,500.	175.00
J9b	500c ultra	700.00	100.00
Nos. J3b-J9b (7)		3,393.	362.50

Type II Frame Inverted - LL Ornament

Type II Frame Inverted: Ornament at LL is is broken with a white gap in center. UL triangle tip aligns horizontally with star center. LR triangle tip and star tip align horizontally.

Wmk. 182
1878-80 Typo. Perf. 11½
Type II Frame Inverted
J3c	3c ultra	21.00	20.00
J4c	5c ultra	22.50	11.50
J5c	10c ultra	275.00	11.00
J6c	20c ultra	325.00	11.00
J7c	50c ultra	600.00	35.00
J8c	100c ultra		2,250.
J9c	500c ultra	700.00	100.00
Nos. J3c-J9c (7)		1,943.	2,438.

Type II Frame Normal
1882-83 Granite Paper
J10	D2	10c ultra	240.00	57.50
		On cover		160.00
J11	D2	20c ultra	575.00	80.00
		On cover		225.00
J12	D2	50c ultra	3,200.	675.00
		On cover		1,500.
J13	D2	100c ultra	1,100.	500.00
		On cover		1,150.
J14	D2	500c ultra	21,000.	325.00
		On cover		3,500.

1882-83 Granite Paper
Type II Frame Inverted
J10a	10c ultra	250.00	60.00
J11a	20c ultra	625.00	90.00
J12a	50c ultra	3,250.	800.00
J13a	100c ultra	1,200.	550.00
J14a	500c ultra	22,500.	350.00

1883-84 Numerals in Red
Type II Frame Inverted
J15	D2	5c blue green	60.00	45.00
		On cover		125.00
J16	D2	10c blue green	110.00	35.00
		On cover		105.00
J17	D2	20c blue green	175.00	30.00
		On cover		135.00
J18	D2	50c blue green	200.00	100.00
		On cover		575.00
J19	D2	100c blue green	575.00	475.00
		On cover		1,600.
J20	D2	500c blue green	1,150.	275.00
		On cover		2,750.
Nos. J15-J20 (6)			2,270.	960.00

1883-84 Numerals in Red
Type II Frame Normal
J15a	5c blue green	175.00	105.00
J16a	10c blue green	275.00	100.00
J17a	20c blue green	500.00	90.00
J18a	50c blue green	550.00	300.00
J19a	100c blue green	1,500.	1,400.
J20a	500c blue green	2,750.	800.00

1884-97 Numerals in Red
Type II Frame Normal
J21	D2	1c olive green	.90	.90
		On cover		20.00
J22	D2	3c olive green	8.00	9.00
		On cover		37.50
J23	D2	5c olive green	2.50	.90
		On cover		10.00
a.		5c yellow green	45.00	15.00
		On cover		55.00
J24	D2	10c olive green	6.75	1.50
		On cover		10.50
a.		10c yellow green	110.00	16.00
		On cover		120.00
J25	D2	20c olive green	13.00	2.25
		On cover		20.00
a.		20c yellow green	190.00	12.00
		On cover		120.00
J26	D2	50c olive green	20.00	5.00
		On cover		55.00
a.		50c yellow green	400.00	125.00
		On cover		500.00
J27	D2	100c olive green	22.50	4.00
		On cover		275.00
a.		100c yellow green	425.00	160.00
		On cover		700.00
J28	D2	500c olive green	175.00	225.00
a.		500c yellow green	800.00	60.00
		On cover		2,250.

Numerous shades of Nos. J21-J28 exist.

1908-09 Wmk. 183
Numerals in Red
J29	D2	1c olive green	.30	1.10
		Never hinged	.35	
		On cover		11.00
J30	D2	5c olive green	.60	.90
		Never hinged	1.00	
		On cover		5.50
J31	D2	10c olive green	1.50	2.25
		Never hinged	2.75	
		On cover		8.50
J32	D2	20c olive green	3.00	5.00
		Never hinged	11.00	
		On cover		22.50
J33	D2	50c olive green	15.00	1.10
		Never hinged	45.00	
		On cover		55.00
J34	D2	100c olive green	30.00	2.25
		Never hinged	55.00	
		On cover		85.00
Nos. J29-J34 (6)			50.40	12.60

 D3

1910 Perf. 11½, 12
Numerals in Red
J35	D3	1c blue green	.25	.25
J36	D3	3c blue green	.25	.25
J37	D3	5c blue green	.25	.25
J38	D3	10c blue green	11.00	.25
J39	D3	15c blue green	.65	1.10
J40	D3	20c blue green	17.50	.25
J41	D3	25c blue green	1.25	.65
J42	D3	30c blue green	1.25	.55
J43	D3	50c blue green	1.50	1.10
Nos. J35-J43 (9)			33.90	4.65

See Nos. S1-S12.

No. J36 Surcharged

1916
J44	D3	5c on 3c bl grn & red	.40	.25

Nos. J35-J36, J43 Surcharged

1924
J45	D3	10c on 1c	.25	8.25
J46	D3	10c on 3c	.25	1.50
J47	D3	20c on 50c	.95	1.50
Nos. J45-J47 (3)			1.45	11.25

 D4

Wmk. 183
1924-26 Typo. Perf. 11½
Granite Paper
J48	D4	5c ol grn & red	.65	.25
J49	D4	10c ol grn & red	2.75	.25
J50	D4	15c ol grn & red ('26)	2.50	.55
J51	D4	20c ol grn & red	6.00	.25
J52	D4	25c ol grn & red	2.75	.55
J53	D4	30c ol grn & red	2.75	.85
J54	D4	40c ol grn & red ('26)	3.75	.70
J55	D4	50c ol grn & red	3.75	.70
Nos. J48-J55 (8)			24.90	4.10

1924 With Grilled Gum
J48a	D4	5c olive green & red	.65	.60
J49a	D4	10c olive green & red	2.50	1.10
J51a	D4	20c olive green & red	4.75	1.50
J52a	D4	25c olive green & red	7.25	65.00
Nos. J48a-J52a (4)			15.15	68.20

See Grilled Gum note after No. 145.

Nos. J50, J53 & J55 Surcharged in Black

1937
J56	D4	5c on 15c	.90	4.25
J57	D4	10c on 30c	.90	1.50
J58	D4	20c on 50c	1.50	5.00
J59	D4	40c on 50c	2.50	12.00
Nos. J56-J59 (4)			5.80	22.75
Set, never hinged			10.50	

 D5

1938 Engr. Unwmk.
J60	D5	5c scarlet	.40	.25
J61	D5	10c scarlet	.55	.25
J62	D5	15c scarlet	1.25	2.25
J63	D5	20c scarlet	.95	.25
J64	D5	25c scarlet	1.40	1.90
J65	D5	30c scarlet	1.40	1.25
J66	D5	40c scarlet	1.60	.45
J67	D5	50c scarlet	1.90	2.25
Nos. J60-J67 (8)			9.45	8.85
Set, never hinged			19.00	

1938 With Grilled Gum
J60a	D5	5c scarlet	.65	1.60
J61a	D5	10c scarlet	.65	1.25
J62a	D5	15c scarlet	1.40	2.50
J63a	D5	20c scarlet	1.25	.55
J64a	D5	25c scarlet	1.40	9.50
J65a	D5	30c scarlet	1.40	2.25
J66a	D5	40c scarlet	2.10	2.10
J67a	D5	50c scarlet	2.50	3.50
Nos. J60a-J67a (8)			11.35	23.25
Set, never hinged			29.00	

See Grilled Gum note after No. 145.

OFFICIAL STAMPS

With Perforated Cross
In 1935 the government authorized the use of regular postage issues perforated with a nine-hole cross for all government departments. Twenty-seven different stamps were so perforated. These were succeeded in 1938 by the cross overprints.

Values for canceled Official Stamps are for those canceled to order. Postally used stamps sell for considerably more. This note does not apply to Nos. 1O1-1O16, 2O27-2O30, 3O23-3O26.

Counterfeit overprints exist of most official stamps.

Official stamps without unused values were not made available to the public unused.

Regular Issues of 1908-36 Overprinted in Black

1938 Unwmk. Perf. 11½
O1	A53	3c olive	.25	.25
O2	A54	5c blue green	.25	.25
O3	A55	10c red violet	.95	.45
O4	A56	15c orange	.25	1.60
O5	A68	20c red	.45	.25
O6	A58	25c brown	.45	1.40
O7	A59	30c ultra	.60	1.00
O8	A60	35c yellow green	.60	1.25
O9	A61	40c gray	.60	1.00

Wmk. 183
With Grilled Gum
O10	A25	50c dp grn & pale grn	.60	1.50
O11	A25	60c brn org & buff	1.25	2.50
O12	A25	70c vio & buff	1.25	4.25
O13	A25	80c sl & buff	1.25	3.25
O14	A36	90c grn & red, *grn*	3.00	3.25
O15	A25	1fr dp cl & pale grn	1.50	3.25
O16	A36	1.20fr brn rose & red, *rose*	1.50	4.50
O17	A36	1.50fr bl & red, *bl*	2.50	6.00
O18	A36	2fr gray blk & red, *gray*	3.00	7.00
Nos. O1-O18 (18)			20.25	42.95
Set, never hinged			65.00	

Nos. O14, O16, O17 and O18 are on surface-colored paper.

1938 Unwmk. With Grilled Gum
O1a	A53	3c olive	4.50	.45
O2a	A54	5c blue green	1.25	.45
O3a	A55	10c red violet	1.50	.55
O4a	A56	15c orange	2.75	1.25
O5a	A68	20c red	1.50	.70
O6a	A58	25c brown	75.00	7.75
O7a	A59	30c ultra	2.50	1.10
O8a	A60	35c yellow green	1.90	1.90
O9a	A61	40c gray	2.50	1.00
Nos. O1a-O9a (9)			93.40	15.15
Set, never hinged			190.00	

See Grilled Gum note after No. 145.

FOR THE WAR BOARD OF TRADE

Regular Issues of 1908-18 Overprinted

1918 Wmk. 183 Perf. 11½, 12
1O1	A26	3c brown org	110.00	225.00
1O2	A26	5c green	10.00	32.50
1O3	A26	7½c gray (I)	300.00	450.00
a.		7½c slate (II)	550.00	950.00
1O4	A28	10c red, *buff*	15.00	40.00
1O5	A28	15c vio, *buff*	12.50	45.00
1O6	A25	20c red & yel	125.00	500.00
1O7	A25	25c dp bl	125.00	500.00
1O8	A25	30c yel brn & pale grn	125.00	450.00
Nos. 1O1-1O8 (8)			822.50	2,242.

Most unused examples of Nos. 1O1-1O8 are reprints made using the original overprint forms.
Counterfeits exist.

Overprinted

1918
1O9	A26	3c brown orange	4.25	35.00
1O10	A26	5c green	12.00	52.50
1O11	A26	7½c gray	4.50	22.50
1O12	A28	10c red, *buff*	45.00	87.50
1O13	A28	15c vio, *buff*		82.50
1O14	A25	20c red & yel	8.75	52.50
1O15	A25	25c dp blue	8.75	52.50
1O16	A25	30c yel brn & pale grn	14.50	87.50
Nos. 1O9-1O16 (8)			180.25	390.00

No. 1O13 was never placed in use.
Fraudulent cancellations are found on Nos. 1O1-1O16.

FOR THE LEAGUE OF NATIONS

Regular Issues Overprinted

On 1908-30 Issues
1922-31 Wmk. 183 Perf. 11½, 12
2O1	A26	2½c ol, buff ('28)		.45
2O2	A26	3c ultra, buff ('30)		8.25
2O3	A26	5c orange, buff		5.50
2O4	A26	5c gray vio, buff ('26)		2.75
2O5	A26	5c red vio, buff ('27)		2.25
2O6	A26	5c dk grn, buff ('31)		25.00
2O7	A26	7½c dp grn, buff ('28)		.55
2O8	A28	10c green, buff		.55
2O9	A28	10c bl grn, buff ('28)		1.10
2O10	A28	10c vio, buff ('31)		2.75
2O11	A28	15c brn red, buff ('28)		1.10
2O12	A28	20c red vio, buff		8.25
2O13	A28	20c car, buff ('26)		2.25
2O14	A28	25c ver, buff		8.25
2O15	A28	25c car, buff		1.10
2O16	A28	25c brn, buff ('27)		17.00
2O17	A28	30c dp bl, buff ('25)		8.25
2O18	A25	30c yel brn & pale grn		14.00
2O19	A25	35c yel grn & yel		10.00
2O20	A25	40c deep blue		1.40
2O21	A25	40c red vio & grn ('28)		14.00
2O22	A25	50c dp grn & pale grn		11.00
2O23	A25	60c brn org & buff	30.00	1.60
2O24	A25	70c vio & buff ('25)		26.00
2O25	A25	80c slate & buff		2.75
2O26	A25	1fr dp cl & pale grn		6.75
2O27	A29	3fr red		32.50

2O28	A30	5fr ultra	60.00	
2O29	A31	10fr dull violet	140.00	
2O30	A31	10fr gray grn ('30)	140.00	
		Nos. 2O1-2O30 (30)	555.35	

1930-44   With Grilled Gum

2O16a	A26	3c ol grn, buff		10.00
		('33)		19.00
2O17a	A28	30c dp bl,buff		425.00
2O22a	A25	50c dp grn & pale grn ('35)	.90	2.25
2O23a	A25	60c brn org & buff ('44)	25.00	225.00
2O24a	A25	70c violet & buff ('32)	1.60	2.25
2O25a	A25	80c slate & buff ('42)	2.75	2.50
2O26a	A25	1fr dp cl & pale grn ('40)		5.25

1935-36   With Grilled Gum

2O31	A36	90c grn & red, grn ('36)		5.00
2O32	A36	1.20fr brn rose & red, rose ('36)	2.75	4.50
	b.	Inverted overprint		4,250.
2O33	A36	1.50fr bl & red, bl	2.75	4.50
2O34	A36	2fr gray blk & red, gray ('36)	2.75	5.25

1922-25   Ordinary Gum

2O31a	A36	90c	14.00
2O32a	A36	1.20fr ('25)	14.00
2O33a	A36	1.50fr ('25)	13.00
2O34a	A36	2fr ('25)	12.00

1928

2O35	A39	5fr blue	87.50

1932   On 1932 Issue

2O36	A41	5c peacock bl	19.00
2O37	A41	10c orange	1.60
2O38	A41	20c cerise	1.60
2O39	A41	30c ultra	55.00
2O40	A41	60c olive brn	15.00

Unwmk.

2O41	A42	1fr ol gray & bl	15.00
		Nos. 2O36-2O41 (6)	107.20

On 1934 Issue
1934-35   Wmk. 183

2O42	A46	3c olive	.25
2O43	A47	5c emerald	.65
2O44	A49	15c orange ('35)	1.50
2O45	A51	25c brown	19.00
2O46	A52	30c ultra	1.60
		Nos. 2O42-2O46 (5)	23.00

1937   On 1936 Issue   Unwmk.

2O47	A53	3c olive	.25	.25
2O48	A54	5c blue green	.25	.25
2O49	A55	10c red violet		1.10
2O50	A56	15c orange	.45	.55
2O51	A57	20c carmine		1.90
2O52	A58	25c brown	.65	1.10
2O53	A59	30c ultra	.65	1.00
2O54	A60	35c yellow green	.65	1.00
2O55	A61	40c gray	.95	1.25
		Nos. 2O47-2O55 (9)	8.40	

1937   With Grilled Gum

2O47a	A53	3c olive	.30
2O48a	A54	5c blue green	.45
2O49a	A55	10c red violet	6.25
2O50a	A56	15c orange	.70
2O51a	A57	20c carmine	2.25
2O52a	A58	25c brown	1.40
2O53a	A59	30c ultra	1.10
2O54a	A60	35c yellow green	4.25
2O55a	A61	40c gray	4.25
		Nos. 2O47a-2O55a (9)	20.95

1937   On 1931 Issue   Wmk. 183

2O56	A40	3fr orange brown	190.00

On 1938 Issue
1938   Unwmk.   Perf. 11½
Granite Paper

2O57	A63	20c red & buff	1.90
2O58	A64	30c blue & lt blue	3.00
2O59	A65	60c brown & buff	5.75
2O60	A66	1fr black & buff	9.25
		Nos. 2O57-2O60 (4)	19.90

Regular Issue of 1938 Overprinted in Black or Red

Granite Paper

2O61	A63	20c red & buff	2.25
2O62	A64	30c blue & lt blue	4.00
2O63	A65	60c brown & buff	7.25
2O64	A66	1fr black & buff (R)	12.50
		Nos. 2O61-2O64 (4)	26.00

Regular Issue of 1938 Overprinted in Black

1939

2O65	A69	3fr brn car, buff	3.25	11.00
2O66	A70	5fr slate bl, buff	5.50	15.00
2O67	A71	10fr green, buff	11.00	32.50
		Nos. 2O65-2O67 (3)	19.75	58.50

FOR THE INTERNATIONAL LABOR BUREAU

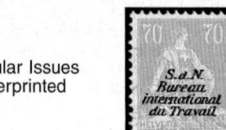

Regular Issues Overprinted

On 1908-30 Issues
1923-30   Wmk. 183   Perf. 11½, 12

3O1	A26	2½c ol grn, buff ('28)		.30
3O2	A26	3c ultra, buff ('30)		1.10
3O3	A26	5c org, buff		.55
3O4	A26	5c red vio, buff ('28)		.20
3O5	A26	7½c dp grn, buff ('28)		.45
3O6	A28	10c grn, buff		.55
3O7	A28	10c bl grn, buff ('28)		1.10
3O8	A28	15c brn red, buff ('28)		1.10
3O9	A28	20c red vio, buff		17.00
3O10	A28	20c car, buff ('27)		5.00
3O11	A28	25c car, buff		1.25
3O12	A28	25c brn, buff ('28)		3.00
3O13	A28	30c dp bl, buff ('25)		2.50
3O14	A25	30c yel brn & pale grn		65.00
3O15	A25	35c yel grn & yel		11.00
3O16	A25	40c deep blue		1.25
3O17	A25	40c red vio & grn ('28)		17.00
3O18	A25	50c dp grn & pale grn		5.00
3O19	A25	60c brn org & buff	1.60	1.90
3O20	A25	70c vio & buff ('24)		26.00
3O21	A25	80c slate & buff	14.00	2.25
3O22	A25	1fr dp cl & pale grn		2.75
3O23	A29	3fr red		25.00
3O24	A30	5fr ultra		37.50
3O25	A31	10fr dull violet		150.00
3O26	A31	10fr gray grn ('30)		150.00
		Nos. 3O1-3O26 (26)		528.75

1937-44   With Grilled Gum

3O18a	A25	50c dp grn & pale grn ('42)	1.75	2.25
3O20a	A25	70c vio & buff	1.75	2.25
3O21a	A25	80c slate & buff ('44)	25.00	175.00
3O22a	A25	1fr dp cl & pale grn ('42)		3.25

1925-42   With Grilled Gum

3O27	A36	90c grn & red, grn ('37)		9.75
	a.	Ordinary gum		5.00
3O28	A36	1.20fr brn rose & red, rose ('42)	14.00	4.00
	a.	Ordinary gum		4.50
3O29	A36	1.50fr bl & red, bl ('37)	2.75	3.00
	a.	Ordinary gum		14.00

3O30	A36	2fr gray blk & red, gray ('36)	3.25	6.25
	a.	Ordinary gum	32.50	
		Nos. 3O27-3O30 (4)	23.00	

3O31	A39	5fr blue	82.50

1932   On 1932 Issue

3O32	A41	5c peacock blue	1.10
3O33	A41	10c orange	.90
3O34	A41	20c cerise	1.25
3O35	A41	30c ultra	7.75
3O36	A41	60c olive brown	7.75

Unwmk.

3O37	A42	1fr ol gray & bl	10.00
		Nos. 3O32-3O37 (6)	28.75

1937   On 1936 Issue

3O38	A53	3c olive	.25	.55
3O39	A54	5c blue green	.25	.55
3O40	A55	10c red violet		2.75
3O41	A56	15c orange	.45	1.10
3O42	A57	20c carmine		2.25
3O43	A58	25c brown	.60	1.40
3O44	A59	30c ultra	.60	1.10
3O45	A60	35c yellow green	.60	1.60
3O46	A61	40c gray	.95	1.90
		Nos. 3O38-3O46 (9)	3.70	13.20

1937   With Grilled Gum

3O38a	A53	3c olive	1.10
3O39a	A54	5c blue green	1.10
3O40a	A55	10c red violet	1.60
3O41a	A56	15c orange	1.90
3O42a	A57	20c carmine	1.60
3O43a	A58	25c brown	2.25
3O44a	A59	30c ultra	2.25
3O45a	A60	35c yellow green	2.75
3O46a	A61	40c gray	2.25
		Nos. 3O38a-3O46a (9)	16.80

1937   On 1931 Issue   Wmk. 183

3O47	A40	3fr orange brown	175.00

On 1934 Issue

3O48	A46	3c olive	5.50

On 1938 Issue
Granite Paper
1938   Unwmk.   Perf. 11½

3O49	A63	20c red & buff	1.60
3O50	A64	30c blue & lt blue	3.25
3O51	A65	60c brown & buff	6.00
3O52	A66	1fr black & buff	8.75
		Nos. 3O49-3O52 (4)	19.60

Regular Issue of 1938 Overprinted in Black or Red

3O53	A63	20c red & buff (Bk)	3.25
3O54	A64	30c bl & lt bl (Bk)	3.25
3O55	A65	60c brn & buff (Bk)	6.50
3O56	A66	1fr blk & buff (R)	7.00
		Nos. 3O53-3O56 (4)	20.00

Regular Issue of 1938 Overprinted in Black

1939

3O57	A69	3fr brn car, buff	4.50	8.25
3O58	A70	5fr slate bl, buff	5.50	15.00
3O59	A71	10fr green, buff	10.00	30.00
		Nos. 3O57-3O59 (3)	20.00	55.25

FRANCHISE STAMPS

These stamps were distributed to many institutions and charitable societies for franking their correspondence.

F1

Control Figures Overprinted in Black

214

Perf. 11½, 12
1911-21   Typo.   Wmk. 183
Blue Granite Paper

S1	F1	2c ol grn & red	.25	.25
S2	F1	3c ol grn & red	2.50	.55
S3	F1	5c ol grn & red	1.10	.25
S4	F1	10c ol grn & red	1.40	.25
S5	F1	15c ol grn & red	21.00	4.00
S6	F1	20c ol grn & red	5.00	.60
		Nos. S1-S6 (6)	31.25	5.90

Without Control Figures

S1a	F1	2c olive green & red	.55	19.00
S2a	F1	3c olive green & red	.55	25.00
S3a	F1	5c olive green & red	4.75	32.50
S4a	F1	10c olive green & red	8.25	50.00
S5a	F1	15c olive green & red	5.25	125.00
S6a	F1	20c olive green & red	9.50	50.00
		Nos. S1a-S6a (6)	28.85	301.50

Control Figures Overprinted in Black

1926

S7	F1	5c ol grn & red	12.50	4.50
S8	F1	10c ol grn & red	7.75	3.25
S9	F1	20c ol grn & red	10.00	3.75
		Nos. S7-S9 (3)	30.25	11.50

Control Figures Overprinted in Black

1927   White Granite Paper

S10	F1	5c green & red	5.00	.40
S11	F1	10c green & red	2.50	.25
	b.	Grilled gum	325.00	725.00
S12	F1	20c green & red	3.50	.30
		Nos. S10-S12 (3)	11.00	.95

Without Control Figures

S10a	F1	5c green & red	32.50	140.00
S11a	F1	10c green & red	32.50	140.00
	c.	Grilled gum	150.00	650.00
S12a	F1	20c green & red	32.50	140.00

Nurse — F2   Nun — F3

J. H. Dunant — F4

Control Figures Overprinted in Black

1935   Perf. 11½

S13	F2	5c turq green	2.25	5.50
	b.	Grilled gum	3.25	.40
S14	F3	10c lt violet	2.25	5.50
	b.	Grilled gum	3.25	.25
S15	F4	20c scarlet	2.25	6.50
	b.	Grilled gum	3.75	.45
		Nos. S13-S15 (3)	6.75	17.50
		Nos. S13b-S15b (3)	10.25	1.10

Without Control Figures

S13a	F2	5c turquoise green	1.40	3.75
	c.	Grilled gum	15.00	1.40
S14a	F3	10c light violet	1.40	3.75
	c.	Grilled gum	15.00	1.40
S15a	F4	20c scarlet	1.40	5.00
	c.	Grilled gum	15.00	1.50
		Nos. S13a-S15a (3)	4.20	12.50
		Nos. S13c-S15c (3)	45.00	4.30

SYRIA

ˈsir-ē-ə

LOCATION — Asia Minor, bordering on Turkey, Iraq, Lebanon, Israel and the Mediterranean Sea
GOVT. — Republic
AREA — 71,498 sq. mi.
POP. — 9,840,000 (est. 1983)
CAPITAL — Damascus

Syria was originally part of the Turkish province of Sourya conquered by British and Arab forces in late 1918 and later partitioned. The British assumed control of the Palestine and Transjordan regions; the French were permitted to occupy the sanjaks of Lebanon, Alaouites and Alexandretta; and the remaining territory, including the vilayets of Damascus and Aleppo, was established as an independent Arab kingdom, under which the first Syrian stamps were issued.

French forces from Beirut deposed King Faisal in July 1920, and two years of military occupation followed until Syria was mandated to France in July 1922. Syrian autonomy was substituted for the mandate in 1934, but full independence was not again achieved until 1946.

10 Milliemes = 1 Piaster
40 Paras = 1 Piaster (Arabian Govt.)
100 Centimes = 1 Piaster (1920)

Issued under French Occupation

Stamps of France, 1900-07, Surcharged

Perf. 14x13½

1919, Nov. 21   Unwmk.
1	A16	1m on 1c gray	250.00	200.00
2	A16	2m on 2c vio brn	600.00	550.00
3	A16	3m on 3c red org	300.00	240.00
4	A20	4m on 15c gray grn	60.00	47.50
5	A22	5m on 5c dp grn	35.00	22.50
6	A22	1p on 10c red	50.00	32.50
7	A22	2p on 25c blue	25.00	15.00
8	A18	5p on 40c red & pale bl	32.50	22.50
9	A18	9p on 50c bis brn & lav	65.00	50.00
10	A18	10p on 1fr cl & ol grn	110.00	80.00
		Nos. 1-10 (10)	1,527.	1,260.

The letters "T.E.O." are the initials of "Territoires Ennemis Occupés." There are two types of the numerals in the surcharges on Nos. 2, 3, 8 and 9.

Stamps of French Offices in Turkey, 1902-03, Surcharged

1919
11	A2	1m on 1c gray	1.50	.80
		Never hinged	2.40	
a.		Inverted surcharge	40.00	
12	A2	2m on 2c violet brn	1.50	.80
		Never hinged	2.40	
a.		Inverted surcharge	40.00	
13	A2	3m on 3c red orange	3.25	1.40
		Never hinged	5.00	
14	A3	4m on 15c pale red	1.50	.80
		Never hinged	2.40	
a.		Inverted surcharge	40.00	
15	A2	5m on 5c green	1.50	.80
		Never hinged	2.40	

Overprinted

16	A5	1p on 25c blue	1.50	.75
		Never hinged	2.40	
a.		Inverted overprint	40.00	

17	A6	2p on 50c bis brn & lav	2.50	1.25
		Never hinged	4.00	
18	A6	4p on 1fr claret & ol grn	4.00	2.50
		Never hinged	5.75	
19	A6	8p on 2fr gray vio & yel	12.50	8.00
		Never hinged	19.00	
a.		"T.E.O." double	110.00	110.00
20	A6	20p on 5fr dk bl & buff	350.00	210.00
		Never hinged	379.75	227.10
		Nos. 11-20 (10)		

On Nos. 17-20 "T.E.O." reads vertically up.
Nos. 1-20 were issued in Beirut and mainly used in Lebanon. Nos. 16-20 were also used in Cilicia.

Stamps of France, 1900-07, Surcharged

1920
21	A16	1m on 1c gray	5.50	4.50
		Never hinged	8.00	
a.		Inverted surcharge	60.00	
b.		Double surcharge	67.50	
22	A16	2m on 2c vio brn	6.50	4.75
		Never hinged	10.00	
a.		Double surcharge	67.50	
b.		Inverted surcharge	60.00	
23	A22	3m on 5c green	13.00	12.00
		Never hinged	21.00	
a.		Double surcharge	82.50	
b.		Inverted surcharge	100.00	
24	A18	20p on 5fr dk bl & buff	475.00	450.00
		Nos. 21-23 (3)	25.00	21.25

The letters "O.M.F." are the initials of "Occupation Militaire Francaise."

Stamps of France, 1900-07, Surcharged in Black or Red

1920
25	A16	1m on 1c gray	1.25	.95
		Never hinged	2.00	
26	A16	2m on 2c violet brn	1.50	1.00
		Never hinged	2.50	
27	A22	3m on 5c green	2.25	2.00
		Never hinged	3.50	
a.		Double surcharge	67.50	
28	A22	5m on 10c red	2.50	2.25
		Never hinged	3.75	
a.		Inverted surcharge	65.00	65.00
b.		Double surcharge	65.00	65.00
29	A18	20p on 5fr dk bl & buff	72.50	70.00
		Never hinged	100.00	
30	A18	20p on 5fr dk bl & buff (R)	300.00	250.00
		Nos. 25-30 (6)	380.00	326.20

Stamps of France, 1900-21, Surcharged in Black or Red

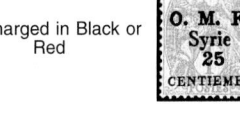

1920-22
31	A16	25c on 1c gray	2.00	1.00
		Never hinged	3.00	
32	A16	50c on 2c vio brn	2.00	1.00
		Never hinged	3.00	
33	A16	75c on 3c red org	2.00	1.00
		Never hinged	3.00	
a.		Inverted surcharge	52.50	52.50
b.		Double surcharge	60.00	60.00
34	A22	1p on 5c green (R)	2.25	2.00
		Never hinged	3.50	
a.		Double surcharge	60.00	60.00
35	A22	1p on 5c green	1.25	1.00
		Never hinged	1.90	
a.		Inverted surcharge	35.00	35.00
b.		Double surcharge	45.00	45.00
36	A22	1p on 20c red brn ('21)	.75	.25
		Never hinged	1.25	
a.		Inverted surcharge	35.00	35.00
b.		Double surcharge	35.00	35.00
37	A22	1.25p on 25c bl ('22)	1.50	.95
		Never hinged	2.25	
a.		Inverted surcharge	40.00	40.00
b.		Double surcharge	37.50	37.50

38	A22	1.50p on 30c org ('22)	1.60	.80
		Never hinged	2.50	
a.		Inverted surcharge	27.50	40.00
39	A22	2p on 10c red	1.25	1.00
		Never hinged	1.90	
a.		Inverted surcharge	50.00	50.00
40	A22	2p on 25c bl (R)	1.25	1.00
		Never hinged	1.90	
a.		Inverted surcharge	45.00	45.00
b.		Double surcharge	35.00	35.00
41	A18	2p on 40c red & pale bl ('21)	1.60	.75
		Never hinged	2.50	
42	A20	2.50p on 50c dl bl ('22)	1.40	1.10
		Never hinged	2.25	
a.		Final "S" of "Piastres" omitted	24.00	24.00
b.		Inverted surcharge	30.00	30.00
c.		Double surcharge	35.00	35.00
43	A22	3p on 25c bl (R)	1.40	1.10
		Never hinged	2.25	
a.		Inverted surcharge	45.00	45.00
44	A18	3p on 60c vio & ultra ('21)	1.75	1.10
		Never hinged	3.50	
a.		Inverted surcharge	37.50	37.50
45	A20	5p on 15c gray grn	2.50	2.25
		Never hinged	3.75	
a.		Double surcharge	140.00	150.00
46	A18	5p on 1fr cl & ol grn ('21)	3.00	1.50
		Never hinged	4.50	
47	A18	10p on 40c red & pale bl	3.75	3.25
		Never hinged	5.50	
48	A18	10p on 2fr org & pale bl ('21)	6.00	3.00
		Never hinged	9.00	
49	A18	25p on 50c bis brn & lav	5.50	4.00
		Never hinged	8.25	
a.		Inverted surcharge	100.00	100.00
50	A18	25p on 5fr dk bl & buff ('21)	110.00	95.00
51	A18	50p on 1fr cl & ol grn	25.00	20.00
		Never hinged	37.50	
a.		"PIASRTES"	1,650.	1,650.
b.		Inverted surcharge	1,700.	1,900.
52	A18	100p on 5fr dk bl & buff (R)	47.50	45.00
		Never hinged	80.00	
53	A18	100p on 5fr dk bl & buff (Bk)	250.00	225.00
a.		"PIASRTES"	1,650.	1,650.
		Nos. 31-53 (23)	475.25	413.05

In first printing, space between "Syrie" and numeral is 2mm, second printing, 1mm. For overprints see Nos. C1-C9.

Surcharged in Black or Red

1920-23
54	A16	10c on 2c violet ('23)	1.40	.90
		Never hinged	2.10	
a.		Inverted surcharge	35.00	35.00
55	A22	10c on 5c org (R) ('23)	1.00	.65
		Never hinged	1.50	
a.		Inverted surcharge	35.00	35.00
56	A16	25c on 1c dk gray	1.10	.90
		Never hinged	1.60	
a.		Inverted surcharge	40.00	40.00
b.		Double surcharge	52.50	52.50
c.		50c on 1c dk gray (error)	4.50	4.50
57	A22	25c on 5c green ('21)	1.10	.60
		Never hinged	1.60	
a.		Inverted surcharge	35.00	35.00
b.		Double surcharge	35.00	35.00
58	A22	25c on 5c orange ('22)	1.00	.80
		Never hinged	1.60	
a.		"CENTIEMES" omitted	37.50	37.50
b.		Inverted surcharge	35.00	35.00
c.		Double surcharge	37.50	37.50
59	A16	50c on 2c vio brn	1.10	.90
		Never hinged	1.60	
a.		Inverted surcharge	35.00	35.00
b.		Double surcharge	45.00	45.00
60	A22	50c on 10c red ('21)	1.25	.55
		Never hinged	2.00	
a.		Inverted surcharge	35.00	35.00
b.		Double surcharge	35.00	35.00
61	A22	50c on 10c green ('22)	1.50	1.25
		Never hinged	2.25	
a.		Inverted surcharge	35.00	35.00
b.		Double surcharge	37.50	37.50
c.		Double surcharge, one inverted	50.00	50.00
62	A16	75c on 3c red orange	3.00	2.00
		Never hinged	6.00	
a.		Inverted surcharge	35.00	35.00
b.		Double surcharge	45.00	45.00
63	A20	75c on 15c sl grn ('21)	1.40	.90
		Never hinged	2.10	
a.		Double surcharge	35.00	35.00
		Nos. 54-63 (10)	13.85	9.45

Preceding Issues Overprinted

1920   Black Overprint
64	A16	25c on 1c sl gray	12.00	10.00
a.		Double overprint	45.00	
65	A16	50c on 2c vio brn	13.00	11.00
a.		Double overprint	45.00	
66	A22	1p on 5c green	11.00	9.00
a.		Double overprint	45.00	
67	A22	2p on 25c blue	18.00	14.50
a.		Double overprint	82.50	
68	A20	5p on 15c gray grn	55.00	47.50
a.		Double overprint	140.00	150.00
69	A18	10p on 40c red & pale bl	80.00	75.00
70	A18	25p on 50c bis brn & lav	225.00	190.00
a.		Double overprint	600.00	
71	A18	50p on 1fr cl & ol grn	650.00	625.00
a.		Double overprint	2,100.	
72	A18	100p on 5fr dk bl & buff	2,000.	1,900.
a.		Double overprint	3,900.	4,300.
		Nos. 64-72 (9)	3,064.	2,882.

Red Overprint
73	A16	25c on 1c sl gray	12.50	10.00
74	A16	50c on 2c vio brn	11.00	8.50
75	A22	1p on 5c green	11.00	8.50
76	A22	2p on 25c blue	9.00	6.50
77	A20	5p on 15c gray grn	55.00	47.50
a.		Double overprint		190.00
78	A18	10p on 40c red & pale bl	85.00	75.00
a.		Double overprint	170.00	
79	A18	25p on 50c bis brn & lav	225.00	180.00
a.		Double overprint	450.00	475.00
80	A18	50p on 1fr cl & ol grn	475.00	425.00
a.		Double surcharge	1,700.	1,900.
81	A18	100p on 5fr dk bl & buff	1,650.	1,650.
a.		Double surcharge	3,500.	3,750.
		Nos. 73-81 (9)	2,533.	2,411.

Nos. 64-81 were used only in the vilayet of Aleppo where Egyptian gold currency was still in use.

A1

Black or Red Surcharge
1921   Perf. 11½
82	A1	25c on ¹⁄₁₀p lt brn	1.25	.85
		Never hinged	1.90	
a.		"25 Centiemes" omitted		
83	A1	50c on ²⁄₁₀p grn	1.25	.85
		Never hinged	1.90	
84	A1	1p on ³⁄₁₀p yel	1.75	.85
		Never hinged	2.50	
a.		"⁹⁄₁₀" for "³⁄₁₀"	12.50	12.50
b.		Inverted surcharge	60.00	60.00
85	A1	1p on 5m rose	2.00	1.10
		Never hinged	3.00	
86	A1	2p on 5m rose	2.50	1.25
		Never hinged	3.25	
a.		Tête bêche pair	160.00	160.00
b.		Inverted surcharge	40.00	40.00
c.		Double surcharge	45.00	45.00
87	A1	3p on 1p gray bl	3.00	1.25
		Never hinged	4.50	
a.		Never hinged	40.00	40.00
88	A1	5p on 2p bl grn	5.00	3.50
		Never hinged	17.50	
a.		Inverted surcharge	45.00	45.00
89	A1	10p on 5p vio brn	11.00	5.75
		Never hinged	20.00	
90	A1	25p on 10p gray (R)	13.00	8.00
		Never hinged	2.00	
a.		Inverted surcharge	45.00	45.00
		Nos. 82-90 (9)	40.75	23.40

Nos. 82-90 are surcharged on stamps of the Arabian Government Nos. 85, 87-93 and have the designs and sizes of those stamps.

Kilis Issue

A2

Sewing Machine Perf. 9
1921   Pelure Paper   Handstamped
91   A2   (1p) violet   50.00 45.00

Issued at Kilis to meet a shortage of the regular issue, caused by the sudden influx of a large number of Armenian refugees from Turkey. The Kilis area was restored to Turkey in Oct. 1923.

Stamps of France, Surcharged

1921-22   Perf. 14x13½
92   A18   2p on 40c red & pale bl   1.25   .90
  a.   Inverted surcharge   35.00 35.00
  b.   Double surcharge   35.00 35.00
  c.   Triple surcharge   82.50
93   A18   2.50p on 50c bis brn & lav ('22) 1.40   1.00
  a.   Double surcharge   37.50 37.50
  b.   2p on 50c bister brown & lavender (error) 82.50 67.50
94   A18   3p on 60c vio & ultra   1.25   .90
  a.   Inverted surcharge   35.00 35.00
  b.   Double surcharge   35.00 35.00
95   A18   5p on 1fr cl & ol grn   7.00   6.00
  a.   Inverted surcharge   40.00 40.00
96   A18   10p on 2fr org & pale bl   15.00 11.00
97   A18   25p on 5fr dk bl & buff   13.00 10.00
    Nos. 92-97 (6)   38.90 29.80

On No. 93 the surcharge reads: "2 PIASTRES 50."
For overprints see Nos. C10-C17.

French Mandate

French Stamps of 1900-23 Surcharged

1923
104   A16   10c on 2c vio brn   .40   .25
  a.   Inverted surcharge   27.50 27.50
  b.   Double surcharge   35.00 35.00
105   A22   25c on 5c orange   .75   .75
  a.   Inverted surcharge   27.50 27.50
106   A22   50c on 10c green   .90   .85
  a.   Inverted surcharge   27.50 27.50
  b.   Double surcharge   35.00 35.00
  c.   25c on 10c green (error)   240.00 240.00
107   A20   75c on 15c sl grn   1.60   1.50
  a.   Inverted surcharge   35.00 35.00
  b.   Double surcharge   37.50 37.50
108   A22   1p on 20c red brn   .75   .70
  a.   Inverted surcharge   27.50 27.50
  b.   Double surcharge   35.00 35.00
109   A22   1.25p on 25c blue   1.40   1.25
  a.   Inverted surcharge   40.00 40.00
  b.   Double surcharge   37.50 37.50
110   A22   1.50p on 30c orange   1.10   .90
  a.   Inverted surcharge   27.50 27.50
111   A22   1.50p on 30c red   1.10   .90
112   A20   2.50p on 50c dl bl   .70   .60
  a.   Inverted surcharge   60.00 60.00
  b.   Double surcharge   35.00 35.00

On Pasteur Stamps of 1923
113   A23   50c on 10c green   2.00   1.75
114   A23   1.50p on 30c red   1.75   1.50
115   A23   2.50p on 50c blue   2.00   1.75

Surcharged

116   A18   2p on 40c red & pale bl   .75   .70
  a.   Inverted surcharge   35.00 35.00
  b.   Double surcharge   37.50 37.50
  c.   "Liabn"   450.00 450.00

---

117   A18   3p on 60c vio & ultra   1.50   1.25
  a.   Inverted surcharge   40.00 40.00
  b.   Double surcharge   75.00 75.00
  c.   "Liabn"   450.00 450.00
118   A18   5p on 1fr cl & ol grn   2.00   1.50
  b.   "Liabn"   450.00 450.00
119   A18   10p on 2fr org & pale bl   7.50   7.00
  a.   "Liabn"   450.00 450.00
120   A18   25p on 5fr dk bl & buff   22.50 20.00
    Nos. 104-120 (17)   48.70 43.15

Stamps of France, 1900-21, Surcharged

1924   Perf. 14x13½
121   A16   10c on 2c vio brn   .40   .25
  a.   Inverted surcharge   35.00 35.00
122   A22   25c on 5c orange   .70   .60
  a.   "25" omitted   24.00
123   A22   50c on 10c green   .70   .60
  a.   Inverted surcharge   35.00 35.00
124   A20   75c on 15c sl grn   .70   .60
125   A22   1p on 20c red brn   .60   .50
  a.   "1 PIASTRES"   24.00
126   A22   1.25p on 25c blue   1.10   .90
127   A22   1.50p on 30c orange   1.10   .90
128   A22   1.50p on 30c red   1.00   .85
129   A20   2.50p on 50c dl bl   1.00   .85

Same on Pasteur Stamps of France, 1923
1924
130   A23   50c on 10c grn   .90   .70
  a.   Inverted surcharge   47.50 47.50
131   A23   1.50p on 30c red   1.40   1.10
132   A23   2.50p on 50c blue   .75   .70
  a.   Inverted surcharge   35.00 35.00
    Nos. 121-132 (12)   10.35 8.55

Olympic Games Issue

Stamps of France, 1924, Surcharged

1924
133   A24   50c on 10c gray grn & yel grn   30.00 27.50
    Never hinged   60.00
134   A25   1.25p on 25c rose & dk rose   30.00 27.50
    Never hinged   60.00
135   A26   1.50p on 30c brn red & blk   30.00 27.50
    Never hinged   60.00
136   A27   2.50p on 50c ultra & dk bl   30.00 27.50
    Never hinged   60.00
    Nos. 133-136 (4)   120.00 110.00

See Nos. 166-169.

Stamps of France 1900-20 Surcharged

137   A18   2p on 40c red & pale bl   .90   .50
    Never hinged   1.75
138   A18   3p on 60c vio & ultra   .70   .65
    Never hinged   1.50
139   A18   5p on 1fr claret & ol grn   3.50   3.25
    Never hinged   7.00
140   A18   10p on 2fr org & pale bl   3.50   3.00
    Never hinged   7.00
141   A18   25p on 5fr dk bl & buff   5.25   4.50
    Never hinged   11.00
    Nos. 137-141 (5)   13.85 11.90

For overprints see Nos. C18-C21.

Stamps of France 1900-21, Surcharged

or

1924-25
143   A16   10c on 2c vio brn   .40   .25
    Never hinged   .80
  a.   Double surcharge   35.00 35.00
  b.   Inverted surcharge   30.00 30.00
144   A22   25c on 5c orange   .40   .25
    Never hinged   .80
  a.   Double surcharge   35.00 35.00
145   A22   50c on 10c green   .75   .50
    Never hinged   1.50
  a.   Double surcharge   35.00 35.00
  b.   Inverted surcharge   30.00 30.00
146   A20   75c on 15c gray grn   .90   .70
    Never hinged   1.75
  a.   Double surcharge   35.00 35.00
  b.   Inverted surcharge   30.00 30.00
147   A22   1p on 20c red brn   .60   .40
    Never hinged   1.25
  a.   Inverted surcharge   26.00 26.00
148   A22   1.25p on 25c blue   .95   .75
    Never hinged   2.00
  a.   Inverted surcharge   30.00 30.00
149   A22   1.50p on 30c red   .90   .70
    Never hinged   2.00
  a.   Double surcharge   35.00 35.00
150   A22   1.50p on 30c orange   26.00 25.00
    Never hinged   52.50
151   A22   2p on 35c violet   1.00   .80
    ('25)
    Never hinged   2.00
152   A18   2p on 40c red & pale bl   .75   .50
    Never hinged   1.50
  a.   Arabic "Piastre" in singular 1.75   1.75
153   A18   2p on 45c grn & bl   5.00   4.00
    ('25)
    Never hinged   10.00
154   A18   3p on 60c vio & ultra   1.10   .75
    Never hinged   2.25
155   A20   3p on 60c lt vio   1.25   .75
    ('25)
    Never hinged   2.50
156   A20   4p on 85c ver   .45   .25
    Never hinged   1.00
157   A18   5p on 1fr cl & ol grn   1.25   .75
    Never hinged   2.50
158   A18   10p on 2fr org & pale bl   2.00   1.50
    Never hinged   4.00
159   A18   25p on 5fr dk bl & buff   2.75   1.50
    Never hinged   5.50
    Nos. 143-159 (17)   46.45 39.35

On No. 152a, the surcharge is as illustrated. The correct fourth line ("2 Piastres" -plural), as it appears on Nos. 151, 152 and 153, has four characters, the third resembling "9."
For overprints see Nos. C22-C25.

Same Surcharge on Pasteur Stamps of France
1924-25
160   A23   50c on 10c green   1.25   1.00
    Never hinged   2.50
161   A23   75c on 15c grn   1.25   1.00
    ('25)
    Never hinged   2.50
162   A23   1.50p on 30c red   1.25   1.00
    Never hinged   2.50
163   A23   2p on 45c red ('25)   1.25   1.00
    Never hinged   2.50
164   A23   2.50p on 50c blue   1.75   1.25
    Never hinged   3.50
165   A23   4p on 75c blue   1.75   1.25
    Never hinged   3.50
    Nos. 160-165 (6)   8.50   6.50

Olympic Games Issue

Stamps of France, 1924, Surcharged in French and Arabic

1924   Same Colors as #133-136
166   A24   50c on 10c   29.00 29.00
    Never hinged   45.00
167   A25   1.25p on 25c   29.00 29.00
    Never hinged   45.00

---

168   A26   1.50p on 30c   29.00 29.00
    Never hinged   45.00
169   A27   2.50p on 50c   29.00 29.00
    Never hinged   45.00
    Nos. 166-169 (4)   116.00 116.00

Ronsard Issue
Same Surcharge on France No. 219
1925
170   A28   4p on 75c bl, *bluish*   1.00   .75

Mosque at Hama A3

Mosque at Damascus A5

View of Merkab A4

Designs: 50c, View of Alexandretta. 75c, View of Hama. 1p, Omayyad Mosque, Damascus. 1.25p, Latakia Harbor. 1.50p, View of Damascus. 2p, View of Palmyra. 2.50p, View of Kalat Yamoun. 3p, Bridge of Daphne. 5p, View of Aleppo. 10p, View of Aleppo. 25p, Columns at Palmyra.

Perf. 12½, 13½
1925   Litho.   Unwmk.
173   A3   10c dark violet   .35   .25
    Never hinged   .55

Photo.
174   A4   25c olive black   .55   .55
    Never hinged   1.50
175   A4   50c yellow green   .50   .25
    Never hinged   .75
176   A4   75c brown orange   .60   .25
    Never hinged   .90
177   A5   1p magenta   .60   .25
    Never hinged   .90
178   A4   1.25p deep green   2.25   1.10
    Never hinged   3.50
179   A4   1.50p rose red   .75   .25
    Never hinged   1.10
180   A4   2p dark brown   2.00   .25
    Never hinged   3.00
181   A4   2.50p peacock blue   1.50   .50
    Never hinged   2.75
182   A4   3p orange brn   1.50   .25
    Never hinged   2.75
183   A4   5p violet   1.25   .25
    Never hinged   2.10
184   A4   10p violet brown   3.50   .30
    Never hinged   5.25
185   A4   25p ultra   5.75   4.50
    Never hinged   8.25
    Nos. 173-185 (13)   21.55 8.95

For surcharges see Nos. 186-206, B1-B12, C26-C45, CB1-CB4.

Surcharged in Black or Red

1926-30
186   A4   1p on 3pi org brn   2.00   .50
    ('30)
187   A4   2p on 1p25 dp grn   1.25   .40
    (R) ('28)
  a.   Double surcharge   16.00 16.00
188   A4   3.50p on 75c org brn   1.00   .35
  a.   Double surcharge   16.00 16.00
189   A4   4p on 25c ol blk   1.50   .35
190   A4   4p on 25c ol blk   1.40   .45
    ('27)
191   A4   4p on 25c ol blk (R)   1.25   .35
    ('28)
192   A4   4.50p on 75c brn org   1.40   .35
193   A4   6p on 2p50 pck bl   1.00   .35
194   A4   7.50p on 2p50 pck bl   1.10   .35
195   A4   7.50p on 2p50 pck bl   .90   .90
    (R) ('28)
  a.   Double surcharge   29.00
196   A4   12p on 1p25 dp grn   1.50   .40
  a.   Surcharge on face and back   50.00 42.50

197	A4	15p on 25p ultra	2.75	.90
198	A4	20p on 1p25 dp grn	2.25	.70
		Nos. 186-198 (13)	21.90	6.35

Size of numerals and arrangement of this surcharge varies on the different denominations.
No. 189 has slanting foot on "4."
No. 190, foot straight.

No. 173 Surcharged in Red

1928

199	A3	05c on 10c dk vio	1.00	.25

Stamps of 1925 Ovptd. in Red or Blue

1929 — *Perf. 13½*

200	A4	50c yellow grn (R)	3.50	2.75
		Never hinged	5.25	
201	A5	1p magenta (Bl)	3.50	2.75
		Never hinged	5.25	
202	A4	1.50p rose red (Bl)	3.50	2.75
		Never hinged	5.25	
203	A4	3p orange brn (Bl)	3.50	2.75
		Never hinged	5.25	
204	A4	5p violet (R)	3.50	2.75
		Never hinged	5.25	
205	A4	10p violet brn (Bl)	3.50	2.75
		Never hinged	5.25	
206	A4	25p ultra (R)	3.50	2.75
		Never hinged	5.25	
		Nos. 200-206 (7)	24.50	19.25

Industrial Exhibition, Damascus, Sept. 1929.

View of Hama — A6

View of Alexandretta — A9

Citadel at Aleppo A10

Great Mosque of Damascus A11

Ruins of Bosra A13

Mosque at Homs A15

View of Sednaya A16

Citadel at Aleppo A17

Ancient Bridge at Antioch A18

Mosque at Damascus A22

Designs: 20c, Great Mosque, Aleppo. 25c, Minaret, Hama. 2p, View of Antioch. 4p, Square at Damascus. 15p, Mosque at Hama. 25p, Monastery of St. Simeon the Stylite (ruins). 50p, Sun Temple (ruins), Palmyra.

Perf. 12x12½

1930-36   Litho.   Unwmk.

208	A6	10c red violet	.50	.25
		Never hinged	1.00	
209	A6	10c vio brn ('33)	.50	.35
		Never hinged	1.00	
209A	A6	10c vio brn, redrawn ('35)	.50	.25
		Never hinged	1.00	
210	A6	20c dark blue	.50	.25
		Never hinged	1.00	
211	A6	20c brn org ('33)	.50	.25
		Never hinged	1.00	
212	A6	25c gray green	.50	.25
		Never hinged	1.00	
213	A6	25c dk bl gray ('33)	.80	.45
		Never hinged	1.60	

Photo.
Perf. 13

214	A9	50c violet	.50	.25
		Never hinged	1.00	
215	A15	75c org red ('32)	.50	.25
		Never hinged	1.00	
216	A10	1p green	.75	.25
		Never hinged	1.50	
217	A10	1p bis brn ('36)	1.75	.40
		Never hinged	3.50	
218	A11	1.50p bister brown	7.50	3.00
		Never hinged	15.00	
219	A11	1.50p dp grn ('33)	1.00	.50
		Never hinged	2.00	
220	A9	2p dark violet	.75	.25
		Never hinged	1.50	
221	A13	3p yellow green	2.00	.70
		Never hinged	4.00	
222	A10	4p yellow orange	.75	.25
		Never hinged	1.50	
223	A15	4.50p rose carmine	1.75	.55
		Never hinged	3.50	
224	A16	6p grnsh black	2.25	.50
		Never hinged	4.50	
225	A17	7.50p dull blue	2.25	.70
		Never hinged	4.50	
226	A18	10p dark brown	2.00	.50
		Never hinged	4.00	
227	A10	15p deep green	3.50	1.00
		Never hinged	7.00	
228	A18	25p violet brown	5.00	1.10
		Never hinged	10.00	
229	A15	50p olive brown	17.50	7.00
		Never hinged	34.00	
230	A22	100p red orange	35.00	15.00
		Never hinged	70.00	
		Nos. 208-230 (24)	88.55	34.25

On No. 209A Arabic inscriptions, upper right, are entirely redrawn with lighter lines. Hyphen added in "Helio-Vaugirard" imprint. Lines in buildings and background more distinct.
On No. 215 the letters of "VAUGIRARD" in the imprint are reversed as in a mirror.
For overprints and surcharges see Nos. 253-268; Nos. 346, M1-M2 in Scott Standard catalogue, Vol. 6.

Autonomous Republic

Parliament Building A23

abu-al-Ala al-Maarri — A24

President Ali Bek el Abed — A25

Saladin — A26

1934, Aug. 2   Engr.   *Perf. 12½*

232	A23	10c olive green	1.50	1.50
		Never hinged	3.00	
233	A23	20c black	1.50	1.40
		Never hinged	3.00	
234	A23	25c red orange	1.75	1.50
		Never hinged	3.50	
235	A23	50c ultra	2.00	1.50
		Never hinged	4.00	
236	A23	75c plum	2.00	1.50
		Never hinged	4.00	
237	A24	1p vermilion	4.50	3.00
		Never hinged	9.00	
238	A24	1.50p green	5.25	3.50
		Never hinged	10.50	
239	A24	2p red brown	5.25	3.50
		Never hinged	10.50	
240	A24	3p Prus blue	5.25	3.50
		Never hinged	10.50	
241	A24	4p brt violet	5.75	3.50
		Never hinged	11.50	
242	A24	4.50p carmine	6.00	3.75
		Never hinged	12.00	
243	A24	5p dark blue	6.00	3.75
		Never hinged	12.00	
244	A24	6p dark brown	6.00	3.75
		Never hinged	12.00	
245	A24	7.50p dark ultra	6.50	3.75
		Never hinged	13.00	
246	A25	10p dark brown	8.50	6.00
		Never hinged	17.00	
247	A25	15p dull blue	12.00	8.50
		Never hinged	24.00	
248	A25	25p rose red	17.50	13.00
		Never hinged	35.00	
249	A26	50p dark brown	30.00	20.00
		Never hinged	60.00	
250	A26	100p lake	45.00	32.50
		Never hinged	90.00	
		Nos. 232-250 (19)	172.25	119.40

Proclamation of the Republic. See Nos. C57-C66. For surcharge see No. M3 in Scott Standard catalogue, Vol. 6.

Stamps of 1930-36 Overprinted in Red or Black

1936, Apr. 15

253	A9	50c violet (R)	2.75	1.50
254	A10	1p bister brn (Bk)	2.75	1.50
255	A9	2p dk violet (R)	2.75	1.50
256	A10	3p yellow grn (Bk)	3.25	1.50
257	A10	4p yellow org (Bk)	3.25	1.50
258	A15	4.50p rose car (Bk)	3.25	1.50
259	A16	6p grnsh blk (R)	4.00	2.00
260	A17	7.50p dull blue (R)	4.75	2.75
261	A18	10p dk brown (Bk)	5.75	3.75
		Nos. 253-261 (9)	32.50	17.50

Industrial Exhibition, Damascus, May 1936. See Nos. C67-C71.

Stamps of 1930 Srchd. in Black

1937-38   *Perf. 13½x13*

262	A10	2.50p on 4p yel org ('38)	.55	.40
263	A22	10p on 100p red orange	1.00	.90

Stamps of 1930-33 Srchd. in Red or Black

1938   *Perf. 13½*

264	A15	25c on 75c org red (Bk)	.50	.25
265	A11	50c on 1.50p dp grn (R)	.60	.30
266	A17	2p on 7.50p dl bl (R)	1.00	.60
267	A17	5p on 7.50p dl bl (R)	1.75	.90
268	A15	10p on 50p ol brn (Bk)	2.25	.95
		Nos. 264-268 (5)	6.10	3.00

President Hashem Bek el Atassi — A27

1938-43   Photo.   Unwmk.

268A	A27	10p dp blue ('42)	1.25	.85
269	A27	12.50p on 10p dp bl (R)	1.50	.90
270	A27	20p dark brown	1.25	.85
		Nos. 268A-270 (3)	4.00	2.60

The 10pi and 20pi exist imperf.

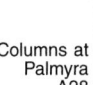

Columns at Palmyra A28

1940   Litho.   *Perf. 11½*

271	A28	5p pale rose	2.00	.65

Exists imperf.

Museum at Damascus — A29

Hotel at Bloudan A30

Kasr-el-Heir A31

1940   Typo.   *Perf. 13x14*

272	A29	10c bright rose	.70	.25
		Never hinged	1.00	
273	A29	20c light blue	.70	.25
		Never hinged	1.00	
274	A29	25c fawn	.75	.25
		Never hinged	1.10	
275	A29	50c ultra	.75	.25
		Never hinged	1.10	

Engr.
Perf. 13

276	A30	1p peacock blue	1.00	.25
		Never hinged	1.50	
277	A30	1.50p chocolate	1.50	.70
		Never hinged	2.25	

278	A30	2.50p dark green	1.00	.30
		Never hinged	1.50	
279	A31	5p violet	1.10	.40
		Never hinged	1.60	
280	A31	7.50p vermilion	2.00	.40
		Never hinged	3.00	
281	A31	50p sepia	3.50	1.25
		Never hinged	5.25	
	Nos. 278-281 (10)		13.00	4.30

For overprints see Nos. 298-299 in Scott
Standard catalogue, Vol. 6.

SEMI-POSTAL STAMPS

Nos. 174-
185 Srchd.
in Red or
Black

1926   Unwmk.   *Perf. 12½, 13½*

B1	A4	25c + 25c ol blk (R)	2.25	2.00
B2	A4	50c + 25c yel grn	2.25	2.00
B3	A4	75c + 25c brown org	2.25	2.00
B4	A5	1p + 50c magenta	2.25	2.00
B5	A4	1.25p + 50c dp grn (R)	2.25	2.00
B6	A4	1.50p + 50c rose red	2.25	2.00
B7	A4	2p + 75c dk brn (R)	2.25	2.00
B8	A4	2.50p + 75c pck bl (R)	2.25	2.00
B9	A4	3p + 1p org brn (R)	2.25	2.00
B10	A4	5p + 1p violet	2.25	2.00
B11	A4	10p + 2p vio brn	2.25	2.00
B12	A4	25p + 5p ultra (R)	2.25	2.00
	Nos. B1-B12 (12)		27.00	24.00
	Set, never hinged		36.00	

On No. B4 the surcharge is set in six lines to
fit the shape of the stamp.
The surcharge was a contribution to the
relief of refugees from the Djebel Druze War.
See Nos. CB1-CB4.

AIR POST STAMPS

Nos. 35, 45, 47
Handstamped in Violet
— a

1920, Dec.   Unwmk.   *Perf. 13½*

C1	A22	1p on 5c	160.00	40.00
C2	A20	5p on 15c	290.00	47.50
C3	A18	10p on 40c	425.00	77.50
	Nos. C1-C3 (3)		875.00	165.00

**Nos. 36, 46, 48 Overprinted Type
"a" in Violet**

1921, June 12

C4	A22	1p on 20c	87.50	40.00
C5	A18	5p on 1fr	425.00	150.00
C6	A18	10p on 2fr	425.00	150.00
	Nos. C4-C6 (3)		937.50	340.00

Excellent counterfeits exist of Nos. C1-C6.

Nos. 36, 46, 48
Overprinted — b

1921, Oct. 5

C7	A22	1p on 20c	60.00	18.50
C8	A18	5p on 1fr	150.00	37.50
a.	Inverted overprint		325.00	240.00
C9	A18	10p on 2fr	200.00	47.50
a.	Double overprint		475.00	400.00
	Nos. C7-C9 (3)		410.00	103.50

Nos. 92, 94-
96 Ovptd.
— c

1922, May 28

C10	A18	2p on 40c	25.00	25.00
a.	Inverted overprint			

C11	A18	3p on 60c	25.00	25.00
C12	A18	5p on 1fr	25.00	25.00
C13	A18	10p on 2fr	25.00	25.00
	Nos. C10-C13 (4)		100.00	100.00

Nos. 116-119 Overprinted Type "c"

1922, Nov. 22

C14	A18	2p on 40c	29.00	29.00
b.	Inverted surcharge			
C15	A18	3p on 60c	29.00	29.00
C16	A18	5p on 1fr	29.00	29.00
C17	A18	10p on 2fr	29.00	29.00
b.	Double overprint			
	Nos. C14-C17 (4)		116.00	116.00

Overprinted "Liabn"

C14a	A18	2p on 40c	400.00	400.00
C15a	A18	3p on 60c	400.00	400.00
C16a	A18	5p on 1fr	400.00	400.00
C17a	A18	10p on 2fr	400.00	400.00

Nos. 137-140 Overprinted Type "c"

1924, Jan. 13

C18	A18	2p on 40c	4.50	4.50
a.	Double overprint		27.50	
C19	A18	3p on 60c	4.50	4.50
a.	Inverted overprint		47.50	
C20	A18	5p on 1fr	4.50	4.50
a.	Inverted overprint		50.00	30.00
C21	A18	10p on 2fr	4.50	4.50
	Nos. C18-C21 (4)		18.00	18.00

Nos. 152,
154, 157-
158
Overprinted

1924, July 17

C22	A18	2p on 40c	7.00	7.00
a.	Inverted overprint		32.50	
C23	A18	3p on 60c	7.00	7.00
a.	Inverted overprint		32.50	
b.	Double overprint		20.00	
C24	A18	5p on 1fr	7.00	7.00
C25	A18	10p on 2fr	7.00	7.00
a.	Inverted overprint		32.50	
	Nos. C22-C25 (4)		28.00	28.00

Regular
Issue of
1925
Overprinted
in Green

1925, Mar. 1

C26	A4	2p dark brown	2.25	2.25
C27	A4	3p orange brown	2.25	2.25
C28	A4	5p violet	2.25	2.25
C29	A4	10p violet brown	2.25	2.25
	Nos. C26-C29 (4)		9.00	9.00

Nos.180,
182, 183-
184 Ovptd.
in Red — f

1926

C30	A4	2p dark brown	2.00	2.00
a.	Inverted overprint		40.00	40.00
C31	A4	3p orange brown	2.00	2.00
C32	A4	5p violet	2.50	2.50
a.	Inverted overprint		40.00	40.00
b.	Double overprint		65.00	65.00
C33	A4	10p violet brown	2.50	2.50
a.	Inverted overprint		40.00	40.00
b.	Double overprint		65.00	65.00
	Nos. C30-C33 (4)		9.00	9.00

Nos. C30-C33 received their first airmail use
June 16, 1929, at the opening of the Beirut-
Marseille line.
For surcharges see Nos. CB1-CB4.

**Regular Issue of 1925 Overprinted
Type "f" in Red or Black**

1929

C34	A4	50c yellow green (R)	1.25	1.25
a.	Inverted overprint		40.00	
b.	Overprinted on face and back		22.50	
c.	Double overprint		40.00	
d.	Double overprint, one inverted		60.00	
e.	Pair, one without overprint			
C35	A5	1p magenta (Bk)	1.75	1.75
a.	Reversed overprint			
b.	Red overprint			
C36	A4	25p ultra (R)	5.50	5.50
a.	Inverted overprint		82.50	
b.	Pair, one without overprint			
	Nos. C34-C36 (3)		8.50	8.50

On No. C35, the overprint is vertical, with
plane nose down.

No. 197 Overprinted Type "f" in Red

1929, July 9

C37	A4	15p on 25p ultra	4.25	4.25
a.	Inverted overprint			

Air Post
Stamps of
1926-29
Ovptd. in
Various
Colors

1929, Sept. 5

C38	A4	50c yellow grn (R)	3.00	3.00
C39	A4	1p magenta (Bl)	3.00	3.00
C40	A4	2p dk brown (V)	3.00	3.00
C41	A4	3p orange brn (Bl)	3.00	3.00
a.	Inverted overprint		70.00	
C42	A4	5p violet (R)	3.00	3.00
C43	A4	10p violet brn (Bl)	3.00	3.00
C44	A4	25p ultra (R)	3.00	3.00
	Nos. C38-C44 (7)		21.00	21.00

Damascus Industrial Exhibition.

AP1

1930, Jan. 30   Red Surcharge

C45	AP1	2p on 1.25p dp grn	3.00	3.00
a.	Inverted surcharge			
b.	Double surcharge		60.00	

Plane over
Homs
AP2

Designs: 1pi, City Wall, Damascus. 2pi,
Euphrates River. 3pi, Temple Ruins, Palmyra.
5pi, Deir-el-Zor. 10pi, Damascus. 15pi,
Aleppo, Citadel. 25pi, Hama. 50pi, Zebdani.
100pi, Telebisse.

1931-33   Photo.   Unwmk.

C46	AP2	50c ocher	1.00	.90
C47	AP2	50c black brn ('33)	1.25	1.00
C48	AP2	1p chestnut brown	1.10	.95
C49	AP2	2p Prus blue	2.75	1.75
C50	AP2	3p blue grn	1.75	1.25
C51	AP2	5p red violet	1.25	1.25
C52	AP2	10p slate grn	1.25	1.25
C53	AP2	15p orange red	2.10	1.50
C54	AP2	25p orange brn	2.75	2.00
C55	AP2	50p black	3.00	2.25
C56	AP2	100p magenta	3.75	2.60
	Nos. C46-C56 (11)		21.95	16.60

Nos. C46 to C56 exist imperforate. Value,
$425.
For overprints see Nos. C67-C71; Nos.
C110-C112, C114-C115, MC1-MC4 in Scott
Standard catalogue, Vol. 6.

Village of
Bloudan
AP12

1934, Aug. 2   Engr.   *Perf. 12½*

C57	AP12	50c yel brown	2.25	2.25
C58	AP12	1p green	2.50	2.50
C59	AP12	2p peacock bl	2.75	2.75
C60	AP12	3p red	3.00	3.00
C61	AP12	5p plum	3.00	3.00
C62	AP12	10p brt violet	27.50	27.50
C63	AP12	15p orange brn	30.00	30.00
C64	AP12	25p dk ultra	35.00	35.00
C65	AP12	50p black	45.00	45.00
C66	AP12	100p red brown	90.00	90.00
	Nos. C57-C66 (10)		241.00	241.00

Proclamation of the Republic. Exist imperf.

Air Post
Stamps of
1931-33
Overprinted
in Red or
Black

1936, Apr. 15   *Perf. 13½x13, 13½*

C67	AP2	50c black brown	5.25	4.75
C68	AP2	1p chnt brown (Bk)	5.25	4.75
C69	AP2	2p Prus blue	5.25	4.75
C70	AP2	3p blue green	5.25	4.75
C71	AP2	5p red violet (Bk)	5.25	4.75
	Nos. C67-C71 (5)		26.25	23.75

Damascus Fair, May 1936.

Syrian
Pavilion at
Paris
Exposition
AP13

1937, July 1   Photo.   *Perf. 13½*

C72	AP13	½p yellow green	2.75	2.75
C73	AP13	1p green	2.75	2.75
C74	AP13	2p lt brown	2.75	2.75
C75	AP13	3p rose red	2.75	2.75
C76	AP13	5p brown orange	2.75	2.75
C77	AP13	10p grnsh black	4.75	4.75
C78	AP13	15p blue	5.25	5.25
C79	AP13	25p dark violet	6.25	6.25
	Nos. C72-C79 (8)		30.00	30.00

Paris International Exposition. Exist imperf.

Ancient
Citadel at
Aleppo
AP14

Omayyad
Mosque
and Minaret
of Jesus at
Damascus
AP15

1937   Engr.   *Perf. 13*

C80	AP14	½p dark violet	.65	.65
C81	AP15	1p black	.65	.65
C82	AP15	2p deep green	.65	.65
C83	AP15	3p deep ultra	.65	.65
C84	AP15	5p rose lake	2.00	2.00
C85	AP15	10p red brown	1.10	1.10
C86	AP14	15p lake brown	4.75	4.75
C87	AP15	25p dark violet	6.00	6.00
	Nos. C80-C87 (8)		16.45	16.45

No. C80 to C87 exist imperforate. Value, set
$175.
For overprint see No. C109 in Scott Standard catalogue, Vol. 6.

Maurice Noguès and Route of France-
Syria Flight — AP16

1938, July   Photo.   *Perf. 11½*

C88	AP16	10p dark green	5.00	4.50
a.	Souv. sheet of 4, perf. 13½		50.00	45.00
b.	Perf. 13½		8.00	8.00

10th anniversary of first Marseille-Beirut
flight, by Maurice Noguès.
No. C88a exists imperf.; value $800.

Bridge at
Deir-el-Zor
AP17

1940   Engr.   *Perf. 13*

C89	AP17	25c brown black	.25	.25
C90	AP17	50c peacock blue	.25	.25
C91	AP17	1p deep ultra	.30	.30
C92	AP17	2p dk orange brn	.45	.45
C93	AP17	5p green	.95	.95
C94	AP17	10p rose carmine	1.40	1.00
C95	AP17	50p dark violet	3.00	2.25
	Nos. C89-C95 (7)		6.60	5.45

Exist imperf.

AIR POST SEMI-POSTAL STAMPS

Nos. C30-C33 Surcharged Like Nos. B1-B12 in Black and Red

1926, Apr. 1		**Unwmk.**	**Perf. 13½**	
CB1	A4	2p + 1p dk brown	3.00	2.75
CB2	A4	3p + 2p org brn	2.75	2.75
CB3	A4	5p + 3p violet	2.75	2.75
CB4	A4	10p + 5p vio brn	2.75	2.75
		Nos. CB1-CB4 (4)	11.25	11.00

The new value is in red and rest of the surcharge in black on Nos. CB1-CB3. The entire surcharge is black on No. CB4.
See note following Nos. B1-B12.

POSTAGE DUE STAMPS

Under French Occupation

French Offices in the Turkish Empire, 1902-03, Surcharged

O. M. F. Syrie Ch. taxe 1 PIASTRE

1920		**Unwmk.**	**Perf. 14x13½**	
J1	A3	1p on 10c rose red	160.00	160.00
J2	A3	2p on 20c brn vio	160.00	160.00
J3	A3	3p on 30c lil	160.00	160.00
J4	A4	4p on 40c red & pale bl	160.00	160.00
		Nos. J1-J4 (4)	640.00	640.00

Postage Due Stamps of France, 1893-1920, Surcharged in Black or Red

O. M. F. Syrie 2 PIASTRES

1920				
J5	D2	1p on 10c brown	3.25	3.25
J6	D2	2p on 20c ol grn (R)	3.25	3.25
a.		"PIASTRE"	900.00	900.00
J7	D2	3p on 30c red	3.25	3.25
a.		"PIASTRE"		
J8	D2	4p on 50c brn vio	4.75	4.75
a.		3p in setting of 4p	525.00	525.00
		Nos. J5-J8 (4)	14.50	14.50
1921-22				
J9	D2	50c on 10c brown	1.40	1.40
a.		"75" instead of "50"	90.00	
b.		"CENTI MES" instead of "CEN-TIEMES"	7.50	
J10	D2	1p on 20c ol grn	1.40	1.40
J11	D2	2p on 30c red	3.25	3.25
J12	D2	3p on 50c brn vio	3.50	3.50
J13	D2	5p on 1fr red brn, straw	5.00	5.00
		Nos. J9-J13 (5)	14.55	14.55

O. M. F. Syrie Dump Taxe 50 CENTIEMES — D3

1921			**Perf. 11½**	
Red Surcharge				
J14	D3	50c on 1p black	3.75	3.75
J15	D3	1p on 1p black	3.75	3.75

O. M. F. Syrie 2 PIASTRES — D4

1922				
J16	D4	2p on 5m rose	10.00	6.50
a.		"AX" of "TAXE" inverted	175.00	175.00
J17	D4	3p on 1p gray bl	15.00	12.00

French Mandate

Postage Due Stamps of France, 1893-1920, Surcharged

Syrie Grand Liban 2 PIASTRES

1923				
J18	D2	50c on 10c brown	1.50	1.50
J19	D2	1p on 20c ol grn	2.25	2.25
J20	D2	2p on 30c red	1.90	1.90
J21	D2	3p on 50c vio brn	1.90	1.90
J22	D2	5p on 1fr red brn, straw	3.75	3.75
		Nos. J18-J22 (5)	11.30	11.30

Postage Due Stamps of France, 1893-1920, Surcharged

SYRIE 1 PIASTRE

1924				
J23	D2	50c on 10c brown	1.00	1.00
J24	D2	1p on 20c ol grn	1.00	1.00
J25	D2	2p on 30c red	1.10	1.10
J26	D2	3p on 50c vio brn	1.50	1.50
J27	D2	5p on 1fr red brn, straw	1.50	1.50
		Nos. J23-J27 (5)	6.10	6.10

Postage Due Stamps of France, 1893-1920, Surcharged

Syrie 2 Piastres

1924				
J28	D2	50c on 10c brown	.75	.75
J29	D2	1p on 20c ol grn	.75	.75
J30	D2	2p on 30c red	1.00	1.00
J31	D2	3p on 50c vio brn	1.40	1.40
J32	D2	5p on 1fr red brn, straw	1.75	1.75
		Nos. J28-J32 (5)	5.65	5.65

Water Wheel at Hama D5

Bridge at Antioch — D6

Designs: 2p, The Tartous. 3p, View of Banias. 5p, Chevaliers' Castle.

1925		**Photo.**	**Perf. 13½**	
J33	D5	50c brown, yel	.25	.25
J34	D6	1p violet, rose	.25	.25
J35	D5	2p black, blue	.55	.55
J36	D5	3p black, red org	1.25	1.25
J37	D5	5p black, bl grn	1.50	1.50
		Nos. J33-J37 (5)	3.80	3.80

D7

Lion — D8

1931				
J38	D7	8p black, gray blue	3.50	3.50
J39	D8	15p black, dull rose	6.00	6.00

ISSUES OF THE ARABIAN GOVERNMENT

The following issues replaced the British Military Occupation (E.E.F.) stamps (Palestine Nos. 2-14) which were used in central and eastern Syria from Nov. 1918 until Jan. 1920.

Turkish Stamps of 1913-18 Handstamped in Various Colors

Also Handstamp Surcharged with New Values as

1 millieme

1 Egyptian piaster

The Seal reads: "Hakuma al Arabie" (The Arabian Government)

			Perf. 11½, 12, 12½, 13½	
1919-20			**Unwmk.**	
1	A24	1m on 2pa red lil (254)	.85	.85
2	A25	1m on 4pa dk brn (255)	.85	.85
3	A26	2m on 5pa vio brn (256)	1.40	1.40
4	A15	2m on 5pa on 10pa gray grn (291)	.95	.95
5	A18	2m on 5pa ocher (304)	22.50	22.50
6	A41	2m on 5pa grn (345)	275.00	250.00
7	A18	2m on 5pa ocher (378)	47.50	47.50
8	A28	4m on 10pa grn (258)	6.50	6.50
9	A28	4m on 10pa grn (271)	.85	.85
10	A22	4m on 10pa bl grn (329)	1.75	1.75
11	A41	4m on 10pa car (346)	37.50	37.50
12	A23	4m on 10pa (415)	7.25	7.25
13	A44	4m on 10pa (424)	1.25	1.25
14	A11	4m on 10pa on 20pa vio brn (B38)	1.25	1.25
15	A41	4m on 10pa car (B42)	.85	.85
16	SP1	4m on 10pa red vio (B46)	1.40	1.40
17	SP1	4m on 10pa on 20pa car rose (B47)	1.40	1.40
19	A21	5pa ocher (317)		
21	A21	20pa car rose (153)	92.50	110.00
22	A29	20pa red (259)	1.40	1.40
23	A29	20pa red (272)	275.00	275.00
24	A17	20pa car (299)	2.75	2.75
25	A21	20pa car rose (318)	2.75	2.75
26	A22	20pa car rose (330)	11.00	11.00
27	A21	20pa car rose (342)	5.00	5.00
28	A41	20pa ultra (347)	2.75	2.75
29	A16	20pa mag (363)	11.00	11.00
30	A17	20pa car (371)		
31	A18	20pa car (373)	7.75	7.75
32	A45	20pa dp rose (425)	3.75	3.75
33	A21	20pa car rose (B8)	2.75	2.75
34	A22	20pa car rose (B33)	2.75	2.75
35	A22	20pa car rose (B36)	13.00	13.00
36	A41	20pa ultra (B43)	.55	.55
37	A16	20pa mag (P140)	2.75	2.75
38	A17	20pa car (P144)	250.00	250.00
39	A21	1pi bl (260)	2.75	2.75
40	A31	1pi on 1½pi car & blk (261)	375.00	375.00
41	A30	1pi bl (273)	92.50	92.50
42	A30	1pi on 1pi bl (273)	125.00	125.00
43	A17	1pi blue (300)	4.75	4.75
44	A18	1pi blue (307)	57.50	57.50

45	A22	1pi ultra (331)	5.75	5.75
46	A21	1pi ultra (343)	10.00	10.00
47	A41	1pi vio & blk (348)	1.75	1.75
48	A18	1pi brt bl (389)	5.75	5.75
49	A46	1pi dl vio (426)	1.75	1.75
50	A47	1pi on 50pa ul-tra (428)	1.10	1.10
51	A21	1pi ultra (B9)	6.00	6.00
52	A22	1pi ultra (B15)	10.00	10.00
53	A18	1pi brt bl (B21)	6.00	6.00
54	A18	1pi blue (B23)	15.00	15.00
55	A22	1pi ultra (B34)	12.50	12.50
56	A41	1pi vio & blk (B44)	2.75	2.75
57	A33	2pi grn & blk (263)	72.50	72.50
58	A13	2pi brn org (289)	2.00	2.00
59	A18	2pi slate (308)	27.50	27.50
60	A18	2pi slate (314)	27.50	27.50
61	A21	2pi bl blk (320)	5.25	5.25
62	A17	2pi org (373)	4.25	4.25
63	A18	5pi brn (310)	12.00	12.00
64	A22	5pi ultra on (333)	23.50	23.50
65	A41	5pi yel brn & blk (349)	4.75	4.75
66	A41	5pi yel brn & blk (418)	4.75	4.75
67	A53	5pi on 2pa Prus bl (547)	7.75	7.75
68	A21	5pi dk vio (B10)	275.00	275.00
69	A17	5pi lil rose (B20)	47.50	47.50
70	A41	5pi yel brn & blk (B45)	4.75	4.75
72	A50	10pi dk grn (431)	130.00	130.00
73	A50	10pi dk vio (432)	110.00	110.00
74	A50	10pi dk vio (432)	375.00	
75	A18	10pi org brn (B2)	350.00	350.00
76	A37	25pi ol grn (267)	350.00	350.00
77	A40	25pi on 200pi grn & blk (287)	500.00	500.00
78	A21	25pi brn (303)	375.00	375.00
79	A51	25pi car, straw (434)	92.50	92.50
81	A52	50pi ind (438)	200.00	200.00

The variety "surcharge omitted" exists on Nos. 1-5, 12-13, 16, 32, 49-50, 67.

A few examples of No. 377 (50pi) and No. 269 (100pi) were overprinted but not regularly issued.

Overprinted

The Inscription reads "Hakum Soria Arabie" (Syrian-Arabian Government)
On Stamp of 1913

83	A26	2m on 5pa vio brn (256)	5.00	5.00

On Stamp of 1916-18

84	A45	20pa dp rose (425)	.55	.55

A1

		Litho.	**Perf. 11½**	
85	A1	5m rose	.55	.55
a.		Tête bêche pair	22.50	10.00
b.		Imperf.		

Independence Issue
Arabic Overprint in Green
"Souvenir of Syrian Independence March 8, 1920"

86	A1	5m rose	250.00	150.00
a.		Tête bêche pair		
b.		Inverted overprint	375.00	375.00

A2

		Litho.		
		Size: 22x18mm		
87	A2	⅒pi lt brn	.25	.25
		Size: 28x22mm		
88	A2	2/10pi yel grn	.30	.25
a.		⅔pi yellow (error)	10.00	10.00
89	A2	3/10pi yellow	.40	.30
90	A2	1pi gray blue	.35	.25
91	A2	2pi blue grn	2.00	1.00

Size: 31x25mm

92	A2	5pi vio brn	2.75	1.50
93	A2	10pi gray	2.75	2.00
		Nos. 86-93 (8)	258.80	155.55

Nos. 86-93 exist imperf.
For overprint see No. J5.

PF1   PF2

Revenue Stamps Surcharged as on Postage Stamps, for Postal Use

1920		Unwmk.	Perf. 11½	
94	PF1	5m on 5pa red	.50	.35
95	PF2	1m on 5pa red	.50	.25
96	PF2	2m on 5pa red	.40	.25
97	PF2	1pi on 5pa red	1.00	.65

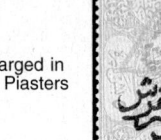

Surcharged in
Syrian Piasters

98	PF2	2pi on 5pa red	.35	.25
99	PF2	3pi on 5pa red	.35	.25
		Nos. 94-99 (6)	3.10	2.00

ISSUES OF THE ARABIAN GOVERNMENT POSTAGE DUE STAMPS

Postage Due Stamps of Turkey, 1914, Handstamped and Surcharged

No. J1   No. J4

1920		Unwmk.	Perf. 12	
J1	D1	2m on 5pa claret	6.75	6.75
J2	D2	20pa red	6.75	6.75
J3	D3	1pi dark blue	6.75	6.75
J4	D4	2pi slate	6.75	6.75
		Nos. J1-J4 (4)	27.00	27.00

Type of Regular Issue
Perf. 11½
Litho.

J5	A2	1pi black	1.25	1.25

TAHITI

tə-'hēt-ē

LOCATION — An island in the South
Pacific Ocean, one of the Society
group
GOVT. — A part of the French
Oceania Colony
AREA — 600 sq. mi.
POP. — 19,029
CAPITAL — Papeete

The stamps of Tahiti were replaced
by those of French Oceania.

100 Centimes = 1 Franc

Covers
**Values are for commercial covers
bearing correct frankings. Philatelic
covers sell for less.**

Counterfeits exist of surcharges and
overprints on Nos. 1-31.

Stamps of French Colonies Surcharged in Black

a   b

c   d

1882		Unwmk.	Imperf.	
1	A8(a)	25c on 35c dk vio, org	425.	350.
		On cover, single franking		6,500.
1A	A8(b)	25c on 35c dk vio, org	4,500.	4,500.
		On cover		—
1B	A8(b)	25c on 40c ver, straw	6,250.	6,750.
		On cover		—

Surcharge Inverted

1c	A8(a)	25c on 35c dk vio, org	500.	450.
1Ad	A8(b)	25c on 35c dk vio, org	4,600.	4,600.
1Be	A8(a)	25c on 40c ver, straw	3,900.	4,100.

Surcharge Reading Up

1f	A8(a)	25c on 35c dk vio, org	525.	475.
1Ag	A8(b)	25c on 35c dk vio, org	4,750.	4,750.

Surcharge Reading Down

1h	A8(a)	25c on 35c dk vio, org	525.	475.
1Ai	A8(b)	25c on 35c dk vio, org	4,600.	4,600.

Double Surcharge, One Inverted

1Bj	A8(a)	25c on 40c ver, straw	7,600.	8,000.

1884			Perf. 14x13½	
2	A9(c)	5c on 20c red, yel grn	300.	240.
		On cover, single franking		9,500.
3	A9(d)	10c on 20c red, yel grn	350.	300.
		On cover, single franking		3,750.
		On wrapper		6,000.

Imperf

4	A8(b)	25c on 1fr brnz grn, straw	750.	650.
		On cover, single franking		9,500.

Covers: Only one cover each is recorded
for Nos. 2 and 4, 8 covers recorded for No. 3.

Surcharge Inverted

2a		5c on 20c red, grn	300.00	240.00
3a		10c on 20c red, grn	340.00	310.00
4a		25c on 1fr brnz grn, straw	750.00	650.00

Surcharge Reading Up

2b		5c on 20c red, grn	300.00	240.00
3b		10c on 20c red, grn	340.00	310.00
4b		25c on 1fr brnz grn, straw	750.00	650.00

Surcharge Reading Down

2c		5c on 20c red, grn	300.00	240.00
3c		10c on 20c red, grn	340.00	310.00
4c		25c on 1fr brnz grn, straw	750.00	650.00

Handstamped in Black

1893			Perf. 14x13½	
5	A9	1c blk, lil bl	950.00	875.00
6	A9	2c brown, buff	3,200.	2,500.
7	A9	4c claret, lav	1,500.	1,250.
8	A9	5c green, grnsh	55.00	47.50
		On cover, single franking		725.00
9	A9	10c black, lav	60.00	52.50
		On cover, single franking		900.00
10	A9	15c blue	60.00	47.50
		On cover, single franking		750.00

11	A9	20c red, green	72.50	65.00
		On cover, single franking		900.00
12	A9	25c yel, straw	8,750.	7,250.
13	A9	25c blk, rose	55.00	47.50
		On cover, single franking		450.00
14	A9	35c violet, org	2,600.	2,200.
15	A9	75c carmine, rose	97.50	67.50
		On cover, single franking		675.00
16	A9	1fr brnz grn, straw	92.50	92.50
		On cover, single franking		750.00

Surcharge Inverted

6a	A9	2c brown, buff	4,000.	3,800.
8a	A9	5c green, grnsh	160.00	140.00
9a	A9	10c black, lav	260.00	225.00
10a	A9	15c blue	240.00	225.00
11a	A9	20c red, green	260.00	240.00
12a	A9	25c yel, straw	10,750.	10,750.
13a	A9	25c blk, rose	240.00	225.00
15a	A9	75c carmine, rose	300.00	260.00
16a	A9	1fr brnz grn, straw	340.00	340.00

Nearly all values of this set are known with
overprint sloping up, sloping down and horizontal. Some occur double. Values the same
as for the normal stamps.

Overprinted in Black

1893				
17	A9	1c blk, lil bl	925.00	800.00
18	A9	2c brn, buff	3,750.	2,750.
19	A9	4c claret, lav	1,850.	1,500.
20	A9	5c grn, grnsh	1,100.	950.00
21	A9	10c black, lav	350.00	350.00
22	A9	15c blue	55.00	50.00
		On cover, single franking		750.00
23	A9	20c red, grn	60.00	55.00
		On cover, single franking		775.00
24	A9	25c yel, straw	50,000.	42,500.
25	A9	25c black, rose	55.00	50.00
		On cover, single franking		450.00
26	A9	35c violet, org	2,600.	2,200.
27	A9	75c carmine, rose	60.00	55.00
		On cover, single franking		675.00
b.		Double overprint	400.00	
28	A9	1fr brnz grn, straw	75.00	60.00
		On cover, single franking		750.00

Inverted Overprint

17a	A9	1c blk, lil bl	1,350.	1,200.
18a	A9	2c brn, buff	4,000.	3,900.
19a	A9	4c claret, lav	2,000.	1,900.
20a	A9	5c grn, grnsh	1,600.	1,500.
21a	A9	10c black, lav	950.	900.
22a	A9	15c blue	250.	225.
23a	A9	20c red, grn	250.	225.
25a	A9	25c black, rose	250.	225.
26a	A9	35c violet, org	3,000.	2,800.
27a	A9	75c carmine, rose	300.	250.
28a	A9	1fr brnz grn, straw	300.	275.

Stamps of French Polynesia Surcharged in Black or Carmine

g   h

1903				
29	A1 (g)	10c on 15c bl (Bk)	11.00	11.00
		On cover, single franking		140.00
a.		Double surcharge	67.50	67.50
b.		Inverted surcharge	72.50	72.50
30	A1 (h)	10c on 25c blk, rose (C)	11.00	11.00
		On cover, single franking		140.00
a.		Double surcharge	67.50	67.50
b.		Inverted surcharge	80.00	80.00
31	A1 (h)	10c on 40c red, straw (Bk)	13.00	13.00
		On cover, single franking		140.00
a.		Double surcharge	80.00	80.00
b.		Inverted surcharge	80.00	80.00
		Nos. 29-31 (3)	35.00	35.00

In the surcharges on Nos. 29-31 there are
two varieties of the "1" in "10," i. e. with long
and short serif.

SEMI-POSTAL STAMPS

Stamps of French
Polynesia Overprinted
in Red

1915		Unwmk.	Perf. 14x13½	
B1	A1	15c blue	300.00	300.00
		On cover, single franking		550.00
a.		Inverted overprint	1,100.	1,000.
B2	A1	15c gray	35.00	35.00
		On cover, single franking		200.00
a.		Inverted overprint	425.00	425.00

Values are for commercial covers bearing
correct frankings. Philatelic covers also exist
and generally sell for less than the values
quoted.

Counterfeits exist.

POSTAGE DUE STAMPS

Counterfeits exist of overprints on
Nos. J1-J26.

Postage Due Stamps of French Colonies Handstamped in Black like Nos. 5-16

1893		Unwmk.	Imperf.	
J1	D1	1c black	400.	400.
J2	D1	2c black	400.	400.
J3	D1	3c black	450.	450.
J4	D1	4c black	450.	450.
J5	D1	5c black	450.	450.
J6	D1	10c black	450.	450.
J7	D1	15c black	450.	450.
J8	D1	20c black	350.	350.
		On cover		8,000.
J9	D1	30c black	450.	450.
J10	D1	40c black	450.	450.
J11	D1	60c black	525.	525.
J12	D1	1fr brown	1,100.	1,100.
J13	D1	2fr brown	1,100.	1,100.
		Nos. J1-J13 (13)	7,025.	7,025.

Surcharge Inverted

J1a	D1	1c black	725.	725.
J2a	D1	2c black	725.	725.
J3a	D1	3c black	725.	725.
J4a	D1	4c black	725.	725.
J5a	D1	5c black	725.	725.
J6a	D1	10c black	725.	725.
J7a	D1	15c black	725.	725.
J8a	D1	20c black	725.	725.
J9a	D1	30c black	725.	725.
J10a	D1	40c black	725.	725.
J11a	D1	60c black	800.	800.
J12a	D1	1fr brown	1,600.	1,600.
J13a	D1	2fr brown	1,600.	1,600.

Surcharge Double

J6b	D1	10c black	1,050.	1,050.
J7b	D1	15c black	1,050.	1,050.

Covers: Only two covers are recorded for
No. J8.

Overprinted in Black like Nos. 17-28

1893				
J14	D1	1c black	2,400.	2,400.
J15	D1	2c black	550.	550.
J16	D1	3c black	550.	550.
J17	D1	4c black	550.	550.
J18	D1	5c black	550.	550.
J19	D1	10c black	550.	550.
J20	D1	15c black	550.	550.
J21	D1	20c black	550.	550.
		On cover, single franking		6,750.
J22	D1	30c black	550.	550.
J23	D1	40c black	550.	550.
J24	D1	60c black	550.	550.
J25	D1	1fr brown	550.	550.
J26	D1	2fr brown	550.	550.
		Nos. J14-J26 (13)	9,000.	9,000.

Surcharge Inverted

J14a	D1	1c black	3,250.	3,250.
J15a	D1	2c black	1,000.	1,000.
J19a	D1	10c black	1,100.	1,100.
J20a	D1	15c black	1,100.	1,100.
J21a	D1	20c black	1,100.	1,100.
J23a	D1	40c black	1,100.	1,100.
J24a	D1	60c black	1,100.	1,100.
J25a	D1	1fr brown	1,100.	1,100.
J26a	D1	2fr brown	1,100.	1,100.

Surcharge Double

J15b	D1	2c black	1,100.	1,100.
J16b	D1	3c black	1,100.	1,100.
J17b	D1	4c black	1,100.	1,100.
J18b	D1	5c black	1,100.	1,100.
J19b	D1	10c black	1,100.	1,100.
J20b	D1	15c black	1,100.	1,100.

J22b	D1	30c black	1,100.	1,100.
J25b	D1	1fr brown	1,100.	1,100.
J26b	D1	2fr brown	1,100.	1,100.

TANGANYIKA

,tan-gə-'nyē-kə

LOCATION — Southeastern Africa bordering on the Indian Ocean
AREA — 362,688 sq. mi.
POP. — 9,404,000 (est. 1961)
CAPITAL — Dar es Salaam

Before World War I, this area formed part of German East Africa It was mandated to Britain after World War I and (in 1946) became a trust territory under the United Nations. In 1935, stamps of the mandate were replaced by those used jointly by Kenya, Uganda and Tanganyika (see Kenya, Uganda and Tanzania).

100 Cents = 1 Rupee
100 Cents = 1 Shilling (1922)
20 Shillings = 1 Pound

Stamps of East Africa & Uganda Protectorates Overprinted

G.E.A.

1921		**Wmk. 4**	**Perf. 14**	
1	A1	12c gray	9.00	110.00
2	A1	15c ultra	7.00	11.00
3	A1	50c dull violet & blk	14.00	100.00

Overprinted

G.E.A.

4	A2	2r black & red, *blue*	42.50	140.00
5	A2	3r gray green & violet	100.00	275.00
7	A2	5r dull violet & ultra	150.00	400.00
		Nos. 1-7 (6)	322.50	1,036.

Overprinted in Red or Black

G.E.A.

1922				
8	A1	1c black (R)	1.25	21.00
9	A1	10c orange (Bk)	2.50	16.00

A3 / Giraffe — A4

		Perf. 14½x14		
1922-25		**Engr.**	**Wmk. 4**	
10	A3	5c dk violet & blk	2.75	.25
11	A3	5c grn & blk ('25)	9.00	1.75
12	A3	10c green & blk	3.25	.95
13	A3	10c yel & blk ('25)	9.00	1.75
14	A3	15c carmine & blk	3.75	.25
15	A3	20c orange & blk	4.25	.25
16	A3	25c black	7.50	7.50
17	A3	25c blue & blk ('25)	4.50	20.00
18	A3	30c blue & blk	5.75	5.75
19	A3	30c dull vio & blk ('25)	6.50	16.00
20	A3	40c brown & black	3.25	5.25
21	A3	50c gray black	5.50	1.75
22	A3	75c bister & black	4.50	21.00
		Perf. 14		
23	A4	1sh green & black	4.75	12.50
a.		Wmk. sideways	8.50	22.00
24	A4	2sh brn vio & blk	5.25	32.50
a.		Wmk. sideways	8.50	22.50
25	A4	3sh blk, wmk. sideways	40.00	37.50
26	A4	5sh red & black	30.00	85.00
a.		Wmk. sideways	60.00	100.00
27	A4	10sh dp blue & blk	85.00	160.00
a.		Wmk. sideways	170.00	375.00
28	A4	£1 orange & black	300.00	475.00
a.		Wmk. sideways	350.00	500.00
		Nos. 10-28 (19)	534.50	884.95

On No. 28 the words of value are in a curve between the circle and "POSTAGE & REVENUE."

King George V
A5 / A6

1927-31				**Typo.**
29	A5	5c green & black	2.00	.25
30	A5	10c yellow & black	2.25	.25
31	A5	15c red & black	2.00	.25
32	A5	20c orange & black	3.00	.25
33	A5	25c ultra & black	4.25	2.25
34	A5	30c dull violet & blk	3.25	3.00
35	A5	30c ultra & blk ('31)	29.00	.35
36	A5	40c brown & black	2.25	7.50
37	A5	50c gray & black	2.90	1.10
38	A5	75c olive grn & blk	2.25	22.50
39	A6	1sh green & black	4.75	3.25
40	A6	2sh violet brn & blk	30.00	6.00
41	A6	3sh black	45.00	85.00
42	A6	5sh scarlet & blk	30.00	24.00
43	A6	10sh ultra & black	85.00	120.00
44	A6	£1 brown org & blk	225.00	400.00
		Nos. 29-44 (16)	472.90	675.95

TANNU TUVA

'tä-nə 'tü-və

(Tuva People's Republic)

LOCATION — Between Siberia and northwestern Mongolia at the sources of the Yenisei, in the basin formed by the Tannu-Ola and Sayan Mountains.
GOVT. — A republic closely identified with Soviet Russia in Asia
AREA — 64,000 sq. mi. (approx.)
POP. — 95,000 (1941 est.)
CAPITAL — Kyzyl

This region, traditionally called Uriankhai, was ruled by the Mongols until the mid-18th century, when it became part of the Chinese Empire. Russia and China struggled for control of the country 1914-21, until it became independent as the Tannu Tuva People's Republic in 1921. In 1944 it was incorporated into the U.S.S.R. as an autonomous region of the Russian Soviet Federated Socialist Republic.

Russian, later Soviet, stamps were used in Tuva prior to 1926 and after 1944.

100 Mongo=1 Tugrik
100 Kopecks = 1 Ruble
100 Kopecks = 1 Tugrik (1934)
100 Kopecks = 1 Aksha (1936)

Watermarks

Wmk. 204 — Stars and Diamonds

Wmk. 170 — Greek Border and Rosettes

Values for covers are for properly franked covers with correct rates, usually addressed to Moscow. Because most have philatelic addresses, some leeway in proper rates is to be expected, and covers that vary slightly from proper rates are generally accepted as commercial covers.

For valuation of covers with multiple franking, see "Catalogue Values for Stamps on Covers" in the Introduction to this catalogue.

Most used examples of Nos. 1-38, 45-52a, 54-92 and C1-C18 on the market are canceled to order, and the used values below are for such stamps.

Tuvan stamps, except for Nos. 117-123 and most of the overprints, were printed by the State Security Printers in Moscow.

Wheel of Truth — A1

1926	**Litho.**	**Wmk. 204**	**Perf. 13½**	
		Size: 20x26mm		
1	A1	1k red	1.50	1.50
		Never hinged	2.50	
		Postal cancel		1.60
		On cover		250.00
2	A1	2k light blue	1.50	1.50
		Never hinged	3.00	
		Postal cancel		1.50
		On cover		250.00
3	A1	5k orange	1.50	1.50
		Never hinged	3.00	
		Postal cancel		1.50
		On cover		250.00
4	A1	8k yel green	2.00	1.75
		Never hinged	3.50	
		Postal cancel		1.50
		On cover		250.00
5	A1	10k violet	2.00	1.75
		Never hinged	4.00	
		Postal cancel		1.50
		On cover		250.00
6	A1	30k dark brown	2.00	1.75
		Never hinged	3.50	
		Postal cancel		1.50
		On cover		250.00
7	A1	50k gray black	2.25	1.75
		Never hinged	4.00	
		Postal cancel		2.00
		On cover		250.00
		Size: 22½x30mm		
		Perf. 10½		
8	A1	1r blue green	6.00	3.00
		Never hinged	11.00	
		Postal cancel		7.50
		On cover		400.00
9	A1	3r red brown	8.00	5.75
		Never hinged	16.00	
		Postal cancel		8.00
		On cover		—
10	A1	5r dark ultra	13.50	8.00
		Never hinged	27.00	
		Postal cancel		13.50
		On cover		—
a.		Imperf, pair	180.00	
		Nos. 1-10 (10)	40.25	28.25
		Set, never hinged	77.50	

Nos. 1-10 have crackled white gum. Reprints can be distinguished by their smooth gum.
Nos. 1-10 in different colors are proofs.

Nos. 7-10 Surcharged in Red or Black

Surcharged in Kyzyl.

1927			**Perf. 13½**	
11	A1	8k on 50k	25.00	12.50
		Never hinged	50.00	
		Postal cancel		27.50
		On cover		275.00
a.		Inverted surcharge	65.00	
b.		Double surcharge	100.00	
		Perf. 10½		
12	A1	14k on 1r	25.00	12.50
		Never hinged	50.00	
		Postal cancel		30.00
		On cover		350.00
a.		Inverted surcharge	75.00	
b.		Double surcharge	85.00	
13	A1	18k on 3r (Bk)	25.00	12.50
		Never hinged	50.00	
		Postal cancel		30.00
		On cover		350.00
a.		Inverted surcharge	90.00	
b.		Double surcharge	75.00	
14	A1	28k on 5r (Bk)	25.00	12.50
		Never hinged	50.00	
		Postal cancel		30.00
		On cover		350.00
a.		Inverted surcharge	90.00	
b.		Double surcharge	75.00	
		Nos. 11-14 (4)	100.00	50.00
		Set, never hinged	200.00	

Nos. 11-14 were surcharged with a shiny ink. Reprints are overprinted with a dull ink and are often smudged.

Tuvan Woman — A3
Map of Tannu Tuva A8
Sheep Herding — A11

Fording a Stream — A13

Tuvan Riding Reindeer — A16

Designs: 2k, Stag. 3k, Mountain goat. 4k, Tuvan and tent. 5k, Tuvan man. 10k, Archery competition. 14k, Camel caravan. 28k, Landscape. 50k, Weaving. 70k, Tuvan on horseback.
Printed in Moscow.

1927		**Litho.**	**Perf. 12½**	
15	A3	1k black, lt brown & red	1.00	.60
		Never hinged	2.00	
		Postal cancel		2.00
		On cover		125.00

16	A3	2k purple, dp brown & green	1.20	.55
		Never hinged	2.40	
		Postal cancel		2.00
		On cover		125.00
17	A3	3k black, bl grn & yellow	2.00	.60
		Never hinged	4.00	
		Postal cancel		9.00
		On cover		125.00
18	A3	4k vio bl & choc	.90	.60
		Never hinged	1.80	
		Postal cancel		1.50
		On cover		125.00
19	A3	5k org, blk & dk bl	.90	.65
		Never hinged	1.80	
		Postal cancel		1.80
		On cover		125.00

Perf. 12½x12

20	A8	8k ol brn, pale bl & red brn	1.00	.65
		Never hinged	2.00	
		Postal cancel		1.00
		On cover		150.00
21	A8	10k black, green & brn red	5.50	1.00
		Never hinged	11.00	
		Postal cancel		1.50
		On cover		200.00
22	A8	14k vio bl & red org	10.00	3.50
		Never hinged	20.00	
		Postal cancel		5.00
		On cover, from		150.00

Perf. 10½

23	A11	18k dk bl & red brn	10.00	5.00
		Never hinged	20.00	
		Postal cancel		10.00
		On cover, from		225.00
a.		Perf 10	70.00	70.00
		Never hinged	140.00	
b.		Perf compund 10, 10½	15.00	8.00
		Never hinged	30.00	
		Postal cancel		15.00
24	A11	28k emer & blk brn	7.25	2.75
		Never hinged	14.50	
		Postal cancel		4.50
		On cover, from		200.00
25	A13	40k rose & bl grn	5.00	2.50
		Never hinged	10.00	
		Postal cancel		5.00
		On cover, from		275.00
a.		Perf 10	8.50	4.00
		Never hinged	17.00	
		Postal cancel		—
b.		Perf 10x10½	9.00	—
		Never hinged	18.00	
		Postal cancel		—
26	A13	50k black, green & red brown	3.50	2.00
		Never hinged	7.00	
		Postal cancel		7.00
		On cover, from		275.00
a.		Perf 10	5.00	2.75
		Never hinged	10.00	
		Postal cancel		5.00
b.		Perf 10x10½	7.00	3.75
		Never hinged	14.00	
		Postal cancel		5.00
27	A13	70k dl red & bis	7.00	4.00
		Never hinged	14.00	
		Postal cancel		10.00
		On cover, from		350.00
28	A16	1r yel brn & vio	16.00	6.75
		Never hinged	32.00	
		Postal cancel		20.00
		On cover, from		350.00
		Nos. 15-28 (14)	71.25	31.15
		Set, never hinged	142.50	

Nos. 15-28 were issued with a crackled white gum. Reprints of the 1k-5k values exist and can be distinguished by their smooth gum.
Nos. 15-28 in different colors are proofs.

Nos. 25-27, 20-22 Surcharged in Various Colors

Surcharged in Moscow.

1932

29	A13	1k on 40k (Bk)	9.00	10.00
		Never hinged	18.00	
		Postal cancel		30.00
		On cover		175.00
a.		Perf 10	10.00	10.00
		Never hinged	20.00	
		Postal cancel		—
b.		Perf 10x10½	10.00	10.00
		Never hinged	20.00	
		Postal cancel		—
30	A13	2k on 50k (Br)	10.00	10.00
		Never hinged	20.00	
		Postal cancel		30.00
		On cover		175.00
a.		Perf 10	10.00	10.00
		Never hinged	20.00	
		Postal cancel		30.00
b.		Perf 10x10½	45.00	25.00
		Never hinged	90.00	
		Postal cancel		35.00
31	A13	3k on 70k (Bl)	10.00	10.00
		Never hinged	20.00	
		Postal cancel		25.00
		On cover		175.00
a.		Inverted surcharge	300.00	
		Never hinged	600.00	

32	A8	5k on 8k (Bk)	10.00	10.00
		Never hinged	20.00	
		Postal cancel		25.00
		On cover		175.00
33	A8	10k (Bk)	10.00	10.00
		Never hinged	20.00	
		Postal cancel		25.00
		On cover		175.00
34	A8	15k 8h 14k (Bk)	15.00	15.00
		Never hinged	30.00	
		Postal cancel		25.00
		On cover		175.00
		Nos. 29-34 (6)	64.00	65.00
		Set, never hinged	128.00	
		#29-34 on philatelic cover		300.00

Issued in connection with the Romanization of the alphabet.
No. 31 with black surcharge was prepared but not issued.

Nos. 20, 22-24 Surcharged in Black

No. 37

No. 38

Surcharged by numbering machine in Kyzyl.

1932-33				**Wmk. 204**
35	A8	10k on 8k	180.00	100.00
		Never hinged	350.00	
		Postal cancel		300.00
36	A8	15k on 14k	300.00	200.00
		Never hinged	600.00	
		Postal cancel		600.00
37	A11	35k on 18k (#23)	150.00	100.00
		Never hinged	275.00	
		Postal cancel		140.00
		On cover		—
a.		Perf 10 (#23a)	150.00	150.00
		Never hinged	300.00	
		Postal cancel		—
b.		Pair, one without surcharge		—
c.		Inverted surcharge	500.00	
38	A11	35k on 28k	150.00	100.00
		Never hinged	275.00	
		Postal cancel		140.00
		On cover		—
a.		Pair, one without surcharge		—
		Nos. 35-38 (4)	780.00	500.00
		Set, never hinged	1,550.	

A19

Revenue Stamps Surcharged

Three types: type 1, figures of value 6.7mm high; type 2, figures of value 6.7mm high, letter "p" lengthened at bottom; type 3, figures of value 5.1mm high.

Surcharged in Kyzyl.

1933				**Perf. 12x12½**
39	A19	15k on 6k org yel, type 1	300.00	150.00
a.		On cover	—	
		"Posta" omitted	—	
40	A19	15k on 6k org yel, type 2	300.00	150.00
a.		On cover	—	
		"Posta" omitted	—	
b.		Inverted surcharge	—	
41	A19	15k on 6k org yel, type 3	500.00	300.00
		On cover	—	
42	A19	35k on 15k red brn, type 1	—	4,000.
		On cover	—	
43	A19	35k on 15k red brn, type 2	—	4,000.
		On cover	—	
44	A19	35k on 15k red brn, type 3	1,500.	800.00
		On cover	—	

Mounted Hunter — A20

Tuvan Inside of Yurt — A21

Tuvan Milking Yak — A22

Die I   Die II

Designs: 2k, Hunter stalking game. 4k, Tractor. 10k, Camel caravan. 15k, Herdsman lassoing reindeer. 20k, Hunter shooting fox with arrow.

Two dies on 10k: Die I, Crown at center top is light and matches the shade of the sky below; Die II, Crown at center top is bold, consistent with rest of design and darker than the sky.

Printed by State Security Printers, Moscow.

1934, Apr.		**Wmk. 170 Photo.**		**Perf. 12**
45	A20	1k red orange	1.50	1.00
		Never hinged	4.00	
		Postal cancel		2.00
		On cover		100.00
46	A20	2k olive green	1.50	1.00
		Never hinged	10.00	
		Postal cancel		6.00
		On cover		100.00
47	A21	3k rose red	1.50	1.00
		Never hinged	5.00	
		Postal cancel		1.50
		On cover		100.00
48	A21	4k slate purple	3.50	1.75
		Never hinged	6.00	
		Postal cancel		3.00
		On cover		100.00
49	A22	5k ultramarine	3.50	1.75
		Never hinged	8.00	
		Postal cancel		2.50
		On cover		100.00
50	A22	10k brown, die II	3.50	1.75
		Never hinged	10.00	
		Postal cancel		8.00
		On cover		125.00
a.		Perf 13¾	25.00	
b.		Perf 11		
c.		10k brown, die I	8.00	2.00
		Never hinged	16.00	
		Postal cancel		8.00
		On cover		150.00
51	A22	15k dark lilac	3.50	1.75
		Never hinged	14.00	
		Postal cancel		3.50
		On cover		100.00
52	A22	20k gray black	4.75	2.75
		Never hinged	20.00	
		Postal cancel		4.00
		On cover		100.00
		Nos. 45-52 (8)	23.25	12.75
		Set, never hinged	50.00	
		Set, imperf	50.00	
		Set, imperf., never hinged	100.00	

Imperf

45a	A20	1k red orange	2.25	1.50
		Never hinged	4.50	
		Postal cancel		4.00
		On cover		100.00
46a	A20	2k olive green	10.00	6.50
		Never hinged	20.00	
		Postal cancel		13.50
47a	A21	3k rose red	2.25	1.25
		Never hinged	4.50	
		Postal cancel		4.00
		On cover		100.00
48a	A21	4k slate purple	4.00	1.75
		Never hinged	8.00	
		Postal cancel		4.50
		On cover		100.00
49a	A22	5k ultramarine	4.00	2.00
		Never hinged	8.00	
		Postal cancel		5.25
		On cover		125.00
50d	A22	10k brown, die II	5.00	3.50
		Never hinged	10.00	
		Postal cancel		8.00
		On cover		150.00
e.		10k brown, die I	8.50	
		Never hinged	18.00	
		Postal cancel		10.00
		On cover		200.00
51a	A22	15k dark lilac	5.00	3.50
		Never hinged	10.00	
		Postal cancel		7.00
		On cover		150.00
52a	A22	20k gray black	17.50	6.00
		Never hinged	35.00	
		Postal cancel		20.00
		Nos. 45a-52a (8)	50.00	26.00
		Set, never hinged	135.00	

Nos. 45a-52a are inscribed "REGISTERED," but were used as regular postage stamps.
Nos. 46, 48 and 50 exist perf 11, and No. 50 also exists perf 11x10. No. 48 exists perf 11½, reportedly as a color trial proof.

No. 51 Surcharged in Black

Surcharged by numbering machine in Kyzyl.

1935				
53	A22	20k on 15k	175.00	325.00
a.		Inverted surcharge		400.00

Map of Tuva — A23

Rocky Outcropping — A24

Designs: 3k, 5k, 10k, Different scenes of Yenisei River. 25k, Bei-kem rapids. 50k, Mounted hunters.
Printed by State Security Printers, Moscow.

1935, Mar.		**Wmk. 170 Photo.**		**Perf. 14**
54	A23	1k yellow orange	2.25	1.75
		Never hinged	2.50	
		Postal cancel		1.50
		On cover		100.00
55	A23	3k deep green	2.25	1.75
		Never hinged	2.50	
		Postal cancel		3.00
		On cover		100.00
56	A23	5k carmine red	3.00	2.00
		Never hinged	3.00	
		Postal cancel		1.50
		On cover		100.00
57	A23	10k violet	3.25	2.00
		Never hinged	3.50	
		Postal cancel		2.00
		On cover		100.00
a.		Perf 14x10x14	35.00	
b.		Pair, imperf between		
58	A24	15k olive green	3.50	2.50
		Never hinged	3.50	
		Postal cancel		2.00
		On cover		100.00
59	A24	25k violet blue	4.00	2.50
		Never hinged	4.00	
		Postal cancel		2.00
		On cover		100.00

60	A24 50k dark brown	5.75	2.75
	Never hinged	6.00	
	Postal cancel		4.00
	On cover		150.00
	Nos. 54-60 (7)	24.00	15.25
	Set, never hinged	45.00	

Nos. 54-60 in different colors, perf and imperf, are proofs.

Badger
A25

Squirrel — A26

Fox — A27

Elk — A28

Yak — A29

Designs: 5k, Ermine. 25k, Otter. 50k, Lynx. 3t, Bactrian camels. 5t, Bear.
Printed by State Security Printers, Moscow.

1935, Mar.

61	A25 1k orange	1.60	1.00
	Never hinged	3.25	
	Postal cancel		2.00
	On cover		100.00
62	A26 3k emerald green	1.60	1.00
	Never hinged	3.25	
	Postal cancel		2.00
	On cover		100.00
a.	Imperf, pair	300.00	
63	A25 5k rose red	1.60	1.10
	Never hinged	4.00	
	Postal cancel		2.00
	On cover		100.00
64	A27 10k crimson red	1.60	1.10
	Never hinged	5.00	
	Postal cancel		2.50
	On cover		100.00
65	A27 25k orange red	2.50	1.20
	Never hinged	5.00	
	Postal cancel		3.00
	On cover		100.00
66	A27 50k deep blue	2.50	1.20
	Never hinged	6.00	
	Postal cancel		3.50
	On cover		125.00
67	A28 1t violet	2.50	1.20
	Never hinged	8.00	
a.	Pair, imperf between	—	
68	A29 2t royal blue	3.50	1.20
	Never hinged	7.00	
69	A29 3t red brown	4.00	1.35
	Never hinged	8.00	
70	A28 5t indigo	5.00	1.75
	Never hinged	10.00	
a.	Imperf, pair	300.00	
b.	Pair, imperf between	—	
	Nos. 61-70 (10)	26.40	12.10
	Set, never hinged	50.00	

Nos. 61-70 in different colors are proofs.

Tuvan Arms — A30

Wrestlers — A31

Herdsman on Bull — A32

Athletic Competitions — A33

Soldiers
A34

Designs: 2k, Pres. Chürmit-Dazhy. 3k, Tuvan with Bactrian camel. 5k, 8k, Archer. 10k, 15k, Spearfishing. 12k, 20k, Bear-hunting. 30k, Camel and train. 40k, 50k, Horse race. 80k, Partisans. 3t, Partisans confiscating cattle. 5t, 1921 battle scene.
Printed by State Security Printers, Moscow.

1936, July   **Perf. 14**

71	A30 1k bronze green	2.00	.70
	Never hinged	3.00	
	Postal cancel		2.00
	On cover		90.00
72	A30 2k dark brown	2.50	1.50
	Never hinged	4.00	
	Postal cancel		3.00
	On cover		100.00
74	A31 4k orange red	—	35.00
	Never hinged		—
75	A31 5k brown purple	5.00	.70
	Never hinged	8.00	
	Postal cancel		2.50
	On cover		90.00
76	A31 6k myrtle green	4.75	.70
	Never hinged	7.50	
	Postal cancel		3.00
	On cover		90.00
77	A31 8k plum	4.75	.70
	Never hinged	7.50	
	Postal cancel		3.00
	On cover		90.00
78	A31 10k rose red	6.00	1.00
	Never hinged	10.00	
	Postal cancel		2.50
	On cover		90.00
79	A31 12k black brown	7.50	1.25
	Never hinged	12.00	
	Postal cancel		4.00
	On cover		90.00

80	A31 15k bronze green	11.00	1.50
	Never hinged	17.00	
	Postal cancel		7.00
	On cover		100.00
81	A31 20k deep blue	11.00	1.20
	Never hinged	14.50	
	Postal cancel		3.00
	On cover		90.00
82	A32 25k orange red	6.00	1.20
	Never hinged	14.50	
	Postal cancel		6.00
	On cover		100.00
83	A32 30k plum	30.00	1.25
	Never hinged	42.50	
	Postal cancel		6.00
	On cover		100.00
84	A32 35k rose red	6.00	1.50
	Never hinged	14.50	
	Postal cancel		4.00
	On cover		100.00
85	A32 40k deep brown	9.00	1.50
	Never hinged	14.50	
	Postal cancel		6.00
	On cover		100.00
86	A32 50k indigo blue	35.00	35.00
	Never hinged	85.00	
	On cover		—
87	A33 70k plum	12.00	2.00
	Never hinged	17.50	
	Postal cancel		5.00
	On cover		125.00
88	A33 80k green	11.00	2.00
	Never hinged	17.00	
	Postal cancel		5.00
	On cover		250.00
89	A34 1a orange red	11.00	2.00
	Never hinged	17.00	
	Postal cancel		4.00
	On cover		125.00
a.	1a rose red (error)		—
90	A34 2a rose red	11.00	3.00
	Never hinged	17.00	
	Postal cancel		10.00
	On cover		250.00
92	A33 5a black brown	15.00	2.50
	Never hinged	17.50	
	Postal cancel		20.00
	On cover		300.00

Perf. 11

72a	A30 2k dark brown	—	50.00
73	A30 3k indigo blue	3.25	.75
	Never hinged	4.75	
	Postal cancel		2.50
74a	A31 4k orange red	3.50	.75
	Never hinged	5.00	
	Postal cancel		3.00
75a	A31 5k brown purple	42.50	—
	Never hinged	85.00	
	Postal cancel		—
76a	A31 6k myrtle green	4.75	.75
	Never hinged	9.50	
	Postal cancel		3.00
78a	A31 10k rose red	5.25	.75
	Never hinged	10.50	
	Postal cancel		2.00
	On cover		90.00
80a	A31 15k bronze green	13.00	1.25
	Never hinged	.26	
	Postal cancel		6.00
81a	A31 20k deep blue	—	—
82a	A32 25k orange red	13.00	.90
	Never hinged	26.00	
	Postal cancel		3.00
84a	A32 35k rose red	13.00	1.25
	Never hinged	26.00	
	Postal cancel		4.00
85a	A32 40k deep brown	7.00	1.50
	Never hinged	14.00	
	Postal cancel		6.00
	On cover		100.00
86a	A32 50k indigo blue	13.00	1.50
	Never hinged	26.00	
	Postal cancel		5.00
	On cover		—
87a	A33 70k plum	9.50	2.50
	Never hinged	20.00	
	Postal cancel		8.00
88a	A33 80k green	9.50	2.50
	Never hinged	19.00	
	Postal cancel		8.00
89b	A34 1a orange red	9.50	3.00
	Never hinged	19.00	
	Postal cancel		8.00
90a	A34 2a rose red	12.00	3.00
	Never hinged	24.00	
	Postal cancel		10.00
91	A33 3a indigo blue	17.50	2.00
	Never hinged	35.00	
	Postal cancel		15.00
	Nos. 71-92 (37)	376.75	168.60
	Set, never hinged	690.00	

15th anniversary of independence.
Imperfs are remainders, later sold by the Soviet Postal Museum.

Values for Nos. 93-98 and 104-116 are for genuine examples. Expertization is essential for these issues.

Issues of 1934-36 Handstamped with Large Numerals and Old Values Obliterated with Bars or Blocks

1938, Aug.

93	A34 5k on 2a (#90a)		400.00
94	AP5 5k on 2a (#C17)		375.00
95	AP1 10k on 1t (#C8)		350.00
96	A24 20k on 50k (#60)		350.00
	On cover		—
97	AP5 30k on 2a (#C17)		350.00
98	AP5 30k on 3a (#C18)		325.00

Types of 1935-36 with Modified Designs and New Colors

1938, Dec.		**Unwmk.**	**Perf. 12½**
99	A25 5k deep green	60.00	—
	Never hinged	90.00	
100	A31 10k indigo (dates removed)	60.00	—
	Never hinged	90.00	
101	AP3 15k red brown ("AIR MAIL," dates removed)	60.00	—
	Never hinged	90.00	
102	A31 20k orange red (dates removed)	85.00	—
	Never hinged	140.00	
103	A33 30k maroon (dates removed)	60.00	—
	Never hinged	90.00	
	Nos. 99-103 (5)	325.00	
	Set, never hinged	500.00	

Some experts believe that these stamps were issued in March 1941.
A few commercial covers exist, dated between 1941 and 1943.

Stamps of 1934-35 Handstamp Surcharged with New Values in Black or Violet at Kyzyl

1939

104	AP1 10k on 1t (#C8)		225.00
a.	10k on 1t, #C8a		—
105	AP1 10k on 1t (#B8) (V)		225.00
106	A24 20k on 50k (#60) (V)		200.00
	On cover		—

Old values obliterated on Nos. 104-106.

Stamps of 1934-36 Handstamp Surcharged with New Values at Kyzyl

1940, Oct.-1941

107	AP1 10k on 1t (#C8)	—	125.00
a.	Double surcharge		—
108	A24 20k on 50k (#60)	—	150.00
109	A27 20k on 50k (#66)	—	350.00
110	A32 20k on 50k (#86a)	—	350.00
111	AP4 20k on 50k (#C14)	—	100.00
112	A33 20k on 70k (#87a)	—	500.00
113	AP4 20k on 75k (#C15)	—	110.00
114	A33 20k on 80k (#88)	—	500.00

The old values are not obliterated on Nos. 107 or 108.

Nos. 91, 92 Handstamp Surcharged with New Values at Kyzyl

1942

115	A33 25k on 3a (#91)	1,200.	—
116	A33 25k on 5a (#92)		

Government House — A35

Exhibition Hall — A36

Tuvan Woman — A37

1942　Typo.　Unwmk.　*Imperf.*

117	A35	25k steel blue	950.00	100.00
118	A36	25k steel blue	950.00	100.00
119	A37	25k steel blue	950.00	150.00
		Nos. 117-119 (3)	2,850.	350.00

21st anniversary of independence.

Nos. 117-119 were printed together in small sheetlets of five (117+119+ 118+117+119), so various se-tenant combinations are possible.

Two additional values, a 25k depicting a Tuvan man and a 50k depicting a soldier on a horse, were prepared, but not issued. A collective proof sheetlet of five, containing Nos. 117-119 and these two values, in the same color as the issued stamps, is also known.

Coat of Arms — A38

Government Building — A39

1943　　Perf. 11 (1 or 2 Sides)
Buff Paper

120	A38	25k slate blue	100.00	—
		Vertical strip of 5	900.00	
121	A38	25k black	100.00	—
		Vertical strip of 5	600.00	
122	A38	25k blue green	90.00	—
123	A39	50k blue green	90.00	—
		Vertical pair, 122 + 123	175.00	
		Nos. 120-123 (4)	380.00	

White Paper

120a	A38	25k slate blue	90.00	—
b.		Strip of 3, imperf between	250.00	
		Sheet of 5	500.00	
121a	A38	25k black	125.00	—
		Vertical strip of five	600.00	
122a	A38	25k blue green	95.00	—
123a	A39	50k blue green	95.00	—
		With gum	175.00	
		Nos. 120a-123a (4)	405.00	

22nd anniversary of independence.

Nos. 120 and 121 were each printed in vertical strips of five, perforated 11 between stamps and imperf on outside edges, so that these stamps may be perforated on top edge only, bottom edge only, or on both top and bottom edges. To make maximum use of limited wartime paper supplies, they were sometimes printed in strips of four. These smaller strips are rare.

Nos. 122 and 123 were printed together in blocks of four, containing a vertical pair of the 25k and a vertical pair of the 50k, perforated internally both vertically and horizontally and imperf on the outer edges. Setenant pairs, Value $225 (#122+123), $275 (#122a+123a).

Nos. 121 and 123a were issued with gum, No. 123a both with and without gum, and the balance of the set without gum.

Used examples and covers exist but are extremely rare.

AIR POST STAMPS

Airplane and Yaks — AP1

Airplane and Capercaillie — AP2

Designs, airplane over: 5k, 15k, Camels. 25k, Argali (wild sheep). 75k, Ox and cart. 2t, Roe deer.
Printed by State Security Printers, Moscow.

Wmk. 170
1934, Apr. 4　Photo.　Perf. 14

C1	AP1	1k orange red	1.40	1.00
		Never hinged	5.00	
		Postal cancel		2.50
		On cover		100.00
C2	AP1	5k emer green	1.40	1.00
		Never hinged	5.00	
		Postal cancel		2.50
		On cover		100.00
C3	AP2	10k purple brown	4.50	3.00
		Never hinged	9.00	
		Postal cancel		3.00
		On cover		100.00
C4	AP1	15k rose red	2.75	1.00
		Never hinged	6.00	
		Postal cancel		3.00
		On cover		100.00
C5	AP2	25k slate purple	2.75	1.00
		Never hinged	6.00	
		Postal cancel		3.50
		On cover		100.00
C6	AP1	50k dp bl green	2.75	1.00
		Never hinged	6.00	
		Postal cancel		4.00
		On cover		100.00
C7	AP2	75k lake	2.75	1.00
		Never hinged	6.00	
		Postal cancel		4.00
		On cover		100.00
C8	AP1	1t royal blue	3.50	2.00
		Never hinged	5.00	
		Postal cancel		5.00
		On cover		100.00
a.		Perf 12½	77.50	—
		Never hinged	155.00	
C9	AP2	2t ultra, 61x31mm	20.00	25.00
		Never hinged	40.00	
		Postal cancel		40.00
		On cover		—
a.		54.5x29mm	40.00	—
		Never hinged	80.00	
		Nos. C1-C9 (9)	41.80	36.00
		Set, never hinged	55.00	

Nos. C1-C9 imperf or perf 11½ and stamps printed in different colors are proofs.

Tuvan Leading Laden Yak — AP3

Horseman and Zeppelin AP4

Seaplane Above Dragon — AP5

Designs: 10k, Tuvan plowing. 50k, Villagers with biplane overhead.
Printed by State Security Printers, Moscow.

1936　　　　　　　　Unwmk.

C10	AP3	5k indigo & beige	3.00	1.50
		Never hinged	4.00	
		On cover		2.00
				100.00
C11	AP3	10k purple & cinnamon	4.50	1.50
		Never hinged	6.00	
		On cover		2.00
				100.00
C12	AP3	15k black brown & pale gray	4.50	1.75
		Never hinged	6.00	
		On cover		2.00
				100.00
C13	AP4	25k plum & cream	6.00	2.50
		Never hinged	10.00	
		On cover		5.00
				100.00
a.		Perf 11	4.50	2.00
		Never hinged	9.00	
		On cover		4.50
b.		Perf compound 14x11	—	
c.		Horiz. pair, perf 11, imperf between	—	
C14	AP4	50k rose red & cream	6.50	2.50
		Never hinged	10.00	
		On cover		7.50
				125.00
C15	AP4	75k emer grn & pale yellow	10.00	4.00
		Never hinged	10.00	
		On cover		10.00
				200.00
C16	AP5	1a blue green & pale bl grn	12.00	5.00
		Never hinged	16.00	
		Postal cancel		—
		On cover		—
C17	AP5	2a rose red & cream	9.50	3.75
		Never hinged	15.00	
		Postal cancel		30.00
		On cover		350.00
C18	AP5	3a dark brown & beige	9.50	3.75
		Never hinged	16.00	
		Postal cancel		35.00
		On cover		400.00
		Nos. C10-C18 (9)	65.50	26.25
		Set, never hinged	120.00	

15th anniversary of independence.

Nos. C10-C18 exist imperf.

TETE

ˈtāt-ə

LOCATION — In southeastern Africa between Nyasaland and Southern Rhodesia.
GOVT. — A district of the Portuguese East Africa Colony.
AREA — 46,600 sq. mi. (approx.)
POP. — 367,000 (approx.)
CAPITAL — Tete

This district was formerly a part of Zambezia. Stamps of Mozambique replaced those of Tete. See Mozambique.

100 Centavos = 1 Escudo

Vasco da Gama Issue of Various Portuguese Colonies Surcharged

1913　　Unwmk.　Perf. 12½, 16
On Stamps of Macao

1	CD20	¼c on ½a bl grn	5.00	5.00
2	CD21	½c on 1a red	2.00	2.10
3	CD22	1c on 2a red vio	2.00	2.10
4	CD23	2½c on 4a yel grn	2.00	2.10
5	CD24	5c on 8a dk blue	2.00	2.10
6	CD25	7½c on 12a vio brn	2.40	3.00

7	CD26	10c on 16a bis brn	2.00	2.10
8	CD27	15c on 24a bister	2.00	2.10
		Nos. 1-8 (8)	19.40	20.60

On Stamps of Portuguese Africa

9	CD20	¼c on 2½r bl grn	6.00	6.10
10	CD21	½c on 5r red	2.00	2.10
11	CD22	1c on 10r red vio	2.00	2.10
12	CD23	2½c on 25r yel grn	2.00	2.10
13	CD24	5c on 50r dk blue	2.00	2.10
14	CD25	7½c on 75r vio brn	2.40	3.00
15	CD26	10c on 100r bis brn	2.00	2.10
16	CD27	15c on 150r bister	2.00	2.10
		Nos. 9-16 (8)	16.40	17.70

On Stamps of Timor

17	CD20	¼c on ½a bl grn	2.00	2.10
18	CD21	½c on 1a red	2.00	2.10
19	CD22	1c on 2a red vio	2.00	2.10
a.		Inverted overprint	30.00	30.00
20	CD23	2½c on 4a yel grn	2.00	2.10
21	CD24	5c on 8a dk blue	2.00	2.10
22	CD25	7½c on 12a vio brn	2.40	3.00
23	CD26	10c on 16a bis brn	2.00	2.10
24	CD27	15c on 24a bister	2.00	2.10
		Nos. 17-24 (8)	16.40	17.70
		Nos. 1-24 (24)	52.20	56.00

Common Design Types pictured following the introduction.

Ceres — A1

1914　　Typo.　Perf. 15x14
Name and Value in Black

25	A1	¼c olive brn	1.40	2.25
		Never hinged	2.00	
26	A1	½c black	1.40	2.25
		Never hinged	2.00	
27	A1	1c blue grn	1.40	2.25
		Never hinged	2.00	
28	A1	1½c lilac brn	1.40	2.25
		Never hinged	2.00	
29	A1	2c carmine	1.40	2.25
		Never hinged	2.00	
30	A1	2½c light vio	1.40	2.25
		Never hinged	2.00	
31	A1	5c deep blue	1.40	2.25
		Never hinged	2.00	
32	A1	7½c yel brn	3.00	3.25
		Never hinged	4.50	
33	A1	8c slate	3.00	3.25
		Never hinged	4.50	
34	A1	10c org brn	3.00	4.00
		Never hinged	4.50	
35	A1	15c plum	4.00	4.50
		Never hinged	6.00	
36	A1	20c yel green	4.00	4.50
		Never hinged	6.00	
37	A1	30c brn, *green*	4.00	4.50
		Never hinged	6.00	
38	A1	40c brn, *pink*	8.00	7.00
		Never hinged	12.00	
39	A1	50c org, *salmon*	10.00	9.00
		Never hinged	15.00	
40	A1	1e grn, *blue*	12.00	10.00
		Never hinged	18.00	
		Nos. 25-40 (16)	60.80	65.75

THAILAND

'ti-,land

(Siam)

LOCATION — Western part of the Malay peninsula in southeastern Asia
GOVT. — Republic
AREA — 198,250 sq. mi.
POP. — 50,000,000 (est. 1984)
CAPITAL — Bangkok

32 Solot = 16 Atts = 8 Sio = 4 Sik = 2 Fuang = 1 Salung

4 Salungs = 1 Tical

100 Satangs (1909) = 1 Tical = 1 Baht (1912)

Watermarks

Wmk. 176 — Chakra

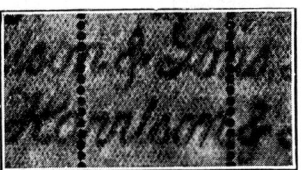

Wmk. 233 — Harrison & Sons, London in Script Letters

King Chulalongkorn
A1   A2

A4

Perf. 14½, 15

1883, Aug. 4	Unwmk.	Engr.
1	A1 1sol blue	14.00	14.00
b.	Imperf., pair		4,500.
2	A1 1att carmine	16.00	16.00
3	A1 1sio vermilion	24.00	24.00
4	A2 1sik yellow	15.00	19.00
5	A4 1sa orange	62.50	62.50
a.	1sa ocher	70.00	70.00
	Nos. 1-5 (5)	131.50	135.50

There are three types of No. 1, differing mainly in the background of the small oval at the top.

A 1 fuang red, of similar design to the foregoing, was prepared but not placed in use. Value, $1,500.

For surcharges see Nos. 6-8, 19.

No. 1 Handstamp Surcharged in Red

a   b

---

c

1 Tical   **1 Tical**
d   e

1885, July 1

6	A1 (a) 1t on 1sol blue	475.	475.
7	A1 (b) 1t on 1sol blue	375.	375.
c.	"1" inverted	1,100.	1,100.
8	A1 (c) 1t on 1sol blue	500.	500.

Surcharges of Nos. 6-8 have been counterfeited.

Types "d" and "e" are typeset *official reprints.*

As is usual with handstamps, double impressions, etc., exist.

King Chulalongkorn — A7

1887-91 Typo. Wmk. 176 Perf. 14

11	A7 1a green ('91)	6.50	2.00
12	A7 2a green & car	6.50	2.00
13	A7 3a grn & blue	12.00	4.00
14	A7 4a grn & org brn	12.00	4.75
15	A7 8a green & yel	12.00	7.00
16	A7 12a lilac & car	17.50	3.50
17	A7 24a lilac & blue	24.00	4.00
18	A7 64a lil & org brn	87.50	29.00
	Nos. 11-18 (8)	178.00	56.25

The design of No. 11 has been redrawn and differs in many minor details from Nos. 12-18.
Issue dates: Nos. 12-18, Apr. 1; No. 11, Feb.
For surcharges see Nos. 20-69, 109, 111, 126.

No. 3 Handstamp Surcharged

1889, Aug. Unwmk. Perf. 15

19	A1 1a on 1sio	19.00	19.00

Three different handstamps were used. Doubles, etc. exist.

Nos. 12 and 13 Handstamp Surcharged

1889-90 Wmk. 176 Perf. 14

20	A7 1a on 2a	4.00	3.00
a.	"1" omitted	275.00	275.00
c.	1st Siamese character invtd.		
d.	First Siamese character omitted	300.00	300.00
21	A7 1a on 3a ('90)	9.00	9.00
a.	Inverted "1"	150.00	150.00

For surcharge see No. 29.

22	A7 1a on 2a grn & car	475.00	475.00

24	A7 1a on 2a grn & car	225.00	225.00

25	A7 1a on 2a grn & car	1,000.	1,000.

26	A7 1a on 3a grn & bl		

Some authorities consider No. 26 a forgery. Doubles, etc., exist in this issue.
Issue dates: Nov. 1889. Sept. 1890.

No. 13 Handstamp Surcharged

1891

27	A7 2a on 3a grn & bl	65.00	65.00

28	A7 2a on 3a grn & bl	55.00	55.00
a.	Double surcharge	250.00	250.00
b.	"2" omitted	250.00	

No. 21 with Additional 2 Att Surcharge

29	A7 2a on 1a on 3a grn & bl	1,500.	1,500.

On No. 29 the 2a surcharge consists of Siamese numeral like No. 27 and English numeral like No. 28.
Most examples of No. 29 show attempts to remove the "1" of the first surcharge.

Typeset Surcharge

30	A7 2a on 3a grn & bl	45.00	45.00

There are 7 types of this surcharge in the setting.
Issued: #27-28, Jan.; #29, Feb.; #30, Mar.

No. 17 Handstamp Surcharged

f   g

1892, Oct.

33	A7 (f) 4a on 24a lil & bl	50.00	50.00
34	A7 (g) 4a on 24a lil & bl	35.00	35.00

Surcharges exist double on Nos. 33-34 and inverted on No. 33.

Nos. 33-34 Handstamp Surcharged in English

1892, Nov.

35	A7 4a on 24a lil & bl	9.00	9.00
c.	Inverted "s"	45.00	45.00

36	A7 4a on 24a lil & bl	14.00	10.00
a.	Inverted "s"	40.00	40.00

37	A7 4a on 24a lil & bl	12.50	12.50

38	A7 4a on 24a lil & bl	15.00	15.00

Numerous inverts., doubles, etc., exist.
Nos. 35 and 37 are surcharged examples of No. 33. Nos. 36 and 38 are surcharged examples of No. 34. The "4 atts" surcharge is small on Nos. 35 and 36, and large on Nos. 37 and 38.

Nos. 18 and 17 Typeset Srchd. in English (Shown) and Siamese

1894

39	A7 1a on 64a lil & org brn	3.50	3.50
a.	Inverted "s"	45.00	45.00
b.	Inverted surcharge	900.00	900.00
d.	Italic "s"	60.00	60.00
e.	Italic "1"	60.00	60.00

40	A7 1a on 64a lil & org brn	2.00	2.00
a.	Inverted capital "S" added to the surcharge	200.00	200.00

h   j

k   l

m

2 Atts.
i

41	A7 (h)	2a on 64a	26.00	26.00
a.		Inverted "s"	42.50	42.50
b.		Double surcharge	100.00	100.00
42	A7 (i)	2a on 64a	3,000.	3,000.
43	A7 (j)	2a on 64a	62.50	62.50
44	A7 (k)	2a on 64a	37.50	37.50
45	A7 (l)	2a on 64a	57.50	57.50
46	A7 (m)	2a on 64a	3.00	3.00
a.		"Att.s"	45.00	45.00

Nos. 41-46 were in one plate of 120 subjects. The quantities were: h, 38; i, 1; j, 8; k, 18; l, 11 and m, 44.

1894, Oct. 12
47	A7	1a on 64a	3.00	3.00
a.		Surcharged on face and back	150.00	
b.		As "a," surcharge on back inverted	200.00	
c.		Double surcharge	475.00	
d.		Inverted surcharge	500.00	
e.		Siamese surcharge omitted	400.00	

See No. 67.

48	A7	2a on 64a	3.00	3.00
a.		"Att"	35.00	35.00
b.		Inverted surcharge	300.00	300.00
c.		Surch. on face and back	400.00	400.00
d.		Surcharge on back inverted	400.00	400.00
e.		Double surcharge	300.00	300.00
f.		Double surch., one inverted	1,100.	1,100.
g.		Inverted "s"	42.50	42.50

1895, July 23
49	A7	10a on 24a lil & bl	7.00	2.00
a.		Inverted "s"	45.00	45.00
b.		Surch. on face and back	175.00	175.00
c.		Surcharge on back inverted	175.00	175.00

No. 16 Surcharged in English (Shown) and Siamese

1896
50	A7	4a on 12a lil & car	15.00	8.00
a.		Inverted "s"	50.00	50.00
b.		Surcharged on face and back	175.00	175.00
c.		Double surcharge on back	175.00	175.00

Two types of surcharge.

Nos. 16-18 Surcharged in English (Shown) and Siamese Antique Surcharges

a   b

c   d

e   f

Atts.
Antique Letters

Atts.
Roman Letters

1898-99
51	A7 (a)	1a on 12a	360.00	360.00
52	A7 (b)	1a on 12a	18.00	7.00
53	A7 (c)	2a on 64a ('99)	30.00	9.00
54	A7 (d)	3a on 12a	12.00	4.00
a.		Double surcharge	350.00	350.00
55	A7 (e)	4a on 12a	12.00	5.00
a.		Double surcharge	350.00	350.00
56	A7 (e)	4a on 24a ('99)	40.00	14.00
57	A7 (f)	10a on 24a ('99)	825.00	825.00
		Nos. 51-57 (7)	1,297.	1,224.

Roman Surcharges

h   i

j   k

l

---

1 Atts.
g

58	A7 (f)	1a on 12a	150.00	150.00
59	A7 (f)	1a on 12a	45.00	20.00
60	A7 (i)	2a on 64a ('99)	35.00	10.00
61	A7 (j)	3a on 12a	85.00	19.00
62	A7 (k)	4a on 12a	40.00	14.00
a.		Double surcharge	175.00	175.00
b.		No period after "Atts."	35.00	35.00
63	A7 (k)	4a on 24a ('99)	60.00	29.00
64	A7 (l)	10a on 24a ('99)	750.00	750.00
		Nos. 58-64 (7)	1,465.	1,292.

In making the settings to surcharge Nos. 51 to 64 two fonts were mixed.

Antique and Roman letters are frequently found on the same stamp. Such stamps sell for more.

Issue dates: Nos. 54-55, 61-62, Feb. 22. Nos. 51-52, 58-59, June 4. Nos. 56-57, 63-64, Oct. 3.

Nos. 16 and 18 Surcharged in English (Shown) and Siamese Surcharged

m   n

o   p

r

1894-99
65	A7 (m)	1a on 12a	20.00	6.00
66	A7 (n)	1a on 12a	20.00	6.00
a.		Inverted "1"	150.00	150.00
b.		Inverted 1st "t"	150.00	150.00
67	A7 (o)	1a on 64a	5.00	5.00
68	A7 (p)	2a on 64a	24.00	8.00
a.		"1 Atts."	500.00	500.00
69	A7 (r)	2a on 64a	24.00	8.00
		Nos. 65-69 (5)	93.00	33.00

Issued: No. 67, 10/12/94; others, 2/14/99.
See No. 47.

A13   A14

1899, Oct.   Typo.   Unwmk.
70	A13	1a dull green	200.	85.
		Postally used		120.
71	A13	2a dl grn & rose	350.	85.
		Postally used		160.
72	A13	3a carmine & blue	600.	125.
		Postally used		260.
73	A13	4a black & grn	2,200.	325.
		Postally used		675.
74	A13	10a carmine & grn	2,500.	500.
		Postally used		975.
		Nos. 70-74 (5)	5,850.	1,120.

The King rejected Nos. 70-74 in 1897, but some were released by mistake to three post offices in Oct. 1899. Used values are for stamps canceled to order at Korat in Dec. 1899.

1899-1904
75	A14	1a gray green	2.00	1.00
76	A14	2a yellow green	2.25	1.25
77	A14	2a scarlet & bl	4.00	2.00
78	A14	3a red & blue	7.00	2.00
79	A14	3a green	20.00	12.00
80	A14	4a dark rose	4.00	1.50
81	A14	4a vio brn & rose	8.00	2.00
82	A14	6a dk rose	35.00	14.00

83	A14	8a dk grn & org	9.00	2.00
84	A14	10a ultra	9.00	3.00
85	A14	12a brn vio & rose	40.00	2.00
86	A14	14a ultra	23.00	18.00
87	A14	24a brn vio & rose	375.00	29.00
88	A14	32a vio brn & bl	66.00	66.00
89	A14	64a brn vio & org brn	70.00	11.00
		Nos. 75-89 (15)	633.25	125.75

Two types of 1a differ in size and shape of Thai "1" are in drawing of spandrel ornaments.
Issue dates: 6a, 14a, 28a, Nos. 77, 79, 81, Jan. 1, 1904; others, Sept. 1899.
For surcharges see Nos. 90-91, 112, 125, 127.

Nos. 78 and 85 With Typewritten Srch. of 6 or 7 Siamese Characters (1 line) in Violet

1902
78a	A14	2a on 3a	5,000.	5,250.
85a	A14	10a on 12a	5,000.	5,250.

Nos. 78a and 85a were authorized provisionals, surcharged and issued by the Battambang postmaster.

Nos. 86 and 88 Surcharged in Black

1905, Feb.
90	A14	1a on 14a	10.00	10.00
a.		No period after "Att"	45.00	45.00
b.		Double surcharge	125.00	125.00
91	A14	2a on 28a	12.00	12.00
a.		Double surcharge	125.00	125.00
b.		No period after "Att"	45.00	45.00

King Chulangkorn — A15

1905-08   Engr.
92	A15	1a orange & green	2.50	1.00
93	A15	2a violet & slate	3.00	1.00
94	A15	2a green ('08)	11.00	4.00
95	A15	3a green	4.00	2.00
96	A15	3a vio & sl ('08)	12.00	6.25
97	A15	4a gray & red	6.00	1.50
98	A15	4a car & rose ('08)	9.50	2.00
99	A15	5a carmine & rose	8.00	3.00
100	A15	8a blk & ol bis	8.75	1.50
101	A15	9a blue ('08)	23.50	9.00
102	A15	12a blue	18.00	4.00
103	A15	18a red brn ('08)	60.00	22.50
104	A15	24a red brown	34.00	8.00
105	A15	1t dp bl & brn org	45.00	10.00
		Nos. 92-105 (14)	245.25	75.75

Issue dates: Dec. 1905, Apr. 1, 1908.
For surcharges and overprints see Nos. 110, 113-117, 128-138, 161-162, B15, B21.

King Chulalongkorn — A16

No. 106

No. 107

No. 108

1907, Apr. 24   **Black Surcharge**
106	A16	10t gray green	600.00	100.00
107	A16	20t gray green	4,750.	350.00
108	A16	40t gray green	3,400.	475.00
		Nos. 106-108 (3)	8,750.	925.00

Counterfeits of Nos. 106-108 exist. In the genuine, the surcharged figures correspond to the Siamese value inscriptions on the basic revenue stamps.

No. 17 Surcharged

1907, Dec. 16
| 109 | A7 | 1a on 24a lil & bl | 4.50 | 1.50 |
| a. | | Double surcharge | 400.00 | |

No. 99 Surcharged

1908, Sept.
| 110 | A15 | 4a on 5a car & rose | 11.00 | 4.00 |

The No. 110 surcharge is found in two spacings of the numerals: normally 15mm apart, and a narrow, scarcer spacing of 13 ½mm.

Nos. 17 and 84 Surcharged in Black

111	A7	2a on 24a lil & bl	4.50	1.20
a.		Inverted surcharge	325.00	325.00
112	A14	9a on 10a ultra	13.50	5.00
a.		Inverted surcharge	325.00	325.00

Jubilee Issue

Nos. 92, 95, 110, 100 and 103 Overprinted in Black or Red

1908, Nov. 11
113	A15	1a	3.25	1.60
a.		Siamese date "137" instead of "127"	950.00	950.00
b.		Pair, one without ovpt.		
114	A15	3a	5.50	3.25
115	A15	4a on 5a	5.50	3.25
a.		Horiz. pair, imperf. btwn.	500.00	
116	A15	8a (R)	21.00	21.00
117	A15	18a	32.50	24.00
		Nos. 113-117 (5)	67.75	53.10

40th year of the reign of King Chulalongkorn. Nos. 113 to 117 exist with a small "i" in "Jubilee."

Statue of King Chulalongkorn A19

1908, Nov. 11   **Engr.**   **Perf. 13½**
118	A19	1t green & vio	52.50	8.00
119	A19	2t red vio & org	72.50	20.00
120	A19	3t pale ol & bl	105.00	16.00
121	A19	5t dl vio & dk grn	160.00	27.50
122	A19	10t bister & car	1,250.	87.50
123	A19	20t gray & red brn	525.00	87.50
124	A19	40t sl bl & blk brn	525.00	300.00
		Nos. 118-124 (7)	2,690.	546.50

The inscription at the foot of the stamps reads: "Coronation Commemoration-Forty-first year of the reign-1908."

Stamps of 1887-1904 Surcharged

1909   **Perf. 14**
125	A14	6s on 6a dk rose	2.50	2.00
126	A7	14s on 12a lil & car	110.00	100.00
127	A14	14s on 14a ultra	20.00	18.00
		Nos. 125-127 (3)	132.50	120.00

Nos. 92-102 Surcharged with Bar and

1909, Aug. 15
128	A15	2s on 1a #92	2.50	1.20
129	A15	2s on 2a #93	60.00	60.00
130	A15	2s on 2a #94	2.75	1.20
a.		"2" omitted	85.00	
131	A15	3s on 3a #95	12.00	7.50
132	A15	3s on 3a #96	4.50	1.00
133	A15	6s on 4a #97	64.00	64.00
134	A15	6s on 4a #98	8.00	2.00
135	A15	6s on 5a #99	12.00	8.75
136	A15	12s on 8a #100	7.00	1.40
137	A15	14s on 9a #101	11.00	3.00
138	A15	14s on 12a #102	22.50	21.00
		Nos. 128-138 (11)	206.25	171.05

King Chulalongkorn — A20

1910   **Engr.**   **Perf. 14x14½**
139	A20	2s org & green	2.50	1.50
140	A20	3s green	2.50	1.50
141	A20	6s carmine	6.50	2.50
142	A20	12s blk & ol brn	12.00	2.50
143	A20	14s blue	20.00	2.50
144	A20	28s red brown	47.50	10.00
		Nos. 139-144 (6)	91.00	20.50

Issue dates: 12s, June 5. Others, May 5. For surcharges see Nos. 163, 223-224.

A21   King Vajiravudh — A22

Printed at the Imperial Printing Works, Vienna

1912   **Perf. 14½**
145	A21	2s brown orange	3.25	1.20
a.		Vert. pair, imperf. btwn.	500.00	500.00
b.		Horiz. pair, imperf. btwn.	500.00	500.00
146	A21	3s yellow green	3.25	1.20
a.		Horiz. pair, imperf. btwn.	500.00	500.00
b.		Vert. pair, imperf. btwn.	500.00	500.00
147	A21	6s carmine rose	4.00	1.50
148	A21	12s gray blk & brn	5.50	2.00
149	A21	14s ultramarine	7.00	2.50
150	A21	28s chocolate	20.00	12.00
151	A22	1b blue & blk	30.00	2.00
a.		Vert. pair, imperf. btwn.	1,250.	1,250.
b.		Horiz. pair, imperf. btwn.	1,250.	1,250.
152	A22	2b car rose & ol brn	35.00	4.00
153	A22	3b yel grn & bl blk	40.00	6.50
154	A22	5b vio & blk	50.00	12.00
155	A22	10b ol grn & vio brn	300.00	95.00
156	A22	20b sl bl & red brn	475.00	95.00
		Nos. 145-156 (12)	973.00	234.90

See Nos. 164-175. For surcharges and overprints see Nos. 157-160, 176-186, 206, B1-B14, B16-B20, B22, B31-B33.

Nos. 147-150 Surcharged in Red or Blue

1914-15
157	A21	2s on 14s (R) ('15)	2.75	.70
a.		Vert. pair, imperf. btwn.	900.00	900.00
b.		Double surcharge	62.50	40.00
158	A21	5s on 6s (Bl)	5.00	.50
a.		Horiz. pair, imperf. btwn.	900.00	900.00
b.		Double surcharge	67.50	67.50
159	A21	10s on 12s (R)	5.00	.50
a.		Double surcharge	67.50	67.50
160	A21	15s on 28s (Bl)	8.50	2.50
		Nos. 157-160 (4)	21.25	4.20

The several settings of the surcharges on Nos. 157-160 show variations in the figures and letters.

Nos. 92-93 Surcharged

1915, Apr. 3
161	A15	2s on 1a org & grn	7.00	5.00
a.		Pair, one without surcharge	350.00	350.00
162	A15	2s on 2a vio & slate	7.00	4.50

No. 143 Surcharged in Red

1916, Oct.
| 163 | A20 | 2s on 14s blue | 4.50 | 2.00 |

Types of 1912 Re-engraved
Printed by Waterlow & Sons, London

1917, Jan. 1   **Perf. 14**
164	A21	2s orange brown	2.50	1.20
165	A21	3s emerald	2.50	2.50
166	A21	5s rose red	4.00	1.20
167	A21	10s black & olive	3.50	1.20
168	A21	15s blue	4.00	1.40
170	A22	1b bl & gray blk	25.00	4.50
171	A22	2b car rose & brn	70.00	35.00
172	A22	3b yellow grn & blk	525.00	275.00
173	A22	5b dp violet & blk	275.00	190.00
174	A22	10b ol gray & vio brn	425.00	32.50
a.		Perf. 12½	500.00	47.50
175	A22	20b sea green & brn	600.00	70.00
a.		Perf. 12½	625.00	85.00
		Nos. 164-175 (11)	1,936.	614.50

The re-engraved design of the satang stamps varies in numerous minute details from the 1912 issue. Four lines of the background appear between the vertical strokes of the "M" of "SIAM" in the 1912 issue and only three lines in the 1917 stamps.

The 1912 stamps with value in bahts are 37½mm high; those of 1917 are 39mm. In the latter issue the king's features, especially the eyes and mouth, are more distinct and the uniform and decorations are more sharply defined.

The 1912 stamps have seven pearls between the earpieces of the crown. On the 1917 stamps there are nine pearls in the same place. Nos. 174 and 175 exist imperforate.

Nos. 164-173 Overprinted in Red

1918, Dec. 2
176	A21	2s orange brown	3.25	3.25
a.		Double overprint	110.00	110.00
177	A21	3s emerald	3.25	3.25
178	A21	5s rose red	4.50	4.50
a.		Double overprint	150.00	150.00
179	A21	10s black & olive	6.75	6.75
180	A21	15s blue	6.75	6.75
181	A22	1b bl & gray blk	27.50	24.00
182	A22	2b car rose & brn	65.00	47.50
183	A22	3b yellow grn & blk	190.00	120.00
184	A22	5b dp vio & blk	400.00	325.00
		Nos. 176-184 (9)	707.00	541.00

Counterfeits of this overprint exist.

Nos. 147-148 Surcharged in Green or Red

1919-20
| 185 | A21 | 5s on 6s (G) | 2.75 | 1.90 |
| 186 | A21 | 10s on 12s (R) ('20) | 6.00 | 1.50 |

Issue dates: 5s, Nov. 11. 10s, Jan. 1.

King
Vajiravudh
A23

Throne Room
A24

1920-26   Engr.   Perf. 14-15, 12½
187 A23 2s brn, *yel* ('21)   3.50   .70
188 A23 3s grn, *grn* ('21)   3.50   .95
189 A23 3s chocolate ('24)   3.25   .70
190 A23 5s rose, *pale rose*   4.50   .70
191 A23 5s green ('22)   34.00   6.00
192 A23 5s dk vio, *lil* ('26)   7.50   .95
193 A23 10s black & org ('21)   7.00   .70
194 A23 15s bl, *bluish* ('21)   8.50   .70
195 A23 15s carmine ('22)   44.00   6.00
196 A23 25s chocolate ('21)   24.00   2.75
197 A23 25s dk blue ('22)   32.50   1.40
198 A23 50s ocher & blk ('21)   32.50   2.00
    Nos. 187-198 (11)   201.50   22.85

For overprints see Nos. 205, B23-B30.

1926, Mar. 5   Perf. 12½
199 A24 1t gray vio & grn   16.00   3.50
200 A24 2t car & org red   35.00   6.00
201 A24 3t ol grn & bl   67.50   25.00
202 A24 5t dl vio & ol grn   95.00   45.00
203 A24 10t red & ol bis   325.00   32.50
204 A24 20t gray bl & brn   375.00   110.00
    Nos. 199-204 (6)   913.50   222.00

This issue was intended to commemorate the fifteenth year of the reign of King Vajiravudh. Because of the King's death the stamps were issued as ordinary postage stamps.

Nos. 195 and 150 with Surcharge similar to 1914-15 Issue in Black or Red

1928, Jan.
205 A23 5s on 15s car   7.00   3.50
206 A21 10s on 28s choc (R)   12.00   2.00

King Prajadhipok
A25   A26

1928   Engr.   Perf. 12½
207 A25 2s deep red
    brown   .65   .65
208 A25 3s deep green   .65   .65
209 A25 5s dark violet   .65   .30
210 A25 10s deep rose   .75   .30
211 A25 15s dark blue   .90   .40
212 A25 25s black & org   4.00   1.00
213 A25 50s brn org & blk   2.00   1.25
214 A25 80s blue & black   4.00   2.50
216 A26 1b dk blue & blk   6.00   2.50
217 A26 2b car rose & blk
    brn   12.00   5.00
218 A26 3b yellow grn &
    blk   12.00   6.00
219 A26 5b dp vio & gray
    blk   20.00   6.75
220 A26 10b ol grn & red
    vio   40.00   10.00
221 A26 20b Prus grn & brn   80.00   18.50
222 A26 40b dk grn & ol brn   160.00   80.00
    Nos. 207-222 (15)   343.60   135.80
    Set, never hinged   500.00

On the single colored stamps, type A25, the lines in the background are uniform; those of the bicolored values are shaded and do not extend to the frame.

Issue dates: 5s, 10s, 2b-40b, Apr. 15; 2s, 3s, 15s, 25s, 50s, May 1; 1b, June 1; 80s, Nov. 15.

For overprints & surcharge see Nos. 300-301, B34 in Scott Standard catalogue, Vol. 6.

Nos. 142, 144
Surcharged in Red or
Blue

1930   Perf. 14
223 A20 10s on 12s blk & ol brn   8.75   2.75
224 A20 25s on 28s red brn (Bl)   30.00   2.25
    Set, never hinged   50.00

King Prajadhipok and Chao P'ya Chakri
A27   A28

Statue of Chao P'ya
Chakri — A29

1932, Apr. 1   Engr.   Perf. 12½
225 A27 2s dark brown   2.00   .40
226 A27 3s deep green   3.25   .85
227 A27 5s dull violet   2.00   .40
228 A28 10s red brn & blk   2.00   .25
229 A28 15s dull blue & blk   9.50   1.50
230 A28 25s violet & black   12.50   2.00
231 A28 50s claret & black   55.00   6.00
232 A29 1b blue black   77.50   15.00
    Nos. 225-232 (8)   163.75   26.40
    Set, never hinged   225.00

150th anniv. of the Chakri dynasty, the founding of Bangkok in 1782, and the opening of the memorial bridge across the Chao Phraya River.

Assembly
Hall,
Bangkok
A30

1939, June 24   Litho.   Perf. 11, 12
233 A30 2s dull red brown   4.50   2.00
234 A30 3s green   9.50   4.00
235 A30 5s dark violet   6.50   .80
236 A30 10s carmine   14.00   .80
237 A30 15s dark blue   35.00   2.00
    Nos. 233-237 (5)   69.50   9.60
    Set, never hinged   90.00

7th anniv. of the Siamese Constitution.

Chakri Palace,
Bangkok — A31

1940   Typo.   Perf. 12½
238 A31 2s dull brown   4.50   1.00
239 A31 3s dp yellow grn   8.00   2.50
    a.   Cliché of 5s in plate of 3s   900.00   725.00
240 A31 5s dark violet   5.50   .50
241 A31 10s carmine   20.00   .50
242 A31 15s dark blue   40.00   1.00
    Nos. 238-242 (5)   78.00   5.50
    Set, never hinged   125.00

Issued: 2s, 3s, 5/13; 5s, 5/24; 15s, 5/28; 10s, 5/30.

SEMI-POSTAL STAMPS

Nos. 164-175
Overprinted in Red

1918, Jan. 11   Unwmk.   Perf. 14
B1 A21 2s orange
    brown   2.40   2.40
B2 A21 3s emerald   2.40   2.40
B3 A21 5s rose red   4.75   4.75
B4 A21 10s black & olive   8.00   8.00
B5 A21 15s blue   8.75   6.00
B6 A22 1b blue & gray
    blk   45.00   32.50
B7 A22 2b car rose &
    brn   65.00   27.50
B8 A22 3b yel grn & blk   100.00   55.00
B9 A22 5b dp vio & blk   250.00   80.00
    a.   Double overprint   775.00   400.00
B10 A22 10b ol grn & vio
    brn   625.00   240.00
B11 A22 20b sea grn &
    brn   2,250.   1,400.
    Nos. B1-B11 (11)   3,361.   1,856.

Excellent counterfeit overprints are known. These stamps were sold at an advance over face value, the excess being given to the Siamese Red Cross Society.

Stamps of 1905-19
Handstamp
Overprinted

1920, Feb.
On Nos. 164, 146, 168
B12 A21 2s (+ 3s) org
    brn   42.50   42.50
B13 A21 3s (+ 2s) green   45.00   45.00
B14 A21 15s (+ 5s) blue   140.00   120.00
On No. 105
B15 A15 1t (+ 25s)   375.00   350.00
On Nos. 185-186
B16 A21 5s on 6s (+ 5s)   62.50   62.50
    a.   Overprint inverted
B17 A21 10s on 12s (+
    5s)   70.00   70.00
    Nos. B12-B17 (6)   735.00   690.00
    Set, never hinged   1,125.

Sold at an advance over face value, the excess being for the benefit of the Wild Tiger Corps. Counterfeits exist.

Stamps of 1905-20
Handstamp
Overprinted

On Nos. 164, 146, 168
B18 A21 2s (+ 3s) org brn   40.00   40.00
B19 A21 3s (+ 2s) green   40.00   40.00
    a.   Pair, one without ovpt.
B20 A21 15s (+ 5s) blue   65.00   65.00
On No. 105
B21 A15 1t (+ 25s)   290.00   290.00
On No. 186
B22 A21 10s on 12s (+ 5s)   65.00   65.00
On No. 190
B23 A23 5s (+ 5s)   100.00   100.00
    Nos. B18-B23 (6)   600.00   600.00
    Set, never hinged   925.00

Sold at an advance over face value, the excess being for the benefit of the Wild Tiger Corps. Counterfeits exist.

Nos. 187-188, 190,
193-194, 196, 198
Overprinted in Blue or
Red

1920, Dec. 21
B24 A23 2s brown, *yel*   15.00   15.00
B25 A23 3s grn, *grn* (R)   15.00   15.00
B26 A23 5s rose, *pale rose*   15.00   15.00
B27 A23 10s blk & org (R)   15.00   15.00
B28 A23 15s bl, *bluish* (R)   30.00   30.00
B29 A23 25s chocolate   100.00   100.00
B30 A23 50s ocher & blk (R)   225.00   225.00
    Nos. B24-B30 (7)   415.00   415.00
    Set, never hinged   625.00

Nos. B12-B30 were sold at an advance over face value, the excess being for the benefit of the Wild Tiger Corps. Counterfeits exist.

Nos. 170-172
Surcharged in Red

1939, Apr. 6   Unwmk.   Perf. 14
B31 A22 5s + 5s on 1b   22.50   22.50
B32 A22 10s + 5s on 2b   27.50   27.50
B33 A22 15s + 5s on 3b   27.50   27.50
    Nos. B31-B33 (3)   77.50   77.50
    Set, never hinged   130.00

Founding of the Intl. Red Cross Soc., 75th anniv.

Bottom line of overprint is different on Nos. B32-B33.

AIR POST STAMPS

Garuda — AP1

1925   Unwmk.   Engr.   Perf. 14, 14½
C1 AP1 2s brown, *yel*   8.00   .50
C2 AP1 3s dark brown   8.00   .50
C3 AP1 5s green   20.00   .55
C4 AP1 10s black & org   32.50   1.00
C5 AP1 15s carmine   8.00   1.50
C6 AP1 25s dark blue   16.00   1.50
C7 AP1 50s brown org &
    blk   60.00   9.00
C8 AP1 1b blue & brown   40.00   11.00
    Nos. C1-C8 (8)   192.50   25.55
    Set, never hinged   290.00

Issue dates: 2s, 50s, Apr. 21; others, Jan. 3.

Nos. C1-C8 received this overprint ("Government Museum 2468") in 1925, but were not issued. The death of King Vajiravudh caused cancellation of the fair at which this set was to have been released.

They were used during 1928 only in the interdepartmental service for accounting purposes of the money-order sections of various Bangkok post offices, and were never sold to the public. Values for set: unused, $1,200; used, $45.

1930-37   Perf. 12½
C9 AP1 2s brown, *yel*   9.50   1.00
C10 AP1 5s green   2.40   .40
C11 AP1 10s black & org   8.00   .40
C12 AP1 15s carmine   32.50   8.00
C13 AP1 25s dark blue ('37)   4.00   1.20
    a.   Vert. pair, imperf. btwn.   450.00
C14 AP1 50s brn org & blk
    ('37)   4.00   2.40
    Nos. C9-C14 (6)   60.40   13.40
    Set, never hinged   90.00

THRACE

'thrās

LOCATION — In southeastern Europe between the Black and Aegean Seas
GOVT. — Former Turkish Province
AREA — 89,361 sq. mi. (approx.)

Thrace underwent many political changes during the Balkan Wars and World War I. It was finally divided among Turkey, Greece and Bulgaria.

100 Lepta = 1 Drachma
40 Paras = 1 Piaster
100 Stotinki = 1 Leva (1919)

Giumulzina District Issue

Turkish Stamps of 1909
(#152-154)8
Surcharged in Blue or
Red

1913		Unwmk.	Perf. 12, 13½	
1	A21	10 l on 20pa rose (Bl)	45.00	45.00
		Never hinged	100.00	
a.		Inverted overprint	170.00	
		Never hinged	250.00	
b.		Double overprint	170.00	
		Never hinged	250.00	
2	A21	25 l on 10pa bl grn	67.50	70.00
		Never hinged	175.00	
a.		Inverted overprint	250.00	
		Never hinged	175.00	
b.		Double overprint	250.00	
		Never hinged	250.00	
3	A21	25 l on 20pa rose (Bl)	67.50	70.00
		Never hinged	140.00	
a.		Inverted overprint	170.00	
		Never hinged	250.00	
b.		Double overprint	170.00	
		Never hinged	250.00	
c.		Béhié ovpt. (#162)	200.00	
		Never hinged	300.00	
4	A21	25 l on 1pi ultra	110.00	115.00
		Never hinged	200.00	
a.		Inverted overprint	220.00	
		Never hinged	290.00	
b.		Double overprint	220.00	
		Never hinged	290.00	
		Nos. 1-4 (4)	290.00	300.00

Counterfeits exist of Nos. 1-4.
Eight other values exist, bearing surcharges differing in color or denomination from Nos. 1-4. These stamps were not issued. Values, each: unused $175; never hinged $350.

Turkish Inscriptions
A1   A2

Type 1

Type 2

1913		Litho.	Imperf.	
		Laid Paper		
		Control Mark in Rose		
		Without Gum		
5	A1	1pi blue, type 1	17.00	17.00
a.		Double print		250.00
b.		Type 2	80.00	75.00
c.		1pi violet, type 1	30.00	25.00
d.		1pi gray, type 1	30.00	25.00
6	A1	2pi violet	17.00	17.00
a.		Double print	500.00	190.00
b.		Type 2		190.00

Wove Paper

c.		2pi blue, type 1	32.50	25.00
d.		2pi gray, type 1	32.50	25.00
7	A2	10pa vermilion	35.00	30.00
a.		10pa red	37.50	35.00
b.		10pa blue	55.00	45.00
c.		10pa violet	55.00	45.00
d.		10pa gray	55.00	45.00
8	A2	20pa blue	35.00	30.00
a.		20pa red	55.00	45.00
b.		20pa violet	55.00	45.00
c.		20pa gray	55.00	45.00
9	A2	1pi violet	37.50	30.00
		Nos. 5-9 (5)	141.50	124.00

Turkish Stamps of
1913 Surcharged in
Red or Black

1913			Perf. 12	
10	A22	1pi on 2pa ol grn (R)	25.00	25.00
		Never hinged	50.00	
10A	A22	1pi on 2pa ol grn	25.00	25.00
		Never hinged	50.00	
11	A22	1pi on 5pa ocher	25.00	25.00
		Never hinged	50.00	
11A	A22	1pi on 5pa ocher (R)	25.00	25.00
		Never hinged	50.00	
12	A22	1pi on 20pa rose	32.50	32.50
		Never hinged	65.00	
13	A22	1pi on 5pi dk vio (R)	65.00	65.00
		Never hinged	140.00	
13A	A22	1pi on 5pi dk vio	65.00	65.00
		Never hinged	140.00	
14	A22	1pi on 10pi dl red	110.00	120.00
		Never hinged	225.00	
15	A22	1pi on 25pi dk grn	475.00	500.00
		Never hinged	1,000.	
		Nos. 10-15 (9)	847.50	882.50

On Nos. 13-15 the surcharge is vertical, reading up. No. 15 exists with double surcharge, one black, one red.
Nos. 10-15 exist with forged surcharges.

Bulgarian Stamps of
1911 Handstamped
Surcharged in Red or
Blue

1913				
16	A20	10pa on 1s myr grn (R)	20.00	20.00
		Never hinged	45.00	
a.		Top ovpt. inverted		100.00
b.		Top ovpt. double		100.00
c.		Top ovpt. omitted		150.00
d.		Bottom ovpt. omitted		150.00
e.		Bottom ovpt. inverted		100.00
17	A21	20pa on 2s car & blk	20.00	20.00
		Never hinged	45.00	
a.		Inverted overprint	60.00	
		Never hinged	100.00	
b.		Inverted overprint, value omitted	85.00	
		Never hinged	160.00	
c.		Text ovpt. omitted, value ovpt. inverted	150.00	
d.		Top ovpt. omitted, value inverted		200.00
e.		Blue ovpt. omitted		175.00
f.		Blue ovpt. inverted		50.00
18	A23	1pi on 5s grn & blk (R)	20.00	20.00
		Never hinged	45.00	
a.		Inverted overprint	125.00	125.00
b.		Top ovpt. inverted	125.00	
19	A22	2pi on 3s lake & blk	28.00	28.00
		Never hinged	55.00	
a.		Inverted overprint	80.00	80.00
		Never hinged	165.00	
20	A24	2½pi on 10s dp red & blk	40.00	40.00
		Never hinged	80.00	
a.		Top ovpt. inverted		165.00
b.		2½pi on 2s		260.00
21	A25	5pi on 15s brn bis	70.00	70.00
		Never hinged	145.00	
a.		Inverted overprint		250.00
b.		Value inverted		250.00
		Nos. 16-21 (6)	198.00	198.00

Same Surcharges on
Greek Stamps

On Issue of 1911

1913			Serrate Roulette 13½	
22	A24	10pa on 1 l grn (R)	22.50	22.50
		Never hinged	45.00	
23	A24	10pa on 1 l grn	23.00	23.00
		Never hinged	45.00	
24	A26	10pa on 5 l grn	110.00	110.00
		Never hinged	225.00	
25	A25	10pa on 25 l ultra (R)	32.50	32.50
		Never hinged	50.00	
26	A25	20pa on 2 l car rose	22.50	22.50
		Never hinged	45.00	
26A	A25	20pa on 30 l car rose		140.00
27	A24	1pi on 3 l ver	22.50	22.50
		Never hinged	45.00	
a.		Value omitted	65.00	65.00
		Never hinged	135.00	
b.		Red overprint	22.50	22.50
		Never hinged	45.00	
27C	A24	1pi on 10 l car rose		550.00
28	A26	2pi on 5 l grn (R)	60.00	60.00
		Never hinged	135.00	
29	A24	2½pi on 10 l car rose	60.00	60.00
		Never hinged	135.00	
30	A25	5pi on 40 l dp bl (R)	110.00	110.00
		Never hinged	190.00	
		Nos. 22-30 (9)	463.00	463.00

On Occupation Stamps of 1912

31	O1	10pa on 1 l brn	20.00	15.00
		Never hinged	40.00	
a.		Value omitted		100.00
b.		Value srch. inverted		50.00
32	O1	20pa on 1 l brn	20.00	15.00
		Never hinged	40.00	
33	O1	1pi on 1 l brn	20.00	15.00
		Never hinged	40.00	
		Nos. 31-33 (3)	60.00	45.00

These surcharges were made with handstamps, two of which were required for each surcharge. The upper handstamp reads "Administration of Autonomous Western Thrace" in old Turkish. The lower handstamp expresses the new value. On horizontal designs, the text appears on the right, and the value appears on the left. On inverted overprints on horizontal stamps, this is reversed.
Nos. 16-33 exist with forged surcharges.
The 2pi on 1 l ovpt. as above was not issued. Value: $350.

OCCUPATION STAMPS

Issued under Allied Occupation

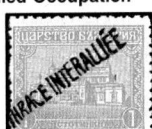

Bulgarian Stamps
of 1915-19
Handstamped in
Violet Blue

The overprint on Nos. N1-N6 is found in four positions: upright, reading from LL to UR; upright, reading from UL to LR; inverted, reading from UR to LL; inverted, LR to UL. On the 1s value, the usual position of the overprint is upright, reading from lower left to upper right; on the rest of the set, the overprint is usually inverted, reading from lower right to upper left.

Perf. 11½, 11½x12, 14

1919			Unwmk.	
		Overprint Inverted, reading from LR to UL		
N1	A43	1s black	3.75	2.50
		Never hinged	9.00	
N2	A43	2s olive green	2.50	2.00
		Never hinged	5.00	
N3	A44	5s green	.85	.85
		Never hinged	1.75	
N4	A44	10s rose	.85	.85
		Never hinged	1.75	
N5	A44	15s violet	.85	.85
		Never hinged	1.75	
N6	A26	25s indigo & black	.85	.85
		Never hinged	1.75	
		Nos. N1-N6 (6)	9.65	7.90
		Nos. N1b-N6 (5)	5.90	5.40

		Overprint Inverted, reading from UR to LL		
N1a	A43	1s black	3.75	2.50
		Never hinged	9.00	
N2a	A43	2s olive green	3.75	2.50
		Never hinged	9.00	
N3a	A44	5s green	8.50	8.50
		Never hinged	17.50	
N4a	A44	10s rose	8.50	8.50
		Never hinged	17.50	
N5a	A44	15s violet	8.50	8.50
		Never hinged	17.50	
N6a	A26	25s indigo & black	8.50	8.50
		Never hinged	17.50	
		Nos. N1a-N6a (6)	41.50	39.00

Overprint Upright, reading from LL to UR

N1b	A43	1s black	2.50	2.00
		Never hinged	5.00	
N2b	A43	2s olive green	3.75	2.50
		Never hinged	9.00	
N3b	A44	5s green	8.50	8.50
		Never hinged	17.50	
N4b	A44	10s rose	8.50	8.50
		Never hinged	17.50	
N5b	A44	15s violet	8.50	8.50
		Never hinged	17.50	
N6b	A26	25s indigo & black	8.50	8.50
		Never hinged	17.50	
		Nos. N1b-N6b (6)	40.25	38.50

Overprint Upright, reading from UL to LR

N1c	A43	1s black	3.75	2.50
		Never hinged	9.00	
N2c	A43	2s olive green	3.75	2.50
		Never hinged	9.00	
N3c	A44	5s green	8.50	8.50
		Never hinged	17.50	
N4c	A44	10s rose	8.50	8.50
		Never hinged	17.50	
N5c	A44	15s violet	8.50	8.50
		Never hinged	17.50	
N6c	A26	25s indigo & black	8.50	8.50
		Never hinged	17.50	
		Nos. N1c-N6c (6)	41.50	39.00

Bulgarian Stamps
of 1911-19
Overprinted in Red
or Black

1919				
N7	A43	1s black (R)	.25	.25
		Never hinged	.50	
a.		Second "L" in "INTERALLIÉE" inverted	5.00	5.00
		Never hinged	7.50	
b.		"F" instead of final "E" in "INTERALLIÉE"	5.00	5.00
		Never hinged	7.50	
N8	A43	2s olive green	.25	.25
		Never hinged	.50	
a.		Second "L" in "INTERALLIÉE" inverted	5.00	5.00
		Never hinged	7.50	
b.		"F" instead of final "E" in "INTERALLIÉE"	5.00	5.00
		Never hinged	7.50	
c.		Inverted ovpt.	40.00	
		Never hinged	80.00	
N9	A44	5s green	.25	.25
		Never hinged	.50	
a.		Second "L" in "INTERALLIÉE" inverted	5.00	5.00
		Never hinged	7.50	
b.		"F" instead of final "E" in "INTERALLIÉE"	5.00	5.00
		Never hinged	7.50	
c.		Inverted ovpt.		
d.		Pair, one without ovpt.	40.00	
e.		Double ovpt.	40.00	
		Never hinged	80.00	
N10	A44	10s rose	.25	.25
		Never hinged	.50	
a.		Second "L" in "INTERALLIÉE" inverted	5.00	5.00
		Never hinged	7.50	
b.		"F" instead of final "E" in "INTERALLIÉE"	5.00	5.00
		Never hinged	7.50	
c.		Inverted ovpt.	30.00	
		Never hinged	45.00	
d.		Pair, one without ovpt.	30.00	
e.		Double ovpt.	45.00	
N11	A44	15s violet	.25	.25
		Never hinged	.50	
a.		Second "L" in "INTERALLIÉE" inverted	5.00	5.00
		Never hinged	7.50	
b.		"F" instead of final "E" in "INTERALLIÉE"	5.00	5.00
		Never hinged	7.50	
N12	A26	25s indigo & black	.25	.25
		Never hinged	.50	
N13	A29	1 l chocolate	5.00	5.00
		Never hinged	10.00	
N14	A37a	2 l brown orange	9.00	9.00
		Never hinged	18.00	
N15	A38	3 l claret	12.00	12.00
		Never hinged	25.00	
a.		Double overprint	25.00	
		Never hinged	50.00	
		Nos. N7-N15 (9)	27.50	27.50

Overprint is vertical, reading up, on Nos. N9-N13.

Bulgarian Stamps of
1919 Overprinted

1920				
N16	A44	5s green	.25	.25
		Never hinged	.50	
a.		Second "e" of "Interalliée" inverted	3.00	3.00
		Never hinged	6.00	
b.		"i" for second "l" in "Interalliée"	3.00	3.00
		Never hinged	6.00	
c.		"r" for "n" in "Interalliée"	3.00	3.00

d.	Never hinged	6.00		
	Imperf, pair	70.00		
	Never hinged	120.00		
N17	A44 10s rose	.25	.25	
	Never hinged	.50		
a.	Second "e" of "Interalliée" inverted	3.00	3.00	
	Never hinged	6.00		
A?	"i" for second "l" in "Interalliée"	3.00	3.00	
	Never hinged	6.00		
c.	"r" for "n" in "Interalliée"	3.00	3.00	
	Never hinged	6.00		
N18	A44 15s violet	.25	.25	
	Never hinged	.50		
a.	Second "e" of "Interalliée" inverted	3.00	3.00	
	Never hinged	6.00		
b.	"i" for second "l" in "Interalliée"	3.00	3.00	
	Never hinged	6.00		
c.	"r" for "n" in "Interalliée"	3.00	3.00	
	Never hinged	6.00		
N19	A44 50s yellow brown, ovpt. reading up	1.50	1.50	
	Never hinged	3.00		
a.	Second "e" of "Interalliée" inverted	3.00	3.00	
	Never hinged	6.00		
b.	"i" for second "l" in "Interalliée"	3.00	3.00	
	Never hinged	6.00		
c.	"r" for "n" in "Interalliée"	3.00	3.00	
	Never hinged	6.00		
d.	Ovpt. reading down	25.00	30.00	
	Never hinged	45.00		
e.	As "d," second "e" of "Interalliée" inverted	3.00	3.00	
	Never hinged	6.00		
f.	As "d," "i" for second "l" in "Interalliée"	3.00	3.00	
	Never hinged	6.00		
g.	As "d," "r" for "n" in "Interalliée"	3.00	3.00	
	Never hinged	6.00		
h.	As "d," imperf, pair	140.00		
	Nos. N16-N19 (4)	2.25	2.25	

Various typographical errors in the overprint are found on all values.

Bulgarian Stamps of 1919 Overprinted

1920 — Perf. 12x11½

N20	A44 5s green	.25	.25	
	Never hinged	.60		
a.	Inverted overprint	32.50	50.00	
	Never hinged	50.00		
b.	Pair, one without ovpt.	42.50	65.00	
	Never hinged	65.00		
c.	Imperf, pair	45.00	65.00	
	Never hinged	65.00		
d.	As "c," inverted overprint	55.00	75.00	
	Never hinged	75.00		
N21	A44 10s rose	.25	.25	
	Never hinged	.60		
a.	Inverted overprint	28.00	37.50	
	Never hinged	37.50		
b.	Double ovpt., one on gum side	45.00	65.00	
	Never hinged	65.00		
c.	Imperf, pair	45.00	65.00	
	Never hinged	65.00		
d.	As "c," inverted overprint	55.00	75.00	
	Never hinged	75.00		
N22	A44 15s violet	.25	.25	
	Never hinged	.60		
a.	Inverted overprint	28.00	37.50	
	Never hinged	37.50		
b.	Imperf, pair	45.00	65.00	
	Never hinged	65.00		
c.	As "c," inverted overprint	55.00	75.00	
	Never hinged	75.00		
N23	A44 25s deep blue	.25	.25	
	Never hinged	.60		
a.	Inverted overprint	28.00	37.50	
	Never hinged	37.50		
b.	Imperf, pair	45.00	65.00	
	Never hinged	65.00		
c.	As "c," inverted overprint	55.00	75.00	
	Never hinged	75.00		
d.	Double ovpt., one on gummed side	45.00		
N24	A44 50s ocher	.25	.25	
	Never hinged	.60		
a.	Inverted overprint	32.50	50.00	
	Never hinged	50.00		
b.	Imperf, pair	45.00	65.00	
	Never hinged	65.00		
c.	As "b," inverted ovpt.	55.00	80.00	

Imperf

N25	A44 30s chocolate	1.50	1.50	
	Never hinged	3.50		
a.	Inverted overprint	32.50	55.00	
	Never hinged	50.00		
b.	Perforated	20.00		
	Never hinged	40.00		
	Nos. N20-N25 (6)	2.75	2.75	

No. N25 is not known without overprint.

ISSUED UNDER GREEK OCCUPATION

Counterfeits exist of Nos. N26-N84.

For Use in Western Thrace

Greek Stamps of 1911-19 Overprinted "Administration Western Thrace" in Greek

Serrate Roulette 13½

1920 Litho. Unwmk.

N26	A24 1 l green	.25	.25	
	Never hinged	.50		
a.	Inverted overprint	20.00		
	Never hinged	40.00		
b.	Double overprint	20.00		
	Never hinged	40.00		
c.	Double overprint, one inverted	75.00		
	Never hinged	140.00		
d.	Ovptd Line 2/Line 3/Line 2	15.00	12.00	
	Never hinged	30.00		
e.	Ovptd Line 1/Line 1/Line 3	15.00	12.00	
	Never hinged	30.00		
N27	A25 2 l rose	.25	.25	
	Never hinged	.50		
a.	Ovptd Line 2/Line 3/Line 2	15.00	12.00	
	Never hinged	30.00		
b.	Ovptd Line 1/Line 1/Line 3	15.00	12.00	
	Never hinged	30.00		
N28	A24 3 l vermilion	.25	.25	
	Never hinged	.50		
a.	Inverted overprint	30.00		
	Never hinged	60.00		
b.	Ovptd Line 2/Line 3/Line 2	15.00	12.00	
	Never hinged	30.00		
c.	Ovptd Line 1/Line 1/Line 3	15.00	12.00	
	Never hinged	30.00		
N29	A26 5 l green	.25	.25	
	Never hinged	.50		
a.	Inverted overprint	25.00		
	Never hinged	50.00		
b.	Double overprint	25.00		
	Never hinged	50.00		
c.	Dbl. ovpt., one inverted	30.00		
	Never hinged	50.00		
N30	A24 10 l rose	.40	.85	
	Never hinged	.60		
N31	A25 15 l dull blue	.40	.75	
	Never hinged	.60		
a.	Inverted overprint	20.00		
	Never hinged	40.00		
b.	Double overprint	20.00		
	Never hinged	40.00		
c.	Dbl. ovpt., one inverted	30.00		
	Never hinged	50.00		
N32	A25 25 l blue	.40	.85	
	Never hinged	.60		
N34	A25 40 l indigo	2.00	4.00	
	Never hinged	4.00		
N35	A26 50 l violet brn	2.00	6.00	
	Never hinged	4.00		
N36	A27 1d ultra	9.00	15.00	
	Never hinged	18.00		
a.	Double overprint	60.00		
	Never hinged	120.00		
N37	A27 2d vermilion	30.00	35.00	
	Never hinged	55.00		
a.	Double overprint	75.00		
	Never hinged	150.00		
	Nos. N26-N37 (11)	45.20	63.45	

The 20 l value with this overprint was not issued. Values: unused $25; never hinged $65.

Engr.

N38	A25 2 l car rose	1.00	1.00	
	Never hinged	2.00		
N39	A24 3 l vermilion	1.00	1.00	
	Never hinged	2.00		
N39A	A25 20 l slate	27.50		
	Never hinged	60.00		
N39B	A25 25 l blue	32.50		
	Never hinged	70.00		
N39C	A25 30 l rose	40.00		
	Never hinged	80.00		
N40	A27 1d ultra	27.50	25.00	
	Never hinged	60.00		
N41	A27 2d vermilion	40.00	35.00	
	Never hinged	80.00		
N42	A27 3d car rose	60.00	80.00	
	Never hinged	125.00		
N43	A27 5d ultra	25.00	30.00	
	Never hinged	50.00		
N44	A27 10d deep blue	25.00	30.00	
	Never hinged	50.00		
a.	Double overprint	300.00		
	Never hinged	500.00		
	Nos. N38-N44 (10)	279.50		

Nos. N38-N44 were not issued. Values for used examples of Nos. N38-N39 and N40-N44 are for cancelled-to-order stamps.

Nos. N42-N44 are overprinted on the reissues of Greece Nos. 210-212. See footnote below Greece No. 213.

Overprinted

N45	A28 25d deep blue	60.00	35.00	
	Never hinged	125.00		

No. N45 was not issued. Used value is for an example canceled-to-order.

With Additional Overprint

Litho.

N46	A24 1 l green	5.00	3.00	
	Never hinged	10.00		
N47	A25 2 l rose	.25	.50	
	Never hinged	.50		
a.	Inverted overprint	65.00		
	Never hinged	90.00		
c.	Double overprint	75.00		
	Never hinged	125.00		
N47B	A26 5 l green	25.00		
	Never hinged	50.00		
N48	A24 10 l rose	.60	.80	
	Never hinged	1.25		
a.	Inverted overprint	17.50		
	Never hinged	35.00		
N49	A25 20 l slate	.60	.80	
	Never hinged	1.25		
a.	Inverted overprint	17.50		
	Never hinged	35.00		
N49B	A25 25 l blue	45.00		
	Never hinged	95.00		
N50	A26 30 l rose (#240)	.65	1.00	
	Never hinged	1.25		

Engr.

N50A	A26 30 l rose (#244)	75.00		
	Never hinged	150.00		
N51	A27 2d vermilion	35.00	30.00	
	Never hinged	75.00		
N52	A27 3d car rose	45.00	30.00	
	Never hinged	90.00		
N53	A27 5d ultra	40.00	32.50	
	Never hinged	85.00		
N54	A27 10d deep blue	35.00	22.50	
	Never hinged	70.00		
	Nos. N46-N54 (12)	307.10	121.10	

Nos. N46, N47B, N49B, N50A, N51, N53 and N54 were not issued. Used values for Nos. N46, N51, N53 and N54 are for canceled-to-order stamps.

For Use in Eastern and Western Thrace

Greek Stamps of 1911-19 Overprinted "Administration Thrace" in Greek

1920 Litho.

N55	A24 1 l green	.25	1.00	
	Never hinged	.50		
a.	Inverted overprint	15.00		
	Never hinged	30.00		
b.	Double overprint	15.00		
	Never hinged	30.00		
N56	A25 2 l rose	.25	.50	
	Never hinged	.50		
a.	Inverted overprint	12.50		
	Never hinged	25.00		
b.	Double overprint	15.00		
	Never hinged	30.00		
c.	Triple overprint	25.00		
	Never hinged	45.00		
d.	Vert. pair, top stamp without ovpt., never hinged	55.00		
N57	A24 3 l vermilion	.25	.50	
	Never hinged	.50		
a.	Inverted overprint	12.50		
	Never hinged	25.00		
b.	Double overprint	15.00		
	Never hinged	30.00		
c.	Double overprint, one inverted	17.50		
	Never hinged	35.00		
N58	A26 5 l green	.25	.50	
	Never hinged	.50		
a.	Inverted overprint	20.00		
	Never hinged	40.00		
b.	Double overprint	35.00		
	Never hinged	70.00		
N59	A24 10 l rose	.50	.75	
	Never hinged	1.00		
a.	Double overprint	85.00		
	Never hinged	165.00		
N59B	A25 15 l dull blue	60.00		
	Never hinged	120.00		
a.	Inverted overprint	60.00		
	Never hinged	100.00		
N60	A25 20 l slate	.65	1.30	
	Never hinged	1.25		
a.	Inverted overprint	17.50		
	Never hinged	35.00		
b.	Double overprint	15.00		
	Never hinged	30.00		
N61	A25 25 l blue	1.75	2.50	
	Never hinged	3.75		
N62	A25 40 l indigo	2.50	7.00	
	Never hinged	5.00		
N63	A26 50 l violet brn	3.00	6.50	
	Never hinged	5.00		
N64	A27 1d ultra	15.00	30.00	
	Never hinged	30.00		
N65	A27 2d vermilion	32.50	45.00	
	Never hinged	65.00		

Engr.

N65A	A25 2 l rose	2.50	4.00	
	Never hinged	5.00		

N66	A24 3 l vermilion	2.50	4.00	
	Never hinged	5.00		
N67	A25 20 l gray lilac	7.50	22.50	
	Never hinged	15.00		
N68	A28 25d deep blue	70.00	100.00	
	Never hinged	140.00		
	Nos. N55-N68 (19)	100.10	220.00	

Nos. N59B and N65A-N68 were not issued. Used values for Nos. N65A-N68 are for canceled-to-order stamps.

With Additional Overprint

Litho.

N68A	A24 1 l green	12.50	6.00	
	Never hinged	25.00		
N69	A25 2 l car rose	.25	.50	
	Never hinged	.50		
a.	Inverted overprint	35.00		
	Never hinged	70.00		
b.	Double overprint	30.00		
	Never hinged	60.00		
N70	A26 5 l green	7.50	8.00	
	Never hinged	15.00		
N71	A25 20 l slate	.25	.50	
	Never hinged	.50		
a.	Double overprint	350.00	325.00	
N72	A26 30 l rose	.25	.50	
	Never hinged	.50		

Engr.

N73	A27 3d car rose	15.00	25.00	
	Never hinged	30.00		
a.	Inverted overprint		—	
N74	A27 5d ultra	25.00	45.00	
	Never hinged	50.00		
N75	A27 10d deep blue	40.00	60.00	
	Never hinged	85.00		
	Nos. N68A-N75 (8)	100.75	145.50	

Nos. N68A, N70 and N74-N75 were not issued. Used values are for canceled-to-order stamps.

Turkish Stamps of 1916-20 Srchd. in Blue, Black or Red

1920 Perf. 11½, 12½

N76	A43 1 l on 5pa org (Bl)	.40	.50	
	Never hinged	.80		
a.	Inverted overprint	35.00	35.00	
	Never hinged	70.00		
b.	Double overprint	30.00	30.00	
	Never hinged	60.00		
c.	Double overprint, one inverted	50.00	50.00	
	Never hinged	100.00		
d.	Double overprint, one on gummed side	35.00		
	Never hinged	70.00		
N77	A32 5 l on 3pi blue	.40	.50	
	Never hinged	.80		
a.	Inverted overprint	100.00	100.00	
	Never hinged	200.00		
b.	Double overprint	70.00	70.00	
	Never hinged	140.00		
N78	A30 20 l on 1pi bl grn	.55	.75	
	Never hinged	1.10		
a.	Inverted overprint	27.50	27.50	
	Never hinged	55.00		
b.	Double overprint	27.50	27.50	
	Never hinged	55.00		
c.	Double overprint, one inverted	40.00	40.00	
	Never hinged	75.00		
d.	Double overprint, one on gummed side	37.50		
	Never hinged	75.00		
N79	A53 25 l on 5pi on 2pa Prus bl (R)	.80	.90	
	Never hinged	1.60		
a.	Inverted overprint	50.00	50.00	
	Never hinged	100.00		
b.	Double overprint	50.00	50.00	
	Never hinged	100.00		
N80	A49 50 l on 5pi bl & blk (R)	6.00	7.00	
	Never hinged	12.00		
N81	A45 1d on 20pa dp rose (Bl)	1.75	1.50	
	Never hinged	3.50		
a.	Double overprint	40.00	40.00	
	Never hinged	80.00		
N82	A22 2d on 10pa on 2pa ol grn (R)	2.50	2.50	
	Never hinged	4.00		
a.	Double overprint	60.00	60.00	
	Never hinged	120.00		
N83	A57 3d on 1pi dp bl (R)	11.00	11.00	
	Never hinged	22.00		
a.	Inverted overprint	60.00	60.00	
	Never hinged	120.00		
b.	Double overprint	65.00	65.00	
	Never hinged	130.00		
N84	A23 5d on 20pa rose	10.00	10.00	
	Never hinged	20.00		
a.	Inverted overprint	75.00	70.00	
	Never hinged	135.00		

b.	Double overprint, one in-verted	75.00	70.00
	Never hinged	135.00	
	Nos. N76-N84 (9)	33.40	34.65

On Nos. N83 and N84, the normal overprint is reading down. On the inverted overprints, it is reading up.

Nos. N77, N78 and N84 are on the 1920 issue with designs modified. Nos. N81, N82 and N83 are on stamps with the 1919 overprints.

POSTAGE DUE STAMPS

Issued under Allied Occupation

1919 Bulgarian Postage Due Stamps Overprinted, Reading Vertically Up

1919		**Unwmk.**	**Perf. 12x11½**	
NJ1	D6	5s emerald	.45	.50
	Never hinged		.90	
a.	Second "L" in "INTERAL-LIÉE" inverted		6.00	6.00
	Never hinged		12.00	
b.	"F" instead of final "E" in "IN-TERALLIÉE"		16.50	11.50
	Never hinged		32.50	
NJ2	D6	10s purple	.90	1.00
	Never hinged		1.75	
a.	Second "L" in "INTERAL-LIÉE" inverted		6.00	6.00
	Never hinged		12.00	
b.	"F" instead of final "E" in "IN-TERALLIÉE"		25.00	16.50
	Never hinged		50.00	
NJ3	D6	50s blue	2.75	3.00
	Never hinged		5.25	
a.	Second "L" in "INTERAL-LIÉE" inverted		52.50	32.50
	Never hinged		100.00	
b.	"F" instead of final "E" in "IN-TERALLIÉE"		52.50	32.50
	Never hinged		100.00	
	Nos. NJ1-NJ3 (3)		4.10	4.50

Type of Bulgarian Postage Due Stamps of 1919-22 Overprinted

1920			**Imperf.**	
NJ4	D6	5s emerald	.25	.50
	Never hinged		.50	
a.	Inverted overprint		40.00	
	Never hinged		60.00	
NJ5	D6	10s deep violet	2.00	2.00
	Never hinged		4.00	
a.	Inverted overprint		40.00	
	Never hinged		60.00	
NJ6	D6	20s salmon	1.00	1.00
NJ7	D6	50s blue	1.50	1.50
	Never hinged		3.00	
			Perf. 12x11½	
NJ8	D6	10s deep violet	1.25	1.25
	Never hinged		2.50	
	Nos. NJ4-NJ8 (5)		6.00	6.25

No. NJ6 issued without gum.

TIBET

tə-'bet

LOCATION — A high tableland in Central Asia
GOVT. — A semi-independent state, nominally under control of China.
AREA — 463,200 sq. mi.
POP. — 1,500,000 (approx.)
CAPITAL — Lhasa

Tibet's postage stamps were valid only within its borders.

6 2/3 Trangka = 1 Sang

Excellent counterfeits of Nos. 1-18 exist. Numerous shades of all values. All stamps issued without gum.

Small bits of foreign matter (inclusions) are to be expected in Native Paper. These do not reduce the value of the stamp unless they have caused serious damage to the design or paper.

A1

1912-50		**Unwmk.**	**Typo.**	**Imperf.**	
		Native Paper			
1	A1	⅛t green		40.00	45.00
2	A1	⅓t blue		40.00	55.00
a.		⅓t ultramarine		50.00	60.00
3	A1	½t violet		40.00	55.00
4	A1	⅔t carmine		50.00	60.00
a.		"POTSAGE"		150.00	175.00
5	A1	1t vermilion		55.00	75.00
6	A1	1s sage green ('50)		100.00	110.00
		Nos. 1-6 (6)		325.00	400.00

The "POTSAGE" error is found on all shades of the ⅔t (positions 6 and 7).
Pin-perf. examples of Nos. 1 and 3 exist.
Issued in sheets of 12.
Beware of private reproductions of #1-5 that were printed in the US around 1986. Sheets of 12 bear "J. Crow Co." imprint. The set of 5 sheets was sold for $5.

Printed Using Shiny Enamel Paint

1920					
1a	A1	⅛t green		60.00	40.00
2b	A1	⅓t blue		500.00	500.00
3d	A1	½t purple		100.00	110.00
4h	A1	⅔t carmine		100.00	110.00
i.		"POTSAGE"		225.00	250.00
5c	A1	1t carmine		350.00	400.00

In some 1920-30 printings, European enamel paint was used instead of ink. It has a glossy surface.

Lion — A2

1914					
7	A2	4t milky blue		750.	850.
a.		4t dark blue		1,100.	1,100.
8	A2	8t carmine rose		165.	175.
a.		8t carmine		1,100.	1,100.

Issued in sheets of 6.

Printed Using Shiny Enamel Paint

1920					
7b	A2	4t blue		1,350.	1,500.
8b	A2	8t carmine		1,350.	1,500.

See note following No. 5c.

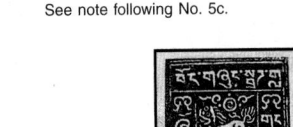

A3

Thin White Native Paper

1933			**Pin-perf.**	
9	A3	½t orange	95.00	100.00
10	A3	⅔t dark blue	95.00	120.00
11	A3	1t rose carmine	95.00	120.00
12	A3	2t scarlet	95.00	120.00
13	A3	4t emerald	95.00	120.00
		Nos. 9-13 (5)	475.00	580.00

Issued in sheets of 12.
Exist imperf.

Heavy Toned Native Paper

1934			**Imperf.**	
14	A3	½t yellow	16.00	18.00
15	A3	⅔t blue	14.00	15.00
16	A3	1t orange ver	14.00	15.00
a.		1t carmine	16.00	18.00
17	A3	2t red	14.00	15.00
a.		2t orange vermilion	14.00	15.00

18	A3	4t green	14.00	15.00
a.		25x25mm instead of 24x24mm	55.00	65.00
		Nos. 14-18 (5)	72.00	78.00

Nos. 14-18 are also known with a private pin-perf.
The ½t and 1t exist printed on both sides.
Issued in sheets of 12.

TIMOR

'tē-ˌmor

LOCATION — The eastern part of Timor island, Malay archipelago
GOVT. — Portuguese Overseas Territory
AREA — 7,330 sq. mi.
POP. — 660,000 (est. 1974)
CAPITAL — Dili

1000 Reis = 1 Milreis
78 Avos = 1 Rupee (1895)
100 Avos = 1 Pataca

Watermark

Wmk. 232 — Maltese Cross

Stamps of Macao Overprinted in Black or Carmine

1885		**Unwmk.**	**Perf. 12½, 13½**	
1	A1	5r black (C)	5.50	1.60
a.		Double overprint	50.00	50.00
b.		Triple overprint	115.00	
2	A1	10r green	8.00	3.50
a.		Overprint on Mozambique stamp	22.50	14.00
b.		Overprinted on Portuguese India stamp	210.00	150.00
3	A1	20r rose, perf. 13½	9.00	4.50
a.		Double overprint	27.50	
		Perf. 12½	9.50	5.00
4	A1	25r violet	3.00	1.10
		Perf. 13½	30.00	17.50
5	A1	40r yellow	6.00	3.00
a.		Double overprint	17.50	
b.		Inverted overprint	21.00	21.00
		Perf. 13½	14.00	11.00
6	A1	50r blue	7.00	2.00
		Perf. 13½	15.00	12.00
7	A1	80r slate	12.50	4.00
8	A1	100r lilac	7.00	1.75
a.		Double overprint	25.00	
b.		Perf. 13½	9.00	3.50
9	A1	200r org, perf. 13½	11.00	4.00
a.		Perf. 12½	12.50	4.75
10	A1	300r brown	8.00	3.50
		Nos. 1-10 (10)	79.00	28.95

The 20r bister, 25r rose and 50r green were prepared for use but not issued.
The reprints are printed on a smooth white chalky paper, ungummed, with rough perforation 13½, and on thin white paper with shiny white gum and clean-cut perforation 13½.

King Luiz — A2

1887		**Embossed**	**Perf. 12½**	
11	A2	5r black	2.50	1.90
12	A2	10r green	4.00	3.00
13	A2	20r bright rose	4.25	3.00
14	A2	25r violet	8.00	3.50
15	A2	40r chocolate	14.00	5.25
16	A2	50r blue	15.00	6.00
17	A2	80r gray	16.50	8.00
18	A2	100r yellow brown	25.00	10.50

19	A2	200r gray lilac	32.50	17.50
20	A2	300r orange	35.00	18.50
		Nos. 11-20 (10)	156.75	77.15

Reprints of Nos. 11, 16, 18 and 19 have clean-cut perforation 13½.
For surcharges see Nos. 34-43, 83-91.

Macao No. 44 Surcharged in Black

1892		**Without Gum**	**Perf. 12½, 13**	
21	A7	30r on 300r orange	10.00	6.75

For surcharge see No. 44.

King Carlos — A3

1894		**Typo.**	**Perf. 11½**	
22	A3	5r yellow	1.25	.65
23	A3	10r red violet	1.75	.65
24	A3	15r chocolate	3.00	.95
25	A3	20r lavender	3.75	1.10
26	A3	25r green	4.50	.80
27	A3	50r light blue	5.75	3.50
a.		Perf. 13½	160.00	125.00
28	A3	75r rose	7.25	2.75
29	A3	80r light green	7.75	4.25
30	A3	100r brown, *buff*	5.75	2.75
31	A3	150r car, *rose*	13.00	8.00
32	A3	200r dk bl, *lt bl*	13.50	10.50
33	A3	300r dk bl, *salmon*	15.00	12.00
		Nos. 22-33 (12)	82.25	47.90

For surcharges and overprints see Nos. 92-102, 120-122, 124-128, 131-133, 183-193, 199.

Stamps of 1887 Surcharged in Red, Green or Black

1895		**Without Gum**	**Perf. 12½**	
34	A2	1a on 5r black (R)	1.00	.85
35	A2	2a on 10r green	1.25	.85
a.		Double surcharge	25.00	
36	A2	3a on 20r brt rose (G)	3.00	1.75
37	A2	4a on 25r violet	6.00	3.00
38	A2	6a on 40r choc	6.00	3.00
39	A2	8a on 50r blue (R)	5.00	2.25
40	A2	13a on 80r gray	15.50	10.00
41	A2	16a on 100r yellow brn	20.00	7.75
42	A2	31a on 200r gray lilac	32.50	20.00
43	A2	47a on 300r org (G)	35.00	22.50
		Nos. 34-43 (10)	122.25	70.05

No. 21 Surcharged

1895		**Without Gum**	**Perf. 12½, 13**	
44	A7	5a on 30r on 300r org	20.00	5.75

Common Design Types pictured following the introduction.

Vasco da Gama Issue
Common Design Types

1898		**Engr.**	**Perf. 14 to 15**	
45	CD20	½a blue green	1.50	.85
46	CD21	1a red	1.50	.85
47	CD22	2a red violet	1.50	.85
48	CD23	4a yellow green	1.50	.85
49	CD24	8a dark blue	3.00	1.25
50	CD25	12a violet brown	3.50	1.40
51	CD26	16a bister brown	4.00	1.90
52	CD27	24a bister	5.00	2.50
		Nos. 45-52 (8)	21.50	10.45

400th anniversary of Vasco da Gama's discovery of the route to India.

For overprints and surcharge see Nos. 148-155.

King Carlos

| | A5 | | A6 |

1898-1903　　Typo.　　Perf. 11½
Name & Value in Black Except #79

53	A5	½a gray	.35	.25
a.		Perf. 12½	2.50	1.75
54	A5	1a orange	.35	.30
a.		Perf. 12½	2.50	1.75
55	A5	2a light green	.35	.30
56	A5	2½a brown	1.25	1.10
57	A5	3a gray violet	1.25	1.10
58	A5	3a gray green ('03)	1.50	1.00
59	A5	4a sea green	1.60	1.00
60	A5	5a rose ('03)	1.50	1.00
61	A5	6a pale yel brn ('03)	1.50	1.00
62	A5	8a blue	2.00	1.10
63	A5	9a red brown ('03)	1.50	1.25
64	A5	10a slate blue ('00)	2.00	1.10
65	A5	10a gray brown ('03)	1.50	1.00
66	A5	12a rose	4.25	3.00
67	A5	12a dull blue ('03)	20.00	10.00
68	A5	13a violet	4.50	3.75
69	A5	13a red lilac ('03)	3.50	1.75
70	A5	15a gray lilac ('03)	5.50	3.75
71	A5	16a dark bl, bl	4.50	3.75
72	A5	20a brn, yelsh ('00)	6.00	3.75
73	A5	22a brn org, pink ('03)	6.00	3.50
74	A5	24a brown, buff	5.50	3.75
75	A5	31a red lil, pinkish	5.50	3.75
76	A5	31a brn, straw ('03)	6.00	3.50
77	A5	47a dk blue, rose	9.00	4.25
78	A5	47a red vio, pink ('03)	8.00	3.50
79	A5	78a blk & red, bl ('00)	12.50	6.75
80	A5	78a dl bl, straw ('03)	20.00	10.00
		Nos. 53-80 (28)	137.40	80.25

Most of Nos. 53-80 were issued without gum.
For surcharges & overprints see #81-82, 104-119, 129-130, 134-147, 195-196.

1899　　　　　　　　Black Surcharge
81	A6	10a on 16a dk bl, bl	3.75	2.50
82	A6	20a on 31a red lil, pnksh	3.75	2.50

Surcharged in Black

1902　　　　　　　On Issue of 1887
83	A2	5a on 25r violet	2.50	1.75
84	A2	5a on 200r gray lil	4.00	2.50
85	A2	6a on 10r blue grn	100.00	50.00
86	A2	6a on 300r orange	3.75	3.50
87	A2	9a on 40r choc	4.50	3.50
88	A2	9a on 100r yel brn	4.50	3.50
89	A2	15a on 20r rose	4.50	3.50
90	A2	15a on 50r blue	100.00	50.00
91	A2	20a on 80r gray	8.75	6.50
		Nos. 83-91 (9)	232.50	124.75

Reprints of Nos. 83-88, 90-91, 104A have clean-cut perf. 13½.

On Issue of 1894
92	A3	5a on 5r yellow	1.90	1.10
a.		Inverted surcharge	40.00	30.00
93	A3	5a on 25r green	2.25	1.10
94	A3	5a on 50r lt blue	2.25	1.40
95	A3	6a on 20r lavender	2.25	1.40
96	A3	9a on 15r choc	2.25	1.40
97	A3	9a on 75r rose	2.25	1.40
98	A3	15a on 10r red vio	4.00	2.25
99	A3	15a on 100r brn, buff	4.00	2.25
100	A3	15a on 300r bl, sal	4.00	2.25
101	A3	22a on 80r lt green	6.00	4.00
102	A3	22a on 200r bl, blue	8.00	4.00

On Newspaper Stamp of 1893
103	N2	6a on 2½r brn	1.00	.85
a.		Inverted surcharge	27.50	27.50
		Nos. 92-103 (12)	40.15	23.40

Nos. 93-97, 99-102 issued without gum.

Stamps of 1898
Overprinted in Black

104	A5	3a gray violet	4.00	1.90
104A	A5	12a rose	6.00	3.75

Reprint noted after No. 91.

No. 67 Surcharged in Black

1905
105	A5	10a on 12a dull blue	8.25	4.25

Stamps of 1898-1903
Overprinted in
Carmine or Green

1911
106	A5	½a gray	.30	.30
a.		Inverted overprint	20.00	20.00
107	A5	1a orange	.30	.30
a.		Perf. 12½	16.00	16.00
108	A5	2a light green	.40	.35
109	A5	3a gray green	.50	.35
110	A5	5a rose (G)	.50	.35
111	A5	6a yel brown	.50	.35
112	A5	9a red brown	.75	.45
113	A5	10a gray brown	.75	.45
114	A5	13a red lilac	.80	.50
115	A5	15a gray lilac	1.60	1.25
116	A5	22a brn org, pink	1.60	1.25
117	A5	31a brown, straw	1.60	1.25
118	A5	47a red vio, pink	3.00	2.50
119	A5	78a dl bl, straw	4.75	3.50
		Nos. 106-119 (14)	17.35	13.15

Preceding Issues
Overprinted in Red

1913　　　　　　Without Gum
On Provisional Issue of 1902
120	A3	5a on 5r yellow	5.00	4.00
121	A3	5a on 25r green	5.00	4.00
122	A3	5a on 50r lt bl	6.00	7.00
123	N2	6a on 2½r brn	6.00	7.00
124	A3	6a on 20r lavender	5.00	4.00
125	A3	9a on 15r choc	5.00	4.00
126	A3	15a on 100r brn, buff	6.00	5.50
127	A3	22a on 80r lt grn	9.00	8.00
128	A3	22a on 200r bl, bl	8.00	7.50

On Issue of 1903
129	A5	3a gray green	6.00	7.50

On Issue of 1905
130	A5	10a on 12a dull bl	6.00	4.00
		Nos. 120-130 (11)	67.00	62.50

Overprinted in Green
or Red

On Provisional Issue of 1902
1913
131	A3	9a on 75r rose (G)	7.00	6.00
132	A3	15a on 10r red vio (G)	6.00	5.00
a.		Inverted overprint	35.00	35.00
133	A3	15a on 300r bl, sal (R)	9.00	8.00
a.		"REUBPLICA"	19.00	19.00
b.		"REPBLICAU"	19.00	19.00

On Issue of 1903
134	A5	5a rose (G)	5.00	4.00
		Nos. 131-134 (4)	27.00	23.00

Stamps of 1898-1903
Overprinted in Red

1913
135	A5	6a yellow brown	5.00	1.75
136	A5	9a red brown	5.00	1.75
137	A5	10a gray brown	5.00	1.75
138	A5	13a violet	7.00	2.50
a.		Inverted overprint	40.00	40.00
139	A5	13a red lilac	6.00	2.50
140	A5	15a gray lilac	6.00	3.25
141	A5	22a brn org, pnksh	7.00	3.50
142	A5	31a red lil, pnksh	8.00	3.50
143	A5	31a brown, straw	10.00	5.50
144	A5	47a blue, pink	11.00	5.50
145	A5	47a red vio, pink	12.00	8.00
146	A5	78a dl bl, straw	15.00	6.50

No. 79 Overprinted in
Red

147	A5	78a blk & red, bl	15.00	8.00
		Nos. 135-147 (13)	112.00	54.00

Vasco da Gama Issue of 1898
Overprinted or Surcharged in Black

1913
148	CD20	½a blue green	.65	.60
149	CD21	1a red	.65	.60
150	CD22	2a red violet	.65	.60
151	CD23	4a yellow green	.65	.60
152	CD24	8a dark blue	1.40	1.10
153	CD25	10a on 12a vio brn	2.50	2.00
154	CD26	16a bister brown	2.00	1.75
155	CD27	24a bister	2.75	2.25
		Nos. 148-155 (8)	11.25	9.50

Ceres — A7

Name and Value in Black
Chalky Paper
1914　　Typo.　　Perf. 15x14
156	A7	½a olive brown	.25	.25
		Never hinged	.40	
157	A7	1a black	.25	.25
		Never hinged	.40	
158	A7	2a blue green	.25	.25
		Never hinged	.40	
159	A7	3a lilac brown	1.00	.75
		Never hinged	1.60	
160	A7	4a carmine	1.00	.75
		Never hinged	1.60	
161	A7	6a light violet	1.00	.75
		Never hinged	1.60	
162	A7	10a deep blue	1.25	.75
		Never hinged	2.00	
163	A7	12a yellow brown	1.50	1.25
		Never hinged	2.40	
164	A7	16a slate	2.25	4.25
		Never hinged	3.50	
165	A7	20a org brown	16.50	6.75
		Never hinged	26.00	
166	A7	40a plum	10.00	5.00
		Never hinged	16.00	
167	A7	58a brown, grn	11.00	7.25
		Never hinged	17.50	
168	A7	76a brown, rose	13.00	7.25
		Never hinged	21.00	

169	A7	1p org, salmon	24.50	12.50
		Never hinged	40.00	
170	A7	3p green, blue	40.00	27.50
		Never hinged	65.00	
		Nos. 156-170 (15)	123.75	75.50

For surcharges see Nos. 200-201, MR1

1920
171	A7	1a black	.60	.45
		Never hinged	1.00	
172	A7	2a blue green	.60	.45
		Never hinged	1.00	

1922-26　　　　Perf. 12x11½
173	A7	½a olive brown	.45	.40
		Never hinged	.70	
174	A7	1a black	.45	.40
		Never hinged	.70	
175	A7	1½a yel grn ('23)	.60	1.10
		Never hinged	1.00	
176	A7	2a blue green	.45	.40
		Never hinged	.70	
177	A7	4a carmine	2.75	2.00
		Never hinged	4.50	
178	A7	7a lt green ('23)	1.75	1.75
		Never hinged	2.75	
179	A7	7½a ultra ('23)	3.25	3.50
		Never hinged	5.25	
180	A7	9a blue ('23)	4.00	6.75
		Never hinged	6.50	
181	A7	11a gray ('23)	4.00	6.75
		Never hinged	6.50	
182	A7	12a yellow brown	2.25	1.90
		Never hinged	3.50	
182A	A7	15a lilac ('23)	9.00	8.00
		Never hinged	14.50	
182B	A7	18a dp blue ('23)	11.00	7.00
		Never hinged	17.50	
182C	A7	19a gray grn ('23)	11.00	6.00
		Never hinged	17.50	
182D	A7	36a turq blue ('23)	10.00	4.75
		Never hinged	16.00	
182E	A7	54a choc ('23)	11.00	8.00
		Never hinged	17.50	
182F	A7	72a brt rose ('23)	17.50	17.50
		Never hinged	28.00	

Glazed Paper
182G	A7	5p car rose ('23)	92.00	60.00
		Never hinged	145.00	
		Nos. 173-182G (17)	181.45	136.20

Preceding Issues
Overprinted in
Carmine

1915　　　　　　　Perf. 11½
On Provisional Issue of 1902
183	A3	5a on 5r yellow	1.00	.55
184	A3	5a on 25r green	1.00	.55
185	A3	5a on 50r lt blue	1.00	.55
186	A3	6a on 20r lavender	1.00	.55
187	A3	9a on 15r chocolate	1.00	.55
188	A3	9a on 75r rose	1.50	.55
189	A3	15a on 10r red vio	1.50	1.50
190	A3	15a on 100r brn, buff	2.00	1.50
191	A3	15a on 300r bl, sal	2.00	3.00
192	A3	22a on 80r lt grn	3.25	2.75
193	A3	22a on 200r bl, bl	5.00	5.00

On No. 103
194	N2	6a on 2½r, perf. 13½	1.00	.55
a.		Perf. 12½	2.00	1.25
b.		Perf. 11½	4.00	1.75

On No. 104
195	A5	3a gray violet	1.00	.60

On No. 105
196	A5	10a on 12a dull bl	1.10	.60
		Nos. 183-196 (14)	23.35	18.80

Type of 1915 with
Additional Surcharge
in Black

Perf. 11½
199	A3	½a on 5a on 50r lt bl	20.00	8.50
a.		Perf. 13½	35.00	12.50

Nos. 178 and 169
Surcharged

1932   *Perf. 12x11½*
200 A7 6a on 72a brt rose   1.50 1.25
   Never hinged   2.40
201 A7 12a on 15a lilac   1.50 1.25
   Never hinged   2.40

"Portugal" and Vasco
da Gama's Flagship
"San Gabriel" — A8

Perf. 11½x12
1935   Typo.   **Wmk. 232**
202 A8 ½a bister   .25   .25
203 A8 1a olive brown   .25   .25
204 A8 2a blue green   .25   .25
205 A8 3a red violet   .60   .60
206 A8 4a black   .60   .30
207 A8 5a gray   .70   .65
208 A8 6a brown   .85   .60
209 A8 7a bright rose   1.00 1.00
210 A8 8a bright blue   1.10 1.10
211 A8 10a red orange   1.60 1.20
212 A8 12a dark blue   2.75 2.10
213 A8 14a olive green   3.25 2.10
214 A8 15a maroon   3.00 2.75
215 A8 20a orange   3.50 2.75
216 A8 30a apple green   5.00 3.00
217 A8 40a violet   9.00 5.00
218 A8 50a olive bister   10.00 5.00
219 A8 1p light blue   24.50 14.00
220 A8 2p brn orange   50.00 25.00
221 A8 3p emerald   67.50 40.00
222 A8 5p dark violet   100.00 52.50
   Nos. 202-222 (21) 285.70 160.40

Common Design Types
1938 Unwmk. Engr. Perf. 13½x13
Name and Value in Black
223 CD34 1a gray green   .25   .25
224 CD34 2a orange brown   .25   .30
225 CD34 3a dk violet brn   .25   .30
226 CD34 4a brt green   .25   .65
227 CD35 5a dk carmine   .25 2.50
228 CD35 6a slate   .45   .25
229 CD35 8a rose violet   .65 1.10
230 CD37 10a brt red violet   .65 1.75
231 CD37 12a red   1.10 2.50
232 CD37 15a orange   1.75 2.50
233 CD36 20a blue   1.75   .80
234 CD36 40a gray black   3.75 1.25
235 CD36 50a brown   3.75 1.25
236 CD38 1p brown carmine   7.50 5.00
237 CD38 2p olive green   17.50 4.00
238 CD38 3p blue violet   22.50 9.50
239 CD38 5p red brown   45.00 14.00
   Nos. 223-239 (17) 107.60 47.90

For overprints see Nos. 245A-245K in Scott
Standard catalogue, Vol. 6.

AIR POST STAMPS

Common Design Type
1938 Unwmk. Engr. Perf. 13½x13
Name and Value in Black
C1 CD39 1a scarlet   .85   .45
C2 CD39 2a purple   .90   .55
C3 CD39 3a orange   .90   .60
C4 CD39 5a ultra   1.00   .65
C5 CD39 10a lilac brown   2.00 1.50
C6 CD39 20a dark green   3.50 1.75
C7 CD39 50a red brown   6.00 4.00
C8 CD39 70a rose carmine 9.00 7.50
C9 CD39 1p magenta   17.50 8.25
   Nos. C1-C9 (9) 41.65 25.25

No. C7 exists with overprint "Exposicao
Internacional de Nova York, 1939-1940" and
Trylon and Perisphere. Counterfeits exist.
For overprints see Nos. C15-C23 in Scott
Standard catalogue, Vol. 6.

POSTAGE DUE STAMPS

D1

1904 Unwmk. Typo. Perf. 12
Without Gum
Name and Value in Black
J1 D1 1a yellow green   .75   .50
J2 D1 2a slate   .75   .50
J3 D1 5a yellow brown   2.50 1.50
J4 D1 6a red orange   2.75 2.25
J5 D1 10a gray brown   3.00 2.00
J6 D1 15a red brown   4.75 3.25
J7 D1 24a dull blue   7.50 6.00
J8 D1 40a carmine   9.00 6.75
J9 D1 50a orange   14.00 8.00
J10 D1 1p dull violet   22.50 15.00
   Nos. J1-J10 (10) 67.50 45.75

Overprinted in
Carmine or Green

1911   **Without Gum**
J11 D1 1a yellow green   .25   .25
J12 D1 2a slate   .30   .25
   a. Inverted overprint
J13 D1 5a yellow brown   .60   .40
J14 D1 6a deep orange   .80   .50
J15 D1 10a gray brown   1.50   .70
J16 D1 15a brown   1.75 1.10
J17 D1 24a dull blue   2.50 2.00
J18 D1 40a carmine (G)   3.25 2.50
J19 D1 50a orange   3.75 2.50
J20 D1 1p dull violet   7.50 7.00
   Nos. J11-J20 (10) 22.20 17.20

Nos. J1-J10
Overprinted in Red
or Green

1913   **Without Gum**
J21 D1 1a yellow green   9.00 9.00
J22 D1 2a slate   9.00 9.00
J23 D1 5a yellow brown   7.00 6.00
J24 D1 6a deep orange   7.00 6.00
   a. Inverted surcharge   30.00
J25 D1 10a gray brown   7.00 6.00
J26 D1 15a red brown   7.00 6.00
J27 D1 24a dull blue   8.00 7.00
J28 D1 40a carmine (G)   8.00 7.00
J29 D1 50a orange   10.00 12.00
J30 D1 1p gray violet   10.00 12.00
   Nos. J21-J30 (10) 82.00 80.00

WAR TAX STAMP

Regular Issue of 1914
Surcharged in Red

1919 Unwmk. Perf. 15x14
Without Gum
MR1 A7 2a on ½a ol brn   30.00 22.50
   Never hinged   45.00
   a. Inverted surcharge 100.00 100.00
   Never hinged   150.00

See note after Macao No. MR2.

NEWSPAPER STAMPS

King Luiz — N1

**Stamps of Macao Surcharged in
Black**
1892 Unwmk. Perf. 12½
Without Gum
P1 N1 2½r on 20r brt rose 2.00   .75
   a. "TIMOR" inverted
P2 N1 2½r on 40r chocolate 2.00   .75
   a. "TIMOR" inverted
   b. Perf. 13½
   c. As "a," perf. 13½   4.50 3.00
P3 N1 2½r on 80r gray   2.00   .75
   a. "TIMOR" inverted
   b. Perf. 13½   18.00 11.50
   Nos. P1-P3 (3)   6.00 2.25

N2   N3

1893-95 Typo. Perf. 11½, 13½
P4 N2 2½r brown   .40   .35
   a. Perf. 12½   2.00 1.50
P5 N3 ½a on 2½r brn ('95) .45   .30

For surcharges see Nos. 103, 123, 194.

POSTAL TAX STAMPS

Pombal Issue
Common Design Types
1925 Unwmk. Perf. 12½
RA1 CD28 2a lake & black   .30   .30
RA2 CD29 2a lake & black   .30   .30
RA3 CD30 2a lake & black   .30   .30
   Nos. RA1-RA3 (3)   .90   .90

**Type of War Tax Stamp of
Portuguese India Overprinted in
Red**

1934-35   *Perf. 12*
RA4 WT1 2a green & blk   6.50 8.00
RA5 WT1 5a green & blk   8.00 8.00
Surcharged in Black
RA6 WT1 7a on ½a rose & blk
   ('35)   10.00 9.00
   Nos. RA4-RA6 (3) 24.50 25.00

The tax was for local education.

**Type of War Tax Stamp of
Portuguese India Overprinted in
Black**

1936   *Perf. 12x11½*
RA7 WT1 10a rose & black   7.00 9.00

1937   *Perf. 11½*
RA8 WT1 10a green & blk   5.50 8.25

POSTAL TAX DUE STAMPS

Pombal Issue
Common Design Types
1925 Unwmk. Perf. 12½
RAJ1 CD28 4a lake & black   .40 1.00
RAJ2 CD29 4a lake & black   .40 1.00
RAJ3 CD30 4a lake & black   .40 1.00
   Nos. RAJ1-RAJ3 (3) 1.20 3.00

TOBAGO

tə-ˈbā-ˌgō

LOCATION — An island in the West Indies lying off the Venezuelan coast north of Trinidad
GOVT. — British Colony
AREA — 116 sq. mi.
POP. — 25,358
CAPITAL — Scarborough (Port Louis)

In 1889 Tobago, then an independent colony, was united with Trinidad under the name of Colony of Trinidad and Tobago. It became a ward of that colony January 1, 1899.

12 Pence = 1 Shilling
20 Shillings = 1 Pound

PRE-STAMP POSTAL MARKINGS

Crowned Circle handstamp types I and V are pictured in the Crowned Circle Handstamps and Great Britain Used Abroad section.

Scarborough

1851-75
A1	I	"Tobago" crowned circle handstamp in red, on cover	1,200.
A2	V	"Tobago" crowned circle handstamp in red, on cover ('75)	5,000.

STAMPS OF GREAT BRITAIN USED IN TOBAGO

Numeral cancellation type A is pictured in the Crowned Circle Handstamps and Great Britain Used Abroad section.

1858-60
A14 (Scarborough)
A3	A	1p rose red (#20)	925.
A4	A	4p rose (#26)	400.
A5	A	6p lilac (#27)	290.
A6	A	1sh green (#28)	2,000.

Issued under British Administration

Queen Victoria
A1   A2

Wmk. Crown and C C (1)
1879   Typo.   Perf. 14
1	A1	1p rose	140.00	95.00
2	A1	3p blue	140.00	80.00
3	A1	6p orange	65.00	80.00
4	A1	1sh green	425.00	80.00
a.	Half used as 6p on cover			
5	A1	5sh slate	900.00	800.00
6	A1	£1 violet	4,500.	

Stamps of the above set with revenue cancellations sell for a small fraction of the price of postally used examples.
Stamps of Type A1, watermarked Crown and C A, are revenue stamps.

1880   Manuscript Surcharge
7	A1	1p on half of 6p org	5,500.	875.

1880
8	A2	½p brown violet	65.00	95.00
9	A2	1p red brown	140.00	70.00
a.	Half used as ½p on cover			2,250.
10	A2	4p yellow green	325.00	35.00
a.	Half used as 2p on cover			2,250.
11	A2	6p bister brown	400.00	125.00
12	A2	1sh bister	100.00	110.00
a.	Imperf.			
	Nos. 8-12 (5)		1,030.	435.00

No. 11 Surcharged in Black

1883
13	A2	2½p on 6p bister brn	95.00	95.00
a.	Double surcharge		4,000.	2,000.

1882-96   Wmk. Crown and C A (2)
14	A2	½p brown vio ('82)	2.25	18.00
15	A2	1p dull green ('90)	1.25	1.00
16	A2	1p red brown ('82)	11.00	3.25
a.	Diagonal half used as ½p on cover			
17	A2	1p rose ('89)	6.50	1.75
18	A2	2½p ultra ('83)	15.00	1.25
a.	2½p dull blue ('83)		65.00	3.75
b.	2½p bright blue		14.00	1.25
19	A2	4p yel grn ('82)	225.00	100.00
20	A2	4p gray ('85)	7.50	4.00
a.	Imperf., pair		2,250.	
21	A2	6p bis brn ('84)	625.00	550.00
a.	Imperf.			
22	A2	6p brn org ('86)	2.75	7.50
23	A2	1sh olive bis ('94)	3.75	25.00
24	A2	1sh brn org ('96)	22.50	90.00

Stamps of 1882-96 Surcharged in Black

Nos. 25-29   No. 30

1886-92
25	A2	½p on 2½p ultra	9.50	24.00
a.	Inverted surcharge			
b.	Pair, one without surcharge		15,000.	
c.	Space between "½" and "PENNY" 3mm		35.00	75.00
d.	Double surcharge		2,500.	2,000.
26	A2	½p on 4p gray	29.00	85.00
a.	Space between "½" and "PENNY" 3mm		75.00	
b.	Double surcharge		3,500.	
27	A2	½p on 6p bis brn	3.75	25.00
a.	Inverted surcharge		3,250.	
b.	Space between "½" and "PENNY" 3mm		30.00	125.00
c.	Double surcharge		3,750.	
28	A2	½p on 6p brn org	150.00	200.00
a.	Space between "½" and "PENNY" 3mm		375.00	450.00
b.	Double surcharge			2,750.
29	A2	1p on 2½ ultra	110.00	22.50
a.	Space between "1" and "PENNY" 4mm		300.00	90.00
b.	Half used as ½p on cover			1,650.
30	A2	2½p on 4p gray	22.50	10.00
a.	Double surcharge		3,500.	3,500.
	Nos. 25-30 (6)		324.75	366.50

Revenue Stamp Type A1 Surcharged in Black

1896
31	A1	½p on 4p lilac & rose	95.00	55.00
a.	Space between "½" and "d"		150.00	82.50
	1½ to 2½mm			

Tobago stamps were replaced by those of Trinidad or Trinidad and Tobago.

TOGO

ˈtō-ˌgō

LOCATION — Western Africa, bordering on the Gulf of Guinea
GOVT. — Republic
AREA — 20,400 sq. mi.
POP. — 2,890,000 (est. 1984)
CAPITAL — Lome

The German Protectorate of Togo was occupied by Great Britain and France in World War I, and later mandated to them. The British area became part of Ghana.

100 Pfennig = 1 Mark
12 Pence = 1 Shilling
100 Centimes = 1 Franc

Watermark

Wmk. 125 — Lozenges

German Protectorate

AREA — 34,934 sq. mi.
POP. — 1,000,368 (1913)

Stamps of Germany Overprinted in Black

1897   Unwmk.   Perf. 13½x14½
1	A9	3pf dark brown	5.50	7.25
	Never hinged	14.50		
	On cover			32.50
a.	3pf yellow brown		9.25	25.00
	Never hinged	27.50		
	On cover			120.00
b.	3pf reddish brown		47.50	140.00
	Never hinged	170.00		
	On cover			325.00
c.	3pf pale gray brown		1,600.	1,200.
	Never hinged	3,600.		
	On cover			1,750.
2	A9	5pf green	5.00	2.90
	Never hinged	8.75		
	On cover			16.00
3	A10	10pf carmine	6.00	3.25
	Never hinged	13.50		
	On cover			16.00
4	A10	20pf ultra	6.00	13.50
	Never hinged	16.00		
	On cover			40.00
5	A10	25pf orange	35.00	60.00
	Never hinged	100.00		
	On cover			175.00
6	A10	50pf red brown	35.00	60.00
	Never hinged	95.00		
	On cover			175.00
	Nos. 1-6 (6)		92.50	146.90

Covers: Value for No. 6 on cover is for overfranked complete covers, usually philatelic.

A3

Kaiser's Yacht, the "Hohenzollern" — A4

1900   Typo.   Perf. 14
7	A3	3pf brown	1.00	1.25
	Never hinged	2.00		
	On cover			55.00
8	A3	5pf green	12.00	2.00
	Never hinged	24.00		
	On cover			20.00
9	A3	10pf carmine	22.00	1.75
	Never hinged	47.50		
	On cover			20.00
10	A3	20pf ultra	1.00	1.50
	Never hinged	4.00		
	On cover			24.00
11	A3	25pf org & blk, yel	1.00	10.00
	Never hinged	4.00		
	On cover			47.50
12	A3	30pf org & blk, sal	1.40	10.00
	Never hinged	4.75		
	On cover			47.50
13	A3	40pf lake & blk	1.00	10.00
	Never hinged	4.00		
	On cover			47.50
14	A3	50pf pur & blk, sal	1.40	7.50
	Never hinged	4.75		
	On cover			40.00
15	A3	80pf lake & blk, rose	2.50	17.00
	Never hinged	5.50		
	On cover			47.50

Engr.
Perf. 14½x14
16	A4	1m carmine	3.50	55.00
	Never hinged	9.50		
	On cover			95.00
17	A4	2m blue	5.50	85.00
	Never hinged	16.00		
	On cover			120.00
18	A4	3m black vio	7.25	150.00
	Never hinged	20.00		
	On cover			190.00

19	A4	5m slate & car	120.00	500.00
	Never hinged	375.00		
	On cover			725.00
	Nos. 7-19 (13)		179.55	851.00

Counterfeit cancellations are found on Nos. 10-19 and 22.

Cover Values for Nos. 11-19 are for overfranked complete covers, usually philatelic.

1909-19   Wmk. 125   Typo.   Perf. 14
20	A3	3pf brown ('19)	.85	
	Never hinged	2.00		
21	A3	5pf green	1.25	2.25
	Never hinged	2.50		
	On cover			16.00
22	A3	10pf carmine ('14)	1.75	110.00
	Never hinged	3.50		
	On cover			650.00

Engr.
Perf. 14½x14
23	A4	5m slate & carmine, (25x17 holes) ('19)	24.00	
	Never hinged	90.00		
a.	5m slate & carmine (26x17 holes) ('15)		26.00	
	Never hinged	110.00		
	Nos. 20-23 (4)		27.85	

Nos. 20 and 23 were never placed in use.

British Protectorate

Nos. 7, 10-19, 21-22 Overprinted or Surcharged

First (Wide) Setting
3mm between Lines
2mm between "Anglo" & "French"
Wmk. 125 (5pf, 10pf); Unwmk.
1914, Oct. 1   Perf. 14, 14½
33	A3	½p on 3pf brown	225.00	175.00
a.	Thin "y" in "penny"		500.00	450.00
34	A3	1p on 5pf green	225.00	175.00
a.	Thin "y" in "penny"		500.00	500.00
35	A3	3pf brown	130.00	100.00
36	A3	5pf green	125.00	100.00
37	A3	10pf carmine	150.00	110.00
a.	Inverted overprint		9,000.	4,000.
b.	Unwmk.			6,250.
38	A3	20pf ultra	37.50	50.00
39	A3	25pf org & blk, yel	37.50	42.50
40	A3	30pf org & blk, sal	42.50	60.00
41	A3	40pf lake & blk	275.00	275.00
42	A3	50pf pur & blk, sal	11,000.	9,000.
43	A3	80pf lake & blk, rose	275.00	300.00
44	A4	1m carmine	5,750.	2,800.
45	A4	2m blue	9,500.	11,000.
a.	Inverted overprint		12,000.	
b.	"Occupation" double		18,000.	13,000.

On Nos. 33-34, the surcharge line ("Half penny" or "One penny") was printed separately and its position varies in relation to the 3-line overprint. On Nos. 46-47, the surcharge and overprint lines were printed simultaneously.

Second (Narrow) Setting
2mm between Lines
2mm between "Anglo" & "French"
1914, Oct.
46	A3	½p on 3pf brown	45.00	30.00
a.	Thin "y" in "penny"		70.00	70.00
b.	"TOG"		475.00	350.00
47	A3	1p on 5pf green	5.00	5.00
a.	Thin "y" in "penny"		15.00	17.50
b.	"TOG"		150.00	125.00
48	A3	3pf brown	5,500.	1,000
a.	"Occupation" omitted			
49	A3	5pf green	1,400.	800.00
50	A3	10pf carmine		3,100.
51	A3	20pf ultra	26.00	14.00
a.	"TOG"			
b.	Vert. pair, #51 & #38		9,000.	
52	A3	25pf org & blk, yel	32.50	35.00
a.	"TOG"		13,750.	
53	A3	30pf org & blk, sal	22.50	32.50
54	A3	40pf lake & blk	5,500.	1,750.
55	A3	50pf pur & blk, sal		7,500.
56	A3	80pf lake & blk, rose	2,750.	2,100.

57	A4	1m carmine	8,500.	4,500.
58	A4	2m blue		10,000.
59	A4	3m black violet		55,000.
60	A4	5m slate & car		55,000.

Third Setting

1¼mm btwn. "Anglo" & "French"
2mm between Lines
"Anglo-French" 15mm Wide

1915, Jan. 7

61	A3	3pf brown	9,000.	3,250.
62	A3	5pf green	225.	150.
63	A3	10pf carmine	225.	150.
64	A3	20pf ultra	1,600.	600.
64A	A3	40pf lake & blk		8,500.
65	A3	50pf pur & blk, sal	15,000.	10,000.

Stamps of Gold Coast
Overprinted Locally

1915, May   Wmk. 3   Perf. 14

66	A7	½p green	.35	2.75
a.		Double overprint	525.00	550.00
67	A8	1p scarlet	.35	.60
a.		Double ovpt.	375.00	500.00
b.		Inverted ovpt.	200.00	275.00
c.		As "b," "Togo" omitted	8,000.	
68	A7	2p gray	.35	1.40
69	A7	2½p ultra	3.00	5.50

Chalky Paper

70	A7	3p violet, yel	3.00	3.75
71	A7	6p dl vio & red vio	2.50	2.00
72	A7	1sh black, grn	2.50	9.00
a.		Double overprint	1,300.	
73	A7	2sh vio & bl, bl	15.00	17.50
74	A7	2sh6p blk & red, bl	5.25	26.00
75	A7	10sh grn & red, grn	50.00	70.00
76	A7	20sh vio & blk, red	150.00	175.00

Surfaced-Colored Paper

77	A7	3p violet, yel	4.50	22.50
78	A7	5sh grn & red, yel	9.25	17.50
		Nos. 66-78 (13)	246.05	353.50

Nos. 66-78 exist with small "F" in "French" and thin "G" in "Togo." Several values are known without the hyphen between "Anglo-French" and all but No. 77 without the first "O" in "Occupation."

Stamps of Gold Coast
Overprinted in London

1916, Apr.   Ordinary Paper

80	A7	½p green	.35	3.00
81	A8	1p scarlet	.35	1.00
a.		Inverted overprint		
82	A7	2p gray	.60	1.75
83	A7	2½p ultra	.70	1.75

Chalky Paper

84	A7	3p violet, yel	4.50	1.50
85	A7	6p dl vio & red vio	2.50	1.25
86	A7	1sh black, grn	5.00	10.00
a.		1sh black, emerald	350.00	750.00
b.		1sh black, bl grn, ol back	9.50	17.50
87	A7	2sh vio & ultra, bl	5.25	9.75
88	A7	2sh6p blk & red, bl	5.25	8.00
89	A7	5sh grn & red, yel	25.00	30.00
90	A7	10sh grn & red, bl grn, ol back	20.00	80.00
a.		10sh green & red, grn	27.50	75.00
91	A7	20sh vio & blk, red	160.00	190.00
		Nos. 80-91 (12)	229.50	338.00

The overprint on Nos. 80-91 is in heavier letters than on Nos. 66-78 and the 2nd and 3rd lines are each ½mm longer. The letter "O" on Nos. 80-91 is narrower and more oval.

Issued under French Occupation
Stamps of German Togo Surcharged

c

d   e

f   g

h   i

**Wmk. Lozenges (5pf and 10pf)
(125), Unwmk. (other values)**

1914   Perf. 14, 14½

151	A3(c+d)	5c on 3pf brn	80.00	80.00
152	A3(c+e)	5c on 3pf brn	75.00	75.00
153	A3(c+f)	5c on 3pf brn	87.50	87.50
154	A3(c+g)	10c on 5pf grn	28.00	28.00
a.		Double surcharge	1,350.	1,350.
155	A3(c+h)	10c on 5pf grn	28.00	28.00
156	A3(c+i)	10c on 5pf grn	55.00	55.00
158	A3(c)	20pf ultra	65.00	65.00
a.		3½mm between "TOGO" and "Occupation"	1,000.	1,000.
159	A3(c)	25pf org & blk, yel	92.50	92.50
160	A3(c)	30pf org & blk, sal	100.00	100.00
161	A3(c)	40pf lake & black	700.00	725.00
162	A3(c)	80pf lake & blk, rose	700.00	725.00
		Nos. 151-162 (11)	2,011.	2,061.

Surcharged or Overprinted in Sans-Serif Type

1915

164	A3	5c on 3pf brown	24,000.	5,250.
165	A3	5pf green	1,200.	525.
166	A3	10pf carmine	1,300.	500.
a.		Inverted overprint	31,000.	19,000.
167	A3	20pf ultra	1,600.	1,200.
168	A3	25pf org & blk, yel	17,250.	8,000.
169	A3	30pf org & blk, sal	17,250.	8,000.
170	A3	40pf lake & blk	17,250.	8,000.
171	A3	50pf pur & blk, sal	24,000.	14,000.
171A	A3	80pf red & blk, rose		65,000.
172	A4	1m carmine		75,000.
173	A4	2m blue	32,000.	26,000.
174	A4	3m black vio		47,500.
175	A4	5m slate & car	47,500.	55,000.

Stamps of Dahomey, 1913-17, Overprinted

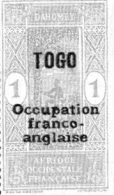

**1916-17   Unwmk.   Perf. 13½x14
Chalky Paper**

176	A5	1c violet & blk	.30	.55
		Never hinged	.55	
		On cover		45.00
a.		Ordinary paper	.30	.40
		Never hinged	.55	
		On cover		45.00
177	A5	2c choc & rose	.30	.55
		Never hinged	.55	
		On cover		45.00
a.		Ordinary paper	.30	.40
		Never hinged	.55	
		On cover		45.00
178	A5	4c black & brn	.55	.90
		Never hinged	.90	
		On cover		45.00
a.		Double overprint	550.00	550.00
b.		Ordinary paper	.55	.35
		Never hinged	.90	
		On cover		45.00
179	A5	5c yel grn & bl grn	.80	.80
		Never hinged	1.20	
		On cover		17.50
a.		Ordinary paper	.80	.80
		Never hinged	1.20	
		On cover		17.50
180	A5	10c org red & rose	.80	.80
		Never hinged	1.20	
		On cover		10.50
a.		Ordinary paper	.80	.65
		Never hinged	1.20	
		On cover		10.50
181	A5	15c brn org & dk vio ('17)	2.00	2.00
		Never hinged	3.25	
		On cover		12.00
182	A5	20c gray & choc	.80	1.20
		Never hinged	1.20	
		On cover		18.00
a.		Ordinary paper	.80	.80
		Never hinged	1.20	
		On cover		18.00
183	A5	25c ultra & dp bl	1.20	1.20
		Never hinged	2.00	
		On cover		21.00
		On cover, single franking		55.00
184	A5	30c choc & vio	1.20	1.60
		Never hinged	2.00	
		On cover		24.00
a.		Ordinary paper	1.20	1.10
		Never hinged	2.00	
		On cover		24.00
185	A5	35c brown & blk	2.00	2.40
		Never hinged	3.25	
		On cover		24.00
		On cover, single franking		45.00
186	A5	40c blk & red org	1.60	2.00
		Never hinged	2.75	
		On cover		27.50
		On cover, single franking		55.00
a.		Ordinary paper	1.60	1.60
		Never hinged	2.75	
		On cover		27.50
187	A5	45c gray & ultra	2.00	2.40
		Never hinged	3.25	
		On cover		35.00
		On cover, single franking		52.50
a.		Ordinary paper	2.00	1.75
		Never hinged	3.25	
		On cover		35.00
188	A5	50c choc & brn	2.00	2.40
		Never hinged	3.25	
		On cover		35.00
		On cover, single franking		72.50
a.		Ordinary paper	2.00	1.90
		Never hinged		3.25
		On cover		35.00
189	A5	75c blue & vio	7.25	8.75
		Never hinged	14.00	
		On cover		40.00
		On cover, single franking		87.50
a.		Ordinary paper	7.25	8.00
		Never hinged	14.00	
		On cover		40.00
190	A5	1fr bl grn & blk	9.50	12.00
		Never hinged	16.00	
		On cover		47.50
		On cover, single franking		110.00
a.		Ordinary paper	9.50	9.50
		Never hinged	16.00	
		On cover		47.50
191	A5	2fr buff & choc	13.50	16.00
		Never hinged	24.00	
		On cover		65.00
		On cover, single franking		120.00
a.		Ordinary paper	13.50	13.50
		Never hinged	24.00	
		On cover		65.00
192	A5	5fr vio & do bl	16.00	18.50
		Never hinged	27.50	
		On cover		75.00
		On cover, single franking		175.00
a.		Ordinary paper	16.00	16.00
		Never hinged	27.50	
		On cover		75.00
		Nos. 176-192 (17)	61.80	74.05

French Mandate

AREA — 21,893 sq. mi.
POP. — 780,497 (1938)

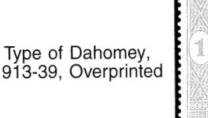

Type of Dahomey,
1913-39, Overprinted

1921

193	A5	1c gray & yel grn	.30	.50
		Never hinged	.50	
		On cover		35.00
a.		Overprint omitted	140.00	140.00
		Never hinged	225.00	
194	A5	2c blue & org	.30	.50
		Never hinged	.50	
		On cover		35.00
195	A5	4c ol grn & org	.30	.50
		Never hinged	.50	
		On cover		35.00
196	A5	5c dull red & blk	.30	.50
		Never hinged	.50	
		On cover		13.50
a.		Overprint omitted	475.00	475.00
		Never hinged	750.00	
197	A5	10c bl grn & yel grn	.70	.80
		Never hinged	.95	
		On cover		27.50
198	A5	15c brown & car	.80	.90
		Never hinged	1.10	
		On cover		16.00
199	A5	20c bl grn & org	1.20	1.20
		Never hinged	2.00	
		On cover		9.50
200	A5	25c slate & org	1.20	1.20
		Never hinged	2.00	
		On cover		8.00
201	A5	30c dp rose & ver	1.60	2.00
		Never hinged	2.40	
		On cover		14.50
		On cover, single franking		27.50
202	A5	35c red brn & yel grn	1.20	1.60
		Never hinged	2.00	
		On cover		4.75
		On cover, single franking		21.00

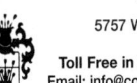

203	A5	40c bl grn & ol	2.00	2.00
	Never hinged		3.25	
	On cover			10.50
	On cover, single franking			14.50
204	A5	45c red brn & ol	1.60	2.00
	Never hinged		2.75	
	On cover			21.00
	On cover, single franking			45.00
205	A5	~~50c dk grn & ol~~	1.60	1.60
	Never hinged		2.75	
	On cover			21.00
	On cover, single franking			47.50
206	A5	75c dl red & ultra	2.00	2.40
	Never hinged		3.25	
	On cover			27.50
	On cover, single franking			40.00
207	A5	1fr gray & ultra	2.00	2.40
	Never hinged		3.25	
	On cover			35.00
	On cover, single franking			80.00
208	A5	2fr ol grn & rose	6.75	7.25
	Never hinged		11.50	
	On cover			40.00
	On cover, single franking			80.00
209	A5	5fr orange & blk	12.00	13.00
	Never hinged		21.00	
	On cover			52.50
	On cover, single franking			92.50
	Nos. 193-209 (17)		35.85	40.35

Stamps and Type of 1921 Surcharged

No. 210　　　　　No. 213

1922-25

210	A5	25c on 15c ol brn & rose red	.55	.65
	Never hinged		.80	
	On cover			10.00
211	A5	25c on 2fr ol grn & rose	.70	.90
	Never hinged		.95	
	On cover			10.00
212	A5	25c on 5fr org & blk	.70	.90
	Never hinged		.95	
	On cover			10.00
a.	"TOGO" omitted		300.00	325.00
	Never hinged		450.00	
213	A5	60c on 75c vio, *pnksh*	1.20	1.60
	Never hinged		2.00	
	On cover			14.50
	On cover, single franking			21.00
a.	"60" omitted		225.00	240.00
	Never hinged		360.00	
214	A5	65c on 45c red brn & ol	1.60	2.00
	Never hinged		2.75	
	On cover			45.00
	On cover, single franking			100.00
a.	"TOGO" omitted		225.00	225.00
	Never hinged		340.00	
215	A5	85c on 75c dull red & ultra	2.40	2.75
	Never hinged		4.50	
	On cover			35.00
	On cover, single franking			72.50
	Nos. 210-215 (6)		7.15	8.80

Issue years: #213, 1922; #211-212, 1924; others, 1925.

Coconut Grove A6

Cacao Trees — A7

Oil Palms A8

1924-38　　　　　　　　　　**Typo.**

216	A6	1c yellow & blk	.25	.40
	Never hinged		.40	
	On cover			24.00
217	A6	2c dp rose & blk	.25	.40
	Never hinged		.40	
	On cover			24.00

218	A6	4c dk blue & blk	.25	.40
	Never hinged		.40	
	On cover			24.00
219	A6	5c dp org & blk	.25	.40
	Never hinged		.40	
	On cover			20.00
220	A6	10c red vio & blk	.25	.40
	Never hinged		.40	
	On cover			10.00
221	A6	15c green & blk	.25	.40
	Never hinged		.40	
	On cover			12.00
222	A7	20c gray & blk	.30	.50
	Never hinged		.45	
	On cover			9.50
223	A7	25c grn & blk, *yel*	.70	.80
	Never hinged		1.00	
	On cover			9.50
224	A7	30c gray grn & blk	.30	.40
	Never hinged		.45	
	On cover			8.00
225	A7	30c dl grn & lt grn ('27)	.80	.80
	Never hinged		1.10	
	On cover			20.00
226	A7	35c lt brown & blk	.80	.95
	Never hinged		1.10	
	On cover			20.00
	On cover, single franking			32.50
227	A7	35c dp bl grn & grn ('38)	.80	.80
	Never hinged		.95	
	On cover			24.00
228	A7	40c red org & blk	.30	.40
	Never hinged		.45	
	On cover			24.00
	On cover, single franking			47.50
229	A7	45c carmine & blk	.30	.40
	Never hinged		.45	
	On cover			13.50
	On cover, single franking			21.00
230	A7	50c ocher & blk, *bluish*	.55	.65
	Never hinged		.80	
	On cover			8.00
231	A7	55c vio bl & car rose ('38)	1.05	1.05
	Never hinged		1.25	
	On cover			8.00
232	A7	60c vio brn & blk, *pnksh*	.30	.40
	Never hinged		.45	
	On cover			24.00
	On cover, single franking			45.00
233	A7	60c dp red ('26)	.50	.70
	Never hinged		.80	
	On cover			24.00
	On cover, single franking			40.00
234	A7	65c gray lil & brn	.70	.80
	Never hinged		1.10	
	On cover			40.00
	On cover, single franking			87.50
235	A7	75c blue & black	.70	.80
	Never hinged		1.10	
	On cover			17.50
	On cover, single franking			27.50
236	A7	80c ind & dl vio ('38)	2.00	2.00
	Never hinged		3.00	
	On cover			40.00
	On cover, single franking			67.50
237	A7	85c brn org & brn	1.25	1.30
	Never hinged		1.90	
	On cover			32.50
	On cover, single franking			80.00
238	A7	90c brn red & cer ('27)	.95	1.20
	Never hinged		1.40	
	On cover			21.00
	On cover, single franking			55.00
239	A8	1fr red brn & blk, *bluish*	.90	.95
	Never hinged		1.40	
	On cover			20.00
	On cover, single franking			45.00
240	A8	1fr blue ('26)	.70	.90
	Never hinged		1.10	
	On cover			27.50
	On cover, single franking			47.50
241	A8	1fr gray lil & grn ('28)	3.25	3.25
	Never hinged		4.75	
	On cover			17.50
	On cover, single franking			24.00
242	A8	1fr dk red & red org ('38)	1.05	1.05
	Never hinged		1.30	
	On cover			32.50
	On cover, single franking			60.00
243	A8	1.10fr vio & dk brn ('28)	4.75	6.50
	Never hinged		8.00	
	On cover			120.00
	On cover, single franking			225.00
244	A8	1.25fr mag & rose ('33)	1.60	2.00
	Never hinged		2.40	
	On cover			20.00
	On cover, single franking			55.00
245	A8	1.50fr bl & lt bl ('27)	.80	.95
	Never hinged		1.20	
	On cover			21.00
	On cover, single franking			47.50
246	A8	1.75fr bis & pink ('33)	9.50	6.00
	Never hinged		16.00	
	On cover			27.50
	On cover, single franking			35.00
247	A8	1.75fr vio bl & ultra ('38)	1.50	1.50
	Never hinged		2.25	
	On cover			24.00
	On cover, single franking			40.00
248	A8	2fr bl blk & blk, *bluish*	1.25	1.30
	Never hinged		1.90	
	On cover			24.00
	On cover, single franking			47.50
249	A8	3fr bl grn & red org ('27)	1.40	1.60
	Never hinged		2.10	
	On cover			25.00
	On cover, single franking			55.00

250	A8	5fr red org & blk, *bluish*	2.10	2.40
	Never hinged		3.25	
	On cover			27.50
	On cover, single franking			55.00
251	A8	10fr ol brn & rose ('26)	2.75	3.25
	Never hinged			
	On cover			32.50
	On cover, single franking			60.00
252	A8	20fr brn red & blk, *yel* ('26)	3.25	4.00
	Never hinged		5.25	
	On cover			40.00
	On cover, single franking			67.50
	Nos. 216-252 (37)		46.60	52.00

For surcharges see No. 253; Nos. 301-302, B8-B9 in Scott Standard catalogue, Vol. 6.

No. 240 Surcharged with New Value and Bars in Red

1926

253	A8	1.25fr on 1fr lt bl	.70	.70
	Never hinged		1.10	
	On cover			40.00
	On cover, single franking			72.50

> Common Design Types pictured following the introduction.

Colonial Exposition Issue
Common Design Types
Engr., "TOGO" Typo. in Black
1931, Apr. 13　　　　**Perf. 12½**

254	CD70	40c deep green	6.50	6.50
	Never hinged		10.50	
	On cover			67.50
255	CD71	50c violet	6.50	6.50
	Never hinged		10.50	
	On cover			55.00
256	CD72	90c red orange	6.50	6.50
	Never hinged		10.50	
	On cover			100.00
	On cover, single franking			140.00
257	CD73	1.50fr dull blue	6.50	6.50
	Never hinged		10.50	
	On cover			87.50
	On cover, single franking			125.00
	Nos. 254-257 (4)		26.00	26.00

Paris International Exposition Issue
Common Design Types
1937　　　　　　　**Perf. 13**

258	CD74	20c deep violet	1.90	1.90
	Never hinged		2.75	
	On cover			67.50
259	CD75	30c dark green	1.90	1.90
	Never hinged		2.75	
	On cover			55.00
260	CD76	40c carmine rose	1.90	1.90
	Never hinged		2.75	
	On cover			52.50
261	CD77	50c dark brown	1.90	1.90
	Never hinged		2.75	
	On cover			47.50
262	CD78	90c red	1.90	1.90
	Never hinged		3.25	
	On cover			67.50
	On cover, single franking			120.00
263	CD79	1.50fr ultra	1.90	1.90
	Never hinged		3.25	
	On cover			60.00
	On cover, single franking			100.00
	Nos. 258-263 (6)		11.40	11.40

Colonial Arts Exhibition Issue
Souvenir Sheet
Common Design Type
1937　　　　　　　**Imperf.**

264	CD77	3fr Prus bl & blk	8.00	9.50
	Never hinged		12.00	
	On cover			72.50
	On cover, single franking			110.00

Caillié Issue
Common Design Type
1939, Apr. 5　　　　**Perf. 12½x12**

265	CD81	90c org brn & org	.95	.95
	Never hinged		1.30	
	On cover			6.50
266	CD81	2fr brt violet	1.10	1.10
	Never hinged		1.60	
	On cover			16.00
	On cover, single franking			27.50
267	CD81	2.25fr ultra & dk bl	1.10	1.10
	Never hinged		1.60	
	On cover			20.00
	On cover, single franking			32.50
	Nos. 265-267 (3)		3.15	3.15

New York World's Fair Issue
Common Design Type
1939, May 10

268	CD82	1.25fr carmine lake	1.25	1.25
	Never hinged		1.60	
	On cover			47.50
	On cover, single franking			92.50
269	CD82	2.25fr ultra	1.25	1.25
	Never hinged		1.60	
	On cover			80.00

SEMI-POSTAL STAMPS

Curie Issue
Common Design Type
1938　**Unwmk.**　**Engr.**　**Perf. 13**

B1	CD80	1.75fr + 50c brt ultra	20.00	20.00
	Never hinged		32.50	

French Revolution Issue
Common Design Type
Photo., Name and Value Typo. in Black
1939

B2	CD83	45c + 25c green	9.50	9.50
	Never hinged		17.50	
	On cover			95.00
B3	CD83	70c + 30c brown	9.50	9.50
	Never hinged		17.50	
	On cover			72.50
B4	CD83	90c + 35c red org	9.50	9.50
	Never hinged		17.50	
	On cover			65.00
B5	CD83	1.25fr + 1fr rose pink	9.50	9.50
	Never hinged		17.50	
	On cover			100.00
	On cover, single franking			150.00
B6	CD83	2.25fr + 2fr blue	9.50	9.50
	Never hinged		10.00	
	On cover			95.00
	On cover, single franking			140.00
	Nos. B2-B6 (5)		47.50	47.50

French Revolution, 150th anniv. Surtax for defense of the colonies.

AIR POST STAMPS

Common Design Type
1940　**Unwmk.**　**Engr.**　**Perf. 12½x12**

C1	CD85	1.90fr ultra	.40	.40
	Never hinged		.55	
	On cover			20.00
C2	CD85	2.90fr dark red	.65	.65
	Never hinged		.95	
	On cover			20.00
C3	CD85	4.50fr dk gray grn	.80	.80
	Never hinged		1.20	
	On cover			24.00
C4	CD85	4.90fr yellow bister	.90	.90
	Never hinged		1.20	
	On cover			27.50
C5	CD85	6.90fr deep orange	1.30	1.30
	Never hinged		2.10	
	On cover			35.00
	Nos. C1-C5 (5)		4.05	4.05

POSTAGE DUE STAMPS

Postage Due Stamps of Dahomey, 1914 Overprinted

1921　**Unwmk.**　　**Perf. 14x13½**

J1	D2	5c green	.70	.95
	Never hinged		1.00	
	On cover			32.50
J2	D2	10c rose	.70	1.00
	Never hinged		1.00	
	On cover			32.50
J3	D2	15c gray	1.45	2.00
	Never hinged		2.30	
	On cover			32.50
J4	D2	20c brown	2.60	2.75
	Never hinged		4.00	
	On cover			35.00
J5	D2	30c blue	3.00	3.25
	Never hinged		4.25	
	On cover			42.50
J6	D2	50c black	2.40	2.75
	Never hinged		3.50	
	On cover			40.00
J7	D2	60c orange	2.40	2.75
	Never hinged		3.50	
	On cover			47.50
J8	D2	1fr violet	4.50	5.25
	Never hinged		6.00	
	On cover			60.00
	Nos. J1-J8 (8)		17.75	20.70

Cotton Field — D3

1925　**Typo.**　**Unwmk.**

J9	D3	2c blue & blk	.25	.40
	Never hinged		.40	
	On cover			25.00

J10	D3	4c dl red & blk	.25 / .40
		Never hinged	.40
		On cover	25.00
J11	D3	5c ol grn & blk	.25 / .40
		Never hinged	.40
		On cover	25.00
J12	D3	10c cerise & blk	.30 / .50
		Never hinged	.45
		On cover	25.00
J13	D3	15c orange & blk	.80 / .95
		Never hinged	1.20
		On cover	30.00
J14	D3	20c red vio & blk	.50 / .65
		Never hinged	.65
		On cover	30.00
J15	D3	25c gray & blk	1.05 / 1.20
		Never hinged	1.40
		On cover	32.50
J16	D3	30c ocher & blk	.50 / .65
		Never hinged	.65
		On cover	32.50
J17	D3	50c brown & blk	1.10 / 1.20
		Never hinged	1.60
		On cover	37.50
J18	D3	60c green & blk	1.10 / 1.20
		Never hinged	1.60
		On cover	42.50
J19	D3	1fr dk vio & blk	1.10 / 1.30
		Never hinged	1.60
		On cover	47.50
		Nos. J9-J19 (11)	7.20 / 8.85

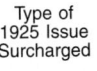

Type of
1925 Issue
Surcharged

1927

J20	D3	2fr on 1fr rose red & vio	6.50 / 7.25
		Never hinged	10.50
		On cover	60.00
J21	D3	3fr on 1fr org brn, blk & ultra	6.50 / 7.25
		Never hinged	10.50
		On cover	67.50

TONGA

ˈtäŋ-gə

LOCATION — A group of islands in the south Pacific Ocean, south of Samoa

GOVT. — Kingdom in British Commonwealth

AREA — 289 sq. mi.

POP. — 98,750 (est. 1983)

CAPITAL — Nuku'alofa

This group, also known as the Friendly Islands, became a British Protectorate in 1900 under the Anglo-German Agreement of 1899.

12 Pence = 1 Shilling
20 Shillings = 1 Pound

Catalogue values for unused stamps in this country are for Never Hinged items, beginning with Scott 87 in the regular postage section.

Watermarks

Wmk. 62 — NZ and Small Star Wide Apart

Wmk. 79 — Turtles

King George I — A1

Perf. 12x11½

1886-92   Typo.   Wmk. 62

1	A1	1p car rose ('87)	11.50 / 4.00
a.		Perf. 12½	450.00 / 7.00
b.		Perf. 12½x10	
2	A1	2p violet ('87)	42.50 / 3.50
a.		Perf. 12½	57.50 / 14.00
3	A1	6p ultra ('88)	57.50 / 2.75
a.		Perf. 12½	67.50 / 4.00
4	A1	6p org yel ('92)	18.00 / 30.00
5	A1	1sh blue grn ('88)	62.50 / 7.25
a.		Perf. 12½	110.00 / 4.50
b.		Half used as 6p on cover	
		Nos. 1-5 (5)	192.00 / 47.50

For surcharges and overprints see #6-9, 24.

Nos. 1 and 2 Surcharged or Overprinted in Black

a   b

1891, Nov. 10   Perf. 12x11½

6	A1(a)	4p on 1p car rose	3.50 / 12.50
a.		No period after "PENCE"	57.50 / 125.00
7	A1(a)	8p on 2p violet	40.00 / 100.00

Type I

1891, Nov. 23   Perf. 12½

Two types of overprint:
I — Solid stars, rays pointed and short.
II — Open-center stars, rays blunt and long.

8	A1(b)	1p car rose (I)	50.00 / 65.00
a.		Overprinted with 3 stars (I)	400.00
b.		Overprinted with 4 stars (I)	550.00
c.		Overprinted with 5 stars (I)	800.00
d.		Type II	50.00 / 65.00
e.		Perf. 12x11½ (I or II)	350.00
9	A1(b)	2p violet (I)	80.00 / 42.50
a.		Type II	80.00 / 42.50
b.		Perf. 12x11½ (I or II)	425.00

Coat of Arms
A4

George I
A5

1892, Nov. 10   Typo.   Perf. 12x11½

10	A4	1p rose	14.00 / 25.00
a.		Diagonal half used as ½p on cover	975.00
11	A5	2p olive gray	27.50 / 18.00
12	A4	4p red brown	55.00 / 80.00
13	A5	8p violet	62.50 / 200.00
14	A5	1sh brown	90.00 / 125.00
		Nos. 10-14 (5)	249.00 / 448.00

For surcharges and overprints see Nos. 15-23, 25-28, 36-37, O1-O10.

Types A4 and A5 Surcharged in Carmine or Black

c   d

e   f

1893

15	A4(c)	½p on 1p ultra (C)	26.00 / 30.00
a.		Surcharge omitted	
16	A4(c)	½p on 1p ultra	50.00 / 55.00
17	A5(d)	2½p on 2p blue grn (C)	21.00 / 13.50
18	A5(d)	2½p on 2p blue grn	19.00 / 19.00
a.		Double surcharge	3,000. / 2,000.
19	A4(e)	5p on 4p org yel	4.50 / 7.50
20	A5(f)	7½p on 8p rose (C)	27.50 / 85.00
		Nos. 15-20 (6)	148.00 / 210.00

Stamps of 1886-92 Surcharged in Blue or Black

g   h

1894

21	A4	½p on 4p red brn (Bl)	2.25 / 8.00
a.		"SURCHARCE"	10.00 / 22.50
b.		Pair, one without surcharge	
c.		"HALF PENNY" omitted	
22	A5	½p on 1sh brn (Bk)	2.75 / 12.50
a.		Double surcharge	310.00
b.		"SURCHARCE"	11.50 / 45.00
c.		As "b," double surcharge	1,000.
23	A5	2½p on 8p vio (Bk)	8.00 / 9.25
a.		No period after "SURCHARGE"	37.50 / 62.50
24	A1	2½p on 1sh blue grn (Bk), perf. 12½	65.00 / 27.50
a.		No period after "SURCHARGE"	200.00
b.		Perf. 12x11½	17.50 / 47.50
		Nos. 21-24 (4)	78.00 / 57.25

Type A5 with Same Surcharges in Carmine

1895   Unwmk.

25	A5(g)	1p on 2p lt blue	50.00 / 30.00
26	A5(h)	1½p on 2p lt bl, perf. 12x11	55.00 / 45.00
a.		Perf. 12	70.00 / 45.00
27	A5(h)	2½p on 2p lt blue	45.00 / 50.00
b.		Without period	250.00 / 250.00
28	A5(h)	7½p on 2p lt bl, perf. 12x11	70.00 / 50.00
a.		Perf. 12	475.00
		Nos. 25-28 (4)	220.00 / 175.00

King George II — A13

1895, Aug. 16   Perf. 12

29	A13	1p gray green	27.50 / 30.00
a.		Diagonal half used as ½p on cover	850.00
b.		Horiz. pair, imperf. btwn.	7,500.
30	A13	2½p dull rose	24.00 / 15.00
31	A13	5p brt blue, perf. 12x11	26.00 / 57.50
a.		Perf. 12	32.50 / 57.50
b.		Perf. 11	400.00
32	A13	7½p yellow	37.50 / 55.00
		Nos. 29-32 (4)	115.00 / 157.50

Type A13 Redrawn and Surcharged "g" or "h" in Black

33	A13(g)	½p on 2½p red	47.50 / 37.50
a.		"SURCHARCE"	85.00 / 70.00
b.		Period after "Postage"	95.00 / 75.00
34	A13(g)	1p on 2½p red	95.00 / 50.00
a.		Period after "Postage"	170.00 / 110.00
35	A13(h)	7½p on 2½p red	62.50 / 75.00
a.		Period after "Postage"	110.00 / 120.00
		Nos. 33-35 (3)	205.00 / 162.50

Nos. 26 and 28 with
Additional Surcharge in
Violet and Black

1896, May   Perf. 12x11

36	A5	½p on 1½p on 2p	500.00
a.		Tongan surch. reading up (C)	475.00 / 475.00
b.		Perf. 12	475.00 / 475.00
c.		As "a," perf. 12	500.00 / 500.00
d.		"Haalf"	3,500.
37	A5	½p on 7½p on 2p	97.50 / 125.00
a.		"Half penny" inverted	3,250.
b.		"Half penny" double	
c.		Tongan surch. reading up	97.50 / 125.00
d.		Tongan surcharge as "c" and double	
e.		"Hafl Penny"	2,200. / 2,500.
f.		"Hafl" only	5,500.
g.		"Hwlf"	
h.		Periods instead of hyphens after words	1,100.
j.		Perf. 12	925.00

 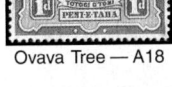

Coat of Arms — A17

Ovava Tree — A18

George II — A19

Prehistoric Trilithon, Tongatabu — A20

Coral Formations A22

Breadfruit A21

View of Haabai A23

Red-breasted Musk Parrot — A24

View of Vavau — A25

Type I   Type II

Two types of 2p:
I — Top of sword hilt shows above "2."
II — No hilt shows.

Wmk. 79 Sideways

		1897-1934	Engr.	Perf. 14
38	A17	½p dark blue	.70	3.00
39	A17	½p green ('34)	1.10	1.40
40	A18	1p dp red & blk	.90	.90
41	A19	2p bis & sep (I)	20.00	7.00
a.		bister & gray, type II	36.00	0.75
42	A19	2½p lt blue & blk	8.00	1.60
a.		"½" without fraction bar	110.00	75.00
43	A20	3p ol grn & blk	4.00	9.75
44	A21	4p dull vio & grn	4.25	4.50
45	A19	5p orange & blk	35.00	16.00
46	A22	6p red	9.00	7.00
47	A19	7½p green & blk	20.00	26.00
a.		Center inverted	6,500.	
48	A19	10p carmine & blk	50.00	55.00
49	A19	1sh red brn & blk	16.00	9.00
a.		"SILENI-E-TAHA" missing second hyphen	350.00	
50	A23	2sh dk ultra & blk	30.00	32.50
51	A24	2sh6p dk violet	65.00	50.00
52	A25	5sh dull red & blk	26.00	32.50
		Nos. 38-52 (15)	289.95	256.15

See Nos. 73-74, 77-78, 80-81. For surcharges see Nos. 63-69.

Stamp of 1897 Overprinted in Black

1899, June 1

53	A18	1p red & black	40.00	72.50
a.		"1889" instead of "1899"	250.00	400.00
b.		Comma omitted after June		
c.		Double overprint		

Marriage of George II to Lavinia, June 1, 1899. The letters "T L" are the initials of Taufa'ahau, the King's family name, and Lavinia.

No. 53 exists with serifed "T" and "L". Some specialists consider it to be an essay or proof.

Queen Salote — A26

Dies of 2p:
Die I — Ball of "2" smaller.
Die II — Ball of "2" larger. "U" has spur at left.

		1920-35	Engr.	Wmk. 79
54	A26	1½p gray blk ('35)	.55	3.50
55	A26	2p violet & sepia	12.00	15.00
56	A26	2p dl vio & blk (I) ('24)	15.00	2.75
a.		Die II	6.00	9.50
57	A26	2½p blue & black	9.00	45.00
58	A26	2½p ultra ('34)	5.00	1.10
59	A26	5p red org & blk	3.75	5.50
60	A26	7½p green & blk	2.00	2.00
61	A26	10p carmine & blk	2.90	5.50
62	A26	1sh red brown & blk	1.40	2.90
		Nos. 54-62 (9)	51.60	83.25

See Nos. 75-76, 79.

Stamps of 1897 Srchd. in Dark Blue or Red

1923

63	A19	2p on 5p org & blk	1.10	1.00
64	A19	2p on 7½p grn & blk	27.50	32.50
65	A19	2p on 10p car & blk	18.00	57.50
66	A19	2p on 1sh red brn & blk	75.00	25.00
a.		"SILENI-E-TAHA" missing second hyphen	600.00	
67	A23	2p on 2sh dk ultra & blk (R)	12.00	7.00
68	A24	2p on 2sh6p dk vio (R)	35.00	7.50

69	A25	2p on 5sh dull red & blk (R)	3.50	2.50
		Nos. 63-69 (7)	172.10	133.00

Queen Salote — A27

Inscribed "1918-1938"

		1938, Oct. 12		Perf. 14
70	A27	1p carmine & blk	.65	4.00
71	A27	2p violet & blk	8.00	8.00
72	A27	2½p ultra & blk	8.00	3.75
		Nos. 70-72 (3)	16.65	10.75
		Set, never hinged	32.00	

Accession of Queen Salote Tupou, 20th anniv.
See Nos. 82-86.

Types of 1897-1920

Die III of 2p:
Foot of "2" longer than in Die II, extending beyond curve of loop.

		1942	Engr.	Wmk. 4
73	A17	½p green	.30	2.75
74	A18	1p scarlet & blk	1.75	2.75
75	A26	2p dull vio & blk (II)	4.50	3.00
a.		Die III	5.50	10.00
76	A26	2½p ultra	1.10	2.00
77	A20	3p green & black	.40	4.25
78	A22	6p orange red	2.00	2.25
79	A26	1sh red brown & gray blk	3.00	3.50
80	A24	2sh6p dk violet	25.00	30.00
81	A25	5sh dull red & brn blk	12.00	60.00
		Nos. 73-81 (9)	50.05	110.50
		Set, never hinged	70.00	

Type of 1938, Inscribed "1918-1943"

		1944, Jan. 25		
82	A27	1p rose car & blk	.25	1.10
83	A27	2p purple & blk	.25	1.10
84	A27	3p dk yel grn & blk	.25	1.10
85	A27	6p red orange & blk	.40	2.00
86	A27	1sh dk red brn & blk	.25	2.00
		Nos. 82-86 (5)	1.40	7.30
		Set, never hinged	2.00	

25th anniv. of the accession of Queen Salote.

> **Catalogue values for unused stamps in this section, from this point to the end of the section, are for Never Hinged items.**

UPU Issue
Common Design Types
Engr.; Name Typo. on 3p, 6p
Perf. 13½, 11x11½

		1949, Oct. 10		Wmk. 4
87	CD306	2½p ultra	.40	.90
88	CD307	3p deep olive	1.75	3.25
89	CD308	6p deep carmine	.55	.55
90	CD309	1sh red brown	.55	.55
		Nos. 87-90 (4)	3.25	5.25

Common Design Types pictured following the introduction.

Queen Salote — A30

		1950, Nov. 1	Photo.	Perf. 12½
91	A28	1p cerise	1.20	3.00
92	A29	5p green	1.20	2.75
93	A30	1sh violet	1.20	3.00
		Nos. 91-93 (3)	3.60	8.75

50th anniv. of the birth of Queen Salote.

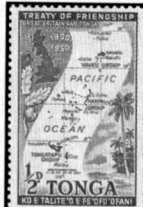

Map and Island Scene — A31

Badges and Royal Palace A32

2½p, Queen Salote & coastal scene. 3p, Queen Salote & ship "Bellona." 5p, Flag of Tonga, island view. 1sh, Arms of Tonga & Great Britain.

Perf. 13x13½ (1p), 13½x13, 12½ (3p)				
		1951, July 2	Engr.	Wmk. 4
94	A31	½p deep green	.30	3.25
95	A32	1p carmine & black	.30	3.25
96	A32	2½p choc & dp grn	.60	3.25
97	A31	3p ultra & org yel	2.75	3.25
98	A32	5p dp green & car	3.75	1.50
99	A32	1sh purple & orange	3.75	1.50
		Nos. 94-99 (6)	11.45	16.00

50th anniv. of the treaty of friendship between Tonga and Great Britain.

OFFICIAL STAMPS

Types of Postage Issue of 1892 Overprinted in Carmine

G.F.B.

Perf. 12x11½				
		1893, Feb. 13		Wmk. 62
O1	A4	1p ultra	11.50	55.00
a.		Half used as ½p on cover		
O2	A5	2p ultra	30.00	62.50
O3	A4	4p ultra	55.00	110.00
O4	A5	8p ultra	100.00	200.00
O5	A5	1sh ultra	110.00	210.00
		Nos. O1-O5 (5)	306.50	637.50

Values are for stamps of good color. Faded and discolored stamps sell for much less.
The overprinted initials stand for "Gaue Faka Buleaga" (On Government Service).

Nos. O1-O5 with Additional Surcharge Handstamped in Black

1893

O6	A4	½p on 1p ultra	20.00	57.50
O7	A5	2½p on 2p ultra	27.50	50.00
O8	A4	5p on 4p ultra	27.50	50.00
O9	A5	7½p on 8p ultra	27.50	92.50
O10	A5	10p on 1sh ultra	32.50	95.00
		Nos. O6-O10 (5)	135.00	345.00

TRANSCAUCASIAN FEDERATED REPUBLICS

ˌtranˌt͡s-ko-ˈkā-zhən ˈfe-də-rāted ri-ˈpə-lĭlĭk

(Armenia, Georgia, Azerbaijan)

LOCATION — In southeastern Europe, south of the Caucasus Mountains between the Black and Caspian Seas
GOVT. — Republic
AREA — 71,255 sq. mi.
POP. — 5,851,000 (approx.)
CAPITAL — Tiflis

The Transcaucasian Federation was made up of the former autonomies of Armenia, Georgia and Azerbaijan. Its stamps were replaced by those of Russia.

100 Kopecks = 1 Ruble

Russian Stamps of 1909-17 Overprinted in Black or Red

		1923	Unwmk.	Perf. 14½x15
1	A15	10k dark blue	4.00	5.00
2	A14	10k on 7k lt bl	4.00	5.00
3	A11	25k grn & gray vio	4.00	5.00
4	A11	35k red brn & grn (R)	4.00	5.00
a.		Double overprint	75.00	75.00
5	A8	50k brn red & grn	4.00	5.00
6	A9	1r pale brn, brn & org	12.00	12.00
7	A12	3½r mar & lt grn	35.00	
		Imperf		
8	A9	1r pale brn, brn & red org	6.50	6.00
		Nos. 1-8 (8)	73.50	
		Nos. 1-6,8 (7)		43.00

No. 7 was prepared but not issued.

Overprinted on Stamps of Armenia Previously Handstamped

a   c

		Perf. 14½x15		
9	A11(c)	25k grn & gray vio	250.00	250.00
10	A8(c)	50k vio & grn vio	250.00	150.00
		Perf. 13½		
11	A9(a)	1r pale brn, brn & org	100.00	50.00
12	A9(c)	1r pale brn, brn & org	150.00	50.00
		Imperf		
13	A9(c)	1r pale brn, brn & red org	35.00	35.00
		Nos. 9-13 (5)	785.00	535.00

Counterfeit overprints exist.

Oil Fields — A1

Soviet Symbols — A2

A28

A29

1923			Perf. 11½	
14	A1	40,000r red violet	3.00	3.50
15	A1	75,000r dark grn	3.00	3.50
16	A1	100,000r blk vio	3.00	3.50
17	A1	150,000r red	3.00	3.50
18	A2	200,000r dull grn	3.00	3.50
19	A2	300,000r blue	3.00	3.50
20	A2	350,000r dark brn	3.00	3.50
21	A2	500,000r rose	3.00	3.50
		Nos. 14-21 (8)	24.00	28.00

Nos. 14-15
Srchd. in
Brown

1923				
22	A1	700,000r on 40,000r	3.00	5.00
a.		Imperf., pair	40.00	
23	A1	700,000r on 75,000r	3.00	5.00
a.		Imperf., pair	40.00	

Types of Preceding Issue with Values in Gold Kopecks

1923, Oct. 24				
25	A2	1k orange	2.50	2.50
26	A2	2k blue green	2.50	2.50
27	A2	3k rose	3.50	2.50
28	A2	4k gray brown	2.25	2.50
29	A1	5k dark violet	2.25	2.50
30	A1	9k deep blue	2.25	2.50
31	A1	18k slate	2.25	2.50
		Nos. 25-31 (7)	17.50	17.50

Nos. 14-21, 25-31 exist imperf. but are not known to have been issued in that condition. Value, $14 each.

TRANSVAAL

tranₜtₛ-'väl

(South African Republic)

LOCATION — Southern Africa
AREA — 110,450 sq. mi.
POP. — 1,261,736 (1904)
CAPITAL — Pretoria

Transvaal was known as the South African Republic until 1877 when it was occupied by the British. The republic was restored in 1884 and continued until 1900 when it was annexed to Great Britain and named "The Transvaal."

12 Pence = 1 Shilling
20 Shillings = 1 Pound

Most unused stamps between Nos. 1-96, 119-122 and 136-137 were issued with gum, but do not expect gum on scarcer stamps as few examples retain their original gum. In many cases removal of the remaining gum may enhance the preservation of the stamps. Otherwise, values for unused stamps are for examples with original gum as defined in the catalogue introduction.

Very fine imperforate stamps will have adequate to large margins. However, rouletted stamps are valued as partly rouletted, with straight edges, and rouletted just into the design, as the rouletting methods were quite inaccurate.

First Republic

Coat of Arms
A1 A2
Mecklenburg Printings
By Adolph Otto, Gustrow
Fine Impressions
Thin Paper

A1 has spread wings on eagle.

1869		Unwmk.		Imperf.
1	A1	1p brown lake	500.00	
a.		1p red	675.00	675.00
2	A1	6p ultra	230.00	230.00
a.		6p ultra	260.00	260.00
3	A1	1sh dark green	800.00	800.00
a.		Tete beche pair		

		Rouletted 15½, 16		
4	A1	1p red	125.00	
a.		1p brown lake	150.00	
b.		1p brick red, "narrow plate"	125.00	
c.		1p vermilion, "narrow plate"	125.00	
5	A1	6p ultra	115.00	115.00
a.		6p pale ultramarine, "narrow plate"	125.00	125.00
6	A1	1sh blue green	150.00	150.00
a.		1sh yellow green	200.00	185.00
b.		1sh deep green	250.00	275.00

Nos. 1-6 were printed from 2 sets of plates, differing in the spacing between the stamps.

The only known example of No. 3a is in a museum.

See Nos. 9-24, 26-33, 35-36, 38-39, 41-42, 43-49, 119, 122. For overprints see Nos. 53-61, 63-66, 68-72, 75-78, 81-83, 86-87, 90-91, 94.

1871-74				
7	A2	3p lilac	92.50	100.00
a.		3p violet	110.00	115.00
8	A2	6p brt ultra ('74)	70.00	27.50
a.		Half used as 3p on cover		1,650.

Many forgeries exist in colors duller or lighter than the genuine stamps.

In forgeries of type A1, all values, the "D" of "EENDRAGT" is not noticeably larger than the other letters and does not touch the top of the ribbon. In type A1 genuine stamps, the "D" is large and touches the ribbon top. The eagle's eye is a dot and its face white on the genuine stamps; the eye is a loop or blob attached to the beak, and the beak is strongly hooked, on the forgeries. Many forgeries of the 1sh have the top line of the ribbon broken above "EENDRAGT."

Forgeries of type A2 usually can be detected only by color.

A sharply struck cancellation of a numeral in three rings is found on many of these forgeries. The similar genuine cancellation is always roughly or heavily struck.

See Nos. 25, 34, 437, 40, 42B, 120-121. For overprints see Nos. 50-52, 62, 67, 73-74, 79-80, 84-85, 88-89, 92-93, 95-96.

Local Printings
(A) By M. J. Viljoen, Pretoria
Poor Impressions,
Overinked and Spotted

1870		Thin Soft Paper		Imperf.
9	A1	1p pink	92.50	
a.		1p rose red	115.00	
b.		1p carmine	80.00	92.50
10	A1	6p dull ultra	375.00	80.00
a.		Tete beche pair		

The only known examples of No. 10a are in museums.

		Rouletted 15½, 16		
11	A1	1p carmine	800.00	300.00
a.		Rouletted 6½		1,100.
12	A1	6p dull ultra	230.00	135.00

Hard Paper, Thick to Medium
Imperf

13	A1	1p carmine	100.00	100.00
a.		1p pale rose red	90.00	
14	A1	6p ultra		
15	A1	1sh gray green	150.00	140.00
a.		1sh dark green		
b.		Tete beche pair	23,000.	
c.		Half used as 6p on cover		2,100.

The existence of No. 14 is questionable.

		Rouletted 15½, 16		
16	A1	1p light carmine	125.00	100.00
a.		1p carmine	62.50	70.00
b.		1p crimson, heavily overinked	175.00	150.00
c.		1p carmine-red, thick paper, yellow smooth gum (May 24, 1870)	125.00	
17	A1	6p ultra	125.00	125.00
a.		Tete beche pair	30,000.	21,000.
b.		6p ultra (thick paper)	125.00	82.50
c.		6p deep ultra, heavily overinked	525.00	200.00
d.		As "b", tete beche pair		
18	A1	1sh dark green	185.00	92.50
a.		1sh gray green	750.00	750.00
b.		1sh deep grn, heavily overinked	600.00	200.00

Nos. 16b, 17c and 18b sometimes are so heavily inked as to be little more than blots of color.

(B) By J. P. Borrius, Potchefstroom
Clearer Impressions Though Often
Overinked

1870		Thick Porous Paper		Imperf.
19	A1	1p black	160.00	135.00
20	A1	6p indigo		

		Rouletted 15½, 16		
21	A1	1p black	25.00	32.50
22	A1	6p gray blue	160.00	70.00
a.		6p indigo	115.00	92.50
b.		6p bright ultra		

Thin Transparent Paper

23	A1	1p black	225.00	750.00
24	A1	1p brt carmine	200.00	62.50
a.		1p deep carmine	80.00	47.50
25	A2	3p gray lilac	125.00	75.00
26	A1	6p ultra	80.00	35.00
27	A1	1sh yellow green	100.00	50.00
a.		1sh deep green	100.00	50.00
b.		Half used as 6p on cover		2,100.

Thick Soft Paper

28	A1	1p dull rose	450.00	85.00
a.		1p brown rose	575.00	140.00
b.		Printed on both sides		
29	A1	6p dull blue	100.00	50.00
a.		6p bright blue	230.00	75.00
b.		6p ultramarine	200.00	75.00
c.		Rouletted 6½		
30	A1	1sh yellow green	975.00	750.00

The paper of Nos. 28 to 30 varies considerably in thickness.

(C) By P. Davis & Son, Natal
Thin to Medium Paper

1874				Perf. 12½
31	A1	1p red	150.00	50.00
a.		1p brownish red	150.00	50.00
32	A1	6p deep blue	200.00	70.00
a.		6p blue	185.00	62.50
b.		Horiz. pair, imperf. between		

(D) By the Stamp Commission, Pretoria
Pelure Paper

1875-76				Imperf.
33	A1	1p pale lilac	70.00	65.00
a.		1p orange red	65.00	32.50
b.		1p brown red	80.00	40.00
c.		Pin perf.	775.00	475.00
34	A2	3p gray lilac	80.00	55.00
a.		3p dull violet	90.00	55.00
b.		Pin perf.		500.00
35	A1	6p blue	77.50	55.00
a.		6p pale blue	77.50	62.50
b.		6p dark blue	82.50	57.50
c.		Tete beche pair, thin opaque paper	20,000.	
d.		Tete beche pair, pelure, transparent paper		
e.		Pin perf.		400.00

The only known examples of No. 35c are in museums.

		Rouletted 15½, 16		
36	A1	1p orange red	450.00	155.00
a.		Rouletted 6½	1,250.	250.00
b.		1p bright red	1,250.	250.00
37	A2	3p dull violet	500.00	165.00
a.		Rouletted 6½	1,100.	320.00
38	A1	6p blue	215.00	130.00
a.		Rouletted 6½	1,275.	140.00

The paper of this group varies slightly in thickness and is sometimes divided into pelure and semipelure. We believe there was only one lot of the paper and that the separation is not warranted.

Thick Hard Paper
Imperf

39	A1	1p orange red ('76)	32.50	25.00
40	A2	3p lilac	425.00	140.00
41	A1	6p deep blue	70.00	25.00
a.		6p blue	115.00	27.50
b.		Tete beche pair		20,000.

		Rouletted 15½, 16		
42	A1	1p orange red ('76)	475.00	175.00
a.		Rouletted 6½ ('75)	700.00	175.00
42B	A2	3p lilac	400.00	
43	A1	6p deep blue	700.00	325.00
a.		6p blue	875.00	125.00
b.		Rouletted 6½ ('75)	750.00	300.00

Soft Porous Paper
Imperf

44	A1	1p orange red	150.00	62.50
45	A1	6p deep blue	225.00	650.00
a.		6p dull blue	400.00	110.00
46	A1	1sh yellow green	460.00	140.00
a.		Half used as 6p on cover		1,850.

		Rouletted 15½, 16		
47	A1	1p orange red		425.00
a.		Rouletted 6½		525.00
48	A1	6p deep blue		185.00
a.		Rouletted 6½		1,275.
49	A1	1sh yellow grn	800.00	400.00
a.		Rouletted 6½		1,400.
b.		Rouletted 15½-16x16½	800.00	400.00

First British Occupation

Stamps and Types of
1875 Overprinted

V. R.

TRANSVAAL

Red Overprint
Pelure Paper

1877		Unwmk.		Imperf.
50	A2	3p lilac	1,500.	210.00
a.		Overprinted on back	3,750.	3,750.
b.		Double ovpt., red and black	7,000.	

		Rouletted 15½, 16		
51	A2	3p lilac	—	1,850.
a.		Rouletted 6½		2,600.

Thin Hard Paper
Imperf

52	A2	3p lilac	1,500.	350.00

Soft Porous Paper

53	A1	6p deep blue	1,850.	210.00
a.		6p deep blue		300.00
b.		Inverted overprint		6,000.
c.		Double overprint	5,250.	1,150.
54	A1	1sh yellow grn	750.00	210.00
a.		Inverted overprint		5,250.
b.		Half used as 6p on cover		2,100.

		Rouletted 15½, 16		
55	A1	6p blue		2,000.
a.		Rouletted 6½		2,750.
56	A1	1sh yellow grn	2,000.	875.00
a.		Rouletted 6½	4,750.	2,750.
b.		As "a.," overprint inverted		7,500.

Black Overprint
Pelure Paper
Imperf

57	A1	1p red	360.00	145.00

		Rouletted 15½, 16		
58	A1	1p red	—	1,350.

Thick Hard Paper
Imperf

59	A1	1p red	35.00	27.50
a.		Inverted overprint	650.00	575.00

		Rouletted 15½, 16		
60	A1	1p red	185.00	57.50
a.		Rouletted 6½	750.00	350.00
b.		Inverted overprint		
c.		Double overprint		1,275.

Soft Porous Paper
Imperf

61	A1	1p red	35.00	40.00
a.		Double overprint		1,400.
62	A2	3p lilac	110.00	52.50
a.		3p deep lilac	200.00	97.50
b.		Inverted overprint		
63	A1	6p dull blue	200.00	100.00
a.		6p bright blue	185.00	35.00
b.		6p dark blue	185.00	250.00
d.		Inverted overprint	1,650.	
e.		Double overprint	4,000.	2,400.
64	A1	6p blue, rose	115.00	55.00
a.		Tete beche pair		
b.		Inverted overprint	140.00	55.00
c.		Overprint omitted	4,000.	2,900.
d.		Half used as 3p on cover		
65	A1	1sh yellow grn	150.00	65.00
a.		Tete beche pair	23,500.	24,000.
b.		Inverted overprint	1,400.	500.00
c.		Half used as 6p on cover		1,750.

The only known examples of No. 64a are in museums.

		Rouletted 15½, 16		
66	A1	1p red	100.00	85.00
a.		Rouletted 6½	750.00	175.00
67	A2	3p lilac	240.00	75.00
a.		Rouletted 6½		875.00
68	A1	6p dull blue	240.00	75.00
a.		Inverted overprint	—	875.00
b.		Rouletted 6½		1,400.
c.		As "a," rouletted 6½		4,750.
69	A1	6p blue, rose	300.00	80.00
a.		Inverted overprint	650.00	80.00
b.		Rouletted 6½		
c.		Tete beche pair		
d.		Overprint omitted		
e.		As "a," rouletted 6½		750.00
f.		As "d," rouletted 6½		
70	A1	1sh yellow grn	325.00	125.00
a.		Inverted overprint	1,400.	575.00
b.		Rouletted 6½	550.00	150.00
c.		As "a," rouletted 6½	1,750.	700.00

In this issue the space between "V. R." and "TRANSVAAL" is normally 8½mm but in position 11 it is 12mm. In this and the following issues there are numerous minor varieties of the overprint, missing periods, etc.

The only known examples of No. 69c are in museums.

Types A1 and A2
Overprinted

V. R.

Transvaal

1877-79				Imperf.
71	A1	1p red, blue	70.00	35.00
a.		"Transvral"	6,500.	2,900.
b.		Inverted overprint	925.00	475.00
c.		Double overprint	4,750.	
d.		Overprint omitted	—	
72	A1	1p red, org ('78)	37.50	24.00
a.		Printed on both sides	—	
b.		Pin perf.		

73	A2	3p lilac, *buff*	75.00	50.00
a.		Inverted overprint		875.00
b.		Pin perf.		
74	A2	3p lilac, *grn* ('79)	175.00	70.00
a.		Inverted overprint		2,350.
b.		Double overprint		
c.		Pin perf.		
75	A1	6p blue, *grn*	115.00	45.00
b.		Tete beche pair		
c.		Inverted overprint		1,275.
d.		Half used as 3p on cover		
76	A1	6p blue, *bl* ('78)	80.00	32.50
b.		Tete beche pair		
c.		Overprint omitted		2,750.
c.		Inverted overprint		1,275.
d.		Half used as 3p on cover		925.00
e.		Double overprint		3,750.
f.		Pin perf.		
		Nos. 71-76 (6)	552.50	256.50

The only known examples of No. 76a are in museums.

Rouletted 15½, 16

77	A1	1p red, *blue*	125.00	45.00
a.		"Transrval"		3,500.
b.		Inverted overprint		
c.		Double overprint		
78	A1	1p red, *org* ('78)	47.50	32.50
a.		Horiz. pair, imperf. vert.		
b.		Rouletted 6½	300.00	115.00
79	A2	3p lilac, *buff*	125.00	32.50
a.		Inverted overprint		3,500.
b.		Vert. pair, imperf. horiz.	875.00	
c.		Rouletted 6½		115.00
80	A2	3p lilac, *grn* ('79)	800.00	175.00
a.		Inverted overprint		
b.		Rouletted 6½	750.00	325.00
81	A1	6p blue, *green*	110.00	32.50
a.		Inverted overprint		750.00
b.		Overprint omitted		4,750.
c.		Tete beche pair	—	
d.		Half used at 3p on cover		800.00
e.		Rouletted 6½	—	1,275.
82	A1	6p blue, *bl* ('78)	325.00	65.00
a.		Inverted overprint	—	1,050.
b.		Overprint omitted	—	4,000.
c.		Tete beche pair	—	
d.		Horiz. pair, imperf. vert.	—	
e.		Half used as 3p on cover		900.00
f.		Double overprint	—	
g.		Rouletted 6½	—	350.00
h.		As "a," rouletted 6½	—	
		Nos. 77-82 (6)	1,532.	382.50

The only known examples of No. 81c are in museums. The existence of No. 82c is questioned.

Types A1 and A2 Overprinted

V. R.
Transvaal

Imperf

83	A1	1p red, *org* ('78)	80.00	52.50
84	A2	3p lilac, *buff* ('78)	92.50	40.00
a.		Pin perf.	875.00	875.00
85	A2	3p lilac, *grn* ('79)	160.00	40.00
a.		Inverted overprint		2,300.
b.		Overprint omitted		
c.		Printed on both sides		1,150.
86	A1	6p blue, *bl* ('78)	160.00	50.00
a.		Tete beche pair	18,000.	
b.		Overprint omitted		800.00
		Nos. 83-86 (4)	492.50	182.50

Rouletted 15½, 16

87	A1	1p red, *org* ('78)	200.00	140.00
a.		Rouletted 6½		350.00
88	A2	3p lilac, *buff* ('78)	210.00	125.00
a.		Vert. pair, imperf. horiz.		
b.		Rouletted 6½		400.00
89	A2	3p lilac, *grn* ('79)	800.00	175.00
a.		Inverted overprint		
b.		Overprint omitted	—	
c.		Rouletted 6½ ('97)		350.00
90	A1	6p blue, *bl* ('78)	500.00	125.00
a.		Tete beche pair	—	1,275.
d.		Rouletted 6½		
e.		As "b," rouletted 6½		400.00

Types A1 and A2 Overprinted

V. R.
Transvaal

1879 — Imperf.

91	A1	1p red, *orange*	55.00	50.00
a.		1p red, *yellow*	57.50	55.00
b.		Small capital "T"	350.00	200.00
92	A2	3p lilac, *green*	52.50	40.00
a.		Small capital "T"	300.00	115.00
93	A2	3p lilac, *blue*	57.50	35.00
a.		Small capital "T"	325.00	110.00
		Nos. 91-93 (3)	165.00	125.00

Rouletted 15½, 16

94	A1	1p red, *yellow*	400.00	240.00
a.		1p red, *orange*	875.00	450.00
b.		Small capital "T"	1,100.	750.00
c.		Rouletted 6½	750.00	750.00
d.		Pin perf.		875.00
95	A2	3p lilac, *green*	875.00	300.00
a.		Small capital "T"		1,000.
b.		Rouletted 6½	1,150.	750.00

96	A2	3p lilac, *blue*	210.00	
a.		Small capital "T"		800.00
b.		Rouletted 6½		950.00
c.		Pin perf.		1,000.

Queen Victoria — A3

1878-80 — Engr. — Perf. 14, 14½

97	A3	½p vermilion ('80)	30.00	100.00
98	A3	1p red brown	19.00	5.25
99	A3	3p claret	30.00	9.25
100	A3	4p olive green	32.50	9.25
101	A3	6p slate	19.00	6.50
a.		Half used as 3p on cover	—	
102	A3	1sh green	140.00	55.00
103	A3	2sh blue	225.00	95.00
		Nos. 97-103 (7)	495.50	280.25

For surcharges see Nos. 104-118, 138-139.

No. 101 Surcharged in Red or Black

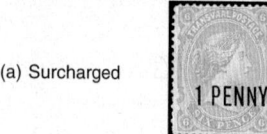

(a) Surcharged — 1 PENNY

1879

104	A3	1p on 6p slate (R)	200.00	95.00
105	A3	1p on 6p slate (Bk)	55.00	27.50

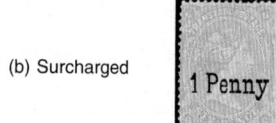

(b) Surcharged — 1 Penny

106	A3	1p on 6p slate (R)	750.00	400.00
107	A3	1p on 6p slate (Bk)	275.00	95.00

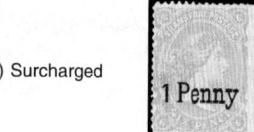

(c) Surcharged — 1 Penny

108	A3	1p on 6p slate (R)	750.00	400.00
109	A3	1p on 6p slate (Bk)	275.00	95.00

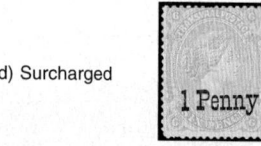

(d) Surcharged — 1 Penny

110	A3	1p on 6p slate (R)	375.00	210.00
111	A3	1p on 6p slate (Bk)	110.00	55.00
a.		Pair, one without surcharge	—	

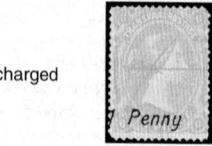

(e) Surcharged — 1 Penny

112	A3	1p on 6p slate (R)	700.00	375.00
113	A3	1p on 6p slate (Bk)	240.00	87.50

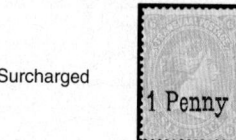

(f) Surcharged — 1 Penny

114	A3	1p on 6p slate (R)	325.00	185.00
115	A3	1p on 6p slate (Bk)	110.00	50.00

(g) Surcharged — **1 Penny**

116	A3	1p on 6p slate (R)	7,000.	1,850.
117	A3	1p on 6p slate (Bk)	700.00	185.00

Surcharge distinctions: a, "PENNY" in gothic capitals. b, "1" has heavy serif at base. c, No serif at base of "1." d, thin serif at base. c, No serif at base of "1." d, Heavy serifs at base of "1" and "p." e, Italics. f, "1" has long, sloping serif at top, thin serif at base. g, Tail of "y" missing.

Second Republic

No. 100 Surcharged — Een Penny

1882 — Unwmk. — Perf. 14, 14½

118	A3	1p on 4p olive grn	20.00	7.00
a.		Inverted surcharge	375.00	250.00

1883 — Perf. 12

119	A1	1p black	8.00	3.00
a.		Imperf.		
b.		Vert. pair, imperf. horiz.	650.00	400.00
c.		Horiz. pair, imperf. vert.	325.00	
120	A2	3p red	17.50	3.50
a.		Horiz. pair, imperf. vert.	—	1,000.
b.		Half used as 1p on cover		750.00
121	A2	3p black, *rose*	32.50	7.50
a.		Half used as 1p on cover		750.00
122	A1	1sh green	80.00	7.00
a.		Tete beche pair	1,150.	185.00
b.		Half used as 6p on cover		550.00
		Nos. 119-122 (4)	138.00	21.00

The so-called reprints of this issue are forgeries. They were made from the counterfeit plates described in the note following No. 8, plus a new false plate for the 3p. The false 3p plate has many small flaws and defects.

Forgeries of No. 120 are in dull orange red, clearly printed on whitish paper, and those of No. 121 in brownish or grayish black on bright rose. Genuine examples of No. 120 lack the orange tint and the paper is yellowish; genuine examples of No. 121 are in black without gray or brown shade, on dull lilac rose paper.

A 6p in slate on white, apparently of this issue, is a late print from the counterfeit plate.

A4

Perf. 13½, 11½x12, 12½, 12½x12

1885-93 — Typo.

123	A4	½p gray	1.75	.25
a.		Imperf. at top and bottom (used strip of 4)	—	
124	A4	1p rose	1.20	.25
125	A4	2p brown	3.00	4.00
126	A4	2p olive bis ('87)	2.40	.25
127	A4	2½p purple ('93)	3.50	.65
128	A4	3p violet	3.75	2.50
129	A4	4p bronze green	5.25	1.50
130	A4	6p blue	4.50	3.75
a.		Imperf.		
131	A4	1sh green	3.75	1.50
132	A4	2sh6p yellow	14.00	3.75
133	A4	5sh steel blue	10.00	6.50
134	A4	10sh pale brown	40.00	13.00
135	A4	£5 dark green ('92)	4,000.	225.00
		Overprinted "Monster" (Specimen)	175.00	
		Nos. 123-134 (12)	93.10	37.90

Reprints of Nos. 123-137, 140-163, 166-174 closely resemble the originals. Paper is whiter; perf. 12½, large holes.

Excellent counterfeits of No. 135 exist.

For overprint and surcharges see Nos. 140-147, 163, 213.

Nos. 120, 122 Surcharged — Halve Penny

1885 — Perf. 12

136	A2	½p on 3p red	8.75	13.00
a.		Surcharge reading down	8.75	13.00

137	A1	½p on 1sh green	32.50	65.00
a.		Surcharge reading down	32.50	65.00
b.		Tete beche pair	1,000.	450.00

Almost all examples of No. 137b have telegraph cancellations. Postally used examples are rare.

Nos. 101, 128 Surcharged in Red or Black

Perf. 14

138	A3	½p on 6p slate	85.00	115.00
139	A3	2p on 6p slate	11.00	17.50
a.		Horiz. pair, imperf. vert.		

Perf. 11½x12, 12½x12

140	A4	½p on 3p vio (Bk)	7.50	7.50
a.		"PRNNY"	55.00	75.00
b.		2nd "N" of "PENNY" invtd.	105.00	115.00

No. 128 Surcharged

No. 141   No. 142

1887

141	A4	2p on 3p violet	2.40	5.00
a.		Double surcharge	210.00	210.00
142	A4	2p on 3p violet	11.50	10.50
a.		Double surcharge	—	400.00

Nos. 126, 130, 131 Surcharged

Nos. 143-144   Nos. 145-146

No. 147

1893 — Red Surcharge

143	A4	½p on 2p olive bis	.90	3.00
a.		Inverted surcharge	3.00	3.50
b.		Bars 14mm apart	1.75	3.75
c.		As "b," inverted	5.75	11.50

Black Surcharge

144	A4	½p on 2p olive bis	1.00	3.00
a.		Inverted surcharge	5.25	5.75
b.		Bars 14mm apart	1.75	3.75
c.		As "b," inverted	23.00	18.50
145	A4	1p on 6p blue	2.00	2.00
a.		Inverted surcharge	2.60	3.00
b.		Double surcharge	65.00	52.50
c.		Pair, one without surcharge	260.00	
d.		Bars 14mm apart	3.00	3.00
e.		As "d," inverted	6.50	5.25
f.		As "d," double		
146	A4	2½p on 1sh green	2.60	6.25
a.		Inverted surcharge	8.00	8.50
b.		Fraction line misplaced "⁹⁄₁₂"	50.00	87.50
c.		As "b," inverted	400.00	350.00
d.		Bars 14mm apart	3.75	8.75
e.		As "d," inverted	11.00	21.00
147	A4	2½p on 1sh green	8.00	7.00
a.		Inverted surcharge	10.00	10.00
b.		Bars 14mm apart	13.00	13.00
c.		As "b," inverted	24.00	24.00
d.		Double surcharge	92.50	105.00
		Nos. 143-147 (5)	14.50	21.25

A13

Wagon with Two Shafts

1894 — Typo. — Perf. 12½

148	A13	½p gray	1.50	.90
149	A13	1p rose	2.40	.25
150	A13	2p olive bister	2.40	.25

151	A13	6p blue	3.25	.60
152	A13	1sh yellow grn	17.50	22.00
		Nos. 148-152 (5)	27.05	24.00

Counterfeits of Nos.148-152 are plentiful.
See note following No. 135 for reprints.

1895-96   **Wagon with Pole**

153	A13	½p gray	1.50	.25
154	A13	1p rose	1.50	.25
155	A13	2p olive bister	1.75	.35
156	A13	3p violet	3.00	1.00
157	A13	4p slate	3.50	1.00
158	A13	6p blue	3.50	1.00
159	A13	1sh green	4.00	1.75
160	A13	5sh slate blue ('96)	20.00	35.00
161	A13	10sh red brown ('96)	20.00	8.00
		Nos. 153-161 (9)	58.75	48.60

Most of the unused examples of Nos. 153-161 now on the market are reprints.
See Nos. 166-174. For surcharge see No. 162.

See note following No. 135 for reprints.

Nos. 159, 127 Surcharged in Red or Green

1895

162	A13	½p on 1sh green (R)	1.75	.25
a.		Inverted surcharge	5.25	5.25
b.		"Pennii" instead of "Penny"	70.00	80.00
c.		Double surcharge	75.00	105.00
163	A4	1p on 2½p pur (G)	.60	.30
a.		Inverted surcharge	20.00	20.00
b.		Surcharge sideways		—
c.		Surcharge on back		4,000.
d.		Space between "1" and "d"	1.50	1.75

A16

1895   **Perf. 11½**

164	A16	6p rose (G)	2.40	2.60
a.		Vertical pair, imperf. between		

Counterfeits of No. 164 are on the 6p dark red revenue stamp of 1898, and have a shiny green ink for the overprint. The false overprint is also found on other revenue denominations, though only the 6p rose was converted to postal use.

Coat of Arms, Wheat Field and Railroad Train — A17

1895, Sept. 6   **Litho.**

165	A17	1p red	2.40	2.60
a.		Imperf.		
b.		Vertical pair, imperf. between	150.00	160.00

Penny Postage in Transvaal. Horiz. pair, imperf. between also exists.
For overprint see No. 245.

Arms Type of 1894 With Pole

1896   **Typo.**   **Perf. 12½**

166	A13	½p green	1.20	.25
167	A13	1p rose & grn	1.20	.25
168	A13	2p brown & grn	1.20	.25
169	A13	2½p ultra & grn	2.40	.25
170	A13	3p red vio & grn	3.00	3.00
171	A13	4p olive & grn	3.00	3.50
172	A13	6p violet & grn	2.00	2.00
173	A13	1sh bister & grn	2.60	.80
174	A13	2sh6p lilac & grn	3.00	3.50
		Nos. 166-174 (9)	19.60	13.80

See note following No. 135 for reprints.
For overprints and surcharges see Nos. 202-212, 214-235, 237-244, 246-251, Cape of Good Hope Nos. N5-N8.

Pietersburg Issue

Date large; "P" in Postzegel large — A18   Date small; "P" in Postzegel large — A19

Date small; "P" in Postzegel small — A20

1901   **Typeset**   *Imperf.*
Initials in Red

175	A18	½p black, *green*	37.50
a.		Initials omitted	125.00
b.		Initials in black	45.00
176	A19	½p black, *green*	50.00
a.		Initials omitted	125.00
b.		Initials in black	52.50
177	A20	½p black, *green*	50.00
a.		Initials omitted	125.00
b.		Initials in black	52.50

Initials in Black

178	A18	1p black, *rose*	5.00
179	A19	1p black, *rose*	6.50
180	A20	1p black, *rose*	8.00
181	A18	2p black, *orange*	7.50
182	A19	2p black, *orange*	20.00
183	A20	2p black, *orange*	25.00
184	A18	4p black, *dull blue*	12.50
185	A19	4p black, *dull blue*	15.00
186	A20	4p black, *dull blue*	40.00
187	A18	6p black, *green*	16.50
188	A19	6p black, *green*	20.00
189	A20	6p black, *green*	55.00
190	A18	1sh black, *yellow*	12.50
191	A19	1sh black, *yellow*	20.00
192	A20	1sh black, *yellow*	30.00

Perf. 11½
Initials in Red

193	A18	½p black, *green*	6.50
194	A19	½p black, *green*	20.00
195	A20	½p black, *green*	15.00

Initials in Black

196	A18	1p black, *rose*	3.00
a.		Horiz. pair, imperf. vert.	65.00
197	A19	1p black, *rose*	3.50
a.		Horiz. pair, imperf. vert.	100.00
198	A20	1p black, *rose*	6.50
a.		Horiz. pair, imperf. vert.	100.00
199	A18	2p black, *orange*	7.50
200	A19	2p black, *orange*	9.50
201	A20	2p black, *orange*	17.00

Nos. 193-201 inclusive are always imperforate on one side.
The setting consisted of 12 stamps of type A18, 6 of type A19, and 6 of type A20. Numerous type-setting varieties exist. The perforated stamps are from the first printing and were put into use first. Used stamps are not valued because all seem to show evidence of having been canceled to order.

Second British Occupation
Issued under Military Authority

Nos. 166-174, 160-161, 135 Overprinted

1900   **Unwmk.**   **Perf. 12½**

202	A13	½p green	.35	.60
a.		"V.I.R."	700.00	
203	A13	1p rose & grn	.35	.50
204	A13	2p brown & grn	4.00	3.00
a.		"V.I.R."	700.00	750.00
205	A13	2½p ultra & grn	1.25	3.00
206	A13	3p red vio & grn	1.25	2.60
207	A13	4p olive & grn	3.75	3.25
a.		"V.I.R."	700.00	
208	A13	6p violet & grn	3.75	2.00
209	A13	1sh bister & grn	3.75	4.50
210	A13	2sh6p hel & grn	4.75	14.00
211	A13	5sh slate blue	9.50	20.00

212	A13	10sh red brown	11.50	22.00
213	A13	£5 dark green	2,500.	925.00
		Nos. 202-212 (11)	44.20	75.45

Nos. 202-213 have been extensively counterfeited. The overprint on the forgeries is clear and clean, with small periods and letters showing completely. In the genuine, letters are worn and lack many or all serifs; the periods are large and oval.
The genuine overprint exists inverted; double; with period missing after "V," after "R," after "I," etc.

Issued in Lydenburg

Nos. 166-169, 171-173 Overprinted in Black

1900

214	A13	½p green	160.00	160.00
215	A13	1p rose & grn	150.00	140.00
216	A13	2p brown & grn	1,400.	1,000.
217	A13	2½p ultra & grn	2,600.	1,050.
218	A13	4p olive & grn	3,750.	1,050.
219	A13	6p violet & grn	3,250.	1,000.
220	A13	1sh bister & grn	5,500.	3,250.

Beware of counterfeits.

No. 167 Surcharged

221	A13	3p on 1p rose & grn	130.00	110.00

Issued in Rustenburg

Nos. 166-170, 172-174 Handstamped in Violet

1900   **Perf. 12½**

223	A13	½p green	175.00	130.00
224	A13	1p rose & grn	130.00	100.00
225	A13	2p brown & grn	375.00	190.00
226	A13	2½p ultra & grn	210.00	130.00
227	A13	3p red vio & grn	300.00	175.00
229	A13	6p violet & grn	1,400.	500.00
230	A13	1sh bister & grn	2,000.	1,100.
231	A13	2sh6p hel & grn	8,000.	

Issued in Schweizer Reneke
Nos. 166-168 and 172 Handstamped "BESIEGED" in Black

1900		**Typo.**	**Perf. 12½**	
232	A13	½p green	290.00	
233	A13	1p rose & green	300.00	
234	A13	2p brown & green	450.00	
235	A13	6p violet & green	1,150.	
		Nos. 232-235 (4)	2,190.	

Same Overprint on Cape of Good Hope No. 59 and Type of 1893
Perf. 14

236	A15	½p green	600.00
236A	A15	1p carmine	600.00

In 1902 five revenue stamps overprinted "V.R.I." are said to have been used postally in Volksrust. There seems to be some doubt that this issue was properly authorized for postal use.

Issued in Wolmaransstad

Nos. 166-173 Handstamped in Blue or Red

1900

237	A13	½p green	290.00	450.00
238	A13	1p rose & grn	200.00	325.00
239	A13	2p brown & grn	2,100.	2,100.

240	A13	2½p ultra & grn (R)	2,100.	
241	A13	3p red vio & grn	3,500.	3,750.
242	A13	4p olive & grn	4,750.	5,250.
243	A13	6p violet & grn	5,250.	5,750.
244	A13	1sh bister & grn	11,000.	

No. 165 Overprinted in Blue

245	A17	1p red	200.00	350.00

Regular Issues
No. 166-168, 170-171, 174 Surcharged or Overprinted

1901-02

246	A13	½p on 2p brn & grn	.80	1.20
247	A13	½p green	.60	1.75
248	A13	1p rose & grn	.60	.25
a.		Overprint "E" omitted	87.50	
249	A13	3p red vio & grn	2.60	4.25
250	A13	4p olive & grn	2.75	6.25
251	A13	2sh6p hel & grn	10.50	30.00
		Nos. 246-251 (6)	17.85	43.70

Excellent counterfeits of Nos. 246-251 are plentiful. See note after No. 213 for the recognition marks of the counterfeits.

Edward VII — A27

Nos. 260, 262 to 267 and 275 to 280 have "POSTAGE" at each side; the other stamps of type A27 have "REVENUE" at the right.

Wmk. Crown and C A (2)

1902-03		**Typo.**	**Perf. 14**	
252	A27	½p gray grn & blk	2.00	.25
253	A27	1p rose & blk	1.50	.25
254	A27	2p violet & blk	5.00	1.50
255	A27	2½p ultra & blk	11.50	1.50
256	A27	3p ol grn & blk	10.50	1.00
257	A27	4p choc & blk	10.50	2.00
258	A27	6p brn org & blk	5.00	1.20
259	A27	1sh ol grn & blk	16.50	20.00
260	A27	1sh red brn & blk	15.00	5.00
261	A27	2sh brown & blk	60.00	70.00
262	A27	2sh yel & blk	17.50	18.50
263	A27	2sh6p black & vio	18.50	17.50
264	A27	5sh vio & blk, yel	35.00	45.00
265	A27	10sh vio & blk, red	75.00	47.50
266	A27	£1 violet & grn	325.00	190.00
267	A27	£5 vio & org	1,650.	750.00
		Nos. 252-266 (15)	608.50	420.90

Issue dates: 3p, 4p, Nos. 260, 262, £1, £5, 1903. Others, Apr. 1, 1902.

1904-09   **Wmk. 3**

268	A27	½p gray grn & blk	10.50	3.50
269	A27	1p rose & blk	8.00	1.20
270	A27	2p violet & blk	15.00	2.40
271	A27	2½p ultra & blk	22.00	10.00
272	A27	3p ol grn & blk	4.00	.60
273	A27	4p choc & blk	5.50	.80
274	A27	6p brn org & blk	13.00	2.40
275	A27	1sh red brn & blk	10.50	4.00
276	A27	2sh yellow & blk	27.50	10.50
277	A27	2sh6p blk & red vio	55.00	10.00
278	A27	5sh vio & blk, yel	29.00	1.75
279	A27	10sh vio & blk, red	80.00	3.50
280	A27	£1 violet & grn	350.00	40.00
		Nos. 268-280 (13)	630.00	87.25

The 2p and 3p are on chalky paper, the 2½p, 4p, 6p and £1 on both chalky and ordinary, and the other values on ordinary paper only.

Issue years: ½p, 1p, 5sh, 1904. 2½p, 6p, 1sh, 1905. 2p, 3p, 4p, 2sh, 1906. 10sh, 1907. £1, 1908. 2sh6p, 1909.

1905-10

281	A27	½p green	3.75	.25
		Booklet pane of 6		
282	A27	1p carmine	1.50	.25
a.		Wmk. 16 (anchor) ('07)	—	375.00
b.		Booklet pane of 6	—	
283	A27	2p dull vio ('10)	4.00	.75
284	A27	2½p ultra ('10)	20.00	10.00
		Nos. 281-284 (4)	28.25	11.25

Wmk. 16 is illustrated in the Cape of Good Hope.

Some of the above stamps are found with the overprint "C. S. A. R." for use by the Central South African Railway, the control mark being applied after the stamps had left the post office.

POSTAGE DUE STAMPS

D1

Wmk. Multiple Crown and C A (3)

1907		Typo.		Perf. 14
J1	D1	½p green & blk	4.00	1.50
		On cover		25.00
J2	D1	1p carmine & blk	4.75	1.00
		On cover		25.00
J3	D1	2p brown org	5.75	1.50
		On cover		90.00
J4	D1	3p blue & blk	8.75	5.00
		On cover		125.00
J5	D1	5p violet & blk	2.75	14.00
		On cover		200.00
J6	D1	6p red brown & blk	5.00	14.00
		On cover		200.00
J7	D1	1sh black & car	14.00	10.00
		On cover		300.00
		Nos. J1-J7 (7)	45.00	47.00

Most canceled examples of Nos. J1-J7 were used outside the Transvaal under the Union of South Africa administration in 1910-16. Values on cover are for commercial usages in the Transvaal, prior to the South African union.

The stamps of Transvaal were replaced by those of South Africa.

TRINIDAD

'tri-nə-ˌdad

LOCATION — West Indies, off the Venezuelan coast
GOVT. — British Colony which became part of the Colony of Trinidad and Tobago in 1889
AREA — 1,864 sq. mi.
POP. — 387,000
CAPITAL — Port of Spain

12 Pence = 1 Shilling
20 Shillings = 1 Pound

PRE-STAMP POSTAL MARKINGS

Crowned Circle handstamp type VII is pictured in the Crowned Circle Handstamps and Great Britain Used Abroad section.

Port of Spain

1850

A1   VII   "Trinidad" crowned circle handstamp in red, on cover   3,100.

Though postage stamps were available in 1851, this handstamp was used on outgoing foreign mail covers which lacked postage stamps until 1858. However, most foreign mail covers did bear an adhesive, and covers with this handstamp and an additional adhesive stamp sell for less.

In 1847 David Bryce, owner of the "Lady McLeod," issued a blue, lithographed, imperf. stamp to prepay his 5-cent rate for carrying letters on his sail-equipped steamer between Port of Spain and San Fernando, another Trinidad port. The stamp pictures the "Lady McLeod" above the monogram "LMcL," expressing no denomination. Value: unused, $50,000; used, $12,500; on cover (pen canceled), $24,000; used stamps canceled by having a corner skinned off, $5,500; cover bearing skinned stamp, $10,000.

Values for unused stamps are for examples with original gum as defined in the catalogue introduction. However, Nos. 9-12 are seldom found with gum, and these are valued without gum.

Values for Nos. 18-26 are for stamps with pin perforations on two or three sides. Stamps with pin perforations on all four sides are not often seen and command large premiums.

Very fine examples of Nos. 27-47 will have perforations touching the design on one or more sides due to the narrow spacing of the stamps on the plates and imperfect perforating methods. These stamps with perfs clear of the design on all four sides are scarce and command substantially higher prices.

"Britannia"
A1   A2

1851-56   Unwmk.   Engr.   Imperf.
Blued Paper

1	A1	(1p) brick red ('56)	200.00	85.00
a.		(1p) brown red ('53)	360.00	77.50
2	A1	(1p) purple brown	20.00	90.00
3	A1	(1p) blue	21.00	72.50
a.		(1p) deep blue, deeply blued paper	175.00	95.00
4	A1	(1p) gray brn ('53)	57.50	90.00
a.		(1p) gray ('52)	90.00	77.50
		Nos. 1-4 (4)	298.50	337.50

1854-57   White Paper

6	A1	(1p) brown red ('57)	3,250.	77.50
7	A1	(1p) gray	55.00	95.00
8	A1	(1p) black violet	32.50	100.00

See Nos. 14, 18, 22, 27, 33, 39, 43, 45, 48, 58. For surcharges see Nos. 62-64.

1852   Litho.
Fine Impressions
Yellowish Paper

9	A2	(1p) blue	11,500.	1,950.
a.		(1p) deep blue	11,500.	1,950.
b.		White paper		1,950.

1853   Bluish Paper

10	A2	(1p) blue	10,000.	2,400.

Same, Lines of Background More or Less Worn

1855-60   Thin Paper

11	A2	(1p) slate blue	5,500.	800.00
12	A2	(1p) blue	5,000.	500.00
a.		(1p) greenish blue		800.00
13	A2	(1p) rose	17.50	750.00
a.		(1p) dull red	17.50	725.00

A3

1859   Engr.   Imperf.
White Paper

14	A1	(1p) dull rose	—	—
15	A3	(1p) gray lilac	125.00	400.00
		4p dull lilac	—	—
16	A3	6p green	15,000.	525.00
17	A3	1sh slate blue	125.00	425.00

Pin-perf. 12½

18	A1	(1p) dull rose red	2,000.	70.00
a.		(1p) lake	2,250.	70.00
19	A3	4p brown lilac		1,250.
a.		4p dull purple	7,500.	1,250.
20	A3	6p deep green	3,500.	250.00
a.		6p yellow green	3,500.	250.00
21	A3	1sh black violet	9,000.	1,750.

Pin-perf. 14

22	A1	(1p) rose red	275.00	35.00
a.		(1p) carmine	325.00	37.50
23	A3	4p brown lilac	250.00	150.00
a.		4p violet	600.00	160.00
b.		4p dull violet	1,650.	125.00
24	A3	6p deep green	800.00	100.00
25	A3	6p yellow green	200.00	160.00
a.		Vert. pair, imperf. between	8,000.	
26	A3	1sh black violet	9,000.	1,150.

1860   Clean-cut Perf. 14 to 15½

27	A1	(1p) dull rose	190.00	67.50
a.		(1p) lake	100.00	40.00
b.		Horiz. pair, imperf. vert.	3,000.	
29	A3	4p violet brown	200.00	95.00
a.		4p dull violet		375.00
30	A3	6p deep green	300.00	175.00
31	A3	6p yellow green	550.00	110.00
32	A3	1sh black violet		

1861   Rough Perf. 14 to 16½

33	A1	(1p) dull rose	170.00	32.50
34	A3	4p gray lilac	750.00	100.00
35	A3	4p brown lilac	325.00	85.00
a.		4p dull violet	750.00	115.00
36	A3	6p green	475.00	85.00
a.		6p blue green	325.00	95.00
37	A3	1sh indigo	1,000.	350.00
a.		1sh purplish blue	1,675.	550.00

Thick Paper

1863   Perf. 11½ to 12

39	A1	(1p) carmine	160.00	25.00
a.		Perf. 11½-12x11	2,000.	600.00
40	A3	4p dull violet	225.00	72.50
41	A3	6p dp blue green	1,350.	100.00
a.		Perf. 11½-12x11		8,000.
42	A3	1sh indigo	2,750.	110.00

Perf. 12½

43	A1	(1p) lake	60.00	25.00

Perf. 13

45	A1	(1p) lake	50.00	25.00
46	A3	6p emerald	500.00	60.00
47	A3	1sh brt violet	4,500.	300.00

1864-72   Wmk. 1   Perf. 12½

48	A1	(1p) red	65.00	3.50
a.		(1p) lake	65.00	7.25
b.		(1p) rose	65.00	3.00
c.		(1p) carmine	70.00	3.75
d.		Imperf., pair	800.00	800.00
49	A3	4p brt violet	150.00	18.00
a.		4p pale violet	250.00	21.00
b.		Imperf.	600.00	
50	A3	4p lilac	200.00	21.00
a.		4p gray lilac		
51	A3	4p gray ('72)	160.00	7.50
52	A3	6p blue green	175.00	9.00
a.		6p emerald	110.00	17.50
53	A3	6p yellow grn	100.00	6.00
a.		6p dp grn	500.00	9.00
b.		Imperf., pair	800.00	
54	A3	1sh purple	200.00	10.00
a.		1sh lilac	150.00	10.00
b.		1sh violet	150.00	10.00
c.		1sh red lilac	160.00	11.00
d.		Imperf.	750.00	
55	A3	1sh orange yel ('72)	175.00	2.00
		Nos. 48-55 (8)	1,225.	77.00

See Nos. 59-61A, 65. For surcharge see No. 67.

Queen
Victoria — A4

1869-94   Typo.   Perf. 12½

56	A4	5sh dull lake	200.00	90.00
a.		Imperf., pair	1,250.	

Perf. 14

57	A4	5sh claret ('94)	67.50	100.00

For overprint see No. O7.

1876   Engr.   Perf. 14

58	A1	(1p) carmine	45.00	2.75
a.		(1p) red	60.00	2.75
b.		(1p) lake	45.00	2.75
c.		Half used as ½p on cover		750.00
59	A3	4p gray	140.00	1.75
60	A3	6p yellow green	120.00	4.00
		6p deep green	150.00	3.00
61	A3	1sh orange yellow	150.00	4.50
		Nos. 58-61 (4)	455.00	13.00

Perf. 14x12½

61A	A3	6p yellow green		6,750.

Value for No. 61A is for stamp with perfs barely touching the design.

Type A1 Surcharged in Black

1879   Wmk. 1   Perf. 14

62	A1	½p lilac	18.00	11.00

Same Surcharge

1882   Wmk. Crown and C A (2)

63	A1	½p lilac	250.00	90.00
64	A1	1p carmine	65.00	2.50
a.		Half used as ½p on cover		675.00

Type of 1859

1882   Wmk. 2

65	A3	4p gray	215.00	13.00

No. 60 Surcharged by pen and ink in Black or Red

1882   Wmk. 1

67	A3	1p on 6p green (R)	14.00	8.00
a.		Half used as ½p on cover		400.00
b.		Black surcharge		1,900.

Counterfeits of No. 67b are plentiful. Various handwriting exists on both 60 and 60a.

A8   A9

1883-84   Typo.   Wmk. 2

68	A7	½p green	9.50	1.50
69	A7	1p rose	20.00	.60
a.		Half used as ½p on cover		950.00
70	A7	2½p ultra	25.00	.70
a.		2½p blue	22.50	.75
71	A7	4p slate	4.00	.70
72	A7	6p olive brn ('84)	70.00	6.50
73	A7	1sh orange brn ('84)	12.00	5.50
		Nos. 68-73 (6)	77.50	15.50

For overprints see Nos. O1-O6.

A7 (illustration)

ONE ONE
Type I   Type II

ONE PENNY:
Type I — Round "O" in "ONE."

Type II — Oval "O" in "ONE."

1896-1904 — Perf. 14

No	Type	Description	Unused	Used
74	A8	½p lilac & green	4.00	.35
75	A8	1p gray grn ('02)	1.00	2.40
76	A8	1p lil & car, type I	4.25	.25
77	A8	1p lil & car, type II ('00)	400.00	4.75
78	A8	1p blk, red, type II ('01)	3.50	.25
a.		Value omitted	36,000.	
79	A8	2½p lilac & ultra	7.25	.25
80	A8	2½p vio & bl, bl ('02)	22.50	.75
81	A8	4p lilac & orange	7.75	22.50
82	A8	4p grn & ultra, buff ('02)	2.25	21.00
83	A8	5p lilac & violet	9.50	16.00
84	A8	6p lilac & black	9.00	6.50
85	A8	1sh grn & org brn	8.25	7.75
86	A8	1sh blk & blk, yel ('04)	22.50	6.50

Wmk. C A over Crown (46)

87	A9	5sh green & org	55.00	90.00
88	A9	5sh lil & red vio ('02)	60.00	77.50
89	A9	10sh grn & blk	250.00	425.00
		Revenue cancel		30.00
90	A9	£1 grn & car	180.00	275.00
		Nos. 74-90 (17)	1,046.	956.75

No. 82 also exists on chalky paper. Values: unused $3.50, used $14. Nos. 88 and 90 exist on both ordinary and chalky paper.
Circular "Registrar General" cancels are revenue usage and of minimal value.
See Nos. 92-104.

Landing of Columbus — A10

1898 — Engr. — Wmk. 1

91	A10	2p gray vio & yel brn	2.50	1.25
		Overprinted "SPECIMEN"	60.00	

400th anniv. of the discovery of the island of Trinidad by Columbus, July 31, 1498.

1904-09 — Wmk. 3 — Chalky Paper

92	A8	½p gray green	9.00	2.25
a.		Ordinary paper	7.00	1.25
93	A8	1p blk, red, type II	11.00	.25
a.		Ordinary paper	11.00	.25
94	A8	2½p vio & bl, bl	27.50	1.10
95	A8	4p blk & car, yel ('06)	5.00	12.00
96	A8	6p lilac & blk ('05)	21.00	18.00
97	A8	6p vio & dp vio ('06)	8.50	15.00
98	A8	1sh blk & bl, yel	24.00	9.50
99	A8	1sh vio & bl, yel	14.00	24.00
100	A8	1sh blk, grn ('06)	2.25	1.50
101	A9	5sh lil & red vio ('07)	70.00	110.00
102	A9	£1 grn & car ('07)	225.00	300.00
		Nos. 92-102 (11)	417.25	493.60

For overprints see Nos. O8-O9.

1906-07

103	A8	1p carmine ('07)	9.50	.25
104	A8	2½p ultramarine	7.00	.25

A11   A12

1909 — Ordinary Paper

105	A11	½p gray green	9.00	.25
106	A12	1p carmine	9.00	.25
107	A11	2½p ultramarine	24.00	3.75
		Nos. 105-107 (3)	42.00	4.25

For overprint see No. O10.

POSTAGE DUE STAMPS

D1

Wmk. Crown and C A (2)
1885, Jan. 1 — Typo. — Perf. 14

J1	D1	½p black	22.50	55.00
J2	D1	1p black	11.00	.25
J3	D1	2p black	42.50	.25
J4	D1	3p black	60.00	.50
J5	D1	4p black	50.00	6.00
J6	D1	5p black	27.50	.70
J7	D1	6p black	47.50	10.00
J8	D1	8p black	65.00	4.00
J9	D1	1sh black	80.00	9.00
		Nos. J1-J9 (9)	406.00	85.70

1906-07 — Wmk. 3

J10	D1	1p black	8.00	.25
J11	D1	2p black	37.50	.25
J12	D1	3p black	15.00	3.25
J13	D1	4p black	15.00	19.00
J14	D1	5p black	17.50	19.00
J15	D1	6p black	7.25	14.00
J16	D1	8p black	16.00	18.00
J17	D1	1sh black	22.50	42.50
		Nos. J10-J17 (8)	138.75	116.25

See Trinidad and Tobago Nos. J1-J16.

OFFICIAL STAMPS

Postage Stamps of 1869-84 Overprinted in Black

O S

1893-94 — Wmk. 2 — Perf. 14

O1	A7	½p green	42.50	65.00
O2	A7	1p rose	45.00	72.50
O3	A7	2½p ultra	55.00	110.00
O4	A7	4p slate	57.50	115.00
O5	A7	6p olive brown	57.50	115.00
O6	A7	1sh orange brown	77.50	160.00

Wmk. Crown and C C (1)
Perf. 12½

O7	A4	5sh dull lake	190.00	750.00
		Nos. O1-O7 (7)	525.00	1,387.

Nos. 92 and 103 Overprinted

OFFICIAL

1909-10 — Wmk. 3 — Perf. 14

O8	A8	½p gray green	2.75	9.00
O9	A8	1p carmine	2.50	10.00
a.		Double overprint		375.00
b.		Inverted overprint	900.00	275.00
c.		Vertical overprint	140.00	160.00

Same Overprint on No. 105

1910

O10	A11	½p gray green	9.50	13.50

Stamps of Trinidad have been superseded by those inscribed "Trinidad and Tobago."

TRINIDAD & TOBAGO

ˈtri-nə-ˌdad and tə-ˈbā-ˌgō

LOCATION — West Indies off the coast of Venezuela
GOVT. — British Colony
AREA — 1,980 sq. mi.
POP. — 1,160,000 (est. 1984)
CAPITAL — Port-of-Spain

The two British colonies of Trinidad and Tobago were united from 1889 until 1899, when Tobago became a ward of the united colony. From 1899 until

1913 postage stamps of Trinidad were used.

12 Pence = 1 Shilling
20 Shillings = 1 Pound
100 Cents = 1 Dollar (1935)

Catalogue values for unused stamps in this country are for Never Hinged items, beginning with Scott 62 in the regular postage section and Scott J9 in the postage due section.

"Britannia"

A1   A2

1913 — Typo. — Wmk. 3 — Perf. 14
Ordinary Paper

1	A1	½p green	3.50	.25
2	A1	1p scarlet	1.75	.25
a.		1p carmine	2.75	.25
4	A1	2½p ultra	8.00	.50

Chalky Paper

5	A1	4p scar & blk, yel	.80	7.00
6	A1	6p red vio & dull vio	11.00	8.00
7	A1	1sh black, emerald	1.75	3.50
a.		1sh black, green	2.00	5.00
b.		1sh black, bl grn, ol back	13.00	10.00
		Nos. 1-2,4-7 (6)	26.80	19.50

1914 — Surface-colored Paper

8	A1	4p scar & blk, yel	2.00	11.00
9	A1	1sh black, green	1.60	12.00

Chalky Paper

10	A2	5sh dull vio & red vio	75.00	110.00
11	A2	£1 green & car	225.00	275.00
		Nos. 8-11 (4)	303.60	408.00

1921-22 — Ordinary Paper — Wmk. 4

12	A1	½p green	3.50	2.75
13	A1	1p scarlet	.75	.40
14	A1	1p brown ('22)	.75	1.90
15	A1	2p gray ('22)	1.25	1.50
16	A1	2½p ultra	1.00	22.50
17	A1	3p ultra ('22)	6.50	.90

Chalky Paper

18	A1	6p red vio & dull vio	4.25	19.00
19	A2	5sh dull vio & red vio	70.00	170.00
20	A2	£1 green & car	170.00	350.00
		Nos. 12-20 (9)	258.00	572.05

For overprints see #B2-B3, MR1-MR13, O1-O5.

"Britannia" and King George V — A3

1922-28 — Ordinary Paper

21	A3	½p green	.55	.25
22	A3	1p brown	.55	.25
23	A3	1½p rose red	2.75	.25
24	A3	2p gray	.55	1.40
25	A3	3p ultra	.55	1.40

Chalky Paper

26	A3	4p red & blk, yel ('28)	3.75	3.75
27	A3	6p red vio & dl vio	2.50	29.00
28	A3	6p red & grn, emer ('24)	1.40	.70
29	A3	1sh blk, emer ('25)	6.25	2.00
30	A3	5sh vio & dull vio	26.00	42.50
31	A3	£1 rose & green	150.00	275.00

Wmk. Multiple Crown and C A (3)
Chalky Paper

32	A3	4p red & blk, yel	3.75	17.00
33	A3	1sh blk, emerald	4.00	11.00
		Nos. 21-33 (13)	202.60	384.50

First Boca — A4

Designs: 2c, Agricultural College. 3c, Mt. Irvine Bay, Tobago. 6c, Discovery of Lake Asphalt. 8c, Queen's Park, Savannah. 12c, Town Hall. 24c, Government House. 48c, Memorial Park. 72c, Blue Basin.

1935-37 — Engr. — Wmk. 4 — Perf. 12

34	A4	1c emer & bl, perf. 12½ ('36)	.40	.25
a.		Perf. 12	.50	1.10
35	A4	2c lt brn & ultra, perf. 12	2.00	1.25
a.		Perf. 12½ ('36)	1.75	.25
36	A4	3c red & black, perf. 12½ ('36)	3.25	.40
a.		Perf. 12	2.75	.40
37	A4	6c bl & brn, perf. 12	5.00	3.00
a.		Perf. 12½ ('37)	13.00	7.50
38	A4	8c red org & yel grn	4.50	4.25
39	A4	12c dk violet & blk	14.00	2.25
a.		Perf. 12½ ('37)	9.50	9.50
40	A4	24c ol grn & blk	8.00	2.75
a.		Perf. 12½ ('37)	22.50	16.00
41	A4	48c slate green	11.00	19.00
42	A4	72c mag & sl grn	40.00	40.00
		Nos. 34-42 (9)	78.15	73.15

Common Design Types pictured following the introduction.

Silver Jubilee Issue
Common Design Type
1935, May 6 — Perf. 11x12

43	CD301	2c black & ultra	.40	1.00
44	CD301	3c car & blue	.40	2.25
45	CD301	6c ultra & brn	2.00	2.50
46	CD301	24c brn vio & ind	9.50	22.00
		Nos. 43-46 (4)	12.30	27.75
		Set, never hinged	22.00	

Coronation Issue
Common Design Type
1937, May 12 — Perf. 13½x14

47	CD302	1c deep green	.25	.25
48	CD302	2c yellow brown	.25	.25
49	CD302	8c deep orange	.50	.50
		Nos. 47-49 (3)	1.00	1.00
		Set, never hinged	1.50	

First Boca — A13

George VI — A14

Various Frames and: 2c, Agricultural College. 3c, Mt. Irvine Bay, Tobago. 4c, Memorial Park. 5c, General Post Office and Treasury. 6c, Discovery of Lake Asphalt. 8c, Queen's Park, Savannah. 12c, Town Hall, San Fernando. 24c, Government House. 60c, Blue Basin.

Perf. 11½x11
1938-41 — Wmk. 4 — Engr.

50	A13	1c emer & blue	.50	.25
51	A13	2c lt brn & ultra	.60	.25
52	A13	3c dk car & blk	7.50	1.00
52A	A13	3c vio brn & bl ('41)	.25	.25
53	A13	4c brown	19.00	2.50
53A	A13	4c red ('41)	.30	.25
54	A13	5c mag ('41)	.30	.25
55	A13	6c brt bl & sep	1.25	.75
56	A13	8c red org & yel grn	1.50	1.00
57	A13	12c dk vio & blk	2.00	.25
58	A13	24c dk ol grn & blk	2.75	.25
59	A13	60c mag & sl grn	7.00	1.75

Perf. 12

60	A14	$1.20 dk grn ('40)	8.50	1.50
61	A14	$4.80 rose pink ('40)	24.00	50.00

Nos. 50-61 (14) 75.45 60.25
Set, never hinged 125.00

Watermark sideways on Nos. 50-59.

> Catalogue values for unused stamps in this section, from this point to the end of the section, are for Never Hinged items.

Peace Issue
Common Design Type
Perf. 13½x14

1946, Oct. 1   Engr.   Wmk. 4

62	CD303	3c brown	.25	.25
63	CD303	6c deep blue	.25	.25

Silver Wedding Issue
Common Design Types
1948, Nov. 22 Photo. Perf. 14x14½

64	CD304	3c red brown	.25	.25

Perf. 11½x11
Engr.

65	CD305	$4.80 rose car	32.50	38.00

UPU Issue
Common Design Types
Engr.; Name Typo. on 6c, 12c
Perf. 13½, 11x11½

1949, Oct. 10   Wmk. 4

66	CD306	5c red violet	.35	.35
67	CD307	6c indigo	1.90	1.90
68	CD308	12c rose violet	.45	.45
69	CD309	24c olive	.45	.45

Nos. 66-69 (4) 3.15 3.15

University Issue
Common Design Types
Inscribed: "Trinidad"

1951, Feb. 16 Engr. Perf. 14x14½

70	CD310	3c chocolate & grn	.25	.25
71	CD311	12c purple & blk	.50	.50

SEMI-POSTAL STAMPS

Emblem of
Red Cross
SP1

Perf. 11, 12
1914, Sept. 18   Typo.   Unwmk.

B1	SP1	(½p) red (on cover)	250.00

This stamp was allowed to pay ½p postage on one day, Sept. 18, 1914, on circulars distributed by the Red Cross. Value on cover is for proper Red Cross usage. Value unused, $15.

No. 2 Overprinted in Red (Cross) and Black (Date)

a   b

1915, Oct. 21   Wmk. 3   Perf. 14

B2	A1 (a) 1p scarlet	2.25	2.25

1916, Oct. 19

B3	A1 (b) 1p scarlet		.80 3.25
a.	Date omitted		

POSTAGE DUE STAMPS

D1

1923-45 Typo. Wmk. 4 Perf. 14

J1	D1	1p black	3.75	3.75
J2	D1	2p black	7.00	1.90
J3	D1	3p black ('25)	7.00	5.00
J4	D1	4p black ('29)	7.00	27.50
J5	D1	5p black ('45)	42.50	110.00
J6	D1	6p black ('45)	75.00	42.50
J7	D1	8p black ('45)	52.50	200.00
J8	D1	1sh black ('45)	90.00	140.00

Nos. J1-J8 (8) 284.75 530.65

> Catalogue values for unused stamps in this section, from this point to the end of the section, are for Never Hinged items.

Denominations in Cents
1947, Sept. 1

J9	D1	2c black	2.50	3.25
J10	D1	4c black	1.50	4.50
J11	D1	6c black	1.90	9.00
J12	D1	8c black	1.90	27.50
J13	D1	10c black	1.90	4.00
J14	D1	12c black	1.90	22.50
J15	D1	16c black	3.50	52.50
J16	D1	24c black	12.50	11.00

Nos. J9-J16 (8) 27.60 134.25

Nos. J9-J16 also exist on chalky paper.

Wmk. 4a (error)

J9a	D1	2c	60.00
J11a	D1	6c	125.00
J14a	D1	12c	150.00

WAR TAX STAMPS

Nos. 1-2 Overprinted

1917   Wmk. 3   Perf. 14

MR1	A1	1p scarlet	4.00	4.25
a.	Invtd. overprint		225.00	300.00

Overprinted

MR2	A1	½p green	1.50	.40
a.	Overprinted on face and back		425.00	
b.	Pair, one without overprint		275.00	
MR3	A1	1p scarlet	1.25	2.25
a.	Pair, one without overprint		425.00	800.00
b.	Double overprint		125.00	

Overprinted

MR4	A1	½p green	.30	6.50
MR5	A1	1p scarlet	.30	1.00

Overprinted

MR6	A1	½p green	.30	3.25
MR7	A1	1p scarlet	3.50	1.25

Overprinted

MR8	A1	½p green	.30	3.25
MR9	A1	1p scarlet	35.00	27.50

Overprinted

MR10	A1	1p scarlet	.80	1.40
a.	Inverted overprint		100.00	100.00

Overprinted

MR11	A1	1p scarlet	1.75	.30
a.	Double overprint		200.00	200.00
b.	Inverted overprint		125.00	125.00

Overprinted

1918

MR12	A1	½p green	.30	2.00
MR13	A1	1p scarlet	.90	1.75
a.	Double overprint		125.00	
b.	Horiz. pair, one without overprint		1,000.	

The War Tax Stamps show considerable variations in the colors, thickness of the paper, distinctness of the watermark, and the gum. Counterfeits exist of the errors of Nos. MR1-MR13.

OFFICIAL STAMPS

Regular Issue of 1913
Overprinted

1913   Wmk. 3   Perf. 14

O1	A1	½p green	1.50	14.00

Same Overprinted

1914

O2	A1	½p green	3.25	20.00

Same Overprinted

1916

O3	A1	½p green	4.00	7.50
a.	Double overprint		50.00	

Same Overprint without Period

1917

O4	A1	½p green	4.75	22.50

Same Overprinted

1917, Aug. 22

O5	A1	½p green	5.00	25.00

The official stamps are found in several shades of green and on paper of varying thickness.

TRIPOLITANIA

tri-ˌpä-lə-'tä-nyə

LOCATION — In northern Africa, bordering on Mediterranean Sea
GOVT. — Italian Colony
AREA — 350,000 sq. mi. (approx.)
POP. — 570,716 (1921)
CAPITAL — Tripoli

Formerly a Turkish province, Tripolitania became part of Italian Libya. See Libya.

100 Centesimi = 1 Lira

Watermark

Wmk. 140 —
Crowns

Propaganda of the Faith Issue
Italian Stamps Overprinted

1923, Oct. 24   Wmk. 140   Perf. 14

1	A68	20c ol grn & brn org	11.00	47.50
		Never hinged	28.00	
		On cover		—
2	A68	30c claret & brn org	11.00	47.50
		Never hinged	28.00	
		On cover		—
a.		Double overprint	2,250.	
		Never hinged	3,500.	
b.		Vert. pair, imperf. btwn and at bottom	1,100.	1,650.
		Never hinged	1,650.	
3	A68	50c vio & brn org	7.50	55.00
		Never hinged	19.00	
		On cover		—
4	A68	1 l blue & brn org	7.50	85.00
		Never hinged	19.00	
		On cover		—
		Nos. 1-4 (4)	37.00	235.00
		Set, never hinged	92.50	

Fascisti Issue

Italian Stamps Overprinted in Red or Black

1923, Oct. 29   Unwmk.

5	A69	10c dk green (R)	15.00	18.50
		Never hinged	37.50	
		On cover		300.00
6	A69	30c dk violet (R)	15.00	18.50
		Never hinged	37.50	
		On cover		300.00
7	A69	50c brown car	15.00	18.50
		Never hinged	37.50	
		On cover		300.00

Wmk. 140

8	A70	1 l blue	15.00	47.50
		Never hinged	37.50	
		On cover		575.00
9	A70	2 l brown	15.00	60.00
		Never hinged	37.50	
		On cover		825.00
a.		Double overprint	1,650.	
		Never hinged	2,500.	
10	A71	5 l blk & bl (R)	15.00	90.00
		Never hinged	37.50	
		On cover		—
		Nos. 5-10 (6)	90.00	253.00
		Set, never hinged	225.00	
		Set on overfranked philatelic cover		750.00

Manzoni Issue
Stamps of Italy, 1923, Overprinted in Red

1924, Apr. 1   Wmk. 140   Perf. 14

11	A72	10c brown red & blk	12.00	75.00
		Never hinged	30.00	
		On cover		—
12	A72	15c blue grn & blk	12.00	75.00
		Never hinged	30.00	
		On cover		—
13	A72	30c black & slate	12.00	75.00
		Never hinged	30.00	
		On cover		—
a.		Imperf.	—	
		Never hinged	—	
14	A72	50c org brn & blk	12.00	75.00
		Never hinged	30.00	
		On cover		—
a.		Line perf. 14	825.00	
		Never hinged	2,100.	
15	A72	1 l blue & blk	75.00	450.00
		Never hinged	185.00	
a.		Line perf. 14	825.00	
		Never hinged	2,100.	
16	A72	5 l violet & blk	500.00	3,000.
		Never hinged	1,225.	
a.		Line perf. 14	2,000.	
		Never hinged	5,000.	
		Nos. 11-16 (6)	623.00	3,750.
		Set, never hinged	1,530.	

On Nos. 15 and 16 the overprint is placed vertically at the left side.
Nos. 11-16 are comb perforated.

Victor Emmanuel Issue

Italy Nos. 175-177 Overprinted

1925-26   Unwmk.   Perf. 11

17	A78	60c brown car	2.25	13.50
		Never hinged	5.50	
		On cover		225.00
18	A78	1 l dark blue	3.00	13.50
		Never hinged	7.50	
		On cover		300.00
a.		Perf. 13½	10.50	42.50
		Never hinged	26.00	
		On cover		375.00

Perf. 13½

19	A78	1.25 l dk blue ('26)	3.75	37.50
		Never hinged	9.25	
		On cover		600.00
a.		Perf. 11	2,000.	2,600.
		Never hinged	4,000.	
		On cover		—
		Nos. 17-19 (3)	9.00	64.50
		Set, #17-19, 18a, 19a, never hinged	4,000.	

Saint Francis of Assisi Issue
Italy Nos. 178-180 Overprinted

1926, Apr. 12   Wmk. 140   Perf. 14

20	A79	20c gray green	2.25	13.50
		Never hinged	5.50	
		On cover		120.00
a.		Vert. pair, one without ovpt.	5,250.	
		Never hinged	8,000.	
21	A80	40c dark violet	2.25	13.50
		Never hinged	5.50	
		On cover		140.00
22	A81	60c red brown	2.25	26.00
		Never hinged	5.50	
		On cover		140.00

Italy No. 182 and Type of A83 Overprinted in Red

Unwmk.

23	A82	1.25 l dark blue	2.25	35.00
		Never hinged	5.50	
		On cover		260.00
24	A83	5 l + 2.50 l ol grn	7.50	67.50
		Never hinged	19.00	
		On cover		—
a.		Horiz. pair, imperf. btwn.	2,250.	
		Never hinged	3,500.	
		Nos. 20-24 (5)	16.50	155.50
		Set, never hinged	25.00	
		Set on overfranked philatelic cover		425.00

Volta Issue

Type of Italy Overprinted

1927, Oct. 10   Wmk. 140   Perf. 14

25	A84	20c purple	4.50	37.50
		Never hinged	11.00	
		On cover		260.00
26	A84	50c deep orange	7.50	26.00
		Never hinged	18.50	
		On cover		260.00
a.		Double overprint	190.00	
		Never hinged	275.00	
b.		As "a," one ovpt. inverted	525.00	
		Never hinged	800.00	
27	A84	1.25 l brt blue	13.50	60.00
		Never hinged	34.00	
		On cover		500.00
		Nos. 25-27 (3)	25.50	123.50
		Set, never hinged	62.50	
		Set on overfranked philatelic cover		350.00

Monte Cassino Issue
Types of Italy Overprinted in Red or Blue

1929, Oct. 14

28	A96	20c dk green (R)	6.00	21.00
		Never hinged	15.00	
		On cover		260.00
29	A96	25c red org (Bl)	6.00	21.00
		Never hinged	15.00	
		On cover		190.00
30	A98	50c + 10c crim (Bl)	6.00	22.50
		Never hinged	15.00	
		On cover		150.00
31	A98	75c + 15c ol brn (R)	6.00	22.50
		Never hinged	15.00	
		On cover		275.00
32	A96	1.25 l + 25c dk vio (R)	13.50	42.50
		Never hinged	34.00	
		On cover		325.00
33	A98	5 l + 1 l saph (R)	13.50	45.00
		Never hinged	34.00	
		On cover		—

Overprinted in Red

Unwmk.

34	A100	10 l + 2 l gray brn	13.50	67.50
		Never hinged	34.00	
		On cover		—
		Nos. 28-34 (7)	64.50	242.00
		Set, never hinged	160.00	
		Set on overfranked philatelic cover		450.00

Royal Wedding Issue

Type of Italy Overprinted

1930, Mar. 17   Wmk. 140

35	A101	20c yellow green	3.00	9.00
		Never hinged	7.50	
		On cover		125.00
36	A101	50c + 10c dp org	2.25	9.00
		Never hinged	5.75	
		On cover		180.00
37	A101	1.25 l + 25c rose red	2.25	18.00
		Never hinged	5.75	
		On cover		280.00
		Nos. 35-37 (3)	7.50	36.00
		Set, never hinged	19.00	
		Set on overfranked philatelic cover		160.00

Ferrucci Issue

Types of Italy Overprinted in Red or Blue

1930, July 26

38	A102	20c violet (R)	6.00	6.00
		Never hinged	15.00	
		On cover		150.00
39	A103	25c dk green (R)	6.00	6.00
		Never hinged	15.00	
		On cover		180.00
40	A103	50c black (R)	6.00	11.00
		Never hinged	15.00	
		On cover		150.00
41	A103	1.25 l deep blue (R)	6.00	21.00
		Never hinged	15.00	
		On cover		350.00
42	A104	5 l + 2 l dp car (Bl)	13.50	45.00
		Never hinged	34.00	
		On cover		—
		Nos. 38-42,C1-C3 (8)	73.50	196.00
		Set, never hinged	180.00	
		Nos. 38-42 on overfranked philatelic cover		260.00

Virgil Issue

Types of Italy Overprinted in Red or Blue

1930, Dec. 4   Photo.

43	A106	15c violet black	1.10	11.50
		Never hinged	2.75	
		On cover		165.00
44	A106	20c orange brown	1.10	4.50
		Never hinged	2.75	
		On cover		100.00
45	A106	25c dark green	1.10	4.50
		Never hinged	2.75	
		On cover		90.00
46	A106	30c lt brown	1.10	4.50
		Never hinged	2.75	
		On cover		95.00
47	A106	50c dull violet	1.10	4.50
		Never hinged	2.75	
		On cover		75.00
48	A106	75c rose red	1.10	9.00
		Never hinged	2.75	
		On cover		190.00
49	A106	1.25 l gray blue	1.10	11.50
		Never hinged	2.75	
		On cover		275.00

Unwmk.
Engr.

50	A106	5 l + 1.50 l dk vio	4.50	45.00
		Never hinged	11.00	
51	A106	10 l + 2.50 l ol brn	4.50	67.50
		Never hinged	11.00	
		Nos. 43-51,C4-C7 (13)	37.70	306.50
		Set, never hinged	90.00	
		Nos. 43-51 on overfranked philatelic cover		450.00

Saint Anthony of Padua Issue

Types of Italy Overprinted in Blue or Red

1931, May 7 Photo. Wmk. 140

52	A116	20c brown (Bl)	1.50	21.00
		Never hinged	3.75	
		On cover		110.00
53	A116	25c green (R)	1.50	7.50
		Never hinged	3.75	
		On cover		110.00
54	A118	30c gray blk (Bl)	1.50	7.75
		Never hinged	3.75	
		On cover		175.00
55	A118	50c dull vio (Bl)	1.50	7.50
		Never hinged	3.75	
		On cover		115.00
56	A120	1.25 l slate bl (R)	1.50	37.50
		Never hinged	3.75	
		On cover		375.00

Overprinted in Red or Black

Unwmk. Engr.

57	A121	75c black (R)	1.50	21.00
		Never hinged	3.75	
		On cover		300.00
58	A122	5 l + 2.50 l dk brn (Bk)	10.50	75.00
		Never hinged	26.00	
		On cover		—
		Nos. 52-58 (7)	19.50	177.00
		Set, never hinged	47.50	
		Set on overfranked philatelic cover		500.00

Native Village Scene A14

1934, Oct. 16 Wmk. 140

73	A14	5c ol grn & brn	5.25	21.00
		Never hinged	13.00	
		On cover		330.00
74	A14	10c brown & black	5.25	21.00
		Never hinged	13.00	
		On cover		280.00
75	A14	20c scar & indigo	5.25	19.00
		Never hinged	13.00	
		On cover		280.00
76	A14	50c purple & brown	5.25	19.00
		Never hinged	13.00	
		On cover		340.00
77	A14	60c org brn & ind	5.25	26.00
		Never hinged	13.00	
		On cover		375.00
78	A14	1.25 l dk bl & grn	5.25	45.00
		Never hinged	13.00	
		On cover		525.00
		Nos. 73-78,C43-C48 (12)	63.00	302.00
		Set, never hinged	155.00	
		Nos. 73-78 on overfranked philatelic cover		350.00

2nd Colonial Arts Exhibition, Naples.

SEMI-POSTAL STAMPS

Many issues of Italy and Italian Colonies include one or more semipostal denominations. To avoid splitting sets, these issues are generally listed as regular postage, airmail, etc., unless all values carry a surtax.

Holy Year Issue

Italian Stamps of 1924 Overprinted in Black or Red

1925 Wmk. 140 Perf. 12

B1	SP4	20c+ 10c dk grn & brn	3.75	22.50
		Never hinged	9.25	
		On cover		200.00
B2	SP4	30c+ 15c dk brn &	3.75	31.00
		Never hinged	9.25	
		On cover		200.00
B3	SP4	50c+ 25c vio & brn	3.75	22.50
		Never hinged	9.25	
		On cover		200.00
B4	SP4	60c+ 30c dp rose & brn	3.75	30.00
		Never hinged	9.25	
		On cover		280.00
B5	SP8	1 l + 50c dp bl & vio (R)	3.75	37.50
		Never hinged	9.25	
		On cover		—
B6	SP8	5 l + 2.50 l org brn & vio (R)	3.75	57.50
		Never hinged	9.25	
		On cover		—
		Nos. B1-B6 (6)	22.50	194.00
		Set, never hinged	55.00	
		Set on overfranked philatelic cover		475.00

Colonial Institute Issue

Peace Substituting Spade for Sword — SP1

1926, June 1 Typo. Perf. 14

B7	SP1	5c + 5c brown	1.10	9.50
		Never hinged	2.75	
		On cover		175.00
B8	SP1	10c + 5c ol brn	1.10	9.50
		Never hinged	2.75	
		On cover		135.00
B9	SP1	20c + 5c bl grn	1.10	9.50
		Never hinged	2.75	
		On cover		105.00
B10	SP1	40c + 5c brn red	1.10	9.50
		Never hinged	2.75	
		On cover		105.00
B11	SP1	60c + 5c orange	1.10	9.50
		Never hinged	2.75	
		On cover		175.00
B12	SP1	1 l + 5c blue	1.10	20.00
		Never hinged	2.75	
		On cover		275.00
		Nos. B7-B12 (6)	6.60	67.50
		Set, never hinged	16.50	
		Set on overfranked philatelic cover		260.00

The surtax was for the Italian Colonial Institute.

Fiera Campionaria Tripoli
See Libya for stamps with this inscription.

Types of Italian Semi-Postal Stamps of 1926 Overprinted like Nos. 17-19

1927, Apr. 21 Unwmk. Perf. 11

B19	SP10	40c + 20c dk brn & blk	3.75	40.00
		Never hinged	9.25	
		On cover		180.00
B20	SP10	60c + 30c brn red & ol brn	3.75	40.00
		Never hinged	9.25	
		On cover		210.00
B21	SP10	1.25 l + 60c dp bl & blk	3.75	60.00
		Never hinged	9.25	
		On cover		375.00
B22	SP10	5 l + 2.50 l dk grn & blk	6.00	92.50
		Never hinged		—
		Nos. B19-B22 (4)	17.25	232.50
		Set, never hinged	42.50	
		Set on overfranked philatelic cover		575.00

The surtax was for the charitable work of the Voluntary Militia for Italian National Defense.

Allegory of Fascism and Victory — SP2

1928, Oct. 15 Wmk. 140

B29	SP2	20c + 5c bl grn	3.25	13.50
		Never hinged	7.50	
		On cover		180.00
B30	SP2	30c + 5c red	3.25	13.50
		Never hinged	7.50	
		On cover		100.00
B31	SP2	50c + 10c pur	3.25	22.50
		Never hinged	7.50	
		On cover		180.00
B32	SP2	1.25 l + 20c dk bl	4.00	30.00
		Never hinged	9.50	
		On cover		500.00
		Nos. B29-B32 (4)	13.75	79.50
		Set, never hinged	32.50	
		Set on overfranked philatelic cover		300.00

46th anniv. of the Societa Africana d'Italia. The surtax aided that society.

Types of Italian Semi-Postal Stamps of 1928 Ovptd.

1929, Mar. 4 Unwmk. Perf. 11

B33	SP10	30c + 10c red & blk	4.50	26.00
		Never hinged	11.00	
		On cover		210.00
B34	SP10	50c + 20c vio & blk	4.50	28.00
		Never hinged	11.00	
		On cover		210.00
B35	SP10	1.25 l + 50c brn & bl	6.75	50.00
		Never hinged	17.00	
		On cover		450.00
B36	SP10	5 l + 2 l ol grn & blk	6.75	97.50
		Never hinged	17.00	
		Nos. B33-B36 (4)	22.50	201.50
		Set, never hinged	55.00	
		Set on overfranked philatelic cover		575.00

The surtax on these stamps was for the charitable work of the Voluntary Militia for Italian National Defense.

Types of Italian Semi-Postal Stamps of 1926, Overprinted in Black or Red Like Nos. B33-B36

1930, Oct. 20

B50	SP10	30c + 10c dp grn & bl grn (Bk)	35.00	52.50
		Never hinged	85.00	
		On cover		300.00
B51	SP10	50c + 10c dk grn & vio (R)	35.00	97.50
		Never hinged	85.00	
		On cover		340.00
B52	SP10	1.25 l + 30c blk brn & red brn (R)	35.00	97.50
		Never hinged	85.00	
		On cover		525.00
B53	SP10	5 l + 1.50 l ind & grn (R)	110.00	260.00
		Never hinged	280.00	
		On cover		—
		Nos. B50-B53 (4)	215.00	507.50
		Set, never hinged	525.00	
		Set on overfranked philatelic cover		1,000.

Ancient Arch — SP3

1930, Nov. 27 Photo. Wmk. 140

B54	SP3	50c + 20c ol brn	3.75	24.00
		Never hinged	9.25	
		On cover		200.00
B55	SP3	1.25 l + 20c dp bl	3.75	24.00
		Never hinged	9.25	
		On cover		280.00
B56	SP3	1.75 l + 20c green	3.75	32.50
		Never hinged	9.25	
		On cover		350.00
B57	SP3	2.55 l + 50c purple	9.00	45.00
		Never hinged	22.50	
		On cover		575.00
B58	SP3	5 l + 1 l deep car	9.00	92.50
		Never hinged	22.50	
		On cover		—
		Nos. B54-B58 (5)	29.25	218.00

Set, never hinged	72.50	
Set on overfranked philatelic cover		350.00

25th anniv. of the Italian Colonial Agricultural Institute. The surtax was for the benefit of that institution.

AIR POST STAMPS

Ferrucci Issue

Type of Italian Air Post Stamps Overprinted in Blue or Red like #38-42

1930, July 26 Wmk. 140 Perf. 14

C1	AP7	50c brown vio (Bl)	6.00	13.50
		Never hinged	15.00	
		On cover		225.00
C2	AP7	1 l dk blue (R)	6.00	18.50
		Never hinged	15.00	
		On cover		375.00
C3	AP7	5 l + 2 l dp car (Bl)	24.00	75.00
		Never hinged	60.00	
		On cover		—
		Nos. C1-C3 (3)	25.00	76.50
		Set, never hinged	90.00	
		Set, on flown cover		425.00

Virgil Issue

Types of Italian Air Post Stamps Overprinted in Red or Blue like #43-51

1930, Dec. 4 Photo.

C4	AP8	50c deep green	2.25	12.00
		Never hinged	5.50	
		On cover		180.00
C5	AP8	1 l rose red	2.25	12.00
		Never hinged	5.50	
		On cover		240.00

Unwmk. Engr.

C6	AP8	7.70 l + 1.30 l dk brn	8.25	60.00
		Never hinged	20.00	
		On cover		575.00
C7	AP8	9 l + 2 l gray	8.25	60.00
		Never hinged	20.00	
		On cover		900.00
		Nos. C4-C7 (4)	17.80	126.00
		Set, never hinged	50.00	
		Set, on flown cover		400.00

Airplane over Columns of the Basilica, Leptis — AP1

Arab Horseman Pointing at Airplane AP2

1931-32 Photo. Wmk. 140

C8	AP1	50c rose car	.75	.25
		Never hinged	1.90	
		On cover		2.50
C9	AP1	60c red org	2.25	10.50
		Never hinged	5.50	
		On cover		165.00
C10	AP1	75c dp bl ('32)	2.25	9.00
		Never hinged	5.50	
		On cover		120.00
C11	AP1	80c dull violet	12.00	16.50
		Never hinged	30.00	
		On cover		240.00
C12	AP2	1 l deep blue	1.50	.25
		Never hinged	3.75	
		On cover		5.50
C13	AP2	1.20 l dk brown	30.00	22.50
		Never hinged	75.00	
		On cover		300.00
C14	AP2	1.50 l org red	13.50	22.50
		Never hinged	34.00	
		On cover		350.00
C15	AP2	5 l green	35.00	35.00
		Never hinged	85.00	
		On cover		750.00
		Nos. C8-C15 (8)	97.25	116.50
		Set, never hinged	210.00	

For surcharges and overprint see Nos. C29-C32.

Agricultural Institute, 25th Anniv. AP3

1931, Dec. 7

C16	AP3	50c	dp blue	3.00	24.00
		Never hinged		7.50	
		On cover			280.00
C17	AP3	80c	violet	3.00	24.00
		Never hinged		7.50	
		On cover			340.00
C18	AP3	1 l	gray black	3.00	35.00
		Never hinged		7.50	
		On cover			450.00
C19	AP3	2 l	deep green	9.00	45.00
		Never hinged		22.50	
		On cover			750.00
C20	AP3	5 l + 2 l	rose red	13.50	92.50
		Never hinged		35.00	
		On cover			—
		Nos. C16-C20 (5)		31.50	220.50
		Set, never hinged		80.00	
		Set, on flown cover			400.00

Graf Zeppelin Issue

Mercury, by Giovanni da Bologna, and
Zeppelin
AP4

Designs: 3 l, 12 l, Mercury. 10 l, 20 l, Guido
Reni's "Aurora." 5 l, 15 l, Arch of Marcus
Aurelius.

1933, May 5

C21	AP4	3 l	dark brown	12.00	120.00
		Never hinged		30.00	
		On cover			400.00
C22	AP4	5 l	purple	12.00	120.00
		Never hinged		30.00	
		On cover			550.00
C23	AP4	10 l	deep green	12.00	225.00
		Never hinged		30.00	
		On cover			825.00
C24	AP4	12 l	deep blue	12.00	240.00
		Never hinged		30.00	
		On cover			1,050.00
C25	AP4	15 l	carmine	12.00	260.00
		Never hinged		30.00	
		On cover			1,050.00
C26	AP4	20 l	gray black	12.00	350.00
		Never hinged		30.00	
		On cover			1,050.00
		Nos. C21-C26 (6)		72.00	1,315.00
		Set, never hinged		180.00	
		Set, on flown cover			4,250.00

For overprints and surcharges see Nos.
C38-C42.

North Atlantic Flight Issue

Airplane,
Lion of St.
Mark
AP7

1933, June 1

C27	AP7	19.75 l	blk & ol brn	20.00	650.00
		Never hinged		47.50	
		On cover			2,600.
C28	AP7	44.75 l	dk bl & lt grn	20.00	650.00
		Never hinged		47.50	
		On cover			2,600.
		Set, never hinged		95.00	
		Set, on flown cover			5,000.

Type of
1931
Ovptd. or
Srchd.

1934, Jan. 20

C29	AP2	2 l on 5 l	org brn	4.50	90.00
		Never hinged		11.00	
		On cover			325.00
C30	AP2	3 l on 5 l	grn	4.50	90.00
		Never hinged		11.00	
		On cover			325.00
C31	AP2	5 l	ocher	4.50	105.00
		Never hinged		11.00	
		On cover			425.00
C32	AP2	10 l on 5 l	rose	6.00	105.00
		Never hinged		19.50	
		On cover			550.00
		Nos. C29-C32 (4)		19.50	390.00
		Set, never hinged		52.50	
		Set, on flown cover			1,675.

For use on mail to be carried on a special
flight from Rome to Buenos Aires.

Types of Libya Airmail
Issue Overprinted in
Black or Red

1934, May 1 — Wmk. 140

C38	AP4	50c	rose red	13.50	160.00
		Never hinged		34.00	
		On cover			400.00
C39	AP4	75c	lemon	13.50	160.00
		Never hinged		34.00	
		On cover			400.00
C40	AP4	5 l + 1 l	brn	13.50	160.00
		Never hinged		34.00	
		On cover			600.00
C41	AP4	10 l + 2 l	dk bl	240.00	850.00
		Never hinged		600.00	
		On cover			
C42	AP5	25 l + 3 l	pur	240.00	850.00
		Never hinged		600.00	
		Nos. C38-C42,CE1-CE2 (7)		547.50	2,500.
		Set, never hinged		1,300.	
		Set, on flown cover			6,000.

"Circuit of the Oases."

Plane
Shadow on
Desert
AP11

Designs: 25c, 50c, 75c, Plane shadow on
desert. 80c, 1 l, 2 l, Camel corps.

1934, Oct. 16 — Photo.

C43	AP11	25c	sl bl & org red	5.25	21.00
		Never hinged		13.00	
		On cover			260.00
C44	AP11	50c	dk grn & ind	5.25	19.00
		Never hinged		13.00	
		On cover			200.00
C45	AP11	75c	dk brn & org red	5.25	19.00
		Never hinged		13.00	
		On cover			280.00
C46	AP11	80c	org brn & ol grn	5.25	21.00
		Never hinged		13.00	
		On cover			340.00
C47	AP11	1 l	scar & ol grn	5.25	26.00
		Never hinged		13.00	
		On cover			375.00
C48	AP11	2 l	dk bl & brn	5.25	45.00
		Never hinged		13.00	
		On cover			525.00
		Nos. C43-C48 (6)		24.00	136.00
		Set, never hinged		77.50	
		Set, on flown cover			425.00

Second Colonial Arts Exhibition, Naples.

AIR POST SEMI-POSTAL STAMPS

King Victor
Emmanuel
III
SPAP1

1934, Nov. 5 — Wmk. 140 — Perf. 14

CB1	SPAP1	25c + 10c	gray grn	9.00	26.00
		Never hinged		22.50	
		On cover			300.00
CB2	SPAP1	50c + 10c	brn	9.00	26.00
		Never hinged		22.50	
		On cover			300.00
CB3	SPAP1	75c + 15c	rose red	9.00	26.00
		Never hinged		22.50	
		On cover			325.00
CB4	SPAP1	80c + 15c	blk brn	9.00	26.00
		Never hinged		22.50	
		On cover			400.00

CB5	SPAP1	1 l + 20c	red brn	9.00	26.00
		Never hinged		22.50	
		On cover			450.00
CB6	SPAP1	2 l + 20c	brt bl	9.00	26.00
		Never hinged		22.50	
		On cover			
CB7	SPAP1	3 l + 25c	pur	26.00	120.00
		Never hinged		65.00	
		On cover			
CB8	SPAP1	5 l + 25c	org	26.00	120.00
		Never hinged		65.00	
		On cover			
CB9	SPAP1	10 l + 30c	rose vio	26.00	120.00
		Never hinged		65.00	
		On cover			
CB10	SPAP1	25 l + 2 l	dp grn	26.00	120.00
		Never hinged		65.00	
		Nos. CB1-CB10 (10)		158.00	636.00
		Set, never hinged		390.00	
		Set, on flown cover			1,800.

65th birthday of King Victor Emmanuel III;
non-stop flight from Rome to Mogadiscio.
For overprint see No. CBO1.

AIR POST SEMI-POSTAL OFFICIAL STAMP

Type of Air Post Semi-Postal Stamps
Overprinted Crown and "SERVIZIO DI
STATO" in Black

1934 — Wmk. 140 — Perf. 14

CBO1	SPAP1	25 l + 2 l	cop red	2,450.	6,000.
		Never hinged		4,850.	
		On cover			9,000.

AIR POST SPECIAL DELIVERY STAMPS

Type of Libya Overprinted in Black
Like Nos. C38-C42

1934, May 1 — Wmk. 140 — Perf. 14

CE1	APSD1	2.25 l	red orange	13.50	160.00
		Never hinged		32.50	
		On cover			800.00
CE2	APSD1	4.50 l + 1 l	dp rose	13.50	160.00
		Never hinged		32.50	
		On cover			—
		Set, never hinged		65.00	

AUTHORIZED DELIVERY STAMP

Authorized Delivery Stamp of Italy
1930, Overprinted like Nos. 38-42

1931, Mar. — Wmk. 140 — Perf. 14

EY1	AD2	10c	reddish brown	18.00	45.00
		Never hinged		45.00	
		On cover			2,000.
a.			dark brown	1,200.	975.00
		Never hinged		1,800.	
		On cover			—

TRISTAN DA CUNHA

ˌtris-tən-də-ˈkü-nə

LOCATION — Group of islands in the
south Atlantic Ocean midway
between the Cape of Good Hope and
South America
GOVT. — A dependency of St. Helena
AREA — 40 sq. mi.
POP. — 325 (1982)

12 Pence = 1 Shilling

Stamps of St.
Helena, 1938-
49,
Overprinted in
Black

1952, Jan. 1 — Wmk. 4 — Perf. 12½

1	A24	½p	purple	.25	2.75
2	A24	1p	blue grn & blk	1.00	1.90
3	A24	1½p	car rose & blk	1.00	1.90
4	A24	2p	carmine & blk	1.00	1.90
5	A24	3p	gray	1.25	1.90
6	A24	4p	ultra	7.00	3.00
7	A24	6p	gray blue	7.00	3.00
8	A24	8p	olive	7.00	7.50
9	A24	1sh	sepia	6.00	2.50
10	A24	2sh6p	deep claret	25.00	17.50
11	A24	5sh	brown	37.50	22.50
12	A24	10sh	violet	60.00	37.50
		Nos. 1-12 (12)		154.00	103.85
		Set, hinged		85.00	

TUNISIA

tü-'nē-zhˌē͟ə

LOCATION — Northern Africa bordering on the Mediterranean Sea
GOVT. — French protectorate
AREA — 63,362 sq. mi.
POP. — 6,966,173 (1984)
CAPITAL — Tunis

100 Centimes = 1 Franc

Covers
Values are for commercial covers bearing correct frankings. Philatelic covers sell for less.

Coat of Arms — A1

Perf. 14x13½

			Unwmk.
1888-97	**Typo.**		
1	A1 1c black, *blue*	5.50	4.75
	Never hinged	10.50	
	On cover		125.00
a.	Horiz. ruled line background	11.00	11.00
	Never hinged	20.00	
	On cover		92.50
2	A1 2c pur brn, *buff*	5.50	4.75
	Never hinged	10.50	
	On cover		125.00
a.	Horiz. ruled line background	12.50	12.50
	Never hinged	20.00	
	On cover		92.50
3	A1 5c green, *grnsh*	37.50	16.00
	Never hinged	72.50	
	On cover		100.00
a.	Horiz. ruled line background	27.50	20.00
	Never hinged	52.50	
	On cover		92.50
4	A1 15c blue, *grysh*	65.00	30.00
	Never hinged	130.00	
5	A1 25c black, *rose*	130.00	80.00
	Never hinged	260.00	
	On cover		325.00
a.	Horiz. ruled line background	375.00	375.00
	On cover		800.00
6	A1 40c red, *straw*	130.00	87.50
	Never hinged	260.00	
	On cover		300.00
7	A1 75c car, *rose*	130.00	95.00
	Never hinged	260.00	
	On cover		600.00
a.	Horiz. ruled line background	175.00	175.00
	Never hinged	360.00	
	On cover		800.00
8	A1 5fr gray vio, *grysh*	575.00	375.00
	On cover		1,300.
a.	Horiz. ruled line background	610.00	575.00
	On cover		1,400.
	Nos. 1-8 (8)	1,078.	693.00

All values exist imperforate. Value, set without gum, $1,200.

Issued: Nos. 1-8, 7/1/88; Nos. 1a//8a, 1897.
Reprints were made in 1893 and some values have been reprinted twice since then. The shades usually differ from those of the originals. Stamps from the 1897 printing are on thicker paper, with white gum instead of grayish, and have a background of horizontal ruled lines.

A2   A3

1888-1902			
9	A2 1c blk, *lil bl*	2.00	1.20
	Never hinged	3.25	
	On cover		67.50
10	A2 2c pur brn, *buff*	2.00	1.20
	Never hinged	3.25	
	On cover		67.50
11	A2 5c grn, *grnsh*	8.00	1.20
	Never hinged	13.50	
	On cover		47.50
12	A2 5c yellow grn ('99)	7.25	1.20
	Never hinged	12.00	
	On cover		12.00
13	A2 10c blk, *lav* ('93)	12.00	2.00
	Never hinged	22.50	
	On cover		27.50
14	A2 10c red ('01)	7.25	1.20
	Never hinged	13.50	
	On cover		9.50
15	A2 15c blue, *grysh*	55.00	1.20
	Never hinged	110.00	
	On cover		45.00
16	A2 15c gray ('01)	11.00	2.40
	Never hinged	21.00	
	On cover		8.00

17	A2 20c red, *grn* ('99)	20.00	2.50
	Never hinged	32.50	
	On cover		40.00
18	A2 25c blk, *rose*	28.00	2.40
	Never hinged	52.50	
	On cover		100.00
19	A2 25c blue ('01)	22.50	3.25
	Never hinged	[...]	
	On cover		40.00
20	A2 35c brown ('02)	55.00	4.00
	Never hinged	110.00	
	On cover		80.00
21	A2 40c red, *straw*	24.00	2.40
	Never hinged	47.50	
	On cover		60.00
22	A2 75c car, *rose*	190.00	92.50
	Never hinged	350.00	
	On cover		400.00
23	A2 75c dp vio, *org* ('93)	35.00	11.00
	Never hinged	65.00	
	On cover		67.50
24	A3 1fr olive, *olive*	40.00	10.50
	Never hinged	72.505	
	On cover		275.00
25	A3 2fr dull violet ('02)	180.00	150.00
	Never hinged	360.00	
	On cover		325.00
26	A3 5fr red lil, *lav*	225.00	87.50
	Bar cancellation		.50
	On cover		400.00

Quadrille Paper

27	A2 15c bl, *grysh* ('93)	52.50	1.20
	Never hinged	100.00	
	On cover		24.00
	Nos. 9-27 (19)	976.50	378.85

For surcharges see Nos. 28, 58-61.
For Nos. 1-8 and 9/27 with perforated "T," see Postage Due stamps.

No. 27 Surcharged in Red

1902			
28	A2 25c on 15c blue	4.00	4.00

Mosque at Kairouan A4

Plowing A5

Ruins of Hadrian's Aqueduct A6

Carthaginian Galley — A7

			Typo.
1906-26			
29	A4 1c blk, *yel*	.25	.25
	Never hinged	.40	
	On cover		20.00
a.	Engraver's name omitted	8.75	8.75
	Never hinged	13.50	
b.	On grayish paper ('17)	.75	.75
	Never hinged	1.25	
	On cover		24.00
30	A4 2c red brn, *straw*	.25	.25
	Never hinged	.40	
	On cover		20.00
a.	Engraver's name omitted	8.75	8.75
	Never hinged	13.50	
b.	On grayish paper ('19)	.75	.75
	Never hinged	1.25	
	On cover		24.00
31	A4 3c lt red ('19)	.25	.25
	Never hinged	.40	
	On cover		11.00
a.	On grayish paper	.30	.30
	Never hinged	.50	
	On cover		12.00
32	A4 5c grn, *grnsh*	.40	.25
	Never hinged	.55	
	On cover		8.00
a.	Engraver's name omitted	10.00	10.00
	Never hinged	16.00	
b.	On grayish paper ('17-'19)	.95	.80
	Never hinged	1.60	
	On cover		9.50
33	A4 5c orange ('21)	.30	.25
	Never hinged	.50	
	On cover		6.00
a.	Engraver's name omitted	8.75	8.75
	Never hinged	13.50	
34	A5 10c red	.40	.40
	Never hinged	.55	
	On cover		6.50

35	A5 10c green ('21)	.50	.40
	Never hinged	.65	
	On cover		17.50
36	A5 15c vio, *pnksh*	1.40	.30
	Never hinged	2.25	
	On cover		12.00
a.	Imperf., pair	175.00	
	Never hinged	[...].00	
b.	On grayish paper ('16, '18)	1.60	.50
	Never hinged	2.50	
	On cover		16.00
37	A5 15c brn, *org* ('23)	.30	.30
	Never hinged	.50	
	On cover		2.40
38	A5 20c brn, *pnksh*	.30	.30
	Never hinged	.50	
	On cover		8.00
a.	Engraver's name omitted	10.00	10.00
	Never hinged	16.00	
b.	On grayish paper ('18)	.75	.75
	Never hinged	1.25	
	On cover		9.50
39	A5 25c deep blue	1.90	.75
	Never hinged	3.25	
	On cover		20.00
	On cover, single franking		32.50
a.	Imperf., pair		
b.	On grayish paper ('17)	3.25	2.00
	Never hinged	5.25	
	On cover		27.50
40	A5 25c violet ('21)	.55	.30
	Never hinged	.75	
	On cover		4.00
41	A6 30c red brn & vio ('19)	1.20	.80
	Never hinged	1.60	
	On cover		12.00
42	A5 30c pale red ('21)	1.20	1.20
	Never hinged	1.75	
	On cover		8.75
43	A6 35c ol grn & brn	10.50	2.40
	Never hinged	17.50	
	On cover		16.00
	On cover, single franking		24.00
44	A6 40c blk brn & red brn	5.25	.80
	Never hinged	9.00	
	On cover		13.50
	On cover, single franking		20.00
45	A5 40c blk, *pnksh* ('23)	1.20	.80
	Never hinged	1.60	
	On cover		3.25
46	A5 40c gray grn ('26)	.25	.25
	Never hinged	.30	
	On cover		2.40
47	A5 50c blue ('21)	.90	.90
	Never hinged	1.45	
	On cover		4.00
	On cover, single franking		5.50
48	A6 60c ol grn & vio ('21)	1.10	.95
	Never hinged	1.40	
	On cover		14.00
	On cover, single franking		9.50
49	A6 60c ver & rose ('25)	.80	.80
	Never hinged	1.20	
	On cover		9.50
	On cover, single franking		16.00
50	A6 75c red brn & red	1.10	.80
	Never hinged	2.00	
	On cover		27.50
	On cover, single franking		40.00
51	A6 75c ver & dl red ('26)	.55	.55
	Never hinged	.65	
	On cover		5.50
	On cover, single franking		8.00
52	A7 1fr red & dk brn	1.20	.80
	Never hinged	2.00	
	On cover		32.50
	On cover, single franking		52.50
53	A7 1fr ind & ultra ('25)	.55	.55
	Never hinged	.80	
	On cover		7.25
	On cover, single franking		12.50
54	A7 2fr brn & ol grn	6.75	2.00
	Never hinged	12.00	
	On cover		40.00
	On cover, single franking		65.00
55	A7 2fr grn & red, *pink* ('25)	1.10	.50
	Never hinged	1.60	
	On cover		9.50
	On cover, single franking		16.00
56	A7 5fr violet & blue	12.00	5.25
	Never hinged	21.00	
	On cover		52.50
	On cover, single franking		80.00
57	A7 5fr gray vio & grn ('25)	1.10	.65
	Never hinged	1.60	
	On cover		17.50
	On cover, single franking		45.00
	Nos. 29-57 (29)	53.55	23.55

The engraver's name, "Puyplat," normally appears in tiny type to the right and below the design.
For surcharges and overprints see Nos. 62-64, 70-73, 115-116, B1-B23, B25-B27, B29-B30, B32-B36, C1-C6.

Stamps and Type of 1888-1902 Surcharged

1908, Sept.			
58	A2 10c on 15c gray, *lt gray* (R)	2.00	2.00
	Never hinged	2.75	
	On cover		5.50
59	A3 35c on 1fr ol, *ol* (R)	4.75	4.75
	Never hinged	9.00	
	On cover		8.00
	On cover, single franking		11.00
60	A3 40c on 2fr dl vio (Bl)	8.75	8.75
	Never hinged	16.50	
	On cover		20.00
	On cover, single franking		32.50

61	A3 75c on 5fr red lil, *lav* (Bl)	6.75	6.75
	Never hinged	14.00	
	On cover		40.00
	On cover, single franking		65.00
	Nos. 58-61 (4)	22.25	22.25

No. 36 Surcharged

1911			
62	A5 10c on 15c vio, *pinkish*	2.00	.80
	Never hinged	3.25	
a.	Inverted surcharge		2,400.
b.	Bars in surcharge omitted	45.00	
	Never hinged	72.50	

No. 34 Surcharged

1917, Mar. 16			
63	A5 15c on 10c red	1.20	.40
	Never hinged	2.00	
	On cover		5.50
a.	"15c" omitted	40.00	
	Never hinged	72.50	
b.	Double surcharge	87.50	
	Never hinged	160.00	
c.	Surcharge bars double	100.00	
	Never hinged	175.00	
d.	Surcharge bars omitted	40.00	
	Never hinged	72.50	

No. 36 Surcharged

1921			
64	A5 20c on 15c vio, *pinkish*	1.20	.40
	Never hinged	1.60	

Arab and Ruins of Dougga — A9

1922-26	**Typo.**	**Perf. 13½x14**	
65	A9 10c green	.25	.25
	Never hinged	.40	
	On cover		16.00
66	A9 10c rose ('26)	.30	.30
	Never hinged	.40	
	On cover		12.00
67	A9 30c rose	1.20	1.20
	Never hinged	1.60	
	On cover		4.75
68	A9 30c lilac ('26)	.50	.50
	Never hinged	.65	
	On cover		2.40
69	A9 50c blue	.80	.80
	Never hinged	1.20	
	On cover		4.00
	On cover, single franking		5.50
	Nos. 65-69 (5)	3.05	3.05

For surcharges see Nos. 117, B24, B28, B31.

Stamps and Type of 1906 Surcharged in Red or Black

a   b

1923-25			
70	A4(a) 10c on 5c grn, *grnsh* (R)	.50	.50
	Never hinged	.65	
	On cover		16.00
a.	Double surcharge	92.50	
	Never hinged	175.00	
b.	Inverted surcharge	130.00	
	Never hinged	175.00	
c.	Double surcharge, one inverted	130.00	
	Never hinged	175.00	
d.	Engraver's name omitted (#32a)	10.00	10.00
	Never hinged	16.00	
71	A5(b) 20c on 15c violet (Bk)	.95	.30
	Never hinged	1.40	
	On cover		4.00
a.	Double surcharge	130.00	

	b.	Never hinged	225.00
		On grayish paper (#36b)	1.60 .50
		Never hinged	2.75
72	A5(b)	30c on 20c yel brn (Bk) ('25)	.50 .50
		Never hinged	.65
		On cover	2.40
	a.	"30" omitted	65.00
		Never hinged	100.00
	b.	Bars omitted	65.00
		Never hinged	100.00
73	A5(b)	50c on 25c blue (R)	.95 .40
		Never hinged	1.40
		On cover	5.50
		On cover, single franking	12.00
	a.	Double surcharge	130.00
		Never hinged	225.00
	b.	Inverted surcharge	120.00
		Never hinged	210.00
		Nos. 70-73 (4)	2.90 1.70

Arab Woman Carrying Water — A10

Grand Mosque at Tunis — A11

Mosque, Tunis — A12

Roman Amphitheater, El Djem (Thysdrus) — A13

1926-46   Typo.   Perf. 14x13½

74	A10	1c lt red	.25 .25
		Never hinged	.40
		On cover	5.50
75	A10	2c olive grn	.25 .25
		Never hinged	.40
		On cover	5.50
76	A10	3c slate blue	.25 .25
		Never hinged	.40
		On cover	4.75
77	A10	5c yellow grn	.25 .25
		Never hinged	.40
		On cover	2.40
78	A10	10c rose	.25 .25
		Never hinged	.40
		On cover	2.40
78A	A12	10c brown ('46)	.25 .25
		Never hinged	.30
		On cover	3.25
79	A11	15c gray lilac	.25 .25
		Never hinged	.40
		On cover	2.40
80	A11	20c deep red	.30 .25
		Never hinged	.50
		On cover	4.75
81	A11	25c gray green	.50 .30
		Never hinged	.65
		On cover	2.40
82	A11	25c lt violet ('28)	.75 .30
		Never hinged	.95
		On cover	2.40
83	A11	30c lt violet	.50 .50
		Never hinged	.65
		On cover	9.50
84	A11	30c blue grn ('28)	.50 .30
		Never hinged	.65
		On cover	8.00
84A	A12	30c dk ol grn ('46)	.25 .25
		Never hinged	.30
		On cover	2.75
85	A11	40c deep brown	.30 .25
		Never hinged	.50
		On cover	2.40
85A	A12	40c lil rose ('46)	.30 .30
		Never hinged	.40
		On cover	2.75
86	A11	45c emerald ('40)	1.10 1.10
		Never hinged	1.40
		On cover	7.25
87	A12	50c black	.30 .25
		Never hinged	.50
		On cover	2.00
88	A12	50c ultra ('34)	.80 .30
		Never hinged	1.00
		On cover	1.25
88B	A12	50c emerald ('40)	.25 .25
		Never hinged	.30
		On cover	6.75
88C	A12	50c lt blue ('46)	.30 .30
		Never hinged	.40
		On cover	2.00
89	A12	60c red org ('40)	.25 .25
		Never hinged	.40
		On cover	4.75
89A	A12	60c ultra ('45)	.25 .25
		Never hinged	.30
		On cover	3.50

90	A12	65c ultra ('38)	.65 .30
		Never hinged	.90
		On cover	1.25
91	A12	70c dark red ('40)	.25 .25
		Never hinged	.30
		On cover	2.00
92	A12	75c vermilion	.50 .50
		Never hinged	.65
		On cover	3.25
93	A12	75c lilac rose ('28)	1.05 .40
		Never hinged	1.40
		On cover	2.40
94	A12	80c blue green	1.00 .90
		Never hinged	1.40
		On cover	9.50
94A	A12	80c blk brn ('40)	.30 .30
		Never hinged	.50
		On cover	1.25
94B	A12	80c emerald ('45)	.50 .30
		Never hinged	.65
		On cover	2.00
95	A12	90c org red ('28)	.40 .40
		Never hinged	.50
		On cover	7.25
		On cover, single franking	16.00
96	A12	90c ultra ('39)	10.00 10.00
		Never hinged	14.00
		On cover	21.00
97	A12	1fr brown violet	.80 .50
		Never hinged	1.00
		On cover	5.50
		On cover, single franking	8.00
97A	A12	1fr rose ('40)	.25 .25
		Never hinged	.40
		On cover	1.25
98	A13	1.05fr dl bl & mag	.75 .55
		Never hinged	.95
		On cover	14.00
		On cover, single franking	21.00
98A	A12	1.20fr blk brn ('45)	.50 .30
		Never hinged	.50
		On cover	2.40
99	A13	1.25fr gray bl & dk bl	.75 .50
		Never hinged	.95
		On cover	14.00
		On cover, single franking	25.00
100	A13	1.25fr car rose ('40)	1.20 1.20
		Never hinged	1.60
		On cover	6.50
		On cover, single franking	17.50
100A	A13	1.30fr bl & vio bl ('42)	.30 .30
		Never hinged	.40
		On cover	2.40
101	A13	1.40fr brt red vio ('40)	1.35 1.35
		Never hinged	1.90
		On cover	4.75
		On cover, single franking	8.00
102	A13	1.50fr bl & dp bl ('28)	1.25 .70
		Never hinged	1.75
		On cover	6.50
		On cover, single franking	13.50
102A	A13	1.50fr rose red & red org ('42)	.55 .55
		Never hinged	.75
		On cover	8.75
		On cover, single franking	16.00
102B	A12	1.50fr rose lil ('46)	.25 .25
		Never hinged	.30
		On cover	1.60
103	A13	2fr rose & ol brn	1.50 .30
		Never hinged	2.25
		On cover	8.75
		On cover, single franking	12.50
104	A13	2fr red orange ('39)	.40 .40
		Never hinged	.55
		On cover	4.00
		On cover, single franking	9.50
104A	A12	2fr Prus grn ('45)	.30 .25
		Never hinged	.40
		On cover	1.25
105	A13	2.25fr ultra ('39)	1.05 1.05
		Never hinged	1.50
		On cover	5.25
		On cover, single franking	17.50
105A	A13	2.40fr red ('46)	.75 .55
		Never hinged	.90
		On cover	6.50
106	A13	2.50fr green ('40)	.90 .90
		Never hinged	1.30
		On cover	5.25
		On cover, single franking	9.50
107	A13	3fr dl bl & org	1.90 .75
		Never hinged	2.75
		On cover	14.50
		On cover, single franking	25.00
108	A13	3fr violet ('39)	.40 .40
		Never hinged	.55
		On cover	2.75
		On cover, single franking	4.00
108A	A13	3fr black brn ('46)	.30 .25
		Never hinged	.40
		On cover	1.25
108B	A13	4fr ultra ('45)	1.10 .65
		Never hinged	1.40
		On cover	3.25
109	A13	5fr red & grn, grnsh	2.75 .90
		Never hinged	3.50
		On cover	35.00
		On cover, single franking	47.50
110	A13	5fr dp red brn ('40)	1.40 1.40
		Never hinged	2.10
		On cover	6.75
		On cover, single franking	14.00
110A	A13	5fr dk green ('46)	.50 .50
		Never hinged	.65
		On cover	1.60

110B	A13	6fr dp ultra ('45)	.80 .50
		Never hinged	1.00
		On cover	2.00
111	A13	10fr brn red & blk, *bluish*	11.00 3.00
		Never hinged	17.50
		On cover	35.00
		On cover, single franking	60.00
112	A13	10fr rose pink ('40)	.90 .90
		Never hinged	1.20
		On cover	8.75
		On cover, single franking	21.00
112A	A13	10fr ver ('46)	.80 .50
		Never hinged	.80
		On cover	5.50
112B	A13	10fr ultra ('46)	.75 .40
		Never hinged	.80
		On cover	5.50
112C	A13	15fr rose lil ('45)	.50 .25
		Never hinged	.65
		On cover	8.00
113	A13	20fr lil & red, *pnksh* ('28)	2.40 1.20
		Never hinged	3.50
		On cover	16.00
		On cover, single franking	32.50
113A	A13	20fr dk green ('45)	.90 .90
		Never hinged	1.20
		On cover	9.50
113B	A13	25fr violet ('45)	.90 .75
		Never hinged	1.10
		On cover	12.00
	a.	No inscriptions below design	11.00 11.00
		Never hinged	16.00
113C	A13	50fr carmine ('45)	1.75 .95
		Never hinged	2.25
		On cover	20.00
113D	A13	100fr car rose ('45)	2.00 1.20
		Never hinged	2.50
		On cover	24.00
		Nos. 74-113D (66)	66.95 44.75

See Nos. 152A-162, 185-189, 199-206 in Scott Standard catalogue, Vol. 6.

For surcharges and overprints see Nos. 114, 118-121, 143-152, B74-B77, B87-B88, B91-B95, B98, C7-C12. Post 1940 listings are in Scott Standard catalogue, Vol. 6.

No. 99 Surcharged with New Value and Bars in Red

1927, Mar. 24

114	A13	1.50fr on 1.25fr	.80 .30
		Never hinged	1.00
		On cover	9.50
		On cover, single franking	60.00

Stamps of 1921-26 Surcharged

1928, May 1

115	A4	3c on 5c orange	.30 .25
		Never hinged	.50
		On cover	6.50
116	A5	10c on 15c brn, *org*	.80 .30
		Never hinged	1.10
		On cover	5.25
	a.	"10c" omitted	120.00
		Never hinged	175.00
	b.	Bars omitted	47.50
		Never hinged	72.50
	c.	Double surcharge	140.00
		Never hinged	210.00
	d.	Pair, #116 + 116c	210.00
		Never hinged	325.00
	e.	Pair #116 + #37	290.00
		Never hinged	425.00
117	A9	25c on 30c lilac	.75 .40
		Never hinged	.950
		On cover	2.40
	a.	Pair #117 + #68	275.00
		Never hinged	400.00
118	A12	40c on 80c bl grn	.80 .50
		Never hinged	1.00
		On cover	2.00
119	A12	50c on 75c ver	.95 .55
		Never hinged	1.20
		On cover	2.00
		Nos. 115-119 (5)	3.60 2.00

No. 83 Surcharged

1929

120	A11	10c on 30c lt violet	1.90 1.10
		Never hinged	2.75

No. 120 exists precanceled only. The value in first column is for a stamp which has not been through the post and has original gum. The value in the second column is for a postally used, gumless stamp. See No. 199a in Scott Standard catalogue, Vol. 6.

No. 85 Surcharged with New Value and Bars

1930

121	A11	50c on 40c dp brn	6.00 .85
		Never hinged	9.25
		On cover	2.00

A14

A15

A16

A17

Perf. 11, 12½, 12½x13

1931-34			**Engr.**
122	A14	1c deep blue	.25 .25
		Never hinged	.40
		On cover	6.00
123	A14	2c yellow brn	.25 .25
		Never hinged	.40
		On cover	6.00
124	A14	3c black	.50 .50
		Never hinged	.65
		On cover	6.00
125	A14	5c yellow grn	.25 .25
		Never hinged	.40
		On cover	4.50
126	A14	10c red	.25 .25
		Never hinged	.40
		On cover	3.50
127	A15	15c dull violet	.75 .65
		Never hinged	.95
		On cover	3.25
128	A15	20c dull brown	.25 .25
		Never hinged	.40
		On cover	3.25
129	A15	25c rose red	.30 .25
		Never hinged	.50
		On cover	2.40
130	A15	30c deep green	.65 .55
		Never hinged	.90
		On cover	10.00
131	A16	40c red orange	.30 .30
		Never hinged	.50
		On cover	2.00
132	A16	50c ultra	.30 .30
		Never hinged	.50
		On cover	1.60
133	A16	75c yellow	2.40 2.10
		Never hinged	3.50
		On cover	4.00
134	A16	90c red	.80 .80
		Never hinged	1.00
		On cover	7.25
		On cover, single franking	16.00
135	A16	1fr olive black	.55 .50
		Never hinged	.75
		On cover	5.00
		On cover, single franking	7.25
136	A16	1fr dk brown ('34)	.55 .50
		Never hinged	.75
		On cover	5.00
		On cover, single franking	7.25
137	A17	1.50fr brt ultra	.95 .75
		Never hinged	1.40
		On cover	6.00
		On cover, single franking	13.50
138	A17	2fr deep brown	.90 .90
		Never hinged	1.25
		On cover	7.25
		On cover, single franking	11.00
139	A17	3fr blue green	10.50 10.50
		Never hinged	16.00
		On cover	21.00
		On cover, single franking	35.00
140	A17	5fr car rose	28.00 22.50
		Never hinged	42.50
		On cover	32.50
		On cover, single franking	52.50
	a.	Perf. 12½	45.00 40.00
		Never hinged	67.50
		On cover	80.00
141	A17	10fr black	52.50 37.50
		Never hinged	80.00
		On cover	80.00
		On cover, single franking	125.00
142	A17	20fr dark brown	65.00 52.50
		Never hinged	110.00
		On cover	110.00
		On cover, single franking	160.00
		Nos. 122-142 (21)	166.20 132.35

For surcharges see Nos. B54-B73.

Nos. 88, 102 Surcharged in Red or Black

1937   *Perf. 14x13½*

143	A12	65c on 50c (R)	.65	.25
		Never hinged	.90	
		On cover		1.25
b.		Double surcharge	120.00	100.00
		Never hinged	175.00	
144	A13	1.75fr on 1.50fr (R)	6.50	1.60
		Never hinged	9.50	
		On cover		4.75
		On cover, single franking		11.00
a.		Double surcharge	110.00	110.00
		Never hinged	160.00	
b.		In pair with unsurcharged stamp	275.00	
		Never hinged	425.00	

1938

145	A12	65c on 50c (Bk)	.90	.30
		Never hinged	1.25	
		On cover		1.25
a.		Double surcharge, one inverted	200.00	200.00
		Never hinged	250.00	
146	A13	1.75fr on 1.50fr (R)	9.50	8.00
		Never hinged	13.50	
		On cover		16.00
		On cover, single franking		32.50

Stamps of 1938-39 Surcharged in Red or Carmine

1940

147	A12	25c on 65c ultra (C)	.25	.25
		Never hinged	.40	
		On cover		4.00
148	A12	1fr on 90c ultra (R)	.55	.55
		Never hinged	.75	
		On cover		1.60
a.		Double surcharge	130.00	
		Never hinged	200.00	

SEMI-POSTAL STAMPS

No. 36 Overprinted in Red

1915, Feb.   Unwmk.   *Perf. 14x13½*

B1	A5	15c vio, *pnksh*	1.60	1.60
		Never hinged	2.40	
		On cover		8.00

No. 32 Overprinted in Red

1916, Feb. 15

B2	A4	5c grn, *grnsh*	2.40	2.40
		Never hinged	3.25	
		On cover		9.50

Types of Regular Issue of 1906 in New Colors and Surcharged

1916, Aug.

B3	A5	10c on 15c brn vio, *bl*	1.30	1.30
		Never hinged	2.00	
		On cover		8.75
B4	A5	10c on 20c brn, *org*	1.50	1.50
		Never hinged	2.40	
		On cover		10.00
B5	A5	10c on 25c bl, *grn*	4.00	4.00
		Never hinged	6.75	
		On cover		13.50
B6	A6	10c on 35c ol grn & vio	8.00	8.00
		Never hinged	14.50	
		On cover		18.00
B7	A6	10c on 40c bis & blk	5.25	5.25
		Never hinged	9.50	
		On cover		17.50
B8	A6	10c on 75c vio brn & grn	12.00	12.00
		Never hinged	21.00	
		On cover		27.50
B9	A7	10c on 1fr red & grn	8.00	8.00
		Never hinged	11.00	
		On cover		27.50
B10	A7	10c on 2fr bis & bl	110.00	110.00
		Never hinged	210.00	
		On cover		200.00
B11	A7	10c on 5fr vio & red	140.00	140.00
		Never hinged	275.00	
		On cover		240.00
		Nos. B3-B11 (9)	290.05	290.05

Nos. B3-B11 were sold at their face value but had a postal value of 10c only. The excess was applied to the relief of prisoners of war in Germany.

Types of Regular Issue of 1906 in New Colors and Surcharged in Carmine

1918

B12	A5	15c on 20c blk, *grn*	2.40	2.40
		Never hinged	4.00	
		On cover		12.00
B13	A5	15c on 25c dk bl, *buff*	2.40	2.40
		Never hinged	4.00	
		On cover		13.50
B14	A6	15c on 35c gray grn & red	3.25	3.25
		Never hinged	5.50	
		On cover		16.00
B15	A6	15c on 40c brn & lt bl	5.50	5.50
		Never hinged	10.50	
		On cover		18.00
B16	A6	15c on 75c red brn & blk	13.00	13.00
		Never hinged	24.00	
		On cover		27.50
B17	A7	15c on 1fr red & vio	35.00	35.00
		Never hinged	60.00	
		On cover		87.50
B18	A7	15c on 2fr bis brn & red	110.00	110.00
		Never hinged	210.00	
		On cover		190.00
B19	A7	15c on 5fr vio & blk	190.00	190.00
		Never hinged	375.00	
		On cover		450.00
		Nos. B12-B19 (8)	361.55	361.55

The different parts of the surcharge are more widely spaced on the stamps of types A6 and A7. These stamps were sold at their face value but had a postal value of 15c only. The excess was intended for the relief of prisoners of war in Germany.

Types of 1906-22 Surcharged

1923

B20	A4	0c on 1c blue	1.20	1.20
		Never hinged	1.75	
		On cover		13.50

B21	A4	0c on 2c ol brn	1.20	1.20
		Never hinged	1.75	
		On cover		13.50
B22	A4	1c on 3c green	1.20	1.20
		Never hinged	1.75	
		On cover		13.50
B23	A4	0c on 5c green	1.20	1.20
		Never hinged	1.75	
		On cover		13.50
B24	A9	3c on 10c vio, *bluish*	1.20	1.20
		Never hinged	1.75	
		On cover		13.50
B25	A5	5c on 15c ol grn	1.20	1.20
		Never hinged	1.75	
		On cover		17.50
B26	A5	5c on 20c bl, *pink*	2.40	2.40
		Never hinged	4.00	
		On cover		21.00
B27	A5	5c on 25c vio, *bluish*	2.40	2.40
		Never hinged	4.00	
		On cover		21.00
B28	A9	5c on 30c orange	2.40	2.40
		Never hinged	3.75	
		On cover		21.00
B29	A6	5c on 35c bl & vio	4.75	4.75
		Never hinged	8.00	
		On cover		24.00
B30	A6	5c on 40c bl & brn	4.75	4.75
		Never hinged	8.00	
		On cover		24.00
B31	A9	10c on 50c blk, *bluish*	6.50	6.50
		Never hinged	11.00	
		On cover		32.50
B32	A6	10c on 60c ol brn & bl	8.75	8.75
		Never hinged	16.00	
		On cover		35.00
B33	A6	10c on 75c vio & lt grn	9.50	9.50
		Never hinged	17.50	
		On cover		40.00
B34	A7	25c on 1fr mar & vio	9.50	9.50
		Never hinged	18.00	
		On cover		40.00
B35	A7	25c on 2fr bl & rose	30.00	30.00
		Never hinged	47.50	
		On cover		72.50
B36	A7	25c on 5fr grn & ol brn	80.00	80.00
		Never hinged	150.00	
		On cover		175.00
		Nos. B20-B36 (17)	168.15	168.15

These stamps were sold at their original values but had postal franking values only to the amounts surcharged on them. The difference was intended to be used for the benefit of wounded soldiers.

This issue was entirely speculative. Before the announced date of sale most of the stamps were taken by postal employees and practically none of them were offered to the public.

Mail Delivery — SP1

Type of Parcel Post Stamps, 1906, with Surcharge in Black

1925, June 7   *Perf. 13½x14*

B37	SP1	1c on 5c brn & red, *pink*	.80	.80
		Never hinged	1.25	
		On cover		8.00
a.		Surcharge omitted	160.00	160.00
		Never hinged	240.00	
B38	SP1	2c on 10c brn & bl, *yel*	.80	.80
		Never hinged	1.25	
		On cover		8.75
B39	SP1	3c on 20c red vio & rose, *lav*	1.60	1.60
		Never hinged	2.40	
		On cover		16.00
B40	SP1	5c on 25c sl grn & rose, *bluish*	1.60	1.60
		Never hinged	2.75	
		On cover		20.00
B41	SP1	5c on 40c rose & grn, *yel*	1.60	1.60
		Never hinged	2.75	
		On cover		20.00
B42	SP1	10c on 50c vio & bl, *lav*	3.25	3.25
		Never hinged	4.75	
		On cover		17.50
B43	SP1	10c on 75c grn & ol, *grnsh*	3.25	3.25
		Never hinged	4.75	
		On cover		16.00
B44	SP1	25c on 1fr bl & grn, *bluish*	3.25	3.25
		Never hinged	4.75	
		On cover		16.00
B45	SP1	25c on 2fr rose & vio, *pnksh*	14.50	14.50
		Never hinged	22.50	
		On cover		35.00

B46	SP1	25c on 5fr red & brn, *lem*	52.50	52.50
		Never hinged	110.00	
		On cover		125.00
		Nos. B37-B46 (10)	83.15	83.15

These stamps were sold at their original values but paid postage only to the amount of the surcharged values. The difference was given to Child Welfare societies.

Tunis-Chad Motor Caravan SP2

1928, Feb.   Engr.   *Perf. 13½*

B47	SP2	40c + 40c org brn	1.60	1.60
		Never hinged	2.40	
		On cover		4.00
B48	SP2	50c + 50c dp vio	2.00	2.00
		Never hinged	2.75	
		On cover		4.00
B49	SP2	75c + 75c dk bl	2.00	2.00
		Never hinged	2.75	
		On cover		4.75
B50	SP2	1fr + 1fr carmine	2.00	2.00
		Never hinged	2.75	
		On cover		6.75
B51	SP2	1.50fr + 1.50fr brt bl	2.00	2.00
		Never hinged	2.75	
		On cover		16.00
B52	SP2	2fr + 2fr dk grn	2.40	2.40
		Never hinged	3.50	
		On cover		10.00
B53	SP2	5fr + 5fr red brn	2.40	2.40
		Never hinged	3.50	
		On cover		17.50
		Nos. B47-B53 (7)	14.40	14.40

The surtax on these stamps was for the benefit of Child Welfare societies.

Nos. 122-135, 137-142 Surcharged in Black

 a

b

1938   *Perf. 11, 12½, 12½x13*

B54	A14(a)	1c + 1c	3.25	3.25
		Never hinged	5.50	
		On cover		6.50
B55	A14(a)	2c + 2c	3.25	3.25
		Never hinged	5.50	
		On cover		6.50
B56	A14(a)	3c + 3c	3.25	3.25
		Never hinged	5.50	
		On cover		6.50
B57	A14(a)	5c + 5c	3.25	3.25
		Never hinged	5.50	
		On cover		6.50
B58	A14(a)	10c + 10c	3.25	3.25
		Never hinged	5.50	
		On cover		6.50
B59	A15(a)	15c + 15c	3.25	3.25
		Never hinged	5.50	
		On cover		6.50
B60	A15(a)	20c + 20c	3.25	3.25
		Never hinged	5.50	
		On cover		6.50
B61	A15(a)	25c + 25c	3.25	3.25
		Never hinged	5.50	
		On cover		6.50
B62	A15(a)	30c + 30c	3.25	3.25
		Never hinged	5.50	
		On cover		6.50
B63	A15(a)	40c + 40c	3.25	3.25
		Never hinged	5.50	
		On cover		6.50
B64	A16(a)	50c + 50c	3.25	3.25
		Never hinged	5.50	
		On cover		6.50
B65	A16(a)	75c + 75c	3.25	3.25
		Never hinged	5.50	
		On cover		6.50
B66	A16(a)	90c + 90c	3.25	3.25
		Never hinged	5.50	
		On cover		6.50
B67	A16(a)	1fr + 1fr	3.25	3.25
		Never hinged	5.50	
		On cover		9.50
B68	A17(b)	1.50fr + 1fr	3.25	3.25
		Never hinged	5.50	
		On cover		7.25
B69	A17(b)	2fr + 1.50fr	5.50	5.50
		Never hinged		
		On cover		9.50
B70	A17(b)	3fr + 2fr	6.50	6.50
		Never hinged	10.50	
		On cover		12.50
B71	A17(b)	5fr + 3fr	24.00	24.00
		Never hinged	35.00	
		On cover		35.00

a.	Perf. 12½	120.00	120.00
	Never hinged	175.00	
	On cover		210.00
B72	A17(b) 10fr + 5fr	52.50	52.50
	Never hinged	80.00	
	On cover		110.00
B73	A17(b) 20fr + 10fr	80.00	80.00
	Never hinged	200.00	
	On cover		190.00
	Nos. B54-B73 (20)	217.25	217.25

50th anniversary of the post office.

AIR POST STAMPS

No. 43
Surcharged
in Red

1919, Apr. Unwmk. Perf. 14x13½

C1	A6 30c on 35c ol grn & brn	1.60	1.60
	Never hinged	2.40	
	On cover		6.00
a.	Inverted surcharge	180.00	
	Never hinged	275.00	
b.	Double surcharge	180.00	
	Never hinged	275.00	
c.	Double inverted surcharge	210.00	
	Never hinged	325.00	
d.	Double surcharge, one inverted	180.00	
	Never hinged	275.00	

Type A6,
Overprinted
in Rose

1920, Apr.

C2	A6 30c ol grn, bl & rose	1.25	1.25
	Never hinged	1.60	
	On cover		4.50
a.	On grayish paper	2.00	2.00
	Never hinged	3.25	
	On cover		6.00

Nos. 53
and 55
Overprinted
in Red

1927, Mar. 24

C3	A7 1fr indigo & ultra	1.25	.80
	Never hinged	1.75	
	On cover		5.25
C4	A7 2fr grn & red, pink	3.50	2.40
	Never hinged	5.50	
	On cover		12.00

Nos. 51
and 57
Srchd. in
Black or
Red

C5	A6 1.75fr on 75c (Bk)	1.25	.80
	Never hinged	1.75	
	On cover		6.00
C6	A7 1.75fr on 5fr (R)	3.50	2.40
	Never hinged	5.50	
	On cover		9.50

Type A13 Ovptd. like #C3-C4 in Blue
1928, Feb.

C7	A13 1.30fr org & lt vio	4.00	1.60
	Never hinged	6.50	
	On cover		6.50
C8	A13 1.80fr gray grn & red	4.75	1.25
	Never hinged	8.00	
	On cover		8.00
C9	A13 2.55fr lil & ol brn	2.40	1.25
	Never hinged	4.00	
	On cover		12.00
	Nos. C7-C9 (3)	11.15	4.10

Type A13 Surcharged like #C5-C6 in Blue

1930, Aug.

C10	A13 1.50fr on 1.30fr org & lt vio	2.75	.95
	Never hinged	4.50	
	On cover		4.75
C11	A13 1.50fr on 1.80fr gray grn & red	4.75	.80
	Never hinged	8.00	
	On cover		4.75

C12	A13 1.50fr on 2.55fr lil & ol brn	9.50	2.40
	Never hinged	16.00	
	On cover		5.25
	Nos. C10-C12 (3)	17.00	4.15

POSTAGE DUE STAMPS

During 1888-1901, postage due stamps were created by perforating regular postage stamps with the letter "T." Generally, panes were folded before perforation, so that the "T" is either upright or inverted on equal numbers of stamps. The high values (75c, 1fr and 5fr) were perforated as needed, not always in full panes, and so examples of these values with inverted "T" command a modest premium.

All values exist perforated with a smaller "T," apparently used in Gafsa. These are rare.

Nos. 1-8 perforated "T"

1888-97

JA1	A1 1c black, blue	7.25	5.50
	Never hinged	14.50	
	On cover		475.00
a.	"T" inverted	7.25	5.50
	Never hinged	14.50	
	On cover		475.00
b.	Horiz. ruled line background ('97)	14.50	14.50
	Never hinged	24.00	
c.	As "b," "T" inverted	14.50	14.50
	Never hinged	24.00	
JA2	A1 2c pur brn, buff	7.25	5.50
	Never hinged	14.50	
	On cover		475.00
a.	"T" inverted	7.25	5.50
	Never hinged	14.50	
	On cover		475.00
b.	Horiz. ruled line background ('97)	17.00	17.00
	Never hinged	30.00	
c.	As "b," "T" inverted	17.00	17.00
	Never hinged	30.00	
JA3	A1 5c green, grnsh	21.00	17.00
	Never hinged	42.50	
	On cover		400.00
a.	"T" inverted	21.00	17.00
	Never hinged	42.50	
	On cover		400.00
b.	Horiz. ruled line background ('97)	25.00	25.00
	Never hinged	45.00	
c.	As "b," "T" inverted	25.00	25.00
	Never hinged	45.00	
JA4	A1 15c blue, grysh	55.00	27.50
	Never hinged	105.00	
	On cover		475.00
a.	"T" inverted	55.00	27.50
	Never hinged	105.00	
	On cover		475.00
JA5	A1 25c black, rose	80.00	52.50
	Never hinged	160.00	
	On cover		600.00
a.	"T" inverted	80.00	52.50
	Never hinged	160.00	
	On cover		600.00
b.	Horiz. ruled line background ('97)	300.00	250.00
	Never hinged	525.00	
c.	As "b," "T" inverted	300.00	250.00
	Never hinged	525.00	
JA6	A1 40c red, straw	60.00	52.50
	Never hinged	120.00	
	On cover		400.00
a.	"T" inverted	60.00	52.50
	Never hinged	120.00	
	On cover		400.00
JA7	A1 75c car, rose	80.00	55.00
	Never hinged	160.00	
a.	"T" inverted	87.50	65.00
	Never hinged	175.00	
b.	Horiz. ruled line background ('97)	170.00	125.00
	Never hinged	330.00	
c.	As "b," "T" inverted	87.50	65.00
	Never hinged	175.00	
JA8	A1 5fr gray vio, grysh	450.00	300.00
a.	"T" inverted	475.00	330.00
b.	Horiz. ruled line background ('97)	475.00	330.00
c.	As "b," "T" inverted	550.00	450.00
	Nos. JA1-JA8 (8)	760.50	515.50

See footnote following No. 8

Nos. 9//27 perforated "T"
1888-1901

JA9	A2 1c blk, lil bl	2.00	2.00
	Never hinged	3.25	
	On cover		400.00
a.	"T" inverted	2.00	2.00
	Never hinged	3.25	
	On cover		400.00
b.	Tête-bêche pair, JA9 & JA9a	7.25	7.25
	Never hinged	13.00	
JA10	A2 2c pur brn, buff	2.75	2.00
	Never hinged	4.75	
	On cover		400.00

---

a.	"T" inverted	2.75	2.00
	Never hinged	4.75	
	On cover		400.00
b.	Tête-bêche pair, JA10 & JA10a	10.50	9.00
	Never hinged	17.50	
JA11	A2 5c grn, grnsh	11.00	2.40
	Never hinged	20.00	
	On cover		350.00
a.	"T" inverted	11.00	2.40
	Never hinged	20.00	
	On cover		350.00
b.	Tête-bêche pair, JA11 & JA11a	40.00	11.00
	Never hinged	70.00	
JA12	A2 5c yellow grn ('99)	8.00	1.25
	Never hinged	15.00	
	On cover		240.00
a.	"T" inverted	8.00	1.25
	Never hinged	15.00	
	On cover		240.00
b.	Tête-bêche pair, JA12 & JA12a	35.00	9.50
	Never hinged	65.00	
JA13	A2 10c blk, lav ('93)	10.50	4.75
	Never hinged	17.50	
	On cover		160.00
a.	"T" inverted	10.50	4.75
	Never hinged	17.50	
	On cover		160.00
b.	Tête-bêche pair, JA13 & JA13a	35.00	17.50
	Never hinged	65.00	
JA14	A2 10c red ('01)	1.60	.80
	Never hinged	3.25	
	On cover		240.00
a.	"T" inverted	1.60	.80
	Never hinged	3.25	
	On cover		240.00
b.	Tête-bêche pair, JA14 & JA14a	8.00	4.75
	Never hinged	14.50	
JA15	A2 15c blue, grysh	17.50	5.50
	Never hinged	32.50	
	On cover		275.00
a.	"T" inverted	17.50	5.50
	Never hinged	32.50	
	On cover		275.00
b.	Tête-bêche pair, JA15 & JA15a	52.50	20.00
	Never hinged	95.00	
JA16	A2 15c gray ('01)	1.60	.80
	Never hinged	3.25	
	On cover		200.00
a.	"T" inverted	1.60	.80
	Never hinged	3.25	
	On cover		200.00
b.	Tête-bêche pair, JA16 & JA16a	8.00	4.75
	Never hinged	14.50	
JA17	A2 20c red, grn ('99)	20.00	5.50
	Never hinged	40.00	
	On cover		275.00
a.	"T" inverted	20.00	5.50
	Never hinged	40.00	
	On cover		275.00
b.	Tête-bêche pair, JA17 & JA17a	65.00	20.00
	Never hinged	120.00	
JA18	A2 25c blk, rose	22.50	6.50
	Never hinged	40.00	
	On cover		275.00
a.	"T" inverted	22.50	6.50
	Never hinged	40.00	
	On cover		275.00
b.	Tête-bêche pair, JA18 & JA18a	65.00	20.00
	Never hinged	100.00	
JA19	A2 25c blue ('01)	3.25	1.20
	Never hinged	6.50	
	On cover		275.00
a.	"T" inverted	3.25	1.20
	Never hinged	6.50	
	On cover		275.00
b.	Tête-bêche pair, JA19 & JA19a	13.00	7.25
	Never hinged	25.00	
JA20	A2 40c red, straw	24.00	6.50
	Never hinged	40.00	
	On cover		325.00
a.	"T" inverted	24.00	6.50
	Never hinged	40.00	
	On cover		325.00
b.	Tête-bêche pair, JA20 & JA20a	72.50	20.00
	Never hinged	125.00	
JA21	A2 75c car, rose	200.00	150.00
	Never hinged	225.00	175.00
JA22	A2 75c dp vio, org ('93)	40.00	12.00
	Never hinged	75.00	
a.	"T" inverted	45.00	13.50
	Never hinged	80.00	
JA23	A3 1fr olive, olive	40.00	12.00
	Never hinged	72.50	
a.	"T" inverted	40.00	12.50
	Never hinged	72.50	
JA24	A3 5fr red lil, lav	175.00	115.00
a.	"T" inverted	200.00	125.00

Quadrille Paper

JA25	A2 15c bl, grysh ('93)	21.00	4.75
	Never hinged	37.50	
	On cover		125.00
a.	"T" inverted	21.00	4.75
	Never hinged	37.50	
	On cover		125.00
b.	Tête-bêche pair, JA25 & JA25a	72.50	20.00
	Never hinged	125.00	
	Nos. JA9-JA25 (17)	600.70	332.95

D1

Perf. 14x13½

1901-03 Unwmk. Typo.

J1	D1 1c black	.55	.50
	Never hinged	.80	
	On cover		40.00
J2	D1 2c orange	1.05	.65
	Never hinged	1.60	
	On cover		40.00
J3	D1 5c blue	.80	.50
	Never hinged	1.25	
	On cover		35.00
a.	On grayish paper ('17)	1.60	1.25
	Never hinged	2.75	
	On cover		40.00
J4	D1 10c brown	.80	.65
	Never hinged	1.25	
	On cover		32.50
J5	D1 20c blue green	4.50	.95
	Never hinged	7.25	
	On cover		32.50
a.	On grayish paper ('18)	5.25	2.00
	Never hinged	8.75	
	On cover		40.00
J6	D1 30c carmine	3.50	.90
	Never hinged	6.00	
	On cover		32.50
a.	On grayish paper ('17)	4.00	1.25
	Never hinged	7.25	
	On cover		40.00
J7	D1 50c brown violet	2.00	.95
	Never hinged	3.25	
	On cover		40.00
a.	On grayish paper ('18)	8.00	2.75
	Never hinged	13.50	
	On cover		47.50
J8	D1 1fr olive green	1.60	.95
	Never hinged	2.75	
	On cover		60.00
J9	D1 2fr carmine, grn	4.50	2.50
	Never hinged	7.50	
	On cover		72.50
J10	D1 5fr blk, yellow	57.50	40.00
	Never hinged	87.50	
	On cover		125.00
	Nos. J1-J10 (10)	76.80	48.55

No. J10 Surcharged in
Blue

1914, Nov.

J11	D1 2fr on 5fr blk, yellow	1.60	1.60
	Never hinged	2.40	
	On cover		65.00

In Jan. 1917 regular 5c postage stamps were overprinted "T" in an inverted triangle and used as postage due stamps.

D2

1922-49

J12	D2 1c black	.30	.30
	Never hinged	.50	
	On cover		32.50
J13	D2 2c black, yellow	.30	.30
	Never hinged	.50	
	On cover		32.50
J14	D2 5c violet brown	.70	.50
	Never hinged	1.05	
	On cover		24.00
J15	D2 10c blue	.55	.50
	Never hinged	.80	
	On cover		24.00
J16	D2 10c yel green ('45)	.25	.25
	Never hinged	.30	
	On cover		20.00
J17	D2 20c orange, yel	.55	.50
	Never hinged	.80	
	On cover		24.00
J18	D2 30c brown ('23)	.55	.30
	Never hinged	.80	
	On cover		27.50
J19	D2 50c rose red	1.05	.50
	Never hinged	1.40	
	On cover		32.50
J20	D2 50c blue vio ('45)	.25	.25
	Never hinged	.30	
	On cover		16.00
J21	D2 60c violet ('28)	1.05	.50
	Never hinged	1.40	
	On cover		40.00
J22	D2 80c bister ('28)	.90	.40
	Never hinged	1.20	
	On cover		52.50
J23	D2 90c orange red ('28)	1.10	.65
	Never hinged	1.60	
	On cover		52.50
J24	D2 1fr green	.65	.30
	Never hinged	.95	
	On cover		52.50
J25	D2 2fr olive grn, straw	1.30	.55
	Never hinged	2.10	
	On cover		60.00
J26	D2 2fr car rose ('45)	.30	.30
	Never hinged	.40	
	On cover		16.00
J27	D2 3fr vio, pink ('29)	.50	.30
	Never hinged	.75	
	On cover		80.00
J28	D2 4fr grnsh bl ('45)	.50	.50
	Never hinged	.65	
	On cover		20.00

J29	D2	5fr violet	.90	.65
		Never hinged	1.20	
		On cover		100.00
J30	D2	10fr cerise ('49)	.50	.50
		Never hinged	.65	
		On cover		24.00
J31	D2	20fr olive gray ('49)	1.40	1.10
		Never hinged	1.75	
		On cover		24.00
		Nos. J12-J31 (20)	13.60	8.95

PARCEL POST STAMPS

Mail Delivery — PP1

1906 Unwmk. Typo. Perf. 13½x14

Q1	PP1	5c grn & vio brn	.80	.65
		Never hinged	1.60	
Q2	PP1	10c org & red	1.20	.80
		Never hinged	2.40	
Q3	PP1	20c dk brn & org	2.00	.80
		Never hinged	4.00	
a.		Center double	525.00	5,500.
Q4	PP1	25c blue & brn	2.75	.80
		Never hinged	6.00	
Q5	PP1	40c gray & rose	3.25	.80
		Never hinged	6.75	
Q6	PP1	50c vio brn & vio	2.75	.80
		Never hinged	6.00	
Q7	PP1	75c bis brn & bl	3.25	.80
		Never hinged	8.00	
Q8	PP1	1fr red brn & red	3.25	.55
		Never hinged	6.75	
Q9	PP1	2fr carmine & bl	9.50	1.20
		Never hinged	18.00	
Q10	PP1	5fr vio & vio brn	27.50	1.60
		Never hinged	47.50	
		Nos. Q1-Q10 (10)	57.00	8.80

Gathering
Dates — PP2

1926

Q11	PP2	5c pale brn & dk bl	.50	.50
		Never hinged	.80	
Q12	PP2	10c rose & vio	.65	.50
		Never hinged	1.20	
Q13	PP2	20c yel grn & blk	.65	.65
		Never hinged	1.20	
Q14	PP2	25c org brn & blk	.65	.65
		Never hinged	1.20	
Q15	PP2	40c dp rose & dp grn	2.75	.65
		Never hinged	4.50	
Q16	PP2	50c lt vio & blk	2.00	.90
		Never hinged	3.25	
Q17	PP2	60c ol & brn red	2.00	.80
		Never hinged	3.25	
Q18	PP2	75c gray vio & bl grn	2.00	.80
		Never hinged	3.25	
Q19	PP2	80c ver & ol brn	2.00	.80
		Never hinged	3.25	
Q20	PP2	1fr Prus bl & dp rose	2.40	.80
		Never hinged	4.00	
Q21	PP2	2fr vio & mag	4.75	.80
		Never hinged	8.00	
Q22	PP2	4fr red & blk	5.25	.80
		Never hinged	8.75	
Q23	PP2	5fr red brn & dp vio	8.00	1.20
		Never hinged	13.50	
Q24	PP2	10fr dl red & grn, grnsh	16.00	1.20
		Never hinged	27.50	
Q25	PP2	20fr yel grn & dp vio, lav	30.00	2.00
		Never hinged	47.50	
		Nos. Q11-Q25 (15)	79.60	13.05

Parcel post stamps were discontinued July 1, 1940.

TURKEY

'tər-kē

LOCATION — Southeastern Europe and Asia Minor, between the Mediterranean and Black Seas
GOVT. — Republic
AREA — 300,947 sq. mi.
POP. — 48,000,000 (est. 1984)
CAPITAL — Ankara

The Ottoman Empire ceased to exist in 1922, and the Republic of Turkey was inaugurated in 1923.

40 Paras = 1 Piaster
40 Paras = 1 Ghurush (1926)
40 Paras = 1 Kurush (1926)
100 Kurush = 1 Lira

> Catalogue values for unused stamps in this country are for Never Hinged items, beginning with Scott 817 in the regular postage section, Scott C1 in the airpost section, and Scott J97 in the postage due section.

Turkish Numerals

"Tughra," Monogram of
Sultan Abdul-Aziz
A1   A2

A3   A4

1863 Unwmk. Litho. Imperf.
Red Band: 20pa, 1pi, 2pi
Blue Band: 5pi
Thin Paper

1	A1	20pa blk, *yellow*	75.00	20.00
a.		Tête bêche pair	250.00	200.00
b.		Without band	100.00	
c.		Green band		
2	A2	1pi blk, *dl vio*	125.00	20.00
a.		1pi black, *gray*	125.00	21.50
b.		Tête bêche pair	400.00	300.00
c.		Without band	140.00	
d.		Design reversed		175.00
e.		1pi blk, *yel* (error)	250.00	150.00
4	A3	2pi blk, *grnsh bl*	115.00	20.00
a.		2pi black, *ind*	115.00	21.50
b.		Tête bêche pair	400.00	300.00
c.		Without band	140.00	
5	A4	5pi blk, *rose*	225.00	45.00
a.		Tête bêche pair	500.00	400.00
b.		Without band	250.00	
c.		Green band	275.00	
d.		Red band	275.00	

Thick, Surface Colored Paper

6	A1	20pa blk, *yellow*	250.00	37.50
a.		Tête bêche pair	450.00	450.00
b.		Design reversed	325.00	325.00
c.		Without band	225.00	225.00
d.		Paper colored through	225.00	225.00
7	A2	1pi blk, *gray*	300.00	35.00
a.		Tête bêche pair	900.00	900.00
b.		Design reversed		
c.		Without band		
d.		Paper colored through	350.00	225.00
		Nos. 1-7 (6)	1,090.	177.50

Full margins: Nos. 1, 2, 4, 5 = 1mm at sides and top, 3mm at bottom (includes part of band); Nos. 6-7 = ¾mm at sides and top, 3¼ at bottom (includes part of band). Height of colored bands is 6mm. Full margins for items without band = 3mm at bottom.

Full margins of first printings: No. 4 = 1mm; No. 5 = ½mm.

The 2pi and 5pi had two printings. In the common printing, the stamps are more widely spaced and alternate horizontal rows of 10 are inverted. In the first and rare printing, the stamps are more closely spaced and no rows are tête bêche.
See Nos. J1-J4.

Crescent and Star,
Symbols of Turkish
Caliphate — A5

Surcharged

1865 Typo. Perf. 12½

8	A5	10pa deep green	11.00	35.00
c.		"1" instead of "10" in each corner	300.00	300.00
9	A5	20pa yellow	7.00	6.00
a.		Star without rays	9.00	6.00
10	A5	1pi lilac	12.50	4.00
a.		Star without rays	20.00	5.00
c.		1pi gray	11.00	3.00
11	A5	2pi blue	6.50	4.00
12	A5	5pi carmine	5.50	4.50
d.		Inverted surcharge		
13	A5	25pi red orange	325.00	250.00

Imperf., Pairs

8b	A5	10pa	125.00	125.00
9b	A5	20pa	125.00	125.00
10b	A5	1pi	100.00	90.00
11a	A5	2pi	100.00	90.00
12b	A5	5pi	150.00	110.00
13a	A5	25pi	900.00	900.00

See Nos. J6-J35. For overprints and surcharges see Nos. 14-52, 64-65, 446-461, 467-468, J71-J77, Eastern Rumelia 1.

Surcharged

1867

14	A5	10pa gray green	9.50	
a.		Imperf., pair	55.00	
15	A5	20pa yellow	15.00	
a.		Imperf., pair	75.00	
16	A5	1pi lilac	20.00	
a.		Imperf., pair	110.00	
b.		Imperf., with surcharge of 5pi	200.00	
17	A5	2pi blue	5.50	45.00
a.		Imperf.		50.00
18	A5	5pi rose	4.50	45.00
a.		Imperf.		50.00
19	A5	25pi orange	3,600.	
		Nos. 14-18 (5)	54.50	

Nos. 14, 15, 16 and 19 were never placed in use.

Surcharged

1869 Perf. 13½

20	A5	10pa dull violet	100.00	12.00
a.		Printed on both sides		
b.		Imperf., pair	90.00	80.00
c.		Inverted surcharge		90.00
d.		Double surcharge		
e.		10pa yellow (error)		300.00
f.		10pa gray brown	60.00	2.10
21	A5	20pa pale green	400.00	14.00
a.		Imperf., pair	450.00	275.00
22	A5	1pi yellow	10.00	2.50
		No gum	2.00	
c.		Inverted surcharge	100.00	
d.		Double surcharge		
e.		Surcharged on both sides		
23	A5	2pi orange red	200.00	10.00
b.		Imperf., pair	125.00	125.00
c.		Printed on both sides		125.00
d.		Inverted surcharge	70.00	70.00
e.		Surcharged on both sides		140.00

24	A5	5pi blue	5.00	10.00
25	A5	5pi gray	30.00	37.50
26	A5	5pi dull rose	37.50	125.00
		Nos. 20-26 (7)	782.50	211.00

Th perf., Perf. 9 to 11 and
Compound

1870-71

27	A5	10pa lilac	550.00	25.00
28	A5	10pa brown	500.00	15.00
a.		10pa brown, *lilac*	3,750.	100.00
b.		10pa purple, *lilac*	3,750.	125.00
c.		10pa gray, *lilac*	5,000.	160.00
29	A5	20pa gray green	75.00	10.00
a.		Printed on both sides		
30	A5	1pi yellow	550.00	10.00
a.		Inverted surcharge	500.00	80.00
b.		Without surcharge		
31	A5	2pi red	8.00	5.00
a.		Imperf.	20.00	20.00
b.		Printed on both sides		40.00
c.		Surcharged on both sides		
32	A5	5pi blue	5.00	12.50
a.		5pi greenish blue	6.00	
33	A5	5pi slate	40.00	50.00
a.		Printed on both sides		80.00
b.		Surcharged on both sides		
34	A5	25pi dull rose	40.00	75.00
		Nos. 27-34 (8)	1,768.	202.50

1873 Perf. 12, 12½

35	A5	10pa dark lilac	475.00	25.00
a.		Inverted surcharge		90.00
36	A5	10pa olive brown	110.00	17.50
a.		10pa bister	110.00	11.00
37	A5	2pi vermilion	3.50	4.50
a.		Surcharged on both sides	22.50	22.50
		Nos. 35-37 (3)	588.50	47.00

Surcharged

1874-75 Perf. 13½

38	A5	10pa red violet	52.50	7.50
a.		Imperf., pair	210.00	50.00
39	A5	20pa yellow green	15.00	5.00
b.		Inverted surcharge	30.00	13.00
c.		Double surcharge		
40	A5	1pi yellow	210.00	30.00
a.		Imperf., pair	100.00	80.00

Perf. 12, 12½

41	A5	10pa red violet	25.00	10.00
a.		Inverted surcharge	45.00	60.00
		Nos. 38-41 (4)	302.50	52.50

Surcharged

1876, Apr. Perf. 13½

42	A5	10pa red lilac	2.00	.50
a.		Inverted surcharge	70.00	
b.		Imperf., pair	15.00	15.00
43	A5	20pa pale green	2.00	.50
b.		Inverted surcharge	70.00	
c.		Imperf., pair	15.00	15.00
44	A5	1pi yellow	2.00	.50
a.		Imperf., pair	27.50	27.50
46	A5	5pi gray blue	1,700.	
47	A5	25pi dull rose	1,700.	
		Nos. 42-44 (3)	6.00	

Nos. 46 and 47 were never placed in use.
See Nos. 64-65.

Surcharged

1876, Jan.

48	A5	¼pi on 10pa violet	3.00	2.50
49	A5	½pi on 20pa yel grn	6.25	2.50
50	A5	1¼pi on 5pa rose	2.25	2.50
a.		Imperf., pair	60.00	
51	A5	2pi on 2pi redsh brn	40.00	7.50
52	A5	5pi on 5pi gray blue	10.00	85.00
		Nos. 48-52 (5)	61.50	100.00

The surcharge on Nos. 48-52 restates in French the value originally expressed in Turkish characters.

The vast majority of No. 51 unused are without gum.

A7

1876, Sept.   Typo.   Perf. 13½

53	A7	10pa black & rose lil	2.00	6.25
54	A7	20pa red vio & grn	62.50	5.00
55	A7	50pa blue & yellow	1.25	10.00
56	A7	2pi black & redsh brn	1.60	5.00
57	A7	5pi red & blue	3.00	12.50
b.		Cliché of 25pi in plate of 5pi	400.00	375.00
58	A7	25pi claret & rose	15.00	85.00
a.			160.00	
		Nos. 53-58 (6)	85.35	123.75

Nos. 56-58 exist perf. 11½, but were not regularly issued.
See Nos. 59-63, 66-91, J36-J38. For overprints see Nos. 462-466, 469-476, J78-J79, P10-P14, Eastern Rumelia 2-40.

1880-84   Perf. 13½

59	A7	5pa black & ol ('81)	3.00	6.50
a.		Imperf.	30.00	
60	A7	10pa black & grn ('84)	3.00	3.50
61	A7	20pa black & rose	55.00	2.00
62	A7	1pi blk & bl (piastres)	75.00	3.00
a.		1pi black & gray blue	85.00	
b.		Imperf.	60.00	
63	A7	1pi blk & bl (piastre) ('81)	110.00	5.00
		Nos. 59-63 (5)	246.00	20.00

A cliché of No. 63 was inserted in a plate of the Eastern Rumelia 1pi (No. 13). This was found in the remainder stock.
Nos. 60-61 and 63 exist perf. 11½, but were not regularly issued.
See Nos. J36-J38.

1881-82

Surcharged like Apr., 1876 Issue

64	A5	20pa gray	4.25	6.25
a.		Inverted surcharge	13.50	
b.		Imperf., pair	25.00	
65	A5	2pi pale salmon	3.00	1.00
a.		Inverted surcharge	22.50	

1884-86   Perf. 11½, 13½

66	A7	5pa lil & pale lil ('86)	200.00	150.00
67	A7	10pa grn & pale grn	1.60	1.25
68	A7	20pa rose & pale rose	2.00	1.25
69	A7	1pi blue & lt blue	2.00	1.25

Perf. 11½

70	A7	2pi ocher & pale ocher	2.25	1.25
71	A7	5pi red brn & pale brn	20.00	25.00
c.		5pi ocher & pale ocher (error)	12.00	12.00

Perf. 11½, 13½

73	A7	25pi blk & pale gray ('86)	300.00	425.00
		Nos. 66-73 (7)	527.85	605.00

Imperf

66a	A7	5pa	60.00	
67a	A7	10pa	40.00	
68b	A7	20pa	40.00	
69b	A7	1pi	40.00	
73a	A7	25pi	150.00	

1886   Perf. 13½

74	A7	5pa black & pale gray	2.00	2.50
75	A7	2pi orange & lt bl	2.00	2.00
76	A7	5pi grn & pale grn	3.00	25.00
77	A7	25pi bis & pale bis	45.00	150.00
		Nos. 74-77 (4)	52.00	179.50

Imperf

74a	A7	5pa	30.00	
75b	A7	2pi	40.00	
76b	A7	5pi	40.00	
77a	A7	25pi	40.00	

Stamps of 1884-86, bisected and surcharged as above, 10pa, 20pa, 1pi and 2pi or surcharged "2" in red are stated to have been made privately and without authority. With the aid of employees of the post office, stamps were passed through the mails.

1888   Perf. 13½

83	A7	5pa green & yellow	2.50	5.00
84	A7	2pi red lilac & bl	1.50	1.50
85	A7	5pi dk brown & gray	5.00	20.00
86	A7	25pi red & yellow	30.00	150.00
		Nos. 83-86 (4)	39.00	176.50

Imperf

83a	A7	5pa	40.00	
84a	A7	2pi	40.00	
85a	A7	5pi	40.00	
86a	A7	25pi	40.00	

Nos. 74-86 exist perf. 11½, but were not regularly issued.

1890   Perf. 11½, 13½

87	A7	10pa green & gray	8.00	1.00
88	A7	20pa rose & gray	1.60	1.00
89	A7	1pi blue & gray	125.00	1.00
90	A7	2pi yellow & gray	2.25	7.50
a.		2pi Olive yel & yel	85.00	7.50
91	A7	5pi buff & gray	5.00	22.50
		Nos. 87-91 (5)	141.85	33.00

Imperf

87a	A7	10pa	20.00	
88a	A7	20pa	20.00	
89a	A7	1pi	100.00	
90b	A7	2pi	100.00	
91a	A7	5pi	25.00	

Arms and Tughra of "El Gazi" (The Conqueror) Sultan Abdul Hamid

A10   A11

A12   A13

A14

1892-98   Typo.   Perf. 13½

95	A10	10pa gray green	2.25	.50
96	A11	20pa violet brn ('98)	1.25	.50
a.		20pa dark pink	7.50	.45
b.		20pa pink	35.00	.45
97	A12	1pi pale blue	110.00	4.00
98	A13	2pi brown org	3.00	1.00
a.		Tête bêche pair	30.00	30.00
99	A14	5pi dull violet	9.00	15.00
a.		Turkish numeral in upper right corner reads "50" instead of "5"	50.00	45.00
		Nos. 95-99 (5)	125.50	21.00

See Nos. J39-J42. For surcharges and overprints see Nos. 100, 288-291, 350, 355-359, 477-478, B38, B41, J80-J82, P25-P34, P36, P121-P122, P134-P137, P153-P154.

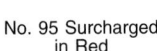

No. 95 Surcharged in Red

1897

100	A10	5pa on 10pa gray grn	3.00	1.25
a.		"Cinq" instead of "Cinq"	20.00	20.00

Turkish stamps of types A11, A17-A18, A21-A24, A26, A28-A39, A41 with or without Turkish overprints and English surcharges with "Baghdad" or "Iraq" are listed under Mesopotamia in Scott Standard catalogue, Vol. 4.
Turkish stamps of types A19 and A21 with Double-headed Eagle and "Shqipenia" handstamp are listed under Albania in Scott Standard catalogue, Vol. 1.

A16

1901   Typo.   Perf. 13¼

For Foreign Postage

102	A16	5pa bister	1.25	.60
103	A16	10pa yellow green	1.25	.60
104	A16	20pa magenta	1.25	.60
a.		Perf. 12	2.50	1.00
105	A16	1pi violet blue	1.50	1.00
106	A16	2pi gray blue	2.50	1.00
107	A16	5pi ocher	8.50	3.50
108	A16	25pi dark green	100.00	30.00
109	A16	50pi yellow	250.00	100.00
		Nos. 102-109 (8)	366.25	137.30

A17

For Domestic Postage

Perf. 13¼

110	A17	5pa purple	1.25	.50
a.		Perf. 12	2.50	1.60
b.		Perf. 12x13¼	3.00	.60
111	A17	10pa green	1.25	.50
a.		Perf. 12	5.00	3.50
b.		Perf. 12x13¼	5.00	1.50
112	A17	20pa carmine	1.25	.50
a.		Perf. 12	3.00	1.60
b.		Perf. 12x13¼	6.00	1.50
113	A17	1pi blue	1.25	.50
a.		Imperf.	20.00	
b.		Perf. 12	4.25	2.25
c.		Perf. 12x13¼	6.00	1.50
114	A17	2pi orange	2.00	.50
115	A17	5pi lilac rose	5.75	1.00
a.		Perf. 12	6.25	2.25

Perf. 13½

116	A17	25pi brown	10.00	2.00
a.		Perf. 12	25.00	8.50
117	A17	50pi yellow brown	37.50	5.00
a.		Perf. 12	55.00	17.00
		Nos. 110-117 (8)	60.25	10.50

Nos. 110-113 exist perf. 12x13½.
See Nos. J43-J46.
For overprints and surcharges see Nos. 165-180, 292-303, 340-341, 361-377, 479-493, B19-B20, B37, P37-P48, P69-P80, P123-P126, P138-P146, P155-P164.

A18

1905   Perf. 12, 13½ and Compound

118	A18	5pa ocher	1.00	.50
119	A18	10pa dull green	1.00	.50
a.		Imperf.	4.00	3.50
120	A18	20pa carmine	1.00	.50
a.		Imperf.	4.00	3.50
121	A18	1pi blue	1.00	.50
122	A18	2pi slate	1.50	.50
123	A18	2½pi red violet	1.50	.50
a.		Imperf.	11.00	9.00
124	A18	5pi brown	2.00	.50
125	A18	10pi orange brn	3.75	.50
126	A18	25pi olive green	12.50	15.00
127	A18	50pi deep violet	50.00	30.00

See Nos. J47-J48. For overprints and surcharges see Nos. 128-131, 181-182, 304-314, 351-354, 378-389, 494-508, B1-B3, B21-B23, B39-B40, P49-P54, P127-P129, P147-P150, P165-P171.

Large "Discount" Overprint in Carmine or Blue

1906

128	A18	10pa dull green (C)	3.00	1.00
129	A18	20pa carmine (Bl)	3.00	1.00
130	A18	1pi blue (C)	3.00	1.00
131	A18	2pi slate (C)	17.50	5.00
		Nos. 118-131 (14)	101.75	57.00

Stamps bearing this overprint were sold to merchants at a discount from face value to encourage the use of Turkish stamps on foreign correspondence, instead of those of the various European powers which maintained post offices in Turkey. The overprint is the Arab "B," for "Béhié," meaning "discount."

A19

1908

132	A19	5pa ocher	1.25	.50
133	A19	10pa blue green	1.75	.30
134	A19	20pa carmine	40.00	.50
135	A19	1pi bright blue	15.00	.50
a.		1pi ultramarine	50.00	10.00
136	A19	2pi blue black	10.00	.50
137	A19	2½pi violet brown	6.00	.50
138	A19	5pi dark violet	80.00	.50
139	A19	10pi red	70.00	2.50
140	A19	25pi dark green	12.00	.50
141	A19	50pi red brown	50.00	35.00

See Nos. J49-J50. For overprints and surcharges see Nos. 142-145, 314B-316B, 390-396, 509-516A, B4-B6, B17, B24-B27, P55-P60, P130-P131, P151, P172, Thrace 15.

Small "Discount" Overprint in Carmine or Blue

142	A19	10pa blue green (C)	7.50	2.50
143	A19	20pa carmine (Bl)	7.50	2.50
144	A19	1pi brt blue (C)	15.00	1.50
145	A19	2pi blue black (C)	25.00	12.50
		Nos. 132-145 (14)	341.00	65.80

A20

Perf. 12, 13½ & Compound

1908, Dec. 17

146	A20	5pa ocher	1.00	.50
147	A20	10pa blue green	1.50	.50
148	A20	20pa carmine	2.00	1.00
149	A20	1pi ultra	3.00	1.00
150	A20	2pi gray black	12.50	15.00
		Nos. 146-150 (5)	20.00	18.00

Imperf

146a	A20	5pa	3.00	3.00
147a	A20	10pa	4.00	4.00
148a	A20	20pa	5.50	5.50
149a	A20	1pi	3.00	3.00

Granting of a Constitution, the date of which is inscribed on the banderol: "324 Temuz 10" (July 24, 1908).
For overprints see Nos. 397, 517.

Tughra and "Reshad" of Sultan Mohammed V — A21

1909, Dec.

151	A21	5pa ocher	1.00	.50
152	A21	10pa blue green	1.00	.50
a.		Imperf.	3.00	3.00
153	A21	20pa carmine rose	1.00	.50
154	A21	1pi ultra	3.00	.50
a.		1pi bright blue	12.50	
155	A21	2pi blue black	3.00	.50
156	A21	2½pi dark brown	90.00	20.00
157	A21	5pi dark violet	12.00	1.00
158	A21	10pi dull red	37.50	1.00
159	A21	25pi dark green	350.00	100.00
160	A21	50pi red brown	150.00	80.00

The 2pa olive green, type A21, is a newspaper stamp, No. P68.

Two types exist for the 10pa, 20pa and 1pi. In the second type, the damaged crescent is restored.

See Nos. J51-J52. For overprints and surcharges see Nos. 161-164, 317-327, 342-343, 398-406, 518-528, 567, B7-B14, B18, B28-B32, P61-P68, P81, P132-P133, P152, P173, Turkey in Asia 67, 72, Thrace 1-4, 13, 13A, 14.

Overprinted in Carmine or Blue

161	A21	10pa blue grn (C)	1.75	.75
a.		Imperf.		
162	A21	20pa car rose (Bl)	1.75	.75
a.		Imperf.		
163	A21	1pi ultra (C)	3.50	2.00
a.		Imperf.	4.00	
b.		1pi bright blue	6.50	3.00
164	A21	2pi blue black (C)	75.00	30.00
a.		Imperf.		
		Nos. 151-164 (14)	730.50	238.00

Stamps of 1901-05 Overprinted in Carmine or Blue

The overprint was applied to 18 denominations in four settings with change of city name, producing individual sets for each city: "MONASTIR," "PRISTINA," "SALONIQUE" and "USKUB."

1911, June 26　　　Perf. 12, 13½

"Monastir"

165	A16	5pa bister	4.50	4.50
166	A16	10pa yel grn	4.50	4.50
167	A16	20pa magenta	9.00	9.00
168	A16	1pi violet blue	9.00	9.00
169	A16	2pi gray blue	9.00	9.00
170	A16	5pi ocher	40.00	60.00
171	A16	25pi dark green	60.00	75.00
172	A16	50pi yellow	100.00	125.00
173	A17	5pa purple	6.00	4.50
174	A17	10pa green	6.00	4.50
175	A17	20pa carmine	9.00	9.00
176	A17	1pi blue	9.00	9.00
177	A17	2pi orange	9.00	9.00
178	A17	5pi lilac rose	40.00	60.00
179	A17	25pi chocolate	85.00	100.00
180	A17	50pi yel brn	100.00	125.00
181	A18	2½pi red violet	65.00	100.00
182	A18	10pi org brn	60.00	60.00
		Nos. 165-182 (18)	625.00	802.00

Sultan's visit to Macedonia. The Arabic overprint reads: "Souvenir of the Sultan's Journey, 1329." Values same for all cities. See Nos. P69-P81.

"Pristina"

165a	A16	5pa bister	1.00	1.00
166a	A16	10pa yel grn	1.00	1.00
167a	A16	20pa magenta	6.00	6.00
168a	A16	1pi violet blue	6.00	6.00
169a	A16	2pi gray blue	6.00	6.00
170a	A16	5pi ocher	35.00	35.00
171a	A16	25pi dark green	60.00	60.00
172a	A16	50pi yellow	100.00	100.00
173a	A17	5pa purple	1.00	1.00
174a	A17	10pa green	1.00	1.00
175a	A17	20pa carmine	6.00	6.00
176a	A17	1pi blue	6.00	6.00
177a	A17	2pi orange	6.00	6.00
178a	A17	5pi lilac rose	40.00	40.00
179a	A17	25pi chocolate	80.00	80.00
180a	A17	50pi yel brn	100.00	100.00
181a	A18	2½pi red violet	60.00	60.00
182a	A18	10pi org brn	60.00	60.00
		Nos. 165a-182a (18)	575.00	575.00

"Salonique"

165b	A16	5pa bister	1.00	1.00
166b	A16	10pa yel grn	1.00	1.00
167b	A16	20pa magenta	6.00	6.00
168b	A16	1pi violet blue	6.00	6.00

169b	A16	2pi gray blue	6.00	6.00
170b	A16	5pi ocher	35.00	35.00
171b	A16	25pi dark green	60.00	60.00
172b	A16	50pi yellow	100.00	100.00
173b	A17	5pa purple	1.00	1.00
174b	A17	10pa green	1.00	1.00
175b	A17	20pa carmine	6.00	6.00
176b	A17	1pi blue	6.00	6.00
177b	A17	2pi orange	6.00	6.00
178b	A17	5pi lilac rose	40.00	40.00
179b	A17	25pi chocolate	80.00	80.00
180b	A17	50pi yel brn	100.00	100.00
181b	A18	2½pi red violet	60.00	60.00
182b	A18	10pi org brn	60.00	60.00
		Nos. 165b-182b (18)	575.00	575.00

"Uskub"

165c	A16	5pa bister	1.00	1.00
166c	A16	10pa yel grn	1.00	1.00
167c	A16	20pa magenta	6.00	6.00
168c	A16	1pi violet blue	6.00	6.00
169c	A16	2pi gray blue	6.00	6.00
170c	A16	5pi ocher	35.00	35.00
171c	A16	25pi dark green	60.00	60.00
172c	A16	50pi yellow	100.00	100.00
173c	A17	5pa purple	1.00	1.00
174c	A17	10pa green	1.00	1.00
175c	A17	20pa carmine	6.00	6.00
176c	A17	1pi blue	6.00	6.00
177c	A17	2pi orange	6.00	6.00
178c	A17	5pi lilac rose	40.00	40.00
179c	A17	25pi chocolate	80.00	80.00
180c	A17	50pi yel brn	100.00	100.00
181c	A18	2½pi red violet	60.00	60.00
182c	A18	10pi org brn	60.00	60.00
		Nos. 165c-182c (18)	575.00	575.00

Sultan's visit to Macedonia. The Arabic overprint reads: "Souvenir of the Sultan's Journey, 1329." See Nos. P69-P81.

General Post Office, Constantinople — A22

1913, Mar. 14　　　Perf. 12

237	A22	2pa olive green	1.00	.50
238	A22	5pa ocher	1.00	.50
239	A22	10pa blue green	1.00	.50
240	A22	20pa carmine rose	1.00	.50
241	A22	1pi ultra	1.00	.50
242	A22	2pi indigo	2.00	.50
243	A22	5pi dull violet	3.50	1.00
244	A22	10pi dull red	6.00	3.00
245	A22	25pi gray green	22.50	22.50
246	A22	50pi orange brown	85.00	125.00

See Nos. J53-J58. For overprints and surcharges see Nos. 247-250, 328-339, 344, 407-414, 529-538, 568, B14-B16, B33-B36, Turkey in Asia 68, Thrace 10, 10A, 11, 11A, 12, N82.

Overprinted in Carmine or Blue

247	A22	10pa blue green (C)	1.00	.50
248	A22	20pa car rose (Bl)	1.00	.50
249	A22	1pi ultra (C)	1.00	.50
250	A22	2pi indigo (C)	17.50	7.50
		Nos. 237-250 (14)	144.50	163.50

Mosque of Selim, Adrianople — A23

1913, Oct. 23　　　Engr.

251	A23	10pa green	1.50	1.00
252	A23	20pa red	2.50	2.00
253	A23	40pa blue	6.00	3.00
		Nos. 251-253 (3)	10.00	6.00

Recapture of Adrianople (Edirne) by the Turks.

See Nos. 592, J59-J62. For overprints and surcharge see Nos. 415-417, 539-540, J59-J62, J67-J70, J83-J86, Thrace N84.

Obelisk of Theodosius in the Hippodrome A24

Column of Constantine A25

Leander's Tower — A26

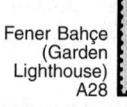

One of the Seven Towers — A27

Fener Bahçe (Garden Lighthouse) A28

The Castle of Europe on the Bosporus A29

Mosque of Sultan Ahmed — A30

Monument to the Martyrs of Liberty A31

Fountains of Suleiman A32

Cruiser "Hamidie" A33

View of Kandili on the Bosporus A34

War Ministry (Later Istanbul University) — A35

Sweet Waters of Europe Park A36

Mosque of Suleiman A37

The Bosporus A38

Mosque of Suleiman A37

Sultan Ahmed's Fountain A39

Sultan Mohammed V — A40

Designs A24-A39: Views of Constantinople.

1914, Jan. 14　　　Litho.

254	A24	2pa red lilac	1.00	.50
255	A25	4pa dark brown	1.00	.50
256	A26	5pa violet brown	1.00	.50
257	A27	6pa dark blue	1.00	.50

Engr.

258	A28	10pa green	2.00	.40
259	A29	20pa red	1.75	.40
260	A30	1pi blue	.75	.50
b.		Booklet pane of 2+2 labels		
261	A31	1½pi car & blk	1.25	.75
262	A32	1¾pi sl & red brn	1.50	1.00
263	A33	2pi green & blk	2.00	.40
264	A34	2½pi org & ol grn	2.00	.50
265	A35	5pi dull violet	4.00	1.00
266	A36	10pi red brown	8.00	1.00
267	A37	25pi olive green	125.00	5.50
268	A38	50pi carmine	8.00	3.00
269	A39	100pi deep blue	75.00	27.50
		Cut cancellation		12.00
270	A40	200pi green & blk	550.00	*400.00*
		Cut cancellation		25.00
		Nos. 254-270 (17)	785.25	443.95

See Nos. 590-591, 593-598.

For overprints and surcharges see Nos. 271-287, 419, 541, 552-553, 574A, 601, 603-604, P174, Turkey in Asia 1-3, 5-9, 73-74, Thrace N77, N78.

Nos. 258-260, 262-263 Ovptd. in Red or Blue

271	A28	10pa green (R)	3.00	.75
272	A29	20pa red (Bl)	10.00	.75
273	A30	1pi blue (R)	3.00	.75
275	A32	1¾pi sl & red brn (Bl)	4.00	1.25
276	A33	2pi green & blk (R)	50.00	5.00
		Nos. 271-276 (5)	70.00	8.50

No. 261
Surcharged

1914, July 23
277 A31 1pi on 1½pi car & blk   3.25 2.50
   a.   "1330" omitted   2.50 1.50
   b.   Double surcharge
   c.   Triple surcharge   5.00 5.00

7th anniv. of the Constitution. The surcharge reads "10 July, 1330, National fête" and has also the numeral "1" at each side, over the original value of the stamp.

Stamps of
1914
Overprinted
in Black or
Red

278 A26 5pa violet brn (Bk) 1.75 .50
279 A28 10pa green (R) 3.25 .50
280 A29 20pa red (Bk) 4.00 .50
281 A30 1pi blue (R) 10.00 1.50
282 A33 2pi grn & blk (R) 15.00 1.50
283 A35 5pi dull violet (R) 50.00 4.25
284 A36 10pi red brown (R) 190.00 65.00
   Nos. 278-284 (7) 274.00 73.75

This overprint reads "Abolition of the Capitulations, 1330".

No. 269 Surcharged

1915
286 A39 10pi on 100pi 62.50 22.50
   a.   Inverted surcharge

No. 270 Surcharged

287 A40 25pi on 200pi 25.00 8.00

Preceding Issues
Overprinted in
Carmine or Black

1915   **On Stamps of 1892**
288 A10 10pa gray green 1.00 .50
   a.   Inverted overprint 7.50 7.50
289 A13 2pi brown orange 1.50 .50
   a.   Inverted overprint 7.50 7.50
290 A14 5pi dull violet 4.00 .50
   a.   On No. 99a 17.00 17.00

On Stamp of 1897
291 A15 5pa on 10pa gray grn 1.00 .50
   a.   Inverted overprint 5.00 5.00
   b.   On No. 100a 10.00 10.00

On Stamps of 1901
292 A16 5pa bister 1.00 .50
293 A16 1pi violet blue 3.00 .50
294 A16 2pi gray blue 2.50 .50
295 A16 5pi ocher 20.00 .50
296 A16 25pi dark green 50.00 20.00
297 A17 5pa purple 1.00 .50
298 A17 10pa green 1.50 .50
299 A17 20pa carmine 1.50 .50
   a.   Inverted overprint 7.50 7.50
300 A17 1pi blue 1.50 .50
   a.   Inverted overprint 5.00 5.00

301 A17 2pi orange 2.00 .50
   a.   Inverted overprint 7.50 7.50
   b.   Double ovpt. (R and Bk) 5.00 5.00
302 A17 5pi lilac rose 2.50 .50
303 A17 25pi brown 12.50 2.00

On Stamps of 1905
304 A18 5pa ocher 1.00 .50
305 A18 10pa dull green 1.00 .50
   a.   Inverted overprint 5.00 5.00
306 A18 20pa carmine 1.00 .50
   a.   Inverted overprint 5.00 5.00
307 A18 1pi brt blue 1.50 .50
   a.   Inverted overprint 5.00 5.00
308 A18 2pi slate 2.50 .50
   a.   Inverted overprint 10.00 10.00
309 A18 2½pi red violet 1.50 .50
310 A18 5pi brown 2.00 .50
   a.   Inverted overprint 10.00 10.00
311 A18 10pi orange brown 12.50 .50
312 A18 25pi olive green 50.00 8.00

On Stamps of 1906
313 A18 10pa dull green 2.00 .50
314 A18 2pi slate 5.00 .50
   a.   Inverted overprint 5.00 5.00

On Stamps of 1908
314B A19 2pi blue black 225.00 50.00
315 A19 2½pi violet brown 5.00 1.50
315A A19 5pi dark violet 100.00 35.00
315B A19 10pi red 15.00 7.50
316 A19 25pi dark green 30.00 5.00
   a.   Inverted overprint 17.00 17.00

With Additional
Overprint

316B A19 2pi blue black 15.00 5.00

On Stamps of 1909
317 A21 5pa ocher 1.00 .50
   a.   Inverted overprint 10.00 10.00
   b.   Double overprint 5.00 5.00
318 A21 20pa car rose 1.25 .75
   a.   Inverted overprint 5.00 5.00
319 A21 1pi ultra 2.00 .50
   a.   Inverted overprint 5.00 5.00
320 A21 2pi blue blk 2.50 .75
321 A21 2½pi dark brn 67.50 25.00
322 A21 5pi dark violet 1.00 .50
   a.   Inverted overprint 6.50 6.50
323 A21 10pi dull red 10.00 .50
324 A21 25pi dark green 1,750. 1,200.

With Additional
Overprint

325 A21 20pa carmine rose 2.00 .50
   a.   Inverted overprint 5.00 5.00
326 A21 1pi ultra 2.00 .50
327 A21 2pi blue black 3.50 .50

On Stamps of 1913
328 A22 5pa ocher 1.00 .50
   a.   Inverted overprint 7.50 7.50
329 A22 10pa blue green 1.00 .50
   a.   Inverted overprint 10.00 10.00
330 A22 20pa carmine rose 1.00 .50
   a.   Inverted overprint 7.50 7.50
331 A22 1pi ultra 1.50 .50
   a.   Inverted overprint 5.00 5.00
332 A22 2pi indigo 2.00 .50
   a.   Inverted overprint 5.00 5.00
333 A22 5pi dull violet 3.00 .50
334 A22 10pi dull red 10.00 .50
   a.   Inverted overprint 10.00 10.00
335 A22 25pi gray green 30.00 20.00

With Additional
Overprint

336 A22 10pa blue green 1.00 .50
337 A22 20pa carmine rose 1.00 .50
338 A22 1pi ultra 2.00 .50
339 A22 2pi indigo 7.50 3.00
   a.   Inverted overprint 10.00 10.00

See Nos. P121-P133.

Stamps of 1901-13
Overprinted

1916
340 A17 5pa purple 1.00 .50
   a.   5pa purple, #P43 80.00 80.00
341 A17 10pa green 1.50 .50
   a.   Double overprint 6.50 6.50
   b.   10pa yellow green, #103 80.00 80.00
342 A21 20pa car rose, #153 2.00 .75
   a.   20pa carmine rose, #162 110.00 110.00
343 A21 1pi ultra 5.50 1.00
344 A22 5pi dull violet 10.00 3.00
   Nos. 340-344 (5) 20.00 5.75

Occupation of the Sinai Peninsula.

Old General Post
Office of
Constantinople
A41

1916, May 29   Litho.   Perf. 13½
345 A41 5pa green .75 .50
   a.   Perf 12½ .75 .50
346 A41 10pa carmine .75 .50
   a.   Perf 12½ .75 .50
347 A41 20pa ultra 1.00 .50
   a.   Perf 12½ 1.00 .50
348 A41 1pi violet & blk 1.50 .75
   a.   Perf 12½ 1.50 1.50
349 A41 5pi yel brn & blk 20.00 2.50
   a.   Perf 12½ 20.00 2.50
   Nos. 345-349 (5) 24.00 4.75

Introduction of postage in Turkey, 50th anniv. For overprints see Nos. 418, B42-B45.

Stamps of 1892-
1905 Overprinted

1916
350 A10 10pa gray grn (R) 2.00 2.00
351 A18 20pa carmine (Bl) 3.75 2.50
352 A18 1pi blue (R) 10.00 5.00
353 A18 2pi slate (Bk) 12.50 2.00
354 A18 2½pi red violet (Bk) 20.00 2.25
   Nos. 350-354 (5) 48.25 13.75

National Fête Day. Overprint reads "10 Temuz 1332" (July 23, 1916).

**Preceding Issues Overprinted or
Surcharged in Red or Black**

     a   b

1916   On Stamps of 1892-98
355 A10(a) 10pa gray green 1.00 .50
355A A11(a) 20pa violet brown 1.00 .50
   b.   Inverted overprint 10.00 10.00
356 A12(a) 1pi gray blue 50.00 50.00
357 A13(a) 2pi brown org 5.00 1.50
358 A14(a) 5pi dull violet 50.00 50.00

On Stamp of 1897
359 A15(b) 5pa on 10pa gray grn .75 .50

On Stamps of 1901
361 A16(a) 5pa bister .75 .50
   a.   Double overprint 7.50 7.50
362 A16(a) 10pa yel grn 1.00 .50
363 A16(a) 20pa magenta .75 .50
364 A16(a) 1pi violet blue 1.00 .50
   a.   Inverted overprint 7.50 7.50
365 A16(a) 2pi gray black 5.00 1.00
366 A16(b) 5pi on 25pi dk grn 55.00 55.00

367 A16(b) 10pi on 25pi dk grn 55.00 55.00
368 A16(a) 25pi dark green 55.00 55.00
369 A17(a) 5pa purple 75.00 50.00
370 A17(a) 10pa green 2.00 1.50
371 A17(a) 20pa carmine .75 .50
   a.   Inverted overprint 7.50 7.50
372 A17(a) 1pi blue 1.00 .50
   a.   Inverted overprint 7.50 7.50
373 A17(a) 2pi orange 1.50 .50
374 A17(b) 10pi on 25pi brown 5.00 1.50
375 A17(b) 10pi on 50pi yel brn 7.50 1.50
376 A17(a) 25pi brown 7.50 1.50
377 A17(a) 50pi red brn 10.00 2.50

On Stamps of 1905
378 A18(a) 5pa ocher .75 .50
379 A18(a) 20pa carmine 1.00 .50
   a.   Inverted overprint 10.00 5.00
380 A18(a) 1pi brt blue 2.00 .50
   a.   Inverted overprint 10.00 10.00
381 A18(a) 2pi slate 1.50 1.00
382 A18(a) 2½pi red violet 7.50 1.50
383 A18(b) 10pi on 25pi ol grn 10.00 3.00
384 A18(b) 10pi on 50pi dp vio 10.00 4.00
385 A18(a) 25pi olive green 10.00 5.00
386 A18(a) 50pi deep violet 7.50 5.00

On Stamps of 1906
387 A18(a) 10pa dull green 1.50 .60
388 A18(a) 20pa carmine 1.50 1.00
389 A18(a) 1pi brt blue 1.50 1.00

On Stamps of 1908
390 A19(a) 2½pi violet brown 67.50 67.50
391 A19(b) 10pi on 25pi dk grn 20.00 12.50
392 A19(b) 10pi on 50pi red brn 67.50 67.50
393 A19(b) 25pi on 50pi red brn 67.50 67.50
394 A19(a) 25pi dark green 15.00 5.00
395 A19(a) 50pi red brown 50.00 50.00

With Additional
Overprint

396 A19(a) 2pi blue black 67.50 67.50

On Stamps of 1908-09
397 A20(a) 5pa ocher 67.50 67.50
398 A21(a) 5pa ocher 1.00 2.50
399 A21(a) 10pa blue green 50.00 50.00
400 A21(a) 20pa carmine rose 50.00 50.00
401 A21(a) 1pi ultra 2.00 1.00
402 A21(a) 2pi blue black 4.00 2.00
403 A21(a) 2½pi dark brown 50.00 50.00
404 A21(a) 5pi dark violet 50.00 50.00

With Additional
Overprint

405 A21(a) 1pi ultra 67.50 67.50
406 A21(a) 2pi blue black 50.00 50.00

On Stamps of 1913
407 A22(a) 5pa ocher 1.00 .75
408 A22(a) 20pa carmine rose 1.50 .50
409 A22(a) 1pi ultra 1.50 .50
410 A22(a) 2pi indigo 3.00 1.00
411 A22(b) 10pi on 50pi org brn 12.50 10.00
412 A22(a) 25pi gray green 7.50 5.00
413 A22(a) 50pi orange brown 15.00 12.50

With Additional
Overprint

414 A22(a) 1pi ultra 2.00 1.00

On Commemorative Stamps of 1913
415 A23(a) 10pa green 1.25 .50
416 A23(a) 20pa red 2.00 .75
417 A23(a) 40pa blue 6.00 2.50

On Commemorative Stamp of 1916
418 A41(a) 5pi yel brn & blk 1.00 .50

No. 277
Surcharged
in Blue

419 A31 60pa on 1pi on 1½pi   3.25   3.50
a. "1330" omitted   40.00   40.00
See Nos. P134-P152, J67-J70.

Turkish
Artillery
A42

Mosque at Orta Köy,
Constantinople — A43

Lighthouse on
Bosporus — A44

Monument to
Martyrs of
Liberty — A45

Map of the
Dardanelles;
Sultan
Mohammed
V — A46

Map of the
Dardanelles
A47

Istanbul
Across the
Golden
Horn
A48

Pyramids of
Egypt
A49

Sentry and
Shell — A51

Sultan
Mohammed
V — A52

1916-18		Typo.	Perf. 12½	
420	A42	2pa violet	1.50	.75
a.		Perf 11½	1.50	.75
421	A43	5pa orange	1.00	.75
a.		Perf 11½	1.50	.75
424	A44	10pa green	1.00	1.00
a.		Perf 11½	1.50	.75
		Engr.		
425	A45	20pa deep rose	1.00	.75
426	A46	1pi dull violet	3.00	.50
		Typo.		
428	A47	50pa ultra	1.50	.50
a.		Perf 11½	12.00	16.00
429	A48	2pi org brn & ind	3.00	.50
a.		Perf 11½	—	
430	A49	5pi pale blue & blk	17.50	2.00
a.		Perf 11½	25.00	2.00
		Engr.		
431	A50	10pi dark green	8.75	5.00
432	A50	10pi dark violet	32.50	2.50
433	A50	10pi dark brown	14.00	2.50
434	A51	25pi carmine, *straw*	2.25	1.50
437	A52	50pi carmine	5.00	5.00
438	A52	50pi indigo	2.00	2.50
439	A52	50pi green, *straw*	2.50	10.00
		Nos. 420-439 (15)	96.50	35.75

For overprints and surcharges see Nos. 541B-541E, 554-560, 565-566, 569-574, 575, 577-578, 579A-580, Turkey in Asia 4, 10, 64-66, Thrace N76, N80, N81. Compare designs A42-A43 with A53-A54.

Forgeries of Nos. 446-545 abound.

**Preceding Issues Overprinted or
Surcharged in Red, Black or Blue**

d   e

f   g

1917		**On Stamps of 1865**		
446	A5(d)	20pa yellow (R)	45.00	67.50
a.		Star without rays (R)	50.00	57.50
447	A5(d)	1pi pearl gray (R)	45.00	67.50
a.		Star without rays (R)	50.00	57.50
448	A5(d)	2pi blue (R)	45.00	67.50
449	A5(d)	5pi carmine (Bk)	45.00	67.50
		On Stamp of 1867		
450	A5(d)	5pi rose (Bk)	45.00	67.50
		On Stamps of 1870-71		
451	A5(d)	2pi red (Bl)	45.00	67.50
452	A5(d)	5pi blue (Bl)	45.00	67.50
453	A5(d)	25pi dull rose (Bl)	45.00	67.50
		On Stamp of 1874-75		
454	A5(d)	10pa red violet (Bl)	45.00	67.50
		On Stamps of April, 1876		
455	A5(d)	10pa red lilac (Bl)	45.00	67.50
a.		10pa red violet (Bl)	50.00	67.50
457	A5(d)	20pa pale green	45.00	67.50
458	A5(d)	1pi yellow (Bl)	45.00	67.50

		On Stamps of January, 1876		
459	A5(d)	¼pi on 10pa rose lil (Bl)	45.00	67.50
460	A5(d)	½pi on 20pa yel grn (R)	45.00	67.50
461	A5(d)	1¾pi on 50pa rose (Bl)	45.00	67.50
		On Stamps of September, 1876		
462	A7(d)	50pa blue & yel	45.00	67.50
463	A7(d)	2pi blk & redsh brn	45.00	67.50
464	A7(d)	25pi claret & rose (Bk)	45.00	67.50
		On Stamps of 1880-84		
465	A7(d)	5pa black & ol (R)	45.00	67.50
466	A7(d)	10pa black & grn (R)	45.00	67.50
		On Stamps of 1881-82		
467	A5(d)	20pa gray (Bl)	45.00	67.50
468	A5(d)	2pi pale sal (Bl)	45.00	67.50
		On Stamps of 1884-86		
469	A7(d)	10pa grn & pale grn (Bk)	45.00	67.50
470	A7(d)	2pi ocher & pale ocher (Bk)	45.00	67.50
471	A7(d)	5pi red brn & pale brn (Bk)	45.00	67.50
		On Stamps of 1886		
472	A7(d)	5pa blk & pale gray (R)	4.00	2.25
a.		Inverted overprint	30.00	30.00
473	A7(d)	2pi org & bl (Bk)	4.50	2.50
a.		Inverted overprint	35.00	35.00
474	A7(d)	5pi grn & pale grn (R)	45.00	67.50
475	A7(d)	25pi bis & pale bis (Bk)	45.00	67.50
		On Stamp of 1888		
476	A7(d)	5pi dk brn & gray (R)	45.00	67.50
		On Stamps of 1892-98		
477	A11(d)	20pa vio brn (R)	4.00	3.00
478	A13(d)	2pi brn org (R)	4.00	3.50
a.		Tête bêche pair	13.50	13.50
		On Stamps of 1901		
479	A16(d)	5pa bister (R)	3.00	3.00
a.		Inverted overprint	20.00	20.00
480	A16(d)	20pa mag (Bk)	2.00	1.50
a.		Inverted overprint	25.00	25.00
481	A16(d)	1pi vio bl (R)	3.00	3.00
a.		Inverted overprint	20.00	20.00
482	A16(d)	2pi gray bl (R)	5.00	5.00
483	A16(d)	5pi ocher (R)	32.50	50.00
484	A16(e)	10pi on 50pi yel (R)	32.50	50.00
485	A16(d)	25pi dk grn (R)	100.00	50.00
486	A17(d)	5pa purple (Bk)	32.50	50.00
487	A17(d)	10pa green (R)	5.00	5.00
488	A17(d)	20pa car (Bk)	2.00	1.50
a.		Inverted overprint	20.00	20.00
489	A17(d)	1pi blue (R)	1.00	.90
490	A17(d)	2pi org (Bk)	3.00	3.00
a.		Inverted overprint	20.00	20.00
491	A17(d)	5pi lil rose (R)	32.50	50.00
492	A17(e)	10pi on 50pi yel brn (R)	45.00	50.00
493	A17(d)	25pi brown (R)	25.00	5.00
		On Stamps of 1905		
494	A18(d)	5pa ocher (R)	2.00	1.00
a.		Inverted overprint	20.00	20.00
495	A18(d)	10pa dl grn (R)	32.50	50.00
496	A18(d)	20pa car (Bk)	1.00	1.00
a.		Double ovpt., one invtd.	35.00	35.00
b.		Inverted overprint	35.00	35.00
497	A18(d)	1pi blue (R)	1.50	1.00
a.		Inverted overprint	35.00	35.00
498	A18(d)	2pi slate (R)	5.00	5.00
499	A18(d)	2½pi red vio (Bk)	5.00	5.00
a.		Inverted overprint	20.00	20.00
500	A18(d)	5pi brown (R)	35.00	45.00
501	A18(d)	10pi orange brn (R)	35.00	50.00
502	A18(e)	10pi on 50pi dp vio (R)	35.00	50.00
503	A18(d)	25pi ol grn (R)	35.00	50.00
		On Nos. 128-131		
504	A18(d)	10pa dl grn (R)	1.50	1.00
a.		Inverted overprint	20.00	20.00
505	A18(d)	20pa car (Bk)	1.00	.75
a.		Double ovpt., one invtd.	20.00	20.00
b.		Inverted overprint	20.00	20.00
506	A18(d)	1pi brt bl (Bk)	1.00	.75
a.		Inverted overprint	20.00	20.00
507	A18(d)	1pi brt bl (R)	1.50	1.25
a.		Inverted overprint	20.00	20.00
508	A18(d)	2pi slate (Bk)	35.00	50.00
		Nos. 494-508 (15)	227.00	311.75

		On Stamps of 1908		
509	A19(d)	5pa ocher (R)	1.50	1.25
510	A19(d)	10pa bl grn (R)	20.00	20.00
510A	A19(d)	1pi brt blue (!)	105.00	110.00
511	A19(d)	2pi bl blk (R)	35.00	50.00
512	A19(d)	2½pi violet brn (Bk)	35.00	35.00
512A	A19(d)	10pi red (R)	*150.00*	225.00
513	A19(e)	10pi on 50pi red brn (R)	35.00	50.00
514	A19(d)	25pi dark green (R)	35.00	50.00

With Additional
Overprint

514A	A19(d)	10pa bl grn (Bk)	150.00	225.00
515	A19(d)	1pi brt bl (R)	35.00	50.00
516	A19(d)	2pi bl blk (R)	5.00	5.00
516A	A19(d)	2pi bl blk (Bk)	65.00	67.50
		On Stamps of 1908-09		
517	A20(d)	5pa ocher (R)	3.00	3.00
518	A21(d)	5pa ocher (R)	2.00	1.50
a.		Double overprint	20.00	20.00
b.		Dbl. ovpt., one inverted	20.00	20.00
519	A21(d)	10pa bl grn (R)	2.00	1.50
520	A21(d)	20pa carmine rose (Bk)	2.00	1.50
a.		Double overprint	35.00	35.00
521	A21(d)	1pi ultra (R)	1.50	1.00
a.		1p bright blue (R)	30.00	30.00
522	A21(d)	2pi bl blk (R)	5.00	5.00
523	A21(d)	2½pi dk brn (Bk)	35.00	50.00
524	A21(d)	5pi dk vio (R)	35.00	50.00
525	A21(d)	10pi dull red (R)	35.00	50.00

With Additional
Overprint

525A	A21(d)	10pa bl grn (Bk)	175.00	225.00
526	A21(d)	1pi ultra (Bk)	125.00	190.00
527	A21(d)	1pi ultra (R)	5.00	4.00
a.		1pi bright blue (R)	125.00	140.00
528	A21(d)	2pi bl blk (Bk)	35.00	50.00
		On Stamps of 1913		
529	A22(d)	5pa ocher (R)	2.50	2.00
530	A22(d)	10pa bl grn (R)	35.00	50.00
531	A22(d)	20pa car rose (Bk)	2.50	2.50
532	A22(d)	1pi ultra (R)	2.50	3.50
533	A22(d)	2pi indigo (R)	3.50	3.50
534	A22(d)	5pi dl vio (R)	35.00	50.00
535	A22(d)	10pi dl red (Bk)	45.00	50.00

With Additional
Overprint

536	A22(d)	10pa bl grn (Bk)	1.50	1.50
a.		Inverted overprint	20.00	20.00
537	A22(d)	1pi ultra (Bk)	3.00	3.00
a.		Inverted overprint	20.00	20.00
538	A22(d)	2pi indigo (Bk)	35.00	100.00
		On Commemorative Stamps of 1913		
539	A23(d)	10pa green (R)	5.00	5.00
a.		Inverted overprint	20.00	20.00
540	A23(d)	40pa blue (R)	7.00	7.00
a.		Inverted overprint	20.00	20.00

On No. 277, with Addition of New Value

541	A31	60pa on 1pi on 1 ½pi (Bk)	8.00 5.00
a.		"1330" omitted	45.00 45.00

On Stamps of 1916-18

541B	A51(f)	25pi car, straw	5.00 5.00
541C	A52(g)	50pi carmine	17.50 17.50
541D	A52(g)	50pi indigo	35.00 50.00
541E	A52(g)	50pi green, straw	15.00 27.50

Ovptd. on Eastern Rumelia No. 12

542	A4(d)	20pa blk & rose (Bl)	35.00 35.00

Ovptd. in Black on Eastern Rumelia #15-17

543	A4(d)	5pa lilac & pale lilac	45.00 45.00
544	A4(d)	10pa green & pale green	45.00 45.00
545	A4(d)	20pa carmine & pale rose	45.00 45.00

Some experts question the status of Nos. 510A, 512A and 525A.
See Nos. J71-J86, P153-P172.

Soldiers in Trench — A52a

1917

545A	A52a	5pa on 1pi red	1.25 .75

It is stated that No. 545A was never issued without surcharge.
See Nos. 548A, 548Af, 602.

Turkish Artillery A53

1917 Typo. Perf. 12½

546	A53	2pa Prussian blue	150.00
a.		Perf 11½	150.00

In type A42 the Turkish inscription at the top is in one group, in type A53 it is in two groups. It is stated that No. 546 was never placed in use. Examples were distributed through the Universal Postal Union at Bern.
For surcharges see Nos. 547-548, Turkey in Asia 69-70.

Surcharged

547	A53	5pi on 2pa Prus bl	15.00 1.75
a.		Inverted surcharge	35.00 15.00
b.		Turkish "5" omitted at lower left	
c.		Perf 11½	15.00 1.75

Surcharged

1918

548	A53	5pi on 2pa Prus blue	15.00 2.00
g.		Inverted surcharge	35.00 20.00

Top line of surcharge on Nos. 547-548 reads "Ottoman Posts."
For surcharge see Thrace No. N79.

No. 545A Surcharged

1918

548A	A52a	2pa on 5pa on 1pi red	2.50 1.75
b.		Double surcharge	20.00 20.00
c.		Inverted surcharge	20.00 20.00
d.		Double surcharge inverted	20.00 20.00
e.		Dbl. surch., one inverted	20.00 20.00
f.		In pair with No. 545A	30.00 30.00

Enver Pasha and Kaiser Wilhelm II on Battlefield A54

St. Sophia and Obelisk of the Hippodrome A55

1918 Typo. Perf. 12, 12½

549	A54	5pa brown red	125.00
550	A55	10pa gray green	125.00

The stamps, of which very few saw postal use, were converted into paper money by pasting on thick yellow paper and reperforating.
Values are for stamps with original gum. Examples removed from the yellow paper are worth $10 each.

Armistice Issue

Overprinted in Black or Red

1919, Nov. 30
On Stamps of 1913

552	A34	2 ½pi org & ol grn	125.00 300.00
553	A38	50pi carmine	125.00 300.00

On Stamps of 1916-18

554	A46	1pi dull violet (R)	7.50 10.00
555	A47	50pa ultra (R), perf 11½	1.00 1.50
a.		Perf 12½	2.00 2.50
556	A48	2pi org brn & ind	1.75 2.00
557	A49	5pi pale bl & blk (R), perf 11½	1.75 2.00
a.		Perf 12½	2.00 3.00
b.		Perf 11½x12½	2.50 4.00
558	A50	10pi dark green (R)	6.25 10.00
559	A51	25pi carmine, straw	6.25 10.00
560	A52	50pi grn, straw (R)	6.25 10.00

Fountain in Desert near Sinai — A56

Sentry at Beersheba — A57

Turkish Troops at Sinai A58

Typo.

562	A56	20pa claret	1.25 2.00
563	A57	1pi blue (R)	125.00 150.00
564	A58	25pi slate blue (R)	125.00 150.00
		Nos. 552-564 (12)	532.00 947.50

The overprint reads: "Souvenir of the Armistice, 30th October 1334." Nos. 562-564 are not known to have been regularly issued without overprint.
See No. J87. For overprints and surcharges see Nos. 576, 579, 582, 583-584, 586, Turkey in Asia 71, Thrace N83.

Stamps of 1911-19 Overprinted in Turkish

"Accession to the Throne of His Majesty, 3rd July 1334-1918," the Tughra of Sultan Mohammed VI and sometimes Ornaments and New Values

Dome of the Rock, Jerusalem — A59

1919

565	A42	2pa violet	1.00 2.50
566	A43	5pa orange	.75 .50
567	A21	5pa on 2pa ol grn	.75 .50
a.		Inverted surcharge	10.00 10.00
568	A22	10pa on 2pa ol grn	1.00 .50
569	A44	10pa green	1.25 1.50
a.		Inverted overprint	25.00 25.00
570	A45	20pa deep rose	1.25 .50
a.		Inverted overprint	12.00 12.00
571	A46	1pi dull violet	1.25 1.00
572	A47	60pa on 50pa ultra	1.25 1.00
573	A48	60pa on 2pi org brn & ind	1.00 .50
574	A48	2pi orange brn & ind	1.00 1.00
574A	A34	2 ½pi orange & ol grn	25.00 37.50
575	A49	5pi pale blue & blk	1.00 1.00
576	A56	10pi on 20pa cl	1.00 1.00
577	A50	10pi dark brown	2.50 2.50
578	A51	25pi carmine, straw	2.00 2.00
579	A57	35pi on 1pi blue	1.50 2.50
579A	A52	50pi carmine	25.00 37.50
580	A52	50pi green, straw	6.00 5.00
581	A59	100pi on 10pa green	6.00 5.00
582	A58	250pi on 25pi sl bl	6.00 5.00
		Nos. 565-582 (20)	86.50 108.50

See note after #586. See #J88-J91.
For overprint and surcharge see Nos. 585, Thrace N82.

Surcharged with Ornaments, New Values and

Perf. 11½, 12½

583	A56	20pa claret	1.75 10.00
584	A57	1pi deep blue	2.50 17.50
585	A59	60pa on 10pa green	1.50 7.50
586	A58	25pi slate blue	9.00 35.00
a.		Inverted overprint	100.00
		Nos. 583-586 (4)	14.75 85.00

#576, 579, 581, 582, 583-586 were prepared in anticipation of the invasion and conquest of Egypt by the Turks. They were not issued at that time but subsequently received various overprints in commemoration of Sultan Mehmet Sadi's accession to the throne (#565-582) and of the 1st anniv. of this event (#583-586).
For surcharge see Thrace No. N83.

Designs of 1913 Modified

1920 Litho. Perf. 11, 12

590	A26	5pa brown orange	1.00 .50

Engr.

591	A28	10pa green	1.00 .50
592	A23	20pa rose	1.00 .50
593	A30	1pi blue green	3.75 .50
594	A32	3pi blue	1.00 .50
595	A34	5pi gray	50.00 .50
596	A36	10pi gray violet	12.50 .50

597	A37	25pi dull violet	5.00 2.50
598	A38	50pi brown	5.00 10.00
		Nos. 590-598 (9)	80.25 16.00

On most stamps of this issue the designs have been modified by removing the small Turkish word at right of the tughra of the Sultan. In the 3pi and 5pi the values have been altered, while for the 25pi the color has been changed.
For surcharges see Thrace Nos. N77, N78, N84.

1921-22 Black Surcharge

600	SP1	30pa on 10pa red vio	1.50 .50
a.		Double surcharge	37.50 37.50
b.		Imperf.	
601	A28	60pa on 10pa green	1.50 .50
a.		Double surcharge	22.50 22.50
602	A52a	4 ½pi on 1pi red	9.00 4.00
a.		Inverted surcharge	20.00 20.00
603	A32	7 ½pi on 3pi blue	15.00 2.00
604	A32	7 ½pi on 3pi bl (R) ('22)	25.00 25.00
a.		Double surcharge	35.00 30.00
		Nos. 600-604 (5)	52.00 9.50

Turkish Stamps of 1916-21 with Greek surcharge as above in blue or black are of private origin.

Issues of the Republic

Crescent and Star — A64

TWO PIASTERS:
Type I — "2" measures 3¼x1¾mm
Type II — "2" measures 2¾x1½mm

FIVE PIASTERS:
Type I — "5" measures 3½x2¼mm
Type II — "5" measures 3x1¾mm

Printed by Ahmed Nazmi, Istanbul
Perf. 13¼x12¾-13¼

1923   Litho.   Thin Paper

605	A64	10pa gray black	.30	.25
		Never hinged	.80	
606	A64	20pa olive yel.	.30	.25
		Never hinged	.80	
607	A64	1pi deep violet	.30	.25
		Never hinged	.80	
a.		Slanting numeral in lower left corner	.50	.25
		Never hinged	1.00	
608	A64	1½pi emerald	.90	.25
		Never hinged	2.00	
a.		1½pi yellow green	.30	.25
		Never hinged	.80	
609	A64	2pi bluish grn (I)	.90	.25
		Never hinged	3.00	
a.		2pi deep green (II)	.90	.25
		Never hinged	3.00	
610	A64	3pi yel brn	.90	.60
		Never hinged	3.00	3.00
611	A64	3¾pi lilac brown	3.00	3.00
		Never hinged	8.00	
612	A64	4½pi carmine	.90	1.20
		Never hinged	3.00	
613	A64	5pi deep purple (I)	4.50	1.75
		Never hinged	10.00	
a.		5pi purple (II)	21.00	1.25
		Never hinged	50.00	
614	A64	7½pi blue	3.00	.60
		Never hinged	10.00	
615	A64	10pi slate	12.00	1.25
		Never hinged	30.00	
a.		10pi blue	16.00	1.25
		Never hinged	40.00	
616	A64	11¼pi dull rose	3.00	2.50
		Never hinged	7.00	
617	A64	15pi brown	15.00	1.25
		Never hinged	40.00	
618	A64	18¾pi myrtle green	4.25	3.75
		Never hinged	10.00	
619	A64	22½pi orange	12.00	2.50
		Never hinged	20.00	
620	A64	25pi black brown	50.00	3.00
		Never hinged	100.00	
621	A64	50pi gray	125.00	5.00
		Never hinged	300.00	
622	A64	100pi dark violet	250.00	11.00
		Never hinged	700.00	
623	A64	500pi deep green	950.00	275.00
		Never hinged	3,000.	
		Cut cancellation		15.00
		Nos. 605-623 (19)	1,436.	313.65
		Set, never hinged	4,250.	

#605-610, 612-617 exist imperf. & part perf.

Printed by Ikdam, Istanbul

1924   Thick Paper   Perf. 11

605b	A64	10pa greenish gray	.90	.25
		Never hinged	2.50	
606b	A64	20pa olive yellow	.90	.25
		Never hinged	2.50	
607b	A64	1pi deep violet	1.75	.25
		Never hinged	4.00	
d.		Slanting numeral in lower left corner	2.00	.25
		Never hinged	5.00	
609b	A64	2pi bluish green (I)	6.00	.90
		Never hinged	15.00	
d.		2pi bluish green (II)	175.00	2.00
		Never hinged	500.00	
610b	A64	3pi yellow brown	150.00	7.50
		Never hinged	450.00	
612b	A64	4½pi carmine	1.50	.60
		Never hinged	3.00	
613b	A64	5pi purple (II)	3.50	.25
		Never hinged	9.00	
614b	A64	7½pi blue	3.50	.60
		Never hinged	9.00	
615b	A64	10pi slate	11.00	12.00
		Never hinged	30.00	
617b	A64	15pi yellow brown	11.00	12.00
		Never hinged	30.00	
		Nos. 605b-617b (10)	190.05	34.60
		Set, never hinged	555.00	

Printed by Ottoman Public Debt Administration, Istanbul

1924-26   Thick Paper   Perf. 12

605c	A64	10pa black	.30	.25
		Never hinged	1.00	
606c	A64	20pa olive yellow	.30	.25
		Never hinged	1.00	
607c	A64	1pi violet	.60	.60
		Never hinged	1.50	
609c	A64	2pi green (II)	3.00	.60
		Never hinged	10.00	
610c	A64	3pi yellow brown	3.50	.60
		Never hinged	10.00	
613c	A64	5pi violet	3.50	1.00
		Never hinged	10.00	
615c	A64	10pi dark blue	60.00	12.00
		Never hinged	250.00	
d.		10pi perf. 13¼x12	60.00	12.00
		Never hinged	275.00	
		Nos. 605c-615c (7)	71.20	15.30
		Set, never hinged	285.00	

Bridge of Sakarya and Mustafa Kemal — A65

1924, Jan. 1   Perf. 12

625	A65	1½pi emerald	.75	.30
626	A65	3pi purple	.90	.50
627	A65	4½pi pale rose	5.00	2.00
628	A65	5pi yellow brown	4.00	2.00
629	A65	7½pi deep blue	5.00	2.00
630	A65	10pi orange	10.00	10.00
631	A65	100pi brown violet	52.50	20.00
632	A65	200pi olive brown	72.50	35.00
		Nos. 625-632 (8)	163.15	71.80
		Set, never hinged	750.00	

Signing of Treaty of Peace at Lausanne.

The Legendary Blacksmith and his Gray Wolf — A66

Sakarya Gorge — A67

Fortress of Ankara — A68

Mustafa Kemal Pasha — A69

1926   A66   Engr.

634	A66	10pa slate	.50	.25
635	A66	20pa orange	.50	.25
636	A66	1g brt rose	.50	.25
637	A67	2g green	1.50	.25
638	A67	2½g gray black	2.00	.25
639	A67	3g copper red	2.50	.25
640	A68	5g lilac gray	4.00	.75
641	A68	6g red	1.00	.25
642	A68	10g deep blue	7.50	.50
643	A68	15g deep orange	10.00	.50
644	A69	25g dk green & blk	15.00	1.25
645	A69	50g carmine & blk	20.00	1.50
646	A69	100g olive grn & blk	35.00	2.00
647	A69	200g brown & blk	90.00	5.50
		Nos. 634-647 (14)	190.00	13.75
		Set, never hinged	800.00	

Stamps of 1926 Overprinted in Black, Silver or Gold

1927, Sept. 9

648	A66	1g brt rose	.50	.50
649	A67	2g green	.50	1.00
650	A67	2½g gray black	1.50	2.00
651	A67	3g copper red	2.00	2.50
652	A68	5g lilac gray	2.50	4.00
653	A68	6g red	1.50	1.50
654	A68	10g deep blue	3.50	3.50
655	A68	15g deep orange	5.00	5.00
656	A69	25g dk green & blk (S)	15.00	20.00
657	A69	50g car & blk (S)	27.50	37.50
658	A69	100g ol grn & blk (G)	60.00	75.00
		Nos. 648-658 (11)	119.50	152.50
		Set, never hinged	425.00	

Agricultural and industrial exhibition at Izmir, Sept. 9-20, 1927.

The overprint reads: "1927" and the initials of "Izmir Dokuz Eylul Sergisi" (Izmir Exhibition, September 9).

Second Izmir Exhibition Issue
Nos. 634-647 Overprinted in Red or Black

On A66-A68

On A69

1928, Sept. 9

659	A66	10pa slate (R)	.50	.40
660	A66	20pa orange	.50	.40
661	A66	1g brt rose	1.00	.50
662	A67	2g green (R)	1.50	1.50
663	A67	2½g gray blk (R)	1.50	1.50
664	A67	3g copper red	1.50	1.50
665	A67	5g lilac gray (R)	2.00	3.00
666	A68	6g red	.50	.50
667	A68	10g deep blue	3.50	3.00
668	A68	15g deep orange	5.00	2.00
669	A69	25g dk grn & blk (R)	15.00	6.25
670	A69	50g car & blk (R)	17.50	20.00
671	A69	100g ol grn & blk (R)	40.00	60.00
672	A69	200g brn & blk (R)	62.50	62.50
		Nos. 659-672 (14)	152.50	153.05
		Set, never hinged	650.00	

The overprint reads "Izmir, September 9, 1928."

Nos. 636, 652, 654 Surcharged in Black (#673) or Red (#674-675)

1929

673	A66	20pa on 1g brt rose	.50	.25
a.		Inverted surcharge	3.50	3.50
674	A68	2½k on 5g lilac gray	1.00	.50
a.		Inverted surcharge	7.50	7.50
675	A68	6k on 10g deep blue	6.00	.75
		Nos. 673-675 (3)	7.50	1.50
		Set, never hinged	40.00	

Railroad Bridge over Kizil Irmak — A70

A71

A72

A73

Latin Inscriptions
Without umlaut over first "U" of "CUMHURIYETI"

1929   Engr.

676	A70	2k gray black	5.00	1.00
677	A70	2½k green	3.00	1.00
678	A70	3k violet brown	4.00	1.50
679	A71	6k dark violet	25.00	1.00
680	A72	12½k deep green	35.00	3.75
681	A73	50k carmine & blk	60.00	8.75
		Nos. 676-681 (6)	132.00	17.00
		Set, never hinged	400.00	

See Nos. 682-691, 694-695, 697, 699. For surcharges & overprints see #705-714, 716-717, 719, 721, 727, 765-766, 770-771, 777, C2, C7.

Sakarya Gorge — A74

Mustafa Kemal Pasha — A75

With umlaut over first "U" of "CUMHURIYETI"

1930

682	A71	10pa green	.25	.25
683	A70	20pa gray violet	.25	.25
684	A71	1k olive green	.50	.50
685	A71	1½k olive black	.50	.40
686	A70	2k dull violet	3.00	.50
687	A70	2½k deep green	2.00	.50
688	A70	3k brown orange	20.00	1.50
689	A71	4k deep rose	7.50	.50
690	A72	5k rose lake	11.50	.50
691	A71	6k indigo	7.50	.50
692	A74	7½k red brown	.25	.25
694	A72	12½k deep ultra	.75	.25
695	A72	15k deep orange	.75	.50
696	A74	17½k dark gray	.75	.50
697	A72	20k black brown	50.00	2.00
698	A72	25k olive brown	1.00	.50
699	A72	30k yellow brown	1.75	1.00
700	A74	40k red violet	1.50	1.00
701	A75	50k red & black	3.50	1.25
702	A75	100k olive grn & blk	3.50	1.25
703	A75	200k dk green & blk	3.75	1.50
704	A75	500k chocolate & blk	17.50	22.50
		Nos. 682-704 (22)	138.00	38.40
		Set, never hinged	600.00	

For surcharges and overprints see Nos. 715, 718, 720, 722-726, 767-769, 772-773, 775-776, 778-780, 823-828, 848-850, C1, C3-C6, C8-C11 (in Scott Standard catalogue, Vol. 6).

Nos. 682-704 Surcharged in Red or Black

a

b

c

1930, Aug. 30

705	A71(a)	10pa on 10pa (R)	.50	1.25
706	A70(b)	10pa on 20pa	.50	1.50
707	A70(b)	20pa on 1ku	1.00	1.50
708	A71(a)	1k on 1½k (R)	.50	1.25
709	A70(b)	1½k on 2k	1.00	1.50
710	A70(b)	2k on 2½k (R)	2.50	2.00
711	A70(b)	2½k on 3k	2.00	1.50
712	A71(a)	3k on 4k	2.00	1.00
713	A72(a)	4k on 5k	2.50	1.00
714	A71(a)	5k on 6k (R)	3.50	4.00
715	A74(a)	6k on 7½k	.75	.50
716	A71(a)	7½k on 12½k (R)	1.25	1.00
717	A72(a)	12½k on 15k	1.25	1.00
718	A74(b)	15k on 17½k (R)	5.00	4.00
719	A72(b)	17½k on 20k (R)	5.00	2.00
720	A74(b)	20k on 25k (R)	7.50	2.00
721	A72(b)	25k on 30k	5.00	2.50
722	A74(b)	30k on 40k	7.50	2.50
723	A75(c)	40k on 50k	15.00	7.50
724	A75(c)	50k on 100k (R)	70.00	16.00
725	A75(c)	100k on 200k (R)	85.00	27.50
726	A75(c)	250k on 500k (R)	75.00	35.00
		Nos. 705-726 (22)	294.25	118.00
		Set, never hinged	1,200.	

Inauguration of the railroad between Ankara and Sivas.

There are numerous varieties in these settings as: "309," "390," "930" inverted, no period after "D," no period after "Y" and raised period before "Y."

No. 685 Surcharged in Red

1931, Apr. 1
727 A71 1k on 1½k olive blk — 1.75 .30

Olive Tree with Roots Extending to All Balkan Capitals — A76

1931, Oct. 20   Engr.   Perf. 12
728 A76 2½k dark green .40 .25
729 A76 4k carmine .50 .25
730 A76 6k steel blue .50 .25
731 A76 7½k dull red .50 .25
732 A76 12k deep orange 1.00 .25
733 A76 12½k dark blue 1.00 .25
734 A76 30k dark violet 1.75 1.50
735 A76 50k dark brown 3.00 .75
736 A76 100k brown violet 6.25 1.50
Nos. 728-736 (9) 14.90 5.25
Set, never hinged 35.00

Second Balkan Conference.

A77   A78

Mustafa Kemal Pasha (Kemal Atatürk) — A79

1931-42   Typo.   Perf. 11½, 12
737 A77 10pa blue green .25 .25
738 A77 20pa deep orange .25 .25
739 A77 30pa brt violet ('38) .25 .25
740 A78 1k dk slate green .25 .25
740A A77 1½k magenta ('42) .55 .25
741 A78 2k dark violet .50 .25
741A A78 2k yel grn ('40) .25 .25
742 A77 2k green .50 .25
743 A78 3k brn org ('38) 1.50 .25
744 A78 4k slate 2.50 .25
745 A78 5k rose red .25 .25
745A A78 5k brown blk ('40) 2.00 .50
746 A78 6k deep blue 3.00 .25
746A A78 6k rose ('40) .80 .30
747 A77 7½k deep rose ('32) .50 .25
747A A78 8k brt blue ('38) 3.50 .25
b. 8k dark blue ('36) 3.50
748 A77 10k black brn ('32) 1.00 .25
748A A77 10k deep blue ('40) 7.00 .60
749 A77 12k bister ('32) 1.00 .25
750 A79 12½k indigo ('32) 1.00 .25
751 A77 15k org yel ('32) 1.00 .25
752 A77 20k olive grn ('32) 1.00 .25
753 A77 25k Prus blue ('32) 2.50 1.00
754 A77 30k magenta ('32) 7.50 .50
755 A79 100k maroon ('32) 200.00 5.50
756 A79 200k purple ('32) 3.75 2.00
757 A79 250k chocolate ('32) 100.00 11.50
Nos. 737-757 (27) 342.60 26.65
Set, never hinged 950.00

See Nos. 1015-1033, 1117B-1126 in Scott Standard catalogue, Vol. 6. For overprints see Nos. 811-816.

Symbolizing 10th Anniversary of Republic — A80

President Atatürk — A81

1933, Oct. 29   Perf. 10
758 A80 1½k blue green 1.25 1.00
759 A80 2k olive brown 1.25 1.00
760 A81 3k dull red 1.25 1.00
761 A81 6k deep blue 1.25 1.00
762 A80 12½k dark blue 3.25 2.50
763 A80 25k dark brown 8.00 5.00
764 A81 50k orange brown 20.00 15.00
Nos. 758-764 (7) 36.25 26.50
Set, never hinged 90.00

10th year of the Turkish Republic. The stamps were in use for three days only.

Nos. 682, 685, 692, 694, 696-698, 702 Overprinted or Surcharged in Red

İzmir 9 Eylül 934 Sergisi

İzmir 9 Eylül 934 Sergisi 2 Kuruş

1934, Aug. 26   Perf. 12
765 A71 10pa green .50 1.00
766 A71 1k on 1½k 1.00 .75
767 A74 2k on 25k 1.50 1.25
768 A74 5k on 7½k 5.00 5.00
769 A74 6k on 17½k 2.50 2.00
770 A72 12½k deep ultra 7.50 5.00
771 A74 15k on 20k 50.00 45.00
772 A74 20k on 25k 35.00 37.50
773 A75 50k on 100k 40.00 37.50
Nos. 765-773 (9) 143.00 135.00
Set, never hinged 600.00

Izmir Fair, 1934.

Nos. 696, 698, 701-704 Surcharged in Black

1936, Oct. 26
775 A74 4k on 17½k 1.00 .50
776 A74 5k on 25k 1.00 .50
777 A73 6k on 50k 1.00 .50
778 A71 10k on 100k 1.75 1.00
779 A75 20k on 200k 5.50 2.00
780 A75 50k on 500k 10.00 3.25
Nos. 775-780 (6) 20.25 7.75
Set, never hinged 75.00

"1926" in Overprint
775a A74 4k on 17½k 6.50 3.75
776a A74 5k on 25k 7.00 3.75
777a A73 6k on 50k 7.00 3.75
778a A75 10k on 100k 9.00 4.50
779a A75 20k on 200k 20.00 10.00
780a A75 50k on 500k 55.00 27.50
Nos. 775a-780a (6) 104.50 53.25
Set, never hinged 250.00

Re-militarization of the Dardanelles.

Hittite Bronze Stag — A82

Thorak's Bust of Kemal Atatürk — A83

1937, Sept. 20   Litho.   Perf. 12
781 A82 3k light violet 1.75 1.25
782 A83 6k blue 3.00 2.00
783 A82 7½k bright pink 4.75 3.75
784 A83 12½k indigo 10.00 7.50
Nos. 781-784 (4) 19.50 14.50
Set, never hinged 40.00

2nd Turkish Historical Congress, Istanbul, Sept. 20-30.

Arms of Turkey, Greece, Romania and Yugoslavia — A84

1937, Oct. 29   Perf. 11½
785 A84 8k carmine 6.75 3.50
786 A84 12½k dark blue 15.00 4.75
Set, never hinged 60.00

The Balkan Entente.

Street in Izmir A85

Fig Tree — A87

30pa, View of Fair Buildings. 3k, Tower, Government Square. 5k, Olive branch. 6k, Woman with grapes. 7½k, Woman picking grapes. 8k, Izmir Harbor through arch. 12k, Statue of Pres. Ataturk. 12½k, Pres. Ataturk.

1938, Aug. 20   Photo.   Perf. 11½
Inscribed: "Izmir Enternasyonal Fuari 1938"
789 A85 10pa dark brown .50 .60
790 A85 30pa purple .75 .50
791 A87 2½k brt green 1.25 1.00
792 A87 3k brown orange 1.25 .50
793 A87 5k olive green 2.25 .75
794 A85 6k brown 5.00 .40
795 A87 7½k scarlet 5.00 2.50
796 A87 8k brown lake 3.50 1.50
797 A87 12k rose violet 6.25 3.50
798 A87 12½k deep blue 10.00 8.50
Nos. 789-798 (10) 35.75 19.75
Set, never hinged 90.00

Izmir International Fair.

President Atatürk Teaching Reformed Turkish Alphabet A95

1938, Nov. 2
799 A95 2½k brt green 1.00 .55
800 A95 3k orange 1.25 .55
801 A95 6k rose violet 1.50 .65
802 A95 7½k deep rose 1.75 1.00
803 A95 8k red brown 2.00 1.10
804 A95 12½k brt ultra 2.50 1.25
Nos. 799-804 (6) 10.00 5.10
Set, never hinged 25.00

Reform of the Turkish alphabet, 10th anniv.

Army and Air Force A96

Atatürk Driving Tractor — A98

3k, View of Kayseri. 7½k, Railway bridge. 8k, Scout buglers. 12½k, President Ataturk.

1938, Oct. 29
Inscribed: "Cumhuriyetin 15 inc yil donumu hatirasi"
805 A96 2½k dark green .60 .35
806 A96 3k red brown .60 .35
807 A98 6k bister .90 .35
808 A96 7½k red 2.00 .90
809 A96 8k rose violet 5.00 2.50
810 A98 12½k deep blue 3.75 1.75
Nos. 805-810 (6) 12.85 6.20
Set, never hinged 30.00

15th anniversary of the Republic.

Stamps of 1931-38 Overprinted in Black

1938, Nov. 21   Perf. 11½x12
811 A78 3k brown orange .75 .35
812 A78 5k rose red .75 .35
813 A78 6k deep blue 1.00 .50
814 A77 7½k deep rose 1.25 .55
815 A78 8k dark blue 3.00 .75
a. 8k bright blue 225.00 150.00
816 A79 12½k indigo 3.75 1.75
Nos. 811-816 (6) 10.50 4.25
Set, never hinged

President Kemal Atatürk (1881-1938). The date is that of his funeral.

Catalogue values for unused stamps in this section, from this point to the end of the section, are for Never Hinged items.

Turkish and American Flags — A102

Presidents Inönü and F. D. Roosevelt and Map of North America A103

Designs: 3k, 8k, Inonu and Roosevelt. 7½k, 12½k, Kemal Ataturk and Washington.

1939, July 15   Photo.   Perf. 14
817 A102 2½k ol grn, red & bl .50 .25
818 A103 3k dk brn & bl grn 1.00 .25
819 A102 6k purple, red & bl 1.00 .25
820 A103 7½k org ver & bl grn 2.00 .40
821 A103 8k dp cl & bl grn 1.50 .40
822 A103 12½k brt bl & bl grn 3.50 .85
Nos. 817-822 (6) 9.50 2.40

US constitution, 150th anniversary.

Nos. 698, 702-704
Surcharged in Black

1939, July 23   Unwmk.   Perf. 13

823	A74	3k on 25k	.40	.25
824	A75	6k on 200k	.65	.50
825	A74	7½k on 25k	.75	.50
826	A75	12k on 100k	1.00	.50
827	A75	12½k on 200k	2.00	.50
828	A75	17½k on 500k	3.00	1.00
		Nos. 823-828 (6)	7.80	3.25

Annexation of Hatay.

Railroad Bridge
A105

Locomotive
A106

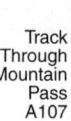

Track
Through
Mountain
Pass
A107

Design: 12½k, Railroad tunnel, Atma Pass.

1939, Oct. 20   Typo.   Perf. 11½

829	A105	3k lt orange red	3.50	3.50
830	A106	6k chestnut	4.00	4.00
831	A107	7½k rose pink	6.00	6.00
832	A107	12½k dark blue	9.00	9.00
		Nos. 829-832 (4)	22.50	22.50

Completion of the Sivas to Erzerum link of the Ankara-Erzerum Railroad.

Atatürk
Residence in
Ankara — A109

Kemal
Atatürk — A110

TÜRKİYE POSTALARI

KEMAL ATATÜRK
1880-1938

A111

Designs: 5k, 6k, 7½k, 8k, 12½k, 17½k, Various portraits of Ataturk, "1880-1938."

1939-40   Photo.

833	A109	2½k brt green	1.00	.50
834	A110	3k dk blue gray	1.00	.50
835	A110	5k chocolate	1.25	.75
836	A110	6k chestnut	1.25	.75
837	A110	7½k rose red	3.75	1.00
838	A110	8k gray green	1.75	
839	A110	12½k brt green	2.00	1.50
840	A110	17½k brt rose	6.50	2.00
		Nos. 833-840 (8)	18.50	8.00

Souvenir Sheet

841	A111	100k blue black	70.00	100.00

Death of Kemal Ataturk, first anniversary.
Size of No. 841: 90x120mm.
Issued: 2½k, 6k, 12½k, 11/11/39; others, 1/3/40.

Namik Kemal
A118

Arms of Turkey,
Greece, Romania
and Yugoslavia
A119

1940, Jan. 3

842	A118	6k chestnut	2.00	.60
843	A118	8k dk olive grn	3.25	1.50
844	A118	12k brt rose red	4.00	2.00
845	A118	12½k brt blue	8.00	3.00
		Nos. 842-845 (4)	17.25	7.10

Birth cent. of Namik Kemal, poet and patriot.

Perf. 11½

1940, Jan. 1   Typo.   Unwmk.

846	A119	8k light blue	3.50	1.00
847	A119	10k deep blue	7.00	2.25

The Balkan Entente.

Nos. 703-704
Surcharged in Red or
Black

1940, Aug. 20   Perf. 12

848	A75	6k on 200k dk grn & blk (R)	.75	1.00
849	A75	10k on 200k dk grn & blk	1.25	1.50
850	A75	12k on 500k choc & blk	2.00	2.50
		Nos. 848-850 (3)	4.00	5.00

13th International Izmir Fair.

Map of
Turkey
and
Census
Figures
A120

1940, Oct. 1   Typo.   Perf. 11½

851	A120	10pa dark blue green	.50	.25
852	A120	3k orange	1.50	1.25
853	A120	6k carmine rose	2.00	1.50
854	A120	10k dark blue	3.00	2.50
		Nos. 851-854 (4)	7.00	5.50

Census of Oct. 20, 1940.

Runner — A121

Pole
Vaulter — A122

Hurdler
A123

Discus
Thrower — A124

1940, Oct. 5

855	A121	3k olive green	2.50	2.50
856	A122	6k rose	7.50	3.50
857	A123	8k chestnut brown	3.50	4.00
858	A124	10k dark blue	5.50	10.00
		Nos. 855-858 (4)	19.00	20.00

11th Balkan Olympics.

Mail
Carriers on
Horseback
A125

Postman of 1840
and
1940 — A126

Old Sailing
Vessel and
Modern
Mailboat — A127

Design: 12k, Post Office, Istanbul.

1940, Dec. 31   Typo.   Perf. 10

859	A125	3k gray green	.75	.50
860	A126	6k rose	1.00	.75
861	A127	10k dark blue	1.50	1.00
862	A127	12k olive brown	2.00	1.50
		Nos. 859-862 (4)	5.25	3.75

Centenary of the Turkish post.

SEMI-POSTAL STAMPS

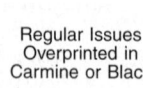

Regular Issues
Overprinted in
Carmine or Black

Overprint reads: "For War Orphans"

Perf. 12, 13½ and Compound

1915   Unwmk.

On Stamps of 1905

B1	A18	10pa dull grn (#119)	1.00	.75
B2	A18	10pi orange brown	12.50	.80

On Stamp of 1906

B3	A18	10pa dull grn (#128)	40.00	25.00

On Stamp of 1908

B4	A19	10pa dull grn	1.50	.75
B5	A19	5pi dark violet	75.00	12.50
		Nos. B1-B5 (5)	130.00	39.80

With Additional
"Discount" Overprint

B6	A19	10pa blue green	240.00	175.00

On Stamps of 1909

B7	A21	10pa blue green	1.00	.75
a.		Inverted overprint	22.50	22.50
b.		Double overprint, one invtd.	30.00	30.00
B8	A21	20pa carmine rose	1.00	.75
a.		Inverted overprint	27.50	27.50
B9	A21	1pi ultra	1.00	.75
B10	A21	5pi dark violet	8.75	1.50
		Nos. B7-B10 (4)	11.75	3.75

See note after No. 131.

With Additional
Overprint

B11	A21	10pa blue green	1.00	.75
b.		Double overprint, one inverted	5.00	5.00
B12	A21	20pa carmine rose	1.50	.75
B13	A21	1pi ultra	2.00	.75

On Stamps of 1913

B14	A22	10pa blue green	1.00	.75
a.		Inverted overprint	22.50	22.50
B15	A22	1pi ultra	1.00	.75
a.		Double overprint	5.00	5.00
		Nos. B11-B15 (5)	6.50	3.75

With Additional
Overprint

B16	A22	10pa blue green	1.75	.75
a.		Inverted overprint	27.50	27.50

On Newspaper Stamp of 1908

B17	A19	10pa blue green	360.00	175.00

On Newspaper Stamp of 1909

B18	A21	10pa blue green	1.75	1.00

Regular Issues
Overprinted in
Carmine or Black

1916   On Stamps of 1901

B19	A17	1pi blue	1.00	.50
a.		Perf. 12	1.50	.75
b.		Perf. 12x13¼	6.00	1.50
B20	A17	5pi lilac rose	10.00	1.50

On Stamps of 1905

B21	A18	1pi brt blue	7.50	2.00
B22	A18	5pi brown	7.50	5.00

On Stamp of 1906

B23	A18	1pi brt blue	1.00	.75

On Stamps of 1908

B24	A19	20pa carmine (Bk)		300.00
B25	A19	10pi red	500.00	200.00

With Additional
Overprint

B26	A19	20pa carmine	8.00	8.00
B27	A19	1pi brt blue (C)	20.00	5.00

On Stamps of 1909

B28	A21	20pa carmine rose	2.00	1.25
B29	A21	1pi ultra	1.50	1.00
B30	A21	10pi dull red	175.00	100.00

With Additional Overprint

B31	A21	20pa carmine rose	1.50	.75
B32	A21	1pi ultra	2.00	1.00

On Stamps of 1913

B33	A22	20pa carmine rose	2.00	1.50
B34	A22	1pi ultra	2.00	1.00
a.		Inverted overprint	5.00	5.00
B35	A22	10pi dull red	22.50	15.00

With Additional Overprint

B36	A22	20pa carmine rose	2.00	1.25

On Newspaper Stamps of 1901

B37	A16	5pi ocher	11.50	6.00
a.		5pa bister, No. P37	150.00	150.00

Regular Issues Surcharged in Black

On Stamp of 1898

B38	A11	10pa on 20pa vio brn	2.00	1.50

On Stamp of 1905

B39	A18	10pa on 20pa carmine	2.00	1.50

On Stamp of 1906

B40	A18	10pa on 20pa carmine	1.50	1.25

On Newspaper Stamp of 1893-99

B41	A11	10pa on 20pa violet brn	2.00	1.50
		Nos. B38-B41 (4)	7.50	5.75

Nos. 346-349 Overprinted

B42	A41	10pa carmine	1.00	.75
a.		Inverted overprint	6.75	6.75
b.		Perf 12½	1.00	.75
B43	A41	20pa ultra	1.00	.75
a.		Inverted overprint	6.75	6.75
b.		Perf 12½	1.00	.75
B44	A41	1pi violet & blk	1.00	.90
a.		Inverted overprint	6.75	6.75
b.		Perf 12½	1.00	.90
B45	A41	5pi yel brn & blk	1.00	.75
a.		Inverted overprint	11.00	11.00
b.		Perf 12½	1.00	.75
		Nos. B42-B45 (4)	4.00	3.15

Nos. B42-B45 formed part of the Postage Commemoration issue of 1916.

A Soldier's Farewell — SP1

1917, Feb. 20   Engr.   Perf. 12½

B46	SP1	10pa red violet	1.25	.50

For surcharges see Nos. 600, B47.

Stamp of Same Design Surcharged

B47	SP1	10pa on 20pa car rose	2.00	.50

Badge of the Society — SP9   School Teacher — SP10

Marie Sklodowska Curie — SP16   Kemal Atatürk — SP23

Designs: 2k+2k, Woman farmer. 2½k+2½k, Typist. 4k+4k, Aviatrix and policewoman. 5k+5k, Women voters. 7½k+7½k, Yildiz Palace, Istanbul. 10k+10k, Carrie Chapman Catt. 12½k+12½k, Jane Addams. 15k+15k, Grazia Deledda. 20k+20k, Selma Lagerlof. 25k+25k, Bertha von Suttner. 30k+30k, Sigrid Undset.

1935, Apr. 17   Photo.   Perf. 11½
Inscribed: "XII Congres Suffragiste International"

B54	SP9	20pa + 20pa brn	.50	.50
B55	SP10	1k + 1k rose car	.75	.50
B56	SP10	2k + 2k sl bl	1.00	.75
B57	SP10	2½k + 2½k yel grn	1.00	.75
B58	SP10	4k + 4k blue	1.50	1.00
B59	SP10	5k + 5k dl vio	2.50	2.00
B60	SP10	7½k + 7½k org red	2.50	2.00
B61	SP16	10k + 10k org	2.50	2.50
B62	SP16	12½k + 12½k dk bl	2.50	2.50
B63	SP16	15k + 15k violet	5.00	5.00
B64	SP16	20k + 20k red org	7.50	6.25
B65	SP16	25k + 25k grn	15.00	14.00
B66	SP16	30k + 30k ultra	90.00	100.00
B67	SP16	50k + 50k dk sl grn	175.00	150.00
B68	SP23	100k + 100k brn car	125.00	140.00
		Nos. B54-B68 (15)	432.25	427.75
		Set, never hinged	750.00	

12th Congress of the Women's Intl. Alliance.

AIR POST STAMPS

Catalogue values for unused stamps in this section are for Never Hinged items.

Nos. 692, 695, 698, 700 Overprinted or Surcharged in Brown or Blue

1934, July 15   Unwmk.   Perf. 12

C1	A74	7½k (Br)	.75	.25
C2	A72	12½k on 15k (Br)	.75	.25
C3	A74	20k on 25k (Br)	.75	.25
C4	A74	25k (Bl)	1.00	.40
C5	A74	40k (Br)	2.25	1.25
		Nos. C1-C5 (5)	5.50	2.40

Regular Stamps of 1930 Surcharged in Brown

1937

C6	A74	4½k on 7½k red brn	5.00	1.00
C7	A72	9k on 15k dp org	40.00	20.00
C8	A74	35k on 40k red vio	10.00	4.25
		Nos. C6-C8 (3)	55.00	25.25

POSTAGE DUE STAMPS

Same Types as Regular Issues of Corresponding Dates

1863   Unwmk.   Imperf.
Blue Band

J1	A1	20pa blk, red brn	100.00	32.50
a.		Tête bêche pair	225.00	225.00
b.		Without band	50.00	
c.		Red band	90.00	45.00
J2	A2	1pi blk, red brn	150.00	22.50
a.		Tête bêche pair	225.00	225.00
b.		Without band	50.00	
J3	A3	2pi blk, red brn	500.00	70.00
a.		Tête bêche pair	650.00	450.00
J4	A4	5pi blk, red brn	300.00	80.00
a.		Tête bêche pair	425.00	425.00
b.		Without band	100.00	
c.		Red band	150.00	
		Nos. J1-J4 (4)	1,050.	205.00

Full margins = 1mm at sides and top, 3mm at bottom (includes part of band). Height of colored bands is 6mm. Full margins for items without band = 3mm at bottom.

1865   Perf. 12½

J6	A5	20pa brown	4.00	5.00
J7	A5	1pi brown	4.00	5.00
b.		Half used as 20pa on cover		
c.		Printed on both sides	25.00	
J8	A5	2pi brown	12.50	25.00
a.		Half used as 1pi on cover		
J9	A5	5pi brown	5.00	30.00
a.		Half used as 2½pi on cover		
J10	A5	25pi brown	45.00	100.00
		Nos. J6-J10 (5)	70.50	165.00

Exist imperf. Values, $60 to $100 each. The 10pa brown is an essay. Value about $2,750.

1867

J11	A5	20pa bister brn	9.00	100.00
J12	A5	1pi bister brn	9.00	
a.		With surcharge of 5pi	13.50	
b.		Imperf., pair	65.00	
J13	A5	2pi fawn	75.00	
J14	A5	5pi fawn	17.50	
J15	A5	25pi bister brn	21,250.	
		Nos. J11-J14 (4)	110.50	

Nos. J12-J15 were not placed in use.

1869   Perf. 13½
With Yellow-Brown Border

J16	A5	20pa bister brn	10.00	10.00
a.		Without surcharge		
J17	A5	1pi bister brn	550.00	20.00
a.		Without surcharge		
J18	A5	2pi bister brn	800.00	20.00
J19	A5	5pi bister brn	2.25	12.50
b.		Without border		
c.		Printed on both sides	15.00	
J20	A5	25pi bister brn		
		Nos. J16-J19 (4)	1,362.	62.50

With Brown Border

Color of border ranges from brown to reddish brown and black brown.

J21	A5	20pa bister brn	125.00	20.00
a.		Inverted surcharge		
b.		Without surcharge		

J22	A5	1pi bister brn	550.00	12.50
a.		Without surcharge		
J23	A5	2pi bister brn	450.00	12.50
b.		Inverted surcharge		
J24	A5	5pi bister brn	2.50	15.00
b.		Without surcharge		
J25	A5	25pi bister brn	37.50	100.00
		Nos. J21-J25 (5)	1,165.	160.00

Pin-perf., Perf. 5 to 11½ and Compound
1871   With Brick Red Border

J26	A5	20pa bister brn	1,250.	50.00
J27	A5	1pi bister brn		5,000.
J28	A5	2pi bister brn	110.00	140.00
J29	A5	5pi bister brn	7.50	25.00

With Black Brown Border

J31	A5	20pa bister brn	150.00	3.50
a.		Half used as 10pa on cover		
b.		Imperf., pair		16.50
c.		Printed on both sides	40.00	40.00
J32	A5	1pi bister brn	225.00	2.50
a.		Half used as 20pa on cover		
c.		Inverted surcharge	50.00	35.00
d.		Printed on both sides		
J33	A5	2pi bister brn	6.00	9.00
a.		Half used as 1pi on cover		
c.		Imperf., pair		16.50
J34	A5	5pi bister brn	2.50	20.00
a.		Half used as 2½pi on cover		
c.		Inverted surcharge		
J35	A5	25pi bister brn	40.00	125.00
a.		Inverted surcharge		
		Nos. J31-J35 (5)	423.50	160.00

1888   Perf. 11½ and 13½

J36	A7	20pa black	4.00	12.50
J37	A7	1pi black	4.00	12.50
J38	A7	2pi black	4.00	15.00
b.		Diagonal half used as 1pi		
		Nos. J36-J38 (3)	12.00	40.00

Imperf

J36a	A7	20pa	11.00
J37a	A7	1pi	11.00
J38a	A7	2pi	11.00

1892   Perf. 13½

J39	A11	20pa black	7.00	12.50
J40	A12	1pi black	25.00	12.50
a.		Printed on both sides		
J41	A13	2pi black	17.50	12.50
		Nos. J39-J41 (3)	49.50	37.50

1901

J42	A11	20pa black, deep rose	2.50	20.00

1901

J43	A17	10pa black, deep rose	4.00	6.00
J44	A17	20pa black, deep rose	3.75	8.75
J45	A17	1pi black, deep rose	3.00	10.00
J46	A17	2pi black, deep rose	2.50	15.00
		Nos. J43-J46 (4)	13.25	39.75

1905   Perf. 12

J47	A18	1pi black, deep rose	3.00	10.00
J48	A18	2pi black, deep rose	4.50	20.00

1908,   Perf. 12, 13½ and Compound

J49	A19	1pi black, deep rose	80.00	7.50
J50	A19	2pi black, deep rose	12.50	45.00

1909

J51	A21	1pi black, deep rose	15.00	50.00
J52	A21	2pi black, deep rose	150.00	175.00
a.		Imperf.	65.00	

1913   Perf. 12

J53	A22	2pa black, deep rose	1.00	.50
J54	A22	5pa black, deep rose	1.00	.50
J55	A22	10pa black, deep rose	1.00	.50
J56	A22	20pa black, deep rose	1.00	.50
J57	A22	1pi black, deep rose	4.50	10.00
J58	A22	2pi black, deep rose	8.00	17.50
		Nos. J53-J58 (6)	16.50	29.50

Adrianople Issue
Nos. 251-253 Surcharged in Black, Blue or Red

1913

J59	A23	2pa on 10pa green (Bk)	3.25	.35
J60	A23	5pa on 20pa red (Bl)	3.25	.35
J61	A23	10pa on 40pa blue (R)	10.00	.80

J62	A23	20pa on 40pa blue (Bk)	32.50 11.00
		Nos. J59-J62 (4)	49.00 12.50

For surcharges see Nos. J67-J70, J83-J86.

D1   D2

D3   D4

1914   **Engr.**

J63	D1	5pa claret	1.25 10.00
J64	D2	20pa red	1.25 10.00
J65	D3	1pi dark blue	1.25 10.00
J66	D4	2pi slate	1.25 10.00
		Nos. J63-J66 (4)	5.00 40.00

For surcharges and overprints see Nos. J87-J91.

Nos. J59 to J62 Surcharged in Red or Black

1916

J67	A23	10pa on 2pa on 10pa (R)	55.00 55.00
J68	A23	20pa on 5pa on 20pa	55.00 55.00
J69	A23	40pa on 10pa on 40pa	55.00 55.00
J70	A23	40pa on 20pa on 40pa (R)	55.00 55.00
		Nos. J67-J70 (4)	220.00 220.00

Preceding Issues Overprinted in Red, Black or Blue

1917   **On Stamps of 1865**

J71	A5	20pa red brn (Bl)	45.00 67.50
J72	A5	1pi red brn (Bl)	45.00 67.50
J73	A5	2pi bis brn (Bl)	45.00 67.50
J74	A5	5pi bis brn (Bl)	45.00 67.50
J75	A5	25pi dk brn (Bl)	45.00 67.50
		Nos. J71-J75 (5)	225.00 337.50

On Stamp of 1869
Red Brown Border

J76	A5	5pi bis brn (R)	45.00 67.50

On Stamp of 1871
Black Brown Border

J77	A5	5pi bis brn	75.00 50.00

On Stamps of 1888

J78	A7	1pi black (R)	45.00 67.50
J79	A7	2pi black (R)	45.00 67.50

On Stamps of 1892

J80	A11	20pa black (R)	2.50 2.50
J81	A12	1pi black (R)	2.50 2.50
J82	A13	2pi black (R)	2.50 2.50
		Nos. J80-J82 (3)	7.50 7.50

Adrianople Issue
On Nos. J59 to J62 with Addition of New Value

J83	A23	10pa on 2pa on 10pa (R)	1.25 1.00
J84	A23	20pa on 5pa on 20pa (Bk)	1.50 1.00
J85	A23	40pa on 10pa on 40pa (Bk)	2.00 1.50
a.		"40pa" double	

J86	A23	40pa on 20pa on 40pa	3.75 3.50
		Nos. J83-J86 (4)	8.50 7.00

Nos. J71-J86 were used as regular postage stamps.

Armistice Issue

No. J65 Overprinted

1919, Nov. 30

J87	D3	1pi dark blue	125.00 150.00

Accession to the Throne Issue
Postage Due Stamps of 1914 Overprinted in Turkish "Accession to the Throne of His Majesty. 3rd July, 1334-1918"

1919

J88	D1	10pa on 5pa claret	25.00 37.50
J89	D2	20pa red	25.00 37.50
J90	D3	1pi dark blue	25.00 37.50
J91	D4	2pi slate	25.00 37.50
		Nos. J88-J91 (4)	100.00 150.00

Railroad Bridge over Kizil Irmak — D5

1926   **Engr.**

J92	D5	20pa ocher	1.25 2.50
J93	D5	1g red	2.00 5.00
J94	D5	2g blue green	3.00 5.00
J95	D5	3g lilac brown	3.50 12.50
J96	D5	5g lilac	6.00 20.00
		Nos. J92-J96 (5)	15.75 45.00
		Set, never hinged	30.00

> **Catalogue values for unused stamps in this section, from this point to the end of the section, are for Never Hinged items.**

Kemal Atatürk — D6

1936   **Litho.**   **Perf. 11½**

J97	D6	20pa brown	.25 .25
J98	D6	2k light blue	.25 .25
J99	D6	3k bright violet	.25 .25
J100	D6	5k Prussian blue	.25 .25
J101	D6	12k bright rose	.35 .25
		Nos. J97-J101 (5)	1.35 1.25

For surcharges see Nos. 1461-1465 in Scott Standard catalogue, Vol. 6.

LOCAL ISSUES

Type I   Type II

Type III   Type IV

Type V   Type VI

During 1873//1882 Turkish stamps with the above overprints were used for local postage in Constantinople (types 1-5) and Mount Athos (type 6).

MILITARY STAMPS

For the Army in Thessaly

Tughra and Bridge at Larissa — M1

1898, Apr. 21   **Unwmk.**   **Perf. 13**

M1	M1	10pa yellow green	10.00 7.50
M2	M1	20pa rose	10.00 7.50
M3	M1	1pi dark blue	10.00 7.50
M4	M1	2pi orange	10.00 7.50
M5	M1	5pi violet	10.00 7.50
		Nos. M1-M5 (5)	50.00 37.50

Issued for Turkish occupation forces to use in Thessaly during the Greco-Turkish War of 1897-98.

Forgeries of Nos. M1-M5 are perf. 11½.

NEWSPAPER STAMPS

N1

Black Overprint

1879   **Unwmk.**   **Perf. 11½ and 13½**

P1	N1	10pa blk & rose lilac	225.00 225.00

Other stamps found with this "IMPRIMES" overprint were prepared on private order and have no official status as newspaper stamps. Counterfeits exist of No. P1.

The 10pa surcharge, on half of 20pa rose and pale rose was made privately. See note after No. 77.

Regular Issue of 1890 Handstamped in Black, Blue or Red

Nos. P10-P29 were overprinted with a single wooden handstamp. Variations in size are due to inking and pressure.

The handstamps on Nos. P10-P29 are found double, inverted and sideways. Counterfeit overprints comprise most of the examples offered for sale in the marketplace.

1891   **Perf. 13½, 11½**

P10	A7	10pa grn & gray	40.00 12.50
a.		Imperf.	22.50 12.50

P11	A7	20pa rose & gray	75.00 15.00
P12	A7	1pi blue & gray	210.00 150.00
P13	A7	2pi yel & gray	525.00 400.00
P14	A7	5pi buff & gray	1,050. 750.00
		Nos. P10-P14 (5)	1,900. 1,327.

Blue Handstamp

P10b	A7	10pa green & gray	210.00 125.00
P11a	A7	20pa rose & gray	340.00 250.00
P12a	A7	1pi blue & gray	425.00 375.00
		Nos. P10b-P12a (3)	975.00 750.00

This overprint on 2pi and 5pi in blue is considered bogus.

Red Handstamp

P10c	A7	10pa green & gray	400.00 325.00
P11b	A7	20pa rose & gray	600.00 450.00
P12b	A7	1pi blue & gray	900.00 1,000.
		Nos. P10c-P12b (3)	1,900. 1,775.

This overprint in red on 2pi and 5pi is considered bogus.
Excellent forgeries of Nos. P10-P14 exist. Certification by a competant authority is suggested.

Same Handstamp on Regular Issue of 1892

1892				**Perf. 13½**
P25	A10	10pa gray green	500.00	100.00
P26	A11	20pa rose	1,250.	375.00
P27	A12	1pi pale blue	110.00	150.00
P28	A13	2pi brown org	200.00	175.00
P29	A14	5pi pale violet	1,800.	1,250.
a.		On No. 99a	500.00	
		Nos. P25-P29 (5)	3,860.	2,050.

Regular Issues of 1892-98 Overprinted in Black

1893-98

P30	A10	10pa gray grn	3.75 2.50
P31	A11	20pa vio brn ('98)	3.00 1.50
a.		20pa dark pink	2.50 1.25
b.		20pa pink	325.00 22.50
P32	A12	1pi pale blue	3.00 1.50
P33	A13	2pi brown org	27.50 12.50
a.		Tete beche pair	22.50
P34	A14	5pi pale violet	85.00 75.00
a.		On No. 99a	140.00 65.00
		Nos. P30-P34 (5)	122.25 93.00

For surcharge and overprints see Nos. B41, P121-P122, P134-P136, P153-P154.

No. 95 Surcharged

1897

P36	A10	5pa on 10pa gray grn	5.00 3.00
a.		"Cniq" instead of "Cinq"	15.00 15.00

For overprint see No. P137.

Nos. 102-107 Overprinted in Black

1901   **Perf. 12, 13½ and Compound**

P37	A16	5pa bister	1.75 1.00
a.		Inverted overprint	
P38	A16	10pa yellow grn	6.25 6.25
P39	A16	20pa magenta	32.50 7.50
P40	A16	1pi violet blue	60.00 22.50
P41	A16	2pi gray blue	125.00 37.50
P42	A16	5pi ocher	300.00 90.00
		Nos. P37-P42 (6)	525.50 164.75

For overprints see Nos. B37, P69-P74, P123, P138-P141, P155-P158.

Same Overprint on Nos. 110-115

1901

P43	A17	5pa purple	8.75 2.00
a.		Perf. 12	50.00 12.50
P44	A17	10pa green	32.50 2.50
a.		Perf. 12	65.00 20.00

P45	A17	20pa carmine	8.75	1.50
a.		Overprinted on back	50.00	7.50
b.		Perf. 12	50.00	7.50
P46	A17	1pi blue	25.00	2.00
a.		Perf. 12	75.00	17.50
P47	A17	2pi orange	87.50	4.00
b.		Inverted overprint	275.00	75.00
a.		Perf. 12	275.00	75.00
P48	A17	5pi lilac rose	160.00	27.50
		Nos. P43-P48 (6)	322.50	39.50

For overprints see Nos. P75-P80, P124-P126, P142-P146, P159-P164.

Same Overprint on Regular Issue of 1905
1905

P49	A18	5pa ocher	2.50	1.00
P50	A18	10pa dull green	30.00	1.50
P51	A18	20pa carmine	2.50	1.25
P52	A18	1pi pale blue	2.50	1.00
P53	A18	2pi slate	70.00	10.00
P54	A18	5pi brown	175.00	20.00
		Nos. P49-P54 (6)	282.50	35.00

For overprints see Nos. P127-P129, P147-P150, P165-P171.

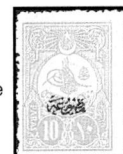

Regular Issue of 1908
Overprinted in Carmine
or Blue

1908

P55	A19	5pa ocher (Bl)	10.00	.50
P56	A19	10pa blue grn (C)	17.50	.50
P57	A19	20pa carmine (Bl)	22.50	1.00
P58	A19	1pi brt blue (C)	100.00	2.50
P59	A19	2pi blue blk (C)	150.00	7.50
P60	A19	5pi dk violet (C)	200.00	17.50
		Nos. P55-P60 (6)	500.00	29.50

For overprints see Nos. B17, P130-P131, P151, P172.

Same Overprint on Regular Issue of 1909
1909

P61	A21	5pa ocher (Bl)	3.50	1.25
a.		Imperf.		
P62	A21	10pa blue grn (C)	8.75	1.50
P63	A21	20pa car rose (Bl)	60.00	1.75
a.		Imperf.		
P64	A21	1pi brt blue (C)	100.00	5.00
P65	A21	2pi blue blk (C)	250.00	30.00
P66	A21	5pi dk violet (C)	500.00	65.00
		Nos. P61-P66 (6)	922.25	104.50

For surcharge and overprints see Nos. B18, P67-P68, P81, P132-P133, P152.

No. 151 Surcharged
in Blue

1910 — Perf. 12, 13½ and Compound

P67	A21	2pa on 5pa ocher	.75	.75

1911 — Perf. 12

P68	A21	2pa olive green	1.00	.50

See No. P173.

Newspaper Stamps of
1901-11 Overprinted in
Carmine or Blue

The overprint was applied to 13 denominations in four settings with change of city name, producing individual sets for each city: "MONASTIR," "PRISTINA," "SALONIQUE" and "USKUB."

1911, June 26 — Perf. 12, 13½
"Monastir"

P69	A16	5pa bister	20.00	22.50
P70	A16	10pa yellow grn	20.00	22.50
P71	A16	20pa magenta	20.00	22.50
P72	A16	1pi violet blue	20.00	22.50
P73	A16	2pi gray blue	25.00	30.00
P74	A16	5pi ocher	50.00	60.00
P75	A17	5pa purple	10.00	12.50
P76	A17	10pa green	10.00	12.50

P77	A17	20pa carmine	10.00	12.50
P78	A17	1pi blue	10.00	12.50
P79	A17	2pi orange	12.00	15.00
P80	A17	5pi lilac rose	30.00	30.00
P81	A21	2pa olive green	3.00	3.75
		Nos. P69-P81 (13)	240.00	278.75

"Pristina"

P69a	A16	5pa bister	5.00	5.00
P70a	A16	10pa yellow grn	5.00	5.00
P71a	A16	20pa magenta	5.00	5.00
P72a	A16	1pi violet blue	5.25	5.25
P73a	A16	2pi gray blue	6.50	6.50
P74a	A16	5pi ocher	13.00	13.00
P75a	A17	5pa purple	5.00	5.00
P76a	A17	10pa green	5.00	5.00
P77a	A17	20pa carmine	5.00	5.00
P78a	A17	1pi blue	6.50	6.50
P79a	A17	2pi orange	6.50	6.50
P80a	A17	5pi lilac rose	13.00	13.00
P81a	A21	2pa olive green	.35	.35
		Nos. P69a-P81a (13)	81.10	81.10

"Salonique"

P69b	A16	5pa bister	5.00	5.00
P70b	A16	10pa yellow grn	5.00	5.00
P71b	A16	20pa magenta	5.00	5.00
P72b	A16	1pi violet blue	5.25	5.25
P73b	A16	2pi gray blue	6.50	6.50
P74b	A16	5pi ocher	13.00	13.00
P75b	A17	5pa purple	5.00	5.00
P76b	A17	10pa green	5.00	5.00
P77b	A17	20pa carmine	5.00	5.00
P78b	A17	1pi blue	6.50	6.50
P79b	A17	2pi orange	6.50	6.50
P80b	A17	5pi lilac rose	13.00	13.00
P81b	A21	2pa olive green	.35	.35
		Nos. P69b-P81b (13)	81.10	81.10

"Uskub"

P69c	A16	5pa bister	5.00	5.00
P70c	A16	10pa yellow grn	5.00	5.00
P71c	A16	20pa magenta	5.00	5.00
P72c	A16	1pi violet blue	5.25	5.25
P73c	A16	2pi gray blue	6.50	6.50
P74c	A16	5pi ocher	13.00	13.00
P75c	A17	5pa purple	5.00	5.00
P76c	A17	10pa green	5.00	5.00
P77c	A17	20pa carmine	5.00	5.00
P78c	A17	1pi blue	6.50	6.50
P79c	A17	2pi orange	6.50	6.50
P80c	A17	5pi lilac rose	13.00	13.00
P81c	A21	2pa olive green	.35	.35
		Nos. P69c-P81c (13)	81.10	81.10

The note after No. 182 will also apply to Nos. P69-P81.

Newspaper Stamps
of 1901-11
Overprinted in
Carmine or Black

1915 — On Stamps of 1893-98

P121	A10	10pa gray green	6.00	.50
a.		Inverted overprint	10.00	10.00
P122	A13	2pi yellow brn	1.50	1.00
a.		Inverted overprint	10.00	10.00

On Stamps of 1901

P123	A16	10pa yellow grn	1.00	.50
P124	A17	5pa purple	1.00	1.00
P125	A17	20pa carmine	2.00	1.00
P126	A17	5pi lilac rose	20.00	5.00

On Stamps of 1905

P127	A18	5pa ocher	2.00	1.00
a.		Inverted overprint	7.50	7.50
P128	A18	2pi slate	17.50	5.00
P129	A18	5pi brown	10.00	.60

On Stamps of 1908

P130	A19	2pi blue blk	1,375.	550.00
P131	A19	5pi dk violet	10.00	1.25

On Stamps of 1909

P132	A21	2pi orange	1.00	.50
P133	A21	5pi dk violet	100.00	35.00
		Nos. P121-P129,P131-P133 (12)	172.00	52.35

Preceding
Newspaper Issues
with additional
Overprint in Red or
Black

1916 — On Stamps of 1893-98

P134	A10	10pa gray green	2.00	.75
P135	A11	20pa violet brn	1.00	.75
P136	A14	5pi dull violet	50.00	50.00

On Stamp of 1897

P137	A10	5pa on 10pa gray grn	.60	.50

On Stamps of 1901

P138	A16	5pa bister	.50	.30
P139	A16	10pa yellow grn	.90	.90
P140	A16	20pa magenta	1.00	.90
a.		Inverted overprint	10.00	10.00
P141	A16	1pi violet blue	1.00	1.00
P142	A17	5pa purple	50.00	50.00
P143	A17	10pa green	50.00	50.00
P144	A17	20pa carmine	1.50	.90
P145	A17	1pi blue	1.50	.90
P146	A17	2pi orange	1.50	.90

On Stamps of 1905

P147	A18	5pa ocher	1.00	.75
P148	A18	10pa dull green	50.00	50.00
P149	A18	20pa carmine	50.00	50.00
P150	A18	1pi pale blue	1.75	1.00

On Stamp of 1908

P151	A19	5pa ocher	62.50	62.50

On Stamp of 1909

P152	A21	5pa ocher	62.50	62.50
		Nos. P134-P152 (19)	389.25	384.55

Preceding
Newspaper Issues
with additional
Overprint in Red or
Black

1917 — On Stamps of 1893-98

P153	A12	1pi gray (R)	2.50	2.00
P154	A11	20pa vio brn (R)	3.75	3.75

On Stamps of 1901

P155	A16	5pa bister (Bk)	1.50	1.25
a.		Inverted overprint	20.00	20.00
P156	A16	10pa yellow grn (R)	1.50	1.25
P157	A16	20pa magenta (Bk)	1.50	1.25
P158	A16	2pi gray blue (R)	40.00	30.00
P159	A17	5pa purple (Bk)	2.25	2.25
a.		Inverted overprint	20.00	20.00
b.		Double overprint	20.00	20.00
c.		Double ovpt., one inverted	25.00	25.00
P160	A17	10pa green (Bk)	22.50	35.00
P161	A17	20pa carmine (Bk)	1.50	1.25
P162	A17	1pi blue (R)	3.00	3.00
P163	A17	2pi orange (Bk)	2.50	2.50
P164	A17	5pi lilac rose (R)	32.50	50.00

On Stamps of 1905

P165	A18	5pa ocher (R)	2.50	2.00
a.		Inverted overprint	10.00	10.00
P166	A18	5pa ocher (Bk)	3.00	2.50
a.		Inverted overprint	10.00	10.00
P167	A18	10pa dull green	2.50	2.00
P168	A18	20pa carmine (Bk)	2.50	2.00
a.		Double overprint	15.00	15.00
P169	A18	1pi blue (R)	2.50	2.00
a.		Inverted overprint	25.00	25.00
P170	A18	2pi slate (R)	32.50	50.00
P171	A18	5pi brown (R)	32.50	50.00

On Stamp of 1908

P172	A19	5pa ocher (R)	32.50	50.00
		Nos. P153-P172 (20)	225.50	294.00

Nos. P153-P172 were used as regular postage stamps.

#P173   #P174

1919 — Blue Surcharge and Red Overprint

P173	A21	5pa on 2pa ol grn	1.25	1.00
a.		Red overprint double	12.50	5.00
b.		Blue surcharge double	12.50	5.00

1920 — Red Surcharge

P174	A25	5pa on 4pa brn	1.25	.50

POSTAL TAX STAMPS

Map of Turkey
and Red
Crescent
PT1

1928 — Unwmk. — Typo. — Perf. 14
Crescent in Red

RA1	PT1	½pi lt brown	.30	.25
RA2	PT1	1pi red violet	.30	.25
RA3	PT1	2½pi orange	.30	.25

Engr. — Various Frames

RA4	PT1	5pi dk brown	.60	.45
RA5	PT1	10pi yellow green	.75	.55
RA6	PT1	20pi slate	1.25	.60
RA7	PT1	50pi dark violet	3.75	1.40
		Nos. RA1-RA7 (7)	7.25	3.75
		Set, never hinged	13.00	

The use of these stamps on letters, parcels, etc. in addition to the regular postage, was obligatory on certain days in each year.

For surcharges see Nos. RA16, RA21-RA22.

Cherubs Upholding
Star — PT2

1932

RA8	PT2	1k ol bis & red	1.00	.30
RA9	PT2	2½k dk brn & red	1.25	.30
RA10	PT2	5k green & red	1.50	.30
RA11	PT2	25k black & red	3.00	1.00
		Nos. RA8-RA11 (4)	6.75	1.90
		Set, never hinged	9.00	

For surcharges and overprints see Nos. RA12-RA15, RA28-RA29, RA36-RA38.

No. RA8 Surcharged

RA12	PT2	20pa on 1k	1.00	.50
RA13	PT2	3k on 1k	1.75	.70
a.		3 "kruus"	2.50	2.50

By a law of Parliament the use of these stamps on letters and telegraph forms, in addition to the regular fees, was obligatory from Apr. 20-30 of each year. The inscription in the tablet at the bottom of the design states that the money derived from the sale of the stamps is devoted to child welfare work.

No. RA8 Surcharged

1933

RA14	PT2	20pa on 1k ol bis & red	1.00	.50
RA15	PT2	3k on 1k ol bis & red	1.75	1.00

No. RA5
Surcharged

RA16 PT1 5k on 10pi yel grn &
          red   1.50   .75
   Nos. RA14-RA16 (3)   4.25 2.25

PT3   PT4

1933   **Perf. 11, 11½**
RA17 PT3 20pa gray vio & red   1.00   .50
RA18 PT4   1k violet & red   1.00   .50
RA19 PT4   5k dk brown & red   2.50   .50
RA20 PT3 15k green & red   3.50   .50
   Nos. RA17-RA20 (4)   8.00 2.00
   Set, never hinged   12.00

   Nos. RA17 and RA20 were issued in
Ankara; Nos. RA18 and RA19 in Izmir.
For overprint see No. RA27.

Nos. RA3,
RA1
Surcharged in
Black

1933-34
RA21 PT1 1k on 2½pi orange   .50   .30
RA22 PT1 5k on ½pi lt brown   1.50   .50

Map of
Turkey
PT5

1934-35   Crescent in Red   Perf. 12
RA23 PT5 ½k blue ('35)   .25   .25
RA24 PT5 1k red brown   .25   .25
RA25 PT5 2½k brown ('35)   .50   .25
RA26 PT5 5k blue green ('35)   1.25   .25
   Nos. RA23-RA26 (4)   2.25 1.00
   Set, never hinged   5.00
   Frame differs from No. RA26.
See Nos. RA30-RA35B.

**Nos. RA17, RA8-RA9 Overprinted
"P.Y.S." in Roman Capitals**
1936   **Perf. 11, 14**
RA27 PT3 20pa gray vio & red   .40   .25
RA28 PT2   1k ol bis & red   .40   .25
RA29 PT2   3k on 2½k dk brn
           & red   .75   .30
   Nos. RA27-RA29 (3)   1.55
   Set, never hinged   12.00

**Type of 1934-35, Inscribed "Türkiye
Kizilay Cemiyeti"**
1938-46   **Perf. 8½-11½**

   Type I — Imprint, "Devlet Basimevi". Cres-
cent red.
   Type II — Imprint, "Alaeddin Kiral Basimevi".
Crescent carmine.
   Type III — Imprint, "Damga Matbaasi". Cres-
cent red.

Crescent in Red or Carmine
RA30 PT5 ½k blue (I)   .50   .25
  a.   Type II   4.00 1.00
  b.   Type III   .50   .25
RA31 PT5 1k red vio (I)   .40   .25
  a.   Type II   6.50 2.00
  b.   Type III   .50   .25
RA32 PT5 2½k orange (I)   .30   .25
  a.   Type III   2.00 1.00
RA33 PT5 5k blue grn (I)   .50   .25
RA33A PT5 5k choc (III)
           ('42)   .25
RA34 PT5 10k pale grn (I)   1.00   .25
  a.   Type III   2.00 1.00

RA35 PT5 20k black (I)   2.50 1.00
RA35A PT5 50k pur (III) ('46)   7.50 1.00
RA35B PT5 1 l blue (III) ('44) 30.00 2.50
   Nos. RA30-RA35B (9)   44.20 6.05
   Set, never hinged   75.00
   For surcharge see No. RA63.

No. RA9 Surcharged
in Black

1938   **Perf. 14**
RA36 PT2 20pa on 2½k   1.00   .50
RA37 PT2   1k on 2½k   1.00   .50

No. RA9 Surcharged
in Black

1938   Unwmk.   Perf. 14
RA37A PT2 20pa on 2½k   1.25   .60
RA37B PT2   1k on 2½k   1.50   .75

**No. RA9 Surcharged "1 Kurus" in
Black**
1939   **Perf. 14**
RA38 PT2 1k on 2½k dk brn &
          red   .50   .50

Child — PT6   Nurse with
                   Child — PT7

1940   Typo.   Perf. 12
Star in Carmine
RA39 PT6 20pa bluish grn   .30   .25
RA40 PT6   1k violet   .30   .25
RA41 PT7   1k lt blue   .30   .25
RA42 PT7 2½k pale red lil   .30   .25
RA43 PT6   3k black   .35   .25
RA44 PT7   5k pale violet   .30   .25
RA45 PT7 10k blue green   1.00   .40
RA46 PT6 15k dark blue   .75   .30
RA47 PT7 25k olive bister   2.50 1.25
RA48 PT7 50k olive gray   6.00 2.50
   Nos. RA39-RA48 (10)   12.10 5.95
   Set, never hinged   30.00

POSTAL TAX AIR POST STAMPS

Air Fund Issues

   These stamps were obligatory on all
air mail for 21 days a year. Tax for the
Turkish Aviation Society: 20pa for a
postcard, 1k for a regular letter, 2 1/2k
for a registered letter, 3k for a telegram,
5k-50k for a package, higher values for
air freight. Postal tax air post stamps
were withdrawn Aug. 21, 1934 and
remainders destroyed later that year.

Biplane
PTAP1

Type PTAP1

**1926   Perf. 11, Pin Perf.
        Unwmk.   Litho.
        Size: 35x25mm**
RAC1 20pa brn & pale grn   3.00   .30
RAC2   1g blue grn & buff   2.00   .30

        Size: 40x29mm
RAC3   5g vio & pale grn   8.00 1.00
RAC4   5g car lake & pale
       grn   35.00 15.00
   Nos. RAC1-RAC4 (4)   48.00 16.60
   Set, never hinged   275.00

PTAP2

PTAP3

1927-29   Type PTAP2
RAC5 20pa dl red & pale
     grn   1.50   .50
RAC6   1k green & yel   1.25   .50
        Type PTAP3
        Perf. 11½
RAC7   2k dp cl & yel grn   1.50   .50
RAC8 2½k red & yel grn   8.00 1.60
RAC9   5k dk bl gray &
       org   1.25   .50
RAC10 10k dk grn & rose   5.00 1.25
RAC11 15k green & yel   5.00 1.00
RAC12 20k ol brn & yel   7.00 2.00
RAC13 50k dk bl & cob bl   10.00 4.50
RAC14 100k car & lt bl   110.00 80.00
   Nos. RAC5-RAC14 (10)   150.50 92.35
   Set, never hinged   825.00

**#RAC1, RAC5, RAC7 and RAC11
Surcharged in Black (RAC15-RAC16,
RAC18-RAC19) or Red (Others)**
1930-31
RAC15   1k ("Bir kurus")
           on RAC1   200.00 75.00
RAC16   1k ("Bir Kurus")
           on RAC5   1.50   .50
RAC17   100pa ("Yuz Para")
           on RAC7   2.00   .75
RAC18   5k ("Bes Kurus")
           on RAC5   8.00 1.50
RAC19   5k ("5 Kurus")
           on RAC5   3.00   .75
RAC20   10k ("On kurus")
           on RAC7   4.00 1.25
RAC21   50k ("Elli kurus")
           on RAC7   12.00 4.00
RAC22   1 l ("Bir lira") on
           RAC7   37.50 9.00
RAC23   5 l ("Bes lira")
           on RAC11   2,000. 400.00
   Nos. RAC15-RAC23 (9)   2,268. 492.75
   Set, never hinged   5,000.

PTAP4   PTAP5

1931-32   Litho.   Perf. 11½
RAC24 PTAP4 20pa black   5.00 1.75
        Typo.
RAC25 PTAP5   1k brown car
              ('32)   2.00   .50
RAC26 PTAP5   5k red ('32)   4.00   .75
RAC27 PTAP5 10k green ('32)   6.00 1.50
   Nos. RAC24-RAC27 (4)   17.00 4.50

PTAP6

1933   Type PTAP6
RAC28 10pa ("On Para") grn   3.50 2.00
RAC29   1k ("Bir Kurus") red   8.00 2.75
RAC30   5k ("Bes Kurus") lil   12.00 3.00
   Nos. RAC28-RAC30 (3)   23.50 7.75

TURKEY IN ASIA
ˈtər-kē in ˈā-zhə

(Anatolia)

40 Paras = 1 Piaster

This designation, which includes all of Turkey in Asia Minor, came into existence during the uprising of 1919, led by Mustafa Kemal Pasha. Actually there was no separation of territory, the Sultan's sovereignty being almost immediately reduced to a small area surrounding Constantinople. The formation of the Turkish Republic and the expulsion of the Sultan followed in 1923. Subsequent issues of postage stamps are listed under Turkey (Republic).

Issues of the Nationalist Government

Turkish Stamps of 1913-18 Surcharged in Black or Red

(The Surcharge reads "Angora 3 Piastres")

1920   **Unwmk.**   **Perf. 12**
On Stamps of 1913

1	A24	3pi on 2pa red lilac	4.75	5.25
2	A25	3pi on 4pa dk brn	37.50	37.50
3	A27	3pi on 6pa dk bl	250.00	150.00

On Stamp of 1916-18

4	A42	3pi on 2pa vio (Bk)	35.00	20.00
		Nos. 1-4 (4)	327.25	212.75

Turkish Stamps of 1913-18 Hstmpd. in Black or Red

(The Srch. reads "Post, Piastre 3")

1921   **On Stamps of 1913**   **Perf. 12**

5	A24	3pi on 2pa red lilac	35.00	25.00
a.		On No. 1	47.50	72.50
b.		As #5, surcharge in red	950.00	
c.		As #5a, surcharge in red	950.00	
6	A25	3pi on 4pa dk brown	30.00	30.00
a.		On No. 2	160.00	175.00
7	A25	3pi on 4pa dk brn (R)	150.00	175.00
a.		On No. 2	160.00	175.00
8	A27	3pi on 6pa dk blue	125.00	150.00
a.		On No. 3	300.00	150.00
9	A27	3pi on 6pa dk bl (R)	62.50	75.00
a.		On No. 3	110.00	140.00

On Stamps of 1916-18

10	A42	3pi on 2pa vio (R)	62.50	75.00
a.		On No. 4	97.50	125.00
		Nos. 5-10 (6)	465.00	530.00

Turkish Revenue Stamps Handstamped in Turkish "Osmanli Postalari, 1336" (Ottoman Post, 1920).

Type a

Dash at upper left is set high. Bottom (date) line is 8½mm long.

Type b

Dash at upper left is set lower. Bottom (date) line is 10mm long.

Type c

Dash at upper left is set lower. Bottom (date) line is 9mm long.

Religious Tribunals Revenue R1

12	R1	1pi grn (a, b, c)	750.00	300.00
13	R1	5pi ultra (a, b)	16,000.	15,500.
14	R1	50pi gray grn (a, b, c)	25.00	35.00
		Cut cancellation		3.00
15	R1	100pi buff (a)	140.00	97.50
a.		100pi yellow (a)	95.00	72.50
		Cut cancellation		7.50
16	R1	500pi org (a)	225.00	150.00
		Cut cancellation		20.00
17	R1	1000pi brn (a)	3,000.	1,750.
		Cut cancellation		175.00

See Nos. 29-32.

Court Costs Revenue R2

Black Overprint

18	R2	10pa grn (b, c)	110.00	100.00
19	R2	1pi ultra (a, c)	—	19,000.
20	R2	5pi rose (c)	17,500.	—
21	R2	50pi ocher (a, b, c)	50.00	50.00
a.		50pi yellow (a, b, c)	12.00	17.00
		Cut cancellation, #21, 21a		2.00
22	R2	100pi brown (a)	150.00	100.00
		Cut cancellation		20.00
23	R2	500pi slate (a)	325.00	325.00
		Cut cancellation		20.00

See Nos. 24, 33-39.

Notary Public Revenue R3

Design R2 Overprinted "Katibi Adliye Masus dur" in Red

24	R3	50pi ocher (a)	1,250.	150.00
		Cut cancellation		20.00

Laborer's Passport Tax Stamp — R4

Notary Public Revenue — R5

Black Overprint

25	R4	2pi emerald (a, c)	—	22,000.
26	R5	100pi yellow brn (a)	1,250.	150.00
		Cut cancellation		30.00

See Nos. 46-48.

Theater Tax Stamp — R6

Land Registry Revenue R7

27	R6	20pa black	5,000.	5,000.
a.		20pa black *grayish*		
28	R7	2pi blue black	6,250.	6,250.

See Nos. 40, 45.

Hejaz Railway Tax Stamp — R8

Black Overprint
Perf. 11½

28A	R8	2pi dk red & bl (b)	1,750.	1,750.

See Nos. 53-57.

Turkish Revenue Stamps Overprinted in Turkish "Osmanli Postalari, 1337" (Ottoman Post, 1921)

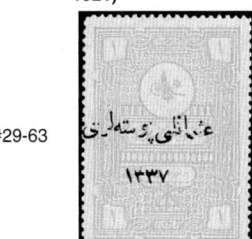

On #29-63

Perf. 12

29	R1	10pa slate	20.00	16.00
a.		Handstamped overprint	100.00	50.00
b.		Double overprint		
30	R1	1pi green	32.50	20.00
a.		Inverted overprint	35.00	22.50
b.		Handstamped overprint	3,500.	3,250.

31	R1	5pi ultra	29.00	14.50
a.		"1337" inverted	100.00	90.00
b.		Half used as 2½pi on cover		
c.		Handstamped overprint	875.00	875.00
		Nos. 29-31 (3)	81.50	50.50

Handstamped Overprint

32	R1	50pi green	7,250.	7,250.

Design R2 Overprinted

33	R2	10pa green	24.50	24.50
a.		Handstamped overprint	3,500.	3,500.
34	R2	1pi ultra	50.00	25.00
a.		Handstamped overprint	875.00	875.00
35	R2	5pi red	24.50	25.00
a.		Inverted overprint		
b.		"1337" inverted	100.00	100.00
c.		Half used as 2½pi on cover		
d.		Handstamped overprint	7,500.	7,500.
e.		5pi rose	72.50	25.00
f.		As "e," handstamped overprint	5,500.	5,500.
36	R2	50pi ocher, handstamped ovpt.	500.00	100.00
		Cut cancellation		20.00
		Nos. 33-36 (4)	599.00	174.50

Design R3 Overprinted
Additional Turkish Overprint in Red or Black

37	R3	10pa green (R)	100.00	60.00
38	R3	1pi ultra (R)	72.50	50.00
39	R3	5pi rose (Bk)	72.50	50.00
a.		"1337" inverted	200.00	200.00
b.		Handstamped overprint	7,000.	7,000.
c.		5pi carmine	100.00	60.00
d.		As "c," handstamped overprint	8,500.	
		Nos. 37-39 (3)	245.00	160.00

Design R7 Overprinted

40	R7	2pi blue black	125.00	110.00
a.		Handstamped overprint	5,500.	5,500.

R12

1921   **Overprinted in Black**   **Perf. 12**

41	R12	5pi green	150.00	125.00
		Cut cancellation		17.50
a.		Handstamped overprint	5,500.	5,000.

Museum Tax Stamp R13

Overprinted in Black

42	R13	1pi ultra	425.00	400.00
a.		Handstamped overprint	5,500.	5,500.
43	R13	5pi deep green	475.00	450.00
a.		Handstamped overprint	5,500.	5,500.

Handstamped Overprint

44	R13	5pi dark vio	7,000.	7,000.

The overprint variety "337" for "1337" exists on Nos. 42-43.

Design R6
Overprinted

Perf. 12, 12½

45	R6	20pa black	12.50	5.00
a.		Date 4½mm high	15.00	
b.		"337" for "1337"	25.00	
c.		Silk paper	725.00	725.00
d.		White paper	15.00	10.00

Design R5
Overprinted

46	R5	10pa green	25.00	25.00
a.		Overprint 21mm long		
b.		"131" for "1337"		
47	R5	1pi ultra	37.50	25.00
a.		"13" for "1337"	50.00	50.00
b.		"131" for "1337"	50.00	50.00
c.		Inverted overprint	90.00	90.00
d.		Handstamped overprint	4,500.	4,500.
48	R5	5pi red	62.50	25.00
a.		Inverted overprint	90.00	90.00
b.		"131" for "1337"	85.00	85.00
c.		Handstamped overprint	4,500.	4,400.
d.		5pi pink	500.00	
e.		As "d," handstamped overprint	5,500.	5,500.
		Nos. 46-48 (3)	125.00	75.00

R16

Perf. 11½, 11½x11
Overprinted in Black

49	R16	10pa pink	4.00	1.50
a.		Imperf.		
b.		Date "1237"	5.00	2.00
d.		Inverted overprint	15.00	
e.		Handstamped overprint	1,950.	1,950.
50	R16	1pi yellow	10.00	5.00
a.		Overprint 18mm long	10.00	5.00
b.		Date "1332"	12.00	
c.		Date "1317"		
d.		Inverted overprint	30.00	
e.		Handstamped overprint	1,950.	1,950.
51	R16	2pi yellow grn	12.50	5.00
a.		Date "1237"	15.00	
b.		Date "1317"		
c.		Imperf.		
d.		Inverted overprint	40.00	9.00
e.		Handstamped overprint		
52	R16	5pi red	20.00	1.00
a.		Horiz. pair, imperf. vert.		
b.		Inverted overprint	25.00	7.50
c.		Double overprint	30.00	12.50
d.		Date "1332"	45.00	
e.		Half used as 2½pi on cover		
f.		Overprint 18mm long	20.00	7.50
g.		Handstamped overprint	1,950.	1,950.
		Nos. 49-52 (4)	46.50	12.50

Design R8 Overprinted
Turkish Inscriptions

20 Paras   1 Piaster

2 Piasters   5 Piasters

1921   Dark Red & Blue   Perf. 11½

53	R8	20pa on 1pi	75.00	75.00
54	R8	1pi on 1pi	7.50	4.00
55	R8	2pi on 1pi	7.50	4.00
a.		Inverted surcharge	25.00	
56	R8	5pi on 1pi	12.00	6.00
		Nos. 53-56 (4)	102.00	89.00

See No. 57.

No. 54 Overprinted

57	R8	1pi on 1pi dk red & bl	50.00	50.00

Hejaz Railway Tax
Stamp — R19

Overprinted in Black

58	R19	1pi grn & brn red	6.00	4.00
a.		Double overprint		
b.		Handstamped overprint		

The errors "1307," "1331" and "2337" occur once in each sheet of Nos. 53-58.

Naval League
Labels — R20

Overprinted in Black

1921   Perf. 12x11½

59	R20	1pa orange	10.00	15.00
a.		Date "1327"	30.00	30.00
60	R20	2pa indigo	10.00	15.00
61	R20	5pa green	12.50	17.50
62	R20	10pa brown	25.00	30.00
63	R20	40pa red brown	175.00	190.00
		Nos. 59-63 (5)	232.50	267.50

The error "2337" occurs on all values of this issue.

The Naval League stamps have pictures of three Turkish warships. They were sold for the benefit of sailors of the fleet but did not pay postage until they were overprinted in 1921.

Turkish Stamps of 1915-20
Overprinted

a

b

The overprints on Nos. 64-77 read "Adana December 1st, 1921." This issue commemorated the withdrawal of the French from Cilicia.

On No. 71 the lines of the overprint are further apart than on Nos. 68-70 and 73-74.

1921   Perf. 12

64	A44 (a)	10pa grn (424)	10.00	7.00
65	A45 (a)	20pa deep rose (425)	10.00	7.00
a.		Inverted overprint	30.00	
66	A51 (a)	25pi car, straw (434)	20.00	25.00
a.		Double overprint		
b.		Inverted overprint	60.00	37.50
		Nos. 64-66 (3)	40.00	39.00

On Newspaper Stamp of 1915

67	A21 (a)	5pa och (P132)	90.00	150.00

On Stamp of 1915

68	A22 (b)	5pa och (328)	350.00	400.00

On Stamps of 1917-18

69	A53 (b)	5pi on 2pa (547)	15.00	17.50
70	A53 (b)	5pi on 2pa (548)	15.00	17.50

On Stamp of 1919

71	A57 (b)	35pi on 1pi bl (Bk; 579)	42.50	50.00
a.		Inverted surcharge	100.00	

On Newspaper Stamp of 1915

72	A21 (b)	5pa och (P132)	200.00	200.00

On No. 72 the overprint is vertical, half reading up and half reading down.

On Stamps of 1920

73	A32 (b)	3pi blue (594)	15.00	12.50
74	A36 (b)	10pi gray vio (596)	20.00	20.00

On Postage Due Stamps of 1914

75	D1 (a)	5pa claret (J63)	350.00	350.00
76	D2 (a)	20pa red (J64)	350.00	400.00
a.		Inverted overprint	750.00	
77	D3 (b)	1pi dk bl (J65)	350.00	400.00
a.		Inverted overprint	750.00	750.00
		Nos. 75-77 (3)	1,050.	1,150.

Withdrawal of the French from Cilicia. Forged overprints exist.

Pact of Revenge,
Burning Village at
Top — A21

Izmir Harbor — A22

Mosque of
Selim,
Adrianople
A23

Mosque of Selim,
Konya — A24

Legendary Gray
Wolf — A26

Soldier — A25

Snake Castle
and Ceyhan
River,
Adana — A27

Parliament
Building at
Sivas — A28

A29

Mosque at
Urfa — A30

Map of
Anatolia
A31

Declaration of Faith
from the
Koran — A32

1922   Litho.   Perf. 11½

78	A21	10pa violet brn	1.00	.25
		Never hinged	2.50	
79	A22	20pa blue grn	1.00	.25
		Never hinged	2.50	
80	A23	1pi dp blue	1.50	.35
		Never hinged	3.25	
81	A24	2pi red brown	3.00	.50
		Never hinged	14.50	
82	A25	5pi dk blue	3.00	.50
		Never hinged	13.50	
83	A26	10pi dk brown	12.50	.75
		Never hinged	50.00	
a.		Vert. pair, imperf between	100.00	
b.		Vert. strip of 3, imperf between	300.00	
84	A27	25pi rose	15.00	2.00
		Never hinged	72.50	
85	A28	50pi indigo	1.50	15.00
		Never hinged	5.00	
86	A29	50pi dk gray	1.50	1.25
		Never hinged	5.00	
87	A30	100pi violet	75.00	8.00
		Never hinged	375.00	
		Cut cancellation		2.00
88	A31	200pi slate	200.00	62.50
		Never hinged	975.00	
		Cut cancellation		9.00
89	A32	500pi green	125.00	27.50
		Never hinged	550.00	
		Cut cancellation		12.00
		Nos. 78-89 (12)	440.00	118.85
		Set, never hinged	2,075.	
		Set, ovptd. "SPECIMEN"	750.00	

Imperf

79a	A22	20pa	25.00	30.00
80a	A23	1pi	15.00	20.00
82a	A25	5pi	15.00	20.00
84a	A27	25pi	35.00	30.00
85a	A28	50pi	27.50	30.00

Stamps of
Type A23
Overprinted

1922

90	A23	1pi deep blue	7.25	15.00
		Never hinged	14.50	

91	A23	5pi deep blue	7.25	20.00
		Never hinged	14.50	
92	A23	10pi brown	7.25	20.00
		Never hinged	14.50	
93	A23	25pi rose	10.00	25.00
		Never hinged	14.50	
94	A23	50pi slate	12.50	25.00
		Never hinged	22.50	
95	A23	100pi violet	17.50	37.50
		Never hinged	35.00	
96	A23	200pi black vio	17.50	50.00
		Never hinged	35.00	
97	A23	500pi blue green	25.00	75.00
		Never hinged	47.50	
		Nos. 90-97 (8)	104.25	267.50
		Set, never hinged	300.00	

Withdrawal of the French from Cilicia and the return of the Kemalist Natl. army. The overprint reads: "Adana, Jan. 5, 1922."

No. 90-97 without overprint were presented to some high government officials.

First Parliament House, Ankara — A33

1922				Litho.
98	A33	5pa violet	.75	2.50
		Never hinged	2.00	
99	A33	10pa green	1.75	2.50
		Never hinged	5.25	
100	A33	20pa pale red	2.50	2.00
		Never hinged	7.00	
101	A33	1pi brown org	12.00	1.50
		Never hinged	40.00	
102	A33	2pi red brown	20.00	4.25
		Never hinged	77.50	
103	A33	3pi rose	6.00	.70
		Never hinged	12.00	
a.		Arabic "13" in right corner	10.00	7.50
b.		Thin grayish paper	55.00	7.50
		Never hinged	210.00	
		Nos. 98-103 (6)	43.00	13.45
		Set, never hinged	140.00	

Nos. 98-103, 103b exist imperf. In 1923 several stamps of Turkey and Turkey in Asia were overprinted in Turkish for advertising purposes. The overprint reads: "Izmir Economic Congress, 17 Feb., 1339."

POSTAGE DUE STAMPS

D1

1922			Litho.	Perf. 11½
J1	D1	20pa dull green	1.00	5.00
		Never hinged	2.50	
a.		Imperf.		—
J2	D1	1pi gray green	1.00	5.00
		Never hinged	2.50	
J3	D1	2pi red brown	2.50	17.50
		Never hinged	7.25	
J4	D1	3pi rose	4.50	25.00
		Never hinged	17.00	
J5	D1	5pi dark blue	6.00	55.00
		Never hinged	24.00	
		Nos. J1-J5 (5)	15.00	
		Set, never hinged	55.00	
		Set, ovptd. "SPECIMEN"	200.00	

TURKS & CAICOS ISLANDS

ˈtərks ənˌd ˈkā-kəs ˈī-ləndz

LOCATION — A group of islands in the West Indies, at the southern extremity of the Bahamas
GOVT. — British colony; a dependency of Jamaica until 1959
AREA — 192 sq. mi.
POP. — 7,436 (1980)
CAPITAL — Grand Turk

12 Pence = 1 Shilling
20 Shillings = 1 Pound

Catalogue values for unused stamps in this country are for Never Hinged items, beginning with Scott 90.

A6

Dependency's Badge — A7

1900-04		Engr.	Wmk. 2	Perf. 14
1	A6	½p green	3.00	4.50
2	A6	1p rose	4.00	.85
3	A6	2p black brown	1.10	1.40
4	A6	2½p gray blue ('04)	2.00	1.10
a.		2½p blue ('00)	9.00	17.50
5	A6	4p orange	4.25	8.00
6	A6	6p violet	2.75	7.50
7	A6	1sh purple brn	3.75	21.00
				Wmk. 1
8	A7	2sh violet	50.00	80.00
9	A7	3sh brown lake	80.00	110.00
		Nos. 1-9 (9)	150.85	234.35

1905-08				Wmk. 3
10	A6	½p green	5.75	.25
11	A6	1p carmine	19.00	.55
12	A6	3p violet, yel ('08)	2.50	7.00
		Nos. 10-12 (3)	27.25	7.80

King Edward VII — A8

1909, Sept. 2				Perf. 14
13	A8	½p yellow green	.85	.45
14	A8	1p carmine	1.40	.45
15	A8	2p gray	5.50	1.60
16	A8	2½p ultra	8.00	4.25
17	A8	3p violet, yel	2.75	2.75
18	A8	4p red, yel	3.75	8.00
19	A8	6p violet	8.00	7.00
20	A8	1sh black, green	8.00	9.50
21	A8	2sh red, grn	45.00	60.00
22	A8	3sh black, red	47.50	45.00
		Nos. 13-22 (10)	130.75	139.00

Turk's-Head Cactus A9

George V A10

1910-11				Wmk. 3
23	A9	¼p claret	2.00	1.10
24	A9	¼p red ('11)	.70	.50
		See Nos. 36, 44.		

1913-16				
25	A10	½p yellow green	.55	2.00
26	A10	1p carmine	1.10	2.50
27	A10	2p gray	2.50	4.00
28	A10	2½p ultra	2.50	3.50
29	A10	3p violet, yel	2.50	12.50
30	A10	4p scarlet, yel	1.10	11.00
31	A10	5p olive grn ('16)	7.50	25.00
32	A10	6p dull violet	2.75	4.00
33	A10	1sh orange	1.75	5.75
34	A10	2sh red, bl grn	18.00	42.00
a.		2sh red, grnsh white ('19)	30.00	80.00
b.		2sh red, emerald ('21)	55.00	80.00
35	A10	3sh black, red	17.50	30.00
		Nos. 25-35 (11)	57.75	142.25

Issued: 5p, 5/18/16; others, 4/1/13.
For overprints see Nos. MR1-MR13.

1921, Apr. 23				Wmk. 4
36	A9	¼p red	4.75	24.00
37	A10	½p green	3.00	6.25
38	A10	1p scarlet	1.10	6.25
39	A10	2p gray	1.10	21.00
40	A10	2½p ultra	2.00	8.50
41	A10	5p olive green	10.00	65.00
42	A10	6p dull violet	7.50	65.00
43	A10	1sh brown orange	12.00	42.50
		Nos. 36-43 (8)	41.45	238.50

A11

A12

Inscribed "Postage"

1922-26				
44	A9	¼p gray black ('26)	1.10	1.25
45	A11	½p green	4.75	4.50
46	A11	1p brown	.65	3.75
47	A11	1½p rose red ('25)	9.00	21.00
48	A11	2p gray	.65	7.00
49	A11	2½p violet, yel	.65	2.40
50	A11	3p ultra	.65	7.00
51	A11	4p red, yel	1.60	21.00
52	A11	5p yellow grn	1.25	30.00
53	A11	6p dull violet	.95	12.00
54	A11	1sh orange	1.10	25.00
55	A11	2sh red, green	2.75	12.50
				Wmk. 3
56	A11	2sh red, green ('25)	35.00	95.00
57	A11	3sh black, red ('25)	7.00	37.50
		Nos. 44-57 (14)	67.10	279.90

Issued: #47, 56-57, 11/24; #44, 10/11; others, 11/20.

Inscribed "Postage and Revenue"

1928, Mar. 1				Wmk. 4
60	A12	½p green	.95	.60
61	A12	1p brown	.95	.90
62	A12	1½p red	.95	4.00
63	A12	2p dk gray	.95	.60
64	A12	2½p vio, yel	.95	6.25
65	A12	3p ultra	.95	8.75
66	A12	6p brown vio	.95	9.25
67	A12	1sh brown org	4.50	9.25
68	A12	2sh red, grn	7.75	45.00
69	A12	5sh green, yel	13.50	45.00
70	A12	10sh violet, bl	62.50	125.00
		Nos. 60-70 (11)	94.90	254.60

Common Design Types pictured following the introduction.

Silver Jubilee Issue
Common Design Type

1935, May 6				Perf. 11x12
71	CD301	½p green & blk	.40	1.00
72	CD301	3p ultra & brn	2.75	5.25
73	CD301	6p ol grn & lt bl	2.10	6.00
74	CD301	1sh brn vio & ind	4.00	4.00
		Nos. 71-74 (4)	9.25	16.25
		Set, never hinged	16.00	

Coronation Issue
Common Design Type

1937, May 12				Perf. 13½x14
75	CD302	½p deep green	.25	.25
76	CD302	2p gray	.45	.65
77	CD302	3p brt ultra	.60	.65
		Nos. 75-77 (3)	1.30	1.55
		Set, never hinged	1.75	

Raking Salt — A13

Salt Industry — A14

1938-45		Wmk. 4		Perf. 12½
78	A13	¼p black	.25	.25
79	A13	½p green	2.40	.25
80	A13	1p brown	.45	.25
81	A13	1½p carmine	.45	.25
82	A13	2p gray	.70	.30
83	A13	2½p orange	2.50	1.10
84	A13	3p ultra	.30	.30
85	A13	6p rose violet	6.00	3.25
85A	A13	6p blk brn ('45)	.25	.25
86	A13	1sh bister	2.40	11.00
86A	A13	1sh dk ol grn ('45)	.25	.25
87	A14	2sh rose car	25.00	17.00

88	A14	5sh green	30.00	25.00
89	A14	10sh dp violet	7.50	8.50
		Nos. 78-89 (14)	78.45	67.95
		Set, never hinged	135.00	

Catalogue values for unused stamps in this section, from this point to the end of the section, are for Never Hinged items.

Peace Issue
Common Design Type

1946, Nov. 4		Engr.	Perf. 13½x14
90	CD303	2p gray black	.25	.25
91	CD303	3p deep blue	.25	.25

Silver Wedding Issue
Common Design Types

1948, Sept. 13	Photo.		Perf. 14x14½
92	CD304	1p red brown	.25	.30
			Perf. 11½x11	
		Engr.; Name Typo.		
93	CD305	10sh purple	15.00	20.00

Dependency's Badge — A17

Flag and Merchant Ship — A18

Map of the Islands A19

Victoria and George VI A20

1948, Dec. 14		Engr.	Perf. 12½
94	A17	½p green	.55	.25
95	A17	2p carmine	.95	.25
96	A18	3p deep blue	.70	.25
97	A19	6p violet	.90	.40
98	A20	2sh ultra & blk	1.40	2.25
99	A20	5sh blue grn & blk	4.00	7.00
100	A20	10sh chocolate & blk	6.25	7.00
		Nos. 94-100 (7)	14.75	17.40

Cent. of political separation from the Bahamas.

UPU Issue
Common Design Types
Engr.; Name Typo. on 3p, 6p
Perf. 13½, 11x11½

1949, Oct. 10				Wmk. 4
101	CD306	2½p red orange	.25	1.50
102	CD307	3p indigo	1.90	1.25
103	CD308	6p chocolate	.75	.75
104	CD309	1sh olive	.75	.50
		Nos. 101-104 (4)	3.65	4.00

Loading Bulk Salt — A21

Dependency's Badge — A22

Designs: 1p, Salt Cay. 1½p, Caicos mail. 2p, Grand Turk. 2½p, Sponge diving. 3p, South Creek. 4p, Map. 6p, Grand Turk Light. 1sh, Government House. 1sh6p, Cockburn Harbor. 2sh, Government offices. 5sh, Salt Loading.

1950, Aug. 2		Engr.	Perf. 12½	
105	A21	½p deep green	.95	.60
106	A21	1p chocolate	.80	1.25
107	A21	1½p carmine	1.40	.90
108	A21	2p red orange	1.00	.60
109	A21	2½p olive green	1.25	.80
110	A21	3p ultra	.60	.60
111	A21	4p rose car & blk	4.00	1.25
112	A21	6p ultra & blk	3.00	.80
113	A21	1sh bl gray & blk	2.50	.60
114	A21	1sh6p red & blk	15.00	5.25
115	A21	2sh ultra & emer	6.50	5.75
116	A21	5sh black & ultra	27.50	11.50
117	A22	10sh purple & blk	30.00	27.50
		Nos. 105-117 (13)	94.50	57.40

WAR TAX STAMPS

Regular Issue of 1913-16 Overprinted

Black Overprint at Bottom of Stamp

1917		Wmk. 3	Perf. 14	
MR1	A10	1p carmine	.25	1.75
a.		Double overprint	200.00	275.00
b.		"TAX" omitted		
c.		Pair, one without ovpt.	700.00	
MR2	A10	3p violet, yel	1.40	5.75
a.		Double overprint	110.00	

Black Overprint at Top or Middle of Stamp

1917				
MR3	A10	1p carmine	.25	1.40
a.		Inverted overprint	55.00	
b.		Double overprint	65.00	77.50
c.		Pair, one without over- print	650.00	
MR4	A10	3p violet, yel	.70	2.00
a.		Double overprint	50.00	60.00
b.		Dbl. ovpt., one inverted	375.00	

Same Overprint in Violet or Red

1918-19				
MR5	A10	1p car (V) ('19)	.50	4.50
a.		Double overprint	24.00	
b.		"WAR" omitted	200.00	
MR6	A10	3p violet, yel (R)	15.00	45.00
a.		Double overprint	375.00	

Regular Issue of 1913-16 Overprinted in Black

1918				
MR7	A10	1p carmine	.25	1.75
MR8	A10	3p violet, yel	4.50	5.00

Same Overprint in Red

1919				
MR9	A10	3p violet, yel	.25	2.75

Regular Issue of 1913-16 Overprinted in Black

MR10	A10	1p carmine	.25	1.10
a.		Double overprint	160.00	190.00
MR11	A10	3p violet, yel	.35	3.00

Regular Issue of 1913-16 Overprinted

MR12	A10	1p carmine	.25	2.75
a.		Double overprint	100.00	
MR13	A10	3p violet, yel	.55	3.00

The bottom two rows of this setting show the words "War" and "Tax" about 1mm farther apart.

TURKS ISLANDS

ˈtərks ˈī-lənds

LOCATION — West Indies, at the southern extremity of the Bahamas
AREA — 616 sq. mi.
POP. — 2,000 (approx.)
CAPITAL — Grand Turk

In 1848 the Turks Islands together with the Caicos group, lying to the northwest, were made a British colony. In 1873 the Colony became a dependency under the government of Jamaica although separate stamp issues were continued. Postage stamps inscribed Turks and Caicos Islands have been used since 1900.

12 Pence = 1 Shilling

PRE-STAMP POSTAL MARKINGS

Crowned Circle handstamp type V is pictured in the Crowned Circle Handstamps and Great Britain Used Abroad section.
Grand Turk

1857				
A1	V	"Turks Islands" crowned circle handstamp, on cover		6,350.

Values for unused stamps are for examples with original gum as defined in the catalogue introduction. Very fine examples of Nos. 1-42 will have generally rough perforations that cut into the design on one or more sides due to the narrow spacing of the stamps on the plates and imperfect perforating methods. Stamps with perfs clear of the design on all four sides are extremely scarce and will command substantially higher prices.

Because of the printing and imperfect perforating methods, stamps are often found scissor separated. Prices will not be adversely affected on those stamps where the scissor cut does not remove the perforations.

Watermark

Wmk. 5 — Small Star

Queen Victoria — A1

Perf. 11½ to 13

1867		Unwmk.		Engr.
1	A1	1p rose	67.50	67.50
2	A1	6p gray black	110.00	140.00
3	A1	1sh slate blue	105.00	67.50
		Nos. 1-3 (3)	282.50	275.00

Perf. 11 to 13x14 to 15

1873-79			Wmk. 5	
4	A1	1p lake	57.50	57.50
5	A1	1p dull red ('79)	62.50	67.50
a.		Horiz. pair, imperf. btwn.	26,000.	
b.		Perf. 11-12	1,100.	
6	A1	1sh violet	5,750.	2,250.

Stamps offered as No. 6 are often examples from which the surcharge has been removed.

Stamps of 1867-79 Surcharged in Black

a   b

c   d

e

12 settings of the ½p, 9 of 2½p, and 6 of 4p.

1881		Unwmk.	Perf. 11 to 13	
7	(a)	½p on 6p gray blk	100.00	170.00
7A	(b)	½p on 6p gray blk	100.00	150.00
8	(b)	½p on 1sh slate bl	140.00	200.00
a.		Double surcharge	8,000.	
8B	(c)	½p on 1sh slate bl	11,000.	
c.		Without fraction bar		

Perf. 11 to 13x14 to 15
Wmk. 5

9	(a)	½p on 1p dull red	150.00	200.00
a.		Double surcharge		
10	(b)	½p on 1p dull red	60.00	150.00
11	(c)	½p on 1p dull red	210.00	275.00
a.		Double surcharge	4,250.	
12	(d)	½p on 1p dull red	260.00	
a.		Without fraction bar	1,150.	
b.		Double surcharge		
13	(e)	½p on 1p dull red	600.00	
14	(a)	½p on 1sh violet	175.00	225.00
a.		Double surcharge	4,000.	
15	(b)	½p on 1sh violet	140.00	225.00
a.		Without fraction bar	625.00	
16	(c)	½p on 1sh violet	105.00	190.00

f

g

h

Perf. 11 to 13
Unwmk.

17	(f)	2½p on 6p gray blk	16,000.	
18	(g)	2½p on 6p gray blk	425.	600.
a.		Horiz. pair, imperf. between	40,000.	
b.		Double surcharge	17,000.	
19	(h)	2½p on 6p gray blk	250.	425.
a.		Double surcharge	16,000.	

---

i

j

Perf. 11 to 13x14 to 15
Wmk. 5

20	(i)	2½p on 1sh violet	4,000.	
21	(h)	2½p on 1sh violet	625.00	950.00
22	(j)	2½p on 1sh violet	9,500.	

k

l

m

n

Perf. 11 to 13
Unwmk.

24	(k)	2½p on 6p gray blk	9,500.	
25	(k)	2½p on 1sh slate bl	27,000.	
26	(l)	2½p on 1sh slate bl	1,500.	
27	(m)	2½p on 1sh slate bl	2,200.	
a.		Without fraction bar	8,000.	
28	(n)	2½p on 1sh slate bl	6,500.	

o

Perf. 11 to 13x14 to 15
Wmk. 5

29	(l)	2½p on 1p dull red	750.00	
30	(o)	2½p on 1p dull red	1,500.	
31	(l)	2½p on 1sh violet	850.00	
a.		Double surcharge of "½"	4,750.	
32	(o)	2½p on 1sh violet	1,350.	
b.		Double surcharge of "½"	9,000.	

p

q

r

Perf. 11 to 13
Unwmk.

33	(p)	4p on 6p gray black	110.00	150.00
34	(q)	4p on 6p gray black	400.00	500.00
35	(r)	4p on 6p gray black	750.00	350.00

Examples of No. 33 with top of "4" painted in are sometimes offered as No. 35.

Perf. 11 to 13x14 to 15
Wmk. 5

36	(r)	4p on 1p dull red	950.00	625.00
a.		Inverted surcharge	3,250.	
37	(p)	4p on 1p dull red	850.00	550.00
a.		Inverted surcharge		
38	(r)	4p on 1sh violet	475.00	750.00
39	(q)	4p on 1sh violet	2,750.	

Wmk. Crown and C C (1)

1881		Engr.	Perf. 14	
40	A1	1p brown red	77.50	105.00
a.		Diagonal half used as ½p on cover		
41	A1	6p olive brown	120.00	175.00
42	A1	1sh slate green	190.00	140.00
		Nos. 40-42 (3)	387.50	420.00

TURKS ISLANDS

A2

1881   **Typo.**
43 A2   4p ultramarine   170.00   67.50

1882-95   **Engr.**   **Wmk. 2**
44 A1   1p orange brn
       ('83)   100.00   35.00
     a.   Half used as ½p on cover   5,000.
45 A1   1p car lake ('89)   3.50   2.25
46 A1   6p yellow brn ('89)   4.50   5.00
47 A1   1sh black brn ('87)   6.00   4.50
     a.   1sh deep brown   6.00   4.50

Typo.
Die A
48 A2   ½p dull green ('85)   6.50   6.00
     a.   ½p blue green ('82)   29.00   29.00
49 A2   2½p red brown ('82)   40.00   16.00
50 A2   4p gray ('84)   38.00   4.00
     a.   Half used as 2p on cover   5,000.

Die B
51 A2   ½p gray green ('94)   3.50   4.50
52 A2   2½p ultra ('93)   3.50   2.75
53 A2   4p dk vio & bl ('95)   11.00   15.00

For descriptions of dies A and B see "Dies of British Colonial Stamps" in table of contents.

1887   **Engr.**   **Perf. 12**
54 A1   1p carmine lake   14.00   3.25

No. 49 Surcharged in Black

1889
55 A2   1p on 2½p red brn   22.00   19.00
     a.   Double surcharge
     b.   Double surcharge, one invert-
         ed
     c.   "One" omitted   1,800.
     d.   Half used as ½p on cover   5,500.

No. 55c caused by the misplacement of the surcharge. Stamps also exist from the same sheet reading "Penny One."

No. 50 Surcharged in Black

Two types of surcharge:
Type I — Upper bar continuous across sheet.
Type II — Upper bar breaks between stamps.

1893
56 A2   ½p on 4p gray (I)   225.00   180.00
     a.   Type II   3,250.   1,450.

This surcharge exists in five settings.

A3

1894   **Typo.**
57 A3   5p olive grn & carmine   10.00   25.00
     a.   Diag. half used as 2½p on cov-
         er   5,000.

UBANGI-SHARI

ü-'ban̠g̠ē 'shär-ē

(Ubangi-Shari-Chad)

LOCATION — In Western Africa, north of the equator
GOVT. — French Colony
AREA — 238,767 sq. mi.

POP. — 833,916
CAPITAL — Bangui

In 1910 French Congo was divided into the three colonies of Gabon, Middle Congo and Ubangi-Shari and officially named "French Equatorial Africa." Under that name in 1934 the group, with the territory of Chad included, became a single administrative unit. See Gabon.

100 Centimes = 1 Franc

Stamps of Middle Congo Ovptd. in Black

1915-22   **Unwmk.**   **Perf. 14x13½**
Chalky Paper
1   A1   1c ol gray & brn   .35   .35
       Never hinged   .55
       On cover   75.00
   a.   Double overprint   225.00
       Never hinged   360.00
   b.   Imperf.   67.50
       Never hinged   100.00
   c.   On ordinary paper   .35   .35
       Never hinged   .55
       On cover   75.00
2   A1   2c violet & brn   .35   .35
       Never hinged   .55
       On cover   75.00
   a.   On ordinary paper   .35   .35
       Never hinged   .55
       On cover   75.00
3   A1   4c blue & brn   .65   .80
       Never hinged   1.10
       On cover   75.00
   a.   On ordinary paper   .55   .55
       Never hinged   1.10
       On cover   75.00
4   A1   5c dk grn & bl   .70   .85
       Never hinged   1.25
       On cover   22.50
   a.   On ordinary paper   1.60   1.60
       Never hinged   3.25
       On cover   25.00
5   A1   5c yel & bl ('22)   1.20   1.60
       Never hinged   2.00
       On cover   25.00
6   A1   10c carmine & bl   1.20   1.20
       Never hinged   6.75
       On cover   14.50
   a.   On ordinary paper   5.25   4.75
       Never hinged   8.75
       On cover   30.00
7   A1   10c dp grn & bl grn
         ('22)   1.20   1.60
       Never hinged   2.00
       On cover   42.50
8   A1   15c brn vio & rose,
         ordinary paper   2.00   2.40
       Never hinged   3.25
       On cover   25.00
9   A1   20c brown & blue   4.00   4.75
       Never hinged   6.75
       On cover   22.50
       On cover, single franking   32.50
   a.   On ordinary paper   4.00
       Never hinged   6.75

Overprinted

10   A2   25c blue & grn   2.00   2.40
       Never hinged   3.25
       On cover   27.50
       On cover, single franking   50.00
11   A2   25c bl grn & gray
         ('22)   1.60   1.60
       Never hinged   2.40
       On cover   12.50
12   A2   30c scarlet & grn   1.60   2.00
       Never hinged   2.75
       On cover   27.50
       On cover, single franking   50.00
13   A2   30c dp rose & rose
         ('22)   1.20   1.60
       Never hinged   2.00
       On cover   37.50
       On cover, single franking   65.00
14   A2   35c vio brn & bl   5.50   6.50
       Never hinged   8.00
       On cover   32.50
       On cover, single franking   67.50
15   A2   40c dl grn & brn   8.00   8.00
       Never hinged   13.50
       On cover   45.00
       On cover, single franking   90.00
16   A2   45c vio & red   8.00   8.00
       Never hinged   13.50
       On cover   55.00
       On cover, single franking   105.00
   a.   On ordinary paper   9.50   7.25
       Never hinged   16.00
       On cover   65.00

17   A2   50c bl grn & red   7.00   7.00
       Never hinged   10.00
       On cover   50.00
       On cover, single franking   105.00
   a.   On ordinary paper   9.50   8.75
       Never hinged   16.00
       On cover   55.00
18   A2   50c blue & grn ('22)   1.20   1.60
       Never hinged   2.00
       On cover   30.00
       On cover, single franking   55.00
19   A2   75c brown & bl   17.50   17.50
       Never hinged   29.00
       On cover   70.00
       On cover, single franking   140.00
20   A3   1fr dp grn & vio   17.50   17.50
       Never hinged   29.00
       On cover   80.00
       On cover, single franking   160.00
21   A3   2fr vio & gray grn   20.00   20.00
       Never hinged   33.00
       On cover   100.00
       On cover, single franking   190.00
22   A3   5fr blue & rose   50.00   50.00
       Never hinged   80.00
       On cover   170.00
       On cover, single franking   275.00
       Nos. 1-22 (22)   152.75 157.60

For surcharges see Nos. B1-B2.

Middle Congo of 1907-22 Ovptd. in Black or Red

1922
23   A1   1c violet & grn   .80   1.20
       Never hinged   1.20
       On cover   75.00
   a.   Overprint omitted   190.00 210.00
       Never hinged   310.00
   b.   Imperf.   45.00
   c.   As "a," imperf   200.00
       Never hinged   325.00
24   A1   2c grn & salmon   .85   1.20
       Never hinged   1.20
       On cover   75.00
25   A1   4c ol brn & brn   1.20   1.60
       Never hinged   2.00
       On cover   75.00
   a.   Overprint omitted   225.00
       Never hinged   360.00
26   A1   5c indigo & rose   1.20   1.60
       Never hinged   2.40
       On cover   21.00
27   A1   10c dp grn & gray grn   2.00   2.40
       Never hinged   3.25
       On cover   45.00
28   A1   15c lt red & dl bl   2.00   2.40
       Never hinged   3.25
       On cover   27.50
29   A1   20c choc & salmon   5.75   6.50
       Never hinged   8.75
       On cover   27.50

Overprinted

30   A2   25c vio & salmon   10.00   11.00
       Never hinged   17.00
       On cover   27.50
31   A2   30c rose & pale rose   3.50   4.00
       Never hinged   5.50
       On cover   40.00
       On cover, single franking   75.00
32   A2   35c vio & grn   6.00   6.00
       Never hinged   9.50
       On cover   35.00
       On cover, single franking   50.00
33   A2   40c ind & vio (R)   6.00   6.00
       Never hinged   9.50
       On cover   35.00
       On cover, single franking   50.00
34   A2   45c choc & vio   6.00   6.00
       Never hinged   9.50
       On cover   65.00
       On cover, single franking   110.00
35   A2   50c dk bl & pale bl   3.25   4.00
       Never hinged   4.75
       On cover   35.00
       On cover, single franking   70.00
36   A2   60c on 75c vio, *pnksh*   4.00   4.75
       Never hinged   7.25
       On cover   40.00
       On cover, single franking   65.00
37   A2   75c choc & sal   6.50   7.25
       Never hinged   10.50
       On cover   70.00
       On cover, single franking   125.00
38   A3   1fr grn & dl bl (R)   12.00   13.00
       Never hinged   19.50
       On cover   90.00
       On cover, single franking   125.00
   a.   Overprint omitted   325.00
       Never hinged   475.00
39   A3   2fr grn & salmon   17.50   17.50
       Never hinged   27.00
       On cover   105.00
       On cover, single franking   190.00

40   A3   5fr grn & ol brn   27.50   27.50
       Never hinged   40.00
       On cover   140.00
       On cover, single franking   225.00
       Nos. 23-40 (18)   116.05 123.90

Nos. 23-29 with Additional Ovpt. in Black, Blue or Red

1924-33
41   A1   1c vio & grn (Bl)   .35   .55
       Never hinged   .55
       On cover   65.00
   a.   "OUBANGUI CHARI" omitted   160.00 160.00
       Never hinged   260.00
42   A1   2c grn & sal (Bl)   .40   .65
       Never hinged   .55
       On cover   65.00
   a.   "OUBANGUI CHARI" omitted   160.00 160.00
       Never hinged   260.00
   b.   Double overprint   175.00
       Never hinged   275.00
43   A1   4c ol brn & brn (Bl)   .40   .65
       Never hinged   .65
       On cover   65.00
   a.   Double overprint (Bl + Bk)   200.00
       Never hinged   325.00
   b.   "OUBANGUI CHARI" omitted   180.00
       Never hinged   290.00
44   A1   5c ind & rose   .40   .65
       Never hinged   .65
       On cover   27.50
   a.   "OUBANGUI CHARI" omitted   150.00
       Never hinged   225.00
45   A1   10c dp grn & gray grn   .80   .95
       Never hinged   1.25
       On cover   20.00
46   A1   10c red org & bl ('25)   .95   1.05
       Never hinged   1.50
       On cover   30.00
47   A1   15c sal & dl bl   .90   .95
       Never hinged   1.40
       On cover   16.00
48   A1   15c sal & dl bl (Bl)
         ('26)   1.20   1.60
       Never hinged   1.60
       On cover   27.50
49   A1   20c choc & salmon
         (Bl)   1.20   1.60
       Never hinged   2.00
       On cover   27.50

On Nos. 41-49 the color in ( ) refers to the overprint "Afrique Equatoriale Francaise."

Overprinted

50   A2   25c vio & salmon
         (Bl)   .85   .85
       Never hinged   1.20
       On cover   14.00
   a.   Imperf.
51   A2   30c rose & pale
         rose (Bl)   .80   1.20
       Never hinged   1.20
       On cover   35.00
       On cover, single franking   70.00
52   A2   30c choc & red
         ('25)   .90   .95
       Never hinged   1.25
       On cover   14.00
   a.   "OUBANGUI CHARI" omit-
       ted   160.00
       Never hinged   260.00
53   A2   30c dk grn & grn
         ('27)   1.60   2.00
       Never hinged   2.75
       On cover   45.00
54   A2   35c vio & grn (Bl)   .85   1.20
       Never hinged   1.20
       On cover   45.00
       On cover, single franking   47.50
   a.   "OUBANGUI CHARI" omit-
       ted   525.00
55   A2   40c ind & vio (Bl)   .85   1.20
       Never hinged   1.20
       On cover   50.00
       On cover, single franking   80.00
56   A2   45c choc & vio (Bl)   1.20   1.60
       Never hinged   2.00
       On cover   16.00
       On cover, single franking   27.50
57   A2   50c dk bl & pale bl
         (R)   .80   .80
       Never hinged   1.20
       On cover   16.00
       On cover, single franking   25.00
58   A2   50c gray & bl vio
         ('25) (R)   1.60   1.75
       Never hinged   2.60
       On cover   14.00
59   A2   60c on 75c dk vio,
         pnksh (R)   .60   .65
       Never hinged   .90
       On cover   21.00
       On cover, single franking   35.00

60 A2 65c org brn & bl
('28) 1.60 *2.00*
  Never hinged 2.75
  On cover 35.00
  On cover, single franking 75.00
61 A2 75c choc & sal (Bl) 2.00 *2.40*
  Never hinged 3.25
  On cover 35.00
  On cover, single franking 80.00
62 A2 75c dp bl & lt bl
('25) (R) 1.20 *1.60*
  Never hinged 1.90
  On cover 21.00
  On cover, single franking 37.50
  a. "OUBANGUI CHARI" omit-
ted 160.00
    Never hinged 260.00
63 A2 75c rose & dk brn
('28) 2.50 *2.75*
  Never hinged 4.00
  On cover 20.00
  On cover, single franking 27.50
64 A2 90c brn red & pink
('30) 5.75 *5.75*
  Never hinged 9.25
  On cover 65.00
  On cover, single franking 150.00
65 A3 1fr grn & ind (Bk +
Bl) ('25) .95 *1.10*
  Never hinged 1.40
  On cover 35.00
  On cover, single franking 70.00
66 A3 1fr grn & ind (R +
Bl) 1.60 *2.40*
  Never hinged 2.75
  On cover 35.00
  On cover, single franking 70.00
67 A3 1.10fr bister & bl
('28) 3.25 *4.00*
  Never hinged 5.25
  On cover 170.00
  On cover, single franking 375.00
68 A3 1.25fr mag & lt grn
('33) 13.00 *13.00*
  Never hinged 20.00
  On cover 50.00
  On cover, single franking 110.00
69 A3 1.50fr ultra & bl
('30) 7.25 *8.00*
  Never hinged 12.00
  On cover 55.00
  On cover, single franking 140.00
70 A3 1.75fr dk brn & dp
buff ('33) 15.00 *15.00*
  Never hinged 23.00
  On cover 45.00
  On cover, single franking 55.00
71 A3 2fr grn & red 1.60 *2.40*
  Never hinged 2.75
  On cover 65.00
  On cover, single franking 125.00
  a. "OUBANGUI CHARI" omit-
ted 1,875. *1,200.*
72 A3 3fr red vio ('30) 5.75 *6.50*
  Never hinged 8.75
  On cover 90.00
  On cover, single franking 170.00
73 A3 5fr grn & ol brn (Bl) 5.25 *6.50*
  Never hinged 8.00
  On cover 70.00
  On cover, single franking 140.00
  Nos. 41-73 (33) 83.35 *94.25*

On Nos. 65, 66 the first overprint color refers to OUBANGUI CHARI.
For surcharges see Nos. 74-81.

**Types of 1924 Issue Surcharged
with New Values in Black or Red**
1925-26
74 A3 65c on 1fr vio & ol 2.00 *2.40*
  Never hinged 3.25
  On cover 80.00
  On cover, single franking 190.00
  a. "65" omitted 160.00
    Never hinged 260.00
75 A3 85c on 1fr vio & ol 2.00 *2.40*
  Never hinged 3.25
  On cover 70.00
  On cover, single franking 140.00
  a. "AFRIQUE EQUATORIALE
FRANCAISE" omitted 160.00
    Never hinged 260.00
  b. Double surcharge 180.00
    Never hinged 275.00
76 A3 1.25fr on 1fr dk bl &
ultra (R) ('26) 1.45 *1.75*
  Never hinged 2.25
  On cover 75.00
  On cover, single franking 160.00
  a. "1f25" omitted 190.00 *125.00*
    Never hinged 290.00

Bars cover old denomination on No. 76.

**Types of 1924 Issue Surcharged
with New Values and Bars**
1927
77 A2 90c on 75c brn red &
rose red 2.40 *3.25*
  Never hinged 4.00
  On cover 70.00
  On cover, single franking 125.00
78 A3 1.50fr on 1fr ultra & bl 2.40 *3.25*
  Never hinged 4.00
  On cover 65.00
  On cover, single franking 110.00
79 A3 3fr on 5fr org brn &
dl red 3.50 *4.00*
  Never hinged 5.50
  On cover 110.00
  On cover, single franking 225.00
80 A3 10fr on 5fr ver & vio 19.00 *21.00*
  Never hinged 27.50
  On cover 160.00
  On cover 300.00

---

81 A3 20fr on 5fr vio & gray 30.00 *35.00*
  Never hinged 47.50
  On cover 190.00
  On cover, single franking 340.00
  Nos. 77-81 (5) 57.30 *66.50*

Common Design Types
pictured following the introduction.

Colonial Exposition Issue
Common Design Types
1931 **Engr.** *Perf. 12½*
Name of Country Typo. in Black
82 CD70 40c deep green 5.50 *5.50*
  Never hinged 9.50
  On cover 110.00
83 CD71 50c violet 5.50 *5.50*
  Never hinged 9.50
  On cover 95.00
84 CD72 90c red orange 5.50 *5.50*
  Never hinged 9.50
  On cover 170.00
  On cover, single franking 225.00
  a. Imperf. 130.00
    Never hinged 200.00
85 CD73l 1.50fr dull blue 5.50 *5.50*
  Never hinged 9.50
  On cover 150.00
  On cover, single franking 200.00
  Nos. 82-85 (4) 22.00 *22.00*

SEMI-POSTAL STAMPS

Regular
Issue of
1915
Surcharged

1916 **Unwmk.** *Perf. 14x13½*
Chalky Paper
B1 A1 10c + 5c car & blue 3.25 *3.50*
  Never hinged 5.50
  On cover 100.00
  a. Inverted surch. 180.00
  b. Double surcharge 180.00
  c. Double surch., one invtd. 130.00 *130.00*
  d. Vertical surcharge 140.00 *140.00*
  e. No period under "C" 20.00 *20.00*
    Never hinged 35.00

Regular
Issue of
1915
Surcharged
in Carmine

B2 A1 10c + 5c car & blue 2.00 *2.40*
  Never hinged 3.25
  On cover 70.00

POSTAGE DUE STAMPS

Postage Due Stamps of
France Overprinted

1928 **Unwmk.** *Perf. 14x13½*
J1 D2 5c light blue 1.60 *2.00*
  Never hinged 2.75
  On cover 105.00
J2 D2 10c gray brown 2.40 *2.40*
  Never hinged 4.00
  On cover 105.00
J3 D2 20c olive green 2.40 *2.40*
  Never hinged 4.00
  On cover 105.00
J4 D2 25c bright rose 2.40 *2.40*
  Never hinged 4.00
  On cover 110.00
J5 D2 30c light red 2.40 *2.40*
  Never hinged 4.00
  On cover 110.00
J6 D2 45c blue green 2.40 *2.40*
  Never hinged 4.00
  On cover 110.00
J7 D2 50c brown violet 2.75 *3.25*
  Never hinged 4.75
  On cover 125.00
J8 D2 60c yellow brown 3.25 *3.50*
  Never hinged 5.50
  On cover 140.00
J9 D2 1fr red brown 4.75 *4.75*
  Never hinged 8.00
  On cover 150.00
J10 D2 2fr orange red 6.50 *7.25*
  Never hinged 12.00
  On cover 170.00

J11 D2 3fr bright violet 6.50 *7.25*
  Never hinged 12.00
  On cover 190.00
  Nos. J1-J11 (11) 37.35 *40.00*

Landscape
D3

Emile Gentil — D4

1930 **Typo.**
J12 D3 5c dp bl & olive .85 *1.20*
  Never hinged 1.25
  On cover 50.00
J13 D3 10c dk red & brn 1.20 *1.60*
  Never hinged 2.00
  On cover 50.00
J14 D3 20c green & brn 1.20 *1.60*
  Never hinged 2.00
  On cover 50.00
J15 D3 25c lt bl & brn 1.60 *2.00*
  Never hinged 2.75
  On cover 55.00
J16 D3 30c bis brn & Prus bl 2.75 *3.25*
  Never hinged 4.00
  On cover 65.00
J17 D3 45c Prus bl & ol 3.50 *4.00*
  Never hinged 5.50
  On cover 65.00
J18 D3 50c red vio & brn 6.00 *6.75*
  Never hinged 9.00
  On cover 70.00
J19 D3 60c gray lil & bl blk 6.50 *7.25*
  Never hinged 10.00
  On cover 75.00
J20 D4 1fr bis brn & bl blk 6.00 *6.75*
  Never hinged 10.00
  On cover 90.00
J21 D4 2fr violet & brown 8.00 *8.00*
  Never hinged 13.00
  On cover 100.00
J22 D4 3fr dp red & brn 8.50 *9.50*
  Never hinged 13.50
  On cover 110.00
  Nos. J12-J22 (11) 46.10 *51.90*

Stamps of Ubangi-Shari were replaced in 1936 by those of French Equatorial Africa.

UGANDA

ü-'gan-də

LOCATION — East Africa, at the Equa-
tor and separated from the Indian
Ocean by Kenya and Tanzania
AREA — 91,343 sq. mi.
POP. — 13,990,000 (est. 1983)
CAPITAL — Kampala

Stamps of 1898-1902 were replaced by those issued for Kenya, Tanganyika and Uganda.

Cowries (50 = 4 Pence)
16 Annas = 1 Rupee (1896)

Unused values for Nos. 2-68 are for stamps without gum. Very fine examples will be evenly cut and will show at least two full typewritten framelines.

A1

A2

Nos. 1-53 were produced with a typewriter by Rev. Ernest Millar of the Church Missionary Society. They were 20-26mm wide, with nine stamps in a horizontal row. Later two more were added to each row, and the stamps became narrower, 16-18mm.
Rev. Millar got a new typewriter in 1895, and the stamps he typed on it have a different

---

appearance. A violet ribbon in the machine, inserted late in 1895, resulted in Nos. 35-53.
Nos. 1-53 are on thin, tough, white paper, laid horizontally with traces of a few vertical lines.

Forgeries of Nos. 1-53 are known.

Without Gum
Wide Letters
Typewritten on Thin Laid Paper
Stamps 20 to 26mm wide
1895 **Unwmk.** *Imperf.*
1 A1 10(c) black 5,750. *3,750.*
2 A1 20(c) black 9,600. *2,350.*
  a. "U A" instead of "U G" 7,750.
3 A1 30(c) black 2,500. *2,000.*
4 A1 40(c) black 7,750. *2,850.*
5 A1 50(c) black 1,800. *1,400.*
  a. "U A" instead of "U G" 10,000.
6 A1 60(c) black 3,250. *2,850.*
**Surcharged with New Value in
Black, Pen-written**
9 A1 10 on 30(c) black 85,000.
10 A1 10 on 50(c) black 85,000.
11 A1 15 on 10(c) black 85,000.
12 A1 15 on 20(c) black 65,000.
13 A1 15 on 40(c) black 85,000.
14 A1 15 on 50(c) black 80,000.
15 A1 25 on 50(c) black 85,000.
16 A1 50 on 60(c) black 85,000.
Stamps 16 to 18mm wide
17 A1 5(c) black 4,000. *1,650.*
18 A1 10(c) black 4,000. *2,000.*
19 A1 15(c) black 2,500. *1,900.*
  a. Verticaly laid paper 6,500.
20 A1 20(c) black 4,000. *1,900.*
  a. Vertically laid paper 8,250.
21 A1 25(c) black 2,000. *2,000.*
22 A1 30(c) black 10,500. *10,000.*
23 A1 40(c) black 10,000. *10,000.*
24 A1 50(c) black 4,750. *5,750.*
25 A1 60(c) black 10,000. *10,000.*
Narrow Letters
Stamps 16 to 18mm wide
26 A2 5(c) black 2,000.
27 A2 10(c) black 2,150.
28 A2 15(c) black 2,150.
29 A2 20(c) black 1,800.
30 A2 25(c) black 2,000.
31 A2 30(c) black 2,250.
32 A2 40(c) black 2,000.
33 A2 50(c) black 2,150.
34 A2 60(c) black 3,200.
35 A2 5(c) violet 900. *825.*
36 A2 10(c) violet 825. *825.*
37 A2 15(c) violet 1,400. *750.*
38 A2 20(c) violet 600. *375.*
  a. "G A" instead of "U G"
  b. Vertically laid paper 3,850.
39 A2 25(c) violet 2,300. *2,000.*
40 A2 30(c) violet 2,850. *1,400.*
41 A2 40(c) violet 2,800. *1,900.*
42 A2 50(c) violet 2,500. *1,900.*
43 A2 100(c) violet 3,250. *3,750.*

As a favor to a philatelist, 35c and 45c denominations were made in black and violet. They were not intended for postal use and no rate called for those denominations.

A3

1896
44 A3 5(c) violet 950. *1,250.*
45 A3 10(c) violet 1,050. *825.*
46 A3 15(c) violet 950. *950.*
47 A3 20(c) violet 500. *275.*
48 A3 25(c) violet 875. *1,150.*
49 A3 30(c) violet 950. *1,050.*
50 A3 40(c) violet 1,100. *1,150.*
51 A3 50(c) violet 950. *1,000.*
52 A3 60(c) violet 2,000. *2,500.*
53 A3 100(c) violet 1,900. *2,500.*

A4

Overprinted "L" in Black
1896 **Typeset** **White Paper**
54 A4 1a black (thin "1") 210. *190.*
  a. Small "O" in "POSTAGE" 1,550. *1,300.*
55 A4 2a black 135. *140.*
  a. Small "O" in "POSTAGE" 615. *675.*
56 A4 3a black 300. *375.*
  a. Small "O" in "POSTAGE" 1,900. *2,250.*

57	A4	4a black	135.	180.
a.		Small "O" in "POSTAGE"		625.

Yellowish Paper

58	A4	8a black	225.	340.
a.		Small "O" in "POSTAGE"	1,675.	2,100.
59	A4	1r black	425.	500.
a.		Small "O" in "POSTAGE"	2,250.	
60	A4	5r black	37,500.	37,500.

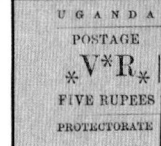

A4a

Without Overprint
White Paper

61	A4a	1a black (thin "1")	125.00	110.00
a.		Small "O" in "POSTAGE"	700.00	675.00
62	A4a	1a black (thick "1")	26.00	30.00
a.		Small "O" in "POSTAGE"	95.00	110.00
63	A4a	2a black	32.50	40.00
a.		Small "O" in "POSTAGE"	110.00	140.00
64	A4a	3a black	32.50	50.00
a.		Small "O" in "POSTAGE"	135.00	200.00
65	A4a	4a black	35.00	42.50
a.		Small "O" in "POSTAGE"	125.00	140.00

Yellowish Paper

66	A4a	8a black	42.50	50.00
a.		Small "O" in "POSTAGE"	155.00	200.00
67	A4a	1r black	95.00	110.00
a.		Small "O" in "POSTAGE"	400.00	475.00
68	A4a	5r black	300.00	400.00
a.		Small "O" in "POSTAGE"	1,000.	1,250.

A5

Queen Victoria — A6

1898-1902 Engr. Wmk. 2 Perf. 14

69	A5	1a red	5.00	4.50
70	A5	1a car rose ('02)	2.50	2.00
71	A5	2a brown	9.25	11.00
72	A5	3a gray	20.00	50.00
a.		3a bluish gray ('02)	21.00	22.50
73	A5	4a dark green	13.00	16.00
74	A5	8a olive gray	15.00	32.50
a.		8a gray green ('02)	32.50	55.00

Wmk. 1

75	A6	1r ultra	60.00	60.00
a.		1r bright blue (02)	72.50	72.50
76	A6	5r brown	110.00	130.00
		Nos. 69-76 (8)	234.75	306.00

A7

1902 Wmk. 2 Black Overprint

77	A7	½a yellow green	3.25	1.90
a.		Inverted overprint	2,200.	
b.		Double overprint	2,500.	
c.		Pair, one without overprint	5,250.	

Red Overprint

78	A7	2½a dark blue	5.00	3.50
a.		Double overprint	650.00	

UKRAINE
yü-'krān

LOCATION — In southeastern Europe, bordering on the Black Sea
GOVT. — Republic
AREA — 170,998 sq. mi.
POP. — 48,760,474 (2001)
CAPITAL — Kiev

Following the collapse of the Russian Empire, a national assembly met at Kiev and declared the Ukrainian National Republic on Jan. 22, 1918. During three years of civil war, the Ukrainian army, as well as Bolshevik, White Russian, Allied and Polish armies, fought back and forth across the country. By November, 1920, Ukraine was finally occupied by Soviet forces and on July 6, 1923, it was incorporated into the Soviet Union. Soviet stamps were used until March 1, 1992, when newly independent Ukraine again began issuing its own stamps.

200 Shahiv = 100 Kopiyok (Kopecks) = 1 Karbovanets (Ruble)
100 Shahiv = 1 Hryvnia

Watermark

Wmk. 116- Crosses and Circles

Republic's Trident Emblem — A1

Ukrainian Peasant — A2

Allegorical Ukraine — A3

Trident — A4

Inscription of Value — A5

1918, July Typo. Imperf.
Thin Paper

1	A1	10sh buff	.35	.40
2	A2	20sh brown	.35	.40
3	A3	30sh ultra	.35	.40
a.		30sh blue	2.75	6.50
4	A4	40sh green	.35	.40
5	A5	50sh red	.35	.40
		Nos. 1-5 (5)	1.75	2.00

The stamps of this issue exist perforated or pin-perforated unofficially.

Forgeries of this set exist on a very thin, glossy paper.

These designs were earlier (April, 1918) utilized for money tokens, printed on thin cardboard, perforated 11½, and bearing an inscription on the reverse "Circulates on par with coins" in Ukrainian. These tokens exist favor canceled but were not postage stamps. Value uncanceled, $6 each.

TRIDENT OVERPRINTS

Stamps of Russia Overprinted in Violet, Black, Blue, Red, Brown or Green

This trident-shaped emblem was taken from the arms of the Grand Prince Volodymyr and adopted as the device of the Ukrainian Republic.

In the early months of independence, Russian stamps were commonly used, but the influx of large quantities of stamps from Russia made it necessary to take measures to protect postal revenue. In August, 1918, local post offices were ordered to send their existing stocks of Russian stamps to regional centers, where they were overprinted with the trident arms. Unoverprinted Russian stamps were declared invalid after October 1, although they were often accepted for use.

Nos. 6-47 represent the basic Russian overprints. Values are for the most common overprint variety.

Following this basic Trident listing are detailed listings for the major regional and city types (Nos. 6a-44s).

The basic Russian stamps to which Trident overprints were applied

A8　　　A9

A11

A12

A13　A14

A15

On Stamps of 1902-03
1918 Wmk. 168 Perf. 13½

6	A12	3½r black & gray	100.00	75.00
7	A12	7r black & yellow	100.00	75.00

On Stamps of 1909-18
Lozenges of Varnish on Face
Perf. 14, 14½x15
Unwmk.

8	A14	1k orange	.25	.35
9	A14	2k green	.25	.35
10	A14	3k red	.25	.35
11	A15	4k carmine	.25	.35
12	A14	5k claret	.25	.35
13	A14	7k light blue	.25	.35
14	A15	10k dark blue	.25	.35
15	A11	14k blue & rose	.25	.35
16	A11	15k red brn & bl	.25	.35
17	A8	20k blue & car	.25	.35
18	A11	25k grn & gray vio	.40	.50
19	A11	35k red brn & grn	.25	.35
20	A8	50k violet & grn	.25	.35
21	A11	70k brown & org	.25	.35

Perf. 13½

22	A9	1r lt brn, brn & org	.55	.75
23	A12	3½r mar & lt grn	1.25	2.50
24	A13	5r dk bl, grn & pale bl	7.50	11.00
25	A12	7r dk grn & pink	9.00	12.00
26	A13	10r scar, yel & gray	13.00	18.00
		Nos. 6-26 (21)	234.95	199.30

On Stamps of 1917
Perf. 14, 14½x15

27	A14	10k on 7k light blue	.75	1.00
28	A11	20k on 14k bl & rose	.75	1.00

On Stamps of 1917-18
Imperf

29	A14	1k orange	.25	.35
30	A14	2k gray green	.25	.35
31	A14	3k red	.25	.35
32	A14	5k carmine	.25	.35
33	A14	5k claret	.90	1.50
34	A11	15k red brn & bl	.25	.35
35	A8	20k bl & car	.75	1.50
36	A11	25k grn & gray vio	60.00	—
37	A11	35k red brn & grn	.25	.35
38	A8	50k violet & grn	.30	.35
39	A11	70k brown & org	.25	.35
40	A9	1r pale brn, brn & red org	.25	.60
41	A12	3½r mar & lt grn	1.00	2.50
42	A13	5r dk bl, grn & pale bl	1.50	3.00
43	A12	7r dk grn & pink	2.50	4.00
44	A13	10r scar, yel & gray	70.00	85.00
		Nos. 29-44 (16)	138.95	100.90

PF1

Russian Stamps AR1-AR3.

Wmk. 171 Litho.
Perf. 14, 14½x14¾

45	PF1	1k red, *buff*	5.00	25.00
46	PF1	5k green, *buff*	20.00	120.00
47	PF1	10k brown, *buff*	35.00	350.00
		Nos. 45-47 (3)	60.00	495.00

Nos. 45-47 were used and accepted as postage stamps during stamp shortages.

REGIONAL ISSUES

Katerynoslav I — Handstamped in black with a rubber device

8a	A14	1k orange	.60	3.50
9a	A14	2k green	.25	.35
10a	A14	3k red	.30	.60
11a	A15	4k carmine	.25	2.50
12a	A14	5k claret	.25	.60
13a	A14	7k light blue	.25	.60
14a	A15	10k dark blue	.25	.35
15a	A11	14k blue & rose	.25	1.25
16a	A11	15k red brn & bl	.25	.25
17a	A8	20k blue & car	.30	.60
18a	A11	25k grn & gray vio	.50	1.25
19a	A11	35k red brn & grn	9.00	15.00
20a	A8	50k violet & grn	.25	.35
21a	A11	70k brown & org	.25	.60
27a	A14	10k on 7k light blue	.25	1.25
28a	A11	20k on 14k bl & rose	.30	2.50
29a	A14	1k orange	.25	.35
30a	A14	2k gray green	6.00	18.00
31a	A14	3k red	.25	.35
32a	A14	5k carmine	120.00	120.00
33a	A14	5k claret	7.00	9.00
34a	A11	15k red brn & bl	.60	2.50
35a	A8	20k bl & car	.90	2.50
37a	A11	35k red brn & grn	3.50	7.00
38a	A8	50k violet & grn	120.00	120.00
39a	A11	70k brown & org	120.00	120.00

Katerynoslav II — Handstamped in black with a rubber device

6a	A12	3½r black & gray	—	360.00
7a	A12	7r black & yellow	120.00	120.00
22a	A9	1r lt brn, brn & org	180.00	240.00
23a	A12	3½r mar & lt grn	15.00	25.00
25a	A12	7r dk grn & pink	25.00	50.00
40a	A9	1r pale brn, brn & red org	2.00	3.00
41a	A12	3½r mar & lt grn	2.50	6.00
42a	A12	7r brn bl, grn & pale brn	50.00	60.00
43a	A12	7r dk grn & pink	150.00	

Kharkiv I — Handstamped in black with a metal device

8b	A14	1k orange	.90	6.00
9b	A14	2k green	2.50	3.50
10b	A14	3k red	.25	.25
11b	A15	4k carmine	1.25	6.00
12b	A14	5k claret	6.00	9.00
13b	A14	7k light blue	30.00	90.00
14b	A15	10k dark blue	3.00	5.00
15b	A11	14k blue & rose	30.00	75.00
16b	A11	15k red brn & bl	.25	.35
17b	A8	20k blue & car	1.50	2.50
18b	A11	25k grn & gray vio	50.00	70.00
19b	A11	35k red brn & grn	.25	.35
20b	A8	50k violet & grn	.25	.35
21b	A11	70k brown & org	.50	2.00
27b	A14	10k on 7k light blue	2.50	3.50
28b	A11	20k on 14k bl & rose	2.00	5.00
29b	A14	1k orange	.25	1.25
30b	A14	2k gray green	1.75	5.00

No	Type	Denom	Unused	Used
31b	A14	3k red	.25	2.00
33b	A14	5k claret	1.25	5.00
34b	A11	15k red brn & bl	6.00	9.00
37b	A11	35k red brn & grn	30.00	90.00
45b	A6	1k red, *buff*	1.00	
46b	A6	5k green, *buff*	8.00	
47b	A6	10k brown, *buff*	2.00	

Kharkiv II — Handstamped in black with a metal device

No	Type	Denom	Unused	Used
6c	A12	3½r black & gray	—	
7c	A12	7r black & yellow	120.00	150.00
9c	A14	2k green	—	
10c	A14	3k red	—	
16c	A11	15k red brn & bl	—	
22c	A9	1r lt brn, brn & org	3.00	18.00
23c	A12	3½r mar & lt grn	30.00	45.00
24c	A13	5r dk bl, grn & pale bl		300.00
25c	A12	7r dk grn & pink	18.00	30.00
26c	A13	10r scar, yel & gray	300.00	240.00
40c	A9	1r pale brn, brn & red org	.25	1.25
41c	A12	3½r mar & lt grn	.50	2.50
42c	A13	5r dk bl, grn & pale bl	1.25	2.50
43c	A12	7r dk grn & pink	18.00	30.00
44c	A13	10r scar, yel & gray	150.00	180.00

Kharkiv III — Handstamped in black with a metal device

No	Type	Denom	Unused	Used
6d	A12	3½r black & gray	180.00	300.00
7d	A12	7r black & yellow	—	300.00
9d	A14	2k green	—	
10d	A14	3k red	—	
16d	A11	15k red brn & bl	—	
22d	A9	1r lt brn, brn & org	7.00	50.00
23d	A12	3½r mar & lt grn	48.00	55.00
24d	A13	5r dk bl, grn & pale bl	—	
25d	A12	7r dk grn & pink	20.00	30.00
26d	A13	10r scar, yel & gray	120.00	150.00
30d	A14	2k gray green	120.00	
40d	A9	1r pale brn, brn & red org	.25	1.25
41d	A12	3½r mar & lt grn	.30	2.50
42d	A13	5r dk bl, grn & pale bl	.60	2.50
43d	A12	7r dk grn & pink	25.00	50.00
44d	A13	10r scar, yel & gray	70.00	70.00

Kiev I — Handstamped in violet with a rubber device

No	Type	Denom	Unused	Used
6e	A12	3½r black & gray	360.00	360.00
7e	A12	7r black & yellow	300.00	180.00
8e	A14	1k orange	.25	.30
9e	A14	2k green	1.25	.90
10e	A14	3k red	3.50	2.50
11e	A15	4k carmine	2.00	2.00
12e	A14	5k claret	.25	.35
13e	A14	7k light blue	18.00	24.00
14e	A14	10k dark blue	.60	.60
15e	A11	14k blue & rose	15.00	18.00
16e	A11	15k red brn	.50	.60
17e	A8	20k blue & car	2.50	1.25
18e	A11	25k grn & gray vio	30.00	24.00
19e	A11	35k red brn & grn	24.00	18.00
20e	A8	50k violet & grn	.25	.35
21e	A11	70k brown & org	.25	.35
22e	A9	1r lt brn, brn & org	6.00	7.50
23e	A12	3½r mar & lt grn	1.25	3.00
24e	A13	5r dk bl, grn & pale bl	50.00	100.00
25e	A12	7r dk grn & pink	48.00	55.00
26e	A13	10r scar, yel & gray	15.00	20.00
27e	A14	10k on 7k light blue	3.50	5.00
28e	A11	20k on 14k bl & rose	.60	.60
29e	A14	1k orange	1.50	2.50
30e	A14	2k gray green	.25	.35
31e	A14	3k red	.25	.35
32e	A15	4k carmine	.25	.35
33e	A14	5k claret	18.00	24.00
34e	A11	15k red brn & bl	4.75	6.00
35e	A8	50k bl & car	18.00	24.00
36e	A11	25k bl & car	—	
37e	A11	35k red brn & grn	.25	.35
38e	A8	50k violet & grn	18.00	15.00
39e	A11	70k brown & org	30.00	35.00
40e	A9	1r pale brn, brn & red org	.60	.60
41e	A12	3½r mar & lt grn	24.00	30.00
42e	A13	5r dk bl, grn & pale bl	.60	1.25
43e	A12	7r dk grn & pink	1.25	1.75
44e	A13	10r scar, yel & gray	300.00	—
45e	PF1	1k red, *buff*	—	
46e	PF1	5k green, *buff*	—	
47e	PF1	10k brown, *buff*	17.00	

Kiev II — Handstamped in violet with a rubber device

No	Type	Denom	Unused	Used
6f	A12	3½r black & gray	48.00	55.00
7f	A12	7r black & yellow	48.00	55.00
8f	A14	1k orange	.25	.35
9f	A14	2k green	.25	.35
10f	A14	3k red	.25	.35
11f	A15	4k carmine	.25	.35
12f	A14	5k claret	.25	.35
13f	A14	7k light blue	12.00	18.00
14f	A15	10k dark blue	.25	.35
15f	A11	14k blue & rose	.30	.50
16f	A11	15k red brn & bl	.25	.35
17f	A8	20k blue & car	.25	.35
18f	A11	25k grn & gray vio	.90	.70
19f	A11	35k red brn & grn	.25	.35
20f	A8	50k violet & grn	.25	.35
21f	A11	70k brown & org	.25	.35
22f	A9	1r lt brn, brn & org	.50	.75
23f	A12	3½r mar & lt grn	.90	2.00
24f	A13	5r dk bl, grn & pale bl	6.00	10.00
25f	A12	7r dk grn & pink	7.00	12.00
26f	A13	10r scar, yel & gray	12.00	15.00
27f	A14	10k on 7k light blue	.25	.35
28f	A11	20k on 14k bl & rose	.25	.35
29f	A14	1k orange	.25	.35
30f	A14	2k gray green	.25	.35
31f	A14	3k red	.25	.35
32f	A15	4k carmine	.75	.90
33f	A14	5k claret	.90	1.50
34f	A11	15k red brn & bl	.25	.35
36f	A11	25k bl & car	50.00	
37f	A11	35k red brn & grn	.25	.35
38f	A8	50k violet & grn		70.00
39f	A11	70k brown & org	.25	.35
40f	A9	1r pale brn, brn & red org	.50	.75
41f	A12	3½r mar & lt grn	1.50	2.00
42f	A13	5r dk bl, grn & pale bl	2.00	2.50
43f	A12	7r dk grn & pink	2.50	3.50
44f	A13	10r scar, yel & gray	50.00	60.00
45f	A6	1k red, *buff*	15.00	
46f	A6	5k green, *buff*	12.00	
47f	A6	10k brown, *buff*	30.00	

Kiev III — Lithographed in black

No	Type	Denom	Unused	Used
6g	A12	3½r black & gray	75.00	150.00
8g	A14	1k orange	.25	.35
9g	A14	2k green	.90	1.25
10g	A14	3k red	.90	1.25
11g	A15	4k carmine	.25	.35
12g	A14	5k claret	.25	.35
13g	A14	7k light blue	2.50	3.00
14g	A15	10k dark blue	3.50	5.00
15g	A11	14k blue & rose	3.50	5.00
16g	A11	15k red brn	.25	.35
17g	A8	20k blue & car	5.00	6.00
18g	A11	25k grn & gray vio	5.00	6.00
19g	A11	35k red brn & grn	.25	.35
20g	A8	50k violet & grn	.25	.35
21g	A11	70k brown & org	.25	.35
23g	A12	3½r mar & lt grn	110.00	120.00
24g	A13	5r dk bl, grn & pale bl	300.00	325.00
25g	A12	7r dk grn & pink	75.00	90.00
26g	A13	10r scar, yel & gray	300.00	325.00
27g	A14	10k on 7k light blue	7.00	12.00
28g	A11	20k on 14k bl & rose	.25	.35
29g	A14	1k orange	.25	.35
30g	A14	2k gray green	.25	.35
31g	A14	3k red	.25	.35
32g	A15	4k carmine	2.50	5.00
33g	A14	5k claret	21.00	18.00
34g	A11	15k red brn & bl	18.00	21.00
37g	A11	35k red brn & grn	24.00	24.00
39g	A11	70k brown & org	18.00	21.00
40g	A9	1r pale brn, brn & red org	.25	5.00
41g	A12	3½r mar & lt grn	75.00	90.00
42g	A13	5r dk bl, grn & pale bl	60.00	90.00
43g	A12	7r dk grn & pink	120.00	150.00

Overinked or worn plates produced impressions where the thin outer line of the trident cannot be distinguished.

Odessa I — Typographed in black

No	Type	Denom	Unused	Used
9h	A14	2k green	.25	.35
11h	A15	4k carmine	50.00	—
12h	A14	5k claret	120.00	—
13h	A14	7k light blue	.30	1.25
14h	A15	10k dark blue	.30	1.75
15h	A11	14k blue & rose	5.00	60.00
16h	A11	15k red brn	.40	.75
17h	A8	20k blue & car	70.00	180.00
19h	A11	35k red brn & grn	.40	.75
20h	A8	50k violet & grn	.30	.60
21h	A11	70k brown & org	13.50	
27h	A14	10k on 7k light blue	6.00	12.00
29h	A14	1k orange	.25	.35
31h	A14	3k red	.25	.35
34g	A11	15k red brn & bl	2.50	5.00
37h	A11	35k red brn & grn	18.00	24.00
38h	A8	50k violet & grn	110.00	180.00
39h	A11	70k brown & org	85.00	100.00

Odessa II — Typographed in black

No	Type	Denom	Unused	Used
8i	A14	1k orange	.25	2.00
9i	A14	2k green	.25	.35
10i	A14	3k red	1.25	3.75
11i	A15	4k carmine	.25	.35
12i	A14	5k claret	.25	.35
13i	A14	7k light blue	.25	.35
14i	A14	10k dark blue	.25	.35
15i	A11	14k blue & rose	.25	.90
16i	A11	15k red brn	.25	.35
17i	A8	20k blue & car	.25	.35
18i	A11	25k grn & gray vio	.40	.90
19i	A11	35k red brn & grn	.25	.35
20i	A8	50k violet & grn	.25	.35
21i	A11	70k brown & org	.40	1.25
27i	A14	10k on 7k light blue	.25	1.20
28i	A11	20k on 14k bl & rose	.25	.40
29i	A14	1k orange	.25	.35
30i	A14	2k gray green	1.25	3.75
31i	A14	3k red	.25	.35
33i	A14	5k claret	15.00	
34i	A11	15k red brn & bl	.25	.35
37i	A11	35k red brn & grn	.25	1.25
38i	A8	50k violet & grn	.25	1.25
39i	A11	70k brown & org	.60	5.00

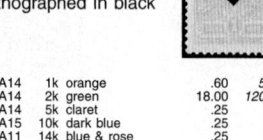

Odessa III — Lithographed in black

No	Type	Denom	Unused	Used
8j	A14	1k orange	.60	5.00
9j	A14	2k green	18.00	120.00
12j	A14	5k claret	.25	.45
14j	A15	10k dark blue	.25	.60
15j	A11	14k blue & rose	.25	.35
16j	A11	15k red brn	.75	3.75
17j	A8	20k blue & car	.25	.40
18j	A11	25k grn & gray vio	3.00	3.75
19j	A11	35k red brn & grn	.25	3.75
20j	A8	50k violet & grn	.25	.35
21j	A11	70k brown & org	.25	.75
27j	A14	10k on 7k light blue	.75	5.50
29j	A14	1k orange	.25	.90
34j	A11	15k red brn & bl	1.80	3.75
37j	A11	35k red brn & grn	.25	1.80
38j	A8	50k violet & grn	.90	5.00
39j	A11	70k brown & org	.60	3.00

Odessa IV — Handstamped in black with a metal device

No	Type	Denom	Unused	Used
6k	A12	3½r black & gray	55.00	60.00
7k	A12	7r black & yellow	150.00	180.00
8k	A14	1k orange	.60	3.00
9k	A14	2k green	.90	2.25
10k	A14	3k red	1.80	2.50
11k	A15	4k carmine	2.75	7.50
12k	A14	5k claret	3.00	7.50
13k	A14	7k light blue	55.00	110.00
14k	A15	10k dark blue	1.25	1.80
15k	A11	14k blue & rose	3.00	4.50
16k	A11	15k red brn	2.25	2.50
17k	A8	20k blue & car	1.30	3.75
18k	A11	25k grn & gray vio	3.00	3.75
19k	A11	35k red brn & grn	3.00	18.00
20k	A8	50k violet & grn	1.80	5.00
21k	A11	70k brown & org	3.75	7.50
22k	A9	1r lt brn, brn & org	1.25	1.80
23k	A12	3½r mar & lt grn	47.50	110.00
24k	A13	5r dk bl, grn & pale bl	9.00	12.00
25k	A12	7r dk grn & pink	9.00	12.00
26k	A13	10r scar, yel & gray	150.00	240.00
27k	A14	10k on 7k light blue	1.25	3.75
28k	A11	20k on 14k bl & rose	2.40	9.00
29k	A14	1k orange	.25	1.80
30k	A14	2k gray green	.90	5.00
31k	A14	3k red	1.25	3.00
32k	A15	4k carmine	110.00	180.00
33k	A14	5k claret	5.00	18.00
34k	A11	15k red brn & bl	1.25	5.00
35k	A8	20k bl & car	110.00	150.00
37k	A11	35k red brn & grn	3.75	15.00
38k	A8	50k violet & grn	7.50	24.00
39k	A11	70k brown & org	35.00	60.00
40k	A9	1r pale brn, brn & red org	.40	.50
41k	A12	3½r mar & lt grn	18.00	9.00
42k	A13	5r dk bl, grn & pale bl	18.00	30.00
43k	A12	7r dk grn & pink	—	
44k	A13	10r scar, yel & gray	150.00	210.00

Odessa V — Handstamped in black with a metal device

No	Type	Denom	Unused	Used
6m	A12	3½r black & gray	210.00	240.00
7m	A12	7r black & yellow	210.00	
8m	A14	1k orange	—	
9m	A14	2k green	90.00	
10m	A14	3k red	180.00	
11m	A15	4k carmine	—	
12m	A14	5k claret	15.00	120.00
13m	A14	7k light blue	—	
14m	A15	10k dark blue	90.00	110.00
15m	A11	14k blue & rose	55.00	
16m	A11	15k red brn	42.50	42.50
17m	A8	20k blue & car	21.00	21.00
18m	A11	25k grn & gray vio	—	
19m	A11	35k red brn & grn	180.00	160.00
20m	A8	50k violet & grn	180.00	160.00
21m	A11	70k brown & org	55.00	160.00
22m	A9	1r lt brn, brn & org	.60	.75
24m	A13	5r dk bl, grn & pale bl		12.00
			—	210.00
25m	A12	7r dk grn & pink	18.00	21.00
26m	A13	10r scar, yel & gray	150.00	120.00
27m	A14	10k on 7k light blue	21.00	21.00
28m	A11	20k on 14k bl & rose	27.50	32.00
29m	A14	1k orange	7.50	7.50
30m	A14	2k gray green	7.50	7.50
31m	A14	3k red	7.50	7.50
33m	A14	5k claret	7.50	7.50
34m	A11	15k red brn & bl	21.00	27.50
37m	A11	35k red brn & grn	—	
38m	A8	50k violet & grn	180.00	
39m	A11	70k brown & org	72.50	60.00
40m	A9	1r pale brn, brn & red org	.50	.50
41m	A12	3½r mar & lt grn	1.80	2.75
42m	A13	5r dk bl, grn & pale bl	110.00	130.00
43m	A12	7r dk grn & pink	—	
44m	A13	10r scar, yel & gray	180.00	180.00

Odessa VI — Handstamped in black with a metal device

No	Type	Denom	Unused	Used
6n	A12	3½r black & gray	240.00	210.00
7n	A12	7r black & yellow	—	
8n	A14	1k orange	100.00	
9n	A14	2k green	5.00	18.00
10n	A14	3k red	120.00	150.00
11n	A15	4k carmine	—	
12n	A14	5k claret	120.00	
13n	A14	7k light blue	150.00	
14n	A15	10k dark blue	2.75	7.00
15n	A11	14k blue & rose	9.00	
16n	A11	15k red brn	35.00	
17n	A8	20k blue & car	45.00	45.00
18n	A11	25k grn & gray vio	35.00	
19n	A11	35k red brn & grn	—	150.00
20n	A8	50k violet & grn	210.00	
21n	A11	70k brown & org	150.00	
22n	A9	1r lt brn, brn & org	.90	1.40
23n	A12	3½r mar & lt grn	2.75	4.50
24n	A13	5r dk bl, grn & pale bl	110.00	240.00
25n	A12	7r dk grn & pink	60.00	240.00
26n	A13	10r scar, yel & gray	120.00	240.00
27n	A14	10k on 7k light blue	35.00	90.00
28n	A11	20k on 14k bl & rose	35.00	42.50
29n	A14	1k orange	9.00	9.00
30n	A14	2k gray green	9.00	9.00
31n	A14	3k red	9.00	9.00
32n	A15	4k carmine	130.00	210.00
33n	A14	5k claret	9.00	9.00
34n	A11	15k red brn & bl	13.00	18.00
35n	A8	20k bl & car	150.00	180.00
38n	A8	50k violet & grn	180.00	
39n	A11	70k brown & org	45.00	45.00
40n	A9	1r pale brn, brn & red org	.50	.75
41n	A12	3½r mar & lt grn	.90	2.25
42n	A13	5r dk bl, grn & pale bl	—	
43n	A12	7r dk grn & pink	—	
44n	A13	10r scar, yel & gray	240.00	

Podillia Ia — Handstamped in black with a metal device

Over 60 additional Podillia trident types and subtypes have been identified by specialists. The majority of these types were made with single-subject overprinting devices composed of non-durable wood or rubber, which quickly deteriorated with use, resulting in subtypes, necessitating the creation of new handstamp types. Because of the rapid wear of the handstamp devices, often only partial trident impressions appear on stamps. The Podillia Ia metal handstamp overprinted far more stamps than any of the wooden or rubber types.

No	Type	Denom	Unused	Used
6o	A12	3½r black & gray	—	
7o	A12	7r black & yellow	110.00	180.00
8o	A14	1k orange	.40	3.75
9o	A14	2k green	.25	.35
10o	A14	3k red	.50	.90
11o	A15	4k carmine	72.50	180.00
12o	A14	5k claret	85.00	3.75
13o	A14	7k light blue	.25	.60
14o	A15	10k dark blue	.50	1.25
15o	A14	14k blue & rose	—	
16o	A11	15k red brn	.25	.35
17o	A8	20k blue & car	.50	.75
18o	A11	25k grn & gray vio	.40	1.25
19o	A11	35k red brn & grn	.35	.35
20o	A8	50k violet & grn	.25	.35
21o	A11	70k brown & org	.25	.35
22o	A9	1r lt brn, brn & org	.40	.60
23o	A12	3½r mar & lt grn	2.50	12.00
24o	A13	5r dk bl, grn & pale bl	25.00	
25o	A12	7r dk grn & pink	25.00	
26o	A13	10r scar, yel & gray	—	
27o	A14	10k on 7k light blue	.25	2.50
28o	A11	20k on 14k bl & rose	1.80	15.00
29o	A14	1k orange	.75	2.50
30o	A14	2k gray green	35.00	
31o	A14	3k red	.25	3.00
33o	A14	5k claret	1.80	
34o	A11	15k red brn & bl	120.00	
37o	A11	35k red brn & grn	—	
38o	A8	50k violet & grn	120.00	47.50

40o A9 1r pale brn, brn & red org .25 .35
41o A12 3½r mar & lt grn 9.00 6.00
42o A13 5r dk bl, grn & pale bl 42.50 30.00
43o A12 7r dk grn & pink 24.00 12.00

Poltava I — Handstamped in violet with a rubber device (kopeck values) or with a metal device (ruble values)

8p A14 1k orange 240.00
9p A14 2k green .25 .35
10p A14 3k red 18.00 24.00
11p A15 4k carmine 18.00 24.00
12p A14 5k claret 9.00 12.00
13p A14 7k light blue 180.00 240.00
14p A15 10k dark blue 12.00 12.00
15p A11 14k blue & rose 240.00
16p A11 15k red brn 6.00 12.00
17p A8 20k blue & car 1.25 2.50
18p A11 25k grn & gray vio 2.50 13.00
19p A11 35k red brn & grn 90.00 75.00
20p A8 50k violet & grn 1.25 1.00
21p A11 70k brown & org .75 .75
22p A9 1r lt brn, brn & org 90.00
24p A13 5r dk bl, grn & pale bl —

25p A12 7r dk grn & pink 13.50 17.00
27p A14 10k on 7k light blue 75.00 50.00
28p A11 20k on 14k bl & rose 20.00 25.00
29p A14 1k orange 3.00 5.00
30p A14 2k gray green 7.50 150.00
31p A14 3k red 1.00 1.50
33p A14 5k claret 130.00 250.00
34p A11 15k red brn & bl 8.00 14.00
35p A8 20k bl & car —
37p A11 35k red brn & grn 7.00 15.00
38p A8 50k violet & grn —
40p A9 1r pale brn, brn & red org 100.00 25.00
41p A12 3½r mar & lt grn —
43p A12 7r dk grn & pink —
44p A13 10r scar, yel & gray —
45p A6 1k red, buff 10.00 15.00
46p A6 5k green, buff 150.00 70.00

Poltava I — Hstmpd. in black with a rubber device (kopeck values) or with a metal device (ruble values)

6q A12 3½r black & gray 300.00
7q A12 7r black & yellow — 300.00
8q A14 1k orange — 250.00
9q A14 2k green 15.00 25.00
10q A14 3k red 20.00 40.00
11q A15 4k carmine 100.00 250.00
12q A15 5k claret 130.00 70.00
13q A14 7k light blue —
14q A15 10k dark blue 100.00 50.00
15q A11 14k blue & rose —
16q A11 15k red brn 5.00 7.50
17q A8 20k blue & car 100.00 50.00
18q A11 25k grn & gray vio — 240.00
19q A11 35k red brn & grn 160.00 100.00
20q A8 50k violet & grn 160.00 70.00
21q A11 70k brown & org 160.00 50.00
22q A9 1r lt brn, brn & org 7.00 4.00
23q A12 3½r mar & lt grn 8.00 10.00
24q A13 5r dk bl, grn & pale bl — 225.00

25q A12 7r dk grn & pink 20.00 25.00
26q A13 10r scar, yel & gray —
27q A14 10k on 7k light blue 160.00 160.00
28q A11 20k on 14k bl & rose 160.00 200.00
29q A14 1k orange 20.00 140.00
30q A14 2k gray green —
31q A14 3k red 27.50 27.50
32q A15 4k carmine —
33q A14 5k claret 200.00 200.00
34q A11 15k red brn & bl 40.00 140.00
35q A8 20k bl & car —
37q A11 35k red brn & grn 200.00 100.00
38q A8 50k violet & grn —
39q A11 70k brown & org —
40q A9 1r pale brn, brn & red org 2.00 2.50
41q A12 3½r mar & lt grn —
42q A13 5r dk bl, grn & pale bl —
43q A12 7r dk grn & pink —
44q A13 10r scar, yel & gray — 260.00
45q A6 1k red, buff —
47q A6 10k brown, buff 325.00

Poltava I — Handstamped in green with a rubber device

9r A14 2k green 200.00
14r A15 10k dark blue —
20r A8 50k violet & grn 160.00 —
21r A11 70k brown & org 160.00 —
27r A14 10k on 7k light blue — 225.00
28r A11 20k on 14k bl & rose —
29r A14 1k orange 250.00
45r A6 1k red, buff —
46r A6 5k green, buff —

Poltava II — Handstamped in black with a rubber device

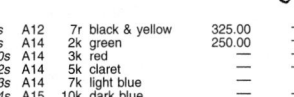

7s A12 7r black & yellow 325.00 —
9s A14 2k green 250.00 —
10s A14 3k red —
12s A14 5k claret —
13s A14 7k light blue —
14s A15 10k dark blue —
16s A11 15k red brn 100.00 225.00
17s A8 20k blue & car —

19s A11 35k red brn & grn 250.00
20s A8 50k violet & grn 130.00 70.00
21s A11 70k brown & org —
22s A9 1r lt brn & org 32.50 25.00
23s A12 3½r mar & lt grn 100.00 75.00
24s A13 5r dk bl, grn & pale bl 160.00 200.00
25s A12 7r dk grn & pink 160.00 140.00
27s A14 10k on 7k light blue — 250.00
28s A11 20k on 14k bl & rose 250.00
29s A14 1k orange —
31s A14 3k red 160.00 200.00
34s A11 15k red brn & bl — 140.00
37s A11 35k red brn & grn — 140.00
40s A9 1r pale brn, brn & red org 14.00 14.00
44s A9 10r scar, yel & gray 250.00 —

The trident overprint was applied by favor to Russia Nos. 88-104, 110-111, the Romanov issue.

For surcharges see Russian Offices in the Turkish Empire Nos. 320-339.

A6

1919, Jan. Litho.
48 A6 20h red & green 10.00 25.00

Because of its high face value, No. 48 was used primarily on money transfer forms or parcel receipts. Used value is for a postally used example.

Nos. 1 and 5 Surcharged

35 к.

1919, Feb. Unwmk. Imperf.
49 A1 35k on 10sh buff 9.00 20.00
50 A5 70k on 50sh red 70.00 50.00
a. Surcharge inverted 60.00

Nos. 49 and 50 were originally believed to have been created by the Soviets in the Ukraine in April, 1919, but more recent research seems to indicate that they were created by the White (Don) Army operating in eastern Ukraine at the request of the Ukrainian government. Correctly franked covers have been recorded from the February-June 1919 period.

Excellent forged surcharges exist.

Ukrainian Soviet Socialist Republic

During 1920/1921, hyperinflation of the ruble created a desperate need for stamps to pay ever-rising postal rates. Many Russian cities and districts surcharged existing stocks of Russian stamps in needed denominations for provisional use.

In June 1920 the national government of the Soviet Ukrainian Republic authorized the Kharkiv post office to create such surcharges for use in the Kharkiv region and in adjacent oblasts. Both unoverprinted Russian stamps and stamps bearing the regional trident overprints of Katerynoslav, Kharkiv and Kyiv were surcharged to raise their face value 100-fold. They were sold at 236 post offices in the Ukraine from June 1920 through Feb. 1921.

In Feb. 1922 three Russian postal savings stamps were surcharged for provisional use by the Kyiv post office, at the direction of the central government. As with the Kharkiv surcharges, these stamps were distributed over a wide area within the country.

KHARKIV ISSUE
Ukrainian and Russian Stamps Handstamp Surcharged

Ukrainian trident overprinted issues and unoverprinted Russian stamps revalued 100-fold by changing denominations from kopecks to rubles.

Two types of overprint: type I, Cyrillic RUB (not including periods) 9.5mmx6.5mm; type II, 8.5mmx6.5mm.

Number of basic Ukrainian or Russian stamp shown in parentheses.

On Katerynoslav Trident Ovpt. Issue of 1918
Type I Reading Upward

1920, June
51 A11 15k red brown & blue (#16a) 75.00 75.00

Kharkiv Trident Ovpt. Issue of 1918

52 A14 1k orange (#8b) 100.00 60.00
53 A14 2k green (#9b) 100.00 65.00
54 A14 3k red (#10b) 80.00 40.00
55 A11 15k red brn & blue (#16b) 40.00 35.00
56 A8 20k blue & car (#17b) 200.00 175.00
a. Surcharge reading downward 300.00 300.00
57 A11 20k on 14k blue & rose (#28b) 170.00 190.00

Imperf
58 A14 1k orange (#29b) 75.00 75.00
a. Surcharge reading downward 120.00 120.00
59 A14 2k green (#30b) 250.00 250.00
60 A14 3k red (#31b) 40.00 40.00

On Kyiv Trident Ovpt. Issue of 1918

 No. 61   No. 63

On Kyiv II Overprint
61 A14 1k orange (#8f) 40.00 40.00

Imperf
62 A14 1k orange (#29f) 40.00 50.00
a. Surcharge reading downward — 50.00

On Kyiv III Overprint
63 A14 3k red (#31g) 15.00 20.00

On Russian Arms Issue of 1909-18

 No. 64

64 A14 1k orange (#73) 50.00 50.00
65 A14 2k green (#74) 10.00 15.00
a. Surcharge reading downward 15.00 20.00
66 A14 3k red (#75) 10.00 15.00
a. Surcharge reading downward 25.00 20.00
67 A15 4k red (#76) 325.00
68 A15 5k claret (#77) 7.00 6.00
a. Surcharge reading downward 20.00 20.00
69 A15 10k dk blue (#79) 15.00 15.00
a. Surcharge reading downward 90.00 100.00
70 A11 15k red brn & blue (#81) 7.00 6.00
a. Surcharge reading downward 10.00 10.00
71 A8 20k blue & car (#82) 10.00 6.00
a. Surcharge reading downward 15.00 12.00

Imperf
72 A14 1k orange (#119) 50.00 36.00
a. Surcharge reading downward 100.00 100.00
73 A14 2k green (#120) 45.00 55.00
74 A14 3k red (#121) 30.00 36.00
75 A14 5k claret (#123) 9.00 7.00
a. Surcharge reading downward 25.00 25.00
76 A11 15k red brn & blue (#125) 120.00 130.00
a. Surcharge reading downward

Type II Reading Upward
On Kharkiv Trident Ovpt. Issue of 1918

 No. 79a

77 A14 3k red (#31b) 35.00 40.00

On Kyiv Trident Ovpt. Issue of 1918
78 A14 1k orange (#29f) 20.00 25.00

On Russian Arms Issue of 1919-18
Perf. 14x14½
79 A14 2k green (#74) 6.00 7.00
a. Surcharge reading downward 12.00 12.00
80 A14 5k claret (#77) 8.00 7.00
a. Surcharge reading downward 15.00 12.00
81 A15 10k dk blue (#79) 18.00 18.00
a. Surcharge reading downward 100.00 115.00
82 A11 15k red brn & blue (#81) 8.00 7.00
a. Surcharge reading downward 12.00 10.00
83 A8 20k blue & car (#82) 8.00 7.00

Imperf
84 A14 2k green (#120) 50.00 60.00

Nos. 51-84 on cover are worth approximately 5 times the total value of the affixed stamps.

KYIV ISSUE

Russian Postal Savings Stamps Handstamp Surcharged

1922, Feb. Wmk. 171
85 7500 (r) on 5k, green, buff 50.00 50.00
a. Surcharge reading downward 60.00 55.00
86 8000 (r) on 5k, green, buff 150.00 90.00
a. Surcharge reading downward 180.00 150.00
87 15000 (r) on 10k, brown, buff 300.00 150.00
a. Surcharge reading downward 450.00 250.00

Nos. 85-87 are normally found on stamps watermarked with a vertical diamond pattern (Wmk. 171) but also exist on paper watermarked sideways, with both upward and downward-reading surcharges. These are rare and are worth approximately 8 times the values shown.

Nos. 85-87 on cover are worth approximately 4 times the total value of the affixed stamps.

Nos. 1-5 surcharged in grivni (hryven) with the Polish eagle were sold as Polish occupation issues. They are of private origin.

Nos. 1-3 and 5 overprinted diagonally as above ("South Russia") are believed to be of private origin.

A lithographed set of 14 stamps (1h-200h) of these types, perf. 11½, was prepared in 1920, but never placed in use. Value, set $5.

All values exist imperf., some with inverted centers. Trial printings exist on various papers, including inverted, multiple, omitted and misaligned center vignettes. These are from the printer's waste.

This set handstamped "VILNA UKRAINA / 1921" and 6 values additionally overprinted "DOPLATA" are of private origin.

In 1923 the Ukrainian government-in-exile in Warsaw prepared an 11-value set, consisting of the 10h, 20h and 40h denominations of the unissued 1920 set surcharged and overprinted with the Cyrillic "UPP," supposedly intended as a Field Post issue for a planned invasion of the Ukraine. The invasion never occurred, and the stamps were never issued. Value $15.

SEMI-POSTAL STAMPS

Ukrainian Soviet Socialist Republic

"Famine" — SP1

Taras H. Shevchenko SP2

"Death" Stalking Peasant — SP3

"Ukraine" Distributing Food — SP4

Perf. 14½x13½, 13½x14½

		1923, June	Litho.		Unwmk.
B1	SP1	10k + 10k gray bl & blk		1.00	5.50
B2	SP2	20k + 20k vio brn & org brn		1.00	5.50
B3	SP3	90k + 30k db & blk, straw		1.00	5.50
B4	SP4	150k + 50k red brn & blk		1.00	5.50
		Nos. B1-B4 (4)		4.00	22.00

Imperf., Pairs

B1a	SP1	10k + 10k	100.00	120.00
B2a	SP2	20k + 20k	100.00	120.00
B3a	SP3	90k + 30k	100.00	120.00
B4a	SP4	150k + 50k	100.00	120.00

The values of these stamps are in karbovanets, which by 1923 converted to rubles at 100 to 1.

**Wmk. 116
Same Colors**

B5	SP1	10k + 10k	50.00	70.00
B6	SP2	20k + 20k	50.00	70.00
a.		Imperf., pair	2,500.	
B7	SP3	90k + 30k	50.00	70.00
B8	SP4	150k + 50k	50.00	70.00
		Nos. B5-B8 (4)	200.00	280.00

MILITARY STAMPS

COURIER FIELD POST ISSUE

Nos. 1-5, 48 Surcharged

1920, Aug. 26

M1	A1	10h on 10sh buff	20.00	—
a.		Inverted surcharge	80.00	
M2	A2	10h on 20sh brown	40.00	—
M3	A3	10h on 30sh ultramarine	50.00	
M4	A4	10h on 40sh green	55.00	
a.		Inverted surcharge	215.00	
M5	A5	10h on 50sh red	50.00	
M6	A1	20h on 10sh buff	55.00	—
M7	A2	20h on 20sh brown	15.00	—
a.		Inverted surcharge	60.00	
M8	A3	20h on 30sh ultramarine	40.00	
a.		Inverted surcharge	160.00	
M9	A4	20h on 40sh green	40.00	
M10	A5	20h on 50sh red	40.00	
a.		Inverted surcharge	160.00	
M11	A1	40h on 10sh buff	200.00	—
M12	A2	40h on 20sh brown	100.00	
M13	A3	40h on 30sh ultramarine	400.00	
M14	A4	40h on 40sh green	200.00	
M15	A5	40h on 50sh red	400.00	
M16	A6	40h on 20hr red & green	—	—

Nos. M1-M16 were prepared to facilitate communications between the Ukrainian government-in-exile at Tarnow, Poland, and its military units in the field.

Only two examples of No. M16 are known, one unused and one used on cover.

Forged surcharges and cancellations exist.

UPPER SENEGAL & NIGER

ˈə-pər ˌse-nə-gäl and ˈnī-jər

LOCATION — In Northwest Africa, north of French Guinea and Ivory Coast
GOVT. — French Colony
AREA — 617,600 sq. mi.
POP. — 2,474,140
CAPITAL — Bamako

In 1921 the name of this colony was changed to French Sudan and postage stamps so inscribed were placed in use.

100 Centimes = 1 Franc

Gen. Louis Faidherbe A1

Oil Palms — A2

Dr. N. Eugène Ballay A3

Perf. 14x13½

		1906-07	Unwmk.		Typo.
		Name of Colony in Red or Blue			
1	A1	1c slate		2.00	2.00
		Never hinged		2.75	
		On cover			125.00
a.		Accent omitted over first "E" of "SÉNEGAL"		9.50	9.50
		Never hinged		20.00	
2	A1	2c brown		2.75	2.40
		Never hinged		3.00	
		On cover			125.00
a.		Accent omitted over first "E" of "SÉNEGAL"		10.00	10.00
		Never hinged		22.50	
3	A1	4c brn, gray bl		6.50	2.75
		Never hinged		4.50	
		On cover			125.00
a.		Accent omitted over first "E" of "SÉNEGAL"		13.50	12.00
		Never hinged		27.50	
4	A1	5c green		7.25	3.25
		Never hinged		13.00	
		On cover			80.00
a.		Accent omitted over first "E" of "SÉNEGAL"		32.50	20.00
		Never hinged		65.00	
5	A1	10c car (B)		7.25	3.25
		Never hinged		11.00	
		On cover			75.00
a.		Accent omitted over first "E" of "SÉNEGAL"		32.50	20.00
		Never hinged		65.00	
6	A1	15c vio ('07)		5.00	5.50
		Never hinged		8.75	
		On cover			100.00
a.		Accent omitted over first "E" of "SÉNEGAL"		27.50	27.50
		Never hinged		55.00	
7	A2	20c black & red, azure		6.50	6.50
		Never hinged		13.00	
		On cover			95.00
8	A2	25c bl, pnksh		20.00	5.00
		Never hinged		40.00	
		On cover			105.00
		On cover, single franking			150.00
9	A2	30c vio brn, pnksh		8.25	6.50
		Never hinged		16.00	
		On cover			105.00
		On cover, single franking			190.00
10	A2	35c blk, yellow		6.50	5.50
		Never hinged		12.00	
		On cover			125.00
		On cover, single franking			190.00
a.		Accent omitted over first "E" of "SÉNEGAL"		32.50	27.50
		Never hinged		65.00	
11	A2	40c car, az (B)		10.50	10.00
		Never hinged		21.00	
		On cover			170.00
		On cover, single franking			275.00
a.		Accent omitted over first "E" of "SÉNEGAL"		55.00	45.00
		Never hinged		115.00	
12	A2	45c brn, grnsh		12.50	13.00
		Never hinged		24.00	
		On cover			170.00
		On cover, single franking			225.00
a.		Accent omitted over first "E" of "SÉNEGAL"		60.00	52.50
		Never hinged		130.00	
13	A2	50c dp vio		12.50	13.00
		Never hinged		24.00	
		On cover			160.00
		On cover, single franking			225.00
a.		Accent omitted over first "E" of "SÉNEGAL"		60.00	52.50
		Never hinged		130.00	
14	A2	75c bl, org		12.50	13.50
		Never hinged		24.00	
		On cover			225.00
		On cover, single franking			375.00
a.		Accent omitted over first "E" of "SÉNEGAL"		60.00	60.00
		Never hinged		130.00	
15	A3	1fr blk, azure		29.00	32.50
		Never hinged		604.00	
		On cover			275.00
		On cover, single franking			450.00
16	A3	2fr bl, pink		52.50	60.00
		Never hinged		110.00	
		On cover			300.00
		On cover, single franking			500.00
17	A3	5fr car, straw (B)		110.00	120.00
		Never hinged		200.00	
		On cover			450.00
		On cover, single franking			625.00
		Nos. 1-17 (17)		311.50	304.65

Camel with Rider — A4

1914-17   Perf. 13½x14

18	A4	1c brn vio & vio	.35	.50
		Never hinged	.50	
		On cover		105.00
19	A4	2c gray & brn vio	.35	.50
		Never hinged	.50	
		On cover		105.00
20	A4	4c black & blue	.35	.50
		Never hinged	.50	
		On cover		105.00
21	A4	5c yel grn & bl grn	1.05	.60
		Never hinged	1.40	
		On cover		55.00
a.		Chalky paper	1.40	.95
		Never hinged	2.40	
22	A4	10c red org & rose	2.75	2.40
		Never hinged	3.50	
		On cover		55.00
a.		Chalky paper	4.50	3.25
		Never hinged	6.75	
23	A4	15c choc & org ('17)	2.00	1.25
		Never hinged	2.90	
		On cover		50.00
a.		Chalky paper	5.50	5.50
		Never hinged	9.50	
24	A4	20c brn vio & blk	2.40	2.40
		Never hinged	4.00	
		On cover		65.00
25	A4	25c ultra & bl	2.00	1.60
		Never hinged	2.75	
		On cover		70.00
		On cover, single franking		160.00
26	A4	30c ol brn & brn	2.00	2.40
		Never hinged	2.75	
		On cover		95.00
		On cover, single franking		170.00
27	A4	35c car rose & vio	3.25	2.75
		Never hinged	5.50	
		On cover		95.00
		On cover, single franking		140.00
28	A4	40c gray & car rose	2.50	1.60
		Never hinged	3.75	
		On cover		100.00
		On cover, single franking		140.00
29	A4	45c bl & ol brn	2.40	2.40
		Never hinged	4.00	
		On cover		105.00
		On cover, single franking		190.00
30	A4	50c black & green	2.75	3.25
		Never hinged	4.50	
		On cover		110.00
		On cover, single franking		200.00
31	A4	75c org & ol brn	2.75	3.25
		Never hinged	4.50	
		On cover		95.00
		On cover, single franking		175.00
32	A4	1fr brown & brn vio	2.75	3.25
		Never hinged	4.50	
		On cover		110.00
		On cover, single franking		225.00
33	A4	2fr green & blue	3.25	4.00
		Never hinged	5.25	
		On cover		140.00
		On cover, single franking		250.00
34	A4	5fr violet & black	13.00	15.00
		Never hinged	22.50	
		On cover		160.00
		On cover, single franking		275.00
		Nos. 18-34 (17)	45.90	47.65

See Upper Volta for types of this issue that escaped overprinting.
For surcharge see No. B1.

SEMI-POSTAL STAMP

Regular Issue of 1914 Surcharged in Red

1915   Unwmk.   Perf. 13½x14

B1	A4	10c + 5c red orange & rose	2.40	2.40
		Never hinged	4.00	
		On cover		100.00

POSTAGE DUE STAMPS

Natives — D1

1906   Unwmk.   Typo.   Perf. 14x13½

J1	D1	5c green, *greenish*	4.00	4.00
		Never hinged	7.25	
		On cover		125.00
J2	D1	10c red brown	8.25	8.00
		Never hinged	16.00	
		On cover		160.00
J3	D1	15c dark blue	11.50	11.50
		Never hinged	24.00	
		On cover		175.00
J4	D1	20c black, *yellow*	15.00	7.50
		Never hinged	30.00	
		On cover		140.00
J5	D1	50c violet	27.50	30.00
		Never hinged	55.00	
		On cover		225.00
J6	D1	60c black, *buff*	22.50	24.00
		Never hinged	45.00	
		On cover		225.00
J7	D1	1fr black, *pinkish*	40.00	45.00
		Never hinged	87.50	
		On cover		350.00
		Nos. J1-J7 (7)	128.75	130.00

D2

1914

J8	D2	5c green	1.25	1.60
		Never hinged	2.00	
		On cover		95.00
J9	D2	10c rose	1.60	2.00
		Never hinged	2.75	
		On cover		95.00
J10	D2	15c gray	1.60	2.00
		Never hinged	2.75	
		On cover		95.00
J11	D2	20c brown	1.60	2.00
		Never hinged	2.75	
		On cover		95.00
J12	D2	30c blue	2.40	2.75
		Never hinged	4.00	
		On cover		100.00
J13	D2	50c black	2.00	2.40
		Never hinged	3.25	
		On cover		120.00
J14	D2	60c orange	7.25	8.00
		Never hinged	12.00	
		On cover		140.00
J15	D2	1fr violet	7.25	8.00
		Never hinged	12.00	
		On cover		160.00
		Nos. J8-J15 (8)	24.95	28.75

Stamps of Upper Senegal and Niger were superceded in 1921 by those of French Sudan.

UPPER SILESIA

'ə-pər si'lē-zh ̧ē-ə

LOCATION — Formerly in eastern Germany and prior to World War I a part of Germany.

A plebiscite held under the terms of the Treaty of Versailles failed to determine the status of the country, the voting resulting about equally in favor of Germany and Poland. Accordingly, the League of Nations divided the territory between Germany and Poland.

100 Pfennig = 1 Mark

100 Fennigi = 1 Marka

Plebiscite Issues

A1

Perf. 14x13½

1920, Feb. 20   Typo.   Unwmk.

1	A1	2½pf slate	.40	.80
		Never hinged	1.10	
		On cover		12.00
2	A1	3pf brown	.40	.85
		Never hinged	1.10	
		On cover		12.00
3	A1	5pf green	.30	.80
		Never hinged	.65	
		On cover		4.00
4	A1	10pf dull red	.40	.90
		Never hinged	1.10	
		On cover		4.00
5	A1	15pf violet	.25	.80
		Never hinged	.65	
		On cover		4.00
6	A1	20pf blue	.25	.80
		Never hinged	.65	
		On cover		4.00
a.		Imperf., pair	275.00	
b.		Half used as 10pf on cover		110.00
c.		20pf prussian blue	1.60	5.75
		Never hinged	4.75	8.00
		On cover		29.00
d.		As "c," half used as 10pf on cover		1,000.
7	A1	50pf violet brn	4.75	8.00
		Never hinged	21.00	
		On cover		32.50
a.		50pf red brown	20.00	50.00
		Never hinged	50.00	
		On cover		160.00
8	A1	1m claret	5.00	11.00
		Never hinged	15.00	
		On cover		50.00
9	A1	5m orange	5.00	11.00
		Never hinged	16.00	
		On cover		150.00
		Nos. 1-9 (9)	16.75	34.95
		Set, never hinged	55.00	

Black Surcharge

	5 Pf.	5 Pf.	5 Pf.	5 Pf.
	I	II	III	IV

10	A1	5pf on 15pf vio (I)	160.00	525.00
		Never hinged	450.00	
		On cover		575.00
a.		Type II		
		Never hinged		
		On cover		675.00
b.		Type III		
		Never hinged		
		On cover		675.00
c.		Type IV		
		Never hinged		
		On cover		675.00
11	A1	5pf on 20pf blue (I)	1.10	3.25
		Never hinged	3.00	
		On cover		11.00
a.		Type II	1.25	3.75
		Never hinged	2.50	
		On cover		15.00
b.		Type III	1.60	4.00
		Never hinged	3.00	
		On cover		19.00
c.		Type IV	2.00	5.00
		Never hinged	3.50	
		On cover		30.00

Red Surcharge

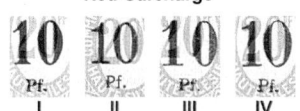

10 Pf.	10 Pf.	10 Pf.	10 Pf.
I	II	III	IV

12	A1	10pf on 20pf bl (I)	1.10	3.25
		Never hinged	3.00	
		On cover		15.00
a.		Type II	1.10	3.25
		Never hinged	2.90	
		On cover		19.00
b.		Type III	1.10	3.25
		Never hinged	3.90	
		On cover		11.00
c.		Type IV	1.10	3.25
		Never hinged	3.90	
		On cover		12.50
d.		Imperf.	60.00	240.00
		On cover	120.00	1,100.

Black Surcharge

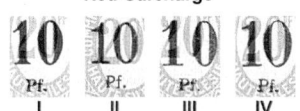

50 Pf.	50 Pf.	50 Pf.	50 Pf.	50 Pf.
Type I	Type II	Type III	Type IV	Type V

13	A1	50pf on 5m org (I), shiny ovpt.	27.50	52.50
		Never hinged	200.00	
		On cover		225.00
a.		Type II	29.00	55.00
		Never hinged	140.00	
		On cover		240.00
b.		Type III	30.00	87.50
		Never hinged	240.00	
		On cover		350.00
c.		Type IV	30.00	87.50
		Never hinged	240.00	
		On cover		350.00
d.		Type V	42.50	120.00
		Never hinged	340.00	

e.		On cover		425.00
		Type I, matte ovpt.	37.50	87.50
		Never hinged	190.00	
		On cover		575.00

Nos. 10-13 are found with many varieties including surcharges inverted, double and double inverted.

Dove with Olive Branch Flying over Silesian Terrain — A2

A3

1920, Mar. 26   Typo.   Perf. 13½x14

15	A2	2½pf gray	.55	.80
		Never hinged	2.25	
		On cover		8.25
16	A2	3pf red brown	.55	.80
		Never hinged	2.25	
		On cover		8.25
17	A2	5pf green	.55	.80
		Never hinged	2.25	
		On cover		4.25
18	A2	10pf dull red	.55	.80
		Never hinged	2.25	
		On cover		5.00
19	A2	15pf violet	.55	.80
		Never hinged	2.25	
		On cover		5.00
20	A2	20pf blue	.80	2.00
		Never hinged	2.25	
		On cover		5.00
21	A2	25pf dark brown	.55	.80
		Never hinged	2.25	
		On cover		8.25
22	A2	30pf orange	.55	.80
		Never hinged	2.25	
		On cover		6.75
23	A2	40pf olive green	.55	2.00
		Never hinged	2.25	
		On cover		6.75

Perf. 14x13½

24	A3	50pf gray	1.00	.80
		Never hinged	3.25	
		On cover		21.00
25	A3	60pf blue	.55	1.60
		Never hinged	3.00	
		On cover		21.00
26	A3	75pf deep green	1.60	2.00
		Never hinged	5.75	
		On cover		25.00
a.		75pf blackish green	825.00	1,250.
		Never hinged	1,650.	
b.		75pf bluish green	1,250.	1,250.
		Never hinged	1,800.	
c.		75pf deep gray green	2,850.	2,450.
		Never hinged	3,250.	
27	A3	80pf red brown	1.60	1.10
		Never hinged	7.50	
		On cover		16.50
28	A3	1m claret	1.60	.80
		Never hinged	7.50	
		On cover		16.50
29	A3	2m dark brown	1.40	.80
		Never hinged	4.75	
		On cover		12.50
30	A3	3m violet	1.40	.80
		Never hinged	4.75	
		On cover		25.00
31	A3	5m orange	4.00	4.50
		Never hinged	12.50	
		On cover		42.50
		Nos. 15-31 (17)	18.35	22.00
		Set, never hinged	67.50	

Nos. 18-28 Overprinted in Black or Red

1921, Mar. 20

32	A2	10pf dull red	4.00	10.00
		Never hinged	18.00	
		On cover		100.00
33	A2	15pf violet	4.00	10.00
		Never hinged	18.00	
		On cover		100.00
34	A2	20pf blue	5.50	14.00
		Never hinged	30.00	
		On cover		100.00
35	A2	25pf dk brn (R)	12.00	32.50
		Never hinged	45.00	
		On cover		125.00
36	A2	30pf orange	10.00	20.00
		Never hinged	50.00	
		On cover		125.00
37	A2	40pf olive grn (R)	11.00	20.00
		Never hinged	45.00	
		On cover		125.00

Overprinted

38	A3	50pf gray (R)	11.00	27.50
		Never hinged	57.50	
39	A3	60pf blue	12.00	22.50
		Never hinged	65.00	
40	A3	75pf deep green	12.00	27.50
		Never hinged	100.00	
a.		75pf blue green	1,650.	1,850.
41	A3	80pf red brown	20.00	35.00
		Never hinged	130.00	
42	A3	1m claret	24.00	65.00
		Never hinged	150.00	
		Nos. 32-42 (11)	125.50	284.00
		Set, never hinged	700.00	

Inverted or double overprints exist on Nos. 32-33, 35-40. Counterfeit overprints exist.

Type of 1920 and Surcharged

1922, Mar.

45	A3	4m on 60pf ol grn	.80	2.00
		Never hinged	3.00	
		On cover		25.00
46	A3	10m on 75pf red	1.25	2.75
		Never hinged	7.00	
		On cover		125.00
47	A3	20m on 80pf orange	6.50	16.00
		Never hinged	23.00	
		On cover		375.00
		Nos. 45-47 (3)	8.55	20.75
		Set, never hinged	32.00	

Stamps of the above design were a private issue not recognized by the Inter-Allied Commission of Government. Value, set of 7, $65 unused, $225 never hinged, $225 used.

OFFICIAL STAMPS

German Stamps of 1905-20 Handstamped in Blue

1920, Feb.   Wmk. 125   Perf. 14, 14½
On Stamps of 1906-19

O1	A22	2pf gray	1.10	1.25
O3	A22	2½pf gray	.55	.65
O4	A16	3pf brown	.55	.65
O5	A16	5pf green	.55	.65
O6	A22	7½pf orange	.55	.65
O7	A16	10pf car rose	.55	.65
O8	A22	15pf dk violet	.55	.65
O9	A16	20pf blue violet	.55	.65
O10	A16	25pf org & blk, *yel*	8.00	6.50
O11	A16	30pf org & blk, *buff*	.55	.65
O12	A22	35pf red brown	.55	.65
O13	A16	40pf lake & blk	.55	.65
O14	A16	50pf vio & blk, *buff*	.55	.65
O15	A16	60pf magenta	.55	.65
O16	A16	75pf green & blk	.55	.65
O17	A16	80pf lake & blk, *rose*	6.50	8.00
O18	A17	1m car rose	1.10	1.25
O19	A21	2m gray blue	5.25	6.50

On National Assembly Stamps of 1919-20

O25	A23	10pf car rose	.90	1.10
O26	A24	15pf choc & bl	1.60	2.00
O27	A25	25pf green & red	3.25	4.00

O28 A25 30pf red vio & red 2.50 3.00

On Semi-Postal Stamps of 1919

O30 A16 10pf + 5pf carmine 6.50 8.00
O31 A22 15pf + 5pf dk vio 6.50 8.00
Nos. O1-O31 (24) 50.35 58.05

Red Handstamp

O5a A16 5pf 10.00 14.00
O8a A22 15pf 6.50 10.00
O9a A16 20pf 6.50 10.00
O13a A16 40pf 20.00 30.00
O16a A16 75pf 20.00 30.00
O26a A24 15pf 1.10 1.25
Nos. O5a-O26a (6) 64.10 95.25

Values of Nos. O1-O31 are for reprints made with a second type of handstamp differing in minor details from the original (example: period after "S" is round instead of the earlier triangular form). Originals are scarce. Counterfeits exist.

Germany No. 65C with this handstamp is considered bogus by experts.

Local Official Stamps of Germany, 1920, Overprinted

1920, Apr.   *Perf. 14*

O32 LO2 5pf green .30 1.00
O33 LO3 10pf carmine .30 1.00
O34 LO4 15pf violet brn .30 1.00
O35 LO5 20pf deep ultra .30 1.00
O36 LO6 30pf orange, *buff* .30 1.00
O37 LO7 50pf violet, *buff* .80 3.00
O38 LO8 1m red, *buff* 6.50 15.00
Nos. O32-O38 (7) 8.80 23.00

Same Overprint on Official Stamps of Germany, 1920-21

1920-21

O39 O1 5pf green 1.00 8.00
O40 O2 10pf carmine .25 1.00
O41 O3 15pf violet brn .25 1.00
O42 O4 20pf deep ultra .25 1.00
O43 O5 30pf orange, *buff* .25 1.00
O44 O6 40pf carmine rose .25 1.00
O45 O7 50pf violet, *buff* .25 1.00
O46 O8 60pf red brown .25 1.00
O47 O9 1m red, *buff* .25 1.00
O48 O10 1.25m dk blue, *yel* .25 1.00
O49 O11 2m dark blue 7.25 12.00
O50 O12 5m brown, *yel* .25 1.00

1922, Feb.   *Wmk. 126*

O51 O11 2m dark blue .25 1.00
Nos. O39-O51 (13) 11.00 31.00

This overprint is found both horizontal, reading upright or inverted, and vertical, reading up or down. These variations generally command no premium over the values above.

The overprint also exists on most values double and double, one inverted, in the above formats, as well as at a 45 degree angle, upreading and downreading, either upright or inverted. These varieties generally sell for 25-100 percent over the value of normal examples.

UPPER VOLTA

LOCATION — Northwestern Africa, north of Gold Coast
GOVT. — French Colony
AREA — 105,869 sq. mi.
POP. — 6,695,500 (est. 1984)
CAPITAL — Ouagadougou

In 1919 the French territory of Upper Volta was detached from the southern section of Upper Senegal and Niger and made a separate colony. In 1933 the colony was divided among its neighbors: French Sudan, Ivory Coast, and Niger Territory.

100 Centimes = 1 Franc

Stamps and Types of Upper Senegal and Niger, 1914-17, Overprinted in Black or Red

1920-28   Unwmk.   *Perf. 13½x14*

1 A4 1c brn vio & vio .25 .40
   Never hinged .40
   On cover 90.00
2 A4 2c gray & brn vio (R) .25 .40
   Never hinged .40
   On cover 90.00
3 A4 4c blk & bl .30 .50
   Never hinged .50
   On cover 90.00
4 A4 5c yel grn & bl grn .90 .80
   Never hinged 1.40
   On cover 45.00
5 A4 5c ol brn & dk brn ('22) .25 .40
   Never hinged .40
   On cover 30.00
6 A4 10c red org & rose 1.40 1.60
   Never hinged 2.40
   On cover 95.00
7 A4 10c yel grn & bl grn ('22) .30 .50
   Never hinged .50
   On cover 50.00
   Complete booklet, 20 #7 9,250.
8 A4 10c claret & bl ('25) .80 .80
   Never hinged .90
   On cover 30.00
   a. Overprint omitted 240.00
   Never hinged 325.00
9 A4 15c choc & org .75 .80
   Never hinged 1.20
   On cover 50.00
   Complete booklet, 20 #9 3,250.
10 A4 20c brn vio & blk (R) 1.10 1.20
   Never hinged 1.75
   On cover 45.00
11 A4 25c ultra & bl 1.40 1.10
   Never hinged 2.10
   On cover 35.00
12 A4 25c blk & bl grn ('22) .75 .75
   Never hinged 1.00
   On cover 14.00
   a. Overprint omitted 200.00
   Never hinged 275.00
13 A4 30c ol brn & brn (R) 2.90 3.50
   Never hinged 4.75
   On cover 65.00
   On cover, single franking 110.00
14 A4 30c red org & rose ('22) 1.50 2.25
   Never hinged 2.40
   On cover 45.00
   On cover, single franking 75.00
15 A4 30c vio & brn red ('25) 1.25 1.60
   Never hinged 1.75
   On cover 16.00
16 A4 30c dl grn & bl grn ('27) 1.25 1.60
   Never hinged 1.75
   On cover 45.00
17 A4 35c car rose & vio 1.00 1.60
   Never hinged 1.50
   On cover 55.00
   On cover, single franking 75.00
18 A4 40c gray & car rose 1.00 1.60
   Never hinged 1.50
   On cover 45.00
   On cover, single franking 65.00
19 A4 45c bl & brn (R) 1.00 1.60
   Never hinged 1.50
   On cover 75.00
   On cover, single franking 125.00
20 A4 50c blk & grn 3.00 3.50
   Never hinged 5.00
   On cover 50.00
   On cover, single franking 125.00
21 A4 50c ultra & bl ('22) 1.20 1.75
   Never hinged 2.10
   On cover 37.50
   On cover, single franking 70.00
22 A4 50c red org & bl ('25) 1.25 1.60
   Never hinged 2.20
   On cover 16.00
   a. Double surcharge, one inverted 1,275. 1,250.
23 A4 60c org red ('26) .80 1.25
   Never hinged 1.10
   On cover 45.00
   On cover, single franking 80.00
24 A4 65c bis & pale bl ('28) 1.60 2.50
   Never hinged 2.50
   On cover 50.00
   On cover, single franking 90.00
25 A4 75c org & brn 1.40 .90
   Never hinged 2.60
   On cover 55.00
   On cover, single franking 140.00
26 A4 1fr brn & brn vio 1.40 2.00
   Never hinged 2.60
   On cover 75.00
   On cover, single franking 170.00
27 A4 2fr grn & bl 1.90 2.40
   Never hinged 3.75
   On cover 90.00
   On cover, single franking 190.00
28 A4 5fr vio & blk (R) 4.00 5.50
   Never hinged 8.50
   On cover 110.00
   On cover, single franking 225.00
Nos. 1-28 (28) 34.90 44.40

No. 9 Surcharged in Various Colors

1922

29 A4 0.01c on 15c (Bk) 1.00 1.60
   Never hinged 1.60
   On cover 75.00
30 A4 0.02c on 15c (Bl) 1.00 1.60
   Never hinged 1.60
   On cover 75.00
31 A4 0.05c on 15c (R) 1.00 1.60
   Never hinged 1.60
   On cover 30.00
Nos. 29-31 (3) 3.00 4.80

Type of 1920 Surcharged

1922

32 A4 60c on 75c vio, *pnksh* .90 1.25
   Never hinged 1.20
   On cover 45.00
   On cover, single franking 70.00

Stamps and Types of 1920 Surcharged with New Value and Bars

1924-27

33 A4 25c on 2fr grn & bl .80 1.00
   Never hinged 1.20
   On cover 20.00
34 A4 25c on 5fr vio & blk .80 1.00
   Never hinged 1.20
   On cover 20.00
35 A4 65c on 45c bl & brn ('25) 1.20 1.60
   Never hinged 1.90
   On cover 90.00
   On cover, single franking 170.00
36 A4 85c on 75c org & brn ('25) 1.60 2.40
   Never hinged 2.50
   On cover 75.00
   On cover, single franking 140.00
37 A4 90c on 75c brn red & sal pink ('27) 1.60 2.40
   Never hinged 2.50
   On cover 75.00
   On cover, single franking 125.00
38 A4 1.25fr on 1fr dp bl & lt bl (R) ('26) 1.25 2.00
   Never hinged 2.00
   On cover 80.00
   On cover, single franking 140.00
39 A4 1.50fr on 1fr dp bl & ultra ('27) 2.75 3.50
   Never hinged 5.00
   On cover 65.00
   On cover, single franking 105.00
40 A4 3fr on 5fr dl red & brn org ('27) 4.50 5.50
   Never hinged 8.50
   On cover 120.00
   On cover, single franking 250.00
41 A4 10fr on 5fr ol grn & lil rose ('27) 14.50 18.50
   Never hinged 26.00
   On cover 125.00
   On cover, single franking 275.00
42 A4 20fr on 5fr org brn & vio ('27) 21.00 28.00
   Never hinged 37.50
   On cover 140.00
   On cover, single franking 300.00
Nos. 33-42 (10) 50.00 65.90

Hausa Chief — A5   Hausa Woman — A6

Hausa Warrior A7

1928   Typo.   *Perf. 13½x14*

43 A5 1c indigo & grn .25 .40
   Never hinged .40
   On cover 70.00
44 A5 2c brn & lil .25 .40
   Never hinged .40
   On cover 70.00
45 A5 4c blk & yel .30 .50
   Never hinged .50
   On cover 70.00
46 A5 5c indigo & gray bl .30 .50
   Never hinged .50
   On cover 45.00
47 A5 10c indigo & pink .90 1.25
   Never hinged 1.20
   On cover 40.00
48 A5 15c brn & brn 1.40 1.90
   Never hinged 2.10
   On cover 25.00
49 A5 20c brn & grn 1.40 1.60
   Never hinged 2.00
   On cover 27.50
50 A6 25c brn & yel 1.90 2.40
   Never hinged 3.00
   On cover 29.00
51 A6 30c dp grn & grn 1.90 2.40
   Never hinged 2.75
   On cover 40.00
52 A6 40c blk & pink 1.90 2.00
   Never hinged 3.50
   On cover 14.00
53 A6 45c brn & blue 2.50 3.25
   Never hinged 5.00
   On cover 35.00
54 A6 50c blk & grn 2.25 2.40
   Never hinged 4.00
   On cover 14.00
55 A6 65c indigo & bl 2.75 3.25
   Never hinged 5.00
   On cover 50.00
56 A6 75c blk & lil 2.40 2.75
   Never hinged 4.00
   On cover 22.50
57 A6 90c brn red & lil 2.75 3.25
   Never hinged 5.00
   On cover 40.00
   On cover, single franking 90.00

Perf. 14x13½

58 A7 1fr brn & grn 2.40 2.75
   Never hinged 4.00
   On cover 30.00
   On cover, single franking 45.00
59 A7 1.10fr indigo & lil 2.75 4.00
   Never hinged 5.00
   On cover 200.00
   On cover, single franking 450.00
60 A7 1.50fr ultra & grysh 3.50 4.50
   Never hinged 6.00
   On cover 40.00
   On cover, single franking 80.00
61 A7 2fr blk & bl 4.00 4.75
   Never hinged 6.00
   On cover 40.00
   On cover, single franking 70.00
62 A7 3fr brn & yel 4.00 4.75
   Never hinged 6.50
   On cover 45.00
   On cover, single franking 100.00
63 A7 5fr brn & lil 4.00 4.75
   Never hinged 6.00
   On cover 50.00
   On cover, single franking 110.00
64 A7 10fr blk & grn 20.00 26.00
   Never hinged 35.00
   On cover 80.00
   On cover, single franking 140.00
65 A7 20fr blk & pink 30.00 32.50
   Never hinged 45.00
   On cover 110.00
   On cover, single franking 200.00
Nos. 43-65 (23) 93.80 112.25

Common Design Types pictured following the introduction.

Colonial Exposition Issue
Common Design Types

1931   Engr.   *Perf. 12½*
Country Name Typo. in Black

66 CD70 40c dp grn 4.00 4.00
   Never hinged 6.50
   On cover 120.00
67 CD71 50c violet 4.75 4.75
   Never hinged 8.00
   On cover 100.00
68 CD72 90c red org 4.75 4.75
   Never hinged 8.00
   On cover 170.00
   On cover, single franking 250.00
69 CD73 1.50fr dull blue 5.50 5.50
   Never hinged 9.50
   On cover 160.00
   On cover, single franking 225.00
Nos. 66-69 (4) 19.00 19.00

POSTAGE DUE STAMPS

Postage Due Stamps of Upper Senegal and Niger, 1914, Overprinted in Black or Red

1920   Unwmk.   *Perf. 14x13½*

J1 D2 5c green .50 .80
   Never hinged .80
   On cover 50.00
J2 D2 10c rose .50 .80
   Never hinged .80
   On cover 50.00
J3 D2 15c gray .65 .80
   Never hinged .95
   On cover 50.00

J4	D2 20c brown (R)	.75	.80
	Never hinged	1.00	
	On cover		55.00
J5	D2 30c blue	.75	.80
	Never hinged	1.00	
	On cover		55.00
J6	D2 50c black (R)	1.25	1.60
	Never hinged	1.75	
	On cover		60.00
J7	D2 60c orange	1.25	1.60
	Never hinged	1.75	
	On cover		75.00
J8	D2 1fr violet	1.75	2.50
	Never hinged	2.40	
	On cover		95.00
	Nos. J1-J8 (8)	7.40	9.70

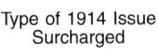

Type of 1914 Issue
Surcharged

1927

J9	D2 2fr on 1fr lilac rose	3.25	4.00
	Never hinged	4.75	
	On cover		125.00
J10	D2 3fr on 1fr orange brn	4.00	4.75
	Never hinged	6.50	
	On cover		140.00

D3

1928 Typo.

J11	D3 5c green	.65	.80
	Never hinged	.80	
	On cover		45.00
J12	D3 10c rose	.80	.80
	Never hinged	1.00	
	On cover		45.00
J13	D3 15c dark gray	1.25	1.60
	Never hinged	1.60	
	On cover		45.00
J14	D3 20c dark brown	1.25	1.60
	Never hinged	1.60	
	On cover		50.00
J15	D3 30c dark blue	1.75	2.50
	Never hinged	3.00	
	On cover		50.00
J16	D3 50c black	3.50	4.00
	Never hinged	5.00	
	On cover		55.00
J17	D3 60c orange	4.50	4.75
	Never hinged	6.75	
	On cover		65.00
J18	D3 1fr dull violet	6.50	7.25
	Never hinged	10.00	
	On cover		75.00
J19	D3 2fr lilac rose	10.50	12.75
	Never hinged	18.00	
	On cover		95.00
J20	D3 3fr orange brn	14.50	18.50
	Never hinged	23.00	
	On cover		105.00
	Nos. J11-J20 (10)	45.20	54.55

URUGUAY

'yur-ə-,gwā

LOCATION — South America, between Brazil and Argentina and bordering on the Atlantic Ocean
GOVT. — Republic
AREA — 72,172 sq. mi.
POP. — 2,991,341 (est. 1983)
CAPITAL — Montevideo

120 Centavos = 1 Real
8 Reales = 1 Peso
100 Centesimos = 1 Peso (1859)
1000 Milesimos = 1 Peso (1898)

Watermarks

Wmk. 187 — R O in Diamond

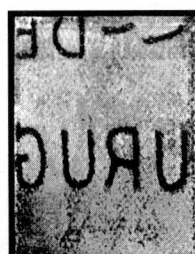
Wmk. 188 —
REPUBLICA O. DEL URUGUAY

Wmk. 189 — Caduceus

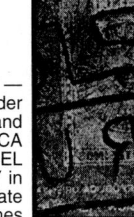
Wmk. 227 — Greek Border and REPUBLICA O. DEL URUGUAY in Alternate Curved Lines

---

GREAT BRITAIN POST OFFICES IN URUGUAY

PRE-STAMP POSTAL MARKINGS
Crowned Circle handstamp type VI is pictured in the Crowned Circle Handstamps and Great Britain Used Abroad section.

1851

A1	VI Crowned Circle handstamp inscribed "PAID AT MONTEVIDEO" in black, on cover	1,100.
A2	VI Crowned Circle handstamp inscribed "PAID AT MONTEVIDEO" in red, on cover	—

STAMPS OF GREAT BRITAIN USED IN MONTEVIDEO
Stamps of Great Britain
Cancelled with "C28" in barred oval
1864-73

A3	1p rose red, plates 73, 92-94, 119, 148, 154, 157, 171 (#33), value from	55.00
A4	2p blue, plate 9 (#29)	65.00
A5	2p blue, plate 13 (#30)	55.00
A6	3p rose (#44)	—
A7	3p rose, plates 4, 5, 7 (#49), value from	70.00
A8	4p rose (#26)	—
A9	4p vermilion,, hair lines (#34c)	—
A10	4p vermilion, plates 7-12 (#43), value from	70.00
A11	6p lilac (#27)	—
A12	6p lilac, plate 4 (#39b)	175.00
A13	6p lilac, plate 5 (#45)	90.00
	Plate 6 (#45)	100.00
A14	6p dull violet, plate 6 (#50)	—
A15	6p violet, plates 8, 9 (#51), value from	80.00
A16	6p brown plate 11 (#59)	—
A17	6p pale buff, plate 11 (#59b)	—
	Plate 12 (#59b)	—
A18	9p straw (#40)	—
A19	9p straw (#46)	—
A20	9p bister (#52)	300.00
A21	10p red brown (#53)	350.00
A22	1sh green (#42)	175.00
A23	1sh green (#48)	150.00
A24	1sh green, plates 4, 5 (#54), value from	80.00
A25	2sh blue (#55)	225.00
A26	5sh rose, plate 1 (#57)	625.00

The British postal agency in Montevideo was closed on July 31, 1875.

CARRIER ISSUES
Issued by Atanasio Lapido, Administrator-General of Posts

A1

A1a

"El Sol de Mayo"
Unwmk.

1856, Oct. 1 Litho. Imperf.

		Litho.	Imperf.
1	A1 60c blue	450.	450.
	On cover		5,000.
a.	60c deep blue	650.	
	On cover		6,500.
b.	60c indigo	1,000.	
c.	60c pale blue	650.	
	On cover		—
2	A1 80c green	500.	500.
	On cover		8,000.
a.	80c deep green	550.	
b.	80c emerald green	600.	
3	A1 1r vermilion	400.	400.
	On cover		11,000.
a.	1r carmine vermilion	450.	

1857, Oct. 1

3B	A1a 60c blue	2,750.	—
	On cover		
c.	60c pale blue	2,750.	—
	On cover		
d.	60c indigo	3,000.	—
	On cover		

Nos. 1-3Bd were spaced very closely on the stone. Very fine examples will have clear margins on three sides and touching or slightly cut into the frames on the fourth (consult the grading illustrations in the catalogue introduction). All genuinely used examples are pen canceled. Certification by a recognized authority is recommended.
Stamps with tiny faults, such as small thin spots, sell for about 75% of the values of sound examples.
See Nos. 410-413.

A2

1858, Mar.

4	A2 120c blue	575.00	650.00
	On cover		7,500.
a.	120c deep blue	600.00	650.00
b.	120c greensih blue	650.00	—
c.	Tête bêche pair	—	—
5	A2 180c green	150.00	200.00
a.	180c deep green	250.00	350.00
b.	180c pale green	140.00	
c.	As "b," thick paper	500.00	
d.	Tête bêche pair	—	—
6	A2 240c dull ver	150.00	1,200.
a.	240c deep vermilion	175.00	
b.	240c brick red	300.00	
c.	180c dl ver in stone of 240c	—	—
d.	Thick paper (dull ver)	—	
e.	240c setenant with a vacant space	5,000.	
	Nos. 4-6 (3)	875.00	2,050.

Nos. 4-6e have been extensively forged. Certification by a recognized authority is recommended.

ISSUES OF THE REPUBLIC

A3

A4

1859, June 26 Thin Numerals

7	A3 60c lilac	50.00	40.00
	On cover		300.00
a.	60c gray lilac	50.00	35.00
	On cover		300.00
8	A3 80c orange	325.00	65.00
	On cover		800.00
a.	80c yellow	450.00	75.00
	On cover		1,500.

9	A3 100c brown lake	110.00	75.00
	On cover		1,500.
a.	100c brown rose	120.00	100.00
	On cover		1,500.
10	A3 120c blue	65.00	30.00
	On cover		250.00
a.	120c slate blue	75.00	25.00
	On cover		600.00
b.	120c greenish blue	75.00	25.00
	On cover		350.00
11	A3 180c green	25.00	30.00
	On cover		1,200.
12	A3 240c vermilion	90.00	90.00
	On cover		1,500.
	Nos. 7-12 (6)	665.00	330.00

Very fine examples of Nos. 7-12 have 1.5mm margins on all sides.

1860 Thick Numerals

13	A4 60c dull lilac	30.00	15.00
	On cover		200.00
a.	60c gray lilac	30.00	15.00
	On cover		250.00
b.	60c brown lilac	30.00	18.00
	On cover		250.00
c.	60c red lilac	120.00	60.00
	On cover		250.00
d.	As "a," fine impression (1st printing)	125.00	45.00
	On cover		350.00
e.	60c chocolate brown	75.00	37.50
	On cover		350.00
14	A4 80c yellow	50.00	25.00
	On cover		400.00
a.	80c orange	100.00	27.50
	On cover		500.00
15	A4 100c rose	100.00	55.00
	On cover		1,200.
a.	100c carmine	110.00	55.00
	On cover		1,200.
16	A4 120c blue	45.00	25.00
	On cover		200.00
17	A4 180c yellow grn	425.00	375.00
	On cover		2,000.
a.	180c deep green	425.00	450.00
	On cover		2,000.
	Nos. 13-17 (5)	650.00	495.00

No. 13 was first printed (1860) in sheets of 192 (16x12) containing 24 types. The impressions are very clear; paper is whitish and of better quality than that of the later printings. In the 1861-62 printings, the layout contains 12 types and the subjects are spaced farther apart.
Very fine examples of Nos. 13-17 have 1.5mm margins on all sides.

Coat of Arms — A5

1864, Apr. 13

18	A5 6c rose	18.00	12.00
	On cover		150.00
a.	6c carmine	40.00	30.00
	On cover		150.00
b.	6c red	40.00	30.00
	On cover		
c.	6c brick red	45.00	30.00
	On cover		1,200.
d.	On laid paper	35.00	25.00
	On cover		
20	A5 6c salmon	500.00	500.00
	On cover		
21	A5 8c green	25.00	25.00
	On cover		750.00
a.	Tête bêche pair	775.00	
b.	8c yellow green	20.00	20.00
	On cover		900.00
c.	8c dark green	20.00	20.00
	On cover		900.00
22	A5 10c yellow	32.50	25.00
	On cover		1,200.
a.	10c ocher	35.00	20.00
	On cover		
23	A5 12c blue	15.00	12.00
	On cover		200.00
a.	12c dark blue	25.00	18.00
	On cover		250.00
b.	12c slate blue	30.00	20.00
	On cover		600.00
c.	12c pale blue	25.00	15.00
	On cover		250.00
d.	On laid paper	30.00	20.00
	On cover		

No. 20, which is on thicker paper, was never placed in use.

Stamps of 1864 Surcharged in Black

1866, Jan. 1

24	A5 5c on 12c blue	30.00	55.00
a.	5c on 12c slate blue	30.00	60.00
b.	Inverted surcharge	150.00	
c.	Double surcharge	150.00	
d.	Pair, one without surcharge		
e.	Triple surcharge	55.00	

25	A5	10c on 8c brt grn	30.00	55.00
a.		10c on 8c dl grn	30.00	55.00
b.		Tête bêche pair	300.00	
c.		Double surcharge	150.00	
26	A5	15c on 10c ocher	35.00	90.00
a.		15c on 10c yellow	35.00	90.00
b.		Inverted surcharge	150.00	
c.		Double surcharge	150.00	
27	A5	20c on 6c rose	40.00	80.00
a.		20c on 6c rose red	37.50	75.00
b.		Inverted surcharge	150.00	
c.		Double surcharge	150.00	
d.		Pair, one without surcharge		
28	A5	20c on 6c brick red	400.00	
a.		Double surcharge	500.00	
		Nos. 24-27 (4)	135.00	280.00

Many counterfeits exist.
No. 28 was not issued.

Coat of Arms and Numeral of Value — A7

A8   A8a

A8b   A8c

Type I

Type II

ONE CENTESIMO:
Type I — The wavy lines behind "CENTESIMO" are clear and distinct. Stamps 4mm apart.
Type II — The wavy lines are rough and blurred. Stamps 3mm apart.

1866, Jan. 10   *Imperf.*

29	A7	1c black (type II)	5.00	7.50
a.		1c black (type I)	5.00	7.50
30	A8	5c blue	6.00	4.00
a.		5c dull blue	5.00	2.50
b.		5c ultramarine	32.50	7.50
c.		Numeral with white flag	25.00	12.00
d.		"ENTECIMOS"	25.00	12.00
e.		"CENTECIMO"	25.00	12.00
f.		"CENTECIMOS" with small "S"	25.00	12.00
g.		Pelure paper	100.00	100.00
h.		Thick paper		
31	A8a	10c yellow green	20.00	7.00
a.		10c blue green	20.00	7.00
b.		"I" of "CENTECIMOS" omitted	27.50	14.00
c.		"CENIECIMOS"	27.50	14.00
d.		"CENTRCIMOS"	27.50	14.00
32	A8b	15c orange yel	30.00	15.00
a.		15c yellow	30.00	15.00
33	A8c	20c rose	35.00	15.00
a.		20c lilac rose	35.00	15.00
b.		Thick paper	37.50	16.00
		Nos. 29-33 (5)	96.00	48.50

See Nos. 34-38. For overprint see No. O11.
Engraved plates were prepared for Nos. 30 to 33 but were not put in use. The stamps were printed from lithographic transfers from the plate. In 1915 a few reprints of the 15c were made from the engraved plate by a California philatelic society, each sheet being numbered and signed by officers of the society; then the plate was defaced.

1866-67   *Perf. 8½ to 13½*

34	A7	1c black	6.50	20.00
35	A8	5c blue	5.00	2.50
a.		5c dark blue	5.00	1.00
b.		Numeral with white flag	25.00	12.00
c.		"ENTECIMOS"	25.00	12.00
d.		"CENTECIMO"	25.00	12.00
e.		"CENTECIMOS" with small "S"	15.00	8.00
f.		Pelure paper	90.00	20.00

36	A8a	10c green	12.00	4.00
a.		10c yellow green	14.00	4.00
b.		"CENIECIMOS"	35.00	14.00
c.		"I" of "CENTECIMOS" omitted	35.00	14.00
d.		"CENTRCIMOS"	35.00	14.00
e.		Pelure paper	90.00	20.00
37	A8b	15c orange yel	21.00	6.00
a.		15c yellow	21.00	10.00
b.		Thin paper	25.00	10.00
38	A8c	20c rose	25.00	10.00
a.		20c brown rose	25.00	10.00
b.		Thin paper	30.00	15.00
c.		Thick paper	30.00	15.00
		Nos. 34-38 (5)	69.50	42.50

A9   A10

A11   A12

1877-79   **Engr.**   *Rouletted 8*

39	A9	1c red brown	.80	.50
40	A10	5c green	1.00	.50
a.		Thick paper	5.00	2.50
41	A11	10c vermilion	2.00	.80
42	A11	20c bister	3.50	1.25
43	A11	50c black	12.50	3.50
43A	A12	1p blue ('79)	50.00	22.50
		Nos. 39-43A (6)	69.80	29.05

The first printing of the 1p had the coat of arms smaller with quarterings reversed. These "error" stamps were not issued, and all were ordered burned. One example is known to have been in a celebrated Uruguayan collection and a few others exist.
See No. 44. For overprints and surcharges see Nos. 52-53, O1-O8, O10, O19.

1880, Nov. 10   **Engr.**   *Rouletted 6*

44	A9	1c brown	.50	.50
a.		Imperf., pair	10.00	
b.		Rouletted 12½	2.50	

Joaquin Suárez — A13

1881, Aug. 25   *Perf. 12½*

45	A13	7c blue	2.50	2.50
a.		Imperf., pair	9.00	9.00

For overprint see No. O9.

A14   Devices from Coat of Arms — A14a

1882, May 15

46	A14	1c green	1.50	1.50
a.		1c yellow green	4.00	2.00
b.		Imperf., pair	13.00	
47	A14a	2c rose	1.25	1.00
a.		Imperf., pair	15.00	

These stamps bear numbers from 1 to 100 according to their position on the sheet.
Counterfeits of Nos. 46 and 47 are plentiful. See Nos. 1132-1133 in Scott Standard catalogue, Vol. 6. For overprints see Nos. 54, O12-O13, O20.

Coat of Arms
A15   A16

Gen. Máximo Santos — A17   General José Artigas — A18

Perf. 12, 12x12½, 12x13, 13x12

1883, Mar. 1

48	A15	1c green	1.50	1.00
49	A16	2c red	2.50	1.50
50	A17	5c blue	2.75	1.75
51	A18	10c brown	5.00	2.50
		Nos. 48-51 (4)	11.75	6.75

Imperf., Pairs

48a	A15	1c	7.00
49a	A16	2c	7.00
50a	A17	5c	6.50
51a	A18	10c	11.00

For overprints see Nos. O14-O18.

No. 40 Overprinted in Black

1883, Sept. 24   *Rouletted 8*

52	A10	5c green	1.00	.75
a.		Double overprint	15.00	15.00
b.		Overprint reading down	6.00	6.00
c.		"Provisorio" omitted	7.00	7.00
d.		"1883" omitted	4.50	4.50

No. 52 with overprint in red is a color essay.

No. 41 Surcharged in Black

1884, Jan. 15

53	A11	1c on 10c ver	.50	.50
a.		Small figure "1"	4.25	4.25
b.		Inverted surcharge	4.25	4.25
c.		Double surcharge	8.00	5.00

No. 47 Overprinted in Black

Perf. 12½

54	A14a	2c rose	.75	.75
a.		Double overprint	14.00	
b.		Imperf., pair	40.00	

A22   A23

Thick Paper

1884, Jan. 25   **Litho.**   **Unwmk.**

55	A22	5c ultra	2.00	1.00
a.		Imperf., pair	7.50	4.00

Thin Paper
Perf. 12½, 13 and Compound

56	A23	5c blue	1.50	.70
a.		Imperf., pair	14.00	

For overprints see Nos. O21-O22.

A24   A24a

A24b   Artigas — A25

Santos — A26   A27

A28

1884-88   **Engr.**   *Rouletted 8*

57	A24	1c gray	.80	.50
58	A24	1c olive	.75	.40
59	A24	1c green	.65	.40
60	A24a	2c vermilion	.40	.25
60A	A24a	2c rose ('88)	.40	.25
61	A24b	5c deep blue	.80	.30
61A	A24b	5c blue, *blue*	2.00	.85
62	A24b	5c violet ('86)	.50	.25
63	A24b	5c lt bl ('88)	.50	.25
64	A25	7c dk brown	2.00	.85
65	A25	7c org ('88)	2.00	.75
66	A26	10c olive brn	.80	.35
67	A27	20c red violet	2.00	1.00
68	A27	20c bis brn ('88)	2.00	1.00
69	A28	25c gray violet	4.00	1.50
70	A28	25c ver ('88)	3.00	1.00
		Nos. 57-70 (16)	22.60	9.90

Water dissolves the blue in the paper of No. 61A.
For overprints see Nos. 73, 98-99, O23-O34, O36-O39, O61.

A29   A30

1887, Oct. 17   **Litho.**   *Rouletted 9*

71	A29	10c lilac	2.50	1.25
a.		10c gray lilac	3.00	1.25

For overprint see No. O40.

1888, Jan. 1   **Engr.**   *Rouletted 8*

72	A30	10c violet	.60	.25

For overprint see No. O35.

No. 62 Overprinted in Black

1889, Oct. 14

73	A24b	5c violet	.40	.40
a.		Inverted overprint	8.00	6.00
b.		Inverted "A" for "V" in "Provisorio"	4.00	4.00

No. 73 with overprint in red is a color essay.

Coat of Arms — A32

Numeral of Value — A33

A34

A35

A36

A37

Justice A38

Mercury A39

A40

Perf. 12½ to 15½ and Compound
1889-1901   Engr.

74	A32	1c green	.50	.25
a.		Imperf., pair	13.00	
75	A32	1c dull bl ('94)	.50	.25
76	A33	2c rose	.50	.25
77	A33	2c red brn ('94)	.55	.25
78	A33	2c org ('99)	.55	.25
79	A34	5c dp blue	.50	.25
80	A34	5c rose ('94)	.55	.25
81	A35	7c bister brn	1.00	.30
82	A35	7c green ('94)	4.75	2.75
83	A35	7c car ('00)	4.00	1.75
84	A36	10c blue grn	3.50	.85
a.		Printed on both sides	20.00	
85	A36	10c org ('94)	3.25	.60
86	A37	20c orange	2.50	.50
87	A37	20c brown ('94)	4.75	1.75
88	A37	20c lt blue ('00)	2.75	.40
a.		20c greenish blue	3.00	.40
89	A38	25c red brown	3.25	.85
90	A38	25c ver ('94)	6.75	3.50
91	A38	25c bis brn ('01)	3.75	.50
92	A39	50c lt blue	7.50	5.00
93	A39	50c lilac ('94)	11.00	5.50
94	A39	50c car ('01)	6.75	1.00
95	A40	1p lilac	18.00	5.00
96	A40	1p lt blue ('94)	25.00	7.00
97	A40	1p dp grn ('01)	20.00	2.25
a.		Imperf., pair	30.00	
		Nos. 74-97 (24)	132.15	41.35

For surcharges and overprints see Nos. 100-101, 142, 180, 185, C1-C3, O41-O60, O89-O91, O108-O109.

Nos. 59 and 62 Overprinted in Red

a   b

1891-92   Rouletted 8

98	A24 (a)	1c green ('92)	.40	.40
a.		Inverted overprint	6.00	6.00
b.		Double overprint	7.75	7.75

c.		Double ovpt., one invtd.	3.00	2.50
d.		"PREVISORIO"	4.00	4.00
99	A24b (b)	5c violet	.25	.25
a.		"1391"	4.00	2.75
b.		Double overprint	4.00	2.75
c.		Inverted overprint	4.00	2.75
d.		Double ovpt., one invtd.	5.00	3.00

Nos. 86 and 81 Surcharged in Black or Red

c   d

Perf. 12½ to 15½ and Compound
1892

100	A37 (c)	1c on 20c org (Bk)	.40	.40
a.		Inverted surcharge	6.00	6.00
101	A35 (d)	5c on 7c bis brn (R)	.40	.40
a.		Inverted surcharge	1.00	1.00
b.		Double surcharge, one invtd.	3.00	3.00
c.		Double surcharge	3.00	3.00
d.		Vertical surcharge	10.00	
e.		"PREVISORIO"	3.00	3.00
f.		"Cinco" omitted	4.50	

No. 101 with surcharge in green is a color essay.

Several surcharge errors of date and misspelling of "Centésimos" exist. Value $15.

A45

A46

Arms A47

Peace A48

1892   Engr.

102	A45	1c green	.50	.25
103	A46	2c rose	.50	.25
104	A47	5c blue	.50	.25
105	A48	10c orange	2.00	.85
		Nos. 102-105 (4)	3.50	1.60

Issued: 1c, 2c, 3/9; 5c, 4/19; 10c, 12/15.

Liberty A49

Arms A50

1894, June 2

106	A49	2p carmine	30.00	17.50
107	A50	3p dull violet	30.00	17.50

Gaucho A51

Solis Theater A52

Locomotive A53

Bull's Head A54

Ceres — A55

Sailing Ship — A56

Liberty — A57

Mercury — A58

Coat of Arms — A59

Montevideo Fortress — A60

Cathedral in Montevideo A61

Perf. 12 to 15½ and Compound
1895-99

108	A51	1c bister	.50	.25
109	A51	1c slate bl ('97)	.50	.25
a.		Printed on both sides	14.00	
110	A52	2c blue	.50	.25
111	A52	2c claret ('97)	.50	.25
112	A53	5c red	.50	.25
113	A53	5c green ('97)	.65	.25
a.		Imperf., pair	3.50	
114	A53	5c grnsh bl ('99)	1.00	.40
115	A54	7c deep green	7.75	2.50
116	A54	7c orange ('97)	3.50	1.25
117	A55	10c brown	2.00	.50
118	A56	20c green & blk	7.00	.85
119	A56	20c cl & blk ('97)	4.75	.60
120	A57	25c red brn & blk	5.50	1.50
a.		Center inverted		2,000.
121	A57	25c pink & bl ('97)	3.50	.60
122	A58	50c blue & blk	7.00	3.50
123	A58	50c grn & brn ('97)	5.00	1.25
124	A59	1p org brn & blk	14.00	5.50
125	A59	1p yel brn & bl ('97)	9.50	3.50
126	A60	2p violet & grn	32.50	20.00
127	A60	2p bis & car ('97)	9.50	2.00
128	A61	3p carmine & blue	32.50	20.00
129	A61	3p lil & car ('97)	12.50	2.50
		Nos. 108-129 (22)	160.65	67.95

All values of this issue exist imperforate but they were not issued in that form.

For overprints and surcharges see Nos. 138-140, 143, 145, 147, O62-O78.

President Joaquin Suárez A62   A63

Statue of President Suárez — A64

Perf. 12½ to 15 and Compound
1896, July 18

130	A62	1c brown vio & blk	.25	.25
131	A63	5c pale bl & blk	.25	.25
132	A64	10c lake & blk	1.00	.30
		Nos. 130-132 (3)	1.50	.80

Dedication of Pres. Suárez statue.
For overprints and surcharge see Nos. 133-135, 144, 146, 152, O79-O81.

Same Overprinted in Red

e   f

1897, Mar. 1

133	A62 (e)	1c brn vio & blk	.40	.40
a.		Inverted overprint	6.00	6.00
134	A63 (e)	5c pale blue & blk	.50	.40
a.		Inverted overprint	9.50	6.00
135	A64 (f)	10c lake & blk	1.00	.60
a.		Inverted overprint	12.00	9.50
b.		Double overprint	7.50	
		Nos. 133-135 (3)	1.90	1.40

"Electricity" — A68

1897-99   Engr.

136	A68	10c red	1.75	.40
137	A68	10c red lilac ('99)	.75	.50

For overprints see Nos. 141, O82-O83.

Regular Issues Overprinted in Red or Blue

1897, Sept. 26

138	A51	1c slate bl (R)	.80	.60
a.		Inverted overprint	4.75	4.75
139	A52	2c claret (Bl)	1.25	1.25
a.		Inverted overprint	4.75	4.75
140	A53	5c green (Bl)	1.75	1.60
a.		Inverted overprint	7.75	7.75
b.		Double overprint		
141	A68	10c red (Bl)	2.75	2.75
a.		Inverted overprint	17.00	17.00
		Nos. 138-141 (4)	6.55	6.20

Commemorating the Restoration of Peace at the end of the Civil War.

Issue for use only on the days of the National Fête, Sept. 26-28, 1897.

Regular Issues Surcharged in Black, Blue or Red

1898, July 25

142	A32	½c on 1c bl (Bk)	.40	.40
a.		Inverted surcharge	3.00	3.00
143	A51	½c on 1c bis (Bl)	.40	.40
a.		Inverted surcharge	3.00	
b.		Double surcharge	2.50	
144	A62	½c on 1c brn vio & blk (R)	.40	.40
145	A52	½c on 2c blue (Bk)	.40	.40
146	A63	½c on 5c pale bl & blk (R)	.40	.40
a.		Double surcharge	6.25	
147	A54	½c on 7c dp grn (R)	.40	.40
		Nos. 142-147 (6)	2.40	2.40

The 2c red brown of 1894 (#77) was also surcharged like #142-147 but was not issued. Value $12.

Liberty — A69

Statue of
Artigas — A70

1898-99   Litho.   Perf. 11, 11½
148 A69 5m rose   .25   .25
149 A69 5m purple ('99)   .25   .25

1899-1900   Engr.   Perf. 12½, 14, 15
150 A70 5m lt blue   .25   .25
151 A70 5m orange ('00)   .25   .25

No. 135 With
Additional Surcharge
in Black

1900, Dec. 1
152 A64 5c on 10c lake & blk   .50   .25
a.   Black bar covering "1897" omit-
     ted   15.00

Cattle — A72

Girl's
Head — A73

Shepherdess — A74

Perf. 13½ to 16 and Compound
1900-10   Engr.
153 A72 1c yellow green   .40   .25
154 A73 5c dull blue   .80   .25
155 A73 5c slate grn ('10)   .80   .25
156 A74 10c gray violet   1.00   .25
     Nos. 153-156 (4)   3.00 1.00

For surcharges and overprints see Nos.
179, 184, O84, O86, O88, O106-O107.

Eros and
Cornucopia
A75

Basket of Fruit
A76

1901, Feb. 11
157 A75 2c vermilion   .50   .25
158 A76 7c brown orange   1.75   .25

For surcharges and overprints see Nos.
197-198, O85, O87, O105.

General
Artigas — A78

Cattle — A79

Eros — A80

Cow — A81

Shepherdess
A82

Numeral
A83

Justice — A84

1904-05   Litho.   Perf. 11½
160 A78 5m orange   .40   .25
a.   5m yellow   .40   .25
161 A79 1c green   .50   .25
a.   Imperf., pair   3.50
162 A80 2c dp orange   .25   .25
a.   2c orange red   .25   .25
b.   Imperf., pair   3.00
163 A81 5c blue   .80   .25
a.   Imperf., pair   3.50
164 A82 10c dk violet ('05)   .50   .25
165 A83 20c gray grn ('05)   2.50   .50
166 A84 25c olive bis ('05)   3.25   .80
     Nos. 160-166 (7)   8.20 2.55

Design of No. 163 measures 17mm by
23mm. See No. 170.
For overprints see Nos. 167-169, O92-O98,
O101-O103.

Overprinted Diagonally
in Carmine or Black

1904, Oct. 15
167 A79 1c green (C)   .40   .40
168 A80 2c deep orange (Bk)   .65   .40
169 A81 5c dark blue (C)   1.25   .60
     Nos. 167-169 (3)   2.30 1.40

End of the Civil War of 1904. In the first
overprinting, "Paz 1904" appears at a 50-
degree angle; in the second, at a 63-degree
angle.

A85

A86

1906, Feb. 23   Litho.   Unwmk.
170 A85 5c dark blue   1.10   .25
a.   Imperf., pair   6.00

Design of No. 170 measures 19¼mm by
25½mm. See No. 163.

1906-07
171 A86 5c deep blue   .30   .30
172 A86 7c orange brn ('07)   .70   .50
173 A86 50c rose   5.00 1.25
     Nos. 171-173 (3)   6.00 2.05

Cruiser "Montevideo" — A87

1908, Aug. 23   Typo.   Rouletted 13
174 A87 1c car & dk grn   2.00 1.50
175 A87 2c green & dk grn   2.00 1.50
176 A87 5c org & dk grn   2.00 1.50
     Nos. 174-176 (3)   6.00 4.50

Center Inverted
174a A87 1c   300.00 300.00
175a A87 2c   300.00 300.00
176a A87 5c   300.00 300.00
     Nos. 174a-176a (3)   900.00 900.00

Imperf., Pairs
174b A87 1c   30.00
175b A87 2c   30.00
176b A87 5c   30.00

Independence of Uruguay, declared Aug.
25, 1825. Counterfeits exist.
For surcharges and overprints see Nos.
186, O99-O100, O104, O110.

View of the Port of Montevideo — A88

Wmk. 187
1909, Aug. 24   Engr.   Perf. 11½
177 A88 2c lt brown & blk   1.25 1.20
178 A88 5c rose red & blk   1.25 1.20

Issued to commemorate the opening of the
Port of Montevideo, Aug. 25, 1909.

Nos. 156, 91
Surcharged

Perf. 14 to 16
1909, Sept. 13   Unwmk.
179 A74 8c on 10c dull vio   .75   .25
a.   "Contesimos"   4.00 2.00
180 A38 23c on 25c bis brn   1.75   .60

Centaur — A89

Wmk. 187
1910, May 22   Engr.   Perf. 11½
182 A89 2c carmine red   .60   .40
183 A89 5c deep blue   .60   .40

Cent. of Liberation Day, May 25, 1810.
The 2c in deep blue and 5c in carmine red
were prepared for collectors.

Stamps of 1900-06 Surcharged

g

h

i

Perf. 14 to 16, 11½
1910, Oct. 6   Unwmk.
Black Surcharge
184 A72 (g) 5m on 1c yel grn   .25   .25
a.   Inverted surcharge   4.50 3.75
Dark Blue Surcharge
185 A39 (h) 5c on 50c dull
              red   .40   .25
a.   Inverted surcharge   4.50 4.50
Blue Surcharge
186 A86 (i) 5c on 50c rose   .80   .45
a.   Double surcharge   20.00
b.   Inverted surcharge   10.00 8.75
     Nos. 184-186 (3)   1.45   .95

Artigas
A90

"Commercial
Progress"
A91

1910, Nov. 21   Engr.   Perf. 14, 15
187 A90 5m dk violet   .25   .25
188 A90 1c dp green   .25   .25
189 A90 2c orange red   .25   .25
190 A90 5c dk blue   .40   .25
191 A90 8c gray blk   .40   .25
192 A90 20c brown   .60   .25
193 A91 23c dp ultra   2.75   .40
194 A91 50c orange   4.00 1.25
195 A91 1p scarlet   7.50 1.25
     Nos. 187-195 (9)   16.25 4.40

See Nos. 199-210. For overprints see Nos.
211-213, O118-O124.

Symbolical of the
Posts — A92

1911, Jan. 6   Wmk. 187   Perf. 11½
196 A92 5c rose car & blk   .80   .60

1st South American Postal Cong., at Montevideo, Jan. 1911.

No. 158 Surcharged
in Red or Dark Blue

Perf. 14 to 16
1911, May 17   Unwmk.
197 A76 2c on 7c brn org (R)   .40   .40
198 A76 5c on 7c brn org (Bl)   .40   .25
a.   Inverted surcharge   8.50 8.50

Centenary of the battle of Las Piedras, won
by the forces under Gen. Jose Gervasio Artigas, May 8, 1811.

Types of 1910
FOUR AND FIVE CENTESIMOS:
Type I — Large numerals about 3mm high.
Type II — Small numerals about 2¼mm
high.

1912-15   Typo.   Perf. 11½
199 A90 5m violet   .25   .25
a.   5m purple   .25   .25
200 A90 5m magenta   .25   .25
a.   5m dull rose   .25   .25
201 A90 1c green ('13)   .25   .25
202 A90 2c brown org   .25   .25
203 A90 2c rose red ('13)   .25   .25
a.   2c deep red ('14)   .25   .25
204 A90 4c org (I) ('14)   .25   .25
a.   4c orange (II) ('15)   .25   .25
b.   4c yellow (II) ('13)   .25   .25
205 A90 5c dull bl (I)   .40   .25
a.   5c blue (II)   .40   .25
206 A90 8c ultra ('13)   .50   .25
207 A90 20c brown ('13)   1.40   .25
a.   20c chocolate   1.40
208 A91 23c dk blue ('15)   3.50   .60
209 A91 50c orange ('14)   3.50 1.50
210 A91 1p vermilion ('15)   10.50 1.25
     Nos. 199-210 (12)   21.30 5.60

Stamps of 1912-15 Overprinted

1913, Apr. 4
211	A90	2c brown orange	.85	.50
a.		Inverted overprint	5.00	4.50
212	A90	4c yellow	.85	.50
213	A90	5c blue	.85	.50
		Nos. 211-213 (3)	2.55	1.50

Cent. of the Buenos Aires Cong. of 1813.

Liberty Extending Peace to the Country — A93

1918, Jan. 3 Litho.
214	A93	2c green & red	.85	.50
215	A93	5c buff & blue	.85	.50

Promulgation of the Constitution.

Statue of Liberty, New York Harbor A94

Harbor of Montevideo A95

Perf. 14, 15, 13½

1919, July 15 Engr.
217	A94	2c carmine & brn	.55	.25
218	A94	4c orange & brn	.55	.25
219	A94	5c blue & brn	.80	.40
220	A94	8c org brn & ind	.80	.40
221	A94	20c ol bis & blk	2.00	.80
222	A94	23c green & blk	4.00	1.25
		Nos. 217-222 (6)	8.70	3.35

Peace at end of World War I.
Perf 13½ used only on 2c, 20c, 23c.

1919-20 Litho. **Perf. 11½**
225	A95	5m violet & blk	.25	.25
226	A95	1c green & blk	.25	.25
227	A95	2c red & blk	.25	.25
228	A95	4c orange & blk	.35	.25
229	A95	5c ultra & slate	.40	.25
230	A95	8c gray bl & lt brn	.50	.25
231	A95	20c brown & blk	1.60	.35
232	A95	23c green & brn	2.75	.65
233	A95	50c brown & blue	5.00	2.00
234	A95	1p dull red & bl	10.00	3.00
		Nos. 225-234 (10)	21.35	7.50

For overprints see Nos. O125-O131.

José Enrique Rodó — A96

Mercury — A97

1920, Feb. 28 Engr. **Perf. 14, 15**
235	A96	2c car & blk	.55	.40
236	A96	4c org & bl	.65	.50
237	A96	5c bl & brn	.75	.55
		Nos. 235-237 (3)	1.95	1.45

Issued to honor José Enrique Rodó, author.
For surcharges see Nos. P2-P4.

1921-22 Litho. **Perf. 11½**
238	A97	5m lilac	.25	.25
239	A97	5m gray blk ('22)	.25	.25
240	A97	1c lt grn	.25	.25
241	A97	1c vio ('22)	.25	.25
242	A97	2c fawn	.40	.25
243	A97	2c red ('22)	.40	.25

244	A97	3c bl grn ('22)	.60	.25
245	A97	4c orange	.40	.25
246	A97	5c ultra	.50	.25
247	A97	5c choc ('22)	.60	.25
248	A97	12c ultra ('22)	2.40	.60
249	A97	36c ol grn ('22)	7.75	2.75
		Nos. 238-249 (12)	14.05	5.85

See Nos. 254-260. For overprint and surcharge see Nos. E1, P1.

Dámaso A. Larrañaga (1771-1848), Bishop, Writer, Scientist and Physician — A98

1921, Dec. 10 Unwmk.
250	A98	5c slate	1.25	1.00

Mercury Type of 1921-22
1922-23 Wmk. 188
254	A97	5m gray blk	.25	.25
255	A97	1c violet ('23)	.25	.25
a.		1c red violet	.25	.25
256	A97	2c pale red	.25	.25
257	A97	2c deep rose ('23)	.30	.25
259	A97	5c yel brn ('23)	.65	.25
260	A97	8c salmon pink ('23)	1.00	.90
		Nos. 254-260 (6)	2.70	2.15

Equestrian Statue of Artigas — A99

Unwmk.
1923, Feb. 26 Engr. **Perf. 14**
264	A99	2c car & sepia	.40	.25
265	A99	5c vio & sepia	.40	.25
266	A99	12c blue & sepia	.40	.25
		Nos. 264-266 (3)	1.20	.75

Southern Lapwing — A100

Perf. 12½, 11½x12½
1923, June 25 Litho. Wmk. 189
Size: 18x22½mm
267	A100	5m gray	.25	.25
268	A100	1c org yel	.25	.25
269	A100	2c lt vio	.25	.25
270	A100	3c gray grn	.40	.25
271	A100	5c lt bl	.40	.25
272	A100	8c rose red	.80	.50
273	A100	12c dp bl	.80	.50
274	A100	20c brn org	2.00	.50
275	A100	36c emerald	4.00	1.75
276	A100	50c orange	6.75	2.75
277	A100	1p brt rose	32.50	20.00
278	A100	2p lt grn	47.50	20.00
		Nos. 267-278 (12)	95.90	47.25

See #285-298, 309-314, 317-323, 334-339.
For surcharges and overprints see Nos. 345-348, O132-O148, P5-P7.

Battle Monument A101

1923, Oct. 12 Wmk. 188 **Perf. 11½**
279	A101	2c dp grn	.55	.40
280	A101	5c scarlet	.55	.40
281	A101	12c dk bl	.55	.40
		Nos. 279-281 (3)	1.65	1.20

Unveiling of the Sarandí Battle Monument by José Luis Zorrilla, Oct. 12, 1923.

"Victory of Samothrace" — A102

Unwmk.
1924, July 29 Typo. **Perf. 11**
282	A102	2c rose	20.00	10.00
283	A102	5c mauve	20.00	10.00
284	A102	12c brt bl	20.00	10.00
		Nos. 282-284 (3)	60.00	30.00

Olympic Games. Sheets of 20 (5x4).
Five hundred sets of these stamps were printed on yellow paper for presentation purposes. They were not on sale at post offices. Value for set, $650.

Lapwing Type of 1923
First Redrawing
Imprint: "A. BARREIRO Y RAMOS"
1924, July 26 Litho. **Perf. 12½, 11½**
Size: 17¼x21½mm
285	A100	5m gray blk	.25	.25
286	A100	1c fawn	.25	.25
287	A100	2c rose lil	.30	.25
288	A100	3c gray grn	.25	.25
289	A100	5c chalky blue	.25	.25
290	A100	8c pink	.50	.25
291	A100	10c turq blue	.40	.25
292	A100	12c slate blue	.50	.25
293	A100	15c lt vio	.50	.25
294	A100	20c brown	.75	.30
295	A100	36c salmon	3.00	.70
296	A100	50c greenish gray	5.00	2.00
297	A100	1p buff	12.00	4.00
298	A100	2p dl vio	20.00	10.00
		Nos. 285-298 (14)	43.95	19.25

Landing of the 33 "Immortals" Led by Juan Antonio Lavalleja — A103

Perf. 11, 11½
1925, Apr. 19 Wmk. 188
300	A103	2c salmon pink & blk	1.40	.80
301	A103	5c lilac & blk	1.40	.80
302	A103	12c blue & blk	1.40	.80
		Nos. 300-302 (3)	4.20	2.40

Cent. of the landing of the 33 Founders of the Uruguayan Republic.

Legislative Palace — A104

Perf. 11½
1925, Aug. 24 Unwmk. Engr.
303	A104	5c vio & blk	1.25	.80
304	A104	12c bl & blk	1.25	.80

Dedication of the Legislative Palace.

General Fructuoso Rivera — A105

Wmk. 188
1925, Sept. 24 Litho. **Perf. 11**
305	A105	5c light red	.50	.40

Centenary of Battle of Rincón. See No. C9.

Battle of Sarandí A106

1925, Oct. 12 **Perf. 11½**
306	A106	2c bl grn	1.25	1.00
307	A106	5c dl vio	1.25	1.00
308	A106	12c dp bl	1.25	1.00
		Nos. 306-308 (3)	3.75	3.00

Centenary of the Battle of Sarandi.

Lapwing Type of 1923
Second Redrawing
Imprint: "Imprenta Nacional"
1925-26 **Perf. 11, 11½, 10½**
Size: 17½x21¾mm
309	A100	5m gray blk	1.00	.25
310	A100	1c dl vio	1.25	.25
311	A100	2c brt rose	1.60	.25
312	A100	3c gray grn	1.25	.40
313	A100	5c dl bl ('26)	2.00	.25
314	A100	12c slate blue	4.00	.40
		Nos. 309-314 (6)	11.10	1.80

The design differs in many small details from that of the 1923-24 issues. These stamps may be readily identified by the imprint and perforation.

Lapwing Type of 1923
Third Redrawing
Imprint: "Imp. Nacional" at center
1926-27 **Perf. 11, 11½, 10½**
Size: 17½x21¾mm
317	A100	5m gray	.40	.25
318	A100	1c lt vio ('27)	2.40	.55
319	A100	2c red	1.75	.40
320	A100	3c gray grn	2.40	.65
321	A100	5c lt bl	.75	.25
322	A100	8c pink ('27)	3.50	.80
323	A100	36c rose buff	8.00	4.00
		Nos. 317-323 (7)	19.20	6.90

These stamps may be distinguished from preceding stamps of the same design by the imprint.

Philatelic Exhibition Issue

Post Office at Montevideo A107

Unwmk.
1927, May 25 Engr. **Imperf.**
330	A107	2c green	4.75	3.50
a.		Sheet of 4	20.00	20.00
331	A107	5c dull red	4.75	3.50
a.		Sheet of 4	20.00	20.00
332	A107	8c dark blue	4.75	3.50
a.		Sheet of 4	20.00	20.00
		Nos. 330-332 (3)	14.25	10.50

Printed in sheets of 4 and sold at the Montevideo Exhibition. Lithographed counterfeits exist.

Lapwing Type of 1923
Fourth Redrawing
Imprint: "Imp. Nacional" at right
Perf. 11, 11½
1927, May 6 Litho. Wmk. 188
Size: 17¾x21¾mm
334	A100	1c gray vio	.40	.25
335	A100	2c vermilion	.40	.25
336	A100	3c gray grn	.80	.35
337	A100	5c blue	.40	.25
338	A100	8c rose	3.00	.80
339	A100	20c gray brn	4.00	1.60
		Nos. 334-339 (6)	9.00	3.50

The design has been slightly retouched in various places. The imprint is in italic capitals and is placed below the right numeral of value.

No. 292 Surcharged in Red

1928, Jan. 13   Unwmk.   Perf. 11½
345 A100 2c on 12c slate blue   2.00 2.00
346 A100 5c on 12c slate blue   2.00 2.00
347 A100 10c on 12c slate blue   2.00 2.00
348 A100 15c on 12c slate blue   2.00 2.00
    Nos. 345-348 (4)   8.00 8.00

Issued to celebrate the inauguration of the railroad between San Carlos and Rocha.

General Rivera — A108

1928, Apr. 19   Engr.   Perf. 12
349 A108 5c car rose   .50   .35
Centenary of the Battle of Las Misiones.

Artigas (7 dots in panels below portrait.) — A109

Imprint: "Waterlow & Sons. Ltd., Londres"

Perf. 11, 12½, 13x13½, 12½x13, 13x12½
1928-43   Size: 16x19½mm
350 A109 5m black   .25   .25
350A A109 5m org ('43)   .25   .25
351 A109 1c dk vio   .25   .25
352 A109 1c brn vio ('34)   .25   .25
352A A109 1c vio bl ('43)   .25   .25
353 A109 2c dp grn   .25   .25
353A A109 2c brn red ('43)   .25   .25
354 A109 3c bister   .25   .25
355 A109 3c dp grn ('32)   .25   .25
355A A109 3c brt grn ('43)   .25   .25
356 A109 5c red   .25   .25
357 A109 5c ol grn ('33)   .25   .25
357A A109 5c dl pur ('43)   .25   .25
358 A109 7c car ('32)   .25   .25
359 A109 8c dk bl   .25   .25
360 A109 8c brn ('33)   .25   .25
361 A109 10c orange   .25   .25
362 A109 10c red org ('32)   .60   .40
363 A109 12c dp bl ('32)   .40   .25
364 A109 15c dl bl   .40   .25
365 A109 17c dk vio ('32)   .80   .25
366 A109 20c ol brn   .65   .25
367 A109 20c red brn ('33)   1.25   .50
368 A109 24c car rose   .90   .35
369 A109 24c yel ('33)   .80   .40
370 A109 36c ol grn ('33)   1.40   .50
371 A109 50c gray   2.40 1.25
372 A109 50c blk ('33)   3.50 1.60
373 A109 50c blk brn ('33)   3.00 1.25
374 A109 1p yel grn   7.00 4.00
     Nos. 350-374 (30)   27.35 15.50

1929-33   Perf. 12½
Size: 22 to 22½x28½ to 29½mm
375 A109 1p ol brn ('33)   6.00   4.00
376 A109 2p dk grn   17.00   9.00
377 A109 2p dl red ('32)   20.00 16.00
378 A109 3p dk bl   25.00 17.00
379 A109 3p blk ('32)   23.00 20.00
380 A109 4p violet   28.00 17.00
381 A109 4p dk ol grn ('32) 23.00 20.00
382 A109 5p car brn   32.50 23.00
383 A109 5p red org ('32)   30.00 20.00
384 A109 10p lake ('33)   92.50 70.00
385 A109 10p dp ultra ('33) 92.50 70.00
    Nos. 375-385 (11)   389.50 286.00

See Nos. 420-423, 462. See type A135.

Equestrian Statue of Artigas — A110

1928, May 1
386 A110 2p Prus bl & choc   16.00   7.75
387 A110 3p dp rose & blk   23.00 12.00

Symbolical of Soccer Victory — A111

1928, July 29
388 A111 2c brn vio   16.00   9.25
389 A111 5c dp red   16.00   9.25
390 A111 8c ultra   16.00   9.25
    Nos. 388-390 (3)   48.00 27.75

Uruguayan soccer victories in the Olympic Games of 1924 and 1928. Printed in sheets of 20, in panes of 10 (5x2).

Gen. Eugenio Garzón — A112

1928, Aug. 25   Imperf.
391 A112 2c red   1.40 1.40
  a.   Sheet of 4   6.50 6.50
392 A112 5c yel grn   1.40 1.40
  a.   Sheet of 4   6.50 6.50
393 A112 8c dp bl   1.40 1.40
  a.   Sheet of 4   6.50 6.50
    Nos. 391-393 (3)   4.20 4.20

Dedication of monument to Garzon. Issued in sheets of 4. Lithographed counterfeits exist.

Black River Bridge A113

Gauchos Breaking a Horse — A114

Peace A115

Montevideo A116

Liberty and Flag of Uruguay A117

Liberty with Torch and Caduceus A118

Statue of Artigas A124

Artigas Dictating Instructions for 1010 Congress A119

Seascape A120

Montevideo Harbor, 1830 — A121

Liberty and Coat of Arms A122

Montevideo Harbor, 1930 — A123

1930, June 16   Perf. 12½, 12
394 A113 5m gray blk   .25   .25
395 A114 1c dk brn   .25   .25
396 A115 2c brn rose   .25   .25
397 A116 3c yel grn   .25   .25
398 A117 5c dk bl   .25   .25
399 A118 8c dl red   .35   .25
400 A119 10c dk vio   .50   .35
401 A120 15c bl grn   .65   .50
402 A121 20c indigo   .80   .65
403 A122 24c red brn   1.10   .80
404 A123 50c org red   3.00   2.00
405 A124 1p black   6.00   3.00
406 A124 2p bl vio   14.00   8.50
407 A124 3p dk red   20.00 14.00
408 A124 4p red org   23.00 19.00
409 A124 5p lilac   35.00 22.50
    Nos. 394-409 (16) 105.65 72.80

Cent. of natl. independence and the promulgation of the constitution.

Type of 1856 Issue
Values in Centesimos
Wmk. 227
1931, Apr. 11   Litho.   Imperf.
410 A1 2c gray blue   3.00   2.00
  a. Sheet of 4   15.00 15.00
411 A1 8c dull red   3.00   2.00
  a. Sheet of 4   15.00 15.00
412 A1 15c blue black 3.00   2.00
  a. Sheet of 4   15.00 15.00
Wmk. 188
413 A1 5c light green 3.00   2.00
  a. Sheet of 4   15.00 15.00
    Nos. 410-413 (4) 12.00   8.00

Sold only at the Philatelic Exhibition, Montevideo, Apr. 11-15, 1931. Issued in sheets of 4.

Juan Zorrilla de San Martin, Uruguayan Poet — A125

1932, June 6   Unwmk.   Perf. 12½
414 A125 1½c brown violet   .25   .25
415 A125 3c green   .25   .25
416 A125 7c dk blue   .25   .25
417 A125 12c lt blue   .40   .25
418 A125 1p deep brown   20.00 13.00
    Nos. 414-418 (5)   21.15 14.00

Semi-Postal Stamp No. B3 Surcharged

1932, Nov. 1   Perf. 12
419 SP1 1½c on 2c + 2c dp grn   .35   .35

Artigas Type of 1928
Imprint: "Imprenta Nacional" at center
1932-35   Litho.   Perf. 11, 12½
Size: 15¾x19¼mm
420 A109 5m lt brown ('35)   .25   .25
421 A109 1c pale violet ('35) .25 .25
422 A109 15m black   .25   .25
423 A109 5c bluish grn ('35) .50   .25
    Nos. 420-423 (4)   1.25 1.00

Gen. J. A. Lavalleja — A126

1933, July 12   Engr.   Perf. 12½
429 A126 15m brown lake   .25   .25

Flag of the Race and Globe — A127

Perf. 11, 11½, 11x11½
1933, Aug. 3   Litho.
430 A127 3c blue green   .50   .25
431 A127 5c rose   .50   .25
432 A127 7c lt blue   .50   .25
433 A127 8c dull red   1.00   .55
434 A127 12c deep blue   .65   .25
435 A127 17c violet   1.75   .80
436 A127 20c red brown   3.50   1.60
437 A127 24c yellow   3.50   1.75
438 A127 36c orange   5.00   2.40
439 A127 50c olive gray   5.50   3.00
440 A127 1p bister   13.00   6.25
    Nos. 430-440 (11)   35.40 17.35

Raising of the "Flag of the Race" and of the 441st anniv. of the sailing of Columbus from Palos, Spain, on his first voyage to America.

Sower — A128

1933, Aug. 28   Unwmk.   Perf. 11½
441 A128 3c blue green   .25   .25
442 A128 5c dull violet   .40   .25
443 A128 7c lt blue   .40   .25
444 A128 8c deep red   .80   .50
445 A128 12c ultra   2.00   1.00
    Nos. 441-445 (5)   3.85   2.25

3rd Constituent National Assembly.

Juan Zorrilla de San Martin — A129

1933, Nov. 9   Engr.   Perf. 12½
446 A129 7c slate   .25   .25

Albatross Flying over Map of the Americas — A130

1933, Dec. 3   Typo.   Perf. 11½
447 A130 3c green, blk & brn   2.75   2.00
448 A130 7c turq bl, brn & blk   1.60   .80
449 A130 12c dk bl, gray & ver   2.40   1.60
450 A130 17c ver, gray & vio   5.00   2.75
451 A130 20c yellow, bl & grn   6.00   3.50
452 A130 36c red, blk & yel   7.75   5.50
    Nos. 447-452 (6)   25.50   16.15

7th Pan-American Conf., Montevideo. Issued in sheets of 6. Value $200. For overprints see Nos. C61-C62.

General Rivera — A131

1934, Feb.   Engr.   Perf. 12½
453 A131 3c green   .25   .25

Stars Representing the Three Constitutions — A132

1934, Mar. 23   Typo.
454 A132 3c yellow grn & grn   .60   .40
455 A132 7c org red & red   .60   .40
456 A132 12c ultra & blue   2.00   .80

Perf. 11½
457 A132 17c brown & rose   2.50   1.25
458 A132 20c yellow & gray   3.50   1.60
459 A132 36c dk vio & bl grn   3.50   1.60
460 A132 50c black & blue   7.00   3.25
461 A132 1p dk car & vio   16.00   6.75
    Nos. 454-461 (8)   35.70   16.05

First Year of Third Republic.

Artigas Type of 1928
Imprint: "Barreiro & Ramos S. A."
1934, Nov. 28   Litho.
462 A109 50c brown black   6.00   2.50

"Uruguay" and "Brazil" Holding Scales of Justice — A133

1935, May 30   Unwmk.   Perf. 11
463 A133 5m brown   .80   .40
464 A133 15m black   .40   .25
465 A133 3c green   .40   .25
466 A133 7c orange   .40   .25
467 A133 12c ultra   .80   .60
468 A133 50c brown   4.00   2.50
    Nos. 463-468 (6)   6.80   4.25

Visit of President Vargas of Brazil.

Florencio Sánchez — A134

1935, Nov. 7
469 A134 3c green   .25   .25
470 A134 7c brown   .25   .25
471 A134 12c blue   .55   .35
    Nos. 469-471 (3)   1.05   .85

Florencio Sanchez (1875-1910), author.

Artigas (6 dots in panels below portrait) — A135

Imprint: "Imprenta Nacional" at center

1936-44   Perf. 11, 12½
474 A135 5m org brn ('37)   .25   .25
475 A135 5m lt brown ('39)   .25   .25
476 A135 1c lt violet ('37)   .25   .25
477 A135 2c dk brown ('37)   .25   .25
478 A135 2c green ('39)   .25   .25
479 A135 5c brt blue ('37)   .25   .25
480 A135 5c bluish grn ('39)   .40   .25
481 A135 12c dull blue ('38)   .25   .25
482 A135 20c fawn   1.40   .35
482A A135 20c rose ('44)   1.00   .40
483 A135 50c brown black   3.00   .80

Size: 21½x28½mm
483A A135 1p brown   8.50   3.00
483B A135 2p blue   14.00   12.00
483C A135 3p gray black   20.00   16.00
    Nos. 474-483C (14)   50.20   34.55

See Nos. 488, and 576 in Scott Standard catalogue, Vol. 6. See type A109.

Power Dam on Black River — A136

1937-38
484 A136 1c dull violet   .25   .25
485 A136 10c blue   .50   .25
486 A136 15c rose   1.25   .65
487 A136 1p choc ('38)   6.25   2.50
    Nos. 484-487 (4)   8.25   3.65

Imprint: "Imprenta Nacional" at right
1938
488 A135 1c bright violet   .40   .25

International Law Congress, 1889 — A137

1939, July 16   Litho.   Perf. 12½
489 A137 1c brown orange   .25   .25
490 A137 2c dull green   .25   .25
491 A137 5c rose ver   .25   .25
492 A137 12c dull blue   .65   .40
493 A137 50c lt violet   2.50   1.50
    Nos. 489-493 (5)   3.90   2.65

50th anniversary of the Montevideo Congress of International Law.

Artigas
A138   A138a

1939-43   Litho.   Unwmk.
Size: 15¾x19mm
494 A138 5m dl brn org ('40)   .25   .25
495 A138 1c lt blue   .25   .25
496 A138 2c lt violet   .25   .25
497 A138 5c violet brn   .25   .25
498 A138 8c rose red   .25   .25
499 A138 10c groon   .50   .25
500 A138 15c dull blue   1.25   .60

Size: 24x29½mm
501 A138 1p dull brn ('41)   2.50   1.00
502 A138 2p dl rose vio ('40)   7.00   3.00
503 A138 4p orange ('43)   9.25   4.00
504 A138 5p ver ('41)   14.00   6.00
    Nos. 494-504 (11)   35.75   16.10

See No. 578 in Scott Standard catalogue, Vol. 6.

Redrawn: Horizontal lines in portrait background
1940-44   Size: 17x21mm
505 A138a 5m brn org ('41)   .25   .25
506 A138a 1c lt blue   .25   .25
507 A138a 2c lt violet ('41)   .25   .25
508 A138a 5c violet brn   .25   .25
509 A138a 8c sal pink ('44)   .25   .25
510 A138a 10c green ('41)   .40   .25
511 A138a 50c olive bis ('42)   6.25   1.75
511A A138a 50c yel grn ('44)   4.75   1.75
    Nos. 505-511A (8)   12.65   5.00

See Nos. 568-575, 577, 601, 632, 660-661 in Scott Standard catalogue, Vol. 6. For surcharges see Nos. 523, 726 in Scott Standard catalogue, Vol. 6.

SEMI-POSTAL STAMPS

Indigent Old Man — SP1

Unwmk.
1930, Nov. 13   Engr.   Perf. 12
B1 SP1 1c + 1c dark violet   .30   .30
B2 SP1 2c + 2c deep green   .30   .30
B3 SP1 5c + 5c red   .45   .45
B4 SP1 8c + 8c gray violet   .45   .45
    Nos. B1-B4 (4)   1.50   1.50

The surtax on these stamps was for a fund to assist the aged.
For surcharge see No. 419.

AIR POST STAMPS

No. 91 Overprinted in Dark Blue, Red or Green

1921-22   Unwmk.   Perf. 14
C1 A38 25c bister brn (Bl)   18.00   15.00
  a.   Black overprint   800.00   800.00
C2 A38 25c bister brn (R)   7.00   7.00
  a.   Inverted overprint   100.00   100.00
C3 A38 25c bister brn (G)
         ('22)   7.00   7.00
    Nos. C1-C3 (3)   32.00   29.00

This overprint, on No. C3, also exists in light yellow green. Value, $85 unused and used. No. C1a was not issued. Some authorities consider it an overprint color trial.

AP2

Wmk. 188
1924, Jan. 2   Litho.   Perf. 11½
C4 AP2 6c dark blue   2.50   2.00
C5 AP2 10c scarlet   3.50   3.00
C6 AP2 20c deep green   5.00   5.00
    Nos. C4-C6 (3)   11.00   10.00

Heron — AP3

1925, Aug. 24   Perf. 12½
Inscribed "MONTEVIDEO"
C7 AP3 14c blue & blk   35.00   25.00
Inscribed "FLORIDA"
C8 AP3 14c blue & blk   35.00   17.50

These stamps were used only on Aug. 25, 1925, the cent. of the Assembly of Florida, on letters intended to be carried by airplane between Montevideo and Florida, a town 60 miles north. The stamps were not delivered to the public but were affixed to the letters and canceled by post office clerks. Later uncanceled stamps came on the market.
One authority believes Nos. C7-C8 served as registration stamps on these two attempted special flights.

Gaucho Cavalryman at Rincón — AP4

1925, Sept. 24   Perf. 11
C9 AP4 45c blue green   17.50

Centenary of Battle of Rincon. Used only on Sept. 24. No. C9 was affixed and canceled by post office clerks.

Albatross — AP5

1926, Mar. 3   Wmk. 188   Imperf.
C10 AP5 6c dark blue   2.00   2.00
C11 AP5 10c vermilion   2.50   2.50
C12 AP5 20c blue green   3.00   3.00
C13 AP5 25c violet   3.50   3.50
    Nos. C10-C13 (4)   11.00   11.00

Excellent counterfeits exist.

1928, June 25   Perf. 11
C14 AP5 10c green   3.00   2.00
C15 AP5 20c orange   5.00   3.00
C16 AP5 30c indigo   5.00   3.00
C17 AP5 38c green   8.50   6.00
C18 AP5 40c yellow   8.50   6.00
C19 AP5 50c violet   10.00   7.50
C20 AP5 76c orange   20.00   17.50
C21 AP5 1p red   20.00   15.00
C22 AP5 1.14p indigo   45.00   35.00
C23 AP5 1.52p yellow   75.00   60.00
C24 AP5 1.90p violet   95.00   75.00
C25 AP5 3.80p red   225.00   170.00
    Nos. C14-C25 (12)   520.00   400.00

Counterfeits of No. C25 exist.

1929, Aug. 23   Unwmk.
C26 AP5 4c olive brown   3.00   3.00

The design was redrawn for Nos. C14-C26. The numerals are narrower, "CENTS" is 1mm high instead of 2½mm and imprint letters touch the bottom frame line.

Pegasus AP6

1929-43   Engr.   Perf. 12½
Size: 34x23mm
C27 AP6 1c red lilac
         ('30)   .40   .40
C28 AP6 1c dk blue
         ('32)   .40   .40
C29 AP6 2c yellow ('30)   .40   .40
C30 AP6 2c olive grn
         ('32)   .40   .40
C31 AP6 4c Prus blue
         ('30)   .70   .70

C32	AP6	4c car rose ('32)	.70 .70
C33	AP6	6c dull vio ('30)	.70 .70
C34	AP6	6c red brown ('32)	.70 .70
C35	AP6	8c red orange	3.00 2.50
C36	AP6	8c gray ('30)	4.00 3.00
C36A	AP6	8c brt green ('43)	2.50 2.00
C37	AP6	16c indigo	2.00 1.50
C38	AP6	16c rose ('30)	3.25 3.00
C39	AP6	24c claret	3.00 2.50
C40	AP6	24c brt violet ('30)	4.25 3.50
C41	AP6	30c bister	3.00 2.75
C42	AP6	30c dk green ('30)	2.00 1.50
C43	AP6	40c dk brown	5.50 5.00
C44	AP6	40c yel org ('30)	6.00 5.00
C45	AP6	60c blue green	5.00 3.25
C46	AP6	60c emerald ('30)	8.50 7.00
C47	AP6	60c dp orange ('31)	3.00 2.00
C48	AP6	80c dk ultra	8.00 7.00
C49	AP6	80c green ('30)	15.00 12.00
C50	AP6	90c light blue	8.00 6.00
C51	AP6	90c dk olive grn ('30)	15.00 12.00
C52	AP6	1p car rose ('30)	10.00 7.50
C53	AP6	1.20p olive grn ('30)	22.00 20.00
C54	AP6	1.20p dp car ('30)	30.00 26.00
C55	AP6	1.50p red brown ('30)	25.00 20.00
C56	AP6	1.50p blk brn ('30)	20.00 15.00
C57	AP6	3p deep red	40.00 35.00
C58	AP6	3p ultra ('30)	30.00 25.00
C59	AP6	4.50p black	75.00 55.00
C60	AP6	4.50p violet ('30)	45.00 35.00
C60A	AP6	10p dp ultra ('43)	17.00 12.00
		Nos. C27-C60A (36)	419.40 336.40

See Nos. C63-C82. For surcharges see Nos. C106-C112, C114 in Scott Standard catalogue, Vol. 6.

Nos. 450, 452 Overprinted in Red

1934, Jan. 1   **Perf. 11½**

C61	A130	17c ver, gray & vio	20.00 15.00
a.		Sheet of 6	140.00
b.		Gray omitted	150.00
c.		Double overprint	150.00
C62	A130	36c red, blk & yel	20.00 15.00
a.		Sheet of 6	140.00

7th Pan-American Conference, Montevideo.

Pegasus Type of 1929
1935   **Engr.**   **Perf. 12½**
Size: 31½x21mm

C63	AP6	15c dull yellow	2.50 2.00
C64	AP6	22c brick red	1.50 1.40
C65	AP6	30c brown violet	2.50 2.00
C66	AP6	37c gray lilac	1.40 1.00
C67	AP6	40c rose lake	2.00 1.40
C68	AP6	47c rose	4.00 3.50
C69	AP6	50c Prus blue	1.40 .80
C70	AP6	52c dp ultra	4.00 3.50
C71	AP6	57c grnsh blue	2.00 1.75
C72	AP6	62c olive green	1.75 .80
C73	AP6	87c gray green	5.00 4.00
C74	AP6	1p olive	3.50 2.25
C75	AP6	1.12p brown red	3.50 2.25
C76	AP6	1.20p bister brn	15.00 12.00
C77	AP6	1.27p red brown	15.00 13.00
C78	AP6	1.62p rose	10.00 9.00
C79	AP6	2p brown rose	17.00 14.00
C80	AP6	2.12p dk slate grn	17.00 14.00
C81	AP6	3p dull blue	15.00 13.00
C82	AP6	5p orange	60.00 60.00
		Nos. C63-C82 (20)	184.05 161.65

Counterfeits exist.
For surcharges, see Nos. C106-C112 in the Scott Standard Catalogue Vol. 6.

Power Dam on Rio Negro — AP7

Imprint: "Imp. Nacional" at center

1937-41   **Litho.**

C83	AP7	20c lt green ('38)	5.50 4.00
C84	AP7	35c red brown ('38)	8.00 6.50
C85	AP7	62c blue grn ('38)	.80 .30
C86	AP7	60c yel org ('38)	2.00 1.50
C86A	AP7	68c pale vio brn ('41)	1.75 .70
C87	AP7	75c violet ('38)	7.50 5.00
C88	AP7	1p dp pink ('38)	2.50 1.75
C89	AP7	1.38p rose ('38)	25.00 20.00
C90	AP7	3p dk blue ('40)	17.00 12.00
		Nos. C83-C90 (9)	70.05 51.75

Imprint at left

C91	AP7	8c pale green ('39)	.60 .50
C92	AP7	20c lt green ('38)	2.00 1.50

For surcharge and overprint see Nos. 545, C120 in Scott Standard catalogue, Vol. 6.

Plane over Sculptured Oxcart — AP8

1939-44   **Perf. 12½**

C93	AP8	20c slate	.50 .40
C94	AP8	20c lt violet ('43)	.80 .80
C95	AP8	20c blue ('44)	.60 .40
C96	AP8	35c red	1.00 .80
C97	AP8	50c brown org	1.00 .30
C98	AP8	75c deep pink	1.10 .25
C99	AP8	1p dp blue ('40)	3.25 .60
C100	AP8	1.38p brt vio	5.50 2.25
C101	AP8	1.38p yel org ('44)	5.00 4.00
C102	AP8	2p blue	8.00 1.40
a.		Perf. 11	7.00 1.10
C103	AP8	5p rose lilac	10.00 2.25
C104	AP8	5p blue grn ('44)	15.00 7.00
C105	AP8	10p rose ('40)	100.00 65.00
		Nos. C93-C105 (13)	151.75 85.45

Counterfeits exist. These differ in design detail and are perfed other than 12.
For surcharges see Nos. C116-C119 in Scott Standard catalogue, Vol. 6.

SPECIAL DELIVERY STAMPS

No. 242 Overprinted

1921, Aug.   **Unwmk.**   **Perf. 11½**

E1	A97	2c fawn	.70 .25
a.		Double overprint	4.25

Caduceus — SD1

Imprint: "IMP. NACIONAL."
1922, Dec. 2   **Litho.**   **Wmk. 188**
Size: 21x27mm

E2	SD1	2c light red	.50 .25

1924, Oct. 1

E3	SD1	2c pale ultra	.50 .25

1928   **Unwmk.**   **Perf. 11**

E4	SD1	2c light blue	.50 .25

Imprint: "IMPRA. NACIONAL."
1928-36   **Wmk. 188**
Size: 16½x19½mm.

E5	SD1	2c black, *green*	.25 .25

Unwmk.

E6	SD1	2c blue green ('29)	.25 .25
		Perf. 11½, 12½	
E7	SD1	2c blue ('36)	.25 .25
		Nos. E5-E7 (3)	.75 .75

LATE FEE STAMPS

Galleon and Modern Steamship — LF1

Wmk. Crossed Keys in Sheet
1936, May 18   **Litho.**   **Perf. 11**

I1	LF1	3c green	.25 .25
I2	LF1	5c violet	.25 .25
I3	LF1	6c blue green	.25 .25
I4	LF1	7c brown	.25 .25
I5	LF1	8c carmine	.50 .50
I6	LF1	12c deep blue	.65 .65
		Nos. I1-I6 (6)	2.15 2.15

POSTAGE DUE STAMPS

D1

1902   **Unwmk.**   **Engr.**   **Perf. 14 to 15**
Size: 21¼x18½mm

J1	D1	1c blue green	.50 .25
J2	D1	2c carmine	.50 .25
J3	D1	4c gray violet	.80 .25
J4	D1	10c dark blue	1.25 .25
J5	D1	20c ocher	2.00 .80
		Nos. J1-J5 (5)	5.05 1.80

Surcharged in Red

1904

J6	D1	1c on 10c dk bl	1.00 1.00
a.		Inverted surcharge	10.00 10.00

1913-15   **Litho.**   **Perf. 11½**
Size: 22½x20mm

J7	D1	1c lt grn	.60 .25
J8	D1	2c rose red	.60 .25
J9	D1	4c dl vio	.80 .25
J10	D1	6c dp brn	1.00 .40
		Size: 21¼x19mm	
J11	D1	10c dl bl	1.00 .40
		Nos. J7-J11 (5)	4.00 1.55

Imprint: "Imprenta Nacional"
1922   **Size: 20x17mm**

J12	D1	1c bl grn	.25 .25
J13	D1	2c red	.25 .25
J14	D1	3c red brn	.50 .25
J15	D1	4c brn vio	.30 .25
J16	D1	5c blue	.50 .25
J17	D1	10c gray grn	.50 .25
		Nos. J12-J17 (6)	2.30 1.50

1926-27   **Wmk. 188**   **Perf. 11**
Size: 20x17mm

J18	D1	1c bl grn ('27)	.50 .25
J19	D1	2c red brn ('27)	.50 .25
J20	D1	5c slate blue	.50 .25
J21	D1	6c light brown	.50 .25
		Nos. J18-J21 (4)	2.00 1.25

1929   **Unwmk.**   **Perf. 10½, 11**

J22	D1	1c blue green	.25 .25
J23	D1	10c gray green	.50 .25

Figure of Value Redrawn (Flat on sides)
1932   **Wmk. 188**

J24	D1	6c yel brn	.50 .25

Imprint: "Casa A. Barreiro Ramos S. A."
1935   **Unwmk.**   **Litho.**   **Perf. 12½**
Size: 20x17mm

J25	D1	4c violet	.50 .25
J26	D1	5c rose	.50 .25

Type of 1935
Imprint: "Imprenta Nacional" at right
1938

J27	D1	1c blue green	.25 .25
J28	D1	2c red brown	.25 .25
J29	D1	3c deep pink	.25 .25
J30	D1	4c light violet	.25 .25
J31	D1	5c blue	.25 .25
J32	D1	8c rose	.25 .25
		Nos. J27-J32 (6)	1.50 1.50

OFFICIAL STAMPS

Regular Issues Handstamped in Black, Red or Blue

Many double and inverted impressions exist of the handstamped overprints on Nos. O1-O83. Prices are the same as for normal stamps or slightly more.

On Stamps of 1877-79
1880-82   **Unwmk.**   **Rouletted 8**

O1	A9	1c red brown	4.00 3.50
O2	A10	5c green	3.00 2.50
O3	A11	20c bister	3.25 3.25
O4	A11	50c black	22.00 22.00
O5	A12	1p blue	22.00 22.00
		Nos. O1-O5 (5)	54.25 53.25

On No. 44
Rouletted 6

O6	A9	1c brown ('81)	6.00 6.00

On Nos. 43-43A
Rouletted 8

O7	A11	50c black (R)	17.00 16.00
O8	A12	1p blue (R)	22.50 20.00

On Nos. 45, 41, 37a
Perf. 12½

O9	A13	7c blue (R) ('81)	4.25 3.25
		Rouletted 8	
O10	A11	10c ver (Bl)	2.00 2.00
		Perf. 13½	
O11	A8b	15c yellow (Bl)	5.00 4.50

1883   **On Nos. 46-47**   **Perf. 12½**

O12	A14	1c green	6.50 6.50
O13	A14a	2c rose	9.50 9.50

On Nos. 50-51
Perf. 12½, 12x12½, 13

O14	A17	5c blue (R)	4.00 4.00
a.		Imperf., pair	4.50
O15	A18	10c brown (Bl)	6.50 6.50
a.		Imperf., pair	6.00

No. 48 Handstamped

1884   **Perf. 12½**

O16	A15	1c green	35.00 32.50

Overprinted Type "a" in Black
On Nos. 48-49
1884   **Perf. 12, 12x12½, 13**

O17	A15	1c green	35.00 32.50
O18	A16	2c red	12.00 9.50

On Nos. 53-56
Rouletted 8

O19	A11	1c on 10c ver	2.00 1.60
a.		Small "1" (No. 53a)	5.00
		Perf. 12½	
O20	A14a	2c rose	6.50 6.50
O21	A22	5c ultra	6.50 6.50
O22	A23	5c blue	5.00 2.00
		Nos. O17-O22 (6)	67.00 58.60

On Stamps of 1884-88

1884-89			Rouletted 8	
O23	A24	1c gray	12.00	5.50
O24	A24	1c green ('88)	2.50	1.60
O25	A24	1c olive grn	3.25	1.75
O26	A24a	2c vermilion	1.00	.60
O27	A24a	2c rose ('88)	2.25	1.25
O28	A24b	5c slate blue	2.25	1.25
O29	A24b	5c slate bl, bl	6.50	5.00
O30	A24b	5c violet ('88)	6.50	5.00
O31	A24b	5c lt blue ('89)	6.50	5.00
O32	A25	7c dk brown	3.25	1.60
O33	A25	7c orange ('89)	3.25	2.25
O34	A26	10c olive brn	2.00	.90
O35	A30	10c violet ('89)	16.00	9.50
O36	A27	20c red violet	3.00	1.60
O37	A27	20c bister brn ('89)	16.00	7.00
O38	A28	25c gray violet	3.50	2.50
O39	A28	25c vermilion ('89)	16.00	7.00
		Nos. O23-O39 (17)	105.75	59.30

The OFICIAL handstamp, type "a," was also applied to No. 73, the 5c violet with "Provisorio" overprint, but it was not regularly issued.

1887	On No. 71	Rouletted 9
O40 A29	10c lilac	5.00

No. O40 was not regularly issued.

On Stamps of 1889-1899
Perf. 12½ to 15 and Compound

1890-1900				
O41	A32	1c green	.80	.25
O43	A32	1c blue ('95)	2.00	2.00
O44	A33	2c rose	.80	.25
O45	A33	2c red brn ('95)	2.50	2.50
O46	A33	2c orange ('00)	.80	.80
O47	A34	5c deep blue	1.50	1.50
O48	A34	5c rose ('95)	2.00	2.00
O49	A35	7c bister brown	1.25	.80
O50	A35	7c green ('95)	25.00	
O51	A36	10c blue green	1.25	.80
O52	A36	10c orange ('95)	25.00	
O53	A37	20c orange	1.25	.80
O54	A37	20c brown ('95)	25.00	
O55	A38	25c red brown	1.25	.80
O56	A38	25c ver ('95)	55.00	
O57	A39	50c lt blue	4.50	4.50
O58	A39	50c lilac ('95)	5.50	5.50
O59	A40	1p lilac	7.00	5.00
O60	A40	1p lt blue ('95)	40.00	22.50

Nos. O50, O52, O54, O56 and O60 were not regularly issued.

1891	On No. 99	Rouletted 8	
O61	A24b 5c violet	1.50	1.25
a.	"1391"	9.00	

On Stamps of 1895-99
Perf. 12½ to 15 and Compound

1895-1900				
O62	A51	1c bister	.60	.60
O63	A51	1c slate blue ('97)	1.25	.55
O64	A52	2c blue	.25	.25
O65	A52	2c claret ('97)	1.25	.55
O66	A53	5c red	.80	.55
O67	A53	5c green ('97)	1.25	.55
O68	A53	5c grnsh blue ('00)	.95	.75
O69	A54	7c deep green	.50	.50
O70	A55	10c brown	.50	.50
O71	A56	20c green & blk	.80	.80
O72	A56	20c claret & blk ('97)	4.50	2.25
O73	A57	25c red brn & blk	.80	.80
O74	A57	25c pink & bl ('97)	4.50	2.25
O75	A58	50c blue & blk	.95	.95
O76	A58	50c grn & brn ('97)	5.75	2.75
O77	A59	1p org brn & blk	4.75	4.75
O78	A59	1p yel brn & bl ('97)	9.25	5.75
a.		Inverted overprint		
		Nos. O62-O78 (17)	38.65	25.10

1897, Sept.	On Nos. 133-135		
O79	A62	1c brown vio & blk	1.25	1.00
O80	A63	5c pale bl & blk	1.75	1.00
O81	A64	10c lake & blk	1.75	1.10
		Nos. O79-O81 (3)	4.75	3.10

Perf. 12½ to 15 and Compound

1897-1900	On Nos. 136-137		
O82	A68	10c red	2.50	1.50
O83	A68	10c red lilac ('00)	1.25	1.25

Regular Issue of 1900-01 Overprinted

1901			Perf. 14 to 16	
O84	A72	1c yellow green	.50	.25
O85	A75	2c vermilion	.65	.25
O86	A73	5c dull blue	.65	.25
O87	A76	7c brown orange	.90	.50

O88	A74	10c gray violet	.95	.55
O89	A37	20c lt blue	8.00	4.00
O90	A38	25c bister brown	1.60	.80
O91	A40	1p deep green	10.50	6.00
a.		Inverted overprint	12.50	8.00
		Nos. O84-O91 (8)	23.75	12.60

Most of the used official stamps of 1901-1928 have been punched with holes of various shapes, in addition to the postal cancellations.

Regular Issue of 1904-05 Overprinted

1905			Perf. 11½	
O92	A79	1c green	.50	.25
O93	A80	2c orange red	.50	.25
O94	A81	5c deep blue	.50	.25
O95	A82	10c dark violet	1.00	.40
O96	A83	20c gray green	3.25	1.00
a.		Inverted overprint		
O97	A84	25c olive bister	2.25	.80
		Nos. O92-O97 (6)	8.00	2.95

Regular Issues of 1904-07 Overprinted

1907, Mar.				
O98	A79	1c green	.25	.25
O99	A86	5c deep blue	.25	.25
O100	A86	7c orange brown	.25	.25
O101	A82	10c dark violet	.25	.25
O102	A83	20c gray green	.40	.35
a.		Inverted overprint	4.00	
O103	A84	25c olive bister	.50	.40
O104	A86	50c rose	.95	.70
		Nos. O98-O104 (7)	2.85	2.45

Regular Issues of 1900-10 Overprinted

1910, July 15			Perf. 14½ to 16	
O105	A75	2c vermilion	8.75	4.00
O106	A73	5c slate green	5.25	3.00
O107	A74	10c gray violet	2.75	1.25
O108	A37	20c grnsh blue	2.75	1.25
O109	A38	25c bister brown	4.50	2.40
		Perf. 11½		
O110	A86	50c rose	6.00	2.50
a.		Inverted overprint	20.00	15.00
		Nos. O105-O110 (6)	30.00	14.40

Peace—O1

1911, Feb. 18			Litho.	
O111	O1	2c red brown	.40	.40
O112	O1	5c dark blue	.40	.40
O113	O1	8c slate	.40	.65
O114	O1	20c gray brown	.55	.95
O115	O1	23c claret	.80	.95
O116	O1	50c orange	1.60	1.25
O117	O1	1p red	4.00	1.50
		Nos. O111-O117 (7)	8.15	5.95

Regular Issue of 1912-15 Overprinted

1915, Sept. 16				
O118	A90	2c carmine	.55	.40
O119	A90	5c dark blue	.55	.40
O120	A90	8c ultra	.55	.40
O121	A90	20c dark brown	1.25	.50
O122	A91	23c dark blue	4.00	3.50

O123	A91	50c orange	6.00	3.50
O124	A91	1p vermilion	8.00	4.00
		Nos. O118-O124 (7)	20.90	12.70

Regular Issue of 1919 Overprinted

1919, Dec. 25				
O125	A95	2c red & black	.80	.40
a.		Inverted overprint	3.50	
O126	A95	5c ultra & blk	.95	.40
O127	A95	8c gray bl & lt brn	.95	.40
a.		Inverted overprint	3.50	
O128	A95	20c brown & blk	2.00	.80
O129	A95	23c green & brn	2.00	.80
O130	A95	50c brown & bl	4.00	2.00
O131	A95	1p dull red & bl	10.00	4.00
a.		Double overprint	15.00	
		Nos. O125-O131 (7)	20.70	8.80

Regular Issue of 1923 Overprinted

1924	Wmk. 189		Perf. 12½	
O132	A100	2c violet	.25	.25
O133	A100	5c light blue	.25	.25
O134	A100	12c deep blue	.30	.25
O135	A100	20c buff	.40	.25
O136	A100	36c blue green	1.75	1.25
O137	A100	50c orange	3.50	2.50
O138	A100	1p pink	6.25	5.00
O139	A100	2p lt green	12.00	10.00
		Nos. O132-O139 (8)	24.70	19.75

Same Overprint on Regular Issue of 1924

1926-27	Unwmk.		Imperf.	
O140	A100	2c rose lilac	.40	.25
O141	A100	5c pale blue	.65	.25
O142	A100	8c pink ('27)	.80	.25
O143	A100	12c slate blue	.95	.25
O144	A100	20c brown	2.00	.40
O145	A100	36c dull rose	3.25	.95
		Nos. O140-O145 (6)	8.05	2.35

Regular Issue of 1924 Overprinted

1928			Perf. 12½	
O146	A100	2c rose lilac	1.50	.95
O147	A100	8c pink	1.50	.50
O148	A100	10c turq blue	2.00	.50
		Nos. O146-O148 (3)	5.00	1.95

Since 1928, instead of official stamps, Uruguay has used envelopes with "S. O." printed on them, and stamps of many issues which are punched with various designs such as star or crescent.

NEWSPAPER STAMPS

No. 245 Surcharged

1922, June 1	Unwmk.	Perf. 11½	
P1	A97 3c on 4c orange	.40	.40
a.	Inverted surcharge	9.50	9.50
b.	Double surcharge	2.50	2.50

Nos. 235-237 Surcharged

1924, June 1			Perf. 14½	
P2	A96	3c on 2c car & blk	.40	.40
P3	A96	6c on 4c red org & bl	.40	.40
P4	A96	9c on 5c bl & brn	.40	.40
		Nos. P2-P4 (3)	1.20	1.20

Nos. 288, 291, 293 Overprinted or Surcharged in Red

1926			Imperf.	
P5	A100	3c gray green	.80	.25
a.		Double overprint	1.00	1.00
P6	A100	9c on 10c turq bl	.95	.40
a.		Double overprint	1.00	1.00
P7	A100	15c light violet	1.25	.50
		Nos. P5-P7 (3)	3.00	1.15

PARCEL POST STAMPS

Mercury — PP1

Imprint: "IMPRENTA NACIONAL"
Inscribed "Exterior"
Size: 20x29½mm
Perf. 11½

1922, Jan. 15	Litho.	Unwmk.	
Q1	PP1 5c grn, straw	.25	.25
Q2	PP1 10c grn, bl gray	.40	.25
Q3	PP1 20c grn, rose	2.10	.55
Q4	PP1 30c grn, grn	2.10	.55
Q5	PP1 50c grn, blue	3.50	.40
Q6	PP1 1p grn, org	5.25	1.60
	Nos. Q1-Q6 (6)	13.60	3.30

Inscribed "Interior"

Q7	PP1 5c grn, straw	.25	.25
Q8	PP1 10c grn, bl gray	.25	.25
Q9	PP1 20c grn, rose	1.00	.25
Q10	PP1 30c grn, grn	1.40	.25
Q11	PP1 50c grn, blue	2.25	.35
Q12	PP1 1p grn, org	6.00	1.25
	Nos. Q7-Q12 (6)	11.15	2.60

Imprint: "IMP. NACIONAL"
Inscribed "Exterior"

1926, Jan. 20		Perf. 11½	
Q13	PP1 20c grn, rose	1.75	.50

Inscribed "Interior"
Perf. 11

Q14	PP1 5c grn, yellow	.40	.25
Q15	PP1 10c grn, bl gray	.50	.25
Q16	PP1 20c grn, rose	1.00	.25
Q17	PP1 30c grn, bl grn	1.75	.40
	Nos. Q13-Q17 (5)	5.40	1.65

Inscribed "Exterior"

1926		Perf. 11½	
Q18	PP1 5c blk, straw	.40	.25
Q19	PP1 10c blk, bl gray	.65	.25
Q20	PP1 20c blk, rose	1.75	.25

Inscribed "Interior"

Q21	PP1 5c blk, straw	.40	.25
Q22	PP1 10c blk, bl gray	.50	.25
Q23	PP1 20c blk, rose	1.00	.25
Q24	PP1 30c blk, bl grn	1.75	.40
	Nos. Q18-Q24 (7)	6.45	1.90

PP2   PP3

Perf. 11, 11½

1927, Feb. 22   **Wmk. 188**

Q25	PP2	1c dp bl	.25	.25
Q26	PP2	2c lt grn	.25	.25
Q27	PP2	4c violet	.25	.25
Q28	PP2	5c red	.25	.25
Q29	PP2	10c dk brn	.40	.25
Q30	PP2	20c orange	.65	.40
	Nos. Q25-Q30 (6)		2.05	1.65

See Nos. Q35-Q38, Q51-Q54 (in Scott Standard catalogue, Vol. 6).

Size: 15x20mm

1928, Nov. 20   **Perf. 11**

Q31	PP3	5c blk, *straw*	.25	.25
Q32	PP3	10c blk, *gray blue*	.25	.25
Q33	PP3	20c blk, *rose*	.50	.25
Q34	PP3	30c blk, *green*	.80	.25
	Nos. Q31-Q34 (4)		1.80	1.00

Type of 1927 Issue

1929-30   **Unwmk.**   **Perf. 11, 12½**

Q35	PP2	1c violet	.25	.25
Q36	PP2	1c ultra ('30)	.25	.25
Q37	PP2	2c bl grn ('30)	.25	.25
Q38	PP2	5c red ('30)	.25	.25
	Nos. Q35-Q38 (4)		1.00	1.00

Nos. Q35-Q38, and possibly later issues, occasionally show parts of a papermaker's watermark.

PP4

1929, July 27   **Wmk. 188**   **Perf. 11**

Q39	PP4	10c orange	.50	.50
Q40	PP4	15c slate blue	.50	.50
Q41	PP4	20c ol brn	.50	.50
Q42	PP4	25c rose red	1.00	.50
Q43	PP4	50c dark gray	2.00	1.00
Q44	PP4	75c violet	8.00	6.00
Q45	PP4	1p gray green	7.50	3.00
	Nos. Q39-Q45 (7)		20.00	12.00

For overprints see Nos. Q57-Q63 in Scott Standard catalogue, Vol. 6.

Ship and Train — PP5

1938-39   **Unwmk.**   **Perf. 12½**

Q46	PP5	10c scarlet	.40	.25
Q47	PP5	20c dk bl	.60	.25
Q48	PP5	30c lt vio ('39)	.95	.25
Q49	PP5	50c green	1.75	.25
Q50	PP5	1p brn org	2.50	1.10
	Nos. Q46-Q50 (5)		6.20	2.10

See Nos. Q70-Q73, Q80, Q88-Q90, Q92-Q93, Q95 in Scott Standard catalogue, Vol. 6.

VATICAN CITY

'va-ti-kən 'si-tē

LOCATION — Western Italy, directly outside the western boundary of Rome

GOVT. — Independent state subject to certain political restrictions under a treaty with Italy

AREA — 108.7 acres

POP. — 1,000 (est.)

100 Centesimi = 1 Lira

Catalogue values for unused stamps in this country are for Never Hinged items, beginning with Scott 68 in the regular postage section, Scott C1 in the airpost section, and Scott E3 in the special delivery section.

Watermark

Wmk. 235 —
Crossed Keys

Papal Arms — A1   Pope Pius XI — A2

Unwmk.
1929, Aug. 1   Engr.   Perf. 14
Surface-Colored Paper

1	A1	5c dk brn & pink	.25	.25
		Never hinged	.40	
		On cover		8.00
2	A1	10c dk grn & lt grn	.25	.35
		Never hinged	.80	
		On cover		4.00
3	A1	20c violet & lilac	.75	.65
		Never hinged	2.60	
		On cover		3.25
4	A1	25c dk bl & lt bl	.95	.75
		Never hinged	3.00	
		On cover		3.25
5	A1	30c indigo & yellow	1.10	.85
		Never hinged	2.75	
		On cover		3.25
6	A1	50c ind & sal buff	1.60	.90
		Never hinged	4.25	
		On cover		3.25
7	A1	75c brn car & gray	2.25	1.50
		Never hinged	6.00	
		On cover		4.00

Photo.
White Paper

8	A2	80c carmine rose	1.60	.50
		Never hinged	4.25	
		On cover		2.40
9	A2	1.25 l dark blue	2.60	1.10
		Never hinged	6.75	
		On cover		4.00
10	A2	2 l olive brown	5.25	2.25
		Never hinged	18.00	
		On cover		12.00
11	A2	2.50 l red orange	4.50	3.75
		Never hinged	14.50	
		On cover		65.00
12	A2	5 l dk green	5.25	12.00
		Never hinged	18.00	
		On cover		80.00
13	A2	10 l olive blk	11.00	17.00
		Never hinged	37.50	
		On cover		100.00
		Nos. 1-13,E1-E2 (15)	74.85	75.35
		Set, never hinged	265.00	

The stamps of Type A1 have, in this and subsequent issues, the words "POSTE VATI-CANE" in rows of colorless letters in the background.

For surcharges and overprints see Nos. 14, 35-40, 61-67, J1-J6, Q1-Q13.

No. 5 Surcharged in Red

1931, Oct. 1

14	A1	25c on 30c ind & yel	3.00	2.25
		Never hinged	10.00	

Arms of Pope Pius XI — A5

Vatican Palace and Obelisk — A6

Vatican Gardens — A7

Pope Pius XI A8

St. Peter's Basilica A9

1933, May 31   Engr.   Wmk. 235

19	A5	5c copper red	.25	.25
		Never hinged	.30	
		On cover		12.00
a.		Imperf., pair	600.00	825.00
20	A6	10c dk brn & blk	.25	.25
		Never hinged	.30	
		On cover		4.75
21	A6	12½c dp grn & blk	.25	.25
		Never hinged	.30	
		On cover		47.50
22	A6	20c orange & blk	.25	.25
		Never hinged	.30	
		On cover		2.40
a.		Vertical pair imperf. between and at bottom	750.00	
23	A6	25c dk olive & blk	.25	.25
		Never hinged	.30	
		On cover		2.40
a.		Imperf., pair	425.00	600.00
24	A7	30c blk & dk brn	.25	.25
		Never hinged	.30	
		On cover		4.00
25	A7	50c vio & dk brn	.25	.25
		Never hinged	.30	
		On cover		4.00
26	A7	75c brn red & dk brn	.25	.25
		Never hinged	.30	
		On cover		4.00
27	A7	80c rose & dk brn	.25	.25
		Never hinged	.30	
		On cover		4.00
28	A8	1 l violet & blk	7.50	7.50
		Never hinged	32.00	
		On cover		24.00
29	A8	1.25 l dk bl & blk	22.50	13.50
		Never hinged	95.00	
		On cover		47.50
30	A8	2 l dk brn & blk	52.50	37.50
		Never hinged	220.00	
		On cover		80.00
31	A8	2.75 l dk vio & blk	67.50	90.00
		Never hinged	270.00	
		On cover		200.00
32	A9	5 l blk brn & dk grn	.25	.25
		Never hinged	.30	
		On cover		32.50
33	A9	10 l dk bl & dk grn	.25	.30
		Never hinged	.30	
		On cover		24.00
34	A9	20 l blk & dp grn	.40	.50
		Never hinged	1.00	
		On cover		95.00
		Nos. 19-34,E3-E4 (18)	153.85	152.70
		Set, never hinged	620.00	

Nos. 8-13 Surcharged in Black

No. 36

No. 36a

1934, June 16   Unwmk.

35	A2	40c on 80c	45.00	20.00
		Never hinged	62.50	
		On cover		80.00
36	A2	1.30 l on 1.25 l	180.00	100.00
		Never hinged	450.00	
		On cover		300.00
a.		Small figures "30" in "1.30"	24,000.	16,000.
		Never hinged	30,000.	
37	A2	2.05 l on 2 l	240.00	32.50
		Never hinged	500.00	
		On cover		95.00
a.		No comma btwn. 2 & 0	550.00	40.00
		Never hinged	1,200.	
38	A2	2.55 l on 2.50 l	150.00	275.00
		Never hinged	375.00	
		On cover		800.00
a.		No comma btwn. 2 & 5	200.00	300.00
		Never hinged	500.00	
39	A2	3.05 l on 5 l	500.00	450.00
		Never hinged	1,200.	
		On cover		1,450.
40	A2	3.70 l on 10 l	450.00	600.00
		Never hinged	1,100.	
		On cover		2,200.
a.		No comma btwn. 3 & 7		
		Nos. 35-40 (6)	1,565.	1,477.
		Set, never hinged	3,680.	

A second printing of Nos. 36-40 was made in 1937. The 2.55 l and 3.05 l of the first printing and 1.30 l of the second printing sell for more.

The status of No. 40a has been questioned. The editors would like to examine an authenticated example of this variety.

Forged surcharges of Nos. 35-40 are plentiful.

Tribonian Presenting Pandects to Justinian I A10

Pope Gregory IX Promulgating Decretals A11

1935, Feb. 1   Photo.

41	A10	5c red orange	4.50	4.50
		Never hinged	20.00	
		On cover		32.50
42	A10	10c purple	4.50	4.50
		Never hinged	20.00	
		On cover		32.50
43	A10	25c green	25.00	35.00
		Never hinged	125.00	
		On cover		120.00
44	A11	75c rose red	65.00	60.00
		Never hinged	310.00	
		On cover		200.00
45	A11	80c dark brown	55.00	42.50
		Never hinged	260.00	
		On cover		140.00
46	A11	1.25 l dark blue	65.00	52.50
		Never hinged	310.00	
		On cover		180.00
		Nos. 41-46 (6)	219.00	199.00
		Set, never hinged	1,045.	

Intl. Juridical Congress, Rome, 1934.

Doves and Bell — A12

Allegory of Church and Bible — A13

St. John Bosco — A14   St. Francis de Sales — A15

1936, June 22

47	A12	5c blue green	1.50	1.50
		Never hinged	7.00	
		On cover		16.00
48	A13	10c black	1.50	1.50
		Never hinged	7.00	
		On cover		16.00
49	A14	25c yellow green	45.00	15.00
		Never hinged	210.00	
		On cover		80.00
50	A12	50c rose violet	1.50	1.50
		Never hinged	7.00	
		On cover		16.00
51	A13	75c rose red	47.50	60.00
		Never hinged	225.00	
		On cover		275.00
52	A14	80c orange brn	2.60	3.00
		Never hinged	12.50	
		On cover		32.50
53	A15	1.25 l dark blue	3.00	3.00
		Never hinged	13.50	
		On cover		32.50
54	A15	5 l dark brown	3.00	7.50
		Never hinged	13.00	
		On cover		80.00
		Nos. 47-54 (8)	105.60	93.00
		Set, never hinged	495.00	

Catholic Press Conference, 1936.

Crypt of St. Cecilia in Catacombs of St. Calixtus A16

Basilica of Sts. Nereus and Achilleus in Catacombs of St. Domitilla A17

1938, Oct. 12   Perf. 14

55	A16	5c bister brown	.40	.40
		Never hinged	1.00	
		On cover		16.00
56	A16	10c deep orange	.40	.40
		Never hinged	1.00	
		On cover		16.00
57	A16	25c deep green	.45	.40
		Never hinged	1.20	
		On cover		12.00
58	A17	75c deep rose	7.50	7.50
		Never hinged	26.00	
		On cover		72.50
59	A17	80c violet	20.00	20.00
		Never hinged	70.00	
		On cover		80.00
60	A17	1.25 l blue	29.00	29.00
		Never hinged	100.00	
		On cover		110.00
		Nos. 55-60 (6)	57.75	57.70
		Set, never hinged	200.00	

Intl. Christian Archaeological Congress, Rome, 1938.

Interregnum Issue

Nos. 1-7 Overprinted in Black

1939, Feb. 20   Perf. 14

61	A1	5c dk brn & pink	26.00	7.50
		Never hinged	100.00	
		On cover		16.00
62	A1	10c dk grn & lt grn	.75	.25
		Never hinged	2.75	
		On cover		2.40
63	A1	20c violet & lilac	.75	.25
		Never hinged	2.75	
		On cover		2.40
64	A1	25c dk bl & lt bl	3.25	5.00
		Never hinged	14.50	
		On cover		32.50
65	A1	30c indigo & yellow	1.25	.25
		Never hinged	5.00	
		On cover		2.40
a.		Pair, one without ovpt.	3,000.	

66	A1	50c indigo & sal buff	1.25	.25
		Never hinged	5.00	
		On cover		2.40
67	A1	75c brn car & gray	1.25	.25
		Never hinged	5.00	
		On cover		2.40
		Nos. 61-67 (7)	34.50	13.75
		Set, never hinged	135.00	

Catalogue values for unused stamps in this section, from this point to the end of the section, are for Never Hinged items.

Coronation of Pope
Pius XII — A18

1939, June 2 **Photo.**

68	A18	25c green	3.00	.40
		On cover		3.25
69	A18	75c rose red	.70	.70
		On cover		16.00
70	A18	80c violet	8.50	4.00
		On cover		16.00
71	A18	1.25 l deep blue	.70	.70
		On cover		16.00
		Nos. 68-71 (4)	12.90	5.80

Coronation of Pope Pius XII, Mar. 12, 1939.

Arms of Pope
Pius XII — A19

Pope Pius XII
A20   A21

Wmk. 235

1940, Mar. 12 **Engr.** **Perf. 14**

72	A19	5c dark carmine	.45	.25
		On cover		12.00
a.		Imperf, pair	1,100.	
73	A20	1 l purple & blk	.45	.25
		On cover		8.00
74	A21	1.25 l slate bl & blk	.45	.25
		On cover		6.50
a.		Imperf, pair	1,100.	1,200.
75	A20	2 l dk brn & blk	2.00	2.00
		On cover		12.00

76	A21	2.75 l dk rose vio & blk	2.50	2.50
		On cover		47.50
		Nos. 72-76 (5)	5.85	5.25

See Nos. 91-98 in Scott Standard catalogue, Vol. 6. For surcharges see Nos. 102-109 in Scott Standard catalogue, Vol. 6.

SEMI-POSTAL STAMPS

Holy Year Issue

Cross and Orb
SP1   SP2

1933 Unwmk. Engr. Perf. 13x13½

B1	SP1	25c + 10c green	4.75	4.75
		Never hinged	14.50	
		On cover		16.00
B2	SP1	75c + 15c scarlet	8.25	16.50
		Never hinged	28.00	
		On cover		47.50
B3	SP2	80c + 20c red brown	30.00	22.50
		Never hinged	115.00	
		On cover		70.00
B4	SP2	1.25 l + 25c ultra	9.00	17.00
		Never hinged	35.00	
		On cover		85.00
		Nos. B1-B4 (4)	52.00	60.75
		Set, never hinged	190.00	

AIR POST STAMPS

Catalogue values for unused stamps in this section are for Never Hinged items.

Statue of St.   Dove of
Peter   Peace over
AP1   Vatican
                         AP2

Elijah's   Our Lady of
Ascent into   Loreto and
Heaven   Angels
AP3   Moving the
                         Holy House
                         AP4

Wmk. 235

1938, June 22 **Engr.** **Perf. 14**

C1	AP1	25c brown	.30	.25
C2	AP2	50c green	.30	.25
C3	AP3	75c lake	.30	.30
C4	AP4	80c dark blue	.30	.45
C5	AP1	1 l violet	.90	.50
C6	AP2	2 l ultra	1.60	.80
C7	AP3	5 l slate blk	3.50	2.50
C8	AP4	10 l dk brown vio	3.50	2.50
		Nos. C1-C8 (8)	10.70	7.55

SPECIAL DELIVERY STAMPS

Pius XI
SD1

Unwmk.

1929, Aug. 1 **Photo.** **Perf. 14**

E1	SD1	2 l carmine rose	20.50	15.00
		Never hinged	82.50	
E2	SD1	2.50 l dark blue	17.00	18.50
		Never hinged	67.50	
		On cover		100.00

For overprints see Nos. Q14-Q15.

Catalogue values for unused stamps in this section, from this point to the end of the section, are for Never Hinged items.

Aerial
View of
Vatican
City
SD2

1933, May 31 **Wmk. 235** **Engr.**

E3	SD2	2 l rose red & brn	.35	.35
E4	SD2	2.50 l dp blue & brn	.35	.55

POSTAGE DUE STAMPS

Nos. 1-3 Overprinted
in Black and Brown

1931, Oct. 1 **Unwmk.** **Perf. 14**

J1	A1	5c dk brown & pink	.35	.75
		Never hinged	1.50	
		On cover		160.00
a.		Double frame	—	
J2	A1	10c dk grn & lt grn	.35	.75
		Never hinged	1.50	
		On cover		160.00
a.		Frame omitted	5,250.	
		Never hinged	6,000.	
J3	A1	20c violet & lilac	1.90	2.25
		Never hinged	7.00	
		On cover		200.00

No. 5 Surcharged

J4	A1	40c on 30c indigo & yel	2.25	6.00
		Never hinged	10.00	
		On cover		160.00

Nos. 10-11 Surcharged

J5	A2	60c on 2 l olive brn	40.00	30.00
		Never hinged	180.00	
		On cover		160.00
J6	A2	1.10 l on 2.50 l red org	11.00	22.50
		Never hinged	35.00	
		On cover		160.00
		Nos. J1-J6 (6)	55.85	62.25
		Set, never hinged	235.00	

In addition to the surcharges, #J4-J6 are overprinted with ornamental frame as on #J1-J3.

No. J5 is valued in the grade of fine.

PARCEL POST STAMPS

Nos. 1-7 Overprinted

1931, Oct. 1 **Unwmk.** **Perf. 14**

Q1	A1	5c dk brown & pink	.25	.55
		Never hinged	.75	
Q2	A1	10c dk grn & lt grn	.25	.55
		Never hinged	.75	
Q3	A1	20c violet & lilac	7.50	2.60
		Never hinged	25.00	
Q4	A1	25c dk bl & lt bl	11.00	5.50
		Never hinged	35.00	
Q5	A1	30c indigo & yel	7.50	5.50
		Never hinged	25.00	
Q6	A1	50c indigo & sal buff	7.50	5.50
		Never hinged	25.00	
Q7	A1	75c brn car & gray	1.50	5.50
		Never hinged	5.50	
a.		Inverted overprint	750.00	
		Never hinged	1,000.	

Nos. 8-13 Overprinted

Q8	A2	80c carmine rose	1.10	5.50
		Never hinged	4.00	
Q9	A2	1.25 l dark blue	1.50	5.50
		Never hinged	5.50	
Q10	A2	2 l olive brown	1.10	5.50
		Never hinged	4.00	
a.		Inverted overprint	750.00	900.00
		Never hinged	1,000.	
Q11	A2	2.50 l red orange	1.90	5.50
		Never hinged	6.50	
a.		Double overprint	750.00	
		Never hinged	1,300.	
b.		Inverted overprint	1,350.	
		Never hinged	2,400.	
Q12	A2	5 l dark green	1.90	5.50
		Never hinged	6.50	
Q13	A2	10 l olive black	1.50	5.50
		Never hinged	5.50	
a.		Double overprint	950.00	
		Never hinged	1,900.	

Nos. E1-E2
Overprinted
Vertically

Q14	SD1	2 l carmine rose	1.50	5.50
		Never hinged	5.50	
Q15	SD1	2.50 l dark blue	1.50	5.50
		Never hinged	5.50	
a.		Inverted overprint	750.00	
		Never hinged	1,300.	
		Nos. Q1-Q15 (15)	47.50	69.70
		Set, never hinged	160.00	

VENEZUELA

ˌve-nə-ˈzwā-lə

LOCATION — Northern coast of South America, bordering on the Caribbean Sea
GOVT. — Republic
AREA — 352,143 sq. mi.
POP. — 15,260,000 (est. 1984)
CAPITAL — Caracas

100 Centavos = 8 Reales = 1 Peso
100 Centesimos = 1 Venezolano (1879)
100 Centimos = 1 Bolivar (1880)

Catalogue values for unused stamps in this country are for Never Hinged items, beginning with Scott 743 in the regular postage section.

GREAT BRITAIN POST OFFICES IN VENEZUELA

LA GUAYRA
Pre-Stamp Postal Markings

Crowned Circle handstamp type II is pictured in the Crowned Circle Handstamps and Great Britain Used Abroad section.

1841
A1 II	"PAID AT LA GUAYRA" crowned circle handstamp in black, on cover	3,000.
	As A1, used as a canceler on British stamp, on cover	4,800.

Stamps of Great Britain Used in La Guayra
Canceled with "C60" in barred oval

1865-80
A2	½p rose red, plate 6 (#58)	—
A3	1p rose red, plates 81, 92, 96, 98, 111, 113, 115, 131, 138, 144, 145, 154, 177, 178, 180, 196 (#33), value from	60.00
A4	1½p lake red, plate 3 (#32)	—
A5	2p blue, plates 13, 14 (#30), value from	60.00
A6	3p rose, plates 14-19 (#61), value from	70.00
A7	4p vermilion, plates 7, 9, 11-14 (#43), value from	60.00
A8	4p vermilion, plate 15 (#69)	325.00
A9	4p pale olive green, plate 15 (#70)	240.00
	Plate 16 (#70)	240.00
A10	6p lilac, plate 5 (#45)	—
A11	6p violet, plates 6, 8 (#51)	—
A12	6p pale buff, plate 11 (#59b)	100.00
	Plate 12 (#59b)	125.00
A13	6p gray, plate 12 (#60)	225.00
A14	6p gray, plates 13-16 (#62), value from	60.00
A15	8p orange (#73)	350.00
A16	9p straw (#40)	—
A17	9p bister (#52)	—
A18	10p red brown (#53)	—
A19	1sh green (#48)	175.00
A20	1sh green, plates 4, 7 (#54)	—
A21	1sh green, plates 8-13 (#64), value from	55.00
A22	2sh blue (#55)	250.00
A23	5sh rose, plate 1 (#57)	525.00
	Plate 2 (#57)	675.00

CIUDAD BOLIVAR
Stamps of Great Britain
Canceled with "D22" in barred oval

1868-79
A30	1p rose red, plate 133 (#33)	250.00
A31	2p blue, plate 13 (#30)	—
A32	3p rose, plate 5 (#49)	—
A33	3p rose, plate 11 (#61)	300.00
A34	4p vermilion, plates 9, 11, 12, 14 (#43), value from	300.00
A35	4p pale olive green, plate 15 (#70)	450.00
	Plate 16 (#70)	450.00
A36	4p gray brown, plate 17 (#84)	1,000.
A37	9p bister (#52)	450.00
A38	10p red brown (#53)	—
A39	1sh green, plates 4, 5, 7 (#54), value from	325.00
A40	1sh green, plates 10, 12, 13 (#64), value from	500.00

A41	2sh blue (#55)	1,000.
A42	5sh rose, plate 1 (#57)	1,750.
	Plate 2 (#57)	2,000.

PORTO CABELLO

1841
A45 II	Crowned circle handstamp inscribed "POR-TO-CABELLO" in red, on cover	3,750.

Earliest known use: Dec. 15, 1841.

A crowned circle handstamp inscribed "MARACAIBO" exists in the General Post Office Proof Books, but no example used on cover has been recorded.

ISSUES OF THE REPUBLIC

Coat of Arms — A1

Fine Impression
No Dividing Line Between Stamps
Unwmk.

1859, Jan. 1   **Litho.**   *Imperf.*
1	A1	½r yellow	60.00	12.00
		On cover		*3,000.*
a.		½r orange		—
		On cover		*750.00*
b.		Greenish paper	225.00	
2	A1	1r blue	450.00	15.00
		On cover		*1,500.*
a.		Half used as ½r on cover		*7,500.*
3	A1	2r red	42.50	15.00
		On cover		*1,500.*
a.		2r dull rose red	55.00	17.00
		On cover		*1,500.*
b.		Half used as 1r on cover		*1,250.*
c.		Greenish paper	225.00	140.00
		Nos. 1-3 (3)	552.50	42.00

Coarse Impression

1859-62   **Thick Paper**
4	A1	½r orange ('61)	12.00	4.00
		On cover		*75.00*
a.		½r yellow ('59)	500.00	30.00
		On cover		*125.00*
b.		½r olive yellow	750.00	35.00
		On cover		*200.00*
c.		Bluish paper	575.00	
d.		½r dull rose (error)	250,000.	350,000.
5	A1	1r blue ('62)	20.00	12.50
		On cover		*2,500.*
a.		1r pale blue	35.00	15.00
		On cover		*2,500.*
b.		1r dark blue	35.00	15.00
		On cover		*2,500.*
c.		Half used as ½r on cover		*7,500.*
d.		Bluish paper	200.00	
6	A1	2r red ('62)	45.00	80.00
		On cover		*1,500.*
a.		2r dull rose	55.00	80.00
		On cover		*1,500.*
b.		Tête bêche pair	10,000.	
c.		Half used as 1r on cover		*400.00*
d.		Bluish paper	225.00	
		Nos. 4-6 (3)	77.00	96.50

In the fine impression, the background lines of the shield are more sharply drawn. In the coarse impression, the shading lines at each end of the scroll inscribed "LIBERTAD" are usually very heavy. Stamps of the coarse impression are closer together, and there is usually a dividing line between them.

Nos. 1-3 exist on thick paper and on bluish paper. Nos. 1-6 exist on pelure paper.

The greenish paper varieties (Nos. 1b and 3c) and the bluish paper varieties were not regularly issued.

Arms — A2

Eagle — A3

1862   **Litho.**
7	A2	¼c green	20.00	*200.00*
		On newsprint		
8	A2	½c dull lilac	8.00	*240.00*
		On newsprint		
a.		½c violet	40.00	210.00
		On newsprint		
9	A2	1c gray brown	42.50	*400.00*
		On newsprint		
		Nos. 7-9 (3)	70.50	*840.00*

Counterfeits are plentiful. Forged cancellations abound on Nos. 7-17.

1863-64
10	A3	½c pale red ('64)	55.00	*400.00*
		On cover		
a.		½c red	60.00	400.00
		On cover		
11	A3	1c slate ('64)	62.50	*160.00*
		On cover		
12	A3	½r orange	7.75	3.50
		On cover		*150.00*
13	A3	1r blue	17.00	8.50
		On cover		*500.00*
a.		1r pale blue	30.00	13.00
		On cover		*600.00*
b.		Half used as ½r on cover		*750.00*
14	A3	2r green	23.00	20.00
		On cover		*2,000.*
a.		2r deep yellow green	30.00	20.00
		On cover		*2,000.*
b.		Quarter used as ½r on cover		*7,500.*
c.		Half used as 1r on cover		*2,000.*

Counterfeits exist.

1865   **Redrawn**
15	A3	½r orange	4.00	*2.50*
		On cover		*3,000.*

The redrawn stamp has a broad "N" in "FEDERACION." "MEDIO REAL" and "FEDERACION" are in thin letters. There are 52 instead of 49 pearls in the circle.
No. 15 in yellow is a postal forgery.

A4

1865-70
16	A4	½c yel grn ('67)	275.00	*300.00*
		On cover		
17	A4	1c bl grn ('67)	275.00	*250.00*
		On cover		
18	A4	½r brn vio (thin paper)	9.50	2.00
		On cover		50.00
19	A4	½r lil rose ('70)	9.50	3.25
		On cover		50.00
a.		½r brownish rose	9.50	3.00
		On cover		50.00
b.		Tête bêche pair	200.00	600.00
		On cover		*5,000.*
20	A4	1r vermilion	45.00	15.00
		On cover		*1,000.*
a.		Half used as ½r on cover		*500.00*
21	A4	2r yellow	160.00	77.50
		On cover		*3,000.*
a.		Half used as 1r on cover		*3,000.*
		Nos. 16-21 (6)	774.00	647.75

This issue is known unofficially rouletted.
Postal forgeries exist of the ½r.
One quarter of #21 used as ½r is a postal forgery.
For overprints see Nos. 37-48.

Overprinted in Very Small Upright Letters "Bolivar Sucre Miranda — Decreto de 27 de Abril de 1870", or "Decreto de 27 de Junio 1870" in Slanting Letters

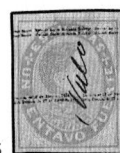

Simón Bolívar — A5

(The "Junio" overprint is continuously repeated, in four lines arranged in two pairs, with the second line of each pair inverted.)

Un	1		Siete	7
Dos	2		Nueve	9
Tres	3		Quince	15
Cuatro	4		Veinte	20
Cinco	5		Cincuenta	50

1871-76   **Litho.**
22	A5	1c yellow	1.50	.40
		On cover		*1,000.*
a.		1c orange	2.10	.45
b.		1c brown orange ('76)	2.10	.30
c.		1c pale buff ('76)	2.10	.45
d.		Laid paper	1.00	.75
23	A5	2c yellow	2.00	.45
		On cover		*1,000.*
a.		2c orange	4.00	.45
b.		2c brown orange	3.50	.75
c.		2c pale buff ('76)	3.50	.45
d.		Laid paper	3.50	.55
e.		Frame inverted	4,000.	3,000.
24	A5	3c yellow	3.00	.75
		On cover		*1,000.*
a.		3c orange	3.00	1.40
b.		3c pale buff ('76)	5.50	1.75
25	A5	4c yellow	4.00	.75
		On cover		*1,000.*
a.		4c orange	4.50	1.25
b.		4c brown orange ('76)	4.50	1.25
c.		4c buff ('76)	4.50	1.25
26	A5	5c yellow	4.00	.75
		On cover		*500.00*
a.		5c orange	4.00	.90
		On cover		*500.00*
b.		5c pale buff ('76)	4.00	.90

c.		On cover	7.50	*500.00*
		Laid paper		.90
27	A5	1r rose	4.00	2.00
		On cover		*1,000.*
a.		1r pale red	4.00	2.00
		On cover		*1,000.*
b.		Laid paper	6.00	2.50
c.		Half used as ½r on cover		*1,500.*
28	A5	2r rose	4.50	2.00
a.		2r pale red	4.50	2.00
b.		Laid paper	12.00	2.50
29	A5	3r rose	6.00	2.00
a.		3r pale red	6.00	2.00
30	A5	5r rose	5.75	1.00
a.		5r pale red	5.75	1.00
31	A5	7r rose	22.50	4.00
a.		7r pale red	22.50	4.00
32	A5	9r green	22.50	4.25
a.		9r olive green	22.50	6.00
33	A5	15r green	55.00	8.50
a.		15r gray green ('76)	55.00	8.50
b.		Frame inverted	8,000.	6,500.
34	A5	20r green	77.50	20.00
a.		Laid paper	110.00	35.00
35	A5	30r green	375.00	110.00
a.		30r gray green ('76)	600.00	160.00
b.		Double overprint		
36	A5	50r green	1,200.	300.00
a.		50r gray green ('76)		
		Nos. 22-34 (13)	212.25	46.85
		Nos. 22-35 (14)	587.25	156.85

These stamps were made available for postage and revenue by official decree, and were the only stamps sold for postage in Venezuela from Mar., 1871 to Aug., 1873.

Due to lack of canceling handstamps, the majority of stamps were canceled with pen marks. Fiscal cancellations were also made with the pen. The values quoted are for pen-canceled stamps.

Different settings were used for the different overprints. Stamps with the upright letters were issued in 1871. Those with the slanting letters in one double line were issued in 1872-73. Those with the slanting overprint in two double lines were issued starting in 1874 from several different settings, those of 1877-78 showing much coarser impressions than the earlier issues. The 7r and 9r are not known with this overprint. Stamps on laid paper (1875) are from a separate setting.

Stamps and Types of 1866-67 Overprinted in Two Lines of Very Small Letters Repeated Continuously

Overprinted "Estampillas de Correo — Contrasena"

1873, July 1
37	A4	½r pale rose	70.00	13.00
		On cover		*2,500.*
a.		½r rose	70.00	13.00
		On cover		*2,500.*
b.		Inverted overprint	175.00	75.00
c.		Tête bêche pair	3,000.	2,000.
38	A4	1r vermilion	85.00	25.00
		On cover		*3,500.*
a.		Inverted overprint		—
b.		Half used as ½r on cover		*5,500.*
39	A4	2r yellow	300.00	125.00
		On cover		—
a.		Inverted overprint		—
b.		Half used as 1r on cover		*12,000.*
		Nos. 37-39 (3)	455.00	163.00

Covers: Only one cover is recorded of No. 39b. Two examples are known on fragments.

Overprinted "Contrasena — Estampillas de Correo"

1873, Nov.
40	A4	1c gray lilac	30.00	32.50
		On cover		
a.		Inverted overprint	6.50	*17.00*
		On cover		*3,000.*
41	A4	2c green	125.00	90.00
		On cover		*3,000.*
a.		Inverted overprint	40.00	50.00
		On cover		*3,000.*
b.		As "a," half used as 1c on cover		*7,500.*
42	A4	½r rose	72.50	13.00
		On cover		100.00
a.		Inverted overprint	30.00	4.00
		On cover		50.00
b.		½r pink	60.00	11.00
		On cover		100.00
43	A4	1r vermilion	85.00	23.00
		On cover		*500.00*
a.		Inverted overprint	35.00	9.00
		On cover		*300.00*
b.		Half used as ½r on cover		*300.00*
44	A4	2r yellow	325.00	160.00
		On cover		*10,000.*
a.		Inverted overprint	110.00	50.00
		On cover		*10,000.*
b.		Half used as 1r on cover		*10,000.*
		Nos. 40-44 (5)	637.50	318.50

Overprinted
"Contrasena —
Estampilla de Correos"

1875

45	A4	½r rose	85.00	10.00
		On cover		200.00
a.		Inverted overprint	125.00	25.00
		On cover		500.00
b.		Double overprint	160.00	90.00
46	A4	1r vermilion	160.00	15.00
		On cover		700.00
a.		Inverted overprint	200.00	80.00
		On cover		2,500.
b.		Tête bêche pair	3,500.	3,000.
c.		Half used as ½r on cover		3,500.

Overprinted
"Estampillas de correo — Contrasena"

1876-77

47	A4	½r rose	77.50	9.25
		On cover		200.00
a.		½r pink	65.00	7.50
		On cover		200.00
b.		Inverted overprint	65.00	7.50
		On cover		200.00
c.		Both lines of overprint read "Contrasena"	75.00	17.50
		On cover		3,500.
d.		Both lines of overprint read "Estampillas de correo"	75.00	17.50
		On cover		3,500.
e.		Double overprint	125.00	35.00
48	A4	1r vermilion ('77)	92.50	23.00
		On cover		700.00
a.		Inverted overprint	85.00	24.00
		On cover		700.00
b.		Tête bêche pair	2,250.	2,500.
c.		Half used as ½r on cover		

On Nos. 47 and 48 "correo" has a small "c" instead of a capital. Nos. 45 and 46 have the overprint in slightly larger letters than the other stamps of the 1873-76 issues.

Overprinted "Decreto de 27 Junio 1870" Twice, One Line Inverted

Simón Bolívar
A6   A7

1879   *Imperf.*

49	A6	1c yellow	4.00	1.00
		Multiple, on cover		
a.		1c orange	5.00	1.50
		Multiple, on cover		1,500.
b.		1c olive yellow	5.50	1.75
		Multiple, on cover		
50	A6	5c yellow	3.50	.50
		On cover		75.00
a.		5c orange	2.50	.75
		On cover		75.00
b.		Double overprint	20.00	10.00
51	A6	10c blue	5.00	.50
		On cover		1,500.
52	A6	30c blue	7.75	1.00
		On cover		3,000.
53	A6	50c blue	7.75	1.00
54	A6	90c blue	40.00	12.00
55	A7	1v rose red	77.50	18.00
56	A7	3v rose red	130.00	55.00
57	A7	5v rose red	225.00	77.50
		Nos. 49-57 (9)	*500.50*	*166.50*

In 1879 and the early part of 1880 there were no regular postage stamps in Venezuela and the stamps inscribed "Escuelas" were permitted to serve for postal as well as revenue purposes. Postally canceled stamps are extremely scarce. Values quoted are for stamps with cancellations of banks or business houses or with pen cancellations. Stamps with pen marks removed are sometimes offered as unused stamps, or may have fraudulent postal cancellations added.

Nos. 49-57 exist without overprint. These are proofs.

Covers: Nos. 53-57 are not known on cover.

A8   A9

1880   *Perf. 11*

58	A8	5c yellow	1.50	.50
		On cover		500.00
a.		5c orange	1.50	.50
		On cover		500.00
b.		Printed on both sides	150.00	85.00
59	A8	10c yellow	2.50	.60
		On cover		1,000.
a.		10c orange	2.50	.60
		On cover, pair		1,000.
60	A8	25c yellow	2.50	.60
		On cover		60.00
a.		25c orange	2.75	.70
		On cover		60.00
b.		Printed on both sides	110.00	52.50
c.		Impression of 5c on back	175.00	90.00
61	A8	50c yellow	4.75	.80
		On cover		2,000.
a.		50c orange	5.25	.85
		On cover		2,000.
b.		Half used as 25c on cover		—
c.		Printed on both sides	150.00	90.00
d.		Impression of 25c on back	150.00	90.00
62	A9	1b pale blue	12.00	1.40
		On cover		3,000.
63	A9	2b pale blue	17.00	1.75
		On cover		5,000.
64	A9	5b pale blue	40.00	5.75
a.		Half used as 2½b on cover		—
65	A9	10b rose red	200.00	70.00
66	A9	20b rose red	1,200.	200.00
67	A9	25b rose red	5,000.	500.00
		Nos. 58-65 (8)	*280.25*	*81.40*

See note on used values below No. 57.
Covers: Nos. 64-67 are not known on cover.

Bolívar — A10

1880   **Litho.**   *Perf. 11*
Thick or Thin Paper

68	A10	5c blue	15.00	7.25
		On cover		200.00
a.		Printed on both sides	225.00	140.00
69	A10	10c rose	20.00	12.00
		On cover		200.00
a.		10c carmine	20.00	12.00
		On cover		250.00
b.		Double impression	90.00	75.00
c.		Horiz. pair, imperf. btwn.	75.00	75.00
70	A10	10c scarlet	20.00	12.00
		On cover		250.00
a.		Horiz. pair, imperf. btwn.	75.00	75.00
71	A10	25c yellow	15.00	7.25
		On cover		250.00
b.		Thick paper	20.00	10.00
		On cover		250.00
72	A10	50c brown	92.50	40.00
		On cover		1,000.
a.		50c deep brown	92.50	.40
		On cover		1,000.
b.		Printed on both sides	225.00	140.00
c.		Half used as 25c on cover		5,000.
73	A10	1b green	140.00	50.00
		On cover		2,000.
a.		Horiz. pair, imperf. btwn.	300.00	300.00
		Nos. 68-73 (6)	*302.50*	*128.50*

Nos. 68 to 73 were used for the payment of postage on letters to be sent abroad and the Escuelas stamps were then restricted to internal use.

Counterfeits of this issue exist in a great variety of shades as well as in wrong colors. They are on thick and thin paper, white or toned, and imperf. or perforated 11, 12 and compound. They are also found tête bêche. Counterfeits of Nos. 68 to 72 inclusive often have a diagonal line across the "S" of "CENTS" and a short line from the bottom of that letter to the frame below it. Originals of No. 73 show parts of a frame around "BOLIVAR."

Simón Bolívar
A11   A12

A13   A14

A15

1882, Aug. 1   Engr.   *Perf. 12*

74	A11	5c blue	.70	.35
		On cover		100.00
75	A12	10c red brown	.70	.35
		On cover		100.00
76	A13	25c yellow brown	1.10	.40
		On cover		20.00
a.		Printed on both sides	50.00	27.50
77	A14	50c green	2.40	.70
		On cover		200.00
a.		Half used as 25c on cover		500.00
78	A15	1b violet	4.50	1.75
		On cover		1,000.
		Nos. 74-78 (5)	*9.40*	*3.55*

Nos. 75-78 exist imperf. Value, set $32.50.
See Nos. 88, 92-95. For surcharges and overprints see Nos. 100-103, 108-112.

A16   A17

A18   A19

A20   A21

A22   A23

1882-88

79	A16	5c blue green	.25	.25
		On cover		100.00
80	A17	10c brown	.25	.25
		On cover		100.00
81	A18	25c orange	.25	.25
		On cover		50.00
82	A19	50c blue	.25	.25
		On cover		200.00
83	A20	1b vermilion	.25	.25
84	A21	3b dull vio ('88)	.25	.25
85	A22	10b dark brn ('88)	1.25	.80
86	A23	20b plum ('88)	1.50	.95
		Nos. 79-86 (8)	*4.25*	*3.25*

By official decree, dated Apr. 14, 1882, stamps of types A11 to A15 were to be used for foreign postage and those of types A16 to A23 for inland correspondence and fiscal use. Issue date: Nos. 79-83, Aug. 1.
See Nos. 87, 89-91, 96-99. For surcharges and overprints see Nos. 104-107, 114-122.

1887-88   Litho.   *Perf. 11*

87	A16	5c gray green	.45	.30
		On cover		100.00
88	A13	25c yellow brown	55.00	22.50
		On cover		100.00
89	A18	25c orange	.70	.45
		On cover		100.00
90	A20	1b orange red ('88)	4.75	.90
		Nos. 87-90 (4)	*60.90*	*24.15*

**   *Perf. 14***

91	A16	5c gray green	95.00	40.00

Stamps of type A16, perf. 11 and 14, are from a new die with "ESCUELAS" in smaller letters. Stamps of the 1887-88 issue, perf. 12,

and a 50c dark blue, perf. 11 or 12, are believed by experts to be from printer's waste. Counterfeits of No. 91 have been made by perforating printers waste of No. 96.

**   Rouletted 8**

92	A11	5c blue	40.00	17.00
		On cover		200.00
93	A13	25c yel brown	15.00	10.00
		On cover		200.00
94	A14	50c green	15.00	10.00
		On cover		500.00
95	A15	1b purple	30.00	20.00
		On cover		500.00
		Nos. 92-95 (4)	*100.00*	*57.00*

1887-88

96	A16	5c green	.25	.25
		On cover		200.00
97	A18	25c orange	.25	.25
		On cover		100.00
98	A19	50c dark blue	1.25	1.10
		On cover		200.00
99	A21	3b purple ('88)	3.50	3.50
		On overfranked cover		1,000.
		Nos. 96-99 (4)	*5.25*	*5.10*

The so-called imperforate varieties of Nos. 92 to 99, and the pin perforated 50c dark blue, type A19, are believed to be from printer's waste.

Stamps of 1882-88
Handstamp
Surcharged in Violet

1892   *Perf. 12*

100	A11	25c on 5c blue	40.00	40.00
101	A12	25c on 10c red brn	16.00	16.00
102	A13	1b on 25c yel brn	16.00	16.00
103	A14	1b on 50c green	20.00	20.00
		Nos. 100-103 (4)	*92.00*	*92.00*

See note after No. 107.

1892

104	A16	25c on 5c bl grn	10.00	6.00
105	A17	25c on 10c brown	10.00	6.00
106	A18	1b on 25c orange	15.00	12.00
107	A19	1b on 50c blue	23.00	12.00
		Nos. 104-107 (4)	*58.00*	*36.00*

Counterfeits of this surcharge abound.

Stamps of 1882-88
Overprinted in Red or
Black

1893

108	A11	5c blue (R)	.55	.25
		On cover		500.00
a.		Inverted overprint	3.25	3.25
b.		Double overprint	16.00	16.00
109	A12	10c red brn (Bk)	.90	.90
		On cover		500.00
a.		Inverted overprint	4.00	4.00
b.		Double overprint	16.00	16.00
110	A13	25c yel brn (R)	.80	.50
		On cover		100.00
a.		Inverted overprint	5.25	5.25
b.		Double overprint	16.00	16.00
c.		25c yel brn (Bk)	500.00	500.00
111	A14	50c green (R)	1.25	.80
		On cover		500.00
a.		Inverted overprint	5.25	5.25
b.		Double overprint	27.50	27.50
112	A15	1b pur (R)	3.25	1.20
		On cover		2,000.
a.		Inverted overprint	10.00	10.00
		Nos. 108-112 (5)	*6.75*	*3.65*

1893

114	A16	5c bl grn (R)	.25	.25
		On cover		500.00
a.		Inverted overprint	3.25	3.25
b.		Double overprint	5.25	5.25
115	A17	10c brn (R)	.25	.25
		On cover		500.00
a.		Inverted overprint	3.25	3.25
b.		Double overprint	3.25	3.25
116	A18	25c org (R)	.25	.25
		On cover		500.00
a.		Inverted overprint	3.25	3.25
117	A18	25c org (Bk)	5.75	2.75
		On cover		500.00
a.		Inverted overprint	8.25	5.00
118	A19	50c blue (R)	.25	.25
		On cover		500.00
a.		Inverted overprint	3.25	3.25
119	A20	1b ver (Bk)	.60	.40
a.		Inverted overprint	4.00	4.00
120	A21	3b dl vio (R)	.90	.40
a.		Double overprint	8.25	8.25
121	A22	10b dk brn (R)	3.50	2.25
a.		Double overprint	10.00	10.00
b.		Inverted overprint	20.00	20.00

122 A23 20b plum (Bk)   3.00   3.00
  a. Double overprint   10.00   20.00
  b. Inverted overprint
    Nos. 114-122 (9)   14.75   9.80
    Counterfeits exist.

Simón Bolívar
A24   A25

1893   **Engr.**
123 A24 5c red brn   .90   .25
  On cover   100.00
124 A24 10c blue   3.25   1.25
  On cover   100.00
125 A24 25c magenta   15.00   .50
  On cover   20.00
126 A24 50c brn vio   4.25   .55
  On cover   50.00
127 A24 1b green   5.75   1.25
  On cover   750.00
  Nos. 123-127 (5)   29.15   3.80

Many shades exist in this issue, but their values do not vary.

1893
128 A25 5c gray   .25   .25
  On cover   100.00
129 A25 10c green   .25   .25
  On cover   100.00
130 A25 25c blue   .25   .25
  On cover   100.00
131 A25 50c orange   .25   .25
  On cover   100.00
132 A25 1b red vio   .25   .25
133 A25 3b red   .55   .25
134 A25 10b dl vio   .90   .80
135 A25 20b red brn   4.25   2.75
  Nos. 128-135 (8)   6.95   5.05

By decree of Nov. 28, 1892, the stamps inscribed "Correos" were to be used for external postage and those inscribed "Instruccion" were for internal postage and revenue purposes.

For surcharge see No. 230.

After July 1, 1895, stamps inscribed "Escuelas" or "Instruccion" were no longer available for postage. Stamps of design A25 in shades different than those listed were printed after 1895.

Landing of Columbus
A26

1893   **Perf. 12**
136 A26 25c magenta   11.00   .60
  On cover   100.00

4th cent. of the discovery of the mainland of South America, also participation of Venezuela in the Intl. Exhib. at Chicago in 1893.

Map of Venezuela
A27

1896   **Litho.**
137 A27 5c yel grn   3.00   2.75
  On cover   250.00
  a. 5c apple green   3.00   2.75
  On cover   250.00
138 A27 10c blue   4.00   5.50
  On cover   250.00
139 A27 25c yellow   4.00   5.50
  On cover   50.00
  a. 25c orange   4.00   5.50
  On cover   50.00
  b. Tête bêche pair   125.00   125.00
       2,000.
140 A27 50c rose red   55.00   25.00
  On cover   500.00
  a. 50c red   52.50   52.50
  On cover   500.00
  b. Tête bêche pair   375.00   375.00
  On cover   500.00
141 A27 1b violet   40.00   27.50
  On cover   1,000.
  Nos. 137-141 (5)   106.00   66.25

Gen. Francisco Antonio Gabriel de Miranda (1752-1816).

These stamps were in use from July 4 to Nov. 4, 1896. Later usage is known.

There are many forgeries of this issue. They include faked errors, imperforate stamps and many tête bêche ones. The paper of the originals is thin, white and semi-transparent. The gum is shiny and crackled. The paper of the reprints is often thick and opaque. The gum is usually dull, smooth, thin and only slightly adhesive.

Bolívar — A28

1899-1901   **Engr.**
142 A28 5c dk grn   1.00   .25
  On cover   50.00
143 A28 10c red   1.25   .40
  On cover   50.00
144 A28 25c blue   1.50   .55
  On cover   75.00
145 A28 50c gray blk   2.00   1.00
  On cover   200.00
146 A28 50c org ('01)   1.75   .50
  On cover   25.00
147 A28 1b yel grn   32.50   15.00
  On cover   1,000.
149 A28 2b orange   400.00   225.00
  On cover
  Nos. 142-147,149 (7)   440.00   242.70

Stamps of 1899 Overprinted in Black

1900
150 A28 5c dk grn   1.25   .40
  On cover   50.00
  a. Inverted overprint   4.75   4.75
151 A28 10c red   1.25   .40
  On cover   50.00
  a. Inverted overprint   6.50   6.50
  b. Double overprint   10.50   10.50
152 A28 25c blue   7.75   1.25
  On cover   50.00
  a. Inverted overprint   13.00   13.00
153 A28 50c gray blk   4.00   .55
  On cover   500.00
  a. Inverted overprint   12.00   12.00
154 A28 1b yel grn   1.75   .80
  On cover   1,000.
  a. Double overprint   13.00   13.00
  b. Inverted overprint   12.00   12.00
155 A28 2b orange   2.75   2.25
  On cover
  a. Inverted overprint   35.00   35.00
  b. Double overprint   32.50   32.50
  Nos. 150-155 (6)   18.75   5.65

Initials are those of R. T. Mendoza. Counterfeit overprints exist, especially of inverted and doubled varieties.

Bolivar Type of 1899-1903 Overprinted

1900
156 A28 5c dk grn   750.00   750.00
  On cover
157 A28 10c red   750.00   750.00
  On cover
158 A28 25c blue   600.00   600.00
  On cover
159 A28 50c yel orange   23.00   1.60
  On cover   30.00
160 A28 1b slate   1.25   1.00
  On cover   200.00
  a. Without overprint   7,000.
  Nos. 156-160 (5)   2,124.   2,102.

Nos. 156-158 Overprinted

1900, Aug. 14
161 A28 5c green   8.00   .55
  On cover   50.00
162 A28 10c red   7.00   1.00
  On cover   50.00

---

163 A28 25c blue   8.00   1.00
  On cover   50.00
  Nos. 161-163 (3)   23.00   2.55

Inverted Overprint
161a A28 5c   9.25   9.25
162a A28 10c   9.25   9.25
163a A28 25c   12.00   12.00
  Nos. 161a-163a (3)   30.50   30.50

Overprint exists on each value without "Castro" or without "1900."

Type of 1893 Surcharged

1904, Jan.   **Perf. 12**
230 A25 5c on 50c green   .80   .60
  On cover   20.00
  a. "Vele"   23.00   23.00
  b. Surcharge reading up   1.00   .50
  c. Double surcharge   18.00   18.00

Gen. José de Sucre — A35   Pres. Cipriano Castro — A37

1904-09   **Engr.**
231 A35 5c bl grn   .50   .25
  On cover   20.00
232 A35 10c carmine   .55   .25
  On cover   20.00
233 A35 15c violet   .90   .40
  On cover   50.00
234 A35 25c dp ultra   6.50   .40
  On cover   10.00
235 A35 50c plum   1.00   .50
  On cover   20.00
236 A35 1b plum   1.10   .50
  On cover   75.00
  Nos. 231-236 (6)   10.55   2.30

Issue date: 15c, Dec. 1909. Others, July 1, 1904.

1905, July 5   **Litho.**   **Perf. 11½**
245 A37 5c vermilion   3.25   3.25
  On cover   100.00
  a. 5c carmine   5.00   5.00
246 A37 10c dark blue   5.50   4.25
  On cover   100.00
247 A37 25c yellow   2.00   1.50
  On cover   100.00
  Nos. 245-247 (3)   10.75   9.00

National Congress. Issued for interior postage only. Valid only for 90 days.

Various part-perforate varieties of Nos. 245-247 exist. Value, $15-$30.

Liberty — A38

1910, Apr. 19   **Engr.**   **Perf. 12**
249 A38 25c dark blue   13.00   .70
  On cover   50.00

Centenary of national independence.

Francisco de Miranda   Rafael Urdaneta
A39   A40

Bolívar — A41

1911   **Litho.**   **Perf. 11½x12**
250 A39 5c dp grn   .50   .25
  On cover   30.00
251 A39 10c carmine   .50   .25
  On cover   30.00
252 A40 15c gray   5.75   .40
  On cover   20.00
253 A40 25c dp bl   3.25   .60
  On cover   20.00
  a. Imperf., pair   40.00   40.00
254 A41 50c purple   3.50   .40
  On cover   30.00
255 A41 1b yellow   3.50   1.50
  On cover   75.00
  Nos. 250-255 (6)   17.00   3.40

The 50c with center in blue was never issued although examples were postmarked by favor.

The centers of Nos. 250-255 were separately printed and often vary in shade from the rest of the design. In a second printing of the 5c and 10c, the entire design was printed at one time.

1913   **Redrawn**
255A A40 15c gray   3.50   2.25
255B A40 25c deep blue   2.00   .65
255C A41 50c purple   2.00   .65
  Nos. 255A-255C (3)   7.50   3.55

The redrawn stamps have two berries instead of one at top of the left spray; a berry has been added over the "C" and "S" of "Centimos"; and the lowest leaf at the right is cut by the corner square.

Simón Bolívar
A42   A43

1914, July   **Engr.**   **Perf. 13½, 14, 15**
256 A42 5c yel grn   37.50   .55
257 A42 10c scarlet   35.00   .50
258 A42 25c dark blue   5.75   .25
  Nos. 256-258 (3)   78.25   1.30

Printed by the American Bank Note Co.

Different frames.

1915-23   **Perf. 12**
259 A43 5c green   4.25   .25
260 A43 10c vermilion   10.00   .60
261 A43 10c claret ('22)   10.00   .60
262 A43 15c dull ol grn   9.25   .60
263 A43 25c ultra   6.50   .25
  a. 25c blue   13.00   .60
264 A43 40c dull green   23.00   11.50
265 A43 50c dp violet   6.50   .80
266 A43 50c ultra ('23)   17.00   4.75
267 A43 75c lt blue   57.50   23.00
  a. 75c greenish blue   57.50   23.00
268 A43 1b dark gray   35.00   5.25
  Nos. 259-268 (10)   179.00   47.90

See Nos. 269-285. For surcharges see Nos. 307, 309-310.

Type of 1915-23 Issue Re-engraved
Printed by Waterlow & Sons, Ltd.

1924-39   **Perf. 12½**
269 A43 5c orange brn   .55   .25
  a. 5c yellow brown   .55   .25
  b. Horiz. pair, imperf. between   25.00   40.00
270 A43 5c green ('39)   12.00   1.00
271 A43 7½c yel grn ('39)   1.25   .40
272 A43 10c dk green   .25   .25
273 A43 10c dk car ('39)   4.00   .25
274 A43 15c olive grn   2.25   .50
275 A43 15c brown ('27)   .30   .25
276 A43 25c ultra   2.25   .25
277 A43 25c red ('28)   .25   .25
  a. Horiz. pair, imperf. btwn.   50.00   85.00
278 A43 40c dp blue ('25)   .55   .25
279 A43 40c slate bl ('39)   7.75   1.25
280 A43 50c dk blue   .55   .25
281 A43 50c dk pur ('39)   7.75   .85
282 A43 1b black   .55   .25
283 A43 3b yel org ('25)   1.75   .25
284 A43 3b red org ('39)   12.00   4.25
285 A43 5b dull vio ('25)   16.00   8.50
  Nos. 269-285 (17)   70.00   19.95

Perf. 14

269c	A43	5c		7.00	2.00
272a	A43	10c		7.00	2.00
274a	A43	15c		8.25	2.75
276a	A43	25c		12.00	4.75
280a	A43	50c		35.00	14.00
282a	A43	1b		42.50	27.00
		Nos. 269c-282a (6)		111.75	52.50

The re-engraved stamps may readily be distinguished from the 1915 issue by the perforation and sometimes by the colors. The designs differ in many minor details which are too minute for illustration or description.

Bolívar and Sucre
A44

Perf. 11½x12, 12

1924, Dec. 1   **Litho.**
286   A44   25c grayish blue   2.75   .55

Redrawn
286A   A44   25c ultra   3.50   .85

Centenary of the Battle of Ayacucho.
The redrawn stamp has a whiter effect with less shading in the faces. Bolívar's ear is clearly visible and the outline of his aquiline nose is broken.

A45   A46

Revenue Stamps Surcharged in Black or Red

1926   **Perf. 12, 12½**

287	A45	5c on 1b ol grn		.65	.40
a.		Double surcharge		8.00	8.00
b.		Pair, one without surcharge		12.00	12.00
c.		Inverted surcharge		8.00	8.00
288	A46	25c on 5c dk brn (R)		.65	.40
a.		Inverted surcharge		8.00	8.00
b.		Double surcharge		8.00	8.00

View of Ciudad Bolívar and General J.V. Gómez — A47

1928, July 21   **Litho.**   **Perf. 12**
289   A47   10c deep green   1.00   .65
a.   Imperf., pair   40.00

25th anniversary of the Battle of Ciudad Bolívar and the foundation of peace in Venezuela.

Simón Bolívar
A48   A49

1930, Dec. 9

290	A48	5c yellow		1.00	.35
291	A48	10c dark blue		1.00	.25
292	A48	25c rose red		1.00	.25
		Nos. 290-292 (3)		3.00	.85

Imperf., Pairs

290a	A48	5c		5.25	5.25
291a	A48	10c		6.50	6.50
292a	A48	25c		10.50	10.50

Death centenary of Simón Bolívar (1783-1830), South American liberator.
Nos. 290-292 exist part-perforate, including pairs imperf. between, imperf. horiz., imperf. vert. Value range, $6-12.

Various Frames
Bluish Winchester Security Paper

1932-38   **Engr.**   **Perf. 12½**

293	A49	5c violet		.50	.25
294	A49	7½c dk green ('37)		1.10	.40
295	A49	10c green		.65	.25
296	A49	15c yellow		1.50	.25
297	A49	22½c dp car ('38)		3.50	.50
298	A49	25c red		1.25	.25
299	A49	37½c ultra ('36)		4.50	2.00
300	A49	40c indigo		4.50	.25
301	A49	50c olive grn		4.50	.40
302	A49	1b lt blue		6.00	.70
303	A49	3b brown		47.50	13.00
304	A49	5b yellow brn		65.00	17.50
		Nos. 293-304 (12)		140.50	35.75

For surcharges see Nos. 308, 318-319, C223 (in Scott Standard catalogue, Vol. 6).

Arms of Bolívar — A50

1933, July 24   **Litho.**   **Perf. 11**
306   A50   25c brown red   3.00   2.40
a.   Imperf., pair   32.50   32.50

150th anniv. of the birth of Simón Bolívar. Valid only to Aug. 21.

Stamps of 1924-32 Surcharged in Black — (Blocks of Surcharge in Color of stamps)

1933

307	A43	7½c on 10c grn		.50	.25
a.		Double surcharge		2.50	2.50
b.		Inverted surcharge		4.25	4.25
308	A49	22½c on 25c (#298)		2.00	.85
309	A43	22½c on 25c (#277)		1.50	1.50
a.		Double surcharge		10.00	10.00
310	A43	37½c on 40c dp bl		2.00	.95
a.		Double surcharge		11.50	11.50
b.		Inverted surcharge		10.00	10.00
		Nos. 307-310 (4)		6.00	3.55

Nurse and Child — A51   River Scene — A52

Gathering Cacao Pods — A53

Cattle Raising A54

Plowing A55

Perf. 11, 11½ or Compound

1937, July 1   **Litho.**

311	A51	5c deep violet		.55	.35
312	A52	10c dk slate grn		.55	.25
313	A53	15c yellow brn		1.00	.55
314	A51	25c cerise		1.00	.25
315	A54	50c yellow grn		6.50	4.25
316	A55	3b orange		12.00	7.75
317	A51	5b lt brown		23.00	15.00
		Nos. 311-317 (7)		44.60	28.50

Nos. 311-317 exist imperforate. Value for set $75. Nos. 311-315 exist in pairs, imperf. between; value range, $20-$30.
For overprints and surcharges see Nos. 321-324, 345; Nos. 376-377, 380-384 in Scott Standard catalogue, Vol. 6.

No. 300 Surcharged in Black

1937, July   **Perf. 12½**

318	A49	25c on 40c indigo		7.75	.95
a.		Double surcharge		16.00	16.00
b.		Inverted surcharge		13.00	13.00
c.		Triple surcharge		32.50	32.50

No. 300 Surcharged

319   A49   25c on 40c indigo   440.00   350.00
a.   Double surcharge

A56

1937, Oct. 28   **Litho.**   **Perf. 10½**
320   A56   25c blue   1.25   .45

Acquisition of the Port of La Guaira by the Government from the British Corporation, June 3, 1937. Exists imperf. See Nos. C64-C65.
A redrawn printing of No. 320, with top inscription beginning "Nacionalización . . ." was prepared but not issued. Value, $40.
For surcharge see No. 385 in Scott Standard catalogue, Vol. 6.

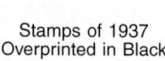

Stamps of 1937 Overprinted in Black

1937, Dec. 17   **Perf. 11, 11½**

321	A51	5c deep violet		5.75	3.25
322	A52	10c dk slate grn		1.75	.75
a.		Inverted overprint		13.00	13.00
323	A51	25c cerise		1.50	.55
a.		Inverted overprint		16.00	16.00
324	A55	3b red orange		375.00	225.00
		Nos. 321-324 (4)		384.00	229.55

Part-perforate pairs exist of Nos. 321-322 and 324. Value range, $12.50 to $125.
See Nos. C66-C78.

Gathering Coffee Beans — A57   Simón Bolívar — A58

Post Office, Caracas — A59

1938   **Engr.**   **Perf. 12**

325	A57	5c green		.40	.25
326	A57	5c deep green		.40	.25
327	A58	10c car rose		.70	.25
328	A58	10c dp rose		.70	.25
329	A59	15c dk violet		1.40	.25
330	A59	15c olive grn		.85	.25
331	A58	25c lt blue		.40	.25
332	A58	25c dk blue		.40	.25
333	A58	37½c dk blue		8.50	4.00
334	A58	37½c lt blue		2.75	.85
335	A59	40c sepia		20.00	7.75
336	A59	40c black		17.00	7.75
337	A57	50c olive grn		27.50	7.75
338	A57	50c dull violet		9.25	.85
339	A58	1b dp brown		12.00	5.50
340	A58	1b black brown		17.00	1.50
341	A57	3b orange		92.50	50.00
342	A59	5b black		15.00	7.75
		Nos. 325-342 (18)		226.75	95.70

See Nos. 400, 412 in Scott Standard catalogue, Vol. 6.

Teresa Carreño — A60   Bolívar Statue — A61

1938, June 12   **Perf. 11½x12**
343   A60   25c blue   5.75   .60

Teresa Carreno, Venezuelan pianist, whose remains were repatriated Feb. 14, 1938.
For surcharge see No. 386 in Scott Standard catalogue, Vol. 6.

1938, July 24   **Perf. 12**
344   A61   25c dark blue   6.50   .60

"The Day of the Worker."
For surcharge see No. 387 in Scott Standard catalogue, Vol. 6.

Type of 1937 Surcharged in Black

1938   **Litho.**   **Perf. 11, 11½**
345   A51   40c on 5b lt brn   8.50   4.50
a.   Inverted surcharge   21.00   21.00

Gen. José I. Paz Castillo, Postmaster of Venezuela, 1859 — A62

1939, Apr. 19 Engr. Perf. 12½
348 A62 10c carmine   2.50 .70

80th anniv. of the first Venezuelan stamp.

View of Ojeda
A63

1939, June 24 Photo.
349 A63 25c dull blue   9.25 .75

Founding of city of Ojeda.

Cristóbal Mendoza
A64

Diego Urbaneja
A65

1939, Oct. 14 Engr. Perf. 13
350 A64 5c green   .40 .25
351 A64 10c dk car rose .40 .25
352 A64 15c dull lilac   1.00 .25
353 A64 25c brt ultra   .80 .25
354 A64 37½c dark blue   15.00 6.25
355 A64 50c lt olive grn 16.00 4.00
356 A64 1b dark brown   6.50 3.50
  Nos. 350-356 (7)   40.10 14.75

Mendoza (1772-1839), postmaster general.

1940-43 Perf. 12
357 A65 5c Prus green   .55 .25
357A A65 7½c dk bl grn ('43) .80 .30
358 A65 15c olive   .95 .30
359 A65 37½c deep blue   1.50 .70
360 A65 40c violet blue   1.10 .35
361 A65 50c violet   6.50 1.75
362 A65 1b dk violet brn   3.50 .90
363 A65 3b scarlet   9.50 3.75
  Nos. 357-363 (8)   24.40 8.30

See Nos. 399, 408, 410-411 in Scott Standard catalogue, Vol. 6. For surcharges see Nos. 396, C226 in Scott Standard catalogue, Vol. 6.

Battle of Carabobo, 1821 — A67

1940, June 13
365 A67 25c blue   6.75 .80

Birth of General JoséAntonio Páez, 150th anniv.

"Crossing the Andes" by Tito Salas — A68

1940, June 13
366 A68 25c dark blue   6.75 .80

Death cent. of General Francisco Santander.

Monument and Urn containing Ashes of Simón Bolívar — A69

Bed where Simón Bolívar was Born — A70

Designs: 15c, "Christening of Bolivar" by Tito Salas. 20c, Bolivar's birthplace, Caracas. 25c, "Bolivar on Horseback" by Salas. 30c, Patio of Bolivar House, Caracas. 37½c, Patio of Bolivar's Birthplace. 50c, "Rebellion of 1812" by Salas.

1940-41
367 A69 5c turq green   .25 .25
368 A69 10c rose pink   .25 .25
369 A69 15c olive   .60 .25
370 A70 20c blue ('41)   1.00 .25
371 A69 25c lt blue   .60 .25
372 A70 30c plum ('41)   1.50 .25
373 A70 37½c dk blue   3.00 1.00
374 A70 50c purple   2.00 .50
  Nos. 367-374 (8)   9.20 3.00

110th anniv. of the death of Simón Bolívar.
See Nos. 397, 398, 403, 405-407, 409 in Scott Standard catalogue, Vol. 6. For surcharges see Nos. 375, 401-402, C224, C237-C238 in Scott Standard catalogue, Vol. 6.

AIR POST STAMPS

Air post stamps of 1930-42 perforated "GN" (Gobierno Nacional) were for official use.

Airplane and Map of Venezuela
AP1   AP2

1930 Unwmk. Litho. Perf. 12
C1 AP1 5c bister brn   .25 .25
C2 AP1 10c yellow   .25 .25
  a. 10c salmon   32.50 32.50
C3 AP1 15c gray   .25 .25
C4 AP1 25c lilac   .25 .25
C5 AP1 40c olive grn   .25 .25
  a. 40c slate blue   45.00
  b. 40c slate green   45.00
C6 AP1 75c dp red   .30 .25
C7 AP1 1b indigo   .45 .25
C8 AP1 1.20b blue grn   .70 .35
C9 AP1 1.70b dk blue   .90 .45
C10 AP1 1.90b blue grn   .90 .50
C11 AP1 2.10b dk blue   1.75 .65
C12 AP1 2.30b vermilion   1.75 .50
C13 AP1 2.50b dk blue   1.75 .50
C14 AP1 3.70b blue grn   1.75 1.10
C15 AP1 10b dull vio   5.25 2.40
C16 AP1 20b gray grn   8.00 4.50
  Nos. C1-C16 (16)   24.75 12.70

Issued: 10b, 6/8; 20b, 6/16; others, 4/5.
Nos. C1-C16 exist imperforate or partly perforated. Value, imperf set $200.
See Nos. C119-C126.

Bluish Winchester Security Paper
1932, July 12 Engr. Perf. 12½
C17 AP2 5c brown   .40 .25
C18 AP2 10c org yel   .40 .25
C19 AP2 15c gray lilac   .40 .25
C20 AP2 25c violet   .40 .25
C21 AP2 40c ol grn   .80 .25
C22 AP2 70c rose   .55 .25
C23 AP2 75c red org   1.00 .25
C24 AP2 1b dk bl   1.10 .25
C25 AP2 1.20b green   2.40 .85
C26 AP2 1.70b red brn   4.75 .55
C27 AP2 1.80b ultra   2.40 .35
C28 AP2 1.90b green   6.00 3.50
C29 AP2 1.95b blue   6.50 2.75
C30 AP2 2b blk brn   4.00 2.25
C31 AP2 2.10b blue   9.50 6.00
C32 AP2 2.30b red   4.00 2.40
C33 AP2 2.50b dk bl   6.00 1.40
C34 AP2 3b dk vio   4.00 .85
C35 AP2 3.70b emerald   8.00 6.00
C36 AP2 4b red org   6.00 1.40
C37 AP2 5b black   6.50 2.40
C38 AP2 8b dk car   13.00 4.75

C39 AP2 10b dk vio   26.00 8.00
C40 AP2 20b grnsh slate   60.00 20.00
  Nos. C17-C40 (24)   176.10 65.45

Pairs imperf. between exist of the 1b (value $150); the 25c and 4b (value $300 each).

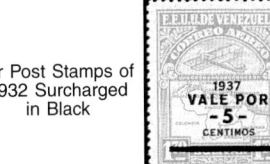

Air Post Stamps of 1932 Surcharged in Black

1937, June 4
C41 AP2 5c on 1.70b red brn   11.00 7.00
C42 AP2 10c on 3.70b emer   11.00 7.00
C43 AP2 15c on 4b red org   5.00 3.50
C44 AP2 25c on 5b blk   5.00 3.50
C45 AP2 1b on 8b dk car   4.00 3.50
C46 AP2 2b on 2.10b bl   30.00 23.00
  Nos. C41-C46 (6)   66.00 47.50

Various varieties of surcharge exist, including double and triple impressions. No. C43 exists in pair imperf. between; value $30 unused, $50 used.

Allegory of Flight
AP3

Allegory of Flight
AP4

National Pantheon at Caracas
AP5

Airplane — AP6   AP7

Perf. 11, 11½ and Compound
1937, July 1   Litho.
C47 AP3 5c brn org   .30 .40
C48 AP4 10c org red   .25 .25
C49 AP5 15c gray blk   .60 .40
C50 AP6 25c dk vio   .60 .40
C51 AP4 40c yel grn   1.10 .55
C52 AP5 70c red   1.10 .40
C53 AP5 75c bister   2.50 1.30
C54 AP5 1b dk gray   1.50 .55
C55 AP4 1.20b pck grn   6.50 4.25
C56 AP5 1.80b dk ultra 3.25 2.00
C57 AP5 1.95b lt ultra 10.00 7.75
C58 AP6 2b chocolate   4.25 1.75
C59 AP6 2.50b gray bl   11.50 11.50
C60 AP4 3b lt vio   6.50 4.50
C61 AP6 3.70b rose red 11.50 15.00
C62 AP5 10b red vio   25.00 15.00
C63 AP5 20b gray grn   30.00 23.00
  Nos. C47-C63 (17)   116.45 90.00

All values exist imperf., and all except the 3.70b part-perf.
Counterfeits exist.
For overprints & surcharges see Nos. C66-C78, C114-C118; Nos. C164-C167, C169-C172, C174-C180 in Scott Standard catalogue, Vol. 6.

1937, Oct. 28   Perf. 11
C64 AP7 70c emerald   1.40 .55
C65 AP7 1.80b ultra   2.25 1.00

Acquisition of the Port of La Guaira by the Government from the British Corporation,

June 3, 1937. Nos. C64-C65 exist imperf. Value, set $275.
A redrawn printing of Nos. C64-C65, with lower inscription beginning "Nacionalización..." was prepared but not issued. Value, $40 each.
For overprints see Nos. C168, C173 in Scott Standard catalogue, Vol. 6.

Air Post Stamps of 1937 Overprinted in Black

1937, Dec. 17   Perf. 11, 11½
C66 AP4 10c org red   1.00 .70
  a. Inverted overprint 15.00 12.00
C67 AP4 25c dk vio   2.00 1.00
C68 AP4 40c yel grn   2.00 1.40
C69 AP3 70c red   1.50 1.00
  a. Inverted overprint 15.00 14.00
  b. Double overprint   20.00 16.00
C70 AP3 1b dk gray   2.00 1.40
  a. Inverted overprint 16.00 13.00
  b. Double overprint   13.00
C71 AP4 1.20b pck grn   30.00 20.00
  a. Double overprint   77.50
C72 AP3 1.80b dk ultra   5.75 2.40
C73 AP5 1.95b lt ultra   7.75 4.25
  a. Inverted overprint 60.00 40.00
C74 AP6 2b chocolate   50.00 23.00
  a. Inverted overprint 100.00 90.00
  b. Double overprint   82.50 82.50
C75 AP6 2.50b gray bl   50.00 19.00
  a. Double overprint   70.00
  b. Inverted overprint 100.00 82.50
C76 AP4 3b lt vio   30.00 12.00
C77 AP5 10b red vio   72.50 40.00
C78 AP3 20b gray   77.50 47.50
  a. Double overprint   150.00 150.00
  Nos. C66-C78 (13)   332.00 173.65

Counterfeit overprints exist on #C77-C78.

View of La Guaira
AP8

National Pantheon
AP9

Oil Wells
AP10

1938-39 Engr. Perf. 12
C79 AP8 5c green   1.00 .50
C80 AP8 5c dk grn   .25 .25
C81 AP9 10c car rose   1.40 .80
C82 AP9 10c scarlet   .25 .25
C83 AP8 12½c dull vio   .60 .55
C84 AP10 15c slate vio   3.00 1.25
C85 AP10 15c dk bl   .85 .25
C86 AP8 25c dk bl   3.00 1.25
C87 AP8 25c bis brn   .25 .25
C88 AP10 30c vio ('39)   2.00 .25
C89 AP9 40c dk vio   3.50 1.25
C90 AP9 40c redsh brn   2.50 .25
C91 AP8 45c Prus grn ('39) 1.00 .25
C92 AP9 50c blue ('39)   1.25 .25
C93 AP10 70c car rose   .85 .25
C94 AP8 75c bis brn   6.00 2.00
C95 AP8 75c ol bis   1.40 .25
C96 AP10 90c red org ('39) 1.00 .25
C97 AP9 1b ol & bis   7.00 2.75
C98 AP9 1b dk vio   1.25 .25
C99 AP10 1.20b orange   20.00 5.75
C100 AP10 1.20b green   2.00 .55
C101 AP8 1.80b ultra   2.00 .55
C102 AP9 1.90b black   5.50 2.75
C103 AP8 1.95b lt bl   4.25 2.50
C104 AP8 2b ol gray   45.00 15.00
C105 AP8 2b car rose   1.75 .70
C106 AP9 2.50b red brn   45.00 20.00
C107 AP9 2.50b orange   10.00 2.75
C108 AP10 3b bl grn   20.00 4.75
C109 AP10 3b ol gray   5.50 2.00
C110 AP8 3.70b gray blk   7.75 5.50

C111 AP10   5b red brn
              ('39)   7.75   2.00
C112 AP9   10b vio brn   20.00   2.40
C113 AP10   20b red org   57.50   25.00
      Nos. C79-C113 (35)   292.35 105.55

See Nos. C227a, C235-C236, C254-C255 in Scott Standard catalogue, Vol. 6.
For surcharge see No. C227 in Scott Standard catalogue, Vol. 6.

Nos. C51, C56, C58-C59, C61 Surcharged

1938, Apr. 15   *Perf. 11, 11½*
C114 AP3   5c on 1.80b   .85   .60
   a.   Inverted surcharge   12.50   7.50
C115 AP6   10c on 2.50b   3.00   1.40
   a.   Inverted surcharge   10.00   7.50
C116 AP6   15c on 2b   1.40   1.10
C117 AP4   25c on 40c   1.75   1.40
C118 AP6   40c on 3.70b   3.50   3.25
      Nos. C114-C118 (5)   10.50   7.75

Plane & Map Type of 1930
White Paper; No Imprint

1938-39   *Engr.*   *Perf. 12½*
C119 AP1   5c dk grn ('39)   .25   .25
C120 AP1   10c org yel ('39)   .55   .25
C121 AP1   12½c rose vio ('39)   1.10   .85
C122 AP1   15c dp bl   .95   .25
C123 AP1   25c brown   1.10   .25
C124 AP1   40c olive ('39)   2.75   .40
C125 AP1   70c rose car ('39)   20.00   7.75
C126 AP1   1b dk bl ('39)   7.75   3.00
      Nos. C119-C126 (8)   34.45 13.00

Monument to Sucre — AP11

Monuments at Carabobo
    AP12   AP13

1938, Dec. 23   *Perf. 13½*
C127 AP11   20c brn blk   .80   .30
C128 AP12   30c purple   1.20   .30
C129 AP13   45c dk bl   1.75   .25
C130 AP11   50c lt ultra   1.50   .25
C131 AP12   70c dk car   26.00   7.50
C132 AP12   90c red org   2.50   .75
C133 AP13   1.35b gray blk   3.00   1.00
C134 AP11   1.40b slate gray   12.00   2.75
C135 AP12   2.25b green   6.00   2.00
      Nos. C127-C135 (9)   54.75 15.10

For surcharge see No. C198 in Scott Standard catalogue, Vol. 6.

Simón Bolívar and Carabobo Monument AP14

1940, Mar. 30   *Perf. 12*
C136 AP14   15c blue   .75   .25
C137 AP14   20c olive bis   .75   .25
C138 AP14   25c red brn   2.75   .40
C139 AP14   40c blk brn   2.25   .25
C140 AP14   1b red lilac   5.00   .55
C141 AP14   2b rose car   11.00   1.40
      Nos. C136-C141 (6)   22.50   3.10

"The Founding of Grand Colombia" AP15

1940, June 13
C142 AP15   15c copper brown   1.25   .45
Founding of the Pan American Union, 50th anniv.

Statue of Simón Bolívar, Caracas — AP16

1940-44
C143 AP16   5c dk grn ('42)   .25   .25
C144 AP16   10c scar ('42)   .25   .25
C145 AP16   12½c dull purple   .75   .30
C146 AP16   15c blue ('43)   .50   .25
C147 AP16   20c bis brn ('44)   .50   .25
C148 AP16   25c bis brn ('42)   .50   .25
C149 AP16   30c dp vio ('43)   .50   .25
C150 AP16   40c blk brn ('43)   .65   .25
C151 AP16   45c turq grn
             ('43)   .65   .25
C152 AP16   50c blue ('44)   .65   .25
C153 AP16   70c rose pink   2.00   .30
C154 AP16   75c ol bis ('43)   7.75   1.60
C155 AP16   90c red org ('43)   1.25   .30
C156 AP16   1b dp red lil
             ('42)   .65   .25
C157 AP16   1.20b dp yel grn
             ('43)   2.50   .75
C158 AP16   1.35b gray blk
             ('42)   10.50   3.50
C159 AP16   2b rose pink
             ('43)   2.00   .25
C160 AP16   3b ol blk ('43)   3.25   .75
C161 AP16   4b black   2.50   .75
C162 AP16   5b red brn ('44)   20.00   8.00
      Nos. C143-C162 (20)   57.60 19.00

See Nos. C232-C234, C239-C253 in Scott Standard catalogue, Vol. 6. For surcharges see Nos. C225, C873 in Scott Standard catalogue, Vol. 6.

REGISTRATION STAMPS

Bolívar — R1

1899, May   Unwmk.   Engr.   Perf. 12
F1   R1   25c yellow brown   3.25   2.75

No. F1 Overprinted

1900
F2   R1   25c yellow brown   2.00   2.00
   a.   Inverted overprint   32.50 32.50
   b.   Double overprint   40.00 40.00

Counterfeit overprints exist, especially of the varieties.

OFFICIAL STAMPS

Coat of Arms — O1

Lithographed, Center Engraved

1898, May 1   Unwmk.   Perf. 12
O1   O1   5c bl grn & blk   .80   .55
O2   O1   10c rose & blk   .95   .85
O3   O1   25c bl & blk   1.50   1.40
O4   O1   50c yel & blk   2.50   2.25
O5   O1   1b vio & blk   2.75   2.50
      Nos. O1-O5 (5)   8.50   7.55

Nos. O4 and O5 Handstamp Surcharged in Magenta or Violet

1899, Nov.
O6   O1   5c on 50c yel & blk   4.75   4.50
O7   O1   5c on 1b vio & blk   20.00 18.00
O8   O1   25c on 50c yel & blk   20.00 18.00
O9   O1   25c on 1b vio & blk   12.00 11.00
      Nos. O6-O9 (4)   56.75 51.50

Inverted Surcharge
O6a   O1   5c on 50c   15.00 15.00
O7a   O1   5c on 1b   40.00 40.00
O8a   O1   25c on 50c   32.50 32.50
O9a   O1   25c on 1b   32.50 32.50
      Nos. O6a-O9a (4)   120.00 120.00

Nos. O6-O9 exist with double surcharge. Value each $18.50-$37.50.
Many of the magenta overprints have become violet. There are intermediate shades.
Counterfeit overprints exist.

Coat of Arms — O3

1900   Litho., Center Engr.
O14   O3   5c bl grn & blk   .40   .40
O15   O3   10c rose & blk   .55   .55
O16   O3   25c bl & blk   .55   .55
O17   O3   50c yel & blk   .55   .55
O18   O3   1b dl vio & blk   .65   .65
      Nos. O14-O18 (5)   2.70   2.70

O4

Imprint: "American Bank Note Co., N.Y."

1904, July   Engr.
O19   O4   5c emerald & blk   .25   .25
O20   O4   10c rose & blk   .65   .65
O21   O4   25c blue & blk   .65   .65
O22   O4   50c red brn & blk   4.25   4.25
   a.   50c claret & black   4.25   4.25
O23   O4   1b red brn & blk   2.00   2.00
   a.   1b claret & black   2.00   2.00
      Nos. O19-O23 (5)   7.80   7.80

No Stars Above Shield — O5

1912   Lithographed in Caracas
O24   O5   5c grn & blk   .55   .30
O25   O5   10c car & blk   .55   .30
O26   O5   25c dk bl & blk   .55   .30
O27   O5   50c pur & blk   .55   .40
   a.   Center double   10.00
O28   O5   1b yel & blk   1.30   .80
      Nos. O24-O28 (5)   3.50   2.10

Perforated Initials

After 1925, Venezuela's official stamps consisted of regular postage stamps, some commemoratives and air post stamps of 1930-42 punched with "GN" (Gobierno Nacional) in large perforated initials.

LOCAL STAMPS FOR THE PORT OF CARUPANO

In 1902 Great Britain, Germany and Italy, seeking compensation for revolutionary damages, established a blockade of La Guaira and seized the custom house. Carúpano, a port near Trinidad, was isolated and issued the following provisionals. A treaty effected May 7, 1903, referred the dispute to the Hague Tribunal.

A1

A2

1902   Typeset   Imperf.
1   A1   5c purple, *orange*   27.00
2   A2   10c black, *orange*   40.00
   a.   Tête bêche pair   82.50
3   A1   25c purple, *green*   32.50
4   A1   50c green, *yellow*   85.00
5   A1   1b blue, *rose*   120.00
      Nos. 1-5 (5)   304.50

A3

1902
6   A3   1b black, *yellow*   200.00
   a.   Tête bêche pair

A4

1903   Handstamped
7   A4   5c carmine, *yellow*   45.00 45.00
8   A4   10c green, *yellow*   92.50 92.50
9   A4   25c green, *orange*   45.00 45.00
10   A4   50c blue, *rose*   45.00 45.00
11   A4   1b violet, *gray*   45.00 45.00
12   A4   2b carmine, *green*   45.00 45.00
13   A4   5b violet, *blue*   45.00 45.00
      Nos. 7-13 (7)   362.50 362.50

Dangerous counterfeits exist of Nos. 1-13.

LOCAL STAMPS FOR THE STATE OF GUAYANA

Revolutionary Steamship "Banrigh" — A1

Control Mark

Control Mark on Block of 4

1903   Typo.   Perf. 12
1	A1	5c	black, *gray*	19.00	19.00
2	A1	10c	black, *orange*	47.50	47.50
3	A1	25c	black, *pink*	19.00	19.00
4	A1	50c	black, *blue*	30.00	30.00
5	A1	1b	black, *straw*	25.00	25.00
		Nos. 1-5 (5)		140.50	140.50

Nos. 1-5 can be found with or without the illustrated control mark which covers four stamps.

Counterfeits include the 10c and 50c in red and are from different settings from the originals. They are on papers differing in colors from the originals. All 5c on granite paper are bogus.

Coat of Arms A2

1903
11	A2	5c	black, *pink*	40.00	
12	A2	10c	black, *orange*	50.00	
13	A2	25c	black, *gray blue*	40.00	
a.		25c black, *blue*		40.00	
14	A2	50c	black, *straw*	40.00	
15	A2	1b	black, *gray*	30.00	
		Nos. 11-15 (5)		200.00	

Postally used examples are very scarce, as are examples having 9 ornaments in horizontal borders. Nos. 11-15 pen canceled sell for same values as unused.

See note on controls after No. 5.

Counterfeits exist of Nos. 11-15. Stamps with 10 ornaments in horizontal borders are counterfeits.

Nos. 1-5, 11-15 were issued by a group of revolutionists and had a limited local use. The dates on the stamps commemorate the declaration of Venezuelan independence and a compact with Spain against Joseph Bonaparte.

VIRGIN ISLANDS

ˈvər-jən ˈī-lənds

LOCATION — West Indies, southeast of Puerto Rico
GOVT. — British colony
AREA — 59 sq. mi.
POP. — 12,034 (1980)
CAPITAL — Road Town

The British Virgin Islands constituted one of the presidencies of the Leeward Islands colony. For many years stamps of Leeward Islands were used concurrently.

The Virgin Islands group is divided between Great Britain and the United States. See Danish West Indies.

12 Pence = 1 Shilling
20 Shillings = 1 Pound
100 Cents = 1 Dollar (1951)

> **Catalogue values for unused stamps in this country are for Never Hinged items, beginning with Scott 88 in the regular postage section.**

PRE-STAMP POSTAL MARKINGS

Crowned Circle handstamp types I and VI are pictured in the Crowned Circle Handstamps and Great Britain Used Abroad section.

1842-58
A1	I	"Tortola" crowned circle handstamp in red, on cover	6,500.
A2	VI	"Tortola" crowned circle handstamp in red, on cover	22,000.

No. A2, in black, was used for the payment of official postage during 1900-18. Value, on cover $1,100.

STAMPS OF GREAT BRITAIN USED IN VIRGIN ISLANDS

Numeral cancellation type A is pictured in the Crowned Circle Handstamps and Great Britain Used Abroad section.

1858-60   A13 (Tortola)
A3	A	1p rose red (#20)	4,250.
A4	A	4p rose (#26)	5,000.
A5	A	6p lilac (#27)	1,600.
A6	A	1sh green (#28)	—

Issued under British Administration

Values for unused stamps are for examples with original gum as defined in the catalogue introduction. However, Nos. 1-2c are valued without gum as the vast majority of examples are found thus.

Virgin and Lamps — A1

St. Ursula — A2

A3

A4

1866   Litho.   Unwmk.   Perf. 12
Toned or White Paper
1	A1	1p green		50.00	65.00
a.		Toned paper		52.50	65.00
c.		Perf. 15x12, toned paper		12,000.	7,750.
2	A3	6p rose		65.00	100.00
a.		Large "V" in "VIRGIN"		375.00	475.00
b.		White paper		100.00	120.00
c.		As "a," white paper		425.00	525.00

Examples offered as No. 1c frequently have forged perfs.

1867-70   Perf. 15
3	A1	1p blue grn		65.00	75.00
		('70)			
4	A1	1p yel grn ('68)		80.00	80.00
a.		Toned paper		92.50	85.00
5	A2	4p lake, *buff*		45.00	65.00
a.		4p lake, *rose*		55.00	75.00
6	A3	6p rose		650.00	650.00
a.		Toned paper ('68)		325.00	375.00
7	A4	1sh rose & blk		300.00	400.00
a.		Toned paper		300.00	400.00
b.		Double lined frame		300.00	400.00
c.		As "b," bluish paper		300.00	400.00

Colored Margins
8	A4	1sh rose & blk		70.00	82.50
a.		White paper		85.00	95.00
b.		Bluish paper		825.00	1,000.
c.		Central figure omitted		225,000.	
		Nos. 3-8 (6)		1,210.	1,352.

Examples of No. 8c have perfs. trimmed on one or two sides.

1878   Wmk. 1   Perf. 14
9	A1	1p green		90.00	110.00

See #16-17, 19-20. For surcharge see #18.

Queen Victoria — A5

1880   Typo.
10	A5	1p green		80.00	95.00
11	A5	2½p red brown		110.00	130.00

1883-84   Wmk. 2
12	A5	½p yellow		92.50	92.50
13	A5	½p green		6.50	13.00
a.		Imperf., pair		1,750.	
14	A5	1p rose		37.50	40.00
15	A5	2½p ultra ('84)		3.00	17.50
		Nos. 12-15 (4)		139.50	163.00

No. 13a probably is a plate proof.

1887   Litho.
16	A2	4p brick red		40.00	70.00
a.		4p brown red		50.00	80.00
17	A3	6p violet		19.00	50.00

No. 8 Handstamp Surcharged in Violet

1888   Unwmk.   Perf. 15
18	A4	4p on 1sh dp rose & blk, toned paper		140.00	175.00
a.		Double surcharge		8,500.	
b.		Inverted surcharge		55,000.	
c.		White paper		200.00	250.00

1889   Wmk. 2   Perf. 14
19	A1	1p carmine		2.75	8.25
20	A4	1sh brown		50.00	80.00
a.		1sh black brown		90.00	110.00

St. Ursula with Sheaf of Lilies A7

Edward VII A8

1899   Engr.
21	A7	½p yellow grn		3.75	.60
a.		"PFNNY"		92.50	140.00
b.		"F" without cross bar		92.50	140.00
c.		Horiz. pair, imperf. between		13,000.	

22	A7	1p red		5.00	2.75
23	A7	2½p ultra		13.00	3.00
24	A7	4p chocolate		4.50	20.00
a.		"PENCF"		825.	1,200.
25	A7	6p dark violet		6.50	3.50
26	A7	7p slate green		12.00	6.50
27	A7	1sh ocher		25.00	37.50
28	A7	5sh dark blue		80.00	95.00
		Nos. 21-28 (8)		149.75	168.85

1904   Typo.   Wmk. 3
29	A8	½p violet & bl grn		1.00	.60
30	A8	1p violet & scar		3.25	.55
31	A8	2p violet & bis		7.75	4.75
32	A8	2½p violet & ultra		3.25	2.75
33	A8	3p violet & blk		4.75	3.25
34	A8	6p violet & brn		3.50	3.25
35	A8	1sh green & scar		6.00	6.50
36	A8	2sh6p violet & blk		35.00	72.50
37	A8	5sh green & ultra		62.50	87.50
		Nos. 29-37 (9)		127.00	181.65

Numerals of 2p, 3p, 1sh and 2sh6p of type A8 are in color on plain tablet.

George V — A9

Die I

For description of dies I and II see "Dies of British Colonial Stamps" in Table of Contents.

1913   Ordinary Paper
38	A9	½p green		3.75	6.00
39	A9	1p scarlet		2.75	17.50
a.		1p carmine		57.50	32.50
40	A9	2p gray		5.50	30.00
41	A9	2½p ultra		11.00	11.00

Chalky Paper
42	A9	3p vio, *yel*		3.25	8.00
43	A9	6p dl vio & red			
		vio		8.00	17.00
44	A9	1sh blk, *green*		3.75	11.00
45	A9	2sh6p blk & red, *bl*		57.50	60.00
46	A9	5sh grn & red, *yel*		45.00	140.00
		Nos. 38-46 (9)		136.50	300.50

Numerals of 2p, 3p, 1sh and 2sh6p of type A9 are in color on plain tablet.

Die II

1921   Wmk. 4
47	A9	½p green		9.50	47.50
48	A9	1p carmine		6.50	30.00

For overprints see Nos. MR1-MR2.

Colony Seal — A10

1922   Wmk. 3
49	A10	3p violet, *yel*		1.10	21.00
50	A10	1sh black, *emerald*		1.00	17.50
51	A10	2sh6p blk & red, *bl*		7.25	14.00
52	A10	5sh grn & red, *yel*		42.50	125.00
		Nos. 49-52 (4)		51.85	177.50

1922-28   Wmk. 4
53	A10	½p green		1.25	3.50
54	A10	1p rose red		.80	.80
55	A10	1p violet ('27)		1.40	5.00
56	A10	1½p rose red			
		('27)		2.10	3.25
57	A10	1½p fawn ('28)		2.25	1.90
58	A10	2p gray		1.40	7.75
59	A10	2½p ultra		3.25	24.00
60	A10	2½p orange ('23)		1.75	2.10
61	A10	3p dl vio, *yel*			
		('28)		3.25	15.00
62	A10	5p dl lil & ol grn		7.75	60.00
63	A10	6p dl vio & red			
		vio		2.10	9.00
a.		6p brown lilac & red violet		2.10	9.00
64	A10	1sh blk, *emer*			
		('28)		3.50	19.00
65	A10	2sh6p blk & red, *bl*			
		('28)		27.50	62.50
66	A10	5sh grn & red,			
		yel ('23)		27.50	95.00
		Nos. 53-66 (14)		85.80	308.80

The ½, 1, 2 and 2½p are on ordinary paper, the others on chalky.

Numerals of 1½p of type A10 are in color on plain tablet.

Common Design Types pictured following the introduction.

Silver Jubilee Issue
Common Design Type

1935, May 6 Engr. Perf. 11x12

69	CD301	1p car & dk blue	1.10	7.00
70	CD301	1½p black & ultra	1.10	6.00
71	CD301	2½p ultra & brn	2.00	5.50
72	CD301	1sh brn vio & ind	17.00	29.00
		Nos. 69-72 (4)	22.20	47.50
		Set, never hinged	32.50	

Coronation Issue
Common Design Type

1937, May 12 Perf. 11x11½

73	CD302	1p dark carmine	.40	2.00
74	CD302	1½p brown	.40	2.00
75	CD302	2½p deep ultra	.40	1.00
		Nos. 73-75 (3)	1.20	5.00
		Set, never hinged	1.75	

King George VI and Seal of the Colony — A11

1938-47 Photo. Perf. 14

76	A11	½p green	.90	.90
77	A11	1p scarlet	1.25	1.00
78	A11	1½p red brown	1.50	1.25
79	A11	2p gray	1.50	1.25
80	A11	2½p ultra	2.00	1.50
81	A11	3p orange	1.25	1.00
82	A11	6p deep violet	3.50	1.00
83	A11	1sh olive bister	2.50	2.00
84	A11	2sh6p sepia	11.00	5.00
85	A11	5sh rose lake	11.00	6.00
86	A11	10sh brt blue ('47)	6.00	11.00
87	A11	£1 gray blk ('47)	7.00	25.00
		Nos. 76-87 (12)	49.40	56.90
		Set, never hinged	70.00	

Catalogue values for unused stamps in this section, from this point to the end of the section, are for Never Hinged items.

Peace Issue
Common Design Type

Perf. 13½x14
1946, Nov. 1 Engr. Wmk. 4

88	CD303	1½p red brown	.25	.25
89	CD303	3p orange	.25	.25

Silver Wedding Issue
Common Design Types

1949, Jan. 3 Photo. Perf. 14x14½

90	CD304	2½p brt ultra	.35	.35

Engr.; Name Typo.
Perf. 11½x11

91	CD305	£1 gray black	18.50	21.00

UPU Issue
Common Design Types
Engr.; Name Typo. on Nos. 93 & 94

1949, Oct. 10 Perf. 13½, 11x11½

92	CD306	2½p ultra	.40	1.75
93	CD307	3p deep orange	1.25	2.00
94	CD308	6p red lilac	.50	.40
95	CD309	1sh olive	.45	.45
		Nos. 92-95 (4)	2.60	4.60

University Issue
Common Design Types

1951 Engr. Perf. 14x14½

96	CD310	3c red brn & gray blk	.40	.40
97	CD311	12c purple & black	1.10	1.40

Map of the Islands A12

1951, Apr. 2 Wmk. 4 Perf. 14½x14

98	A12	6c red orange	.50	1.25
99	A12	12c purple	1.00	.50
100	A12	24c olive grn	.65	1.00
101	A12	$1.20 carmine	2.50	1.50
		Nos. 98-101 (4)	4.65	4.25

Restoration of the Legislative Council, 1950.

Sombrero Lighthouse — A13

Map of Jost van Dyke — A14

Designs: 3c, Sheep. 4c, Map, Anegada. 5c, Cattle. 8c, Map, Virgin Gorda. 12c, Map, Tortola. 24c, Badge of the Presidency. 60c, Dead Man's Chest. $1.20, Sir Francis Drake Channel. $2.40, Road Town. $4.80, Map, Virgin Islands.

1952, Apr. 15 Perf. 12½x13, 13x12½

102	A13	1c gray black	.40	2.00
103	A14	2c deep green	.85	.25
104	A14	3c choc & gray blk	.45	1.25
105	A14	4c red	.70	1.60
106	A14	5c gray blk & rose lake	1.40	.70
107	A14	8c ultra	.85	1.25
108	A14	12c purple	1.25	1.60
109	A13	24c dk brown	1.00	.25
110	A14	60c blue & ol grn	4.00	11.00
111	A14	$1.20 ultra & blk	6.00	12.00
112	A14	$2.40 hn brn & dk grn	175.00	16.00
113	A14	$4.80 rose car & bl	19.00	19.00
		Nos. 102-113 (12)	50.90	66.90

WAR TAX STAMPS

Regular Issue of 1913 Overprinted

1916-17 Wmk. 3 Perf. 14
Die I

MR1	A9	1p scarlet	.55	8.00
a.		1p carmine	2.50	21.00
MR2	A9	3p violet, yellow	4.50	26.00

WALLIS & FUTUNA ISLANDS
'wä-ləs and fə-'tü-nə 'ī-ləndz

LOCATION — Group of islands in the South Pacific Ocean, northeast of Fiji
GOVT. — French Overseas Territory
AREA — 106 sq. mi.
POP. — 13,000 (est. 1984)
CAPITAL — Mata-Utu, Wallis Island

100 Centimes = 1 Franc

New Caledonia Stamps of 1905-28 Overprinted in Black or Red

1920-28 Unwmk. Perf. 14x13½

1	A16	1c black, green	.30	.30
		Never hinged	.45	
		On cover		125.00
a.		Double overprint	175.00	
		Never hinged	240.00	
2	A16	2c red brown	.30	.30
		Never hinged	.45	
		On cover		125.00
3	A16	4c blue, org	.50	.50
		Never hinged	.75	
		On cover		125.00
4	A16	5c green	.50	.50
		Never hinged	.75	
		On cover		65.00
5	A16	5c dull blue ('22)	.40	.55
		Never hinged	.65	
		On cover		110.00

6	A16	10c rose	.65	.65
		Never hinged	1.00	
		On cover		50.00
7	A16	10c green ('22)	.90	.90
		Never hinged	1.20	
		On cover		50.00
8	A16	10c red, pink ('25)	2.25	2.25
		Never hinged	3.00	
		On cover		50.00
9	A16	15c violet	1.10	1.10
		Never hinged	1.60	
		On cover		50.00
10	A17	20c gray brown	1.00	1.25
		Never hinged	1.40	
		On cover		65.00
11	A17	25c blue, grn	1.50	1.50
		Never hinged	2.25	
		On cover		75.00
		On cover, single franking		200.00
12	A17	25c red, yel ('22)	1.00	1.00
		Never hinged	1.25	
		On cover		45.00
13	A17	30c brown, org	1.60	2.00
		Never hinged	2.40	
		On cover		80.00
		On cover, single franking		225.00
14	A17	30c dp rose ('22)	1.50	1.75
		Never hinged	2.40	
		On cover		50.00
15	A17	30c red orange ('25)	.85	.85
		Never hinged	1.10	
		On cover		45.00
16	A17	30c lt green ('27)	2.40	3.25
		Never hinged	3.75	
		On cover		65.00
17	A17	35c black, yel (R)	1.00	1.00
		Never hinged	1.40	
		On cover		105.00
		On cover, single franking		275.00
18	A17	40c rose, grn	1.25	1.50
		Never hinged	1.60	
		On cover		95.00
		On cover, single franking		140.00
19	A17	45c violet brn, pnksh	1.60	2.00
		Never hinged	2.40	
		On cover		95.00
		On cover, single franking		175.00
20	A17	50c red, org	1.75	2.10
		Never hinged	2.50	
		On cover		105.00
		On cover, single franking		225.00
21	A17	50c dark blue ('22)	2.00	2.40
		Never hinged	2.90	
		On cover		65.00
		On cover, single franking		160.00
22	A17	50c dark gray ('25)	2.60	3.25
		Never hinged	4.00	
		On cover		90.00
		On cover, single franking		200.00
23	A17	65c deep blue ('28)	7.50	7.50
		Never hinged	10.50	
		On cover		80.00
		On cover, single franking		175.00
24	A17	75c olive green	2.50	2.60
		Never hinged	4.00	
		On cover		125.00
		On cover, single franking		275.00

Nos. 113, 115-116 Overprinted

25	A18	1fr blue, yel grn	5.25	5.25
		Never hinged	7.50	
		On cover		125.00
		On cover, single franking		275.00
a.		Triple overprint	200.00	
		Never hinged	280.00	
b.		Double overprint	200.00	
		Never hinged	280.00	
c.		Pair, one stamp without overprint	525.00	
26	A18	1.10fr orange brn ('28)	5.50	7.25
		Never hinged	7.00	
		On cover		175.00
		On cover, single franking		30.00
27	A18	2fr carmine, bl	8.50	8.50
		Never hinged	12.00	
		On cover		140.00
		On cover, single franking		300.00
28	A18	5fr black, org (R)	17.00	17.00
		Never hinged	26.00	
		On cover		200.00
		On cover, single franking		400.00
		Nos. 1-28 (28)	73.20	79.00

No. 9 Surcharged in Various Colors

1922

29	A16	0.01c on 15c violet (Bk)	.75	.95
		Never hinged	1.10	
		On cover		160.00
30	A16	0.02c on 15c violet (Bl)	.75	.95
		Never hinged	1.10	
		On cover		125.00
31	A16	0.04c on 15c violet (G)	.75	.95
		Never hinged	1.10	
		On cover		125.00
32	A16	0.05c on 15c violet (R)	.75	.95
		Never hinged	1.10	
		On cover		105.00
		Nos. 29-32 (4)	3.00	3.80

Stamps and Types of 1920 Surcharged in Black or Red

1924-27

33	A18	25c on 2fr car, bl	1.00	1.00
		Never hinged	1.50	
		On cover		55.00
34	A18	25c on 5fr black, org	1.00	1.00
		Never hinged	1.50	
		On cover		55.00
35	A17	65c on 40c rose red, grn ('25)	1.75	2.00
		Never hinged	2.40	
		On cover		80.00
		On cover, single franking		200.00
36	A17	85c on 75c ol grn ('25)	1.40	1.60
		Never hinged	2.10	
		On cover		95.00
		On cover, single franking		225.00
37	A17	90c on 75c dp rose ('27)	2.25	2.75
		Never hinged	3.25	
		On cover		80.00
		On cover, single franking		225.00
38	A18	1.25fr on 1fr dp bl (R; '26)	1.10	1.40
		Never hinged	1.60	
		On cover		105.00
		On cover, single franking		190.00
39	A18	1.50fr on 1fr dp bl, bl ('27)	5.50	5.50
		Never hinged	7.25	
		On cover		125.00
		On cover, single franking		375.00
a.		Double surcharge	300.00	
		Never hinged	410.00	
b.		Surcharge omitted	290.00	
		Never hinged	390.00	
40	A18	3fr on 5fr red vio ('27)	9.00	8.00
		Never hinged	10.50	
		On cover		140.00
		On cover, single franking		400.00
a.		Surcharge omitted	240.00	
		Never hinged	325.00	
b.		Double surcharge	325.00	
		Never hinged	410.00	
41	A18	10fr on 5fr ol, lav ('27)	42.50	42.50
		Never hinged	47.50	
		On cover		160.00
		On cover, single franking		425.00
42	A18	20fr on 5fr vio rose, yel ('27)	50.00	50.00
		Never hinged	62.50	
		On cover		250.00
		On cover, single franking		550.00
		Nos. 33-42 (10)	115.50	115.75

New Caledonia Stamps and Types of 1928-40 Overprinted as in 1920

1930-40 Perf. 13½, 14x13, 14x13½

43	A19	1c brn vio & indigo	.25	.25
		Never hinged	.40	
		On cover		105.00
a.		Double overprint	200.00	
		Never hinged	260.00	
44	A19	2c dk brn & yel grn	.25	.25
		Never hinged	.40	
		On cover		95.00
45	A19	3c brn vio & ind ('40)	.25	.25
		Never hinged	.35	
		On cover		105.00
46	A19	4c org & Prus grn	.25	.25
		Never hinged	.40	
		On cover		95.00
47	A19	5c Prus bl & dp ol	.30	.40
		Never hinged	.45	
		On cover		90.00
48	A19	10c gray lil & dk brn	.30	.40
		Never hinged	.45	
		On cover		80.00
49	A19	15c yel brn & dp bl	.30	.40
		Never hinged	.45	
		On cover		75.00
50	A19	20c brn red & dk brn	.60	.70
		Never hinged	.90	
		On cover		65.00
51	A19	25c dk grn & dk brn	1.10	1.25
		Never hinged	1.50	
		On cover		45.00
52	A20	30c gray grn & bl grn	1.10	1.25
		Never hinged	1.50	
		On cover		65.00
53	A20	35c Prus grn & dk grn ('38)	1.10	1.25
		Never hinged	1.50	
		On cover		75.00
a.		Without overprint	200.00	
		Never hinged	47.50	
54	A20	40c brt red & olive	1.10	1.10
		Never hinged	1.50	
		On cover		45.00
55	A20	45c dp bl & red org	1.10	1.25
		Never hinged	1.50	
		On cover		65.00
56	A20	45c bl grn & dl grn ('40)	.90	1.00
		Never hinged	1.20	
		On cover		75.00
57	A20	50c violet & brn	1.10	1.10
		Never hinged	1.50	
		On cover		40.00

58	A20	55c bl vio & rose red ('38)		2.40	2.75
		Never hinged		3.50	
		On cover			75.00
59	A20	60c vio bl & car ('40)		.75	.90
		Never hinged		1.00	
		On cover			65.00
60	A20	65c org brn & bl		2.00	2.00
		Never hinged		2.90	
		On cover			75.00
61	A20	70c dp rose & brn ('38)		1.40	1.60
		Never hinged		1.75	
		On cover			75.00
62	A20	75c Prus bl & ol gray		3.00	3.00
		Never hinged		4.00	
		On cover			70.00
63	A20	80c dk cl & grn ('38)		1.40	1.60
		Never hinged		1.75	
		On cover			70.00
64	A20	85c green & brown ('38)		3.75	4.00
		Never hinged		5.25	
		On cover			70.00
65	A20	90c dp red & brt red		2.40	2.75
		Never hinged		3.40	
		On cover			75.00
		On cover, single franking			160.00
66	A20	90c ol grn & rose red ('39)		1.10	1.25
		Never hinged		1.40	
		On cover			40.00
67	A21	1fr dp ol & sal red		4.00	4.75
		Never hinged		5.25	
		On cover			105.00
		On cover, single franking			190.00
68	A21	1fr rose red & dk car ('38)		2.40	2.75
		Never hinged		3.25	
		On cover			80.00
		On cover, single franking			145.00
69	A21	1fr brn red & grn ('40)		.80	.80
		Never hinged		1.10	
		On cover			45.00
70	A21	1.10fr dp grn & brn		40.00	40.00
		Never hinged		52.50	
		On cover			225.00
		On cover, single franking			375.00
71	A21	1.25fr brn red & grn ('33)		3.75	3.50
		Never hinged		4.50	
		On cover			70.00
		On cover, single franking			190.00
72	A21	1.25fr rose red & dk car ('39)		1.10	1.25
		Never hinged		1.20	
		On cover			65.00
		On cover, single franking			190.00
73	A21	1.40fr dk bl & red org ('40)		1.10	1.40
		Never hinged		1.40	
		On cover			65.00
		On cover, single franking			145.00
74	A21	1.50fr dp bl & bl		1.25	1.50
		Never hinged		1.90	
		On cover			75.00
		On cover, single franking			145.00
75	A21	1.60fr dp grn & brn ('40)		1.60	2.00
		Never hinged		2.00	
		On cover			75.00
		On cover, single franking			160.00
76	A21	1.75fr dk bl & red org ('33)		16.00	16.00
		Never hinged		22.00	
		On cover			125.00
		On cover, single franking			225.00
77	A21	1.75fr vio bl ('38)		2.50	2.75
		Never hinged		3.50	
		On cover			90.00
		On cover, single franking			190.00
78	A21	2fr red org & brn		2.00	1.90
		Never hinged		3.00	
		On cover			95.00
		On cover, single franking			225.00
79	A21	2.25fr vio bl ('39)		2.50	2.40
		Never hinged		3.25	
		On cover			75.00
		On cover, single franking			160.00
80	A21	2.50fr brn & lt brn ('40)		2.00	2.40
		Never hinged		2.75	
		On cover			90.00
		On cover, single franking			200.00
81	A21	3fr magenta & brn		2.00	2.00
		Never hinged		2.75	
		On cover			95.00
		On cover, single franking			190.00
82	A21	5fr dk bl & brn		2.50	2.60
		Never hinged		3.75	
		On cover			105.00
		On cover, single franking			225.00
83	A21	10fr vio & brn, pnksh		3.50	3.50
		Never hinged		5.50	
		On cover			105.00
		On cover, single franking			225.00
84	A21	20fr red & brn, yel		5.25	5.25
		Never hinged		7.75	
		On cover			125.00
		On cover, single franking			275.00
		Nos. 43-84 (42)		122.45	127.70

For overprints see Nos. 94-126 in Scott Standard catalogue, Vol. 6.

Common Design Types pictured following the introduction.

Colonial Exposition Issue
Common Design Types

1931, Apr. 13 Engr. Perf. 12½
Name of Country Typo. in Black

85	CD70	40c deep green		8.75	8.75
		Never hinged		13.00	
		On cover			125.00
86	CD71	50c violet		8.75	8.75
		Never hinged		13.00	
		On cover			105.00
87	CD72	90c red orange		8.75	8.75
		Never hinged		13.00	
		On cover			170.00
		On cover, single franking			225.00
88	CD73	1.50fr dull blue		8.75	8.75
		Never hinged		13.00	
		On cover			160.00
		On cover, single franking			200.00
		Nos. 85-88 (4)		35.00	35.00

Colonial Arts Exhibition Issue
Common Design Type
Souvenir Sheet

1937 Imperf.

89	CD78	3fr red violet		28.50	37.50
		Never hinged		45.00	
		On cover			200.00
		On cover, single franking			300.00

New York World's Fair Issue
Common Design Type

1939, May 10 Engr. Perf. 12½x12

90	CD82	1.25fr carmine lake		3.00	3.00
		Never hinged		4.50	
		On cover			95.00
		On cover, single franking			170.00
91	CD82	2.25fr ultramarine		3.00	3.00
		Never hinged		4.50	
		On cover			95.00
		On cover, single franking			160.00

SEMI-POSTAL STAMPS

French Revolution Issue
Common Design Type
Unwmk.

1939, July 5 Photo. Perf. 13
Name and Value Typo. in Black

B1	CD83	45c + 25c green		19.00	19.00
		Never hinged		30.00	
		On cover			170.00
B2	CD83	70c + 30c brown		19.00	19.00
		Never hinged		30.00	
		On cover			125.00
B3	CD83	90c + 35c red org		19.00	19.00
		Never hinged		30.00	
		On cover			95.00
B4	CD83	1.25fr + 1fr rose pink		19.00	19.00
		Never hinged		30.00	
		On cover			170.00
		On cover, single franking			250.00
B5	CD83	2.25fr + 2fr blue		19.00	19.00
		Never hinged		30.00	
		On cover			160.00
		On cover, single franking			225.00
		Nos. B1-B5 (5)		95.00	95.00
		Set, never hinged		150.00	

POSTAGE DUE STAMPS

Postage Due Stamps of New Caledonia, 1906, Overprinted in Black or Red

1920 Unwmk. Perf. 13½x14

J1	D2	5c ultra, azure		1.00	1.00
		Never hinged		1.60	
		On cover			125.00
J2	D2	10c brn, buff		1.10	1.10
		Never hinged		1.75	
		On cover			125.00
J3	D2	15c grn, grnsh		1.10	1.10
		Never hinged		1.75	
		On cover			125.00
J4	D2	20c blk, yel (R)		1.50	1.50
		Never hinged		2.60	
		On cover			145.00
a.		Double overprint		200.00	
		Never hinged		290.00	
J5	D2	30c carmine rose		1.50	1.50
		Never hinged		2.60	
		On cover			160.00
J6	D2	50c ultra, straw		2.40	2.40
		Never hinged		4.00	
		On cover			170.00
J7	D2	60c olive, azure		2.90	2.90
		Never hinged		4.75	
		On cover			190.00
a.		Double overprint		200.00	
		Never hinged		290.00	
J8	D2	1fr grn, cream		3.75	3.75
		Never hinged		6.50	
		On cover			225.00
		Nos. J1-J8 (8)		15.25	15.25

Type of 1920 Issue Surcharged

1927

J9	D2	2fr on 1fr brt vio		17.50	17.50
		Never hinged		27.50	
		On cover			300.00
J10	D2	3fr on 1fr org brn		17.50	17.50
		Never hinged		27.50	
		On cover			340.00

Postage Due Stamps of New Caledonia, 1928, Overprinted as in 1920

1930

J11	D3	2c sl bl & dp brn		.25	.25
		Never hinged		.40	
		On cover			160.00
J12	D3	4c brn red & bl grn		.25	.25
		Never hinged		.40	
		On cover			160.00
J13	D3	5c red org & bl blk		.25	.25
		Never hinged		.40	
		On cover			125.00
J14	D3	10c mag & Prus bl		.25	.25
		Never hinged		.40	
		On cover			95.00
J15	D3	15c dl grn & scar		.35	.35
		Never hinged		.50	
		On cover			95.00
J16	D3	20c maroon & ol grn		.75	.75
		Never hinged		1.00	
		On cover			105.00
J17	D3	25c bis brn & sl bl		.75	.75
		Never hinged		1.00	
		On cover			105.00
J18	D3	30c bl grn & ol grn		1.40	1.40
		Never hinged		1.90	
		On cover			105.00
J19	D3	50c lt brn & dk red		.85	.85
		Never hinged		1.20	
		On cover			125.00
J20	D3	60c mag & brt rose		1.40	1.40
		Never hinged		1.90	
		On cover			140.00
J21	D3	1fr dl bl & Prus grn		1.40	1.40
		Never hinged		2.00	
		On cover			160.00
J22	D3	2fr dk red & ol grn		1.40	1.40
		Never hinged		2.00	
		On cover			175.00
J23	D3	3fr vio & brn		1.40	1.40
		Never hinged		2.00	
		On cover			200.00
		Nos. J11-J23 (13)		10.70	10.70

WESTERN UKRAINE

ˈwes-tərn yü-ˈkrān

LOCATION — In Eastern Central Europe
GOVT. — A former short-lived independent State

A provisional government was established in 1918 in the eastern part of Austria-Hungary but the area later came under Polish administration.

100 Shahiv (Sotykiv) = 1 Hryvnia
100 Heller = 1 Krone

Forgeries of almost all Western Ukraine stamps are plentiful. Particularly dangerous forgeries have been noted for the Kolomyia Issue and for the First and Second Stanyslaviv Issues.

Lviv Issue

Austria Nos. 145-146, 148, 169 Overprinted

Nos. 1-4A are handstamped with an octagonal overprint that reads "ZAKHIDNO UKR.

NARODNA REPUBLYKA" ("Western Ukrainian National Republic"), framing the image of a rearing crowned lion.

1918, Nov. 20

1	A37	3h		55.00	425.00
a.		Inverted overprint		150.00	
2	A37	5h light green		50.00	325.00
a.		Inverted overprint		150.00	
3	A37	10h magenta		50.00	325.00
a.		Inverted overprint		150.00	
4	A42	20h dark green		35.00	350.00
a.		Inverted overprint		150.00	
4A	A42	20h light green		240.00	900.00
		Nos. 1-4A (5)		430.00	2,325.

This issue was in circulation for only two days before Lviv was captured by the Poles on Nov. 22. No examples of Nos. 1-4A used in Lviv are known.

The Western Ukrainian National Republic (ZUNR) government evacuated to the city of Ternopil, which became the provisional capital. ZUNR postal operations were set up in other Western Ukrainian cities, and the Lviv Issue was used in Stanyslaviv (earliest known cancellation date, Dec. 8), Khodoriv and Kolomyia.

Nos. 1-4 exist in pairs with both normal and inverted overprints. Value $325.

Overprints in other colors (green, red and violet) are known, but these are probably proofs. Violet-black overprints are likely transitional color impressions.

Kolomyia Issue

Austria Nos. 168, 145, 147, 149 Surcharged

Kolomyia is the main town of the Pokutia region of southwestern Ukraine. Cut off from ZUNR postal officials and in urgent need of basic value stamps, the Kolomyia postmaster obtained permission from the District Military Command to surcharge remaining Austrian postage stamps to either 5 or 10 sotyks, the equivalent of 5 or 10 heller. These stamps were produced on Dec. 10, under very strict security, by preparing two distinct plates (one for each value) that overprinted 25 stamps at a time (5x5 quarter sections of the Austrian 100-stamp panes). The stamps were placed on sale two days later.

1918, Dec. 12 Unwmk. Perf. 12½

5	A42	5sot on 15h dl red		90.00	120.00
a.		Inverted overprint		600.00	725.00
b.		Double overprint		1,500.	1,600.
6	A37	10sot on 3h vio		90.00	120.00
7	A37	10sot on 6h dp org		1,650.	1,250.
8	A37	10sot on 12h lt bl		1,750.	1,500.
		Nos. 5-8 (4)		3,580.	2,990.

10 sotyk on 15 heller values are essays; only six were produced.

All inverted surcharges on Nos. 6-8 are forgeries. Double surcharges are forgeries.

First Stanyslaviv Issue

Austrian Stamps of 1916-18 Surcharged in Shahiv (shown) and Hryvnia Currency

At the end of December, 1918, the national government again moved, this time to the city of Stanyslaviv (present-day Ivano-Frankivsk). A shortage of qualified postal personnel resulted in a considerable delay in the creation of new ZUNR postage stamps. In the interim, remaining unoverprinted Austrian stamps were used. Finally, on March 18, 1919, 20 different available Austrian definitive stamps were typograph surcharged at the Weidenfeld Printing Shop in Stanyslaviv.

1919, Mar. 18

9	A37	3sh on 3h bright violet		17.00	22.50
10	A37	5sh on 5h light green		17.00	22.50
11	A37	6sh on 6h deep orange		32.50	55.00
12	A37	10sh on 10h mag		27.50	37.50

13	A37	12sh on 12h lt blue	27.50	37.50
a.		Double overprint	300.00	425.00
b.		Double overprint, one on reverse	500.00	210.00
14	A42	15sh on 15h dull red	27.50	37.50
15	A42	20sh on 20h deep green	27.50	37.50
16	A42	30sh on 30h dull violet	100.00	100.00
17	A39	40sh on 40h olive green	27.50	37.50
18	A39	50sh on 50h dark green	27.50	37.50
19	A39	60sh on 60h deep blue	27.50	37.50
20	A39	80sh on 80h orange brown	27.50	37.50
a.		Inverted overprint	300.00	425.00
21	A39	1hr on 1k car, *yel*	40.00	45.00
22	A40	2hr on 2k lt blue	40.00	50.00
23	A40	3hr on 3k claret (on #161)	3,250.	3,250.
24	A40	3hr on 3k car rose (on #165)	100.00	82.50
25	A40	3hr on 3k car rose (on #173)	80.00	80.00
26	A40	4hr on 4k dk grn (on #162)	800.00	700.00
27	A40	4hr on 4k yel grn (on #166)	75.00	55.00
28	A40	10hr on 10k deep violet	800.00	800.00
a.		Double overprint	3,000.	3,500.
		Nos. 9-28 (20)	5,571.	5,562.

The 25sh on 25h, type A42, in both light and dull blue shades, never received this overprint. All such stamps are fantasies.

Second Stanyslaviv Issue

The overprinting of a second issue of postage stamps in Stanyslaviv was undertaken in early May. Stamps from several different Austrian stamp series were utilized to create four distinct sets. Most of the stamps available were Austrian postage due, charity or field post stamps.

Postage Due Stamps of Bosnia, 1904 Surcharged but without Asterisks

1919, May 5

29	D1	1sh on 1h blk, red & yel	32.50	40.00
a.		Inverted overprint	100.00	65.00
b.		Double overprint	90.00	60.00
30	D1	2sh on 2h blk, red & yel	15.00	15.00
a.		Inverted overprint	85.00	150.00
31	D1	3sh on 3h blk, red & yel	17.50	35.00
a.		Inverted overprint	25.00	45.00
32	D1	4sh on 4h blk, red & yel	125.00	125.00
a.		Inverted overprint	175.00	175.00
b.		Double overprint	300.00	300.00
33	D1	5sh on 5h blk, red & yel	3,250.	3,500.
34	D1	6sh on 6h blk, red & yel	600.00	600.00
a.		Inverted overprint	900.00	900.00
b.		Double overprint	750.00	750.00
35	D1	7sh on 7h blk, red & yel	25.00	27.50
a.		Inverted overprint	37.50	42.50
36	D1	8sh on 8h blk, red & yel	25.00	30.00
a.		Inverted overprint	50.00	60.00
b.		Vertical overprint	750.00	950.00
c.		As "b," double overprint	950.00	1,100.
37	D1	10sh on 10h blk, red & yel	1,250.	1,400.
38	D1	15sh on 15h blk, red & yel	625.00	625.00
a.		Inverted overprint	750.00	800.00
39	D1	20sh on 20h blk, red & yel	6,250.	
a.		Double overprint	7,750.	17,000.
40	D1	50sh on 50h blk, red & yel	350.00	375.00
a.		Inverted overprint	550.00	600.00

Nos. 29-40 were created by overprinting Bosnian 1904 postage due stamps, which had been brought to Stanyslaviv by a Ukrainian military officer returning from the Serbian front. The same printing cliché was used as for the First Stanyslaviv Issue, but the asterisk obliterators were removed.

Most of the overprinting was made using 50-stamp panes (half of a sheet). After one half of the pane (25 positions) was overprinted, it would apparently be turned over and its second half overprinted with the same 25-position block, but as an inverted impression. After overprinting, the pane was torn into two equal 25-stamp halves.

A corrected block was utilized in overprinting, resulting in two types of surcharges on No. 29 (shahiv to shaha) and on Nos. 32, 34 and 38 (shahiv to shahi).

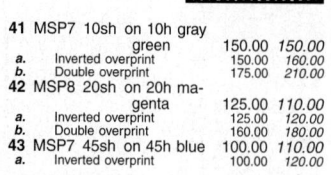

Austrian Military Semipostal Stamps of 1918 Srchd.

41	MSP7	10sh on 10h gray green	150.00	150.00
a.		Inverted overprint	150.00	160.00
b.		Double overprint	175.00	210.00
42	MSP8	20sh on 20h magenta	125.00	110.00
a.		Inverted overprint	125.00	120.00
b.		Double overprint	160.00	180.00
43	MSP7	45sh on 45h blue	100.00	110.00
a.		Inverted overprint	100.00	120.00

Nos. 41-43 were printed in the same manner as Nos. 29-40.

Austrian Military Stamps of 1917 Srchd.

44	M3	1sh on 1h grnsh blue		
45	M3	2sh on 2h red orange	100.00	100.00
a.		Inverted overprint	125.00	125.00
b.		Double overprint	210.00	210.00
46	M3	3sh on 3h olive gray	175.00	190.00
a.		Double overprint	750.00	750.00
47	M3	5sh on 5h olive grn	275.00	275.00
48	M3	6sh on 6h violet	150.00	175.00
49	M3	10sh on 10h org brn	900.00	1,000.
50	M3	12sh on 12h blue	550.00	600.00
a.		Inverted overprint	650.00	725.00
51	M3	15sh on 15h brt rose	500.00	600.00
a.		Inverted overprint	625.00	725.00
52	M3	20sh on 20h red brown	16.50	20.00
a.		Inverted overprint	82.50	140.00
b.		Double overprint	47.50	55.00
53	M3	25sh on 25h ultra	3,250.	3,900.
54	M3	30sh on 30h slate	1,000.	1,200.
55	M3	40sh on 40h olive bis	850.00	850.00
56	M3	50sh on 50h deep green	9.00	9.00
a.		Inverted overprint	20.00	20.00
b.		Double overprint	55.00	55.00
57	M3	60sh on 60h car rose	950.00	950.00
58	M3	80sh on 80h dull blue	47.50	47.50
a.		Inverted overprint	80.00	85.00
59	M3	90sh on 90h dk vio	950.00	1,000.
60	M4	2hr on 2k rose, *straw*	15.00	17.50
a.		Inverted overprint	27.50	35.00
b.		Imperforate	3,000.	
61	M4	3hr on 3k blue, *grn*	22.50	25.00
a.		Inverted overprint	27.50	30.00
b.		Double overprint	60.00	65.00
62	M4	4hr on 4k rose, *grn*	22.50	25.00
a.		Inverted overprint	50.00	30.00
b.		Double overprint	60.00	65.00
63	M4	10hr on 10k dl violet, *gray*	35,000.	35,000.

Two examples of No. 63 were printed, and neither was ever postally used. The "used" example was cut from a document prepared by the Western Ukrainian economic bureau (Ekonomat) to display the stamps that made up the First, Second and Third Stanyslaviv issues. The specimen stamps on this document were tied with a double-ring bureau cancel that somewhat resembles a regular double-ring postal cancellation.

About half of this issue, where several sheets were available for printing, was overprinted in the manner of Nos. 29-43.

Austrian Stamps of 1916-18 Surcharged

64	A38	15sh on 36h vio (on #J61)	350.00	450.00
a.		Double overprint	450.00	500.00
65	A38	50sh on 42h choc (on #J63)	5,000.	5,500.
66	A37	3sh on 3h brt violet (on #145)	190.00	190.00
67	A37	5sh on 5h lt green (on #146)	190.00	190.00
a.		Inverted overprint	290.00	290.00
68	A37	6sh on 6h deep org (on #147)	725.00	725.00
69	A37	10sh on 10h magenta (on #148)	210.00	210.00
a.		Inverted overprint	250.00	250.00
70	A37	12sh on 12h lt blue (on #149)	425.00	425.00
71	A38	15sh on 15h rose red (on #150)	190.00	190.00
a.		Inverted overprint	225.00	225.00
72	A42	15sh on 15h dull red (on #168)	210.00	210.00
73	A42	30sh on 30h dull violet (on #171)	190.00	190.00
a.		Double overprint	350.00	350.00
74	A39	40sh on 40h ol grn (on #154)	300.00	300.00
75	M3	50sh on 50h dp grn (on #M61)	475.00	475.00

The two bars in the surcharge were originally created to obliterate the "PORTO" on Nos. 64 and 65 but were subsequently retained for Nos. 66-75.

Third Stanyslaviv Issue

Austrian Stamps of 1916-18 Overprinted

1919, May

76	A37	3h brt violet	.50	1.00
77	A37	5h light green	.50	1.00
78	A37	6h deep orange	.50	1.00
79	A37	10h magenta	.50	1.00
80	A37	12h light blue	.50	1.00
81	A42	15h dull red	.50	1.00
82	A42	20h deep green	.50	1.00
83	A42	25h blue	.50	1.00
84	A42	30h dull vio	.50	1.00
85	A39	40h olive green	.75	1.25
86	A39	50h dark green	.75	1.25
87	A39	60h deep blue	.75	1.25
88	A39	80h orange brn	1.00	1.60
89	A39	90h red violet	1.00	1.60
90	A39	1k car, *yel*	1.25	4.00
91	A40	2k light blue	2.00	6.00
92	A40	3k carmine rose	2.50	7.50
93	A40	4k yellow grn	12.00	16.00
94	A40	10k deep violet	16.00	50.00
		Nos. 76-94 (19)	42.50	99.10

Issued: 3h-10h, 15h, 25h-40h, 60h-1k, 5/8; balance of set, 5/13.

A definitive set for Western Ukraine was ordered from the Austrian State Printing Office in March, 1919. Because of the time involved in designing and printing these stamps, Nos. 76-94 were overprinted in Vienna as a provisional issue and were delivered in two shipments. Because travel into and out of Stanyslaviv was becoming more difficult as the month wore on, it was not known whether or not the second shipment, which included the higher values, would arrive. Because of this, the Fourth Stanyslaviv Issue, Nos. 95-103, were overprinted locally.

Fourth Stanislaviv Issue

Austrian Military Stamps of 1917-18 Surcharged in Black

1919, May			**Perf. 12½**	
95	M3	2hr on 2k rose, *straw*	15.00	15.00
a.		Perf 11½	130.00	150.00

96	M3	3hr on 2k rose, *straw*	13.00	16.00
a.		Perf 11½	130.00	160.00
97	M3	3hr on 3k grn, *blue*	125.00	175.00
a.		"5" instead of "3" at left in overprint	1,500.	
98	M3	4hr on 2k rose, *straw*	15.00	16.00
99	M3	4hr on 4k rose, *grn*	1,300.	1,900.
100	M3	5hr on 2k rose, *straw*	20.00	22.50
a.		Inverted surcharge	300.00	
101	M3	10hr on 10h dp grn	30.00	40.00
a.		Double surcharge	175.00	

Austrian Postage Due Stamps of 1916 Srchd., but without Rosettes and Numerals

102	D5	1hr ultra	140.00	210.00
103	D5	5hr ultra	1,400.	2,100.

REGISTRATION STAMPS

Kolomyia Issue

RS1

Without Gum

1918-19		**Unwmk. Typeset**		***Imperf.***
F1	RS1	30sot black, *rose*	250.00	175.00
F2	RS1	50sot black, *rose* ('19)	120.00	150.00

No. F1 was printed on Dec. 10 and issued Dec. 12, 1918, along with the regular Kolomyia Issue (Nos. 5-8). On Dec. 19, the ZUNR government approved an increase in the registered letter rate to 50 sotyks, effective January 1, 1919. Because of communication disruptions, the Kolomyia post office did not learn of this decree until about January 7, when it ordered new values in the higher denomination (No. F2). F1 continued to be used, usually in combination with 20h of Austrian stamps, until supplies were exhausted, at which point No. F2 was put into use. A second printing of the 50sot value was made in late March. Variations in paper color — from light pink to deep rose — as well as paper thickness occurred in the 30-sot and both of the 50-sot printings.

Nos. F1-F2a were typographed in vertical panes of five stamps by the Wilhelm Brauner Print Ship in Kolomyia.

Forgeries exist.

OCCUPATION STAMPS

Romanian Occupation of Pokutia

Only the stamps listed below were officially created. Soon after the Romanian occupation ended on Aug. 20, 1919, the C.M.T. handstamps fell into the hands of speculators, and some 37 other Austrian stamps were overprinted. None of these privately-created stamps are known on authentic covers.

Austrian Stamps Surcharged in Dark Violet Blue

1919, June 14 Unwmk. *Perf. 12½*
On Stamps of 1916-18

N1	A37	40h on 5h lt grn	4.50	*5.50*
N2	A42	60h on 15h dl red	5.50	*6.50*
N3	A42	60h on 20h dp grn	2.25	*3.25*
a.		Inverted overprint	3,000.	
b.		Double overprint	25.00	
N4	A42	60h on 25h blue	12.00	*13.00*
a.		Inverted overprint	60.00	
b.		Double overprint	82.50	
N5	A42	60h on 30h dl vio	14.00	*15.00*
N6	A39	1k 20h on 50h dk grn	5.50	*6.50*
N7	A39	1k 20h on 60h dp bl	10.00	*12.00*
N8	A39	1k 20h on 1k car, yel	19.00	*21.00*

On Austrian Postage Due Stamps of 1910-1917

N9	D4	40h on 5h rose red	21.00	*22.50*
N10	D3	1k 20h on 25h carmine	175.00	*350.00*
N11	D4	1k 20h on 25h rose red	175.00	*350.00*
N12	D4	1k 20h on 30h rose red	1,400.	*1,400.*
N13	A38	1k 20h on 50h on 42h choc	1,500.	*1,500.*

Arms of Kiev — Arms of Ukraine

Arms of Galicia

First Definitive Issue, May 1919: Lithographed at the Austrian State Printing Office on unwatermarked white paper. Inscribed: "Ukrainska Narodnia Republyka Zakhidnia Oblast." ("Ukrainian National Republic Western Province"). Set of 12 values (four of each design), perf 11½ or imperf. Not issued. Value, set of 12: perf $350; imperf $550.

Second Definitive Issue, May 1919: Lithographed at the Austrian State Printing Office on unwatermarked white paper. Inscribed: "Ukrainska Narodnia Respublika Z.O." ("Ukrainian National Republic W(estern) P(rovince)"). Design incorporates the heraldic arms of Ukraine (trident), Kiev (Archangel Michael) and Lviv (lion rampant). 10, 20 and 50 sotyk values imperf; 1 and 10 krone values perf 11½. Not issued. Value, set of 5, $6. Also exists on cream-colored paper.

YEMEN

ˈye-mən

LOCATION — Arabian Peninsula, south of Saudi Arabia and bordering on the Red Sea
GOVT. — Kingdom
AREA — 73,300 sq. mi.
CAPITAL — San'a

40 Bogaches = 1 Imadi

Watermarks

Wmk. 127 — Quatrefoils

Wmk. 258 — Arabic Characters and Y G Multiple

For Domestic Postage

A1

Crossed Daggers and Arabic Inscriptions A2

1926 Unwmk. Typo. *Imperf.*
Laid Paper
Without Gum

1	A1	2½b black	60.00	60.00
2	A1	2½b black, *orange*	60.00	60.00
3	A2	5b black	60.00	60.00
		Nos. 1-3 (3)	180.00	180.00

No. 2 is known rouletted 7½ or 9.
Type A1 differs from A2 primarily in the inscription in the left dagger blade.
All come on wove paper. Beware of forgeries, especially those on wove paper.

For Foreign and Domestic Postage

Arabic Inscriptions
A3   A4

1930-31 Wmk. 127 *Perf. 14*

7	A3	½b orange ('31)	.30	.25
8	A3	1b green	.40	.30
9	A3	1b yellow grn ('31)	.35	.25
10	A3	2b olive grn	.40	.35
11	A3	2b olive brn ('31)	.35	.25
12	A3	3b dull vio ('31)	.40	.35
13	A3	4b red	.60	.50
14	A3	4b deep rose ('31)	.50	.40
15	A3	5b slate gray ('31)	.90	.50
16	A4	6b dull blue	1.25	1.00
17	A4	6b dp ultra ('31)	1.00	.75
18	A4	8b lilac rose ('31)	1.40	1.00
19	A4	10b lt brown	2.00	1.40
20	A4	10b brn org ('31)	1.75	1.00
21	A4	20b yel grn ('31)	4.50	2.50

22	A4	1i red brn & lt bl	8.00	6.00
23	A4	1i lil rose & yel grn ('31)	8.00	6.00
		Nos. 7-23 (17)	32.10	22.80

Some values exist imperforate.
For surcharges and overprints see No. 30; Nos. 59-62, 166-167, 169-171, 174-176, 246-246P in Scott Standard catalogue, Vol. 6.

Flags of Saudi Arabia, Yemen and Iraq — A5

1939 Litho. Wmk. 258 *Perf. 12½*

24	A5	4b dl rose & ultra	.80	.50
25	A5	6b slate bl & ultra	.80	.50
26	A5	10b fawn & ultra	1.40	.75
27	A5	14b olive & ultra	2.25	1.25
28	A5	20b yel grn & ultra	3.25	1.75
29	A5	1i claret & ultra	6.50	3.50
		Nos. 24-29 (6)	15.00	8.25

2nd anniv. of the Arab Alliance. Nos. 24-29 exist imperforate. Value set, $20.
For overprints see Nos. C29-C29D in Scott Standard catalogue, Vol. 6.

a   b

Five types of surcharge:
All genuine surcharges are 12-13mm x 15-16mm and were made from steel handstamps.
a. "YEMEN" ½mm from left frameline and ½mm above bottom frameline.
b. "YEMEN" ½mm from left frameline and 1½mm above bottom frameline.
c. "YEMEN" 1½mm from left frameline and ½mm above bottom frameline. Found only on Types A13 and D1.
d. Arabic "4" at the center of the surcharge has been replaced with two vertical strokes. Usually blurred and found only on Type A9.
e. Arabic "4" has been replaced by a pair of crescents. Found only on Type A13.
Values of surcharged stamps are for ordinary examples. Clear, legible surcharges command a premium. Beware of fraudulent rubber-stamped surcharges in violet or grey black ink.

1939 Wmk. 127 *Perf. 14*
No. 7 Handstamped Type "a" in Black

30	A3	4b on ½b orange	*15.00*	*12.50*

See Nos. 44-48, 59-67, 82, 86-87 in Scott Standard catalogue, Vol. 6.

A6

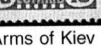

A7

1940 Wmk. 258 Litho. *Perf. 12½*

31	A6	½b ocher & ultra	.25	.25
32	A6	1b lt grn & rose red	.25	.25
33	A6	2b bis brn & vio	.25	.25
34	A6	3b dl vio & ultra	.25	.25
35	A6	4b rose & yel grn	.35	.30
36	A6	5b dk gray grn & bis brn	.40	.35
37	A7	6b ultra & yel org	.45	.45
38	A7	8b claret & dull bl	.55	.50
39	A7	10b brn org & yel grn	.75	.75
40	A7	14b gray grn & vio	.95	.80
41	A7	18b emerald & blk	1.10	.90
42	A7	20b yel ol & cerise	1.50	1.50
43	A7	1i vio rose, yel grn & brn red	2.75	2.50
		Nos. 31-43 (13)	9.80	9.05
		Set, never hinged	20.00	

No. 36 was used as a 4b stamp in 1957.
For surcharges see Nos. 44-47 in Scott Standard catalogue, Vol. 6.

YUGOSLAVIA

yü-gō-'slä-vē-ə

LOCATION — Southern Europe, bordering on the Adriatic Sea
GOVT. — Kingdom
AREA — 98,766 sq. mi.
POP. — 22,850,000 (est. 1983)
CAPITAL — Belgrade

On December 1, 1918, Bosnia and Herzegovina, Croatia, Dalmatia, Montenegro, Serbia and Slovenia united to form a kingdom which was later called Yugoslavia. Other listings may be found under all.

100 Heller = 1 Krone
(Bosnia & Herzegovina)

100 Filler = 1 Krone
(Croatia-Slavonia)

100 Paras = 1 Dinar (General Issues)

> Catalogue values for unused stamps in this country are for Never Hinged items, beginning with Scott RA1 in the postal tax section, and Scott RAJ1 in the postal tax due section.

> Counterfeits exist of most of the 1918-19 overprints for Bosnia and Herzegovina, Croatia-Slavonia and Slovenia.

BOSNIA AND HERZEGOVINA

Stamps of Bosnia and Herzegovina, 1910, Overprinted or Surcharged in Black or Red

a

b

c

	1918		Unwmk.		Perf. 12½
1L1	A4(a)	3h olive green	.40	.80
1L2	A4(b)	5h dk grn (R)	.40	.40
1L3	A4(a)	10h carmine	.40	.40
1L4	A4(a)	20h dk brn (R)	.40	.40
1L5	A4(a)	25h deep blue (R)	.40	.40
1L6	A4(b)	30h green	.40	.40
1L7	A4(b)	40h orange	.40	.40
1L8	A4(b)	45h brown red	.40	.40
1L9	A4(b)	50h dull violet	.55	.80
1L10	A4(a)	60h on 50h dl vio	.40	.40
1L11	A4(b)	80h on 6h org brown	.40	.40
1L12	A4(a)	90h on 35h myr green	.40	.40
1L13	A5(c)	2k gray green	.40	.40
1L14	A4(b)	3k on 3h ol grn	2.00	2.75

1L15	A5(c)	4k on 1k mar	4.00	4.75
1L16	A4(b)	10k on 2h vio	6.00	6.75
		Nos. 1L1-1L16 (16)	17.35	20.25

Inverted and double overprints and assorted varieties exist on the stamps for Bosnia and Herzegovina.

Bosnian Girl — A1

1918		Typo.	Perf. 11½	
1L17	A1	2h ultramarine	.40	.40
1L18	A1	6h violet	.80	1.20
1L19	A1	10h rose	.40	.40
1L20	A1	20h green	.40	.40
		Nos. 1L17-1L20 (4)	2.00	2.40

Imperforate stamps of this type (A1) are newspaper stamps of Bosnia.
See Nos. 1L21-1L22, 1L43-1L45.

Bosnia and Herzegovina Nos. P1-P2 (Nos. 1L17-1L18, Imperf.) Srchd.

1918			Imperf.	
1L21	A1	3h on 2h ultra	.40	.40
a.		Double surcharge	14.00	
1L22	A1	5h on 6h violet	.40	.40
a.		Double surcharge	14.00	

Stamps of Bosnia and Herzegovina, 1906-17, Ovptd. or Srchd. in Black or Red

d

e

KRALJEVSTVO S. H. S.
f

1919			Perf. 12½	
1L25	A23(d)	3h claret	.40	.80
1L26	A23(e)	5h green	.40	.40
1L27	A23(e)	10h on 6h dark gray	.40	.40
1L28	A24(d)	20h on 35h myr green	.40	.40
1L29	A24(d)	25h ultra	.40	.40
1L30	A23(d)	30h orange red	.40	.40
1L31	A24(d)	45h olive brn	.40	.40
1L32	A27(d)	45h on 80h org brown	.40	.40
a.		Perf. 11½	1.40	1.60
1L33	A24(e)	50h slate blue	100.00	100.00
1L34	A24(e)	50h on 72h dk blue (R)	.40	.40
1L35	A24(d)	60h brown violet	.40	.40
1L36	A27(e)	80h orange brown	.40	.40
a.		Perf. 11½	35.00	30.00
1L37	A27(d)	90h dark violet	.40	.40
a.		Perf. 11½	3.50	2.75
1L38	A17(f)	2k gray green	.40	.40
a.		Imperf.	35.00	
b.		Perf. 9½	4.50	5.00
1L39	A26(d)	3k car, green	.40	.55
1L40	A28(e)	4k car, green	1.75	2.50
1L41	A26(d)	5k dk vio, gray	1.75	2.75
1L42	A28(e)	10k dk vio, gray	3.25	4.00
		Nos. 1L25-1L42 (18)	112.35	115.40

Nos. 1L32, 1L36, 1L37, 1L40 and 1L42 have no bars in the overprint.
Nos. 1L25 to 1L42 exist with inverted overprint or surcharge.

Bosnia and Herzegovina Nos. P2-P4 (Nos. 1L18-1L20, Imperf.) Srchd.

1920			Imperf.	
1L43	A1	2h on 6h violet	200.00	180.00
1L44	A1	2h on 10h rose	50.00	50.00
1L45	A1	2h on 20h green	10.00	10.00
		Nos. 1L43-1L45 (3)	260.00	240.00

SEMI-POSTAL STAMPS ISSUES FOR BOSNIA AND HERZEGOVINA

Leading Blind Soldier — SP1

Wounded Soldier — SP2

Semi-Postal Stamps of Bosnia and Herzegovina, 1918 Overprinted

1918		Unwmk.	Perf. 12½, 13	
1LB1	SP1	10h greenish bl	.80	1.00
a.		Overprinted as No. 1LB2	52.50	52.50
1LB2	SP2	15h red brown	2.00	2.40
a.		Overprinted as No. 1LB1	47.50	47.50

Bosnian Semi-Postal Stamps of 1916 Overprinted like No. 1LB2

1LB3	SP1	5h green	125.00	175.00
a.		Overprinted as No. 1LB1	375.00	375.00
1LB4	SP2	15h magenta	100.00	125.00
		Nos. 1LB1-1LB4 (4)	227.80	303.00

Inverted and double overprints exist on Nos. 1LB1-1LB4.

Regular Issue of Bosnia, 1906 Surcharged in Black

Mail Wagon SP3

Bridge at Mostar SP4

Scene near Sarajevo — SP5

1919				
1LB5	SP3	10h + 10h on 40h org red	1.25	2.00
1LB6	SP4	20h + 10h on 20h dk brown	.60	1.75
1LB7	SP5	45h + 15h on 1k mar	4.75	4.75
		Nos. 1LB5-1LB7 (3)	6.60	8.50

Nos. 1LB5-1LB7 exist with surcharge inverted. Value each $7.50.

SPECIAL DELIVERY STAMPS ISSUES FOR BOSNIA AND HERZEGOVINA

Lightning
SD1   SD2

Bosnian Special Delivery Stamps Overprinted in Black

1918		Unwmk.	Perf. 12½, 13	
1LE1	SD1	2h vermilion	6.00	6.00
a.		Inverted overprint	35.00	
b.		Overprinted as No. 1LE2	47.50	47.50
1LE2	SD2	5h deep green	3.25	3.25
a.		Inverted overprint	18.00	
b.		Overprinted as No. 1LE1	47.50	47.50

POSTAGE DUE STAMPS ISSUES FOR BOSNIA AND HERZEGOVINA

Postage Due Stamps of Bosnia and Herzegovina, 1916, Overprinted in Black or Red

a

b

1918		Unwmk.	Perf. 12½, 13	
1LJ1	D2 (a)	2h red	.25	.25
1LJ2	D2 (b)	4h red	.55	.55
1LJ3	D2 (a)	5h red	.25	.25
1LJ4	D2 (b)	6h red	.90	.90
1LJ5	D2 (a)	10h red	.25	.25
1LJ6	D2 (b)	15h red	6.75	6.75
1LJ7	D2 (a)	20h red	.25	.25
1LJ8	D2 (b)	25h red	.55	.55
1LJ9	D2 (a)	30h red	.55	.55
1LJ10	D2 (b)	40h red	.25	.25
1LJ11	D2 (a)	50h red	1.20	1.20

c

d

1LJ12	D2 (c)	1k dark blue (R)	.55	.55
1LJ13	D2 (d)	3k dark blue (R)	.40	.40
		Nos. 1LJ1-1LJ13 (13)	12.70	12.70

Nos. 1LJ1-1LJ13 exist with overprint double or inverted. Value $3 to $7.
Nos. 1LJ1-1LJ11 exist with type "b" overprint instead of type "a," and vice versa. Value, each $10.

Stamps of Bosnia and Herzegovina, 1900-04, Surcharged

e

f

1919				
1LJ14	A2 (e)	2h on 35h blue	.55	.80
1LJ15	A2 (e)	5h on 45h grnsh bl	.95	1.20
1LJ16	A2 (f)	10h on 10 red	.25	.25
1LJ17	A2 (f)	15h on 40h org	.40	.50
1LJ18	A2 (f)	20h on 5h green	.25	.25
1LJ19	A2 (e)	25h on 20h pink	.40	.55

1LJ20 A2 (f) 30h on 30h bis
brn .40 .55
1LJ21 A2 (e) 1k on 50h red lil .25 .55
1LJ22 A2 (e) 3k on 25h blue .50 .55

Postage Due Stamps of Bosnia and Herzegovina, 1904 Surcharged

g   h

1LJ23 D1 (g) 40h on 6h blk,
red & yel .25 .25
1LJ24 D1 (h) 50h on 8h blk,
red & yel .25 .25
1LJ25 D1 (h) 200h blk, red &
grn 8.00 6.75
1LJ26 D1 (h) 4k on 7h blk,
red & yel .40 .55
Nos. 1LJ14-1LJ26 (13) 12.85 13.00

Nos. 1LJ14-1LJ26 exist with overprint double or inverted. Value, $3 to $6.

CROATIA-SLAVONIA

Stamps of Hungary Overprinted in Blue

A1

| 1918 | Wmk. 137 | Perf. 15 |
On Stamps of 1913

2L1 A1 6f olive green 1.10 2.00
2L2 A1 50f lake, *blue* 1.20 2.00

A2   A3

On Stamps of 1916

2L3 A2 10f violet 100.00 *140.00*
2L4 A3 15f red 100.00 *140.00*

A4

On Hungary Nos. 106-107
White Numerals

2L4A A4 10f rose 1,600. *1,600.*
2L5 A4 15f violet 150.00 150.00
 a. Inverted overprint

On Stamps of 1916-18
Colored Numerals

2L6 A4 2f brown orange .40 .40
2L7 A4 3f red lilac .40 .40
2L8 A4 5f green .40 .40
2L9 A4 6f greenish blue .40 .40
2L10 A4 10f rose red 16.00 12.00
2L11 A4 15f violet .40 .40
2L12 A4 20f gray brown .40 .40
2L13 A4 25f dull blue .40 .40
2L14 A4 35f brown .40 .40
2L15 A4 40f olive green .40 .80

The overprints and surcharges for Croatia-Slavonia exist inverted, double, double inverted, in wrong colors, on wrong stamps, on back, in pairs with one lacking overprint, etc.

A5

A6

2L16 A5 50f red vio & lilac .40 .40
2L17 A5 75f brt bl & pale bl .40 .40
2L18 A5 80f grn & pale grn .40 .40
2L19 A6 1k red brown & cl .40 .40
2L20 A6 2k olive brn & bis .40 .40
2L21 A6 3k dark vio & ind .40 .40
2L22 A6 5k dk brn & lt brn 2.50 3.00
2L23 A6 10k vio brn & vio 16.00 16.00

Stamps of Hungary Overprinted in Blue, Black or Red

A7   A8

2L24 A7 10f scarlet (Bl) .40 .40
2L25 A7 20f dark brown (Bk) .40 .40
2L26 A7 25f deep blue (R) .40 .80
2L27 A8 40f olive green (Bl) .40 .40
 Nos. 2L6-2L27 (22) 42.10 39.40

Many other stamps of the 1913-18 issues of Hungary, the Semi-Postal Stamps of 1915-16 and Postage Due Stamps were surreptitiously overprinted but were never sold through the post office.

Freedom of Croatia-
Slavonia
A9

| 1918 | Unwmk. | Litho. | Perf. 11½ |
2L28 A9 10f rose 6.50 4.00
2L29 A9 20f violet 6.50 4.00
2L30 A9 25f blue 12.00 8.00
2L31 A9 45f greenish blk 95.00 55.00
 Nos. 2L28-2L31 (4) 120.00 71.00

Independence of Croatia, Slavonia and Dalmatia.
#2L28-2L31 exist imperforate, but were not officially issued in this condition.
Excellent counterfeits of #2L28-2L31 exist.

Allegory of Youth with
Freedom Standard
A10   A11

Falcon, Symbol of
Liberty — A12

| 1919 | | Perf. 11½ |
2L32 A10 2f brn orange .25 .40
2L33 A10 3f violet .25 .50
2L34 A10 5f green .25 .25
2L35 A11 10f red .25 .25
2L36 A11 20f black brown .25 .25
2L37 A11 25f deep blue .25 .25
2L38 A11 45f dark ol grn .25 .25
2L39 A12 1k carmine rose .25 .25
2L40 A12 3k dark violet .80 .95
2L41 A12 5k deep brown 1.20 .80
 Nos. 2L32-2L41 (10) 4.00 4.15

| | | Perf. 12½ |
2L32a A10 2f 2.90 2.90
2L33a A10 3f 2.90 2.90
2L34a A10 5f 15.00 15.00
2L35a A11 10f 2.90 2.90
2L36a A11 20f 2.90 2.90
 Nos. 2L32a-2L36a (5) 26.60 26.60

#2L32-2L41 exist imperf. Value, set $25.

SEMI-POSTAL STAMPS ISSUES FOR CROATIA-SLAVONIA

SP1   SP2

SP3

| 1918 | Wmk. 137 | Perf. 15 |
2LB1 SP1 10f + 2f rose red .40 2.75
2LB2 SP2 15f + 2f dull violet .40 .40
2LB3 SP3 40f + 2f brn carmine .40 .85
 Nos. 2LB1-2LB3 (3) 1.20 4.00

SPECIAL DELIVERY STAMP ISSUE FOR CROATIA-SLAVONIA

SD1

Hungary No. E1 Overprinted in Black

| 1918 | Wmk. 137 | Perf. 15 |
2LE1 SD1 2f gray green & red .25 .25

POSTAGE DUE STAMPS ISSUES FOR CROATIA-SLAVONIA

D1

Postage Due Stamps of Hungary Overprinted in Blue

| 1918 | Wmk. Crown (136) | Perf. 15 |
2LJ1 D1 50f green & blk 650.00 650.00
  Wmk. Double Cross (137)
2LJ2 D1 1f green & red 40.00 40.00
 a. Inverted overprint
2LJ3 D1 2f green & red 1.20 1.20
2LJ4 D1 10f green & red 1.20 1.20
2LJ5 D1 12f green & red 160.00 160.00
2LJ6 D1 15f green & red .80 .80
2LJ7 D1 20f green & red .80 .80
2LJ8 D1 30f green & red 2.00 2.00
2LJ9 D1 50f green & blk 65.00 65.00
 Nos. 2LJ2-2LJ9 (8) 271.00 271.00

NEWSPAPER STAMPS ISSUES FOR CROATIA-SLAVONIA

N1   N2

Hungary No. P8 Overprinted in Black

| 1918 | Wmk. 137 | Imperf. |
2LP1 N1 (2f) orange .40 .40

| 1919 | Litho. | Unwmk. |
2LP2 N2 2f yellow orange .25 1.20

SLOVENIA

Chain Breaker
A1   A2

3, 5, 10, 15f: Chain on right wrist is short, extending only about half way to the frame.
10f: Numerals are 8½mm high.
20, 25, 30, 40f: Distant mountains show faintly between legs of male figure.
40f: Numerals 7mm high. The upright strokes of the "4" extend to the same height; the "0" is 3mm wide.

| 1919 | Unwmk. | Perf. 11½ |
Lithographed at Ljubljana
Fine Impression

3L1 A1 3f violet .25 .25
3L2 A1 5f green .25 .25
3L3 A1 10f carmine rose .40 .25
3L4 A1 15f blue .25 .25
3L5 A2 20f brown .65 .25
3L6 A2 25f blue .30 .25
3L7 A2 30f lilac rose .30 .25
3L8 A2 40f bister .30 .25
 Nos. 3L1-3L8 (8) 2.70 2.00

Various stamps of this series exist imperforate and part perforate. Many shades exist.
See Nos. 3L9-3L17, 3L24-3L28. For surcharges see Nos. 3LJ15-3LJ32.

Allegories of Freedom
A3   A4

King Peter I — A5

3, 5, 15f: The chain on the right wrist touches the bottom tablet.
10f: Numerals are 7½mm high.
15f: Curled end of loin cloth appears above letter "H" in the bottom tablet.
20, 25, 30, 40f: The outlines of the mountains have been redrawn and they are more distinct than on the lithographed stamps.
40f: Numerals 8mm high. The left slanting stroke of the "4" extends much higher than the main vertical stroke. The "0" is 2½mm wide and encloses a much narrower space than on the lithographed stamp.

| 1919-20 | | Perf. 11½ |
Typographed at Ljubljana and Vienna
Coarse Impression

3L9 A1 3f violet .25 .25
3L10 A1 5f green .30 .25
3L11 A1 10f red .25 .25
3L12 A1 15f blue 1.60 .25
3L13 A2 20f brown .55 .25
3L14 A2 25f blue .50 .25
3L15 A2 30f carmine rose .55 .25
3L16 A2 30f dp red 2.75 .90
3L17 A2 40f orange .55 .25
3L18 A3 50f green .55 .25
 a. 50f dark green 3.50 1.10
 b. 50f olive green 3.50 1.10
3L19 A3 60f dark blue .85 .25
 a. 60f violet blue .85 .25
3L20 A4 1k vermilion .55 .25
 a. 1k red orange .55 .25
3L21 A4 2k blue .55 .25
 a. 2k dull ultramarine .90 .25

3L22	A5	5k brown lake	.80	.25
a.		5k lake	12.00	1.60
b.		5k dull red	.60	.25
3L23	A5	10k deep ultra	3.25	.90
		Nos. 3L9-3L23 (15)	13.85	5.05

Nos. 3L9-3L23 exist imperf. Value, set $90.
Many of the series exist part perforate.
Many shades exist of lower values.
See Nos. 3L29-3L32, 3L40-3L41.

Serrate Roulette 13½

3L24	A1	5f light grn	.25	.25
3L25	A1	10f carmine	.25	.25
3L26	A1	15f slate blue	.30	.25
3L27	A2	20f dark brown	.65	.25
a.		Serrate x straight roul.	.65	.25
3L28	A2	30f car rose	.30	.25
a.		Serrate x straight roul.	.70	.25
3L29	A3	50f green	.30	.25
3L30	A3	60f dark blue	.95	.40
a.		60f violet blue	2.25	1.10
3L31	A4	1k vermilion	1.40	.40
a.		1k rose red	1.40	.40
3L32	A4	2k blue	9.00	2.75
		Nos. 3L24-3L32 (9)	13.40	5.05

Roulette x Perf. 11½

3L24a	A1	5f	150.00	150.00
3L25a	A1	10f	55.00	55.00
3L26a	A1	15f	175.00	175.00
3L28b	A2	30f	55.00	55.00
3L29a	A3	50f	5.25	4.00
3L30b	A3	60f	55.00	55.00
3L31b	A4	1k	55.00	55.00

Thick Wove Paper

1920		**Litho.**	**Perf. 11½**	
3L40	A5	15k gray green	7.25	14.50
3L41	A5	20k dull violet	1.40	2.40

On Nos. 3L40-3L41 the horizontal lines
have been removed from the value tablets.
They are printed over a background of pale
brown wavy lines.

Chain
Breaker
A7

Freedom
A8

King Peter
I — A9

Pale red wavy
lines

Dinar Values:
Type I — Size: 21x30½mm.
Type II — Size: 22x32½mm.

Thin to Thick Wove Paper

1920		**Serrate Roulette 13½**		
3L42	A7	5p olive green	.25	.25
3L43	A7	10p green	.25	.25
3L44	A7	15p brown	.25	.25
3L45	A7	20p carmine	.40	.40
3L46	A7	25p chocolate	.40	.25
3L47	A8	40p dark violet	.25	.25
3L48	A8	45p yellow	.25	.25
3L49	A8	50p dark blue	.25	.25
3L50	A8	60p red brown	.25	.25
3L51	A9	1d dark brown (I)	.25	.25
		Perf. 11½		
3L52	A9	2d gray vio (II)	.25	.25
3L53	A9	4d grnsh black (I)	.30	.30
3L54	A9	6d olive brn (II)	.25	.25
3L55	A9	10d brown red (II)	.25	.25
		Nos. 3L42-3L55 (14)	3.90	4.25

The 2d and 6d have a background of pale
red wavy lines, the 10d of gray lines.
Counterfeits exist of No. 3L45.

POSTAGE DUE STAMPS ISSUES FOR SLOVENIA

D1

Ljubljana Print
Numerals 9½mm high

1919		**Litho.**	**Unwmk.**	**Perf. 11½**	
3LJ1	D1	5f carmine		.25	.25
3LJ2	D1	10f carmine		.25	.25
3LJ3	D1	20f carmine		.25	.25
3LJ4	D1	50f carmine		.25	.25

Nos. 3LJ1-3LJ4 were also printed in scarlet
and dark red.

Numerals 8mm high

3LJ5	D1	1k dark blue	.45	.30
3LJ6	D1	5k dark blue	.65	.50
3LJ7	D1	10k dark blue	.90	.75
		Nos. 3LJ1-3LJ7 (7)	3.00	2.55

Vienna Print

1920		**Numerals 11 to 12 mm high**		
3LJ8	D1	5f red	.25	.25
3LJ9	D1	10f red	.25	.25
3LJ10	D1	20f red	.25	.25
3LJ11	D1	50f red	1.25	.85

Numerals 7mm high

3LJ12	D1	1k Prussian blue	1.10	.70
a.		1k dark blue	5.00	4.50
3LJ13	D1	5k Prussian blue	1.60	1.25
a.		5k dark blue	8.00	6.75
3LJ14	D1	10k Prussian blue	3.75	3.25
a.		10k dark blue	14.00	15.00
		Nos. 3LJ8-3LJ14 (7)	8.45	6.80

Nos. 3LJ8-3LJ14 exist imperf. Value, set
$40.

No. 3L4 Surcharged
in Red

1920		**On Litho. Stamps**		**Perf. 11½**	
3LJ15	A1	5p on 15f blue		.25	.25
3LJ16	A1	10p on 15f blue		.60	.80
3LJ17	A1	20p on 15f blue		.25	.25
3LJ18	A1	50p on 15f blue		.25	.25
		Nos. 3LJ15-3LJ18 (4)		1.35	1.55

Nos. 3L7, 3L12,
3L26, 3L28, 3L28a
Surcharged in Dark
Blue

3LJ19	A2	1d on 30f lil rose	.25	.25
3LJ20	A2	3d on 30f lil rose	.25	.25
3LJ21	A2	8d on 30f lil rose	1.60	.80
		Nos. 3LJ19-3LJ21 (3)	2.10	1.30

On Typographed Stamps

3LJ22	A1	5p on 15f pale bl	12.00	12.00
3LJ23	A1	10p on 15f pale bl	35.00	25.00
3LJ24	A1	20p on 15f pale bl	11.00	4.00
3LJ25	A1	50p on 15f pale bl	6.00	7.00
		Nos. 3LJ22-3LJ25 (4)	64.00	38.50
3LJ26	A1	5p on 15f slate bl	2.75	.50
3LJ27	A1	10p on 15f slate bl	8.50	3.25
3LJ28	A1	20p on 15f slate bl	2.75	.50
3LJ29	A1	50p on 15f slate bl	2.75	.50
3LJ30	A2	1d on 30f dp rose	2.75	.65
a.		Serrate x straight roulette	7.00	4.50
3LJ31	A2	3d on 30f dp rose	5.75	1.75
a.		Serrate x straight roulette	8.00	5.50
3LJ32	A2	8d on 30f dp rose	125.00	6.50
a.		Serrate x straight roulette	125.00	7.50
		Nos. 3LJ26-3LJ32 (7)	150.25	13.65

The para surcharges were printed in sheets
of 100, ten horizontal rows of ten. There were:
5p three rows, 10p one row, 20p three rows,
50p three rows. The dinar surcharges were in
a setting of 50, arranged in vertical rows of

---

five. There were: 1d five rows, 3d three rows,
8d two rows.

NEWSPAPER STAMPS ISSUES FOR SLOVENIA

Eros — N1

Ljubljana Print

1919		**Unwmk.**	**Litho.**	**Imperf.**	
3LP1	N1	2f gray		.25	.25
3LP2	N1	4f gray		.25	.40
3LP3	N1	6f gray		3.50	4.00
3LP4	N1	10f gray		.25	.25
3LP5	N1	30f gray		.25	.40
		Nos. 3LP1-3LP5 (5)		4.50	5.30

See Nos. 3LP6-3LP13. For surcharges see
Nos. 3LP14-3LP23, 4LB1-4LB5.

N2

1920			**Vienna Print**	
3LP6	N2	2f gray	.25	.25
3LP7	N2	4f gray	6.50	10.00
3LP8	N2	6f gray	1.75	2.75
3LP9	N2	10f gray	14.00	21.00
3LP10	N2	2f blue	.25	.30
3LP11	N2	4f blue	.25	.25
3LP12	N2	6f blue	125.00	125.00
3LP13	N2	10f blue	.25	.25
		Nos. 3LP6-3LP13 (8)	148.25	159.80

Nos. 3LP1, 3LP10 Surcharged

a

b

On Ljubljana Print

3LP14	N1 (a)	2p on 2f gray	.25	.40
3LP15	N1 (a)	4p on 2f gray	.25	.40
3LP16	N1 (a)	6p on 2f gray	.40	.65
3LP17	N1 (b)	2p on 2f gray	.65	.80
3LP18	N1 (b)	30p on 2f gray	.65	.85

On Vienna Print

3LP19	N1 (a)	2p on 2f blue	.25	.25
3LP20	N1 (a)	4p on 2f blue	.25	.25
3LP21	N1 (a)	6p on 2f blue	.25	.25
3LP22	N1 (b)	2p on 2f blue	.25	.25
3LP23	N1 (b)	30p on 2f blue	.25	.25
		Nos. 3LP14-3LP23 (10)	3.45	4.35

The five surcharges were arranged in a setting of 100, in horizontal rows of ten. There
were: 2p three rows, 4p three rows, 6p two
rows, 10p one row and 30p one row. The
sheets were perforated 11½ horizontally
between the groups of the different values.

SEMI-POSTAL STAMPS ISSUE FOR CARINTHIA PLEBISCITE

SP1

Nos. 3LP2, 3LP1 Surcharged With Various Designs in Dark Red

1920				
4LB1	SP1	5p on 4f gray	.25	.25
4LB2	SP1	15p on 4f gray	.25	.25
4LB3	SP1	25p on 4f gray	.25	.55
4LB4	SP1	45p on 2f gray	.25	1.20
4LB5	SP1	50p on 2f gray	.25	1.40
4LB6	SP1	2d on 2f gray	2.00	6.00
		Nos. 4LB1-4LB6 (6)	3.25	9.65

Nos. 4LB1 to 4LB6 have a different
surcharge on each stamp but each includes
the letters "K.G.C.A." which signify Carinthian
Governmental Commission, Zone A.
Sold at three times face value for the benefit
of the Plebiscite Propaganda Fund.

GENERAL ISSUES

For Use throughout the Kingdom

King
Alexander — A1

King Peter
I — A2

Unwmk.

1921, Jan. 16		**Engr.**	**Perf. 12**	
1	A1	2p olive brown	.25	.25
2	A1	5p deep green	.25	.25
3	A1	10p carmine	.25	.25
4	A1	15p violet	.25	.25
5	A1	20p black	.25	.25
6	A1	25p dark blue	.25	.25
7	A1	50p olive green	.25	.25
8	A1	60p vermilion	.25	.25
9	A1	75p purple	.25	.25
10	A2	1d orange	.25	.25
11	A2	2d olive bister	.30	.25
12	A2	4d dark green	.60	.25
13	A2	5d carmine rose	2.50	.25
14	A2	10d red brown	12.00	.55
		Nos. 1-14 (14)	17.90	3.80
		Set, never hinged	32.50	

Exist imperf. Value, set $125.
For surcharge see No. 27.

Nos. B1-B3 Surcharged in Black, Brown, Green or Blue

a

b

1922-24				
15	SP1(a)	1d on 10p	.25	.25
16	SP2(b)	1d on 15p ('24)	.25	.25
17	SP3(a)	1d on 25p (Br)	.25	.25
18	SP2(b)	3d on 15p (G)	.80	.25
a.		Blue surcharge	1.20	1.20
19	SP2(b)	8d on 15p (G)	1.60	.25
a.		Double surcharge	35.00	30.00
b.		9d on 15p (error)	130.00	
20	SP2(b)	20d on 15p	10.00	1.00
21	SP2(b)	30d on 15p (Bl)	27.50	2.50
		Nos. 15-21 (7)	40.65	4.75
		Set, never hinged	60.00	

A3

1923, Jan. 23   **Engr.**

22	A3	1d red brown	2.00	.25
23	A3	5d carmine	3.75	.25
24	A3	8d violet	6.75	.25
25	A3	20d green	27.50	.75
26	A3	30d red orange	72.50	2.75
		Nos. 22-26 (5)	112.50	4.25
		Set, never hinged	250.00	

For surcharge see No. 28.

Nos. 8 and 24
Surcharged in Black
or Blue

1924, Feb. 18

27	A1	20p on 60p ver	.25	.25
28	A3	5d on 8d violet (Bl)	8.00	.60
		Set, never hinged	17.50	

The color of the surcharge on No. 28 varies, including blue, blue black, greenish black and black.

A4

A5

1924, July 1   **Perf. 14**

29	A4	20p black	.25	.25
30	A4	50p dark brown	.25	.25
31	A4	1d carmine	.25	.25
32	A4	2d myrtle green	.25	.25
33	A4	3d ultramarine	.25	.25
34	A4	5d orange brown	1.40	.25
35	A5	10d dark violet	12.50	.25
36	A5	15d olive green	7.50	.25
37	A5	20d vermilion	7.50	.25
38	A5	30d deep green	7.50	1.25
		Nos. 29-38 (10)	37.65	3.50
		Set, never hinged	80.00	

No. 33 Surcharged

1925, June 5

39	A4	25p on 3d ultramarine	.35	.25
40	A4	50p on 3d ultramarine	.35	.25
		Set, never hinged	1.60	

King Alexander — A6

1926-27   **Typo.**   **Perf. 13**

41	A6	25p deep green	.25	.25
42	A6	50p olive brown	.25	.25
43	A6	1d scarlet	.25	.25
44	A6	2d slate black	.25	.25
45	A6	3d slate blue	.30	.25
46	A6	4d red orange	.50	.25
47	A6	5d violet	.80	.25
48	A6	8d black brown	5.25	.25
49	A6	10d olive brown	4.00	.25
50	A6	15d brown ('27)	15.00	.25
51	A6	20d dark vio ('27)	17.50	.25
52	A6	30d orange ('27)	65.00	.45
		Nos. 41-52 (12)	109.35	3.20
		Set, never hinged	240.00	

For overprints and surcharges see Nos. 53-62, 87-101, B5-B16.

Nos. B7-B16
Overprinted over the
Red Surcharge

1928, July

53	A6	1d scarlet	.25	.25
a.		Surcharge "0.50" inverted		
54	A6	2d black	.50	.25
55	A6	3d deep blue	.80	.50
56	A6	4d red orange	2.00	.60
57	A6	5d bright vio	1.60	.25
58	A6	8d black brown	6.50	.95
59	A6	10d olive brown	12.50	.25
60	A6	15d brown	95.00	3.00
61	A6	20d violet	47.50	3.00
62	A6	30d orange	125.00	9.50
		Nos. 53-62 (10)	291.65	18.55
		Set, never hinged	725.00	

King Alexander — A7

With Imprint at Foot

1931-34   **Perf. 12½**

63	A7	25p black	.25	.25
64	A7	50p green	.25	.25
65	A7	75p slate green	.40	.25
66	A7	1d red	.25	.25
67	A7	1.50d pink	.80	.25
68	A7	1.75d dp rose ('34)	1.60	.35
69	A7	3d slate blue	6.00	.25
70	A7	3.50d ultra ('34)	2.40	.35
71	A7	4d deep orange	3.00	.25
72	A7	5d purple	3.00	.25
73	A7	10d dark olive	12.00	.25
74	A7	15d deep brown	12.00	.25
75	A7	20d dark violet	24.00	.25
76	A7	30d rose	12.00	.45
		Nos. 63-76 (14)	77.95	3.90
		Set, never hinged	175.00	

Type of 1931 Issue
Without Imprint at Foot

1932-33

77	A7	25p black	.25	.25
78	A7	50p green	.25	.25
79	A7	1d red	.25	.25
80	A7	3d slate bl ('33)	1.00	.25
81	A7	4d deep org ('33)	3.50	.25
82	A7	5d purple ('33)	5.25	.25
83	A7	10d dk olive ('33)	17.00	.25
84	A7	15d deep brn ('33)	27.50	.25
85	A7	20d dark vio ('33)	35.00	.25
86	A7	30d rose ('33)	45.00	.35
		Nos. 77-86 (10)	135.00	2.60
		Set, never hinged	225.00	

See Nos. 102-115.

Nos. 41 to 52
Overprinted

1933, Sept. 5   **Perf. 13**

87	A6	25p deep green	.25	.25
88	A6	50p olive brown	.25	.25
89	A6	1d scarlet	.75	.25
90	A6	2d slate black	3.25	.70
91	A6	3d slate blue	3.00	.25
92	A6	4d red orange	2.00	.25
93	A6	5d violet	4.00	.25
94	A6	8d black brown	9.25	1.40
95	A6	10d olive brown	16.00	.25
96	A6	15d brown	24.00	1.75
97	A6	20d dark violet	32.50	.80
98	A6	30d orange	32.50	.80
		Nos. 87-98 (12)	127.75	7.20
		Set, never hinged	240.00	

Semi-Postal Stamps of 1926
Overprinted like Nos. 87 to 98 and
Four Bars over the Red Surcharge of
1926

1933, Sept. 5

99	A6	25p green	.80	.25
100	A6	50p olive brown	.80	.25
101	A6	1d scarlet	2.40	.50
		Nos. 99-101 (3)	4.00	1.00
		Set, never hinged	8.00	

Nos. 99-101 exist with double impression of bars. Value, each $5.50 unused, $4.50 used.

King Alexander Memorial Issue
Type of 1931-34 Issues
Borders in Black

1934, Oct. 17

102	A7	25p black	.25	.25
103	A7	50p green	.25	.25
104	A7	75p slate green	.25	.25
105	A7	1d red	.25	.25
106	A7	1.50d pink	.25	.25
107	A7	1.75d deep rose	.25	.25
108	A7	3d slate blue	.25	.25
109	A7	3.50d ultramarine	.25	.25
110	A7	4d deep orange	.40	.25
111	A7	5d purple	.60	.25
112	A7	10d dark olive	2.00	.25
113	A7	15d deep brown	4.00	.25
114	A7	20d dark violet	12.00	.25
115	A7	30d rose	10.00	.40
		Nos. 102-115 (14)	31.00	3.65
		Set, never hinged	50.00	

Cyrillic Characters
Latin and Cyrillic inscriptions are transposed within some sets. In some sets some stamps are inscribed in Latin, others in Cyrillic. This will be mentioned only if it is necessary to identify otherwise identical stamps.

King Peter II — A10

1935-36   **Perf. 13x12½**

116	A10	25p brown black	.25	.25
117	A10	50p yel orange	.25	.25
118	A10	75p turq green	.25	.25
119	A10	1d brown red	.25	.25
120	A10	1.50d scarlet	.25	.25
121	A10	1.75d cerise	.25	.25
122	A10	2d magenta ('36)	.25	.25
123	A10	3d brn orange	.25	.25
124	A10	3.50d ultramarine	.40	.25
125	A10	4d yellow grn	1.20	.25
126	A10	4d slate blue ('36)	.25	.25
127	A10	10d bright vio	1.20	.25
128	A10	15d brown	1.20	.25
129	A10	20d bright blue	4.75	.25
130	A10	30d rose pink	2.40	.25
		Nos. 116-130 (15)	13.40	3.75
		Set, never hinged	25.00	

For overprints see Nos. N12, N14, N29 in Scott Standard catalogue, Vol. 6.

King Alexander — A11		Nikola Tesla — A12

1935, Oct. 9   **Perf. 12½x11½, 11½**

131	A11	75p turq green	.30	.40
132	A11	1.50d scarlet	.30	.40
133	A11	1.75d dark brown	.35	.80
134	A11	3.50d ultramarine	2.00	2.40
135	A11	7.50d rose carmine	1.25	2.00
		Nos. 131-135 (5)	4.20	6.00

Death of King Alexander, 1st anniv.

1936, May 28   **Litho.**   **Perf. 12½x11½**

136	A12	75p yel grn & dk brn	.40	.25
137	A12	1.75d dull blue & indigo	.40	.25
		Set, never hinged	2.00	

80th birthday of Nikola Tesla (1856-1943), electrical inventor.

Memorial Church, Oplenac — A13	Coats of Arms of Yugoslavia, Greece, Romania and Turkey — A14

1937, July 1

138	A13	3d Prussian grn	1.00	.50
a.		Perf. 12½	15.00	24.00
		Never hinged	30.00	
139	A13	4d dark blue	1.00	1.20
		Set, never hinged	4.00	

"Little Entente," 16th anniversary.

Perf. 11, 11½, 12½

1937, Oct. 29   **Photo.**

140	A14	3d peacock grn	1.25	.40
141	A14	4d ultramarine	1.75	1.25
		Set, never hinged	5.50	

Balkan Entente.

King Peter II — A16

1939-40   **Typo.**   **Perf. 12½**

142	A16	25p black ('40)	.25	.25
143	A16	50p orange ('40)	.25	.25
144	A16	1d yellow grn	.25	.25
145	A16	1.50d red	.25	.25
146	A16	2d dp mag ('40)	.25	.25
147	A16	3d dull red brn	.25	.25
148	A16	4d ultra	.25	.25
148A	A16	5d dk blue ('40)	.25	.25
148B	A16	5.50d dk vio brn ('40)		.50
149	A16	6d slate blue	1.00	.25
150	A16	8d sepia	1.20	.25
151	A16	12d bright vio	1.75	.25
152	A16	16d dull violet	2.40	.25
153	A16	20d blue ('40)	2.40	.25
154	A16	30d brt pink ('40)	5.50	.55
		Nos. 142-154 (15)	16.75	4.05
		Set, never hinged	35.00	

For overprints and surcharges see Nos. N1-N11, N13, N15-N28, N30-N35 in Scott Standard catalogue, Vol. 6; Croatia 1-25 in Scott Standard catalogue, Vol. 2; Serbia 2N1-2N30 in Scott Standard catalogue, Vol. 6.

Arms of Yugoslavia, Greece, Romania and Turkey	
A17	A18

1940, June 1

155	A17	3d ultramarine	.80	.50
156	A18	3d ultramarine	.80	.50
a.		Pair, #155-156	6.00	12.00
157	A17	4d dark blue	.80	.50
158	A18	4d dark blue	.80	.50
a.		Pair, #157-158	6.00	12.00
		Nos. 155-158 (4)	3.20	2.00
		Set, never hinged	7.50	
		Pairs, never hinged	30.00	

Balkan Entente.

Bridge at
Obod
A19

1940, Sept. 29 — Litho.

159 A19 5.50d slate grn & dull grn 2.00 3.25
Never hinged 3.75

Zagreb Phil. Exhib.; 500th anniv. of Johann Gutenberg's invention of printing. The first press in the Yugoslav area was located at Obod in 1493.

SEMI-POSTAL STAMPS

Giving Succor to Wounded SP1

Wounded Soldier SP2

Symbolical of National Unity — SP3

Unwmk.
1921, Jan. 30 — Engr. — Perf. 12

B1 SP1 10p carmine .25 .25
B2 SP2 15p violet brown .25 .25
B3 SP3 25p light blue .25 .25
  Nos. B1-B3 (3) .75 .75

Nos. B1-B3 were sold at double face value, the excess being for the benefit of invalid soldiers.
Exist imperf. Value $35.
For surcharges see Nos. 15-21.

This overprint was applied to 500,000 examples of No. B1 in 1923 and they were given to the Society for Wounded Invalids (Uprava Ratnih Invalida) which sold them for 2d a piece. These overprinted stamps had no franking power, but some were used through ignorance.

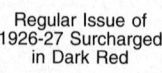
Regular Issue of 1926-27 Surcharged in Dark Red

1926, Nov. 1 — Perf. 13

B5 A6 25p + 25p green .25 .25
B6 A6 50p + 50p olive brn .25 .25
B7 A6 1d + 50p scarlet .25 .25
B8 A6 2d + 50p black .25 .25
B9 A6 3d + 50p slate blue .25 .25
B10 A6 4d + 50p red org .30 .25
B11 A6 5d + 50p brt vio .50 .25
B12 A6 8d + 50p black brn 1.00 .25
B13 A6 10d + 1d olive brn 2.00 .25
B14 A6 15d + 1d brown 8.00 1.00
B15 A6 20d + 1d dark vio 12.00 .55
B16 A6 30d + 1d orange 27.50 3.25
  a. Double surcharge
  Nos. B5-B16 (12) 52.55 7.05

The surtax on these stamps was intended for a fund for relief of sufferers from floods.
For overprints see Nos. 99-101.

Cathedral at Duvno SP4

King Tomislav SP6

Kings Tomislav and Alexander SP5

Perf. 12½, 11½x12
1929, Nov. 1 — Typo.

B17 SP4 50p (+ 50p) olive green .25 .25
B18 SP5 1d (+ 50p) red .60 .40
B19 SP6 3d (+ 1d) blue 1.60 1.10
  Nos. B17-B19 (3) 2.45 1.75

Millenary of the Croatian kingdom. The surtax was used to create a War Memorial Cemetery in France and to erect a monument to Serbian soldiers who died there.
No. B18 exists imperf. Value $400.

View of Dobropolje SP7

War Memorial — SP8

View of Kajmaktchalan SP9

1931, Apr. 1 — Perf. 12½, 11½

B20 SP7 50p + 50p blue grn .25 .25
B21 SP8 1d + 1d scarlet .25 .25
B22 SP9 3d + 3d deep blue .75 .75
  Nos. B20-B22 (3) 1.25 1.25

The surtax was added to a fund for a War Memorial to Serbian soldiers who died in France during World War I.

SP10

SP12

SP11

Black Overprint
1931, Nov. 1 — Perf. 12½, 11½x12

B23 SP10 50p (+ 50p) olive grn .25 .25
B24 SP11 1d (+ 50p) red .25 .25
B25 SP12 3d (+ 1d) blue .30 .30
  Nos. B23-B25 (3) .80 .80

Surtax for War Memorial fund.

Rower on Danube at Smederevo SP13

Bled Lake SP14

Danube near Belgrade SP15

View of Split Harbor SP16

Zagreb Cathedral — SP17

Prince Peter — SP18

1932, Sept. 2 — Litho. — Perf. 11½

B26 SP13 75p + 50p dl grn & lt blue .60 1.20
B27 SP14 1d + ½d scar & lt blue .60 1.20
B28 SP15 1½d + ½d rose & green .80 1.60
B29 SP16 3d + 1d bl & lt bl 1.60 2.40
B30 SP17 4d + 1d red org & lt blue 8.00 17.00
B31 SP18 5d + 1d dl vio & li-lac 8.00 14.00
  Nos. B26-B31 (6) 19.60 37.40

European Rowing Championship Races, Belgrade.

King Alexander SP19

Prince Peter SP20

1933, May 25 — Typo. — Perf. 12½

B32 SP19 50p + 25p black 6.00 12.00
B33 SP19 75p + 25p yel grn 6.00 12.00
B34 SP19 1.50d + 50p rose 6.00 12.00
B35 SP19 3d + 1d bl vio 6.00 12.00

B36 SP19 4p + 1d dk grn 6.00 12.00
B37 SP19 5d + 1d orange 6.00 12.00
  Nos. B32-B37 (6) 36.00 72.00

11th Intl. Congress of P.E.N. (Poets, Editors and Novelists) Clubs, Dubrovnik, May 25-27.
The labels at the foot of the stamps are printed in either Cyrillic or Latin letters and each bears the amount of a premium for the benefit of the local P.E.N. Club at Dubrovnik.

1933, June 28

B38 SP20 75p + 25p slate grn .25 .25
B39 SP20 1½d + ½d deep red .25 .25

60th anniv. meeting of the National Sokols (Sports Associations) at Ljubljana, July 1.

Eagle Soaring over City — SP22

Athlete and Eagle — SP23

1934, June 1 — Perf. 12½

B40 SP22 75p + 25p green 4.00 9.00
B41 SP22 1.50d + 50p car 6.00 9.50
B42 SP22 1.75d + 25p brown 10.00 9.50
  Nos. B40-B42 (3) 20.00 28.00

20th anniversary of Sokols of Sarajevo.

1934, June 1

B43 SP23 75p + 25p Prus grn 2.40 4.75
B44 SP23 1.50d + 50p car 2.40 4.75
B45 SP23 1.75d + 25p choc 10.00 14.50
  Nos. B43-B45 (3) 14.80 24.00

60th anniversary of Sokols of Zagreb.

Mother and Children
SP24   SP25

Perf. 12½x11½
1935, Dec. 25 — Photo.

B46 SP24 1.50d + 1d dk brn & brown 1.25 1.20
  a. Perf. 11½ 12.00 14.50
B47 SP25 3.50d + 1.50d bright ultra & bl 2.00 2.90

The surtax was for "Winter Help."

Queen Mother Marie SP26

Prince Regent Paul SP27

1936, May 3 — Litho.

B48 SP26 75p + 25p grnsh bl .25 .40
B49 SP26 1.50d + 50p rose pink .25 .45
B50 SP26 1.75d + 75p brown 1.25 1.25
B51 SP26 3.50d + 1d brt bl 1.60 2.75
  Nos. B48-B51 (4) 3.35 4.85

1936, Sept. 20 — Typo.

B52 SP27 75p + 50p turq grn & red .40 .35
B53 SP27 1.50d + 50p cer & red .40 .35

Surtax for the Red Cross.

Princes Tomislav and Andrej
SP28 SP29

Perf. 11½x12½, 12½x11½

1937, May 1
B54	SP28	25p + 25p red brn	.25	.25
B55	SP28	75p + 75p emerald	.25	.40
B56	SP29	1.50d + 1d org red	.30	.65
B57	SP29	2d + 1d magenta	.60	1.20
		Nos. B54-B57 (4)	1.40	2.50

Souvenir Sheet

National Costumes — SP30

1937, Sept. 12   **Perf. 14**
B57A	SP30	Sheet of 4	4.75	10.00
		Never hinged	9.50	
b.		1d blue green	1.00	1.75
c.		1.50d bright violet	1.00	1.75
d.		2d rose red	1.00	1.75
e.		4d dark blue	1.00	1.75

1st Yugoslavian Phil. Exhib., Belgrade. Sold only at the exhibition post office at 15d each.

SP31   SP32

Perf. 11½x12½, 12½x11½

1938, May 1   **Photo.**
B58	SP31	50p + 50p dark brn	.25	.30
B59	SP32	1d + 1d dk green	.25	.35
B60	SP31	1.50d + 1.50d scar	.50	.40
B61	SP32	2d + 2d magenta	1.25	.80
		Nos. B58-B61 (4)	2.25	1.85

Surtax for the benefit of Child Welfare. For overprints see Nos. B75-B78.

Bridge and Anti-aircraft Lights — SP33

1938, May 28   **Perf. 11½x12½**
B62	SP33	1d + 50p dk grn	.40	.80
B63	SP33	1.50d + 1d scarlet	.60	1.20
a.		Perf. 11½	17.50	27.50
B64	SP33	2d + 1d rose vio	1.25	2.40
a.		Perf. 11½	18.00	35.00
B65	SP33	3d + 1.50d dp bl	2.00	4.00
		Nos. B62-B65 (4)	4.25	8.40

Intl. Aeronautical Exhib., Belgrade.

Cliff at Demir-Kapiya — SP34

Modern Hospital SP35

Runner Carrying Torch — SP36   Alexander I — SP37

Perf. 11½x12½, 12½x11½

1938, Aug. 1
B66	SP34	1d + 1d slate grn & dp grn	.45	.40
B67	SP35	1.50d + 1.50d scar	.70	.55
B68	SP36	2d + 2d claret & dp rose	1.60	3.25
B69	SP37	3d + 3d dp bl	1.60	3.25
		Nos. B66-B69 (4)	4.35	7.45

The surtax was to raise funds to build a hospital for railway employees.

Runner SP38   Shot-Putter SP41

Hurdlers SP39

Pole Vaulter SP40

1938, Sept. 11
B70	SP38	50p + 50p org brn	1.40	2.50
B71	SP39	1d + 1d sl grn & dp grn	1.40	2.50
B72	SP40	1.50d + 1.50d rose & dk mag	1.40	2.50
B73	SP41	2d + 2d dk blue	2.75	5.00
		Nos. B70-B73 (4)	6.95	12.50

Ninth Balkan Games.

Stamps of 1938 Overprinted in Black

a   b

1938, Oct. 1
B75	SP31(a)	50p + 50p dk brn	.40	.55
B76	SP32(b)	1d + 1d dk grn	.40	.80
B77	SP31(a)	1.50d + 1.50d scar	.60	1.20
B78	SP32(b)	2d + 2d mag	1.25	2.40
		Nos. B75-B78 (4)	2.65	4.95

Surtax for the benefit of Child Welfare.

Postriders SP43

1d+1d, Rural mail delivery. 1.50d+1.50d, Mail train. 2d+2d, Mail bus. 4d+4d, Mail plane.

1939, Mar. 15   **Photo.**   **Perf. 11½**
B79	SP43	50p + 50p buff, bis & brown	.30	.55
B80	SP43	1d + 1d sl grn & dp green	.30	.55
B81	SP43	1.50d + 1.50d red, cop red & brn car	2.00	2.00
B82	SP43	2d + 2d dp plum & rose lilac	2.00	2.75
B83	SP43	4d + 4d ind & sl bl	2.40	4.00
		Nos. B79-B83 (5)	7.00	9.85

Centenary of the present postal system in Yugoslavia. The surtax was used for the Railway Benevolent Association.
The Cyrillic and Latin inscriptions are transposed on Nos. B82 and B83.

Child Eating SP48

Children at Seashore — SP49

Boy Planing Board SP50

Children in Crib — SP51

1939, May 1   **Perf. 12½**
B84	SP48	1d + 1d blk & dp bl green	.50	1.00
B85	SP49	1.50d + 1.50d org brn & sal	2.00	3.25
a.		Perf. 11½	80.00	160.00
B86	SP50	2d + 2d mar & vio rose	1.40	2.90
B87	SP51	4d + 4d ind & royal blue	1.40	2.90
		Nos. B84-B87 (4)	5.30	10.05

The surtax was for the benefit of Child Welfare.

Czar Lazar of Serbia — SP52

Milosh Obilich — SP53

1939, June 28   **Perf. 11½**
B88	SP52	1d + 1d sl grn & bl grn	1.60	1.60
B89	SP53	1.50d + 1.50d mar & brt car	1.60	1.60

Battle of Kosovo, 550th anniversary.

Training Ship "Jadran" SP54

Designs: 1d+50p, Steamship "King Alexander." 1.50d+1d, Freighter "Triglan." 2d+1.50d, Cruiser "Dubrovnik."

1939, Sept. 6   **Engr.**
B90	SP54	50p + 50p brn org	.40	.80
B91	SP54	1d + 50p dull grn	.80	1.60
B92	SP54	1.50d + 1d dp rose	1.25	2.40
B93	SP54	2d + 1.50d dark bl	2.00	4.00
		Nos. B90-B93 (4)	4.45	8.80

Yugoslav Navy and Merchant Marine. The surtax aided a Marine Museum.
Nos. B90-B93 also exist with a small "S" engraver's mark. Set value NH, $160. Location of the mark: On No. B90, above the base of the bowsprit. On No. B91, at the top of the smoke plume just below the "B" in the country name. On No. B92, at the top left of the large numeral "1". On No. B93, in the curve of the numeral "2".

Motorcycle and Sidecar — SP58

Racing Car SP59

Motorcycle SP60

1280 YUGOSLAVIA

Racing Car
SP61

1939, Sept. 3   **Photo.**
B94	SP58	50p + 50p multi	.50	.80
B95	SP59	1d + 1d multi	1.00	1.60
B96	SP60	1.50d + 1.50d multi	1.40	2.40
B97	SP61	2d + 2d multi	2.50	4.00
		Nos. B94-B97 (4)	5.40	8.80

Automobile and Motorcycle Races, Belgrade. The surtax was for the Race Organization and the State Treasury.

Unknown
Soldier
Memorial
SP62

1939, Oct. 9   **Perf. 12½**
B98	SP62	1d + 50p sl grn & green	1.00	1.60
B99	SP62	1.50d + 1d red & rose red	1.00	1.60
B100	SP62	2d + 1.50d dp cl & vio rose	1.25	2.40
B101	SP62	3d + 2d dp bl & bl	2.50	4.00
		Nos. B98-B101 (4)	5.75	9.60

Assassination of King Alexander, 5th anniv. The surtax was used to aid World War I invalids.

Postman
Delivering
Mail — SP64

Postman Emptying
Mail Box — SP65

Parcel Post
Delivery
Wagon
SP66

Parcel Post
SP67

Repairing
Telephone
Wires — SP68

1940, Jan. 1
B102	SP64	50p + 50p brn & deep org	.60	1.00
B103	SP65	1d + 1d sl grn & blue grn	.60	1.00
B104	SP66	1.50d + 1.50d red brn & scar	1.00	2.40
B105	SP67	2d + 2d dl vio & red lilac	1.25	2.40
B106	SP68	4d + 4d sl bl & bl	4.00	6.50
		Nos. B102-B106 (5)	7.45	13.30

The surtax was used for the employees of the Postal System in Belgrade.

Croats'
Arrival at
Adriatic in
640
SP69

King
Tomislav — SP70

Death of Matija
Gubec — SP71

Anton and
Stjepan
Radic
SP72

Map of
Yugoslavia
SP73

1940, Mar. 1   **Typo.**   **Perf. 11½**
B107	SP69	50p + 50p brn org	.40	.55
B108	SP70	1d + 1d green	.40	.55
B109	SP71	1.50d + 1.50d brt red	1.25	.55
B110	SP72	2d + 2d dk cerise	2.00	2.40
B111	SP73	4d + 2d dark blue	2.00	2.75
		Nos. B107-B111 (5)	6.05	6.80

The surtax was used for the benefit of postal employees in Zagreb.

Children
Playing in
Snow
SP74

Children at
Seashore — SP75

1940, May 1   **Photo.**   **Perf. 11½, 12½**
B112	SP74	50p + 50p brn org & org yellow	.25	.40
B113	SP75	1d + 1d sl grn & dk green	.25	.40
B114	SP74	1.50d + 1.50d brn red & scarlet	.60	.80
B115	SP75	2d + 2d mar & vio rose	1.00	1.60
		Nos. B112-B115 (4)	2.10	3.20

The surtax was for Child Welfare.

Nos. C11-C14
Surcharged in
Carmine

Perf. 11½x12½, 12½x11½
1940, Dec. 23
B116	AP6	50p + 50p on 5d	.25	.25
B117	AP7	1d + 1d on 10d	.25	.40
a.		Perf. 12½	40.00	40.00
B118	AP8	1.50d + 1.50d on 20d	.80	1.40
B119	AP9	2d + 2d on 30d	.90	1.75
		Nos. B116-B119 (4)	2.20	3.80

The surtax was used to fight tuberculosis. For surcharges see Nos. NB1-NB4 in Scott Standard catalogue, Vol. 6.

AIR POST STAMPS

Dubrovnik
AP1

Lake Bled
AP2

Falls of
Jaice — AP3

Church at
Oplenac — AP4

Bridge at
Mostar — AP5

Perf. 12½
1934, June 15   **Typo.**   **Unwmk.**
C1	AP1	50p violet brown	.25	.25
C2	AP2	1d green	.25	.25
C3	AP3	2d rose red	.50	.30
C4	AP4	3d ultramarine	1.10	.45
C5	AP5	10d vermilion	2.50	4.00
		Nos. C1-C5 (5)	4.60	5.25

Border in Black

King Alexander Memorial Issue
1935, Jan. 1
| C6 | AP4 | 3d ultramarine | 3.25 | 4.75 |

St. Naum
Convent — AP6

Port of
Rab — AP7

Sarajevo
AP8

Ljubljana
AP9

Perf. 11½x12½, 12½x11½
1937, Sept. 12   **Photo.**
C7	AP6	50p brown	.25	.25
a.		Perf. 12½	.25	.25
C8	AP7	1d yellow grn	.25	.25
a.		Perf. 12½	.25	.25
C9	AP8	2d blue gray	.25	.25
a.		Perf. 12½	.25	.25
C10	AP9	2.50d rose red	.25	.25
a.		Perf. 12½	.25	.25
C11	AP6	5d brn violet	.25	.25
a.		Perf. 12½	.25	.25
C12	AP7	10d brown lake	.50	.25
a.		Perf. 12½	.70	.25
C13	AP8	20d dark green	5.25	8.00
a.		Perf. 12½	.70	1.00
C14	AP9	30d ultramarine	18.00	27.50
a.		Perf. 12½	1.00	1.75
		Nos. C7-C14 (8)	25.00	37.00

For surcharges see Nos. B116-B119; Nos. NB1-NB4, NC1-NC8 in Scott Standard catalogue, Vol. 6.

Cathedral
of Zagreb
AP10

Bridge at
Belgrade
AP11

1940, Aug. 15   **Litho.**   **Perf. 12½**
| C15 | AP10 | 40d Prus grn & pale green | 4.50 | 3.50 |
| C16 | AP11 | 50d slate bl & gray bl | 4.50 | 5.00 |

For overprints see Nos. NC9-NC10 in Scott Standard catalogue, Vol. 6.

POSTAGE DUE STAMPS

King
Alexander — D1

1921   **Typo.**   **Unwmk.**   **Perf. 11½**
Red or Black Surcharge
| J1 | D1 | 10p on 5p green (R) | .25 | .25 |
| J2 | D1 | 30p on 5p green (Bk) | .25 | .25 |

D2   D3

1921-22   Typo.   Perf. 11½, Rough

J3	D2	10p rose	.25	.25
J4	D2	30p yellow green	.25	.25
J5	D2	50p violet	.25	.25
J6	D2	1d brown	.30	.25
J7	D2	2d blue	.40	.25
J8	D3	5d orange	2.00	.25
J9	D3	10d violet brown	6.00	.45
a.		Cliche of 10p in sheet of 10d	190.00	—
J10	D3	25d pink	35.00	1.60
J11	D3	50d green	30.00	1.60
		Nos. J3-J11 (9)	74.45	5.15

1924   Perf. 9, 10½, 11½, Clean-cut

J12	D3	10p rose red	.25	.25
J13	D3	30p yellow green	.35	.40
J14	D3	50p violet	.25	.25
J15	D3	1d brown	.25	.25
J16	D3	2d deep blue	.50	.25
J17	D3	5d orange	1.60	.25
J18	D3	10d violet brown	10.00	.25
J19	D3	25d pink	65.00	1.25
J20	D3	50d green	47.50	1.25
		Nos. J12-J20 (9)	125.70	4.40

Nos. J19-J20 do not exist perf 9. Nos. J18-J20 do not exist perf 11½.

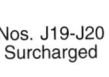

Nos. J19-J20
Surcharged

1928

J21	D3	10d on 25d pink	3.25	.40
J22	D3	10d on 50d green	3.25	.40
a.		Inverted surcharge	30.00	18.00

A second type of "1" in surcharge has flag projecting horizontally. Value, each: $24 never hinged; $12 unused; $3.25 used.

Coat of Arms — D4

1931   Typo.   Perf. 12½
With Imprint at Foot

J23	D4	50p violet	1.40	.25
J24	D4	1d deep magenta	3.00	.25
J25	D4	2d deep blue	9.50	.25
J26	D4	5d orange	2.00	.25
J27	D4	10d chocolate	10.00	1.25
		Nos. J23-J27 (5)	25.90	2.25

For overprints see Nos. NJ1-NJ13 in Scott Standard catalogue, Vol. 6; Croatia 26-29, J1-J5 in Scott Standard catalogue, Vol. 2.

1932   Without Imprint at Foot

J28	D4	50p violet	.25	.25
J29	D4	1d deep magenta	.25	.25
J30	D4	2d deep blue	.25	.25
J31	D4	5d orange	.25	.25
J32	D4	10d chocolate	.25	.25
		Nos. J28-J32 (5)	1.25	1.25

Numeral of
Value — D5

Overprint in Green, Blue or Maroon

1933   Perf. 9, 10½, 11½

J33	D5	50p vio (G)	.25	.25
a.		Perf. 10½		.30
J34	D5	1d brown (Bl)	.25	.25
a.		Perf. 10½	2.00	1.40

J35	D5	2d blue (M)	.25	.25
a.		Perf. 10½	1.00	1.25
J36	D5	5d orange (Bl)	.80	.25
J37	D5	10d violet brn (Bl)	4.00	.25
		Nos. J33-J37 (5)	5.55	1.25

POSTAL TAX STAMPS

> Catalogue values for unused stamps in this section are for Never Hinged items.

The tax was for the Red Cross or The Olympic Fund unless otherwise noted.

Red Cross
Emblem — PT1

Unwmk.

1933, Sept. 17   Litho.   Perf. 13

RA1	PT1 50p dark blue & red	.65	.25

Obligatory on inland letters during Red Cross Week, Sept. 17-23.
See No. RAJ1.

Dr. Vladen
Djordjevic — PT2

1936, Sept. 20   Typo.   Perf. 12

RA2	PT2 50p brn blk & red	.40	.25

Obligatory on inland letters during Red Cross Week, Sept. 20-26.

Aiding the
Wounded
PT3

1938, Sept. 18   Litho.   Perf. 12½

RA3	PT3 50p dk bl, red, yel & grn	.40	.25

1940, Sept. 15   Redrawn

RA4	PT3 50p slate blue & red	.55	.25

The inscription at the upper right of this stamp and the numerals of value are in smaller characters.
Obligatory on all letters during the second week of September.

POSTAL TAX DUE STAMPS

> Catalogue values for unused stamps in this section are for Never Hinged items.

Type of Postal Tax Stamp Inscribed "PORTO"

1933   Unwmk.   Litho.   Perf. 12½

RAJ1	PT1 50p dull grn & red	1.00	.25
a.	Perf. 11½	20.00	8.00

ZAMBEZIA

zam-ˈbē-zē-ə

LOCATION — A former district of the Mozambique Province in Portuguese East Africa
GOVT. — Part of the Portuguese East Africa Colony

The districts of Quelimane and Tete were created from Zambezia. Eventually stamps of Mozambique came into use. See Quelimane and Tete.

1000 Reis = 1 Milreis

King Carlos
A1   A2

Perf. 11½, 12½, 13½

1894   Typo.   Unwmk.

1	A1	5r yellow	.25	.25
2	A1	10r red violet	.75	.45
3	A1	15r chocolate	1.50	.65
a.		Perf. 12½	27.50	19.00
4	A1	20r lavender	1.50	.65
5	A1	25r blue green	2.00	1.25
a.		Perf. 11½	30.00	30.00
6	A1	50r lt blue	2.50	1.25
7	A1	75r carmine	5.00	3.25
a.		Perf. 11½	50.00	35.00
8	A1	80r yellow grn	7.00	2.50
9	A1	100r brown, buff	6.00	1.75
10	A1	150r car, rose	8.00	3.00
11	A1	200r dk blue, bl	9.00	3.00
a.		Perf. 11½	200.00	150.00
b.		Perf. 13½	32.50	24.00
12	A1	300r dk bl, salmon	15.00	4.50
a.		Perf. 11½	25.00	20.00
		Nos. 1-12 (12)	58.50	22.50

For surcharges and overprints see Nos. 36-47, 73-74, 77-81, 84-88.

1898-1903   Perf. 11½
Name and Value in Black or Red (500r)

13	A2	2½r gray	.45	.45
14	A2	5r orange	.45	.45
15	A2	10r lt green	.75	.50
16	A2	15r brown	1.25	1.00
17	A2	15r gray grn ('03)	1.60	1.40
18	A2	20r gray violet	1.25	1.00
19	A2	25r sea green	1.25	1.00
20	A2	25r carmine ('03)	1.00	.85
21	A2	50r blue	1.25	1.10
22	A2	50r brown ('03)	4.00	2.25
23	A2	65r dull bl ('03)	10.00	5.50
24	A2	75r rose	20.00	5.25
25	A2	75r lilac ('03)	3.25	2.75
26	A2	80r violet	5.00	3.00
27	A2	100r dk bl, bl	2.00	2.00
28	A2	115r org brn, pink ('03)	15.00	7.25
29	A2	130r brn, straw ('03)	15.00	7.25
30	A2	150r brn, buff	6.00	3.50
31	A2	200r red vio, pnksh	6.00	3.50
32	A2	300r dk bl, rose	8.00	3.50
33	A2	400r dull bl, straw ('03)	12.00	8.50
34	A2	500r blk, bl ('01)	20.00	6.75
35	A2	700r vio, yelsh ('01)	30.00	8.75
		Nos. 13-35 (23)	165.50	77.50

For surcharges and overprints see Nos. 49-68, 72, 82-83, 93-107.

Stamps of 1894
Surcharged

1902   Perf. 11½, 12½

36	A1	65r on 10r red vio	10.00	7.00
37	A1	65r on 15r choc	10.00	7.00
38	A1	65r on 20r lav	10.00	7.00
39	A1	65r on 300r bl, sal	10.00	7.00
40	A1	115r on 5r yel	10.00	7.00
41	A1	115r on 25r bl grn	10.00	7.00
42	A1	115r on 80r yel grn	10.00	7.00
43	A1	130r on 75r car	7.00	7.00
44	A1	130r on 150r car, rose	5.25	5.25
45	A1	400r on 50r lt bl	2.00	3.25
46	A1	400r on 100r brn, buff	2.00	3.50
47	A1	400r on 200r bl, bl	2.00	3.50

Same Surcharge on No. P1

48	N1	130r on 2½r brn	9.00	7.00
		Nos. 36-48 (13)	97.25	78.50

Stamps of 1898
Overprinted

1902   Perf. 11½

49	A2	15r brown	2.00	1.40
50	A2	25r sea green	2.00	1.40
51	A2	50r blue	2.00	1.40
52	A2	75r rose	6.00	3.75
		Nos. 49-52 (4)	12.00	7.95

No. 23 Surcharged in
Black

1905

53	A2	50r on 65r dull blue	6.50	4.00

Stamps of 1898-1903
Overprinted in
Carmine or Green

1911

54	A2	2½r gray	.35	.25
55	A2	5r orange	.35	.25
56	A2	10r light green	.40	.25
a.		Inverted overprint	15.00	12.50
57	A2	15r gray green	.40	.25
58	A2	20r gray violet	.50	.30
59	A2	25r carmine (G)	1.50	.50
60	A2	50r brown	.40	.35
61	A2	75r lilac	1.25	.90
62	A2	100r dk bl, bl	1.25	.90
63	A2	115r org brn, pink	1.25	.90
64	A2	130r brown, straw	1.25	.90
65	A2	200r red vio, pnksh	1.25	.90
66	A2	400r dull bl, straw	2.10	1.10
67	A2	500r blk & red, bl	2.10	1.10
68	A2	700r violet, yelsh	2.25	1.50
		Nos. 54-68 (15)	16.60	10.35

Stamps of 1902-05
Overprinted in
Carmine or Green

1914   Without Gum

72	A2	50r on 65r dl bl	4,000.	1,200.
73	A1	115r on 5r yellow	2.00	1.50
74	A1	115r on 25r bl grn	2.00	1.50
75	A1	115r on 80r yel grn	2.00	1.50
76	N1	130r on 2½r brn (G)	2.00	1.50
a.		Carmine overprint	22.50	22.50
77	A1	130r on 75r car	2.50	1.50
a.		Perf. 12½	5.50	7.00
78	A1	130r on 150r car, rose	2.50	1.50
79	A1	400r on 50r lt bl	3.00	3.00
a.		Perf. 12½	11.00	11.00
80	A1	400r on 100r brn, buff	3.00	2.50
81	A1	400r on 200r bl, bl	3.00	2.50

On Nos. 51-52

82	A2	50r blue	1.50	1.50
83	A2	75r rose	1.50	1.50
		Nos. 73-83 (11)	25.00	20.00

Preceding Issues
Overprinted in
Carmine

1915   On Surcharged Issue of 1902

84	A1	115r on 5r yellow	.85	.45
85	A1	115r on 25r bl grn	.85	.45
86	A1	115r on 80r lt grn	.85	.45
87	A1	130r on 75r carmine	.85	.45
a.		Perf. 12½	4.50	2.25
88	A1	130r on 150r car, rose	.85	.45
92	N1	130r on 2½r (down)	.85	.45

On Nos. 51, 53

93	A2	50r blue	.85	.50
a.		"Republica" inverted	15.00	15.00
94	A2	50r on 65r dull bl	3.50	4.50
		Nos. 84-94 (8)	9.45	7.70

Stamps of 1898-1903
Overprinted Locally
in Carmine

1917   **Without Gum**

95	A2	2½r gray	1.50	3.00
96	A2	5r orange	9.00	6.50
97	A2	10r light green	9.00	6.00
98	A2	15r gray green	8.00	6.50
99	A2	20r gray violet	9.00	6.50
100	A2	25r sea green	13.50	15.00
101	A2	100r blue, *blue*	4.00	2.75
102	A2	115r org brn, *pink*	4.00	2.75
103	A2	130r brown, *straw*	4.00	2.75
104	A2	200r red vio, *pnksh*	4.00	2.75
105	A2	400r dull bl, *straw*	4.50	3.50
106	A2	500r blk & red, *bl*	6.00	3.75
107	A2	700r vio, *yelsh*	10.00	5.25
		Nos. 95-107 (13)	86.50	67.00

NEWSPAPER STAMP

N1

1894   **Unwmk.**   **Typo.**   *Perf. 12½*

P1	N1	2½r brown	.60	.35

For overprints and surcharges see Nos. 76, 92.

ZANZIBAR

ˈzan-zə-ˌbär

LOCATION — Group of islands about twenty miles off the coast of Tanganyika in East Africa
GOVT. — British protectorate
AREA — 1,044 sq. mi. (approx.)
POP. — 354,360 (est. 1967)
CAPITAL — Zanzibar

Before 1895, unoverprinted stamps of India were used in Zanzibar.

12 Pies = 1 Anna
16 Annas = 1 Rupee
100 Cents = 1 Rupee (1908)
100 Cents = 1 Shilling (1935)

Catalogue values for unused stamps in this country are for Never Hinged items, beginning with Scott 201 in the regular postage section and Scott J18 in the postage due section.

Watermarks

Wmk. 47 —   Wmk. 71 —
Multiple Rosette   Rosette

Stamps of British India
Overprinted

On Stamps of 1882-95

1895   **Wmk. Star (39)**   *Perf. 14*
Blue Overprint

1	A17	½a green	*30,000.*	*6,250.*
2	A19	1a violet brn	*3,500.*	*600.*
a.		"Zanzibar"		*28,500.*

1895-96   **Black Overprint**

3	A17	½a green	5.00	5.00
a.		"Zanzibar"	*1,450.*	*800.00*
b.		"Zanibar"	*1,450.*	*1,900.*
c.		"Zapzibar"		
d.		Double overprint, one albino	250.00	
4	A19	1a violet brn	5.25	4.25
a.		"Zanzibar"		*4,000.*
b.		"Zanibar"	*1,900.*	*2,250.*
5	A20	1a6p bister brn	5.50	4.25
a.		"Zanzibar"	*4,500.*	*1,200.*
b.		"Zanibar"	*2,000.*	
c.		"Zanibar"	*1,800.*	*1,750.*
d.		"Zapzibar"	*125.00*	*125.00*
6	A21	2a ultra	10.00	9.00
a.		"Zanzibar"	*8,500.*	*3,500.*
b.		"Zanibar"	*6,750.*	*2,500.*
c.		"Zapzibar"	*150.00*	*160.00*
d.		Double overprint	310.00	
e.		Double overprint, one albino	280.00	
f.		2a pale blue	9.50	8.50
7	A28	2a6p green	10.00	5.50
a.		"Zanzibar"	*8,500.*	*1,800.*
b.		"Zanibar"	*800.00*	*1,400.*
c.		"Zapzibar"		
d.		"Zanzipar"	*1,250.*	
e.		Second "z" italic	400.00	575.00
f.		Double overprint, one albino	280.00	
8	A22	3a orange	13.50	17.50
a.		"Zanzibar"	*1,150.*	*2,150.*
b.		"Zanibar"	*7,500.*	*8,000.*
9	A23	4a olive grn	22.50	20.00
a.		"Zanzibar"	*11,500.*	*4,750.*

10	A25	8a red vio	36.00	30.00
a.		"Zanzibar"	*11,500.*	*9,000.*
11	A26	12a vio, *red*	20.00	11.50
a.		"Zanzibar"	*11,500.*	*5,000.*
12	A27	1r gray	125.00	100.00
a.		"Zanzibar"	*10,500.*	*6,750.*
13	A29	1r car rose & grn	22.50	30.00
a.		Vertical overprint	475.00	
14	A30	2r brn & rose	125.00	135.00
a.		"Zanziba"	*32,500.*	—
b.		Inverted "r"	4,500.	5,500.
c.		Pair, one without overprint		
15	A30	3r grn & brn	95.00	105.00
a.		"Zanziba"	*32,500.*	
b.		Inverted "r"	*6,750.*	*6,750.*
16	A30	5r vio & blue	105.00	97.50
a.		"Zanziba"	*32,500.*	
b.		Inverted "r"	5,000.	6,000.
c.		Dbl. ovpt., one invtd.	950.00	
d.		Double overprint, one albino	1,600.	

On Stamp of 1873-76
Wmk. Elephant's Head (38)

17	A14	6a bister	22.50	12.50
a.		"Zanzidar"	*11,500.*	*4,000.*
b.		"Zanzibarr"	*7,240.*	*4,400.*
c.		"Zanibar"	*900.00*	*1,400.*
d.		"Zapzibar"		
e.		Double overprint		
f.		Double overprint, one albino	190.00	
g.		Triple overprint, one albino	250.00	
		Nos. 3-17 (15)	622.75	587.00

Nos. 4-6 Surcharged

    (a)   (b)

a   b

    (c)   (d)

c   d

e   f

1896   **Wmk. Star (39)**
Black Surcharge

18	(a)	2½a on 1a	200.00	110.00
19	(b)	2½a on 1a	525.00	350.00
a.		Inverted "1" in "½"	3,250.	—
20	(c)	2½a on 1a	225.00	125.00

Red Surcharge

21	(a)	2½a on 1a	275.00	725.00
22	(b)	2½a on 1a	500.00	1,050.
23	(c)	2½a on 1a	310.00	725.00
24	(a)	2½a on 1a6p	85.00	60.00
a.		"Zanzidar"	*1,700.*	*1,450.*
b.		"Zanzibar"	*5,250.*	*2,250.*
d.		Inverted "1" in "½"	*1,250.*	*1,000.*
24C	(b)	2½a on 1a6p	250.00	550.00
25	(c)	2½a on 1a6p	145.00	350.00
26	(d)	2½a on 1a6p	200.00	175.00
a.		Inverted "1" in "½"	*1,750.*	*1,400.*
b.		Roman "I" in "½"	*1,000.*	*1,000.*
c.		"Zanzibar" double, one albino	350.00	
27	(e)	2½a on 1a6p	475.00	400.00
c.		"Zanzibar" double, one albino	875.00	
27A	(f)	2½a on 1a6p	*27,500.*	18,000.
28	(a)	2½a on 2a	160.00	360.00
28A	(b)	2½a on 2a	340.00	625.00
29	(c)	2½a on 2a	180.00	425.00
30	(d)	2½a on 2a	80.00	47.50
a.		Inverted "1" in "½"	500.00	325.00
b.		Roman "I" in "½"	300.00	180.00
c.		"Zanzibar" double, one albino	190.00	
d.		"Zanzibar" triple, two albino	350.00	
31	(e)	2½a on 2a	225.00	125.00
b.		Inverted "1" in "½"	4,000.	2,000.
c.		"2" in "½" omitted	17,500.	
d.		"2" for "2½"	25,000.	
e.		"1" of "½" omitted	17,500.	7,500.
f.		"Zanzibar" double, one albino	600.00	
31A		2½a on 2a	5,750.	2,800.

Certain type varieties are found in the word "Zanzibar" on Nos. 1 to 31A viz: Inverted "q" for "b," broken "p" for "n," "i" without dot, small second "z" and tall second "z." These varieties are found on all values from ½a to 1r inclusive and the tall "z" is also found on the 2r, 3r and 5r.

Stamps of British East
Africa, 1896,
Overprinted in Black or
Red

1896   **Wmk. Crown and C A (2)**

32	A8	½a yellow grn	42.50	25.00
33	A8	1a carmine	42.50	19.00
a.		Double overprint	825.00	1,000.
b.		Double overprint, one albino	350.00	
34	A8	2½a dk blue (R)	100.00	52.50
a.		Inverted "S" in "ANNAS"	—	600.00
35	A8	4½a orange	55.00	65.00
36	A8	5a dark ocher	70.00	45.00
a.		"r" omitted	—	4,400.
37	A8	7½a lilac	60.00	70.00
		Nos. 32-37 (6)	370.00	276.50

Sultan Seyyid Hamed-bin-Thwain

A2   A3

1896, Sept. 20   **Engr.**   **Wmk. 71**

38	A2	½a yel grn & red	4.50	2.00
39	A2	1a indigo & red	4.00	1.75
40	A2	2a red brn & red	3.75	.85
41	A2	2½a ultra & red	17.50	1.60
42	A2	3a slate & red	19.00	10.00
43	A2	4a dk green & red	12.00	6.00
44	A2	4½a orange & red	8.75	7.00
45	A2	5a bister & red	9.25	4.00
a.		Half used as 2½a on cover		*4,900.*
46	A2	7½a lilac & red	6.50	6.50
47	A2	8a ol gray & red	13.50	9.00
48	A3	1r ultra & red	24.00	12.00
49	A3	2r green & red	32.50	13.00
50	A3	3r violet & red	36.00	13.00
51	A3	4r lake & red	27.50	20.00
52	A3	5r blk brn & red	38.00	20.00
		Nos. 38-52 (15)	256.75	126.70

No. 43 Surcharged in Red

1897

53	A2	(a) 2½a on 4a	100.00	*55.00*
54	A2	(b) 2½a on 4a	325.00	*300.00*
55	A2	(c) 2½a on 4a	120.00	*82.50*
		Nos. 53-55 (3)	545.00	437.50

1898   **Engr.**   **Wmk. 47**

56	A2	½a yel grn & red	1.75	.45
57	A2	1a indigo & red	6.00	1.40
58	A2	2a red brn & red	9.25	2.25
58A	A2	2½a ultra & red	5.50	.45
59	A2	3a slate & red	8.25	.75
60	A2	4a dk grn & red	4.25	1.25
60A	A2	4½a orange & red	15.00	1.25
61	A2	5a bister & red	22.50	2.25
61A	A2	7½a lilac & red	17.50	3.50
61B	A2	8a ol gray & red	22.00	3.25
		Nos. 56-61B (10)	112.00	16.80

Sultan Seyyid Hamoud-bin-Mahommed-bin-Said

A4   A5

1899-1901

62	A4	½a yel grn & red	3.00	.65
63	A4	1a indigo & red	5.00	.25
64	A4	1a car & red ('01)	3.75	.25
65	A4	2a red brn & red	4.50	.75
66	A4	2½a ultra & red	4.50	.75
67	A4	3a slate & red	6.50	3.00
68	A4	4a dk green & red	6.00	3.25
69	A4	4½a orange & red	20.00	9.25
70	A4	4½a ind & red ('01)	22.00	14.50
71	A4	5a bister & red	6.50	2.40
72	A4	7½a lilac & red	6.50	*7.00*
73	A4	8a ol gray & red	6.50	*5.50*

Wmk. 71

74	A5	1r ultra & red	24.00	17.50
75	A5	2r green & red	27.50	24.00
76	A5	3r violet & red	50.00	52.50

77	A5	4r lilac rose & red	75.00	77.50
78	A5	5r gray brown & red	85.00	95.00
		Nos. 62-78 (17)	356.25	314.05

For surcharges see Nos. 94-98.

A6

Monogram of
Sultan Ali bin
Hamoud — A7

1904, June 8   Typo.   Wmk. 47

79	A6	½a emerald	3.00	1.00
80	A6	1a rose red	3.00	.25
81	A6	2a bister brown	5.00	.50
82	A6	2½a ultra	5.00	.40
83	A6	3a gray	6.00	2.50
84	A6	4a blue green	4.50	1.75
85	A6	4½a black	5.00	2.75
86	A6	5a ocher	7.50	1.90
87	A6	7½a violet	9.25	8.75
88	A6	8a olive green	6.50	5.50
89	A7	1r ultra & red	37.50	27.50
90	A7	2r green & red	45.00	55.00
91	A7	3r violet & red	65.00	100.00
92	A7	4r magenta & red	75.00	120.00
93	A7	5r olive & red	75.00	120.00
		Nos. 79-93 (15)	352.25	447.80

**Nos. 69-70, 72-73 Surcharged in
Black or Lake**

g

h

i

1904

94	A4 (g)	1a on 4½a	5.00	6.00
95	A4 (g)	1a on 4½a (L)	6.00	24.00
96	A4 (h)	2a on 4a (L)	19.00	24.00
97	A4 (i)	2½a on 7½a	17.50	25.00
	a.	"Hiaf"	16,000.	
98	A4 (i)	2½a on 8a	29.00	40.00
	a.	"Hiaf"	15,000.	10,000.
		Nos. 94-98 (5)	76.50	119.00

Sultan Ali bin Hamoud
A8   A9

Palace of the
Sultan — A11

1908-09   Engr.   Wmk. 47

99	A8	1c gray ('09)	2.75	.35
100	A8	3c yellow grn	9.00	.25
101	A8	6c carmine	11.00	.25
102	A8	10c org brn ('09)	7.00	2.25
103	A8	12c violet	19.00	3.25

104	A9	15c ultra	18.00	.45
105	A9	25c brown	8.50	1.10
106	A9	50c dp green	10.00	7.00
107	A9	75c slate ('09)	16.00	17.50
108	A10	1r yellow green	42.50	14.00
109	A10	2r violet	21.00	18.00
110	A10	3r yellow brown	35.00	57.50
111	A10	4r red	75.00	100.00
112	A10	5r blue	65.00	90.00
113	A11	10r brn & dk grn	200.00	350.00
114	A11	20r yel grn & blk	550.00	800.00
115	A11	30r dk brn & blk	650.00	950.00
116	A11	40r org brn & blk	850.00	
117	A11	50r lilac & blk	750.00	
118	A11	100r blue & blk	1,100.	
119	A11	200r black & brn	1,500.	
		Nos. 99-112 (14)	339.75	311.90

It is probable that Nos. 118 and 119 were
used only for fiscal purposes.

Sultan
Khalifa bin
Harub — A12

Dhow — A13

Dhow — A14

1913   Perf. 14

120	A12	1c gray	.50	.50
121	A12	3c yellow grn	1.50	.60
122	A12	6c carmine	1.75	.25
123	A12	10c brown	1.25	3.25
124	A12	12c violet	1.40	.40
125	A12	15c ultra	3.25	.40
126	A12	25c black brn	1.40	2.50
127	A12	50c dk green	3.75	7.00
128	A12	75c dk gray	2.75	5.00
129	A13	1r yellow grn	19.00	16.00
130	A13	2r dk violet	15.00	32.50
131	A13	3r orange	22.50	50.00
132	A13	4r red	35.00	80.00
133	A13	5r blue	50.00	50.00
134	A14	10r brown & grn	190.00	375.00
135	A14	20r yel grn & blk	350.00	650.00
136	A14	30r dk brn & blk	375.00	800.00
137	A14	40r orange & blk	600.00	1,000.
138	A14	50r dull vio & blk	600.00	1,100.
139	A14	100r blue & blk	750.00	
140	A14	200r black & brn	1,100.	
		Nos. 120-134 (15)	349.05	623.40

1914-22   Wmk. 3

141	A12	1c gray	.90	.30
142	A12	3c yellow grn	1.40	.25
143	A12	6c carmine	1.00	.25
144	A12	8c vio, yel ('22)	1.00	6.50
145	A12	10c dk grn, yel ('22)	.85	.40
146	A12	15c ultra	1.50	7.50
148	A12	50c dark green	5.00	6.50
149	A12	75c deep gray	3.50	35.00
150	A13	1r yellow grn	5.50	4.00
151	A13	2r dark violet	12.00	13.00
152	A13	3r brown org	25.00	50.00
153	A13	4r red	22.50	95.00
154	A13	5r blue	19.00	72.50
155	A14	10r brown & grn	200.00	700.00
		Nos. 141-155 (14)	299.15	991.20

1921-29   Wmk. 4

156	A12	1c gray	.30	9.00
157	A12	3c yellow grn	3.25	5.50
158	A12	3c orange ('22)	.40	.25
159	A12	4c green ('22)	.60	2.50
160	A12	6c carmine	.40	.55
161	A12	6c vio, bl ('22)	.45	.25
162	A12	10c lt brown	.80	15.00
163	A12	12c violet	.50	.35
164	A12	12c carmine ('22)	.50	.50
165	A12	15c ultra	.80	14.00
166	A12	20c dk blue ('22)	1.25	.40
167	A12	25c black brn	.90	26.00
168	A12	50c blue green	2.75	6.50
169	A12	75c dark gray	3.25	65.00
170	A13	1r yellow grn	7.00	4.00
171	A13	2r dk violet	4.50	15.00
172	A13	3r ocher	5.50	8.50
173	A13	4r red	17.50	45.00
174	A13	5r blue	24.00	75.00
175	A14	10r brown & grn	190.00	450.00
176	A14	20r green & blk	400.00	750.00
177	A14	30r dk brn & blk ('29)	350.00	750.00
		Nos. 156-175 (20)	264.65	743.30

Sultan Khalifa bin
Harub ("CENTS" with
Serifs) — A15

1926-27

184	A15	1c brown	1.00	.25
185	A15	3c yellow org	.30	.25
186	A15	4c deep green	.30	.25
187	A15	6c dark violet	.35	.25
188	A15	8c slate	1.10	5.50
189	A15	10c olive green	1.10	.45
190	A15	12c deep red	3.00	.25
191	A15	20c ultra	.65	.40
192	A15	25c violet, yel	12.00	3.00
193	A15	50c claret	4.50	.50
194	A15	75c olive brown	30.00	40.00
		Nos. 184-194 (11)	54.30	51.20

> **Catalogue values for unused
> stamps in this section, from this
> point to the end of the section, are
> for Never Hinged items.**

"CENTS"
without
Serifs — A16

Dhow — A17

Dhow — A18

1936   Perf. 14

201	A16	5c deep green	.25	.25
202	A16	10c black	.25	.25
203	A16	15c carmine	.30	1.25
204	A16	20c brown org	.25	.25
205	A16	25c violet, yel	.25	.25
206	A16	30c ultra	.25	.25
207	A16	40c black brown	.25	.25
208	A16	50c claret	.50	.25
209	A17	1sh yellow grn	.75	.25
210	A17	2sh dark violet	2.50	2.50
211	A17	5sh red	24.00	8.00
212	A17	7.50sh blue	40.00	35.00
213	A18	10sh brn & grn	40.00	30.00
		Nos. 201-213 (13)	109.55	78.75

For overprints see Nos. 222-223.

A19

1936, Dec. 9

214	A19	10c olive grn & blk	4.25	.35
215	A19	20c red violet & blk	6.50	2.75
216	A19	30c deep ultra & blk	19.00	.65
217	A19	50c red orange & blk	20.00	5.50
		Nos. 214-217 (4)	49.75	9.25

Reign of Sultan Khalifa bin Harub, 25th
anniv.

A20

Dhow & Map Showing Zanzibar & Muscat.

Perf. 14

1944, Nov. 20   Engr.   Wmk. 4

218	A20	10c violet blue	1.00	5.00
219	A20	20c brown orange	1.50	3.75
220	A20	50c Prus green	1.50	.40
221	A20	1sh dull purple	1.50	1.00
		Nos. 218-221 (4)	5.50	10.15

200th anniv. of the Al Busaid Dynasty.

Nos. 202 and 206
Overprinted in Red

1946, Nov. 11

222	A16	10c black	.25	.50
223	A16	30c ultra	.40	.50

Victory of the Allied Nations in WW II.

Common Design Types
pictured following the introduction.

Silver Wedding Issue
Common Design Types
1949, Jan. 10   Photo.   Perf. 14x14½

224	CD304	20c orange	.60	1.50

**Engraved; Name Typographed
Perf. 11½x11**

225	CD305	10sh light brown	29.00	36.50

UPU Issue
Common Design Types
**Engr.; Name Typo. on 30c, 50c
Perf. 13½, 11x11½**

1949, Oct. 10   Wmk. 4

226	CD306	20c red orange	.45	3.75
227	CD307	30c indigo	2.50	2.00
228	CD308	50c red lilac	1.25	3.25
229	CD309	1sh blue green	1.25	4.50
		Nos. 226-229 (4)	5.45	13.50

Sultan Khalifa bin
Harub — A21

Seyyid
Khalifa
Schools
A22

Perf. 12x12½, 13x12½

1952, Aug. 26   Engr.

230	A21	5c black	.25	.25
231	A21	10c red orange	.25	.25
232	A21	15c green	2.00	3.00
233	A21	20c carmine	.75	.75
234	A21	25c plum	1.10	.25
235	A21	30c blue green	1.10	.25
236	A21	35c ultra	1.00	5.00
237	A21	40c chocolate	1.00	2.00
238	A21	50c purple	3.25	.25
239	A22	1sh choc & bl grn	.75	.25
240	A22	2sh claret & ultra	3.00	2.75
241	A22	5sh carmine & blk	3.00	6.50
242	A22	7.50sh emer & gray	27.50	27.50
243	A22	10sh gray blk & rose red	12.00	15.00
		Nos. 230-243 (14)	56.95	64.00

POSTAGE DUE STAMPS

D1

Rouletted 10

				Unwmk.
1931		**Typeset**		
		Thin Paper		
		Without Gum		
J1	D1	1c blk, *orange*	12.50	150.00
		On cover		1,000.
J2	D1	2c blk, *orange*	5.50	80.00
		On cover		600.00
J3	D1	3c blk, *orange*	5.75	65.00
		On cover		600.00
J3A	D1	6c blk, *orange*		8,000.
		On cover		10,000.
J4	D1	9c blk, *orange*	3.25	35.00
		On cover		500.00
J4A	D1	12c blk, *orange*	15,000.	12,000.
		On cover		12,500.
J4B	D1	12c blk, *green*	1,600.	675.00
		On cover		6,000.
J5	D1	15c blk, *orange*	3.25	42.50
		On cover		500.00
J6	D1	18c blk, *orange*	27.50	90.00
		On cover		750.00
a.		18c black, *salmon*	5.00	75.00
		On cover		600.00
J7	D1	20c blk, *orange*	4.50	80.00
		On cover		600.00
J8	D1	21c blk, *orange*	4.00	50.00
		On cover		500.00
J8A	D1	25c blk, *orange*	19,000.	17,000. —
		On cover		
J8B	D1	25c blk, *magenta*	3,250.	1,500.
		On cover		9,000.
J9	D1	31c blk, *orange*	11.00	110.00
		On cover		2,500.
J10	D1	50c blk, *orange*	24.00	250.00
		On cover		5,000.
J11	D1	75c blk, *orange*	80.00	600.00
		On cover		6,000.

The variety "cent.s" occurs once on each sheet of Nos. J3 to J11 inclusive.

Insufficiently prepaid
Postage due.
25 cents.

D2

				Rouletted 5
1931-33				
		Thick Paper		
J12	D2	2c blk, *salmon*	25.00	37.50
		On cover		650.00
J13	D2	3c blk, *rose*	4.00	65.00
		On cover		1,000.
J14	D2	6c blk, *yellow*	4.00	40.00
		On cover		450.00
J15	D2	12c blk, *blue*	5.00	32.50
		On cover		450.00
J16	D2	25c blk, *pink*	11.00	130.00
		On cover		1,000.
J17	D2	25c blk, *dull violet*	25.00	80.00
		On cover		850.00
		Nos. J12-J17 (6)	74.00	385.00

Catalogue values for unused stamps in this section, from this point to the end of the section, are for Never Hinged items.

D3

			Wmk. 4	Perf. 14
1936		**Typo.**		
J18	D3	5c violet	8.50	14.00
		On cover		275.00
J19	D3	10c carmine	6.50	3.25
		On cover		275.00
J20	D3	20c green	2.50	6.50
		On cover		325.00
J21	D3	30c brown	16.00	24.00
		On cover		500.00
J22	D3	40c ultra	10.00	30.00
		On cover		500.00
J23	D3	1sh gray	15.00	37.50
		On cover		1,250.
		Nos. J18-J23 (6)	58.50	115.25

Chalky paper was introduced in 1956 for the 5c, 30c, 40c, 1sh, and in 1962 for the 10c, 20c. Value for set of 6, unused $3.25, used $110.
See note after No. 300a in Scott Standard catalogue, Vol. 6.

ZULULAND

'zü-ˌlü-ˌland

LOCATION — Northeastern part of Natal, South Africa
GOVT. — British Colony
AREA — 10,427 sq. mi.

POP. — 230,000 (estimated 1900)
CAPITAL — Eshowe

12 Pence = 1 Shilling
20 Shillings = 1 Pound

Stamps of Great Britain Overprinted

			Wmk. 30	Perf. 14
1888-93				
1	A54	½p vermilion	7.00	3.00
2	A40	1p violet	30.00	6.00
3	A56	2p green & red	26.00	50.00
4	A57	2½p vio, *bl* ('91)	37.50	22.50
5	A58	3p violet, *yel*	29.00	25.00
6	A59	4p green & brn	60.00	75.00
7	A61	5p lil & bl ('93)	100.00	150.00
8	A62	6p vio, *rose*	20.00	20.00
9	A63	9p blue & lil ('92)	120.00	130.00
10	A65	1sh green ('92)	150.00	170.00
		Wmk. 31		
11	A51	5sh rose ('92)	700.00	800.00
		Nos. 1-10 (10)	579.50	651.50

Natal No. 66 Overprinted

			Wmk. 2
1888-94			
12	A14	½p green, no period	28.50	47.50
a.		Period after "Zululand"	62.50	95.00
b.		As "a," double overprint	1,500.	1,750.
c.		As "a," invtd. overprint	1,400.	
d.		As "a," pair, one without ovpt.	7,500.	
e.		As No. 12, double overprint	1,600.	1,750.

Natal No. 71 Ovptd. Like Nos. 1-11

13	A11	6p violet ('94)	70.00	62.50

A1

1891

14	A1	1p lilac	3.75	3.50

By proclamation of the Governor of Zululand, dated June 27th, 1891, No. 14 was declared to be a postage stamp.

A2

			Typo.
1894-96			
15	A2	½p lilac & grn	6.00	5.50
16	A2	1p lilac & rose	6.00	3.00
17	A2	2½p lilac & blue	16.00	9.75
18	A2	3p lilac & brn	10.00	4.00
19	A2	6p lilac & blk	22.50	25.00
20	A2	1sh green	50.00	45.00
21	A2	2sh6p grn & blk ('96)	90.00	110.00
22	A2	4sh grn & car rose	150.00	225.00
23	A2	£1 violet, *red*	600.00	650.00
24	A2	£5 vio & blk, *red*	5,750.	1,900.
		Nos. 15-23 (9)	950.50	1,077.

Numerals of Nos. 19-24 are in color on plain tablet. Dangerous forgeries of No. 24 exist.
Purple or violet cancellations are not necessarily revenue cancels. 14 of the 17 post offices and agencies used violet as well as black postal cancellations.
Zululand was annexed to Natal in Dec. 1897 and separate stamps were discontinued June 30, 1898.

Scott International Album

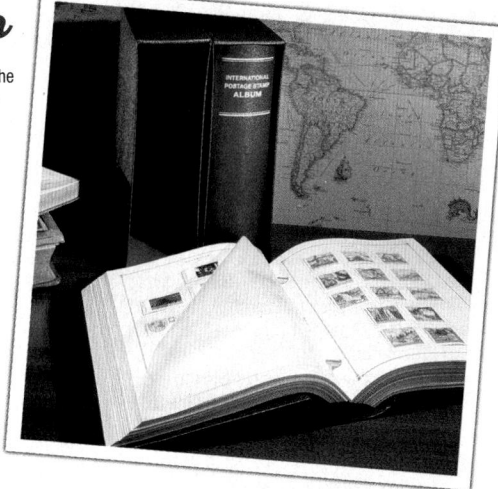

Prices have never been so low on selected album parts. It is a wonderful opportunity to collect internationally. The Ultimate Album for Worldwide Collectors! Pick a period in history and embark on a philatelic adventure. With the International Album, the whole world is divided chronologically into more than 40 parts. From the classic era of philately to present day, the International is one of the broadest and far reaching worldwide albums available. *Binders are sold separately.*

- More than 16,000 pages with spaces for over 220,000 stamps.
- Pages printed on 2 sides.

Item	Part	Binder		Retail	AA*
801A140	1A1	(1840-1940)	Regular	$150.00	$120.00
801A240	1A2	(1840-1940)	Regular	$150.00	$120.00
801B140	1B1	(1840-1940)	Regular	$150.00	$120.00
801B240	1B2	(1840-1940)	Regular	$150.00	$120.00
802P149	2A	(1940-49)	Regular	$150.00	$120.00
802P249	2B	(1940-49)	Regular	$150.00	$120.00
803P155	3A	(1949-55)	Regular	$150.00	$120.00
803P255	3B	(1949-55)	Regular	$150.00	$120.00
804P159	4A	(1956-60)	Regular	$150.00	$120.00
804P259	4B	(1956-60)	Regular	$150.00	$120.00
805P063	5	(1960-63)	Jumbo	$75.00	$55.00
805P165	5A	(1963-65)	Jumbo	$150.00	$120.00
806P066	6	(1965-66)	Jumbo	$75.00	$55.00
806P168	6A	(1966-68)	Jumbo	$75.00	$55.00
807P171	7A	(1968-71)	Jumbo	$75.00	$55.00
807P271	7B	(1968-71)	Jumbo	$75.00	$55.00
808P173	8A	(1971-73)	Regular	$75.00	$55.00
808P273	8B	(1971-73)	Regular	$75.00	$55.00
809P074	9	(1973-74)	Regular	$150.00	$120.00
810P075	10	(1974-75)	Jumbo	$75.00	$55.00
811P076	11	(1975-76)	Jumbo	$150.00	$120.00
812P077	12	(1976-77)	Jumbo	$150.00	$120.00
813P078	13	(1977-78)	Jumbo	$150.00	$120.00
814P078	14	(1978)	Regular	$150.00	$120.00
815P079	15	(1979)	Regular	$150.00	$120.00
816P080	16	(1980)	Jumbo	$150.00	$120.00
817P081	17	(1981)	Regular	$150.00	$120.00
818P082	18	(1982)	Regular	$150.00	$120.00
819P083	19	(1983)	Regular	$150.00	$120.00
820P084	20	(1984)	Jumbo	$60.00	$44.00
821P085	21	(1985)	Jumbo	$150.00	$120.00
822P186	22A	(1986)	Regular	$60.00	$44.00
822P286	22B	(1986)	Regular	$60.00	$44.00
823P187	23A	(1987)	Regular	$60.00	$44.00
823P287	23B	(1987)	Regular	$150.00	$120.00
824P188	24A	(1988)	Regular	$60.00	$44.00
824P288	24B	(1988)	Regular	$60.00	$44.00
825P189	25A	(1989)	Regular	$60.00	$44.00
825P289	25B	(1989)	Regular	$60.00	$44.00
826P190	26A	(1990)	Regular	$60.00	$44.00
826P290	26B	(1990)	Regular	$60.00	$44.00
827P191	27A	(1991)	Regular	$60.00	$44.00
827P291	27B	(1991)	Regular	$60.00	$44.00
828P192	28A	(1992)	Regular	$60.00	$44.00
828P292	28B	(1992)	Regular	$60.00	$44.00
829P193	29A	(1993)	Regular	$60.00	$44.00
829P293	29B	(1993)	Regular	$60.00	$44.00
830P194	30A	(1994)	Regular	$60.00	$44.00
830P294	30B	(1994)	Regular	$60.00	$44.00
831P195	31A	(1995)	Regular	$60.00	$44.00
831P295	31B	(1995)	Regular	$60.00	$44.00
832P196	32A	(1996)	Regular	$60.00	$44.00
832P296	32B	(1996)	Regular	$60.00	$44.00
833P197	33A	(1997)	Regular	$60.00	$44.00
833P297	33B	(1997)	Regular	$60.00	$44.00
834P198	34A	(1998)	Regular	$60.00	$44.00
834P298	34B	(1998)	Regular	$60.00	$44.00
835P199	35A	(1999)	Regular	$60.00	$44.00
835P299	35B	(1999)	Regular	$60.00	$44.00
836P100	36A	(2000)	Regular	$150.00	$120.00
836P200	36B	(2000)	Regular	$60.00	$44.00
837P101	37A	(2001)	Regular	$60.00	$44.00
837P201	37B	(2001)	Regular	$150.00	$120.00
838P102	38A	(2002)	Regular	$60.00	$44.00

Item	Part	Binder		Retail	AA*
838P202	38B	(2002)	Regular	$60.00	$44.00
839P103	39A	(2003)	Regular	$60.00	$44.00
839P203	39B	(2003)	Regular	$60.00	$44.00
840P104	40A	(2004)	Regular	$60.00	$44.00
840P204	40B	(2004)	Regular	$60.00	$44.00
841P105	41A	(2005)	Regular	$60.00	$44.00
841P205	41B	(2005)	Regular	$60.00	$44.00
842P106	42A	(2006)	Regular	$135.00	$99.99
842P206	42B	(2006)	Regular	$99.99	$72.50
843P107	43A	(2007)	Regular	$99.99	$72.50
843P207	43B	(2007)	Regular	$99.99	$72.50
844P108	44A	(2008)	Jumbo	$125.00	$89.99
844P208	44B	(2008)	Jumbo	$125.00	$89.99
845P109	45A	(2009)	Jumbo	$135.00	$99.99
845P209	45B	(2009)	Jumbo	$135.00	$99.99
846P110	46A	(2010)	Regular	$135.00	$99.99
846P210	46B	(2010)	Regular	$135.00	$99.99
847P111	47A	(2011)	Regular	$135.00	$99.99
847P211	47B	(2011)	Regular	$135.00	$99.99
848P112	48A	(2012)	Regular	$135.00	$99.99
848P212	48B	(2012)	Regular	$135.00	$99.99
800PC72*	People's Republic of China			$49.99	$39.99
800BOH*	Bosnia & Herzegovina 1879-2007			$49.99	$39.99

* Indicates a special order item. May take 4-6 weeks for delivery.

INTERNATIONAL SERIES BINDERS AND SLIPCASES
Attractive, blue two-post binder is available in two sizes. Features distinctive silver embossed spine. **Binder will hold International pages only.** Labels available for all parts. For a complete list see amosadvantage.com

Item		Retail	AA*
800B001	Regular Binder Holds 300 pages	$52.99	$40.99
800B002	Jumbo Binder Holds 400 pages.	$52.99	$40.99
800BC01	Regular Binder Slipcase	$32.99	$26.99
800BC02	Jumbo Binder Slipcase	$32.99	$26.99
8__LB01	International Label(s)	$2.29	$1.69

AmosAdvantage.com
1-800-572-6885

ORDERING INFORMATION

**AA prices apply to paid subscribers of Amos Hobby titles, or for orders placed online.
Prices, terms and product availability subject to change.*

Shipping & Handling:
United States: 10% of order total. Minimum charge $7.99 Maximum charge $45.00.
Canada: 20% of order total. Minimum charge $19.99 Maximum charge $200.00.
Foreign orders are shipped via FedEx Economy Intl. and billed actual freight.

Illustrated Identifier

This section pictures stamps or parts of stamp designs that will help identify postage stamps that do not have English words on them.

Many of the symbols that identify stamps of countries are shown here as well as typical examples of their stamps.

See the Index and Identifier in this catalogue for stamps with inscriptions such as "sen," "posta," "Baja Porto," "Helvetia," "K.S.A.", etc.

The 190-page *Linn's Stamp Identifier* includes more than 2,000 inscriptions and more than 500 large stamp illustrations.

The book is available from Linn's Stamp News, P.O. Box 29, Sidney, OH 45365-0029.

1. HEADS, PICTURES AND NUMERALS

GREAT BRITAIN

Great Britain stamps never show the country name, but, except for postage dues, show a picture of the reigning monarch.

Victoria

Edward VII   George V   Edward VIII

George VI

Some George VI stamps are surcharged in annas, new paisa or rupees. These are listed under Oman.

VICTORIA

Queen Victoria

INDIA

Other stamps of India show this portrait of Queen Victoria and the words "Service" and "Annas."

AUSTRIA

YUGOSLAVIA

(Also BOSNIA & HERZEGOVINA if imperf.)

BOSNIA & HERZEGOVINA

Denominations also appear in top corners instead of bottom corners.

HUNGARY

Another stamp has posthorn facing left.

BRAZIL

AUSTRALIA

Kangaroo and Emu

SWITZERLAND

2. ORIENTAL INSCRIPTIONS

CHINA

Any stamp with this one character is from China (Imperial, Republic or People's Republic).

This character appears in a four-character overprint on stamps of Manchukuo. These stamps are local provisionals, which are unlisted. Other overprinted Manchukuo stamps show this character but have more than four characters in the overprints. These are listed in People's Republic of China.

Some Chinese stamps show the Sun.

Most stamps of Republic of China show this series of characters.

Chinese stamps without China character

REPUBLIC OF CHINA

MANCHUKUO

Temple   Emperor Pu-Yi

          政郵國

The first 3 characters are common to many Manchukuo stamps.

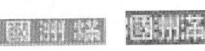

The last 3 characters are common to other Manchukuo stamps.

Orchid Crest

Manchukuo stamp without these elements

JAPAN

Chrysanthemum Crest   Country Name

Japanese stamps without these elements

The number of characters in the center and the design of dragons on the sides will vary.

KOREA

Yin Yang appears on some stamps.

THAILAND

Country Name

King Chulalongkorn   King Prajadhipok and Chao P'ya Chakri

3. CENTRAL AND EASTERN ASIAN INSCRIPTIONS

INDIA - FEUDATORY STATES

Alwar   Bhor

Bundi

Similar stamps come with different designs in corners and differently drawn daggers (at center of circle).

Dhar   Faridkot

Hyderabad

Similar stamps exist with straight line frame around stamp, and also with different central design, which is inscribed "Postage" or "Post & Receipt."

Hyderabad

Indore

Jammu & Kashmir

Text and thickness of ovals vary. Some stamps have flower devices in corners.

Jhalawar

A similar stamp has the central figure in an oval.

Kotah

Nandgaon

Nowanuggur

Poonch

Similar stamps exist in various sizes.

Rajpeepla

Soruth

Tonk

NEPAL

Similar stamps are smaller, have squares in upper corners and have five or nine characters in central bottom panel.

TANNU TUVA

GEORGIA

This inscription is found on other pictorial stamps.

ARMENIA

The four characters are found somewhere on pictorial stamps. On some stamps, only the middle two are found.

---

4. AFRICAN INSCRIPTIONS

ETHIOPIA

5. ARABIC INSCRIPTIONS

AFGHANISTAN

Many early Afghanistan stamps show Tiger's head. Many of these have ornaments protruding from outer ring; others show inscriptions in black.

Arabic Script

Mosque Gate & Crossed Cannons
The four characters are found somewhere on pictorial stamps. On some stamps only the middle two are found.

EGYPT

IRAN

Country Name

Royal Crown

SAUDI ARABIA

Tughra (Central design)

THRACE   YEMEN

TURKEY

Star & Crescent is a
device found on many
Turkish stamps, but is
also found on stamps
from other Arabic
areas (see Pakistan-
Bahawalpur).

 Tughra. Similar tughras
can be found on stamps of
Turkey in Asia, Afghanistan
and Saudi Arabia.

Mohammed V

Mustafa Kemal

Plane, Star and Crescent

TURKEY IN ASIA

Other Turkey in Asia pictorials show
star & crescent.
Other stamps show tughra
shown under Turkey.

6. GREEK INSCRIPTIONS

GREECE

Country Name in various styles
(Some Crete stamps overprinted with the
Greece country name are listed in Crete.)

Lepta

Drachma   Drachmas   Lepton
Abbreviated Country Name

Other forms of country name

No country name

CRETE

Country Name

These words are
on other stamps.

Grosion

Crete stamps with a surcharge that have
the year "1922" are listed under Greece.

EPIRUS   ### IONIAN ISLANDS

Country Name

7. CYRILLIC INSCRIPTIONS

RUSSIA

Postage Stamp

Imperial Eagle

Postage in various styles

Abbreviation Abbreviation   Russia
for Kopeck   for Ruble

 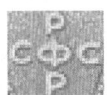

Abbreviation for Russian Soviet
Federated Socialist Republic
RSFSR stamps were overprinted (see below).

Abbreviation for Union of Soviet
Socialist Republics

This item is footnoted in Latvia.

RUSSIA - Army of the North

"OKCA"

RUSSIA - Wenden

RUSSIAN OFFICES IN THE TURKISH EMPIRE

These letters appear on other stamps of the Russian offices.

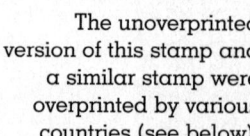

The unoverprinted version of this stamp and a similar stamp were overprinted by various countries (see below).

ARMENIA

FAR EASTERN REPUBLIC

Country Name

SOUTH RUSSIA

Country name

FINLAND

Circles and Dots on stamps similar to Imperial Russia issues

BATUM

Forms of country name

TRANSCAUCASIAN FEDERATED REPUBLICS

Abbreviation for country name

ROMANIA

UKRAINE

The trident appears on many stamps, usually as an overprint.

Abbreviation for Ukrainian Soviet Socialist Republic

WESTERN UKRAINE

Abbreviation for country name

AZERBAIJAN

 Abbreviation for Azerbaijan Soviet Socialist Republic

MONTENEGRO

Country name in various forms

 Abbreviation for country name

 No country name (A similar Montenegro stamp without country name has same vignette.)

SERBIA

Country name in various forms

Abbreviation for country name

No country name

YUGOSLAVIA

Showing country name

No country name

BULGARIA

Country name   Postage

Stotinka

Stotinki (plural) Abbreviation for Stotinki

Country Name in various forms and styles

No country name

 Abbreviation for Lev, leva

MONGOLIA

No country name

INDEX AND IDENTIFIER

Postage stamps that do not have English words on them are shown in the Illustrated Identifier.

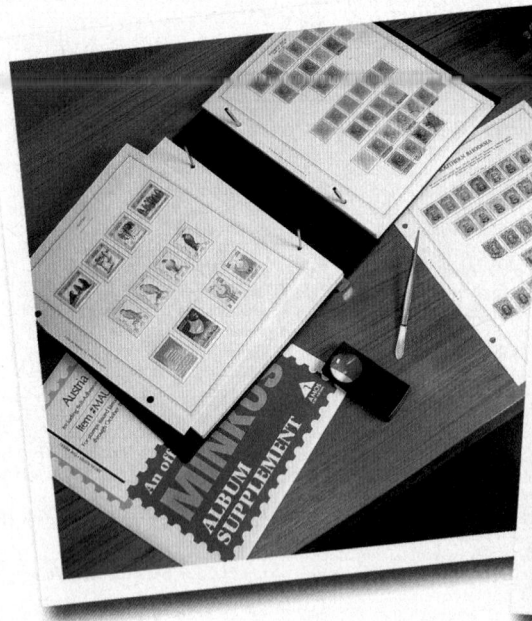

MINKUS
Album Series

The Minkus album line is now available through Amos Hobby Publishing.
The supplement schedule is listed below. Pages are punched to fit 2 or 3-ring binders.
Sold as page units only. Binders, slipcases and labels sold separately.
For more information album contents visit our web site at www.amosadvantage.com.

FEBRUARY
Global Part 1
Global Part 2
All American Regular & Commemoratives

MARCH
All American Part 3 United Nations
U.N Singles
U.N. Imprint Blocks
U.N. Postal Stationery

APRIL
All American Part 2 Postal Stationery
All American Part 4 Booklet Panes
All American Part 5 Sheetlets
All American Part 7 Postal Cards
U.S. Commemoratives
U.S. Plate Blocks
U.S. Regular Issues
U.S. Booklet Panes
U.S. Postal Stationery
U.S. Sheetlets

MAY
Albania
Austria
Bulgaria
Canada
Croatia
France
French Andorra
Germany
Gibraltar
Great Britain, Ireland
Guernsey, Jersey, Isle Of Man
Hong Kong
Ireland
Monaco
Romania
Serbia & Montenegro
Singapore
Slovenia

JUNE
Denmark
Egypt
Finland
Greece
Israel Singles
Israel Plate Blocks
Israel Tab Singles
Korea
Liechtenstein
Norway
Sweden
Switzerland

JULY
Bangladesh
India
Italy
Japan
Pakistan
People's Republic of China
Portugal/Azores/Maderia
San Marino
Spain
Sri Lanka
Thailand
Vatican City

AUGUST
Armenia
Azerbaijan
Belarus
Belgium
Czech Republic & Slovakia
Georgia
Hungary
Kazakhstan
Kyrgyzstan
Latvia, Lithuania, Estonia
Luxembourg
Moldova
Netherlands
Poland
Russia
Tajikistan
Turkmenistan
Ukraine
Uzbekistan

SEPTEMBER
Argentina
Australia
Brazil
Chile
Colombia
Dominican Republic
Haiti
Mexico
New Zealand
Venezuela

DECEMBER
All American Part 6 Plate No. Coils
U.S. Plate No. Coils

SCOTT.
911 Vandemark Road
Sidney OH 45365
1-800-572-6885
amosadvantage.com

INDEX TO ADVERTISERS 2015 CLASSIC SPECIALIZED

2015 CLASSIC SPECIALIZED DEALER DIRECTORY YELLOW PAGE LISTINGS

This section of your Scott Catalogue contains advertisements to help you conveniently find what you need, when you need it...!

Accessories

BROOKLYN GALLERY COIN & STAMP, INC.
8725 4th Ave.
Brooklyn, NY 11209
PH: 718-745-5701
FAX: 718-745-2775
info@brooklyngallery.com
www.brooklyngallery.com

Appraisals

COLONIAL STAMP COMPANY
5757 Wilshire Blvd. PH #8
Los Angeles, CA 90036
PH: 323-933-9435
FAX: 323-939-9930
Toll Free in North America
PH: 877-272-6693
FAX: 877-272-6694
info@colonialstampcompany.com
www.colonialstampcompany.com

DR. ROBERT FRIEDMAN & SONS STAMP & COIN BUYING CENTER
2029 W. 75th St.
Woodridge, IL 60517
PH: 800-588-8100
FAX: 630-985-1588
drbobstamps@comcast.net
www.drbobfriedmanstamps.com

PHILIP WEISS AUCTIONS
74 Merrick Rd
Lynbrook, NY 11563
PH: 516-594-0731
FAX: 516-594-9414
phil@prwauctions.com
www.prwauctions.com

Asia

DANIEL F. KELLEHER AUCTIONS LLC
PMB 44
60 Newtown Rd
Danbury, CT 06810
PH: 203-297-6056
FAX: 203-297-6059
info@kelleherauctions.com
www.kelleherauctions.com

THE STAMP ACT
PO Box 1136
Belmont, CA 94002
PH: 650-703-2342
PH: 650-592-3315
FAX: 650-508-8104
thestampact@sbcglobal.net

Auctions

COLONIAL STAMP COMPANY
5757 Wilshire Blvd. PH #8
Los Angeles, CA 90036
PH: 323-933-9435
FAX: 323-939-9930
Toll Free in North America
PH: 877-272-6693
FAX: 877-272-6694
info@colonialstampcompany.com
www.colonialstampcompany.com

DANIEL F. KELLEHER AUCTIONS LLC
PMB 44
60 Newtown Rd
Danbury, CT 06810
PH: 203-297-6056
FAX: 203-297-6059
info@kelleherauctions.com
www.kelleherauctions.com

DUTCH COUNTRY AUCTIONS
4115 Concord Pike
Wilmington, DE 19803
PH: 302-478-8740
FAX: 302-478-8779
auctions@dutchcountryauctions.com
www.dutchcountryauctions.com

PHILIP WEISS AUCTIONS
74 Merrick Rd
Lynbrook, NY 11563
PH: 516-594-0731
FAX: 516-594-9414
phil@prwauctions.com
www.prwauctions.com

R. MARESCH & SON LTD.
5th Floor - 6075 Yonge St.
Toronto, ON M2M 3W2
CANADA
PH: 416-363-7777
FAX: 416-363-6511
www.maresch.com

Auctions-Mail Bid

DANIEL F. KELLEHER AUCTIONS LLC
PMB 44
60 Newtown Rd
Danbury, CT 06810
PH: 203-297-6056
FAX: 203-297-6059
info@kelleherauctions.com
www.kelleherauctions.com

Auctions - Public

ALAN BLAIR AUCTIONS, L.L.C.
Suite 1
5405 Lakeside Ave.
Richmond, VA 23228-6060
PH: 800-689-5602
FAX: 804-262-9307
alanblair@verizon.net
www.alanblairstamps.com

DANIEL F. KELLEHER AUCTIONS LLC
PMB 44
60 Newtown Rd
Danbury, CT 06810
PH: 203-297-6056
FAX: 203-297-6059
info@kelleherauctions.com
www.kelleherauctions.com

Australia

ARON R. HALBERSTAM PHILATELISTS, LTD.
PO Box 150168
Van Brunt Station
Brooklyn, NY 11215-0168
PH: 718-788-397
arh@arhstamps.com
www.arhstamps.com

Australia

COLONIAL STAMP COMPANY
5757 Wilshire Blvd. PH #8
Los Angeles, CA 90036
PH: 323-933-9435
FAX: 323-939-9930
Toll Free in North America
PH: 877-272-6693
FAX: 877-272-6694
info@colonialstampcompany.com
www.colonialstampcompany.com

Australian States

COLONIAL STAMP COMPANY
5757 Wilshire Blvd. PH #8
Los Angeles, CA 90036
PH: 323-933-9435
FAX: 323-939-9930
Toll Free in North America
PH: 877-272-6693
FAX: 877-272-6694
info@colonialstampcompany.com
www.colonialstampcompany.com

Austria

HENRY GITNER PHILATELISTS, INC.
PO Box 3077-S
Middletown, NY 10940
PH: 845-343-5151
PH: 800-947-8267
FAX: 845-343-0068
hgitner@hgitner.com
www.hgitner.com

Belgium

**HENRY GITNER
PHILATELISTS, INC.**
PO Box 3077-S
Middletown, NY 10940
PH: 845-343-5151
PH: 800-947-8267
FAX: 845-343-0068
hgitner@hgitner.com
www.hgitner.com

Bermuda

**ARON R. HALBERSTAM
PHILATELISTS, LTD.**
PO Box 150168
Van Brunt Station
Brooklyn, NY 11215-0168
PH: 718-788-397
arh@arhstamps.com
www.arhstamps.com

COLONIAL STAMP COMPANY
5757 Wilshire Blvd. PH #8
Los Angeles, CA 90036
PH: 323-933-9435
FAX: 323-939-9930
Toll Free in North America
PH: 877-272-6693
FAX: 877-272-6694
info@colonialstampcompany.com
www.colonialstampcompany.com

British Asia

COLONIAL STAMP COMPANY
5757 Wilshire Blvd. PH #8
Los Angeles, CA 90036
PH: 323-933-9435
FAX: 323-939-9930
Toll Free in North America
PH: 877-272-6693
FAX: 877-272-6694
info@colonialstampcompany.com
www.colonialstampcompany.com

**DANIEL F. KELLEHER
AUCTIONS LLC**
PMB 44
60 Newtown Rd
Danbury, CT 06810
PH: 203-297-6056
FAX: 203-297-6059
info@kelleherauctions.com
www.kelleherauctions.com

THE STAMP ACT
PO Box 1136
Belmont, CA 94002
PH: 650-703-2342
PH: 650-592-3315
FAX: 650-508-8104
thestampact@sbcglobal.net

British Commonwealth

**ARON R. HALBERSTAM
PHILATELISTS, LTD.**
PO Box 150168
Van Brunt Station
Brooklyn, NY 11215-0168
PH: 718-788-397
arh@arhstamps.com
www.arhstamps.com

British Commonwealth

**DANIEL F. KELLEHER
AUCTIONS LLC**
PMB 44
60 Newtown Rd
Danbury, CT 06810
PH: 203-297-6056
FAX: 203-297-6059
info@kelleherauctions.com
www.kelleherauctions.com

Buying

**DR. ROBERT FRIEDMAN &
SONS STAMP & COIN BUYING
CENTER**
2029 W. 75th St.
Woodridge, IL 60517
PH: 800-588-8100
FAX: 630-985-1588
drbobstamps@comcast.net
www.drbobfriedmanstamps.com

Canada

CANADA STAMP FINDER
54 Soccavo Crescent
Brampton, ON L6Y 0W3
PH: 905-488-6109
Toll Free in North America
PH: 877-412-3106
FAX: 323-215-2635
info@canadastampfinder.com
www.canadastampfinder.com

Canada

COLONIAL STAMP COMPANY
5757 Wilshire Blvd. PH #8
Los Angeles, CA 90036
PH: 323-933-9435
FAX: 323-939-9930
Toll Free in North America
PH: 877-272-6693
FAX: 877-272-6694
info@colonialstampcompany.com
www.colonialstampcompany.com

Cape of Good Hope

COLONIAL STAMP COMPANY
5757 Wilshire Blvd. PH #8
Los Angeles, CA 90036
PH: 323-933-9435
FAX: 323-939-9930
Toll Free in North America
PH: 877-272-6693
FAX: 877-272-6694
info@colonialstampcompany.com
www.colonialstampcompany.com

China

**DANIEL F. KELLEHER
AUCTIONS LLC**
PMB 44
60 Newtown Rd
Danbury, CT 06810
PH: 203-297-6056
FAX: 203-297-6059
info@kelleherauctions.com
www.kelleherauctions.com